ISSN 0360-2796

BIBLIOGRAPHIC GUIDE TO
GOVERNMENT PUBLICATIONS—U.S.
1981

Volume 2
N—Z

G.K. HALL & CO.
70 Lincoln Street, Boston, Massachusetts

Copyright © 1982 by G.K.Hall & Co.
All rights reserved.
Manufactured in the United States of America
ISBN 0–8161–6957–8

Nadeau, Robert L., 1944- Readings from the new book on nature : physics and metaphysics in the modern novel / Robert L. Nadeau. Amherst : University of Massachusetts Press, 1981. p. cm. Bibliography: p. Includes index. ISBN 0-87023-331-9 :   LC Card 81-2625   DDC 813/.54/09356 19
1. American fiction - 20th century - History and criticism. 2. Physics in literature. 3. Literature and science. I. Title.
PS374.P45 N3

Naff, Thomas. The Middle East challenge, 1980-1985 /. Carbondale , c1981. p. cm. ISBN 0-8093-1042-2 LC Card 81-5651 DDC 320.956 19
DS63.1 .M486

Nafziger, R. H. (Ralph H.) Haas, L. A. (Larry A.) Low pressure leaching of Duluth complex matte /. Avondale, Md. , 1981. p. cm. LC Card 80-606897   DDC 622 s 669/.7332 19
TN23 .U43 TN799.N6

Nafziger, Ralph H. (joint author) Spironello, Victor R. An evaluation of used aluminum smelter potlining as a substitute for fluorspan in cupola ironmelting /. [Avondale, Md.] [1981] p. cm. LC Card 80-606836   DDC 622 s 672.2/4 19
TN23 .U43 TN707

Nahm, Andrew C. The United States and Korea . Kalamazoo , 1979. 262 p. ; LC Card 78-65924   DDC 327.730519 19
E183.8.K6 U54

Nailing up the home sweet home /. Walker, Jeanne Murray. [Cleveland] , Oberlin, Ohio , c1980. 60 p. ; ISBN 0-914946-24-2 (pbk.) :   LC Card 80-68027 DDC 811/.54 19
PS3573.A425336 N3

Nair, Balakrishnan K. Schenck, George K. SIC-based demand information system for nonfuel minerals /. Washington , 1981. p. cm.   LC Card 81-607810   DDC 622 s 025/.06553 19
TN295 .U4 HD9506.A2

Najita, Joyce M. Guide to statutory provisions in public sector collective bargaining : characteristics, functions, and powers of administering agencies / by Joyce M. Najita and Helene S. Tanimoto. Honolulu, Hawaii (2425 Campus Rd., Honolulu 96822) : Industrial Relations Center, University of Hawaii at Manoa, c1981. v, 237 p. ; 23 cm. (Occasional publication / Industrial Relations Center, University of Hawaii at Manoa ; no. 137) "March 1981." Includes bibliographical references. LC Card 81-138923 DDC 344.73/0189041353 347.304189041353 19
1. Collective labor agreements - Government employees - United States - States. I. Tanimoto, Helene S. II. Series: Occasional publication (University of Hawaii at Manoa. Industrial Relations Center) , no. 137. III. Title.
KF3409.P77 Z9536

Nakagawa, Yukio, 1918- McCall, Wade W. (Wade Wiley), 1920- Growing plants without soil /. Honolulu [1981] p. cm. LC Card 81-6716 -   DDC 631.5/85 19
SB126.5 .M38

Nakano, Richard Toshitaka, 1939- (joint author) Kratky, B. A., 1944- Protecting lettuce plants from preemergence herbicide damage /. [Honolulu] [1980] 7 p. : LC Card 80-26589   DDC 635/.529 19
SB608.L523 K7

Nakayama, T. O. M. (Tommy O. M.), 1928- Chi, Chia-hsiung, 1943- Inhibition of Cellulomonas sp. by heat-treated sugarcane bagasse and rice straw /. Honolulu , 1981. p. cm. LC Card 81-4120 DDC 632/.32 19
QR160 .C47

NALOXONE - CONGRESSES.
Satellite Conference on Naltrexone, Richmond, 1976. Narcotic antagonists, naltrexone . Rockville, Md. , Springfield, Va.] 1976. x, 181 p. : LC Card 76-40692 DDC 615/.7822 19
RC568.H4 S27 1976

NAMES, GEOGRAPHICAL - UNITED STATES.
Werner, Pamela A. A survey of national geocoding systems. [Cambridge, Mass.], 1974. xi, 344 p. LC Card 76-51887
NYPL [JFF 80-1538]

NAMES, PERSONAL (CATALOGING)
Valk, Barbara G. HAPI thesaurus and name authority, 1975-1977 /. Los Angeles , c1979. 113 p. ; ISBN 0-87903-403-3 LC Card 79-620062   DDC 980/.005 19
Z1605.H162 V34 F1408

NAMIBIA - FOREIGN RELATIONS.
United States. Congress. House. Committee on Foreign Affairs. Subcommittee on Africa. Namibia update . Washington , 1981. iv, 35 p. :   LC Card 81-600962 DDC 968.8/03 19
KF27 .F625 1980h

Namibia - Government. see **Namibia - Politics and government.**

NAMIBIA - POLITICS AND GOVERNMENT.
United States. Congress. House. Committee on Foreign Affairs. Subcommittee on Africa. Namibia update . Washington , 1981. iv, 35 p. :   LC Card 81-600962 DDC 968.8/03 19
KF27 .F625 1980h

Namibia update . United States. Congress. House. Committee on Foreign Affairs. Subcommittee on Africa. Washington , 1981. iv, 35 p. : LC Card 81-600962   DDC 968.8/03 19
KF27 .F625 1980h

NANNIPPUS PHLEGON.
MacFadden, Bruce J. Nannippus phlegon (Mammalia, Equidae) from the Pliocene (Blancan) of Florida /. Gainesville (Museum Rd., University of Florida, Gainesville, FL 32611) , 1980. 37 p. : LC Card 81-621398 DDC 569/.72 19
QE882.U6 M28

Nannippus phlegon (Mammalia, Equidae) from the Pliocene (Blancan) of Florida /. MacFadden, Bruce J. Gainesville (Museum Rd., University of Florida, Gainesville, FL 32611) , 1980. 37 p. : LC Card 81-621398 DDC 569/.72 19
QE882.U6 M28

Nantucket . Massachusetts. Water Quality and Research Section. Westborough , 1978. 50 p. : LC Card 79-623987 DDC 363.7/3942/0974497 19
TD224.M4 M39 1978a

NANTUCKET (MASS.) - MAPS.
United States. Soil Conservation Service. Nantucket County, Massachusetts /. Lanham, MD , 1980. 1 map : LC Card 81-690021
G3762.N3 1979 .U5

NAPLES (ITALY) - EARTHQUAKE, 1980.
Pell, Claiborne, 1918- Earthquake in Italy . Washington , 1980. vii, 17 p. : LC Card 80-604120 DDC 363.3/495 19
DG851 .P44

NAPOLEONIC WARS. see **FRANCE - HISTORY - REVOLUTION, 1789-1799.**

Narayanan, Rangesan. An economic evaluation of the salinity impacts from energy development : the case of the Upper Colorado River Basin / by Rangesan Narayanan, Sumol Padungchai, A. Bruce Bishop. Logan, Utah : Utah Water Research Laboratory, Utah State University, 1979. x, 71 p. : ill. ; 28 cm. (Water resources planning series . UWRL/P-79/07) Bibliography: p. 65-68. LC Card 80-622072 DDC 363.7/394 19
1. Energy facilities - Environmental aspects - Colorado River watershed. 2. Energy facilities - Colorado River watershed - Water-supply. 3. Irrigation water - Colorado River watershed - Quality. 4. Saline waters - Colorado River watershed. I. Padungchai, Sumol, joint author. II. Bishop, A. Bruce, joint author. III. Title. IV. Series.
TD195.E5 N37

NARCOTIC ADDICTION. see **NARCOTIC HABIT.**

Narcotic addiction over a quarter of a century in a major American city, 1950-1977 . Friends Medical Science Research Center. [Rockville, Md.] , 1980. vi, 92 p. : LC Card 80-601276 DDC 362.2/93/097526 19
HV5833.B2 F74 1980

NARCOTIC ADDICTS - ADDRESSES, ESSAYS, LECTURES.
Documentation Associates Information Services Incorporated. Research issues update, 1978 /. Rockville, Md. , Washington , 1979. xvii, 308 p. : LC Card 79-601820 DDC 362.2/93/072 19
HV5809 .D62 1979a

NARCOTIC ADDICTS - ALCOHOL USE.
Barr, Harriet Linton. The problem-drinking drug addict /. [Rockville, Md.] , 1978. vii, 52 p. : LC Card 79-602286 DDC 362.2/938 19
HV5831.P4 A5 1978a

NARCOTIC ADDICTS - FAMILY RELATIONSHIPS.
Addicted women . Rockville, Md. [1979] vi, 130 p. : LC Card 80-601626 DDC 616.86/3/0088042 19
RC566 .A32

NARCOTIC ADDICTS - MASSACHUSETTS - STATISTICS.
Roy, Marjorie Brown. Drug defendants in Massachusetts, 1978 /. Boston , 1979. 31 leaves ; LC Card 79-623946 DDC 364.1/77/09744 19
HV5831.M4 A5 1979

NARCOTIC ADDICTS - PENNSYLVANIA - ALCOHOL USE.
Barr, Harriet Linton. The problem-drinking drug addict /. [Rockville, Md.] , 1978. vii, 52 p. : LC Card 79-602286 DDC 362.2/938 19
HV5831.P4 A5 1978a

NARCOTIC ADDICTS - PSYCHOLOGY.
Addicted women . Rockville, Md. [1979] vi, 130 p. : LC Card 80-601626 DDC 616.86/3/0088042 19
RC566 .A32

NARCOTIC ADDICTS - REHABILITATION - BIBLIOGRAPHY.
New York (State). Drug Abuse Control Commission. Bureau of Social Science Research. Annotated bibliography of research reports. New York [1973] 31 p. LC Card 77-100005 *NYPL [*ZT-1250]*

NARCOTIC ADDICTS - REHABILITATION - IOWA.
Iowa. Dept. of Substance Abuse. Iowa, criminal justice system and substance abuse /. Des Moines, Iowa [1979?] 58 p. ; LC Card 80-621464 DDC 364.1/77/09777 19
HV9305.I8 I56 1979

NARCOTIC ADDICTS - REHABILITATION - NEW YORK (CITY) - CASE STUDIES.
Friedman, Lucy N. The wildcat experiment . Rockville, Md. , Washington [1978] ix, 147 p. ; LC Card 79-602059 DDC 362.2/9386 19
HV5833.N45 F74

NARCOTIC ADDICTS - REHABILITATION - UNITED STATES.
System Sciences, inc. Evaluation of treatment alternatives to street crime . [Washington] , 1979. xii, 150 p. ; LC Card 79-602081 DDC 362.2/937/0973 19
HV5825 .S94 1979

NARCOTIC HABIT - ADDRESSES, ESSAYS, LECTURES.
Documentation Associates Information Services Incorporated. Research issues update, 1978 /. Rockville, Md. , Washington , 1979. xvii, 308 p. : LC Card 79-601820 DDC 362.2/93/072 19
HV5809 .D62 1979a

NARCOTIC HABIT - MARYLAND - BALTIMORE - CASE STUDIES.
Friends Medical Science Research Center. Narcotic addiction over a quarter of a century in a major American city, 1950-1977 . [Rockville, Md.] , 1980. vi, 92 p. : LC Card 80-601276 DDC 362.2/93/097526 19
HV5833.B2 F74 1980

NARCOTIC HABIT - PSYCHOLOGICAL ASPECTS.
Addicted women . Rockville, Md. [1979] vi, 130 p. : LC Card 80-601626 DDC 616.86/3/0088042 19
RC566 .A32

NARCOTIC LAWS.
United States. Dept. of State. The global legal framework for narcotics and prohibitive substances . Washington, D.C. , 1979. 86, 14 p. ; LC Card 79-603788
K5282 .U54 *NYPL [JLF 81-316]*

NARCOTIC TRADE. see NARCOTICS, CONTROL OF.

NARCOTIC TRAFFIC. see NARCOTICS, CONTROL OF.

NARCOTICS AND CRIME - MASSACHUSETTS - STATISTICS.
Roy, Marjorie Brown. Drug defendants in Massachusetts, 1978 /. Boston , 1979. 31 leaves ; LC Card 79-623946 DDC 364.1/77/09744 19
HV5831.M4 A5 1979

NARCOTICS, CONTROL OF - FLORIDA.
United States. Congress. Senate. Committee on Banking, Housing and Urban Affairs. Banks and narcotics money flow in south Florida . Washington , 1980. v, 245 p. ; LC Card 80-603356 DDC 346.73/082 19
KF26 .B39 1980j

NARCOTICS, CONTROL OF - GEORGIA.
United States. Congress. House. Select Committee on Narcotics Abuse and Control. Interdiction of drug trafficking in Georgia . Washington , 1980. iii, 17 p. ; LC Card 80-603853 DDC 363.4/5/09758 19
HV8079.N3 U53 1980

United States. Congress. House. Select Committee on Narcotics Abuse and Control. Interdiction of drug trafficking in Georgia . Washington , 1980. iv, 266 p. ; LC Card 80-603326 DDC 363.4/5/09758 19
KF27.5 .N3 1980b

NARCOTICS, CONTROL OF - INTERNATIONAL COOPERATION.
United States. Congress. House. Select Committee on Narcotics Abuse and Control. The use of paraquat to eradicate illicit marihuana crops and the health implications of paraquat-contaminated marihuana on the U. S. market . Washington , 1980. iii, 99 p. : LC Card 80-602592 DDC 363.4/5 19
RA1242.P34 U54 1980

NARCOTICS, CONTROL OF - MASSACHUSETTS - STATISTICS.
Roy, Marjorie Brown. Drug defendants in Massachusetts, 1978 /. Boston , 1979. 31 leaves ; LC Card 79-623946 DDC 364.1/77/09744 19
HV5831.M4 A5 1979

NARCOTICS, CONTROL OF - MEXICO.
United States. Congress. House. Select Committee on Narcotics Abuse and Control. The use of paraquat to eradicate illicit marihuana crops and the health implications of paraquat-contaminated marihuana on the U. S. market . Washington , 1980. iii, 99 p. : LC Card 80-602592 DDC 363.4/5 19
RA1242.P34 U54 1980

NARCOTICS, CONTROL OF - NEW YORK (CITY)
New York (State). Temporary State Commission of Investigation. Interim report concerning the operations of Special Narcotics Parts of the Supreme Court. New York [1973] 21 leaves *NYPL [*XME-9454]*

NARCOTICS, CONTROL OF - NEW YORK (N.Y.)
Padavan, Frank. Heroin--new sources/new users . [Albany, N.Y. , 1980] 36 p. : LC Card 81-621128 DDC 362.2/93 19
HV5822.H4 P32

NARCOTICS, CONTROL OF - UNITED STATES.
United States. Congress. House. Select Committee on Narcotics Abuse and Control. Drug abuse in the Armed Forces of the United States . Washington , 1980. iii, 144 p. : LC Card 80-601999 DDC 353.0084/29 19
KF27.5 .N3 1979g

United States. Congress. House. Select Committee on Narcotics Abuse and Control. Drug paraphernalia . Washington , 1980. iii, 46 p. : LC Card 80-604119 DDC 381/.4568 19
HV5825 .U563 1980

United States. Congress. House. Select Committee on Narcotics Abuse and Control. Federal drug strategy . Washington , 1980. iii, 164 p. : LC Card 81-601321 DDC 363.4/5/0973 19
KF27.5 .N3 1980f

United States. Congress. House. Select

Committee on Narcotics Abuse and Control. Increased heroin supply and decreased Federal funds . Washington , 1980. iii, 144 p. : LC Card 80-603349 DDC 362.2/93/0973 19
KF27.5 .N3 1980c

United States. Congress. House. Select Committee on Narcotics Abuse and Control. Increased heroin supply and decreased federal funds . Washington , 1980 [i.e. 1981] iii, 76 p. : LC Card 81-601275 DDC 362.2/9356/0973 19
HV5822.H4 U53 1980

United States. Congress. House. Select Committee on Narcotics Abuse and Control. Oversight on federal drug strategy--1979 . Washington , 1980 [i.e. 1981] iv, 63 p. : LC Card 81-601283 DDC 363.4/5/0973 19
HV5825 .U563 1981

United States. Congress. House. Select Committee on Narcotics Abuse and Control. The use of paraquat to eradicate illicit marihuana crops and the health implications of paraquat-contaminated marihuana on the U. S. market . Washington , 1980. iii, 99 p. : LC Card 80-602592 DDC 363.4/5 19
RA1242.P34 U54 1980

United States. Congress. Senate. Committee on Appropriations. Subcommittee on Departments of State, Justice, and Commerce, the Judiciary, and Related Agencies. Federal drug enforcement and supply control efforts . Washington , 1980. iii, 325, vi p. : LC Card 80-603504 DDC 353.0076/5 19
KF26 .A659 1979b

United States. Congress. Senate. Committee on Rules and Administration. To create a Select Committee on Narcotics Abuse and Control . Washington , 1980. iv, 224 p. : LC Card 80-602455 DDC 353.0076/5 19
KF26 .R8 1980

United States. Congress. Senate. Committee on the Judiciary. Subcommittee on Criminal Justice. Drug control program of the Federal Government . Washington , 1980. iv, 157 p. : LC Card 80-602793 DDC 363.4/5/0973 19
KF26 .J8377 1979

United States. Congress. Senate. Committee on the Judiciary. Subcommittee on Criminal Justice. Forfeiture of narcotics proceeds . Washington , 1981. iii, 165 p. ; LC Card 81-600972 DDC 363.4/5 19
KF26 .J8377 1980h

NARCOTICS - JURISPRUDENCE. see NARCOTIC LAWS.

NARCOTICS - PERIODICALS.
Bulletin on narcotics. v. 1- ; Oct. 1949- New York [etc.] LC Card 53-18079 *NYPL [VTYA (United Nations. Secretariat. Social Affairs Dept. Bulletin on narcotics)]*

Narragansett Bay . Hale, Stuart O., 1917- Narragansett, RI [1980] ix, 122 p. : ISBN 0-938412-19-1 (pbk.) : LC Card 80-52813 DDC 974.5 19
F87.N2 H34

NARRAGANSETT BAY REGION, R.I. - DESCRIPTION AND TRAVEL.
Hale, Stuart O., 1917- Narragansett Bay . Narragansett, RI [1980] ix, 122 p. : ISBN 0-938412-19-1 (pbk.) : LC Card 80-52813 DDC 974.5 19
F87.N2 H34

NARRAGANSETT BAY REGION, R.I. - HISTORY.
Hale, Stuart O., 1917- Narragansett Bay . Narragansett, RI [1980] ix, 122 p. : ISBN 0-938412-19-1 (pbk.) : LC Card 80-52813 DDC 974.5 19
F87.N2 H34

NARRATIVE, FIRST PERSON. see FIRST PERSON NARRATIVE.

NASA's biomedical research program /. Ahn, Chung-Hae. Washington, D.C. , 1981. p. cm. LC Card 81-607969 DDC 616.9/80214 19
RC1150 .A35

Nash, A. E. Keir. Understanding and planning for ORV recreation : the 1978-79 Washington offroad recreation survey / by A. E. Keir Nash with Marguerite Bou-Raad Nash for Interagency Committee for Outdoor Recreation, State of Washington. Tumwater, Wash. : The Committee, 1979 v, 159 p. : ill. ; 28 cm.

Includes bibliographical references. LC Card 79-625837 DDC 338.3/4 19
1. Outdoor recreation - Washington (State). 2. All terrain vehicles - Washington (State) - Recreational use. 3. Recreational surveys - Washington (State). I. Nash, Marguerite Bou-Raad, joint author. II. Washington (State). Interagency Committee for Outdoor Recreation. III. Title.
GV191.42.W2 N37

Nash, Marguerite Bou-Raad. (joint author) Nash, A. E. Keir. Understanding and planning for ORV recreation . Tumwater, Wash. , 19. v, 159 p. : LC Card 79-625837 DDC 338.3/4 19
GV191.42.W2 N37

Nash, Norman Frederick, 1936- Illinois. University at Urbana-Champaign. Library. Rare Book Room. The Renaissance at Illinois . [Urbana Ill.] , c1980. 58 p. : LC Card 80-622396 DDC 011/.44/0977366 19
Z6207.R4 I43 1980 CB361

Nashat, Guity, 1937- The origins of modern reform in Iran / by Guity Nashat. Urbana : University of Illinois Press, c1981. p. cm. Based on the author's thesis (Ph.D.--University of Chicago, 1973) presented under the title: the beginnings of modernization in Iran. Bibliography: p. Includes index. ISBN 0-252-00822-7 LC Card 81-3343 DDC 955/.04 19
1. Iran - History - 19th century. 2. Husayn Khān Mushir al-Dawlah, 1827 or 8-1881. 3. Statesmen - Iran - Biography. I. Title.
DS307 .N26

Nashua River . Bilger, Michael D. Westborough, Mass. [1978] iv leaves, 45 p. : LC Card 79-624432 DDC 363.7/3942/097443 19
TD225.N2 B54

Nashua River. Massachusetts. Division of Water Pollution Control. Water Quality Section. Nashua River basin . Westborough [1975] 38 p. : LC Card 79-620604 DDC 363.7/3942/097443 19
TD225.N2 M37 1975

Nashua River. Massachusetts. Water Quality and Research Section. Nashua River basin . Westborough, Mass. [1978] 31 p. : LC Card 79-620603 DDC 363.7/3942/097444 19
TD225.N2 M38 1978

Nashua River basin. Chesebrough, Eben W. Baseline water quality surveys of selected lakes and ponds in the Nashua River basin, 1977 /. Westborough, Mass. [1978] 141 p. : LC Card 79-620602 DDC 363.7/3942/097443 19
TD225.N2 C47

Nashua River basin . Massachusetts. Division of Water Pollution Control. Water Quality Section. Westborough [1975] 38 p. : LC Card 79-620604 DDC 363.7/3942/097443 19
TD225.N2 M37 1975

Nashua River basin . Massachusetts. Water Quality and Research Section. Westborough, Mass. [1978] 31 p. : LC Card 79-620603 DDC 363.7/3942/097444 19
TD225.N2 M38 1978

NASHVILLE (TENN.) - INTELLECTUAL LIFE.
Young, Thomas Daniel, 1919- Waking their neighbors up . Athens , c1982. p. cm. ISBN 0-8203-0600-2 LC Card 81-14736 DDC 810/.9/975 19
PS261 .Y63

Nassau County, N. Y. Sheriff's Dept.
Annual report. [Mineola] illus., ports. 28 cm.
1. Nassau County, N. Y. Sheriff's Dept. - Periodicals.
NYPL [JLM 80-1080]

NASSAU COUNTY, N. Y. SHERIFF'S DEPT. - PERIODICALS.
Nassau County, N. Y. Sheriff's Dept. Annual report. [Mineola] ***NYPL [JLM 80-1080]***

NASSAU COUNTY (N.Y.) - LIBRARIES.
Feinberg, Richard P. A union list of microform collections in Nassau and Suffolk County libraries /. Stony Brook, N.Y. , Bellport, N.Y. , 1980. viii, 220 p. ; LC Card 81-111481 DDC 011/.36 19
Z1033.M5 F43

Nathan (Robert R.) Associates, Washington, D. C. Assessment and evaluation of the impact of archetypal national health insurance plans on U. S. health manpower requirements / prepared for Division of Manpower Intelligence, Bureau

of Health Manpower Education, National Institutes of Health by Lien-fu Huang and Elwood W. Shomo. [Bethesda, Md.] : U. S. Dept. of Health, Education, and Welfare, Public Health Service, Health Resources Administration, Bureau of Health Resources Development, 1974. xviii, 117 p. : ill. ; 28 cm. Cover title: The Impact of Archetypal national health insurance plans on U. S. Health Manpower Requirements. "DHEW Publication no. (HRA) 75-1." Bibliography: p. 114-117.
1. Medical personnel - United States - Supply and distribution. 2. Medical personnel - United States - Utilization. 3. Insurance, Health - United States. I. Huang, Lien-fu. II. Shomo, Elwood Warren. III. United States. Bureau of Health Resources Development. Division of Manpower Intelligence. IV. Title. V. Title: Impact of archetypal national health insurance plans on U. S. health manpower requirements.
NYPL [JLF 80-904]

Nathanson, Stanley N. Ultrasystems, inc. Evaluation and analysis of the Cleff job matching system: final report /. - Irvine, Calif. , 1975. 2 v. in 1 : ***NYPL [*XME-9380]***

National Academy of Education. Prejudice and pride : the Brown decision after twenty-five years, May 17, 1954-May 17, 1979 : report from the National Academy of Education / Stephen K. Bailey, rapporteur ; panel contributors, Lascelles Anderson ... [et al.]. [Washington] : U. S. Dept. of Health, Education, and Welfare, Education Division, 1979. 37 p. ; 28 cm. Bibliography: p. 35-37. LC Card 79-602965 DDC 344.73/0798 19
1. Discrimination in education - Law and legislation - United States - Addresses, essays, lectures. I. Bailey, Stephen Kemp. II. Title.
KF4155.A2 N38

National Academy of Engineering. Environmental Studies Board. see Environmental Studies Board.

National Academy of Public Administration. LEAA Criminal Justice Planning Panel.
Criminal justice planning in the governing process : a review of nine states : report of a panel of the National Academy of Public Administration. [Washington] : Law Enforcement Assistance Administration, U. S. Dept. of Justice, 1979. ca. 200 p. in various pagings ; 28 cm. Includes bibliography. LC Card 79-602883
1. Criminal justice, Administration of - Planning - United States - Case studies. 2. Criminal justice, Administration of - Planning - United States. I. United States. Law Enforcement Assistance Administration. II. Title.
HV8138 .N269 1979

National Academy of Sciences report . United States. Congress. House. Committee on Science and Technology. Washington , 1980. iii, 147 p. : LC Card 80-603067 DDC 333.79/0973 19
KF27 .S39 1980b

National Academy of Sciences report on healthful diets . United States. Congress. House. Committee on Agriculture. Subcommittee on Domestic Marketing, Consumer Relations, and Nutrition. Washington , 1980. iii, 312 p. ; LC Card 80-603777 DDC 613.2 19
KF27 .A3336 1980

National Academy of Sciences (U. S.). Committee on Scholarly Communication with the People's Republic of China. Rural health in the People's Republic of China . [Bethesda, Md.] , Washington, D.C. , 1980 [i.e. 1981] ix, 207 p. : LC Card 81-601104 DDC 362.1/0425 19
RA771.7.C6 R87

National Academy of Sciences (U. S.). Institute of Medicine. Committee on Health Planning Goals and Standards. Health planning in the United States / Committee on Health Planning Goals and Standards, Institute of Medicine, National Academy of Sciences. Washington, D.C. : National Academy Press, 1981- p. cm. Bibliography: v. 1, p. ISBN 0-309-03144-3 (v. 1) LC Card 81-9534 DDC 362.1/06 19
1. Health planning - United States. 2. Medical policy - United States. I. Title.
RA395.A3 N285 1981

National Academy of Sciences, Washington, D. C. Environmental Studies Board. see Environmental Studies Board.

National Advisory Council on Equality of Educational Opportunity. see United States. National Advisory Council on Equality of Educational Opportunity.

National Advisory Neurological and Communicative Disorders and Stroke Council (U. S.)
Panel on Communicative Disorders (U. S.) Report of the Panel on Communicative Disorders to the National Advisory Neurological and Communicative Disorders and Stroke Council, National Institute of Neurological and Communicative Disorders and Stroke. [Bethesda, Md.] [1979] xvii, 351 p. ; LC Card 80-601219 DDC 616.85/5/0072073 19
RC423 .P24 1979

Panel on Convulsive and Neuromuscular Disorders (U. S.) Report of the Panel on Convulsive and Neuromuscular Disorders to the National Advisory Neurological and Communicative Disorders and Stroke Council, National Institute of Neurological and Communicative Disorders and Stroke. [Bethesda, Md.] [1979] xiii, 124 p. : LC Card 80-601220 DDC 616.7/4/0072073 19
RC925.5 .P26 1979

National Advisory Neurological and Communicative Disorders and Stroke Council (United States). Task Force on Basic Science. Report of the Task Force on Basic Science to the National Advisory Neurological and Communicative Disorders and Stroke Council. [Washington, D.C.] : U. S. Dept. of Health, Education, and Welfare, Public Health Service, National Institutes of Health, 1979. ix, 129 p. ; 28 cm. (NIH publication ; no. 79-1920) "Prepared for the National Institute of Neurological and Communicative Disorders and Stroke." LC Card 80-601253 DDC 612.8/072073 19
1. Neurology - Research - United States. I. National Institute of Neurological and Communicative Disorders and Stroke. II. Series: United States. National Institutes of Health. Publication, 79-1920.
QP356 .N28 1979

National Aeronautics and Space Administration. see United States. National Aeronautics and Space Administration.

National Affairs, Bureau of, Washington, D. C. see Bureau of National Affairs, Washington, D. C.

A national agenda for the eighties . United States. President's Commission for a National Agenda for the Eighties. Washington , 1980. 214 p. ; LC Card 81-356 DDC 973.926 19
HC106.7 .U577 1980

National Agricultural Library. see United States. National Agricultural Library.

National Agricultural Library (U. S.) Guide to sources for agricultural and biological research /. Berkeley , c1981. p. cm. ISBN 0-520-03226-8 LC Card 76-7753 DDC 016.63 19
Z5071 .G83 S493

National Air and Space Museum.
Aircraft of the National Air and Space Museum, Smithsonian Institution / compiled by Claudia M. Oakes. Washington, D.C. : Smithsonian Institution Press, 1981. p. cm. LC Card 81-607991 DDC 629.133/074/0153 19
1. National Air and Space Museum. 2. Airplanes - Catalogs. I. Oakes, Claudia M. II. Title.
TL506.U6 W455 1981

Crouch, Tom D. The Blériot XI, the story of a classic aircraft /. Washington, D.C. , 1981. p. cm. ISBN 0-87474-345-1 LC Card 81-607931 DDC 629.133/343 19
TL686.B6 C76

Space science comes of age . Washington , 1981. xiii, 194 p. : ISBN 0-87474-508-X : LC Card 80-28966 DDC 500.5/09 19
QB500 .S62

NATIONAL AIR AND SPACE MUSEUM.
National Air and Space Museum. Aircraft of the National Air and Space Museum, Smithsonian Institution /. Washington, D.C. , 1981. p. cm. LC Card 81-607991 DDC 629.133/074/0153 19
TL506.U6 W455 1981

National and international energy stabilization policies /. Askari, Hossein. Austin, Tex. [1980] 14, [8] p. ; LC Card 80-622514 DDC 333.79/0973

19
HD9502.U52 A79

National Archives and Records Service documents preservation program and trust fund operation . United States. Congress. House. Committee on Government Operations. Subcommittee on Government Information and Individual Rights. Washington , 1980. v, 913 p. ; LC Card 80-602891 DDC 353.0071/46 19
KF27 .G6628 1979a

The National Archives and Records Service in 1978 /. United States. National Archives and Records Service. [Washington, D.C.] [1979?] 20 p. : LC Card 80-601808 DDC 027.5753 19
CD3023 .U54 1979a

The National Archives celebrates the bicentennial /. United States. General Services Administration. Washington, D. C. , 1975. 15 p. ; *NYPL [*XME-9265]*

National Arthritis Advisory Board. see **United States. National Arthritis Advisory Board.**

National Asphalt Pavement Association. Bright, Richard. Early hardening of asphalt in hot bituminous paving mixtures . [Raleigh] , 1966. vi, 70 p. : LC Card 80-508397 DDC 625.8/5 s 625.8/5 19
TE270 .B67 pt. 2

Bright, Richard. The effect of viscosity of asphalt on the properties of bituminous paving mixtures /. [Raleigh] , 1966. 2 v. : LC Card 80-508426 DDC 625.8/5 19
TE270 .B67

Bright, Richard. Hardening of asphalt in hot bituminous base, binder, and sand mixtures . [Raleigh] , 1966. vi, 83 p. : LC Card 80-508398 DDC 625.8/5 s 625.8/5 19
TE270 .B67 pt. 1

A national assessment of case disposition and classification in the juvenile justice system. Smith, Charles P., 1931- Washington, D.C. , 1979-80. 3 v. : LC Card 80-600043 DDC 364.3/6/0973 19
HV9104 .S6

A national assessment of serious juvenile crime and the juvenile justice system . National Juvenile Justice System Assessment Center (United States) [Washington, D.C.] [1980] 4 v. : LC Card 80-602691 DDC 364.3/6/0973 19
HV9104 .N23 1980

National Association of Extradition Officials (U. S.) Maine. Attorney General's Office. The extradition law report, 1979-1980 /. [Augusta] [1980] xxii, 176 leaves (leaf 176 blank) ; LC Card 80-624020 DDC 345.73/052 347.30552 19
KF9635.A59 M34

National Association of Housing and Redevelopment Officials. (Old Catalog form: National Association of Housing Officials) Designing rehab programs : a local government guidebook / prepared by National Association of Housing and Redevelopment Offic[i]als under contract H-2626 for the U. S. Department of Housing and Urban Development, Office of Policy Development and Research. [Washington, D.C.] : The Office : for sale by the Supt. of Docs., U. S. Govt. Print. Off., 1980. iv, 90, [75] p. : ill. ; 28 cm. "October 1979." LC Card 80-602368 DDC 352.7/5/0973 19
1. Housing rehabilitation - United States. 2. Housing rehabilitation - United States - Finance. I. United States. Dept. of Housing and Urban Development. Office of Policy Development and Research. II. Title.
HD7293 .N3325 1980

National Association of State Directors of Law Enforcement Training. National Symposium on Job-Task Analysis in Criminal Justice, Dallas, 1978. National Symposium on Job-Task Analysis in Criminal Justice . Washington, D.C. , 1979. ix, 465 p. ; LC Card 79-603983 DDC 363.2/2 19
HV8143 .N39 1978

National Association of State Drug Abuse Program Coordinators. TASC, an approach for dealing with the substance abusing offender : guidelines for the development of a treatment alternatives to street crime project / prepared by the National Association of State Drug Abuse Program Coordinators, Inc. Washington : Law Enforcement Assistance

Administration, U. S. Dept. of Justice, 1978 [i.e. 1979] iv, 77, [83] p. : forms ; 28 cm. "Prepared for the Law Enforcement Assistance Administration, Department of Justice, under contract no. J-LEAA-035-75." LC Card 79-602048
1. Drug abuse and crime - United States. 2. Drug abuse - Treatment - United States. 3. Criminal justice, Administration of - United States. 4. Alcoholism and crime - United States. I. United States. Law Enforcement Assistance Administration. II. Title.
HV5825 .N32 1979

National automotive research act . United States. Congress. House. Committee on Interstate and Foreign Commerce. Subcommittee on Energy and Power. Washington , 1980. v, 136 p. ; LC Card 80-602959 DDC 343.73/078629222 19
KF27 .I5542 1980a

National Black Health Providers Task Force on High Blood Pressure Education and Control (U. S.) Final report of the National Black Health Providers Task Force on High Blood Pressure Education and Control. [Bethesda, Md.?] : U. S. Dept. of Health and Human Services, Public Health Service, National Institutes of Health, National Heart, Lung, and Blood Institute, 1980. xiv, 356 p. ; 28 cm. (NIH publication. no. 80-1474) Oct. 1980. Item 507-E-1 Includes bibliographical references. LC Card 80-604146 DDC 362.1/96132/008996073 19
1. Hypertension - United States - Prevention. 2. Afro-Americans - Health and hygiene. I. National Heart, Lung, and Blood Institute. II. Series: DHHS publication, no. (NIH) 80-1474. III. Title.
RA645.H9 N35 1980

Review and response to the final report of the National Black Health Providers Task Force on High Blood Pressure Education and Control. [Bethesda, Md.?] , 1980. vii, 57 p. : LC Card 80-604145 DDC 362.1/9613205/08996073 19
RC685.H8 R43

National Bureau of Standards authorization. United States. Congress. House. Committee on Science and Technology. Subcommittee on Science, Research, and Technology. 1981 National Bureau of Standards authorization . Washington , 1980. iii, 424 p. : LC Card 80-602738 DDC 353.0072/23682/1 19
KF27 .S399 1980a

National Cancer Institute. see **United States. National Cancer Institute.**

National Cancer Institute Symposium on Biohazards and Zoonotic Problems of Primate Procurement, Quarantine, and Research, Frederick Cancer Research Center, 1975. Biohazards and zoonotic problems of primate procurement, quarantine, and research : proceedings of a cancer research safety symposium, conducted at Frederick Cancer Research Center, Frederick, Maryland, March 19, 1975 / scientific editor, M. L. Simmons. [Bethesda, Md. : U. S. Dept. of Health, Education, and Welfare, Public Health Service, National Institutes of Health], 1975. 137 p. : ill. ; 28 cm. (Cancer research safety monograph series . v. 2) DHEW publication ; no. (NIH) 76-890 Includes bibliographies. LC Card 76-600529 DDC 614.4/3 19
1. Primates as carriers of disease - Congresses. 2. Zoonoses - Prevention - Congresses. 3. Primates - Diseases - Congresses. 4. Primates as laboratory animals - Safety measures - Congresses. I. Simmons, M. L. II. United States. National Cancer Institute. III. Title: Biohazards and zoonotic problems of primate procurement ... IV. Series. V. Series: United States. Dept. of Health, Education and Welfare. DHEW publication, no. (NIH) 76-890.
RA641.P7 N37 1975

National Cancer Institute (U. S.) Shimkin, Michael Boris, 1912- Science and cancer /. [Bethesda? Md.] , 1980. viii, 109 p. : LC Card 80-603983 DDC 616.99/4 19
RC263 .S48 1980

National cancer program; Director's report and annual plan. United States. National Cancer Institute. 1979- [Bethesda, Md.]
NYPL [JLM 80-1047]

National Capital Planning Commission. N. C. P. C. see **United States. National Capital Planning Commission.**

National Cartographic Information Center. Aerial photography summary record system. no. 3- ; Aug. 1979- [Reston, Va.]. *NYPL [Map. Div.]*

NATIONAL CEMETERIES, AMERICAN. United States. Congress. House. Committee on Veterans' Affairs. Subcommittee on Compensation, Pension, Insurance, and Memorial Affairs. Review of the operation of the overseas cemeteries and memorials administered by the American Battle Monuments Commission and Arlington National Cemetery, also H.R 6355 and H.R. 6356 . Washington , 1980. iii, 52 p. ; LC Card 80-603070 DDC 343.73/0256 19
KF27 .V43 1980

NATIONAL CEMETERIES - LAW AND LEGISLATION - UNITED STATES. United States. Congress. House. Committee on Veterans' Affairs. Subcommittee on Compensation, Pension, Insurance, and Memorial Affairs. Review of the national cemetery system administered by the Veterans' Administration, also H.R. 6146 . Washington , 1980. iii, 36 p. ; LC Card 80-603344 DDC 353.0086 19
KF27 .V43 1980c

United States. Congress. House. Committee on Veterans' Affairs. Subcommittee on Compensation, Pension, Insurance, and Memorial Affairs. Review of the operation of the overseas cemeteries and memorials administered by the American Battle Monuments Commission and Arlington National Cemetery, also H.R 6355 and H.R. 6356 . Washington , 1980. iii, 52 p. ; LC Card 80-603070 DDC 343.73/0256 19
KF27 .V43 1980

NATIONAL CEMETERIES - UNITED STATES. Heimbuch, Raymond J. Evaluation of alternative interment methods for national cemeteries. Washington, D.C. , 1980. 214 p. in various pagings : LC Card 81-600537 DDC 353.0086 19
UB393 .H44

United States. Congress. House. Committee on Veterans' Affairs. Subcommittee on Compensation, Pension, Insurance, and Memorial Affairs. Review of the national cemetery system administered by the Veterans' Administration, also H.R. 6146 . Washington , 1980. iii, 36 p. ; LC Card 80-603344 DDC 353.0086 19
KF27 .V43 1980c

National Center for Appropriate Technology. (United States.) NCAT brief .
(3) Quammen, David, 1948- Appropriate jobs . Butte, Mont. , c1980. 14 p. : LC Card 80-138213 DDC 331.12/0973 19
HC103.7 .Q35

National Center for Education Statistics. Bulletin. Mar. 1979- Washington.
NYPL [Econ. Div.]

The condition of education for Hispanic Americans / by George H. Brown ... [et al.]. [Washington] : U. S. Dept. of Health, Education, and Welfare, Education Division, National Center for Education Statistics : for sale by the Supt. of Docs., U. S. Govt. Print. Off., [1980] xviii, 268 p. : ill. ; 26 cm. Includes bibliographical references. LC Card 80-602546 DDC 371.97/68/073 19
1. Hispanic Americans - Education. I. Brown, George Haskell, 1922-. II. Title.
LC2669 .N37 1980

Crain, Robert L. The influence of high school racial composition on Black college attendance and test performance /. [Washington] , 1978, c1979 printing. xix, 143 p. ; LC Card 79-601911 *LC146 .C72 1978* *NYPL [JLF 81-370]*

Directory of Federal agency education data tapes /. [Washington, D.C.] [1980] ix, 229 p. : LC Card 80-602708 *L901 .F4165 1980* *NYPL [JFF 81-84]*

Eckland, Bruce Kent. A capsule description of young adults four and one-half years after high school /. [Washington, D.C.] , 1979. ix, 34 p. : LC Card 80-601549 DDC 305.2/3/0973 19
HQ799.7 .E3

Mushkin, Selma J., 1913- Indicators of youth

unemployment and education in industrialized nations /. [Washington] , 1978. v, 181 p. : LC Card 79-602354
HD6270 .M87   ***NYPL [JLG 81-24]***

Research Triangle Institute. Center for Educational Research and Evaluation. Tabular summary of the third follow-up questionnaire data /. [Washington] , 1978. 4 v. ; LC Card 79-602292
LA229 .R46 1978a

Sponsored reports series - National Center for Education Statistics.
Eckland, Bruce Kent. A capsule description of young adults four and one-half years after high school /. [Washington, D.C.] , 1979. ix, 34 p. : LC Card 80-601549 DDC 305.2/3/0973 19
HQ799.7 .E3

Williams, Jeffrey W. Students and schools /. [Washington] , 1979. viii, 85 p. : LC Card 79-602036
LC69 .W54   ***NYPL [JLF 81-365]***

National Center for Educational Statistics.
Veltman, Calvin J. The role of language characteristics in the socioeconomic attainment process of Hispanic origin men and women /. [Washington, D.C.?] , 1980. iv, 103 p. ; LC Card 81-601023 DDC 305.8/68073 19
E184.S75 V44

National Center for Health Services Research.
Emergency medical services systems research project abstracts. [Hyattsville, Md.]
NYPL [JLM 80-873]

Experiments in interviewing techniques . Ann Arbor , 1979. 444 p. : ISBN 0-87944-247-6 LC Card 79-53851
RA408.5 .E96   ***NYPL [JLF 81-173]***

NCHSR research proceedings series.
Symposium on a Review and Critique of Cost Accounting for Pharmaceutical Services, New York, 1977. Cost accounting for pharmaceutical services . Hyattsville, Md. [1980] v, 70 p. : LC Card 80-602830 DDC 362.1/7 19
RS92 .S96 1977

NCHSR research report series.
Sudman, Seymour. Health care surveys using diaries /. Hyattsville, Md. [1980] vii, 123, [173] p. : LC Card 80-600121 DDC 362.1/0723 19
RA408.5 .S9

National Center for Health Services Research and Development. Boston Consulting Group. Financial planning in ambulatory health programs /. [Washington] , 1973. xi, 243 p.;
NYPL [JLF 80-714]

National Center for Health Statistics. see United States. National Center for Health Statistics.

National Center for Health Statistics (U. S.)
Feller, Barbara A. Health characteristics of persons with chronic activity limitation . Hyattsville, Md. , 1981. p. cm. ISBN 0-8406-0229-4 LC Card 81-11249 DDC 312/.0973 s 312/.3 19
RA407.3 .A346 no. 137 RA644.6

Foster, Jean. Family planning visits by teenagers, United States, 1978 /. Hyattsville, Md. , 1981. p. cm. ISBN 0-8406-0227-8 LC Card 81-11090 DDC 362.1/1/0973 s 362.1/2 19
RA407.3 .A349 no. 58 HQ766.5.U5

Hing, Esther. Use of health services by women 65 years and over. Hyattsville, Md. [1981] p. cm. LC Card 81-607865 DDC 362.1/1/0973 s 362.1/9/0880565 19
RA407.3 .A349 no. 59 RA408.W65

Schoenborn, Charlotte A. Basic data from Wave I of the National survey of personal health practices and consequences . Hyattsville, Md. , 1981. p. cm. ISBN 0-8406-0230-8 LC Card 81-11274 DDC 614.4/273 19
RA407.3 .S36

Taffel, Selma. Interval between births, United States, 1970-1977 . Hyattsville, Md. [1981] p. cm. ISBN 0-8406-0223-5 LC Card 81-9575 DDC 312/.1/73 s 312/.1/73 19
HA211 .A3 no. 39 HB902

National Center for Productivity and Quality of Working Life.

Directory of productivity and quality of working life centers. Washington : National Center for Productivity and Quality of Working Life, 1978. viii, 68 p. ; 27 cm. Includes bibliographical references. LC Card 79-602026
1. Industrial productivity centers - United States - Directories. 2. Labor and laboring classes - Research - United States - Directories. I. Title. II. Title: Quality of working life centers.
HC110.I52 N37 1978a

Productivity and job security : attrition--benefits and problems. Washington : National Center for Productivity and Quality of Working Life : for sale by Supt. of Docs., U. S. Govt. Print. Off., 1977. vii, 116 p. ; 24 cm. Bibliography: p. 111-116. LC Card 77-604826
1. Job security - United States - Case studies. 2. Unemployment, Technological - United States - Case studies. 3. Collective labor agreements - United States - Case studies. I. Title.
HD6331.2.U5 N37 1977

Starting a labor-management committee in your organization : some pointers for action. Washington : National Center for Productivity and Quality of Working Life : for sale by the Supt. of Docs., U. S. Govt. Print. Off., 1978. 55 p. ; 27 cm. Bibliography: p. 47-50. LC Card 78-603560
1. Labor-management committees - United States. 2. Industrial productivity - United States. I. Title.
HD6490.L33 N37 1978

National Center for Research in Vocational Education (U. S.) Career and labor market information . Columbus, Ohio , Washington, D.C. [1980] v, 71 p. ; LC Card 80-602937 DDC 331.12/0973 19
HD5724 .C33

National Center for the Study of Collective Bargaining in Higher Education. Douglas, Joel M. Contract development in higher education . [New York] , c1980. iv leaves, 363 p. : LC Card 80-139146 DDC 331.89/0413712/0973 19
LB2335.885.U6 D68

National Center on Child Abuse and Neglect.
National Conference on Child Abuse and Neglect, 2d, Houston, Tex., 1977. Child abuse and neglect . [Washington] 1978. 2 v. : LC Card 78-603476
HV881 .N35 1977   ***NYPL [JLM 81-191]***

Selected readings on mother-infant bonding. [Washington, D.C. , 1979] 115 p. : LC Card 79-604305 DDC 306.8/7 19
HQ759 .S44

NATIONAL CHARACTERISTICS, AMERICAN - ADDRESSES, ESSAYS, LECTURES.
Boorstin, Daniel Joseph, 1914- The fertile verge . Washington , 1980. 19 p. ; ISBN 0-8444-0357-1 (pbk.) LC Card 80-27815 DDC 973 19
E169.1 .B693

NATIONAL CHARACTERISTICS, GREEK.
Herzfeld, Michael, 1947- Ours once more . Austin , 1981. p. cm. ISBN 0-292-76018-3 LC Card 81-10398 DDC 398/.09495 19
GR170 .H47

National Clearinghouse for Alcohol Information.
Occupational alcoholism programs bibliography / developed by National Clearinghouse for Alcohol Information, U. S. Department of Health, Education, and Welfare, Public Health Service, Alcohol, Drug Abuse, and Mental Health Administration, National Institute on Alcohol Abuse and Alcoholism. Rockville, Md. : The Clearinghouse, 1980. iii, 42 p. ; 24 cm. (DHEW publication ; no. (ADM) 80-943) LC Card 80-602280 DDC 016.6583/822 19
1. Alcoholism and employment - Bibliogrpahy. I. Series: United States. Dept. of Health, Education and Welfare. DHEW publication, no. (ADM) 80-943. II. Title.
Z7164.C81 N257 1980 HF5549.5.A4

National Clearinghouse for Human Genetic Diseases. Clinical genetic service centers : a national listing. [Rockville, Md.] : U. S. Dept. of Health and Human Services, Public Health Service, Health Services Administration, Bureau of Community Health Services, [1980] iii, 117 p. ; 29 cm. (DHHS publication ; no. (HSA) 80-5135) Cover title. LC Card 80-602604 DDC 362.1/96042/02573 19
1. Medical genetics - United States - Societies, etc. -

Directories. 2. Genetic counseling - United States - Directories. I. Series: United States. Dept. of Health and Human Services. DHHS publication, no. (HSA) 80-5135. II. Title.
RB155 .N37 1980

National Clearinghouse for Smoking and Health. Program Research Branch.
Teenage smoking. Green, Dorothy E. Teenage smoking : immediate and long-term patterns / prepared by Dorothy E. Green, Chilton Research Services. Washington, D.C. [1979] ix, 259 p. ; LC Card 80-601231 DDC 362.2/9 19
HV5745 .G74

National Clearinghouse on Aging. Human resource issues in the field of aging : the nursing home industry. Rev. [Washington, D.C.] : U. S. Dept. of Health, Education, and Welfare, Office of Human Development Services, Administration on Aging, National Clearinghouse on Aging : for sale by the Supt. of Docs., U. S. Govt. Print. Off., [1980] v, 20 p. : graphs ; 27 cm. (AoA occasional papers in gerontology ; no. 1) HEW publication ; no. (OHDS) 80-20093 "Prepared by Chester Levine." Published in 1976 under title: Manpower needs in the field of aging. Includes bibliographical references. LC Card 80-602117 DDC 331.12/913621/60973 19
1. Nursing homes - United States - Employees - Supply and demand - Statistics. 2. Nursing homes - United States - Statistics. I. Levine, Chester. II. Series: United States. Administration on Aging. AoA occasional papers in gerontology , no. 1. III. Title.
RA997 .N375 1980

National Clearinghouse on Domestic Violence.
Domestic violence: information series. June, 1980 Rockville, Md.   ***NYPL [Per. Div.]***

National Climatic Center. Butson, Keith D. Selective guide to climatic data sources . Washington [1979] xvi, 142 p. : LC Card 80-602294 DDC 551.5 s 016.5516 19
Z6685 .U64 no. 4.11 1979 Z6683.C5 QC981

The national coal production, distribution, and utilization act of 1980 . United States. Congress. Senate. Committee on Energy and Natural Resources. Washington , 1980. iv, 435 p. : LC Card 80-603714 DDC 343.73/07752 347.3037752 19
KF26 .E55 1980d

National Coastal Ecosystems Team.
Beak Consultants, Portland, Or. Biological impacts of minor shoreline structures on the coastal environment . Washington, D.C. [1980- v. : LC Card 80-602540 DDC 574.5/2638 19
QH541.5.C65 B4 1980

Environmental planning for offshore oil and gas /. [Washington] , 1978. 5 v. in 9 : LC Card 78-601850
TD195.P4 E58   ***NYPL [JSK 81-30]***

Miglarese, John V. Ecological characterization of the sea island coastal region of South Carolina and Georgia . [Washington, D.C.] [1979] x, 35 p. : LC Card 80-601523 DDC 574.5/267/09757 19
QH105.S6 M53

Peterson, Charles Henry. The ecology of intertidal flats of North Carolina . Slidell, LA , 1979 [i.e. 1980] vi, 73 p. : LC Card 80-601522 DDC 574.5/2636 19
QH105.N8 P45

Rowlett, Richard A. Observations of marine birds and mammals in the northern Chesapeake Bight /. [Washington, D.C.] , 1980. xii, 87 p. : LC Card 80-602344 DDC 598.2975 19
QL683.A87 R68

Willdan Associates. Mississippi Deltaic Plain Region ecological characterization . [Washington] [1980- v. <1> : LC Card 80-603159 DDC 330.9763/3063 19
HC108.N42 W54 1980

National Coastal Ecosystems Team (U. S.) Texas barrier islands region ecological characterization . Washington, D.C.?] , 1980. 2 v. : LC Card 81-600915 DDC 333.91/09764/1 19
QH105.T4 T52

National Collection of Fine Arts. see Smithsonian Institution. National Collection of Fine Arts.

National College of Criminal Defense Lawyers and Public Defenders. The National journal of criminal defense. v. 1- spring 1975- [Houston,] LC Card 75-646015
NYPL [JLM 80-803]

National Commission for Employment Policy (United States.).
Special report - National Commission for Employment Policy .
(no. 35) Ginzberg, Eli, 1911- Tell me about your school . Washington, D.C. [1979] 79 p. ; LC Card 80-602363 DDC 371.8/1 19
LA339.N5 G48

National Commission for Manpower Policy, the first five years, 1974-1979 : a report / [compiled] by Eli Ginzberg. Washington, D.C. : National Commission for Employment Policy, 1979 [i.e. 1980] ii, 166 p. ; 28 cm. (Special report - National Commission for Employment Policy ; no. 36) LC Card 80-602132 DDC 353.0083/06 19
1. United States. National Commission for Manpower Policy. 2. Manpower policy - United States - History - Sources. I. Ginzberg, Eli, 1911-. II. United States. National Commission for Manpower Policy. III. Series: United States. National Commission for Employment Policy. Special report - National Commission for Employment Policy , no. 36.
HD5724 .N22

National Commission for the Protection of Human Subjects of Biomedical and Behavioral Research. see United States. National Commission for the Protection of Human Subjects of Biomedical and Behavioral Research.

Bibliographic series. see Bibliographic series.
Bibliographic series. see Bibliographical series.

National Commission on Libraries and Information Science. see United States. National Commission on Libraries and Information Science.

National Commission on Productivity and Work Quality. International City Management Association. Jurisdictional guide to productivity improvement projects . Washington , 1975. 1 v. ;
NYPL [JLF 80-1181]

National Commission on Water Quality. The Chesapeake Bay . Gloucester Point, Va. [1975] 2 v. : LC Card 80-621270 DDC 363.7/3942/0916347 19
TD223.1 .C44

National Committee Against Discrimination in Housing. Guide to fair housing law enforcement by metro fair housing centers and other local fair housing groups / prepared by the National Committee Against Discrimination in Housing, Inc. [Washington, D.C.] : U. S. Dept. of Housing and Urban Development, Office of Policy Development and Research, 1979. 64 p. ; 28 cm. "July 1979." "HUD-PDR-491." Bibliography: p. 52. LC Card 80-601837 DDC 363.5/1 19
1. Discrimination in housing - United States. I. Title.
HD7288.76.U5 N37 1979

National Community Development Association. United States Conference of Mayors. The private development process . [Washington] [1979] iii, 49 p. ; LC Card 79-601943
HD259 .U53 1979

National Conference of Senior Officials to Consider Unesco Recommendations on Physical Education and Sport, Washington, D.C., 1977. Report of the National Conference of Senior Officials to Consider Unesco Recommendations on Physical Education and Sport, held in Washington, D.C., November 16-18, 1977. [Washington] : U. S. Dept. of Health, Education, and Welfare, Office of Education, 1979. vii, 143 p. ; 27 cm. LC Card 80-601246 DDC 613.7 19
1. Physical education and training - Congresses. 2. Sports - Congresses. I. United States. Office of Education.
GV205 .N234 1977

National Conference of State Legislatures. Strengthening the legislative process : an agenda for improvement : recommendations. Denver, Colo. (1124 17th St., Suite 1500, Denver 80202) : National Conference of State Legislatures, [1980?] 32 p. ; 23 x 11 cm. Cover title. LC Card 81-621044 DDC 328.73 19

1. Legislative bodies - United States - States. I. Title.
JK2495 .N37 1980

Transferable development rights . [Trenton] [1979?] xi, 340 p. ; LC Card 80-622361 DDC 346.7304/5 19
KF5698.5.A75 T7

National Conference of States on Building Codes and Standards.
National Conference of States on Building Codes & Standards. NBS/NCSBCS Joint Conference on Research and Innovation in the Building Regulatory Process, 3d, Annapolis, 1978. Research and innovation in the building regulatory process . Washington , 1979. x, 360 p. : LC Card 79-600090 DDC 602/.18 s 343.73/07869 19
QC100 .U57 no. 552 KF5701

Silver, Larry. Directory of State building codes & regulations /. Mclean, Va. , c1980. ca. 100 p. in various pagings : LC Card 80-124004 DDC 016.3467304/5 016.34730645 19
KF5701.Z95 S5

National Conference on Career Education, Commissioner's. see Commissioner's National Conference on Career Education, Houston, Tex., 1976.

National Conference on Child Abuse and Neglect, 2d, Houston, Tex., 1977. Child abuse and neglect : issues on innovation and implementation : proceedings of the second annual National Conference on Child Abuse and Neglect, April 17-20, 1977 / edited by Michael L. Lauderdale, Rosalie N. Anderson, Stephen E. Cramer. [Washington : National Center on Child Abuse and Neglect, Children's Bureau, Administration for Children, Youth, and Families, Office of Human Development Services, U. S. Dept. of Health, Education, and Welfare], 1978. 2 v. : ill. ; 27 cm. (DHEW publication (OHDS) 78-30147-78-30148) Includes bibliographies. LC Card 78-603476
1. Child abuse - United States - Congresses. 2. Child abuse - Services - United States - Congresses. I. Lauderdale, Michael L. II. Anderson, Rosalie N. III. Cramer, Stephen E. IV. National Center on Child Abuse and Neglect. V. Title.
HV881 .N35 1977   NYPL [JLM 81-191]

National Conference on Diabetes : Current Status and Future Directions, Reston, Va., 1979. Report of the National Conference on Diabetes : Current Status and Future Directions, October 9-12, 1979, Sheraton International Conference Center, Reston, Virginia : appendix to the third Annual report of the National Diabetes Advisory Board / sponsored by the National Diabetes Advisory Board. [Bethesda, Md.] : U. S. Dept. of Health and Human Services, Public Health Service, National Institutes of Health, [1980] xxx, 170 p. ; 28 cm. (NIH publication ; no. 80-2073) "April 1980." Bibliography: p. 109-111. LC Card 80-602553 DDC 616.4/62 19
1. Diabetes - Congresses. 2. Diabetes - Research - United States - Congresses. I. United States. National Diabetes Advisory Board. Annual report. II. United States. National Diabetes Advisory Board. III. Series: United States. National Institutes of Health. Publication, no. 80-2073.
RC660 .N37 1979

National Conference on Health Promotion Programs in Occupational Settings, Washington, D.C., 1979. Proceedings of the National Conference on Health Promotion Programs in Occupational Settings, January 17, 18, and 19, 1979 / conference coordinator and editor, Alice M. McGill, editorial board members, James E. Bernstein ... [et al.]. Washington, D.C. : U. S. Dept. of Health, Education, and Welfare, Public Health Service, Office of the Assistant Secretary for Health, [1979] xii, 69 p. ; 23 cm. LC Card 80-600621 DDC 362.1/0883317 19
1. Industrial hygiene - United States - Congresses. I. McGill, Alice M. II. Bernstein, James E. III. United States. Office of the Assistant Secretary for Health. IV. Title.
HD7654 .N28 1979

National Conference on Measurements of Laser Emissions for Regulatory Purposes, Rockville, Md., 1974. National Conference on Measurements of Laser Emissions for Regulatory Purposes : proceedings of a conference held in Rockville, Maryland, June

4-7, 1974 / edited by Robert H. James ; cosponsored by National Bureau of Standards and U. S. Dept. of Health, Education, and Welfare, Public Health Service, Food and Drug Administration, Bureau of Radiological Health. [Rockville, Md.] : The Bureau ; Washington : for sale by the Supt. of Docs., U. S. Govt. Print. Off., 1976 i.e. 1977. vii, 255 p. : ill. ; 27 cm. (HEW publication. (FDA) 76-8037) LC Card 77-602983 DDC 535.5/8 19
1. Laser beams - Measurement - Standards - Congresses. I. James, Robert H. II. United States. National Bureau of Standards. III. United States. Bureau of Radiological Health. IV. Series: United States. Dept. of Health, Education and Welfare. DHEW publication, (FDA) 76-8037.
QC689.5.L37 N37 1974

National Conference on Medical Education in Alcohol and Drug Abuse, Washington, D.C., 1977. Alcohol and drug abuse in medical education /. Rockville, Md. , Washington, D.C. , 1980. ix, 131 p. ; LC Card 80-602242 DDC 616.86/007/11 19
RC565 .A37

National Conference on Mental Health Issues Related to Sudden Infant Death Syndrome, Baltimore, Md., 1977. Mental health issues in grief counseling : summary of proceedings, National Conference on Mental Health Issues Related to Sudden Infant Death Syndrome, February 23-25, 1977, Friendship International Hotel, Baltimore, Maryland / Stanley E. Weinstein, editor and conference coordinator. Rockville, Md. : U. S. Dept. of Health, Education, and Welfare, Public Health Service, Health Services Administration, Bureau of Community Health Services ; Washington, D.C. : for sale by the Supt. of Docs., U. S. Govt. Print. Off., 1979 i.e. 1980. 133 p. ; 28 cm. (DHEW publication ; no. (HSA) 80-5264) Includes bibliographies. LC Card 80-602299 DDC 362.8/286 19
1. Sudden death in infants - Psychological aspects - Congresses. 2. Bereavement - Psychological aspects - Congresses. 3. Grief - Congresses. 4. Parent and child - Congresses. 5. Counseling - Congresses. I. Weinstein, Stanley E. II. Series: United States. Dept. of Health, Education and Welfare. DHEW publication, no. (HSA) 80-5264. III. Title.
RJ59 .N37 1977

National Conference on Numerical Methods in Heat Transfer. Proceedings. 1st- ; 1979- [College Park, Md.] "Sponsored jointly by the office of Naval Research and the Department of Mechanical Engineering, University of Maryland at College Park."
1. Heat - Transmission - Congresses. 2. Numerical analysis - Congresses. I. United States. Office of Naval Research. II. Maryland. University. Dept. of Mechanical Engineering.   NYPL [JSP 81-105]

National Conference on Regulatory Aspects of Building Rehabilitation, National Bureau of Standards, 1978. Proceedings of the National Conference on Regulatory Aspects of Building Rehabilitation, held at the National Bureau of Standards, October 30, 1978 / Sandra A. Berry, editor. [Washington, D.C.] : U. S. Dept. of Commerce, National Bureau of Standards : for sale by the Supt. of Docs., U. S. Govt. Print. Off., 1979. ix, 201, 30 p. : ill. ; 26 cm. (NBS special publication ; 549) LC Card 79-600095 DDC 602.18 s 343.73/078690/24 19
1. Building laws - United States - Congresses. 2. Buildings - United States - Repair and reconstruction - Congresses. I. Berry, Sandra A. II. Series: United States. National Bureau of Standards Special publication, 549. III. Title.
QC100 .U57 no. 549 KF5701

National Conference on the Interagency R&D Program, 4th, Washington, D.C., 1979. Energy/environment IV : proceedings of the Fourth National Conference on the Interagency Energy/Environment R&D Program, June 7 & 8, 1979, Shoreham Americana Hotel, Washington, DC / sponsored by the Office of Energy, Minerals, and Industry within the Environmental Protection Agency's Office of Research and Development. [Cincinnati, Ohio] : EPA, 1980. v, 330 : ill. ; 28 cm. (The Energy / environment R & D decision series) "EPA 600/9-79-040." "October 1979." Includes bibliographical references and index. LC Card 80-602220 DDC 333.79/0973 19
1. Energy development - United States - Congresses. 2. Environmental protection - United States - Congresses.

7

GOVERNMENT PUBLICATIONS - U.S.: 1981
National Endowment for the Arts Composer/Librettist Program.

I. United States. Environmental Protection Agency. Office of Energy, Minerals, and Industry. II. Series: Energy/environment R&D decision series. III. Title.
TJ163.15 .N37 1979

National Conference on the Interagency Energy / Environment R&D Program.
Energy/environment: proceedings. Washington. illus. 28 cm. (The Energy / environment R & D decision series) "EPA". Conference for 1979- sponsored by U. S. Environmental Portection Agency, Office of Research and Development, Office of Energy, Mineralsand Industry.
1. Energy policy - Environmental aspects - United States - Congresses. 2. Energy facilities - Environmental aspects - United States - Congresses. I. United States. Environmental Protection Agency. Office of Energy, Minerals, and Industry. II. National Conference on the Interagency Energy / Environment R&D Program. Proceedings. III. Title. NYPL [JLM 80-1115]

Proceedings. National Conference on the Interagency Energy / Environment R&D Program. Energy/environment: proceedings. Washington. NYPL [JLM 80-1115]

National Conference on the Interagency R&D Program, 2d Washington, D.C., 1977.
Energy/environment II / Second Annual Conference on the Interagency R&D Program, June 6 and 7, 1977, Sheraton Park Hotel, Washington, D.C.; sponsored by the Office of Energy, Minerals, and Industry within the Environmental Protection Agency's Office of Research and Development. [Cincinnati] : EPA, 1977. v, 563 p., [1] leaf of plates : ill. ; 28 cm. (The Energy / environment R & D decision series) "EPA-600/9-77-012." "EPA-335." Includes bibliographies and index. LC Card 78-603659
1. Energy development - United States - Congresses. 2. Environmental protection - United States - Congresses. I. United States. Environmental Protection Agency. Office of Energy, Minerals, and Industry. II. Title.
TJ163.15 .N37 1977   NYPL [JLF 81-191]

National Conference on Weights and Measures.
Model state laws and regulations / adopted by the National Conference on Weights and Measures. 1979 ed. Washington, D.C. : U. S. Dept. of Commerce, National Bureau of Standards : for sale by the Supt. of Docs., U. S. Govt. Print. Off., [1980] 119 p. in various pagings : maps ; 28 cm. (NBS handbook ; 130) LC Card 79-600214   DDC 343.73/075/02632 19
1. Weights and measures - Law and legislation - United States - States. I. Series: United States. National Bureau of Standards. Handbook, 130. II. Title.
KF1665.Z95 N37 1979

NATIONAL CONSCIOUSNESS. see NATIONALISM.

NATIONAL CONSUMER COOPERATIVE BANK - EMPLOYEES.
United States. Congress. Senate. Committee on Banking, Housing and Urban Affairs. Nominations of Robert E. Herzstein, Frank B. Sollars, Alexis M. Herman, and Alfred R. Marane . Washington , 1980. iii, 78 p. ;   LC Card 80-603063   DDC 353.82 19
KF26 .B39 1980i

United States. Congress. Senate. Committee on Banking, Housing and Urban Affairs. Nomination of Wayman D. Palmer . Washington , 1980. ii, 13 p. ;   LC Card 80-603651   DDC 353.0082/52045 19
KF26 .B39 1980p

National Consumers Foundation (United States.)
Illinois. Office of Consumer Services. A consumer's guide to proceedings before the Illinois Commerce Commission /. [Springfield, IL] 1979. iii, 55 p. :   LC Card 80-621523   DDC 343.773/0929 19
KFI1485.1 .A823

National Cooperative Highway Research Program.
Report .
(222) Virginia. University. Civil Engineering Dept. Bridges on secondary highways and local roads . Washington, D.C. , 1980. 132 p. :   ISBN 0-309-03025-0 (pbk.)   LC Card 80-51497   DDC 625.7 s 624.2 19
TE7 .N25 no. 222 TG153

Summary of progress through 1980 / National Cooperative Highway Research Program. Washington, D.C. (2101 Constitution Avenue, N.W., Washington 20418) : Transportation Research Board, National Research Council,

National Academy of Sciences--National Academy of Engineering, 1980. 168 p. ; 28 cm.   LC Card 81-123734   DDC 625.7/072073 19
1. Highway research - United States. I. Title.
TE23 .N24 1980

National Council of State Boards of Nursing (U. S.) Examination Committee. The State board test pool examination for registered nurse licensure /. Chicago, Ill. , 1981. 122 p. ;   ISBN 0-914091-02-6 (pbk.) :   LC Card 81-6107   DDC 610.73/076 19
RT55 .S73

NATIONAL COUNCIL OF STATE BOARDS OF NURSING (U. S.) - EXAMINATIONS - STUDY GUIDES.
The State board test pool examination for registered nurse licensure /. Chicago, Ill. , 1981. 122 p. ;   ISBN 0-914091-02-6 (pbk.) :   LC Card 81-6107   DDC 610.73/076 19
RT55 .S73

National Council of State Committees for Children and Youth. The States report on children and youth. [Washington? 1960] 232 p. 20 cm. Summary report prepared for the Golden Anniversary White House Conference on Children and Youth.   LC Card 60-61000
1. Child welfare - United States. 2. Youth - United States. I. Golden Anniversary White House Conference on Children and Youth, Washington, D. C., 1960. II. Title. NYPL [JLD 80-3271]

National Council of Teachers of English. United States Postal Service. All about letters /. [Washington, D.C.] [c1979] 64 p. :   LC Card 79-600199   DDC 808.6 19
BJ2101 .U54 1979

National Council on Radiation Protection and Measurements.
Influence of dose and its distribution in time on dose-response relationships for low-let radiations : recommendations of the National Council on Radiation Protection and Measurements. Washington, D.C. : NCRP, 1980. vi, 216 p. : graphs ; 23 cm. (NCRP report. no. 64) Bibliography: p. 177-200. Includes index.   ISBN 0-913392-48-0 (pbk.)   LC Card 80-81304   DDC 591.19/15 19
1. Ionizing radiation - Physiological effect. 2. Ionizing radiation - Dose-response relationship. I. Series: National Council on Radiation Protection and Measurements. NCRP report, no. 64. II. Title.
QP82.2.I53 N37 1980

Management of persons accidentally contaminated with radionuclides : recommendations of the National Council on Radiation Protection and Measurements. Washington, D.C. : NCRP, 1980, c1979. vi, 205 ; 23 cm. (NCRP report ; no. 65) Bibliography: p. 166-192. Includes index.   ISBN 0-913392-49-9 (pbk.)   LC Card 79-91648   DDC 616.9/897 19
1. Radioactive substances - Toxicology. 2. Radioisotopes - Toxicology. I. Series: National Council on Radiation Protection and Measurements. NCRP report, no. 65. II. Title.
RA1231.R2 N26 1979

NCRP report.
(no. 64) National Council on Radiation Protection and Measurements. Influence of dose and its distribution in time on dose-response relationships for low-let radiations . Washington, D.C. , 1980. vi, 216 p. :   ISBN 0-913392-48-0 (pbk.)   LC Card 80-81304   DDC 591.19/15 19
QP82.2.I53 N37 1980

(no. 65) National Council on Radiation Protection and Measurements. Management of persons accidentally contaminated with radionuclides . Washington, D.C. , 1980, c1979. vi, 205 ;   ISBN 0-913392-49-9 (pbk.)   LC Card 79-91648   DDC 616.9/897 19
RA1231.R2 N26 1979

National Council on the Aging. Directory of senior centers and clubs. 1974- Washington.   LC Card 75-643610   NYPL [JLM 80-1123]

National Credit Union Administration. see United States. National Credit Union Administration.

NATIONAL CRIME INFORMATION CENTER (UNITED STATES.)
United States. Congress. Office of Technology Assessment. A preliminary assessment of the National Crime Information Center and the

Computerized Criminal History System. Washington [1978] vii, 84 p. ;   LC Card 78-600164   DDC 025/.06364973 19
HV6791 .U52 1978

National Criminal Justice Reference Service. Cain, Anthony A. Restitution . [Washington, D.C.] [1979 i.e. 1980] vii, 61 p. ;   LC Card 80-601596   DDC 364.6/8 19
HV8688 .C34

NATIONAL DANCES. see FOLK DANCING.

NATIONAL DEBTS. see DEBTS, PUBLIC.

National defense funding levels for fiscal year 1981 . United States. Congress. House. Committee on Armed Services. Subcommittee on Investigations. Washington , 1980. ii, 27 p. ;   LC Card 80-602709   DDC 355.6/22/0973 19
KF27 .A753 1980a

National Defense Transportation Association. Defense transportation journal. v. 23, no. 5- ; Sept./Oct. 1967- [Washington]   NYPL [JSP 81-117 & VWA (Defense transportation journal)]

National Defense University.
National Security Affairs Conference, 6th, National Defense University, 1979. Continuity and change in the eighties and beyond . [Washington, D.C.] , 1979. xiii, 222 p. ;   LC Card 80-601820   DDC 355/.033073 19
UA23 .N248 1979

National Defense University. Research Directorate. Daleski, Richard J. Defense management in the 1980s . Washington, D.C. , 1980. vi, 57 p. :   LC Card 81-600682   DDC 355.6/0973 19
UA23.6 .D34

NATIONAL DEVELOPMENT BANK (U. S.)
United States. Congress. House. Committee on Banking, Finance and Urban Affairs. Subcommittee on General Oversight and Renegotiation. Oversight hearings on National Development Bank legislation . Washington , 1980. iii, 220 p. :   LC Card 81-600651   DDC 346.73/0822 347.306822 19
KF27 .B563 1980

National development plan 1962-68 .
International Bank for Reconstruction and Development. [Washington] , 1966. 44 leaves in various foliations ;   LC Card 78-107098   DDC 338.91 s 354.6690072 19
HG3881 .I602 no. Af-47a HJ2184.7

National Diabetes Information Clearinghouse (U. S.) Diet and nutrition for people with diabetes : selected annotations / prepared by the National Diabetes Information Clearinghouse. [Bethesda, Md.] : U. S. Dept. of Health, Education, and Welfare, Public Health Service, National Institutes of Health, National Institute of Arthritis, Metabolism, and Digestive Diseases, 1979. iii, 58 p. ; 28 cm. (NIH publication ; no. 80-1872) Includes index.   LC Card 80-601526   DDC 016.6164/620654 19
1. Diabetes - Diet therapy - Bibliography. 2. Diabetics - Nutrition - Bibliography. 3. Diabetes - Information services - United States - Directories. I. Series: United States. National Institutes of Health. Publication, no. 80-1872. II. Title.
Z6664.D5 N37 1979 RC662

National directory of drug abuse and alcoholism treatment programs. National Institute on Drug Abuse. Rockville, Md. , Washington, D.C. , 1979. xi, 350 p. ;   LC Card 80-601556   DDC 362.2/9 19
HV5825 .N35 1979

National District Attorneys Association. Prosecutor's responsibility in spouse abuse cases. Washington, D.C. , 1980. 13, 24 [13] p. ;   LC Card 80-602608   DDC 345.73/04555 19
KF9322.A75 P76

National Endowment for the Arts. American Music Center, New York. Compositions, libretti, and translations supported by the National Endowment for the Arts Composer/Librettist Program. New York [1978] 35 p. ;   LC Card 78-109449
ML120.U5 A468

The Cultural post. no. [1]- ; Mar. 1975- [Washington]   NYPL [*ZAN-5360]

National Endowment for the Arts Composer/Librettist Program. American Music Center, New York. Compositions, libretti, and translations supported by the National Endowment for the Arts Composer/Librettist Program. New York [1978] 35 p. ; LC Card 78-109449

ML120.U5 A468

National Endowment for the Arts. Research Division.
Audience development : an examination of selected analysis and prediction techniques applied to symphony and theatre attendance in four southern cities. Washington, D.C. : National Endowment for the Arts, Research Division, 1981. 47 p. ; 28 cm. (National Endowment for the Arts Research Division report ;#14) Bibliography: p. 45-46. ISBN 0-89062-097-0 (pbk.) LC Card 80-600125 DDC 790.2/068/8 19
1. Theater audiences. 2. Public relations - Performing arts. 3. Southern States - Amusements. I. Series: National Endowment for the Arts. Research Division. Research Division report, #14. II. Title.
PN1590.A9 N3 1981

Research Division report.
(#14) National Endowment for the Arts. Research Division. Audience development . Washington, D.C. , 1981. 47 p. ; ISBN 0-89062-097-0 (pbk.) LC Card 80-600125 DDC 790.2/068/8 19
PN1590.A9 N3 1981

National Endowment for the Humanities.
Bicentennial reading, viewing, listening : a program for the American Issues Forum / sponsored by the National Endowment for the Humanities and the American Library Association. Chicago : American Library Association, [1976] [12] p. ; 29 cm. Microfilm.
1. United States - Bibliography. 2. United States - History - Bibliography. I. American Library Association. II. American Issues Forum. III. Title.
NYPL [*ZH-661]

Epstein, Helen, 1947- A study in American pluralism through oral histories of holocaust survivors /. [New York] [1977?] 157, xciv leaves ; LC Card 77-153163
E184.J5 E613   **NYPL [*PXY 80-4926]**

Humanities; newsletter of the National Endowment of the Humanities. v. [1]-8, no. 4; winter 1969/70-June 1978 (incomplete) Washington.   **NYPL [JFM 80-62]**

Pennsylvania. Historical and Museum Commission. Guide to the microfilm of the records of Pennsylvania's revolutionary governments, 1775-1790 (record group 27) in the Pennsylvania State Archives, 54 rolls . Harrisburg , 1978 [c1979] vii, 351 p. ; LC Card 79-624725
E263.P4 P37 1979   **NYPL [ISC 80-2758]**

National Endowment for the Humanities. American Issues Forum. see American Issues Forum.

NATIONAL ENDOWMENT FOR THE HUMANITIES - PERIODICALS.
Humanities; newsletter of the National Endowment of the Humanities. v. [1]-8, no. 4; winter 1969/70-June 1978 (incomplete) Washington.   **NYPL [JFM 80-62]**

National Energy Information Center. Monthly petroleum product price report. Washington.
NYPL [JLM 80-1101]

National Energy Security Corporation . United States. Congress. House. Committee on Interstate and Foreign Commerce. Subcommittee on Energy and Power. Washington , 1980. iv, 559 p. ; LC Card 80-602005 DDC 346.7304/67915 19
KF27 .I5542 1979y

NATIONAL ENERGY SECURITY CORPORATION (U. S.)
United States. Congress. House. Committee on Interstate and Foreign Commerce. Subcommittee on Energy and Power. National Energy Security Corporation . Washington , 1980. iv, 559 p. ; LC Card 80-602005 DDC 346.7304/67915 19
KF27 .I5542 1979y

National Engineering Laboratory (United States). Center for Fire Safety. Conference on Fire Safety for the Handicapped, National Bureau of Standards, 1979. Fire and life safety for the handicapped . Washington, D.C. , 1980. ix, 144 p. ; LC Card 80-600082 DDC 602/.18 s 362.4/38

19
QC100 .U57 no. 585 TH9112

National Environmental Satellite Service. see United States. National Environmental Satellite Service.

National evaluation program : Series B .
(no. 1) System Sciences, inc. Evaluation of treatment alternatives to street crime . [Washington] , 1979. xii, 150 p. ; LC Card 79-602081 DDC 362.2/937/0973 19
HV5825 .S94 1979

National experience in the formulation and implementation of population policy, 1960-1976 /. United Nations. Dept. of Economic and Social Affairs. New York , 1978- v. ; LC Card 78-109255 DDC 300 s 304.6 19
JX1977 .A2 ST/ESA/SER.R/19, etc.

National experience in the formulation and implementation of population policy, 1960-1976 . United Nations. Dept. of International Economic and Social Affairs. New York , 1979. iv, 43 p., [1] leaf of plates : LC Card 80-112443 DDC 300 s 304.6/09598 19
JX1977 .A2 ST/ESA/SER.R/32

A national export policy . Chamber of Commerce of the United States of America. International Dept. Washington, D.C. , c1981. iii, 49 p. ; ISBN 0-89834-037-3 (pbk.) : LC Card 81-67315 DDC 382/.63/0973 19
HF1455 .C47 1981

National Family and Reproductive Health Association. A directory of national health, education, and social service organizations concerned with youth / prepared by National Family Planning and Reproductive Health Association staff ; Vita Threatt-Ellis, project director ; Joanne Barnes, research associate. Rockville, Md. : U. S. Dept. of Health, Education, and Welfare, Public Health Service, Health Services Administration, Bureau of Community Health Services, [1979] 56 p. ; 28 cm. "Grant no. FP-T-300013-01-0." "August 31, 1979." LC Card 80-601714
1. Youth - Services for - United States - Directories. I. Threatt-Ellis, Vita. II. Barnes, Joanne. III. United States. Health Services Administration. Bureau of Community Health Services. IV. Title.
HV741 .N316 1979   **NYPL [JLF 80-1557]**

National Fertilizer Development Center, Muscle Shoals, Ala. see United States. National Fertilizer Development Center, Muscle Shoals, Ala.

NATIONAL FILM BOARD OF CANADA.
Richard, Valliere T., 1952- Norman McLaren, manipulator of movement . Newark [N.J.] , c1981. p. cm. ISBN 0-87413-192-8 LC Card 80-53998 DDC 791.43/023/0924
NC1766.C32 M357 1981

National Fire Academy. Fire investigation handbook /. [Washington, D.C.?] , 1980. ix, 187 p. ; LC Card 80-600095 DDC 363.3/765 19
TH9180 .F48

National Fire Data Center (U. S.) Fire in the United States : deaths, injuries, dollar loss, and incidents at the national, state, and local levels. 1978 ed. Washington : U. S. Dept. of Commerce, U. S. Fire Administration, National Fire Data Center : for sale by the Supt. of Docs., U. S. Govt. Print. Off., 1978. xxi, 252 p. : ill. ; 27 cm. Bibliography: p. 233-235. Includes index. LC Card 79-602273
1. Fires - United States - Statistics. I. Title.
TH9448 .N28 1978

National Fire Data Center (United States.)
Munson, Michael J. Indirect costs of residential fires /. [Washington] , 1979 [i.e. 1980] vi, 30 p. : LC Card 80-602415 DDC 363.3/79 19
TH9445.D9 M86

National Fire Safety and Research Office. see United States. National Fire Safety and Research Office.

National food review. NFR-1- ; 1978-[Washington National Economic Analysis Division of the Economics, Statistics, and Cooperatives Service, U. S. Dept. of Agriculture] illus. 26-28 cm. Quarterly. Supersedes: United States. Dept. of Agriculture. Economic Research Service. National food situation. LC Card 78-643276
1. Produce Trade - United States - Periodicals. 2. Food industry and trade - United States - Periodicals. I.

United States. Dept. of Agriculture. Economics, Statistics, and Cooperatives Service. National Economic Analysis Division.   **NYPL [JLM 80-1081]**

National food situation. United States. Dept. of Agriculture. Economic Research Service. NFS-96-161; May 1961-Sept. 1977. [Washington] 66 no. in 3 v. LC Card 59-33311
NYPL [M-10 6174]

National Foreign Assessment Center (U. S.)
The Cuban economy . Washington, D.C. , 1981. vii, 54 p. : LC Card 81-601904 DDC 330.97291/064 19
HC152.5 .C8

Directory of officials of the Socialist Republic of Vietnam . Washington, D.C. , 1980. xii, 204 p. ; LC Card 81-600559 DDC 354.597002 19
JQ821 .D48

OECD countries . Washington, D.C. [1980] iv, 56 p. ; LC Card 80-604134 DDC 331.13/7 19
HD5707.5 .O43

The OECD steel industries : difficult years ahead / United States of America, Central Intelligence Agency, National Foreign Assessment Center. Washington, D.C. : The Center, [1980] v, 15 p. : graphs ; 27 cm. (A Research paper / United States of America, Central Intelligence Agency, National Foreign Assessment Center) "October 1980." "ER 80-10513." LC Card 80-603610 DDC 338.4/7669142 19
1. Steel industry and trade. I. Series: Research paper (National Foreign Assessment Center (U. S.). II. Title.
HD9510.5 .N26 1980

Some perspectives on oil availability for the non-OPEC LDCs . Washington, D.C. , 1980. viii, 48 p. : LC Card 80-603931 DDC 333.8/23211/091724 19
HD9560.5 .S62

NATIONAL FOUNDATION FOR THE ARTS AND THE HUMANITIES - APPROPRIATIONS AND EXPENDITURES.
United States. Congress. House. Committee on Education and Labor. Subcommittee on Postsecondary Education. Reauthorization of the National Foundation for the Arts and the Humanities act and the Museum services act . Washington , 1980. xii, 1105 p. : LC Card 80-603480 DDC 353.0072/236854 19
KF27 .E369 1980a

NATIONAL FOUNDATION ON THE ARTS AND THE HUMANITIES.
United States. Congress. House. Committee on Education and Labor. Subcommittee on Postsecondary Education. Field hearings on the reauthorization of the National Foundation for the Arts and the Humanities act and the Museum services act . Washington , 1980. xi, 1151 p. : LC Card 80-603320 DDC 353.0085/4 19
KF27 .E369 1980

National Foundation on the Arts and the Humanities. Federal Council on the Arts and the Humanities. see Federal Council on the Arts and the Humanities.

National Foundation on the Arts and the Humanities. National Endowment for the Arts. see National Endowment for the Arts.

National Gallery of Art (Mellon Gallery) Washington, D. C. see United States. National Gallery of Art.

National Gallery of Art of the Smithsonian Institution. see Smithsonian Institution. National Collection of Fine Arts.

National Gallery of Art (U. S.) Thompson, Robert Farris. The four moments of the sun . Washington , 1981. p. cm. ISBN 0-89468-003-X LC Card 81-14033 DDC 730/.09675/10740153 19
NB1099.C6 T5

National gas survey . United States. Federal Power Commission. Transmission, Distribution, and Storage Technical Advisory Task Force on Rate Design. Washington , 1977. ca. 250 p. : LC Card 78-601032
HD9581.U5 U53 1977

National Geophysical and Solar-Terrestrial Data Center. Berry, George W. Thermal springs list for the United States /. Boulder, Colo. , Boulder, Colo. (Code D64, 325 Broadway, Boulder, Colo. 80303) , 1980. 59 p. : LC Card

81-600521   DDC 553.7 19
GB1198.2 .B47

National Guard strength and armories . New York (State). Legislative Commission on Expenditure Review. Albany, N.Y. [1980] S-4, ii, 46 p. :   LC Card 80-621855   DDC 355.3/7/09747 19
UA361 .A52 1980

The National Guard tort claims act . United States. Congress. Senate. Committee on the Judiciary. Subcommittee on the Constitution. Washington , 1980. v, 780 p. ;   LC Card 80-603086   DDC 343.73/013 19
KF26 .J8359 1980

National health insurance working papers -- Department of Health and Human Services. Developing the national health plan . [Washington, D.C.?] , 1980. 2 v. :   LC Card 81-601466   DDC 368.4/2/00973 19
HD7102.U4 D4

National Health Planning Information Center. Mental health planning : an annotated bibliography. [Washington] : U. S. Dept. of Health, Education, and Welfare, Public Health Service, Health Resources Administration, Bureau of Health Planning, National Health Planning Information Center : for sale by the Supt. of Docs., U. S. Govt. Print. Off., [1978] v, 159 p. ; 28 cm. (Health planning bibliography series . 11) DHEW publication ; no. (HRA) 79-14001 "Prepared by Rita Fox." "HRP-0301101." "October 1978."   LC Card 80-601593   DDC 362.2/068 19
1. Mental health planning - Bibliography. I. Fox, Rita, 1920-. II. Series. III. Series: United States. Dept. of Health, Education and Welfare. DHEW publication, no. (HRA) 79-14001. IV. Title.
Z6664.N5 N34 1978 RA790

National Health Service Corps. see United States. National Health Service Corps.

NATIONAL HEALTH SERVICE CORPS (U. S.)
United States. Congress. Senate. Committee on Labor and Human Resources. Subcommittee on Health and Scientific Research. Oversight of the National Health Service Corps . Washington , 1980. iv, 167 p. :   LC Card 81-600609   DDC 362.1/0973 19
KF26 .L274 1980l

National Heart, Lung, and Blood Institute. National Black Health Providers Task Force on High Blood Pressure Education and Control (U. S.) Final report of the National Black Health Providers Task Force on High Blood Pressure Education and Control. [Bethesda, Md.?] , 1980. xiv, 356 p. ;   LC Card 80-604146   DDC 362.1/96132/008996073 19
RA645.H9 N35 1980

Review and response to the final report of the National Black Health Providers Task Force on High Blood Pressure Education and Control. [Bethesda, Md.?] , 1980. vii, 57 p. :   LC Card 80-604145   DDC 362.1/9613205/08996073 19
RC685.H8 R43

National Heart, Lung, and Blood Institute. Division of Lung Diseases. National Heart, Lung, and Blood Institute. Division of Lung Diseases. Task Force on Epidemiology of Respiratory Diseases. Report of Task Force on Epidemiology of Respiratory Diseases . [Bethesda, Md.?] , 1980. vii, 244 p. :   LC Card 81-600681   DDC 614.5/92/00973 19
RA645.R4 N37 1980

National Heart, Lung, and Blood Institute. Division of Lung Diseases. Task Force on Epidemiology of Respiratory Diseases. Report of Task Force on Epidemiology of Respiratory Diseases : state of knowledge, problems, needs / Division of Lung Diseases, National Heart, Lung, and Blood Institute. [Bethesda, Md.?] : U. S. Dept. of Health and Human Services, Public Health Service, National Institutes of Health, 1980. vii, 244 p. : ill., 1 map ; 28 cm. (NIH publication. no. 81-2019) Cover title: Epidemiology of respiratory diseases. Spine title: Task force report on epidemiology of respiratory diseases. "October 1980." Includes bibliographical references.   LC Card 81-600681   DDC 614.5/92/00973 19
1. Respiratory organs - Diseases - United States. 2. Respiratory organs - Diseases - Research - United States. 3. Epidemiology - Research - United States. 4. Lung diseases - United States. 5. Epidemiology - United

States. I. National Institutes of Health (U. S.). II. National Heart, Lung, and Blood Institute. Division of Lung Diseases. III. Title. IV. Title: Task force report on epidemiology of respiratory diseases. V. Title: Epidemiology of respiratory diseases. VI. Series: DHHS publication, no. (NIH) 81-2019.
RA645.R4 N37 1980

National Heart, Lung, and Blood Institute. Hypertension Task Force. Report of the Hypertension Task Force. [Bethesda, Md.] : U. S. Dept. of Health, Education, and Welfare, Public Health Service, National Institutes of Health ; [Washington, D.C. : for sale by the Supt. of Docs., U. S. Govt. Print. Off.], 1979. 9 v. ; 28 cm. (NIH publication ; nos. 79-1623-79-1631) Includes bibliographical references. CONTENTS. - v. 1. General summary and recommendations.--v. 2. Scientific summary and recommendations.--v. 3. Current research and recommendations from the task force subgroups on local and systemic hemodynamics.--v. 4. Current research and recommendations from the task force subgroups on neural control of the circulation, vascular smooth muscle: nerve terminals.--v. 5. Current research and recommendations from the task force subgroups on hypertensive vascular disease, vascular smooth muscle: contractile apparatus.--v. 6. Current research and recommendations from the task force subgroups on pediatrics, genetics.--v. 7. Current research and recommendations from the task force subgroups on prostaglandins, kallikrein-kinin.--v. 8. Current research and recommendations from the task force subgroups on renin-angiotensin-aldosterone, salt and water.--v. 9. Current research and recommendations from the task force subgroups on therapeutics, pregnancy, obesity.   LC Card 80-601819   DDC 616.1/32/072073 19
1. Hypertension - Research - United States. I. Series: United States. National Institutes of Health. Publication, nos. 79-1623-79-1631.
RC685.H8 N38 1979

National Heart, Lung, and Blood Institute. Office of the Director. Joint US-USSR Symposium on Hypertension, 1st, Sochi, Russia, 1978. Proceedings /. [Bethesda, Md.] , Washington, D.C. [1979] xiv, 436 p. :   LC Card 80-601230   DDC 616.1/32 19
RC685.H8 J64 1978

National heritage policy act of 1979 . United States. Congress. Senate. Committee on Energy and Natural Resources. Subcommittee on Parks, Recreation, and Renewable Resources. Washington , 1980. iv, 517 p. :   LC Card 80-603718   DDC 344.73/094 19
KF26 .E5565 1980d

The national highway safety needs report . United States. Dept. of Transportation. Washington , 1976. 148 p. in various pagings :   LC Card 76-601953
HE5614.2 .U56 1976   NYPL [JLF 80-1698]

National HMO census of prepaid plans. United States. Office of Health Maintenance Organization. Rockville, Md. [Washington, D.C.] [1979] 34 p., [3] leaves of plates :   LC Card 80-602548   DDC 368.3/82/00973 19
HG9396 .U55 1979

National household pesticide usage study, 1976-1977 . Savage, Eldon P. Washington, D.C. [1979] cover 1980. ix, 126 p. :   LC Card 80-603384   DDC 363.7/384 19
TX325 .S28

NATIONAL INCOME - UNITED STATES - ACCOUNTING.
United States. Advisory Committee on Gross National Product Data Improvement. Gross national product data improvement project report . Washington , 1979. xii, 204 p. ;   LC Card 79-602253
HC110.I5 U48 1979   NYPL [JLF 81-487]

National Indian civil rights issues. United States. Commission on Civil Rights. Hearing before the United States Commission on Civil Rights . [Washington] [1979- v. ;   LC Card 79-604247   DDC 323.1/197/073 19
E93 .U53 1979a

National Information Center for Special Education Materials. NICSEM mini-index to special education materials : personal and social development for moderately and severely handicapped students. 1st ed. Los Angeles, CA : National Information Center for Educational Media, University of Southern California, 1980. xiv, 53 p. : ill. ; 27 cm.   ISBN

0-89320-046-8 (pbk.) :   LC Card 80-82541   DDC 371.9 19
1. Handicapped children - Education - Audio-visual aids - Indexes. 2. Handicapped children - Education - Classification. 3. Classification - Books - Education. I. Title.
LC4023 .N37 1980a

National Institute for Advance Studies (U. S.) Summary of national hearings of the White House Conference on Families / prepared for White House Conference on Families. Washington, D.C. : National Institute for Advanced Studies, [1980] ca. 150 p. in various pagings ; 28 cm. "April 10, 1980." On cover: National hearings summary.   LC Card 80-602558   DDC 362.8/2/0973 19
1. Family policy - United States - Congresses. I. White House Conference on Families, Washington, D.C., 1979. II. Title.
HQ536 .N39 1980

National Institute for Advanced Studies (U. S.) Viano, Emilio. Victim/witness services . [Washington, D.C.] , 1979. 69 p. ;
HV6250.3.U5 V49   NYPL [JLF 81-398]

National Institute for Juvenile Justice and Delinquency Prevention. National Juvenile Justice System Assessment Center (U. S.) A preliminary national assessment of the status offender and the juvenile justice system . [Washington, D.C.] [1980] xv, 221 p. :   LC Card 80-600044   DDC 364.3/6/0973 19
HV9104 .N23 1980a

National Juvenile Justice System Assessment Center (United States) A national assessment of serious juvenile crime and the juvenile justice system . [Washington, D.C.] [1980] 4 v. :   LC Card 80-602691   DDC 364.3/6/0973 19
HV9104 .N23 1980

Smith, Charles P., 1931- A national assessment of case disposition and classification in the juvenile justice system. Washington, D.C. , 1979-80. 3 v. :   LC Card 80-600043   DDC 364.3/6/0973 19
HV9104 .S6

Smith, Charles P., 1931- A preliminary national assessment of child abuse and neglect and the juvenile justice system . [Washington, D.C.] [1980] c1979. xiv, 154 p. ;   LC Card 80-600045   DDC 362.7/044 19
HV741 .S55 1980

Weis, Joseph G. Jurisdiction and the elusive status offender . Washington, D.C. [1980] c1979. ix, 135 p. :   LC Card 80-602845   DDC 364.3/6/0973 19
HV9104 .W447

National Institute for Occupational Safety and Health. Conference on Occupational Stress, Los Angeles, 1978. New developments in occupational stress . Los Angeles, Calif. [1979] v, 120 p. ;   LC Card 80-621405   DDC 158.7 19
HF5548.85 .C65 1978

NIOSH publications catalog. Cincinnati. 28 cm. (DHHS (NIOSH) publication) Vols. for 1980- published by the institute's Division of Technical Services.
1. National Institute for Occupational Safety and Health - Bibliography - Periodicals. 2. Industrial hygiene - Bibliography - Periodicals. 3. Industrial safety - Bibliography - Periodicals. I. National Institute for Occupational Safety and Health. Division of Technical Services. II. Title.   NYPL [JLM 81-42]

NIOSH research report. Assessment of deep body temperature of workers in hot jobs /. Cincinnati , Washington , 1976. v, 52 p. :   LC Card 80-511613   DDC 612/.014462 19
RC963.5.H4 A88

NIOSH technical report. Occupational exposure to talc containing asbestos . Cincinnati, Ohio , Washington, D.C. , 1980. xiii, 106 p. :   LC Card 80-602295   DDC 363.1/79 19
RC965.A7 O22

Yokel, Felix Y. Recommended technical provisions for construction practice in shoring and sloping of trenches and excavations /. Washington, DC [1980] xvi, 68 p. :   LC Card 80-600068   DDC 690/.02/18 s 624.1/52 19
TA435 .U58 no. 127 TA770

BIBLIOGRAPHIC GUIDE

National Institute for Occupational Safety and Health. (cont.)

10

Yokel, Felix Y. Soil classification for construction practice in shallow trenching /. Washington, D.C. [1980] xiv, 76 p. : LC Card 80-600014 DDC 690/.02/18 s 624.1/51/012 19
TA435 .U58 no. 121 TA710

NATIONAL INSTITUTE FOR OCCUPATIONAL SAFETY AND HEALTH.
United States. Congress. House. Committee on Interstate and Foreign Commerce. Subcommittee on Oversight and Investigations. Data transfer restrictions impede epidemiological research . Washington , c1980 [i.e. 1981] v, 32 p. ; LC Card 81-600797 DDC 363.1/1/0723 19
RA652.4 .U54 1981

NATIONAL INSTITUTE FOR OCCUPATIONAL SAFETY AND HEALTH - BIBLIOGRAPHY - PERIODICALS.
National Institute for Occupational Safety and Health. NIOSH publications catalog. Cincinnati.
NYPL [JLM 81-42]

National Institute for Occupational Safety and Health. Division of Technical Services.
National Institute for Occupational Safety and Health. NIOSH publications catalog. Cincinnati.
NYPL [JLM 81-42]

National Institute for Occupational Safety and Health. Technical Services, Division of. see National Institute for Occupational Safety and Health. Division of Technical Services.

National Institute of Allergy and Infectious Diseases (U. S.) Wilson, Elaine Blume. At the edge of life . [Bethesda, Md.?] , Washington, D.C. , 1980. 75 p. : LC Card 80-604128 DDC 616.9/25 19
RC114.5 .W54

National Institute of Arthritis, Metabolism, and Digestive Diseases. Office of the Associate Director for Arthritis, Bone, and Skin Diseases. Progress against the rheumatic diseases (1967-1977) : a report to the Senate Committee on Appropriations / Office of the Associate Director for Arthritis, Bone, and Skin Diseases, National Institute of Arthritis, Metabolism, and Digestive Diseases. [Bethesda, Md.] : U. S. Dept. of Health, Eudcation [sic] and Welfare, Public Health Service, National Institutes of Health, 1978. vii, 39 p. ; 27 cm. (DHEW publication. no. (NIH) 79-1600) LC Card 79-602034 DDC 616.7/23/0072073 19
1. Rheumatism - Research - United States. I. United States. Congress. Senate. Committee on Appropriations. II. Series: United States. Dept. of Health, Education and Welfare. DHEW publication, no. (NIH) 79-1600. III. Title.
RC927 .N38 1978

National Institute of Dental Research. see United States. National Institute of Dental Research.

National Institute of Drug Abuse.
NIDA research monograph series .
(25) Behavioral analysis and treatment of substance abuse /. Rockville, Md. , Washington, D.C. , 1979. viii, 256 p. : LC Card 79-600111 DDC 616.86 19
RC563.2 .B42

National Institute of Education.
Bose, Christine E. The relationship between women's studies, career development, and vocational choice /. Washington, D.C. , 1980. xi, 59 p. ; LC Card 80-602291 DDC 305.4/2/072073 19
HQ1181.U5 B67

Education finance and organization research perspectives for the future . Washington, D.C. [1980] v, 274 p. : LC Card 80-602666 DDC 379.73 19
LB2825 .E25

Gross, Ronald. Future directions for open learning . Washington, D.C. : [Lincoln, Neb.] : x, 82 p. : LC Card 80-601828 DDC 378/.1554/0973 19
LC6251 .G75

JWK International Corporation. Summary and recommendations . Washington , 1978. iii leaves, 46, 5, 227 p. ; LC Card 78-602799
E184.O6 J18 1978 NYPL [JLF 81-294]

Lawyers' Committee for Civil Rights Under

Law. State legal standards for the provision of public education . Washington , 1978. 153 p. ; LC Card 79-600821
KF4120 .L37 NYPL [JLF 81-35]

McCoy, Marilyn. Higher education financing in the fifty states . Washington , 1979. xvii, 221 p. : LC Card 78-21570
LB2342 .M18 1979 NYPL [JLG 81-15]

School crime and disruption . Washington , 1978. v, 195 p. ; LC Card 79-602563
LB3249 .S37 NYPL [JLF 81-295]

Testing, teaching, and learning . Washington, D.C. , 1979. vii, 391, [43] p. : LC Card 80-601554 DDC 371.2/6/0973 19
LB3051 .T443

National Institute of Education. Program on Educational Policy and Organization. Green, Dorothy E. Teenage smoking . Washington, D.C. [1979] ix, 259 p. ; LC Card 80-601231 DDC 362.2/9 19
HV5745 .G74

NATIONAL INSTITUTE OF HANDICAPPED RESEARCH - EMPLOYEES.
United States. Congress. Senate. Committee on Labor and Human Resources. Nomination . Washington , 1980. ii, 76 p. ; LC Card 80-603359 DDC 353.0084/4 19
KF26 .L27 1980f

National Institute of Justice (U. S.)
Brousseau, Bill. Affirmative action, equal employment opportunity in the criminal justice system . [Washington, D.C.] [1980] vii, 49 p. ; LC Card 80-602931 DDC 016.33113/3 19
HV8143 .B76

Caplan, Marc H. Police manpower management . Washington, D.C. , 1980. vii, 50 p. ; LC Card 81-601200 DDC 350.74/068/ 19
HV8141 .C34

Newman, Oscar. Factors influencing crime and instability in urban housing developments /. Washington, D.C. , 1980. xiii, 302 p. : LC Card 81-600762 DDC 364.2/2 19
HD7293 .N485

Petersilia, Joan. The prison experience of career criminals /. Washington, D.C. , 1980. xviii, 87 p. : LC Card 81-601009 DDC 365/.66 19
HV9304 .P44

Rubinstein, Michael L. Alaska bans plea bargaining /. Washington, D.C. , 1980. viii, 312 p. : LC Card 81-601045 DDC 345.798/072 347.980572 19
KFA1778.5 .R8

National Institute of Justice (U. S.). Office of Development, Testing, and Dissemination. Carrow, Deborah. Crime victim compensation /. [Washington, D.C.] [1980] i, 235 p. : LC Card 80-602243 DDC 362.8/8 19
HV6250.3.U5 C37

National Institute of Justice (United States.) Levine, Mark. Standards of care in adult and juvenile correctional institutions . Washington, D.C. , 1980. vii, 40 p. ; LC Card 80-602119 DDC 016.365/973/0218 19
HV9304 .L44

National Institute of Justice (United States.). Office of Development, Testing, and Dissemination.
Nelson, Elmer K. Unification of community corrections /. Washington, D.C. , 1980. vi, 164 p. : LC Card 80-602244 DDC 364.6/8 19
HV9304 .N45

Program models - National Institute of Justice, Office of Development, Testing, and Dissemination.
Nelson, Elmer K. Unification of community corrections /. Washington, D.C. , 1980. vi, 164 p. : LC Card 80-602244 DDC 364.6/8 19
HV9304 .N45

National Institute of Law Enforcement and Criminal Justice.
Abt Associates. Arson prevention and control /. [Washington, D.C.] [1980] vii, 167 p. : LC Card 80-601661 DDC 364.4/6 19
HV6638 .A27 1980

Allen, Harry E. Critical Issues in Adult Probation . Washington, D.C. , 1979. vii, 289 p. ; LC Card 79-604144 DDC 364.6/3/0973 19
HV9304 .A64

Arson and arson investigation . [Washington] ,

1977. xvii, 132 p. : LC Card 78-601941
HV8079.A7 A77 NYPL [JLF 81-179]

Boston, Guy D. Crime against the elderly . [Washington] , 1977. vii, 81 p. ; LC Card 78-601970
HV6250.4.A34 B66

Boston, Guy D. Techniques for project evaluation . [Washington] , 1977. vii, 70 p. ; LC Card 79-602173 DDC 364/.973/072 19
HV8138 .B587

Burpo, John H. Police unions in the civil service setting /. Washington D.C. , 1979. v, 38 p. ; LC Card 80-601834 DDC 352/.005173/0973 19
HV7936.P47 B87

Cain, Anthony A. Restitution . [Washington, D.C.] [1979 i.e. 1980] vii, 61 p. ; LC Card 80-601596 DDC 364.6/8 19
HV8688 .C34

Carrow, Deborah. Rape, guidelines for a community response /. [Washington, D.C.] [1980] iii, 296 p. : LC Card 80-601822 DDC 362.8/8 19
HV6561 .C37

Colton, Kent W. Police and computer technology . Washington, D.C. [1979] vii, 68 p. ; LC Card 80-601840 DDC 363.2/028/54 19
HV7936.A8 C58

Corruption in land use and building regulation : program for the study of corruption in local government / U. S. Department of Justice, Law Enforcement Assistance Administration, National Institute of Law Enforcement and Criminal Justice. [Washington, D.C.] : The Institute : for sale by the Supt. of Docs., U. S. Govt. Print. Off., 1979. 2 v. ; 28 cm. Includes bibliographies. CONTENTS. - v. 1. An integrated report of conclusions.--v. 2. Appendix: case studies of corruption and reform. LC Card 79-604180
1. Zoning - United States. 2. Zoning law - United States. 3. Land use - Law and legislation - United States. 4. Building laws - United States. 5. Corruption investigation - United States. I. Title.
HT169.7 .N35 1979

Crime and disruption in schools : a selected bibliography / compiled by Robert Rubel ... [et al.]. Washington, D.C. : United States Dept. of Justice, Law Enforcement Assistance Administration, National Institute of Law Enforcement and Criminal Justice : for sale by the Supt. of Docs., U. S. Govt. Print. Off., 1979. vii, 104 p. : ill. ; 26 cm. LC Card 80-601518 DDC 371.5/8/0973 19
1. School violence - United States. 2. School vandalism - United States. I. Rubel, Robert J. II. Title.
LB3013.3 .N375 1979

Epstein, Sidney. Guidelines for police performance appraisal, promotion and placement procedures. [Washington] , 1973. xiii, 57 p. ; LC Card 74-167251
NYPL [JLF 80-658]

Fletcher, Thomas W., 1924- An anticorruption strategy for local governments . Washington, D.C. , 1979. xi, 55 p. ; LC Card 79-603981
JS401 .F57 NYPL [JLF 81-280]

Fowler, Floyd J. Reducing residential crime and fear . Washington, D.C. , 1979. xxiii, 309 p. : LC Card 80-601262 DDC 364.4/0458/097463 19
HV6795.H3 F68

Greisinger, George W. Civil service systems . Washington, D.C. [1979] xxii, 141, [64] p. : LC Card 80-601604 DDC 352.2/0973 19
HV7935 .G73

Guidelines for developing an injury and damage reduction program in municipal police departments. A manual of recommended methods for managing and operating an injury and damage reduction program. Washington, 1973. 122 p.: illus. 26 cm. LC Card 75-102799
1. Accidents. 2. Police. I. Title.
NYPL [JLF 80-592]

Illegal corporate behavior /. [Washington] , 1979. xxxii, 314 p. ; LC Card 79-603988 DDC 364.1/68/0973 19
HV6769 .I44

Kansas City, Mo. Police Dept. Response time analysis /. Washington , 1978. 2 v. : LC Card 79-603050
HV8148.K22 K34 1978

Ku, Richard. A university's approach to delinquency prevention . [Washington] , 1977. ii, 128 p. ; LC Card 77-602177
HV9106.U7 K8   **NYPL** *[JLF 81-166]*

Lyman, Theodore R. Prevention, detection, and correction of corruption in local government . Washington , 1978. vi, 83 p. ; LC Card 79-603441
JS401 .L95   **NYPL** *[JLF 81-328]*

Miller, Herbert S. Plea bargaining in the United States /. [Washington] , 1978. liii, 311, 64, [14] p. : LC Card 79-602258
KF9654 .M54   **NYPL** *[JLF 81-304]*

Program plan. Washington. 27 cm. For earlier years, see its: Program and project. Plan.
1. Law enforcement - United States - Periodicals.
         NYPL *[JLM 80-921]*

Publications of the National Institute of Law Enforcement and Criminal Justice : a comprehensive bibliography / compiled by John Ferry, Marjorie Kravitz, Ollie Smith ; National Criminal Justice Reference Service. [Washington] : The Institute : for sale by the Supt. of Docs., U. S. Govt. Print. Off., 1978. vii, 230 p. ; 26 cm. Includes indexes. LC Card 79-601977 DDC 016.364/973 19
1. Law enforcement - United States - Bibliography. 2. Criminal justice, Administration of - United States - Bibliography. 3. National Institute of Law Enforcement and Criminal Justice - Bibliography. I. Ferry, John. II. Kravitz, Marjorie. III. Smith, Ollie L. IV. United States. National Criminal Justice Reference Service. V. Title.
Z7164.P76 N37 HV8138

Ruegg, Rosalie T. The police patrol car . Washington , 1978. xvii, 117 p. ; LC Card 77-13244
QC100 .U57 no. 480-15 HV7936.V4
         NYPL *[*XME-9526]*

Shanley, Mark. International policing . [Washington] , 1978. vii, 97 p. ; LC Card 78-602822
Z7164.P76 S5 HV7921 **NYPL** *[JLF 80-1418]*

System Sciences, inc. Evaluation of treatment alternatives to street crime . [Washington] , 1979. xii, 150 p. ; LC Card 79-602081 DDC 362.2/937/0973 19
HV5825 .S94 1979

Whitcomb, Debra. Focus on robbery . [Washington] , 1979. iii, 76 p. : LC Card 79-602932 DDC 363.2/52 19
HV8145.W2 W45

NATIONAL INSTITUTE OF LAW ENFORCEMENT AND CRIMINAL JUSTICE - BIBLIOGRAPHY.
National Institute of Law Enforcement and Criminal Justice. Publications of the National Institute of Law Enforcement and Criminal Justice . [Washington] , 1978. vii, 230 p. ; LC Card 79-601977 DDC 016.364/973 19
Z7164.P76 N37 HV8138

National Institute of Law Enforcement and Criminal Justice. Model Program Development Division.
Lyman, Theodore R. Prevention, detection, and correction of corruption in local government . Washington , 1978. vi, 83 p. ; LC Card 79-603441
JS401 .L95   **NYPL** *[JLF 81-328]*

Managing criminal warrants / prepared by James P. Gannon ... [et al.]. Washington : U. S. Dept. of Justice, Law Enforcement Assistance Administration, National Institute of Law Enforcement and Criminal Justice, Office of Development, Testing, and Dissemination, Model Program Development Division : for sale by the Supt. of Docs., U. S. Govt. Print. Off., 1978. vii, 92 p. : ill. ; 27 cm. (Program models) Bibliography: p. 60-61. LC Card 79-602012
1. Arrest - United States. 2. Warrants (Law) - United States. I. Gannon, James P. II. Title.
KF9625 .N37   **NYPL** *[JLF 81-324]*

National Institute of Law Enforcement and Criminal Justice. Program for the Study of Corruption in Local Government. Manikas, Peter. Establishing a citizens' watchdog group /. [Washington, D.C.] , 1979. xii, 129 p. ; LC Card 79-604009
JK2249 .M36   **NYPL** *[JLF 81-343]*

National Institute of Mental Health. see United States. National Institute of Mental Health.

National Institute of Mental Health (U. S.)
Monahan, John, 1946- The clinical prediction of violent behavior /. Rockville, Md. (5600 Fishers Lane, Rockville, Md. 20857) , Washington, D.C. , 1980 i.e.1981. xi, 134 p. : LC Card 81-601072 DDC 616.85/82 19
RC569.5.V55 M64

Special report . Rockville, Md. , Washington, D.C. , 1981. 160 p. : LC Card 81-601423 DDC 616.89/82 19
RC514 .S68

Summerlin, Florence A. Religion and mental health . Rockville, Md. (5600 Fishers Lane, Rockville, Md. 20857) , Washington, D.C. , 1980. 401 p. in various pagings ; LC Card 81-601117 DDC 016.3622 19
Z6664.N5 S94 RA790

National Institute of Mental Health (U. S.). Division of Scientific and Public Information.
Attitudes toward the mentally ill . Rockville, Md. (5600 Fisher Lane, Rockville, Md., 20857) , Washington, D.C. , 1980. ix, 76 p. ; LC Card 80-600135 DDC 362.2/042 19
RC455.2.P85 A85

Runck, Bette. Biofeedback . Rockville, Md. (5600 Fishers Lane, Rockville, Md. 20857) , 1980. xi, 99 p. ; LC Card 80-600134 DDC 615.8/51 19
RC489.B53 R86

National Institute of Neurological and Communicative Disorders and Stroke.
National Advisory Neurological and Communicative Disorders and Stroke Council (United States). Task Force on Basic Science. Report of the Task Force on Basic Science to the National Advisory Neurological and Communicative Disorders and Stroke Council. [Washington, D.C.] , 1979. ix, 129 p. ; LC Card 80-601253 DDC 612.8/072073 19
QP356 .N28 1979

NINCDS monograph .
(no. 22) The Neurological bases of language disorders in children . Bethesda, Md. , Washington, D.C. , 1980. viii, 196 p. : LC Card 80-602387 DDC 618.92/855 19
RJ496.L35 N48

Panel on Convulsive and Neuromuscular Disorders (U. S.) Report of the Panel on Convulsive and Neuromuscular Disorders to the National Advisory Neurological and Communicative Disorders and Stroke Council, National Institute of Neurological and Communicative Disorders and Stroke. [Bethesda, Md.] [1979] xiii, 124 p. : LC Card 80-601220 DDC 616.7/4/0072073 19
RC925.5 .P26 1979

Panel on Inflammatory, Demyelinating and Degenerative Diseases (U. S.) Report of the Panel on Inflammatory, Demyelinating, and Degenerative Diseases to the National Advisory Neurological and Communicative Disorders and Stroke Council [prepared for the] National Institute of Neurological and Communicative Disorders and Stroke. [Bethesda, Md.] [1979] ix, 129 p. ; LC Card 80-601215 DDC 616.8/072073 19
RC346 .P275 1979

National Institute of Senior Centers. Directory of senior centers and clubs. 1974- Washington. LC Card 75-643610 **NYPL** *[JLM 80-1123]*

National Institute on Aging. The Older woman . [Bethesda, Md.] , Washington, D.C. , 1979. 51 p. ; LC Card 79-604218
HQ1064.U5 O42   **NYPL** *[JLF 81-395]*

National Institute on Alcohol Abuse and Alcoholism.
National Institute on Drug Abuse. National directory of drug abuse and alcoholism treatment programs. Rockville, Md. , Washington, D.C. , 1979. xi, 350 p. ; LC Card 80-601556 DDC 362.2/9 19
HV5825 .N35 1979

Research monograph - National Institute on Alcohol Abuse and Alcoholism .
(1) Alcoholism and alcohol abuse among women, research issues . Rockville, Md. , Washington, D.C. [1980] xvii, 256 p. ; LC Card 79-600166 DDC 362.2/92/088042 19
HV5137 .A42

A selected guide to audio-visual materials on alochol and alcoholism / National Institute on Alcohol Abuse and Alcoholism. Rockville, Md. : NIAAA, 1975. viii, 34 p. : ill. ; 26 cm. (DHEW publications. no. (ADM) 75-32) Microfiche (neg.) 1 sheet. 11 x 15 cm. (NYPL FSN 34,773 Cover title. LC Card 79-42259
1. Alcohol - Physiological effect - Film catalogs. 2. Alcoholism - Film catalogs. I. Title.
         NYPL *[*XME-8890]*

The whole college catalog about drinking. Rockville, Md. : U. S. Dept. of Health, Education, and Welfare, Public Health Service, Alcohol, Drug Abuse, and Mental Health Administration, National Institute on Alcohol Abuse and Alcoholism ; Washington : for sale by the Supt. of Docs., U. S. Govt. Print. Off., [1976] xii, 129 p. : ill. ; 26 cm. (DHEW publication ; no. (ADM) 76-361) Bibliography: p. 123. LC Card 76-603043 DDC 362.2/9286/088375 19
1. Alcoholism - United States - Prevention. 2. Youth - United States - Alcohol use - Prevention. 3. Universities and colleges - United States - Curricula. I. Series: United States. Dept. of Health, Education and Welfare. DHEW publication, no. (ADM) 76-361. II. Title.
HV5292 .N33 1976

National Institute on Alcohol Abuse and Alcoholism. Division of Extramural Research. Alcoholism and alcohol abuse among women, research issues . Rockville, Md. , Washington, D.C. [1980] xvii, 256 p. ; LC Card 79-600166 DDC 362.2/92/088042 19
HV5137 .A42

National Institute on Alcohol Abuse and Alcoholism. Laboratory of Epidemiology and Population Studies. Normative approaches to the prevention of alcohol abuse and alcoholism . Rockville, Md. , Washington D.C. [1980] xiv, 238 p. ; LC Card 79-600168 DDC 362.2/9286 19
HV5288 .N67

National Institute on Alcohol Abuse and Alcoholism. National Clearinghouse for Alcohol Information. see National Clearinghouse for Alcohol Information.

National Institute on Alcohol Abuse and Alcoholism. State Assistance Branch. State plan profiles, 1979-1980. [Rockville, Md.] : State Assistance Branch, National Institute on Alcohol Abuse and Alcoholism, Alcohol, Drug Abuse, and Mental Health Administration, [1980] iv, 232 p. ; 28 cm. LC Card 80-602308
1. Alcoholism - United States - Prevention. 2. Federal aid to alcoholism programs - United States. I. Title.
HV5035 .N37 1980

National Institute on Drug Abuse.
Characteristics of the drug-abusing woman. Rockville, Md. , Washington [1979] vii, 82 p. ; LC Card 79-602768
RC564 .C47   **NYPL** *[JLF 81-407]*

Documentation Associates Information Services Incorporated. Drug users and driving behaviors /. Rockville, Md. , Washington , 1977. xi, 173 p. ; LC Card 77-604394
HE5620.D65 D62 1977 **NYPL** *[JLF 81-178]*

Documentation Associates Information Services Incorporated. International drug use /. Rockville, Md. , Washington , 1978 i.e. 1979. xxv, 199 p. ; LC Card 79-601922 DDC 362.2/93 19
HV5809 .D62 1979

Documentation Associates Information Services Incorporated. Research issues update, 1978 /. Rockville, Md. , Washington , 1979. xvii, 308 p. : LC Card 79-601820 DDC 362.2/93/072 19
HV5809 .D62 1979a

Drug users and the criminal justice system /. Rockville, Md. , Washington , 1977. xv, 150 p. ; LC Card 77-604248 DDC 362.2/93/0973 19
HV5825 .D7775

Fishburne, Patricia M. National survey on drug abuse : main findings 1979 /. Rockville, Md. , 1980. 279 p. in various pagings, [9] leaves of plates :   **NYPL** *[JLF 81-136]*

N. I. D. A. research monograph series. see National Institute on Drug Abuse. NIDA research monograph series.

National directory of drug abuse and alcoholism treatment programs. Rev. 1979. Rockville,

Md. : U. S. Dept. of Health, Education, and Welfare, Public Health Service, Alcohol, Drug Abuse, and Mental Health Administration, National Institute on Drug Abuse : National Institute on Alcohol Abuse and Alcoholism ; Washington, D.C. : for sale by the Supt. of Docs., U. S. Govt. Print. Off., 1979. xi, 350 p. ; 28 cm. (DHEW publication ; no. (ADM) 79-321) Published in 1976 under title: National directory of drug abuse treatment programs. LC Card 80-601556 DDC 362.2/9 19
1. Drug abuse - Treatment - United States - Directories. I. National Institute on Alcohol Abuse and Alcoholism. II. Series: United States. Dept. of Health, Education and Welfare. DHEW publication, no. (ADM) 79-321. III. Title.
HV5825 .N35 1979

National Institute on Drug Abuse training grants directory. Rockville, Md..
                              NYPL [JLM 81-16]

NIDA research monograph .
(27) Committee on Problems of Drug Dependence. Problems of drug dependence, 1979 . Rockville, Md. , Washington, D.C. , 1979. xiii, 483 p. : LC Card 80-600008 DDC 362.2/93/0973 19
HV5825 .C617 1979

NIDA research monograph series.
([no.] 20) Self-administration of abused substances . Rockville, Md. , 1978. ix, 246 p. : LC Card 78-63094
RC564 .S44   NYPL [JLM 76-1439 [no.] 20]

(no. 9) Satellite Conference on Naltrexone, Richmond, 1976. Narcotic antagonists, naltrexone . Rockville, Md. , Springfield, Va.] 1976. x, 181 p. : LC Card 76-40692 DDC 615/.7822 19
RC568.H4 S27 1976

(26) The Behavioral aspects of smoking /. Rockville, Md. , Washington, D.C. , 1979. vii, 192 p. ; LC Card 79-600141 DDC 362.2/9 19
HV5740 .B43

(29) Drug abuse deaths in nine cities . Rockville, Md. , Washington, D.C. , 1980. xi, 176 p. ; LC Card 80-600013 DDC 362.2/932/0973 19
HV5825 .D7733

(6) Williams, Jay R. Effects of labeling the "drug-abuser". Rockville, Md. , Springfield, Va. , 1976. v, 39 p. ; LC Card 76-3101 DDC 364.1/77/019 19
HV5824.Y68 W55

Referral strategies for polydrug abusers / National Institute on Drug Abuse. Rockville, Md. : U. S. Dept. of Health, Education, and Welfare, Public Health Service, Alcohol, Drug Abuse, and Mental Health Administration, [1977] viii, 60 p. ; 24 cm. (National polydrug collaborative project treatment manual . 3) Services research monograph series DHEW publication ; no. (ADM) 77-515 "Primary authors, Betsy S. Comstock ... [and] Grace Dammann." Bibliography: p. 60. LC Card 78-602531 DDC 362.2/938 19
1. Drug abuse - Treatment - United States. I. Comstock, Betsy S. II. Dammann, Grace. III. Series. IV. Series: United States. Dept. of Health, Education and Welfare. DHEW publication, no. (ADM) 77-515. V. Title.
HV5825 .N35 1977

Research issues - National Institute on Drug Abuse .
(18) Drug users and the criminal justice system /. Rockville, Md. , Washington , 1977. xv, 150 p. ; LC Card 77-604248 DDC 362.2/93/0973 19
HV5825 .D7775

(22)) Documentation Associates Information Services Incorporated. Research issues update, 1978 /. Rockville, Md. , Washington , 1979. xvii, 308 p. : LC Card 79-601820 DDC 362.2/93/072 19
HV5809 .D62 1979a

(23) Documentation Associates Information Services Incorporated. International drug use /. Rockville, Md. , Washington , 1978 i.e. 1979. xxv, 199 p. ; LC Card 79-601922 DDC 362.2/93 19
HV5809 .D62 1979

(25) Spotts, James V. Use and abuse of amphetamine and its substitutes /. Rockville,

Md. , Washington, D.C. , 1980. xvi, 560 p. ; LC Card 80-601718 DDC 362.2/9 19
RC568.A45 S68

(27) Austin, Gregory A. Guide to the drug research literature /. Rockville, Md. , Washington, D.C. , 1979. xx, 397 p. ; LC Card 80-601861 DDC 016.61686/3 19
RC564 .A96

Self-administration of abused substances . Rockville, Md. , 1978. ix, 246 p. : LC Card 78-63094
RC564 .S44   NYPL [JLM 76-1439 [no.] 20]

Services research report - National Institute on Drug Abuse.
Simpson, Dennis Dwayne, 1943- Alcohol and illicit drug use . [Rockville, Md.] , Washington , 1977. iv, 21 p. ; LC Card 77-603897 DDC 362.2/922/0973 19
HV5292 .S53

South Dakota. Division of Drugs and Substances Control. NIDA State plan for drug abuse prevention for the State of South Dakota . [Pierre] [1979] 223 p. : LC Card 80-621620 DDC 362.2/937/09783 19
HV5831.S66 A5 1979a

SRI International. Consequences of alcohol & marijuana use . Rockville, Md. , Washington, D.C. , 1980. xii, 227 p. : LC Card 80-601619 DDC 616.86/1 19
RC564 .S18 1980

Statistical series: quarterly report. Series G. no. 1- ; Rockville, Md.   *NYPL [Econ. Div.]*

Statistical series. Series A. no. 1- Rockville, Md., 1977-   *NYPL [Econ. Div.]*

Technical paper - National Institute on Drug Abuse.
Rufener, Brent L. Management effectiveness measures for NIDA drug abuse treatment programs /. Rockville, Md. , Washington, D.C. , 1977. 2 v. ; LC Card 80-603129 DDC 362.2/9386/0973 19
RC564 .R83

Workshop on Synthetic Estimates, Princeton, N. J., 1978. Synthetic estimates for small areas . Rockville, Md. , Washington , 1979. viii, 282 p. : LC Card 79-600067
RC563.2 .W67 1978

NATIONAL INSTITUTE ON DRUG ABUSE.
Rufener, Brent L. Management effectiveness measures for NIDA drug abuse treatment programs /. Rockville, Md. , Washington, D.C. , 1977. 2 v. ; LC Card 80-603129 DDC 362.2/9386/0973 19
RC564 .R83

National Institute on Drug Abuse. Division of Research.
Behavioral analysis and treatment of substance abuse /. Rockville, Md. , Washington, D.C. , 1979. viii, 256 p. : LC Card 79-600111 DDC 616.86 19
RC563.2 .B42

Drug abuse deaths in nine cities . Rockville, Md. , Washington, D.C. , 1980. xi, 176 p. ; LC Card 80-600013 DDC 362.2/932/0973 19
HV5825 .D7733

Foltz, Rodger L. GC/MS assays for abused drugs in body fluids /. Rockville, Md. (5600 Fishers Lane, Rockville, Md. 20857) , Washington, D.C. , 1980. ix, 202 p. ; LC Card 80-600143 DDC 616.86/3 19
RS190.P78 F64

National Institute on Drug Abuse. Division of Resource Development. Services Research Branch. see National Institute on Drug Abuse. Services Research Branch.

National Institute on Drug Abuse. Office of Medical and Professional Affairs. SRI International. Consequences of alcohol & marijuana use . Rockville, Md. , Washington, D.C. , 1980. xii, 227 p. : LC Card 80-601619 DDC 616.86/1 19
RC564 .S18 1980

National Institute on Drug Abuse. Services Research Branch.
Burt Associates. Family therapy . Rockville, Md. , Washington, D.C. , 1980. v, 41 p. ; LC Card 80-601770 DDC 616.89/156 19
RC488.5 .B82 1980

Nonurban drug abuse programs : a descriptive

study. [Rockville, Md.] : U. S. Dept. of Health, Education, and Welfare, Public Health Service, Alcohol, Drug Abuse, and Mental Health Administration, National Institute on Drug Abuse ; Washington : for sale by the Supt. of Docs., U. S. Govt. Print. Off., 1978. 27 p. ; 27 cm. (Services research report) DHEW publication ; no. (ADM) 78-636 Bibliography: p. 21. LC Card 78-602308 DDC 362.2/93/0973 19
1. Drug abuse - United States. 2. Rural population - Drug use. 3. Drug abuse surveys - United States. I. Series: National Institute on Drug Abuse. Services Research Branch. Services Research report. II. Title.
HV5825 .N35 1978b

Services Research administrative report.
Barr, Harriet Linton. The problem-drinking drug addict /. [Rockville, Md.] , 1978. vii, 52 p. ; LC Card 79-602286 DDC 362.2/938 19
HV5831.P4 A5 1978a

Texas Christian University, Fort Worth. Institute of Behaviorial Research. Comparative effectiveness of drug abuse treatment modalities. [Washington, D.C.] [1979] vi, 55 p. ; LC Card 79-601884 DDC 362.2/93 19
RC564 .T49 1979

Services Research monograph series.
Addicted women . Rockville, Md. [1979] vi, 130 p. : LC Card 80-601626 DDC 616.86/3/0088042 19
RC566 .A32

Burt Associates. Family therapy . Rockville, Md. , Washington, D.C. , 1980. v, 41 p. ; LC Card 80-601770 DDC 616.89/156 19
RC488.5 .B82 1980

Mason, Terry. Inhalant use and treatment /. Rockville, Md. , Washington , 1979. vii, 62 p. ; LC Card 79-603028 DDC 362.2/93 19
RC568.S64 M37

Services Research report.
Friends Medical Science Research Center. Narcotic addiction over a quarter of a century in a major American city, 1950-1977 . [Rockville, Md.] , 1980. vi, 92 p. : LC Card 80-601276 DDC 362.2/93/097526 19
HV5833.B2 F74 1980

National Institute on Drug Abuse. Services Research Branch. Nonurban drug abuse programs . [Rockville, Md.] , Washington , 1978. 27 p. ; LC Card 78-602308 DDC 362.2/93/0973 19
HV5825 .N35 1978b

Symposium on Comprehensive Health Care for Addicted Families and Their Children, New York, N.Y., 1976. Symposium on Comprehensive Health Care for Addicted Families and Their Children, May 20 & 21, 1976, New York, New York /. Rockville, Md. [1977] ix, 122 p. ; LC Card 77-603390
RG580.D76 S93 1976   NYPL [JLF 81-175]

Workshop for Ethnographers and Single State Agency Policymakers and Planners, Chicago, 1979. Ethnography . Rockville, Md. , 1980. xvi, 128 p. ; LC Card 80-602292 DDC 362.2/9 19
HV5809 .W67 1979

National Institute on Drug Abuse training grants directory. Rockville, Md., National Institute on Drug Abuse. 27 cm. Annual.
1. Drug abuse - Study and teaching - United States - Directories. I. National Institute on Drug Abuse. II. Title: Training grants directory.
                         NYPL [JLM 81-16]

National Institutes of Health. see United States. National Institutes of Health.

National Institutes of Health (U. S.)
National Heart, Lung, and Blood Institute. Division of Lung Diseases. Task Force on Epidemiology of Respiratory Diseases. Report of Task Force on Epidemiology of Respiratory Diseases . [Bethesda, Md.?] , 1980. vii, 244 p. : LC Card 81-600681 DDC 614.5/92/00973 19
RA645.R4 N37 1980

Rural health in the People's Republic of China . [Bethesda, Md.] , Washington, D.C. , 1980 [i.e. 1981] ix, 207 p. : LC Card 81-601104 DDC 362.1/0425 19
RA771.7.C6 R87

Selected bibliography of essential hypertension /. Bethesda, Md. , 1980. 24 p. ; LC Card

81-600700   DDC 016.6161/32 19
Z6664.H9 S44 RC685.H8

Selected bibliography on ethnic and racial
factors in hypertension /. Bethesda, Md. , 1980.
10 p. ;   LC Card 81-600730   DDC 016.6161/32071
19
Z6664.H9 S45 RC685.H8

Shimkin, Michael Boris, 1912- Science and
cancer /. [Bethesda? Md.] , 1980. viii, 109 p. :
LC Card 80-603983   DDC 616.99/4 19
RC263 .S48 1980

National Intelligence Act of 1980 . United States.
Congress. Senate. Select Committee on
Intelligence. Washington , 1980. vi, 658 p. :
LC Card 81-600623   DDC 344.73/052 347.30452
19
KF26.5 .I5 1980

**National Invitational Symposium on the King
Decision (1980 : Wayne State University)**
Black English and the education of Black
children and youth : proceedings of the
National Invitational Symposium on the King
Decision / edited, with an introduction by
Geneva Smitherman. Detroit, Mich. : Center
for Black Studies, Wayne State University,
c1981. 441 p. : ill., ports. ; 22 cm. "Sponsored by
the Center for Black Studies, Wayne State University,
February 21-23, 1980." Includes bibliographies.   LC
Card 80-85071   DDC 371.97/96073 19
*1. Afro-Americans - Education - Congresses. 2. Black
English - Study and teaching - United States -
Congresses. I. Smitherman, Geneva. II. Wayne State
University. Center for Black Studies.*
LC2771 .N37 1981

The National journal of criminal defense. v. 1-
spring 1975- [Houston,] National College of
Criminal Defense Lawyers and Public
Defenders. 26 cm. Semiannual.   LC Card
75-646015
*1. Defense (Criminal procedure) - United States -
Periodicals. 2. Criminal procedure - United States -
Periodicals. I. National College of Criminal Defense
Lawyers and Public Defenders.*
                                    NYPL [JLM 80-803]

**National Juvenile Justice System Assessment
Center (U. S.)**
A preliminary national assessment of the status
offender and the juvenile justice system : role
conflicts, constraints, and information gaps / by
Charles P. Smith ... [et al.]. [Washington,
D.C.] : U. S. Dept. of Justice, Law
Enforcement Assistance Administration, Office
of Juvenile Justice and Delinquency Prevention,
[1980] c1979. xv, 221 p. : ill. ; 28 cm. (Reports
of the national juvenile justice assessment centers) At
head of title: National Institute for Juvenile Justice and
Delinquency Prevention. Title on spine: The status
offender. "Prepared by the National Juvenile Justice
System Assessment Center." "April 1980." Bibliography:
p. 211-221.   LC Card 80-600044   DDC 364.3/6/0973
19
*1. Status offenders - United States. 2. Juvenile justice,
Administration of - United States. I. Smith, Charles P.,
1931-. II. National Institute for Juvenile Justice and
Delinquency Prevention. III. Title. IV. Title: Status
offender. V. Series.*
HV9104 .N23 1980a

Smith, Charles P., 1931- A national assessment
of case disposition and classification in the
juvenile justice system. Washington, D.C. ,
1979-80. 3 v. :   LC Card 80-600043   DDC
364.3/6/0973 19
HV9104 .S6

**National Juvenile Justice System Assessment
Center (United States)** A national
assessment of serious juvenile crime and the
juvenile justice system : the need for a rational
response / by Charles P. Smith ... [et al.].
[Washington, D.C.] : U. S. Dept. of Justice,
Law Enforcement Assistance Administration,
Office of Juvenile Justice and Delinquency
Prevention, National Institute for Juvenile
Justice and Delinquency Prevention : for sale
by the Supt. of Docs., U. S. Govt. Print. Off.,
[1980] 4 v. : ill. ; 28 cm. (Reports of the national
juvenile justice assessment centers) "April 1980."
Includes bibliographies. CONTENTS. - v. 1.
Summary.--v. 2. Definition, characteristics of incidents
and individuals, and relationship to substance abuse.--v.
3. Legislation, jurisdiction, program interventions, and
confidentiality of juvenile records.--v. 4. Economic
impact.   LC Card 80-602691   DDC 364.3/6/0973 19
1. Juvenile delinquency - United States - Collected

works. *2. Juvenile justice, Administration of - United
States - Collected works. I. Smith, Charles P., 1931-. II.
National Institute for Juvenile Justice and Delinquency
Prevention. III. Title. IV. Series.*
HV9104 .N23 1980

National League for Nursing. Guidelines for
volunteer participation in childhood
immunization programs. New York : National
League for Nursing, c1980. xv, 333 p. : ill. ; 28
cm. "Pub. no. 52-1800." "Supported under contract
200-77-0725 from the Center for Disease Control."
Errata slip inserted. Includes bibliographies.   LC Card
80-132263
*1. Immunization of children. 2. Volunteer workers in
immunization. 3. Immunization of children - United
States. I. Center for Disease Control. II. Title.*
RJ240 .N37 1980   *NYPL [JLF 81-445]*

**National League for Protection of Colored
Women. see National Urban League.**

National League of Cities.
NLC urban observatory research report.
(no. 35) Miller, Mary Lenn. Affirmative
action planning. [Garland, Tex.], 1977. 121
p.;   *NYPL [JLF 80-1394]*

**Urban observatory research report. see
National League of Cities. NLC urban
observatory research report.**

**National League on Urban Conditions among
Negroes. see National Urban League.**

National level bibliographic record--films /.
Library of Congress. Processing Service.
Washington, D.C. (Building 159, Navy Yard
Annex, Washington, D.C. 20541) , 1981. p. cm.
LC Card 81-607956   DDC 025.3/47/02854 19
Z695.66 .L57 1981

NATIONAL LIBERATION MOVEMENTS -
AFRICA.
United States. Congress. House. Committee on
Armed Services. Delegation to Africa. Report
of the delegation to Africa . Washington , 1980.
iii, 29 p. ;   LC Card 80-601793   DDC 355/.03306
19
DT30 .U58 1980

National Library of Medicine (U. S.) Centenary
of Index medicus, 1879-1979 /. Bethesda, Md. ,
Washington, D.C. , 1980. vii, 115 p. ;   LC Card
80-603763   DDC 610/.5 19
Z6659.5 .C45 R119

**National Library Service for the Blind and
Physically Handicapped.**
Libros parlantes, 1980. 3d ed. Washington :
Library of Congress, 1980. p. cm. Previous
editions published by the Service under its earlier name:
United States. Library of Congress. Division for the
Blind and Physically Handicapped. Spanish and English.
Cumulative catalog of the Library of Congress
collection of Spanish-language recorded and braille
materials for Spanish-speaking people distributed to
cooperating libraries, 1973-1980.   ISBN 0-8444-0345-8
LC Card 80-23606   DDC 011/.63 19
*1. Talking books - Bibliography - Catalogs. 2.
Blind-Books and reading - Bibliography - Catalogs. I.
Title.*
Z5347 .U59 1980

Music & musicians: large-print scores and books
catalog. Washington. 28 cm. Continues: United
States. Library of Congress. Division of the Blind and
Physically Handicapped. Music & musicians: large-print
scores and books catalog (not in the library).   LC Card
79-640268
*1. Blind, Music for the - Bibliography - Catalogs. I.
Title. II. Title: Large-print scores and books catalog.*
                                    NYPL [JMM 80-46]

News. Washington. Continues: United States.
Library of Congress. Division for the Blind and
Physically Handicapped. News (not in the library)
                                    NYPL [Econ. Div.]

National longitudinal study. Crain, Robert L. The
influence of high school racial composition on
Black college attendance and test performance
/. [Washington] , 1978, c1979 printing. xix, 143
p. ;   LC Card 79-601911
LC146 .C72 1978   *NYPL [JLF 81-370]*

**National Longitudinal Surveys of Mature Women,
Conference on the. see Conference on the
National Longitudinal Surveys of Mature
Women, United States Department of Labor,
1978.**

**National Manpower Institute. Center for
Education and Work.** Barton, Paul E.
Between two worlds. Washington, 1978. 4 v.;
                                    NYPL [JLF 80-1274]

**National Manpower Institute. Education and
Work, Center for. see National Manpower
Institute. Center for Education and Work.**

**National Marine Fisheries Service. see United
States. National Marine Fisheries Service.**

National market system, five year status report .
United States. Congress. House. Committee on
Interstate and Foreign Commerce.
Subcommittee on Oversight and Investigations.
Washington , 1980. vii, 105 p. ;   LC Card
80-603861   DDC 332.64/273 19
HG4910 .U54 1980

National Measurement Laboratory (U. S.)
Standard reference materials : a reference
method for the determination of lithium in
serum / Rance A. Velapoldi ... [et al], National
Measurement Laboratory, National Bureau of
Standards ; with the cooperation of a
committee of experts, George N. Bowers ... [et
al]. Washington, D.C. : U. S. Dept. of
Commerce, National Bureau of Standards : for
sale by the Supt. of Docs., U. S. Govt. Print.
Off., 1980. xiv, 99 p. : ill. ; 26 cm. (Standard
reference materials) NBS special publication ; 260-69
"Issued July 1980." Includes bibliographical references.
LC Card 80-600091   DDC 602/.18 s 616.07/56
19
*1. Serum - Analysis - Standards. 2. Lithium - Analysis -
Standards. 3. Flame spectroscopy. 4. Atomic absorption
spectroscopy. I. Velapoldi, R. A. II. Bowers, George N.
III. Title. IV. Title: A reference method for the
determination of lithium in serum. V. Series: United
States. National Bureau of Standards. Standard
reference materials.*
QC100 .U57 no. 260-69 RB46

Symposium on Accuracy in Powder Diffraction,
National Bureau of Standards, 1979. Accuracy
in powder diffraction . [Washington, D.C.]
[1980] x, 572 p. :   LC Card 80-600010   DDC
602/.18 s 548/.83 19
QC100 .U57 no. 567 QC482.D5

Ultrasonic tissue characterization II .
Washington , 1979. xi, 362 p. :   LC Card
79-600026   DDC 602/.18 s 616.07/543 19
QC100 .U57 no. 525 RC78.7.U4

**National Measurement Laboratory (U. S.).
Center for Radiation Research.**
International Conference on Nuclear Cross
Sections for Technology (1979 : University of
Tennessee) Nuclear cross sections for
technology . [Washington, D.C.?] , 1980. xvi,
1039 p. :   LC Card 80-600128   DDC 602/.18 s
539.7/54 19
QC100 .U57 no. 594 QC794.6.C7

Spencer, L. V. (Lewis Van Clief), 1924-
Structure shielding against fallout gamma rays
from nuclear detonations /. [Washington,
D.C.?] , 1980. xvi, 967 p :   LC Card 80-600120
DDC 602/.18 s 363.1/89 19
QC100 .U57 no. 570 UF787

**National Measurement Laboratory (U. S.). Time
and Frequency Division.** Time and frequency
users' manual / edited by George Kamas,
Sandra L. Howe ; Time and Frequency
Division, National Measurement Laboratory,
National Bureau of Standards. Washington,
D.C. : U. S. Dept. of Commerce, National
Bureau of Standards : for sale by the Supt. of
Docs., U. S. Govt. Print. Off., 1979. xvi, 248
p. : ill. ; 27 cm. (NBS special publication ; 559)
Includes bibliographical references and indexes.   LC
Card 79-600169   DDC 602/.18 s 529/.7 19
*1. Time measurements - Handbooks, manuals, etc. 2.
Radio frequency - Handbooks, manuals, etc. I. Kamas,
George. II. Howe, Sandra L. III. Series: United States.
National Bureau of Standards Special publication, 559.
IV. Title.*
QC100 .U57 no. 559 QB209

The national military command structure .
Steadman, Richard C. Washington , 1978. iii,
79 p. ;   LC Card 79-602790
UA23.3 .S73

National monthly medicaid statistics. Sept. 1978-
Baltimore. At head of title: Health care financing
program statistics. Published by the Health Care
Financing Administration.

I. United States. Health Care Financing Administration.
II. Title: Health care financing program statistics.
NYPL [Econ. Div.]

National Municipal League. Partnership within
the states . Urbana , 1976. vi, 311 p. ;   LC Card
77-622179
JS348 .P25   **NYPL [*XME-9431]**

National Museum of American Art. Isham,
Sheila, 1927- East and West, painting/poems /.
Washington, D.C. , c1981. [40] p. :   LC Card
81-66   DDC 759.13 19
ND1457.C56 I832 1981

National Museum of American Art (U. S.)
Nosanow, Barbara Shissler. More than land or
sky . Washington, D.C. , 1981. p. cm.   LC Card
81-13566   DDC 709/.74/074014 19
N6516 .N67

National Museum of American History (U. S.)
Harris, Elizabeth M. In touch . Washington,
D.C. , 1981. p. cm.   LC Card 81-2489   DDC
686.2/82/09034 19
HV1721 .H37

Warner, Deborah Jean. Perfect in her place .
Washington, D.C. , 1981. p. cm.   LC Card
81-607826   DDC 331.4/0973 19
HD6095 .W198

**NATIONAL MUSEUM OF AMERICAN
HISTORY (U. S.) - EXHIBITIONS.**
Harris, Elizabeth M. In touch . Washington,
D.C. , 1981. p. cm.   LC Card 81-2489   DDC
686.2/82/09034 19
HV1721 .H37

**National Museum of Canada. see National
Museums of Canada.**

National Museum of History and Technology.
(Old Catalog form: Museum of History and
Technology, Washington, D. C.)
Marshall, Howard W. Buckaroos in Paradise .
Washington , 1980. xvi, 95 p. :   ISBN
0-8444-0348-2   LC Card 80-23261   DDC
979.3/54 19
F847.H8 M37

National Museums of Canada. (Old Catalog form:
Ottawa National Museum of Canada)
Archaeological whale bone--a northern
resource . Fayetteville, ARK , 1979. xx, 558
p. :   LC Card 80-624409   DDC 971.9/5 19
E99.E7 A73

**National Ocean Policy Study. see United States.
Congress. Senate. National Ocean Policy
Study.**

National Ocean Survey. (Old Catalog form:
United States. National Ocean Survey)
Surface water temperature and density, Atlantic
Coast : North and South America /U. S. Dept.
of Commerce, National Oceanic and
Atmospheric Administration, National Ocean
Survey. - 4th ed. Rockville, Md. : National
Ocean Survey ; Washington, D. C. : for sale by
the Supt. of Docs., U. S. Govt. Print. Off.,
1973. 109 p. : ill., maps ; 26 cm. (Its: NOS
publication. 31-1) Chiefly tables. First-2d editions
published under title: Surface water temperature and
salinity, Atlantic coast, North and South America;
1st-3d editions issued by United States Coast &
Geodetic Survey.
*1. Ocean temperature - Atlantic Ocean. 2. Sea-water -
Density. I. Title.*   **NYPL [JSF 81-4]**

**National Ocean Survey. Cnastal Zone
Management, Office of. see National Ocean
Survey. Office of Coastal Zone Management.**

**National Ocean Survey. Office of Coastal Zone
Management.** United States. Geological
Survey. Coastal mapping handbook /.
Washington , 1978. vi, 199 p. :   LC Card
78-600000
GB452.2 .U54 1978
             NYPL [Map Div. 81-155]

National Park Foundation. Richard T. Greener .
[Washington, D. C.] , 1980. 16 p. :
             NYPL [Sc F 80-218]

**NATIONAL PARKS AND RESERVES -
ADMINISTRATION. see NATIONAL
PARKS AND RESERVES -
MANAGEMENT.**

**NATIONAL PARKS AND RESERVES -
MANAGEMENT.**
New Jersey. Pinelands Commission. Draft
comphrehensive management plan for the

Pinelands National Reserve. New Lisbon, N.
J. , 1980. 2 v. :   **NYPL [JLF 80-1614]**

**NATIONAL PARKS AND RESERVES - NEW
JERSEY.**
New Jersey. Pinelands Commission. Draft
comphrehensive management plan for the
Pinelands National Reserve. New Lisbon, N.
J. , 1980. 2 v. :   **NYPL [JLF 80-1614]**

**NATIONAL PARKS AND RESERVES -
UNITED STATES.**
Harris, David V. The geologic story of the
national parks and monuments /. Fort Collins,
Colo. (271 S.W. Aylesworth, Fort Collins
80523) , 1980. xvi, 322 p., [3] p. of plates :
   LC Card 81-112429   DDC 557.3 19
QE77 .H368 1980

Readings on the protection and management of
marine and submerged resources of the national
parks . Washington , 1980. ix, 157 p. :   LC Card
80-603550   DDC 333.91/0973 19
QH91.75.U6 R4

United States. Congress. House. Committee on
Interior and Insular Affairs. Subcommittee on
National Parks and Insular Affairs. To establish
a barrier islands protection system .
Washington , 1980. vii, 650 p. :   LC Card
80-603095   DDC 346.7304/6784 19
KF27 .I5365 1980

United States. Congress. Senate. Committee on
Energy and Natural Resources. Subcommittee
on Parks, Recreation, and Renewable
Resources. Barrier island protection system .
Washington , 1980. iii, 465 p. :   LC Card
80-604056   DDC 346.7304/6784 347.30646784
19
KF26 .E5565 1980e

United States. Congress. Senate. Committee on
Energy and Natural Resources. Subcommittee
on Parks, Recreation, and Renewable
Resources. Biscayne National Park, Florida ;
Valley Forge National Historical Park,
Pennsylvania; Vietnam Veterans Memorial ; and
Salinas National Monument in New Mexico .
Washington , 1980. iii, 195 p. :   LC Card
80-602956   DDC 346.7304/6783/0262 19
KF26 .E5565 1980

United States. Congress. Senate. Committee on
Energy and Natural Resources. Subcommittee
on Parks, Recreation, and Renewable
Resources. Various parks and Bureau of Land
Management related legislation . Washington ,
1980. iii, 194 p. :   LC Card 81-600804   DDC
346.7304/6783/0262 347.306467830262 19
KF26 .E5565 1980h

**NATIONAL PARKS AND RESERVES -
UNITED STATES - HISTORY.**
Tweed, William C. Recreation site planning and
improvement in national forests, 1891-1942 /.
Washington, D.C. , 1980 [i.e. 1981] vi, 29 p. :
   LC Card 81-601100   DDC 333.78/3/0973 19
GV191.4 .T83

National Passive Solar Conference. Proceedings.
Newark, Del., American Section, International
Solar Energy Society. illus. 28 cm. Sponsored by
U. S. Dept. of Energy, Office of Conservation And
Solar Applications, Passive Systems Development
Program.
*1. Solar energy - Congresses. I. International Solar
Energy Society. American Section. II. United States.
Dept. of Energy. Office of Conservation and Solar
Applications. Passive Systems Development Program.*
             NYPL [JSP 80-342]

National perspective. United States. Congress.
Senate. Committee on Governmental Affairs.
Subcommittee on Intergovernmental Relations.
Nonprofit organization participation in the
federal aid system . Washington , 1980. 2 v. ;
   LC Card 81-600646   DDC 361.3/7/0973 19
KF26 .G6738 1980d

**National Petroleum Council. Committee on
Unconventional Gas Sources.** Interim
summary, unconventional gas sources /
National Petroleum Council, Committee on
Unconventional Gas Sources ; John F. Bookout,
chairman. [Washington] : The Council, c1980.
20, 7, 11 p. : graphs ; 28 cm. "June 1980."   LC
Card 80-139029   DDC 553.2/85/0973 19
*1. Gas, Natural. I. Title. II. Title: Unconventional gas
sources.*
TN880 .N29 1980

National Petroleum Reserve--Alaska. Derksen,

Dirk V. Use of wetland habitats by birds in the
National Petroleum Reserve--Alaska /.
Washington, D.C. , 1981. p. cm.   LC Card
81-607937   DDC 639.9/784109798 19
S914 .A3 no.141 QL684A4

**NATIONAL PLANNING. see ECONOMIC
POLICY.**

**National policy objectives and the adequacy of
our current navy forces .** United States.
Congress. House. Committee on Armed
Services. Subcommittee on Seapower and
Strategic and Critical Materials. Washington ,
1980 [i.e. 1981] ii, 137 p. :   LC Card 81-601761
DDC 359/.03/0973 19
KF27 .A769 1979e

**National polydrug collaborative project treatment
manual .**
(3) National Institute on Drug Abuse. Referral
strategies for polydrug abusers /. Rockville, Md.
[1977] viii, 60 p. ;   LC Card 78-602531   DDC
362.2/938 19
HV5825 .N35 1977

National port assessment, 1980-1990 . United
States. Office of Port and Intermodal
Development. [Washington] [1980] ix, 127 p. :
   LC Card 80-603149   DDC 387.1/0973 19
HE553 .U644 1980a

National Portrait Gallery, Washington, D. C.
Hussey, Jeannette M. The code duello in
America /. Washington , 1980. p. cm.   LC Card
80-607828   DDC 394/.8 19
CR4595.U5 H87

Pachter, Marc. Champions, heroes of American
sport /. [Washington] , New York [1981] p.
cm.   ISBN 0-8109-1602-9 (Abrams) :   LC Card
80-28934   DDC 796/.092/2 B 19
GV697.A1 P28

**NATIONAL PORTRAIT GALLERY,
WASHINGTON, D.C. - EXHIBITIONS.**
Pachter, Marc. Champions, heroes of American
sport /. [Washington] , New York [1981] p.
cm.   ISBN 0-8109-1602-9 (Abrams) :   LC Card
80-28934   DDC 796/.092/2 B 19
GV697.A1 P28

The national power grid study. United States.
Dept. of Energy. Office of Utility Systems.
Washington, D.C. [Springfield, Va. , 1980] 2
v. :   LC Card 80-601760   DDC 363.6/2 19
TK23 .U52 1980

**National priorities for the investigation and
prosecution of white collar crime .** Tompkins,
Joseph B. Washington, D.C. , 1980. x, 50, 21-a
p. ;   LC Card 80-603918   DDC 364.1/68/0973 19
HV8079.W47 T65

**National prisoner statistics special report;
SD-NPS-SR.** United States. National Criminal
Justice Information and Statistics Service.
Washington.   **NYPL [JLM 81-137]**

**NATIONAL PRODUCT, GROSS. see GROSS
NATIONAL PRODUCT.**

**NATIONAL PRODUCTIVITY COUNCIL
(UNITED STATES.)**
United States. Congress. House. Committee on
Banking, Finance and Urban Affairs.
Subcommittee on Economic Stabilization.
Productivity performance and the American
economy . Washington , 1980. iv, 318 p. :   LC
Card 80-603669   DDC 338/.06/0973 19
KF27 .B542 1980a

National publications act of 1980 . United States.
Congress. House. Committe on House
Administration. Washington , 1980. iv, 179 p. ;
   LC Card 80-601753   DDC 343.73/0998 19
KF32 .H6 1980

National publications act of 1980 . United States.
Congress. House. Committee on Government
Operations. Legislation and National Security
Subcommittee. Washington , 1980. iii, 277 p. ;
   LC Card 80-603037   DDC 343.73/0998 19
KF27 .G6676 1980e

The National Publications Act of 1980 . United
States. Congress. House. Committee on Rules.
Subcommittee on Rules of the House.
Washington , 1980. iii, 126 p. ;   LC Card
81-600621   DDC 343.73/0998 347.303998 19
KF27 .R8737 1980

**National Railroad Passenger Corporation. see
Amtrak.**

National Referral Center (U. S.) A Directory of information resources in the United States . Washington, D.C. , 1981. p. cm. ISBN 0-8444-0372-5 LC Card 81-607045 DDC 550/.72073 19
QE47.A1 D58

National Research Council. Alternatives for the Reduction of Chlorofluorocarbon Emissions, Committee on. see National Research Council. Committee on Alternatives for the Reduction of Chlorofluorocarbon Emissions.

National Research Council. Board on Science and Technology for International Development. Panel on Microbial Processes. Microbial processes : promising technologies for developing countries : report of an ad hoc panel of the Advisory Committee on Technology Innovation, Board on Science and Technology for International Development, Commission on International Relations, National Research Council. Washington, D.C. : National Academy of Sciences, 1979. xii, 198 p. : ill. ; 23 cm. Includes bibliographies. LC Card 79-91534 DDC 660/.62 19
1. Industrial microbiology. 2. Underdeveloped areas - Technological innovations. I. Title.
QR53 .N35 1979

National Research Council. Committee on Alternatives for the Reduction of Chlorofluorocarbon Emissions. National Research Council. Committee on Impacts of Stratospheric Change. Protection against depletion of stratospheric ozone by chlorofluorocarbons /. Washington, D.C. , 1979. xvii, 392 p. : ISBN 0-309-02947-3 LC Card 79-57247
TD887.C47 N37 1979 NYPL [JSE 81-221]

National Research Council. Committee on Impacts of Stratospheric Change. Protection against depletion of stratospheric ozone by chlorofluorocarbons / Committee on Impacts of Stratospheric Change, Assembly of Mathematical and Physical Sciences, Committee on Alternatives for the Reduction of Chlorofluorocarbon Emissions, Committee on Sociotechnical Systems. Washington, D.C. : National Academy of Sciences, 1979. xvii, 392 p. : ill. ; 23 cm. Includes bibliographies. ISBN 0-309-02947-3 LC Card 79-57247
1. Chlorofluorocarbons - Environmental aspects. 2. Atmospheric ozone. 3. Stratosphere. 4. Air - Pollution. 5. Aerosols - Environmental aspects. I. National Research Council. Committee on Alternatives for the Reduction of Chlorofluorocarbon Emissions. II. Title.
TD887.C47 N37 1979 NYPL [JSE 81-221]

National Research Council. Committee on Nuclear and Alternative Energy Systems. ENERGY IN TRANSITION, 1985-2010. United States. Congress. House. Committee on Science and Technology. National Academy of Sciences report . Washington , 1980. iii, 147 p. : LC Card 80-603067 DDC 333.79/0973 19
KF27 .S39 1980b

United States. Congress. Senate. Committee on Energy and Natural Resources. Energy in transition, 1985-2010 . Washington , 1980. iii, 61 p. ; LC Card 80-602968 DDC 333.79 19
KF26 .E55 1980c

National Research Council. Committee on Nutrition, Brain Development, and Behavior. International Nutrition Conference on the Behavioral Effects of Energy and Protein Deficits, Washington, D.C., 1977. Behavioral effects of energy and protein deficits . [Bethesda, Md.] , Washington , 1979. vii, 370 p. : LC Card 79-604003 DDC 155.9/16 19
RJ399.M26 I57 1977

National Research Council. Committee on Surface Mining and Reclamation. Mining and processing of oil shale and tar sands : a working paper prepared for the Committee on Surface Mining and Reclamation, Board on Mineral and Energy Resources, Commission on Natural Resources, National Research Council. Washington, D.C. : National Academy of Sciences, 1980. xiv, 222 p. : ill. ; 28 cm. Appendix 2 to the Committee's Surface mining of non-coal minerals. Bibliography: p. 187-208. ISBN 0-309-03037-4 (pbk.) LC Card 80-146216 DDC 333.8/23 19
1. Oil-shale industry - Environmental aspects - United States. 2. Oil sands extraction plants - Environmental

aspects - United States. I. National Research Council. Committee on Surface Mining and Reclamation. Surface mining of non-coal minerals. II. Title.
TD195.O4 N37 1980

Surface mining of non-coal minerals. National Research Council. Committee on Surface Mining and Reclamation. Mining and processing of oil shale and tar sands : a working paper prepared for the Committee on Surface Mining and Reclamation, Board on Mineral and Energy Resources, Commission on Natural Resources, National Research Council. Washington, D.C. , 1980. xiv, 222 p. : ISBN 0-309-03037-4 (pbk.) LC Card 80-146216 DDC 333.8/23 19
TD195.O4 N37 1980

National Research Council. Committee to Study the Human Health Effects of Subtherapeutic Antibiotic Use in Animal Feeds. The effects on human health of subtherapeutic use of antimicrobials in animal feeds / Committee to Study the Human Health Effects of Subtherapeutic Antibiotic Use in Animal Feeds, Division of Medical Sciences, Assembly of Life Sciences, National Research Council. Washington, D.C. : National Academy of Sciences, 1980. xvi, 376 p. : ill. ; 28 cm. Includes bibliographies. ISBN 0-309-03044-7 LC Card 80-81486 DDC 616.9/2 19
1. Bacterial diseases - Transmission. 2. Antibiotics in animal nutrition. 3. Antibiotic residues - Hygienic aspects. 4. Drug resistance in micro-organisms. 5. Meat - Microbiology. I. Title.
RA644.B32 N37 1980

National Research Council. Division of Biology and Agriculture. Food and Nutrition Board. see National Research Council. Food and Nutrition Board.

National Research Council. Division of Engineering. Maritime Transportation Research Board. see National Research Council. Maritime Transportation Research Board.

NATIONAL RESEARCH COUNCIL. FOOD AND NUTRITION BOARD. United States. Congress. House. Committee on Agriculture. Subcommittee on Domestic Marketing, Consumer Relations, and Nutrition. National Academy of Sciences report on healthful diets . Washington , 1980. iii, 312 p. ; LC Card 80-603777 DDC 613.2 19
KF27 .A3336 1980

National Research Council. Maritime Transportation Research Board. Symposium on Piloting and VTS Systems, Washington, D.C., 1979. Proceedings /. Washington, D.C. , 1980. ix, 233 p. ; LC Card 80-126646 DDC 387.1/66 19
VK1645 .S95 1979

National Research Council. Nuclear and Alternative Energy Systems, Committee on. see National Research Council. Committee on Nuclear and Alternative Energy Systems.

National Research Council of Canada. (Old Catalog form: Canada. Scientific and Industrial Research, Honorary Advisory Council for.)

National Research Council of Canada. Division of Chemistry (1969/70-) Symposium on Accuracy in Powder Diffraction, National Bureau of Standards, 1979. Accuracy in powder diffraction . [Washington, D.C.] [1980] x, 572 p. : LC Card 80-600010 DDC 602/.18 s 548/.83 19
QC100 .U57 no. 567 QC482.D5

National Research Council. Transportation Research Board. Automobile Inspection, Maintenance & Repair Conference, National Academy of Sciences, 1979. Automobile Inspection, Maintenance & Repair Conference . [Washington] [1979] iv, 126 p. : LC Card 80-601649 DDC 629.28/25 19
TL154 .A82 1979

Bibliography on project evaluation and priority programming criteria. Washington, D.C. : Transportation Research Board, National Academy of Sciences, 1980. 35 p. ; 28 cm. (Transportation research circular . no. 213 0097-8515) LC Card 80-112146 DDC 016.62904 19
1. Transportation - Planning - Bibliography. I. Title. II. Series.
Z5853.T7 N37 1980 TA1145

Concrete pavements and pavement overlays / Transportation Research Board, Commission on Sociotechnical Systems, National Research Council. Washington, D.C. : National Academy of Sciences, 1980. iv, 48 p. : ill. ; 28 cm. (Transportation research record . 756 0361-1981) Reports prepared for the 59th annual meeting of the Transportation Research Board. Includes bibliographical references. ISBN 0-309-03070-6 LC Card 80-607869 DDC 380.5 s 625.8/4 19
1. Pavements, Concrete - Addresses, essays, lectures. 2. Pavements, Asphalt concrete - Addresses, essays, lectures. I. Title. II. Series.
TE7 .H5 no. 756 TE278

Design of sedimentation basins. Washington, D.C. : Transportation Research Board, National Research Council, 1980. 53 p. : ill. ; 28 cm. (Synthesis of highway practice . 70 0547-5570) Prepared by W. O. Ree. "Research sponsored by the American Association of State Highway and Transportation Officials in cooperation with the Federal Highway Administration." Bibliography: p. 38-39. ISBN 0-309-03027-7 (pbk.) : LC Card 80-52843 DDC 625.7/34 19
1. Settling basins - Design and construction. 2. Sedimentation and deposition - Environmental aspects. 3. Road construction - Environmental aspects. I. Ree, William Oscar, 1913-. II. Title. III. Series.
TD439 .N37 1980

Motor vehicle size and weight regulations, enforcement, and permit operations. Washington, D.C. : Transportation Research Board, National Research Council, [1980] 45 p. : ill. ; 28 cm. (Synthesis of highway practice . 68 0547-5570) "Research sponsored by the American Association of State Highway and Transportation Officials, in cooperation with the Federal Highway Administration." "April 1980." Includes bibliographical references. ISBN 0-309-03019-6 (pbk.) : LC Card 80-66742 DDC 629.2/24 19
1. Trucks - United States - Weight. 2. Trucks - Law and legislation - United States. I. American Association of State Highway and Transportation Officials. II. United States. Federal Highway Administration. III. Title. IV. Series.
TL230 .N27 1980

National Research Council. Transportation Research Board. Steering Committee for the Study of Methods to Increase Use of Safety Belts. Study of methods for increasing safety belt use : report of a committee convened by the Transportation Research Board, National Academy of Sciences. Washington : U. S. Govt. Print. Off., 1980. ix, 22 p. ; 24 cm. At head of title: 96th Congress, 2d session. Committee print. "96-40." "March 1980." "Printed for the use of the Committee on Public Works and Transportation. LC Card 80-602588 DDC 363.1/2572 19
1. Automobiles - Seat belts. I. United States. Congress. House. Committee on Public Works and Transportation. II. Title.
TL159 .N34 1980

National Research Council (U. S.). Transportation Research Board. Advances in urban transportation planning /. Washington, D.C. , 1980. iv, 22 p. : ISBN 0-309-03115-X (pbk.) LC Card 81-4761 DDC 380.5 s 388.4/068 19
TE7 .H5 no. 771 HE305

National Research Council (U. S.) Transportation Research Board. Alternative work schedules . Washington, D.C. , 1980. 54 p. : ISBN 0-309-03153-2 (pbk.) : LC Card 80-54556 DDC 388.4/13143/0973 19
HE308 .A62

Application of pavement design models. Washington, D.C. : Transportation Research board, Commission on Sociotechnical Systems, National Research Council, National Academy of Sciences, 1980. p. cm. (Transportation research record . 766) Reports presented at the 59th annual meeting of the Transportation Research Board. ISBN 0-309-03109-5 LC Card 81-1639 DDC 380.5 s 625.8 19
1. Pavements - Design and construction - Addresses, essays, lectures. I. Title. II. Series.
TE7 .H5 no. 766 TE251

Asphalt--materials, mixes, and construction /. Washington, D.C. , 1981. p. cm. ISBN 0-309-03122-2 LC Card 81-38324 DDC 380.5 s 625.8/5 19
TE7 .H5 no. 777 TE270

Consumer perspectives in travel choice and interactive travel data collection. Washington,

D.C. : Transportation Research Board, Commission on Sociotechnical Systems, National Research Council, National Academy of Sciences, 1980. iv, 33 p. : ill. ; 28 cm. (Transportation research record . 765) Reports presented at the 59th annual meeting of the Transportation Research Board. Includes bibliographical references. ISBN 0-309-03108-7 LC Card 81-1664 DDC 380.5 s 388.4 19
1. Choice of transportation - Addresses, essays, lectures. 2. Commuters - Attitudes - Addresses, essays, lectures. 3. Transportation planning - Evaluation - Addresses, essays, lectures. I. Title. II. Series.
TE7 .H5 no. 765 HE336.C5

Direction finding from arterials to destinations : research / sponsored by the American Association of State Highway and Transportation Officials in cooperation with the Federal Highway Administration. Washington, D.C. : Transportation Research Board, National Research Council, 1980. 50 p. : ill. ; 28 cm. (Synthesis of highway practice, 0547-5570 . 71) "September 1980." Includes bibliographical references. ISBN 0-309-03031-5 (pbk.) : LC Card 80-54090 DDC 388.3/122 19
1. Traffic signs and signals - United States. I. American Association of State Highway and Transportation Officials. II. United States. Federal Highway Administration. III. Title. IV. Series.
TE228 .N32 1980

Grade crossings, devices, visibility, and freeway operations /. Washington, D.C. , 1980. iv, 49 p. : ISBN 0-309-03117-6 LC Card 81-4730 DDC 380.5 s 625.7/94 19
TE7 .H5 no. 773 TE228

Guideway snow and ice control and roadside maintenance /. Washington, D.C. [1981] p. cm. ISBN 0-309-03121-4 LC Card 81-3965 DDC 380.5 s 625.7/63 19
TE7 .H5 no. 776 TE220.5

Human factors and motorist information needs /. Washington, D.C. , 1980. p. cm. ISBN 0-309-03172-9 LC Card 81-9482 DDC 380.5 s 388.3/12 19
TE7 .H5 no. 782 HE332

National Seminar on Asphalt Pavement Recycling (1980 : Dallas-Fort Worth Regional Airport) Proceedings of the National Seminar on Asphalt Pavement Recycling. Washington, D.C. , 1981. p. cm. ISBN 0-309-03101-X LC Card 81-607072 DDC 380.5 s 666/.893 19
TE7 .H5 no. 780 TE270

Paratransit 1980 /. Washington, D.C. , 1981. p. cm. ISBN 0-309-03123-0 LC Card 81-38318 DDC 380.5 s 388.4/132 19
TE7 .H5 no. 778 HE308

Transportation energy--data, forecasting, policy, and models. Washington, D.C. : Transportation Research Board, Commission on Sociotechnical Systems, National Research Council, National Academy of Sciences, 1980. v, 108 p. : ill. ; 28 cm. (Transportation research record . 764) Reports presented at the 59th annual meeting of the Transportation Research Board. ISBN 0-309-03107-9 LC Card 81-1665 DDC 380.5 s 333.79 19
1. Transportation and state - Addresses, essays, lectures. 2. Energy policy - Addresses, essays, lectures. 3. Transportation - Energy consumption - Addresses, essays, lectures. I. Title. II. Series.
TE7 .H5 no. 764 HE152.6

NATIONAL RESOURCES. see NATURAL RESOURCES.

NATIONAL SCHOOL LUNCH PROGRAM.
Hippler, Arthur E. A study to determine causes of decline in the national school lunch program in Alaska /. Anchorage [1979] 119, 15, 28 leaves : LC Card 80-623189 DDC 371.7/16/09798 19
LB3479.U6 H56

National Science Foundation. see United States. National Science Foundation.

National Science Foundation authorization.
United States. Congress. House. Committee on Science and Technology. Subcommittee on Science, Research, and Technology. 1981 National Science Foundation authorization . Washington , 1980. iv, 853 p. : LC Card 80-603468 DDC 353.0072/236855 19
KF27 .S399 1980c

National Science Foundation authorization act for fiscal years 1981 and 1982 . United States.

Congress. Senate. Committee on Labor and Human Resources. Subcommittee on Health and Scientific Research. Washington , 1980. iv, 132 p. : LC Card 80-602713 DDC 353.0072/236855 19
KF26 .L274 1980a

National Science Foundation (U. S.)
Berry, Richard M. Employment patterns of academic scientists and engineers, 1973-78. [Washington, D.C.] , 1980. v, 15 p. : LC Card 80-603833 DDC 331.12/515/0973 19
Q149.U5 B47

Moehle, Jack P. Experiments to study earthquake response of R/C structures with stiffness interruptions . Urbana, Ill. [1980] xiii, 421 p. : LC Card 80-624330 DDC 693.8/52 19
TA683 .M66

NATIONAL SCIENCE FOUNDATION (U. S.)
United States. Congress. House. Committee on Science and Technology. Posture hearings (NSF, NBS, and FEMA) . Washington , 1980. iii, 200 p. : LC Card 80-604103 DDC 353.008 19
KF27 .S39 1980f

National Science Foundation (U. S.). Division of International Programs. Science policy . [Washington, D.C.?] , 1980. 2 v. ; LC Card 80-604130 DDC 507/.2073 19
Q127.U6 S319

NATIONAL SCIENCE FOUNDATION (U. S.) - OFFICIALS AND EMPLOYEES.
United States. Congress. Senate. Committee on Labor and Human Resources. Nomination . Washington , 19. ii 28 p. : LC Card 80-604090 DDC 353.0085/5 19
KF26 .L27 1980m

NATIONAL SEA GRANT PROGRAM.
United States. Congress. Senate. Committee on Labor and Human Resources. Subcommittee on Education, Arts, and Humanities. Reauthorization of the national sea grant college program . Washington , 1980. iii, 204 p. ; LC Card 80-603079 DDC 346.7304/695 19
KF26 .L2735 1980a

The national security adviser . United States. Congress. Senate. Committee on Foreign Relations. Washington , 1980. v, 243 p. : LC Card 80-602957 DDC 353.03/1 19
KF26 .F6 1980n

National Security Affairs Conference, 6th, National Defense University, 1979.
Continuity and change in the eighties and beyond : proceedings of the National Security Affairs Conference, 23-25 July 1979, National Defense University. [Washington, D.C.] : NDU Press, 1979. xiii, 222 p. ; 27 cm. Conference sponsors: National Defense University and Assistant Secretary of Defense (International Security Affairs) Includes bibliographical references. LC Card 80-601820 DDC 355/.033073 19
1. United States - National security - Congresses. 2. United States - Military policy - Congresses. I. National Defense University. II. United States. Assistant Secretary of Defense (International Security Affairs). III. Title.
UA23 .N248 1979

National security affairs monograph .
(79-5) Cole, Brady M. Procurement of Naval ships . Washington, D.C. , 1979. vi, 52 p. (p. 52 advertisements) : LC Card 79-604212 DDC 338.7/6238/200973 19
VM299.6 .C64

National security affairs monograph series .
(no. 80-3) Heaton, William R. A united front against hegemonism . Washington, DC , 1980. vi, 55 p. ; LC Card 80-601629 DDC 327.51 19
DS779.27 .H4

(79-5) Cole, Brady M. Procurement of Naval ships . Washington, D.C. , 1979. vi, 52 p. (p. 52 advertisements) : LC Card 79-604212 DDC 338.7/6238/200973 19
VM299.6 .C64

(80-3) Heaton, William R. A united front against hegemonism . Washington, DC , 1980. vi, 55 p. ; LC Card 80-601629 DDC 327.51 19
DS779.27 .H4

(80-5) Malone, Daniel K. ROLAND, a case for or against NATO standardization? /. Washington, DC , 1980. ix, 120 p. ; LC Card 80-602358 DDC 358/.175/091821 19
UF530 .M26

(80-7) Ennis, Harry F. Peacetime industrial preparedness for wartime ammunition production /. Washington, D.C. [1980] vi, 122 p. : LC Card 80-603600 DDC 355.2/6/0973 19
HC110.D4 E56

(80-8) Daleski, Richard J. Defense management in the 1980s . Washington, D.C. , 1980. vi, 57 p. : LC Card 81-600682 DDC 355.6/0973 19
UA23.6 .D34

National Seminar on Asphalt Pavement Recycling (1980 : Dallas-Fort Worth Regional Airport) Proceedings of the National Seminar on Asphalt Pavement Recycling. Washington, D.C. : Transportation Research Board, National Academy of Sciences, 1981. p. cm. (Transportation research record . 780) ISBN 0-309-03101-X LC Card 81-607072 DDC 380.5 s 666/.893 19
1. Pavements, Asphalt - Recycling - Congresses. I. National Research Council (U. S.) Transportation Research Board. II. Title. III. Series.
TE7 .H5 no. 780 TE270

National Serials Data Program. Grosch, Audrey N., 1934- Conversion of the Minnesota Union List of Serials (MULS) to National Serials Data Program (NSDP) requirements . Washington, D.C. [1973?] 52 leaves : LC Card 80-622843 DDC 025/.04 19
Z692.S5 G76

NATIONAL SERIALS DATA PROGRAM.
Grosch, Audrey N., 1934- Conversion of the Minnesota Union List of Serials (MULS) to National Serials Data Program (NSDP) requirements . Washington, D.C. [1973?] 52 leaves : LC Card 80-622843 DDC 025/.04 19
Z692.S5 G76

NATIONAL SERVICE - LAW AND LEGISLATION - UNITED STATES.
United States. Congress. House. Committee on Education and Labor. Subcommittee on Select Education. Proposed Presidential Commission on National Service Act of 1980 . Washington , 1980. iii, 69 p. ; LC Card 80-604048 DDC 344.73/03137 347.3043137 19
KF27 .E373 1980c

United States. Congress. Senate. Committee on Labor and Human Resources. Subcommittee on Child and Human Development. Presidential Commission on National Service and National Commission on Volunteerism . Washington , 1980. v, 606 p. : LC Card 80-604000 DDC 361.3/7/0973 19
KF26 .L273 1980a

NATIONAL SERVICE - UNITED STATES.
Slackman, Joel N. Costs of the National Service Act (H.R. 2206) . [Washington, D.C.] , c1980. xii, 42 p. ; LC Card 81-600733 DDC 355.2/236/0973 19
HD6273 .S57

United States. Congress. Senate. Committee on Labor and Human Resources. Subcommittee on Child and Human Development. Presidential Commission on National Service and National Commission on Volunteerism . Washington , 1980. v, 606 p. : LC Card 80-604000 DDC 361.3/7/0973 19
KF26 .L273 1980a

National Sickle Cell Disease Program.
Directory of national, Federal, and local sickle cell disease programs / Sickle Cell Disease Branch, Division of Blood Diseases and Resources, National Heart, Lung, and Blood Institute. Bethesda, Md. : United States Dept. of Health, Education, and Welfare, Public Health Service, National Institutes of Health, [1978] 30 p. ; 24 cm. (DHEW publication ; no. (NIH) 78-714) LC Card 79-601535 DDC 362.1/96152700973 19
1. Sickle cell anemia - Hospitals - United States - Directories. 2. Sickle cell anemia - United States - Societies, etc. - Directories. 3. Community health services - United States - Directories. I. Series: United States. Dept. of Health, Education and Welfare. DHEW publication, no. (NIH) 78-714. II. Title.
RC641.7/S5 N36 1978

Prenatal approaches to the diagnosis of fetal hemoglobinopathies . [Bethesda, Md.] , 1980. xiii, 259 p. : LC Card 80-602909 DDC 618.3/2 19
RG629.H45 P73

National Ski Areas Association. United States. Forest Service. Planning considerations for winter sports resort development /. [Washington] , 1973. iii, 53 p. :
NYPL [JLF 79-1344]

National ski patrol system recognition act of 1979 . United States. Congress. House. Committee on the Judiciary. Subcommittee on Administrative Law and Governmental Relations. Washington , 1980. iii, 62 p. ;   LC Card 81-600585   DDC 344.73/0476 347.304476 19
KF27 .J832 1980g

NATIONAL SKI PATROL SYSTEM (U. S.) United States. Congress. House. Committee on the Judiciary. Subcommittee on Administrative Law and Governmental Relations. National ski patrol system recognition act of 1979 . Washington , 1980. iii, 62 p. ;   LC Card 81-600585   DDC 344.73/0476 347.304476 19
KF27 .J832 1980g

National Strategy Conference on Improving Service Delivery to the Rural Elderly (1979 : Des Moines, Iowa) Improving services for the rural elderly : summary report and recommendations of the National Strategy Conference on Improving Service Delivery to the Rural Elderly, Des Moines, Iowa, January 28-February 2, 1979. Washington, D.C. : Farmers Home Administration, U. S. Dept. of Agriculture, [1980] ix, 62 p. ; 23 cm. "Prepared for the Farmers Home Administration under contract no. 53-3157-9-27 by Dwight Jensen Associates"--T.p. verso. "October 1980." Bibliography: p. [59]-62.   LC Card 80-69618   DDC 362.6/0973 19
1. Rural aged - Services for - United States - Congresses. I. United States. Farmers Home Administration. II. Dwight Jensen Associates. III. Title.
HV1465 .N36 1979

National Survey (Firm) 1978 Highway map of Orleans County, New York. Chester, Vt., c1978. col. map. 55 x 70 cm. Scale ca. 1:63,360. Includes index and location map. Text and illus. on verso. Distributed by County Superintendent of Highways.
1. Orleans County, N. Y. - Maps. 2. Orleans County, N. Y. - Road maps. I. Orleans County, N. Y. County Superintendent of Highways.
NYPL [Map Div. 80-3303]

National survey of food stamp and food distribution program recipients. United States. Food and Nutrition Service. Washington, 1974. v, 47 p.   *NYPL [JLE 81-549]*

National survey on drug abuse : main findings 1979 /. Fishburne, Patricia M. Rockville, Md. , 1980. 279 p. in various pagings, [9] leaves of plates :   *NYPL [JLF 81-136]*

National Survey Research Group, New York. Survey report on the economic impact of D2 lands restrictions and the public view of alternative uses of State capital expenditures to offset such effects / conducted by National Survey Research Group, inc., in collaboration with Rowan Group Inc. for the State of Alaska, Legislative Affairs Agency. Juneau, Alaska : The Agency, [1980] i, 49 p. : graphs ; 28 cm. "February, 1980." LC Card 80-622486   DDC 333.1/09798 19
1. Alaska - Public lands - Public opinion. 2. Alaska - Economic policy - Public opinion. 3. Public opinion - Alaska. I. Rowan Group. II. Alaska. Legislative Affairs Agency. III. Title.
HD243.A3 N37 1980

National Symposium on Job-Task Analysis in Criminal Justice, Dallas, 1978. National Symposium on Job-Task Analysis in Criminal Justice : proceedings, November 12-14, 1978, Dallas, Texas / project coordinator, Larry A. Giddings ; proceedings editor, Diana Sooy ; co-sponsoring agencies, National Association of State Directors of Law Enforcement Training, Texas Commission on Law Enforcement, Officer Standards, and Education. Washington, D.C. : Law Enforcement Assistance Administration, U. S. Dept. of Justice, 1979. ix, 465 p. ; 28 cm. Convened by LEAA's Office of Criminal Justice Education and Training. Bibliography: p. 267-277.   LC Card 79-603983   DDC 363.2/2 19
1. Police - United States - Congresses. 2. Job analysis - Congresses. 3. Police - United States - Job descriptions - Congresses. 4. Police training - United States - Congresses. I. Giddings, Larry A. II. Sooy, Diana. III. National Association of State Directors of

Law Enforcement Training. IV. Texas. Commission on Law Enforcement Officer Standards and Education. V. United States. Law Enforcement Assistance Administration. Office of Criminal Justice Education and Training.
HV8143 .N39 1978

National Symposium on Waterborne Transmission of Giardiasis, Cincinnati, 1978. Waterborne transmission of giardiasis : proceedings of a symposium September 18-20, 1978 / sponsored by the Health Effects Research Laboratory and the Municipal Envirnomental Research Laboratory ; edited by W. Jakubowski and J. C. Hoff. Cincinnati : U. S. Environmental Protection Agency, Office of Research and Development, Environmental Research Center ; Springfield, Va. : National Technical Information Service, 1979. xiv, 306 p. : ill. ; 24 cm. "EPA-600/9-79-001." Includes bibliographical references.   LC Card 79-603744   DDC 614.5/3 19
1. Giardiasis - Congresses. 2. Giardia - Congresses. 3. Giardiasis - Transmission - Congresses. 4. Waterborne infection - Congresses. I. Jakubowski, Walter. II. Hoff, John C. III. Health Effects Research Laboratory, Cincinnati, Ohio. IV. Municipal Environmental Research Laboratory. V. Title.
RC145 .N37 1978

National Technology Foundation Act of 1980. United States. Congress. House. Committee on Science and Technology. Subcommittee on Science, Research, and Technology. H.R. 6910 . Washington , 1981. iii, 887 p. :   LC Card 81-601618   DDC 344.73/095 347.30495 19
KF27 .S399 1980i

NATIONAL TECHNOLOGY FOUNDATION (U. S.) United States. Congress. House. Committee on Science and Technology. Subcommittee on Science, Research, and Technology. H.R. 6910 . Washington , 1981. iii, 887 p. :   LC Card 81-601618   DDC 344.73/095 347.30495 19
KF27 .S399 1980i

National Training and Information Center. Home mortgage disclosure act and reinvestment strategies : A guidebook / for U. S. Department of Housing and Urban Development, Office of Policy Development and Research, by National Training and Information Center under contract number H-2666. [Washington] : HUD, 1979. ii, 94 p. : ill. ; 28 cm.   LC Card 79-603975
1. Mortgage loans - United States. 2. Discrimination in mortgage loans - United States. I. United States. Dept. of Housing and Urban Development. Office of Policy Development and Research. II. Title.
HG2040.5.U5 N43 1979
NYPL [JLF 81-232]

National Transportation Safety Board authorization . United States. Congress. Senate. Committee on Commerce, Science, and Transportation. Washington , 1980. iii, 26 p. ;   LC Card 80-602102   DDC 353.0072/236875 19
KF26 .C69 1980h

National Urban League. National Urban League Entrepreneurial Development Program : final report. [New York] : The League, 1972. 54 p. in various pagings ; 28 cm. "... Accomplished ... under contract with the Economic Development Administration." On cover: Economic Development Administration. Technical Assistance Project. U. S. Department of Commerce.
1. Minority business enterprises - United States. 2. Afro-American business enterprises. I. United States. Economic Development Administration. II. Title.
NYPL [JLF 80-1689]

National Urban League Entrepreneurial Development Program . National Urban League. [New York] , 1972. 54 p. in various pagings ;   *NYPL [JLF 80-1689]*

National Urban League (for Social Service among Negroes) see National Urban League.

NATIONAL URBAN LEAGUE - HISTORY - SOURCES. Schomburg Center for Research in Black Culture. Records. 1924-1979. 53 boxes.
NYPL [Sc Rare MSS-44]

National Urban League. Research Dept. The black aged in New York State : a graphic analysis prepared for the New York State Conference on the Black Aged, June 27-28, 1974 / by National Urban League Research

Dept. and New York City Office for the Aging. New York : [s. n., 1974?] 14 p. : all ill. ; 28 cm. Microfiche (neg.) 1 sheet. 11 x 15 cm. (NYPL FSN Sc 017,807) Cover title. Includes bibliographical references.
1. Afro-American aged - New York (State). I. New York (City). Office for the Aging. II. Title.
NYPL [Sc Micro F-8063]

National urban recreation study . United States. Heritage Conservation and Recreation Service. [Washington , 1978] 184 p. :   LC Card 78-602420
GV53 .U54 1978

NATIONAL VISITOR CENTER. United States. Congress. House. Committee on Public Works and Transportation. Subcommittee on Public Buildings and Grounds. To amend the National Visitor Center Facilities Act of 1968 . Washington , 1980. iii, 34 p. :   LC Card 81-600581   DDC 344.73/09 347.3049 19
KF27 .P8964 1979e

National Weather Service. see United States. National Weather Service.

National wildlife refuges . United States. Congress. House. Committee on Merchant Marine and Fisheries. Subcommittee on Fisheries and Wildlife Conservation and the Environment. Washington , 1980. vii, 584 p. :   LC Card 80-602809   DDC 346.7304/695 19
KF27 .M447 1979f

National workers' compensation standards act of 1979 . United States. Congress. House. Committee on Education and Labor. Subcommittee on Labor Standards. Washington , 1980. vi, 815 p. :   LC Card 80-603427   DDC 344.73/021 19
KF27 .E348 1980c

National workers' compensation standards act of 1979 . United States. Congress. Senate. Committee on Labor and Human Resources. Washington , 1980. vi, 794 p. :   LC Card 80-602897   DDC 344.73/021 19
KF26 .L27 1979y

National Workshop on Auto Theft Prevention, New York, 1978. National Workshop on Auto Theft Prevention : compendium of proceedings, New York Hilton Hotel, October 3-6, 1978 / sponsored by the New York State Senate Committee on Transportation. Albany : The Senate, [1979] 167 p., [1] leaf of plates : ill. ; 26 cm. Bibliography: p. 167.   LC Card 79-623519
1. Automobile theft - United States - Prevention - Congresses. 2. Automobile theft investigation - United States - Congresses. I. New York (State). Legislature. Senate. Committee on Transportation.
HV6658 .N37 1978   *NYPL [JLF 80-1515]*

National Youth Workers Alliance, Washington, D. C. Runaway youth program directory / prepared for the Office of Juvenile Justice and Delinquency Prevention, LEAA, U. S. Department of Justice by the National Youth Workers Alliance. [Washington, D.C.] : The Office, [1979] 109 p. : map ; 23 cm. "August 1979." LC Card 79-604199
1. Runaway youth - Services for - United States - Directories. I. United States. Law Enforcement Assistance Administration. Office of Juvenile Justice and Delinquency Prevention. II. Title.
HV1431 .N37 1979   *NYPL [JLD 81-606]*

NATIONALISM AND NATIONALITY. see NATIONALISM.

NATIONALISM - BIBLIOGRAPHY. Bentley, G. Carter. Ethnicity and nationality . Seattle [1981] p. cm. ISBN 0-295-95853-7 LC Card 81-51280 DDC 016.3058 19
Z5118.E84 B46 GN495.6

NATIONALISM - GREECE. Herzfeld, Michael, 1947- Ours once more . Austin , 1981. p. cm. ISBN 0-292-76018-3 LC Card 81-10398 DDC 398/.09495 19
GR170 .H47

NATIONALISM - UNITED STATES - HISTORY. Lipow, Arthur. Authoritarian socialism in America . Berkeley , c1981. p. cm. ISBN 0-520-04005-8 LC Card 79-65763 DDC 320.5/31/0973 19
HX86 .L73

Nations Unies. see United Nations.

The Nation's use of health resources, 1979 /.

Haupt, Barbara J. [Washington] [1980] x, 169 p. ; LC Card 80-602252 DDC 362.1/0973 19
RA410.53 .H38

The nationwide boating survey. United States. Coast Guard. Office of Boating Safety. Recreational boating in the Continental United States in 1973 and 1976 . Washington, D.C. [1979] vii, 121, [131] p. : LC Card 79-602077
GV776.A2 U54 1979

Native American series .
(no. 4) Oandasan, William. A branch of California redwood /. Los Angeles, CA , c1980. p. cm. ISBN 0-935626-03-4 LC Card 81-3518 DDC 811/.54 19
PS3565.A5 B7

Native American women and equal opportunity . United States. Women's Bureau. [Washington, D.C.] , 1979. vii, 81 p. : LC Card 80-600536
E98.W8 U54 1979 **NYPL [HBC 81-449]**

Native Americans in films. O'Connor, John E. The Hollywood Indian . Trenton, N.J. , c1980. xvi, 79 p. : ISBN 0-938766-00-7 (pbk.) LC Card 80-620048 DDC 791.43/09/093520397 19
PN1995.9.I48 O33

Native basketry of Western North America . Jones, Joan Megan. Springfield , 1978. viii, 63 p. : ISBN 0-89792-075-9 LC Card 79-625517 DDC 069/.09773/56 s 746.41/2/08997078 19
AM101 .I373 no. 3 E78.W5

Native names of Mexican birds . Birkenstein, Lillian R. Washington , 1981. p. cm. LC Card 80-606886 DDC 333.95/4 s 598.2972/014 19
S914 .A3 no. 138 QL686

Natividad, Alberto. A Drug terminology--general glossary, English-Spanish/Spanish-English . [Los Angeles] [1980] vi, 134 p. ; LC Card 80-135304 DDC 616.86/3/00326 19
RC564 .D783

NATO. see North Atlantic Treaty Organization.

NATO--a status report : a report to the Committee on Foreign Relations, United States Senate. Washington : U. S. G.P.O., 1980. viii, 24 p. ; 24 cm. At head of title: 96th Congress, 2d session. Committee print. Report of a trip, Aug. 7-16, 1980, by a delegation of U. S. Senators led by Howard H. Baker, Jr. "October 1980." LC Card 80-603869 DDC 355/.031/091821 19
1. North Atlantic Treaty Organization. I. Baker, Howard H. (Howard Henry), 1925-. II. United States. Congress. Senate. Committee on Foreign Relations.
UA646.3 .N225

Nato Advanced Study Institute on Atomic and Molecular Processes in Controlled Thermonuclear Fusion, Castéra-Verduzan, France, 1979. Atomic and molecular physics in controlled thermonuclear fusion / edited by M. R. C. McDowell and A. M. Ferendeci. New York : Plenum Press, c1980. xii, 493 p. : graphs ; 26 cm. (NATO advanced study institutes series. Series B: physics. v. 53) "Lectures presented at the NATO Advanced Study Institute on Atomic and Molecular Processes in Controlled Thermonuclear Fusion, held at Chateau de Bonas, Castera-Verduzan, Gers, France, August 13-24, 1979." Includes bibliographical references and indexes. ISBN 0-306-40424-9 LC Card 80-238
1. Controlled fusion - Congresses. 2. Fusion reactors - Congresses. 3. Collisions (Nuclear physics) - Congresses. I. McDowell, M. R. C. II. Ferendeci, A. M. III. North Atlantic Treaty Organization. IV. Title. V. Title: Molecular processes. VI. Series.
QC791.7 .N37 1979 **NYPL [JSF 81-175]**

Nato Advanced Study Institute on Field Theoretical Methods in Particle Physics, University of Kaiserslautern, 1979. Field theoretical methods in particle physics / edited by Werner Rühl. New York : Published in cooperation with NATO Scientific Affairs Division [by] Plenum Press, c1980. ix, 598 p. : graphs ; 26 cm. (NATO advanced study institutes series. Series B: physics. v. 55) "Lectures presented at the NATO Advanced Study Institute on Kaiserslautern, Kaiserslautern, German Federal Republic, August 13-24, 1979." Includes bibliographical references and index.
ISBN 0-306-40444-3 LC Card 80-11773
1. Field theory (Physics) - Congresses. 2. Particles (Nuclear physics) - Congresses. I. Rühl, Werner. II. North Atlantic Treaty Organization. III. Title. IV. Series.
QC793.3.F5 N37 1979 **NYPL [JSF 80-1051]**

Nato Advanced Study Institute on Nondestructive Evaluation of Semiconductor Materials and Devices, Villa Tuscolano, Italy, 1978. Nondestructive evaluation of semiconductor materials and devices : [lectured presented at the NATO Advanced Study Institute on Nondestructive Evaluation of Semiconductor Materials and Devices, held at the Villa Tuscolano, Italy, September 19-29, 1978] / edited by Jay N. Zemel. New York : Plenum Press, c1979. xi, 782 p. : ill. ; 26 cm. (NATO advanced study institutes series. Series B: physics. v. 46) Incudes bibliographical references and index. "Published in cooperation with NATO Scientific Affairs Division." ISBN 0-306-40293-9 LC Card 79-16499
1. Semiconductors - Testing - Congresses. I. Zemel, Jay N. II. North Atlantic Treaty Organization. Division of Scientific Affairs. III. Title. IV. Series.
TK7871.85 .N376 1978 **NYPL [JSF 80-961]**

NATO advanced study institutes series. Series B: physics.
(v. 46) Nato Advanced Study Institute on Nondestructive Evaluation of Semiconductor Materials and Devices, Villa Tuscolano, Italy, 1978. Nondestructive evaluation of semiconductor materials and devices . New York , c1979. xi, 782 p. : ISBN 0-306-40293-9 LC Card 79-16499
TK7871.85 .N376 1978 **NYPL [JSF 80-961]**

(v. 53) Nato Advanced Study Institute on Atomic and Molecular Processes in Controlled Thermonuclear Fusion, Castéra-Verduzan, France, 1979. Atomic and molecular physics in controlled thermonuclear fusion /. New York , c1980. xii, 493 p. : ISBN 0-306-40424-9 LC Card 80-238
QC791.7 .N37 1979 **NYPL [JSF 81-175]**

(v. 55) Nato Advanced Study Institute on Field Theoretical Methods in Particle Physics, University of Kaiserslautern, 1979. Field theoretical methods in particle physics /. New York , c1980. ix, 598 p. : ISBN 0-306-40444-3 LC Card 80-11773
QC793.3.F5 N37 1979 **NYPL [JSF 80-1051]**

(v. 44) Cargèse Summer Institute on Recent Developments in Gravitation, 1978. Recent developments in gravitation, Cargèse, 1978 /. New York , c1979. viii, 596 p. : ISBN 0-306-40198-3 LC Card 79-9174
QC178 .C18 1978

NATO after Afghanistan . Lunn, Simon. Washington , 1980. ix, 64 p. ; LC Card 80-603855 DDC 355/.031/091821 19
UA646.3 .L85

NATO and Western security in the 1980's--the European perception . United States. Congress. House. Committee on Foreign Affairs. Washington , 1980. viii, 78 p. : LC Card 80-601730 DDC 355/.03304 19
UA646 .U48 1980

NATO collaboration and the U. S. arms export control issue. United States. General Accounting Office. No easy choice . Washington, D.C. , 1981. vii, 84 p. : LC Card 81-600892 DDC 382/.456234/0973 19
HD9743.U6 U59 1981

Nato Conference on Fjord Oceanography, Victoria, B.C., 1979. Fjord oceanography : [proceedings of the NATO Conference on Fjord Oceanography, held in Victoria, British Columbia, Canada, June 4-8, 1979, and sponsored by the NATO Special Program Panel on Marine Sciences] / edited by Howard J. Freeland and David M. Farmer and Colin D. Levings. New York : Published in coordination with NATO Scientific Affairs Division by Plenum Press, c1980. xiv, 715 p. : ill. ; 26 cm. (NATO conference series; IV, Marine sciences. v. 4) Includes bibliographies and indexes. ISBN 0-306-40439-7 LC Card 80-12273
1. Fjords - Congresses. 2. Oceanography - Congresses. 3. Marine ecology - Congresses. I. Freeland, Howard J. II. Farmer, David M. III. Levings, Colin D. IV. North Atlantic Treaty Organization. Division of Scientific Affairs. V. Nato Special Program Panel on Marine Sciences. VI. Title.
GC28 .N37 1979 **NYPL [JSF 80-1088]**

Nato conference series. Series 1: Ecology.
(v.1) Conference on the Functions of Living Plant Collections in Conservation and Conservation-Orientated Research and Public

Education, Kew, Eng., 1975. Conservation of threatened plants . New York , c1976. xvi, 336 p. : ISBN 0-306-32801-1 LC Card 76-20762
QK86.A1 C66 1975 **NYPL [JSK 77-181 v.1]**

NATO Scientific Affairs Division. see North Atlantic Treaty Organization. Division of Scientific Affairs.

Nato Special Program Panel on Marine Sciences. Nato Conference on Fjord Oceanography, Victoria, B.C., 1979. Fjord oceanography . New York , c1980. xiv, 715 p. : ISBN 0-306-40439-7 LC Card 80-12273
GC28 .N37 1979 **NYPL [JSF 80-1088]**

NATO support agreements . United States. Congress. Senate. Committee on Armed Services. Subcommittee on Procurement Policy and Reprograming. Washington , 1980. iii, 17 p. ; LC Card 80-603045 DDC 341.7/2 19
KF26 .A768 1980

NATO, task of adaptation /. Strausz-Hupé, Robert, 1903- [Columbia] , 1978. 18 p. ; LC Card 79-622644 DDC 341.7/2 19
JX1393.N67 S77

A Natural area survey .
(no. 10) Fresno Canyon. [Austin] , 1976. 144 p., [1] leaf of plates : LC Card 80-623781 DDC 508.764/933 19
QH105.T4 F73

(no. 12) Bofecillos Mountains. [Austin] , 1976. 181 p. : LC Card 80-623783 DDC 508.764/933 19
QE168.B63 B63

(no. 14) Enchanted Rock. [Austin] , 1979. 166 p., [1] leaf of plates : LC Card 80-623785 DDC 508.764/62 19
QH105.T4 E52

(pt. 3) Mount Livermore and Sawtooth Mountain /. [Austin] , 1973. 84 p., [1] leaf of plates : LC Card 80-623871 DDC 508.764/934 19
QH105.T4 M68

A natural area survey of ten northwestern Missouri counties /. Iffrig, Greg F. [Jefferson City] , 1979. 75 leaves : LC Card 80-621252 DDC 333.78/09778/1 19
QH76.5.M8 I34

NATURAL AREAS - IDAHO.
Rabe, Fred W. Aquatic natural areas in Idaho /. Moscow, Idaho [1977] 103 p., [7] leaves of plates : LC Card 80-621482 DDC 333.95/2/09796 19
QH76.5.I2 R33

NATURAL AREAS - LAW AND LEGISLATION - UNITED STATES.
United States. Congress. Senate. Committee on Energy and Natural Resources. Subcommittee on Parks, Recreation, and Renewable Resources. National heritage policy act of 1979 . Washington , 1980. iv, 517 p. : LC Card 80-603718 DDC 344.73/094 19
KF26 .E5565 1980d

NATURAL AREAS - MISSOURI.
Iffrig, Greg F. A natural area survey of ten northwestern Missouri counties /. [Jefferson City] , 1979. 75 leaves : LC Card 80-621252 DDC 333.78/09778/1 19
QH76.5.M8 I34

NATURAL AREAS - TEXAS - DAVIS MOUNTAINS.
Mount Livermore and Sawtooth Mountain /. [Austin] , 1973. 84 p., [1] leaf of plates : LC Card 80-623871 DDC 508.764/934 19
QH105.T4 M68

NATURAL AREAS - TEXAS - LLANO CO.
Enchanted Rock. [Austin] , 1979. 166 p., [1] leaf of plates : LC Card 80-623785 DDC 508.764/62 19
QH105.T4 E52

NATURAL AREAS - TEXAS - PRESIDIO CO.
Fresno Canyon. [Austin] , 1976. 144 p., [1] leaf of plates : LC Card 80-623781 DDC 508.764/933 19
QH105.T4 F73

Natural bridges of Tennessee /. Corgan, James X. Nashville , 1979. viii, 102 p. ; LC Card 79-626059 DDC 557.68 s 551.4 19
QE165 .A2 no. 80 GB565.T4

NATURAL BRIDGES - TENNESSEE.
Corgan, James X. Natural bridges of Tennessee /. Nashville , 1979. viii, 102 p. ; LC Card

79-626059 DDC 557.68 s 551.4 19
QE165 .A2 no. 80 GB565.T4

NATURAL CHILDBIRTH - ADDRESSES, ESSAYS, LECTURES.
Childbirth, alternatives to medical control /. Austin , 1981. p. cm. ISBN 0-292-71072-0 : LC Card 81-11644 DDC 362.1/982 19
RG940 .C47

Natural disaster survey report .
(80-1) United States. National Oceanic and Atmospheric Administration. Red River Valley tornadoes of April 10, 1979 . Rockville, Md. [1980] v, 60 p., [2] leaves of plates : LC Card 80-601568 DDC 363.3/492 19
QC955.5.T4 U54 1980

NATURAL DISASTERS - CONNECTICUT.
Connecticut. Office of Civil Preparedness. Hazard analysis and mitigation. [Hartford] [1978?] 67 p. : LC Card 79-622876 DDC 363.3/4/09746 19
GB5010 .C66 1978

NATURAL DISASTERS - OREGON - BENTON CO.
Bela, James L. Geologic hazards of eastern Benton County, Oregon /. Portland, Or. , 1979. viii, 122 p. : LC Card 80-622942 DDC 553/.09795 s 624.1/51/0979534 19
QE155 .A3 no. 98 QE156.B46

NATURAL DISASTERS - UNITED STATES - INFORMATION SERVICES.
Hays, Walter W. Program and plans of the U. S. Geological Survey for producing information needed in national seismic hazards and risk assessment, fiscal years 1980-84 /. [Arlington, Va.] , 1979. iv, 40 p. : LC Card 80-602831 DDC 557.3 s 363.3/495 19
QE75 .C5 no. 816 QE535.2.U6

NATURAL GAS. see GAS, NATURAL.

Natural gas issues, 1979 . United States. Congress. House. Committee on Interstate and Foreign Commerce. Subcommittee on Energy and Power. Washington , 1980. iii, 289 p. : LC Card 80-602780 DDC 333.8/233/0973 19
KF27 .I5542 1979ae

Natural gas plan needed to provide greater protection for highpriority and critical uses . United States. General Accounting Office. Washington, D.C. , 1981. v, 46 p. ; LC Card 81-601431 DDC 333.8/233/0973 19
HD9581.U5 U54 1981

Natural gas supplies . United States. Congress. House. Committee on Interstate and Foreign Commerce. Subcommittee on Oversight and Investigations. Washington , 1975- v. : LC Card 75-602828
KF27 .I5547 1975

Natural gas transmission system optimization [by] George Dantzig [and others] With contributions by Gunther Buerk [and others] New York, American Gas Association [1970] iv, 276 p. illus. 28 cm. Report of research performed at the Operations Research Center of the University of California at Berkeley under contract with the Pipeline Research Committee of the American Gas Association under the association's project NX-37. Bibliography: p. 276. LC Card 76-124102 *1. Gas, Natural - Pipe lines - Mathematical models. 2. Electronic data processing - Gas, Natural - Pipe lines. I. Dantzig, George Bernard, 1914-. II. California. University. Operations Research Center. III. American Gas Association. Pipeline Research Committee. IV. Title.*
TN880.5 .N37 **NYPL [JSF 80-864]**

NATURAL HISTORY - FOX RIVER, WIS. AND ILL.
Snearley, K. E. Environmental inventory of the Chain of Lakes and Fox River region of Illinois /. [Antioch] , 1977. ix, 185 p., [5] leaves of plates (4 fold.) : LC Card 78-620605 DDC 574.9773/2 19
QH105.I3 S65

NATURAL HISTORY - GEORGIA - SAPELO ISLAND.
Teal, Mildred. Portrait of an island /. Athens, Ga. [1981] p. cm. ISBN 0-8203-0585-5 LC Card 81-7631 DDC 574.9758/737 19
QH105.G4 T4 1981

NATURAL HISTORY - GREAT FALLS, POTOMAC RIVER - GUIDE-BOOKS.
Reed, John Calvin, 1930- The river and the

rocks . Washington , 1980. vii, 75 p. : LC Card 80-600023 DDC 557.3 s 557.52 19
QE75 .B9 no. 1471 QE122.G7

NATURAL HISTORY - ILLINOIS - CHAIN O'LAKES REGION.
Snearley, K. E. Environmental inventory of the Chain of Lakes and Fox River region of Illinois /. [Antioch] , 1977. ix, 185 p., [5] leaves of plates (4 fold.) : LC Card 78-620605 DDC 574.9773/2 19
QH105.I3 S65

NATURAL HISTORY - LAKE CHAMPLAIN WATERSHED.
Lake Champlain Basin Study (United States.) Shaping the future of Lake Champlain . [Boston, Mass.] [1979] x, 124, 45 p. ; LC Card 80-622025 DDC 333.91/6316/097454 19
TD225.L252 L34 1979

NATURAL HISTORY - MINNESOTA - CROW RIVER REGION.
Kucera, Thomas. River survey report of North Fork Crow River and Crow River /. [St. Paul] , 1977. 79 p. : LC Card 78-620652 DDC 597.092/9776/5 19
QL628.M6 K83

NATURAL HISTORY - NEBRASKA.
McCarraher, D. Bruce. Nebraska's sandhills lakes /. Lincoln , 1977. 67 p. : LC Card 77-623677 DDC 574.5/2636 19
QH105.N2 M32

The natural history of H.G. Wells /. Reed, John Robert, 1938- Athens, c1981. p. cm. ISBN 0-8214-0628-0 LC Card 81-11261 DDC 823/.912 19
PR5778.P5 R4 1981

NATURAL HISTORY - OKLAHOMA - OSAGE COUNTY (OKLA.)
Mathews, John Joseph, 1895- Talking to the moon /. Norman [Okla.] [1981] c1945. viii, 243 p. ; ISBN 0-8061-1611-0 LC Card 81-137822 DDC 976.6/2505/0924 19
E99.O8 M298 1981

NATURAL HISTORY - OREGON - ROGUE RIVER.
Purdom, William B. Guide to the geology and lore of the wild reach of the Rogue River, Oregon /. Eugene , 1977. 67 p. : LC Card 77-622970 DDC 917.95/2 19
QH1 .O7 no. 22 QH105.O7

NATURAL HISTORY - TEXAS - BOFECILLOS MOUNTAINS.
Bofecillos Mountains. [Austin] , 1976. 181 p. : LC Card 80-623783 DDC 508.764/933 19
QE168.B63 B63

NATURAL HISTORY - TEXAS - DAVIS MOUNTAINS.
Mount Livermore and Sawtooth Mountain /. [Austin] , 1973. 84 p., [1] leaf of plates : LC Card 80-623871 DDC 508.764/934 19
QH105.T4 M68

NATURAL HISTORY - TEXAS - LLANO CO.
Enchanted Rock. [Austin] , 1979. 166 p., [1] leaf of plates : LC Card 80-623785 DDC 508.764/62 19
QH105.T4 E52

NATURAL HISTORY - TEXAS - PRESIDIO CO.
Fresno Canyon. [Austin] , 1976. 144 p., [1] leaf of plates : LC Card 80-623781 DDC 508.764/933 19
QH105.T4 F73

Natural increase differentials, 1960-1975 /. Arkansas. University. Population and Employment Studies Section. Little Rock, Ark. , 1976. 17 p. : LC Card 77-622036 DDC 312/.8/09767 19
HA256 .A7 1976

NATURAL MONUMENTS - UNITED STATES.
Harris, David V. The geologic story of the national parks and monuments /. Fort Collins, Colo. (271 S.W. Aylesworth, Fort Collins 80523) , 1980. xvi, 322 p., [3] p. of plates : LC Card 81-112429 DDC 557.3 19
QE77 .H368 1980

NATURAL PHILOSOPHY. see PHYSICS.

Natural Resource Policies in Relation to Economic Development and International Cooperation, Wisconsin Seminar on. see Wisconsin Seminar on Natural Resource

Policies in Relation to Economic Development and International Cooperation, University of Wisconsin--Madison, 1977-1978.

NATURAL RESOURCES.
Global 2000 Study (U. S.) The global 2000 report to the President--entering the twenty-first century . Washington, D.C. , 1980- v. <1-2> : LC Card 80-602859 DDC 333.7 19
HC79.E5 G59 1980b

NATURAL RESOURCES - ALASKA.
Gudgel-Holmes, Dianne. Ethnohistory of four interior Alaskan waterbodies /. [Anchorage, Alaska] [1979] 148 p. : LC Card 80-623266 DDC 979.8/4 19
F910 .G78

NATURAL RESOURCES - ALASKA - CONGRESSES.
Alaska Science Conference, 29th, University of Alaska, Fairbanks, 1978. Alaska fisheries . [Fairbanks , 1979] ix, 796 p. : LC Card 80-622119 DDC 639/.2/09798 19
SH222.A4 A64 1978

Natural resources and environment in the Bureau of Oceans and International Environmental and Scientific Affairs . United States. Congress. House. Committee on Science and Technology. Subcommittee on Science, Research, and Technology. Washington , 1980. iii, 159 p. ; LC Card 80-603700 DDC 353.0085/5 19
KF27 .S399 1980e

NATURAL RESOURCES - CALIFORNIA.
California. Dept. of Forestry. California's forest resources . [Sacramento, CA] , 1979. ca. 500 p. in various pagings : LC Card 80-622914 DDC 333.75/09794 19
SD144.C2 C3 1979

Natural Resources Center (Conn.) Henney, Louise H. Natural resources information directory for the State of Connecticut, 1980 /. [Hartford, CT] [1980] ii, 39 p. : LC Card 80-623121 DDC 333.7/025/746 19
HC107.C8 H453

NATURAL RESOURCES - CONGRESSES.
Wisconsin Seminar on Natural Resource Policies in Relation to Economic Development and International Cooperation, University of Wisconsin--Madison, 1977-1978. Resources and development . Madison , London , c1980. xv, 500 p. ; ISBN 0-299-08250-4 : LC Card 80-10577
HC55 .W57 1977a **NYPL [JLE 80-3198]**

NATURAL RESOURCES - CONSERVATION. see CONSERVATION OF NATURAL RESOURCES.

Natural resources information directory for the State of Connecticut, 1980 /. Henney, Louise H. [Hartford, CT] [1980] ii, 39 p. : LC Card 80-623121 DDC 333.7/025/746 19
HC107.C8 H453

NATURAL RESOURCES - INFORMATION SERVICES - CONNECTICUT - DIRECTORIES.
Henney, Louise H. Natural resources information directory for the State of Connecticut, 1980 /. [Hartford, CT] [1980] ii, 39 p. : LC Card 80-623121 DDC 333.7/025/746 19
HC107.C8 H453

NATURAL RESOURCES - LAW AND LEGISLATION - NEW JERSEY.
New Jersey. Legislature. General Assembly. Committee on Agriculture and Environment. Public hearing before Assembly Agriculture and Environment Committee, on Assembly no. 1818 (Natural resources bond issue) . [Trenton] [1980] 24, 6 p. ; LC Card 80-623796 DDC 344.749/046 347.490446 19
KFN1811.4 .A3 1980a

NATURAL RESOURCES - LOUISIANA - NEW ORLEANS REGION - COLLECTED WORKS.
Willdan Associates. Mississippi Deltaic Plain Region ecological characterization . [Washington] [1980- v. <1> : LC Card 80-603195 DDC 330.9763/3063 19
HC108.N42 W54 1980

NATURAL RESOURCES - MICHIGAN.
Michigan. Dept. of Natural Resources. Michigan's forest resources, 1979 . [Lansing, Mich.] [1980?] xv, 134 p., [1] leaf of plates :

LC Card 80-621232   DDC 333.75/09774 19
HC107.M5 M4343 1980

**NATURAL RESOURCES - MISSISSIPPI -
GULF REGION - COLLECTED WORKS.**
Willdan Associates. Mississippi Deltaic Plain
Region ecological characterization .
[Washington] [1980- v. <1> :   LC Card
80-603195   DDC 330.9763/3063 19
HC108.N42 W54 1980

**NATURAL RESOURCES - MISSISSIPPI
RIVER - DELTA - COLLECTED WORKS.**
Willdan Associates. Mississippi Deltaic Plain
Region ecological characterization .
[Washington] [1980- v. <1> :   LC Card
80-603195   DDC 330.9763/3063 19
HC108.N42 W54 1980

**NATURAL RESOURCES - NEW YORK
(STATE) - CLASSIFICATION.**
New York (State). Office of Planning Services.
LUNR classification manual. Albany , 1974. 23
p. ;   *NYPL [*XME-9096]*

**NATURAL RESOURCES - NEW YORK
(STATE) - PERIODICALS.**
The Conservationist. v. 14, no. 5- ; Apr./May
1960- Albany.
             *NYPL [*ZAN-T5219 & M-10 5488]*

**NATURAL RESOURCES - VIRGINIA -
INFORMATION SERVICES - VIRGINIA.**
Virginia. General Assembly. Joint Subcommittee
Studying the Virginia Resource Information
System. Report of the Joint Subcommittee
Studying the Virginia Resource Information
System (VARIS) to the Governor and the
General Assembly of Virginia. Richmond ,
1980. 134 p. ;   LC Card 80-622729   DDC
300/.9755 s 025/.063337/09755 19
J87 .V9 1980c no. 20 HC107.V8

NATURAL SCENERY. see LANDSCAPE.

**NATURAL SCIENCE. see PHYSICS;
SCIENCE.**

Natural soil groups, St. Marys County, Maryland
/. United States. Soil Conservation Service.
[Lanham? Md.] [1981] 1 map : LC Card
81-693031
G3843.S3J3 1981 .U5

Natural soil groups, Worcester County, Maryland
/. United States. Soil Conservation Service.
[Lanham? Md.] [1980?] 1 map : LC Card
81-693029
G3843.W6J3 1980 .U5

**NATURAL WATER CHEMISTRY. see WATER
CHEMISTRY.**

NATURALISM IN LITERATURE.
Pizer, Donald. Twentieth-century American
literary naturalism . Carbondale , c1982. p. cm.
ISBN 0-8093-1027-9 LC Card 81-5606 DDC
813/.5/0912 19
PS374.N29 P5

NATURALIZATION - UNITED STATES.
United States. Immigration and Naturalization
Service. Basic guide to naturalization /.
[Washington, D.C.] , 1980] 115 p. : LC Card
80-603228   DDC 323.6/23/0973 19
KF4819 .K316

NATURE.
Bailey, Liberty Hyde, 1858-1954. The holy
earth /. Ithaca, N.Y. , 1980. 112 p., [1] leaf of
plates : ISBN 0-9605314-6-7 (pbk.) LC Card
80-27854   DDC 333.7/01 19
S521 .B16 1980

**The nature and distribution of subsidence
problems affecting HUD and urban areas (task
A)** /. HRB-Singer, inc., State College, Pa.
Energy and Natural Resources Program Dept.
[Washington, D.C.] , 1979. x, 113 p. ; LC Card
79-603258
TH1094 .H17 1979   *NYPL [JSF 81-154]*

Nature Conservancy (United States.) Klein,
Robert, 1947- Long term protection of Maine's
critical areas . Augusta, Va. , Arlington, Va. ,
1978. 85, [118] p. : LC Card 80-620928 DDC
333.7/2/09741 19
HC107.M23 E54

NATURE CONSERVATION - ALASKA.
United States. Heritage Conservation and
Recreation Service. A proposal for protection of
eleven Alaskan rivers /. [Washington, D.C.]
[1980] ca. 200 p. in various pagings : LC Card

80-602406   DDC 333.78/45/09798 19
QH76.5.A4 U56 1980

**NATURE CONSERVATION - ALASKA -
MANAGEMENT.**
United States. Dept. of the Interior. Final
environmental supplement . Washington
[1978?] ca. 600 p. in various pagings : LC Card
79-601643
QH76.5.A4 U54 1978   *NYPL [JLF 81-375]*

**NATURE CONSERVATION - FLORIDA -
EVERGLADES NATIONAL PARK.**
United States. National Park Service. Denver
Service Center. Final environmental statement,
FES-78-7 . [Denver] [1978] vii, 211 p. : LC
Card 79-601941   DDC 333.91/8/0975939 19
QH76.5.F6 U54 1978

NATURE CONSERVATION - MINNESOTA.
Minnesota. Environmental Quality Board.
Potential critical areas inventory. St. Paul ,
1979. [77] p. in various pagings, [2] fold. leaves
of plates : LC Card 79-625262 DDC
333.78/09776 19
QH76.5.M6 M57 1979

NATURE CONSERVATION - MONTANA.
Utter, Jack. Wild river management . Bozeman,
MT [1980] xiii, 117 leaves : LC Card 80-623137
DDC 333.78/45 19
TD224.M9 U88

NATURE CONSERVATION - SNAKE RIVER.
United States. National Park Service. Snake
River . [Washington] [1980] viii, 302 p. : LC
Card 80-602290   DDC 333.78/45/097961 19
QH76.5.S62 U54 1980

**NATURE CONSERVATION - UNITED
STATES - DIRECTORIES.**
Liaison conservation directory for endangered
and threatened species /. Washington, D.C. ,
1980. v, 129 p. : LC Card 81-601550 DDC
333.95/16/0973 19
QH35 .L49 1980

**NATURE CONSERVATION - WASHINGTON
(STATE)**
Washington (State). Water Resources
Management Division. Policy Development
Section. Cedar-Sammamish Basin instream
resources protection program, including
proposed administrative rules, and supplemental
environmental impact statement . Olympia,
Wash. , 1979. 148 p. in various pagings : LC
Card 79-625825   DDC 333.91/0216/0979777 19
TD224.W2 W38 1979

**NATURE, EFFECT OF MAN ON. see MAN -
INFLUENCE ON NATURE.**

The nature of the youth employment problem .
Lerman, Robert I. [Washington, D.C.]
[Springfield, Va.] 1980. 105, 4 p. ; LC Card
80-602227   DDC 331.3/4137973 19
HD6273 .L46

**NATURE PROTECTION. see NATURE
CONSERVATION.**

**NATUROPATHS - LICENSES -
CALIFORNIA.**
California. Legislature. Assembly. Subcommittee
on Health Personnel. Hearing on naturopaths,
November 18, 1980, Sacramento, California /.
Sacramento (Box 90, State Capitol, Sacramento,
CA 95814) [1980] 64 p. ; LC Card 81-621551
DDC 353.97940082/43 19
KFC10.4 .H43 1980

Nault, Michael J. Bibliography and index of
theses and dissertations on the geology of
Louisiana / by Michael J. Nault. Baton Rouge,
La. : Dept. of Natural Resources, Louisiana
Geological Survey, [1980] iv, 36 leaves : maps ;
28 cm. (Resources information series . no. 2)
"July 1980." Includes indexes. LC Card 80-623624 DDC
016.55763 19
*1. Geology - Louisiana - Bibliography. 2. Dissertations,
Academic - United States - Bibliography. I. Title. II.
Series.*
Z6034.U5 L86 QE117

NAUTICAL ALMANACS.
The Astronomical almanac. 1981- Washington.
LC Card 80-647548   *NYPL [JSP 81-85]*

United States. Nautical Almanac Office.
American ephemeris and nautical almanac.
1855-1980. Washington. 126 v. LC Card
70-35435   *NYPL [ONR (United States.
Nautical Almanac Office. American
ephemeris and nautical almanac)]*

**NAUTICAL CHARTS - NEW HAMPSHIRE -
SAUNAPEE, LAKE.**
New Hampshire. Division of Safety Services.
Navigation chart, Lake Sunapee /. [Concord?
N.H.] , 1978. 1 map : LC Card 81-692836
G3742.S93P5 1978 .N4

NAVAHO INDIAN RESERVATION - MAPS.
Nielson, Woodrow. Soil survey of Navajo
Indian Reservation, San Juan County, Utah /.
[Washington] [1980] viii, 119 p., [12] fold.
leaves of plates : LC Card 80-602348 DDC
631.4/7/79259 19
S599.U8 N53

**NAVAHO INDIANS - GOVERNMENT
RELATIONS.**
United States. Congress. House. Committee on
Interior and Insular Affairs. Subcommittee on
Energy and the Environment. Mill tailings dam
break at Church Rock, New Mexico .
Washington , 1980. iv, 232 p. : LC Card
80-601962   DDC 622/.8 19
KF27 .I518 1979i

NAVAHO INDIANS - HANDICAPPED.
Haskins, James, 1941- He will lift up his head .
[Washington] [1978?] 55 p. : LC Card
79-602502
E99.N3 H33   *NYPL [HBC 81-604]*

NAVAHO INDIANS - LEGENDS.
Women versus men . Lincoln , 1982. p. cm.
ISBN 0-8032-2319-6 LC Card 81-7433 DDC
299/.72 19
E99.N3 W74

**NAVAHO INDIANS - RELIGION AD
MYTHOLOGY.**
Women versus men . Lincoln , 1982. p. cm.
ISBN 0-8032-2319-6 LC Card 81-7433 DDC
299/.72 19
E99.N3 W74

**NAVAHO INDIANS - TEXTILE INDUSTRY
AND FABRICS - CATALOGS.**
Maxwell Museum of Anthropology.
Southwestern weaving . Albuquerque , 1981. p.
cm. ISBN 0-8263-0587-3 LC Card 81-8143 DDC
746.1/4/08997079074018961 19
E78.S7 M35 1981

NAVAJO INDIANS - HISTORY.
Brusse, David M. A history of the Chaco
Navajos /. Albuquerque, N.M. , Washington,
D.C. , 1980. viii, 542 p. : LC Card 81-601717
DDC 978.9/8200497 19
E99.N3 B76

**NAVAL ADMINISTRATION. see UNITED
STATES. NAVY.**

**NAVAL ART AND SCIENCE - HISTORY -
20TH CENTURY.**
Vlahos, Michael, 1951- The blue sword .
Newport, R.I. , Washington, D.C. , 1980 [i.e.
1981] p. cm. LC Card 81-9654 DDC
359/.07/1173 19
V420 .V55

**NAVAL ART AND SCIENCE - HISTORY -
BIBLIOGRAPHY.**
Schultz, Charles R. Bibliography of maritime
and naval history periodical articles published
1976-1977 /. College Station , 1979. 90 p. ;
LC Card 79-624012   DDC 016.3875/09 19
Z6837 .S38 VK15

**NAVAL CONSTRUCTION. see SHIP-
BUILDING.**

**Naval Education and Training Program
Development Center.**
Gunner's mate G 1 & C. [Rev. 1980].
[Pensacola, Fla. : Naval Education and Training
Program Development Center ; Washington,
D.C. : U. S. Govt. Print. Off., 1980] ca. 500 p.
in various pagings : ill. ; 27 cm. (Rate training
manual and nonresident career course) Cover title.
"Prepared by the Naval Education and Training
Program Development Center ... for the Chief of Naval
Education and Training." "NAVEDTRA 10186-D."
Previous editions by the U. S. Bureau of Naval
Personnel. Includes index. LC Card 80-603250
DDC 623/.553 19
*1. United States. Navy - Gunner's mates. 2. United
States. Navy - Ordnance and ordnance stores. 3. Naval
gunnery. I. United States. Bureau of Naval Personnel.
Gunner's mate G 1 & C. II. United States. Chief of
Naval Education and Training. III. Title.*
VF160 .N38 1980

Human behavior and leadership / Naval

Education and Training Support Command ; [prepared by the Naval Education and Training Program Development Center, Pensacola, Florida, for the Chief of Naval Education and Training]. [Washington?] : The Command, [1977] i.e. 1978. iii, 163, [51] p. : ill. ; 27 cm. (Rate training manual and nonresident career course) Cover title. "Revised 1977." "NAVEDTRA 10058-B." Previous ed. by U. S. Naval Training Command. Bibliography: p. 158-160. Includes index.   LC Card 78-601716   DDC 158/.4/024359 19
1. Leadership. 2. Psychology, Military. 3. United States. Navy - Petty officers. I. United States. Naval Education and Training Support Command. II. United States. Chief of Naval Education and Training. III. United States. Naval Training Command. Human behavior and leadership. IV. Title.
VB203 .N38 1978

Machinist's mate 3 & 2. Rev. [Washington, D.C. : Naval Education and Training Support Command : U. S. Govt. Print. Off., 1978]. iv, 399, iii, 106 p., [3] fold. leaves of plates : ill. (some col.) ; 27 cm. (Rate training manual and nonresident career course) Cover title. "NAVEDTRA 10524-E." Edition of 1972 issued by United States Naval Training Command. Includes index.   LC Card 80-601617   DDC 623.8/72 19
1. United States. Navy - Machinist's mates. 2. Marine engines - Maintenance and repair. I. United States. Naval Training Command. Machinist's mate 3 & 2. II. Title.
VG803 .N38 1978

United States. Naval Education and Training Command. Gunner's Mate M 1 & C /. [Pensacola, Fla. , Washington, D.C. , 1979] iii, 329, 75 p., [1] fold. leaf of plates :   LC Card 80-601852   DDC 623.4/519 19
VF347 .U56 1979

NAVAL EDUCATION - UNITED STATES.
United States. Congress. House. Committee on Merchant Marine and Fisheries. Ad Hoc Select Subcommittee on Maritime Education and Training. Sea training at maritime academies oversight . Washington, 1980 [i.e. 1981] iv, 246 p. :   LC Card 81-600941   DDC 623.88/07073 19
KF27 .M458 1980

NAVAL EDUCATION - UNITED STATES - PERIODICALS.
Campus; the Navy education training monthly. Pensacola.   LC Card 75-640835
          NYPL [JLM 80-1068]

NAVAL GUNNERY.
Naval Education and Training Program Development Center. Gunner's mate G 1 & C. [Pensacola, Fla. , Washington, D.C. , 1980] ca. 500 p. in various pagings :   LC Card 80-603250   DDC 623/.553 19
VF160 .N38 1980

NAVAL HISTORY - BIBLIOGRAPHY.
Schultz, Charles R. Bibliography of maritime and naval history periodical articles published 1976-1977 /. College Station , 1979. 90 p. ;
   LC Card 79-624012   DDC 016.3875/09 19
Z6837 .S38 VK15

NAVAL HISTORY - CONGRESSES.
United States Naval Academy History Symposium, 3rd, 1977. Changing interpretations and new sources in naval history . New York , 1980. xi, 471 p. :   ISBN 0-8240-9517-0 :   LC Card 80-5
D27 .U63 1977   ***NYPL [JFE 81-505]***

NAVAL MUSEUMS - UNITED STATES - DIRECTORIES.
Bartis, Peter. Maritime folklife resources . Washington, D.C. , 1980. iii, 129 p. ;   LC Card 80-602335   DDC 390/.4/6238 19
GR105 .B37

Naval nuclear propulsion program--1980 . United States. Congress. House. Committee on Armed Services. Procurement and Military Nuclear Systems Subcommittee. Washington , 1980. vi, 246, iv p. :   LC Card 80-602476   DDC 343.73/0194 19
KF27 .A7657 1980

NAVAL POLICY. see SEA-POWER.

NAVAL POWER. see UNITED STATES. NAVY.

Naval research logistics quarterly. v. 1- ; Mar. 1954- [Washington] Office of Naval Research. 26 cm. Microfilm. "Navexos P-1278." INDEXES:

Vols. 1-15, Mar. 1954-1968, precedes v. 1. Vols. 1-20, Mar. 1954-1973, precedes v. 20.
1. Navy-yards and naval stations - Periodicals. 2. Transportation, Military - Periodicals. I. United States. Office of Naval Research.   ***NYPL [*ZAN-5064]***

Naval Safety Center. Fathom. Norfolk, Va..
         NYPL [Sci. & Tech. Div.]

NAVAL WAR COLLEGE (U. S.) - HISTORY - 20TH CENTURY.
Vlahos, Michael, 1951- The blue sword . Newport, R.I. , Washington, D.C. , 1980 [i.e. 1981] p. cm.   LC Card 81-9654   DDC 359/.07/1173 19
V420 .V55

Naval Weapons Center.
   Administrative publication - Naval Weapons Center .
     (200) Iroquois Research Institute. A land use history of Coso Hot Springs, Inyo County, California /. China Lake, Calif. , 1979. xiv, 232 p., [2] leaves of plates (1 fold.) :   LC Card 79-602009   DDC 979.4/87 19
     E99.P2 I7 1979

Naval Weapons Center. Public Works Dept.
Iroquois Research Institute. A land use history of Coso Hot Springs, Inyo County, California /. China Lake, Calif. , 1979. xiv, 232 p., [2] leaves of plates (1 fold.) :   LC Card 79-602009   DDC 979.4/87 19
E99.P2 I7 1979

NAVAL WEAPONS SYSTEMS. see UNITED STATES. NAVY - WEAPONS SYSTEMS.

NAVIGATION, AERIAL. see NAVIGATION (AERONAUTICS)

NAVIGATION (AERONAUTICS)
Barnett, Irene P. Air navigation /. Maxwell Air Force Base, Ala. , 1978. v, 135 p. :   LC Card 79-603385   DDC 629.132/51 19
TL586 .B316

NAVIGATION - ALASKA - HISTORY.
Mohr, Joan Antonson. Alaska and the sea . Anchorage, Ala. , 1979. iii, 104 p. :   LC Card 80-622124   DDC 387/.009798 19
VK24.A4 M63

NAVIGATION - BIBLIOGRAPHY - CATALOGS.
United States. Coast Guard Auxiliary. Auxiliary bibliography of publications. [Washington] , 1979. ii, 95 p. ;   LC Card 79-602683
Z7514.B6 U54 1979 VM321

Navigation chart, Lake Sunapee /. New Hampshire. Division of Safety Services. [Concord? N.H.] , 1978. 1 map :   LC Card 81-692836
G3742.S93P5 1978 .N4

NAVIGATION CHARTS. see NAUTICAL CHARTS.

NAVIGATION - HANDBOOKS, MANUALS, ETC.
(1981) Tobin, Wallace E. The mariner's pocket companion /. Annapolis, Md. [1981] c1974. p. cm.   ISBN 0-87021-381-4 :   LC Card 79-84797   DDC 623.88/02/02 19
VK155 .T6 1981

NAVIGATION - HISTORY - BIBLIOGRAPHY.
Schultz, Charles R. Bibliography of maritime and naval history periodical articles published 1976-1977 /. College Station , 1979. 90 p. ;
   LC Card 79-624012   DDC 016.3875/09 19
Z6837 .S38 VK15

NAVIGATION - LAW AND LEGISLATION. see MARITIME LAW.

NAVIGATION LAWS. see MARITIME LAW.

NAVIGATION - MAPS. see NAUTICAL CHARTS.

Navigation user charges impact the transportation of agricultural products / James Binkley ... [et al.]. Blacksburg, Va. : Virginia Water Resources Research Center, Virginia Polytechnic Institute and State University, [1979] viii, 97 p. : ill. ; 23 cm. (Bulletin - Virginia Water Resources Research Center ; 121) Author statement from label mounted on t.p. "October 1979." "Project B-082-VA." Bibliography: p. 63-67.   LC Card 79-626057   DDC 551.4/8 s 386/.242 19
1. Inland water transportation - United States - Rates. 2. Farm produce - United States - Transportation. I. Binkley, James K. II. Series: Virginia Polytechnic

Institute and State University. Water Resources Research Center. Bulletin, 121.
TD201 .V57 no. 121 HE629

NAVIGATORS. see DISCOVERIES (IN GEOGRAPHY)

NAVVIES. see LABOR AND LABORING CLASSES.

NAVY. see SEA-POWER.

NAVY-YARDS AND NAVAL STATIONS - PERIODICALS.
Naval research logistics quarterly. v. 1- ; Mar. 1954- [Washington]   ***NYPL [*ZAN-5064]***

Naylor, Robert K.
(joint author) Kale, Balkrishna Damodar, 1925- Wisconsin population and households, March 1979 /. Madison, Wis. , 1980. 20 p. ;   LC Card 80-623861   DDC 312/.09775 19
HA716 .K345
(joint author) Kale, Balkrishna Damodar, 1925- Wisconsin population by age and sex, 1958-1990 /. Madison, Wis. [1979] 10 p. :   LC Card 79-625835   DDC 312/.8/09775 19
HA716 .K35

NBS building science series .
(v. 129) Chapman, Robert E. Cost estimation and cost variability in residential rehabilitation /. Washington, D.C. , 1980. x, 109 p. :   LC Card 80-600174   DDC 690/.0218 s 690/.8/0286 19
TA435 .U58 vol. 129 HD7293

(123) Knab, Lawrence I. The effect of moisture on the thermal conductance of roofing systems /. [Washington] , 1980. x, 46 p. :   LC Card 80-600031   DDC 690/.0218 s 690/.15 19
TA435 .U58 no. 123 TH2401

(124) Hurricane wind speeds in the United States /. Washington, D.C. [1980] viii, 30, 11 p. :   LC Card 80-600039   DDC 690/.02/18 s 551.5/52 19
TA435 .U58 no. 124 QC933

NBS monograph .
(166) Barth, James R. Evaluating the impact of securities regulation on venture capital markets /. Washington, D.C. , 1980. iv, 38 p. :   LC Card 80-600036   DDC 602.18 s 332/.0414 19
QC100 .U556 no. 166 HG4963

NBS special publication .
(v 594) International Conference on Nuclear Cross Sections for Technology (1979 : University of Tennessee) Nuclear cross sections for technology . [Washington, D.C.?] , 1980. xvi, 1039 p. :   LC Card 80-600128   DDC 602/.18 s 539.7/54 19
QC100 .U57 no. 594 QC794.6.C7

(250) United States. National Bureau of Standards. Office of Measurement Services. Calibration and related measurement services of the National Bureau of Standards /. Washington , 1978. vii, 100 p. ;   LC Card 79-603214   DDC 602/.8/7 19
T50 .U57 1978

(558) Marshall, Harold E. Efficient allocation of research funds . Washington, D.C. [1979] viii, 47 p. :   LC Card 79-600210   DDC 602/.18 s 338.4/569/0072073 19
QC100 .U57 no. 558 TH23

(560) United States-Japan Cooperative Program in Natural Resources. Panel on Wind and Seismic Effects. Wind and seismic effects . Washington, D.C. , c1980. 604 p. in various pagings :   LC Card 79-600134   DDC 602/.18 s 624.1/76 19
QC100 .U57 no. 560 TA654.5

(570) Spencer, L. V. (Lewis Van Clief), 1924- Structure shielding against fallout gamma rays from nuclear detonations /. [Washington, D.C.?] , 1980. xvi, 967 p :   LC Card 80-600120   DDC 602/.18 s 363.1/89 19
QC100 .U57 no. 570 UF787

(581) Roundtable Discussion of Radon in Buildings, National Bureau of Standards, 1979. Radon in buildings . Washington, D.C. [1980] x, 77 p. :   LC Card 80-600069   DDC 602/.18 s 628.5/35 19
QC100 .U57 no. 581 TD885.5.R33

(585) Conference on Fire Safety for the Handicapped, National Bureau of Standards, 1979. Fire and life safety for the handicapped . Washington, D.C. , 1980. ix, 144 p. :   LC Card

80-600082 DDC 602/.18 s 362.4/38 19
QC100 .U57 no. 585 TH9112

(589) Workshop on Eddy Current
Nondestructive Testing, (1977 : National
Bureau of Standards) Eddy current
nondestructive testing . Washington, D.C. ,
1981. viii, 158 p. : LC Card 80-600172 DDC
602/.18 s 620.1/67 19
QC100 .U57 no. 589 TA417.35

(601) Implant retrieval . Washington, D.C. ,
1981. xi, 776 : LC Card 80-600194 DDC 602/.18
s 617/.307 19
QC100 .U57 no. 601 RD755.5

**NBS/NCSBCS Joint Conference on Research
and Innovation in the Building Regulatory
Process, 3d, Annapolis, 1978.** Research and
innovation in the building regulatory process :
proceedings of the third annual NBS/NCSBCS
Joint Conference, held in Annapolis, Maryland,
on September 12, 1978, in conjunction with the
eleventh annual meeting of the National
Conference of States on Building Codes and
Standards, inc. (NCSBCS) / Patrick W. Cooke,
editor ; sponsored by U. S. Department of
Commerce, National Bureau of Standards and
National Conference of States on Building
Codes and Standards (NCSBCS). Washington :
The Bureau : for Sale by the Supt. of Docs., U.
S. Govt. Print. Off., 1979. x, 360 p. : ill. ; 27
cm. (NBS special publication ; 552) LC Card
79-600090 DDC 602/.18 s 343.73/07869 19
*1. Building laws - United States - Congresses. I. Cooke,
Patrick W. II. United States. National Bureau of
Standards. III. National Conference of States on
Building Codes and Standards. IV. Series: United States.
National Bureau of Standards Special publication, 552.
V. Title.*
QC100 .U57 no. 552 KF5701

**Near coastal zone, Persian Gulf and Gulf of
Oman.** United States. Naval Oceanography
Command Detachment, Asheville, N.C.
Climatic study of the Persian Gulf and Gulf of
Oman . [Washington] [1980] viii, 125 p. : LC
Card 80-602634 DDC 551.69165/35 19
QC994.5 .U53 1980

NEAR EAST - COMMERCE.
Kirkland, Jack J. Market potential of the
Middle East /. [Pullman] , 1980. 82 p. : LC
Card 80-622499 DDC 330.956/04 19
HF3756.Z5 K57

NEAR EAST - ECONOMIC CONDITIONS.
Kirkland, Jack J. Market potential of the
Middle East /. [Pullman] , 1980. 82 p. : LC
Card 80-622499 DDC 330.956/04 19
HF3756.Z5 K57

**NEAR EAST - FOREIGN ECONOMIC
RELATIONS - ADDRESSES, ESSAYS,
LECTURES.**
Africa, the Middle East, and the new
international economic order /. New York ,
1980. xx, 162 p. ; ISBN 0-08-025117-X LC Card
80-14688
HF1611 .A55 1980   *NYPL [Sc E 81-32]*

**NEAR EAST - FOREIGN RELATIONS -
UNITED STATES.**
United States. Congress. Senate. Committee on
Foreign Relations. U. S. Middle East policy .
Washington , 1980. iii, 55 p. ; LC Card
80-602819 DDC 327.73056 19
KF26 .F6 1980g

**Near East - Government. see Near East - Politics
and government.**

**NEAR EAST - LIBRARY RESOURCES -
WASHINGTON (D.C.) - DIRECTORIES.**
Dorr, Steven R. Scholars' guide to Washington,
D.C., for Middle Eastern studies /. Washington,
D.C. , 1981. p. cm. ISBN 0-87474-372-9 LC
Card 81-607073 DDC 956/.00720753 19
Z3013.6 .D67 DS61.9.U6

NEAR EAST - MAPS.
(1973) Defense Mapping Agency. Topographic
Center. Middle East briefing map. [Washington,
D.C., 1973] col. map 91 x 83 cm. Scale
1:1,500,000. Relief shown by shading. "11-73." Series
1308." "Stock no. 1308XMEBRMAP*03."
G7420 1973 .D4 NYPL [Map. Div. 80-3395]

(1980) United States. Central Intelligence
Agency. The eastern Mediterranean.
[Washington , 1980] 1 map : LC Card 81-692535
G7420 1980 .U51

(1980) United States. Central Intelligence
Agency. Southwest Asia. [Washington , 1980] 1
map : LC Card 81-692534
G7420 1980 .U5

**NEAR EAST - POLITICS AND
GOVERNMENT - 1945- - ADDRESSES,
ESSAYS, LECTURES.**
The Middle East challenge, 1980-1985 /.
Carbondale , c1981. p. cm. ISBN 0-8093-1042-2
LC Card 81-5651 DDC 320.956 19
DS63.1 .M486

NEAR EAST - STRATEGIC ASPECTS.
United States. Congress. Senate. Committee on
Foreign Relations. U. S. security interests and
policies in Southwest Asia . Washington , 1980.
iii, 368 p. : LC Card 80-603283 DDC
355/.033056 19
KF26 .F6 1980p

United States-European communities relations .
Washington [D.C.] , 1979. x, 44 p. ; LC Card
80-603969 DDC 337/.09/047 19
HF1411 .U64

Nebesky, William E. An economic evaluation of
the potential for recycling waste materials in
Anchorage, Alaska : final report to the House
Finance Committee of the Alaska State
Legislature / by William E. Nebesky.
Fairbanks : Institute of Social and Economic
Research, University of Alaska, [1980] xiv, 156
p. ; 28 cm. "May 1, 1980." Bibliography: p. 155-156.
LC Card 80-623358 DDC 363.7/28 19
*1. Recycling (Waste, etc.) - Economic aspects -
Alaska - Anchorage. I. Alaska. Legislature. House of
Representatives. Finance Committee. II. Title.*
TD794.5 .N43

Nebiker, Walter. State of Rhode Island and
Providence Plantations, preliminary survey
report, Town of Glocester / [author : Walter
Nebiker]. Providence, R. I. : Historical
Preservation Commission, 1980. iv, 62 leaves,
[14] leaves of plates : ill. (some folded; 28 cm.
Title on cover: Historic and architectural resources of
Glocester, Rhode Island: a preliminary report.
Bibliography: leaves 60-61.
*1. Glocester, R. I. - Building. 2. Historic buildings -
Rhode Island - Glocester. I. Rhode Island. Historical
Preservation Commission. II. Title. III. Title: Historic
and architectural resources of Glocester, Rhode Island:
a preliminary report.*
NYPL [IQK (Glocester) 81-780]

Nebraska.
Nebraska real estate license laws and rules and
regulations / State of Nebraska. Lincoln, Neb.
(301 Centennial Mall, South, P.O. Box 94667,
Lincoln 68509) : Nebraska Real Estate
Commission, 1980. 41 p. in various pagings ; 22
cm. Cover title. "Issued July 19, 1980." LC Card
80-624276 DDC 346.78204/37 347.8206437 19
*1. Real estate agents - Licenses - Nebraska. I.
Nebraska. Real Estate Commission. II. Title.*
KFN282.R4 A3 1980

**Nebraska. Agricultural Experiment Station,
Lincoln.**
Miscellaneous publication .
(MP 39) Wilhite, Donald A. Drought in the
Great Plains . [Lincoln] [1980] 75 p. ; LC
Card 80-624036 DDC 016.363/492 19
Z6683.D7 W54 QC929.D8

Report - Agricultural Experiment Station .
(no. 95) Lamphear, F. Charles. Economic
integration and Nebraska's
agricultural-industrial complex /. [Lincoln] ,
1979. 32 p. ; LC Card 79-625580 DDC
338.1/09782 19
HD9007.N2 L35

NEBRASKA - ANTIQUITIES.
Grange, Roger T. Salvage archeology in the
Red Willow Reservoir, Nebraska /. Lincoln,
Neb. , 1980. xi, 236 p., [1] leaf of plates : LC
Card 80-624104 DDC 978.2 s 978.2/83 19
F661 .N32 no. 9 E78.N3
NYPL [HBA no. 9]

**Nebraska - Archaeology. see Nebraska -
Antiquities.**

Nebraska. Commission on Aging. Bolton,
Christopher R. The determination of
gerontology education appropriate to aging
related occupational roles . [Lincoln] , 1978.
115 leaves / ; LC Card 79-621870 DDC
362.6/07/11 19
HV1451 .B64

Nebraska. Conservation and Survey Division. see
Nebraska. University. Conservation and
Survey Division.

**Nebraska Coordinating Commission for
Postsecondary Education.**
Analysis of the State student incentive grant
programs for 1977-78 / Nebraska Coordinating
Commission for Postsecondary Education.
Lincoln : The Commission, 1979. 17 leaves ; 28
cm. Cover title. LC Card 79-623374 DDC
378/.3/09782 19
1. Student aid - Nebraska. I. Title.
LB2337.5.N2 N4 1979

Fall headcount enrollments in Nebraska
institutions of postsecondary education, 1973
through 1979 . Lincoln, Neb. (P.O. Box 95005,
301 Centennial Mall South, Lincoln 68509)
[1980] iv, 30 p. : LC Card 80-624294 DDC
378/.1059/782 19
LC148 .F34

**Nebraska. Court Rules. Workmen's
Compensation Court.** Rules of procedure of
the Nebraska Workmen's Compensation Court.
Lincoln, Neb. : The Court, [1978] 23 p. ; 22
cm. Cover title. LC Card 78-111321 DDC
344.782/021/0269 19
*1. Workmen's compensation - Nebraska. 2. Nebraska.
Workmen's Compensation Court. 3. Court rules -
Nebraska. I. Title.*
KFN342.A435 A2 1978

**Nebraska. Dept. of Correctional Services.
Research and Planning Section.** Adult male
prisoners, July 1, 1978-June 30, 1979 :
summary statistics of felony prisoners and
parolees. Lincoln, Neb. : Dept. of Correctional
Services, Division of Administrative Services,
Research and Planning Section, 1979. 129 p. ;
28 cm. Cover title: Statistical report, fiscal year
1978-79. Tables. LC Card 80-621736 DDC
365/.44/09782 19
1. Prisoners - Nebraska - Statistics. I. Title.
HV7277 .A6 1979

Nebraska. Dept. of Environmental Control. Rules
and regulations pertaining to compost sites,
effective date, October 30, 1978 / State of
Nebraska, Department of Environmental
Control. [Lincoln] : The Dept., [1978] 16 p. in
various pagings ; 21 cm. Includes index. LC Card
79-625022 DDC 344.782/04626 347.82044626
19
1. Compost - Law and legislation - Nebraska. I. Title.
KFN359.R3 A32 1978

Nebraska. Dept. of Health. Rule 30, regulations
and standards for hospitals : effective date,
April 23, 1979. Lincoln, Neb. : State of
Nebraska, Dept. of Health, [1979] 51 p. :
forms ; 22 cm. Cover title. LC Card 81-621038
DDC 344.782/03211 347.82043211 19
*1. Hospitals - Law and legislation - Nebraska. I. Title.
II. Title: Regulations and standards for hospitals.*
KFN361.A433 A2 1979

Nebraska. Dept. of Personnel. Rules &
regulations, Nebraska state personnel system.
[Lincoln, Neb. (P.O. Box 94905, 301
Centennial Mall South, Lincoln, Neb. 68509)] :
Nebraska Dept. of Personnel, [1980] [56] p. ;
28 cm. Cover title. "July 30, 1980." LC Card
80-624216 DDC 342.782/068 347.820268 19
1. Civil service - Nebraska. I. Title.
KFN435.A435 A2 1980

Nebraska. Dept. of Public Welfare.
Minimum standards for licensing foster homes
caring for children / Nebraska Department of
Public Welfare. Lincoln : The Dept., 1980 13
p. : forms ; 28 cm. Cover title. "DSS-PAM-0865
Rev. 6/80." LC Card 80-624214 DDC
344.782/032733 347.820432733 19
1. Foster home care - Licenses - Nebraska. I. Title.
KFN350.C4 A32 1980

**Nebraska. Dept. of Public Welfare. Division of
Research and Statistics.** Where are the
children? / [Prepared by the Division of
Research and Statistics]. [Lincoln] : Nebraska
Dept. of Public Welfare, [1976]. 88 p. : ill. ; 28
cm. Microfiche (neg.) NTIS 1 sheet. 11 x 15 cm. (PB
282 532) Cover title. Includes bibliographical references.
LC Card 78-621978
1. Foster home care - Nebraska - Statistics. I. Title.
*HV875 .N27 1976   NYPL [*XME-9432]*

**Nebraska. Dept. of Public Welfare. Research and
Statistics, Division of.** see Nebraska. Dept.
of Public Welfare. Division of Research and

Statistics.

Nebraska. Dept. of Roads. (Old Catalog form: Nebraska. Roads, Dept. of)
Focus on Nebraska highways. [Lincoln, 1974?]
36 p.: *NYPL [JLF 80-597]*
Supplemental specifications to standard specifications for highway construction, series 1973 / State of Nebraska, Department of Roads. [Lincoln] : The Dept., [1978?] 104 p. : ill. ; 29 cm. Cover title. LC Card 79-625491 DDC 625.7/0218 19
1. Roads - Standards - Nebraska. 2. Roads - Design - Standards - Nebraska. 3. Road construction - Contracts and specifications - Nebraska. I. Title.
TE24.N2 N43 1978

Nebraska. Division of Rehabilitation Services.
Three-year interim state plan for Nebraska Rehabilitation Services, fiscal years 1980-81-82. [Lincoln : The Division, 1979?] iv, 64 p. ; 30 cm. Cover title. LC Card 80-622103 DDC 362/.0425 19
1. Vocational rehabilitation - Nebraska. I. Title.
HD7256.U6 N34 1979

Nebraska. Division of Social Service.
DSS pamphlet .
(365) Nebraska. Division of Social Services. Minimum standards for licensing day care centers caring for children. Lincoln [1978?] 34 p. ; LC Card 80-623525 DDC 344.782/032712 19
KFN282.D3 A32 1978

Nebraska. Division of Social Services.
Minimum standards for licensing day care centers caring for children. Lincoln : Division of Social Services, Nebraska Dept. of Public Welfare, [1978?] 34 p. ; 22 cm. (DSS pamphlet . 365, rev. 4/78) LC Card 80-623525 DDC 344.782/032712 19
1. Day care centers - Licenses - Nebraska. I. Series: Nebraska. Division of Social Service. DSS pamphlet , 365. II. Title.
KFN282.D3 A32 1978

Rules for family day care : effective date, November 15, 1978. [Lincoln] : Nebraska Dept. of Public Welfare, [1978] 15 p. ; 22 cm. Cover title. LC Card 80-620953 DDC 344.782/032712 347.820432712 19
1. Day care centers - Law and legislation - Nebraska. I. Title. II. Title: Family day care.
KFN282.D3 A32 1978a

Nebraska energy conservation plan . Nebraska. Energy Office. [Lincoln, Neb.] [1978] ca. 250 p. in various pagings ; LC Card 80-623054 DDC 333.79/16/09782 19
TJ163.4.U6 N42 1978

Nebraska. Energy Office.
McCoy, Patrick T. Legal obstacles to car/vanpooling in Nebraska /. Lincoln, Neb. [1978] 14, 16 p. ; LC Card 80-623554 DDC 343.782/0982 347.8203982 19
KFN298 .M32

Nebraska energy conservation plan : for Department of Energy funding for the 1978 Federal fiscal year / prepared by Nebraska Energy Office. [Lincoln, Neb.] : The Office, [1978] ca. 250 p. in various pagings ; 30 cm. "March 1978." LC Card 80-623054 DDC 333.79/16/09782 19
1. Energy conservation - Nebraska. 2. Energy policy - Nebraska. I. Title.
TJ163.4.U6 N42 1978

Nebraska. Game and Parks Commission.
McCarraher, D. Bruce. Nebraska's sandhills lakes /. Lincoln , 1977. 67 p. : LC Card 77-623677 DDC 574.5/2636 19
QH105.N2 M32

Van Velson, Rodney C. The McConaughy rainbow . Lincoln, Nebraska , 1978. 83 p. : LC Card 79-626007 DDC 639.3/755 19
QL638.S2 V36

Nebraska. Geological Survey. Geologic bedrock map of Nebraska, by the Nebraska Geological Survey. Compiled by Raymond R. Burchett. Lincoln, Conservation and Survey Division, University of Nebraska, 1969. col. map 45 x 80 cm. Scale 1:1,000,000; 1 in. equals approx. 16 miles. Relief shown by spot heights. Includes "Geologic cross section along southern Nebraska border" and "Composite lithologic section." LC Card 77-697028
1. Geology - Nebraska - Maps. 2. Nebraska - Maps. I. Burchett, R. R. II. Nebraska. University. Conservation

and Survey Division. III. Title. IV. Title: Bedrock map of Nebraska.
G4191.C5 1969 .N4
NYPL [Map Div. 81-3032]

NEBRASKA - HISTORY - MANUSCRIPTS - CATALOGS.
Nebraska State Historical Society. Manuscript Division. A guide to the Manuscript Division of the State archives, Nebraska State Historical Society Lincoln , 1974. viii, 292 p. : LC Card 74-623165 DDC 978.2 s 016.9782 19
CD3354 .N42a no. 5 Z1307 F666

NEBRASKA - HISTORY - SOURCES - BIBLIOGRAPHY - CATALOGS.
Nebraska State Historical Society. Manuscript Division. A guide to the Manuscript Division of the State archives, Nebraska State Historical Society Lincoln , 1974. viii, 292 p. : LC Card 74-623165 DDC 978.2 s 016.9782 19
CD3354 .N42a no. 5 Z1307 F666

Nebraska individual family grant program : statistical summary, March flood 1978. [Lincoln, Neb. : Military Dept. of Nebraska, State Civil Defense Agency, 1978] [16] leaves ; 27 cm. Cover title. "October 1978." Chiefly tables. LC Card 79-621874 DDC 363.3/49382/09782 19
1. Disaster relief - Nebraska - Finance - Statistics. I. Nebraska. State Civil Defense Agency.
HV555.U62 N377

Nebraska. Laws, statutes, etc. Public accountancy act of 1957, as amended : rules of professional conduct, rules and regulations. Lincoln, Neb. : Nebraska State Board of Public Accountancy, [1979] 48 p. ; 23 cm. At head of title: State of Nebraska. "October 1979." LC Card 80-623309 DDC 346.782/06648/02632 19
1. Accountants - Legal status, laws, etc. - Nebraska. I. Nebraska. State Board of Public Accountancy. II. Title.
KFN329.A25 A32 1979

Nebraska. Legislature.
Nebraska unicameral, eighty-sixth legislature, second session : section index to bills introduced, LB 598 through LB 986 and carried-over bills, February 1, 1980 / [compiled by Patrick J. O'Donnell, clerk of the Legislature, Gloria Peterson, index clerk. [Lincoln : State of Nebraska, 1980] 14 p. ; 22 cm. Stamped on cover: Nebraska Publications Clearinghouse, Nebraska Library Commission, Lincoln, Nebraska. LC Card 80-623547 DDC 348.782/01 347.82081 19
1. Bills, Legislative - Nebraska - Indexes. I. O'Donnell, Patrick J. II. Nebraska Publications Clearinghouse. III. Title. IV. Title: Section index to bills introduced, LB 598 through LB 986 and carried-over bills.
KFN10 .L43

O'Donnell, Patrick J. Nebraska unicameral, Eighty-sixth Legislature, second session . [Lincoln, Neb.] [1980] 71 p. ; LC Card 80-623519 DDC 348.782/01 347.82081 19
KFN10 .O36

Nebraska. Legislature. Judiciary Committee.
Deviant sexual behavior : Judiciary Committee interim report, Legislative Resolution 207, introduced by Senator Duis. [Lincoln] : The Committee, [1978?] 291 leaves : ill. ; 28 cm. Caption title. Includes bibliographies. LC Card 80-624459 DDC 363.4/8/09782 19
1. Sex offenders - Legal status, laws, etc. - Nebraska. 2. Sex offenders - Nebraska. 3. Sexual deviation - Nebraska. I. Title.
KFN11.72 .J8 1978

Nebraska Library Commission. ILL directory / Nebraska Library Commission. Lincoln, Neb. : NLC, 1980. [30] p. ; 28 cm. LC Card 80-622026 DDC 027.0782 19
1. Inter-library loans - Nebraska. 2. Libraries - Nebraska - Directories. I. Title.
Z713.5.U6 N36 1980

NEBRASKA - MAPS.
(1966) United States. Soil Conservation Service. Nebraska /. Lincoln, Nebr. , 1966. 1 map ; LC Card 81-691016
G4190 1966 .U5

(1969) Nebraska. Geological Survey. Geologic bedrock map of Nebraska. Lincoln, 1969. col. map 45 x 80 cm. Scale 1:1,000,000; 1 in. equals approx. 16 miles. Relief shown by spot heights. Includes "Geologic cross section along southern Nebraska border" and "Composite lithologic section." LC Card

77-697028
G4191.C5 1969 .N4
NYPL [Map Div. 81-3032]

Nebraska. Natural Resources Commission.
Engberg, R. A. A statistical analysis of the quality of surface water in Nebraska /. Washington , 1981. p. cm. LC Card 81-2161 DDC 553.7/9/09782 19
TD224.N18 E5

University of Nebraska-Lincoln. Remote Sensing Center. General land use in Nebraska--summer 1973. [Lincoln] 1974. col. map 43 x 76 cm. Scale ca. 1:1,000,000. Relief shown by spot heights. Includes text. LC Card 78-691032
G4191.G4 1973 .U5
NYPL [Map Div. 81-3033]

Nebraska. Office of Planning and Programming. see Nebraska. State Office of Planning and Programming.

Nebraska. Planning and Programming, State Office of. see Nebraska. State Office of Planning and Programming.

Nebraska public school finance study : a study of equal educational opportunity and school tax equity in Nebraska, July 1978 / directed by C. Cale Hudson for the Nebraska State Department of Education. Lincoln, Neb. : The Dept., [197-] xii, 292 p. : graphs ; 28 cm. Includes bibliographical references. LC Card 80-620533 DDC 379.1/3/09782 19
1. Education - Nebraska - Finance. 2. Educational equalization - Nebraska. I. Hudson, Charles Cale. II. Nebraska. State Dept. of Education.
LB2826.N25 N48

Nebraska. Public Welfare, Dept. of. see Nebraska. Dept. of Public Welfare.

Nebraska Publications Clearinghouse. Nebraska. Legislature. Nebraska unicameral, eighty-sixth legislature, second session . [[Lincoln , 1980] 14 p. ; LC Card 80-623547 DDC 348.782/01 347.82081 19
KFN10 .L43

Nebraska. Real Estate Commission. Nebraska. Nebraska real estate license laws and rules and regulations /. Lincoln, Neb. (301 Centennial Mall, South, P.O. Box 94667, Lincoln 68509) , 1980. 41 p. in various pagings ; LC Card 80-624276 DDC 346.78204/37 347.8206437 19
KFN282.R4 A3 1980

Nebraska real estate license laws and rules and regulations /. Nebraska. Lincoln, Neb. (301 Centennial Mall, South, P.O. Box 94667, Lincoln 68509) , 1980. 41 p. in various pagings ; LC Card 80-624276 DDC 346.78204/37 347.8206437 19
KFN282.R4 A3 1980

Nebraska. Roads, Dept. of. see Nebraska. Dept. of Roads.

Nebraska. Special Education Branch. Putting the puzzle together : the education of prekindergarten handicapped children in Nebraska / prepared by Special Education Branch, Nebraska Department of Education. Lincoln, Neb. : The Branch, [1979] ii, 28 p. : ill. ; 29 cm. Cover title. "February, 1979." LC Card 79-625369 DDC 371.9/09782 19
1. Handicapped children - Education (Preschool) - Nebraska. I. Title.
LC4032.N4 N42 1979

Nebraska. State Board of Nursing. Rules and regulations governing the renewal and reinstatement of nurses' licenses, 1979. Lincoln, Neb. : Nebraska State Board of Nursing, [1980] 9 p. : forms ; 22 cm. LC Card 80-622055 DDC 344.782/0414 347.82044414 19
1. Nurses - Licenses - Nebraska. I. Title.
KFN326.5.N81 A32 1980

Nebraska. State Board of Public Accountancy.
Nebraska. Laws, statutes, etc. Public accountancy act of 1957, as amended . Lincoln, Neb. [1979] 48 p. ; LC Card 80-623309 DDC 346.782/06648/02632 19
KFN329.A25 A32 1979

Nebraska. State Civil Defense Agency. Nebraska individual family grant program . [Lincoln, Neb. , 1978] [16] leaves ; LC Card 79-621874 DDC 363.3/49382/09782 19
HV555.U62 N377

Nebraska. State Dept. of Education.
Identification supplement to rule 3 : ideas for

identification of gifted/talented in the areas of creativity, leadership, visual and performing arts, psychomotor ability. Lincoln : Nebraska State Dept. of Education, [1979?] 63 p. : forms ; 28 cm. Cover title. Bibliography: p. 55.   LC Card 80-620684   DDC 371.95 19
1. Gifted children - Identification. 2. Ability - Testing. I. Title.
HQ773.5 .N4 1979

Nebraska public school finance study . Lincoln, Neb. [197-] xii, 292 p. :   LC Card 80-620533   DDC 379.1/3/09782 19
LB2826.N25 N48

Rule 51, the State Department of Education rule on development of reimbursable local special education programs for handicapped children. Lincoln, Neb. : Commissioner of Education, [1978?] iii, 48, a-d p. ; 28 cm. Cover title. Includes index.   LC Card 80-622035   DDC 371.9/09782 19
1. Handicapped children - Education - Nebraska - Finance. I. Title: Rule on development of reimbursable local special education programs for handicapped children.
LC4032.N4 N43 1978

Nebraska State Historical Society. Bulletin.
(no. 5) Nebraska State Historical Society. Manuscript Division. A guide to the Manuscript Division of the State archives, Nebraska State Historical Society Lincoln , 1974. viii, 292 p. :   LC Card 74-623165   DDC 978.2 s 016.9782 19
CD3354 .N42a no. 5 Z1307 F666

Publications in anthropology. For additional listing of contents, see Old Catalog.
(no. 9) Grange, Roger T. Salvage archeology in the Red Willow Reservoir, Nebraska /. Lincoln, Neb. , 1980. xi, 236 p., [1] leaf of plates :   LC Card 80-624104   DDC 978.2 s 978.2/83 19
F661 .N32 no. 9 E78.N3
NYPL [HBA no. 9]

(no. 9) Grange, Roger T. Salvage archeology in the Red Willow Reservoir, Nebraska /. Lincoln, Neb. , 1980. xi, 236 p., [1] leaf of plates :   LC Card 80-624104   DDC 978.2 s 978.2/83 19
F661 .N32 no. 9 E78.N3
NYPL [HBA no. 9]

Nebraska State Historical Society. Manuscript Division.
A guide to the Manuscript Division of the State archives, Nebraska State Historical Society Lincoln : The Society, 1974. viii, 292 p. : ill. ; 28 cm. (Bulletin - Nebraska State Historical Society ; no. 5) Includes index.   LC Card 74-623165   DDC 978.2 s 016.9782 19
1. Nebraska - History - Manuscripts - Catalogs. 2. Nebraska - History - Sources - Bibliography - Catalogs. 3. Nebraska State Historical Society. Manuscript Division - Catalogs. I. Series: Nebraska State Historical Society. Bulletin, no. 5. II. Title.
CD3354 .N42a no. 5 Z1307 F666

NEBRASKA STATE HISTORICAL SOCIETY. MANUSCRIPT DIVISION - CATALOGS.
Nebraska State Historical Society. Manuscript Division. A guide to the Manuscript Division of the State archives, Nebraska State Historical Society Lincoln , 1974. viii, 292 p. :   LC Card 74-623165   DDC 978.2 s 016.9782 19
CD3354 .N42a no. 5 Z1307 F666

Nebraska. State Office of Planning and Programming.
University of Nebraska-Lincoln. Remote Sensing Center. General land use in Nebraska--summer 1973. [Lincoln] 1974. col. map 43 x 76 cm. Scale ca. 1:1,000,000. Relief shown by spot heights. Includes text.   LC Card 78-691032
G4191.G4 1973 .U5
NYPL [Map Div. 81-3033]

University of Nebraska--Lincoln. Water Resources Research Institute. A cost-benefit presentation of several artificial recharge schemes in the Upper Big Blue River Basin . Lincoln, Neb. [1975] 40 leaves :   LC Card 79-623375   DDC 333.91/04153/09782 19
TD404 .U54 1975

Nebraska technical series .
(no. 2) Van Velson, Rodney C. The McConaughy rainbow . Lincoln, Nebraska , 1978. 83 p. :   LC Card 79-626007   DDC 639.3/755

19
QL638.S2 V36

Nebraska unicameral, eighty-sixth legislature, second session . Nebraska. Legislature. [[Lincoln , 1980] 14 p. ;   LC Card 80-623547   DDC 348.782/01 347.82081 19
KFN10 .L43

Nebraska unicameral, Eighty-sixth Legislature, second session . O'Donnell, Patrick J. [Lincoln, Neb.] [1980] 71 p. ;   LC Card 80-623519   DDC 348.782/01 347.82081 19
KFN10 .O36

Nebraska. University. Conservation and Soil Survey. see Nebraska. University. Conservation and Survey Division.

Nebraska. University. Conservation and Survey Division. Nebraska. Geological Survey. Geologic bedrock map of Nebraska. Lincoln, 1969. col. map 45 x 80 cm. Scale 1:1,000,000; 1 in. equals approx. 16 miles. Relief shown by spot heights. Includes "Geologic cross section along southern Nebraska border" and "Composite lithologic section."   LC Card 77-697028
G4191.C5 1969 .N4
NYPL [Map Div. 81-3032]

Nebraska Water Resources Center. NWRC publication .
(no. 7) Nebraska Water Resources Center. Water resources publications related to the State of Nebraska. [Lincoln] [1979] 129 p. ;   LC Card 80-621398   DDC 016.33391/009782 19
Z7935 .N4 1979 TC424.N2

Water resources publications related to the State of Nebraska. 4th ed. [Lincoln] : Nebraska Water Resources Center, Institute of Agriculture and Natural Resources, University of Nebraska-Lincoln, [1979] 129 p. ; 28 cm. (NWRC publication ; no. 7) "November 1979." Third ed. (1975) by the Center under its previous name, Water Resources Research Institute, University of Nebraska--Lincoln. Includes indexes.   LC Card 80-621398   DDC 016.33391/009782 19
1. Water resources development - Nebraska - Bibliography. 2. Water quality management - Nebraska - Bibliography. I. University of Nebraska--Lincoln. Water Resources Research Institute. Water resources publications related to the State of Nebraska. II. Series: Nebraska Water Resources Center. NWRC publication , no. 7. III. Title.
Z7935 .N4 1979 TC424.N2

Nebraska water survey paper .
(no. 47) Souders, Vernon L. Geology and groundwater supplies of Box Butte County, Nebraska /. [Lincoln] [1980] vii, 205 p. :   LC Card 80-623050   DDC 553/.7/09782 s 551.7/9/0978294 19
GB1025.N2 N42 no. 47 QE136.B67

NEBRASKA. WORKMEN'S COMPENSATION COURT.
Nebraska. Court Rules. Workmen's Compensation Court. Rules of procedure of the Nebraska Workmen's Compensation Court. Lincoln, Neb. [1978] 23 p. ;   LC Card 78-111321   DDC 344.782/021/0269 19
KFN342.A435 A2 1978

Nebraska. Workmen's Compensation Court. Research and Statistics Division.
Occupational injuries and illnesses in Nebraska by industry, 1977, including 1976 tabulations / State of Nebraska, Nebraska Workmen's Compensation Court, Research and Statistics Division. [Lincoln, Neb.] : The Division, [197-?] vi, 66 p. : ill. ; 28 cm.   LC Card 80-622042   DDC 312/.43/09782 19
1. Industrial accidents - Nebraska - Statistics. 2. Occupational diseases - Nebraska - Statistics. I. Title.
HD7262.5.U62 N23 1970

Nebraska's sandhills lakes /. McCarraher, D. Bruce. Lincoln , 1977. 67 p. :   LC Card 77-623677   DDC 574.5/2636 19
QH105.N2 M32

NEBULAE, EXTRAGALACTIC. see GALAXIES.

Neches Basin. Texas. Dept. of Water Resources. Projected land use maps year 2000, Neches Basin. Austin, Tex. , 1978. [9] leaves :   LC Card 80-675294   DDC 912/.133373/30976415 19
G1372.N4G4 T4 1978

Need for more effective regulation of direct additives to food . United States. General

Accounting Office. Washington, D.C. [1980] vi, 42 p. ;   LC Card 80-603222   DDC 353.0077/82 19
KF3879.P7 A836

Needham, Rodney. Circumstantial deliveries / Rodney Needham. Berkeley : University of California Press, c1981. p. cm. (Quantum books) Essays previously published: 1978-1980. Bibliography: p. Includes index. CONTENTS. - Rehearsal -- Essential perplexities -- Physiological symbols -- Inner states as universals -- Characteristics of religion -- Existential quandaries.   ISBN 0-520-04389-8   LC Card 81-1247   DDC 128 19
1. Ethnology - Philosophy - Addresses, essays, lectures. 2. Classification, Primitive - Addresses, essays, lectures. 3. Ethopsychology - Addresses, essays, lectures. I. Title.
GN345 .N43

NEEDLEWORK - TEXAS - HISTORY - 20TH CENTURY.
LaCoste, Janet Shook. Watercolor, wax & wool . [San Antonio] , c1980. [88] p. :   ISBN 0-933164-81-5 (pbk.)   LC Card 80-82780   DDC 746.44/2/0924 19
NK9198.L3 A4 1980

NEEL, FRANK H., 1916-
United States. Congress. Senate. Committee on Commerce, Science, and Transportation. Nominations--Amtrak . Washington , 1980. iii, 24 p. ;   LC Card 80-602501   DDC 353.0087/5 19
KF26 .C69 1980m

Neeley, Jeffrey. United States. International Trade Commission. Leather wearing apparel from Uruguay . Washington, D.C. , 1980. ii, 9, 47 p. ;   LC Card 81-600775   DDC 382/.4568522/0973 19
HF2651.L45 U64 1980

Neenan, P. H. Impact of the food stamp and expanded food and nutrition education programs on food expenditure and nutrient intake of low income rural Florida households / P. H. Neenan and C. G. Davis. Gainesville : Agriculture Experimental Stations, Institute of food and Agricultural sciences, University of Florida, 1978. xii, 79 p. : graphs ; 24 cm. (Bulletin - Agricultural Experimental Stations, University of Florida ; 805) Bibliography: p. 77-79.   LC Card 79-626209   DDC 363.8/82/09759 19
1. Food stamp program - Florida - Case studies. 2. Nutrition - Study and teaching - Florida - Case studies. I. Davis, Carlton G., joint author. II. Series: Florida. Agricultural Experiment Station, Gainesville. Bulletin , 805. III. Title.
HV696.F6 N37

Neff, Don J. Forage preferences of trained mule deer on the Beaver Creek watersheds / Don J. Neff. Phoenix : Arizona Game and Fish Dept., 1974. iv, 61 p. : ill. ; 23 cm. (Special report - Arizona Game and Fish Department . no. 4) Bibliography: p. 34-37.   LC Card 78-621556   DDC 599.73/57 19
1. Deer - Food. 2. Deer - Training. 3. Mule deer. 4. Mammals - Arizona - Beaver Creek watershed. I. Series: Arizona. Game and Fish Commission. Special report - Arizona Game and Fish Commission , no. 4. II. Title.
QL737.U55 N38

NEGOTIABLE INSTRUMENTS - UNITED STATES.
United States. Congress. Senate. Committee on the Judiciary. Subcommittee on Improvements in Judicial Machinery. Preference section of the Bankruptcy Code, S. 3023 . Washington , 1981. iii, 34 p. ;   LC Card 81-601155   DDC 346.73/078/0262 347.306780262 19
KF26 .J855 1980e

NEGOTIATION.
United States. Central Intelligence Agency. National Foreign Assessment Center. Soviet strategy and tactics in economic and commercial negotiations with the United States /. Washington , 1979. v, 11 p. ;   LC Card 79-602793
*HF1456.5.R9 U54 1979   NYPL [*XME-9336]*

NEGROES (UNITED STATES) see AFRO-AMERICANS.

Neher, Michael A. Heavy metal accumulation and its effect on the biota of an industrial settling pond : completion report, OWRT project no. A-102-MONT / Michael A. Neher and George F. Weisel. Bozeman : Montana University Joint Water Resources Research Center, 1977. viii, 96, 2 p., [1] leaf of plates : ill. ; 28 cm.

(MUJWRRC report . no. 90) Bibliography: p. 75-79.
LC Card 79-624616   DDC 574.5/26322 19
1. Heavy metals - Environmental aspects. 2. Settling basins. 3. Aquatic organisms - Effect of water pollution on. I. Weisel, George Ferdinand, 1915- joint author. II. Series: Montana University Joint Water Resources Research Center. Report , no. 90. III. Title.
QH545.H42 N44

Neher, R. E. Soil survey of Luna County, New Mexico / United States Department of Agriculture, Soil Conservation Service, in cooperation with New Mexico Agricultural Experiment Station. [Washington, D.C. : National Cooperative Soil Survey], 1980. iii, 80 p., [81] folded leaves of plates : ill. ; 28 cm. Cover title. Prepared by Raymond E. Neher and William A. Buchanan. "Issued May 1980"--P. i. Bibliography: p. 78.   LC Card 80-603368   DDC 631.4/7/78968 19
1. Soils - New Mexico - Luna County - Maps. I. Buchanan, William Albert, 1908-. II. United States. Soil Conservation Service. III. New Mexico Agricultural Experiment Station. IV. Title.
S599.N6 N4

NEIGHBORHOOD.
Cohen, Rick. Partnerships for neighborhood preservation . [Harrisburg] , 1978. vii, 200 p. ; LC Card 79-622460   DDC 307.7/6/0973 19
HN90.C6 C626

United States. National Commission on Neighborhoods. People, building neighborhoods . [Washington?] , Washington [1979] xi, 358 p. ;   LC Card 79-602955
HN90.C6 U66 1979

NEIGHBORHOOD - CASE STUDIES.
Joint Center for Urban Studies. The behavioral foundations of neighborhood change /. Washington [1979] 205 p. ;   LC Card 79-601949
HT123 .J63 1979   *NYPL [JLF 81-252]*

NEIGHBORHOOD GOVERNMENT - OHIO - CLEVELAND.
Griffin, Burt W. Cities within a city . Cleveland, Ohio , c1981. viii, 133 p. :   LC Card 81-135043   DDC 352/.000473/0977132 19
JS773 .G74

NEIGHBORHOOD IMPROVEMENTS PROGRAMS. see COMMUNITY DEVELOPMENT, URBAN.

Neighborhood mobilization . Henig, Jeffrey R., 1951- New Brunswick, N.J. , c1981. p. cm. ISBN 0-8135-0933-5 :   LC Card 81-5234   DDC 307.7/6/0977311 19
HT177.C5 H45

Neily, Rupert. Enforcement manual for the proposed Pittston Oil Refinery : final draft / by Rupert Neily. Augusta, Me. : Dept. of Environmental Protection, [1980] ca. 650 p. in various pagings : ill. ; 28 cm. Cover title. "March 1980." LC Card 80-622764   DDC 353.974/0082/42 19
1. Petroleum refineries - Environmental aspects - Maine - Eastport. 2. Petroleum - Refining - Waste disposal - Law and legislation - Maine. I. Maine. Dept. of Environmental Protection. II. Title.
TD195.P4 N44

Neiser, Brent. Kentucky. Legislative Research Commission. Committee for Program Review and Investigation. Program evaluation, Kentucky State Fire and Tornado Insurance Fund /. Frankfort, KY. [1981] viii, 82 p. ;   LC Card 81-621577   DDC 353.97690071/3 19
HG9778.K4 K46 1981

NEKTON - NORTH CAROLINA - ALBEMARLE SOUND.
Hester, Joseph M. Nekton population dynamics in the Albemarle Sound and Neuse River estuaries /. Raleigh , 1975. 129 p.   LC Card 75-622760   DDC 592 19
QH105.N8 H47

NEKTON - NORTH CAROLINA - NEUSE RIVER ESTUARY.
Hester, Joseph M. Nekton population dynamics in the Albemarle Sound and Neuse River estuaries /. Raleigh , 1975. 129 p.   LC Card 75-622760   DDC 592 19
QH105.N8 H47

Nekton population dynamics ... Hester, Joseph M. Nekton population dynamics in the Albemarle Sound and Neuse River estuaries /. Raleigh , 1975. 129 p. :   LC Card 75-622760,

DDC 592 19
QH105.N8 H47

Nelson, Anne H. Women as third-party neutrals . Ithaca , 1978. vi, 55 p. ;   ISBN 0-87546-066-6 :   LC Card 78-620003   DDC 331.89/14/02373 19
HD6058 .W6894

Nelson, Ben A. The Star lake archaeological project . Carbondale , c1982. p. cm.   ISBN 0-8093-0949-1   LC Card 81-13596   DDC 978.9/83 19
E78.N65 S75

Nelson, Cary. Our last first poets : vision and history in contemporary American poetry / Cary Nelson. Urbana : University of Illinois Press, c1981. p. cm. Includes index.   ISBN 0-252-00885-5   LC Card 81-5082   DDC 811/.54/09 19
1. American poetry - 20th century - History and criticism. 2. Free verse. 3. Politics and literature - United States. I. Title.
PS325 .N4

Nelson, Daniel N., 1948- Communist legislatures in comparative perspective /. Albany , 1982. p. cm.   ISBN 0-87395-566-8   LC Card 81-9189   DDC 328/.3/091717 19
JC474 .C64 1982

Nelson, David Charles, 1943- Annual performance report for Russian River red salmon study / by David C. Nelson. Juneau : Alaska Dept. of Fish and Game, Sport Fish Division, [1977?] 54 p. : ill. ; 28 cm. (Anadromous fish studies . AFS 44-3) At head of title: Volume 18. Study AFS 44-3. Cover title: Russian River red salmon studies. Bibliography: p. 51-53.   LC Card 78-621575   DDC 597/.55 19
1. Sockeye salmon. 2. Fishery management - Alaska - Russian River. 3. Fishing surveys - Alaska - Russian River. 4. Fishing - Alaska - Russian River - Statistics. I. Title. II. Title: Russian River red salmon studies. III. Series.
QL638.S2 N449

Nelson, David D. Validation of selection procedures for welfare specialists / David D. Nelson. [St. Paul] : Minnesota Dept. of Personnel, Division of Recruitment and Selection, 1976. 46 p. ; 28 cm. (Technical report - Minnesota Department of Personnel, Division of Recruitment and Selection ; no. 20) Bibliography: p. 46.   LC Card 77-622755   DDC 361/.0076 19
1. Social service - Minnesota - Examinations. I. Series: Minnesota. Dept. of Personnel. Division of Recruitment and Selection. Technical report - Minnesota Department of Personnel, Division of Recruitment and Selection , no. 20. II. Title.
HV98.M65 N44

Nelson, DeVaughn R. Cook, John R. (John Richard), 1950- Occupational exposure to ionizing radiation in the United States . Washington, D.C. , 1980 [i.e. 1981] xi, 74, [68] p. :   LC Card 81-601500   DDC 363.1/79 19
RC965.R25 C66

Nelson, Elizabeth Ness. Women's studies as a catalyst for faculty development / Elizabeth Ness Nelson, Kathryn H. Brooks. Washington, D.C. : U. S. Dept. of Health, Education, and Welfare, National Institute of Education, Program on Teaching and Learning : for sale by the Supt. of Docs., U. S. Govt. Print. Off., 1980. xii, 43 p. ; 23 cm. (Women's studies monograph series) Bibliography: p. 33-35.   LC Card 80-602285   DDC 378/.12/0973 19
1. Universitities and colleges - United States - Faculty. 2. Women's studies - United States. I. Brooks, Kathryn H., joint author. II. Title. III. Series.
LB2331.72 .N44

Nelson, Elmer K. Unification of community corrections / E. K. Nelson, Jr., Robert Cushman, Nora Harlow. Washington, D.C. : U. S. Dept. of Justice, National Institute of Justice, Office of Development, Testing, and Dissemination : for sale by Supt. of Docs., U. S. Govt. Print. Off., 1980. vi, 164 p. : ill. ; 28 cm. (Program models - National Institute of Justice, Office of Development, Testing, and Dissemination) "April 1980." Bibliography: p. 162-164.   LC Card 80-602244   DDC 364.6/8 19
1. Community-based corrections - United States. 2. Corrections - United States. I. Cushman, Robert, joint author. II. Harlow, Nora, joint author. III. National Institute of Justice (United States). Office of Development, Testing, and Dissemination. IV. Series: National Institute of Justice (United States). Office of

Development, Testing, and Dissemination. Program models - National Institute of Justice, Office of Development, Testing, and Dissemination. V. Title.
HV9304 .N45

Nelson, Harold D. Ethiopia, a country study /. Washington, D.C.] 1981. p. cm.   LC Card 81-7928   DDC 963/.06 19
DT378 .E73 1981

Nelson, Kathryn P. Recent suburbanization of Blacks, how much, who, and where / prepared for the Office of Economic Affairs, the Office of Policy Development and Research, Department of Housing and Urban Development by Kathryn P. Nelson. [Washington] : The Office, 1979. 34 p. : ill. ; 27 cm. "HUD-PDR-378(2)." Bibliography: p. 32-34.   LC Card 79-602959
1. Afro-Americans - Housing. 2. Residential mobility - United States. 3. Suburbs - United States. I. United States. Dept. of Housing and Urban Development. Office of Policy Development and Research. II. Title.
HD7288.72.U5 N44

Nelson, Martha. A guide to collections on women in the New York area / compiled by Martha Nelson & Jan Clausen; the Center for the Study of Women and Sex Roles. Graduate School, CUNY. [New York: CUNY, 1980?] 17 p.; 28 cm. Cover title. Additional sources: p. 1.
1. Women - Library resources - New York (City) - Directories. I. Clausen, Jan. II. New York (City), City University of New York. Center for the Study of Women and Sex Roles. III. Title.
NYPL [JLF 81-437]

Nelson-Moore, James L. Radioactive mineral occurrences of Colorado and bibliography / by James L. Nelson-Moore, Donna Bishop Collins and A. L. Hornbaker. Denver, Colo. : Colorado Geological Survey, Dept. of Natural Resources, State of Colorado, 1978. ix, 1054 p. (2 fold.) : maps (12 fold. in pocket) ; 29 cm. (Bulletin - Colorado Geological Survey, State of Colorado ; 40)   LC Card 80-621968   DDC 557.88 s 553.4/93/09788 19
1. Radioactive substances - Colorado. 2. Radioactive substances - Colorado - Bibliography. I. Collins, Donna Bishop, joint author. II. Hornbaker, A. L., joint author. III. Colorado. Geological Survey. IV. Series: Colorado. Geological Survey. Bulletin , 40. V. Title.
QE91 .A4 no. 40 QE364.2.R3

Nelson, Nancy. Washington (State). Dept. of Ecology. Shorelands Division. Overview, coastal aquatic management policies of Washington State and federal agencies /. Olympia, Wash. [1980] 29 p. ;   LC Card 80-624143   DDC 333.91/7/09797 19
HT393.W3 W3 1980

Nelson, Paul E., 1927- Fusarium . University Park, PA [1981] p. cm.   ISBN 0-271-00293-X :   LC Card 81-47174   DDC 632/.34 19
SB741.F9 F87

Nelson, Sally. Idaho. University. Dept. of Agricultural Economics and Applied Statistics. Publications and graduate theses in agricultural economics and applied statistics, July 1977-July 1978 /. Moscow, Idaho [1978] 20 leaves ;   LC Card 80-620584   DDC 016.3381 19
Z5074.E3 I36 1978 HD1775.I2

Nelson, Theodore A. Measuring markets : a guide to the use of Federal and State statistical data. [Updated version]. [Washington] : U. S. Dept. of Commerce, Industry, and Trade Administration, 1979. iv, 101 p. ; 21 x 27 cm. Bibliography: p. 88-97.   LC Card 79-603999
1. Market surveys - United States. 2. Marketing research - United States. 3. United States - Statistical services. I. United States. Industry and Trade Administration. II. Title.
HF5415.3 .N44 1979

Nelson, Theresa. Hazard analysis of injuries relating to cribs : full size cribs (1504), portable cribs (1529) / Theresa Nelson. Washington : U. S. Consumer Product Safety Commission, Bureau of Epidemiology, 1975. 66 p. ; 27 cm. Cover title: Hazard analysis, cribs. "NIIC-1504-75-H007." Includes bibliographical references.   LC Card 76-600895
1. Cribs (Children's furniture) - Accidents. 2. Infants - Wounds and injuries - Case studies. I. United States. Consumer Product Safety Commission. Bureau of Epidemiology. II. Title.
TS886.5.C74 N44   *NYPL [JLF 80-1346]*

NEMATOCIDES - ENVIRONMENTAL ASPECTS - CALIFORNIA.
California. Legislature. Assembly. Ad Hoc Committee on Water Contamination. Transcript /. [Sacramento, Calif.] [1979] 350 p. : LC Card 80-621897 DDC 344.794/046343 347.940446343 19
KFC10.4 .W35 1979

California. Legislature. Assembly. Ad Hoc Committee on Water Contamination. Transcript (investigation into DBCP) . Sacramento, CA , 1980. 140 p. : LC Card 80-623739 DDC 363.7/394 19
KFC10.4 .W35 1980

NEMATODE DISEASES OF PLANTS - BIBLIOGRAPHY.
O'Bannon, J. H. Bibliography of nematodes of citrus . Washington , 1979. 11 p. ; LC Card 79-602330 DDC 016.634/35965182 19
Z5354.P3 C636 Suppl SB608.C5

NEOBOMOLOCHUS - CLASSIFICATION.
Cressey, Roger F., 1930- Parasitic copepods from the Gulf of Mexico and Caribbean Sea, I . Washington , 1981. p. cm. LC Card 81-9055 DDC 591 s 595.3/4 19
QL1 .S54 no. 339 QL444.C73

NEOCLASSICISM (ART)
Starobinski, Jean. [1789, les emblèmes de la raison. English.] 1789, the emblems of reason /. Charlottesville , 1981. p. cm. ISBN 0-8139-0915-5 LC Card 81-13135 DDC 709/.44 19
NX452.5.N4 S7

NEPAL - PHOTO MAPS.
World Bank. Agriculture and Rural Development Dept. Resource Planning Unit. Nepal /. Washington, D.C. , 1980. 1 remote sensing image on 2 sheets : LC Card 81-692612
G7761.A4 1980 .W6

Neponset River . Massachusetts. Division of Water Pollution Control. Water Quality Section. Westborough [1976] 38, A-U p. : LC Card 77-622675 DDC 363.7/3942/097447 19
TD224.M4 M36 1976h

NERVOUS SYSTEM - DISEASES - RESEARCH - UNITED STATES.
Panel on Inflammatory, Demyelinating and Degenerative Diseases (U. S.) Report of the Panel on Inflammatory, Demyelinating, and Degenerative Diseases to the National Advisory Neurological and Communicative Disorders and Stroke Council [prepared for the] National Institute of Neurological and Communicative Disorders and Stroke. [Bethesda, Md.] [1979] ix, 129 p. ; LC Card 80-601215 DDC 616.8/072073 19
RC346 .P275 1979

NESS COUNTY (KAN.) - ADMINISTRATIVE AND POLITICAL DIVISIONS - MAPS.
United States. Soil Conservation Service. Township, school, and hospital district map, Ness County, Kansas /. Lincoln, Nebr. , 1979. 1 map : LC Card 81-691149
G4203.N5F7 1979 .U5

Nesselroad, Paul E. (joint author) Layton, Ronald A. Estimated annual costs, production, and income for selected livestock and crop enterprises, eastern West Virginia. [Morgantown] 1970. 92 p. LC Card 80-515026 DDC 338.1/09754 19
S561.6.W4 L39

NET NATIONAL PRODUCT. see NATIONAL INCOME.

The net-winged midges of eastern North America, with notes on new taxonomic characters in the family Blephariceridae (Diptera) /. Hogue, Charles Leonard. Los Angeles , 1978. 41 p. : LC Card 78-104487 DDC 574 s 595.77/1 19
Q11 .L52 no. 291 QL537.B56

NETHERLANDS - BIOGRAPHY - PORTRAITS - EXHIBITIONS.
Wilson, William Henry, 1939- Dutch seventeenth century portraiture, the golden age /. Sarasota, Fla. , c1980. [185] p. : ISBN 0-916758-03-6 (pbk.) LC Card 80-53473 DDC 704.9/42/0942074015961 19
N7607 .W54

NETS (GEODESY) - CONGRESSES.
International Symposium on Problems Related to the Redefinition of North American Geodetic Networks, 2d, Arlington, Va., 1978. Proceedings /. [Rockville, Md.] , Washington , 1979. xiii, 645 p. : LC Card 78-15124
QB301 .I66 1978 NYPL [JSE 81-179]

NETSC location, Broomall, Pennsylvania /. United States. Soil Conservation Service. Lanham, MD , 1980. 1 map : LC Card 81-690189
G3824.B84A1 1980 .U5

NETWORK ANALYSIS (PLANNING)
(1978) Jones, Lynne McCallister. Studying egocentric networks by mass survey /. [Berkeley] , 1978. v, 77 p. : LC Card 78-622144 DDC 301/.0723 19
HN29 .J63

NETWORK THEORY. see SYSTEM ANALYSIS.

NETWORKS, COMPUTER. see COMPUTER NETWORKS.

Networks for networkers . Conference on Networks for Networkers, Indianapolis, 1979. New York, N.Y. , London , 1980. xvi, 444 p. : ISBN 0-7201-1599-X ; LC Card 80-40016
*Z674.8 .C66 1979 NYPL [*R-*HB 80-3875]*

Networks for Networkers, Conference on. see Conference on Networks for Networkers, Indianapolis, 1979.

Neuberg am Rhein . Karch, Dieter. Lincoln, Neb. , c1978. x, 215 p. :
*NYPL [*EA N363 new series no. 59]*

NEUBURG - DESCRIPTION.
Karch, Dieter. Neuberg am Rhein . Lincoln, Neb. , c1978. x, 215 p. :
*NYPL [*EA N363 new series no. 59]*

Neugarten, Bernice Levin, 1916- Extending the human life span . [Chicago] , Washington [1977] v, 70 p. : LC Card 77-604795
*HQ1064.U5 E9 NYPL [*XME-9403]*

Neugebauer, Marcia. Symposium on Space Missions to Comets, Goddard Space Flight Center, 1977. Space missions to comets . [Washington] , 1979. v, 226 p. : LC Card 79-604295 DDC 523.6 19
QB721 .S97 1977

Neuhaus, William B. Urban abandonment and property tax delinquency / prepared by William B. Neuhaus. Frankfort, Ky. : Legislative Research Commission, 1978. iii, 22 p. ; 21 cm. (Research report / Legislative Research Commission . no. 149) Bibliography: p. 19-21. LC Card 79-621078 DDC 343.76905/4 347.690354 19
1. Real property tax - Kentucky. 2. Tax-sales - Kentucky. 3. Abandonment of property - Kentucky. 4. Tax-sales - Missouri - St. Louis. I. Series: Kentucky. Legislative Research Commission. Research report , no. 149. II. Title.
KFK1679 .N48

Neuman, Dennis R. (joint author) Munshower, Frank F. The effects of stack emissions on the range resource in the vicinity of Colstrip, Montana . Bozeman , 1977, cover 1978. ix, 196 p. : LC Card 78-623223 DDC 574.5/2643 19
QH545.C57 M86

Neuman, Robert W. Davis, Hester A., 1930- Archeological and historical resources of the Red River Basin. [Fayetteville] 1970. ix, 194 p. LC Card 77-633171 DDC 976.6/6 19
E99.C12 D4 NYPL [ITV 74-585]

Neumann, George R. (joint author) Kiefer, Nicholas M., 1951- The effect of alternative partial benefits formulas on beneficiary part-time work behavior. Washington, D.C. , 1979. v, 70 p. : LC Card 80-602692 DDC 368.4/4/00973 s 331.25/723 19
HD7096.U5 U637 no. 79-6

Neumann, Richard, 1952- (joint author) DiPillo, Salvatore A. Connecticut occupational staffing patterns . [Hartford] [1980] 86 p. : LC Card 80-623517 DDC 331.12/5/09746 19
HD5725.C8 D553

Neumeier, L. A. (joint author) McIlwain, J. F. Consolidation of an iron-base superalloy by powder metallurgy techniques /. Washington, D.C. [1981] p. cm. LC Card 80-607851 DDC 622 s 672.3/7 19
TN23 .U43 TN697.I7

The Neurological bases of language disorders in children : methods and directions for research : a symposium held at the National Institutes of Health, January 16-17, 1978 / Christy L. Ludlow and Mary Ellen Doran-Quine, editors. Bethesda, Md. : U. S. Dept. of Health, Education, and Welfare, Public Health Service, National Institutes of Health, National Institute of Neurological and Communicative Disorders and Stroke ; Washington, D.C. : for sale by the Supt. of Docs., U. S. Govt. Print. Off., 1980. viii, 196 p. : ill. ; 28 cm. (NINCDS monograph ; no. 22) NIH publication ; no. 79-440 "August 1979." Includes bibliographies. LC Card 80-602387 DDC 618.92/855 19
1. Language disorders in children - Congresses. 2. Language and languages - Physiological aspects - Congresses. 3. Brain - Congresses. 4. Children - Language - Research - Congresses. I. Ludlow, Christy L. II. Doran-Quine, Mary Ellen. III. Series: National Institute of Neurological and Communicative Disorders and Stroke. NINCDS monograph , no. 22.
RJ496.L35 N48

NEUROLOGY - RESEARCH - UNITED STATES.
National Advisory Neurological and Communicative Disorders and Stroke Council (United States). Task Force on Basic Science. Report of the Task Force on Basic Science to the National Advisory Neurological and Communicative Disorders and Stroke Council. [Washington, D.C.] , 1979. ix, 129 p. ; LC Card 80-601253 DDC 612.8/072073 19
QP356 .N28 1979

NEUROMUSCULAR DISEASES - RESEARCH - UNITED STATES.
Panel on Convulsive and Neuromuscular Disorders (U. S.) Report of the Panel on Convulsive and Neuromuscular Disorders to the National Advisory Neurological and Communicative Disorders and Stroke Council, National Institute of Neurological and Communicative Disorders and Stroke. [Bethesda, Md.] [1979] xiii, 124 p. : LC Card 80-601220 DDC 616.7/4/0072073 19
RC925.5 .P26 1979

Nevada.
Rules for state personnel administration, effective January 1980. Carson City, Nev. (Capitol Complex, Room 200, Blasdel Building, Carson City 89710) : Dept. of Administration, Personnel Division, [1980] p. 309-442 : forms ; 28 cm. Cover title. LC Card 81-621067 DDC 353.9793001 19
1. Civil serivce - Nevada. I. Title.
KFN1035.A434 A2 1980

Nevada. Agricultural Experiment Station, Reno.
Candland, David M. Soil survey of Big Smoky Valley Area, Nevada, part of Nye County /. [Washington] 1980. iii, 140 p. [2] fold. leaves of plates : LC Card 80-601637 DDC 631.4/7/79334 19
S599.N425 C36

Quality monitoring of flows from irrigation water and surface runoff in Carson Valley, Nevada, 1976 irrigation season / J. C. Guitjens ... [et al.]. Reno : Max C. Fleischmann College of Agriculture, University of Nevada, [1979] iv, 130 p. (p. 129-130 blank) : ill. ; 28 cm. "December 1979." "R131." Chiefly tables. Bibliography: p. 10. LC Card 79-625751 DDC 363.7/3942/0979359 19
1. Irrigation water - Nevada - Carson Valley - Quality. 2. Runoff - Nevada - Carson Valley. I. Guitjens, J. C. II. Max C. Fleischmann College of Agriculture. Cooperative Extension Service. III. Title.
TC824.N3 N48 1979

Nevada allied health education and manpower : a study relating allied health education programs to projected employment requirements for allied health personnel in Nevada / consultant, Karen S. Winkler ; project management, Nevada State Comprehensive Health Planning. Carson City, Nev. : State of Nevada, Comprehensive Health Planning, 1976. 98 p. : map ; 29 cm. Includes bibliographical references. LC Card 80-621254 DDC 331.12/3161 19
1. Paramedical education - Nevada. 2. Allied health personnel - Nevada - Supply and demand. I. Winkler, Karen S. II. Nevada. State Comprehensive Health Planning.
R847.6.N3 N48

NEVADA - ANTIQUITIES.
McClellan, Carole. The archeology of Lake Mead National Recreation Area . Tucson, Ariz. [Washington, D.C.?] , 1980. x,188 p. : LC Card

81-600707   DDC 979.3/12 19
F788 .M163

Nevada - Archaeology. see Nevada - Antiquities.

**NEVADA. BUDGET DIVISION - AUDITING
AND INSPECTION.**
Nevada. Legislative Auditor. State of Nevada,
Department of Administration, Budget Division,
audit report, fiscal year ended June 30, 1977.
Carson City, Nev. [197-] 18 leaves ;   LC Card
78-623421   DDC 353.97930072/32 19
HJ2053.N4 N44 1970z

**Nevada. Bureau of Mines and Geology.
Bulletin .**
(91) Garside, Larry J. Thermal waters of
Nevada /. Reno , 1979. 163 p. :   LC Card
80-621826   DDC 553.7 19
GB1199.7.N3 G37

(92) Bonham, Harold F. Geology of the
Tonopah, Lone Mountain, Klondike, and
Northern Mud Lake quadrangles, Nevada /.
Reno , 1979. 141 p. :   LC Card 80-621827
DDC 557.93/34 19
QE138.N9 B66

(93) Papke, Keith G. Fluorspar in Nevada /.
Reno , 1979. 77 p. :   LC Card 80-621828
DDC 553.6 19
TN948.F6 P36

(94) Mifflin, Martin D. Pluvial lakes and
estimated pluvial climates of Nevada /.
Reno , 1979. 57 p. :   LC Card 80-621829
DDC 551.48/2/09793 19
QC884 .M53

**Nevada. Conservation and Natural Resources,
State Dept. of. see Nevada. State Dept. of
Conservation and Natural Resources.**

Nevada. Constitution. Bushnell, Eleanore. The
Nevada constitution: origin and growth /
Eleanore Bushnell ; with Don W. Driggs. Reno,
1980. x, 221 p.   ISBN 0-87417-034-6
KFN1002.Z9 B8 1972
NYPL [IBO (Nevada) 80-3141]

**The Nevada constitution: origin and growth /
Eleanore Bushnell ; with Don W. Driggs.**
Bushnell, Eleanore. Reno, 1980. x, 221 p.
ISBN 0-87417-034-6
KFN1002.Z9 B8 1972
NYPL [IBO (Nevada) 80-3141]

NEVADA - CONSTITUTIONAL LAW.
Bushnell, Eleanore. The Nevada constitution:
origin and growth / Eleanore Bushnell ; with
Don W. Driggs. Reno, 1980. x, 221 p.   ISBN
0-87417-034-6
KFN1002.Z9 B8 1972
NYPL [IBO (Nevada) 80-3141]

**Nevada. Dept. of Conservation and Natural
Resources. see Nevada. State Dept. of
Conservation and Natural Resources.**

**NEVADA. DEPT. OF ENERGY - AUDITING
AND INSPECTION.**
Nevada. Legislative Auditor. State of Nevada,
Department of Energy audit report, fiscal year
ended June 30, 1979. Carson City, Nev. [1980]
23 leaves ;   LC Card 80-621823   DDC
353.97930072/32 19
HD9502.U53 N464 1980

**Nevada. Dept. of Highways. Planning Survey
Division.** Transportation systems : project
selection and funding / prepared by State of
Nevada, Department of Highways, Planning
Survey & Program-Project Management
Divisions. [Carson City] : The Divisions, 1978.
iii, 31 leaves, [1] leaf of plates : map ; 28 cm.
Cover title. At head of title: State of Nevada. LC
Card 80-620633   DDC 380.5/068 19
*1. Transportation and state - Nevada. 2.
Transportation - Nevada. 3. Roads - Nevada. I.
Nevada. Dept. of Highways. Program-Project
Management Division. II. Title.*
HE213.N3 N48 1978

**Nevada. Dept. of Highways. Program-Project
Management Division.** Nevada. Dept. of
Highways. Planning Survey Division.
Transportation systems . [Carson City] , 1978.
iii, 31 leaves, [1] leaf of plates :   LC Card
80-620633   DDC 380.5/068 19
HE213.N3 N48 1978

Nevada. Dept. of Motor Vehicles. Nevada. Dept.
of Transportation. Safety Section. 1978 Nevada
fatal traffic accident report /. [Carson City?]
[1979?] 34, 44 leaves, [6] leaves of plates (1

fold.) :   LC Card 80-623180   DDC 312/.274/09793
19
HE5614.3.N42 N47 1979

**Nevada. Dept. of Occupational Safety and
Health.**
Rules 60-66, rules of procedure of Occupational
Safety and Health Review Board ; Rule 67,
rules of occupational safety and health
recordkeeping requirements ; Rule 68, rules for
inspections, citations, and proposed penalties ;
Rule 69, rules of practice for variances,
limitations, variations, tolerances, and
exemptions / Department of Occupational
Safety and Health. Carson City, Nev. : The
Dept., [1980] vi, 50 p. ; 23 cm. "Adopted pursuant
to the Nevada Administrative procedure act and
chapter 591 of the statutes of Nevada 1973. Effective
December 20, 1979." LC Card 80-622837   DDC
344.793/0465 19
*1. Industrial safety - Law and legislation - Nevada. 2.
Industrial hygiene - Law and legislation - Nevada. 3.
Nevada. Occupational Safety and Health Review
Board - Rules and practice. I. Nevada. Occupational
Safety and Health Review Board. II. Title.*
KFN935.A443 A2 1980

Rules 60-66, rules of procedure of Occupational
Safety and Health Review Board ; Rule 67,
rules of occupational safety and health
recordkeeping requirements ; Rule 68, rules for
inspections, citations, and proposed penalties ;
Rule 69, rules of practice for variances /
Department of Occupational Safety and Health.
Carson City, Nev. (515 East Musser St., Carson
City 89714) : The Dept., [1981] vi, 50 p. ; 23
cm. "Adopted pursuant to the Nevada Administrative
Procedure Act and chapter 591 of the statutes of
Nevada 1973. Effective January 9, 1981." LC Card
81-622215   DDC 344.793/0465/02636
347.930446502636 19
*1. Industrial safety - Law and legislation - Nevada. 2.
Industrial hygiene - Law and legislation - Nevada. I.
Nevada. Occupational Safety and Health Review Board.
II. Title.*
KFN935.A444 A2 1981

Nevada. Dept. of Transportation. Safety Section.
1978 Nevada fatal traffic accident report /
prepared by State of Nevada, Department of
Transportation, Planning Survey Division,
Safety Section, in cooperation with Nevada
Department of Motor Vehicles and the Federal
Highway Administration. [Carson City?] : The
Section, [1979?] 34, 44 leaves, [6] leaves of
plates (1 fold.) : ill. ; 28 cm. Cover title.   LC
Card 80-623180   DDC 312/.274/09793 19
*1. Traffic accidents - Nevada - Statistics. 2. Violent
deaths - Nevada - Statistics. I. Nevada. Dept. of Motor
Vehicles. II. United States. Federal Highway
Administration. III. Title.*
HE5614.3.N42 N47 1979

Nevada. Division of Environmental Protection.
Nevada. State Environmental Commission.
State of Nevada air quality regulations adopted
by Nevada State Environmental Commission ;
administered by Department of Conservation
and Natural Resources, Division of
Environmental Protection. [Carson City, Nev.]
[1980] ca. 100 p. in various pagings ;   LC Card
80-622609   DDC 344.793/046342 19
KFN958.A436 A2 1980

**NEVADA. DIVISION OF STATE LANDS -
AUDITING AND INSPECTION.**
Nevada. Legislative Auditor. State of Nevada,
Department of Conservation and Natural
Resources, Division of State Lands audit report,
fiscal year ended June 30, 1977. Carson City,
Nev. [1977?] 21 leaves ;   LC Card 78-623424
DDC 353.97930072/32 19
HD243.N4 N47 1977

Nevada. Division of State Parks. Eckbo, Dean,
Austin & Williams. Nevada state-wide trails
study . [Carson City] [1978] 48, [16] leaves :
LC Card 80-620874   DDC 790/.09793 19
GV191.42.N27 E24

Nevada. Division of Water Planning. Gilbert (J.
B.) & Associates. Water conservation in
Nevada . Carson City [1979] xvii, 273 p. :   LC
Card 80-622041   DDC 333.91/16/09793 19
TD224.N2 G54 1979

Nevada. Division of Water Resources.
Rush, F. Eugene. Geohydrology of Smith
Valley, Nevada, with special reference to the
water-use period, 1953-72 /. [Carson City] ,
1976. 95 p. :   LC Card 80-623615   DDC

553.7/09793/58 19
GB705.N3 R87

Schroer, C. V. Nevada streamflow
characteristics /. Carson City [1978] 478 p. :
LC Card 80-623614   DDC 551.48/3/09793 19
GB1225.N3 S37

Utah. Division of Water Resources. Specific
problem analysis summary report . [Salt Lake
City] , 1977. 87 p., [1] leaf of plates :   LC Card
80-620890   DDC 333.9/1/09792 19
TC423.6 .U82 1977

**NEVADA - EXECUTIVE DEPARTMENTS -
MANAGEMENT - DATA PROCESSING.**
Nevada. Legislative Commission. Data
processing by Nevada state government.
[Carson City] [1980] v, 26 p. :   LC Card
81-621355   DDC 353.97930071 19
JK8549.A8 N49 1980

**Nevada. Governor's Committee on Employment
of the Handicapped.** Rights handbook for the
handicapped / Governor's Committee on
Employment of the Handicapped, Nevada
Rehabilitation Division, Bureau of
Governmental Research, University of Nevada.
[Carson City] : The Committee, 1977. iv, 80
p. ; 28 cm. Includes bibliographical references. LC
Card 79-621844   DDC 346.79301/3 19
*1. Handicapped - Law and legislation - Nevada. I.
Nevada. Rehabilitation Division. II. Nevada. University.
Bureau of Governmental Research. III. Title.*
KFN691.H3 A837

**Nevada. Highway Planning Division. see Nevada.
Dept. of Highways. Planning Survey
Division.**

NEVADA - HISTORY.
Bancroft, Hubert Howe, 1832-1918. History of
Nevada, 1540-1888 /. Reno, Nev. , 1981. p.
cm.   ISBN 0-87417-068-0   LC Card 81-13145
DDC 979.3/01 19
F841 .B2 1981

Nevada. Legislative Auditor.
State of Nevada, Department of Administration,
Budget Division, audit report, fiscal year ended
June 30, 1977. Carson City, Nev. : Legislative
Auditor, [197-] 18 leaves ; 28 cm. Cover title.
LC Card 78-623421   DDC 353.97930072/32 19
*1. Nevada. Budget Division - Auditing and inspection.
I. Title.*
HJ2053.N4 N44 1970z

State of Nevada, Department of Conservation
and Natural Resources, Division of State Lands
audit report, fiscal year ended June 30, 1977.
Carson City, Nev. : Legislative Auditor, [1977?]
21 leaves ; 28 cm. Cover title.   LC Card 78-623424
DDC 353.97930072/32 19
*1. Nevada. Division of State Lands - Auditing and
inspection. 2. Legislative auditing - Nevada. I. Title.*
HD243.N4 N47 1977

State of Nevada, Department of Energy audit
report, fiscal year ended June 30, 1979. Carson
City, Nev. : Nevada Legislature, Legislative
Auditor, [1980] 23 leaves ; 28 cm. Cover title.
LC Card 80-621823   DDC 353.97930072/32 19
*1. Nevada. Dept. of Energy - Auditing and inspection.
I. Title.*
HD9502.U53 N464 1980

State of Nevada, Office of Labor Commissioner
audit report : fiscal year ended June 30, 1978.
Carson City, Nevada : Legislative Auditor,
[1979?] 19 leaves : forms ; 28 cm. Cover title. At
head of title: Nevada Legislature. LC Card 80-621822
DDC 353.97930072/32 19
1. Nevada. Office of Labor Commissioner.
HD8083.N3 N37 1979

State of Nevada Public Service Commission
audit report, fiscal year ended June 30, 1978.
Carson City, Nev. : Legislative Auditor, [1978]
33 leaves ; 29 cm. Cover title. LC Card 78-623423
DDC 353.97930072/32 19
*1. Nevada. Public Service Commission - Auditing and
inspection. I. Title.*
HD2767.N29 N47 1978

State of Nevada Public Works Board audit
report, fiscal year ended June 30, 1978. Carson
City, Nev. : Legislative Auditor, [1979?] 26
leaves ; 28 cm. Cover title. LC Card 80-621821
DDC 353.97930072/32 19
*1. Nevada. State Public Works Board - Appropriations
and expenditures. I. Title.*
TA24.N3 N48 1979

Nevada. Legislative Commission.
Availability of liability and employee group insurance to local government. [Carson City] : Legislative Commission of the Legislative Counsel Bureau, State of Nevada, 1978. ii, 103 p. ; 29 cm. (Bulletin - Legislative Commission of the Legislative Counsel Bureau, State of Nevada ; no. 79-11) Cover title. LC Card 78-624286 DDC 346.793/0865 19
1. Insurance, Government risks - Nevada. I. Series: Nevada. Legislative Counsel Bureau. Bulletin , 79-11. II. Title.
KFN799.G6 A25 1978

Data processing by Nevada state government. [Carson City] : Legislative Commission of the Legislative Counsel Bureau, State of Nevada, [1980] v, 26 p. : ill. ; 28 cm. (Bulletin / Legislative Commission of the Legislative Counsel Bureau, State of Nevada . no. 81-13) Cover title. "October 1980." LC Card 81-621355 DDC 353.97930071 19
1. Administrative agencies - Nevada - Management - Data processing. 2. Nevada - Executive departments - Management - Data processing. 3. Electronic data processing departments - Security measures. I. Series: Bulletin (Nevada. Legislative Commission) , no. 81-13. II. Title.
JK8549.A8 N49 1980

Effects of tax relief measures. [Carson City] : Legislative Commission of the Legislative Counsel Bureau, State of Nevada, [1980] vii, 42 p. ; 28 cm. (Bulletin / Legislative Commission of the Legislative Counsel Bureau, State of Nevada . no. 81-18) Cover title. "December 1980." LC Card 81-621361 DDC 343.79304 347.93034 19
1. Taxation - Law and legislation - Nevada. 2. Property tax - Law and legislation - Nevada. I. Series: Bulletin (Nevada. Legislative Commission) , no. 81-18. II. Title.
KFN1070 .A25 1980

Federal funding in local programs / Legislative Commission of the Legislative Counsel Bureau, State of Nevada. [Carson City] : The Commission, [1980] iv, 41 p. ; 28 cm. (Bulletin / Legislative Commission of the Legislative Counsel Bureau, State of Nevada . no. 81-19) Cover title. Chiefly tables. "October 1980." LC Card 81-621358 DDC 336.1/85 19
1. Grants-in-aid - Nevada - Statistics. 2. Grants-in-aid - United States - Statistics. 3. Local finance - Nevada - Statistics. I. Series: Bulletin (Nevada. Legislative Commission) , no. 81-19. II. Title.
HJ565 .N48 1980

Juvenile crime and abuse of alcohol / Legislative Commission of the Legislative Counsel Bureau, State of Nevada. [Carson City] : The Commission, [1980] viii, 37 p. ; 28 cm. (Bulletin / Legislative Commission of the Legislative Counsel Bureau, State of Nevada . no. 81-10) Cover title. "October 1980." LC Card 81-621352 DDC 364.3/6/09793 19
1. Alcoholism and crime - Prevention. 2. Youth - Nevada - Alcohol use - Prevention. 3. Juvenile delinquency - Nevada - Prevention. I. Series: Bulletin (Nevada. Legislative Commission) , no. 81-10. II. Title.
HV5053 .N48 1980

Libraries and other systems for storing information. [Carson City, Nev.] : Legislative Commission of the Legislative Counsel Bureau, State of Nevada, [1980] xviii, 202 p. ; 28 cm. (Bulletin / Legislative Commission of the Legislative Counsel Bureau, State of Nevada . no. 81-15) Cover title. LC Card 81-621357 DDC 025/.04 19
1. Information services - Nevada. 2. Information storage and retrieval systems. 3. Libraries - Nevada. I. Series: Bulletin (Nevada. Legislative Commission) , no. 81-15. II. Title.
Z674.5.U5 N48 1980

Prevention of child abuse. [Carson City] : Legislative Commission of the Legislative Counsel Bureau, State of Nevada, [1980] vi, 78 p. : ill. ; 28 cm. (Bulletin / Legislative Commission of the Legislative Counsel Bureau, State of Nevada . no. 81-12) Cover title. "October 1980." Bibliography: p. 23-24. LC Card 81-621354 DDC 362.7/1 19
1. Child abuse - Nevada - Prevention. I. Series: Bulletin (Nevada. Legislative Commission) , no. 81-12. II. Title.
HV742.N3 N48 1980

Statewide master plan for fire protection. [Carson City] : Legislative Commission of the Legislative Counsel Bureau, State of Nevada, [1980] ix, 65 p. ; 28 cm. (Bulletin / Legislative Commission of the Legislative Counsel Bureau, State of Nevada . no. 81-17) Cover title. "October 1980." LC Card 81-621360 DDC 363.3/77/09793 19

1. Fire prevention - Nevada. I. Series: Bulletin (Nevada. Legislative Commission) , no. 81-17. II. Title.
TH9504 .N34 1980

Sunset review. [Carson City, Nev.] : Legislative Commission of the Legislative Counsel Bureau, State of Nevada, [1980] 238 p. in various pagings : ill. ; 28 cm. (Bulletin / Legislative Commission of the Legislative Counsel Bureau, State of Nevada . no. 81-21) Cover title. Includes bibliographical references. LC Card 81-621606 DDC 353.979307/6 19
1. Sunset reviews of government programs - Nevada. I. Series: Bulletin (Nevada. Legislative Commission) , no. 81-21. II. Title.
JK8538 1980 .N486

Nevada. Legislative Counsel Bureau. Bulletin .
(79-11) Nevada. Legislative Commission. Availability of liability and employee group insurance to local government. [Carson City] , 1978. ii, 103 p. ; LC Card 78-624286 DDC 346.793/0865 19
KFN799.G6 A25 1978

Nevada. Legislative Counsel Bureau. Legislative Commission. see Nevada. Legislative Commission.

Nevada occupational information use and needs assessment . Fox, Warren H. Reno, Nev. [1979] 141, 96 p. ; LC Card 80-620637 DDC 025/.06331702 19
HB2615.N3 F69

Nevada. Occupational Safety and Health Review Board.
Nevada. Dept. of Occupational Safety and Health. Rules 60-66, rules of procedure of Occupational Safety and Health Review Board ; Rule 67, rules of occupational safety and health recordkeeping requirements ; Rule 68, rules for inspections, citations, and proposed penalties ; Rule 69, rules of practice for variances, limitations, variations, tolerances, and exemptions /. Carson City, Nev. [1980] vi, 50 p. ; LC Card 80-622837 DDC 344.793/0465 19
KFN935.A443 A2 1980

Nevada. Dept. of Occupational Safety and Health. Rules 60-66, rules of procedure of Occupational Safety and Health Review Board ; Rule 67, rules of occupational safety and health recordkeeping requirements ; Rule 68, rules for inspections, citations, and proposed penalties ; Rule 69, rules of practice for variances, limitations, variations, tolerances, and exemptions /. Carson City, Nev. (515 East Musser St., Carson City 89714) [1981] vi, 50 p. ; LC Card 81-622215 DDC 344.793/0465/02636 347.930446502636 19
KFN935.A444 A2 1981

NEVADA. OCCUPATIONAL SAFETY AND HEALTH REVIEW BOARD - RULES AND PRACTICE.
Nevada. Dept. of Occupational Safety and Health. Rules 60-66, rules of procedure of Occupational Safety and Health Review Board ; Rule 67, rules of occupational safety and health recordkeeping requirements ; Rule 68, rules for inspections, citations, and proposed penalties ; Rule 69, rules of practice for variances, limitations, variations, tolerances, and exemptions /. Carson City, Nev. [1980] vi, 50 p. ; LC Card 80-622837 DDC 344.793/0465 19
KFN935.A443 A2 1980

NEVADA - OCCUPATIONS - INFORMATION SERVICES.
Fox, Warren H. Nevada occupational information use and needs assessment . Reno, Nev. [1979] 141, 96 p. ; LC Card 80-620637 DDC 025/.06331702 19
HB2615.N3 F69

NEVADA. OFFICE OF LABOR COMMISSIONER.
Nevada. Legislative Auditor. State of Nevada, Office of Labor Commissioner audit report . Carson City, Nevada [1979?] 19 leaves : LC Card 80-621822 DDC 353.97930072/32 19
HD8083.N3 N37 1979

NEVADA - PUBLIC LANDS.
United States. Congress. House. Committee on Interior and Insular Affairs. Subcommittee on Public Lands. The MX missile system . Washington , 1980. vii, 906 p. ; LC Card 80-603306 DDC 358/.174/0973 19
KF27 .I544 1979a

NEVADA. PUBLIC SERVICE COMMISSION - AUDITING AND INSPECTION.
Nevada. Legislative Auditor. State of Nevada Public Service Commission audit report, fiscal year ended June 30, 1977. Carson City, Nev. [1978] 33 leaves ; LC Card 78-623423 DDC 353.97930072/32 19
HD2767.N29 N47 1978

Nevada. Rehabilitation Division. Nevada. Governor's Committee on Employment of the Handicapped. Rights handbook for the handicapped /. [Carson City] , 1977. iv, 80 p. ; LC Card 79-621844 DDC 346.79301/3 19
KFN691.H3 A837

Nevada. State Board of Architecture. Rules & regulations / Nevada State Board of Architecture. Las Vegas, Nev. (800 E. Sahara Ave., Suite 2, Las Vegas 89104) : The Board, 1980. [30] p. ; 20 cm. Cover title. LC Card 81-621037 DDC 344.793/0176172 347.9304176172 19
1. Architects - Legal status, laws, etc. - Nevada. I. Title. II. Title: Rules and regulations.
KFN929.A7 A32 1980

Nevada. State Comprehensive Health Planning. Nevada allied health education and manpower . Carson City, Nev. , 1976. 98 p. : LC Card 80-621254 DDC 331.12/3161 19
R847.6.N3 N48

State of Nevada allied health manpower inventory and planning estimates for 1975 and 1980. [Carson City] : State of Nevada, Comprehensive Health Planning, [1975] 133 p. ; 28 cm. "May, 1975." Chiefly tables. LC Card 80-623229 DDC 331.12/9161/09793 19
1. Allied health personnel - Nevada - Supply and demand - Statistics. 2. Allied health personnel - Employment - Nevada - Statistics. I. Title. II. Title: Allied health manpower inventory and planning estimates for 1975 and 1980.
RA410.8.N3 N48 1975

Nevada. State Dept. of Conservation and Natural Resources. (Old Catalog form: Nevada. Conservation and Natural Resources, Dept. of)
Regulations governing pier construction, deposit of fill, dredging, or alteration of Lake Tahoe shoreline, adopted September 24, 1979 / State of Nevada, Department of Conservation and Natural Resources. [Carson City, Nev.] : The Dept., [1979] 8 p. ; 28 cm. LC Card 80-622985 DDC 346.793/57046917 19
1. Shore protection - Law and legislation - Tahoe, Lake. 2. Piers - Law and legislation - Tahoe, Lake. I. Title.
KFN1051.8.A434 A2 1979

Water resources bulletin .
(no. 44) Harrill, J. R. Pumping and depletion of ground-water storage in Las Vegas Valley, Nevada, 1955-74 /. [Carson City] , 1976. vii, 70 p. ; LC Card 80-623616 DDC 333.91/2/0979313 19
GB705.N3 A35 no. 44 TD224.N2

Nevada. State Dept. of Conservation and Natural Resources. Division of Water Resources. see Nevada. Division of Water Resources.

Nevada. State Dept. of Education. Vocational-Technical and Adult Education Branch.
A survey of adult and continuing educaton programs in Nevada. Carson City. tables. 29 cm. Annual. Report year ends June 30. Title varies: 1970/71-1971/72, A survey of continuing education programs in Nevada. At head of title; 1972/73- , State Board Education.
1. Vocational education - Nevada - Periodicals. I. Nevada. State Dept. of Education. Vocational-Technical and Adult Education Branch. A survey of continuing education programs in Nevada. II. Title. III. Title: A survey of continuing education programs in Nevada.
NYPL [JLM 80-726]

A survey of continuing education programs in Nevada. Nevada. State Dept. of Education. Vocational-Technical and Adult Education Branch. A survey of adult and continuing educaton programs in Nevada. Carson City.
NYPL [JLM 80-726]

Nevada. State Environmental Commission. State of Nevada air quality regulations adopted by Nevada State Environmental Commission ; administered by Department of Conservation and Natural Resources, Division of Environmental Protection. [Carson City, Nev.] : The Commission, [1980] ca. 100 p. in various

pagings ; 28 cm. Cover title. "April 1980." LC Card 80-622609 DDC 344.793/046342 19
1. Air - Pollution - Law and legislation - Nevada. I. Nevada. Division of Environmental Protection. II. Title.
KFN958.A436 A2 1980

Nevada. State Museum, Carson City.
Occasional papers .
(no. 4) Price, John A., 1933- The Washo Indians . [Carson City, Nev.] c1980. vi, 82 p., [2] leaves of plates : LC Card 80-623850 DDC 970.004/97 19
E99.W38 P74

NEVADA. STATE PUBLIC WORKS BOARD - APPROPRIATIONS AND EXPENDITURES.
Nevada. Legislative Auditor. State of Nevada Public Works Board audit report, fiscal year ended June 30, 1978. Carson City, Nev. [1979?] 26 leaves ; LC Card 80-621821 DDC 353.97930072/32 19
TA24.N3 N48 1979

Nevada state-wide trails study . Eckbo, Dean, Austin & Williams. [Carson City] [1978] 48, [16] leaves : LC Card 80-620874 DDC 790/.09793 19
GV191.42.N27 E24

Nevada streamflow characteristics /. Schroer, C. V. Carson City [1978] 478 p. : LC Card 80-623614 DDC 551.48/3/09793 19
GB1225.N3 S37

Nevada studies in history and political science.
For other vols. in this series, see Old Catalog.
(no. 8) Bushnell, Eleanore. The Nevada constitution: origin and growth / Eleanore Bushnell ; with Don W. Driggs. Reno, 1980. x, 221 p. ISBN 0-87417-034-6
KFN1002.Z9 B8 1972
         NYPL [IBO (Nevada) 80-3141]

Nevada. Taxicab Authority. Rules and regulations governing service and safety of operations of taxicabs under the jurisdiction of the Taxicab Authority of Nevada / State of Nevada, Taxicab Authority. Carson City : SPO, [197-] 16 p. ; 23 cm. "General order number 3." LC Card 79-625366 DDC 343.793/0982 19
1. Taxicabs - Nevada. I. Title.
KFN900.T3 A32 1979

Nevada. University. Bureau of Governmental Research. (Old Catalog form: Nevada. University. Governmental (Research, Bureau of))
Nevada. Governor's Committee on Employment of the Handicapped. Rights handbook for the handicapped /. [Carson City] , 1977. iv, 80 p. ; LC Card 79-621844 DDC 346.79301/3 19
KFN691.H3 A837

Nevada. University. Governmental Research, Bureau of. see **Nevada. University. Bureau of Governmental Research.**

Nevada. University. Library. Rendall, Marian K. A guide to some research collections in the University Library /. Reno, 1971. ca. 140 p.;
         NYPL [JFF 80-473]

NEVADA. UNIVERSITY. LIBRARY.
Rendall, Marian K. A guide to some research collections in the University Library /. Reno, 1971. ca. 140 p.;   *NYPL [JFF 80-473]*

Nevada. University, Reno. see **University of Nevada, Reno.**

Nevada. Water Resources, Division of. see **Nevada. Division of Water Resources.**

Nevé, Richard A. Development of a chemical assay for saxitoxin or paralytic shellfish poison (PSP) : a report to the Alaska State legislature / by Richard A. Nevé and Paul B. Reichardt. Fairbanks : Institute of Marine Science, University of Alaska, 1978. iv, 23 leaves : ill. ; 28 cm. Includes bibliographies. LC Card 78-623526 DDC 634/.9 19
1. Saxitoxin - Analysis. 2. Colorimetric analysis. 3. Fluorimetry. I. Reichardt, Paul B., joint author. II. Alaska. Legislature. III. Title.
QP632.S27 N48

Neville, Robert C. Reconstruction of thinking / Robert C. Neville. Albany : State University of New York Press, 1981. p. cm. Bibliography: p. Includes index. ISBN 0-87395-494-7 LC Card 81-5347 DDC 128/.3 19
1. Thought and thinking. I. Title.
B105.T54 N48

New alien identification system . United States. General Accounting Office. [Washington] 1979. iii, 40 p. ; LC Card 79-602501 DDC 353.0081/7 19
JV6505 1979 .G45

New America .
(v. 4, no. 1) Cuentos Chicanos /. Albuquerque, N.M. , c1980. 109 p. : LC Card 81-110854 DDC 813/.01/08868 19
PS647.M49 C8

New and expanding industry. Indiana. Dept. of Commerce. Economic Research Division. Indianapolis.   *NYPL [JLM 80-877]*

A new approach is needed for weapon systems coproduction programs between the United States and its allies . United States. General Accounting Office. [Washington, D.C.] 1979. v, 29 p. ; LC Card 79-603384 DDC 355.8/2/0973 19
UF533 .U52 1979

The New braille musician. Washington. 27 cm. Irregular. Supersedes The Braille musician (not in the library) Began publication in Sept. 1969. Issued by the Division for the Blind and Physically Handicapped, Library of Congress. "Includes reviews of recent acquisitions and a table of contents for each of the braille editions." Superseded by The Musical mainstream. LC Card 70-608593
1. Music - Periodicals. 2. Blind, Periodicals for the. 3. Blind, Music for the. I. United States. Library of Congress. Division for the Blind and Physically Handicapped.   *NYPL [JMM 80-45]*

New Brunswick, N. J. Agricultural Experiment Station. see **New Jersey. Agricultural Experiment Station, New Brunswick.**

New Brunswick, N. J. Rutgers University. see **Rutgers University, New Brunswick, N. J.**

NEW BUSINESS ENTERPRISES - UNITED STATES.
United States. Congress. House. Committee on Science and Technology. Innovation . Washington , 1980. v, 228 p. ; LC Card 80-602110 DDC 338/.06 19
KF27 .S39 1979f

NEW CASTLE COUNTY (DEL.) - MAPS.
United States. Soil Conservation Service. New Castle County, Delaware /. Hyattsville, MD , 1979. 1 map : LC Card 81-690013
G3833.N4 1979 .U5

New concerns in educational administration.
Bloomington, Ind. : School of Education, Indiana University, 1980. iii, 117 p. : ill. ; 23 cm. (Viewpoints in teaching and learning . v. 56, no. 2 0160-8398) Includes bibliographies. LC Card 80-128415 DDC 371.2/00973 19
1. School management and organization - United States - Addresses, essays, lectures. I. Series.
LB2805 .N487

The new conservationists . Ohio. Division of Civilian Conservation. [Columbus, Ohio] [1979?] ix, 41 p. : LC Card 80-623069 DDC 331.3/8133372/09771 19
HD6274.O3 O33 1979

A new constitutional convention for Alaska? . Fischer, Victor. [Anchorage? Alaska , 1980] iii, 49 leaves ; LC Card 80-623893 DDC 342.969/0292 349.6902292 19
KFH403 .F57

"A new decade--the outlook for financial management" . Financial Management Conference, 9th, Washington, D.C., 1980. [Washington, D.C.] , 1980. i, 64 p. : LC Card 80-602663 DDC 351.72 19
HJ257.2 .F55 1980

New developments in occupational stress. Conference on Occupational Stress, Los Angeles, 1978. Los Angeles, Calif. [1979] v, 120 p. ; LC Card 80-621405 DDC 158.7 19
HF5548.85 .C65 1978

New directions for corrections .
(v. 1) Punishment, perspectives in a civilized society . Arlington, Tex. [1977?] iv, 129 p. : LC Card 80-621841 DDC 364.6/0973 19
HV9471 .P86

(v. 2) Restitution and victims of crime . Arlington, Tex. [1977?] iv, 86 p. : LC Card 80-621838 DDC 364.6/8 19
HV6250.2 .R47

(v. 5) Rehabilitation, what part of corrections? .

Arlington, Tex. [1977?] vi, 152 p. : LC Card 80-621842 DDC 364.6/01 19
HV9303 .R43

New directions for nuclear R.D. & D., post-INFCE . United States. Congress. House. Committee on Science and Technology. Subcommittee on Energy Research and Production. Washington , 1980. iii, 401 p. : LC Card 80-604001 DDC 363.1/79 19
KF27 .S3936 1980b

New directions in rural preservation. Washington, D.C. : U. S. Dept. of the Interior, Heritage Conservation and Recreation Service, Division of State Plans and Grants : For sale by the Supt. of Docs., U. S. G.P.O., [1980?] xi, 115 p. : ill. ; 28 cm. (Preservation planning series) HCRS publication ; no. 45 S/N 024-016-00146-0 Item 624-E-9 Includes bibliographies. LC Card 81-601043 DDC 307.7/2/0973 19
1. United States - Rural conditions. 2. Farms - Conservation and restoration. 3. Rural development - United States. I. United States. Heritage Conservation and Recreation Service. Division of State Plans and Grants. II. Series.
HN59 .N398

NEW ENGLAND - HISTORY - COLONIAL PERIOD, CA. 1600-1775 - COLLECTED WORKS.
Smith, John, 1580-1631. [Works. 1983.] The complete works of Captain John Smith (1580-1631) /. Chapel Hill , c1983. p. cm. ISBN 0-8078-1525-X LC Card 81-10364 DDC 975.5/02 19
F229 .S59 1983

New England River Basins Commission. see **United States. New England River Basins Commission.**

New England writers series.
Miller, Perry, 1905-1963. Jonathan Edwards /. Amherst , 1981, c1949. p. cm. ISBN 0-87023-328-9 : LC Card 81-4496 DDC 285.8/092/4 19
BX7260.E3 M5 1981

NEW ENGLANDERS IN CALIFORNIA - ADDRESSES, ESSAYS, LECTURES.
Hart, James David, 1911- New Englanders in Nova Albion . Boston , 1976. vi, 34 p. : LC Card 76-52   *NYPL [*KSD 80-202 no. 3]*

New Englanders in Nova Albion . Hart, James David, 1911- Boston , 1976. vi, 34 p. : LC Card 76-52   *NYPL [*KSD 80-202 no. 3]*

A new genus and species of Chelid turtle from Queensland, Australia /. Legler, John M. Los Angeles, Calif. , 1980. 18 p. : LC Card 80-138331 DDC 574 s 597.92 19
Q11 .L52 no. 324 QL666.C535

The new global fishing regime . United States. Central Intelligence Agency. National Foreign Assessment Center. Washington, D.C. [1980] iv, 7 p., 3 fold. leaves of plates : LC Card 80-602918 DDC 338.3/727 19
SH331 .U48 1980

New Hampshire. Agricultural Experiment Station, Durham.
Research report .
(no. 73) Luloff, A. E. New Hampshire's population . Durham, N.H. [1978?] iv, 37 : LC Card 79-622912 DDC 312/.8/09742 19
HA516 .L84

(no. 76) Dammann, J. C. Economies in fuel wood supply firms in New Hampshire /. Durham, N.H. [1979] ii, 23 p. : LC Card 80-620870 DDC 338.4/366265/09742 19
HD9757.N4 D35

(no. 81) A Survey of the town forest resources in New Hampshire /. Durham, N.H. [1980] ii, 18 p. : LC Card 80-622912 DDC 333.75/09742 19
SD566.N4 S87

Station bulletin .
(513) McDonnell, Mark J. The flora of Plum Island, Essex County, Massachusetts /. Durham, N.H. [1979] ii, 110 p. : LC Card 80-621366 DDC 581.9744/5 19
QK166 .M28

Timber values of town forests / by J.P. Barrett ... [et al.]. Durham, N.H. : New Hampshire Agricultural Experiment Station, University of New Hampshire, [1979] ii, 44 p. : ill. ; 29 cm. (Research report - New Hampshire

Agricultural Experiment Station . no. 77) Cover title. "October 1979." Bibliography: p. 22. LC Card 80-622381 DDC 333.1/1 19
1. Community forests - New Hampshire. 2. Timber - New Hampshire. 3. Cities and towns - New Hampshire. I. Barrett, James P. II. Title. III. Title: Town forests. IV. Series: New Hampshire. Agricultural Research Station, Durham. Research report , no. 77.
SD428.N45 N48 1979

New Hampshire. Agricultural Research Station, Durham.
Research report .
(no. 77) New Hampshire. Agricultural Experiment Station, Durham. Timber values of town forests /. Durham, N.H. [1979] ii, 44 p. : LC Card 80-622381 DDC 333.1/1 19
SD428.N45 N48 1979

New Hampshire. Dept. of Employment Security. New Hampshire employment by occupations to 1985. Frye, Richard M. New Hampshire employment by occupation, projected to 1990 / Wesley S. Noyes, Jr., supervisor ; Richard M. Frye, research analyst. [Concord, N.H.] [Washington] , 1979. 161 p. in various pagings : LC Card 80-621985 DDC 331.12/3/09742 19
HD5725.N4 F79 1979

New Hampshire. Dept. of Employment Security. Economic Analysis and Reporting Section.
New Hampshire staffing patterns in manufacturing industries : an occupational employment statistics survey / conducted by the Economic Analysis and Reports [sic] Section, New Hampshire Department of Employment Security, in cooperation with the U. S. Bureau of Labor Statistics and the Employment and Training Administration. [Concord] : The Dept., 1977. i, 218 p. : graphs ; 28 cm. (People at work) Cover title: Manufacturing occupations, 1977. LC Card 79-620965 DDC 331.12/57/09742 19
1. Labor supply - New Hampshire Statistics. 2. New Hampshire - Occupations - Statistics. I. Title. II. Title: Manufacturing occupations, 1977. III. Series: People at work (Concord).
HD5725.N4 N45 1977

New Hampshire staffing patterns in selected nonmanufacturing industries, 1978 : an occupation employment statistics survey / conducted by the Economic Analysis and Reports Section, New Hampshire Department of Employment Security, in cooperation with the U. S. Bureau of Labor Statistics and the Employment and Training Administration. [Concord, N.H.] : The Section, 1979. i, 172 p. : graphs ; 28 cm. LC Card 80-621986 DDC 331.12/5/09742 19
1. Labor supply - New Hampshire Statistics. 2. New Hampshire - Occupations - Statistics. I. United States. Bureau of Labor Statistics. II. United States. Employment and Training Administration. III. Title.
HD5725.N4 N45 1979

New Hampshire. Dept. of Health and Welfare.
Biennial report. [Concord] illus. 28 cm.
1. Mental health services - New Hampshire - Periodicals. 2. Public welfare - New Hampshire - Periodicals. 3. Public health - New Hampshire - Periodicals. I. Title.   **NYPL [JLM 80-829]**

New Hampshire. Dept. of Public Works and Highways. Planning and Economics Division.
State of New Hampshire general highway maps / prepared by the New Hampshire Department of Public Works and Highways, Planning and Economics Division, in cooperation with the United States Department of Transportation, Federal Highway Administration. [Concord] : New Hampshire Dept. of Public Works and Highways, [1977?] [78] leaves of plates : maps ; 46 x 61 cm. (County series) Cover title. Scale of maps 1:63,360 or 1˝ = 1 mile. Includes index. LC Card 79-625810 DDC 912/.742
1. New Hampshire - Road maps. I. Title.
G1221.P2 N4 1977

New Hampshire. Division of Safety Services.
Navigation chart, Lake Sunapee / New Hampshire Dept. of Safety, Division of Safety Services ; printed through the courtesy of the Lake Saunapee Protective Association. 1st rev. ed. [Concord? N.H.] : The Division, 1978. 1 map : col. ; 65 x 38 cm. Relief shown by spot heights. Includes text, list of buoys, and inset. LC Card 81-692836
1. Nautical charts - New Hampshire - Saunapee, Lake.

I. Lake Sunapee Protective Association. II. Title.
G3742.S93P5 1978 .N4

New Hampshire employment by occupation, projected to 1990 /. Frye, Richard M. [Concord, N.H.] [Washington] , 1979. 161 p. in various pagings : LC Card 80-621985 DDC 331.12/3/09742 19
HD5725.N4 F79 1979

New Hampshire. Health and Welfare, Dept. of. see New Hampshire. Dept. of Health and Welfare.

NEW HAMPSHIRE - HISTORY, LOCAL.
Trementozzi, Miriam, 1947- Preservation, an ethic for planning /. Concord, N.H. , 1980. p. cm. LC Card 80-26731 DDC 363.6/9 19
E159 .T795

NEW HAMPSHIRE - OCCUPATIONS.
Frye, Richard M. New Hampshire employment by occupation, projected to 1990 /. [Concord, N.H.] [Washington] , 1979. 161 p. in various pagings : LC Card 80-621985 DDC 331.12/3/09742 19
HD5725.N4 F79 1979

NEW HAMPSHIRE - OCCUPATIONS - STATISTICS.
New Hampshire. Dept. of Employment Security. Economic Analysis and Reporting Section. New Hampshire staffing patterns in manufacturing industries . [Concord] , 1977. i, 218 p. : LC Card 79-620965 DDC 331.12/57/09742 19
HD5725.N4 N45 1977

New Hampshire. Dept. of Employment Security. Economic Analysis and Reporting Section. New Hampshire staffing patterns in selected nonmanufacturing industries, 1978 . [Concord, N.H.] , 1979. i, 172 p. : LC Card 80-621986 DDC 331.12/5/09742 19
HD5725.N4 N45 1979

NEW HAMPSHIRE - POPULATION - STATISTICS.
Luloff, A. E. New Hampshire's population . Durham, N.H. [1978?] iv, 37 : LC Card 79-622912 DDC 312/.8/09742 19
HA516 .L84

NEW HAMPSHIRE - ROAD MAPS.
New Hampshire. Dept. of Public Works and Highways. Planning and Economics Division. State of New Hampshire general highway maps /. [Concord] [1977?] [78] leaves of plates : LC Card 79-625810 DDC 912/.742
G1221.P2 N4 1977

New Hampshire staffing patterns in manufacturing industries . New Hampshire. Dept. of Employment Security. Economic Analysis and Reporting Section. [Concord] , 1977. i, 218 p. : LC Card 79-620965 DDC 331.12/57/09742 19
HD5725.N4 N45 1977

New Hampshire staffing patterns in selected nonmanufacturing industries, 1978 . New Hampshire. Dept. of Employment Security. Economic Analysis and Reporting Section. [Concord, N.H.] , 1979. i, 172 p. : LC Card 80-621986 DDC 331.12/5/09742 19
HD5725.N4 N45 1979

New Hampshire. University. Agricultural Experiment Station. see New Hampshire. Agricultural Experiment Station, Durham.

New Hampshire. University. Art Galleries. see New Hampshire. University. University Art Galleries.

New Hampshire. University. University Art Galleries.
Olney, Susan Faxon. Two American impressionists . Durham, N.H. , c1980. 22 p. : LC Card 80-80237 DDC 759.13 19
ND237.B4595 A4 1980

Weeks, Edwin Lord, 1849-1903. The art of Edwin Lord Weeks, 1849-1903 [exhibition]/. Durham, N. H. , 1976. 34 p.:
NYPL [3-MCX+ W39 80-1385]

New Hampshire's population /. Luloff, A. E. Durham, N.H. [1978?] iv, 37 : LC Card 79-622912 DDC 312/.8/09742 19
HA516 .L84

NEW HAVEN COUNTY, CONN. - MAPS.
(1979) United States. Soil Conservation Service. New Haven County, Connecticut /. Lanham,

MD , 1979. 1 map : LC Card 81-690030
G3783.N3 1978 .U5

New Jersey.
Results of the general election held November 4, 1975, for the office of 80 members of the General Assembly and six public questions / State of New Jersey ; J. Edward Crabiel, Secretary of State. [Trenton] : The State, [1975?] 10 p. ; 31 cm. LC Card 78-103094 DDC 324.9749/043 19
1. Elections - New Jersey - Statistics. I. New Jersey. Office of the Secretary of State. II. Title.
JK3593 1975 .N48 1975

New Jersey. Agricultural Experiment Station, New Brunswick. Hole, Thornton J. F. Soil survey of Ocean County, New Jersey /. [Washington] [1980] vii, 102 p., [35] fold. leaves of plates : LC Card 80-602312 DDC 631.4/7/74948 19
S599.N5 H64

New Jersey. Attorney General's Office. Motor Vehicle Service Delivery Task Force. see New Jersey. Motor Vehicle Service Delivery Task Force.

New Jersey Basic Skills Council.
Report to the Board of Higher Education on the results of the New Jersey college basic skills placement testing, May 1, 1978-September 28, 1978 / New Jersey Basic Skills Council. [Trenton, N.J.] : The Council, [1978] 54 p. : graphs ; 29 cm. "November 17, 1978." LC Card 80-622754 DDC 379.1/54/09749 19
1. Competency-based education - New Jersey. I. New Jersey. Board of Higher Education. II. Title.
LC1032.5.N5 N48 1978

Report to the Board of Higher Education on the results of the New Jersey college basic skills placement testing, May 1, 1978-September 28, 1978, aggregated according to sending high schools / New Jersey Basic Skills Council. [Trenton? N.J.] : The Council, [1978] [76] p. in various pagings : graphs ; 29 cm. "December 15, 1978." LC Card 80-622753 DDC 370/.9749 19
1. Basic education - New Jersey - Statistics. 2. Universities and colleges - New Jersey - Examinations - Statistics. 3. Education, Secondary - New Jersey - Directories. I. Title.
LC1035.7.N5 N48 1978

NEW JERSEY (BATTLESHIP, BB-62)
United States S. New Jersey Battleship Commission (N.J.) Report of the U. S. S. New Jersey Battleship Commission (created by JR-6 of 1975). [Trenton, N.J.? , 1977?] 28, 4 p. ; LC Card 80-620534 DDC 359.3/252 19
VA65.N5 U22 1977

New Jersey. Board of Higher Education. New Jersey Basic Skills Council. Report to the Board of Higher Education on the results of the New Jersey college basic skills placement testing, May 1, 1978-September 28, 1978 /. [Trenton, N.J.] [1978] 54 p. : LC Card 80-622754 DDC 379.1/54/09749 19
LC1032.5.N5 N48 1978

New Jersey. Budget and Accounting, Division of. see New Jersey. Division of Budget and Accounting.

New Jersey. Bureau of Coastal Planning and Development.
Rutgers University, New Brunswick, N.J. Center for Coastal and Environmental Studies. Comparison of natural and altered estuarine systems . [New Brunswick, N.J.] [1979] xv, 247 p. : LC Card 80-623603 DDC 574.5/26365 19
QH105.N5 R87 1979

Rutgers University, New Brunswick, N.J. Center for Coastal and Environmental Studies. Comparison of natural and altered estuarine systems . [New Brunswick, N.J.] [1979] 2 v. : LC Card 80-623604 DDC 574.5/26365 19
QH105.N5 R87 1979a

New Jersey. Bureau of Local Management Services. New Jersey state aid catalog for local governments. 1972- [Trenton]   **NYPL [JLM 81-65]**

New Jersey. Cabinet Committee on Urban Policy. An assessment of New Jersey's urban programs / prepared by Cabinet Committee on Urban Policy. Trenton : The Committee, 1978. 192 p. in various pagings ; 28 cm. Includes bibliographies. LC Card 79-623364

31

GOVERNMENT PUBLICATIONS - U.S.: 1981
New Jersey. Dept. of Labor and Industry. Division of Planning

1. *Urban policy - New Jersey. I. Title.*
HT123.5.N5 N46 1978

New Jersey. Capital Budgeting and Planning, Commission on. see New Jersey. Commission on Capital Budgeting and Planning.

New Jersey. Coastal Planning and Development, Bureau of. see New Jersey. Bureau of Coastal Planning and Development.

New Jersey. Coastal Zone Management, Office of. see New Jersey. Office of Coastal Zone Management.

New Jersey. Commission of Investigation.
Interim report and recommendations of the State of New Jersey Commission of Investigation on incorrect injury leave practices in the counties. [Trenton, N.J. : The Commission, 1979?] 64 p. ; 28 cm. Cover title. Includes bibliographical references. LC Card 79-623334 DDC 352/.005164/09749 19
1. *Sick leave - New Jersey. 2. Workmen's compensation - New Jersey. 3. Insurance, Accident - New Jersey. I. Title. II. Title: Incorrect injury leave practices in the counties.*
HD5115.6.U52 N56 1979

Report and recommendations of the State of New Jersey Commission of Investigation on the investigation of sudden death cases. [Trenton, N.J.] : The Commission, [1979?] 169, 2, 6 p. ; 28 cm. Cover title. LC Card 80-620967 DDC 363.2/5 19
1. *Murder - New Jersey - Case studies. 2. Homicide investigation - New Jersey - Case studies. 3. Sudden death - New Jersey - Case studies.*
HV6533.N23 N48 1979

Report and recommendations of the State of New Jersey, Commission of Investigation on questionable practices and procedures by local, county, and other public bodies in the purchase and administration of public insurance programs. [Trenton, N.J.] : The Commission, [1980?] 367 p. : ill. ; 28 cm. LC Card 80-623824 DDC 350.82/56/09749 19
1. *Insurance, Government risks - New Jersey. 2. Corruption (in politics) - New Jersey. I. Title.*
HG8215.N5 N48 1980

Report and recommendations on the misuse of public funds in the operation of non-public schools for handicapped children / State Commission of Investigation of New Jersey. [Trenton] : The Commission, [1978] 211 p. ; 28 cm. LC Card 78-623079
1. *Federal aid to private schools - New Jersey. 2. Handicapped children - Education - Finance - New Jersey. I. Title.*
LB2827.5.N5 N48 1978
NYPL [JLF 80-1650]

New Jersey. Commission on Capital Budgeting and Planning. Summary report and recommendations. Trenton. 29 cm. Annual.
1. *Capital budget - New Jersey - Periodicals.*
NYPL [JLM 80-719]

New Jersey. Commission on Income Maintenance. Final report of the Commission on Income Maintenance : report to the Governor and the legislature (pursuant to P.L. 1975, c. 359). [Franklin, N.J.] : The Commission, [1980] iii leaves, 50 p. ; 28 cm. Cover title. "June 13, 1980." LC Card 80-623829 DDC 362.5/82 19
1. *New Jersey. Commission on Income Maintenance. 2. Income maintenance programs - New Jersey. I. Title.*
HC107.N53 I513 1980

NEW JERSEY. COMMISSION ON INCOME MAINTENANCE.
New Jersey. Commission on Income Maintenance. Final report of the Commission on Income Maintenance . [Franklin, N.J.] [1980] iii leaves, 50 p. ; LC Card 80-623829 DDC 362.5/82 19
HC107.N53 I513 1980

New Jersey. Commission on Individual Liberty and Personal Privacy. Public hearing before Commission on Individual Liberty and Personal Privacy, re: confidentiality and access to medical records, held November 8, 1978, Rutgers Law School, Newark, New Jersey. [Trenton] : The Commission, [1978] 21 p. : 28 cm. Microfiche (neg.) 1 sheet. 11 x 15 cm. (NYPL FSN 35,561) Cover title. LC Card 79-624641
1. *Medical records - Law and legislation - New Jersey. 2. Confidential communications - Physicians - New*

Jersey. I. Title.
KFN2167.R4 A84   NYPL [*XME-9450]

New Jersey. Commission on Sex Discrimination in the Statutes.
Public hearing before Commission on Sex Discrimination in the Statutes held June 2, 1979, Senate Conference Room, State House, Trenton, New Jersey. [Trenton, N.J.] : The Commission, [1979] 2, 74, 84 p. ; 28 cm. Cover title. LC Card 79-625604 DDC 344.749/014133 19
1. *Sex discrimination in employment - Law and legislation - New Jersey. 2. Sex discrimination against women - Law and legislation - New Jersey.*
KFN2134.5.D5 A876

Public hearing before Commission on Sex Discrimination in the Statutes on marriage and family law : held February 26, 1980, Burlington County Vocational School, Mount Holly, New Jersey. [Trenton] : The Commisssion, [1980] 37, 15, 134 p. : ill. ; 28 cm. Cover title. LC Card 80-622456 DDC 346.74901/5 19
1. *Domestic relations - New Jersey. 2. Marriage law - New Jersey. 3. Married women - New Jersey. 4. Sex discrimination - Law and legislation - New Jersey. I. Title.*
KFN1894 .A83

Public hearing before Commission on Sex Discrimination in the Statutes on sex discrimination in marriage and family law : held, February 13, 1980, Labor Education Center Auditorium, Rutgers University, New Brunswick, New Jersey. [Trenton] : The Commission, [1980] 39, 19, 43 p. : ill. ; 28 cm. LC Card 80-622457 DDC 346.74901/5 19
1. *Domestic relations - New Jersey. 2. Marriage law - New Jersey. 3. Married women - New Jersey. 4. Sex discrimination - Law and legislation - New Jersey. I. Title.*
KFN1894 .A84

New Jersey. Committee on Urban policy, Cabinet. see New Jersey. Cabinet Committee on Urban Policy.

New Jersey Conference of Social Work. Interracial Committee. Survey of Negro life in New Jersey : community reports / Interracial Committee, New Jersey Conference of Social Work [and the New Jersey Department of Insitiutions and Agencies]. Trenton, N. J. : The Committee, 1932. 18 v. ; 28 cm. Microfilm. Numbers 9-22 published in Newark. CONTENTS. - no. 2. Montclair. - no. 3 Englewood. - no. 4. The Oranges. - no. 5. Hackensack. - no. 6. Passaic and Paterson. - no. 8. Monmouth County. - n0. 9. Morristown. - no. 10. Bayonne. - no. 11. Princeton. - no. 13. Small Negro communities. - no. 14. Atlantic City. - no. 15. New Brunswick and Perth Amboy. - n0 16. Cape May County. - no. 17. Camden. - no. 18. Salem County. - no. 19. Newark. - n0 21. Trenton. - no. 22. Pleasantville.
1. *Afro-Americans - New Jersey. I. New Jersey. Dept. of Institutions and Agencies. II. Title.*
NYPL [Sc Micro R-3667]

New Jersey. County and Municipal Government Study Commission. Public hearing before County and Municipal Government Study Commission on draft report "The development of libraries and networks" : held January 11, 1980, Assembly Chamber, State House, Trenton, New Jersey. Trenton, N.J. : The Commission, [1980] 36, 38 p. ; 28 cm. Cover title. LC Card 80-621672 DDC 027.0749 19
1. *Libraries - New Jersey. 2. Library information networks - New Jersey.*
Z674.4 .N48 1980

NEW JERSEY. DEPT. OF COMMERCE AND ECONOMIC DEVELOPMENT.
New Jersey. Legislature. Senate. State Government Federal and Interstate Relations and Veterans Affairs Committee. Public hearing before Senate State Government Committee on S-874, a bill to create a Department of Commerce and Economic Development, held March 10, 1980, Archive Room, State Library, Trenton, New Jersey. [Trenton, N.J.] [1980] 27 p. ; LC Card 80-622530 DDC 343.749/07 19
KFN1811.3 .S7 1980

New Jersey. Dept. of Community Affairs. Division of Planning. New Jersey. Laws, statutes, etc. Planning, environmental and related enabling legislation. [Trenton] , 1980. 66 p. ; LC Card 80-622986 DDC 344.749/046 19
KFN2154 .A3 1980

New Jersey. Dept. of Education. see New Jersey. State Dept. of Education.

New Jersey. Dept. of Environmental Protection. (Old Catalog form: New Jersey. Environmental Protection, Dept. of) Rules and regulations on licensing of superintendents or operators of public water supply systems, public water treatment plants, and public sewage treatment plants. Rev. [Trenton] : New Jersey State Dept. of Environmental Protection, 1973. 19 p. ; 22 cm. Cover title. LC Card 79-624793 DDC 344.749/0176281 19
1. *Water-supply engineers - Licenses - New Jersey. I. Title.*
KFN2129.E61 A32 1973

Seminar on Industrial Pretreatment, Federal, State, and Local Government Perspectives and Industry's Interests, New Jersey Institute of Technology, 1979. Proceedings . [Trenton] [1980] vii, 73 p. ; LC Card 80-620966 DDC 628.1/683 19
TD896 .S45 1979

New Jersey. Dept. of Environmental Protection. Bureau of Coastal Planning and Development. see New Jersey. Bureau of Coastal Planning and Development.

New Jersey. Dept. of Environmental Protection. Office of Coastal Zone Management. see New Jersey. Office of Coastal Zone Management.

New Jersey. Dept. of Higher Education. Research note - New Jersey Department of Higher Education .
(79-4) O'Connor, Linda. Profile of full-time first-time freshmen enrolled in N.J. colleges, fall 1977 and fall 1978 /. [Trenton] [1979] ii, [77] p. ; LC Card 80-621678 DDC 378/.1059749 19
LA331.5 .O28

(79-5) O'Connor, Linda. Enrollments of students in N.J. colleges and universities by age category, fall 1977 and fall 1978 /. [Trenton] [1979] [47] p. ; LC Card 80-621679 DDC 378/.1059/749 19
LC144.N5 O26

(79-7) O'Connor, Linda. Applications/admissions information, by sector for fall 1977, by institution for fall 1978 . [Trenton] [1979] [42] p. ; LC Card 80-621681 DDC 378/.1056/09749 19
LB2351.3.N5 O26

New Jersey. Dept. of Higher Education. Office of Research.
O'Connor, Linda. Applications/admissions information, by sector for fall 1977, by institution for fall 1978 . [Trenton] [1979] [42] p. ; LC Card 80-621681 DDC 378/.1056/09749 19
LB2351.3.N5 O26

O'Connor, Linda. Enrollments of students in N.J. colleges and universities by age category, fall 1977 and fall 1978 /. [Trenton] [1979] [47] p. ; LC Card 80-621679 DDC 378/.1059/749 19
LC144.N5 O26

O'Connor, Linda. Profile of full-time first-time freshmen enrolled in N.J. colleges, fall 1977 and fall 1978 /. [Trenton] [1979] ii, [77] p. ; LC Card 80-621678 DDC 378/.1059749 19
LA331.5 .O28

New Jersey. Dept. of Human Services. Task Force on the Juvenile Code. see New Jersey. Task Force on the Juvenile Code.

New Jersey. Dept. of Institutions and Agencies. (Old Catalog form: New Jersey. Institutions and Agencies Dept.)
New Jersey Conference of Social Work. Interracial Committee. Survey of Negro life in New Jersey . Trenton, N. J. , 1932. 18 v. ;
NYPL [Sc Micro R-3667]

New Jersey. Dept. of Labor and Industry. Division of Planning and Research. (Old Catalog form: New Jersey. Labor and Industry Dept. Planning and Research Division)
Annual planning information and occupational supply and demand report: Long Branch-Asbury Park labor area. Red Bank. 28 cm. Cover title. Title varies: 1979, Annual planning information: Long Branch-Asbury Park labor area.
1. *Labor supply - New Jersey - Long Branch -*

BIBLIOGRAPHIC GUIDE

New Jersey. Dept. of Labor and Industry. Division of Planning

32

Statistics. 2. Labor supply - New Jersey - Asbury Park - Statistics. I. New Jersey. Dept. of Labor and Industry. Division of Planning and Research. Annual planning information: Long Branch-Asbury Park labor area. II. Title. *NYPL [JLM 80-1120]*

Annual planning information: Long Branch-Asbury Park labor area. New Jersey. Dept. of Labor and Industry. Division of Planning and Research. Annual planning information and occupational supply and demand report: Long Branch-Asbury Park labor area. Red Bank. *NYPL [JLM 80-1120]*

Characteristics of occupational injuries and illnesses in New Jersey, 1977 : information from the Supplementary Data System. [Trenton] : New Jersey Dept. of Labor and Industry, Division of Planning and Research, 1979. v, 59 p. : graphs ; 28 cm. Cover title. LC Card 80-622360 DDC 312./.43/09749 19
1. Industrial accidents - New Jersey - Statistics. 2. Industrial hygiene - New Jersey - Statistics. I. Title.
HD7262.5.U62 N44 1979

Charpentier, Thomas. Occupational employment in selected service industries in New Jersey. Trenton, N.J. , 1980. v, 230 p. : LC Card 80-624024 DDC 331.12/51/0009749 19
HD5718.S452 U53

New Jersey employment and the economy: New Brunswick-Perth Amboy-Sayreville labor area. Aug. 1980- Trenton. *NYPL [Econ. Div.]*

New Jersey employment and the economy: Trenton labor area. June 1980- Trenton. *NYPL [Econ. Div.]*

New Jersey employment and the economy: Vineland-Millville-Bridgeton labor area. June 1980- Trenton. *NYPL [Econ. Div.]*

Occupational employment in selected construction industries in New Jersey. Trenton : New Jersey Dept. of Labor and Industry, Division of Planning and Research, 1979. iii, 98 p. ; 28 cm. Cover title. "Prepared ... by Thomas Charpentier, Thomas Marx, and William Jacobsen." LC Card 80-621724 DDC 331.12/524/09749 19
1. Construction workers - New Jersey - Supply and demand - Statistics. 2. New Jersey - Occupations - Statistics. 3. Construction workers - Job descriptions. I. Charpentier, Thomas. II. Marx, Thomas. III. Jacobsen, William. IV. Title.
HD5718.B92 U546 1979

Occupational employment in selected finance-insurance-real estate industries in New Jersey. Trenton, N.J. : New Jersey Dept. of Labor and Industry, Division of Planning and Research, 1979. iii, 112 p. : graphs ; 28 cm. Cover title. LC Card 80-623798 DDC 331.12/513321/09749 19
1. Insurance companies - New Jersey - Employees - Supply and demand - Statistics. 2. Real estate business - New Jersey - Employees - Supply and demand - Statistics. 3. Financial institutions - New Jersey - Employees - Supply and demand - Statistics. I. Title.
HD5718.I482 U55 1979

Seidel, Laurence H. The veteran in New Jersey, 1978 . Trenton, N.J. , 1979. 16, [7] leaves : LC Card 80-620973 DDC 355.1/154/09749 19
UB358.N5 S4

New Jersey. Dept. of Labor and Industry. Economic Research, Office of. *see* **New Jersey. Dept. of Labor and Industry. Office of Economic Research.**

New Jersey. Dept. of Labor and Industry. Office of Economic Research.
Dale, John D. An economic profile of Monmouth County /. [Trenton, N.J.] [1980] xi, 153 p. : LC Card 80-622708 *HC107.N52 M663* *NYPL [JLF 80-1656]*

Kahn, Hannah W. An economic profile of Hudson County, New Jersey /. [Trenton, N.J.] , 1979. ix, 144 p. : LC Card 80-620869 *HC107.N52 H834*

Ryle, Patricia M. An economic profile of Bergen County, New Jersey /. [Trenton, N.J.] [1980] xviii, 152 p., [1] fold. leaf of plates : LC Card 80-622725 DDC 330.9749/21043 19 *HC107.N53 B477*

New Jersey. Dept. of Labor and Industry. Planning and Research, Division of. *see* **New Jersey. Dept. of Labor and Industry. Division of Planning and Research.**

New Jersey. Dept. of the Public Advocate.
Annual report. [Trenton, N. J.] 28 cm. Vols. for 1977 - include the annual report of the Office of the Public Defender. LC Card 77-643225
1. Public defenders - New Jersey - Periodicals. 2. Ombudsman - New Jersey - Periodicals. I. New Jersey. Office of the Public Defender. Annual report.
NYPL [JLM 80-1143]

New Jersey. Dept. of Transportation. (Old Catalog form: New Jersey. Transportation Dept.)
Four years of highway accomplishments, January 1, 1970-December 31, 1973 / New Jersey Department of Transportation. [Trenton] : The Dept., [1974?] 75 p. ; 22x28 cm.
1. Roads - New Jersey - Statistics. I. Title.
NYPL [JLF 80-998]

New Jersey motor bus contract assistance : a review and analysis of the current program / New Jersey Department of Transportation. [Trenton] : The Dept., [1979] viii leaves, 61 p. : graphs ; 28 cm. "January 9, 1979." LC Card 79-623830 DDC 388.4/1322 19
1. Motor bus lines - New Jersey. 2. Motor bus lines - New Jersey - Finance. 3. Subsidies - New Jersey. I. Title.
HE5633.N5 N45 1979

New Jersey State rail plan for rail transportation and local rail services : 1979 update. [Trenton] : New Jersey Dept. of Transportation, 1979. vii, 153, 135 p. : ill. ; 28 cm. Cover title. Bibliography: p. 132-135 (3d group) LC Card 80-620740 DDC 385/.068 19
1. Railroads - New Jersey. 2. Railroads - New Jersey - Passenger traffic. 3. Transportation planning - New Jersey. I. Title.
HE2771.N5 N48 1979

New Jersey. Division of Budget and Accounting. (Old Catalog form: New Jersey. Treasury Dept. Budget and Accounting Division).
State of New Jersey financial report year ended June 30, 1979. [Trenton, N.J.] : Dept. of the Treasury, Division of Budget and Accounting, 1979?] 53 p. ; 22 x 28 cm. LC Card 80-621346 DDC 353.97490072/31 19
1. Finance, Public - New Jersey - Statistics. I. Title.
HJ585 .N36 1979

New Jersey. Division of Fish, Game, and Shellfisheries.
Rutgers University, New Brunswick, N.J. Center for Coastal and Environmental Studies. Comparison of natural and altered estuarine systems . [New Brunswick, N.J.] [1979] xv, 247 p. : LC Card 80-623603 DDC 574.5/26365 19
QH105.N5 R87 1979

Rutgers University, New Brunswick, N.J. Center for Coastal and Environmental Studies. Comparison of natural and altered estuarine systems . [New Brunswick, N.J.] [1979] 2 v. : LC Card 80-623604 DDC 574.5/26365 19
QH105.N5 R87 1979a

New Jersey. Division of Legislative Information and Research. Confidentiality of legislative research papers : a survey / by the Division of Legislative Information and Research, Office of Legislative Services, State of New Jersey. [Trenton] : The Division, 1978. 68 p. ; 28 cm. "[Prepared by P.P. Guzzo] September 2, 1976. Revised: October 27, 1978." LC Card 79-622026 DDC 328.73/0773 19
1. Bill drafting - United States - States. 2. Legislation - Research - United States - States. 3. Legislative reference bureaus - United States - States. 4. Public records - United States - States - Access control. I. Guzzo, Peter P. II. Title.
KF4950.Z95 N48

New Jersey. Division of Local Government Services. Bureau of Local Management Services. *see* **New Jersey. Bureau of Local Management Services.**

NEW JERSEY. DIVISION OF MOTOR VEHICLES.
New Jersey. Motor Vehicle Service Delivery Task Force. Report of the Motor Vehicle Service Delivery Task Force. [Trenton, N.J.] , 1979. iii, 58, 67 p. ; LC Card 80-623765 DDC 353.97490087/834 19
HE5633.N5 N47 1979

New Jersey. Division of Rural Resources. State Soil Conservation Committee. *see* **New Jersey. State Soil Conservation Committee.**

New Jersey. Division of Taxation. Local Property and Public Utility Branch.
New Jersey. Division of Taxation. Research and Statistics Section. Coefficients of deviation . Trenton , 1978. xiii, 77 p. ; LC Card 78-622220 *HJ4121.N5 D58 1978* *NYPL [JLF 81-12]*

New Jersey. Division of Taxation. Research Section. Coefficients of deviation . Trenton , 1980. xiii, 77 p. ; LC Card 80-622291 DDC 336.22/2 19
HJ4121.N42 N48 1980

New Jersey. Division of Taxation. Research and Statistics Section.
Coefficients of deviation : a measure of property assessment uniformity : a study / by Research Section and Local Property and Public Utility Branch of the Division. Trenton : State of New Jersey, Dept. of the Treasury, Division of Taxation, 1978. xiii, 77 p. ; 22 x 28 cm. Cover title. Chiefly tables. LC Card 78-622220
1. Property tax - New Jersey. I. New Jersey. Division of Taxation. Local Property and Public Utility Branch. II. Title.
HJ4121.N5 D58 1978 *NYPL [JLF 81-12]*

The optional double weighting of the sales factor in the corporation business tax allocation formula : a feasibility study (pursuant to Senate Concurrent resolution 3024) / prepared by the Research and Statistics Section, Division of Taxation. [Trenton] : State of New Jersey, Dept. of the Treasury, Division of Taxation, [1978] 2, 15, [14] p. ; 29 cm. Cover title. "June 1978." LC Card 79-623338 DDC 353.97490072/44 19
1. Corporations - Taxation - New Jersey. I. Title.
HJ4655.N34 N48 1978

Owner occupied housing statistics from homestead rebate and income tax data match : a study / by the Research and Statistics Section, State of New Jersey, Department of the Treasury, Division of Taxation. [Trenton] : The Section, 1980. iii, 495 p. ; 28 cm. Cover title. Tables.
1. Property tax - New Jersey - Statistics. 2. Income - New Jersey - Statistics. 3. Housing - New Jersey - Statistics. I. Title.
HJ4121.N52 N48 1979 *NYPL [JLF 80-1606]*

Owner occupied housing statistics from homestead rebate and income tax data match : a study / by the Research and Statistics Section, State of New Jersey, Department of the Treasury, Division of Taxation. [Trenton] : The Section, [1980] iii, 84, 176-495 p. : ill. ; 27 cm. Cover title. Tables. "April 1980." LC Card 80-623728 DDC 336.22/09749 19
1. Property tax - New Jersey - Statistics. 2. Income - New Jersey - Statistics. 3. Housing - New Jersey - Statistics. I. Title.
HJ4121.N52 N48 1980a

New Jersey. Division of Taxation. Research Section. Coefficients of deviation : a measure of property assessment uniformity : a study / by Research Section and Local Property and Public Utility Branch of the Division. Trenton : State of New Jersey, Dept. of the Treasury, Division of Taxation, 1980. xiii, 77 p. ; 22 x 28 cm. Cover title. Chiefly tables. LC Card 80-622291 DDC 336.22/2 19
1. Property tax - New Jersey - Statistics. I. New Jersey. Division of Taxation. Local Property and Public Utility Branch. II. Title.
HJ4121.N42 N48 1980

New Jersey. Division of Youth and Family Services. Bureau of Licensing.
Listing of licensed child care centers: Central region. Trenton. 28 cm.
1. Day care centers - New Jersey - Directories. I. Title.
NYPL [JLM 80-847]

Listing of licensed child care centers: Metropolitan region. Trenton. 28 cm.
1. Day care centers - New Jersey - Directories. I. Title.
NYPL [JLM 80-848]

Listing of licensed child care centers: Northern region. Trenton. 28 cm.
1. Day care centers - New Jersey - Directories. I. Title.
NYPL [JLM 80-849]

Listing of licensed child care centers: Southern region. Trenton. 28 cm.
1. Day care centers - New Jersey - Directories. I. Title.
NYPL [JLM 80-850]

NEW JERSEY - ECONOMIC CONDITIONS.
New Jersey. Legislature. General Assembly.
Task Force on the Impact of the 1980
Recession. Public hearing before Assembly Task
Force on the Impact of the 1980 Recession .
[Trenton] [1980] 37, 24 p. ;   LC Card 80-623795
     DDC 330.9749/043 19
KFN1811.4 .I56 1980

New Jersey. Legislature. Joint Economic
Committee. A program to improve the business
climate of New Jersey . [Trenton , 1980] v, 165
p. ;   LC Card 80-624028   DDC 332.6/7322749 19
KFN1811.62 .E25 1980

New Jersey. Education Committee (Senate) see
New Jersey. Legislature. Senate. Committee
on Education.

New Jersey. Education, State Dept. of. see New
Jersey. State Dept. of Education.

**New Jersey employment and the economy: New
Brunswick-Perth Amboy-Sayreville labor area.**
Aug. 1980- Trenton. Issued by the New Jersey
Dept. of Labor and Industry, Division of Planning and
Research.
*I. New Jersey. Dept. of Labor and Industry. Division of
Planning and Research.*   **NYPL [Econ. Div.]**

**New Jersey employment and the economy:
Trenton labor area.** June 1980- Trenton. Issued
by the New Jersey Dept. of Labor and Industry,
Division of Planning and Research.
*I. New Jersey. Dept. of Labor and Industry. Division of
Planning and Research.*   **NYPL [Econ. Div.]**

**New Jersey employment and the economy:
Vineland-Millville-Bridgeton labor area.** June
1980- Trenton. Issued by the New Jersey Dept. of
Labor and Industry, Division of Planning and Research.
*I. New Jersey. Dept. of Labor and Industry. Division of
Planning and Research.*   **NYPL [Econ. Div.]**

New Jersey. Employment Security Council. Final
report on the New Jersey unemployment
compensation program / New Jersey
Employment Security Council. [Trenton] : New
Jersey Dept. of Labor and Industry, 1979. 66
p. ; 28 cm. Cover title.   LC Card 79-623832
1. Insurance, Unemployment - New Jersey. I. Title.
HD7096.U6 N564 1979
     NYPL [JLF 80-1314]

New Jersey. Environmental Protection, Dept. of.
see New Jersey. Dept. of Environmental
Protection.

New Jersey. Executive Dept. Governor's
Conference on the Future of the New Jersey
Shore, Point Pleasant, N.J., 1979. The future of
the New Jersey shore . New Brunswick, N.J. ,
1980. ix, 113 p. ;   LC Card 80-623449   DDC
     333.91/7/09749 19
HT393.N5 G68 1979

**NEW JERSEY - FULL EMPLOYMENT
     POLICIES.**
New Jersey. Legislature. Joint Economic
Committee. A program to improve the business
climate of New Jersey . [Trenton , 1980] v, 165
p. ;   LC Card 80-624028   DDC 332.6/7322749 19
KFN1811.62 .E25 1980

New Jersey. Governor, 1911-13 (Wilson) Vetoes
of Woodrow Wilson, / Governor of New
Jersey, session of legislature, 1912. [Trenton ;
1912.] 35 l.
*1. Veto - New Jersey. 2. New Jersey - Politics and
government 1865-1950. 3. Wilson, Woodrow, Pres. U.
S., 1856-1924. I. Title.*   **NYPL [*ZT-1251]**

**New Jersey. Hazardous Waste Advisory
     Commission.** Report of Governor Brendan
Byrne's Hazardous Waste Advisory
Commission. Trenton, N.J. : The Commission,
[1980] 70, [36] p. : ill. ; 28 cm. Cover title:
Report of the Hazardous Waste Advisory Commission
to Governor Brendan Byrne. "January 1980." Includes
bibliographical references.   LC Card 80-621669   DDC
     363.7/28 19
*1. Hazardous wastes - New Jersey. 2. Hazardous
wastes - Law and legislation - New Jersey. I. Title.*
TD811.5 .N48 1980

New Jersey. Health, State Dept. of. see New
Jersey. State Dept. of Health.

New Jersey Historical Commission. Petrick,
Barbara, 1935- Mary Philbrook . Trenton, N.J.
[1981] p. cm.   ISBN 0-89743-052-2   LC Card
     81-11285   DDC 305.4/2/0924 B 19
HQ1413.P49 P47

**NEW JERSEY - HISTORY -
     BIBLIOGRAPHY.**
Abrams, H. Leon. A partial working
bibliography on the Amerindians of New Jersey
/. Greeley, Colo. , 1980. 10 leaves ;
     NYPL [HBA 80-381 no. 41]

**New Jersey. Individual Liberty and Personal
Privacy, Commission on.** see New Jersey.
Commission on Individual Liberty and
Personal Privacy.

New Jersey. Institutions and Agencies, Dept. of.
see New Jersey. Dept. of Institutions and
Agencies.

New Jersey. Investigation, Commission of. see
New Jersey. Commission of Investigation.

New Jersey. Judiciary Committee (Senate) see
New Jersey. Legislature. Senate. Judiciary
Committee.

**New Jersey. Law Revision and Legislative
Services Commission.** Transferable
development rights . [Trenton] [1979?] xi, 340
p. ;   LC Card 80-622361   DDC 346.7304/5 19
KF5698.5.A75 T7

New Jersey. Laws, statutes, etc. (Old Catalog
form: New Jersey. Statutes)
Planning, environmental and related enabling
legislation. Rev. ed. [Trenton] : State of New
Jersey, Dept. of Community Affairs, Division of
Planning, 1980. 66 p. ; 28 cm.   LC Card
     80-622986   DDC 344.749/046 19
*1. Environmental law - New Jersey. 2. Regional
planning - Law and legislation - New Jersey. 3. Local
government - New Jersey. I. New Jersey. Dept. of
Community Affairs. Division of Planning. II. Title.*
KFN2154 .A3 1980

NEW JERSEY. LEGISLATURE.
New Jersey. Legislature. Senate. State
Government Federal and Interstate Relations
and Veterans Affairs Committee. Public hearing.
Trenton, N. J. , 1977. 35, 13 p. ;
     NYPL [JLG 80-143]

**New Jersey. Legislature. Ethical Standards, Joint
Legislative Committee on.** see New Jersey.
Legislature. Joint Legislative Committee on
Ethical Standards.

**New Jersey. Legislature. General Assembly. Ad
Hoc Committee to Study Automobile
Insurance Reform.** Ad hoc committee report
on automobile insurance reform in the State of
New Jersey. [Trenton : The Committee], 1979.
iv, 40 leaves, p. 41-112 ; 28 cm. Cover title.
Includes bibliographical references.   LC Card
     79-623345   DDC 346.749/086232 19
*1. Insurance, Automobile - New Jersey. 2. Insurance,
No-fault automobile - New Jersey. I. Title.*
KFN1811.82 .A93 1979

**New Jersey. Legislature. General Assembly.
Automobile Insurance Reform, Ad Hoc
Committee to Study.** see New Jersey.
Legislature. General Assembly. Ad Hoc
Committee to Study Automobile Insurance
Reform.

**New Jersey. Legislature. General Assembly.
Banking and Insurance Committee.**
New Jersey. Legislature. Senate. Labor,
Industry and Professions Committee. Public
hearing before Senate Labor, Industry and
Professions Committee and Assembly Banking
and Insurance Committee on S-975 and A-755
(a bill to provide for the licensing and
regulation of mortgage bankers, mortgage
brokers, and mortgage solicitors by the
Commissioner of Banking) . [Trenton] [1980]
9, 38, 27 p. ;   LC Card 80-622489   DDC
     346.74904/364 19
KFN1811.3 .L3 1980

New Jersey. Legislature. Senate. Labor,
Industry and Professions Committee. Public
hearing before Senate Labor, Industry and
Professions Committee and Assembly Banking
and Insurance Committee on S-975 and A-755.
[Trenton, 1980] 38, 27 p.   **NYPL [JLF 81-84]**

**New Jersey. Legislature. General Assembly.
Banking and Insurance Committee. Ad Hoc
Committee to Study Automobile Insurance
Reform.** see New Jersey. Legislature.
General Assembly. Ad Hoc Committee to
Study Automobile Insurance Reform.

**New Jersey. Legislature. General Assembly.
Committee on Agriculture and Environment.**

Public hearing before Assembly Agriculture and
Environment Committee, on A-966 (the
Radiation emergency response act), held April
8, 1980, Assembly Chamber, State House,
Trenton, New Jersey. [Trenton] : The
Committee, [1980] 79 p. in various pagings ; 28
cm. Cover title.   LC Card 80-623636   DDC
     344.749/0472 19
*1. Radioactive substances - Safety regulations - New
Jersey. 2. Nuclear facilities - Safety regulations - New
Jersey. I. Title.*
KFN1811.4 .A3 1980

Public hearing before Assembly Agriculture and
Environment Committee on Assembly
resolution no. 3017 : an investigation
concerning the suitability of existing sites for
the storage of hazardous or chemical wastes in
this state, held May 9, 1979, Assembly
Chamber, State House, Trenton, New Jersey.
[Trenton] : The Committee, [1979] 32, 93 p. ;
28 cm. Cover title.   LC Card 79-624638
1. Hazardous wastes - New Jersey. I. Title.
KFN1811.4 .A3 1979

Public hearing before Assembly Agriculture and
Environment Committee on Assembly no.
3037 : prescribes the conditions under which a
public utility may operate nuclear powerplants :
held April 9, 1979, Assembly Chamber,
Trenton, New Jersey. [Trenton] : The
Committee, [1979] 4, 56, 21 p. ; 28 cm.   LC
     Card 79-624766
*1. Atomic power-plants - Law and legislation - New
Jersey. 2. Atomic power - Law and legislation - New
Jersey. I. Title.*
KFN1811.4 .A3 1979a   **NYPL [JLF 80-1295]**

Public hearing before Assembly Agriculture and
Environment Committee, on Assembly no. 1818
(Natural resources bond issue) : held June 19,
1980, Assembly Chamber, State House,
Trenton, New Jersey. [Trenton] : The
Committee, [1980] 24, 6 p. ; 28 cm. Cover title.
     LC Card 80-623796   DDC 344.749/046
     347.490446 19
*1. Environmental law - New Jersey. 2. Natural
resources - Law and legislation - New Jersey. 3. State
bonds - New Jersey. 4. Environmental policy - New
Jersey - Finance. I. Title.*
KFN1811.4 .A3 1980a

**New Jersey. Legislature. General Assembly.
Committee on Banking and Insurance.** see
New Jersey. Legislature. General Assembly.
Banking and Insurance Committee.

**New Jersey. Legislature. General Assembly.
Committee on Institutions, Health &
Welfare.**
New Jersey. Legislature. Senate. Institutions,
Health and Welfare Committee. Joint Senate
and Assembly Institutions, Health and Welfare
Committee meeting on food poisoning outbreak
at Marlboro Psychiatric Hospital, held
November 5, 1979, Marlboro Psychiatric
Hospital, Marlboro, New Jersey. [Trenton :
Senate Committee : 47 p. ;   LC Card 80-621984
     DDC 363.1/9265/0974946 19
KFN1811.3 .I47 1979b

New Jersey. Legislature. Senate. Institutions,
Health and Welfare Committee. Joint Senate
and Assembly Institutions, Health and Welfare
Committee meeting on food poisoning outbreak
at Marlboro Psychiatric Hospital, held March 6,
1980, Marlboro Psychiatric Hospital, Marlboro,
New Jersey. [Trenton , 1980] 36 p. ;   LC Card
     80-623830   DDC 363.1/92 19
KFN1811.3 .I47 1980a

Public hearing before Assembly Institutions,
Health, and Welfare Committee on A-1823
(Institutional bond issue) : held June 19, 1980,
Room 217, State House, Trenton, New Jersey.
[Trenton] : The Committee, [1980] 3 v. ; 28
cm. Cover title.   LC Card 80-623827   DDC 336.3/1
     19
*1. State bonds - New Jersey. 2. Public institutions -
New Jersey. I. Title.*
KFN1811.4 .I58 1980

Public hearing before Assembly Institutions,
Health, and Welfare Committee on allegations
of abuse at New Lisbon State School, held May
25, 1979, Multipurpose Building, New Lisbon
State School, New Lisbon, New Jersey.
[Trenton?] : The Committee, [1979?] 30, 70 p. ;
28 cm. Cover title.   LC Card 80-620972   DDC
     362.2/1/0974961 19
1. New Lisbon State School. 2. Mental health

facilities - New Jersey - New Lisbon - Employees. 3.
Mentally handicapped - New Jersey - New Lisbon -
Abuse of. I. Title: Allegations of abuse at New Lisbon
State School.
KFN1811.4 .I58 1979b

Public hearing before Assembly Institutions,
Health, and Welfare Committee on allegations
of abuse at New Lisbon State School, held
April 20, 1979 ... New Lisbon State School,
New Lisbon, New Jersey. [Trenton, N.J.] : The
Committee, [1979] 87, 4 p. ; 28 cm. Cover title.
Includes index. LC Card 79-625977 DDC
362.3/09749 19
1. New Lisbon State School. 2. Mental health
facilities - New Jersey - Employees. I. Title.
KFN1811.4 .I58 1979a

**New Jersey. Legislature. General Assembly.
Committee on State Government.** Public
hearing before sub-Committee of Assembly
State Government Committee on the impact of
casino gaming, held July 26, 1979, Commission
Chambers, Atlantic City Hall, Atlantic City,
New Jersey. [Trenton] : The Committee, [1979]
42, 7 p. : graphs ; 28 cm. Cover title. LC Card
80-622488 DDC 353.97490076 19
1. Gambling - New Jersey. 2. Gambling - Licenses -
New Jersey. I. Title.
KFN1811.4 .S78 1979b

**New Jersey. Legislature. General Assembly.
Committee on Taxation.** Report on
assessment, equalization, and revaluation /
General Assembly Committee on Taxation.
[Trenton] : The Committee, [1977?] 41 p. ; 28
cm. Microfilm. Cover title. LC Card 78-621479
1. Property tax - New Jersey. I. Title.
HJ4121.N5 N46 1977   NYPL [*ZT-1263]

**New Jersey. Legislature. General Assembly.
Committee on Transportation and
Communications.** see New Jersey.
Legislature. General Assembly.
Transportation and Communications
Committee.

**New Jersey. Legislature. General Assembly.
Committee to Study Automobile Insurance
Reform, Ad Hoc.** see New Jersey.
Legislature. General Assembly. Ad Hoc
Committee to Study Automobile Insurance
Reform.

**New Jersey. Legislature. General Assembly.
County Government Committee.** Public
hearing before Assembly County Government
Committee on mandated costs of caps
legislation : held March 10, 1980, Senate
Chamber, State House, Trenton, New Jersey.
[Trenton] : The Committee, [1980] 27, 3 p. ; 28
cm. Cover title. LC Card 80-622531 DDC
343.749/03 19
1. County government - New Jersey. 2. Local finance -
New Jersey. 3. Local taxation - New Jersey. I. Title.
KFN1811.4 .C68 1980

**New Jersey. Legislature. General Assembly.
County Government Commmittee.** Public
hearing before Assembly County Government
Committee on mandated costs of caps
legislation : held March 13, 1980, Assembly
Chamber, State House, Trenton, New Jersey.
[Trenton] : The Committee, [1980] 40, 5 p. ; 28
cm. Cover title. LC Card 80-623641 DDC
352.1/232/09749 19
1. Government spending policy - New Jersey. 2. Local
finance - New Jersey. I. Title.
KFN1811.4 .C68 1980a

**New Jersey. Legislature. General Assembly.
Energy and Natural Resources Committee.**
Public hearing before Assembly Energy and
Natural Resources Committee on A-1825, Dune
and shorefront protection act. [Trenton], The
Committee, [1980] 2 v. ; 28 cm. Cover title.
Hearings held Jul. 14, 1980 in Toms River, N.J. and
Jul. 21, 1980 in Brant Beach, N.J. Includes indexes.
LC Card 80-623987 DDC 346.74904/6917
347.490646917 19
1. Shore protection - Law and legislation - New Jersey.
2. Sand-dunes - Law and legislation - New Jersey. I.
Title.
KFN1811.4 .E53 1980

Public hearing before Assembly Energy and
Natural Resources Committee on AR-13,
co-generation of electricity, held March 27,
1980, Assembly Chamber, State House,
Trenton, New Jersey. Trenton, N.J. : The
Committee, [1980] 27, 4 p. ; 28 cm. Cover title.

LC Card 80-624084   DDC 343.749/0929
347.4903929 19
1. Cogeneration of electric power and heat - New
Jersey. 2. Energy policy - New Jersey. I. Title.
KFN1811.4 .E53 1980a

Public hearing before Assembly Energy and
Natural Resources Committee on Assembly, no.
728 (Blue Acres Bond issue) held March 20,
1978, Wayne Township Municipal Building,
Wayne, New Jersey. [Trenton] : The
Committee, [1978?] 38 p. ; 28 cm. Cover title.
LC Card 79-624644   DDC 343.749/0924
347.4903924 19
1. Water-supply - Law and legislation - New Jersey. 2.
Water-supply - New Jersey - Finance. 3. Watershed
management - New Jersey. I. Title.
KFN1811.4 .E53 1978b

**New Jersey. Legislature. General Assembly.
Institutions, Health & Welfare, Committee
on.** see New Jersey. Legislature. General
Assembly. Committee on Institutions,
Health & Welfare.

**New Jersey. Legislature. General Assembly.
Judiciary, Law, Public Safety & Defense
Committee.** Public hearing before special
subcommittee of the Assembly Judiciary, Law,
Public Safety and Defense Committee on
current practices in New Jersey liquor industry
and question of price deregulation. [Trenton] :
The Committee, [1979] 2 v. ; 28 cm. Cover title.
Hearings held May 29, 1979 at Montclair State College,
and May 31, 1979 at Glassboro State College. Includes
index. LC Card 79-625827 DDC 353.97490076/1
19
1. Liquor traffic - New Jersey. 2. Liquor traffic -
Prices - New Jersey. I. Title. II. Title: Current practices
in New Jersey liquor industry and question of price
deregulation.
KFN1811.4 .J78 1979b

**New Jersey. Legislature. General Assembly.
Labor Committee.**
New Jersey. Legislature. Senate. Labor,
Industry and Professions Committee. Public
hearing before the Senate Labor, Industry &
Proffessions [sic] Committee and the Assembly
Labor Committee on workers' compensation,
administrative aspects . [Trenton] [1979] 30
p. ; LC Card 79-625599
KFN1811.3 .L3 1979   NYPL [*XMF-13771]

Public hearing before Assembly Labor
Committee, on unemployment compensation :
held March 3, 1980- County Administration
Building, Jersey City, New Jersey. [Trenton] :
The Committee, [1980]- v. ; 28 cm. Cover title.
LC Card 80-622509 DDC 368.4/4/009749 19
1. Insurance, Unemployment - New Jersey. I. Title.
KFN1811.4 .L24 1980

**New Jersey. Legislature. General Assembly.
Labor Committee: Business Concerns,
Subcommittee on.** see New Jersey.
Legislature General Assembly. Labor
committee. Subcommittee on Business
Concerns.

**New Jersey. Legislature General Assembly.
Labor committee. Subcommittee on Business
Concerns.**
Public hearing before Subcommittee on Business
Concerns of the Assembly Labor Committee re:
job training. [Trenton:"bs. n.], 1979. 29, 1x-14x;
28 cm. Microfiche (neg.) 1 sheet. 11 x 15 cm. (NYPL
FSN 35,316) Cover title. "Held October 23, 1979 ...
State House."
1. Occupational training - New Jersey. I. Title.
NYPL [*XME-9334]

Public hearing before Subcommittee on Business
Concerns of the Assembly Labor Committee, re
job training : held October 23, 1979, Senate
Chamber, State House, Trenton, New Jersey.
[Trenton : The Subcommittee, 1980] 14 p. :
ill. ; 28 cm. Cover title. LC Card 80-621236 DDC
331.25/924/09749 19
1. Occupational training - New Jersey. I. Title.
KFN1811.4 .L243 1979

**New Jersey. Legislature. General Assembly.
Legislative Oversight Committee.**
Public hearing before Assembly Legislative
Oversight Committee on energy crisis.
Trenton : The Committee, [1979] 3 v. ; 28 cm.
Cover title. LC Card 80-620968
1. Energy policy - New Jersey. 2. Energy
conservation - New Jersey.
KFN1811.4 .L4 1979   NYPL [JLM 80-473]

Public hearing before Assembly Legislative
Oversight Committee on the licensing of casino
employees : held October 29, 1979, Casino
Control Commission Office, Tennessee Ave.
and Boardwalk, Atlantic City, New Jersey.
[Trenton, N.J.] : The Committee, [1979] 86 p. ;
29 cm. LC Card 80-620969 DDC 353.97490076 19
1. Gambling - Licenses - New Jersey. I. Title.
KFN1811.4 .L4 1979a

**New Jersey. Legislature. General Assembly.
Municipal Government Committee.**
Public hearing before Assembly Municipal
Government Committee on Assembly bill 1819
(storm water management) : held May 18,
1979...Hackensack, New Jersey. [Trenton] : The
Committee, [1979?] 3,60 p. ; 28 cm. Cover title.
LC Card 80-621670 DDC 346.74904/691
347.49064691 19
1. Storm sewers - Law and legislation - New Jersey. 2.
Storm water retention basins - Law and legislation -
New Jersey. I. Title.
KFN1811.4 .M8 1979c

The state uniform construction code : report of
the Committee on Municipal Government of
the General Assembly (pursuant to Assembly
resolution 58 of 1978) January 3, 1980.
[Trenton] : The Committee, [1980] ii, 34 p. ; 28
cm. Cover title. LC Card 80-624085 DDC
343.749/07869 347.49037869 19
1. Building laws - New Jersey. I. Title.
KFN1811.82 .M86 1980

**New Jersey. Legislature. General Assembly.
Revenue, Finance, and Appropriations
Committee.**
Public hearing before Assembly Revenue,
Finance and Appropriations Committee on
Assembly concurrent resolution no. 139 O[i.e.
A]CR (use of casino gambling revenues to assist
senior citizens and disabled) held June 30,
1980, Assembly Majority Conference Room,
State House, Trenton, New Jersey. [Trenton] :
The Committee, [1980] 3, 32 p. ; 28 cm. Cover
title. LC Card 80-623450
1. Gambling - New Jersey. 2. Old age assistance - New
Jersey. 3. Public welfare - Law and legislation - New
Jersey. I. Title. II. Title: Use of casino gambling
revenues to assist senior citizens and disabled.
KFN1811.4 .R45 1980

Public hearing before Assembly Revenue,
Finance, and Appropriations Committee on
ACR-29 : held May 27, 1980, Assembly
Chamber, State House, Trenton, New Jersey.
[Trenton] : The Committee, [1980] 3, 9, 23 p. ;
28 cm. Cover title. LC Card 80-623639 DDC
343.74905/4 347.490354 19
1. Real property tax - New Jersey - Deductions. 2.
Aged - Taxation - New Jersey. 3. Handicapped -
Taxation - New Jersey. I. Title.
KFN1811.4 .R45 1980a

**New Jersey. Legislature. General Assembly.
State Government, Federal and Interstate
Relations, and Veterans' Affairs Committee.**
Public hearing before Assembly State
Government, Federal and Interstate Relations,
and Veterans Affairs Committee on Assembly
bill No. 1201 : an act to amend the "Casino
control act," approved June 2, 1977 (P.L. 1977,
c. 110) and P.L. 1978, c. 7, supplementary
thereto, and repealing sections 21 to 30 of P.L.
1978, c. 7 : held April 9, 1980, Assembly
Chamber, State House, Trenton, New Jersey.
[Trenton] : The Committee, [1980] 10, 32, 4
p. ; 28 cm. Cover title. LC Card 80-622529 DDC
344.749/0542 19
1. Gambling - New Jersey. I. Title.
KFN1811.4 .S78 1980

Public hearings before Assembly State
Government, Federal and Interstate Relations
and Veterans Affairs Committee on Assembly
bill 1081 held March 3, 1980, Assembly
Chamber, State House, Trenton, New Jersey.
[Trenton, N.J.] : The Committee, [1980] 122 p.
in various pagings ; 28 cm. Cover title. LC Card
80-622532 DDC 344.749/0542 19
1. Gambling - New Jersey.
KFN1811.4 .S78 1980a

**New Jersey. Legislature. General Assembly.
State Government, Federal Interstate
Relations, and Veterans' Affairs Committee.**
Public hearing before Assembly State
Government, Federal and Interstate Relations
and Veterans Affairs Committee on ACR-117,
held June 11, 1980, Assembly Chamber, State

GOVERNMENT PUBLICATIONS - U.S.: 1981

35

New Jersey. Legislature. Senate. State Government Federal and

House, Trenton, New Jersey. [Trenton, N.J.] :
The Committee, [1980] 5, 10, 9 p. ; 28 cm.
Cover title. Includes index.   LC Card 80-623799
DDC 342.749/044 347.490244 19
*1. Bills, Legislative - New Jersey. 2. Legislation - New
Jersey.*
KFN1811.4 .S78 1980b

**New Jersey. Legislature. General Assembly. Task
Force on the Impact of the 1980 Recession.**
Public hearing before Assembly Task Force on
the Impact of the 1980 Recession : held May
22, 1980 .... [Trenton] : The Task Force, [1980]
37, 24 p. ; 29 cm. Cover title.   LC Card 80-623795
DDC 330.9749/043 19
1. New Jersey - Economic conditions. I. Title.
KFN1811.4 .I56 1980

**New Jersey. Legislature. General Assembly.
Taxation, Committee on. see New Jersey.
Legislature. General Assembly. Committee
on Taxation.**

**New Jersey. Legislature. General Assembly.
Transportation and Communications
Committee.** Public hearing before
subcommittee of Assembly Transportation and
Communications Committee to investigate the
transportation of radioactive cargo on highways
within New Jersey (created pursuant to
Assembly Resolution 3003), held August 21,
1979, Freeholders' Chambers, Bergen County
Administration Building, Hackensack, New
Jersey. [Trenton] : The Committee, [1979?] 59,
10 p. ; 28 cm. Cover title.   LC Card 80-622508
DDC 343.749/093 19
*1. Radioactive substances - Transportation - Law and
legislation - New Jersey. 2. Transportation,
Automotive - Law and legislation - New Jersey. 3.
Radioactive substances - New Jersey - Transportation.
4. Transportation, Automotive - New Jersey - Freight.
I. Title.*
KFN1811.4 .T7 1979

**New Jersey. Legislature. Joint Economic
Committee.** A program to improve the
business climate of New Jersey : report of the
Legislative Joint Economic Committee.
[Trenton : The Committee, 1980] v, 165 p. ; 28
cm. Cover title. "May 1, 1980." Includes bibliographical
references.   LC Card 80-624028   DDC
332.6/7322749 19
*1. New Jersey - Economic conditions. 2. Industry and
state - New Jersey. 3. New Jersey - Full employment
policies. I. Title.*
KFN1811.62 .E25 1980

**New Jersey. Legislature. Joint Legislative
Committee on Ethical Standards.**
Report. Trenton. 28 cm.
*1. New Jersey. Legislature. Joint Legislative Committee
on Ethical Standards. - Periodicals.*
NYPL [JLM 81-54]

**NEW JERSEY. LEGISLATURE. JOINT
LEGISLATIVE COMMITTEE ON
ETHICAL STANDARDS. -
PERIODICALS.**
New Jersey. Legislature. Joint Legislative
Committee on Ethical Standards. Report.
Trenton.   **NYPL [JLM 81-54]**

**New Jersey. Legislature. Legislative Oversight
Committee. see New Jersey. Legislature.
General Assembly. Legislative Oversight
Committee.**

**New Jersey. Legislature. Senate. Agriculture
Committee.** Public hearing before Senate
Agriculture Committee on Senate no. 450 :
"Right to farm act", held April 18, Trenton,
New Jersey. [Trenton] : The Committee, [1980]
48, 10 p. ; 28 cm. Cover title.   LC Card 80-621240
DDC 346.74904/676/0262 19
*1. Land use, Rural - Law and legislation - New Jersey.
2. Agricultural laws and legislation - New Jersey. I.
Title.*
KFN1811.3 .A35 1979

**New Jersey. Legislature. Senate. Committee on
Education.** (Old Catalog form: New Jersey.
Education Committee (Senate))
Public hearing before Senate Education
Committee on the impact of spending
limitations on local school districts : held
September 18, 1979, Essex County College,
Newark, New Jersey. [Trenton : The
Committee, 1979?] 134 p. in various pagings ;
28 cm. Cover title. Includes index.   LC Card
80-621237   DDC 379.1/222/09749 19
1. School districts - New Jersey - Finance. 2.

*Intergovernmental fiscal relations - New Jersey. 3.
Local finance - New Jersey. I. Title.*
KFN1811.3 .E3 1979a

**New Jersey. Legislature. Senate. Committee on
Energy and Environment.** Public hearing
before Senate Energy and Environment
Committee on implementation of the Pinelands
protection act (P.L. 1979, chapter 111) : held
February 6, 1980, Pemberton, New Jersey.
[Trenton, N.J.] : The Committee, [1980] 44, 32,
148 p. : ill. ; 28 cm. Cover title.   LC Card
80-622507   DDC 353.7490082/326 19
*1. Land use - New Jersey - Pine Barrens. 2. Land use -
Law and legislation - New Jersey - Pine Barrens. I.
Title.*
KFN1811.3 .E5 1980

**New Jersey. Legislature. Senate. Committee on
Law, Public Safety and Defense.** Public
hearing before Senate Law, Public Safety, and
Defense Committee on Senate bill no. 1631
(adoption revision) : held February 23, 1977,
Senate Chamber, State House, Trenton, New
Jersey. [Trenton] : The Committee, [1977] 11,
12 p. ; 29 cm. Microfiche (neg.) NTIS. 1 sheet. 11 x
15 cm. (PB-275 048) Cover title.   LC Card 77-622937
1. Adoption - New Jersey.
*KFN1811.3 .L39 1977   NYPL [*XME-9410]*

**New Jersey. Legislature. Senate. Committee on
Revenue, Finance and Appropriations. see
New Jersey. Legislature. Senate. Revenue,
Finance and Appropriations Committee.**

**New Jersey. Legislature. Senate. Education,
Committee on. see New Jersey. Legislature.
Senate. Committee on Education.**

**NEW JERSEY. LEGISLATURE. SENATE -
ELECTIONS.**
New Jersey. Legislature. Senate. Judiciary
Committee. Public hearing before Senate
Judiciary Committee on SCR #83 (proposes to
amend the Constitution of New Jersey to
provide that the members of the New Jersey
Senate be elected every year in which a
gubernatorial election is held) . [Trenton]
[1980] 3, 3 p. ;   LC Card 80-623640   DDC
342.749/055 347.490225 19
KFN1811.3 .J8 1980a

**New Jersey. Legislature. Senate. Energy and
Environment, Committee on. see New Jersey.
Legislature. Senate. Committee on Energy
and Environment.**

**New Jersey. Legislature. Senate. Institutions,
Health and Welfare Committee.**
Joint Senate and Assembly Institutions, Health
and Welfare Committee meeting on food
poisoning outbreak at Marlboro Psychiatric
Hospital, held November 5, 1979, Marlboro
Psychiatric Hospital, Marlboro, New Jersey.
[Trenton : Senate Committee : 47 p. ; 29 cm.
Cover title.   LC Card 80-621984   DDC
363.1/9265/0974946 19
*1. Food poisoning - New Jersey - Marlboro. 2.
Marlboro Psychiatric Hospital. I. New Jersey.
Legislature. General Assembly. Committee on
Institutions, Health & Welfare. II. Title.*
KFN1811.3 .I47 1979b

Joint Senate and Assembly Institutions, Health
and Welfare Committee meeting on food
poisoning outbreak at Marlboro Psychiatric
Hospital, held March 6, 1980, Marlboro
Psychiatric Hospital, Marlboro, New Jersey.
[Trenton : s.n., 1980] 36 p. ; 28 cm. Cover title.
LC Card 80-623830   DDC 363.1/92 19
*1. Marlboro Psychiatric Hospital. 2. Food poisoning -
New Jersey - Marlboro. I. New Jersey. Legislature.
General Assembly. Committee on Institutions, Health &
Welfare. II. Title.*
KFN1811.3 .I47 1980a

Public hearing before Senate Institutions,
Health, and Welfare Committee, on Senate bill
no. 352 (An act concerning the involuntary
commitment of persons for treatment of mental
disorders), held June 26, 1980, State House,
Trenton, New Jersey. [Trenton, N.J.] : The
Committee, 1980] 17, 29, 9 p. ; 28 cm. Cover
title.   LC Card 80-623454   DDC 344.749/044 19
*1. Insane - Commitment and detention - New Jersey. I.
Title.*
KFN1811.3 .I47 1980

**New Jersey. Legislature. Senate. Judiciary
Committee.** (Old Catalog form: New Jersey.
Judiciary Committee (Senate))
Public hearing before Senate Judiciary

Committee ... held June 30, 1980, room 223,
State House, Trenton, New Jersey. Trenton,
N.J. : The Committee, [1980] [40], 40, 58 p. ;
28 cm. Cover title. Hearing on SCR-4, SCR-7,
SCR-45, SCR-78 & S-81 & S-828 (Initiative and
referendum) Includes index.   LC Card 80-623800
DDC 328/.2 19
1. Referendum - New Jersey. I. Title.
KFN1811.3 .J8 1980

Public hearing before Senate Judiciary
Committee on SCR #83 (proposes to amend
the Constitution of New Jersey to provide that
the members of the New Jersey Senate be
elected every year in which a gubernatorial
election is held) : held April 10, 1980, State
House, Trenton, New Jersey. [Trenton] : The
Committee, [1980] 3, 3 p. ; 28 cm. Cover title.
LC Card 80-623640   DDC 342.749/055
347.490225 19
1. New Jersey. Legislature. Senate - Elections. I. Title.
KFN1811.3 .J8 1980a

**New Jersey. Legislature. Senate. Labor, Industry
and Professions Committee.**
Public hearing before Senate Labor, Industry
and Professions Committee and Assembly
Banking and Insurance Committee on S-975
and A-755 (a bill to provide for the licensing
and regulation of mortgage bankers, mortgage
brokers and mortgage solicitors by the
commissioner of Banking) held March 19, 1980.
[Trenton: The Committee, 1980] 38, 27 p. 28
cm. Cover title.
*1. Mortgages - Law and legislation - New Jersey. I.
New Jersey. Legislature. General Assembly. Banking
and Insurance Committee. II. Title.*
NYPL [JLF 81-84]

Public hearing before Senate Labor, Industry
and Professions Committee and Assembly
Banking and Insurance Committee on S-975
and A-755 (a bill to provide for the licensing
and regulation of mortgage bankers, mortgage
brokers, and mortgage solicitors by the
Commissioner of Banking) : held March 19,
1980, Senate Chamber, State House, Trenton,
New Jersey. [Trenton] : The Committees,
[1980] 9, 38, 27 p. ; 28 cm. Cover title. LC Card
80-622489   DDC 346.74904/364 19
*1. Mortgage banks - New Jersey. 2. Mortgage loans -
New Jersey. I. New Jersey. Legislature. General
Assembly. Banking and Insurance Committee. II. Title.*
KFN1811.3 .L3 1980

Public hearing before the Senate Labor,
Industry & Proffessions [sic] Committee and the
Assembly Labor Committee on workers'
compensation, administrative aspects : held
April 19, 1979, Assembly Chamber, State
House, Trenton, New Jersey. [Trenton] : Senate
Labor, Industry & Professions Committee,
[1979] 30 p. ; 28 cm. Microfiche (neg.) 1 sheet. 11
x 15 cm. (NYPL FSN 35,554) Cover title.   LC Card
79-625599
*1. Workmen's compensation - New Jersey. I. New
Jersey. Legislature. General Assembly. Labor
Committee. II. Title.*
*KFN1811.3 .L3 1979   NYPL [*XMF-13771]*

**New Jersey. Legislature. Senate. Law, Public
Safety and Defense, Committee on. see New
Jersey. Legislature. Senate. Committee on
Law, Public Safety and Defense.**

**New Jersey. Legislature. Senate. Revenue,
Finance and Appropriations Committee.**
Public hearing before Senate Revenue, Finance,
and Appropriations Committee on SCR 90,
held May 28, 1980, Assembly Chamber, State
House, Trenton, New Jersey. [Trenton] : The
Committee, [1980] 13 p. ; 28 cm. Cover title.
LC Card 80-623722   DDC 343.749/054
347.490354 19
*1. Real property tax - New Jersey - Deductions. 2.
Aged - Taxation - New Jersey. 3. Handicapped -
Taxation - New Jersey. I. Title.*
KFN1811.3 .R48 1980

**New Jersey. Legislature. Senate. State
Government Federal and Interstate Relations
and Veterans Affairs Committee.**
Public hearing, before Senate State
Government, Federal and Interstate Relations
and Veterans Affairs Committee on Senate
concurrent resolution no. 101 (proposing a
constitutional amendment to provide for a
unicameral legislature) Trenton, N. J. : The
Committee, 1977. 35, 13 p. ; 28 cm.
1. New Jersey. Legislature.   **NYPL [JLG 80-143]**

BIBLIOGRAPHIC GUIDE

New Jersey. Legislature. Senate. State Government Federal and

36

Public hearing before Senate State Government Committee on S-874, a bill to create a Department of Commerce and Economic Development, held March 10, 1980, Archive Room, State Library, Trenton, New Jersey. [Trenton, N.J.] : The Committee, [1980] 27 p. ; 28 cm. Cover title. Includes index. LC Card 80-622530 DDC 343.749/07 19
1. New Jersey. Dept. of Commerce and Economic Development. I. Title.
KFN1811.3 .S7 1980

New Jersey. Library Development Bureau. 1980 public-area library guide. [Trenton, N.J. : New Jersey State Library, 1980] ii, 102 p. ; 23 cm. LC Card 80-622726 DDC 027.4/025/749 19
1. Public libraries - New Jersey - Directories. I. Title.
Z732.N6 N53 1980

New Jersey. Local Finance Board. Report. [Trenton?] 28 cm. Annual.
1. New Jersey. Local Finance Board - Periodicals. 2. Local finance - New Jersey - Statistics - Periodicals.
NYPL [JLM 80-689]

NEW JERSEY. LOCAL FINANCE BOARD - PERIODICALS.
New Jersey. Local Finance Board. Report. [Trenton?] **NYPL [JLM 80-689]**

New Jersey. Local Management Services, Bureau of. see New Jersey. Bureau of Local Management Services.

NEW JERSEY - MAPS.
(1978) United States. Geological Survey. State of New Jersey /. Reston, Va. , 1978. 1 map : 61 x 53 cm. Scale 1:500,000; 1 in. equals approx. 8 miles. Title in right lower margin: New Jersey, base map with highways and contours, shaded, relief. "Lambert conformal conic projection, standard parallels 33° and 45°." Relief shown by contours, spot heights, and shading. Date under population legend: 1974.
G3810 1974 .U51
NYPL [Map Div. 80-3383]

NEW JERSEY - MAPS, TOPOGRAPHIC.
United States. Geological Survey. State of New Jersey /. Reston, Va. , 1978. 1 map : 61 x 53 cm. Scale 1:500,000; 1 in. equals approx. 8 miles. Title in right lower margin: New Jersey, base map with highways and contours, shaded, relief. "Lambert conformal conic projection, standard parallels 33° and 45°." Relief shown by contours, spot heights, and shading. Date under population legend: 1974.
G3810 1974 .U51
NYPL [Map Div. 80-3383]

New Jersey motor bus contract assistance . New Jersey. Dept. of Transportation. [Trenton] [1979] viii leaves, 61 p. : LC Card 79-623830 DDC 388.4/1322 19
HE5633.N5 N45 1979

New Jersey. Motor Vehicle Service Delivery Task Force. Report of the Motor Vehicle Service Delivery Task Force. [Trenton, N.J.] : Office of the Attorney General, 1979. iii, 58, 67 p. ; 28 cm. Cover title. LC Card 80-623765 DDC 353.97490087/834 19
1. Automobiles - New Jersey - Registration. 2. Automobile license plates - New Jersey. 3. Automobile drivers' licenses - New Jersey. 4. New Jersey. Division of Motor Vehicles. I. Title.
HE5633.N5 N47 1979

New Jersey. Motor Vehicles, Division of. see New Jersey. Division of Motor Vehicles.

New Jersey. Natural Resource Council. New Jersey. Office of Environmental Analysis. Index, lands subject to investigation for areas now or formerly below mean high water /. [Trenton, N.J.] [1979] [150] leaves : LC Card 79-625373 DDC 912/.1333918/09749 19
G1256.G4 N4 1979

NEW JERSEY - OCCUPATIONS - STATISTICS.
Charpentier, Thomas. Occupational employment in selected service industries in New Jersey. Trenton, N.J. , 1980. v, 230 p. : LC Card 80-624024 DDC 331.12/51/0009749 19
HD5718.S452 U53

New Jersey. Dept. of Labor and Industry. Division of Planning and Research. Occupational employment in selected construction industries in New Jersey. Trenton , 1979. iii, 98 p. ; LC Card 80-621724 DDC 331.12/524/09749 19
HD5718.B92 U546 1979

New Jersey. Office of Coastal Zone Management.
Rutgers University, New Brunswick, N.J. Center for Coastal and Environmental Studies. The coastal geomorphology of New Jersey. New Brunswick [1977] 2 v. : LC Card 80-623995 DDC 333.91/7/09749 19
GB459.4 .R87 1977

Rutgers University, New Brunswick, N.J. Center for Coastal and Environmental Studies. Onshore support bases for OCS oil and gas development . New Brunswick, N.J. [1977] xvi, 234 p. : LC Card 80-622533 DDC 338.2/7282/09749 19
TN872.N5 R87 1977

New Jersey. Office of Environmental Analysis. Index, lands subject to investigation for areas now or formerly below mean high water / prepared for the Natural Resource Council by State of New Jersey, Department of Environmental Protection, Office of Environmental Analysis. [Trenton, N.J.] : The Office, [1979] [150] leaves : chiefly maps ; 36 cm. "June 1979." Errata sheet inserted. On map sheets: Photography and index by Mark Hurd Aerial Surveys Inc. LC Card 79-625373 DDC 912/.1333918/09749 19
1. Submerged lands - New Jersey - Maps. 2. Submerged lands - New Jersey - Indexes. I. New Jersey. Natural Resource Council. II. Title. III. Title: Lands subject to investigation for areas now or formerly below mean high water.
G1256.G4 N4 1979

New Jersey. Office of Policy and Planning. A proposal for the development of the New Jersey fisheries industry : a working paper. Trenton, N.J. : Office of Policy and Planning, [1979?] 74 leaves : ill. ; 28 cm. (Staff report - Governor's Office of Policy and Planning, State of New Jersey) LC Card 80-620739 DDC 338.3/72709749 19
1. Fisheries - Economic aspects - New Jersey. 2. Fisheries - New Jersey - Planning. 3. Fishery policy - New Jersey. I. Series: New Jersey. Office of Policy and Planning. Staff report - Governor's Office of Policy and Planning, State of New Jersey. II. Title.
SH222.N5 N48 1979

Staff report - Governor's Office of Policy and Planning, State of New Jersey.
New Jersey. Office of Policy and Planning. A proposal for the development of the New Jersey fisheries industry . Trenton, N.J. [1979?] 74 leaves : LC Card 80-620739 DDC 338.3/72709749 19
SH222.N5 N48 1979

New Jersey. Office of the Public Defender. Annual report. New Jersey. Dept. of the Public Advocate. Annual report. [Trenton, N. J.] LC Card 77-643225 **NYPL [JLM 80-1143]**

New Jersey. Office of the Secretary of State. New Jersey. Results of the general election held November 4, 1975, for the office of 80 members of the General Assembly and six public questions /. [Trenton] [1975?] 10 p. ; LC Card 78-103094 DDC 324.9749/043 19
JK3593 1975 .N48 1975

New Jersey. Palisades Interstate Park Commission. see Palisades Interstate Park Commission (New York and New Jersey)

New Jersey. Pinelands Commission. Draft comphrehensive management plan for the Pinelands National Reserve (National Parks and Recreation Act, 1978) and Pinelands area (New Jersey Pinelands Protection Act, 1979) / State of New Jersey, Pinelands Commission. New Lisbon, N. J. : The Commisssion, 1980. 2 v. : ill., maps ; 28 cm. Includes bibliography.
1. Pine Barrens. 2. National parks and reserves - New Jersey. 3. National parks and reserves - Management. I. Title.
NYPL [JLF 80-1614]

NEW JERSEY - POLITICS AND GOVERNMENT 1865-1950.
New Jersey. Governor, 1911-13 (Wilson) Vetoes of Woodrow Wilson, /. [Trenton ; 1912.] 35 l. **NYPL [*ZT-1251]**

New Jersey. Port Authority of New York and New Jersey. see Port Authority of New York and New Jersey.

New Jersey. Port of New York Authority. see Port of New York Authority.

New Jersey portraits .
(4) Petrick, Barbara, 1935- Mary Philbrook . Trenton, N.J. [1981] p. cm. ISBN 0-89743-052-2 LC Card 81-11285 DDC 305.4/2/0924 B 19
HQ1413.P49 P47

New Jersey. Public Advocate, Dept. of. see New Jersey. Dept. of the Public Advocate.

New Jersey. Public Broadcasting Authority. Instructional television programming (secondary). Trenton. 23 cm.
1. Television broadcasting - New Jersey - Periodicals. 2. Television in education - New Jersey - Periodicals. I. Title.
NYPL [MWGB 81-12]

New Jersey. Sex discrimination in the Statutes, Commission on. see New Jersey. Commission on Sex Discrimination in the Statutes.

New Jersey state aid catalog for local governments. 1972- [Trenton] 28 cm. Irregular. Issued by the New Jersey Division of Local Government Services (1979- , by the division's Bureau of Local Management Services). Title varies: 1972-76, Catalogue of state programs of assistance to New Jersey local governments
1. Economic assistance, Domestic - New Jersey - Directories. I. New Jersey. Bureau of Local Management Services. II. Title: Catalogue of state programs of assistance to New Jersey local governments. **NYPL [JLM 81-65]**

New Jersey. State College, Montclair. Anthropology Club. Exhibition : ancient art from Ecuador ; Sprague Library, Special Collections Room, March 1 - April 1 1973. [Montclair] : The College, 1973. [11] p. ; ill.; 28 cm. Microfilm. Cover title. Catalog of an exhibition of works from the collection of an anonymous collector whose holdings have been cataloged by the Anthropology Club of Montclair State College.
1. Ecuador - Antiquities - Exhibitions. 2. Indians of South America - Ecuador - Antiquities. I. New Jersey. State College, Montclair. Sprague Library. II. Title. III. Title: Ancient art from Ecuador.
NYPL [*ZH-661]

New Jersey. State College, Montclair. Library. see New Jersey. State College, Montclair. Sprague Library.

New Jersey. State College, Montclair. Sprague Library. New Jersey. State College, Montclair. Anthropology Club. Exhibition : ancient art from Ecuador . [Montclair] , 1973. [11] p. ; **NYPL [*ZH-661]**

New Jersey. State Dept. of Education. (Old Catalog form: New Jersey. Education, State Dept. of)
New Jersey. Study Commission on Adolescent Education. Between the times . [Trenton, N.J.] [1978] 2 v. : LC Card 80-623250 DDC 373.749 19
LA331 .N36 1978

New Jersey. State Dept. of Education. Bureau of Planning. Planning handbooks for local districts. Trenton, N. J. **NYPL [JLM 81-301]**

New Jersey. State Dept. of Education. Division of Field Services. Bureau of Planning. see New Jersey. State Dept. of Education. Bureau of Planning.

New Jersey. State Dept. of Education. Division of Research, Planning and Evaluation. Planning handbooks for local districts. Trenton, N. J. **NYPL [JLM 81-301]**

New Jersey. State Dept. of Education. Division of Research, Planning and Evaluation. Bureau of Planning. see New Jersey. State Dept. of Education. Bureau of Planning.

New Jersey. State Dept. of Education. Library Development Bureau. see New Jersey. Library Development Bureau.

New Jersey. State Dept. of Education. Planning, Bureau of. see New Jersey. State Dept. of Education. Bureau of Planning.

New Jersey. State Dept. of Education. Research, Planning and Evaluation, Division of. see New Jersey. State Dept. of Education. Division of Research, Planning and Evaluation.

New Jersey. State Dept. of Education. State Library, Trenton. see New Jersey. State Library, Trenton.

New Jersey. State Dept. of Health. (Old Catalog form: New Jersey. Health Dept.)

Manual of standards for hospital facilities.
[Trenton] : New Jersey State Dept. of Health,
[1979] vi, [75], 106 p. : forms ; 29 cm.
Accompanied by amendments: 4 leaves. "October 1979."
 LC Card 80-621987 DDC 362.1/1/09749 19
*1. Hospitals - Law and legislation - New Jersey. 2.
Hospitals - Licenses - New Jersey. I. Title.*
KFN2161 .A4 1979

**New Jersey. State Legislature. General Assembly.
Committee on Agriculture and Environment.**
Public hearing before Assembly Agriculture and
Environment Committee on AR-51 : a
resolution to study aerial spraying of Sevin to
control gypsy moths : held October 2, 1980,
Assembly Chamber, State House, Trenton, New
Jersey. Trenton, N.J. : The Committee, [1980]
2, 74, 112 p. : ill. ; 28 cm. Cover title. LC Card
 81-620749 DDC 344.749/04633 347.49044633
 19
*1. Gypsy moth - Control - New Jersey. 2. Carbaryl -
Toxicology. 3. Aerial spraying and dusting in forestry -
Environmental aspects - New Jersey. I. Title.*
KFN1811.4 .A3 1980b

**New Jersey. State Legislature. General Assembly.
Committee on Institutions, Health &
Welfare.** New Jersey. State Legislature.
Senate. Institutions, Health, and Welfare
Committee. Public hearing before Senate
Institutions, Health, and Welfare Committee
and Assembly Institutions, Health, and Welfare
Committee on rooming house fire in Bradley
Beach . [Trenton? , 1980?] 40, 35, 6 p. ; LC
 Card 80-623979 DDC 362.1/6 19
KFN1811.3 .I47 1980b

**New Jersey. State Legislature. General Assembly.
Judiciary, Law, Public Safety, and Defense
Committee.**
Committee meeting before Assembly Judiciary,
Law, Public Safety, and Defense Committee on
A-1079 (Racketeer Influenced and Corrupt
Organizations Act) : held October 30, 1980,
Room 219, State House, Trenton, New Jersey.
[Trenton] : The Committee, [1980] 18, 22, 36
p. ; 28 cm. Cover title. LC Card 81-621304 DDC
 345.749 347.4905 19
*1. Racketeering - New Jersey. 2. Organized crime -
New Jersey. 3. Corporation law - New Jersey -
Criminal provisions. I. Title. II. Title: Racketeer
Influenced and Corrupt Organizations Act.*
KFN1811.4 .J78 1980a

Status report of the Assembly Judiciary, Law,
Public Safety, and Defense Committee, Task
Force on Juvenile Justice. Trenton, N.J. : The
Committee, [1980] ii, 12 p. ; 28 cm. "May 8,
1980." LC Card 80-624424 DDC 345.749/08
 347.49058 19
*1. Juvenile justice, Administration of - New Jersey. I.
Title.*
KFN1811.82 .J83 1980

**New Jersey. State Legislature. General Assembly.
Judiciary, Law, Public Safety, and Defense
Committee. Subcommittee on ACR-99.**
**New Jersey. State Legislature. General Assembly.
Judiciary, Law, Public Safety, and Defense
Committee. Subcommittee on Juvenile
Justice.** Public hearing before Subcommittee
on ACR-99 (amending the Constitution of the
State of New Jersey to permit the Legislature
to authorize by law and to regulate, control,
and license the conduct, operation, and play of
amusement games) of Assembly Judiciary, Law,
Public Safety, and Defense Committee : held
May 8, 1980, Seaside Heights Municipal
Building, Seaside Heights, New Jersey.
[Trenton] : The Subcommittee, [1980] 4, 12 p. ;
28 cm. Cover title. LC Card 80-623977 DDC
 344.749/0542 347.4904542 19
*1. Gambling - New Jersey. 2. Bingo - Law and
legislation - New Jersey. 3. Lotteries - Law and
legislation - New Jersey. I. Title.*
KFN1811.4 .J782 1980

Report of the Assembly Judiciary, Law, Public
Safety, and Defense Committee, Juvenile
Justice Subcommittee, on juvenile violence,
vandalism, and the juvenile justice system /.
Trenton, N.J. [1980] ii, 30 p. ; LC Card
 80-624394 DDC 364.3/6/09749 19
HV9105.N5 R46

**New Jersey. State Legislature. General Assembly.
Revenue, Finance, and Appropriations
Committee.** Public hearing before Assembly
Revenue, Finance, and Appropriations
Committee on Assembly Resolution Number 50

(memorializes Congress to transfer funding from
unnecessary military spending to domestic
spending for human services) : held October 8,
1980, Council Chambers, City Hall, Newark,
New Jersey. [Trenton] : The Committee, [1980]
49, 23x p. ; 28 cm. Cover title. LC Card
 81-621305 DDC 353.97490084 19
*1. Public welfare - New Jersey. 2. Public welfare -
United States. 3. United States - Military policy. I.
Title.*
KFN1811.4 .R45 1980b

**New Jersey. State Legislature. Senate.
Committee on Law, Public Safety, and
Defense.** Public hearing before Senate Law,
Public Safety, and Defense Committee, on
Passaic Valley Sewerage Commission : held
June 13, 1980, Council Chambers, City Hall,
Paterson, New Jersey. [Trenton : The
Committee, 1980] 46, 16 p. ; 28 cm. Cover title.
"Water quality monitoring program / Passaic River
Coalition": p. 2-13 (2nd group) Includes index. LC
 Card 80-624390 DDC 352.6/2/097493 19
*1. Passaic Valley Sewerage Commission (N.J.). I.
Passaic Valley Sewerage Commission (N.J.). II. Passaic
River Coalition. III. Title.*
KFN1811.3 .L39 1980

**New Jersey. State Legislature. Senate.
Institutions, Health, and Welfare Committee.**
Public hearing before Senate Institutions,
Health, and Welfare Committee and Assembly
Institutions, Health, and Welfare Committee on
rooming house fire in Bradley Beach : held
August 7, 1980, Majority Conference Room,
State House, Trenton, New Jersey. [Trenton? :
s.n., 1980?] 40, 35, 6 p. ; 28 cm. Cover title.
Includes index. LC Card 80-623979 DDC 362.1/6
 19
*1. Bradley Beach (N.J.) - Fire, 1980. 2. Rest homes -
New Jersey - Fires and fire prevention. I. New Jersey.
State Legislature. General Assembly. Committee on
Institutions, Health & Welfare. II. Title.*
KFN1811.3 .I47 1980b

**New Jersey. State Legislature. Senate.
Institutions, Health, and Welfare Committee.
Sub-committee on Health Care Costs.** Public
hearing before Sub-committee on Health Care
Costs of the Senate Institutions, Health, and
Welfare Committee on scope and extent of
health insurance coverage in New Jersey : held
September 4, 1980, Senate Chamber, State
House, Trenton, New Jersey. [Trenton] : The
Sub-committee, [1980] 47, [47] p. ; 28 cm.
Cover title. Includes index. LC Card 80-624339
 DDC 344.749/022 347.490422 19
1. Insurance, Health - New Jersey. I. Title.
KFN1811.3 .I474 1980

**New Jersey. State Legislature. Senate. State
Government, Federal and Interstate
Relations, and Veterans Affairs Committee.**
Public hearing before Senate State Government,
Federal and Interstate Relations, and Veterans
Affairs Committee on S-1396 and S-1397
(amending the Legislative Activities Disclosure
Law), held, October 23, 1980, Assembly
Chamber, State House, Trenton, New Jersey.
[Trenton] : The Committee, [1980] 9, 15, 4 p. ;
29 cm. Cover title. LC Card 81-620747 DDC
 342.749/052 347.490252 19
*1. Lobbying - Law and legislation - New Jersey. 2.
Elections - New Jersey - Campaign funds. I. Title.*
KFN1811.3 .S7 1980a

**New Jersey. State Legislature. Senate.
Transportation and Communications
Committee.** Public hearing before
sub-Committee of the Senate Transportation
and Communications Committee on role and
responsibilities of the Port Authority of New
York and New Jersey : held December 15,
1980, Freeholders Room, Bergen County
Administration Building, Hackensack, New
Jersey. [Trenton, N.J.] : The Committee, [1981]
75, 33 p. ; 28 cm. Cover title. Bibliography: p. 24-26
(2nd group) LC Card 81-621896 DDC
 353.97490087/71 19
*1. Port Authority of New York and New Jersey. I.
Title.*
KFN1811.3 .T73 1980

**New Jersey. State Library and Public Record
Office, Trenton. see New Jersey. State
Library, Trenton.**

**New Jersey. State Library, Trenton. (Old
Catalog form: New Jersey. State Library and**

Public Record Office, Trenton)
A developing State plan for library services.
Trenton, N.J. : State of New Jersey, Dept. of
Education, State Library, [1980] 33 p. ; 28 cm.
"January 1980." Bibliography: p. 26-28. LC Card
 80-622115 DDC 027.0749 19
1. Libraries - New Jersey. I. Title.
Z678.4.N5 N48 1980

New Jersey State Museum. O'Connor, John E.
The Hollywood Indian . Trenton, N.J. , c1980.
xvi, 79 p. : ISBN 0-938766-00-7 (pbk.) LC Card
 80-620048 DDC 791.43/09/093520397 19
PN1995.9.I48 O33

**New Jersey. State Museum, Trenton. (Old
Catalog form: New Jersey State Museum,
Trenton)**
Taft, Lisa Factor. Herman Carl Mueller .
Trenton, N.J. , c1979. 48 p. : LC Card
 79-622661
NK4670.7.M833 A4 1979

**New Jersey State rail plan for rail
transportation and local rail services .** New
Jersey. Dept. of Transportation. [Trenton] ,
1979. vii, 153, 135 p. : LC Card 80-620740
 DDC 385/.068 19
HE2771.N5 N48 1979

New Jersey. State Soil Conservation Committee.
Hole, Thornton J. F. Soil survey of Ocean
County, New Jersey /. [Washington] [1980]
vii, 102 p., [35] fold. leaves of plates : LC Card
 80-602312 DDC 631.4/7/74948 19
S599.N5 H64

**New Jersey. State University, New Brunswick.
see Rutgers University, New Brunswick, N.
J.**

**New Jersey. Statutes. see New Jersey. Laws,
statutes, etc.**

**New Jersey. Study Commission on Adolescent
Education.** Between the times : report of the
New Jersey Study Commission on Adolescent
Education. [Trenton, N.J.] : The Commission,
[1978] 2 v. : ill. ; 28 cm. Vol. 1 (xiii, 146 p.) is
reprinted in its entirety in v. 2, with p. [147]-243 of
additional material. "Prepared for Fred G. Burke, New
Jersey Commissioner of Education." Bibliography: p.
127-146. LC Card 80-623250 DDC 373.749 19
*1. Education, Secondary - New Jersey - Collected
works. 2. Adolescence - Collected works. I. New
Jersey. State Dept. of Education. II. Title.*
LA331 .N36 1978

New Jersey. Task Force on the Juvenile Code.
Juvenile justice in New Jersey: an assessment of
the new Juvenile Code: executive summary /
Dale Dannefer and Joseph DeJames. Trenton:
Dept. of Human Services, 1979. 20 p.; 28 cm.
Microfiche (neg.) 1 sheet. 11 x 15 cm. (NYPL FSN
35,314) "The research project was carried out by the
former Task Force on the Juvenile Code ..."
*1. Children - Legal status, laws, etc. - New Jersey. I.
DeJames, Joseph. II. Dannefer, Dale. III. Title.*
NYPL [*XME-9341]

**New Jersey. Taxation, Committee on. see New
Jersey. Legislature. General Assembly.
Committee on Taxation.**

**New Jersey. Transportation, Dept. of. see New
Jersey. Dept. of Transportation.**

**New Jersey. Treasury Dept. Cabinet Committee
on Urban Policy. see New Jersey. Cabinet
Committee on Urban Policy.**

**New Jersey. Treasury Dept. Division of Budget
and Accounting. see New Jersey. Division of
Budget and Accounting.**

**New Jersey. University, New Brunswick. see
Rutgers University, New Brunswick, N. J.**

**New Jersey. Urban Policy, Cabinet Committee
on. see New Jersey. Cabinet Committee on
Urban Policy.**

**New Jersey's productivity improvement
investment account.** Berry, Frances Stokes.
Lexington, Ky. (P.O. Box 11910, Lexington
40578) , 1980. 12 p. : LC Card 81-144027 DDC
 353.97490001/47 19
JK3560.L3 B47

NEW LISBON STATE SCHOOL.
New Jersey. Legislature. General Assembly.
Committee on Institutions, Health & Welfare.
Public hearing before Assembly Institutions,
Health, and Welfare Committee on allegations
of abuse at New Lisbon State School, held May

25, 1979, Multipurpose Building, New Lisbon State School, New Lisbon, New Jersey. [Trenton?] [1979?] 30, 70 p. ; LC Card 80-620972 DDC 362.2/1/0974961 19
KFN1811.4 .I58 1979b

New Jersey. Legislature. General Assembly. Committee on Institutions, Health & Welfare. Public hearing before Assembly Institutions, Health, and Welfare Committee on allegations of abuse at New Lisbon State School, held April 20, 1979 ... New Lisbon State School, New Lisbon, New Jersey. [Trenton, N.J.] [1979] 87, 4 p. ; LC Card 79-625977 DDC 362.3/09749 19
KFN1811.4 .I58 1979a

A new marsupial frog (Hylidae, Gastrotheca) from the Andes of Ecuador /. Duellman, William Edward, 1930- Lawrence, Kan. [1980] 13 p. : LC Card 80-622163 DDC 597.8/7 19
QL668.E24 D8315

New Mexican review. see **Santa Fe New Mexican.**

New Mexico ACT and SAT results, 1978-79 /. Nochumson, Bayla S. Santa Fe, N.M. [1980] v, 35 p. : LC Card 80-623171 DDC 378/.1664 19
LB2353.42 .N6

New Mexico Agricultural Experiment Station. Neher, R. E. Soil survey of Luna County, New Mexico /. [Washington, D.C.] 1980. iii, 80 p., [81] folded leaves of plates : LC Card 80-603368 DDC 631.4/7/78968 19
S599.N6 N4

New Mexico. Agricultural Experiment Station, University Park. Sammis, Theodore W. Demonstration of irrigation return flow water quality in the Mesilla Valley, New Mexico /. Las Cruces, N.M. [1980] ix, 149 p. : LC Card 80-623166 DDC 333.91/009789 s 631.7 19
GB705.N6 N64 no. 117 TC824.N6

United States. Soil Conservation Service. Soil survey of Chaves County, New Mexico, southern part /. [Washington] [1980] iv, 143 p., [90] fold. leaves of plates : LC Card 80-602510 DDC 631.4/7/78943 19
S599.N6 U54 1980

NEW MEXICO - ANTIQUITIES. Berman, Mary Jane. Cultural resources overview of Socorro, New Mexico /. Albuquerque, N.M. : Santa Fe, N.M. : v, 128 p. : LC Card 80-602245 DDC 978.9/62 19
E78.N65 B36

Lister, Robert H. Chaco Canyon . Albuquerque , 1981. p. cm. ISBN 0-8263-0574-1 : LC Card 80-54566 DDC 978.9/82 19
E78.N65 L57

The Star lake archaeological project . Carbondale , c1982. p. cm. ISBN 0-8093-0949-1 LC Card 81-13596 DDC 978.9/83 19
E78.N65 S75

New Mexico - Archaelogy. see **New Mexico - Antiquities.**

New Mexico. Attorney General's Office. Parker, Alfred L. A study of the New Mexico liquor control act /. [Albuquerque, N.M.] , 1980. 173, 39 p. : LC Card 80-624137 DDC 363.4/1/09789 19
HV5086.N6 P37

Report of the Attorney General on the February 2 and 3, 1980 riot at the Penitentiary of New Mexico. [Santa Fe] : State of New Mexico, Office of the Attorney General, 1980- v. : ill. ; 28 cm. Includes index. LC Card 80-623176 DDC 365/.641 19
1. New Mexico. Penitentiary, Santa Fé - Collected works. 2. Prison riots - New Mexico - Santa Fé - Collected works. I. Title.
HV9475.N62 N46 1980

New Mexico basic skills plan /. New Mexico. Dept. of Education. Superintendent's Basic Skills Task Force. [Santa Fe] [1977] 18, 13, [11] p. ; LC Card 80-620749 DDC 370/.7/3209789 19
LC1032.5.N6 N48 1977

NEW MEXICO - BIOGRAPHY. Poe, Sophie A. (Sophie Alberding), 1862- Buckboard days /. Albuquerque , 1981, c1936. p. cm. ISBN 0-8263-0572-5 : LC Card 80-54565

DDC 978.9/04/0922 B 19
F786.P8 P63 1981

New Mexico. Board of Educational Finance-- Commission of Postsecondary Education. Factbook on New Mexico public two-year community colleges and vocational schools, 1978-79. Santa Fe, N.M. : State of New Mexico, Board of Educational Finance--Commission on Postsecondary Education, [1979] vi, 90 p. : graphs ; 28 cm. Cover title: Public community colleges and vocational schools factbook. LC Card 80-622001 DDC 379.1/552/09789 19
1. Vocational education - New Mexico. 2. Community colleges - New Mexico. I. Title. II. Title: Public community colleges and vocational schools factbook.
LC1046.N45 N47 1979

New Mexico. Bureau of Mines and Mineral Resources. (Old Catalog form: New Mexico. Institute of Mining and Technology, Socorro. Mines and Mineral Resources Bureau.) Chapin, Charles Edward, 1932- Coal, uranium, oil, and gas potential of the Riley-Puertecito area, Socorro County, New Mexico /. Socorro [1979] v, 33 p., [3] fold. leaves of plates : LC Card 79-626216 DDC 553.2/09789/62 19
TN805.N6 C47

Circular . (169) Clemons, Russell E. Geology of Good Sight Mountains and Uvas Valley, southwest New Mexico /. Socorro , 1979. 32 p. : LC Card 80-620987 DDC 553/.09789 s 557.89/68 19
TN24.N6 A235 no. 169 QE144.G66

Memoir . (35) Condie, Kent C. Geology and geochemistry of Precambrian rocks, central and south-central New Mexico /. Socorro , 1979. 58 p. : LC Card 80-622498 DDC 551.7/1/09789 19
QE653 .C653

New Mexico certification requirements /. New Mexico. Dept. of Education. Santa Fe, N.M. [1978] vi, 64 p. ; LC Card 79-625368 DDC 379.1/57/09789 19
LB1772.N6 N48 1978

New Mexico Coal Surface Mining Commission. New Mexico. Mining and Minerals Division. State of New Mexico surface coal mining regulations, Rule 80-1 /. Santa Fe, N.M. [1980] xvi, 262 p. ; LC Card 80-624203 DDC 346.78904/68 347.8906468 19
KFN3855.5.A435 A2 1980

NEW MEXICO - COMMERCE - DIRECTORIES. New Mexico. Dept. of Development. New Mexico export manufacturers directory. Santa Fe, N.M. [1976?] [27] p. ; LC Card 80-622755 DDC 382/.6/0294789 19
HD9727.N6 N45 1976

NEW MEXICO - COMMERCE - HANDBOOKS, MANUALS, ETC. New Mexico. International Trade Development Section. New Mexico export handbook. Santa Fe, N.M. [1980] 70 p. : LC Card 80-623172 DDC 382/.6/025789 19
HF3161.N6 N64 1980

New Mexico. Commission on the Status of Women. Young, Tasia. Report of the Southwest Consultation on the Educational Needs of Rural Girls and Women, convened by the Information Resources Committee, Advisory Council on Women's Educational Programs in Santa Fe, New Mexico, September 10 and 11, 1976 /. Albuquerque [1976?] 25 leaves ; LC Card 79-623319 DDC 376/.9789 19
LC1758.N6 Y68

New Mexico. Constitution. The Constitution of the state of New Mexico : as adopted January 21, 1911, and as subsequently amended by the people in general and special elections, 1912 through 1980. [Santa Fe] : Shirley Hooper, Secretary of State, [1981] 98 p. ; 16 cm. "January, 1981." LC Card 81-621910 DDC 342.789/023 347.890223 19
1. New Mexico - Constitutional law. I. New Mexico. Secretary of State. II. Title.
KFN4001 1911 .A37

NEW MEXICO - CONSTITUTIONAL LAW. New Mexico. Constitution. The Constitution of the state of New Mexico . [Santa Fe] [1981]

98 p. ; LC Card 81-621910 DDC 342.789/023 347.890223 19
KFN4001 1911 .A37

NEW MEXICO - CONSTITUTIONAL LAW - AMENDMENTS. New Mexico. Legislative Council Service. Constitutional amendments proposed by the Legislature in 1975 and 1976 and arguments for and against. Santa Fe , 1976. ii, 39 p. ; LC Card 81-461635 DDC 342.789/035 347.890235 19
KFN4001 1911.A7 N48

New Mexico. Cultural Properties Review Committee. Kessell, John L. The missions of New Mexico since 1776 /. Albuquerque , 1980. xii, 276 p., [6] leaves of plates : ISBN 0-8263-0514-8 : LC Card 79-4934
F797 .K47 **NYPL [IWSB 80-3227]**

New Mexico. Dept. of Development. (Old Catalog form: New Mexico. Development, Dept. of) New Mexico export manufacturers directory. Santa Fe, N.M. : New Mexico Dept. of Development, State of New Mexico, [1976?] [27] p. ; 28 cm. LC Card 80-622755 DDC 382/.6/0294789 19
1. New Mexico - Manufactures - Directories. 2. New Mexico - Commerce - Directories. 3. Foreign trade promotion - New Mexico - Directories. I. Title.
HD9727.N6 N45 1976

New Mexico. Dept. of Education. (Old Catalog form: New Mexico. Education Dept.) New Mexico certification requirements / compiled by Jacqueline Gutierrez. Santa Fe, N.M. : State Dept. of Education, [1978] vi, 64 p. ; 29 cm. "May 1978." LC Card 79-625368 DDC 379.1/57/09789 19
1. Teachers - Certification - New Mexico. I. Gutierrez, Jacqueline. II. Title.
LB1772.N6 N48 1978

New Mexico. Dept. of Education. Evaluation, Assessment, and Testing Unit. Nochumson, Bayla S. New Mexico's standardized test results . Santa Fe., N.M. , 1979. ii, 38 p. : LC Card 80-621725 DDC 371.2/6/09789 19
LB3052.N6 N6

Young, William Russell, 1949- New Mexico dropout study, 1977-78 and 1978-79 /. Santa Fe, N.M. [1980] [24] p. ; LC Card 80-623587 DDC 373.12913/09789 19
LC144.N6 Y68

New Mexico. Dept. of Education. Superintendent's Basic Skills Task Force. New Mexico basic skills plan / prepared by Superintendent's Basic Skills Task Force. [Santa Fe] : New Mexico Dept. of Education, [1977] 18, 13, [11] p. ; 28 cm. "Revised August 1977." Includes bibliography. LC Card 80-620749 DDC 370/.7/3209789 19
1. Competency-based education - New Mexico. I. Title.
LC1032.5.N6 N48 1977

New Mexico. Dept. of Insurance. Directory of insurance companies / issued by the Department of Insurance of the State Corporation Commission. Santa Fe, N.M. : The Dept., 1979. 96 p. ; 22 x 28 cm. "November 1, 1979." LC Card 80-621677 DDC 368/.0025/789 19
1. Insurance - New Mexico - Directories. I. Title.
HG8526.N6 N48 1979

New Mexico. Development, Dept. of. see **New Mexico. Dept. of Development.**

New Mexico dropout study, 1977-78 and 1978-79 /. Young, William Russell, 1949- Santa Fe, N.M. [1980] [24] p. ; LC Card 80-623587 DDC 373.12913/09789 19
LC144.N6 Y68

New Mexico. Dry Cleaning Board. Rules and regulations. 1952. New Mexico. Laws, statutes, etc. State law and rules and regulations applicable to the dry cleaning industry : chapter 198, laws of 1941, otherwise known as sections 51-2101 to 2116, inclusive, New Mexico statutes 1941 annotated. Santa Fe, N.M. [1952] 35 p. ; LC Card 79-119739 DDC 343.789/07866712/02632 347.8903786671202632 19
KFN3882.L38 A32 1952

New Mexico. Education, Dept. of. see **New Mexico. Dept. of Education.**

**New Mexico. Employment Security Dept.
Research and Statistics Section.** Veterans in
New Mexico / prepared by the Research and
Statistics Section. Alburquerque, N.M. : The
Section, 1978. 34 leaves : ill. ; 28 cm. LC Card
79-626217 DDC 355.1/15/09789 19
1. Veterans - New Mexico. I. Title.
UB358.N6 N42 1978

New Mexico. Energy and Minerals Dept. Zinder
(H.) and Associates, inc. Report to the New
Mexico Energy and Minerals Department of
storage and alternative options for increasing
the availability of natural gas. Socorro, N.M.
[1979] 61, [61] p. : LC Card 80-622030 DDC
333.8/23311/09789 19
TN881.N6 Z52 1979

**New Mexico Energy Institute at New Mexico
Institute of Mining & Technology.**
Budding, Antonius Jacob, 1922- Geology and
oil characteristics of the Santa Rosa tar sands,
Guadalupe County, New Mexico . Socorro,
N.M. [1979] 18 p., [1] leaf of plates : LC Card
80-622029 DDC 553.2/82/0978925 19
TN872.N6 B82

Zinder (H.) and Associates, inc. Report to the
New Mexico Energy and Minerals Department
of storage and alternative options for increasing
the availability of natural gas. Socorro, N.M.
[1979] 61, [61] p. : LC Card 80-622030 DDC
333.8/23311/09789 19
TN881.N6 Z52 1979

**New Mexico Energy Institute at New Mexico
State University.**
An appraisal study of the geothermal resources
of Arizona and adjacent areas in New Mexico
and Utah and their value for desalination and
other uses / by Chandler A. Swanberg ... [et
al.]. Las Cruces, N.M. : New Mexico Energy
Institute, New Mexico State University, [1977]
vii, 76 leaves, [12] leaves of plates : ill. ; 28 cm.
(NMEI report . no. 006) "July 1977." Bibliography:
leaves 18-21. LC Card 80-623249 DDC 553.7 19
*1. Geothermal resources - Arizona. 2. Geothermal
resources - New Mexico. 3. Geothermal resources -
Utah. 4. Saline water conversion. I. Swanberg, Chandler
A. II. Series: New Mexico Energy Institute at New
Mexico State University. NMEI report , no. 006. III.
Title.*
GB1199.5 .N48 1977

NMEI report .
(no. 006) New Mexico Energy Institute at
New Mexico State University. An appraisal
study of the geothermal resources of Arizona
and adjacent areas in New Mexico and Utah
and their value for desalination and other
uses /. Las Cruces, N.M. [1977] vii, 76
leaves, [12] leaves of plates : LC Card
80-623249 DDC 553.7 19
GB1199.5 .N48 1977

**New Mexico. Environment Improvement Division.
Occupational Health and safety Section.
Data Management Unit.** 1978 characteristics
of New Mexico high hazard industries, mobile
worksites / Environmental Improvement
Division, Occupational Health and safety, data
Management ; prepared by Robert L. Edgar ...
[et al.]. Santa Fe, N.M. : The Division, [1979]
113 p. ; 28 cm. "October 1979." LC Card
80-621997 DDC 312/.43/09789 19
*1. Industrial accidents - New Mexico - Statistics. I.
Edgar, Robert L. II. Title. III. Title: Characteristics of
New Mexico high hazard industries, mobile worksites.*
HD7262.5.U62 N66 1979

**New Mexico. Environmental Improvement
Agency. Water Supply Regulation Section.
New Mexico public water supplies chemical
data, 1974.** New Mexico. Environmental
Improvement Division. Water Supply Section.
Chemical quality of New Mexico community
water supplies, 1980 : a compilation of
chemical and physical data / Environmental
Improvement Division, Water Supply
Section ; Francisco N. Garcia, program
manager ; Steven T. Pierce, environmental
scientist. [Santa Fe] [1980] 256 p. ; LC Card
80-624082 DDC 363.6/1 19
TD224.N6 N47 1980

**New Mexico. Environmental Improvement
Division. Occupational Health and Safety
Section. Data Management Unit.** 1978
characteristics of New Mexico high hazard
industries : fixed worksites / Environmental
Improvement Division, Occupational Health

and Safety - Data Management ; prepared by
Robert L. Edgar ... [et al.]. Santa Fe, N.M. :
The Unit, [1979] 144 p. : ill. ; 28 cm. "October
1979." Chiefly tables. Includes index. LC Card
80-622292 DDC 312/.43/09789 19
*1. Occupational diseases - New Mexico - Statistics. 2.
Industrial accidents - New Mexico - Statistics. I. Edgar,
Robert L. II. Title.*
RC964 .N46 1979a

**New Mexico. Environmental Improvement
Division. Water Supply Section.** Chemical
quality of New Mexico community water
supplies, 1980 : a compilation of chemical and
physical data / Environmental Improvement
Division, Water Supply Section ; Francisco N.
Garcia, program manager ; Steven T. Pierce,
environmental scientist. [Santa Fe] : The
Section, [1980] 256 p. ; 28 cm. Ed. for 1974
entered under the Section's earlier name, Water Supply
Regulation Section, with title: New Mexico public water
supplies chemical data, 1974. Chiefly tables. LC Card
80-624082 DDC 363.6/1 19
*1. Water quality - New Mexico - Statistics. 2. Drinking
water - New Mexico - Statistics. I. Garcia, Francisco N.
II. Pierce, Steven T. III. New Mexico. Environmental
Improvement Agency. Water Supply Regulation
Section. New Mexico public water supplies chemical
data, 1974. IV. Title.*
TD224.N6 N47 1980

**NEW MEXICO - EXECUTIVE
DEPARTMENTS.**
New Mexico. Governor's Committee on
Reorganization of State Government. Final
report /. Santa Fe, N.M. [1970] ix, 202 p. :
LC Card 80-623230 DDC 353.978907/3 19
JK8038 1970 .N48

New Mexico export handbook. New Mexico.
International Trade Development Section. Santa
Fe, N.M. [1980] 70 p. : LC Card 80-623172
DDC 382/.6/025789 19
HF3161.N6 N64 1980

New Mexico export manufacturers directory.
New Mexico. Dept. of Development. Santa Fe,
N.M. [1976?] [27] p. ; LC Card 80-622755
DDC 382/.6/0294789 19
HD9727.N6 N45 1976

New Mexico. General Construction Bureau. 1979
New Mexico uniform building code. [Sante Fe,
N.M.] : Commerce and Industry Dept.,
Construction Industries Division, General
Construction Bureau, [1980] ca. 150 p. ; 28 cm.
Cover title. LC Card 80-622976 DDC
343.789/07869/002632 19
1. Building laws - New Mexico. I. Title.
KFN4059.A1 A32 1980

**New Mexico. Governor's Committee on
Reorganization of State Government.** Final
report / Governor's Committee, Reorganization
of State Government. Santa Fe, N.M. : The
Committee, [1970] ix, 202 p. : ill. ; 28 cm. "1
January 1970." On cover: New Mexico's statutory
executive agencies and how they grew. Includes index.
LC Card 80-623230 DDC 353.978907/3 19
*1. Administrative agencies - New Mexico. 2. New
Mexico - Executive departments. I. Title: New Mexico's
statutory executive agencies and how they grew.*
JK8038 1970 .N48

The New Mexico historical review. v. 1- ; 1926-
Santa Fe, N. M. plates, ports. 23 cm. Quarterly.
Published by the Historical Society of New Mexico
(with the School of American Research, 1927-July,
1929; with the University of New Mexico, Oct.
1929-1960.) INDEXES: Vols. 1-15, 1926-40. 1 v.
*1. New Mexico - History - Periodicals. I. New Mexico
Historical Society. II. New Mexico. University. III.
Santa Fe, N. M. School of American Research.*
             *NYPL [IAA (New Mexico historical
                                     review.)]*

New Mexico Historical Society. The New
Mexico historical review. v. 1- ; 1926- Santa
Fe, N. M.   *NYPL [IAA (New Mexico
                                 historical review.)]*

**NEW MEXICO - HISTORY - WAR WITH
MEXICO, 1845-1848 - PERSONAL
NARRATIVES.**
Gibson, George Rutledge, 1810 (ca.)-1885.
Over the Chihuahua and Santa Fe trails,
1847-1848 . Albuquerque , c1981. p. cm. ISBN
0-8263-0590-3 ; LC Card 81-52054 DDC
973.6/2 19
E411 .G44

NEW MEXICO - HISTORY - 1848-
Poe, Sophie A. (Sophie Alberding), 1862-
Buckboard days /. Albuquerque , 1981, c1936.
p. cm. ISBN 0-8263-0572-5 : LC Card 80-54565
DDC 978.9/04/0922 B 19
F786.P8 P63 1981

**NEW MEXICO - HISTORY - 1848- -
SOURCES.**
New Mexico (Ter.). Legislative Assembly.
House of Representatives. State of New
Mexico: House [proceedings], 1907. [Santa Fe,
1907] 43 leaves;   *NYPL [*ZT-1265]*

NEW MEXICO - HISTORY, LOCAL.
Kessell, John L. The missions of New Mexico
since 1776 /. Albuquerque , 1980. xii, 276 p.,
[6] leaves of plates : ISBN 0-8263-0514-8 : LC
Card 79-4934
F797 .K47   *NYPL [IWSB 80-3227]*

NEW MEXICO - HISTORY - PERIODICALS.
The New Mexico historical review. v. 1- ;
1926- Santa Fe, N. M.   *NYPL [IAA (New
                          Mexico historical review.)]*

New Mexico. Human Rights Commission.
Rules and regulations / New Mexico Human
Rights Commission. [Santa Fe] : The
Commission, [1980] 11 p. ; 22 cm. "Effective
February 18, 1980." LC Card 80-623550 DDC
342.789/085/02636 347.89028502636 19
*1. Civil rights - New Mexico. 2. New Mexico. Human
Rights Commission - Rules and practice.*
KFN4011.A435 A2 1980

**NEW MEXICO. HUMAN RIGHTS
COMMISSION - RULES AND
PRACTICE.**
New Mexico. Human Rights Commission.
Rules and regulations /. [Santa Fe] [1980] 11
p. ; LC Card 80-623550 DDC 342.789/085/02636
347.89028502636 19
KFN4011.A435 A2 1980

**New Mexico. Institute of Mining and Technology,
Socorro. Bureau of Mines and Mineral
Resources.** see New Mexico. Bureau of
Mines and Mineral Resources.

**New Mexico. Institute of Mining and Technology,
Socorro. Geophysical Research Center.**
Davis, Paul, 1950- Spring characteristics of the
western Roswell artesian basin . Las Cruces,
N.M. [1980] viii, 93 p. : LC Card 80-623165
DDC 333.91/009789 s 551.49/8 19
GB705.N6 N64 no. 116 GB1198.3.N6

Gross, Gerardo Wolfgang. Paul Spring, an
investigation of recharge in the Roswell (N.M.)
artesian basin /. Las Cruces, N.M. [1979] 135
p. : LC Card 80-622504 DDC 551.49/09789/43 19
GB705.N6 N64 no. 113 GB1199.3.N6

**New Mexico. International Trade Development
Section.** New Mexico export handbook. Santa
Fe, N.M. : International Trade Development
Section, New Mexico Commerce and Industry
Dept., [1980] 70 p. : ill. ; 28 cm. "March 1980."
Includes index. LC Card 80-623172 DDC
382/.6/025789 19
*1. New Mexico - Commerce - Handbooks, manuals,
etc. 2. Foreign trade promotion - New Mexico -
Handbooks, manuals, etc. I. Title.*
HF3161.N6 N64 1980

New Mexico. Laws, statutes, etc. (Old Catalog
form: New Mexico. Statutes)
Gross receipts and compensating tax act. New
Mexico. Taxation and Revenue Dept. Gross
receipts & compensating tax regulations /
Taxation & Revenue Dept. [Santa Fe, N.M.]
[1980] x, 174, 58 p. ; LC Card 80-623312
DDC 343.78906/8 19
KFN4080.A434 A2 1980

Laws of the State of New Mexico. Portales, N.
M., Bishop Print. and Litho Co. 23 cm. Spine
title, 1979- : Laws of New Mexico.
I. Title.   *NYPL [JLL 80-237]*

State law and rules and regulations applicable
to the dry cleaning industry : chapter 198, laws
of 1941, otherwise known as sections 51-2101
to 2116, inclusive, New Mexico statutes 1941
annotated. Santa Fe, N.M. : New Mexico Dry
Cleaning Board, [1952] 35 p. ; 23 x 10 cm.
Cover title. "July 1, 1952." LC Card 79-119739
DDC 343.789/07866712/02632
347.8903786671202632 19
*1. Cleaning and dyeing industry - Law and legislation -
New Mexico. I. New Mexico. Dry Cleaning Board.*

Rules and regulations. 1952. II. Title.
KFN3882.L38 A32 1952

New Mexico. Legislative Council Service.
Constitutional amendments proposed by the
Legislature in 1975 and 1976 and arguments for
and against. Santa Fe : New Mexico Legislative
Council Service, 1976. ii, 39 p. ; 28 cm. LC
Card 81-461635 DDC 342.789/035 347.890235
19
1. New Mexico - Constitutional law - Amendments. I.
Title: Constitutional amendments proposed by the
Legislature in 1975 and 1976 ...
KFN4001 1911.A7 N48

New Mexico. Legislature. Legislative Council
Service. Legislative handbook / compiled by
New Mexico Legislative Council Service. Santa
Fe, N.M. : The Service, [1981] ca. 200 p. : ill. ;
29 cm. "January, 1981." LC Card 81-621463 DDC
328.789/05 19
1. New Mexico. Legislature - Rules and practice. I.
Title.
KFN4021.5.R8 A25 1981

NEW MEXICO. LEGISLATURE - RULES
AND PRACTICE.
New Mexico. Legislature. Legislative Council
Service. Legislative handbook /. Santa Fe, N.M.
[1981] ca. 200 p. : LC Card 81-621463 DDC
328.789/05 19
KFN4021.5.R8 A25 1981

NEW MEXICO - MANUFACTURES -
DIRECTORIES.
New Mexico. Dept. of Development. New
Mexico export manufacturers directory. Santa
Fe, N.M. [1976?] [27] p. ; LC Card 80-622755
DDC 382/.6/0294789 19
HD9727.N6 N45 1976

New Mexico. Mines and Mineral Resources,
Bureau of. see New Mexico. Bureau of
Mines and Mineral Resources.

New Mexico. Mining and Minerals Division.
State of New Mexico surface coal mining
regulations, Rule 80-1 / adopted by the New
Mexico Coal Surface Mining Commission, May
15, 1980 ; administered and enforced by the
Mining and Minerals Division of the Energy
and Minerals Department. Santa Fe, N.M. :
The Division, [1980] xvi, 262 p. ; 28 cm. "Rule
80-1 supersedes Rule 79-1 filed July 11, 1979, by the
Mining and Minerals Division of the Energy and
Minerals Department." "July 1980." LC Card
80-624203 DDC 346.78904/68 347.8906468 19
1. Strip mining - Law and legislation - New Mexico. 2.
Coal mines and mining - Law and legislation - New
Mexico. I. New Mexico Coal Surface Mining
Commission. II. Title.
KFN3855.5.A435 A2 1980

New Mexico. Motor Transportation Division.
Rules and regulations. [Santa Fe, N.M.
(P.E.R.A. Bldg., P.O. Box 1028, Santa Fe
87503)] : Motor Transportation Division, State
of New Mexico, Transportation Dept., [1980] ii,
57 p. : ill. ; 28 cm. Cover title. LC Card
81-621088 DDC 343.789/0944/02636
347.890394402636 19
1. Transportation, Automotive - Law and legislation -
New Mexico. 2. Motor vehicles - Law and legislation -
New Mexico. I. Title.
KFN3897.A433 A2 1980

NEW MEXICO. PENITENTIARY, SANTA FÉ -
COLLECTED WORKS.
New Mexico. Attorney General's Office. Report
of the Attorney General on the February 2 and
3, 1980 riot at the Penitentiary of New Mexico.
[Santa Fe] , 1980- v. : LC Card 80-623176 DDC
365/.641 19
HV9475.N62 N46 1980

NEW MEXICO - PUBLIC LANDS -
ECONOMIC ASPECTS.
Gray, James R. Estimated benefits and costs of
state ownership of Bureau of Land Management
lands in New Mexico /. Las Cruces, N.M.
[1980] 20 p. ; LC Card 80-623254 DDC
333.1/09789 19
HD243.N5 G7

New Mexico. Secretary of State. (Old Catalog
form: New Mexico. State, Secretary of)
New Mexico. Constitution. The Constitution of
the state of New Mexico . [Santa Fe] [1981]
98 p. ; LC Card 81-621910 DDC 342.789/023
347.890223 19
KFN4001 1911 .A37

New Mexico. State Agency on Aging. State plan
on aging under Title III of the Older Americans
Act for New Mexico, fiscal years 1981-83.
[Santa Fe, N.M. (440 Saint Michael's Dr.,
Santa Fe 87503) , 1980] 126 p. in various
pagings ; LC Card 81-620578 DDC 362.6/09789
19
HQ1064.U6 N283

New Mexico. State Board of Examiners for
Architects. Architectural law and rules and
regulations / the New Mexico Board of
Examiners for Architects. [Santa Fe] : The
Board, [1955] 15 p. ; 24 x 11 cm. Cover title.
"July 1, 1955." LC Card 79-119877 DDC
344.789/0176172 347.8904176172 19
1. Architects - Legal status, laws, etc. - New Mexico. 2.
Architects - Certification - New Mexico. I. Title.
KFN3929.A7 A32 1955

New Mexico. State Bureau of Mines and
Mineral Resources. see New Mexico. Bureau
of Mines and Mineral Resources.

New Mexico. State Dept. of Education. see New
Mexico. Dept. of Education.

New Mexico. State Health Planning and
Development Bureau. New Mexico State
medical facilities plan, 1978-79 / State Health
Planning and Development Division, [1979]
[Santa Fe] : Health and Environment Dept.,
Health Planning and Development Division,
[1979] 290 p. in various pagings : ill. ; 28 cm.
Cover title. LC Card 79-624737 DDC
362.1/1/09789 19
1. Health facilities - Planning - New Mexico. 2. Health
facilities - New Mexico - Statistics. 3. Hospitals - New
Mexico - Statistics. 4. Hospital utilization - New
Mexico - Statistics. I. Title.
RA981.N6 N48 1979

New Mexico State medical facilities plan,
1978-79 /. New Mexico. State Health Planning
and Development Bureau. [Santa Fe] [1979]
290 p. in various pagings : LC Card 79-624737
DDC 362.1/1/09789 19
RA981.N6 N48 1979

New Mexico state plan on aging, fiscal years
1981-83. State plan on aging under Title III of
the Older Americans Act for New Mexico,
fiscal years 1981-83. [Santa Fe, N.M. (440
Saint Michael's Dr., Santa Fe 87503) , 1980]
126 p. in various pagings ; LC Card 81-620578
DDC 362.6/09789 19
HQ1064.U6 N283

New Mexico. State, Secretary of. see New
Mexico. Secretary of State.

New Mexico State University. Agricultural
Economics Dept. Energy requirements for
agricultural production in New Mexico :
principal investigator, Neil A. Patrick ; final
report by Neil A. Patrick ... [et al.]
(Department of Agricultural Economics, New
Mexico State University). [Las Cruces] : New
Mexico Energy Institute at New Mexico State
University, [1979] v, 44 p. ; 28 cm. "May 1979."
"NMEI 29." Bibliography: p. 44. LC Card 79-625597
DDC 333.79/13 19
1. Agriculture - New Mexico - Energy consumption. I.
Patrick, Neil A. II. Title.
S494.5.E5 N47 1979

New Mexico State University. Dept. of
Agricultural Engineering.
Consumptive use and yields of crops in New
Mexico /. Las Cruces, N.M. [1979] vi, 108 p. :
LC Card 80-622505 DDC 333.91/009789 s
631.7 19
GB705.N6 N64 no. 115 S600.7.E93

Sammis, Theodore W. Demonstration of
irrigation return flow water quality in the
Mesilla Valley, New Mexico /. Las Cruces,
N.M. [1980] ix, 149 p. : LC Card 80-623166
DDC 333.91/009789 s 631.7 19
GB705.N6 N64 no. 117 TC824.N6

New Mexico State University. Dept. of
Agronomy. Wierenga, Petrus Johannes. Soil
salinity and cotton yields as affected by surface
and trickle irrigation . Las Cruces, N.M.
[1979] vi, 212 p. : LC Card 80-622502 DDC
333.91/009789 s 631.4/16 19
GB705.N6 N64 no. 106 S616.U6

New Mexico State University. Range
Improvement Task Force. Gray, James R.
Estimated benefits and costs of state ownership
of Bureau of Land Management lands in New

Mexico /. Las Cruces, N.M. [1980] 20 p. ;
LC Card 80-623254 DDC 333.1/09789 19
HD243.N5 G7

New Mexico State University. Water Resources
Research Institute.
Consumptive use and yields of crops in New
Mexico /. Las Cruces, N.M. [1979] vi, 108 p. :
LC Card 80-622505 DDC 333.91/009789 s
631.7 19
GB705.N6 N64 no. 115 S600.7.E93

Davis, Paul, 1950- Spring characteristics of the
western Roswell artesian basin . Las Cruces,
N.M. [1980] viii, 93 p. : LC Card 80-623165
DDC 333.91/009789 s 551.49/8 19
GB705.N6 N64 no. 116 GB1198.3.N6

Gross, Gerardo Wolfgang. Paul Spring, an
investigation of recharge in the Roswell (N.M.)
artesian basin /. Las Cruces, N.M. [1979] 135
p. : LC Card 80-622504 DDC 551.49/09789/43 19
GB705.N6 N64 no. 113 GB1199.3.N6

Wierenga, Petrus Johannes. Soil salinity and
cotton yields as affected by surface and trickle
irrigation . Las Cruces, N.M. [1979] vi, 212
p. : LC Card 80-622502 DDC 333.91/009789 s
631.4/16 19
GB705.N6 N64 no. 106 S616.U6

WRRI report .
(no. 106) Wierenga, Petrus Johannes. Soil
salinity and cotton yields as affected by
surface and trickle irrigation . Las Cruces,
N.M. [1979] vi, 212 p. : LC Card 80-622502
DDC 333.91/009789 s 631.4/16 19
GB705.N6 N64 no. 106 S616.U6

(no. 108) Hain, Kathleen E. The survival of
enteric viruses in septic tanks and septic tank
drain fields /. Las Cruces, N.M. [1979] x, 73
p. : LC Card 80-622272 DDC 628/.742 19
GB705.N6 N64 no. 108 QR4

(no. 110) Brandvold, D. K. Chemical and
biological survey of the Upper Gila River
system in New Mexico . Las Cruces, N.M.
[1979] iii, 48 p. ; LC Card 80-622273 DDC
333.91/009789 s 628.1/686789/692 19
GB705.N6 N64 no. 110 QH105.N6

(no. 113) Gross, Gerardo Wolfgang. Paul
Spring, an investigation of recharge in the
Roswell (N.M.) artesian basin /. Las Cruces,
N.M. [1979] 135 p. : LC Card 80-622504
DDC 551.49/09789/43 19
GB705.N6 N64 no. 113 GB1199.3.N6

(no. 114) Taylor, Robert Gay, 1940- Effects
of bacteria on nitrate and nitrite
concentrations in groundwater of the Ogallala
aquifer /. Las Cruces, N.M. [1979] vii, 20
leaves : LC Card 80-622275 DDC 333.91/09789
s 628.1/68 19
GB705.N6 N64 no. 114 TD224.N6

(no. 115) Consumptive use and yields of
crops in New Mexico /. Las Cruces, N.M.
[1979] vi, 108 p. : LC Card 80-622505 DDC
333.91/009789 s 631.7 19
GB705.N6 N64 no. 115 S600.7.E93

(no. 116) Davis, Paul, 1950- Spring
characteristics of the western Roswell artesian
basin . Las Cruces, N.M. [1980] viii, 93 p. :
LC Card 80-623165 DDC 333.91/009789 s
551.49/8 19
GB705.N6 N64 no. 116 GB1198.3.N6

(no. 117) Sammis, Theodore W.
Demonstration of irrigation return flow water
quality in the Mesilla Valley, New Mexico /.
Las Cruces, N.M. [1980] ix, 149 p. : LC
Card 80-623166 DDC 333.91/009789 s 631.7 19
GB705.N6 N64 no. 117 TC824.N6

New Mexico. Statutes. see New Mexico. Laws,
statutes, etc.

New Mexico. Taxation and Revenue Dept.
A checklist of New Mexico State and local
taxes, permits, and licenses. Santa Fe, N.M. :
Tax Research and Statistics Office, Taxation
and Revenue Dept., [1979] 39 p. ; 23 x 10 cm.
Cover title. LC Card 80-623253 DDC
353.97890072/4/0025 19
1. Taxation - New Mexico. 2. Fees, Administration -
New Mexico. 3. Tax administration and procedure -
New Mexico. I. Title.
HJ2423 .A7 1979

Gross receipts & compensating tax regulations /
Taxation & Revenue Dept. [Santa Fe, N.M.] :
The Dept., [1980] x, 174, 58 p. ; 30 cm. Cover

title. "Pertaining to the New Mexico gross receipts and compensating tax act." Includes index. LC Card 80-623312 DDC 343.78906/8 19
1. Business tax - New Mexico. 2. Use tax - New Mexico. I. New Mexico. Laws, statutes, etc. Gross receipts and compensating tax act. II. Title.
KFN4080.A434 A2 1980

New Mexico (Ter.). House of Representatives.
see New Mexico (Ter.). Legislative Assembly. House of Representatives.

New Mexico (Ter.). Legislative Assembly. House of Representatives. (Old Catalog form: New Mexico (Ter.). House.)
State of New Mexico: House [proceedings], 1907. [Santa Fe: s. n., 1907] 43 leaves; 36 cm. Microfilm. Original paged according to legislative days. Composed of clippings from the Santa Fe New Mexican. Cover title.
1. New Mexico (Ter.). Legislative Assembly. House of Representatives. 2. New Mexico - History - 1848- - Sources. I. Santa Fe New Mexican.
*NYPL [*ZT-1265]*

NEW MEXICO (TER.). LEGISLATIVE ASSEMBLY. HOUSE OF REPRESENTATIVES.
New Mexico (Ter.). Legislative Assembly. House of Representatives. State of New Mexico: House [proceedings], 1907. [Santa Fe, 1907] 43 leaves; *NYPL [*ZT-1265]*

New Mexico. University.
The New Mexico historical review. v. 1- ; 1926- Santa Fe, N. M. *NYPL [IAA (New Mexico historical review.)]*

Symposium on Cultural Resources Management and Remote Sensing, Tucson, Ariz. 1978. Remote sensing and non-destructive archeology /. Washington, DC , 1978. vii, 71 p. : LC Card 80-602610 DDC 930.1/028 19
CC76.4 .S9 1978

New Mexico. University. Bureau of Business & Economic Research. Parker, Alfred L. A study of the New Mexico liquor control act /. [Albuquerque, N.M.] , 1980. 173, 39 p. : LC Card 80-624137 DDC 363.4/1/09789 19
HV5086.N6 P37

New Mexico. University. Business & Economic Research, Bureau of. see New Mexico. University. Bureau of Business & Economic Research.

New Mexico. University. Division of Government Research. Bureau of Business & Economic Research. see New Mexico. University. Bureau of Business & Economic Research.

New Mexico. University. Division of Public Administration. Rehabilitation, what part of corrections? . Arlington, Tex. [1977?] vi, 152 p. : LC Card 80-621842 DDC 364.6/01 19
HV9303 .R43

New Mexico. University. Institute of Meteoritics.
Special publication .
(no. 19) Fodor, R. V. Catalog of lithic fragments in LL-group chondrites /. Albuquerque, N.M. , 1978. 38 p. : LC Card 80-621989 DDC 549/.112 19
QB755 .F53

New Mexico. University. Latin American Institute. The Problem of the undocumented worker /. [Albuquerque] [1979?] iii, 89 p. : LC Card 80-601248 DDC 331.6/2/72073 19
HD8081.M6 P76

New Mexico. University. Maxwell Museum of Anthropology. see Maxwell Museum of Anthropology.

New Mexico's standardized test results . Nochumson, Bayla S. Santa Fe., N.M. , 1979. ii, 38 p. : LC Card 80-621725 DDC 371.2/6/09789 19
LB3052.N6 N6

New Mexico's statutory executive agencies and how they grew. New Mexico. Governor's Committee on Reorganization of State Government. Final report /. Santa Fe, N.M. [1970] ix, 202 p. : LC Card 80-623230 DDC 353.978907/3 19
JK8038 1970 .N48

A new nonparasitic species of the holarctic lamprey genus Lethenteron Creaser and Hubbs, 1922, (Petromyzonidae) from northwestern North America, with notes on other species of the same genus /. Vladykov, Vadim Dmitrij, 1898- [Fairbanks] 1978. 74 p. : LC Card 78-622997 DDC 574 s 597/.2 19
QH1 .A258 no. 19 QL638.25.P48

New Orleans. Bureau of Governmental Research. see Bureau of Governmental Research, New Orleans.

New Orleans. Charter. Bureau of Governmental Research, New Orleans. Referendum : proposed Charter change /. New Orleans , 1964. 16 l. ;
*NYPL [*ZT-1245]*

NEW ORLEANS - CHARTERS.
Bureau of Governmental Research, New Orleans. Referendum : proposed Charter change /. New Orleans , 1964. 16 l. ;
*NYPL [*ZT-1245]*

New Orleans. Louisiana State Museum. see Louisiana State Museum, New Orleans.

NEW ORLEANS METROPOLITAN AREA - ECONOMIC CONDITIONS.
Klaasen, Thomas A. Venture capital and the New Orleans economy /. [New Orleans] , 1980. 30 leaves ; LC Card 80-622446 DDC 330 s 332/.04154 19
HC107.L8 L58 no. 34 HG3729.U5

NEW ORLEANS REGION - ECONOMIC CONDITIONS - COLLECTED WORKS.
Willdan Associates. Mississippi Deltaic Plain Region ecological characterization . [Washington] [1980- v. <1> : LC Card 80-603195 DDC 330.9763/3063 19
HC108.N42 W54 1980

NEW ORLEANS - SOCIAL LIFE AND CUSTOMS - ADDRESSES, ESSAYS, LECTURES.
Huber, Leonard Victor, 1903- Creole collage . Lafayette, La. , c1980. 138 p. : LC Card 79-57462 DDC 976.3/3500441 19
F379.N59 C874

New Orleans. Southern Forest Experiment Station. see United States. Southern Forest Experiment Station, New Orleans.

New routes capital construction program . New York (State). Division of Audits and Accounts. Albany [1980] 30, [12] leaves ; LC Card 80-622249 DDC 353.97470072/32 19
HE4491.N68 N48 1980

New school districts in rural Alaska . University of Alaska, Fairbanks. Center for Northern Educational Research. Fairbanks , 1978. v, 247 p., [1] fold. leaf of plates : LC Card 78-622541 DDC 370.19/346 19
LC5147.A4 U54 1978

New serial holdings, 1977 /. Tucker, Jane C. [Washington] [Springfield, Va.] 1977. vi, 232 p. ; LC Card 77-602720
Z7403 .T79 Q158.5   *NYPL [JSF 81-153]*

New species of frogs ... Lynch, John D. New species of frogs (leptodactylidae, Eleutherodactylus) from the Amazonian lowlands of Ecuador /. Lawrence , 1974. 22 p. : LC Card 74-623647 DDC 597.8/7 19
QL668.E257 L936

A new species of Lampropholis (Lacertilia, Scincidae) from the rainforests of northeastern Queensland /. Greer, Allen E. Ann Arbor, Mich. [1980] 12 p. : LC Card 80-622058 DDC 597.95 19
QL666.L28 G73

A new species of Liolaemus (Sauria: Iguanidae) from the Andean Mountains of the southern Mendoza volcanic region of Argentina /. Cei, José Miguel, 1918- Lawrence , 1978. 6 p. : LC Card 79-621682 DDC 597.95 19
QL666.L25 C44

A new systematic arrangement for Philodryas serra (Schlegel) and Philodryas pseudoserra Amaral (Serpentes : Colubridae) /. Thomas, Robert A. Austin , 1977. 20 p. : LC Card 78-621007 DDC 574 s 597.96 19
AM101 .T474 no. 27 QL666.O636

NEW TOWNS - FRANCE - PARIS REGION.
Underhill, Jack A. French national urban policy and the Paris region new towns . [Washington] [1980] 131 p. : LC Card 80-602925 DDC

307.7/6/0944 19
HT165.P37 U52

NEW YORK (CITY) - AFRO-AMERICAN AGED.
New York (City). Office for the Aging. Research Dept. Selected findings on the black elderly from The elderly in the inner city. New York [1974] 15 p.; *NYPL [*ZT-1250]*

NEW YORK (CITY) - AGED - ADDRESSES, ESSAYS, LECTURES.
Cantor, Marjorie H. The elderly in the inner city of New York. New York [1973] 29 leaves ; *NYPL [*XME-9046]*

NEW YORK (CITY) - AGED - PERIODICALS.
New York (City). Office for the Aging. Lay advocacy training program annual report. 1972/73- New York. *NYPL [JLM 80-981]*

New York (City). Agency for Child Development. Medical and Health Research Association of New York City. The New York City infant day care study . Rockville, Md. [1979] 195 p. ; LC Card 79-602030
HV859.N5 M43 1979   *NYPL [JLF 81-486]*

New York (City). Aging, Office for the. see New York (City). Office for the Aging.

NEW YORK (CITY) - ALCOHOLISM - STATISTICS - PERIODICALS.
New York (City). Office of Chief Medical Examiner. Report to the mayor of the poisonings from the consumption of alcohol or the denatured alcohol. 1925/26. New York. 1 v. *NYPL [*ZAN-T5201]*

New York (City) American Society of Mechanical Engineers. see American Society of Mechanical Engineers.

NEW YORK (CITY) - ARCHITECTURE - GUIDE-BOOKS.
New York (City). Landmarks Preservation Commission. A guide to New York City landmarks /. New York , c1979. viii, 82 p. : *NYPL [IRGV 80-2827]*

New York (City). Audit and Control, Bureau of. see New York (City). Bureau of Audit and Control.

New York (City). Aviation and Marine, Dept. of. see New York (City). Dept. of Marine and Aviation.

New York (City). Battery Park City. see Battery Park City, New York (City)

New York (City). Board of Coroners. (Old Catalog form: New York (City). Borough of Manhattan. Coroner's Board)
Report. New York. 24-29 cm. Microfilm. Ceased publication with 1917.
1. New York (City) - Statistics, Vital - Periodicals.
*NYPL [*ZAN-T5203]*

New York (City). Board of Education. (Old Catalog form: New York (City). Education Dept.
Annual meeting. [Proceedings] New York. 23 cm.
1. New York (City). Board of Education - Periodicals.
NYPL [JLL 80-199]

Chancellor's report on programs and problems affecting integration of the New York City public schools. New York, 1974. 36 p. charts. 28 cm. Microfilm. Cover title: Programs and problems affecting integration of the New York City public schools. "Irving Anker, chancellor." Includes bibliographical references. LC Card 77-27109
1. Segregation in education - New York (City). I. Anker, Irving. II. Title.   *NYPL [*Z-3211]*

Facts and figures. New York. illus. 10 x 15 cm. Cover title, 1969/70- : New York City public schools facts and figures.
1. Education - New York (City) - Handbooks, manuals, etc. 2. Education - New York (City) - Statistics - Yearbooks. I. New York (City). Board of Education. New York City public schools facts and figures. II. Title. III. Title: New York City public schools facts and figures.   *NYPL [JLK 80-174]*

New York City public schools facts and figures. New York (City). Board of Education. Facts and figures. New York.
NYPL [JLK 80-174]

NEW YORK (CITY). BOARD OF EDUCATION - ADMINISTRATION.
New York (State). Temporary State Commission of Investigation. Report of the

BIBLIOGRAPHIC GUIDE

New York (City). Board of Education. Community School Board.

42

New York State Commission of Investigation of an investigation of certain contracting practices and procedures of the New York City Board of Education and related matters. New York [1975?] 41, 3 leaves ; LC Card 78-620962 DDC 353.97470085/1 19
L183.N5 B53 1975

New York (City). Board of Education. Community School Board. District 6. see **New York (City). Community School Board. District 6.**

NEW YORK (CITY). BOARD OF EDUCATION - PERIODICALS.
New York (City). Board of Education. Annual meeting. [Proceedings] New York.
NYPL [JLL 80-199]

New York (City). Board of Estimate and Apportionment. (Old Catalog form: New York (City). Estimate Board)
In the matter of the establishment of a new "use district" to be known as the "retail district" : memorandum in favor of the inclusion of the west side of Madison Avenue from Madison Square to 38th Street in the proposed "retail district" zone / [prepared by] House, Grossman & Vorhaus [and presented] before the Board of Estimate and Apportionment of the City of New York [by] Moses H. Grossman, of Counsel. New York : M. B. Brown, [1929?] ii, 90 p. : ill. (some col.), plans ; 32 cm. Cover title.
1. Zoning - New York (City). 2. New York (City) - City planning. 3. City planning - New York (State). I. Grossman, Moses Henry, 1873-1942. II. Title.
NYPL [JLG 80-226]

NEW YORK (CITY) - BRIDGES.
Triborough Bridge and Tunnel Authority. Triborough Bridge and Tunnel Authority facilities. New York, 1973. 25 p.:
NYPL [JSE 80-724]

New York (City). Bureau of Audit and Control.
Audit report on over-time incurred by uniformed employees of the New York City Fire Department, January 1, 1975 to June 30, 1978/Office of the Comptroller, City of New York, Bureau of Audit and Control. [New York]: The Bureau, [1978] 19 leaves; 28 cm. Microfiche (neg.) 1 sheet. 11 x 15 cm. (NYPL FSN 34,803 Caption title.
1. Fire fighters - New York (City). 2. Overtime - New York (City). I. Title. II. Title: Over-time incurred by uniformed employees of the New York City Fire Department. *NYPL [*XME-9059]*

Report on the failure of hospitals to take action on adverse determinations issued by the New York County Health Services Review Organization/ Office of the Comptroller, City of New York, Bureau of Audit and Control. New York: The Bureau, 1978. ix, 13 l.; 28 cm. Microfilm. Caption title.
1. Hospital care - New York City). 2. Hospitals - New York (City) - Administration. I. Title.
NYPL [*ZT-1265]

NEW YORK (CITY). BUREAU OF HEALTH CARE SERVICES - AUDITING AND INSPECTION.
New York (State). Division of Audits and Accounts. New York City Health Department Medicaid provider restitutions, January 1, 1969 to April 30, 1977. [Albany] , 1978. 2, 10 leaves ; LC Card 79-620527 DDC 352.1/72 19
HD7102.U5 N66 1978a

New York (City). Bureau of Municipal Investigation and Statistics. (Old Catalog form: New York (City). Municipal Investigation and Statistics Bureau)
New York City Health and Hospitals Corporation: report on financial audit and management survey. New York. 29 cm. Report year ends June 30. Prepared by its Division of Management Audits.
1. New York (City). Health and Hospitals Corporation - Accounting - Periodicals. 2. New York (City) Health and Hospitals Corporation - Management - Periodicals. I. Title.
NYPL [JLM 81-2]

New York (City). Bureau of Municipal Statistics. see **New York (City). Bureau of Municipal Investigation and Statistics.**

New York (City). Bureau of Records. see **New York (City) Dept. of Health Bureau of Records and Statistics.**

New York (City). Bureau of Records and Statistics. see **New York (City) Dept. of Health Bureau of Records and Statistics.**

New York (City). Bureau of Records of Vital Statistics. see **New York (City) Dept. of Health Bureau of Records and Statistics.**

New York (City). Bureau of Vital Records and Statistics. see **New York (City) Dept. of Health Bureau of Records and Statistics.**

New York (City). Bureau of Vital Statistics. see **New York (City) Dept. of Health Bureau of Records and Statistics.**

New York (City). Chief Medical Examiner, Office of. see **New York (City). Office of Chief Medical Examiner.**

New York (City). Child Development, Agency for. see **New York (City). Agency for Child Development.**

New York (City). City Commission for the United Nations and for the Consular Corps.
Register of foreign consulates and associated government offices in New York. New York. 23 cm.
1. Diplomatic and consular service in the United States - Registers. 2. New York (City) - Directories. I. Title.
NYPL [*R-Econ. 80-806 & JLL 80-238]

New York (City). City Commission on Human Rights. (Old Catalog form: New York (City). Human Rights, Commission on)
Paul, Alice. Economic investment and the future of neighborhoods. [New York], 1977. iii, 111 p.;
NYPL [JLF 80-1388]

NEW YORK (CITY) - CITY PLANNING.
Alexander Cooper Associates. Battery Park City draft summary report 2nd 1979 master plan /. New York , 1979. 97 p. :
NYPL [IRH 80-1028]

From landfill to park. New York, 1974. 45 p.:
NYPL [*ZI-281]

New York (City). Board of Estimate and Apportionment. In the matter of the establishment of a new "use district" to be known as the "retail district" . New York [1929?] ii, 90 p. : *NYPL [JLG 80-226]*

New York (City). City Planning Commission. Plan for New York City, 1969. Cambridge, Mass. [c1969] 6 v. ISBN 0-262-64004-X (v. 1) varies LC Card 78-89854
HT168.N5 A5

New York (City). Housing and Development Administration. Office of Programs and Policies. Summary of government housing activities in New York City /. [New York] [1974?] ca. 160 leaves in various pagings;
NYPL [JLF 80-1475]

New York (City). Office of Lower Manhattan Development. Special Greenwich Street Development District /. New York [1971] 55 p.: *NYPL [JLF 80-1634]*

New York (City). City Planning Commission.
Greenpoint : striking a balance between industry & housing / New York City Planning Commission. New York : The Commission, 1974. 80 p. : ill., maps ; 22 x 28 cm. LC Card 79-51179
1. City planning - New York (State). 2. Greenpoint, Brooklyn - City planning. I. Title.
NYPL [IRM (Greenpoint) 80-1108]

Plan for New York City, 1969; a proposal. Cambridge, Mass., MIT Press [c1969] 6 v. illus. (part col.), col. maps. 43 x 44 cm. CONTENTS. - 1. Critical issues.--2. The Bronx.--3. Brooklyn.--4. Manhattan.--5. Queens.--6. Staten Island. ISBN 0-262-64004-X (v. 1) varies LC Card 78-89854
1. City planning - New York (State). 2. New York (City) - City planning. 3. New York (City) - Social conditions. I. Title.
HT168.N5 A5

New York (City). City Planning Dept. see **New York (City). Dept. of City Planning.**

New York (City), City University of New York. Center for the Study of Women and Sex Roles. Nelson, Martha. A guide to collections on women in the New York area /. [New York, 1980?] 17 p.; *NYPL [JLF 81-437]*

NEW YORK (CITY). CITY UNIVERSITY OF NEW YORK - FINANCE.

New York (State). Division of Audits and Accounts. Tuition assistance program receivables and payables of the City University of New York, fiscal year ended June 30, 1978 /. Albany [1980] 3, 24 leaves ; LC Card 80-622250 DDC 379.1/22/097471 19
LD3835 .N49 1980

NEW YORK (CITY). CITY UNIVERSITY OF NEW YORK - FRESHMAN - STATISTICS.
Kramer, Rena. Characteristics of enrollees and non-enrollees among freshmen/. New York, 1974. 19 leaves; *NYPL [*ZT-1254]*

New York (City). City University of New York. Office of Program and Policy Research. Kramer, Rena. Characteristics of enrollees and non-enrollees among freshmen/. New York, 1974. 19 leaves; *NYPL [*ZT-1254]*

New York (City). City University of New York. Office of Urban Policy and Programs. Brief biographical sketches of appointed officials of the executive branch of the government of the City of New York/ prepared by the Office of Urban Policy and Programs, the Graduate school and University Center, the City University of New York. New York : The Office, 1974. [88] p. ; 22 cm.
1. New York (City) - Officials and employees - Biography. I. Title. *NYPL [JFD 80-9607]*

New York (City). (City University of New York. Program and Policy Research, Office of. see **New York (City). City University of New York. Office of Program and Policy Research.**

New York (City). City University of New York. Queens College. see **Queens College, Flushing, N. Y.**

New York (City). City University of New York. Research Foundation. Muller, Charlotte Feldman, 1921- Study of physician reimbursement under medicare and medicaid /. [Washington] 1979- v. : LC Card 80-601289 DDC 338.4/33621/0973 19
R728.5 .M84

New York (City). City University of New York. Urban Policy and Programs, Office of. see **New York (City). City University of New York. Office of Urban Policy and Programs.**

NEW YORK (CITY) - COLLECTIVE LABOR AGREEMENTS - HOSPITALS - PERIODICALS.
New York (City). Office of Municipal Labor Relations. [Agreement between the City of New York and related public employers, the New York City Health and Hospitals Corporation, and the Doctors Council. New York]
NYPL [JLM 80-1128]

NEW YORK (CITY) - COLLECTIVE LABOR AGREEMENTS - PHYSICIANS - PERIODICALS.
New York (City). Office of Municipal Labor Relations. [Agreement between the City of New York and related public employers, the New York City Health and Hospitals Corporation, and the Doctors Council. New York]
NYPL [JLM 80-1128]

NEW YORK (CITY) - COLLEGE STUDENTS' SOCIO-ECONOMIC STATUS.
Kramer, Rena. Characteristics of enrollees and non-enrollees among freshmen/. New York, 1974. 19 leaves; *NYPL [*ZT-1254]*

New York (City). Commission for the United Nations and for the Consular Corps. see **New York (City). City Commission for the United Nations and for the Consular Corps.**

New York (City). Commission on Human Rights. see **New York (City). City Commission on Human Rights.**

NEW YORK (CITY) - COMMUNITY DEVELOPMENT, URBAN.
Paul, Alice. Economic investment and the future of neighborhoods. [New York], 1977. iii, 111 p.; *NYPL [JLF 80-1388]*

New York (City). Community School Board. District 6. Tell me, child. New York, c1980. 134 p.: *NYPL [JFD 81-25]*

New York (City). Community School District 6. see **New York (City). Community School Board. District 6.**

New York (City). Comptroller's office. Bureau of Audit and Control. see New York (City). Bureau of Audit and Control.

New York (City). Comptroller's Office. Bureau of Municipal Investigation and Statistics. see New York (City). Bureau of Municipal Investigation and Statistics.

New York (City). Cooper-Hewitt Museum of Decorative Arts and Design. see Cooper-Hewitt Museum of Decorative Arts and Design.

New York (City). Coroners, Board of. see New York (City). Board of Coroners.

NEW YORK (CITY) - CRIME AND CRIMINALS - STATISTICS.
New York (City). Police Dept. Crime Analysis Section. Statistical report: Complaints and arrests. New York.   *NYPL [JLM 80-898]*

New York (City). Cultural Affairs, Dept. of. see New York (City). Dept. of Cultural Affairs.

NEW YORK (CITY) - DAY CARE CENTERS.
Medical and Health Research Association of New York City. The New York City infant day care study . Rockville, Md. [1979] 195 p. ;   LC Card 79-602030
HV859.N5 M43 1979   NYPL [JLF 81-486]

New York (City). Dept. of City Planning. (Old Catalog form: New York (City). City Planning Dept.)
From landfill to park. New York, 1974. 45 p.:
*NYPL [*ZI-281]*

Kingsbridge, Marble Hill: the state of the community / [City of New York, Department of City Planning]. [New York]: The Department, 1977. 14 p.: ill.; 28 cm. Microfilm. "NYC DCP 77-16." Victor Marrero, Chairman.
*1. Kingsbridge, New York (City) - Social conditions. 2. Marble Hill, New York (City) - Social conditions. I. Marrero, Victor. II. Title.   NYPL [*ZT-1265]*

New York (City). Dept. of Consumer Affairs.
Consumer issues and actions affecting the handicapped . [New York] [1974] 130 p. ;
NYPL [JLF 81-590]

New York (City). Dept. of Correction. House of Detention for Women. see New York (City). House of Detention for Women.

New York (City). Dept. of Cultural Affairs.
Funding news. winter, 1980- New York.
NYPL [Econ. Div.]

New York (City). Dept. of Health. (Old Catalog form: New York (City). Health Dept.)
Births and infant mortality, tuberculosis cases and deaths. 1932-33. New York. 2 v. illus. 29 cm. Microfilm.
1. Infants - Mortality - New York (City) - Statistics - Periodicals. 2. Tuberculosis - New York (City) - Statistics - Periodicals. I. Title.
*NYPL [*ZAN-T5294]*

Epitome of the births, marriages, stillbirths, and deaths. 1879. New York. illus. 27 cm. Microfilm.
*1. New York (City) - Statistics, Vital - Periodicals. I. Title.   NYPL [*ZAN-T5300]*

Medical and Health Research Association of New York City. The New York City infant day care study . Rockville, Md. [1979] 195 p. ;   LC Card 79-602030
HV859.N5 M43 1979   NYPL [JLF 81-486]

New York (City). Dept. of Health. Bureau of Records. see New York (City) Dept. of Health Bureau of Records and Statistics.

New York (City) Dept. of Health Bureau of Records and Statistics.
Condensed quarterly report. June, 1902- Sept. 1912 (incomplete). [New York] 31 cm.
Microfilm. Issued by the bureau under its earlier name: Bureau of Records. Ceased publication with Sept. 1912?
1. New York (City) - Statistics, Vital - Periodicals.
*NYPL [*ZAN-T5208]*

Reported mortality, together with the actual mortality. 1877-80, 1883. [New York] 35 cm. Microfilm. Annual. Name of issuing body as: Bureau of Vital Statistics. Ceased publication with 1883?
*I. Title.   NYPL [*ZAN-T5209]*

Weekly mortality from the principal causes of death. 1876-77. New York. tables. 41 x 54 cm. Microfilm. Ceased publication in 1877.
*1. New York (City) - Statistics, Vital - Periodicals. I. Title.   NYPL [*ZAN-T5293]*

New York (City). Dept. of Health. Bureau of Records of Vital Statistics. see New York (City) Dept. of Health Bureau of Records and Statistics.

New York (City). Dept. of Health. Bureau of Vital Records and Statistics. see New York (City) Dept. of Health Bureau of Records and Statistics.

New York (City). Dept. of Health. Bureau of Vital Statistics. see New York (City) Dept. of Health Bureau of Records and Statistics.

New York (City). Dept. of Health. Records and Statistics, Bureau of. see New York (City) Dept. of Health Bureau of Records and Statistics.

New York (City). Dept. of Highways. (Old Catalog form: New York (City). Highways Dept.)
Bettigole (N. H.) Company. Inspection & report, Fresh Kills Bridge at Richmond Avenue, Borough of Richmond /. New York, 1974. 44 leaves, 8 folded leaves of plates:
NYPL [JSF 80-922]

Hardesty & Hanover, firm, engineers, New York. Capital project TD-4 : remote control of movable bridges/. [New York] , 1974. iii, 114 p., 17 leaves of plates :   *NYPL [JSF 80-410]*

New York (City). Dept. of Marine and Aviation. (Old Catalog form: New York (City). Marine and Aviation Dept.)
Bechtel Corporation. Hunts Point Food Center. New York , 1968. 20 p. :
NYPL [JLG 80-158]

New York (City). Dept. of Personnel. (Old Catalog form: New York (City). Personnel, Dept. of)
Annual report under executive order 109 - employee safety program. New York. 30 cm.
1. Safety regulations - New York (City) - Periodicals. I. Title. II. Title: Employee safety program.
NYPL [JLM 80-702]

Work experience programs & supportive services administered by Department of Personnel. New York. 22 x 36 cm.
1. Occupational training - New York (City) - Periodicals. I. Title.   NYPL [JLN 80-76]

NEW YORK (CITY). DEPT. OF SOCIAL SERVICES - AUDITING AND INSPECTION.
New York (State). Division of Audits and Accounts. New York City Health Department Medicaid provider restitutions, January 1, 1969 to April 30, 1977. [Albany] , 1978. 2, 10 leaves ;   LC Card 79-620527   DDC 352.1/72 19
HD7102.U5 N66 1978a

NEW YORK (CITY) - DESCRIPTION.
New York (City). Landmarks Preservation Commission. A guide to New York City landmarks /. New York , c1979. viii, 82 p. :
NYPL [IRGV 80-2827]

NEW YORK (CITY) - DESCRIPTION - 1951- - GUIDE-BOOKS.
The ultimate guide to shopping in New York /. [New York] , c1979. 48 p. :
NYPL [IRGV 80-2533]

NEW YORK (CITY) - DIRECTORIES.
New York (City). City Commission for the United Nations and for the Consular Corps. Register of foreign consulates and associated government offices in New York. New York.
*NYPL [*R-Econ. 80-806 & JLL 80-238]*

NEW YORK (CITY) - DISCRIMINATION IN MORTGAGE LANDING.
Paul, Alice. Economic investment and the future of neighborhoods. [New York], 1977. iii, 111 p.;   *NYPL [JLF 80-1388]*

New York (City). Division of Vital Statistics. see New York (City) Dept. of Health Bureau of Records and Statistics.

New York (City). Downtown Brooklyn Development, Office of. see New York (City). Office of Downtown Brooklyn Development.

New York (City). Education Dept. see New York (City). Board of Education.

NEW YORK (CITY) - EDUCATION - FINANCE.
New York (State). Division of Audits and Accounts. State financial assistance due New York City for City University community

colleges, fiscal year ended June 30, 1975. [Albany] [1979] 3, 27 leaves ;   LC Card 80-620516   DDC 379.1/22/097471 19
LB2826.5.N5 N46 1979

NEW YORK (CITY) - EDUCATION - HANDBOOKS, MANUALS, ETC.
New York (City). Board of Education. Facts and figures. New York.   *NYPL [JLK 80-174]*

NEW YORK (CITY) - EDUCATION - STATISTICS - YEARBOOKS.
New York (City). Board of Education. Facts and figures. New York.   *NYPL [JLK 80-174]*

New York (City). Engineering Foundation. see Engineering Foundation, New York.

New York (City). Estimate and Apportionment, Board of. see New York (City). Board of Estimate and Apportionment.

New York (City). Executive Office of the Mayor. see New York (City). Office of the Mayor.

New York (City). Exposition and Convention Center (Proposed) see New York Exposition and Convention Center (Proposed)

New York (City). Federal Reserve Bank. see Federal Reserve Bank of New York.

NEW YORK (CITY) - FINANCE, PUBLIC - ACCOUNTING.
United States. General Accounting Office. New York City's efforts to improve its accounting systems, Department of the Treasury . [Washington] , 1977. 29 p. ;   LC Card 77-601736
*HJ9777.N42 N48 1977   NYPL [*XME-9396]*

NEW YORK (CITY) - FIRE FIGHTERS.
New York (City). Bureau of Audit and Control. Audit report on over-time incurred by uniformed employees of the New York City Fire Department. [New York] [1978] 19 leaves;
*NYPL [*XME-9059]*

New York (City). General Grant National Memorial. see General Grant National Memorial.

New York (City) - Government. see New York (City) - Politics and government.

New York (City). Greenwich Street Development District. see Special Greenwich Street Development District, New York (City)

NEW YORK (CITY) - HANDICAPPED AS CONSUMERS - CONGRESSES.
Consumer issues and actions affecting the handicapped . [New York] [1974] 130 p. ;
NYPL [JLF 81-590]

New York (City). Handicapped, Office for the. see New York (City). Office for the Handicapped.

New York (City). Harlem, Mayor's Commission on Conditions in. see New York (City). Mayor's Commission on Conditions in Harlem.

New York (City). Health and Hospitals Corporation.
New York (City). Office of Municipal Labor Relations. [Agreement between the City of New York and related public employers, the New York City Health and Hospitals Corporation, and the Doctors Council. New York]
NYPL [JLM 80-1128]

NEW YORK (CITY). HEALTH AND HOSPITALS CORPORATION.
New York (State). Division of Audits and Accounts. Control of hospital inpatient nursing costs under the Medicaid Program, New York City Health and Hospitals Corporation. Albany [1980] 4, 2 leaves, 32 p. ;   LC Card 80-622789   DDC 362.1/1/068 19
RT86.74.N48 N48 1980

NEW YORK (CITY). HEALTH AND HOSPITALS CORPORATION - ACCOUNTING - PERIODICALS.
New York (City). Bureau of Municipal Investigation and Statistics. New York City Health and Hospitals Corporation: report on financial audit and management survey. New York.   *NYPL [JLM 81-2]*

NEW YORK (CITY) HEALTH AND HOSPITALS CORPORATION - MANAGEMENT - PERIODICALS.
New York (City). Bureau of Municipal Investigation and Statistics. New York City Health and Hospitals Corporation: report on

financial audit and management survey. New York. *NYPL [JLM 81-2]*

New York City Health and Hospitals Corporation: report on financial audit and management survey. New York (City). Bureau of Municipal Investigation and Statistics. New York. *NYPL [JLM 81-2]*

New York City Health Department Medicaid provider restitutions, January 1, 1969 to April 30, 1977. New York (State). Division of Audits and Accounts. [Albany] , 1978. 2, 10 leaves ; LC Card 79-620527   DDC 352.1/72 19
HD7102.U5 N66 1978a

New York (City). Health Dept. see New York (City). Dept. of Health.

New York (City). Highways, Dept. of. see New York (City). Dept. of Highways.

NEW YORK (CITY) - HOSPITAL CARE.
New York (City). Bureau of Audit and Control. Report on the failure of hospitals to take action on adverse determinations issued by the New York County Health Services Review Organization/. New York, 1978. ix, 13 l.;
*NYPL [*ZT-1265]*

New York (State). Division of Audits and Accounts. Control of hospital inpatient nursing costs under the Medicaid Program, New York City Health and Hospitals Corporation. Albany [1980] 4, 2 leaves, 32 p. ;   LC Card 80-622789
DDC 362.1/1/068 19
RT86.74.N48 N48 1980

NEW YORK (CITY) - HOSPITALS - ADMINISTRATION.
New York (City). Bureau of Audit and Control. Report on the failure of hospitals to take action on adverse determinations issued by the New York County Health Services Review Organization/. New York, 1978. ix, 13 l.;
*NYPL [*ZT-1265]*

NEW YORK (CITY) - HOSPITALS - COSTS.
New York (State). Division of Audits and Accounts. Control of hospital inpatient nursing costs under the Medicaid Program, New York City Health and Hospitals Corporation. Albany [1980] 4, 2 leaves, 32 p. ;   LC Card 80-622789
DDC 362.1/1/068 19
RT86.74.N48 N48 1980

NEW YORK (CITY). HOUSE OF DETENTION FOR WOMEN.
New York (City). Office of the Mayor. Report by deputy mayor Edward F. Cavanagh, jr. to Mayor Robert F. Wagner regarding the Women's House of Detention. [New York] 1965. 9 p. ;   *NYPL [*ZT-1247]*

NEW YORK (CITY) - HOUSING.
New York (City). Housing and Development Administration. Office of Programs and Policies. Summary of government housing activities in New York City /. [New York] [1974?] ca. 160 leaves in various pagings;
NYPL [JLF 80-1475]

New York (City). Housing and Development Administration. Office of Programs and Policies. Summary of government housing activities in New York City / Housing & Development Administration, Office of Programs and Policies. [New York] : The Office, [1974?] ca. 160 leaves in various pagings; 28 cm.
1. Housing - New York (City). 2. New York (City) - City planning. 3. City planning - New York (State). I. Title.   *NYPL [JLF 80-1475]*

New York (City). Human Resources Administration.
HRA basic facts. New York.
NYPL [JLM 80-980]

NEW YORK (CITY). HUMAN RESOURCES ADMINISTRATION.
New York (State). Division of Audits and Accounts. Comprehensive health plan offered by the Health Insurance Plan of Greater New York (HIP) to certain medicaid recipients, New York City Human Resources Administration. [Albany] [1979] 7, 56, 18 p. ;   LC Card 80-622253   DDC 362.1/0425 19
RA413.3.H4 N48 1979

New York (City). Human Resources Administration. Agency for Child Development. see New York (City). Agency for Child Development.

NEW YORK (CITY). HUMAN RESOURCES ADMINISTRATION - AUDITING AND INSPECTION.
New York (State). Division of Audits and Accounts. Client relocation and related payments, New York City Human Resources Administration. [Albany] , 1979. 4, 27 leaves ;
LC Card 79-624387   DDC 352.7/5/097471 19
HV87.N5 N46 1979

NEW YORK (CITY). HUMAN RESOURCES ADMINISTRATION - DIRECTORIES.
HRA basic facts. New York.
NYPL [JLM 80-980]

New York (City). Human Rights, Commission on. see New York (City). City Commission on Human Rights.

New York (City). Hunts Point Food Center. see Hunts Point Food Center.

The New York City infant day care study . Medical and Health Research Association of New York City. Rockville, Md. [1979] 195 p. ;   LC Card 79-602030
HV859.N5 M43 1979   *NYPL [JLF 81-486]*

NEW YORK (CITY) - INFANTS - MORTALITY - STATISTICS - PERIODICALS.
New York (City). Dept. of Health. Births and infant mortality, tuberculosis cases and deaths. 1932-33. New York. 2 v.
*NYPL [*ZAN-T5294]*

New York (City). Intermediate School 201 Complex. ... We come to dedicate a school / Arthur A. Schomburg Intermediate School. [New York : The School, 196-?]. 33 leaves ; 36 cm. Microfilm. English, with Spanish translations. CONTENTS: The African American digs up his past / Arthur A. Schomburg. - Arthur A. Schomburg and the Schomburg Collection. - A new chant / James E. Campbell.
1. New York (City). Intermediate School 201 Complex. I. Title.   *NYPL [Sc Micro R-3667]*

NEW YORK (CITY). INTERMEDIATE SCHOOL 201 COMPLEX.
New York (City). Intermediate School 201 Complex. ... We come to dedicate a school /. [New York , 196-?]. 33 leaves ;
NYPL [Sc Micro R-3667]

NEW YORK (CITY) - INVESTMENT BANKING.
Paul, Alice. Economic investment and the future of neighborhoods. [New York], 1977. iii, 111 p.;   *NYPL [JLF 80-1388]*

New York (City). Kennedy Galleries. see Kennedy Galleries, inc., New York.

NEW YORK (CITY) - LABOR SUUPPLY - STATISTICS.
United States. Bureau of Labor Statistics. Some aspects of the ghetto labor market in New York. New York, 1971. 21 p.   LC Card 72-601109
HD5726.N5 A54 1971b   *NYPL [*ZT-1264]*

New York (City). Landmarks Preservation Commission. A guide to New York City landmarks / Landmarks Preservation Commission of the City of New York ; text, Ellen W. Kramer ; editor, Patricia W. Rich. New York : The Commission, c1979. viii, 82 p. : plans ; 22 cm. Cover title. "Supplement to 1979 Landmarks guide", 1 sheet. 28 cm. fold. and inserted. Includes index.
1. New York (City) - Description. 2. Architecture - New York (City) - Guide-books. I. Kramer, Ellen W. II. Title.   *NYPL [IRGV 80-2827]*

New York (City). Lower Manhattan Development, Office of. see New York (City). Office of Lower Manhattan Development.

New York (City). Management and Budget, Office of. see New York (City). Office of Management and Budget.

New York (City). Marine and Aviation Dept. see New York (City). Dept. of Marine and Aviation.

New York (City). Mayor. Executive Office. see New York (City). Office of the Mayor.

New York (City). Mayor's Commission on Conditions in Harlem. (Old Catalog form: New York (City) Harlem, Mayor's Commission on conditions in).
Ford, James W., 1893- The causes and the remedies for the March 19th outbreak in Harlem /. [New York, 1935]. 23 p.
NYPL [Sc Micro F-1246]

New York (City). Mayor's Office. see New York (City). Office of the Mayor.

New York (City). Mayor's Office for the Handicapped. see New York (City). Office for the Handicapped.

New York (City). Medical and Health Research Association. see Medical and Health Research Association of New York City.

NEW YORK (CITY) - MEDICAL CARE.
New York (State). State Study Commission for New York City. Task Force on Health and Hospitals. Health care needs and the New York City Health and Hospitals Corporation. - New York , 1973. iv, 183 p. ;
NYPL [JLF 80-1463]

NEW YORK (CITY) - MINORITIES - EMPLOYMENT - STATISTICS.
United States. Bureau of Labor Statistics. Some aspects of the ghetto labor market in New York. New York, 1971. 21 p.   LC Card 72-601109
HD5726.N5 A54 1971b   *NYPL [*ZT-1264]*

New York (City). Municipal Investigation and Statistics, Bureau of. see New York (City). Bureau of Municipal Investigation and Statistics.

New York (City). Municipal Labor Relations, Office of. see New York (City). Office of Municipal Labor Relations.

NEW YORK (CITY) - MUNICIPAL SERVICES.
New York (City). Office of Neighborhood Government. Integrating city services. New York , 1974. 70 p. ;   *NYPL [JLF 80-1266]*

NEW YORK (CITY) - NARCOTICS, CONTROL OF.
New York (State). Temporary State Commission of Investigation. Interim report concerning the operations of Special Narcotics Parts of the Supreme Court. New York [1973] 21 leaves   *NYPL [*XME-9454]*

New York (City). National Municipal League. see National Municipal League.

New York (City). Neighborhood Government, Office of. see New York (City). Office of Neighborhood Government.

NEW YORK (CITY) - OCCUPATIONAL TRAINING - PERIODICALS.
New York (City). Dept. of Personnel. Work experience programs & supportive services administered by Department of Personnel. New York.   *NYPL [JLN 80-76]*

NEW YORK CITY OFF-TRACK BETTING CORPORATION - AUDITING AND INSPECTION.
New York (State). Division of Audits and Accounts. Profitability of branch offices, New York City Off-Track Betting Corporation /. Albany , 1980. 21, [11] leaves ;   LC Card 80-621875   DDC 352.93/6 19
SF332.5.N7 N48 1980

New York (City). Office for the Aging.
Cantor, Marjorie H. The elderly in the inner city of New York. New York [1973] 29 leaves ;   *NYPL [*XME-9046]*

The elderly in the inner city. New York (City). Office for the Aging. Research Dept. Selected findings on the black elderly from The elderly in the inner city: a study/conducted by the Research Department of the New New York [1974] 15 p.;   *NYPL [*ZT-1250]*

Lay advocacy training program annual report. 1972/73- New York. 28 cm. Report year ends June 30. Cover title: Lay advocate training program annual report.
1. Aged - New York (City) - Periodicals. I. Title.
NYPL [JLM 80-981]

National Urban League. Research Dept. The black aged in New York State . New York [1974?] 14 p. :   *NYPL [Sc Micro F-8063]*

New York (City). Office for the Aging. Research Dept. Selected findings on the black elderly from The elderly in the inner city: a study/conducted by the Research Department of the New New York: The Office, [1974] 15

p.; 28 cm. (Facts for action) Microfilm. "Prepared for New York State Seminar on the Black Aged, June 27-28, 1974, New York." Cover title.
1. Afro-American aged - New York (City). I. New York (City). Office for the Aging. The elderly in the inner city. II. Title. NYPL [*ZT-1250]

New York (City). Office for the Handicapped. Consumer issues and actions affecting the handicapped . [New York] [1974] 130 p. ;
NYPL [JLF 81-590]

New York (City). Office of Chief Medical Examiner. Report to the mayor on the poisonings from the consumption of alcohol or the denatured alcohol. 1925/26. New York. 1 v. 24 cm. Microfilm. No more published?
1. Alcoholism - New York (City) - Statistics - Periodicals. I. Title. NYPL [*ZAN-T5201]

New York (City). Office of Downtown Brooklyn Development. Atlantic Avenue, Special Zoning District / the Office of the Mayor, the Office of Downtown Brooklyn Development ; Abraham D. Beame, Mayor. Brooklyn, N. Y. : The Office, 1974. 47 p. : ill. ; 21 x 28 cm.
1. Brooklyn - Streets. 2. Brooklyn - City planning. 3. City planning - New York (State). I. Title. II. Title: Special Zoning District. NYPL [IRH 80-2879]

New York (City). Office of Economic Development. Report on economic conditions in New York City. Jan./June, 1980- New York.
NYPL [Econ. Div.]

New York (City). Office of Lower Manhattan Development. Special Greenwich Street Development District / Office of Lower Manhattan Development, Office of the Mayor, City of New York. New York: The Office, [1971] 55 p.: ill., 28 cm. Cover title.
1. City planning - New York (State). 2. New York (City) - City planning. 3. Special Greenwich Street Development District, New York (City). I. Title. NYPL [JLF 80-1634]

New York (City). Office of Management and Budget. Report on economic conditions in New York City. Jan./June, 1980- New York.
NYPL [Econ. Div.]

New York (City). Office of Municipal Labor Relations. [Agreement between the City of New York and related public employers, the New York City Health and Hospitals Corporation, and the Doctors Council. New York] 28 cm.
1. Collective labor agreements - Hospitals - New York (City) - Periodicals. 2. Collective labor agreements - Physicians - New York (City) - Periodicals. I. New York (City). Health and Hospitals Corporation. II. Doctors Council. III. Title.
NYPL [JLM 80-1128]

New York (City). Office of Neighborhood Government. Integrating city services: the role of the district manager / Office of Neighborhood Government, City of New York. New York : The Office, 1974. 70 p. ; 28 cm. Cover title.
1. Municipal services - New York (City). 2. New York (City) - Politics and government. I. Title.
NYPL [JLF 80-1266]

New York (City). Office of the Mayor. (Old Catalog form: New York (City). Mayor's Office)
Report by deputy mayor Edward F. Cavanagh, jr. to Mayor Robert F. Wagner regarding the Women's House of Detention. [New York : Office of the Mayor] 1965. 9 p. ; 36 cm.
Microfilm. Caption title.
1. New York (City). House of Detention for Women. I. Cavanagh, Edward F. II. Title. NYPL [*ZT-1247]

New York (City). Office of the Mayor. Office for the Aging. see New York (City). Office for the Aging.

New York (City). Office of the Mayor. Office for the Handicapped. see New York (City). Office for the Handicapped.

New York (City). Office of the Mayor. Office of Downtown Brooklyn Development. see New York (City). Office of Downtown Brooklyn Development.

NEW YORK (CITY) - OFFICIALS AND EMPLOYEES - BIOGRAPHY.
New York (City). City University of New York. Office of Urban Policy and Programs. Brief biographical sketches of appointed officials

of the executive branch of the government of the City of New York/. New York , 1974. [88] p. ;
NYPL [JFD 80-9607]

NEW YORK (CITY) - OVERTIME.
New York (City). Bureau of Audit and Control. Audit report on over-time incurred by uniformed employees of the New York City Fire Department. [New York] [1978] 19 leaves;
NYPL [*XME-9059]

New York (City). Parks, Recreation and Cultural Affairs Administration. Dept. of Cultural Affairs. see New York (City). Dept. of Cultural Affairs.

New York (City). Parks, Recreation and Cultural Affairs Administration. Landmarks Preservation Commission. see New York (City). Landmarks Preservation Commission.

New York (City). Pennsylvania Avenue landfill site. see Pennsylvania Avenue landfill site, New York (City)

New York (City). Personnel, Dept. of. see New York (City). Dept. of Personnel.

New York (City). Planning Commission. see New York (City). City Planning Commission.

New York (City). Police Dept. Crime Analysis Section.
Complaints and arrests. New York (City). Police Dept. Crime Analysis Section. Statistical report: Complaints and arrests. New York. NYPL [JLM 80-898]

Statistical report: Complaints and arrests. New York. 28 cm. Monthly.
1. Crime and criminals - New York (City) - Statistics. I. New York (City). Police Dept. Crime Analysis Section. Complaints and arrests.
NYPL [JLM 80-898]

New York (City). Police Dept. Office of Management Analysis. Crime Analysis Section. see New York (City). Police Dept. Crime Analysis Section.

New York (City). Police Dept. Office of Programs and Policies. Crime Analysis Section. see New York (City). Police Dept. Crime Analysis Section.

NEW YORK (CITY) - POLITICS AND GOVERNMENT.
New York (City). Office of Neighborhood Government. Integrating city services. New York , 1974. 70 p. ; NYPL [JLF 80-1266]

NEW YORK (CITY) - POOR - MEDICAL CARE.
New York (State). Division of Audits and Accounts. Comprehensive health plan offered by the Health Insurance Plan of Greater New York (HIP) to certain medicaid recipients, New York City Human Resources Administration. [Albany] [1979] 7, 56, 18 p. ; LC Card 80-622253 DDC 362.1/0425 19
RA413.3.H4 N48 1979

New York (City) Population Council. see Population Council, New York.

New York (City). Port Authority of New York and New Jersey. see Port Authority of New York and New Jersey.

New York (City). Port of New York Authority. see Port of New York Authority.

New York (City). Public Library. Research Libraries.
Dictionary catalog of the Research Libraries of the New York Public Library, 1911-1971. [New York] : New York Public Library, Astor, Lenox, and Tilden Foundations ; [Boston] : distributed by G. K. Hall, c1979- v. <1-200, 321-360> ; 37 cm. ISBN 0-8161-0320-8 (set)
LC Card 80-146184 DDC 019/.1/097471 19
1. New York (City). Public Library. Research Libraries - Catalogs.
Z881 .N59 1979

NEW YORK (CITY). PUBLIC LIBRARY. RESEARCH LIBRARIES - CATALOGS.
New York (City). Public Library. Research Libraries. Dictionary catalog of the Research Libraries of the New York Public Library, 1911-1971. [New York] [Boston] , c1979- v. <1-200, 321-360> ; ISBN 0-8161-0320-8 (set)
LC Card 80-146184 DDC 019/.1/097471 19
Z881 .N59 1979

New York City public schools facts and figures.

New York (City). Board of Education. Facts and figures. New York. NYPL [JLK 80-174]

New York (City). Queens College. see Queens College, Flushing, N. Y.

New York (City). Records and Statistics, Bureau of. see New York (City) Dept. of Health Bureau of Records and Statistics.

New York (City). Records, Bureau of. see New York (City) Dept. of Health Bureau of Records and Statistics.

New York (City). Records of Vital Statistics, Bureau of. see New York (City) Dept. of Health Bureau of Records and Statistics.

NEW YORK (CITY) - RELOCATION (HOUSING)
New York (State). Division of Audits and Accounts. Client relocation and related payments, New York City Human Resources Administration. [Albany] , 1979. 4, 27 leaves ;
LC Card 79-624387 DDC 352.7/5/097471 19
HV87.N5 N46 1979

NEW YORK (CITY) - SAFETY REGULATIONS - PERIODICALS.
New York (City). Dept. of Personnel. Annual report under executive order 109 - employee safety program. New York.
NYPL [JLM 80-702]

NEW YORK (CITY) - SEGREGATION IN EDUCATION.
New York (City). Board of Education. Chancellor's report on programs and problems affecting integration of the New York City public schools. New York, 1974. 36 p. LC Card 77-27109 NYPL [*Z-3211]

NEW YORK (CITY) - SHOPPING - DIRECTORIES.
The ultimate guide to shopping in New York /. [New York] , c1979. 48 p. :
NYPL [IRGV 80-2533]

NEW YORK (CITY) - SOCIAL CONDITIONS.
New York (City). City Planning Commission. Plan for New York City, 1969. Cambridge, Mass. [c1969] 6 v. ISBN 0-262-64004-X (v. 1) varies LC Card 78-89854
HT168.N5 A5

New York (City). Special Greenwich Street Development District. see Special Greenwich Street Development District, New York (City)

NEW YORK (CITY) - STATISTICS, VITAL - PERIODICALS.
New York (City). Board of Coroners. Report. New York. NYPL [*ZAN-T5203]

New York (City). Dept. of Health. Epitome of the births, marriages, stillbirths, and deaths. 1879. New York. NYPL [*ZAN-T5300]

New York (City) Dept. of Health Bureau of Records and Statistics. Condensed quarterly report. June, 1902- Sept. 1912 (incomplete). [New York] NYPL [*ZAN-T5208]

New York (City) Dept. of Health Bureau of Records and Statistics. Weekly mortality from the principal causes of death. 1876-77. New York. NYPL [*ZAN-T5293]

NEW YORK (CITY). SUPREME COURT. SPECIAL NARCOTICS PARTS.
New York (State). Temporary State Commission of Investigation. Interim report concerning the operations of Special Narcotics Parts of the Supreme Court. New York [1973] 21 leaves NYPL [*XME-9454]

New York City Transit Authority. (Old Catalog form: New York (City). Transit Authority)
Bronx bus map. New York, c1977. col. map 46 x 46 cm. Scale not given. Text and guide to hours and frequency of service on verso.
1. Bronx (Borough) - Maps. 2. Motor bus lines - New York (State) - Bronx (Borough) - Maps. I. Manhattan & Bronx Surface Transit Operating Authority. II. Metropolitan Transportation Authority. III. Title.

Brooklyn bus map. New York, 1976, c1974. col. map 46 x 46 cm. Scale not given. Includes two insets. On verso: chart of hours of service and diagram of "Culture bus loop II".
1. Brooklyn - Maps. 2. Motor bus lines - New York (State) - Brooklyn - Maps. I. Metropolitan Transportation Authority.
NYPL [Map Div. 80-3368]

Manhattan bus map. New York, c1980. col. map 28 x 85 cm. Scale not given. Oriented with north toward upper right. Includes text. 17 routh maps, 16 schematic diagrams of routes, and text on verso.
1. Manhattan (Borough) - Maps. 2. Motor bus lines - New York (State) - Manhattan (Borough) - Maps. I. Manhattan & Bronx Surface Transit Operating Authority. II. Metropolitan Transportation Authority.
NYPL [Map Div. 80-3370]

Staten Island bus map. New York, c1977. col. map, 46 x 46 cm. Scale not given. Oriented with north toward upper left. Text, guides to hours and frequency of service, route digram of Staten Island rapid transit, and Staten Island ferry schedule on verso. Text, guides to hours and frequency of service, route diagramof Staten Island rapid transit, and Staten Island ferry schedule on verso.
1. Staten Island, N. Y. - Maps. 2. Motor bus lines - New York (State) - Staten Island - Maps. I. Metropolitan Transportation Authority.
NYPL [Map Div. 80-3371]

NEW YORK CITY TRANSIT AUTHORITY.
New York (State). Division of Audits and Accounts. New routes capital construction program . Albany [1980] 30, [12] leaves ; LC Card 80-622249 DDC 353.97470072/32 19
HE4491.N68 N48 1980

NEW YORK (CITY) - TRANSIT SYSTEMS - AUDITING AND INSPECTION.
New York (State). Division of Audits and Accounts. New routes capital construction program . Albany [1980] 30, [12] leaves ; LC Card 80-622249 DDC 353.97470072/32 19
HE4491.N68 N48 1980

NEW YORK (CITY) - TRANSIT SYSTEMS - FINANCE.
Bigel, Jack. Financing New York's public transit system . New York, N.Y. , c1980. 2 v. (vii, 168 leaves) : LC Card 80-128796 DDC 388.4/042 19
HE4491.N65 B53

New York (State). Division of Audits and Accounts. New routes capital construction program . Albany [1980] 30, [12] leaves ; LC Card 80-622249 DDC 353.97470072/32 19
HE4491.N68 N48 1980

NEW YORK (CITY) - TRANSIT SYSTEMS - RATES.
New York Railways Corporation. Local and joint passenger tariff No. 1. New York, 1925. [30] leaves;
NYPL [JSF 79-584]

New York (City). Transportation Administration. Regional Plan Association, New York. Transportation and economic opportunity. [New York, 1973] 206 p. *NYPL [JLF 81-23]*

[Report]. [New York]. illus. 28 cm.
1. New York (City). Transportation Administration - Periodicals. NYPL [JLM 80-899]

New York (City). Transportation Administration. Dept. of Highways. see New York (City). Dept. of Highways.

NEW YORK (CITY). TRANSPORTATION ADMINISTRATION - PERIODICALS.
New York (City). Transportation Administration. [Report]. [New York].
NYPL [JLM 80-899]

New York (City). Triborough Bridge and Tunnel Authority. see Triborough Bridge and Tunnel Authority.

NEW YORK (CITY) - TUBERCULOSIS - STATISTICS - PERIODICALS.
New York (City). Dept. of Health. Births and infant mortality, tuberculosis cases and deaths. 1932-33. New York. 2 v.
*NYPL [*ZAN-T5294]*

NEW YORK (CITY) - TUNNELS.
Triborough Bridge and Tunnel Authority. Triborough Bridge and Tunnel Authority facilities. New York, 1973. 25 p.:
NYPL [JSE 80-724]

New York (City). United Nations and for the Consular Corps. City Commission for the. see New York (City). Commission for the United Nations and for the Consular Corps.

NEW YORK (CITY) - URBAN TRANSPORTATION.
Regional Plan Association, New York. Transportation and economic opportunity. [New York, 1973] 206 p. *NYPL [JLF 81-23]*

New York (City). Vital Records and Statistics, Bureau of. see New York (City) Dept. of Health Bureau of Records and Statistics.

New York (City). Vital Statistics, Bureau of. see New York (City) Dept. of Health Bureau of Records and Statistics.

New York (City). Vital Statistics, Division of. see New York (City) Dept. of Health Bureau of Records and Statistics.

NEW YORK (CITY) - WATER SUPPLY.
Quirk, Lawler & Matusky Engineers. Hydraulic analysis of the New York City water supply system /. Tappan, N. Y. , 1974. xviii, 82, A1-A9 p. : *NYPL [JSF 80-751]*

New York (City). William E. Wiener Oral History Library. see William E. Wiener Oral History Library.

NEW YORK (CITY) - WOMEN - LIBRARY RESOURCES - DIRECTORIES.
Nelson, Martha. A guide to collections on women in the New York area /. [New York, 1980?] 17 p.; *NYPL [JLF 81-437]*

New York (City). Women's House of Detention. see New York (City). House of Detention for Women.

NEW YORK (CITY) - YOUTH.
New York (City). Youth Board. The summer of 1962 . New York , 1962. iv, 64 p. ;
NYPL [JLF 80-1632]

New York (City). Youth Board. The summer of 1962 : a report to the Mayor on New York City's program of vigilance and services for youth / New York City Youth Board. New York : The Board, 1962. iv, 64 p. ; 28 cm.
1. Youth - New York (City). I. Title.
NYPL [JLF 80-1632]

NEW YORK (CITY) - ZONING.
New York (City). Board of Estimate and Apportionment. In the matter of the establishment of a new "use district" to be known as the "retail district" . New York [1929?] ii, 90 p. : *NYPL [JLG 80-226]*

New York City's efforts to improve its accounting systems, Department of the Treasury . United States. General Accounting Office. [Washington] , 1977. 29 p. ; LC Card 77-601736
*HJ9777.N42 N48 1977 NYPL [*XME-9396]*

New York Convention Center Development Corporation. New York Exposition and Convention Center : draft environmental impact statement /. [[New York] 1980. 2 v. :
NYPL [JSF 80-851]

New York Exposition and Convention Center : draft environmental impact statement / [prepared on behalf of New York Convention Center Development Corporation by Parsons Brinckerhoff Quade & Douglas, Inc. in association with Urbitran Associates, Inc. [New York : The Corporation], 1980. 2 v. : ill., maps ; 28 cm. The draft accepted by CCDC, Jan. 7, 1980 and issued for comments by the general public. "Notice of completion of draft Environmental impact statement," 5 leaves, inserted. Includes bibliographical references.
1. New York Exposition and Convention Center (Proposed). 2. Environmental impact statements. I. Parsons Brinckerhoff Quade & Douglas, Inc. II. New York Convention Center Development Corporation.
NYPL [JSF 80-851]

NEW YORK EXPOSITION AND CONVENTION CENTER (PROPOSED)
New York Exposition and Convention Center : draft environmental impact statement /. [[New York] 1980. 2 v. : *NYPL [JSF 80-851]*

New York magazine. The ultimate guide to shopping in New York /. [New York] , c1979. 48 p. : *NYPL [IRGV 80-2533]*

New York Medical College, Flower and Fifth Avenue Hospitals. Center for Comprehensive Health Practice. Symposium on Comprehensive Health Care for Addicted Families and Their Children, New York, N.Y., 1976. Symposium on Comprehensive Health Care for Addicted Families and Their Children, May 20 & 21, 1976, New York, New York /. Rockville, Md. [1977] ix, 122 p. ; LC Card 77-603390
RG580.D76 S93 1976 NYPL [JLF 81-175]

NEW YORK (N.Y.) - CITY PLANNING.
Danielson, Michael N. New York, the politics of urban regional development /. Berkeley , c1981. p. cm. ISBN 0-520-04371-5 LC Card 81-7480 DDC 307.7/6 19
HT393.N7 D3

NEW YORK POINT SYSTEM. see BLIND - PRINTING AND WRITING SYSTEMS.

New York Public Library. Map Division. Dictionary catalog of the Map Division. Bibliographic guide to maps and atlases. Boston. *NYPL [Map. Div. 81-27]*

New York Public Library. Research Libraries. Bibliographic guide to maps and atlases. Boston.
NYPL [Map. Div. 81-27]

New York Public Library. Schomburg Center for Research in Black Culture. see Schomburg Center for Research in Black Culture.

New York Railways Corporation. Local and joint passenger tariff No. 1: Borough of Manhattan, New York City, N. Y. / New York Railways Corporation. New York: The Corporation, 1925. [30] leaves; 29 cm. "Effective May 1, 1925." "Issued under order of Public Service Commission, First District, State of New York."
1. New York (City) - Transit systems - Rates. I. New York (State). Public Service Commission. 1st District. II. Title. NYPL [JSF 79-584]

NEW YORK REGION - POLITICS AND GOVERNMENT.
Danielson, Michael N. New York, the politics of urban regional development /. Berkeley , c1981. p. cm. ISBN 0-520-04371-5 LC Card 81-7480 DDC 307.7/6 19
HT393.N7 D3

New York Sea Grant Institute. Lake Ontario atlas. Albany, N.Y. , 197<6. v. <2-3, 5-7> : LC Card 80-119579 DDC 551.48/2/097479 19
GB1627.G81 L34

New York (State). Adirondack Park Agency. Adirondack Park land use and development plan and recommendations for implementation. Submitted to Governor Nelson A. Rockefeller and members of the New York State Legislature. [Ray Brook, N. Y.] 1973. iii, 35 p. 31 cm. Microfilm. Cover title.
*1. Adirondack Park, N. Y. 2. Land use - New York (State). I. Title. NYPL [*ZT-1264]*

New York (State). Advisory Committee on Sentencing. see New York (State). Executive Advisory Committee on Sentencing.

NEW YORK (STATE) - AERIAL PHOTOGRAPHS - CATALOGS.
New York (State). Map Information Unit. Inventory of aerial photography and other remotely sensed imagery of New York State. Albany , c1979. 181 p. : LC Card 79-124244
F120 .N46 1979 NYPL [JSF 81-134]

New York State American Revolution Bicentennial Commission. New York State Archives. Local records on microfilm in the New York State Archives. Albany, N.Y. , 1979. xi, 41 p. ; LC Card 80-622762 DDC 027.5747 19
Z1317 .N74 1979 F119

New York State Archives. Local records on microfilm in the New York State Archives. Albany, N.Y. : New York State American Revolution Bicentennial Commission : New York State Archives, State Education Dept., 1979. xi, 41 p. ; 23 cm. LC Card 80-622762 DDC 027.5747 19
1. New York (State) - History - Sources - Bibliography - Microform catalogs. 2. Documents on microfilm - New York (State) - Catalogs. 3. New York State Archives - Microform catalogs. I. New York State American Revolution Bicentennial Commission. II. Title.
Z1317 .N74 1979 F119

NEW YORK STATE ARCHIVES - MICROFORM CATALOGS.
New York State Archives. Local records on microfilm in the New York State Archives. Albany, N.Y. , 1979. xi, 41 p. ; LC Card 80-622762 DDC 027.5747 19
Z1317 .N74 1979 F119

NEW YORK (STATE). ARMY NATIONAL GUARD - AUDITING AND INSPECTION.
New York (State). Legislative Commission on Expenditure Review. National Guard strength

and armories . Albany, N.Y. [1980] S-4, ii, 46 p. : LC Card 80-621855 DDC 355.3/7/09747 19
UA361 .A52 1980

New York (State). Arts, Council on the. see New York (State). State Council on the Arts.

New York (State). Assembly. see New York (State). Legislature. Assembly.

New York State Assembly Conference on Growth Industries for New York's Future (1980 : Albany, N.Y.) McNamee, Dardis. Growth industries for New York's future /. [Albany, N.Y.] [1979?] 48 p. : LC Card 81-621125 DDC 338.09747 19
HC107.N7 M35

New York (State). Board of Estimate and Control. (Old Catalog form: New York (State). Estimate and Control Board) New York (State). Governor. Executive budget. [Albany] *NYPL [*R-Econ. 81-299 & TIB (New York (State). Governor. Executive budget)]*

New York (State). Board of Regents of the University of the State of New York. see New York (State). University.

New York (State) Bureau of Field Financial Services. see New York (State). Division of Educational Management Services.

New York (State). Bureau of School and Categorical Programs Evaluation. New York (State). University. Division of Research. Project ideas . Albany [1978] iv, 33 p. ; LC Card 79-621882 DDC 371.9/09747 19
LC4092.N7 N4 1978

New York (State). Capital District Regional Planning Commission. see Capital District Regional Planning Commission.

NEW YORK (STATE) - CENSUS, 1970. New York (State). Office of Planning Services. Data and Systems Bureau. Selected 1970 census statistics for New York State minor civil divisions. [Albany?, 1973] 1 v. (loose-leaf) *NYPL [*R-Econ. 78 4041]*

New York (State). Child Welfare, Temporary State Commission on. see New York (State). Temporary State Commission on Child Welfare.

New York State College of Agriculture and Life Sciences. Phosphorus managemnt strategies or lakes . Ann Arbor, Mich. , 1980. vi, 490 p. : ISBN 0-250-40332-3 LC Card 79-55150
TD223.3 .P48

New York (State). Commerce Dept. see New York (State). Dept. of Commerce.

New York (State) .Commission of Investigation. see New York (State). Temporary State Commission of Investigation.

New York (State). Commission on Cable Television. Cable communications in New York State : an agenda for government involvement : (docket no. 90112). Albany, N.Y. : New York State, Commission on Cable Television, 1979. xii, 222 p. : ill. ; 28 cm. LC Card 80-622826 DDC 384.55/56/09747 19
1. Telecommunication policy - New York (State). 2. Community antenna television - New York (State). I. Title.
HE7791.N7 N48 1979

New York (State). Committee for Jobs and Energy Independence. Energy Assembly, Albany, N.Y., 1978. An Energy Assembly /. [Albany, N.Y.] [1978]. iv, 12, 90, [40] p. : LC Card 80-621930 DDC 333.79/09747 19
HD9502.U53 N5234 1978

New York State comprehensive planning assistance program . New York (State). Executive Dept. Division of Housing and Community Renewal. New York, N.Y. [1978] ca. 100 p. in various pagings : LC Card 80-621895 DDC 363.5/8/09747 19
HD7303.N7 N393 1978

New York (State). Conservation Dept. The Conservationist. v. 14, no. 5- ; Apr./May 1960- Albany. *NYPL [*ZAN-T5219 & M-10 5488]*

New York (State). Consumer Protection Board. see New York (State). State Consumer Protection Board.

New York (State). Council on Health Care Financing. Interim report to the Governor and the New York State Legislature, March 31, 1979 / Council on Health Care Financing. [Albany] : The Council, [1979] 50 p. ; 28 cm. Cover title. LC Card 80-621874 DDC 353.97470084/1045 19
1. Hospitals - New York (State) - Finance. 2. New York (State). Council on Health Care Financing. 3. Hospitals - Finance - Law and legislation - New York (State). I. Title.
RA981.N7 N46 1979

NEW YORK (STATE). COUNCIL ON HEALTH CARE FINANCING. New York (State). Council on Health Care Financing. Interim report to the Governor and the New York State Legislature, March 31, 1979 /. [Albany] [1979] 50 p. ; LC Card 80-621874 DDC 353.97470084/1045 19
RA981.N7 N46 1979

New York (State). Council on the Arts. see New York (State). State Council on the Arts.

New York State county maps and atlas. New York (State). Dept. of Transportation. Albany, N. Y. [1974?] [46] l. *NYPL [Map Div. 79-131]*

New York (State). Court for the Correction of Errors. see New York (State). Court for the Trial of Impeachments and Correction of Errors.

New York (State). Court for the Trial of Impeachments and Correction of Errors. (Old Catalog form: New York (State). Courts. Court for the Trial of Impeachments and Correction of Errors) In the Court for the Correction of Errors. The People on the relation of Norris L. Martin and John Dikeman, vs. the President and Trustees of the village of Brooklyn. Error book. [Albany, N. Y., 1834] 16 p. 20 cm. F. B. Cutting, attorney for the plaintiffs. Cover title. Provenance: Peter Gansevoort, Nov. 29, 1834, Writ of error, no. 3 (Inscription) // Points on the part of the defendants in error, fold. leaf inserted. GANSEVOORT-LANSING COLL.
1. Brooklyn - Streets - Adams Street. 2. Compensation (Law) - New York (State) - Brooklyn - Cases. I. Martin, Norris L., plaintiff in error. II. Dikeman, John, plaintiff in error. III. Cutting, F. B. IV. Brooklyn, defendant in error. V. Title.
NYPL [*KF 1834 80-200]

New York (State). Courts. Court for the Trial of Impeachments and Correction of Errors. see New York (State). Court for the Trial of Impeachments and Correction of Errors.

New York (State). Data and Systems Bureau. see New York (State). Office of Planning Services. Data and Systems Bureau.

New York (State). Dept. of Commerce. (Old Catalog form: New York (State). Commerce Dept.) Seminar on Investing in America, New York, 1973. Investing in America . [New York] 1973. 1 v. (various pagings) ; *NYPL [JLE 80-1704]*

The ultimate guide to shopping in New York /. [New York] , c1979. 48 p. : *NYPL [IRGV 80-2533]*

NEW YORK (STATE). DEPT. OF COMMERCE - FINANCE. New York (State). Division of Audits and Accounts. Financial and operating practices, New York State Department of Commerce, Albany, New York, December 31, 1978. [Albany] [1979] 11 leaves, 75 p., 57 leaves ; LC Card 79-626155 DDC 353.97470072 19
HF3161.N7 N55 1979

New York (State). Dept. of Conservation. see New York (State). Conservation Dept.

New York (State). Dept. of Education, State. see New York (State). University.

New York (State). Dept. of Environmental Conservation. Bulletin .
(74) Eissler, Benjamin B. Low-flow data and frequency analysis of streams in New York, excluding New York City and Long Island /. Albany, N.Y. , 1979. v, 176 p. : LC Card 80-622145 DDC 551.48/3/09747 19
GB1225.N7 E37

New York (State). Dept. of Health. (Old Catalog form: New York (State). Health Board) Hoff, Margaret B. Birthweight, gestation, and infant mortality by race, sex, and age at death, New York State excluding New York City, 1968-1970 /. Albany , 1976. 47 p. : LC Card 79-625689 DDC 312/.1/747 19
RJ60.U52 N43

Induced terminations of pregnancy recorded in New York State 1978 : with five year summary, 1974-1978 / New York State Department of Health. [Albany] : The Dept., [1979 or 1980] 48 p. : graphs ; 28 cm. LC Card 80-621894 DDC 363.4/6/09747 19
1. Abortion - New York (State) - Statistics. I. Title.
HQ767.5.U5 N48 1979

NEW YORK (STATE). DEPT. OF HEALTH. New York (State). Division of Audits and Accounts. Control of hospital inpatient nursing costs under the Medicaid Program, New York City Health and Hospitals Corporation. Albany [1980] 4, 2 leaves, 32 p. ; LC Card 80-622789 DDC 362.1/1/068 19
RT86.74.N48 N48 1980

New York (State). Dept. of Health. Division of Laboratories and Research. Simpson, Karl W. Common larvae of Chironomidae (Diptera) from New York State streams and rivers . Albany, N.Y. , 1980, c1979. v, 105 p. : LC Card 80-624096 DDC 595.77/1 19
QL537.C456 S55

New York (State) Dept. of Labor. Division of Research and Statistics. (Old Catalog form: New York (State). Labor Dept. Research and Statistics Division) JOBFLO; a report on demand occupations: New York City. Oct. 1979- Albany, N. Y.
NYPL [Econ. Div.]

New York (State). Dept. of Labor. Research and Statistics, Division of. see New York (State) Dept. of Labor. Division of Research and Statistics.

New York (State). Dept. of Labor. Workmen's Compensation Board. see New York (State). Workmen's Compensation Board.

New York (State). Dept. of Motor Vehicles. (Old Catalog form: New York (State). Motor Vehicles, Dept. of) Motor vehicle inspection regulations / State of New York, [Department of Motor Vehicles]. [Albany] : The Dept., [1979?] ii, 36 p. ; 28 cm. LC Card 80-623041 DDC 343.747/0944 347.4703944 19
1. Motor vehicles - Inspection - New York (State). I. Title.
KFN5470.A432 A2 1979

Rules and regulations for conducting a drivers' school and private service bureau. [Albany] : New York State Dept. of Motor Vehicles, [1977?] 18, 3, 3 p. ; 28 cm. "CR-76/77 (12/77)." LC Card 80-622375 DDC 353.97470087/832 19
1. Automobile driver education - Law and legislation - New York (State). I. Title.
KFN5475 .A4 1977

New York (State). Dept. of Motor Vehicles. Division of Research and Development. (Old Catalog form: New York (State). Motor Vehicles, Dept. of. Research and Development, Division of) An interim evaluation of the New York State alcohol and drug rehabilitation program. [Albany] : New York State Dept. of Motor Vehicles, Division of Research and Development, 1978. 125 p. ; 28 cm. LC Card 79-625328 DDC 364.6/8 19
1. Drinking and traffic accidents - New York (State). 2. Alcoholics - Rehabilitation - New York (State). I. Title.
HE5620.D7 N417 1978

McNaughton, D. Comparison of alternate modes of drinking driver rehabilitation/Jefferson County study /. [Albany] [1979] ca. 100 leaves in various foliations : LC Card 80-621876 DDC 363.1/251 19
HE5620.D7 M26

New York (State). Dept. of Motor Vehicles. Research and Development, Division of. see New York (State). Dept. of Motor Vehicles. Division of Research and Development.

New York (State). Dept. of Public Service. Anderson, Shirley R. New York State home insulation and energy conservation act

program . Albany , 1979. 29 p. ; LC Card 80-622156 DDC 333.79 19
TJ163.5.D86 A52

Symposium on Productivity and Managerial Assessment, Albany, 1975. Public utility productivity . Albany [1975?] xv, 256 p. : LC Card 75-41898
HD2766 .S95 1975   **NYPL [*XME-9419]**

O.R. report .
(A-3) Hausgaard, Olaf. An energy almanac, New York State, 1960-1980 /. Albany , 1976. ii, 19, [25] p. ; LC Card 76-623699 DDC 330.9747/005 s 333.79/13/09747 19
H62.5.U5 N57a no. A-3 HD9502.U53N52

New York (State). Dept. of Public Service. Research, Office of. see **New York (State). Dept. of Public Service. Office of Research.**

New York (State). Dept. of State. (Old Catalog form: New York (State). State Department) New York (State). Legislature. Administrative Regulations Review Committee. The State register . [Albany] 1978. 58 leaves ; LC Card 79-625699 DDC 342.747/06 347.47026 19
KFN5010.62 .A35 1978c

Urban Development Corporation. A step-by-step guide to resources for economic development /. New York, N.Y. , c1980. 208 p. ; LC Card 80-620009 DDC 353.0082/09747 19
HC107.N73 P6385 1980

New York (State). Dept. of State. Committee on Public Access to Records. Report to the legislature on the Open meetings law / State of New York, Committee on Public Access to Records. Albany, N.Y. : Dept. of State, [1977] 12 p. ; 28 cm. Caption title. LC Card 80-622378 DDC 342.747/0664 347.4702064 19
1. New York (State) - Executive departments - Public meetings. 2. Administrative agencies - New York (State) - Public meetings. I. Title.
KFN5747.P83 A86 1977

NEW YORK (STATE). DEPT. OF TAXATION AND FINANCE. AUDIT DIVISION - AUDITING AND INSPECTION.
New York (State). Division of Audits and Accounts. Financial and operating practices, Department of Taxation and Finance, Audit Division, miscellaneous taxes, Albany, New York, as of March 31, 1979 /. Albany [1980] 5, 31, 8 leaves ; LC Card 80-622160 DDC 353.97470072/4 19
HJ3325.3 .N48 1980

New York (State). Dept. of Transportation.
Eissler, Benjamin B. Summary and evaluation of crest-stage-gage data in New York. Albany, N. Y., 1974. 24 p.   **NYPL [JSF 81-23]**

New York State county maps and atlas. Albany, N. Y. [1974?] [46] l. col. maps. 28 x 44 cm. Scale 1:250,000 Cover title.
1. New York (State) - Maps. I. Title.
    NYPL [Map Div. 79-131]

New York (State). Dept. of Transportation. Map Information Unit. see **New York (State). Map Information Unit.**

New York (State). Dept. of Public Service. Office of Research.
Hausgaard, Olaf. An energy almanac, New York State, 1960-1980 /. Albany , 1976. ii, 19, [25] p. ; LC Card 76-623699 DDC 330.9747/005 s 333.79/13/09747 19
H62.5.U5 N57a no. A-3 HD9502.U53N52

New York (State). Deputy Attorney General for Nursing Homes, Health & Social Services.
Analysis of New York's profit-making long-term care facilities / Charles J. Hynes, Deputy Attorney General for Nursing Homes, Health & Social Services. [Albany] : The Deputy Attorney General, 1978. i, 65 p. : graph ; 28 cm. LC Card 79-623522 DDC 364.1/63 19
1. Nursing homes, Proprietary - New York (State) - Rates. 2. Nursing homes, Proprietary - New York (State) - Accounting. 3. Medicaid fraud - New York (State). I. Title.
RA997.5.N7 N45 1978

NEW YORK (STATE) - DESCRIPTION AND TRAVEL - 1951-
New York (State). Office of Parks and Recreation. Interim report to the Legislature . Albany, N.Y. , 1978. 28 p. : LC Card 80-621341 DDC 353.97470086/3 19
F120 .N48 1978

New York (State). Division of Audits and Accounts.
Audit report - Division of Audits and Accounts .
(AL-St-10-79) New York (State). Division of Audits and Accounts. New York State Higher Education Services Corporation operating practices concerning the interest and default revolving guarantee account, Albany, New York, October 31, 1977. [Albany] [1979] 51 leaves in various foliations ; LC Card 79-625693 DDC 378.3/.09747 19
LA337.5 .N45 1979

(AL-St-11-79) New York (State). Division of Audits and Accounts. Financial and operating practices, New York State Department of Commerce, Albany, New York, December 31, 1978. [Albany] [1979] 11 leaves, 75 p., 57 leaves ; LC Card 79-626155 DDC 353.97470072 19
HF3161.N7 N55 1979

(AL-St-12-79) New York (State). Division of Audits and Accounts. Financial and operating practices, New York State, Division of Criminal Justice Services, Albany, New York, September 30, 1978. [Albany] [1980] 50 p., 29, 3 leaves ; LC Card 80-621892 DDC 353.97470074 19
HV7282 .A6 1980

(AL-St-44-79) New York (State). Division of Audits and Accounts. Financial and operating practices, Department of Taxation and Finance, Audit Division, miscellaneous taxes, Albany, New York, as of March 31, 1979 /. Albany [1980] 5, 31, 8 leaves ; LC Card 80-622160 DDC 353.97470072/4 19
HJ3325.3 .N48 1980

(NY-AUTH-10-80) New York (State). Division of Audits and Accounts. Profitability of branch offices, New York City Off-Track Betting Corporation /. Albany , 1980. 21, [11] leaves ; LC Card 80-621875 DDC 352.93/6 19
SF332.5.N7 N48 1980

(NY-AUTH-18-78) New York (State). Division of Audits and Accounts. Report no. 7, the New York State Mitchell-Lama program . [Albany] , 1978. 65 leaves ; LC Card 79-622401 DDC 353.97470072/32 19
HD268.N5 N26 1978

(NY-AUTH-30-79) New York (State). Division of Audits and Accounts. New routes capital construction program . Albany [1980] 30, [12] leaves ; LC Card 80-622249 DDC 353.97470072/32 19
HE4491.N68 N48 1980

(NY-AUTH-34-80) New York (State). Division of Audits and Accounts. The financial viability of Starrett City under the New York State Mitchell-Lama Program. Albany [1980] 32 p., [15] leaves p. ; LC Card 80-622788 DDC 363.5/8 19
HD7288.85.U62 N75 1980

(NY-AUTH-8-80) New York (State). Division of Audits and Accounts. Interstate Sanitation Commission . Albany [1980] 2, 18, [11] leaves ; LC Card 80-622786 DDC 353.9/3772/0974 19
TD171 .N55 1980

(NY-ST-10-79) New York (State). Division of Audits and Accounts. Financial and operating practices, Council on the Arts, April 1, 1974-September 30, 1978. [Albany] , 1979. 30, [8] leaves ; LC Card 79-624388 DDC 353.97470085 19
NX24.N7 N48 1979

(NY-ST-5-79) New York (State). Division of Audits and Accounts. Review of treatment records documenting Medicaid billings at Office of Mental Health outpatient facilities in New York City. [Albany] , 1979. 2, 8, [6] leaves ; LC Card 79-625695 DDC 353.97470082/56 19
HD7102.U5 N66 1979

(NYC-28-79) New York (State). Division of Audits and Accounts. Comprehensive health plan offered by the Health Insurance Plan of Greater New York (HIP) to certain medicaid recipients, New York City Human Resources Administration. [Albany] [1979] 7, 56, 18

p. ; LC Card 80-622253 DDC 362.1/0425 19
RA413.3.H4 N48 1979

(NYC-34-77) New York (State). Division of Audits and Accounts. Review of New York City audits of supplemental welfare funds. Albany [1980] 4, 20 leaves ; LC Card 80-622251 DDC 352.94/4/097471 19
HV86 .N77 1980

(NYC-34-78) New York (State). Division of Audits and Accounts. State financial assistance due New York City for City University community colleges, fiscal year ended June 30, 1975. [Albany] [1979] 3, 27 leaves ; LC Card 80-620516 DDC 379.1/22/097471 19
LB2826.5.N5 N46 1979

(NYC-37-79) New York (State). Division of Audits and Accounts. Implementation of the New York State tuition assistance program at community colleges of the City University of New York, July 1, 1976--December 31, 1978. Albany [1980] 4, 29 leaves ; LC Card 80-621893 DDC 378.3/09747/1 19
LD3853 .N48 1980

(NYC-38-79) New York (State). Division of Audits and Accounts. Tuition assistance program receivables and payables of the City University of New York, fiscal year ended June 30, 1978 /. Albany [1980] 3, 24 leaves ; LC Card 80-622250 DDC 379.1/22/097471 19
LD3835 .N49 1980

(NYC-39-79) New York (State). Division of Audits and Accounts. Client relocation and related payments, New York City Human Resources Administration. [Albany] , 1979. 4, 27 leaves ; LC Card 79-624387 DDC 352.7/5/097471 19
HV87.N5 N46 1979

(NYC-54-79) New York (State). Division of Audits and Accounts. Control of hospital inpatient nursing costs under the Medicaid Program, New York City Health and Hospitals Corporation. Albany [1980] 4, 2 leaves, 32 p. ; LC Card 80-622789 DDC 362.1/1/068 19
RT86.74.N48 N48 1980

(NYC-61-77) New York (State). Division of Audits and Accounts. New York City Health Department Medicaid provider restitutions, January 1, 1969 to April 30, 1977. [Albany] , 1978. 2, 10 leaves ; LC Card 79-620527 DDC 352.1/72 19
HD7102.U5 N66 1978a

Client relocation and related payments, New York City Human Resources Administration. [Albany] : Office of the State Comptroller, Division of Audits and Accounts, 1979. 4, 27 leaves ; 29 cm. (Audit report - Division of Audits and Accounts ; NYC-39-79) LC Card 79-624387 DDC 352.7/5/097471 19
1. New York (City). Human Resources Administration - Auditing and inspection. 2. Relocation (Housing) - New York (City). I. Series: New York (State). Division of Audits and Accounts. Audit report - Division of Audits and Accounts , NYC-39-77. II. Title.
HV87.N5 N46 1979

Comprehensive health plan offered by the Health Insurance Plan of Greater New York (HIP) to certain medicaid recipients, New York City Human Resources Administration. [Albany] : Office of the State Comptroller, Division of Audits and Accounts, [1979] 7, 56, 18 p. ; 30 cm. (Audit report - Division of Audits and Accounts ; NYC-28-79) "December 20, 1979." LC Card 80-622253 DDC 362.1/0425 19
1. Health Insurance Plan of Greater New York. 2. Medicaid - New York (City). 3. Poor - Medical care. 4. New York (City). Human Resources Administration. I. Series: New York (State). Division of Audits and Accounts. Audit report - Division of Audits and Accounts , NYC-28-79. II. Title.
RA413.3.H4 N48 1979

Control of hospital inpatient nursing costs under the Medicaid Program, New York City Health and Hospitals Corporation. Albany : State of New York, Office of the State Comptroller, Division of Audits and Accounts, [1980] 4, 2 leaves, 32 p. ; 28 cm. (Audit report - Office of the State Comptroller, Division of Audits and Accounts ; NYC-54-79) "Report filed May 1, 1980."

LC Card 80-622789   DDC 362.1/1/068 19
1. Nursing - New York (City) - Costs. 2. New York
(City) - Hospitals - Costs. 3. Hospital care - New York
City. 4. New York (City). Health and Hospitals
Corporation. 5. Medicaid - New York (State). 6. New
York (State). Dept. of Health. I. Series: New York
(State). Division of Audits and Accounts. Audit report -
Division of Audits and Accounts , NYC-54-79. II.
Title.
RT86.74.N48 N48 1980

Financial and operating practices, Council on
the Arts, April 1, 1974-September 30, 1978.
[Albany] : Office of the State Comptroller,
Division of Audits and Accounts, 1979. 30, [8]
leaves ; 30 cm. (Audit report - Division of Audits
and Accounts ; NY-ST-10-79)   LC Card 79-624388
DDC 353.97470085 19
1. New York (State). State Council on the Arts. 2.
Arts - New York (State) - Management. I. Series: New
York (State). Division of Audits and Accounts. Audit
report - Division of Audits and Accounts ,
NY-ST-10-79. II. Title.
NX24.N7 N48 1979

Financial and operating practices, Department
of Taxation and Finance, Audit Division,
miscellaneous taxes, Albany, New York, as of
March 31, 1979 / Division of Audits and
Accounts. Albany : State of New York, Office
of the State Comptroller, [1980] 5, 31, 8
leaves ; 29 cm. (Audit report - Division of Audits
and Accounts ; AL-St-44-79) "Report filed March 14,
1980."   LC Card 80-622160   DDC 353.97470072/4
19
1. New York (State). Dept. of Taxation and Finance.
Audit Division - Auditing and inspection. 2. Tax
collection - New York (State). 3. Tax administration
and procedure - New York (State). 4. Tax auditing -
New York (State). I. Series: New York (State). Division
of Audits and Accounts. Audit report - Division of
Audits and Accounts , AL-St-44-79. II. Title.
HJ3325.3 .N48 1980

Financial and operating practices, New York
State Department of Commerce, Albany, New
York, December 31, 1978. [Albany] : Office of
the State Comptroller, Division of Audits and
Accounts, [1979] 11 leaves, 75 p., 57 leaves ;
29 cm. (Audit report . AL-St-11-79) "Report filed:
July 10, 1979."   LC Card 79-626155   DDC
353.97470072 19
1. New York (State). Dept. of Commerce - Finance. I.
Series: New York (State). Division of Audits and
Accounts. Audit report - Division of Audits and
Accounts , AL-St-11-79. II. Title.
HF3161.N7 N55 1979

Financial and operating practices, New York
State, Division of Criminal Justice Services,
Albany, New York, September 30, 1978.
Albany : State of New York, Office of the State
Comptroller, Division of Audits and Accounts,
[1980] 50 p., 29, 3 leaves ; 29 cm. (Audit report -
Division of Audits and Accounts ; AL-St-12-79)   LC
Card 80-621892   DDC 353.97470074 19
1. New York (State). Division of Criminal Justice
Services - Auditing and inspection. I. Series: New York
(State). Division of Audits and Accounts. Audit report -
Division of Audits and Accounts , AL-St-12-79. II.
Title.
HV7282 .A6 1980

The financial viability of Starrett City under the
New York State Mitchell-Lama Program.
Albany : State of New York, Office of the State
Comptroller, Division of Audits and Accounts,
[1980] 32 p., [15] leaves p. ; 29 cm. (Audit
report - Division of Audits and Accounts ;
NY-AUTH-34-80) "Report filed April 30, 1980."   LC
Card 80-622788   DDC 363.5/8 19
1. Rental housing - New York (City) - Finance. I.
Series: New York (State). Division of Audits and
Accounts. Audit report - Division of Audits and
Accounts , NY-AUTH-34-80. II. Title.
HD7288.85.U62 N75 1980

Implementation of the New York State tuition
assistance program at community colleges of
the City University of New York, July 1,
1976--December 31, 1978. Albany : State of
New York, Office of the State Comptroller,
Division of Audits and Accounts, [1980] 4, 29
leaves ; 29 cm. (Audit report - Division of Audits
and Accounts ; NYC-37-79) "March 7, 1980."   LC
Card 80-621893   DDC 378.3/09747/1 19
1. New York University - Finance. 2. Student aid -
New York (State). I. Series: New York (State). Division
of Audits and Accounts. Audit report - Division of

Audits and Accounts , NYC-37-79. II. Title.
LD3853 .N48 1980

Interstate Sanitation Commission : financial
condition and operating procedures, July 1,
1977 to June 30, 1978. Albany : State of New
York, Office of the State Comptroller, Division
of Audits and Accounts, [1980] 2, 18, [11]
leaves ; 28 cm. (Audit report - Division of Audits
and Accounts . NY-AUTH-8-80) "Report filed: May 6,
1980."   LC Card 80-622786   DDC 353.9/3772/0974
19
1. Interstate Sanitation Commission. I. Series: New
York (State). Division of Audits and Accounts. Audit
report - Division of Audits and Accounts ,
NY-AUTH-8-80. II. Title.
TD171 .N55 1980

New routes capital construction program : New
York City Transit Authority / Division of
Audits and Accounts. Albany : State of New
York, Office of the State Comptroller, Division
of Audits and Accounts, [1980] 30, [12]
leaves ; 29 cm. (Audit report - Division of Audits
and Accounts ; NY-AUTH-30-79) "February 7, 1980."
LC Card 80-622249   DDC 353.97470/72/32 19
1. New York (City) - Transit systems - Auditing and
inspection. 2. New York (City) - Transit systems -
Finance. 3. New York City Transit Authority. I. Series:
New York (State). Division of Audits and Accounts.
Audit report - Division of Audits and Accounts ,
NY-AUTH-30-79. II. Title.
HE4491.N68 N48 1980

New York City Health Department Medicaid
provider restitutions, January 1, 1969 to April
30, 1977. [Albany] : Office of the State
Comptroller, Division of Audits and Accounts,
1978. 2, 10 leaves ; 30 cm. (Audit report -
Division of Audits and Accounts . NYC-61-77)   LC
Card 79-620527   DDC 352.1/72 19
1. Medicaid - New York (City). 2. New York (City).
Dept. of Social Services - Auditing and inspection. 3.
New York (City). Bureau of Health Care Services -
Auditing and inspection. I. Series: New York (State).
Division of Audits and Accounts. Audit report -
Division of Audits and Accounts , NYC-61-77. II.
Title.
HD7102.U5 N66 1978a

New York State Higher Education Services
Corporation operating practices concerning the
interest and default revolving guarantee
account, Albany, New York, October 31, 1977.
[Albany] : Office of the State Comptroller,
Division of Audits and Accounts, [1979] 51
leaves in various foliations ; 30 cm. (Audit
report - Division of Audits and Accounts ; Al-St-10-79)
"Report filed: August 9, 1979."   LC Card 79-625693
DDC 378.3/.09747 19
1. New York State Higher Education Services
Corporation. I. Series: New York (State). Division of
Audits and Accounts. Audit report - Division of Audits
and Accounts , AL-St-10-79. II. Title.
LA337.5 .N45 1979

Profitability of branch offices, New York City
Off-Track Betting Corporation / State of New
York, Office of the State Comptroller, Division
of Audits and Accounts. Albany : The Division,
1980. 21, [11] leaves ; 29 cm. (Audit report -
Division of Audits and Accounts ; NY-AUTH-10-80)
LC Card 80-621875   DDC 352.93/6 19
1. New York City Off-Track Betting Corporation -
Auditing and inspection. I. Series: New York (State).
Division of Audits and Accounts. Audit report -
Division of Audits and Accounts , NY-AUTH-10-80. II.
Title.
SF332.5.N7 N48 1980

Report no. 7, the New York State
Mitchell-Lama program : supervision of
development costs of co-op city by the Division
of Housing and Community Renewal.
[Albany] : Office of the State Comptroller,
Division of Audits and Accounts, 1978. 65
leaves ; 30 cm. (Audit report - Division of Audits
and Accounts . NY-AUTH-18-78)   LC Card
79-622401   DDC 353.97470072/32 19
1. Real estate development - New York (City). 2. New
York (State). Executive Dept. Division of Housing and
Community Renewal. 3. Construction industry - New
York (City) - Auditing and inspection. I. Title: New
York State Mitchell-Lama program. II. Series: New
York (State). Division of Audits and Accounts. Audit
report - Division of Audits and Accounts ,
NY-AUTH-18-78.
HD268.N5 N26 1978

Review of New York City audits of

supplemental welfare funds. Albany : State of
New York, Office of the State Comptroller,
Division of Audits and Accounts, [1980] 4, 20
leaves ; 29 cm. (Audit report - Division of Audits
and Accounts . NYC-34-77) "Report filed: March 25,
1980."   LC Card 80-622251   DDC 352.94/4/097471
19
1. Public welfare - New York (State) - Auditing and
inspection. I. Series: New York (State). Division of
Audits and Accounts. Audit report - Division of Audits
and Accounts , NYC-34-77. II. Title.
HV86 .N77 1980

Review of treatment records documenting
Medicaid billings at Office of Mental Health
outpatient facilities in New York City.
[Albany] : Office of the State Comptroller,
Division of Audits and Accounts, 1979. 2, 8,
[6] leaves ; 29 cm. (Audit report - Division of
Audits and Accounts . NY-ST-5-79)   LC Card
79-625695   DDC 353.97470082/56 19
1. Medicaid - New York (City). 2. Psychiatric
hospitals - New York (City) - Outpatient services. 3.
Psychiatry - New York (City) - Medical records. I.
Series: New York (State). Division of Audits and
Accounts. Audit report - Division of Audits and
Accounts , NY-ST-5-79. II. Title.
HD7102.U5 N66 1979

State financial assistance due New York City
for City University community colleges, fiscal
year ended June 30, 1975. [Albany] : Office of
the State Comptroller, Division of Audits and
Accounts, [1979] 3, 27 leaves ; 30 cm. (Audit
report - Division of Audits and Accounts ; NYC-34-78)
"Report filed: September 28, 1979."   LC Card
80-620516   DDC 379.1/22/097471 19
1. Education - New York (City) - Finance. I. Series:
New York (State). Division of Audits and Accounts.
Audit report - Division of Audits and Accounts ,
NYC-34-78. II. Title.
LB2826.5.N5 N46 1979

Tuition assistance program receivables and
payables of the City University of New York,
fiscal year ended June 30, 1978 / Division of
Audits and Accounts. Albany : State of New
York, Office of the State Comptroller, [1980] 3,
24 leaves ; 29 cm. (Audit report - Division of Audits
and Accounts ; NYC-38-79) "Report filed March 14,
1980."   LC Card 80-622250   DDC 379.1/22/097471
19
1. New York (City). City University of New York -
Finance. 2. Student aid - New York (City). I. Series:
New York (State). Division of Audits and Accounts.
Audit report - Division of Audits and Accounts ,
NYC-38-79. II. Title.
LD3835 .N49 1980

**NEW YORK (STATE). DIVISION OF
CRIMINAL JUSTICE SERVICES -
AUDITING AND INSPECTION.**
New York (State). Division of Audits and
Accounts. Financial and operating practices,
New York State, Division of Criminal Justice
Services, Albany, New York, September 30,
1978. Albany [1980] 50 p., 29, 3 leaves ;   LC
Card 80-621892   DDC 353.97470074 19
HV7282 .A6 1980

**New York (State). Division of Educational
Management Services.** (Old Catalog form:
New York (State). University. Educational
Management Services, Division of)
Program budgeting for school districts :
supplement to Handbook 3, budgeting /
[prepared by August E. Cerrito]. Albany :
University of the State of New York, State
Education Dept., Division of Educational
Management Services, 1973. v, 61 p. ; 28 cm.
Bibliography: p. 61.   LC Card 79-625622   DDC
379.1/22/09747 19
1. Public schools - New York (State) - Business
management. I. Cerrito, August E. II. New York
(State). Division of Educational Management Services.
School business management handbook. III. Title.
LB2823.5 .N34 1973

School business management handbook. New
York (State). Division of Educational
Management Services. Program budgeting for
school districts : supplement to Handbook 3,
budgeting / [prepared by August E. Cerrito].
Albany , 1973. v, 61 p. ;   LC Card 79-625622
DDC 379.1/22/09747 19
LB2823.5 .N34 1973

**New York (State). Division of Equalization and
Assessment.**
Adams, Sylvia. The classified real property tax .

Albany, NY [1980] 41 p. ; LC Card 80-622879
DDC 336.22/09747 19
HJ4181 .A67

Full value programs during the 1970's. Albany, NY : Division of Equalization and Assessment, [1979] 14 p. ; 28 cm. Cover title. "September 1979."
LC Card 80-621877 DDC 336.22/2 19
1. Real property tax - New York (State) - Statistics. I. Title.
HJ4249 .N44 1979a

Kupferman, Michael E. Classified real property tax systems in the United States /. Albany, N.Y. [1980] 65, xv p. ; LC Card 80-622877
DDC 336.22/2 19
HJ4181 .K86

McCord, Thomas. State agricultural preservation programs . Albany, NY [1979] iii, 49, 5 p. : LC Card 80-622880 DDC 353.9/372421 19
HJ4181 .M32

Patenaude, John J. Report on proposed State assessments of all public utility real property in New York State /. Albany, N.Y. [1980] 10 p. ;
LC Card 80-621854 DDC 336.22/2 19
HD2767.N74 P37

New York (State). Division of Equalization and Assessment. Office of Program Analysis & Development. McCord, Thomas. The quality of assessment practices in New York State . Albany, N.Y. [1980] 20 p. : LC Card 80-622878
DDC 336.22/2 19
HJ4249 .M33

New York (State). Division of Housing and Community Renewal. see New York (State). Executive Dept. Division of Housing and Community Renewal.

New York (State). Division of Human Rights. see New York (State). State Division of Human Rights.

New York (State). Division of Land Resources and Forest Management. Resources Program Development. The environmental control industry in New York State : an assessment of prospects for the private sector. [Albany] : Resources Program Development, Division of Land Resources and Forest Management, New York State Dept. of Environmental Conservation, [1979] iv, 73 p. ; 28 cm. "January 1979." Prepared by R.C. Kiddle, with contributions by R.H. Miller. LC Card 80-622827 DDC 338.4/7628/09747 19
1. Sanitary engineering - Economic aspects - New York (State). 2. Refuse and refuse disposal - Economic aspects - New York (State). 3. Environmental protection - Economic aspects - New York (State). I. Kiddle, Robert C. II. Miller, Ronald Herman, 1939-. III. Title.
TD24.N7 N47 1979

New York (State). Division of School Business Management. see New York (State). Division of Educational Management Services.

New York (State). Division of the Humanities and the Arts. Fifteen under forty. [Albany, N.Y., 1970] 1 v. (unpaged) LC Card 72-633963
ND238.N5 F5

New York (State). Drug Abuse Control Commission. Bureau of Program Planning. New York (State). Drug Abuse Control Commission. Bureau of Social Science Research. Annotated bibliography of research reports. New York [1973] 31 p. LC Card 77-100005 *NYPL [*ZT-1250]*

New York (State). Drug Abuse Control Commission. Bureau of Social Science Research. Annotated bibliography of research reports [by] Bureaus of Social Science Research and Program Planning. New York [1973] 31 p. 28 cm. Microfilm. LC Card 77-100005
1. Drug abuse - Bibliography. 2. Narcotic addicts - Rehabilitation - Bibliography. I. New York (State). Drug Abuse Control Commission. Bureau of Program Planning. II. Title. *NYPL [*ZT-1250]*

New York (State). Drug Abuse Control Commission. Program Planning, Bureau of. see New York (State). Drug Abuse Control Commission. Bureau of Program Planning.

New York (State). Drug Abuse Control Commission. Social Science Research, Bureau of. see New York (State). Drug

Abuse Control Commission. Bureau of Social Science Research.

New York (State). Economic Development Board. Household projections for New York State counties. [Albany, N. Y. : The Board], 1976. [8] p., [87] leaves ; 29 cm. Cover title. Chiefly tables.
1. Households - New York (State) - Statistics. 2. Population forecasting - New York (State). I. Title.
*NYPL [*R-Econ. 80-4783]*

NEW YORK (STATE) - ECONOMIC POLICY. New York (State). Legislature. Senate. Standing Committee on Commerce and Economic Development. Plain talk about improving the economy of New York /. Albany, N.Y. [1980] 196 p. ; LC Card 81-620511 DDC 338.9747 19
HC107.N7 N3743 1980

New York (State). Education Dept. see New York (State). University.

New York (State). Educational Management Services, Division of. see New York (State). Division of Educational Management Services.

New York State Energy Research and Development Authority. 1979 NYSERDA passive solar design awards / State of New York, New York State Energy Research and Development Authority (NYSERDA) ; [editor, designer, and illustrator, Leonard F. Tantillo]. Albany, N.Y. : The Authority, [c1980] vii, 72 p. : ill. ; 22 x 28 cm. Bibliography: p. 67-68. Includes index. LC Card 80-128412 DDC 728/.68 19
1. Solar houses - New York (State) - Design and construction. 2. Solar energy - New York (State) - Passive systems. I. Tantillo, Leonard F. II. Title. III. Title: Passive solar design awards.
TH7414 .N48 1980

New York (State). Environmental Conservation, Dept. of. see New York (State). Dept. of Environmental Conservation.

New York (State). Estimate and Control Board. see New York (State). Board of Estimate and Control.

New York (State). Executive Advisory Committee on Sentencing. Crime and punish in New York: an inquiry into sentencing and the criminal justice system, report / to Governor Hugh L. Carey, prepared by the Executive Advisory Committee on Sentencing. [Albany] : The Committee, 1979. 2 v. ; 23 cm. Vol. 2: has subtitle Appendix. Robert M. Morgenthau, chairmain. Bibliography: [v. 2], p. 339-352.
1. Sentences (Criminal procedure) - New York (State). 2. Criminal justice, Administration of - New York (State). I. Morgenthau, Robert M. II. Title.
NYPL [JLE 80-2963]

Crime and punishment in New York : an inquiry into sentencing and the criminal justice system : report to Governor Hugh L. Carey / prepared by the Executive Advisory Committee on Sentencing. [Albany] : The Committee, [1979] xvii, 214 p. ; 23 cm. "March 1979." Includes bibliographical references. LC Card 80-622706 DDC 345.747/0772 19
1. Sentences (Criminal procedure) - New York (State). 2. Criminal justice, Administration of - New York (State). I. Title.
KFN6172 .A873

NEW YORK (STATE) - EXECUTIVE DEPARTMENTS - PUBLIC MEETINGS. New York (State). Dept. of State. Committee on Public Access to Records. Report to the legislature on the Open meetings law /. Albany, N.Y. [1977] 12 p. ; LC Card 80-622378 DDC 342.747/0664 347.4702664 19
KFN5747.P83 A86 1977

New York (State). Executive Dept. Division of Housing and Community Renewal. (Old Catalog form: New York (State). Housing and Community Renewal, Division of) New York State comprehensive planning assistance program : a survey of efforts to implement state housing policy. New York, N.Y. : Division of Housing and Community Renewal, [1978] ca. 100 p. in various pagings : forms ; 28 cm. Cover title. LC Card 80-621895 DDC 363.5/8/09747 19
1. Housing policy - New York (State). 2. Housing - Law and legislation - New York (State). 3. Public housing - New York (State). 4. Housing - New York

(State) - Finance. I. Title.
HD7303.N7 N393 1978

NEW YORK (STATE). EXECUTIVE DEPT. DIVISION OF HOUSING AND COMMUNITY RENEWAL. New York (State). Division of Audits and Accounts. Report no. 7, the New York State Mitchell-Lama program . [Albany] , 1978. 65 leaves ; LC Card 79-622401 DDC 353.97470072/32 19
HD268.N5 N26 1978

New York (State). Executive Dept. Economic Development Board. Demographic projections for New York State counties : preliminary. [Albany, N. Y. : The Board], 1975. 1 v. (unpaged) ; 29 cm. Cover title. Chiefly tables.
1. Population forecasting - New York (State). 2. New York (State) - Population - Statistics. I. Title.
*NYPL [*R-Econ. 80-4592]*

New York (State). Executive Dept. Housing and Community Renewal, Division of. see New York (State). Executive Dept. Division of Housing and Community Renewal.

NEW YORK (STATE) - GENEALOGY - BIBLIOGRAPHY - MICROFORM CATALOGS. Genealogical Society of Utah. Descriptive inventory of the New York collection /. Salt Lake City , 1980. xliii, 249 p. ; ISBN 0-87480-170-2 (pbk.) LC Card 79-92984 DDC 016.929/1/0720747 19
Z1317 .G45 1980 F118

New York (State). Governor.
The budget and recommendations. New York (State). Governor. Executive budget. [Albany]
*NYPL [*R-Econ. 81-299 & TIB (New York (State). Governor. Executive budget)]*

Executive budget. [Albany] 28 cm. Annual. Report year for 1916/17 ends Oct. 1; for 1917/18-1942/43 ends June 30; for 1943/44- ends Mar. 31. Vols. for 1923/24-1926/27 issued by the Board of Estimate and Control. At head of title, 1969/70- : State of New York. Title varies: 1916/17, Revision of desired appropriations; 1917/18-1918/19, The Governor's compilation of appropriations; 1920/21, Message from the Governor transmitting statement of appropriations; 1923/24-1926/27, The budget and recommendations; 1928/29-1931/32, Message from the Governor and the budget containing financial reports and recommendations for appropriations. Vols. for 1932/33-1958/59 issued in 2 pts.
1. Budget - New York (State) - Periodicals. I. New York (State). Board of Estimate and Control. II. New York (State). Governor. Revision of desired appropriations. III. New York (State). Governor. The Governor's compilation of appropriations. IV. New York (State). Governor. Message from the Governor transmitting statement of appropriations. V. New York (State). Governor. The budget and recommendations. VI. New York (State). Governor. Message from the Governor and the budget containing financial reports and recommendations for appropriations. VII. Title.
*NYPL [*R-Econ. 81-299 & TIB (New York (State). Governor. Executive budget)]*

The Governor's compilation of appropriations. New York (State). Governor. Executive budget. [Albany] *NYPL [*R-Econ. 81-299 & TIB (New York (State). Governor. Executive budget)]*

Message from the Governor and the budget containing financial reports and recommendations for appropriations. New York (State). Governor. Executive budget. [Albany] *NYPL [*R-Econ. 81-299 & TIB (New York (State). Governor. Executive budget)]*

Message from the Governor transmitting statement of appropriations. New York (State). Governor. Executive budget. [Albany] *NYPL [*R-Econ. 81-299 & TIB (New York (State). Governor. Executive budget)]*

Revision of desired appropriations. New York (State). Governor. Executive budget. [Albany] *NYPL [*R-Econ. 81-299 & TIB (New York (State). Governor. Executive budget)]*

New York (State). Governor, 1975- (Carey) Message to the Legislature, January 4, 1978 /

Hugh L. Carey, Governor. [Albany] : State of
New York, [1978] 24 p. ; 23 cm. Cover title.
   LC Card 80-621851   DDC 353.974703/5 19
*1. New York (State) - Politics and government -
1951- - Addresses, essays, lectures. I. Title.*
J87 .N72 1978 Ja4

State of the health message : special message to
the legislature, February 27, 1980 / Hugh L.
Carey, Governor. [Albany] : State of New
York, [1980] 25 p. ; 22 cm. Cover title.   LC Card
80-623008   DDC 362.1/09747 19
*1. Medical policy - New York (State). 2. Medical care -
New York (State). 3. Public health - New York (State).
I. Title.*
RA395.A4 N76213 1980

**New York (State). Governor's Commission on
Libraries.** New York (State). State
University, Albany. Library service now in New
York State . Albany, N.Y. , 1978. 112 p. :   LC
   Card 80-622246   DDC 027.0747 19
Z678.4.N7 N5 1978

**New York (State). Health Dept. see New York
(State). Dept. of Health.**

**NEW YORK STATE HIGHER EDUCATION
SERVICES CORPORATION.**
New York (State). Division of Audits and
Accounts. New York State Higher Education
Services Corporation operating practices
concerning the interest and default revolving
guarantee account, Albany, New York, October
31, 1977. [Albany] [1979] 51 leaves in various
foliations ;   LC Card 79-625693   DDC
   378.3/.09747 19
LA337.5 .N45 1979

**New York State Higher Education Services
Corporation operating practices concerning the
interest and default revolving guarantee
account, Albany, New York, October 31, 1977.**
New York (State). Division of Audits and
Accounts. [Albany] [1979] 51 leaves in various
foliations ;   LC Card 79-625693   DDC
   378.3/.09747 19
LA337.5 .N45 1979

**NEW YORK (STATE) - HISTORY, LOCAL -
SOURCES - BIBLIOGRAPHY -
MICROFORM CATALOGS.**
Genealogical Society of Utah. Descriptive
inventory of the New York collection /. Salt
Lake City , 1980. xliii, 249 p. ;   ISBN
   0-87480-170-2 (pbk.)   LC Card 79-92984   DDC
   016.929/1/0720747 19
Z1317 .G45 1980 F118

**NEW YORK (STATE) - HISTORY -
SOCIETIES, ETC.**
New York (State) State Museum, Albany.
Survey of museums and historical societies in
New York State. Albany , 1979. vii, 67 p. ;
   LC Card 80-621017   DDC 974.7/006/0747 19
F116 .N273 1979

**NEW YORK (STATE) - HISTORY -
SOURCES - BIBLIOGRAPHY -
MICROFORM CATALOGS.**
New York State Archives. Local records on
microfilm in the New York State Archives.
Albany, N.Y. , 1979. xi, 41 p. ;   LC Card
80-622762   DDC 027.5747 19
Z1317 .N74 1979 F119

**New York State home insulation and energy
conservation act program .** Anderson, Shirley
R. Albany , 1979. 29 p. ;   LC Card 80-622156
   DDC 333.79 19
TJ163.5.D86 A52

**New York (State). Human Rights, State Division
of. see New York (State). State Division of
Human Rights.**

**New York (State). Humanities and the Arts,
Division of the. see New York (State).
Division of the Humanities and the Arts.**

**NEW YORK (STATE). INDIAN
COMMISSION.**
Upton, Helen M. The Everett report in
historical perspective . Albany, N.Y. , c1980.
xiii, 248 p. :   LC Card 80-623134   DDC
   974.7/00497 19
E99.I7 U75

**NEW YORK (STATE) - INDUSTRIES -
CONGRESSES.**
McNamee, Dardis. Growth industries for New
York's future /. [Albany, N.Y.] [1979?] 48 p. :

   LC Card 81-621125   DDC 338.09747 19
HC107.N7 M35

**New York (State) Investigation, Temporary
State Commission of. see New York (State).
Temporary State Commission of
Investigation.**

**New York (State). Joint Labor/Management
Committee.** 1978 report to the Governor and
the legislature, January 1, 1978-October 15,
1978 / State of New York, Joint
Labor/Management Committee. [Albany] : The
Committee, [1979] 11, [33] p. ; 28 cm. Cover
title.   LC Card 79-624386   DDC 344.747/021 19
*1. Employers' liability - New York (State). 2.
Workmen's compensation - New York (State). 3.
Products liability - New York (State). I. Title.*
KFN5010.62 .L3 1979

New York (State). Laws, statutes, etc. (Old
Catalog form: New York (State). Statutes)
Excerpts from New York State education law,
rules of the Board of Regents, and regulations
of the Commissioner of Education pertaining to
public and free association libraries, library
systems, trustees, and librarians. Albany :
University of the State of New York, State
Education Dept., Division of Library
Development, 1979. iv, 59 p. ; 28 cm.
*1. Library legislation - New York (State). I. New York
(State). University. Rules of the Board of Regents and
regulations of the Commissioner of Education
pertaining to public and free association libraries, library
systems, trustees, and librarians. II. New York (State).
State Library, Albany. Division of Library
Development. III. Title.*
KFN5675 .A3 1973   NYPL [JFF 80-1211]

Judiciary law--court acts pamphlet : 1979-80
black book. New York, N.Y. : M. Bender,
c1979. ca. 800 p. in various pagings ; 24 cm.
Includes index.   LC Card 80-143134   DDC
   347.747/01/02632 19
1. Courts - New York (State). I. Title.
KFN5950 .A3 1979

**New York (State). Legislative Commission on
Energy Systems.**
Conference on Wood Chips for Fuel and
Energy, Clarkson College, 1978. Conference on
Wood Chips for Fuel and Energy, Clarkson
College, Potsdam, New York, January 11, 1978
/. [Albany, N.Y.] [1978] 181 p. :   LC Card
   80-621929   DDC 662/.65 19
TP324 .C66 1978

Energy Assembly, Albany, N.Y., 1978. An
Energy Assembly /. [Albany, N.Y.] [1978]. iv,
12, 90, [40] p. :   LC Card 80-621930   DDC
   333.79/09747 19
HD9502.U53 N5234 1978

**New York (State). Legislative Commission on
Expenditure Review.**
CETA programs in New York State : program
audit, August 1979 / Legislative Commission
on Expenditure Review. [Albany, N.Y.] : The
Commission, 1979. 8, iii, 92 p. : ill. ; 28 cm. At
head of title: The Legislature--State of New York.
Cover title.   LC Card 80-621029
*1. Public service employment - New York (State). I.
New York (State). Legislature. II. Title.*
HD5725.N7 N44 1979   NYPL [JLF 81-122]

Delinquency prevention and youth development
programs : program audit / Legislative
Commission on Expenditure Review. [Albany,
N.Y.] : The Commission, [1980] 4, ii, 68 p. ; 28
cm. Cover title. "May 1980." Includes bibliographical
references.   LC Card 80-622881   DDC
   364.3/6/09747 19
*1. Juvenile delinquency - New York (State). 2. Youth -
Services for - New York (State). I. Title.*
HV9105.N7 N44 1980

Drinking driver program : program audit, May
1979 / Legislative Commission on Expenditure
Review. Albany, N.Y. : The Commission,
[1979] 3, ii, 46 p. : ill. ; 28 cm. Cover title. At
head of title: The Legislature, State of New York.
Includes bibliographical references.   LC Card
79-625048
*1. Drinking and traffic accidents - New York (State). I.
Title.*
HE5620.D7 N42 1979   NYPL [JLF 81-242]

Energy use in state facilities : program audit,
June 1980 / Legislative Commission on
Expenditure Review. [Albany] : The
Commission, [1980] 6, ii, 50 p. ; graphs ; 28
cm. Cover title.   LC Card 80-623042   DDC 333.79

   19
*1. Public buildings - New York (State) - Energy
conservation. 2. Public buildings - New York (State) -
Energy consumption. I. Title.*
TJ163.5.B84 N48 1980

National Guard strength and armories :
program audit, March 1980 / Legislative
Commission on Expenditure Review. Albany,
N.Y. : The Commission, [1980] S-4, ii, 46 p. :
ill. ; 29 cm. Cover title. At head of title: The
Legislature, State of New York.   LC Card 80-621855
   DDC 355.3/7/09747 19
*1. New York (State). Army National Guard - Auditing
and inspection. 2. Armories - New York (State) -
Auditing and inspection. I. Title.*
UA361 .A52 1980

Occupational education in secondary schools :
program audit, July 1980 / Legislative
Commission on Expenditure Review. Albany,
N.Y. : The Commission, [1980] 5, ii, 70 p. :
ill. ; 28 cm. Cover title. At head of title: The
Legislature--State of New York.   LC Card 80-623681
   DDC 373.2/09747 19
1. Vocational education - New York (State). I. Title.
LC1046.N5 N48 1980

School food programs : program audit, 5.1.78 /
Legislative Commission on Expenditure Review.
Albany : The Commission, 1978. 5, ii, 50 p. :
graphs ; 28 cm. Cover title. At head of title: The
Legislature--State of New York. Includes bibliographical
references.   LC Card 79-621326   DDC
   371.7/16/09747 19
1. School children - Food - New York (State). I. Title.
LB3479 .U55 1978

**New York (State). Legislature.
The clerk's manual of rules, forms and laws for
the regulation of business in the Senate
and Assembly of the State of New York.**
New York (State). Legislature. The clerk's
manual of rules, statutes, procedures and
precedents applicable to the ordinary business
of the Legislature of the State of New York.
Albany.   *NYPL [SEFB(New York (State).
Legislature. Clerk's manual of rules, forms
and laws ...)]*

The clerk's manual of rules, procedures and
precedents applicable to the ordinary business
of the Legislature of the State of New York.
Albany. 26 cm. For earlier file, see its: The clerk's
manual of rules, statutes, procedures and precedents
applicable to the ordinary business of the Legislature of
the State of New York. Cover title, 1979- ; Legislative
procedures manual, Senate and Assembly.
*1. New York (State). Legislature - Rules and practice -
Handbooks, manuals, etc. I. New York (State).
Legislature. Legislative procedures manual, Senate and
Assembly. II. Title.*   *NYPL [JLM 80-897]*

The clerk's manual of rules, statutes, procedures
and precedents applicable to the ordinary
business of the Legislature of the State of New
York. Albany. 15-23 cm. Annual, 1858-1945;
biennial (slightly irregular), 1946/47-1967/70. Title
varies: 1858-1946/47, The clerk's manual of rules,
forms and laws for the regulation of business in the
Senate and Assembly of the State of New York (varies
slightly); 1948/49, The clerk's manual of rules,
procedures and precedents of the Legislature of the
State of New York. For later file, see its: The clerk's
manual of rules, procedures and precedents applicable
to the ordinary business of the Legislature of the State
of New York.
*1. New York (State). Legislature - Rules and practice -
Handbooks, manuals, etc. I. New York (State).
Legislature. The clerk's manual of rules, forms and laws
for the regulation of business in the Senate and
Assembly of the State of New York. II. Title.*
     *NYPL [SEFB(New York (State).
Legislature. Clerk's manual of rules, forms
and laws ...)]*

**Legislative procedures manual, Senate and
Assembly.** New York (State). Legislature.
The clerk's manual of rules, procedures and
precedents applicable to the ordinary business
of the Legislature of the State of New York.
Albany.   *NYPL [JLM 80-897]*

New York (State). Legislative Commission on
Expenditure Review. CETA programs in New
York State . [Albany, N.Y.] , 1979. 8, iii, 92
p. :   LC Card 80-621029
HD5725.N7 N44 1979   NYPL [JLF 81-122]

**New York (State). Legislature. Administrative
Regulations Review Committee.** The State
register : an administrative journal for New

York State : a background report and proposal / prepared by the State-Assembly Administrative Regulations Review Committee in cooperation with the Department of State. [Albany : The Committee], 1978. 58 leaves ; 28 cm. LC Card 79-625699 DDC 342.747/06 347.47026 19
1. New York State register. 2. Administrative law - New York (State). I. New York (State). Dept. of State. II. Title.
KFN5010.62 .A35 1978c

New York (State). Legislature. Assembly. (Old Catalog Form: New York (State). Assembly) McNamee, Dardis. Growth industries for New York's future /. [Albany, N.Y.] [1979?] 48 p. : LC Card 81-621125 DDC 338.09747 19
HC107.N7 M35

Schiff, Arthur. The impact of food stamp reform on the Northeast /. [[Albany] 1977. 17 p. : LC Card 79-624025 DDC 363.8 19
KF3745.F62 S34

New York (State). Legislature. Assembly. Office of the Speaker. Small business, New York's forgotten majority. [Albany, N.Y.] : Office of the Speaker, New York State Assembly, [1980] 103 p. : ill. ; 28 cm. "February 21, 1980." Includes bibliographical references. LC Card 81-621131 DDC 338.6/42/09747 19
1. Small business - Government policy - New York (State). 2. Industry and state - New York (State). I. Title.
HD2346.U52 N556 1980

New York (State). Legislature. Assembly. Science and Technology Staff. Linking science and technology to public policy . [Albany] [1979] viii, 156 p. (p. 155-156 blank) : ISBN 0-915194-03-1 LC Card 78-22608 DDC 353.9/172 19
Q127.U6 L56

New York (State). Legislature. Assembly. Standing Committee on Labor. Compilation of public hearing testimony on Assembly bill no. 7 : "The Workers' compensation reform act of 1979," April 20, 1979, New York City / New York State Assembly, Standing Committee on Labor. [Albany, N.Y.] : The Committee, [1979?] 151 p. : ill. ; 29 cm. LC Card 80-621872 DDC 344.747/021 19
1. Workmen's compensation - New York (State). I. Title.
KFN5010.4 .L3 1979

New York (State). Legislature. Assembly. Task Force on School Finance and Real Property Taxation. The legislative response to the property tax crisis : an analysis of public policy approaches to classification / New York State Assembly Task Force on School Finance and Real Property Taxation ; staff for this report, Edwin Margolis, counsel to the Majority ... [et al.]. Albany, N.Y. (The Capitol, Albany 12248) : The Task Force, [1979] 66 p. : ill. ; 28 cm. "September 1979." LC Card 81-621126 DDC 336.22/2 19
1. Real property tax - New York (State). I. Margolis, Edwin. II. Title.
HJ4249 .N444 1979

New York (State). Legislature. Domestic Slavery, Joint Committee on So Much of the Governor's Message as Relates to. see New York (State). Legislature. Joint Committee on So Much of the Governor's Message as Relates to Domestic Slavery.

New York (State). Legislature. Joint Committee on So Much of the Governor's Message as Relates to Domestic Slavery. Report of the joint committee of the Senate and Assembly on so much of the Governor's message as relates to domestic slavery : in Senate, May 18, 1836. [Albany? : s. n., 1836]. 5 p. ; 24 cm. Microfiche (neg.) 1 sheet. 11 x 15 cm. (NYPL FSN 017,855) Legislature, 1836. Senate. Doc. 106. Submitted by Mr. Mack. LC Card CA26-298
1. Slavery in the United States. 2. Abolitionists - United States. I. Mack, Ebenezer.
        NYPL [Sc Micro F-9174]

New York (State). Legislature. Joint Legislative Task Force to Study and Evaluate the Pari-Mutuel Racing and Breeding Industry in New York State.
New York (State). Legislature. Joint Legislative Task Force to Study and Evaluate the Pari-Mutuel Racing and Breeding Industry in

New York State. Advisory Council. An examination of the regional off-track betting system in New York State : an analysis / prepared by the staff of the Joint Legislative Task Force to Study and Evaluate the Pari-Mutuel Racing and Breeding Industry in New York State. [Albany, N.Y. : The Task Force, 1979] 71 p. : ill. ; 28 cm. LC Card 80-621095 DDC 353.97470076 19
1. Horse race betting - New York (State). I. Title.
SF332.5.N7 N49 1979

New York (State). Legislature. Joint Legislative Task Force to Study and Evaluate the Pari-Mutuel Racing and Breeding Industry in New York State. Advisory Council. The racing and breeding industry views itself . Albany, N.Y. [1979] vi, 187 p. ; LC Card 81-622047 DDC 338.4/7984/009747 19
SF335.U6 N697 1979

The racing and breeding industry views itself : problems, priorities, and recommendations : a report / submitted by the Advisory Council to the Joint Legislative Task Force to Study and Evaluate the Pari-Mutuel Racing and Breeding Industry in New York State. Albany, N.Y. : The Task Force, [1979] vi, 187 p. ; 28 cm. LC Card 81-622047 DDC 338.4/7984/009747 19
1. Horse-racing - New York (State) - Finance. 2. Horse breeding - New York (State) - Finance. 3. Horse race betting - New York (State). I. Title. New York (State). Legislature. Joint Legislative Task Force to Study and Evaluate the Pari-Mutuel Racing and Breeding Industry in New York State. II. Title.
SF335.U6 N697 1979

New York (State). Legislature. Legislative Commission on Expenditure Review. State subsidized low rent public housing . Albany, N.Y. (111 Washington Ave., Albany 12210) [1980] 10, iii, 92 p. : LC Card 81-621642 DDC 363.5/8 19
HD7288.78.U52 N77

New York (State). Legislature. Legislative Commission on Science & Technology. Cline, James G. The status of alternative energy technologies, March 1980 /. Albany, N.Y. (Assembly P.O. Box 167, Albany 12248) [1980] 23 p. ; LC Card 81-621009 DDC 333.79/09747 19
TJ163.25.U6 C59

NEW YORK (STATE). LEGISLATURE - OFFICIALS AND EMPLOYEES.
Gleason, Eugene J. Executive dominance in New York State. [Albany, 1974] 33 p. LC Card 78-64398   **NYPL [JLF 80-538]**

NEW YORK (STATE). LEGISLATURE - RULES AND PRACTICE - HANDBOOKS, MANUALS, ETC.
New York (State). Legislature. The clerk's manual of rules, procedures and precedents applicable to the ordinary business of the Legislature of the State of New York. Albany.
        NYPL [JLM 80-897]

New York (State). Legislature. The clerk's manual of rules, statutes, procedures and precedents applicable to the ordinary business of the Legislature of the State of New York. Albany.   **NYPL [SEFB(New York (State). Legislature. Clerk's manual of rules, forms and laws ...)]**

New York (State). Legislature. Senate. Committee on Transportation.
National Workshop on Auto Theft Prevention, New York, 1978. National Workshop on Auto Theft Prevention . Albany [1979] 167 p., [1] leaf of plates : LC Card 79-623519
HV6658 .N37 1978   **NYPL [JLF 80-1515]**

Public transportation safety : a serious problem in New York State : a report / by the New York State Senate Committee on Transportation. [Albany] : The Committee, [1979] 16 p. ; 28 cm. Cover title. "June 1, 1979." LC Card 80-622830 DDC 363.1/25 19
1. Traffic safety - New York (State). 2. Local transit - New York (State). I. Title.
HE5614.3.N5 N48 1979

New York (State). Legislature. Senate. Mental Hygiene and Addiction Control Committee.
Padavan, Frank. Heroin--new sources/new users . [Albany, N.Y. , 1980] 36 p. : LC Card 81-621128 DDC 362.2/93 19
HV5822.H4 P32

New York (State). Legislature. Senate. Minority Task Force on Criminal Justice. The criminal must pay! : Restitution in New York State / New York State Senate Minority Task Force on criminal Justice. [Albany] : The Task force, [1980] 51 p. ; 28 cm. LC Card 80-622773 DDC 344.747/03288 19
1. Restitution - New York (State). I. Title.
KFN5010.72 .C73 1980

New York (State). Legislature. Senate. Standing Committee on Cities and City of New York.
Certiorari : a report on administrative and judicial review of real property assessments / New York State Senate Standing Committee on Cities and City of New York ; John E. Flynn, chairman. [Albany, N.Y.] : The Committee, 1980. 119 p. ; 28 cm. (State of New York legislative document) Bibliography: p. 114. LC Card 80-624086 DDC 353.7470072/421 19
1. Real property tax - New York (State). 2. Assessment - New York (State). 3. Tax protests and appeals - New York (State). 4. Real property tax - New York (N.Y.). I. Flynn, John E. II. Title. III. Series.
KFN5010.72 .C57 1980

New York (State). Legislature. Senate. Standing Committee on Commerce and Economic Development. Plain talk about improving the economy of New York / New York State Senate Standing Committee on Commerce and Economic Development. Albany, N.Y. : The Committee, [1980] 196 p. ; 28 cm. "May 1980." Includes bibliographical references. LC Card 81-620511 DDC 338.9747 19
1. New York (State) - Economic policy. I. Title.
HC107.N7 N3743 1980

New York (State). Legislature. Senate. Task Force on Critical Problems.
A business permit assistance program for New York State / New York Senate Research Service, Task Force on Critical Problems. Albany, N.Y. : The Task Force, [1978] 79 p. ; 28 cm. "March 1978." Bibliography: p. 37. LC Card 80-622153 DDC 353.97470082/4046 19
1. Business enterprises - Licenses - New York (State). 2. Licenses - New York (State). I. Title.
HD3630.U7 N647 1978

The popular interest versus the public interest ... : a report on the popular initiative / New York Senate Research Service, Task Force on Critical Problems. Albany, N.Y. : The Task Force, [1979] iv, 83 p. ; 29 cm. "May, 1979." Includes bibliographical references. LC Card 80-622244 DDC 328/.2 19
1. Referendum - New York (State). 2. Referendum - United States. I. Title.
JF495 .N582 1979

New York (State). Legislature. Senate. Transportation, Committee on. see New York (State). Legislature. Senate. Committee on Transportation.

New York State Library data base users manual. New York (State). State Library, Albany. Albany, N.Y. , 1979. iii, 31 p. ; LC Card 80-621015 DDC 027.5/09747 19
Z674.5.U52 A426 1979

New York (State). Map Information Unit. Inventory of aerial photography and other remotely sensed imagery of New York State. 2d ed., 1968-79. Albany : Map Information Unit, New York State Dept. of Transportation, c1979. 181 p. : ill. ; 28 cm. Chiefly tables. Bibliography: p. 179. LC Card 79-124244
1. New York (State) - Aerial photographs - Catalogs. I. Title.
F120 .N46 1979   **NYPL [JSF 81-134]**

NEW YORK (STATE) - MAPS.
(1974) New York (State). Dept. of Transportation. New York State county maps and atlas. Albany, N. Y. [1974?] [46] l.
        NYPL [Map Div. 79-131]

New York (State). Medical School Enrollment and Physician Manpower, Regents Task Force on. see New York (State). Regents Task Force on Medical School Enrollment and Physician Manpower.

New York (State). Metropolitan Transportation Authority. see Metropolitan Transportation Authority.

New York State Mitchell-Lama program. New York (State). Division of Audits and Accounts. Report no. 7, the New York State

Mitchell-Lama program . [Albany] , 1978. 65 leaves ; LC Card 79-622401 DDC 353.97470072/32 19
HD268.N5 N26 1978

New York (State). Motor vehicle, Dept. of. see New York (State). Dept. of Motor Vehicles.

New York (State). Museum, Albany. see New York (State) State Museum, Albany.

New York (State). Museum and Science Service. Bulletin .
(no. 430a-) Mosquitoes of New York. Albany, N.Y. , 1979- v. 1 : LC Card 80-622492 DDC 595.77/1 19
QL536 .M698

New York (State). Office for Education of Children with Handicapping Conditions.
Train-a-champ . Albany, N.Y. , c1979. vii, 95 p. : LC Card 81-119267 DDC 371.9/044 19
GV445 .T73

New York (State). Office of Court Administration. Committee on Criminal Jury Instructions (New York) Criminal jury instructions, New York /. [New York, N.Y.] , c1979- v. <3> : LC Card 79-620044 DDC 345.747/075 347.470575 19
KFN6171.A65 C65

New York (State). Office of Drug Abuse Services. Bureau of Social Science Research and Program Evaluation. Drug abuse prevention : the awareness, experience, and opinions of junior and senior high school students in New York State survey : report no. 2 of winter 1974/75 / Richard Dembo ... [et al.]. [Albany] : New York State Office of Drug Abuse Services, Bureau of Social Science Research and Program Evaluation, 1976. 33 p. ; 28 cm. Microfiche (neg.) 1 sheet. 11 x 15 cm. (PB-273 755) LC Card 77-622761
1. Youth - New York (State) - Drug use. 2. Drug abuse - New York (State) - Prevention. 3. Drug abuse - Study and teaching - New York (State). 4. High school students - New York (State) - Attitudes. I. Dembo, Richard. II. Title.
HV5824.Y68 N76 1976 **NYPL [*XME-9523]**

New York (State). Office of ESC Educational Opportunity Programs. New York (State). University. Division of Research. Project ideas . Albany [1978] iv, 33 p. ; LC Card 79-621882 DDC 371.9/09747 19
LC4092.N7 N4 1978

New York (State). Office of Health Systems Management. New York (State). Office of Public Health. Safe, effective, and therapeutically equivalent prescription drugs . Albany [1978?] xiv, 122 p. ; LC Card 79-621906 DDC 615/.1 19
RS51 .N484 1978

New York (State). Office of Mental Retardation and Developmental Disabilities. Deinstitutionalization in New York State : an update from the New York State Office of Mental Retardation and Developmental Disabilities. [Albany : The Office, 1978] 28 leaves ; 28 cm. Cover title. "November 1978." LC Card 80-621300 DDC 362.3/85/09747 19
1. Mental retardation services - New York (State). I. Title.
HV3006.N69 N485 1978

New York (State). Office of Parks and Recreation. Interim report to the Legislature : New York Urban Cultural Park System. Albany, N.Y. : New York State Parks & Recreation, 1978. 28 p. : ill. ; 32 cm. Cover title. LC Card 80-621341 DDC 353.97470086/3 19
1. Historic sites - New York (State). 2. Parks - New York (State) - Description and travel - 1951-. I. Title.
F120 .N48 1978

New York (State). Office of Planning Services. Candeub, Fleissig & Associates. Comprehensive policy plan for the city of Tonawanda, N. Y. /. Albany, N. Y. , 1975. v, 158 p. :
NYPL [JLF 80-1232]

LUNR classification manual: land use and natural resource inventory of New York State / Albany : The Office, 1974. 23 p. ; 22 cm. Microfiche (neg.) 1 sheet. 11 x 15 cm. (NYPL FSN 35,056) Cover title.
1. Land use - New York (State) - Classification. 2.

Natural resources - New York (State) - Classification. I. Title. II. Title: Land use and natural resource inventory.
NYPL [*XME-9096]

New York (State). Office of Planning Services. Data and Systems Bureau. Selected 1970 census statistics for New York State minor civil divisions. [Albany?, 1973] 1 v. (loose-leaf) 22 x 29 cm. Caption-title.
1. New York (State) - Census, 1970. 2. New York (State) - Population - Statistics. I. Title.
NYPL [*R-Econ. 78 4041]

New York (State). Office of Public Health. Safe, effective, and therapeutically equivalent prescription drugs : statutory authority, section 206(o) Public health law (chapter 776 of the laws of 1977) effective April 1, 1978 : certified or approved by the Commissioner of the Federal Food & Drug Administration. Albany : New York State Dept. of Health, Office of Public Health : New York State Dept. of Health, Office of Health Systems Management : available from Health Education Service, [1978?] xiv, 122 p. ; 22 cm. Errata slip inserted. Includes index. LC Card 79-621906 DDC 615/.1 19
1. Drugs - Generic substitution - Dictionaries. 2. Drugs - Therapeutic equivalency - Dictionaries. 3. Drugs - Dictionaries. I. New York (State). Office of Health Systems Management. II. Title. III. Title: Therapeutically equivalent prescription drugs.
RS51 .N484 1978

New York (State). Office of Urban School Services. New York (State). University. Division of Research. Project ideas . Albany [1978] iv, 33 p. ; LC Card 79-621882 DDC 371.9/09747 19
LC4092.N7 N4 1978

New York (State). Palisades Interstate Park Commission. see Palisades Interstate Park Commission (New York and New Jersey)

New York (State). Parks and Recreation, Office of. see New York (State). Office of Parks and Recreation.

New York (State). Parks and Recreation, State Council of. see New York (State). State Council of Parks and Recreation.

New York (State). Planning Services, Office of. see New York (State). Office of Planning Services.

NEW YORK (STATE) - POLITICS AND GOVERNMENT - 1951- - ADDRESSES, ESSAYS, LECTURES.
New York (State). Governor, 1975- (Carey) Message to the Legislature, January 4, 1978 /. [Albany] [1978] 24 p. ; LC Card 80-621851 DDC 353.974703/5 19
J87 .N72 1978 Ja4

NEW YORK (STATE) - POPULATION - STATISTICS.
New York (State). Executive Dept. Economic Development Board. Demographic projections for New York State counties . [Albany, N. Y.] 1975. 1 v. (unpaged) ;
NYPL [*R-Econ. 80-4592]

New York (State). Office of Planning Services. Data and Systems Bureau. Selected 1970 census statistics for New York State minor civil divisions. [Albany?, 1973] 1 v. (loose-leaf)
NYPL [*R-Econ. 78 4041]

New York (State). Port Authority of New York and New Jersey. see Port Authority of New York and New Jersey.

New York (State). Port of New York Authority. see Port of New York Authority.

NEW YORK (STATE) - PUBLIC LANDS - TAXATION.
Dorn, Alan D. Taxation of New York State owned lands /. Albany, N.Y. [1980] 36 p. : LC Card 80-622831 DDC 336.22/5 19
HJ9288 .D67

New York (State). Public Service Commission. 1st District. New York Railways Corporation. Local and joint passenger tariff No. 1. New York, 1925. [30] leaves;
NYPL [JSF 79-584]

New York (State). Public Service, Dept. of. see New York (State). Dept. of Public Service.

New York (State). Racing and Wagering Board. see New York (State). State Racing and Wagering Board.

New York State Racing and Wagering Board drug medication study . Boyd, Joseph H. [Albany] , 1976. 69 leaves ; LC Card 78-621360 DDC 636.1/089558 19
SF951 .B79

New York State real property tax circuit breaker relief /. Boyd, Donald, 1955- Albany, NY [1979] iii, 38 p. ; LC Card 80-622832 DDC 336.22 19
HJ4249 .B69

New York (State). Regents Task Force on Medical School Enrollment and Physician Manpower. Interim report and synopsis of the findings to date of the Regents Task Force on Medical School Enrollment and Physician Manpower to the Regents of the University of the State of New York. Albany : The Task Force, 1974. vi, 90 p. : graphs ; 28 cm. Includes bibliographical references.
1. Medical education - New York (State). 2. Medical colleges - New York (State). 3. Physicians - New York (State) - Supply and demand. I. New York (State). University. **NYPL [JFF 81-279]**

NEW YORK STATE REGISTER.
New York (State). Legislature. Administrative Regulations Review Committee. The State register . [Albany] 1978. 58 leaves ; LC Card 79-625699 DDC 342.747/06 347.47026 19
KFN5010.62 .A35 1978c

New York (State). Revise the Social Services Law, State Temporary Commission to. see New York (State). State Temporary Commission to Revise the Social Services Law.

New York (State). St. Lawrence-Eastern Ontario Commission. Evaluation of shore structures and shore erodibility : St. Lawrence River, New York State / submitted to Saint Lawrence Seaway Development Corporation by St. Lawrence-Eastern Ontario Commission. Massena, N.Y. : U. S. Dept. of Transportation, St. Lawrence Seaway Development Corp. ; Watertown, N.Y. : The Commission, 1977. vi, 165 p. : ill. ; 28 cm. Includes bibliographical references. LC Card 80-621706 DDC 627/.12 19
1. Shore protection - St. Lawrence River. 2. Erosion - St. Lawrence River. I. St. Lawrence Seaway Development Corporation. II. Title.
TC225.S138 N48 1977

New York (State). Sentencing, Executive Advisory Committee on. see New York (State). Executive Advisory Committee on Sentencing.

New York (State). Social Services Law, State Temporary Commission to Revise the. see New York (State). State Temporary Commission to Revise the Social Services Law.

New York (State). State Board of Equalization and Assessment. Educational finance and the New York State real property tax : full value assessing and equalization / State Board of Equalization and Assessment. Albany, NY : The Board, 1979. 56 p. ; 28 cm. Cover title. LC Card 80-621873 DDC 379.1/3 19
1. Real property tax - New York (State). 2. Assessment - New York (State). 3. Education - New York (State) - Finance. I. Title.
HJ4249 .N45 1979

New York (State). State Cabinet of Natural History. see New York (State) State Museum, Albany.

New York (State). State College of Agriculture and Life Sciences. see New York State College of Agriculture and Life Sciences.

New York (State). State Consumer Protection Board. The profits of failure : the proprietary vocational school industry in New York State : a report / by the New York State Consumer Protection Board. Albany, N.Y. : The Board, [1978] 114 p. ; 28 cm. Cover title. Includes bibliographical references. LC Card 80-621030
1. Vocational education - New York (State). 2. Trade schools - New York (State). I. Title.
LC1046.N5 N48 1978 **NYPL [JLF 80-1578]**

New York (State). State Council of Parks and Recreation. People, resources, recreation, 1978 : New York statewide comprehensive recreation plan. [Albany] : State of New York, New York State Office of Parks & Recreation, State Council of Parks & Recreation, [1978]

364 p. : ill., maps (1 fold. in pocket) ; 30 cm.
"March 1978." LC Card 80-623046 DDC
353.0085/09747 19
1. Outdoor recreation - New York (State) - Planning. I. Title.
GV191.42.N7 N48 1978

NEW YORK (STATE). STATE COUNCIL ON THE ARTS. (Old Catalog form: New York (State). Arts, Council on the)
New York (State). Division of Audits and Accounts. Financial and operating practices, Council on the Arts, April 1, 1974-September 30, 1978. [Albany] , 1979. 30, [8] leaves ; LC Card 79-624388 DDC 353.97470085 19
NX24.N7 N48 1979

New York (State). State Department. see New York (State). Dept. of State.

New York (State). State, Dept. of. see New York (State). Dept. of State.

New York (State). State Dept. of Education. see New York (State). University.

New York (State). State Division of Human Rights. (Old Catalog form: New York (State). Human Rights, Division of)
Official human rights agencies in New York State. New York. 28 cm.
1. Civil rights - New York (State) - Directories. I. Title.
NYPL [JLM 80-711]

New York (State). State Library, Albany.
Gehring, Charles. A guide to Dutch manuscripts relating to New Netherland in United States repositories /. Albany , 1978. ix, 138 p. ; LC Card 79-624962
Z1361.D8 G45 E184.D9 NYPL [IF 80-2567]

Miscellaneous publication. no. 2- ; June 1977-Albany. *NYPL [Econ. Div.]*
New York State Library data base users manual. Albany, N.Y. : University of the State of New York, State Education Dept., New York State Library, 1979. iii, 31 p. ; 28 cm.
Errata sheet inserted. LC Card 80-621015 DDC 027.5/09747 19
1. New York (State). State Library, Albany. Database Services. 2. Bibliographical services - New York (State). 3. Machine-readable bibliographic data. I. Title.
Z674.5.U52 A426 1979

NEW YORK (STATE). STATE LIBRARY, ALBANY. DATABASE SERVICES.
New York (State). State Library, Albany. New York State Library data base users manual. Albany, N.Y. , 1979. iii, 31 p. ; LC Card 80-621015 DDC 027.5/09747 19
Z674.5.U52 A426 1979

New York (State). State Library, Albany. Division of Library Development. New York (State). Laws, statutes, etc. Excerpts from New York State education law, rules of the Board of Regents, and regulations of the Commissioner of Education pertaining to public and free association libraries, library systems, trustees, and librarians. Albany , 1979. iv, 59 p. ;
KFN5675 .A3 1973 NYPL [JFF 80-1211]

New York (State). State Library, Albany. Legislative and Governmental Services. Holt, Dorothy. State legislatures . Albany, N.Y. [1980] 9 p. ; LC Card 80-622699 DDC 016.32873 19
Z7164.R4 H6 JK2488

New York (State) State Museum, Albany.
New York, the State of art. [Albany , 1977?] 59 p. : LC Card 80-622455 DDC 709/.747/074014743 19
N6530.N7 N48

Survey of museums and historical societies in New York State. Albany : University of the State of New York, State Education Dept., New York State Museum, Cultural Education Center, 1979. vii, 67 p. ; 28 cm. Includes bibliographical references. LC Card 80-621017 DDC 974.7/006/0747 19
1. New York (State) - History - Societies, etc. 2. Museums - New York (State). I. Title.
F116 .N273 1979

Wissig, George C. Bedrock geology of the Ossining quadrangle, New York /. Albany , 1979. 1 portfolio ; LC Card 80-621857 DDC 557.47/277 19
QE146.W35 W53

New York (State). State Museum and Science Service.

Bulletin .
(no. 430a) Means, Robert G. The genus Aedes Meigen, with identification keys to genera of Culicidae /. Albany, N.Y. , 1979. x, 221 p. : LC Card 80-621820 DDC 595.77/1 s 595.77/1 19
QL536 .M698 Pt. 1

(no. 432) McCabe, Timothy Lee. A reclassification of the Polia complex for North America (Lepidoptera: Noctuidae) /. Albany, N.Y. [1980] vi, 141 p. : LC Card 80-623061 DDC 595.78/1 19
QL561.N7 M27

(no. 433) Baird, Gordon C. Sedimentary relationships of Portland Point and associated Middle Devonian rocks in central and western New York /. Albany, N.Y. [1979] iv, 24 p. : LC Card 79-625700 DDC 551.7/4 19
QE665 .B23

(no. 435) Mitchell, Richard Sheppard, 1938-Magnoliaceae through Ceratophyllaceae of New York State /. Albany, N.Y. , 1979. vi, 62 p. : LC Card 80-621817 DDC 581.9747 19
QK177 .M67

New York (State). State Racing and Wagering Board. Boyd, Joseph H. New York State Racing and Wagering Board drug medication study . [Albany] , 1976. 69 leaves ; LC Card 78-621360 DDC 636.1/089558 19
SF951 .B79

New York (State). State Study Commission for New York City. Task Force on Health and Hospitals. Health care needs and the New York City Health and Hospitals Corporation / Task Force on Health and Hospitals. - New York : The Temporary State Commission to Make a Study of the Governmental Operation of the City of New York, 1973. iv, 183 p. ; 28 cm.
1. Medical care - New York (City).
NYPL [JLF 80-1463]

New York (State). State Temporary Commission to Revise the Social Services Law.
Children in need : an assessment of the foster care program in New York State / New York State Temporary Commission to Revise the Social Services Law ; William T. Smith, II, chairman. Albany, N.Y. : The Commission, 1978. iii, 55 p. ; 28 cm. (Interim study report - New York State Temporary Commission to Revise the Social Services Law ; no. 7) Includes bibliographical references. LC Card 79-623521 DDC 362.7/33/09747 19
1. Foster home care - New York (State) - Evaluation. I. Smith, William T., 1916-. II. Series: New York (State). State Temporary Commission to Revise the Social Services Law. Interim Study report , no. 7. III. Title.
KFN5600.A73 S7 no. 7 HV875

Interim Study report .
(no. 7) New York (State). State Temporary Commission to Revise the Social Services Law. Children in need . Albany, N.Y. , 1978. iii, 55 p. ; LC Card 79-623521 DDC 362.7/33/09747 19
KFN5600.A73 S7 no. 7 HV875

New York (State). State University, Albany.
Library service now in New York State : a background paper / prepared for the Governor's Commission on Libraries. Albany, N.Y. : University at Albany, 1978. 112 p. : ill. ; 28 cm. Cover title. Prepared by A. E. Prentice and J. L. Connor. Bibliography: p. 103-110. Includes index. LC Card 80-622246 DDC 027.0747 19
1. Libraries - New York (State). I. Prentice, Ann E. II. Connor, Jean L. III. New York (State). Governor's Commission on Libraries. IV. Title.
Z678.4.N7 N5 1978

Symposium on Productivity and Managerial Assessment, Albany, 1975. Public utility productivity . Albany [1975?] xv, 256 p. : LC Card 75-41898
*HD2766 .S95 1975 NYPL [*XME-9419]*

New York (State). State University, Albany. Art Gallery. Stankiewicz, Richard, 1922- The sculpture of Richard Stankiewicz . [Albany, N.Y. , 1979] [28] p. : LC Card 80-621808 DDC 730/.92/4 19
NB237.S5793 A4 1979

New York (State). State University, Albany. Graduate School of Public Affairs.
Gleason, Eugene J. Executive dominance in

New York State. [Albany, 1974] 53 p. LC Card 78-64398 *NYPL [JLF 80-538]*

New York (State). State University, Albany. Graduate School of Public Affairs. Comparative Development Studies Center.
Baaklini, Abdo I. The politics of legislation in New York State . [Albany] [1979] viii, 102 p. (p. 99-102 blank) ; ISBN 0-915194-04-X LC Card 78-22606 DDC 328.747/077 19
KFN5723.Z9 B3

Linking science and technology to public policy . [Albany] [1979] viii, 156 p. (p. 155-156 blank) : ISBN 0-915194-03-1 LC Card 78-22608 DDC 353.9/172 19
Q127.U6 L56

New York (State). State University, Albany. Library and Information Sciences, School of. see New York (State). State University, Albany. School of Library and Information Science.

New York (State). State University, Albany. Productivity Research Project for State Government. Motivating state government productivity improvement programs . [Albany] [1975] iii, 127 p. : LC Card 76-623355
*JK2465 .M68 NYPL [*XME-9545]*

New York (State). State University, Albany. Public Affairs, Graduate School of. see New York (State). State University, Albany. Graduate School of Public Affairs.

New York (State). State University, Albany. School of Library and Information Science.
Schenectady County : a guide to the municipal records / School of Library and Information Science, State University of New York at Albany. Albany : School of Library and Info. Sciences, Univ. of New York, 1977. [136] p. ; 28 cm.
1. Municipal government - New York (State) - Schenectady County - Records and correspondence - Directories. 2. Archives - New York (State) - Schenectady County. - Directories. I. Title.
NYPL [JLF 80-1434]

New York (State). State University at Binghamton. Social Policy Institute. Local planning and special revenue sharing : a report /submitted by the Social Policy Institute of the State University of New York at Binghamton to the Institute for Public Policy Alternatives. [Albany?] : Institute for Public Policy Alternatives, State University of New York, 1975. i, 37 leaves ; 28 cm. LC Card 76-623363 DDC 331.11/09747 19
1. Manpower policy - New York (State). 2. Occupational training - New York (State). 3. Revenue sharing - New York (State). I. New York (State). State University. Institute for Public Policy Alternatives. II. Title.
HD5725.N7 N47 1975

New York (State). State University at Stony Brook. Library.
Poetry tapes at Stony Brook : an annotated catalog / compiled and annotated by Joseph A. Lipari ; project director, Esther J. Walls. Stony Brook, N.Y. : University Libraries, State University of New York at Stony Brook, c1980. iv, 80 p. ; 22 cm. Includes index. LC Card 80-152658 DDC 016.80881 19
1. Poetry - Phonotape catalogs. 2. Poetry - Video tape catalogs. 3. New York (State). State University at Stony Brook. Library - Catalogs. I. Lipari, Joseph A. II. Title.
PN1064 .N4 1980

NEW YORK (STATE). STATE UNIVERSITY AT STONY BROOK. LIBRARY - CATALOGS.
New York (State). State University at Stony Brook. Library. Poetry tapes at Stony Brook . Stony Brook, N.Y. , c1980. iv, 80 p. ; LC Card 80-152658 DDC 016.80881 19
PN1064 .N4 1980

New York (State). State University at Stony Brook. Marine Sciences Research Center. Special report .
(12) Surficial sediments and seagrasses of eastern Great South Bay, N.Y. /. Stony Brook, N.Y. , 1978. ii, 30 p. ; LC Card 80-620917 DDC 551.46/146 19
GC383 .S87

New York (State). State University. College of Education, Oswego. see New York State. State University College, Oswego.

New York State. State University College, Oswego.
Historical sketches relating to the first quarter century of the State Normal and Training School at Oswego, N. Y. Oswego, N. Y., R. J. Oliphant, job printer, bookbinder and stationer, 1888. 303 p., 1 l. front., pl., ports. 23 cm. On cover: First quarter century, 1887. State Normal and Training School, Oswego, N. Y. Historical sketches. List of teachers and biographical sketches: p. [131]-202. "Necrological report": p. [204]-208. "Alphabetical list of graduates ... for the first twenty-five years": p. [209]-233. "History of graduates ... to July 6th, 1886, inclusive: p. [234]-306. LC Card 34-17567
1. New York (State). State University College, Oswego - History. I. Title. **NYPL [JFD 79-5928]**

NEW YORK (STATE). STATE UNIVERSITY COLLEGE, OSWEGO - HISTORY.
New York State. State University College, Oswego. Historical sketches relating to the first quarter century of the State Normal and Training School at Oswego, N. Y. Oswego, N. Y., 1888. 303 p., 1 l. LC Card 34-17567
NYPL [JFD 79-5928]

New York (State). State University. Institute for Public Policy Alternatives. New York (State). State University at Binghamton. Social Policy Institute. Local planning and special revenue sharing . [Albany?] , 1975. i, 37 leaves ; LC Card 76-623363 DDC 331.11/09747 19
HD5725.N7 N47 1975

NEW YORK (STATE) - STATISTICS, MEDICAL.
Occupational exposure to talc containing asbestos . Cincinnati, Ohio , Washington, D.C. , 1980. xiii, 106 p. : LC Card 80-602295 DDC 363.1/79 19
RC965.A7 O22

New York (State). Statutes. see New York (State). Laws, statutes, etc.

New York (State). Task Force on Health and Hospitals. see New York (State). State Study Commission for New York City. Task Force on Health and Hospitals.

New York (State). Task Force on Medical School Enrollment and Physician Manpower, Regents. see New York (State). Regents Task Force on Medical School Enrollment and Physician Manpower.

New York (State). Temporary Commission to Revise the Social Services Law. see New York (State). State Temporary Commission to Revise the Social Services Law.

New York (State). Temporary State Commission of Investigation.
Interim report concerning the operations of Special Narcotics Parts of the Supreme Court. New York [1973] 21 leaves 28 cm. Microfiche (neg.) 1 sheet. 11 x 15 cm. (NYPL FSN 35,558) Cover title.
1. New York (City). Supreme Court. Special Narcotics Parts. 2. Narcotics, Control of - New York (City). I. Title. **NYPL [*XME-9454]**

Life and death at the Bronx Psychiatric Center / State of New York, Commission of Investigation. New York : The Commission, 1977. 67 p. ; 28 cm. Cover title. Includes bibliographical references. LC Card 77-622769 DDC 362.2/1/09747275 19
1. Mentally ill - Abuse of. 2. Mentally handicapped - Abuse of. 3. Bronx Psychiatric Center. I. Title.
RC445.N7 N435

Report of the New York State Commission of Investigation of an investigation of certain contracting practices and procedures of the New York City Board of Education and related matters. New York : The Commission, [1975?] 41, 3 leaves ; 28 cm. Cover title. LC Card 78-620962 DDC 353.97470085/1 19
1. New York (City). Board of Education - Administration. 2. Educational accountability - New York (State) - New York (City). 3. Conflict of interests (Public office) - New York (State) - New York (City).
L183.N5 B53 1975

New York (State). Temporary State Commission on Child Welfare. Training curriculum on freeing children for adoption / by the Temporary State Commission on Child Welfare. [New York : The Commission, 1979] 139 p. ; 28 cm. Cover title. LC Card 80-622702 DDC

346.74701/78 19
1. Parent and child (Law) - New York (State). 2. Custody of children - New York (State). 3. Adoption - New York (State). I. Title.
KFN5130 .A837

New York (State). Temporary State Commission to Revise the Social Services Law. see New York (State). State Temporary Commission to Revise the Social Services Law.

New York (State). Transportation, Dept. of. see New York (State). Dept. of Transportation.

New York (State). University.
Federal legislation and education in New York State. Albany : University of the State of New York, State Education Dept., [1980] 89 p. ; 23 cm. "February 1980." LC Card 80-623411 DDC 344.747/07 19
1. Federal aid to education - New York (State). I. Title.
LB2826.N7 N42 1980

The master plan. Rev. 1960. Albany [1961] 72 p. diagrs., tables. 26 cm.
1. Education and state - New York (State). 2. Universities and colleges - New York (State).
NYPL [JFF 78-1282]

New York (State). Regents Task Force on Medical School Enrollment and Physician Manpower. Interim report and synopsis of the findings to date of the Regents Task Force on Medical School Enrollment and Physician Manpower to the Regents of the University of the State of New York. Albany , 1974. vi, 90 p. : **NYPL [JFF 81-279]**

Position paper. no. 1-20; Nov. 1967-Nov. 1973. [Albany, State Education Dept.] 20 no. in 1 v. 23 cm. Irregular. Cover title. No more published?
1. Education - New York (State) - Periodicals.
NYPL [JLL 80-322]

Rules of the Board of Regents and regulations of the Commissioner of Education pertaining to public and free association libraries, library systems, trustees, and librarians. New York (State). Laws, statutes, etc. Excerpts from New York State education law, rules of the Board of Regents, and regulations of the Commissioner of Education pertaining to public and free association libraries, library systems, trustees, and librarians. Albany , 1979. iv, 59 p. ;
KFN5675 .A3 1973 **NYPL [JFF 80-1211]**

New York (State). University. Commissioner of Education. see New York (State). University. Office of the President of the University and Commissioner of Education.

New York (State). University. Division of Educational Management Services. see New York (State). Division of Educational Management Services.

New York (State). University. Division of Research. (Old Catalog form: New York (State). University. Research Division)
Project ideas : noteworthy practices found in New York State's locally devised compensatory education projects / prepared by the Division of Research and Bureau of School and Categorical Programs Evaluation for the Office of ESC Education Opportunity Programs and Office of Urban School Services. Albany : University of the State of New York, State Education Dept., [1978] iv, 33 p. ; 14 x 22 cm. "June 1978." LC Card 79-621882 DDC 371.9/09747 19
1. Compensatory education - New York (State). 2. Project method in teaching. I. New York (State). Bureau of School and Categorical Programs Evaluation. II. New York (State). Office of ESC Educational Opportunity Programs. III. New York (State). Office of Urban School Services. IV. Title.
LC4092.N7 N4 1978

New York (State). University. Noncollegiate Sponsored Instruction, Office on. see New York (State). University. Office on Noncollegiate Sponsored Instruction.

New York (State). University. Office of the President of the University and Commissioner of Education. Report of the Commissioner of Education, Gordon M. Ambach, to the New York State Legislature on library pilot projects, organized under chapter 787, Laws of 1978, New York State, covering the period December 15, 1978 - August 31, 1979. Albany, NY : University of the State of

New York, State Education Dept., [1977?] iii, 44, [19] p. ; 28 cm. LC Card 80-622745 DDC 027.8/09747 19
1. School libraries - New York (State). 2. Library cooperation - New York (State). I. Ambach, Gordon M.
Z675.S3 N53 1977

New York (State). University. Office on Noncollegiate Sponsored Instruction. A guide to educational programs in noncollegiate organizations. Albany : Office on Noncollegiate Sponsored Instruction, the University of the State of New York ; 1974. iv, 54 p. ; 28 cm.
1. Professional education - United States - Directories. 2. Technical education - United States - Directories. 3. Education, Higher - United States - Directories. I. Title.
NYPL [JFF 80-552]

New York (State). University. President of the University and Commissioner of Education. see New York (State). University. Office of the President of the University and Commissioner of Education.

New York (State). University. Regents Task Force on Medical School Enrollment and Physician Manpower. see New York (State). Regents Task Force on Medical School Enrollment and Physician Manpower.

New York (State). University. Research, Division of. see New York (State). University. Division of Research.

New York (State). University. State Museum. see New York (State) State Museum, Albany.

New York (State.) Urban Development Corporation. see Urban Development Corporation.

New York (State). Workmen's Compensation Board.
Research and statistics bulletin . (no. 32) New York (State). Workmen's Compensation Board. Work accidents in nonprofit membership organizations /. [Albany?] [1976] v, 63 p. ; LC Card 80-622882 DDC 368.4/1/009747 s 363.1/1/09747 19
HD7816.U7 N687 no. 32 HD7262.5.U6

Work accidents in nonprofit membership organizations / State of New York, Workmen's Compensation Board. [Albany?] : The Board, [1976] v, 63 p. ; 28 cm. (Research & statistics bulletin ; no. 32) Cover title. Chiefly tables. LC Card 80-622882 DDC 368.4/1/009747 s 363.1/1/09747 19
1. Industrial accidents - New York (State) - Statistics. 2. Workmen's compensation - New York (State) - Statistics. I. Series: New York (State). Workmen's Compensation Board. Research and statistics bulletin , no. 32. II. Title.
HD7816.U7 N687 no. 32 HD7262.5.U6

New York Stock Exchange. Conference on U. S. Competitiveness (1980 : Harvard University) Conference on U. S. Competitiveness . Washington , 1980. viii, 109 p. ; LC Card 80-603876 DDC 382/.0973 19
HF1436 .C65 1980

New York, the politics of urban regional development /. Danielson, Michael N. Berkeley , c1981. p. cm. ISBN 0-520-04371-5 LC Card 81-7480 DDC 307.7/6 19
HT393.N7 D3

New York, the State of art. [Albany : New York State Museum, 1977?] 59 p. : ill. (some col.) ; 26 cm. Catalog of the exhibition held Oct. 8-Nov. 27, 1977 at the New York State Museum. Descriptive catalog (22 p.) inserted. LC Card 80-622455 DDC 709/.747/074014743 19
1. Art, American - New York (State) - Exhibitions. I. New York (State) State Museum, Albany.
N6530.N7 N48

NEW YORK UNIVERSITY. ART COLLECTION - EXHIBITIONS.
A Handbook of twentieth century art. - Storrs, Conn. , 1973. 71, iv p. :
NYPL [3-MAVZ (New York) 80-2266]

NEW YORK UNIVERSITY - FINANCE.
New York (State). Division of Audits and Accounts. Implementation of the New York State tuition assistance program at community colleges of the City University of New York, July 1, 1976--December 31, 1978. Albany

[1980] 4, 29 leaves ; LC Card 80-621893 DDC
378.3/09747/1 19
LD3853 .N48 1980

**New York University. Grey Art Gallery & Study
Center. see Grey Art Gallery & Study
Center.**

**New York University. School of Commerce,
Accounts and Finance.** Final report, New
York University-University of Lagos Project.
[New York : School of Commerce], New York
University, [1970] 45 leaves ; 28 cm. LC Card
80-503704 DDC 650/.07/106691 19
*1. Business education - Nigeria - Lagos (City). 2.
University of Lagos. I. United States. Agency for
International Development. II. University of Lagos. III.
Title.*
HF1176.N62 L334 1970

**Newark Chamber of Commerce. see Newark, N.
J. Chamber of Commerce.**

Newark industrial directory. Newark, N. J. 28
cm. Published by Newark Chamber of Commerce.
Ceased publication with 1964?
*1. Commerce - New Jersey - Newark - Directories. I.
Newark, N. J. Chamber of Commerce.*
NYPL [M-10 2272]

Newark, N. J. Chamber of Commerce. (Old
Catalog form: Newark Chamber of
Commerce.)
Newark industrial directory. Newark, N. J.
NYPL [M-10 2272]

NEWARK, N.J. - CENSUS - MAPS.
United States. Bureau of the Census. Urban
atlas, tract data for standard metropolitan
statistical areas . Washington, D.C. , 1974 [i.e.
1975] [30] p. : LC Card 80-600863 DDC
912/.1312/0974932
G1257.N5E25 U5 1975

NEWAYGO COUNTY (MICH.) - MAPS.
United States. Soil Conservation Service.
Newaygo County, Michigan /. Lincoln, Nebr. ,
1976. 1 map ; LC Card 81-691402
G4113.N4 1976 .U5

**NEWDEGATE, CHARLES NEWDIGATE, 1816-
1887.**
Arnstein, Walter L. Protestant versus Catholic
in Mid-Victorian England . Columbia , 1982. p.
cm. ISBN 0-8262-0354-X LC Card 81-11451
DDC 274.2/081 19
BX1493 .A86

Newlon, Howard. (joint author) Pawlett, Nathaniel
Mason. The route of the Three Notch'd Road .
Charlottesville, Va. [1980] vi, 26 p. : LC Card
80-620018 DDC 388.1/09755/4 19
HE356.V8 P39

Newman, D. Paul. (joint author) Fellingham, John
C. Agency and monitoring costs in a general
equilibrium setting /. [Austin] , 1978. 24, [4]
p. ; LC Card 79-621441 DDC 657/.45/0724 19
HF5667 .F46

Newman, Debra L. United States. National
Archives and Records Service. Selected
documents pertaining to black workers among
the records of the Department of Labor and its
component bureaus, 1902-1969 /. Washington ,
1977. viii, 55 p. ; LC Card 77-12904
Z1361.N39 U63 1977 E185.8
NYPL [Sc F 81-48]

Newman, Oscar. Factors influencing crime and
instability in urban housing developments /
Oscar Newman, Karen A. Franck. Washington,
D.C. : U. S. Dept. of Justice, National Institute
of Justice : For sale by the Supt. of Docs., U.
S. G.P.O. , 1980. xiii, 302 p. : ill., charts ; 28
cm. "Institute for Community Design Analysis"--t.p.
verso. "August 1980." "Grant number
76-NI-99-0036-S-2"--t.p. verso. S/N 027-000-01025-3
Item 718-A Bibliography: p. 297-302. LC Card
81-600762 DDC 364.2/2 19
*1. Dwellings - United States - Security measures. 2.
Public housing - United States - Security measures. 3.
Crime prevention and architectural design - United
States. I. Franck, Karen A. II. National Institute of
Justice (U. S.). III. Institute for Community Design
Analysis (New York, N.Y.). IV. Title.*
HD7293 .N485

Newman, Sumner. Utah. Office of the Legislative
Auditor General. A performance audit of
electronic repair dealer registration in Utah .
[Salt Lake City] [1979] ii, 14, 3 leaves ; LC

Card 79-626149 DDC 353.97920082/42 19
HC107.U83 C637 1979

Newman, T. Stell. The Lapakahi project : a
progress report on archaeological research / by
T. Stell Newman. [Honolulu] : Dept. of Land
and Natural Resources, Division of State Parks,
State of Hawaii, 1968. 7 leaves ; 28 cm. (State
archaeological journal ; 68-2) LC Card 80-506633
DDC 996.9/1 19
*1. Man, Prehistoric - Hawaii - Kohala Mountain region.
2. Hawaiians - Antiquities. 3. Kohala Mountain region,
Hawaii - Antiquities. 4. Hawaii - Antiquities. I. Hawaii.
Division of State Parks. II. Series: Hawaii state
archaeological journal, 68-2. III. Title.*
GN875.H3 N48

**NEWS. see Northeastern United States Water
Supply Study.**

**NEWSPAPERS - BIBLIOGRAPHY - UNION
LISTS.**
Hawaii State Library. Serials holdings list .
[Honolulu] , 1979. vi, 184 p. ; LC Card
79-624871 DDC 011/.34 19
Z6945 .H4 1979 PN4801

**Newspapers on microfilm in the Washington
State Library /.** Washington (State). State
Library, Olympia. [Olympia] [1980] iii, 86 p. ;
LC Card 80-622614 DDC 011/.35 19
Z6952.W31 W23 1980 PN4897.W3

Newton, Judith Lowder. Women, power, and
subversion : social strategies in British fiction,
1778-1860 / by Judith Lowder Newton.
Athens : University of Georgia Press, c1981. p.
cm. Bibliography: p. Includes index. ISBN
0-8203-0564-2 LC Card 81-1068 DDC
823/.009/9287 19
*1. English fiction - Women authors - History and
criticism. 2. Women in literature. 3. Power (Social
sciences) in literature. 4. Feminism and literature. 5.
English fiction - 19th century - History and criticism. I.
Title.*
PR830.W62 N4

NEZ PERCÉ INDIANS - BIOGRAPHY.
Gidley, M. (Mick) Kopet . Seattle [1981] p.
cm. ISBN 0-295-95794-8 : LC Card 80-54428
DDC 970.004/97 B 19
E99.N5 J5828

NEZ PERCÉ INDIANS - HISTORY.
Gidley, M. (Mick) Kopet . Seattle [1981] p.
cm. ISBN 0-295-95794-8 : LC Card 80-54428
DDC 970.004/97 B 19
E99.N5 J5828

Ngoc Lung, Hoang. see Lung, Hoang Ngoc.

**Niagara County, N. Y. Economic Development
and Planning Dept.** Highway map of Niagara
County, New York, "Rainbow Country" U. S.
A. Issued by: Niagara County Economic
Development and Planning Department.
Lockport, N. Y., 1978. col. map. 44 x 53 cm.
on sheet 69 x 57 cm. Scale ca. 1:105,000. "R. W. S.
3/76." Folded title: Highways in Rainbow Country,
Niagara County, New York, U. S. A. Includes text and
illus. On verso: City of Lockport. - City of North
Tonawanda. - City of Niagara Falls. - [inset of
downtown] Niagara Falls, U. S. A.
*1. Niagara County, N. Y. - Maps. 2. Niagara County,
N. Y. - Road maps. NYPL [Map Div. 80-3317]*

NIAGARA COUNTY, N. Y. - MAPS.
(1978) Niagara County, N. Y. Economic
Development and Planning Dept. Highway map
of Niagara County, New York. Lockport, N.
Y., 1978. col. map. 44 x 53 cm. on sheet 69 x
57 cm. Scale ca. 1:105,000. "R. W. S. 3/76." Folded
title: Highways in Rainbow Country, Niagara County,
New York, U. S. A. Includes text and illus. On verso:
City of Lockport. - City of North Tonawanda. - City of
Niagara Falls. - [inset of downtown] Niagara Falls, U.
S. A. *NYPL [Map Div. 80-3317]*

NIAGARA COUNTY, N. Y. - ROAD MAPS.
Niagara County, N. Y. Economic Development
and Planning Dept. Highway map of Niagara
County, New York. Lockport, N. Y., 1978. col.
map. 44 x 53 cm. on sheet 69 x 57 cm. Scale ca.
1:105,000. "R. W. S. 3/76." Folded title: Highways in
Rainbow Country, Niagara County, New York, U. S. A.
Includes text and illus. On verso: City of Lockport. -
City of North Tonawanda. - City of Niagara Falls. -
[inset of downtown] Niagara Falls, U. S. A.
NYPL [Map Div. 80-3317]

NICARAGUA - FOREIGN RELATIONS.
United States. Congress. House. Committee on
Foreign Affairs. Subcommittee on

Inter-American Affairs. Review of the
Presidential certification of Nicaragua's
connection to terrorism . Washington , 1980. iii,
50, p. ; LC Card 80-603450 DDC
353.0089/097285 19
KF27 .F646 1980d

Nice, D. Stephen. Children of military families .
Washington , 1978. x, 188 p. : LC Card
79-602509 DDC 362.8/2 19
RJ501.A2 C47

**Nichi-Bei Yüko Kikin. see Japan-United States
Friendship Commission.**

Nicholls, David B. Digital evaluation and failure
analysis data / prepared by David B. Nicholls,
under contract to Rome Air Development
Center. Griffiss Air Force Base, NY :
Reliability Analysis Center, 1980. 2 v. ; 27 cm.
(Microcircuit device reliability . MDR-15) "Summer
1980." Errata slip inserted. LC Card 80-144504
DDC 621.381/73/0278 19
*1. Digital integrated circuits - Reliability - Tables. 2.
Digital integrated circuits - Testing. I. United States.
Air Development Center, Rome, N. Y. II. Reliability
Analysis Center. III. Title. IV. Series.*
TK7874 .N48

Nichols, David, 1947- Oversight of the structure
and management of the Department of Energy .
Washington , 1980 [i.e. 1981] iii, 434 p. : LC
Card 81-601669 DDC 353.87 19
TJ163.25.U6 O93

Nichols, Margaret Irby. Handbook of reference
sources / by Margaret Irby Nichols. 3rd ed.
Austin, Tex. : Texas State Library, Library
Development Division, 1981. ix, 429 p. ; 28
cm. Includes indexes. LC Card 81-149285 DDC
011/.02 19
1. Reference books - Bibliography. I. Title.
Z711 .N53 1981

Nichols, Ralph. Additional early Miocene
mammals from the Lemhi Valley of Idaho /
Ralph Nichols. [Pocatello] : Idaho State
University Museum of Natural History, 1979.
12 p. : ill. ; 23 cm. (Tebiwa . no. 17) Bibliography:
p. 10. LC Card 79-624993 DDC 500 s 569 19
*1. Mammals, Fossil. 2. Paleontology - Miocene. 3.
Paleontology - Idaho - Lemhi Co. I. Title. II. Series.*
E78.I18 T43 no. 17 QE881

Nichols, Thomas Everett. (joint author) Johnson,
Marc A. Grain movements to and from North
Carolina grain handling and processing firms,
1977 /. Raleigh, N.C. , 1979. 43 p. : LC Card
80-622293 DDC 338.1 s 380.1/4131/09756 19
S97 .Z4 no. 59 HE199.5.G7

Nicholson, John C. Soil survey of Goochland
County, Virginia / [by John C. Nicholson,
Thomas R. Burruss, and David L. Jones] ;
United States Department of Agriculture, Soil
Conservation Service, in cooperation with the
Virginia Polytechnic Institute and State
University. [Washington] : The Service, 1980.
ix, 137 p., [22] fold. leaves of plates : ill.,
maps ; 29 cm. Cover title. "Issued February 1980."
Bibliography: p. 74. LC Card 80-601854 DDC
631.4/7/755455 19
*1. Soils - Virginia - Goochland Co. - Maps. I. Burruss,
Thomas R., joint author. II. Jones, David L., joint
author. III. United States. Soil Conservation Service. IV.
Virginia Polytechnic Institute and State University. V.
Title.*
S599.V8 N52

**NICKEL-CADMIUM BATTERIES -
RECYCLING.**
Wilson, D. A. (Donald A.) A pyrometallurgical
method for processing Ni-Cd scrap batteries .
[Washington, D.C.] [1981] p. cm. LC Card
81-10151 DDC 622 s 669/.56 19
TN23 .U43 TN799.N6

NICKEL - ELECTROMETALLURGY.
Mussler, R. E. (Ralph E.) Electrowinning of
nickel and cobalt from domestic laterite
processing . [Avondale, MD] [1981] p. cm.
LC Card 81-607807 DDC 622 s 669/.733 19
TN23 .U43 TN799.N6

NICKEL - METALLURGY.
Haas, L. A. (Larry A.) Low pressure leaching
of Duluth complex matte /. Avondale, Md. ,
1981. p. cm. LC Card 80-606897 DDC 622 s
669/.7332 19
TN23 .U43 TN799.N6

Nilsen, D. N. Solvent extraction of nickel and
copper from laterite-ammoniacal leach liquors /.

Avondale, MD , 1981. p. cm. LC Card 81-38488 DDC 622 s 669/.7332 19
TN23 .U43 TN799.N6

Wilson, D. A. (Donald A.) A pyrometallurgical method for processing Ni-Cd scrap batteries /. [Washington, D.C.] [1981] p. cm. LC Card 81-10151 DDC 622 s 669/.56 19
TN23 .U43 TN799.N6

NICKEL SULPHIDE.
Schaefer, Seth C. Electrochemical determination of Gibbs energies of formation of cobalt and nickel sulfides /. Washington, D.C. [1981] p. cm. LC Card 81-10082 DDC 622 s 546/.62357 19
TN23 .U43 QD555.5

Nicol, Davidson. The United Nations and decision-making . New York [c1978] 2 v. : LC Card 79-126238 DDC 354.1/03 19
JX1977 .U4257

Nicolet, Claude, 1930-
[Métier de citoyen dans la Rome républicaine. English]
The world of the citizen in republican Rome / C. Nicolet ; translated by P.S. Falla. Berkeley : University of California Press, 1980. 435 p. ; 24 cm. Translation of: Le métier de citoyen dans la Rome republicaine. Bibliography: p. [423]-428. Includes index. ISBN 0-520-03545-3 LC Card 77-80474 DDC 323.6/0937 19
1. Citizenship - Rome. 2. Rome - Politics and government - 510-30 B.C. I. Title.
DG83.1 .N513 1980b

NICOTIANA.
Gerstel, Dan U. Cytoplasmic male sterility in Nicotiana . [Raleigh] , 1980. 31 p. ; LC Card 80-622299 DDC 633.7/1 19
QK495.S7 G47

NICSEM mini-index to special education materials . National Information Center for Special Education Materials. Los Angeles, CA , 1980. xiv, 53 p. : ISBN 0-89320-046-8 (pbk.) : LC Card 80-82541 DDC 371.9 19
LC4023 .N37 1980a

Nida. see National Institute on Drug Abuse.

NIDA Research monograph .
(v. 32) Foltz, Rodger L. GC/MS assays for abused drugs in body fluids /. Rockville, Md. (5600 Fishers Lane, Rockville, Md. 20857) , Washington, D.C. , 1980. ix, 202 p. : LC Card 80-600143 DDC 616.86/3 19
RS190.P78 F64

(26) The Behavioral aspects of smoking /. Rockville, Md. , Washington, D.C. , 1979. vii, 192 p. ; LC Card 79-600141 DDC 362.2/9 19
HV5740 .B43

(29) Drug abuse deaths in nine cities /. Rockville, Md. , Washington, D.C. , 1980. xi, 176 p. ; LC Card 80-600013 DDC 362.2/932/0973 19
HV5825 .D7733

(30) Theories on drug abuse . Rockville, Md. . xli, 488 p. : LC Card 80-600058 DDC 616.86/3 19
RC564 .T5

NIDA State plan for drug abuse prevention for the State of South Dakota . South Dakota. Division of Drugs and Substances Control. [Pierre] [1979] 223 p. : LC Card 80-621620 DDC 362.2/937/09783 19
HV5831.S66 A5 1979a

Niebauer, H. J. Recent fluctuations in meteorological and oceanographic parameters in Alaska waters / by H. J. Niebauer. Fairbanks, Alaska : Alaska Sea Grant Program, University of Alaska, [1980] iv, 34 p. : ill. ; 28 cm. (Alaska sea grant report. 79-12) IMS report ; 79-2 "February 1980." Bibliography: p. 32-34. LC Card 80-623130 DDC 551.46 551.46/634 19
1. Meteorology, Maritime - Alaska, Gulf of. 2. Meteorology, Maritime - Bering Sea. 3. Ocean temperature - Alaska, Gulf of. 4. Ocean temperature - Bering Sea. 5. Ice - Alaska, Gulf of. 6. Ice - Bering Sea. I. Alaska Sea Grant Program. II. Series: University of Alaska, Fairbanks. Institute of Marine Science. Institute of Marine Science report ; 79-2. III. Title.
GC1 .A497 no. 79-2 QC994.6

Nielson, Woodrow. Soil survey of Navajo Indian Reservation, San Juan County, Utah / [by Woodrow Nielson and Austin J. Erickson] ; United States Department of Agriculture, Soil Conservation Service, and United States

Department of the Interior, Bureau of Indian Affairs, in cooperation with the Utah Agricultural Experiment Station. [Washington] : The Service, [1980] viii, 119 p., [12] fold. leaves of plates : ill. (some col.) ; 29 cm. Cover title. LC Card 80-602348 DDC 631.4/7/79259 19
1. Soils - Utah - San Juan Co. - Maps. 2. Soils - Navaho Indian Reservation - Maps. 3. Navaho Indian Reservation - Maps. I. Erickson, Austin J., joint author. II. United States. Soil Conservation Service. III. United States. Bureau of Indian Affairs. IV. Utah. Agricultural Experiment Station, Logan. V. Title.
S599.U8 N53

Nigbor, M. T. (Michael T.) Case history of a pilot scale acidic in situ uranium leaching experiment / by M.T. Nigbor, W.H. Engelmann, and D. R. Tweeton. Avondale, MD : U. S. Dept. of the Interior, Bureau of Mines, 1981. p. cm. (Report of investigations) Bibliography: p. LC Card 81-607873 DDC 622 s 622/.34932 19
1. Uranium mines and mining. 2. In situ processing (Mining). I. Engelmann, W. H. (William H.). II. Tweeton, Daryl R. III. Series: Report of investigations (United States. Bureau of Mines). IV. Title.
TN23 .U43 TN799.U7

NIGER.
France. Ambassade. United States. Service de presse et d'information. The Republic of Niger . New York , 1960. 32 p. : LC Card 62-37711
NYPL [Sc Micro R-3644]

Nigeria . United States. Bureau of International Commerce. [Washington] , 1976. v, 190 p. : LC Card 76-602544
HC517.N48 U53 1976   NYPL [JLF 81-313]

NIGERIA - APPROPRIATIONS AND EXPENDITURES.
International Bank for Reconstruction and Development. National development plan 1962-68 . [Washington] , 1966. 44 leaves in various foliations ; LC Card 78-107098 DDC 338.91 s 354.6690072 19
HG3881 .I602 no. Af-47a HJ2184.7

NIGERIA - ECONOMIC CONDITIONS.
United States. Bureau of International Commerce. Nigeria . [Washington] , 1976. v, 190 p. : LC Card 76-602544
HC517.N48 U53 1976   NYPL [JLF 81-313]

NIGERIA - ECONOMIC POLICY.
International Bank for Reconstruction and Development. National development plan 1962-68 . [Washington] , 1966. 44 leaves in various foliations ; LC Card 78-107098 DDC 338.91 s 354.6690072 19
HG3881 .I602 no. Af-47a HJ2184.7

NIGERIA - POPULATION - BIBLIOGRAPHY.
Lucas, David. Population in Nigeria : a select bibliography / David Lucas and John McWilliam. Chapel Hill , 1974. 15 p. ; LC Card 77-155614 DDC 016.3046/09669 19
Z7164.D3 L82 HB3666.7.A3

Nikodem, Zdenek D. Nuclear power regulation / prepared by Zdenek D. Nikodem, Andrew W. Reynolds, R. Gene Clark. Washington, D.C. : U. S. Dept. of Energy, Energy Information Administration, Assistant Administrator for Applied Analysis : [Available from Supt. of Docs., U. S.G.P.O.], 1980. xxvi, 230 p. : ill. ; 28 cm. (Energy policy study . v. 10) "DOE/EIA-0201/10." "May 1980." Includes bibliographical references. LC Card 80-603213 DDC 343.73/0925 347.303925 19
1. Atomic power-plants - Law and legislation - United States. 2. Atomic power - Law and legislation - United States. I. Reynolds, Andrew W. II. Clark, R. Gene. III. Title. IV. Series.
KF2138 .N54

NILE PERCH.
Thompson, Kenneth W. Analysis of potential environmental factors, especially thermal, which would influence the survivorship of exotic Nile perch if introduced into artificially heated reservoirs in Texas /. [Austin] , 1977. 37 p. : LC Card 78-620720 DDC 639.9/7758 19
QL638.C34 T48

Nilsen, D. N. Solvent extraction of nickel and copper from laterite-ammoniacal leach liquors / by D.N. Nilsen, R.E. Siemens, and S.C. Rhoads. Avondale, MD : United States Dept. of the Interior, Bureau of Mines, 1981. p. cm. (Report of investigations / United States Department of

the Interior, Bureau of Mines) Bibliography: p. LC Card 81-38488 DDC 622 s 669/.7332 19
1. Nickel - Metallurgy. 2. Copper - Metallurgy. 3. Laterite. 4. Solvent extraction. I. Siemens, R. E. (Richard E.). II. Rhoads, S. C. III. Series: Report of investigations (United States. Bureau of Mines). IV. Title.
TN23 .U43 TN799.N6

NIMBUS (METEOROLOGICAL SATELLITES)
Knight, Keith Shelburne. Atmospheric structure determined from satellite data /. Washington, D.C. [Springfield, Va.] 1981. x, 95 p. : LC Card 81-601075 DDC 551.5/14 19
QC879.59.A .K58

Nine-digit zip codes . United States. Congress. Senate. Committee on Governmental Affairs. Subcommittee on Energy, Nuclear Proliferation, and Federal Services. Washington , 1981. iii, 274 p. : LC Card 81-610629 DDC 383/.145 19
KF26 .G6728 1980d

Nine essays on Rómulo Gallegos / edited and with a foreword by Hugo Rodríguez-Alcalá. Riverside, CA : Latin American Studies Program, University of California, [1979] ii, 215 p. : ill. ; 28 cm. (Commemorative series - Latin American Studies Program ; no. 3) "December 1979." English and Spanish. Includes bibliographical references. LC Card 80-621557 DDC 863 19
1. Gallegos, Rómulo, Pres. Venezuela, 1884-1969. Doña Bárbara - Addresses, essays, lectures. 2. Gallegos, Rómulo, Pres. Venezuela, 1884-1969. Brizna de raja en el viento - Addresses, essays, lectures. 3. Gallegos, Rómulo, Pres. Venezuela, 1884-1969. Pobre negro - Addresses, essays, lectures. I. Rodríguez-Alcalá, Hugo. II. Series: California. University, Riverside. Latin American Studies Program. Commemorative series - Latin American Studies Program , no. 3.
PQ8549.G24 D6296

Nineteen eighty campaign instructions.
Washington (State). Public Disclosure Commission. 1980 campaign instructions . Olympia, Wash. (403 Evergreen Plaza, FJ-42, Olympia 98504) , 1980. vi, 49 p. : LC Card 80-623468 DDC 324.7/8/09797 19
JK1991.5.W37 W38 1980

1980 census of population: alphabetical index of industries and occupations. United States. Bureau of the Census. 1st- ed. Washington, 1980-
*NYPL [*R-Econ. 81-164 & JLM 81-159]*

1980 census of population: classified index of industries and occupations. United States. Bureau of the Census. 1st- ed. Washington, 1980-
*NYPL [*R-Econ. 81-163 & JLM 81-158]*

Nineteen eighty, Leaves of grass at 125. 1980, Leaves of grass at 125 . Detroit , 1980. 78 p., [1] leaf of plates : LC Card 81-136978 DDC 811/.3 19
PS3231 .A515

Nineteen eighty-one agricultural outlook.
Agricultural Outlook Conference (1980 : Washington, D.C.) 1981 agricultural outlook . Washington , 1981. vi, 565 p. : LC Card 81-601003 DDC 338.1/0973 19
HD1755 .A38 1980

1974 followup of disabled & nondisabled adults /. United States. Social Security Administration. Office of Research and Statistics. Washington , 1979. 2 v. in 1 ;   *NYPL [JLF 80-1201]*

Nineteenth-century fiction.
Tennyson, G. B. An index to Nineteenth-century fiction, volumes 1-30, summer 1945-March 1976 /. Berkeley , c1977. viii, 195 p. : ISBN 0-520-03334-5 LC Card 77-71900 DDC 823/.8/09 19
PR873.T762 T4 1977

NINETEENTH-CENTURY FICTION - INDEXES.
Tennyson, G. B. An index to Nineteenth-century fiction, volumes 1-30, summer 1945-March 1976 /. Berkeley , c1977. viii, 195 p. : ISBN 0-520-03334-5 LC Card 77-71900 DDC 823/.8/09 19
PR873.T762 T4 1977

Nineteenth-century photography in Philadelphia. Philadelphia. Library Company. New York [Philadelphia, Pa.] , c1980. xxviii, 226 p. : ISBN 0-486-23932-2 : LC Card 79-54401
TR25.P5 P47 1980   NYPL [MFW 81-102]

NIOSH publications catalog. National Institute for Occupational Safety and Health. Cincinnati. *NYPL [JLM 81-42]*

Nishimoto, R. K. (Roy Katsuto), 1944-
Effects of Polado on several horticultural crops / R.K. Nishimoto. Honolulu : Hawaii Institute of Tropical Agriculture and Human Resources, University of Hawaii, 1981. p. cm. (Research series / Hawaii Institute of Tropical Agriculture and Human Resources, 0197-9310) Bibliography: p. LC Card 81-2796 DDC 633.6/14 19
1. Vegetables - Wounds and injuries. 2. Plants, Effect of glyphosate on. I. Title. II. Title: Polado on several horticultural crops. III. Series: Research series (Hawaii Institute of Tropical Agriculture and Human Resources) .
SB608.V4 N57

Modes of action of selected herbicides /. Honolulu, Hawaii [1981] p. cm. LC Card 81-2376 DDC 632/.953 19
SB951.4 .M62

Nishimura, Brian. Determining the inland extent of Hawaii's coastal zone boundaries / by Brian Nishimura. [Honolulu] : Pacific Urban Studies and Planning Program, University of Hawaii, [1978] vii, 169 p. : maps ; 28 cm. (Technical supplement - Hawaii Coastal Zone Management Program . no. 14) "September, 1978." Prepared for the State of Hawaii Dept. of Planning and Urban Development. Bibliography: p. 165-169. LC Card 80-623816 DDC 333.91/7/09969 19
1. Coastal zone management - Hawaii. I. Hawaii. University, Honolulu. Pacific Urban Studies and Planning Program. II. Hawaii. Dept. of Planning and Economic Development. III. Series: Hawaii Coastal Zone Management Program. Technical supplement - Hawaii Coastal Zone Management Program , no. 14. IV. Title.
HT393.H3 N57

Nishimura, Charles H.
Economic security for older persons in Hawaii : some issues, problems, and opportunities / Charles H. Nishimura, Gail M. Kaito, Lianne L. U. Lai, researchers. Honolulu, Hawaii : Legislative Reference Bureau, [1980] x, 192 p. : ill. ; 28 cm. (Report - Legislative Reference Bureau . no. 1, 1980) Includes bibliographical references. LC Card 80-622005 DDC 027.6/5 s 362.6/3 19
1. Old age assistance - Hawaii. 2. Income maintenance programs - Hawaii. 3. Aged - Hawaii - Economic conditions. I. Kaito, Gail M., joint author. II. Lai, Lianne L. U., joint author. III. Hawaii. Legislative Reference Bureau. IV. Series: Hawaii. Legislative Reference Bureau. Report - State of Hawaii, Legislative Reference Bureau , 1980, no. 1. V. Title.
KFH20 .H38 1980 no. 1 HV1468.H3

The feasibility of integrating human services in Hawaii : some issues, problems, and opportunities / Charles H. Nishimura, Stanley K. Okinaka, researchers. Honolulu : Legislative Reference Bureau, 1978. xiii, 262 p. : ill. ; 28 cm. (Report - Legislative Reference Bureau, State of Hawaii ; no. 1, 1978) Includes bibliographies and indexes. LC Card 78-624136 DDC 027.6/5 s 361/.9969 19
1. Social service - Hawaii. 2. Social service - United States. I. Okinaka, Stanley K., joint author. II. Series: Hawaii. Legislative Reference Bureau. Report - Legislative Reference Bureau , 1978, no. 1. III. Title.
KFH20 .H38 1978, no. 1 HV98.H3

Nissen, William I. (joint author) Crane, Stanley R. Hydrogen sulfide generation by reaction of natural gas, sulfur, and steam /. [Avondale Md.] [1981] p. cm. LC Card 80-606831 DDC 622 s 628.5/32 19
TN23 .U43 TP245.S9

Nitocra affinis. Ustach, Joseph F. Effects of sub-lethal oil levels on the reproduction of a copepod, Nitocra affinis /. [Raleigh] 1977. 16 leaves : LC Card 79-623524 DDC 595.3/4 19
QL444.C74 U87

NITRATES - ENVIRONMENTAL ASPECTS - NORTH DAKOTA - STATISTICS.
North Dakota. State Dept. of Health. Nutrient levels in North Dakota streams, 1972-1978 /. [Bismarck, N.D.] [1980] 86 p. : LC Card 80-622821 DDC 363.7/3942/09784 19
TD224.N9 N65 1980

NITRILOTRIACETIC ACID.
United States. Congress. House. Committee on Interstate and Foreign Commerce. Subcommittee on Oversight and Investigations.

EPA's action concerning nitrilotriacetic acid (NTA) . Washington , 1980. iv, 393 p. ; LC Card 80-603817 DDC 363.1/79 19
KF27 .I5547 1980r

NITRITES.
United States. Dept. of Agriculture. Economics, Statistics, and Cooperatives Service. An analysis of a ban on nitrite use in curing bacon. Washington , Springfield, Va. , 1979. iv, 23 p. ; LC Card 79-602021 DDC 338.1/0973 s 363.1/929 19
HD1759 .U56a no. 48 HD9435.U52

NITRITES - TOXICOLOGY.
United States. Congress. House. Committee on Agriculture. USDA/FDA announcement on nitrites and related issues . Washington , 1980. iv, 221 p. : LC Card 81-600861 DDC 363.1/92 19
KF27 .A3 1980c

NITROGEN - ENVIRONMENTAL ASPECTS - TEXAS - TRINITY RIVER WATERSHED.
Trinity River Authority of Texas. Planning and Environmental Management Division. Low flow nutrient loss in the mid-Trinity River ; Runoff-related pollutant loadings in the mid-Trinity River /. [Austin] , 1978. iii, 72, iv, 73 p. : LC Card 80-622543 DDC 363.7/3942/097642 19
TD224.T4 T74 1978

NIXON, RICHARD MILHOUS, 1913- - IMPEACHMENT.
Columbia Broadcasting System, inc. CBS News. CBS News special report: "Impeachment, the Committee votes". [New York, 1974] 12 leaves; *NYPL [*XMB-1400]*

Njeru, Enos Hudson Nthia. Land adjudication and its implications for the social organization of the Mbere / by Enos Hudson Nthia Njeru. Madison, Wis. : Land Tenure Center, University of Wisconsin-Madison, [1978] i, 38 p. ; 28 cm. (A Research paper - Land Tenure Center, University of Wisconsin-Madison . no. 73 0084-0815) "November 1978." Bibliography: p. 30. LC Card 80-623243 DDC 333 s 306/.3 19
1. Mbere (African people) - Land tenure. 2. Land tenure - Kenya. I. Series: Wisconsin. University--Madison. Land Tenure Center. Research paper , no. 73. II. Title.
HD107 .W52 no. 73 DT433.545.M34

The NLRB and arbitration . Truesdale, John C., 1921- Amherst , 1979. 18 p. ; LC Card 80-624267 DDC 344.73/0189143 347.304189143 19
KF3372.Z9 T78

No easy choice . United States. General Accounting Office. Washington, D.C. , 1981. vii, 84 p. : LC Card 81-600892 DDC 382/.456234/0973 19
HD9743.U6 U59 1981

No moving parts /. Deal, Susan Strayer. Boise, Idaho , c1980. vii, 50 p. ; ISBN 0-916272-15-X (pbk.) LC Card 80-67909 DDC 811/.54 19
PS3554.E134 N6

No-property-tax cities after Proposition 13 . Worcester, Ellen. Sacramento, CA , Sacramento, CA (Box 90, State Capitol, Sacramento, CA 95814) [1980] iii, 52 p. ; LC Card 81-620796 DDC 352.1/352/09794 19
HJ4121.C22 W67

No time for mud pies . United States. National Commission on the International Year of the Child. Children's Advisory Panel. [Washington, D.C.] , Auburn, AL [1980] 31 p. : LC Card 80-600049 DDC 323.3 19
HQ789 .U55 1980

No. 44, the mysterious stranger . Twain, Mark, 1835-1910. Berkeley [1981] c1969. p. cm. ISBN 0-520-04544-0 LC Card 81-40326 DDC 813/.4 19
PS1322 .M97 1981

NOAA/NCAR Boulder Atmospheric Observatory.
Project Phoenix . [Boulder, Colo.] , Washington, D.C. [1979] xiv, 281 p. : LC Card 80-602120 DDC 551.5/072 19
QC869 .P76

Report - NOAA/NCAR Boulder Atmospheric Observatory .
(no. 1) Project Phoenix . [Boulder, Colo.] , Washington, D.C. [1979] xiv, 281 p. : LC Card 80-602120 DDC 551.5/072 19
QC869 .P76

NOBEL PRIZES.
United States. Congress. House. Committee on Science and Technology. Outlooks from Nobel Prize winners . Washington , 1981. iii, 66 p. : LC Card 81-601401 DDC 607/.2/73 19
KF27 .S39 1980i

NOBLE METALS. see PRECIOUS METALS.

Noble, Stedman. (joint author) Ayres, Robert U. Economic impact of mass production of alternative low emissions automotive power systems /. Springfield, Va. , 1977. 244 p. : *NYPL [JLF 80-387]*

Nochumson, Bayla S.
New Mexico ACT and SAT results, 1978-79 / prepared by Bayla S. Nochumson. Santa Fe, N.M. : New Mexico State Dept. of Education, Evaluation, Assessment, and Testing Unit, [1980] v, 35 p. : ill. ; 28 cm. LC Card 80-623171 DDC 378/.1664 19
1. Universities and colleges - New Mexico - Entrance examinations - Statistics. 2. American College Testing Program. 3. Scholastic apititude test. I. Title.
LB2353.42 .N6

New Mexico's standardized test results : CTBS and SFTAA for the 1978-1979 school year / prepared by Bayla S. Nochumson, Carroll L. Hall. Santa Fe , N.M. : Evaluation, Assessment, and Testing Unit, New Mexico State Dept. of Education, 1979. ii, 38 p. : graphs ; 29 cm. LC Card 80-621725 DDC 371.2/6/09789 19
1. Educational tests and measurements - New Mexico. 2. Ability - Testing. 3. Scholastic aptitude tests. I. Hall, Carroll L., joint author. II. New Mexico. Dept. of Education. Evaluation, Assessment, and Testing Unit. III. Title.
LB3052.N6 N6

NOCTUIDAE - CLASSIFICATION.
McCabe, Timothy Lee. A reclassification of the Polia complex for North America (Lepidoptera: Noctuidae) /. Albany, N.Y. [1980] vi, 141 p. : LC Card 80-623061 DDC 595.78/1 19
QL561.N7 M27

Noggle, Burl. Working with history : the Historical Records Survey in Louisiana and the nation, 1936-1942 / Burl Noggle. Baton Rouge : Louisiana State University Press, c1981. p. cm. Bibliography: p. ISBN 0-8071-0881-2 : LC Card 81-5789 DDC 976.3 19
1. Louisiana Historical Records Survey. 2. Historical Records Survey (U. S.). 3. Louisiana - History - Sources. 4. United States - History - Sources. I. Title.
F369 .N63

NOISE.
(1974) United States. Office of Noise Abatement and Control. Information on levels of environmental noise requisite to protect public health and welfare with an adequate margin of safety. Washington, 1974. ca 159 p. in various pagings: LC Card 76-11078 *NYPL [JSF 80-574]*

NOISE CONTROL - LAW AND LEGISLATION - UNITED STATES.
United States. Environmental Protection Agency. Office of Noise Abatement and Control. Official docket for proposed revision to rail carrier noise emission regulation /. Washington, 1980. 1 v.; *NYPL [JLM 81-95]*

Noise control of diesel-powered underground mining machines, 1979 / compiled by R. C. Martholomae ... [et al.]. Washington, D.C. : U. S. Dept. of the Interior, Bureau of Mines, [1981] p. cm. (Information circular / Bureau of Mines) Bibliography: p. LC Card 80-607181 DDC 622 s 622/.2 19
1. Mining machinery - Noise. 2. Diesel motor - Noise. 3. Noise - Physiological effect. I. Bartholomae, R. C. II. Series: United States. Bureau of Mines. Information circular , .
TN295 .U4 TN345

NOISE - PHYSIOLOGICAL EFFECT.
Noise control of diesel-powered underground mining machines, 1979 /. Washington, D.C. [1981] p. cm. LC Card 80-607181 DDC 622 s 622/.2 19
TN295 .U4 TN345

NOISE POLLUTION - ARIZONA - TUCSON.
Conley, Vesta B. Daytime noise environment in Tucson, Arizona. Tucson, 1973. iii, 78 p.
NYPL [JSF 80-132]

NOISE POLLUTION - MEASUREMENT - STANDARDS - ILLINOIS.
Illinois. Environmental Protection Agency. Measurement procedures for enforcement of noise pollution control regulations (parts 1 & 2). [Springfield] , 1980. 18 p. : LC Card 80-623335 DDC 363.7/463 19
TD894 .I48 1980

NOISE PREVENTION. see NOISE CONTROL.

Nokleberg, Warren J.
Stratiform zinc-lead deposits in the Drenchwater Creek area, Howard Pass quadrangle, northwestern Brooks Range, Alaska / by Warren J. Nokleberg and Gary R. Winkler. Menlo Park, CA : U. S. Geological Survey, 1981. p. cm. (Geological Survey professional paper . 1209) Shorter contributions to general geology Bibliography: p. LC Card 81-607994 DDC 553.4/4/097987 19
1. Zinc ores - Alaska - Drenchwater Creek region. 2. Lead ores - Alaska - Drenchwater Creek region. I. Winkler, G. R. II. Title. III. Series.
TN483.A64 N64

Stratigraphy and structure of the Strawberry mine roof pendant, central Sierra Nevada, California / by Warren J. Nokleberg. Washington : U. S. Govt. Print. Off., 1980. p. cm. (Shorter contributions to general geology) Geological Survey professional paper . Bibliography: p. Includes index. LC Card 80-607173 DDC 551.7/6/097944 19
1. Geology, Stratigraphic - Mesozoic. 2. Roof pendants (Geology). 3. Geology - Sierra Nevada Mountains. I. Series: United States. Geological Survey. Shorter contributions to general geology. II. Title.
QE675 .N64

Nolting, Donald H. Electric fish screen efficiency, Willow Creek Reservoir / by Donald H. Nolting. Denver : State of Colorado, Dept. of Game and Fish, 1962. iv, 24 p. : ill. ; 28 cm. (Technical bulletin - State of Colorado, Department of Game and Fish . no. 11) Bibliography: p. 24. LC Card 81-464857 DDC 639.9/7755 19
1. Fish screens - Colorado - Willow Creek. 2. Trout - Mortality. 3. Fishes - Effect of dams on. 4. Reservoirs - Environmental aspects - Colorado - Willow Creek. I. Title. II. Title: Willow Creek Reservoir. III. Series: Colorado. Game and Fish Dept. Technical bulletin , no. 11.
SH157.85.F54 N64

Nolting, Louvan E. The structure and functions of the U. S.S.R. State Committee for Science and Technology / by Louvan E. Nolting. [Washington, D.C.] : U. S. Dept. of Commerce, Bureau of the Census, [1979] iv, 53 p. ; 28 cm. (Foreign economic report. 19) "November, 1979." Bibliography: p. 44-53. LC Card 80-602662 DDC 354.470085/5 19
1. Soviet Union. Gosudarstvennyĭ komitet po nauke i tekhnike. I. Title. II. Series.
Q127.S696 N64 *NYPL [JLM 78-229 19]*

Nomejko, Irene M.
(joint author) O'Connor, Linda. Applications/admissions information, by sector for fall 1977, by institution for fall 1978 . [Trenton] [1979] [42] p. ; LC Card 80-621681 DDC 378/.1056/09749 19
LB2351.3.N5 O26

O'Connor, Linda. Degrees conferred by N.J. colleges and universities by race, sex, and major program category, F.Y. 1979 /. [Trenton, N.J.] [1980] [86] p. ; LC Card 80-624027 DDC 378/.24/09749 19
LB2381 .O27

(joint author) O'Connor, Linda. Profile of full-time first-time freshmen enrolled in N.J. colleges, fall 1977 and fall 1978 /. [Trenton] [1979] ii, [77] p. ; LC Card 80-621678 DDC 378/.1059749 19
LA331.5 .O28

Nomimations of Robert E. Herzstein, Frank B. Sollars, Alexis M. Herman, and Alfred R. Marane . United States. Congress. Senate. Committee on Banking, Housing and Urban Affairs. Washington , 1980. iii, 78 p. ; LC Card 80-603063 DDC 353.82 19
KF26 .B39 1980i

Nomination . United States. Congress. Senate. Committee on Labor and Human Resources. Washington , 1980. ii, 41 p. ; LC Card 80-603645 DDC 353.001/04 19
KF26 .L27 1980n

Nomination . United States. Congress. Senate. Committee on Labor and Human Resources. Washington , 19. ii 28 p. ; LC Card 80-604090 DDC 353.0085/5 19
KF26 .L27 1980m

Nomination . United States. Congress. Senate. Committee on Labor and Human Resources. Washington , 1980. ii, 46 p. ; LC Card 80-602975 DDC 353.0084 19
KF26 .L27 1980d

Nomination . United States. Congress. Senate. Committee on Labor and Human Resources. Washington , 1980. 114 p. ; LC Card 81-601605 DDC 353.844 19
KF26 .L27 1981a

Nomination . United States. Congress. Senate. Committee on Labor and Human Resources. Washington , c1981. ii, 378 p. : LC Card 81-600954 DDC 353.83
KF26 .L27 1981

Nomination . United States. Congress. Senate. Committee on Labor and Public Welfare. Washington , 1976. iii, 70 p. : LC Card 76-601909
KF26 .L3 1975o

Nomination--deputy secretary of commerce . United States. Congress. Senate. Committee on Commerce, Science, and Transportation. Washington , 1981. iii, 8 p. ; LC Card 81-601776 DDC 353.82 19
KF26 .C69 1981c

Nomination--deputy secretary of transportation . United States. Congress. Senate. Committee on Commerce, Science, and Transportation. Washington , 1981. iii, 25 p. ; LC Card 81-600981 DDC 353.86 19
KF26 .C69 1981

Nomination--DOT . United States. Congress. Senate. Committee on Commerce, Science, and Transportation. Washington , 1980. iii, 13 p. ; LC Card 80-602746 DDC 353.86 19
KF26 .C69 1980n

Nomination--National Transportation Board . United States. Congress. Senate. Committee on Commerce, Science, and Transportation. Washington , 1980. iii, 8 p. ; LC Card 80-602720 DDC 353.0087/5 19
KF26 .C69 1980k

Nomination of Admiral B.R. Inman . United States. Congress. Senate. Select Committee on Intelligence. Washington , 1981. iii, 36 p. ; LC Card 81-601774 DDC 327.1/2/06073 19
KF26.5 .I5 1981

Nomination of Albert Carnesale . United States. Congress. Senate. Committee on Environment and Public Works. Washington , 1980. iii, 138 p. ; LC Card 80-603300 DDC 353.0087/22 19
KF26 .E6 1980f

Nomination of Alexander M. Haig, Jr. . United States. Congress. Senate. Committee on Foreign Relations. Washington , 1981. 2 v. ; LC Card 81-600880 DDC 353.1 19
KF26 .F6 1981

Nomination of Barbara S. Thomas . United States. Congress. Senate. Committee on Banking, Housing and Urban Affairs. Washington , 1980. ii, 61 p. ; LC Card 80-603679 DDC 353.0082/58 19
KF26 .B39 1980s

Nomination of Caspar W. Weinberger to be Secretary of Defense . United States. Congress. Senate. Committee on Armed Services. Washington , 1981. iii, 61 p. ; LC Card 81-600831 DDC 353.6 19
KF26 .A7 1981

Nomination of Charles W. Snodgrass . United States. Congress. Senate. Committee on Armed Services. Washington , 1980. ii, 7 p. ; LC Card 80-602952 DDC 353.63 19
KF26 .A7 1980b

Nomination of Curtis A. Hessler . United States. Congress. Senate. Committee on Finance. Washington , 1980. iii, 22 p. ; LC Card

80-603001 DDC 353.2 19
KF26 .F5 1980c

Nomination of David A. Stockman . United States. Congress. Senate. Committee on Governmental Affairs. Washington , 1981. iii, 169 p. ; LC Card 81-601411 DDC 353.0071 19
KF26 .G67 1981a

Nomination of David C. Jones . United States. Congress. Senate. Committee on Armed Services. Washington , 1980. ii, 64 p. ; LC Card 81-603324 DDC 355.3/3042/0973 19
KF26 .A7 1980e

Nomination of Donald I. Hovde . United States. Congress. Senate. Committee on Banking, Housing and Urban Affairs. Washington , 1981. iii, 49 p. ; LC Card 81-601780 DDC 353.85 19
KF26 .B39 1981b

Nomination of Edmund S. Muskie . United States. Congress. Senate. Committee on Foreign Relations. Washington , 1980. iii, 44 p. ; LC Card 80-602965 DDC 353.1 19
KF26 .F6 1980j

Nomination of Edwin L. Harper . United States. Congress. Senate. Committee on Governmental Affairs. Washington , 1981. iii, 25 p. ; LC Card 81-601771 DDC 353.0071 19
KF26 .G67 1981b

Nomination of Frank C. Carlucci III to be Deputy Secretary of Defense . United States. Congress. Senate. Committee on Armed Services. Washington , 1981. ii, 45 p. ; LC Card 81-600832 DDC 353.6 19
KF26 .A7 1981a

Nomination of George Vernon Orr, Jr., to be secretary of the Air Force . United States. Congress. Senate. Committee on Armed Services. Washington , 1981. ii, 12 p. ; LC Card 81-601412 DDC 353.63 19
KF26 .A7 1981b

Nomination of Henry Bowen Frazier III . United States. Congress. Senate. Committee on Governmental Affairs. Washington , 1980. iii, 24 p. ; LC Card 80-602712 DDC 353.0083/2 19
KF26 .G67 1980b

Nomination of Jack R. Borsting . United States. Congress. Senate. Committee on Armed Services. Washington , 1980. 6 p. ; LC Card 80-603338 DDC 353.6 19
KF26 .A7 1980d

Nomination of James Bert Thomas, Jr. . United States. Congress. Senate. Committee on Governmental Affairs. Washington , 1980 [i.e. 1981] iii, 33 p. ; LC Card 81-601163 DDC 353.844 19
KF26 .G67 1980n

Nomination of James L. Malone . United States. Congress. Senate. Committee on Foreign Relations. Washington , 1981. iii, 80 p. ; LC Card 81-601860 DDC 353.1 19
KF26 .F6 1981d

Nomination of Jeane J. Kirkpatrick . United States. Congress. Senate. Committee on Foreign Relations. Washington , 1981. iii, 110 p. ; LC Card 81-601348 DDC 353.1 19
KF26 .F6 1981a

Nomination of John F. Lehman, Jr., to be Secretary of the Navy . United States. Congress. Senate. Committee on Armed Services. Washington , 1981. ii, 30 p. ; LC Card 81-601340 DDC 353.7 19
KF26 .A7 1981c

Nomination of John O. Marsh, Jr., to be secretary of the Army . United States. Congress. Senate. Committee on Armed Services. Washington , 1981. iii, 22 p. ; LC Card 81-601158 DDC 353.62 19
KF26 .A7 1981d

Nomination of John S. Hassell, Jr. . United States. Congress. Senate. Committee on Environment and Public Works. Washington , 1980. iii, 39 p. ; LC Card 80-603010 DDC 353.0086/42 19
KF26 .E6 1980e

Nomination of John S. R. Shad . United States. Congress. Senate. Committee on Banking, Housing and Urban Affairs. Washington , 1981. ii, 34 p. ; LC Card 81-601937 DDC 353.0082/58 19
KF26 .B39 1981h

Nomination of Justice William Patrick Clark .
United States. Congress. Senate. Committee on
Foreign Relations. Washington , 1981. iii, 84
p. :   LC Card 81-601174   DDC 353.1 19
KF26 .F6 1981c

Nomination of Karen Hastie Williams . United
States. Congress. Senate. Committee on
Governmental Affairs. Washington , 1980. iii,
73 p. ;   LC Card 80-602444   DDC 353.0071/2 19
KF26 .G67 1980a

Nomination of Lyle E. Gramley . United States.
Congress. Senate. Committee on Banking,
Housing and Urban Affairs. Washington, D.C. ,
1980. iii, 124 p. :   LC Card 80-602772   DDC
353.0082/5 19
KF26 .B39 1980g

**Nomination of Michael Cardenas to be
administrator of the Small Business
Administration .** United States. Congress.
Senate. Select Committee on Small Business.
Washington , 1981. iii, 64 p. ;   LC Card
81-602263   DDC 353.0082/048 19
KF26.5 .S6 1981c

Nomination of Murray L. Weidenbaum . United
States. Congress. Senate. Committee on
Banking, Housing and Urban Affairs.
Washington , 1981. iii, 114 p. ;   LC Card
81-601619   DDC 353.0082 19
KF26 .B39 1981a

Nomination of Ray A. Barnhart . United States.
Congress. Senate. Committee on Environment
and Public Works. Washington , 1981. iii, 38
p. ;   LC Card 81-601612   DDC 353.0086/42 19
KF26 .E6 1981

Nomination of Richard S. Schweiker . United
States. Congress. Senate. Committee on
Finance. Washington , c1981. iii, 39 p. ;   LC
Card 81-600829   DDC 353.842 19
KF26 .F5 1981

Nomination of Richard T. Pratt . United States.
Congress. Senate. Committee on Banking,
Housing and Urban Affairs. Washington , 1981.
iii, 49 p. ;   LC Card 81-601950   DDC 353.0082/5
19
KF26 .B39 1981d

Nomination of Samuel R. Pierce, Jr. . United
States. Congress. Senate. Committee on
Banking, Housing and Urban Affairs.
Washington , 1981. iii, 95 p. ;   LC Card
81-601350   DDC 353.85 19
KF26 .B39 1981c

Nomination of Stephen M. Goldfeld . United
States. Congress. Senate. Committee on
Banking, Housing and Urban Affairs.
Washington , 1980. ii, 23 p. ;   LC Card
80-603302   DDC 353.09/3 19
KF26 .B39 1980l

**Nomination of Thomas W. Fredericks to
Assistant Secretary of the Interior .** United
States. Congress. Senate. Select Committee on
Indian Affairs. Washington , 1980. iii, 126 p. ;
LC Card 80-603457   DDC 353.3 19
KF26.5 .I4 1980n

Nomination of Wayman D. Palmer . United
States. Congress. Senate. Committee on
Banking, Housing and Urban Affairs.
Washington , 1980. ii, 13 p. ;   LC Card
80-603651   DDC 353.0082/52045 19
KF26 .B39 1980p

Nomination of William C. Gardner . United
States. Congress. Senate. Committee on
Governmental Affairs. Washington , 1980. iii,
26 p. ;   LC Card 80-603340   DDC 353.008/8/09753
19
KF26 .G67 1980h

Nomination of William E. Brock III . United
States. Congress. Senate. Committee on
Finance. Washington , 1981. ii, 43 p. ;   LC Card
81-601985   DDC 353.0082/7 19
KF26 .F5 1981c

Nomination of William J. Casey . United States.
Congress. Senate. Select Committee on
Intelligence. Washington , 1981. iv, 51 p. ;   LC
Card 81-601604   DDC 327.1/2/06073 19
KF26.5 .I5 1981a

Nomination--secretary of commerce . United
States. Congress. Senate. Committee on
Commerce, Science, and Transportation.
Washington , 1981. iii, 46 p. ;   LC Card

81-600818   DDC 353.82 19
KF26 .C69 1981a

Nomination--Secretary of Transportation . United
States. Congress. Senate. Committee on
Commerce, Science, and Transportation.
Washington , 1981. iii, 54 p. ;   LC Card
81-600815   DDC 353.86 19
KF26 .C69 1981e

**Nomination to be a member of the Postal Rate
Commission and nominations to be governors
of the U. S. Postal Service .** United States.
Congress. Senate. Committee on Governmental
Affairs. Washington , 1980. iii, 78 p. ;   LC Card
80-603489   DDC 353.0087/3 19
KF26 .G67 1980j

Nominations--Amtrak . United States. Congress.
Senate. Committee on Commerce, Science, and
Transportation. Washington , 1980. iii, 24 p. ;
LC Card 80-602501   DDC 353.0087/5 19
KF26 .C69 1980m

Nominations--assistant secretaries of commerce .
United States. Congress. Senate. Committee on
Commerce, Science, and Transportation.
Washington , 1981. iii, 4 p. ;   LC Card 81-602035
DDC 353.82 19
KF26 .C69 1981h

Nominations--August . United States. Congress.
Senate. Committee on Commerce, Science, and
Transportation. Washington , 1980. iii, 48 p. ;
LC Card 80-603804   DDC 353.0082 19
KF26 .C69 1980s

**Nominations--Department of Commerce and
Federal Maritime Commission .** United States.
Congress. Senate. Committee on Commerce,
Science, and Transportation. Washington ,
1980. iii, 81 p. ;   LC Card 80-601935   DDC
353.82 19
KF26 .C69 1979ak

**Nominations--Departments of Commerce and
Transportation .** United States. Congress.
Senate. Committee on Commerce, Science, and
Transportation. Washington , 1981. iii, 5 p. ;
LC Card 81-601952   DDC 353.82 19
KF26 .C69 1981g

Nominations--DOT . United States. Congress.
Senate. Committee on Commerce, Science, and
Transportation. Washington , 1981. iii, 35 p. ;
LC Card 81-601783   DDC 353.86 19
KF26 .C69 1981b

NOMINATIONS FOR OFFICE - MISSOURI.
Missouri. Office of the Secretary of State.
Certification of candidates /. [Jefferson City,
Mo. , 1980] 30 p. ;   LC Card 80-623055   DDC
324.5/4/09778 19
JK2075 .M8 1980

**Nominations of Abraham Katz, William J.
Driver, and John L. Palmer .** United States.
Congress. Senate. Committee on Finance.
Washington , 1980. iii, 19 p. ;   LC Card
80-602760   DDC 353.842 19
KF26 .F5 1980b

**Nominations of Dorothy Sellers and Ricardo M.
Urbina .** United States. Congress. Senate.
Committee on Governmental Affairs.
Washington , 1980. iii, 34 p. ;   LC Card
81-600816   DDC 353.008/8/09753 19
KF26 .G67 1980m

**Nominations of Fred C. Ikle, to be under
secretary of defense for policy, and William H.
Taft, IV, to be general counsel of the
Department of Defense .** United States.
Congress. Senate. Committee on Armed
Services. Washington , 1981. ii, 24 p. ;   LC
Card 81-602261   DDC 353.6 19
KF26 .A7 1981f

**Nominations of Herta Lande Seidman and
Stephen J. Friedman .** United States. Congress.
Senate. Committee on Banking, Housing and
Urban Affairs. Washington , 1980. iii, 53 p. :
LC Card 80-602446   DDC 353.82 19
KF26 .B39 1980c

**Nominations of John E. Chapoton, Roscoe L.
Egger, Jr., and Paul C. Roberts .** United States.
Congress. Senate. Committee on Finance.
Washington , 1981. iii, 40 p. ;   LC Card
81-601602   DDC 353.2 19
KF26 .F5 1981d

**Nominations of Michael Blumenfeld, John A.
Bushnell, John W. Clark, Clifford B. O'Hara,
William Sidell, Robinson O. Everett, and
William E. Peacock .** United States. Congress.
Senate. Committee on Armed Services.
Washington , 1980. ii, 49 p. ;   LC Card
80-602497   DDC 353.0087/6444 19
KF26 .A7 1980c

**Nominations of Norman B. Ture and Beryl
Wayne Sprinkel .** United States. Congress.
Senate. Committee on Finance. Washington ,
1981. iii, 17 p. ;   LC Card 81-601959   DDC 353.2
19
KF26 .F5 1981e

**Nominations of Philip D. Winn, John J. Knapp,
Emanuel S. Savas, and Arthur E. Teele, Jr., .**
United States. Congress. Senate. Committee on
Banking, Housing and Urban Affairs.
Washington , 1981. iii, 136 p. ;   LC Card
81-601958   DDC 353.85 19
KF26 .B39 1981f

**Nominations of Ralph Raikes and William D.
Wampler .** United States. Congress. Senate.
Committee on Agriculture, Nutrition, and
Forestry. Washington , 1980. iii, 31 p. :   LC
Card 80-604017   DDC 353.0082/33045 19
KF26 .A35 1980c

**Nominations of Robert E. Herzstein, C. Moxley
Featherston, William M. Fay, Charles R.
Simpson, Edna Parker, and Sheldon V.
Ekman .** United States. Congress. Senate.
Committee on Finance. Washington , 1980. iii,
80 p. ;   LC Card 80-603685   DDC 353.0072/4 19
KF26 .F5 1980f

**Nonagricultural wage and salary employment in
Ohio [and various metropolitan areas] Table
RS-790-1.** Ohio. Bureau of Employment
Services. Division of Research and Statistics.
Columbus.   *NYPL [M-11 2926]*

**Nondestructive evaluation of semiconductor
materials and devices .** Nato Advanced Study
Institute on Nondestructive Evaluation of
Semiconductor Materials and Devices, Villa
Tuscolano, Italy, 1978. New York , c1979. xi,
782 p. :   ISBN 0-306-40293-9   LC Card 79-16499
TK7871.85 .N376 1978   *NYPL [JSF 80-961]*

**Nondestructive Evaluation of Semiconductor
Materials and Devices, Nato Advanced
Study Institute on. see Nato Advanced Study
Institute on Nondestructive Evaluation of
Semiconductor Materials and Devices, Villa
Tuscolano, Italy, 1978.**

Nondiscrimination in insurance . United States.
Congress. House. Committee on Interstate and
Foreign Commerce. Subcommittee on
Consumer Protection and Finance.
Washington , 1981. iv, 425 p. :   LC Card
81-601385   DDC 346.73/086 347.30686 19
KF27 .I554 1980j

Nondiscrimination in Insurance Act, S. 2477 .
United States. Congress. Senate. Committee on
the Judiciary. Subcommittee on Antitrust,
Monopoly, and Business Rights. Washington ,
1980 [i.e. 1981] iii, 416 p. :   LC Card 81-601316
DDC 346.73/086 347.30686 19
KF26 .J835 1980e

**Non-Federal financing of water resources
development :** proceedings of a conference held
on January 4, 1978 at the Sheraton
Inn-Portland International Airport / sponsored
by the state water resource agencies of Idaho,
Oregon, and Washington, and by the water
research institute or center in each of the three
states. Corvallis: Oregon State University, 1978.
80 p. ; 28 cm. Includes bibliographical references.
LC Card 79-621887
*1. Water resources development - Northwest, Pacific -
Finance - Congresses. I. Idaho. University. Water
Resources Research Institute. II. Oregon Water
Resources Research Institute. III. State of Washington
Water Research Center.*
HD1695.N74 N66   *NYPL [JLF 80-1601]*

**NONFERROUS METALS -
ELECTROMETALLURGY.**
Cole, Ernest R. Insoluble anodes for
electrowinning zinc and other metals /.
Washington [1981] p. cm.   LC Card 80-607823
DDC 622 s 669/.52 19
TN23 .U43 TN796

NONFORMAL EDUCATION.
Vella, Jane Kathryn, 1931- Learning to listen .

Amherst, MA , c1979. vii, 58 p. : ISBN
0-932288-57-X (pbk.) LC Card 80-131689
DDC 374 19
LC5219 .V44

Wedemeyer, Charles A. Learning at the back
door . Madison , 1981. p. cm. ISBN
0-299-08560-0 : LC Card 80-52301 DDC 374
19
LC45.3 .W43

**NON-FORMAL EDUCATION - ECONOMIC
ASPECTS - UNITED STATES -
EVALUATION.**
United States. Science and Education
Administration. Extension. Evaluation of
economic and social consequences of
cooperative extension programs /. Washington,
D.C. , 1980. xiii, 188 p. : LC Card 80-601705
DDC 378/.104/0973 19
LC45.4 .U54 1980

**NON-FORMAL EDUCATION - SOCIAL
ASPECTS - UNITED STATES -
EVALUATION.**
United States. Science and Education
Administration. Extension. Evaluation of
economic and social consequences of
cooperative extension programs /. Washington,
D.C. , 1980. xiii, 188 p. : LC Card 80-601705
DDC 378/.104/0973 19
LC45.4 .U54 1980

**NONFOSSIL FUELS. see SYNTHETIC
FUELS.**

**NONLINEAR MECHANICS -
MATHEMATICAL MODELS -
CONGRESSES.**
Research in nonlinear structural and solid
mechanics . Washington, D.C. [Springfield,
Va.] 1980. viii, 289 p. : LC Card 81-601087
DDC 624.1/71/0724 19
TA646 .R38

Nonmetropolitan America in transition / edited
by Amos H. Hawley and Sara Mills Mazie.
Chapel Hill : University of North Carolina
Press, c1981. p. cm. Includes index. CONTENTS. -
An overview / Amos H. Hawley and Sara Mills
Mazie -- The deconcentration of population: Diversity
in post-1970 population trends / David L. Brown and
Calvin L. Beale. Residential preferences in the United
States / James J. Zuiches. Local perspectives on
community growth / Mark Baldassare -- The changing
structure of economic opportunity: Agriculture and the
community / Olaf F. Larson. Manufacturing industry /
Thomas E. Till. The service sector / Mark David
Menchik. The availability of passenger transportation /
Arthur Saltzman and Lawrence W. Newlin. Energy and
location / Irving Hoch -- The differential access to
opportunity: Unemployment and underemployment /
Vernon M. Briggs, Jr. Poverty / Stephen F. Seninger
and Timothy M. Smeeding. Poverty / Candace Howes
and Ann R. Markusen. The Black population / John R.
Moland, Jr. The Mexican-American population / Marta
Tienda -- The distribution of amenities: Housing supply
and demand / Wilbur R. Thompson and James
Mikesell. The provision of community services /
Stephen P. Coelen and William F. Fox. Health and
health services / Roger A. Rosenblatt -- Growth,
environmental impact, and planning: Land-use trends /
Marion Clawson. Environmental quality and protection
/ Frederick H. Buttel. Local governments / Alvin D.
Sokolow. Fiscal status of local government / Thomas F.
Stinson. Public institutions and the planning process /
Pat Choate. ISBN 0-8078-1490-3 LC Card 81-3511
DDC 307.7/2/0973 19
*1. Cities and towns - United States - Addresses, essays,
lectures. 2. Urban policy - United States - Addresses,
essays, lectures. 3. United States - Social conditions -
1960- - Addresses, essays, lectures. 4. United States -
Population - Addresses, essays, lectures. 5. Migration,
Internal - United States - Addresses, essays, lectures. I.
Hawley, Amos Henry. II. Mazie, Sara Mills, 1941-.*
HT123 .N65

**NONPROFESSIONALS IN SOCIAL
SERVICE. see PARAPROFESSIONALS
IN SOCIAL SERVICE.**

**NONPROFIT CORPORATIONS. see
CORPORATIONS, NONPROFIT.**

**Nonprofit organization participation in the
federal aid system** . United States. Congress.
Senate. Committee on Governmental Affairs.
Subcommittee on Intergovernmental Relations.
Washington , 1980. 2 v. ; LC Card 81-600646
DDC 361.3/7/0973 19
KF26 .G6738 1980d

**NONPROLIFERATION, NUCLEAR. see
NUCLEAR NONPROLIFERATION.**

The Non-proliferation Treaty . United States.
Congress. Senate. Committee on Foreign
Relations. Subcommittee on Arms Control,
Oceans, International Operations, and
Environment. Washington , 1980. iii, 99 p. :
LC Card 80-603656 DDC 327.1/74 19
KF26 .F6286 1980

**NONTARIFF DISTORTIONS OF TRADE. see
NONTARIFF TRADE BARRIERS.**

NONTARIFF TRADE BARRIERS.
Sullivan, Daniel E. Minerals and the Tokyo
Round of the MTN /. Washington [1981] p.
cm. LC Card 81-607909 DDC 622 s 382/.42 19
TN295 .U4 HD9506.A2

NONTARIFF TRADE BARRIERS - JAPAN.
United States. Congress. Senate. Select
Committee on Small Business. Impact of
non-tariff barriers on the ability of small
business to export to Japan . Washington ,
1980. iii, 424 p. : LC Card 80-603719 DDC
382/.64 19
KF26.5 .S6 1980r

Nonurban drug abuse programs . National
Institute on Drug Abuse. Services Research
Branch. [Rockville, Md.] , Washington , 1978.
27 p. ; LC Card 78-602308 DDC 362.2/93/0973
19
HV5825 .N35 1978b

NON-WAGE PAYMENTS - UNITED STATES.
Huck, Daniel F. Alternative approaches to
adjusting compensation for federal bluecollar
employees /. [Washington, D.C.] , 1980. xxii,
59 p. ; LC Card 80-604160 DDC 353.001/2 19
JK776 .H8

**NON-WAGE PAYMENTS - UNITED STATES -
PERIODICALS.**
United States. Office of Labor-Management and
Welfare-Pension Reports. Characteristics of
plans on file under the Welfare and pension
plans disclosure act. [Washington]
NYPL [JLM 80-866]

**NOONAN, N. D. - ECONOMIC
CONDITIONS.**
Lemmerman, Kathe L. Columbus / Noonan
study . Denver , 1974. xiii, 104, [48] p. :
NYPL [JLF 81-30]

Noor, Ahmed Khairy, 1938- Research in
nonlinear structural and solid mechanics .
Washington, D.C. [Springfield, Va.] 1980. viii,
289 p. : LC Card 81-601087 DDC 624.1/71/0724
19
TA646 .R38

**NORAD. see North American Air Defense
Command.**

**Nord-Atlantik-Pakt-Organisation. see North
Atlantic Treaty Organization.**

Nordstrom, Karl F. Rutgers University, New
Brunswick, N.J. Center for Coastal and
Environmental Studies. The coastal
geomorphology of New Jersey. New Brunswick
[1977] 2 v. : LC Card 80-623995 DDC
333.91/7/09749 19
GB459.4 .R87 1977

Nordstrom, Paul E. South Dakota recreational
trails plan, January 1, 1980 / prepared by Paul
E. Nordstrom, David G. Johnson ; with the
cooperation of the 1979 South Dakota
Recreational Trails Committee ; prepared for
the Parks and Recreation Division of the South
Dakota Dept. of Game, Fish, and Parks.
[Pierre, S.D.] : The Division, [1979?] 178 p. :
ill. ; 28 cm. Includes bibliographical references. LC
Card 80-622746 DDC 790/.09783 19
*1. Outdoor recreation - South Dakota - Planning. 2.
Trails - South Dakota - Planning. 3. Recreational
surveys - South Dakota. I. Johnson, David G., 1950-
joint author. II. South Dakota. Recreational Trails
Committee. III. South Dakota. Division of Parks &
Recreation. IV. Title.*
GV191.42.S8 N67

**Norfolk, Va. Naval Safety Center. see Naval
Safety Center.**

Norge. see Norway.

Normal diet, adolescence /. Tuckermanty,
Elizabeth. Columbus, Ohio (456 Clinic Dr.,
Columbus 43210) , c1980. 31 p. : LC Card

81-620941 DDC 613.2/088055 19
RJ235 .T83

Normal diet, age of dependency /. Cox, Janice
Hovasi. Columbus, Ohio (456 Clinic Dr.,
Columbus 43210) , c1980. 34 p. : LC Card
81-620939 DDC 613.2/6 19
RJ216 .C69

Normal diet, age of parental control /.
Tuckermanty, Elizabeth. Columbus, Ohio (456
Clinic Dr., Columbus 43210) , c1980. 31 p. :
LC Card 81-620940 DDC 613.2/6 19
RJ206 .T83

Normal diet, geriatrics /. Molleson, Ann L.
Columbus, Ohio (456 Clinic Dr., Columbus
43210) , c1980. 23 p. : LC Card 81-620943
DDC 613.2/0880565 19
TX361.A3 M64

Normal diet, pregnancy and lactation /. Cox,
Janice Hovasi. Columbus, Ohio (456 Clinic Dr.,
Columbus 43210) , c1980. 47 p. : LC Card
81-620942 DDC 618.2/4 19
RG559 .C68

NORMAN, LINDSAY D.
United States. Congress. Senate. Committee on
Energy and Natural Resources. Lindsay D.
Norman, Jr., and John D. Hughes
nominations . Washington , 1980. iii, 123 p. :
LC Card 80-603780 DDC 353.0082/327 19
KF26 .E55 1980g

Norman McLaren, manipulator of movement .
Richard, Valliere T., 1952- Newark [N.J.] ,
c1981. p. cm. ISBN 0-87413-192-8 LC Card
80-53998 DDC 791.43/023/0924
NC1766.C32 M357 1981

**Normative approaches to the prevention of
alcohol abuse and alcoholism** : proceedings of a
symposium, April 26-28, 1977, San Diego,
California / sponsored by Laboratory of
Epidemiology and Population Studies, Division
of Intramural Research, NIAAA ; edited by
Thomas C. Harford, Douglas A. Parker, and
Lillian Light. Rockville, Md. : U. S. Dept. of
Health, Education, and Welfare, Public Health
Service, Alcohol, Drug Abuse, and Mental
Health Administration, National Institute on
Alcohol Abuse and Alcoholism ; Washington
D.C. : for sale by the Supt. of Docs., U. S.
Govt. Print. Off., [1980] ix, 238 p. ; 24 cm.
(Research monograph - National Institute on Alcohol
Abuse and Alcoholism . no. 3) DHEW publication ; no.
(ADM) 79-847 Bibliography: p. 215-236. Includes
index. LC Card 79-600168 DDC 362.2/286 19
*1. Alcoholism - United States - Congresses. 2.
Alcoholism - United States - Prevention - Congresses. I.
Harford, Thomas C. II. Parker, Douglas A. III. Light,
Lillian. IV. National Institute on Alcohol Abuse and
Alcoholism. Laboratory of Epidemiology and Population
Studies.*
HV5288 .N67

Norris, James N. Articulated coralline algae of
the Gulf of California, Mexico / James N.
Norris and H. William Johansen. Washington :
Smithsonian Institution Press, 1981- p. cm.
(Smithsonian contributions to the marine sciences . no.
7) Bibliography: p. Includes index. CONTENTS. - 1.
Amphiroa Lamouroux. LC Card 81-607063 DDC
589.4/1 19
*1. Corallinaceae. 2. Algae - Mexico - California, Gulf
of. I. Johansen, H. William. II. Title. III. Series.*
QK569.C8 N67

Norsk . Stokker, Kathleen, 1946- Madison, Wis. ,
1981. p. cm. ISBN 0-299-08690-9 : LC Card
81-50827 DDC 439.8/282/421 19
PD2623 .S86

**NORTH AMERICA - ANTIQUITIES -
ADDRESSES, ESSAYS, LECTURES.**
Cultural resources remote sensing /.
Washington, D.C. , 1980. ix, 390 p. : LC Card
81-601114 DDC 973/.028 19
E77.9 .C84

**North America - Archaeology. see Indians of
North America - Antiquities.**

**NORTH AMERICAN AIR DEFENSE
COMMAND.**
United States. Congress. House. Committee on
Armed Services. Strategic warning system false
alerts . Washington , 1980. ii, 30 p. : LC Card
80-603048 DDC 358/.17/0973 19
KF27 .A7 1980c

North American economic interdependence .

United States. Congress. Senate. Committee on
Finance. Subcommittee on International Trade.
Washington , 1979. iii, 110 p. ;   LC Card
   80-601405   DDC 337.1/7 19
KF26 .F554 1979j

North American fauna .
(no. 73) Faanes, Craig A. Birds of the St. Croix
River Valley, Minnesota and Wisconsin /.
Washington, D.C. , 1981. 196 p. :   LC Card
   81-607022   DDC 596.097 s 598.29775/1 19
QL155 .A4 no. 73 QL683.S23

North American tortoises : conservation and
ecology / edited by R. Bruce Bury in
cooperation with World Wildlife Fund.
Washington, D.C. : U. S. Dept. of the Interior,
Fish and Wildlife Service, 1981. p. cm. (Wildlife
research report . 12)   LC Card 81-607867   DDC
   597.92 19
*1. Gopherus. 2. Reptiles - North America. I. Bury, R.
Bruce. II. World Wildlife Fund. III. Series.*
QL666.C584 N67

NORTH ATLANTIC ASSEMBLY.
United States. Library of Congress. Foreign
Affairs and National Defense Division. The role
of the North Atlantic Assembly /. Washington ,
1979. vii, 55 p. ;   LC Card 80-601029   DDC
   341.24/3 19
JX1393.N67 U519 1979

North Atlantic Treaty Organization.
Cargèse Summer Institute on Recent
Developments in Gravitation, 1978. Recent
developments in gravitation, Cargèse, 1978 /.
New York , c1979. viii, 596 p. :   ISBN
   0-306-40198-3   LC Card 79-9174
QC178 .C18 1978

Nato Advanced Study Institute on Atomic and
Molecular Processes in Controlled
Thermonuclear Fusion, Castéra-Verduzan,
France, 1979. Atomic and molecular physics in
controlled thermonuclear fusion /. New York ,
c1980. xii, 493 p. :   ISBN 0-306-40424-9   LC
   Card 80-238
QC791.7 .N37 1979   NYPL [JSF 81-175]

Nato Advanced Study Institute on Field
Theoretical Methods in Particle Physics,
University of Kaiserslautern, 1979. Field
theoretical methods in particle physics /. New
York , c1980. ix, 598 p. :   ISBN 0-306-40444-3
   LC Card 80-11773
QC793.3.F5 N37 1979   NYPL [JSF 80-1051]

**NORTH ATLANTIC TREATY
ORGANIZATION.**
Hillier, Pat. U. S. ground forces . [Washington,
D.C.] , 1980. xxiii, 87 p. :   LC Card 81-600683
   DDC 355/.033073 19
UA23 .H513

Kaplan, Lawrence S. A community of interests .
Washington, D.C. , 1980. xii, 251 p. :   LC Card
   81-600535   DDC 355/.032/4 19
UA12 .K28

NATO--a status report . Washington , 1980.
viii, 24 p. ;   LC Card 80-603869   DDC
   355/.031/091821 19
UA646.3 .N225

Strausz-Hupé, Robert, 1903- NATO, task of
adaptation /. [Columbia] , 1978. 18 p. ;   LC
   Card 79-622644   DDC 341.7/2 19
JX1393.N67 S77

United States. Congress. House. Committee on
Foreign Affairs. NATO and Western security in
the 1980's--the European perception .
Washington , 1980. viii, 78 p. :   LC Card
   80-601730   DDC 355/.03304 19
UA646 .U48 1980

United States. Congress. House. Committee on
Foreign Affairs. Subcommittee on Europe and
the Middle East. United States-Western
European relations in 1980 . Washington ,
1980. xi, 320 p. :   LC Card 80-603423   DDC
   327.7304 19
KF27 .F64214 1980b

United States. Congress. Senate. Committee on
Armed Services. Subcommittee on Procurement
Policy and Reprograming. NATO support
agreements . Washington , 1980. iii, 17 p. ;   LC
   Card 80-603045   DDC 341.7/2 19
KF26 .A768 1980

United States. General Accounting Office. The
multinational F-16 aircraft program .
[Washington] 1979. v, 32 p. ;   LC Card

79-603054   DDC 358.4/183/0973 19
UF533 .U52 1979a

**North Atlantic Treaty Organization. Advisory
Group for Aerospace Research and
Development.** (Old Catalog form: North
Atlantic Treaty Organization. Aeronautical
Research and Development, Advisory Group
for)
How to obtain information in different fields of
science and technology: a user's guide / North
Atlantic Treaty Organization, Advisory Group
for Aerospace Research and Development.
Langley Field, Va.: National Distribution
Centre; United States NASA, 1974. 1 v. of
various pagings; 30 cm. (AGARD lecture series. no.
69) Includes bibliographies.
*1. Science - Information services. 2. Technology -
Information services. I. United States. National
Aeronautics and Space Administration. II. Title.*
                          NYPL [JSG 80-127]

**North Atlantic Treaty Organization. Aerospace
Research and Development, Advisory Group
for. see North Atlantic Treaty Organization.
Advisory Group for Aerospace Research and
Development.**

**NORTH ATLANTIC TREATY
ORGANIZATION - ARMED FORCES -
WEAPONS SYSTEMS - STANDARDS.**
Malone, Daniel K. ROLAND, a case for or
against NATO standardization? /. Washington,
DC , 1980. ix, 120 p. ;   LC Card 80-602358
   DDC 358/.175/091821 19
UF530 .M26

**North Atlantic Treaty Organization. Division of
Scientific Affairs.** (Old Catalog form: North
Atlantic Treaty Organization. Scientific
Affairs Division)
Nato Advanced Study Institute on
Nondestructive Evaluation of Semiconductor
Materials and Devices, Villa Tuscolano, Italy,
1978. Nondestructive evaluation of
semiconductor materials and devices . New
York , c1979. xi, 782 p. :   ISBN 0-306-40293-9
   LC Card 79-16499
TK7871.85 .N376 1978   NYPL [JSF 80-961]

Nato Conference on Fjord Oceanography,
Victoria, B.C., 1979. Fjord oceanography . New
York , c1980. xiv, 715 p. :   ISBN 0-306-40439-7
   LC Card 80-12273
GC28 .N37 1979   NYPL [JSF 80-1088]

**North Atlantic Treaty Organization. Eco-
Sciences, Special Program Panel on. see
North Atlantic Treaty Organization. Special
Program Panel on Eco-Sciences.**

**North Atlantic Treaty Organization. Economics
Directorate.**
Regional development in the USSR .
Newtonville, Mass. , 1979. 294 p. (p. 294
blank) :   ISBN 0-89250-115-4   LC Card 79-91195
HT395.R8 R43   NYPL [JLE 80-2914]

Regional development in the USSR .
Newtonville, Mass. , 1979. 294 p. (p. 294
blank) :   ISBN 0-89250-115-4   LC Card 79-91195
HT395.R8 R43

**North Atlantic Treaty Organization. Information
Directorate.**
Regional development in the USSR .
Newtonville, Mass. , 1979. 294 p. (p. 294
blank) :   ISBN 0-89250-115-4   LC Card 79-91195
HT395.R8 R43   NYPL [JLE 80-2914]

Regional development in the USSR .
Newtonville, Mass. , 1979. 294 p. (p. 294
blank) :   ISBN 0-89250-115-4   LC Card 79-91195
HT395.R8 R43

**North Atlantic Treaty Organization. Marine
Sciences, Special Program Panel on. see
North Atlantic Treaty Organization. Special
Program Panel on Marine Sciences.**

**NORTH ATLANTIC TREATY
ORGANIZATION - MILITARY POLICY.**
Lunn, Simon. NATO after Afghanistan .
Washington , 1980. ix, 64 p. ;   LC Card
   80-603855   DDC 355/.031/091821 19
UA646.3 .L85

**NORTH ATLANTIC TREATY
ORGANIZATION - NORWAY.**
Amundsen, Kirsten. Norway, NATO, and the
forgotten Soviet challenge /. Berkeley , c1981.
vi, 50 p. :   ISBN 0-87725-514-8 (pbk.) :   LC Card

81-80337   DDC 355/.0330481 19
UA750 .A56

**North Atlantic Treaty Organization. Office of
the Scientific Adviser. see North Atlantic
Treaty Organization. Division of Scientific
Affairs.**

**North Atlantic Treaty Organization. Scientific
Affairs Division. see North Atlantic Treaty
Organization. Division of Scientific Affairs.**

**NORTH ATLANTIC TREATY
ORGANIZATION - SPAIN.**
Dreisonstok, Thomas F. Spain and NATO.
Carlisle Barracks, Pa., 1971. iii, 52 leaves.
                        *NYPL [*XME-9305]*

**North Atlantic Treaty Organization. Special
Program Panel on Eco-Sciences.** Conference
on the Functions of Living Plant Collections in
Conservation and Conservation-Orientated
Research and Public Education, Kew, Eng.,
1975. Conservation of threatened plants . New
York , c1976. xvi, 336 p. :   ISBN 0-306-32801-1
   LC Card 76-20762
QK86.A1 C66 1975   NYPL [JSK 77-181 v.1]

**North Atlantic Treaty Organization. Special
Program Panel on Marine Sciences.** Marine
natural products chemistry . New York , c1977.
x, 433 p. :   ISBN 0-306-32921-2   LC Card
   76-58470
QH91.8.B5 M37   NYPL [JSF 80-872]

**North Carolina. Administrative Office of the
Courts.**
Brannon, Joan G. The judicial system in North
Carolina /. Raleigh, N.C. , 1977. 32 p. :   LC
   Card 80-621864   DDC 347.752/01 19
KFN7910.Z9 B7

North Carolina. State University, Raleigh.
School of Design. 100 courts . [Raleigh, N.C.]
[1978] 2 v. :   LC Card 80-621917   DDC
   725/.15/09756 19
NA4472.N8 N67 1978

**NORTH CAROLINA AGRICULTURAL AND
TECHNICAL STATE UNIVERSITY -
MAPS.**
North Carolina Agricultural and Technical State
University. Physical Plant Dept. North Carolina
Agricultural and Technical State University,
Greensboro, North Carolina /. [Greensboro]
[1978] 1 map ;   LC Card 81-690418
G3904.G7:2N5 1978 .N6

**North Carolina Agricultural and Technical State
University. Physical Plant Dept.** North
Carolina Agricultural and Technical State
University, Greensboro, North Carolina /
Physical Plant Department ; campus layout
drawn by J.W. Chow, date June 6, 1975. Rev.
1978. [Greensboro] : The Dept., [1978] 1 map ;
28 x 44 cm. Oriented with north toward the upper
right.   LC Card 81-690418
*1. North Carolina Agricultural and Technical State
University - Maps. I. Chow, J. W.*
G3904.G7:2N5 1978 .N6

**North Carolina. Agricultural Experiment Station.
Technical bulletin .**
(no. 256) Rutz, D. A. Factors affecting
production of the mosquito, Culex
quinquefasciatus (=fatigans) from anaerobic
animal waste lagoons /. [Raleigh] , 1978. 32
p. :   LC Card 80-622296   DDC 630 s 614.4/323
   19
S97 .E25 no. 256 RA640

**North Carolina. Agricultural Experiment Station,
Raleigh.** King, John M. Soil survey of
Henderson County, North Carolina /.
[Washington, D.C. , 1980] viii, 89 p., [15] fold.
leaves of plates :   LC Card 80-602311   DDC
   631.4/7/75692 19
S599.N8 K55

**North Carolina. Agricultural Research Service.
Technical bulletin - Agricultural Research
Service .**
(no. 258) Marin, Carmen M. Tobacco
literature, a bibliography /. Raleigh [1979]
iii, 362 p. ;   LC Card 80-621376   DDC
   016.6337/1 19
Z7882 .M37 SB273

(no. 259) Smith, Clyde Fuhriman, 1913- An
annotated list of Aphididae (Homoptera) of
the Caribbean islands and South and Central
America /. [Raleigh] , 1979. 131 p. ;   LC

63

GOVERNMENT PUBLICATIONS - U.S.: 1981
North Carolina. Division of Archives and History. Archaeology

Card 80-621377   DDC 595.7/52 19
QL527.A64 S64

(no. 263) Gerstel, Dan U. Cytoplasmic male
sterility in Nicotiana . [Raleigh] , 1980. 31
p. ;   LC Card 80-622299   DDC 633.7/1 19
QK495.S7 G47

North Carolina airport system plan . North
Carolina. Dept. of Transportation. Office of the
Assistant Secretary for Planning. Raleigh
[1979] 2 v. : LC Card 80-622937   DDC
387.7/36/09757 19
HE9797.5.U52 N86 1979

**NORTH CAROLINA - ANTIQUITIES -
BIBLIOGRAPHY - CATALOGS.**
Hargrove, Thomas H. A guide to research
papers in the archaeology of North Carolina on
file with the Archaeology Branch of the North
Carolina Division of Archives and History /.
Raleigh , 1980. ii, 105 p. ;   LC Card 80-622594
DDC 016.9756 19
Z1319 .H37 F256

**North Carolina Archeological Council.
Publication - North Carolina Archeological
Council** .
(13) Hargrove, Thomas H. A guide to
research papers in the archaeology of North
Carolina on file with the Archaeology Branch
of the North Carolina Division of Archives
and History /. Raleigh , 1980. ii, 105 p. ;
LC Card 80-622594   DDC 016.9756 19
Z1319 .H37 F256

**North Carolina. Archives and History, Division
of. see North Carolina. Division of Archives
and History.**

North Carolina. Bicycle Program. Hunter,
William W. Mopeds, an analysis of 1976-1978
North Carolina accidents /. Chapel Hill, N.C.
[1979] 194 p. in various pagings :   LC Card
80-622241   DDC 363.1/259 19
HE5614.3.N6 H86

North Carolina. Board of Architecture.
Architectural practice act, Professional
corporation act, rules of the State Board /
North Carolina Board of Architecture. 7th
combined ed. [Raleigh, N.C.] : The Board,
1980. 39 p. ; 23 cm. Cover title. Sixth ed. published
in 1977 under title: Architectural practice act and
related statutes, regulations of the State Board.   LC
Card 80-622691   DDC 344.756//0176172 19
1. Architects - Legal status, laws, etc. - North Carolina.
I. Title.
KFN7729.A7 A3 1980

**North Carolina. Board of Public Welfare. see
North Carolina. State Board of Public
Welfare.**

**NORTH CAROLINA. BOARD OF WATER
WELL CONTRACTOR EXAMINERS.**
North Carolina. Governmental Evaluation
Commission. Governmental Evaluation
Commission report on North Carolina Board of
Water Well Contractor Examiners. Raleigh,
N.C. [1978?] ii, 21 p. ;   LC Card 79-626103
DDC 353.9755082//325 19
TD224.N8 N675 1978

**North Carolina. Bureau of Employment Security
Research.**
Labor supply and demand, North Carolina,
1980 / prepared by Bureau of Employment
Security Research. [Raleigh, N.C.] :
Employment Security Commission of North
Carolina, [1980] 81 p. ; 28 cm. Bibliography: p.
80-81. LC Card 80-623291   DDC 331.12/09756 19
1. North Carolina - Occupations. 2. Labor supply -
North Carolina. 3. Job vacancies - North Carolina. I.
Title.
HD5725.N8 N64 1980a

North Carolina wage rates and weekly earnings
in selected occupations. 1973- Raleigh. 28 cm.
Biennial. Formed by the union of its North Carolina
occupational wage rates in production jobs, and its
North Carolina weekly earnings in nonproduction
occupations (latter title not in the library).
1. Wages - North Carolina - Periodicals. I. Title.
NYPL [JLM 81-14]

North Carolina youth : labor market statistics /
Employment Security Commission, [Bureau of
Employment Security Research]. Raleigh,
N.C. : The Bureau, [1979] ii, 83 p. ; 28 cm. (A
Labor market information publication of the Bureau of
Employment Security Research) "July, 1979."   LC
Card 80-623680   DDC 331.3/412/09756 19

1. Youth - Employment - North Carolina. 2. Manpower
policy - North Carolina. I. North Carolina. Employment
Security Commission. II. Series: Labor market
information publication (Raleigh). III. Title.
HD6274.N8 N83 1979

Occupational employment in nonmanufacturing,
North Carolina, 1978 / prepared by Bureau of
Employment Security Research. Raleigh, N.C. :
Employment Security Commission of North
Carolina, [1980] iv, 57 p. : graphs ; 28 cm. (A
Labor market information publication) "January 1980."
LC Card 80-623030   DDC 331.12/5/09756 19
1. Labor supply - North Carolina. 2. North Carolina -
Occupations. I. Series: Labor market information
publication (Raleigh). II. Title.
HD5725.N8 N64 1980

Projections to 1982 . Raleigh, N.C. [1979] 17
v. ;   LC Card 80-622695   DDC 331.12/09756 19
HD5725.N8 P76

North Carolina. Chronic Disease Branch.
Epilepsy in North Carolina : resources and
recommendations. Raleigh, N.C. : Chronic
Disease Branch, Division of Health Services,
Dept. of Human Resources, 1977. 286, [65] p. :
ill. ; 29 cm. Includes bibliographical references.   LC
Card 79-622838   DDC 362.1//96853009756 19
1. Epilepsy - North Carolina. 2. Epileptics - Services
for - North Carolina. I. Title.
RA645.E64 N67 1977

**North Carolina. Community Planning Division.
see North Carolina. Division of Community
Planning.**

**North Carolina. Council on the Status of
Women.** Aftermath : a report on sexual
assault in North Carolina. Raleigh : Dept. of
Administration, North Carolina Council on the
Status of Women, 1978. xvii, 37 p. ; 28 cm.
LC Card 79-624323   DDC 364.1/532//0756 19
1. Rape - North Carolina. 2. Rape victims - Services
for - North Carolina. I. Title.
HV6565.N8 N67 1978

North Carolina. County Court (Gates Co.) Gates
County, North Carolina, court minutes /
Marilyn Poe Laird, Vivian Poe Jackson, Judith
Krause Reid. [Calumet Park, Il.] : Poe
Publishers, [1979?- v. : map ; 28 cm. Includes
indexes.   LC Card 80-100182
1. Court records - North Carolina - Gates County. 2.
Gates County, N. C. - Genealogy. I. Laird, Marilyn
Poe. II. Jackson, Vivian Poe. III. Reid, Judith Krause.
IV. Title.
KFN7916.G38 A7 1779

**North Carolina. Courts, Administrative Office of
the. see North Carolina. Administrative
Office of the Courts.**

**North Carolina. Dept. of Administration.
Division of Policy Development.** Balanced
growth in North Carolina : a technical report.
[Raleigh] : Division of Policy Development,
Dept. of Administration, State of North
Carolina, [1979] 331 p. : ill. ; 22 x 30 cm.
"December 1979."   LC Card 80-622591   DDC
338.9756 19
1. North Carolina - Economic conditions. 2. Economic
zoning - North Carolina. I. Title.
HC107.N8 N634 1979

**North Carolina. Dept. of Conservation and
Development. Community Planning Division.
see North Carolina. Division of Community
Planning.**

**North Carolina. Dept. of Conservation and
Development. Division of Community
Planning. see North Carolina. Division of
Community Planning.**

**North Carolina. Dept. of Crime Control and
Public Safety.** A crime control agenda for
North Carolina : a comprehensive crime control
report to the Governor and the 1979 General
Assembly, and matters to consider in the future
/ J. Phil Carlton, secretary, Department of
Crime Control and Public Safety. [Raleigh,
N.C.] : The Dept., 1978. 562 p. : ill. ; 28 cm.
LC Card 80-622242   DDC 364/.9756 19
1. Law enforcement - North Carolina. 2. Crime
prevention - North Carolina. I. Carlton, John Phil,
1938-. II. Title.
HV7283 .A6 1978

**North Carolina. Dept. of Cultural Resources.
Division of Archives and History. see North
Carolina. Division of Archives and History.**

**North Carolina. Dept. of Cultural Resources.
Division of State Library. see North
Carolina. Division of State Library.**

**North Carolina. Dept. of Human Resources.
Division of Facility Services. Licensure and
Certification Section.**
Rules and regulations for the licensing of home
health agencies. Raleigh, N.C. : North Carolina
Dept. of Human Resources, Division of Facility
Services, Licensure and Certification Section,
[1980] 14 p. ; 23 cm. "August 1, 1980."   LC Card
81-621294   DDC 344.756//03214 347.56043214
19
1. Home care services - Law and legislation - North
Carolina. I. Title.
KFN7763.H65 A32 1980

Rules and regulations for the licensing of
nursing homes and home for the aged beds
when licensed as a part of a nursing home.
Raleigh, N.C. (P.O. Box 12200, Raleigh
27605) : North Carolina Dept. of Human
Resources, Division of Facility Services,
Licensure and Certification Section, [1980] 34
p. ; 23 cm. "August 1, 1980."   LC Card 81-621297
DDC 344.756//03216 347.56043216 19
1. Nursing homes - Licenses - North Carolina. 2. Old
age homes - Licenses - North Carolina. I. Title.
KFN7763.N8 A32 1980

**North Carolina. Dept. of Human Resources.
Division of Social Services. Special report.**
no. 46- ; Oct. 1979- Raleigh.
NYPL [Econ. Div.]

**North Carolina. Dept. of Motor Vehicles. State
Highway Patrol. see North Carolina. State
Highway Patrol.**

**North Carolina. Dept. of Transportation and
Highway Safety. State Highway Patrol. see
North Carolina. State Highway Patrol.**

**North Carolina. Dept. of Transportation. Office
of the Assistant Secretary for Planning.**
North Carolina airport system plan : technical
report / prepared by N.C. Department of
Transportation, Office of Assistant Secretary for
Planning ... [et al.]. Raleigh : The Office, [1979]
2 v. : ill. ; 22 x 28 cm.   LC Card 80-622937
DDC 387.7/36/09757 19
1. Airports - North Carolina. 2. Aeronautics,
Commercial - North Carolina. I. Title.
HE9797.5.U52 N86 1979

Smith (Wilbur) and Associates. North Carolina
rail plan, 1979 /. [Raleigh] [1979] 300 p. in
various pagings, [2] leaves of plates :   LC Card
80-621028   DDC 385/.09756 19
TF24.N8 S64 1979

**North Carolina. Division of Archives and
History.**
Mitchell, Thornton W. Preliminary guide to
records relating to Blacks in the North Carolina
State Archives /. [Raleigh] [1980] 14 p. ;   LC
Card 80-623389   DDC 975.6 s
016.9756//00496073 19
F251 .N67a no. 17 Z1361.N39 E185.93.N6

Records relating to Tennessee in the North
Carolina State archives / by C.F.W. Coker and
George Stevenson. Rev. Raleigh, N.C. : State of
North Carolina, Dept. of Cultural Resources,
Division of Archives and History, 1980. 7 p. :
ill. ; 28 cm. (Archives information circular . no. 3)
Caption title.   LC Card 80-623026   DDC 975.6 s
016.9768 19
1. North Carolina. Division of Archives and History -
Catalogs. 2. Tennessee - History - Sources -
Bibliography - Catalogs. I. Coker, Charles F. W. II.
Stevenson, George, 1936-. III. Title. IV. Series.
F251 .N67a no. 3, 1980 CD3424

Smith, Herbert McKelden, 1951- Architectural
resources . Raleigh, N.C. , 1979. 177 p. :   LC
Card 80-622823   DDC 720/.9756/62 19
NA730.N82 G847

Stevenson, George, 1936- A select bibliography
for genealogical research in North Carolina /.
Raleigh, N.C. , c1980. 18 p. ;   LC Card
80-623027   DDC 975.6 s 016.929/1/09756 19
F251 .N67a no. 10, 1980 Z1319 F253

**North Carolina. Division of Archives and History.
Archaeology Branch.**
Hargrove, Thomas H. A guide to research
papers in the archaeology of North Carolina on
file with the Archaeology Branch of the North
Carolina Division of Archives and History /.
Raleigh , 1980. ii, 105 p. ;   LC Card 80-622594

BIBLIOGRAPHIC GUIDE

North Carolina. Division of Archives and History. Archaeology   *64*

DDC 016.9756 19
Z1319 .H37 F256

**NORTH CAROLINA. DIVISION OF
ARCHIVES AND HISTORY.
ARCHAEOLOGY BRANCH - CATALOGS.**
Hargrove, Thomas H. A guide to research
papers in the archaeology of North Carolina on
file with the Archaeology Branch of the North
Carolina Division of Archives and History /.
Raleigh , 1980. ii, 105 p. ;   LC Card 80-622594
DDC 016.9756 19
Z1319 .H37 F256

**NORTH CAROLINA. DIVISION OF
ARCHIVES AND HISTORY -
CATALOGS.**
Mitchell, Thornton W. Preliminary guide to
records relating to Blacks in the North Carolina
State Archives /. [Raleigh] [1980] 14 p. ;   LC
Card 80-623389   DDC 975.6 s
016.9756/00496073 19
F251 .N67a no. 17 Z1361.N39 E185.93.N6

North Carolina. Division of Archives and
History. Records relating to Tennessee in the
North Carolina State archives /. Raleigh, N.C. ,
1980. 7 p. :   LC Card 80-623026   DDC 975.6 s
016.9768 19
F251 .N67a no. 3, 1980 CD3424

North Carolina. Division of Community Planning.
(Old Catalog form: North Carolina.
Conservation and Development Dept.
Community Planning Division)
Community facilities plan, Louisburg, N. C. /
[prepared by State of North Carolina,
Department of Conservation and Development,
Division of Community Planning]. [Raleigh? N.
C. : The Division, 1963]. 22 leaves ; 28 cm.
Microfilm. Cover title.
*1. Municipal services - North Carolina - Louisburg. I.
Title.*   **NYPL [*ZT-1250]**

North Carolina. Division of Marine Fisheries.
Sampair, James L. Buried oyster shell resource
evaluation of the eastern region of the
Albemarle Sound /. Raleigh , 1976. iii, 47 p. :
LC Card 78-623214   DDC 553.5 19
SH379.5 .S25

**North Carolina. Division of Mineral Resources.
Special publication .**
(4) Randazzo, Anthony F. Petrography and
stratigraphy of the Carolina Slate Belt, Union
County, North Carolina /. Raleigh , 1972. iii
leaves, 38 p., [1] fold leaf of plates :   LC Card
80-623227   DDC 553/.09756 s 552.09756/755
19
QE147 .A32 no. 4 QE445.N8

**North Carolina. Division of Services for the
Blind.** Technology and the handicapped:
telecommunication services in the rehabilitation
of the blind . Raleigh , 1977. v leaves, 163 p. :
LC Card 79-623503   DDC 362.4/183 19
HV1701 .T43

**North Carolina. Division of State Budget and
Management. Research snd Planning
Services. Demographic Research.** North
Carolina township estimates and projections.
Raleigh, N.C. (116 W. Jones St., Raliegh
27611) , 1979. [46] p. ;   LC Card 80-623292
DDC 312/.8/09756 19
HA555 .N67

North Carolina. Division of State Library.
Checklist of official North Carolina
publications. v. 1, no. 1- ; Jan./June 1980-
Raleigh. Supersedes: North Carolina. State Library,
Raleigh. North Carolina Publications; a checklist of
official state publications.
I. Title.   **NYPL [Econ. Div.]**

North Carolina. Division of the State Library.
see **North Carolina. Division of State
Library.**

North Carolina dog law manual. North Carolina.
Laws, statutes, etc. 1979 supplement to North
Carolina dog law manual /. [Chapel Hill]
[1979?] 47 p. ;   LC Card 80-623111   DDC
346.75604/7 19
KFN7484.5.D63 A3 1979 Suppl

**NORTH CAROLINA - ECONOMIC
CONDITIONS.**
North Carolina. Dept. of Administration.
Division of Policy Development. Balanced
growth in North Carolina . [Raleigh] [1979]
331 p. :   LC Card 80-622591   DDC 338.9756 19
HC107.N8 N634 1979

NORTH CAROLINA - ECONOMIC POLICY.
North Carolina. State Goals and Policy Board.
A balanced growth policy for North Carolina .
[Raleigh?] , 1978. v, 52, 15 p. :   LC Card
79-625002   DDC 338.9756 19
HC107.N8 N645 1978

**North Carolina. Employment Security
Commission.**
North Carolina. Bureau of Employment
Security Research. North Carolina youth .
Raleigh, N.C. [1979] ii, 83 p. ;   LC Card
80-623680   DDC 331.3/412/09756 19
HD6274.N8 N83 1979

Projections to 1982 . Raleigh, N.C. [1979] 17
v. ;   LC Card 80-622695   DDC 331.12/09756 19
HD5725.N8 P76

**North Carolina. Employment Security
Commission. Bureau of Employment Security
Research.** see **North Carolina. Bureau of
Employment Security Research.**

**North Carolina. Employment Security Research,
Bureau of.** see **North Carolina. Bureau of
Employment Security Research.**

North Carolina. Energy Division. Energy
consumption in North Carolina, 1960-1977 /
North Carolina Energy Division. Raleigh : The
Division, [1978?] 29 leaves ; 28 cm.   LC Card
80-623032   DDC 333.79/13/09756 19
*1. Energy consumption - North Carolina - Statistics. 2.
Energy policy - North Carolina - Statistics. I. Title.*
HD9502.U53 N674 1978

**NORTH CAROLINA - GENEALOGY -
BIBLIOGRAPHY.**
Stevenson, George, 1936- A select bibliography
for genealogical research in North Carolina /.
Raleigh, N.C. , c1980. 18 p. ;   LC Card
80-623027   DDC 975.6 s 016.929/1/09756 19
F251 .N67a no. 10, 1980 Z1319 F253

North Carolina. General Assembly.
North Carolina. General Assembly. Committee
on Retirement Benefits in Addition to Salary.
Report to the 1979 General Aasembly of North
Carolina, second session, 1980 /. [Raleigh ,
1980] 74 p. in various pagings /   LC Card
80-624247   DDC 353.9756005 19
JK4160 .N666 1980

North Carolina. Legislative Research
Commission. Administration rules . [Raleigh]
[1980] i, 11, [63] p. ;   LC Card 80-623286   DDC
348.756/025 19
KFN7890 .A25 1980

North Carolina. Legislative Research
Commission. Administrative rules . Raleigh,
N.C. (State Legislative Building, Raleigh
27611) , 1980. iii, 13, [97] p. :   LC Card
81-621511   DDC 342.756/066 347.560266 19
KFN7840 .A25 1980

North Carolina. Legislative Research
Commission. Alcoholic beverage control laws .
[Raleigh, N.C.] [1980] 6, [6] p. ;   LC Card
80-623337   DDC 344.756/0541 19
KFN7775 .A25 1980

North Carolina. Legislative Research
Commission. Alien landholding . Raleigh, N.C.
(Room 2126, 2226, State Legislative Bldg.,
Raleigh, N.C. 27611) [1981] 42 p. in various
pagings :   LC Card 81-621648   DDC 346.75604/32
347.5606432 19
KFN7512.5 .A25 1981

North Carolina. Legislative Research
Commission. Alternative work schedules .
Raleigh (State Legislative Building, Raleigh
27611) [1981] 48 p. in various pagings :   LC
Card 81-621513   DDC 342.73/0686 347.302686
19
KFN7835 .A25 1981

North Carolina. Legislative Research
Commission. Drivers' education and school bus
drivers' programs . Raleigh, N.C. (Room 2126,
2226, State Legislative Bldg., Raleigh, N.C.
27611) [1981] 86 p. in various pagings ;   LC
Card 81-621691   DDC 629.28/32/0712756 19
TL152.66.U5 N67 1981

North Carolina. Legislative Research
Commission. Gasohol production and
distribution . [Raleigh] [1980] iv, 16, [29] p. :
LC Card 80-623287   DDC 338.4/7662669 19
KFN7691.G37 A25 1980

North Carolina. Legislative Research
Commission. Hydroelectric generation of

power . [Raleigh, N.C.] [1980] 16, [4] p. :   LC
Card 80-623336   DDC 363.6/2 19
TK1424.N8 N67 1980

North Carolina. Legislative Research
Commission. Police traffic radar . [Raleigh]
[1980] 11, [36] p. :   LC Card 80-623288   DDC
363.2/52 19
KFN7697.8 .A25 1980

North Carolina. Legislative Research
Commission. Revenue laws . [Raleigh] [1980]
ix, 31, [51] p. ;   LC Card 80-623283   DDC
343.75604 19
KFN7870 .A25 1980

**North Carolina. General Assembly. Committee
on Retirement Benefits in Addition to
Salary.** Report to the 1979 General
Aasembly of North Carolina, second session,
1980 / Committee on Retirement Benefits in
Addition to Salary. [Raleigh : State of North
Carolina, Legislative Services Commission,
1980] 74 p. in various pagings ; 28 cm. "June 5,
1980"--p. iii.   LC Card 80-624247   DDC 353.9756005
19
*1. Civil service pensions - North Carolina. 2. Civil
service pensioners - Employment - North Carolina. 3.
North Carolina - Officials and employees - Salaries,
allowances, etc. 4. Retirement income - North Carolina.
I. North Carolina. General Assembly. II. Title.*
JK4160 .N666 1980

**North Carolina. General Assembly. Legislative
Research Commission.** see **North Carolina.
Legislative Research Commission.**

**North Carolina. Geological Survey Section.
Bulletin - North Carolina, Geological Survey
Section.**
Parker, John Marson, 1906- Geology and
mineral resources of Wake County /.
Raleigh , 1979. xi, 122 p., 4 leaves of plates
(3 fold.) :   LC Card 80-621007   DDC 557.56/55
19
QE148.W25 P37

Parker, John Marson, 1906- Geology and
mineral resources of Wake County /. Raleigh ,
1979. xi, 122 p., 4 leaves of plates (3 fold.) :
LC Card 80-621007   DDC 557.56/55 19
QE148.W25 P37

**North Carolina. Geology and Mineral Resources
Section.
Bulletin - North Carolina, Geology and
Mineral Resources Section .**
(85) Sampair, James L. Buried oyster shell
resource evaluation of the eastern region of
the Albemarle Sound /. Raleigh , 1976. iii,
47 p. :   LC Card 78-623214   DDC 553.5 19
SH379.5 .S25

**North Carolina. Governmental Evaluation
Commission.**
Governmental Evaluation Commission report
on North Carolina Board of Registration for
Professional Engineers and Land Surveyors.
Raleigh, N.C. : The Commission, [1979] v, 37
p. ; 28 cm. Cover title.   LC Card 79-626110   DDC
353.97560082/42 19
*1. North Carolina. State Board of Registration for
Professional Engineers and Land Surveyors. I. Title.*
TA157 .N55 1979

Governmental Evaluation Commission report
on North Carolina Board of Water Well
Contractor Examiners. Raleigh, N.C. : The
Commission, [1978?] ii, 21 p. ; 28 cm. Cover
title.   LC Card 79-626103   DDC 353.9755082/325 19
*1. North Carolina. Board of Water Well Contractor
Examiners. I. Title.*
TD224.N8 N675 1978

Governmental Evaluation Commission report
on North Carolina State Board of Examiners of
Electrical Contractors. Raleigh, N.C. : The
Commission, [1979?] v, 26 p. ; 28 cm. Cover
title.   LC Card 79-626116   DDC 353.97560082/42 19
*1. North Carolina. State Board of Examiners of
Electrical Contractors. 2. Electricians - Licences -
North Carolina. 3. Electric contracting - North
Carolina. I. Title.*
HD9697.A3 U55 1979

Governmental Evaluation Commission report
on regulation of employment agencies. Raleigh,
N.C. : The Commission, [1979?] iv, 29 p. ; 28
cm. Cover title.   LC Card 79-626118   DDC
353.97560083/3 19
1. Employment agencies - North Carolina. 2. Industry

GOVERNMENT PUBLICATIONS - U.S.: 1981

65

North Carolina. Legislative Study Commission on Alternatives for

and state - North Carolina. I. Title.
HD5876.N8 N68 1979

North Carolina. Governor's Highway Safety Program. Hunter, William W. Mopeds, an analysis of 1976-1978 North Carolina accidents /. Chapel Hill, N.C. [1979] 194 p. in various pagings : LC Card 80-622241 DDC 363.1/259 19
HE5614.3.N6 H86

North Carolina. Governor's Primary Care Task Force. Report of the Governor's Primary Care Task Force / submitted to the Governor, March 1979. [Raleigh : The Task Force, 1979] ii, 23 p. ; 28 cm. LC Card 80-622769 DDC 362.1/09756 19
1. Medicine, State - North Carolina - Planning. 2. Ambulatory medical care - North Carolina - Planning. I. Title.
RA412.5.U6 N8 1979

North Carolina. Health Coordinating Council. The North Carolina State health plan / prepared by the North Carolina Health Coordinating Council. [Raleigh] : The Council, [1979] 431 p. ; 27 cm. "April 11, 1979." Includes bibliographical references. LC Card 80-621910 DDC 362.1/09756 19
1. Health planning - North Carolina. 2. Medical policy - North Carolina. 3. Public health - North Carolina. 4. Medical care - North Carolina. I. Title.
RA395.A4 N795 1979

North Carolina. Highway Patrol. see **North Carolina. State Highway Patrol.**

NORTH CAROLINA - HISTORY - SOURCES - BIBLIOGRAPHY - CATALOGS.
Mitchell, Thornton W. Preliminary guide to records relating to Blacks in the North Carolina State Archives /. [Raleigh] [1980] 14 p. ; LC Card 80-623389 DDC 975.6 s
016.9756/00496073 19
F251 .N67a no. 17 Z1361.N39 E185.93.N6

North Carolina. Laws, statutes, etc. (Old Catalog form: North Carolina. Statutes)
North Carolina radiation protection act. North Carolina. Radiation Protection Commission. North Carolina regulations for protection against radiation / adopted by the North Carolina Radiation Protection Commission, effective February 1, 1980. Raleigh, N.C. [1980] 170 p. ; LC Card 80-622690 DDC 344.756/0472 19
KFN7780.A8 A32 1980

1979 supplement to North Carolina dog law manual / compiled by Patrice Solberg. [Chapel Hill] : Institute of Government, University of North Carolina at Chapel Hill, [1979?] 47 p. ; 25 cm. Cover title. LC Card 80-623111 DDC 346.75604/7 19
1. Dogs - Law and legislation - North Carolina. I. Solberg, Patrice. II. Title. III. Title: North Carolina dog law manual.
KFN7484.5.D63 A3 1979 Suppl

North Carolina. Legislative Council. Report to the General Assembly of North Carolina : corporate tax structures of other states, the preservation of historic sites, mental institution employees, 1963 House bill 1122, municipal school transportation. [Raleigh, N.C.] : Legislative Council, 1965. 56 leaves ; 28 cm. Cover title. LC Card 80-623220 DDC 349.756 19
1. Law - North Carolina.
KFN7420 .L392

North Carolina. Legislative Research Commission.
Administration rules : report to the 1979 General Assembly of North Carolina, second session, 1980 / Legislative Research Commission. [Raleigh] : The Commission, [1980] i, 11, [63] p. ; 28 cm. LC Card 80-623286 DDC 348.756/025 19
1. Administrative procedure - North Carolina. 2. Legislative oversight - North Carolina. I. North Carolina. General Assembly. II. Title.
KFN7890 .A25 1980

Administrative rules : report to the 1981 General Assembly of North Carolina / Legislative Research Commission. Raleigh, N.C. (State Legislative Building, Raleigh 27611) : The Commission : Available through the Legislative Library, 1980. iii, 13, [97] p. : forms ; 28 cm. Cover title. LC Card 81-621511 DDC 342.756/066 347.560266 19
1. Administrative procedure - North Carolina. 2.

Administrative acts - North Carolina. 3. Legislative oversight - North Carolina. I. North Carolina. General Assembly. II. Title.
KFN7840 .A25 1980

Aging : interim report to the 1979 General Assembly of North Carolina, second session, 1980 / Legislative Research Commission. Raleigh, N.C. : The Commission, [1980] ii, 18, [14] p. ; 28 cm. LC Card 80-623284 DDC 344.756/0326 19
1. Aged - Legal status, laws, etc. - North Carolina. I. Title.
KFN7491.A3 A25 1980

Alcoholic beverage control laws : interim report to the 1979 General Assembly of North Carolina, second session, 1980. [Raleigh, N.C.] : Legislative Research Commission : available through the Legislative Library, [1980] 6, [6] p. ; 28 cm. Cover title. LC Card 80-623337 DDC 344.756/0541 19
1. Liquor laws - North Carolina. 2. Alcohol as fuel - Law and legislation - North Carolina. I. North Carolina. General Assembly. II. Title.
KFN7775 .A25 1980

Alien landholding : report to the 1981 General Assembly of North Carolina / Legislative Research Commission. Raleigh, N.C. (Room 2126, 2226, State Legislative Bldg., Raleigh, N.C. 27611) : The Commission : Available through the Legislative Library, [1981] 42 p. in various pagings : map ; 28 cm. LC Card 81-621648 DDC 346.75604/32 347.5606432 19
1. Real property - North Carolina - Foreign ownership. I. North Carolina. General Assembly. II. Title.
KFN7512.5 .A25 1981

Alternative work schedules : report to the 1981 General Assembly of North Carolina / Legislative Research Commission. Raleigh (State Legislative Building, Raleigh 27611) : The Commission : Available through Legislative Library, [1981] 48 p. in various pagings : form ; 29 cm. LC Card 81-621513 DDC 342.73/0686 347.302686 19
1. Civil service - North Carolina. 2. Hours of labor - North Carolina. I. North Carolina. General Assembly. II. Title.
KFN7835 .A25 1981

Drivers' education and school bus drivers' programs : report to the 1981 General Assembly of North Carolina / Legislative Research Commission. Raleigh, N.C. (Room 2126, 2226, State Legislative Bldg., Raleigh, N.C. 27611) : The Commission : Available through the Legislative Library, [1981] 86 p. in various pagings ; 28 cm. LC Card 81-621691 DDC 629.28/32/0712756 19
1. Automobile driver education - North Carolina. 2. Bus driving - Study and teaching - North Carolina. I. North Carolina. General Assembly. II. Title.
TL152.66.U5 N67 1981

Gasohol production and distribution : report to the 1979 General Assembly of North Carolina, second session, 1980 / Legislative Research Commission. [Raleigh] : The Commission, [1980] iv, 16, [29] p. : ill. ; 28 cm. LC Card 80-623287 DDC 338.4/7662669 19
1. Gasohol - Law and legislation - North Carolina. 2. Gasohol. I. North Carolina. General Assembly. II. Title.
KFN7691.G37 A25 1980

Housing and building codes : report to the 1979 General Assembly of North Carolina / Legislative Research Commission. Raleigh, N.C. : The Commission, [1979] 8, [15] p. ; 28 cm. LC Card 79-624368 DDC 344.756/063635 19
1. Building laws - North Carolina. 2. Housing - Law and legislation - North Carolina. I. Title.
KFN7859 .A25 1979

Hydroelectric generation of power : interim report to the 1979 General Assembly of North Carolina, second session, 1980. [Raleigh, N.C.] : Legislative Research Commission : available through the Legislative Library, [1980] 16, [4] p. : map ; 28 cm. Cover title. LC Card 80-623336 DDC 363.6/2 19
1. Hydroelectric power plants - North Carolina. 2. Electric utilities - North Carolina. 3. Energy policy - North Carolina. I. North Carolina. General Assembly. II. Title.
TK1424.N8 N67 1980

Law enforcement officers salary continuation plan : report to the 1979 General Assembly of North Carolina, second session, 1980 /

Legislative Research Commission. [Raleigh] : The Commission, [1980] iv, 12, [60] p. : graphs ; 28 cm. Cover title. LC Card 80-623281 DDC 331.2/813632/09756 19
1. Police - Salaries, pensions, etc. - North Carolina. I. Title.
KFN7835.8.S7 A25 1980

Management of waste and other environmental programs : report to the 1981 General Assembly of North Carolina / Legislative Research Commission. Raleigh, N.C. (Room 2126, 2226, State Legislative Building, Raleigh 27611) : The Commission, [1981] 14, [4] p. ; 28 cm. Cover title. LC Card 81-621654 DDC 363.7/28 19
1. Environmental protection - North Carolina. I. Title.
TD171.3.N8 N67 1981

Police traffic radar : report to the 1979 General Assembly of North Carolina, second session, 1980 / Legislative Research Commission. [Raleigh] : The Commission, [1980] 11, [36] p. : ill. ; 28 cm. LC Card 80-623288 DDC 363.2/52 19
1. Radar in speed limit enforcement - Law and legislation - North Carolina. I. North Carolina. General Assembly. II. Title.
KFN7697.8 .A25 1980

Public school facility needs : report to the 1979 General Assembly of North Carolina, second session, 1980 / Legislative Research Commission. Raleigh, N.C. : The Commission, [1980] i, 26, [96] p. ; 28 cm. Cover title. LC Card 80-622592 DDC 371.6/2/09756 19
1. School facilities - North Carolina - Planning. I. Title.
LB3241.3.N8 N67 1980

Revenue laws : report to the 1979 General Assembly of North Carolina, second session, 1980 / Legislative Research Commission. [Raleigh] : The Commission : available through the Legislative Library, [1980] x, 31, [51] p. ; 29 cm. Cover title. LC Card 80-623283 DDC 343.75604 19
1. Taxation - Law and legislation - North Carolina. I. North Carolina. General Assembly. II. Title.
KFN7870 .A25 1980

Rights of adopted children : report to the 1981 General Assembly of North Carolina / Legislative Research Commission. Raleigh (State Legislative Building, Raleigh 27611) : The Commission : Available through the Legislative Library, [1981] 19, [23] p. ; 28 cm. LC Card 81-621509 DDC 346.75601/78 347.5606178 19
1. Adoption - North Carolina. 2. Children, Adopted - Legal status, laws, etc. - North Carolina. I. Title.
KFN7504.5 .A25 1981

School finance studies : report to the 1981 General Assembly of North Carolina / Legislative Research Commission. Raleigh, N.C. (State Legislative Building, Raleigh 27611) : The Commission : Available through the Legislative Library, [1981] v, 10, [21] p. ; 28 cm. LC Card 81-621656 DDC 379.1/22/09756 19
1. Education - North Carolina - Finance. I. Title.
LB2826.N8 N67 1981

State revenue sharing : interim report to the 1979 General Assembly of North Carolina, second session, 1980 / Legislative Research Commission. [Raleigh] : The Commission : available through the Legislative Library, [1980] 17, [148] p. ; 28 cm. Cover title. LC Card 80-623285 DDC 336.1/85 19
1. Revenue sharing - North Carolina. I. Title.
HJ615 .N67 1980

Temporary employees retirement : report to the 1981 General Assembly of North Carolina / Legislative Research Commission. Raleigh (State Legislative Building, Raleigh 27611) : The Commission : Available through the Legislative Library, [1981] viii, 7, [25] p. ; 28 cm. LC Card 81-621507 DDC 344.756/012529 347.560412529 19
1. Civil service pensions - Law and legislation - North Carolina. 2. Employees, Temporary - Pensions - North Carolina. I. Title.
KFN7835.5 .A25 1981

North Carolina. Legislative Study Commission on Alternatives for Water Management.
Alternatives for water management : report of the legislative study commission to the North Carolina General Assembly. [Raleigh, N.C.] : State of North Carolina, [1980] ca. 100 p. in

various pagings ; 28 cm. "March 1980." Includes a bibliography.　LC Card 80-622778　DDC 333.91/15/09756 19
1. Water resources development - North Carolina. 2. Water-supply - North Carolina - Management. I. Title.
TC424.N8 N59 1980

North Carolina lighthouses /. Stick, David, 1919-
Raleigh , 1980. xi, 85 p. :　ISBN 0-86526-144-X (pbk.) :　LC Card 80-622599　DDC 387.1/55 19
VK1024.N8 S74

NORTH CAROLINA - MAPS.
(1974) Triangle J Council of Governments. North Carolina Region J inventory and atlas /. Research Triangle Park, N.C. , 1974. [272] p. :　LC Card 80-675218　DDC 912/.756
G1300 .T7 1974

NORTH CAROLINA - MILITIA - HISTORY - SOURCES.
Duplin County, N. C. Militia. Courts-martial. Minutes of the regimental courts-martial, Duplin County Militia, North Carolina, 1784-1853. Rose Hill, N. C., 1979. 157 leaves:
NYPL [APR (Duplin Co., N. C.) 80-1096]

NORTH CAROLINA - OCCUPATIONS.
North Carolina. Bureau of Employment Security Research. Labor supply and demand, North Carolina, 1980 /. [Raleigh, N.C.] [1980] 81 p. ;　LC Card 80-623291　DDC 331.12/09756 19
HD5725.N8 N64 1980a

North Carolina. Bureau of Employment Security Research. Occupational employment in nonmanufacturing, North Carolina, 1978 /. Raleigh, N.C. [1980] iv, 57 p. :　LC Card 80-623030　DDC 331.12/5/09756 19
HD5725.N8 N64 1980

NORTH CAROLINA - OCCUPATIONS - STATISTICS.
Projections to 1982 . Raleigh, N.C. [1979] 17 v. ;　LC Card 80-622695　DDC 331.12/09756 19
HD5725.N8 P76

NORTH CAROLINA - OFFICIALS AND EMPLOYEES - SALARIES, ALLOWANCES, ETC.
North Carolina. General Assembly. Committee on Retirement Benefits in Addition to Salary. Report to the 1979 General Aasembly of North Carolina, second session, 1980 /. [Raleigh , 1980] 74 p. in various pagings ;　LC Card 80-624247　DDC 353.9756005 19
JK4160 .N666 1980

North Carolina Population Center. see **Carolina Population Center.**

NORTH CAROLINA - POPULATION - STATISTICS.
North Carolina township estimates and projections. Raleigh, N.C. (116 W. Jones St., Raliegh 27611) , 1979. [46] p. ;　LC Card 80-623292　DDC 312/.8/09756 19
HA555 .N67

North Carolina. Public Welfare, State Board of. see **North Carolina. State Board of Public Welfare.**

North Carolina. Radiation Protection Commission. North Carolina regulations for protection against radiation / adopted by the North Carolina Radiation Protection Commission, effective February 1, 1980. Raleigh, N.C. : N.C. Dept. of Human Resources, Division of Facility Services, Radiation Protection Section, [1980] 170 p. ; 22 cm. Cover title. Regulations promulgated under the North Carolina radiation protection act.　LC Card 80-622690　DDC 344.756/0472 19
1. Radioactive substances - Law and legislation - North Carolina. 2. Radioactive substances - Safety regulations - North Carolina. I. North Carolina. Radiation Protection Section. II. North Carolina. Laws, statutes, etc. North Carolina radiation protection act. III. Title.
KFN7780.A8 A32 1980

North Carolina. Radiation Protection Section. North Carolina. Radiation Protection Commission. North Carolina regulations for protection against radiation /. Raleigh, N.C. [1980] 170 p. ;　LC Card 80-622690　DDC 344.756/0472 19
KFN7780.A8 A32 1980

North Carolina rail plan, 1979 /. Smith (Wilbur) and Associates. [Raleigh] [1979] 300 p. in

various pagings, [2] leaves of plates :　LC Card 80-621028　DDC 385/.09756 19
TF24.N8 S64 1979

North Carolina Region J inventory and atlas /. Triangle J Council of Governments. Research Triangle Park, N.C. , 1974. [272] p. :　LC Card 80-675218　DDC 912/.756
G1300 .T7 1974

North Carolina regulations for protection against radiation /. North Carolina. Radiation Protection Commission. Raleigh, N.C. [1980] 170 p. ;　LC Card 80-622690　DDC 344.756/0472 19
KFN7780.A8 A32 1980

North Carolina sheriffs' civil duties. Brannon, Joan G. Handling writs of execution /. [Chapel Hill] , 1980. 122 p. :　LC Card 81-621397　DDC 347.756/077 347.560777 19
KFN7951 .B73

North Carolina. State Board of Charities and Public Welfare. see **North Carolina. State Board of Public Welfare.**

NORTH CAROLINA. STATE BOARD OF EXAMINERS OF ELECTRICAL CONTRACTORS.
North Carolina. Governmental Evaluation Commission. Governmental Evaluation Commission report on North Carolina State Board of Examiners of Electrical Contractors. Raleigh, N.C. [1979?] v, 26 p. ;　LC Card 79-626116　DDC 353.97560082/42 19
HD9697.A3 U55 1979

North Carolina. State Board of Public Welfare. (Old Catalog form: North Carolina. Public Welfare, State Board of.)
Capital punishment in North Carolina. Raleigh, N.C. : N.C. State Board of Charities and Public Welfare, 1929. 173 p. : ill. ; 23 cm. (Special bulletin - N.C. State Board of Charities and Public Welfare ; no. 10)　LC Card 80-502322　DDC 361/.9756 s 364.6/6/09756 19
1. Capital punishment - North Carolina. 2. Prisoners - North Carolina - Case studies. I. Series: North Carolina. State Board of Public Welfare. Special bulletin , no. 10. II. Title.
HV86 .N84 no. 10 HV8699.U6N8

Special bulletin .
(no. 10) North Carolina. State Board of Public Welfare. Capital punishment in North Carolina. Raleigh, N.C. , 1929. 173 p. :　LC Card 80-502322　DDC 361/.9756 s 364.6/6/09756 19
HV86 .N84 no. 10 HV8699.U6N8

North Carolina. State Board of Refrigeration Examiners. North Carolina State Board of Refrigeration Examiners register, as of February 28, 1979 : G.S. 87, article 5--references. Raleigh, N.C. : The Board, [1979] 33 p. ; 22 x 10 cm.　LC Card 79-625627　DDC 353.97560082/42 19
1. Refrigeration industry - Licenses - North Carolina. 2. Air conditioning industry - Licenses - North Carolina.
HD9999.A53 U554 1979

NORTH CAROLINA. STATE BOARD OF REGISTRATION FOR PROFESSIONAL ENGINEERS AND LAND SURVEYORS.
North Carolina. Governmental Evaluation Commission. Governmental Evaluation Commission report on North Carolina Board of Registration for Professional Engineers and Land Surveyors. Raleigh, N.C. [1979] v, 37 p. ;　LC Card 79-626110　DDC 353.97560082/42 19
TA157 .N55 1979

North Carolina. State Commission on Higher Education Facilities. Facilities inventory and utilization manual for the State of North Carolina. 4th ed. Raleigh, N.C. : University of North Carolina, North Carolina State Commission on Higher Education Facilities, [1979] ix, 163 p. : ill. ; 28 cm. Earlier ed. published in 1969 under title: Facilities inventory and utilization study, fall of 1968, for the State of North Carolina. At head of title: Higher education comprehensive planning program. "October 1979." Includes index.　LC Card 80-621138　DDC 378/.196/09756 19
1. College facilities - North Carolina. I. Title. II. Title: Higher education comprehensive planning program.
LB3223 .N582 1979

North Carolina. State Goals and Policy Board. A balanced growth policy for North Carolina : a

proposal for public discussion. [Raleigh?] : State Goals and Policy Board, State of North Carolina, 1978. v, 52, 15 p. : map ; 28 cm. Cover title.　LC Card 79-625002　DDC 338.9756 19
1. North Carolina - Economic policy. I. Title.
HC107.N8 N645 1978

The North Carolina State health plan /. North Carolina. Health Coordinating Council. [Raleigh] [1979] 431 p. ;　LC Card 80-621910　DDC 362.1/09756 19
RA395.A4 N795 1979

North Carolina. State Highway Commission. Bright, Richard. Early hardening of asphalt in hot bituminous paving mixtures . [Raleigh] , 1966. vi, 70 p. :　LC Card 80-508397　DDC 625.8/5 s 625.8/5 19
TE270 .B67 pt. 2

Bright, Richard. The effect of viscosity of asphalt on the properties of bituminous paving mixtures /. [Raleigh] , 1966. 2 v. :　LC Card 80-508426　DDC 625.8/5 19
TE270 .B67

Bright, Richard. Hardening of asphalt in hot bituminous base, binder, and sand mixtures . [Raleigh] , 1966. vi, 83 p. :　LC Card 80-508398　DDC 625.8/5 s 625.8/5 19
TE270 .B67 pt. 1

North Carolina. State Highway Patrol.
Activity report and performance record. North Carolina. State Highway Patrol. Zone operations report. 1964-74 (incomplete). [Raleigh]　　　*NYPL [JLM 80-855]*

Field operations report. North Carolina. State Highway Patrol. Zone operations report. 1964-74 (incomplete). [Raleigh]
NYPL [JLM 80-855]

Line operations report. North Carolina. State Highway Patrol. Zone operations report. 1964-74 (incomplete). [Raleigh]
NYPL [JLM 80-855]

Zone operations report. 1964-74 (incomplete). [Raleigh] 28 cm. Semiannual, with cumulative Dec. issue. Issued by its Enforcement Division, 1964-71. Title varies: 1964-June, 1965, Activity report and performance record; Dec. 1965-1970, Report; 1971, June, 1973, Field operations report; Dec. 1972, Line operations report. Ceased publication with Dec. 1974?
1. Police, State - North Carolina - Statistics - Periodicals. I. North Carolina. State Highway Patrol. Enforcement Division. II. North Carolina. State Highway Patrol. Activity report and performance record. III. North Carolina. State Highway Patrol. Field operations report. IV. North Carolina. State Highway Patrol. Line operations report. V. Title.
NYPL [JLM 80-855]

North Carolina. State Highway Patrol. Enforcement Division. North Carolina. State Highway Patrol. Zone operations report. 1964-74 (incomplete). [Raleigh]
NYPL [JLM 80-855]

North Carolina. State Library, Division of. see **North Carolina. Division of State Library.**

North Carolina State of the University of North Carolina, Raleigh. see **North Carolina. State University, Raleigh.**

North Carolina State University. Dept. of Entomology. Movement of highly mobile insects . Raleigh, N.C. [1979] xii, 456 p. :　LC Card 80-624277　DDC 595.78/04525 19
QL551.S85 M68

North Carolina. State University, Raleigh. Southeast Conference on Urban Stormwater Management, North Carolina State University, 1979. Urban stormwater management . [Raleigh, N.C.] [1980] vi, 252 p. :　LC Card 80-623271　DDC 363.6/1 19
TD657 .S68 1979

North Carolina. State University, Raleigh. Center for Marine and Coastal Studies.
Report - Center for Marine and Coastal Studies, North Carolina State University . (no. 77-9) Boc, Stanley J. An analysis of beach overwash along North Carolina's coast /. Raleigh , 1977. 17, [7] leaves of plates (6 fold.) :　LC Card 77-624232　DDC 551.4/57/09756 19
GB459.4 .B6

North Carolina. State University, Raleigh. Center for Occupational Education. A prospectus for a vocational education policy

GOVERNMENT PUBLICATIONS - U.S.: 1981

67   North Dakota. Dept. of Accounts and Purchases. Central

resource center. Raleigh : Center for Occupational Education, North Carolina State University at Raleigh, 1975. 47 leaves ; 28 cm.
    LC Card 79-622866   DDC 370.11/3/09756 19
1. Vocational education - North Carolina. I. Title.
LC1046.N8 N68 1975

North Carolina. State University, Raleigh. Dept. of Botany. Response of phytoplankton to water quality in the Chowan River system / by A.M. Witherspoon ... [et al.] ; Department of Botany, North Carolina State University. [Raleigh, N.C.] : Water Resources Research Institute of the University of North Carolina, [1979] xv, 204 p. : ill. ; 28 cm. (Report - Water Resources Research Institute of the University of North Carolina . no. 129) "April 1979." "UNC-WRRI-79-129." "Project no. B-091-NC, agreement no. 14-34-0001-6104." Bibliography: p. 143-144.   LC Card 79-626203   DDC 589.4 19
1. Freshwater algae - North Carolina - Chowan River. 2. Water quality - North Carolina - Chowan River. 3. Freshwater phytoplankton - North Carolina - Chowan River. 4. Bacteriology - North Carolina - Chowan River. 5. Water bloom - North Carolina - Chowan River. 6. Chowan River, N.C. I. Witherspoon, A. M. II. Series: University of North Carolina (System). Water Resources Research Institute. Report , no. 129. III. Title.
HD1694.N8 N6 no. 129 QK571.5.N8

North Carolina. State University, Raleigh. Dept. of Food Science. International Conference on UHT Processing and Aseptic Packaging of Milk and Milk Products, North Carolina State University, 1979. International Conference on UHT Processing and Aseptic Packaging of Milk and Milk Products, November 27-29, 1979 . Raleigh, N.C. , c1980. iv, 230 p. :   LC Card 80-120778   DDC 637 19
SF250.5 .I56 1979

North Carolina. State University, Raleigh. School of Design. 100 courts : a report on North Carolina judicial facilities : a project of the School of Design, North Carolina State University at Raleigh for the Administrative Office of the Courts, State of North Carolina / Robert P. Burns, project director. [Raleigh, N.C.] : The Office, [1978] 2 v. : ill. ; 28 cm. Bibliography: v. 1, p. 225-227. CONTENTS. - v. 1. The statewide perspective.--v. 2. The county perspective.
    LC Card 80-621917   DDC 725/.15/09756 19
1. Court-houses - North Carolina. I. Burns, Robert Paschal, 1933-. II. North Carolina. Administrative Office of the Courts. III. Title.
NA4472.N8 N67 1978

North Carolina. State University, Raleigh. Sea Grant Program. Onslow Bay physical/dynamical experiments, summer-fall, 1975 . [Raleigh] 1978. xxiv, 170 p. :   LC Card 78-623321   DDC 551.46/148 19
GC512.N8 O56

NORTH CAROLINA - STATISTICS.
Triangle J Council of Governments. North Carolina Region J inventory and atlas /. Research Triangle Park, N.C. , 1974. [272] p. :   LC Card 80-675218   DDC 912/.756
G1300 .T7 1974

North Carolina. Statutes. see North Carolina. Laws, statutes, etc.

North Carolina. Task Force on Public Telecommunications. Interconnections for North Carolina and beyond : the report of the North Carolina Task Force on Public Telecommunications to Governor James B. Hunt, Jr. [Raleigh: The Task Force, 1979] vi, 114 p. : ill. ; 28 cm. Letter of transmittal dated April 4, 1979. Includes bibliographical references.   LC Card 80-620760
1. Telecommunication - North Carolina. 2. Telecommunication policy - North Carolina. I. Title.
HE7791.N8 N67 1979

North Carolina township estimates and projections. Raleigh, N.C. (116 W. Jones St., Raliegh 27611) : Demographic Research and Planning Services, Division of State Budget and Management, 1979. [46] p. ; 28 cm.   LC Card 80-623292   DDC 312/.8/09756 19
1. North Carolina - Population - Statistics. 2. Population forecasting - North Carolina. I. North Carolina. Division of State Budget and Management. Research snd Planning Services. Demographic Research.
HA555 .N67

North Carolina. Unemployment Compensation Commission. see North Carolina. Employment Security Commission.

North Carolina. University.
Studies in the Germanic languages and literatures. For additional listing of contents, see Old Catalog.
(no. 96) Murphy, G. Ronald, 1938- Brecht and the Bible . Chapel Hill , 1980. 104 p. ;
    ISBN 0-8078-8096-5   LC Card 80-20207
PT2603.R397 Z7856   **NYPL [RKA no. 96]**

North Carolina. University. Bureau of Community Drama. Selden, Samuel, 1899- First principles of play direction. Chapel Hill, N. C. [1937] 57 p.   LC Card 38-28085
                            NYPL [MWEO 81-10]

North Carolina. University. Community Drama, Bureau of. see North Carolina. University. Bureau of Community Drama.

North Carolina. University. Population Center. see Carolina Population Center.

North Carolina. University. State University, Raleigh. see North Carolina. State University, Raleigh.

North Carolina wage rates and weekly earnings in selected occupations. North Carolina. Bureau of Employment Security Research. 1973- Raleigh.   **NYPL [JLM 81-14]**

North Carolina youth . North Carolina. Bureau of Employment Security Research. Raleigh, N.C. [1979] ii, 83 p. ;   LC Card 80-623680   DDC 331.3/412/09756 19
HD6274.N8 N83 1979

North Coastal water quality survey, 1976 /.
Massachusetts. Water Quality and Research Section. Westborough, Mass. [1978] v, 53 p. :
    LC Card 79-620601   DDC 363.7/3942/097445 19
TD224.M4 M39 1978c

North Coastal, 1976. Massachusetts. Water Quality and Research Section. North Coastal water quality survey, 1976 /. Westborough, Mass. [1978] v, 53 p. :   LC Card 79-620601   DDC 363.7/3942/097445 19
TD224.M4 M39 1978c

North Dakota.
Constitution of North Dakota (updated through January 1, 1981) : renumbered pursuant to NDCC section 46-03-11.1. [Bismarck] : North Dakota Legislative Council, 1981. iv, 56 p. : ill. ; 22 cm. Cover title.   LC Card 81-621137   DDC 342.784/023 347.840223 19
1. North Dakota - Constitutional law. I. North Dakota. Legislative Council. II. Title.
KFN9001 1889 .A34

North Dakota. Administration on Aging.
State/area plan on aging for the State of North Dakota for fiscal year 1978 / Administration on Aging. [Bismark] : The Administration, [1977] ii, 118 p. : diagrs. ; 28 cm. Cover title.   LC Card 79-623544   DDC 362.6/09784 19
1. North Dakota. Administration on Aging. I. Title.
HV1468.N9 N67 1977

NORTH DAKOTA. ADMINISTRATION ON AGING.
North Dakota. Administration on Aging. State/area plan on aging for the State of North Dakota for fiscal year 1978 /. [Bismark] [1977] ii, 118 p. :   LC Card 79-623544   DDC 362.6/09784 19
HV1468.N9 N67 1977

North Dakota. Agricultural Experiment Station, Fargo.
Agricultural economics report .
(no. 125) Voelker, Stanley W. A functional classification of agricultural trade centers in North Dakota /. Fargo [1978] 51 p. :   LC Card 78-623601   DDC 338.1 s 381/.41/09784 19
SB205.S7 N64 no. 125 HT123.5.N9

Bacteriological analyses of Lake Metigoshe water and sediments / by M. Bromel ... [et al.]. Fargo : Agricultural Experiment Station, North Dakota State University, 1978. ii, 14 p. : ill. ; 28 cm. (Bulletin - Agricultural Experiment Station, North Dakota State University . 507) Cover title. Bibliography: p. 14.   LC Card 79-625005   DDC 363.7/3942/0978461 19
1. Sanitary microbiology - North Dakota - Metigoshe Lake. 2. Water quality - North Dakota - Metigoshe Lake. 3. Eutrophication - North Dakota - Metigoshe

Lake. I. Bromel, M. II. Series: North Dakota. Agricultural Experiment Station, Fargo. Bulletin , 507. III. Title.
QR48 .N67 1978

Bulletin .
(no. 509) Environmental, economic & social impacts of a coal gasification plant in western North Dakota /. Fargo, N.D. [1980] xii, 160 p. (p. 160 blank) :   LC Card 80-622684   DDC 338.4/7665772/0978482 19
TD195.G3 E58

(507) North Dakota. Agricultural Experiment Station, Fargo. Bacteriological analyses of Lake Metigoshe water and sediments /. Fargo , 1978. ii, 14 p. :   LC Card 79-625005   DDC 363.7/3942/0978461 19
QR48 .N67 1978

Research report .
(no. 71) North Dakota. Agricultural Experiment Station, Fargo. Water as a parameter for development of energy resources in the Upper Great Plains . Fargo, N.D. [1978] ii, 144 p. :   LC Card 79-625649   DDC 630 s 333.8/22/0978 19
S99 .A5a no. 71 HD9502.U53N683

Water as a parameter for development of energy resources in the Upper Great Plains : socioeconomic effects of alternative patterns of coal-based energy development : research project technical completion report / by Norman E. Toman ... [et al.]. Fargo, N.D. : North Dakota Agricultural Experiment Station, North Dakota State University of Agriculture and Applied Science, [1978] ii, 144 p. : ill. ; 28 cm. (Research report - North Dakota Agricultural Experiment Station . no. 71) "December 1978." Bibliography: p. 133-134.   LC Card 79-625649   DDC 630 s 333.8/22/0978 19
1. Energy policy - North Dakota. 2. Energy policy - Montana. 3. Energy policy - Wyoming. 4. Coal - North Dakota. 5. Coal - Montana. 6. Coal - Wyoming. I. Toman, Norman E. II. Series: North Dakota. Agricultural Experiment Station, Fargo. Research report , no. 71. III. Title.
S99 .A5a no. 71 HD9502.U53N683

North Dakota. Auditor's Office.
Audit report, Commissioner of Insurance, Bismarck, North Dakota : expanded scope review and financial review for the years ended June 30, 1979, 1978, and 1977 / Office of State Auditor. Bismarck, N.D. : State of North Dakota, [1980] 77, 61 p. ; 29 cm. Cover title. "Client code #408." Appendix A (1 p.) inserted.   LC Card 80-623717   DDC 353.97840082/55 19
1. North Dakota. Dept. of Insurance - Auditing and inspection. I. Title.
HG8538.N9 N92 1980

Audit report, Governor's Office, Bismarck, North Dakota : examination for the years ended June 30, 1979, June 30, 1978 / Office of State Auditor. Bismarck, N.D. : State of North Dakota, [1979?] 24 leaves ; 28 cm. Cover title. "Client code #103."   LC Card 80-623331   DDC 353.978403/1 19
1. North Dakota. Governor's Office - Accounting. 2. North Dakota. Governor's Office - Appropriations and expenditures. I. Title.
JK6452 1979 .N67

North Dakota central personnel compensation plan, July, 1979-June, 1981. North Dakota. Dept. of Accounts and Purchases. Central Personnel Division. Bismarck, N.D. [1979] 120 p. in various pagings;   LC Card 80-621617   DDC 353.9784001/23 19
JK6457 .N64 1979

NORTH DAKOTA - CONSTITUTIONAL LAW.
North Dakota. Constitution of North Dakota (updated through January 1, 1981) . [Bismarck] , 1981. iv, 56 p. :   LC Card 81-621137   DDC 342.784/023 347.840223 19
KFN9001 1889 .A34

North Dakota. Dept. of Accounts and Purchases. Central Personnel Division. North Dakota central personnel compensation plan, July, 1979-June, 1981. Bismarck, N.D. : Dept. of Accounts & Purchases, Central Personnel Division, [1979] 120 p. in various pagings ; 28 cm. Cover title.   LC Card 80-621617   DDC 353.9784001/23 19
1. North Dakota - Officials and employees - Salaries, allowances, etc. 2. Civil service positions - North

North Dakota. Dept. of Insurance - Auditing and inspection.

BIBLIOGRAPHIC GUIDE

68

Dakota - Classification. I. Title.
JK6457 .N64 1979

NORTH DAKOTA. DEPT. OF INSURANCE -
AUDITING AND INSPECTION.
North Dakota. Auditor's Office. Audit report,
Commissioner of Insurance, Bismarck, North
Dakota . Bismarck, N.D. [1980] 77, 61 p. ;
  LC Card 80-623717   DDC 353.97840082/55 19
HG8538.N9 N92 1980

North Dakota. Dept. of Public Instruction.
Statutory requirements for all schools (K-12).
Bismarck, N.D. : Dept. of Public Instruction,
[1979?] 8 p. ; 22 cm. Cover title. LC Card
  80-623544   DDC 344.784/071 19
1. Educational law and legislation - North Dakota. I.
Title.
KFN8990 .A868

North Dakota. Dept. of Social Service. Social
Service Board. see North Dakota. Social
Service Board.

North Dakota. Dept. of State. 1980 handbook of
duties for county and precinct election officials
/ by Ben Meier, Secretary of State. [Bismarck,
N.D]. : State of North Dakota [Dept. of State,
1980] 27 p. : maps ; 28 cm. Cover title. LC Card
  80-623814   DDC 324.6/09784 19
1. Elections - North Dakota - Handbooks, manuals, etc.
I. Meier, Ben. II. Title.
JK2023.N9 N93 1980

North Dakota. Division of Fisheries. Ragan,
James E. Water quality of selected North
Dakota lakes /. [Bismarck, N.D.] , 1978. [112]
p. : LC Card 79-626040   DDC 553.7/8/09784 19
TD224.N9 R33

NORTH DAKOTA - ECONOMIC POLICY.
North Dakota. State University of Agriculture
and Applied Science, Fargo. Center for
Economic Development. A program of
management and technical assistance in EDA
designated areas in North Dakota . Fargo, N.
D. , 1974. 70 p. :   *NYPL [JLF 80-1351]*

North Dakota economic studies. For additional
listing of contents, see Old Catalog.
(no. 24) Ramsett, David E. A conceptual model
for the coal severance tax /. [Grand Forks]
[1979] iii, 49 p. : LC Card 80-622818   DDC
  336.2/78622334/0973 19
HD9540.8.U5 R35   *NYPL [TAA no. 24]*

(no. 25) Reed, Jeffrey A. North Dakota farm
labor market . [Grand Forks] [1979] iii, 54 p. ;
  LC Card 80-622819   DDC 331.12/53/09784 19
HD1527.N85 R43   *NYPL [TAA no. 25]*

(no. 26) Dobesh, Larry J. Cost of equity
determinants for electric utilities /. [Grand
Forks] [1979] v, 45 p. : LC Card 80-622685
  DDC 338.4/336362 19
HD9685.U5 D5   *NYPL [TAA no. 26]*

NORTH DAKOTA - EXECUTIVE
DEPARTMENT - DIRECTORIES.
The Structure of North Dakota state
government . Bismarck, ND [1979] 76 leaves
in various foliations ; LC Card 80-622720 DDC
  353.978404 19
JK6431 1979 .S77

NORTH DAKOTA - EXECUTIVE
DEPARTMENTS.
North Dakota. State Library Commission.
Legislative history of North Dakota State
agencies . Bismarck , 1978. xiii, 473 p. ; LC
  Card 79-621511
KFN9040 .A84   *NYPL [JLF 80-1257]*

North Dakota farm labor market . Reed, Jeffrey
A. [Grand Forks] [1979] iii, 54 p. ; LC Card
  80-622819   DDC 331.12/53/09784 19
HD1527.N85 R43   *NYPL [TAA no. 25]*

North Dakota. Game and Fish Dept.
Report - North Dakota State Game and Fish
Department .
  (no. 1059A) Ragan, James E. Water quality
  of selected North Dakota lakes /. [Bismarck,
  N.D.] , 1978. [112] p. : LC Card 79-626040
  DDC 553.7/8/09784 19
TD224.N9 R33

North Dakota. Geological Survey.
Bluemle, John P. Geologic highway map of
North Dakota. [Bismarck] 1977. col. map Scale
1:1,000,000. Relief shown by spot heights. Includes text
and geologic cross section along 47 1/2' N latitude.
       NYPL [Map Div. 81-3029]

Bulletin .
  (71, pt. 3) Hutchinson, Rickard D.
  Ground-water resources of Ramsey County,
  North Dakota /. Bismarck, N.D. , 1980. 36
  p. : LC Card 80-622721   DDC 553.7/9/09784 s
    553.7/9/0978436 19
GB705.N9 A25 no. 26, pt. 3 GB1025.N9

  (72, pt. 3) Ackerman, D. J. Ground-water
  resources of Morton County, North Dakota
  /. Bismarck, N.D. , 1980. v, 51 p. : LC Card
    80-622722   DDC 553.7/9/09784 s
    553.7/9/0978485 19
GB705.N9 A25 no. 27, pt. 3 GB1025.N9

  (75, pt. 2) Burkart, M. R. Ground-water data
  for Sheridan County, North Dakota /.
  Bismark, N.D. , 1980. iv, 302 p. : LC Card
    80-622724   DDC 557.84 s 553.7/9/0978476 19
GB705.N9 A25 no. 32, pt. 2 GB1025.N9

  (76, pt. 2) Anna, Lawrence O. Ground-water
  data for Billings, Golden Valley, and Slope
  Counties, North Dakota /. Bismarck, N.D. ,
  1980. v, 241 p. : LC Card 80-623714   DDC
    553.7/9/09784 s 553.7/9/0978494 19
GB705.N9 A25 no. 29, pt. 2 GB1025.N9

Hutchinson, Rickard D. Ground-water resources
of Ramsey County, North Dakota /. Bismarck,
N.D. , 1980. 36 p. : LC Card 80-622721   DDC
  553.7/9/09784 s 553.7/9/0978436 19
GB705.N9 A25 no. 26, pt. 3 GB1025.N9

Report of investigations .
  (no. 70) Groenewold, Gerald H. Geologic
  and hydrogeologic conditions affecting land
  use in the Bismarck-Mandan area /. [Grand
  Forks] , 1980. iv, 42 p. : LC Card 80-623715
    DDC 557.84 s 624.1/51/0978477 19
TN24.N9 A3 no. 70 QE150.B57

NORTH DAKOTA. GOVERNOR'S OFFICE -
ACCOUNTING.
North Dakota. Auditor's Office. Audit report,
Governor's Office, Bismarck, North Dakota .
Bismarck, N.D. [1979?] 24 leaves ; LC Card
  80-623331   DDC 353.978403/1 19
JK6452 1979 .N67

NORTH DAKOTA. GOVERNOR'S OFFICE -
APPROPRIATIONS AND
EXPENDITURES.
North Dakota. Auditor's Office. Audit report,
Governor's Office, Bismarck, North Dakota .
Bismarck, N.D. [1979?] 24 leaves ; LC Card
  80-623331   DDC 353.978403/1 19
JK6452 1979 .N67

North Dakota grain and oilseed transportation
statistics, 1978-79 /. Griffin, Gene C. Fargo,
N.D. , 1979. iii, 70 p. : LC Card 80-621931
  DDC 388.044 19
HE2321.G7 G74

North Dakota history. v. 12- ; 1945- Bismarck.
illus., maps (part fold.), plates, ports. 23-28 cm.
Quarterly (some issues combined). For earlier file,
whose numbering it continues, see (in Old Catalog)
North Dakota historical quarterly. Published by the
State Historical Society of North Dakota.
1. North Dakota - History - Periodicals. I. North
Dakota. State Historical Society.
       NYPL [IAA (North Dakota history)]

NORTH DAKOTA - HISTORY -
PERIODICALS.
North Dakota history. v. 12- ; 1945- Bismarck.
       NYPL [IAA (North Dakota history)]

The North Dakota quarterly. V. 24- ;
WINTER, 1956- Grand Forks.

North Dakota. Laws, statutes. etc.
Crime victims reparations act. 1979. North
Dakota. Laws, statutes. etc. [Workmen's
compensation act.] North Dakota Workmen's
compensation act and Crime victims
reparations act and rules of procedure,
effective July 1, 1979 / issued by Bronald
Thompson, chairman, Quentin Retterath,
Loretta Jennings ; Richard J. Gross, counsel.
[Bismarck] [1979] 105 p. ; LC Card
  80-621922   DDC 344.784/021/02632 19
KFN8942.A335 A2 1979

[North Dakota energy conversion and
transmission facility siting act]
Energy conversion and transmission facility
siting / North Dakota Public Service
Commission. [Bismarck, ND] : The
Commission, [1979] 20, 24 leaves ; 28 cm.
Cover title. CONTENTS. - Siting act.--Rules and

regulations. LC Card 80-622198 DDC
  343.784/092 19
1. Energy facilities - Location - Law and legislation -
North Dakota. I. North Dakota. Public Service
Commission. II. Title.
KFN8886.A334 A2 1979

[Workmen's compensation act]
North Dakota Workmen's compensation act
and Crime victims reparations act and rules
of procedure, effective July 1, 1979 / issued
by Bronald Thompson, chairman, Quentin
Retterath, Loretta Jennings ; Richard J.
Gross, counsel. [Bismarck] : State of North
Dakota, [1979] 105 p. ; 22 cm. LC Card
  80-621922   DDC 344.784/021/02632 19
1. Workmen's compensation - North Dakota. 2.
Reparation - North Dakota. I. Thompson, Bronald. II.
Retterath, Quentin. III. Jennings, Loretta. IV. North
Dakota. Laws, statutes, etc. Crime victims reparations
act. 1979. V. North Dakota. Workmen's compensation
Bureau. Rules of procedure. 1979. VI. Title.
KFN8942.A335 A2 1979

North Dakota. Legislative Council.
North Dakota. Constitution of North Dakota
(updated through January 1, 1981) .
[Bismarck] , 1981. iv, 56 p. : LC Card 81-621137
  DDC 342.784/023 347.840223 19
KFN9001 1889 .A34

State agency rules mandated by or related to
Federal statutes or regulations / prepared by
the Legislative Council staff for the
Administrative Rules Committee. [Bismarck] :
The Council, [1979] 5, [12] p. ; 28 cm. Caption
title. "November 1979." LC Card 80-623546 DDC
  342.784/0664 19
1. Administrative law - North Dakota. 2.
Administrative law - United States. I. North Dakota.
Legislative Council. Administrative Rules Committee.
II. Title.
KFN9040 .A25 1979

North Dakota. Legislative Council.
Administrative Rules Committee. North
Dakota. Legislative Council. State agency rules
mandated by or related to Federal statutes or
regulations /. [Bismarck] [1979] 5, [12] p. ;
  LC Card 80-623546   DDC 342.784/0664 19
KFN9040 .A25 1979

North Dakota. Library Commission. see North
Dakota. State Library Commission.

NORTH DAKOTA - MAPS.
(1977) Bluemle, John P. Geologic highway map
of North Dakota. [Bismarck] 1977. col. map
Scale 1:1,000,000. Relief shown by spot heights.
Includes text and geologic cross section along 47 1/2'
N latitude.   *NYPL [Map Div. 81-3029]*

NORTH DAKOTA - OFFICIALS AND
EMPLOYEES - DIRECTORIES.
Directory: federal, state, county, city and
special district officials in North Dakota. Grand
Forks, N. D.   *NYPL [JLM 80-691]*

NORTH DAKOTA - OFFICIALS AND
EMPLOYEES - SALARIES,
ALLOWANCES, ETC.
North Dakota. Dept. of Accounts and
Purchases. Central Personnel Division. North
Dakota central personnel compensation plan,
July, 1979-June, 1981. Bismarck, N.D. [1979]
120 p. in various pagings ; LC Card 80-621617
  DDC 353.9784001/23 19
JK6457 .N64 1979

NORTH DAKOTA - POPULATION -
STATISTICS.
Voelker, Stanley W. Population changes within
census county divisions of North Dakota,
1950-1970 /. Fargo, N.D. [Washington] ,
1971. 23 leaves, [4] leaves of plates : LC Card
  80-621261   DDC 312/.8/09784 19
HA566 .V63

North Dakota. Postsecondary Education
Commission. McKinney, Thomas Harry.
Governance and financing of school district
junior colleges and educational centers in North
Dakota . Bismarck, N.D. , 1978. 141 p. in
various pagings : LC Card 79-623536 DDC
  378.784 19
LB2327 .M24

North Dakota. Public Service Commission.
Griffin, Gene C. North Dakota grain and
oilseed transportation statistics, 1978-79 /.
Fargo, N.D. , 1979. iii, 70 p. : LC Card

80-621931   DDC 388.044 19
HE2321.G7 G74

North Dakota. Laws, statutes, etc. [North Dakota energy conversion and transmission facility siting act.] Energy conversion and transmission facility siting /. [Bismarck, ND] [1979] 20, 24 leaves ;   LC Card 80-622198   DDC 343.784/092 19
KFN8886.A334 A2 1979

The North Dakota quarterly. V. 24- ; WINTER, 1956- Grand Forks, University of North Dakota Press. illus., ports. 23-27 cm. For earlier file, whose numbering it continues, see (in Old Catalog): North Dakota. University. The quarterly journal. Issued by the University of North Dakota. INDEXES: - Vols. 24-26, winter, 1956-autumn, 1958, with v. 26. (Includes index to v. 16-23, Nov. 1925-spring/summer 1933, of the Quarterly journal of the University of North Dakota).
1. North Dakota - History - Periodicals. I. North Dakota. University. II. North Dakota. University. The quarterly journal (Indexes).

North Dakota. Regional Environmental Assessment Program.
REAP reports .
(no. 79-14) Whitman, Warren C. Analysis of grassland vegetation on selected key areas in southwestern North Dakota . [Bismarck [1979]] x, 199 p. :   LC Card 80-622820   DDC 581.5/2643/09784 19
QK179 .W83

(no. 79-2) Reigh, Robert C. Fishes of the western tributaries of the Missouri River in North Dakota . [Bismarck, N.D.] [1979] xi, 207 p. :   LC Card 80-622780   DDC 597.092/9784/7 19
QL628.N9 R44

North Dakota. Social Service Board. Children born out of wedlock in North Dakota . [Bismarck, N.D. Box 7, Bismarck, 58505)] [1980] 75 p. :   LC Card 80-624223   DDC 362.7/044 19
HQ999.U6 C49

North Dakota. State Dept. of Health. Nutrient levels in North Dakota streams, 1972-1978 / by North Dakota State Health Department and Soil Conservation Committee. [Bismarck, N.D.] : The Dept., [1980] 86 p. : chiefly graphs ; 28 cm. Cover title. "February 1980."   LC Card 80-622821   DDC 363.7/3942/09784 19
1. Water - Pollution - North Dakota - Statistics. 2. Phosphates - Environmental aspects - North Dakota - Statistics. 3. Nitrates - Environmental aspects - North Dakota - Statistics. I. North Dakota. State Soil Conservation Committee. II. Title.
TD224.N9 N65 1980

North Dakota. State Engineer. Rules and regulations of the North Dakota State Engineer governing the drainage of water. [Bismarck, N.D. : State Engineer, 1979] iii, 15, [7] p. : ill. ; 22 cm. Cover title.   LC Card 80-622991   DDC 343.784/07862754/02636 19
1. Drainage laws - North Dakota. I. Title.
KFN9051.A434 A2 1979

North Dakota. State Historical Society. North Dakota history. v. 12- ; 1945- Bismarck.
NYPL [IAA (North Dakota history)]

North Dakota. State Library Commission. (Old Catalog form: North Dakota. Library Commission)
Legislative history of North Dakota State agencies : a compendium of North Dakota State agencies, their organization, function & legislative history. Bismarck : State Library Commission, 1978. xiii, 473 p. ; 29 cm. Includes index.   LC Card 79-621511
1. Administrative agencies - North Dakota. 2. North Dakota - Executive departments. I. Title.
KFN9040 .A84   **NYPL [JLF 80-1257]**

The Structure of North Dakota state government . Bismarck, ND [1979] 76 leaves in various foliations ;   LC Card 80-622720   DDC 353.978404 19
JK6431 1979 .S77

North Dakota. State Soil Conservation Committee. North Dakota. State Dept. of Health. Nutrient levels in North Dakota streams, 1972-1978 /. [Bismarck, N.D.] [1980] 86 p. :   LC Card 80-622821   DDC 363.7/3942/09784 19
TD224.N9 N65 1980

North Dakota. State University of Agriculture and Applied Science, Fargo. (Old Catalog form: North Dakota. State University, Fargo.)
Little Missouri Grasslands study, Southwestern North Dakota. Fargo, 1973. 27 p.:
NYPL [*XME-8720]

North Dakota. State University of Agriculture and Applied Science, Fargo. Agricultural Economics, Dept. of. see North Dakota. State University of Agriculture and Applied Science, Fargo. Dept. of Agricultural Economics.

North Dakota. State University of Agriculture and Applied Science, Fargo. Center for Economic Development. A program of management and technical assistance in EDA designated areas in North Dakota : final report : February 16, 1972 - June 30, 1974 grant period [prepared by the] Center for Economic Development, North Dakota State University, Fargo, under grant from the Economic Development Administration. Fargo, N. D. : The Center, 1974. 70 p. : ill., map ; 28 cm. "Technical Assistance project 05-06-09452."
1. North Dakota - Economic policy. 2. Regional planning - North Dakota. I. United States. Economic Development Administration. II. Title.
NYPL [JLF 80-1351]

North Dakota. State University of Agriculture and Applied Science, Fargo. Dept. of Agricultural Economics. Voelker, Stanley W. A functional classification of agricultural trade centers in North Dakota /. Fargo [1978] 51 p. :   LC Card 78-623601   DDC 338.1 s 381/.41/09784 19
SB205.S7 N64 no. 125 HT123.5.N9

North Dakota. State University of Agriculture and Applied Science, Fargo. Little Missouri Grasslands study.
Conference on Mining and Power Production, Dickinson State College, 1973. Conference on Mining and Power Production /. Fargo, N.D. , 1973. v, 130 p., [8] leaves of plates :   LC Card 80-621258   DDC 333.8/2215/097848 19
TN805.N9 C66 1973

Interim report-Little Missouri Grasslands study, North Dakota State University.
(no. 5) Conference on Mining and Power Production, Dickinson State College, 1973. Conference on Mining and Power Production /. Fargo, N.D. , 1973. v, 130 p., [8] leaves of plates :   LC Card 80-621258   DDC 333.8/2215/097848 19
TN805.N9 C66 1973

North Dakota. State University of Agriculture and Applied Science, Fargo. Upper Great Plains Transportation Institute. see Upper Great Plains Transportation Institute.

North Dakota. State University of Agriculture and Applied Science, Fargo. Water Resources Research Institute.
Research report .
(no. WI-221-043-77) Moran, Stephen R. Hydrogeology of the Lake Metigoshe basin, North Dakota and Manitoba /. Fargo , 1977. v, 59 leaves :   LC Card 79-621837   DDC 553.7/9/0978461 19
GB1025.N9 M67

North Dakota. State University of Agriculture and Applied Sciences, Fargo. Agricultural Economics, Dept. of. see North Dakota. State University of Agriculture and Applied Sciences, Fargo. Dept. of Agricultural Economics.

North Dakota. State University of Agriculture and Applied Sciences, Fargo. Dept. of Agricultural Economics. Voelker, Stanley W. Population changes within census county divisions of North Dakota, 1950-1970 /. Fargo, N.D. [Washington] , 1971. 23 leaves, [4] leaves of plates :   LC Card 80-621261   DDC 312/.8/09784 19
HA566 .V63

North Dakota. State Water Commission. see North Dakota. State Water Conservation Commission.

North Dakota. State Water Conservation Commission. (Old Catalog form: North Dakota. Water Conservation Commission)
Anna, Lawrence O. Ground-water data for Billings, Golden Valley, and Slope Counties,

North Dakota /. Bismarck, N.D. , 1980. v, 241 p. :   LC Card 80-623714   DDC 553.7/9/09784 s 553.7/9/0978494 19
GB705.N9 A25 no. 29, pt. 2 GB1025.N9

North Dakota. State Wheat Commission. Griffin, Gene C. North Dakota grain and oilseed transportation statistics, 1978-79 /. Fargo, N.D. , 1979. iii, 70 p. :   LC Card 80-621931   DDC 388.044 19
HE2321.G7 G74

North Dakota Study Group on Evaluation.
Churchill, Edith H. E. Children's language and thinking . Grand Forks, N.D. , 1977. 60 p. :   LC Card 77-72096   DDC 370.15/2 19
LB1117 .C54

Hull, Bill. Teachers' seminars on children's thinking . Grand Forks, N.D. , 1978. 56 p. ;   LC Card 78-52231   DDC 370.15/2 19
LB1117 .H95

Olson, Ruth Anne. Evaluation as interaction in support of change /. Grand Forks, N.D. , 1980. 33 p. ;   LC Card 80-85357   DDC 371.1/44/09784 19
LB2838 .O47

North Dakota. University.
The North Dakota quarterly. V. 24- ; WINTER, 1956- Grand Forks.

The quarterly journal (Indexes) The North Dakota quarterly. V. 24- ; WINTER, 1956- Grand Forks.

North Dakota. University. Bureau of Business and Economic Research. (Old catalog form: North Dakota. University. Economic and Business Research, Bureau of.)
Ramsett, David E. A conceptual model for the coal severance tax /. [Grand Forks] [1979] iii, 49 p. :   LC Card 80-622818   DDC 336.2/78622334/0973 19
HD9540.8.U5 R35   **NYPL [TAA no. 24]**

Reed, Jeffrey A. North Dakota farm labor market . [Grand Forks] [1979] iii, 54 p. ;   LC Card 80-622819   DDC 331.12/53/09784 19
HD1527.N85 R43   **NYPL [TAA no. 25]**

North Dakota. University. Bureau of Economic and Business Research. see North Dakota. University. Bureau of Business and Economic Research.

North Dakota. University. Bureau of Educational Research and Services.
A general report : the financing of elementary and secondary education in North Dakota, "the FESEND project" / by Richard Hill ... [et al.]. Grand Forks, N.D. : Bureau of Educational Research and Services, University of North Dakota, 1979. iii, 90 p. ; 23 cm.   LC Card 80-621578   DDC 379.1/13/09784 19
1. Education - North Dakota - Finance. I. Hill, Richard, 1932-. II. Title.
LB2826.N9 N68 1979

Report - Bureau of Educational Research and Services .
(no. 9) Kranz, Bella. Multi-dimensional screening device (MDSD) for the identification of gifted/talented children /. Grand Forks , 1978. 66 p. ;   LC Card 79-622441   DDC 371.95/2 19
HQ773.5 .K7

North Dakota. University. Bureau of Governmental Affairs. Directory: federal, state, county, city and special district officials in North Dakota. Grand Forks, N. D.
NYPL [JLM 80-691]

North Dakota. University. Business and Economic Research, Bureau of. see North Dakota. University. Bureau of Business and Economic Research.

North Dakota. University. Economic and Business Research, Bureau of. see North Dakota. University. Bureau of Business and Economic Research.

North Dakota. University. Governmental Affairs, Bureau of. see North Dakota. University. Bureau of Governmental Affairs.

North Dakota. University. Institute for Ecological Studies.
Research report - Institute for Ecological Studies, University of North Dakota .
(no. 20) Casey, Timothy J. Chemical and biological investigations of mice and deer in

North Dakota. University. Institute for Ecological Studies. (cont.)

BIBLIOGRAPHIC GUIDE

70

the vicinity of two coal-fired power plants near Stanton, North Dakota /. Grand Forks , 1976. viii, 58 p. : LC Card 77-621848 DDC 599.02/4 19
QH545.C57 C37

(no. 27) Kannowski, Paul Bruno, 1927-Invertebrates of southwestern North Dakota . Grand Forks, N.D. [1978] x, 255 p. : LC Card 80-622687 DDC 592/.0526404/097848 19
QL197 .K36 1978

Special publication - Institute for Ecological Studies, University of North Dakota .
(no. 4) Steinhaus, Virginia S. A list of vertebrates of southeastern North Dakota /. Grand Forks, N.D. [1979] 29 p. : LC Card 80-622451 DDC 596.09784 19
QL197 .S88

(no. 5) Steinhaus, Virginia S. A list of vertebrates of southcentral North Dakota /. Grand Forks, N.D. [1979] 30 p. : LC Card 80-622452 DDC 596.09784 19
QL197 .S87

(no. 6) Steinhaus, Virginia S. A list of vertebrates of northwestern North Dakota /. Grand Forks, N.D. [1979] 28 p. ; LC Card 80-622453 DDC 596.09784/7 19
QL197 .S86

(no. 7) Steinhaus, Virginia S. A list of vertebrates of northcentral North Dakota /. Grand Forks, N.D. [1979] 29 p. ; LC Card 80-622454 DDC 596.09784 19
QL197 .S85

North Dakota. Water Conservation Commission. see **North Dakota. State Water Conservation Commission.**

North Dakota Workmen's compensation act and Crime victims reparations act and rules of procedure, effective July 1, 1979 /. North Dakota. Laws, statutes, etc. [Workmen's compensation act.] [Bismarck] [1979] 105 p. ; LC Card 80-621922 DDC 344.784/021/02632 19
KFN8942.A335 A2 1979

North Dakota. Workmen's compensation Bureau. Rules of procedure. 1979. North Dakota. Laws, statutes, etc. [Workmen's compensation act.] North Dakota Workmen's compensation act and Crime victims reparations act and rules of procedure, effective July 1, 1979 / issued by Bronald Thompson, chairman, Quentin Retterath, Loretta Jennings ; Richard J. Gross, counsel. [Bismarck] [1979] 105 p. ; LC Card 80-621922 DDC 344.784/021/02632 19
KFN8942.A335 A2 1979

North half Shoshone National Forest, Wyoming. United States. Forest Service. Rocky Mountain Region. Shoshone National Forest, Wyoming. [Denver] 1969. col. map on sheet 66 x 92 cm. Scale 1:126,720; 1/2″ = 1 mile. Folded title: North half Shoshone National Forest, Wyoming. Printed on both sides of sheet. Relief shown by hachures and spot heights. "Polyconic projection ... Sixth principal meridian, Wind River meridian." "Forest visitors map." "Forest Service map, class A." Includes col. illus., text, index to "Forest Service recreation sites," 2 key maps, and "Vicinity map." LC Card 74-696308
G4262.S5 1969 .U5

NYPL [Map Div. 80-3348]

North, Jeannette H. Immigration literature : abstracts of demographic, economic, and policy studies / United States Department of Justice, Immigration and Naturalization Service, Office of Planning, Evaluation, and Budgeting ; compiled by Jeannette H. North, Susan J. Grodsky. Washington : The Office : for sale by Supt. of Docs., U. S. Govt. Print. Off., 1979. viii, 89 p. ; 26 cm. LC Card 79-604155
1. United States - Emigration and immigration - Abstracts. 2. Emigration and immigration - Economic aspects - United States - Abstracts. I. Grodsky, Susan J., joint author. II. United States. Immigration and Naturalization Service. Office of Planning, Evaluation, and Budgeting. III. Title.
JV6455 .N67 **NYPL [JLF 81-424]**

NORTH MANHATTAN PROJECT - HISTORY - SOURCES.
Schomburg Center for Research in Black Culture. Records. 1924-1979. 53 boxes.
NYPL [Sc Rare MSS-44]

The North Pacific cretaceous Trigoniid genus Yaadia /. Saul, Louella Rankin. Berkeley , 1978. 65 p., 12 leaves of plates : ISBN 0-520-09582-0 LC Card 77-84990 DDC 564/.11 19
QE812.T74 S28

North Pacific Fur Seal Protection Act . United States. Congress. House. Committee on Foreign Affairs. Subcommittee on Asian and Pacific Affairs. Washington , 1980 [i.e. 1981] v, 152 p. : LC Card 81-600859 DDC 346.7304/6959 347.30646959 19
KF27 .F638 1979i

NORTH PACIFIC OCEAN - BATHYMETRIC MAPS.
California. University. Scripps Institution of Oceanography, La Jolla. Bathymetric atlas of the North Pacific Ocean /. Bay St. Louis, MS , 1978. [174] p. (1 fold.) : LC Card 80-675283 DDC 912/.155146/54 19
G2862.N6C2 C3 1978

North River. Massachusetts. Division of Water Pollution Control. Water Quality Section. North River basin . Westborough , 1975. 16 p. : LC Card 78-621331 DDC 363.7/3942/0974482 19
TD224.M4 M36 1975i

North River. Massachusetts. Division of Water Pollution Control. Water Quality Section. North River basin . Westborough [1976] 22 p. : LC Card 79-620607 DDC 363.7/3942/0974482 19
TD224.M4 M36 1976i

North River . Massachusetts. Water Quality and Research Section. Westborough , 1977. 53 p. : LC Card 79-622379 DDC 363.7/3942/0974482 19
TD224.M4 M39 1977i

North River basin . Massachusetts. Division of Water Pollution Control. Water Quality Section. Westborough , 1975. 16 p. : LC Card 78-621331 DDC 363.7/3942/0974482 19
TD224.M4 M36 1975i

North River basin . Massachusetts. Division of Water Pollution Control. Water Quality Section. Westborough [1976] 22 p. : LC Card 79-620607 DDC 363.7/3942/0974482 19
TD224.M4 M36 1976i

North River basin . Massachusetts. Water Quality and Research Section. North River . Westborough , 1977. 53 p. : LC Card 79-622379 DDC 363.7/3942/0974482 19
TD224.M4 M39 1977i

North Slope Borough, Alaska. Commission on History and Culture. Qiñiqtuagaksrat utuqqanaat iñuuniaġninisiqun : the traditional land use inventory for the mid-Beaufort Sea. Barrow, Alaska : North Slope Borough, Commission on History and Culture, c1980- v. : ill. ; 24 x 29 cm. Bibliography: p. 207. ISBN 0-936052-00-7 (v. 1) LC Card 80-80683 DDC 970.004/97 19
1. Eskimos - Alaska. 2. Eskimos - Beaufort Sea region. I. Title. II. Title: The traditional land use inventory for the mid-Beaufort Sea.
E99.E7 N64 1980

North-South dialog . United States. Congress. House. Committee on Foreign Affairs. Subcommittee on International Economic Policy and Trade. Washington , 1980. iii, 267 p. ; LC Card 80-603478 DDC 337/.09/048 19
KF27 .F6465 1980a

North Texas. Vines, Robert A., 1907- Trees of north Texas /. Austin , c1981. p. cm. ISBN 0-292-78018-4 : LC Card 81-1644 DDC 582.1609764 19
QK484.T4 V53

NORTHAMPTON COUNTY (VA.) - GENEALOGY.
Mihalyka, Jean Merritt. Gravestone inscriptions in Northampton County, Virginia /. Richmond, Va. , 1980. xxxiii, 99 p. : ISBN 0-88490-092-4 (pbk.) LC Card 81-621014 DDC 929.5/09755/15 19
F232.N85 M53

Northbook . Morgan, Frederick, 1922- Urbana , c1982. p. cm. ISBN 0-252-00947-9 LC Card 81-14664 DDC 811/.54 19
PS3563.O83 N6

Northeast Anthropological Association. Ecological anthropology of the Middle Connecticut River Valley /. Amherst , 1979. iv,

161 p. : LC Card 80-621530 DDC 974 19
F12.C7 E26

Northeast corridor completion act of 1979 . United States. Congress. Senate. Committee on Commerce, Science, and Transportation. Subcommittee on Surface Transportation. Washington , 1980. iii, 89 p. ; LC Card 80-602086 DDC 343.73/095 347.30395 19
KF26 .C698 1980

Northeast corridor improvement project . United States. Congress. House. Committee on Interstate and Foreign Commerce. Subcommittee on Transportation and Commerce. Washington , 1980. iii, 161 p. ; LC Card 80-603407 DDC 343.73/0958 347.303958 19
KF27 .I5589 1980g

Northeast energy policy, 1978 . Northeastern Legislative Energy Staff. Albany, N.Y. [1978] 8 leaves ; LC Card 80-621219 DDC 346.7404/679 19
KF2120.Z95 N67

Northeast Missouri State University. The Chariton review. v. 1- ; spring 1975- [Kirksville] LC Card 75-645643   **NYPL [JFL 80-223]**

Northeastern Forest Experiment Station, Broomall, Pa. Powell, Douglas S. The forest resources of Maryland /. Broomall, Pa. , 1980. 103 p. : LC Card 80-601810 DDC 333.75/0974 s 333.75/11/09752 19
SD11 .A455494 no. 61 SD144.M3

Northeastern Legislative Energy Staff. Energy policy making in the Northeast : a directory of state programs and institutions. [Albany, N.Y.] : Northeastern Legislative Leaders Energy Project, [1977] 102 p., [10] fold. leaves of plates ; 28 cm. Cover title. "September 1977." "NSF/RA-770213." LC Card 78-624417 DDC 353.9/3823/02574 19
1. Energy policy - Northeastern States - Directories. I. Title.
HD9502.U53 A1167 1977

Northeast energy policy, 1978 : significant energy laws enacted during the 1978 State legislative sessions in the ten Northeastern States. Albany, N.Y. : Northeastern Legislative Leaders Energy Project, [1978] 8 leaves ; 28 cm. "NSF/RA-78-0288." "November 1978." LC Card 80-621219 DDC 346.7404/679 19
1. Energy conservation - Law and legislation - Northeastern States. 2. Energy facilities - Law and legislation - Northeastern States. 3. Energy policy - Northeastern States. I. Title.
KF2120.Z95 N67

Northeastern Political Science Association. Gleason, Eugene J. Executive dominance in New York State. [Albany, 1974] 53 p. LC Card 78-64398   **NYPL [JLF 80-538]**

NORTHEASTERN STATES - ANTIQUITIES - CONGRESSES.
Conference on Northeastern Archaeology, University of Massachusetts, 1979. Proceedings of the Conference on Northeastern Archaeology /. Amherst , 1980. vi, 219 p. : LC Card 80-623704 DDC 974 19
F106 .C75 1979

Northeastern United States Water Supply Study. Quirk, Lawler & Matusky Engineers. Hydraulic analysis of the New York City water supply system /. Tappan, N. Y. , 1974. xviii, 82, A1-A9 p. :   **NYPL [JSF 80-751]**

Northern Arizona University. Libraries. Chicano bibliography : a guide to Chicano materials in the NAU Libraries / by Carlos Greth and the editors of Discovery.Rev. ed. [Flagstaff] : Northern Arizona University Libraries, 1980. vii, 36 p. : ill. ; 23 cm. (Discovery series ; no. 1) Ed. of 1974 published under title: Chicano materials. LC Card 80-622441 DDC 016.973/046872 19
1. Mexican Americans - Bibliography - Catalogs. 2. Northern Arizona University. Libraries - Catalogs. I. Greth, Carlos. II. Title.
Z1361.M4 N67 1980 E184.M5

NORTHERN ARIZONA UNIVERSITY. LIBRARIES - CATALOGS.
Northern Arizona University. Libraries. Chicano bibliography . [Flagstaff] , 1980. vii, 36 p. : LC Card 80-622441 DDC 016.973/046872 19
Z1361.M4 N67 1980 E184.M5

NORTHERN FUR SEAL.
United States. Congress. House. Committee on
Foreign Affairs. Subcommittee on Asian and
Pacific Affairs. North Pacific Fur Seal
Protection Act . Washington , 1980 [i.e. 1981]
v, 152 p. : LC Card 81-600859 DDC
346.7304/6959 347.30646959 19
KF27 .F638 1979i

United States. National Oceanic and
Atmospheric Administration. The story of the
Pribilof fur seals. [Washington] [1976] 34 p. :
LC Card 77-601364 DDC 333.95/9 19
SH361 .U75 1976

**NORTHERN FUR SEAL - LAW AND
LEGISLATION - UNITED STATES.**
United States. Congress. House. Committee on
Foreign Affairs. Subcommittee on Asian and
Pacific Affairs. North Pacific Fur Seal
Protection Act . Washington , 1980 [i.e. 1981]
v, 152 p. : LC Card 81-600859 DDC
346.7304/6959 347.30646959 19
KF27 .F638 1979i

United States. Congress. House. Committee on
Merchant Marine and Fisheries. Subcommittee
on Fisheries and Wildlife Conservation and the
Environment. Dinsell-Johnson fund--N. Pacific
fur seal . Washington , 1980. vii, 540 p. : LC
Card 81-600826 DDC 343.7305/585333954
347.3035585333954 19
KF27 .M447 1980c

Northern Great Plains Resources Program.
Lemmerman, Kathe L. Columbus / Noonan
study . Denver , 1974. xiii, 104, [48] p. :
                        NYPL [JLF 81-30]

**Northern Great Plains Resources Program. Socio-
Economic and Cultural Aspects Work Group.**
Twomey, James P. Governmental programs,
resources and regulatory powers available to
assist localities during coal development . -
Denver , 1974. i, 29, [65] p. ;
                        NYPL [JLF 80-707]

Northern lights . Ludvigson, Susan. Baton
Rouge , 1981. p. cm. ISBN 0-8071-0879-0 LC
Card 81-6039 DDC 811/.54 19
PS3562.U27 N6

Northern Resource Management. State land
disposal policy study / prepared for the State of
Alaska Legislative Finance Division by
Northern Resource Management ; project team,
David Hanson, Robert Klein, Vincent
McClelland. [Juneau, Alaska] : The Division,
[1980] 90, [38] p. : graphs ; 28 cm. "March
1980." LC Card 80-623199 DDC 333.1/6/09798 19
*1. Alaska - Public lands. I. Alaska. Legislative Finance
Division. II. Title.*
HD243.A3 N67 1980

**NORTHERN TIER PIPELINE, WASH.-
MINN.**
Thompson, Larry S. The effects of
large-diameter underground crude-oil pipelines
on wildlife . Helena, Mont. [1979] vii, 55 p. :
LC Card 80-622216 DDC 333.79/09786 s
333.95/9 19
TJ163.25.U6 M653 1979, no. 2 TD195.P5

**NORTHERN TIER REGIONAL PLANNING
COMMISSION.**
Intergovernmental Organization for Planning. A
case study of the northern tier region of
northeastern Pennsylvania. Eugene, Or., 1971.
58 l.   *NYPL [JLF 80-1285]*

Northrup, Incorporated. Blake, Floyd.
Development and demonstration of low cost
heliostats . [Austin] [1979] xv, 74 p. : LC Card
80-620769 DDC 621.47 19
TJ810 .B5

Northrup, James P. Old age, handicapped, and
Vietnam-era antidiscrimination legislation / by
James P. Northrup. Philadelphia : Industrial
Research Unit, Wharton School, University of
Pennsylvania, c1978. vii, 92 p. ; 23 cm.
Supplement to no. 14, Labor relations and public policy
series. Includes bibliographical references. ISBN
0-89546-008-4 LC Card 78-70927 DDC
344.73/01133 347.3041133 19
*1. Discrimination in employment - Law and legislation -
United States. 2. Aged - Employment - United States.
3. Handicapped - Employment - United States. 4.
Veterans - Employment - United States. I. Series: Labor
relations and public policy series, report no. 14
(Supplement). II. Title.*
KF3464 .N6 Suppl

NORTHWEST, PACIFIC - HISTORY.
Scheuerman, Richard D. The Volga Germans .
Moscow, Idaho , c1980. 245 p. : ISBN
0-89301-073-1 LC Card 80-52314 DDC 979.5
19
F855.2.R85 S33

**NORTHWEST, PACIFIC - HISTORY -
PERIODICALS.**
Pacific Northwest quarterly. v. 1- ; Oct. 1906-
Seattle. LC Card 80-30966
            *NYPL [IAA(Pacific Northwest
                        quarterly)]*

**NORTHWEST, PACIFIC - INDUSTRIES -
ENERGY CONSUMPTION.**
Hassoun, Hussein. Industrial energy
consumption studies /. Salem , 1978- v. ; LC
Card 79-622416 DDC 333.79/13 19
HC107.A19 H37

**Northwest Regional Energy Conference, Seattle,
1978.** Proceedings of the Northwest Regional
Energy Conference, May 31-June 1, 1978,
Seattle, Washington / co-sponsors, Central
Washington University [and] U. S. Department
of Energy, Assistant Secretary for
Intergovernmental and Institutional Relations,
Office of Education, Business, and Labor
Affairs ; edited by Anne S. Denman and Dale
R. Comstock. [Washington] : The Dept., 1978.
vii, 201 p. ; 23 cm. LC Card 79-602539
*1. Energy policy - Northwest, Pacific - Congresses. I.
Denman, Anne S. II. Comstock, Dale R. III. Central
Washington University. IV. United States. Dept. of
Energy. Office of Education, Business, and Labor
Affairs. V. Title.*
HD9502.U53 A1964 1978
                        NYPL [JLE 81-480]

**Northwest River-Indian Creek watershed,
Chesapeake City, Virginia** . United States. Soil
Conservation Service. Lanham, MD , 1980. 1
map : LC Card 81-690292
G3882.N67 1979 .U5

**NORTHWEST RIVER WATERSHED (VA.
AND N.C.) - MAPS, TOPOGRAPHIC.**
United States. Soil Conservation Service.
Northwest River-Indian Creek watershed,
Chesapeake City, Virginia . Lanham, MD ,
1980. 1 map : LC Card 81-690292
G3882.N67 1979 .U5

**Northwest salmon enhancement program--salmon
interception** . United States. Congress. House.
Committee on Merchant Marine and Fisheries.
Subcommittee on Fisheries and Wildlife
Conservation and the Environment.
Washington , 1980. v, 512 p. : LC Card
80-603908 DDC 343.73/07692755
347.3037692755 19
KF27 .M447 1979h

**NORTHWEST TERRITORIES -
ANTIQUITIES - ADDRESSES, ESSAYS,
LECTURES.**
Archaeological whale bone--a northern
resource . Fayetteville, ARK , 1979. xx, 558
p. : LC Card 80-624409 DDC 971.9/5 19
E99.E7 A73

**Northwest Territories - Archaeology. see
Northwest Territories - Antiquities.**

Northwestern University, Evanston, Ill. Land
economics; a journal of planning, housing &
public utilities. v. 1- ; 1925- Chicago [etc.] LC
Card 26-19201   *NYPL [*ZAN-T4596]*

**NORTON, ANDRE - CRITICISM AND
INTERPRETATION - ADDRESSES,
ESSAYS, LECTURES.**
Yoke, Carl B. Roger Zelazny and Andre
Norton, proponents of individualism /.
Columbus , 1979. 26 p. ; LC Card 80-137489
DDC 813/.54 19
PS374.S35 Y6

Norton, Daniel R. Ground temperature
measurements. Washington : U. S.G.P.O., 1980.
p. cm. (Geological Survey professional paper . 1203)
Includes bibliographies. CONTENTS. - Pallmann
technique / by Daniel R. Norton and Irving
Friedman -- Evaluation of the Pallmann technique in
two geothermal areas of west-central Nevada / by F.H.
Olmsted, Irving Friedman, and Daniel R. Norton --
Ground temperatures in and near Yellowstone National
Park / by Irving Friedman and Daniel R. Norton. LC
Card 81-607982 DDC 551.1/4 19
*1. Earth temperature - Measurement - Addresses,
essays, lectures. I. Friedman, Irving, 1920-. II. Olmsted,*

F. H. (Franklin Howard), 1921-. III. Title. IV. Series.
QE509 .N67

Norton, Herman Albert. Religion in Tennessee,
1777-1945 / Herman A. Norton. 1st ed. :
Knoxville : University of Tennessee Press :
Tennessee Historical Commission, c1981. p. cm.
(Tennessee three star books) Bibliography: p. Includes
index. ISBN 0-87049-317-5 : LC Card 81-1562
DDC 280/.09768 19
1. Tennessee - Church history. I. Title.
BR555.T2 N67

**NORWAY - FOREIGN RELATIONS -
SOVIET UNION.**
Amundsen, Kirsten. Norway, NATO, and the
forgotten Soviet challenge /. Berkeley , c1981.
vi, 50 p. : ISBN 0-87725-514-8 (pbk.) : LC Card
81-80337 DDC 355/.0330481 19
UA750 .A56

NORWAY - NATIONAL SECURITY.
Amundsen, Kirsten. Norway, NATO, and the
forgotten Soviet challenge /. Berkeley , c1981.
vi, 50 p. : ISBN 0-87725-514-8 (pbk.) : LC Card
81-80337 DDC 355/.0330481 19
UA750 .A56

**Norway, NATO, and the forgotten Soviet
challenge /.** Amundsen, Kirsten. Berkeley ,
c1981. vi, 50 p. : ISBN 0-87725-514-8 (pbk.) :
LC Card 81-80337 DDC 355/.0330481 19
UA750 .A56

NORWEGIAN LANGUAGE - GRAMMAR.
Stokker, Kathleen, 1946- Norsk . Madison,
Wis. , 1981. p. cm. ISBN 0-299-08690-9 : LC
Card 81-50827 DDC 439.8/282/421 19
PD2623 .S86

Norwood, Janet Lippe. Women in the labor
force : some new data series / [Janet L.
Norwood and Elizabeth Waldman].
[Washington, D.C.] : The U. S. Dept. of Labor,
Bureau of Labor Statistics, 1979. 9 p. : ill. ; 28
cm. (Report - U. S. Bureau of Labor Statistics ; 575)
Includes bibliographical references. LC Card
80-601713 DDC 331.1/0973 s 331.4/12/0973 19
*1. Women - Employment - United States - Statistics. I.
Waldman, Elizabeth, joint author. II. Series: United
States. Bureau of Labor Statistics. Report, 575. III.
Title.*
HD8051 .A7876 no. 575 HD6094

Norwood, Richard H. A cultural resource
overview of the Eureka, Saline, Panamint, and
Darwin region, east central California / by
Richard H. Norwood and Charles S. Bull ;
written in collaboration with Emma Lou Davis ;
with a section by Ronald Quinn ; prepared for
the United States Department of Interior,
Bureau of Land Management, California Desert
Planning Staff ; Eric W. Ritter, general editor.
Riverside, Calif. : Bureau of Land Management,
California, 1980. 219, [26] p. : ill., maps ; 28
cm. (Cultural resources publications.
Anthropology--history) "Contract No.
YA-512-CT7-226." 629-E-5 Bibliography: p. 186-219.
LC Card 81-601926 DDC 979.4/87 19
*1. California - Antiquities. 2. Deserts - California. 3.
California - History, Local. 4. Indians of North
America - California - Antiquities. I. Bull, Charles S. II.
Davis, Emma Lou. III. Ritter, Eric W. IV. United
States. Bureau of Land Management. Desert Planning
Staff. V. Title. VI. Series.*
F863 .N67

Nosanow, Barbara Shissler. More than land or
sky : art from Appalachia / Barbara Shissler
Nosanow. Washington, D.C. : Published for the
National Museum of American Art by the
Smithsonian Institution Press, 1981. p. cm.
"Published on the occasion of an exhibition organized
by the National Museum of American Art, Smithsonian
Institution, Washington, D.C., and shown there October
30, 1981-January 3, 1982, before traveling to museums
through-out the thirteen-state Appalachian region"--T.p.
verso. LC Card 81-13566 DDC 709/.74/074014 19
*1. Art, American - Appalachian region - Exhibitions. I.
National Museum of American Art (U. S.). II. Title.*
N6516 .N67

NOSOLOGY.
The International classification of diseases, 9th
revision, clinical modification . [Washington,
D.C.?] , 1980. 3 v. ; LC Card 81-601048 DDC
616/.0012 19
RB115 .I49 1980

Nossman, Waters, Krueger, Marsh & Riordan.
Summary: an evaluation of the options of the
U. S. Government in its relationship to U. S.

firms in international petroleum affairs: a report prepared for the Federal Energy Administration / Nossman, Waters, Krueger March & Riordan; Robert B. Krueger, project director ... Los Angeles: Nossman, Waters, Krueger, Marsh & Riordan, 1975. 122 p.; 28 cm. Cover title.
1. Petroleum industry and trade. 2. United States - Foreign economic relations. 3. Petroleum industry and trade - United States. I. Krueger, Robert B. II. United States. Federal Energy Administration. III. Title. IV. Title: Evaluation of the options of the U. S. Government in its relationship to U. S. firms in international petroleum affairs.
NYPL [JLF 80-599]

A note on simplification orderings /. Dershowitz, Nachum. Urbana, Ill. [1979] 8 p. ;   LC Card 80-621698   DDC 001.64 s 511 19
QA76 .I4 no. 986 QA76.9.A96

Notes illustrating the military geography of the United States, 1813-1880 /. United States. Adjutant-General's Office. Austin , c1979. xii, 203 p. :   ISBN 0-292-75515-5   LC Card 79-63158
UA26 .A2 1979   **NYPL [IBM 81-609]**

Notes on the use of the Viven-Bessières rifle grenade /. France. Ministère de la guerre. Washington, 1918. 12 p.:   **NYPL [*ZV-179]**

Notes toward a bibliography of sources relating to Fort Ross State Historic Park, California /. Hussey, John A. Sacramento, CA [1979] xv, 150 p. :   LC Card 80-621182   DDC 016.9794/18 19
Z1262.F67 H87 F869.F664

Nõukogude Liidu Kommunistlik Partei. see Kommunisticheskaiã partiiã Sovetskogo Soĩuza.

Noun, Louise R. Eberle, Abastenia St. Leger, 1878- Abastenia St. Leger Eberle, sculptor (1878-1942) . [Des Moines] , c1980. 21, [8] p., [15] leaves of plates :   LC Card 80-66884   DDC 730/.92/4 19
NB237.E2 A4 1980

NOVA SCOTIA - DESCRIPTION AND TRAVEL.
Salusbury, John, 1707-1762. Expeditions of honour . Newark , London , c1981. p. cm.
ISBN 0-87413-169-3   LC Card 81-11537   DDC 971.6/01 19
F1038 .S2 1981

NOVA SCOTIA - HISTORY - 1713-1763.
Salusbury, John, 1707-1762. Expeditions of honour . Newark , London , c1981. p. cm.
ISBN 0-87413-169-3   LC Card 81-11537   DDC 971.6/01 19
F1038 .S2 1981

Novalis, Carol M., 1948- (joint author. 0700) Patrick, Ruth J. A study of library cooperatives, networks, and demonstration projects . New York , 1980. p. cm.   ISBN 0-89664-313-1 :   LC Card 79-20231
Z731 .P34

Novels of the 1740s /. Beasley, Jerry C. Athens Ga. , c1982. p. cm.   ISBN 0-8203-0590-1   LC Card 81-10390   DDC 823/.5/09 19
PR851 .B4 1982

NOW ACCOUNTS - ARKANSAS.
Adams, Jack E. The potential impact of negotiable order of withdrawal accounts on the banking industry in Arkansas . Fayetteville, Ark. [1979] iv, 55 leaves ;   LC Card 80-622482   DDC 332.1/09767 19
HG1660.U5 A28

NOW ACCOUNTS - LAW AND LEGISLATION - UNITED STATES.
United States. Congress. House. Committee on Banking, Finance and Urban Affairs. Subcommittee on Financial Institutions Supervision, Regulation and Insurance. Regulation Q and related measures . Washington , 1980. v, 1013 p. :   LC Card 80-602494   DDC 346.73/082 19
KF27 .B544 1980a

Nowicke, Joan W. Pollen morphology and phylogenetic relationships of the Berberidaceae / Joan W. Nowicke and John J. Skvarla. Washington : Smithsonian Institution Press, 1981. p. cm. (Smithsonian contributions to botany ; no. 50) Bibliography: p.   LC Card 80-21960   DDC 581 s 583/.117 19
1. Berberidaceae. 2. Palynotaxonomy. I. Skvarla, John J., joint author. II. Series: Smithsonian Institution.

Smithsonian contributions to botany , no. 50. III. Title.
QK1 .S2747 no. 50 QK495.B45

NOZZLES.
Johnson, D. I. (Donald I.) Investigation of a flow-turn/nozzle device to improve the cutting ability of a borehole mining tool /. Washington, D.C. [1981] p. cm.   LC Card 81-607848   DDC 622 s 681./76 19
TN23 .U43 TN281.5

NRC oversight . United States. Congress. House. Committee on Government Operations. Environment, Energy, and Natural Resources Subcommittee. Washington , 1980 [i.e. 1981] iii, 152 p. ;   LC Card 81-601389   DDC 353.0087/22 19
KF27 .G655 1980g

NRC views and analysis of the recommendations of the President's Commission on the Accident at Three Mile Island /. United States. Office of Nuclear Reactor Regulation. Washington, D.C. , 1979. 51 p. in various pagings ;   LC Card 80-601286   DDC 363.1/79 19
TK1343 .U57 1979

NSRDS-NBS.
(71) Ledbetter, H. M. Physical and mechanical properties of selected technological alloys /. Washington , 1981. p. cm.   LC Card 81-14053   DDC 602/.18 s 620.1/6 19
QC100 .U573 no. 71 TA460

Nuckton, Carole Frank. (joint author) French, Ben C. Marketing order program alternatives . [Davis] , 1978. v, 110 p. :   LC Card 78-623151   DDC 338.1/09794 s 381/.41/09794 19
HD9000.1 .C3 no. 78-2 HD9007.C2

Nuclear accident and recovery at Three Mile Island : a report / prepared by the Subcommittee on Nuclear Regulation for the Committee on Environment and Public Works, U. S. Senate. Washington : U. S. G.P.O., 1980. vii, 423 p. : ill. ; 26 cm. At head of title: 96th Congress, 2d session. Committee print. On cover: Report to the United States Senate, nuclear accident and recovery at Three Mile Island, a special investigation. "Serial no. 96-14." "June 1980" Item 1045 Includes bibliographical references.   LC Card 81-600709   DDC 363.1/79 19
1. Atomic power-plants - Pennsylvania - Accidents. 2. Three Mile Island Nuclear Power Plant, Pa. I. United States. Congress. Senate. Committee on Environment and Public Works. Subcommittee on Nuclear Regulation.
TK1344.P4 N82

Nuclear accident and recovery at Three Mile Island . United States. Congress. Senate. Committee on Environment and Public Works. Subcommittee on Nuclear Regulation. Washington , 1980. vii, 423 p. :   LC Card 80-603139   DDC 363.1/79 19
TK1345.H37 U5 1980

Nuclear and hazardous waste problems in New Hampshire . United States. Congress. Senate. Committee on Appropriations. Subcommittee on HUD-Independent Agencies. Washington , 1980 [i.e. 1981] iii, 122 p. ;   LC Card 81-601754   DDC 363.7/28 19
KF26 .A6486 1980b

NUCLEAR COLLISIONS. see COLLISIONS (NUCLEAR PHYSICS)

The nuclear crisis and State and local governments . United States. Congress. House. Committee on the Budget. Task Force on State and Local Government. Washington , 1980. iii, 34 p. ;   LC Card 80-601148   DDC 353.97470082/65621483/0289 19
KF27 .B879 1979a

Nuclear cross sections for technology . International Conference on Nuclear Cross Sections for Technology (1979 : University of Tennessee) [Washington, D.C.?] , 1980. xvi, 1039 p. :   LC Card 80-600128   DDC 602/.18 s 539.7/54 19
QC100 .U57 no. 594 QC794.6.C7

NUCLEAR ENERGY. see ATOMIC ENERGY.

Nuclear energy in Oklahoma, 1979. Oklahoma. State Legislative Council. [Oklahoma City] [1980] [44] leaves ;   LC Card 80-623906   DDC 333.79/24/09766 19
HD9698.U53 O56 1980

Nuclear energy's dilemma . United States. General Accounting Office. [Washington] ,

1977. xvii, 73 p. :   LC Card 77-603908
TD898 .U54 1977

NUCLEAR ENGINEERING.
(1980) United States. Congress. House. Committee on Science and Technology. Subcommittee on Energy Research and Production. New directions for nuclear R.D. & D., post-INFCE . Washington , 1980. iii, 401 p. :   LC Card 80-604001   DDC 363.1/79 19
KF27 .S3936 1980b

NUCLEAR EXPORTS. see NUCLEAR NONPROLIFERATION.

Nuclear exports, international safety and environmental issues . United States. Congress. House. Committee on Foreign Affairs. Subcommittee on International Economic Policy and Trade. Washington , 1980. iii, 226 p. ;   LC Card 80-603801   DDC 363.1/79 19
KF27 .F6465 1979f

NUCLEAR FACILITIES - DEFENSE MEASURES.
Ramberg, Bennett. Destruction of nuclear energy facilities in war . Lexington, Mass. , c1980. xvi, 203 p. :   LC Card 80-7691
UA929.95.A87 R35   **NYPL [JLE 81-179]**

NUCLEAR FACILITIES - MILITARY ASPECTS.
Ramberg, Bennett. Destruction of nuclear energy facilities in war . Lexington, Mass. , c1980. xvi, 203 p. :   LC Card 80-7691
UA929.95.A87 R35   **NYPL [JLE 81-179]**

NUCLEAR FACILITIES - SAFETY REGULATIONS - NEW JERSEY.
New Jersey. Legislature. General Assembly. Committee on Agriculture and Environment. Public hearing before Assembly Agriculture and Environment Committee, on A-966 (the Radiation emergency response act), held April 8, 1980, Assembly Chamber, State House, Trenton, New Jersey. [Trenton] [1980] 79 p. in various pagings ;   LC Card 80-623636   DDC 344.749/0472 19
KFN1811.4 .A3 1980

NUCLEAR FACILITIES - UNITED STATES - SAFETY MEASURES.
United States. Congress. House. Committee on Government Operations. Environment, Energy, and Natural Resources Subcommittee. Nuclear Regulatory Commission--the Rogovin report . Washington , 1980. iii, 90 p. ;   LC Card 80-602901   DDC 363.1/79 19
KF27 .G655 1980b

NUCLEAR FUELS.
(1980) United States. Congress. House. Committee on Science and Technology. Subcommittee on Energy Research and Production. New directions for nuclear R.D. & D., post-INFCE . Washington , 1980. iii, 401 p. :   LC Card 80-604001   DDC 363.1/79 19
KF27 .S3936 1980b

NUCLEAR FUELS - CONGRESSES.
International Meeting on Advanced LMFBR Fuels, Tucson, Ariz., 1977. Advanced LMFBR fuels . Hinsdale, Ill. , c1977. xi, 694 p. :   LC Card 77-88497
TK9360 .I63 1977   **NYPL [JSD 80-865]**

NUCLEAR FUELS - INDIA.
United States. Congress. House. Committee on Foreign Affairs. Resolutions of disapproval pertaining to the shipment of nuclear fuel to India . Washington , 1980. iii, 170 p. ;   LC Card 80-603439   DDC 353.0089 19
KF27 .F6 1980g

United States. Congress. Senate. Committee on Foreign Relations. The Tarapur nuclear fuel export issue . Washington , 1980. iii, 134 p. :   LC Card 80-602987   DDC 382/.4562148335/0973 19
KF26 .F6 1980l

NUCLEAR INDUSTRIES. see ATOMIC ENERGY INDUSTRIES.

NUCLEAR MEDICINE - UNITED STATES.
United States. Congress. House. Committee on Science and Technology. Subcommittee on Energy Research and Production. Low-level nuclear waste burial grounds . Washington , 1980. iii, 100 p. :   LC Card 80-601955   DDC 363.7/28 19
KF27 .S3936 1979l

NUCLEAR NONPOOLIFERATION.
United States. Library of Congress. Congressional Research Service. Alternative breeding cycles for nuclear power . Washington , 1980. xx, 124 p. :   LC Card 80-603560   DDC 333.79/24/0973 19
TK9203.B7 U53 1980

NUCLEAR NONPROLIFERATION.
United States. Congress. House. Committee on Foreign Affairs. Resolutions of disapproval pertaining to the shipment of nuclear fuel to India . Washington , 1980. iii, 170 p. ;   LC Card 80-603439   DDC 353.0089 19
KF27 .F6 1980g

United States. Congress. House. Committee on Foreign Affairs. Subcommittee on International Security and Scientific Affairs. Department of Energy fiscal year 1981 budget . Washington , 1980. iii, 46 p. ;   LC Card 80-603009   DDC 353.0082/236823 19
KF27 .F64825 1980d

United States. Congress. House. Committee on Science and Technology. Subcommittee on Energy Research and Production. New directions for nuclear R.D. & D., post-INFCE . Washington , 1980. iii, 401 p. :   LC Card 80-604001   DDC 363.1/79 19
KF27 .S3936 1980b

United States. Congress. Senate. Committee on Foreign Relations. India-Pakistan nuclear issues . Washington , 1980. iii, 19 p. ;   LC Card 80-602998   DDC 327.73054 19
KF26 .F6 1980K

United States. Congress. Senate. Committee on Foreign Relations. The Tarapur nuclear fuel export issue . Washington , 1980. iii, 134 p. :   LC Card 80-602987   DDC 382/.4562148335/0973 19
KF26 .F6 1980l

United States. Congress. Senate. Committee on Foreign Relations. Subcommittee on Arms Control, Oceans, International Operations, and Environment. The Non-proliferation Treaty . Washington , 1980. iii, 99 p. :   LC Card 80-603656   DDC 327.1/74 19
KF26 .F6286 1980

United States-European communities relations . Washington [D.C.] , 1979. x, 44 p. ;   LC Card 80-603969   DDC 337./09/047 19
HF1411 .U64

United States. General Accounting Office. U. S. nuclear non-proliferation policy: impact on exports and nuclear industry could not be determined . Washington, D.C. , 1980. vi, 78 p. ;   LC Card 80-603954   DDC 382/.4562345119/0973 19
HD9698.U52 U55 1980b

United States. Library of Congress. Environment and Natural Resources Policy Division. Nuclear proliferation factbook /. Washington , 1980. xi, 531 p. :   LC Card 80-603879   DDC 327.1/74 19
JX1974.73 .U55 1980

NUCLEAR NONPROLIFERATION - ADDRESSES, ESSAYS, LECTURES.
Reader on nuclear nonproliferation /. Washington , 1980. x, 344 p. :   LC Card 81-600802   DDC 327.1/74 19
JX1974.73 .R4

NUCLEAR PHYSICS - STATISTICAL METHODS - CONGRESSES.
Proceedings of the NEACRP meeting of a Monte Carlo study group. Argonne, Ill. [1974] 363 l.   *NYPL [*XMQ-2014]*

Nuclear plant shutdowns . United States. Congress. House. Committee on Interior and Insular Affairs. Subcommittee on Energy and the Environment. Washington , 1980. v, 346 p. :   LC Card 80-603454   DDC 363.1/79 19
KF27 .I518 1979j

NUCLEAR POLLUTION. see RADIOACTIVE POLLUTION.

NUCLEAR POWER. see ATOMIC POWER.

Nuclear power regulation /. Nikodem, Zdenek D. Washington, D.C. , 1980. xxvi, 230 p. :   LC Card 80-603213   DDC 343.73/0925 347.303925 19
KF2138 .N54

NUCLEAR-POWERED SHIPS. see ATOMIC SHIPS.

NUCLEAR PROLIFERATION. see NUCLEAR NONPROLIFERATION.

Nuclear proliferation factbook /. United States. Library of Congress. Environment and Natural Resources Policy Division. Washington , 1980. xi, 531 p. :   LC Card 80-603879   DDC 327.1/74 19
JX1974.73 .U55 1980

Nuclear-pumped lasers: proceedings of a workshop held at NASA Langley Research Center, Hampton, Va., July 25-26, 1979. [Washington]: NASA, Scientific and Technical Information Branch, 1979. vi, 136 p.: ill.; 27 cm. (United States. National Aeronautics and Space Administration. NASA conference publications. NASA-CP. 2107) Includes bibliographies.
1. Lasers - Congresses. 2. Atomic power - Congresses. I. United States, Langley Research Center, Hampton, Va. II. Series.   *NYPL [JSF 80-528]*

Nuclear reactor safety . Okrent, David. Madison , 1981. p. cm.   ISBN 0-299-08350-0 :   LC Card 80-53958   DDC 621.48/35 19
TK9152 .O35

NUCLEAR REACTOR SUPPLY INDUSTRY. see ATOMIC ENERGY INDUSTRIES.

NUCLEAR REACTORS.
(1980) Irradiation of samples for $^{40}Ar/^{39}Ar$ dating using the Geological Survey TRIGA reactor /. Washington , 1980. p. cm.   LC Card 80-607859   DDC 551.7/01 19
QE508 .I77

NUCLEAR REACTORS - ENVIRONMENTAL ASPECTS.
United States. Congress. House. Committee on Foreign Affairs. Subcommittee on International Economic Policy and Trade. Nuclear exports, international safety and environmental issues . Washington , 1980. iii, 226 p. ;   LC Card 80-603801   DDC 363.1/79 19
KF27 .F6465 1979f

NUCLEAR REACTORS - FINLAND.
Wydler, John W. Oversight of energy development in northern Europe . Washington , 1980. v, 45 p. :   LC Card 80-603051   DDC 333.79/24 19
TJ163.25.E853 W93

NUCLEAR REACTORS - FUEL. see NUCLEAR FUELS.

NUCLEAR REACTORS - RELIABILITY - CONGRESSES.
International Conference on Nuclear Systems Reliability Engineering and Risk Assessment, Gatlinburg, Tenn., 1977. Nuclear systems reliability engineering and risk assessment . Philadelphia , 1977. xi, 849 p. :   LC Card 77-91478
TK9152 .I48 1977   *NYPL [JSF 81-47]*

NUCLEAR REACTORS - SAFETY MEASURES.
(1980) United States. Congress. House. Committee on Foreign Affairs. Subcommittee on International Economic Policy and Trade. Nuclear exports, international safety and environmental issues . Washington , 1980. iii, 226 p. ;   LC Card 80-603801   DDC 363.1/79 19
KF27 .F6465 1979f

NUCLEAR REACTORS - SAFETY MEASURES - CONGRESSES.
International Conference on Nuclear Systems Reliability Engineering and Risk Assessment, Gatlinburg, Tenn., 1977. Nuclear systems reliability engineering and risk assessment . Philadelphia , 1977. xi, 849 p. :   LC Card 77-91478
TK9152 .I48 1977   *NYPL [JSF 81-47]*

NUCLEAR REACTORS - SAFETY REGULATIONS - UNITED STATES - HISTORY.
Okrent, David. Nuclear reactor safety . Madison , 1981. p. cm.   ISBN 0-299-08350-0 :   LC Card 80-53958   DDC 621.48/35 19
TK9152 .O35

NUCLEAR REACTORS - SWEDEN.
Wydler, John W. Oversight of energy development in northern Europe . Washington , 1980. v, 45 p. :   LC Card 80-603051   DDC 333.79/24 19
TJ163.25.E853 W93

NUCLEAR REACTORS - UNITED STATES - SAFETY MEASURES - HISTORY.
Okrent, David. Nuclear reactor safety . Madison , 1981. p. cm.   ISBN 0-299-08350-0 :   LC Card 80-53958   DDC 621.48/35 19
TK9152 .O35

Nuclear Regulatory Commission authorizations for fiscal year 1981 . United States. Congress. House. Committee on Interior and Insular Affairs. Subcommittee on Energy and the Environment. Washington , 1980. iv, 503 p. :   LC Card 80-603512   DDC 353.0072/2368722 19
KF27 .I518 1980

The Nuclear Regulatory Commission, more aggressive leadership needed . United States. General Accounting Office. [Washington, D.C. , 1980] vii, 93 p. ;   LC Card 80-601236   DDC 353.0087/22 19
HD9698.U52 U55 1980a

Nuclear Regulatory Commission--the Rogovin report . United States. Congress. House. Committee on Government Operations. Environment, Energy, and Natural Resources Subcommittee. Washington , 1980. iii, 90 p. ;   LC Card 80-602901   DDC 363.1/79 19
KF27 .G655 1980b

NUCLEAR RESEARCH - UNITED STATES.
United States. Congress. House. Committee on Science and Technology. Subcommittee on Energy Research and Production. New directions for nuclear R.D. & D., post-INFCE . Washington , 1980. iii, 401 p. :   LC Card 80-604001   DDC 363.1/79 19
KF27 .S3936 1980b

United States. Congress. House. Committee on Science and Technology. Subcommittee on Energy Research and Production. Quests with U. S. accelerators--50 years, the high energy physics and nuclear physics research programs . Washington , c1980 [i.e. 1981] iii, 463 p. :   LC Card 81-601187   DDC 539.7/072073 19
KF27 .S3936 1980d

United States. General Accounting Office. Increasing costs, competition may hinder U. S. position of leadership in high energy physics . Washington, D.C. , 1980. v, 222 p. :   LC Card 80-603949   DDC 539.7/6/072073 19
QC793.4 .U54 1980

Nuclear safeguards . United States. Library of Congress. Congressional Research Service. Washington , 1980. xi, 50 p. ;   LC Card 80-602868   DDC 363.1/79 19
HD9698.U52 U57 1980a

Nuclear safety research and development act of 1980. United States. Congress. House. Committee on Science and Technology. Subcommittee on Energy Research and Production. H.R. 7190, Nuclear safety research and development act of 1980 . Washington , 1980. iii, 93 p. ;   LC Card 80-603021   DDC 343.73/0925 19
KF27 .S3936 1980

NUCLEAR SHIELDING. see SHIELDING (RADIATION)

NUCLEAR SHIPS. see ATOMIC SHIPS.

Nuclear siting and licensing process (Limerick Atomic Power Station, Pa.) . United States. Congress. House. Committee on Interior and Insular Affairs. Subcommittee on Energy and the Environment. Washington , 1980. iv, 305 p. :   LC Card 80-600605   DDC 343.73/0925 347.303925 19
KF27 .I518 1980c

Nuclear spent fuel storage in the Pacific . United States. Congress. House. Committee on Interior and Insular Affairs. Subcommittee on National Parks and Insular Affairs. Washington , 1980. iv, 233 p. :   LC Card 80-602767   DDC 344.73/04622 19
KF27 .I5365 1979b

Nuclear systems reliability engineering and risk assessment . International Conference on Nuclear Systems Reliability Engineering and Risk Assessment, Gatlinburg, Tenn., 1977. Philadelphia , 1977. xi, 849 p. :   LC Card 77-91478
TK9152 .I48 1977   *NYPL [JSF 81-47]*

Nuclear Systems Reliability Engineering and Risk Assessment, International Conference on. see International Conference on Nuclear

Systems Reliability Engineering and Risk Assessment, Gatlinburg, Tenn., 1977.

Nuclear war strategy . United States. Congress. Senate. Committee on Foreign Relations. Washington , 1981. iii, 40 p. ; LC Card 81-601145 DDC 355/.0217/0973 19
KF26 .F6 1980s

NUCLEAR WARFARE. see ATOMIC WARFARE.

Nuclear waste disposal . United States. Congress. House. Committee on Interstate and Foreign Commerce. Subcommittee on Energy and Power. Washington , 1980. iii, 240 p. : LC Card 80-603993 DDC 344.73/04622 347.3044622 19
KF27 .I5542 1980j

Nuclear waste management reorganization act of 1979 . United States. Congress. Senate. Committee on Governmental Affairs. Subcommittee on Energy, Nuclear Proliferation, and Federal Services. Washington , 1980. iv, 772 p. : LC Card 80-602895 DDC 344.73/04622 19
KF26 .G6728 1979m

Nuclear Waste Research, Development, and Demonstration Act of 1980. United States. Congress. House. Committee on Science and Technology. Subcommittee on Energy Research and Production. H.R. 7418--Nuclear Waste Research, Development, and Demonstration Act of 1980 . Washington , 1980. iii, 118 p. : LC Card 80-604068 DDC 344.73/04622 347.3044622 19
KF27 .S3936 1980a

NUCLEAR WEAPONS. see ATOMIC WEAPONS.

Nueces Basin. Texas. Dept. of Water Resources. Projected land use maps year 2000, Nueces Basin. Austin, Tex. , 1978. [13] leaves : LC Card 80-675295 DDC 912/.133373/3097641 19
G1372.N8G4 T4 1978

Nuechterlein, Donald Edwin, 1925- The President's program directors the Assistant Secretaries . Charlottesville, Va. [1977]. iii, 112 p. : LC Card 77-603586
JK518 .P75

Nugent, Nell Marion. Cavaliers and pioneers : abstracts of Virginia land patents and grants : supplement, Northern Neck grants, no. 1, 1690-1692 / abstracted by Nell Marion Nugent ; indexed by Susan Bracey Sheppard. Richmond : Virginia State Library, 1980. iii, 18 p. ; 23 cm. (Virginia State Library publications . no. 47 0083-6524) Includes index. ISBN 0-88490-088-6 (pbk.) LC Card 80-141230 DDC 929/.3755 19
1. Virginia - Genealogy. 2. Land grants - Virginia. I. Series: Virginia. State Library, Richmond. Publications, no. 47. II. Title.
F225 .N842 1934 Suppl.

NUISANCES - NORTH CAROLINA.
Lawrence, David M. 1979 legislation, self-dealing, fire lanes, and agricultural nuisances /. [Chapel Hill] , 1979. 6 p. ; LC Card 79-625895 DDC 342.756/09 s 349.756 347.56029 s 347.56
KFN7830.A15 L6 no. 16

Nulty, Michael L. Ecology of caddisflies (Trichoptera:Hydropsychidae) in a Neosho River riffle / by Michael L. Nulty. Emporia, Kan. : Emporia State University, 1980. 30 p. : ill. ; 23 cm. (The Emporia State research studies . v. 28, no. 3) "This study originated as a master's thesis .. at Emporia State University." Bibliography: p. 28-30. LC Card 80-622260 DDC 595.7/45 19
1. Hydropsychidae - Ecology. 2. Insects - Ecology. 3. Insects - Neosho River - Ecology. I. Title. II. Series.
QL518.H94 N84

Number of active employer accounts, covered workers, taxable wages and contributions under Ohio Unemployment Compensaton Law, Ohio Bureau of Employment Services, since 1936. Columbus : Division of Research and Statistics, Ohio Bureau of Employment Services, [1978] 15 leaves ; 22 x 28 cm. Microfilm. Caption title.
1. Insurance, Unemployment - Ohio - Statistics. 2. Wages - Ohio - Statistics. I. Ohio. Bureau of Employment Services. Division of Research and Statistics. II. Title. *NYPL [*ZT-1259]*

Number of active employer accounts, covered workers, total wages, taxable wages and contributions under Ohio Employment Compensation Law. Ohio. Bureau of Employment Services. Division of Research and Statistics. Columbus, 1977. 14 leaves;
*NYPL [*ZT-1264]*

Numbers, Ronald L. Wisconsin medicine . Madison, Wis. , 1981. ix, 212 p. : ISBN 0-299-08430-2 : LC Card 80-52297 DDC 362.1/09775 19
R357 .W57

A Numerator and denominator for measuring change : the Census Bureau. Washington : The Bureau : for sale by the Supt. of Docs., U. S. Govt. Print. Off., 1975. 195 p. : ill. ; 29 cm. (Technical paper - U. S. Bureau of the Census ; 37) Includes index. LC Card 75-619192 DDC 001.4/33 19
1. United States. Bureau of the Census. 2. United States - Statistical services - Congresses. 3. Social indicators - United States - Congresses. I. Series: United States. Bureau of the Census. Technical paper , 37.
HA37 .U52 1975

NUMERICAL ANALYSIS - CONGRESSES.
National Conference on Numerical Methods in Heat Transfer. Proceedings. 1st- ; 1979- [College Park, Md.] *NYPL [JSP 81-105]*

NUMERICAL DIFFERENTIATION - DATA PROCESSING.
Speelpenning, B. Compiling fast partial derivatives of functions given by algorithms /. Urbana, Ill. [1980] v, 75 p. : LC Card 80-623652 DDC 001.64 s 519.4 19
QA76 .I4 no. 1002 QA299

Numerical index of position classifications. Kentucky. Dept. of Personnel. Division of Classification. [Frankfort] , 1979. 81 leaves ; LC Card 80-622392 DDC 353.9769001/03/016 19
JK5357 .K46 1979

NUMERICAL INTEGRATION.
(1980) Gear, Charles William. Automatic multirate methods for ordinary differential equations /. Urbana, Ill. [1980] 14 p. ; LC Card 80-622966 DDC 001.64 s 515.3/52 19
QA76 .I4 no. 1000 QA372

Numerical Methods in Heat Transfer, National Conference on. see National Conference on Numerical Methods in Heat Transfer.

Nunnallee, Edmund Pierce. (joint author) Thorne, Richard E. A portable hydroacoustic data acquisition system for fish stock assessment /. Seattle [1972] ii, 14 leaves : LC Card 81-462262 DDC 639/.2 19
SH344.23.E3 T48

Nunnally, Nelson R. Use of fluvial processes to minimize adverse effects of stream channelization / by Nelson R. Nunnally, Edward Keller. [Raleigh, N.C.] : Water Resources Research Institute of the University of North Carolina, 1979. viii, 115 p. : ill. ; 28 cm. (Report - Water Resources Research Institute of the University of North Carolina ; no. 144) Errata slip inserted. "Project no. B-089-NC; agreement no. 14-34-0001-6103." Includes bibliographies. LC Card 80-620990 DDC 333.91/009756 s 627/.12 19
1. Stream conservation. 2. Stream channelization - Environmental aspects. 3. Stream conservation - North Carolina - Mecklenburg Co. 4. Stream channelization - Environmental aspects - North Carolina - Mecklenburg Co. I. Keller, Edward A., 1942- joint author. II. University of North Carolina (System). Water Resources Research Institute. III. Series: University of North Carolina (System). Water Resources Research Institute. Report ; no. 144. IV. Title.
HD1694.N8 N6 no. 144 TC424.N8

Nurco, David. Friends Medical Science Research Center. Narcotic addiction over a quarter of a century in a major American city, 1950-1977 . [Rockville, Md.] , 1980. vi, 92 p. : LC Card 80-601276 DDC 362.2/93/097526 19
HV5833.B2 F74 1980

Nurse planning information series. 1- Hyattsville, Md., 1977- 26 cm. (DHEW publication (HRA)) Irregular. At head of title: U. S. Dept. of Health, Education, and Welfare, Public Health Service, Health Resources Administration, Bureau of Health Manpower, Division of Nursing.
1. Nursing - Research - Collected works. I. United States. Health Resources Administration. Division of Nursing. *NYPL [JLM 81-4]*

Nurse planning information series . (13) Franklin Research Center. Continuing education in nursing . Hyattsville, Md. [1980] x, 196 p. ; LC Card 80-602706 DDC 610.73/07/15 19
Z5818.N8 F7 1980 RT76

NURSE PRACTITIONERS - EMPLOYMENT - UNITED STATES - STATISTICS.
Longitudinal study of nurse practitioners . Hyattsville, Md. , Washington, D.C. , 1980. xv, 221 p. : LC Card 80-602207 DDC 610.73/0692 19
RT82.8 .L67

NURSE PRACTITIONERS - UNITED STATES - LONGITUDINAL STUDIES.
Longitudinal study of nurse practitioners . Hyattsville, Md. , Washington, D.C. , 1980. xv, 221 p. : LC Card 80-602207 DDC 610.73/0692 19
RT82.8 .L67

NURSE PRACTITIONERS - UNITED STATES - STATISTICS.
Longitudinal study of nurse practitioners . Hyattsville, Md. , Washington, D.C. , 1980. xv, 221 p. : LC Card 80-602207 DDC 610.73/0692 19
RT82.8 .L67

Nurse shortage and its impact on care for the elderly . United States. Congress. House. Select Committee on Aging. Subcommittee on Health and Long-Term Care. Washington , 1981 [i.e. 1980] iii, 127 p. : LC Card 81-601169 · DDC 362.1/6 19
KF27.5 .A355 1980f

Nursery stock for nonindustrial private forest lands in Oregon. Oregon. Dept. of Forestry. Salem, Or. [1979] x, 35, [22] p. : LC Card 79-623541 DDC 634.9/564/09795 19
SD398.42.O7 O73 1979

NURSERY STOCK - OREGON.
Oregon. Dept. of Forestry. Nursery stock for nonindustrial private forest lands in Oregon. Salem, Or. [1979] x, 35, [22] p. : LC Card 79-623541 DDC 634.9/564/09795 19
SD398.42.O7 O73 1979

NURSES - CALIFORNIA - SUPPLY AND DEMAND.
United States. Congress. House. Committee on Ways and Means. Subcommittee on Health. Issues affecting the financing and operation of hospitals . Washington , c1980 [i.e. 1981] iv, 178 p. : LC Card 81-601137 DDC 362.1/09794 19
KF27 .W344 1980f

NURSES - LICENSES - NEBRASKA.
Nebraska. State Board of Nursing. Rules and regulations governing the renewal and reinstatement of nurses' licenses, 1979. Lincoln, Neb. [1980] 9 p. : LC Card 80-622055 DDC 344.782/0414 347.8204414 19
KFN326.5.N81 A32 1980

NURSES - OKLAHOMA - STATISTICS.
Oklahoma. Board of Nurse Registration and Nursing Education. Report of nurse population in Oklahoma, 1979 /. Oklahoma City, Okla. [1980] [11] p. : LC Card 80-623277 DDC 331.12/5161073/09766 19
RT5.O5 O32 1980

NURSES - UNITED STATES - SUPPLY AND DEMAND.
United States. Congress. House. Select Committee on Aging. Subcommittee on Health and Long-Term Care. Nurse shortage and its impact on care for the elderly . Washington , 1981 [i.e. 1980] iii, 127 p. : LC Card 81-601169 DDC 362.1/6 19
KF27.5 .A355 1980f

NURSES - UNITED STATES - SUPPLY AND DEMAND - MATHEMATICAL MODELS.
Doyle, Timothy C. The impact of health system changes on the nation's requirements for registered nurses in 1985 /. Hyattsville, Md. , Washington , 1978. vi, 71 p. : LC Card 79-602562
RT86.73 .D68 *NYPL [JLF 81-185]*

Nursing and rest home law and rules. Ohio. Laws, statutes, etc. [Nursing home and rest home licensure law.] [Columbus] [1978?] 18 p. ; LC Card 80-622700 DDC 344.771/03216 19
KFO363.N8 A3 1978

Nursing arts practice. Nursing skills and procedures /. Columbus, Ohio , Reston, Va. ,

c1979. x, 1077 p. : LC Card 81-103544 DDC
610.73/02/02 19
RT62 .N8 1979

NURSING - EXAMINATIONS, QUESTIONS, ETC.
The State board test pool examination for
registered nurse licensure /. Chicago, Ill. , 1981.
122 p. ; ISBN 0-914091-02-6 (pbk.) : LC Card
81-6107 DDC 610.73/076 19
RT55 .S73

NURSING HOME ADMINISTRATORS - MICHIGAN - STATISTICS.
Michigan. Cooperative Health Information
System. Licensed health occupations . Lansing,
Mich. , 1978. 41 p. : LC Card 80-622888 DDC
331.12/913621609774 19
RA997.5.M5 M52 1978

NURSING HOME ADMINISTRATORS - SUPPLY AND DEMAND - ARKANSAS - STATISTICS - PERIODICALS.
Arkansas health manpower statistics: nursing
home administrators. 1978- Little Rock.
NYPL [JLM 80-1086]

NURSING HOME AND ADMINISTRATORS - TEXAS - STATISTICS.
Texas. Bureau of State Health Planning &
Resource Development. Data Collection and
Analysis Division. Texas health manpower
report . Austin, Tex. , 1978. 101 p. : LC Card
80-623855 DDC 331.12/9136216068 19
RA997.5.T4 T432 1978

NURSING HOME CARE - MAINE - PLANNING.
Maine. Bureau of Health Planning and
Development. Rehabilitation and maintenance
program plan . [Augusta, Me.] [1980] iii, 156
p. : LC Card 80-622394 DDC 362.1/9897/009741
19
RA564.8 .M34 1980

NURSING HOME CARE - OHIO.
Ohio. Nursing Home Commission. A program
in crisis, blueprint for action . Columbus, Ohio
[1979] xix, 233 p. : LC Card 80-621848 DDC
362.1/6/09771 19
RA997.5.O3 O38 1979

NURSING HOMES - CALIFORNIA - UTILIZATION.
Chandler, Daniel, 1940- Facilitating access to
skilled nursing facilities for indigent patients /.
Sacramento, Calif. , 1980. 51 p. ; LC Card
80-623746 DDC 362.1/6/09794 19
RA997.5.C3 C47

NURSING HOMES - CONNECTICUT.
United States. Congress. House. Select
Committee on Aging. Subcommittee on Health
and Long-Term Care. Problems of nursing
home bed availability and placement .
Washington , 1980. iii, 63 p. ; LC Card
80-603433 DDC 362.1/6 19
KF27.5 .A355 1980b

NURSING HOMES - EMPLOYEES - IN-SERVICE TRAINING - AUDIO-VISUAL AIDS.
Kelly, Mary Margaret. Films for in-service
education in long-term care facilities /. Denton,
Tex. , 1980. ii, 39 leaves ; LC Card 80-622861
DDC 362.6/1 19
RA999.I5 K44

NURSING HOMES - LAW AND LEGISLATION - ILLINOIS.
Illinois. Dept. of Public Health. Minimum
standards, rules and regulations for classification
and licensure of intermediate care facilities,
skilled nursing facilities. [Springfield] [1980] x,
319, [13] p. ; LC Card 80-622572 DDC
344.773/03216 19
KFI1563.N8 A32 1980

Illinois. Dept. of Public Health. Minimum
standards, rules and regulations for classification
and licensure of skilled nursing facilities and
intermediate care facilities. [Springfield] [1980]
1 v. (various pagings) : LC Card 81-621482
DDC 344.773/03216 347.73043216 19
KFI1563.N8 A32 1980a

NURSING HOMES - LAW AND LEGISLATION - OHIO.
Ohio. Laws, statutes, etc. [Nursing home and
rest home licensure law.] Nursing and rest
home law and rules. [Columbus] [1978?] 18
p. ; LC Card 80-622700 DDC 344.771/03216 19
KFO363.N8 A3 1978

Ohio. Nursing Home Commission. A program
in crisis, blueprint for action . Columbus, Ohio
[1979] xix, 233 p. : LC Card 80-621848 DDC
362.1/6/09771 19
RA997.5.O3 O38 1979

NURSING HOMES - LICENSES - NORTH CAROLINA.
North Carolina. Dept. of Human Resources.
Division of Facility Services. Licensure and
Certification Section. Rules and regulations for
the licensing of nursing homes and home for
the aged beds when licensed as a part of a
nursing home. Raleigh, N.C. (P.O. Box 12200,
Raleigh 27605) [1980] 34 p. ; LC Card
81-621297 DDC 344.756/03216 347.56043216
19
KFN7763.N8 A32 1980

NURSING HOMES - MISSOURI - COSTS.
Missouri. Division of Budget and Planning.
Reimbursement alternatives for long-term
nursing care in Missouri. [Jefferson City]
[1979] 130 p. ; LC Card 80-620611 DDC
362.1/6/0681 19
RA997.5.M8 M55 1979

NURSING HOMES - MISSOURI - RATES.
Missouri. Division of Budget and Planning.
Reimbursement alternatives for long-term
nursing care in Missouri. [Jefferson City]
[1979] 130 p. ; LC Card 80-620611 DDC
362.1/6/0681 19
RA997.5.M8 M55 1979

NURSING HOMES - MISSOURI - STATISTICS.
Missouri Center for Health Statistics. Missouri
nursing homes, 1978 /. Jefferson City [1979]
viii, 25 p. : LC Card 80-622280 DDC
362.1/6/09778 19
RA997.5.M8 M56 1979

NURSING HOMES - OHIO.
Ohio. Nursing Home Commission. A program
in crisis, blueprint for action . Columbus, Ohio
[1979] xix, 233 p. : LC Card 80-621848 DDC
362.1/6/09771 19
RA997.5.O3 O38 1979

NURSING HOMES - OKLAHOMA - DIRECTORIES.
Oklahoma. Health Facilities Service. Licensure
Division. 1980 directory of licensed long-term
care facilities. [Oklahoma City, Okla.] [1980]
38 p. ; LC Card 80-622402 DDC 362.1/6/025766
19
RA997.5.O5 O43 1980

NURSING HOMES, PROPRIETARY - NEW YORK (STATE) - ACCOUNTING.
New York (State). Deputy Attorney General
for Nursing Homes, Health & Social Services.
Analysis of New York's profit-making long-term
care facilities /. [Albany] , 1978. i, 65 p. : LC
Card 79-623522 DDC 364.1/63 19
RA997.5.N7 N45 1978

NURSING HOMES, PROPRIETARY - NEW YORK (STATE) - RATES.
New York (State). Deputy Attorney General
for Nursing Homes, Health & Social Services.
Analysis of New York's profit-making long-term
care facilities /. [Albany] , 1978. i, 65 p. : LC
Card 79-623522 DDC 364.1/63 19
RA997.5.N7 N45 1978

NURSING HOMES - UNITED STATES - EMPLOYEES - SUPPLY AND DEMAND - STATISTICS.
National Clearinghouse on Aging. Human
resource issues in the field of aging .
[Washington, D.C.] [1980] v, 20 p. : LC Card
80-602117 DDC 331.12/913621/60973 19
RA997 .N375 1980

NURSING HOMES - UNITED STATES - FINANCE - STATISTICS.
Bloom, Barbara, 1950- Utilization patterns and
financial characteristics of nursing homes in the
United States, 1977 /. Hyattsville, Md. , 1981.
p. cm. ISBN 0-8406-0215-4 LC Card 80-606876
DDC 362.1/1/0973 s 362.1/6/0973 19
RA407.3 .A349 no. 53 RA997

NURSING HOMES - UNITED STATES - PHARMACEUTICAL SERVICES.
United States. Congress. House. Select
Committee on Aging. Drug abuse in nursing
homes . Washington , 1980. iv, 131 p. ; LC
Card 80-603430 DDC 362.1/6 19
KF27.5 .A3 1980d

NURSING HOMES - UNITED STATES - STATISTICS.
National Clearinghouse on Aging. Human
resource issues in the field of aging .
[Washington, D.C.] [1980] v, 20 p. : LC Card
80-602117 DDC 331.12/913621/60973 19
RA997 .N375 1980

Strahan, Genevieve W. Inpatient health
facilities statistics, United States, 1978 /.
Hyattsville, Md. , 1980. p. cm. ISBN
0-8406-0204-9 LC Card 80-607845 DDC
362.1/1/0973 19
RA981.A2 S78

NURSING HOMES - UNITED STATES - UTILIZATION - STATISTICS.
Bloom, Barbara, 1950- Utilization patterns and
financial characteristics of nursing homes in the
United States, 1977 /. Hyattsville, Md. , 1981.
p. cm. ISBN 0-8406-0215-4 LC Card 80-606876
DDC 362.1/1/0973 s 362.1/6/0973 19
RA407.3 .A349 no. 53 RA997

Zappolo, Aurora. Discharges from nursing
homes . Hyattsville, Md. , 1981. p. cm. ISBN
0-8406-0216-2 LC Card 81-607016 DDC
362.1/6/0973 19
RA997 .Z36

NURSING HOMES - WASHINGTON (STATE) - DIRECTORIES.
Washington (State). Office of Nursing Home
Affairs. Survey Section. Directory of licensed
nursing homes. Olympia.
NYPL [JLM 80-846]

NURSING HOMES - WASHINGTON (STATE) - UTILIZATION.
Community-based care systems for the
functionally disabled . Olympia, Wash. , 1979.
xiv, 339 p. : LC Card 79-620045 DDC
362.1/4/09797 19
RA645.36.W2 C65

NURSING - LAW AND LEGISLATION - ILLINOIS.
Illinois. Laws, statutes, etc. The Illinois nursing
act . Springfield , 1961. 19 p. ; LC Card
81-453496 DDC 344.773/0414/02632 19
KFI1526.5.N8 A32 1961

NURSING - LAW AND LEGISLATION - UNITED STATES.
Becker, Dorothy D. Health professions
legislation /. [Hyattsville, Md?] , 1980. 1 v. in
various pagings ; LC Card 81-601013 DDC
344.73/041 347.30441 19
KF2905 .A372

NURSING LITERATURE SEARCHING. see INFORMATION STORAGE AND RETRIEVAL SYSTEMS - NURSING.

NURSING - NEW YORK (CITY) - COSTS.
New York (State). Division of Audits and
Accounts. Control of hospital inpatient nursing
costs under the Medicaid Program, New York
City Health and Hospitals Corporation. Albany
[1980] 4, 2 leaves, 32 p. ; LC Card 80-622789
DDC 362.1/1/068 19
RT86.74.N48 N48 1980

Nursing procedures for the practical nurse.
Nursing skills and procedures /. Columbus,
Ohio , Reston, Va. , c1979. x, 1077 p. : LC
Card 81-103544 DDC 610.73/02/02 19
RT62 .N8 1979

NURSING - RESEARCH - COLLECTED WORKS.
Nurse planning information series. 1-
Hyattsville, Md., 1977- *NYPL [JLM 81-4]*

Nursing skills and procedures / [edited and
distributed by the Trade and Industrial
Education, Instructional Materials Laboratory,
the Ohio State University, College of
Education]. Columbus, Ohio : The Laboratory ;
Reston, Va. : Reston Pub. Co., c1979. x, 1077
p. : ill. ; 28 cm. "A complete revision of the former
manuals titled Nursing arts practice and Nursing
procedures for the practical nurse"--acknowledgement.
LC Card 81-103544 DDC 610.73/02/02 19
1. Practical nursing - Handbooks, manuals, etc. I. Ohio
State University. Instructional Materials Laboratory. II.
Nursing arts practice. III. Nursing procedures for the
practical nurse.
RT62 .N8 1979

NURSING - STUDY AND TEACHING (CONTINUING EDUCATION) - ABSTRACTS.

Franklin Research Center. Continuing education in nursing . Hyattsville, Md. [1980] x, 196 p. ;
LC Card 80-602706 DDC 610.73/07/15 19
Z5818.N8 F7 1980 RT76

NURSING - STUDY AND TEACHING (CONTINUING EDUCATION) - BIBLIOGRAPHY.
Franklin Research Center. Continuing education in nursing . Hyattsville, Md. [1980] x, 196 p. ;
LC Card 80-602706 DDC 610.73/07/15 19
Z5818.N8 F7 1980 RT76

NURSING - STUDY AND TEACHING (CONTINUING EDUCATION) - UNITED STATES - STATISTICS.
Longitudinal study of nurse practitioners .
Hyattsville, Md. , Washington, D.C. , 1980. xv, 221 p. : LC Card 80-602207 DDC 610.73/0692 19
RT82.8 .L67

NURSING - STUDY AND TEACHING (GRADUATE) - UNITED STATES - STATISTICS.
Longitudinal study of nurse practitioners .
Hyattsville, Md. , Washington, D.C. , 1980. xv, 221 p. : LC Card 80-602207 DDC 610.73/0692 19
RT82.8 .L67

NURSING - UNITED STATES - STATISTICS.
United States. Veterans Administration. Survey of factors relating to job satisfaction among VA nurses . [Washington] , 1973. 20, [45] p. :
NYPL [JLF 80-1691]

Nutrient and drug interactions /. Molleson, Ann L. Columbus, Ohio (456 Clinic Dr., Columbus 43210) , c1980. 28 p. ; LC Card 81-620938
DDC 615/.7045 19
RM302 .M64

Nutrient content of foods, nutritional supplements, and food fallacies /.
Gallagher-Allred, Charlette R. Columbus, Ohio (456 Clinic Dr., Columbus 43210) , c1980. 40 p. : LC Card 81-620936 DDC 641.1 19
TX551 .G26

Nutrient kinetics of phytoplankton in the Pamlico River, North Carolina /. Kuenzler, Edward J. [Raleigh] [1979] xxii, 163 p. : LC Card 79-626205 DDC 333.91/009756 s 589.4 19
HD1694.N8 N6 no. 139 QK571.5.N8

Nutrient levels in North Dakota streams, 1972-1978 /. North Dakota. State Dept. of Health. [Bismarck, N.D.] [1980] 86 p. : LC Card 80-622821 DDC 363.7/3942/09784 19
TD224.N9 N65 1980

NUTRIENT SUPPLEMENTS. see DIETARY SUPPLEMENTS.

NUTRITION.
(1980) Latanick, Maureen Rogan. Appraisal of nutritional status /. Columbus, Ohio (456 Clinic Dr., Columbus 43210) , c1980. 40 p. : LC Card 81-620937 DDC 616.3/9075 19
RC621 .L37

(1980) Molleson, Ann L. Nutrient and drug interactions /. Columbus, Ohio (456 Clinic Dr., Columbus 43210) , c1980. 28 p. ; LC Card 81-620938 DDC 615/.7045 19
RM302 .M64

(1980) United States. General Accounting Office. What foods should Americans eat? . [Washington, D.C. , 1980] iv, 92 p. ; LC Card 80-602052 DDC 641.1/07/1073 19
TX353 .U495 1980

NUTRITION AND STATE. see NUTRITION POLICY.

NUTRITION - BIBLIOGRAPHY.
United States. National Agricultural Library. Food and Nutrition Information and Educational Materials Center. Index to the proceedings of 10 USDA-Land-Grant university seminars. [Washington, 1974] xiii, 27 p.
*NYPL [*Z-3211]*

NUTRITION DISORDERS - DIAGNOSIS.
Latanick, Maureen Rogan. Appraisal of nutritional status /. Columbus, Ohio (456 Clinic Dr., Columbus 43210) , c1980. 40 p. : LC Card 81-620937 DDC 616.3/9075 19
RC621 .L37

NUTRITION DISORDERS - RESEARCH - UNITED STATES.
The Biomedical and behavioral basis of clinical nutrition . [Bethesda, Md.] , Washington, D.C. , 1979. xii, 217 p. ; LC Card 80-601711 DDC

616.3/9 19
RC620.5 .B52

NUTRITION DISORDERS - TEXAS - PREVENTION - CONGRESSES.
Food & fitness . [Austin, Tex.] [1979?] vi, 105 p. ; LC Card 80-621074 DDC 362.1/9639 19
RA645.N87 F66

NUTRITION EXTENSION WORK - TEXAS - CONGRESSES.
Food & fitness . [Austin, Tex.] [1979?] vi, 105 p. ; LC Card 80-621074 DDC 362.1/9639 19
RA645.N87 F66

NUTRITION IN PREGNANCY. see PREGNANCY - NUTRITIONAL ASPECTS.

Nutrition in primary care .
(1) Gallagher-Allred, Charlette R. Nutrient content of foods, nutritional supplements, and food fallacies /. Columbus, Ohio (456 Clinic Dr., Columbus 43210) , c1980. 40 p. : LC Card 81-620936 DDC 641.1 19
TX551 .G26

(10) Bossetti, Brenda. Dietary management in diabetes mellitus /. Columbus, Ohio (456 Clinic Dr., Columbus 43210) , c1980. 51 p. : LC Card 81-620945 DDC 616.4/620654 19
RC662 .B67

(11) Molleson, Ann L. Dietary management in hypertension /. Columbus, Ohio (456 Clinic Dr., Columbus 43210) , c1980. 28 p. : LC Card 81-620946 DDC 616.1/320654 19
RC685.H8 M56

(12) Gallagher-Allred, Charlette R. Dietary management in hyperlipidemia /. Columbus, Ohio (456 Clinic Dr., Columbus 43210) , c1980. 20 p. : LC Card 81-620947 DDC 616.3/9970654 19
RC632.H87 G34

(13) Stein, Joan Z. Dietary management in gastrointestinal diseases /. Columbus, Ohio (456 Clinic Dr., Columbus 43210) , c1980. 28 p. ; LC Card 81-620948 DDC 616.3/30654 19
RC802 .S69

(14) Hurley, Roberta Smith. Dietary management for alcoholic patients /. Columbus, Ohio (456 Clinic Dr., Columbus 43210) , c1980. 15 p. ; LC Card 81-620949 DDC 616.86/10654 19
RC565 .H86

(16) Latanick, Maureen Rogan. An office strategy for nutrition-related patient education and compliance /. Columbus, Ohio (456 Clinic Dr., Columbus 43210) , c1980. 23 p. ; LC Card 81-620951 DDC 613.2/07/15 19
R727.4 .L37

(2) Latanick, Maureen Rogan. Appraisal of nutritional status /. Columbus, Ohio (456 Clinic Dr., Columbus 43210) , c1980. 40 p. : LC Card 81-620937 DDC 616.3/9075 19
RC621 .L37

(3) Molleson, Ann L. Nutrient and drug interactions /. Columbus, Ohio (456 Clinic Dr., Columbus 43210) , c1980. 28 p. ; LC Card 81-620938 DDC 615/.7045 19
RM302 .M64

(4) Cox, Janice Hovasi. Normal diet, age of dependency /. Columbus, Ohio (456 Clinic Dr., Columbus 43210) , c1980. 34 p. : LC Card 81-620939 DDC 613.2/6 19
RJ216 .C69

(5) Tuckermanty, Elizabeth. Normal diet, age of parental control /. Columbus, Ohio (456 Clinic Dr., Columbus 43210) , c1980. 31 p. : LC Card 81-620940 DDC 613.2/6 19
RJ206 .T83

(6) Tuckermanty, Elizabeth. Normal diet, adolescence /. Columbus, Ohio (456 Clinic Dr., Columbus 43210) , c1980. 31 p. : LC Card 81-620941 DDC 613.2/088055 19
RJ235 .T83

(7) Cox, Janice Hovasi. Normal diet, pregnancy and lactation /. Columbus, Ohio (456 Clinic Dr., Columbus 43210) , c1980. 47 p. : LC Card 81-620942 DDC 618.2/4 19
RG559 .C68

(8) Molleson, Ann L. Normal diet, geriatrics /. Columbus, Ohio (456 Clinic Dr., Columbus 43210) , c1980. 23 p. : LC Card 81-620943

DDC 613.2/0880565 19
TX361.A3 M64

Nutrition labeling and information amendments of 1979 to the Federal food, drug, and cosmetic act . United States. Congress. Senate. Committee on Labor and Human Resources. Subcommittee on Health and Scientific Research. Washington , 1980. v, 738 p. : LC Card 80-602890 DDC 344.73/04232 19
KF26 .L274 1980b

NUTRITION - LAW AND LEGISLATION - UNITED STATES.
United States. Congress. Senate. Committee on Labor and Human Resources. Subcommittee on Health and Scientific Research. Nutrition labeling and information amendments of 1979 to the Federal food, drug, and cosmetic act . Washington , 1980. v, 738 p. : LC Card 80-602890 DDC 344.73/04232 19
KF26 .L274 1980b

Nutrition needs of the elderly . United States. Congress. Senate. Committee on Agriculture, Nutrition, and Forestry. Subcommittee on Nutrition. Washington , 1981. iv, 122 p. ; LC Card 81-601607 DDC 362.1/9897639 19
KF26 .A3559 1980b

NUTRITION OF CHILDREN. see CHILDREN - NUTRITION; INFANTS - NUTRITION.

NUTRITION OF PLANTS. see PLANTS - NUTRITION.

NUTRITION POLICY - TEXAS - CONGRESSES.
Food & fitness . [Austin, Tex.] [1979?] vi, 105 p. ; LC Card 80-621074 DDC 362.1/9639 19
RA645.N87 F66

NUTRITION POLICY - UNITED STATES.
United States. General Accounting Office. What foods should Americans eat? . [Washington, D.C. , 1980] iv, 92 p. ; LC Card 80-602052 DDC 641.1/07/1073 19
TX353 .U495 1980

Nutrition research methods and technology .
United States. Congress. House. Committee on Science and Technology. Subcommittee on Science, Research, and Technology. Washington , 1979. iv, 415 p. : LC Card 80-602711 DDC 613.2/072073 19
KF27 .S399 1979q

NUTRITION - RESEARCH - UNITED STATES.
United States. Congress. House. Committee on Science and Technology. Subcommittee on Science, Research, and Technology. Nutrition research methods and technology . Washington , 1979. iv, 415 p. : LC Card 80-602711 DDC 613.2/072073 19
KF27 .S399 1979q

United States. Joint Council on Food and Agricultural Sciences. Ad Hoc Committee on Human Nutrition. Human nutrition programs . Washington, D.C. [1980] v, 120, [21] p. : LC Card 80-601855 DDC 613.2/07/073 19
TX367 .U56 1980

NUTRITION - STUDY AND TEACHING.
Latanick, Maureen Rogan. An office strategy for nutrition-related patient education and compliance /. Columbus, Ohio (456 Clinic Dr., Columbus 43210) , c1980. 23 p. ; LC Card 81-620951 DDC 613.2/07/15 19
R727.4 .L37

NUTRITION - STUDY AND TEACHING - CALIFORNIA.
United States. Congress. House. Committee on Agriculture. Subcommittee on Domestic Marketing, Consumer Relations, and Nutrition. Expanded food and nutrition education program (Los Angeles, Calif.) . Washington , 1980. iii, 106 p. ; LC Card 80-604023 DDC 362.1/9639 19
KF27 .A3336 1980a

NUTRITION - STUDY AND TEACHING - FLORIDA - CASE STUDIES.
Neenan, P. H. Impact of the food stamp and expanded food and nutrition education programs on food expenditure and nutrient intake of low income rural Florida households /. Gainesville , 1978. xii, 79 p. : LC Card 79-626209 DDC 363.8/82/09759 19
HV696.F6 N37

NUTRITION - STUDY AND TEACHING - UNITED STATES.
Synectics Corporation. The Expanded Food and Nutrition Education Program . [Washington] [1979] xi, 131 p. : LC Card 79-601895 DDC 641.1/07/073 19
TX364 .S96 1979

United States. Joint Council on Food and Agricultural Sciences. Ad Hoc Committee on Human Nutrition. Human nutrition programs . Washington, D.C. [1980] v, 120, [21] p. : LC Card 80-601855 DDC 613.2/07/073 19
TX367 .U56 1980

NUTRITION SURVEYS - SIERRA LEONE.
Michigan. State University, East Lansing. Dept. of Agricultural Economics. Household food consumption in rural Sierra Leone /. East Lansing, Mich. , 1979. x, 111 p. : LC Card 80-621811 DDC 362.1/9639 19
TX360.S5 M52 1979

NUTRITION - UNITED STATES.
United States. Congress. House. Committee on Science and Technology. Subcommittee on Science, Research, and Technology. Nutrition research methods and technology . Washington , 1979. iv, 415 p. : LC Card 80-602711 DDC 613.2/072073 19
KF27 .S399 1979q

United States. Congress. Senate. Committee on Agriculture, Nutrition, and Forestry. Subcommittee on Nutrition. Trends in the American diet . Washington , 1980. iii, 66 p. ; LC Card 80-602728 DDC 362.1/9639/073 19
KF26 .A3559 1980

Nutritional quality of infant formula . United States. Congress. House. Committee on Interstate and Foreign Commerce. Subcommittee on Health and the Environment. Washington , 1980. ii, 212 p. ; LC Card 80-602521 DDC 344.73/04232 19
KF27 .I5543 1980c

NUTRITIONALLY INDUCED DISEASES - CONGRESSES.
Food & fitness . [Austin, Tex.] [1979?] vi, 105 p. ; LC Card 80-621074 DDC 362.1/9639 19
RA645.N87 F66

Nyberg, Randy. (joint author) Walzer, Norman. Revenue sharing in Illinois municipalities /. Springfield, IL [1979] 6, 47, [67] p. : LC Card 80-623316 DDC 336.1/85 19
HJ9227 .W345

Nyblade, Carl. Five year intertidal community change, San Juan Islands, 1974-1978, and the intertidal benthos of North Puget Sound, summer 1978 / Carl F. Nyblade. Olympia, Wash. : Baseline Study Program, Washington State Dept. of Ecology, [1979] v, 137 p. : maps ; 28 cm. "August 1979." Bibliography: p. 131-137. LC Card 80-622613 DDC 591.92/632 19
1. Intertidal fauna - Washington (State) - San Juan Islands. 2. Intertidal fauna - Washington (State) - Puget Sound. 3. Intertidal zonation - Washington (State) - San Juan Islands. 4. Intertidal zonation - Washington (State) - Puget Sound. 5. Benthos - Washington (State) - San Juan Islands. 6. Benthos - Washington (State) - Puget Sound. I. Title.
QL212 .N9

Nybo, James H. Montana. Energy Division. Montana renewable energy viability project . Helena, Mont. , 1980. v, 103 p. : LC Card 80-622559 DDC 333.79 19
TJ163.25.U6 M653 1980

Nygren, Edward J. Corcoran Gallery of Art. Of time and place . Washington, D.C. , 1981. p. cm. ISBN 0-86528-010-X LC Card 81-607836 DDC 704.9/42/0973074013 19
N6510 .C69 1981

NYPUM program evaluation. Virginia. Dept. of Corrections. Bureau of Research, Reporting and Evaluation. [Richmond] , 1977. 171 p. ; LC Card 79-621982 DDC 365/.9755462 19
HV9105.V7 V5 1977

Nyrop, Richard F. Peru, a country study /. Washington, D.C. , 1981, c1980. p. cm. LC Card 81-3456 DDC 985/.063 19
F3408 .P4647 1981

Nyserda. see New York State Energy Research and Development Authority.

O. A. S. see Organization of American States.

O and C lands. Richardson, Elmo. BLM's

billion-dollar checkerboard . Santa Cruz, Calif. , Washington, D.C. , c1980. x, 200 p. : LC Card 81-600781 DDC 333.75/09795 19
SD566.O7 R5

O. C. D. E. see Organization for Economic Cooperation and Development.

O. E. A. see Organization of American States.

O. E. C. D. see Organization for Economic Cooperation and Development.

O. H. I. see United States. Office for Handicapped Individuals.

O. M. B. E. see United States. Office of Minority Business Enterprise.

O. M. S. see World Health Organization.

O. P. E. C. see Organization of Petroleum Exporting Countries.

O. P. I. C. see Overseas Private Investment Corporation.

O. R. C. see Olympus Research Corporation.

O. T. A. see United States. Congress. Office of Technology Assessment.

O. T. A. N. see North Atlantic Treaty Organization.

OAHU - POPULATION.
Cohn, Rebecca W. Differential fertility in Hawaii . [Honolulu, Hawaii] [1980] 24 p. : LC Card 80-622655 DDC 304.6/09969 s 304.6/3/099693 19
HB3525.H3 H33a no. 32 HB935.H3

OAK PARK, CALIF. - ANTIQUITIES - ADDRESSES, ESSAYS, LECTURES.
The Archeology of Oak Park, Ventura County, California /. Los Angeles , 1978. 2 v. : LC Card 80-621558 DDC 979.4/92 19
E99.C815 A7

Oak Ridge National Laboratory. International Conference on Nuclear Cross Sections for Technology (1979 : University of Tennessee) Nuclear cross sections for technology . [Washington, D.C.?] , 1980. xvi, 1039 p. : LC Card 80-600128 DDC 602/.18 s 539.7/54 19
QC100 .U57 no. 594 QC794.6.C7

Oak Ridge National Laboratory Life Sciences Symposium, 1st, Oak Ridge, Tenn., 1978.
Synthetic fossil fuel teachnology, potential health and environmental effects : proceedings of the First Annual Oak Ridge National Laboratory Life Sciences Symposium, September 25-28, 1978 / edited by K. E. Cowser, C. R. Richmond. Ann Arbor, Mich. : Ann Arbor Science Publishers, c1980. xiii, 288 p. : ill. ; 29 cm. "Sponsored by the Oak Ridge National Laboratory, Department of Energy." Includes bibliographies. LC Card 80-68338
1. Fossil fuels - Congresses. 2. Synthetic fuels - Congresses. I. Cowser, Kenneth E. II. Richmond, Chester R. III. United States. National Laboratory, Oak Ridge, Tenn. IV. Title. **NYPL [JSF 81-116]**

Oak Ridge, Tenn. National Laboratory. see United States. National Laboratory, Oak Ridge, Tenn.

Oakes, Claudia M. National Air and Space Museum. Aircraft of the National Air and Space Museum, Smithsonian Institution /. Washington, D.C. , 1981. p. cm. LC Card 81-607991 DDC 629.133/074/0153 19
TL506.U6 W455 1981

Oakes, William J. Mayer- see Mayer-Oakes, William J., 1923-

Oakland, Calif. Museum. see Oakland Museum.

Oakland Museum.
Thomas Hill, the grand view /. Oakland, Calif. , 1980. 64 p. : LC Card 80-82938 DDC 759.13 19
ND237.H615 A4 1980

Oakland Museum. Art Dept. Thomas Hill, the grand view /. Oakland, Calif. , 1980. 64 p. : LC Card 80-82938 DDC 759.13 19
ND237.H615 A4 1980

Oandasan, William. A branch of California redwood / by William Oandasan. Los Angeles, CA : American Indian Studies Center, University of California, c1980. p. cm. (Native American series ; no. 4) ISBN 0-935626-03-4 LC Card 81-3518 DDC 811/.54 19
I. Title. II. Series.
PS3565.A5 B7

O'Bannon, J. H. Bibliography of nematodes of citrus : supplement / [by J. H. O'Bannon, R. P. Esser, and R. N. Inserra]. Washington : Science and Education Administration, U. S. Dept. of Agriculture, 1979. 11 p. ; 26 cm. Includes indexes. LC Card 79-602330 DDC 016.634/35965182 19
1. Citrus fruits - Diseases and pests - Bibliography. 2. Nematode diseases of plants - Bibliography. 3. Plant nematodes - Bibliography. I. Esser, R. P., joint author. II. Inserra, R. N., joint author. III. Title.
Z5354.P3 C636 Suppl SB608.C5

OBESITY - CONGRESSES.
Behavioral analysis and treatment of substance abuse /. Rockville, Md. , Washington, D.C. , 1979. viii, 256 p. : LC Card 79-600111 DDC 616.86 19
RC563.2 .B42

Self-administration of abused substances . Rockville, Md. , 1978. ix, 246 p. : LC Card 78-63094
RC564 .S44   **NYPL [JLM 76-1439 [no.] 20]**

Obeyesekere, Ranjini. An Anthology of modern writing from Sri Lanka /. Tucson, Ariz. [1981], c1979. p. cm. ISBN 0-8165-0702-3 : LC Card 81-1140 DDC 891/.487/08 19
PK2871.E1 A5

Obion County, Tennessee /. United States. Soil Conservation Service. Fort Worth, Tex. , 1980. 1 map : LC Card 81-692275
G3963.O2J4 1980 .U5

O'Brien, David M. Theright of privacy--its constitutional & social dimensions : a comprehensive bibliography / compiled by David M. O'Brien. Austin : Tarlton Law Library, School of Law, University of Texas, 1980. vi, 55 p. ; 28 cm. (Tarlton Law Library legal bibliography series ; #213) ISBN 0-935630-04-X (pbk.) LC Card 80-622796 DDC 016.34273/0858 19
1. Privacy, Right of - United States - Bibliography. I. Series: Tarlton Law Library. Tarlton Law Library legal bibliography series ; no. 21. II. Title.
KF1262.A1 O25

O'Brien, Richard J. Basic data on spirometry in adults 25-74 years of age, United States, 1971-75 / Richard J. O'Brien and Terence A. Drizd. Hyattsville, Md. : U. S. Dept. of Health and Human Services, Public Health Service, Office of Health Research, Statistics, and Technology, National Center for Health Statistics, 1980. p. cm. (Vital and health statistics : Series 11, Data from the National Health Survey ; no. 222) DHHS publication ; no. (PHS) 81-1672 Includes bibliographical references. LC Card 80-607829 DDC 312/.0973 s 312/.6 19
1. Spirometry. 2. Health surveys - United States. I. Drizd, Terence, joint author. II. Series: United States. National Center for Health Statistics. Vital and health statistics : Series 11, Data from National Health Survey, data from the health examination survey , no. 222. III. Title.
RA407.3 .A347 no. 222 RC734.S65

O'Brien, Robert Thomas, 1925- (joint author) Hain, Kathleen E. The survival of enteric viruses in septic tanks and septic tank drain fields /. Las Cruces, N.M. [1979] x, 73 p. : LC Card 80-622272 DDC 628/.742 19
GB705.N6 N64 no. 108 QR48

O'BRIEN, WILLIAM SMITH, 1803-1864.
Touhill, Blanche M. (Blanche Marie), 1931- William Smith O'Brien and his Irish revolutionary companions in penal exile /. Columbia , 1981. p. cm. ISBN 0-8262-0339-6 LC Card 81-1899 DDC 941.5081/092/4 19
DA952.O22 T68

Observations of marine birds and mammals in the northern Chesapeake Bight /. Rowlett, Richard A. [Washington, D.C.] , 1980. xii, 87 p. : LC Card 80-602344 DDC 598.2975 19
QL683.A87 R68

Observations of Sacramento River bank erosion, 1977-1979. California. Dept. of Water Resources. Northern District. [Sacramento, Calif.] [1979] x, 58 p. : LC Card 80-621717 DDC 551.3/52/097945 19
GB565.C2 C34 1979

Observations on the use of energy in social structure analysis /. Adams, Richard Newbold, 1924- [Austin] , 1979. ii, 76 leaves ; LC Card

79-624609 DDC 303.4/83 19
TJ163.2 .A3

Obsidian hydration dates for Klamath prehistory
/. Aikens, C. Melvin. [Pocatello] , 1978. 17 p. :
LC Card 78-623053 DDC 500 s 979.5/2 19
E78.I18 T43 no. 11 E99.K7

**OBSTETRICS - SOCIAL ASPECTS -
ADDRESSES, ESSAYS, LECTURES.**
Childbirth, alternatives to medical control /.
Austin , 1981. p. cm. ISBN 0-292-71072-0 : LC
Card 81-11644 DDC 362.1/982 19
RG940 .C47

Occasional papers in Latin American studies.
El Intelectual y el estado, Venezuela-Chile /.
College Park, Md. , 1980. 69 p. ; LC Card
80-54441 DDC 305.5/5 19
HM213 .I54

Occasional publications in Maine archaeology .
(no. 1) Willoughby, Charles Clark, 1857-1943.
Indian antiquities of the Kennebec Valley /.
Augusta, Me. , c1980. 128 p., [22] leaves of
plates : ISBN 0-913764-13-2 LC Card 81-119254
DDC 974.1/22 19
E78.M2 W54 1980

OCCULT SCIENCES.
Philosophy of science and the occult /.
Albany , 1981. p. cm. ISBN 0-87395-572-2 LC
Card 81-13552 DDC 001.9/01 19
BF1411 .P49

OCCULTISM. see OCCULT SCIENCES.

**OCCUPATION, CHOICE OF. see
VOCATIONAL GUIDANCE.**

**OCCUPATION DISEASES. see
OCCUPATIONAL DISEASES.**

The Occupation of Japan : economic policy and
reform : the proceedings of a symposium
sponsored by the MacArthur Memorial, April
13-15, 1978 / edited by Lawrence H. Redford.
Norfolk, Va. : The Memorial, 1980. x, 382 p. ;
28 cm. Bibliography: p. 338-361. Includes index. LC
Card 80-144161 DDC 338.952 19
1. Japan - Economic policy - 1945- - Congresses. 2.
Japan - History - Allied occupation, 1945-1952 -
Congresses. I. Redford, Lawrence H. II. MacArthur
Memorial.
HC462.9 .O23

Occupational alcoholism programs bibliography
/. National Clearinghouse for Alcohol
Information. Rockville, Md. , 1980. iii, 42 p. ;
LC Card 80-602280 DDC 016.6583/822 19
Z7164.C81 N257 1980 HF5549.5.A4

**OCCUPATIONAL ASPIRATIONS. see
VOCATIONAL INTERESTS.**

**Occupational demand, supply, and wages in West
Virginia** /. Clay, Rex J. [Charleston, W. Va.]
[1980] iv leaves, 424 p. ; LC Card 80-621755
DDC 331.12/09754 19
HD5725.W4 C52

Occupational developments magazine. V. 1, NO.
2- ; FALL, 1979/WINTER, 1980- Indianapolis.
Supersedes Manpower developments. Issued by the
Indiana Office of Manpower Development.
I. Indiana. Office of Manpower Development.
                                    NYPL [Econ. Div.]

OCCUPATIONAL DISEASES - MAINE.
Maine. Laws, statutes, etc. [Workers'
compensation act.] Maine Workers'
compensation act and Occupational disease law
/. Augusta, Me. , 1979. 66 p. ; LC Card
80-622036 DDC 344.741/021/02632 19
KFM342.A3329 A2 1979

**OCCUPATIONAL DISEASES - MAINE -
STATISTICS.**
Maine. Bureau of Labor. Research and Statistics
Division. Characteristics of work-related injuries
and illnesses in Maine . Augusta, Me. [1979]
76 p. ; LC Card 80-621340 DDC 363.1/1209741
19
RC964 .M25 1979

**OCCUPATIONAL DISEASES -
MASSACHUSETTS - STATISTICS.**
Massachusetts. Dept. of Labor and Industries.
Division of Statistics. 1972-1975 occupational
injury and illness survey /. Boston, Mass.
[1979] 17 p. : LC Card 80-621949 DDC
312/.39803/09744 19
RC964 .M39 1979

**OCCUPATIONAL DISEASES - NEBRASKA -
STATISTICS.**

Nebraska. Workmen's Compensation Court.
Research and Statistics Division. Occupational
injuries and illnesses in Nebraska by industry,
1977, including 1976 tabulations /. [Lincoln,
Neb.] [197-?] vi, 66 p. : LC Card 80-622042
DDC 312/.43/09782 19
HD7262.5.U62 N23 1970

**OCCUPATIONAL DISEASES - NEW
MEXICO - STATISTICS.**
New Mexico. Environmental Improvement
Division. Occupational Health and Safety
Section. Data Management Unit. 1978
characteristics of New Mexico high hazard
industries . Santa Fe, N.M. [1979] 144 p. :
LC Card 80-622292 DDC 312/.43/09789 19
RC964 .N46 1979a

**OCCUPATIONAL DISEASES - NEW YORK
(STATE) - STATISTICS.**
Occupational exposure to talc containing
asbestos . Cincinnati, Ohio , Washington, D.C. ,
1980. xiii, 106 p. : LC Card 80-602295 DDC
363.1/79 19
RC965.A7 O22

**OCCUPATIONAL DISEASES - RESEARCH -
UNITED STATES.**
United States. Congress. House. Committee on
Interstate and Foreign Commerce.
Subcommittee on Oversight and Investigations.
Data transfer restrictions impede
epidemiological research . Washington , c1980
[i.e. 1981] v, 32 p. ; LC Card 81-600797 DDC
363.1/1/0723 19
RA652.4 .U54 1981

**OCCUPATIONAL DISEASES - SOUTH
DAKOTA - STATISTICS.**
South Dakota. State Dept. of Health. Division
of Public Health Statistics. Reported
occupational injuries and illnesses, South
Dakota, 1972 and 1973 . Pierre , 1974. 37 p. ;
LC Card 81-472623 DDC 312/.39803/09783 19
RC964 .S667 1974

**OCCUPATIONAL DISEASES - UNITED
STATES.**
Cook, John R. (John Richard), 1950-
Occupational exposure to ionizing radiation in
the United States . Washington, D.C. , 1980
[i.e. 1981] x, 74, [68] p. : LC Card 81-601500
DDC 363.1/79 19
RC965.R25 C66

United States. Dept. of Labor. Office of the
Assistant Secretary for Policy, Evaluation and
Research. An interim report to Congress on
occupational diseases . [Washington] [1980]
138 p. ; LC Card 80-602704 DDC 363.1/1/0973
19
RC964 .U54 1980

**OCCUPATIONAL DISEASES - UNITED
STATES - CONGRESSES.**
Lost in the workplace . [Washington, D.C.]
[1980?] 468 p. ; LC Card 80-601645 DDC
363.1/1/0973 19
HD7265.5.U5 L67

**OCCUPATIONAL DISEASES - UNITED
STATES - STATISTICS.**
United States. Dept. of Labor. Office of the
Assistant Secretary for Policy, Evaluation and
Research. An interim report to Congress on
occupational diseases . [Washington] [1980]
138 p. ; LC Card 80-602704 DDC 363.1/1/0973
19
RC964 .U54 1980

**OCCUPATIONAL DISEASES -
WASHINGTON (STATE) - STATISTICS.**
Washington (State). Dept. of Labor and
Industries. Division of Safety. Management
Information Section. 1976 occupational injury
and illness survey /. [Olympia] [1978] 43 p. :
LC Card 79-624249 DDC 312/.39803/09797 19
RC964 .W36 1978

Washington (State). Dept. of Labor and
Industries. Division of Safety. Management
Information Section. 1977 occupational injury
and illness survey /. Olympia , 1979. 46 p. :
LC Card 80-620759 DDC 362.1/1/09797 19
RC964 .W36 1979

Occupational earnings in all metropolitan area.
July 1979- [Washington], Bureau of Labor
Statistics.
I. United States. Bureau of Labor Statistics.
                                    NYPL [Econ. Div.]

Occupational education in secondary schools .

New York (State). Legislative Commission on
Expenditure Review. Albany, N.Y. [1980] 5, ii,
70 p. : LC Card 80-623681
LC1046.N5 N48 1980

**Occupational employment estimates for selected
nonmanufacturing industries, 1978** /.
Wisconsin. Dept. of Industry, Labor and
Human Relations. Bureau of Administration,
Planning, and Analysis. [Madison, Wis.] [1980]
iv, 212 p. : LC Card 80-623196 DDC
331.12/51/0009775 19
HD5725.W5 W55 1980

**Occupational employment in manufacturing
industries, 1977** /. United States. Bureau of
Labor Statistics. Washington, D.C. [1980] vi,
91 p., [1] leaf of plates : LC Card 80-602314
DDC 331.12/57/0973 19
HD5724 .U625 1980a

**Occupational employment in nonmanufacturing
industries** . South Dakota. Dept. of Labor.
Research and Statistics. Aberdeen, S.D. , 1979.
i, 38 leaves ; LC Card 80-621189 DDC
331.12/51/09783 19
HD5725.S8 S63 1979a

**Occupational employment in nonmanufacturing,
North Carolina, 1978** /. North Carolina.
Bureau of Employment Security Research.
Raleigh, N.C. [1980] iv, 57 p. : LC Card
80-623030 DDC 331.12/5/09756 19
HD5725.N8 N64 1980

**Occupational employment in selected
construction industries in New Jersey.** New
Jersey. Dept. of Labor and Industry. Division
of Planning and Research. Trenton , 1979. iii,
98 p. ; LC Card 80-621724 DDC
331.12/524/09749 19
HD5718.B92 U546 1979

**Occupational employment in selected
finance-insurance-real estate industries in New
Jersey.** New Jersey. Dept. of Labor and
Industry. Division of Planning and Research.
Trenton, N.J. , 1979. iii, 112 p. : LC Card
80-623798 DDC 331.12/513321/09749 19
HD5718.I482 U55 1979

**Occupational employment in selected
nonmanufacturing industries.** Keitt, Barbara L.
Washington, D.C. , 1981. vi, 78 p. ; LC Card
81-601842 DDC 331.12/5/0973 19
HD5724 .K42

**Occupational employment in selected
non-manufacturing industries of Colorado,
1978.** Colorado. Division of Employment and
Training. Denver, Colo. , 1980. ix, 151 p. ; LC
Card 80-621967 DDC 331.12/5/09788 19
HD5725.C6 C58 1980

**Occupational employment in selected service
industries in New Jersey.** Charpentier, Thomas.
Trenton, N.J. , 1980. v, 230 p. : LC Card
80-624024 DDC 331.12/51/0009749 19
HD5718.S452 U53

**Occupational employment of selected
manufacturing industries, Wyoming, 1977** /.
Wyoming. Employment Security Commission
Research and Analysis Section. Casper, Wyo.
[197-?] 19 leaves : LC Card 80-622021 DDC
331.12/57/09787 19
HD5725.W9 W96 1970

**Occupational employment of selected
nonmanufacturing industries in Tennessee, 1975**
/. Tennessee. Dept. of Employment Security.
Research and Statistics Section. [Nashville]
[1977] i, 61 leaves : LC Card 78-621484 DDC
331.12/5/09768 19
HD5725.T4 T413 1977c

Occupational employment statistics . Virginia.
Employment Commission. Manpower Research
Division. [Richmond] [1980] ix, 198 p. : LC
Card 80-622341 DDC 331.12/5/09755 19
HD5725.V8 V53 1980

Occupational employment statistics . West
Virginia. Dept. of Employment Security.
Research and Statistics Section. [Charleston]
[1975?] 78 p. ; LC Card 76-622476
HD5725.W4 W38b no. 100-C
                                    NYPL [JLF 80-1513]

**Occupational employment statistics for Michigan
regulated industries** /. Michigan. Employment
Security Commission. Detroit, Mich. [1980] ii,
38 p. : LC Card 80-623990 DDC

331.12513636/09774 19
HD5725.M5 M44 1980

Occupational employment statistics, non-manufacturing industries, Alaska, 1978 /.
Van Houten, John. [Juneau] , 1979. 68 p. : LC Card 80-620795   DDC 331.12/51/0009798 19
HD5725.A4 V32

Occupational employment trends in the State of Oregon, 1977-1985 /. Oregon. Employment Division. Research and Statistics Section. [Salem, Or.] [1979] 157 p. ; LC Card 80-621879   DDC 331.12/3/09795 19
HD5725.O7 O67 1979

Occupational exposure to ionizing radiation in the United States . Cook, John R. (John Richard), 1950- Washington, D.C. , 1980 [i.e. 1981] x, 74, [68] p. : LC Card 81-601500   DDC 363.1/79 19
RC965.R25 C66

Occupational exposure to talc containing asbestos : morbidity, mortality, and environmental studies of miners and millers. Cincinnati, Ohio : U. S. Dept. of Health, Education, and Welfare, Public Health Service, Center for Disease Control, National Institute for Occupational Safety and Health ; Washington, D.C. : for sale by the Supt. of Docs., U. S. Govt. Print. Off., 1980. xiii, 106 p. : ill. ; 28 cm. (NIOSH technical report) DHEW publication ; no. (NIOSH) 80-115 "February, 1980." Includes bibliographical references. CONTENTS. - Dement, J. M. and Zumwalde, R. D. Environmental study.-- Gamble, J. F., Fellner, W., and DeMeo, M. J. Cross sectional morbidity study.--Brown, D. P. and Wagoner, J. K. Retrospective cohort study of mortality. LC Card 80-602295   DDC 363.1/79 19
1. Asbestos industry - Hygienic aspects - New York (State). 2. Talc - Toxicology. 3. Occupational diseases - New York (State) - Statistics. 4. New York (State) - Statistics, Medical. I. Dement, John M. II. Series: National Institute for Occupational Safety and Health. NIOSH technical report.
RC965.A7 O22

OCCUPATIONAL FORECASTING. see EMPLOYMENT FORECASTING.

Occupational health hazards of older workers in New Mexico . United States. Congress. Senate. Special Committee on Aging. Washington , 1980. iv, 95 p. ; LC Card 80-602736   DDC 363.1/1962234932 19
KF26.5 .A3 1979h

Occupational injuries and illnesses in Nebraska by industry, 1977, including 1976 tabulations /. Nebraska. Workmen's Compensation Court. Research and Statistics Division. [Lincoln, Neb.] [197-?] vi, 66 p. : LC Card 80-622042   DDC 312/.43/09782 19
HD7262.5.U62 N23 1970

Occupational needs in the Mississippi Appalachian region, 1974-1985 /. Mississippi. Employment Security Commission. Research and Statistics Dept. [Jackson] , 1977. v, 30 p. ; LC Card 78-621707   DDC 331.12/3/097629 19
HD5725.M7 M57 1977b

An occupational profile of selected nonmanufacturing industries in Massachusetts, 1978 /. McNulty, John T. Boston, Ma [1980] ii, 99 leaves : LC Card 80-622439   DDC 331.12/5/09744 19
HD5725.M4 M34

Occupational profiles of selected government employment in Oregon, 1975. Oregon. Employment Division. Research and Statistics Section. [Salem] [1976] 84 p. ; LC Card 79-623888
HD8011.O7 O74 1976   NYPL [JLF 80-1498]

Occupational profiles of selected regulated industries in Oregon, 1976 /. Oregon. Employment Division. Research and Statistics Section. [Salem] [1979?] 54 p. ; LC Card 80-622149   DDC 331.12/5138/009795 19
HD5718.T72 U58 1979

Occupational program survey report /. Maryland. Alcoholism Control Administration. Baltimore , 1977. 13, [4] leaves ; LC Card 79-621085   DDC 658.3/822 19
HV5297.M3 M37 1977

OCCUPATIONAL RETRAINING - CALIFORNIA - CONTRA COSTA COUNTY.

United States. Employment and Training Administration. Layoff time training . Berley, CA., 1977. v, 115, [1] p. ;
HD5701 .U53 no. 61 HD5718.C272
         *NYPL [*XME-9433]*

OCCUPATIONAL RETRAINING - UNITED STATES.
United States. Congress. Senate. Committee on Labor and Human Resources. Workers and the evolving economy of the eighties . Washington , 1981. iv, 387 p. : LC Card 81-601377   DDC 331.12/042/0973 19
KF26 .L27 1980s

OCCUPATIONAL RETRAINING - VERMONT.
Mattson, Robert E. Final upgrading report. [Montpelier, Vt.] 1973. xiv, 126 p.
         *NYPL [*XME-9292]*

Occupational safety and health . United States. Dept. of Labor. Library. [Washington] , 1978 i.e. 1979. vii, 648 p. ; LC Card 79-603966
Z7914.S17 U54 1979 T55

Occupational Safety and Health Administration's impact on small business . United States. Occupational Safety and Health Administration. Policy Analysis and Integration Staff. [Washington] , 1976. v, 55, [71] p. : LC Card 77-602353
*HD7654 .U55 1976   NYPL [*XME-9522]*

Occupational Safety and Health Improvements Act of 1980 . United States. Congress. Senate. Committee on Labor and Human Resources. Washington , 1980. vii, 1170 p. : LC Card 81-600656   DDC 344.73/0465 347.304465 19
KF26 .L27 1980l

Occupational Safety and Health Review Commission. see United States. Occupational Safety and Health Review Commission.

Occupational staffing patterns of selected nonmanufacturing industries in Pennsylvania . Pennsylvania. Office of Employment Security. Research and Statistics Division. Harrisburg, Pa. [1980] iii, 326 p. ; LC Card 80-622719   DDC 331.12/5/09748 19
HD5725.P4 P458 1980

Occupational staffing patterns of selected regulated industries in Pennsylvania. Pennsylvania. Bureau of Employment Security. Research and Statistics Division. [Harrisburg] , 1979. ii, 73 p. ; LC Card 79-624037
HD5725.P4 P45 1979   NYPL [JLF 80-1646]

Occupational supply and demand /. Wilson, James Rollo, 1949- [Juneau] [1979] 30 p. ; LC Card 80-622142   DDC 331.12/09798 19
HD5725.A4 W55

OCCUPATIONAL TRAINING - CALIFORNIA.
Wiederanders, Mark R. Job survival skills of youthful offenders . [Washington] , 1978. 105 p. ; LC Card 79-621769   DDC 331.3/4 19
HV9288 .W53

OCCUPATIONAL TRAINING - HAWAII - DIRECTORIES.
A Directory of employment training resources in Hawaii. 1978- Honululu.
         NYPL [JLM 81-41]

OCCUPATIONAL TRAINING - LAW AND LEGISLATION - UNITED STATES.
United States. Congress. House. Committee on Education and Labor. Subcommittee on Elementary, Secondary, and Vocational Education. Truth in testing act of 1979, the Educational testing act of 1979 . Washington , 1980. viii, 1194 p. : LC Card 80-601862   DDC 344.73/07 19
KF27 .E3364 1979r

United States. Congress. Senate. Committee on Labor and Human Resources. Subcommittee on Education, Arts, and Humanities. Youth Act of 1980 . Washington , 1980. vi, 681 p. : LC Card 80-604088   DDC 344.73/01342592 347.3041342592 19
KF26 .L2735 1980b

United States. Congress. Senate. Committee on Labor and Human Resources. Subcommittee on Employment, Poverty, and Migratory Labor. Youth employment and welfare reform jobs, 1980 . Washington , 1980. vi, 892 p. : LC Card 81-600874   DDC 344.73/01342592

347.3041342592 19
KF26 .L2737 1980b

OCCUPATIONAL TRAINING - MASSACHUSETTS - CONGRESSES.
Human Resources Development: Governor's Conference for Employers, Boston, 1978. Proceedings /. [Boston] [1978] 28 p. (p. 27-28 blank), [1] fold. leaf of plates : LC Card 79-623425   DDC 331.25/92/09744 19
HD5715.3.M4 H85 1978

OCCUPATIONAL TRAINING - MONTANA.
Montana. Division of Employment Security. Youth in Montana labor force /. Helena, Mont. [1980] v leaves, 87, [74] p. ; LC Card 80-622327   DDC 331.3/412/09786 19
HD6274.M7 M66 1980

OCCUPATIONAL TRAINING - NEW JERSEY.
New Jersey. Legislature General Assembly. Labor committee. Subcommittee on Business Concerns. Public hearing before Subcommittee on Business Concerns of the Assembly Labor Committee re: job training. [Trenton:"bs. n.], 1979. 29, 1x-14x;   *NYPL [*XME-9334]*

New Jersey. Legislature General Assembly. Labor committee. Subcommittee on Business Concerns. Public hearing before Subcommittee on Business Concerns of the Assembly Labor Committee, re job training . [Trenton , 1980] 14 p. : LC Card 80-621236   DDC 331.25/924/09749 19
KFN1811.4 .L243 1979

OCCUPATIONAL TRAINING - NEW YORK (CITY) - PERIODICALS.
New York (City). Dept. of Personnel. Work experience programs & supportive services administered by Department of Personnel. New York.   *NYPL [JLN 80-76]*

OCCUPATIONAL TRAINING - NEW YORK (STATE)
New York (State). State University at Binghamton. Social Policy Institute. Local planning and special revenue sharing . [Albany?] , 1975. i, 37 leaves ; LC Card 76-623363   DDC 331.11/09747 19
HD5725.N7 N47 1975

OCCUPATIONAL TRAINING - UNITED STATES.
Barton, Paul E. Between two worlds. Washington, 1978. 4 v.;
         NYPL [JLF 80-1274]

OCCUPATIONAL TRAINING - UNITED STATES - CORRUPT PRACTICES.
United States. Congress. House. Committee on Government Operations. Manpower and Housing Subcommittee. CETA's vulnerability to fraud and abuse . Washington , 1980. iv, 251 p. ; LC Card 80-604021   DDC 353.0083 19
KF27 .G6678 1980g

Occupational trends, 1978-1984, Arkansas . Arkansas. Employment Security Division. Research and Analysis Section. Little Rock, Ark. [1980] v leaves, 105 p. ; LC Card 80-622649   DDC 331.12/09767 19
HD5725.A8 A49 1980

Occupation/industry research publication. Massachusetts. Division of Employment Security. Job Market Research Service. Employment and wages State summary, 1978. [Boston] [1979?] 21 leaves ; LC Card 80-621279   DDC 331.12/5/09744 19
HD5725.M4 M37 1979

Meisner, Charlotte. Variety and distribution of occupations in Massachusetts. Boston, MA. [1980] ii, 61 p. ; LC Card 80-623644   DDC 331.12/5/09744 19
HB2615.M4 M44

Winer, Elliot A. Employment requirements for Massachusetts by occupation, by industry, 1976-1985 /. Boston, MA [1979] 58 leaves : LC Card 80-623635   DDC 331.12/3/09744 19
HD5725.M4 W56

OCCUPATIONS - CHOICE. see VOCATIONAL GUIDANCE.

OCCUPATIONS, DANGEROUS.
Virginia. Dept. of Labor and Industry. Virginia rules and regulations declaring hazardous occupations, as promulgated by Commissioner, Virginia Department of Labor and Industry, effective date November 1, 1979 /. Richmond,

Va. [1979] 16, [5] p. ; LC Card 80-622803
DDC 344.755/0134 19
KFV2735.5.A435 A2 1979

OCCUPATIONS - DISEASES. see
OCCUPATIONAL DISEASES.

OCCUPATIONS - HYGIENIC ASPECTS. see
INDUSTRIAL HYGIENE.

Occupations in Idaho, 1976-1985. Idaho. Dept. of
Employment, Planning, Research, and
Evaluation Bureau. [Boise] [1979] 55 p. : LC
Card 79-626027 DDC 331.12/09796 19
HD5725.I23 I28 1979

OCCUPATIONS - LICENSES - CALIFORNIA.
Schutz, Howard G. Regulating occupations in
California ; the role of public members on State
boards /. [Berkeley] , 1980. ix, 22 p. ; ISBN
0-87772-276-5 LC Card 80-15719
HD3630.U7 S38

OCCUPATIONS - LICENSES - OREGON.
Oregon. Employment Division. Licensed
occupations in Oregon /. [Salem] [1977] 65
p. ; LC Card 79-625475 DDC 353.97950082/4046
19
HD3630.U7 O72 1977

**Occurrence and distribution of human bacterial
pathogens in Virginia surface waters /.** Wendt,
Stephen L. Blacksburg, Va. , 1979. vii, 68 p. :
LC Card 79-625812 DDC 333.91/009755 s
363.7/394 19
TD201 .V57 no. 118 TD224.V8

**Occurrence, quality, and quantity of ground
water in Wilbarger County, Texas /.** Price,
Robert Donald, 1926- Austin, Tex. , 1979. viii,
229 p., [4] leaf of plates (3 fold.) : LC Card
80-621331 DDC 333.91/009764 s
553.7/9/09764746 19
TD224.T4 A333 no. 240 GB1025.T4

OCEAN CIRCULATION.
MODE-1 Scientific Council. Mid-Ocean
Dynamics Experiment - One. Washington,
1973. 38 p.: *NYPL [JSF 80-781]*

**OCEAN CURRENTS - ATLANTIC COAST
(UNITED STATES)**
Walton, Todd L. Littoral drift estimates along
the coastline of Florida /. Gainesville , 1976. ii,
41, [89] p. : LC Card 77-622038 DDC 551.46/34
19
GC272 .W34

**OCEAN CURRENTS - FLORIDA - GULF
REGION.**
Walton, Todd L. Littoral drift estimates along
the coastline of Florida /. Gainesville , 1976. ii,
41, [89] p. : LC Card 77-622038 DDC 551.46/34
19
GC272 .W34

Ocean dumping . United States. Congress. House.
Committee on Merchant Marine and Fisheries.
Subcommittee on Fisheries and Wildlife
Conservation and the Environment.
Washington , 1975- v. : LC Card 75-603626
KF27 .M447 1975e

Ocean dumping . United States. Congress. House.
Committee on Merchant Marine and Fisheries.
Subcommittee on Oceanography. Washington ,
1980. viii, 404 p. : LC Card 80-603809 DDC
344.73/04626 347.3044626 19
KF27 .M473 1980b

OCEAN ENERGY RESOURCES.
Baham Corporation. Renewable ocean energy
sources /. Washington, D.C. , 1978- v. : LC
Card 80-502142 DDC 333.91/64 19
TK1056 .B33 1978

United States. Congress. Office of Technology
Assessment. Renewable ocean energy sources.
Washington , 1978- v. : LC Card 78-600053
DDC 333.91/64 19
TJ163.2 .U48 1978

OCEAN MINERAL RESOURCES. see
MARINE MINERAL RESOURCES.

**OCEAN MINING - LAW AND
LEGISLATION - UNITED STATES.**
United States. Congress. House. Committee on
Foreign Affairs. The status of the Third United
Nations Conference on the Law of the Sea,
spring 1980 . Washington , 1980. iii, 84 p. ;
LC Card 80-602730 DDC 341.4/5 19
KF27 .F6 1980c

United States. Congress. House. Committee on
Foreign Affairs. Subcommittee on International

Economic Policy and Trade. Deep seabed hard
mineral resources act . Washington , 1980. iv,
271 p. ; LC Card 80-602899 DDC 346.7304/685
19
KF27 .F6465 1980

United States. Congress. Senate. Committee on
Foreign Relations. Subcommittee on Arms
Control, Oceans, International Operations, and
Environment. Law of the sea negotiations .
Washington , 1981. iii, 301 p. ; LC Card
81-601946 DDC 341.4/5 19
KF26 .F6286 1981

OCEAN MINING - PACIFIC OCEAN.
Khalafalla, S. E. Selective extraction of metals
from Pacific sea nodules with dissolved sulfur
dioxide /. Avondale, Md. , 1980. p. cm. LC
Card 80-606861 DDC 622 s 669/.028/3 19
TN23 .U43 TN291.5

OCEAN POLLUTION. see **MARINE
POLLUTION.**

OCEAN - RESEARCH. see
OCEANOGRAPHIC RESEARCH.

OCEAN ROUTES. see **TRADE ROUTES.**

Ocean shipping act of 1979 . United States.
Congress. Senate. Committee on Commerce,
Science, and Transportation. Subcommittee on
Merchant Marine and Tourism. Washington ,
1979. v, 707 p. : LC Card 80-602185 DDC
343.73/0968 19
KF26 .C695 1979d

**OCEAN TEMPERATURE - ALASKA, GULF
OF.**
Niebauer, H. J. Recent fluctuations in
meteorological and oceanographic parameters in
Alaska waters /. Fairbanks, Alaska [1980] iv,
34 p. : LC Card 80-623130 DDC 551.46
551.46/634 19
GC1 .A497 no. 79-2 QC994.6

**OCEAN TEMPERATURE - ATLANTIC
OCEAN.**
National Ocean Survey. Surface water
temperature and density, Atlantic Coast .
Rockville, Md. , Washington, D. C. , 1973. 109
p. : *NYPL [JSF 81-4]*

OCEAN TEMPERATURE - BERING SEA.
Niebauer, H. J. Recent fluctuations in
meteorological and oceanographic parameters in
Alaska waters /. Fairbanks, Alaska [1980] iv,
34 p. : LC Card 80-623130 DDC 551.46
551.46/634 19
GC1 .A497 no. 79-2 QC994.6

Ocean thermal energy conversion . United States.
Congress. House. Committee on Merchant
Marine and Fisheries. Subcommittee on
Oceanography. Washington , 1980. vii, 495 p. :
LC Card 80-602723 DDC 346.7304/68 19
KF27 .M473 1979a

Ocean thermal energy conversion. United States.
Congress. House. Subcommittee on Science and
Technology. Subcommittee on Energy
Development and Applications. H.R. 7474 .
Washington , 1980 [i.e. 1981] iii, 68 p. : LC
Card 81-600876 DDC 346.7304/68 347.306468
19
KF27 .S3934 1980j

Ocean thermal energy conversion act of 1980 .
United States. Congress. Senate. Committee on
Commerce, Science, and Transportation.
Washington , 1980. iv, 164 p. : LC Card
80-603076 DDC 346.7304/688 347.3064688 19
KF26 .C69 1980o

OCEAN THERMAL POWER PLANTS.
Baham Corporation. Renewable ocean energy
sources /. Washington, D.C. , 1978- v. : LC
Card 80-502142 DDC 333.91/64 19
TK1056 .B33 1978

United States. Congress. Office of Technology
Assessment. Recent developments in ocean
thermal energy. Washington, D.C. , 1980. 32
p. : LC Card 80-600074 DDC 621.31/243 19
TK1056 .U52 1980

**OCEAN THERMAL POWER PLANTS -
ENVIRONMENTAL ASPECTS.**
United States. Dept. of Energy. Office of
Energy Technology. Environmental
development plan ocean thermal energy
conversion. Washington , Springfield, Va. ,
1979. vii, 48 p. ; LC Card 79-603982 DDC
333.91/4 19
TD195.E4 U522 1979

**OCEAN THERMAL POWER PLANTS -
HAWAII.**
United States. Congress. House. Committee on
Merchant Marine and Fisheries. Subcommittee
on Oceanography. Ocean thermal energy
conversion . Washington , 1980. vii, 495 p. :
LC Card 80-602723 DDC 346.7304/68 19
KF27 .M473 1979a

**OCEAN THERMAL POWER PLANTS - LAW
AND LEGISLATION - UNITED STATES.**
United States. Congress. House. Committee on
Merchant Marine and Fisheries. Subcommittee
on Oceanography. Ocean thermal energy
conversion . Washington , 1980. vii, 495 p. :
LC Card 80-602723 DDC 346.7304/68 19
KF27 .M473 1979a

United States. Congress. House. Committee on
Science and Technology. Subcommittee on
Energy Development and Applications. H.R.
7474 . Washington , 1980 [i.e. 1981] iii, 68 p. :
LC Card 81-600876 DDC 346.7304/68
347.306468 19
KF27 .S3934 1980j

United States. Congress. Senate. Committee on
Commerce, Science, and Transportation. Ocean
thermal energy conversion act of 1980 .
Washington , 1980. iv, 164 p. : LC Card
80-603076 DDC 346.7304/688 347.3064688 19
KF26 .C69 1980o

OCEAN THERMAL POWER SYSTEMS. see
OCEAN THERMAL POWER PLANTS.

OCEAN TRANSPORTATION. see **SHIPPING.**

OCEAN TRAVEL.
Analysis of the North American cruise industry
/. [Washington, D.C.?] [1980] v, 145 p. : LC
Card 80-604175 DDC 387.5/42 19
G550 .A56

OCEAN WAVES - NORTH CAROLINA.
Boc, Stanley J. An analysis of beach overwash
along North Carolina's coast /. Raleigh , 1977.
17, [7] leaves of plates (6 fold.) : LC Card
77-624232 DDC 551.4/57/09756 19
GB459.4 .B6

OCEANIAN AMERICANS - CIVIL RIGHTS.
Civil rights issues of Asian and Pacific
Americans . [Washington, D.C.] , 1980. xiii,
834, 20 p. ; LC Card 80-602622 DDC
323.1/195/073 19
E184.O6 C58

Oceanic linguistics special publications .
(no. 18) Lichtenberk, Frantisek, 1945- A
grammar of Manam /. Honolulu, HI , c1981. p.
cm. ISBN 0-8248-0764-2 LC Card 81-11362
DDC 499/.12 19
PL6254.M291 L5

OCEANIC MIXING - DATA PROCESSING.
Machemehl, Jerry L. Flow dynamics and
sediment movement in Lockwoods Folly Inlet,
North Carolina /. [Raleigh] , 1977. viii, 139 p. :
LC Card 78-622678 DDC 551.46/148 19
GC299 .M33

**OCEANIC MIXING - MATHEMATICAL
MODELS.**
Machemehl, Jerry L. Flow dynamics and
sediment movement in Lockwoods Folly Inlet,
North Carolina /. [Raleigh] , 1977. viii, 139 p. :
LC Card 78-622678 DDC 551.46/148 19
GC299 .M33

Oceanic sound scattering prediction / edited by
Neil R. Andersen and Bernard J. Zahuranec.
New York : Plenum Press, c1977. xii, 859 p. :
ill. ; 26 cm. (Marine science. v. 5) Proceedings of a
symposium conducted by the Ocean Science and
Technology Division of the Office of Naval Research
held in Monterey, Calif. Nov. 10-14, 1975. Includes
bibliographies index. ISBN 0-306-35505-1 LC Card
77-3445
*1. Underwater acoustics - Congresses. 2. Sound-waves -
Scattering - Congresses. 3. Bioacoustics - Congresses. 4.
Marine biology - Congresses. I. Andersen, Neil R. II.
Zahuranec, Bernard J. III. United States. Office of
Naval Research. Ocean Science and Technology
Division.*
QC242 .O25 *NYPL [JSF 81-96]*

**OCEANOGRAPHIC RESEARCH - LAW AND
LEGISLATION - UNITED STATES.**
United States. Congress. Senate. Committee on
Labor and Human Resources. Subcommittee on
Education, Arts, and Humanities.
Reauthorization of the national sea grant

college program . Washington , 1980. iii, 204 p. ; LC Card 80-603079 DDC 346.7304/695 19
KF26 .L2735 1980a

OCEANOGRAPHIC RESEARCH - UNITED STATE.
United States. Congress. House. Committee on Science and Technology. Subcommittee on Natural Resources and Environment. Research and development programs of the National Oceanic and Atmospheric Adminstration . Washington , 1979, [i.e. 1980] iii, 229 p. ; LC Card 80-602771 DDC 353.0082/32 19
KF27 .S398 1979i

OCEANOGRAPHIC RESEARCH - UNITED STATES.
United States. Congress. House. Committee on Merchant Marine and Fisheries. Subcommittee on Oceanography. Sea grant programs . Washington , 1976. 2 v. ; LC Card 76-602454
KF27 .M473 1976
　　　　　　NYPL [JLE 77-2823 & JLL 81-82]

OCEANOGRAPHIC SUBMERSIBLES.
Vadus, Joseph R. International status and utilization of undersea vehicles, 1976 /. Rockville, Md. , Washington [1976] 29 p. : LC Card 80-497559 DDC 387.2/7 19
GC67 .V32

OCEANOGRAPHY AND STATE - CONGRESSES.
Marine Sciences and Ocean Policy Symposium, University of California, Santa Barbara, 1979. Marine Sciences and Ocean Policy Symposium . [Santa Barbara] , 1979. xviii, 318 p. : ISBN 0-937202-00-2 LC Card 80-51564 DDC 333.91/64 19
GC64 .M37 1979

OCEANOGRAPHY AND STATE - UNITED STATES.
United States. Interagency Committee on Ocean Pollution Research, Development, and Monitoring. Reports of the Subcommittees on National Needs and Problems, Data Collection, Storage, and Distribution, Monitoring, Research and Development . [Washington, D.C.] , Springfield, VA , 1979. v, 177 p. : LC Card 80-601835 DDC 363.7/394 19
GC511 .U625 1979

OCEANOGRAPHY - BIBLIOGRAPHY.
California. University. Scripps Institution of Oceanography, La Jolla. Bibliography of the SIO reference series, 1979 /. La Jolla, Calif. [1980] ii, 4 p. ; LC Card 80-622917 DDC 016.55146 19
Z6004.P6 C24 1980 GC11

OCEANOGRAPHY - BIBLIOGRAPHY - CATALOGS.
United States. Office of Naval Research. Ocean Science and Technology Division. Report availability notice : Summer 1974 . Arlington, VA. , 1974. ii, 308 p. ; *NYPL [JSF 80-767]*

OCEANOGRAPHY - CONGRESSES.
Nato Conference on Fjord Oceanography, Victoria, B.C., 1979. Fjord oceanography . New York , c1980. xiv, 715 p. : ISBN 0-306-40439-7 LC Card 80-12273
GC28 .N37 1979　　　　*NYPL [JSF 80-1088]*

OCEANOGRAPHY - INFORMATION SERVICES - UNITED STATES - DIRECTORIES.
A Directory of information resources in the United States . Washington, D.C. , 1981. p. cm. ISBN 0-8444-0372-5 LC Card 81-607045 DDC 550/.72073 19
QE47.A1 D58

OCEANOGRAPHY - NORTH CAROLINA - DRUM INLET.
Blankinship, Paul R. A flow study of Drum Inlet, North Carolina /. Raleigh , 1976. 56 p. : LC Card 77-624531 DDC 551.46/09 19
GC512.N8 B55

OCEANOGRAPHY - NORTH CAROLINA - ONSLOW BAY.
Onslow Bay physical/dynamical experiments, summer-fall, 1975 . [Raleigh] 1978. xxiv, 170 p. ; LC Card 78-623321 DDC 551.46/148 19
GC512.N8 O56

OCEANOGRAPHY - RESEARCH. see OCEANOGRAPHIC RESEARCH.

OCEANOGRAPHY - STUDY AND TEACHING (HIGHER) - VIRGINIA.

Virginia. State Council of Higher Education. Graduate marine science education in Virginia . Richmond, Va. [1978] 3, v, 155 p. ; LC Card 79-624103 DDC 551.46/007/11755 19
GC31.6 .V575 1978

OCEANOLOGY. see OCEANOGRAPHY.

Ochiltree County Historical Survey Committee.
Wheatheart of the plains . [Perrytown?, Tex.] , 1969. 653 p. : LC Card 81-100404 DDC 976.4/81506/0922 B 19
F392.O2 W45

OCHILTREE COUNTY (TEX.) - BIOGRAPHY.
Wheatheart of the plains . [Perrytown?, Tex.] , 1969. 653 p. : LC Card 81-100404 DDC 976.4/81506/0922 B 19
F392.O2 W45

OCHILTREE COUNTY (TEX.) - HISTORY.
Wheatheart of the plains . [Perrytown?, Tex.] , 1969. 653 p. : LC Card 81-100404 DDC 976.4/81506/0922 B 19
F392.O2 W45

OCHOCO CREEK WATERSHED, OR.
Berndt, H. W. Forest land use and streamflow in central Oregon /. Portland, Or. , 1970. 15 p. : LC Card 71-608738 DDC 634.9/09795 s 553.7/09795/83 19
SD11 .A45614 no. 93 SD387.M8

O'Connor, Frank R. An analysis of future petroleum development on the Alaskan Outer Continental Shelf, Kodiak area / by Frank R. O'Connor and Patrick L. Dobey. [Juneau] : State of Alaska, Dept. of Natural Resources, Division of Geological & Geophysical Survey[s], [1976] iii, 23, 4 leaves, [2] fold. leaves of plates : ill. ; 28 cm. "A study for the Department of Community and Regional Affairs, Community Planning Division." "June 1976." Bibliography: leaf 23. LC Card 80-622388 DDC 338.2/7282/097894 19
1. Petroleum in submerged lands - Alaska. 2. Continental shelf - Alaska. I. Dobey, Patrick L., joint author. II. Alaska. Division of Geological and Geophysical Surveys. III. Alaska. Division of Community Planning. IV. Title.
TN872.A7 O34

O'Connor, John E. The Hollywood Indian : stereotypes of native Americans in films / John E. O'Connor ; foreword by Lorraine E. Williams. Trenton, N.J. : New Jersey State Museum, c1980. xvi, 79 p. : ill. ; 22 x 28 cm. Bibliography: p. 75-56. Includes index. ISBN 0-938766-00-7 (pbk.) LC Card 80-620048 DDC 791.43/09/093520397 19
1. Indians in motion pictures. 2. Moving-pictures - United States - History. I. New Jersey State Museum. II. Title. III. Title: Native Americans in films.
PN1995.9.I48 O33

O'Connor, Kristina M. (joint author) Goldsmith, Scott. Historic and projected oil and gas consumption /. [Juneau?] , 1980. 55 leaves ; LC Card 80-622464 DDC 338.2/728/09798 19
HD9567.A4 G63

O'Connor, Linda.
Applications/admissions information, by sector for fall 1977, by institution for fall 1978 : statistical compilations / prepared by Linda O'Connor, Irene Nomejko. [Trenton] : New Jersey Dept. of Higher Education, Office of Research, [1979] [42] p. ; 28 cm. (Research note - New Jersey Department of Higher Education ; 79-7) "October 1979." Tables. LC Card 80-621681 DDC 378/.1056/09749 19
1. Universities and colleges - New Jersey - Admission - Statistics. I. Nomejko, Irene M., joint author. II. New Jersey. Dept. of Higher Education. Office of Research. III. Series: New Jersey. Dept. of Higher Education. Research note - New Jersey Department of Higher Education , 79-7. IV. Title.
LB2351.3.N5 O26

Degrees conferred by N.J. colleges and universities by race, sex, and major program category, F.Y. 1979 / prepared by Linda O'Connor, Irene Nomejko. [Trenton, N.J.] : New Jersey Dept. of Higher Education, Office of Research, [1980] [86] p. ; 28 cm. (Research note / New Jersey Department of Higher Education . 80-7) Cover title. "April 1980." LC Card 80-624027 DDC 378/.24/09749 19
1. Degrees, Academic - New Jersey - Statistics. I. Nomejko, Irene M. II. Series: Research note (New

Jersey. Dept. of Higher Education) , 80-7. III. Title.
LB2381 .O27

Enrollments of students in N.J. colleges and universities by age category, fall 1977 and fall 1978 / prepared by Linda O'Connor, Leslie Scarlata. [Trenton] : New Jersey Dept. of Higher Education, Office of Research, [1979] [47] p. ; 28 cm. (Research note - New Jersey Department of Higher Education ; 79-5) "November 1979." Tables. LC Card 80-621679 DDC 378/.1059/749 19
1. College attendance - New Jersey - Statistics. I. Scarlata, Leslie, joint author. II. New Jersey. Dept. of Higher Education. Office of Research. III. Series: New Jersey. Dept. of Higher Education. Research note - New Jersey Department of Higher Education , 79-5. IV. Title.
LC144.N5 O26

Profile of full-time first-time freshmen enrolled in N.J. colleges, fall 1977 and fall 1978 / prepared by Linda O'Connor, Irene Nomejko. [Trenton] : New Jersey Dept. of Higher Education, Office of Research, [1979] ii, [77] p. ; 28 cm. (Research note - New Jersey Department of Higher Education ; 79-4) "August 1979." Tables. LC Card 80-621678 DDC 378/.1059749 19
1. College freshmen - New Jersey - Statistics. I. Nomejko, Irene M., joint author. II. New Jersey. Dept. of Higher Education. Office of Research. III. Series: New Jersey. Dept. of Higher Education. Research note - New Jersey Department of Higher Education , 79-4. IV. Title.
LA331.5 .O28

October report on the current fuel situation from the Energy Information Administration . United States. Congress. Senate. Committee on Energy and Natural Resources. Subcommittee on Energy Regulation. Washington , 1980. iii, 217 p. : LC Card 80-602534 DDC 338.4/766535827/0973 19
KF26 .E5535 1979m

ODLE, ROBERT CHARLES, 1944-
United States. Congress. Senate. Committee on Energy and Natural Resources. Johnson, Odle, and Heffelfinger nominations . Washington , 1981. iii, 140 p. : LC Card 81-601965 DDC 353.87 19
KF26 .E55 1981d

Odle, Sara J. Stimulating government utilization of sheltered workshops /. Memphis [1977] xiv, 319 p. : LC Card 78-622547
HD7256.U5 S83　　　　*NYPL [JLE 81-488]*

O'Donnell, Patrick J.
Nebraska. Legislature. Nebraska unicameral, eighty-sixth legislature, second session . [[Lincoln , 1980] 14 p. : LC Card 80-623547 DDC 348.782/01 347.82081 19
KFN10 .L43

Nebraska unicameral, Eighty-sixth Legislature, second session : subject index to legislative bills / compiled by Patrick J. O'Donnell, Gloria Peterson. [Lincoln, Neb.] : The Legislature, [1980] 71 p. ; 22 cm. "February 1, 1980." "Includes bills 598 through 986 inclusive with all bills carried over from the Eighty-sixth Legislature, first session." "03-01-02-80." LC Card 80-623519 DDC 348.782/01 347.82081 19
1. Bills, Legislative - Nebraska - Indexes. I. Peterson, Gloria, 1934- joint author. II. Nebraska. Legislature. III. Title.
KFN10 .O36

O'Donnell, Sheryl R. Changing perspectives on menopause /. Austin , c1981. p. cm. ISBN 0-292-71069-0 : LC Card 81-11714 DDC 612/.665 19
RG186 .C45

ODOR CONTROL.
Osag, T. R. Control of odors from inedibles-rendering plants /. Research Triangle Park, N. C., 1974. vi, 51 p. in various pagings.
　　　　NYPL [JSF 80-793]

OECD countries : unemployment in the 1970s and perspectives for the 1980s : a research paper / National Foreign Assessment Center. Washington, D.C. : Central Intelligence Agency : Document Expediting (DOCEX) Project, Exchange and Gift Division, Library of Congress [distributor], [1980] iv, 56 p. ; 27 cm. "November 1980." "Research for this project was completed on 1 October 1980." Chiefly tables. "ER 80-10579." LC Card 80-604134 DDC 331.13/7 19
1. Employment forecasting. 2. Unemployment. 3.

Organisation for Economic Co-operation and
Development. I. United States. Central Intelligence
Agency. II. National Foreign Assessment Center (U.
S.).
HD5707.5 .O43

The OECD steel industries . National Foreign
Assessment Center (U. S.) Washington, D.C.
[1980] v, 15 p. :   LC Card 80-603610   DDC
338.4/7669142 19
HD9510.5 .N26 1980

OECOLOGY. see ECOLOGY.

Of time and place . Corcoran Gallery of Art.
Washington, D.C. , 1981. p. cm.   ISBN
0-86528-010-X   LC Card 81-607836   DDC
704.9/42/0973074013 19
N6510 .C69 1981

Off-track betting in Massachusetts .
Pugh-Roberts Associates. Cambridge, Mass. ,
1976. ix, 35 leaves :   LC Card 77-621719
SF332.5.M4 P83 1976   **NYPL [*XME-9421]**

**Offenders admitted to the Mutual Agreement
Program, calendar year 1978.** Wisconsin.
Division of Corrections. Office of Systems and
Evaluation. Madison, Wis. , 1979. 25 p. ;   LC
Card 80-620784   DDC 365/.66/09775 19
HV8369 .W62 1979

**OFFENSES AGAINST PROPERTY - UNITED
STATES.**
United States. General Accounting Office.
From quantity to quality . [Washington] [1980]
iv, 41 p. ;   LC Card 80-602224   DDC 363.2/5 19
HV6658 .U55 1980

United States. Law Enforcement Assistance
Administration. Criminal Conspiracies Division.
What happened . Washington, D.C. , 1979. 62
p. in various pagings ;   LC Card 79-602151   DDC
364.1/62 19
HV6635 .U54 1979

**OFFENSES AGAINST PROPERTY - UNITED
STATES - DATA PROCESSING.**
Walsh, Marilyn E. Computerized tracking of
stolen office equipment . Washington , 1979. vi,
107 p. :   LC Card 79-602794   DDC 363.2/5 19
HV6658 .W295

**OFFICE BUILDINGS - MICHIGAN - ANN
ARBOR - ENVIRONMENTAL
ENGINEERING - PSYCHOLOGICAL
ASPECTS.**
Marans, Robert W. Evaluating built
environments . [Ann Arbor] , 1981. p. cm.
ISBN 0-87944-272-7 :   LC Card 81-6709   DDC
725/.1 19
TH6025 .M37

**OFFICE EQUIPMENT. see OFFICE
EQUIPMENT AND SUPPLIES.**

**OFFICE EQUIPMENT AND SUPPLIES -
DATA PROCESSING.**
Walsh, Marilyn E. Computerized tracking of
stolen office equipment . Washington , 1979. vi,
107 p. :   LC Card 79-602794   DDC 363.2/5 19
HV6658 .W295

**OFFICE EQUIPMENT AND SUPPLIES
INDUSTRY - UNITED STATES.**
United States. Congress. House. Committee on
Small Business. Subcommittee on Special Small
Business Problems. Problems of U. S. office
machine dealers . Washington, D.C. , 1980. iii,
92 p. :   LC Card 80-603808   DDC 381/.4568 19
KF27 .S686 1980

**OFFICE LANDSCAPING. see OFFICE
LAYOUT.**

OFFICE LAYOUT.
Suffolk County, N. Y. Planning Commission.
Suffolk County office study. Hauppauge, N. Y.,
1974. 33 p.   **NYPL [JLF 81-19]**

OFFICE LEASES - UNITED STATES.
United States. Congress. Senate. Committee on
Environment and Public Works. Leasing of
unoccupied space . Washington , 1980. ii, 83
p. ;   LC Card 80-601863   DDC 353.0071/23 19
KF26 .E6 1980j

**OFFICE MACHINES. see OFFICE
EQUIPMENT AND SUPPLIES.**

Office of elected attorney general . Pennsylvania.
General Assembly. Task Force on Office of
Elected Attorney General. Harrisburg , 1978.
vii, 54 p. ;   LC Card 79-622493
KFP11.62 .O4 1978   **NYPL [JLF 80-1517]**

**Office of Government Ethics and Federal
post-employment restrictions :** legislative
history of Title IV and V of the Ethics in
Government Act of 1979 [i.e. 1978] as
amended / [compiled by] Committee on
Governmental Affairs, United States Senate.
Washington : U. S. G.P.O., 1980. vi, 304 p. ;
24 cm. At head of title: 96th Congress, 2d session.
Committee print. Includes bibliographical references.
   LC Card 80-603840   DDC 342.73/068 347.30268
19
*1. United States. Ethics in Government Act of 1978.
Title 4-5. 2. United States. Office of Government
Ethics. 3. United States - Officials and employees,
Retired - Employment. I. United States. Congress.
Senate. Committee on Governmental Affairs.*
KF4568.A315 A15 1980

Office of Science and Technology Policy . United
States. Congress. Senate. Committee on
Commerce, Science, and Transportation.
Subcommittee on Science, Technology, and
Space. Washington , 1980. iii, 72 p. ;   LC Card
80-603897   DDC 353.0085/5 19
KF26 .C697 1980g

OFFICE PLANNING. see OFFICE LAYOUT.

OFFICE PRACTICE - AUTOMATION.
Guidance on requirements analysis for office
automation systems. Washington, D.C. , c1980.
125 p. in various pagings :   LC Card 80-600179
   DDC 602/.18 s 651.8/4 19
QC100 .U57 no. 500-72 HF5548.2

**OFFICE RECORDS. see BUSINESS
RECORDS.**

**An office strategy for nutrition-related patient
education and compliance /.** Latanick, Maureen
Rogan. Columbus, Ohio (456 Clinic Dr.,
Columbus 43210) , c1980. 23 p. ;   LC Card
81-620951   DDC 613.2/07/15 19
R727.4 .L37

**OFFICE SUPPLIES. see OFFICE
EQUIPMENT AND SUPPLIES.**

**OFFICES - LOCATION - NEW YORK (STATE)
- SUFFOLK COUNTY.**
Suffolk County, N. Y. Planning Commission.
Suffolk County office study. Hauppauge, N. Y.,
1974. 33 p.   **NYPL [JLF 81-19]**

**Official docket for proposed revision to rail
carrier noise emission regulation /.** United
States. Environmental Protection Agency.
Office of Noise Abatement and Control.
Washington, 1980. 1 v.;   **NYPL [JLM 81-95]**

Official guide to the Smithsonian. Smithsonian
Institution. Washington, D.C. , 1981. p. cm.
   LC Card 80-607800   DDC 069/.09753 19
Q11 .S79 1981

**Official human rights agencies in New York
State.** New York (State). State Division of
Human Rights. New York.
                                NYPL [JLM 80-711]

**Official list of embalmers, funeral directors, and
funeral homes** . Connecticut. State Dept. of
Health Services. Hartford, Conn. [1979] 65 p. ;
   LC Card 80-623116   DDC 363.7/5/025746 19
RA622.A7 C66 1979

**OFFICIAL PUBLICATIONS. see
GOVERNMENT PUBLICATIONS.**

**Official publications of French West Africa,
1946-1958.** United States. Library of Congress.
General Reference and Bibliography Division.
Washington, D. C., 1961. x, 208 p. ;
                                NYPL [Sc F 80-133]

OFFICIAL SECRETS - UNITED STATES.
United States. Congress. Senate. Select
Committee on Intelligence. Intelligence
identities protection legislation . Washington ,
1980. iii, 118 p. ;   LC Card 81-600614   DDC
344.73/0176132712 347.304176132712 19
KF26.5 .I5 1980a

**Official State multiple list for elementary
schools, K-8** . Perry, Gerald K. Charleston,
W.Va. [1980] iv, 42, 10 p. ;   LC Card 80-621060
   DDC 016.3701/56/09754 19
Z5817 .P47 LB3047.5.W4

**OFFICIALS AND EMPLOYEES,
INTERNATIONAL. see
INTERNATIONAL OFFICIALS AND
EMPLOYEES.**

**OFFSHORE DRILLING (PETROLEUM) see
OIL WELL DRILLING, SUBMARINE.**

**OFFSHORE GAS FIELDS. see GAS,
NATURAL, IN SUBMERGED LANDS.**

**OFFSHORE GAS INDUSTRY -
ENVIRONMENTAL ASPECTS - UNITED
STATES.**
Environmental planning for offshore oil and gas
/. [Washington] , 1978. 5 v. in 9 :   LC Card
78-601850
TD195.P4 E58   **NYPL [JSK 81-30]**

**OFFSHORE OIL FIELDS. see PETROLEUM
IN SUBMERGED LANDS.**

**OFFSHORE OIL INDUSTRY -
ENVIRONMENTAL ASPECTS - UNITED
STATES.**
Environmental planning for offshore oil and gas
/. [Washington] , 1978. 5 v. in 9 :   LC Card
78-601850
TD195.P4 E58   **NYPL [JSK 81-30]**

**OFFSHORE WATER POLLUTION. see
MARINE POLLUTION.**

OGALLALA FORMATION.
Taylor, Robert Gay, 1940- Effects of bacteria
on nitrate and nitrite concentrations in
groundwater of the Ogallala aquifer /. Las
Cruces, N.M. [1979] vii, 20 leaves :   LC Card
80-622275   DDC 333.91/09789 s 628.1/68 19
GB705.N6 N64 no. 114 TD224.N6

O'Gara, Kevin. California. Dept. of Industrial
Relations. Division of Labor Statistics and
Research. California sawmills and planing mills
industry . San Francisco , 1978. v, 26 p. ;   LC
Card 79-623207   DDC 312/.43/09794 19
RC965.W6 C28 1978

**OGLALA INDIANS - MYTHOLOGY. see
OGLALA INDIANS - RELIGION AND
MYTHOLOGY.**

**OGLALA INDIANS - RELIGION AND
MYTHOLOGY.**
Powers, William K. Yuwipi, vision and
experience in Oglala ritual /. Lincoln , c1982.
p. cm.   ISBN 0-8032-3663-8   LC Card 81-10501
   DDC 299/.74 19
E99.O3 P683

**OGLALA INDIANS - RITES AND
CEREMONIES.**
Powers, William K. Yuwipi, vision and
experience in Oglala ritual /. Lincoln , c1982.
p. cm.   ISBN 0-8032-3663-8   LC Card 81-10501
   DDC 299/.74 19
E99.O3 P683

Oglesby, Clarkson Hill, 1908- (joint author)
Bishop, A. Bruce. Socio-economic and
community factors in planning urban freeways.
[Washington] 1970. xiii, 216 p.   LC Card
73-610102
HE356.C2 B5   **NYPL [JLF 81-276]**

**Ohio Agricultural Research and Development
Center.**
Ernst, James Edgar. Soil survey of Seneca
County, Ohio. [Washington, D.C.?] , 1980. vii,
143 p., 81 folded p. of plates :   LC Card
80-604150   DDC 631.4/7/77124 19
S599.O3 E77

Kerr, James W. Soil survey of Pickaway
County, Ohio /. [Washington, D.C.] [1980] vii,
172 p., [36] fold. leaves of plates :   LC Card
80-602251   DDC 631.4/7/771815 19
S599.O3 K47

Kilmer, Richard Lee, 1943- The impact of
regulation on transportation efficiency /.
Columbus , 1974. 13, 3, 5 p. ;
                                NYPL [*XME-9249]

Lerch, Norbert K. Soil survey of Butler County,
Ohio /. [Washington] [1980] vii, 175 p., [38]
fold. leaves of plates   LC Card 80-602516   DDC
631.4/7/77175 19
S599.O3 L36

McLoda, N. A. Soil survey of Franklin County,
Ohio /. [Washington] [1980] viii, 188 p., [37]
fold. leaves of plates :   LC Card 80-602372   DDC
631.4/7/77156 19
S599.O3 M32

Redmond, Charles Edward, 1932- Soil survey
of Ashland County, Ohio /. [Washington]
[1980] vii, 179 p., [31] fold. leaves of plates :
   LC Card 80-602507   DDC 631.4/7/77129 19
S599.O3 R39

Research circular.
(255) Weiss, Michael J. An annotated

bibliography of the genus Stelidota Erichson
(Coleoptera: Nitidulidae, Nitidulinae) /.
Wooster, Ohio [1980] 37 p. ; LC Card
80-623557 DDC 016.59576/43 19
Z5858.S74 W44 QL596.N58

**Ohio. Agriculture, Dept. of. see Ohio. Dept. of
Agriculture.**

Ohio authors.
Hughes, James M. Louis Bromfield, Ohio and
self-discovery /. Columbus , 1979. 22 p. ; LC
Card 80-137468 DDC 813/.52 19
PS3503.R66 Z76

Lindsay, Clarence B. Hart Crane, an
introduction /. Columbus , 1979. 30 p. ; LC
Card 80-137513 DDC 811/.52 19
PS3505.R272 Z75

Robinson, Anna T. Nikki Giovanni .
Columbus , 1979. 25 p. ; LC Card 80-137505
DDC 811/.54 19
PS3557.I55 Z87

Sweeney, Gerard M. Sherwood Anderson,
wanderer and myth-maker /. Columbus , 1979.
23 p. ; LC Card 80-137471 DDC 813/.52 B 19
PS3501.N4 Z855

Throne, Marilyn. Walter Havighurst, novelist of
the heartland /. Columbus , 1979. 20 p. ; LC
Card 80-137524 DDC 813/.54 19
PS3515.A8694 Z89

Yoke, Carl B. Roger Zelazny and Andre
Norton, proponents of individualism /.
Columbus , 1979. 26 p. ; LC Card 80-137489
DDC 813/.54 19
PS374.S35 Y6

Ohio Biological Survey.
Biological notes .
(no. 12) Buchanan, Forest W. The breeding
birds of Carroll and northern Jefferson
Counties, Ohio . Columbus, Ohio , 1980. vii,
50 p. : LC Card 80-623347 DDC 598.29771/67
19
QL684.O3 B83 1980

**Ohio. Bureau of Employment Services. Division
of Research and Statistics.**
Average employment, total payroll, and average
weekly earnings of educational local
government employees covered under Ohio
unemployment compensation law, by county.
RS 203.8. Columbus. 28 cm. Annual.
*1. Ohio - Officials and employees - Salaries, allowances,
etc. - Statistics - Periodicals. 2. Labor supply - Ohio -
Statistics - Periodicals. 3. Wages - Ohio - Statistics -
Periodicals. I. Ohio. Bureau of Employment Services.
Division of Research and Statistics. RS 203.8.*
NYPL [JLM 81-22]

Average hourly earnings of production workers
in Ohio [and various metropolitan areas] Table
RS-790-4. Columbus. 28 cm. Annual. Issued by the
Bureau of Unemployment Compensation, Division of
Research and Statistics, 1965. Issued in parts.
*1. Wages - Ohio - Statistics - Periodicals. I. Ohio.
Bureau of Unemployment Compensation. Division of
Research and Statistics. II. Ohio. Bureau of
Employment Services. Division of Research and
Statistics. Table RS-790-4. III. Title.*
NYPL [JLM 80-999]

Average manufacturing employment in Ohio
and eight large countie's subject to Ohio
Unemployment Compensation Law, 1959
through 1978 / Division of Research and
Statistics; Ohio Bureau of Employment
Services. Columbus : The Division, 1979. 1
leaf ; 28 cm. Microfiche (neg.) 1 sheet. 11 x 15 cm.
(NYPL FSN 35,050)
1. Insurance, Unemployment - Ohio - Statistics. I. Title.
NYPL [*XME-9166]

Average number of workers covered under
Ohio unemployment compensation law, by
industrial division and county. RS 203.1-B.
Columbus. 28 cm. Annual.
*1. Labor supply - Ohio - Statistics - Periodicals. I.
Ohio. Bureau of Employment Services. Division of
Research and Statistics. RS 203.1-B. II. Title.*
NYPL [JLM 81-27]

Average weekly earnings of production workers
in Ohio [and various metropolitan areas] Table
RS-790-2. Columbus. 28 cm. Annual. Issued by the
Bureau of Unemployment Compensation, Division of
Research and Statistics, 1965. Issued in parts.
*1. Wages - Ohio - Statistics - Periodicals. I. Ohio.
Bureau of Unemployment Compensation. Division of*

Research and Statistics. II. Ohio. Bureau of
Employment Services. Division of Research and
Statistics. Table RS-790-2. III. Title.
NYPL [JLM 80-997]

Average weekly earnings of workers under Ohio
unemployment compensation law, by industrial
division and county. RS 203.3-B. Columbus. 28
cm. Annual.
*1. Wages - Ohio - Statistics - Periodicals. I. Ohio.
Bureau of Employment Services. Division of Research
and Statistics. RS 203.3-B. II. Title.*
NYPL [JLM 81-26]

Average weekly earnings of workers under Ohio
Unemployment Compensation Law, by
industrial division since 1939 / State of Ohio,
Bureau of Employment Services, [Division of
Research and Statistics] Columbus: The
Division, 1979. 2 leaves; 22 x 28 cm. Microfilm.
Caption title.
*1. Wages - Ohio - Statistics. 2. Insurance,
Unemployment - Ohio - Statistics. I. Title.*
NYPL [*ZT-1265]

Average weekly hours of production workers in
Ohio [and various metropolitan areas] Table
RS-790-3. Columbus. 28 cm. Annual. Issued by the
Bureau of Unemployment Compensation, Division of
Research and Statistics, 1965. Issued in parts.
*1. Hours of labor - Ohio - Statistics - Periodicals. I.
Ohio. Bureau of Unemployment Compensation.
Division of Research and Statistics. II. Ohio. Bureau of
Employment Services. Division of Research and
Statistics. Table RS-790-3. III. Title.*
NYPL [JLM 80-995]

Employers, workers, total and taxable payroll,
and contributions under Ohio Unemployment
Compensation Law since 1938 / Bureau of
Employment Services, [Division of Research
and Statistics] Columbus : The Division, 1979.
2 leaves ; 22 x 28 cm. Microfilm. Caption title.
*1. Insurance, Unemployment - Ohio - Statistics. 2.
Wages - Ohio - Statistics. I. Title.*
NYPL [*ZT-1264]

Employment, payroll, and earnings under the
Ohio unemployment compensation law by
county, 1972 through 1978. Columbus :
Division of Research and Statistics, Ohio
Bureau of Employment Services, [1979?] 90
leaves ; 28 cm. At head of title: Ohio Labor market
information. LC Card 80-623537 DDC
331.12/5/09771 19
*1. Labor supply - Ohio - Statistics. 2. Wages - Ohio -
Statistics. 3. Insurance, Unemployment - Ohio -
Statistics. I. Title. II. Title: Ohio labor market
information.*
HD5725.O3 O37 1979a

Employment, payroll, and earnings under the
Ohio unemployment compensation law by
county, 1972 through 1979. Columbus :
Division of Research and Statistics, Ohio
Bureau of Employment Services, [1980] 90
leaves ; 29 cm. (Ohio labor market information)
Chiefly tables. LC Card 80-623675 DDC
331.12/5/09771 19
*1. Labor supply - Ohio - Statistics. 2. Wages - Ohio -
Statistics. 3. Insurance, Unemployment - Ohio. I. Title.
II. Series.*
HD5725.O3 O37 1980

Nonagricultural wage and salary employment in
Ohio [and various metropolitan areas] Table
RS-790-1. Columbus. 28 cm. Annual. Issued by the
Bureau of Unemployment Compensation, Division of
Research and Statistics, 1963-65. Issued in parts.
*1. Labor supply - Ohio - Statistics - Periodicals. I.
Ohio. Bureau of Unemployment Compensation.
Division of Research and Statistics. II. Ohio. Bureau of
Employment Services. Division of Research and
Statistics. Table RS-790-1. III. Title.*
NYPL [M-11 2926]

Number of active employer accounts, covered
workers, taxable wages and contributions under
Ohio Unemployment Compensaton Law.
Columbus [1978] 15 leaves ;
NYPL [*ZT-1259]

Number of active employer accounts, covered
workers, total wages, taxable wages and
contributions under Ohio Employment
Compensation Law, Ohio Bureau of
Employment Services, since 1936/[Division of
Research and Statistics, Ohio Bureau of
Employment Services] Columbus: The Division,
1977. 14 leaves ; 22 x 28 cm. Microfilm. Caption
title.

1. Insurance, Unemployment - Ohio - Statistics. 2.
Wages - Ohio - Statistics. I. Title.
NYPL [*ZT-1264]

Payrolls and contributions under Ohio
unemployment compensation law, by industry.
RS 203.2-1. Columbus. 28 cm. Annual.
*1. Wages - Ohio - Statistics - Periodicals. 2. Insurance,
Unemployment - Ohio - Statistics - Periodicals. I. Ohio.
Bureau of Employment Services. Division of Research
and Statistics. RS 203. 2-1. II. Title.*
NYPL [JLM 81-28]

RS 203. 2-1. Ohio. Bureau of Employment
Services. Division of Research and Statistics.
Payrolls and contributions under Ohio
unemployment compensation law, by
industry. RS 203.2-1. Columbus.
NYPL [JLM 81-28]

RS 203.1. Ohio. Bureau of Employment
Services. Division of Research and Statistics.
Workers covered under Ohio unemployment
compensation law, by industrial group. RS
203.1. Columbus. NYPL [JLM 81-25]

RS 203.1-B. Ohio. Bureau of Employment
Services. Division of Research and Statistics.
Average number of workers covered under
Ohio unemployment compensation law, by
industrial division and county. RS 203.1-B.
Columbus. NYPL [JLM 81-27]

RS 203.8. Ohio. Bureau of Employment
Services. Division of Research and Statistics.
Average employment, total payroll, and
average weekly earnings of educational local
government employees covered under Ohio
unemployment compensation law, by county.
RS 203.8. Columbus. NYPL [JLM 81-22]

RS 203.3-B. Ohio. Bureau of Employment
Services. Division of Research and Statistics.
Average weekly earnings of workers under
Ohio unemployment compensation law, by
industrial division and county. RS 203.3-B.
Columbus. NYPL [JLM 81-26]

Table RS-790-2. Ohio. Bureau of Employment
Services. Division of Research and Statistics.
Average weekly earnings of production
workers in Ohio [and various metropolitan
areas] Table RS-790-2. Columbus.
NYPL [JLM 80-997]

Table RS-790-3. Ohio. Bureau of Employment
Services. Division of Research and Statistics.
Average weekly hours of production workers
in Ohio [and various metropolitan areas]
Table RS-790-3. Columbus.
NYPL [JLM 80-995]

Table RS-790-4. Ohio. Bureau of Employment
Services. Division of Research and Statistics.
Average hourly earnings of production
workers in Ohio [and various metropolitan
areas] Table RS-790-4. Columbus.
NYPL [JLM 80-999]

Table RS-790-1. Ohio. Bureau of Employment
Services. Division of Research and Statistics.
Nonagricultural wage and salary employment
in Ohio [and various metropolitan areas]
Table RS-790-1. Columbus.
NYPL [M-11 2926]

Workers covered under Ohio unemployment
compensation law, by industrial group. RS
203.1. Columbus. 28 cm. Annual. Issued in parts,
one for each county.
*1. Labor supply - Ohio - Statistics - Periodicals. I.
Ohio. Bureau of Employment Services. Division of
Research and Statistics. RS 203.1. II. Title.*
NYPL [JLM 81-25]

**Ohio. Bureau of Employment Services. Research
and Statistics, Division of. see Ohio. Bureau
of Employment Services. Division of
Research and Statistics.**

**Ohio. Bureau of Unemployment Compensation.
Division of Research and Statistics.**
Ohio. Bureau of Employment Services. Division
of Research and Statistics. Average hourly
earnings of production workers in Ohio [and
various metropolitan areas] Table RS-790-4.
Columbus. NYPL [JLM 80-999]

Ohio. Bureau of Employment Services. Division
of Research and Statistics. Average weekly
earnings of production workers in Ohio [and
various metropolitan areas] Table RS-790-2.
Columbus. NYPL [JLM 80-997]

Ohio. Bureau of Employment Services. Division

BIBLIOGRAPHIC GUIDE

Ohio. Bureau of Unemployment Compensation. Division of   **84**

of Research and Statistics. Average weekly
hours of production workers in Ohio [and
various metropolitan areas] Table RS-790-3.
Columbus.   ***NYPL [JLM 80-995]***

Ohio. Bureau of Employment Services. Division
of Research and Statistics. Nonagricultural wage
and salary employment in Ohio [and various
metropolitan areas] Table RS-790-1. Columbus.
    NYPL [M-11 2926]

Ohio. Dept. of Administrative Services. Ohio.
Governor's Task Force on Women in State
Government. Governor's Task Force on
Women in State Government. [Columbus ,
1978?] vi, 100 p. :   LC Card 80-117284   DDC
  353.9771001/04 19
JK5560.5.W6 O34 1978

Ohio. Dept. of Agriculture. (Old Catalog form:
  Ohio. Agriculture Dept.)
Agricultural land use in Ohio. [Columbus :
Dept. of Agriculture, State of Ohio, [1979] 97
p. : ill. ; 29 cm. Cover title. Prepared by J. H.
Sitterley and G. W. Volk. "March 1979." LC Card
  80-621589   DDC 333.76/13/09771 19
*1. Land use, Rural - Ohio. 2. Agriculture - Ohio. I.
Sitterley, John H. II. Volk, Garth W. III. Title.*
HD211.O3 O37 1979

**Ohio. Dept. of Economic and Community
  Development.** Prototype Incorporated. State
of Ohio unified correctional master plan.
[Columbus, Ohio] [1979] 241 p. in various
pagings :   LC Card 80-621188   DDC 364.6/09771
  19
HV9305.O2 P76 1979

Ohio. Dept. of Health.
  Nursing homes and rest homes. 1978? Ohio.
  Laws, statutes, etc. [Nursing home and rest
  home licensure law.] Nursing and rest home
  law and rules. Rev. to May 10, 1977.
  [Columbus] [1978?] 18 p. ;   LC Card
  80-622700   DDC 344.771/03216 19
  KFO363.N8 A3 1978

  Ohio. Laws, statutes, etc. Ohio public health
  manual, annotated. [Columbus] , 1980. 858 p. :
    LC Card 80-623836   DDC 344.771/04/02632 19
  KFO354 .A3 1980

**Ohio. Dept. of Natural Resources. Division of
  Water. see Ohio. Division of Water.**

**Ohio. Dept. of Public Welfare. Bureau of
  Research and Statistics.** Characteristics of
Ohio's recipients of aid to dependent children :
1975 study / [prepared by Bureau of Research
and Statistics, Ohio Department of Public
Welfare]. Columbus : The Department, [1977]
iii, 19 p. : graphs ; 29 cm.   LC Card 78-621688
  DDC 362.7/13/09771 19
1. Child welfare - Ohio. I. Title.
HV742.O3 O36 1977

Ohio. Dept. of Rehabilitation and Correction.
Prototype Incorporated. State of Ohio unified
correctional master plan. [Columbus, Ohio]
[1979] 241 p. in various pagings :   LC Card
  80-621188   DDC 364.6/09771 19
HV9305.O2 P76 1979

Ohio. Dept. of Taxation. (Old Catalog form: Ohio.
  Taxation Dept.)
Property taxes : Real estate and public utility ;
amount of taxes and special assessments levied
currently and delinquent taxes from former
years in Ohio cities, by city. Columbus.
    NYPL [JLM 80-1035]

Ohio. Division of Civilian Conservation. The new
conservationists : working for the earth : the
YCC in Ohio, 1971-79. [Columbus, Ohio] :
Ohio Dept. of Natural Resources, Division of
Civilian Conservation, [1979?] ix, 41 p. : ill. ;
28 cm.   LC Card 80-623069   DDC
  331.3/8133372/09771 19
1. Youth Conservation Corps (Ohio). I. Title.
HD6274.O3 O33 1979

Ohio. Division of Geological Survey.
  Report of investigations.
    (no. 111) Quinn, Michael J. Glacial geology
    of Champaign County, Ohio /. Columbus ,
    1979. iii, 17 p. :   LC Card 80-622747   DDC
    557.71 s 551.7/92/09771465 19
    QE151 .A186 no. 111 QE697

    (no. 112) White, George Willard, 1903-
    Glacial geology of Ashtabula County, Ohio /.
    Columbus , 1979. iv, 48 p. :   LC Card

80-622748   DDC 557.71 s 551.7/92/0977134 19
QE151 .A186 no. 112 QE697

  (no. 113) Stith, David A. Chemical
composition, stratigraphy, and depositional
environments of the Black River Group
(Middle Ordovician), southwestern Ohio /.
Columbus , 1979. iv, 36 p. :   LC Card
80-622410   DDC 557.71 s 551.7/31 19
QE151 .A186 no. 113 QE660

Ohio. Division of Lands and Soil.
Ernst, James Edgar. Soil survey of Seneca
County, Ohio. [Washington, D.C.?] , 1980. vii,
143 p., 81 folded p. of plates :   LC Card
80-604150   DDC 631.4/7/77124 19
S599.O3 E77

An inventory of Ohio soils, Madison County.
[Columbus, Ohio] : Ohio Dept. of Natural
Resources, Division of Lands and Soil, 1979. 48
p. (p. 46-48 blank) : ill. (1 fold. in pocket) ; 28
cm. (Progress report - Ohio Department of Natural
Resources, Division of Lands and Soil ; no. 57) Report
by J. C. Gerken and R. J. Scherzinger. LC Card
  80-621013   DDC 631.4/9771 s 631.4/977155 19
*1. Soils - Ohio - Madison Co. I. Gerken, J. C. II.
Scherzinger, R. J. III. Series: Ohio. Division of Lands
and Soil. Progress report , no. 57. IV. Title.*
S599.O3 A25 no. 57

Kerr, James W. Soil survey of Pickaway
County, Ohio /. [Washington, D.C.] [1980] vii,
172 p., [36] fold. leaves of plates :   LC Card
80-602251   DDC 631.4/7/771815 19
S599.O3 K47

Lerch, Norbert K. Soil survey of Butler County,
Ohio /. [Washington] [1980] vii, 175 p., [38]
fold. leaves of plates :   LC Card 80-602516   DDC
  631.4/7/77175 19
S599.O3 L36

McLoda, N. A. Soil survey of Franklin County,
Ohio /. [Washington] [1980] viii, 188 p., [37]
fold. leaves of plates :   LC Card 80-602372   DDC
  631.4/7/77156 19
S599.O3 M32

Progress report .
  (no. 57) Ohio. Division of Lands and Soil.
  An inventory of Ohio soils, Madison County.
  [Columbus, Ohio] , 1979. 48 p. (p. 46-48
  blank) :   LC Card 80-621013   DDC 631.4/9771 s
  631.4/977155 19
  S599.O3 A25 no. 57

Redmond, Charles Edward, 1932- Soil survey
of Ashland County, Ohio /. [Washington]
[1980] vii, 179 p., [31] fold. leaves of plates :
  LC Card 80-602507   DDC 631.4/7/77129 19
S599.O3 R39

**Ohio. Division of Surveillance and Water Quality
  Standards.** Water quality study of the Ottawa
River, Allen and Putnam Counties, Ohio / G.
L. Martin ... [et al.]. [Columbus] : Ohio
Environment Protection Agency, Office of
Wastewater Pollution Control, Division of
Surveillance and Water Quality Standards,
1979. 35, [35] p., [4] leaves of plates : ill. ; 29
cm. On cover: Ohio EPA water quality survey.
Bibliography: p. 33-35 (1st group)   LC Card 80-621710
  DDC 363.7/3942/09771 19
*1. Water quality - Ohio - Ottawa River Watershed. I.
Martin, George Lloyd, 1919-. II. Title. III. Title: Ohio
EPA water quality survey. IV. Title: Water quality
survey.*
TD224.O3 O254 1979

Ohio. Division of Water.
Callahan, Charles C. Principles of water rights
law in Ohio /. [Columbus, Ohio] [1979] xiii,
48 p. :   LC Card 80-622377   DDC 346.77104/691
  19
KFO446 .C34 1979

Schmidt, James J. Ground-water resources of
Knox County /. Columbus , 1980. 1 map :   LC
  Card 81-691460
G4083.K6C34 1980 .S3

Schmidt, James J. Ground-water resources of
Pickaway County /. Columbus , 1980. 1 map :
  LC Card 81-691459
G4083.P5C34 1980 .S3

Schmidt, James J. Ground-water resources of
Ross County /. Columbus , 1980. 1 map :   LC
  Card 81-691461
G4083.R6C34 1980 .S3

**Ohio. Economic and Community Development,
  Dept. of. see Ohio. Dept. of Economic and**

Community Development.

Ohio election statistics. Ohio. Secretary of State.
Columbus.   ***NYPL [SEH (Ohio. State,
  Secretary of. Vote for state officers, etc.,
  polled at the annual election)]***

Ohio EPA water quality survey. Ohio. Division
of Surveillance and Water Quality Standards.
Water quality study of the Ottawa River, Allen
and Putnam Counties, Ohio /. [Columbus] ,
1979. 35, [35] p., [4] leaves of plates :   LC Card
  80-621710   DDC 363.7/3942/09771 19
TD224.O3 O254 1979

OHIO - GENEALOGY.
Records of Black and Mulatto persons [in
Ohio]. [1804-57] 1 reel.   ***NYPL [*ZI-276]***

**Ohio. Governor's Task Force on School
  Discipline.** Report / Governor's Task Force
on School Discipline. [Columbus, Ohio] : The
Task Force, [1980] 16 p. ; 26 cm. Cover title.
Includes bibliographical references.   LC Card
  80-622226   DDC 371.5/09771 19
1. School discipline - Ohio.
LB3012 .O33 1980

**Ohio. Governor's Task Force on Women in State
  Government.** Governor's Task Force on
Women in State Government. [Columbus :
Ohio Dept. of Administrative Services, 1978?]
vi, 100 p. : ill. ; 28 cm. Cover title. Bibliography: p.
98-100.   LC Card 80-117284   DDC 353.9771001/04
  19
*1. Women in the civil service - Ohio. I. Ohio. Dept. of
Administrative Services. II. Title.*
JK5560.5.W6 O34 1978

**Ohio. Health, Dept. of. see Ohio. Dept. of
  Health.**

OHIO IN LITERATURE.
Baker, William D. William Dean Howells .
Columbus , 1979. 24 p. ;   LC Card 80-138752
  DDC 818/.409 19
PS2033 .B3

Hughes, James M. Louis Bromfield, Ohio and
self-discovery /. Columbus , 1979. 22 p. ;   LC
  Card 80-137468   DDC 813/.52 19
PS3503.R66 Z76

Ohio labor market information. Ohio. Bureau of
Employment Services. Division of Research and
Statistics. Employment, payroll, and earnings
under the Ohio unemployment compensation
law by county, 1972 through 1978. Columbus
[1979?] 90 leaves ;   LC Card 80-623657   DDC
  331.12/5/09771 19
HD5725.O3 O37 1979a

Ohio labor market information.
Ohio. Bureau of Employment Services. Division
of Research and Statistics. Employment,
payroll, and earnings under the Ohio
unemployment compensation law by county,
1972 through 1979. Columbus [1980] 90
leaves ;   LC Card 80-623675   DDC 331.12/5/09771
  19
HD5725.O3 O37 1980

Ohio. Laws, statutes, etc.
  [Nursing home and rest home licensure law]
  Nursing and rest home law and rules. Rev. to
  May 10, 1977. [Columbus] : Ohio Dept. of
  Health, [1978?] 18 p. ; 28 cm. Cover title.
  Nursing homes and rest homes rules: p. 5-18.
  Published in 1974 under title: Nursing and rest home
  law and regulations.   LC Card 80-622700   DDC
  344.771/03216 19
  *1. Nursing homes - Law and legislation - Ohio. 2. Rest
  homes - Law and legislation - Ohio. I. Ohio. Dept. of
  Health. Nursing homes and rest homes. 1978?. II. Title.*
  KFO363.N8 A3 1978

  Ohio public health manual, annotated. 1980 ed.
  [Columbus] : Dept. of Health, State of Ohio,
  1980. 858 p. ; 27 cm. Includes index.
  CONTENTS. - Ohio revised code sections affecting or
  of interest to health officials; complete to April 1,
  1980.--Ohio administrative code rules of the Dept. of
  Health; complete to April 1, 1980.   LC Card
  80-623836   DDC 344.771/04/02632 19
  *1. Public health laws - Ohio. I. Ohio. Dept. of Health.
  II. Title.*
  KFO354 .A3 1980

**Ohio Multitype Interlibrary Cooperation
  Committee.** Ohio regional library and
information systems, as proposed by the Ohio
Multitype Interlibrary Cooperation Committee.
[Columbus, : State Library of Ohio, 1979] 21

p. ; 22 cm. Cover title. "June 1979." Includes bibliographical references. LC Card 80-621374 DDC 021.6/4/09771 19
1. Ohio Regional Library and Information System. I. Title.
Z674.82.O36 O36 1979

Ohio. Nursing Home Commission. A program in crisis, blueprint for action : final report of the Ohio Nursing Home Commission. Columbus, Ohio : The Commission, [1979] xix, 233 p. : ill. ; 29 cm. Includes bibliographical references. LC Card 80-621848 DDC 362.1/6/09771 19
1. Nursing homes - Ohio. 2. Nursing home care - Ohio. 3. Nursing homes - Law and legislation - Ohio. I. Title.
RA997.5.O3 O38 1979

OHIO - OFFICIALS AND EMPLOYEES - SALARIES, ALLOWANCES, ETC. - STATISTICS - PERIODICALS.
Ohio. Bureau of Employment Services. Division of Research and Statistics. Average employment, total payroll, and average weekly earnings of educational local government employees covered under Ohio unemployment compensation law, by county. RS 203.8. Columbus. *NYPL [JLM 81-22]*

Ohio public health manual, annotated. Ohio. Laws, statutes, etc. [Columbus] , 1980. 858 p. ; LC Card 80-623836 DDC 344.771/04/02632 19
KFO354 .A3 1980

OHIO REGIONAL LIBRARY AND INFORMATION SYSTEM.
Ohio Multitype Interlibrary Cooperation Committee. Ohio regional library and information systems, as proposed by the Ohio Multitype Interlibrary Cooperation Committee. [Columbus, , 1979] 21 p. ; LC Card 80-621374 DDC 021.6/4/09771 19
Z674.82.O36 O36 1979

Ohio regional library and information systems, as proposed by the Ohio Multitype Interlibrary Cooperation Committee. Ohio Multitype Interlibrary Cooperation Committee. [Columbus, , 1979] 21 p. ; LC Card 80-621374 DDC 021.6/4/09771 19
Z674.82.O36 O36 1979

Ohio River basin study area, Ohio. United States. Soil Conservation Service. Average annual precipitation in inches, 1931-60, southwest Ohio River basin study area, Ohio /. Lincoln, Nebr. , 1978. 1 map : LC Card 81-691036
G4081.C88 1960 .U5

Ohio River basin study area, Ohio. United States. Soil Conservation Service. P.L. 566 watershed status, southwest Ohio River basin study area, Ohio /. Lincoln, Nebr. , 1978. 1 map : LC Card 81-691040
G4081.C315 1978 .U5

Ohio River navigation . United States. Army. Corps of Engineers. Ohio River Division. Cincinnati, Ohio [1979] 64 p. : LC Card 80-601829 DDC 386/.32/0977 19
TC625.O3 U54 1979

OHIO RIVER - NAVIGATION - HISTORY.
United States. Army. Corps of Engineers. Ohio River Division. Ohio River navigation . Cincinnati, Ohio [1979] 64 p. : LC Card 80-601829 DDC 386/.32/0977 19
TC625.O3 U54 1979

Ohio. Secretary of State. (Old Catalog form: Ohio. State, Secretary of.)
Ohio election statistics. Columbus. 25 cm. Annual, 1890-1905; biennial, 1908- Title varies: 1890-1930, Vote for state officers ... polled in the several counties of the state of Ohio (varies slightly).
1. Elections - Ohio - Statistics - Periodicals. I. Ohio. Secretary of State. Vote for state officers ... polled in the several counties of the state of Ohio. II. Title.
NYPL [SEH (Ohio. State, Secretary of. Vote for state officers, etc., polled at the annual election)]

Vote for state officers ... polled in the several counties of the state of Ohio. Ohio. Secretary of State. Ohio election statistics. Columbus. *NYPL [SEH (Ohio. State, Secretary of. Vote for state officers, etc., polled at the annual election)]*

Ohio. State, Secretary of. see **Ohio. Secretary of State.**

Ohio. State University, Bowling Green. (Old Catalog form: Ohio. Bowling Green State

University, Bowling Green.)
Journal of American culture. v. 1- Spring 1978- [Bowling Green, Ohio] LC Card 79-642570
NYPL [JFL 80-314]

Ohio. State University, Bowling Green. Office of Continuing Education, Regional and Summer Programs. Financial aid for the non-traditional, part-time student . [Bowling Green, Ohio] , c1980. vii, 56 leaves ; LC Card 80-129745 DDC 378.3/0973 19
LB2337.5.O3 F56

Bibliographies of famous philosophers. see **Bibliographies of famous philosophers.**

Ohio. State University, Columbus.
The Journal of higher education. v. 1- ; 1930- [Columbus, Ohio] LC Card 32-99
*NYPL [*ZAN-3244]*

Ohio. State University, Columbus. Center for Human Resource Research. Choice mechanisms in the migration decision. Columbus] 1974. vii, 129 p.
NYPL [JLF 80-1365]

Ohio. State University, Columbus. College of Law. Callahan, Charles C. Principles of water rights law in Ohio /. [Columbus, Ohio] [1979] xiii, 48 p. : LC Card 80-622377 DDC 346.77104/691 19
KFO446 .C34 1979

Ohio. State University, Columbus. Cooperative Extension Service. Henderson, Dennis R. Feeder calf production and marketing patterns, southeast Ohio/. [Columbus], 1974. iii, 41 leaves; *NYPL [*ZT-1260]*

Ohio. State University, Columbus. Dept. of Agricultural Economics and Rural Sociology. Henderson, Dennis R. Feeder calf production and marketing patterns, southeast Ohio/. [Columbus], 1974. iii, 41 leaves; *NYPL [*ZT-1260]*

Kilmer, Richard Lee, 1943- The impact of regulation on transportation efficiency /. Columbus , 1974. 13, 3, 5 p. ; *NYPL [*XME-9249]*

Ohio. State University, Columbus. Dept. of Sociology. Disaster Research Center. see **Ohio. State University, Columbus. Disaster Research Center.**

Ohio. State University, Columbus. Disaster Research Center. Tierney, Kathleen J. Crisis intervention programs for disaster victims . Rockville, Md. , Washington [1979] xvi, 203 p. ; LC Card 79-603002 DDC 362.2 19
HV555.U6 T53

Ohio. State University, Columbus. Human Resource Research, Center for. see **Ohio. State University, Columbus. Center for Human Resource Research.**

Ohio. State University, Columbus. Mershon Center for Education in National Security. (Old Catalog form: Mershon center for Education in National Security)
Stein, Janice Gross. Rational decision-making . Columbus , c1980. xv, 399 p. : ISBN 0-8142-0312-4 LC Card 80-13589
DS119.2 .S73 *NYPL [JLE 81-169]*

Ohio. State University, Columbus. Program for the Study of Crime and Delinquency. Allen, Harry E. Critical Issues in Adult Probation . Washington, D.C. , 1979. vii, 289 p. ; LC Card 79-604144 DDC 364.6/3/0973 19
HV9304 .A64

Ohio. State University, Columbus. School of Public Administration. Program for the Study of Crime and Delinquency. see **Ohio. State University, Columbus. Program for the Study of Crime and Delinquency.**

Ohio State University. Instructional Materials Laboratory. Nursing skills and procedures /. Columbus, Ohio , Reston, Va. , c1979. x, 1077 p. : LC Card 81-103544 DDC 610.73/02/02 19
RT62 .N8 1979

Ohio. State University, Kent. Library Science, School of. see **Ohio. State University, Kent. School of Library Science.**

Ohio. State University, Kent. School of Library Science. (Old Catalog form: Ohio. State University, Kent. Library Science, School of)
Wynar, Lubomyr Roman, 1932- Guide to ethnic museums, libraries, and archives in the

United States /. Kent, Ohio , 1978. xvi, 378 p. ; LC Card 78-624077
E184.A1 W95

Ohio State University. Marching Band. Script Ohio, 1878-79--1978-79 /. Columbus, Ohio , c1979. 223 p. : LC Card 80-153680 DDC 785/.06/277157 19
ML1311 .S4

OHIO STATE UNIVERSITY. MARCHING BAND.
Script Ohio, 1878-79--1978-79 /. Columbus, Ohio , c1979. 223 p. : LC Card 80-153680 DDC 785/.06/277157 19
ML1311 .S4

Ohio. Taxation, Dept. of. see **Ohio. Dept. of Taxation.**

Ohio University, Athens. Dept. of English. Milton quarterly. v. 1- ; [Mar.] 1967- Athens, Ohio. LC Card 76-644374
*NYPL [*ZAN-4347]*

Ohio Valley Historic Indian Conference. Ethnohistory. Tucson [etc.]. LC Card 57-43343
NYPL [HBB (Ethnohistory)]

Ohio. Water, Division of. see **Ohio. Division of Water.**

Ohio's self-help natural gas program . United States. Congress. House. Committee on Interstate and Foreign Commerce. Subcommittee on Energy and Power. Washington , 1980. iii, 171 p. : LC Card 80-603775 DDC 333.8/23315/09771 19
KF27 .I5542 1980k

Ohls, James C. (joint author) Munson, Michael J. Indirect costs of residential fires /. [Washington] , 1979 [i.e. 1980] vi, 30 p. : LC Card 80-602415 DDC 363.3/79 19
TH9445.D9 M86

Ohno, Kate. Bainbridge, Robert C. Wilson historic buildings inventory, Wilson, North Carolina /. [Raleigh?] , 1980. iv, 244 p. : LC Card 81-621389 DDC 975.6/43 19
F264.W74 B34

OIL. see **PETROLEUM.**

OIL AND GAS LAW. see **PETROLEUM LAW AND LEGISLATION.**

OIL AND GAS LEASES - ALASKA.
Alaska. Legislature. House of Representatives. Interim Committee on Oil and Gas Leasing Policy. In the Legislature of the State of Alaska, Eleventh Legislature, second session . Anchorage, Alaska [1980] 215 p. ; LC Card 80-622471 DDC 346.79804/68232 19
KFA1211.82 .O35 1980

OIL AND GAS LEASES - BEAUFORT SEA.
Alaska. Legislature. House of Representatives. Interim Committee on Oil and Gas Leasing Policy. In the Legislature of the State of Alaska, Eleventh Legislature, second session . Anchorage, Alaska [1980] 215 p. ; LC Card 80-622471 DDC 346.79804/68232 19
KFA1211.82 .O35 1980

OIL AND GAS LEASES - MEXICO, GULF OF.
Final environmental impact statement . [Washington, D.C.?] : New Orleans, La. (Hale Boggs Federal Building, New Orleans, La. 70130) : xiiii [sic], 227 p. : LC Card 81-601099 DDC 333.8/231/0976 19
TD195.P4 F56

OIL AND GAS LEASES - MIDDLE ATLANTIC STATES.
Draft environmental impact statement : proposed 1981 outer continental shelf oil gas lease sale offshore the Mid-Atlantic States /. [New York] , 1980. 1 v. of various pagings : *NYPL [JSG 81-43]*

OIL AND GAS LEASES - NEW MEXICO.
United States. Congress. Senate. Committee on Energy and Natural Resources. Subcommittee on Energy Resources and Materials Production. Reinstatement of oil and gas lease, New Mexico 33955 . Washington , 1980. iii, 32 p. ; LC Card 80-603814 DDC 346.78904/6823 347.890646823 19
KF26 .E5543 1980d

Oil and gas leases on Indian lands . United States. Congress. Senate. Select Committee on Indian Affairs. Washington , 1981- v. <1 > : LC Card 81-601766 DDC 346.7304/6823

347.30646823 19
KF26.5 .I4 1981

OIL AND GAS LEASES - UNITED STATES.
United States. Bureau of Land Management.
Final environmental statement . [Washington]
[1980] viii, 384, [257] p. :   LC Card 80-601418
DDC 333.33/9 19
HD9566 .U52 1980

United States. Congress. Senate. Committee on
Energy and Natural Resources. Subcommittee
on Energy Resources and Materials Production.
Federal oil and gas leasing act of 1979 .
Washington , 1980. iii, 259 p. :   LC Card
80-601767   DDC 346.7304/6823 19
KF26 .E5543 1979a

United States. Congress. Senate. Subcommittee
on Energy Resources and Materials Production.
Production of oil from tar sand and other
hydrocarbon deposits . Washington , 1980. iii,
142 p. :   LC Card 81-600562   DDC 343.73/0772
347.303772 19
KF26 .E5543 1980h

United States. Congress. Senate. Select
Committee on Indian Affairs. Oil and gas leases
on Indian lands . Washington , 1981- v. <1
> :   LC Card 81-601766   DDC 346.7304/6823
347.30646823 19
KF26.5 .I4 1981

United States. General Accounting Office.
Actions needed to increase federal onshore oil
and gas exploration and development .
Washington, D.C. , 1981. xi, 203 p. ;   LC Card
81-601214   DDC 353.0082/388 19
HD9566 .U543 1981

United States. General Accounting Office.
Policy needed to guide natural gas regulation
on Federal lands . [Washington] , 1979. vii, 71
p. :   LC Card 79-602690   DDC 353.0087/23 19
HD9581.U5 U54 1979

OIL-BEARING SANDS. see OIL SANDS.

OIL FIELDS - IRAN - MAPS.
United States. Central Intelligence Agency.
Iraq-Iran central and southern border areas.
[Washington , 1980] 1 map :   LC Card 81-692540
G7611.F2 1980 .U5

OIL FIELDS - IRAQ - MAPS.
United States. Central Intelligence Agency.
Iraq-Iran central and southern border areas.
[Washington , 1980] 1 map :   LC Card 81-692540
G7611.F2 1980 .U5

OIL FIELDS - NEAR EAST - MAPS.
United States. Central Intelligence Agency.
Middle East area oilfields and facilities.
[Washington , 1980] 1 map :   LC Card 81-692536
G7421.H8 1980 .U5

**OIL FIELDS, OFFSHORE. see PETROLEUM
IN SUBMERGED LANDS.**

OIL-FUEL. see PETROLEUM AS FUEL.

Oil import fees . United States. Congress. House.
Committee on Ways and Means. Subcommittee
on Trade. Washington , 1980. iv, 443 p. :   LC
Card 80-603505   DDC 353.0082/75 19
KF27 .W348 1980d

**OIL INDUSTRIES - UNITED STATES -
STATISTICS.**
Stocks of grains, oilseeds, and hay .
Washington, D.C. , 1981. 71 p. ;   LC Card
81-601041   DDC 338.1/0973 s 338.1/731/0973
19
HD1751 .A5 no. 649 HD9034

United States. Economics, Statistics, and
Cooperatives Service. U. S. fats and oils
statistics, 1963-78. [Washington, D.C.] [1980]
iv, 104 p. ;   LC Card 80-601591   DDC 338.1/0973
s 338.1/7385/0973 19
HD1751 .A5 no. 631 HD9490.U6

OIL LEASES. see OIL AND GAS LEASES.

**OIL POLLUTION DAMAGES, LIABILITY
FOR. see LIABILITY FOR OIL
POLLUTION DAMAGES.**

**OIL POLLUTION OF THE SEA -
ENVIRONMENTAL ASPECTS.**
Ustach, Joseph F. Effects of sub-lethal oil levels
on the reproduction of a copepod, Nitocra
affinis /. [Raleigh] 1977. 16 leaves :   LC Card
79-623524   DDC 595.3/4 19
QL444.C74 U87

**OIL ROYALTIES. see OIL AND GAS
LEASES.**

Oil sands . Cox, Christopher H. [Golden, CO]
[1980] 12 p. :   LC Card 80-142733   DDC 553 s
553.2/82 19
TN1 .M534 vol. 23, no. 4 TN870.5

OIL SANDS.
Cox, Christopher H. Oil sands . [Golden, CO]
[1980] 12 p. :   LC Card 80-142733   DDC 553 s
553.2/82 19
TN1 .M534 vol. 23, no. 4 TN870.5

**OIL SANDS EXTRACTION PLANTS -
ENVIRONMENTAL ASPECTS - UNITED
STATES.**
National Research Council. Committee on
Surface Mining and Reclamation. Mining and
processing of oil shale and tar sands .
Washington, D.C. , 1980. xiv, 222 p. :   ISBN
0-309-03037-4 (pbk.)   LC Card 80-146216
DDC 333.8/23 19
TD195.O4 N37 1980

**OIL SANDS - LAW AND LEGISLATION -
UNITED STATES.**
United States. Congress. Senate. Committee on
Energy and Natural Resources. Subcommittee
on Energy Resources and Materials Production.
Production of oil from tar sand and other
hydrocarbon deposits . Washington , 1980. iii,
142 p. :   LC Card 81-600562   DDC 343.73/0772
347.303772 19
KF26 .E5543 1980h

**OIL SANDS - NEW MEXICO - SANTA ROSA
REGION.**
Budding, Antonius Jacob, 1922- Geology and
oil characteristics of the Santa Rosa tar sands,
Guadalupe County, New Mexico . Socorro,
N.M. [1979] 18 p., [1] leaf of plates :   LC Card
80-622029   DDC 553.2/82/0978925 19
TN872.N6 B82

OIL SEEPAGE - CALIFORNIA.
Hodgson, Susan F. Onshore oil & gas seeps in
California /. Sacramento , 1980. iv, 97 p. :   LC
Card 80-623064   DDC 553.2/8/09794 19
TN872.C2 H57

**OIL-SHALE INDUSTRY -
ENVIRONMENTAL ASPECTS - UNITED
STATES.**
National Research Council. Committee on
Surface Mining and Reclamation. Mining and
processing of oil shale and tar sands .
Washington, D.C. , 1980. xiv, 222 p. :   ISBN
0-309-03037-4 (pbk.)   LC Card 80-146216
DDC 333.8/23 19
TD195.O4 N37 1980

**OIL-SHALE INDUSTRY - LAW AND
LEGISLATION - UNITED STATES.**
United States. Congress. Senate. Committee on
Energy and Natural Resources. Subcommittee
on Energy Resources and Materials Production.
Oil shale leasing . Washington , 1980. iii, 143
p. :   LC Card 80-604059   DDC 343.73/077
347.30377 19
KF26 .E5543 1980g

Oil shale leasing . United States. Congress.
Senate. Committee on Energy and Natural
Resources. Subcommittee on Energy Resources
and Materials Production. Washington , 1980.
iii, 143 p. :   LC Card 80-604059   DDC 343.73/077
347.30377 19
KF26 .E5543 1980g

OIL-SHALES.
Peng, Syd S., 1939- Stress distribution and
pillar design in oil shale retorts /. Avondale,
Md. , 1981. p. cm.   LC Card 81-607827   DDC
622 s 622/.3382 19
TN23 .U43 TN858

United States. Congress. Office of Technology
Assessment. An assessment of oil shale
technologies. Washington, D.C. , 1980. vii, 517
p. :   LC Card 80-600101
TN858 .U54 1980   *NYPL   [JSF 80-1073]*

OIL-SHALES - COLORADO - TESTING.
Dolinar, Dennis R. Mechanical properties of oil
shale and overlying strata, Naval oil shale
reserve, Anvil Points, Colorado /. [Washington,
D.C.] , 1981. p. cm.   LC Card 81-607870   DDC
622/.18282/097881 19
TN23 .U43 TN859.U52C6

**OIL SPILL DAMAGES, LIABILITY FOR. see
LIABILITY FOR OIL POLLUTION**

DAMAGES.

OIL SPILLS - DATA PROCESSING.
The Oilspill risk analysis model of the U. S.
Geological Survey /. Washington [1981] p. cm.
LC Card 80-606812   DDC 363.7/394
GC1085 .O44

**OIL SPILLS - ENVIRONMENTAL ASPECTS -
UNITED STATES.**
United States. Maritime Administration. United
States Department of Commerce final
environmental impact statement . [Washington]
[1979] ca. 350 p. in various pagings :   LC Card
79-602128   DDC 333.91/1/0973 19
TD427.P4 U58 1979

OIL SPILLS - MATHEMATICAL MODELS.
The Oilspill risk analysis model of the U. S.
Geological Survey /. Washington [1981] p. cm.
LC Card 80-606812   DDC 363.7/394
GC1085 .O44

OIL TANKERS. see TANKERS.

OIL WELL DRILLING, SUBMARINE.
(1974) United States. National Science
Foundation. Deep sea drilling project.
[Washington, D. C.] 1974. 19 p.   LC Card
75-44202   *NYPL   [JSF 80-400]*

**OIL WELL DRILLING, SUBMARINE -
ENVIRONMENTAL ASPECTS - MEXICO,
GULF OF.**
Final environmental impact statement .
[Washington, D.C.?] : New Orleans, La. (Hale
Boggs Federal Building, New Orleans, La.
70130) : xiiii [sic], 227 p. :   LC Card 81-601099
DDC 333.8/231/0976 19
TD195.P4 F56

**OIL WELL DRILLING, SUBMARINE -
ENVIRONMENTAL ASPECTS - MIDDLE
ATLANTIC STATES.**
Draft environmental impact statement :
proposed 1981 outer continental shelf oil gas
lease sale offshore the Mid-Atlantic States /.
[New York] , 1980. 1 v. of various pagings :
NYPL   [JSG 81-43]

**OIL WELL MAINTENANCE. see OIL
WELLS - MAINTENANCE AND REPAIR.**

**OIL WELL SERVICING. see OIL WELLS -
MAINTENANCE AND REPAIR.**

**OIL WELL WORKOVER. see OIL WELLS -
MAINTENANCE AND REPAIR.**

**OIL WELLS - EQUIPMENT AND
SUPPLIES - REPAIRING. see OIL
WELLS - MAINTENANCE AND REPAIR.**

**OIL WELLS - MAINTENANCE AND
REPAIR.**
A Primer of oil-well service and workover.
Austin, Tex. , Dallas, Tex. , 1979. v, 106 p. :
LC Card 80-154730   DDC 622/.3382 19
TN871 .P7164 1979

**OIL WELLS - REPAIRING. see OIL WELLS -
MAINTENANCE AND REPAIR.**

**OIL WELLS - SERVICING. see OIL WELLS -
MAINTENANCE AND REPAIR.**

**OIL WELLS - WORKOVER. see OIL WELLS -
MAINTENANCE AND REPAIR.**

OILSEEDS.
Mattil, K. F. Review and comparative analysis
of oilseed raw materials and processes suitable
for the production of protein products for
human consumption. New York , 1974. viii, 36
p. :   LC Card 81-465132   DDC 300 s 664/.64 19
JX1977 .A2 ID/126 (ID/WG.120/10/Rev. 1)

**OILSEEDS - TRANSPORTATION -
STATISTICS.**
Griffin, Gene C. North Dakota grain and
oilseed transportation statistics, 1978-79 /.
Fargo, N.D. , 1979. iii, 70 p. :   LC Card
80-621931   DDC 388.044 19
HE2321.G7 G74

**The Oilspill risk analysis model of the U. S.
Geological Survey** / by Richard A. Smith ... [et
al.]. Washington : U. S. Geological Survey,
[1981] p. cm. (Geological Survey professional paper .
1227) Bibliography: p.   LC Card 80-606812   DDC
363.7/394
*1. Oil spills - Mathematical models. 2. Oil spills - Data
processing. I. Smith, Richard A. II. Series.*
GC1085 .O44

Oinas, Felix J. Folklore, nationalism, and politics
/. Columbus, Ohio , 1978. 189 p. ;   ISBN

0-89357-043-5 (pbk.)   LC Card 80-123925
GR41.5 .F64   **NYPL [JFE 80-3942]**

Okanogan County Conservation District, Okanogan County, Washington. United States. Soil Conservation Service. Historical districts, Okanogan County Conservation District, Okanogan County, Washington /. Portland, Or. , 1980. 1 map :   LC Card 81-691539
G4283.O3E635 1980 .U5

O'Keefe, Thomas J. (joint author) Cole, Ernest R. Insoluble anodes for electrowinning zinc and other metals /. Washington [1981] p. cm.   LC Card 80-607823   DDC 622 s 669/.52 19
TN23 .U43 TN796

Okinaka, Stanley K. (joint author) Nishimura, Charles H. The feasibility of integrating human services in Hawaii . Honolulu , 1978. xiii, 262 p. :   LC Card 78-624136   DDC 027.6/5 s 361/.9969 19
KFH20 .H38 1978, no. 1 HV98.H3

Oklahoma.
[Public Accountancy Act of 1968]
Public Accountancy Act of 1968 (as amended 1980) ; and, Rules of general application (as amended September 25, 1980). [Oklahoma City, Okla.] : Oklahoma State Board of Public Accountancy, [1980] 56 p. ; 22 cm. Cover title.   LC Card 81-621472   DDC 346.766/063 347.660663 19
1. Accountants - Legal status, laws, etc. - Oklahoma. I. Oklahoma State Board of Public Accountancy. Rules of general application (as amended September 25, 1980). 1980. II. Title.
KFO1529.A25 A32 1980

Oklahoma, a history of five centuries /. Gibson, Arrell Morgan. Norman , c1981. p. cm.   ISBN 0-8061-1758-3   LC Card 81-40284   DDC 976.6 19
F694 .G49 1981

Oklahoma. Ad Valorem Tax Division. 1980 Oklahoma personal property valuation schedule / Oklahoma Tax Commission ; compiled by Ad Valorem Tax Division. [Oklahoma City] : The Division, [1980] 98 p. ; 28 cm. Cover title. Includes index.   LC Card 80-621907   DDC 343.76605/42 19
1. Taxation of personal property - Oklahoma - Statistics. 2. Assessment - Oklahoma - Statistics. I. Title.
HJ4591.O5 O37 1980

Oklahoma. Agricultural Experiment Station, Stillwater.
Bulletin .
(B-743) Riffe, Don A. Hedging strategies to protect the financial position of cattle feeders and lenders /. [Stillwater] , 1979. 39 p. :   LC Card 79-625381   DDC 338.4/36213/0724 19
HD9433.U4 R54

Burgess, Dent Louis, 1913- Soil survey of Marshall County, Oklahoma /. [Washington, D. C. , 1980] vii, 92 p., [20] fold. leaves of plates :   LC Card 80-602509   DDC 631.4/7/76661 19
S599.O4 B88

Research report .
(P-755) Mapp, Harry P. The impact of increased energy costs on water use and agricultural output in the Oklahoma Panhandle /. [Stillwater] , 1977. 72 p. :   LC Card 77-623893   DDC 338.1/3/0976613 19
HD1739.O5 M36

(P-776) Kletke, Darrel D. Farmland investment value appraisal and purchase feasibility analyses . [Stillwater] , 1978. 83 p. ;   LC Card 78-624315   DDC 333.33/5/0973 19
HD1393 .K56 1978

Richardson, James W. An application of optimal control techniques to agricultural policy analysis /. [Stillwater, Okla.] , 1979. 41 p. :   LC Card 79-625383   DDC 338.1/873 19
HD1765 1979 .R52

Technical bulletin .
(T-154) Richardson, James W. An application of optimal control techniques to agricultural policy analysis /. [Stillwater, Okla.] , 1979. 41 p. ;   LC Card 79-625383   DDC 338.1/873 19
HD1765 1979 .R52

OKLAHOMA - ANTIQUITIES.
Oklahoma Highway Archaeological Survey. An archaeological survey of U. S. 69, Pittsburg, Atoka, and Bryan Counties, Oklahoma /.

[Norman] , 1976. v, 158 p. :   LC Card 77-621832   DDC 976.6/6 19
E78.O45 O48 1976

Oklahoma - Archaeology. see Oklahoma - Antiquities.

OKLAHOMA - BIOGRAPHY.
Oklahoma memories /. Norman , 1981. p. cm.   ISBN 0-8061-1689-7   LC Card 81-2777   DDC 976.6 19
F693 .O37

Oklahoma. Board of Nurse Registration and Nursing Education. Report of nurse population in Oklahoma, 1979 / Oklahoma Board of Nurse Registration and Nursing Education. Oklahoma City, Okla. : The Board, [1980] [11] p. : map ; 28 cm. Tables.   LC Card 80-623277   DDC 331.12/5161073/09766 19
1. Nurses - Oklahoma - Statistics. I. Title.
RT5.O5 O32 1980

Oklahoma City. Resource Analysis & Management Group. see Resource Analysis & Management Group, Oklahoma City.

Oklahoma Co., Okla. Election Board. Election manual 80 for county precinct officials. [Oklahoma City] : Oklahoma County Election Board, [1980] iv, 54 p. : ill. ; 22 cm. Cover title.   LC Card 80-623107   DDC 324.6/09766/38 19
1. Elections - Oklahoma - Oklahoma Co. - Handbooks, manuals, etc. I. Title.
JK2023.O5 O57 1980

Oklahoma comprehensive water plan. Oklahoma. Water Resources Board. [Oklahoma City] , 1980. ii, 248 p. :   LC Card 80-623045   DDC 333.91/009766 s 333.91/15/09766 19
TD224.O5 A3 no. 94 TC424.O5

Oklahoma. Constitution. Constitution of the State of Oklahoma, as amended to January 1, 1980. St. Paul, Minn. : West Pub. Co., c1980. iii, 98 p. (p. 94-98 blank for "Notes") ; 25 cm.   LC Card 80-622784   DDC 342.766/023 19
1. Oklahoma - Constitutional law. I. Title.
KFO1601 1907 .A53

OKLAHOMA - CONSTITUTIONAL LAW.
Oklahoma. Constitution. Constitution of the State of Oklahoma, as amended to January 1, 1980. St. Paul, Minn. , c1980. iii, 98 p. (p. 94-98 blank for "Notes") ;   LC Card 80-622784   DDC 342.766/023 19
KFO1601 1907 .A53

Oklahoma. Delegation to the White House Conference on Balanced National Growth and Economic Development, Washington, D. C., 1978. Report and recommendations to the Governor from the Oklahoma Delegation to the White House Conference on Balanced National Growth and Economic Development. [Oklahoma City] : Dept. of Economic and Community Affairs, 1978. 12, 2 [i.e. 3] leaves ; 29 cm.   LC Card 79-620770   DDC 338.9766 19
1. Oklahoma - Economic policy. 2. White House Conference on Balanced National Growth and Economic Development, Washington, D. C., 1978. I. Oklahoma. Dept. of Economic and Community Affairs. II. Title.
HC107.O5 O44 1978

Oklahoma. Dept. of Economic and Community Affairs.
Oklahoma. Delegation to the White House Conference on Balanced National Growth and Economic Development, Washington, D.C., 1978. Report and recommendations to the Governor from the Oklahoma Delegation to the White House Conference on Balanced National Growth and Economic Development. [Oklahoma City] , 1978. 12, 2 [i.e. 3] leaves ;   LC Card 79-620770   DDC 338.9766 19
HC107.O5 O44 1978

Oklahoma. Dept. of Economic and Community Affairs. Children's Services Coordination Project. Voices of Oklahoma families . [Oklahoma City] , 1978. ix, 300 p. :   LC Card 79-621197   DDC 362.7/1/09766 19
HV742.O5 O35 1978

Oklahoma. Dept. of Economic and Community Affairs. Children's Services Coordination Project. Voices of Oklahoma families : a needs assessment report for the Department of Institutions, Social and Rehabilitative Services / conducted by the Department of Economic and Community Affairs through the cooperative efforts of Margaret Wines, director, Children's

Services Coordination Project ... [et al.]. [Oklahoma City] : Dept. of Institutions, Social and Rehabilitative Services, 1978. ix, 300 p. : ill. ; 28 cm. Bibliography: p. 239-241.   LC Card 79-621197   DDC 362.7/1/09766 19
1. Child welfare - Oklahoma. I. Wines, Margaret. II. Oklahoma. Dept. of Institutions, Social and Rehabilitative Services. III. Oklahoma. Dept. of Economic and Community Affairs. IV. Title.
HV742.O5 O35 1978

Oklahoma. Dept. of Education. see Oklahoma. State Dept. of Education.

Oklahoma. Dept. of Highways. Planning Division. Oklahoma Highway Archaeological Survey. An archaeological survey of U. S. 69, Pittsburg, Atoka, and Bryan Counties, Oklahoma /. [Norman] , 1976. v, 158 p. :   LC Card 77-621832   DDC 976.6/6 19
E78.O45 O48 1976

Oklahoma. Dept. of Human Services. Statistical bulletin. 1980- Oklahoma City. Supersedes: Oklahoma. Dept. of Institutions, Social and Rehabilitative Services. Monthly bulletin.
NYPL [Econ. Div.]

Oklahoma. Dept. of Institutions, Social and Rehabilitative Services. (Old Catalog form: Oklahoma. Institutions, Social and Rehabilitative Services, Dept. of)
Oklahoma. Dept. of Economic and Community Affairs. Children's Services Coordination Project. Voices of Oklahoma families . [Oklahoma City] , 1978. ix, 300 p. :   LC Card 79-621197   DDC 362.7/1/09766 19
HV742.O5 O35 1978

Oklahoma. Dept. of Libraries. Archives and Records Division.
Guide to Oklahoma state archives / compiled and edited by Thomas W. Kremm, with editorial assistance from H. Glenn Jordan. Oklahoma City, Okla. : Archives and Records Division, Oklahoma Dept. of Libraries, 1980- v. 1 ; 28 cm. Includes index.   LC Card 80-622713   DDC 016.9766 19
1. Oklahoma. Dept. of Libraries. Archives and Records Division - Catalogs. 2. Oklahoma - History - Sources - Bibliography - Catalogs. I. Kremm, Thomas W. II. Jordan, H. Glenn. III. Title.
CD3454 .O38 1980a

Guide to special collections of the Oklahoma State Archives / compiled and edited by Thomas W. Kremm under the direction of Marietta Malzer. Oklahoma City, Okla. : Archives and Records Division, Oklahoma Dept. of Libraries, 1980. v, 32 leaves ; 28 cm. Includes index.   LC Card 80-622712   DDC 016.9766 19
1. Oklahoma. Dept. of Libraries. Archives and Records Division - Catalogs. 2. Oklahoma - History - Sources - Bibliography - Catalogs. I. Kremm, Thomas W. II. Title.
CD3454 .O38 1980

OKLAHOMA. DEPT. OF LIBRARIES. ARCHIVES AND RECORDS DIVISION - CATALOGS.
Oklahoma. Dept. of Libraries. Archives and Records Division. Guide to Oklahoma state archives /. Oklahoma City, Okla. , 1980- v. 1 ;   LC Card 80-622713   DDC 016.9766 19
CD3454 .O38 1980a

Oklahoma. Dept. of Libraries. Archives and Records Division. Guide to special collections of the Oklahoma State Archives /. Oklahoma City, Okla. , 1980. v, 32 leaves ;   LC Card 80-622712   DDC 016.9766 19
CD3454 .O38 1980

Oklahoma. Division of State Parks.
Rules & regulations / Oklahoma Tourism & Recreation Department, Division of State Parks. Rev. May 1979. [Oklahoma City, Okla.] : The Division, [1979] 19 p. ; 18 cm. Cover title.   LC Card 80-622622   DDC 346.766/046783 19
1. Recreation areas - Law and legislation - Oklahoma. 2. Parks - Law and legislation - Oklahoma. I. Title.
KFO1652.5.A435 A2 1979

Rules & regulations / Oklahoma Tourism & Recreation Department, Division of State Parks. Rev. [Oklahoma City, Okla.] : The Division, 1980. 19 p. : ill. ; 18 cm. Cover title.   LC Card 80-623108   DDC 346.766/046783 19
1. Parks - Law and legislation - Oklahoma. 2. Recreation areas - Law and legislation - Oklahoma. I. Title.
KFO1652.5.A439 A2 1980

OKLAHOMA - ECONOMIC POLICY.
Oklahoma. Delegation to the White House
Conference on Balanced National Growth and
Economic Development, Washington, D.C.,
1978. Report and recommendations to the
Governor from the Oklahoma Delegation to the
White House Conference on Balanced National
Growth and Economic Development.
[Oklahoma City] , 1978. 12, 2 [i.e. 3] leaves ;
  LC Card 79-620770   DDC 338.9766 19
HC107.O5 O44 1978

**Oklahoma. Education, State Dept. of. see
    Oklahoma. State Dept. of Education.**

**Oklahoma Employment Security Commission.
    Research and Planning.** Oklahoma population
estimates . [Oklahoma City, Okla.] [1980] 22
p. : LC Card 80-624236   DDC 312/.8/09766 19
HA585 .O46

**Oklahoma. Employment Security Commission.
    Research and Planning Division.**
Descriptions of jobs studied in the Oklahoma
Occupational Wage Survey Series. [Oklahoma
City] : Research & Planning, Oklahoma
Employment Security Commission, 1973. [8],
47 p. ; 28 cm. Cover title. At head of title: Job
descriptions.
*1. Job descriptions. 2. Oklahoma - Occupations -
Classifications. I. Title.*   **NYPL   [JLF 80-1364]**

Oklahoma population estimates. [Oklahoma
City?].   **NYPL   [JLM 80-721]**

Oklahoma population estimates : July 1, 1978
data for State, SMSA'S, counties, selected
cities. [Oklahoma City] : Oklahoma
Employment Security Commission, Research
and Planning, [1979] 24 p. : ill. ; 28 cm.
"Released September 1979." Includes bibliographical
references.   LC Card 80-621544   DDC 312/.8/09766
  19
1. Oklahoma - Population - Statistics. I. Title.
HA583 .E48 1979

Youth in the labor force. [Oklahoma City,
Okla.] : Oklahoma Employment Security
Commission, Research and Planning, [1979?] 15
p. : ill. ; 28 cm. "The compilation, analysis, and
narrative description of data ... by Roger Jacks." Chiefly
tables.   LC Card 80-620522   DDC 331.3/4125/09766
  19
*1. Youth - Employment - Oklahoma - Statistics. I.
Jacks, Roger. II. Title.*
HD6274.O5 O34 1979

OKLAHOMA - ETHNIC RELATIONS.
Phillips, Glenn S. Race relations in Oklahoma
/. Oklahoma City, Okla. , 1979. 81 p. ; LC
  Card 80-621086   DDC 305.8/009766 19
F705.A1 P48

Oklahoma. Forestry Division.
Miller, Robert L. Water quality management in
Ouachita Highland headwaters of Oklahoma .
[Oklahoma City] , 1980. xxvi, 109 p. : LC Card
  80-623044   DDC 363.7/39456/097666 19
TD224.O5 M54

**Resource bulletin - Oklahoma State
    Department of Agriculture, Forestry
    Division .**
(1) Miller, Robert L. Water quality
management in Ouachita Highland
headwaters of Oklahoma . [Oklahoma City] ,
1980. xxvi, 109 p. : LC Card 80-623044   DDC
363.7/39456/097666 19
TD224.O5 M54

OKLAHOMA - GENEALOGY.
Baker, Jack D. Cherokee emigration rolls,
1817-1835 /. Oklahoma City , c1977. 67
leaves ; LC Card 77-156017
E99.C5 B27

**Oklahoma. Geological Survey.
    Bulletin .**
(128) Shelton, John W. Geology and mineral
resources of Noble County, Oklahoma /.
Norman , 1979. v, 66 p. : LC Card 80-621935
DDC 557.66 s 557.66/27 19
QE153 .A2 no. 128 QE154.N58

**Oklahoma. Health Facilities Service. Licensure
    Division.** 1980 directory of licensed long-term
care facilities. [Oklahoma City, Okla.] : State
Dept. of Health, Health Facilities Service,
Licensure Division, State of Oklahoma, [1980]
38 p. ; 29 cm. "April 1980." Cover title. LC Card
  80-622402   DDC 362.1/6/025766 19
1. Nursing homes - Oklahoma - Directories. I. Title. II.

Title: Directory of licensed long-term care facilities.
RA997.5.O5 O43 1980

Oklahoma. Health Planning Commission.
Oklahoma. State Health Coordinating Council.
1980 Oklahoma State health plan /. [Oklahoma
City , 1980] v, 842 p. : LC Card 80-622403
DDC 362.1/09766 19
RA395.A4 O535 1980

Oklahoma Highway Archaeological Survey. An
archaeological survey of U. S. 69, Pittsburg,
Atoka, and Bryan Counties, Oklahoma /
prepared by staff, Oklahoma Highway
Archaeological Survey ; compiled and edited by
David R. Lopez and Kenneth D. Keith ;
contributions by James M. Briscoe ... [et al.].
[Norman] : The Survey, 1976. v, 158 p. : ill. ;
28 cm. (Papers in highway archaeology ; no. 2) At
head of title: Oklahoma Department of Highways,
Planning Division. On cover: U. S. 69 project,
Oklahoma. Bibliography: p. 149-158.   LC Card
  77-621832   DDC 976.6/6 19
*1. Indians of North America - Oklahoma - Atoka
County - Antiquities. 2. Indians of North America -
Oklahoma - Bryan County - Antiquities. 3. Indians of
North America - Oklahoma - Pittsburg County -
Antiquities. 4. Atoka County, Okla. - Antiquities. 5.
Bryan County, Okla. - Antiquities. 6. Pittsburg County,
Okla. - Antiquities. 7. Interstate 69 - Oklahoma. 8.
Oklahoma - Antiquities. I. Lopez, David R. II. Keith,
Kenneth D. III. Briscoe, James M. IV. Oklahoma.
Dept. of Highways. Planning Division. V. Title: An
archaeological survey of U. S. 69, Pittsburg, Atoka, and
Bryan Counties ... VI. Title: U. S. 69 project,
Oklahoma. VII. Series: Papers in highway archaeology ,
no. 2.*
E78.O45 O48 1976

OKLAHOMA - HISTORY.
Gibson, Arrell Morgan. Oklahoma, a history of
five centuries /. Norman , c1981. p. cm. ISBN
  0-8061-1758-3 LC Card 81-40284   DDC 976.6
  19
F694 .G49 1981

Shirley, Glenn. Heck Thomas, frontier marshal
/. Norman , 1981, c1962. p. cm. ISBN
  0-8061-1664-1 LC Card 81-40293   DDC
  976.6/04/0924 B 19
F698.T48 S48 1981

**OKLAHOMA - HISTORY - SOURCES -
    BIBLIOGRAPHY - CATALOGS.**
Oklahoma. Dept. of Libraries. Archives and
Records Division. Guide to Oklahoma state
archives /. Oklahoma City, Okla. , 1980- v. 1 ;
  LC Card 80-622713   DDC 016.9766 19
CD3454 .O38 1980a

Oklahoma. Dept. of Libraries. Archives and
Records Division. Guide to special collections
of the Oklahoma State Archives /. Oklahoma
City, Okla. , 1980. v, 32 leaves ; LC Card
  80-622712   DDC 016.9766 19
CD3454 .O38 1980

Oklahoma. Human Rights Commission. Phillips,
Glenn S. Race relations in Oklahoma /.
Oklahoma City, Okla. , 1979. 81 p. ; LC Card
  80-621086   DDC 305.8/009766 19
F705.A1 P48

**Oklahoma. Institutions, Social and Rehabilitative
    Services, Dept. of. see Oklahoma. Dept. of
    Institutions, Social and Rehabilitative
    Services.**

**Oklahoma. Legislative Council. see Oklahoma.
    State Legislative Council.**

Oklahoma. Legislature. Oklahoma. State
Legislative Council. Division of Research and
Reference Services. Legislative highlights of the
first session, Thirty-seventh Oklahoma
Legislature, 1979 (as of the recess of June 1) /.
[Oklahoma City?] [1979] 34 p. ; LC Card
  80-623059   DDC 348.766/01 19
KFO1215.2 1979

**The Oklahoma manual for real estate brokers
    and sales associates /.** Oklahoma. Real Estate
Commission. Oklahoma City, Okla. , 1978. xiii,
77 p. : LC Card 80-623214   DDC 333.33/09766 19
HD266.O5 O37 1978

Oklahoma memories / edited by Anne Hodges
Morgan and Rennard Strickland. 1st ed.
Norman : University of Oklahoma Press, 1981.
p. cm. Includes bibliographical references and index.
  ISBN 0-8061-1689-7 LC Card 81-2777   DDC
  976.6 19
1. Oklahoma - Biography. 2. Oklahoma - Social life and

*customs. 3. Frontier and pioneer life - Oklahoma. I.
Morgan, Anne Hodges, 1940-. II. Strickland, Rennard.*
F693 .O37

**OKLAHOMA - OCCUPATIONS -
    CLASSIFICATIONS.**
Oklahoma. Employment Security Commission.
Research and Planning Division. Descriptions
of jobs studied in the Oklahoma Occupational
Wage Survey Series. [Oklahoma City] , 1973.
[8], 47 p. ;   **NYPL   [JLF 80-1364]**

**OKLAHOMA - OFFICIALS AND
    EMPLOYEES - SALARIES,
    ALLOWANCES, ETC.**
Oklahoma. State Personnel Board. Classification
and compensation plan. Okla[homa] City, Okla.
[1980] 40 leaves ; LC Card 80-623079   DDC
353.9766001/03 19
JK7157 .O37 1980

Oklahoma population estimates. [Oklahoma
City?], Oklahoma Employment Security
Commission, Research and Planning Division.
27 cm. Annual. Report year ends June 30. "Data for
state, SMSA'S, counties, selected cities."
*1. Oklahoma - Population - Periodicals. I. Oklahoma.
Employment Security Commission. Research and
Planning Division.*   **NYPL   [JLM 80-721]**

Oklahoma population estimates : July 1, 1979
data for state, SMSA's, counties, selected cities.
[Oklahoma City, Okla.] : Oklahoma
Employment Security Commission, Research
and Planning, [1980] 22 p. : ill., maps ; 28 cm.
(Job service) Cover title. "Released June 1980." LC
  Card 80-624236   DDC 312/.8/09766 19
*1. Oklahoma - Population - Statistics. I. Oklahoma
Employment Security Commission. Research and
Planning. II. Series: Job service (Oklahoma
Employment Security Commission. Research and
Planning).*
HA585 .O46

Oklahoma population estimates . Oklahoma.
Employment Security Commission. Research
and Planning Division. [Oklahoma City] [1979]
24 p. : LC Card 80-621544   DDC 312/.8/09766 19
HA583 .E48 1979

**OKLAHOMA - POPULATION -
    PERIODICALS.**
Oklahoma population estimates. [Oklahoma
City?].   **NYPL   [JLM 80-721]**

OKLAHOMA - POPULATION - STATISTICS.
Oklahoma. Employment Security Commission.
Research and Planning Division. Oklahoma
population estimates . [Oklahoma City] [1979]
24 p. : LC Card 80-621544   DDC 312/.8/09766 19
HA583 .E48 1979

Oklahoma population estimates . [Oklahoma
City, Okla.] [1980] 22 p. : LC Card 80-624236
DDC 312/.8/09766 19
HA585 .O46

OKLAHOMA - RACE RELATIONS.
Phillips, Glenn S. Race relations in Oklahoma
/. Oklahoma City, Okla. , 1979. 81 p. ; LC
  Card 80-621086   DDC 305.8/009766 19
F705.A1 P48

Oklahoma. Real Estate Commission. The
Oklahoma manual for real estate brokers and
sales associates / edited and compiled by G.
Douglas Fox. Rev. Oklahoma City, Okla. :
Oklahoma Real Estate Commission, 1978. xiii,
77 p. : ill. ; 28 cm. On cover: Real estate manual.
Published in 1969 under title: The Oklahoma manual
for real estate brokers and salesmen. LC Card
  80-623214   DDC 333.33/09766 19
*1. Real estate business - Oklahoma - Handbooks,
manuals, etc. 2. Real estate business - Law and
legislation - Oklahoma. I. Fox, G. Douglas, 1933-. II.
Title. III. Title: Real estate manual.*
HD266.O5 O37 1978

**OKLAHOMA - SOCIAL LIFE AND
    CUSTOMS.**
Oklahoma memories /. Norman , 1981. p. cm.
  ISBN 0-8061-1689-7 LC Card 81-2777   DDC
  976.6 19
F693 .O37

**Oklahoma. Special Committee on Criminal
    Justice System.** Final report and
recommendations / Special Committee on
Criminal Justice System. [Oklahoma City] :
State Legislative Council, Research and
Reference Services Division, 1978. 207 p. ; 29
cm. "Submitted to the second session of the thirty-sixth
legislature. "April 1978." LC Card 78-622606   DDC

364/.9766 19
1. Criminal justice, Administration of - Oklahoma. I. Oklahoma. State Legislative Council. Research and Reference Services Division.
HV7286 .A6 1978

OKLAHOMA. STATE AGENCY FOR SURPLUS PROPERTY - AUDITING AND INSPECTION.

Oklahoma. State Legislative Council. Post-Audit Section. Performance audit, State Agency for Surplus Property, a division of the State Board of Public Affairs /. [Oklahoma City] [1980] 35 p. ; LC Card 80-622935 DDC 353.97660071/3045 19
JK1669.O5 O34 1980

Oklahoma State Board of Public Accountancy. Rules of general application (as amended September 25, 1980). 1980. Oklahoma. [Public Accountancy Act of 1968.] Public Accountancy Act of 1968 (as amended 1980) ; and, Rules of general application (as amended September 25, 1980). [Oklahoma City, Okla.] [1980] 56 p. ; LC Card 81-621472 DDC 346.766/063 347.660663 19
KFO1529.A25 A32 1980

Oklahoma. State Dept. of Education. (Old Catalog form: Oklahoma. Education Dept.) Suggested guidelines for local education agency compliance with Section 504 of the Rehabilitation Act of 1973 /. [Oklahoma City, Okla.] [ca. 1979] 83 p. : LC Card 80-624295 DDC 362.4/0483 19
NA2545.P5 S8

Oklahoma. State Dept. of Vocational and Technical Education. FY 1978-79 cost per program report : area vocational-technical schools / State Department of Vocational and Technical Education. Stillwater, Okla. : The Dept., [1979] 78 leaves ; 36 cm. Cover title. Tables. LC Card 80-622152 DDC 379.1/552/09766 19
1. Vocational education - Oklahoma - Finance - Statistics. I. Title. II. Title: Cost per program report.
LC1046.O5 O6 1979

Oklahoma. State Health Coordinating Council. 1980 Oklahoma State health plan / [Oklahoma State Health Coordinating Council]. [Oklahoma City : Oklahoma Health Planning Commission, 1980] v, 842 p. : ill. ; 28 cm. Includes bibliographical references. LC Card 80-622403 DDC 362.1/09766 19
1. Health planning - Oklahoma. 2. Medical policy - Oklahoma. 3. Public health - Oklahoma. 4. Medical care - Oklahoma. I. Oklahoma. Health Planning Commission. II. Title.
RA395.A4 O535 1980

Oklahoma. State Legislative Council. (Old Catalog form: Oklahoma. Legislative Council.) Nuclear energy in Oklahoma, 1979 [Oklahoma City] : Oklahoma Legislative Council, [1980] [44] leaves ; 28 cm. Cover title. Includes bibliography. LC Card 80-623906 DDC 333.79/24/09766 19
1. Atomic energy industries - Oklahoma. 2. Atomic power - Law and legislation - Oklahoma. I. Title.
HD9698.U53 O56 1980

Statistical data on the Oklahoma Legislature : statistical data on legislative measures, 1971-1980, and workload of the Senate and House of Representatives, second session, 37th Legislature, 1980 / prepared by Eldon L. Chowning. Oklahoma City, Okla. (305 State Capitol, Oklahoma City, Okla.) : State Legislative Council, [1980] 16 leaves ; 28 cm. "July 1980." Tables. LC Card 80-624227 DDC 328.766/077 19
1. Legislation - Oklahoma - Statistics. I. Chowning, Eldon L. II. Title.
KFO1215.2 1980

A Summary digest of laws enacted by the second regular session and the first extraordinary session of the Thirty-seventh Oklahoma Legislature, 1980 /. Oklahoma City, Okla. (305 State Capitol, Oklahoma City, Okla.) , 1980. vi leaves, 221 p. ; LC Card 80-624215 DDC 348.766/026 347.660826 19
KFO1225.5 1980

Oklahoma. State Legislative Council. Division of Fiscal Services. Oklahoma. State Legislative Council. Division of Research and Reference Services. Legislative

highlights of the first session, Thirty-seventh Oklahoma Legislature, 1979 (as of the recess of June 1) /. [Oklahoma City?] [1979] 34 p. ; LC Card 80-623059 DDC 348.766/01 19
KFO1215.2 1979

Statistical data on the Oklahoma Legislature : workload of the Senate and House of Representatives, 1979 / prepared by Eldon L. Chowning, legislative fiscal analyst, Fiscal Services Division. Oklahoma City, Okla. : State Legislative Council, [1979] 12 leaves ; 28 cm. "July 1979." LC Card 80-623058 DDC 328.766/077 19
1. Legislation - Oklahoma - Statistics. I. Chowning, Eldon L. II. Title.
KFO1215.2 1979a

A Summary digest of laws enacted by the second regular session and the first extraordinary session of the Thirty-seventh Oklahoma Legislature, 1980 /. Oklahoma City, Okla. (305 State Capitol, Oklahoma City, Okla.) , 1980. vi leaves, 221 p. ; LC Card 80-624215 DDC 348.766/026 347.660826 19
KFO1225.5 1980

Oklahoma. State Legislative Council. Division of Research and Reference Services. Legislative highlights of the first session, Thirty-seventh Oklahoma Legislature, 1979 (as of the recess of June 1) / prepared by Division of Research and Reference Services and Division of Fiscal Services of the State Legislative Council ; project coordinated by James B. Croy ; summaries contributed by Mary Brooks ... [et al.]. [Oklahoma City?] : The Council, [1979] 34 p. ; 28 cm. "June 1979." LC Card 80-623059 DDC 348.766/01 19
1. Legislation - Oklahoma. 2. Bills, Legislative - Oklahoma. I. Croy, James B. II. Oklahoma. Legislature. III. Oklahoma. State Legislative Council. Division of Fiscal Services. IV. Title.
KFO1215.2 1979

A Summary digest of laws enacted by the second regular session and the first extraordinary session of the Thirty-seventh Oklahoma Legislature, 1980 /. Oklahoma City, Okla. (305 State Capitol, Oklahoma City, Okla.) , 1980. vi leaves, 221 p. ; LC Card 80-624215 DDC 348.766/026 347.660826 19
KFO1225.5 1980

Oklahoma. State Legislative Council. Post-Audit Section. Performance audit, State Agency for Surplus Property, a division of the State Board of Public Affairs / submitted to Subcommittee on Fiscal Operations by Postaudit Section, Fiscal Services Division, State Legislative Council. [Oklahoma City] : The Council, [1980] 35 p. ; 28 cm. LC Card 80-622935 DDC 353.97660071/3045 19
1. Oklahoma. State Agency for Surplus Property - Auditing and inspection. 2. Surplus government property - Oklahoma. I. Oklahoma. State Legislative Council. Subcommittee on Fiscal Operations. II. Title: Performance audit, State Agency for Surplus Property.
JK1669.O5 O34 1980

Oklahoma. State Legislative Council. Research and Reference Services Division. Oklahoma. Special Committee on Criminal Justice System. Final report and recommendations /. [Oklahoma City] , 1978. 207 p. ; LC Card 78-622606 DDC 364/.9766 19
HV7286 .A6 1978

Oklahoma. State Legislative Council. Special Committee on Health Care Delivery System. Final report and recommendations / State Legislative Council, Research and Reference Services Division, Special Committee on Health Care Delivery System. [Oklahoma City?] : The Council, 1979. 2 v. : ill. ; 28 cm. Includes bibliographical references. LC Card 79-623655 DDC 362.1/09766 19
1. Medical care - Oklahoma. 2. Medical care - Law and legislation - Oklahoma. 3. Central State Griffin Memorial Hospital.
RA395.A4 O536

Findings and recommendations / State Legislative Council, Research and Reference Services Division, Special Committee on Health Care Delivery System. [Oklahoma City] : The Division, [1980] 223 p. : ill. ; 28 cm. "May 22, 1980." LC Card 80-623080 DDC 362.1/09766 19
1. Medical care - Oklahoma. 2. Mental health services - Oklahoma. 3. Medical laws and legislation - Oklahoma. 4. Oklahoma. State Legislative Council. Special

Committee on Health Care Delivery System. I. Title.
RA395.A4 O536 1980

OKLAHOMA. STATE LEGISLATIVE COUNCIL. SPECIAL COMMITTEE ON HEALTH CARE DELIVERY SYSTEM.

Oklahoma. State Legislative Council. Special Committee on Health Care Delivery System. Findings and recommendations /. [Oklahoma City] [1980] 223 p. : LC Card 80-623080 DDC 362.1/09766 19
RA395.A4 O536 1980

Oklahoma. State Legislative Council. Subcommittee on Fiscal Operations. Oklahoma. State Legislative Council. Post-Audit Section. Performance audit, State Agency for Surplus Property, a division of the State Board of Public Affairs /. [Oklahoma City] [1980] 35 p. ; LC Card 80-622935 DDC 353.97660071/3045 19
JK1669.O5 O34 1980

Oklahoma. State Personnel Board. Classification and compensation plan. Okla[homa] City, Okla. : Oklahoma State Personnel Board, [1980] 40 leaves ; 28 cm. Cover title. "Reporting date February 15, 1980." Tables. LC Card 80-623079 DDC 353.9766001/03 19
1. Oklahoma - Officials and employees - Salaries, allowances, etc. 2. Civil service positions - Oklahoma - Classification. I. Title.
JK7157 .O37 1980

Oklahoma. State Regents for Higher Education. Division of Fiscal Affairs. Land, buildings, and equipment in the Oklahoma State system of higher education for 1977-78 and 1978-79 / prepared by Division of Fiscal Affairs. Oklahoma City : Oklahoma State Regents for Higher Education, [1979] 6 leaves ; 22 x 36 cm. "December 1979." LC Card 80-622950 DDC 378/.196/09766 19
1. College facilities - Oklahoma - Statistics. I. Title.
LB3223.4.O5 O43 1979a

Oklahoma. State University of Agriculture and Applied Science, Stillwater. School of Civil Engineering. Technical publication . (no. 22) Ellifritt, Duane S. An inventory of historic engineering sites in Oklahoma /. Stillwater, Okla. [1974] 21, [12] leaves : LC Card 80-130043 DDC 624 s 624/.09766 19
TA7 .O47 no. 22 TA24.O5

Oklahoma Tax Commission. Monthly research and statistical bulletin. Jan. 1970, Feb-July, 1971. Oklahoma City. 28 cm. Issues for Feb.-July, 1971 called v. 2, no. 1-6, Ceased publication with July, 1971?
1. Sales tax - Oklahoma - Statistics - Periodicals. I. Title. **NYPL [JLM 80-920]**

Oklahoma. University. J. Willis Stovall Museum. Contributions from the Stovall Museum, University of Oklahoma . (no. 5) Gardner, Joan S. The conservation of fragile specimens from the Spiro Mound, LeFlore County, Oklahoma . Norman, Okla. , 1980. iv, 75 leaves : LC Card 80-623068 DDC 976.6/79 19
E78.O45 G34

Oklahoma. University. Office of Research Administration. Reid, George Willard, 1917- Final report on the Governor's Conference on Research and Development Priorities for the State of Oklahoma /. [Norman, Okla. , 1973] 293 p. in various pagings : LC Card 80-621267 DDC 338.9766 19
T176 .R4

Oklahoma. University. Research Administration, Office of. *see* **Oklahoma. University. Office of Research Administration.**

Oklahoma. Water Resources Board. Oklahoma comprehensive water plan. [Oklahoma City] : Oklahoma Water Resources Board, 1980. ii, 248 p. : ill. ; 28 cm. (Publication - Oklahoma Water Resources Board . 94) Bibliography: p. 246-247. Includes index. LC Card 80-623045 DDC 333.91/009766 s 333.91/15/09766 19
1. Water resources development - Oklahoma. I. Series: Oklahoma. Water Resources Board. Publication , 94. II. Title.
TD224.O5 A3 no. 94 TC424.O5

Oklahoma's water quality standards, 1976. Oklahoma City, Okla. : Oklahoma Water

Resources Board, [197-?] 91 p. : ill. ; 28 cm.
(Publication - Oklahoma Water Resources Board ; 79)
Bibliography: p. 10. Includes index.   LC Card
    80-622277   DDC 333.91/009766 s
    363.7/39462/09766 19
1. Water quality - Standards - Oklahoma. I. Series:
Oklahoma. Water Resources Board. Publication , 79. II.
Title.
TD224.O5 A3 no. 79

Publication .
    (79) Oklahoma. Water Resources Board.
    Oklahoma's water quality standards, 1976.
    Oklahoma City, Okla. [197-?] 91 p. : LC
    Card 80-622277   DDC 333.91/009766 s
    363.7/39462/09766 19
TD224.O5 A3 no. 79

    (90) Oklahoma. Water Resources Board.
    Rules, regulations, and modes of procedure /.
    [Oklahoma City] [1979] iii, 73 p. ; LC Card
    80-621865   DDC 333.91/009766 s 333.91/00766
    s 346.76604/691/002636 347.66064691002636 19
TD224.O5 A3 no. 90 KFO1646

    (94) Oklahoma. Water Resources Board.
    Oklahoma comprehensive water plan.
    [Oklahoma City] , 1980. ii, 248 p. :   LC Card
    80-623045   DDC 333.91/009766 s
    333.91/15/09766 19
TD224.O5 A3 no. 94 TC424.O5

Rules, regulations, and modes of procedure /
Oklahoma Water Resources Board. 1979
revision. [Oklahoma City] : The Board, [1979]
iii, 73 p. ; 28 cm. (Publication - Oklahoma Water
Resources Board . 90) LC Card 80-621865   DDC
333.91/009766 s 333.91/00766 s
346.76604/691/002636 347.66064691002636 19
1. Water - Law and legislation - Oklahoma. 2.
Oklahoma. Water Resources Board - Rules and
practice. I. Series: Oklahoma. Water Resources Board.
Publication , 90. II. Title.
TD224.O5 A3 no. 90 KFO1646

OKLAHOMA. WATER RESOURCES BOARD -
RULES AND PRACTICE.
Oklahoma. Water Resources Board. Rules,
regulations, and modes of procedure /.
[Oklahoma City] [1979] iii, 73 p. ; LC Card
80-621865   DDC 333.91/009766 s 333.91/00766
s 346.76604/691/002636 347.66064691002636 19
TD224.O5 A3 no. 90 KFO1646

Oklahoma Water Resources Research Institute.
Westphal, Joseph W. Commitments, priorities,
and organizational options for water resource
planning in Oklahoma /. [Stillwater] [1979]
xix, 346 p. :   LC Card 80-622933   DDC
333.91/15/09766 19
TC424.O5 W47

Oklahoma's water quality standards, 1976.
Oklahoma. Water Resources Board. Oklahoma
City, Okla. [197-?] 91 p. :   LC Card 80-622277
DDC 333.91/009766 s 363.7/39462/09766 19
TD224.O5 A3 no. 79

Okrent, David. Nuclear reactor safety : on the
history of the regulatory process / David
Okrent. Madison : University of Wisconsin
Press, 1981. p. cm. Bibliography: p. Includes index.
    ISBN 0-299-08350-0 :   LC Card 80-53958
    DDC 621.48/35 19
1. Nuclear reactors - United States - Safety measures -
History. 2. Nuclear reactors - Safety regulations -
United States - History. 3. United States. Atomic
Energy Commission. Advisory Committee on Atomic
Safeguards - History. I. Title.
TK9152 .O35

Oksenberg, Lois. Experiments in interviewing
techniques . Ann Arbor , 1979. 444 p. :   ISBN
0-87944-247-6   LC Card 79-53851
RA408.5 .E96   ***NYPL [JLF 81-173]***

Okudara, Jon T. Hawaii. Legislative Reference
Bureau. Guide to government in Hawaii /.
Honolulu, 1973. iv, 122 p.:
    NYPL [IXS 80-1670]

Okuma, Angelo. Geology of the carbonate rocks
of Path Valley, Franklin County, Pennsylvania /
Angelo Okuma. [Harrisburg] : Commonwealth
of Pennsylvania, State Planning Board, Bureau
of Topographic and Geologic Survey, 1970. 1
portfolio ([1] fold. leaf : col. map) ; 28 cm.
(Progress report - Commonwealth of Pennsylvania,
State Planning Board, Bureau of Topographic and
Geologic Survey . 179) Title from portfolio. Includes
bibliography.   LC Card 74-621157   DDC 557.48 s
    557.48/44 19

1. Geology, Stratigraphic - Ordovician. 2. Geology,
Stratigraphic - Silurian. 3. Rocks, Carbonate. 4.
Geology - Pennsylvania - Franklin Co. I. Series:
Pennsylvania. Topographic and Geologic Survey.
Progress report , 179. II. Title.
QE157 .A293 no. 179 QE660

OLD AGE ASSISTANCE - HAWAII.
Nishimura, Charles H. Economic security for
older persons in Hawaii . Honolulu, Hawaii
[1980] x, 192 p. :   LC Card 80-622005   DDC
    027.6/5 s 362.6/3 19
KFH20 .H38 1980 no. 1 HV1468.H3

OLD AGE ASSISTANCE - INDIANA.
Indiana. State Commission on the Aging and
Aged. State plan on aging for the State of
Indiana for fiscal year 1980. [Indianapolis, Ind.]
[1979] ca. 50 p. in various pagings ;   LC Card
    80-621779   DDC 362.6/09772 19
HV1468.I6 I47 1979

OLD AGE ASSISTANCE - NEW JERSEY.
New Jersey. Legislature. General Assembly.
Revenue, Finance, and Appropriations
Committee. Public hearing before Assembly
Revenue, Finance and Appropriations
Committee on Assembly concurrent resolution
no. 139 O[i.e. A]CR (use of casino gambling
revenues to assist senior citizens and disabled)
held June 30, 1980, Assembly Majority
Conference Room, State House, Trenton, New
Jersey. [Trenton] [1980] 3, 32 p. ;   LC Card
    80-623450
KFN1811.4 .R45 1980

United States. Congress. House. Select
Committee on Aging. Subcommittee on Human
Services. Reauthorization of the Older
Americans Act, 1981 . Washington , 1980- v.
<1> ;   LC Card 80-603785   DDC 353.0084/6 19
KF27.5 .A36 1980c

OLD AGE ASSISTANCE - NORTH
       CAROLINA.
Strickland, Lucy. The law and the elderly in
North Carolina /. [Chapel Hill], 1980. x, 154
p. ;   LC Card 81-620519   DDC 344.765/0326
    347.6504326 19
KFN7491.A3 S75 1980

OLD AGE ASSISTANCE - UNITED STATES.
United State. Congress. House. Select
Committee on Aging. Older Americans Act .
Washington, D.C. , 1979. v, 124 p. ;   LC Card
    80-603981   DDC 344.73/0326 347.304326 19
KF3737 .A25 1979

United States. Congress. House. Select
Committee on Aging. Subcommittee on Human
Services. Reauthorization of the Older
Americans Act, 1981 . Washington , 1980- v.
<1> ;   LC Card 80-603785   DDC 353.0084/6 19
KF27.5 .A36 1980c

United States. Congress. Senate. Special
Committee on Aging. The proposed fiscal 1981
budget . Washington , 1980. ii, 18 p. :   LC Card
    80-601777   DDC 362.6/3/0973 19
HV1461 .U63 1980

United States. Library of Congress.
Congressional Research Service. Federal
responsibility to the elderly . Washington ,
1979. iii, 16 p. :   LC Card 79-600867   DDC
    362.6/3/0973 19
HV1461 .U645 1979

OLD AGE ASSISTANCE - UNITED STATES -
       BIBLIOGRAPHY.
Mubarak, Jill. Gerontology and the law . Los
Angeles, Calif. , 1979. xiv, 102 p. ;   LC Card
    79-123375   DDC 016.34473/0326 19
KF390.A4 M8

OLD AGE ASSISTANCE - UNITED STATES -
       CONGRESSES.
Institute on Minority Aging, 3d, San Diego
State University, 1975. Minority aging and the
legislative process. - San Diego , c1977. xxi, 96
p. :   ***NYPL [JLF 80-1458]***

OLD AGE ASSISTANCE - UNITED STATES -
       STATES.
State offices on aging . Washington , 1980. vii,
37 p. ;   LC Card 81-600673   DDC 362.6/0973 19
KF3737.Z95 S73

OLD AGE ASSISTANCE - VERMONT.
Giguere, Gregory C. The elderly of Vermont .
Waterbury, Vt. [1979] 43 p. in various
pagings :   LC Card 80-621071   DDC 362.6/09743

19
HV1468.V4 G53

Old age, handicapped, and Vietnam-era
antidiscrimination legislation /. Northrup,
James P. Philadelphia , c1978. vii, 92 p. ;
    ISBN 0-89546-008-4   LC Card 78-70927   DDC
    344.73/01133 347.3041133 19
KF3464 .N6 Suppl

OLD AGE HOMES - LICENSES - NORTH
       CAROLINA.
North Carolina. Dept. of Human Resources.
Division of Facility Services. Licensure and
Certification Section. Rules and regulations for
the licensing of nursing homes and home for
the aged beds when licensed as a part of a
nursing home. Raleigh, N.C. (P.O. Box 12200,
Raleigh 27605) [1980] 34 p. ;   LC Card
    81-621297   DDC 344.756/03216 347.56043216
    19
KFN7763.N8 A32 1980

OLD AGE HOMES - MAINE -
       DIRECTORIES.
Maine. Division of Licensing and Certification.
Maine licensed boarding homes for the aged
directory /. [Augusta] [1979] 21 p. ;   LC Card
    80-620930   DDC 361.6/1/025741 19
HV1450 .M34 1979

OLD AGE HOMES - NEW YORK (STATE)
Close, Beatrice A. Private proprietary homes for
adults . [Albany] [1979] 132 p. ;   LC Card
    79-625315   DDC 362.6/1/09747 19
HV1468.N7 C55

OLD AGE HOMES - UNITED STATES -
       STATES - STATISTICS.
United States. Health Care Financing
Administration. Office of Policy, Planning, and
Research. Selected characteristics of the living
arrangements and institutionalization of the
elderly in the States, HEW regions, and the
United States . Washington , 1978. vii, 501 p. :
    LC Card 79-603338
HD7287.8 .U5 1978   ***NYPL [JLF 81-290]***

OLD AGE HOMES - UNITED STATES -
       STATISTICS.
United States. Health Care Financing
Administration. Office of Policy, Planning, and
Research. Selected characteristics of the living
arrangements and institutionalization of the
elderly in the States, HEW regions, and the
United States . Washington , 1978. vii, 501 p. :
    LC Card 79-603338
HD7287.8 .U5 1978   ***NYPL [JLF 81-290]***

OLD AGE HOMES - VIRGINIA.
Virginia. General Assembly. Joint Legislative
Audit & Review Commission. Homes for adults
in Virginia /. [Richmond, Va.] [1979] iv, 73
p. :   LC Card 80-622566   DDC 362.6/1/09755 19
HV1468.V8 V5 1979

OLD AGE HOMES - WASHINGTON (STATE)
Washington (State). Center for Health Statistics.
Boarding homes in Washington State, 1978 /.
Olympia, Wash. [1979] iv, 23 p. :   LC Card
    80-621771   DDC 362.6/1/09797 19
HV1468.W2 W35 1979

OLD AGE PENSIONS.
Torrey, Barbara Boyle. An international
comparison of pension systems /. [Washington,
D.C.] , 1980. v, 52, [46] p. ;   LC Card 80-602549
    DDC 331.25/2 19
HD7105.3 .T67

OLD AGE PENSIONS - COST-OF-LIVING
       ADJUSTMENTS - MONTANA.
Montana. Legislature. Interim Study Committee
on Public Systems. Coping with inflation .
Helena, Mont. (Room 138, State Capitol,
Helena 59620) , 1980. i, 28, [38] p. ;   LC Card
    81-621342   DDC 353.9786005 19
HD7106.U5 M59 1980

OLD AGE PENSIONS - FRANCE.
Horlick, Max. Private pension plans in West
Germany and France /. Washington, D.C. ,
c1980. v, 70 p. ;   LC Card 80-600176   DDC
    368.4/3/00973 331.25/2/0943 19
HD7123 .A39 no. 55 HD7106.F8

OLD AGE PENSIONS - GERMANY, WEST.
Horlick, Max. Private pension plans in West
Germany and France /. Washington, D.C. ,
c1980. v, 70 p. ;   LC Card 80-600176   DDC
    368.4/3/00973 331.25/2/0943 19
HD7123 .A39 no. 55 HD7106.F8

OLD AGE PENSIONS - KANSAS.
United States. Congress. Senate. Special
Committee on Aging. Retirement benefits, are
they fair and are they enough? . Washington ,
1981. iii, 74 p. ;　LC Card 81-602039　DDC
331.25/2/0973 19
KF26.5 .A3 1980j

OLD AGE PENSIONS - LAW AND
LEGISLATION - MONTANA.
Montana. Legislature. Interim Study Committee
on Public Systems. Coping with inflation .
Helena, Mont. (Room 138, State Capitol,
Helena 59620) , 1980. i, 28, [38] p. ;　LC Card
81-621342　DDC 353.9786005 19
HD7106.U5 M59 1980

OLD AGE PENSIONS - MONTANA -
EFFECT OF INFLATION ON.
Montana. Legislature. Interim Study Committee
on Public Systems. Coping with inflation .
Helena, Mont. (Room 138, State Capitol,
Helena 59620) , 1980. i, 28, [38] p. ;　LC Card
81-621342　DDC 353.9786005 19
HD7106.U5 M59 1980

OLD AGE PENSIONS - TAXATION -
UNITED STATES.
United States. Congress. House. Select
Committee on Aging. Subcommittee on
Retirement Income and Employment. Oversight
on recommendations of 1979 Social Security
Advisory Council . Washington , 1980. iv, 208
p. ;　LC Card 80-603006　DDC 368.4/00973 19
KF27.5 .A374 1980

United States. Congress. House. Select
Committee on Aging. Subcommittee on
Retirement Income and Employment. Social
security . Washington , 1980. v, 39 p. :　LC
Card 80-603864　DDC 353.0082/56 19
HD7125 .U537 1980a

OLD AGE PENSIONS - UNITED STATES.
Koitz, David. Summary of recommendations
and surveys on social security and pension
policies . Washington , 1980. vii, 48 p. ;　LC
Card 80-603856　DDC 368.4/3/00973 19
HD7125 .K59

Meier, Elizabeth L. Retirement income goals /.
Washington, D.C. [1980] v, 60 p. ;　LC Card
80-602550　DDC 331.25/2/0973 19
HD7106.U5 M37

United States. Congress. House. Select
Committee on Aging. Retirement, the broken
promise . Washington , 1981. iii, 91 p. ;　LC
Card 81-601334　DDC 331.25/2/0973 19
KF27.5 .A3 1980j

United States. Congress. Senate. Committee on
Finance. Subcommittee on Social Security.
Social security retirement test . Washington ,
1980. iv, 305 p. ;　LC Card 80-603289　DDC
344.73/023 19
KF26 .F568 1980a

United States. Congress. Senate. Special
Committee on Aging. Retirement benefits, are
they fair and are they enough? . Washington ,
1981. iii, 74 p. ;　LC Card 81-602039　DDC
331.25/2/0973 19
KF26.5 .A3 1980j

United States. President's Commission on
Pension Policy. An interim report /.
Washington, D.C. (736 Jackson Place, N.W.,
Washington, D.C. 20006) , 1980. 66 p. in
various pagings ;　LC Card 81-600721　DDC
331.25/2/0973 19
HD7106.U5 U644 1981

OLD AGE PENSIONS - UNITED STATES -
PERIODICALS.
United States. Social Security Administration.
Office of the Actuary. Actuarial study.
[Washington?]　　　　**NYPL [JLM 81-126]**

United States. Social Security Board. Office of
the Actuary. Actuarial study. no. [1]-19
(incomplete). [Washington?] 1937-44.
　　　　NYPL [SIW (U. S. Social Security
　　　　Board. Actuary Office. Actuarial study)]

OLD AGE - RESEARCH.
An In-depth analysis of the needs assessment of
the elderly, 1976, Washington State . [Salem] ,
1978. 117 xvii p. ;　LC Card 79-621901　DDC
362.6/09797 19
HQ1064.U6 W295

OLD AGE, SURVIVORS AND DISABILITY
INSURANCE. see SOCIAL SECURITY.

An old capital and a new president /. Fallows,
James M. Bloomington, Ind. , c1979. 16 p. ;
　　　　LC Card 80-140042　DDC 973.926/092/4 19
E873 .F34

Old Dominion University. Dept. of University
Police. Old Dominion University / Old
Dominion University, Department of University
Police. Rev. June 1978. [Richmond, Va.] : The
Dept., [1978] 1 view ; 25 x 33 cm., folded to
28 x 22 cm. Bird's-eye-view. Oriented with north
toward the lower right. Includes list of buildings and
departments. Text of "Motor vehicle regulations 78-79"
on verso. "1942 Security 7/78." LC Card 81-690416
1. Old Dominion University - Description - Aerial -
Maps.
G3884.N6:2O4A3 1978 .O4

OLD DOMINION UNIVERSITY -
DESCRIPTION - AERIAL - MAPS.
Old Dominion University. Dept. of University
Police. Old Dominion University /. [Richmond,
Va.] [1978] 1 view ;　LC Card 81-690416
G3884.N6:2O4A3 1978 .O4

Old English poetry : essays on style / edited by
Daniel G. Calder. Berkeley : University of
California Press, c1979. vii, 174 p. ; 24 cm.
(California. University. University at Los Angeles.
Center for medieval and renaissance studies.
Contributions. 10) "Based on papers delivered at a
symposium on Old English poetry held in Los Angeles,
March 31 to April 2, 1977 [and] co-sponsored by the
Center for Medieval and Renaissance Studies and the
Department of English." Bibliography: p. 58-65.
Includes index.　ISBN 0-520-03830-4　LC Card
78-65473
1. Anglo-Saxon poetry - History and criticism -
Congresses. 2. Anglo-Saxon language - Style -
Congresses. I. Calder, Daniel Gillmore. II. California.
University. University at Los Angeles. Center for
Medieval and Renaissance Studies. III. California.
University. University at Los Angeles. Dept. of English.
IV. Series.
PR201 .O4　　　　**NYPL [JFE 81-565]**

OLD RED SANDSTONE (GEOLOGY) see
GEOLOGY, STRATIGRAPHIC -
DEVONIAN.

OLD STONE AGE. see PALEOLITHIC
PERIOD.

Old West Regional Commission.
Future development projections and hydrologic
modeling in the Yellowstone River Basin,
Montana /. Helena, MT , 1977. xi, 141 p. :
　　　　LC Card 80-623619　DDC 333.91/009786/3 19
TC424.M9 F87

Hinz, Tom. The effect of altered streamflow on
migratory birds of the Yellowstone River Basin,
Montana /. Helena , 1977. x, 107 p. :　LC Card
78-623506　DDC 598.2/525 19
QL683.Y44 H56

Older Americans Act . United State. Congress.
House. Select Committee on Aging.
Washington, D.C. , 1979. v, 124 p. ;　LC Card
80-603981　DDC 344.73/0326 347.304326 19
KF3737 .A25 1979

Older Americans act of 1965, as amended .
United States. Laws, statutes, etc. Washington,
D.C. [1979] viii, 173 p. ;　LC Card 80-602137
　　　　DDC 344.73/0326/02632 19
KF3737 .A3 1979

The Older woman : continuities and
discontinuities : report of the National Institute
on Aging and the National Institute of Mental
Health Workshop, September 14-16, 1978.
[Bethesda, Md.] : U. S. Dept. of Health,
Education, and Welfare, Public Health Service,
National Institutes of Health ; Washington,
D.C. : for sale by the Supt. of Docs., U. S.
Govt. Print. Off, 1979. 51 p. ; 27 cm. (NIH
publication. no.79-1897)　LC Card 79-604218
1. Aged women - United States - Congresses. I.
National Institute on Aging. II. United States. National
Institute of Mental Health.
HQ1064.U5 O42　　　　**NYPL [JLF 81-395]**

Older workers in small towns . Goudy, Willis J.
Ames, Iowa [1977] viii, 205 p. :　LC Card
80-623924　DDC 331.3/98/09777 19
HD6281.I8 G68

O'Leary, Brian, 1940- Ames Summer Study on
Space Settlements and Industrialization Using
Nonterrestrial Materials, Ames Research
Center, 1977. Space resources and space
settlements . Washington, D.C. , 1979. x, 288

p. :　LC Card 79-603821　DDC 629.44/2 19
TL795.7 .A45 1977

O'Leary, William. Family planning statistics, 1965
to 1973 : Africa, Asia, Latin America / by
William O'Leary, Eugene Vandrovec, and Gary
Lewis. Washington : U. S. Dept. of Commerce,
Social and Economic Statistics Administration,
Bureau of the Census, International Statistical
Programs Center : for sale by the Supt. of
Dcos., U. S. Govt. Print. Off., 1975. 74 p., [1]
fold. leaf of plates ; 28 cm. Includes
bibliographical references.　LC Card 75-600039　DDC
363.9/6/091724 19
1. Underdeveloped areas - Birth control - Statistics. I.
Vandrovec, Eugene, joint author. II. Lewis, Gary, joint
author. III. Title.
HQ766.7 .O43

Olga Fisch collection. Muratorio, Ricardo. A
feast of color, Corpus Christi dance costumes of
Ecuador . Washington, D.C. , 1981. p. cm.
　　　　ISBN 0-86528-008-8　LC Card 80-29379　DDC
793.3/19866 19
GT4995.C6 M87

OLIGOCENE PERIOD. see GEOLOGY,
STRATIGRAPHIC - OLIGOCENE;
PALEONTOLOGY - OLIGOCENE.

Olin, Jacqueline S. Archaeological ceramics .
Washington, D.C. , 1982. p. cm.　LC Card
81-9128　DDC 930.1/028/5 19
CC79.5.P6 A73

OLIVE INDUSTRY AND TRADE - MEXICO.
Emerson, L. P. Bill. Mexico's expanding olive
industry /. [Washington, D.C.] [foreword 1980]
14 p. :　LC Card 80-602696　DDC 338.1 s
338.1/7463/0972 19
S21 .Z2383 no. 294 HD9019.O4M6

OLIVE - MARKETING - LAW AND
LEGISLATION - UNITED STATES.
United States. Congress. House. Committee on
Agriculture. Subcommittee on Domestic
Marketing, Consumer Relations, and Nutrition.
Marketing orders for walnuts and olives and
Freestone Peach Research and Education Act .
Washington , 1980. iii, 74 p. ;　LC Card
80-604106　DDC 343.73/08514/0262
347.30385140262 19
KF27 .A3336 1980b

OLIVE-OIL - LAW AND LEGISLATION.
United Nations Conference on Olive Oil,
Geneva, 1978. United Nations Conference on
Olive Oil, 1978. New York , 1978. iii, 7 p. ;
　　　　LC Card 79-110907　DDC 300 s
341.7/5475664362 19
JX1977 .A2 TD/OLIVE OIL.6/10 K3947.O43

Oliveira, Ronald A. An examination of dynamic
relationships--and the lack thereof--among U. S.
lumber prices, U. S. housing starts, U. S. log
exports to Japan, and Japanese housing starts /
[Ronald A. Oliveira and Gerald W. Whittaker].
Corvallis : Agricultural Experiment Station,
Oregon State University, [1979] 34 p. ; 28 cm.
(Special report - Agricultural Experiment Station,
Oregon State University ; 565) Cover title. "December
1979." Bibliography: p. 24. LC Card 80-621302
　　　　DDC 338.4/7674/00973 19
1. Lumber trade - United States - Mathematical models.
2. Housing - United States - Mathematical models. 3.
Housing - Japan - Mathematical models. I. Whittaker,
Gerald W., joint author. II. Oregon. Agricultural
Experiment Station, Corvallis. III. Series: Oregon.
Agricultural Experiment Station, Corvallis. Special
report, 565. IV. Title.
HD9755 .O44

Olm, Jane. Bibliography on juvenile delinquency
in Texas / prepared for the Task Force of
Juvenile Delinquency by Jane Olm. [Austin] :
University of Texas, School of Law, Criminal
Justice Reference Library, [1970] 34 leaves ; 28
cm. (Tarlton Law Library legal bibliography . no. 3)
Cover title. "November 1970." LC Card 80-622265
DDC 016.345764/08 016.34764058 19
1. Juvenile justice, Administration of - Texas -
Bibliography. 2. Juvenile delinquency - Texas -
Bibliography. I. Texas. Task Force on Juvenile
Delinquency. II. Texas. University at Austin. Criminal
Justice Reference Library. III. Series: Tarlton Law
Library. Tarlton Law Library legal bibliography series ,
no. 3. IV. Title.
KFT1795.A1 O4

Olmsted, F. H. (Franklin Howard), 1921-
Norton, Daniel R. Ground temperature
measurements. Washington , 1980. p. cm.　LC

Card 81-607982   DDC 551.1/4 19
QE509 .N67

Olmsted Park System, Jamaica Pond boathouse, Jamaica Plain, Massachusetts . White, Richard, 1924- Washington, D.C. , 1979. 51 p. :   LC Card 80-601622   DDC 690/.587/0288 19
TH2401 .W47

Olney, Susan Faxon. Two American impressionists : Frank W. Benson and Edmund C. Tarbell / [Susan Faxon Olney] Durham, N.H. : University of New Hampshire, University Art Galleries, c1980. 22 p. : ill. ; 24 x 24 cm. Cover title. Includes catalog of an exhibition held at University Art Galleries, University of New Hampshire, Durham, Mar. 12-Apr. 26, 1979. Includes bibliographical references. LC Card 80-80237   DDC 759.13 19
1. Benson, Frank Weston, 1862-1951 - Exhibitions. 2. Tarbell, Edmund Charles, 1862-1938 - Exhibitions. 3. Impressionism (Art) - Massachusetts - Exhibitions. I. Benson, Frank Weston, 1862-1951. II. Tarbell, Edmund Charles, 1862-1938. III. New Hampshire. University. University Art Galleries. IV. Title.
ND237.B4595 A4 1980

OLOMANA SCHOOL - EVALUATION.
University of Hawaii at Manoa. Social Welfare Development & Research Center. Evaluation & report of progress, 1972-73. [Manoa] [1973] viii, 78, [33] leaves ;   LC Card 80-494222   DDC 365/.42/099693 19
HV9106.K182 H348 1973

Olpere, Daniel P. Pennsylvania. Bureau of Local Government Services. Information Services Division. Catalog of State aids to local governments /. Harrisburg [1976] ca. 300 p. in various pagings :   LC Card 80-622718   DDC 353.97480072/5 19
HJ665 .P33 1976

Olsen, David L., 1933- Whooping Crane Recovery Team. Whooping crane recovery plan, January 1980 /. [Albuquerque, N.M. , 1980] vi, 206 p. :   LC Card 80-602324   DDC 639.9/7831 19
QL696.G84 W48 1980

Olsen, Diana. Florida. State University, Tallahassee. Art Gallery. Precolumbian exhibition, the John and Mary Carter collection of Peruvian precolumbian artifacts and textiles /. [Tallahassee] , c1978. 127 p. :   LC Card 80-116225   DDC 985/.01/074015988 19
F3429.3.A7 F56 1978

Olsgaard, John N. Union list of items received by South Dakota Federal document depositories / compiled by John N. Olsgaard and Marcia A. Jones. Vermillion, S.D. : I. D. Weeks Library, University of South Dakota, c1980. 107 leaves ; 22 x 37 cm.   LC Card 80-623201   DDC 015.73 19
1. United States - Government publications - Bibliography - Union lists. 2. Catalogs, Union - South Dakota. 3. Libraries, Depository - South Dakota. I. Jones, Marcia A., joint author. II. Title.
Z1223.Z7 O55 J83

Weeks (I. D.) Library. Energy, a bibliography and index of related materials at the University of South Dakota /. Vermillion , c1978. 546 p. ;   LC Card 79-621285
Z5853.P83 W4 1978 TJ163.2

NYPL [JLF 80-1563]

OLSON, CHARLES, 1910-1970 - SOCIETIES, PERIODICALS, ETC.
Olson; the journal of the Charles Olson Archives. no. 1- ; spring 1974- [Storrs] LC Card 77-643320   *NYPL [JFL 80-224]*

Olson-Elliott and Associates. Thompson, Larry S. The effects of large-diameter underground crude-oil pipelines on wildlife . Helena, Mont. [1979] vii, 55 p. :   LC Card 80-622216   DDC 333.79/09786 s 333.95/9 19
TJ163.25.U6 M653 1979, no. 2 TD195.P5

Olson, Jerry Chipman, 1917- Alkalic rocks and resources of thorium and associated elements in the Powderhorn District, Gunnison County, Colorado / by Jerry C. Olson and David C. Hedlund. Washington : U. S. Govt. Print. Off., 1980. p. cm. (Geology and resources of thorium in the United States) Geological Survey professional paper ; 1049-C Bibliography: p.   LC Card 80-607811   DDC 552/.1 19
1. Alkalic igneous rocks. 2. Intrusions (Geology) - Colorado - Gunnison Co. 3. Thorium ores - Colorado - Gunnison Co. I. Hedlund, David Carl, 1924- joint

author. II. Series. III. Series: United States. Geological Survey. Professional paper, 1049-C. IV. Title.
QE462.A4 O44

Olson, Kent D. Iowa. State University of Science and Technology, Ames. Center for Agricultural and Rural Development. Estimated impacts of two environmental alternatives in agriculture . Ames , 1977. viii, 112 p. :   LC Card 79-621027
HD1765 1980 .I56 1977

NYPL [JLF 81-142]

Olson, Ruth Anne. Evaluation as interaction in support of change / Ruth Anne Olson ; North Dakota Study Group on Evaluation. Grand Forks, N.D. : University of North Dakota, 1980. 33 p. ; 26 cm. Bibliography: p. 32-33.   LC Card 80-85357   DDC 371.1/44/09784 19
1. Teachers - Rating of - North Dakota - Case studies. I. North Dakota Study Group on Evaluation. II. Title.
LB2838 .O47

Olson, Storrs L.
Fossil vertebrates from the Bahamas . Washington , 1982. p. cm.   LC Card 81-13543   DDC 560 s 566/.097296 19
QE701 .S56 no. 48 QE841

The relationships of the Pedionomidae (Aves, Charadriiformes) / Storrs L. Olson and David W. Steadman. Washington : Smithsonian Institution Press, 1981. p. cm. (Smithsonian contributions to zoology . no. 337) Bibliography: p.   LC Card 81-412   DDC 591 s 598/.33 19
1. Pedionomus torquatus - Classification. 2. Pedionomus torquatus - Anatomy. 3. Birds - Classification. 4. Birds - Anatomy. I. Steadman, David W., joint author. II. Title. III. Title: Pedionomidae (Aves, Charadriiformes). IV. Series. V. Series: Smithsonian Institution. Smithsonian contributions to zoology , no. 337.
QL1 .S54 no. 337 QL696.C465

Olson; the journal of the Charles Olson Archives. no. 1- ; spring 1974- [Storrs, University of Connecticut Library]. illus. 23 cm. Semiannual.   LC Card 77-643320
1. Olson, Charles, 1910-1970 - Societies, periodicals, etc. I. Connecticut. University. Library.

NYPL [JFL 80-224]

Olson, Theodore M. Ground water resources of Five Mile Prairie, Spokane County, Washington / by Theodore M. Olson. Olympia, Wash. : State of Washington, Dept. of Ecology, Water Resources Information System, [1979] iv, 30 p. : ill., maps (3 fold. in pocket) ; 28 cm. (WRIS technical bulletin ; no. 23) "August 1979." Bibliography: p. 21-22.   LC Card 80-621127   DDC 553.7/9/0979737 19
1. Water, Underground - Washington (State) - Spokane Co. I. Series: Water Resources Information System. WRIS technical bulletin , no. 23. II. Title.
GB1025.W2 O47

Olton, Jean S. The Town of Colonie . Colonie, N.Y. , 1980. 190 p. :   LC Card 81-141419   DDC 974.7/42 19
F129.C692 T68

OLYMPIC GAMES, MOSCOW, 1980.
United States. Congress. House. Committee on Banking, Finance and Urban Affairs. Subcommittee on Consumer Affairs. Medals for the 1980 U. S. summer Olympic team . Washington , 1980. iii, 15 p. ;   LC Card 80-602976   DDC 344.73/099 347.30499 19
KF27 .B535 1980e

United States. Congress. House. Committee on Foreign Affairs. U. S. participation in the 1980 summer Olympic games . Washington , 1980. iii, 88 p. ;   LC Card 80-602748   DDC 796.4/8/0947431 19
KF27 .F6 1980d

United States. Congress. House. Committee on Interstate and Foreign Commerce. Subcommittee on Transportation and Commerce. Alternatives to the Moscow Olympics . Washington , 1980. iii, 83 p. ;   LC Card 80-602442   DDC 353.0085/8 19
KF27 .I5589 1980a

United States. Congress. Senate. Committee on Foreign Relations. 1980 summer Olympics boycott . Washington , 1980. iii, 97 p. ;   LC Card 80-602014   DDC 796.4/8/094731 19
KF26 .F6 1980d

Olympus Research Corporation. Education service and work : the multi-funded approach. [Washington] : Federal Interagency Committee on Education, Sub-Committee on Education

and Work ; for sale by the Supt. of Docs., U. S. Govt. Print. Off., 1977. 99 p. ; 23 cm. "Prepared by Olympus Research Corporation (ORC) pursuant to ... contract no. 300-76-0537 from the Office of Education, U. S. Department of Health, Education and Welfare." Bibliography: p. 91-94.   LC Card 78-600742
1. Education, Cooperative - United States - Directories. 2. Vocational rehabilitation - United States - Directories. I. United States. Federal Interagency Committee on Education. Sub-Committee on Education and Work. II. Title.
LB1029.C6 O48 1977   NYPL [JFE 81-723]

O'Malley, Nancy. (joint author) Lynn, Warren M. Cultural resource survey of Choke Canyon Reservoir, Live Oak and McMullen Counties, Texas /. Austin , 1977. xiv, 273 p. :   LC Card 78-622852   DDC 976.4/447 19
F392.F92 L96

O'Malley, Patrick M. (joint author) Johnston, Lloyd. Drugs and the class of '78 . Rockville, Md. , Washington , 1979. xxi, 335 p. :   LC Card 79-604015   DDC 362.2/9 19
HV5824.Y68 J622

OMAN - ADMINISTRATIVE AND POLITICAL DIVISIONS - MAPS.
United States. Central Intelligence Agency. Oman regions. [Washington , 1980] 1 map :   LC Card 81-692531
G7561.F7 1980 .U5

OMAN, GULF OF - CLIMATE - CHARTS, DIAGRAMS, ETC.
United States. Naval Oceanography Command Detachment, Asheville, N.C. Climatic study of the Persian Gulf and Gulf of Oman . [Washington] [1980] viii, 125 p. :   LC Card 80-602634   DDC 551.69165/35 19
QC994.5 .U53 1980

Oman regions. United States. Central Intelligence Agency. [Washington , 1980] 1 map :   LC Card 81-692531
G7561.F7 1980 .U5

Oman tribes. United States. Central Intelligence Agency. [Washington , 1980] 1 map :   LC Card 81-692532
G7561.E1 1980 .U5

OMBUDSMAN - NEW JERSEY - PERIODICALS.
New Jersey. Dept. of the Public Advocate. Annual report. [Trenton, N. J.] LC Card 77-643225   *NYPL [JLM 80-1143]*

Omnibus antiterrorism act of 1979 . United States. Congress. Senate. Committee on Governmental Affairs. Washington , 1979. iv, 448 p. ;   LC Card 80-602011   DDC 345.73/023 19
KF26 .G67 1979am

Omnibus Geothermal Energy Commercialization Act of 1979 . United States. Congress. Senate. Committee on Energy and Natural Resources. Washington , 1980. iii, 69 p. ;   LC Card 80-604105   DDC 346.7304/688 347.3064688 19
KF26 .E55 1980m

Omnibus maritime regulatory reform, revitalization, and reorganization act . United States. Congress. House. Committee on Ways and Means. Washington , 1980. iii, 144 p. :   LC Card 80-602429   DDC 343.73/096 19
KF27 .W3 1980b

Omnibus Maritime Regulatory Reform Revitalization and Reorganization Act of 1980 . United States. Congress. House. Committee on the Judiciary. Subcommittee on Monopolies and Commercial Law. Washington , 1980 [i.e. 1981] iii, 160 p. ;   LC Card 81-601640   DDC 343.73/096 347.30396 19
KF27 .J8663 1980a

OMNIBUS SERVICE. see MOTOR BUS LINES.

Omnibus territorial legislation--1980 . United States. Congress. Senate. Committee on Energy and Natural Resources. Washington , 1980. iv, 679 p. :   LC Card 81-600632   DDC 349.73 347.3 19
KF26 .E55 1980l

The omnipresent debate . Harris, Wendell V. DeKalb , c1981. p. cm.   LC Card 80-8663   DDC 828/.8/08 19
PR778.P55 H3

OMÓLION, GREECE - ANTIQUITIES.
Miller, Stella G. Two groups of Thessalian gold /. Berkeley , c1979. xiii, 78 p., [16] leaves of

plates : ISBN 0-520-09580-4 LC Card 77-80473
DF261.O57 M54   **NYPL** *[L-11 622 v. 188]*

Omólion, Greece - Archaeology. see Omólion, Greece - Antiquities.

On-line image recognition using radial profiles /. Robinson, Colan Michael, 1952- Urbana, Ill. [1980] vii leaves, 104 p. : LC Card 80-623656 DDC 001.6/4 s 621.3819/598 19
QA76 .I4 no. 1023 TA1650

On "Stratification in a dual economy" /. Hauser, Robert Mason. [Madison, Wis.] [1980] 29, [3] p. ; LC Card 80-622908 DDC 339.2/0973 19
HC110.I5 H36

On teaching philosophy / George S. Maccia, guest editor. Bloomington, Ind. : School of Education, Indiana University, 1980. v. 93 p. ; 23 cm. (Viewpoints in teaching and learning, 0160-8398 . v. 56, no. 4) Includes bibliographies. CONTENTS. - Can moral education be divorced from philosophical inquiry? / Matthew Lipman and Ann Margaret Sharp -- The teaching of philosophy in social studies / James P. Shaver -- Philosophy and the high school curriculum / Grant Wiggins -- Teaching philosophy in a two-year college / James F. Perry -- Teaching moral criticism in the sciences / Elizabeth Steiner and Ruth Hitchcock -- Forum / Christine I. Bennett -- Media exchange / Gary J. Anglin -- Legislation / David H. Florio. LC Card 81-620733 DDC 371.1/02 19
1. Teaching - Addresses, essays, lectures. I. Maccia, George S. II. Series.
LB41 .O576

On the complexity of inferring join dependencies /. Maier, David, 1953- Urbana, Ill. [1979] 23 p. ; LC Card 80-622080 DDC 001.64 s 001.64/2 19
QA76 .I4 no. 985 QA76.9.D3

On the linkage of solar ultraviolet radiation to skin cancer . Cutchis, Pythagoras. Washington, D.C. , 1978. xiv, 146, [13] p. : LC Card 79-602135 DDC 616.99/477071 19
RC280.S5 C83

ONE-ACT PLAYS - PROMPTBOOKS AND TYPESCRIPTS. see DRAMA - PROMPTBOOKS AND TYPESCRIPTS, ONE-ACT.

One Hundred and Twelve Workshop, 112 Greene Street, 1970-1978. 112 Workshop, 112 Greene Street, 1970-1978 . New York , 1981. p. cm. ISBN 0-8147-1037-9 : LC Card 78-71391 DDC 700/.6/07471 19
NX511.N4 A16

$1,050,000 into the pockets of the American tobacco trust. Cannon, Joseph Gurney, 1836-1926. [Washington? D. C. , 1900] 16 p. ;
NYPL *[Arents S 1607]*

One Twelve Workshop, 112 Greene Street, 1970-1978. 112 Workshop, 112 Greene Street, 1970-1978 . New York , 1981. p. cm. ISBN 0-8147-1037-9 : LC Card 78-71391 DDC 700/.6/07471 19
NX511.N4 A16

O'Neal, Dave. Illinois. Governor's Jail and Detention Standards Review Committee. Report of the Governor's Jail and Detention Standards Review Committee /. [Springfield, Ill.] [1979] ca. 200 p. in various pagings ; LC Card 80-623376 DDC 353.97730084/95 19
HV8332 .I32 1979

O'Neil, Eileen. (joint author) Bolton, Christopher R. The determination of gerontology education appropriate to aging related occupational roles . [Lincoln] , 1978. 115 leaves ; LC Card 79-621870 DDC 362.6/07/11 19
HV1451 .B64

O'Neill, Eugene Gladstone, 1888-1953. Complete scripts of Eugene O'Neill's one-act plays of the sea / directed by William Challee; sets and costumes by Perry Watkins. New York: Lafayette Theatre, 1937. 1 v. (various pagings): ill.; 29 cm. Typescript. Includes cast list and mounted photographs. Produced at the Lafayette Theatre, N. Y. C., on Oct. 29, 1937, as a Federal Theatre Project. CONTENTS. - Moon of the Caribbees. - In the zone. - Bound east for Cardiff. - The long voyage home.
1. American drama. 2. Drama - Promptbooks and typescripts, One-act. I. Federal Theatre Project. II. Title.   **NYPL** *[NCOF+ 79-920]*

O'Neill, Gerard K. Ames Summer Study on Space Settlements and Industrialization Using

Nonterrestrial Materials, Ames Research Center, 1977. Space resources and space settlements . Washington, D.C. , 1979. x, 288 p. : LC Card 79-603821 DDC 629.44/2 19
TL795.7 .A45 1977

Ong, Paul M. Asians in Washington : a statistical profile / prepared by Paul M. Ong, Joanne T. Fujita, Sam Chin with assistance from Kai Fujita. Olympia : Washington State Commission on Asian American Affairs, 1976. vii. 69 p. : ill. ; 28 cm. Microfilm (neg.) NTIS. 1 sheet. 11 x 15 cm. (PB-268748) Bibliography: p. 68-69. LC Card 77-621579
1. Asian Americans - Washington (State) - Statistics. 2. Washington (State) - Population - Statistics. I. Fujita, Joanne T., joint author. II. Chin, Sam, joint author. III. Washington (State). Commission on Asian American Affairs. IV. Title.
F900.O6 O53   **NYPL** *[*XME-9406]*

Online literature searching and databases. Environmental Research Center, Cincinnati. Library. Cincinnati.   **NYPL** *[JFM 80-262]*

Onshore oil & gas seeps in California /. Hodgson, Susan F. Sacramento , 1980. iv, 97 p. : LC Card 80-623064 DDC 553.2/8/09794 19
TN872.C2 H57

Onshore support bases for OCS oil and gas development . Rutgers University, New Brunswick, N.J. Center for Coastal and Environmental Studies. New Brunswick, N.J. [1977] xvi, 234 p. : LC Card 80-622533 DDC 338.2/7282/09749 19
TN872.N5 R87 1977

Onslow Bay physical/dynamical experiments, summer-fall, 1975 : data report / by L.J. Pietrafesa ... [et al.]. [Raleigh : Sea Grant Program, North Carolina State University], 1978. xxiv, 170 p. : ill. ; 28 cm. (UNC sea grant publication . UNC-SG-77-07) Report - Center for Marine and Coastal Studies ; no. 78-04 Bibliography: p. 169-170. LC Card 78-623321 DDC 551.46/148 19
1. Oceanography - North Carolina - Onslow Bay. I. Pietrafesa, Leonard J. II. North Carolina. State University, Raleigh. Sea Grant Program. III. Series: Sea grant publication (Raleigh) , UNC-SG-77-07.
GC512.N8 O56

ONTARIO COUNTY, N. Y. - ADMINISTRATIVE AND POLITICAL DIVISIONS - MAPS. Kemmer, Paul. Highway map of Ontario County, New York /. Canandaigua, N. Y., 1978. col. map 41 x 44 cm. Scale ca. 1:135,000 At head of title: William Sage, County Supt. of Hwys. Revised by Anthony Priano, 1977. Shows township and municipal boundaries. Includes location map within Rochester - Genesee Regional Transportation District. On verso: list of town and state highways and county roads.   **NYPL** *[Map Div. 80-3340]*

Ontario County, N. Y. Highway Dept. Kemmer, Paul. Highway map of Ontario County, New York /. Canandaigua, N. Y., 1978. col. map 41 x 44 cm. Scale ca. 1:135,000 At head of title: William Sage, County Supt. of Hwys. Revised by Anthony Priano, 1977. Shows township and municipal boundaries. Includes location map within Rochester - Genesee Regional Transportation District. On verso: list of town and state highways and county roads.   **NYPL** *[Map Div. 80-3340]*

ONTARIO COUNTY, N. Y. - MAPS. (1978) Kemmer, Paul. Highway map of Ontario County, New York /. Canandaigua, N. Y., 1978. col. map 41 x 44 cm. Scale ca. 1:135,000 At head of title: William Sage, County Supt. of Hwys. Revised by Anthony Priano, 1977. Shows township and municipal boundaries. Includes location map within Rochester - Genesee Regional Transportation District. On verso: list of town and state highways and county roads.   **NYPL** *[Map Div. 80-3340]*

ONTARIO COUNTY, N. Y - ROAD MAPS. Kemmer, Paul. Highway map of Ontario County, New York /. Canandaigua, N. Y., 1978. col. map 41 x 44 cm. Scale ca. 1:135,000 At head of title: William Sage, County Supt. of Hwys. Revised by Anthony Priano, 1977. Shows township and municipal boundaries. Includes location map within Rochester - Genesee Regional Transportation District. On verso: list of town and state highways and county roads.   **NYPL** *[Map Div. 80-3340]*

ONTARIO, LAKE. Lake Ontario atlas. Albany, N.Y. , 197<6. v. <2-3, 5-7> : LC Card 80-119579 DDC

551.48/2/097479 19
GB1627.G81 L34

ONTOLOGY. Kaminsky, Jack, 1922- Essays in linguistic ontology /. Carbondale , c1982. p. cm. ISBN 0-8093-1044-9 LC Card 81-14411 DDC 111 19
B808.5 .K35

OPEC. see Organization of Petroleum Exporting Countries.

OPEN-CAST MINING. see STRIP MINING.

OPEN-CUT MINING. see STRIP MINING.

Open file reference report . (79-1) Alaska. Division of Forest, Land, and Water Management. Water Management Section. Federal lands in Alaska and their reserved water rights . Anchorage, Alaska [1979] 222 leaves in various foliations : LC Card 80-622413 DDC 346.79804/691 347.98064691 19
KFA1646 .A844

OPEN-PIT MINING. see STRIP MINING.

Open space policy . Foresta, Ronald A., 1944- New Brunswick, N.J. , c1981. p. cm. ISBN 0-8135-0923-8 : LC Card 81-2513 DDC 333.78/4 19
HT393.N5 F67

Open space preservation . Daugherty, Arthur Berry, 1936- Washington , Springfield, Va. , 1978. v, 32 p. ; LC Card 79-601799 DDC 338.1/0973 s 336.24/216 19
HD1759 .U56a no. 32 HJ4653.C73

OPEN SPACES - NEW JERSEY. Foresta, Ronald A., 1944- Open space policy . New Brunswick, N.J. , c1981. p. cm. ISBN 0-8135-0923-8 : LC Card 81-2513 DDC 333.78/4 19
HT393.N5 F67

OPEN SPACES - UNITED STATES. Daugherty, Arthur Berry, 1936- Open space preservation . Washington , Springfield, Va. , 1978. v, 32 p. ; LC Card 79-601799 DDC 338.1/0973 s 336.24/216 19
HD1759 .U56a no. 32 HJ4653.C73

United States. Heritage Conservation and Recreation Service. National urban recreation study . [Washington , 1978] 184 p. : LC Card 78-602420
GV53 .U54 1978

OPEN SPACES - VIRGINIA. Bertelsen, Michael K. Landowner supply-response behavior and the land conversion process in the rural urban fringe /. Blacksburg [1980] vi, 69 p. : LC Card 80-623705 DDC 081 s 333.76/13/09755 19
AS36 .V512 no. 155 HD211.V8

OPERATING STATEMENTS. see FINANCIAL STATEMENTS.

Operation and effects of the generalized system of preferences . United Nations. Conference on Trade and Development. New York , 1979. vi, 146 p. ; LC Card 80-121468 DDC 300 s 382.7/53 19
JX1977 .A2 TD/B/C.5/61

Operation of the generalized system of preferences . United States. Congress. House. Committee on Ways and Means. Subcommittee on Trade. Washington , 1980. iii, 111 p. ; LC Card 80-603343 DDC 353.0082/7 19
KF27 .W348 1980c

Operation of the International Tin Agreement /. Witzig, Thomas J. [Avondale, Md.] , 1981. p. cm. LC Card 81-607844 DDC 622 s 338.2/7453 19
TN295 .U4 HD9539.T5

Operation of the U. S. Employment Service . United States. Congress. House. Committee on Government Operations. Manpower and Housing Subcommittee. Washington , 1976. iv, 359 p. : LC Card 76-603085
KF27 .G6678 1976b

Operation of wastewater treatment plants : a field study training program / prepared by California State University, Sacramento (formerly Sacramento State College), Department of Civil Engineering, in cooperation with the California Water Pollution Control Association, for the Environmental Protection Agency, Office of Water Program Operations,

Municipal Permits and Operations Division.2nd ed. Sacramento : The University, <1980- > v. <3 > : ill. ; 28 cm. Includes bibliographical references and index. LC Card 81-114782 DDC 628.3 19

1. Sewage disposal plants. I. California State University, Sacramento. Dept. of Civil Engineering. II. California Water Pollution Control Association. III. United States. Environmental Protection Agency. Office of Water Program Operations. Municipal Permits and Operations Division.
TD746 .O64 1980

Operation Ranch Hand . Buckingham, William A. Washington, D.C. , 1981. p. cm. LC Card 81-11244 DDC 959.704/348 19
DS559.8.C5 B82

OPERATIONAL ANALYSIS. see OPERATIONS RESEARCH.

Operational and support costs of the Navy's F/A-18 can be substantially reduced . United States. General Accounting Office. Washington, D.C. [1980] iii, 58 p., [1] leaf of plates : LC Card 80-602400 DDC 358.4/183 19
VG93 .U54 1980

Operational applications of satellite snowcover observations . Workshop on Operational Applications of Satellite Snowcover Observations, Sparks, Nev., 1979. Washington, D.C. , 1980. vi, 301 p. : LC Card 80-602361 DDC 551.57/846 19
GB2601.72.A83 W67 1979

Operational civil remote sensing systems . United States. Congress. House. Committee on Science and Technology. Subcommittee on Space Science and Applications. Washington , 1980. iii, 315 p. : LC Card 80-603708 DDC 338.4/76213678 19
KF27 .S3995 1980a

Operational guide to white-collar crime enforcement.
Becker, Jay. The investigation of computer crime /. Washington, D.C. [1980] ii, 73 p. ; LC Card 80-602307 DDC 363.2/5 19
HV8079.W47 B4 1980

OPERATIONAL RESEARCH. see OPERATIONS RESEARCH.

Operational review--management and use of consultants by the state agencies. Virginia. General Assembly. Joint Legislative Audit & Review Commission. Management and use of consultants by state agencies /. [Richmond, Va.] , 1980. iv, 73 p. : LC Card 80-623858 DDC 353.975507/22 19
JK3949.C7 V54 1980

OPERATIONS RESEARCH.
(1980) United States. General Accounting Office. Models, data, and war . [Washington, D.C.] , 1980. v, 153 p. : LC Card 80-601429 DDC 355/.0335/73072 19
UA23 .U475 1980

(1981) Beyer, Jan E. Aquatic ecosystems . Seattle, c1981. ix, 315 p. : ISBN 0-295-95719-0 : LC Card 79-57217 DDC 574.5/263/0724 19
QH541.5.W3 B48 1981

OPERATIONS, SURGICAL - CLASSIFICATION.
The International classification of diseases, 9th revision, clinical modification . [Washington, D.C.?] , 1980. 3 v. ; LC Card 81-601048 DDC 616/.0012 19
RB115 .I49 1980

OPIATES. see NARCOTICS.

OPIC services for U. S. investors in China . United States. Congress. House. Committee on Foreign Affairs. Washington , 1981. iii, 68 p. ; LC Card 81-600814 DDC 332.6/7373/051 19
KF27 .F6 1980o

OPILIONES - CLASSIFICATION.
Shear, William A. A review of the Cyphophthalmi of the United States and Mexico, with a proposed reclassification of the suborder (Arachnida, Opiliones) /. New York, N.Y. , 1980. 34 p. : LC Card 80-147274 DDC 591 s 595.4/3 19
QL1 .A436 no. 2705 QL458.4

Opinion Research Corporation, Princeton, N. J. Kirschner Associates. Longitudinal evaluation of the National Nutrition Program for the Elderly . [Washington, D.C.] [1980] xiv, 333

p. : LC Card 80-601632 DDC 362.6/3 19
HV696.F6 K57 1980

Opinions of the Attorney General and report to the Governor of Virginia. Virginia. Attorney General's Office. Richmond. **NYPL [XMZ (Virginia. Law Dept. Annual report)]**

Opinions of the Maryland State Board of Education, June 1964 through January 1978. Maryland. State Board of Education. Baltimore, Md. , 1979. vii, 801 p. ; LC Card 80-621495 DDC 344.752/07/02642 19
KFM1590.A56 E35

Opler, Paul A. The leafmining moths of the genus Cameraria associated with Fagaceae in California (Lepidoptera, Gracillariidae) / Paul A. Opler and Donald R. Davis. Washington : Smithsonian Institution Press, 1981. p. cm. (Smithsonian contributions to zoology ; no. 333) Bibliography: p. LC Card 80-26743 DDC 591 s 595.78/1 19

1. Cameraria - Classification. 2. Cameraria - Host plants. 3. Fagaceae - Diseases and pests. 4. Insects - Classification. 5. Insects - California - Classification. I. Davis, Donald Ray, joint author. II. Series: Smithsonian Institution. Smithsonian contributions to zoology , no. 333. III. Title.
QL1 .S54 no. 333 QL561.G7

Oppenheimer, Kenneth R. Stanford Research Institute. SRI International. Cost effectiveness of marine fire protection programs . [Washington] , 1978. xvii, 212 p. : LC Card 79-602278
VK1258 .S18 1979   **NYPL [JLF 81-262]**

Opportunities in Illinois State government . Jones, John Herbert. [Springfield] [1979] viii, 34 p. ; LC Card 80-621144 DDC 300/.9773 s 353.977309/3/025 19
JK5774 .A3 no. 150 JK5749.C7

Opportunities in State government. Jones, John Herbert. Opportunities in Illinois State government . [Springfield] [1979] viii, 34 p. ; LC Card 80-621144 DDC 300/.9773 s 353.977309/3/025 19
JK5774 .A3 no. 150 JK5749.C7

OPTICAL MASERS. see LASERS.

OPTICAL MATERIALS - CONGRESSES.
Topical Conference on Basic Optical Properties of Materials, Gaithersburg, Md., 1980. Basic optical properties of materials . Washington, D.C. [1980] x, 241 p. : LC Card 80-600038 DDC 602/.18 s 620.1/1295 19
QC100 .U57 no. 574 QC374

OPTICAL PATTERN RECOGNITION.
(1980) Robinson, Colan Michael, 1952- On-line image recognition using radial profiles /. Urbana, Ill. [1980] vii leaves, 104 p. : LC Card 80-623656 DDC 001.6/4 s 621.3819/598 19
QA76 .I4 no. 1023 TA1650

Optical Society of America. Topical Conference on Basic Optical Properties of Materials, Gaithersburg, Md., 1980. Basic optical properties of materials . Washington, D.C. [1980] x, 241 p. : LC Card 80-600038 DDC 602/.18 s 620.1/1295 19
QC100 .U57 no. 574 QC374

Optical spectra of nonmetallic inorganic transient species in aqueous solution /. Hug, Gordon L. Washington [1981] vi, 159 p. : LC Card 80-606826 DDC 602/.18 s 543/.0858 19
QC100 .U573 no. 69 QC454.A2

OPTICAL TRADE - LAW AND LEGISLATION - UNITED STATES - STATES.
State restrictions on vision care providers . [Washington, D.C.?] , 1980. xix, 289 p. ; LC Card 81-600519 DDC 343.73/078681411 347.30378681411 19
KF2036.E93 Z957

OPTICS, FIBER. see FIBER OPTICS.

The optimal number of response alternatives for a scale . Cox, Eli Peace. Austin, Tex. [1980] 43, [8] p. ; LC Card 80-624133 DDC 300/.1/5195 19
H61 .C68

Optimal risk-based design of hydraulic structures . Tung, Yeou-Koung. Austin, Tex. [1980] xix, 396 p. : LC Card 80-624307 DDC 627 19
TC153 .T86

Optimal risk-based design of water resource engineering projects. Tung, Yeou-Koung. Optimal risk-based design of hydraulic structures . Austin, Tex. [1980] xix, 396 p. : LC Card 80-624307 DDC 627 19
TC153 .T86

OPTIMIZATION (MATHEMATICS) see MATHEMATICAL OPTIMIZATION.

OPTIMIZATION TECHNIQUES. see MATHEMATICAL OPTIMIZATION.

OPTIMIZATION THEORY. see MATHEMATICAL OPTIMIZATION.

The optional double weighting of the sales factor in the corporation business tax allocation formula . New Jersey. Division of Taxation. Research and Statistics Section. [Trenton] [1978] 2, 15, [14] p. ; LC Card 79-623338 DDC 353.97490072/44 19
HJ4655.N34 N48 1978

Options in public education . Chicago. Dept. of Program Development/Alternative Schools. Chicago, Ill. , c1979. xv, 175 p. : LC Card 80-122328 DDC 371/.01025/77311 19
L903.I3 C48 1979

OPTOMETRISTS - ARKANSAS - STATISTICS - PERIODICALS.
Arkansas health manpower statistics: optometrists. 1978- Little Rock.
NYPL [JLM 80-1087]

OPTOMETRISTS - MICHIGAN - STATISTICS.
Michigan. Cooperative Health Information System. Licensed health occupations . Lansing , 1979. 36 p. (p. 36 blank) : LC Card 79-624666 DDC 331.12/916177509774 19
RE943.M5 M5 1979

OPTOMETRISTS - MISSOURI - SUPPLY AND DEMAND.
Hurley, Patrick. Missouri health manpower analyses . [Jefferson City] , 1977. x, 120 p. : LC Card 77-624251 DDC 331.12/3161775/09778 19
RE943.M53 H87

OPTOMETRISTS - MISSOURI - SUPPLY AND DEMAND - STATISTICS.
Hurley, Patrick. Missouri health manpower analyses . [Jefferson City] , 1977. x, 120 p. : LC Card 77-624251 DDC 331.12/3161775/09778 19
RE943.M53 H87

OPTOMETRISTS - UNITED STATES - SUPPLY AND DEMAND.
United States. Health Resources Administration. Bureau of Health Manpower. Supply of optometrists in the United States . [Bethesda? Md.] , 1978. iii, 23 p. ; LC Card 79-603959 DDC 331.12/916177/00973 19
RE959 .U54 1978

OPTOMETRISTS - UNITED STATES - SUPPLY AND DEMAND - STATISTICS.
United States. Health Resources Administration. Bureau of Health Manpower. Supply of optometrists in the United States . [Bethesda? Md.] , 1978. iii, 23 p. ; LC Card 79-603959 DDC 331.12/916177/00973 19
RE959 .U54 1978

OPTOMETRY - ECONOMIC ASPECTS - UNITED STATES.
United States. Federal Trade Commission. Bureau of Economics. Economic report [on] effects of restrictions on advertising and commercial practice in the professions . Washington, D.C. [1980] viii, 120 p. : LC Card 80-602861 DDC 338.4/761775/0973 19
RE959.3 .U53 1980

OPTOMETRY - STUDY AND TEACHING - THE WEST.
Welsh, Wayne. A performance audit of the WICHE student exchange program . [Salt Lake City] , 1978. iii, 45 leaves ; LC Card 78-622932 DDC 370.19/62 19
R847.6.U8 W44

OPTOMETRY - UNITED STATES - PRACTICE.
United States. Federal Trade Commission. Bureau of Economics. Economic report [on] effects of restrictions on advertising and commercial practice in the professions . Washington, D.C. [1980] viii, 120 p. : LC

Card 80-602861   DDC 338.4/761775/0973 19
RE959.3 .U53 1980

Opyrchal, Anthony M. Economic significance of the Florida phosphate industry : an input-output (I-O) analysis / by Anthony M. Opyrchal and Kung-Lee Wang. [Washington, D.C.] : U. S. Dept. of the Interior, Bureau of Mines, [1981] p. cm. (Information circular / Bureau of Mines) Bibliography: p.   LC Card 80-606892   DDC 622 s 338.2/764 19
1. Phosphate industry - Florida. I. Wang, Kung-Lee, joint author. II. Series: United States. Bureau of Mines. Information circular . III. Title.
TN295 .U4 HD9484.P5U5

ORAL HABITS - CONGRESSES.
Oral motor behavior . [Bethesda, Md.] , 1979. vi, 261 p. :   LC Card 79-604290   DDC 617/.522 19
RK480 .O7

ORAL HISTORY.
First person America /. New York , 1980. xxv, 287 p. :   ISBN 0-394-41397-0 :   LC Card 80-7660
E169 .56   NYPL [ILH 81-601]

ORAL HISTORY - BIBLIOGRAPHY - CATALOGS.
California. University. Regional Oral History Office. Catalogue of the Regional Oral History Office, 1954-1979 /. Berkeley , 1980. xiii, 119 p., [4] leaves of plates :   ISBN 0-9604164-0-4 (pbk.) :   LC Card 80-65525   DDC 016.9794 19
Z1261 .C117 1980 F861

Oral motor behavior : impact on oral conditions and dental treatment : workshop proceedings, May 16-17, 1979 / co-sponsored by National Institute of Dental Research ... [et al.] ; edited by Patricia Bryant, Elliot Gale, John Rugh. [Bethesda, Md.] : U. S. Dept. of Health, Education, and Welfare, Public Health Service, National Institutes of Health, 1979. vi, 261 p. : ill. ; 27 cm. (NIH publication ; no. 79-1845) "August 1979." Includes bibliographies.   LC Card 79-604290   DDC 617/.522 19
1. Mastication disorders - Congresses. 2. Oral habits - Congresses. 3. Malocclusion - Etiology - Congresses. 4. Jaws - Muscles - Congresses. 5. Dentures - Congresses. I. Bryant, Patricia. II. Gale, Elliot V., 1938-. III. Rugh, John. IV. United States. National Institute of Dental Research. V. Series: United States. National Institutes of Health. Publication, no. 79-1845.
RK480 .O7

ORANGE COUNTY (VT.) - MAPS.
United States. Soil Conservation Service. Orange County, Vermont /. Lanham, MD , 1979. 1 map :   LC Card 81-690025
G3753.O6 1977 .U5

ORANGE JUICE INDUSTRY - BRAZIL.
Wilson, John Harvard, 1953- Brazil's orange juice industry /. [Washington, D.C.] , 1980. ii, 17 p. :   LC Card 80-602547   DDC 338.1 s 338.4/766363 19
S21 .Z2383 no. 295 HD9348.5.O723B6

Orbach, Michael K. United States fisheries systems and social science : a bibliography of work and directory researchers / editors, Michael K. Orbach, Valerie R. Harper. Washington, D.C. : U. S. Dept. of Commerce, National Oceanic and Atmospheric Administration, National Marine Fisheries Service : for sale by the Supt. of Docs., U. S. Govt. Print. Off., 1979. v, 162 p. : map ; 28 cm. Bibliography: p. 147-153.   LC Card 80-601229   DDC 016.3383/714/0973 19
1. Fishermen - Socio-economic status - United States - Bibliography. 2. Fisheries - Social aspects - United States - Bibliography. 3. Fisheries - Economic aspects - United States - Bibliography. 4. Fishing villages - United States - Bibliography. 5. Fisheries - Social aspects - Research - United States - Directories. 6. Fisheries - Economic aspects - Research - United States - Directories. I. Harper, Valerie R., joint author. II. Title.
Z5974.U5 O72 HD8039.F66

ORBITING ASTRONOMICAL OBSERVATORIES - CONGRESSES.
Scientific research with the space telescope . [Huntsville, Ala.] , Washington, D.C. [1979] xii, 327 p. :   LC Card 80-601618   DDC 520 19
QB61 .S33

ORBITING VEHICLES. see SPACE STATIONS.

ORCHID CULTURE.
(1981) Rentoul, J. N., 1909- Growing orchids .

Seattle [1981] c1980. p. cm.   ISBN 0-295-95839-1   LC Card 81-3023   DDC 635.9/3415 19
SB409 .R4 1981

Orden, David.
Cooperative extension small-farm programs in the South : an inventory and evaluation / David Orden, Steven T. Buccola, Patricia Klobus Edwards. Blacksburg : Virginia Polytechnic Institute and State University, [1980] xii, 86 p. : ill. ; 28 cm. (Bulletin - Research Division, Virginia Polytechnic Institute and State University . 153) Bibliography: p. 77-79.   LC Card 80-622494   DDC 081 s 341/.683/0975 19
1. Farms, Small - Government policy - Southern States. 2. Agricultural extension work - Government policy - Southern States. I. Buccola, Steven T., joint author. II. Edwards, Patricia Klobus, joint author. III. Series: Virginia Polytechnic Institute and State University. Research Division. Bulletin , 153. IV. Title.
AS36 .V512 no. 153 HD1476.U5

Small farm programs : implications from a study in Virginia / by David Orden and Dennis K. Smith. Blacksburg : Virginia Polytechnic Institute and State University, 1978. xvi, 200 p. : graphs ; 26 cm. (Research Division bulletin ; 135) Bibliography: p. 191-194.   LC Card 79-623060   DDC 081 s 338.1/8755 19
1. Farms, Small - United States. 2. Agriculture and state - United States. 3. Farms, Small - Virginia. I. Smith, Dennis K., joint author. II. Series: Virginia Polytechnic Institute and State University. Research Division. Bulletin , 135. III. Title.
AS36 .V512 no. 135 HD1476.U5

Order without government . Thomas, David John, 1945- Urbana , c1981. p. cm.   ISBN 0-252-00888-X   LC Card 81-1818   DDC 980/.004/98 19
F2380.1.A7 T48

ORDNANCE, NAVAL - TESTING.
Young, George Anthony, 1919- Effects of the explosion of 45 tons of TNT under water at a depth scaled to test Baker /. White Oak, Md. , 1954. ix, 154 p. :   LC Card 80-514235   DDC 662/.27 19
VF540 .Y68

ORDOVICIAN FORMATION. see GEOLOGY, STRATIGRAPHIC - ORDOVICIAN; PALEONTOLOGY - ORDOVICIAN.

ORE CARRIERS - COST OF OPERATION.
Andrews, Benjamin V. Relative costs of U. S. and foreign nodule transport ships /. Rockville, Md. , 1978. vi, 70 p. :   LC Card 78-602299
HE746 .A75

ORE-DRESSING.
Dahlin, D. C. (David Clifford), 1951- Beneficiation of potential platinum resources from southeastern Alaska /. Washington, D.C. [1981] p. cm.   LC Card 81-607026   DDC 622 s 622/.3424 19
TN23 .U43 TN538.P53

Peterson, R. E. (Roy Ernest), 1926- Benefication of a hemaititic taconite by reduction roasting, magnetic separation, and flotation /. Washington [1981] p. cm.   LC Card 81-3883   DDC 622 s 622/.341 19
TN23 .U43 TN538.I7

Peterson, R. E. (Roy Ernest), 1926- Reduction roasting and beneficiation of a hematitic-geothitic taconite /. [Washington, D.C.] [1981] p. cm.   LC Card 80-606877   DDC 622 s 669/.141 19
TN23 .U43 TN538.I7

Salisbury, H. B. Beneficiation of low-grade California chromite ores /. [Avondale, Md.] , 1981. p. cm.   LC Card 81-607307   DDC 622 s 622/.34643 19
TN23 .U43 TN538.C57

ORE TREATMENT. see ORE-DRESSING.

Oregon.
[Laws, etc]
Criminal code of Oregon and selected laws relating to juvenile court proceedings, alcoholic liquors, and controlled substances. Salem, Or. : Legislative Counsel Committee, 1980. 375 p. ; 22 cm. "Text reprinted from Oregon revised statutes." Includes index.   LC Card 81-145570   DDC 345.795/002632 347.9505002632 19
1. Criminal law - Oregon. 2. Criminal procedure - Oregon. 3. Juvenile courts - Oregon. I. Oregon.

Legislative Assembly. Legislative Counsel Committee. II. Title.
KFO2961 .A3 1980

Oregon, a statistical profile. Oregon. Dept. of Economic Development. Research and Agency Liaison Division. Portland , 1978. vi, 49, [3] p. :   LC Card 79-623551
HC107.O7 O48 1978   NYPL [JLF 80-1437]

Oregon. Accountancy, State Board of. see Oregon. State Board of Accountancy.

OREGON - ADMINISTRATIVE AND POLITICAL DIVISIONS.
Mattis, James. Boundary determination procedures for Oregon local governments. [Eugene] , 1979-1980. 2 v. :   LC Card 80-623933   DDC 349.795 s 342.795/09 349.795 s 347.95029 19
KFO2831.A7 L34 no. 16 KFO2830

Oregon. University. Bureau of Governmental Research and Service. Local government boundary commissions . [Eugene] , 1978. iii, 112 p. :   LC Card 78-622792
JS451 .O7 1978a   NYPL [JLF 80-1445]

Oregon administrative rules /. Oregon. Dept. of Education. Salem, Or. [1979- 1 v. :   LC Card 80-621418   DDC 371.2/009795 19
LB2809.O7 O73 1979

Oregon. Agricultural Experiment Station, Corvallis.
Oliveira, Ronald A. An examination of dynamic relationships--and the lack thereof--among U. S. lumber prices, U. S. housing starts, U. S. log exports to Japan, and Japanese housing starts /. Corvallis [1979] 34 p. ;   LC Card 80-621302   DDC 338.4/7674/00973 19
HD9755 .O44

Special report.
(565) Oliveira, Ronald A. An examination of dynamic relationships--and the lack thereof--among U. S. lumber prices, U. S. housing starts, U. S. log exports to Japan, and Japanese housing starts /. Corvallis [1979] 34 p. ;   LC Card 80-621302   DDC 338.4/7674/00973 19
HD9755 .O44

(572) Moe, Debra K. Wheat acreage response to changes in prices and government programs in Oregon and Washington /. Corvallis , 1980. 55 p. :   LC Card 80-622276   DDC 338.1/7311/09795 19
HD9049.W5 U4456

Station circular .
(675) Conklin, Frank S. An evaluation of expected private losses from selected public policies for reducing open field burning, Willamette Valley, Oregon /. Corvallis [1979] 78 p. ;   LC Card 80-620510   DDC 363.7/392 19
TD884 .C74

OREGON - ANTIQUITIES - ADDRESSES, ESSAYS, LECTURES.
Aikens, C. Melvin. Obsidian hydration dates for Klamath prehistory /. [Pocatello] , 1978. 17 p. :   LC Card 78-623053   DDC 500 s 979.5/2 19
E78.I18 T43 no. 11 E99.K7

Oregon Arts Commission. Folk art of the Oregon country /. [Salem?] , c1980. 128 p. :   LC Card 80-622779   DDC 745/.09795/074013 19
NK805.O7 F64

Oregon. Board of Higher Education, State. see Oregon. State Board of Higher Education.

Oregon. Board of Police Standards and Training.
Policies and procedures manual / State of Oregon, Board on Police Standards and Training. [1979 revision]. [Salem, Or.] : The Board, [1979]- 1 v. : ill. ; 28 cm. Cover title. Loose-leaf for updating.   LC Card 80-623340   DDC 363.2/09795 19
1. Police - Standards - Oregon - Collected works. 2. Police training - Oregon - Collected works. I. Title.
HV7571.O7 B6 1979

Oregon. Bureau of Labor. (Old Catalog form: Oregon. Labor Bureau.)
Divorced women in Portland : a report on an inquiry / Oregon Bureau of Labor. [Salem] : The Bureau, 1978. 83 p. : ill. ; 28 cm. Errata slip inserted. Includes bibliographical references.   LC Card 79-623549   DDC 305.4/8 19
1. Divorcees - Oregon - Portland - Economic

BIBLIOGRAPHIC GUIDE

Oregon. Bureau of Labor and Industries. Technical Assistance

96

conditions. I. Title.
HQ836.P8 O73 1978

**Oregon. Bureau of Labor and Industries.
Technical Assistance Unit.** A handbook of
Oregon wage and hour laws. [Salem, Or.] :
Oregon Bureau of Labor and Industries,
Technical Assistance Unit, 1980. iv, 41 p. ; 22
cm. Cover title. Includes index. LC Card 80-623410
  DDC 344.795/0121 347.9504121 19
1. Wages - Oregon. 2. Hours of labor - Oregon. I. Title.
KFO2734 .A853

Oregon community profiles /. Oregon. Dept. of
Economic Development. [Portland, Or.]
[1978?- <75 > pamphlet ; LC Card 78-623103
  DDC 979.5 19
HN79.O7 O73 1978

Oregon. Dept. of Economic Development.
[Oregon community profiles / prepared by the
Department of Economic Development, State
of Oregon. Portland, Or.] : The Dept., [1978?-
<75 > pamphlet ; 28 cm. Each pamphlet devoted
to a separate city of Oregon. LC Card 78-623103
  DDC 979.5 19
1. Social surveys - Oregon. I. Title.
HN79.O7 O73 1978

The Oregon economy . Salem, Or. (155 Cottage
St. N.E., Salem) [1980?] 16 p. ; LC Card
  80-623280 DDC 330.9795/043 19
HC107.O7 O625

**Oregon. Dept. of Economic Development.
Research and Agency Liaison Division.**
Oregon, a statistical profile. Portland : State of
Oregon, Dept. of Economic Development,
Research and Agency Liaison Division, 1978.
vi, 49, [3] p. : graphs ; 29 cm. Bibliography: p.
[51-52] LC Card 79-623551
1. Oregon - Economic conditions. I. Title.
HC107.O7 O48 1978   **NYPL [JLF 80-1437]**

Oregon. Dept. of Education.
Due process hearing handbook. Salem : Oregon
Dept. of Education, [1980] iv, 75 p. ; 28 cm.
"Verne A. Duncan, State Superintendent of Public
Instruction." "January 1980." Includes bibliographical
references. LC Card 80-622701 DDC 344.795/0791
  19
*1. Handicapped children - Education - Law and
legislation - Oregon. I. Duncan, Verne A. II. Title.*
KFO2795.9.H3 A833

Oregon administrative rules / Oregon
Department of Education. Salem, Or. : The
Dept., [1979- 1 v. : forms ; 28 cm. Loose-leaf for
updating. LC Card 80-621418 DDC 371.2/009795
  19
*1. School management and organization - Oregon. 2.
Oregon - Dept. of Education. I. Title.*
LB2809.O7 O73 1979

Oregon State plan for Title 1, Migrant
education, 1980. [Salem : Oregon State Dept. of
Education, 1979?] 56, [28] p. : forms ; 28 cm.
  LC Card 80-623912 DDC 371.96/75/09795 19
*1. Children of migrant laborers - Education - Oregon. I.
Title.*
LC5152.O7 O73 1979

OREGON. DEPT. OF EDUCATION.
Oregon. Dept. of Education. Oregon
administrative rules /. Salem, Or. [1979- 1 v. :
  LC Card 80-621418 DDC 371.2/009795 19
LB2809.O7 O73 1979

Oregon. Dept. of Employment. (Old Catalog form:
  Oregon. Employment, Dept. of)
Oregon's labor force trends. v. 7, no. 6- v. 8,
no. 1, 3-11, v. 9-17, no. 9, 11- v. 21; Apr.-Nov.
1965, Jan.-Sept., Nov. 1966-July, Sept.
1975-1979. Salem.   **NYPL [M-11 4968]**

Oregon. Dept. of Energy.
Hassoun, Hussein. Industrial energy
consumption studies /. Salem , 1978- v. ; LC
  Card 79-622416 DDC 333.79/13 19
HC107.A19 H37

Oregon. State University, Corvallis. Federal
Cooperative Extension Service. Oregon Energy
Extension Service State plan /. [Corvallis]
[1980] 38 p. ; LC Card 80-621871 DDC
  630/.9795 s 333.79/16/09795 19
S105 .E43 no. 569 TJ163.4.U6

Oregon. Dept. of Fish and Wildlife.
A statewide comprehensive plan for fish and
wildlife on the national forests in the State of
Oregon : FY--1981-1985. [Portland] : Oregon
Dept. of Fish and Wildlife, [1979?] 84 p. : ill. ;

28 cm. Cover title. Prepared jointly by the Oregon
Dept. of Fish and Wildlife and the Pacific Northwest
Region of the U. S. Forest Service. LC Card
80-621380
*1. Wildlife management - Oregon. 2. Fishery
management - Oregon. 3. Forest reserves - Oregon -
Recreational use. I. United States. Forest Service.
Pacific Northwest Region. II. Title.*
SK439 .O75 1979   **NYPL [JLF 81047]**

**Oregon. Dept. of Fish and Wildlife. Research and
Development Section.** Oregon rainbow and
cutthroat trout evaluation / [prepared by John
R. Moring and Robert M. Hooton]. [Portland] :
Research and Development Section, Oregon
Dept. of Fish and Wildlife, 1978. 27 leaves :
ill. ; 28 cm. (Federal aid progress reports : Fisheries)
Cover title. "F-94-R." LC Card 79-621865 DDC
  597/.55 19
*1. Cutthroat trout. 2. Fishes - Oregon - Willamette
River watershed. I. Moring, John R. II. Hooton, Robert
M. III. Title. IV. Series.*
QL638.S2 O73 1978

Oregon. Dept. of Forestry.
Nursery stock for nonindustrial private forest
lands in Oregon. Salem, Or. : Dept. of Forestry,
[1979] x, 35, [22] p. : map ; 28 cm. "February
1979." Bibliography: p. 33. LC Card 79-623541
  DDC 634.9/564/09795 19
*1. Forest nurseries - Oregon. 2. Nursery stock -
Oregon. 3. Wood-lots - Oregon. I. Title.*
SD398.42.O7 O73 1979

The Oregon forest practices act : chemical
rules & guidelines. [Salem] : Oregon State
Forestry Dept., 1978. ii, 22 p. : ill. ; 28 cm.
Cover title. LC Card 80-622824 DDC
  346.79504/675 19
*1. Forestry law and legislation - Oregon. 2. Chemicals -
Law and legislation - Oregon. 3. Pesticides - Law and
legislation - Oregon. I. Title.*
KFO2649 .A836

**Oregon. Dept. of Geology and Mineral
Industries.** White, Craig. Geology and
geochemistry of Mt. Hood volcano /. Portland,
Or. (1069 State Office Bldg., Portland, Or.
97201) , 1980. iii, 26 p. : LC Card 80-624065
  DDC 552/.22/0979561 19
QE461 .W48

**Oregon. Dept. of Human Resources. Employment
Division. see Oregon. Employment Division.**

Oregon. Dept. of Justice. The Attorney General's
model rules of procedure under the
Administrative procedure act, effective
December 3, 1979 / James A. Redden,
Attorney General. Salem, Or. : Attorney
General, [1979?] iii, 143 p. : forms ; 23 cm.
Cover title. LC Card 80-622995 DDC 342.795/066
  19
*1. Administrative procedure - Oregon. I. Redden, James
A. II. Title. III. Title: Model rules of procedure under
the Administrative procedure act.*
KFO2840 .A825 1979

OREGON - ECONOMIC CONDITIONS.
GMA Research Corporation. Alternate use and
marketing study: southwest portion of the
Umatilla Army Depot /. [Pendleton], 1974. 75
l.:   **NYPL [JLF 80-198]**

Oregon. Dept. of Economic Development.
Research and Agency Liaison Division. Oregon,
a statistical profile. Portland , 1978. vi, 49, [3]
p. : LC Card 79-623551
HC107.O7 O48 1978   **NYPL [JLF 80-1437]**

The Oregon economy . Salem, Or. (155 Cottage
St. N.E., Salem) [1980?] 16 p. ; LC Card
  80-623280 DDC 330.9795/043 19
HC107.O7 O625

Oregon. Legislative Assembly. Committee on
Trade and Economic Development. Economic
development handbook /. Salem, Or. , 1976. iii,
165 p. : LC Card 79-625087
HC107.O7 O54 1976   **NYPL [JLE 81-337]**

**Oregon. Economic Development, Dept of. see
Oregon. Dept. of Economic Development.**

OREGON - ECONOMIC POLICY.
Oregon. Legislative Assembly. Committee on
Trade and Economic Development. Economic
development handbook /. Salem, Or. , 1976. iii,
165 p. : LC Card 79-625087
HC107.O7 O54 1976   **NYPL [JLE 81-337]**

The Oregon economy : decade of the seventies,
with comparisons to the Nation and the sixties.

Salem, Or. (155 Cottage St. N.E., Salem) :
Dept. of Economic Development, [1980?] 16
p. ; 28 cm. LC Card 80-623280 DDC
  330.9795/043 19
*1. Oregon - Economic conditions. I. Oregon. Dept. of
Economic Development.*
HC107.O7 O625

Oregon. Elections Division.
Candidates and political parties manual /
compiled and published by Norma Paulus,
Secretary of State, Elections Division. [Salem,
Or.] : The Division, 1980. 42 p. : forms ; 28
cm. Cover title. LC Card 80-623672 DDC
  324.6/09795 19
*1. Elections - Oregon - Handbooks, manuals, etc. I.
Paulus, Norma. II. Title.*
JK2023.O7 O73 1980

Contributions and expenditures reporting and
campaign finance regulations, 1975-1976.
[Salem : Secretary of State, 1976?] 16, 21 p. :
forms ; 28 cm. Cover title. "Chapter 260: 1975
replacement part: Campaign finance regulation, election
offenses": p. 1-21 (2d group) LC Card 77-620693
  DDC 324.7/8/09795 19
*1. Elections - Oregon - Campaign funds. I. Oregon.
Laws, statutes, etc. Oregon revised statutes. Chapter
260. 1976. II. Title.*
KFO2820.85.C2 A32 1976

Contributions and expenditures reporting and
campaign finance regulations, 1980 / compiled
and published by Norma Paulus, Secretary of
State, Elections Division. [Salem, Or.] : The
Division, [1980] 23 p., p. 833-851 : forms ; 28
cm. Cover title. LC Card 80-623899 DDC
  342.795/078/02636 347.95027802636 19
*1. Elections - Oregon - Campaign funds. I. Paulus,
Norma. II. Title.*
KFO2820.85.C2 A32 1980

**Oregon - Employees. see Oregon - Officials and
  employees.**

**Oregon. Employment, Dept. of. see Oregon. Dept.
  of Employment.**

Oregon. Employment Division.
Licensed occupations in Oregon / prepared by
State of Oregon, Employment Division,
Department of Human Resources. Rev. Sept.
1977. [Salem] : The Division, [1977] 65 p. ; 28
cm. Includes index. LC Card 79-625475 DDC
  353.97950082/4046 19
*1. Occupations - Licenses - Oregon. 2. Oregon -
Occupations. I. Title.*
HD3630.U7 O72 1977

Oregon women at work. [Salem : State of
Oregon Employment Division, Dept. of Human
Resources], 1977. 71 p. ; 28 cm. Microfiche. (neg.)
NTIS. 1 sheet. 11 x 15 cm. (PB-285 445) A labor
market information publication of the State of Oregon
Employment Division, Department of Human Resources.
Cover title. LC Card 78-621381
1. Women - Employment - Oregon - Statistics. I. Title.
HD6096.O7 O73 1977   **NYPL [*XME-9535]**

**Oregon. Employment Division. Research and
Statistics Section.**
Occupational employment trends in the State of
Oregon, 1977-1985 / prepared by Research and
Statistics Section, State of Oregon, Employment
Division, Department of Human Resources.
[Salem, Or.] : The Division, [1979] 157 p. ; 28
cm. Includes bibliographical references. LC Card
  80-621879 DDC 331.12/3/09795 19
*1. Employment forecasting - Oregon. 2. Labor supply -
Oregon. 3. Job vacancies - Oregon. 4. Oregon -
Occupations. I. Title.*
HD5725.O7 O67 1979

Occupational profiles of selected government
employment in Oregon, 1975. [Salem] : State of
Oregon, Employment Division, Dept. of Human
Resources, [1976] 84 p. ; 28 cm. "RS pub 24
(9-76)." LC Card 79-623888
*1. Oregon - Officials and employees. 2. Employment
forecasting - Oregon. I. Title.*
HD8011.O7 O74 1976   **NYPL [JLF 80-1498]**

Occupational profiles of selected regulated
industries in Oregon, 1976 / prepared by
Research and Statistics Section. [Salem] : State
of Oregon, Employment DIvision, Dept. of
Human Resources, [1979?] 28 p. : ill. ; 28 cm. Cover
title. "RS pub 34(5-79)" LC Card 80-622149 DDC
  331.12/5138/009795 19
*1. Transport workers - Oregon - Supply and demand. 2.
Communication and traffic - Oregon - Employees -*

Supply and demand. 3. *Oregon - Occupations.* I. *Title.*
HD5718.T72 U58 1979

Oregon labor trends. Feb. 1980- [Salem].
NYPL [Econ. Div.]

Oregon special unemployment assistance program and transition benefits / prepared by State of Oregon, Employment Division, Department of Human Resources, Research and Statistics. [Salem, Or. : The Division, 1980] 30 p. ; 28 cm. Cover title. LC Card 80-622704 DDC 368.4/4/009795 19
1. Insurance, Unemployment - Oregon. I. Title.
HD7096.U6 O734 1980

Oregon's labor force trends. v. 7, no. 6- v. 8, no. 1, 3-11, v. 9-17, no. 9, 11- v. 21; Apr.-Nov. 1965, Jan.-Sept., Nov. 1966-July, Sept. 1975-1979. Salem. **NYPL [M-11 4968]**

Oregon Energy Extension Service State plan /. Oregon. State University, Corvallis. Federal Cooperative Extension Service. [Corvallis] [1980] 38 p. : LC Card 80-621871 DDC 630/.9795 s 333.79/16/09795 19
S105 .E43 no. 569 TJ163.4.U6

Oregon. Energy Planning Program. Isaak, David. Solar system economics /. Salem, Or. , 1980. 119, [24] p. : LC Card 80-623275 DDC 338.4/362147/09795 19
HD9681.U63 O75

Oregon. Executive Dept. Regulatory requirements for business, construction, land development. 1980-81 ed. Salem, Or. : State of Oregon, Executive Dept., [1980] 30, 2, 14 p. ; 28 cm. Cover title. Includes indexes. LC Card 80-623339 DDC 342.795/0664 19
1. Trade regulation - Oregon - Indexes. 2. Building laws - Oregon - Indexes. 3. Land use - Law and legislation - Oregon - Indexes. I. Title.
KFO2630 .A46 1980

Oregon. Executive Dept. Personnel Division. Oregon. Executive Dept. Personnel Division. Compensation and Classification Services Unit. Management service compensation plan, effective April 1, 1980 /. [Salem, Or.] [1980?] 92 p. ; LC Card 80-622739 DDC 353.9795001/23 19
JK9057 .O73 1980a

Oregon. Executive Dept. Personnel Division. Compensation and Classification Services Unit. Management service compensation plan, effective April 1, 1980 / issued by the Personnel Division ; prepared by Compensation and Classification Services Unit. [Salem, Or.] : State of Oregon, Executive Dept., [1980?] 92 p. ; 28 cm. LC Card 80-622739 DDC 353.9795001/23 19
1. Oregon - Officials and employees - Salaries, allowances, etc. I. Oregon. Executive Dept. Personnel Division. II. Title.
JK9057 .O73 1980a

Representable compensation plan : effective April 1, 1980 / prepared by Compensation and Classification Services Unit. [Salem, Or.] : State of Oregon, Executive Dept., Personnel Division, [1980] 97 p. ; 28 cm. LC Card 80-622740 DDC 353.9795001/23 19
1. Oregon - Officials and employees - Salaries, allowances, etc. - Statistics. I. Title.
JK9057 .O73 1980

Oregon. Fish and Wildlife, Dept. of. see Oregon. Dept. of Fish and Wildlife.

The Oregon forest practices act . Oregon. Dept. of Forestry. [Salem] , 1978. ii, 22 p. : LC Card 80-622824 DDC 346.79504/675 19
KFO2649 .A836

Oregon. Forestry, Dept. of. see Oregon. Dept. of Forestry.

Oregon - Government employees. see Oregon - Officials and employees.

Oregon. Governor's Commission for Women. Miller, Marilyn G. Domestic violence in Oregon /. [Salem] [1979] 43, [20] p. ; LC Card 80-621297 DDC 362.8/2 19
HV6626 .M54

Oregon. Governor's Commission on Youth. Report on the opinions and experiences of Oregon youth. Salem : Governor's Commission on Youth, 1976. 51, 10 p. ; 29 cm. Microfiche (neg.) NTIS. 1 sheet. 11 x 15 cm. (PB-268 775) LC Card 77-621410

1. Youth - Oregon. 2. Youth - Oregon - Attitudes. I. Title.
HQ796 .O647 1976 **NYPL [*XME-9430]**

Oregon. Higher Education, State Board of. see Oregon. State Board of Higher Education.

Oregon Historical Society. Folk art of the Oregon country /. [Salem?] , c1980. 128 p. : LC Card 80-622779 DDC 745/.09795/074013 19
NK805.O7 F64

OREGON - INDUSTRIES - ENERGY CONSUMPTION. Hassoun, Hussein. Industrial energy consumption studies /. Salem , 1978- v. ; LC Card 79-622416 DDC 333.79/13 19
HC107.A19 H37

Oregon. Information and Referral Task Force. Oregon Information and Referral Task Force report. Salem : State Community Services Program, Dept. of Human Resources, 1978. ca. 300 p. in various pagings ; 28 cm. Includes index. LC Card 79-620753 DDC 361/.007 19
1. Social service - Information services - Oregon - Directories. 2. Oregon. Information and Referral Task Force. I. Title.
HV86 .O84 1978

OREGON. INFORMATION AND REFERRAL TASK FORCE. Oregon. Information and Referral Task Force. Oregon Information and Referral Task Force report. Salem , 1978. ca. 300 p. in various pagings ; LC Card 79-620753 DDC 361/.007 19
HV86 .O84 1978

Oregon Information and Referral Task Force report. Oregon. Information and Referral Task Force. Salem , 1978. ca. 300 p. in various pagings ; LC Card 79-620753 DDC 361/.007 19
HV86 .O84 1978

Oregon. Labor, Bureau of. see Oregon. Bureau of Labor.

Oregon labor trends. Feb. 1980- [Salem], Research and Statistics Section, Employment Division. Supersedes Oregon's labor force trends. I. *Oregon. Employment Division. Research and Statistics Section.* **NYPL [Econ. Div.]**

Oregon. Law Enforcement Council. Recidivism of adult offenders : a pilot recidivism study in eleven Oregon counties [Salem, Ore.] : Oregon Law Enforcement Council, [1980] ii, 22 p. : ill. ; 22 cm. Author: Pamela Erickson Gervais. Includes bibliographical references. LC Card 80-622692 DDC 364.3/09795 19
1. Recidivists - Oregon. I. Gervais, Pamela. II. Title.
HV6793.O7 O73 1980

Oregon. Laws, statutes, etc. Oregon revised statutes. Chapter 260. 1976. Oregon. Elections Division. Contributions and expenditures reporting and campaign finance regulations, 1975-1976. [Salem , 1976?] 16, 21 p. : LC Card 77-620693 DDC 324.7/8/09795 19
KFO2820.85.C2 A32 1976

Oregon. Legislative Assembly. Committee on Trade and Economic Development. Economic development handbook / compiled by the Legislative Committee on Trade and Economic Development. Salem, Or. : The Committee, 1976. iii, 165 p. : ill. ; 23 cm. Includes indexes. LC Card 79-625087
1. Oregon - Economic conditions. 2. Oregon - Economic policy. I. Title.
HC107.O7 O54 1976 **NYPL [JLE 81-337]**

Oregon. Legislative Assembly. Interim Committee on the Judiciary. Proposed Oregon Evidence Code : report of the Legislative Interim Committee on the Judiciary. Salem, Or. (347 State Capitol, Salem 97310) : The Committee, [1980] xv, 230 p. ; 28 cm. "December 1980." LC Card 81-621515 DDC 347.795/06 347.95076 19
1. Evidence (Law) - Oregon. I. Title.
KFO2940 .A25 1980

Oregon. Legislative Assembly. Legislative Counsel Committee. Oregon. [Laws, etc.] Criminal code of Oregon and selected laws relating to juvenile court proceedings, alcoholic liquors, and controlled substances. Salem, Or. , 1980. 375 p. ; LC Card 81-145570 DDC 345.795/002632 347.9505002632 19
KFO2961 .A3 1980

Oregon. Legislative Assembly. Legislative Research.
Staff sunset review .
(80:4) Oregon. Legislative Assembly. Legislative Research. Well drillers and contractors . Salem, Or. (S-420 State Capitol, Salem 97310) [1980] iv, 40 p. ; LC Card 81-620549 DDC 344.795/017627114 347.950417627114 19
KFO2849 .A25 1980

Well drillers and contractors : prepared pursuant to chapter 842, Oregon laws, 1977. Salem, Or. (S-420 State Capitol, Salem 97310) : Legislative Research, [1980] iv, 40 p. ; 28 cm. (Staff sunset review . 80:4) Cover title. "April 1980." Includes bibliographical references. LC Card 81-620549 DDC 344.795/017627114 347.950417627114 19
1. Wells - Law and legislation - Oregon. 2. Well drillers - Licenses - Oregon. I. Series: Oregon. Legislative Assembly. Legislative Research. Staff sunset review , 80:4. II. Title.
KFO2849 .A25 1980

Oregon. Legislative Assembly. Legislative Task Force on Hospice. Report and recommendations / Legislative Task Force on Hospice. [Salem, Or.] : The Task Force, [1980] v, 59 p. ; 28 cm. Cover title. Written by Mary Lou Jacobs. "August 1980." LC Card 81-620893 DDC 362.1/9 19
1. Terminal care - Oregon. 2. Terminal care facilities - Oregon. 3. Terminal care facilities - Law and legislation - Oregon. I. Jacobs, Mary Lou. II. Title.
R726.8 .O73 1980

Oregon. Legislative Assembly. Senate. Interim Task Force on Intergovernmental Coordination. Report of the Senate Interim Task Force on Intergovernmental Coordination. [Salem, Or. (447 State Capitol, Salem, Or. 97310)] : The Task Force, [1979] xiv, 103 p. ; 28 cm. "December 1979." LC Card 81-620891 DDC 352.0795 19
1. Local government - Oregon. 2. Metropolitan government - Oregon. 3. Special districts - Oregon. I. Title.
JS451 .O7 1979

Oregon. Legislative Assembly. Senate. Interim Task Force on Regulation of the Motor Carrier Industry. Report of the Senate Interim Task Force on Regulation of the Motor Carrier Industry : submitted to members of the Sixty-first Legislative Assembly in accordance with House Joint Resolution 52, Sixtieth Legislative Assembly. [Salem] : The Task Force, [1980] xi, 135 p. : ill. ; 28 cm. "January 1980." Includes bibliographical references. LC Card 80-623673 DDC 343.795/09483 19
1. Transportation, Automotive - Law and legislation - Oregon.
KFO2411.72 .R33 1980

Oregon. Legislative Assembly. Trade and Economic Development, Committee on. see Oregon. Legislative Assembly. Committee on Trade and Economic Development.

OREGON - MAPS.
(1979) United States. Bureau of Land Management. Oregon, proposed initial inventory, roadless areas and islands which do not have wilderness characteristics /. [Portland] , 1979. 3 maps : 61 x 94 cm. and 94 x 61 cm. Scale 1:500,000. Relief shown by spot heights. Includes index map. LC Card 79-695513
G4291.G4 s500 .U5
NYPL [Map Div. 81-3037]

(1979) United States. Geological Survey. Oregon, base map with highways and contours /. Reston, Va. , 1979. 1 map : LC Card 81-691602
G4290 1979 .U5

Oregon. Mental Health Division. Manpower Development Office. Job analysis in the human services : an annotated bibliography / State of Oregon, Department of Human Resources, Mental Health Division ; prepared by Manpower Development Office. Salem, Ore. : The Office, [1980] 66 p. ; 22 cm. "January, 1980." Bibliography: p. 63-66. LC Card 80-622587 DDC 016.6583/06 19
1. Job analysis - Bibliography. I. Title.
Z7164.C81 O74 1980 HF5549.5.J6

OREGON - OCCUPATIONS.
Oregon. Employment Division. Licensed

occupations in Oregon /. [Salem] [1977] 65 p. ; LC Card 79-625475 DDC 353.97950082/4046 19
HD3630.U7 O72 1977

Oregon. Employment Division. Research and Statistics Section. Occupational employment trends in the State of Oregon, 1977-1985 /. [Salem, Or.] [1979] 157 p. ; LC Card 80-621879 DDC 331.12/3/09795 19
HD5725.O7 O67 1979

Oregon. Employment Division. Research and Statistics Section. Occupational profiles of selected regulated industries in Oregon, 1976 /. [Salem] [1979?] 54 p. ; LC Card 80-622149 DDC 331.12/5138/009795 19
HD5718.T72 U58 1979

OREGON - OFFICIALS AND EMPLOYEES.
Oregon. Employment Division. Research and Statistics Section. Occupational profiles of selected government employment in Oregon, 1975. [Salem] [1976] 84 p. ; LC Card 79-623888
HD8011.O7 O74 1976   ***NYPL [JLF 80-1498]***

OREGON - OFFICIALS AND EMPLOYEES - SALARIES, ALLOWANCES, ETC.
Oregon. Executive Dept. Personnel Division. Compensation and Classification Services Unit. Management service compensation plan, effective April 1, 1980 /. [Salem, Or.] [1980?] 92 p. ; LC Card 80-622739 DDC 353.9795001/23 19
JK9057 .O73 1980a

OREGON - OFFICIALS AND EMPLOYEES - SALARIES, ALLOWANCES, ETC. - STATISTICS.
Oregon. Executive Dept. Personnel Division. Compensation and Classification Services Unit. Representable compensation plan . [Salem, Or.] [1980] 97 p. ; LC Card 80-622740 DDC 353.9795001/23 19
JK9057 .O73 1980

Oregon, proposed initial inventory, roadless areas and islands which do not have wilderness characteristics /. United States. Bureau of Land Management. [Portland] , 1979. 3 maps : 61 x 94 cm. and 94 x 61 cm. Scale 1:500,000. Relief shown by spot heights. Includes index map. LC Card 79-695513
G4291.G4 s500 .U5
     NYPL [Map Div. 81-3037]

Oregon rainbow and cutthroat trout evaluation /. Oregon. Dept. of Fish and Wildlife. Research and Development Section. [Portland] , 1978. 27 leaves ; LC Card 79-621865 DDC 597/.55 19
QL638.S2 O73 1978

Oregon. Real Estate Division. Directory of licensed billing, factoring, collection, and debt consolidation agencies, as of October 1, 1979. [Salem] : Dept. of Commerce, Real Estate Division, [1979] 26 p. ; 28 cm. Cover title: Credit agency directory, 1979-1980. LC Card 80-621878 DDC 332.7 19
1. Credit management - Oregon - Directories. I. Title.
HG3754.5.U6 O73 1979

Oregon. Renewable Resources Program. Isaak, David. Solar system economics /. Salem, Or. , 1980. 119, [24] p. : LC Card 80-623275 DDC 338.4/362147/09795 19
HD9681.U63 O75

Oregon. Secretary of State. Elections Division. see Oregon. Elections Division.

Oregon special unemployment assistance program and transition benefits /. Oregon. Employment Division. Research and Statistics Section. [Salem, Or. , 1980] 30 p. ; LC Card 80-622704 DDC 368.4/4/009795 19
HD7096.U6 O734 1980

Oregon State Bar. Continuing Legal Education. Worker's compensation / Oregon State Bar, Continuing Legal Education ; co-sponsored by Section on Workers' Compensation. [Portland] : Oregon State Bar, Continuing Legal Education, [1980] xiii, 196, 36 p. : forms ; 23 cm. LC Card 81-620533 DDC 344.795/021 347.950421 19
1. Workers' compensation - Law and legislation - Oregon. I. Oregon State Bar. Section on Workers' Compensation. II. Title.
KFO2742 .O74

Oregon State Bar. Section on Workers' Compensation. Oregon State Bar. Continuing Legal Education. Worker's compensation /. [Portland] [1980] xiii, 196, 36 p. : LC Card 81-620533 DDC 344.795/021 347.950421 19
KFO2742 .O74

Oregon. State Board of Accountancy. Newsletter and roster of certified public accountants, public accountants, accountants authorized to conduct municipal audits. [Salem] 28 cm. Annual. For earlier years, see its: Certified public accountants, public accountants, professional corporations, and accountants authorized to conduct municipal audits in Oregon. Report year ends Sept. 30th.
1. Accountants - Oregon - Directories.
     NYPL [JLM 81-160]

Oregon. State Board of Chiropractic Examiners. Licentiate report of Oregon State Board of Chiropractic Examiners. [Salem] : Orgeon State Health Division, 1979. 12 p. ; 28 cm. Cover title. LC Card 80-621381 DDC 615.5/34/025795 19
1. Chiropractors - Oregon - Directories. 2. Oregon. State Board of Chiropractic Examiners. I. Title.
RZ233 .O73 1979

OREGON. STATE BOARD OF CHIROPRACTIC EXAMINERS.
Oregon. State Board of Chiropractic Examiners. Licentiate report of Oregon State Board of Chiropractic Examiners. [Salem] , 1979. 12 p. ; LC Card 80-621381 DDC 615.5/34/025795 19
RZ233 .O73 1979

Oregon. State Board of Higher Education. (Old Catalog form: Oregon. Higher Education Dept.)
Biennial report of the director of libraries. Eugene [etc.] 29 cm. For later years, see: Oregon. State Board of Higher Education. Interinstitutional Library Council. Biennial report.
1. Libraries, University and college - Oregon - Periodicals. I. Title.   ***NYPL [M-10 605]***

Oregon. State Board of Radiologic Technology. 1980 directory of licensees / Oregon State Board of Radiologic Technology. Portland, Or. : The Board, [1980] 77 p. : map ; 22 cm. Cover title: 1980 directory of licensed radiologic technologists. LC Card 80-622693 DDC 616.07/57/025795 19
1. Radiologic technologists - Oregon - Directories. I. Title. II. Title: 1980 directory of licensed radiologic technologists. III. Title: Directory of licensed radiologic technologists.
R895.A4 O73 1980

Oregon. State Dept. of Geology and Mineral Industries.
Bulletin .
(100) Ramp, Lenin. Geology and mineral resources of Josephine County, Oregon /. Portland, Or. , 1979. iv, 45 p. : LC Card 80-622943 DDC 553/.09795 s 557.95/25 19
QE155 .A3 no. 100 QE156.J67

(98) Bela, James L. Geologic hazards of eastern Benton County, Oregon /. Portland, Or. , 1979. viii, 122 p. : LC Card 80-622942 DDC 553/.09795 s 624.1/51/0979534 19
QE155 .A3 no. 98 QE156.B46

Oregon. State Forestry Dept. see Oregon. Dept. of Forestry.

Oregon State plan for Title 1, Migrant education, 1980. Oregon. Dept. of Education. [Salem , 1979?] 56, [28] p. : LC Card 80-623912 DDC 371.96/75/09795 19
LC5152.O7 O73 1979

Oregon. State System of Higher Education. see Oregon. State Board of Higher Education.

Oregon State University. Agricultural Experiment Station. Lovell, Burrell B. Soil survey of Malheur County, Oregon, northeastern part /. [Washington, D.C.] 1980. viii, 94 p., [22] folded leaves of plates : LC Card 80-603621 DDC 631.4/7/79597 19
S599.O7 L68

Oregon. State University, Corvallis. Environmental Health Sciences Center. Terrestrial microcosms and environmental chemistry . [Washington] [1978?] xv, 147 p. : LC Card 79-601829 DDC 574.5/264 19
QH541.2 .T45

Oregon. State University, Corvallis. Federal Cooperative Extension Service.
Holst, David. Effects of the 1977 drought on eastern Oregon ranches /. [Corvallis] [1979] 25

p. : LC Card 79-625679 DDC 630/.9795 s 338.1/4 19
S105 .E43 no. 555 S600.7.D76

Oregon Energy Extension Service State plan / prepared for Oregon Department of Energy and US Department of Energy by Oregon State University Extension Service ; Owen D. Osborne, energy program leader. [Corvallis] : The Extension Service, [1980] 38 p. : ill. ; 28 cm. (Special report - Oregon State University Extension Service ; 569) "January 1980." Includes bibliographical references. LC Card 80-621871 DDC 630/.9795 s 333.79/16/09795 19
1. Energy conservation - Oregon. 2. Energy policy - Oregon. I. Osborne, Owen D. II. Oregon. Dept. of Energy. III. United States. Dept. of Energy. IV. Series: Oregon. State University, Corvallis. Federal Cooperative Extension Service. Special report , 569. V. Title.
S105 .E43 no. 569 TJ163.4.U6

Special report .
(555) Holst, David. Effects of the 1977 drought on eastern Oregon ranches /. [Corvallis] [1979] 25 p. : LC Card 79-625679 DDC 630/.9795 s 338.1/4 19
S105 .E43 no. 555 S600.7.D76

(569) Oregon. State University, Corvallis. Federal Cooperative Extension Service. Oregon Energy Extension Service State plan /. [Corvallis] [1980] 38 p. : LC Card 80-621871 DDC 630/.9795 s 333.79/16/09795 19
S105 .E43 no. 569 TJ163.4.U6

Oregon. State University, Corvallis. Forest Research Laboratory.
Research bulletin .
(25-26) Animal damage to coniferous plantations in Oregon and Washington /. Corvallis, Or. , 1979. 2 v. : LC Card 80-623387 DDC 634.9 s 634.9/7547 19
SD12 .O87 no. 25-26 SB608.D6

Oregon. State University, Corvallis. Water Resources Research Institute.
Water research progress at OSU . [Corvallis, Or.] , 1979. 101 p. : LC Card 79-626121 DDC 551.48 19
GB658.7 .W37

WRRI .
(54) Seidler, Ramon J. Health significance of Klebsiella pneumoniae in drinking water emanating from redwood tanks /. Corvallis, Or. , 1977. 81 p. : LC Card 78-624331 DDC 333.91/009795 s 628.1/3 19
HD1694.O7 A13 no. 54 QR48

(57) Bella, David A. Environment, technology, and future generations /. Corvallis , 1978. ii, 36 p. ; LC Card 79-625127 DDC 333.91/009795 s 363.7/05 19
HD1694.O7 A13 no. 57 TD170

Oregon. Tax Court. Research Division. Rules, Regular Division / Oregon Tax Court. Rev. July 1, 1980. Salem, Or. : The Court, [1980] iv, 61 p. ; 28 cm. LC Card 80-623341 DDC 343.79504/0269 19
1. Tax courts - Oregon. 2. Court rules - Oregon. I. Title.
KFO2871.5.A437 A2 1980

Oregon. Teacher Standards and Practices Commission. Discrimination and the Oregon educator. Salem, Or. [1980] viii, 37 p. ; LC Card 80-623412 DDC 370.19/342/09795 19
LC212.22.O7 D57 1980

Oregon. University. Bureau of Governmental Research and Service. (Old Catalog form: Oregon. University. Governmental Research and Service, Bureau of)
Henke, Joseph T. A case study of Greater Egypt Regional Planning and Development Commission /. Eugene, 1971. 48 l. LC Card 76-106858   ***NYPL [JLF 80-1283]***

Henke, Joseph T. A case study of Windham Regional Planning and Development Commission, Vermont /. Eugene, Or., 1970. 69 l. LC Card 73-101271   ***NYPL [JLF 80-1288]***

Intergovernmental Organization for Planning. A case study of the northern tier region of northeastern Pennsylvania. Eugene, Or., 1971. 58 l.   ***NYPL [JLF 80-1285]***

Local government boundary commissions : the Oregon experience. [Eugene] : Bureau of Governmental Research and Service, University

of Oregon, 1978. iii, 112 p. ; 28 cm. Principal
author, Ken Tollenaar. Includes bibliographical
references.   LC Card 78-622792
*1. Local government - Oregon. 2. Oregon -
Administrative and political divisions. I. Tollenaar,
Kenneth C. II. Title.*
JS451 .O7 1978a   **NYPL [JLF 80-1445]**

Transfer of municipal court jurisdiction in
Oregon. [Eugene, Ore.] : Bureau of
Governmental Research and Service, School of
Community Service and Public Affairs,
University of Oregon, [1980] 77 p. ; 29 cm.
   LC Card 80-622705   DDC 347.795/01 19
*1. Municipal courts - Oregon. 2. District courts -
Oregon. 3. Jurisdiction - Oregon. I. Title.*
KFO2918 .O73

**Oregon. University. Governmental Research and
Service, Bureau of.** see **Oregon. University.
Bureau of Governmental Research and
Service.**

Oregon. University. Museum of Art. Folk art of
the Oregon country /. [Salem?] , c1980. 128
p. :   LC Card 80-622779   DDC 745/.09795/074013
   19
NK805.O7 F64

**Oregon. University. Museum of Natural History.
Bulletin.**
   (no. 22) Purdom, William B. Guide to the
   geology and lore of the wild reach of the
   Rogue River, Oregon /. Eugene , 1977. 67
   p. :   LC Card 77-622970   DDC 917.95/2 19
QH1 .O7 no. 22 QH105.O7

   (no. 23) Gustafson, Eric Paul. The vertebrate
   faunas of the Pliocene Ringold Formation,
   south-central Washington /. Eugene, Or. ,
   1978. 62 p. :   LC Card 79-625683   DDC
   574.979 s 566/.09797/51 19
QH1 .O7 no. 23 QE841

**Oregon. University. School of Community
Service and Public Affairs. Bureau of
Governmental Research and Service.** see
**Oregon. University. Bureau of Governmental
Research and Service.**

Oregon. Water Policy Review Board. Final report
to the Pacific Northwest Regional Commission
on Oregon's drought and conservation activities
/ Oregon Water Resources Department,
respectfully submitted by the Water Policy
Review Board. [Salem, Or.] : The Dept., [1979]
74 p. : ill. ; 28 cm.   LC Card 80-621882   DDC
   333.91/16/09795 19
*1. Water conservation - Oregon. 2. Droughts - Oregon.
I. Pacific Northwest Regional Commission. II. Title.*
TD224.O7 O72 1979

Oregon. Water Resources Dept. Rules and
regulations prescribing general standards for the
construction and maintenance of water wells in
Oregon. [Salem, Or.] : Water Resources Dept.,
[1979] 27 p., [17] leaves of plates : ill. ; 29 cm.
At head of title: State of Oregon. Cover title.   LC
   Card 80-623342   DDC 353.97950087/1 19
1. Wells - Law and legislation - Oregon. I. Title.
KFO2849.A435 A2 1979

Oregon Water Resources Research Institute.
Non-Federal financing of water resources
development . Corvallis, 1978. 80 p. ;   LC Card
   79-621887
HD1695.N74 N66   **NYPL [JLF 80-1601]**

Oregon wilderness act of 1979 . United States.
Congress. Senate. Committee on Energy and
Natural Resources. Subcommittee on Parks,
Recreation, and Renewable Resources.
Washington , 1980. vii, 696 p. :   LC Card
   80-603319   DDC 346.7304/6782/0262 19
KF26 .E5565 1979j

Oregon women . Leasher, Evelyn M. Corvallis,
1980, c1981. viii, 54 p. ;   ISBN 0-87071-138-5
   (pbk.)   LC Card 81-122472   DDC
   016.3054/09795 19
HQ1438.O7 L4

Oregon women at work. Oregon. Employment
Division. [Salem] 1977. 71 p. ;   LC Card
   78-621381
HD6096.O7 O73 1977   **NYPL [*XME-9535]**

Oregon. Youth, Governor's Commission on. see
Oregon. Governor's Commission on Youth.

Oregon's labor force trends. v. 7, no. 6- v. 8, no.
1, 3-11, v. 9-17, no. 9, 11- v. 21; Apr.-Nov.
1965, Jan.-Sept., Nov. 1966-July, Sept.
1975-1979. Salem. illus. 28 cm. Monthly. Report

year ends Oct. 31. For earlier file, whose numbering it
continues, see (in Old Catalog): Oregon's labor market.
Prepared by the Research and Statistics Division of
Oregon's Dept. of Employment, Apr. 1955-July 1969;
by the Research and Statistics Section of Oregon's
Employment Division, Aug. 1969-Oct. 1979.
Superseded by Oregon labor trends.
*1. Labor supply - Oregon - Statistics - Periodicals. I.
Oregon. Dept. of Employment. II. Oregon. Employment
Division. Research and Statistics Section.*
                                      NYPL [M-11 4968]

ORES - DRESSING. see **ORE-DRESSING.**

ORES, MAGNETIC SEPARATION OF. see
MAGNETIC SEPARATION OF ORES.

ORES - MONTANA.
Bennetts, J. (John) Preparation of platinum
flotation concentrate from stillwater complex
ore /. Avondale, Md. [1981] p. cm.   LC Card
   80-606913   DDC 622 s 622/.3424 19
TN23 .U43 TN523

ORGANIC CHEMISTRY. see **CHEMISTRY,
ORGANIC.**

ORGANIC COMPOUNDS.
White, J. C. (Jack C.) Removal of organic
contaminants from aluminum chloride solutions
/. Avondale, Md. , 1981. p. cm.   LC Card
   81-607812   DDC 622 s 622/.34926 19
TN23 .U43 TP245.A4

**ORGANIC COMPOUNDS -
ENVIRONMENTAL ASPECTS -
ILLINOIS.**
Economic impact of incorporating RACT 1
guidelines for VOC emissions into the Illinois
air pollution control regulations (R78-3 and
R78-4) /. Chicago IL , 1979. xxii, 137, [125]
p. :   LC Card 79-624233   DDC 363.7/39262/09773
   19
TD885.5.O74 E28

ORGANIC GEOCHEMISTRY.
Hatcher, Patrick G. The organic geochemistry
of Mangrove Lake, Bermuda /. Rockville, Md. ,
1978. vi, 92 p. :   LC Card 78-601738   DDC
   551.46 s 551.9/097299 19
GC1 .U42c no. 10 GB1657.B47

**The organic geochemistry of Mangrove Lake,
Bermuda /.** Hatcher, Patrick G. Rockville,
Md. , 1978. vi, 92 p. :   LC Card 78-601738
   DDC 551.46 s 551.9/097299 19
GC1 .U42c no. 10 GB1657.B47

**Organisation de coopèration et de développement
économiques.** see **Organization for Economic
Cooperation and Development.**

Organisation des Etats américains. see
Organization of American States.

Organisation des Nations Unies. see **United
Nations.**

**Organisation des Nations Unies pour l'éducation,
la science et la culture.** see **United Nations
Educational, Scientific and Cultural
Organization.**

Organisation du Traité de l'Atlantique-Nord. see
North Atlantic Treaty Organization.

Organisation du Traité de Varsovie. see
Organizatsiia stran Varshavskogo dogovora.

**ORGANISATION FOR ECONOMIC CO-
OPERATION AND DEVELOPMENT.**
OECD countries . Washington, D.C. [1980] iv,
56 p. ;   LC Card 80-604134   DDC 331.13/7 19
HD5707.5 .O43

Organisation mondiale de la santé. see **World
Health Organization.**

Organismo internacional de energía atómica. see
International Atomic Energy Agency.

**Organização de Cooperação e de
Desenvolvimento Econômicos.** see
**Organization for Economic Cooperation and
Development.**

Organização dos Estados Americanos. see
Organization of American States.

**Organización de cooperación y desarrollo
económicos.** see **Organization for Economic
Cooperation and Development.**

**Organización de las Naciones Unidas para la
Educación, la Ciencia y la Cultura.** see
**United Nations Educational, Scientific and
Cultural Organization.**

Organización de los Estados Americanos. see
Organization of American States.

Organización Mundial de la Salud. see **World
Health Organization.**

**ORGANIZACIÓN OBRERA
REVOLUCIONARIA
PUERTORRIQUEÑA.**
United States. Congress. Senate. Committee on
the Judiciary. Subcommittee to Investigate the
Administration of the Internal Security Act and
Other Internal Security Laws. The Puerto Rican
Revolutionary Workers Organization .
Washington , 1976. v, 47, viii p. ;   LC Card
   76-601803   DDC 322.4/2/0973 19
HV6432 .U54 1976

**Organization and administration of the United
States Tax Court** . United States. Congress.
House. Committee on Ways and Means.
Washington , 1980. iii, 38 p. ;   LC Card
   80-602486   DDC 343.7304/0269 19
KF27 .W3 1980d

**Organization and functions, Department of
Conservation /.** California. Dept. of
Conservation. Sacramento, Calif. , 1964. 15 p. :
                                      NYPL [*ZT-1245]

**Organization for Economic Cooperation and
Development. Committee on Reactor
Physics.** Proceedings of the NEACRP
meeting of a Monte Carlo study group.
Argonne, Ill. [1974] 363 l.
                                      NYPL [*XMQ-2014]

**Organization for Economic Cooperation and
Development. International Energy Agency.**
see **International Energy Agency.**

**Organization for Economic Cooperation and
Development. Nuclear Energy Agency.
Committee on Reactor Physics.** see
**Organization for Economic Cooperation and
Development. Committee on Reactor
Physics.**

**Organization for Economic Cooperation and
Development. Reactor Physics, Committee
on.** see **Organization for Economic
Cooperation and Development. Committee
on Reactor Physics.**

ORGANIZATION, INDUSTRIAL. see
INDUSTRIAL ORGANIZATION.

Organization of American States.
América en cifras. 1960-77 (incomplete)
Washington.   **NYPL [SDG (America)
                           (America en cifras)]**

Documentos oficiales .
   (OEA/ser.J/IX, CEPCIECC/doc.92, rev.1,
   add. 1) Inter-American Council for
   Education, Science, and Culture. Permanent
   Executive Committee. Anexos al Informe
   final de la sexta reunión de la CEPCIECC,
   del 13 al 17 de noviembre de 1972,
   Washington, D.C. = Appendices to the Final
   report of the sixth meeting of CEPCIECC,
   November 13 through 17, 1972, Washington,
   D.C. /. Washington [1972 or 1973] iv, 269
   p. :   LC Card 81-470412   DDC 341.24/5 s
   341.7/6727 19
F1402 .A169 OEA/ser.J/IX,
   CEPCIECC/doc.92, rev. 1, add. 1 F1408.4

   (OEA/Ser. A/19 (SEPF)) Inter-American
   convention on conflict of laws concerning
   checks. Convención interamericana sobre
   conflictos de leyes en materia de cheques =.
   Washington , 1975. iii, 8 p. ;   LC Card
   81-463811   DDC 341.24/5 s 341.7/51 19
F1402 .A169 OEA/Ser. A/19 (SEPF)

   (OEA/Ser. A/20 (SEPF)) Inter-American
   convention on international commercial
   arbitration. Convención interamericana sobre
   arbitraje comercial internacional =.
   Washington , 1975. iii, 12 p. ;   LC Card
   81-463810   DDC 341.24/5 s 341.5/22/0265 19
F1402 .A169 OEA/Ser. A/20 (SEPF)

   (OEA/Ser. A/21 (SEPF)) Inter-American
   convention on letters rogatory. Convención
   interamericana sobre exhortos o cartas
   rogatorias =. Washington , 1975. iii, 20 p. ;
   LC Card 81-463813   DDC 341.24/5 s
   341.7/8/0265 19
F1402 .A169 OEA/Ser. A/21 (SEPF)

   (OEA/Ser. A/22 (SEPF)) Inter-American
   convention on the taking of evidence abroad.
   Convención interamericana sobre recepción

de pruebas en el extranjero =. Washington , 1975. iii, 20 p. ;　LC Card 81-463809　DDC 341.24/5 s 341.7/8/0265 19
F1402 .A169 OEA/Ser. A/22 (SEPF)

(OEA/Ser. A/23 (SEPF)) Inter-American convention on the legal regime of powers of attorney to be used abroad. Convención interamericana sobre régimen legal de poderes para ser utilizados en el extranjero =. Washington , 1975. iii, 16 p. ;　LC Card 81-463812　DDC 341.24/5 s 341.7/8/0265 19
F1402 .A169 OEA/Ser. A/23 (SEPF)

(OEA/Ser. A/30 (SEPF)) Inter-American convention on proof of and information on foreign law. Convención interamericana sobre prueba e información acerca del derecho extranjero . Washington, D.C. , 1979. iii, 27 p. ;　LC Card 80-113645　DDC 341.24/5 s 341.7/8/0265 19
F1402 .A169 OEA/Ser. A/30 (SEPF)

(OEA/Ser. A/34-OEA/Ser.A/34, Add. 1) United States. Treaties, etc. Panama, Sept. 7, 1977. Tratados sobre el Canal de Panamá suscritos entre la República de Panamá y los Estados Unidos de América =. Washington, D.C. , 1979. 2 v. :　LC Card 80-121836　DDC 341.4/46/02667307287 19
JX1398.72 1979 .U54 1977

(OEA/Ser. P/I.1 ref. 5) Organization of American States. General Assembly. Reglamento de la Asamblea General . Washington, D.C. , 1978. v, 30 p. ;　LC Card 80-142828　DDC 341.24/5 s 341.24/5 19
F1402 .A169 OEA/Ser. P/I.1 rev. 5 F1402.A4

(OEA/Ser.Y/II.l) Organization of American States. Manual de clasificación para la Serie de documentos oficiales de la OEA . Washington, D.C. , 1979. viii, 121 p. :　LC Card 79-111656　DDC 341.24/5 s 025.4/2 19
F1402 .A169 OEA/Ser.Y/II.1 Z697.G7

Documents oficiales .
(OEA/ser. G CP/ACTA 324/78) Organization of American States. Permanent Council. Acta de la sesión ordinaria celebrada el 3 de mayo de 1978 . Washington, D.C. , 1978. v, 268 p. ;　LC Card 79-108138　DDC 341.24/5 19
F1402 .A169 OEA/Ser. G CP/ACTA 324/78

Manual de clasificación para la Serie de documentos oficiales de la OEA : un manual para el mantenimiento de la Serie / Organización de los Estados Amercanos [sic]. Washington, D.C. : Secretaría General, Organización de los Estados Americanos, 1979. viii, 121 p. : diagr. ; 28 cm. (Serie de documentos oficiales de la OEA ; OEA/Ser.Y/II.l) On t.p.: Adm.　LC Card 79-111656　DDC 341.24/5 s 025.4/2 19
1. Classification - Books - Government publications. 2. Organization of American States. I. Series: Organization of American States. Documentos oficiales ,
OEA/Ser.Y/II.l. II. Title.
F1402 .A169 OEA/Ser.Y/II.1 Z697.G7

Official record : OEA/Ser. L .
(V/II.49, doc. 19, corr. 1) Inter-American Commission on Human Rights. Report on the situation of human rights in Argentina /. Washington, D.C. [1980] iii, 266 p. ;　ISBN 0-8270-1099-0 (pbk.) :　LC Card 80-128497　DDC 341.24/5 s 323.4/0983 19
F1405.5 1959 .O7 OEA/Ser.L ; V/II.49, doc. 19, corr. 1 JC599.A7

ORGANIZATION OF AMERICAN STATES.
Organization of American States. Manual de clasificación para la Serie de documentos oficiales de la OEA . Washington, D.C. , 1979. viii, 121 p. :　LC Card 79-111656　DDC 341.24/5 s 025.4/2 19
F1402 .A169 OEA/Ser.Y/II.l Z697.G7

Organization of American States. Permanent Council. Acta de la sesión ordinaria celebrada el 3 de mayo de 1978 . Washington, D.C. , 1978. v, 268 p. ;　LC Card 79-108138　DDC 341.24/5 19
F1402 .A169 OEA/Ser. G CP/ACTA 324/78

Organization of American States. Biblioteca Conmemorativa de Colón. see Columbus Memorial Library.

Organization of American States. Columbus Memorial Library. see Columbus Memorial Library.

Organization of American States. Council. Inter-American Economic and Social Council. see Inter-American Economic and Social Council.

Organization of American States. Dept. of Educational Affairs. Educational deficits in the Caribbean = Los déficits educativos en el Caribe. [Washington, D.C.] : Organization of American States, Dept. of Educational Affairs, [1979] viii, 128 p. : ill. ; 28 cm. (Atlas series ; no. 2) Collection of monographs and studies of education "79-XIII-007-S." Bibliography: p. 108.　LC Card 80-132005　DDC 371.9/67/09729 19
1. Socially handicapped children - Education - Caribbean area. 2. Illiteracy - Caribbean area. 3. Underdeveloped areas - Education. I. Title. II. Title: Los déficits educativos en el Caribe. III. Series: Atlas series (Washington, D.C.) , no. 2.
LC4095.C37 O73 1979

Organization of American States. Dept. of External Cooperation. International Trade Unit. see Organization of American States. International Trade Unit.

Organization of American States. Dept. of Publications. Columbus Memorial Library. see Columbus Memorial Library.

Organization of American States. Dept. of Publicatons. Biblioteca Conmemorativa de Colón. see Columbus Memorial Library.

Organization of American States. Dept. of Scientific Affairs. Programa Regional de Desarrollo Científico y Tecnológico. see Programa Regional de Desarrollo Científico y Tecnológico.

Organization of American States. General Assembly.
Reglamento de la Asamblea General : aprobado en el primer período extraordinario de sesiones el 7 de julio de 1970, incluye las reformas en el tercer, cuarto, séptimo y octavo períodos ordinarios de sesiones / Organización de los Estados Americanos, Asamblea General. Washington, D.C. : Secretaría General de la Organización de los Estados Americanos, 1978. v, 30 p. ; 28 cm. ([Documentos oficiales] - Organización de los Estados Americanos . OEA/Ser. P/I.1 rev. 5)　LC Card 80-142828　DDC 341.24/5 s 341.24/5 19
1. Organization of American States. General Assembly - Rules and practice. I. Series: Organization of American States. Documentos oficiales , OEA/Ser. P/I.1 ref. 5. II. Title.
F1402 .A169 OEA/Ser. P/I.1 rev. 5 F1402.A4

ORGANIZATION OF AMERICAN STATES. GENERAL ASSEMBLY - RULES AND PRACTICE.
Organization of American States. General Assembly. Reglamento de la Asamblea General . Washington, D.C. , 1978. v, 30 p. ;　LC Card 80-142828　DDC 341.24/5 s 341.24/5 19
F1402 .A169 OEA/Ser. P/I.1 rev. 5 F1402.A4

Organization of American States. General Secretariat.
Al libertador general San Martín . Washington, D.C. [1978] vii, 51 p., [1] leaf of plates :　LC Card 80-145557　DDC 980/.02/0924 B 19
F2235.4 .A677

Synthesis of economic performance in Latin America. 1978- Washington.
NYPL　[JLM 80-785]

Tribute to Picasso : [exhibition], Organization of American States, October 25, 1973, Washington, D.C. = Homenaje a Picasso. [Washington : Organization of American States, General Secretariat, 1973] [33] p. : ill. (some col.) ; 23 cm. Cover title.　LC Card 75-328387
1. Paintings, Latin America - Exhibitions. 2. Paintings, Modern - 20th century - Latin America - Exhibitions. 3. Picasso, Pablo, 1881-1973. I. Title. II. Title: Homenaje a Picasso.
ND202 .O73 1973

Organization of American States. General Secretariat. Biblioteca Conmemorativa de Colón. see Columbus Memorial Library.

Organization of American States. General Secretariat. Columbua Memorial Library. see Columbus Memorial Library.

Organization of American States. Inter-American Commission on Human Rights. see Inter-

American Commission on Human Rights.

Organization of American States. Inter-American Council for Education, Science, and Culture. see Inter-American Council for Education, Science, and Culture.

Organization of American States. International Trade and Export Development Program. U. S. market profiles, series III / International Trade and Export Development Program. Washington, D.C. : [Published for] CIES [by] General Secretariat, Organization of American States, [1980] 19 v. : ill. ; 28 cm. Cover title. CONTENTS. - [1] Apricot paste and pulp.--[2] Bleached beeswax.--[3] Cigarette lighters (non-precious metal).--[4] Coconut meat.--[5] Compressors.--[6] Costume jewelry.--[7] Crystallized ginger.--[8] Environmental and industrial process controls.--[9] Fruit paste and pulp of cashew apple, mamey colorado, sopodilla, soursop, and sweetsop.--[10] Guitars.--[11] Honey.--[12] Knives, fork[s], and spoons with silver-plated handles.--[13] Leather desk accessories of a box-like construction.--[14] Meat sauce.--[15] Non-standard wood moulding.--[16] Orange marmalade.--[17] Shoe polishes and cleaners.--[18] Steel pipe fittings.--[19] Wooden household utensils.　ISBN 0-8270-1011-7 (pbk. : v. 1) :　LC Card 80-498362　DDC 658.8/35/0973 19
1. Market surveys - United States. I. Inter-American Economic and Social Council. II. Title.
HC110.C6 O73 1980

Organization of American States. International Trade Unit. Smith, Bryant D. The impact of trade policy on exports in oil rich countries . Washington , 1975. ix, 136 p. :　LC Card 80-469796
HF3436.5 .S63

Organization of American States. Library Development Program. Cuadernos bibliotecológicos .
(no. 62) Shepard, Marietta Daniels, 1913- ... A solicitud de los países ... . Washington, D.C. , 1974. 27 p. ;　LC Card 80-121848　DDC 020 s 021.6/4 19
Z674 .P182 no. 62 Z738

Organization of American States. Pan American Health Organization. see Pan American Health Organization.

Organization of American States. Permanent Council. Acta de la sesión ordinaria celebrada el 3 de mayo de 1978 : aprobada en la sesión del 7 de junio de 1978 / [Organización de los Estados Americanos, Consejo Permanente]. Washington, D.C. : Secretaría General de la Organización de los Estados Americanos, 1978. v, 268 p. ; 28 cm. ([Documentos oficiales] - Organización de los Estados Americanos ; OEA/Ser. G CP/ACTA 324/78) Documents presented at a meeting.　LC Card 79-108138　DDC 341.24/5 19
1. Organization of American States. I. Series: Organization of American States. Documents oficiales , OEA/ser. G CP/ACTA 324/78. II. Title.
F1402 .A169 OEA/Ser. G CP/ACTA 324/78

Organization of American States. Secretaría General. see Organization of American States. General Secretariat.

ORGANIZATION OF PETROLEUM EXPORTING COUNTRIES.
Fleisis, Heywood W. The effect of OPEC oil pricing on output, prices, and exchange rates in the United States and other industrial countries /. [Washington, D.C.] , 1981. xx, 107 p. :　LC Card 81-601242　DDC 338.2/3 19
HD9560.4 .F58

United States. General Accounting Office. Changes needed to improve government's knowledge of OPEC financial influence in the United States . [Washington] 1979. vi, 71 p. ;　LC Card 80-600965　DDC 332.6/73/0973 19
HG4910 .U5434 1979a

ORGANIZATION OF PETROLEUM EXPORTING COUNTRIES - ECONOMIC ASSISTANCE.
United Nations. Conference on Trade and Development. Secretariat. Financial solidarity for development . New York , 1979. 2 v. ;　LC Card 80-125802　DDC 300 s 338.91 19
JX1977 .A2 TD/B/C.7/31

ORGANIZATION OF PETROLEUM EXPORTING COUNTRIES - STATISTICS.
The PIMS U. S.-OPEC petroleum report, year

1973. Washington, D.C. [1974] 26 p. : LC Card 80-603212 DDC 382/.42282/0973 19
HD9560.4 .P48

Organization, role, and staffing of State budget offices /. Kentucky. University. Bureau of Business Research. Lexington, Ky. , 1961, 1965 printing. vi, 122 p. ; LC Card 80-506084 DDC 353.9/3722 19
HJ2053.A1 K46 1961

ORGANIZATION, SOCIAL. see SOCIAL STRUCTURE.

ORGANIZATIONAL CHANGE - RESEARCH.
Pethia, Robert F. The case for a multivariate treatment of situational diversity, complexity, change, and relatedness in studies of organizational design /. Austin, Tex. [1980] 19 p. : LC Card 80-623771 DDC 302.3/5 19
HM131 .P393

ORGANIZATIONAL EFFECTIVENESS.
United Nations. Dept. of Technical Co-operation for Development. Handbook on the improvement of administrative management in public administration . New York , 1979. vii, 67 p. : LC Card 80-119207 DDC 300 s 350.007/5/091724 19
JX1977 .A2 ST/ESA/SER.E/19

United States. General Accounting Office. Evaluating a performance measurement system . [Washington, D.C. [1980] 24 p. ; LC Card 80-602699 DDC 353.07/6 19
JK468.P75 U56 1980

Zammuto, Raymond F. Assessing organizational effectiveness . Albany , 1982. p. cm. ISBN 0-87395-552-8 LC Card 81-9130 DDC 658.4/01 19
HD58.9 .Z35

Organizational forms for effecting patient and material movement /. Emerzian, A. D. Joseph. [Atlanta] , 1976. vii leaves, 78 p. ; LC Card 76-622515 DDC 362.1/1/068 19
RA975.5.P39 E47

ORGANIZATIONAL INNOVATION. see ORGANIZATIONAL CHANGE.

Organizational systems for national planning /. United Nations. Dept. of Technical Co-operation for Development. New York , 1979. vi, 177 p. : LC Card 79-123608 DDC 300 s 338.9/009172/4 19
JX1977 .A2 ST/ESA/SER.E/18

Organizations engaged in preparing standards for dental materials and therapeutic agents with a list of standards /. Paffenbarger, George Corbly, 1902- [Washington, D.C.] [1980] iii, 51 p. ; LC Card 80-600041 DDC 602/.18 s 362.1/7 19
QC100 .U57 no. 571 RK681

ORGANIZATSIIA STRAN VARSHAVSKOGO DOGOVORA.
Hillier, Pat. U. S. ground forces . [Washington, D.C.] , 1980. xxiii, 87 p. : LC Card 81-600683 DDC 355/.033073 19
UA23 .H513

ORGANIZED CAMPS. see CAMPS.

Organized crime and use of violence . United States. Congress. Senate. Committee on Governmental Affairs. Permanent Subcommittee on Investigations. Washington , 1980- v. : LC Card 80-603084 DDC 364.1/06/073 19
KF26 .G674 1980a

ORGANIZED CRIME - INFORMATION SERVICES - UNITED STATES.
United States. General Accounting Office. The interstate organized crime index . [Washington, D.C.] , 1979. ii, 53 p. ; LC Card 79-602616 DDC 353.0075 19
HV8079.O73 U54 1979

ORGANIZED CRIME - NEW JERSEY.
New Jersey. State Legislature. General Assembly. Judiciary, Law, Public Safety, and Defense Committee. Committee meeting before Assembly Judiciary, Law, Public Safety, and Defense Committee on A-1079 (Racketeer Influenced and Corrupt Organizations Act) . [Trenton] [1980] 18, 22, 36 p. ; LC Card 81-621304 DDC 345.749 347.4905 19
KFN1811.4 .J78 1980a

ORGANIZED CRIME - PENNSYLVANIA.
Pennsylvania. Crime Commission (1968-) A decade of organized crime . St. Davids, Pa. ,

c1980. xii, 279 p. : ISBN 0-937972-00-2 (pbk.) LC Card 80-620035 DDC 364.1/06/0748 19
HV7288 .A6 1980

ORGANIZED CRIME - UNITED STATES.
United States. Congress. Senate. Committee on Governmental Affairs. Permanent Subcommittee on Investigations. Organized crime and use of violence . Washington , 1980- v. : LC Card 80-603084 DDC 364.1/06/073 19
KF26 .G674 1980a

Organizing for development . President's Reorganization Project (U. S.) Washington, D.C. , 1979. viii, 66, [36] p. : LC Card 81-601244 DDC 338.973 19
HC110.P63 P73 1979

Organizzazione del Trattato dell'Atlantico del Nord. see North Atlantic Treaty Organization.

Organizzazione del Trattato Nord Atlantico. see North Atlantic Treaty Organization.

ORGANOCHLORINE COMPOUNDS - ENVIRONMENTAL ASPECTS - SOUTH CAROLINA.
Blus, Lawrence J. Breeding biology and relation of pollutants to black skimmers and gull-billed terns in South Carolina /. Washington, D.C. , 1980. p. cm. LC Card 80-607954 DDC 639.9/79/0973 s 598/.338 19
SK361 .A256 no. 230 QL696.C479

ORGANOFLUORINE COMPOUNDS.
(1979) Screening of selected fluoroaromatic compounds for use as agrichemicals, I /. Urbana, Ill. [1979] 17 p. : LC Card 80-622082 DDC 557.73 s 632/.952 19
QE105 .A45 no. 508 SB952.F55

ORGANOHALOGEN COMPOUNDS - ENVIRONMENTAL ASPECTS.
Bonner, William P. Effects of wastewater process operation on organics in potable water supplies /. Knoxville , 1978. ix, 109 leaves : LC Card 79-624195 DDC 628.1/62 19
TD758.5.O75 B66

Orientation Conference for Louisiana Legislators (1980 :Baton Rouge, La.) A Workbook of informational data . Baton Rouge, LA (P.O. Box 44012, Baton Rouge 70804) [1980?] xi leaves, 212 p. : LC Card 81-620884 DDC 353.9763 19
HJ465 .W67

ORIGIN AND DESTINATION TRAFFIC SURVEYS - NEW YORK METROPOLITAN AREA - PERIODICALS.
Trans-Hudson vehicular origin and destination survey. [New York]. **NYPL [JLM 80-891]**

The Origins of Chinese civilization / edited by David N. Keightley ; with contributions by Noel Barnard ... [et al.]. Berkeley : University of California Press, c1981. p. cm. Includes bibliographies and index. ISBN 0-520-04229-8 LC Card 81-4595 DDC 931 19
1. China - Civilization - To 221 B.C. I. Keightley, David N. II. Barnard, Noel.
DS741.65 .O74

The origins of modern reform in Iran /. Nashat, Guity, 1937- Urbana , c1981. p. cm. ISBN 0-252-00822-7 LC Card 81-3343 DDC 955/.04 19
DS307 .N26

ORISKANY FORMATION. see GEOLOGY, STRATIGRAPHIC - DEVONIAN.

Orleans County, N. Y. County Superintendent of Highways. National Survey (Firm) 1978 Highway map of Orleans County, New York. Chester, Vt., c1978. col. map. 55 x 70 cm. Scale ca. 1:63,360. Includes index and location map. Text and illus. on verso. Distributed by County Superintendent of Highways. **NYPL [Map Div. 80-3303]**

Orleans County, N. Y. Highways, Superintendent of. see Orleans County, N. Y. County Superintendent of Highways.

ORLEANS COUNTY, N. Y. - MAPS.
(1978) National Survey (Firm) 1978 Highway map of Orleans County, New York. Chester, Vt., c1978. col. map. 55 x 70 cm. Scale ca. 1:63,360. Includes index and location map. Text and illus. on verso. Distributed by County Superintendent of Highways. **NYPL [Map Div. 80-3303]**

ORLEANS COUNTY, N. Y. - ROAD MAPS.
National Survey (Firm) 1978 Highway map of Orleans County, New York. Chester, Vt., c1978. col. map. 55 x 70 cm. Scale ca. 1:63,360. Includes index and location map. Text and illus. on verso. Distributed by County Superintendent of Highways. **NYPL [Map Div. 80-3303]**

Orleans County, N. Y. Superintendent of Highways. see Orleans County, N. Y. County Superintendent of Highways.

Orleans, Leo A. China's population policies and population data : review and update / prepared for the Committee on Foreign Affairs, U. S. House of Representatives ; by the Congressional Research Service, Library of Congress. Washington : U. S. G.P.O., 1981. v, 32 p. ; 24 cm. At head of title: 97th Congress, 1st session. Committee print. Item 1017-A, 1017-B (microfiche) Includes bibliographical references. LC Card 81-601675 DDC 304.6/0951 19
1. China - Population. 2. China - Population policy. I. United States. Congress. House. Committee on Foreign Affairs. II. Library of Congress. Congressional Research Service. III. Title.
HB3654.A3 O74

ORLÉANS, LOUIS PHILIPPE JOSEPH, DUC D', 1747-1793.
Kelly, George Armstrong, 1932- Victims, authority, and terror . Chapel Hill , c1982. p. cm. ISBN 0-8078-1495-4 LC Card 81-10298 DDC 944.04 19
DC138 .K35

Orlins, Robert I. (joint author) Baumhoff, Martin A. An archaeological assay on Dry Creek, Sonoma County, California /. Berkeley , 1979. xi, 244 p. : LC Card 80-620631 DDC 979.4/18 19
E51 .C2 no. 40 E78.C15

ORNAMENTAL WOODY PLANTS - ALASKA.
Epps, Alan C. Landscape plant materials for Alaska /. [Fairbanks] [Washington] , c1979. iii, 66 p. : LC Card 80-623301 DDC 635.9/77/09798 19
SB435.52.A4 E66

ORNITHOLOGY - TECHNIQUE.
Johnston, Richard F. Replication of habitat profiles for birds /. Lawrence , 1979. 11 p. : LC Card 79-624990 DDC 598.2/5 19
QL677.5 .J63

OROGENY - CANADA - CONGRESSES.
"The Caledonides in the USA" . [Blacksburg, Va.] , 1980. iv, 329, 19 p. : LC Card 81-134431 DDC 551.7/32/0973 19
QE661 .C34

OROGENY - EUROPE - CONGRESSES.
"The Caledonides in the USA" . [Blacksburg, Va.] , 1980. iv, 329, 19 p. : LC Card 81-134431 DDC 551.7/32/0973 19
QE661 .C34

OROGENY - UNITED STATES - CONGRESSES.
"The Caledonides in the USA" . [Blacksburg, Va.] , 1980. iv, 329, 19 p. : LC Card 81-134431 DDC 551.7/32/0973 19
QE661 .C34

O'Rourke, Andrew Desmond, 1938- (joint author) Kirkland, Jack J. Market potential of the Middle East /. [Pullman] , 1980. 82 p. : LC Card 80-622499 DDC 330.956/04 19
HF3756.Z5 K57

ORR, GEORGE VERNON, 1916-
United States. Congress. Senate. Committee on Armed Services. Nomination of George Vernon Orr, Jr., to be secretary of the Air Force . Washington , 1981. ii, 12 p. ; LC Card 81-601412 DDC 353.63 19
KF26 .A7 1981b

Orr, James A.
(joint author) Aho, C. Michael, 1949- Demographic and occupational characteristics of workers in trade-sensitive industries /. [Washington, D.C.] [Springfield, Va.] 1980. 17, [15] p. ; LC Card 80-602632 DDC 331.11/4 19
HD5710.75.U6 A37

(joint author) Bayard, Thomas O. Trade and employment effects of tariff reductions agreed to in the MTN /. [Washington, D.C.] [Springfield, Va.] 1980. 11, [31] p. ; LC Card 80-602631 DDC 382.7 19
HF1757 .B39

ORTHOPEDIC IMPLANTS - COMPLICATIONS AND SEQUELAE - CONGRESSES.
Implant retrieval . Washington, D.C. , 1981. xi, 776 :   LC Card 80-600194   DDC 602/.18 s 617/.307 19
QC100 .U57 no. 601 RD755.5

ORTHOPEDIC IMPLANTS - MATERIALS - CORROSION - CONGRESSES.
Implant retrieval . Washington, D.C. , 1981. xi, 776 :   LC Card 80-600194   DDC 602/.18 s 617/.307 19
QC100 .U57 no. 601 RD755.5

ORTHOPEDIC IMPLANTS - MATERIALS - DETERIORATION - CONGRESSES.
Implant retrieval . Washington, D.C. , 1981. xi, 776 :   LC Card 80-600194   DDC 602/.18 s 617/.307 19
QC100 .U57 no. 601 RD755.5

Orwell, George, 1903-1950.
Politics and the English language. Lewis, Flossie, 1942- The involuntary conversion of a 727 or crash! : some ways and means to deflate the inflated style with a new look at Orwell's "Politics and the English language" / by Flossie Lewis (Florence C. Lewis) ; [cover design, Gene Izuno]. Berkeley, Calif. , c1979. iv, 35 p. ;   LC Card 80-155340   DDC 808/.042 19
PE1421 .L4

POLITICS AND THE ENGLISH LANGUAGE - ADDRESSES, ESSAYS, LECTURES.
Lewis, Flossie, 1942- The involuntary conversion of a 727 or crash! . Berkeley, Calif. , c1979. iv, 35 p. ;   LC Card 80-155340   DDC 808/.042 19
PE1421 .L4

Ory, Norma R. Bookbinding, a living art : June 11-September 7, 1980, Masterson Junior Gallery, the Museum of Fine Arts, Houston, September 18-October 19, 1980, the Humanities Research Center, the University of Texas at Austin / pref. by William C. Agee ; catalogue by Norma R. Ory. Houston, Tex. : The Museum, c1980. 48 p. : ill. ; 23 x 31 cm. Exhibition organized by N.R. Org; co-curated by Decherd Turner. Bibliography: p. 48.   ISBN 0-89090-004-3 (pbk.)   LC Card 80-83065   DDC 686.3/074064/1411 19
1. Bookbinding - Exhibitions. 2. Houston, Tex. - Exhibitions. I. Turner, Decherd. II. Houston, Tex. Museum of Fine Arts. III. Texas. University at Austin. Humanities Research Center. IV. Title.
Z269 .O79

ORYZA - BIBLIOGRAPHY.
Eastin, E. F. Selected bibliography of red rice and other wild rices (Oryza spp.) /. College Station , 1979. 59 p. ;   LC Card 79-625846   DDC 016.6331/87 19
Z5356.R43 E25 SB615.R4

Osag, T. R. Control of odors from inedibles-rendering plants / T. R. Osag and G. B. Crane. Research Triangle Park, N. C., U. S. Environmental Protection Agency, Office of Air and Waste Management, Office of Air Quality Planning and Standards, 1974. vi, 51 p. in various pagings. ill. 26 cm. "EPA-450/1-74-006."
1. Odor control. 2. Rendering works. I. Crane, George B., joint author. II. United States. Environmental Protection Agency. Office of Air Quality Planning and Standards. III. Title.   **NYPL [JSF 80-793]**

OSAGE INDIANS - BIOGRAPHY.
Mathews, John Joseph, 1895- Talking to the moon /. Norman [Okla.] [1981] c1945. viii, 243 p. ;   ISBN 0-8061-1611-0   LC Card 81-137822   DDC 976.6/2505/0924 19
E99.O8 M298 1981

Osborne, John C., 1928- Grimmelshausen, Hans Jakob Christoph von, 1625-1676. [Seltzame Springinsfeld. English.] The singular life story of heedless Hopalong /. Detroit , 1981. p. cm.   ISBN 0-8143-1688-3   LC Card 81-10446   DDC 833/.5 19
PT1731.S7 E5 1981

Osborne, Owen D. Oregon. State University, Corvallis. Federal Cooperative Extension Service. Oregon Energy Extension Service State plan /. [Corvallis] [1980] 38 p. :   LC Card 80-621871   DDC 630/.9795 s 333.79/16/09795 19
S105 .E43 no. 569 TJ163.4.U6

Osga, Glenn A. An investigation of the riding experiences of MSF rider course participants in South Dakota / by Glenn A. Osga ; prepared by Human Factors Laboratory, University of South Dakota. Pierre, S.D. : Office of State and Community Programs, Division of Highway Safety, South Dakota Dept. of Public Safety, [1980] xi, 231 leaves : forms ; 28 cm. (Report / Human Factors Laboratory, University of South Dakota . no. HFL-80-2) "August 1980; final report"--Cover. Bibliography: leaves 198-203.   LC Card 80-624202   DDC 629.28/475/0715 19
1. Motorcycling - Study and teaching - South Dakota. I. University of South Dakota. Human Factors Laboratory. II. Series: Report (University of South Dakota. Human Factors Laboratory) , no. HFL-80-2. III. Title.
TL440.5 .O83

Oshiro, Ernest M. (Ernest Masao), 1949- Application of an input-output linear programming model in land use planning for Molokai / Ernest M. Oshiro and Harold L. Baker. Honolulu, Hawaii : Hawaii Institute of Tropical Agriculture and Human Resources, University of Hawaii, [1981] p. cm. (Research report / Hawaii Institute of Tropical Agriculture and Human Resources, University of Hawaii, 0073-0998 . 246) Bibliography: p.   LC Card 81-4464   DDC 333.76/17/0996924 19
1. Land use, Rural - Hawaii - Molokai - Planning - Linear programming. I. Baker, Harold L. II. Series: Reaearch report (Hawaii Institute of Tropical Agriculture and Human Resources) , 246. III. Title.
HD211.H3 O84

OSMOREGULATION.
Ellis, Robert W. Effect of mercury on osmotic regulation and protein kinetics in the crayfish, Pacifastacus leniusculus /. Boise, Idaho , 1979. 30, [4] leaves :   LC Card 79-626025   DDC 595.3/841 19
QL444.M33 E44

Ospina, Enrique. Disaggregated econometric analysis of U. S. slaughter beef supply / Enrique Ospina and C. Richard Shumway. College Station, Tex. : Texas Agricultural Experiment Station, Texas A&M University System, [1980] 57 p. ; 23 cm. (Technical monograph - The Texas Agricultural Experiment Station ; 9) Bibliography: p. 54-55.   LC Card 80-621501   DDC 338.1/76213/0973 19
1. Cattle trade - United States - Mathematical models. 2. Beef cattle - United States - Mathematical models. 3. Beef packers - Mathematical models. I. Shumway, C. Richard, joint author. II. Series: Texas. Agricultural Experiment Station, College Station. Technical monograph - The Texas Agricultural Experiment Station , 9. III. Title.
HD9433.U4 O84

Ostenson, Thomas K. (joint author) Voelker, Stanley W. Population changes within census county divisions of North Dakota, 1950-1970 /. Fargo, N.D. [Washington] , 1971. 23 leaves, [4] leaves of plates :   LC Card 80-621261   DDC 312/.8/09784 19
HA566 .V63

OSTEOPATHS - MICHIGAN - STATISTICS.
Michigan. Cooperative Health Information System. Licensed health occupations, Michigan physicians (M.D. and D.O.) 1976. Lansing, Mich. [1976] 57 p. :   LC Card 80-622891   DDC 331.12/916109774 19
RA410.8.M5 M49 1976

OSTEOPATHS - SUPPLY AND DISTRIBUTION - ARKANSAS - STATISTICS - PERIODICALS.
Arkansas health manpower statistics: osteopaths. 1978- Little Rock.
                           NYPL [JLM 80-1078]

OSTEOPATHS - VERMONT - STATISTICS.
Vermont. Dept. of Health. Division of Public Health Statistics. Physicians in Vermont, 1979. Burlington, Vt. [1980] iv, 45 p. :   LC Card 80-623433   DDC 331.12/9161/09743 19
RA410.8.V5 V47 1980

OSTEOPATHS - WASHINGTON (STATE) - STATISTICS.
Starzyk, Patricia M. Allopathic and osteopathic physicians in Washington State, 1978 /. Olympia, Wash. [197-?] 54 p. :   LC Card 80-624428   DDC 331.12/9161/09797 19
RA410.8.W2 S73

Osterholm, Michael T. (joint author) Singer, Rexford D. Ground water quality in southeastern Minnesota /. Minneapolis, Minn. [1980] vi, 79, 64 leaves :   LC Card 80-622728   DDC 553.7/9/097761 19
TD224.M6 S56

Osterkamp, W. R. Perennial-streamflow characteristics related to channel geometry and sediment in the Missouri River basin / by W.R. Osterkamp and E.R. Hedman. [Reston, Va.?] : U. S. Geological Survey, [1981] p. cm. (Geological Survey professional paper) Bibliography: p.   LC Card 81-607905   DDC 551.48/3/0978 19
1. Stream measurements - Missouri Valley. 2. River channels - Missouri Valley. 3. Sediment transport - Missouri Valley. I. Hedman, E. R. II. Title. III. Series.
GB1227.M7 O84

Osterndorf, Logan. Mushkin, Selma J., 1913- Indicators of youth unemployment and education in industrialized nations /. [Washington] , 1978. v, 181 p. :   LC Card 79-602354
HD6270 .M87   **NYPL [JLG 81-24]**

OSTRES. see OYSTERS.

Ostroff, Eugene. Western views and Eastern visions / by Eugene Ostroff. Washington : Published by the Smithsonian Institution Traveling Exhibition Service with the cooperation of the United States Geological Survey, 1981. 118 p. : ill. ; 28 cm. Prepared in conjunction with an exhibition presented by the Smithsonian Institution Traveling Exhibition Service. Bibliography: p. 116-118.   ISBN 0-86528-005-3 (pbk.)   LC Card 81-70   DDC 779/.9978 19
1. Photography - The West - History - Exhibitions. I. Smithsonian Institution. Traveling Exhibition Service. II. Title.
TR23.6 .O87

Ostrom, Elinor. Policing metropolitan America / by Elinor Ostrom, Roger B. Parks, and Gordon P. Whitaker. [Washington] : National Science Foundation : for sale by the Supt. of Docs., U. S. Govt. Print. Off., [1977] viii, 49 p. : ill. ; 27 cm. Microfiche (neg.) NTIS. 1 sheet. 11 x 15 cm. (PB 270 028 "NSF/RA-770001." "Report prepared for National Science Foundation, Research Applications Directorate, RANN--Research Applied to National Needs." Bibliography: p. 48-49.   LC Card 77-603798
1. Police - United States. 2. Police administration - United States. I. Parks, Roger B., joint author. II. Whitaker, Gordon P., joint author. III. United States. National Science Foundation. Research Applied to National Needs Program. IV. Title.
HV8138 .O76   **NYPL [*XME-9420]**

Oswalt, Wendell H. Historic settlements along the Kuskokwim River, Alaska / by Wendell H. Oswalt. Juneau, Alaska : Alaska Division of State Libraries and Museums, Dept. of Education, 1980. 104 p. : ill. ; 28 cm. (Alaska State Library historical monograph ; no. 7) Bibliography: p. 96-104.   LC Card 80-623186   DDC 979.8/4 19
1. Kuskokwim Valley, Alaska - History, Local. 2. Land settlement - Alaska - Kuskokwim Valley - History. I. Series: Historical monographs (Juneau) , no. 7. II. Title.
F912.K85 O85

Oswego, N. Y. State University College. see New York State. State University College, Oswego.

Ota. see United States. Congress. Office of Technology Assessment.

OTA Oceans Program. Energy from open ocean kelp farms /. Washington , 1980. ix, 82 p. :   LC Card 80-603976   DDC 333.95/3 19
TP360 .E54

OTA Seminar on the Discrete Address Beacon System (DABS), Washington, D.C., 1980. Proceedings of the OTA Seminar on the Discrete Address Beacon System (DABS). Washington, D.C. : Congress of the U. S., Office of Technology Assessment, [1980] vii, 46 p. ; 26 cm. (OTA background paper ; OTA-BP-T-4) "July 1980."   LC Card 80-600093   DDC 387.7/4042/0973 19
1. Radio air traffic control systems - Congresses. I. Series: United States. Congress. Office of Technology Assessment. OTA background paper , OTA-BP-T-4.
TL696.R25 O18 1980

Otelsberg, Jonah. (joint author) Muller, Charlotte Feldman, 1921- Study of physician reimbursement under medicare and medicaid /.

[Washington] 1979- v. : LC Card 80-601289
DDC 338.4/33621/0973 19
R728.5 .M84

Other nations, other peoples . Pike, Lewis W.
[Washington, D.C.] , 1979. xxiii, 139 p. : LC
Card 80-600989 DDC 370.19/6 19
LC1099 .P54

Otis, Ted. Some economic aspects of air pollution
in Montana / Ted Otis, John Duffield and
Mike Ruby. Helena, Mont. : Air Quality
Bureau, Montana Dept. of Health and
Environmental Sciences, [1979] ii, 94 p. ; 28
cm. "November 1979." Bibliography: p. 78-84. LC
Card 80-622032 DDC 338.4/73637392/09786
19
1. Air - Pollution - Economic aspects - Montana. I.
Duffield, John, joint author. II. Ruby, Mike, joint
author. III. Montana. Air Quality Bureau. IV. Title.
HC107.M93 A45

Ott, Mary Diederich. Women's participation in
first-professional degree programs in medicine,
dentistry, veterinary medicine, and law, 1969-70
through 1974-75 / by Mary Diederich Ott.
[Washington] : U. S. Dept. of Health,
Education, and Welfare, Education Division,
National Center for Education Statistics : for
sale by the Supt. of Docs., U. S. Govt. Print.
Off., 1976. viii, 21 p. : ill. ; 26 cm. "NCES
76-023." LC Card 77-601995 DDC 610/.7/1173 19
1. Women medical students - United States - Statistics.
2. Women dental students - United States - Statistics. 3.
Women veterinary students - United States - Statistics.
4. Women law students - United States - Statistics. 5.
Professional education of women - United States -
Statistics. I. Title: Women's participation in
first-professional degree programs ...
R745 .O87

Otter, Augustine J. Soil survey of Calumet and
Maitowoc Counties, Wisconsin / [by Augustine
J. Otter] ; United Sstates Department of
Agriculture, Soil Conservation Service, in
cooperation with Research Division of the
College of Agricultural and Life Sciences,
University of Wisconsin. [Washington, D.C. :
The Service] 1980. vii, 176 p., [64] fold. leaves
of plates : ill. ; 28 cm. Cover title. Bibliography: p.
102. LC Card 80-602383 DDC 631.4/7/77566 19
1. Soils - Wisconsin - Calumet Co. - Maps. 2. Soils -
Wisconsin - Manitowoc County - Maps. I. United
States. Soil Conservation Service. II. Wisconsin.
University, Madison. College of Agricultural and Life
Sciences. Research Division. III. Title.
S599.W5 O86

Our Constitution and government. United States.
Immigration and Naturalization Service. [1st]-
ed. Washington, 1940-   *NYPL [Pub. Cat.*
80-967 & IB (United States. Immigration
and Naturalization Service. Our
Constitution and government.)]

Our last first poets . Nelson, Cary. Urbana ,
c1981. p. cm. ISBN 0-252-00885-5 LC Card
81-5082 DDC 811/.54/09 19
PS325 .N4

Our Massachusetts State government : a
collection of essays / edited by George S.
Perry, Jr. [Boston] : Massachusetts Dept. of
Education : Massachusetts Teachers
Association, c1978. 158 p. ; 21 cm. Addendum
slip inserted. Includes bibliographies. LC Card
80-620701 DDC 320.9744 19
1. Massachusetts - Politics and government - Addresses,
essays, lectures. I. Perry, George Sylva, 1954-.
JK3119 .O95

Ours once more . Herzfeld, Michael, 1947-
Austin , 1981. p. cm. ISBN 0-292-76018-3 LC
Card 81-10398 DDC 398/.09495 19
GR170 .H47

**Out-of-state institutions operating in Virginia,
1978-79.** Virginia. State Council of Higher
Education. [Richmond] [1979] 42 p. ; LC Card
80-622044 DDC 378.73 19
LA227.3 .V57 1979

Out of this struggle : the Filipinos in Hawaii /
edited by Luis V. Teodoro, Jr. ; foreword by
Danilo E. Ponce ; drawings by Francisco
"Corky" Trinidad. Honolulu : Published for the
Filipino 75th Anniversary Commemoration
Commission by the University Press of Hawaii,
c1981. p. cm. Bibliography: p. ISBN 0-8248-0747-2
LC Card 81-714 DDC 996.9/0049921 19
1. Filipino Americans - Hawaii - History. 2. Hawaii -
Race relations. I. Teodoro, Luis V., 1941-. II. Filipino

75th Anniversary Commemoration Commission. III.
Title: Filipinos in Hawaii.
DU624.7.F4 O9

OUTBURSTS, ROCK. see ROCK BURSTS.

**OUTDOOR RECREATION - BLACK HILLS
NATIONAL FOREST - MAPS.**
United States. Forest Service. Rocky Mountain
Region. Black Hills Nacional Forest, South
Dakota, Wyoming, 1972. [Denver] 1976. col.
map on sheet 114 x 66 cm. Scale 1:126,720; 1/2″
= 1 mile. Printed on both sides of sheet. Relief shown
by hachures and spot heights. "Polyconic projection.
Black Hills meridian, sixth principal meridian." "Forest
visitors map." Includes map keys, "Vicinity maps," text,
col. illus., "Recreation site directory," and "Pactola
Reservoir vicinity map," "Sheridan Lake vicinity map,"
and "Deerfield Lake vicinity map." Includes map keys,
"Vicinity map," text, col. illus., "Recreation site
directory," and "Pactola Reservoir vicinity map,"
"Sheridan Lake vicinity map," and "Deerfield Lake
vicinity map."
G4182.B51 1972 .U5
                            NYPL [Map Div. 80-3419]

OUTDOOR RECREATION - CALIFORNIA.
California. Dept. of Parks and Recreation.
CORRP 74 . Sacramento , 1974. x, 188 p. :
LC Card 75-620931
GV191.42.C2 C34 1974
                              NYPL [JFF 80-1472]

**OUTDOOR RECREATION - CALIFORNIA -
COSTS.**
California. Dept. of Finance. Program
Evaluation Unit. Review of Davis-Dolwig
allocation methodology . [Sacramento] [1979]
xviii, 85 p. : LC Card 80-620662 DDC
333.78/09794 19
GV191.42.C2 C33 1979

**OUTDOOR RECREATION - CALIFORNIA -
PLANNING.**
Troy, Richard E. California State park system
plan, 1980 . Sacramento, Calif. [1980] viii, 239
p. : LC Card 80-622915 DDC 333.78/3/09794 19
GV191.42.C2 T76

**OUTDOOR RECREATION - COLORADO -
ARAPAHO NATIONAL FOREST - MAPS.**
United States. Forest Service. Rocky Mountain
Region. Arapaho National Forest, Colorado,
1974. [Denver] 1977. col. map on sheet 66 x
107 cm. Scale 1:126,720; 11/2″ = 1 mile. Printed on
both sides of sheet. Relief shown by hachures and sport
heights. "Polyconic projection." "Sixth principal
meridian." "Forest visitors map."
                            NYPL [Map Div. 80-3424]

**OUTDOOR RECREATION - COLORADO -
GRAND MESA NATIONAL FOREST -
MAPS.**
United States. Forest Service. Rocky Mountain
Region. Grand Mesa National Forest, Colorado,
1976. [Denver] 1976. col. map 65 x 90 cm.
Scale 1:126,720; 1/2″ = 1 mile. Relief shown by
hachures and spot heights. "Polyconic projection." "Sixth
principal and Ute meridians." "Forest visitors map."
Includes map of "Fruita Division," location map, "Index
to Geological Survey topographic maps," recreation
index, text, and col. illus. On verso: map of "Grand
Mesa lakes country," scale ca. 1:42,500; key map; text;
col. illus. LC Card 77-694720
G4312.G6 1976 .U5
                            NYPL [Map Div. 80-3420]

**OUTDOOR RECREATION - COLORADO -
GUNNISON NATIONAL FOREST -
MAPS.**
United States. Forest Service. Rocky Mountain
Region. Gunnison National Forest, Colorado.
[Denver], 1976. col. map on sheet 143 x 66 cm.
Scale 1:126,720; 1/2″ = 1 mile. Printed on both sides
of sheet. Relief shown by hachures and spot heights.
"Polyconic projection." "New Mexico and sixth principal
meridians." Includes inset of "Black Canyon of the
Gunnison National Monument," 2 vicinity maps, "Index
to Geological Survey topographical maps," recreation
indexes, text, and col. illus. LC Card 77-694719
G4312.G8 1976 .U5
                            NYPL [Map Div. 80-3349]

**OUTDOOR RECREATION - COLORADO -
RIO GRANDE NATIONAL FOREST -
MAPS.**
United States. Forest Service. Rocky Mountain
Region. Rio Grande National Forest, Colorado,
1975. [Denver] 1975] col. map on sheet 142 x
67 cm. Scale 1:126,720; 1/2″ = 1 mile. Folded title:
Rio Grande National Forest, Colorado. Printed on both

sides of sheet. "Polyconic projection. New Mexico and
sixth principal meridians." Relief shown by hachures
and spot heights. "Forest visitors map." Includes key
maps, "Vicinity map," recreation indexes, text, and col.
illus. LC Card 76-690740
G4312.R5 1975 .U5
                            NYPL [Map Div. 80-3418]

**OUTDOOR RECREATION - COLORADO -
ROOSEVELT NATIONAL FOREST -
MAPS.**
United States. Forest Service. Rocky Mountain
Region. Roosevelt National Forest, Colorado.
[Denver] 1974. col. map on sheet 66 x 92 cm.
Scale 1:126,720; 1/2″ = 1 mile. Printed on both sides
of sheet. "Polyconic projection. Sixth principal
meridian." Relief shown by hachures and spot heights.
"Forest Service map class A." "Forest visitors map."
Includes text, 2 recreation directories, "Vicinity map," 2
key maps, and col. illus. LC Card 76-690738
G4312.R66 1974 .U5
                            NYPL [Map Div 80-3346]

**OUTDOOR RECREATION - COLORADO -
SAN ISABEL NATIONAL FOREST -
MAPS.**
United States. Forest Service. Rocky Mountain
Region. San Isabel National Forest, Colorado.
[Denver] 1972. col. map on sheet 115 x 66 cm.
Scale 1:126,720; 1/2″ = 1 mile. Printed on both sides
of sheet. Relief shown by hachures and spot heights.
"Polyconic projection ... New Mexico and sixth
principal meridians." "Forest Service map." "Forest
visitors map." Includes col. illus., text, map keys, listings
of "Forest Service recreation sites," index to "Points of
interest," and "Vicinity map." "Reprinted 1978." LC
Card 74-696335
G4312.S2 1972 .U5
                            NYPL [Map Div. 80-3362]

**OUTDOOR RECREATION - COLORADO -
SAN JUAN NATIONAL FOREST -
MAPS.**
United States. Forest Service. Rocky Mountain
Region. San Juan National Forest, Colorado.
[Denver], 1974. col. map. on sheet 66 x 105
cm. Scale 1:126,720; 1/2″ = 1 mile. Printed on both
sides of sheet. Relief shown by hachures and spot
heights. "Polyconic projection." "New Mexico principal
meridian." "Reprinted 1976." "Forest visitors map."
"Forest Service map class A." Includes inset of Mesa
Verde National Park, 2 map keys, "Vicinity map,"
"Recreation directory," text, and col. illus.
                            NYPL [Map Div. 80-3365]

**OUTDOOR RECREATION - COLORADO -
UNCOMPAHGRE NATIONAL FOREST -
MAPS.**
United States. Forest Service. Rocky Mountain
Region. Uncompahgre National Forest,
Colorado. [Denver] 1972. col. map on sheet 65
x 97 cm. Scale 1:126,720; 1/2″ = 1 mile. Printed on
both sides of sheet. Relief shown by hachures and spot
heights. "New Mexico, Sixth, Ute principal meridians."
Includes text, col. illus., "Vicinity map," "Map key[s],"
and "Recreation site directory." "Reprinted 1976."
"Polyconic projection." LC Card 75-690673
G4312.U6 1972 .U5
                            NYPL [Map Div. 80-3364]

**OUTDOOR RECREATION - COLORADO -
WHITE RIVER NATIONAL FOREST -
MAPS.**
United States. Forest Service. Rocky Mountain
Region. White River National Forest, Colorado.
[Denver] 1973. col. map on sheet 66 x 143 cm.
Scale 1:126,720; 1/2″ = 1 mile. Relief shown by
hachures and spot heights. Printed on both sides of
sheet. "Polyconic projection. Sixth principal meridian."
"Forest visitors map." Includes col. illus., text, "Key
map," "Vicinity map," "Recreation directory," and
indexes to "Ski areas" and "Points of interest." "Forest
Service map class A." LC Card 75-690675
G4312.W5 1973 .U5
                            NYPL [Map Div. 80-3350]

**OUTDOOR RECREATION - HELLS
CANYON NATIONAL RECREATION
AREA - MAPS.**
United States. Forest Service. Pacific Northwest
Region. Wallowa-Whitman National Forest
[north half] Oregon. Portland , 1979. 1 map :
on sheet 66 x 102 cm. Scale ca. 1:126,720. Relief
shown by hachures and spot heights. Map printed on
both sides of sheet. Map includes Hells Canyon
National Recreation Area, Oregon-Idaho.
G4292.W31 1975 .U53
                            NYPL [Map Div. 80-3406]

OUTDOOR RECREATION - INDIANA.
Indiana. Division of Outdoor Recreation.
Master plan 1978+ . Indianapolis , 1978. 80
p. : LC Card 79-625222 DDC 771/.558/09772 19
HD211.I6 I53 1978

**OUTDOOR RECREATION - MARYLAND -
SUGAR LOAF MOUNTAIN - GUIDE-
BOOKS.**
Sugarloaf Regional Trails (Project) Circling
historic landscapes . Silver Spring, Md. , c1980.
99 p. : LC Card 80-117883 DDC 917.52/87 19
GV191.42.M3 S93 1980

**OUTDOOR RECREATION - MICHIGAN -
MAPS.**
Michigan. Dept. of Natural Resources. [County
highway maps of Michigan] Lansing, Mich.,
1969-1979. 97 col. maps each on sheet 36 x 45
cm. of 45 x 36 cm. Scale ca. 1:165,000. Relief
shown by spot heights and hachures. Shows public
parks, camp grounds and other recreation areas.
NYPL [Map Div. 80-3417]

**OUTDOOR RECREATION - NEVADA -
PLANNING.**
Eckbo, Dean, Austin & Williams. Nevada
state-wide trails study . [Carson City] [1978]
48, [16] leaves : LC Card 80-620874 DDC
790/.09793 19
GV191.42.N27 E24

**OUTDOOR RECREATION - NEW YORK
(STATE) - PLANNING.**
New York (State). State Council of Parks and
Recreation. People, resources, recreation, 1978 .
[Albany] [1978] 364 p. : LC Card 80-623046
DDC 353.0085/09747 19
GV191.42.N7 N48 1978

**OUTDOOR RECREATION -
PENNSYLVANIA - MERCER COUNTY -
MAPS.**
Mercer County (Pa.). Tourist Promotion
Agency. Mercer County, rainbow's end,
outdoor activity guide . Sharon, Pa. [1980?] 2
maps on 1 sheet : LC Card 81-690457
G3823.M4E63 1980 .M4

**OUTDOOR RECREATION - SOUTH
DAKOTA - BUFFALO GAP NATIONAL
GRASSLAND - MAPS.**
United States. Forest Service. Rocky Mountain
Region. Buffalo Gap national Grassland, South
Dakota. [Denver] 1974. col. map on sheet 65 x
120 cm. Scale 1:126,720; 1/2″ = 1 mile. Printed on
both sides of sheet. "Polyconic projection. Black Hills
meridian and sixth principal meridian." Relief shown by
hachures and spot heights. "Forest Service map class
A." "Grassland visitors map." Includes text, col. illus.,
"Recreation directory," "Map key," and "Vicinity map."
LC Card 77-691258
G4182.B82 1974 .U5
NYPL [Map Div. 80-3351]

**OUTDOOR RECREATION - SOUTH
DAKOTA - PLANNING.**
Nordstrom, Paul E. South Dakota recreational
trails plan, January 1, 1980 /. [Pierre, S.D.]
[1979?] 178 p. : LC Card 80-622746 DDC
790/.09783 19
GV191.42.S8 N67

**OUTDOOR RECREATION - UNITED
STATES.**
How effective are your community recreation
services? [Washington] , 1973. 189 p. in various
pagings :   *NYPL [JFF 80-1149]*

**OUTDOOR RECREATION - VERMONT -
PLANNING.**
Vermont. Agency of Environmental
Conservation. Division of Planning. Vermont
State comprehensive outdoor recreation plan .
[Montpelier] , 1978. ca. 500 p. in various
pagings, [17] fold. leaves of plates (8 fold. in
pocket) : LC Card 80-622420 DDC 790/.09743 19
GV191.42.V5 V48 1978

**OUTDOOR RECREATION - WASHINGTON
(STATE)**
Nash, A. E. Keir. Understanding and planning
for ORV recreation . Tumwater, Wash. , 19. v,
159 p. : LC Card 79-625837 DDC 338.3/4 19
GV191.42.W2 N37

**OUTDOOR RECREATION - WASHINGTON
(STATE) - CONGRESSES.**
Recreation '76 Conference, University of
Washington, 1976. Recreation '76 Conference
proceedings, February 23 and 24, 1976,
University of Washington /. Seattle , Pullman

[1976] iv, 114 p. : LC Card 77-623136 DDC
333.78/4 19
GV191.42.W2 R42 1976

**OUTDOOR RECREATION - WASHINGTON
(STATE) - WHITMAN COUNTY - MAPS.**
United States. Soil Conservation Service.
Historical and recreational sites, Whitman
County, Washington /. Portland, Or. , 1977. 1
map : LC Card 81-691525
G4283.W6E635 1977 .U5

**OUTDOOR RECREATION - WYOMING -
BIGHORN NATIONAL FOREST - MAPS.**
United States. Forest Service. Rocky Mountain
Region. Bighorn National Forest, Wyoming.
[Denver], 1974. col. map. on sheet 65 x 103
cm. Scale 1:126,720; 1/2″ = 1 mile. Printed on both
sides of sheet. Relief Shawn by hachures and spot
heights. "Polyconic projection." "Sixth principal
meridian." Includes location map, 2 map Keys, 2
indexes to recreation areas, text, and col. illus.
NYPL [Map Div. 80-3361]

**OUTDOOR RECREATION - WYOMING -
MEDICINE BOW NATIONAL FOREST -
MAPS.**
United States. Forest Service. Rocky Mountain
Region. Medicine Bow National Forest,
Wyoming. [Denver] 1973. col. map on sheet 65
x 114 cm. Scale 1:126,720; 1/2″ = 1 mile. Folded
title: The Medicine Bow National Forest in Wyoming.
Printed on both sides of sheet. Relief shown by
hachures and spot heights. "Polyconic projection ...
Sixth principal meridian." "Forest visitors map." "Forest
Service map, class A." Includes col. illus., text, index to
"Points of interest," "Recreation directory," 2 key maps,
and location map.   LC Card 74-696309
G4262.M4 1973 .U5
NYPL [Map Div. 80-3343]

**OUTDOOR RECREATION - WYOMING -
SHOSHONE NATIONAL FOREST -
MAPS.**
United States. Forest Service. Rocky Mountain
Region. Shoshone National Forest, Wyoming.
[Denver] 1969. col. map on sheet 66 x 92 cm.
Scale 1:126,720; 1/2″ = 1 mile. Folded title: North
half Shoshone National Forest, Wyoming. Printed on
both sides of sheet. Relief shown by hachures and spot
heights. "Polyconic projection ... Sixth principal
meridian, Wind River meridian." "Forest visitors map."
"Forest Service map, class A." Includes col. illus., text,
index to "Forest Service recreation sites," 2 key maps,
and "Vicinity map."   LC Card 74-696308
G4262.S5 1969 .U5
NYPL [Map Div. 80-3348]

United States. Forest Service. Rocky Mountain
Region. Shoshone National Forest, Wyoming.
[Denver] 1971. col. map on sheet 67 x 92 cm.
Scale 1:126,720; 1/2″ = 1 mile. Folded title: Shoshone
National Forest, Wyoming, south half. Printed on both
sides of sheet. Relief shown by hachures and spot
heights. "Polyconic projection ... Sixth principal
meridian, Wind River meridian." "Forest visitors map."
"Forest Service map, class A." Includes col. illus., text,
indexes to "Forest Service recreation sites," and "State
recreation sites," 2 key maps, and "Vicinity map." LC
Card 74-696307
G4262.S5 1971 .U5
NYPL [Map Div. 80-3347]

**Outer Continental Shelf oil and gas activities in
the mid-Atlantic and their onshore impacts .**
Macpherson, George S. Reston, VA [1980]
viii, 63 p. : LC Card 80-129968 DDC
338.2/728/0974 19
TN872.A5 M32

**Outer Continental Shelf Environmental
Assessment Program.** Environmental
assessment of the Alaskan continental shelf .
[Rockville, Md.?] , 1980. xv, 313 p. : LC Card
81-600735 DDC 574.5/2636/09798 19
QH105.A4 E586

**OUTER SPACE - COLONIES. see SPACE
COLONIES.**

**OUTER SPACE - EXPLORATION -
CONGRESSES.**
Symposium on Space Missions to Comets,
Goddard Space Flight Center, 1977. Space
missions to comets . [Washington] , 1979. v,
226 p. : LC Card 79-604295 DDC 523.6 19
QB721 .S97 1977

**OUTER SPACE - EXPLORATION -
ECONOMIC ASPECTS - UNITED
STATES.**
Wolken, Lawrence C. The exploration and

colonization of space . College Station, Tex. ,
c1980. 28 p. ; LC Card 81-621410 DDC 919.9/04
19
HC110.O93 W64

**OUTER SPACE - EXPLORATION -
POLITICAL ASPECTS - UNITED
STATES.**
Wolken, Lawrence C. The exploration and
colonization of space . College Station, Tex. ,
c1980. 28 p. ; LC Card 81-621410 DDC 919.9/04
19
HC110.O93 W64

**OUTLAWS - SOUTHWEST, OLD -
BIOGRAPHY.**
Penick, James L. The great western land
pirate . Columbia , 1981. p. cm. ISBN
0-8262-0342-6 LC Card 81-1779 DDC
364.1/5/0924 B 19
F396.M95 P46

An outline of state and local taxes in Virginia.
Virginia. Division of Industrial Development.
Richmond, Va. [1977] iii leaves, 18 p. ; LC
Card 80-621940 DDC 336.2/009755 19
HF2438 .A7 1977

**The outlook for housing in Japan to the year
2000 /.** Ueda, Michihiko. [Portland, Or.?] ,
c1980. 25 p. : LC Card 81-600898 DDC
634.9/09795 s 363.5/0952 19
SD11 .A45614 no. 276 HD7367.A3

The outlook for transportation energy . Halstead,
Woodrow J. Charlottesville, Va. [1978?] v, 21
p. : LC Card 79-625794 DDC 333.79 19
TJ163.5.T7 H34

Outlooks from Nobel Prize winners . United
States. Congress. House. Committee on Science
and Technology. Washington , 1981. iii, 66 p. :
LC Card 81-601401 DDC 607/.2/73 19
KF27 .S39 1980i

**Outreach programs of the land grant university,
which publics should they serve? :** Proceedings
of a conference on the campus of Kansas State
University, July 14 and 15, 1978 / organized
by the Colloquium on Alternatives for Human
Survival ; funded by the Kansas Committee for
the Humanities ... [et al.] ; edited by Jan L.
Flora and Jim Converse. [Manhattan :
Agricultural Experiment Station, Kansas State
University, 1979] 246 p. ; 28 cm. "June 1979."
Includes bibliographical references. LC Card
80-622898 DDC 378/.054/0973 19
*1. State universities and colleges - United States. 2.
Agricultural research - United States. I. Flora, Jan L.,
1941-. II. Converse, Jim. III. Colloquium on
Alternatives for Human Survival.*
LB2329.5 .O9

OUTSIDE BROKERS. see BROKERS.

Outstanding claims against Cuba . United States.
Congress. House. Committee on Foreign
Affairs. Subcommittee on International
Economic Policy and Trade. Washington ,
1980. iii, 21 p. ; LC Card 80-603106 DDC
327.7291073 19
KF27 .F6465 1979e

Ouzts, W. Glenn. Land use/land cover maps of
Texas / compiled and interpreted by W. Glenn
Ouzts. Austin : Texas Dept. of Water
Resources, 1977, 1978 printing. 47 leaves : col.
maps ; 28 x 43 cm. Scale of maps 1:500,000. On all
maps: "Prepared by the Texas Department of Water
Resources." "For additional copies ... contact TNRIS,
P.O. Box 13087, Austin, Texas 78711." "LP-62." LC
Card 80-675250 DDC 912/.133373/09764
*1. Land use - Texas - Maps. I. Texas Dept. of Water
Resources. II. Title.*
G1371.G4 O9 1978

OVARIES - TUMORS.
Scully, Robert E. Tumors of the ovary and
maldeveloped gonads /. Washington, D.C. ,
1979. 413 p. : LC Card 80-602599 DDC
616.99/2 s 616.99/465 19
RD651 .A8 fasc. 16 RC280.O8

**Over the Chihuahua and Santa Fe trails,
1847-1848 .** Gibson, George Rutledge, 1810
(ca.)-1885. Albuquerque , c1981. p. cm. ISBN
0-8263-0590-3 : LC Card 81-52054 DDC
973.6/2 19
E411 .G44

Over-the-counter drugs. United States. Food and
Drug Administration. Preamble compilation:
over-the-counter drugs. Mar. 1936/Mar. 1978-

Washington.
NYPL [*R-Econ. 80-2052 & JLL 80-360]

Over-time incurred by uniformed employees of the New York City Fire Department. New York (City). Bureau of Audit and Control. Audit report on over-time incurred by uniformed employees of the New York City Fire Department. [New York] [1978] 19 leaves;
NYPL [*XME-9059]

Overall plan, Buffalo-Red River Watershed District . Minnesota. Water Resources Board. [St. Paul] , 1979. iii, iv, 85 p. :   LC Card 79-624540   DDC 333.91/009776/9 19
HD1694.M6 M58 1979

Overcash, Michael R.
Characterization and land application of seafood industry wastewaters / by Michael R. Overcash, Dhiraj Pal. Raleigh : Water Resources Research Institute of the University of North Carolina, [1980] ix, 34 leaves : ill. ; 28 cm. (WRRI report . no. 142) "UNC-WRRI-80-142." "Project no. B-100-NC; agreement no. 14-34-0001-7173." "April 1980." on cover "August 1980." Bibliography: leaves 32-33.   LC Card 80-623929   DDC 664/.94996 19
1. Sewage as fertilizer - United States. 2. Seafood processing - United States - Waste disposal. I. Pal, Dhiraj, joint author. II. Series: University of North Carolina (System). Water Resources Research Institute. WRRI report , no. 142. III. Title.
TD774 .O92

(joint author) Pal, Dhiraj. Assessment of land treatment technology for petroleum refinery solid wastes /. [Raleigh, N.C.] [1980] vi, 30 leaves, [1] leaf of plates :   LC Card 80-623569   DDC 333.91/009756 s 628.5/46 19
HD1694.N8 N6 no. 141 TD899.P4

Overcoming world hunger . United States. Presidential Commission on World Hunger. Washington, DC [1980] xiii, 251 p. ;   LC Card 80-600057   DDC 338.1/9 19
HD9000.5 .U55 1980a

Overcrowding in Texas prisons. Texas. Legislature. House of Representatives. Study Group. Austin , 1979. 23 p. ;   LC Card 79-624889   DDC 365/.6 19
HV8363 .T42 1979

OVERHEAD ELECTRIC LINES. see ELECTRIC LINES - OVERHEAD.

OVERHEAD POWER LINES. see ELECTRIC LINES - OVERHEAD.

OVERLAND JOURNEYS TO THE PACIFIC.
Russell, Marian Sloan, 1845-1937. Land of enchantment . Albuquerque [1981] c1954. xiv, 163 p. :   ISBN 0-8263-0571-7 :   LC Card 80-54564   DDC 917.8 19
F786 .R96 1981

Overseas beneficiaries . United States. Veterans Administration. Washington , 1980. xviii, 403 p. ;   LC Card 80-602866   DDC 355.1/151/0973 19
UB373 .U54 1980

Overseas business reports. United States. Industry and Trade Administration. OBR 77-62- ; Nov. 1977- Washington.   *NYPL [JLM 80-840]*

Overseas Private Investment Corporation . United States. Congress. Senate. Committee on Foreign Relations. Washington , 1980. iv, 246 p. :   LC Card 80-604067   DDC 346.73/07 347.3067 19
KF26 .F6 1980q

OVERSEAS PRIVATE INVESTMENT CORPORATION.
United States. Congress. House. Committee on Foreign Affairs. OPIC services for U. S. investors in China . Washington , 1981. iii, 68 p. ;   LC Card 81-600814   DDC 332.6/7373/051 19
KF27 .F6 1980o

United States. Congress. House. Committee on Foreign Affairs. Subcommittee on International Economic Policy and Trade. Review of activities of the Overseas Private Investment Corporation . Washington , 1980. iii, 111 p. ;   LC Card 80-602111   DDC 353.0082 19
KF27 .F6465 1979d

United States. Congress. Senate. Committee on Foreign Relations. Overseas Private Investment Corporation . Washington , 1980. iv, 246 p. :   LC Card 80-604067   DDC 346.73/07 347.3067 19
KF26 .F6 1980q

United States. Congress. Senate. Committee on Foreign Relations. S. 1916 . Washington , 1980. iii, 32 p. ;   LC Card 80-601997   DDC 346.51/07 19
KF26 .F6 1980a

Oversight . United States. Congress. House. Committee on Science and Technology. Subcommittee on Energy Development and Applications. Washington , 1980 [i.e. 1981] iii, 234 p. :   LC Card 81-600865   DDC 338.1/7665772 19
KF27 .S3934 1980g

Oversight, alcohol fuels . United States. Congress. House. Committee on Science and Technology. Subcommittee on Energy Development and Applications. Washington , 1980. iii, 115 p. :   LC Card 80-603693   DDC 338.4/7662669 19
KF27 .S3934 1980d

Oversight and reauthorization of action agency, 1979 . United States. Congress. House. Committee on Education and Labor. Subcommittee on Select Education. Washington , 1980. vii, 1719 p. :   LC Card 80-603281   DDC 353.0072/23684 19
KF27 .E373 1979f

Oversight--biomass . United States. Congress. House. Committee on Science and Technology. Subcommittee on Energy Development and Applications. Washington , 1980. iii, 175 p. :   LC Card 80-603030   DDC 338.4/76628 19
KF27 .S3934 1980

Oversight, DOE solar and conservation programs . United States. Congress. House. Committee on Science and Technology. Subcommittee on Energy Development and Applications. Washington , 1980. iii, 210 p. :   LC Card 81-600834   DDC 353.0082/3 19
KF27 .S3934 1980e

Oversight hearing on employment impact of current and proposed economic policies . United States. Congress. House. Committee on Education and Labor. Subcommittee on Employment Opportunities. Washington , c1980 [i.e. 1981] iii, 51 p. ;   LC Card 81-601627   DDC 339.5/0973 19
KF27 .E3366 1980c

Oversight hearing on Federal library programs . United States. Congress. House. Committee on Education and Labor. Subcommittee on Elementary, Secondary, and Vocational Education. Washington , 1980. iii, 71 p. :   LC Card 80-603097   DDC 353.0085/2 19
KF27 .E3364 1980c

Oversight hearing on the Architectural and Transportation Barriers Compliance Board . United States. Congress. House. Committee on Education and Labor. Subcommittee on Select Education. Washington , 1981. iii, 219 p. :   LC Card 81-601157   DDC 353.0086/2 19
KF27 .E373 1980f

Oversight hearing on the child labor provisions of the Fair labor standards act . United States. Congress. House. Committee on Education and Labor. Subcommittee on Labor Standards. Washington , 1980. iv, 196 p. :   LC Card 80-603516   DDC 353.0083/82 19
KF27 .E348 1980b

Oversight hearing on the federal enforcement of equal employment opportunity laws . United States. Congress. House. Committee on Education and Labor. Subcommittee on Employment Opportunities. Washington , 1980. iv, 98 p. :   LC Card 80-604008   DDC 353.001/04 19
KF27 .E3366 1980a

Oversight hearing on the impact of inflation on rehabilitation services . United States. Congress. House. Committee on Education and Labor. Subcommittee on Select Education. Washington , 1980. iii, 50 p. :   LC Card 80-603046   DDC 362/.0425 19
KF27 .E373 1980a

Oversight hearing to receive testimony on Agent Orange . United States. Congress. House. Committee on Veterans' Affairs. Subcommittee on Medical Facilities and Benefits. Washington , 1980. iii, 121 p. ;   LC Card 80-602984   DDC 363.7/384 19
KF27 .V459 1980

Oversight hearing, United States Metric Board . United States. Congress. House. Committee on

Science and Technology. Subcommittee on Science, Research, and Technology. Washington , 1980. iii, 34 ;   LC Card 80-602077   DDC 353.0082/1 19
KF27 .S399 1979m

Oversight hearings on Depository Institutions Deregulation Committee . United State. Congress. House. Committee on Banking, Finance, and Urban Affairs. Subcommittee on Financial Institutions Supervision, Regulation and Insurance. Washington , 1980. vi, 582 p. :   LC Card 81-600873   DDC 353.0082/52 19
KF27 .B544 1980c

Oversight hearings on employment programs for veterans and veterans' preference in federal employment . United States. Congress. House. Committee on Veterans' Affairs. Subcommittee on Education, Training, and Employment. Washington , 1981. iii, 221 p. :   LC Card 81-601161   DDC 354.1/154/0973 19
KF27 .V436 1980b

Oversight hearings on Indian education . United States. Congress. House. Committee on Education and Labor. Subcommittee on Elementary, Secondary, and Vocational Education. Washington , 1980 [i.e. 1981] iv, 252 p. :   LC Card 81-601356   DDC 353.0085/1/08897 19
KF27 .E3364 1980j

Oversight hearings on National Development Bank legislation . United States. Congress. House. Committee on Banking, Finance and Urban Affairs. Subcommittee on General Oversight and Renegotiation. Washington , 1980. iii, 220 p. :   LC Card 81-600651   DDC 346.73/0822 347.306822 19
KF27 .B563 1980

Oversight hearings on OSHA--occupational safety and health for Federal employees . United States. Congress. House. Committee on Education and Labor. Subcommittee on Health and Safety. Washington , 1980- v. :   LC Card 80-602740   DDC 353.001/6 19
KF27 .E3394 1979a

Oversight hearings on section 14(C) of the Fair Labor Standards Act . United States. Congress. House. Committee on Education and Labor. Subcommittee on Labor Standards. Washington , 1980. v, 540 p. :   LC Card 80-603995   DDC 353.0083/6 19
KF27 .E348 1980d

Oversight hearings on the Currency and Foreign Transactions Reporting Act . United States. Congress. House. Committee on Banking, Finance and Urban Affairs. Subcommittee on General Oversight and Renegotiation. Washington , 24 cm. iii, 130 p. :   LC Card 81-600959   DDC 353.0082/52 19
KF27 .B563 1980a

Oversight hearings on the Export-Import Bank . United States. Congress. House. Committee on Banking, Finance and Urban Affairs. Subcommittee on International Trade, Investment and Monetary Policy. Washington , 1980. iii. 143 p. :   LC Card 81-600657   DDC 353.0082/52 19
KF27 .B577 1980a

Oversight hearings on the Federal employees' compensation act . United States. Congress. House. Committee on Education and Labor. Subcommittee on Labor Standards. Washington, D.C. , 1980- v. :   LC Card 80-603447   DDC 353.0082/56 19
KF27 .E348 1980a

Oversight hearings on the Federal mine safety and health amendments act of 1977 . United States. Congress. House. Committee on Education and Labor. Subcommittee on Health and Safety. Washington, D.C. , 1980. v. <1-3> :   LC Card 80-602787   DDC 353.0082/382/0289 19
KF27 .E3394 1979

Oversight hearings on the implementation of title XI, Public Law 95-561 . United States. Congress. House. Committee on Education and Labor. Subcommittee on Elementary, Secondary, and Vocational Education. Washington , 1980. iii, 47 p. :   LC Card 80-604010   DDC 371.97/97/0795 19
KF27 .E3364 1980f

Oversight hearings on the Longshoremen's and harbor workers' compensation act . United States. Congress. House. Committee on Education and Labor. Subcommittee on Labor Standards. Washington , 1980. viii, 1231 p. :
LC Card 80-603416   DDC 353.0082/56 19
KF27 .E348 1979d

Oversight hearings on the Longshoremen's and Harbor Workers' Compensation Act. Supplement . United States. Congress. House. Committee on Education and Labor. Subcommittee on Labor Standards. Washington , 1980. v, 57 p. ;   LC Card 80-604153   DDC 344.73/0217 347.304217 19
KF27 .E348 1979d Suppl

Oversight hearings on Title I--Child Abuse Prevention and Treatment and Adoption Reform Act of 1978 . United States. Congress. House. Committee on Education and Labor. Subcommittee on Select Education. Washington , c1981. iv, 376 p. :   LC Card 81-601885   DDC 353.0084/7 19
KF27 .E373 1980f

Oversight in the recruitment and retention of Veterans' Administration physicians and dentists, and H.R. 6153 . United States. Congress. House. Committee on Veterans' Affairs. Subcommittee on Medical Facilities and Benefits. Washington , 1981. iv, 168 p. :   LC Card 81-601384   DDC 353.001/31 19
KF27 .V459 1980c

Oversight of Department of Justice Public Integrity Section . United States. Congress. Senate. Committee on the Judiciary. Washington , 1980. iii, 12 p. ;   LC Card 81-600613   DDC 353.5 19
KF26 .J8 1980h

Oversight of energy development in Africa and the Middle East . United States. Congress. House. Committee on Science and Technology. Washington , 1980. v, 132 p. :   LC Card 80-602581   DDC 333.79/15/096 19
TJ163.25.A4 U54 1980

Oversight of energy development in northern Europe . Wydler, John W. Washington , 1980. v, 45 p. :   LC Card 80-603051   DDC 333.79/24 19
TJ163.25.E853 W93

Oversight of energy development in South America . Wydler, John W. Washington , 1980. v, 167 p. :   LC Card 80-603265   DDC 333.79/098 19
TJ163.25.S65 W92

Oversight of GPO's direct deal printing procurement system . United States. Congress. Senate. Committee on Governmental Affairs. Washington , 1980. iii, 94 p. :   LC Card 80-602743   DDC 353.0081/9 19
KF26 .G67 1980c

Oversight of Indian health services in the Pacific Northwest and Alaska . United States. Congress. Senate. Select Committee on Indian Affairs. Washington , c1980 [i.e. 1981] iv, 124 p. :   LC Card 81-601184   DDC 353.0081/497/09795 19
KF26.5 .I4 1980r

Oversight of Labor Department's investigation of Teamsters central states pension fund . United States. Congress. Senate. Committee on Government Affairs. Permanent Subcommittee on Investigations. Washington , 1981. v, 521 p. :   LC Card 81-601398   DDC 332.6/7254 19
KF26 .G674 1980f

Oversight of Older Americans Act administration . United States. Congress. House. Select Committee on Aging. Washington , 1980. iii, 43 p. :   LC Card 80-604046   DDC 353.0084/6 19
KF27.5 .A3 1980f

Oversight of SBA's management assistance programs . United States. Congress. Senate. Select Committee on Small Business. Subcommittee on Government Regulation and Paperwork. Washington , 1980. iii, 201 p. :   LC Card 80-602431   DDC 353.0082/048 19
KF26.5 .S629 1979b

Oversight of the administration of the Federal Freedom of Information Act . United States. Congress. Senate. Committee on Government Affairs. Subcommittee on Intergovernmental Relations. Washington , 1980 [i.e. 1981] iv,

543, p. ;   LC Card 81-600809   DDC 353.0081/1 19
KF26 .G6738 1980c

Oversight of the General Services Administration . United States. Congress. Senate. Committee on the Judiciary. Subcommittee on Limitations of Contracted and Delegated Authority. Washington , 1980. iii, 89 p. :   LC Card 80-604043   DDC 353.0071 19
KF26 .J857 1979a

Oversight of the Indian Child Welfare Act . United States. Congress. Senate. Select Committee on Indian Affairs. Washington , 1980. iii, 148 p. :   LC Card 80-604076   DDC 353.0084/7/08997 19
KF26.5 .I4 1980q

Oversight of the Legal Services Corporation, 1980 . United States. Congress. Senate. Committee on Labor and Human Resources. Subcommittee on Employment, Poverty, and Migratory Labor. Washington , 1980. iv, 324 p. ;   LC Card 80-602105   DDC 353.0084/5 19
KF26 .L2737 1980

Oversight of the National Health Service Corps . United States. Congress. Senate. Committee on Labor and Human Resources. Subcommittee on Health and Scientific Research. Washington , 1980. iv, 167 p. :   LC Card 81-600609   DDC 362.1/0973 19
KF26 .L274 1980l

Oversight of the structure and management of the Department of Energy : staff report / Committee on Governmental Affairs, United States Senate. Washington : U. S. G.P.O. : For sale by the Supt. of Docs., U. S. G.P.O., 1980 [i.e. 1981] iii, 434 p. : ill. ; 24 cm. At the head of title: 96th Congress, 2d session. Committee print. Authors: David Nichols and others. "December 1980." S/N 052-070-05553-7 Item 1037-A Bibliography: p. 251-255.   LC Card 81-601669   DDC 353.87 19 1. *United States. Dept. of Energy. Management.* 2. *Energy policy - United States.* I. Nichols, David, 1947-. II. *United States. Congress. Senate. Committee on Governmental Affairs.*
TJ163.25.U6 O93

Oversight of the Taiwan relations act . United States. Congress. Senate. Committee on Foreign Relations. Subcommittee on East Asian and Pacific Affairs. Washington , 1980. iii, 44 p. ;   LC Card 80-602822   DDC 327.73051/249 19
KF26 .F6354 1980a

Oversight of VA pacemaker policy . United States. Congress. Senate. Committee on Veterans' Affairs. Washington , 1980. iii, 190 p. :   LC Card 80-604040   DDC 355.1/156/0973 19
KF26 .V4 1980b

Oversight on activities of the VA's Inspector General . United States. Congress. Senate. Committee on Veterans' Affairs. Washington , 1980. iii, 212 p. ;   LC Card 81-600655   DDC 353.0081/2 19
KF26 .V4 1980d

Oversight on admission policies to VA medical care facilities . United States. Congress. House. Committee on Veterans' Affairs. Washington, D.C. , 1980. vi, 373 p. :   LC Card 80-601953   DDC 353.0081/2 19
KF27 .V4 1979f

Oversight on Civil Aeronautics Board . United States. Congress. Senate. Committee on Commerce, Science, and Transportation. Subcommittee on Aviation. Washington , 1980. iii, 57 p. :   LC Card 80-603444   DDC 353.0087/7712 19
KF26 .C692 1980

Oversight on Education for all handicapped children act, 1979 . United States. Congress. Senate. Committee on Labor and Human Resources. Subcommittee on the Handicapped. Washington , 1980. vi, 1215 p. :   LC Card 80-601923   DDC 353.0085/1 19
KF26 .L2739 1979b

Oversight on Education for all handicapped children act, 1980 . United States. Congress.

Senate. Committee on Labor and Human Resources. Subcommittee on the Handicapped. Washington , 1980. iii, 156 p. :   LC Card 80-602464   DDC 353.0085/1 19
KF26 .L2739 1980

Oversight on efforts to reduce infant mortality and to improve pregnancy outcome . United States. Congress. Senate. Committee on Labor and Human Resources. Subcommittee on Child and Human Development. Washington , 1980 [i.e. 1981] v, 700 p. :   LC Card 81-601360   DDC 362.1/982/00973 19
KF26 .L273 1980c

Oversight on federal drug strategy--1979 . United States. Congress. House. Select Committee on Narcotics Abuse and Control. Washington , 1980 [i.e. 1981] iv, 63 p. :   LC Card 81-601283   DDC 363.4/5/0973 19
HV5825 .U563 1981

Oversight on financially distressed hospitals . United States. Congress. Senate. Committee on Labor and Human Resources. Subcommittee on Health and Scientific Research. Washington , 1980. iv, 172 p. ;   LC Card 80-603458   DDC 362.1/04252 19
KF26 .L274 1980f

Oversight on GAO report . United States. Congress. House. Committee on the Judiciary. Subcommittee on Civil and Constitutional Rights. Washington , 1980. iii, 131 p. ;   LC Card 81-600610   DDC 353.0081/1 19
KF27 .J847 1980b

Oversight on issues affecting Hispanics and migrant and seasonal farmworkers . United States. Congress. Senate. Committee on Labor and Human Resources. Subcommittee on Employment, Poverty, and Migratory Labor. Washington , 1981. iii, 127 p. ;   LC Card 81-601138   DDC 353.0083/6 19
KF26 .L2737 1980c

Oversight on programs for the deaf and hearing impaired, 1980 . United States. Congress. Senate. Committee on Labor and Human Resources. Subcommittee on the Handicapped. Washington , 1980. iv, 238 p. ;   LC Card 80-602742   DDC 362.4/28/0973 19
KF26 .L2739 1980a

Oversight on recommendations of 1979 Social Security Advisory Council . United States. Congress. House. Select Committee on Aging. Subcommittee on Retirement Income and Employment. Washington , 1980. iv, 208 p. :   LC Card 80-603006   DDC 368.4/00973 19
KF27.5 .A374 1980

Oversight on Resources planning act . United States. Congress. Senate. Committee on Agriculture, Nutrition, and Forestry. Subcommittee on Environment, Soil Conservation, and Forestry. Washington , 1980. iii, 144 p. :   LC Card 80-600839   DDC 353.0082/338 19
KF26 .A3543 1979f

Oversight on the Commodity Futures Trading Commission . United States. Congress. Senate. Committee on Agriculture, Nutrition, and Forestry. Subcommittee on Agricultural Research and General Legislation. Washington , 1980. iii, 135 p. ;   LC Card 80-602999   DDC 332.63/28 19
KF26 .A3534 1980c

Oversight on the Federal coal leasing program . United States. Congress. Senate. Committee on Energy and Natural Resources. Subcommittee on Energy Resources and Materials Production. Washington , 1980. iii, 315 p. :   LC Card 80-603709   DDC 353.0071/32 19
KF26 .E5543 1980c

Oversight on the Full employment and balanced growth act . United States. Congress. House. Committee on Education and Labor. Subcommittee on Employment Opportunities. Washington , 1979. v, 234 p. :   LC Card 80-603323   DDC 353.0083 19
KF27 .E3366 1980

Oversight on the Longshoremen's and Harbor Workers' Compensation Act, 1980 . United States. Congress. Senate. Committee on Labor and Human Resources. Washington , 1981. v, 472 p. :   LC Card 81-601328   DDC 353.0082/56 19
KF26 .L27 1980t

Oversight on the Surface Mining Control and Reclamation Act of 1977 . United States. Congress. House. Committee on Interior and Insular Affairs. Subcommittee on Energy and the Environment. Washington , 1981. vi, 621 p. ;   LC Card 81-601889   DDC 353.0082/382 19
KF27 .I518 1980d

Oversight report on the administration of the Endangered species act and the Convention on International Trade in Endangered Species of Wild Fauna and Flora /. United States. Congress. House. Committee on Merchant Marine and Fisheries. Subcommittee on Fisheries and Wildlife Conservation and the Environment. Washington , 1980. ii, 28 p. ;
      LC Card 80-602275   DDC 353.0082/328 19
QL84.2 .U55 1980

Oversight report on the U. S.-Canada East Coast fishery agreement and boundary treaty /. United States. Congress. House. Committee on Merchant Marine and Fisheries. Subcommittee on Fisheries and Wildlife Conservation and the Environment. Washington , 1980. ii, 23 p. ;
      LC Card 80-601727   DDC 342.73/0413 347.302413 19
LAW

Oversight study of the Florida Department of Agriculture and Consumer Services /. Florida. Legislature. Senate. Committee on Agriculture. [Tallahassee] [1978] ii, 84 leaves ;   LC Card 81-620852   DDC 353.97590082/33 19
S451.F6 F54 1978

Oversight, Western solar energy activities . United States. Congress. House. Committee on Science and Technology. Subcommittee on Energy Development and Applications. Washington , 1980. iii, 127 p. ;   LC Card 80-603333   DDC 333.79/23/0978 19
KF27 .S3934 1980b

Overstreet, Robin M. Marine maladies? : Worms, germs, and other symbionts from the northern Gulf of Mexico / by Robin M. Overstreet. [Ocean Springs, Miss.] : Mississippi-Alabama Sea Grant Consortium, c1978. 140 p. : ill. ; 26 cm. "Conducted in cooperation with the U. S. Department of Commerce, NOAA, Office of Sea Grant, under grant no. 04-7-158-44017 and National Marine Fisheries Service, under PL 88-309, project no. 2-262-R." "MASGP-78-021." Bibliography: p. 122-137.
      LC Card 78-112833   DDC 591.52/49 19
1. Parasites - Fishes. 2. Parasites - Shellfish. 3. Fishes - Mexico, Gulf of - Diseases. 4. Shellfish - Mexico, Gulf of - Diseases. I. Mississippi-Alabama Sea Grant Program. II. Title.
SH175 .O94

OVERTIME - NEW YORK (CITY)
New York (City). Bureau of Audit and Control. Audit report on over-time incurred by uniformed employees of the New York City Fire Department. [New York] [1978] 19 leaves;
                        *NYPL [*XME-9059]*

OVERTIME - UNITED STATES.
United States. Wage and Hour and Public Contracts Division. [Interpretative bulletin of the Fair labor standards act of 1938. Part 776. Subpart A. Coverage of wage-hour law.] Coverage of wage-hour law . Washington, D.C. , 1950. x, 29 p. ;   LC Card 80-116713   DDC 344.73/0121 347.304121 19
KF3489 .A36

Overview, coastal aquatic management policies of Washington State and federal agencies /. Washington (State). Dept. of Ecology. Shorelands Division. Olympia, Wash. [1980] 29 p. ;   LC Card 80-624143   DDC 333.91/7/09797 19
HT393.W3 W3 1980

An overview of crime in Arizona . Arizona. State Justice Planning Agency. Statistical Analysis Center. Phoenix, Ariz. [1980] 37 p. :   LC Card 80-623187   DDC 364/.9791 19
HV7252 .A6 1980

An overview of nutrition programs in Virginia /. Virginia. Dept. of Intergovernmental Affairs. Office of Human Resources. [Richmond] , 1978. 93, [2] p. ;   LC Card 79-621946   DDC 363.8/8/09755 19
HV696.F6 V57 1978

Ovrufskiĭ, G. D. (joint author) Gabovich, Rafail Davidovich. Fluorine in stomatology and hygiene =. Bethesda, Md. , Washington , 1977.

---

vi, 1028 p. :   LC Card 78-600559   DDC 612/.3924 19
RK331 .G313

Owen, Edward S., 1946- Playing and coaching wheelchair basketball / Edward S. Owen. Urbana : University of Illinois Press, c1982. p. cm. Bibliography: p. Includes index.   ISBN 0-252-00867-7   LC Card 81-10456   DDC 796.32/38 19
1. Wheelchair basketball. 2. Wheelchair basketball - Coaching. I. Title.
GV886.5 .O93

Owen, John B. (joint author) Reigh, Robert C. Fishes of the western tributaries of the Missouri River in North Dakota . [Bismarck, N.D.] [1979] xi, 207 p. :   LC Card 80-622780   DDC 597.092/9784/7 19
QL628.N9 R44

Owens, Charles. (joint author) Hickman, Glenn L. Soil survey of Mobile County, Alabama /. [Washington] , 19. vii, 134 p., [60] fold. leaves of plates :   LC Card 80-603367   DDC 631.4/7/76122 19
S599.A4 H53

Owens, James Patrick, 1924- Mixon, Robert B. Uranium-series dating of mollusks and corals and age of Pleistocene deposits, Chesapeake Bay area, Virginia and Maryland /. Washington , 1981. p. cm.   LC Card 81-607014   DDC 551.7/92/097521 19
QE697 .M7

Owens, Joseph. Aristotle, the collected papers of Joseph Owens / edited by John R. Catan. Albany : State University of New York Press, [1981] p. cm. Companion vol. to the author's St. Thomas Aquinas on the existence of God. "Complete bibliography of Joseph Owens, C.Ss.R.": Includes bibliographical references and indexes. CONTENTS. - Aristotle, teacher of those who know -- Aristotle on categories -- The Aristotelian conception of the sciences -- Matter and predication in Aristotle -- The grounds of universality in Aristotle -- The universality of the sensible in the Aristotelian noetic -- Aristotle, cognition a way of being -- Aristotelian soul as cognitive of sensibles, intelligibles, and self -- A note on Aristotle, de Anima 3.4.429b9 -- Aristotle's definition of soul -- The Aristotelian argument for the material principle of bodies -- Teleology of nature in Aristotle -- The grounds of ethical universality in Aristotle -- Nature and ethical norm in Aristotle -- Aristotelian ethics, medicine, and the changing nature of man.
      ISBN 0-87395-534-X   LC Card 81-7602   DDC 185 19
1. Aristotle - Addresses, essays, lectures. I. Catan, John R. II. Title.
B485 .O82

OWENS VALLEY - HISTORY.
Camp and community . Fullerton , c1977. xvi, 233 p. :   ISBN 0-930046-00-5   LC Card 77-75817
D769.8.A6 C23
                        NYPL [IXH (Manzanar) 80-2530]

Owensby, Clenton E., 1940- (joint author) Launchbaugh, John L. Kansas rangelands, their management based on a half century of research /. Manhattan [1978?] 56 p. :   LC Card 80-621772   DDC 633.2/02/09781 19
SF85.35.K3 L38

Ownbey, J. W. United States. Naval Oceanography Command Detachment, Asheville, N.C. Guide to standard weather summaries and climatic services /. [Asheville, N.C.] 1980. ix, 92, 102, [6] p. ;   LC Card 80-601710   DDC 551.6 19
QC982.5.U6 U53 1980

Owner occupied housing statistics from homestead rebate and income tax data match . New Jersey. Division of Taxation. Research and Statistics Section. [Trenton] , 1980. iii, 495 p. ;
HJ4121.N52 N48 1979
                        NYPL [JLF 80-1606]

Owner occupied housing statistics from homestead rebate and income tax data match . New Jersey. Division of Taxation. Research and Statistics Section. [Trenton] [1980] iii, 84, 176-495 p. ;   LC Card 80-623728   DDC 336.22/09749 19
HJ4121.N52 N48 1980a

OWNERSHIP. see PROPERTY.

Ownership and efficiency in urban buses /. Feibel, Charles. Washington, D.C. , 1980. 19

---

p. ;   LC Card 80-114661   DDC 388.4/042 19
HE5613 .F44

OXIDATION LAGOONS. see SEWAGE LAGOONS.

OXIDATION PONDS. see SEWAGE LAGOONS.

Oxley, Frances E. (joint author) Petto, Anthony C. Environmental regulations and other factors influencing industrial plant migrations /. Chicago, Ill. [1979] xxi, 106 p. ;   LC Card 79-626019   DDC 338.6/042/0977 19
HC107.A14 P47

OXYGEN IN THE BODY - CONGRESSES.
Biochemical and clinical aspects of oxygen . New York , 1979. xix, 866 p. :   ISBN 0-12-164380-8   LC Card 79-23522
QP535.O1 B54   *NYPL [JSE 80-1264]*

OXYGEN - PHYSIOLOGICAL EFFECT - CONGRESSES.
Biochemical and clinical aspects of oxygen . New York , 1979. xix, 866 p. :   ISBN 0-12-164380-8   LC Card 79-23522
QP535.O1 B54   *NYPL [JSE 80-1264]*

OXYGEN STEELMAKING. see STEEL - METALLURGY - OXYGEN PROCESSES.

OYSTER FISHERIES - LOUISIANA.
Breithaupt, Rob L. A study of the southern oyster drill (Thais haemastoma) distribution and density on the oyster seed grounds /. New Orleans, La. [1979] vii, 20 p. :   LC Card 80-621329   DDC 639/.411/09763 19
QL430.5.M9 B73

OYSTER SHELL.
Sampair, James L. Buried oyster shell resource evaluation of the eastern region of the Albemarle Sound /. Raleigh , 1976. iii, 47 p. :   LC Card 78-623214   DDC 553.5 19
SH379.5 .S25

OYSTERS.
United States. Office of Fisheries Development. A comprehensive review of the commercial oyster industries in the United States /. Washington , 1977. vi, 63 p. ;   LC Card 77-602004
HD9472.O83 U56   *NYPL [*XME-9429]*

OZARK MOUNTAIN REGION - POPULATION.
Campbell, Rex R. Population change in the Ozarks region, 1970-1975 . [Washington] , 1978. v, 29 p. :   LC Card 80-622359   DDC 304.6/2/097671 19
HB3517 .C35

OZARK MOUNTAIN REGION - POPULATION - STATISTICS.
United States. Ozarks Regional Commission. Missouri, socioeconomic strata health analysis . [Washington] , 1975. xi, 432 p. :   LC Card 78-622054   DDC 362.1/09778 19
RA407.4.M8 U54 1975

OZARK MOUNTAIN REGION - STATISTICS, MEDICAL.
United States. Ozarks Regional Commission. Missouri, socioeconomic strata health analysis . [Washington] , 1975. xi, 432 p. :   LC Card 78-622054   DDC 362.1/09778 19
RA407.4.M8 U54 1975

OZARK MOUNTAIN REGION - STATISTICS, VITAL.
United States. Ozarks Regional Commission. Missouri, socioeconomic strata health analysis . [Washington] , 1975. xi, 432 p. :   LC Card 78-622054   DDC 362.1/09778 19
RA407.4.M8 U54 1975

Ozarks Regional Commission. see United States. Ozarks Regional Commission.

OZONE, ATMOSPHERIC. see ATMOSPHERIC OZONE.

Ozone, chlorine dioxide, and chloramines as alternatives to chlorine for disinfection of drinking water . United States. Environmental Protection Agency. Water Supply Research Division. Cincinnati, Ohio [1977] 1979 printing. 84 p. :   LC Card 80-601552   DDC 628.1/66 19
TD459 .U54 1977

OZONE - ENVIRONMENTAL ASPECTS - LOUISIANA.
Louisiana. Dept. of Natural Resources. Louisiana State implementation plan revisions

for ozone abatement. Baton Rouge, LA [1978?]
ca. 150 p. ; LC Card 80-622129 DDC
363.7/39256/09763 19
TD887.H93 L68 1978

OZONE - TOXICOLOGY.
Health effects of ozone and other
photochemical oxidants in the Chicago area /.
Chicago, IL , 1979. vi, 83 p. : LC Card
80-621150 DDC 615.9/02 19
RA577.O97 H4

OZONE - TOXICOLOGY - ILLINOIS - CHICAGO REGION.
Health effects of ozone and other
photochemical oxidants in the Chicago area /.
Chicago, IL , 1979. vi, 83 p. : LC Card
80-621150 DDC 615.9/02 19
RA577.O97 H4

P. A. H. O. see Pan American Health Organization.

P. B. G. C. see Pension Benefit Guaranty Corporation.

P. C. M. R. see United States. President's Committee on Mental Retardation.

PDE directory. Pennsylvania. Dept. of Education.
[Harrisburg] *NYPL [JLK 80-194]*

P. E. C. see Palestine Economic Corporation.

P. H. S. see United States. Public Health Service.

P. I. C. G. see International Geological Correlation Programme.

P. P. R. O. see Public Policy Research Organization.

PVC. see POLYVINYL CHLORIDE.

PACEMAKER, ARTIFICIAL (HEART)
United States. Congress. Senate. Committee on
Veterans' Affairs. Oversight of VA pacemaker
policy . Washington , 1980. iii, 190 p. : LC
Card 80-604040 DDC 355.1/156/0973 19
KF26 .V4 1980b

Pachter, Marc. Champions, heroes of American
sport / written and edited by Marc Pachter,
with Amy Henderson, Jeannette Hussey, and
Margaret C. S. Christman ; introd. by Red
Smith. [Washington] : National Portrait Gallery,
Smithsonian Institution ; New York : H. N.
Abrams, [1981] p. cm. "[Catalog of] an exhibition at
the National Portrait Gallery, July 1 to September 6,
1981, sponsored by Philip Morris, Incorporated."
ISBN 0-8109-1602-9 (Abrams) : LC Card
80-28934 DDC 796/.092/2 B 19
*1. Athletes - United States - Portraits - Exhibitions. 2.
Athletes - United States - Biography. 3. Washington,
D.C. - Exhibitions. 4. National Portrait Gallery,
Washington, D.C. - Exhibitions. I. National Portrait
Gallery, Washington, D. C. II. Philip Morris
Incorporated. III. Title.*
GV697.A1 P28

PACIFASTACUS LENIUSCULUS - EFFECT OF WATER POLLUTION ON.
Ellis, Robert W. Effect of mercury on osmotic
regulation and protein kinetics in the crayfish,
Pacifastacus leniusculus /. Boise, Idaho , 1979.
30, [4] leaves : LC Card 79-626025 DDC
595.3/841 19
QL444.M33 E44

PACIFASTACUS LENIUSCULUS - PHYSIOLOGY.
Ellis, Robert W. Effect of mercury on osmotic
regulation and protein kinetics in the crayfish,
Pacifastacus leniusculus /. Boise, Idaho , 1979.
30, [4] leaves : LC Card 79-626025 DDC
595.3/841 19
QL444.M33 E44

**Pacific / Asian American Families and HEW-
related Issues, Conference on.** see
Conference on Pacific/Asian American
Families and HEW-related Issues, Airlie
House, 1978.

PACIFIC AREA - ECONOMIC CONDITIONS - CONGRESSES.
Pacific Basin Development Conference,
Honolulu, 1980. Economic growth and
development through unity . [Honolulu] [1980]
339 p. : LC Card 80-603217 DDC 338.99 19
HC681 .P27 1980

PACIFIC AREA - ECONOMIC POLICY - CONGRESSES.
Pacific Basin Development Conference,

Honolulu, 1980. Economic growth and
development through unity . [Honolulu] [1980]
339 p. : LC Card 80-603217 DDC 338.99 19
HC681 .P27 1980

**Pacific Basin Development Conference, Honolulu,
1980.** Economic growth and development
through unity : final report, February 17-20,
1980, Kuilima, Hawaii / Pacific Basin
Development Conference. [Honolulu] : The
Conference, [1980] 339 p. : ill. ; 28 cm. Cover
title. LC Card 80-603217 DDC 338.99 19
*1. Pacific area - Economic policy - Congresses. 2.
Pacific area - Economic conditions - Congresses. I.
Title.*
HC681 .P27 1980

Pacific basin energy . United States. Congress.
Senate. Committee on Energy and Natural
Resources. Washington , 1980. iv, 546 p. : LC
Card 81-600636 DDC 346.7304/679
347.3064679 19
KF26 .E55 1980i

**Pacific Coast canned fruits f.o.b. price
relationships 1945-75** . Hoos, Sidney Samuel,
1911- [Berkeley, Calif.] [1975] ii, 31 p. ; LC
Card 80-623213 DDC 338.4/36648 19
HD9247.A18 H65 1975

PACIFIC HALIBUT - AGE.
Southward, G. Morris. Sampling landings of
halibut for age composition /. Seattle , 1976. 31
p. : LC Card 81-456583 DDC 639/.2758 s 597/.5
19
SH351.H2 I54 no. 58 QL638.P7

PACIFIC HALIBUT - MIGRATION.
Best, Edgar Allan, 1925- Distribution and
abundance of juvenile halibut in the
southeastern Bering Sea /. Seattle , 1977. 23
p. : LC Card 81-456584 DDC 639/.2758 s 597/.5
19
SH351.H2 I54 no. 62 QL638.P7

**Pacific herring (Clupea pallasii) harvest
statistics ...** Blankenbeckler, Dennis. Pacific
herring (Clupea pallasii) harvest statistics and a
summary of hydroacoustical surveys conducted
in Southeastern Alaska during the fall, winter,
and spring of 1975-1976 /. Juneau [1976] 95
p. : LC Card 77-620582 DDC 639/.09798 s
333.95/6 19
SH11 .A7252a no. 28 SH351.H5

PACIFIC ISLANDS (TER.) - MAPS.
(1975) United States. Geological Survey. Trust
Territory of the Pacific Islands. [Washington]
1975. col. map 64 x 128 cm. Scale 1:4,000,000.
Depths shown by gradient tints. "Lambert conformal
conic projection based on standard parallels 6° and 30°."
"Compiled and edited for the Trust Territory of the
Pacific Islands by the U. S. Geological Survey from
charts compiled by the U. S. Air Force, U. S. Army,
and various other sources to 1973." Includes location
map. Insets: Yap Islands.--Rota.--Saipan and
Tinian.--Truk Islands.--Palau Islands.--Kwajalein
Atoll.--Ponape Islands.--Majuro and Arno Atolls. LC
Card 78-691550
G9405 1973 .U5

**Pacific Northwest Forest and Range Experiment
Station (Portland, Or.)** Ueda, Michihiko.
The outlook for housing in Japan to the year
2000 /. [Portland, Or.?] , c1980. 25 p. : LC
Card 81-600898 DDC 634.9/09795 s
363.5/0952 19
SD11 .A45614 no. 276 HD7367.A3

Pacific Northwest Laboratory, Richland, Wash.
see Battelle Memorial Institute, Columbus,
Ohio. Pacific Northwest Laboratory,
Richland, Wash.

Pacific Northwest quarterly. v. 1- ; Oct. 1906-
Seattle. illus. 25 cm. Publication suspended Oct.
1908-Apr. 1912. Official journal of the Washington
State Historical Society, 1955- . Title varies: 1906-35,
The Washington historical quarterly. Vols. for 1906-35
issued by Washington University State Historical
Society; 1936-52 by University of Washington; 1953-56
by University of Washington Press; 1957- by University
of Washington cooperating with Washington State
Historical Society. LC Card 80-30966
*1. Northwest, Pacific - History - Periodicals. I.
Washington State Historical Society. II. Washington
(State). University. Washington University State
Historical Society. III. Washington (State). University.
IV. Title: Washington historical quarterly.*
*NYPL [IAA(Pacific Northwest
quarterly)]*

Pacific Northwest Regional Commission.
Harding, Roger A. Forest inventory with
Landsat . Olympia , 1978. ix, 221 p. : LC Card
79-621899 DDC 634.9/285 19
SD387.R4 H37

Oregon. Water Policy Review Board. Final
report to the Pacific Northwest Regional
Commission on Oregon's drought and
conservation activities /. [Salem, Or.] [1979]
74 p. : LC Card 80-621882 DDC 333.91/16/09795
19
TD224.O7 O72 1979

**Pacific Northwest River Basins Commission. see
United States. Pacific Northwest River
Basins Commission.**

**Pacific Northwest Seminar on Clinical
Laboratory Planning and Design.** Pacific
Northwest Seminar on Clinical Laboratory
Planning and Design, Seattle, 1956. [Olympia,
Wash., 1967?] 1 v. (various pagings) LC Card
81-462890 DDC 610/.28 19
RB36 .P32 1967

**Pacific Northwest Seminar on Clinical
Laboratory Planning and Design, Seattle,
1956.** Pacific Northwest Seminar on Clinical
Laboratory Planning and Design. Edited by
Marilyn McCrum. [Olympia, Wash., Dept. of
Health, 1967?] 1 v. (various pagings) illus. 28
cm. On cover: Clinical laboratory planning & design.
Sponsored by the University of Washington, Division of
Environmental Health, and others. Includes
bibliographical references. LC Card 81-462890 DDC
610/.28 19
*1. Medical laboratories - Planning - Congresses. I.
McCrum, Marilyn, ed. II. Washington (State).
University. Division of Environmental Health. III. Title.
IV. Title: Clinical laboratory planning & design.*
RB36 .P32 1967

PACIFIC OCEAN - MAPS - EXHIBITIONS.
California State University, Fullerton. Library.
The grand ocean . [Fullerton] , c1979. 24 p. :
LC Card 79-623761 DDC 912/.1964/074019496
19
GA383 .C34 1979

**Pacific regional report. see United States. Bureau
of Labor Statistics. Pacific Regional Office.
Regional report.**

PACIFIC SALMON.
Robinson, E. Thomas. Accounting for Alaska
nonprofit salmon enhancement facilities,
including a chart of accounts /. Fairbanks ,
1978. xii, 67 p. : LC Card 79-623795 DDC
639.3/755 19
SH35.A62 R62

University of Alaska, Fairbanks. Institute of
Marine Science. Some aspects of the carrying
capacity of Prince William Sound, Alaska, for
hatchery released pink and chum salmon fry /.
Fairbanks , 1978. ix, 98 p. : LC Card 78-624148
DDC 551.46 s 639.3/755 19
GC1 .A497 no. 78-3 SH167.S17

PACIFIC SALMON - ALASKA - EGGS - MARKETING.
Alaska. Dept. of Fish and Game. Sale of roe
from subsistence-caught salmon in the
Artic-Yukon-Kuskokwim region, 1974-1977 .
[Juneau] , 1978. ii, 36 leaves : LC Card
78-624006 DDC 333.95/6 19
SH222.A4 A33 1978

PACIFIC SALMON - ALASKA - SALCHA RIVER.
Dinneford, W. Bruce. Third interim report of
the commercial fish-technical evaluation study,
Salcha River /. Anchorage, Alaska , 1977. vi,
88 p. : LC Card 79-625783 DDC 597/.55 19
QL638.S2 D56

PACIFIC SALMON - CONGRESSES.
Workshop on the Estuarine Survival of Salmon,
Juneau, Alaska, 1979. Proceedings of the
Workshop on the Estuarine Survival of Salmon,
Juneau, Alaska, February 8, 1979 /. Fairbanks,
Alaska , 1979. 38 p. ; LC Card 80-621846 DDC
597/.55 19
QL638.S2 W67 1979

PACIFIC SALMON - EGGS - MARKETING.
Alaska. Dept. of Fish and Game. Sale of roe
from subsistence-caught salmon in the
Artic-Yukon-Kuskokwim region, 1974-1977 .
[Juneau] , 1978. ii, 36 leaves : LC Card
78-624006 DDC 333.95/6 19
SH222.A4 A33 1978

PACIFIC SALMON FISHERIES - WASHINGTON (STATE) - STATISTICS.
Miller, Marc C. Trends in catch timing and distribution of the Washington commercial troll salmon fishery, 1960-1975 /. [Olympia, Wash.] , 1979. iii, 56 p. : LC Card 80-620830 DDC 338.3/72755 19
SH222.W2 M54

PACIFIC SETTLEMENT OF INTERNATIONAL DISPUTES.
United States Commission on Proposals for the National Academy of Peace and Conflict Resolution. Interim report of the U. S. Commission on Proposals for the National Academy of Peace and Conflict Resolution . Washington , 1980. iii, 16, vii p. ; LC Card 80-604123 DDC 327.1/72/071173 19
JX1963 .U14 1980

Pacific Telecommunications Conference, Honolulu, 1979. Pacific Telecommunications Conference : papers and proceedings of a conference held January 8 and 9, 1979, at the Ilikai Hotel, Honolulu, Hawaii / edited by Dan J. Wedemeyer and David L. Jones ; sponsored by Communications Society of the Institute of Electrical and Electronics Engineers, Department of Planning and Economic Development, State of Hawaii, Hawaii Tele-Communications Association, in cooperation with Institute of Electrical and Electronics Engineers, Hawaii Section [and] Office of Telecommunications, State of Alaska ; organized by Department of Electrical Engineering, University of Hawaii [and] Social Science Research Institute, University of Hawaii ; logistics by Office of Management Programs, College of Business Administration, University Of Hawaii. Honolulu : PTC, 1979. ca. 500 p. in various pagings : ill. ; 28 cm. Includes bibliographical references. LC Card 79-110059
1. Telecommunication - Pacific area - Congresses. I. Wedemeyer, Dan J. II. Jones, David L. III. University of Hawaii at Manoa. Dept. of Electrical Engineering. IV. university of Hawaii at Manoa. Social Science Research Institute.
TK5102.3.P32 P32 1979
NYPL [JLF 80-1628]

Pack, Janet Rothenberg. United States. Advisory Commission on Intergovernmental Relations. Regional growth. Washington, D.C. [1980- v. <1- > : LC Card 80-603208 DDC 361.6/0973 19
HT392 .U5 1980

Packaged fluid milk sales in federal milk order markets. United States. Agricultural Marketing Service. [Washington] LC Card 77-643112
NYPL [JLM 80-754]

Packard, Randall M., 1945- Chiefship and cosmology : an historical study of political competition / Randall M. Packard. Bloomington : Indiana University Press, c1981. p. cm. (African systems of thought) Based of the author's thesis (Ph.D.) Includes bibliographical references and index. ISBN 0-253-30831-3 LC Card 81-47013 DDC 967.5/17 19
1. Bashi (African people) - Kings and rulers. 2. Bashi (African people) - Politics and government. I. Title.
DT650.B366 P3

PACKING (MINING) see MINE FILLING.

PACKING (TRANSPORTATION) see BACKPACKING.

Packwood, Bob. United States. Congress. Senate. Committee on Commerce, Science, and Transportation. The goals of the Committee on Commerce, Science, and Transportation for the first session of the 97th Congress /. Washington , 1981. vii, 47 p. ; LC Card 81-601277 DDC 328.73/07652 19
JK1240.C57 U54 1981

Padavan, Frank. Heroin--new sources/new users : findings and recommendations on the present heroin epidemic and the shifting patterns of heroin abuse : a report / by Frank Padavan. [Albany, N.Y. : New York State Senate, Mental Hygiene and Addiction Control Committee, 1980] 36 p. : ill. ; 28 cm. "June 1980." LC Card 81-621128 DDC 362.2/93 19
1. Heroin. 2. Heroin habit - Treatment - New York (State). 3. Narcotics, Control of - New York (N.Y.). I. New York (State). Legislature. Senate. Mental Hygiene and Addiction Control Committee. II. Title.
HV5822.H4 P32

PADRE ISLAND, TEX.
Land and water resources, historical changes, and dune criticality . Austin, Tex. , 1978. v, 46 p. : LC Card 79-623595 DDC 553/.09764 s 551.4/57/0976447 19
QE167 .T42 no. 92 GB459.4

Padungchai, Sumol. (joint author) Narayanan, Rangesan. An economic evaluation of the salinity impacts from energy development . Logan, Utah , 1979. x, 71 p. : LC Card 80-622072 DDC 363.7/394 19
TD195.E5 N37

Paffenbarger, George Corbly, 1902- Organizations engaged in preparing standards for dental materials and therapeutic agents with a list of standards / G. C. Paffenbarger, R. W. Rupp, Margaret Malmstedt. [Washington, D.C.] : U. S. Dept. of Commerce, National Bureau of Standards : for sale by the Supt. of Docs., U. S. Govt. Print. Off., [1980] iii, 51 p. ; 27 cm. (NBS special publication ; 571) "Issued April 1980." LC Card 80-600041 DDC 602/.18 s 362.1/7 19
1. Dental instruments and apparatus - Standards. 2. Dental materials - Standards. 3. Materia medica, Dental - Standards. 4. Dentistry - Standards - Societies, etc. I. Rupp, R. W., joint author. II. Malmstedt, Margaret, joint author. III. Series: United States. National Bureau of Standards Special publication, 571. IV. Title.
QC100 .U57 no. 571 RK681

Page, Steven J.
Effectiveness of wet cutter bars in reducing salt mine dust / by Steven J. Page, Charles W. Urban, and Jon C. Volkwein. Washington : U. S. Dept. of the Interior, Bureau of Mines, [1980] p. cm. (Report of investigations / Bureau of Mines) Bibliography: p. LC Card 80-607782 DDC 622 s 622/.3632 19
1. Salt mines and mining - Dust control. 2. Mining machinery - Cutter bars. I. Urban, Charles W., joint author. II. Volkwein, Jon C., joint author. III. Series: United States Bureau of Mines. Report of investigations . IV. Title.
TN23 .U43 TN312

Evaluation of the use of foam for dust control on face drills and crushers / by Steven J. Page. [Washington, D.C.] : United States Dept. of the Interior, Bureau of Mines, [1981] p. cm. (Report of investigations) Bibliography: p. LC Card 81-4727 DDC 622 s 622/.8 19
1. Gypsum mines and mining - Dust control. 2. Foam. I. Series: Report of investigations (United States. Bureau of Mines). II. Title.
TN23 .U43 TN312

Volkwein, Jon C. Canopy air curtain dust reductions on a gathering-arm loader /. [Avondale, Md.] [1981] p. cm. LC Card 81-10148 DDC 622 s 622/.2 19
TN23 .U43 TN312

Page, William Frank, 1948- (joint author) Seiling, Virginia. Health characteristics of veterans and nonveterans . Washington, D.C. [1980] v, 75 p. : LC Card 80-602055 DDC 362.1/9 19
RA408.M4 S44

PAH-UTE INDIANS. see PAIUTE INDIANS.

Pahlman, John E. (joint author) Khalafalla, S. E. Selective extraction of metals from Pacific sea nodules with dissolved sulfur dioxide /. Avondale, Md. , 1980. p. cm. LC Card 80-606861 DDC 622 s 669/.028/3 19
TN23 .U43 TN291.5

Pai, Hsien-yung, 1937-
[Yu yüan ching meng. English]
Wandering in the garden, waking from a dream / Pai Hsien-yung ; translated by the author and Patia Yasin ; edited by George Kao. Bloomington : Indiana University Press, c1982 p. cm. (Chinese literature in translation) Translation of: Yu yüan ching meng. ISBN 0-253-19981-6 LC Card 81-47165 DDC 895.1/35 19
1. Pai, Hsien-yung, 1937- - Translations, English. I. Kao, George. II. Title. III. Series.
PL2892.A345 A24

PAI, HSIEN-YUNG, 1937- - TRANSLATIONS, ENGLISH.
Pai, Hsien-yung, 1937- [Yu yüan ching meng. English] Wandering in the garden, waking from a dream /. Bloomington , c19. p. cm. ISBN 0-253-19981-6 LC Card 81-47165 DDC 895.1/35 19
PL2892.A345 A24

Paige, J. I. (Jack I.) Introduction of sulfur into copper converter slags to produce copper matte / by J.I. Paige and W.E. Anable. Washington, D.C. : U. S. Dept. of the Interior, Bureau of Mines, 1981. p. cm. (Report of investigations) Bibliography: p. LC Card 81-607890 DDC 622 s 669/.3 19
1. Copper - Electrometallurgy. 2. Mattes. 3. Sulphur. 4. Slag. I. Anable, W. E. II. Series: Report of investigations (United States. Bureau of Mines). III. Title.
TN23 .U43 TN780

Pailthorp, Keith. (joint author) Fischer, Norman M. Research in Washington higher education /. [Olympia] , 1978. 112 p. : LC Card 79-623622
LB1028 .F484
NYPL [JFF 80-1521]

Paine, Judith. Theodate Pope Riddle, her life and work. [Washington?] : National Park Service, 1979. [26] p. : ill. ; 20 x 26 cm. Exhibition at the Theodore Roosevelt Birthplace, New York, May 24-Sept. 1, 1979. Bibliography: p. [26] LC Card 79-52952
1. Riddle, Theodate Pope, 1868-1946 - Exhibitions. 2. Architects - United States - Biography. I. Riddle, Theodate Pope, 1868-1946. II. United States. National Park Service. III. Title.
NA737.R53 A4 1979
NYPL [3-MQZ (Riddle) 81-627]

PAINTERS - MISSISSIPPI - BIOGRAPHY.
Tucker, Cynthia Grant. Kate Freeman Clark . Jackson, MS [1981] p. cm. ISBN 0-87805-136-8 LC Card 81-4516 DDC 759.13 B 19
ND237.C555 T8

PAINTING, AMERICAN - CATALOGS.
United States. National Gallery of Art. American paintings. Washington , 1980. 311 p. : LC Card 80-11221
ND205 .U54 1980   ***NYPL [3-MAVY (Washington, D. C.) 80-2649]***

PAINTING, AMERICAN - CONNECTICUT - EXHIBITIONS.
Connecticut and American impressionism . Storrs, c1980. 184 p. :
NYPL [MCW 80-2001]

PAINTING, AMERICAN - EXHIBITION.
Florida. University, Gainsville. University Gallery. The Gallery Guild, in cooperation with the University Gallery, are pleased to present the American scene . [Gainesville] [1979?] [63] p. : LC Card 79-623238 DDC 759.13/074/015979 19
ND212 .F563 1979

PAINTING, AMERICAN - EXHIBITIONS.
Cropsey, Jasper francis, 1823-1900. Jasper F. Cropsey 1823-1900. College Park , 1968. vi, 65 p. : ***NYPL [MCX C935 81-873]***

Fifteen under forty. [Albany, N.Y., 1970] 1 v. (unpaged) LC Card 72-633963
ND238.N5 F5

PAINTING, CHINESE - T'ANG-FIVE DYNASTIES, 618-960 - INDEXES.
Cahill, James Francis, 1926- An index of early Chinese painters and paintings . Berkeley , c1980. x, 391 p. ; ISBN 0-520-03576-3 LC Card 77-85755 DDC 759.951/016 19
ND1043.3 .C3

PAINTING, CHINESE - SUNG-YÜAN DYNASTIES, 960-1368 - INDEXES.
Cahill, James Francis, 1926- An index of early Chinese painters and paintings . Berkeley , c1980. x, 391 p. ; ISBN 0-520-03576-3 LC Card 77-85755 DDC 759.951/016 19
ND1043.3 .C3

PAINTING, ITALIAN - WASHINGTON, D. C. - CATALOGS.
United States. National Gallery of Art. Catalogue of the Italian paintings /. Washington , c1979. 2 v. : LC Card 79-4410
ND611 .U54 1979
NYPL [MAVY (Washinton, D. C.) 81-62]

PAINTING, MODERN - 19TH CENTURY - CONNECTICUT - EXHIBITIONS.
Connecticut and American impressionism . Storrs, c1980. 184 p. :
NYPL [MCW 80-2001]

PAINTING, MODERN - 19TH CENTURY - UNITED STATES - EXHIBITIONS.
Cropsey, Jasper francis, 1823-1900. Jasper F. Cropsey 1823-1900. College Park , 1968. vi, 65 p. : ***NYPL [MCX C935 81-873]***

**PAINTING, MODERN - 20TH CENTURY -
UNITED STATES - EXHIBITIONS.**
Florida. University, Gainsville. University
Gallery. The Gallery Guild, in cooperation with
the University Gallery, are pleased to present
the American scene . [Gainesville] [1979?] [63]
p. :   LC Card 79-623238   DDC 759.13/074/015979
19
ND212 .F563 1979

**PAINTING - WASHINGTON, D. C. -
CATALOGS.**
United States. National Gallery of Art.
American paintings. Washington , 1980. 311
p. :   LC Card 80-11221
ND205 .U54 1980   *NYPL [3-MAVY
(Washington, D. C.) 80-2649]*

**PAINTINGS, LATIN AMERICA -
EXHIBITIONS.**
Organization of American States. General
Secretariat. Tribute to Picasso . [Washington ,
1973] [33] p. :   LC Card 75-328387
ND202 .O73 1973

**PAINTINGS, MODERN - 20TH CENTURY -
LATIN AMERICA - EXHIBITIONS.**
Organization of American States. General
Secretariat. Tribute to Picasso . [Washington ,
1973] [33] p. :   LC Card 75-328387
ND202 .O73 1973

PAIUTE INDIANS.
Iroquois Research Institute. A land use history
of Coso Hot Springs, Inyo County, California /.
China Lake, Calif. , 1979. xiv, 232 p., [2] leaves
of plates (1 fold.) :   LC Card 79-602009   DDC
979.4/87 19
E99.P2 I7 1979

Pajestka, Jozef. United Nations. Dept. of
Technical Co-operation for Development.
Organizational systems for national planning /.
New York , 1979. vi, 177 p. :   LC Card
79-123608   DDC 300 s 338.9/009172/4 19
JX1977 .A2 ST/ESA/SER.E/18

**PAKISTAN - FOREIGN RELATIONS -
UNITED STATES.**
United States. Congress. Senate. Committee on
Foreign Relations. India-Pakistan nuclear
issues . Washington , 1980. iii, 19 p. ;   LC Card
80-602998   DDC 327.73054 19
KF26 .F6 1980K

Pakistan major ethnic groups. United States.
Central Intelligence Agency. [Washington ,
1980] 1 map :   LC Card 81-692533
G7641.E1 1980 .U5

Pakistan's cotton industry /. Petges, Richard.
[Washington, D.C.] [1980] 20 p. :   LC Card
80-602637   DDC 338.1 s 338.1/7351/095491 19
S21 .Z2383 no. 296 HD9086.P3

Pal, Dhiraj.
Assessment of land treatment technology for
petroleum refinery solid wastes / by Dhiraj Pal,
Michael R. Overcash. [Raleigh, N.C.] : Water
Resources Research Institute, University of
North Carolina, [1980] vi, 30 leaves, [1] leaf of
plates : ill. ; 28 cm. (Report - Water Resources
Institute of the University of North Carolina . no. 141)
"July 1980." "Project no. B-100-NC; Agreement no.
14-34-0001-7173." Includes bibliographical references.
LC Card 80-623569   DDC 333.91/009756 s
628.5/46 19
*1. Petroleum refineries - Waste disposal. 2. Petroleum -
Biodegradation. I. Overcash, Michael R., joint author.
II. Series: University of North Carolina (System). Water
Resources Research Institute. Report , no. 141. III.
Title.*
HD1694.N8 N6 no. 141 TD899.P4

(joint author) Overcash, Michael R.
Characterization and land application of seafood
industry wastewaters /. Raleigh [1980] ix, 34
leaves :   LC Card 80-623929   DDC 664/.94996 19
TD774 .O92

**PALEO-INDIANS - NORTH AMERICA -
IMPLEMENTS.**
Goodyear, Albert C. A hypothesis for the use
of cryptocrystalline raw materials among
Paleo-Indian groups of North America /.
Columbia, S.C. [1979] 15 leaves ;   LC Card
80-621583   DDC 970.01/1 19
E98.I4 G66

**PALEOANTHROPOLOGY. see MAN,
PREHISTORIC.**

PALEOBOTANY - BIBLIOGRAPHY.
Watt, Arthur Dwight, 1921- Index of generic
names of fossil plants, 1974-1978 .
Washington , 1981. p. cm.   LC Card 80-606811
DDC 557.3 s 561/.014 19
QE75 .B9 no. 1517 QE903

**PALEOBOTANY - CHINA - KWANGSI
(PROVINCE)**
Early and Middle Devonian charophytes of
eastern Guangxi, China /. Louisville, Ky. ,
c1980. iv, 16 p., leaves 17-18 :   LC Card
80-623043   DDC 561/.93 19
QE955 .E25

PALEOBOTANY - CRETACEOUS.
Hueber, Francis M. Megaspores and a
palynomorph from the lower Potomac Group in
Virginia /. Washington , 1982. p. cm.   LC Card
81-607852   DDC 560 s 561/.13 19
QE701 .S56 no. 49 QE996

PALEOBOTANY - DEVONIAN.
Early and Middle Devonian charophytes of
eastern Guangxi, China /. Louisville, Ky. ,
c1980. iv, 16 p., leaves 17-18 :   LC Card
80-623043   DDC 561/.93 19
QE955 .E25

**PALEOBOTANY - DILUVIAL. see
PALEOBOTANY - RECENT.**

**PALEOBOTANY - ENGLAND - SILWOOD
LAKE.**
Spicer, Robert A., 1950- The sorting and
deposition of allochthonous plant material in a
modern environment at Silwood Lake, Silwood
Park, Berkshire, England /. Washington , 1981.
v, 77 p. :   LC Card 80-607854   DDC 560/.1/78 19
QE931.3 .S64

**PALEOBOTANY - HOLOCENE. see
PALEOBOTANY - RECENT.**

**PALEOBOTANY - ILLINOIS - CATALOGS
AND COLLECTIONS.**
Janssen, Raymond Ellsworth, 1903- Leaves and
stems from fossil forests . Springfield, Ill. ,
1979. 190 p. :   ISBN 0-89792-077-5   LC Card
80-622162   DDC 561/.074/017356 19
QE937.I5 J29 1979

PALEOBOTANY - NOMENCLATORS.
Watt, Arthur Dwight, 1921- Index of generic
names of fossil plants, 1974-1978 .
Washington , 1981. p. cm.   LC Card 80-606811
DDC 557.3 s 561/.014 19
QE75 .B9 no. 1517 QE903

**PALEOBOTANY - POSTGLACIAL. see
PALEOBOTANY - RECENT.**

PALEOBOTANY - RECENT.
Spicer, Robert A., 1950- The sorting and
deposition of allochthonous plant material in a
modern environment at Silwood Lake, Silwood
Park, Berkshire, England /. Washington , 1981.
v, 77 p. :   LC Card 80-607854   DDC 560/.1/78 19
QE931.3 .S64

**PALEOBOTANY - SENONIAN. see
PALEOBOTANY - CRETACEOUS.**

PALEOBOTANY - VIRGINIA.
Hueber, Francis M. Megaspores and a
palynomorph from the lower Potomac Group in
Virginia /. Washington , 1982. p. cm.   LC Card
81-607852   DDC 560 s 561/.13 19
QE701 .S56 no. 49 QE996

PALEOCLIMATOLOGY - NEVADA.
Mifflin, Martin D. Pluvial lakes and estimated
pluvial climates of Nevada /. Reno , 1979. 57
p. :   LC Card 80-621829   DDC 551.48/2/09793 19
QC884 .M53

**PALEOETHNOGRAPHY. see MAN,
PREHISTORIC.**

PALEOGEOGRAPHY - UNITED STATES.
Imlay, Ralph Willard, 1908- Jurassic
paleobiogeography of the conterminous United
States in its continental setting /. Washington ,
1980. v, 134 p. :   LC Card 80-600017   DDC
560/.176 19
QE681 .I48

**PALEOLIMNOLOGY - ENGLAND -
SILWOOD LAKE.**
Spicer, Robert A., 1950- The sorting and
deposition of allochthonous plant material in a
modern environment at Silwood Lake, Silwood
Park, Berkshire, England /. Washington , 1981.
v, 77 p. :   LC Card 80-607854   DDC 560/.1/78 19
QE931.3 .S64

PALEOLITHIC PERIOD.
Dreiman, Richard N. Methods in artifact
analysis . Berkeley [1979] 79 p. :   LC Card
80-623478   DDC 930.1 s 930.1/2 19
E51 .C2 no. 42 GN772.A1

PALEONTOLOGY - ALASKA.
Imlay, Ralph Willard, 1908- Early Jurassic
ammonites from Alaska /. Washington , 1981.
iv, 49 p., 12 leaves of plates :   LC Card
81-607901   DDC 564/.53 19
QE807.A5 I585

**PALEONTOLOGY - BAHAMAS -
ADDRESSES, ESSAYS, LECTURES.**
Fossil vertebrates from the Bahamas .
Washington , 1982. p. cm.   LC Card 81-13543
DDC 560 s 566/.097296 19
QE701 .S56 no. 48 QE841

**PALEONTOLOGY - BIGHORN RIVER
WATERSHED, WYO. AND MONT.**
Bown, Thomas M. A review of the Proteutheria
and Insectivora of the Willwood Formation
(Lower Eocene), Bighorn Basin, Wyoming /.
Washington , 1981. p. cm.   LC Card 81-607068
DDC 557.3 s 569/.12 19
QE75 .B9 no. 1523 QE882.I5

PALEONTOLOGY - CALIFORNIA.
Saul, Louella Rankin. The North Pacific
cretaceous Trigoniid genus Yaadia /. Berkeley ,
1978. 65 p., 12 leaves of plates :   ISBN
0-520-09582-0   LC Card 77-84990   DDC
564/.11 19
QE812.T74 S28

PALEONTOLOGY - CAMBRIAN.
Miller, James Frederick, 1943- Taxonomic
revisions of some Upper Cambrian and Lower
Ordovician conodonts with comments on their
evolution /. Lawrence, Kan. , 1980. 39 p., [2]
leaves of plates :   LC Card 80-623003   DDC 560 s
562/.2 19
QE701 .K33 no. 99 QE899

Rowell, A. J. Inarticulate brachiopods of the
Lower and Middle Cambrian Pioche shale of
the Ploche District, Nevada /. Lawrence, Kan. ,
1980. 26 p., [4] leaves of plates :   LC Card
80-621789   DDC 560 s 564/.8 19
QE701 .K33 no. 98 QE797.I5

PALEONTOLOGY - CARBONIFEROUS.
Mapes, Royal H. Carboniferous and Permian
Bactritoidea (Cephalopoda) in North America /.
Lawrence, Kan. , 1979. ii, 75 p., [20] leaves of
plates :   LC Card 79-625202   DDC 560 s 564/.5 19
QE701 .K3 no. 64 QE806

PALEONTOLOGY - CRETACEOUS.
Saul, Louella Rankin. The North Pacific
cretaceous Trigoniid genus Yaadia /. Berkeley ,
1978. 65 p., 12 leaves of plates :   ISBN
0-520-09582-0   LC Card 77-84990   DDC
564/.11 19
QE812.T74 S28

PALEONTOLOGY - EOCENE.
Bown, Thomas M. A review of the Proteutheria
and Insectivora of the Willwood Formation
(Lower Eocene), Bighorn Basin, Wyoming /.
Washington , 1981. p. cm.   LC Card 81-607068
DDC 557.3 s 569/.12 19
QE75 .B9 no. 1523 QE882.I5

Dockery, David T. The invertebrate
macropaleontology of the Clarke County,
Mississippi, area /. Jackson, Miss. , 1980. 387
p. :   LC Card 80-623808   DDC 562/.09762/673 19
QE770 .D62

PALEONTOLOGY - FLORIDA.
MacFadden, Bruce J. Nannippus phlegon
(Mammalia, Equidae) from the Pliocene
(Blancan) of Florida /. Gainesville (Museum
Rd., University of Florida, Gainesville, FL
32611) , 1980. 37 p. :   LC Card 81-621398   DDC
569/.72 19
QE882.U6 M28

PALEONTOLOGY - IDAHO - LEMHI CO.
Nichols, Ralph. Additional early Miocene
mammals from the Lemhi Valley of Idaho /.
[Pocatello] , 1979. 12 p. :   LC Card 79-624993
DDC 500 s 569 19
E78.I18 T43 no. 17 QE881

PALEONTOLOGY - JURASSIC.
(1980) Imlay, Ralph Willard, 1908- Jurassic
paleobiogeography of the conterminous United
States in its continental setting /. Washington ,
1980. v, 134 p. :   LC Card 80-600017   DDC

560/.176 19
QE681 .I48

(1981) Imlay, Ralph Willard, 1908- Early
Jurassic ammonites from Alaska /.
Washington , 1981. iv, 49 p., 12 leaves of
plates : LC Card 81-607901   DDC 564/.53 19
QE807.A5 I585

(1981) Imlay, Ralph Willard, 1908- Jurassic
(Oxfordian and Late Callovian) ammonites from
the western interior region of the United States
/. Washington , 1981. p. cm.   LC Card 81-607015
DDC 564/.53/0978 19
QE807.A5 I593

**PALEONTOLOGY - KANSAS - WALLACE
CO.**
Bennett, Debra K. The fossil fauna from Lost
and Found Quarries (Hemphillian, latest
Miocene), Wallace County, Kansas /.
Lawrence , 1979. 24 p. :   LC Card 79-624442
DDC 569/.09781/123 19
QE881 .B49

**PALEONTOLOGY - LOWER SILURIAN. see
PALEONTOLOGY - ORDOVICIAN.**

**PALEONTOLOGY - MEXICO - SAN MIGUEL
DE ALLENDE REGION.**
Dalquest, Walter Woelber, 1917- Late
Hemphillian mammals of the Ocote local fauna,
Guanajuato, Mexico /. Austin, Tex. , 19. 25 p. :
LC Card 80-622865   DDC 574 s 569 19
AM101 .T474 no. 32 QE881

PALEONTOLOGY - MIDWAY ISLANDS.
Wells, John West, 1907- Fossil corals from
Midway atoll /. Washington , 1981. p. cm.   LC
Card 81-607875   DDC 563/.6/099699 19
QE778 .W43

PALEONTOLOGY - MIOCENE.
Allison, Richard C., 1935- A late Oligocene or
earliest Miocene molluscan fauna from Sitkinak
Island, Alaska /. Menlo Park, CA (345
Middlefield Rd., MS 51 Bldg. 5, Menlo Park
94025) [1981] p. cm.   LC Card 81-607925   DDC
564/.09798/4 19
QE801 .A44

Bennett, Debra K. The fossil fauna from Lost
and Found Quarries (Hemphillian, latest
Miocene), Wallace County, Kansas /.
Lawrence , 1979. 24 p. :   LC Card 79-624442
DDC 569/.09781/123 19
QE881 .B49

Nichols, Ralph. Additional early Miocene
mammals from the Lemhi Valley of Idaho /.
[Pocatello] , 1979. 12 p. :   LC Card 79-624993
DDC 500 s 569 19
E78.I18 T43 no. 17 QE881

Poore, Richard Z. Biostratigraphy and
paleoecology of the upper Miocene (Messinian)
and lower Pliocene (?) Cerro de Almendral
section, Alermía Basin, southern Spain /.
Washington , 1981. iii, 11 p., [2] leaves of
plates :   LC Card 80-607164   DDC
551.7/86/094681 19
QE694 .P67

**PALEONTOLOGY - MISSISSIPPI - CLARKE
CO.**
Dockery, David T. The invertebrate
macropaleontology of the Clarke County,
Mississippi, area /. Jackson, Miss. , 1980. 387
p. :   LC Card 80-623808   DDC 562/.09762/673 19
QE770 .D62

**PALEONTOLOGY - NEVADA - PIOCHE
REGION.**
Rowell, A. J. Inarticulate brachiopods of the
Lower and Middle Cambrian Pioche shale of
the Ploche District, Nevada /. Lawrence, Kan. ,
1980. 26 p., [4] leaves of plates :   LC Card
80-621789   DDC 560 s 564/.8 19
QE701 .K33 no. 98 QE797.I5

PALEONTOLOGY - NORTH AMERICA.
Harrison, Jessica A. A review of the extinct
wolverine, Plesiogulo (Carnivora, Mustelidae)
from North America /. City of Washington ,
1981. p. cm.   LC Card 81-607075   DDC 560 s
569/.74 19
QE701 .S56 no. 46 QE882.C15

Mapes, Royal H. Carboniferous and Permian
Bactritoidea (Cephalopoda) in North America /.
Lawrence, Kan. , 1979. ii, 75 p., [20] leaves of
plates :   LC Card 79-625202   DDC 560 s 564/.5 19
QE701 .K3 no. 64 QE806

PALEONTOLOGY - OLIGOCENE.
Allison, Richard C., 1935- A late Oligocene or
earliest Miocene molluscan fauna from Sitkinak
Island, Alaska /. Menlo Park, CA (345
Middlefield Rd., MS 51 Bldg. 5, Menlo Park
94025) [1981] p. cm.   LC Card 81-607925   DDC
564/.09798/4 19
QE801 .A44

Dockery, David T. The invertebrate
macropaleontology of the Clarke County,
Mississippi, area /. Jackson, Miss. , 1980. 387
p. :   LC Card 80-623808   DDC 562/.09762/673 19
QE770 .D62

PALEONTOLOGY - ORDOVICIAN.
Miller, James Frederick, 1943- Taxonomic
revisions of some Upper Cambrian and Lower
Ordovician conodonts with comments on their
evolution /. Lawrence, Kan. , 1980. 39 p., [2]
leaves of plates :   LC Card 80-623003   DDC 560 s
562/.2 19
QE701 .K33 no. 99 QE899

PALEONTOLOGY - OREGON.
Saul, Louella Rankin. The North Pacific
cretaceous Trigoniid genus Yaadia /. Berkeley ,
1978. 65 p., 12 leaves of plates :   ISBN
0-520-09582-0   LC Card 77-84990   DDC
564/.11 19
QE812.T74 S28

PALEONTOLOGY - PERMIAN.
Mapes, Royal H. Carboniferous and Permian
Bactritoidea (Cephalopoda) in North America /.
Lawrence, Kan. , 1979. ii, 75 p., [20] leaves of
plates :   LC Card 79-625202   DDC 560 s 564/.5 19
QE701 .K3 no. 64 QE806

PALEONTOLOGY - PLIOCENE.
Dalquest, Walter Woelber, 1917- Late
Hemphillian mammals of the Ocote local fauna,
Guanajuato, Mexico /. Austin, Tex. , 19. 25 p. :
LC Card 80-622865   DDC 574 s 569 19
AM101 .T474 no. 32 QE881

Gustafson, Eric Paul. The vertebrate faunas of
the Pliocene Ringold Formation, south-central
Washington /. Eugene, Or. , 1978. 62 p. :   LC
Card 79-625683   DDC 574.979 s 566/.09797/51
19
QH1 .O7 no. 23 QE841

Harrison, Jessica A. A review of the extinct
wolverine, Plesiogulo (Carnivora, Mustelidae)
from North America /. City of Washington ,
1981. p. cm.   LC Card 81-607075   DDC 560 s
569/.74 19
QE701 .S56 no. 46 QE882.C15

MacFadden, Bruce J. Nannippus phlegon
(Mammalia, Equidae) from the Pliocene
(Blancan) of Florida /. Gainesville (Museum
Rd., University of Florida, Gainesville, FL
32611) , 1980. 37 p. :   LC Card 81-621398   DDC
569/.72 19
QE882.U6 M28

Poore, Richard Z. Biostratigraphy and
paleoecology of the upper Miocene (Messinian)
and lower Pliocene (?) Cerro de Almendral
section, Alermía Basin, southern Spain /.
Washington , 1981. iii, 11 p., [2] leaves of
plates :   LC Card 80-607164   DDC
551.7/86/094681 19
QE694 .P67

**PALEONTOLOGY - SILURIAN, LOWER. see
PALEONTOLOGY - ORDOVICIAN.**

PALEONTOLOGY - UNITED STATES.
United States. Federal Highway Administration.
Office of Environmental Policy. The
consideration of archeology and paleontology in
the Federal-aid highway program.
[Washington] , 1979. 79 p. :   LC Card 79-602652
E159.5 .U54 1978   NYPL [HBC 81-515]

PALEONTOLOGY - WEST (U. S.)
Imlay, Ralph Willard, 1908- Jurassic (Oxfordian
and Late Callovian) ammonites from the
western interior region of the United States /.
Washington , 1981. p. cm.   LC Card 81-607015
DDC 564/.53/0978 19
QE807.A5 I593

**PALEOZOIC PERIOD. see GEOLOGY,
STRATIGRAPHIC - PALEOZOIC.**

PALESTINE - ECONOMIC CONDITIONS.
Palestine Economic Corporation. Memorandum
/. New York [1947] 16 p. ;
*NYPL [*XMH-1601]*

Palestine Economic Corporation. Memorandum /
submitted by the Palestine Economic
Corporation to the United Nations Special
Committee on Palestine. New York : The
Corporation, [1947] 16 p. ; 23 cm. Microfiche
(neg.) 1 sheet. 11 x 15 cm. (NYPL FSN 34,499) Cover
title.
*1. Jewish-Arab relations. 2. Palestine - Economic
conditions. I. United Nations. General Assembly.
Special Committee on Palestine. II. Title.*
*NYPL [*XMH-1601]*

**PALESTINE PROBLEM, 1917- see JEWISH-
ARAB RELATIONS.**

**Palisades Interstate Park Commission (New
York and New Jersey)** (Old Catalog form:
New York (State). Palisades Interstate Park
Commission)
Composite annual report. 1959- Bear Mountain,
N. Y. illus. 23-28 cm. Combines, for more
convenient use, the separate reports made by the
commission to the states of New York and New Jersey
on Palisades Interstate Park activities.   LC Card
A60-9592
1. Palisades Interstate Park - Periodicals.
NYPL [JLM 81-72]

**PALISADES INTERSTATE PARK -
PERIODICALS.**
Palisades Interstate Park Commission (New
York and New Jersey) Composite annual
report. 1959- Bear Mountain, N. Y.   LC Card
A60-9592   *NYPL [JLM 81-72]*

Palm, David. Health care expenditures in
Nebraska, selected years, 1966-1976 / by David
Palm, Arthur Chan. Lincoln, Neb. : State
Health Planning and Development Agency,
Nebraska Dept. of Health, [1979] ix, 47 p. ; 28
cm. "July 1979." Bibliography: p. 46-47.   LC Card
80-620751   DDC 338.4/33621/09782 19
*1. Medical care, Cost of - Nebraska - Statistics. I.
Chan, Arthur, joint author. II. Title.*
RA410.54.N2 P34

Palmer, Colin A., 1942- Human cargoes : the
British slave trade to Spanish America,
1700-1739 / Colin Palmer. Urbana : University
of Illinois Press, c1981. xv, 183 p. : 2 maps ; 24
cm. (Blacks in the new world) Bibliography: p.
171-177. Includes index.   ISBN 0-252-00846-4 :   LC
Card 81-3326   DDC 3-82/.44/0941 19
*1. Slave-trade - Great Britain - History - 18th century.
2. Slave-trade - Africa - History - 18th century. 3.
Slave-trade - Latin America - History - 18th century. 4.
South Sea Company - History - 18th century. I. Title.
II. Series.*
HT1161 .P34

Palmer, Edith, 1940- The Austrian banking
system under the 1979 statute / by Edith
Palmer. Washington, D.C. : Law Library,
Library of Congress, 1980. 130 p. ; 28 cm.
"Bundesgesetz vom 24. Jänner 1979 über das
Kreditwesen (Kreditwesengesetz--KWG)": p. 113-130.
Includes bibliographical references.   LC Card
80-600156   DDC 346.436/082 19
*1. Banking law - Austria. I. Austria. Laws, statutes, etc.
Kreditwesengesetz. 1980. II. Title.*
LAW

PALMER, JOHN LOGAN.
United States. Congress. Senate. Committee on
Finance. Nominations of Abraham Katz,
William J. Driver, and John L. Palmer .
Washington , 1980. iii, 19 p. ;   LC Card
80-602760   DDC 353.842 19
KF26 .F5 1980b

Palmer, Ted. The evaluation of juvenile diversion
projects : final report / by Ted Palmer, Marvin
Bohnstedt, Roy Lewis. [Sacramento] : Dept. of
the Youth Authority, 1978. xx, 366 p. ; 29 cm.
Bibliography: p. 364-366.   LC Card 79-623204
*1. Pre-trial intervention - California - Evaluation. 2.
Juvenile corrections - California - Evaluation. I.
Bohnstedt, Marvin, joint author. II. Lewis, Roy V., joint
author. III. California. Dept. of the Youth Authority.
IV. Title.*
HV9105.C2 P34   NYPL [JLF 81-140]

PALMER, WAYMAN DUBOIS, 1927-
United States. Congress. Senate. Committee on
Banking, Housing and Urban Affairs.
Nomination of Wayman D. Palmer .
Washington , 1980. ii, 13 p. ;   LC Card
80-603651   DDC 353.0082/52045 19
KF26 .B39 1980p

Palmour, Karen P. University of Georgia.
International Trade and Development Center. A

small business export development program /.
Athens, Ga. , c1980. 24 p. : LC Card 80-624106
DDC 658.8/48 19
HF1009.5 .U55 1980

Palmquist, Raymond B. Impact of highway
improvements on property values in
Washington / [Raymond B. Palmquist] ;
prepared for Washington State Transportation
Commission, in cooperation with U. S.
Department of Transportation, Federal Highway
Administration. Olympia, WA : Social and
Economic Planning Section, Public
Transportation and Planning Division, Dept. of
Transportation, [1980] 247 p. : ill. ; 29 cm.
"March 1980." "Research project HR-564." Bibliography:
p. 185-188. LC Card 80-622759 DDC
333.33/2/09797 19
1. Real property - Valuation - Washington (State) -
Mathematical models. 2. Highway planning -
Washington (State) - Mathematical models. I.
Washington (State). Transportation Commission. II.
United States. Federal Highway Administration. III.
Washington (State). Planning and Public Transportation
Division. Social and Economic Planning Section. IV.
Title.
HD266.W2 P34

Paltridge, James Gilbert. Mid-career education
and training : community support systems /
James Gilbert Paltridge, Mary C. Regan, Dawn
G. Terkla. Davis, Calif. : Institute of
Governmental Affairs, University of California,
1979. v, 93 leaves : diagrs. ; 28 cm. (California
studies in community policy and change. no. 6)
Bibliography: leaves 92-93. LC Card 80-623848
DDC 374 19
1. Career education - United States. 2. Continuing
education - United States. I. Regan, Mary, 1930- joint
author. II. Terkla, Dawn G., joint author. III. Title. IV.
Series.
LC1037.5 .P33   **NYPL** *[JLM 77-672 no. 6]*

Paludan, Phillip S., 1938- Victims : a true story
of the Civil War / by Phillip Shaw Paludan.1st
ed. Knoxville : University of Tennessee Press,
c1981. p. cm. Includes bibliographical references and
index. ISBN 0-87049-316-7 LC Card 81-2578
DDC 973.7/33 19
1. Shelton Laurel Valley (N.C.) - Massacre, 1863. 2.
United States - History - Civil War, 1861-1865 -
Prisoners and prisons. I. Title.
F262.M25 P34

PALYNOLOGY.
(1982) Hueber, Francis M. Megaspores and a
palynomorph from the lower Potomac Group in
Virginia /. Washington , 1982. p. cm. LC Card
81-607852 DDC 560 s 561/.13 19
QE701 .S56 no. 49 QE996

PALYNOTAXONOMY.
Nowicke, Joan W. Pollen morphology and
phylogenetic relationships of the Berberidaceae
/. Washington , 1981. p. cm. LC Card 80-21960
DDC 581 s 583/.117 19
QK1 .S2747 no. 50 QK495.B45

PAMLICO RIVER, N.C.
Kuenzler, Edward J. Nutrient kinetics of
phytoplankton in the Pamlico River, North
Carolina /. [Raleigh] [1979] xxii, 163 p. : LC
Card 79-626205 DDC 333.91/009756 s 589.4 19
HD1694.N8 N6 no. 139 QK571.5.N8

Pan American Health Organization.
Control de las infecciones entéricas.
Washington, 1964. 83 p. map. 26 cm. (Its
Publicaciones científicas. no. 100) English ed. published
under title: Control of gastrointestinal diseases. At head
of title: Discusiones tecnicas, XIV Reunión del Consejo
Directivo de la OPS, Washington, D.C., septiembre de
1963. Includes bibliographical references. LC Card
80-495685
1. Diarrhea - Prevention - Congresses. 2. Intestines -
Infections - Prevention - Congresses. 3. Diarrhea -
Latin America - Prevention - Congresses. 4. Diarrhea in
children - Latin America - Congresses. I. Title. II.
Series.
RA10 .P252 no. 100a RA644.D9

Control of gastrointestinal diseases; ideas for
the formulation of a plan for the control of
gastrointestinal diseases, including
environmental sanitation measures,
epidemiology, health education, and early
diagnosis and treatment. Washington, 1964. iii,
77 p. 26 cm. (Its Scientific publication. no. 100)
Consists of the working documents for the technical
discussions at the 14th meeting of the PAHO Directing
Council, Washington, D.C., Sept. 1963. Includes

bibliographical references. LC Card 81-458187 DDC
362.1/09181/2 s 614.5/933 19
1. Diarrhea - Prevention - Congresses. 2. Intestines -
Infections - Prevention - Congresses. 3. Diarrhea -
Latin America - Prevention - Congresses. 4. Diarrhea in
children - Latin America - Congresses. I. Series: Pan
American Health Organization. Publicaciones
científicas , no. 100. II. Title.
RA10 .P252 no. 100 RA644.D9

Directorio de psiquiatras de America Latina =
Directory of psychiatrists in Latin America.
Washington, D.C. : Organización Panamericana
de la Salud, Oficina Sanitaria Panamericana,
Oficina Regional de la Organización Mundial
de la Salud, 1968. cxi, 558, 10 p. ; 24 cm.
(Publicación científica - Organización Panamericana de
la Salud . no. 163) Pref. and introd. in Spanish and
English. Includes index. LC Card 80-140541 DDC
362.1/09181/2 s 616.89/0025/8 19
1. Psychiatrists - Latin America - Directories. I. Title.
II. Title: Directory of psychiatrists in Latin America.
III. Series: Pan American Health Organization.
Publicaciones científicas , no. 163.
RA10 .P252 no. 163 RC335

Publicaciones científicas .
(no. 100) Pan American Health Organization.
Control of gastrointestinal diseases.
Washington, 1964. iii, 77 p. LC Card
81-458187 DDC 362.1/09181/2 s 614.5/933 19
RA10 .P252 no. 100 RA644.D9

(no. 163) Pan American Health Organization.
Directorio de psiquiatras de America Latina
=. Washington, D.C. , 1968. cxi, 558, 10 p. ;
LC Card 80-140541 DDC 362.1/09181/2 s
616.89/0025/8 19
RA10 .P252 no. 163 RC335

(no. 293) Seminario sobre Organización de
Servicios para el Retrasado Mental,
Cartagena, Colombia, 1973. Seminario sobre
Organización de Servicios para el Retrasado
Mental . Washington , 1974. iii, 100 p. ; LC
Card 80-513008
RA10 .P252 no. 293 RC569.9

(no. 350) Torres-Anjel, Manuel J.
Enterotoxigenic Clostridium perfringens type
A in selected humans . Washington , 1977.
32 p. ; LC Card 78-102859 DDC 362.1/09181/2
s 615.9/52995 19
RA10 .P252 no. 350 QR201.C54

(no. 386) Burke, Mary. Inter-American
investigation of mortality in childhood .
Washington, D.C. , 1979. v, 145 p. : ISBN
92-75-11386-6 (pbk.) : LC Card 80-132481
DDC 362.1/09181/2 s 304.6/4 19
RA10 .P252 no. 386 HB1323.C5

**Pan American Union. Biblioteca Conmemorativa
de Colón. see Columbus Memorial Library.**

**Pan American Union. Dept. of Cultural Affairs.
Biblioteca Conmemorativa de Colón. see
Columbus Memorial Library.**

**Pan American Union. Dept. of Cultural Affairs.
Columbus Memorial Library. see Columbus
Memorial Library.**

Pan American Union. Dept. of Statistics. (Old
Catalog form: Pan American Union. Statistics
Division)
América en cifras. 1960-77 (incomplete)
Washington.   **NYPL** *[SDG (America)*
(America en cifras)]

**Pan American Union. Dept. of Scientific Affairs.
Programa Regional de Desarrollo Científico
y Tecnológico. see Programa Regional de
Desarrollo Científico y Tecnológico.**

**Pan American Union. Inter-American Economic
and Social Council. see Inter-American
Economic and Social Council.**

**Pan American Union. Library. see Columbus
Memorial Library.**

**Pan American Union. Statistics, Dept. of. see
Pan American Union. Dept. of Statistics.**

**Pan American Union. Statistics Division. see Pan
American Union. Dept. of Statistics.**

PANAMA CANAL.
United States. Congress. House. Committee on
Merchant Marine and Fisheries. Subcommittee
on Panama Canal. Panama Canal oversight .
Washington , 1980. iii, 158 p. : LC Card
80-603322 DDC 353.0087/6444 19
KF27 .M475 1980a

**Panama Canal Commission authorization fiscal
year 1981 .** United States. Congress. Senate.
Committee on Armed Services. Washington ,
1980 [i.e. 1981] ii, 32 p. ; LC Card 81-600852
DDC 353.0072/234 19
KF26 .A7 1980f

**PANAMA CANAL - ENVIRONMENTAL
ASPECTS.**
United States. Congress. House. Committee on
Merchant Marine and Fisheries. Subcommittee
on Panama Canal. Panama Canal oversight .
Washington , 1980. iii, 158 p. : LC Card
80-603322 DDC 353.0087/6444 19
KF27 .M475 1980a

Panama Canal oversight . United States.
Congress. House. Committee on Merchant
Marine and Fisheries. Subcommittee on Panama
Canal. Washington , 1980. iii, 158 p. : LC Card
80-603322 DDC 353.0087/6444 19
KF27 .M475 1980a

PANAMA CANAL TREATIES, 1977.
United States. Congress. House. Committee on
Merchant Marine and Fisheries. Subcommittee
on Panama Canal. Panama Canal oversight .
Washington , 1980. iii, 158 p. : LC Card
80-603322 DDC 353.0087/6444 19
KF27 .M475 1980a

United States. General Accounting Office.
Background information bearing upon Panama
Canal treaty implementing legislation .
[Washington] [1979] 62 p. ; LC Card 79-602532
DDC 353.0087/6444 19
JX1398.73 .U54 1979

United States. General Accounting Office.
Implementing the Panama Canal treaty of
1977--good planning but many issues remain .
Washington, D.C. , 1980. vii, 101 p. : LC Card
80-602506 DDC 353.0087/6444 19
JX1398.73 .U54 1980

United States. Treaties, etc. Panama, Sept. 7,
1977. Tratados sobre el Canal de Panamá
suscritos entre la República de Panamá y los
Estados Unidos de América =. Washington,
D.C. , 1979. 2 v. : LC Card 80-121836 DDC
341.4/46/02667307287 19
JX1398.72 1979 .U54 1977

Panama Canal Zone. see Canal Zone.

PANAMA CITY, FLA. - HARBOR.
United States. Board of Engineers for Rivers
and Harbors. The ports of Panama City &
Pensacola, FL and Pascagoula & Gulfport, MS
/. Washington , Fort Belvoir, VA , 1979. vi,
130 p. : LC Card 80-603371 DDC 387.1/09759/95
19
HE554.A4 U53 1979

Panel on Communicative Disorders (U. S.)
Report of the Panel on Communicative
Disorders to the National Advisory
Neurological and Communicative Disorders and
Stroke Council, National Institute of
Neurological and Communicative Disorders and
Stroke. [Bethesda, Md.] : U. S. Dept. of Health,
Education, and Welfare, Public Health Service,
National Institutes of Health, [1979] xvii, 351
p. ; 28 cm. (NIH publication ; no. 79-1914) "June 1,
1979." LC Card 80-601219 DDC 616.85/5/0072073
19
1. Communicative disorders. 2. Communicative
disorders - Research - United States. I. National
Advisory Neurological and Communicative Disorders
and Stroke Council (U. S.). II. Series: United States.
National Institutes of Health. Publication, no. 79-1914.
III. Title.
RC423 .P24 1979

**Panel on Convulsive and Neuromuscular
Disorders (U. S.)** Report of the Panel on
Convulsive and Neuromuscular Disorders to the
National Advisory Neurological and
Communicative Disorders and Stroke Council,
National Institute of Neurological and
Communicative Disorders and Stroke.
[Bethesda, Md.] : U. S. Dept. of Health,
Education, and Welfare, Public Health Service,
National Institutes of Health, [1979] xiii, 124
p. : ill. ; 28 cm. (NIH publication ; no. 79-1913)
"June 1, 1979." LC Card 80-601220 DDC
616.7/4/0072073 19
1. Neuromuscular diseases - Research - United States.
2. Epilepsy - Research - United States. 3. Medical
policy - United States. I. National Advisory
Neurological and Communicative Disorders and Stroke
Council (U. S.). II. National Institute of Neurological

and Communicative Disorders and Stroke. III. Series:
United States. National Institutes of Health. Publication,
no. 79-1913. IV. Title.
RC925.5 .P26 1979

**Panel on Energy, Natural Resources, and the
Environment (U. S.)**
Energy, natural resources, and the environment
in the eighties : report of the Panel on energy,
Natural Resources, and the Environment.
Washington : President's Commission for a
National Agenda for the Eighties : For sale by
The Supt. of Docs., U. S. G.P.O., 1980. 57 p. ;
23 cm.   LC Card 81-649   DDC 333.79/0973 19
*1. Energy policy - United States. 2. Power resources -
United States. 3. Environmental policy - United States.
I. Title.*
HD9502.U52 P35 1981

Energy, natural resources, and the environment
in the eighties : report of the Panel on Energy,
Natural Resources, and the Environment.
Washington : President's Commission for a
National Agenda for the Eighties, 1981. p. cm.
   LC Card 80-649   DDC 333.79/0973 19
*1. Energy policy - United States. 2. Power resources -
United States. I. Title.*
HD9502.U52 P35 1981

**Panel on Inflammatory, Demyelinating and
Degenerative Diseases (U. S.)** Report of the
Panel on Inflammatory, Demyelinating, and
Degenerative Diseases to the National Advisory
Neurological and Communicative Disorders and
Stroke Council [prepared for the] National
Institute of Neurological and Communicative
Disorders and Stroke. [Bethesda, Md.] : U. S.
Dept. of Health, Education, and Welfare, Public
Health Service, National Institutes of Health,
[1979] ix, 129 p. ; 28 cm. (NIH publication ; no.
79-1916) "June 1, 1979." LC Card 80-601215   DDC
616.8/072073 19
*1. Nervous system - Diseases - Research - United
States. 2. Medical policy - United States. I. National
Institute of Neurological and Communicative Disorders
and Stroke. II. Series: United States. National Institutes
of Health. Publication, no. 79-1916.*
RC346 .P275 1979

**Panel on the American Economy: Employment,
Productivity, and Inflation (U. S.)** The
American economy--employment, productivity,
and inflation in the eighties : report of the
Panel on the American Economy--Employment,
Productivity, and Inflation, President's
Commission for a National Agenda for the
Eighties. Washington : The Commission : For
sale by the The Supt. of Docs., U. S. G.P.O.,
1980. 82 p. ; 23 cm.   LC Card 81-357   DDC
330.973/0926 19
*1. United States - Economic policy - 1971-. 2.
Industrial productivity - United States. 3. Labor
supply - United States. 4. Inflation (Finance) - United
States. I. Title.*
HC106.7 .P345 1981

A panel study of income dynamics. Michigan.
University. Survey Research Center. Wave 1- ;
1968- Ann Arbor.   ***NYPL [M-11 5247]***

Panichas, George Andrew. The courage of
judgment : essays in criticism, culture, and
society / George A. Panichas ; with a foreword
by Austin Warren.1st ed. Knoxville : University
of Tennessee Press, c1981. p. cm. Includes index.
   ISBN 0-87049-325-6 :   LC Card 81-4050   DDC
809 19
*1. Literature - History and criticism - Addresses, essays,
lectures. I. Title.*
PN511 .P158

Pannell, James P., 1926- Soil survey of Rio
Grande County area, Colorado / [by James P.
Pannell, James M. Yenter, and Tom S.
Bargsten] ; United States Department of
Agriculture, Soil Conservation Service, in
cooperation with Colorado Agricultural
Experiment Station. [Washington] : The
Service, 1980. iv, 89 p., [2] fold. leaves of
plates : ill. maps ; 29 cm. Cover title. "Issued
February 1980." Bibliography: p. 87. Includes index.
   LC Card 80-602320   DDC 631.4/7/78837 19
*1. Soils - Colorado - Rio Grande County - Maps. I.
Yenter, James M., joint author. II. Bargsten, Tom S.,
joint author. III. United States. Soil Conservation
Service. IV. Colorado. Agricultural Experiment Station,
Fort Collins. V. Title.*
S599.C6 P36

**PANNONIA - ANTIQUITIES - ADDRESSES,
   ESSAYS, LECTURES.**

The Archaeology of Roman Pannonia /.
Lexington, Ky. , Budapest , c1980. 506 p.,
clxvii p. of plates :   ISBN 963-05-1886-4
   (Akadémiai Kiadó)   LC Card 77-80463   DDC
939/.8 19
DG59.P2 A73

Panza, Giuliano F. International Association of
Seismology and the Physics of the Earth's
Interior. European Seismological Commission.
Working Group on Statistical Methods.
Bibliography of statistical aspects of seismicity
/. Boulder, Colo. , 1978. iv, 74 p. ;   LC Card
79-603198   DDC 551 s 551.2/2/072 19
QE500 .W67a no. 13 Z6033.E1 QE539

Paone, James. Johnson, Wilton. Land utilization
and reclamation in the mining industry,
1930-80 /. [Avondale, MD] [1981] p. cm.   LC
   Card 81-38489   DDC 622 s 333.73 19
TN295 .U4 TN23

**PAPAGO INDIAN RESERVATION, ARIZ. -
   ANTIQUITIES.**
Vogler, Lawrence. Reports on data recovery
operations at two sites in the Papago Indian
Reservation, Arizona . [Tucson, Ariz.] [1978]
v, 45, v, 44, leaves :   LC Card 80-622637   DDC
979.1/77 19
E99.H68 V63

Paper ballot . Illinois. State Board of Elections.
[Springfield, Ill. , 1980?] 60 p. :   LC Card
80-621476   DDC 324.6/5/09773 19
KFI1620.3 .A836

**PAPER MAKING AND TRADE -
   ADDRESSES, ESSAYS, LECTURES.**
Appropriate industrial technology for paper
products and small pulp mills. New York ,
1979. xiii, 149 p. :   LC Card 80-108650   DDC
300 s 338.4/7676 19
JX1977 .A2 ID/232/3, no. 3

**PAPER - MANUFACTURE. see PAPER
   MAKING AND TRADE.**

**PAPER - TRADE AND STATISTICS. see
   PAPER MAKING AND TRADE.**

[Papers] Specialists' Session on Chemical Kinetics
Calculations, University of California, 1968.
Berkeley, Calif. 1968. 1 v. (various pagings)
   NYPL [JSF 75-122]

Papers in administration.
(no. 1) Boyer, Edward C. Collective bargaining
for municipal employees. [Laramie], 1973. iii,
34 p.;   ***NYPL [JLM 75-1268 no. 1]***

Papers in highway archaeology .
(no. 2) Oklahoma Highway Archaeological
Survey. An archaeological survey of U. S. 69,
Pittsburg, Atoka, and Bryan Counties,
Oklahoma /. [Norman] , 1976. v, 158 p. :   LC
Card 77-621832   DDC 976.6/6 19
E78.O45 O48 1976

(no. 3) Briscoe, James M. The plantation site
(Mi-63) . [Oklahoma City] , 1977. xii, 276 p.,
[1] fold. leaf of plates :   LC Card 79-621192
DDC 976.6/74 19
E99.C13 B74

**Papers in international studies. Southeast Asia
   series .**
(no. 57) Siregar, Susan Rodgers. Adat, Islam,
and Christianity in a Batak homeland /.
Athens, Ohio , 1981. p. cm.   ISBN 0-89680-110-1
   LC Card 81-11073   DDC 959.8/1 19
DS632.B3 S57

(no. 58) Van Esterik, Penny. Cognition and
design production in Ban Chiang painted
pottery /. [Athens, Ohio] , 1981. p. cm.   ISBN
0-89680-078-4   LC Card 81-11172   DDC
738.3/7 19
NK4156.6.B36 V37

Paperwork and red tape . United States. Office of
Management and Budget. Washington , 1979.
133 p. in various pagings ;
   NYPL [JLE 81-478]

Paperwork and redtape reduction act of 1979 .
United States. Congress. Senate. Committee on
Governmental Affairs. Subcommittee on
Federal Spending Practices and Open
Government. Washington , 1980. iii, 190 p. ;
   LC Card 80-602188   DDC 342.73/066 19
KF26 .G6732 1979h

PAPHIOPEDILUM.
Rentoul, J. N., 1909- Growing orchids . Seattle
[1981] c1980. p. cm.   ISBN 0-295-95839-1 LC

Card 81-3023   DDC 635.9/3415 19
SB409 .R4 1981

Papke, Keith G. Fluorspar in Nevada / Keith G.
Papke. 1st ed. Reno : Mackay School of Mines,
University of Nevada, 1979. 77 p. : ill., maps (2
fold. col. in pocket) ; 28 cm. (Bulletin - Nevada
Bureau of Mines and Geology ; 93) Bibliography: p.
74-75. Includes index.   LC Card 80-621828   DDC
553.6 19
*1. Fluorspar - Nevada. I. Series: Nevada. Bureau of
Mines and Geology. Bulletin , 93. II. Title.*
TN948.F6 P36

Papp, John F. Structure study of a
CF_2Br_2-inhibited methane flame--the effect of
CF_2Br_2 on composition, net reaction rates, and
rate coefficients / by John F. Papp, Charles P.
Lazzara, Joan C. Biordi. [Washington] : United
States Dept. of the Interior, Bureau of Mines,
1981. p. cm. (Report of investigations / Bureau of
Mines) Bibliography: p.   LC Card 80-606846   DDC
622 s 628.9/223 19
*1. Flame. 2. Methane. 3. Dibromodifluoromethane. 4.
Chemical inhibitors. I. Lazzara, Charles P. II. Biordi,
Joan C. III. Series: United States Bureau of Mines.
Report of investigations . IV. Title.*
TN23 .U43 QD516

**PAPUA NEW GUINEA - ADMINISTRATIVE
   AND POLITICAL DIVISIONS - MAPS.**
[United State. Central Intelligence Agency]
Papua and New Guinea administrative
divisions. [Washington , 1970] 1 map :   LC
Card 81-692529
G8161.F7 1970 .U5

**PAPUA NEW GUINEA - SOCIAL LIFE AND
   CUSTOMS - ADDRESSES, ESSAYS,
   LECTURES.**
Rituals of manhood . Berkeley , c1981. p. cm.
   ISBN 0-520-04448-7 LC Card 81-1807 DDC
392/.14 19
GN671.N5 R55

**"Par Force" (Reef Bay) Estate Great House and
Reef Bay Sugar Factory in Virgin Islands
National Park.** Hatch, Charles E. [Washington]
1969. iii, 18 l.   LC Card 80-503016   DDC
972.97/22 19
F2136.9.R43 H37 1969

Paradigm lost? Kegley, Charles W. The
comparative study of foreign policy .
[Columbia] , 1980. 36 p. ;   LC Card 81-620735
DDC 327/.072 19
JX1291 .K427

**Paradise Inn, Mount Rainier National Park,
Washington /.** Snow, David E. [Denver]
[1979?] vii, 153 p. :   LC Card 79-603743   DDC
728/.5/0288 19
TX941.P37 S64

**PARADISE VALLEY, NEV. - SOCIAL LIFE
   AND CUSTOMS - EXHIBITIONS.**
Marshall, Howard W. Buckaroos in Paradise .
Washington , 1980. xvi, 95 p. :   ISBN
0-8444-0348-2 LC Card 80-23261 DDC
979.3/54 19
F847.H8 M37

**PARAGUAY - HISTORY - SOURCES -
   BIBLIOGRAPHY.**
California. University. Riverside. Library.
Godoi-Díaz Pérez Collection. Research guide to
the Godoi-Díaz Pérez Collection in the Library
of the University of California, Riverside /.
Riverside , 1973. 60 p. ;
   NYPL [HLM 81-769]

Paralegals, a selected bibliography /. Cain,
Anthony A. Washington, D.C. , 1978 [i.e.
1979] vii, 40 p. ;   LC Card 79-603300   DDC
016.34/0023 19
KF320.L4 C34

**Paralic to fluvial record of an early Cretaceous
marine transgression--Longford Member, Kiowa
Formation, north-central Kansas /.** Franks,
Paul C. [Lawrence, Kan.] [1979] 55 p. :   LC
Card 80-621776   DDC 557.81 s 551.7/7 19
QE113 .A2 no. 219 QE686

**Parallel compilation in a multiprocessor
environment /.** Mickunas, M. Dennis. Urbana,
Ill. [1979] 29 p. :   LC Card 80-621699   DDC
001.64 s 001.64/2 19
QA76.I4 no. 991 QA76.6

**PARALLEL PROCESSING (ELECTRONIC
   COMPUTERS)**
Mickunas, M. Dennis. Parallel compilation in a

multiprocessor environment /. Urbana, Ill.
[1979] 29 p. :   LC Card 80-621699   DDC 001.64 s
001.64/2 19
QA76 .14 no. 991 QA76.6

PARAMEDICAL EDUCATION - NEVADA.
Nevada allied health education and manpower .
Carson City, Nev. , 1976. 98 p. :   LC Card
80-621254   DDC 331.12/3161 19
R847.6.N3 N48

PARAPROFESSIONALS IN SOCIAL
SERVICE - VERMONT.
Stanfield, Robert E. The uses of
paraprofessionals in the delivery of manpower
and social services through public service
employment. [Montpelier, Vt.] 1973. xiii, 64 p.
                              *NYPL [*XME-9293]*

PARAPSYCHOLOGY. see PSYCHICAL
RESEARCH.

PARAQUAT - TOXICOLOGY.
United States. Congress. House. Select
Committee on Narcotics Abuse and Control.
The use of paraquat to eradicate illicit
marihuana crops and the health implications of
paraquat-contaminated marihuana on the U. S.
market . Washington , 1980. iii, 99 p. :   LC
Card 80-602592   DDC 363.4/5 19
RA1242.P34 U54 1980

PARASITES - BIRDS.
McDonald, Malcolm Edwin, 1915- Key to
trematodes reported in waterfowl /.
Washington, D.C. , 1981. p. cm.   LC Card
81-607044   DDC 333.95/4/0973 s 639.9/741 19
S914 .A3 no. 142 QL391.P7

PARASITES - CATALOGS AND
COLLECTIONS.
Salley, E. Jean. Checklist of types in the U. S.
national parasite collection /. [Washington] ,
1978. iv, 233 p. ;   LC Card 78-602796   DDC
591.52/49/0740153 19
QL757 .S23

PARASITES - FISHES.
Overstreet, Robin M. Marine maladies? .
[Ocean Springs, Miss.] , c1978. 140 p. :   LC
Card 78-112833   DDC 591.52/49 19
SH175 .O94

PARASITES - MAN. see MEDICAL
PARASITOLOGY.

PARASITES - SHELLFISH.
Overstreet, Robin M. Marine maladies? .
[Ocean Springs, Miss.] , c1978. 140 p. :   LC
Card 78-112833   DDC 591.52/49 19
SH175 .O94

PARASITES - UNITED STATES - CATALOGS
AND COLLECTIONS.
Salley, E. Jean. Checklist of types in the U. S.
national parasite collection /. [Washington] ,
1978. iv, 233 p. ;   LC Card 78-602796   DDC
591.52/49/0740153 19
QL757 .S23

Parasitic copepods from the Gulf of Mexico and
Caribbean Sea, I . Cressey, Roger F., 1930-
Washington , 1981. p. cm.   LC Card 81-9055
DDC 591 s 595.3/4 19
QL1 .S54 no. 339 QL444.C73

PARATRANSIT SERVICES - UNITED
STATES - ADDRESSES, ESSAYS,
LECTURES.
Paratransit 1980 /. Washington, D.C. , 1981. p.
cm.   ISBN 0-309-03123-0   LC Card 81-38318
DDC 380.5 s 388.4/132 19
TE7 .H5 no. 778 HE308

Paratransit 1980 / Transportation Research
Board, Commission on Sociotechnical Systems,
National Research Council. Washington, D.C. :
National Academy of Sciences, 1981. p. cm.
(Transportation research record . 778)   ISBN
0-309-03123-0   LC Card 81-38318   DDC 380.5
s 388.4/132 19
1. Paratransit services - United States - Addresses,
essays, lectures. I. National Research Council (U. S.)
Transportation Research Board. II. Series.
TE7 .H5 no. 778 HE308

PARENT AND CHILD - CONGRESSES.
National Conference on Mental Health Issues
Related to Sudden Infant Death Syndrome,
Baltimore, Md., 1977. Mental health issues in
grief counseling . Rockville, Md. , Washington,
D.C. , 1979 i.e. 1980. 133 p. ;   LC Card
80-602299   DDC 362.8/286 19
RJ59 .N37 1977

PARENT AND CHILD (LAW) - NEW YORK
(STATE)
New York (State). Temporary State
Commission on Child Welfare. Training
curriculum on freeing children for adoption /.
[New York , 1979] 139 p. ;   LC Card 80-622702
DDC 346.74701/78 19
KFN5130 .A837

Parental kidnaping prevention act of 1979, S.
105 . United States. Congress. Senate.
Committee on the Judiciary. Subcommittee on
Criminal Justice. Washington , 1980. iv, 156
p. ;   LC Card 80-602799   DDC 345.73/0254 19
KF26 .J8377 1980c

Parental kidnaping prevention act of 1979,
S.105 . United States. Congress. Senate.
Committee on the Judiciary. Subcommittee on
Criminal Justice. Washington , 1980. iii, 378
p. ;   LC Card 80-602982   DDC 345.73/0254 19
KF26 .J8377 1980b

Parental kidnaping, 1979 . United States.
Congress. Senate. Committee on Labor and
Human Resources. Subcommittee on Child and
Human Development. Washington , 1979. iv,
285 p. :   LC Card 80-600739   DDC 364.1/54 19
KF26 .L273 1979d

PARENTAL REJECTION.
Evoy, John J. The rejected . University Park
[1981] p. cm.   ISBN 0-271-00285-9 :   LC Card
81-47172   DDC 155.9/24 19
RC455.4.F3 E96

Pargeter, J. K. (John K.) DeBarbadillo, John J.,
1942- Process for recovering chromium and
other metals from superalloy scrap /. Avondale,
Md. [1981] p. cm.   LC Card 81-6102   DDC 622
s 669/.734 19
TN23 .U43 TN799.C5

PARI-MUTUEL BETTING - LAW AND
LEGISLATION - INDIANA.
Indiana. Legislative Council. Interim Study
Committee on Racing. Interim Study
Committee on Racing . Indianapolis [1976] ii,
133, p. ;   LC Card 77-622132
KFI3384 .A25 1976   *NYPL [*XME-9538]*

PARI-MUTUEL BETTING - LAW AND
LEGISLATURE - FLORIDA.
Florida. Legislature. Senate. Committee on
Commerce. A review of the Thoroughbred
Racing Advisory Committee in the Department
of Business Regulation /. [Tallahassee] [1980]
i, 18 p. ;   LC Card 81-621207   DDC 344.759/099
347.590499 19
KFF384 .A25 1980

PARIS, TREATY OF, 1898.
Johnston, William Andrew, 1871- History up to
date . New York , 1899. 257 p. :
                              *NYPL [*ZH-665]*

Park, Edward.
Disposition of royalty oil and gas. 1980.
Goldsmith, Scott. Historic and projected oil
and gas consumption / for the Alaska
Royalty Oil and Gas Development Advisory
Board, by Scott Goldsmith and Kristina
O'Connor. [Juneau?] , 1980. 55 leaves ;   LC
Card 80-622464   DDC 338.2/728/09798 19
HD9567.A4 G63

PARKE COUNTY (IND.) - MAPS.
United States. Soil Conservation Service. Parke
County, Indiana /. Lincoln, Nebr. , 1980. 1
map :   LC Card 81-691257
G4093.P2 1980 .U5

Parker, Alfred L. A study of the New Mexico
liquor control act / prepared for the Office of
the Attorney General ... [et al.] by Alfred L.
Parker, with Leo Carbajal ... [et al.].
[Albuquerque, N.M.] : Bureau of Business and
Economic Research, Institute for Applied
Research Services, University of New Mexico,
1980. 173, 39 p. : ill. ; 28 cm.   LC Card
80-624137   DDC 363.4/1/09789 19
1. Liquor laws - New Mexico. 2. License system - New
Mexico. I. New Mexico. Attorney General's Office. II.
New Mexico. University. Bureau of Business &
Economic Research. III. Title.
HV5086.N6 P37

Parker and Ipswich Rivers . Massachusetts.
Water Quality and Research Section.
Westborough, Mass. [1977] 13 p. :   LC Card
79-620594   DDC 363.7/3942/097445 19
TD224.M4 M368 1977a

Parker, Bruce C. (joint author) Wendt, Stephen L.
Occurrence and distribution of human bacterial
pathogens in Virginia surface waters /.
Blacksburg, Va. , 1979. vii, 68 p. :   LC Card
79-625812   DDC 333.91/009755 s 363.7/394 19
TD201 .V57 no. 118 TD224.V8

Parker, Cecil. (joint author) Fuller, Stephen.
Economics of grain sorghum production and
marketing /. College Station, Tex. , 1979. iii, 43
p. ;   LC Card 80-620821   DDC 338.1/73174/09764
19
HD9049.S6 U53

Parker, Douglas A. Normative approaches to the
prevention of alcohol abuse and alcoholism .
Rockville, Md. , Washington D.C. [1980] ix,
238 p. ;   LC Card 79-600168   DDC 362.2/9286 19
HV5288 .N67

Parker, Gary W. A history of Marine Medium
Helicopter Squadron 161 / by Gary W. Parker.
Washington : History and Museums Division,
Headquarters, U. S. Marine Corps : for sale by
the Supt. of Docs., U. S. Govt. Print. Off.,
1978. vii, 47 P. : ill. ; 27 cm. Includes
bibliographical references.   LC Card 79-601669
1. United States. Marine Medium Helicopter Squadron
161 - History. I. United States. Marine Corps. History
and Museums Division. II. Title.
VG94.6.M38 P37   *NYPL [JFF 81-182]*

Parker, Harry W. Alternative energy sources for
agricultural applications including gasification of
fibrous residues : final report / Harry W. Parker
and Lyndell H. Holmes ; prepared for Texas
Energy Advisory Council, Energy Development
Fund. [Austin] : Texas Energy Advisory
Council, [1979] xi, 101 p. : ill. ; 28 cm. (Report -
Texas Energy Advisory Council, Energy Development
Fund . # EDF-018) "August 31, 1979." Bibliography:
p. 99-101.   LC Card 80-620767   DDC 333.79/38 19
1. Renewable energy sources. 2. Agricultural wastes -
Recycling. 3. Gas-producers. 4. Agriculture. I. Holmes,
Lyndell H., joint author. II. Series: Texas. Energy
Development Fund. Report - Texas Energy Advisory
Council, Energy Development Fund , # EDF-018. III.
Title.
TJ163.2 .P362

Parker, James W. Friendship Cemetery,
Columbus, Mississippi : tombstone inscriptions
and burial records /. Columbus , 1979. 2 v. (xii,
358 p.) :
                    NYPL [APR (Columbus, Miss.) 81-100]

Parker, John, 1923- Windows into China : the
Jesuits and their books, 1580-1730 / by John
Parker. Boston : Trustees of the Public Library
of the City of Boston, 1978. xi, 36 p. :
facsims. ; 22 cm. (Maury A. Bromsen lecture in
humanistic bibliography [copy 2] no. 5) One of 1350
copies designed by the Stinehour Press and printed by
the Meriden Gravure Company.   LC Card 77-13191
1. Missions - China - Addresses, essays, lectures. 2.
Jesuits - Missions - Addresses, essays, lectures. 3.
Chinese rites - Addresses, essays, lectures. I. Title. II.
Series.   *NYPL [*KSD 80-202 no. 5]*

Parker, John Leon, 1912- Soil survey of
Stillwater County area, Montana / [by John L.
Parker, Gordon L. Decker, and Michael T.
Jackson] ; United States Department of
Agriculture, Soil Conservation Service, in
cooperation with Montana Agricultural
Experiment Station. [Washington, D.C.] : The
Service, [1980] vii, 131, 98, [4] p., [1] fold. leaf
of plates : maps ; 28 cm. Cover title. Bibliography:
p. 61 (2d group)   LC Card 80-603196   DDC
631.4/7/786651 19
1. Soils - Montana - Stillwater Co. - Maps. I. Decker,
Gordon L., joint author. II. Jackson, Michael T., joint
author. III. United States. Soil Conservation Service. IV.
Montana. Agricultural Experiment Station, Bozeman. V.
Title.
S599.M9 P37

Parker, John Marson, 1906- Geology and mineral
resources of Wake County / by John M. Parker
III. Raleigh : North Carolina, Dept. of Natural
Resources and Community Development,
Divison of Land Resources, Geological Survey
Section, 1979. xi, 122 p., 4 leaves of plates (3
fold.) : ill. ; 28 cm. (Bulletin - North Carolina,
Geological Survey Section ; 86) Bibliography: p.
114-122.   LC Card 80-621007   DDC 557.56/55 19
1. Geology - North Carolina - Wake Co. 2. Mines and
mineral resources - North Carolina - Wake Co. I. North
Carolina. Geological Survey Section. II. Series: North
Carolina. Geological Survey Section. Bulletin - North

Carolina, Geological Survey Section. III. Title.
QE148.W25 P37

Parker River study, 1968 /. McAnespie, Robert
C. Boston [1969] [11] p. : LC Card 80-118014
DDC 363.7/3942/097445 19
TD224.M4 M27

Parkinson, Robert J. (joint author) McLoda, N. A.
Soil survey of Franklin County, Ohio /.
[Washington] [1980] viii, 188 p., [37] fold.
leaves of plates : LC Card 80-602372 DDC
631.4/7/77156 19
S599.O3 M32

**Parks and Open Land Advisory Committee,
Hunterdon County, N. J. see Hunterdon
County, N. J. Parks and Open Land
Advisory Committee.**

PARKS - BRITISH COLUMBIA.
United States. National Park Service. An
inventory of international park possibilities:
Point Roberts, Boundary Bay, San Juan and
Gulf Islands Archipelago. [Washington?] 1973.
87 l. LC Card 81-461454 DDC 333.78/3/0979773
19
SB482.W2 U54 1973

PARKS - CALIFORNIA - GUIDE-BOOKS.
California coastal access guide /. Berkeley ,
c1981. p. cm. ISBN 0-520-04576-9 LC Card
81-14667 DDC 917.94/0453 19
F859.3 .C26

PARKS - CALIFORNIA - MENDOCINO CO.
Sullenberger, Martha. Dogholes and donkey
engines . Sacramento, CA [1980] iv, 133 p. :
LC Card 80-623070 DDC 363.6/9/0979415 19
F868.M5 S94

PARKS - CALIFORNIA - PLANNING.
Troy, Richard E. California State park system
plan, 1980 . Sacramento, Calif. [1980] viii, 239
p. : LC Card 80-622915 DDC 333.78/3/09794 19
GV191.42.C2 T76

PARKS - CANADA.
United States. National Park Service. An
inventory of international park possibilities:
Point Roberts, Boundary Bay, San Juan and
Gulf Islands Archipelago. [Washington?] 1973.
87 l. LC Card 81-461454 DDC 333.78/3/0979773
19
SB482.W2 U54 1973

Parks, Evalyn C.
(joint author) Allen, Harry E. Critical Issues in
Adult Probation . Washington, D.C. , 1979. vii,
289 p. ; LC Card 79-604144 DDC 364.6/3/0973
19
HV9304 .A64

(joint author) Carlson, Eric Walfred, 1944-
Critical issues in adult probation . Washington,
D.C. , 1979. vii, 492 p. ; LC Card 79-603823
DDC 364.6/3/0973 19
HV9304 .C34

Parks, John T. (joint author) Corgan, James X.
Natural bridges of Tennessee /. Nashville ,
1979. viii, 102 p. ; LC Card 79-626059 DDC
557.68 s 551.4 19
QE165 .A2 no. 80 GB565.T4

**PARKS - LAW AND LEGISLATION -
OKLAHOMA.**
Oklahoma. Division of State Parks. Rules &
regulations /. [Oklahoma City, Okla.] [1979]
19 p. ; LC Card 80-622622 DDC 346.766/046783
19
KFO1652.5.A435 A2 1979

Oklahoma. Division of State Parks. Rules &
regulations /. [Oklahoma City, Okla.] , 1980.
19 p. : LC Card 80-623108 DDC 346.766/046783
19
KFO1652.5.A439 A2 1980

**PARKS - NEW JERSEY - HUNTERDON
COUNTY.**
Hunterdon County, N. J. Parks and Open Land
Advisory Committee. The Hunterdon County
Park and Open Space Plan /. [Flemington, N.
J.] 1972. 83, [4] p.: ***NYPL [JLF 79-1725]***

PARKS - NEW YORK (STATE)
New York (State). Office of Parks and
Recreation. Interim report to the Legislature .
Albany, N.Y. , 1978. 28 p. : LC Card 80-621341
DDC 353.97470086/3 19
F120 .N48 1978

**PARKS - NEW YORK (STATE) - MONROE
COUNTY.**

Monroe County, N. Y. Dept. of Parks. Program
compare. Rochester, N. Y., 1966. 118 p.:
NYPL [JLF 81-3]

Parks, Roger B. (joint author) Ostrom, Elinor.
Policing metropolitan America /. [Washington]
[1977] viii, 49 p. : LC Card 77-603798
HV8138 .O76 ***NYPL [*XME-9420]***

PARKS - UNITED STATES.
United States. National Park Service. An
inventory of international park possibilities:
Point Roberts, Boundary Bay, San Juan and
Gulf Islands Archipelago. [Washington?] 1973.
87 l. LC Card 81-461454 DDC 333.78/3/0979773
19
SB482.W2 U54 1973

PARKS - WASHINGTON (STATE)
United States. National Park Service. An
inventory of international park possibilities:
Point Roberts, Boundary Bay, San Juan and
Gulf Islands Archipelago. [Washington?] 1973.
87 l. LC Card 81-461454 DDC 333.78/3/0979773
19
SB482.W2 U54 1973

**PARKS - WASHINGTON (STATE) - POINT
ROBERTS.**
United States. National Park Service. An
inventory of international park possibilities:
Point Roberts, Boundary Bay, San Juan and
Gulf Islands Archipelago. [Washington?] 1973.
87 l. LC Card 81-461454 DDC 333.78/3/0979773
19
SB482.W2 U54 1973

**PARKS - WISCONSIN - WOOD COUNTY -
MAPS.**
United States. Soil Conservation Service. Public
and private parks and recreation areas, Wood
County, Wisconsin /. Lincoln, Nebr. , 1978. 1
map : LC Card 81-691238
G4123.W9G52 1978 .U5

Parlamento europeo. see European Parliament.

Parlement européen. see European Parliament.

**PARLIAMENTARY LAW. see
PARLIAMENTARY PRACTICE.**

PARLIAMENTARY PRACTICE.
Mason, Paul, 1898- Manual of legislative
procedure for legislative and other
governmental bodies /. Sacramento, CA , 1979.
674 p. ; LC Card 80-622491 DDC 060.42 19
JF515 .M33 1979

PARLIAMENTS. see LEGISLATIVE BODIES.

Parma. Biblioteca palatina. MSS. (Hebr. 482)
Berechiah ben Natronai, ha-Nakdan, 12th cent.
The ethical treatises of Berachya . New York,
1973. lv, 361, ix, 153 p. ISBN 0-405-05253-7
LC Card 73-2187
BJ1287.B4 E5 1973 ***NYPL [*PMK 80-982]***

Parmer, Coleen K. Census bibliography /
compiled by Coleen K. Parmer. [Bowling
Green, Ohio : Bowling Green State University,
197-] 80, [1] p. ; 28 cm. (BGSU Library
bibliographic series . no. 75) Cover title. LC Card
80-108176 DDC 016.3173 19
1. United States - Census - Bibliography. I. Title. II.
Series.
Z7553.C3 P37 HA215

PAROLE - ALASKA.
Alaska. Board of Parole. Parole guidelines for
Alaska /. [Juneau, Ala.] [1979] iv, 130, [207]
p. ; LC Card 80-622140 DDC 364.6/2/09798 19
HV9305.A3 A48 1979

PAROLE - CALIFORNIA - EVALUATION.
Star, Deborah. Summary parole . [Sacramento]
[1979] x, 193 p. : LC Card 80-620661 DDC
364.6/09794 s 364.6/2/09794 19
HV9305.C3 A32 no. 60

Parole guidelines for Alaska /. Alaska. Board of
Parole. [Juneau, Ala.] [1979] iv, 130, [207] p. ;
LC Card 80-622140 DDC 364.6/2/09798 19
HV9305.A3 A48 1979

PAROLE - HAWAII.
Hawaii. University, Honolulu. Social Welfare
Development and Research Center. The Adult
Furlough Center . [Honolulu] , 1974. iv, 18,
[18] leaves ; LC Card 77-621669
HV9305.H3 H38 1974 ***NYPL [*XME-9423]***

PAROLE - MASSACHUSETTS - STATISTICS.
Farrow, Carolyn. 1977 Parole Board releases
from State institutions /. [Boston] [1979?] 74
leaves ; LC Card 80-620625 DDC 364.6/2./09744

19
HV9305.M4 F37

Parot, Joseph John, 1940- Polish Catholics in
Chicago, 1850-1920 : a religious history /
Joseph John Parot. DeKalb : Northern Illinois
University Press, c1981. p. cm. Includes
bibliographical references and index. ISBN
0-87580-081-5 LC Card 81-11297 DDC
282/.0899185077311 19
1. Catholic Church - Illinois - Chicago region - History.
2. Polish Americans - Illinois - Chicago region -
Religion. 3. Polish National Catholic Church of
America - Illinois - Chicago region - History. 4.
Chicago region (Ill.) - Church history. I. Title.
BX1418.C4 P37

Parr, Marilyn K., 1947- United States. Library of
Congress. Manuscript Division. Members of
Congress . Washington , 1980. xiii, 217 p. :
ISBN 0-8444-0272-9
Z1236 .U613 1979 E176 ***NYPL [JLE 81-85]***

Parrett, Charles. Floods of May 1978 in
southeastern Montana and northeastern
Wyoming /. Washington [1981] p. cm. LC
Card 81-607843 DDC 551.48/9/097863 19
GB1399.4.M9 F46

Parrish, Richard H. Climatic variation and
exploitation in the Pacific mackerel fishery / by
Richard H. Parrish and Alec D. MacCall. La
Jolla, Calif. : State of California, Resources
Agency, Dept. of Fish and Game, 1978. 110
p. : graphs ; 23 cm. (Fish bulletin . 167)
Bibliography: p. 92-96. LC Card 79-623023 DDC
597/.05222 19
1. Mackerel fisheries - California. 2. Chub mackerel. 3.
Fish populations - Statistical methods. 4. Fisheries -
Climatic factors. I. MacCall, Alec D., joint author. II.
Series: California. Dept. of Fish and Game. Fish
bulletin , 167. III. Title.
SH351.M2 P37

Parrott, Charles A., 1944- Historic buildings
access for the disabled : technical report /
Charles A. Parrott. Washington, D.C. :
Technical Preservation Services Division,
Heritage Conservation and Recreation Service,
1980. p. cm. (Heritage Conservation and Recreation
Service publication ; no. 46) TPS reports "April 1980."
Bibliography: p. LC Card 80-23427 DDC 720/.42
19
1. Historic buildings - United States - Access for the
physically handicapped. I. Series: United States.
Heritage Conservation and Recreation Service. HCRS
publication, no. 46. II. Title.
NA2545.P5 P37

Parsons Brinckerhoff Quade & Douglas, Inc.
New York Exposition and Convention Center :
draft environmental impact statement /. [[New
York] 1980. 2 v. : ***NYPL [JSF 80-851]***

Parsons, Carl. Summary of housing and
socio-economic data : Black River-St. Lawrence
region / Carl Parsons and Roseanne Murphy.
Springfield, Va. : Available from RPB and
National Technical Information Service, 1974.
vi, 106 p. : ill., maps ; 28 cm. "Technical series
report no. 12, 1974." "1975 printing." Chiefly tables.
"Performing organization: Black River-St. Lawrence
Regional Planning Board.
1. Housing - St. Lawrence Valley - Statistics. 2. St.
Lawrence Valley - Economic conditions - Statistics. I.
Murphy, Roseanne. II. Black River-St. Lawrence
Regional Planning Board. III. Title.
NYPL [JLF 81-31]

Parsons, William P. (joint author) Hall, Thomas L.
Schools of public health . [Washington] [1980]
vi, 58 p. ; LC Card 80-602405 DDC 614/.07/1173
19
RA440.7.U6 H34

**PART-TIME EMPLOYMENT - UNITED
STATES.**
Kiefer, Nicholas M., 1951- The effect of
alternative partial benefits formulas on
beneficiary part-time work behavior.
Washington, D.C. , 1979. v, 70 p. : LC Card
80-602692 DDC 368.4/4/00973 s 331.25/723 19
HD7096.U5 U637 no. 79-6

United States. Congress. Senate. Committee on
Governmental Affairs. Subcommittee on
Governmental Efficiency and the District of
Columbia. Status of implementation of the
Part-Time Career Employment Act of 1978 .
Washington , 1980 [i.e. 1981] iv, 77 p. : LC
Card 81-601317 DDC 353.001/4 19
KF26 .G6735 1980d

PART-TIME WORK. see PART-TIME EMPLOYMENT.

Parti communiste (bolchevik) de l'U. R. S. S. see **Kommunisticheskaĭa partiĭa Sovetskogo Soĭuza.**

PARTIAL EQUILIBRIUM (ECONOMICS) see **EQUILIBRIUM (ECONOMICS)**

A partial working bibliography on the Amerindians of New Jersey /. Abrams, H. Leon. Greeley, Colo. , 1980. 10 leaves ;
    NYPL [HBA 80-381 no. 41]

A partial working bibliography on the Amerindians of New York /. Abrams, H. Leon. Greeley, Colo. , 1979. 22 leaves ; LC Card 80-622303 DDC 909/.09812 s 016.9747/00497 19
    GN4 .U53 no. 22 Z1209.2.U52N65

PARTIALLY SEEING. see VISUALLY HANDICAPPED.

PARTICIPATION, POLITICAL. see **POLITICAL PARTICIPATION.**

PARTICLE ACCELERATORS - UNITED STATES.
United States. Congress. House. Committee on Science and Technology. Subcommittee on Energy Research and Production. Quests with U. S. accelerators--50 years, the high energy physics and nuclear physics research programs . Washington , c1980 [i.e. 1981] iii, 463 p. : LC Card 81-601187 DDC 539.7/072073 19
    KF27 .S3936 1980d

PARTICLE SIZE DETERMINATION - CONGRESSES.
Microbeam Analysis Society. Characterization of particles . Washington, D.C. [1980] vi, 223 p. : LC Card 80-600033 DDC 602/.18 s 620/.43 19
    QC100 .U57 no. 533 TA418.8

PARTICLES - ENVIRONMENTAL ASPECTS - ILLINOIS.
Arnold, Edward, 1941- Identification of sources causing TSP non-attainment . Chicago , 1979. vii, 132, [65] p. : LC Card 79-626018 DDC 363.7/3921/09773393 19
    TD883.5.I45 A8

Cohen, Alan S., 1944- Economic impact of sulfur dioxide and particulate matter regulations in Illinois, R77-15 /. Chicago, IL , 1979. xii, 123 p. : LC Card 80-620893 DDC 363.7/387 19
    TD885.5.S8 C63

Equitable Environmental Health, inc. The economic impact of proposed regulations to reduce particulate emissions from steel mills and industrial fugitive sources, R78-10 and R78-11 /. Chicago, IL , 1979. 241 p. in various pagings : LC Card 79-624236 DDC 363.7/392 19
    TD884.5 .E68 1978

PARTICLES (NUCLEAR PHYSICS) - CONGRESSES.
Nato Advanced Study Institute on Field Theoretical Methods in Particle Physics, University of Kaiserslautern, 1979. Field theoretical methods in particle physics /. New York , c1980. ix, 598 p. : ISBN 0-306-40444-3 LC Card 80-11773
    QC793.3.F5 N37 1979 NYPL [JSF 80-1051]

PARTICLES (NUCLEAR PHYSICS) - RESEARCH - UNITED STATES.
United States. Congress. House. Committee on Science and Technology. Subcommittee on Energy Research and Production. Quests with U. S. accelerators--50 years, the high energy physics and nuclear physics research programs . Washington , c1980 [i.e. 1981] iii, 463 p. : LC Card 81-601187 DDC 539.7/072073 19
    KF27 .S3936 1980d

United States. General Accounting Office. Increasing costs, competition may hinder U. S. position of leadership in high energy physics . Washington, D.C. , 1980. v, 222 p. : LC Card 80-603949 DDC 539.7/6/072073 19
    QC793.4 .U54 1980

Partido Comunista Ruso. see **Kommunisticheskaĭa partiĭa Sovetskogo Soĭuza.**

Parties, candidates, and voters in Japan : six quantitative studies / edited by John Creighton Campbell. Ann Arbor : Center for Japanese studies, University of Michigan, 1981. p. cm. (Michigan papers in Japanese studies . no. 2) ISBN 0-939512-07-6 : LC Card 81-6190 DDC

324/.0952 19
1. Political parties - Japan - Addresses, essays, lectures. 2. Elections - Japan - Addresses, essays, lectures. I. Campbell, John Creighton. II. Series.
    JQ1698.A1 P37

PARTIES, POLITICAL. see POLITICAL PARTIES.

Partito comunista di Cecoslovacchia. see **Komunistická strana Československa.**

Partnership within the states : local self-government in the Federal system / edited by Stephanie Cole. Urbana : Institute of Government and Public Affairs, University of Illinois, 1976. vi, 311 p. ; 28 cm. (Toward '76) Microfiche (neg.) NTIS. 4 sheets. 11 x 15 cm. (PB 269 834) Proceedings of a conference held in Chicago, Nov. 19-20, 1975, co-sponsored by the U. S. Advisory Commission on Intergovernmental Relations and the National Municipal League. Includes bibliographical references. LC Card 77-622179
1. Municipal home rule - Congresses. 2. Federal government - United States - Congresses. I. Cole, Stephanie. II. United States. Advisory Commission on Intergovernmental Relations. III. National Municipal League.
    JS348 .P25   *NYPL [*XME-9431]*

Partnerships for neighborhood preservation /. Cohen, Rick. [Harrisburg] , 1978. vii, 200 p. ; LC Card 79-622460 DDC 307.7/6/0973 19
    HN90.C6 C626

Party activists in Virginia . Abramowitz, Alan. Charlottesville , 1981. x, 106 p. ; LC Card 81-142700 DDC 324.5/6/09755 19
    JK2295.V83 A24

PASCAGOULA, MISS. - HARBOR.
United States. Board of Engineers for Rivers and Harbors. The ports of Panama City & Pensacola, FL and Pascagoula & Gulfport, MS /. Washington , Fort Belvoir, VA , 1979. vi, 130 p. : LC Card 80-603371 DDC 387.1/09759/95 19
    HE554.A4 U53 1979

Pasco Volunteers Conference, Columbia Basin College, 1976. Pasco Volunteers Conference : final report. Olympia: Office of Voluntary Action, 1976. 19 p.; 28 cm. Microfiche (neg.) 1 sheet. 11 x 15 cm. (NYPL FSN, 35,079) Conference sponsored by Office of Voluntary Action, State of Washington; conference held at Columbia Basin College in Pasco, Washington, June 25-26, 1976.
1. Volunteer workers in social service - Washington (State) - Congresses. I. Washington (State). Office of Community Development. Office of Voluntary Action.
    *NYPL [*XME-9108]*

Paskin, S. (joint author) McNaughton, D. Comparison of alternate modes of drinking driver rehabilitation/Jefferson County study /. [Albany] [1979] ca. 100 leaves in various foliations : LC Card 80-621876 DDC 363.1/251 19
    HE5620.D7 M26

Pasley, Beverley. Capital District Regional Planning Commission. Capital district region industrial facilities survey. Albany. [1974] 23 leaves ; LC Card 78-28990 *NYPL [*ZT-1254]*

Pasour, E. C. Land use and land-use planning in North Carolina / E. C. Pasour, Jr., Kuo-Ching Lin. Raleigh, N.C. : Dept. of Economics and Business, North Carolina State University, 1979. 63 p. : ill. ; 23 cm. (Economics information report . no. 58) Bibliography: p. 53-55. LC Card 80-621098 DDC 338.1 s 333.76/13/09756 19
1. Land use, Rural - North Carolina. 2. Land use - North Carolina - Planning. I. Lin, Kuo-Ching, joint author. II. Title. III. Series.
    S97 .Z4 no. 58 HD211.N8

Passaic River Coalition. New Jersey. State Legislature. Senate. Committee on Law, Public Safety, and Defense. Public hearing before Senate Law, Public Safety, and Defense Committee, on Passaic Valley Sewerage Commission . [Trenton , 1980] 46, 16 p. ; LC Card 80-624390 DDC 352.6/2/097493 19
    KFN1811.3 .L39 1980

Passaic Valley Sewerage Commission (N.J.) New Jersey. State Legislature. Senate. Committee on Law, Public Safety, and Defense. Public hearing before Senate Law, Public Safety, and Defense Committee, on Passaic Valley Sewerage Commission . [Trenton , 1980] 46, 16 p. ; LC

Card 80-624390 DDC 352.6/2/097493 19
    KFN1811.3 .L39 1980

PASSAIC VALLEY SEWERAGE COMMISSION (N.J.)
New Jersey. State Legislature. Senate. Committee on Law, Public Safety, and Defense. Public hearing before Senate Law, Public Safety, and Defense Committee, on Passaic Valley Sewerage Commission . [Trenton , 1980] 46, 16 p. ; LC Card 80-624390 DDC 352.6/2/097493 19
    KFN1811.3 .L39 1980

PASSAMAQUODDY INDIANS - PERIODICALS.
Maine. Agent Passamaquody Indians. Report of agent of the Passamaquoddy tribe of Indians. Augusta.   *NYPL [*ZAN-H394]*

Passey, Anders J. Tanzania, land use and agricultural diversification /. [Washington] [1968?] 90 p. : LC Card 81-462748 DDC 338.1/09678 19
    S473.T35 T36

The passive judiciary . Goldstein, Abraham S. Baton Rouge , c1981. p. cm. ISBN 0-8071-0856-1 : LC Card 81-11749 DDC 345.73/05042 347.3055042 19
    KF9640 .G64

Passive restraints . Flynn, Lois. [Washington, D.C.] , Springfield, Va. [1979] iii leaves, 190 p. ; LC Card 80-602367 DDC 016.6292/76 19
    Z5173.S2 F58 TL242

Passive Solar Conference. see National Passive Solar Conference.

Passive solar design awards. New York State Energy Research and Development Authority. 1979 NYSERDA passive solar design awards /. Albany, N.Y. [c1980] vii, 72 p. : LC Card 80-128412 DDC 728/.68 19
    TH7414 .N48 1980

PASSIVE SOLAR HEATING SYSTEMS. see SOLAR HEATING - PASSIVE SYSTEMS.

PASSPORTS - UNITED STATES.
United States. Congress. House. Committee on the Judiciary. Subcommittee on Immigration, Refugees, and International Law. Waiver of nonimmigrant visa requirements . Washington , 1980. iv, 146 p. ; LC Card 80-603043 DDC 342.73/082 19
    KF27 .J8645 1980a

Pastoral care in alcoholism/alcohol abuse /. United States. Naval Education and Training Command. [Pensacola, Fla.] 1980. iii, 164 p. : LC Card 80-603166 DDC 362.2/9286 19
    BV4460.5 .U54 1980

PASTORAL LITERATURE - HISTORY AND CRITICISM - ADDRESSES, ESSAYS, LECTURES.
Survivals of pastoral /. Lawrence , 1979. x, 150 p. ; LC Card 80-621786 DDC 809/.9145 19
    PN56.P3 S9

PASTORAL PSYCHOLOGY - BIBLIOGRAPHY.
Summerlin, Florence A. Religion and mental health . Rockville, Md. (5600 Fishers Lane, Rockville, Md. 20857) , Washington, D.C. , 1980. 401 p. in various pagings ; LC Card 81-601117 DDC 016.3622 19
    Z6664.N5 S94 RA790

Pastron, Allen G. The Archeology of Oak Park, Ventura County, California /. Los Angeles , 1978. 2 v. : LC Card 80-621558 DDC 979.4/92 19
    E99.C815 A7

PASTURAGE. see GRAZING.

PASTURES - SOUTH DAKOTA - MAPS.
United States. Soil Conservation Service. Pasture production and soil loss areas, western South Dakota river basins /. Lincoln, Nebr. , 1979. 1 map : LC Card 81-691116
    G4181.J67 1979 .U5

PASTURES - TROPICS - BIBLIOGRAPHY.
A Selected bibliography of Centrosema, Desmodium, Stylosanthes and other tropical and subtropical pasture legumes [microform] /. Honolulu , 1981. p. cm. LC Card 81-2533 DDC 016.6333 19
    Z5074 .L3 SB203.3.T76

Patenaude, John J. Report on proposed State assessments of all public utility real property in

New York State / prepared by John J. Patenaude. Albany, N.Y. : Division of Equalization and Assessment, [1980] 10 p. ; 28 cm. Cover title. "April 1980." LC Card 80-621854 DDC 336.22/2 19
1. Public utilities - Taxation - New York (State). 2. Real property tax - New York (State). I. New York (State). Division of Equalization and Assessment. II. Title.
HD2767.N74 P37

Patent and trademark forms booklet /. United States. Patent and Trademark Office. Washington , 1979 [i. e. 1980] 1 v. :
NYPL [*VBE 81-231]

Patent and Trademark Law Amendments of 1980 /. United States. Congress. House. Committee on Government Operations. Legislation and National Security Subcommittee. Washington , 1980. iii, 218 p. ; LC Card 80-604009 DDC 346.7304/86 347.306486 19
KF27 .G6676 1980i

PATENT LAWS AND LEGISLATION - UNITED STATES.
United States. Congress. House. Committee on Government Operations. Legislation and National Security Subcommittee. Patent and Trademark Law Amendments of 1980 . Washington , 1980. iii, 218 p. ; LC Card 80-604009 DDC 346.7304/86 347.306486 19
KF27 .G6676 1980i

PATENT LAWS AND LEGISLATION - UNITED STATES - FORMS.
United States. Patent and Trademark Office. Patent and trademark forms booklet /. Washington , 1979 [i. e. 1980] 1 v. :
NYPL [*VBE 81-231]

PATENT LAWYERS - DIRECTORIES.
Directory of patent attorneys and agents. McLean, Va.. *NYPL [*VBL 81-125]*

PATENT LAWYERS - UNITED STATES - DIRECTORIES.
Directory of patent attorneys and agents. McLean, Va.. *NYPL [*VBL 81-125]*

Patent profiles.
United States. Patent and Trademark Office. Office of Technology Assessment and Forecast. Solar energy. [Washington, D.C.] [1980] iii, 190 p. : LC Card 80-601594 DDC 621.47/0272 19
TJ810 .U63 1980

United States. Patent and Trademark Office. Office of Technology Assessment and Forecast. Synthetic fuels. Washington, D.C. [1979] iii, 230 p. : LC Card 80-601527 DDC 662/.66/0272 19
TP360 .U63 1979

PATENTS AND GOVERNMENT-DEVELOPED INVENTIONS - UNITED STATES.
United States. Congress. House. Committee on Science and Technology. Subcommittee on Science, Research, and Technology. Government patent policy . Washington , 1979. iii, 221 p. ; LC Card 80-602808 DDC 353.0082/4 19
KF27 .S399 1979r

United States. Congress. House. Committee on Science and Technology. Subcommittee on Science, Research, and Technology. H.R. 5715, Government Patent Policy Act of 1980 . Washington , 1980. iii, 184 p. : LC Card 80-603795 DDC 346.7304/86 347.306486 19
KF27 .S399 1980h

PATENTS, GOVERNMENT-OWNED - UNITED STATES.
United States. Congress. House. Committee on Science and Technology. Subcommittee on Science, Research, and Technology. Government patent policy . Washington , 1979. iii, 221 p. ; LC Card 80-602808 DDC 353.0082/4 19
KF27 .S399 1979r

PATENTS - UNITED STATES.
United States. Patent and Trademark Office. U. S. design patents. Nov. 9, 1842- Woodbridge, Conn.. *NYPL [*XFR-10]*

PATENTS - UNITED STATES - CLASSIFICATION.
United States. Patent and Trademark Office. Concordance, United States patent classification

to international patent classification. [Washington, D.C.] , Washington , 1980. 148 p. ; LC Card 79-603986 DDC 608.773/012 19
T223.F4 U54 1980

PATERNITY - CALIFORNIA.
California. Legislature. Assembly. Committee on Judiciary. Blood tests in paternity litigation . Sacramento, CA [1980] iii, 178 p. : LC Card 81-621366 DDC 346.79401/78 347.9406178 19
KFC10.4 .J8 1980

PATERNITY TESTING.
California. Legislature. Assembly. Committee on Judiciary. Blood tests in paternity litigation . Sacramento, CA [1980] iii, 178 p. : LC Card 81-621366 DDC 346.79401/78 347.9406178 19
KFC10.4 .J8 1980

PATH PASCAL (COMPUTER PROGRAM LANGUAGE)
Campbell, Ronald H. A practical implementation of path expressions /. Urbana, Ill. [1980] 25 p. ; LC Card 80-623653 DDC 001.64 s 001.64/24 19
QA76 .I4 no. 1008 QA76.73.P217

The Pathfinder or, The inland sea /. Cooper, James Fenimore, 1789-1851. Albany , c1981. xxvi, 569 p., [6] leaves of plates : ISBN 0-87395-365-7 LC Card 79-15598 DDC 813/.2 19
PS1410.A2 R8

PATHOGENIC BACTERIA. see BACTERIA, PATHOGENIC.

PATHOLOGICAL PSYCHOLOGY. see PSYCHOLOGY, PATHOLOGICAL.

Pathways to military service for men and women. United States. Office of the Assistant Secretary of Defense (Manpower, Reserve Affairs, and Logistics) [Washington] , 1978. 68 p. ; LC Card 78-603689
UB147 .U49 1978

PATIENT COMPLIANCE.
Latanick, Maureen Rogan. An office strategy for nutrition-related patient education and compliance /. Columbus, Ohio (456 Clinic Dr., Columbus 43210) , c1980. 23 p. ; LC Card 81-620951 DDC 613.2/07/15 19
R727.4 .L37

PATIENT EDUCATION.
Latanick, Maureen Rogan. An office strategy for nutrition-related patient education and compliance /. Columbus, Ohio (456 Clinic Dr., Columbus 43210) , c1980. 23 p. ; LC Card 81-620951 DDC 613.2/07/15 19
R727.4 .L37

PATIENTS, EDUCATION OF. see PATIENT EDUCATION.

Patients in public institutions for the mentally retarded, 1967. United States. National Institute of Mental Health. Biometry Branch. Survey and Reports Section. Chevy Chase, Md. , Washington , 1969. ii, 79 p. ; LC Card 81-452003 DDC 362.3/850973 19
RC570.5.U6 U65 1969

Patients' reasons for visiting physicians . Cypress, Beulah K. Hyattsville, Md. [1981] p. cm. ISBN 0-8406-0225-1 LC Card 81-607915 DDC 362.1/1/0973 362.1 19
RA407.3 .A349 no. 56 RA410.7

Patriarche, Mercer H. (joint author) Tanner, Howard A. Shaping the world's finest freshwater fishery /. Lansing, Mich. [1980] 86 p. : LC Card 80-622892 DDC 333.95/6/09744 19
SH464.G7 T36

Patrick County Project. McCombs, Dorothy F. The Appalachian region of Virginia . Blacksburg, Va. , 1981. p. cm. LC Card 81-11487 DDC 016.9755 19
Z1345 .M36 F226

Patrick, Neil A.
Gopalakrishnan, Chennat. Energy in Western agriculture . Honolulu , 1981. p. cm. LC Card 81-628 DDC 333.79/13 19
S494.5.E5 G66

New Mexico State University. Agricultural Economics Dept. Energy requirements for agricultural production in New Mexico . [Las Cruces] [1979] v, 44 p. ; LC Card 79-625597 DDC 333.79/13 19
S494.5.E5 N47 1979

Patrick, Ruth J. A study of library cooperatives, networks, and demonstration projects : final report / by Ruth J. Patrick, Joseph Casey, Carol M. Novalis ; program executive, Steven M. Frankel ; for the Office of Planning, Budgeting, and Evaluation, United States Office of Education pursuant to contract no. 300-76-0464. New York : K. G. Saur Pub., 1980. p. cm. Bibliography: p. Bibliography: CONTENTS. - v. 1. Findings and recommendations.--v. 2. Case study reports. ISBN 0-89664-313-1 : LC Card 79-20231
1. Library cooperation - United States - Case studies. 2. Library information networks - United States - Case studies. 3. Library science - Research - United States - Case studies. I. Casey, Joseph, 1949- joint author. 0700. II. Novalis, Carol M., 1948- joint author. 0700. III. United States. Office of Education. Office of Planning, Budgeting, and Evaluation. IV. Title.
Z731 .P34

Patrides, C. A. Approaches to Sir Thomas Browne . Columbia, MO , c1982. p. cm. ISBN 0-8262-0357-4 LC Card 81-13017 DDC 828/.409 19
PR3327 .A9 1982

Patronsky, Mark C. Wisconsin. Legislature. Legislative Council. Case and opinion review. Madison, Wis. [1980] 4 v. ; LC Card 81-621133 DDC 347.775/012 347.750712 19
KFW2807 .A25 1980

PATTERN PERCEPTION.
(1980) Michalski, Ryszard Stanisław, 1937- Knowledge acquisition through conceptual clustering . Urbana, Ill. [1980] 40 p. : LC Card 80-623657 DDC 001.64 s 519.5/35 19
QA76 .I4 no. 1026 QA278

Patterns of crime and delinquency in Massachusetts, 1979-1978 /. Roy, Marjorie Brown. Boston [1980] 18 leaves ; LC Card 80-623647 DDC 364.1/09744 19
HV6793.M4 R69

Patterns of geographic variation in Florida snakes /. Christman, Steven P. Gainesville , 1980. p. 158-256 : LC Card 81-621400 DDC 574 s 597.95/09759 19
QH1 .F6 vol. 25, no. 3 QL666.O6

Patterns of urban and rural population growth. United Nations. Dept. of International Economic and Social Affairs. New York , 1980. ix, 175 p. : LC Card 80-138417 DDC 081 s 304.6/2 19
JX1977 .A2 ST/ESA/SER.A/68 HB1951

Patterson Associates. Hazardous wastes management in Illinois / by Patterson Associates, inc. Chicago, IL : State of Illinois, Institute of Natural Resources, 1979. v, 97 p. : forms ; 28 cm. (Document - Illinois Institute of Natural Resources ; no. 79/32) Includes bibliographical references. LC Card 80-621151 DDC 363.7/28 19
1. Hazardous wastes - Illinois. I. Series: Illinois Institute of Natural Resources. Document - Illinois Institute of Natural Resources , no. 79/32. II. Title.
TD811.5 .P37 1979

Patterson, Harrold P. Development of a health status index for Texas counties / by Harrold P. Patterson. Austin, Tex. : Texas Dept. of Health, Bureau of State Health Planning and Resource Development, [1978] iv, 69 p. : maps ; 28 cm. (Technical report - Bureau of State Health Planning and Resource Development ; no. 5) "April 1978." LC Card 79-623634 DDC 362.1/09764 19
1. Health status indicators - Texas. 2. Health planning - Texas. I. Series: Texas. Bureau of State Health Planning & Resource Development. Technical report - Bureau of State Health Planning and Resource Development , no. 5. II. Title.
RA407.4.T45 P37

Patterson, Terry. Kentucky business and personal taxes / [research and writing, Terry Patterson ; editorial review, Kentucky Department of Revenue]. [Frankfort] : Kentucky Dept. of Commerce, [1978] 24 p. ; 28 cm. "Prepared by the Kentucky Department of Commerce, Division of Research and Planning." "June 1978." Bibliography: p. 23-24. LC Card 80-620588 DDC 353.97690072/4 19
1. Taxation - Kentucky. 2. Business enterprises - Taxation - Kentucky. I. Kentucky. Dept. of Revenue. II. Kentucky. Dept. of Commerce. Division of Research and Planning. III. Title.
HJ2408 .P37

Paul, A. J. (joint author) Feder, Howard M. A preliminary survey of the benthos of Resurrection Bay and Aialik Bay, Alaska /. Fairbanks, Alaska , 1979. iii, 53 p. : LC Card 80-623129   DDC 551.46 s 591.9798/3 19
GC1 .A497 R78-7 QL161

Paul, Alice. Economic investment and the future of neighborhoods: an analysis, including testimony and recommendations based on hearings held by the New York City Commission on Human Rights / report prepared by Alice Paul and Ken Baker. [New York]: New York City Commission on Human Rights, 1977. iii, 111 p.; 28 cm.
1. Discrimination in mortgage loans - New York (City).
2. Community development, Urban - New York (City).
3. Investment banking - New York (City). I. Baker, Ken, joint author. II. New York (City). City Commission on Human Rights. III. Title.
                              NYPL [JLF 80-1388]

Paul Spring, an investigation of recharge in the Roswell (N.M.) artesian basin /. Gross, Gerardo Wolfgang. Las Cruces, N.M. [1979] 135 p. : LC Card 80-622504   DDC 551.49/09789/43 19
GB705.N6 N64 no. 113 GB1199.3.N6

Paul Strand archive /. Arizona. University. Center for Creative Photography. Tucson, Ariz. , c1980. 25 p. : LC Card 80-144141   DDC 770/.92/4 19
TR140.S7345 A73 1980

Paulk, Herschel Leverne, 1934- Soil survey of Candler, Evans, and Tattnall Counties, Georgia / [by Herschel L. Paulk] ; U. S. Department of Agriculture, Soil Conservation Service, in cooperation with University of Georgia, College of Agriculture, Agricultural Experiment Stations. [Washington] : The Service, [1980] viii, 96 p., [42] fold. leaves of plates : ill. ; 29 cm. Cover title. Bibliography: p. 52.   LC Card 80-601838   DDC 631.4/7/75877 19
1. Soils - Georgia - Candler Co. - Maps. 2. Soils - Georgia - Evans Co. - Maps. 3. Soils - Georgia - Tattnall Co. - Maps. I. United States. Soil Conservation Service. II. Georgia. Agricultural Experiment Stations. III. Title.
S599.G4 P315

Paulson, D. L. (Danton L.) Hebble, T. L. (Terry L.) Recovery of principal metal values from electrolytic zinc waste /. Avondale, MD [1981] p. cm.   LC Card 81-10044   DDC 622 s 669/.52 19
TN23 .U43 TN796

Paulson, Gerald A. (joint author) Mitsch, William J. The Momence Wetlands of the Kankakee River in Illinois . Chicago , 1979. vi, 55 p. :   LC Card 79-624911   DDC 333.91/8/0977363 19
QH105.I3 M57

Paulson, Oscar L. Hydrologic and biologic characteristics of natural channels in coastal marsh of Mississippi /. Mississippi State, Miss. , 1977. iii, 22 leaves :   LC Card 79-625357   DDC 551.46/09 19
QH105.M7 H9

Paulus, Norma.
Oregon. Elections Division. Candidates and political parties manual /. [Salem, Or.] , 1980. 42 p. :   LC Card 80-623672   DDC 324.6/09795 19
JK2023.O7 O73 1980

Oregon. Elections Division. Contributions and expenditures reporting and campaign finance regulations, 1980 /. [Salem, Or.] [1980] 23 p., p. 833-851 :   LC Card 80-623899   DDC 342.795/078/02636 347.95027802636 19
KFO2820.85.C2 A32 1980

Pautler, Paul A. (joint author) Kass, David I. Physician control of Blue Shield plans . [Washington, D.C.] [1979] v, 139 p. ;   LC Card 80-601542   DDC 368.3/8 19
RA413.3.B49 K37

PAVEMENTS, ASPHALT.
Bright, Richard. Early hardening of asphalt in hot bituminous paving mixtures . [Raleigh] , 1966. vi, 70 p. :   LC Card 80-508397   DDC 625.8/5 s 625.8/5 19
TE270 .B67 pt. 2

Bright, Richard. Hardening of asphalt in hot bituminous base, binder, and sand mixtures . [Raleigh] , 1966. vi, 83 p. : LC Card 80-508398   DDC 625.8/5 s 625.8/5 19
TE270 .B67 pt. 1

PAVEMENTS, ASPHALT - COLLECTED WORKS.
Bright, Richard. The effect of viscosity of asphalt on the properties of bituminous paving mixtures /. [Raleigh] , 1966. 2 v. :   LC Card 80-508426   DDC 625.8/5 19
TE270 .B67

PAVEMENTS, ASPHALT CONCRETE - ADDRESSES, ESSAYS, LECTURES.
National Research Council. Transportation Research Board. Concrete pavements and pavement overlays /. Washington, D.C. , 1980. iv, 48 p. :   ISBN 0-309-03070-6   LC Card 80-607869   DDC 380.5 s 625.8/4 19
TE7 .H5 no. 756 TE278

PAVEMENTS, ASPHALT - CONGRESSES.
Asphalt--materials, mixes, and construction /. Washington, D.C. , 1981. p. cm.   ISBN 0-309-03122-2   LC Card 81-38324   DDC 380.5 s 625.8/5 19
TE7 .H5 no. 777 TE270

PAVEMENTS, ASPHALT - RECYCLING - CONGRESSES.
National Seminar on Asphalt Pavement Recycling (1980 : Dallas-Fort Worth Regional Airport) Proceedings of the National Seminar on Asphalt Pavement Recycling. Washington, D.C. , 1981. p. cm.   ISBN 0-309-03101-X   LC Card 81-607072   DDC 380.5 s 666/.893 19
TE7 .H5 no. 780 TE270

PAVEMENTS, BITUMINOUS.
Bright, Richard. Early hardening of asphalt in hot bituminous paving mixtures . [Raleigh] , 1966. vi, 70 p. :   LC Card 80-508397   DDC 625.8/5 s 625.8/5 19
TE270 .B67 pt. 2

Bright, Richard. Hardening of asphalt in hot bituminous base, binder, and sand mixtures . [Raleigh] , 1966. vi, 83 p. :   LC Card 80-508398   DDC 625.8/5 s 625.8/5 19
TE270 .B67 pt. 1

PAVEMENTS, BITUMINOUS - COLLECTED WORKS.
Bright, Richard. The effect of viscosity of asphalt on the properties of bituminous paving mixtures /. [Raleigh] , 1966. 2 v. :   LC Card 80-508426   DDC 625.8/5 19
TE270 .B67

PAVEMENTS, CONCRETE - ADDRESSES, ESSAYS, LECTURES.
National Research Council. Transportation Research Board. Concrete pavements and pavement overlays /. Washington, D.C. , 1980. iv, 48 p. :   ISBN 0-309-03070-6   LC Card 80-607869   DDC 380.5 s 625.8/4 19
TE7 .H5 no. 756 TE278

PAVEMENTS - DESIGN AND CONSTRUCTION - ADDRESSES, ESSAYS, LECTURES.
National Research Council (U. S.) Transportation Research Board. Application of pavement design models. Washington, D.C. , 1980. p. cm.   ISBN 0-309-03109-5   LC Card 81-1639   DDC 380.5 s 625.8 19
TE7 .H5 no. 766 TE251

Pavlides, Louis, 1921-
The central Virginia volcanic-plutonic belt : an island arc of Cambrian(?) age / by Louis Pavlides. Washington : U. S.G.P.O. , 1981. p. cm. (Geological Survey professional paper ; 1231-A.) Bibliography: p.   LC Card 81-607018   DDC 552/.1 19
1. Rocks, Igneous. 2. Geology, Stratigraphic - Cambrian. 3. Island arcs - Virginia. 4. Geology - Virginia. I. Series. II. Series: Geological Survey professional paper ; 1231-A. III. Title.
QE461 .P328

Middle and upper Paleozoic granitic rocks in the Piedmont near Fredericksburg, Virginia . Washington , 1981. p. cm.   LC Card 81-607861   DDC 552/.3 19
QE462.G7 M48

Pawlett, Nathaniel Mason. The route of the Three Notch'd Road : a preliminary report / by Nathaniel Mason Pawlett and Howard H. Newlon, Jr. Charlottesville, Va. : Virginia Highway & Transportation Research Council, [1980] vi, 26 p. : ill., maps (1 fold. in pocket) ; 28 cm. (Historic roads of Virginia) "January 1976, revised June 1980." "VHTRC 76-R32."   LC Card 80-620018   DDC 388.1/09755/4 19

1. Roads - Virginia. 2. Highway law - Virginia. I. Newlon, Howard, joint author. II. Title. III. Title: Three Notch'd Road.
HE356.V8 P39

PAWNEE NATIONAL GRASSLAND - MAPS.
(1969) United States. Forest Service. Rocky Mountain Region. Pawnee National Grassland, Colorado. [Denver] 1969. col. map 55 x 101 cm. Scale 1:126,720; 1/2″ = 1 mile. "Polyconic projection; 1927 North American Datum. Sixth principal meridian." "Forest Service map." Includes source diagram and key map. Text and illus. on verso. "Reprinted 1977."   LC Card GM69-1310
G4312.P3 1969 .U5
                              NYPL [Map Div. 80-3367]

Pawns in a triangle of hate . Gardiner, C. Harvey (Clinton Harvey) Seattle , c1981. p. cm.   ISBN 0-295-95855-3   LC Card 81-51278   DDC 940.53/1 19
D769.8.A6 G37

Pay and price standards . United States. Council on Wage and Price Stability. Washington , 1979. 95 p. in various pagings ;   LC Card 79-603044
KF6067 .A88   *NYPL [JLF 81-439]*

Paying for social security . Chaikind, Stephen. [Washington, D.C.], 1981. xix, 47 p. ;   LC Card 81-601225   DDC 353.0082/56 19
HD7125 .C47

Paylore, Patricia. Caldwell, Mary. The Sonoran Desert . Tucson, Ariz. [1976] ca. 400 p. :   LC Card 79-625338   DDC 016.9172/170954 19
Z7408.S59 C34 QH104.5.S58

Payment of attorneys' fees in tax litigation . United States. Congress. House. Committee on Ways and Means. Subcommittee on Select Revenue Measures. Washington , 1980 [i.e. 1981] iii, 111 p. ;   LC Card 81-600811   DDC 343.7304/0269 347.30340269 19
KF27 .W3468 1980d

Payment of taxes under protest . Montana. Legislature. Revenue Oversight Committee. Helena, Mont. (Room 138, State Capitol, Helena 59620) [1980] i, 27 p. ;   LC Card 81-621340   DDC 353.97860072/4 19
KFM9471.5 .A25 1980

Paynter, Robert. Ecological anthropology of the Middle Connecticut River Valley /. Amherst , 1979. iv, 161 p. :   LC Card 80-621530   DDC 974 19
F12.C7 E26

PAYROLL TAX (SOCIAL SECURITY) see **SOCIAL SECURITY TAXES.**

Payrolls and contributions under Ohio unemployment compensation law, by industry. RS 203.2-1. Ohio. Bureau of Employment Services. Division of Research and Statistics. Columbus.   *NYPL [JLM 81-28]*

PBB general population study : final report, September 30, 1979. [Lansing : Michigan Dept. of Public Health, 1979] 269 p. in various pagings : ill. ; 28 cm. Cover title. Reports by University of Michigan, School of Public Health, Environmental Sciences Laboratory, Mt. Sinai School of Medicine, and Wayne State University, School of Medicine. Includes bibliographical references.   LC Card 80-621045   DDC 363.1/79 19
1. Polybrominated biphenyls - Toxicology - Michigan. 2. Health surveys - Michigan. 3. Michigan - Statistics, Medical. I. Michigan. University. School of Public Health. II. Mount Sinai School of Medicine. Environmental Sciences Laboratory. III. Wayne State University. School of Medicine.
RA1242.P69 P16

PCB's, dangers associated with their storage and use . United States. Congress. House. Committee on Interstate and Foreign Commerce. Subcommittee on Oversight and Investigations. Washington , 1980. iv, 704 p. :   LC Card 80-602788   DDC 363.1/79 19
KF27 .I5547 1979s

PEACE.
United States Commission on Proposals for the National Academy of Peace and Conflict Resolution. Interim report of the U. S. Commission on Proposals for the National Academy of Peace and Conflict Resolution . Washington , 1980. iii, 16, vii p. ;   LC Card 80-604123   DDC 327.1/72/071173 19
JX1963 .U14 1980

PEACE OFFICERS - OKLAHOMA - BIOGRAPHY.
Shirley, Glenn. Heck Thomas, frontier marshal /. Norman , 1981, c1962. p. cm. ISBN 0-8061-1664-1 LC Card 81-40293 DDC 976.6/04/0924 B 19
F698.T48 S48 1981

Peacetime industrial preparedness for wartime ammunition production /. Ennis, Harry F. Washington, D.C. [1980] vi, 122 p. : LC Card 80-603600 DDC 355.2/6/0973 19
HC110.D4 E56

PEACH - LAW AND LEGISLATION - UNITED STATES.
United States. Congress. House. Committee on Agriculture. Subcommittee on Domestic Marketing, Consumer Relations, and Nutrition. Marketing orders for walnuts and olives and Freestone Peach Research and Education Act . Washington , 1980. iii, 74 p. ; LC Card 80-604106 DDC 343.73/08514/0262 347.30385140262 19
KF27 .A3336 1980b

PEACHES - SOUTH CAROLINA - STATISTICS.
South Carolina Crop and Livestock Reporting Service. South Carolina fruit tree survey, 1978 . [Clemson, S.C.] [Washington] [1979] 26 p. : LC Card 80-621005 DDC 338.1 s 338.1/7411/09757 19
HD1775.S6 S6 no. 404 SB320.7.S6

Peacock, Richard D. SPEED2, a computer program for the reduction of data from automatic data acquisition systems / Richard D. Peacock and John M. Smith. [Washington, D.C.] : U. S. Dept. of Commerce, National Bureau of Standards : for sale by Supt. of Docs., U. S. Govt. Print. Off., [1979] 58, 68, 22, [7] p. ; 27 cm. (NBS technical note. 1108) "Issued September 1979." Includes bibliographical references. LC Card 79-603987 DDC 602/.18 s 001.6 19
1. Data reduction - Computer programs. 2. SPEED2 (Computer program). I. Smith, John Melvin, 1937- joint author. II. Series: United States. National Bureau of Standards. Technical note , 1108. III. Title.
QC100 .U5753 no. 1108 QA276

PEAK LOAD - ECONOMIC ASPECTS - WISCONSIN.
Wisconsin. Public Service Commission. Accounts and Finance Division. Periods of peak demand for utility service . [Madison, Wis.] [1979] iii, 30 p. : LC Card 79-626145 DDC 363.6/09775 s 338.4/736362 19
HD2767.W6 A37 no. 59a HD9685.U6W6

PEANUTS - UNITED STATES.
United States. Congress. House. Committee on Agriculture. Subcommittee on Oilseeds and Rice. 1980 support price for peanuts . Washington , 1980. iii, 70 p. ; LC Card 80-601929 DDC 338.1/8 19
KF27 .A367 1980

United States. Congress. Senate. Committee on Agriculture, Nutrition, and Forestry. Increase in minimum level price support on 1980 and 1981 quota peanuts . Washington , 1980. iii, 80 p. ; LC Card 80-602531 DDC 343.73/0763368 19
KF26 .A35 1980a

United States. Tariff Commission. Peanuts . Washington, 1955. 42 l. LC Card 55-60610
NYPL [JLF 75-1381]

PEAR - PACKING - ECONOMIC ASPECTS - CALIFORNIA - LAKE CO.
Stollsteimer, John F. Regional efficiency in the organization of agricultural processing facilities . [Berkeley] , 1975. 148 p. : LC Card 76-622988 DDC 338.1 s 664/.80413 19
HD1407 .C27 no. 35 SB373

Pearce, Roy Harvey. Progress and its discontents /. Berkeley , c1982. p. cm. ISBN 0-520-04478-9 LC Card 81-11643 DDC 303.4 19
HM101 .P89

Pearse, Gary A. Inventory and cataloging : annual performance report for Study no. G-I / Gary A. Pearse, Kenneth T. Alt. Juneau : Alaska Dept. of Fish and Game, Sport Fish Division, [1978] 76 p. : ill. ; 28 cm. (Sport fish investigations of Alaska) On cover: Volume 19. July 1, 1977-June 30, 1978. "Federal aid in fish restoration." Includes bibliographies. LC Card 79-621586 DDC 333.95/6/09798 19

1. Fishes - Alaska. 2. Limnology - Alaska. I. Alt, Kenneth T., joint author. II. Alaska. Division of Sport Fish. III. Title. IV. Series.
QL628.A4 P42

Pearson, Helen Wallenstein. Theories on drug abuse . Rockville, Md. . xli, 488 p. : LC Card 80-600058 DDC 616.86/3 19
RC564 .T5

PEAT INDUSTRY - ENVIRONMENTAL ASPECTS - MIDDLE WEST.
Camp, Dresser & McKee. Environmental Sciences Division. Effect of peat mining on fish and other aquatic organisms in the Upper Midwest /. Washington, DC [1981] p. cm. LC Card 81-607838 DDC 622/.331 19
SH177.P4 C35 1981

Peat, Marwick, Mitchell and Company. State of Montana, Boulder River School and Hospital : report on audit, fiscal year ended June 30, 1976 / conducted under contract by Peat, Marwick, Mitchell & Co. Helena : Office of the Legislative Auditor, State of Montana, [1977] iv, 35 leaves ; 28 cm. LC Card 78-621802 DDC 353.97860072/32 19
1. Boulder River School and Hospital - Accounting.
RC445.M9 B686

PEATLANDS - MIDDLE WEST.
Camp, Dresser & McKee. Environmental Sciences Division. Effect of peat mining on fish and other aquatic organisms in the Upper Midwest /. Washington, DC [1981] p. cm. LC Card 81-607838 DDC 622/.331 19
SH177.P4 C35 1981

Peavy, Howard S. The effects of non-sewered subdivisions on ground water quality / by Howard S. Peavy, Craig E. Brawner, Phillip E. Stark. Bozeman, MT : Dept. of Civil Engineering and Engineering Mechanics, Montana State University for the Water Quality Bureau, State Dept. of Health & Environmental Science, [1980?] iv, 65, 22 p. : ill., maps (6 fold. in pocket) ; 29 cm. Bibliography: p. 18-22, (3d group) LC Card 80-623175 DDC 363.7/394 19
1. Water, Underground - Pollution - Montana. 2. Septic tanks - Environmental aspects - Montana. I. Brawner, Craig E., joint author. II. Stark, Phillip E., joint author. III. Montana. Water Quality Bureau. IV. Title.
TD224.M9 P33

Peckham, Richard D.
(joint author) Chlupach, Robert S. Lake and stream investigations . Juneau [1978] 88 p. ; LC Card 79-621585 DDC 333.95/6/09798 19
QL628.A4 C48

Sport fish investigations of Alaska . Juneau [1977] 115 p. : LC Card 78-621554 DDC 333.95/6/09798 19
QL628.A4 S67

Pecorella, Patricia A. Survey-guided development: a consultant manual for human resources management specialists / [prepared by Patricia A. Pecorella, Doris L. Hausser, and Anne L. Wissler]. [Washington?] : Dept. of the Navy, Bureau of Naval Personnel, Human Resources Management Division, 1974. 1 v. (various pagings) ; 26 cm. "NAVPERS 15264." Cover title. Includes bibliography.
1. Personnel management. I. Hausser, Doris L., joint author. II. Wissler, Anne L., joint author. III. United States. Bureau of Naval Personnel. Human Resources Management Division. IV. Title.
NYPL [JLF 81-585]

PEDAGOGY. see EDUCATION; TEACHING.

Pedde, Lawrence D. United States. Bureau of Reclamation. Metric manual /. Denver , 1978. xvii, 278 p. : ISBN 0-8103-1020-1
QC92.U54 U53 1980   *NYPL [JSE 81-281]*

Pedersen, Paul, 1936- Counseling across cultures /. Honolulu , 1981. p. cm. ISBN 0-8248-0725-1 (pbk.) : LC Card 81-2961 DDC 616.89/14 19
BF637.C6 C63 1981

Pediatric care program plan. Maine. Bureau of Health Planning and Development. [Augusta] [1979] v, 75, [27] p. : LC Card 80-622813 DDC 362.1/98920009741 19
RJ102.5.M2 M34 1979

PEDIATRIC NEPHROLOGY - JUVENILE LITERATURE.
Someone special . Minneapolis, Minn. , 1981. p. cm. ISBN 0-940210-00-2 LC Card 81-51347

DDC 618.92/61 19
RJ476.K5 S65

PEDIATRIC RESPIRATORY DISEASES - MONTANA - LONGITUDINAL STUDIES.
Montana. Air Quality Bureau. Pulmonary function testing of elementary school children . Helena, Mont. [1979] p. : LC Card 80-620864 DDC 618.92/24 19
RJ433.5.P8 M66 1979

Pedionomidae (Aves, Charadriiformes) Olson, Storrs L. The relationships of the Pedionomidae (Aves, Charadriiformes) /. Washington , 1981. p. cm. LC Card 81-412 DDC 591 s 598/.33 19
QL1 .S54 no. 337 QL696.C465

PEDIONOMUS TORQUATUS - ANATOMY.
Olson, Storrs L. The relationships of the Pedionomidae (Aves, Charadriiformes) /. Washington , 1981. p. cm. LC Card 81-412 DDC 591 s 598/.33 19
QL1 .S54 no. 337 QL696.C465

PEDIONOMUS TORQUATUS - CLASSIFICATION.
Olson, Storrs L. The relationships of the Pedionomidae (Aves, Charadriiformes) /. Washington , 1981. p. cm. LC Card 81-412 DDC 591 s 598/.33 19
QL1 .S54 no. 337 QL696.C465

PELINNAÍON, GREECE.
Miller, Stella G. Two groups of Thessalian gold /. Berkeley , c1979. xiii, 78 p., [16] leaves of plates : ISBN 0-520-09580-4 LC Card 77-80473
DF261.O57 M54   *NYPL [L-11 622 v. 188]*

Pell, Claiborne, 1918-
Earthquake in Italy : a report to the Committee on Foreign Relations, United States Senate / by Claiborne Pell. Washington : U. S. G.P.O., 1980. vii, 17 p. : ill., maps ; 24 cm. At head of title: 96th Congress, 2d session. Committee print. "December 1980." LC Card 80-604120 DDC 363.3/495 19
1. Naples (Italy) - Earthquake, 1980. I. United States. Congress. Senate. Committee on Foreign Relations. II. Title.
DG851 .P44

Earthquake in the Azores : a tragedy and the American response : a report to the Committee on Foreign Relations, United States Senate, May 1980 / by Claiborne Pell. Washington : U. S. Govt. Print. Off., 1980. vii, 21 p. : ill. ; 24 cm. At head of title: Committee print. 96th Congress, 2d session. LC Card 80-603275 DDC 363.3/495 19
1. Disaster relief - Azores. 2. Economic assistance, American - Azores. 3. Earthquakes - Azores. I. United States. Congress. Senate. Committee on Foreign Relations. II. Title.
HV555.A96 P44

PELTIER HEAT. see THERMOELECTRIC APPARATUS AND APPLIANCES.

Pelzman, Joseph. Aho, C. Michael, 1949- Assessing the changing structure of world trade /. Washington, D.C. , Springfield, Va. , 1980. 34 [i.e. 82] p. ; LC Card 81-600792 DDC 382/.45/000973 19
HF3031 .A59

PEMON INDIANS. see ARECUNA INDIANS.

Penaeoid and Sergestoid shrimps (Crustacea. Huff, James Alan, 1949- St. Petersburg, Fla. , 1979. 102 p. : LC Card 80-622670 DDC 574/.92/34 s 595.3/843/09759 19
QH92.3 .M45 vol. 5, pt. 4 QL444.M33

PENAEUS.
Bishop, J. M. Biological observations on commercial penaeid shrimps caught by bottom trawl in South Carolina estuaries, February 1973-January 1975 /. [Charleston] [197-] xi, 97 p. : LC Card 80-621322 DDC 595.3/843 19
QL444.M33 B57

The Penal code of the State of California . California. Laws, statutes, etc. Los Angeles , c1978. viii, 1201 p. ;
KFC1100.A335 A2 1979
     NYPL [JLE 80-2779]

PENAL CODES. see CRIMINAL LAW.

PENAL LAW. see CRIMINAL LAW.

PENALTIES (CRIMINAL LAW) see PUNISHMENT.

PENALTIES (INTERNATIONAL LAW) see SANCTIONS (INTERNATIONAL LAW)

Pendleton, Ind. Reformatory. see Indiana Reformatory, Pendleton.

The Pendleton reflector. v. 2, no. 180-v. 74, no. 6; Jan. 31, 1964-June 11, 1971 (incomplete). Pendleton, Ind. illus., 39 cm. Microfilm. Frequency varies. Occasional errors in numbering. "The Pendleton reflector is written edited, and published by the inmates of the Indiana Reformatory."
1. Prison periodicals. I. Indiana Reformatory, Pendleton.
NYPL [*ZAN-2109]

Peng, Samuel S. Research Triangle Institute. Center for Educational Research and Evaluation. Tabular summary of the third follow-up questionnaire data /. [Washington] , 1978. 4 v. ; LC Card 79-602292
LA229 .R46 1978a

Peng, Syd S., 1939- Stress distribution and pillar design in oil shale retorts / by Syd S. Peng and Richard E. Thill. Avondale, Md. : U. S. Dept. of the Interior, Bureau of Mines, 1981. p. cm. (Report of investigations) Bibliography: p. LC Card 81-607827 DDC 622 s 622/.3382 19
1. Oil-shales. 2. In situ processing (Mining). 3. Rock mechanics. I. Thill, Richard E. II. Series: Report of investigations (United States. Bureau of Mines). III. Title.
TN23 .U43 TN858

Penick, James L. The great western land pirate : John A. Murrell in legend and history / James L. Penick, Jr. Columbia : University of Missouri Press, 1981. p. cm. Bibliography: p. Includes index. ISBN 0-8262-0342-6 LC Card 81-1779 DDC 364.1/5/0924 B 19
1. Murrell, John A. 2. Crime and criminals - Southwest, Old - History. 3. Southwest, Old - History. 4. Outlaws - Southwest, Old - Biography. 5. Southwest, Old - Biography. I. Title.
F396.M95 P46

Penn Center. Philadelphia. City Planning Commission. [Philadelphia] 1952. 22 p. LC Card 81-471288
HT177.P47 P44 1952

PENN SCHOOL, ST. HELENA ISLAND, S. C. - SOURCES.
University of North Carolina at Chapel Hill. Library. Southern Historical Collection. Guide to the microfilm edition of the Penn School papers, 1862-1976 . [Chapel Hill , 1977] 42 p. ;
NYPL [Sc F 80-196]

Penner, Harold L. Soil survey of Sedgwick County, Kansas / [by Harold L. Penner and William A. Wehmueller] ; United States Department of Agriculture, Soil Conservation Service, in cooperation with Kansas Agricultural Experiment Station. [Washington : Soil Conservation Service, 1979] vii, 126 p., [41] fold. leaves of plates : ill. ; 29 cm. Cover title. Includes bibliographical references and index. LC Card 79-603621 DDC 631.4/7/78186 19
1. Soils - Kansas - Sedgwick Co. - Maps. I. Wehmuller, William A., joint author. II. United States. Soil Conservation Service. III. Kansas. Agricultural Experiment Station, Manhattan. IV. Title.
S599.K2 P44

Pennsylvania. Agriculture, Dept. of. see Pennsylvania. Dept. of Agriculture.

Pennsylvania archives.
Pennsylvania. Historical and Museum Commission. Guide to the published archives of Pennsylvania, covering the 138 volumes of Colonial records and Pennsylvania archives, series I-IX /. Harrisburg , 1976. v, 91 p. ; LC Card 79-623725 DDC 016.9748 19
F146.C622 P46 1976

Pennsylvania. Archives and Manuscripts, Division of. see Pennsylvania. Division of Archives and Manuscripts.

PENNSYLVANIA ARCHIVES - HISTORY.
Pennsylvania. Historical and Museum Commission. Guide to the published archives of Pennsylvania, covering the 138 volumes of Colonial records and Pennsylvania archives, series I-IX /. Harrisburg , 1976. v, 91 p. ; LC Card 79-623725 DDC 016.9748 19
F146.C622 P46 1976

PENNSYLVANIA ARCHIVES - INDEXES.
Pennsylvania. Historical and Museum Commission. Guide to the published archives of Pennsylvania, covering the 138 volumes of Colonial records and Pennsylvania archives, series I-IX /. Harrisburg , 1976. v, 91 p. ; LC

Card 79-623725 DDC 016.9748 19
F146.C622 P46 1976

PENNSYLVANIA. ATTORNEY GENERAL'S OFFICE.
Pennsylvania. General Assembly. Task Force on Office of Elected Attorney General. Office of elected attorney general . Harrisburg , 1978. vii, 54 p. ; LC Card 79-622493
KFP11.62 .O4 1978   **NYPL [JLF 80-1517]**

PENNSYLVANIA AVENUE LANDFILL SITE, NEW YORK (CITY)
From landfill to park. New York, 1974. 45 p.:
NYPL [*ZI-281]

Pennsylvania. Board of Pardons.
Rules / Board of Pardons, Commonwealth of Pennsylvania. [Harrisburg, Pa.] : The Board, [1980] 16 p. ; 23 x 9 cm. Cover title. "Effective March 17, 1969. Revised February 1, 1980." LC Card 80-623113 DDC 345.748/077/02636 19
1. Pennsylvania. Board of Pardons - Rules and practice.
KFP592.A433 A2 1980

PENNSYLVANIA. BOARD OF PARDONS - RULES AND PRACTICE.
Pennsylvania. Board of Pardons. Rules /. [Harrisburg, Pa.] [1980] 16 p. ; LC Card 80-623113 DDC 345.748/077/02636 19
KFP592.A433 A2 1980

Pennsylvania. Bureau of Employment Security. Research and Statistics Division.
Occupational staffing patterns of selected regulated industries in Pennsylvania (SIC's-401, 42, 45, and 48, excluding 483) : [Harrisburg] : The Division, 1979. ii, 73 p. ; 29 cm. (Occupational employment statistics) Bibliography: p. 72. LC Card 79-624037
1. Labor supply - Pennsylvania - Statistics. 2. Pennsylvania - Occupations - Statistics. 3. Labor supply - Pennsylvania - Pittsburgh metropolitan area - Statistics. 4. Pittsburgh metropolitan area - Occupations - Statistics. I. United States. Bureau of Labor Statistics. II. United States. Employment and Training Administration. III. Title.
HD5725.P4 P45 1979   **NYPL [JLF 80-1646]**

Pennsylvania. Bureau of International Commerce.
Pennsylvania. Dept. of Commerce. Bureau of Statistics, Research and Planning. Pennsylvania manufacturing exports /. [Harrisburg] [1978?] [71] leaves : LC Card 80-622589 DDC 382/.45/0009748 19
HF3161.P4 P45 1978

Pennsylvania. Bureau of Local Government Services. Information Services Division.
Catalog of State aids to local governments / Information Services Division, Bureau of Local Government Services, Department of Community Affairs. 4th ed. Harrisburg : DCA, [1976] ca. 300 p. in various pagings : ill. ; 28 cm. A revision of the 1965 ed. issued by Better Government Associates under title: State aids to local government. "Prepared by D. P. Olpere." LC Card 80-622718 DDC 353.9748000072/5 19
1. Grants-in-aid - Pennsylvania. 2. Intergovernmental fiscal relations - Pennsylvania. I. Olpere, Daniel P. II. Better Government Associates. State aids to local government. III. Title.
HJ665 .P33 1976

Citizen's guide to Pennsylvania local government. Pennsylvania. Dept. of Community Affairs. Information Services Center. Citizen's guide to Pennsylvania local government / Information Services Center, Department of Community Affairs. 3d ed. Harrisburg [1980] c1979. vi, 62 p. ; LC Card 80-622365 DDC 352.0748 19
JS451 .P2 1980

Pennsylvania. Bureau of Management Services. see Pennsylvania. Office of Administration. Bureau of Management Services.

Pennsylvania. Bureau of Special Education.
Stewart, Gerald. Statistical and expenditure data for intermediate unit operated programs and services for exceptional children, 1976-77 /. Harrisburg , Pa. , 1978. 28 p. ; LC Card 80-623258 DDC 371.9/09748 19
LC4032.P4 S73

Pennsylvania. Bureau of Topographic and Geologic Survey. see Pennsylvania. Topographic and Geologic Survey.

Pennsylvania. Bureau of Transportation Planning Statistics. Pennsylvania traffic volume map / prepared by the Pennsylvania Department of

Transportation, Bureau of Transportation Planning Statistics, in cooperation with the U. S. Department of Transportation, Federal Highway Administration. [Harrisburg] : The Bureau, 1979. 1 map : photocopy ; 74 x 105 cm. In right lower margin: Type 14, statewide traffic volume map. Includes 15 insets. LC Card 81-692949
1. Traffic flow - Pennsylvania - Maps. I. Title.
G3821.P21 1979 .P4

Pennsylvania. Bureau of Water Quality Management. Publication.
(no. 36) Brezina, Edward R. An aquatic biological investigation of Stony Creek, Dauphin and Lebanon Counties, Pennsylvania /. Harrisburg , 1974. 27 p. ; LC Card 75-623487 DDC 363.6/1 s 574.92/9/74818 19
TD224.P4 P45A no. 36 QH105.P4

Pennsylvania (Colony). Provincial Council. Minutes. Pennsylvania. Historical and Museum Commission. Guide to the published archives of Pennsylvania, covering the 138 volumes of Colonial records and Pennsylvania archives, series I-IX / by Henry Howard Eddy ; finding media prepared by Martha L. Simonetti. Harrisburg , 1976. v, 91 p. ; LC Card 79-623725 DDC 016.9748 19
F146.C622 P46 1976

PENNSYLVANIA - COMMERCE.
Pennsylvania. Dept. of Commerce. Bureau of Statistics, Research and Planning. Pennsylvania manufacturing exports /. [Harrisburg] [1978?] [71] leaves : LC Card 80-622589 DDC 382/.45/0009748 19
HF3161.P4 P45 1978

Pennsylvania. Commission on Crime and Delinquency. Division of Criminal Justice Statistics. Kunkle, John H. Plea negotiation in Pennsylvania . [Harrisburg] [1979] ii, 105, [76] p. : LC Card 80-622816 DDC 345.748/072 19
KFP578.5 .K86

Pennsylvania. Community Affairs, Dept. of. see Pennsylvania. Dept. of Community Affairs.

Pennsylvania. Crime Commission (1968-) A decade of organized crime : 1980 report / Pennsylvania Crime Commission. St. Davids, Pa. : The Commission, c1980. xii, 279 p. : ill. ; 28 cm. Errata slip inserted. Includes bibliographical references and indexes. ISBN 0-937972-00-2 (pbk.) LC Card 80-620035 DDC 364.1/06/0748 19
1. Organized crime - Pennsylvania. I. Title.
HV7288 .A6 1980

Pennsylvania. Dept. of Agriculture. (Old Catalog form: Pennsylvania. Agriculture Dept.) Pennsylvania. Governor's Office of Policy and Planning. The socio-economic impact of the Three Mile Island accident . Harrisburg, Pa. [1980] iii, 162, [43] p., [1] folded leaf of plates : LC Card 81-621645 DDC 330.9748/18 19
HD9698.U54 M476 1980

Pennsylvania. Dept. of Commerce. Bureau of Statistics, Research and Planning.
Assessment of Pennsylvania's business community : manufacturing and mining, 1972-1977 / prepared by Bureau of Statistics, Research, and Planning. [Harrisburg] : Pennsylvania Dept. of Commerce, [1980] 53 p. ; 28 cm. Tables. "May 1980." LC Card 80-622817 DDC 338.09748 19
1. Pennsylvania - Manufactures - Statistics. 2. Mineral industries - Pennsylvania - Statistics. 3. Labor supply - Pennsylvania - Statistics. I. Title.
HD9727.P415 P46 1980

Pennsylvania manufacturing exports / prepared for the Bureau of International Commerce by the Bureau of Statistics, Research, and Planning ; Carol M. Wilson, editor. [Harrisburg] : Pennsylvania Dept. of Commerce, Bureau of International Commerce, [1978?] [71] leaves : maps ; 22 cm. LC Card 80-622589 DDC 382/.45/0009748 19
1. Pennsylvania - Commerce. 2. Foreign trade promotion - Pennsylvania. I. Wilson, Carol M. II. Pennsylvania. Bureau of International Commerce. III. Title.
HF3161.P4 P45 1978

Pennsylvania. Dept. of Community Affairs. (Old Catalog form: Pennsylvania. Community Affairs, Dept. of)
Cohen, Rick. Partnerships for neighborhood preservation . [Harrisburg] , 1978. vii, 200 p. ;

GOVERNMENT PUBLICATIONS - U.S.: 1981

121   Pennsylvania. General Assembly. Legislative Budget and Finance

LC Card 79-622460   DDC 307.7/6/0973 19
HN90.C6 C626

A housing program for Pennsylvania,
1975-1990: prepared for governor Milton J.
Shapp / by the Pennsylvania Dept. of
Community Affairs, A. L. Hydeman, Jr.,
Secretary. [Harrisburg]: Commonwealth of
Pennsylvania, Dept. of Community Affairs,
1974. ii, 156 p. ; 28 cm. "August 1974" Includes
bibliography: p. 153-155.
1. Housing policy - Pennsylvania. I. Title.
                              NYPL [JLF 80-1279]

Reversing regional decline : an analysis and
strategy. [Harrisburg] : Commonwealth of
Pennsylvania, Department of Community
Affairs, [1976] 13, [8] leaves : ill. ; 28 cm.
Microfiche (neg.) NTIS. 1 sheet. 11 x 15 cm.
(PB-273-447) Cover title. Includes bibliographical
references.   LC Card 76-624629
1. Intergovernmental fiscal relations - United States. 2.
Regional planning - United States. I. Title.
HJ275 .P45 1976   NYPL [*XME-9553]

PENNSYLVANIA. DEPT. OF COMMUNITY AFFAIRS.

Pennsylvania. General Assembly. Legislative
Budget and Finance Committee. Study of State
fees . Harrisburg, Pa. [1979] vi, 89 p. ; LC
Card 80-622146   DDC 353.97480072/6 19
HT167.5.P4 P46 1979

**Pennsylvania. Dept. of Community Affairs.
Information Services Center.**
Citizen's guide to Pennsylvania local
government / Information Services Center,
Department of Community Affairs. 3d ed.
Harrisburg : The Department, [1980] c1979. vi,
62 p. ; 23 cm. Second ed. (1975) by Information
Services Division, Bureau of Local Government
Services, Pennsylvania. "February 1980." Bibliography:
p. 60-62. LC Card 80-622365 DDC 352.0748 19
1. Local government - Pennsylvania. I. Pennsylvania.
Bureau of Local Government Services. Information
Services Division. Citizen's guide to Pennsylvania local
government. II. Title.
JS451 .P2 1980

Taxation manual / Information Services Center,
Department of Community Affairs. 1st ed.
Harrisburg, Pa. : The Center, c1979. iv, 88 p. ;
28 cm. LC Card 80-622479   DDC 343.74804/3 19
1. Local taxation - Pennsylvania. I. Title.
KFP490 .A855

Township supervisors handbook / Information
Services Center, Department of Community
Affairs. 2d ed. Harrisburg : The Dept., [1980]
v, 52 p. : diagrs. ; 28 cm. First ed., prepared by
Local Government Research Corp., published in 1976
under title: Handbook for newly elected township
supervisors. "April 1980." LC Card 80-622716 DDC
352/.0072/09748 19
1. Local government - Pennsylvania - Handbooks,
manuals, etc. I. Local Government Research
Corporation. Handbook for newly elected township
supervisors. II. Title.
JS451 .P1 1980a

Pennsylvania. Dept. of Education. (Old Catalog
form: Pennsylvania. Education, Dept. of)
Brehman, George E. A tabular summation of
1977-78 higher education equal opportunity
program survey findings /. Harrisburg, PA ,
1979. iv, 41 p. ; LC Card 80-621911 DDC
378.748 19
LA355.5 .B73

Cober, John Gordon, 1915- Final annual report
to the General Assembly on the intermediate
unit system, 1976-77-1977-78 /. Harrisburg, PA
[1980] vi, 120 p. ; LC Card 80-622342 DDC
372.9748 19
LA355 .C63

The environmental impact of electrical power
generation: nuclear and fossil; a minicourse for
secondary schools and adult education.
Harrisburg, Pennsylvania Dept. of Education,
1973. v, 89 p. illus. 28 cm. (PDE Working paper)
Bibliography: p. 81-84.
1. Electric power. 2. Atomic power-plants. 3. Electric
power-plants. I. Title.   NYPL [JSF 80-262]

Estimates of school district subsidies payable
1979-80 : basic instruction subsidy, health
services subsidy, nonpublic transportation
subsidy, vocational education subsidy.
[Harrisburg] : Pennsylvania Dept. of Education,
1979. v, 20 leaves ; 22 x 28 cm. Cover title.
"Provisions of H.B. 140--conference report. LC Card

80-621560   DDC 379.1/3/09748 19
1. Education - Pennsylvania - Finance - Statistics. 2.
Public health - Pennsylvania - Finance - Statistics. 3.
Transportation - Pennsylvania - Finance - Statistics. 4.
State aid to education - Pennsylvania - Statistics. I.
Title.
LB2826.P4 P373 1979

Methods and costs of tax collection in school
districts in Pennsylvania. [Harrisburg, Pa. : s.n.,
1977?] 70 p. in various pagings ; 28 cm. Cover
title. Study conducted by Pennsylvania Dept. of
Education and Dept. of Revenue. Tables. LC Card
80-621623   DDC 352.1/3/09748 19
1. Tax collection - Pennsylvania - Costs - Statistics. 2.
Local taxation - Pennsylvania - Statistics. I.
Pennsylvania. Dept. of Revenue. II. Title.
HJ9306 .P42 1977

PDE directory. [Harrisburg] 22 cm.
1. Education - Pennsylvania - Directories. I. Title.
                              NYPL [JLK 80-194]

Pennsylvania regulations and guidelines
concerning safety in the school science
laboratory. Harrisburg : Pennsylvania Dept. of
Education, 1978. [67] p. ; 28 cm. LC Card
80-621921   DDC 344.748/075 347.480475 19
1. Physical laboratories - Safety regulations -
Pennsylvania. 2. Schools - Safety regulations -
Pennsylvania. I. Title.
KFP380.A1 A3 1978

Programs approved for teacher education in
Pennsylvania colleges and universities.
Harrisburg, PA : Pennsylvania Dept. of
Education, 1979. ii, 102 leaves ; 28 cm. Tables.
      LC Card 80-621835   DDC 370/.7/309748 19
1. Teachers, Training of - Pennsylvania - Statistics. 2.
Universities and colleges - Pennsylvania - Statistics. I.
Title.
LB2167.P4 P46 1979

Teacher strike report, 1977-78, Pennsylvania
public schools. [Harrisburg, PA] : Pennsylvania
Dept. of Education, [1978] 23 [7], leaves ; 29
cm. "June 1978." LC Card 80-622147 DDC
331.89/2813711/009748 19
1. Strikes and lockouts - Teachers - Pennsylvania. I.
Title.
LB2844.47.U62 P466

Teacher strike report, 1978-79, Pennsylvania
public schools. [Harrisburg, PA] : Pennsylvania
Dept. of Education, [1979] 27, [15] leaves :
map ; 28 cm. "June 1979." LC Card 80-622148
DDC 331.89/2813711/009748 19
1. Strikes and lockouts - Teachers - Pennsylvania. I.
Title.
LB2844.47.U62 P4662

**Pennsylvania. Dept. of Education. Bureau of
Information Systems. Division of Research.**
Senier, John K. S. Annual occupational
withdrawal rates for Pennsylvania and the
major labor market areas /. Harrisburg, Pa. ,
1974. iv, 51 p. ; LC Card 80-621271 DDC
331.12/09748 19
HD5725.P4 S46

**Pennsylvania. Dept. of Education. Division of
Research.** Cober, John Gordon, 1915- Cost of
teaching different subjects. [Harrisburg] 1973. v,
13 p.;   NYPL [*Z-3215]

**Pennsylvania. Dept. of Education. Research,
Division of. see Pennsylvania. Dept. of
Education. Division of Research.**

**Pennsylvania. Dept. of Environmental Resources.
State Conservation Commission. see
Pennsylvania. State Conservation
Commission.**

**Pennsylvania. Dept. of Environmental Resources.
Topographic and Geologic Survey. see
Pennsylvania. Topographic and Geologic
Survey.**

Pennsylvania. Dept. of Revenue. (Old Catalog
form: Pennsylvania. Revenue dept.)
Pennsylvania. Dept. of Education. Methods and
costs of tax collection in school districts in
Pennsylvania. [Harrisburg, Pa. , 1977?] 70 p. in
various pagings ; LC Card 80-621623 DDC
352.1/3/09748 19
HJ9306 .P42 1977

Pennsylvania. Division of Acute Care. Directory
of licensed/approved hospitals in Pennsylvania.
[Harrisburg, Pa.] : Pennsylvania Dept. of
Health, Office of Quality Assurance, Division
of Acute Care, [1976?] iii, 61 p. ; 28 cm. Cover

title. LC Card 80-622478 DDC 362.1/1/025748 19
1. Hospitals - Pennsylvania - Directories. I. Title.
RA977 .P46 1976

**Pennsylvania. Division of Archives and
Manuscripts.**
Descriptive list of the map collection in the
Pennsylvania State Archives : catalogue of maps
in the principal map collection (MG 11) /
compiler, Martha L. Simonetti ; editors, Donald
H. Kent, Harry E. Whipkey. Harrisburg :
Commonwealth of Pennsylvania, Pennsylvania
Historical and Museum Commission, 1976. 178
p. ; 24 cm. LC Card 77-623410
1. Pennsylvania - Maps - Bibliography - Catalogs. 2.
Pennsylvania. Division of Archives and Manuscripts. I.
Simonetti, Martha L. II. Kent, Donald H. III. Whipkey,
Harry E. IV. Pennsylvania. Historical and Museum
Commission. V. Title.
Z6027.U5 P46 1976 GA447
                              NYPL [Map Div. 81-152]

McBride, David, 1949- The Afro-American in
Pennsylvania . Harrisburg , 1979. vii, 36 p. :
      LC Card 79-625708
Z1361.N39 M27 E185.93.P41

PENNSYLVANIA. DIVISION OF ARCHIVES AND MANUSCRIPTS.
Pennsylvania. Division of Archives and
Manuscripts. Descriptive list of the map
collection in the Pennsylvania State Archives .
Harrisburg , 1976. 178 p. ; LC Card 77-623410
Z6027.U5 P46 1976 GA447
                              NYPL [Map Div. 81-152]

PENNSYLVANIA. DIVISION OF ARCHIVES AND MANUSCRIPTS - CATALOGS.
McBride, David, 1949- The Afro-American in
Pennsylvania . Harrisburg , 1979. vii, 36 p. :
      LC Card 79-625708
Z1361.N39 M27 E185.93.P41

**Pennsylvania. Division of Planning and Program
Evaluation.** Community service center
recidivism evaluation / prepared by Division of
Planning and Program Evaluation, Office of the
Budget. [Harrisburg, Pa.] : The Office, [1976]
44 p. ; 28 cm. Cover title. "March 1976."
Bibliography: p. 31-32. LC Card 80-622329 DDC
364.3 19
1. Recidivists - Pennsylvania. 2. Pre-release programs
for prisoners - Pennsylvania - Evaluation. 3.
Community-based corrections - Pennsylvania -
Evaluation. I. Title.
HV9305.P3 P43 1976

**Pennsylvania. Education, Dept. of. see
Pennsylvania. Dept. of Education.**

**Pennsylvania. General Assembly. Joint State
Government Commission.** (Old Catalog form:
Pennsylvania. Joint State Government
Commission.
Local school tax reform : a proposal to reduce
property and nuisance taxes. Harrisburg, Pa. :
General Assembly of the Commonwealth of
Pennsylvania, Joint State Government
Commission, 1980. vii, 37 p. ; 28 cm. Includes
bibliographical references. LC Card 80-622333   DDC
336.22/2 19
1. Local taxation - Pennsylvania. I. Title.
HJ9306 .P425 1980

Private detectives and security business :
proposed Title 22 Pennsylvania consolidated
statutes. Harrisburg, Pa. : General Assembly of
the Commonwealth of Pennsylvania, Joint State
Government Commission, [1980] ix, 47 p. ; 28
cm. "April 1980." LC Card 80-622714 DDC
344.748/017613632 19
1. Detectives - Legal status, laws, etc. - Pennsylvania. 2.
Police, Private - Pennsylvania. I. Title.
KFP282.D47 A25 1980

**Pennsylvania. General Assembly. Joint State
Government Commission. Task Force on
Office of Elected Attorney General. see
Pennsylvania. General Assembly. Task Force
on Office of Elected Attorney General.**

**Pennsylvania. General Assembly. Legislative
Budget and Finance Committee.
Report of Legislative Budget and Finance
Committee .**
(# 6) Pennsylvania. General Assembly.
Legislative Budget and Finance Committee.
Study of State fees . Harrisburg, Pa. [1979]
vi, 89 p. ; LC Card 80-622146 DDC
353.97480072/6 19
HT167.5.P4 P46 1979

(#4) Pennsylvania. General Assembly. Legislative Budget and Finance Committee. Study of State fees . Harrisburg, PA. , 1978. iv, 33 p. ; LC Card 79-621202 DDC 353.97480085/8 19
KFP11.62 .B8 1978

Study of State fees : fees of Pennsylvania Harness Racing Commission. Harrisburg, PA. : Legislative Budget and Finance Committee, 1978. iv, 33 p. ; 28 cm. (Report of Legislative Budget and Finance Committee . #4) LC Card 79-621202 DDC 353.97480085/8 19
1. Pennsylvania. State Harness Racing Commission. 2. Harness racing - Licenses - Pennsylvania. I. Title. II. Title: Fees of Pennsylvania Harness Racing Commission. III. Series: Pennsylvania. General Assembly. Legislative Budget and Finance Committee. Report of Legislative Budget and Finance Committee , #4.
KFP11.62 .B8 1978

Study of State fees : fees of the Department of Community Affairs. Harrisburg, Pa. : Legislative Budget and Finance Committee, [1979] vi, 89 p. ; 29 cm. (Report of Legislative Budget and Finance Committee ; # 6) "July 1979." Includes index. LC Card 80-622146 DDC 353.97480072/6 19
1. Pennsylvania. Dept. of Community Affairs. 2. Fees, Administrative - Pennsylvania. I. Series: Pennsylvania. General Assembly. Legislative Budget and Finance Committee. Report of Legislative Budget and Finance Committee , # 6. II. Title.
HT167.5.P4 P46 1979

Wrap-up report of Legislative Budget and Finance Committee study of State fees / Legislative Budget and Finance Committee. Harrisburg, Pa. : The Committee, [1980] viii, 83 p. ; 29 cm. Summary sheet inserted. Includes bibliographical references. LC Card 80-622330 DDC 353.97480072/6 19
1. Fees, Administrative - Pennsylvania. 2. Licenses - Pennsylvania. I. Title.
KFP11.62 .B8 1980

Pennsylvania. General Assembly. Task Force on Office of Elected Attorney General. Office of elected attorney general : final report. / [General Assembly of the Commonwealth of Pennsylvania, Joint State Government Commission, Task Force on Office of Elected Attorney General] Harrisburg : The Commission, 1978. vii, 54 p. ; 28 cm. LC Card 79-622493
1. Pennsylvania. Attorney General's Office. 2. Attorneys-general - Pennsylvania. I. Title.
KFP11.62 .O4 1978   *NYPL [JLF 80-1517]*

Pennsylvania geology. Harrisburg, Topographic and Geologic Survey. illus. 23 cm. Bimonthly. LC Card 70-15808
1. Geology - Pennsylvania - Periodicals. I. Pennsylvania. Topographic and Geologic Survey.
NYPL [JSP 80-358]

Pennsylvania. Governor's Commission on Three Mile Island. Legal Subcommittee. Legal aspects of the Three Mile Island accident : report of the Legal Subcommittee to the Governor's Commission on Three Mile Island. Harrisburg, Pa. : The Subcommittee, [1980] ii leaves, 69 p. ; 28 cm. Includes bibliographical references. LC Card 80-621928 DDC 344.748/0472 19
1. Three Mile Island Nuclear Power Plant, Pa. 2. Atomic power-plants - Law and legislation - Pennsylvania. 3. Atomic power-plants - Pennsylvania - Accidents. I. Title.
KFP290 .A87

Pennsylvania. Governor's Council on Drug and Alcohol Abuse. Office of Research and Evaluation. Rush, Thomas Vale. The prevalence and intensity of alcohol and illicit drug use in Pennsylvania. [Harrisburg] v.
NYPL [JLF 79-928]

Pennsylvania. Governor's Council on Drug and Alcohol Abuse. Research and Evaluation, Office of. see **Pennsylvania. Governor's Council on Drug and Alcohol Abuse. Office of Research and Evaluation.**

Pennsylvania. Governor's Office of Policy and Planning. The socio-economic impact of the Three Mile Island accident : final report / prepared by Governor's Office of Policy and Planning, in cooperation with the Department of Agriculture ... [et al.]. Harrisburg, Pa. : The Office, [1980] iii, 162, [43] p., [1] folded leaf of

plates : col. map ; 28 cm. LC Card 81-621645 DDC 330.9748/18 19
1. Metropolitan Edison Company. 2. Three Mile Island Nuclear Power Plant, Pa. 3. Atomic power-plants - Accidents - Economic aspects - Pennsylvania. 4. Atomic power-plants - Accidents - Social aspects - Pennsylvania. I. Pennsylvania. Dept. of Agriculture. II. Title.
HD9698.U54 M476 1980

Pennsylvania. Governor's Study Commission on Public Employe Relations. Recommendations for legislative and administrative change to the public sector collective bargaining laws of Pennsylvania / prepared by Governor's Study Commission on Public Employe Relations, Benjamin R. Jones, chairman. [Harrisburg] : The Commission, 1978. ii, 76 p. : ports. ; 28 cm. LC Card 78-623470 DDC 344.748/01890413539 19
1. Collective labor agreements - Government employees - Pennsylvania. I. Jones, Benjamin R. II. Title.
KFP332.8.P77 A84

Pennsylvania. Harness Racing Commission. see **Pennsylvania. State Harness Racing Commission.**

Pennsylvania. Health Data Center. A profile of Pennsylvania hospitals. [Harrisburg] : Pennsylvania Dept. of Health, Bureau of Health Data Systems, Health Data Center, [1980] iv leaves, 35 p. ; 22 x 28 cm. Cover title. Tables. LC Card 80-623420 DDC 362.1/1/09748 19
1. Hospitals - Pennsylvania - Statistics. 2. Hospitals - Pennsylvania - Directories. I. Title.
RA981.P4 P39 1980

Pennsylvania. Historical and Museum Commission.
Guide to the microfilm of the records of Pennsylvania's revolutionary governments, 1775-1790 (record group 27) in the Pennsylvania State Archives, 54 rolls : a microfilm project / sponsored by the National Endowment for the Humanities ; Harry E. Whipkey and Roland M. Baumann, project director, Martha L. Simonetti, assistant project director ; Roland M. Baumann, editor, Douglas H. West, editorial associate. Harrisburg : Commonwealth of Pennsylvania, Pennsylvania Historical and Museum Commission, 1978 [c1979] vii, 351 p. ; 24 cm. Title on spine: Guide to microfilm of Pennsylvania's revolutionary governments, 1775-1790. LC Card 79-624725
1. Pennsylvania - Politics and government - Revolution, 1775-1783 - Sources - Microform catalogs. 2. Pennsylvania - Politics and government - 1775-1865 - Sources - Microform catalogs. 3. Pennsylvania. Historical and Museum Commission - Microform Catalogs. I. Whipkey, Harry E. II. Baumann, Roland M. III. Simonetti, Martha L. IV. National Endowment for the Humanities. V. Title. VI. Title: Records of Pennsylvania's revolutionary governments, 1775-1790. VII. Title: Guide to microfilm of Pennsylvania's revolutionary governments, 1775-1790.
E263.P4 P37 1979   *NYPL [ISC 80-2758]*

Guide to the published archives of Pennsylvania, covering the 138 volumes of Colonial records and Pennsylvania archives, series I-IX / by Henry Howard Eddy ; finding media prepared by Martha L. Simonetti. Harrisburg : Commonwealth of Pennsylvania, Pennsylvania Historical and Museum Commission, 1976. v, 91 p. ; 23 cm. The Colonial records include the minutes of the Provincial Council of the Colony of Pennsylvania and the Supreme Executive Council of the State of Pennsylvania. Reprint of the 1949 ed. published by the Commission, Harrisburg. Bibliography: p. 91. LC Card 79-623725 DDC 016.9748 19
1. Colonial records of Pennsylvania - Indexes. 2. Pennsylvania archives - Indexes. 3. Pennsylvania - History - Sources - Indexes. 4. Pennsylvania - History - Colonial period, ca. 1600-1775 - Sources - Indexes. 5. Pennsylvania - History - Revolution, 1775-1783 - Sources - Indexes. 6. Colonial records of Pennsylvania - History. 7. Pennsylvania archives - History. I. Eddy, Henry Howard. II. Simonetti, Martha L. III. Pennsylvania (Colony). Provincial Council. Minutes. IV. Pennsylvania. Supreme Executive Council. Minutes. V. Pennsylvania archives. VI. Title.
F146.C622 P46 1976

Pennsylvania. Division of Archives and Manuscripts. Descriptive list of the map collection in the Pennsylvania State Archives .

Harrisburg , 1976. 178 p. ; LC Card 77-623410
Z6027.U5 P46 1976
NYPL [Map Div. 81-152]

PENNSYLVANIA. HISTORICAL AND MUSEUM COMMISSION - MICROFORM CATALOGS.
Pennsylvania. Historical and Museum Commission. Guide to the microfilm of the records of Pennsylvania's revolutionary governments, 1775-1790 (record group 27) in the Pennsylvania State Archives, 54 rolls . Harrisburg , 1978 [c1979] vii, 351 p. ; LC Card 79-624725
E263.P4 P37 1979   NYPL [ISC 80-2758]

PENNSYLVANIA - HISTORY - COLONIAL PERIOD, CA. 1600-1775 - SOURCES - INDEXES.
Pennsylvania. Historical and Museum Commission. Guide to the published archives of Pennsylvania, covering the 138 volumes of Colonial records and Pennsylvania archives, series I-IX /. Harrisburg , 1976. v, 91 p. ; LC Card 79-623725 DDC 016.9748 19
F146.C622 P46 1976

PENNSYLVANIA - HISTORY - REVOLUTION, 1775-1783 - SOURCES - INDEXES.
Pennsylvania. Historical and Museum Commission. Guide to the published archives of Pennsylvania, covering the 138 volumes of Colonial records and Pennsylvania archives, series I-IX /. Harrisburg , 1976. v, 91 p. ; LC Card 79-623725 DDC 016.9748 19
F146.C622 P46 1976

PENNSYLVANIA - HISTORY - SOURCES - INDEXES.
Pennsylvania. Historical and Museum Commission. Guide to the published archives of Pennsylvania, covering the 138 volumes of Colonial records and Pennsylvania archives, series I-IX /. Harrisburg , 1976. v, 91 p. ; LC Card 79-623725 DDC 016.9748 19
F146.C622 P46 1976

Pennsylvania. Joint State Government Commission. see **Pennsylvania. General Assembly. Joint State Government Commission.**

Pennsylvania. Local Government Commission. Cable television in the Commonwealth of Pennsylvania, analysis and recommendations. Harrisburg, PA : Commonwealth of Pennsylvania, Local Government Commission, [1979] 109, [7] p. : maps ; 28 cm. Cover title. Prepared by M. P. Gasbarre and M. A. Zywen. "November, 1979." Bibliography: p. [114]-[116] LC Card 80-622151
1. Community antenna television - Pennsylvania. I. Gasbarre, Michael P. II. Zywen, Mark A. III. Title.
HE8700.7.C6 P45 1979

PENNSYLVANIA - MANUFACTURES - STATISTICS.
Pennsylvania. Dept. of Commerce. Bureau of Statistics, Research and Planning. Assessment of Pennsylvania's business community . [Harrisburg] [1980] 53 p. ; LC Card 80-622817 DDC 338.09748 19
HD9727.P415 P46 1980

Pennsylvania manufacturing exports /.
Pennsylvania. Dept. of Commerce. Bureau of Statistics, Research and Planning. [Harrisburg] [1978?] [71] leaves : LC Card 80-622589 DDC 382/.45/0009748 19
HF3161.P4 P45 1978

PENNSYLVANIA - MAPS.
(1977) United States. Geological Survey. State of Pennsylvania. Reston, Va., 1977. col. map 62 x 104 cm. Scale 1:500,000; 1 in. equals approx. 8 miles. Alternate title: Pennsylvania, base map with highways and contours, shaded relief. "Lambert conformal conic projection." Relief shown by contours, spot heights, and shading. In bottom margin: 1975.
G3820 1975 .U5 NYPL [Map Div. 80-3384]

PENNSYLVANIA - MAPS - BIBLIOGRAPHY - CATALOGS.
Pennsylvania. Division of Archives and Manuscripts. Descriptive list of the map collection in the Pennsylvania State Archives . Harrisburg , 1976. 178 p. ; LC Card 77-623410
Z6027.U5 P46 1976 GA447
NYPL [Map Div. 81-152]

PENNSYLVANIA - MAPS, TOPOGRAPHIC.
United States. Geological Survey. State of
Pennsylvania. Reston, Va., 1977. col. map 62 x
104 cm. Scale 1:500,000; 1 in. equals approx. 8 miles.
Alternate title: Pennsylvania, base map with highways
and contours, shaded relief. "Lambert conformal conic
projection." Relief shown by contours, spot heights, and
shading. In bottom margin: 1975.
G3820 1975 .U5   NYPL [Map Div. 80-3384]

**Pennsylvania. Municipal Statistics and Records
Division.** A tale of 51 Pennsylvania cities /
prepared by Municipal Statistics and Records
Division, Bureau of Local Government Services,
Department of Community Affairs.
[Harrisburg] : The Division, [1975?] 16 p. ;
22-28 cm. Microfilm. Tables.
1. Local finance - Pennsylvania - Statistics. I. Title.
*NYPL [*ZT-1263]*

**Pennsylvania. Northern Tier Regional Planning
Commission. see Northern Tier Regional
Planning Commission.**

**PENNSYLVANIA - OCCUPATIONS -
STATISTICS.**
Pennsylvania. Bureau of Employment Security.
Research and Statistics Division. Occupational
staffing patterns of selected regulated industries
in Pennsylvania. [Harrisburg] , 1979. ii, 73 p. ;
LC Card 79-624037
HD5725.P4 P45 1979   NYPL [JLF 80-1646]

Pennsylvania. Office of Employment Security.
Research and Statistics Division. Occupational
staffing patterns of selected nonmanufacturing
industries in Pennsylvania . Harrisburg, Pa.
[1980] iii, 326 p. ; LC Card 80-622719 DDC
331.12/5/09748 19
HD5725.P4 P458 1980

Senier, John K. S. Annual occupational
withdrawal rates for Pennsylvania and the
major labor market areas /. Harrisburg, Pa. ,
1974. iv, 51 p. ; LC Card 80-621271 DDC
331.12/09748 19
HD5725.P4 S46

**Pennsylvania. Office of Administration. Bureau of
Management Services.** Statistical-research
bulletin. v. 1, issue 1, v. 2-4 ; [Mar. 1972?],
Mar. 1973-1974. Harrisburg, Pa. 28 cm.
Quarterly. Ceased publication with 1974?
1. Pennsylvania - Statistics - Bibliography - Periodicals.
2. Pennsylvania - Statistical services - Periodicals. I.
Title.   *NYPL [JLM 80-57]*

**Pennsylvania. Office of Basic Education. Division
of Child Nutrition.** Barr, Phyllis. School
lunch recipe book /. Harrisburg, PA (333
Market St., Harrisburg PA 17126) [1980]
c1979. 340 p. ; LC Card 80-624454 DDC
641.5/71 19
TX820 .B34 1980

**Pennsylvania. Office of Budget and
Administration.** Medical assistance cost
containment. [Harrisburg] : Commonwealth of
Pennsylvania, Office of Budget and
Administration, [1980] xi, 28 p. ; 28 cm. Cover
title. "January 1980." LC Card 80-622144 DDC
338.4/3362104252/09748 19
1. Medicaid - Pennsylvania - Costs. I. Title.
HD7102.U5 P42 1980

**Pennsylvania. Office of Employment Security.
Research and Statistics Division.**
Occupational staffing patterns of selected
nonmanufacturing industries in Pennsylvania :
survey period--second quarter 1978 / prepared
by the Research and Statistics Division of the
Pennyslvania Office of Employment Security, in
cooperation with the Bureau of Labor Statistics
and the Employment and Training
Administration of the U. S. Department of
Labor. Harrisburg, Pa. : The Division, [1980]
iii, 326 p. ; 28 cm. (Occupation employment
statistics) "Issued July 1980." Bibliography: p. 325. LC
Card 80-622719 DDC 331.12/5/09748 19
1. Labor supply - Pennsylvania - Statistics. 2.
Pennsylvania - Occupations - Statistics. I. United States.
Bureau of Labor Statistics. II. United States.
Employment and Training Administration. III. Title.
HD5725.P4 P458 1980

**PENNSYLVANIA - POLITICS AND
GOVERNMENT - 1775-1865 - SOURCES -
MICROFORM CATALOGS.**
Pennsylvania. Historical and Museum
Commission. Guide to the microfilm of the
records of Pennsylvania's revolutionary
governments, 1775-1790 (record group 27) in

the Pennsylvania State Archives, 54 rolls .
Harrisburg , 1978 [c1979] vii, 351 p. ; LC Card
79-624725
E263.P4 P37 1979   NYPL [ISC 80-2758]

**PENNSYLVANIA - POLITICS AND
GOVERNMENT - REVOLUTION, 1775-
1783 - SOURCES - MICROFORM
CATALOGS.**
Pennsylvania. Historical and Museum
Commission. Guide to the microfilm of the
records of Pennsylvania's revolutionary
governments, 1775-1790 (record group 27) in
the Pennsylvania State Archives, 54 rolls .
Harrisburg , 1978 [c1979] vii, 351 p. ; LC Card
79-624725
E263.P4 P37 1979   NYPL [ISC 80-2758]

**PENNSYLVANIA - RACE RELATIONS -
SOURCES - BIBLIOGRAPHY -
CATALOGS.**
McBride, David, 1949- The Afro-American in
Pennsylvania . Harrisburg , 1979. vii, 36 p. ;
LC Card 79-625708
Z1361.N39 M27 E185.93.P41

**Pennsylvania regulations and guidelines
concerning safety in the school science
laboratory.** Pennsylvania. Dept. of Education.
Harrisburg , 1978. [67] p. ; LC Card 80-621291
DDC 344.748/075 347.480475 19
KFP380.A1 A3 1978

**Pennsylvania. Revenue, Dept. of. see
Pennsylvania. Dept. of Revenue.**

Pennsylvania. State Conservation Commission.
United States. Soil Conservation Service.
General soil map, Armstrong County,
Pennsylvania /. [Lanham, Md.] [1980?] 1
map : LC Card 81-690078
G3823.A6J3 1974 .U5

**PENNSYLVANIA. STATE HARNESS
RACING COMMISSION.** (Old Catalog
form: Pennsylvania. Harness Racing
Commission)
Pennsylvania. General Assembly. Legislative
Budget and Finance Committee. Study of State
fees . Harrisburg, PA. , 1978. iv, 33 p. ; LC
Card 79-621202 DDC 353.97480085/8 19
KFP11.62 .B8 1978

**Pennsylvania. State University. Agriculture,
College of. see Pennsylvania. State
University. College of Agriculture.**

**Pennsylvania. State University. College of
Agriculture.** (Old Catalog form: Pennsylvania.
State University. Agriculture, College of)
United States. Soil Conservation Service.
General soil map, Armstrong County,
Pennsylvania /. [Lanham, Md.] [1980?] 1
map : LC Card 81-690078
G3823.A6J3 1974 .U5

**PENNSYLVANIA STATE UNIVERSITY.
COLLEGE OF ENGINEERING.**
Bezilla, Michael. Engineering education at Penn
State . University Park , 1981. p. cm. ISBN
0-271-00287-5 : LC Card 81-47170 DDC
620/.007/1174853 19
T171.P54 B49

**Pennsylvania. State University. Institute for
Research on Human Resources.** The
bituminous coal industry, a forecast :
manpower, government policy, technology /
Elchanan Cohn ... [et al.]. University Park, Pa :
Institute for Research on Human Resources,
Pennsylvania State University, 1975. xx, 333
p. : ill. ; 23 cm. Includes bibliographical references.
LC Card 80-622230
1. Coal trade - United States. 2. Bituminous coal -
United States. 3. Manpower policy - United States -
Mathematical models. I. Cohn, Elchanan. II. Title.
HD9546 .P44 1975   NYPL [JLE 81-186]

**PENNSYLVANIA - STATISTICAL SERVICES -
PERIODICALS.**
Pennsylvania. Office of Administration. Bureau
of Management Services. Statistical-research
bulletin. v. 1, issue 1, v. 2-4 ; [Mar. 1972?],
Mar. 1973-1974. Harrisburg, Pa.
NYPL [JLM 80-57]

**PENNSYLVANIA - STATISTICS -
BIBLIOGRAPHY - PERIODICALS.**
Pennsylvania. Office of Administration. Bureau
of Management Services. Statistical-research
bulletin. v. 1, issue 1, v. 2-4 ; [Mar. 1972?],
Mar. 1973-1974. Harrisburg, Pa.
NYPL [JLM 80-57]

**Pennsylvania. Supreme Executive Council.
Minutes.** Pennsylvania. Historical and Museum
Commission. Guide to the published archives
of Pennsylvania, covering the 138 volumes of
Colonial records and Pennsylvania archives,
series I-IX / by Henry Howard Eddy ;
finding media prepared by Martha L.
Simonetti. Harrisburg , 1976. v, 91 p. ; LC
Card 79-623725 DDC 016.9748 19
F146.C622 P46 1976

**Pennsylvania. TMI Advisory Panel on Health
Research Studies.** Health-related behavioral
impact of the Three Mile Island nuclear
incident . [Harrisburg] [1980- v. : LC Card
80-622808 DDC 363.1/79 19
BF789.D5 H42

Pennsylvania. Topographic and Geologic Survey.
Pennsylvania geology. Harrisburg. LC Card
70-15808   *NYPL [JSP 80-358]*

Progress report .
(179) Okuma, Angelo. Geology of the
carbonate rocks of Path Valley, Franklin
County, Pennsylvania /. [Harrisburg] , 1970.
1 portfolio ([1] fold. leaf : col. map) ; LC
Card 74-621157 DDC 557.48 s 557.48/44 19
QE157 .A293 no. 179 QE660

(180) Clark, John H. Geology of the
carbonate rocks in western Franklin County,
Pennsylvania /. [Harrisburg] , 1970. 1
portfolio ([1] fold. leaf : col. map) ; LC Card
74-621156 DDC 557.48 s 557.48/44 19
QE157 .A293 no. 180 QE656

Pennsylvania traffic volume map /. Pennsylvania.
Bureau of Transportation Planning Statistics.
[Harrisburg] , 1979. 1 map : LC Card 81-692949
G3821.P21 1979 .P4

**PENNSYLVANIAN EPOCH. see GEOLOGY,
STRATIGRAPHIC - PENNSYLVANIAN.**

PENOBSCOT INDIANS - PERIODICALS.
Maine. Agent Penobscot Tribe of Indians.
Report of agent of the Penobscot tribe of
Indians. Augusta. LC Card 20-18367
*NYPL [*ZAN-H399]*

PENOLOGY. see PUNISHMENT.

PENSACOLA, FLA. - HARBOR.
United States. Board of Engineers for Rivers
and Harbors. The ports of Panama City &
Pensacola, FL and Pascagoula & Gulfport, MS
/. Washington , Fort Belvoir, VA , 1979. vi,
130 p. : LC Card 80-603371 DDC 387.1/09759/95
19
HE554.A4 U53 1979

**Pensacola, Fla. Naval Education and Training
Program Development Center. see Naval
Education and Training Program
Development Center.**

Pensieri /. Leopardi, Giacomo, 1798-1837.
[Pensieri. English & Italian.] Baton Rouge ,
c1981. p. cm. ISBN 0-8071-0885-5 : LC Card
81-11745 DDC 851/.7 19
PQ4708.P6 E5 1981

**PENSION APPROPRIATION BILLS
(UNITED STATES) see PENSIONS,
MILITARY - UNITED STATES.**

**PENSION BENEFIT GUARANTY
CORPORATION.**
United States. Congress. Joint Committee on
Taxation. Description of legislation relating to
Pension Benefit Guaranty Corporation plan
termination insurance for multiemployer
pension plans . Washington , 1980. iii, 56 p. ;
LC Card 80-602420 DDC 344.73/01252 19
KF3512 .A25 1980b

United States. Congress. Senate. Committee on
Finance. Subcommittee on Private Pension
Plans and Employee Fringe Benefits. Pension
plan termination insurance for multiemployer
pension plans . Washington , 1980. iii, 315 p. ;
LC Card 80-602745 DDC 344.73/01252 19
KF26 .F565 1980

The pension game . United States. Dept. of
Justice. Task Force on Sex Discrimination.
Washington , 1979. 78 p. ; LC Card 79-602270
HD6080.2.U5 U52 1979   NYPL [Jlf 81-399]

**Pension plan termination insurance for
multiemployer pension plans .** United States.
Congress. Senate. Committee on Finance.
Subcommittee on Private Pension Plans and
Employee Fringe Benefits. Washington , 1980.

iii, 315 p. ; LC Card 80-602745 DDC
344.73/01252 19
KF26 .F565 1980

PENSION TRUSTS - UNITED STATES.
United States. Congress. House. Committee on
Ways and Means. Subcommittee on Oversight.
Review of progress on Teamsters' Central States
pension fund reform . Washington , 1980. iii,
236 p. ; LC Card 80-602733 DDC 331.25/22 19
KF27 .W345 1980b

United States. Congress. Joint Committee on
Taxation. Description of legislation relating to
Pension Benefit Guaranty Corporation plan
termination insurance for multiemployer
pension plans . Washington , 1980. iii, 56 p. ;
      LC Card 80-602420 DDC 344.73/01252 19
KF3512 .A25 1980b

United States. Congress. Senate. Committee on
Finance. Subcommittee on Private Pension
Plans and Employee Fringe Benefits. Pension
plan termination insurance for multiemployer
pension plans . Washington , 1980. iii, 315 p. ;
      LC Card 80-602745 DDC 344.73/01252 19
KF26 .F565 1980

United States. Congress. Senate. Committee on
Government Affairs. Permanent Subcommittee
on Investigations. Oversight of Labor
Department's investigation of Teamsters central
states pension fund . Washington , 1981. v, 521
p. : LC Card 81-601398 DDC 332.6/7254 19
KF26 .G674 1980f

United States. Office of Management and
Budget. Administration of the Employee
retirement income security act, ERISA .
[Washington, D.C.] [1980] xvi, 81 p. ; LC
      Card 80-601600 DDC 353.0083/5 19
KF3512 .A863

PENSION TRUSTS - UNITED STATES - INVESTMENTS.
United States. Congress. Senate. Select
Committee on Small Business. The investment
of pension funds in farmland . Washington ,
1980. iii, 350 p. : LC Card 80-603904 DDC
332.63/242 19
KF26.5 .S6 1980o

PENSIONS, MILITARY - UNITED STATES.
United States. Congress. House. Committee on
Armed Services. Subcommittee on Military
Compensation. Benefits for survivors of retired
military personnel, S. 91 . Washington , 1981
[i.e. 1981] ii, 130 p. ; LC Card 81-600805 DDC
343.73/0112 347.303112 19
KF27 .A76392 1980b

United States. Congress. House. Committee on
Armed Services. Subcommittee on Military
Compensation. Hearing on H.R. 2817, H.R.
3677, and H.R. 6270, legislation related to
benefits for former spouse of a military retiree,
before the Military Compensation
Subcommittee of the Committee on Armed
Services, House of Representatives, Ninety-sixth
Congress, second session, May 28, 1980.
Washington , 1980 [i.e. 1981] ii, 126 p. : LC
      Card 81-600974 DDC 343.73/0112 347.303112
19
KF27 .A76392 1980c

United States. Congress. House. Committee on
Post Office and Civil Service. Subcommittee on
Compensation and Employee Benefits.
Minimum benefit provision of the disability
retirement program . Washington , 1980. iii, 35
p. ; LC Card 80-602789 DDC 353.005 19
KF27 .P638 1980a

United States. Congress. House. Committee on
Post Office and Civil Service. Subcommittee on
Compensation and Employee Benefits.
Retirement appeals, military leave, and
quadrennial pay commission . Washington ,
1980. iii, 20 p. ; LC Card 80-602189 DDC
343.73/011 19
KF27 .P638 1980

United States. Congress. House. Committee on
Veterans' Affairs. Subcommittee on
Compensation, Pension, Insurance, and
Memorial Affairs. Hearings on H.R. 4367 and
H.R. 6688 . Washington , 1980. iv, 353 p. :
      LC Card 80-603310 DDC 343.73/011 19
KF27 .V43 1980b

United States. Congress. House. Committee on
Veterans' Affairs. Subcommittee on
Compensation, Pension, Insurance, and

Memorial Affairs. Review of compensation and
DIC programs . Washington , 1980. iii, 93 p. ;
      LC Card 80-603330 DDC 343.73/0112 19
KF27 .V43 1980a

United States. Veterans Administration.
Overseas beneficiaries . Washington , 1980.
xviii, 403 p. ; LC Card 80-602866 DDC
355.1/151/0973 19
UB373 .U54 1980

United States. Veterans Administration. Study
of former prisoners of war . Washington , 1980.
v, 181 p. ; LC Card 80-602576 DDC
35.1/156/0973 19
UB369 .U57 1980

United States. Veterans Administration. Office
of Planning and Program Evaluation. Study of
former prisoners of war /. Washington, D.C. ,
1980. iii, 181 p. ; LC Card 80-602667 DDC
355.1/15 19
UB369 .U57 1980a

PENSIONS - UNITED STATES.
United States. President's Commission on
Pension Policy. An interim report /. Chicago,
Ill. , 1980. 51, [13] p. : LC Card 80-132555
DDC 331.25/2/0973 19
HD7106.U5 U644 1980a

PENSIONS - UNITED STATES - PERIODICALS.
United States. Office of Labor-Management and
Welfare-Pension Reports. Characteristics of
plans on file under the Welfare and pension
plans disclosure act. [Washington]
                                    NYPL   [JLM 80-866]

The people and art of the Philippines /.
University of California, Los Angeles. Museum
of Cultural History. Los Angeles , c1981. p.
cm. LC Card 81-2328 DDC 709/.599/074013 19
N7327 .U54 1981

People at work (Concord)
New Hampshire. Dept. of Employment
Security. Economic Analysis and Reporting
Section. New Hampshire staffing patterns in
manufacturing industries . [Concord] , 1977. i,
218 p. : LC Card 79-620965 DDC
331.12/57/09742 19
HD5725.N4 N45 1977

The people book. Vermont. State Planning Office.
Montpelier, Vt. , 1978. v, 70 p. : LC Card
79-623073 DDC 312/.8/09743 19
HA673 .S72 1978

People, building neighborhoods . United States.
National Commission on Neighborhoods.
[Washington?] , Washington [1979] xi, 358 p. :
      LC Card 79-602955
HN90.C6 U66 1979

People, dwellings & neighborhoods . Tri-State
Regional Planning Commission. New York ,
1978. x, 45 p. : LC Card 79-620973
HD7304.N5 T73 1978   NYPL   [JLF 80-1583]

People power . United States. Office of Consumer
Affairs. Consumer Information Division.
[Washington] [1980] ix, 411 p. :
                                    NYPL   [JLF 80-1637]

People, resources, recreation, 1978 . New York
(State). State Council of Parks and Recreation.
[Albany] [1978] 364 p. : LC Card 80-623046
DDC 353.0085/09747 19
GV191.42.N7 N48 1978

PEOPLE'S BANKS. see BANKS AND BANKING, COOPERATIVE.

The People's Republic of China and the U. S. : a
primer on developing trade relations. Atlanta,
Ga. : Georgia World Congress Institute, [1979]
v, 118 p. ; 29 cm. (Conference series - Georgia
World Congress Institute ; no. 5) Proceedings of a
conference held Mar. 1-2, 1979, at the Georgia World
Congress Center. LC Card 80-622176 DDC
382/.0951/073 19
*1. United States - Commerce - China - Congresses. 2.
China - Commerce - United States - Congresses. 3.
United States - Foreign economic relations - China -
Congresses. 4. China - Foreign economic relations -
United States - Congresses. 5. China - Economic
conditions - 1976- - Congresses. I. Series: Georgia
World Congress Institute. Conference series - Georgia
World Congress Institute , no. 5.*
HF3128 .P46

Peoples Republic of China, 1949- see **China
(People's Republic of China, 1949-)**

PEOPLES TEMPLE.
United States. Congress. House. Committee on
Foreign Affairs. Staff Investigative Group. The
assassination of Representative Leo J. Ryan and
the Jonestown, Guyana, tragedy . Washington ,
1979. xv, 782 p. : LC Card 80-600543
E840.8.R88 U48 1979

United States. Congress. House. Committee on
Foreign Affairs. Subcommittee on International
Operations. Review of the implementation of
recommendations relating to the death of
Representative Leo J. Ryan . Washington ,
1980. iii, 78 p. ; LC Card 80-603637 DDC
364.1/524/098811 19
KF27 .F647 1980a

**Per capita payments to Indians by tribal
governments** . United States. Congress. Senate.
Select Committee on Indian Affairs.
Washington , 1980. iii, 8 p. ; LC Card 80-603107
DDC 342.73/0872 347.302872 19
KF26.5 .I4 1980k

**Percina gymnocephala, a new percid fish of the
subgenus Alvordius, from the New River in
North Carolina, Virginia, and West Virginia** /.
Beckham, Eugene C. Baton Rouge, La. , 1980.
11 p. : LC Card 80-623109 DDC 591 s 597/.58 19
QL3 .L67 no. 57 QL638.P4

PERCINA GYMNOCEPHALA - CLASSIFICATION.
Beckham, Eugene C. Percina gymnocephala, a
new percid fish of the subgenus Alvordius, from
the New River in North Carolina, Virginia, and
West Virginia /. Baton Rouge, La. , 1980. 11
p. : LC Card 80-623109 DDC 591 s 597/.58 19
QL3 .L67 no. 57 QL638.P4

Pere Marquette Lake, 1975. Michigan. Dept. of
Natural Resources. Water Quality Division.
Biological survey of Pere Marquette Lake, 1975
/. [Lansing] , 1978. 11, 24 p. : LC Card
78-622591 DDC 628.1/6836/0977461 19
QH105.M5 M54 1978

**Perennial-streamflow characteristics related to
channel geometry and sediment in the Missouri
River basin** /. Osterkamp, W. R. [Reston, Va.?]
[1981] p. cm. LC Card 81-607905 DDC
551.48/3/0978 19
GB1227.M7 O84

Perera, Lakshmi. Sri Lanka. [New York, N.Y.
(485 Lexington Ave., New York 10017)] :
United Nations Fund for Population Activities,
[1980] 30 p. ; 22 cm. (Population profiles . 13)
Cover title. "April 1980." ISBN 0-89714-011-7 (pbk.) :
      LC Card 80-138983 DDC 304.6/09549/3 19
*1. Sri Lanka - Population. I. United Nations Fund for
Population Activities. II. Series: Population profiles
(United Nations Fund for Population Activities) , 13.
III. Title.*
HB3636.8.A3 P47

Perfect in her place . Warner, Deborah Jean.
Washington, D.C. , 1981. p. cm. LC Card
81-607826 DDC 331.4/0973 19
HD6095 .W198

PERFORATED CARD SYSTEMS. see PUNCHED CARD SYSTEMS.

Performance appraisal, promise and peril /.
Gruenfeld, Elaine F. Ithaca, N.Y. , 1981. 68
p. ; ISBN 0-87546-088-7 : LC Card 81-3920
DDC 658.3/125 19
HF5549.5.R3 G66
                                    NYPL   [JLM 76-840 no. 25]

**Performance audit, Department of Game--Fish
program** . Washington (State). Legislature.
Budget Committee. Olympia , 1979. vi, 90 p. :
      LC Card 79-626054 DDC 353.97970072/32 s
353.97970082/362 19
HJ11 .W2453 no. 79-3 SH222.W2

**A performance audit of electronic repair dealer
registration in Utah** . Utah. Office of the
Legislative Auditor General. [Salt Lake City]
[1979] ii, 14, 3 leaves ; LC Card 79-626149
DDC 353.97920082/42 19
HC107.U83 C637 1979

**A performance audit of mental health programs
funded by the State of Utah.** Utah. Office of
the Legislative Auditor General. [Salt Lake
City] , 1976. 177 p. : LC Card 77-621216 DDC
353.97920084/2045 19
RA790.65.U8 U86 1976

A performance audit of the Division of Fine Arts
/. Utah. Office of the Legislative Auditor

General. [Salt Lake City] , 1980. 39, 8 p. ;   LC
Card 80-621609 DDC 353.97920085/4 19
NX24.U8 U7938 1980

**A performance audit of the Division of
Purchasing in the Department of Finance** /.
Utah. Office of the Legislative Auditor General.
[Salt Lake City] (412 State Capitol, Salt Lake
City, 84114) [1980] ii, 62, 4 p. ;   LC Card
80-623434 DDC 353.97920071/2 19
JK8488.A1 U86 1980

**A performance audit of the Motor Vehicle
Business Administration** /. Utah. Office of the
Legislative Auditor General. [Salt Lake City]
[1980] 48, 13 p. ;   LC Card 80-621605 DDC
353.97920087/834 19
HD9710.U53 U88 1980

**A performance audit of the State Department of
Insurance** /. Utah. Office of the Legislative
Auditor General. [Salt Lake City] [1980] iii, 42
p. :   LC Card 80-622523 DDC 353.97920082/55 19
HG8538.U8 U85 1980

**A performance audit of the Utah Schools for the
Deaf and Blind** /. Utah. Office of the
Legislative Auditor General. [Salt Lake City,
Utah] , 1979. iii, 41, 10 leaves ;   LC Card
79-626146 DDC 371.91/1/09792 19
HV2561.U82 U857 1979

**A performance audit of the WICHE student
exchange program** . Welsh, Wayne. [Salt Lake
City] , 1978. iii, 45 leaves ;   LC Card 78-622932
DDC 370.19/62 19
R847.6.U8 W44

**Performance audit, State Agency for Surplus
Property.** Oklahoma. State Legislative Council.
Post-Audit Section. Performance audit, State
Agency for Surplus Property, a division of the
State Board of Public Affairs /. [Oklahoma
City] [1980] 35 p. ;   LC Card 80-622935 DDC
353.97660071/3045 19
JK1669.O5 O34 1980

**PERFORMANCE AWARDS - UNITED
STATES.**
United States. Congress. House. Committee on
Post Office and Civil Service. Subcommittee on
Compensation and Employee Benefits. Incentive
and performance awards program .
Washington , 1980. iii, 138 p. ;   LC Card
81-600582 DDC 353.001/47 19
KF27 .P638 1980m

**PERFORMANCE AWARDS - UNITED
STATES - PERIODICALS.**
United States. Civil Service Commission. Office
of Incentive Systems. Progress through
achievements. 1976/77- Washington. LC Card
79-643386   **NYPL [JLM 80-1092]**

PERFORMANCE - BIBLIOGRAPHY.
United States. Defense Documentation Center.
Performance measurement /. Alexandria, Va.,
1976. 1 v. (various pagings)
NYPL [*XME-9314]

Performance measurement /. United States.
Defense Documentation Center. Alexandria,
Va., 1976. 1 v. (various pagings)
NYPL [*XME-9314]

Performance of concrete in marine environment.
International Conference on Performance of
Concrete in Marine Environment, St. Andrew's,
N. B., 1980. Detroit , c1980. vii, 627 p. :   LC
Card 80-67890
TA440 .I525 1980

**Performance of the Community Services
Administration** . United States. Congress.
House. Committee on Government Operations.
Manpower and Housing Subcommittee.
Washington , 1981. iv, 354 p. ;   LC Card
81-601643 DDC 353.0084 19
KF27 .G6678 1979g

**Performance of the Occupational Safety and
Health Administration** . United States.
Congress. House. Committee on Government
Operations. Manpower and Housing
Subcommittee. Washington , 1977. iv, 163 p. ;
LC Card 80-603631 DDC 353.008/3/0289 19
KF27 .G6678 1977f

PERFORMANCE RATING (OF EMPLOYEES)
see **EMPLOYEES, RATING OF.**

**A performance review of the Alaska State Board
of Parole, May 9, 1979.** Alaska. Division of
Legislative Audit. Juneau, Alaska [1979] 27

p. ;   LC Card 79-625953   DDC 353.97980084/93 19
HV9305.A3 A53 1979

**A performance review of the Division of
Occupational Safety and Health, Department
of Labor.** Alaska. Division of Legislative Audit.
[Juneau] , 1979. 45 p., p. 46a-tt, p. 47a-d : LC
Card 80-622122 DDC 353.97980078 19
HD7262.5.U62 A52 1979

**A performance review of the Office of the
Governor, Alaska State Commission for Human
Rights.** Alaska. Division of Legislative Audit.
Juneau, Alaska [1979] 23, [10] p. ;   LC Card
80-622205 DDC 353.97980081/1 19
JC599.U52 A34 1979

**A performance review of the Office of the
Governor, Division of Policy Development and
Planning.** Alaska. Division of Legislative Audit.
Juneau, Alaska [1979?] 20 leaves, leaves a-n ;
LC Card 80-622202 DDC 353.979807/2 19
HC107.A45 A4584 1979

**PERFORMING ARTS - PUBLIC
RELATIONS. see PUBLIC RELATIONS -
PERFORMING ARTS.**

**PERFORMING ARTS - UNITED STATES -
PERIODICALS.**
The Cultural post. no. [1]- ; Mar. 1975-
[Washington]   **NYPL [*ZAN-5360]**

**PERIDOTITE - ALASKA - SORENSON,
MOUNT, REGION.**
Geology of an alpine-type peridotite in the
Mount Sorenson area, east central Alaska .
Washington , 1981. p. cm. LC Card 81-607942
DDC 552/.3 19
QE462.P45 G46

**PERIDOTITE - MICHIGAN, UPPER
PENINSULA.**
The Yellow Dog peridotite and a possible
buried igneous complex of lower Keweenawan
age in the northern peninsula of Michigan /.
Lansing, Mich. , 1979. v, 31 p. :   LC Card
80-622270 DDC 557.74 s 552/.3 19
QE125 .A417 no. 24 QE462.P45

Perinatal casualty report, Kansas, 1975-1976 /.
Kansas. Bureau of Registration and Health
Statistics. [Topeka, Kan.] [1979] vi, 92 p. :
LC Card 80-621775 DDC 362.1/9832 19
RG632.U62 K34

Perinatal mortality and prematurity in Missouri
/. Schramm, Wayne F. Jefferson City [1979]
ix, 68 p. :   LC Card 80-621734 DDC 362.1/9832
19
RG632.U62 M57

**PERINATAL MORTALITY - KANSAS -
STATISTICS.**
Kansas. Bureau of Registration and Health
Statistics. Perinatal casualty report, Kansas,
1975-1976 /. [Topeka, Kan.] [1979] vi, 92 p. :
LC Card 80-621775 DDC 362.1/9832 19
RG632.U62 K34

**PERINATAL MORTALITY - MISSOURI -
STATISTICS.**
Schramm, Wayne F. Perinatal mortality and
prematurity in Missouri /. Jefferson City
[1979] ix, 68 p. :   LC Card 80-621734 DDC
362.1/9832 19
RG632.U62 M57

PERINATAL MORTALITY - TEXAS.
Texas Infant Mortality Task Force. Texas
Infant Mortality Task Force report /.
Washington , 1980. iv, 77 p. :   LC Card
80-602575 DDC 362.1/9832/009764141 19
RJ60.U52 T497

**PERINATAL MORTALITY - TEXAS -
HARRIS CO.**
Texas Infant Mortality Task Force. Texas
Infant Mortality Task Force report /.
Washington , 1980. iv, 77 p. :   LC Card
80-602575 DDC 362.1/9832/009764141 19
RJ60.U52 T497

**Periodic reports of agricultural economics and
statistics.** Washington, U. S. Dept. of
Agriculture. 26 cm. Title varies slightly.
*1. United States. Dept. of Agriculture - Bibliography. I.
United States. Dept. of Agriculture.*
NYPL [JLM 80-812]

Periodicals bank holdings list, 1980 /. Iowa.
State Library, Des Moines. Des Moines, Iowa
[1980] 75 p. ;   LC Card 80-621804 DDC 011/.34
19
Z6945 .I685 1980 PN4832

**PERIODICALS - BIBLIOGRAPHY -
CATALOGS.**
Iowa. State Library, Des Moines. Periodicals
bank holdings list, 1980 /. Des Moines, Iowa
[1980] 75 p. ;   LC Card 80-621804 DDC 011/.34
19
Z6945 .I685 1980 PN4832

**PERIODICALS - BIBLIOGRAPHY - UNION
LISTS.**
Hawaii State Library. Serials holdings list .
[Honolulu] , 1979. vi, 184 p. ;   LC Card
79-624871 DDC 011/.34 19
Z6945 .H4 1979 PN4801

South Dakota union list of serials, including
colleges of mid-America /. Brookings, S.D. ,
1979. viii, 728 p. :   LC Card 79-626200 DDC
011/.34 19
Z6945 .S612 1979 PN4832

**PERIODICALS - UNION LISTS. see
PERIODICALS - BIBLIOGRAPHY -
UNION LISTS.**

Periods of peak demand for utility service .
Wisconsin. Public Service Commission.
Accounts and Finance Division. [Madison,
Wis.] [1979] iii, 30 p. :   LC Card 79-626145
DDC 363.6/09775 s 338.4/736362 19
HD2767.W6 A37 no. 59a HD9685.U6W6

PERMAFROST. see FROZEN GROUND.

**PERMANENT EDUCATION. see
CONTINUING EDUCATION.**

**PERMANENT MAGNETS. see MAGNETS,
PERMANENT.**

**PERMIAN FORMATION. see GEOLOGY,
STRATIGRAPHIC - PERMIAN;
PALEONTOLOGY - PERMIAN.**

Permit directory . Massachusetts. Dept. of
Environmental Quality Engineering. [Boston]
[1980] iii, 60 p. :   LC Card 80-623543 DDC
344.744/046 19
KFM2754 .A836

Permits handbook for coal development /.
Wayman, Cooper H. Golden, CO , c1981. xxiii,
616 p. :   ISBN 0-918062-40-3 :   LC Card 80-22500
DDC 353.0082/327 19
KF1830 .W39

Peroff, Kathleen A. Gautreaux housing
demonstration : an evaluation of its impact on
participating households / U. S. Department of
Housing and Urban Development, Office of
Policy Development & Research, Division of
Policy Studies ; Kathleen A. Peroff, Cloteal L.
Davis, Ronald Jones, in collaboration with
Richard T. Curtin ... [et al.]. Washington, D.C. :
The Office : for sale by the Supt. of Docs., U.
S. Govt. Print. Off., [1979] x, 202 p. : ill. ; 28
cm. "December 1979." Includes bibliographical
references. LC Card 80-602934 DDC 363.5/1 19
*1. Public housing - Illinois - Chicago metropolitan area.
2. Discrimination in housing - Illinois - Chicago
metropolitan area. 3. Gautreaux, Dorothy. I. Davis,
Cloteal L., joint author. II. Jones, Ronald, 1945- joint
author. III. United States. Dept. of Housing and Urban
Development. Office of Policy Development and
Research. Division of Policy Studies. IV. Title.*
HD7288.78.U52 C46

PEROMYSCUS MANICULATUS.
Radwan, M. A., 1926- Impregnating and
coating with endrin to protect Douglas-fir seed
from rodents /. Portland, Or., 1970. 17 p. :   LC
Card 77-608734 DDC 634.9/0979 s
634.9/75466 19
SD11 .A45614 no. 94 SB608.D6

Perrin, William Henry, d. 1892?.
History of Alexander, Union, and Pulaski
counties, Illinois. Public Library, Winnetka,
Ill. Genealogy Projects Committee. An index
to the names of persons appearing in History
of Alexander, Union and Pulaski counties,
Illinois. (Edited by William Henry Perrin.
Chicago ... 1883) Thomson, Ill. [1973] 129 p.;
LC Card 75-116464   **NYPL [IVF
(Alexander) (Perrin, W. H. History of
Alexander, Union ... counties, Ill. Index)]**

Perry, George Sylva, 1954- Our Massachusetts
State government . [Boston] , c1978. 158 p. ;
LC Card 80-620701 DDC 320.9744 19
JK3119 .O95

Perry, Gerald K. Official State multiple list for
elementary schools, K-8 : group III, social
studies, art, and music, optional subjects,

applied music, applied art, and the humanities, July 1, 1980-June 30, 1985 / prepared by Gerald K. Perry. Charleston, W.Va. : Division of Instructional Learning Systems, Bureau of Learning Systems, West Virginia Dept. of Education, [1980] iv, 42, 10 p. ; 28 cm. LC Card 80-621060   DDC 016.3791/56/09754 19
1. Textbooks - West Virginia - Bibliography. I. West Virginia. Division of Instructional Learning Systems. II. Title.
Z5817 .P47 LB3047.5.W4

Perry, William, 1954- Maine. Bureau of Health Planning and Development. Distribution of primary care physicians in Maine, July 1, 1979 /. [Augusta, Me.] [1979] 67 p. ; LC Card 80-621729   DDC 331.11/1 19
RA410.8.M2 M34 1979a

Persia. see Iran.

PERSIAN GULF - CLIMATE - CHARTS, DIAGRAMS, ETC.
United States. Naval Oceanography Command Detachment, Asheville, N.C. Climatic study of the Persian Gulf and Gulf of Oman . [Washington] [1980] viii, 125 p. : LC Card 80-602634   DDC 551.69165/35 19
QC994.5 .U53 1980

PERSIAN GULF REGION - STRATEGIC ASPECTS.
United States. Congress. House. Committee on Foreign Affairs. Subcommittee on Europe and the Middle East. U. S. interests in, and policies toward, the Persian Gulf, 1980 . Washington , 1980. iv, 471 p. ; LC Card 80-603806   DDC 355/.0330536 19
KF27 .F64214 1980c

United States. Congress. Senate. Committee on Foreign Relations. U. S. security interests and policies in Southwest Asia . Washington , 1980. iii, 368 p. : LC Card 80-603283   DDC 355/.033056 19
KF26 .F6 1980p

Persistent peoples : cultural enclaves in perspective / George Pierre Castile and Gilbert Kushner, editors ; contributing authors, William Y. Adams ... [et al.]. Tucson, Ariz. : University of Arizona Press, c1981. p. cm. Bibliography: p. Includes index. ISBN 0-8165-0744-9 : LC Card 81-10476   DDC 305.8 19
1. Ethnic groups - Addresses, essays, lectures. 2. Ethnicity - Addresses, essays, lectures. I. Castile, George Pierre. II. Kushner, Gilbert. III. Adams, William Yewdale, 1927- .
GN495.4 .P45

PERSONAL AIRCRAFT. see AIRPLANES, PRIVATE.

PERSONAL AIRPLANES. see AIRPLANES, PRIVATE.

Personal assistants for handicapped federal employees . United States. Congress. House. Committee on Post Office and Civil Service. Subcommittee on Civil Service. Washington , 1980. iii, 84 p. : LC Card 80-604075   DDC 342.73/068 347.30268
KF27 .P635 1980c

Personal files in the U. S. Air Force historical collection. Albert F. Simpson Historical Research Center. [Maxwell Air Force Base, Ala.] , 1975. 29 p. ; LC Card 79-602942   DDC 016.3584/00973 19
Z6725.U5 A59 1975 UG633

PERSONAL HEALTH. see HEALTH.

PERSONAL INJURIES - UNITED STATES.
United States. Interagency Task Force on Compensation and Liability for Releases of Hazardous Substances. The superfund concept . [Washington] , 1979. 315 p. in various pagings : LC Card 79-603356   DDC 344.73/04632 19
KF1298 .A83

Personal liability of public officials, under Federal law /. Hardy, Paul T., 1953- Athens, Ga. , c1980. p. cm. ISBN 0-89854-068-2 : LC Card 80-28931   DDC 342.73/068 19
KF1306.A2 H37 1980b

PERSONAL LIBERTY. see LIBERTY.

Personal property taxation in Virginia localities. Inflation and the Virginia income tax ; Personal property taxation in Virginia localities ; Transportation taxation in Virginia. Richmond, Va. , 1979. x, 210 p. ; LC Card 80-623840   DDC

336.2/009755 19
HJ4655.V88 I64

PERSONAL RAPID TRANSIT.
United States. Congress. Office of Technology Assessment. Impact of advanced group rapid transit technology. Washington, D.C. [1980] viii, 58 p. : LC Card 80-600001
HE305 .U555 1980   **NYPL [JLF 80-1368]**

PERSONNEL ADMINISTRATION. see PERSONNEL MANAGEMENT.

Personnel bibliography series. United States. Office of Personnel Management. Library. no. 103- ; 1979- Washington.
NYPL [JLM 80-974]

PERSONNEL MANAGEMENT.
Pecorella, Patricia A. Survey-guided development. [Washington?] , 1974. 1 v. (various pagings) ;   **NYPL [JLF 81-585]**

United States. Civil Service Commission. Bureau of Intergovernmental Personnel Programs. Guidelines for qualitative evaluations of personnel operations in state and local governments. [Washington] 1974. 21 p.
NYPL [*XME-9074]

PERSONNEL MANAGEMENT - DATA PROCESSING.
Carpenter, James B. Relative validity of two item formats for obtaining length of service data from job inventories/. Brooks Air Force Base, Tex., 1973. 4 leaves.
NYPL [*XME-9684]

PERSONNEL MANAGEMENT - HANDBOOKS, MANUALS, ETC.
United States. Office of Personnel Management. Manager's handbook. [Washington, D.C.] [1979] viii, 252 p. ; LC Card 80-601755   DDC 353.1 19
HF5549 .U445 1979

Personnel management reform; progress in state and local governments. v. 1, no. 2- ; Aug. 1980- [Washington] Issued by Office of Intergovernmental Personnel Programs of the Office of Personnel Management.
I. United States. Office of Personnel Management. Office of Intergovernmental Personnel Programs.
NYPL [Econ. Div.]

PERSONNEL MANAGEMENT - STUDY AND TEACHING - UNITED STATES.
United States. Civil Service Commission. Bureau of Training. Personnel Management Training Center. Instructors' guide for workshop in employee development /. [Washington?] , 1973. 305 p. in various pagings :
NYPL [JLF 80-1341]

PERSONNEL MANAGEMENT - UNITED STATES.
United States. Congress. House. Committee on Education and Labor. Subcommittee on Labor-Management Relations. Pressures in today's workplace . Washington , 1981. vii, 62 p. ; LC Card 81-601273   DDC 658.3/00973 19
HD8072.5 .U54 1981

United States. General Accounting Office. An evaluation of the Intergovernmental personnel act of 1970 . [Washington, D.C. , 1979] v, 96 p. : LC Card 80-602660   DDC 350.1/0973 19
JK765 .U57 1979

Westin, Alan F. Computer science & technology . Washington , 1979. xxiv, 439 p. : LC Card 79-600081   DDC 602.18 s 658.3/00973 19
QC100 .U57 no. 500-50 HF5549.2.U5

PERSONNEL MANAGEMENT - UNITED STATES - BIBLIOGRAPHY - PERIODICALS.
United States. Office of Personnel Management. Library. Personnel bibliography series. no. 103- ; 1979- Washington.
NYPL [JLM 80-974]

Personnel pamphlet series .
(no. 1) Loevi, F. J. (Francis J.) Day-to-day labor-management relations under E.O. 11491 /. [Washington, D.C.] , 1975. viii, 43 p. ; LC Card 81-469428   DDC 658.3/155 19
HD6972.5 .L63 1975

Personnel procedure . Hawaii. Dept. of Education. Personnel Management, Certification, and Development Branch. [Honolulu, Hawaii] [1979] 17, [11] p. : LC

Card 80-621552   DDC 344.969/078 19
KFH395.95 .A83

PERSONNEL RECORDS IN EDUCATION - LAW AND LEGISLATION - IDAHO.
Guidelines for the management of student records . Boise, Idaho , 1980. vii, 27 p. : LC Card 80-624210   DDC 344.796/079 347.960479 19
KFI392.5 .G83 1980

PERSONNEL RECORDS - UNITED STATES - DATA PROCESSING.
Westin, Alan F. Computer science & technology . Washington , 1979. xxiv, 439 p. : LC Card 79-600081   DDC 602.18 s 658.3/00973 19
QC100 .U57 no. 500-50 HF5549.2.U5

Personnel series, handbook P. United States Postal Service. 40- ; Oct. 1980- [Washington]
NYPL [Econ. Div.]

PERSONNEL SERVICE IN EDUCATION - CALIFORNIA.
California. Statewide Task Force on School Counseling. Report of Statewide Task Force on School Counseling /. [Sacramento] [1979] iii, 41 p. ; LC Card 80-621961   DDC 371.4/09794 19
LB1027.5 .C347 1979

Persons who may object to unlawful searches seizures . Cannaday, Kenneth S. Chapel Hill, N.C. (P.O. Box 990, Chapel Hill 27514) [1981], c1978. 10 p. ; LC Card 81-621675   DDC 347.756 s 345.73/0552 347.5607 s 347.5605552 19
KFN7908.A15 U6 no. 81/01 KF9662

Perspectives for communities and organizations on plant closings and job dislocations /. Root, Kenneth. Ames, Iowa [1979] iv, 32 leaves ; LC Card 80-623164   DDC 338.6/042 19
HD5708.55.U6 R66

Perspectives on medicaid and medicare management. Sept. 1979- Baltimore, Medicaid/Medicare, Management Institute, Improvements Promotion Division. (United States. Health Care Financing Administration. HCFA [publication]) Supersedes Journal for medicaid management.   LC Card 80-648067
I. Medicaid/Medicare Management Institute. Improvements Promotion Division.
NYPL [Econ. Div.]

Perspectives on NATO's southern flank : Senate delegation report, April 3-13, 1980 : a report to the Committee on Foreign Relations, United States Senate. Washington : U. S. Govt. Print. Off., 1980. v, 46 p. ; 24 cm. "June 1980." At head of title: 96th Congress, 2d session. Committee print.   LC Card 80-603559   DDC 355/.0330182/2 19
1. Mediterranean region - Strategic aspects. 2. Indian Ocean - Strategic aspects. I. United States. Congress. Senate. Committee on Foreign Relations. II. Title: Senate delegation report.
UA646.55 .P47

Perspectives; the civil rights quarterly. v. 12, no. 1- ; spring 1980- Washingotn. For earlier file, whose numbering it continues, see Civil rights digest. Issued by the U. S. Commission on Civil Rights.
I. United States. Commission on Civil Rights.
NYPL [Econ. Div.]

Perth Amboy /. Herbert H. Smith Associates. [West Trenton, N. J., 1963) 2 v. :
NYPL [JLF 80-1151]

PERTH AMBOY, N. J. CITY PLANNING.
Herbert H. Smith Associates. Perth Amboy /. [West Trenton, N. J., 1963) 2 v. :
NYPL [JLF 80-1151]

Perth Amboy, N. J. City Planning Board. Herbert H. Smith Associates. Perth Amboy /. [West Trenton, N. J., 1963) 2 v. :
NYPL [JLF 80-1151]

Perth Amboy, N. J. Planning Board. see Perth Amboy, N. J. City Planning Board.

PERU.
Peru, a country study /. Washington, D.C. , 1981, c1980. p. cm. LC Card 81-3456   DDC 985/.063 19
F3408 .P4647 1981

Peru, a country study / Foreign Area Studies, the American University ; edited by Richard F. Nyrop. 3rd ed. Washington, D.C. : American University, Foreign Area Studies : For sale by the Supt. of Docs., U. S.G.P.O, 1981, c1980. p. cm. (Area handbook series) Revision of: Area

handbook for Peru. 1972. "Research completed 1979." "DA Pam 550.42"--Verso t.p. Bibliography: p. Includes index.   LC Card 81-3456   DDC 985/.063 19
1. Peru. I. Nyrop, Richard F. II. American University, Washington, D. C. Foreign Area Studies. III. Area Handbook for Peru.
F3408 .P4647 1981

PERU - HISTORY - TO 1820 - ARCHIVAL RESOURCES - LATIN AMERICA.
Hanke, Lewis. Guía de las fuentes en hispanoamérica para el estudio de la administración virreinal española en México y en el Perú, 1535-1700 /. Washington, D.C. , 1980. x, 523 p. ;   ISBN 0-8270-1091-5 :   LC Card 81-115511   DDC 972 19
Z1426 .H36 F1231

Peru shelter sector assessment. United States. Agency for International Development. Office of Housing. [Washington, D.C.] , 1979. xii, 60, 15, [23] p. :   LC Card 80-602028   DDC 363.5/0985 19
HD7329.A3 U53 1979

Perzak, F. J. (Frank J.) Kubala, T. A. (Theodore A.) Electric ignition of lycopodium powder /. Avondale, MD [1981] p. cm.   LC Card 81-9944   DDC 622 s 628.9/22 19
TN23 .U43 QD516

Pesoado, Pedro. Soil survey of Richland County, Montana. [Washington, D.C.?] : U. S. Dept of Agriculture, Soil Conservation Service, C1980. iv, 71 p., 142 folded p. of plates : ill., maps (1 col.) ; 28 cm. Authors: Pedro Pesoado, Jr., and Lester C. Brockmann. "In cooperation with Montana Agricultural Experiment Station." "Issued August 1980"--p. i. Item 102-B-26 Bibliography: p. 68-69.   LC Card 80-604152   DDC 631.4/7/78623 19
1. Soils - Montana - Richland County - Maps. I. Brockmann, Lester C. II. United States. Soil Conservation Service. III. Montana Agricultural Experiment Station. IV. Title.
S599.M57 P47

Pessemier, Edgar A., 1922- Store image and positioning / by Edgar A. Pessemier. West Lafayette, Ind. : Institute for Research in the Behavioral, Economic, and Management Sciences, Krannert Graduate School of Management, Purdue University, [1979] 16, [2], 7 p. (p. [1]-7, 3d group, advertisements) : ill. ; 28 cm. (Paper - Institute for Research in the Behavioral, Economic, and Management Sciences, Krannert Graduate School of Management : no. 709) "October 1979." Bibliography: p. [17]-[18]   LC Card 80-621467   DDC 658/.001/9 s 658.8/374 19
1. Consumers' preferences. 2. Consumers. 3. Motivation research (Marketing). 4. Positioning (Advertising). I. Series: Krannert Graduate School of Management. Institute for Research in the Behavioral, Economic, and Management Sciences. Paper - Institute for Research in the Behavioral, Economic, and Management Sciences, Krannert Graduate School of Management , no. 709. II. Title.
HD6483 .P8 no. 709 HF5415.3

PEST CONTROL, INTEGRATED.
Sill, Webster H., 1916- Plant protection . Ames, Iowa [1981] p. cm.   ISBN 0-8138-1665-3   LC Card 81-12323   DDC 632 19
SB950 .S54

PEST CONTROL - LAW AND LEGISLATION - LOUISIANA.
Louisiana. Laws, statutes, etc. Louisiana, Structural pest control law ; Rules and regulations. Baton Rouge, La. [1980?] 25 p. ;   LC Card 80-623022   DDC 344.763/046 19
KFL282.I5 A3 1980

PEST CONTROL - OREGON - WILLAMETTE VALLEY.
Conklin, Frank S. An evaluation of expected private losses from selected public policies for reducing open field burning, Willamette Valley, Oregon /. Corvallis [1979] 78 p. ;   LC Card 80-620510   DDC 363.7/392 19
TD884 .C74

PESTICIDES - CALIFORNIA.
California. State Water Resources Control Board. Significance of pesticides from irrigated agriculture in California /. [Sacramento, CA] , 1977, 1979 printing. vi, 152, [98] leaves of plates :   LC Card 80-621350   DDC 628.1/68/09794 s 632/.95/09794 19
TD224.C3 A47 no. 62 SB950.2.C2

PESTICIDES - ENVIRONMENTAL ASPECTS - CALIFORNIA.

California. State Water Resources Control Board. Significance of pesticides from irrigated agriculture in California /. [Sacramento, CA] , 1977, 1979 printing. vi, 152, [98] leaves of plates :   LC Card 80-621350   DDC 628.1/68/09794 s 632/.95/09794 19
TD224.C3 A47 no. 62 SB950.2.C2

PESTICIDES - ILLINOIS.
Enviromental Health Resource Center. A report on pesticide use and regulatory programs in Illinois /. Chicago, IL [1979] x, 169 p. :   LC Card 80-621689   DDC 363.1/79 19
SB970.4.U5 E57 1979

PESTICIDES - ILLINOIS - STATISTICS.
Conley, Dennis M. Fertilizer and pesticide use by Illinois agriculture /. Urbana, Ill. [1979] 35 p. :   LC Card 80-623956   DDC 338.1/62 19
S633.3.I3 C66

PESTICIDES - LAW AND LEGISLATION - CALIFORNIA.
California. Structural Pest Control Act, with Rules and regulations . Sacramento, Calif. , 1980. 60 p. ;   LC Card 81-621018   DDC 344.794/04633 347.94044633 19
KFC641.5.P63 A3 1980

California. State Water Resources Control Board. Significance of pesticides from irrigated agriculture in California /. [Sacramento, CA] , 1977, 1979 printing. vi, 152, [98] leaves of plates :   LC Card 80-621350   DDC 628.1/68/09794 s 632/.95/09794 19
TD224.C3 A47 no. 62 SB950.2.C2

PESTICIDES - LAW AND LEGISLATION - FLORIDA.
Florida. Legislature. Senate. Committee on Agriculture. A review of the Pesticide Technical Council in the Department of Agriculture and Consumer Services /. [Tallahassee] [1980] i, 21, [7] p. ;   LC Card 81-621222   DDC 344.759/04633 347.59044633 19
KFF380.P4 A25 1980

PESTICIDES - LAW AND LEGISLATION - ILLINOIS.
Enviromental Health Resource Center. A report on pesticide use and regulatory programs in Illinois /. Chicago, IL [1979] x, 169 p. :   LC Card 80-621689   DDC 363.1/79 19
SB970.4.U5 E57 1979

PESTICIDES - LAW AND LEGISLATION - OREGON.
Oregon. Dept. of Forestry. The Oregon forest practices act . [Salem] , 1978. ii, 22 p. :   LC Card 80-622824   DDC 346.79504/675 19
KFO2649 .A836

PESTICIDES - LAW AND LEGISLATION - UNITED STATES.
United States. Congress. House. Committee on Agriculture. Subcommittee on Department Investigations, Oversight, and Research. Extension of Federal insecticide, fungicide, and rodenticide act . Washington , 1980. iii, 209 p. ;   LC Card 80-603325   DDC 344.73/04633 19
KF27 .A33265 1980a

PESTICIDES - NEBRASKA - STATISTICS.
Johnson, Bruce B. Agricultural crop pesticide usage in Nebraska, 1978 /. [Lincoln] [1979] iv, 30, [11] p. :   LC Card 80-621253   DDC 632/.95/09782 19
SB950.2.N4 J63

PESTICIDES POLICY - ILLINOIS.
Enviromental Health Resource Center. A report on pesticide use and regulatory programs in Illinois /. Chicago, IL [1979] x, 169 p. :   LC Card 80-621689   DDC 363.1/79 19
SB970.4.U5 E57 1979

PESTICIDES - TOXICOLOGY - UNITED STATES.
United States. Congress. House. Committee on Education and Labor. Subcommittee on Labor Standards. Oversight hearing on the child labor provisions of the Fair labor standards act . Washington , 1980. iv, 196 p. :   LC Card 80-603516   DDC 353.0083/82 19
KF27 .E348 1980b

United States. Congress. House. Committee on Interstate and Foreign Commerce. Subcommittee on Oversight and Investigations. Involuntary exposure to agent orange and other toxic spraying . Washington , 1980. iv, 256 p. :   LC Card 80-602744   DDC 363.1/79 19
KF27 .I5547 1979r

PESTICIDES - UNITED STATES.
Savage, Eldon P. National household pesticide usage study, 1976-1977 . Washington, D.C. [1979] cover 1980. ix, 126 p. :   LC Card 80-603384   DDC 363.7/384 19
TX325 .S28

PESTS - CONTROL. see PEST CONTROL.

PESTS - EXTERMINATION. see PEST CONTROL.

Peter W. Rodino Institute of Criminal Justice. Juvenile justice reform. Jersey City, N.J. (2039 Kennedy Blvd., Jersey City 07305) , 1980. 60 p. ;   LC Card 81-112897   DDC 345.73/08 347.3058 19
KF9779.A2 J88

Peters, Susan D. The Photographer's hand /. Washington, D.C. , c1980. p. cm.   LC Card 80-27845   DDC 779/.09/047074013 19
TR646.U5 P45

Petersilia, Joan.
Criminal careers of habitual felons / by Joan Petersilia, Peter W. Greenwood, Marvin Lavin. [Washington] : National Institute of Law Enforcement and Criminal Justice, Law Enforcement Assistance Administration : for sale by the Supt. of Docs., U. S. Govt. Print. Off., 1978. xxvi, 161 p. : forms ; 27 cm. Includes bibliographical references.   LC Card 79-602505   DDC 364.3/09794 19
1. Recidivists - California. 2. Crime and criminals - California. 3. Criminal justice, Administration of - California. I. Greenwood, Peter W., joint author. II. Lavin, Marvin, joint author. III. Title.
HV6793.C2 P47 1978

The prison experience of career criminals / by Joan Petersilia, Paul Honig ; with the assistance of Charles Hubay, Jr. Washington, D.C. : U. S. Dept. of Justice, National Institute of Justice : For sale by the Supt. of Docs., U. S. G.P.O., 1980. xviii, 87 p. : charts ; 28 cm. "November 1980. "Grant number 77-NI-99-0072, awarded to the Rand Corporation"--T.p. verso. S/N 027-000-01071-7 Item 718-A Bibliography: p. 85-87.   LC Card 81-601009   DDC 365/.66 19
1. Recidivists - United States. 2. Rehabilitation of criminals - United States. 3. Prisoners - United States. I. Honig, Paul, 1953-. II. Hubay, Charles, 1947-. III. Rand Corporation. IV. National Institute of Justice (U. S.). V. Title.
HV9304 .P44

Peterson, Arthur R.
Fish and wildlife survey of the St. Louis River / by Arthur R. Peterson. [St. Paul] : Minnesota Dept. of Natural Resources, Division of Fish and Wildlife, Ecological Services Section, [1979] vii, 103 p., [25] leaves of plates : ill. ; 28 cm. (Special publication - Division of Fish and Wildlife, Ecological Services Section ; no. 127) "May 1979." Bibliography: p. 103.   LC Card 80-621233   DDC 574.5/26323/09776 19
1. Stream ecology - Minnesota - St. Louis River. 2. Fishes - Minnesota - St. Louis River. I. Series: Minnesota. Division of Fish and Wildlife. Ecological Services Section. Special publication - Division of Fish and Wildlife, Ecological Services Section , no. 127. II. Title.
QH105.M55 P48

Kucera, Thomas. River survey report of North Fork Crow River and Crow River /. [St. Paul] , 1977. 79 p. :   LC Card 78-620652   DDC 597.092/9776/5 19
QL628.M6 K83

Peterson, Charles Henry. The ecology of intertidal flats of North Carolina : a community profile / by Charles H. Peterson, Nancy M. Peterson ; project officers, Carroll L. Cordes, Martha W. Young ; prepared for National Coastal Ecosystems Team, U. S. Fish and Wildlife Service. Slidell, LA : The Service, 1979 [i.e. 1980] vi, 73 p. : ill. ; 28 cm. Cover title: Biological services program. "FWS/OBS-79/39." Bibliography: p. 65-73.   LC Card 80-601522   DDC 574.5/2636 19
1. Tidal flat ecology - North Carolina. I. Peterson, Nancy M., joint author. II. Cordes, Carroll L. III. Young, Martha W. IV. National Coastal Ecosystems Team. V. Title. VI. Title: Biological services program.
QH105.N8 P45

Peterson, Frank L. (joint author) Petty, Susan. Hawaiian waste injection practices and problems /. Honolulu, Hawaii [1979] viii, 104 p. :   LC Card 80-621493   DDC 553.7/09969 s

627/.56 19
TC1 .H36 no. 123 TD760

Peterson, Gary R., 1948- Cobalt
availability--domestic : a minerals availability
system appraisal / by Gary R. Peterson, Donald
I. Bleiwas, and Paul R. Thomas. Washington,
D.C. : U. S. Dept. of the Interior, Bureau of
Mines, 1981. p. cm. (Information circular)
Bibliography: p.   LC Card 81-607981   DDC 622 s
553.4/8
1. Cobalt industry - United States. I. Bleiwas, Donald I.
II. Thomas, Paul R. III. Series: Information circular
(United States. Bureau of Mines) ,. IV. Title.
TN295 .U4 HD9539.C463U5

Peterson, Gloria, 1934- (joint author) O'Donnell,
Patrick J. Nebraska unicameral, Eighty-sixth
Legislature, second session . [Lincoln, Neb.]
[1980] 71 p. ;   LC Card 80-623519   DDC
348.782/01 347.82081 19
KFN10 .O36

Peterson, John, Ph.D. Massachusetts. Dept. of
Elder Affairs. A conceptual framework for
planning and the development of services for
the aging population of Massachusetts. Boston
[1978] 95 leaves ;   LC Card 80-623700   DDC
362.6/09744 19
HQ1064.U6 M44 1978

Peterson, Kent A. Tweeton, Daryl R. Selection of
lixiviants for in situ uranium leaching /.
Avondale, MD [1981] p. cm.   LC Card 81-6103
DDC 622 s 622/.34932 19
TN295 .U4 TN490.U7

Peterson, Nancy M. (joint author) Peterson,
Charles Henry. The ecology of intertidal flats of
North Carolina . Slidell, LA , 1979 [i.e. 1980]
vi, 73 p. :   LC Card 80-601522   DDC 574.5/2636
19
QH105.N8 P45

Peterson, Norman V. (joint author) Ramp, Lenin.
Geology and mineral resources of Josephine
County, Oregon /. Portland, Or. , 1979. iv, 45
p. :   LC Card 80-622943   DDC 553/.09795 s
557.95/25 19
QE155 .A3 no. 100 QE156.J67

Peterson, R. E. (Roy Ernest), 1926-
Beneficiation of a hematitic taconite by
reduction roasting, magnetic separation, and
flotation / by R.E. Peterson and A.F. Colombo.
Washington : U. S. Dept. of the Interior,
Bureau of Mines, [1981] p. cm. (Report of
investigations / United States Dept. of the
Interior, Bureau of Mines) Bibliography: p.   LC Card 81-3883
DDC 622 s 622/.341 19
1. Ore-dressing. 2. Taconite. I. Colombo, A. F. (Arthur
F.). II. Series: Report of investigations (United States.
Bureau of Mines). III. Title.
TN23 .U43 TN538.I7

Reduction roasting and beneficiation of a
hematitic-geothitic taconite / R. E. Peterson
and A. F. Colombo. [Washington, D.C.] : U. S.
Dept. of the Interior, Bureau of Mines, [1981]
p. cm. (Report of investigations) Bibliography: p.   LC
Card 80-606877   DDC 622 s 669/.141 19
1. Ore-dressing. 2. Iron - Metallurgy. 3. Taconite -
Minnesota - Mesaba Range. I. Colombo, A. F. (Arthur
F.). II. Series: Report of investigations (United States.
Bureau of Mines). III. Title.
TN23 .U43 TN538.I7

Peterson, Ralph. Workshop on Operational
Applications of Satellite Snowcover
Observations, Sparks, Nev., 1979. Operational
applications of satellite snowcover observations .
Washington, D.C. , 1980. iv, 301 p. :   LC Card
80-602361   DDC 551.57/846 19
GB2601.72.A83 W67 1979

Peterson, Russell D. Gulf of Mexico Coastal
Ecosystems Workshop, Port Aransas, Tex.,
1979. Proceedings of the Gulf of Mexico
Coastal Ecosystems Workshop /. [Washington]
[1980] vi, 214 p. :   LC Card 80-603154   DDC
333.91/7/0916364 19
QH105.T4 G84 1979

Peterson, William H. Economic education .
Knoxville , c1982. p. cm.   ISBN 0-87049-333-7 :
LC Card 81-11449   DDC 330/.07/073 19
HB74.8 .E25

Petges, Richard. Pakistan's cotton industry / [by
Richard Petges]. [Washington, D.C.] : United
States Dept. of Agriculture, Foreign
Agricultural Service [1980] 20 p. : map ; 28 cm.
(FAS-M ; 296) Cover title.   LC Card 80-602637

DDC 338.1 s 338.1/7351/095491 19
1. Cotton growing - Pakistan. 2. Cotton manufacture -
Pakistan. 3. Cotton trade - Pakistan. I. Series: United
States. Foreign Agricultural Service (1953-) FAS-M ,
296. II. Title.
S21 .Z2383 no. 296 HD9086.P3

Pethia, Robert F. The case for a multivariate
treatment of situational diversity, complexity,
change, and relatedness in studies of
organizational design / Robert F. Pethia.
Austin, Tex. : Graduate School of Business,
University of Texas at Austin ; distributed by
Bureau of Business Research, University of
Texas at Austin, [1980] 19 p. : ill. ; 28 cm.
(Working paper / Graduate School of Business, the
University of Texas at Austin . 80-15) "July 1980."
Bibliography: p. 19.   LC Card 80-623771   DDC
302.3/5 19
1. Organizational change - Research. I. Series: Texas.
University at Austin. Graduate School of Business.
Working paper - Graduate School of Business,
University of Texas at Austin , 80-15. II. Title.
HM131 .P393

Petner, Joseph N. (joint author) Churchill, Edith
H. E. Children's language and thinking . Grand
Forks, N.D. , 1977. 60 p. :   LC Card 77-72096
DDC 370.15/2 19
LB1117 .C54

Petrick, Barbara, 1935- Mary Philbrook : the
radical feminist in New Jersey / Barbara
Petrick. Trenton, N.J. : New Jersey Historical
Commission, [1981] p. cm. (New Jersey portraits ;
4) Bibliography: p.   ISBN 0-89743-052-2   LC Card
81-11285   DDC 305.4/2/0924 B 19
1. Philbrook, Mary. 2. Feminists - New Jersey -
Biography. I. New Jersey Historical Commission. II.
Title. III. Series.
HQ1413.P49 P47

Petro, Peter G. Symposium . Washington , 1977.
ix, 141 p. ;   LC Card 77-601861
HD5875 .S95   **NYPL [*XME-9409]**

PETROCHEMICALS. see PETROLEUM
PRODUCTS.

Petroglyphs and pictographs of Utah /.
Castleton, Kenneth Bitner, 1903- Salt Lake
City , 1978-1979. 2 v. :   LC Card 78-53941
DDC 709/.01/1309792 19
E78.U55 C37

PETROGLYPHS - UTAH.
Castleton, Kenneth Bitner, 1903- Petroglyphs
and pictographs of Utah /. Salt Lake City ,
1978-1979. 2 v. :   LC Card 78-53941   DDC
709/.01/1309792 19
E78.U55 C37

Petrography and stratigraphy of the Carolina
Slate Belt, Union County, North Carolina /.
Randazzo, Anthony F. Raleigh , 1972. iii
leaves, 38 p., [1] fold leaf of plates :   LC Card
80-623227   DDC 553/.09756 s 552.09756/755
19
QE147 .A32 no. 4 QE445.N8

PETROLEUM.
(1980) Safer, Arnold E. A strategy of oil
proliferation . Washington , 1980. vii, 20 p. ;
LC Card 80-603267   DDC 333.8/23215 19
TN870 .S22

PETROLEUM AS FUEL.
Barton-Aschman Associates. Petroleum shortage
response program for the State of Illinois .
Springfield, Ill. [1979] viii, 73 p. ;   LC Card
80-622395   DDC 333.8/23217/09773 19
TP355 .B33 1979

United States. Congress. Senate. Committee on
Energy and Natural Resources. Subcommittee
on Energy Regulation. October report on the
current fuel situation from the Energy
Information Administration . Washington ,
1980. iii, 217 p. :   LC Card 80-602534   DDC
338.4/766553827/0973 19
KF26 .E5535 1979m

PETROLEUM AS FUEL - ECONOMIC
ASPECTS - ILLINOIS.
Illinois Institute of Natural Resources. Heating
oil status report. Springfield, Ill. [1979] 6, [6]
p. :   LC Card 80-623374   DDC 338.4/76655384 19
HD9567.I3 I36 1979

PETROLEUM AS FUEL - PRICES -
NORTHEASTERN STATES.
United States. Congress. House. Committee on
Ways and Means. Subcommittee on Public

Assistance and Unemployment Compensation.
Fuel assistance legislation . Washington , 1980.
iv, 102 p. ;   LC Card 80-601970   DDC
344.73/032583 19
KF27 .W3464 1979g

PETROLEUM AS FUEL - PRICES - UNITED
STATES.
United States. Congress. House. Committee on
Government Operations. Environment, Energy,
and Natural Resources Subcommittee. Home
heating oil price and supply issues, the
Department of Energy's record . Washington ,
1980. iii, 216 p. ;   LC Card 80-603000   DDC
338.4/36655384 19
KF27 .G655 1980

PETROLEUM - BIODEGRADATION.
Pal, Dhiraj. Assessment of land treatment
technology for petroleum refinery solid wastes
/. [Raleigh, N.C.] [1980] vi, 30 leaves, [1] leaf
of plates :   LC Card 80-623569   DDC
333.91/009756 s 628.5/46 19
HD1694.N8 N6 no. 141 TD899.P4

PETROLEUM - BIODETERIORATION. see
PETROLEUM - BIODEGRADATION.

PETROLEUM - CALIFORNIA.
Hallmark, Fred O. Unconventional petroleum
resources in California /. Sacramento , 1980. iv,
17 p. :   LC Card 80-621718   DDC 553.2/82 19
TN872.C2 H28

PETROLEUM CONSERVATION - UNITED
STATES.
United States. Congress. Senate. Committee on
Finance. Subcommittee on Taxation and Debt
Management Generally. Special oil taxes .
Washington , 1980 [i.e. 1981] iii, 222 p. :   LC
Card 81-601139   DDC 336.2/783338232/0973
19
KF26 .F5695 1980j

PETROLEUM - GEOLOGY - ALASKA -
ALASKA PENINSULA.
Alaska. Division of Geological and Geophysical
Surveys. Tertiary formations and associated
Mesozoic rocks in the Alaska Peninsula area,
Alaska, and their petroleum-reservoir and
source-rock potential /. Anchorage, Alaska ,
1979. iv, 65 p. :   LC Card 80-622183   DDC
553/.09798 s 553.2/82/0997984 19
QE83 .A25 no. 62 QE691

PETROLEUM - GEOLOGY - ATLANTIC
COAST (UNITED STATES)
Structural framework, stratigraphy, and
petroleum geology of the area of oil and gas
lease Sale no. 49 on the U. S. Atlantic
Continental Shelf and slope /. Arlington, Va. ,
1980. v, 101 p. :   LC Card 80-600090   DDC 557.3
s 553.2/82/0974 19
QE75 .C5 no. 812 QE78.3

PETROLEUM - GEOLOGY - NEW MEXICO -
EDDY CO.
Foster, Roy W. Geology of Loco Hills sand,
Loco Hills field, Eddy County, New Mexico /.
Socorro [1976] 177 p. :   LC Card 80-623789
DDC 557.89/42 19
QE144.E3 F67

PETROLEUM - GEOLOGY - TEXAS - TEXAS
PANHANDLE.
Handford, C. Robertson. Lower Permian facies
of the Palo Duro Basin, Texas . [Austin] , 1980.
iv, 31 p. :   LC Card 80-623707   DDC 553/.09764 s
551.7/5609764/8 19
QE167 .T42 no. 102 QE674

The petroleum import fee, Department of Energy
Oversight . United States. Congress. House.
Committee on Government Operations.
Environment, Energy, and Natural Resources
Subcommittee. Washington , 1980. iii, 271 p. :
LC Card 80-602747   DDC 382/.42282/0973 19
KF27 .G655 1980a

PETROLEUM IN SUBMERGED LANDS -
ALASKA.
O'Connor, Frank R. An analysis of future
petroleum development on the Alaskan Outer
Continental Shelf, Kodiak area /. [Juneau]
[1976] iii, 23, 4 leaves, [2] fold. leaves of
plates :   LC Card 80-622388   DDC
338.2/7282/097894 19
TN872.A7 O34

PETROLEUM IN SUBMERGED LANDS -
MEXICO, GULF OF - MATHEMATICAL
MODELS.
Drew, Lawrence J. Estimation of the future

rates of oil and gas discoveries in the western Gulf of Mexico /. Washington , 1981. p. cm.
LC Card 81-6768   DDC 553.2/8/09726 19
TN872.A5 D73

PETROLEUM IN SUBMERGED LANDS - MIDDLE ATLANTIC STATES.
Macpherson, George S. Outer Continental Shelf oil and gas activities in the mid-Atlantic and their onshore impacts . Reston, VA [1980] viii, 63 p. :   LC Card 80-129968   DDC 338.2/728/0974 19
TN872.A5 M32

PETROLEUM IN SUBMERGED LANDS - NEW JERSEY.
Rutgers University, New Brunswick, N.J. Center for Coastal and Environmental Studies. Onshore support bases for OCS oil and gas development . New Brunswick, N.J. [1977] xvi, 234 p. :   LC Card 80-622533   DDC 338.2/7282/09749 19
TN872.N5 R87 1977

PETROLEUM INDUSTRY AND TRADE.
Nossman, Waters, Krueger, Marsh & Riordan. Summary: an evaluation of the options of the U. S. Government in its relationship to U. S. firms in international petroleum affairs. Los Angeles, 1975. 122 p.;   *NYPL [JLF 80-599]*

Pugash, James Z. The geopolitics of oil . Washington , 1980. v. 89 p. ;   LC Card 80-604126   DDC 333.8/232 19
HD9560.5 .P76

United States. Central Intelligence Agency. Office of Economic Research. The world oil market in the years ahead . Washington , 1979. ix, 80 p. :   LC Card 79-603266
HD9565.6 .U53 1979

United States. Congress. House. Committee on Government Operations. Environment, Energy, and Natural Resources Subcommittee. Effect of Iraqi-Iranian conflict on U. S. energy policy . Washington , 1981. iii, 70 p. :   LC Card 81-600850   DDC 333.79/0973 19
KF27 .G655 1980e

United States. Congress. House. Permanent Select Committee on Intelligence. Subcommittee on Oversight. Intelligence on the world energy outlook and its policy implications . Washington , 1980. iii, 235 p. :   LC Card 80-603479   DDC 333.79 19
KF27.5 .I55 1979a

United States. Congress. Office of Technology Assessment. World petroleum availability, 1980-2000. Washington, D.C. [1980] vii, 77 p. :   LC Card 80-600164   DDC 338.2/7282 19
HD9560.5 .U62 1980

United States. Congress. Senate. Committee on Energy and Natural Resources. Geopolitics of oil . Washington , 1980. 2 v. :   LC Card 80-603788   DDC 333.8/232/0973 19
KF26 .E55 1980j

United States. Congress. Senate. Committee on Energy and Natural Resources. World petroleum outlook--1981 . Washington , 1981. iii, 152 p. :   LC Card 81-601403   DDC 333.8/232 19
KF26 .E55 1981e

United States. Congress. Senate. Committee on Energy and Natural Resources. Subcommittee on Energy Regulation. July report on the current fuel situation from the Energy Information Administration . Washington , 1980. iii, 176 p. :   LC Card 80-602079   DDC 338.4/7665538/0973 19
KF26 .E5535 1979n

PETROLEUM INDUSTRY AND TRADE - ALASKA.
Goldsmith, Scott. Historic and projected oil and gas consumption /. [Juneau?] , 1980. 55 leaves ;   LC Card 80-622464   DDC 338.2/728/09798 19
HD9567.A4 G63

United States. Office of Minerals Policy and Research Analysis. Final report of the 105(b) economic and policy analysis /. [Washington] , 1980. vii, 145 p. :   LC Card 80-601683   DDC 333.8/2315/097987 19
HD9567.A4 U565 1980

PETROLEUM INDUSTRY AND TRADE - ALASKA - STATISTICS - PERIODICALS.
Alaska. Oil and Gas Conservation Commission.

Bulletin. 1979- Anchorage.   *NYPL [JLM 80-1049]*

PETROLEUM INDUSTRY AND TRADE - ENVIRONMENTAL ASPECTS - ALASKA.
Derksen, Dirk V. Use of wetland habitats by birds in the National Petroleum Reserve--Alaska /. Washington, D.C. , 1981. p. cm.   LC Card 81-607937   DDC 639.9/784109798 19
S914 .A3 no.141 QL684A4

PETROLEUM INDUSTRY AND TRADE - ENVIRONMENTAL ASPECTS - UNITED STATES.
United States. Dept. of Energy. Motor gasoline deregulation and the gasoline tilt . [Washington] , 1979- v. ;   LC Card 79-602143
HD9579.G4 U52 1979a

PETROLEUM INDUSTRY AND TRADE - GOVERNMENT POLICY - UNITED STATES.
United States. General Accounting Office. Actions needed to increase federal onshore oil and gas exploration and development . Washington, D.C. , 1981. xi, 203 p. ;   LC Card 81-601214   DDC 353.0082/388 19
HD9566 .U543 1981

PETROLEUM INDUSTRY AND TRADE. - ILLINOIS.
Illinois. General Assembly. Legislative Investigating Commission. Self service gasoline marketing practices in Illinois . Chicago, Ill. [1980] ix, 94 p. ;   LC Card 80-622131   DDC 381/.4566553827/09773 19
HD9567.I3 I34 1980

Illinois Institute of Natural Resources. Heating oil status report. Springfield, Ill. [1979] 6, [6] p. :   LC Card 80-623374   DDC 338.4/76655384 19
HD9567.I3 I36 1979

PETROLEUM INDUSTRY AND TRADE - LAW. see PETROLEUM LAW AND LEGISLATION.

PETROLEUM INDUSTRY AND TRADE - PRICES. see PETROLEUM PRODUCTS - PRICES.

PETROLEUM INDUSTRY AND TRADE - STATISTICS.
The PIMS U. S.-OPEC petroleum report, year 1973. Washington, D.C. [1974] 26 p. :   LC Card 80-603212   DDC 382/.42282/0973 19
HD9560.4 .P48

PETROLEUM INDUSTRY AND TRADE - TEXAS.
Prindle, David F. (David Forrest), 1948- Petroleum politics and the Texas Railroad Commission /. Austin , 1981. p. cm.   ISBN 0-292-76474-X   LC Card 81-7535   DDC 353.97640087/5/06 19
HD9567.T3 P74

PETROLEUM INDUSTRY AND TRADE - UNITED STATES.
Delaney, James B. The state of competition in gasoline marketing . Washington, D.C. [Springfield, Va.] 1980- v. :   LC Card 80-602541   DDC 338.6/048 19
HD9565 .D44

Gold, Fern R. Access to oil . [Washington , 1977. xiii, 113 p. ;   LC Card 78-600524
HD9566 .G64   *NYPL [JLE 81-460]*

Library of Congress. Congressional Research Service. Petroleum industry involvement in alternative sources of energy /. Washington , 1977. 385 p., [1] folded leaf of plates :   LC Card 81-601738   DDC 333.79/0973 19
HD9565 .L48 1977

Nossman, Waters, Krueger, Marsh & Riordan. Summary: an evaluation of the options of the U. S. Government in its relationship to U. S. firms in international petroleum affairs. Los Angeles, 1975. 122 p.;   *NYPL [JLF 80-599]*

Profitability of major oil companies . College Station, Tex. , c1980. 16 p. ;   LC Card 81-621414   DDC 338.7/6223382/0973 19
HD9565 .P75

United States. Congress. House. Committee on Government Operations. Environment, Energy, and Natural Resources Subcommittee. Department of Energy's emergency energy conservation programs . Washington , 1980 [i.e. 1981] iii, 200 p. :   LC Card 81-600860   DDC 333.79/17/0973 19
KF27 .G655 1980f

United States. Congress. House. Committee on Small Business. Petroleum products . Washington , 1980. v, 99 p. :   LC Card 80-602595   DDC 338.4/766553/0973 19
KF32 .S6 1980

United States. Congress. Senate. Committee on Energy and Natural Resources. Subcommittee on Energy Regulation. Federal gasoline allocation process . Washington , 1980. iii, 207 p. :   LC Card 80-603652   DDC 353.0082/6566553827 19
KF26 .E5535 1980d

United States. Congress. Senate. Committee on the Judiciary. Subcommittee on Antitrust, Monopoly, and Business Rights. Why gasoline prices remain high . Washington , 1980 [i.e. 1981] i, 52 p. :   LC Card 81-600930   DDC 338.4/366553827/0973 19
KF26 .J835 1980c

United States. Dept. of Energy. Final report to the President on oil supply shortages during 1979. Washington, D.C. [1980] 58 p. :   LC Card 80-602863   DDC 338.2/7282/0973 19
HD9566 .U533 1980

PETROLEUM INDUSTRY AND TRADE - UNITED STATES - ENERGY CONSERVATION.
United States. General Accounting Office. How the petroleum refining industry approaches energy conservation--a case study . [Washington, D.C.] [1980] v, 60 p. ;   LC Card 80-602620   DDC 333.79 19
TP690.2.U6 U54 1980

PETROLEUM INDUSTRY AND TRADE - UNITED STATES - FINANCE.
Ryan, Paul, 1930- An analysis of petroleum company investments in non-petroleum energy sources /. Washington, D.C. [Springfield, VA , 1979] 2 v. :   LC Card 80-601258   DDC 332.6/7254 19
HD9565 .R9

Petroleum industry involvement in alternative sources of energy /. Library of Congress. Congressional Research Service. Washington , 1977. 385 p., [1] folded leaf of plates :   LC Card 81-601738   DDC 333.79/0973 19
HD9565 .L48 1977

Petroleum Industry Monitoring System (U. S.)
The PIMS U. S.-OPEC petroleum report, year 1973. Washington, D.C. [1974] 26 p. :   LC Card 80-603212   DDC 382/.42282/0973 19
HD9560.4 .P48

PETROLEUM - IRAN - PIPE LINES - MAPS.
United States. Central Intelligence Agency. Iraq-Iran central and southern border areas. [Washington , 1980] 1 map :   LC Card 81-692540
G7611.F2 1980 .U5

PETROLEUM - IRAQ - PIPE LINES - MAPS.
United States. Central Intelligence Agency. Iraq-Iran central and southern border areas. [Washington , 1980] 1 map :   LC Card 81-692540
G7611.F2 1980 .U5

PETROLEUM - JURISPRUDENCE. see PETROLEUM LAW AND LEGISLATION.

PETROLEUM - LAW. see PETROLEUM LAW AND LEGISLATION.

PETROLEUM LAW AND LEGISLATION - TEXAS.
Prindle, David F. (David Forrest), 1948- Petroleum politics and the Texas Railroad Commission /. Austin , 1981. p. cm.   ISBN 0-292-76474-X   LC Card 81-7535   DDC 353.97640087/5/06 19
HD9567.T3 P74

PETROLEUM LAW AND LEGISLATION - UNITED STATES.
United States. Congress. House. Committee on Interstate and Foreign Commerce. Subcommittee on Energy and Power. Enforcement of major refiner cases . Washington , 1981. iii, 883 p. ;   LC Card 81-601792   DDC 346.7304/68232/0262 347.30646823220262 19
KF27 .I5542 1980q

United States. Congress. House. Committee on Interstate and Foreign Commerce. Subcommittee on Energy and Power. Gasoline marketing practices . Washington , 1981. iv, 470 p. :   LC Card 81-601363   DDC

Petroleum law and legislation - United States. (cont.) **BIBLIOGRAPHIC GUIDE**

130

343.73/088566553827 347.30388566553827 19
KF27 .I5542 1980r

United States. Congress. House. Committee on Interstate and Foreign Commerce. Subcommittee on Oversight and Investigations. DOE gasoline allocation regulations and enforcement . Washington , 1980. iii, 216 p. :
LC Card 80-604027 DDC 353.0082/6566553827 19
KF27 .I5547 1980m

United States. Congress. House. Committee on Small Business. Subcommittee on Antitrust and Restraint of Trade Activities Affecting Small Business. Small Business Motor Fuel Marketer Preservation Act-H.R. 6722 . Washington , 1980. vii, 835 p. : LC Card 80-604087 DDC 343.73/078629287 347.30378629287 19
KF27 .S6335 1980b

United States. Congress. Senate. Committee on Energy and Natural Resources. Extending the antitrust exemption in the Energy Policy and Conservation Act . Washington , 1981. iii, 42 p. : LC Card 81-601762 DDC 343.73/072 347.30372 19
KF26 .E55 1981c

United States. Congress. Senate. Committee on Energy and Natural Resources. Subcommittee on Energy Regulation. Limiting oil imports . Washington , 1980. iii, 221 p. : LC Card 80-602100 DDC 343.73/0872282/0262 19
KF26 .E5535 1979l

United States. Congress. Senate. Committee on Energy and Natural Resources. Subcommittee on Energy Research and Development. Energy supply act (Title VIII) . Washington , 19. iv, 391 p. : LC Card 80-602175 DDC 346.7304/679/0262 19
KF26 .E554 1979e

United States. Congress. Senate. Committee on the Judiciary. Subcommittee on Antitrust, Monopoly, and Business Rights. Gasohol competition act of 1979, S. 2251 . Washington , 1980. iii, 201 p. : LC Card 80-603339 DDC 343.73/078662669 19
KF26 .J835 1980

United States. Congress. Senate. Committee on the Judiciary. Subcommittee on Antitrust, Monopoly, and Business Rights. International Energy Agreement, S. 1413 . Washington , 1980 [i.e. 1981] iii, 175 p. ; LC Card 81-600938 DDC 341.7/5472282/0973 19
KF26 .J835 1979o

United States. Congress. Senate. Committee on the Judiciary. Subcommittee on Antitrust, Monopoly, and Business Rights. Small Business Motor Fuel Marketer Preservation Act of 1980 . Washington , 1981. v, 491 p. : LC Card 81-601869 DDC 343.73/088566553827 347.30388566553827 19
KF26 .J835 1980d

PETROLEUM - NEAR EAST - PIPE LINES - MAPS.
United States. Central Intelligence Agency. Middle East area oilfields and facilities. [Washington , 1980] 1 map : LC Card 81-692536
G7421.H8 1980 .U5

PETROLEUM - NEW MEXICO - SOCORRO CO.
Chapin, Charles Edward, 1932- Coal, uranium, oil, and gas potential of the Riley-Puertecito area, Socorro County, New Mexico /. Socorro [1979] v, 33 p., [3] fold. leaves of plates : LC Card 79-626216 DDC 553.2/09789/62 19
TN805.N6 C47

PETROLEUM - PIPE LINES - ENVIRONMENTAL ASPECTS - MONTANA.
Thompson, Larry S. The effects of large-diameter underground crude-oil pipelines on wildlife . Helena, Mont. [1979] vii, 55 p. :
LC Card 80-622216 DDC 333.79/09786 s 333.95/9 19
TJ163.25.U6 M653 1979, no. 2 TD195.P5

PETROLEUM - PIPE LINES - ENVIRONMENTAL ASPECTS - TEXAS - GULF REGION.
Texas. Environmental Management Program. Pipelines and natural resources of the Texas coast /. [Austin, Tex.] [1980] vi, 266 p. : LC Card 80-622734 DDC 388.5 19
TD195.P5 T49 1980

Petroleum politics and the Texas Railroad Commission /. Prindle, David F. (David Forrest), 1948- Austin , 1981. p. cm. ISBN 0-292-76474-X LC Card 81-7535 DDC 353.97640087/5/06 19
HD9567.T3 P74

PETROLEUM - PRICES.
Fleisis, Heywood W. The effect of OPEC oil pricing on output, prices, and exchange rates in the United States and other industrial countries /. [Washington, D.C.] , 1981. xx, 107 p. : LC Card 81-601242 DDC 338.2/3 19
HD9560.4 .F58

PETROLEUM - PRICES - UNITED STATES.
Jelinek, Robert Vincent, 1926- Costs of synthetic fuels in relation to oil prices . Washington , 1981. xiii, 129 p. : LC Card 81-601665 DDC 338.4/366266/0973 19
HD9564 .J44

United States. Congress. House. Committee on Interstate and Foreign Commerce. Subcommittee on Oversight and Investigations. Cost to consumers of deregulation of crude oil . Washington , 1980. iii, 72 p. : LC Card 80-604045 DDC 338.2/3 19
KF27 .I5547 1980l

United States. Congress. House. Committee on Interstate and Foreign Commerce. Subcommittee on Oversight and Investigations. Stripper oil miscertification . Washington , 1980. iii, 63 p. : LC Card 80-604004 DDC 338.2/3 19
KF27 .I5547 1980j

PETROLEUM - PRICES - UNITED STATES - STATISTICS - PERIODICALS.
Monthly petroleum product price report. Washington. NYPL [JLM 80-1101]

Petroleum product price report. Monthly petroleum product price report. Washington. NYPL [JLM 80-1101]

Petroleum products . United States. Congress. House. Committee on Small Business. Washington , 1980. v, 99 p. : LC Card 80-602595 DDC 338.4/766553/0973 19
KF32 .S6 1980

PETROLEUM PRODUCTS - ILLINOIS.
Illinois Institute of Natural Resources. Illinois petroleum shortage response plan /. [Springfield] [1979] vi, 20 p. ; LC Card 80-622188 DDC 333.79/09773 19
HD9502.U53 I456 1979

PETROLEUM PRODUCTS - PRICES.
Askari, Hossein. National and international energy stabilization policies /. Austin, Tex. [1980] 14, [8] p. ; LC Card 80-622514 DDC 333.79/0973 19
HD9502.U52 A79

PETROLEUM PRODUCTS - PRICES - STATISTICS.
The PIMS U. S.-OPEC petroleum report, year 1973. Washington, D.C. [1974] 26 p. : LC Card 80-603212 DDC 382/.42282/0973 19
HD9560.4 .P48

PETROLEUM PRODUCTS - PRICES - UNITED STATES.
The Case of the billion dollar stripper . Washington , 1980. v, 29 p. : LC Card 80-603868 DDC 338.2/3 19
HD9564 .C38

Jelinek, Robert Vincent, 1926- Costs of synthetic fuels in relation to oil prices . Washington , 1981. xiii, 129 p. : LC Card 81-601665 DDC 338.4/366266/0973 19
HD9564 .J44

United States. Congress. House. Committee on Government Operations. Commerce, Consumer, and Monetary Affairs Subcommittee. Adequacy of COWPS enforcement of price standards for petroleum products . Washington , 1980. iii, 280 p. : LC Card 80-602969 DDC 353.0082/62282044 19
KF27 .G634 1980a

United States. Congress. House. Committee on Interstate and Foreign Commerce. Subcommittee on Energy and Power. Enforcement of major refiner cases . Washington , 1981. iii, 883 p. ; LC Card 81-601792 DDC 346.7304/68232/0262 347.3064682320262 19
KF27 .I5542 1980q

PETROLEUM PRODUCTS - PRICES - UNITED STATES - STATISTICS - PERIODICALS.
Monthly petroleum product price report. Washington. NYPL [JLM 80-1101]

PETROLEUM PRODUCTS - UNITED STATES.
United States. Congress. House. Committee on Small Business. Petroleum products . Washington , 1980. v, 99 p. : LC Card 80-602595 DDC 338.4/766553/0973 19
KF32 .S6 1980

United States. Congress. Senate. Committee on Energy and Natural Resources. Subcommittee on Energy Regulation. July report on the current fuel situation from the Energy Information Administration . Washington , 1980. iii, 176 p. : LC Card 80-602079 DDC 338.4/7665538/0973 19
KF26 .E5535 1979n

United States. Dept. of Energy. Final report to the President on oil supply shortages during 1979. Washington, D.C. [1980] 58 p. : LC Card 80-602863 DDC 338.2/7282/0973 19
HD9566 .U533 1980

PETROLEUM REFINERIES - ENVIRONMENTAL ASPECTS - MAINE - EASTPORT.
Neily, Rupert. Enforcement manual for the proposed Pittston Oil Refinery . Augusta, Me. [1980] ca. 650 p. in various pagings : LC Card 80-622764 DDC 353.974/0082/42 19
TD195.P4 N44

PETROLEUM REFINERIES - GOVERNMENT POLICY - UNITED STATES.
United States. Congress. House. Committee on Interstate and Foreign Commerce. Subcommittee on Energy and Power. Eomestic refinery policy--oversight . Washington , 1981. iii, 208 p. : LC Card 81-601359 DDC 338.4/766553/0973 19
KF27 .I5542 1980o

PETROLEUM REFINERIES - IRAN - MAPS.
United States. Central Intelligence Agency. Iraq-Iran central and southern border areas. [Washington , 1980] 1 map : LC Card 81-692540
G7611.F2 1980 .U5

PETROLEUM REFINERIES - IRAQ - MAPS.
United States. Central Intelligence Agency. Iraq-Iran central and southern border areas. [Washington , 1980] 1 map : LC Card 81-692540
G7611.F2 1980 .U5

PETROLEUM REFINERIES - LAW AND LEGISLATION - NORTH CAROLINA.
Grant, Cy. A study of federal and state legislation concerning the construction of proposed oil refineries /. Raleigh, NC (105 1911 Bldg. North Carolina State University, Raleigh 27650) , 1980. 23, 4 p. : LC Card 80-624348 DDC 343.756/0772 347.5603772 19
KFN7658.R43 G72

PETROLEUM REFINERIES - LAW AND LEGISLATION - UNITED STATES.
Grant, Cy. A study of federal and state legislation concerning the construction of proposed oil refineries /. Raleigh, NC (105 1911 Bldg. North Carolina State University, Raleigh 27650) , 1980. 23, 4 p. : LC Card 80-624348 DDC 343.756/0772 347.5603772 19
KFN7658.R43 G72

PETROLEUM REFINERIES - NEAR EAST - MAPS.
United States. Central Intelligence Agency. Middle East area oilfields and facilities. [Washington , 1980] 1 map : LC Card 81-692536
G7421.H8 1980 .U5

PETROLEUM REFINERIES - UNITED STATES.
United States. Congress. House. Committee on Interstate and Foreign Commerce. Subcommittee on Energy and Power. Eomestic refinery policy--oversight . Washington , 1981. iii, 208 p. : LC Card 81-601359 DDC 338.4/766553/0973 19
KF27 .I5542 1980o

United States. Library of Congress. Congressional Research Service. U. S. refineries . Washington , 1980. v, 169 p. : LC Card 80-603551 DDC 665.5/3/0973 19
TP690.3 .U538 1980

PETROLEUM REFINERIES - WASTE DISPOSAL.

Pal, Dhiraj. Assessment of land treatment technology for petroleum refinery solid wastes /. [Raleigh, N.C.] [1980] vi, 30 leaves, [1] leaf of plates : LC Card 80-623569 DDC 333.91/009756 s 628.5/46 19
HD1694.N8 N6 no. 141 TD899.P4

PETROLEUM - REFINING - WASTE DISPOSAL - LAW AND LEGISLATION - MAINE.

Neily, Rupert. Enforcement manual for the proposed Pittston Oil Refinery . Augusta, Me. [1980] ca. 650 p. in various pagings : LC Card 80-622764 DDC 353.974/0082/42 19
TD195.P4 N44

PETROLEUM - RESERVES.

United States. Congress. Senate. Committee on Energy and Natural Resources. World petroleum outlook--1981 . Washington , 1981. iii, 152 p. : LC Card 81-601403 DDC 333.8/232 19
KF26 .E55 1981e

PETROLEUM - RESERVES - LAW AND LEGISLATION - UNITED STATES.

United States. Congress. House. Committee on Interstate and Foreign Commerce. Subcommittee on Energy and Power. Filling the strategic petroleum reserve, oversight, and H.R. 7252, use of the naval petroleum reserves . Washington , 1980. iv, 410 p. : LC Card 81-600602 DDC 346.7304/6823216 347.30646823216 19
KF27 .I5542 1980l

PETROLEUM SHIPPING TERMINALS - IRAN - MAPS.

United States. Central Intelligence Agency. Iraq-Iran central and southern border areas. [Washington , 1980] 1 map : LC Card 81-692540
G7611.F2 1980 .U5

PETROLEUM SHIPPING TERMINALS - IRAQ - MAPS.

United States. Central Intelligence Agency. Iraq-Iran central and southern border areas. [Washington , 1980] 1 map : LC Card 81-692540
G7611.F2 1980 .U5

PETROLEUM SHIPPING TERMINALS - NEAR EAST - MAPS.

United States. Central Intelligence Agency. Middle East area oilfields and facilities. [Washington , 1980] 1 map : LC Card 81-692536
G7421.H8 1980 .U5

Petroleum shortage response program for the State of Illinois . Barton-Aschman Associates. Springfield, Ill. [1979] viii, 73 p. ; LC Card 80-622395 DDC 333.8/23217/09773 19
TP355 .B33 1979

PETROLEUM - STORAGE.

United States. Strategic Petroleum Reserve Office. Strategic petroleum reserve . [Washington] , 1976- v. : LC Card 77-602345
TP692.5 .U627 1976a

PETROLEUM - TAXATION - UNITED STATES.

Resource Analysis & Management Group, Oklahoma City. The effects of the crude oil windfall profits tax on recoverable crude oil resources and production therefrom /. Oklahoma City, Okla. , 1980. v, 46 leaves : LC Card 80-82957 DDC 338.2/7282/0973 19
HD9560.8.U5 R47 1980

United States. Congress. Senate. Committee on Finance. Subcommittee on Taxation and Debt Management Generally. Small royalty owners exemption from the windfall profit tax . Washington , 1980. vii, 442 p. ; LC Card 81-600593 DDC 343.7305/244 347.3035244 19
KF26 .F5695 1980d

United States. Congress. Senate. Committee on Finance. Subcommittee on Taxation and Debt Management Generally. Special oil taxes . Washington , 1980 [i.e. 1981] iii, 222 p. : LC Card 81-601139 DDC 336.2/783338232/0973 19
KF26 .F5695 1980j

PETROLEUM - TRADE AND STATISTICS.
see PETROLEUM INDUSTRY AND TRADE.

PETROLEUM - UNITED STATES.

United States. Congress. House. Committee on

Armed Services. Subcommittee on Investigations. Department of Defense petroleum requirements and supplies . Washington , 1980. iii, 17 p. ; LC Card 80-603555 DDC 355.2/4/0973 19
UC263 .U517 1980

PETROLEUM - UNITED STATES - RESERVES.

United States. Congress. House. Committee on Armed Services. Subcommittee on Investigations. Department of Defense petroleum requirements and supplies . Washington , 1980. iii, 651 p. : LC Card 80-602946 DDC 355.2/43/0973 19
KF27 .A753 1979c

United States. Congress. Senate. Committee on Energy and Natural Resources. Subcommittee on Energy Resources and Materials Production. Strategic petroleum reserve and the naval petroleum reserve . Washington , 1980. iii, 65 p. ; LC Card 80-602779 DDC 333.8/23211/0973 19
KF26 .E5543 1980a

United States. Congressional Budget Office. An evaluation of the strategic petroleum reserve . Washington , 1980. xv, 36 p. : LC Card 80-602590 DDC 333.8/2311/0973 19
HD9502.U52 U512 1980a

PETROLEUM - UNITED STATES - RESERVES - FINANCE.

Holt, Barry J. Financing options for the strategic petroleum reserve /. [Washington, D.C.] , 1981. xv, 40 p. ; LC Card 81-601992 DDC 353.0072/22538 19
HD9565 .H6

PETROLEUM - UNITED STATES - STORAGE.

United States. Congress. House. Committee on Armed Services. Subcommittee on Investigations. Department of Defense petroleum requirements and supplies . Washington , 1980. iii, 651 p. : LC Card 80-602946 DDC 355.2/43/0973 19
KF27 .A753 1979c

United States. Congress. Senate. Committee on Energy and Natural Resources. Subcommittee on Energy Resources and Materials Production. Strategic petroleum reserve and the naval petroleum reserve . Washington , 1980. iii, 65 p. ; LC Card 80-602779 DDC 333.8/23211/0973 19
KF26 .E5543 1980a

United States. Congress. Senate. Committee on Governmental Affairs. Permanent Subcommittee on Investigations. Energy security . Washington , 1980. iii, 154 p. : LC Card 80-603907 DDC 333.79/0973 19
KF26 .G674 1980d

United States. General Accounting Office. Factors influencing the size of the U. S. strategic petroleum reserve . [Washington, D.C. , 1979] iii, 42 p. ; LC Card 79-602708 DDC 333.8/23211/0973 19
TP692.5 .U624 1979

United States. General Accounting Office. U. S. strategic petroleum reserve at a turning point . Washington, D.C. , 1980. iv p., 28 leaves : LC Card 80-601078 DDC 333.8/23211/0973 19
TP692.5 .U624 1980

PETROLEUM - UNITED STATES - STORAGE - FINANCE.

Holt, Barry J. Financing options for the strategic petroleum reserve /. [Washington, D.C.] , 1981. xv, 40 p. ; LC Card 81-601992 DDC 353.0072/22538 19
HD9565 .H6

PETROLEUM - UNITED STATES - STORAGE - PERIODICALS.

United States. Strategic Petroleum Reserve Office. Annual strategic petroleum reserve report. [Washington]. LC Card 78-645585
NYPL [JSP 80-382]

PETROLEUM WASTE - LAW AND LEGISLATION - UNITED STATES.

United States. Congress. Senate. Committee on Environment and Public Works. Recycling of used oil . Washington , 1980. iii, 111 p. ; LC Card 80-603011 DDC 346.73/04622 19
KF26 .E6 1980d

PETROLEUM WASTE - RECYCLING - NORTH CAROLINA.

Howard, Dick, 1937- Waste oil, North Carolina's recovered resource /. [Lexington, Ky.] , c1980. 8 p. : LC Card 80-139998 DDC 353.9 s 363.7/28 19
JS308 .C6 no. 687 TP687

PETROLEUM WASTE - RECYCLING - UNITED STATES.

United States. Congress. Senate. Committee on Environment and Public Works. Recycling of used oil . Washington , 1980. iii, 111 p. ; LC Card 80-603011 DDC 346.73/04622 19
KF26 .E6 1980d

Petrologic and structural studies in the northwestern Sierra Nevada.
Hietanen, Anna Martta, 1909- The Feather River area as a part of the Sierra Nevada suture system in California . Washington , 1981. p. cm. LC Card 80-606891 DDC 551.8/709794 19
QE90.F4 H5

PETROLOGY - NORTH CAROLINA - UNION COUNTY.

Randazzo, Anthony F. Petrography and stratigraphy of the Carolina Slate Belt, Union County, North Carolina /. Raleigh , 1972. iii leaves, 38 p., [1] fold leaf of plates : LC Card 80-623227 DDC 553/.09756 s 552.09756/755 19
QE147 .A32 no. 4 QE445.N8

Petrology of the Eagle Sandstone, Bearpaw Mountains area, north-central Montana /.
Gautier, Donald L. Washington [1981] p. cm. LC Card 81-607963 DDC 557.3 s 552/.5 19
QE75 .B9 no. 1521 QE471.15.S25

Pettinger, Lawrence R. Digital classification of landsat data for vegetation and land cover mapping in the Blackfoot River watershed, southeastern Idaho : a case study, including step-by-step procedures for computer-assisted analysis of landsat digital data, with emphasis on assessment of classification accuracy and generation of output products / by Lawrence R. Pettinger. Washington : U. S. Govt. Print. Off., 1980. p. cm. (Geological Survey professional papers . 1219) Bibliography: p. LC Card 80-606816 DDC 581.9/028 19
1. Vegetation mapping - Remote sensing - Data processing. 2. Vegetation classification - Idaho - Blackfoot River watershed. 3. Botany - Blackfoot River watershed. 4. Landsat satellites. 5. Blackfoot River watershed, Idaho. I. Title. II. Title: Classification of landsat data for vegetation and land cover mapping in the Blackfoot River watershed, southeastern Idaho. III. Title: Land cover mapping in the Blackfoot River watershed, southeastern Idaho. IV. Series: United States. Geological Survey. Professional paper, 1219.
QK63 .P47

Petto, Anthony C. Environmental regulations and other factors influencing industrial plant migrations / by Anthony C. Petto, Frances E. Oxley, and William J. Stanley. Chicago, Ill. : State of Illinois, Institute of Natural Resources, [1979] xxi, 106 p. ; 28 cm. (Document - Illinois Institute of Natural Resources ; no. 79/24) "August 1979." Bibliography: p. 98-100. LC Card 79-626019 DDC 338.6/042/0977 19
1. Industries, Location of - Middle West. 2. Industries, Location of - Illinois. I. Oxley, Frances E., joint author. II. Stanley, William J., joint author. III. Series: Illinois Institute of Natural Resources. Document - Illinois Institute of Natural Resources , no. 79/24. IV. Title.
HC107.A14 P47

Petty, A. V. Recycling of waste magnesite-chrome refractories from copper smelting furnaces / by A.V. Petty, Jr., and E. Martin. Avondale, MD : United States Dept. of the Interior, Bureau of Mines, [1981] p. cm. (Bureau of Mines report of investigations) Bibliography: p. LC Card 81-607818 DDC 622 s 669/.734 19
1. Chromium. 2. Refractory materials - Recycling. 3. Copper - Metallurgy - Waste disposal. I. Martin, E. (Eddie). II. Series: Report of investigations (United States. Bureau of Mines). III. Title.
TN23 .U43 TN799.C5

Petty, Susan. Hawaiian waste injection practices and problems / by Susan Petty, Frank L. Peterson. Honolulu, Hawaii : Water Resources Research Center, University of Hawaii, [1979] viii, 104 p. : ill. ; 28 cm. (Technical report - Water Resources Research Center, University of Hawaii ; no. 123) "Project completion report for evaluation of waste

injection problems in Hawai'i. Principal investigator: Frank L. Peterson. Project period: 1 January 1978 to 31 December 1978." "January 1979." Errata slip inserted. Includes bibliographies. LC Card 80-621493 DDC 553.7/09969 s 627/.56 19
1. Sewage disposal in the ground - Hawaii. 2. Sewage disposal in the ground - Environmental aspects - Hawaii. I. Peterson, Frank L., joint author. II. Series: Hawaii. University, Honolulu. Water Resources Research Center , no. 123. III. Title.
TC1 .H36 no. 123 TD760

Pfeiffenberger, C. L. (joint author) McCord, Thomas. Business property taxes and exemptions in New York State . Albany, NY [1980] xi, 101 p. : LC Card 80-622828 DDC 336.22/5 19
HJ4249 .M3

(joint author) McCord, Thomas. State agricultural preservation programs . Albany, NY [1979] iii, 49, 5 p. : LC Card 80-622880 DDC 353.9/372421 19
HJ4181 .M32

Pfeiffer, Anne. Financing for industry in Missouri / prepared by Anne Pfeiffer. Jefferson City, Mo. : Missouri Division of Commerce and Industrial Development, Dept. of Consumer Affairs, Regulation, and Licensing, [1979] 35 p. ; 28 cm. "June 1979." LC Card 79-625948 DDC 338.6/041 19
1. Industrial development bonds - Missouri. 2. Corporations - Missouri - Finance. I. Title.
HG4949 .P45

Pfister, Linda A. Career and labor market information . Columbus, Ohio , Washington, D.C. [1980] v, 71 p. ; LC Card 80-602937 DDC 331.12/0973 19
HD5724 .C33

Pflieger, William L. The fishes of Missouri / by William L. Pflieger ; Mark Sullivan, editor ; Lynne Taylor, artist. [Jefferson City] : Missouri Dept. of Conservation, 1975, viii, 343 p., [2] leaves of plates : ill. (some col.), maps ; 28 cm. Includes bibliographical references and index. LC Card 81-620611 DDC 597.092/9778 19
1. Fishes - Missouri. 2. Fishes - Missouri - Identification. 3. Fishing - Missouri. I. Sullivan, Mark, 1932-. II. Taylor, Lynne. III. Title.
QL628.M8 P47

Pham, Tu Duc. Labor force growth and employment expansion in Hawaii / Tu Duc Pham and Bertrand M. Renaud. [Honolulu, Hawaii] : Hawaii Agricultural Experiment Station, University of Hawaii, [1979] 38, [1] p. : ill. ; 23 cm. (Research bulletin - Hawaii Agricultural Experiment Station, University of Hawaii. 154 0073-098X) Bibliography: p. 38-[39] LC Card 80-623585 DDC 331.12/09969 19
1. Labor supply - Hawaii. 2. Employment forecasting - Hawaii. I. Renaud, Bertrand M., joint author. II. Series: Hawaii. Agricultural Experiment Station, Honolulu. Research bulletin , 154. III. Title.
HD5725.H3 P45

PHARMACEUTICAL INDUSTRY. see DRUG TRADE.

The pharmaceutical industry in India . Jawaharlal Nehru University. [New York] [1977] iv, 49 p. ; LC Card 81-479945 DDC 300 s 338.4/76151/09543 19
JX1977 .A2 TD/B/C.6/20

PHARMACEUTICAL POLICY - UNITED STATES.
United States. Congress. Office of Technology Assessment. A review of selected Federal vaccine and immunization policies . Washington , 1979. xvi, 208 p. : LC Card 79-600165 DDC 614.4/7/0973 19
RA638 .U48 1979

United States. Dept. of Health, Education, and Welfare. Review Panel on New Drug Regulation. Final report /. [Washington] , 1977. 117, [85] p. ; LC Card 77-602914
RA401.A3 U52 1977   *NYPL [JLF 81-208]*

PHARMACEUTICAL POLICY - UNITED STATES - STATES.
United States. Food and Drug Administration. Division of Federal-State Relations. State Services Branch. State programs and services in food and drug control /. Rockville, Md. , 1978. xiv, 68 p. : LC Card 79-600638 DDC 353.0077/82 19
TX531 .U536 1978

PHARMACEUTICAL RESEARCH - UNITED STATES.
United States. Dept. of Health, Education, and Welfare. Review Panel on New Drug Regulation. Final report /. [Washington] , 1977. 117, [85] p. ; LC Card 77-602914
RA401.A3 U52 1977   *NYPL [JLF 81-208]*

PHARMACEUTICAL SERVICES - ACCOUNTING.
Symposium on a Review and Critique of Cost Accounting for Pharmaceutical Services, New York, 1977. Cost accounting for pharmaceutical services . Hyattsville, Md. [1980] v, 70 p. : LC Card 80-602830 DDC 362.1/7 19
RS92 .S96 1977

PHARMACEUTICAL SERVICES - GEORGIA - CONGRESSES.
Georgia Conference for the Southeastern Region Mental Health Pharmacists, University of Georgia, 1978. Proceedings /. Athens [1978?] 59 p. : LC Card 80-620708 DDC 362.2 19
RA790.65.G4 G49 1978

PHARMACISTS - GEORGIA - CONGRESSES.
Georgia Conference for the Southeastern Region Mental Health Pharmacists, University of Georgia, 1978. Proceedings /. Athens [1978?] 59 p. : LC Card 80-620708 DDC 362.2 19
RA790.65.G4 G49 1978

Pharmacists in Washington State, 1977 /. Starzyk, Patricia M. Olympia, Wash. [1979] 39 p. : LC Card 80-621514 DDC 331.11/916151/09797 19
RS67.U7 W37

PHARMACISTS - SUPPLY & DISTRIBUTION - ARKANSAS - STATISTICS - PERIODICALS.
Arkansas health manpower statistics: pharmacists. 1978- Little Rock. LC Card 80-1903   *NYPL [JLM 80-1076]*

PHARMACISTS - WASHINGTON (STATE) - STATISTICS.
Starzyk, Patricia M. Pharmacists in Washington State, 1977 /. Olympia, Wash. [1979] 39 p. : LC Card 80-621514 DDC 331.11/916151/09797 19
RS67.U7 W37

PHARMACY - LAW AND LEGISLATION - UNITED STATES.
United States. Congress. House. Committee on Interstate and Foreign Commerce. Subcommittee on Health and the Environment. Drug regulation reform--oversight . Washington , 1980- v. <1- > ; LC Card 80-603639 DDC 353.0077/84 19
KF27 .I5543 1980j

Phase II incremental pricing of natural gas . United States. Congress. House. Committee on Interstate and Foreign Commerce. Subcommittee on Energy and Power. Washington , 1980. iv, 389 p. ; LC Card 80-603476 DDC 343.73/08556657 19
KF27 .I5542 1980d

Phaup, Marvin. Iden, George. The productivity problem . [Washington, D.C.] , 1981. xvii, 137 p. ; LC Card 81-600899 DDC 331.11/8/0973 19
HC110.C3 I32

Phay, Robert E. The public library : a guide book for North Carolina library trustees / Robert E. Phay. ; [cover design by Sarah S. McMillan].Rev. ed. [Chapel Hill] : Institute of Government, University of North Carolina at Chapel Hill, 1980. 69 p. : forms ; 26 cm. Bibliography: p. [43]-46. LC Card 81-620731 DDC 021.8/2/09756 19
1. Libraries - Trustees. 2. Public libraries - North Carolina. I. University of North Carolina at Chapel Hill. Institute of Government. II. Title.
Z681.5 .P45 1980

PHENOMENOLOGY - ADDRESSES, ESSAYS, LECTURES.
Heidegger, Martin, 1889-1976. [Grundprobleme der Phänomenologie. English.] The basic problems of phenomenology /. Bloomington , c1981. p. cm. ISBN 0-253-17686-7 LC Card 80-8379 DDC 142/.7 19
B3279.H48 G7813

PHENOXY GROUPS.
United States. Congress. House. Committee on Agriculture. Subcommittee on Forests. Phenoxy

herbicides in forest management . Washington , 1980. iii, 152 p. : LC Card 80-602796 DDC 333.75/16/0978 19
KF27 .A348 1980

Phenoxy herbicides in forest management . United States. Congress. House. Committee on Agriculture. Subcommittee on Forests. Washington , 1980. iii, 152 p. : LC Card 80-602796 DDC 333.75/16/0978 19
KF27 .A348 1980

PHILADELPHIA - BIOGRAPHY - PORTRAITS.
Philadelphia. Library Company. Nineteenth-century photography in Philadelphia . New York [Philadelphia, Pa.] , c1980. xxviii, 226 p. : ISBN 0-486-23932-2 : LC Card 79-54401
TR25.P5 P47 1980   *NYPL [MFW 81-102]*

Philadelphia. City Planning Commission. Penn Center; redevelopment area plan. [Philadelphia] 1952. 22 p. illus. 28 cm. LC Card 81-471288
1. Urban renewal - Pennsylvania - Philadelphia. I. Title.
HT177.P47 P44 1952

PHILADELPHIA. CONGRESS HALL.
Anderson, Susan H. The most splendid carpet /. Philadelphia , Washington , 1978. x, 93 [3] p. : LC Card 79-602679
NK3012.S46 A52   *NYPL [3-MOP 81-683]*

PHILADELPHIA. CONGRESS HALL. SENATE CHAMBER CARPET.
Anderson, Susan H. The most splendid carpet /. Philadelphia , Washington , 1978. x, 93 [3] p. : LC Card 79-602679
NK3012.S46 A52   *NYPL [3-MOP 81-683]*

Philadelphia. Dept. of Public Welfare. Proposed child protective service plan / Philadelphia Department of Public Welfare, Philadelphia County children and youth agency. [Philadelphia]: The Dept., 1979. iii, 42 leaves; 28 cm. Microfilm.
1. Child abuse - Pennsylvania. I. Title.
*NYPL [*ZT-1264]*

Philadelphia. Dept. of Records. (Old Catalog form: Philadelphia, Records Dept. of.) Annual report. Philadelphia, Dept. of Records. 28 cm. Report year ends June 30. LC Card 72-625479
1. Public records - Pennsylvania - Philadelphia - Periodicals.   *NYPL [JLM 80-1135]*

PHILADELPHIA - DESCRIPTION - VIEWS.
Philadelphia. Library Company. Nineteenth-century photography in Philadelphia . New York [Philadelphia, Pa.] , c1980. xxviii, 226 p. : ISBN 0-486-23932-2 : LC Card 79-54401
TR25.P5 P47 1980   *NYPL [MFW 81-102]*

Philadelphia Geriatric Center. Lawton, Mortimer Powell. Social and medical services in housing for the aged /. Rockville, Md. , Washington, D.C. , 1980. vii, 112 p. ; LC Card 80-603249 DDC 363.5/9 19
HD7287.92.U54 L383

Philadelphia. Library Company. (Old Catalog form: Library Company of Philadelphia) A flock of beautiful birds : the ornithological Collection of Louise Elkins Sinkler. Philadelphia : Library Co. of Philadelphia, 1977. 43 p. : ill. ; 23 cm. LC Card 77-155254
1. Birds - Pictorial works. 2. Sinkler, Louise E. - Art Collections. I. Title.
QL674 .P34 1977   *NYPL [JFE 80-3586]*

Nineteenth-century photography in Philadelphia : 250 historic prints from the Library Company of Philadelphia / by Kenneth Finkel. New York : Dover Publications ; [Philadelphia, Pa.] : Library Company of Philadelphia, c1980. xxviii, 226 p. : ill. ; 29 cm. Bibliography: p. [221] Includes index. ISBN 0-486-23932-2 : LC Card 79-54401
1. Photography - Pennsylvania - Philadelphia - History. 2. Philadelphia - Description - Views. 3. Philadelphia - Biography - Portraits. I. Finkel, Kenneth. II. Title.
TR25.P5 P47 1980   *NYPL [MFW 81-102]*

PHILADELPHIA (PA.) - PARKS.
United States. National Park Service. Division of Publications. Independence, Independence National Historical Park /. Washington, D.C. , 1981. p. cm. LC Card 81-607080 DDC 917.48/11 19
F158.65.I3 U54 1981

PHILADELPHIA (PA.) - STREETS.
Lopez, Claude Anne. Benjamin Franklin's "good house" /. Washington, D.C. , 1981. p. cm. LC Card 81-607929 DDC 974.8/11 19
E302.6.F8 L78

Philadelphia. Planning Commission. see Philadelphia. City Planning Commission.

Philadelphia. Public Welfare, Dept. of. see Philadelphia. Dept. of Public Welfare.

Philadelphia. Records, Dept. of. see Philadelphia. Dept. of Records.

Philadelphia. Temple University. Institute for Survey Research. LoSciuto, Leonard A. Professional and paraprofessional drug abuse counselors . Rockville, Md. , 1979. v, 244 p. ; LC Card 79-604153 DDC 362.2/9386 19
HV5825 .L67

Philadelphia - Views. see Philadelphia - Description - Views.

PHILANTHIDAE - CLASSIFICATION.
Krombein, Karl V. Biosystematic studies of Ceylonese wasps, VIII . Washington , 1981. p. cm. LC Card 81-607805 DDC 591 s 595.79/8 19
QL1 .S54 no. 343 QL568.P5

PHILANTHROPY. see SOCIAL SERVICE.

Philbrick, Marianne. Cooper, James Fenimore, 1789-1851. Wyandotté, or, The hutted knoll . Albany , c1981. p. cm. ISBN 0-87395-414-9 LC Card 81-1132 DDC 813/.2 19
PS1419 .W7 1981

Philbrick, Thomas. Cooper, James Fenimore, 1789-1851. Wyandotté, or, The hutted knoll . Albany , c1981. p. cm. ISBN 0-87395-414-9 LC Card 81-1132 DDC 813/.2 19
PS1419 .W7 1981

PHILBROOK, MARY.
Petrick, Barbara, 1935- Mary Philbrook . Trenton, N.J. [1981] p. cm. ISBN 0-89743-052-2 LC Card 81-11285 DDC 305.4/2/0924 B 19
HQ1413.P49 P47

Philip Morris Incorporated. Pachter, Marc. Champions, heroes of American sport /. [Washington] , New York [1981] p. cm. ISBN 0-8109-1602-9 (Abrams) : LC Card 80-28934 DDC 796/.092/2 B 19
GV697.A1 P28

PHILIPPINE ISLANDS - INDUSTRIES.
Philippines industrial development strategy and policies. Washington, D.C. , 1980. ix, 301 p. ; LC Card 80-141445 DDC 338.9599 19
HC455 .P53

PHILIPPINES - ANTIQUITIES - EXHIBITIONS.
University of California, Los Angeles. Museum of Cultural History. The people and art of the Philippines /. Los Angeles , c1981. p. cm. LC Card 81-2328 DDC 709/.599/074013 19
N7327 .U54 1981

PHILIPPINES - CIVILIZATION - EXHIBITIONS.
University of California, Los Angeles. Museum of Cultural History. The people and art of the Philippines /. Los Angeles , c1981. p. cm. LC Card 81-2328 DDC 709/.599/074013 19
N7327 .U54 1981

Philippines industrial development strategy and policies. Washington, D.C. : East Asia and Pacific Regional Office, World Bank, 1980. ix, 301 p. ; 27 cm. (A World Bank country study) Based on the findings of a mission that visited the Philippines in Feb. 1979; Barend A. de Vries, chief of mission. LC Card 80-141445 DDC 338.9599 19
1. Philippine Islands - Industries. 2. Industry and state - Philippine Islands. I. De Vries, Barend A. II. International Bank for Reconstruction and Development. East Asia and Pacific Regional Office. III. Series: World Bank country study.
HC455 .P53

Philipstown, N. Y. Town Board. Bryan & Panico, Inc. Road construction specifications . Philipstown, N. Y. , 1974. 35 leaves in various pagings . *NYPL [JSF 81-54]*

Phillips, Allan R. Monson, Gale. Annotated checklist of the birds of Arizona /. Tucson, Ariz. , 1981. p. cm. LC Card 81-11687 DDC 598.29791 19
QL684.A6 M64 1981

Phillips, David Atlee, 1952- McClellan, Carole. The archeology of Lake Mead National Recreation Area . Tucson, Ariz. [Washington, D.C.?] , 1980. x,188 p. : LC Card 81-600707 DDC 979.3/12 19
F788 .M163

Phillips, Diana Buder. Sunset 1979. Austin, Tex. : House Study Group, Texas House of Representatives, 1979. 5, [15] p. ; 28 cm. (Sunset report . no. 8) LC Card 80-620628 DDC 328.764/07456 19
1. Sunset reviews of government programs - Texas. I. Texas. Legislature. House of Representatives. Study Group. II. Title. III. Series.
JK4838 1979 .P48

Phillips, Dorothy. Train-a-champ . Albany, N.Y. , c1979. vii, 95 p. : LC Card 81-119267 DDC 371.9/044 19
GV445 .T73

Phillips, E. L. (Earl L.) Laboratory analysis of pozzolan (fly ash) concrete / by E.L. Phillips. Washington : U. S. Dept. of the Interior, Bureau of Mines, 1981. p. cm. (Report of investigations / United States Department of the Interior, Bureau of Mines) LC Card 81-607036 DDC 622 s 622/.4 19
1. Pozzuolanas - Analysis. I. Series: Report of investigations (United States. Bureau of Mines). II. Title.
TN23 .U43 TP882

Phillips, Gary L. Fishes of the Minnesota region / Gary L. Phillips, William D. Schmid, James C. Underhill. Minneapolis : University of Minnesota Press, 1982. p. cm. Bibliography: p. Includes index. ISBN 0-8166-0979-9 : LC Card 81-14693 DDC 597.092/9776 19
1. Fishes - Minnesota. I. Schmid, William D. II. Underhill, James Campbell. III. Title.
QL628.M6 P47

Phillips, Glenn S. Race relations in Oklahoma / [conducted and prepared by Glenn S. Phillips, Keven Virgilio]. Oklahoma City, Okla. : Oklahoma Human Rights Commission, 1979. 81 p. ; 28 cm. Includes bibliographical references. LC Card 80-621086 DDC 305.8/009766 19
1. Oklahoma - Race relations. 2. Minorities - Oklahoma. 3. Oklahoma - Ethnic relations. I. Virgilio, Keven, joint author. II. Oklahoma. Human Rights Commission. III. Title.
F705.A1 P48

Phillips, S. Albert. Kentucky. Laws, statutes, etc. The banking laws of Kentucky /. [Frankfort , 1926?] 44 p. ; LC Card 80-512032 DDC 346.769/082/02632 19
KFK1365 .A3 1926

PHILOSOPHERS - FRANCE - BIOGRAPHY - ADDRESSES, ESSAYS, LECTURES /.
Simone Weil, interpretations of a life /. Amherst , 1981. p. cm. ISBN 0-87023-343-2 : LC Card 81-7460 DDC 194 19
B2430.W474 S617

The philosophers of Greece /. Brumbaugh, Robert Sherrick, 1918- Albany, N.Y. [1982] p. cm. ISBN 0-87395-550-1 LC Card 81-9120 DDC 180 19
B171 .B78 1982

PHILOSOPHICAL ANALYSIS. see ANALYSIS (PHILOSOPHY)

PHILOSOPHY, ANALYTICAL. see ANALYSIS (PHILOSOPHY)

PHILOSOPHY, ANCIENT.
Brumbaugh, Robert Sherrick, 1918- The philosophers of Greece /. Albany, N.Y. [1982] p. cm. ISBN 0-87395-550-1 LC Card 81-9120 DDC 180 19
B171 .B78 1982

Frischer, Bernard. The sculpted word /. Berkeley , c1982. p. cm. ISBN 0-520-04190-9 LC Card 81-13143 DDC 187 19
B573 .F74

PHILOSOPHY, ANCIENT - ADDRESSES, ESSAYS, LECTURES.
Anscombe, G. E. M. (Gertrude Elizabeth Margaret) From Parmenides to Wittgenstein /. Minneapolis , c1981. p. cm. ISBN 0-8166-1078-9 : LC Card 81-4317 DDC 192 s 190 19
B1618 .A571 1981, vol. 1 B171

PHILOSOPHY, ANCIENT - HISTORY.
Dihle, Albrecht. The theory of will in classical

antiquity /. Berkeley , c1982. p. cm. ISBN 0-520-04059-7 LC Card 81-7424 DDC 128/.3 19
B187.F7 D54

PHILOSOPHY AND SCIENCE. see SCIENCE - PHILOSOPHY.

PHILOSOPHY - BIBLIOGRAPHY.
Lapointe, François. Edmund Husserl and his critics, an international bibliography (1894-1979) . Bowling Green, Ohio , c1980. 351 p. ; ISBN 0-912632-42-9 LC Card 80-83172 DDC 016.193 19
Z8429.4 .L36 B3279.H94

PHILOSOPHY, ENGLISH - 19TH CENTURY.
Harris, Wendell V. The omnipresent debate . DeKalb , c1981. p. cm. LC Card 80-8663 DDC 828/.8/08 19
PR778.P55 H3

PHILOSOPHY, GREEK. see PHILOSOPHY, ANCIENT.

PHILOSOPHY IN LITERATURE.
Reed, John Robert, 1938- The natural history of H.G. Wells /. Athens , c1981. p. cm. ISBN 0-8214-0628-0 LC Card 81-11261 DDC 823/.912 19
PR5778.P5 R4 1981

PHILOSOPHY, JEWISH - ADDRESSES, ESSAYS, LECTURES.
Altmann, Alexander, 1906- Essays in Jewish intellectual history /. Hanover, N.H. , 1981. x, 324 p. ; ISBN 0-87451-192-5 : LC Card 80-54471 DDC 296 19
BM45 .A45

PHILOSOPHY, MEDIEVAL - ADDRESSES, ESSAYS, LECTURES.
Altmann, Alexander, 1906- Essays in Jewish intellectual history /. Hanover, N.H. , 1981. x, 324 p. ; ISBN 0-87451-192-5 : LC Card 80-54471 DDC 296 19
BM45 .A45

PHILOSOPHY, MODERN - ADDRESSES, ESSAYS, LECTURES.
Anscombe, G. E. M. (Gertrude Elizabeth Margaret) From Parmenides to Wittgenstein /. Minneapolis , c1981. p. cm. ISBN 0-8166-1078-9 : LC Card 81-4317 DDC 192 s 190 19
B1618 .A571 1981, vol. 1 B171

PHILOSOPHY, MORAL. see ETHICS.

PHILOSOPHY, NATURAL. see PHYSICS.

PHILOSOPHY OF LITERATURE. see LITERATURE - PHILOSOPHY.

Philosophy of science and the occult / edited by Patrick Grim. Albany : State University of New York Press, 1981. p. cm. (SUNY series in philosophy) Includes bibliographies. ISBN 0-87395-572-2 LC Card 81-13552 DDC 001.9/01 19
1. Occult sciences. 2. Psychical research. 3. Unidentified flying objects. 4. Science - Philosophy. I. Grim, Patrick. II. Series.
BF1411 .P49

PHILOSOPHY OF TEACHING. see EDUCATION - PHILOSOPHY.

PHILOSOPHY - PERIODICALS.
The Southern Journal of philosophy. v. 1- ; spring, 1963- Memphis. LC Card 68-7760
*NYPL [*ZAN-3214]*

PHILOSOPHY, ROMAN. see PHILOSOPHY, ANCIENT.

Philpot, Wilbertine P. United States. Health Resources Administration. Bureau of Health Manpower. Minorities & women in the health fields . [Hyattsville, Md.] , Washington , 1978. xiii, 122 p. : LC Card 79-602970
R693 .U55 1978   *NYPL [JLF 81-355]*

Phipps, Antony A. Homebuyer's information package : a guidebook for buying and owning a home / prepared by Abt Associates ; Antony A. Phipps and Norma F. Moseley, authors ; for the Office of Policy Development and Research, U. S. Department of Housing and Urban Development. [Washington, D.C.?] : The Office : For sale by the Supt. of Docs., U. S. G.P.O., 1979. 1 v. (loose-leaf) : ill. (some col.), forms ; 28 cm. "February 1979"--P. 4 of cover. "Contract H-2646." "HUD-PDR-370"--P. 4 of cover. [S/N 023-000-00508-5] S/N 023-000-00508-5 LC Card 81-600743 DDC 643/.12 19

BIBLIOGRAPHIC GUIDE

Phoenix, Ariz. Heard Museum of Anthropology and Primitive

134

1. Home ownership - United States. 2. House buying - United States. 3. Abt Associates. I. Moseley, Norma F. II. United States. Dept. of Housing and Urban Development. Office of Policy Development and Research. III. Title.
HD1379 .P468

Phoenix, Ariz. Heard Museum of Anthropology and Primitive Art. see **Heard Museum of Anthropology and Primitive Art, Phoenix, Ariz.**

The phoenix of the Western world . Brundage, Burr Cartwright, 1912- Norman , c1981. p. cm.
ISBN 0-8061-1773-7   LC Card 81-40278   DDC 299/.78 19
F1219.76.R45 B78

Phosphate and tripolyphosphate adsorption by clay minerals and estuarine sediments /. Lake, Carol A. Blacksburg , 1977. v, 58 p. :   LC Card 77-624071   DDC 333.91/009755 s 551.46/09 19
TD201 .V57 no. 109 GC97.8.V8

PHOSPHATE INDUSTRY - FLORIDA.
Opyrchal, Anthony M. Economic significance of the Florida phosphate industry .
[Washington, D.C.]   [1981] p. cm.   LC Card 80-606892   DDC 622 s 338.2/764 19
TN295 .U4 HD9484.P5U5

PHOSPHATE INDUSTRY - FLORIDA - EQUIPMENT AND SUPPLIES.
Stanley, Donald A. Treatment of Florida surface waters for use in phosphate beneficiation /. [Washington, D.C.] [1981] p. cm.   LC Card 80-606882   DDC 622 s 661/.43 19
TN23 .U43

PHOSPHATE INDUSTRY - FLORIDA - WASTE DISPOSAL.
Brandt, Luther Warren, 1920- Dewatering Florida phosphatic clay wastes by a moving screen method /. [Washington] [1981] p. cm.
LC Card 80-607788   DDC 622 s 622/.364 19
TN23 .U43 TD899.P45

PHOSPHATE LEASES - FLORIDA - MANATEE COUNTY - MAPS.
United States. Soil Conservation Service. Manatee County, Florida, phosphate holdings /. Fort Worth, Tex. , 1980. 1 map :   LC Card 81-690257
G3933.M3H5 1980 .U5

PHOSPHATE ROCK.
Good, Philip C. Direct preparation of phosphoric acid from intermediate-grade western phosphatic shale /. [Washington] , 1981. p. cm.   LC Card 80-606841   DDC 622 s 661/.25 19
TN23 .U43 TP217.P5

PHOSPHATES - ENVIRONMENTAL ASPECTS - NORTH CAROLINA - UNIVERSITY LAKE.
Kuenzler, Edward J. Phosphorus dynamics in a North Carolina Piedmont reservoir /. Raleigh, N.C. [1980] xii, 56 p. :   LC Card 80-622281
DDC 333.91/009756 s 628.1/32 19
HD1694.N8 N6 no. 154 TD427.P56

PHOSPHATES - ENVIRONMENTAL ASPECTS - NORTH DAKOTA - STATISTICS.
North Dakota. State Dept. of Health. Nutrient levels in North Dakota streams, 1972-1978 /. [Bismarck, N.D.] [1980] 86 p. :   LC Card 80-622821   DDC 363.7/3942/09784 19
TD224.N9 N65 1980

PHOSPHATES - FLORIDA.
Beneficiation of high-magnesium phosphate from southern Florida /. Avondale, Md. , 1981. p. cm. LC Card 81-12298   DDC 622/.4629 19
TN23 .U43

PHOSPHATES - VIRGINIA.
Lake, Carol A. Phosphate and tripolyphosphate adsorption by clay minerals and estuarine sediments /. Blacksburg , 1977. v, 58 p. :   LC Card 77-624071   DDC 333.91/009755 s 551.46/09 19
TD201 .V57 no. 109 GC97.8.V8

PHOSPHORIC ACID.
Good, Philip C. Direct preparation of phosphoric acid from intermediate-grade western phosphatic shale /. [Washington] , 1981. p. cm.   LC Card 80-606841   DDC 622 s 661/.25 19
TN23 .U43 TP217.P5

Phosphorus dynamics in a North Carolina Piedmont reservoir /. Kuenzler, Edward J. Raleigh, N.C. [1980] xii, 56 p. :   LC Card 80-622281   DDC 333.91/009756 s 628.1/32 19
HD1694.N8 N6 no. 154 TD427.P56

PHOSPHORUS - ENVIRONMENTAL ASPECTS - GREAT LAKES - CONGRESSES.
Phosphorus managemnt strategies or lakes . Ann Arbor, Mich. , 1980. vi, 490 p. :   ISBN 0-250-40332-3   LC Card 79-55150
TD223.3 .P48

PHOSPHORUS - ENVIRONMENTAL ASPECTS - TEXAS - TRINITY RIVER WATERSHED.
Trinity River Authority of Texas. Planning and Environmental Management Division. Low flow nutrient loss in the mid-Trinity River ; Runoff-related pollutant loadings in the mid-Trinity River /. [Austin] , 1978. iii, 72, iv, 73 p. :   LC Card 80-622543   DDC 363.7/3942/097642 19
TD224.T4 T74 1978

PHOSPHORUS - ENVIRONMENTAL ASPECTS - WASHINGTON (STATE) - WASHINGTON, LAKE - MATHEMATICAL MODELS.
Stochastic analysis of water quality /. Logan [1979] viii, 75 p. :   LC Card 80-621125   DDC 628.1/61 19
TD367 .S8

Phosphorus export from rural Maine watersheds /. Schroeder, David C. [Orono, Me.] [1979] iv, 42 leaves :   LC Card 80-623370   DDC 363.7/394 19
TD427.P56 S37

Phosphorus managemnt strategies or lakes : proceedings of the 1979 conference sponsored by the New York State College of Agriculture and Life Sciences, a Statutory College of the State University at Cornell University, [and] the International Joint Commission (U. S. and Canada) / edited by Raymond C. Loehr, Colleen S. Martin, Walter Rast. Ann Arbor, Mich. : Ann Arbor Science, 1980. vi, 490 p. : ill. ; 24 cm. Includes bibliographical references and index.   ISBN 0-250-40332-3   LC Card 79-55150
1. Water quality management - Great Lakes - Congresses. 2. Phosphorus - Environmental aspects - Great Lakes - Congresses. 3. Sewage disposal in rivers, lakes, etc. - Great Lakes - Congresses. I. Loehr, Raymond C. II. Martin, Colleen S. III. Rast, Walter. IV. New York State College of Agriculture and Life Sciences.
TD223.3 .P48

PHOTOCHEMICAL AIR POLLUTION. see **PHOTOCHEMICAL SMOG.**

PHOTOCHEMICAL SMOG - ILLINOIS - CHICAGO REGION.
Health effects of ozone and other photochemical oxidants in the Chicago area /. Chicago, IL , 1979. vi, 83 p. :   LC Card 80-621150   DDC 615.9/02 19
RA577.O97 H4

PHOTOCHEMICAL SMOG - LOUISIANA.
Louisiana. Dept. of Natural Resources. Louisiana State implementation plan revisions for ozone abatement. Baton Rouge, LA [1978?] ca. 150 p. ;   LC Card 80-622129   DDC 363.7/39256/09763 19
TD887.H93 L68 1978

PHOTOCHEMISTRY.
(1974) Garvin, David, 1923- Chemicl kinetics data survey VII. Washington, 1974. 101 p.
NYPL [JSF 80-995]

PHOTOGRAPHERS - FRANCE - BIOGRAPHY.
Davis, Keith F., 1952- Désiré Charnay, expeditionary photographer /. Albuquerque , c1981. p. cm.   ISBN 0-8263-0592-X :   LC Card 81-52052   DDC 770/.92/4 B 19
TR140.C46 D38

The Photographer's hand / organized by Susan Dodge Peters for the Smithsonian Institution Traveling Exhibition Service, 1980-1982 ; [catalog editor, Mei Su Teng]. Washington, D.C. : The Service, c1980. p. cm. Bibliography: p.   LC Card 80-27845   DDC 779/.09/047074013 19
1. Photography, Handworked - Exhibitions. 2. Cliché-verri - Exhibitions. I. Peters, Susan D. II. Teng, Mei Su. III. Smithsonian Institution. Traveling

Exhibition Service.
TR646.U5 P45

A photographic legacy /. Counts, I. Wilmer. Bloomington, Ind. , c1979. 72 p. :
NYPL [IT 80-2223]

PHOTOGRAPHY.
Stapp, William F., 1945- Picture it! /. Washington, D.C. , 1981. 95 p. :   ISBN 0-86528-004-5   LC Card 80-28867   DDC 770 -19
TR149 .S68

PHOTOGRAPHY - AESTHETICS. see **PHOTOGRAPHY, ARTISTIC.**

PHOTOGRAPHY - ANIMATED PICTURES. see **CINEMATOGRAPHY; MOVING-PICTURES.**

PHOTOGRAPHY, ARTISTIC.
Yavno, Max. The photography of Max Yavno /. Berkeley, Calif. , c1981. ca. 150 p. :   ISBN 0-520-04238-7 (pbk.)   LC Card 80-6060   DDC 779/.092/4 19
TR654 .Y35

PHOTOGRAPHY, ARTISTIC - EXHIBITIONS.
Davies, Hugh Marlais. 1948- Al Souza /. [Amherst] , c1979. [24] p. :   LC Card 79-4894
TR647 .S69 1979
NYPL [MFX (Souza) 80-2495]

Invented images /. [Santa Barbara] , 1980. 76 p. :   LC Card 79-620046
TR646.U6 S3654   *NYPL [MFW 81-808]*

Sommer, Frederick, 1905- Frederick Sommer at seventy-five . Long Beach , 1980. [72] p. :   LC Card 80-310
TR647 .S62 1980
NYPL [MFX (Sommer) 81-836]

PHOTOGRAPHY, DOCUMENTARY - EXHIBITIONS.
Deal, Fiskin, Hernandez, McGowan, Mudford, Rice . Long Beach , c1980. p. cm.   ISBN 0-936270-01-2   LC Card 80-24842   DDC 779/.4/097949074019493 19
TR820.5 .D4

PHOTOGRAPHY, HANDWORKED - EXHIBITIONS.
The Photographer's hand /. Washington, D.C. , c1980. p. cm.   LC Card 80-27845   DDC 779/.09/047074013 19
TR646.U5 P45

PHOTOGRAPHY - HISTORY.
Stapp, William F., 1945- Picture it! /. Washington, D.C. , 1981. 95 p. :   ISBN 0-86528-004-5   LC Card 80-28867   DDC 770 19
TR149 .S68

PHOTOGRAPHY IN ASTRONAUTICS. see **SPACE PHOTOGRAPHY.**

PHOTOGRAPHY - MOVING-PICTURES. see **CINEMATOGRAPHY; MOVING-PICTURES.**

The photography of Max Yavno /. Yavno, Max. Berkeley, Calif. , c1981. ca. 150 p. :   ISBN 0-520-04238-7 (pbk.)   LC Card 80-6060   DDC 779/.092/4 19
TR654 .Y35

PHOTOGRAPHY - PENNSYLVANIA - PHILADELPHIA - HISTORY.
Philadelphia. Library Company. Nineteenth-century photography in Philadelphia . New York [Philadelphia, Pa.] , c1980. xxviii, 226 p. :   ISBN 0-486-23932-2 :   LC Card 79-54401
TR25.P5 P47 1980   *NYPL [MFW 81-102]*

PHOTOGRAPHY, PICTORIAL. see **PHOTOGRAPHY, ARTISTIC.**

PHOTOGRAPHY - THE WEST - HISTORY - EXHIBITIONS.
Ostroff, Eugene. Western views and Eastern visions /. Washington , 1981. 118 p. :   ISBN 0-86528-005-3 (pbk.)   LC Card 81-70   DDC 779/.9978 19
TR23.6 .O87

PHOTOGRAPHY, TRAVEL. see **TRAVEL PHOTOGRAPHY.**

PHOTOLYSIS (CHEMISTRY) see **PHOTOCHEMISTRY.**

**PHOTONUCLEAR REACTIONS -
CONGRESSES.**
International Symposium on Lepton and Photon
Interactions at High Energies, 9th, Batavia, Ill.,
1979. Proceedings of the 1979 International
Symposium on Lepton and Photon Interactions
at High Energies, August 23-29, 1979 /.
Batavia, Ill. , 1979. x, 621, 11 p. : LC Card
80-602047 DDC 539.7/211 19
QC794.8.W4 I58 1979

The phototropic woman /. Thomas, Annabel,
1929- Iowa City , c1981. p. cm. ISBN
0-87745-113-3 LC Card 81-10469 DDC
813/.54 19
PS3570.H557 P5

**PHOTOVOLTAIC POWER GENERATION -
GOVERNMENT POLICY - UNITED
STATES.**
United States. Congress. House. Committee on
Science and Technology. Subcommittee on
Energy Development and Applications. Solar
photovoltaic program . Washington , 1980. iii,
161 p. : LC Card 80-603425 DDC
338.4/762131244/0973 19
KF27 .S3934 1980c

**PHREATOPHYTES - ARIZONA - GILA
RIVER WATERSHED.**
Evapotranspiration before and after clearing
phreatophytes, Gila River Flood Plain, Graham
County, Arizona /. Washington , 1981. p. cm.
LC Card 81-607801 DDC 551.57/2 19
QC915.7.U5 E9

PHTHISIS. see TUBERCULOSIS.

Phucas, Charles B. Symposium on International
Standards Information and Isonet, National
Bureau of Standards, 1979. Symposium on
International Standards Information and
ISONET . Washington, D.C. [1980] vii, 59 p. :
LC Card 80-600073 DDC 602/.18 s
389/.6/0601 19
QC100 .U57 no. 579 T59.A1

**Physical and mechanical properties of selected
technological alloys** /. Ledbetter, H. M.
Washington , 1981. p. cm. LC Card 81-14053
DDC 602/.18 s 620.1/6 19
QC100 .U573 no. 71 TA460

**PHYSICAL CHEMISTRY. see CHEMISTRY,
PHYSICAL AND THEORETICAL.**

**PHYSICAL DISTRIBUTION OF GOODS -
MATHEMATICAL MODELS.**
Deuermeyer, Bryan L. A model for the analysis
of system service level in warehouse-retailer
distribution systems . West Lafayette, Ind.
[1979] 33, [16], 9 leaves : LC Card 80-621782
DDC 658/.001/9 s 658.7/81 19
HD6483 .P8 no. 716 HF5429

**PHYSICAL EDUCATION AND TRAINING -
CONGRESSES.**
National Conference of Senior Officials to
Consider Unesco Recommendations on Physical
Education and Sport, Washington, D.C., 1977.
Report of the National Conference of Senior
Officials to Consider Unesco Recommendations
on Physical Education and Sport, held in
Washington, D.C., November 16-18, 1977.
[Washington] , 1979. vii, 143 p. ; LC Card
80-601246 DDC 613.7 19
GV205 .N234 1977

**PHYSICAL EDUCATION FOR
HANDICAPPED CHILDREN -
LOUISIANA.**
Stokes, Billy Ray. Physical education for the
handicapped . [Baton Rouge] , 1978. vi, 152
p. ; LC Card 80-620856 DDC 371.9/044 19
L154 .B32 no. 1506 GV445

**PHYSICAL EDUCATION FOR MENTALLY
HANDICAPPED CHILDREN -
CONGRESSES.**
Train-a-champ . Albany, N.Y. , c1979. vii, 95
p. : LC Card 81-119267 DDC 371.9/044 19
GV445 .T73

Physical education for the handicapped . Stokes,
Billy Ray. [Baton Rouge] , 1978. vi, 152 p. ;
LC Card 80-620856 DDC 371.9/044 19
L154 .B32 no. 1506 GV445

**Physical elements and mobilization of human
resources** . United Nations Conference on
Human Settlements, Vancouver, B.C., 1976.
[New York?] 1976. 92 p. ; LC Card 80-514948

DDC 300 s 361.6 19
JX1977 .A2 A/CONF.70/A/3

**PHYSICAL FITNESS CENTERS - LAW AND
LEGISLATION - UNITED STATES.**
United States. Federal Trade Commission.
Report of the presiding officer on proposed
trade regulation rule . [Washington] , 1979. ii,
213 p. ; LC Card 79-602972 DDC 344.73/099 19
KF2042.P49 A877

**PHYSICAL GEOGRAPHY - FENWICK
ISLAND.**
Dolan, Robert. Geographical analysis of
Fenwick Island, Maryland, a Middle Atlantic
coast barrier island /. Washington, D.C. , 1980.
24 p. : LC Card 79-600212 DDC 333.7 19
GB126.M3 D64

**PHYSICAL GEOGRAPHY - TEXAS - TRAVIS
CO.**
Austin, Tex. Dept. of Planning. Austin
tomorrow, environment . Austin, Tex. , 1974.
xiv, 303 p. : LC Card 81-459302 DDC
363.7/009764/31 19
TD181.T42 T722 1974

**PHYSICAL LABORATORIES - SAFETY
REGULATIONS - PENNSYLVANIA.**
Pennsylvania. Dept. of Education. Pennsylvania
regulations and guidelines concerning safety in
the school science laboratory. Harrisburg ,
1978. [67] p. ; LC Card 80-621291 DDC
344.748/075 347.480475 19
KFP380.A1 A3 1978

**PHYSICAL LABORATORIES - UNITED
STATES - DIRECTORIES.**
Leedy, K. O. Catalog of Federal metrology and
calibration capabilities /. [Gaithersburg, Md.] ,
Washington , 1979. iii, 48 p. : LC Card
79-600075 DDC 602/.18 s 530.8/025/73 19
QC100 .U57 no. 546 QC51.U6

**PHYSICAL LABORATORIES - UNITED
STATES - SAFETY MEASURES.**
Gerlovich, Jack A. Better science through
safety /. Ames, Iowa , 1981. x, 145 p. : ISBN
0-8138-1780-3 LC Card 81-126506 DDC
502/.8/9 19
QC51.U6 G47

**PHYSICAL OCEANOGRAPHY. see
OCEANOGRAPHY.**

Physical therapists in Washington State, 1978 /.
Starzyk, Patricia M. Olympia, Wash. [1978?]
35 p. : LC Card 80-621085 DDC
331.1/2916158/09797 19
RM699.3.U6 S8

**PHYSICAL THERAPISTS - TEXAS -
STATISTICS.**
Texas. Bureau of State Health Planning &
Resource Development. Division of Data
Collection and Analysis. Texas health
manpower report . Austin, Tex. [1979?] 127
p. : LC Card 80-622320 DDC
331.12/9161582/09794 19
RM699.3.U6 T49 1979

**PHYSICAL THERAPISTS - WASHINGTON
(STATE) - STATISTICS.**
Starzyk, Patricia M. Physical therapists in
Washington State, 1978 /. Olympia, Wash.
[1978?] 35 p. : LC Card 80-621085 DDC
331.1/2916158/09797 19
RM699.3.U6 S8

**PHYSICALLY HANDICAPPED -
EMPLOYMENT - UNITED STATES.**
United States. Congress. House. Committee on
Post Office and Civil Service. Subcommittee on
Civil Service. Personal assistants for
handicapped federal employees . Washington ,
1980. iii, 84 p. : LC Card 80-604075 DDC
342.73/068 347.30268 19
KF27 .P635 1980c

**PHYSICALLY HANDICAPPED - HOME
CARE - WASHINGTON (STATE)**
Community-based care systems for the
functionally disabled . Olympia, Wash. , 1979.
xiv, 339 p. : LC Card 79-620045 DDC
362.1/4/09797 19
RA645.36.W2 C65

**PHYSICALLY HANDICAPPED - SERVICES
FOR - LAW AND LEGISLATION -
UNITED STATES.**
United States. Congress. House. Committee on
Post Office and Civil Service. Subcommittee on
Civil Service. Personal assistants for

handicapped federal employees . Washington ,
1980. iii, 84 p. : LC Card 80-604075 DDC
342.73/068 347.30268
KF27 .P635 1980c

**PHYSICALLY HANDICAPPED -
TRANSPORTATION - CASE STUDIES.**
Public Technology, inc. Elderly and
handicapped transportation . Washington, D.C.
[1979] 121 p. : LC Card 80-601590 DDC
362.4/0483 19
HQ1063.5 .P8 1979

**PHYSICALLY HANDICAPPED - UNITED
STATES - BIOGRAPHY.**
Hearst, James, 1900- My shadow below me /.
Ames, Iowa , c1981. p. cm. ISBN 0-8138-1136-8
LC Card 81-14265 DDC 811/.52 19
PS3515.E146 Z47

**PHYSICALLY HANDICAPPED - UNITED
STATES - STATISTICS.**
Feller, Barbara A. Health characteristics of
persons with chronic activity limitation .
Hyattsville, Md. , 1981. p. cm. ISBN
0-8406-0229-4 LC Card 81-11249 DDC
312/.0973 s 312/.3 19
RA407.3 .A346 no. 137 RA644.6

**PHYSICALLY HANDICAPPED - UNITED
STATES - TRANSPORTATION.**
Booz, Allen and Hamilton, inc. Transportation
Consulting Division. Planning for the phase-in
of fixed-route accessible buses : interim report
/. Washington , 1980. 1 v. :
NYPL [JLM 80-1153]

United States. Congress. House. Committee on
Education and Labor. Subcommittee on Select
Education. Oversight hearing on the
Architectural and Transportation Barriers
Compliance Board . Washington , 1981. iii, 219
p. : LC Card 81-601157 DDC 353.0086/2 19
KF27 .E373 1980d

Physician control of Blue Shield plans . Kass,
David I. [Washington, D.C.] [1979] v, 139 p. ;
LC Card 80-601542 DDC 368.3/8 19
RA413.3.B49 K37

**PHYSICIAN EXTENDERS. see PHYSICIANS'
ASSISTANTS.**

Physician reimbursement under medicare :
current policy, trends, and issues /
Subcommittee on Health of the Committee on
Ways and Means, U. S. House of
Representatives. Washington : U. S. G.P.O.,
1980 [i.e. 1981] vii, 58 p. ; 24 cm. At head of
title: 96th Congress, 2d session. Committee print.
WMCP: 96-77. Prepared with the assistance of the
Congressional Research Service, Library of Congress.
"December 23, 1980." Item 1028 Includes
bibliographical references. LC Card 81-600995 DDC
338.4/33621/0973 19
*1. Medicare. 2. Medical fees - United States. I. United
States. Congress. House. Committee on Ways and
Means. Subcommittee on Health. II. Library of
Congress. Congressional Research Service.*
HD7102.U4 P49

**PHYSICIAN SERVICES UTILIZATION -
UNITED STATES - STATISTICS.**
Cypress, Beulah K. Patients' reasons for visiting
physicians . Hyattsville, Md. [1981] p. cm.
ISBN 0-8406-0225-1 LC Card 81-607915 DDC
362.1/1/0973 362.1 19
RA407.3 .A349 no. 56 RA410.7

**PHYSICIAN SUPPORT PERSONNEL. see
PHYSICIANS' ASSISTANTS.**

**PHYSICIAN'S ASSISTANTS - LEGAL
STATUS, LAWS, ETC. - CALIFORNIA.**
California. Laws, statutes, etc. Extracts of the
business and professions code and rules and
regulations relating to physician's assistants /.
Sacramento, Calif. , 1979. 48, [2] p. ; LC Card
80-621368 DDC 344.794/0412 347.9404412 19
KFC546.5.P48 A32 1979

**PHYSICIANS' ASSOCIATES. see
PHYSICIANS' ASSISTANTS.**

**PHYSICIANS, FOREIGN - LICENSES -
UNITED STATES.**
United States. Congress. House. Committee on
the Judiciary. Subcommittee on Immigration,
Refugees, and International Law. Admission of
alien physicians for graduate medical
education . Washington , 1980. iii, 250 p. ; LC
Card 80-603068 DDC 344.73/07684 19
KF27 .J8645 1980

Physicians in Vermont, 1979. Vermont. Dept. of
Health. Division of Public Health Statistics.
Burlington, Vt. [1980] iv, 45 p. : LC Card
80-623433 DDC 331.12/9161/09743 19
RA410.8.V5 V47 1980

**PHYSICIANS - KENTUCKY - SUPPLY AND
DEMAND.**
Kentucky. Professional Schools Admissions
Committee. A plan to provide professional
education and services to underserved areas of
the State . Frankfort, Ky. , 1979. x, 48 p. ; LC
Card 80-620638 DDC 344.769/011231
347.690411231 19
KFK1325 .A25 1979

**PHYSICIANS - LEGAL STATUS, LAWS, ETC.
see MEDICAL LAWS AND
LEGISLATION.**

**PHYSICIANS - MAINE - SUPPLY AND
DEMAND - STATISTICS.**
Maine. Bureau of Health Planning and
Development. Distribution of primary care
physicians in Maine, July 1, 1979 /. [Augusta,
Me.] [1979] 67 p. ; LC Card 80-621729 DDC
331.11/1 19
RA410.8.M2 M34 1979a

PHYSICIANS - MICHIGAN - STATISTICS.
Michigan. Cooperative Health Information
System. Licensed health occupations, Michigan
physicians (M.D. and D.O.) 1976. Lansing,
Mich. [1976] 57 p. : LC Card 80-622891 DDC
331.12/916109774 19
RA410.8.M5 M49 1976

**PHYSICIANS - NEW YORK (STATE) -
SUPPLY AND DEMAND.**
New York (State). Regents Task Force on
Medical School Enrollment and Physician
Manpower. Interim report and synopsis of the
findings to date of the Regents Task Force on
Medical School Enrollment and Physician
Manpower to the Regents of the University of
the State of New York. Albany , 1974. vi, 90
p. :   *NYPL [JFF 81-279]*

**PHYSICIANS - SALARIES, PENSIONS, ETC.
- LAW AND LEGISLATION - UNITED
STATES.**
United States. Congress. House. Committee on
Veterans' Affairs. Subcommittee on Medical
Facilities and Benefits. Oversight in the
recruitment and retention of Veterans'
Administration physicians and dentists, and
H.R. 6153 . Washington , 1981. iv, 168 p. :
LC Card 81-601384 DDC 353.001/31 19
KF27 .V459 1980c

**PHYSICIANS - SALARIES, PENSIONS, ETC.
- UNITED STATES.**
United States. Congress. House. Committee on
Armed Services. Subcommittee on Military
Compensation. Hearings on H.R. 5168, H.R.
7626, and S. 1454, miscellaneous military
personnel management and military
compensation legislation, before the Military
Compensation Subcommittee of the Committee
on Armed Services, House of Representatives,
Ninety-sixth Congress, second session,
September 10, November 15, December 4,
1979, February 22, June 4, 11, and 19, 1980.
Washington , 1980 [i.e. 1981] ii, 127 p. ; LC
Card 81-600976 DDC 343.73/013 347.30313 19
KF27 .A76392 1979b

PHYSICIANS - UNITED STATES.
Kass, David I. Physician control of Blue Shield
plans . [Washington, D.C.] [1979] v, 139 p. ;
LC Card 80-601542 DDC 368.3/8 19
RA413.3.B49 K37

**PHYSICIANS - UNITED STATES -
STATISTICS.**
Budde, Norbert W. Characteristics of
physicians . [Hyattsville, Md.] [1979- -v. ; LC
Card 80-602072
RA410.7 .B82   *NYPL [JLM 81-120]*

PHYSICIANS - VERMONT - STATISTICS.
Vermont. Dept. of Health. Division of Public
Health Statistics. Physicians in Vermont, 1979.
Burlington, Vt. [1980] iv, 45 p. : LC Card
80-623433 DDC 331.12/9161/09743 19
RA410.8.V5 V47 1980

**PHYSICIANS - WASHINGTON (STATE) -
STATISTICS.**
Starzyk, Patricia M. Allopathic and osteopathic
physicians in Washington State, 1978 /.
Olympia, Wash. [197-?] 54 p. : LC Card

80-624428 DDC 331.12/9161/09797 19
RA410.8.W2 S73

**PHYSICS - COMPUTER PROGRAMS -
BIBLIOGRAPHY.**
United States. National Technical Information
Service. A directory of computer software
applications, physics, 1970-May 1978.
Springfield, Va. , c1978. vii, 208, 114 p. ; LC
Card 80-602674
Z7144.C74 U54 1978 QC52
    NYPL [JSF 81-190]

PHYSICS - HISTORY.
Heilbron, J. L. Elements of early modern
physics /. Berkeley , c1981. p. cm. ISBN
0-520-04554-8 LC Card 81-40327 DDC
537/.09032 19
QC507 .H482

PHYSICS IN LITERATURE.
Nadeau, Robert L., 1944- Readings from the
new book on nature . Amherst , 1981. p. cm.
ISBN 0-87023-331-9 : LC Card 81-2625 DDC
813/.54/09356 19
PS374.P45 N3

Physics of Fiber Optics, Conference on the. see
**Conference on the Physics of Fiber Optics,
University of Rhode Island, 1978.**

**PHYSIOGRAPHY. see GEOLOGY;
GEOMORPHOLOGY; PHYSICAL
GEOGRAPHY.**

**The physiological basis for spacecraft
environmental limits** /. Walisora, J. M.
Washington, D.C. [Springfield, Va.] c1979.
xvii, 217 p. : LC Card 81-600766 DDC 612/.0145
19
RC1150 .W34

**PHYSIOLOGICAL EFFECT OF LIGHT ON
PLANTS. see PLANTS, EFFECT OF
LIGHT ON.**

**PHYSIOLOGICAL EFFECT OF MERCURY.
see MERCURY - PHYSIOLOGICAL
EFFECT.**

**PHYSIOLOGICAL THERAPEUTICS. see
THERAPEUTICS, PHYSIOLOGICAL.**

**PHYSIOTHERAPY. see THERAPEUTICS,
PHYSIOLOGICAL.**

**PHYTOGEOGRAPHY - COLORADO -
CHAFFEE COUNTY - MAPS.**
United States. Soil Conservation Service. Land
use and natural plant communities, Chaffee
County, Colorado /. Portland, Or. , 1979. 1
map : LC Card 81-691557
G4313.C2G4 1979 .U5

**PHYTOGEOGRAPHY - COLORADO -
CUSTER COUNTY - MAPS.**
United States. Soil Conservation Service. Land
use and natural plant communities, Custer
County, Colorado /. Portland, Or. , 1979. 1
map : LC Card 81-691555
G4313.C8G4 1979 .U5

**PHYTOGEOGRAPHY - COLORADO - EAGLE
COUNTY - MAPS.**
United States. Soil Conservation Service. Land
use and natural plant communities, Eagle
County, Colorado /. Portland, Or. , 1979. 1
map on 2 sheets : LC Card 81-691548
G4313.E2G4 1978 .U5

**PHYTOGEOGRAPHY - COLORADO -
JEFFERSON COUNTY - MAPS.**
United States. Soil Conservation Service. Land
use and natural plant communities, Jefferson
County, Colorado /. Portland, Or. , 1980. 1
map : LC Card 81-691558
G4313.J4G4 1979 .U5

**PHYTOGEOGRAPHY - COLORADO - LAKE
COUNTY - MAPS.**
United States. Soil Conservation Service. Land
use and natural plant communities, Lake
County, Colorado /. Portland, Or. , 1979. 1
map : LC Card 81-691554
G4313.L2G4 1978 .U5

**PHYTOGEOGRAPHY - COLORADO - SAN
MIGUEL COUNTY - MAPS.**
United States. Soil Conservation Service. Land
use and natural plant communities, San Miguel
County, Colorado /. Portland, Or. , 1979. 1
map on 2 sheets : LC Card 81-691549
G4313.S4G4 1978 .U5

**PHYTOGEOGRAPHY - COLORADO -
SUMMIT COUNTY - MAPS.**

United States. Soil Conservation Service. Land
use and natural plant communities, Summit
County, Colorado /. Portland, Or. , 1979. 1
map : LC Card 81-691545
G4313.S8G4 1978 .U5

**PHYTOGEOGRAPHY - COLORADO -
TELLER COUNTY - MAPS.**
United States. Soil Conservation Service. Land
use and natural plant communities, Teller
County, Colorado /. Portland, Or. , 1979. 1
map : LC Card 81-691544
G4313.T4G4 1978 .U5

**PHYTOGEOGRAPHY - MADAGASCAR -
MAPS.**
United States. Central Intelligence Agency.
Madagascar. [Washington, 1973] col. map 48 x
33 cm. Scale 1:3,465,000. Relief shown by shading
and spot heights. "501245." Includes location map,
comparative area map, and maps of "Population," "Tribal
groups," "Economic activity," and "Vegetation." LC
Card 75-690371
G8460 1973 .U51
    NYPL [Map Div. 81-3036]

PHYTOGEOGRAPHY - NEW YORK (STATE)
Mitchell, Richard Sheppard, 1938-
Magnoliaceae through Ceratophyllaceae of New
York State /. Albany, N.Y. , 1979. vi, 62 p. :
LC Card 80-621817 DDC 581.9747 19
QK177 .M67

**PHYTOGEOGRAPHY - NORTH DAKOTA -
MAPS.**
Whitman, Warren C. Analysis of grassland
vegetation on selected key areas in
southwestern North Dakota . [Bismarck
[1979?] x, 199 p. : LC Card 80-622820 DDC
581.5/2643/09784 19
QK179 .W83

**PHYTOGEOGRAPHY - SOUTH DAKOTA -
MAPS.**
United States. Soil Conservation Service. South
Dakota, natural vegetation /. Lincoln, Nebr. ,
1974. 1 map : LC Card 81-691111
G4181.D2 1974 .U5

United States. Soil Conservation Service. South
Dakota natural vegetation /. Lincoln, Nebr. ,
1976. 1 map : LC Card 81-691110
G4181.D2 1976 .U5

PHYTOGEOGRAPHY - TANZANIA - MAPS.
United States. Central Intelligence Agency.
Tanzania. [Washington, 1970] col. map 42 x 43
cm. on sheet 44 x 80 cm. Scale 1:3,220,000. Relief
shown by shading and spot heights. "76839." Includes
location map, comparative area map, and maps of
"Population," "Economic activity," "Ethnic groups," and
"Vegetation." LC Card GM70-4480
G8440 1970 .U51
    NYPL [Map Div. 80-3387]

PHYTOGRAPHY. see BOTANY.

PHYTOLOGY. see BOTANY.

Phytopathogenic fungi . Brown, Merton F.
[Columbia, Mo.] , c1979. vii, 355 p., : LC Card
79-91283 DDC 589.2/044 19
QK601 .B84

**PHYTOPLANKTON - NORTH CAROLINA -
PAMLICO RIVER.**
Kuenzler, Edward J. Nutrient kinetics of
phytoplankton in the Pamlico River, North
Carolina /. [Raleigh] [1979] xxii, 163 p. : LC
Card 79-626205 DDC 333.91/009756 s 589.4 19
HD1694.N8 N6 no. 139 QK571.5.N8

**PHYTOSOCIOLOGY. see PLANT
COMMUNITIES.**

Pícaros, madmen, naïfs, and clowns . Riggan,
William, 1946- Norman , c1981. p. cm. ISBN
0-8061-1714-1 : LC Card 81-2791 DDC
809.3/923 19
PN3383.P64 R5

PICASSO, PABLO, 1881-1973.
Organization of American States. General
Secretariat. Tribute to Picasso . [Washington ,
1973] [33] p. : LC Card 75-328387
ND202 .O73 1973

PICEANCE VALLEY - ANTIQUITIES.
Grady, James, 1931- Environmental factors in
archaeological site locations /. Denver, Colo. ,
1980. xvii, 372 p. : LC Card 80-602060 DDC
978.8/1 19
E78.C6 G7 1980

Pickard, Jerome Percival, 1916- Appalachian Regional Commission. Appalachia . Washington, D.C. , 1979. 92 p. : LC Card 80-602657 DDC 330.974/043 19
HC107.A127 A66 1979

Picket fence planning in California. Waldhorn, Steven A. Sacramento , 1976-77. Xll, 62 p.
JS451.C25 W34 **NYPL [*XME-9440]**

Pickle, Joe, 1910- Caylor, H. W. (Harvey Wallace), b. 1867. H.W. Caylor, frontier artist /. College Station , c1981. 125 p. : ISBN 0-89096-108-5 : LC Card 80-6112 DDC 759.13 19
ND237.C384 A4 1981

PICK'S DISEASE OF THE BRAIN. see PRESENILE DEMENTIA.

PICTORIAL PHOTOGRAPHY. see PHOTOGRAPHY, ARTISTIC.

Picture it! /. Stapp, William F., 1945- Washington, D.C. , 1981. 95 p. : ISBN 0-86528-004-5 LC Card 80-28867 DDC 770 19
TR149 .S68

Pieper, Mary J. (joint author) Morton, Robert A. Shorelines changes on Mustang Island and North Padre Island (Aransas Pass to Yarborough Pass) . Austin , 1977. 45 p. : LC Card 78-621044 DDC 553/.09764 s 551.3/6/09764113 19
TN24.T4 T38 no. 77-1 GB459.4

PIERCE, CHARLES SANDERS, 1839-1914. Apel, Karl Otto. [Der Denkweg von Charles S. Peirce. English.] Charles S. Peirce . Amherst, Mass. , c1981. p. cm. ISBN 0-87023-177-4 : LC Card 81-3337 DDC 191 19
B945.P44 A7513

Pierce, Francis. United States. Congressional Budget Office. Indexing the individual income tax for inflation /. [Washington, D.C.] [1980] xv, 81 p. ; LC Card 80-603390 DDC 336.24/2/0973 19
HJ4637 .U53 1980

Pierce, Ken. A history of the Abenaki people / Ken Pierce. [Burlington] : University of Vermont, Instructional Development Center, c1977. 75 p. : maps ; 22 cm. Bibliography: p. 67-75. LC Card 81-134344 DDC 974/.00497 19
1. Abnaki Indians - History. I. Title.
E99.A13 P53

Pierce, Kenneth Lee. (joint author) Colman, Steven M. Weathering rinds on andesitic and basaltic stones as a Quaternary age indicator, Western United States /. Washington , 1981. iv, 56 p. : LC Card 80-607840 DDC 551.7/9/0978 19
QE696 .C656

PIERCE, SAMUEL R., 1922- United States. Congress. Senate. Committee on Banking, Housing and Urban Affairs. Nomination of Samuel R. Pierce, Jr. . Washington , 1981. iii, 95 p. ; LC Card 81-601350 DDC 353.85 19
KF26 .B39 1981c

Pierce, Steven T. New Mexico. Environmental Improvement Division. Water Supply Section. Chemical quality of New Mexico community water supplies, 1980 . [Santa Fe] [1980] 256 p. ; LC Card 80-624082 DDC 363.6/1 19
TD224.N6 N47 1980

Pierman, Brian C. (joint author) Adler, Sanford C. A history of walkway slip-resistance research at the National Bureau of Standards /. [Washington] , 1979. iv, 31 p. : LC Card 79-600179 DDC 602/.18 s 698/.9 19
QC100 .U57 No. 565 TA418.72

PIERS - LAW AND LEGISLATION - TAHOE, LAKE. Nevada. State Dept. of Conservation and Natural Resources. Regulations governing pier construction, deposit of fill, dredging, or alteration of Lake Tahoe shoreline, adopted September 24, 1979 /. [Carson City, Nev.] [1979] 8 p. ; LC Card 80-622985 DDC 346.793/57046917 19
KFN1051.8.A434 A2 1979

Pietrafesa, Leonard J. Onslow Bay physical/dynamical experiments, summer-fall, 1975 . [Raleigh] 1978. xxiv, 170 p. : LC Card 78-623321 DDC 551.46/148 19
GC512.N8 O56

PIG. see SWINE.

Piggford, Roland R. A survey of non-resident lending and borrowing activity in Massachusetts / Roland R. Piggford. Boston, MA : Massachusetts Board of Library Commissioners, [1979] i, 150, 7 p. : graphs ; 21 x 28 cm. On cover: Data for Massachusetts, a special report." "November 1979." LC Card 80-622848 DDC 025.6/09744 19
1. Libraries - Massachusetts - Circulation, loans - Statistics. I. Massachusetts. Board of Library Commissioners. II. Title. III. Title: Data for Massachusetts, a special report.
Z732.M41 P53

PIGS. see SWINE.

Pikasso, Pablo. see Picasso, Pablo, 1881-1973.

Pike, David, 1950- German writers in Soviet exile, 1933-1945 / David Pike. Chapel Hill : University of North Carolina Press, c1981. p. cm. Bibliography: p. Includes index. ISBN 0-8078-1492-X LC Card 81-10394 DDC 830/.9/00912 B 19
1. Authors, German - 20th century - Political and social views. 2. Germans - Soviet Union. 3. Authors, German - 20th century - Biography. 4. German literature - Soviet Union - History and criticism. 5. Kommunisticheskaiă Partiiă Sovetskogo Soiŭza - Purges. 6. Terrorism - Soviet Union. I. Title.
PT405 .P46

Pike, Douglas Eugene, 1924- Vietnam's foreign relations, 1975-78 : report / prepared for the Subcommittee on Asian and Pacific Affairs of the Committee on Foreign Affairs, U. S. House of Representatives by the Foreign Affairs and National Defense Division, Congressional Research Service, Library of Congress. Washington : U. S. G.P.O., 1979. vii, 21 p. ; 24 cm. At head of title: 96th Congress, 1st session. Committee print. "June 1979." Includes bibliographical references. LC Card 80-603974 DDC 327.597 19
1. Vietnam - Foreign relations. I. United States. Congress. House. Committee on Foreign Affairs. Subcommittee on Asian and Pacific Affairs. II. Library of Congress. Foreign Affairs and National Defense Division. III. Title.
DS559.912 P54

Pike, Fredrick B. The Spanish Civil War, 1936-39 . Lincoln , c1982. p. cm. ISBN 0-8032-1961-X LC Card 81-14644 DDC 946.081 19
DP269.8.P8 S6

Pike, Lewis W. Other nations, other peoples : a survey of student interests, knowledge, attitudes, and perceptions / by Lewis W. Pike and Thomas S. Barrows ; with Margaret H. Mahoney and Ann Jungeblut. [Washington, D.C.] : U. S. Dept. of Health, Education, and Welfare, Office of Education : for sale by the Supt. of Docs., U. S. Govt. Print. Off., 1979. xxiii, 139 p. : ill. ; 27 cm. (HEW publication ; no. (OE) 78-19004) "Contract no. OEC-0-72-4618." Bibliography: p. 48. LC Card 80-600989 DDC 370.19/6 19
1. Intercultural education. I. Barrows, Thomas S., joint author. II. Series: United States. Dept. of Health, Education and Welfare. DHEW publication, no. (OE) 78-19004. III. Title.
LC1099 .P54

PIKE NATIONAL FOREST, COLO. - MAPS. (1970) United States. Forest Service. Rocky Mountain Region. Pike National Forest, Colorado; west-[east] half. [Denver] 1970. 2 col. maps on sheet 106 x 65 cm. Scale 1:126,720; 1/2" = 1 mile. Printed on both sides of sheet. "Reprinted 1977." "Polyconic projection, 1927 North American datum." Relief shown by hachures and spot heights. Forest Service map. Includes text, col. illus., index to recreation sites, and location map. LC Card GM72-1927
G4312.P48 1970 .U5
NYPL [Map Div. 80-3344]

Pilla, Thomas V. United States. Commission on Civil Rights. Western Regional Office. Puerto Ricans in California . [Washington, D.C.] , 1980. vii, 19 p. ; LC Card 80-601602 DDC 323.1/1687295/0794 19
F870.P85 U54 1980

PILLARING (MINING) - MATHEMATICAL MODELS. Kripakov, Nicholas P. Analysis of pillar stability on steeply pitching seam using the finite element method /. Washington, D.C. [1981] p.

cm. LC Card 80-606871 DDC 622 s 622/.28 19
TN23 .U43 TN292

Pilot aging study . United States. Congress. House. Committee on Science and Technology. Washington , 1980 [i.e. 1981] iii, 63 p. ; LC Card 81-601375 DDC 331.25 19
KF27 .S3975 1980a

PILOT CHARTS. see NAUTICAL CHARTS.

PILOT GUIDES - MALACCA, STRAIT OF. Defense Mapping Agency. Hydrographic Center. Sailing directions (enroute) for the Strait of Malacca and Sumatera. [Washington] , 1978- 1 v. : LC Card 78-603700
VK931 .D43 1978 **NYPL [JFF 81-152]**

PILOT GUIDES - PHILIPPINE ISLANDS. Defense Mapping Agency. Hydrographic/Topographic Center. Sailing directions (enroute) for the Philippines. Washington, D.C. , 1979- 1 v. : LC Card 80-603979 DDC 623.89/29599 19
VK911 .D43 1979

PILOT GUIDES - SOUTH CHINA SEA. Defense Mapping Agency. Hydrographic/Topographic Center. Sailing directions (enroute) for the South China Sea and Gulf of Thailand. Washington, D.C. , 1979- 1 v. : LC Card 80-600971 DDC 623.89/29597 19
VK905 .D43 1979

PILOT GUIDES - SUMATRA. Defense Mapping Agency. Hydrographic Center. Sailing directions (enroute) for the Strait of Malacca and Sumatera. [Washington] , 1978- 1 v. : LC Card 78-603700
VK931 .D43 1978 **NYPL [JFF 81-152]**

PILOT GUIDES - THAILAND, GULF OF. Defense Mapping Agency. Hydrographic/Topographic Center. Sailing directions (enroute) for the South China Sea and Gulf of Thailand. Washington, D.C. , 1979- 1 v. : LC Card 80-600971 DDC 623.89/29597 19
VK905 .D43 1979

PILOT GUIDES - TONKIN GULF. Defense Mapping Agency. Hydrographic/Topographic Center. Sailing directions (enroute) for the South China Sea and Gulf of Thailand. Washington, D.C. , 1979- 1 v. : LC Card 80-600971 DDC 623.89/29597 19
VK905 .D43 1979

PILOTLESS AIRCRAFT. see GUIDED MISSILES.

PILOTS AND PILOTAGE - CONGRESSES. Symposium on Piloting and VTS Systems, Washington, D.C., 1979. Proceedings /. Washington, D.C. , 1980. ix, 233 p. ; LC Card 80-126646 DDC 387.1/66 19
VK1645 .S95 1979

PILOTS AND PILOTAGE - LAW AND LEGISLATION - LOUISIANA - NEW ORLEANS. Louisiana. Board of River Port Pilot Commissioners for the Port of New Orleans. Commissioners' rules /. [New Orleans, La.] [1980] [16] p. ; LC Card 80-623405 DDC 343.763/350967 19
KFL312.N4 A32 1980

Piltz, Rick. Energy conservation. Austin, Tex. (P.O. Box 2910, Austin 78769) : House Study Group, Texas House of Representatives, [1981] vii, 58 p. ; 28 cm. (House Study Group special legislative report . no. 69) "March 30, 1981." Bibliography: p. 56-58. LC Card 81-622292 DDC 333.79/16/09764 19
1. Energy conservation - Texas. I. Texas. Legislature. House of Representatives. Study Group. II. Series: Special legislative report (Texas. Legislature. House of Representatives. Study Group) , no. 69. III. Title.
HD9502.U53 T455

The PIMS U. S.-OPEC petroleum report, year 1973. Washington, D.C. : Petroleum Industry Monitoring System, Federal Energy Administration, Office of Policy and Analysis, [1974] 26 p. : graphs ; 27 cm. Cover title. "July 1, 1974." LC Card 80-603212 DDC 382/.42282/0973 19
1. Petroleum industry and trade - Statistics. 2. Organization of Petroleum Exporting Countries - Statistics. 3. Petroleum products - Prices - Statistics. I. Petroleum Industry Monitoring System (U. S.).
HD9560.4 .P48

PINE BARRENS.
New Jersey. Pinelands Commission. Draft comphrehensive management plan for the Pinelands National Reserve. New Lisbon, N. J. , 1980. 2 v. :   *NYPL [JLF 80-1614]*

Pine Bluff, Ark. Agricultural, Mechanical and Normal College. see Arkansas. Agricultural, Mechanical and Normal College, Pine Bluff.

PINEAPPLE - HAWAII - MOLOKAI - SOILS.
Dissipation of phytotoxic diuron residues in Hawaii pineapple soils /. Honolulu [1981] p. cm.   LC Card 81-6945   DDC 632/.954 19
S592.6.H47 D57

Pinelands. see Pine Barrens.

PINK SALMON.
University of Alaska, Fairbanks. Institute of Marine Science. Some aspects of the carrying capacity of Prince William Sound, Alaska, for hatchery released pink and chum salmon fry /. Fairbanks , 1978. ix, 98 p. :   LC Card 78-624148   DDC 551.46 s 639.3/755 19
GC1 .A497 no. 78-3 SH167.S17

PINKERTON, ALLAN, 1819-1884 - EXHIBITIONS.
Voss, Frederick. We never sleep . Washington, D.C. , 1981. p. cm.   LC Card 81-607851   DDC 363.2/89/0973 19
HV8087.P75 V67

PINKERTON'S NATIONAL DETECTIVE AGENCY - HISTORY - EXHIBITIONS.
Voss, Frederick. We never sleep . Washington, D.C. , 1981. p. cm.   LC Card 81-607851   DDC 363.2/89/0973 19
HV8087.P75 V67

The piñon pine . Lanner, Ronald M. Reno , 1981, c1980. p. cm.   ISBN 0-87417-065-6   LC Card 81-119   DDC 585/.2 19
QK494.5.P66 L36 1981

PINYON PINES - SOUTHWEST, NEW.
Lanner, Ronald M. The piñon pine . Reno , 1981, c1980. p. cm.   ISBN 0-87417-065-6   LC Card 81-119   DDC 585/.2 19
QK494.5.P66 L36 1981

Pioneer and Historical Society of the State of Michigan. see Michigan State Historical Society.

Pioneer missionary to the Bering Strait Eskimos . Renner, Louis L., 1926- Portland, Ore. , 1979. xv, 207 p. :   ISBN 0-8323-0343-7 : LC Card 79-53362
E99.E7 L257   *NYPL [JFE 80-4064]*

PIONEERS - MINNESOTA - BIOGRAPHY.
Bost, Théodore, 1834-1920. A frontier family in Minnesota . Minneapolis , c1981. p. cm.   ISBN 0-8166-1032-0 :   LC Card 81-10401   DDC 977.6/5 B 19
F606 .B75313

PIONEERS - NEW MEXICO - BIOGRAPHY.
Poe, Sophie A. (Sophie Alberding), 1862- Buckboard days /. Albuquerque , 1981, c1936. p. cm.   ISBN 0-8263-0572-5 :   LC Card 80-54565   DDC 978.9/04/0922 B 19
F786.P8 P63 1981

PIONEERS - SOUTHWEST, NEW - BIOGRAPHY.
Russell, Marian Sloan, 1845-1937. Land of enchantment . Albuquerque [1981] c1954. xiv, 163 p. :   ISBN 0-8263-0571-7 :   LC Card 80-54564   DDC 917.8 19
F786 .R96 1981

PIPE LINES - BRITISH COLUMBIA - MAPS.
British Columbia. Ministry of Mines and Petroleum Resources. Pipelines of British Columbia /. [Victoria] [1978] 1 map ; 73 x 92 cm. Scale 1:1,900,800; 30 miles to 1 in. Photocopy. "May 1978." Inset: Fort St. John area. LC Card 79-691292
G3511.P4 1978 .B7
       NYPL [Map Div. 81-3030]

PIPE LINES, GAS, NATURAL. see GAS, NATURAL - PIPE LINES.

PIPE LINES - NEBRASKA - LITTLE NEMAHA RIVER WATERSHED - MAPS.
United States. Soil Conservation Service. Mines, utilities, and pipeline map, upper Little Nemaha watershed, Lancaster, Cass, and Otoe Counties, Nebraska /. Lincoln, Nebr. , 1979. 1 map : LC

Card 81-691086
G4192.L5H1 1978 .U5

PIPE LINES, PETROLEUM. see PETROLEUM - PIPE LINES.

PIPELINES. see PIPE LINES.

Pipelines and natural resources of the Texas coast /. Texas. Environmental Management Program. [Austin, Tex.] [1980] vi, 266 p. : LC Card 80-622734   DDC 388.5 19
TD195.P5 T49 1980

Pipelines of British Columbia /. British Columbia. Ministry of Mines and Petroleum Resources. [Victoria] [1978] 1 map ; 73 x 92 cm. Scale 1:1,900,800; 30 miles to 1 in. Photocopy. "May 1978." Inset: Fort St. John area. LC Card 79-691292
G3511.P4 1978 .B7
       NYPL [Map Div. 81-3030]

Pipes and tubes of iron or steel from Japan . United States. International Trade Commission. Washington, D.C. [1980] ii, 29, 37 p. ;   LC Card 80-602337   DDC 382/.4567283/0973 19
HF2651.S76 U54 1980a

Pitruzzello, Ronald. (joint author) Steahr, Thomas E. Cause of death and socioeconomic structures of towns in Connecticut /. Storrs , 1976. 43 p. :   LC Card 76-624113   DDC 304.6/4/09746 19
RA407.4.C6 S73

Pitt, William D. (joint author) McManus, Benny R. Tennessee agribusiness /. Knoxville [1979] 38 p. (p. 38 blank for "Notes") :   LC Card 80-622069   DDC 338.1/09768 19
HD9007.T2 M32

Pitts, Griff. Counseling theories, developing counselors /. Lanham, MD [1981] p. cm.   ISBN 0-8191-1476-6 :   LC Card 80-6319   DDC 158/.3 19
BF637.C6 C655

Pitts, J. J. Soil survey of Marion County, South Carolina / [by James J. Pitts] ; United States Department of Agriculture, Soil Conservation Service, in cooperation with South Carolina Agricultural Experiment Station and South Carolina Land Resources Conservation Commission. [Washington] : The Service, 1980. vii, 99 p., [27] fold. leaves of plates : ill. ; 28 cm. Cover title. "Issued July 1980." Bibliography: p. 49.   LC Card 80-603206   DDC 631.4/7/75786 19
1. Soils - South Carolina - Marion Co. - Maps. I. United States. Soil Conservation Service. II. South Carolina. Agricultural Experiment Station, Clemson. III. South Carolina. Land Resources Conservation Commission. IV. Title.
S599.S58 P58

PITTSBURG COUNTY, OKLA. - ANTIQUITIES.
Oklahoma Highway Archaeological Survey. An archaeological survey of U. S. 69, Pittsburg, Atoka, and Bryan Counties, Oklahoma /. [Norman] , 1976. v, 158 p. :   LC Card 77-621832   DDC 976.6/6 19
E78.O45 O48 1976

Pittsburgh. Carnegie-Mellon University. see Carnegie-Mellon University.

PITTSBURGH METROPOLITAN AREA - OCCUPATIONS - STATISTICS.
Pennsylvania. Bureau of Employment Security. Research and Statistics Division. Occupational staffing patterns of selected regulated industries in Pennsylvania. [Harrisburg] , 1979. ii, 73 p. ; LC Card 79-624037
HD5725.P4 P45 1979   *NYPL [JLF 80-1646]*

PITTSBURGH. POST OFFICE.
Mail damage reduction and service improvement pilot program for the Pittsburgh Post Office . Morgantown [1974?] 64 leaves ;   LC Card 77-623863   DDC 383/.14/0974886 19
HE6497.D35 M34

Pittsburgh Research Center. Bureau of Mines Technology Transfer Seminars (1980 : Pittsburgh, Pa., etc.) Mine safety education and training seminar . Washington, D.C. [1981] p. cm.   LC Card 81-607813   DDC 622 s 622/.8/071 19
TN295 .U4

Pittsburgh. University. Black Community Education Research and Development, Dept. of. see Pittsburgh. University. Dept. of Black Community Education Research and Development.

Pittsburgh. University. Dept. of Black Community Education Research and Development. Daniel, Jack L. What can you do with a major in Black studies /. [Pittsburgh] , 1973. vii [i. e. iii], 21 leaves :
       NYPL [Sc Micro R-3643]

PIUTE INDIANS. see PAIUTE INDIANS.

Pizer, Donald. Twentieth-century American literary naturalism : an interpretation / by Donald Pizer. Carbondale : Southern Illinois University Press, c1982. p. cm. (Crosscurrents/modern critiques/new series) Bibliography: p. Includes index.   ISBN 0-8093-1027-9   LC Card 81-5606   DDC 813/.5/0912 19
1. American fiction - 20th century - History and criticism. 2. Naturalism in literature. I. Title.
PS374.N29 P5

PL-566 watershed projects. United States. Soil Conservation Service. Missouri, status of PL-566 watershed projects /. Lincoln, Nebr. , 1979. 1 map :   LC Card 81-691209
G4161.C315 1979 .U5

PL-566 watershed projects. United States. Soil Conservation Service. Missouri, status of PL-566 watershed projects /. Lincoln, Nebr. , 1980. 1 map :   LC Card 81-691208
G4161.C315 1980 .U5

PLACE-NAMES. see NAMES, GEOGRAPHICAL.

The place of poetry . Clausen, Christopher, 1942- Lexington , 1981. p. cm.   ISBN 0-8131-1429-2 :   LC Card 80-5172   DDC 821/.009 19
PS303 .C57

Placek, P. L. Feed grade versus extraction correlations on uranium ores from New Mexico /. Avondale, Md. , 1981. p. cm.   LC Card 80-607857   DDC 622 s 622/.34932 19
TN23 .U43 TN490.U7

Placer gold mining in Washington /. Moen, Wayne S. Olympia , 1979. 21 p. :
       *NYPL [*ZQ-577]*

Placing minority women in professional jobs /. Glover, Robert W. Washington , 1978. vii, 75 p. ;   LC Card 78-600751
HD5701 .U53 no. 55 HD6053.6.U5
       NYPL [Sc F 81-49]

Plain folk : the life stories of undistinguished Americans / edited and with an introduction by David M. Katzman and William M. Tuttle, Jr. Urbana : University of Illinois Press, c1981. p. cm. Edited essays from the Independent published between 1902 and 1906. Includes bibliographical references.   ISBN 0-252-00884-7   LC Card 81-3026   DDC 973.91/1/0922 B 19
1. United States - Social life and customs - 1865-1918 - Addresses, essays, lectures. 2. Labor and laboring classes - United States - History - 20th century - Addresses, essays, lectures. 3. United States - Biography - Addresses, essays, lectures. I. Katzman, David M. II. Tuttle, William M., 1937-. III. Independent (New York, N.Y.).
E168 .P7

Plain talk about improving the economy of New York /. New York (State). Legislature. Senate. Standing Committee on Commerce and Economic Development. Albany, N.Y. [1980] 196 p. ;   LC Card 81-620511   DDC 338.9747 19
HC107.N7 N3743 1980

Plan de développement pour la région Sud-Ouest. Development and Resources Corporation. [A development plan for the Southwest region; a report. French.] New York, 1968. 1 v. (various pagings) LC Card 81-468759   DDC 338.9666/8 19
HC1025 .D4814 1968

Plan for New York City, 1969. New York (City). City Planning Commission. Cambridge, Mass. [c1969] 6 v.   ISBN 0-262-64004-X (v. 1) varies   LC Card 78-89854
HT168.N5 A5

Plan for vocational rehabilitation services, fiscal years, 1978-1980. Illinois. Division of Vocational Rehabilitation. [Springfield] [1977] v, 105 p. :   LC Card 78-621657   DDC 362.4/0484 19
HV1555.I3 I4 1977

A plan to provide professional education and services to underserved areas of the State . Kentucky. Professional Schools Admissions Committee. Frankfort, Ky. , 1979. x, 48 p. ;   LC Card 80-620638   DDC 344.769/011231

347.690411231 19
KFK1325 .A25 1979

PLANETARY GEARING. see GEARING, PLANETARY.

Planification de programmes nationaux de nutrition . American Technical Assistance Corporation. [Washington, D.C.] [1973] 2 v. : LC Card 80-136136 DDC 362.1/9639 19
TX359 .A43 1973

PLANING-MILLS - CALIFORNIA - ACCIDENTS - STATISTICS.
California. Dept. of Industrial Relations. Division of Labor Statistics and Research. California sawmills and planing mills industry . San Francisco , 1978. v, 26 p. ; LC Card 79-623207 DDC 312/.43/09794 19
RC965.W6 C28 1978

PLANKTON POPULATIONS.
Lei, Chi-hsiang. Population dynamics and production of Daphnia ambigua in a fish pond, Kansas /. [Lawrence] , 1980. p. [687]-715 : LC Card 80-621787 DDC 500 s 591.5/26322 19
Q1 .K17 vol. 51, no. 25 QL143

Planned Parenthood Federation of America. Alan Guttmacher Institute. see Alan Guttmacher Institute.

Planner's data book for Bergen County.
Hackensack, N. J., County Planning Board, County of Bergen. 28 cm. (Bergen County, N. J. Planning Board. Technical report)
1. Regional planning - New Jersey - Bergen County - Collected works. I. Bergen County, N. J. Planning Board. II. Series.   **NYPL [JLM 81-199]**

Planning & development review. v. 1-2, no. 6; 1978-79. Chicago, Dept. of Planning, City and Community Development. 2 v. in 1 illus. 28 cm. Monthly (irregular) Supersedes Urban renewal review. For later file, which continues its numbering, see Planning in review.
1. City planning - Illinois - Chicago - Periodicals. I. Chicago. Dept. of Planning, City and Community Development.   **NYPL [JLM 80-1121]**

Planning and zoning handbook. Hotaling, Robert B. Michigan townships planning and zoning handbook/. East Lansing (27 Kellogg Center for Continuing Education, MSU, East Lansing 48824) , 1980. xii, 208 p. : LC Card 80-620046 DDC 346.77404/5 347.740645 19
KFM4658 .H67

PLANNING, CITY. see CITY PLANNING.

Planning, conservation, and regulation : issues for the 80s : proceedings of a workshop held in Laramie, Wyoming, November 9, 1979 / Susan Morgenstern, editor. [Cheyenne] : Wyoming Dept. of Economic Planning and Development, Office of the Chief of State Planning, [1980] v, 108 p. : ill. ; 28 cm. "March 1980." Sponsored by the Department of Economic Planning and Development, the Public Service Commission, and the Energy Conservation Office. LC Card 80-622619 DDC 333.79/09787 19
1. Energy policy - Wyoming - Congresses. 2. Energy conservation - Wyoming - Congresses. I. Morgenstern, Susan. II. Wyoming. State Dept. of Economic Planning and Development. III. Wyoming. Public Service Commission. IV. Wyoming. Energy Conservation Office.
HD9502.U53 W85

Planning considerations for winter sports resort development /. United States. Forest Service. [Washington] , 1973. iii, 53 p. :
         NYPL [JLF 79-1344]

PLANNING, ECONOMIC. see ECONOMIC POLICY.

PLANNING, EDUCATIONAL. see EDUCATIONAL PLANNING.

Planning, environmental and related enabling legislation. New Jersey. Laws, statutes, etc. [Trenton] , 1980. 66 p. ; LC Card 80-622986 DDC 344.749/046 19
KFN2154 .A3 1980

Planning, for a change . Dale, Duane, 1946- Amherst , c1978. 88 p. : LC Card 79-624733
JK1764 .D35   **NYPL [JLF 81-311]**

Planning for exterior work on the First Parish Church, Portland, Maine, using photographs as project documentation. Washington, D.C. : Heritage Conservation and Recreation Service, Technical Preservation Services, U. S. Dept. of the Interior : for sale by the Supt. of Docs., U. S. Govt. Print. Off., 1979. 55 p. : ill. ; 28 cm. (Preservation case studies) HCRS publication ; no. 20 CONTENTS. - Hecker, J. C. A preliminary survey of the building.--Doughty, S. W. Architect's specifications for project work. LC Card 80-601858 DDC 726/.5/0288 19
1. Portland, Me. First Parish Church. 2. Churches - Maine - Portland - Conservation and restoration. I. Hecker, John C. II. Doughty, Sylvanus W. III. Series. IV. Series: United States. Heritage Conservation and Recreation Service. HCRS publication, no. 20.
NA5235.P7 P57

Planning for the future. South Dakota. State Library Commission. South Dakota State Library . Pierre, S.D. , 1979. 50 p. : LC Card 80-621618 DDC 027.0783 19
Z678.4.S8 S68 1979

Planning for the phase-in of fixed-route accessible buses : interim report /. Booz, Allen and Hamilton, inc. Transportation Consulting Division. Washington , 1980. 1 v. :
         NYPL [JLM 80-1153]

Planning for trilateral scientific and technological cooperation by Egypt, Israel, and the United States : letter of transmittal from the President of the United States and text of the report on a plan for United States participation in trilateral scientific and technological cooperation .... Washington : U. S. G.P.O., 1980. vii, 49 p. ; 24 cm. At head of title: 96th Congress, 2d session. Committee print. "Printed for the use of the Committee on Foreign Affairs." LC Card 80-603873 DDC 327.1/7 19
1. Science and state - United States. 2. Technology and state - United States. 3. Science and state - Egypt. 4. Science and state - Israel. 5. Science - International cooperation. 6. Technology - International cooperation. I. United States. President (1977-1981 : Carter). II. United States. Congress. House. Committee on Foreign Affairs.
Q127.U6 P53

Planning for wildlife in cities and suburbs /. Leedy, Daniel L. [Washington] , 1978. vii, 64 p. : LC Card 79-603493 DDC 639.9/09173/2 19
QH541.5.C6 L43 1978

Planning handbooks for local districts. Trenton, N. J. Issues for 1974 published by the New Jersey State Dept. of Education, Bureau of Planning; for 1975- by the dept's Division of Research, Planning and Evaluation.
1. Educational planning - New Jersey - Collected works. 2. Education - New Jersey - Collected works. I. New Jersey. State Dept. of Education. Bureau of Planning. II. New Jersey. State Dept. of Education. Division of Research, Planning and Evaluation.
         NYPL [JLM 81-301]

PLANNING - HANDBOOKS, MANUALS, ETC.
Dale, Duane, 1946- Planning, for a change . Amherst , c1978. 88 p. : LC Card 79-624733
JK1764 .D35   **NYPL [JLF 81-311]**

Planning in review. v. 3, no. 2- ; June 1980- Chicago. Issued by the Chicago Dept. of Planning.
I. Chicago. Dept. of Planning.
         NYPL [Econ. Div.]

Planning information for vocational education, State of Iowa, fiscal year 1981. Iowa. Dept. of Job Service. Labor Market Information Unit. Des Moines, Iowa [1980] 112 p. : LC Card 80-622458 DDC 373.2/46/09777 19
LC1046.I8 I65 1980

PLANNING, NATIONAL. see ECONOMIC POLICY.

PLANNING, STATE. see ECONOMIC POLICY.

Planning U. S. general purpose forces . United States. Congressional Budget Office. Washington , 1977. xxiii, 95 p. : LC Card 77-603153
UA26.E27 U54 1977

PLANT AND EQUIPMENT INVESTMENTS. see CAPITAL INVESTMENTS.

PLANT AND OFFICE LAYOUT. see OFFICE LAYOUT.

PLANT ASSOCIATIONS. see PLANT COMMUNITIES.

PLANT-BREEDING - HAWAII - CONGRESSES.
Crop improvement in Hawaii--past, present,

future . [Honolulu] [1981] p. cm. LC Card 81-4885 DDC 631.5/3/09969 19
SB123 .C82

PLANT CLASSIFICATION. see BOTANY - CLASSIFICATION.

PLANT COMMUNITIES.
Davis, Graham J. Responses of submersed vascular plant communities to environmental change . Washington, D.C. , 1980. x, 70 p. : LC Card 80-607178 DDC 581.5/2623 19
QK930 .D38

PLANT COMMUNITIES - MONTANA - YELLOW WATER TRIANGLE.
Jorgensen, Henry E. Vegetation of the Yellow Water Triangle, Montana /. [Helena] , 1979. vii, 57 p. : LC Card 79-626265 DDC 581.5/2643/09786 19
QK171 .J67

PLANT CONSERVATION - CONGRESSES.
Conference on the Functions of Living Plant Collections in Conservation and Conservation-Orientated Research and Public Education, Kew, Eng., 1975. Conservation of threatened plants . New York , c1976. xvi, 336 p. : ISBN 0-306-32801-1 LC Card 76-20762
QK86.A1 C66 1975 NYPL [JSK 77-181 v.1]

PLANT CYTOTAXONOMY.
Chromosome numbers in Compositae, XII. Washington , 1981. p. cm. LC Card 81-607855 DDC 581 s 5831.55 19
QK1 .S2747 no. 52 QK495.C74

PLANT EVOLUTION. see PLANTS - EVOLUTION.

PLANT GROWTH. see GROWTH (PLANTS)

PLANT INTRODUCTION - HAWAII - CONGRESSES.
Crop improvement in Hawaii--past, present, future . [Honolulu] [1981] p. cm. LC Card 81-4885 DDC 631.5/3/09969 19
SB123 .C82

Plant juice protein and moisture expression from organic materials : a bibliography, addenda to R2386 published May, 1976 / by H. W. Ream ... [et al.]. Madison : Research Division, College of Agricultural and Life Sciences, University of Wisconsin--Madison, [1978] 17 p. ; 28 cm. "R2386-1." Addition to the publication of the same title by the Research Division, College of Agricultural and Life Sciences, University of Wisconsin--Madison. LC Card 79-625898 DDC 016.664/6 19
1. Plant proteins - Bibliography. 2. Extraction (Chemistry) - Bibliography. I. Ream, H. W. II. Wisconsin. University, Madison. College of Agricultural and Life Sciences. Research Division. III. Wisconsin. University--Madison. College of Agricultural and Life Sciences. Research Division. Plant juice protein and moisture expression from organic materials.
Z5524.P83 P53 TP453.P7

PLANT NEMATODES - BIBLIOGRAPHY.
O'Bannon, J. H. Bibliography of nematodes of citrus . Washington , 1979. 11 p. ; LC Card 79-602330 DDC 016.634/35965182 19
Z5354.P3 C636 Suppl SB608.C5

PLANT NUTRITION. see PLANTS - NUTRITION.

Plant nutrition, magnesium and hypomagnesemia in animals /. Hannaway, D. B. Lexington, Ky [1980] 90 p. ; LC Card 80-623110 DDC 581.1/3354 19
QK753.M27 H36

PLANT POPULATIONS.
Demography and evolution in plant populations /. Berkeley , 1980. xiv, 222 p. : ISBN 0-520-03931-9 LC Card 79-64486 DDC 581.5/248 19
QK910 .D45

PLANT POPULATIONS - ANDES.
Smith, Alan P. Growth and population dynamics of Espeletia (Compositae) in the Venezuelan Andes /. Washington , 1981. p. cm. LC Card 81-607061 DDC 581 s 583/.55 19
QK1 .S2747 no. 48 QK495.C74

PLANT POPULATIONS - VENEZUELA.
Smith, Alan P. Growth and population dynamics of Espeletia (Compositae) in the Venezuelan Andes /. Washington , 1981. p. cm. LC Card 81-607061 DDC 581 s 583/.55 19
QK1 .S2747 no. 48 QK495.C74

Plant protection . Sill, Webster H., 1916- Ames, Iowa [1981] p. cm. ISBN 0-8138-1665-3 LC Card 81-12323 DDC 632 19
SB950 .S54

PLANT PROTEINS - BIBLIOGRAPHY.
Plant juice protein and moisture expression from organic materials . Madison [1978] 17 p. ; LC Card 79-625898 DDC 016.664/6 19
Z5524.P83 P53 TP453.P7

PLANT SHUTDOWNS - LAW AND LEGISLATION - UNITED STATES.
United States. Congress. House. Committee on Education and Labor. Subcommittee on Labor-Management Relations. Hearings on plant closing problems . Washington , 1980. vi, 500 p. ; LC Card 81-600603 DDC 344.73/0125 347.304125 19
KF27 .E347 1980f

United States. Congress. House. Committee on Education and Labor. Subcommittee on Labor-Management Relations. Hearings on plant closing problems . Washington , 1981. iv, 152 p. ; LC Card 81-601623 DDC 343.73/0742 347.303742 19
KF27 .E347 1980h

PLANT SHUTDOWNS - UNITED STATES.
Root, Kenneth. Perspectives for communities and organizations on plant closings and job dislocations /. Ames, Iowa [1979] iv, 32 leaves ; LC Card 80-623164 DDC 338.6/042 19
HD5708.55.U6 R66

United States. Congress. Senate. Committee on Labor and Human Resources. Workers and the evolving economy of the eighties . Washington , 1981. iv, 387 p. : LC Card 81-601377 DDC 331.12/042/0973 19
KF26 .L27 1980s

PLANT SOCIETIES. see PLANT COMMUNITIES.

PLANT-SOIL RELATIONSHIPS.
(1980) Hannaway, D. B. Plant nutrition, magnesium and hypomagnesemia in animals /. Lexington, Ky [1980] 90 p. ; LC Card 80-623110 DDC 581.1/3354 19
QK753.M27 H36

PLANT TAXONOMY. see BOTANY - CLASSIFICATION.

Plant Variety Protection Act . United States. Congress. Senate. Committee on Agriculture, Nutrition, and Forestry. Subcommittee on Agricultural Research and General Legislation. Washington , 1980. iv, 211 p. : LC Card 80-604101 DDC 346.7304/86 347.306486 19
KF26 .A3534 1980d

Plant variety protection act amendments . United States. Congress. House. Committee on Agriculture. Subcommittee on Department Investigations, Oversight, and Research. Washington , 1980. v, 330 p. ; LC Card 80-603003 DDC 346.7304/86 19
KF27 .A33265 1979e

PLANTATION CROPS. see TROPICAL CROPS.

The plantation site (Mi-63) . Briscoe, James M. [Oklahoma City] , 1977. xii, 276 p., [1] fold. leaf of plates : LC Card 79-621192 DDC 976.6/74 19
E99.C13 B74

PLANTATION SITE, OKLA.
Briscoe, James M. The plantation site (Mi-63) . [Oklahoma City] , 1977. xii, 276 p., [1] fold. leaf of plates : LC Card 79-621192 DDC 976.6/74 19
E99.C13 B74

PLANTING. see AGRICULTURE.

PLANTS AND SOIL. see PLANT-SOIL RELATIONSHIPS.

PLANTS - CLASSIFICATION. see BOTANY - CLASSIFICATION.

PLANTS, CULTIVATED - HAWAII - VARIETIES - CONGRESSES.
Crop improvement in Hawaii--past, present, future . [Honolulu] [1981] p. cm. LC Card 81-4885 DDC 631.5/3/09969 19
SB123 .C82

PLANTS, CULTIVATED - VARIETIES - LAW AND LEGISLATION - UNITED STATES.
United States. Congress. House. Committee on Agriculture. Subcommittee on Department Investigations, Oversight, and Research. Plant variety protection act amendments . Washington , 1980. v, 330 p. ; LC Card 80-603003 DDC 346.7304/86 19
KF27 .A33265 1979e

United States. Congress. Senate. Committee on Agriculture, Nutrition, and Forestry. Subcommittee on Agricultural Research and General Legislation. Plant Variety Protection Act . Washington , 1980. iv, 211 p. : LC Card 80-604101 DDC 346.7304/86 347.306486 19
KF26 .A3534 1980d

PLANTS, DESERT. see DESERT FLORA.

PLANTS, EFFECT OF CARBOLIC ACID ON.
Bofill, Jordi. Uptake and release of phenol by algal cells /. Austin, Tex. [1979] vii leaves, 49 p. : LC Card 80-622520 DDC 589.3/133 19
QK565 .B57

PLANTS, EFFECT OF DIURON ON - HAWAII - MOLOKAI.
Dissipation of phytotoxic diuron residues in Hawaii pineapple soils /. Honolulu [1981] p. cm. LC Card 81-6945 DDC 632/.954 19
S592.6.H47 D57

PLANTS, EFFECT OF FLUE GASES ON.
Munshower, Frank F. The effects of stack emissions on the range resource in the vicinity of Colstrip, Montana . Bozeman , 1977, cover 1978. ix, 196 p. : LC Card 78-623223 DDC 574.5/2643 19
QH545.C57 M86

PLANTS, EFFECT OF GLYPHOSATE ON.
Nishimoto, R. K. (Roy Katsuto), 1944- Effects of Polado on several horticultural crops /. Honolulu , 1981. p. cm. LC Card 81-2796 DDC 633.6/14 19
SB608.V4 N57

PLANTS, EFFECT OF HERBICIDES ON.
Modes of action of selected herbicides /. Honolulu, Hawaii [1981] p. cm. LC Card 81-2376 DDC 632/.953 19
SB951.4 .M62

United States. Congress. House. Committee on Agriculture. Subcommittee on Forests. Phenoxy herbicides in forest management . Washington , 1980. iii, 152 p. : LC Card 80-602796 DDC 333.75/16/0978 19
KF27 .A348 1980

PLANTS, EFFECT OF LIGHT ON.
Davis, Graham J. Responses of submersed vascular plant communities to environmental change . Washington, D.C. , 1980. x, 70 p. : LC Card 80-607178 DDC 581.5/2623 19
QK930 .D38

PLANTS, EFFECT OF MAGNESIUM ON.
Hannaway, D. B. Plant nutrition, magnesium and hypomagnesemia in animals /. Lexington, Ky [1980] 90 p. ; LC Card 80-623110 DDC 581.1/3354 19
QK753.M27 H36

PLANTS, EFFECT OF POLYOXYMETHYLENE ON.
Shigo, Alex L., 1930- Some effects of paraformaldehyde on wood surrounding tapholes in sugar maple trees /. Upper Darby, Pa. , 1970. 11 p. : LC Card 81-460882 DDC 634.9/0974 s 633.6/49 19
SD11 .A455493 no. 161 SB608.S913

PLANTS, EFFECT OF SHADE ON.
Ruth, Robert H. Effect of shade on germination and growth of salmonberry /. Portland, Or. , 1970. 10 p. : LC Card 70-608740 DDC 634.9/09795 s 634/.711 19
SD11 .A45614 no. 96 QK495.R78

PLANTS, EFFECT OF STRESS ON.
Davis, Graham J. Responses of submersed vascular plant communities to environmental change . Washington, D.C. , 1980. x, 70 p. : LC Card 80-607178 DDC 581.5/2623 19
QK930 .D38

PLANTS - EVOLUTION.
Demography and evolution in plant populations /. Berkeley , 1980. xiv, 222 p. : ISBN 0-520-03931-9 LC Card 79-64486 DDC 581.5/248 19
QK910 .D45

Plants for California landscapes . California. Dept. of Water Resources. [Sacramento, Calif.] [1979] vi, 127 p. : LC Card 80-621393 DDC 635.9/52 19
SB472.32.U6 C34 1979

PLANTS - GROWTH. see GROWTH (PLANTS)

PLANTS - NUTRITION.
(1980) Hannaway, D. B. Plant nutrition, magnesium and hypomagnesemia in animals /. Lexington, Ky [1980] 90 p. ; LC Card 80-623110 DDC 581.1/3354 19
QK753.M27 H36

Plants of Deep Canyon and the central Coachella Valley, California /. Zabriskie, Jan G., 1947- Riverside , c1979. 175 p. : LC Card 79-63644 DDC 581.9794/97 19
QK149 .Z32

PLANTS, ORNAMENTAL - CALIFORNIA - DROUGHT RESISTANCE.
California. Dept. of Water Resources. Plants for California landscapes . [Sacramento, Calif.] [1979] vi, 127 p. : LC Card 80-621393 DDC 635.9/52 19
SB472.32.U6 C34 1979

PLANTS - PATENTS.
United States. Congress. House. Committee on Agriculture. Subcommittee on Department Investigations, Oversight, and Research. Plant variety protection act amendments . Washington , 1980. v, 330 p. ; LC Card 80-603003 DDC 346.7304/86 19
KF27 .A33265 1979e

United States. Congress. Senate. Committee on Agriculture, Nutrition, and Forestry. Subcommittee on Agricultural Research and General Legislation. Plant Variety Protection Act . Washington , 1980. iv, 211 p. : LC Card 80-604101 DDC 346.7304/86 347.306486 19
KF26 .A3534 1980d

PLANTS, PROTECTION OF.
Kratky, B. A., 1944- Protecting lettuce plants from preemergence herbicide damage /. [Honolulu] [1980] 7 p. : LC Card 80-26589 DDC 635/.529 19
SB608.L523 K7

Sill, Webster H., 1916- Plant protection . Ames, Iowa [1981] p. cm. ISBN 0-8138-1665-3 LC Card 81-12323 DDC 632 19
SB950 .S54

PLANTS, PROTECTION OF - PERIODICALS.
Convention of International Trade in Endangered Species of Wild Fauna and Flora. Annual report by the United States of America. 1977- Washington . *NYPL [JLM 80-800]*

PLANTS - SOILLESS CULTURE. see HYDROPONICS.

Plantz, Merritt A. (Merritt Alexander), 1921- Soil survey of Keya Paha County, Nebraska. [Washington, D.C.?] , 1980. ix, 224 p., 62 folded p. of plates : LC Card 81-600561 DDC 631.4/7/782725 19
S599.N2 S63

PLASMA CONFINEMENT.
Fusion energy, an overview of magnetic confinement approach, its objectives, and pace . Washington , 1980. xiv, 182 p. : LC Card 81-600666 DDC 621.48/4 19
TK9204 .F87

PLASMA CONTAINMENT. see PLASMA CONFINEMENT.

PLASMA CONTROL. see PLASMA CONFINEMENT.

PLASMA ISOLATION. see PLASMA CONFINEMENT.

Plass, W. T. Seminar on the Role of Overburden Analysis in Surface Mining (1980 : Wheeling, W. VA.) Proceedings of Seminar on the Role of Overburden Analysis in Surface Mining, Wheeling, W. Va., May 6-7, 1980 /. Washington , 1981. p. cm. LC Card 81-607049 DDC 622 s 622/.31 19
TN295 .U4 TD195.S75

PLASTIC COATING - CONGRESSES.
Powder Coatings Conference, Cleveland, 1972. Powder Coatings Conference proceedings. Cleveland , 1973. 146 leaves :
NYPL [JSF 81-290]

PLASTIC INDUSTRIES. see PLASTICS INDUSTRY AND TRADE.

PLASTIC POWDERS - CONGRESSES.
Powder Coatings Conference, Cleveland, 1972.
Powder Coatings Conference proceedings.
Cleveland , 1973. 146 leaves :
    NYPL [JSF 81-290]

The plastics industry /. Gordian Associates. Oak
Ridge, Tenn. , 1977. v, 31 p. ; ISBN
    0-87079-202-4 : LC Card 77-12044 DDC
    338.4/5 19
TP1120 .G59 1977

PLASTICS INDUSTRY AND TRADE.
(1977) Gordian Associates. The plastics
industry /. Oak Ridge, Tenn. , 1977. v, 31 p. ;
    ISBN 0-87079-202-4 : LC Card 77-12044
    DDC 338.4/5 19
TP1120 .G59 1977

**PLASTICS INDUSTRY AND TRADE -
    ENERGY CONSUMPTION.**
Gordian Associates. The plastics industry /.
Oak Ridge, Tenn. , 1977. v, 31 p. ; ISBN
    0-87079-202-4 : LC Card 77-12044 DDC
    338.4/5 19
TP1120 .G59 1977

Platão. see Plato.

PLATE TECTONICS.
Hietanen, Anna Martta, 1909- The Feather
River area as a part of the Sierra Nevada suture
system in California . Washington , 1981. p.
cm. LC Card 80-606891 DDC 551.8/709794 19
QE90.F4 H5

PLATINUM GROUP.
Bennetts, J. (John) Preparation of platinum
flotation concentrate from stillwater complex
ore /. Avondale, Md. [1981] p. cm. LC Card
    80-606913 DDC 622 s 622/.3424 19
TN23 .U43 TN523

PLATINUM ORES - ALASKA.
Dahlin, D. C. (David Clifford), 1951-
Beneficiation of potential platinum resources
from southeastern Alaska /. Washington, D.C.
[1981] p. cm. LC Card 81-607026 DDC 622 s
    622/.3424 19
TN23 .U43 TN538.P53

PLATO.
Brumbaugh, Robert Sherrick, 1918- Process
metaphysics and educational theory /. Albany ,
1981. p. cm. ISBN 0-87395-574-9 LC Card
    81-14329 DDC 370/.1 19
LB85.P7 B78

PLATO - KNOWLEDGE, THEORY OF.
Moline, Jon, 1937- Plato's theory of
understanding /. Madison, Wis. , 1981. p. cm.
    ISBN 0-299-08660-7 : LC Card 81-50826
    DDC 121 19
B398.K7 M64

Platon. see Plato.

Plato's theory of understanding /. Moline, Jon,
1937- Madison, Wis. , 1981. p. cm. ISBN
    0-299-08660-7 : LC Card 81-50826 DDC 121
    19
B398.K7 M64

Platt, Rutherford H. Intergovernmental
management of floodplains / Rutherford H.
Platt, with the assistance of George M.
McMullen ... [et al.] ; special consultant, Jon A.
Kusler. [Boulder] : Institute of Behavioral
Science, University of Colorado, 1980. xv, 317
p. : ill. ; 23 cm. (Monograph - Program on
Technology, Environment, and Man ; # 30) Includes
bibliographies. LC Card 80-82675 DDC
    350.82/329/0973 19
    *1. Floodplains - United States - Management. 2. Water
    resources development - United States. 3. Land use -
    United States - Planning. I. Series: Colorado.
    University. Program on Technology, Environment, and
    Man. Monograph - Program on Technology,
    Environment, and Man, University of Colorado , #30.
    II. Title.*
HD1694 .A5126 1980

**Platte County Extension Homemaker's Council
    (Wyo.)** Wyoming Platte County heritage /
Platte County Extension Homemaker's Council.
Wheatland, Wyo. : The Council, c1981. p. cm.
Includes index. LC Card 81-2567 DDC 978.7/17 19
    *1. Platte County (Wyo.) - History. 2. Platte County
    (Wyo.) - Biography. I. Title.*
F767.P5 P58 1981

PLATTE COUNTY (WYO.) - BIOGRAPHY.
Platte County Extension Homemaker's Council
(Wyo.) Wyoming Platte County heritage /.

Wheatland, Wyo. , c1981. p. cm. LC Card
    81-2567 DDC 978.7/17 19
F767.P5 P58 1981

PLATTE COUNTY (WYO.) - HISTORY.
Platte County Extension Homemaker's Council
(Wyo.) Wyoming Platte County heritage /.
Wheatland, Wyo. , c1981. p. cm. LC Card
    81-2567 DDC 978.7/17 19
F767.P5 P58 1981

PLATYHELMINTHES - IDENTIFICATION.
McDonald, Malcolm Edwin, 1915- Key to
trematodes reported in waterfowl /.
Washington, D.C. , 1981. p. cm. LC Card
    81-607044 DDC 333.95/4/0973 s 639.9/741 19
S914 .A3 no. 142 QL391.P7

Plaut, Thomas R. The gross regional product of
Texas and its regions / Thomas R. Plaut and
Mildred C. Anderson. Austin : Bureau of
Business Research, University of Texas at
Austin, c1981. xi, 54 p. : ill. ; 23 cm.
Bibliography: p. [53]-54. ISBN 0-87755-244-4 (pbk.)
    LC Card 80-68661 DDC 339.3764 19
    *1. Texas - Economic conditions. I. Anderson, Mildred
    C. II. Title.*
HC107.T4 P58

Plaxico, James Sam, 1924- (joint author) Kletke,
Darrel D. Farmland investment value appraisal
and purchase feasibility analyses . [Stillwater] ,
1978. 83 p. ; LC Card 78-624315 DDC
    333.33/5/0973 19
HD1393 .K56 1978

PLAY.
Recommendations for child play areas /.
[Milwaukee] [1980?] vi, 808 leaves : LC Card
    80-153214 DDC 711/.558 19
GV423 .R33

The play of musement /. Sebeok, Thomas Albert,
1920- Bloomington , c1981. p. cm. ISBN
    0-253-39994-7 LC Card 80-8846 DDC 001.51
    19
P99 .S33

**Playa Lake monitoring for the Llano Estacado
    total water management study** . Texas. Dept. of
Water Resources. [Austin] , 1980. 18 leaves, [2]
leaves of plates : LC Card 80-621333 DDC
    553.7/8/0723 19
TD224.T4 T36 1980

**PLAYAS - TEXAS - LUBBOCK CO. - DATA
    PROCESSING.**
Texas. Dept. of Water Resources. Playa Lake
monitoring for the Llano Estacado total water
management study . [Austin] , 1980. 18 leaves,
[2] leaves of plates : LC Card 80-621333 DDC
    553.7/8/0723 19
TD224.T4 T36 1980

**PLAYAS - TEXAS - LUBBOCK CO. -
    MATHEMATICAL MODELS.**
Texas. Dept. of Water Resources. Playa Lake
monitoring for the Llano Estacado total water
management study . [Austin] , 1980. 18 leaves,
[2] leaves of plates : LC Card 80-621333 DDC
    553.7/8/0723 19
TD224.T4 T36 1980

PLAYGROUNDS - ABSTRACTS.
Hill, Ann B. Abstracts on child play areas and
child support facilities /. Milwaukee [Wis.] ,
Milwaukee, WI (P.O. Box 413, Milwaukee,
Wis. 53201) c1978. v, 102 leaves : LC Card
    81-106795 DDC 790/.06/8 19
GV423 .H54

PLAYGROUNDS - BIBLIOGRAPHY.
Moore, Gary T. Bibliography on children and
the physical environment . Milwaukee [Wis.] ,
Milwaukee, WI (P.O. Box 413, Milwaukee,
Wis. 53201) [1979] v, 143 p. ; LC Card
    81-106815 DDC 016.3052/3 19
Z7164.C5 M68 HQ767.9

PLAYGROUNDS - PLANNING.
Recommendations for child play areas /.
[Milwaukee] [1980?] vi, 808 leaves : LC Card
    80-153214 DDC 711/.558 19
GV423 .R33

Playing and coaching wheelchair basketball /.
Owen, Edward S., 1946- Urbana , c1982. p. cm.
    ISBN 0-252-00867-7 LC Card 81-10456 DDC
    796.32/38 19
GV886.5 .O93

Plea bargaining in the United States /. Miller,
Herbert S. [Washington] , 1978. liii, 311, 64,

[14] p. : LC Card 79-602258
KF9654 .M54   *NYPL [JLF 81-304]*

PLEA BARGAINING - PENNSYLVANIA.
Kunkle, John H. Plea negotiation in
Pennsylvania . [Harrisburg] [1979] ii, 105, [76]
p. : LC Card 80-622816 DDC 345.748/072 19
KFP578.5 .K86

PLEA BARGAINING - UNITED STATES.
Miller, Herbert S. Plea bargaining in the United
States /. [Washington] , 1978. liii, 311, 64, [14]
p. : LC Card 79-602258
KF9654 .M54   *NYPL [JLF 81-304]*

Plea negotiation in Pennsylvania . Kunkle, John
H. [Harrisburg] [1979] ii, 105, [76] p. : LC
    Card 80-622816 DDC 345.748/072 19
KFP578.5 .K86

PLEAS OF GUILTY - UNITED STATES.
Goldstein, Abraham S. The passive judiciary .
Baton Rouge , c1981. p. cm. ISBN
    0-8071-0856-1 : LC Card 81-11749 DDC
    345.73/05042 347.3055042 19
KF9640 .G64

Pleasants, James A. (joint author) Watts, Gordon
P. The Monitor . [Kure Beach, N.C.] [1978?]
[87] leaves ; LC Card 80-622593 DDC
    016.9737/52 19
Z1242 .W37 E595.M7

Pleck, Joseph H. (joint author) Grady, Kathleen E.
The male sex role . Rockville, Md. ,
Washington, D.C. , 1979. x, 196 p. ; LC Card
    79-604183 DDC 016.3053 19
Z7164.S42 G7 HQ1075

**PLEIOCENE PERIOD. see GEOLOGY,
    STRATIGRAPHIC - PLIOCENE;
    PALEONTOLOGY - PLIOCENE.**

**Pleistocene and Holocene fluvial history of
    Uphapee Creek, Macon County, Alabama** /.
Markewich, Helaine W. Reston, VA [1981] p.
cm. LC Card 81-607035 DDC 557.3 s
    551.7/9/0976/49 19
QE75 .B9 no. 1522 QE696

**Pleistocene drainage reversal in the Upper Tuttle
    Creek reservoir area of Kansas** /. Chelikowsky,
Joseph Rudolph, 1907- Lawrence , 1976. 10 p. :
    LC Card 76-623731 DDC 557.81 s
    551.48/09781 19
QE113 .A2 no. 211, pt. 1 GB565.K2

**The Pleistocene geology of Amchitka Island
    Aleutian Islands, Alaska** /. Gard, Leonard
Meade, 1923- Washington , 1980. iv, 38 p. :
    LC Card 80-607888 DDC 557.3 s
    551.7/92/097984 19
QE75 .B9 no. 1478 QE84.A38

**PLEISTOCENE PERIOD. see GEOLOGY,
    STRATIGRAPHIC - PLEISTOCENE.**

Plenge, Manuel A. Type specimens of birds in the
Museo de Historia Natural "Javier Prado,"
Lima, Peru / by Manuel A. Plenge. Baton
Rouge : Louisiana State University, 1979. 13
p. ; 23 cm. (Occasional papers of the Museum of
Zoology ; no. 53) Caption title. Bibliography: p. 11-13.
    LC Card 79-623920 DDC 591 s
    598/.074/098525 19
    *1. Birds - Catalogs and collections. 2. Type specimens
    (Natural history). 3. Lima. Universidad de San Marcos.
    Museo de Historia Natural "Javier Prado". I. Lima.
    Universidad de San Marcos. Museo de Historia Natural
    "Javier Prado". II. Series: Louisiana State University,
    Baton Rouge. Museum of Zoology. Occasional papers
    of the Museum of Zoology , no. 53. III. Title.*
QL3 .L67 no. 53 QL677.2

PLEOSCHISMA - CLASSIFICATION.
Kornicker, Louis S., 1919- A restudy of the
Ostracode genus Pleoschisma Brady, 1890
(Myodocopina) /. Washington, D.C. , 1981. iii,
16 p. : LC Card 80-607813 DDC 591 s 595.3/3 19
QL1 .S54 no. 332 QL444.O85

PLESIOGULO.
Harrison, Jessica A. A review of the extinct
wolverine, Plesiogulo (Carnivora, Mustelidae)
from North America /. City of Washington ,
1981. p. cm. LC Card 81-607075 DDC 560 s
    569/.74 19
QE701 .S56 no. 46 QE882.C15

Pleszkun, Andrew R. (joint author) Hannon, Bruce
M. Dollar, energy, and labor cost
differential--leaded vs. unleaded gasoline .
Chicago, IL [1980] vii, 162 p. : LC Card
    80-622965 DDC 338.4/366553827/0973 19
HD9579.G4 H35

Plevin, Amy J. (joint author) Simpson, Clinton H. The development of a methodology for transportation safety planning in Virginia /. Charlottesville, Va. [1980] 37, [24] p. ; LC Card 80-622408 DDC 363.1/206/09755 19
HE5614.3.V8 S57

PLIOCENE PERIOD. see GEOLOGY, STRATIGRAPHIC - PLIOCENE; PALEONTOLOGY - PLIOCENE.

Plog Research, inc. Self-administration of abused substances . Rockville, Md. , 1978. ix, 246 p. : LC Card 78-63094
RC564 .S44   **NYPL** *[JLM 76-1439 [no.] 20]*

PLOTTING CHARTS.
United States. Central Intelligence Agency. World plotting series /. Washington [1976] 7 maps : 77 x 59 cm. or smaller. Scale 1:18,000,000. "Lambert conformal conic, standard parallels 37°N and 65°N." "This map is designed to be used in conjunction with automated cartographic systems." 540931-540937. Includes "Index to sheets." "Series 1147." LC Card 79-691244
G3201.A1 s18000 .U6
     NYPL *[Map. Div. 80-3396]*

Plous, Phyllis. Invented images /. [Santa Barbara] , 1980. 76 p. : LC Card 79-620046
TR646.U6 S3654   **NYPL** *[MFW 81-808]*

Plum culture in Hawaii /. Yee, Warren, 1921- Honolulu , 1981. p. cm. LC Card 81-6824 DDC 634/.22/09969 19
SB377 .Y43

PLUM - HAWAII.
Yee, Warren, 1921- Plum culture in Hawaii /. Honolulu , 1981. p. cm. LC Card 81-6824 DDC 634/.22/09969 19
SB377 .Y43

PLUM ISLAND, MASS.
McDonnell, Mark J. The flora of Plum Island, Essex County, Massachusetts /. Durham, N.H. [1979] ii, 110 p. : LC Card 80-621366 DDC 581.9744/5 19
QK166 .M28

PLUMBISM. see LEAD-POISONING.

PLUMERIA.
Hawaiian plumerias /. Honolulu , 1981. p. cm. LC Card 81-6746 DDC 635.9/77375 19
SB413.P56 H38

Plummer, John F. (John Francis), 1944- Vox feminae . Kalamazoo, Mich. , 1981. viii, 223 p. ; ISBN 0-918720-12-5 (pbk.) : LC Card 81-3981 DDC 809.1/9352042 19
CB351 .S83 vol. 15 PN691

Plummer, Ralph W.
Mail damage reduction and service improvement pilot program for the Pittsburgh Post Office . Morgantown [1974?] 64 leaves ; LC Card 77-623863 DDC 383/.14/0974886 19
HE6497.D35 M34

Proceedings, West Virginia University-United States Postal Service workshop . Morgantown [1973?] 50 p. ; LC Card 77-623862 DDC 383/.14/0973 19
HE6497.D35 P76

United States Postal Service damage reduction program . Morgantown , 1975. 99 leaves ; LC Card 77-623861 DDC 383/.14/0973 19
HE6497.D35 U52

Pluta, Joseph E. Economic and business issues of the 1980's /. [Austin] , c1980. vii, 235 p. : ISBN 0-87755-242-8 (pbk.) LC Card 80-137600 DDC 330.9764/063 19
HC107.T4 E27

Pluvial lakes and estimated pluvial climates of Nevada /. Mifflin, Martin D. Reno , 1979. 57 p. : LC Card 80-621829 DDC 551.48/2/09793 19
QC884 .M53

PLUVIAL PERIODS - NEVADA.
Mifflin, Martin D. Pluvial lakes and estimated pluvial climates of Nevada /. Reno , 1979. 57 p. : LC Card 80-621829 DDC 551.48/2/09793 19
QC884 .M53

PLYMOUTH COUNTY (MASS.) - MAPS.
United States. Soil Conservation Service. Plymouth County, Massachusetts /. Lanham, MD , 1980. 1 map : LC Card 81-690018
G3763.P5 1980 .U5

PNEUMOCOCCAL VACCINE - UNITED STATES.

United States. Congress. Office of Technology Assessment. A review of selected Federal vaccine and immunization policies . Washington , 1979. xvi, 208 p. : LC Card 79-600165 DDC 614.4/7/0973 19
RA638 .U48 1979

PNEUMOCONIOSIS. see LUNGS - DUST DISEASES.

PNEUMOKONIOSIS. see LUNGS - DUST DISEASES.

PNEUMONIA, PNEUMOCOCCAL - UNITED STATES - PREVENTIVE INOCULATION - COST EFFECTIVENESS.
United States. Congress. Office of Technology Assessment. A review of selected Federal vaccine and immunization policies . Washington , 1979. xvi, 208 p. : LC Card 79-600165 DDC 614.4/7/0973 19
RA638 .U48 1979

Poch, George A. Soil survey of Olmsted County, Minnesota / [by George A. Poch] ; United States Department of Agriculture, Soil Conservation Service, in cooperation with Minnesota Agricultural Experiment Station. [Washington, D.C.] : The Service, [1980] ix, 202 p., [53] fold. leaves of plates : ill. ; 28 cm. Cover title. Bibliography: p. 115. Includes index. LC Card 80-602323 DDC 631.4/7/776155 19
1. Soils - Minnesota - Olmsted Co. - Maps. I. United States. Soil Conservation Service. II. Minnesota. Agricultural Experiment Station, St. Anthony Park. III. Title.
S599.M45 P62

Podell, Lawrence. (joint author) Kramer, Rena. Characteristics of enrollees and non-enrollees among freshmen/. New York, 1974. 19 leaves;
*NYPL [*ZT-1254]*

PODIATRISTS - LAW AND LEGISLATION - KANSAS.
Kansas. Laws, statutes, etc. Kansas statutes relating to the practice of podiatry (chiropody) . [Topeka, Kan.] , 1953. 8 p. ; LC Card 81-478968 DDC 344.781/041 347.810441 19
KFK326.5.P62 A32 1953

PODIATRISTS - TEXAS - STATISTICS.
Texas. Bureau of State Health Planning & Resource Development. Data Collection and Analysis Division. Texas health manpower reports . Austin, Tex. [1979?] 47 p. : LC Card 80-622795 DDC 331.12/91617585009764 19
RD563 .T49 1979

PODIATRY - STUDY AND TEACHING - THE WEST.
Welsh, Wayne. A performance audit of the WICHE student exchange program . [Salt Lake City] , 1978. iii, 45 leaves ; LC Card 78-622932 DDC 370.19/62 19
R847.6.U8 W44

POE, JOHN WILLIAM, 1850-1923.
Poe, Sophie A. (Sophie Alberding), 1862- Buckboard days /. Albuquerque , 1981, c1936. p. cm. ISBN 0-8263-0572-5 : LC Card 80-54565 DDC 978.9/04/0922 B 19
F786.P8 P63 1981

Poe, Sophie A. (Sophie Alberding), 1862- Buckboard days / by Sophie A. Poe ; edited by Eugene Cunningham ; introduction by Sandra L. Myres. Albuquerque : University of New Mexico Press, 1981, c1936. p. cm. Reprint. Originally published : Caldwell, Idaho : Caxton Printers, 1936. Includes index. ISBN 0-8263-0572-5 : LC Card 80-54565 DDC 978.9/04/0922 B 19
1. Poe, John William, 1850-1923. 2. Poe, Sophie A. (Sophie Alberding), 1862-. 3. Frontier and pioneer life - New Mexico. 4. New Mexico - History - 1848-. 5. Pioneers - New Mexico - Biography. 6. New Mexico - Biography. I. Cunningham, Eugene, 1896-1957. II. Title.
F786.P8 P63 1981

POE, SOPHIE A. (SOPHIE ALBERDING), 1862-
Poe, Sophie A. (Sophie Alberding), 1862- Buckboard days /. Albuquerque , 1981, c1936. p. cm. ISBN 0-8263-0572-5 : LC Card 80-54565 DDC 978.9/04/0922 B 19
F786.P8 P63 1981

Poet and critic; a magazine of verse, a workshop in print, a forum of opinion. v. 1- ; fall, 1964- Ames, Dept. of English and Speech, Iowa State University. illus. 23 cm. Microfilm. Three no. a year. Supersedes (in old Catalog): Poet & critic; a folder of poetry and criticism. Issued by the Dept. of English

and Speech, Iowa State University.
1. Poetry - Periodicals. I. Iowa. State University of Science and Technology, Ames. Dept. of English and Speech.   **NYPL** *[*ZAN-4509]*

POETICS.
Todorov, Tzvetan, 1939- [Poétique. English.] Introduction to poetics /. Minneapolis , 1981. p. cm. ISBN 0-8166-1008-8 : LC Card 81-3073 DDC 808.1 19
PN1043 .T613

POETRY AND SCIENCE. see LITERATURE AND SCIENCE.

POETRY AND SOCIETY. see LITERATURE AND SOCIETY.

POETRY, MEDIEVAL - HISTORY AND CRITICISM - ADDRESSES, ESSAYS, LECTURES.
Vox feminae . Kalamazoo, Mich. , 1981. viii, 223 p. ; ISBN 0-918720-12-5 (pbk.) : LC Card 81-3981 DDC 809.1/9352042 19
CB351 .S83 vol. 15 PN691

POETRY, MODERN - 20TH CENTURY - HISTORY AND CRITICISM - COLLECTED WORKS.
Carruth, Hayden, 1921- [Selections.] Working papers . Athens , c1981. p. cm. ISBN 0-8203-0583-9 LC Card 81-4404 DDC 809/.04 19
PN771 .C336

POETRY - PERIODICALS.
Poet and critic; a magazine of verse, a workshop in print, a forum of opinion. v. 1- ; fall, 1964- Ames.   **NYPL** *[*ZAN-4509]*

POETRY - PHONOTAPE CATALOGS.
New York (State). State University at Stony Brook. Library. Poetry tapes at Stony Brook . Stony Brook, N.Y. , c1980. iv, 80 p. ; LC Card 80-152658 DDC 016.80881 19
PN1064 .N4 1980

Poetry tapes at Stony Brook . New York (State). State University at Stony Brook. Library. Stony Brook, N.Y. , c1980. iv, 80 p. ; LC Card 80-152658 DDC 016.80881 19
PN1064 .N4 1980

POETRY - TECHNIQUE. see POETICS.

POETRY - VIDEO TAPE CATALOGS.
New York (State). State University at Stony Brook. Library. Poetry tapes at Stony Brook . Stony Brook, N.Y. , c1980. iv, 80 p. ; LC Card 80-152658 DDC 016.80881 19
PN1064 .N4 1980

POETS, AMERICAN - 19TH CENTURY - BIOGRAPHY - ADDRESSES, ESSAYS, LECTURES.
1980, Leaves of grass at 125 . Detroit , 1980. 78 p., [1] leaf of plates : LC Card 81-136978 DDC 811/.3 19
PS3231 .A515

POETS, AMERICAN - 20TH CENTURY - BIOGRAPHY.
Hearst, James, 1900- My shadow below me /. Ames, Iowa , c1981. p. cm. ISBN 0-8138-1136-8 LC Card 81-14265 DDC 811/.52 19
PS3515.E146 Z47

Hearst, James, 1900- Time like a furrow . Iowa City , 1981. p. cm. ISBN 0-89033-004-2 : LC Card 81-13736 DDC 818/.5203 B 19
PS3515.E146 Z475

Lindsay, Clarence B. Hart Crane, an introduction /. Columbus , 1979. 30 p. ; LC Card 80-137513 DDC 811/.52 19
PS3505.R272 Z75

POETS, AMERICAN - 20TH CENTURY - CORRESPONDENCE.
Frost, Robert, 1874-1963. Robert Frost and Sidney Cox . Hanover, N.H. , 1981. xiv, 297 p. ; ISBN 0-87451-195-X : LC Card 80-54464 DDC 811/.52 B 19
PS3511.R94 Z523 1981

Pogany, D. Z. The potential economic impact of solar heated residences in Illinois, 1976-2000 / [D. Z. Pogany, J. E. Dunwoody]. [Springfield] : Illinois Dept. of Business and Economic Development, Division of Energy, 1976. viii, 101 p. : ill. ; 28 cm. Microfiche (neg.) NTIS 2 sheets. 11 x 15 cm. (PB 265489) Cover title. Includes bibliographical references. LC Card 77-622518
1. Solar houses - Illinois. 2. Dwellings - Energy consumption. I. Dunwoody, J. E., joint author. II.

Illinois. Division of Energy. III. Title.
HD7303.I3 P64   NYPL [*XME-9620]

POINT FOUR PROGRAM. see TECHNICAL ASSISTANCE, AMERICAN.

POISONS, ECONOMIC. see PESTICIDES.

POKER.
Hayano, David M. Poker faces . Berkeley , c1982. p. cm.   ISBN 0-520-04492-4   LC Card 81-11549   DDC 306/.4 19
HV6713 .H39

Poker faces . Hayano, David M. Berkeley , c1982. p. cm.   ISBN 0-520-04492-4   LC Card 81-11549   DDC 306/.4 19
HV6713 .H39

Polado on several horticultural crops. Nishimoto, R. K. (Roy Katsuto), 1944- Effects of Polado on several horticultural crops /. Honolulu , 1981. p. cm.   LC Card 81-2796   DDC 633.6/14 19
SB608.V4 N57

POLAND - HISTORY - PIAST PERIOD, 960-1386.
Manteuffel, Tadeusz, 1902-1970. [Polska w okresie prawa książęcego, 963-1194. English.] The formation of the polish state . Detroit , 1981. p. cm.   ISBN 0-8143-1682-4   LC Card 81-11583   DDC 943.8/02 19
DK4212 M3613

POLAR EXPEDITIONS. see ANTARCTIC REGIONS.

POLARITY IN LITERATURE.
Thurin, Erik Ingvar. Emerson as priest of Pan . Lawrence , c1981. p. cm.   ISBN 0-7006-0216-X :   LC Card 81-4818   DDC 814/.3 19
PS1642.S47 T5

POLIA - CLASSIFICATION.
McCabe, Timothy Lee. A reclassification of the Polia complex for North America (Lepidoptera: Noctuidae) /. Albany, N.Y. [1980] vi, 141 p. :   LC Card 80-623061   DDC 595.78/1 19
QL561.N7 M27

POLICE.
National Institute of Law Enforcement and Criminal Justice. Guidelines for developing an injury and damage reduction program in municipal police departments. Washington, 1973. 122 p.:   LC Card 75-102799
NYPL [JLF 80-592]

POLICE ADMINISTRATION - UNITED STATES.
Burpo, John H. Police unions in the civil service setting /. Washington D.C. , 1979. v, 38 p. ;   LC Card 80-601834   DDC 352/.005173/0973 19
HV7936.P47 B87

Greisinger, George W. Civil service systems . Washington, D.C. [1979] xxii, 141, [64] p. :   LC Card 80-601604   DDC 352.2/0973 19
HV7935 .G73

Koepsell, Terry W. Small police agency consolidation . [Washington] , 1979. xii, 102 p. ;   LC Card 79-603014   DDC 352.2/0973 19
HV7921 .K63

Ostrom, Elinor. Policing metropolitan America /. [Washington] [1977] viii, 49 p. :   LC Card 77-603798
HV8138 .O76   NYPL [*XME-9420]

POLICE ADMINISTRATION - UNITED STATES - ABSTRACTS.
Caplan, Marc H. Police manpower management . Washington, D.C. , 1980. vii, 50 p. ;   LC Card 81-601200   DDC 350.74/068/ 19
HV8141 .C34

Police and computer technology . Colton, Kent W. Washington, D.C. [1979] vii, 68 p. ;   LC Card 80-601840   DDC 363.2/028/54 19
HV7936.A8 C58

POLICE - ARIZONA - HANDBOOKS, MANUALS, ETC.
Arizona Prosecuting Attorneys' Advisory Council. Law enforcement officer's manual . [Phoenix, Ariz.] [c1979- 1 v. ;   LC Card 80-148419   DDC 345.791/05 347.91055 19
KFA2975 .A96

POLICE - BIBLIOGRAPHY.
Shanley, Mark. International policing . [Washington] , 1978. vii, 97 p. ;   LC Card 78-602822
Z7164.P76 S5 HV7921 NYPL [JLF 80-1418]

POLICE-COMMUNITY RELATIONS. see PUBLIC RELATIONS - POLICE.

Police-community relations in the city of Wichita and Sedgwick County . United States. Commission on Civil Rights. Kansas Advisory Committee. Washington, D.C. [1980] xi, 95 p. :   LC Card 80-603162   DDC 363.2/2/0978186 19
HV7936.P8 U53 1980

POLICE - JOB STRESS - ABSTRACTS.
Duncan, J. T. Skip. Police stress . [Washington, D.C.] , 1979. vii, 94 p. ;   LC Card 79-603991   DDC 016.3632/2/019 19
HV7936.J63 D86

Police-juvenile diversion . Shepherd, Jack R. Washington, D.C. , 1980. x, 77, [91] p. :   LC Card 81-601094   DDC 364.6/8 19
HV9105.M5 S5 1980

POLICE - KANSAS - COMPLAINTS AGAINST.
United States. Commission on Civil Rights. Kansas Advisory Committee. Police-community relations in the city of Wichita and Sedgwick County . Washington, D.C. [1980] xi, 95 p. :   LC Card 80-603162   DDC 363.2/2/0978186 19
HV7936.P8 U53 1980

POLICE - KANSAS - RECRUITING.
United States. Commission on Civil Rights. Kansas Advisory Committee. Police-community relations in the city of Wichita and Sedgwick County . Washington, D.C. [1980] xi, 95 p. :   LC Card 80-603162   DDC 363.2/2/0978186 19
HV7936.P8 U53 1980

POLICE - LABOR PRODUCTIVITY - ABSTRACTS.
Freimund, Justus. Police productivity /. [Washington] , 1978. vii, 47 p. ;   LC Card 79-602774   DDC 331.11/8 19
HV7936.P7 F73

Police manpower management . Caplan, Marc H. Washington, D.C. , 1980. vii, 50 p. ;   LC Card 81-601200   DDC 350.74/068/ 19
HV8141 .C34

The police patrol car . Ruegg, Rosalie T. Washington , 1978. xvii, 117 p. ;   LC Card 77-13244
QC100 .U57 no. 480-15 HV7936.V4
NYPL [*XME-9526]

POLICE, PRIVATE - FLORIDA.
Florida. Legislature. Senate. Governmental Operations Committee. A review of the Private Security Advisory Council in the Department of State /. [Tallahassee] [1980] i, 28 p. ;   LC Card 81-621187   DDC 353.97590074 19
KFF282.D47 A25 1980

POLICE, PRIVATE - PENNSYLVANIA.
Pennsylvania. General Assembly. Joint State Government Commission. Private detectives and security business . Harrisburg, Pa. [1980] ix, 47 p. ;   LC Card 80-622714   DDC 344.748/017613632 19
KFP282.D47 A25 1980

Police productivity /. Freimund, Justus. [Washington] , 1978. vii, 47 p. ;   LC Card 79-602774   DDC 331.11/8 19
HV7936.P7 F73

POLICE - SALARIES, PENSIONS, ETC. - NORTH CAROLINA.
North Carolina. Legislative Research Commission. Law enforcement officers salary continuation plan . [Raleigh] [1980] iv, 12, [60] p. :   LC Card 80-623281   DDC 331.2/813632/09756 19
KFN7835.8.S7 A25 1980

POLICE - SALARIES, PENSIONS, ETC. - UNITED STATES.
United States. Congress. House. Committee on Education and Labor. Subcommittee on Labor Standards. Hearings on a death benefit for Federal law enforcement officers and firefighters . Washington , 1980. iv, 161 p. ;   LC Card 80-602763   DDC 344.73/023 19
KF27 .E348 1980

POLICE - SALARIES, PENSIONS, ETC. - VIRGINIA.
Virginia. Retirement Study Commission. Report of the Virginia Retirement Study Commission to the Governor and the General Assembly of Virginia. Richmond , 1980. 129 p. ;   LC Card 80-623142   DDC 300/.9755 s 353.9755005 19
J87 .V9 1980c no. 31 JK3960.P4

POLICE SERVICES FOR JUVENILES - MICHIGAN.
Shepherd, Jack R. Police-juvenile diversion . Washington, D.C. , 1980. x, 77, [91] p. :   LC Card 81-601094   DDC 364.6/8 19
HV9105.M5 S5 1980

POLICE - STANDARDS - OREGON - COLLECTED WORKS.
Oregon. Board of Police Standards and Training. Policies and procedures manual /. [Salem, Or.] [1979]- 1 v. :   LC Card 80-623340   DDC 363.2/09795 19
HV7571.O7 B6 1979

POLICE, STATE - NORTH CAROLINA - STATISTICS - PERIODICALS.
North Carolina. State Highway Patrol. Zone operations report. 1964-74 (incomplete). [Raleigh]   NYPL [JLM 80-855]

Police stress . Duncan, J. T. Skip. [Washington, D.C.] , 1979. vii, 94 p. ;   LC Card 79-603991   DDC 016.3632/2/019 19
HV7936.J63 D86

Police traffic radar . North Carolina. Legislative Research Commission. [Raleigh] [1980] 11, [36] p. :   LC Card 80-623288   DDC 363.2/52 19
KFN7697.8 .A25 1980

Police training . Ferry, John. Washington, D.C. [1980] vii, 38 p. ;   LC Card 80-602850   DDC 363.2/2/0715 19
HV8143 .F47

POLICE TRAINING - BIBLIOGRAPHY.
Shanley, Mark. International policing . [Washington] , 1978. vii, 97 p. ;   LC Card 78-602822
Z7164.P76 S5 HV7921 NYPL [JLF 80-1418]

POLICE TRAINING - LAW AND LEGISLATION - VERMONT.
Vermont Criminal Justice Training Council. Rules and regulations /. [Montpelier?] [1979?] 24 p. ;   LC Card 80-623937   DDC 345.743/052 347.430552 19
KFV435.8.S7 A32 1979

POLICE TRAINING - OREGON - COLLECTED WORKS.
Oregon. Board of Police Standards and Training. Policies and procedures manual /. [Salem, Or.] [1979]- 1 v. :   LC Card 80-623340   DDC 363.2/09795 19
HV7571.O7 B6 1979

POLICE TRAINING - UNITED STATES - ABSTRACTS.
Ferry, John. Police training . Washington, D.C. [1980] vii, 38 p. ;   LC Card 80-602850   DDC 363.2/2/0715 19
HV8143 .F47

POLICE TRAINING - UNITED STATES - CONGRESSES.
National Symposium on Job-Task Analysis in Criminal Justice, Dallas, 1978. National Symposium on Job-Task Analysis in Criminal Justice . Washington, D.C. , 1979. xx, 465 p. ;   LC Card 79-603983   DDC 363.2/2 19
HV8143 .N39 1978

Police unions in the civil service setting /. Burpo, John H. Washington D.C. , 1979. v, 38 p. ;   LC Card 80-601834   DDC 352/.005173/0973 19
HV7936.P47 B87

POLICE - UNITED STATES.
Epstein, Sidney. Guidelines for police performance appraisal, promotion and placement procedures. [Washington] , 1973. xiii, 57 p. ;   LC Card 74-167251
NYPL [JLF 80-658]

Ostrom, Elinor. Policing metropolitan America /. [Washington] [1977] viii, 49 p. :   LC Card 77-603798
HV8138 .O76   NYPL [*XME-9420]

POLICE - UNITED STATES - ABSTRACTS.
Brousseau, Bill. Affirmative action, equal employment opportunity in the criminal justice system . [Washington, D.C.] [1980] vii, 49 p. ;   LC Card 80-602931   DDC 016.33113/3 19
HV8143 .B76

POLICE - UNITED STATES - COMPLAINTS AGAINST.
United States. Commission on Civil Rights. Federal Bureau of Investigation--Indian reservations police abuse . Washington, D.C. [1979] iii, 69 p. ;   LC Card 80-601782   DDC

323.1/197/073 19
E93 .U53 1979

POLICE - UNITED STATES - CONGRESSES.
National Symposium on Job-Task Analysis in
Criminal Justice, Dallas, 1978. National
Symposium on Job-Task Analysis in Criminal
Justice . Washington, D.C. , 1979. ix, 465 p. ;
LC Card 79-603983　DDC 363.2/2 19
HV8143 .N39 1978

**POLICE - UNITED STATES - DATA
PROCESSING.**
Colton, Kent W. Police and computer
technology . Washington, D.C. [1979] vii, 68
p. ;　LC Card 80-601840　DDC 363.2/028/54 19
HV7936.A8 C58

**POLICE - UNITED STATES - JOB
DESCRIPTIONS - CONGRESSES.**
National Symposium on Job-Task Analysis in
Criminal Justice, Dallas, 1978. National
Symposium on Job-Task Analysis in Criminal
Justice . Washington, D.C. , 1979. ix, 465 p. ;
LC Card 79-603983　DDC 363.2/2 19
HV8143 .N39 1978

**POLICE - UNITED STATES - LABOR
PRODUCTIVITY - ABSTRACTS.**
Freimund, Justus. Police productivity /.
[Washington] , 1978. vii, 47 p. ;　LC Card
79-602774　DDC 331.11/8 19
HV7936.P7 F73

**POLICE VEHICLES - COST
EFFECTIVENESS.**
Ruegg, Rosalie T. The police patrol car .
Washington , 1978. xvii, 117 p. ;　LC Card
77-13244
QC100 .U57 no. 480-15 HV7936.V4
NYPL [*XME-9526]

**POLICE VEHICLES - COST OF
OPERATION.**
Ruegg, Rosalie T. The police patrol car .
Washington , 1978. xvii, 117 p. ;　LC Card
77-13244
QC100 .U57 no. 480-15 HV7936.V4
NYPL [*XME-9526]

POLICE VEHICLES - EONOMIC ASPECTS.
Ruegg, Rosalie T. The police patrol car .
Washington , 1978. xvii, 117 p. ;　LC Card
77-13244
QC100 .U57 no. 480-15 HV7936.V4
NYPL [*XME-9526]

**Policies and administrative procedures for the
education of handicapped students.** Texas.
Education Agency. Dept. of Special Education.
Austin, Tex. [1979] xii, 179 p. ;　LC Card
80-621337　DDC 371.9/09764 19
LC4032.T5 T49 1979

**Policies and practices of the child protective
services system in Cook County /.** Brown, H.
Frederick. [Chicago, Ill.] [1978] 30, 16 p. :
LC Card 80-623540　DDC 344.773/10327044
347.73104327044 19
KFI1799.C62 C7215

Policies and procedures manual /. Oregon. Board
of Police Standards and Training. [Salem, Or.]
[1979]- 1 v. :　LC Card 80-623340　DDC
363.2/09795 19
HV7571.O7 B6 1979

Policies on human settlements in Bolivia . United
States Habitat and Human Settlements
Foundation. [New York] 1977. 55 p. ;　LC
Card 80-117387　DDC 363.5/8/0984 19
HD7322.A3 U54 1977

Policing metropolitan America /. Ostrom, Elinor.
[Washington] [1977] viii, 49 p. :　LC Card
77-603798
HV8138 .O76　　　**NYPL [*XME-9420]**

Policy and procedures manual /. South Dakota.
Office of Cultural Preservation. [Pierre] [1980]
48 leaves ;　LC Card 80-152347　DDC
353.97830085/9 19
F652 .S68 1980

**Policy conflict--energy, environmental, and
materials .** United States. General Accounting
Office. [Washington, D.C.] [1980] iv, 38 p. ;
LC Card 80-602621　DDC 333.8/232 19
HD9502.U52 U55 1980

the policy matrix papers. Massachusetts.
Metropolitan Area Planning Council. The policy
matrix paper[s] . Boston , 1977. 160 p. :　LC
Card 79-621114　DDC 307.7/6/0974461 19
HT394.B6 M365 1977

**Policy needed to guide natural gas regulation on
Federal lands .** United States. General
Accounting Office. [Washington] , 1979. vii, 71
p. :　LC Card 79-602690　DDC 353.0087/23 19
HD9581.U5 U54 1979

Policy papers in international affairs.
(no. 14) Amundsen, Kirsten. Norway, NATO,
and the forgotten Soviet challenge /. Berkeley ,
c1981. vi, 50 p. :　ISBN 0-87725-514-8 (pbk.) :
LC Card 81-80337　DDC 355/.0330481 19
UA750 .A56

**Policy plan for Kansas Department of Education,
fiscal year 1980.** Kansas. State Dept. of
Education. Topeka, Kan. [1979] 89 p., [1] leaf
of plates :　LC Card 80-622954　DDC
371.2/07/09781 19
LB2809.K2 K36 1979

POLICY SCIENCES - CONGRESSES.
Case studies and a dialogue on the role of
geographic analysis in public policy /.
[[Urbana-Champaign] [1979] 51 p. :　LC Card
80-621477　DDC 361.6/1 19
H22 .C37

**POLICY SCIENCES - COST
EFFECTIVENESS - CONGRESSES.**
Workshop on Research Needed to Improve the
Quality of Socioeconomic Data Used in
Regulatory Decisionmaking, Library of
Congress, 1979. Workshop on Research Needed
to Improve the Quality of Socioeconomic Data
Used in Regulatory Decisionmaking .
Washington , 1980. xiii, 296 p. ;　LC Card
80-602262　DDC 361.6/1/072073 19
H22 .W67 1979

**POLISH AMERICANS - ILLINOIS -
CHICAGO REGION - RELIGION.**
Parot, Joseph John, 1940- Polish Catholics in
Chicago, 1850-1920 . DeKalb , c1981. p. cm.
ISBN 0-87580-081-5　LC Card 81-11297　DDC
282/.0899185077311 19
BX1418.C4 P37

Polish Catholics in Chicago, 1850-1920 . Parot,
Joseph John, 1940- DeKalb , c1981. p. cm.
ISBN 0-87580-081-5　LC Card 81-11297　DDC
282/.0899185077311 19
BX1418.C4 P37

**POLISH NATIONAL CATHOLIC CHURCH
OF AMERICA - ILLINOIS - CHICAGO
REGION - HISTORY.**
Parot, Joseph John, 1940- Polish Catholics in
Chicago, 1850-1920 . DeKalb , c1981. p. cm.
ISBN 0-87580-081-5　LC Card 81-11297　DDC
282/.0899185077311 19
BX1418.C4 P37

The political animal . Rauch, Leo. Amherst,
MA , c1981. p. cm.　ISBN 0-87023-338-6 :　LC
Card 81-3070　DDC 320/.01/09 19
JA83 .R34

**A political atlas of Louisiana gubernatorial
elections /.** Wildgen, John K. [New Orleans] ,
1979. 14 leaves :　LC Card 79-625553　DDC
330.9763 s 912/.13249763 19
HC107.L8 L58 no.30 G1361.F9

**Political consciousness and American democracy
/.** Lea, James F. Jackson , 1981. p. cm.　ISBN
0-87805-150-3　LC Card 81-13133　DDC
323/.042/0973 19
JK1764 .L4

POLITICAL ECONOMY. see ECONOMICS.

POLITICAL ETHICS.
Gunn, Elizabeth M. Ethics and the public
service . Norman, Okla. [1980] 47 p. ;　LC
Card 80-623689　DDC 016.35 19
Z7164.A2 G86 JF1525.E8

POLITICAL ETHICS - BIBLIOGRAPHY.
Gunn, Elizabeth M. Ethics and the public
service . Norman, Okla. [1980] 47 p. ;　LC
Card 80-623689　DDC 016.35 19
Z7164.A2 G86 JF1525.E8

**POLITICAL PARTICIPATION - ILLINOIS -
DIRECTORIES.**
Jones, John Herbert. Opportunities in Illinois
State government . [Springfield] [1979] viii, 34
p. ;　LC Card 80-621144　DDC 300/.9773 s
353.977309/3/025 19
JK5774 .A3 no. 150 JK5749.C7

**POLITICAL PARTICIPATION - UNITED
STATES.**
Lea, James F. Political consciousness and
American democracy /. Jackson , 1981. p. cm.

ISBN 0-87805-150-3　LC Card 81-13133　DDC
323/.042/0973 19
JK1764 .L4

United States. Advisory Commission on
Intergovernmental Relations. Citizen
participation in the American Federal system /.
Washington, D.C. [1980] v, 357 p. ;　LC Card
80-602148　DDC 323/.042/0973 19
JK1764 .U54 1980

**POLITICAL PARTICIPATION - UNITED
STATES - HANDBOOKS, MANUALS,
ETC.**
Dale, Duane, 1946- How to make citizen
involvement work . Amherst , c1978. iii, 92 p. :
LC Card 79-624734
JK1764 .D34　　　**NYPL [JLF 80-1677]**

Dale, Duane, 1946- Planning, for a change .
Amherst , c1978. 88 p. :　LC Card 79-624733
JK1764 .D35　　　**NYPL [JLF 81-311]**

POLITICAL PARTICIPATION - VIRGINIA.
Abramowitz, Alan. Party activists in Virginia .
Charlottesville , 1981. x, 106 p. ;　LC Card
81-142700　DDC 324.5/6/09755 19
JK2295.V83 A24

**POLITICAL PARTIES - JAPAN -
ADDRESSES, ESSAYS, LECTURES.**
Parties, candiates, and voters in Japan . Ann
Arbor , 1981. p. cm.　ISBN 0-939512-07-6 :　LC
Card 81-6190　DDC 324/.0952 19
JQ1698.A1 P37

POLITICAL PARTIES - VIRGINIA.
Abramowitz, Alan. Party activists in Virginia .
Charlottesville , 1981. x, 106 p. ;　LC Card
81-142700　DDC 324.5/6/09755 19
JK2295.V83 A24

**POLITICAL PLATFORMS. see POLITICAL
PARTIES.**

POLITICAL PRISONERS.
United States. Congress. House. Committee on
Foreign Affairs. Subcommittee on International
Organizations. Human rights and the
phenomenon of disappearances . Washington ,
1980. viii, 636 p. ;　LC Card 80-603094　DDC
323.4/3 19
KF27 .F648 1979g

POLITICAL PRISONERS - RUSSIA.
United States. Congress. House. Committee on
Foreign Affairs. Subcommittee on International
Organizations. Human rights and the detention
of Andrei Sakharov, update . Washington ,
1980. iii, 35 p. ;　LC Card 80-602958　DDC
323.4/0947 19
KF27 .F648 1980a

POLITICAL SCIENCE. Here and with local
subdivision are entered works on the
discipline of political science. Works on the
politics of particular countries, regions, cities,
etc., are entered under the name of the place
subdivided by Politics and government.

**POLITICAL SCIENCE - ADDRESSES,
ESSAYS, LECTURES.**
Anscombe, G. E. M. (Gertrude Elizabeth
Margaret) Ethics, religion, and politics /.
Minneapolis , c1981. p. cm.　ISBN
0-8166-1082-7 :　LC Card 81-4315　DDC 192 s
170 19
B1618 .A571 1981, vol. 3 BJ1012

POLITICAL SCIENCE - HISTORY.
Rauch, Leo. The political animal . Amherst,
MA , c1981. p. cm.　ISBN 0-87023-338-6 :　LC
Card 81-3070　DDC 320/.01/09 19
JA83 .R34

**POLITICAL SCIENCE IN LITERATURE. see
POLITICS IN LITERATURE.**

POLITICAL SCIENCE RESEARCH.
United States. Congress. Office of Technology
Assessment. Technology assessment in business
and government . - [Washington] , 1977. xii, 32
[i. e. 33] p. :　　　**NYPL [*XME-9383]**

**POLITICAL SOCIALIZATION - UNITED
STATES.**
Lea, James F. Political consciousness and
American democracy /. Jackson , 1981. p. cm.
ISBN 0-87805-150-3　LC Card 81-13133　DDC
323/.042/0973 19
JK1764 .L4

POLITICAL SOCIOLOGY.
Waisman, Carlos H. (Carlos Horacio), 1943-
Modernization and the working class . Austin ,

c1982. p. cm. ISBN 0-292-75065-X LC Card
81-10397 DDC 306/.2 19
HD8031 .W34

**POLITICIANS - UNITED STATES -
ICONOGRAPHY - EXHIBITIONS.**
Lilly Library, Indiana University, Bloomington.
Wendell Lewis Willkie, 1892-1944 .
Bloomington , 1980. 24 p. : LC Card 80-140105
DDC 016.973917/092/4 19
Z881.I42 P8 no. 32 E748.W7

**POLITICS AND EDUCATION -
BIBLIOGRAPHY.**
Hastings, Anne H. The study of politics and
education . [Eugene, Or.] , 1980. ix, 291 p. ;
LC Card 80-129023 DDC 016.37973 19
Z5815.U5 H37 LC89

**POLITICS AND LITERATURE - UNITED
STATES.**
Nelson, Cary. Our last first poets . Urbana ,
c1981. p. cm. ISBN 0-252-00885-5 LC Card
81-5082 DDC 811/.54/09 19
PS325 .N4

Rosen, Robert C., 1947- John Dos Passos,
politics and the writer /. Lincoln , c1981. p.
cm. ISBN 0-8032-3860-6 LC Card 81-1928 DDC
813/.52 19
PS3507.O743 Z79

POLITICS IN LITERATURE.
Rosen, Robert C., 1947- John Dos Passos,
politics and the writer /. Lincoln , c1981. p.
cm. ISBN 0-8032-3860-6 LC Card 81-1928 DDC
813/.52 19
PS3507.O743 Z79

**The Politics of agrarian change in Asia and Latin
America** / edited by Howard Handelman.
Bloomington : Indiana University Press, c1981.
p. cm. "Originally country study papers presented to
the second project seminar, held at the AUFS Institute
of World Affairs Conference Center in Salisbury,
Connecticut, September 16-18, 1979"--Pref. "Published
in association with the American Universities Field
Staff." Includes bibliographical references.
CONTENTS. - An Indian farm lobby, the Kisian
Sammelan / Marcus Franda -- The farmers federation
of Thailand / Brewster Grace -- Rural mobilization for
modernization in South Korea / Albert Ravenholt --
Ecuadorian agrarian reform / Howard Handelman --
Food policy decision-making in Colombia / Thomas G.
Sanders -- Peasants, landlords, and bureaucrats, the
politics of agrarian reform in Peru / Howard
Handelman -- Agrarian reform and the international
consensus. ISBN 0-253-34548-0 LC Card 81-47565
DDC 338.1/85 19
*1. Land reform - Asia - Case studies. 2. Land reform -
Latin America - Case studies. 3. Agricultural price
supports - Asia - Case studies. 4. Agricultural price
supports - Latin America - Case studies. I. Handelman,
Howard, 1943-. II. American Universities Field Staff.
HD1333.A78 P64*

Politics of Education Association. Hastings, Anne
H. The study of politics and education .
[Eugene, Or.] , 1980. ix, 291 p. ; LC Card
80-129023 DDC 016.37973 19
Z5815.U5 H37 LC89

The politics of Indian removal . Green, Michael
D., 1941- Lincoln , c1982. p. cm. ISBN
0-8032-2109-6 LC Card 81-14670 DDC
970.004/97 19
E99.C9 G74

The politics of legislation in New York State .
Baaklini, Abdo I. [Albany] [1979] viii, 102 p.
(p. 99-102 blank) ; ISBN 0-915194-04-X LC
Card 78-22606 DDC 328.747/077 19
KFN5723.Z9 B3

POLK, JAMES K. (JAMES KNOX), 1795-1849.
Williams, Frank Broyles, 1913- Tennessee's
presidents /. Knoxville , c1981. p. cm. ISBN
0-87049-321-3 : LC Card 81-3391 DDC
973/.09/92 B 19
E176.1 .W7225

Pollard, David D. Delaney, Paul T. Deformation
of host rocks and flow of magma during growth
of minette dikes and breccia-bearing intrusions
near Ship Rock, New Mexico /. Washington ,
1981. p. cm. LC Card 81-6769 DDC 551.8/8 19
QE611.5.U6 D44

POLLEN.
Michener, Charles Duncan, 1918- Pollen
manipulation and related activities and
structures in bees of the family Apidae /.
[Lawrence] 1978. p. 576-601 : LC Card

79-621073 DDC 500 s 595.79/9 19
Q1 .K17 vol. 51, no. 19 QL568.A6

**Pollen manipulation and related activities and
structures in bees of the family Apidae /.**
Michener, Charles Duncan, 1918- [Lawrence]
1978. p. 576-601 : LC Card 79-621073 DDC 500
s 595.79/9 19
Q1 .K17 vol. 51, no. 19 QL568.A6

**Pollen morphology and phylogenetic
relationships of the Berberidaceae /.** Nowicke,
Joan W. Washington , 1981. p. cm. LC Card
80-21960 DDC 581 s 583/.117 19
QK1 .S2747 no. 50 QK495.B45

POLLS. see ELECTIONS.

**POLLUTION - ECONOMIC ASPECTS -
UNITED STATES.**
The Economic impact of pollution control.
[Washington?] 1972. 332 p. LC Card 72-601528
TD180 .E25   **NYPL [JLF 81-274]**

**POLLUTION - ENVIRONMENTAL
ASPECTS.**
United States. Library of Congress.
Congressional Research Service. Effects of
chronic exposure to low-level pollutants in the
environment . Washington , 1975. ii, 402 p. ;
LC Card 75-603631
QH545.A1 U54 1975   **NYPL [JSE 81-285]**

**POLLUTION - ENVIRONMENTAL
ASPECTS - CONGRESSES.**
Biological evaluation of environmental impacts .
Washington, D.C. , 1980. iv, 237 p. : LC Card
80-604147 DDC 333.951/028 19
QH545.A .B564

POLLUTION - INDIANA.
Indiana. Environmental Management Board.
Report on the environment . Indianapolis, Ind. ,
1977. xii, 96 p. : LC Card 80-622166 DDC
363.7/009772 19
TD171.3.I6 I52 1977

**POLLUTION - MEASUREMENT -
COMPUTER PROGRAMS - CATALOGS.**
A Directory of computer software applications:
environmental pollution & control. [Springfield,
Va.]   **NYPL [JSP 81-8]**

POLLUTION - MINNESOTA.
Minnesota. Environmental Quality Board.
Potential critical areas inventory. St. Paul ,
1979. [77] p. in various pagings, [2] fold. leaves
of plates : LC Card 79-625262 DDC
333.78/09776 19
QH76.5.M6 M57 1979

Pollution of interstate waters. United States.
Public Health Service. [Washington] 1959. 2 v.
LC Card 75-80621   **NYPL [JSF 81-65]**

**POLLUTION OF WATER. see WATER -
POLLUTION.**

POLLUTION - TEXAS - TRAVIS CO.
Austin, Tex. Dept. of Planning. Austin
tomorrow, an environmental . Austin, Tex. , 1974.
xiv, 303 p. : LC Card 81-459302 DDC
363.7/009764/31 19
TD181.T42 T722 1974

POLLUTION - TOXICOLOGY.
United States. Library of Congress.
Congressional Research Service. Effects of
chronic exposure to low-level pollutants in the
environment . Washington , 1975. ii, 402 p. ;
LC Card 75-603631
QH545.A1 U54 1975   **NYPL [JSE 81-285]**

**POLLUTION - TOXICOLOGY - NEW YORK
(STATE) - NIAGARA FALLS.**
United States. Congress. House. Committee on
Interstate and Foreign Commerce.
Subcommittee on Oversight and Investigations.
Love Canal, health studies and relocation .
Washington , 1980. v, 71 p. : LC Card
80-604042 DDC 363.7/28 19
KF27 .I5547 1980o

**POLYBROMINATED BIPHENYLS -
TOXICOLOGY - MICHIGAN.**
PBB general population study . [Lansing , 1979]
269 p. in various pagings : LC Card 80-621045
DDC 363.1/79 19
RA1242.P69 P16

Polychlorinated biphenyls : regulations and
substitutes : a compliance manual for the U. S.
mining industry / by R. A. Westin ... [et al.].
[Washington, D.C.] : U. S. Dept. of the
Interior, Bureau of Mines, 1981. p. cm.

(Information circular / Bureau of Mines) Bibliography:
p. LC Card 80-607190 DDC 622 s 363.1/79 19
*1. Polychlorinated biphenyls - Handbooks, manuals, etc.
2. Electricity in mining - Handbooks, manuals, etc. I.
Westin, Robert A. II. Series: United States. Bureau of
Mines. Information circular .
TN295 .U4 T55.3.H3*

**POLYCHLORINATED BIPHENYLS -
ENVIRONMENTAL ASPECTS.**
Griffin, Robert A. Attenuation of water--soluble
polychlorinated biphenyls by earth materials /.
Urbana, Ill. [1980] iii, 98 p. : LC Card
80-622556 DDC 557.73 s 628.5/5 19
QE105 .A32 no. 86 TD879.P64

**POLYCHLORINATED BIPHENYLS -
ENVIRONMENTAL ASPECTS -
MISSISSIPPI RIVER WATERSHED.**
URS Company, Seattle, Wash. Dynamics of
polychlorinated biphenyls in the upper
Mississippi River . Columbia, Mo. ,
Washington , 1978- v. : LC Card 79-602554
DDC 363.7/394 19
TD427.P65 U18 1978

**POLYCHLORINATED BIPHENYLS -
ENVIRONMENTAL ASPECTS - UNITED
STATES.**
United States. Congress. House. Committee on
Interstate and Foreign Commerce.
Subcommittee on Oversight and Investigations.
PCB's, dangers associated with their storage
and use . Washington , 1980. iv, 704 p. : LC
Card 80-602788 DDC 363.1/79 19
KF27 .I5547 1979s

United States. Congress. House. Committee on
Merchant Marine and Fisheries. Dredge spoil
disposal and PCB contamination . Washington ,
1980. v, 698 p. : LC Card 81-600658 DDC
363.7/28 19
KF27 .M4 1980

**POLYCHLORINATED BIPHENYLS -
HANDBOOKS, MANUALS, ETC.**
Polychlorinated biphenyls . [Washington,
D.C.] , 1981. p. cm. LC Card 80-607190 DDC
622 s 363.1/79 19
TN295 .U4 T55.3.H3

**POLYCHLORINATED BIPHENYLS -
STORAGE.**
United States. Congress. House. Committee on
Interstate and Foreign Commerce.
Subcommittee on Oversight and Investigations.
PCB's, dangers associated with their storage
and use . Washington , 1980. iv, 704 p. : LC
Card 80-602788 DDC 363.1/79 19
KF27 .I5547 1979s

**POLYCHLORINATED BIPHENYLS -
TOXICOLOGY.**
United States. Congress. House. Committee on
Interstate and Foreign Commerce.
Subcommittee on Oversight and Investigations.
PCB's, dangers associated with their storage
and use . Washington , 1980. iv, 704 p. : LC
Card 80-602788 DDC 363.1/79 19
KF27 .I5547 1979s

**POLYCHLORINATED BIPHENYLS -
TOXICOLOGY - UNITED STATES.**
United States. Congress. House. Committee on
Merchant Marine and Fisheries. Dredge spoil
disposal and PCB contamination . Washington ,
1980. v, 698 p. : LC Card 81-600658 DDC
363.7/28 19
KF27 .M4 1980

**Polymeric concentration determined by drag
reduction /.** Zatko, Jalna R. [Avondale, MD]
[1981] p. cm. LC Card 81-607021 DDC 622 s
622/.7 19
TN23 .U43 QD381.8

**POLYMERS AND POLYMERIZATION -
ANALYSIS.**
(1981) Zatko, Jalna R. Polymeric concentration
determined by drag reduction /. [Avondale,
MD] [1981] p. cm. LC Card 81-607021 DDC
622 s 622/.7 19
TN23 .U43 QD381.8

**POLYOXYMETHYLENE - PHYSIOLOGICAL
EFFECT.**
Shigo, Alex L., 1930- Some effects of
paraformaldehyde on wood surrounding
tapholes in sugar maple trees /. Upper Darby,
Pa. , 1970. 11 p. : LC Card 81-460882 DDC
634.9/0974 s 633.6/49 19
SD11 .A455493 no. 161 SB608.S913

POLYVINYL CHLORIDE.
Gordian Associates. The plastics industry /.
Oak Ridge, Tenn. , 1977. v, 31 p. ; ISBN
0-87079-202-4 : LC Card 77-12044 DDC
338.4/5 19
TP1120 .G59 1977

Polyzoides, Stephanos. Courtyard housing in Los
Angeles : a typological study / Stephanos
Polyzoides, Roger Sherwood, and James Tice ;
photography by Julius Shulman. Berkeley :
University of California Press, c1982. p. cm.
Includes bibliographical references and index. ISBN
0-520-04251-4 LC Card 80-6057 DDC
728/.09794/94 19
*1. Courtyard houses - California - Los Angeles. I.
Sherwood, Roger. II. Tice, James. III. Shulman, Julius.
IV. Title.*
NA7238.L6 P6

Pomeroy, John S., 1929-
Landslides in the Greater Pittsburgh region,
Pennsylvania / by John S. Pomeroy.
Washington : U. S.G.P.O., 1981. p. cm.
(Geological Survey professional paper . 1229)
Bibliography: p. LC Card 81-607013 DDC 551.3 19
*1. Landslides - Pennsylvania - Pittsburgh region. I.
Title. II. Series.*
QE599.U5 P64

Mass movement in two selected areas of
western Washington County, Pennsylvania / by
John S. Pomeroy. Washington : U. S. Govt.
Print. Off., 1981. p. cm. (Shorter contributions to
general geology) Geological Survey professional paper ;
1170-E Bibliography: p. LC Card 80-607835 DDC
551.3 19
*1. Mass-wasting - Pennsylvania - Washington Co. I.
Series: United States. Geological Survey. Shorter
contributions to general geology. II. Title.*
QE599.U5 P65

Pomeroy, Roger. (joint author) Greer, T. Vernon.
Sugars and sirups from Canada . Washington,
D.C. , 1980. [1980] ii, 17, 66 p. ; LC Card 80-602338
DDC 382/.4136/0973 19
HF2651.S8 U55

POMO INDIANS - ANTIQUITIES.
Baumhoff, Martin A. An archaeological assay
on Dry Creek, Sonoma County, California /.
Berkeley , 1979. xi, 244 p. : LC Card 80-620631
DDC 979.4/18 19
E51 .C2 no. 40 E78.C15

Pompeo, Mary Jo. (joint author) Kelly, Mary
Margaret. Films for in-service education in
long-term care facilities /. Denton, Tex. , 1980.
ii, 39 leaves ; LC Card 80-622861 DDC 362.6/1
19
RA999.I5 K44

POMPEY, THE GREAT, 106-48 B.C.
Greenhalgh, P. A. L. Pompey, the Roman
Alexander / Columbia , 1981, c1980. xix, 267
p., [4] p. of plates : ISBN 0-8262-0335-3 LC
Card 80-54460 DDC 937/.05/0924 B 19
DG258 .G73 1981

Pompey, the Roman Alexander /. Greenhalgh, P.
A. L. Columbia , 1981, c1980. xix, 267 p., [4]
p. of plates : ISBN 0-8262-0335-3 LC Card
80-54460 DDC 937/.05/0924 B 19
DG258 .G73 1981

**PONDEROSA PINE - WOUNDS AND
    INJURIES - OREGON.**
Animal damage to coniferous plantations in
Oregon and Washington /. Corvallis, Or. ,
1979. 2 v. : LC Card 80-623387 DDC 634.9 s
634.9/7547 19
SD12 .O87 no. 25-26 SB608.D6

**PONDEROSA PINE - WOUNDS AND
    INJURIES - WASHINGTON (STATE)**
Animal damage to coniferous plantations in
Oregon and Washington /. Corvallis, Or. ,
1979. 2 v. : LC Card 80-623387 DDC 634.9 s
634.9/7547 19
SD12 .O87 no. 25-26 SB608.D6

PONDS - MASSACHUSETTS.
Massachusetts. Water Quality and Research
Section. Compilation of lakes, ponds, and
reservoirs relative to the Massachusetts Lake
Classification Program /. Westborough, Mass. ,
1976. 124 p. ; LC Card 79-623986 DDC
551.48/2/09744 19
GB1625.M3 M37 1976

PONY EXPRESS - HISTORY.
Fike, Richard E. The pony express stations of
Utah in historical perspective /. [Salt Lake

City] [Washington, D.C.] 1979. iii, 113 p. :
LC Card 79-602930 DDC 917.92/0433 19
HE6375.P65 F54

**The pony express stations of Utah in historical
perspective /.** Fike, Richard E. [Salt Lake City]
[Washington, D.C.] 1979. iii, 113 p. : LC Card
79-602930 DDC 917.92/0433 19
HE6375.P65 F54

Pool, Danny L. (joint author) Hill, S. D.
Electrowinning of zinc from zinc chloride in
monopolar and bipolar fused-salt cells /.
Washington [1981] p. cm. LC Card 80-607820
DDC 622 s 669/.52 19
TN23 .U43 TN796

Poor and without heat . Design Alternatives, inc.
[Washington] , 1979] vi, 55 p. : LC Card
80-601856 DDC 363.5/8 19
HD7293 .D45 1979

**POOR - CONNECTICUT - ENERGY
    ASSISTANCE.**
Connecticut. General Assembly. Legislative
Program Review and Investigations Committee.
Weatherization assistance for low income
persons . [Hartford, CT] (Legislative Office
Building, 18 Trinity St., Hartford 06115)
[1980] vii, 124 p. ; LC Card 81-621601 DDC
353.97460084/5045 19
HC107.C83 P6325 1980

**POOR-ENERGY ASSISTANCE - LAW AND
    LEGISLATION - MAINE.**
Maine. Division of Community Services. Rules,
chapter 1, home heating crisis assistance
program as amended 1/28/80 by amendment
number 1 ... /. [Augusta, Me.] [1980] ii, 25
leaves ; LC Card 80-623905 DDC 344.741/03263
347.41043263 19
KFM351.E53 A32 1980

**POOR - ENERGY ASSISTANCE - LAW AND
    LEGISLATION - UNITED STATES.**
United States. Congress. House. Committee on
Education and Labor. Subcommittee on Human
Resources. Economic opportunity amendments
of 1980 . Washington , 1980. v, 441 p. ; LC
Card 80-603732 DDC 344.73/0636358
347.304636358 19
KF27 .E34 1980a

United States. Congress. Senate. Committee on
Labor and Human Resources. Subcommittee on
Aging. Home energy assistance act .
Washington , 1980- v. ; LC Card 80-602480
DDC 344.73/03263 19
KF26 .L2716 1979

**POOR - HOSPITAL CARE - ILLINOIS -
    CHICAGO.**
United States. Congress. House. Committee on
Ways and Means. Subcommittee on Health.
Problems facing financially troubled hospitals .
Washington , 1980. vi, 584 p. : LC Card
80-603721 DDC 338.4/336211/0973 19
KF27 .W344 1980b

**POOR - HOSPITAL CARE - NEW YORK
    (CITY)**
United States. Congress. House. Committee on
Ways and Means. Subcommittee on Health.
Problems facing financially troubled hospitals .
Washington , 1980. vi, 584 p. : LC Card
80-603721 DDC 338.4/336211/0973 19
KF27 .W344 1980b

**POOR - HOSPITAL CARE - TENNESSEE -
    MEMPHIS.**
United States. Congress. House. Committee on
Ways and Means. Subcommittee on Health.
Problems facing financially troubled hospitals .
Washington , 1980. vi, 584 p. : LC Card
80-603721 DDC 338.4/336211/0973 19
KF27 .W344 1980b

**POOR - HOSPITAL CARE - TEXAS -
    FINANCE.**
Texas. Advisory Commission on
Intergovernmental Relations. Medically indigent
costs affecting local governments . [Austin,
Tex.] [1980] 26 p. : LC Card 80-623837 DDC
362.1/9 19
RA981.T4 T33 1980

**POOR - HOSPITAL CARE - UNITED
    STATES.**
United States. Congress. House. Committee on
Ways and Means. Subcommittee on Health.
The hospital financing crisis . Washington ,
1980. v, 160 p. ; LC Card 80-603696 DDC

338.4/336211/0973 19
KF27 .W344 1980c

United States. Congress. Senate. Committee on
Labor and Human Resources. Subcommittee on
Health and Scientific Research. Oversight on
financially distressed hospitals . Washington ,
1980. iv, 172 p. ; LC Card 80-603458 DDC
362.1/04252 19
KF26 .L274 1980f

**POOR - HOSPITAL CARE - UNITED
    STATES - FINANCE.**
Background information for hearings on
problems facing financially troubled hospitals /.
Washington , 1980. ii, 9 p. ; LC Card 81-600741
DDC 338.4/336211/0973 19
RA981.A2 B3

POOR - MAINE - STATISTICS.
Maine. State Planning Office. Indicators of
poverty. [Augusta, Me. , 1980] [22] p. ; LC
Card 80-621545 DDC 339.4/6/09741 19
HC107.M23 P625 1980

POOR - MEDICAL CARE - CALIFORNIA.
Chandler, Daniel, 1940- Facilitating access to
skilled nursing facilities for indigent patients /.
Sacramento, Calif. , 1980. 51 p. ; LC Card
80-623746 DDC 362.1/6/09794 19
RA997.5.C3 C47

**POOR - MEDICAL CARE - CALIFORNIA -
    COSTS.**
California. County Health Care Costs Study.
Health care costs and services in California
counties . Sacramento, Calif. , 1978. xx, 136
p. : LC Card 78-623918
RA412.5.U6 C29 1978   NYPL [JLF 81-148]

POOR - MEDICAL CARE - INDIANA.
Indiana. Unemployment Relief Commission.
Services, facilities, and costs of medical care
and hospitalization for township relief cases /.
Indianapolis , 1941. 11, [19] leaves ; LC Card
80-500265 DDC 362.1/9 19
RA418.5.P6 I54 1941

**POOR - MEDICAL CARE - INDIANA -
    COSTS.**
Indiana. Unemployment Relief Commission.
Services, facilities, and costs of medical care
and hospitalization for township relief cases /.
Indianapolis , 1941. 11, [19] leaves ; LC Card
80-500265 DDC 362.1/9 19
RA418.5.P6 I54 1941

**POOR - MEDICAL CARE - TEXAS -
    FINANCE.**
Texas. Advisory Commission on
Intergovernmental Relations. Medically indigent
costs affecting local governments . [Austin,
Tex.] [1980] 26 p. : LC Card 80-623837 DDC
362.1/9 19
RA981.T4 T33 1980

**POOR - NORTHEASTERN STATES -
    ENERGY ASSISTANCE.**
United States. Congress. House. Committee on
Ways and Means. Subcommittee on Public
Assistance and Unemployment Compensation.
Fuel assistance legislation . Washington , 1980.
iv, 102 p. ; LC Card 80-601970 DDC
344.73/032583 19
KF27 .W3464 1979g

**POOR - SERVICES FOR - WASHINGTON
    (STATE) - DIRECTORIES.**
Washington (State). Office of Community
Development. A brief survey of CSA-related
anti-poverty organizations in Washington State.
[Olympia] , 1978. 64 p. ; LC Card 79-621288
HV86 .W365 1978a   NYPL [JLF 81-121]

POOR - UNITED STATES.
Michigan. University. Survey Research Center.
A panel study of income dynamics. Wave 1- ;
1968- Ann Arbor.   NYPL [M-11 5247]

**POOR - UNITED STATES - ENERGY
    ASSISTANCE.**
Design Alternatives, inc. Poor and without
heat . [Washington] , 1979] vi, 55 p. : LC Card
80-601856 DDC 363.5/8 19
HD7293 .D45 1979

United States. Congress. House. Committee on
Appropriations. Subcommittee on Departments
of Labor, and Health, Education, and Welfare,
and Related Agencies. Departments of Labor
and Health, Education, and Welfare, and
Related Agencies appropriations for 1981 .
Washington , 1979. ii, 55, i p. ; LC Card

80-602536 DDC 353.0072/23682/56 19
KF27 .A652 1980a

United States. Congress. House. Committee on Education and Labor. Subcommittee on Human Resources. Federal efforts to aid low-income and elderly individuals affected by life-threatening heat conditions . Washington , 1980 [i.e. 1981] iii, 53 p. :   LC Card 81-601392 DDC 362.5/8 19
KF27 .E34 1980c

Poore, Richard Z. Biostratigraphy and paleoecology of the upper Miocene (Messinian) and lower Pliocene (?) Cerro de Almendral section, Alermía Basin, southern Spain / by Richard Z. Poore and Sean Murphy Stone ; prepared in cooperation with the Empresa Nacional de Investigaciones Mineras of Spain. Washington : U. S. Govt. Print. Off., 1981. iii, 11 p., [2] leaves of plates : ill. ; 29 cm. (Shorter contributions to general geology) Geological Survey professional paper ; 774-F Bibliography: p. 9. Includes index. LC Card 80-607164 DDC 551.7/86/094681 19
1. Geology, Stratigraphic - Miocene. 2. Geology, Stratigraphic - Pliocene. 3. Paleontology - Miocene. 4. Paleontology - Pliocene. 5. Geology - Spain - Almería (Province). I. Stone, Sean Murphy, joint author. II. Empresa Nacional Adaro de Investigaciones Mineras. III. Series: United States. Geological Survey. Shorter contributions to general geology. IV. Title.
QE694 .P67

Pope, Dudley. Life in Nelson's Navy / by Dudley Pope. Annapolis, Md. : Naval Institute Press, 1981. ix, 279 p. : ill. ; 22 cm. Bibliography: p. [265]-273. Includes index. ISBN 0-87021-346-6 : LC Card 80-82726 DDC 359.1/0941 19
1. Great Britain. Royal Navy - History - 18th century. 2. Great Britain. Royal Navy - History - 19th century. 3. Great Britain - History, Naval. I. Title.
VA454 .P66 1981

Pope John Paul II at the United Nations. United Nations. Dept. of Public Information. New York , 1980. 64 p. :   LC Card 80-146375 DDC 282/.092/4 19
BX1378.5 .U54 1980

POPES - VOYAGES AND TRAVELS - NEW YORK (CITY).
United Nations. Dept. of Public Information. Pope John Paul II at the United Nations. New York , 1980. 64 p. :   LC Card 80-146375 DDC 282/.092/4 19
BX1378.5 .U54 1980

Popko, Edward. Squatter settlements and housing policy : experiences with sites-and-services in Colombia / by Edward S. Popko. [Washington, D.C.?] : Agency for International Development, Office of Housing ; Cambridge, Mass. : Department of Urban Studies and Planning, Massachusetts Institute of Technology, 1980. vi, 200 p. : ill., forms, 1 plan ; 28 cm. (Occasional paper series) "March 30, 1980." Bibliography: p. 195-200. LC Card 81-600768 DDC 363.5/8/09861 19
1. Squatter settlements - Colombia. 2. Housing policy - Colombia. I. United States. Agency for International Development. Office of Housing. II. Massachusetts Institute of Technology. Dept. of Urban Studies and Planning. III. Series: Occasional paper series (United States. Agency for International Development. Office of Housing). IV. Title.
HD7325.A3 P658

POPLAR RIVER POWER PROJECT.
Montana. Bureau of Air Quality. Scientific and Engineering Advisory Panel on Poplar River Air Quality. Issue paper /. Helena, Mont. [1979] 32 p. :   LC Card 80-621735 DDC 363.7/392 19
TD883.5.M6 M66 1979

Popp, Carl John, 1941- (joint author) Brandvold, D. K. Chemical and biological survey of the Upper Gila River system in New Mexico . Las Cruces, N.M. [1979] iii, 48 p. ;   LC Card 80-622273 DDC 333.91/009789 s 628.1/686789/692 19
GB705.N6 N64 no. 110 QH105.N6

Popp, John T. Investigation of the gas content of coal seams in the vicinity of Charleston, Illinois / by John T. Popp, Dennis D. Coleman, Robert A. Keogh, Illinois State Geological Survey. Chicago, IL. : State of Illinois, Institute of Natural Resources, 1979. v leaves, 36 p. : ill. ; 28 cm. (Document - State of Illinois, Institute of

Natural Resources ; no. 79/38) "Project no. 6..047." Includes bibliographies. LC Card 80-621153 DDC 553.2/85 19
1. Coal mines and mining - Illinois - Charleston region. 2. Mine gases. I. Coleman, Dennis D., joint author. II. Keogh, Robert A., joint author. III. Illinois. State Geological Survey. IV. Series: Illinois Institute of Natural Resources. Document - Illinois Institute of Natural Resources , no. 79/38. V. Title.
TN805.I3 P66

Poppe, Barbara B. Directory of world seismograph stations. Volume I, The Americas / Boulder, Colo. : The Center : U. S. Dept. of Commerce, NationalOceanic and Atmospheric Administration, Environmental Data and Information Service, 1980- v. <1, pt. 1 > : charts, maps ; 28 cm. (Report SE . v. 25) "U. S. Dept. of Interior, Geological Survey." "October 1980. CONTENTS. - pt. 1. United States, Canada, Bermuda LC Card 80-603927 DDC 551 s 551.2/2/2025 19
1. Seismological stations - United States - Directories. 2. Seismological stations - Canada - Directories. 3. Seismological stations - Bermuda Islands - Directories. I. United States. National Oceanic and Atmospheric Administration. Environmental Data and Information Service. II. United States. Geological Survey. III. World Data Center A for Solid Earth Geophysics. IV. Title. V. Series.
QE500 .W67a no. 25 QE540.U6

POPULAR ARTS. see POPULAR CULTURE.

POPULAR CULTURE.
Becker, Howard Saul, 1928- Art worlds /. Berkeley, c1981. p. cm. ISBN 0-520-04386-3 LC Card 81-2694 DDC 700/.1/03 19
NX180.S6 B42

Popular Culture Association. Journal of American culture. v. 1- Spring 1978- [Bowling Green, Ohio]   LC Card 79-642570
           NYPL [JFL 80-314]

The popular interest versus the public interest ... . New York (State). Legislature. Senate. Task Force on Critical Problems. Albany, N.Y. [1979] iv, 83 p. ;   LC Card 80-622244 DDC 328/.2 19
JF495 .N582 1979

POPULATION.
United Nations. Dept. of International Economic and Social Affairs. Patterns of urban and rural population growth. New York , 1980. ix, 175 p. :   LC Card 80-138417 DDC 081 s 304.6/2 19
JX1977 .A2 ST/ESA/SER.A/68 HB1951

United States. Congress. Senate. Committee on Foreign Relations. World population trends . Washington , 1980. iv, 346 p. :   LC Card 80-603894 DDC 304.6 19
KF26 .F6 1980r

Population and energy . United States. Congress. House. Committee on Science and Tecnology. Subcommittee on Energy Research and Production. Washington , 1981. iii, 154 p. :   LC Card 81-601357 DDC 333.79/13/0973 19
KF27 .S3936 1980f

Population and Hawaii's future . Hawaii. Commission on Population and the Hawaiian Future. Honolulu [1977] ii, 65 p. :   LC Card 77-624063
HB3525.H3 H32 1977   *NYPL [JLF 81-118]*

Population and labor force projections for Massachusetts /. Steller, Mary-Ellen. Boston , 1980. 45 leaves :   LC Card 80-623457 DDC 312/.8/09744 19
HB3525.M4 S77

POPULATION ASSISTANCE.
United Nations. Dept. of Technical Co-operation for Development. Demographic evaluation and analysis of population census data . New York , 1980. iv, 30 p. ;   LC Card 80-130816 DDC 300 s 304.6/0723 19
JX1977 .A2 ST/ESA/SER.E/22

POPULATION ASSISTANCE, AMERICAN.
United States. Congress. Senate. Committee on Foreign Relations. World population trends . Washington , 1980. iv, 346 p. :   LC Card 80-603894 DDC 304.6 19
KF26 .F6 1980r

POPULATION ASSISTANCE - CONGRESSES.
Consultation on population assistance

co-ordination, Geneva, 15-16 March 1979. [New York, N.Y.] [1979] 38 p. ;   LC Card 80-106090
HB884.5 .C66

Population change in the Ozarks region, 1970-1975 . Campbell, Rex R. [Washington] , 1978. v, 29 p. :   LC Card 80-622359 DDC 304.6/2/097671 19
HB3517 .C35

Population changes within census county divisions of North Dakota, 1950-1970 /. Voelker, Stanley W. Fargo, N.D. [Washington] , 1971. 23 leaves, [4] leaves of plates :   LC Card 80-621261 DDC 312/.8/09784 19
HA566 .V63

POPULATION - COLLECTED WORKS.
United Nations. Dept. of Economic and Social Affairs. National experience in the formulation and implementation of population policy, 1960-1976 /. New York , 1978- v. ;   LC Card 78-109255 DDC 300 s 304.6 19
JX1977 .A2 ST/ESA/SER.R/19, etc.

POPULATION - CONGRESSES.
United Nations. Ad Hoc Group of Experts on Demographic Projections. Prospects of population, methodology, and assumptions . New York , 1979. iv, 292 p. :   LC Card 79-127715 DDC 300 s 304.6 19
JX1977 .A2 ST/ESA/SER.A/67

Population Council, New York. International Programs. Maternal and child health/family planning program . New York, N.Y. , 1980. v, 341 p. :   LC Card 80-143941 DDC 362.1/982/0091724 19
RG940 .M368

Population dose and health impact of the accident at the Three Mile Island Nuclear Station . United States. Ad Hoc Interagency Population Dos Assessement Group. Washington , 1979. 77, [16] p. :   LC Card 79-602730
RA569 .U46 1979

Population dynamics and catch susceptibility of smallmouth buffalo in Rough River Reservoir /. Hoyt, Robert D. [Frankfort, Ky.] , 1976. vii, 67 p. :   LC Card 79-624983 DDC 639/.2 s 597/.52 19
SH222.K4 A3 no. 62 QL638.C27

Population dynamics and production of Daphnia ambigua in a fish pond, Kansas /. Lei, Chi-hsiang. [Lawrence] , 1980. p. [687]-715 :   LC Card 80-621787 DDC 500 s 591.5/26322 19
Q1 .K17 vol. 51, no. 25 QL143

Population estimates by county, Arkansas . Arkansas. University. Industrial Research and Extension Center. Little Rock, Ark. , 1975. 6 leaves ;   *NYPL [*XME-9187]*

POPULATION FORECASTING.
Wilkie, Jane. Evaluation of discontinuities in regional population projections/. Amherst , 1973. 21, iii p. ;   *NYPL [*ZT-1259]*

POPULATION FORECASTING - ARKANSAS.
Arkansas. University. Industrial Research and Extension Center. Population estimates by county, Arkansas . Little Rock, Ark. , 1975. 6 leaves ;   *NYPL [*XME-9187]*

POPULATION FORECASTING - CONGRESSES.
United Nations. Ad Hoc Group of Experts on Demographic Projections. Prospects of population, methodology, and assumptions . New York , 1979. iv, 292 p. :   LC Card 79-127715 DDC 300 s 304.6 19
JX1977 .A2 ST/ESA/SER.A/67

POPULATION FORECASTING - CONNECTICUT.
Connecticut. Office of Policy & Management. Division of Comprehensive Planning. Population projections for Connecticut municipalities and regions to the year 2000 /. Hartford, Conn. [1980] 26 p. :   LC Card 80-621972 DDC 312/.8/09746 19
HA283 .O33 1980

POPULATION FORECASTING - ILLINOIS.
Illinois. Bureau of the Budget. Uniform demographic and economic data, 1970-2000 : summary /. [Springfield] , 1973. 68 p. :
           NYPL [JLF 81-5]

POPULATION FORECASTING - ILLINOIS - STATISTICS - PERIODICALS.
Illinois population projections : summary and by county 1970-2025. [Springfield] LC Card 75-622431   *NYPL [JLM 80-991]*

POPULATION FORECASTING - MASSACHUSETTS.
Steller, Mary-Ellen. Population and labor force projections for Massachusetts /. Boston , 1980. 45 leaves : LC Card 80-623457 DDC 312/.8/09744 19
HB3525.M4 S77

POPULATION FORECASTING - MISSOURI.
Missouri Center for Health Statistics. Missouri population estimates by county, by age, by sex, 1971-1978. Jefferson City [1979] 4, [7] p. ;
LC Card 80-621947 DDC 312/.8/09778 19
HA476 .M57 1979

POPULATION FORECASTING - NEW YORK (STATE)
New York (State). Economic Development Board. Household projections for New York State counties. [Albany, N. Y.] 1976. [8] p., [87] leaves ;   *NYPL [*R-Econ. 80-4783]*

New York (State). Executive Dept. Economic Development Board. Demographic projections for New York State counties. [Albany, N. Y.] 1975. 1 v. (unpaged) ;
*NYPL [*R-Econ. 80-4592]*

POPULATION FORECASTING - NORTH CAROLINA.
North Carolina township estimates and projections. Raleigh, N.C. (116 W. Jones St., Raliegh 27611) , 1979. [46] p. ; LC Card 80-623292 DDC 312/.8/09756 19
HA555 .N67

POPULATION FORECASTING - VERMONT.
Vermont. State Planning Office. The people book. Montpelier, Vt. , 1978. v, 70 p. : LC Card 79-623073 DDC 312/.8/09743 19
HA673 .S72 1978

POPULATION FORECASTING - WASHINGTON (STATE)
Washington (State). Office of Financial Management. Forecasting and Support Services Division. State and county population forecasts by age and sex, 1980-2000. [Olympia] [1980] [31] p. ; LC Card 80-622047 DDC 312/.8/09797 19
HA693 .W36 1980

POPULATION, FOREIGN. see EMIGRATION AND IMMIGRATION.

Population in Nigeria : a select bibliography / David Lucas and John McWilliam. Lucas, David. Chapel Hill , 1974. 15 p. ; LC Card 77-155614 DDC 016.3046/09669 19
Z7164.D3 L82 HB3666.7.A3

The population of Hawaii, 1977 . United States. Bureau of the Census. [Honolulu] [1978] 12 p. ; LC Card 80-623123 DDC 319.69 s 304.6/2/09969 19
HA329.1 .A25 no. 125 HB3525.H3

The population of Hawaii, 1979 . United States. Bureau of the Census. [Honolulu, Hawaii] [1980] 4, [7] p. ; LC Card 80-622660 DDC 319.69 s 312/.8/09969 19
HA329.1 .A25 no. 136 HA329.2

POPULATION POLICY.
United States. Congress. Senate. Committee on Foreign Relations. World population trends . Washington , 1980. iv, 346 p. : LC Card 80-603894 DDC 304.6 19
KF26 .F6 1980r

POPULATION POLICY - COLLECTED WORKS.
United Nations. Dept. of Economic and Social Affairs. National experience in the formulation and implementation of population policy, 1960-1976 /. New York , 1978- v. ; LC Card 78-109255 DDC 300 s 304.6 19
JX1977 .A2 ST/ESA/SER.R/19, etc.

Population program and policy design series.
(no. 3) Asayesh, Homa Ghasemi-Gonabadi. Iran population and family planning studies . Chapel Hill , 1971. 76 leaves ; LC Card 81-451969 DDC 016.3046/0955 19
Z7164.D3 A72 HB3636.4.A3

Population projection series .
(PPS-5) Maine. State Planning Office. Historical population data for Maine municipalities.

[Augusta, Me. , 1980] [18] p. ; LC Card 80-621546 DDC 312/.8/09741 19
HA413 .S75 1980

POPULATION PROJECTIONS. see POPULATION FORECASTING.

Population projections for Connecticut municipalities and regions to the year 2000 /. Connecticut. Office of Policy & Management. Division of Comprehensive Planning. Hartford, Conn. [1980] 26 p. : LC Card 80-621972 DDC 312/.8/09746 19
HA283 .O33 1980

Population redistribution and changes in housing tenure status in the United States /. Chi, Peter S. K. [Washington, D.C.] [1980] 27 p. ; LC Card 80-601677 DDC 304.8/2/0973 19
HD7287.82.U6 C45

Population research. CPR population research. [Bethesda, Md.]   *NYPL [JLM 81-10]*

POPULATION RESEARCH - COLLECTED WORKS.
United States. Bureau of the Census. International population reports. Series P-95. [Washington]   *NYPL [SDG (U. S. Census Bureau. International population reports. Series P-95)]*

POPULATION, RURAL. see RURAL POPULATION.

POPULATION - STATISTICS.
International Demographic Data Center (U. S.) International population dynamics, 1950-79 . Washington, D.C. [1980] iv, 258 p. ; LC Card 80-602932 DDC 312/.8 19
HA155 .I57 1980

Population studies (New York) ; no. 67.
United Nations. Ad Hoc Group of Experts on Demographic Projections. Prospects of population, methodology, and assumptions . New York , 1979. iv, 292 p. : LC Card 79-127715 DDC 300 s 304.6 19
JX1977 .A2 ST/ESA/SER.A/67

POPULISM - LATIN AMERICA - ADDRESSES, ESSAYS, LECTURES.
Latin American populism in comparative perspective /. Albuquerque , c1981. p. cm. ISBN 0-8263-0580-6 : LC Card 80-54572 DDC 320.98 19
JL966 .L36

Porcella, R. L. Compilation of strong-motion records from the August 6, 1979 Coyote Lake earthquake /. [Washington, D.C.] [1979] vii, 71 p. : LC Card 80-621634 DDC 551.2/2/0979473 19
QE535.2.U6 C65

PORK INDUSTRY AND TRADE - UNITED STATES.
United States. Dept. of Agriculture. Economics, Statistics, and Cooperatives Service. An analysis of a ban on nitrite use in curing bacon. Washington , Springfield, Va. , 1979. iv, 23 p. ; LC Card 79-602021 DDC 338.1/0973 s 363.1/929 19
HD1759 .U56a no. 48 HD9435.U52

PORNOGRAPHY - SOCIAL ASPECTS - ILLINOIS.
Illinois. General Assembly. Legislative Investigating Commission. Sexual exploitation of children . Chicago, Ill. (300 W. Washington St., Chicago 60606) [1980] ix, 317 p. : LC Card 80-624398 DDC 362.7/1 19
HQ72.U53 I34 1980

Port Authority of New York and New Jersey. (Old catalog form: Port of New York Authority)
Trans-Hudson vehicular origin and destination survey. [New York]. *NYPL [JLM 80-891]*

PORT AUTHORITY OF NEW YORK AND NEW JERSEY.
New Jersey. State Legislature. Senate. Transportation and Communications Committee. Public hearing before sub-Committee of the Senate Transportation and Communications Committee on role and responsibilities of the Port Authority of New York and New Jersey . [Trenton, N.J.] [1981] 75, 33 p. ; LC Card 81-621896 DDC 353.97490087/71 19
KFN1811.3 .T73 1980

Port Authority of New York and New Jersey. Planning and Development Dept. Economic impact of the U. S. merchant marine and shipbuilding industries : an input-output analysis / prepared for U. S. Dept. of Commerce, Maritime Administration, [by] The Port of New York and New Jersey Planning and Development Dept. New York: Port of New York and New Jersey Planning and Development Dept., 1977. viii, 272 p.; 28 cm. Microfiche (neg.) NTIS. 3 sheets. 11 x 15 cm. (PB 272 518) "MA-GEN-970-78004."
1. Merchant marine - United States - Mathematical models. 2. Ship-building - United States - Mathematical models. 3. United States - Economic conditions - 1971-. 4. Interindustry economics. I. United States. Maritime Administration. II. Title.
HE746 .C48   *NYPL [*XME-9407]*

Port Authroity of NY & NJ. see Port Authority of New York and New Jersey.

Port development and related maritime matters . United States. Congress. House. Committee on Merchant Marine and Fisheries. Washington , 1980 [i.e. 1981] iv, 585 p. : LC Card 81-601880 DDC 353.0087/71 19
KF27 .M4 1980a

The port of Boston, Massachusetts /. United States. Board of Engineers for Rivers and Harbors. Washington , Ft. Belvoir, Va. , 1979. vi, 91 p. : LC Card 79-603481
HE554.B6 U53 1979

The port of Buffalo, New York /. Water Resources Support Center (U. S.) Washington , Fort Belvoir, VA , 1980. vi, 55 p. : LC Card 80-601613 DDC 386/.8/0974797 19
HE554.B8 W37 1980

Port of New York Authority. Trans-Hudson vehicular origin and destination survey. [New York].   *NYPL [JLM 80-891]*

Port safety and liquefied gas safety and siting . United States. Congress. House. Committee on Merchant Marine and Fisheries. Subcommittee on Coast Guard and Navigation. Washington , 1979. vii, 748 p. : LC Card 80-601892 DDC 343.73/0967 19
KF27 .M434 1979e

Port series. [New series]. United States. Board of Engineers for Rivers and Harbors. no. 1- Washington, 1946- illus., maps (fold. in pocket)
NYPL [VDNA (United States. Rivers and Harbors, Board of Engineers. Port series. [New series].]

PORT TERMINALS. see MARINE TERMINALS.

Portable electric typewriters from Japan . United States. International Trade Commission. Washington, D.C. [1980] ii, 15, A-41 p. ; LC Card 80-602317 DDC 382/.4568161 19
HD9802.J32 U5 1980

A portable hydroacoustic data acquisition system for fish stock assessment /. Thorne, Richard E. Seattle [1972] ii, 14 leaves : LC Card 81-462262 DDC 639/.2 19
SH344.23.E3 T48

Porter, John F. (joint author) Broder, Josef M. An economic analysis of rural court consolidation in Georgia /. [Athens, Ga.] [1980] 21 p. : LC Card 80-623190 DDC 347.758/012 19
KFG516.C55 B76

Porter, Lawrence Delpino, 1932- Processed data from the strong-motion records of the Santa Barbara earthquake of 13 August 1978 : final results / by L. D. Porter, J. T. Ragsdale, R. D. McJunkin (Office of Strong-Motion Studies, California Division of Mines and Geology). Sacramento, CA : The Division, 1979. 3 v. : ill. ; 28 cm. (Special report - California Division of Mines and Geology ; 144) Bibliography: v. 3, p. 81-82. LC Card 80-622289 DDC 557.94 s 551.2/2/0979491 19
1. Santa Barbara, Calif. - Earthquake, 1978 - Charts, diagrams, etc. I. Ragsdale, J. T., joint author. II. McJunkin, R. D., joint author. III. California. Office of Strong-Motion Studies. IV. Series: California. Division of Mines and Geology. Special report , 144. V. Title.
TN24.C2 A33 no. 144 QE535.2.U6

Porter, Nancy M. The effectiveness of women's studies teaching / Nancy M. Porter, Margaret T. Eileenchild. Washington, D.C. : U. S. Dept. of Health, Education, and Welfare, National

Institute of Education, Program on Teaching and Learning : for sale by the Supt. of Docs., U. S. Govt. Print. Off., [1980] ix, 76 p. ; 23 cm. (Women's studies monograph series) Bibliography: p. 65-73. LC Card 80-602283 DDC 305.4/07/073 19
1. Women's studies - United States - Evaluation. I. Eileenchild, Margaret T., joint author. II. Title. III. Series.
HQ1181.U5 P67

Portland Art Association, Portland, Or. Museum of Art. see **Portland, Or. Art Museum.**

Portland Art Museum, Portland, Or. see **Portland, Or. Art Museum.**

PORTLAND, ME. FIRST PARISH CHURCH.
Planning for exterior work on the First Parish Church, Portland, Maine, using photographs as project documentation. Washington, D.C. , 1979. 55 p. : LC Card 80-601858 DDC 726/.5/0288 19
NA5235.P7 P57

Portland, Me. Portland Museum of Art. see **Portland Museum of Art.**

Portland Museum of Art. Hewitt, Karen. Educational toys in America, 1800 to the present /. Burlington, Vt. , c1979. 141 p. : LC Card 80-131686 DDC 688.7/25 19
LB1029.T6 H48

Portland, Or. Art Museum. (Old Catalog form: Portland art museum, Portland, Ore.)
Invented images /. [Santa Barbara] , 1980. 76 p. : LC Card 79-620046
TR646.U6 S3654 ***NYPL [MFW 81-808]***

PORTLAND, OR. - BRIDGES.
United States. Congress. House. Committee on Public Works and Transportation. Subcommittee on Surface Transportation. Proposed third bridge crossing on the Columbia River between Vancouver, Washington, and Portland, Oregon . Washington , 1980. iii, 89 p. : LC Card 80-603449 DDC 388.1/32/0979549 19
KF27 .P8966 1980

Portnoy, Alice W.
Scholars as contractors . Washington , 1979. 265 p. in various pagings : LC Card 79-603005
CC136 .S36 ***NYPL [JLF 81-76]***

Workshop on Management Techniques Applied to Archeology, Texas Tech University, 1977. Scholars as managers, or how can the managers do it better . Washington , 1978. vii, 21 p., [2] leaves of plates : LC Card 79-602641
CC51 .W67 1977

Portrait of an island /. Teal, Mildred. Athens, Ga. [1981] p. cm. ISBN 0-8203-0585-5 LC Card 81-7631 DDC 574.9758/737 19
QH105.G4 T4 1981

PORTRAITS, DUTCH - EXHIBITIONS.
Wilson, William Henry, 1939- Dutch seventeenth century portraiture, the golden age /. Sarasota, Fla. , c1980. [185] p. : ISBN 0-916758-03-6 (pbk.) LC Card 80-53473 DDC 704.9/42/0942074015961 19
N7607 .W54

PORTRAITS, GROUP - NETHERLANDS - EXHIBITIONS.
Wilson, William Henry, 1939- Dutch seventeenth century portraiture, the golden age /. Sarasota, Fla. , c1980. [185] p. : ISBN 0-916758-03-6 (pbk.) LC Card 80-53473 DDC 704.9/42/0942074015961 19
N7607 .W54

PORTRAITS - LOUISIANA - NEW ORLEANS - CATALOGS.
Louisiana State Museum, New Orleans. The Louisiana Portrait Gallery /. New Orleans , c1979- v. <1> : LC Card 80-624103 DDC 704.9/42/074016335 19
N7593.8.L8 L68 1979

PORTS. see **HARBORS.**

The ports of Baton Rouge and Lake Charles, Louisiana /. Water Resources Support Center (U. S.) Washington , Fort Belvoir, VA , 1979. vi, 114 p., [1] leaf of plates : LC Card 80-601764 DDC 387.1/09763/18 19
TC225.B37 W37 1979

PORTS OF ENTRY - UNITED STATES.
United States. General Accounting Office. A single agency needed to manage port-of-entry inspections--particularly at U. S. airports,

Department of Justice, Department of the Treasury, Department of Agriculture, Department of Health, Education, and Welfare. [Washington] 1973. 33 p. LC Card 73-602073 DDC 353.007 19
HE9797.5.U5 U52 1973

Ports of Hawaii : Honolulu, Port Allen, Nawiliwili, Kahului, Kaunakakai, Kawaihae, Hilo / prepared by the Water Resources Support Center.Rev. 1980. Washington : U. S. G.P.O. ; Fort Belvoir, Va. : For sale by Water Resources Support Center, 1980. vi, 78 p. : ill., maps (2 folded in pocket) ; 26 cm. (Port series . no. 50) Earlier ed. published in 1971 under title: Ports of the Hawaiian Islands. LC Card 80-603619 DDC 387.1/09969 19
1. Harbors - Hawaii. I. Water Resources Support Center (U. S.). II. Title: Ports of the Hawaiian Islands. III. Series: Port series (United States. Army. Corps of Engineers) , no. 50.
HE554.A6 P63 1980

The ports of Panama City & Pensacola, FL and Pascagoula & Gulfport, MS /. United States. Board of Engineers for Rivers and Harbors. Washington , Fort Belvoir, Va. , 1979. vi, 130 p. : LC Card 80-603371 DDC 387.1/09759/95 19
HE554.A4 U53 1979

Ports of the Hawaiian Islands. Ports of Hawaii . Washington , Fort Belvoir, Va. , 1980. vi, 78 p. : LC Card 80-603619 DDC 387.1/09969 19
HE554.A6 P63 1980

PORTUGUESE LITERATURE - WOMEN AUTHORS - HISTORY AND CRITICISM - BIBLIOGRAPHY.
Alarcón, Norma. Bibliography of Hispanic women writers /. Bloomington, IN. , c1980. iv, 86 p. ; LC Card 80-138062 DDC 016.86/09/9287 19
Z1609.L7 A45 PQ6055

The Portuguese manuscripts collection of the Library of Congress . United States. Library of Congress. Washington , 1980. xi, 187 p. ; ISBN 0-8444-0329-6 LC Card 80-607039
Z6621.U582 P68 ***NYPL [JFE 81216]***

Portuguese West Africa. see **Angola.**

Posadas, Dionisio. Introducción a la electroquímica / por Dionisio Posadas. Washington, D.C. : Secretaría General de la Organización de los Estados Americanos, Programa Regional de Desarrollo Científico y Tecnológico, 1980. vii, 136 p. : ill. ; 23 cm. (Série de química . monografiá no. 22) Bibliography: p. 131-132. ISBN 0-08-270122-0 (pbk.) : LC Card 81-119707 DDC 540 s 541.3/7 19
1. Electrochemistry. I. Title. II. Series.
QD1 .S303 no. 22 QD553

POSITIONING (ADVERTISING)
Pessemier, Edgar A., 1922- Store image and positioning /. West Lafayette, Ind. [1979] 16, [2], 7 p. (p. [1]-7, 3d group, advertisements) : LC Card 80-621467 DDC 658/.001/9 s 658.8/374 19
HD6483 .P8 no. 709 HF5415.3

Possible amendments to the "1916 Antidumping act" . United States. Congress. Senate. Committee on Finance. Subcommittee on International Trade. Washington , 1980. iii, 148 p. ; LC Card 80-603689 DDC 344.73/04626 19
KF26 .F554 1980c

Possible effects on the atmosphere of large-scale helium extraction from the atmosphere /. Morrison, Robert Eugene, 1930- Washington , 1979. vii, 14 p. ; LC Card 79-603780 DDC 333.9/2 19
TD888.G37 M67

Post, Robert C. Yankee enterprise, the rise of the American system of manufactures . Washington. D.C. , 1981. p. cm. ISBN 0-87474-631-0 LC Card 81-607315 DDC 338.0973 19
HC103 .Y36

POSTAL LIFE INSURANCE. see **INSURANCE, LIFE.**

Postal service act of 1980 . United States. Congress. Senate. Committee on Governmental Affairs. Subcommittee on Energy, Nuclear Proliferation, and Federal Services. Washington , 1980. v, 669 p. : LC Card 80-603728 DDC 343.73/0992/0262 347.3039920262 19
KF26 .G6728 1980b

POSTAL SERVICE - EMPLOYEES - LEGAL STATUS, LAWS, ETC. - UNITED STATES.
United States. Congress. Senate. Committee on Governmental Affairs. Subcommittee on Energy, Nuclear Proliferation, and Federal Services. Postal service act of 1980 . Washington , 1980. v, 669 p. : LC Card 80-603728 DDC 343.73/0992/0262 347.3039920262 19
KF26 .G6728 1980b

POSTAL SERVICE - LAW AND LEGISLATION - UNITED STATES.
United States. Congress. House Committee on Post Office and Civil Service. Subcommittee on Postal Personnel and Modernization. Improvement in administering false representation statute . Washington , 1980. iii, 18 p. ; LC Card 80-603694 DDC 343.73/0992 347.303992 19
KF27 .P6677 1980b

United States. Congress. Senate. Committee on Governmental Affairs. Annual report of the Postmaster General . Washington , 1980. iii, 19 p. ; LC Card 80-602955 DDC 353.0087/3/06 19
KF26 .G67 1980d

United States. Congress. Senate. Committee on Governmental Affairs. Subcommittee on Energy, Nuclear Proliferation, and Federal Services. Postal service act of 1980 . Washington , 1980. v, 669 p. : LC Card 80-603728 DDC 343.73/0992/0262 347.3039920262 19
KF26 .G6728 1980b

POSTAL SERVICE - UNITED STATES.
United States. Congress. House. Committee on Post Office and Civil Service. Implications of proposed reductions in Postal Service appropriations . Washington , 1980. iii, 90 p. ; LC Card 80-602977 DDC 383/.4973 19
KF27 .P6 1980

United States. Congress. Senate. Committee on Governmental Affairs. Annual report of the Postmaster General . Washington , 1980. iii, 19 p. ; LC Card 80-602955 DDC 353.0087/3/06 19
KF26 .G67 1980d

POSTAL SERVICE - UNITED STATES - AIR MAIL. see **AIR MAIL SERVICE - UNITED STATES.**

POSTAL SERVICE - UNITED STATES - DAMAGED MAIL - CONGRESSES.
Proceedings, West Virginia University-United States Postal Service workshop . Morgantown [1973?] 50 p. ; LC Card 77-623862 DDC 383/.14/0973 19
HE6497.D35 P76

POSTAL SERVICE - UNITED STATES - DAMAGED MAIL - PREVENTION.
United States Postal Service damage reduction program . Morgantown , 1975. 99 leaves ; LC Card 77-623861 DDC 383/.14/0973 19
HE6497.D35 U52

POSTAL SERVICE - UNITED STATES - DAMAGED MAIL - PREVENTION - CASE STUDIES.
Mail damage reduction and service improvement pilot program for the Pittsburgh Post Office . Morgantown [1974?] 64 leaves ; LC Card 77-623863 DDC 383/.14/0974886 19
HE6497.D35 M34

POSTAL SERVICE - UNITED STATES - EMPLOYEES - DISEASES AND HYGIENE.
United States. Congress. House Committee on Post Office and Civil Service. Subcommittee on Postal Personnel and Modernization. Health and safety in the postal service . Washington , 1981. iii, 132 p. ; LC Card 81-601394 DDC 353.001/61 19
KF27 .P6677 1980c

United States. Congress. House Committee on Post Office and Civil Service. Subcommittee on Postal Personnel and Modernization. Safety and health within U. S. Postal Service . Washington , 1980. vi, 392 p. : LC Card 80-603078 DDC 363.1/193834973 19
KF27 .P6677 1980a

POSTAL SERVICE - UNITED STATES - EQUIPMENT AND SUPPLIES.
United States. Congress. House Committee on Post Office and Civil Service. Subcommittee on

Postal Personnel and Modernization. Electronic message service systems . Washington , 1980. iv, 317 p. : LC Card 80-602988 DDC 384.1/4 19
KF27 .P6677 1980

POSTAL SERVICE - UNITED STATES - RATES.
United States Postal Service. Board of Governors. Action of the Governors under 39 U. S. C. [Washington] [1977?] 802 p. in various pagings. *NYPL [*XME-9307]*

POSTAL SERVICE - UNITED STATES - SAFETY MEASURES.
United States. Congress. House Committee on Post Office and Civil Service. Subcommittee on Postal Personnel and Modernization. Health and safety in the postal service . Washington , 1981. iii, 132 p. : LC Card 81-601394 DDC 353.001/61 19
KF27 .P6677 1980c

United States. Congress. House Committee on Post Office and Civil Service. Subcommittee on Postal Personnel and Modernization. Safety and health within U. S. Postal Service . Washington , 1980. vi, 392 p. : LC Card 80-603078 DDC 363.1/193834973 19
KF27 .P6677 1980a

POSTAL SERVICE - UNITED STATES - UNMAILABLE MATTER. see POSTAL SERVICE - LAW AND LEGISLATION - UNITED STATES.

POST-ATTACK REHABILITATION OF INDUSTRY. see WAR DAMAGE, INDUSTRIAL.

Poston, Susan L. California. University. University at Los Angeles. Library. The Latin American collections in the UCLA Library . [Los Angeles] , 1973. 20 p., [3] leaves of plates : LC Card 80-620845 DDC 980/.0072079494 19
Z1610 .C34 1973 F1408

POST-RETIREMENT EMPLOYMENT. see UNITED STATES - OFFICIALS AND EMPLOYEES, RETIRED - EMPLOYMENT.

Post-revolutionary Cuba in a changing world . Gonzalez, Edward. Santa Monica, CA , 1975. ix, 78 p. ; LC Card 80-468852
AS36.R3 R-1844 F1788
                    NYPL [HOF 80-3135]

Postsecondary educational supply and occupational demand in Texas for the period of 1977-1983 . Texas. State 1202 Commission. Austin, Tex. [1978] 119 p. : LC Card 79-620962 DDC 331.12/09764 19
HD5725.T5 T38 1978

Postsecondary issues . Georgia. Governor's Committee on Postsecondary Education. Atlanta, Ga. [1979] 63 p. : LC Card 80-621982 DDC 378/.107 19
LA261.5 .G46 1979

Posture hearings (EPA and NOAA) . United States. Congress. House. Committee on Science and Technology. Washington , 1980. iii, 70 p. ; LC Card 80-604052 DDC 353.0082/321 19
KF27 .S39 1980e

Posture hearings (NASA and FAA) . United States. Congress. House. Committee on Science and Technology. Washington , 1980. iii, 107 p. ; LC Card 80-602953 DDC 353.0085/6 19
KF27 .S39 1980

Posture hearings (NSF, NBS, and FEMA) . United States. Congress. House. Committee on Science and Technology. Washington , 1980. iii, 200 p. ; LC Card 80-604103 DDC 353.008 19
KF27 .S39 1980f

POTABLE WATER. see DRINKING WATER.

POTASH.
Thompson, Philip, 1950- Development of a continuous flotation process for removal of insoluble slimes from potash ore /. Washington [1980] p. cm. LC Card 80-607785 DDC 622/.3636 19
TN23 .U43

POTATO INDUSTRY - LAW AND LEGISLATION - UNITED STATES.
United States. Congress. Senate. Committee on Agriculture, Nutrition, and Forestry. Subcommittee on Agricultural Research and General Legislation. To prohibit futures trading

of potatoes on commodity exchanges . Washington , 1980. v, 257 p. : LC Card 80-601327 DDC 343.73/08513491/0262 19
KF26 .A3534 1979e

Potential critical areas inventory. Minnesota. Environmental Quality Board. St. Paul , 1979. [77] p. in various pagings, [2] fold. leaves of plates : LC Card 79-625262 DDC 333.78/09776 19
QH76.5.M6 M57 1979

Potential displacement of oil by nuclear energy and coal in electric utilities . United States. Congress. House. Committee on Interstate and Foreign Commerce. Subcommittee on Oversight and Investigations. Washington , 1981. iii, 394 p. : LC Card 81-601364 DDC 333.79/3215/0973 19
KF27 .I5547 1980s

Potential economic and environmental impacts of alternative sediment control policies /. Campbell, Joseph C. Ames, Iowa [1979] viii leaves, 91 p. : LC Card 80-623102 DDC 333.76/16/0973 19
TD427.S33 C35

The potential economic impact of solar heated residences in Illinois, 1976-2000 /. Pogany, D. Z. [Springfield] , 1976. viii, 101 p. : LC Card 77-622518
HD7303.I3 P64   *NYPL [*XME-9620]*

Potential efficiencies through coordination of milk assembly and milk manufacturing plant location in the northeastern United States /. Buccola, Steven T. Blacksburg, Va. , 1979. viii, 64 p. : LC Card 79-625090 DDC 081 s 381/.4171/0974 19
AS36 .V512 no. 149 HD9282.U5A115

Potential for hydroelectric power generation, Island of Ponape, Ponape District, Trust Territory of the Pacific. Brown, Russell Ray, 1941- Washington , 1979. v, 83 p. : LC Card 80-601032 DDC 333.91/4 19
TK1524.P66 B76

Potential for improved automobile fuel economy between 1985 and 1995 . United States. Congress. Senate. Committee on Energy and Natural Resources. [Washington , 1980] iii, 516 p. : LC Card 80-603426 DDC 333.8/232 19
KF26 .E55 1980e

Potential for renewable resource alcohol fuels. United States. Congress. Joint Economic Committee. Subcommittee on Energy. Alcohol fuels policy . Washington , 1980. 2 v. : LC Card 80-604078 DDC 338.4/7662669 19
KF25 .E245 1980

The potential impact of negotiable order of withdrawal accounts on the banking industry in Arkansas . Adams, Jack E. Fayetteville, Ark. [1979] iv, 55 leaves ; LC Card 80-622482 DDC 332.1/09767 19
HG1660.U5 A28

Potential irrigation water erosion hazard, Grant County, Washington /. United States. Soil Conservation Service. Portland, Or. , 1977. 1 map : LC Card 81-691513
G4283.G7J4 1977 .U5

Potential waste disposal areas, northern Los Angeles County /. California. Dept. of Water Resources. Southern District. [Sacramento] [1979] vii, 58 p. : LC Card 80-621404 DDC 363.7/28 19
TD811.5 .C34 1979

Poth, Leonard A. The economic impact of the mineral industry of South Dakota / prepared under the direction of Leonard A. Poth and Earl Hoskins. Vermillion, S.D. : Business Research Bureau, School of Business, University of South Dakota, [1978] 135 p. : ill. ; 28 cm. (Bulletin - Business Research Bureau, University of South Dakota ; no. 126) "October 1978." "Study ... conducted for the United States Bureau of Mines." Includes bibliographies. LC Card 80-622563 DDC 330 s 338.2/09783 19
1. Mines and mineral resources - South Dakota. 2. Mineral industries - South Dakota. I. Hoskins, Earl R., joint author. II. United States. Bureau of Mines. III. Series: South Dakota. University. Business Research Bureau. Bulletin , no. 126. IV. Title.
HF5006 .S6 no. 126 HD9506.U63S5

Potomac River Basin water quality, 1978-1979 /. Rasin, V. James. Rockville, Md. (1055 1st St.,

Rockville 20850) [1980] vii, 77, 22 p. : LC Card 80-624161 DDC 363.7/3942/0972 19
TD225.P74 R373

POTOMAC RIVER - SHORELINES - LAW AND LEGISLATION.
United States. Congress. Senate. Committee on Energy and Natural Resources. Subcommittee on Parks, Recreation, and Renewable Resources. Preservation and protection of the Potomac River shoreline . Washington , 1980. iii, 79 p. ; LC Card 80-602980 DDC 346.7304/6784 19
KF26 .E5565 1980b

Potter, Ted. Kentucky. University. Art Museum. Kentucky art, 1980 . Lexington, Ky. , c1980. 20 p. : LC Card 80-144144 DDC 709/.769/074016947 19
N6530.K4 K46 1980

POTTERY - 20TH CENTURY - MINNESOTA - EXHIBITIONS.
Minnesota pottery, a potter's view . Minneapolis [1981] 32 p. : LC Card 81-50237 DDC 738/.09776/0740176579 19
NK4025.M6 M56

POTTERY - 20TH CENTURY - UNITED STATES - EXHIBITIONS.
Centering on contemporary clay . Iowa City, Iowa , c1981. 68 p. : LC Card 81-50916 DDC 730/.0973/0740177655 19
NK4008 .C46

Pottery, a notebook for new potters / developed and published by the Smithsonian Institution Traveling Exhibition Service. Washington, D.C. : The Service, [1981] p. cm. Bibliography: p. ISBN 0-86528-009-6 LC Card 81-5828 DDC 738.1 19
1. Pottery craft. I. Smithsonian Institution. Traveling Exhibition Service.
TT920 .P6

POTTERY, AMERICAN - EXHIBITIONS.
Centering on contemporary clay . Iowa City, Iowa , c1981. 68 p. : LC Card 81-50916 DDC 730/.0973/0740177655 19
NK4008 .C46

POTTERY, AMERICAN - GEORGIA.
Rinzler, Ralph. The Meaders family, north Georgia potters /. Washington, D.C. , 1981. p. cm. LC Card 81-607995 DDC 738/.092/2 B 19
NK4210.M35 R56

POTTERY, AMERICAN - MINNESOTA - EXHIBITIONS.
Minnesota pottery, a potter's view . Minneapolis [1981] 32 p. : LC Card 81-50237 DDC 738/.09776/0740176579 19
NK4025.M6 M56

POTTERY - ANALYSIS - CONGRESSES.
Archaeological ceramics . Washington, D.C. , 1982. p. cm. LC Card 81-9128 DDC 930.1/028/5 19
CC79.5.P6 A73

POTTERY, ANCIENT - EXHIBITIONS.
Los Angeles County Museum of Art. Ancient bronzes, ceramics, and seals . Los Angeles, Calif. , c1981. p. cm. ISBN 0-87587-100-3 LC Card 81-1270 DDC 730/.093 19
NK7907 .L67 1981

POTTERY CRAFT.
Pottery, a notebook for new potters /. Washington, D.C. [1981] p. cm. ISBN 0-86528-009-6 LC Card 81-5828 DDC 738.1 19
TT920 .P6

POTTERY MAKING (HANDICRAFT) see POTTERY CRAFT.

POTTERY, PREHISTORIC - AEGEAN SEA REGION.
Rutter, Jeremy B. Ceramic change in the Aegean Early Bronze Age . [Los Angeles] [c1979] 37 p. : ISBN 0-917956-11-7 LC Card 80-620674 DDC 738.3/09391 19
GN778.22.G8 R87

POTTERY, PREHISTORIC - GREECE.
Rutter, Jeremy B. Ceramic change in the Aegean Early Bronze Age . [Los Angeles] [c1979] 37 p. : ISBN 0-917956-11-7 LC Card 80-620674 DDC 738.3/09391 19
GN778.22.G8 R87

POTTERY - THAILAND - BAN CHIANG.
Van Esterik, Penny. Cognition and design production in Ban Chiang painted pottery /.

[Athens, Ohio] , 1981. p. cm. ISBN
0-89680-078-4 LC Card 81-11172 DDC
738.3/7 19
NK4156.6.B36 V37

Potvin, Judy. (joint author) Welch, Barbara. The
voluntary water quality monitoring project
report, 1979 /. [Augusta] [1980] 136 p. : LC
Card 80-623367 DDC 363.7/3942/09741 19
TD224.M2 W44

**POULTRY INDUSTRY - UNITED STATES -
PERIODICALS.**
United States. Dept. of Agriculture. Economic
Research Service. Poultry and egg situation.
PES. 213-296; May 1961-1977. [Washington]
NYPL [M-10 6134]

Pound, Ezra, 1885-1972.
Cantos. Terrell, Carroll Franklin. A companion
to the Cantos of Ezra Pound / by Carroll F.
Terrell. Orono , Berkeley , c1988- v. <1> ;
ISBN 0-520-03687-5 (University of Calif. Press)
LC Card 78-54802 DDC 811/.52 19
PS3531.O82 C289

CANTOS.
Terrell, Carroll Franklin. A companion to the
Cantos of Ezra Pound /. Orono , Berkeley ,
c1988- v. <1> ; ISBN 0-520-03687-5
(University of Calif. Press) LC Card 78-54802
DDC 811/.52 19
PS3531.O82 C289

POVERTY - ALASKA.
Alaska. Dept. of Community and Regional
Affairs. Everybody needs somebody /. Juneau,
Alaska [1979?] 36 p. : LC Card 79-625245
DDC 362.5/09798 19
HV98.A4 A39 1979

POVERTY RESEARCH.
Alaska. Dept. of Community and Regional
Affairs. Everybody needs somebody /. Juneau,
Alaska [1979?] 36 p. : LC Card 79-625245
DDC 362.5/09798 19
HV98.A4 A39 1979

POVERTY - STATISTICS.
Maine. State Planning Office. Indicators of
poverty. [Augusta, Me. , 1980] [22] p. ; LC
Card 80-621545 DDC 339.4/6/09741 19
HC107.M23 P625 1980

POW. United States. Veterans Administration.
Office of Planning and Program Evaluation.
Study of former prisoners of war /.
Washington, D.C. , 1980. iii, 181 p. ; LC Card
80-602667 DDC 355.1/15 19
UB369 .U57 1980a

POW/MIA's . United States. Congress. House.
Committee on Foreign Affairs. Subcommittee
on Asian and Pacific Affairs. Washington ,
1980. v, 49 p. ; LC Card 80-603653 DDC
959.704/37 19
KF27 .F638 1980a

Powder Coatings Conference, Cleveland, 1972.
Powder Coatings Conference proceedings, the
Cleveland State University/Division of
Continuing Education, November 17, 1972.
Cleveland : Cleveland State University, 1973.
146 leaves : ill. ; 28 cm. Includes bibliographies.
*1. Plastic powders - Congresses. 2. Plastic coating -
Congresses. I. Cleveland State University. Division of
Continuing Education. II. Title.*
NYPL [JSF 81-290]

Powder Coatings Conference proceedings. Powder
Coatings Conference, Cleveland, 1972.
Cleveland , 1973. 146 leaves :
NYPL [JSF 81-290]

**POWDER METAL PROCESS. see POWDER
METALLURGY.**

POWDER METALLURGY.
McIlwain, J. F. Consolidation of an iron-base
superalloy by powder metallurgy techniques /.
Washington, D.C. [1981] p. cm. LC Card
80-607851 DDC 622 s 672.3/7 19
TN23 .U43 TN697.I7

**POWDERED PLASTICS. see PLASTIC
POWDERS.**

**POWDERS - OPTICAL PROPERTIES -
MEASUREMENT - CONGRESSES.**
Symposium on Accuracy in Powder Diffraction,
National Bureau of Standards, 1979. Accuracy
in powder diffraction . [Washington, D.C.]
[1980] x, 572 p. : LC Card 80-600010 DDC
602/.18 s 548/.83 19
QC100 .U57 no. 567 QC482.D5

Powell, Douglas S. The forest resources of
Maryland / [by Douglas S. Powell and Neal P.
Kingsley]. Broomall, Pa. : Forest Service, U. S.
Dept. of Agriculture, Northeastern Forest
Experiment Station, 1980. 103 p. : ill. ; 26 cm.
(Forest Service resource bulletin NE . 61) "ODC
(752):905.2." Cover title. Bibliography: p. 40. LC Card
80-601810 DDC 333.75/0974 s
333.75/11/09752 19
*1. Forests and forestry - Maryland. 2. Timber -
Maryland. I. Kingsley, Neal P., joint author. II.
Northeastern Forest Experiment Station, Broomall, Pa.
III. Title.*
SD11 .A455494 no. 61 SD144.M3

Powell, Mary Lucas. Bioarchaeology of the
McCutchan-McLaughlin site (34Lt-11) :
biophysical and mortuary variability in eastern
Oklahoma / by Mary Lucas Powell and J.
Daniel Rogers. Norman, Okla. : Oklahoma
Archeological Survey, 1980. vi, 98 p. : ill. ; 28
cm. (Studies in Oklahoma's past. no. 5) Bibliography:
p. 91-98. LC Card 80-622411 DDC 976.6/76 19
*1. McCutchan-McLaughlin site, Okla. 2. Indians of
North America - Oklahoma - Anthropometry. 3.
Indians of North America - Oklahoma - Mortuary
customs. I. Rogers, J. Daniel, joint author. II. Title. III.
Series.*
E78.O45 P66   *NYPL [HBA no. 5]*

**Power and process: a commentary on eminent
domain and condemnation.** MacBride, Dexter
D. [Washington, 1979] x, 84 p. LC Card
70-77921
KF5599 .Z9M3   *NYPL [JLD 80-3601]*

**POWER, BALANCE OF. see BALANCE OF
POWER.**

**POWER DISTRIBUTION, ELECTRIC. see
ELECTRIC POWER DISTRIBUTION.**

**POWER, LEGISLATIVE. see LEGISLATIVE
POWER.**

POWER (MECHANICS) - BIBLIOGRAPHY.
Weeks (I. D.) Library. Energy, a bibliography
and index of related materials at the University
of South Dakota /. Vermillion , c1978. 546 p. ;
LC Card 79-621285
Z5853.P83 W4 1978 TJ163.2
NYPL [JLF 80-1563]

POWER (MECHANICS) - CONGRESSES.
Symposium on Biotechnology in Energy
Production and Conservation, 1st, Gatlinburg,
Tenn., 1978. Biotechnology in energy
production and conservation . New York ,
c1979. vi, 513 p. : ISBN 0-471-05745-2 (pbk.)
LC Card 80-128733
TJ163.7 .S97 1978   *NYPL [JSE 80-1362]*

POWER (MECHANICS) - INDEXES.
Weeks (I. D.) Library. Energy, a bibliography
and index of related materials at the University
of South Dakota /. Vermillion , c1978. 546 p. ;
LC Card 79-621285
Z5853.P83 W4 1978 TJ163.2
NYPL [JLF 80-1563]

The power of power politics . Vasquez, John A.,
1945- New Brunswick, N.J. , c1981. p. cm.
ISBN 0-8135-0919-X : LC Card 81-5849 DDC
327/.072 19
JX1291 .V38

POWER-PLANTS - ALASKA - MAPS.
Conwell, Cleland N. Energy resource map of
Alaska /. College, AK , 1977. 1 map : 82 x 118
cm. Scale 1:2,500,000. "Base by U. S. Geological
Survey: Alaska, Map E, 1954." Insets: [Cook Inlet
area]--[Aleutian Islands]--Oil and gas regions and
provinces. LC Card 79-692512
G4371.H1 1977 .C6
NYPL [Map Div. 81-3049]

**POWER-PLANTS, ATOMIC. see ATOMIC
POWER-PLANTS.**

**POWER-PLANTS, ELECTRIC. see ELECTRIC
POWER-PLANTS.**

**POWER PLANTS, HYDROELECTRIC. see
HYDROELECTRIC POWER PLANTS.**

**POWER-PLANTS, STEAM. see STEAM
POWER-PLANTS.**

**POWER POLITICS. see BALANCE OF
POWER.**

**POWER PRODUCTION, ELECTRIC. see
ELECTRIC POWER PRODUCTION.**

**Power program of the Tennessee Valley
Authority .** United States. Congress. Senate.

Committee on Appropriations. Subcommittee on
Energy and Water Development. Washington ,
1981. iii, 192 p. : LC Card 81-601951 DDC
353.0082/3/09768 19
KF26 .A6469 1980b

POWER RESOURCES.
(1979) United Nations. Economic Commission
for Europe. Energy reserves and supplies in the
ECE region . New York , 1979. vi, 74 p. : LC
Card 80-125171 DDC 333.79/11/094 19
JX1977 .A2 E/ECE/984

POWER RESOURCES - ALASKA - MAPS.
Conwell, Cleland N. Energy resource map of
Alaska /. College, AK , 1977. 1 map : 82 x 118
cm. Scale 1:2,500,000. "Base by U. S. Geological
Survey: Alaska, Map E, 1954." Insets: [Cook Inlet
area]--[Aleutian Islands]--Oil and gas regions and
provinces. LC Card 79-692512
G4371.H1 1977 .C6
NYPL [Map Div. 81-3049]

POWER RESOURCES - BIBLIOGRAPHY.
United States. Dept. of Housing and Urban
Development. Office of International Affairs.
Housing and urban development energy
research abroad . [Washington, D.C.] , 1980. i,
27 p. : LC Card 80-601814 DDC 016.33379 19
Z5853.P83 U525 1980 TJ163.2

Weeks (I. D.) Library. Energy, a bibliography
and index of related materials at the University
of South Dakota /. Vermillion , c1978. 546 p. ;
LC Card 79-621285
Z5853.P83 W4 1978 TJ163.2
NYPL [JLF 80-1563]

POWER RESOURCES - CANADA.
United States. General Accounting Office.
Prospects for cooperation and trade of energy
resources between the United States and
Canada . [Washington, D.C. , 1979] iii, 33 p. ;
LC Card 80-600527 DDC 333.79/0971 19
HD9502.C32 U56 1979

**POWER RESOURCES - ENVIRONMENTAL
ASPECTS - UNITED STATES -
CONGRESSES.**
Transcript from the national hearing on the
Federal nonnuclear energy RD&D program .
Washington, D.C. , 1980. xv, 161 p. ; LC Card
81-600788 DDC 333.79/15/0973 19
TD195.E49 T7

POWER RESOURCES - EUROPE.
United Nations. Economic Commission for
Europe. Energy reserves and supplies in the
ECE region . New York , 1979. vi, 74 p. : LC
Card 80-125171 DDC 333.79/11/094 19
JX1977 .A2 E/ECE/984

POWER RESOURCES - IDAHO.
Finn, Mark W. Idaho energy facts /. Boise, ID
[1980] viii, 186, 20 p. : LC Card 80-623630
DDC 333.79/09796 19
HD9502.U53 I23

POWER RESOURCES - INDEXES.
Weeks (I. D.) Library. Energy, a bibliography
and index of related materials at the University
of South Dakota /. Vermillion , c1978. 546 p. ;
LC Card 79-621285
Z5853.P83 W4 1978 TJ163.2
NYPL [JLF 80-1563]

**POWER RESOURCES - INFORMATION
SERVICES - UNITED STATES -
CONGRESSES.**
United States. Library of Congress.
Congressional Research Service. Energy
information . Washington , 1980. ix, 114 p. ;
LC Card 80-602583 DDC 333.79/07 19
TJ163.17 .U54 1980

**POWER RESOURCES - LAW AND
LEGISLATION - UNITED STATES.**
Compilation of the Energy Security Act of
1980, and 1980 amendments to the Defense
Production Act of 1950 /. Washington , 1980.
3 v. (v. 2252 p.) ; LC Card 80-603878 DDC
346.7304/679 347.3064679 19
KF2120.A32 A15 1980

United States. Laws, statutes, etc. Compilation
of energy-related legislation /. Washington ,
1979. 3 v. ; LC Card 79-603457
KF2120 .A3 1979

**POWER RESOURCES - LAW AND
LEGISLATION - WASHINGTON (STATE)**
Washington (State). Legislature. Senate. Energy
and Utilities Committee. Major energy

legislation of the 1979 legislative session /. Olympia, WA [1979] 26 p. : LC Card 80-621222 DDC 346.79704/679/02638 19
KFW11.72 .E53 1979

Watson, Richard H. Energy, transition to the '80s . Olympia, WA [1980] 52 p., [2] leaves : LC Card 80-623469 DDC 346.7304/679 19
KFW286 .W38

POWER RESOURCES - LAW AND LEGISLATION - WISCONSIN.
Wisconsin. Legislative reference bureau. Wisconsin's outlook on energy /. Madison, Wis. [1980] 17 p. ; LC Card 80-624141 DDC 300/.9775 s 346.77504/679 300/.9775 s 347.75064679 19
KFW2415 .L4 80-4 KFW2686

POWER RESOURCES - MISSOURI - COSTS.
Missouri. Division of Energy. Missouri energy costs in the 1970s . Jefferson City, Mo. [1980] 20 leaves : LC Card 80-623049 DDC 338.4/36655/09778 19
HD9502.U53 M8955 1980

POWER RESOURCES - PRICES - UNITED STATES.
United States. Congress. Joint Economic Committee. Subcommittee on Energy. Impact of energy prices and inflation on American families . Washington , 1981. iii, 74 p. : LC Card 81-601606
KF25 .E245 1980a

POWER RESOURCES - RESEARCH - FLORIDA.
Florida. Governor's Energy Office. Toward a comprehensive energy research and development program for Florida /. [Tallahassee, Fla.] [1979] 21, 8, 221 p. ; LC Card 80-621492 DDC 333.79/0720759 19
TJ163.25.U6 F55 1979

POWER RESOURCES - RESEARCH - UNITED STATES - FINANCE.
United States. Congressional Budget Office. Federal energy research . Washington , 1976. xvi, 77 p. : LC Card 77-602336 DDC 333.79/15/0973 19
TJ163.25.U6 U513 1976a

POWER RESOURCES - SOCIAL ASPECTS.
Adams, Richard Newbold, 1924- Observations on the use of energy in social structure analysis /. [Austin] , 1979. ii, 76 leaves ; LC Card 79-624609 DDC 303.4/83 19
TJ163.2 .A3

POWER RESOURCES - UNITED STATES.
Panel on Energy, Natural Resources, and the Environment (U. S.) Energy, natural resources, and the environment in the eighties . Washington , 1980. 57 p. ; LC Card 81-649 DDC 333.79/0973 19
HD9502.U52 P35 1981

Panel on Energy, Natural Resources, and the Environment (U. S.) Energy, natural resources, and the environment in the eighties . Washington , 1981. p. cm. LC Card 80-649 DDC 333.79/0973 19
HD9502.U52 P35 1981

United States. Congress. Office of Technology Assessment. Alternative energy futures. Washington, D.C. [1980- 1 v. : LC Card 80-600046
TJ163.25.U6 U49 1980

NYPL [JLM 80-1009]

United States. Congress. Senate. Committee on Governmental Affairs. Permanent Subcommittee on Investigations. Energy security . Washington , 1980. iii, 154 p. : LC Card 80-603907 DDC 333.79/0973 19
KF26 .G674 1980d

UnitedStates. Congress. Senate. Special Committee on Aging. Energy and the aged . Washington , 1980. iii, 40 p. : LC Card 80-601941 DDC 363.6/2 19
KF26.5 .A3 1979f

POWER RESOURCES - UNITED STATES - COSTS.
United States. Congress. House. Committee on Interstate and Foreign Commerce. Subcommittee on Oversight and Investigations. Impact of energy inflation . Washington , 1980. iii, 315 p. : LC Card 80-602823 DDC 332.4/1/0973 19
KF27 .I5547 1979u

POWER RESOURCES - UNITED STATES - FINANCE.
Ryan, Paul, 1930- An analysis of petroleum company investments in non-petroleum energy sources /. Washington, D.C. [Springfield, VA , 1979] 2 v. : LC Card 80-601258 DDC 332.6/7254 19
HD9565 .R9

United States. Congress. House. Committee on Appropriations. Subcommittee on Energy and Water Development. Energy and water development appropriations for 1982 . Washington , 1981. 2 v. (2710, xviii p.) ; LC Card 81-601647 DDC 353.0072/236823 19
KF27 .A64 1981

POWER RESOURCES - VIRGINIA.
Line, Lloyd E. Energy in the 80's . Richmond, Va. (310 Turner Rd., Richmond, 23225) [1980] xviii, 203 p. : LC Card 81-622013 DDC 333.79/09755 19
TJ163.25.U6 L56

POWER RESOURCES - WASHINGTON (STATE)
Watson, Richard H. Energy, transition to the '80s . Olympia, WA [1980] 52 p., [2] leaves : LC Card 80-623469 DDC 346.7304/679 19
KFW286 .W38

POWER RESOURCES - WEST (U. S.) - ADDRESSES, ESSAYS, LECTURES.
Energy resource recovery in arid lands /. Albuquerque , c1981. p. cm. ISBN 0-8263-0564-4 LC Card 80-54573 DDC 333.79/0978 19
TJ163.25.U6 E54

POWER (SOCIAL SCIENCES) IN LITERATURE.
Newton, Judith Lowder. Women, power, and subversion . Athens , c1981. p. cm. ISBN 0-8203-0564-2 LC Card 81-1068 DDC 823/.009/9287 19
PR830.W62 N4

POWER SUPPLY. see POWER RESOURCES.

POWER TRANSMISSION, ELECTRIC. see ELECTRIC POWER TRANSMISSION.

Powerplant Fuel Conservation Act of 1980 . United States. Congress. House. Committee on Interstate and Foreign Commerce. Subcommittee on Energy and Power. Washington , 1980. iv, 623 p. : LC Card 80-604038 DDC 346.7304/67916/0262 347.3064679160262 19
KF27 .I5542 1980i

Powerplant fuels conservation act of 1980 . United States. Congress. Senate. Committee on Energy and Natural Resources. Subcommittee on Energy Regulation. Washington , 1980. iv, 1228 p. : LC Card 80-603723 DDC 346.7304/6793216 347.30646793216 19
KF26 .E5527 1980

Powers, Edward A., 1941- (joint author) Goudy, Willis J. Older workers in small towns . Ames, Iowa [1977] viii, 205 p. : LC Card 80-623924 DDC 331.3/98/09777 19
HD6281.I8 G68

Powers, Jane VanDeMark. Adolescent health care services in Michigan : needs for program modification / researched & written by Jane VanDeMark Powers ; with direction & assistance from Sheila J. Ward ; secretary, Nancy J. Miller ; Bureau of Personal Health Services, Michigan Dept. of Public Health ; sponsored by Evaluation Branch, Planning & Evaluation, Dept. of Health, Education & Welfare. Lansing : The Bureau, 1978. vi, 159 p. : ill. ; 28 cm. "Purchase order RO-V-1009-77." Includes bibliographies. LC Card 79-620710 DDC 362.1/9 19
1. Youth - Medical care - Michigan. 2. Youth - Medical care - Michigan - Kent Co. I. Ward, Sheila J. II. Michigan. Bureau of Personal Health Services. III. Title.
RJ102.5.M5 P68

Powers, William K. Yuwipi, vision and experience in Oglala ritual / William K. Powers. Lincoln : University of Nebraska Press, c1982. p. cm. Bibliography: p. Includes index. ISBN 0-8032-3663-8 LC Card 81-10501 DDC 299/.74 19
1. Oglala Indians - Religion and mythology. 2. Oglala Indians - Rites and ceremonies. 3. Indians of North America - Great Plains - Religion and mythology. 4. Indians of North America - Great Plains - Rites and ceremonies. I. Title.
E99.O3 P683

Poynter Center.
Fallows, James M. An old capital and a new president /. Bloomington, Ind. , c1979. 16 p. : LC Card 80-140042 DDC 973.926/092/4 19
E873 .F34

Poynter Center. Citizen and the News Project. The Classroom and the newsroom /. Bloomington, Ind. , 1979. 140 p. ; LC Card 80-140151 DDC 070/.07 19
PN4888.S6 C58

Pozo-Ledezma, Leo F. United States. Dept. of Housing and Urban Development. Office of International Affairs. Housing and urban development planning in Mexico . Washington, D.C. [1980] 54 p. ; LC Card 80-602924 DDC 307.7/6/0972 19
Z7164.H8 U4495 1980 HD7306.A3

POZZUOLANAS - ANALYSIS.
Phillips, E. L. (Earl L.) Laboratory analysis of pozzolan (fly ash) concrete /. Washington , 1981. p. cm. LC Card 81-607036 DDC 622 s 622/.4 19
TN23 .U43 TP882

Practical construction law . Griffin, Harry L. [Washington, D.C.] (1120 Twentieth St., NW, Washington 20036) , c1981. vii, 405 p. ; LC Card 81-129626 DDC 343.73/07869 347.3037869 19
KF902 .G74 1981

A practical implementation of path expressions /. Campbell, Ronald H. Urbana, Ill. [1980] 25 p. ; LC Card 80-623653 DDC 001.64 s 001.64/24 19
QA76 .I4 no. 1008 QA76.73.P217

PRACTICAL NURSING - HANDBOOKS, MANUALS, ETC.
Nursing skills and procedures /. Columbus, Ohio , Reston, Va. , c1979. x, 1077 p. : LC Card 81-103544 DDC 610.73/02/02 19
RT62 .N8 1979

PRACTICAL NURSING - STUDY AND TEACHING - LAW AND LEGISLATION - TEXAS.
Texas. State Board of Vocational Nurse Examiners. Minimum standards for Vocational nurse education. Austin, Tex. , 1979. iii, 26 p. ; LC Card 80-622928 DDC 344.764/0414 19
KFT1526.5.P66 A32 1979

Practice book revisions /. Connecticut. Superior Court. Rules Committee. East Hartford, Conn. , 1980. i, 31 p. ; LC Card 80-138409 DDC 347.746/05 19
KFC4130 .C6 1980 Suppl

The Practice of management : selected recent references. [Washington, D.C.] : U. S. Dept. of Labor, Office of the Assistant Secretary for Administration and Management, Library : For sale by the Supt. of Docs., U. S. G.P.O., 1980. ii, 101 p. ; 28 cm. "May 1980." S/N 029-000-00406-4 LC Card 80-604143 DDC 016.658 19
1. Management - Bibliography. I. United States. Dept. of Labor. Library.
Z7164.O7 P68 HD30.5

Pradl, Gordon M. Expectation and cohesion / by Gordon M. Pradl. Berkeley, Calif. : Bay Area Writing Project, University of California, c1979. iii, 29 p. ; 23 cm. (Curriculum publication / University of California, Berkeley, Bay Area Writing Project . no. 7) Bibliography: p. 29. LC Card 80-155392 DDC 808/.042 19
1. English language - Style. 2. English language - Semantics. I. Bay Area Writing Project. II. Series: Curriculum publication , no. 7. III. Title.
PE1421 .P7

PRAGMATISM.
Apel, Karl Otto. [Der Denkweg von Charles S. Peirce. English.] Charles S. Peirce . Amherst, Mass. , c1981. p. cm. ISBN 0-87023-177-4 : LC Card 81-3337 DDC 191 19
B945.P44 A7513

Prairie pothole region. Establishment of seeded grasslands for wildlife habitat in the prairie pothole region /. Washington, D.C. , 1981. p. cm. LC Card 81-607001 DDC 639.9/79/0973 s 639.9/79 19
SK361 .A256 no. 234

PRAIRIES - UNITED STATES.
Establishment of seeded grasslands for wildlife habitat in the prairie pothole region /.

Washington, D.C. , 1981. p. cm. LC Card
81-607001 DDC 639.9/79/0973 s 639.9/79 19
SK361 .A256 no. 234

Pratt (Enoch) Free Library, Baltimore. see
Enoch Pratt Free Library, Baltimore.

Pratt, Richard T. An economic analysis of the
"due on sale" clause in the California mortgage
market / prepared by Richard T. Pratt and Tim
S. Campbell. [West Lafayette, Ind.] : Credit
Research Center, Krannert Graduate School of
Management, Purdue University, 1979, c1978.
ii, 29 p. : ill. ; 23 cm. (Monograph / Credit
Research Center, Krannert Graduate School of
Management, Purdue University . no. 14) Includes
bibliographical references. LC Card 81-621404 DDC
332.7/22/09794 19
1. Mortgage loans - California. I. Campbell, Timothy S.
II. Series: Monograph (Krannert Graduate School of
Management. Credit Research Center) , no. 14. III.
Title.
HG2040.5.U6 C35 1979

PRATT, RICHARD THOMAS, 1937-
United States. Congress. Senate. Committee on
Banking, Housing and Urban Affairs.
Nomination of Richard T. Pratt . Washington ,
1981. iii, 49 p. ; LC Card 81-601950 DDC
353.0082/5 19
KF26 .B39 1981d

**Prayer in public schools and buildings--federal
court jurisdiction** . United States. Congress.
House. Committee on the Judiciary.
Subcommittee on Courts, Civil Liberties, and
the Administration of Justice. Washington ,
1981. iv, 976 p. ; LC Card 81-601626 DDC
344.73/0796 347.304796 19
KF27 .J857 1980a

PRC Energy Analysis Company. Solar energy
commercialization for African countries /
prepared by PRC Energy Analysis Company for
U. S. Department of Energy, Assistant
Secretary for Conservation and Solar
Applications, Office of Solar Applications and
Commercialization. [Washington] : The Office ;
Springfield, Va. : available from National
Technical Information Service, U. S. Dept. of
Commerce, [1978] ix, 103 p. : ill. ; 28 cm.
"December 1978." "HCP/CS-2522." "Contract no.
EG-77-C-01-2522." Includes bibliographical references.
LC Card 79-602118 DDC 333.79/23/0967 19
1. Solar energy - Africa. I. United States. Dept. of
Energy. Office of Solar Applications and
Commercialization. II. Title.
TJ810 .P27 1978

**PRE-CAMBRIAN PERIOD. see GEOLOGY,
STRATIGRAPHIC - PRE-CAMBRIAN.**

Precambrian rocks. Condie, Kent C. Geology and
geochemistry of Precambrian rocks, central and
south-central New Mexico /. Socorro , 1979.
58 p. : LC Card 80-622498 DDC 551.7/1/09789
19
QE653 .C653

PRECAST CONCRETE CONSTRUCTION.
United States. Dept. of Housing and Urban
Development. Office of Policy Development
and Research. Design and construction of
large-panel concrete structures . [Washington]
[1979] xii, 49 p. : ISBN 0-08-931238-3 LC Card
79-603976 DDC 693.8/52 19
TA658.44 .U52 1979

**PRECIOUS METALS - LAW AND
LEGISLATION - UNITED STATES.**
United States. Congress. Senate. Committee on
Banking, Housing and Urban Affairs. Margin
requirements for transactions in financial
instruments . Washington , 1980. vii, 850 p. :
LC Card 80-603509 DDC 346.73/0922 19
KF26 .B39 1980r

PRECIOUS METALS - RECYCLING.
Salisbury, H. B. Recovery of copper and
associated precious metals from electronic scrap
/. Washington [1981] p. cm. LC Card
80-607807 DDC 622 s 699/.3 19
TN23 .U43 no. 8500 TD812.5.C66

**PRECIPITATION (METEOROLOGY) -
ILLINOIS.**
Changnon, Stanley Alcide. Review of Illinois
summer precipitation conditions /. Urbana ,
1980. 160 p. : LC Card 80-623561 DDC
551.57/72/773 19
QC925.1.U8 I325

**PRECIPITATION (METEOROLOGY) -
KENTUCKY - KENTUCKY RIVER
WATERSHED - MAPS.**
United States. Soil Conservation Service.
Average annual precipitation, Kentucky River
Basin . Fort Worth, Tex. , 1980. 1 map : LC
Card 81-692250
G3952.K44C3 1980 .U5

**PRECIPITATION (METEOROLOGY) -
NORTHERN HEMISPHERE - MAPS.**
Aeronautical Chart and Information Center (U.
S.) Annual precipitation chart . St. Louis
[1959] 1 map : LC Card 81-690546
G3211.C88 1959 .A3

**PRECIPITATION (METEOROLOGY) -
OHIO - MAPS.**
United States. Soil Conservation Service.
Average annual precipitation in inches, 1931-60,
southwest Ohio River basin study area, Ohio /.
Lincoln, Nebr. , 1978. 1 map : LC Card
81-691036
G4081.C88 1960 .U5

**PRECIPITATION (METEOROLOGY) -
SOUTH DAKOTA - MAPS.**
United States. Soil Conservation Service. South
Dakota, average annual precipitation (inches)
1941-70 /. Lincoln, Nebr. , 1976. 1 map : LC
Card 81-691114
G4181.C88 1970 .U5

**PRECIPITATION (METEOROLOGY) -
WASHINGTON (STATE) - ENTIAT
RIVER WATERSHED - MAPS.**
United States. Soil Conservation Service.
Precipitation and runoff, Entiat River Basin,
Chelan County, Washington /. Portland, Or. ,
1979. 1 map : LC Card 81-691528
G4282.E5C88 1978 .U5

**PRECIPITATION (METEOROLOGY) -
WASHINGTON (STATE) - FRANKLIN
COUNTY - MAPS.**
United States. Soil Conservation Service.
Precipitation map, Franklin County
Conservation District, Franklin County,
Washington /. Portland, Or. , 1980. 1 map :
LC Card 81-691510
G4283.F7C88 1980 .U5

**PRECIPITATION (METEOROLOGY) -
WASHINGTON (STATE) - GRANT
COUNTY - MAPS.**
United States. Soil Conservation Service.
General precipitation, Grant County,
Washington /. Portland, Or. , 1978. 1 map :
LC Card 81-691511
G4283.G7C88 1978 .U5

**PRECIPITATION (METEOROLOGY) -
WASHINGTON (STATE) - WALLA
WALLA COUNTY - MAPS.**
United States. Soil Conservation Service.
Average annual precipitation, Walla Walla
County Soil Conservation District, Walla Walla
County, Washington /. Portland, Or. , 1979. 1
map : LC Card 81-691505
G4283.W3C88 1979 .U5

PRECISION CASTING.
Calvert, Eugene D. An investment mold for
titanium casting /. Washington [1981] p. cm.
LC Card 80-607847 DDC 622 s 673/.7322255
19
TN23 .U43 TS562

**Preclinical and clinical testing by the
pharmaceutical industry, 1980--DMSO** . United
States. Congress. Senate. Subcommittee on Labor
and Human Resources. Subcommittee on
Health and Scientific Research. Washington ,
1980. iii, 103 p. ; LC Card 81-600617 DDC
363.1/9464 19
KF26 .L274 1980n

**Precolumbian exhibition, the John and Mary
Carter collection of Peruvian precolumbian
artifacts and textiles** /. Florida. State
University, Tallahassee. Art Gallery.
[Tallahassee] , c1978. 127 p. : LC Card
80-116225 DDC 985/.01/074015988 19
F3429.3.A7 F56 1978

**PREDATOR CONTROL - ENVIRONMENTAL
ASPECTS - THE WEST.**
United States. Fish and Wildlife Service.
Predator damage in the West . [Washington] ,
1978. vii, 168 p. : LC Card 79-602347 DDC
636.08/3 19
SF810.7.C88 U54 1978

**PREDATOR CONTROL - GOVERNMENT
POLICY - UNITED STATES.**
United States. Congress. Senate. Committee on
Environment and Public Works. Animal
damage control program . Washington , 1980.
iv, 595 p. : LC Card 80-603724 DDC 639.9/6 19
KF26 .E6 1980i

**PREDATOR CONTROL - LAW AND
LEGISLATION - UNITED STATES.**
United States. Congress. House. Committee on
Agriculture. Subcommittee on Department
Investigations, Oversight, and Research. Animal
damage control act of 1980 . Washington ,
1980. iv, 305 p. ; LC Card 80-602972 DDC
343.73/0766083 19
KF27 .A33265 1980

Predator Control Summit, Austin, Tex., 1980.
Proceedings of the Predator Control Summit,
January 15, 1980, Austin, Texas / sponsored by
the Texas Department of Agriculture, Reagan
V. Brown, Commissioner. Austin, Tex. : The
Dept., [1980] 45 p. ; 28 cm. Bibliography: p. 45.
LC Card 80-622863 DDC 636.08/3 19
1. Predator control - United States - Congresses. 2.
Predator control - Texas - Congresses. I. Texas. Dept.
of Agriculture.
SF810.6.U6 P74 1980

**PREDATOR CONTROL - TEXAS -
CONGRESSES.**
Predator Control Summit, Austin, Tex., 1980.
Proceedings of the Predator Control Summit,
January 15, 1980, Austin, Texas /. Austin, Tex.
[1980] 45 p. ; LC Card 80-622863 DDC 636.08/3
19
SF810.6.U6 P74 1980

**PREDATOR CONTROL - UNITED STATES -
CONGRESSES.**
Predator Control Summit, Austin, Tex., 1980.
Proceedings of the Predator Control Summit,
January 15, 1980, Austin, Texas /. Austin, Tex.
[1980] 45 p. ; LC Card 80-622863 DDC 636.08/3
19
SF810.6.U6 P74 1980

Predator damage in the West . United States.
Fish and Wildlife Service. [Washington] , 1978.
vii, 168 p. : LC Card 79-602347 DDC 636.08/3
19
SF810.7.C88 U54 1978

**PREDICTION, EARTHQUAKES. see
EARTHQUAKE PREDICTION.**

**PREDICTION OF CRIMINAL BEHAVIOR.
see CRIMINAL BEHAVIOR,
PREDICTION OF.**

**Pre-employment security procedures of the
intelligence agencies** . United States. Congress.
House. Permanent Select Committee on
Intelligence. Subcommittee on Oversight.
Washington , 1980. iv, 213 p. ; LC Card
80-602800 DDC 353.0074 19
KF27.5 .I55 1979

**PREFABRICATED CONCRETE
CONSTRUCTION. see PRECAST
CONCRETE CONSTRUCTION.**

**Preference section of the Bankruptcy Code, S.
3023** . United States. Congress. Senate.
Committee on the Judiciary. Subcommittee on
Improvements in Judicial Machinery.
Washington , 1981. iii, 34 p. ; LC Card
81-601155 DDC 346.73/078/0262
347.306780262 19
KF26 .J855 1980e

**PREFERENTIAL DUTY. see TARIFF
PREFERENCES.**

**PREFERENTIAL TARIFF. see TARIFF
PREFERENCES.**

Pregill, Gregory K. Fossil vertebrates from the
Bahamas . Washington , 1982. p. cm. LC Card
81-13543 DDC 560 s 566/.097296 19
QE701 .S56 no. 48 QE841

PREGNANCY - NUTRITIONAL ASPECTS.
Cox, Janice Hovasi. Normal diet, pregnancy
and lactation /. Columbus, Ohio (456 Clinic
Dr., Columbus 43210) , c1980. 47 p. : LC Card
81-620942 DDC 618.2/4 19
RG559 .C68

**PREGNANT WOMEN - UNITED STATES -
DRUG USE.**
United States. Congress. House. Select
Committee on Narcotics Abuse and Control.
The use of drugs during pregnancy .

Washington , 1980. iii, 99 p. ; LC Card
80-602790 DDC 362.8/2 19
KF27.5 .N3 1980

**PREHISTORIC ANTIQUITIES. see MAN,
PREHISTORIC.**

**Prehistoric butchering techniques in the lower
granite reservoir, southeastern Washington /.**
Lyman, R. Lee. [Pocatello] , 1978. 25 p. : LC
Card 79-620641 DDC 979.7/4 19
E78.I18 T43 no. 13 E78.W3

**PREHISTORIC MAN. see MAN,
PREHISTORIC.**

Prejudice and pride . National Academy of
Education. [Washington] , 1979. 37 p. ; LC
Card 79-602965 DDC 344.73/0798 19
KF4155.A2 N38

**Preliminary analysis of aircraft accident data:
United States civil aviation.** United States.
National Transportation Safety Board.
Washington.   *NYPL [JLM 80-909]*

**A preliminary analysis of the IRS tax
administration system.** United States. Congress.
Office of Technology Assessment. -
Washington , Springfield, Va. , 1977. x, 206 p. ;
     NYPL [*XME-9377]

**A preliminary archaeological survey for the
Conquista project in Gonzales, Atascosa, and
Live Oak Counties, Texas /.** McGraw, A.
Joachim. [San Antonio] , 1979. iii, 31 leaves ;
LC Card 80-620819 DDC 976.4/445 19
E78.T4 M317

**The preliminary archeological inventory of the
Savannah River Plant, Aiken and Barnwell
Counties, South Carolina /.** Hanson, Glen T.
Columbia , 1978. viii, 166 p. : LC Card
79-620819 DDC 975.7/75 19
E78.S6 H38

**A preliminary assessment of the National Crime
Information Center and the Computerized
Criminal History System.** United States.
Congress. Office of Technology Assessment.
Washington [1978] vii, 84 p. ; LC Card
78-600164 DDC 025/.06364973 19
HV6791 .U52 1978

**Preliminary checklist of the vascular flora of
Connecticut (growing without cultivation) /.**
Dowhan, Joseph J. Hartford, Conn. , 1979. x,
176 p. ; LC Card 80-620747 DDC 557.46 s
582.09746 19
QE93 .A1165 no. 8 QK151

**Preliminary guide to records relating to Blacks
in the North Carolina State Archives /.**
Mitchell, Thornton W. [Raleigh] [1980] 14 p. ;
LC Card 80-623389 DDC 975.6 s
016.9756/00496073 19
F251 .N67a no. 17 Z1361.N39 E185.93.N6

**Preliminary inventory of the cartographic records
of the Soil Conservation Service /.** United
States. National Archives and Records Service.
Washington , 1981. p. cm. LC Card 81-3988
DDC 016.3530082/326 19
CD3026 .A32 no. 195 CD3038

**Preliminary inventory of the Pueblo records
created by field offices of the Bureau of Indian
Affairs** . United States. National Archives and
Records Service. Washington , 1980. vii, 34 p. ;
LC Card 80-607174 DDC 016.973 s
016.3231/197/073 19
CD3026 .A32 no. 192 Z1210.P8 E99.P9

**Preliminary inventory of the records of St.
Elizabeths Hospital** . United States. National
Archives and Records Service. Washington ,
1981. p. cm. LC Card 81-607004 DDC 016.973 s
016.3622/1/09753 19
*CD3026 .A32 no. 193 Z6675.H75
RC445.W19W37*

**Preliminary inventory of the records of the
Civilian Conservation Corps** . United States.
National Archives and Records Service.
Washington , 1980. vii, 23 p. ; LC Card
80-28921 DDC 016.973 s 016.3337/2/0973 19
CD3026 .A32 no. 11, 1980 CD3035

**A preliminary national assessment of child abuse
and neglect and the juvenile justice system** .
Smith, Charles P., 1931- [Washington, D.C.]
[1980] c1979. xiv, 154 p. ; LC Card 80-600045
DDC 362.7/044 19
HV741 .S55 1980

**A preliminary national assessment of the status
offender and the juvenile justice system** .
National Juvenile Justice System Assessment
Center (U. S.) [Washington, D.C.] [1980]
c1979. xv, 221 p. : LC Card 80-600044 DDC
364.3/6/0973 19
HV9104 .N23 1980a

**A preliminary report on the revitalization of the
Federal Contract Compliance Program.** United
states. Office of Federal Contract Compliance
Programs. Task Force. Washington , 1977. xxix,
301 p. ; LC Card 78-602378
KF3464 .A86   *NYPL [JLF 81-198]*

**A preliminary survey of the benthos of
Resurrection Bay and Aialik Bay, Alaska /.**
Feder, Howard M. Fairbanks, Alaska , 1979. iii,
53 p. : LC Card 80-623129 DDC 551.46 s
591.9798/3 19
GC1 .A497 R78-7 QL161

Premature mortality, Texas, 1978. Texas. Bureau
of State Health Planning & Resource
Development. Division of Data Collection and
Analysis. Austin, Tex. [1980] ix, 21 p. : LC
Card 80-622852 DDC 304.6/4/09764 19
HB1355.T4 T49 1980

PREMIUMS (RETAIL TRADE)
Vredenburg, Harvey L. Trading stamps in the
service station. Iowa City, Iowa, 1959. v, 34
p. :   *NYPL [*XME-9742]*

**Prenatal approaches to the diagnosis of fetal
hemoglobinopathies** : an international research
workshop designed to update knowledge in
prenatal diagnosis and laboratory methodologies
of hemoglobinopathies, February 23-24, 1978,
Los Angeles, California / sponsored by Sickle
Cell Disease Branch, Division of Blood
Diseases and Resources, National Heart, Lung,
and Blood Institute, National Institutes of
Health, and Martin Luther King Jr. General
Hospital, [and] Charles R. Drew Postgraduate
Medical School ; editors, Yuet W. Kan, Clarice
D. Reid. [Bethesda, Md.] : U. S. Dept. of
Health and Human Services, Public Health
Service, National Institutes of Health, 1980.
xiii, 259 p. : ill. ; 28 cm. (NIH publication. no.
80-1529) "May 1980." Includes bibliographical
references. LC Card 80-602909 DDC 618.3/2 19
*1. Hemoglobinopathy in children - Diagnosis -
Congresses. 2. Fetus - Diseases - Diagnosis -
Congresses. 3. Fetal blood - Analysis - Congresses. I.
Kan, Yuet W. II. Reid, Clarice D. III. National Sickle
Cell Disease Program. IV. Martin Luther King Jr.
General Hospital. V. Charles R. Drew Postgraduate
Medical School. VI. Series: United States. National
Institutes of Health. Publication, no. 80-1529.*
RG629.H45 P73

PRENATAL CARE - CONGRESSES.
Symposium on Comprehensive Health Care for
Addicted Families and Their Children, New
York, N.Y., 1976. Symposium on
Comprehensive Health Care for Addicted
Families and Their Children, May 20 & 21,
1976, New York, New York /. Rockville, Md.
[1977] ix, 122 p. : LC Card 77-603390
RG580.D76 S93 1976   *NYPL [JLF 81-175]*

**PRENATAL CARE - MISSOURI -
STATISTICS.**
Schramm, Wayne F. Perinatal mortality and
prematurity in Missouri /. Jefferson City
[1979] ix, 68 p. : LC Card 80-621734 DDC
362.1/9832 19
RG632.U62 M57

Prentice, Ann E. New York (State). State
University, Albany. Library service now in New
York State . Albany, N.Y. , 1978. 112 p. : LC
Card 80-622246 DDC 027.0747 19
Z678.4.N7 N5 1978

Prentki, Richard T. Aquatic plants, lake
management, and ecosystem consequences of
lake harvesting . Madison, WI [1979] 435 p. :
LC Card 80-621513 DDC 632/.58/091692 19
SB614 .A687

**PREPAID GROUP MEDICAL PRACTICE. see
HEALTH MAINTENANCE
ORGANIZATIONS.**

Prepaid health plans: /. United States. Congress.
Senate. Committee on Government Operations.
Permanent Subcommittee on Investigations.
Washington, 1977. 1 v.: *NYPL [JLE 81-117]*

**PREPAID LEGAL SERVICES - UNITED
STATES - COSTS.**

United States. General Accounting Office.
Quality civil legal services for the poor and
near poor are possible through improved
productivity . [Washington, D.C. , 1979] iii, 23
p. ; LC Card 80-600508 DDC 362.5/8 19
KF336 .A718

**PREPAID MEDICAL CARE. see INSURANCE,
HEALTH.**

**Preparation of platinum flotation concentrate
from stillwater complex ore /.** Bennetts, J.
(John) Avondale, Md. [1981] p. cm. LC Card
80-606913 DDC 622 s 622/.3424 19
TN23 .U43 TN523

**The preparation of teachers for schools in
culturally deprived neighborhoods /.** Bridge
Project. Flushing, N. Y. , 1965. xviii, 400 p. ;
LC Card 67-61064   *NYPL [Sc F 80-191]*

**Preparations for the 32d International Whaling
Commission meeting** . United States. Congress.
House. Committee on Foreign Affairs.
Subcommittee on International Organizations.
Washington , 1980. iii, 155 p. ; LC Card
80-602734 DDC 333.95/6 19
KF27 .F648 1980

Preparing for disasters . California. Legislature.
Assembly. Committee on Governmental
Organization. Subcommittee on Emergency
Planning and Disaster Relief. [Sacramento,
CA] , 1980. a-e, 29, [7] leaves ; LC Card
80-621899 DDC 363.3/48/09794 19
HV555.U62 C34 1980

**Prepublication review and secrecy requirements
imposed upon federal employees** . United
States. Congress. House. Committee on the
Judiciary. Subcommittee on Civil and
Constitutional Rights. Washington , 1981. iii,
100 p. ; LC Card 81-601753 DDC 353.0071/45 19
KF27 .J847 1980g

**PRE-RELEASE PROGRAMS FOR
PRISONERS - PENNSYLVANIA -
EVALUATION.**
Pennsylvania. Division of Planning and Program
Evaluation. Community service center
recidivism evaluation /. [Harrisburg, Pa.]
[1976] 44 p. ; LC Card 80-622329 DDC 364.3 19
HV9305.P3 P43 1976

**PRESCRIBED BURNING - ECONOMIC
ASPECTS - OREGON - WILLAMETTE
VALLEY.**
Conklin, Frank S. An evaluation of expected
private losses from selected public policies for
reducing open field burning, Willamette Valley,
Oregon /. Corvallis [1979] 78 p. ; LC Card
80-620510 DDC 363.7/392 19
TD884 .C74

**PRESCRIBED BURNING -
ENVIRONMENTAL ASPECTS -
OREGON - WILLAMETTE VALLEY.**
Conklin, Frank S. An evaluation of expected
private losses from selected public policies for
reducing open field burning, Willamette Valley,
Oregon /. Corvallis [1979] 78 p. ; LC Card
80-620510 DDC 363.7/392 19
TD884 .C74

PRESENILE DEMENTIA.
United States. Congress. Senate. Committee on
Labor and Human Resources. Subcommittee on
Aging. Impact of Alzheimer's disease on the
nation's elderly . Washington , 1980 [i.e. 1981]
vi, 199 p. ; LC Card 81-601182 DDC
362.1/989768983 19
KF26 .L2716 1980

The present state of the American economy .
United States. Congress. Senate. Committee on
the Budget. Washington , 1981- v. <1 > : LC
Card 81-600968 DDC 338.973 19
KF26 .B8 1981

**A presentation of oral testimony received at
hearings of the Special District[s]
Subcommittee** . Illinois. General Assembly.
House of Representatives. Counties and
Townships Committee. Special Districts
Subcommittee. [Springfield] [1980] xiv, 134
p. : LC Card 80-623558 DDC 352/.0073 19
KFI1211.4 .C686 1979

**PRE-SENTENCE INVESTIGATION
REPORTS - GREAT BRITAIN.**
Shroff, Kersi B. Individualized sentencing and
the use of social inquiry (presentence) reports
in England /. Washington , 1978. 20 p. ; LC

Card 78-600143   DDC 345.42/0772 19
KD8406 .S55

PRE-SENTENCE INVESTIGATION REPORTS - WASHINGTON (STATE) - SEATTLE - STATISTICAL METHODS.
Lichtenstein, Karen. Assessment of variables used in presentence recommendations and court decisions /. Olympia, Wash. [1980] vii, 29 p. : LC Card 80-623909   DDC 345.797/77077/0723 347.977705770723 19
KFX2379.89 .L52

Preservation, an ethic for planning /.
Trementozzi, Miriam, 1947- Concord, N.H. , 1980. p. cm.   LC Card 80-26731   DDC 363.6/9 19
E159 .T795

Preservation and protection of the Potomac River shoreline . United States. Congress. Senate. Committee on Energy and Natural Resources. Subcommittee on Parks, Recreation, and Renewable Resources. Washington , 1980. iii, 79 p. ;   LC Card 80-602980   DDC 346.7304/6784 19
KF26 .E5565 1980b

Preservation case studies.
Guthrie, Susan. Main Street historic district, Van Buren, Arkansas . Washington, D.C. , 1980. 31 p. :   LC Card 80-603967   DDC 363.6/9/0976735 19
F419.V36 G87

Planning for exterior work on the First Parish Church, Portland, Maine, using photographs as project documentation. Washington, D.C. , 1979. 55 p. :   LC Card 80-601858   DDC 726/.5/0288 19
NA5235.P7 P57

White, Richard, 1924- Olmsted Park System, Jamaica Pond boathouse, Jamaica Plain, Massachusetts . Washington, D.C. , 1979. 51 p. :   LC Card 80-601622   DDC 690/.587/0288 19
TH2401 .W47

Preservation/Design Group. Hudson-Mohwak Industrial Gateway, inc. Some interesting buildings, sites, and natural features in the Hudson-Mohawk Urban Cultural Park /. [Troy? N.Y.] [1979] 1 map :   LC Card 81-692835
G3802.H87E635 1979 .H8

PRESERVATION OF FORESTS. see NATURAL RESOURCES.

PRESERVATION OF HISTORICAL RECORDS. see ARCHIVES.

PRESERVATION OF STREAMS AND RIVERS. see STREAM CONSERVATION.

Preservation plan and program for Caddoan Mounds State Historic Site, Cherokee County, Texas /. Texas. Historic Sites and Restoration Branch. [Austin, Tex.] [1978] 73, 25 p. : LC Card 79-622483   DDC 333.78/3 19
E99.C12 T48 1978

Preservation planning series.
New directions in rural preservation. Washington, D.C. [1980?] xi, 115 p. :   LC Card 81-601043   DDC 307.7/2/0973 19
HN59 .N398

Presidential Commission on National Service and National Commission on Volunteerism . United States. Congress. Senate. Committee on Labor and Human Resources. Subcommittee on Child and Human Development. Washington , 1980. v, 606 p. :   LC Card 80-604000   DDC 361.3/7/0973 19
KF26 .L273 1980a

Presidential recommendations for Selective Service reform. United States. President, 1977- (Carter) Selective Service reform . Washington , 1980. ix, 62 p. ;   LC Card 80-601724   DDC 343.73/0122 19
KF7263 .A25 1980

President's cash management initiatives /. United States. Treasury Dept. Washington , 1980. vi, 94 p. ;   LC Card 80-601795   DDC 353.0072/4 19
HJ3252 .U58 1980

President's cash management initiatives in the fiscal year 1981 budget . United States. Congress. House. Committee on Ways and Means. Washington , 1980. iv, 197 p. :   LC Card 80-602770   DDC 353.0072/6 19
KF27 .W3 1980f

President's Committee on Mental Retardation. see United States. President's Committee on

Mental Retardation.

President's economic revitalization program .
United States. Congress. House. Committee on the Budget. Washington , 1980. iii, 205 p. :   LC Card 80-604100   DDC 338.973 19
KF27 .B8 1980c

The President's environmental program, 1979.
Washington, D.C. : Council on Environmental Quality, Executive Office of the President : for sale by the Supt. of Docs., U. S. Govt. Print. Off., [1979] v, 57 p. ; 26 cm. Includes a fact sheet, executive orders, and Presidential message on the environment.   LC Card 80-148627   DDC 363.7/00973 19
1. Environmental protection - United States. 2. Environmental policy - United States. I. United States. President, 1977- (Carter). II. United States. Council on Environmental Quality.
TD171 .P734

President's National Commission on Productivity and Work Quality. see National Commission on Productivity and Work Quality.

The President's new anti-inflation program .
United States. Congress. Joint Economic Committee. Washington , 1980. iii, 172 p. ;   LC Card 80-603703   DDC 332.4/15/0973 19
KF25 .E2 1980e

The President's program directors the Assistant Secretaries : a symposium, U. S. Civil Service Commission, Federal Executive Institute, Charlottesville, Virginia, December 8-9, 1976 / edited by Thomas P. Murphy, Donald E. Nuechterlein, Ronald J. Stupak. Charlottesville, Va. : U. S. The Institute, [1977]. iii, 112 p. : ill. ; 23 cm.   LC Card 77-603586
1. Presidents - United States - Staff. 2. Government executives - United States. I. Murphy, Thomas P., 1931-. II. Nuechterlein, Donald Edwin, 1925-. III. Stupak, Ronald J. IV. Federal Executive Institute. V. Title.
JK518 .P75

President's proposal for withholding on interest and dividends . United States. Congress. House. Committee on Ways and Means. Washington , 1980. v, 310 p. :   LC Card 80-603348   DDC 353.0072/44 19
KF27 .W3 1980k

President's Reorganization Project (U. S.)
Organizing for development : final report : reorganization study of federal community and economic development programs. Washington, D.C. : President's Reorganization Project, Office of Management and Budget, 1979. viii, 66, [36] p. : 4 charts ; 28 cm. "Local Development Reorganization Project"--P. 2 of cover. "February 1979." Item 854   LC Card 81-601244   DDC 338.973 19
1. Economic assistance, Domestic - United States. 2. Federal aid to community development - United States. 3. Community development - United States. I. Local Development Reorganization Project (U. S.). II. Title. III. Title: Reorganization study of federal community and economic development programs.
HC110.P63 P73 1979

PRESIDENTS - UNITED STATES - BIOGRAPHY.
Williams, Frank Broyles, 1913- Tennessee's presidents /. Knoxville, c1981. p. cm.   ISBN 0-87049-321-3 :   LC Card 81-3391   DDC 973/.09/92 B 19
E176.1 .W7225

PRESIDENTS - UNITED STATES - ELECTION - 1976.
Massachusetts. Electoral College, 1976. Proceedings of the Electoral College of Massachusetts, December 13, 1976 /. [Boston] [1977?] 34 p. :   LC Card 80-621942   DDC 324.9744043 19
JK529 .M37 1976

PRESIDENTS - UNITED STATES - POWERS. see EXECUTIVE POWER - UNITED STATES.

PRESIDENTS - UNITED STATES - PRESS CONFERENCES.
Commission on Presidential Press Conference (U. S.) Report of the Commission on Presidential Press Conferences. [Charlottesville] [Washington, D.C. , c1981] 9 p. ;   ISBN 0-8191-1461-8 (pbk.) :   LC Card 81-140872   DDC 353.03/5 19
JK518 .C62 1981

PRESIDENTS - UNITED STATES - STAFF.
The President's program directors the Assistant Secretaries . Charlottesville, Va. [1977]. iii, 112 p. :   LC Card 77-603586
JK518 .P75

PRESS AND POLITICS - GREAT BRITAIN - HISTORY - 19TH CENTURY.
Koss, Stephen E. The rise and fall of the political press in Britain . Chapel Hill [1981] p. cm.   ISBN 0-8078-1483-0   LC Card 81-1707   DDC 072 19
PN5124.P6 K6 1981

PRESS LAW - UNITED STATES.
United States. Congress. House. Committee on Interstate and Foreign Commerce. Subcommittee on Communications. Prohibited renewal considerations and crossownership restrictions . Washington , 1980. iii, 98 p. ;   LC Card 80-602804   DDC 343.73/09945 19
KF27 .I5537 1980b

PRESS MONOPOLIES - UNITED STATES.
United States. Congress. House. Committee on Small Business. Subcommittee on General Oversight and Minority Enterprise. Media concentration . Washington , 1980- v. :   LC Card 80-603015   DDC 302.2/3 19
KF27 .S64 1980a

Pressler, Larry, 1942- U. S. senators from the prairie / by Larry Pressler ; with a foreword by W.O. Farber ; and introductory notes by Howard H. Baker, Jr. and George McGovern. 1st ed. Washington, D.C. : United States Senate, [1980] p. cm. Bibliography: p. Includes index. A historical analysis of their role in national and state politics accompanies biographical sketches and excerpts from speeches of South Dakota's 23 United States Senators.   ISBN 0-88249-033-8 :   LC Card 80-25220   DDC 328.73/092/2 B 920 19
1. Legislators - United States - Biography. 2. United States. Congress. Senate - Biography. 3. United States - Politics and government - 20th century - Sources. 4. South Dakota - Biography. I. Title.
E747 .P83

PRESSURE VESSELS - STANDARDS - VERMONT.
Vermont. Dept. of Labor and Industry. Boiler and pressure vessel rules . [Montpelier, Vt. , 1980] 28 leaves ;   LC Card 80-623908   DDC 363.1/89 19
TJ263.5 .V47 1980

Pressures in today's workplace . United States. Congress. House. Committee on Education and Labor. Subcommittee on Labor-Management Relations. Washington , 1981. vii, 62 p. ;   LC Card 81-601273   DDC 658.3/00973 19
HD8072.5 .U54 1981

PRESSURIZED CONTAINERS. see PRESSURE VESSELS.

PRESTON COUNTY (W.VA.) - MAPS.
United States. Soil Conservation Service. Preston County, West Virginia /. Lanham, MD , 1980. 1 map :   LC Card 81-690036
G3893.P7 1978 .U5

Preston, James, 1941- Mother worship . Chapel Hill , c1981. p. cm.   ISBN 0-8078-1471-7   LC Card 81-3336   DDC 306/.6 19
BL325.M6 M67

PRE-TRIAL INTERVENTION - CALIFORNIA - EVALUATION.
Palmer, Ted. The evaluation of juvenile diversion projects . [Sacramento] , 1978. xx, 366 p. ;   LC Card 79-623204
HV9105.C2 P34   *NYPL [JLF 81-140]*

PRE-TRIAL INTERVENTION - ILLINOIS - CHAMPAIGN.
Ku, Richard. A university's approach to delinquency prevention . [Washington] , 1977. ii, 128 p. :   LC Card 77-602177
HV9106.U7 K8   *NYPL [JLF 81-166]*

PRE-TRIAL INTERVENTION - ILLINOIS - URBANA.
Ku, Richard. A university's approach to delinquency prevention . [Washington] , 1977. ii, 128 p. :   LC Card 77-602177
HV9106.U7 K8   *NYPL [JLF 81-166]*

PRE-TRIAL INTERVENTION - MICHIGAN.
Shepherd, Jack R. Police-juvenile diversion . Washington, D.C. , 1980. x, 77, [91] p. :   LC Card 81-601094   DDC 364.6/8 19
HV9105.M5 S5 1980

PRE-TRIAL PROCEDURE - NORTH CAROLINA.
Farb, Robert L. The public's right to attend criminal proceedings in North Carolina /. Chapel Hill, N.C. [1980], c1978. 10 p. ; LC Card 80-622371 DDC 347.756 s 345.756/05 19
KFN7908.A15 U6 no. 80/01 KFN7910.5.C6

PRE-TRIAL PROCEDURE - TEXAS - CONGRESSES.
Legal Assistants Seminar on Civil Litigation, Houston, Tex., 1979. Legal Assistants Seminar on Civil Litigation, Houston, November 30-December 1, 1979 /. [Austin] [1979] ca. 250 p. in various pagings : LC Card 80-621743 DDC 347.764/07 19
KFT1738.A2 L43 1979

PRE-TRIAL RELEASE - UNITED STATES.
United States. Congress. Senate. Committee on the Judiciary. Subcommittee on Criminal Justice. Pretrial service agencies . Washington , c1981. iii, 112 p. : LC Card 81-600953 DDC 347.73/72 347.30772 19
KF26 .J8377 1980i

PRE-TRIAL RELEASE - WISCONSIN.
Wisconsin. Legislative Council. Issues relating to pretrial release pursuant to the issuance of a citation or summons /. Madison, Wis. [1980] 54 p. ; LC Card 80-624139 DDC 347.775/072 347.750772 19
KFW2976.6 .A25 1980

Pretrial service agencies . United States. Congress. Senate. Committee on the Judiciary. Subcommittee on Criminal Justice. Washington , c1981. iii, 112 p. : LC Card 81-600953 DDC 347.73/72 347.30772 19
KF26 .J8377 1980i

PRE-TRIAL SERVICE AGENCIES - UNITED STATES.
United States. Congress. Senate. Committee on the Judiciary. Subcommittee on Criminal Justice. Pretrial service agencies . Washington , c1981. iii, 112 p. : LC Card 81-600953 DDC 347.73/72 347.30772 19
KF26 .J8377 1980i

The prevalence and intensity of alcohol and illicit drug use in Pennsylvania. Rush, Thomas Vale. [Harrisburg] 1977 2 v. *NYPL [JLF 79-928]*

Prevention, detection, and correction of corruption in local government . Lyman, Theodore R. Washington , 1978. vi, 83 p. ; LC Card 79-603441
JS401 .L95 *NYPL [JLF 81-328]*

Prevention of child abuse. Nevada. Legislative Commission. [Carson City] [1980] vi, 78 p. : LC Card 81-621354 DDC 362.7/1 19
HV742.N3 N48 1980

PREVENTION OF CRIME. see CRIME PREVENTION.

Prevention of developmental disabilities in Illinois : options to guide state prevention efforts. [Springfield, Ill.] : Illinois Bureau of the Budget, Office of Planning, 1979. 142 p. : ill. ; 28 cm. "Prepared for the Governor's Planning Council on Developmental Disabilities"--Cover. Bibliography: p. 134-142. LC Card 80-623961 DDC 362.1/9892 19
1. Child health services - Illinois. 2. Infant health services - Illinois. 3. Maternal health services - Illinois. 4. Developmental disabilities - Illinois - Prevention. 5. Developmental disabilities - Government policy - Illinois. I. Illinois. Bureau of the Budget. Office of Planning. II. Illinois Governor's Planning Council on Developmental Disabilities.
RJ102.5.I3 P73

PREVENTION OF DISEASE. see MEDICINE, PREVENTIVE.

Prevention of dust explosions in grain elevators--an achievable goal . United States. Dept. of Agriculture. Office of the Special Coordinator for Grain Elevator Safety and Security. [Washington] [1980] xii, 172 p. : LC Card 80-601550 DDC 363.1/89 19
TH9445.G7 U54 1980

PREVENTION OF FIRES. see FIRE PREVENTION.

PREVENTION OF JUVENILE DELINQUENCY. see JUVENILE DELINQUENCY - PREVENTION.

PREVENTIVE HEALTH SERVICES - UNITED STATES.
Institute of Medicine. Healthy people .

Washington , 1979. viii, 484 p. : LC Card 79-603264
RA445 .I57 1979 *NYPL [JLD 80-3780]*

PREVENTIVE MEDICINE. see MEDICINE, PREVENTIVE.

Preview of Mexico's vegetable production for export /. Emerson, L. P. Bill. [Washington, D.C.] [1980] 74 p. : LC Card 80-603534 DDC 338.1/75/0972 19
HD9220.M42 E43

Priano, Anthony. Kemmer, Paul. Highway map of Ontario County, New York /. Canandaigua, N. Y., 1978. col. map 41 x 44 cm. Scale ca. 1:135,000 At head of title: William Sage, County Supt. of Hwys. Revised by Anthony Priano, 1977. Shows township and municipal boundaries. Includes location map within Rochester - Genesee Regional Transportation District. On verso: list of town and state highways and county roads.
NYPL [Map Div. 80-3340]

PRIBILOF ISLANDS.
United States. National Oceanic and Atmospheric Administration. The story of the Pribilof fur seals. [Washington] [1976] 34 p. : LC Card 77-601364 DDC 333.95/9 19
SH361 .U75 1976

Pribula, George.
(joint author) Simon, Edward, 1946- Delaware occupational employment statistics . Newark, DE [1979?] iii, 76 p. ; LC Card 80-621965 DDC 331.12/57/09751 19
HD5725.D3 S53

(joint author) Simon, Edward, 1946- Delaware occupational employment statistics . Newark, DE [1980] iv, 65 p. ; LC Card 80-622179 DDC 331.12/51/0009751 19
HD5725.D3 S54

PRICE CONTROL. see PRICE REGULATION.

PRICE DISCRIMINATION - UNITED STATES.
United States. Congress. Senate. Select Committee on Small Business. Customer pickup proposals and their impact on small business and the Robinson-Patman act . Washington , 1980. iii, 266 p. : LC Card 80-602985 DDC 338.5/2 19
KF26.5 .S6 1980d

Price, Eleonore B. From waste to energy--the recycling connection : a legislative outlook / prepared for the Washington State Senate Energy and Utilities Committee by Eleonore B. Price. [Olympia, Wash.] : The Committee, [1980] v leaves, 112 p. ; 28 cm. "November, 1980." Bibliography: p. 90-99. LC Card 81-621765 DDC 363.7/28 19
1. Recycling (Waste, etc.) - Washington (State). I. Washington (State). Legislature. Senate. Energy and Utilities Committee. II. Title.
TD794.5 .P73

PRICE FIXING. see PRICE REGULATION.

PRICE INDEXES.
United Nations. Statistical Office. Methods used in compiling the United Nations price indexes for basic commodities in international trade /. New York , 1979. vi, 115 p. ; LC Card 80-106353 DDC 300 s 338.5/28 19
JX1977 .A2 ST/STAT/Ser.M/29/rev. 2 HB225

PRICE INDICES. see PRICE INDEXES.

Price, John A., 1933- The Washo Indians : history, life cycle, religion, technology, economy, and modern life / by John A. Price ; Donald R. Tuohy, editor. [Carson City, Nev.] : Nevada State Museum, c1980. vi, 82 p., [2] leaves of plates : ill. ; 29 cm. (Occasional papers - Nevada State Museum ; no. 4) "April 1980." Bibliography: p. 76-81. LC Card 80-623850 DDC 970.004/97 19
1. Washo Indians. I. Tuohy, Donald R. II. Series: Nevada. State Museum, Carson City. Occasional papers , no. 4. III. Title.
E99.W38 P74

PRICE POLICY, GOVERNMENTAL. see PRICE REGULATION.

PRICE REGULATION - CHINA - HISTORY.
Wang, Tong-eng, 1933- Economic policies and price stability in China /. Berkeley , c19. xvi, 146 p. : ISBN 0-912966-24-6 (pbk.) : LC Card 80-620008 DDC 338.5/26/0951 19
HB236.C55 W36 *NYPL [*OVA no. 16]*

PRICE REGULATION - UNITED STATES.
The Case of the billion dollar stripper . Washington , 1980. v, 29 p. : LC Card 80-603868 DDC 338.2/3 19
HD9564 .C38

United States. Congress. House. Committee on Interstate and Foreign Commerce. Subcommittee on Energy and Power. Enforcement of major refiner cases . Washington , 1981. iii, 883 p. ; LC Card 81-601792 DDC 346.7304/68232/0262 347.30646823320262 19
KF27 .I5542 1980q

United States. Congress. House. Committee on Interstate and Foreign Commerce. Subcommittee on Oversight and Investigations. Cost to consumers of deregulation of crude oil . Washington , 1980. iii, 72 p. : LC Card 80-604045 DDC 338.2/3 19
KF27 .I5547 1980l

Price, Robert Donald, 1926-
(joint author) Muller, Daniel A. Ground-water availability in Texas . Austin, Tex. [1979] vii, 77 p. : LC Card 80-620811 DDC 333.91/009764 s 553.7/9/09764 19
TD224.T4 A333 no. 238 GB1025.T4

Occurrence, quality, and quantity of ground water in Wilbarger County, Texas / by Robert D. Price. Austin, Tex. : Texas Dept. of Water Resources, 1979. viii, 229 p., [4] leaf of plates (3 fold.) : ill. ; 28 cm. (Report - Texas Department of Water Resources ; 240) Bibliography: p. 99-101. LC Card 80-621331 DDC 333.91/009764 s 553.7/9/09764746 19
1. Water, Underground - Texas - Wilbarger Co. 2. Water-supply - Texas - Wilbarger Co. I. Series: Texas. Dept. of Water Resources. Report - Texas Department of Water Resources , 240. II. Title.
TD224.T4 A333 no. 240 GB1025.T4

PRICE STABILIZATION, GOVERNMENTAL. see PRICE REGULATION.

Price volatility in the silver futures market . United States. Congress. Senate. Committee on Agriculture, Nutrition, and Forestry. Subcommittee on Agricultural Research and General Legislation. Washington , 1980. iv, 619 p. ; LC Card 80-602947 DDC 332.63/28 19
KF26 .A3534 1980a

PRICE-WAGE POLICY. see WAGE-PRICE POLICY.

Prices and purchasing power parities in Latin America, 1960-1972 /. Salazar-Carrillo, Jorge. Washington, D.C. , 1978. ca. 350 p. in various pagings ; LC Card 80-134989 DDC 338.5/2/098 19
HB235.L25 S34

PRICES AND WAGES. see WAGE-PRICE POLICY.

PRICES, FOOD. see FOOD PRICES.

PRICES - INDEX NUMBERS. see PRICE INDEXES.

PRICES - INDEXES. see PRICE INDEXES.

PRICES - LATIN AMERICA.
Salazar-Carrillo, Jorge. Prices and purchasing power parities in Latin America, 1960-1972 /. Washington, D.C. , 1978. ca. 350 p. in various pagings ; LC Card 80-134989 DDC 338.5/2/098 19
HB235.L25 S34

PRICES - REGULATION. see PRICE REGULATION.

The pricing structure of local telephone service . Alleman, James H. [Boulder, Colo.] , 1977. 21 p. ; LC Card 77-602916 DDC 384.6/3 19
HE8825 .A6

PRIDE, INC.
United States. Congress. Senate. Committee on Appropriations. Subcommittee on HUD-Independent Agencies. Management of HUD's multi-family properties, the Cliffton Terrace case . Washington , 1980. iii, 375, vi p. ; LC Card 80-602962 DDC 353.0086/5043/09753 19
KF26 .A6486 1979b

Priest-Jones, Janet. (joint author) Bose, Christine E. The relationship between women's studies, career development, and vocational choice /. Washington, D.C. , 1980. xi, 59 p. ; LC Card

80-602291   DDC 305.4/2/072073 19
HQ1181.U5 B67

PRIMARIES - GEORGIA - STATISTICS.
Georgia. Secretary of State. Consolidated vote .
Atlanta , 1974. 174 p. ;   LC Card 79-311170
JK2075.G5 G46 1974   ***NYPL [JLF 81-94]***

PRIMARIES - ILLINOIS.
Illinois. State Board of Elections. Paper ballot .
[Springfield, Ill. , 1980?] 60 p. ;   LC Card
80-621476   DDC 324.6/5/09773 19
KFI1620.3 .A836

PRIMARIES - MISSOURI.
Missouri. Office of the Secretary of State.
Certification of candidates /. [Jefferson City,
Mo. , 1980] 30 p. ;   LC Card 80-623055   DDC
324.5/4/09778 19
JK2075 .M8 1980

Primary forest products industry & timber use,
Minnesota, 1973 /. Blyth, James E. St. Paul ,
1979. 34 p. :   LC Card 79-602962   DDC
333.75/0977 s 338.1/7498/09776 19
SD11 .A45533 no. 39 HD9757.M6

PRIMARY PRODUCTIVITY - KANSAS -
KANSAS RIVER.
Marzolf, G. Richard. Kansas River limnology .
Manhattan , 1979. 56 p. :   LC Card 79-625208
DDC 574.5/26323/09781 19
QH105.K3 M37

PRIMATES AS CARRIERS OF DISEASE -
CONGRESSES.
National Cancer Institute Symposium on
Biohazards and Zoonotic Problems of Primate
Procurement, Quarantine, and Research,
Frederick Cancer Research Center, 1975.
Biohazards and zoonotic problems of primate
procurement, quarantine, and research .
[Bethesda, Md.] 1975. 137 p. :   LC Card
76-600529   DDC 614.4/3 19
RA641.P7 N37 1975

PRIMATES AS LABORATORY ANIMALS -
SAFETY MEASURES - CONGRESSES.
National Cancer Institute Symposium on
Biohazards and Zoonotic Problems of Primate
Procurement, Quarantine, and Research,
Frederick Cancer Research Center, 1975.
Biohazards and zoonotic problems of primate
procurement, quarantine, and research .
[Bethesda, Md.] 1975. 137 p. :   LC Card
76-600529   DDC 614.4/3 19
RA641.P7 N37 1975

PRIMATES - DISEASES - CONGRESSES.
National Cancer Institute Symposium on
Biohazards and Zoonotic Problems of Primate
Procurement, Quarantine, and Research,
Frederick Cancer Research Center, 1975.
Biohazards and zoonotic problems of primate
procurement, quarantine, and research .
[Bethesda, Md.] 1975. 137 p. :   LC Card
76-600529   DDC 614.4/3 19
RA641.P7 N37 1975

A Primer of oil-well service and workover. 3rd
ed. Austin, Tex. : Petroleum Extension Service,
University of Texas at Austin ; Dallas, Tex. :
Association of Oilwell Servicing Contractors,
1979. v, 106 p. : ill. ; 28 cm.   LC Card 80-154730
DDC 622/.3382 19
1. Oil wells - Maintenance and repair. I. University of
Texas at Austin. Petroleum Extension Service. II.
Association of Oilwell Servicing Contractors.
TN871 .P7164 1979

Primeras tragedias españolas /. Bermúdez,
Jéronimo, 16th cent. [Chapel Hill] , Madrid,
España , 1975. 223 p. ;   ISBN 84-7039-219-0
(Editorial Castalia)   LC Card 80-123086   DDC
862/.3 19
PQ6279.B47 P7 1975

PRINCE GEORGES COUNTY, MD. - MAPS.
(1979) United States. Soil Conservation Service.
Prince Georges County, Maryland /.
Hyattsville, MD , 1979. 1 map :   LC Card
81-690002
G3843.P7 1977 .U5

Princeton, N. J. Opinion Research Corporation.
see Opinion Research Corporation, Princeton,
N. J.

Princeton University.
Munson, Michael J. Indirect costs of residential
fires /. [Washington] , 1979 [i.e. 1980] vi, 30
p. :   LC Card 80-602415   DDC 363.3/79 19
TH9445.D9 M86

Princeton University. Center of International
Studies. Ramberg, Bennett. Destruction of
nuclear energy facilities in war . Lexington,
Mass. , c1980. xvi, 203 p. :   LC Card 80-7691
UA929.95.A87 R35   ***NYPL [JLE 81-179]***

Principles, objectives, and curricula for programs
in the education of gifted and talented pupils :
kindergarten through grade twelve.
Sacramento : California State Dept. of
Education, 1979. xiv, 114 p. ; 23 cm. Title on
spine: Education of gifted and talented pupils.
Edition for 1971 published under title: Principles, objectives,
and curricula for programs in the education of mentally
gifted minors. Bibliography: p. 106-112.   LC Card
80-620650   DDC 371.95 19
1. Gifted children - Education. I. California. Dept. of
Education. II. Title. III. Title: Education of gifted and
talented pupils.
LC3993 .P74 1979

Principles of water resources planning (phase II)
/. Whipple, William, 1909- [New Brunswick]
[1978] 26 leaves ;   LC Card 79-623366   DDC
333.91 19
TC409 .W48

Principles of water rights law in Ohio /.
Callahan, Charles C. [Columbus, Ohio] [1979]
xiii, 48 p. :   LC Card 80-622377   DDC
346.77104/691 19
KFO446 .C34 1979

Prindle, David F. (David Forrest), 1948-
Petroleum politics and the Texas Railroad
Commission / by David F. Prindle. 1st ed.
Austin : University of Texas Press, 1981. p. cm.
(The Elma Dill Russell Spencer Foundation series. no.
12) Includes bibliographical references and index.
ISBN 0-292-76474-X   LC Card 81-7535   DDC
353.97640087/5/06 19
1. Petroleum industry and trade - Texas. 2. Energy
development - Texas. 3. Petroleum law and legislation -
Texas. 4. Energy development - Law and legislation -
Texas. 5. Railroad commission of Texas. I. Title.
HD9567.T3 P74

PRINEVILLE RESERVOIR (ORE.)
United States. Congress. Senate. Committee on
Energy and Natural Resources. Subcommittee
on Energy Research and Development.
Crooked River Project Act of August 6, 1956 .
Washington , 1980. iii, 82 p. ;   LC Card
80-603805   DDC 346.7304/6916 347.30646916
19
KF26 .E554 1980b

PRINTING FOR THE BLIND. see BLIND -
PRINTING AND WRITING SYSTEMS.

PRINTING, PUBLIC - UNITED STATES.
United States. Congress. House. Committe on
House Administration. National publications act
of 1980 . Washington , 1980. iv, 179 p. ;   LC
Card 80-601753   DDC 343.73/0998 19
KF32 .H6 1980

United States. Congress. House. Committee on
Government Operations. Legislation and
National Security Subcommittee. National
publications act of 1980 . Washington , 1980.
iii, 277 p. ;   LC Card 80-603037   DDC
343.73/0998 19
KF27 .G6676 1980e

United States. Congress. House. Committee on
Rules. Subcommittee on Rules of the House.
The National Publications Act of 1980 .
Washington , 1980. iii, 126 p. ;   LC Card
81-600621   DDC 343.73/0998 347.303998 19
KF27 .R8737 1980

United States. Congress. Senate. Committee on
Governmental Affairs. Oversight of GPO's
direct deal printing procurement system .
Washington , 1980. iii, 94 p. ;   LC Card
80-602743   DDC 353.0081/9 19
KF26 .G67 1980c

PRIORITIES, INDUSTRIAL - UNITED
STATES.
United States. Congress. House. Committee on
Armed Services. Capability of U. S. defense
industrial base . Washington , 1980 [i.e. 1981]
ii, 1796, ii p. :   LC Card 81-600988   DDC
355.2/6/0973 19
KF27 .A7 1980K

PRISON ADMINISTRATION - UNITED
STATES - COLLECTED WORKS.
United States. General Accounting Office. The
Department of Justice can do more to help
improve conditions at State and local

correctional facilities . Washington, D.C. , 1980.
v, 52 p. ;   LC Card 80-603948   DDC 365/.7/0973
19
HV9471 .U53 1980a

The prison experience of career criminals /.
Petersilia, Joan. Washington, D.C. , 1980. xviii,
87 p. :   LC Card 81-601009   DDC 365/.66 19
HV9304 .P44

PRISON FURLOUGHS - HAWAII.
Hawaii. University, Honolulu. Social Welfare
Development and Research Center. The Adult
Furlough Center . [Honolulu] , 1974. iv, 18,
[18] leaves ;   LC Card 77-621669
HV9305.H3 H38 1974   ***NYPL [*XME-9423]***

Prison grievance mechanisms manual /. Keating,
J. Michael, 1939- [Washington] , 1979, c1977.
vii, 62 p. ;   LC Card 79-602345   DDC 365/.643
HV9469 .K4 1979

Prison industries . Johnson, Carolyn, 1948-
[Washington] , 1978. vii, 32 p. ;   LC Card
79-602384   DDC 016.365/65/0973 19
HV8925 .J63

PRISON INDUSTRIES - ILLINOIS.
Becker, Reynold E. Report to the House of
Representatives /. [Springfield] [1980] 20 p. ;
LC Card 80-623320   DDC 365/.65/09773 19
HV8929.I42 B43

PRISON INDUSTRIES - UNITED STATES -
ABSTRACTS.
Johnson, Carolyn, 1948- Prison industries .
[Washington] , 1978. vii, 32 p. ;   LC Card
79-602384   DDC 016.365/65/0973 19
HV8925 .J63

PRISON PERIODICALS.
The Pendleton reflector. v. 2, no. 180-v. 74, no.
6; Jan. 31, 1964-June 11, 1971 (incomplete).
Pendleton, Ind.   ***NYPL [*ZAN-2109]***

PRISON RIOTS - NEW MEXICO - SANTA
FÉ - COLLECTED WORKS.
New Mexico. Attorney General's Office. Report
of the Attorney General on the February 2 and
3, 1980 riot at the Penitentiary of New Mexico.
[Santa Fe] , 1980- v. :   LC Card 80-623176   DDC
365/.641 19
HV9475.N62 N46 1980

PRISONERS - CALIFORNIA - STATISTICS.
California. Dept. of Corrections. Management
Information Section. California prisoners, 1977
and 1978 . Sacramento, Calif. [1979?] vii, 157
p. :   LC Card 80-623512   DDC 364.3/09794 19
HV7254 .A6 1979

PRISONERS - DENTAL CARE - UNITED
STATES.
United States. General Accounting Office. A
Federal strategy is needed to help improve
medical and dental care in prisons and jails .
[Washington, D.C.] , 1978. v, 74 p. :   LC Card
79-603770   DDC 365/.66 19
HV8843 .U54 1978

PRISONERS - HEALTH AND HYGIENE -
UNITED STATES - COLLECTED
WORKS.
United States. General Accounting Office. The
Department of Justice can do more to help
improve conditions at State and local
correctional facilities . Washington, D.C. , 1980.
v, 52 p. ;   LC Card 80-603948   DDC 365/.7/0973
19
HV9471 .U53 1980a

PRISONERS - LEGAL STATUS, LAWS, ETC. -
UNITED STATES.
Keating, J. Michael, 1939- Prison grievance
mechanisms manual /. [Washington] , 1979,
c1977. vii, 62 p. ;   LC Card 79-602345   DDC
365/.643
HV9469 .K4 1979

PRISONERS - LEGAL STATUS, LAWS, ETC. -
UNITED STATES - COLLECTED
WORKS.
United States. General Accounting Office. The
Department of Justice can do more to help
improve conditions at State and local
correctional facilities . Washington, D.C. , 1980.
v, 52 p. ;   LC Card 80-603948   DDC 365/.7/0973
19
HV9471 .U53 1980a

PRISONERS - MASSACHUSETTS.
Metzler, Charles, 1951- Trends in commitments
to correctional institutions . [Boston] [1979]
[24] leaves :   LC Card 80-620620   DDC

365/.4/09744 19
HV9305.M4 M476

PRISONERS - MEDICAL CARE - UNITED STATES.
United States. General Accounting Office. A Federal strategy is needed to help improve medical and dental care in prisons and jails . [Washington, D.C.] , 1978. v, 74 p. : LC Card 79-603770 DDC 365/.66 19
HV8843 .U54 1978

PRISONERS - NEBRASKA - STATISTICS.
Nebraska. Dept. of Correctional Services. Research and Planning Section. Adult male prisoners, July 1, 1978-June 30, 1979 . Lincoln, Neb. , 1979. 129 p. ; LC Card 80-621736 DDC 365/.44/09782 19
HV7277 .A6 1979

PRISONERS - NORTH CAROLINA - CASE STUDIES.
North Carolina. State Board of Public Welfare. Capital punishment in North Carolina. Raleigh, N.C. , 1929. 173 p. : LC Card 80-502322 DDC 361/.9756 s 364.6/6/09756 19
HV86 .N84 no. 10 HV8699.U6N8

PRISONERS OF WAR - UNITED STATES.
United States. Veterans Administration. Study of former prisoners of war . Washington , 1980. v, 181 p. ; LC Card 80-602576 DDC 35.1/156/0973 19
UB369 .U57 1980

United States. Veterans Administration. Office of Planning and Program Evaluation. Study of former prisoners of war /. Washington, D.C. , 1980. iii, 181 p. ; LC Card 80-602667 DDC 355.1/15 19
UB369 .U57 1980a

PRISONERS - PENSIONS - UNITED STATES.
United States. Congress. House. Committee on Ways and Means. Subcommittee on Social Security. Receipt of Social Security benefits by persons incarcerated in penal institutions . Washington , 1980. iv, 96 p. ; LC Card 80-603715 DDC 368.4/00880692 19
KF27 .W347 1980b

PRISONERS' PERIODICALS. see PRISON PERIODICALS.

PRISONERS, POLITICAL. see POLITICAL PRISONERS.

PRISONERS - SERVICES FOR - WASHINGTON (STATE)
Sykes, Thomas M. An analysis of program needs of prison inmates in Washington State /. Olympia, Wash. [1980] xxi, 139 p. ; LC Card 80-620028 DDC 365/.66/09797 19
HV9475.W2 S93

PRISONERS - UNITED STATES.
Petersilia, Joan. The prison experience of career criminals /. Washington, D.C. , 1980. xviii, 87 p. : LC Card 81-601009 DDC 365/.66 19
HV9304 .P44

PRISONERS - UNITED STATES - STATISTICS - COLLECTED WORKS.
United States. National Criminal Justice Information and Statistics Service. National prisoner statistics special report; SD-NPS-SR. Washington.   *NYPL [JLM 81-137]*

PRISONERS - VIRGINIA - STATISTICS.
Virginia. Dept. of Corrections. Bureau of Research, Reporting, and Evaluation. Reporting Section. The Virginia State penal system, felons committed, fiscal years 1972-1976 ; the Virginia State penal system, felons confined, fiscal years 1972-1976 /. [Richmond] [1977?] 17 p. ; LC Card 80-623252 DDC 364.3/09755 19
HV8366 .V82 1977

PRISONERS - WASHINGTON (STATE)
Sykes, Thomas M. An analysis of program needs of prison inmates in Washington State /. Olympia, Wash. [1980] xxi, 139 p. ; LC Card 80-620028 DDC 365/.66/09797 19
HV9475.W2 S93

PRISONERS - WISCONSIN.
Wisconsin. Division of Corrections. Office of Systems and Evaluation. Offenders admitted to the Mutual Agreement Program, calendar year 1978. Madison, Wis. , 1979. 25 p. ; LC Card 80-620784 DDC 365/.66/09775 19
HV8369 .W62 1979

PRISONERS - WISCONSIN - STATISTICS.
Wisconsin. Division of Corrections. Office of Policy, Planning, and Budget. Adult admissions and releases . Madison, Wis. [1980] 30 p. : LC Card 80-623463 DDC 364.3/7/09775 19
HV8369 .W62 1979a

Wisconsin. Division of Corrections. Office of Systems and Evaluation. Offenders admitted to the Mutual Agreement Program, calendar year 1978. Madison, Wis. , 1979. 25 p. ; LC Card 80-620784 DDC 365/.66/09775 19
HV8369 .W62 1979

PRISONS - CALIFORNIA.
California. Legislature. Joint Advisory Committee on State Prison Facilities and Incarceration Alternatives. Report of the Joint Advisory Committee on State Prison Facilities and Incarceration Alternatives. [Sacramento, Calif. (Rm. 6001, State Capitol, Sacramento 95812)] [1978] 41 p. ; LC Card 81-620647 DDC 365/.9794 19
HV9475.C2 C35 1978

PRISONS - EMPLOYEES.
United States. Dept. of the Army. Human self-development in confinement /. Washington, 1973. 24 p.;   *NYPL [*XM-13534]*

PRISONS - LAW AND LEGISLATION - CALIFORNIA.
California. Laws, statutes, etc. Laws and guidelines for local detention facilities. [Sacramento] , 1974. 1 v. (loose-leaf) ;   *NYPL [JLD 79-3793]*

PRISONS - MICHIGAN - OVERCROWDING.
Michigan. Joint Legislative/Executive Task Force on Prison Overcrowding. Report of the Joint Legislative/Executive Task Force on Prison Overcrowding. [Lansing, Mich. , 1980] iii leaves, 24, [85] p. : LC Card 80-624338 DDC 365/.646 19
HV8342 .M53 1980

PRISONS, MILITARY - UNITED STATES.
United States. Dept. of the Army. Human self-development in confinement /. Washington, 1973. 24 p.;   *NYPL [*XM-13534]*

PRISONS - OFFICIALS AND EMPLOYEES. see PRISONS - EMPLOYEES.

PRISONS - STANDARDS - CALIFORNIA.
California. Legislature. Joint Advisory Committee on State Prison Facilities and Incarceration Alternatives. Report of the Joint Advisory Committee on State Prison Facilities and Incarceration Alternatives. [Sacramento, Calif. (Rm. 6001, State Capitol, Sacramento 95812)] [1978] 41 p. ; LC Card 81-620647 DDC 365/.9794 19
HV9475.C2 C35 1978

PRISONS - STANDARDS - ILLINOIS.
Illinois. Governor's Jail and Detention Standards Review Committee. Report of the Governor's Jail and Detention Standards Review Committee /. [Springfield, Ill.] [1979] ca. 200 p. in various pagings ; LC Card 80-623376 DDC 353.97730084/95 19
HV8332 .I32 1979

PRISONS - STANDARDS - UNITED STATES - ABSTRACTS.
Levine, Mark. Standards of care in adult and juvenile correctional institutions . Washington, D.C. , 1980. vii, 40 p. ; LC Card 80-602119 DDC 016.365/973/0218 19
HV9304 .L44

PRISONS - TEXAS - OVERCROWDING.
Texas. Legislature. House of Representatives. Study Group. Overcrowding in Texas prisons. Austin , 1979. 23 p. ; LC Card 79-624889 DDC 365/.6 19
HV8363 .T42 1979

PRISONS - UNITED STATES.
Keating, J. Michael, 1939- Prison grievance mechanisms manual /. [Washington] , 1979, c1977. vii, 62 p. ; LC Card 79-602345 DDC 365/.643
HV9469 .K4 1979

Privacy and public records . Searcy, Seth S. Austin , 1977. xv, 82 p. ; LC Card 77-623845
KFT1662.5.P8 S4   *NYPL [*XME-9391]*

Privacy and security of criminal history information : analyses of State privacy legislation : 1979 supplement / [prepared by SEARCH Group, inc.]. Washington, D.C. :

National Criminal Justice Information and Statistics Service, Law Enforcement Assistance Administration, U. S. Dept. of Justice : for sale by the Supt. of Docs., U. S. Govt. Print. Off., c1979. xi, 545 p. ; 28 cm. LC Card 80-601565 DDC 342.73/0858 19
1. Criminal registers - United States - States. 2. Privacy, Right of - United States - States. I. Search Group. II. United States. National Criminal Justice Information and Statistics Service. Privacy and security of criminal history information.
KF9751.Z95 N37 Suppl

Privacy and security of criminal history information . Trubow, George B. [Washington] , 1978. 73 p. ; LC Card 79-602370 DDC 342.73/0858 347.302858 19
KF9751 .T78

Privacy protection act . United States. Congress. Senate. Committee on the Judiciary. Washington , 1980. iv, 233 p. ; LC Card 80-602900 DDC 342.73/0853 19
KF26 .J8 1980b

PRIVACY, RIGHT OF.
Stallings, Wayne. Confidentially and public access policy for local government /. Chapel Hill, 1972. v, 32, 17 p.   *NYPL [*XME-9237]*

PRIVACY, RIGHT OF - CALIFORNIA.
California. Intergovernmental Board on Electronic Data Processing. Guidelines establishing requirements for security and confidentiality of information systems. Sacramento , 1974. iii, 74 p. ;   *NYPL [JFF 80-550]*

PRIVACY, RIGHT OF - ILLINOIS.
Sokolik, Stanley Lewis, 1928- Protecting the privacy of Illinois citizens . Springfield, Ill. [1979] vii, 88 p. ; LC Card 80-623377 DDC 323.44/8/09773 19
JC596.2.U5 S65

PRIVACY, RIGHT OF - NORTH DAKOTA.
Skeen, David. Disclosure of criminal and traffic records . Grand Forks, N.D. [1980] i, 22, 3 p. ; LC Card 81-620708 DDC 320.9784 s 345.73/056 320.9784 s 347.30556 19
JK6401 .N65 no. 58 KFN9192.5

PRIVACY, RIGHT OF - TEXAS.
Searcy, Seth S. Privacy and public records . Austin , 1977. xv, 82 p. ; LC Card 77-623845
KFT1662.5.P8 S4   *NYPL [*XME-9391]*

PRIVACY, RIGHT OF - UNITED STATES.
Searcy, Seth S. Privacy and public records . Austin , 1977. xv, 82 p. ; LC Card 77-623845
KFT1662.5.P8 S4   *NYPL [*XME-9391]*

Trubow, George B. Privacy and security of criminal history information . [Washington] , 1978. 73 p. ; LC Card 79-602370 DDC 342.73/0858 347.302858 19
KF9751 .T78

United States. Congress. House. Committee on Post Office and Civil Service. Subcommittee on Census and Population. Confidentiality of shippers' export declaration . Washington , 1980. iii, 62 p. ; LC Card 80-602741 DDC 343.73/0878 19
KF27 .P632 1980

United States. Congress. House. Committee on Ways and Means. Subcommittee on Oversight. Review of taxpayer privacy issues . Washington , 1980. iii, 185 p. ; LC Card 80-603900 DDC 323.44/83/0973 19
KF27 .W345 1980g

United States. Congress. Senate. Committee on Government Operations. Staff study of computer security in Federal programs /. Washington , 1977. v, 2,8 p. ; LC Card 79-602721
JK468.A8 U47 1977   *NYPL [JLE 81-477]*

United States. Congress. Senate. Committee on the Judiciary. Privacy protection act . Washington , 1980. iv, 233 p. ; LC Card 80-602900 DDC 342.73/0853 19
KF26 .J8 1980b

United States. Congress. Senate. Committee on the Judiciary. Subcommittee on Criminal Laws and Procedures. The erosion of law enforcement intelligence and its impact on the public security . Washington , 1978. iii, 179 p. ; LC Card 79-600797 DDC 363.2/52 19
HV8141 .U52 1978

Westin, Alan F. Computer science &

technology . Washington , 1979. xxiv, 439 p. :
LC Card 79-600081 DDC 602.18 s 658.3/00973
19
QC100 .U57 no. 500-50 HF5549.2.U5

**PRIVACY, RIGHT OF - UNITED STATES -
BIBLIOGRAPHY.**
O'Brien, David M. Theright of privacy--its
constitutional & social dimensions . Austin ,
1980. vi, 55 p. ; ISBN 0-935630-04-X (pbk.) LC
Card 80-622796 DDC 016.34273/0858 19
KF1262.A1 O25

**PRIVACY, RIGHT OF - UNITED STATES -
PUBLIC OPINION.**
United States. Congress. House. Committee on
Government Operations. Subcommittee on
Government Information and Individual Rights.
Public reaction to privacy issues . Washington ,
c1980 [i.e. 1981] iii, 153 p. ; LC Card 81-600838
DDC 323.44/8/0973 19
KF27 .G6628 1979c

**PRIVACY, RIGHT OF - UNITED STATES -
STATES.**
Privacy and security of criminal history
information . Washington, D.C. , c1979. xi, 545
p. ; LC Card 80-601565 DDC 342.73/0858 19
KF9751.Z95 N37 Suppl

**PRIVATE AIRPLANES. see AIRPLANES,
PRIVATE.**

Private detectives and security business .
Pennsylvania. General Assembly. Joint State
Government Commission. Harrisburg, Pa.
[1980] ix, 47 p. ; LC Card 80-622714 DDC
344.748/017613632 19
KFP282.D47 A25 1980

The private development process . United States
Conference of Mayors. [Washington] [1979] iii,
49 p. ; LC Card 79-601943
HD259 .U53 1979

Private higher education in Maryland .
Maryland. Committee to Study Private Higher
Education in Maryland. Annapolis , 1973. 159
p. in various pagings : LC Card 77-621589
*LB2342 .M344 1973   NYPL [*XME-9542]*

**PRIVATE INTERNATIONAL LAW. see
CONFLICT OF LAWS.**

**Private pension plans in West Germany and
France /.** Horlick, Max. Washington, D.C. ,
c1980. v, 70 p. ; LC Card 80-600176 DDC
368.4/3/00973 331.25/2/0943 19
HD7123 .A39 no. 55 HD7106.F8

**PRIVATE PROPERTY, RIGHT OF. see
RIGHT OF PROPERTY.**

Private proprietary homes for adults . Close,
Beatrice A. [Albany] [1979] 132 p. ; LC Card
79-625315 DDC 362.6/1/09747 19
HV1468.N7 C55

**PRIVATE SCHOOLS - CONNECTICUT -
STATISTICS.**
Connecticut. State Dept. of Education. Division
of Educational Administration. Bureau of
Research, Planning, and Evaluation.
Connecticut nonpublic schools, October 1, 1979
/. [Hartford] [1980] iii, 35 p. : LC Card
80-623577 DDC 371./02/09746 19
LC50.C6 C66 1980

**PRIVATE SCHOOLS - LAW AND
LEGISLATION - HAWAII.**
Hawaii. Dept. of Education. Personnel
Management, Certification, and Development
Branch. Personnel procedure . [Honolulu,
Hawaii] [1979] 17, [11] p. : LC Card 80-621552
DDC 344.969/078 19
KFH395.95 .A83

PRIVILEGED DEBTS. see BANKRUPTCY.

PROBABILITIES.
(1980) Development of a probability based load
criterion for American national standard A58 .
[Washington, D.C.] , 1980. v, 222 p. : LC Card
80-600067 DDC 602/.18 s 690/.21 19
QC100 .U57 no. 577 TH845

**Probability of earthquake occurrence in the
vicinity of the Chena Flood Control Dam near
Fairbanks, Alaska .** Davis, T. Neil. Fairbanks ,
1978. i, 18 leaves, [10] leaves of plates : LC
Card 79-622804 DDC 551.2/2/097986 19
QE535.2.U6 D38

**PROBATE LAW AND PRACTICE -
CALIFORNIA.**
California probate workflow manual, revised /.

Berkeley, Calif. , c1980- 2 v. (loose-leaf) : LC
Card 79-53359 DDC 346.79405/2 347.940652
19
KFC205 .C34 1980

PROBATE LAW AND PRACTICE - MAINE.
Maine. Probate Law Revision Commission.
Report to the 109th Maine Legislature and
summary of the Commission's study and
recommendations concerning Maine probate law
/. [Augusta, Me.] [1978] 2, 51 p. ; LC Card
80-622558 DDC 346.74105/2 19
KFM144 .A868

PROBATION.
Friday, Paul C. Critical issues in adult
probation . [Washington, D.C.] , 1979. 108 p. ;
LC Card 79-603822 DDC 364.6/3 19
HV9278 .F73

PROBATION - STANDARDS - TEXAS.
Texas Adult Probation Commission. Standards
for adult probation services in Texas. [Austin,
Tex.] [1980] iii leaves, 20 p. ; LC Card
80-623900 DDC 364.6/3/09764 19
HV9305.T4 T5 1980

PROBATION - UNITED STATES.
Allen, Harry E. Critical Issues in Adult
Probation . Washington, D.C. , 1979. vii, 289
p. ; LC Card 79-604144 DDC 364.6/3/0973 19
HV9304 .A64

Carlson, Eric Walfred, 1944- Critical issues in
adult probation . Washington, D.C. , 1979. vii,
492 p. ; LC Card 79-603823 DDC 364.6/3/0973
19
HV9304 .C34

The problem-drinking drug addict /. Barr, Harriet
Linton. [Rockville, Md.] , 1978. vii, 52 p. : LC
Card 79-602286 DDC 362.2/938 19
HV5831.P4 A5 1978a

**Problem location map, Limestone-Muddy Creek
watershed, portions of Duplin, Jones, and
Onslow Counties, North Carolina.** United
States. Soil Conservation Service. Fort Worth,
Tex. , 1979. 1 map : LC Card 81-692265
G3902.L48G4 1979 .U5

**The problem of disposing of nuclear low-level
waste .** United States. General Accounting
Office. [Washington, D.C.] , 1980. vii, 30 p. ;
LC Card 80-601696 DDC 363.7/28 19
TD898 .U54 1980

The Problem of the undocumented worker /
edited by Robert S. Landmann. [Albuquerque] :
Latin American Institute, University of New
Mexico, [1979?] iii, 89 p. : ill. ; 28 cm. Papers
presented at a 2-day workshop seminar held at the
University of New Mexico's D. H. Lawrence Ranch
conference facility. Includes bibliographical references
and index. LC Card 80-601248 DDC
331.6/2/72073 19
*1. Alien labor, Mexican - United States - Congresses. 2.
Aliens, Illegal - Employment - United States -
Congresses. I. Landmann, Robert S. II. New Mexico.
University. Latin American Institute.*
HD8081.M6 P76

Problem, solving . Brightman, Harvey J. Atlanta,
Ga. , 1980. ix, 242 p. : ISBN 0-88406-131-0 :
LC Card 80-25078 DDC 658.4/03 19
HD30.29 .B74

PROBLEM SOLVING.
Brightman, Harvey J. Problem, solving .
Atlanta, Ga. , 1980. ix, 242 p. : ISBN
0-88406-131-0 : LC Card 80-25078 DDC
658.4/03 19
HD30.29 .B74

**Problems affecting low-rent public housing
projects .** Jones, Ronald, 1945- [Washington,
D.C.] [1979] x, 317 p. : LC Card 80-600612
HD7293 .J66

Problems facing financially troubled hospitals .
United States. Congress. House. Committee on
Ways and Means. Subcommittee on Health.
Washington , 1980. vi, 584 p. : LC Card
80-603721 DDC 338.4/336211/0973 19
KF27 .W344 1980b

**Problems in assessing the cancer risks of
low-level ionizing radiation exposure .** United
States. General Accounting Office. Washington,
D.C. , 1981. 2 v. : LC Card 81-600890 DDC
616.99/4071 19
RC268.55 .U54 1981

Problems in urban centers . United States.
Congress. House. Committee on the District of

Columbia. Washington , 1980 [i.e. 1981] ix,
936, x p. : LC Card 81-601760 DDC 361.6/09753
19
KF27 .D5 1980

Problems of drug dependence, 1979 . Committee
on Problems of Drug Dependence. Rockville,
Md. , Washington, D.C. , 1979. xiii, 483 p. :
LC Card 80-600008 DDC 362.2/93/0973 19
HV5825 .C617 1979

**Problems of nursing home bed availability and
placement .** United States. Congress. House.
Select Committee on Aging. Subcommittee on
Health and Long-Term Care. Washington ,
1980. iii, 63 p. ; LC Card 80-603433 DDC
362.1/6 19
KF27.5 .A355 1980b

**Problems of rural elderly households in Powell
County, Kentucky /.** Larson, Donald Keith,
1932- [Washington] [Springfield, Va. , 1978]
iii, 25 p. ; LC Card 81-451882 DDC
362.6/09769/585 19
HV1468.K4 L37

Problems of U. S. office machine dealers . United
States. Congress. House. Committee on Small
Business. Subcommittee on Special Small
Business Problems. Washington, D.C. , 1980. iii,
92 p. : LC Card 80-603808 DDC 381/.4568 19
KF27 .S686 1980

**Problems Related to the Redefinition of North
American Geodetic Networks, International
Symposium. see International Symposium on
Problems Related to the Redefinition of
North American Geodetic Networks, 2d,
Arlington, Va., 1978.**

Problems with the 1980 census . United States.
Congress. House. Committee on Government
Operations. Commerce, Consumer, and
Monetary Affairs Subcommittee. Washington ,
1980. iii, 174 p. ; LC Card 80-602783 DDC
353.0081/9 19
KF27 .G634 1980

Problems with the 1980 census count . United
States. Congress. House. Committee on
Government Operations. Commerce, Consumer,
and Monetary Affairs Subcommittee.
Washington , 1980. vi, 284 p. ; LC Card
80-604022 DDC 001.43/3 19
KF27 .G634 1980e

**Procedural difficulties encountered by smaller
business in dealing with the IRS .** United
States. Congress. Senate. Select Committee on
Small Business. Subcommittee on Taxation,
Financing, and Investment. Washington , 1980.
iii, 172 p. ; LC Card 80-603483 DDC 353.0072/4
19
KF26.5 .S686 1980

**Procedure employed to determine use-vaue of
agricultural land in Virginia with estimate
use-values for 57 jurisdictions authorizing
use-value taxation for the tax-year 1979 /.**
Tsang, C. Steve. Richmond, Va. [197-] vii, 53,
[12] p. ; LC Card 80-621172 DDC 336.22/2 19
HJ4277 .T75

PROCEDURE (LAW) - IOWA.
Iowa. Clerks' Manual Advisory Committee. A
manual for clerks of the Iowa District Courts.
[Iowa City] [Des Moines?] , 1979. ca. 200 p.
in various pagings : LC Card 80-622629 DDC
347.777/016 19
KFI4715 .A83

PROCEDURE (LAW) - WISCONSIN.
Wisconsin. Dept. of Administration. Office of
Program and Management Analysis. 1977 status
report on judicial reform in Wisconsin .
Madison , 1977. 45, 31 p. : LC Card 78-621327
DDC 347.775/01 19
KFW2908 .A812

**Procedures for determining ranges of use-values
for agriculture, horticulture, forest, and open
space land in Virginia with 1979 suggested
use-values.** Tsang, C. Steve. Procedure
employed to determine use-vaue of agricultural
land in Virginia with estimate use-values for 57
jurisdictions authorizing use-value taxation for
the tax-year 1979 /. Richmond, Va. [197-] vii,
53, [12] p. ; LC Card 80-621172 DDC 336.22/2
19
HJ4277 .T75

Procedures for licensing insurance adjusters /.
Texas. State Board of Insurance. [Austin, Tex.]

[1980?] 16 leaves ; LC Card 80-622804 DDC 346.764/086014 19
KFT1385 .A846

Procedures for the certification of operators of wastewater treatment works. Illinois. Environmental Protection Agency. [Springfield, Ill. , 1980] 29 p. : LC Card 80-623066 DDC 353.97730087/1 19
TD524.I3 I44 1980

Procedures to adjust 1980 census counts have limitations . United States. General Accounting Office. Washington, D.C. , 1980. v, 37 p. ; LC Card 81-600763 DDC 353.0081/9 19
HA201 1980

Procedures to be followed for the placement of children with special needs in educational programs . Sawyer, Ann L. Chapel Hill [1979] 58 p. ; LC Card 81-621674 DDC 344.756/0791 347.5604791 19
KFN7795.9.H3 S28

Proceeding of the annual Climate Diagnostics Workshop. Climate Diagnostics Workshop. [Washington, etc.]. LC Card 79-640997
NYPL [JSP 80-293]

Proceedings. Workshop on Switching Requirements and R & D for Fusion Reactors, Palo Alto, Calif., 1976. Palo Alto , 1977. 1 v. of various pagings : *NYPL [JSF 80-697]*

Proceedings of a Conference on Neutrons from Electron Medical Accelerators . Conference on Neutrons from Electron Medical Accelerators, National Bureau of Standards, 1979. Washington , 1979. vii, 175 p. ; LC Card 79-600133 DDC 602/.18 s 615.8/422 19
QC100 .U57 no. 554 RM849

Proceedings of Seminar on the Role of Overburden Analysis in Surface Mining, Wheeling, W. Va., May 6-7, 1980 /. Seminar on the Role of Overburden Analysis in Surface Mining (1980 : Wheeling, W. VA.) Washington , 1981. p. cm. LC Card 81-607049 DDC 622 s 622/.31 19
TN295 .U4 TD195.S75

Proceedings of the centennial celebration of the first meeting of the General Assembly of the state of South Carolina. Columbia, S. C. Centennial Celebration Committee. Columbia, S. C., 18. 40 p. *NYPL [*ZI-277]*

Proceedings of the International symposium on Computer-Assisted Cartography . Auto-Carto, 2d, Reston, Va., 1975. [Suitland, Md.] [Falls Church, Va.] [1975?] 614 p. : LC Card 79-117745
GA108.7 .A95 1975
NYPL [Map Div. 81-153]

Proceedings of the National Conference on Health Promotion Programs in Occupational Settings, January 17, 18, and 19, 1979 /. National Conference on Health Promotion Programs in Occupational Settings, Washington, D.C., 1979. Washington, D.C. [1979] xii, 69 p. ; LC Card 80-600621 DDC 362.1/0883317 19
HD7654 .N28 1979

Proceedings of the National Conference on Regulatory Aspects of Building Rehabilitation, held at the National Bureau of Standards, October 30, 1978 /. National Conference on Regulatory Aspects of Building Rehabilitation, National Bureau of Standards, 1978. [Washington, D.C.] , 1979. ix, 201, 30 p. : LC Card 79-600095 DDC 602.18 s 343.73/078690/24 19
QC100 .U57 no. 549 KF5701

Proceedings of the National Seminar on Asphalt Pavement Recycling. National Seminar on Asphalt Pavement Recycling (1980 : Dallas-Fort Worth Regional Airport) Washington, D.C. , 1981. p. cm. ISBN 0-309-03101-X LC Card 81-607072 DDC 380.5 s 666/.893 19
TE7 .H5 no. 780 TE270

Proceedings of the NEACRP meeting of a Monte Carlo study group, July 1-3, 1974, Argonne, Illinois ... /compiled by Cyrilia Hytry. Argonne, Ill. : Argonne National Laboratory, [1974] 363 l. Microfiche (neg.) NTIS. 4 sheets 11 x 15 cm. (ANL-75-2) NEACRP-L-118. "Sponsored by the Nuclear Energy Agency Committee on Reactor Physics." Includes bibliographies.
1. Nuclear physics - Statistical methods - Congresses. 2.

Monte Carlo method - Congresses. I. Organization for Economic Cooperation and Development. Committee on Reactor Physics. II. United States. Argonne National Laboratory, Lemont, Ill. III. Hytry, Cyrilia.
*NYPL [*XMQ-2014]*

Proceedings of the Northwest Regional Energy Conference, May 31-June 1, 1978, Seattle, Washington /. Northwest Regional Energy Conference, Seattle, 1978. [Washington] , 1978. vii, 201 p. ; LC Card 79-602539
HD9502.U53 A1964 1978
NYPL [JLE 81-480]

Proceedings of the seventh symposium, psychology in the Department of Defense, 16 April-18 April 1980. Colorado Springs, Colo. : Dept. of Behavioral Sciences and Leadership, U. S. Air Force Academy ; [Springfield, Va. (5285 Port Royal Rd., Springfield 22151) : National Technical Information Service, U. S. Dept. of Commerce distributor], 1980. xxiv, 635 p. : ill. ; 28 cm. Cover title: Psychology in the Department of Defense. "USAFA-TR-80-12"--Cover. LC Card 80-604141 DDC 355/.001/9 19
1. Psychology, Military - Congresses. 2. United States - Armed Forces - Personnel management - Congresses. 3. Psychology - Congresses. I. United States. Air Force Academy. Dept. of Behavioral Sciences and Leadership. II. Symposium on Psychology in the Dept. of Defense (7th : 1980 : Colorado Springs, Colo.). III. Title: Psychology in the Department of Defense.
U22.3 .P712

Proceedings of the Texas postsecondary education outlook, 1980-1985 : Joe C. Thompson Conference Center, December 9-10, 1979, Austin, Texas / sponsored by University of Texas System, Institute of Higher Education Management. [Austin] : The Institute, c1979. xv, 166 p. : graphs ; 28 cm. On spine: The Texas postsecondary education outlook, 1980-1985. LC Card 80-623590 DDC 378.764 19
1. State universities and colleges - Texas - Congresses. I. University of Texas System. Institute of Higher Education Management. II. Title: Texas postsecondary education outlook, 1980-1985.
LB2329.5 .P76

Proceedings of the Workshop on the Estuarine Survival of Salmon, Juneau, Alaska, February 8, 1979 /. Workshop on the Estuarine Survival of Salmon, Juneau, Alaska, 1979. Fairbanks, Alaska , 1979. 38 p. ; LC Card 80-621846 DDC 597/.55 19
QL638.S2 W67 1979

Proceedings of the 1979 Iroquois Pottery Conference /. Iroquois Pottery Conference (1979 : Rochester Museum and Science Center) Rochester, N.Y. , 1980. vii, 207 p. : LC Card 80-52736 DDC 970.004/97
E99.I7 I74 1979

PROCESS ENGINEERING (MANUFACTURES) see MANUFACTURING PROCESSES.

Process for recovering chromium and other metals from superalloy scrap /. DeBarbadillo, John J., 1942- Avondale, Md. [1981] p. cm. LC Card 81-6102 DDC 622 s 669/.734 19
TN23 .U43 TN799.C5

Process metaphysics and educational theory /. Brumbaugh, Robert Sherrick, 1918- Albany , 1981. p. cm. ISBN 0-87395-574-9 LC Card 81-14329 DDC 370/.1 19
LB85.P7 B78

Processed data from the strong-motion records of the Santa Barbara earthquake of 13 August 1978 /. Porter, Lawrence Delpino, 1932- Sacramento, CA , 1979. 3 v. : LC Card 80-622289 DDC 557.94 s 551.2/2/0979491 19
TN24.C2 A33 no. 144 QE535.2.U6

PROCESSES, MANUFACTURING. see MANUFACTURING PROCESSES.

PROCESSING, INDUSTRIAL. see MANUFACTURING PROCESSES.

Proctor, Richard M. Surface design for fabric / Richard M. Proctor and Jennifer F. Lew. Seattle : University of Washington Press, c1982. p. cm. Bibliography: p. Includes index. ISBN 0-295-95874-X LC Card 81-7420 DDC 677/.022 19
1. Textile design. I. Lew, Jennifer F. II. Title.
TS1475 .P76

Procurement law case book : special text of the

Judge Advocate General's School, U. S. Army. [Charlottesville] : The School, 1957 [i.e. 1958] iii, 390 p. ; 27 cm. Cover title. "ST 27-151." LC Card 79-107788 DDC 346.73/023 347.30623 19
1. Public contracts - United States - Cases. 2. Defense contracts - United States - Cases. 3. Government purchasing - United States - Cases. I. United States. Judge Advocate General's School, Charlottesville, Va.
KF845 .P76 1958

Procurement of Naval ships . Cole, Brady M. Washington, D.C. , 1979. vi, 52 p. (p. 52 advertisements) : LC Card 79-604212 DDC 338.7/6238/200973 19
VM299.6 .C64

The prodigal daughter . McAlexander, Hubert Horton. Baton Rouge , c1981. p. cm. ISBN 0-8071-0862-6 : LC Card 81-4766 DDC 813/.4 B 19
PS2358 .M37

PRODUCE EXCHANGES. see COMMODITY EXCHANGES.

PRODUCE TRADE - CALIFORNIA.
French, Ben C. Marketing order program alternatives . [Davis] , 1978. v, 110 p. : LC Card 78-623151 DDC 338.1/09794 s 381/.41/09794 19
HD9000.1 .C3 no. 78-2 HD9007.C2

PRODUCE TRADE - LAW AND LEGISLATION - UNITED STATES.
United States. Congress. House. Committee on Agriculture. Subcommittee on Domestic Marketing, Consumer Relations, and Nutritions. Agricultural Bargaining Act . Washington , 1980. vi, 464 p. ; LC Card 80-604049 DDC 343.73/0851/0262 347.3038510262 19
KF27 .A3336 1979c

PRODUCE TRADE - UNDERDEVELOPED AREAS. see UNDERDEVELOPED AREAS - PRODUCE TRADE.

PRODUCE TRADE - UNITED STATES.
United States. Dept. of Agriculture. U. S. agricultural export development efforts /. Washington , 1980. v, 36 p. : LC Card 80-603056 DDC 382/.41/0973 19
HD9006 .U557 1980

PRODUCE TRADE - UNITED STATES - PERIODICALS.
National food review. NFR-1- ; 1978- [Washington] LC Card 78-643276
NYPL [JLM 80-1081]

United States. Dept. of Agriculture. Economic Research Service. Foreign agricultural trade of the United States. June, 1961-1977 (incomplete) Washington.

United States. Dept. of Agriculture. Economic Research Service. National food situation. NFS-96-161; May 1961-Sept. 1977. [Washington] 66 no. in 3 v. LC Card 59-33311
NYPL [M-10 6174]

PRODUCER GAS. see GAS-PRODUCERS.

Product and professional liability; proceedings of the first symposium in the University of Missouri-Columbia, College of Engineering series ... held at the University of Missouri-Columbia, November 6-7, 1967. Edited by Donald L. Gibson. [Columbia, 1967?] 138 l. illus. 28 cm. (University of Missouri-Columbia. College of Engineering. Engineering extension series. no. 10) Sponsored by the Dept. of Mechanical and Aerospace Engineering, University of Missouri-Columbia, the Missouri Society of Professional Engineers, the University of Missouri School of Law, and the Extension Division of the University of Missouri-Columbia. LC Card 74-632752 DDC 620 s 346.7303/82 19
1. Products liability - United States - Congresses. 2. Malpractice - United States - Congresses. 3. Engineers - Malpractice - United States - Congresses. I. Gibson, Donald L., ed. II. University of Missouri--Columbia. Dept. of Mechanical and Aerospace Engineering. III. Series: Missouri. University. College of Engineering. Engineering extension series, no. 10.
TA7 .M538 no. 10 KF1296

Product liability . United States. Congress. House. Committee on Interstate and Foreign Commerce. Subcommittee on Consumer Protection and Finance. Washington , 1980. v, 1019 p. : LC Card 81-600641 DDC 346.7303/82 347.306382 19
KF27 .I554 1980i

PRODUCT LIABILITY. see PRODUCTS LIABILITY.

Product liability insurance ratemaking . United States. Congress. House. Committee on Small Business. Subcommittee on General Oversight and Minority Enterprise. Washington , 1980. iii, 45 p. ; LC Card 80-604047 DDC 368.5 19
KF27 .S64 1980e

Product liability, legislative hearings . United States. Congress. House. Committee on Interstate and Foreign Commerce. Subcommittee on Consumer Protection and Finance. Washington , 1980. v, 1019 p. : LC Card 80-603466 DDC 346.7303/82 19
KF27 .I554 1979i

PRODUCT QUALITY. see QUALITY OF PRODUCTS.

PRODUCT RECALL - LAW AND LEGISLATION - UNITED STATES.
United States. Congress. House. Committee on Interstate and Foreign Commerce. Subcommittee on Consumer Protection and Finance. Tire recall . Washington , 1979. iii, 36 p. ; LC Card 80-600683 DDC 346.7303/82 19
KF27 .I554 1979e

PRODUCT SAFETY - LAW AND LEGISLATION - UNITED STATES.
United States. Congress. House. Committee on Interstate and Foreign Commerce. Subcommittee on Consumer Protection and Finance. Product liability, legislative hearings . Washington , 1980. v, 1019 p. : LC Card 80-603466 DDC 346.7303/82 19
KF27 .I554 1979i

PRODUCT SAFETY - LAW AND LEGISLATION - UNITED STATES - CONGRESSES.
Radioactivity in consumer products /. Washington , Springfield, Va. , 1978. xi, 509 p. : LC Card 79-602786
RA569 .R29

PRODUCT SAFETY - UNITED STATES - STATISTICS.
Kessler, Eileen. Consumer product-related injuries treated in hospital emergency rooms, contiguous United States, January 1, 1976-December 31, 1976 /. Washington , 1978. i, 63 p. : LC Card 78-602486
TS175 .K47

Product system productivity research. General Electric Company. Automation and Control Laboratory. Washington, 1976. 3 v.
*NYPL [*XME-9310]*

PRODUCTION. see INDUSTRY.

PRODUCTION-LINE METHODS. see ASSEMBLY-LINE METHODS.

Production of oil from tar sand and other hydrocarbon deposits . United States. Congress. Senate. Committee on Energy and Natural Resources. Subcommittee on Energy Resources and Materials Production. Washington , 1980. iii, 142 p. : LC Card 81-600562 DDC 343.73/0772 347.303772 19
KF26 .E5543 1980h

PRODUCTION PROCESSES. see MANUFACTURING PROCESSES.

PRODUCTIVE LIFE SPAN. see LIFE SPAN, PRODUCTIVE.

Productivity . United States. Bureau of Labor Statistics. Washington, D.C. , 1980. iv, 166 p. ; LC Card 80-603243 DDC 016.338/06 19
Z7164.L1 U6672 1980 HC110.I52

PRODUCTIVITY, AGRICULTURAL. see AGRICULTURAL PRODUCTIVITY.

Productivity and cost control for the small and medium-sized firm /. Steffy, Wilbert. Ann Arbor , 1980. vii, 170 p. : LC Card 80-622255 DDC 338.1/6 19
HD56 .S75

Productivity and inflation . Freund, William Curt, 1926- Washington , 1980. v, 14 p. ; LC Card 80-602572 DDC 332.4/1 19
HG229 .F655

Productivity and job security . National Center for Productivity and Quality of Working Life. Washington , 1977. vii, 116 p. ; LC Card 77-604826
HD6331.2.U5 N37 1977

Productivity and Managerial Assessment, Symposium on. see Symposium on Productivity and Managerial Assessment, Albany, 1975.

PRODUCTIVITY, INDUSTRIAL. see INDUSTRIAL PRODUCTIVITY.

Productivity measures for selected industries, 1954-79. Washington, D.C. : U. S. Dept. of Labor, Bureau of Labor Statistics : For sale by the Supt. of Docs., U. S. G.P.O., 1981. v, 206 p. : 97 charts ; 28 cm. (Bulletin . 2093) Authors: Andrew Campbell ... [et al.]. "April 1981." S/N 029-001-02572-6 Item 768-A-1 Bibliography: p. 204-206. LC Card 81-601923 DDC 338/.06/0973 19
1. Industrial productivity - United States - Statistics. I. Campbell, Andrew, 1920-. II. United States. Bureau of Labor Statistics. III. Series: Bulletin (United States. Bureau of Labor Statistics) , 2093.
HC110.I52 P75

PRODUCTIVITY OF CAPITAL. see CAPITAL PRODUCTIVITY.

PRODUCTIVITY OF LABOR. see LABOR PRODUCTIVITY.

Productivity performance and the American economy . United States. Congress. House. Committee on Banking, Finance and Urban Affairs. Subcommittee on Economic Stabilization. Washington , 1980. iv, 318 p. : LC Card 80-603669 DDC 338/.06/0973 19
KF27 .B542 1980a

The productivity problem . Iden, George. [Washington, D.C.] , 1981. xvii, 137 p. ; LC Card 81-600899 DDC 331.11/8/0973 19
HC110.C3 I32

Productivity, the foundation of growth : studies / prepared for the use of the Special Study on Economic Change of the Joint Economic Committee, Congress of the United States. Washington : U. S. G.P.O. : For sale by the Supt. of Docs., U. S. G.P.O., 1980. v, 128 p. ill. ; 23 cm. (Special study on economic change . v. 10) At head of title: 96th Congress, 2d session. Joint committee print. "December 29, 1980. S/N 052-070-05511-1 Item 1000 Includes bibliographical references LC Card 81-601972 DDC 338/.06/0973 19
1. Industrial productivity - United States. 2. United States - Economic conditions - 1971-. I. United States. Congress. Joint Economic Committee. II. Series.
HC110.I52 P77

PRODUCTS, COMMERCIAL. see COMMERCIAL PRODUCTS.

PRODUCTS, DAIRY. see DAIRY PRODUCTS.

PRODUCTS LIABILITY - NEW YORK (STATE)
New York (State). Joint Labor/Management Committee. 1978 report to the Governor and the legislature, January 1, 1978-October 15, 1978 /. [Albany] [1979] 11, [33] p. ; LC Card 79-624386 DDC 344.747/021 19
KFN5010.62 .L3 1979

PRODUCTS LIABILITY - UNITED STATES.
United States. Congress. House. Committee on Interstate and Foreign Commerce. Subcommittee on Consumer Protection and Finance. Product liability . Washington , 1980. v, 1019 p. : LC Card 81-600641 DDC 346.7303/82 347.306382 19
KF27 .I554 1980i

United States. Congress. House. Committee on Interstate and Foreign Commerce. Subcommittee on Consumer Protection and Finance. Product liability, legislative hearings . Washington , 1980. v, 1019 p. : LC Card 80-603466 DDC 346.7303/82 19
KF27 .I554 1979i

United States. Dept. of Commerce. Task Force on Product Liability and Accident Compensation. Uniform product liability act . [Washington] , 1979. 44 p. ; LC Card 80-601839 DDC 346.7303/82 19
KF1296 .A8168

United States. Interagency Task Force on Product Liability. Interagency Task Force on Product Liability . [Washington] , 1977. 1 v. (various pagings);   *NYPL [*XME-9329]*

PRODUCTS LIABILITY - UNITED STATES - CONGRESSES.
Product and professional liability. [Columbia,

1967?] 138 l. LC Card 74-632752 DDC 620 s 346.7303/82 19
TA7 .M538 no. 10 KF1296

PRODUCTS, MANUFACTURED. see MANUFACTURES.

PRODUCTS, WASTE. see WASTE PRODUCTS.

Professional and paraprofessional drug abuse counselors . LoSciuto, Leonard A. Rockville, Md. , 1979. v, 244 p. ; LC Card 79-604153 DDC 362.2/9386 19
HV5825 .L67

PROFESSIONAL EDUCATION OF WOMEN - UNITED STATES - STATISTICS.
Ott, Mary Diederich. Women's participation in first-professional degree programs in medicine, dentistry, veterinary medicine, and law, 1969-70 through 1974-75 /. [Washington] , 1976. viii, 21 p. : LC Card 77-601995 DDC 610/.7/1173 19
R745 .O87

PROFESSIONAL EDUCATION - UNITED STATES - DIRECTORIES.
New York (State). University. Office on Noncollegiate Sponsored Instruction. A guide to educational programs in noncollegiate organizations. Albany , 1974. iv, 54 p. ;
NYPL [JFF 80-552]

Professional leave, fiscal 1978, Washington public colleges and universities. State of Washington, Council for Postsecondary Education ; project officer, Jackie M. Johnson. Washington (State). Council for Postsecondary Education. [Olympia] , 1978. 52 p. ; LC Card 79-623052
LB2331.7 .W37 1978

Professional minority consulting firms. United States. Environmental Protection Agency. Procurement and Contracts Management Division. Washington.   *NYPL [*R-Econ. 80-2054 & JLM 80-1149]*

Professional motor vehicle theft and chop shops . United States. Congress. Senate. Committee on Governmental Affairs. Permanent Subcommittee on Investigations. Washington , 1980. vi, 491 p. : LC Card 80-601876 DDC 364.1/62 19
KF26 .G674 1979b

PROFESSIONAL STANDARDS REVIEW ORGANIZATION (MEDICINE) - UNITED STATES.
United States. Congress. House. Committee on Ways and Means. Subcommittee on Health. Professional standards review organization program . Washington , 1980. vii, 459 p. : LC Card 81-600622 DDC 362.1/068 19
KF27 .W344 1980e

Professional standards review organization program . United States. Congress. House. Committee on Ways and Means. Subcommittee on Health. Washington , 1980. vii, 459 p. : LC Card 81-600622 DDC 362.1/068 19
KF27 .W344 1980e

Professional standards review organization, program evaluation. United States. Health Care Financing Administration. Office of Research, Demonstrations, and Statistics. [Washington]
NYPL [JLM 81-32]

PROFESSIONAL STANDARDS REVIEW ORGANIZATIONS (MEDICINE) - UNITED STATES.
United States. Congress. House. Committee on Interstate and Foreign Commerce. Subcommittee on Oversight and Investigations. Wasted health dollars . Washington , 1980. iv, 155 p. : LC Card 80-603470 DDC 353.0077 19
KF27 .I5547 1980f

PROFESSIONAL STANDARDS REVIEW ORGANIZATIONS (MEDICINE) - UNITED STATES - COST EFFECTIVENESS.
Koretz,Daniel M. The impact of PSROs on health care-costs . [Washington, D.C.] , 1971 [i.e. 1981] xvi, 56 p. ; LC Card 81-600900 DDC 362.1/1/0973 19
RA399.A3 K6

PROFESSIONAL STANDARDS REVIEW ORGANIZATIONS (MEDICINE) - UNITED STATES - EVALUATION - PERIODICALS.
United States. Health Care Financing Administration. Office of Research, Demonstrations, and Statistics. Professional

standards review organization; program evaluation. [Washington] **NYPL [JLM 81-32]**

The professionalization of young hockey players /. Vaz, Edmund W. Lincoln , c1982. p. cm. ISBN 0-8032-4652-8 LC Card 81-12938 DDC 796.96/2 19
GV847 .V39

PROFESSIONS - CHOICE. see VOCATIONAL GUIDANCE.

PROFESSIONS - LAW AND LEGISLATION - KENTUCKY.
Kentucky. Professional Schools Admissions Committee. A plan to provide professional education and services to underserved areas of the State . Frankfort, Ky. , 1979. x, 48 p. ; LC Card 80-620638 DDC 344.769/011231 347.690411231 19
KFK1325 .A25 1979

PROFESSIONS - UNITED STATES.
Johnson, Gordon C. Metropolitan professional sexual differentiation . [Madison] [1979] 27 p. ; LC Card 80-622903 DDC 331.11/4 19
HD8038.U5 J6

Professors, presidents, and politicians . Cross, George Lynn. Norman , c1981. p. cm. ISBN 0-8061-1781-8 LC Card 81-40288 DDC 378.766/37 19
LD4323 .C75

Proficiency assessment in California : 1980 status report on implementation of California's Pupil Proficiency Law : a report / prepared by the Department of Education's Office of Program Evaluation and Research in response to a request by the California Legislature. Sacramento, CA (721 Capitol Mall, Sacramento 95814) : The Department, 1980. viii, 82 p. ; 28 cm. LC Card 81-621861 DDC 371.2/6/09794 19
1. Competency-Based educational tests - California. I. California. State Dept. of Education. Office of Program Evaluation and Research.
LC1034 .P76

A profile analysis of Minnesota counties. United States. Bureau of the Census. [Washington, D.C.] , 1979. ix, 79 p. : LC Card 79-603984
HA453 .U54 1979 **NYPL [JLF 81-266]**

A profile of characteristics distinguishing between program completers and program non-completers. Williams, Lawrence T. [Boston] , 1980. 20 leaves ;
NYPL [*ZT-1263]

Profile of economic region; Indiana labor market. Indiana. Employment Security Division. Research and Statistics Section. Indiana labor market ; profile of economic [Indianapolis]
NYPL [JLM 80-715]

Profile of electric power plant construction work force /. Leholm, Arlen. Fargo , 1976. ii, 53 p. : LC Card 77-621855 DDC 338.1/0212 s 331.11/99054 19
HD1407 .A33 no. 22 HD8039.B92U5

Profile of full-time first-time freshmen enrolled in N.J. colleges, fall 1977 and fall 1978 /. O'Connor, Linda. [Trenton] [1979] ii, [77] p. ; LC Card 80-621678 DDC 378/.1059749 19
LA331.5 .O28

A profile of Pennsylvania hospitals. Pennsylvania. Health Data Center. [Harrisburg] [1980] iv leaves, 35 p. ; LC Card 80-623420 DDC 362.1/1/09748 19
RA981.P4 P39 1980

Profiles of scheduled air carrier airport operations. United States. Aviation Forecast Branch. [Washington] **NYPL [JLM 80-1140]**

Profiles of scheduled air carrier departure and arrival operations for top 100 U. S. airports. United States. Aviation Forecast Branch. NOV. 1978- Washington. **NYPL [Econ. Div.]**

PROFIT AND LOSS STATEMENTS. see FINANCIAL STATEMENTS.

PROFIT-SHARING TRUSTS. see INVESTMENT TRUSTS.

PROFIT - UNITED STATES.
Profitability of major oil companies . College Station, Tex. , c1980. 16 p. ; LC Card 81-621414 DDC 338.7/6223382/0973 19
HD9565 .P75

United States. Congress. Senate. Committee on Armed Services. Subcommittee on Procurement

Policy and Reprograming. Vinson-Trammell act repeal or revision . Washington , 1980. iii, 171 p. ; LC Card 80-603036 DDC 346.73/023 19
KF26 .A768 1980a

Profitability of branch offices, New York City Off-Track Betting Corporation /. New York (State). Division of Audits and Accounts. Albany , 1980. 21, [11] leaves ; LC Card 80-621875 DDC 352.93/6 19
SF332.5.N7 N48 1980

Profitability of major oil companies : normal returns or windfall profits? / Gerald D. Keim ... [et al.]. College Station, Tex. : Center for Education and Research in Free Enterprise, Texas A&M University, c1980. 16 p. ; 23 cm. (Research monograph series / Center for Education and Research in Free Enterprise, Texas A&M University . no. 4) LC Card 81-621414 DDC 338.7/6223382/0973 19
1. Petroleum industry and trade - United States. 2. Profit - United States. I. Keim, Gerald D. II. Series: Research monograph series (Texas A & M University. Center for Education and Research in Free Enterprise) , no. 4.
HD9565 .P75

The profits of failure . New York (State). State Consumer Protection Board. Albany, N.Y. [1978] 114 p. ; LC Card 80-621030
LC1046.N5 N48 1978 **NYPL [JLF 80-1578]**

Program and financial plan fiscal years 1980, 1981, and 1985. Illinois. Division of Vocational Rehabilitation. [Springfield, Ill.] [1979] 35 p. ; LC Card 80-621705 DDC 362/.0425 19
HV1555.I3 I4 1979

Program and financial plan for state vocational rehabilitation agencies. United States. Rehabilitation Services Administration. Washington. LC Card 78-645637
NYPL [JLM 80-870]

Program and fiscal review of state comic book law (chapter 19.18 RCW). Washington (State). Legislature. Legislative Budget Committee. Olympia , 1980. iii, 7 p. ; LC Card 80-624258 DDC 353.97970072/32 s 343.797/08557415 353.97970072/32 s 347.97038557415 19
HJ11 .W2453 no. 80-5 KFW271.B64

Program and plans of the U. S. Geological Survey for producing information needed in national seismic hazards and risk assessment, fiscal years 1980-84 /. Hays, Walter W. [Arlington, Va.] , 1979. iv, 40 p. : LC Card 80-602831 DDC 557.3 s 363.3/495 19
QE75 .C5 no. 816 QE535.2.U6

A program audit of equal employment opportunity in Utah State Government /. Utah. Office of the Legislative Auditor General. [Salt Lake City] , 1979. ii, 58 p. : LC Card 79-624189 DDC 353.9792001/04 19
JK8460.A33 U82 1979

Program budgeting for school districts . New York (State). Division of Educational Management Services. Albany , 1973. v, 61 p. ; LC Card 79-625622 DDC 379.1/22/09747 19
LB2823.5 .N34 1973

Program compare. Monroe County, N. Y. Dept. of Parks. Rochester, N. Y., 1966. 118 p.:
NYPL [JLF 81-3]

Program de Estudios Conjuntos sobre Integración Económica Latinoamericana. Salazar-Carrillo, Jorge. Prices and purchasing power parities in Latin America, 1960-1972 /. Washington, D.C. , 1978. ca. 350 p. in various pagings ; LC Card 80-134989 DDC 338.5/2/098 19
HB235.L25 S34

Program evaluation, Kentucky Bureau for the Blind /. Kentucky. Legislative Research Commission. Committee for Program Review and Investigation. Frankfort, Ky. [1980] xiii, 151 p. ; LC Card 81-621574 DDC 353.97690084/4 19
HV1796.K5 C65 1980

Program evaluation, Kentucky State Fire and Tornado Insurance Fund /. Kentucky. Legislative Research Commission. Committee for Program Review and Investigation. Frankfort, KY. [1981] viii, 82 p. ; LC Card 81-621577 DDC 353.97690071/3 19
HG9778.K4 K46 1981

A program in crisis, blueprint for action . Ohio.

Nursing Home Commission. Columbus, Ohio [1979] xix, 233 p. : LC Card 80-621848 DDC 362.1/6/09771 19
RA997.5.O3 O38 1979

Program memorandum: employment/. Hawaii. [Honolulu], 1977. 30, 7 p.
NYPL [*XME-9682]

Program needs of prison inmates. Sykes, Thomas M. An analysis of program needs of prison inmates in Washington State /. Olympia, Wash. [1980] xxi, 139 p. ; LC Card 80-620028 DDC 365/.66/09797 19
HV9475.W2 S93

A program of management and technical assistance in EDA designated areas in North Dakota . North Dakota. State University of Agriculture and Applied Science, Fargo. Center for Economic Development. Fargo, N. D. , 1974. 70 p. : **NYPL [JLF 80-1351]**

Program Planners, inc. Bigel, Jack. Financing New York's public transit system . New York, N.Y. , c1980. 2 v. (vii, 168 leaves) : LC Card 80-128796 DDC 388.4/042 19
HE4491.N65 B53

Program planning report for 1978-79 fiscal year /. California. Dept. of Corrections. [Sacramento] [1978] 4 v. : LC Card 79-625532 DDC 365/.9794 19
HV9305.C2 C267 1978

A program to improve the business climate of New Jersey . New Jersey. Legislature. Joint Economic Committee. [Trenton , 1980] v, 165 p. ; LC Card 80-624028 DDC 332.6/7322749 19
KFN1811.62 .E25 1980

Programa de Transporta Marítimo OEA/CEPAL. Bibliografía sobre transporte en Chile / preparado por el Programa de Transporte Marítimo OEA/CEPAL. [New York] : Naciones Unidas, Consejo Económico y Social, 1977. 66 p. ; 28 cm. ([Document] - Naciones Unidas ; E/CEPAL/L.170) "Limitado." At head of title: CEPAL, Comisión Económica para América Latina. LC Card 80-119987
1. Transportation - Chile - Bibliography. I. United Nations. Economic Commission for Latin America. II. Series: United Nations. [Document] E/CEPAL/L.170. III. Title.
Z7164.T8 P76 1977 HE234.A1

Programa Regional de Desarrollo Científico y Tecnológico.
Aspectos organizacionales de la política científica y tecnológica en América Latina : situación y perspectivas del proyecto multinacional : reunión de coordinación, Washington, D.C., 20 al 24 de noviembre de 1978. Washington, D.C. : Programa Regional de Desarrollo Científico y Tecnológico, Departamento de Asuntos Científicos, Secretaría General de la Organización de los Estados Americanos, [1979?] iii, 66 p. ; 28 cm. (Estudios sobre el desarrollo científico y tecnológico . no. 35) "79-XXII-A-0145" LC Card 79-119687
1. Science and state - Latin America. 2. Technology and state - Latin America. 3. Research - Latin America - Management. 4. Research - International cooperation. I. Title. II. Series.
Q127.L38 P76 1979

Determinación de prioridades de desarrollo cientificotecnológico a nivel nacional. Washington, D.C. : Programa Regional de Desarrollo Científico y tecnológico, Departamento de Asuntos Científicos, Secretaría General de la Organización de los Estados Americanos, 1974. iii, 94 p. : ill. ; 28 cm. (Estudios sobre el desarrollo científico y tecnológico . no. 16) Prepared by J.C. Gamba. Bibliography: p. 89-92. LC Card 80-123437
1. Technology and state - Latin America. 2. Latin America - Economic conditions. I. Gamba, Juan Carlos. II. Title. III. Series.
T24.A1 P76 1974

Silva, Mauricio, Ing. Informe sobre el estudio "Análisis del proceso evolutivo y de las soluciones autónomas en el Proyecto San José del Pino" /. [Washington] , 1977. v, 39, [73] p. : LC Card 80-117186
HD7313.S3 S54

Programme des Nations Unies pour le développement. see United Nations. Development Programme.

Programme des Nations Unies pour l'environnement. see United Nations. Environment Programme.

Programme international de correlation géologique. see International Geological Correlation Programme.

PROGRAMMING LANGUAGES (ELECTRONIC COMPUTERS) For individual computer languages see the name of the language, e.g. COBOL (Computer program language).
(1980) Treu, Siegfried. A testbed for providing uniformity to user-computer interaction languages /. [Washington, D.C.] , 1980. 72 p. in various pagings : LC Card 80-603146 DDC 602/.18 s 001.64/24 19
QC100 .U57 no. 500-63 QA76.7

PROGRAMMING LANGUAGES (ELECTRONIC COMPUTERS) - BIBLIOGRAPHY.
Brodie, Michael L. Computer science & technology . [Washington, D.C.] , 1980. x, 75 p. ; LC Card 80-600052 DDC 602/.18 s 016.00164/2 19
QC100 .U57 no. 500-59 Z5643.D36 QA76.9.D3

PROGRAMS, ACADEMIC. see DISSERTATIONS, ACADEMIC.

Programs approved for teacher education in Pennsylvania colleges and universities. Pennsylvania. Dept. of Education. Harrisburg, PA , 1979. ii, 102 leaves ; LC Card 80-621835 DDC 370/.7/309748 19
LB2167.P4 P46 1979

PROGRAMS, COMPUTER. see COMPUTER PROGRAMS.

Programs for older Americans : evaluations by academic gerontologists / edited by Gordon F. Streib. Gainesville : Published for the Center for Gerontological Studies and Programs by University Presses of Florida, 1981. p. cm. (Research series . v. 1) Bibliography: p. ISBN 0-8130-0705-4 LC Card 81-11645 DDC 305.2/6/0973 19
1. Gerontology - Research - United States - Case studies. 2. Aged, Services for - United States - Evaluation. I. Streib, Gordon Franklin, 1918-. II. University of Florida. Center for Gerontological Studies and Programs. III. Series: Research series (University of Florida. Center for Gerontological Studies and Programs).
HQ1064.U5 P73

Programs of developmental studies in Missouri State-supported institutions of higher education /. Sanders, Nell S. [Jefferson City] [1978] 65 leaves : LC Card 79-621793 DDC 379.1/54/09778 19
LC1032.5.M8 S26

Progress against the rheumatic diseases (1967-1977) . National Institute of Arthritis, Metabolism, and Digestive Diseases. Office of the Associate Director for Arthritis, Bone, and Skin Diseases. [Bethesda, Md.] , 1978. vii, 39 p. ; LC Card 79-602034 DDC 616.7/23/0072073 19
RC927 .N38 1978

Progress and its discontents / edited by Gabriel A. Almond, Marvin Chodorow, and Roy Harvey Pearce ; sponsored by the Western Center of the American Academy of Arts and Sciences. Berkeley : University of California Press, c1982. p. cm. Papers based on a conference held in Palo Alto, Calif., Feb. 1979. Includes bibliographical references and index. ISBN 0-520-04478-9 LC Card 81-11643 DDC 303.4 19
1. Progress - Congresses. I. Almond, Gabriel Abraham, 1911-. II. Chodorow, Marvin. III. Pearce, Roy Harvey. IV. American Academy of Arts and Sciences. Western Center.
HM101 .P89

PROGRESS - CONGRESSES.
Progress and its discontents /. Berkeley , c1982. p. cm. ISBN 0-520-04478-9 LC Card 81-11643 DDC 303.4 19
HM101 .P89

Progress report and preliminary 1981-83 agenda. United States Radiation Policy Council. Washington, D.C. (Room 3026, New Executive Office Building, 726 Jackson Place, N.W., Washington, D.C., 20503) , 1980. 177 p. in

various pagings ; LC Card 81-600523 DDC 353.0075 19
RA569 .U17 1980

Progress toward a free appropriate public education. United States. Bureau of Education for the Handicapped. State Program Implementation Studies Branch. 1979- [Washington] LC Card 79-643307
NYPL [JLM 80-747]

Progressive masks . Holmes, Oliver Wendell, 1841-1935. Newark , c1982. p. cm. ISBN 0-87413-188-X LC Card 80-54787 DDC 347.73/2634 347.3073534 19
KF8745.H6 A44

PROGRESSIVISM (UNITED STATES POLITICS)
Holmes, Oliver Wendell, 1841-1935. Progressive masks . Newark , c1982. p. cm. ISBN 0-87413-188-X LC Card 80-54787 DDC 347.73/2634 347.3073534 19
KF8745.H6 A44

PROGRESSIVISM (UNITED STATES POLITICS) - SOURCES - BIBLIOGRAPHY - CATALOGS.
Library of Congress. Manuscript Division. The La Follette family collection. Washington , 1981. p. cm. ISBN 0-8444-0360-1 LC Card 81-1165 DDC 016.97391/092/2 19
CD3029.5.L2 L52 1981

Prohibited renewal considerations and crossownership restrictions . United States. Congress. House. Committee on Interstate and Foreign Commerce. Subcommittee on Communications. Washington , 1980. iii, 98 p. ; LC Card 80-602804 DDC 343.73/09945 19
KF27 .I5537 1980b

PROJECT APOLLO.
(1980) Geology of the Apollo 16 area, Central Lunar Highlands . Washington , 1980. p. cm. LC Card 80-607170 DDC 559.9/1 19
QB592 .G47

Project for Grrk-Turkish Economic Cooperation. see Greek-Turkish Economic Cooperation Project.

Project formulation and evaluation series . (no. 3) Hansen, John R. Guide to practical project appraisal . New York , 1978. viii, 121 p. : LC Card 78-111887 DDC 300 s 658.4/04 19
JX1977 .A2 ID/SER.H/3

Project ideas . New York (State). University. Division of Research. Albany [1978] iv, 33 p. ; LC Card 79-621882 DDC 371.9/09747 19
LC4092.N7 N4 1978

PROJECT MANAGEMENT. see INDUSTRIAL PROJECT MANAGEMENT.

PROJECT MANAGEMENT, INDUSTRIAL. see INDUSTRIAL PROJECT MANAGEMENT.

Project map, Baker River watershed, Grafton County, New Hampshire /. United States. Soil Conservation Service. [Lanham? Md.] [1979?] 1 map : LC Card 81-690286
G3742.B33N22 1979 .U5

Project map, Carney Creek watershed, Choctaw County, Oklahoma. United States. Soil Conservation Service. Fort Worth, Tex. , 1980. 1 map : LC Card 81-692268
G4022.C38N22 1980 .U5

Project map, Elm Creek (1250) watershed, portions of Coleman, Runnels, and Taylor Counties, Texas. United States. Soil Conservation Service. Fort Worth, Tex. , 1979. 1 map : LC Card 81-692267
G4032.E62 1978 .U5

Project map, Limestone-Muddy Creek watershed, portions of Duplin, Jones, and Onslow Counties, North Carolina. United States. Soil Conservation Service. Fort Worth, Tex. , 1979. 1 map : LC Card 81-692266
G3902.L48 1979 .U5

Project map, Los Olmos Creek watershed, Jim Hogg and Starr Counties, Texas. United States. Soil Conservation Service. Temple, Tex. [1979] 1 map : LC Card 81-692271
G4032.L67N22 1979 .U5

Project map, Meadow Creek watershed, Fayette County, West Virginia, Drainage Area 6530 AC /. United States. Soil Conservation Service. Lanham, MD , 1980. 1 map : LC Card

81-690287
G3892.M4N22 1978 .U5

Project map, Spring Creek watershed, Colbert and Franklin Counties, Alabama /. United States. Soil Conservation Service. Fort Worth, Tex. , 1979. 1 map : LC Card 81-692287
G3972.S6N22 1979 .U5

PROJECT METHOD IN TEACHING.
New York (State). University. Division of Research. Project ideas . Albany [1978] iv, 33 p. ; LC Card 79-621882 DDC 371.9/09747 19
LC4092.N7 N4 1978

PROJECT NETWORKS. see NETWORK ANALYSIS (PLANNING)

Project Phoenix : the September 1978 field operation / W. H. Hooke, editor. [Boulder, Colo.] : NOAA/NCAR Boulder Atmospheric Observatory ; Washington, D.C. : for sale by the Supt. of Docs., U. S. Govt. Print. Off., [1979] xiv, 281 p. : ill. ; 29 cm. (Report - NOAA/NCAR Boulder Atmospheric Observatory ; no. 1) Includes bibliographical references. LC Card 80-602120 DDC 551.5/072 19
1. Project PHOENIX. I. Hooke, William H. II. NOAA/NCAR Boulder Atmospheric Observatory. III. Series: NOAA/NCAR Boulder Atmospheric Observatory. Report - NOAA/NCAR Boulder Atmospheric Observatory , no. 1.
QC869 .P76

PROJECT PHOENIX.
Project Phoenix . [Boulder, Colo.] , Washington, D.C. [1979] xiv, 281 p. : LC Card 80-602120 DDC 551.5/072 19
QC869 .P76

Project S. H. A. R. E. see Project SHARE.

Project SHARE.
Care of the terminally ill . Rockville, Md. (P.O. Box 2309, Rockville, Md., 20852) , 1980. v, 23 p. ; LC Card 81-601199 DDC 362.1/9 19
R726.8 .C373

Issues in domestic violence / Project Share. [Rockville, Md.] : The Project, [1980] v, 25 p. ; 27 cm. (Human services bibliography series) DHEW publication ; no. OS-76-130 "May 1980." LC Card 80-602672 DDC 362.8/3 19
1. Wife abuse - United States - Abstracts. 2. Abused wives - Services for - United States - Abstracts. I. Series. II. Series: United States. Dept. of Health, Education and Welfare. DHEW publication, no. OS-76-130. III. Title.
HV6626 .P76 1980

The Project Share collection, 1976-1979. Rockville, Md. : Project Share, [1979] vii, 891 p., 28 cm. Includes index. LC Card 80-601833 DDC 361.3/068 19
1. Social work administration - United States - Abstracts. I. Title.
HV91 .P763 1979

The Project Share collection, 1976-1979. Project SHARE. Rockville, Md. [1979] vii, 891 p., 28 cm. LC Card 80-601833 DDC 361.3/068 19
HV91 .P763 1979

Project Squid. Project Squid Workshop on Gas Turbine Combustor Design Problems, Purdue University, 1978. Gas turbine combustor design problems /. Washington , c1980. xvi, 431 p. : ISBN 0-89116-177-5 LC Card 79-22350
TJ778 .P74 1978 ***NYPL [JSE 81-58]***

Project Squid Workshop on Gas Turbine Combustor Design Problems, Purdue University, 1978. Gas turbine combustor design problems / edited by Arthur H. Lefebvre. Washington : Hemisphere Pub. Corp., c1980. xvi, 431 p. : ill. ; 24 cm. At head of title: A Project Squid workshop. Includes bibliographical references and index. Sponsored by the Air Force Office of Scientific Research, Naval Air Systems Command, and Office of Naval Research (Power Program). ISBN 0-89116-177-5 LC Card 79-22350
1. Gas-Turbines - Combustion chambers - Design and construction - Congresses. I. Lefebvre, Arthur Henry, 1923-. II. Project Squid. III. United States. Air Force. Office of Scientific Research. IV. United States. Naval Air Systems Command. V. United States. Office of Naval Research. VI. Title.
TJ778 .P74 1978 ***NYPL [JSE 81-58]***

PROJECT-TEACHING. see PROJECT METHOD IN TEACHING.

PROJECT VOYAGER.
United States. National Aeronautics and Space

Administration. Voyager 1, encounter with Jupiter. [Washington] , 1979. 43 p. : LC Card 79-602497
QB661 .U54 1979a   **NYPL [JSF 81-36]**

Projected changes in Northeastern skiing participation and supply capacity as influenced by a changing economy /. Kottke, Marvin Walter. Storrs, Conn. [1980] 38 p. ; LC Card 80-624079   DDC 796.93/0974 19
GV854.5.N58 K67

Projected land use maps year 2000, Brazos Basin. Texas. Dept. of Water Resources. Austin, Tex. , 1978. [19] leaves : LC Card 80-675289   DDC 912/.133373/3097641 19
G1372.B7G4 T4 1978

Projected land use maps year 2000, Canadian Basin. Texas. Dept. of Water Resources. Austin, Tex. , 1978. [7] leaves : LC Card 80-675290   DDC 912/.133373/3097661 19
G1372.C3G4 T4 1978

Projected land use maps year 2000, Colorado Basin. Texas. Dept. of Water Resources. Austin, Tex. , 1978. [15] leaves : LC Card 80-675288   DDC 912/.133373/3097641 19
G1372.C55G4 T4 1978

Projected land use maps year 2000, Guadalupe Basin. Texas. Dept. of Water Resources. Austin, Tex. , 1978. [7] leaves : LC Card 80-675292   DDC 912/.133373/3097641 19
G1372.G8G4 T4 1978

Projected land use maps year 2000, Lavaca Basin. Texas. Dept. of Water Resources. Austin, Tex. , 1978. [4] leaves : LC Card 80-675293   DDC 912/.133373/309764255 19
G1372.L3G4 T4 1978

Projected land use maps year 2000, Neches Basin. Texas. Dept. of Water Resources. Austin, Tex. , 1978. [9] leaves : LC Card 80-675294   DDC 912/.133373/30976415 19
G1372.N4G4 T4 1978

Projected land use maps year 2000, Nueces Basin. Texas. Dept. of Water Resources. Austin, Tex. , 1978. [13] leaves : LC Card 80-675295   DDC 912/.133373/3097641 19
G1372.N8G4 T4 1978

Projected land use maps year 2000, Red Basin. Texas. Dept. of Water Resources. Austin, Tex. , 1978. [11] leaves : LC Card 80-675296   DDC 912/.133373/3097642 19
G1372.R4G4 T4 1978

Projected land use maps year 2000, Rio Grande Basin. Texas. Dept. of Water Resources. Austin, Tex. , 1978. [18] leaves : LC Card 80-675297   DDC 912/.133373/3097644 19
G1372.R5G4 T4 1978

Projected land use maps year 2000, Sabine Basin. Texas. Dept. of Water Resources. Austin, Tex. , 1978. [10] leaves : LC Card 80-675298   DDC 912/.133373/309764179 19
G1372.S15G4 T4 1978

Projected land use maps year 2000, San Antonio Basin. Texas. Dept. of Water Resources. Austin, Tex. , 1978. [5] leaves : LC Card 80-675299   DDC 912/.133373/3097641 19
G1372.S22G4 T4 1978

Projected land use maps year 2000, San Jacinto Basin. Texas. Dept. of Water Resources. Austin, Tex. , 1978. [4] leaves : LC Card 80-675300   DDC 912/.133373/309764141 19
G1372.S24G4 T4 1978

Projected land use maps year 2000, Sulphur Basin. Texas. Dept. of Water Resources. Austin, Tex. , 1978. [4] leaves : LC Card 80-675301   DDC 912/.133373/3097642 19
G1372.S8G4 T4 1978

Projected land use maps year 2000, Trinity Basin. Texas. Dept. of Water Resources. Austin, Tex. , 1978. [11] leaves : LC Card 80-675302   DDC 912/.133373/309764 19
G1372.T8G4 T4 1978

Projected 1980 overall agricultural employment by regions, commodities, and related sectors /. Schluter, Gerald E. Ames, Iowa [1975] v leaves, 85 p. : LC Card 80-623869   DDC 331.12/33/0973 19
HD5718.A272 U67

PROJECTILE POINTS - KLAMATH VALLEY - ADDRESSES, ESSAYS, LECTURES.
Aikens, C. Melvin. Obsidian hydration dates for

Klamath prehistory /. [Pocatello] , 1978. 17 p. : LC Card 78-623053   DDC 500 s 979.5/2 19
E78.I18 T43 no. 11 E99.K7

Projections of employment by industry and occupation, 1980-1985 . California. Employment Data and Research Division. [Sacramento, CA] , 1978- v.<1-2> ; LC Card 79-621759   DDC 331.12/3/09794 19
HD5725.C2 C228 1978

Projections of employment by industry and occupation, 1980-1985, State of California. California. Employment Data and Research Division. Sacramento, Calif. , 1979. 75 p. : LC Card 80-125165   DDC 331.12/3/09794 19
HD5725.C2 C228 1979a

Projections to 1982 : employment and job needs by occupation for nonagricultural wage and salary workers : planning region A-[R] / prepared by Bureau of Employment Security Research. Raleigh, N.C. : Employment Security Commission of North Carolina, [1979] 17 v. ; 29 cm. "July 1979."   LC Card 80-622695   DDC 331.12/09756 19
1. Employment forecasting - North Carolina - Statistics. 2. Labor supply - North Carolina - Statistics. 3. Job vacancies - North Carolina - Statistics. 4. North Carolina - Occupations - Statistics. I. North Carolina. Bureau of Employment Security Research. II. North Carolina. Employment Security Commission. III. Title.
HD5725.N8 P76

Projections to 1982 by occupation and industry, West Virginia /. West Virginia. Dept. of Employment Security. Labor and Economic Research Section. Charleston, W. Va. , 1979. i leaf, 99 p. ; LC Card 80-620829   DDC 331.12/3/09754 19
HD5725.W4 W38 1979a

PROLIFERATION, NUCLEAR. see NUCLEAR NONPROLIFERATION.

Promoting health/preventing disease : objectives for the nation. [Washington, D.C.?] : U. S. Dept. of Health and Human Services, Public Health Service, Office of the Assistant Secretary for Health, 1980. xiv, 197 p. ; 28 cm. "November 1980"--Prelim p. Item 485   LC Card 80-604164   DDC 362.1/0973 19
1. Public health - United States. 2. Medicine, Preventive - United States. 3. Medical policy - United States. I. United States. Office of the Assistant Secretary for Health and Surgeon General.
RA445 .P7

PROMOTIONS, SCHOOL. see GRADING AND MARKING (STUDENTS)

PROPAGANDA, RUSSIAN.
United States. Congress. House. Permanent Select Committee on Intelligence. Subcommittee on Oversight. Soviet covert action (the forgery offensive) . Washington , 1980. iii, 245 p. : LC Card 80-603647   DDC 327.1/2/0947 19
KF27.5 .I55 1980b

PROPERTY.
Umbeck, John R., 1945- A theory of property rights . Ames , 1981. p. cm.   ISBN 0-8138-1675-0   LC Card 81-1141   DDC 323.4/6 19
HB711 .U52

PROPERTY, HORIZONTAL. see CONDOMINIUM (HOUSING)

PROPERTY INSURANCE. see INSURANCE, PROPERTY.

PROPERTY, REAL. see REAL PROPERTY.

PROPERTY, RIGHT OF. see RIGHT OF PROPERTY.

Property tax administration . Ward, Keith J. Auburn, Ala. [1980] xiv, 167 p. : LC Card 80-622123   DDC 353.97610072/42 19
HJ4121.A22 W37

PROPERTY TAX - ALABAMA.
Ward, Keith J. Property tax administration . Auburn, Ala. [1980] xiv, 167 p. : LC Card 80-622123   DDC 353.97610072/42 19
HJ4121.A22 W37

The property tax and economic development. Rhode Island. Statewide Planning Program. Providence, R.I. [1980] x, 132 p. ; LC Card 80-622770   DDC 361.6/09745 s 336.22/09745 19
HT393.R5 R45b no. 36D HJ4121.R42

PROPERTY TAX - ARIZONA.
Arizona. Citizens' Commission on Tax Reform and School Finance. Final report of the Citizens' Commission on Tax Reform and school Finance . [Phoenix] , 1979. 72 p. in various pagings ; LC Card 80-621566   DDC 379.1/3/09791 19
LB2826.A6 A7 1979

PROPERTY TAX - CALIFORNIA.
Worcester, Ellen. No-property-tax cities after Proposition 13 . Sacramento, CA , Sacramento, CA (Box 90, State Capitol, Sacramento, CA 95814) [1980] iii, 52 p. ; LC Card 81-620796   DDC 352.1/352/09794 19
HJ4121.C22 W67

PROPERTY TAX - CALIFORNIA - BIBLIOGRAPHY.
Heckart, Ronald J. Proposition 13 in the 1978 California primary . Berkeley [1981] p. cm.   LC Card 80-27111   DDC 016.33622/09794 19
Z7164.T23 H4 HJ4121.C22

PROPERTY TAX - CONNECTICUT.
McEachern, William A. An analysis of Connecticut's 1979 school finance formula /. Storrs, Conn. , c1980. 91, 11 p. ; ISBN 0-931176-78-6 (pbk.)   LC Card 80-623844   DDC 379.1/222/09746 19
HD251 .R283 no. 32 LB2826.C8

PROPERTY TAX CREDIT - NEW YORK (STATE)
Boyd, Donald, 1955- New York State real property tax circuit breaker relief /. Albany, NY [1979] iii, 38 p. ; LC Card 80-622832   DDC 336.22 19
HJ4249 .B69

PROPERTY TAX - ILLINOIS.
Heins, A. James. Property taxes in Illinois /. [Urbana, Ill.] [1980] 11 p. : LC Card 80-622897   DDC 336.22/09773 19
HJ4121.I33 H44

PROPERTY TAX - KANSAS - STATISTICS.
Kansas. State Dept. of Education. 1979 mill levies of the 306 unified school districts of Kansas. Topeka [1979] 40 p. ; LC Card 80-622607   DDC 379.1/22/09781 19
LB2826.K2 K38 1979b

PROPERTY TAX - LAW AND LEGISLATION - NEVADA.
Nevada. Legislative Commission. Effects of tax relief measures. [Carson City] [1980] vii, 42 p. ; LC Card 81-621361   DDC 343.79304 347.93034 19
KFN1070 .A25 1980

PROPERTY TAX - MAINE - STATISTICS.
Municipal valuation return . [Augusta, Me. , 1979?] ca. 150 leaves in various foliations ; LC Card 80-623459   DDC 336.22/2/09741 19
HJ9249 .M86

PROPERTY TAX - MICHIGAN.
Verburg, Kenneth. Michigan local property tax primer /. East Lansing [1980] vi, 55 p. ; LC Card 80-620026   DDC 361.6/09774 s 343.77405/4 361.6/09774 s 347.740354 19
JK5801 .M48 no. B25 KFM4691.P7

PROPERTY TAX - NEW JERSEY.
Documentation of the crisis in public education in New Jersey, 1975-1976. Trenton , 1978. 2 v. ; LC Card 79-623344   DDC 379.749 19
KFN2190 .D6

New Jersey. Division of Taxation. Research and Statistics Section. Coefficients of deviation . Trenton , 1978. xiii, 77 p. ; LC Card 78-622220
HJ4121.N5 D58 1978   **NYPL [JLF 81-12]**

New Jersey. Legislature. General Assembly. Committee on Taxation. Report on assessment, equalization, and revaluation /. [Trenton] [1977?] 41 p. ; LC Card 78-621459
HJ4121.N5 N46 1977   **NYPL [*ZT-1263]**

PROPERTY TAX - NEW JERSEY - STATISTICS.
New Jersey. Division of Taxation. Research and Statistics Section. Owner occupied housing statistics from homestead rebate and income tax data match . [Trenton] [1980] iii, 84, 176-495 p. ; LC Card 80-623728   DDC 336.22/09749 19
HJ4121.N52 N48 1980a

New Jersey. Division of Taxation. Research and Statistics Section. Owner occupied housing statistics from homestead rebate and income tax

data match . [Trenton] , 1980. iii, 495 p. ;
HJ4121.N52 N48 1979
NYPL [JLF 80-1606]

New Jersey. Division of Taxation. Research
Section. Coefficients of deviation . Trenton ,
1980. xiii, 77 p. ; LC Card 80-622291 DDC
336.22/2 19
HJ4121.N42 N48 1980

**PROPERTY TAX - OHIO - STATISTICS -
PERIODICALS.**
Property taxes : Real estate and public utility ;
amount of taxes and special assessments levied
currently and delinquent taxes from former
years in Ohio cities, by city. Columbus.
NYPL [JLM 80-1035]

PROPERTY TAX - RHODE ISLAND.
Rhode Island. Statewide Planning Program.
Land use and eocnomic development
perspectives of Rhode Island property taxes.
Providence, R.I. [1980] xviii, 165 p. ; LC Card
80-622771 DDC 336.22/09745 19
HJ4121.R42 R46 1980

Rhode Island. Statewide Planning Program. The
property tax and economic development.
Providence, R.I. [1980] x, 132 p. ; LC Card
80-622770 DDC 361.6/09745 s 336.22/09745
19
HT393.R5 R45b no. 36D HJ4121.R42

PROPERTY TAX - TEXAS.
Texas. State Property Tax Board. General
appraisal manual . [Austin, Tex.] [1980?] 1 v. ;
LC Card 80-622895 DDC 353.97640072/421 19
KFT1691.P7 A85

PROPERTY TAX - UNITED STATES.
United States. Federal Council on the Aging.
The impact of the tax structure on the elderly.
Washington , 1975. iv, 119 p. ; LC Card
76-601234
HJ4653.A82 U55 1975 **NYPL [JLF 80-1411]**

Property taxation (ACA 55-Mori), housing
program incentives . California. Legislature.
Assembly. Committee on Housing and
Community Development. Sacramento, CA
[1979] ii, 95, [21] p. : LC Card 80-621896 DDC
338.4/33335/09794 19
KFC10.4 .H67 1979a

Property taxes in Illinois /. Heins, A. James.
[Urbana, Ill.] [1980] 11 p. : LC Card 80-622897
DDC 336.22/09773 19
HJ4121.I33 H44

Property taxes : Real estate and public utility ;
amount of taxes and special assessments levied
currently and delinquent taxes from former
years in Ohio cities, by city. Columbus, Ohio
Dept. of Taxation. 22 x 28 cm.
1. Property tax - Ohio - Statistics - Periodicals. I. Ohio.
Dept. of Taxation. **NYPL [JLM 80-1035]**

A proposal for protection of eleven Alaskan
rivers /. United States. Heritage Conservation
and Recreation Service. [Washington, D.C.]
[1980] ca. 200 p. in various pagings : LC Card
80-602406 DDC 333.78/45/09798 19
QH76.5.A4 U56 1980

A proposal for the development of the New
Jersey fisheries industry . New Jersey. Office
of Policy and Planning. Trenton, N.J. [1979?]
74 leaves : LC Card 80-620739 DDC
338.3/72709749 19
SH222.N5 N48 1979

Proposals to balance the budget . United States.
Congress. House. Committee on the Budget.
Washington , 1980. iv, 281 p. ; LC Card
80-602724 DDC 353.0072/22 19
KF7 .B8 1980a

Proposals to restructure the financing of private
health insurance . United States. Congress.
House. Committee on Ways and Means.
Subcommittee on Health. Washington , 1980.
iii, 273 p. : LC Card 80-602814 DDC 344.73/022
19
KF27 .W344 1980

Proposals to stimulate health care competition .
United States. Congress. Senate. Committee on
Finance. Subcommittee on Health.
Washington , 1980. iv, 462 p. ; LC Card
80-602729 DDC 344.73/022 19
KF26 .F5538 1980

The proposed Alaska General Stock Ownership
Corporation (AGOSC) /. Arlon R. Tussing &
Associates. [Juneau? Alaska] [1980] vi, 64 p. ;

LC Card 80-622651 DDC 338.7/6223382/09798
19
HG183.A4 A74 1980

Proposed amendments to Florida constitution to
be on ballot on October 7, 1980, and on
November 4, 1980, elections /. Dauer,
Manning Julian, 1909- [Gainesville] , 1980. 20
p. ; LC Card 80-623606 DDC 300/.9759 s
342.759/04 19
JK4401 .A33 no. 63 KFF401 1968

Proposed amendments to the Indiana juvenile
code (P.L. 136) . Indiana. Judicial Study
Commission. Juvenile Justice Division.
Indianapolis, Ind. , 1978. v, 92 p. ; LC Card
80-622379 DDC 345.772/08/0262
347.720580262 19
KFI3596 .A84

Proposed changes to military compensation .
United States. Congress. Senate. Committee on
Armed Services. Subcommittee on Manpower
and Personnel. Washington , 1980. iii, 101 p. ;
LC Card 80-602795 DDC 355.6/4/0973 19
KF26 .A7548 1980

Proposed child protective service plan /.
Philadelphia. Dept. of Public Welfare.
[Philadelphia], 1979. iii, 42 leaves;
NYPL [*ZT-1264]

Proposed Community Energy Efficiency Act .
United States. Congress. Senate. Committee on
Energy and Natural Resources. Subcommittee
on Energy Conservation and Supply.
Washington , c1981. iv, 186 p. ; LC Card
81-600952 DDC 346.7304/67916 347.306467916
19
KF26 .E553 1980e

Proposed Constitution of the State of Texas.
[Austin : Secretary of State of the State of
Texas, 1975?] 23 p. ; 36 cm. Includes the text of
the 1976 Proposed Constitution of the State of Texas,
as ammended by the 64th session of the Texas
Legislature: p. 12-20. LC Card 76-620741 DDC
342/.764/023 19
1. Texas - Constitutional law. I. Texas. Legislature.
Proposed Constitution of the State of Texas. 1975.
KFT1601 1876 .A25456

Proposed constitutional amendments analyzed .
Texas. Legislative Council. [Austin? Tex.]
[1980?] 24 p. ; LC Card 80-622923 DDC
342.764/035 19
KFT1601 1876.A88 A45

Proposed domestic livestock grazing program for
the Challis Planning Unit . United States.
Bureau of Land Management. [Washington] ,
1977. 1 v. (various pagings) :
NYPL [JLF 80-1442]

Proposed earthquake safety programs and
activities of the Department of Conservation,
fiscal years 1982 through 1986 /. Davis, James
F. Sacramento, CA , 1980. vi, 38 p. ; LC Card
80-623482 DDC 557.94 s 551.2/2/09794 19
QE89 .A1117 no. 57 QE535.2.U6

The proposed fiscal 1981 budget . United States.
Congress. Senate. Special Committee on Aging.
Washington , 1980. ii, 18 p. : LC Card
80-601777 DDC 362.6/3/0973 19
HV1461 .U63 1980

Proposed five-year OCS oil and gas lease sale
schedule, March 1980-February 1985. United
States. Bureau of Land Management. Final
environmental statement . [Washington] [1980]
viii, 384, [257] p. : LC Card 80-601418 DDC
333.33/9 19
HD9566 .U52 1980

Proposed general revenue sharing extension .
United States. Congress. Senate. Committee on
Finance. Subcommittee on Revenue Sharing,
Intergovernmental Revenue Impact, and
Economic Problems. Washington , 1980. iv, 650
p. : LC Card 80-603507 DDC 343.73/034 19
KF26 .F567 1980

Proposed medical facilities planning annex to the
Texas state health plan /. Texas. Statewide
Health Coordinating Council. [Austin] [1980]
ca. 200 p. in various pagings : LC Card
80-624127 DDC 362.1/1/09764 19
RA395.A4 T4886 1980 Suppl

Proposed Oregon Evidence Code . Oregon.
Legislative Assembly. Interim Committee on
the Judiciary. Salem, Or. (347 State Capitol,
Salem 97310) [1980] xv, 230 p. ; LC Card

81-621515 DDC 347.795/06 347.95076 19
KFO2940 .A25 1980

The proposed plan of the State of Texas for
technical assistance and energy conservation
measures available to schools, hospitals, units
of local government, and public care
institutions /. Keeran, Duane. [Austin] [1979]
xv, 64 p. ; LC Card 80-621353 DDC
333.79/09764 19
HD9502.U53 T43

Proposed Presidential Commission on National
Service Act of 1980 . United States. Congress.
House. Committee on Education and Labor.
Subcommittee on Select Education.
Washington , 1980. iii, 69 p. ; LC Card
80-604048 DDC 344.73/03137 347.3043137 19
KF27 .E373 1980c

Proposed residential energy efficiency plan .
United States. Congress. Senate. Committee on
Finance. Washington , 1979. iii, 74 p. ; LC
Card 80-600624 DDC 346.7304/67916/0262 19
KF26 .F5 1979l

Proposed revisions, Texas State implementation
plan, regulations . Texas. Air Control Board.
[Austin?] [1980] 113 p. in various pagings ;
LC Card 80-622987 DDC 344.764/046342 19
KFT1558 .A82

Proposed revisions to ocean dumping criteria .
United States. Environmental Protection
Agency. Oil and Special Materials Control
Division. Washington , 1977. 2 v. ;
NYPL [JSF 80-969]

Proposed settlement of Maine Indian land
claims . United States. Congress. Senate. Select
Committee on Indian Affairs. Washington ,
1980 LC Card 81-601172 DDC 346.74104/32/08897
347.410643208897 19
KF26.5 .I4 1980w

Proposed third bridge crossing on the Columbia
River between Vancouver, Washington, and
Portland, Oregon . United States. Congress.
House. Committee on Public Works and
Transportation. Subcommittee on Surface
Transportation. Washington , 1980. iii, 89 p. :
LC Card 80-603449 DDC 388.1/32/0979549 19
KF27 .P8966 1980

Proposed Veterans' Administration budget for
fiscal year 1982 . United States. Congress.
House. Committee on Veterans' Affairs.
Washington , 1981. iii 87 p. : LC Card
81-601758 DDC 353.0072/236812 19
KF27 .V4 1981a

Proposition 13 assessment issues . Doerr, David
R. [Sacramento CA] , 1980] 1 v. (various
pagings) : LC Card 81-620793 DDC
333.33/2/09794 19
HJ4121.C22 D63

Proposition 13 in the 1978 California primary .
Heckart, Ronald J. Berkeley [1981] p. cm. LC
Card 80-27111 DDC 016.33622/09794 19
Z7164.T23 H4 HJ4121.C22

PROPOXYPHENE NEPSYLATA.
United States. Congress. House. Committee on
Interstate and Foreign Commerce.
Subcommittee on Health and the Environment.
Propoxyphene--oversight . Washington , 1980.
iii, 187 p. ; LC Card 80-604112 DDC 362.2/93 19
KF27 .I5543 1980m

Propoxyphene--oversight . United States.
Congress. House. Committee on Interstate and
Foreign Commerce. Subcommittee on Health
and the Environment. Washington , 1980. iii,
187 p. ; LC Card 80-604112 DDC 362.2/93 19
KF27 .I5543 1980m

**PROSECUTION - UNITED STATES -
DECISION MAKING.**
Goldstein, Abraham S. The passive judiciary .
Baton Rouge , c1981. p. cm. ISBN
0-8071-0856-1 ; LC Card 81-11749 DDC
345.73/05042 347.3055042 19
KF9640 .G64

Prosecutor's responsibility in spouse abuse cases.
Washington, D.C. : U. S. Dept. of Justice, Law
Enforcement Assistance Administration : for
sale by the Supt. of Docs., U. S. Govt. Print.
Off., 1980. 13, 24 [13] p. ; 28 cm. Cover title.
"March, 1980." Conference organized by the National
District Attorneys Association and the Center for
Women Policy Studies, held at Memphis, Tenn., Sept.

25-28, 1978. Includes bibliography. LC Card
80-602608 DDC 345.73/04555 19
*1. Wife abuse - United States - Congresses. 2. Conjugal
violence - Law and legislation - United States -
Congresses. I. National District Attorneys Association.
II. Center for Women Policy Studies.*
KF9322.A75 P76

**PROSPECTING - MEXICO, GULF OF -
MATHEMATICAL MODELS.**
Drew, Lawrence J. Estimation of the future
rates of oil and gas discoveries in the western
Gulf of Mexico /. Washington , 1981. p. cm.
LC Card 81-6768 DDC 553.2/8/09726 19
TN872.A5 D73

**Prospects for cooperation and trade of energy
resources between the United States and
Canada** . United States. General Accounting
Office. [Washington, D.C. , 1979] iii, 33 p. :
LC Card 80-600527 DDC 333.79/0971 19
HD9502.C32 U56 1979

**Prospects for human services programs in the
economic and social climate of the eighties** .
United States. Congress. House. Committee on
the Budget. Task Force on Human and
Community Resources. Washington , 1980. iii,
103 p. : LC Card 80-603013 DDC 361/.973 19
KF27 .B848 1980

**Prospects of population, methodology, and
assumptions** . United Nations. Ad Hoc Group
of Experts on Demographic Projections. New
York , 1979. iv, 292 p. : LC Card 79-127715
DDC 300 s 304.6 19
JX1977 .A2 ST/ESA/SER.A/67

**A prospectus for a vocational education policy
resource center.** North Carolina. State
University, Raleigh. Center for Occupational
Education. Raleigh , 1975. 47 leaves ; LC Card
79-622866 DDC 370.11/3/09756 19
LC1046.N8 N68 1975

Prosser, L. J. (Leonard J.) Methane drainage
study utilizing an underground pipeline,
Marianna mine 58 / by L.J. Prosser, Jr., G.L.
Finfinger, and J. Cervik. [Washington, D.C.] :
United States Dept. of the Interior, Bureau of
Mines, [1981] p. cm. (Report of investigations)
Bibliography: p. LC Card 81-1765 DDC 622 s
622/.8 19
*1. Coal mines and mining - Safety measures. 2. Mine
ventilation. 3. Methane. I. Finfinger, Gerald L. II.
Cervik, Joseph. III. Series: Report of investigations
(United States. Bureau of Mines). IV. Title.*
TN23 U43 TN295

PROSTHESIS.
Bell, Trudy. Technologies for the handicapped
and the aged . [Washington] , 1979. iii, 43 p. :
LC Card 80-601228 DDC 617 19
R856 .B4

PROSTHETICS. see PROSTHESIS.

PROSTITUTION, JUVENILE - ILLINOIS.
Illinois. General Assembly. Legislative
Investigating Commission. Sexual exploitation
of children . Chicago, Ill. (300 W. Washington
St., Chicago 60606) [1980] ix, 317 p. : LC
Card 80-624398 DDC 362.7/1 19
HQ72.U53 I34 1980

**Protecting lettuce plants from preemergence
herbicide damage** /. Kratky, B. A., 1944-
[Honolulu] [1980] 7 p. : LC Card 80-26589
DDC 635/.529 19
SB608.L523 K7

Protecting people at work : a reader in
occupational safety and health. Washington,
D.C. : U. S. Dept. of Labor : for sale by the
Supt. of Docs., U. S. Govt. Print. Off., 1980.
361, [3] p. : ill. ; 21 cm. Bibliography: p.
[363]-[364] LC Card 80-602208 DDC 363.1/0973
19
*1. Industrial safety - United States - Addresses, essays,
lectures. 2. Industrial hygiene - United States -
Addresses, essays, lectures. I. United States. Dept. of
Labor.*
HD7262.5.U6 P76

Protecting the privacy of Illinois citizens .
Sokolik, Stanley Lewis, 1928- Springfield, Ill.
[1979] vii, 88 p. ; LC Card 80-623377 DDC
323.44/8/09773 19
JC596.2.U5 S65

**Protection against depletion of stratospheric
ozone by chlorofluorocarbons** /. National
Research Council. Committee on Impacts of

Stratospheric Change. Washington, D.C. , 1979.
xvii, 392 p. : ISBN 0-309-02947-3 LC Card
79-57247
TD887.C47 N37 1979   *NYPL [JSE 81-221]*

**PROTECTION OF ENVIRONMENT. see
ENVIRONMENTAL PROTECTION.**

**PROTECTION OF NATURE. see NATURE
CONSERVATION.**

**PROTECTION OF PLANTS. see PLANTS,
PROTECTION OF.**

Protection of Shareholders' Rights Act of 1980 .
United States. Congress. Senate. Committee on
Banking, Housing and Urban Affairs.
Subcommittee on Securities. Washington , 1981.
iv, 479 p. : LC Card 81-601417 DDC
346.73/0666 347.306666 19
KF26 .B3954 1980b

**PROTECTION OF WILD FLOWERS. see
PLANTS, PROTECTION OF.**

PROTEIDS. see PROTEINS.

PROTEIN METABOLISM.
Ellis, Robert W. Effect of mercury on osmotic
regulation and protein kinetics in the crayfish,
Pacifastacus leniusculus /. Boise, Idaho , 1979.
30, [4] leaves : LC Card 79-626025 DDC
595.3/841 19
QL444.M33 E44

PROTEINS.
(1974) Mattil, K. F. Review and comparative
analysis of oilseed raw materials and processes
suitable for the production of protein products
for human consumption. New York , 1974. viii,
36 p. : LC Card 81-465132 DDC 300 s 664/.64 19
JX1977 .A2 ID/126 (ID/WG.120/10/Rev. 1)

**PROTEROZOIC PERIOD. see GEOLOGY,
STRATIGRAPHIC - PRE-CAMBRIAN.**

Protess, David. (joint author) Manikas, Peter.
Establishing a citizens' watchdog group /.
[Washington, D.C.] , 1979. xii, 129 p. ; LC
Card 79-604009
JK2249 .M36   *NYPL [JLF 81-343]*

**Protestant versus Catholic in Mid-Victorian
England** . Arnstein, Walter L. Columbia , 1982.
p. cm. ISBN 0-8262-0354-X LC Card 81-11451
DDC 274.2/081 19
BX1493 .A86

**Protestant versus Catholic in Mid-Victorian
England.** Arnstein, Walter L. Protestant versus
Catholic in Mid-Victorian England . Columbia ,
1982. p. cm. ISBN 0-8262-0354-X LC Card
81-11451 DDC 274.2/081 19
BX1493 .A86

PROTEUTHERIA.
Bown, Thomas M. A review of the Proteutheria
and Insectivora of the Willwood Formation
(Lower Eocene), Bighorn Basin, Wyoming /.
Washington , 1981. p. cm. LC Card 81-607068
DDC 557.3 s 569/.12 19
QE75 .B9 no. 1523 QE882.I5

Proto-Athabaskan verb stem variation /. Leer,
Jeff. [Fairbanks, Alaska] 1979- [c1980- v. ;
LC Card 80-622238 DDC 497/.2 19
PM641 .L4

PROTO-ATHAPASCAN LANGUAGE - VERB.
Leer, Jeff. Proto-Athabaskan verb stem
variation /. [Fairbanks, Alaska] 1979- [c1980-
v. ; LC Card 80-622238 DDC 497/.2 19
PM641 .L4

**Protocol to the MTN customs valuation
agreement** . United States. Congress. Senate.
Committee on Finance. Subcommittee on
International Trade. Washington , 1980. 23 p. ;
LC Card 80-602438 DDC 353.0082/7 19
KF26 .F554 1980a

Prototype Incorporated. State of Ohio unified
correctional master plan. [Columbus, Ohio] :
Ohio Dept. of Rehabilitation & Correction,
[1979] 241 p. in various pagings : ill. ; 28 cm.
Cover title. Prepared for the Ohio Dept. of
Rehabilitation and Correction and the Ohio Dept. of
Economic and Community Development. Includes a
bibliography. LC Card 80-621188 DDC
364.6/09771 19
*1. Corrections - Ohio. I. Ohio. Dept. of Rehabilitation
and Correction. II. Ohio. Dept. of Economic and
Community Development. III. Title.*
HV9305.O2 P76 1979

PROTOZOA - ATLANTIC OCEAN.
Cifelli, Richard. Textural observations on some
living species of planktonic foraminifera /.
Washington , 1982. p. cm. LC Card 81-607840
DDC 560 s 592.1/304471 19
QE701 .S56 no. 45 QL368.F6

PROTOZOA - DEVELOPMENT.
Cifelli, Richard. Textural observations on some
living species of planktonic foraminifera /.
Washington , 1982. p. cm. LC Card 81-607840
DDC 560 s 592.1/304471 19
QE701 .S56 no. 45 QL368.F6

PROTOZOA - MORPHOLOGY.
Cifelli, Richard. Textural observations on some
living species of planktonic foraminifera /.
Washington , 1982. p. cm. LC Card 81-607840
DDC 560 s 592.1/304471 19
QE701 .S56 no. 45 QL368.F6

Provenzano, George. (joint author) Ewing, Ben B.
Economic impact of a proposed change in lead
effluent standards /. Chicago, IL [1980] vi, 83
p. ; LC Card 80-623378 DDC 363.7/394 19
TD427.H45 E92

**PROVIDENCE AND THRIFT. see SAVING
AND THRIFT.**

Providencia : a case study in economic censuses /
International StatisticalPrograms Center.[Rev.
Apr. 1980] [Washington, D.C.?] : U. S. Dept. of
Commerce, Bureau of the Census, 1980. xiii,
327 p. : maps, forms ; 28 cm. "Prepared under a
Resources Support Services Agreement with the Office
of International Training, U. S. Agency for International
Development." Item 146 LC Card 80-603922 DDC
330.9861/8 19
*1. Economic surveys. 2. Industrial surveys. 3.
Underdeveloped areas. 4. Underdeveloped areas -
Industries. I. United States. Bureau of the Census. II.
International Statistical Programs Center (U. S.). III.
United States. Agency for International Development.
Office of International training.*
HC28 .P83 1980

**Providing additional civil and criminal penalties
for aviation safety violations** . United States.
Congress. House. Committee on Public Works
and Transportation. Subcommittee on Aviation.
Washington , 1980. iv, 314 p. ; LC Card
81-600604 DDC 343.73/0975 347.303975 19
KF27 .P89624 1980o

**Providing greater flexibility for the armed forces
in ordering reserves to active duty** . United
States. Congress. Senate. Committee on Armed
Services. Subcommittee on Manpower and
Personnel. Washington , 1980 [i.e. 1981] iii, 32
p. ; LC Card 81-600808 DDC 343.73/012
347.30312 19
KF26 .A7548 1980b

Provine, Dorothy S. United States. National
Archives and Records Service. Preliminary
inventory of the records of St. Elizabeths
Hospital . Washington , 1981. p. cm. LC Card
81-607004 DDC 016.973 s 016.3622/1/09753
19
*CD3026 .A32 no. 193 Z6675.H75
RC445.W19W37*

Prucha, Francis Paul.
  **Bibliographical guide to the history of Indian-
  white relations in the United States.**
  Prucha, Francis Paul. Indian-white relations
  in the United States : a bibliography of works
  published 1975-1980 / Francis Paul Prucha.
  Lincoln, Neb. , c1982. p. cm. ISBN
  0-8032-3665-4 LC Card 81-14722 DDC
  016.3231/197073 19
  Z1209.2.U5 P67 Suppl E93

  Indian-white relations in the United States : a
  bibliography of works published 1975-1980 /
  Francis Paul Prucha. Lincoln, Neb. : University
  of Nebraska Press, c1982. p. cm. Supplement to:
  A bibliographical guide to the history of Indian-white
  relations in the United States / Francis Paul Prucha.
  Chicago : University of Chicago Press, 1977. Includes
  index. ISBN 0-8032-3665-4 LC Card 81-14722
  DDC 016.3231/197073 19
  *1. Indians of North America - Government relations -
  Bibliography. I. Prucha, Francis Paul. Bibliographical
  guide to the history of Indian-white relations in the
  United States. II. Title.*
  Z1209.2.U5 P67 Suppl E93

**Prudhoe Bay project final environmental impact
statement** . United States. Federal Energy
Regulatory Commission. Office of Pipeline and

Producer Regulation. Washington, D.C. , 1980.
xv, 416 p. :   LC Card 80-603226   DDC
  333.8/2331/09798 19
TD195.G3 U55 1980

**PRUNE INDUSTRY - CALIFORNIA -
    STATISTICS.**
California Prune Advisory Board. The
California prune industry marketing program,
1972-1976. [San Francisco] , 1978. xxi, 33 p. ;
  LC Card 80-620543   DDC 338.4/766480421 19
HD9259.P73 U53 1978

Pryor, David. United States. General Accounting
Office. Controls over DOD's management
support service contracts need strengthening .
Washington, D.C. , 1981. v, 76 p. ;   LC Card
  81-601728   DDC 355.6/211/0973 19
UC263 .U54 1981

PSEUDOMONADACEAE.
Robinton, Elizabeth Dorothy. The Mill River
and its floodplain in Northampton and
Williamsburg, Massachusetts . Amherst [1972?]
vii leaves, 72 p. :   LC Card 80-497906   DDC
  581.5/26323 19
QK166 .R67

PSITHYRUS.
Bumble bees and cuckoo bumble bees of
California (Hyenoptera, Apidae) /. Berkeley,
CA , 1981. p. cm.   ISBN 0-520-09645-2 LC Card
  81-10422   DDC 595.7/09794 s 595.79/909794
  19
QL475.C3 C3 vol. 23 QL568.A6

Psuty, Norbert P. Rutgers University, New
Brunswick, N.J. Center for Coastal and
Environmental Studies. Comparison of natural
and altered estuarine systems . [New
Brunswick, N.J.] [1979] 2 v. :   LC Card
  80-623604   DDC 574.5/26365 19
QH105.N5 R87 1979a

PSYCHAGOGY. see PSYCHOTHERAPY.

Psychiatric drug study /. Gee, Susan.
Washington, D.C. , 1979- v. <1> :   LC Card
  79-604263   DDC 616.89/18 19
RM315 .G43

**PSYCHIATRIC HOSPITAL CARE -
    MICHIGAN.**
Michigan. Select Panel on Abuse in Michigan
Mental Health Institutions. Report of the Select
Panel on Abuse in Michigan Mental Health
Institutions. [Lansing] , 1978. iii, 77 leaves ;
  LC Card 78-622912   DDC 362.2/1 19
RC445.M48 M52 1978

**PSYCHIATRIC HOSPITALS - NEW YORK
    (CITY) - OUTPATIENT SERVICES.**
New York (State). Division of Audits and
Accounts. Review of treatment records
documenting Medicaid billings at Office of
Mental Health outpatient facilities in New York
City. [Albany] , 1979. 2, 8, [6] leaves ;   LC
  Card 79-625695   DDC 353.97470082/56 19
HD7102.U5 N66 1979

**PSYCHIATRIC HOSPITALS - UNITED
    STATES - COLLECTED WORKS.**
Mental health statistics; Series A: mental health
facilities report. Rockville, Md..
                                    NYPL [JLM 80-1073]

**PSYCHIATRIC HOSPITALS -
    WASHINGTON (D.C.) - HISTORY -
    SOURCES - CATALOGS.**
United States. National Archives and Records
Service. Preliminary inventory of the records of
St. Elizabeths Hospital . Washington , 1981. p.
cm.   LC Card 81-607004   DDC 016.973 s
  016.3622/1/09753 19
*CD3026 .A32 no. 193 Z6675.H75
    RC445.W19W37*

**PSYCHIATRISTS - LATIN AMERICA -
    DIRECTORIES.**
Pan American Health Organization. Directorio
de psiquiatras de America Latina =.
Washington, D.C. , 1968. cxi, 558, 10 p. ;   LC
  Card 80-140541   DDC 362.1/09181/2 s
  616.89/0025/8 19
RA10 .P252 no. 163 RC335

**PSYCHIATRY AND RELIGION -
    BIBLIOGRAPHY.**
Summerlin, Florence A. Religion and mental
health . Rockville, Md. (5600 Fishers Lane,
Rockville, Md. 20857) , Washington, D.C. ,
1980. 401 p. in various pagings ;   LC Card

  81-601117   DDC 016.3622 19
Z6664.N5 S94 RA790

**PSYCHIATRY - NEW YORK (CITY) -
    MEDICAL RECORDS.**
New York (State). Division of Audits and
Accounts. Review of treatment records
documenting Medicaid billings at Office of
Mental Health outpatient facilities in New York
City. [Albany] , 1979. 2, 8, [6] leaves ;   LC
  Card 79-625695   DDC 353.97470082/56 19
HD7102.U5 N66 1979

**PSYCHIATRY, TRANSCULTURAL -
    CONGRESSES.**
Counseling across cultures /. Honolulu , 1981.
p. cm.   ISBN 0-8248-0725-1 (pbk.) :   LC Card
  81-2961   DDC 616.89/14 19
BF637.C6 C63 1981

PSYCHICAL RESEARCH.
Philosophy of science and the occult /.
Albany , 1981. p. cm.   ISBN 0-87395-572-2 LC
  Card 81-13552   DDC 001.9/01 19
BF1411 .P49

PSYCHOANALYSIS.
Wurmser, Leon. The mask of shame /.
Baltimore , c1981. p. cm.   ISBN 0-8018-2527-X
  LC Card 81-964   DDC 152.4 19
BF575.S45 W87

PSYCHOANALYSIS AND LITERATURE.
King, Walter N. Hamlet's search for meaning /.
Athens, Ga. , 1982. p. cm.   ISBN 0-8203-0597-9
  LC Card 81-12979   DDC 822.3/3 19
PR2807 .K48

PSYCHODIAGNOSTICS.
Monahan, John, 1946- The clinical prediction
of violent behavior /. Rockville, Md. (5600
Fishers Lane, Rockville, Md. 20857) ,
Washington, D.C. , 1980 i.e.1981. xi, 134 p. :
  LC Card 81-601072   DDC 616.85/82 19
RC569.5.V55 M64

PSYCHOLINGUISTICS, DEVELOPMENTAL.
    see LANGUAGE ACQUISITION.

**PSYCHOLOGICAL ASSESSMENT. see
    PSYCHODIAGNOSTICS.**

**PSYCHOLOGICAL MEASUREMENT. see
    PSYCHOMETRICS.**

**PSYCHOLOGICAL SCALING. see
    PSYCHOMETRICS.**

**PSYCHOLOGICAL STATISTICS. see
    PSYCHOMETRICS.**

**PSYCHOLOGICAL TESTS -
    MATHEMATICAL MODELS.**
Brown, Keith Cates, 1933- Modeling the group
admissions process . West Lafayette, Ind. ,
1978. 17, 7 p. ;   LC Card 78-623489   DDC
  658/.001/9 s 302.3/4 19
HD6483 .P8 no. 668 HM133

PSYCHOLOGICAL WARFARE.
United States. Congress. House. Committee on
Foreign Affairs. Subcommittee on International
Organizations and Movements. Behavioral
sciences and the national security .
Washington , 1965. vi, 1OR, iii, 203 p. :   LC
  Card 80-503601   DDC 327.73 s 327.1/1 19
E840.2 .A3 no. 4 E846

**PSYCHOLOGISTS - LEGAL STATUS, LAWS,
    ETC. - VIRGINIA.**
Regulations of the Boards . Richmond, Va. (2
South Ninth St., P.O. Box 1-X, Richmond, Va.
23202), [1977?] 36 p. ;   LC Card 80-623907
  DDC 344.755/0176115 347.5504176115 19
KFV2726.5.P73 A3 1977

**PSYCHOLOGISTS - SOUTH DAKOTA -
    DIRECTORIES.**
South Dakota. Board of Examiners of
Psychologists. Directory of licensed
psychologists and associate psychologists /.
[Pierre?] , 1979. [7] p. ;   LC Card 79-625660
  DDC 150/.25/783 19
BF30 .S68 1979

**PSYCHOLOGY, ABNORMAL. see
    PSYCHOLOGY, PATHOLOGICAL.**

**PSYCHOLOGY AND RELIGION -
    BIBLIOGRAPHY.**
Summerlin, Florence A. Religion and mental
health . Rockville, Md. (5600 Fishers Lane,
Rockville, Md. 20857) , Washington, D.C. ,
1980. 401 p. in various pagings ;   LC Card
  81-601117   DDC 016.3622 19
Z6664.N5 S94 RA790

PSYCHOLOGY - CONGRESSES.
Proceedings of the seventh symposium,
psychology in the Department of Defense, 16
April-18 April 1980. Colorado Springs, Colo.
[Springfield, Va. (5285 Port Royal Rd.,
Springfield 22151)] 1980. xxiv, 635 p. :   LC
  Card 80-604141   DDC 355/.001/9 19
U22.3 .P712

PSYCHOLOGY - DATA PROCESSING.
Freiherr, Gregory. The seeds of artificial
intelligence . Bethesda, Md. , Washington, D.C.
[1980] 74 p. :   LC Card 80-602247   DDC 001.64
  19
R858 .F73

Psychology in the Department of Defense.
Proceedings of the seventh symposium,
psychology in the Department of Defense, 16
April-18 April 1980. Colorado Springs, Colo.
[Springfield, Va. (5285 Port Royal Rd.,
Springfield 22151)] 1980. xxiv, 635 p. :   LC
  Card 80-604141   DDC 355/.001/9 19
U22.3 .P712

**PSYCHOLOGY - MATHEMATICAL
    MODELS.**
Hirshfeld, Stephen F. Algebraic systems ;
applications in the behavioral and social
sciences /. Alexandria, Va. , 1978. 119 p. ;
                                    NYPL [JLF 80-1630]

**PSYCHOLOGY - MEASUREMENT. see
    PSYCHOMETRICS.**

**PSYCHOLOGY, MEDICAL. see
    PSYCHOLOGY, PATHOLOGICAL.**

PSYCHOLOGY, MILITARY.
Naval Education and Training Program
Development Center. Human behavior and
leadership . [Washington?] [1977] i.e. 1978.
iii, 163, [51] p. :   LC Card 78-601716   DDC
  158/.4/024359 19
VB203 .N38 1978

PSYCHOLOGY, MILITARY - CONGRESSES.
Proceedings of the seventh symposium,
psychology in the Department of Defense, 16
April-18 April 1980. Colorado Springs, Colo.
[Springfield, Va. (5285 Port Royal Rd.,
Springfield 22151)] 1980. xxiv, 635 p. :   LC
  Card 80-604141   DDC 355/.001/9 19
U22.3 .P712

**PSYCHOLOGY OF LEARNING. see
    LEARNING, PSYCHOLOGY OF.**

PSYCHOLOGY, PATHOLOGICAL.
Evoy, John J. The rejected . University Park
[1981] p. cm.   ISBN 0-271-00285-9 :   LC Card
  81-47172   DDC 155.9/24 19
RC455.4.F3 E96

**PSYCHOLOGY, PATHOLOGICAL -
    ECONOMIC ASPECTS - CONGRESSES.**
Conference on Mental Health and the
Economy, Hunt Valley, Md., 1978. Mental
health and the economy . Kalamazoo, Mich.
[1979] viii, 423 p. :   ISBN 0-911558-69-1 LC
  Card 79-25809
RC455 .C625 1978   NYPL [JLE 80-2456]

**PSYCHOLOGY, PATHOLOGICAL - SOCIAL
    ASPECTS - CONGRESSES.**
Conference on Mental Health and the
Economy, Hunt Valley, Md., 1978. Mental
health and the economy . Kalamazoo, Mich.
[1979] viii, 423 p. :   ISBN 0-911558-69-1 LC
  Card 79-25809
RC455 .C625 1978   NYPL [JLE 80-2456]

**PSYCHOLOGY - SCALING. see
    PSYCHOMETRICS.**

**PSYCHOLOGY, SOCIAL. see SOCIAL
    PSYCHOLOGY.**

**PSYCHOLOGY - STATISTICS. see
    PSYCHOMETRICS.**

PSYCHOMETRICS.
Cox, Eli Peace. The optimal number of
response alternatives for a scale . Austin, Tex.
[1980] 43, [8] p. ;   LC Card 80-624133   DDC
  300/.1/5195 19
H61 .C68

**PSYCHOMETRY (PSYCHOPHYSICS) see
    PSYCHOMETRICS.**

**PSYCHOPATHOLOGY. see PSYCHOLOGY,
    PATHOLOGICAL.**

**PSYCHOPATHY. see PSYCHOLOGY,
    PATHOLOGICAL.**

PSYCHOPHARMACOLOGICAL RESEARCH.
United States. Psychopharmacology Research
Branch. The documentation of clinical
psychotropic drug trials. Rockville, Md. [1973]
2 v.   *NYPL [JSK 80-137]*

PSYCHOPHARMACOLOGY - CONGRESSES.
Workshop on Behavioral Toxicology, National
Institutes of Health, 1975. Proceedings /.
[Bethesda, Md.] [1976?] v, 109 p. :   LC Card
77-601979
RA1191 .W67 1975   *NYPL [JSF 81-141]*

PSYCHOPHARMACOLOGY - RESEARCH.
see **PSYCHOPHARMACOLOGICAL
RESEARCH.**

PSYCHOTHERAPY.
Wurmser, Leon. The mask of shame /.
Baltimore , c1981. p. cm.   ISBN 0-8018-2527-X
LC Card 81-964   DDC 152.4 19
BF575.S45 W87

PSYCHOTROPIC DRUGS.
Gee, Susan. Psychiatric drug study /.
Washington, D.C. , 1979- v. <1> :   LC Card
79-604263   DDC 616.89/18 19
RM315 .G43

PSYCHOTROPIC DRUGS - ANALYSIS.
Foltz, Rodger L. GC/MS assays for abused
drugs in body fluids /. Rockville, Md. (5600
Fishers Lane, Rockville, Md. 20857) ,
Washington, D.C. , 1980. ix, 202 p. :   LC Card
80-600143   DDC 616.86/3 19
RS190.P78 F64

**PSYCHOTROPIC DRUGS - UNITED
STATES.**
United States. Congress. House. Select
Committee on Narcotics Abuse and Control.
Diversion of licit drugs to illegal markets .
Washington , 1980. iii, 90 p. :   LC Card
80-601949   DDC 363.4/5 19
KF27.5 .N3 1979i

PTYCHOCHEILUS LUCIUS - HABITAT.
Holden, Paul B. Habitat requirements of
juvenile Colorado River squawfish /. [Fort
Collins, Colo.] , Washington , 1978. 71 p. :   LC
Card 79-602765   DDC 639.9/77092/9792 19
QL638.C94 H64

PTYCHOPTERIDAE.
Byers, George William, 1923- Summer crane
flies of Lake Itasca vicinity, Minnesota /.
[Lawrence] , 1979. p. 604-613 ;   LC Card
79-622728   DDC 500 s 595.77/1 19
Q1 .K17 vol. 51, no. 20 QL537.T5

**PUBERTY RITES - PAPUA NEW GUINEA -
ADDRESSES, ESSAYS, LECTURES.**
Rituals of manhood . Berkeley , c1981. p. cm.
ISBN 0-520-04448-7   LC Card 81-1807   DDC
392/.14 19
GN671.N5 R55

Public acceptance of women in politics .
Levenson, Rosaline. Chico, Calif. [1980] 31
p. ;   LC Card 80-622812   DDC 320/.088042 19
HQ1391.U5 L48

Public accountancy act of 1957, as amended .
Nebraska. Laws, statutes, etc. Lincoln, Neb.
[1979] 48 p. ;   LC Card 80-623309   DDC
346.782/06648/02632 19
KFN329.A25 A32 1979

**Public Accountancy Act of 1968 (as amended
1980) ; and, Rules of general application (as
amended September 25, 1980).** Oklahoma.
[Public Accountancy Act of 1968.] [Oklahoma
City, Okla.] [1980] 56 p. ;   LC Card 81-621472
DDC 346.766/063 347.660663 19
KFO1529.A25 A32 1980

PUBLIC ACCOUNTANTS. see
ACCOUNTANTS.

PUBLIC ACCOUNTING. see **FINANCE,
PUBLIC - ACCOUNTING.**

**Public acquisition costs of recreation land to the
year 2000** / [written by Hall Winslow ; with
the aid of Frank Occhipinti and Thomas
Hernandez ; under the supervision of Richard
S. DeTurk]. New York : Planning Division,
Tri-State Transportation Commission, 1968. 23
p. ; 28 cm. (Tri-State Transportation Commission.
Open space series. no. 9) Microfilm. "Interim technical
report, 4098-9111." Includes bibliographical references.
*1. Recreation areas - Middle Atlantic States - Costs. 2.
Recreation areas - Planning - Middle Atlantic States. I.
Winslow, Hall. II. Tri-State Transportation Commission.
Planning Division.*   *NYPL [*ZT-1244]*

**Public acts of the General Assembly of the State
of Georgia.** Georgia. Laws, statutes, etc.
Atlanta, Ga. , 1899. 329 p. ;   LC Card 79-118475
DDC 348.758/023 19
KFG25.2 1896

PUBLIC ADMINISTRATION.
Gunn, Elizabeth M. Ethics and the public
service . Norman, Okla. [1980] 47 p. ;   LC
Card 80-623689   DDC 016.35 19
Z7164.A2 G86 JF1525.E8

United Nations. Dept. of Technical
Co-operation for Development. Handbook on
the improvement of administrative management
in public administration . New York , 1979. vii,
67 p. :   LC Card 80-119207   DDC 300 s
350.007/5/091724 19
JX1977 .A2 ST/ESA/SER.E/19

**PUBLIC ADMINISTRATION -
BIBLIOGRAPHY.**
Gunn, Elizabeth M. Ethics and the public
service . Norman, Okla. [1980] 47 p. ;   LC
Card 80-623689   DDC 016.35 19
Z7164.A2 G86 JF1525.E8

**PUBLIC ADMINISTRATION - COST
EFFECTIVENESS - CONGRESSES.**
Workshop on Research Needed to Improve the
Quality of Socioeconomic Data Used in
Regulatory Decisionmaking, Library of
Congress, 1979. Workshop on Research Needed
to Improve the Quality of Socioeconomic Data
Used in Regulatory Decisionmaking .
Washington , 1980. xiii, 296 p. ;   LC Card
80-602262   DDC 361.6/1/072073 19
H22 .W67 1979

**PUBLIC ADMINISTRATION - FORMS,
BLANKS, ETC.**
Washington (State). Legislature. Budget
Committee. State forms management program
/. Olympia [1979] v, 57 p. ;   LC Card 79-626055
DDC 353.97970072/32 s 353.97970071/4 19
HJ11 .W2453 no. 79-4 JK9249.P36

**PUBLIC ADMINISTRATION - RESEARCH -
UNITED STATES - CONGRESSES.**
Public Management Research Conference,
Brookings Institution, 1979. Setting public
management research agendas . [Washington,
D.C.] [1980] iv, 95 p. :   LC Card 80-602841
DDC 350/.00072/073 19
JF1338.A2 P85 1979

Public aid cost control. Illinois. General
Assembly. House of Representatives.
Democratic Staff. [Springfield, Ill.] [1980] 28
p. :   LC Card 80-623563   DDC 353.97730084 19
HV86 .I37 1980a

**Public assistance programs in the State of
Washington .** Washington (State). Dept. of
Social and Health Services. Division of Analysis
and Information Services. Olympia, Wash.
[1979] iv, 151 p. ;   LC Card 79-625823   DDC
361.6/09797 19
HV86 .W365 1979

**Public assistance recipients & cash payments by
state & county.** [Washington] 20-28 cm. (SSA
publication) Annual. Title varies slightly. Issued by the
Office of Research and Statistics of the Social Security
Administration.   LC Card 78-640797
*1. Public welfare - United States - Statistics -
Periodicals. 2. Child welfare - United States -
Statistics - Periodicals. I. United States. Social Security
Administration. Office of Research and Statistics.*
NYPL [JLM 81-20]

**Public assistance recipients and cash payments
by State and county-February 1979.** United
States. Social Security Administration. Office of
Research and Statistics. Washington, D.C. ,
1980. v, 85 p. ;   LC Card 80-600053   DDC
361/.973/0212 19
HV85 .U54 1980

Public assistance statistics. United States. Social
Security Administration. Office of Research and
Statistics. Mar. 1977- [Washington]   LC Card
77-643177   *NYPL [JLM 80-970]*

**Public attitudes toward community wastewater
reclamation and reuse options /.** Bruvold,
William H. Davis, Calif. , 1979. v, 51 p. ;   LC
Card 80-621184   DDC 333.91/009794 s 363.6/1
19
GB705.C2 C27 no. 179 TD429

**Public auditing techniques for performance
improvement .** United Nations/INTOSAI

Seminar on Government Auditing, Vienna,
1979. New York , 1980. iii, 108 p. ;   LC Card
80-130822   DDC 300 s 351.72/32 19
JX1977 .A2 ST/ESA/SER.E/20

Public building needs . United States. Congress.
House. Committee on Public Works and
Transportation. Subcommittee on Public
Buildings and Grounds. Washington , 1980. vi,
430 p. :   LC Card 81-600628   DDC 353.0086/2 19
KF27 .P8964 1980

**PUBLIC BUILDINGS - ILLINOIS - ENERGY
CONSERVATION.**
Illinois Institute of Natural Resources. Illinois
State plan, energy conservation in institutions .
[Springfield, Ill.] [Springfield, Va. , 1979 or
1980] ii, 76 p. :   LC Card 80-622576   DDC 333.79
19
TJ163.5.B84 I43 1979

**PUBLIC BUILDINGS - NEW YORK (STATE) -
ENERGY CONSERVATION.**
New York (State). Legislative Commission on
Expenditure Review. Energy use in state
facilities . [Albany] [1980] 6, ii, 50 p. :   LC
Card 80-623042   DDC 333.79 19
TJ163.5.B84 N48 1980

**PUBLIC BUILDINGS - NEW YORK (STATE) -
ENERGY CONSUMPTION.**
New York (State). Legislative Commission on
Expenditure Review. Energy use in state
facilities . [Albany] [1980] 6, ii, 50 p. :   LC
Card 80-623042   DDC 333.79 19
TJ163.5.B84 N48 1980

Public buildings proposals . United States.
Congress. Senate. Committee on Environment
and Public Works. Washington , 1980. iv, 318
p. :   LC Card 80-603295   DDC 353.0086/2 19
KF26 .E6 1980g

**Public community colleges and vocational schools
factbook.** New Mexico. Board of Educational
Finance--Commission of Postsecondary
Education. Factbook on New Mexico public
two-year community colleges and vocational
schools, 1978-79. Santa Fe, N.M. [1979] vi, 90
p. :   LC Card 80-622001   DDC 379.1/552/09789 19
LC1046.N45 N47 1979

PUBLIC CONTRACTS - UNITED STATES.
Consultants and contractors . Washington, D.C.
[1977] viii, 610 p. :   LC Card 81-601555   DDC
353/.0722 19
JK468.C7 C666

United States. Congress. House. Committee on
Government Operations. Government Activities
and Transportation Subcommittee. Amending
the Federal Property and Administrative
Services Act of 1949 . Washington , 1980. iii,
224 p. :   LC Card 80-604062   DDC
346.73/023/0262 347.30230262 19
KF27 .G6626 1980a

United States. Congress. House. Committee on
Government Operations. Legislation and
National Security Subcommittee. Limitation on
yearend obligations . Washington , 1980. iv,
237 p. :   LC Card 80-602718   DDC 342.73/068 19
KF27 .G6676 1980c

United States. Congress. House. Committee on
Small Business. Subcommittee on General
Oversight and Minority Enterprise. Contracting
out/government competition . Washington ,
1980. iv, 276 p. :   LC Card 81-600619   DDC
353.0071/1 19
KF27 .S64 1980i

United States. Congress. House. Committee on
Small Business. Subcommittee on General
Oversight and Minority Enterprise. Task Force
on Minority Enterprise. Minority truckers
participation in Federal procurement contracts .
Washington , 1980. iv, 107 p. ;   LC Card
80-603017   DDC 346.73/023 19
KF27 .S64 1980c

United States. Congress. House. Committee on
Small Business. Subcommittee on General
Oversight and Minority Enterprise. Small
business preferential procurement programs .
Washington , 1980 [i.e. 1981] iii, 640 p. :   LC
Card 81-600845   DDC 353.0071/2 19
KF27 .S64 1980l

United States. Congress. House. Committee on
the Budget. Task Force on Government
Efficiency. Consultant and service contracts .
Washington , 1980 [i.e. 1981] iii, 140 p. ;   LC

Card 81-600948 DDC 353.0071/1 19
KF27 .B847 1980

United States. Congress. Senate. Committee on Governmental Affairs. Consultant Reform Act of 1980 . Washington , 1981. iv, 668 p. ; LC Card 81-601616 DDC 342.73/068 347.30268 19
KF26 .G67 1980o

United States. Congress. Senate. Committee on Governmental Affairs. Oversight of GPO's direct deal printing procurement system . Washington , 1980. iii, 94 p. : LC Card 80-602743 DDC 353.0081/9 19
KF26 .G67 1980c

United States. Congress. Senate. Committee on Governmental Affairs. Subcommittee on Civil Service and General Services. Federal consulting service contracts . Washington , 1980- v. ; LC Card 80-603411 DDC 353.09/3 19
KF26 .G6724 1980

United States. Congress. Senate. Committee on Governmental Affairs. Subcommittee on Federal Spending Practices and Open Government. Continued oversight of the Small Business Association's [i.e. Administration's] 8 (a) program . Washington , 1980. iii, 105 p. ; LC Card 80-603071 DDC 353.0082/048 19
KF26 .G6732 1979j

United States. Congress. Senate. Committee on the Judiciary. Subcommittee on Limitations of Contracted and Delegated Authority. Federal use of contractors and consultants . Washington , 1981. iv, 342 p. ; LC Card 81-601757 DDC 353/.0722 19
KF26 .J857 1980

United States. Congress. Senate. Select Committee on Small Business. H.R. 5612, to amend the Small Business Act to extend the current SBA 8(a) pilot program . Washington , 1980. iii, 211 p. : LC Card 80-604024 DDC 346.73/0652 347.306652 19
KF26.5 S6 1980u

United States. Dept. of Health, Education, and Welfare. Cost principles and procedures for establishing indirect cost and other rates for grants and contracts with the Department of Health, Education, and Welfare . Washington , 1974. vii, 64 p. ; *NYPL [JLF 80-867]*

United States. General Accounting Office. Contracting for computer software development serious problems require management attention to avoid wasting additional millions . [Washington, D.C.] , 1979. v, 84 p. ; LC Card 79-604267 DDC 353.0071/1 19
JK468.A8 U5 1979a

United states. Office of Federal Contract Compliance Programs. Task Force. A preliminary report on the revitalization of the Federal Contract Compliance Program. Washington , 1977. xxix, 301 p. ; LC Card 78-602378
KF3464 .A86 *NYPL [JLF 81-198]*

PUBLIC CONTRACTS - UNITED STATES - CASES.
Procurement law case book . [Charlottesville] , 1957 [i.e. 1958] iii, 390 p. ; LC Card 79-107788 DDC 346.73/023 347.30623 19
KF845 .P76 1958

PUBLIC CONTRACTS - UNITED STATES - CONGRESSES.
Scholars as contractors . Washington , 1979. 265 p. in various pagings : LC Card 79-603005
CC136 .S36 *NYPL [JLF 81-76]*

Stimulating government utilization of sheltered workshops /. Memphis [1977] xiv, 319 p. : LC Card 78-622547
HD7256.U5 S83 *NYPL [JLE 81-488]*

Workshop on Management Techniques Applied to Archeology, Texas Tech University, 1977. Scholars as managers, or how can the managers do it better . Washington , 1978. vii, 21 p., [2] leaves of plates : LC Card 79-602641
CC51 .W67 1977

PUBLIC CORPORATIONS. see CORPORATIONS.

Public debt limit . United States. Congress. Senate. Committee on Finance. Subcommittee on Taxation and Debt Management Generally. Washington , 1980 [i.e. 1981] iii, 27 p. ; LC Card 81-601333 DDC 336.3/46/0973 19
KF26 .F5695 1980i

Public debt limit--1981 . United States. Congress. Senate. Committee on Finance. Subcommittee on Taxation and Debt Management. Washington , 1981. iii, 86 p. ; LC Card 81-600957 DDC 336.3/46/0973 19
KF26 .F5694 1981

PUBLIC DEBTS. see DEBTS, PUBLIC.

PUBLIC DEFENDERS - NEW JERSEY - PERIODICALS.
New Jersey. Dept. of the Public Advocate. Annual report. [Trenton, N. J.] LC Card 77-643225 *NYPL [JLM 80-1143]*

PUBLIC DOCUMENTS. see GOVERNMENT PUBLICATIONS.

Public easements under the Alaska native claims settlement act . Joint Federal-State Land Use Planning Commission for Alaska. Anchorage, Alaska , 1979. 181 p. ; LC Card 79-624668 DDC 346.79804/32/08997 19
KFA1650 .J64

PUBLIC ENTERPRISES. see GOVERNMENT BUSINESS ENTERPRISES.

PUBLIC FINANCE. see FINANCE, PUBLIC.

Public full-time professional staff average salaries for the 1978-79 school year. Maine. Dept. of Educational and Cultural Services. Division of Planning and Management Information. Local Administrative Unit. State of Maine public full-time professional staff average salaries for the 1978-79 school year /. [Augusta] [1979?] iv, 47 p. ; LC Card 79-622302 DDC 331.2/813711/009741 19
LB2842.2 .M338 1979

The Public grain warehouse and warehouse receipts act ; Rules and regulations. Illinois. Laws, statutes, etc. Springfield, Ill. [1973?] 13 p. ; LC Card 80-622697 DDC 343.773/07631 19
KFI1484.A335 A2 1973

PUBLIC HEALTH ADMINISTRATION - ILLINOIS.
Illinois. Dept. of Public Health. 1981 plan, phase 1, 1979-81. [Springfield] [1980] 153, 21 p. : LC Card 80-623321 DDC 353.9773008/41 19
RA54 .D45 1980

PUBLIC HEALTH ADMINISTRATION - NORTH CAROLINA.
Kaiser, Donald L. (Donald Lance), 1945- The empirical examination of administrative roles in local health departments /. Chapel Hill, NC , c1981. p. cm. ISBN 0-89055-309-2 LC Card 81-9806 DDC 362.1/068 19
RA5 .K34

PUBLIC HEALTH ADMINISTRATION - RESEARCH.
Kaiser, Donald L. (Donald Lance), 1945- The empirical examination of administrative roles in local health departments /. Chapel Hill, NC , c1981. p. cm. ISBN 0-89055-309-2 LC Card 81-9806 DDC 362.1/068 19
RA5 .K34

PUBLIC HEALTH ADVISORY GROUPS - UNITED STATES.
Little (Arthur D.) inc. An evaluation of the operation of subarea advisory councils /. [Hyattsville, Md.] [Springfield, Va.] 1979. x, 299 p. ; LC Card 79-603995
RA395.A3 L57 1979 *NYPL [JLF 81-358]*

PUBLIC HEALTH - ALASKA.
Alaska. Statewide Health Coordinating Council. Approved State health plan for Alaksa; /. Juneau, Alaska , 1980. 455 p. in various pagings : LC Card 80-622664 DDC 362.1/09798 19
RA395.A4 A45 1980

Public health and safety effects of high-voltage overhead transmission lines . Banks, Robert S. Minneapolis , 1977. 180 p. in various pagings : LC Card 81-456124 DDC 363.1/89 19
RA569.3 .B36

PUBLIC HEALTH - CALIFORNIA.
California. County Health Care Costs Study. Health care costs and services in California counties . Sacramento, Calif. , 1978. xx, 136 p. : LC Card 78-623918
RA412.5.U6 C29 1978 *NYPL [JLF 81-148]*

PUBLIC HEALTH - DICTIONARIES.
Health resources dictionary /. Baltimore, Md. (501 Saint Paul Pl., Suite 1000, Baltimore, Md., 21202) , c1980. 93 p. ; LC Card 81-101546

DDC 362.1/032/1 19
RA423 .H45

PUBLIC HEALTH - HAWAII.
Hawaii. Dept. of Health. State functional plan for health . [Honolulu] [1980] xiv, 280, [110] p. : LC Card 80-623119 DDC 362.1/09969 19
RA395.A4 H32 1980

Hawaii. Statewide Health Coordinating Council. Hawaii State health plan. [Honolulu] [1980] ca. 400 p. in various pagings : LC Card 80-622185 DDC 362.1/09969 19
RA395.A4 H34 1980

PUBLIC HEALTH - ILLINOIS - FINANCE.
Illinois. Dept. of Public Health. 1980 plan, phase 1, 1978-80 /. [Springfield, Ill.] [1980] 101 p. : LC Card 80-623062 DDC 353.97730084/1 19
RA447.I3 I44 1980

PUBLIC HEALTH - INDIANA.
Indiana. Statewide Health Coordinating Council. Indiana plan for health, 1979-1984 /. Indianapolis, IN [1979- v. <1, pt. A-B> ; LC Card 80-623458 DDC 362.1/09772 19
RA395.A4 I653 1979

PUBLIC HEALTH LABORATORIES - UNITED STATES - DIRECTORIES.
Directory of personnel responsible for radiological health programs. Rockville, Md..
  NYPL [JLL 80-243]

PUBLIC HEALTH LAWS, INTERNATIONAL.
United States. Congress. Senate. Committee on Labor and Human Resources. Subcommittee on Health and Scientific Research. International Health Act of 1980 . Washington , 1980. iii, 147 p. ; LC Card 81-600608 DDC 344.73/04 347.3044 19
KF26 .L274 1980k

PUBLIC HEALTH LAWS - MASSACHUSETTS.
Massachusetts. Laws, statutes, etc. Manual of laws pertaining to public health, 1980. Boston [1980] cx, 2214 p. ; LC Card 80-122554 DDC 344.744/04/02632 19
KFM2754 .A3 1980

PUBLIC HEALTH LAWS - OHIO.
Ohio. Laws, statutes, etc. Ohio public health manual, annotated. [Columbus] , 1980. 858 p. ; LC Card 80-623836 DDC 344.771/04/02632 19
KFO354 .A3 1980

PUBLIC HEALTH LAWS - SOUTH DAKOTA.
South Dakota. Legislature. Health Rules Sunset Committee. Final report of the Health Rules Sunset Committee /. Pierre, S.D. [1980] iii, 26 p. ; LC Card 80-622825 DDC 344.783/04 19
KFS3011.62 .H43 1980

PUBLIC HEALTH LAWS - UNITED STATES.
Becker, Dorothy D. Health professions legislation . [Hyattsville, Md?] , 1980. 1 v. in various pagings ; LC Card 81-601013 DDC 344.73/041 347.30441 19
KF2905 .A372

United States. Compilation of selected acts within the jurisdiction of the Committee on Energy and Commerce /. Washington , 1981. 4 v. ; LC Card 81-601845 DDC 344.73/04/02632 347.304402632 19
KF3775 .A3 1981

United States. Laws, statutes, etc. Compilation of selected acts within the jurisdiction of the Committee on Interstate and Foreign Commerce . Washington , 1980- v. ; LC Card 80-601741 DDC 344.73/04/02632 19
KF3775 .A3 1980

PUBLIC HEALTH - LOUISIANA.
Louisiana. Division of Health Planning and Development. Louisiana revised 1980 State health plan. [Baton Rouge, La. , Springfield, Va. , 1980] iv, 182 p. ; LC Card 80-622412 DDC 362.1/09763 19
RA395.A4 L835 1980

PUBLIC HEALTH - NEW HAMPSHIRE - PERIODICALS.
New Hampshire. Dept. of Health and Welfare. Biennial report. [Concord]
  NYPL [JLM 80-829]

PUBLIC HEALTH - NEW YORK (STATE)
New York (State). Governor, 1975- (Carey) State of the health message . [Albany] [1980] 25 p. ; LC Card 80-623008 DDC 362.1/09747 19
RA395.A4 N76213 1980

PUBLIC HEALTH - NORTH CAROLINA.
North Carolina. Health Coordinating Council.
The North Carolina State health plan /.
[Raleigh] [1979] 431 p. ; LC Card 80-621910
DDC 362.1/09756 19
RA395.A4 N795 1979

**PUBLIC HEALTH - OHIO - CLEVELAND
REGION.**
Metropolitan Health Planning Corporation.
Health systems plan, 1980. Cleveland, Ohio
(908 Standard Bldg., Cleveland 44113) , c1979.
xvi, 151 p. : LC Card 81-159152 DDC
362.1/09771/3 19
RA395.A4 O25 1979

PUBLIC HEALTH - OKLAHOMA.
Oklahoma. State Health Coordinating Council.
1980 Oklahoma State health plan /. [Oklahoma
City , 1980] v, 842 p. : LC Card 80-622403
DDC 362.1/09766 19
RA395.A4 O535 1980

**PUBLIC HEALTH - PENNSYLVANIA -
FINANCE - STATISTICS.**
Pennsylvania. Dept. of Education. Estimates of
school district subsidies payable 1979-80 .
[Harrisburg] , 1979. v, 20 leaves ; LC Card
80-621560 DDC 379.1/3/09748 19
LB2826.P4 P373 1979

**PUBLIC HEALTH PERSONNEL - TRAINING
OF - UNITED STATES.**
United States. Health Resources Administration.
Bureau of Health Manpower. A report on
public and community health personnel .
Washington, D.C. , 1980. viii, 220 p. ; LC Card
80-602370 DDC 331.12/913621 19
RA440.9 .U47 1980

**PUBLIC HEALTH PERSONNEL - UNITED
STATES.**
United States. Health Resources Administration.
Bureau of Health Manpower. A report on
public and community health personnel .
Washington, D.C. , 1980. viii, 220 p. ; LC Card
80-602370 DDC 331.12/913621 19
RA440.9 .U47 1980

**PUBLIC HEALTH PERSONNEL - UNITED
STATES - DIRECTORIES.**
Directory of personnel responsible for
radiological health programs. Rockville, Md..
NYPL [JLL 80-243]

**PUBLIC HEALTH PERSONNEL - UNITED
STATES - SUPPLY AND DEMAND.**
United States. Health Resources Administration.
Bureau of Health Manpower. A report on
public and community health personnel .
Washington, D.C. , 1980. viii, 220 p. ; LC Card
80-602370 DDC 331.12/913621 19
RA440.9 .U47 1980

PUBLIC HEALTH - PLANNING. see
HEALTH PLANNING.

PUBLIC HEALTH SERVICES. see PUBLIC
HEALTH.

PUBLIC HEALTH - SOUTH DAKOTA.
South Dakota. Statewide Health Coordinating
Council. South Dakota state plan for health,
1980-1985. [Pierre, S.D.] , 1980. 334 p. in
various pagings : LC Card 80-623024 DDC
362.1/09783 19
RA395.A4 S68 1980

**PUBLIC HEALTH - STUDY AND TEACHING
(GRADUATE) - UNITED STATES -
STATISTICS.**
Hall, Thomas L. Schools of public health .
[Washington] [1980] vi, 58 p. ; LC Card
80-602405 DDC 614/.07/1173 19
RA440.7.U6 H34

PUBLIC HEALTH - SURVEYS. see HEALTH
SURVEYS.

PUBLIC HEALTH - TEXAS.
Texas. Statewide Health Coordinating Council.
The Texas state health plan /. [Austin] [1980]
ca. 300 p. in various pagings : LC Card
80-623084 DDC 362.1/09764 19
RA395.A4 T4886 1980

PUBLIC HEALTH - UNITED STATES.
Institute of Medicine. Healthy people .
Washington , 1979. viii, 484 p. : LC Card
79-603264
RA445 .I57 1979   **NYPL [JLD 80-3780]**

Promoting health/preventing disease .
[Washington, D.C.?] , 1980. xiv, 197 p. ; LC

Card 80-604164 DDC 362.1/0973 19
RA445 .P7

PUBLIC HEALTH - VIRGINIA.
Virginia. Statewide Health Coordinating
Council. State health plan, Commonwealth of
Virginia /. [Richmond, Va.] [1979] 2 v. : LC
Card 80-620762 DDC 362.1/09755 19
RA395.A4 V88 1979

**PUBLIC HEALTH - WASHINGTON (STATE) -
INFORMATION SERVICES -
WASHINGTON (STATE) -
DIRECTORIES.**
Health Policy Analysis Program (Wash.) The
yellow pages . Seattle, Wash. [1978] v, 80
leaves ; LC Card 79-621291 DDC 362.1/09797 19
RA407.4.W3 H4 1978

**PUBLIC HEALTH - WASHINGTON (STATE) -
STATISTICAL SERVICES -
DIRECTORIES.**
Health Policy Analysis Program (Wash.) The
yellow pages . Seattle, Wash. [1978] v, 80
leaves ; LC Card 79-621291 DDC 362.1/09797 19
RA407.4.W3 H4 1978

**Public hearing before Assembly Agriculture and
Environment Committee, on A-966 (the
Radiation emergency response act), held April
8, 1980, Assembly Chamber, State House,
Trenton, New Jersey.** New Jersey. Legislature.
General Assembly. Committee on Agriculture
and Environment. [Trenton] [1980] 79 p. in
various pagings ; LC Card 80-623636 DDC
344.749/0472 19
KFN1811.4 .A3 1980

**Public hearing before Assembly Agriculture and
Environment Committee on AR-51 .** New
Jersey. State Legislature. General Assembly.
Committee on Agriculture and Environment.
Trenton, N.J. [1980] 2, 74, 112 p. : LC Card
81-620749 DDC 344.749/04633 347.49044633
19
KFN1811.4 .A3 1980b

**Public hearing before Assembly Agriculture and
Environment Committee on Assembly no.
3037 .** New Jersey. Legislature. General
Assembly. Committee on Agriculture and
Environment. [Trenton] [1979] 4, 56, 21 p. ;
LC Card 79-624766
KFN1811.4 .A3 1979a   **NYPL [JLF 80-1295]**

**Public hearing before Assembly Agriculture and
Environment Committee on Assembly
resolution no. 3017 .** New Jersey. Legislature.
General Assembly. Committee on Agriculture
and Environment. [Trenton] [1979] 32, 93 p. ;
LC Card 79-624638
KFN1811.4 .A3 1979

**Public hearing before Assembly Agriculture and
Environment Committee, on Assembly no. 1818
(Natural resources bond issue) .** New Jersey.
Legislature. General Assembly. Committee on
Agriculture and Environment. [Trenton] [1980]
24, 6 p. ; LC Card 80-623796 DDC 344.749/046
347.490446 19
KFN1811.4 .A3 1980a

**Public hearing before Assembly County
Government Committee on mandated costs of
caps legislation .** New Jersey. Legislature.
General Assembly. County Government
Committee. [Trenton] [1980] 27, 3 p. ; LC
Card 80-622531 DDC 343.749/03 19
KFN1811.4 .C68 1980

**Public hearing before Assembly County
Government Committee on mandated costs of
caps legislation .** New Jersey. Legislature.
General Assembly. County Government
Commmittee. [Trenton] [1980] 40, 5 p. ; LC
Card 80-623641 DDC 352.1/232/09749 19
KFN1811.4 .C68 1980a

**Public hearing before Assembly Energy and
Natural Resources Committee on A-1825, Dune
and shorefront protection act.** New Jersey.
Legislature. General Assembly. Energy and
Natural Resources Committee. [Trenton] [1980]
2 v. ; LC Card 80-623987 DDC 346.74904/6917
347.490646917 19
KFN1811.4 .E53 1980

**Public hearing before Assembly Energy and
Natural Resources Committee on AR-13,
co-generation of electricity, held March 27,
1980, Assembly Chamber, State House,
Trenton, New Jersey.** New Jersey. Legislature.
General Assembly. Energy and Natural

Resources Committee. Trenton, N.J. [1980] 27,
4 p. ; LC Card 80-624084 DDC 343.749/0929
347.4903929 19
KFN1811.4 .E53 1980a

**Public hearing before Assembly Energy and
Natural Resources Committee on Assembly,
no. 728 (Blue Acres Bond issue) held March
20, 1978, Wayne Township Municipal Building,
Wayne, New Jersey.** New Jersey. Legislature.
General Assembly. Energy and Natural
Resources Committee. [Trenton] [1978?] 38
p. ; LC Card 79-624644 DDC 343.749/0924
347.4903924 19
KFN1811.4 .E53 1978b

**Public hearing before Assembly Institutions,
Health, and Welfare Committee on A-1823
(Institutional bond issue) .** New Jersey.
Legislature. General Assembly. Committee on
Institutions, Health & Welfare. [Trenton]
[1980] 3 v. ; LC Card 80-623827 DDC 336.3/1
19
KFN1811.4 .I58 1980

**Public hearing before Assembly Institutions,
Health, and Welfare Committee on allegations
of abuse at New Lisbon State School, held
April 20, 1979 ... New Lisbon State School,
New Lisbon, New Jersey.** New Jersey.
Legislature. General Assembly. Committee on
Institutions, Health & Welfare. [Trenton, N.J.]
[1979] 87, 4 p. ; LC Card 79-625977 DDC
362.3/09749 19
KFN1811.4 .I58 1979a

**Public hearing before Assembly Labor
Committee, on unemployment compensation .**
New Jersey. Legislature. General Assembly.
Labor Committee. [Trenton] [1980]- v. ; LC
Card 80-622509 DDC 368.4/4/009749 19
KFN1811.4 .L24 1980

**Public hearing before Assembly Legislative
Oversight Committee on the licensing of casino
employees .** New Jersey. Legislature. General
Assembly. Legislative Oversight Committee.
[Trenton, N.J.] [1979] 86 p. ; LC Card
80-620969 DDC 353.97490076 19
KFN1811.4 .L4 1979a

**Public hearing before Assembly Municipal
Government Committee on Assembly bill 1819
(storm water management) .** New Jersey.
Legislature. General Assembly. Municipal
Government Committee. [Trenton] [1979?]
3,60 p. ; LC Card 80-621670 DDC 346.74904/691
347.49064691 19
KFN1811.4 .M8 1979c

**Public hearing before Assembly Revenue,
Finance, and Appropriations Committee on
ACR-29 .** New Jersey. Legislature. General
Assembly. Revenue, Finance, and
Appropriations Committee. [Trenton] [1980] 3,
9, 23 p. ; LC Card 80-623639 DDC 343.74905/4
347.490354 19
KFN1811.4 .R45 1980a

**Public hearing before Assembly Revenue,
Finance, and Appropriations Committee on
Assembly Resolution Number 50 (memorializes
Congress to transfer funding from unnecessary
military spending to domestic spending for
human services) .** New Jersey. State
Legislature. General Assembly. Revenue,
Finance, and Appropriations Committee.
[Trenton] [1980] 49, 23x p. ; LC Card
81-621305 DDC 353.97490084 19
KFN1811.4 .R45 1980b

**Public hearing before Assembly State
Government, Federal and Interstate Relations,
and Veterans Affairs Committee on Assembly
bill No. 1201 .** New Jersey. Legislature.
General Assembly. State Government, Federal
and Interstate Relations, and Veterans' Affairs
Committee. [Trenton] [1980] 10, 32, 4 p. ;
LC Card 80-622529 DDC 344.749/0542 19
KFN1811.4 .S78 1980

**Public hearing before Assembly Task Force on
the Impact of the 1980 Recession .** New
Jersey. Legislature. General Assembly. Task
Force on the Impact of the 1980 Recession.
[Trenton] [1980] 37, 24 p. ; LC Card 80-623795
DDC 330.9749/043 19
KFN1811.4 .I56 1980

Public hearing before Commission on Individual Liberty and Personal Privacy, re: confidentiality and access to medical records, held November 8, 1978, Rutgers Law School, Newark, New Jersey. New Jersey. Commission on Individual Liberty and Personal Privacy. [Trenton] [1978] 21 p. : LC Card 79-624641
KFN2167.R4 A84 **NYPL [*XME-9450]**

Public hearing before Commission on Sex Discrimination in the Statutes on marriage and family law . New Jersey. Commission on Sex Discrimination in the Statutes. [Trenton] [1980] 37, 15, 134 p. : LC Card 80-622456 DDC 346.74901/5 19
KFN1894 .A83

Public hearing before Commission on Sex Discrimination in the Statutes on sex discrimination in marriage and family law . New Jersey. Commission on Sex Discrimination in the Statutes. [Trenton] [1980] 39, 19, 43 p. : LC Card 80-622457 DDC 346.74901/5 19
KFN1894 .A84

Public hearing before Senate Agriculture Committee on Senate no. 450 . New Jersey. Legislature. Senate. Agriculture Committee. [Trenton] [1980] 48, 10 p. : LC Card 80-621240 DDC 346.74904/676/0262 19
KFN1811.3 .A35 1979

Public hearing before Senate Education Committee on the impact of spending limitations on local school districts . New Jersey. Legislature. Senate. Sub-committee on Education. [Trenton , 1979?] 134 p. in various pagings ; LC Card 80-621237 DDC 379.1/222/09749 19
KFN1811.3 .E3 1979a

Public hearing before Senate Energy and Environment Committee on implementation of the Pinelands protection act (P.L. 1979, chapter 111) . New Jersey. Legislature. Senate. Committee on Energy and Environment. [Trenton, N.J.] [1980] 44, 32, 148 p. : LC Card 80-622507 DDC 353.7490082/326 19
KFN1811.3 .E5 1980

Public hearing before Senate Institutions, Health, and Welfare Committee and Assembly Institutions, Health, and Welfare Committee on rooming house fire in Bradley Beach . New Jersey. State Legislature. Senate. Institutions, Health, and Welfare Committee. [Trenton? , 1980?] 40, 35, 6 p. ; LC Card 80-623979 DDC 362.1/6 19
KFN1811.3 .I47 1980b

Public hearing before Senate Institutions, Health, and Welfare Committee, on Senate bill no. 352 (An act concerning the involuntary commitment of persons for treatment of mental disorders), held June 26, 1980, State House, Trenton, New Jersey. New Jersey. Legislature. Senate. Institutions, Health and Welfare Committee. [Trenton, N.J.] , 1980] 17, 29, 9 p. ; LC Card 80-623454 DDC 344.749/044 19
KFN1811.3 .I47 1980

Public hearing before Senate Judiciary Committee ... held June 30, 1980, room 223, State House, Trenton, New Jersey. New Jersey. Legislature. Senate. Judiciary Committee. Trenton, N.J. [1980] [40], 40, 58 p. ; LC Card 80-623800 DDC 328/.2 19
KFN1811.3 .J8 1980

Public hearing before Senate Judiciary Committee on SCR #83 (to amend the Constitution of New Jersey to provide that the members of the New Jersey Senate be elected every year in which a gubernatorial election is held) . New Jersey. Legislature. Senate. Judiciary Committee. [Trenton] [1980] 3, 3 p. ; LC Card 80-623640 DDC 342.749/055 347.490225 19
KFN1811.3 .J8 1980a

Public hearing before Senate Labor, Industry and Professions Committee and Assembly Banking and Insurance Committee on S-975 and A-755 (a bill to provide for the licensing and regulation of mortgage bankers, mortgage brokers, and mortgage solicitors by the Commissioner of Banking) . New Jersey. Legislature. Senate. Labor, Industry and Professions Committee. [Trenton] [1980] 9, 38, 27 p. ; LC Card 80-622489 DDC 346.74904/364 19
KFN1811.3 .L3 1980

Public hearing before Senate Labor, Industry and Professions Committee and Assembly Banking and Insurance Committee on S-975 and A-755. New Jersey. Legislature. Senate. Labor, Industry and Professions Committee. [Trenton, 1980] 38, 27 p. **NYPL [JLF 81-84]**

Public hearing before Senate Law, Public Safety, and Defense Committee, on Passaic Valley Sewerage Commission . New Jersey. State Legislature. Senate. Committee on Law, Public Safety, and Defense. [Trenton , 1980] 46, 16 p. ; LC Card 80-624390 DDC 352.6/2/097493 19
KFN1811.3 .L39 1980

Public hearing before Senate Revenue, Finance, and Appropriations Committee on SCR 90, held May 28, 1980, Assembly Chamber, State House, Trenton, New Jersey. New Jersey. Legislature. Senate. Revenue, Finance and Appropriations Committee. [Trenton] [1980] 13 p. ; LC Card 80-623722 DDC 343.749/054 347.490354 19
KFN1811.3 .R48 1980

Public hearing before Senate State Government Committee on S-874, a bill to create a Department of Commerce and Economic Development, held March 10, 1980, Archive Room, State Library, Trenton, New Jersey. New Jersey. Legislature. Senate. State Government Federal and Interstate Relations and Veterans Affairs Committee. [Trenton, N.J.] [1980] 27 p. ; LC Card 80-622530 DDC 343.749/07 19
KFN1811.3 .S7 1980

Public hearing before Senate State Government, Federal and Interstate Relations, and Veterans Affairs Committee on S-1396 and S-1397 (amending the Legislative Activities Disclosure Act and the Campaign Contributions Reporting Law), held, October 23, 1980, Assembly Chamber, State House, Trenton, New Jersey. New Jersey. State Legislature. Senate. State Government, Federal and Interstate Relations, and Veterans Affairs Committee. [Trenton] [1980] 9, 15, 4 p. ; LC Card 81-620747 DDC 342.749/052 347.490252 19
KFN1811.3 .S7 1980a

Public hearing before special subcommittee of the Assembly Judiciary, Law, Public Safety and Defense Committee on current practices in New Jersey liquor industry and question of price deregulation. New Jersey. Legislature. General Assembly. Judiciary, Law, Public Safety & Defense Committee. [Trenton] [1979] 2 v. ; LC Card 79-625827 DDC 353.97490076/1 19
KFN1811.4 .J78 1979b

Public hearing before sub-Committee of Assembly State Government Committee on the impact of casino gaming, held July 26, 1979, Commission Chambers, Atlantic City Hall, Atlantic City, New Jersey. New Jersey. Legislature. General Assembly. Committee on State Government. [Trenton] [1979] 42, 7 p. : LC Card 80-622488 DDC 353.97490076 19
KFN1811.4 .S78 1979b

Public hearing before subcommittee of Assembly Transportation and Communications Committee to investigate the transportation of radioactive cargo on highways within New Jersey (created pursuant to Assembly Resolution 3003), held August 21, 1979, Freeholders' Chambers, Bergen County Administration Building, Hackensack, New Jersey. New Jersey. Legislature. General Assembly. Transportation and Communications Committee. [Trenton] [1979?] 59, 10 p. ; LC Card 80-622508 DDC 343.749/093 19
KFN1811.4 .T7 1979

Public hearing before sub-Committee of the Senate Transportation and Communications Committee on role and responsibilities of the Port Authority of New York and New Jersey . New Jersey. State Legislature. Senate. Transportation and Communications Committee. [Trenton, N.J.] [1981] 75, 33 p. ; LC Card 81-621896 DDC 353.97490087/71 19
KFN1811.3 .T73 1980

Public hearing before Subcommittee on ACR-99 (amending the Constitution of the State of New Jersey to permit the Legislature to authorize by law and to regulate, control, and license the conduct, operation, and play of amusement games) of Assembly Judiciary, Law, Public Safety, and Defense Committee . New Jersey. State Legislature. General Assembly. Judiciary, Law, Public Safety, and Defense Committee. Subcommittee on ACR-99. [Trenton] [1980] 4, 12 p. ; LC Card 80-623977 DDC 344.749/0542 347.4904542 19
KFN1811.4 .J782 1980

Public hearing before Subcommittee on Business Concerns of the Assembly Labor Committee re: job training. New Jersey. Legislature General Assembly. Labor committee. Subcommittee on Business Concerns. [Trenton:"bs. n.], 1979. 29, 1x-14x; **NYPL [*XME-9334]**

Public hearing before Subcommittee on Business Concerns of the Assembly Labor Committee, re job training . New Jersey. Legislature General Assembly. Labor committee. Subcommittee on Business Concerns. [Trenton , 1980] 14 p. : LC Card 80-621236 DDC 331.25/924/09749 19
KFN1811.4 .L243 1979

Public hearing before Sub-committee on Health Care Costs of the Senate Institutions, Health, and Welfare Committee on scope and extent of health insurance coverage in New Jersey . New Jersey. State Legislature. Senate. Institutions, Health, and Welfare Committee. Sub-committee on Health Care Costs. [Trenton] [1980] 47, [47] p. ; LC Card 80-624339 DDC 344.749/022 347.490422 19
KFN1811.3 .I474 1980

Public hearing before the Senate Labor, Industry & Proffessions [sic] Committee and the Assembly Labor Committee on workers' compensation, administrative aspects . New Jersey. Legislature. Senate. Labor, Industry and Professions Committee. [Trenton] [1979] 30 p. ; LC Card 79-625599
KFN1811.3 .L3 1979 **NYPL [*XMF-13771]**

Public hearing on economic statistical indicators, indexing, proposed Federal Trade Commission, consumer credit rules and credit union, interest rates and costs of funds . California. Legislature. Assembly. Committee on Finance, Insurance, and Commerce. Sacramento, CA (Box 90, Sacramento 95814) [1980] 220 p. : LC Card 81-621157 DDC 332.7/09794 19
KFC10.4 .F56 1980

Public hearing on Indian children . California. Legislature. Assembly. Committee on Human Resources. Sacramento, CA [1979] ii, 133 p. ; LC Card 80-623743 DDC 344.794/032733/08997 19
KFC10.4 .H8 1979

Public hearing on permanent funding for domestic violence centers (AB 1946, Moore), Tuesday, October 23, 1979 ... Los Angeles, California /. California. Legislature. Assembly. Committee on Human Resources. Sacramento, CA [1979?] 198 p. : LC Card 80-623516 DDC 362.8/283 19
KFC10.4 .H8 1979a

PUBLIC HOUSING - ILLINOIS - CHICAGO METROPOLITAN AREA.
Peroff, Kathleen A. Gautreaux housing demonstration . Washington, D.C. [1979] x, 202 p. : LC Card 80-602934 DDC 363.5/1 19
HD7288.78.U52 C46

PUBLIC HOUSING - NEW YORK (STATE)
New York (State). Executive Dept. Division of Housing and Community Renewal. New York State comprehensive planning assistance program . New York, N.Y. [1978] ca. 100 p. in various pagings : LC Card 80-621895 DDC 363.5/8/09747 19
HD7303.N7 N393 1978

PUBLIC HOUSING - NEW YORK (STATE) - FINANCE.
State subsidized low rent public housing . Albany, N.Y. (111 Washington Ave., Albany 12210) [1980] 10, iii, 92 p. : LC Card 81-621642 DDC 363.5/8 19
HD7288.78.U52 N77

PUBLIC HOUSING - TEXAS.
Texas. Dept. of Community Affairs. Texas State housing plan /. [Austin , 1978] 137 p. : LC

Card 80-622869 DDC 363.5/8 19
HD7303.T4 T495 1978

PUBLIC HOUSING - UNITED STATES.
Jones, Ronald, 1945- Problems affecting
low-rent public housing projects . [Washington,
D.C.] [1979] x, 317 p. ; LC Card 80-600612
HD7293 .J66

Residents' satisfaction in HUD-assisted
housing . Washington [1979] ca. 200 p. in
various pagings : LC Card 79-601946
HD7293 .R372   **NYPL [JLF 81-344]**

**PUBLIC HOUSING - UNITED STATES -
COLLECTED WORKS.**
Rouse, W. Victor. Crime in public housing .
Washington, D.C. , 1978 [i.e. 1979- v. ; LC
Card 79-603818
HV6791 .R67

**PUBLIC HOUSING - UNITED STATES -
MANAGEMENT.**
United States. Congress. Senate. Committee on
Appropriations. Subcommittee on
HUD-Independent Agencies. Management of
HUD's multi-family properties, the Cliffton
Terrace case . Washington , 1980. iii, 375, vi
p. ; LC Card 80-602962 DDC
353.0086/5043/09753 19
KF26 .A6486 1979b

**PUBLIC HOUSING - UNITED STATES -
SECURITY MEASURES.**
Newman, Oscar. Factors influencing crime and
instability in urban housing developments /.
Washington, D.C. , 1980. xiii, 302 p. ; LC Card
81-600762 DDC 364.2/2 19
HD7293 .N485

PUBLIC HYGIENE. see PUBLIC HEALTH.

PUBLIC INSTITUTIONS - NEW JERSEY.
New Jersey. Legislature. General Assembly.
Committee on Institutions, Health & Welfare.
Public hearing before Assembly Institutions,
Health, and Welfare Committee on A-1823
(Institutional bond issue) . [Trenton] [1980] 3
v. ; LC Card 80-623827 DDC 336.3/1 19
KFN1811.4 .I58 1980

**PUBLIC INSTITUTIONS - TEXAS - ENERGY
CONSERVATION.**
Keeran, Duane. The proposed plan of the State
of Texas for technical assistance and energy
conservation measures available to schools,
hospitals, units of local government, and public
care institutions /. [Austin] [1979] xv, 64 p. ;
LC Card 80-621353 DDC 333.79/09764 19
HD9502.U53 T43

PUBLIC LAW - CALIFORNIA.
California. Laws, statutes, etc. Government
code . - North Highlands, Calif. [1980?] 2 v.
(xix, 1351 p.) :   **NYPL [JLE 80-2785]**

Public law 480 aid for refugees . United States.
Congress. Senate. Committee on Agriculture,
Nutrition, and Forestry. Subcommittee on
Foreign Agricultural Policy. Washington , 1980.
iii, 29 p. ; LC Card 80-602524 DDC
344.73/03287 19
KF26 .A3549 1980

**PUBLIC LIBRARIANS - CERTIFICATION -
TEXAS.**
Texas. State Board of Library Examiners.
Report to the Sunset Advisory Commission /.
[Austin] [1979] 67 leaves ; LC Card 80-620788
DDC 021.8/2 19
Z682.2.U5 T49 1979

**PUBLIC LIBRARIES - NEW JERSEY -
DIRECTORIES.**
New Jersey. Library Development Bureau. 1980
public-area library guide. [Trenton, N.J. , 1980]
ii, 102 p. ; LC Card 80-622726 DDC
027.4/025/749 19
Z732.N6 N53 1980

PUBLIC LIBRARIES - NORTH CAROLINA.
Phay, Robert E. The public library . [Chapel
Hill] , 1980. 69 p. : LC Card 81-620731 DDC
021.8/2/09756 19
Z681.5 .P45 1980

PUBLIC LIBRARIES - WISCONSIN.
Ross, Judith, 1947- Wisconsin public library
building survey for handicapped accessibility /.
Madison, WI [1979] 16, 2 p. ; LC Card
80-621510 DDC 727/.8/04209775 19
Z711.92.P5 R67

The public library . Phay, Robert E. [Chapel
Hill] , 1980. 69 p. : LC Card 81-620731 DDC

021.8/2/09756 19
Z681.5 .P45 1980

Public library usage in Illinois . Elrick and
Lavidge. Springfield , 1977. 31 p. : LC Card
78-620783 DDC 302.2/3 19
HE8700.7.A8 E57 1977 suppl

**Public Library, Winnetka, Ill. Genealogy
Projects Committee.**
An index to the names of persons appearing in
History of Alexander, Union and Pulaski
counties, Illinois. (Edited by William Henry
Perrin. Chicago ... 1883) Thomson, Ill. :
Heritage House [1973] 129 p.; 28 cm. LC Card
75-116464
*1. Alexander County, Ill. - History. 2. Union County,
Ill. - History. 3. Pulaski County, Ill. - History. I. Perrin,
William Henry, d. 1892? History of Alexander, Union,
and Pulaski counties, Illinois. II. Title. III. Title: History
of Alexander, Union and Pulaski counties, Illinois.*
**NYPL [IVF (Alexander) (Perrin, W. H.
History of Alexander, Union ... counties,
Ill. Index)]**

An index to the names of persons appearing in
The History of Gallatin, Saline, Hamilton,
Franklin and Williamson Counties, Illinois.
(Chicago, The Goodspeed Pub. Co., 1887).
Thomson, Ill. : Heritage House [c1973] 122 p. ;
28 cm.
*1. Gallatin County, Ill. - Genealogy. 2. Saline County,
Ill. - Genealogy. 3. Williamson County, Ill. -
Genealogy. 4. Franklin County, Ill. - Genealogy. 5.
Williamson County, Ill. - Genealogy. I. Title. II. Title:
History of Gallatin, Saline, Hamilton, Franklin and
Williamson Counties, Illinois.*
NYPL [APR (Gallatin Co., Ill.) 80-1987]

Public Management and Research, inc. Viano,
Emilio. Victim/witness services . [Washington,
D.C.] , 1979. 69 p. ;
HV6250.3.U5 V49   **NYPL [JLF 81-398]**

**Public Management Research Conference,
Brookings Institution, 1979.** Setting public
management research agendas : integrating the
sponsor, producer, and user : proceedings for
[sic] the Public Management Research
Conference, November 19-20, 1979, Brookings
Institution, Washington, D.C. / co-sponsored by
the General Accounting Office ... [et al.].
[Washington, D.C.] : U. S. Office of Personnel
Management, [1980] iv, 95 p. : ports. ; 28 cm.
(OPM document ; 127-53-1) "February 1980."
Bibliography: p. 59-60. LC Card 80-602841 DDC
350/.00072/073 19
*1. Public administration - Research - United States -
Congresses. I. United States. General Accounting
Office. II. Series: United States. Office of Personnel
Management. OPM document , 127-53-1. III. Title.*
JF1338.A2 P85 1979

PUBLIC OPINION - ALASKA.
National Survey Research Group, New York.
Survey report on the economic impact of D2
lands restrictions and the public view of
alternative uses of State capital expenditures to
offset such effects /. Juneau, Alaska [1980] i,
49 p. : LC Card 80-622486 DDC 333.1/09798 19
HD243.A3 N37 1980

PUBLIC OPINION - UNITED STATES.
Attitudes toward the mentally ill . Rockville,
Md. (5600 Fisher Lane, Rockville, Md.,
20857) , Washington, D.C. , 1980. ix, 76 p. ;
LC Card 80-600135 DDC 362.2/042 19
RC455.2.P85 A85

Baldassare, Mark. The growth dilemma .
Berkeley , c1981. p. cm. ISBN 0-520-04302-2
LC Card 81-1449 DDC 304.6/2/0973 19
HB3505 .B298

Campbell, Angus, 1910- The sense of well-being
in America . New York , c1981. xiii, 263 p. ;
ISBN 0-07-009683-X LC Card 80-14379
HN59 .C29   **NYPL [JLE 81-367]**

DuBow, Fred. Reactions to crime . Washington,
D.C. , 1980. viii, 90 p. ; LC Card 80-602129
DDC 364.1/01/9 19
HV6791 .D82

Turner, Thomas Reed, 1941- Beware the people
weeping . Baton Rouge , c1982. p. cm. ISBN
0-8071-0986-X . LC Card 81-14252 DDC
973.7/092/4 19
E457.5 .T96

United States. Congress. House. Committee on
Government Operations. Subcommittee on
Government Information and Individual Rights.

Public reaction to privacy issues . Washington ,
c1980 [i.e. 1981] iii, 153 p. ; LC Card 81-600838
DDC 323.44/8/0973 19
KF27 .G6628 1979c

**The public papers of Governor Bert T. Combs,
1959-1963 /.** Combs, Bert T., 1911- Lexington ,
c1979. xxvi, 539 p., [1] leaf of plates : ISBN
0-8131-0604-4 : LC Card 78-58103
J87 .K417 1959   **NYPL [ITY 80-2687]**

**Public participation practices of the U. S. Army
Corps of Engineers /.** Crist, Charles E. Fort
Collins, Colo. , 1979. vi, 123 p. ; LC Card
79-626247 DDC 333.91/15/0973 19
TC423 .C76

Public personnel management . United States.
Office of Personnel Management. Library.
Washington , 1979. 77 p. ; LC Card 79-601906
Z7164.C6 U66 1979 JK765
NYPL [JLF 81-315]

Public policy & chronic disease : a forum /
sponsored by the National Arthritis Advisory
Board. [Washington] : U. S. Dept. of Health,
Education, and Welfare, Public Health Service,
National Institutes of Health, 1979. x, 122 p. :
ill. ; 28 cm. (NIH publication. no. 79-1896) LC
Card 79-602729
*1. Chronic diseases - United States. 2. Chronically ill -
Care and treatment - United States. 3. Arthritis -
United States. 4. Medical policy - United States. I.
United States. National Arthritis Advisory Board.*
RA644.6 .P82   **NYPL [JLF 81-366]**

Public policy and the frail elderly . United
States. Federal Council on the Aging.
Washington, D.C. , 1979. viii, 170 p. ; LC Card
80-600607
HV1457 .U52 1979   **NYPL [JLF 81-261]**

**Public policy for the management of groundwater
in the coastal plain of North Carolina /.**
Sherwani, Jabbar K. [Raleigh, N.C.] [1980] xv,
63 p. : LC Card 80-623572 DDC 333.91/009756 s
333.91/04/09756 19
HD1694.N8 N6 no. 158 TD224.N8

**PUBLIC POLICY MANAGEMENT. see
POLICY SCIENCES.**

Public Policy Research Organization. Matthews,
Joseph R. A survey of EDP performance
measurement for local government . - Irvine,
Calif. , 1975. iii, 31 p. :   **NYPL [*XME-9422]**

Public reaction to privacy issues . United States.
Congress. House. Committee on Government
Operations. Subcommittee on Government
Information and Individual Rights.
Washington , c1980 [i.e. 1981] iii, 153 p. ; LC
Card 81-600838 DDC 323.44/8/0973 19
KF27 .G6628 1979c

PUBLIC RECORDS.
International Records Management Federation.
Retention Standards Committee. International
records retention survey . Racine, WI , c1980.
17 p. ; LC Card 80-137617 DDC 651.5/1 19
HF5736 .I57 1980

PUBLIC RECORDS - ACCESS CONTROL.
Stallings, Wayne. Confidentially and public
access policy for local government /. Chapel
Hill , 1972. v, 32, 17 p.   **NYPL [*XME-9237]**

**PUBLIC RECORDS - LAW AND
LEGISLATION - TEXAS.**
Searcy, Seth S. Privacy and public records .
Austin , 1977. xv, 82 p. ; LC Card 77-623845
KFT1662.5.P8 S4   **NYPL [*XME-9391]**

**PUBLIC RECORDS - LAW AND
LEGISLATION - UNITED STATES.**
Searcy, Seth S. Privacy and public records .
Austin , 1977. xv, 82 p. ; LC Card 77-623845
KFT1662.5.P8 S4   **NYPL [*XME-9391]**

United States. Congress. House. Committee on
Government Operations. Legislation and
National Security Subcommittee. The
Congressional reports elimination act of 1980 .
Washington , 1980. iii, 66 p. ; LC Card
80-603104 DDC 342.73/066 19
KF27 .G6676 1980d

United States. Congress. House. Committee on
Government Operations. Legislation and
National Security Subcommittee. National
publications act of 1980 . Washington , 1980.
iii, 277 p. ; LC Card 80-603037 DDC
343.73/0998 19
KF27 .G6676 1980e

PUBLIC RECORDS - PENNSYLVANIA - PHILADELPHIA - PERIODICALS.
Philadelphia. Dept. of Records. Annual report.
Philadelphia. LC Card 72-625479
           NYPL [JLM 80-1135]

PUBLIC RECORDS - PRESERVATION. see **ARCHIVES.**

PUBLIC RECORDS - UNITED STATES.
United States. Commission on Federal Paperwork. Records management in Federal agencies . Washington , 1977. 66 p. : LC Card 78-601367
JK468.P76 U5 1977b   *NYPL [JLE 81-453]*

PUBLIC RECORDS - UNITED STATES - STATES - ACCESS CONTROL.
New Jersey. Division of Legislative Information and Research. Confidentiality of legislative research papers . [Trenton] , 1978. 68 p. ; LC Card 79-622026 DDC 328.73/0773 19
KF4950.Z95 N48

PUBLIC RELATIONS.
Gordon, Robbie. We interrupt this program . Amherst , 1980, c1978. 117 p. : LC Card 79-624735
HM263 .G63   *NYPL [JLF 81-53]*

PUBLIC RELATIONS - BUSINESS. see **PUBLIC RELATIONS.**

PUBLIC RELATIONS - CHARITIES. see **PUBLIC RELATIONS - SOCIAL SERVICE.**

PUBLIC RELATIONS - INDUSTRY. see **PUBLIC RELATIONS.**

PUBLIC RELATIONS - PERFORMING ARTS.
National Endowment for the Arts. Research Division. Audience development . Washington, D.C. , 1981. 47 p. ; ISBN 0-89062-097-0 (pbk.)
  LC Card 80-600125 DDC 790.2/068/8 19
PN1590.A9 N3 1981

PUBLIC RELATIONS - POLICE.
United States. Commission on Civil Rights. Kansas Advisory Committee. Police-community relations in the city of Wichita and Sedgwick County . Washington, D.C. [1980] xi, 95 p. : LC Card 80-603162 DDC 363.2/2/0978186 19
HV7936.P8 U53 1980

PUBLIC RELATIONS - SOCIAL SERVICE.
Gordon, Robbie. We interrupt this program . Amherst , 1980, c1978. 117 p. : LC Card 79-624735
HM263 .G63   *NYPL [JLF 81-53]*

Public representation on boards and Blue Shield allowances . United States. General Accounting Office. Washington, D.C. , 1980. v, 96 p. ; LC Card 81-600715 DDC 362.1/0681 19
RA413.3.B5 U55 1980

Public school facility needs . North Carolina. Legislative Research Commission. Raleigh, N.C. [1980] i, 26, [96] p. ; LC Card 80-622592 DDC 371.6/2/09756 19
LB3241.3.N8 N67 1980

Public school transportation. Texas. School Transportation Section. Austin, Tex. , 1980. vi, 57 p. : LC Card 80-622617 DDC 371.8/72/09764 19
LB2864 .T42 1980

PUBLIC SCHOOL - UNITED STATES - HISTORY - 19TH CENTURY.
Soltow, Lee. The rise of literacy and the common school in the United States . Chicago , 1981. p. cm. ISBN 0-226-76812-0 LC Card 81-7464 DDC 428.4 19
LC151 .S64

PUBLIC SCHOOLS - NEW JERSEY - CAMDEN COUNTY.
Blaustein, Albert P., 1921- Civil rights U. S. A.. [Washington, D. C., 1964] v, 55 p. : LC Card 64-60745   *NYPL [Sc D 80-371]*

PUBLIC SCHOOLS - NEW YORK (STATE) - BUSINESS MANAGEMENT.
New York (State). Division of Educational Management Services. Program budgeting for school districts . Albany , 1973. v, 61 p. ; LC Card 79-625622 DDC 379.1/22/09747 19
LB2823.5 .N34 1973

PUBLIC SCHOOLS - OHIO - CLEVELAND - HISTORY.
Freese, Andrew. Early history of the Cleveland

public schools. Cleveland, 1876. 128 p. LC Card 60-15972   *NYPL [JFE 80-3409]*

PUBLIC SECURITIES. see **SECURITIES.**

PUBLIC SERVICE CORPORATIONS. see **PUBLIC UTILITIES.**

PUBLIC SERVICE EMPLOYMENT - KENTUCKY - HISTORY - SOURCES - BIBLIOGRAPHY - CATALOGS.
Kentucky. Division of Archives and Records Management. Harry E. Bullock papers . Frankfort, Ky. , 1979. iv, 7 leaves ; LC Card 79-623426 DDC 016.3628/5 19
Z7164.L1 K4 1979 HD5725.K4

PUBLIC SERVICE EMPLOYMENT - NEW YORK (STATE)
New York (State). Legislative Commission on Expenditure Review. CETA programs in New York State . [Albany, N.Y.] , 1979. 8, iii, 92 p. : LC Card 80-621029
HD5725.N7 N44 1979 *NYPL [JLF 81-122]*

PUBLIC SERVICE EMPLOYMENT - UNITED STATES.
United States. General Accounting Office. Antirecession assistance--an evaluation . [Washington] 1977. v, 128 p. : LC Card 77-604896
HD5724 .U629 1977 *NYPL [JLF 81-298]*

United States. General Accounting Office. More benefits to jobless can be attained in public service employment, Department of Labor . Washington , 1977. x, 99 p. ; LC Card 77-601735
HD5724 .U629 1977a *NYPL [*XME-9418]*

PUBLIC SERVICE EMPLOYMENT - UNITED STATES - CONGRESSES.
Conference on Evaluation of the Economic Stimulus Package, Brookings Institution, 1977. Conference report on evaluating the 1977 economic stimulus package /. [Washington] , 1978. iii, 127 p. ; LC Card 79-602314
HC106.7 .C665 1977 *NYPL [JLF 81-172]*

PUBLIC SERVICE EMPLOYMENT - UNITED STATES - CORRUPT PRACTICES.
United States. Congress. House. Committee on Government Operations. Manpower and Housing Subcommittee. CETA's vulnerability to fraud and abuse . Washington , 1980. iv, 251 p. ; LC Card 80-604021 DDC 353.0083 19
KF27 .G6678 1980g

PUBLIC SERVICE EMPLOYMENT - VERMONT.
Burleson, Erica. The role of the coach in public service employment. [Montpelier, Vt.] 1973. ix, 43 p.   *NYPL [*XME-9294]*

Burleson, Richard A. SWP versus PEP. [Montpelier, Vt.] 1973. xi, 77 p.
    *NYPL [*XME-9290]*

Mattson, Robert E. Considerations in the selection of public service employers. [Montpelier, Vt.] 1973. xiii, 51 p.
    *NYPL [*XME-9291]*

Mattson, Robert E. An evaluation of individualized and pool slot development for public service employment. [Montpelier, Vt.] 1973. xv, 32 p.   *NYPL [*XME-9289]*

Stanfield, Robert E. The uses of paraprofessionals in the delivery of manpower and social services through public service employment. [Montpelier, Vt.] 1973. xiii, 64 p.
    *NYPL [*XME-9293]*

PUBLIC SERVICES. see **MUNICIPAL SERVICES.**

PUBLIC SERVITUDES - ALASKA.
Joint Federal-State Land Use Planning Commission for Alaska. Public easements under the Alaska native claims settlement act . Anchorage, Alaska , 1979. 181 p. : LC Card 79-624668 DDC 346.79804/32/08997 19
KFA1650 .J64

Public Technology, inc.
Elderly and handicapped transportation : eight case studies / prepared by Public Technology, inc., secretariat to the Urban Consortium for Technology Initiatives. Washington, D.C. : U. S. Dept. of Transportation, Urban Mass Transportation Administration, Office of the Secretary, [1979] 121 p. : ill. ; 28 cm. LC Card 80-601590 DDC 362.4/0483 19

1. Aged - Transportation - Case studies. 2. Physically handicapped - Transportation - Case studies. I. Title.
HQ1063.5 .P8 1979

Elderly and handicapped transportation : information sourcebook / prepared by Public Technology, Inc. ... Secretariat to the Urban Consortium for Technology Initiatives. Washington: U. S. Govt. Print. Off., 1979 28 p.; 28 cm. Microfiche (neg.) 1 sheet. 11 x 15 cm. (NYPL FSN 35,080) "Supported by U. S. Department of Transportation, Urban Mass Transportation Administration, Office of Service and Methods Demonstration and Office of the Secretary, Office of Intergovernmental Affairs."
1. Aged - Transportation. 2. Handicapped - Transportation. I. Urban Consortium for Technology Initiatives. II. United States. Dept. of Transportation. III. Title.   *NYPL [*XME-9106]*

Public transportation . Rothenberg, Morris Jerome, 1934- [Washington, D.C.] [1980] viii, 200, [160] p. : LC Card 80-602279 DDC 388.4/0973 19
HE308 .R67

Public transportation in Washington State.
Washington (State). Planning and Public Transportation Division. Olympia, Wash. [1980] iii, 126, [67] p., [1] leaf of plates : LC Card 80-623197 DDC 380.5/068 19
HE213.W2 W36 1980

Public transportation safety . New York (State). Legislature. Senate. Committee on Transportation. [Albany] [1979] 16 p. ; LC Card 80-622830 DDC 363.1/25 19
HE5614.3.N5 N48 1979

PUBLIC USE - UNITED STATES.
Althaus, Helen F. Public trust rights /. [Washington] , 1978. xxxix, 421 p. ; LC Card 80-602930 DDC 346.7304/691 19
KF5571 .A94

PUBLIC UTILITIES - ADDRESSES, ESSAYS, LECTURES.
Applications of economic principles in public utility industries /. [Ann Arbor] , c1981. ix, 155 p. ; ISBN 0-87712-211-3 LC Card 81-936 DDC 338.4/33636/0973 19
HD2763 .A66

PUBLIC UTILITIES - CALIFORNIA - DEFENSE MEASURES.
California. Office of Emergency Services. Utilities Division. Disaster preparedness for California utilities. [Sacramento] , 1978. 13 leaves ; LC Card 79-622089 DDC 353.97940075/4 19
UA929.95.P93 C34 1978

PUBLIC UTILITIES - GEORGIA.
Georgia. General Assembly. House of Representatives. Public Utilities Study Committee. Report of the Public Utilities Study Committee of the House of Representatives. [Atlanta , 1979] iii, 31, [7] p. ; LC Card 80-623324 DDC 343.758/09 347.58039 19
KFG11.82 .P8 1979

Georgia. Public Service Commission. Utility rules of the Georgia Public Service Commission, effective January 1, 1976 . Atlanta, Ga. [1976?] 126 p. ; LC Card 77-620988 DDC 343.758/09/02636 19
KFG285.A433 A2 1976

PUBLIC UTILITIES - LAW. see **PUBLIC UTILITIES.**

PUBLIC UTILITIES - NEBRASKA - LITTLE NEMAHA RIVER WATERSHED - MAPS.
United States. Soil Conservation Service. Historical, utilities, and quarries map, lower Little Nemaha watershed, Johnson, Nemaha, Otoe, and Richardson Counties, Nebraska /. Lincoln, Nebr. , 1979. 1 map : LC Card 81-691089
G4192.L5E635 1979 .U5

United States. Soil Conservation Service. Mines, utilities, and pipeline map, upper Little Nemaha watershed, Lancaster, Cass, and Otoe Counties, Nebraska /. Lincoln, Nebr. , 1979. 1 map : LC Card 81-691086
G4192.L5H1 1978 .U5

PUBLIC UTILITIES - PERIODICALS.
Land economics; a journal of planning, housing & public utilities. v. 1- ; 1925- Chicago [etc.] LC Card 26-19201
    *NYPL [*ZAN-T4596]*

PUBLIC UTILITIES - RATES - ADDRESSES, ESSAYS, LECTURES.
Applications of economic principles in public utility industries /. [Ann Arbor] , c1981. ix, 155 p. ; ISBN 0-87712-211-3 LC Card 81-936 DDC 338.4/33636/0973 19
HD2763 .A66

PUBLIC UTILITIES - TAXATION - NEW YORK (STATE)
Patenaude, John J. Report on proposed State assessments of all public utility real property in New York State /. Albany, N.Y. [1980] 10 p. ; LC Card 80-621854 DDC 336.22/2 19
HD2767.N74 P37

PUBLIC UTILITIES - TAXATION - UNITED STATES.
United States. Congress. House. Committee on Ways and Means. Accounting treatment of the investment tax credit and accelerated depreciation for public utility ratemaking purposes . Washington , 1980. iv, 136 p. ; LC Card 80-603022 DDC 343.7305/267 19
KF27 .W3 1980g

PUBLIC UTILITIES - UNITED STATES - ADDRESSES, ESSAYS, LECTURES.
Applications of economic principles in public utility industries /. [Ann Arbor] , c1981. ix, 155 p. ; ISBN 0-87712-211-3 LC Card 81-936 DDC 338.4/33636/0973 19
HD2763 .A66

PUBLIC UTILITIES - UNITED STATES - CONGRESSES.
Symposium on Productivity and Managerial Assessment, Albany, 1975. Public utility productivity . Albany [1975?] xv, 256 p. : LC Card 75-41898
HD2766 .S95 1975   *NYPL [*XME-9419]*

PUBLIC UTILITIES - UNITED STATES - RATES.
United States. Congress. House. Committee on Ways and Means. Accounting treatment of the investment tax credit and accelerated depreciation for public utility ratemaking purposes . Washington , 1980. iv, 136 p. ; LC Card 80-603022 DDC 343.7305/267 19
KF27 .W3 1980g

Public utility productivity . Symposium on Productivity and Managerial Assessment, Albany, 1975. Albany [1975?] xv, 256 p. : LC Card 75-41898
HD2766 .S95 1975   *NYPL [*XME-9419]*

PUBLIC UTILITY REGULATION. see PUBLIC UTILITIES.

Public water supplies /. Illinois. Pollution Control Board. [Springfield , 1979] 22 p. ; LC Card 80-621932 DDC 353.97730082322 s 344.773/046343 19
KFI1554 .A4 1972 chap. 6 KFI1556

PUBLIC WELFARE ADMINISTRATION - QUALITY CONTROL.
United States. Social and Rehabilitation Service. Office of Quality Control Management. Training for federal quality control review /. Washington D. C. , 1974. 167 p. ;
NYPL [JLF 81-28]

PUBLIC WELFARE - CALIFORNIA.
Iseri, Joyce. Low-income single mothers and public assistance programs /. [Sacramento, Calif.] [1980] iii, 53 leaves ; LC Card 81-621365 DDC 362.8/282/09794 19
HV699 .I75

PUBLIC WELFARE - FEDERAL AID. see FEDERAL AID TO PUBLIC WELFARE.

PUBLIC WELFARE - LAW AND LEGISLATION - ILLINOIS.
Illinois. Commission to Revise and Rewrite the Public Aid Code. Report to the Illinois General Assembly on code revision /. [Springfield, Ill.] (612 South Second St., Springfield 62706) [1980] 1v. (various pagings) ; LC Card 81-621938 DDC 344.773/03 347.73043 19
KFI1549 .A25 1980

PUBLIC WELFARE - LAW AND LEGISLATION - NEW JERSEY.
New Jersey. Legislature. General Assembly. Revenue, Finance, and Appropriations Committee. Public hearing before Assembly Revenue, Finance and Appropriations Committee on Assembly concurrent resolution no. 139 O[i.e. A]CR (use of casino gambling

revenues to assist senior citizens and disabled) held June 30, 1980, Assembly Majority Conference Room, State House, Trenton, New Jersey. [Trenton] [1980] 3, 32 p. ; LC Card 80-623450
KFN1811.4 .R45 1980

PUBLIC WELFARE - LAW AND LEGISLATION - SOUTH DAKOTA.
1974 administrative rules of South Dakota, Title 67, Department of Social Services . [Pierre] [1976?] 396 p. ; LC Card 80-126719 DDC 344.783/03 19
KFS3349.A434 A2 1976

PUBLIC WELFARE - LAW AND LEGISLATION - UNITED STATES.
United States. Congress. Joint Economic Committee. A model income supplement bill. Washington, 1974. v, 62 p.;
NYPL [JLE 81-116]

United States. Congress. Senate. Committee on Labor and Human Resources. Subcommittee on Employment, Poverty, and Migratory Labor. Youth employment and welfare reform jobs, 1980 . Washington , 1980. vi, 892 p. : LC Card 81-600874 DDC 344.73/01342592 347.3041342592 19
KF26 .L2737 1980b

PUBLIC WELFARE - MAINE - PERIODICALS.
Maine. Dept. of Human Services. Title XX comprehensive annual services program plan. [Augusta] 28 cm. LC Card 79-642723
NYPL [JLM 80-1072]

PUBLIC WELFARE - MASSACHUSETTS.
United States. Social and Rehabilitation Service. Assistance Payments Administration. Child support payments control, Massachusetts and Washington. [Washington] [1974] 100 p. :
NYPL [JLF 80-1363]

PUBLIC WELFARE - MICHIGAN - STATISTICS - PERIODICALS.
Michigan. Dept. of Social Services. Assistance payments statistics. Lansing.
NYPL [JLM 80-1129]

PUBLIC WELFARE - NEW HAMPSHIRE - PERIODICALS.
New Hampshire. Dept. of Health and Welfare. Biennial report. [Concord]
NYPL [JLM 80-829]

PUBLIC WELFARE - NEW JERSEY.
New Jersey. State Legislature. General Assembly. Revenue, Finance, and Appropriations Committee. Public hearing before Assembly Revenue, Finance, and Appropriations Committee on Assembly Resolution Number 50 (memorializes Congress to transfer funding from unnecessary military spending to domestic spending for human services) . [Trenton] [1980] 49, 23x p. ; LC Card 81-621305 DDC 353.97490084 19
KFN1811.4 .R45 1980b

PUBLIC WELFARE - NEW YORK (STATE) - AUDITING AND INSPECTION.
New York (State). Division of Audits and Accounts. Review of New York City audits of supplemental welfare funds. Albany [1980] 4, 20 leaves ; LC Card 80-622251 DDC 352.94/4/097471 19
HV86 .N77 1980

PUBLIC WELFARE - UNITED STATES.
New Jersey. State Legislature. General Assembly. Revenue, Finance, and Appropriations Committee. Public hearing before Assembly Revenue, Finance, and Appropriations Committee on Assembly Resolution Number 50 (memorializes Congress to transfer funding from unnecessary military spending to domestic spending for human services) . [Trenton] [1980] 49, 23x p. ; LC Card 81-621305 DDC 353.97490084 19
KFN1811.4 .R45 1980b

United States. Congress. House. Committee on the Budget. Task Force on Human and Community Resources. Prospects for human services programs in the economic and social climate of the eighties . Washington , 1980. iii, 103 p. : LC Card 80-603013 DDC 361/.973 19
KF27 .B848 1980

PUBLIC WELFARE - UNITED STATES - CASE STUDIES.
United States. Congress. Joint Economic

Committee. How public welfare benefits are distributed in low-income areas. Washington , 1973. x, 144 p.;   *NYPL [JLE 81-118]*

PUBLIC WELFARE - UNITED STATES - STATES.
United States. Congress. Joint Economic Committee. Welfare in the 70's. Washington, 1974. ix, 300 p.;   *NYPL [JLE 81-115]*

PUBLIC WELFARE - UNITED STATES - STATES - STATISTICS.
United States. Social Security Administration. Office of Research and Statistics. Public assistance recipients and cash payments by State and county-February 1979. Washington, D.C. , 1980. v, 85 p. ; LC Card 80-600053 DDC 361/.973/0212 19
HV85 .U54 1980

PUBLIC WELFARE - UNITED STATES - STATISTICS - PERIODICALS.
Public assistance recipients & cash payments by state & county. [Washington] LC Card 78-640797   *NYPL [JLM 81-20]*

United States. Social Security Administration. Office of Research and Statistics. Public assistance statistics. Mar. 1977- [Washington] LC Card 77-643177   *NYPL [JLM 80-970]*

PUBLIC WELFARE - VIRGINIA - PLANNING.
Virginia. Office of the Secretary of Human Resources. The effects of services integration in Virginia at the local and state level /. Richmond [1978] 58 p. ; LC Card 79-624121 DDC 361.6/09755 19
HV86 .V86 1978

PUBLIC WELFARE - WASHINGTON (STATE)
Washington (State). Dept. of Social and Health Services. Division of Analysis and Information Services. Public assistance programs in the State of Washington . Olympia, Wash. [1979] iv, 151 p. ; LC Card 79-625823 DDC 361.6/09797 19
HV86 .W365 1979

Public works as a countercyclical tool . United States. Congress. Joint Economic Committee. Washington , 1980. iii, 86 p. : LC Card 80-603664 DDC 339.5/22 19
KF25 .E2 1980f

A Publication of the Franklin K. Lane Memorial Fund, Institute of Governmental Studies, University of California, Berkeley.
Danielson, Michael N. New York, the politics of urban regional development /. Berkeley , c1981. p. cm. ISBN 0-520-04371-5 LC Card 81-7480 DDC 307.7/6 19
HT393.N7 D3

Publication of the North Carolina Biological Survey .
(#1980-12) Atlas of North American freshwater fishes, 1980-et seq. / . [Raleigh, N.C.] , c1980. x, 854 p. : ISBN 0-917134-03-6 : LC Card 80-620039 DDC 597.092/97 19
QL625 .A84

Publications and data tapes of the National Center for Health Statistics available from the National Technical Information Service. United States. National Center for Health Statistics. Hyattsville, Md. , 1978. 260 p. ; LC Card 79-602913
Z7553.M43 U54 1978 RA407.3
NYPL [JLF 81-340]

Publications and graduate theses in agricultural economics and applied statistics, July 1977-July 1978 /. Idaho. University. Dept. of Agricultural Economics and Applied Statistics. Moscow, Idaho [1978] 20 leaves ; LC Card 80-620584 DDC 016.3381 19
Z5074.E3 I36 1978 HD1775.I2

Publications and patents with abstracts.
July/Dec. 1970- [New Orleans, La.] 27 cm. Semiannual. For earlier file, see: United States. Agricultural Research Service. Southern Utilization Research and Development Division. Publications and patents. Published by the U. S. Agricultural Research Service, Southern Marketing and Nutrition Research Division July/Dec. 1970-Jan./June, 1972; by the service's Southern Regional Research Center, July/Dec. 1972-Jan./June, 1977; by the U. S. Dept. of Agriculture, Science and Education Administration, Southern Regional Research Center, July/Dec. 1977-
1. Agricultural processing - Abstracts - Periodicals. 2. Agricultural processing - Patents - Periodicals. 3. Farm

produce - Abstracts - Periodicals. I. United States. Agricultural Research Service. Southern Marketing and Nutrition Research Division. II. United States. Agricultural Research Service. Southern Regional Research Center. III. United States. Science and Education Administration. Southern Regional Research Center. **NYPL [*VA 80-314]**

Publications in archaeology (Austin, Tex.) .
(report no. 14-15) Two sites in Uvalde County. [Austin, Tex.] [1979] vi, 15, vi, 19 p., : LC Card 80-622621 DDC 976.4/432 19
E78.T4 T89

Publications in architecture and urban planning .
(rept. R78-4) Hill, Ann B. Abstracts on child play areas and child support facilities /. Milwaukee [Wis.] , Milwaukee, WI (P.O. Box 413, Milwaukee, Wis. 53201) , c1978. v, 102 leaves : LC Card 81-106795 DDC 790/.06/8 19
GV423 .H54

(rept. R79-2) Community Design Center (Milwaukee, Wis.) Recommendations for child care centers /. Milwaukee , 1979. 453 leaves in various foliations : LC Card 80-153764 DDC 362.7/12 19
HV851 .C65 1979

(rept. R79-3) Moore, Gary T. Bibliography on children and the physical environment . Milwaukee [Wis.] , Milwaukee, WI (P.O. Box 413, Milwaukee, Wis. 53201) [1979] v, 143 p. ; LC Card 81-106815 DDC 016.3052/3 19
Z7164.C5 M68 HQ767.9

Publications of the National Institute of Law Enforcement and Criminal Justice . National Institute of Law Enforcement and Criminal Justice. [Washington] , 1978. vii, 230 p. ; LC Card 79-601977 DDC 016.364/973 19
Z7164.P76 N37 HV8138

Publications on ethnicity and nationality of the School of International Studies, University of Washington .
(v. 3) Bentley, G. Carter. Ethnicity and nationality . Seattle [1981] p. cm. ISBN 0-295-95853-7 LC Card 81-51280 DDC 016.3058 19
Z5118.E84 B46 GN495.6

PUBLICITY.
Gordon, Robbie. We interrupt this program . Amherst , 1980, c1978. 117 p. : LC Card 79-624735
HM263 .G63 **NYPL [JLF 81-53]**

The public's right to attend criminal proceedings in North Carolina /. Farb, Robert L. Chapel Hill, N.C. [1980], c1978. 10 p. , : LC Card 80-622371 DDC 347.756 s 345.756/05 19
KFN7908.A15 U6 no. 80/01 KFN7910.5.C6

Puckett, Larry J. Dendroclimatic estimates of a drought index for northern Virginia / by Larry J. Puckett. Washington, D.C. : U. S. Geological Survey, [1981] p. cm. (Geological Survey water-supply paper ; 2080) Includes bibliographies. LC Card 80-607816 DDC 551.6/4 19
1. Drought forecasting - Virginia. 2. Dendroclimatology - Virginia. 3. Trees - Growth. I. Title. II. Title: Drought index. III. Series: United States. Geological Survey. Water supply paper , 2080.
QC929.D8 P84

Puckett, Stephen M. Wisconsin. Division of Corrections. Office of Policy, Planning, and Budget. Adult admissions and releases . Madison, Wis. [1980] 30 p. : LC Card 80-623463 DDC 364.3/7/09775 19
HV8369 .W62 1979a

PUEBLO INDIANS - ANTIQUITIES - CONSERVATION AND RESTORATION.
The Archeology and stabilization of the Dominguez and Escalante ruins. Denver , 1979. ix, 496 p. : LC Card 79-603760
E99.P9 A72 **NYPL [HBC 81-508]**

PUEBLO INDIANS - GOVERNMENT RELATIONS - BIBLIOGRAPHY - CATALOGS.
United States. National Archives and Records Service. Preliminary inventory of the Pueblo records created by field offices of the Bureau of Indian Affairs . Washington , 1980. vii, 34 p. ; LC Card 80-607174 DDC 016.973 s 016.3231/197/073 19
CD3026 .A32 no. 192 Z1210.P8 E99.P9

The Puerto Rican Revolutionary Workers Organization . United States. Congress. Senate.

Committee on the Judiciary. Subcommittee to Investigate the Administration of the Internal Security Act and Other Internal Security Laws. Washington , 1976. v, 47, viii p. ; LC Card 76-601803 DDC 322.4/2/0973 19
HV6432 .U54 1976

Puerto Ricans in California . United States. Commission on Civil Rights. Western Regional Office. [Washington, D.C.] , 1980. vii, 19 p. ;
  LC Card 80-601602 DDC 323.1/1687295/0794 19
F870.P85 U54 1980

PUERTO RICANS IN CALIFORNIA - CIVIL RIGHTS.
United States. Commission on Civil Rights. Western Regional Office. Puerto Ricans in California . [Washington, D.C.] , 1980. vii, 19 p. ; LC Card 80-601602 DDC 323.1/1687295/0794 19
F870.P85 U54 1980

PUERTO RICO.
Puerto Rico. Office of the Commonwealth of Puerto Rico, Washington, D. C. Puerto Rico /. Washington, D. C. [1951] 47 p. : LC Card 51-62958 **NYPL [Sc F 81-13]**

Puerto Rico. Commonwealth of Puerto Rico, Office of the, Washington, D. C. see **Puerto Rico. Office of the Commonwealth of Puerto Rico, Washington, D. C.**

PUERTO RICO - ECONOMIC CONDITIONS - 1952-
United States. Dept. of Commerce. Interagency Study Group. Economic study of Puerto Rico . [Washington] , 1979. 2 v. : LC Card 80-601545 DDC 330.97295/053 19
HC154.5 .U54 1979

Puerto Rico. Office of the Commonwealth of Puerto Rico, Washington, D. C. Puerto Rico / Office of the Government of Puerto Rico. Washington, D. C. : The Office, [1951] 47 p. : ill. ; 27 cm. Bibliography: p. 45-47. LC Card 51-62958
1. Puerto Rico. **NYPL [Sc F 81-13]**

PUERTO RICO TARIFF BILL OF 1900 - SPEECHES IN CONGRESS.
Cannon, Joseph Gurney, 1836-1926. $1,050,000 into the pockets of the American tobacco trust. [Washington? D. C. , 1900] 16 p. ;
  NYPL [Arents S 1607]

Puerto Rico. University. Mayagüez University Campus. College of Agricultural Sciences.
Gierbolini, Roberto E. Soil survey of Ponce area of southern Puerto Rico /. [Washington] [1979] iii, 80 p., [22] fold. leaves of plates : LC Card 80-602349 DDC 631.4/7/72957 19
S599.25.P832 P663

Pugash, James Z. The geopolitics of oil : staff report / printed at the request of the Committee on Energy and Natural Resources, United States Senate. Washington : U. S. G.P.O. : For sale by the Supt. of Docs., U. S. G.P.O., 1980. v. 89 p. ; 24 cm. At head of title: 96th Congress, 2d session. Committee print. "James Z. Pugash ... wrote the report with Gina Despres"--p. iv. "Publication no. 96-119." "December 1980." Includes bibliographical references. LC Card 80-604126 DDC 333.8/232 19
1. Petroleum industry and trade. 2. World politics - 1975-1985. I. Despres, Gina. II. United States. Congress. Senate. Committee on Energy and Natural Resources. III. Title.
HD9560.5 .P76

Puget Sound books.
Chasan, Daniel Jack. The water link . Seattle , 1981. p. cm ISBN 0-295-95782-4 (University of Washington Press) : LC Card 81-11457 DDC 333.91/64 19
HC107.W22 P838

PUGET SOUND REGION (WASH.) - INDUSTRIES - HISTORY.
Chasan, Daniel Jack. The water link . Seattle , 1981. p. cm ISBN 0-295-95782-4 (University of Washington Press) : LC Card 81-11457 DDC 333.91/64 19
HC107.W22 P838

Pugh, Olin S. Commercial banking trends, 1950-1979 : a survey of United States and South Carolina developments / by Olin S. Pugh. [Columbia] : Division of Research, College of Business Administration, University of South Carolina, 1980. viii, 86 p. ; 23 cm.

(Occasional studies - Division of Research, College of Business Administration, the University of South Carolina . no. 13) LC Card 80-622707 DDC 332.1/2/0973 19
1. Banks and banking - United States. 2. Banks and banking - South Carolina. I. Series: South Carolina. University. College of Business Administration. Division of Research. Occasional studies - Division of Research, College of Business Administration, the University of South Carolina , no. 13. II. Title.
HG2491 .P79

Pugh-Roberts Associates. Off-track betting in Massachusetts : a report submitted to the Legislative Committee on Government Regulations : final report. Cambridge, Mass. : Pugh-Roberts Associates, 1976. ix, 35 leaves : graphs ; 30 cm. Microfiche (neg.) NTIS. 1 sheet. 11 x 15 cm. (PB 269 632) LC Card 77-621719
1. Horse race betting - Massachusetts. 2. Horse-racing - Massachusetts. I. Massachusetts. General Court. Committee on Government Regulations. II. Title.
SF332.5.M4 P83 1976 **NYPL [*XME-9421]**

PULASKI COUNTY, ILL. - HISTORY.
Public Library, Winnetka, Ill. Genealogy Projects Committee. An index to the names of persons appearing in History of Alexander. Thomson, Ill. [1973] 129 p.; LC Card 75-116464
  NYPL [IVF (Alexander) (Perrin, W. H. History of Alexander, Union ... counties, Ill. Index)]

PULASKI, KAZIMIERZ, 1747-1779 - BIBLIOGRAPHY.
Hoskins, Janina W. Casimir Pulaski, 1747-1779 . [Washington , 1979] 24 p. : LC Card 79-124952
Z8716.5 .H67 E207.P8 **NYPL [JFE 80-4304]**

Pulich, Warren. Gulf of Mexico Coastal Ecosystems Workshop, Port Aransas, Tex., 1979. Proceedings of the Gulf of Mexico Coastal Ecosystems Workshop /. [Washington] [1980] vi, 214 p. : LC Card 80-603154 DDC 333.91/7/0916364 19
QH105.T4 G84 1979

Pulmonary function testing of elementary school children . Montana. Air Quality Bureau. Helena, Mont. [1979] 73 p. : LC Card 80-620864 DDC 618.92/24 19
RJ433.5.P8 M66 1979

PULMONARY FUNCTION TESTS - MONTANA.
Montana. Air Quality Bureau. Pulmonary function testing of elementary school children . Helena, Mont. [1979] 73 p. : LC Card 80-620864 DDC 618.92/24 19
RJ433.5.P8 M66 1979

Pulmonary toxicology of respirable particles . Hanford Life Sciences Symposium, 19th, Richland, Wash., 1979. Oak Ridge, Tenn. , 1980. xi, 676 p. : ISBN 0-87079-121-4 LC Card 80-22907 DDC 616.2/44 19
RC756 .H3 1979

PULMONARY TUBERCULOSIS. see TUBERCULOSIS.

PUMA HUNTING - COLORADO - CANON CITY.
Currier, Mary Jean P. Mountain lion population and harvest near Canon City, Colorado, 1974-1977 /. [Denver] , 1977. vi, 12 p. : LC Card 78-621470 DDC 639.9/7974428 19
QL737.C23 C83

PUMAS.
Currier, Mary Jean P. Mountain lion population and harvest near Canon City, Colorado, 1974-1977 /. [Denver] , 1977. vi, 12 p. : LC Card 78-621470 DDC 639.9/7974428 19
QL737.C23 C83

Pumpage of water in Louisiana, 1975 /. Cardwell, George T., 1922- Baton Rouge, La. , 1979. iv, 15 p. : LC Card 80-620624 DDC 333.91/13/09763 19
TD224.L8 C37

Pumped-slurry backfilling of abandoned coal mine workings for subsidence control at Rock Springs, Wyoming /. Colaizzi, Gary J. Washington , 1981. p. cm. LC Card 80-39876 DDC 622 s 622/.334 19
TN295 .U4 TN319

Pumping and depletion of ground-water storage in Las Vegas Valley, Nevada, 1955-74 /. Harrill, J. R. [Carson City] , 1976. vii, 70 p. :

LC Card 80-623616   DDC 333.91/2/0979313 19
GB705.N3 A35 no. 44 TD224.N2

PUNCH-CARD SYSTEMS. see PUNCHED CARD SYSTEMS.

PUNCHED CARD SYSTEMS - BUSINESS. see PUNCHED CARD SYSTEMS.

PUNCHED CARD SYSTEMS - NAMES, GEOGRAPHICAL.
Werner, Pamela A. A survey of national geocoding systems. [Cambridge, Mass.], 1974. xi, 344 p.   LC Card 76-51887
NYPL [JFF 80-1538]

PUNCHED TAPES. see DATA TAPES.

Punishment chart for crimes of general interest in the Superior Courts of North Carolina /. Drennan, James C. [Chapel Hill] , 1978. ix, 40 p. ;   LC Card 78-624325   DDC 345.756/077 19
KFN7983.2.Z9 D73

PUNISHMENT IN CRIME DETERRENCE - UNITED STATES.
Bailey, William C., 1944- Deterrence and the celerity of the death penalty . [Madison] . 46 p. ;   LC Card 79-625417   DDC 364.6/6/0973 19
HV8699.U5 B34

PUNISHMENT - NORTH CAROLINA.
Drennan, James C. Punishment chart for crimes of general interest in the Superior Courts of North Carolina /. [Chapel Hill] , 1978. ix, 40 p. ;   LC Card 78-624325   DDC 345.756/077 19
KFN7983.2.Z9 D73

Farb, Robert L. The impact of Baldasar v. Illinois on uncounseled misdemeanor convictions in North Carolina /. Chapel Hill, N.C. , 1980, c1978. 4 p. ;   LC Card 80-622793   DDC 347.756 s 345.756/056 19
KFN7908.A15 U6 no. 80/04 KFN7978

Punishment, perspectives in a civilized society : Center for Social Work Research, University of Texas at Austin, January 17-20, 1977 / conference convener, Chester A. Chiles ; editors, Isabelle Collora, Douglas W. Denton, Georgann [sic] English ; [co-sponsored by Center for Social Work Research, University of Texas at Austin, and Institute of Urban Studies, Research and Service Programs Division, University of Texas at Arlington]. Arlington, Tex. : The Institute, [1977?] iv, 129 p. : ill. ; 22 cm. (New directions for corrections . v. 1) Includes bibliographies.   LC Card 80-621841   DDC 364.6/0973 19
1. Punishment - United States - Congresses. I. Collora, Isabelle. II. Denton, Douglas W. III. English, Georgeann. IV. Texas. University at Austin. Center for Social Work Research. V. Texas. University at Arlington. Institute of Urban Studies. Research and Service Programs Division. VI. Series.
HV9471 .P86

PUNISHMENT - UNITED STATES - CONGRESSES.
Punishment, perspectives in a civilized society . Arlington, Tex. [1977?] iv, 129 p. :   LC Card 80-621841   DDC 364.6/0973 19
HV9471 .P86

Pupil appraisal handbook /. Louisiana. Bureau of Pupil Appraisal. [Baton Rouge] , 1978. 80 leaves ;   LC Card 79-621593   DDC 370/.9763 s 371.9 19
L154 .B32 no. 1508 RJ50

Purcell, Wayne D. (joint author) Riffe, Don A. Hedging strategies to protect the financial position of cattle feeders and lenders /. [Stillwater] , 1979. 39 p. :   LC Card 79-625381   DDC 338.4/36213/0724 19
HD9433.U4 R54

PURCHASING POWER - LATIN AMERICA.
Salazar-Carrillo, Jorge. Prices and purchasing power parities in Latin America, 1960-1972 /. Washington, D.C. , 1978. ca. 350 p. in various pagings ;   LC Card 80-134989   DDC 338.5/2/098 19
HB235.L25 S34

Purdie, Hazel. Georgia bibliography : county history / compiled by Hazel Purdie.2d ed. [Atlanta] : Readers Services, Division of Public Library Services, Georgia Dept. of Education, 1979. v, 107 p. : map ; 29 cm. Includes indexes.   LC Card 80-622190   DDC 016.9758 19
1. Georgia - History, Local - Bibliography - Catalogs. 2. Georgia. Division of Public Library Services - Catalogs. I. Georgia. Division of Public Library Services. Readers

Services. II. Title.
Z1273 .P87 1979 F286

Purdom, William B. Guide to the geology and lore of the wild reach of the Rogue River, Oregon / by William B. Purdom. Eugene : Museum of Natural History, University of Oregon, 1977. 67 p. : ill. (some col.) ; 27 cm. (Bulletin - Museum of Natural History, University of Oregon . no. 22) Bibliography: p. 62-63.   LC Card 77-622970   DDC 917.95/2 19
1. Natural history - Oregon - Rogue River. 2. Geology - Oregon - Rogue River - Guide-books. 3. Rogue River, Or. - Guide-books. I. Title. II. Title: Wild reach of the Rogue River, Oregon. III. Series: Oregon. University. Museum of Natural History. Bulletin, no. 22.
QH1 .O7 no. 22 QH105.O7

Purdue University. Agricultural Experiment Station. Smallwood, Benjamin F. Soil survey of Marshall County, Indiana. [Washington, D.C.?] , 1980. vii, 136 p., 63 folded p. of plates :   LC Card 81-601062   DDC 631.4/7/77288 19
S599.I63 S6

Purdue University, Lafayette, Ind. Agricultural Experiment Station. see Purdue University. Agricultural Experiment Station, Lafayette.

Purdue University, Lafayette, Ind. Center for Information and Numerical Data Analysis and Synthesis. Electronic properties research literature retrieval guide, 1972-1976 : a comprehensive compilation of scientific and technical literature / by the Center for Information and Numerical Data Analysis and Synthesis (CINDAS), Purdue University ; editors, J. F. Chaney, T. M. Putnam. New York : IFI/Plenum, c1979. 4 v. ; 29 cm. Includes indexes. CONTENTS. - v. 1. Elements.--v. 2. Inorganic and intermetallic compounds.--v. 3. Alloys and cermets.--v. 4. Mixtures, rocks and minerals, composites and systems, polymers.   ISBN 0-306-68010-6   LC Card 79-16082
1. Materials - Electric properties - Bibliography. I. Chaney, James F. II. Putnam, Thomas Milton, 1945-. III. Title.
Z5853.M38 P82 1979 QC527.5
NYPL [JSF 81-252]

Purdue University, Lafayette, Ind. Engineering Experiment Station. Joint Highway Research Project. Yamin, Hadi. Relationship of highway development and city development for non-metropolitan places in Indiana . West Lafayette, Ind. , 1979. xii, 175 leaves :   LC Card 80-620933   DDC 388.1/1 19
TE24.I6 Y35

Purdue University, Lafayette, Ind. Institute for Research in the Behavioral, Economic and Management Sciences.
Paper.
(no. 728) Evans, Gerald. Multiple objectives and uncertainty in long range energy generation expansion planning /. West Lafayette, Ind. , 1980. 26, [11] p. :   LC Card 80-622434   DDC 658/.001/9 s 363.6/2 19
HD6483 .P8 no. 728 HD9685.A2

PURE FOOD. see FOOD ADULTERATION AND INSPECTION; FOOD LAW AND LEGISLATION.

PURIFICATION OF WATER. see WATER - PURIFICATION.

PURÍSIMA CONCEPCIÓN MISSION (CALIFORNIA) (Old Catalog form: Purísima Concepción Mission, Cal.)
Hageman, Fred C. An archeological and restoration study of Mission La Purísima Concepción . Santa Barbara, Calif. , Glendale, Calif. , 1980. xxxi, 307 p. :   LC Card 79-64806
F869.P89 H33   *NYPL [IXH (Purísima Concepción Mission) 81-684]*

Pushkarev, Boris. Urban rail in America : an exploration of criteria for fixed-guideway transit / Boris S. Pushkarev with Jeffrey M. Zupan and Robert S. Cumella. Bloomington : Indiana University Press, c1981. p. cm. "A Regional Plan Association book." Includes bibliographical references and index.   ISBN 0-253-37555-X   LC Card 81-47293   DDC 388.4/2/0973 19
1. Local transit - United States. 2. Local transit - United States - Planning. I. Zupan, Jeffrey M. II. Cumella, Robert S. III. Title.
HE4451 .P87

Putnam County, N. Y. Planning Board. Bryan & Panico, Inc. Road construction specifications . Philipstown, N. Y. , 1974. 35 leaves in various pagings :   *NYPL [JSF 81-54]*

Putnam, Lee A., 1920- Cochran, Rex. Soil survey of Grayson County, Texas /. [Washington? , 1980] vii, 141 p., [41] leaves of plates :   LC Card 80-602304   DDC 631.4/7/764557 19
S599.T4 C593

Putnam, Thomas Milton, 1945- Purdue University, Lafayette, Ind. Center for Information and Numerical Data Analysis and Synthesis. Electronic properties research literature retrieval guide, 1972-1976 . New York , c1979. 4 v. ;   ISBN 0-306-68010-6   LC Card 79-16082
Z5853.M38 P82 1979 QC527.5
NYPL [JSF 81-252]

Putting rehabilitation knowledge to use . Muthard, John E., 1917- Gainesville, Fla. , 1980. vii, 80 p. ;   LC Card 80-622447   DDC 362/.0425 s 362/.0425 19
RM930.A1 F55 no. 11 HD7256.U5

Putting the puzzle together . Nebraska. Special Education Branch. Lincoln, Neb. [1979] ii, 28 p. :   LC Card 79-625369   DDC 371.9/09782 19
LC4032.N4 N42 1979

Putz, Paul. Historic sites of South Dakota . [Vermillion, S.D.] , 1980. x, 126 p. :   LC Card 80-623927   DDC 917.83/0433 19
F652 .H57

Pyles, Rebecca A. (joint author) Duellman, William Edward, 1930- A new marsupial frog (Hylidae, Gastrotheca) from the Andes of Ecuador /. Lawrence, Kan. [1980] 13 p. :   LC Card 80-622163   DDC 597.8/7 19
QL668.E24 D8315

A pyrometallurgical method for processing Ni-Cd scrap batteries /. Wilson, D. A. (Donald A.) [Washington, D.C.] [1981] p. cm.   LC Card 81-10151   DDC 622 s 669/.56 19
TN23 .U43 TN799.N6

Pyrometallurgical recovery of chromium from scrap metals : laboratory studies / by C.L. Kusik ... [et al.] [Avondale, Md.] : U. S. Dept. of the Interior, Bureau of Mines, [1981] p. cm. (Report of investigations / Bureau of Mines) Bibliography: p.   LC Card 81-10147   DDC 622 s 669/.734 19
1. Chromium - Metallurgy. 2. Pyrometallurgy. 3. Scrap metals - Recycling. I. Kusik, Charles L. II. Series: Report of investigations (United States. Bureau of Mines).
TN23 .U43 TN799.C5

PYROMETALLURGY.
Pyrometallurgical recovery of chromium from scrap metals . [Avondale, Md.] [1981] p. cm.   LC Card 81-10147   DDC 622 s 669/.734 19
TN23 .U43 TN799.C5

Wilson, D. A. (Donald A.) A pyrometallurgical method for processing Ni-Cd scrap batteries /. [Washington, D.C.] [1981] p. cm.   LC Card 81-10151   DDC 622 s 669/.56 19
TN23 .U43 TN799.N6

Qiñiqtuagaksrat utuqqanaat iñuuniaġninisiqun . North Slope Borough, Alaska. Commission on History and Culture. Barrow, Alaska , c1980- v. :   ISBN 0-936052-00-7 (v. 1)   LC Card 80-80683   DDC 970.004/97 19
E99.E7 N64 1980

QUACKS AND QUACKERY - UNITED STATES.
United States. Congress. House. Select Committee on Aging. Frauds against the elderly . Washington , 1980 [i.e. 1981] iii, 144 p. :   LC Card 81-600945   DDC 364.1/63 19
KF27.5 .A3 1980m

Quadratic algorithms for minimizing joins in restricted relational expressions /. Sagiv, Yehoshua. Urbana, Ill. [1979] 38 p. ;   LC Card 80-622081   DDC 001.64 s 519.7 19
QA76 .I4 no. 992 QA76.9.D3

QUADRATURE, MECHANICAL. see NUMERICAL INTEGRATION.

QUAILS - NEBRASKA - LITTLE NEMAHA RIVER WATERSHED - MAPS.
United States. Soil Conservation Service. Quail population, upper Little Nemaha watershed, Lancaster, Cass, and Otoe Counties, Nebraska /. Lincoln, Nebr. , 1979. 1 map ;   LC Card

81-691091
G4192.L5D4 1978 .U51

Quality assurance technical development program course catalog. United States. Defense Logistics Agency. Alexandria Va.
NYPL [JLM 80-723]

Quality civil legal services for the poor and near poor are possible through improved productivity . United States. General Accounting Office. [Washington, D.C. , 1979] iii, 23 p. ; LC Card 80-600508 DDC 362.5/8 19
KF336 .A718

QUALITY CONTROL - STUDY AND TEACHING - HANDBOOKS, MANUALS, ETC.
United States. Defense Logistics Agency. Quality assurance technical development program course catalog. Alexandria Va.
NYPL [JLM 80-723]

QUALITY CONTROL - UNITED STATES.
United States. Congress. House. Committee on Ways and Means. Subcommittee on Trade. Quality of production and improvement in the workplace . Washington , 1980 [i.e. 1981] iii, 186 p. : LC Card 81-600833 DDC 338/.06 19
KF27 .W348 1980k

Quality monitoring of flows from irrigation water and surface runoff in Carson Valley, Nevada, 1976 irrigation season /. Nevada. Agricultural Experiment Station, Reno. Reno [1979] ix, 130 p. (p. 129-130 blank) : LC Card 79-625751 DDC 363.7/3942/0979359 19
TC824.N3 N48 1979

The quality of American life in the eighties .
United States. Panel on the Quality of American Life. Washington , 1980. 140 p. : LC Card 81-281 DDC 361.6/1/0973 19
HN60 .U545 1980

The quality of assessment practices in New York State . McCord, Thomas. Albany, N.Y. [1980] 20 p. : LC Card 80-622878 DDC 336.22/2 19
HJ4249 .M33

Quality of drinking water--1980 . United States. Congress. House. Committee on Interstate and Foreign Commerce. Subcommittee on Health and the Environment. Washington, 1980. vii, 714 p. : LC Card 80-604005 DDC 363.6/1 19
KF27 .I5543 1980n

QUALITY OF FOREST SITES. see FOREST SITE QUALITY.

QUALITY OF LIFE - BRAZIL.
Brazil, human resources special report. [Washington, D.C.] 1979. 578 p. in various pagings, [1] fold. leaf of plates : LC Card 80-143532 DDC 304.6/0981 19
HB3563 .B735

The quality of life concept . Booz, Allen Public Administration Services, inc. [Washington] , 1973. 1 v. (various pagings).
*NYPL [*XME-9624]*

QUALITY OF LIFE - CONGRESSES.
United Nations Conference on Human Settlements, Vancouver, B.C., 1976. Global review of human settlements. [New York?] 1976. 237 p. : LC Card 80-515666 DDC 330 s 307.7/6 19
JX1977 .A2 A/CONF.70/A/1

QUALITY OF LIFE - UNITED STATES.
United States. Panel on the Quality of American Life. The quality of American life in the eighties . Washington , 1980. 140 p. : LC Card 81-281 DDC 361.6/1/0973 19
HN60 .U545 1980

Quality of production and improvement in the workplace . United States. Congress. House. Committee on Ways and Means. Subcommittee on Trade. Washington , 1980 [i.e. 1981] iii, 186 p. : LC Card 81-600833 DDC 338/.06 19
KF27 .W348 1980k

QUALITY OF PRODUCTS.
United States. Congress. House. Committee on Ways and Means. Subcommittee on Trade. Quality of production and improvement in the workplace . Washington , 1980 [i.e. 1981] iii, 186 p. : LC Card 81-600833 DDC 338/.06 19
KF27 .W348 1980k

QUALITY OF WATER. see WATER QUALITY.

Quality of working life centers. National Center for Productivity and Quality of Working Life.

Directory of productivity and quality of working life centers. Washington , 1978. viii, 68 p. ; LC Card 79-602026
HC110.I52 N37 1978a

Quammen, David, 1948- Appropriate jobs : common goals of labor & appropriate technology / by David Quammen ; editor, Brian Mertz. Butte, Mont. : National Center for Appropriate Technology, c1980. 14 p. : ill. ; 28 cm. (NCAT brief . 3) Bibliography: p. 13-14. LC Card 80-138213 DDC 331.12/0973 19
1. Renewable energy sources - United States. 2. Labor supply - United States. 3. Technology - United States. I. Mertz, Brian. II. Series: National Center for Appropriate Technology. (United States.) NCAT brief , 3. III. Title.
HC103.7 .Q35

A quantitative sampling program of benthic communities in nearshore subtidal areas within the Rosario Strait region of Northern Puget Sound, Washington State (1976) /. Smith, Gary Frederick. [Olympia] [1979] vi, 105 p. : LC Card 80-622612 DDC 591.9797/7 19
QH105.W2 S65

Quantities and costs of wood biomass in Idaho /. Johnson, Leonard R. Moscow, Idaho , 1979. 10 p. : LC Card 79-624515 DDC 333.79/38 19
TP360 .J58

QUANTITY COOKERY.
Barr, Phyllis. School lunch recipe book /. Harrisburg, PA (333 Market St., Harrisburg PA 17126) [1980] c1979. 340 p. : LC Card 80-624454 DDC 641.5/71 19
TX820 .B34 1980

QUANTITY OF MONEY. see MONEY SUPPLY.

QUARRIES AND QUARRYING - ENVIRONMENTAL ASPECTS - ALABAMA - CALHOUN CO.
Moore, James D. Effect of quarry blasting on ground-water quality in a limestone terrane in Calhoun County, Alabama /. Auburn, Ala. [1979] vi, 72 p. : LC Card 79-625904 DDC 333.91/009761 s 628.1/683 19
TC1 .A85 no. 38 TD224.A2

QUARRIES AND QUARRYING - NEBRASKA - LITTLE NEMAHA RIVER WATERSHED - MAPS.
United States. Soil Conservation Service. Historical, utilities, and quarries map, lower Little Nemaha watershed, Johnson, Nemaha, Otoe, and Richardson Counties, Nebraska /. Lincoln, Nebr. , 1979. 1 map : LC Card 81-691089
G4192.L5E635 1979 .U5

QUARRIES AND QUARRYING - OREGON - BY-PRODUCTS.
Martinez, G. M. (George M.) Recovery of byproduct heavy minerals from Oregon and Washington sand and gravel operations /. Washington , 1981. p. cm. LC Card 81-6080 DDC 622 s 622/.751 19
TN23 .U43 TN939

QUARRIES AND QUARRYING - WASHINGTON (STATE) - BY-PRODUCTS.
Martinez, G. M. (George M.) Recovery of byproduct heavy minerals from Oregon and Washington sand and gravel operations /. Washington , 1981. p. cm. LC Card 81-6080 DDC 622 s 622/.751 19
TN23 .U43 TN939

QUARTZ - STANDARDS.
Mavrodineanu, Radu, 1910- Metal-on-quartz filters as a standard reference material for spectrophotometry--SRM 2031 /. [Washington, D.C.] [1980] xiii, 110 p. : LC Card 79-600192 DDC 602/.18 s 681/.414 19
QC100 .U57 no. 260-68 QC465

A quasi three-dimensional finite-difference ground-water flow model with a field application /. Achmad, Grufron. Baltimore, Md. , 1979. iv, 22, [35] p. : LC Card 80-621644 DDC 557.52 s 551.49/0724 19
QE121 .A23 no. 33 TC176

Quaternary faulting in East Texas /. Collins, Edward W. Austin, Tex. , 1980. iii, 20 p. : LC Card 80-621660 DDC 553/.09764 s 551.8/7/09764 19
TN24.T4 T38 no. 80-1 QE606.5.U6

QUATERNARY PERIOD. see GEOLOGY, STRATIGRAPHIC - QUATERNARY.

QUECHUA INDIANS - ASTRONOMY.
Urton, Gary, 1946- At the crossroads of the earth and the sky . Austin , c1981. p. cm. ISBN 0-292-70349-X LC Card 81-4331 DDC 520/.985/37 19
F2230.2.K4 U77 1981

QUECHUA INDIANS - PHILOSOPHY.
Urton, Gary, 1946- At the crossroads of the earth and the sky . Austin , c1981. p. cm. ISBN 0-292-70349-X LC Card 81-4331 DDC 520/.985/37 19
F2230.2.K4 U77 1981

Queens College, Flushing, N. Y. (Old Catalog form: New York (City). Queens college) African art at Queens College. [Flushing, N. Y. , 1969] [28] p. :
NYPL [Sc Micro F-8095]

Bridge Project. The preparation of teachers for schools in culturally deprived neighborhoods /. Flushing, N. Y. , 1965. xviii, 400 p. ; LC Card 67-61064 *NYPL [Sc F 80-191]*

Queens College, New Brunswick, N. J. see Rutgers University, New Brunswick, N. J.

Quemado Lakes. Brandvold, D. K. Chemical and biological survey of the Upper Gila River system in New Mexico . Las Cruces, N.M. [1979] iii, 48 p. ; LC Card 80-622273 DDC 333.91/009789 s 628.1/686789/692 19
GB705.N6 N64 no. 110 QH105.N6

Questions of cinema /. Heath, Stephen. Bloomington , c1981. p. cm. ISBN 0-253-15913-X LC Card 81-47524 DDC 791.43/01 19
PN1995 .H397

Quests with U. S. accelerators--50 years, the high energy physics and nuclear physics research programs . United States. Congress. House. Committee on Science and Technology. Subcommittee on Energy Research and Production. Washington , c1980 [i.e. 1981] iii, 463 p. : LC Card 81-601187 DDC 539.7/072073 19
KF27 .S3936 1980d

QUETZALCOATL.
Brundage, Burr Cartwright, 1912- The phoenix of the Western world . Norman , c1981. p. cm. ISBN 0-8061-1773-7 LC Card 81-40278 DDC 299/.78 19
F1219.76.R45 B78

QUETZALCOHUATL. see QUETZALCOATL.

Quien sabe? . University of California, Los Angeles. Chicano Studies Research Center. Los Angeles, Calif. , 1981. p. cm. ISBN 0-89551-000-6 LC Card 81-10156 DDC 016.973/046872 19
Z1361.M4 U55 1981 E184.M5

Quindry, Kenneth E. The Tennessee constitutional spending limitation : history of spending limitations and the budgetary effects of Tennessee's Proposal nine / Kenneth E. Quindry, Barabara S. Haskew, and Niles Schoening. Knoxville : Center for Business and Economic Research, College of Business Administration, University of Tennessee, 1979. vii, 69 p. : ill. ; 28 cm. At head of title: Contract completion report. LC Card 80-621169 DDC 336.3/9/09768 19
1. Taxation - Tennessee. 2. Tennessee - Appropriations and expenditures. 3. Government spending policy - Tennessee. I. Haskew, Barbara S., joint author. II. Schoening, Niles, joint author. III. Title.
HJ2434 .Q56

QUININE SULFATE - OPTICAL PROPERTIES - STANDARDS.
Velapoldi, R. A. A Fluorescence standard reference material, quinine sulfate dihydrate /. Washington, D.C. , 1980. xvi, 122 p. : LC Card 79-600119 DDC 602/.18 s 535/.35 19
QC100 .U57 no. 260-64 QC477

Quinn, Michael J. Glacial geology of Champaign County, Ohio / by Michael J. Quinn and Richard P. Goldthwait ; [cartographers, R. Anne Berry and James A. Brown]. Columbus : State of Ohio, Dept. of Natural Resources, Division of Geological Survey, 1979. iii, 17 p. : ill., fold. map ; 29 cm. (Report of investigations - State of Ohio, Division of Geological Survey ; no. 111) Bibliography: p. 16-17. Map inserted. LC Card

80-622747 DDC 557.71 s 551.7/92/09771465
19
*1. Glacial epoch - Ohio - Champaign County. I.
Goldthwait, Richard Parker, 1911-. II. Series: Ohio.
Division of Geological Survey. Report of
investigations , no. 111. III. Title.*
QE151 .A186 no. 111 QE697

Quinn, Rodney S. Maine. Dept. of State. Election
laws & procedures handbook, 1980 /. [Augusta]
[1980] 71 p. : LC Card 81-621247 DDC
342.741/07 347.41027 19
KFM420 .A873

Quirk, Lawler & Matusky Engineers. Hydraulic
analysis of the New York City water supply
system / Quirk, Lawler & Matusky Engineer.
Tappan, N. Y. : Quirk, Lawler & Matusky
Engineers, 1974. xviii, 82, A1-A9 p. : ill. ; 27
cm. At head of title: North Atlantic Division, U. S.
Army Corps of Engineers. On cover: Northeastern
United States Water Supply Study. "Contract no.
DACW 52-73-C-009."
*1. Water supply - New York (City). I. Northeastern
United States Water Supply Study. II. United States.
Army. Corps of Engineers. North Atlantic Division. III.
Title.*   **NYPL [JSF 80-751]**

**QUITO REGION (ECUADOR) - RURAL
  CONDITIONS.**
Cushner, Nicholas P. Farm and factory .
Albany, N.Y. [1982] p. cm. ISBN 0-87395-570-6
LC Card 81-13537 DDC 338.1/09866/13 19
HD1890.Q5 C87

R.B. Kitaj / organized by Joe Shannon.
Washington, D.C. : Smithsonian Institution
Press : For sale by the Supt. of Docs., U. S.
G.P.O., 1981. p. cm. Catalog of a traveling
exhibition held at Hirshhorn Museum and Sculpture
Garden, Smithsonian Institution, Washington, D.C.,
Cleveland Museum of Art, and Städtische Kunsthalle
Düsseldorf, Sept. 17, 1981-Mar. 21, 1982. Bibliography:
p. LC Card 81-607809 DDC 759.13 19
*1. Kitaj, R. B. - Exhibitions. I. Kitaj, R. B. II. Shannon,
Joe. III. Hirshhorn Museum and Sculpture Garden. IV.
Cleveland Museum of Art. V. Städtische Kunsthalle
Düsseldorf.*
N6537.K53 A4 1981

**R. E. A. see United States. Rural Electrification
  Administration.**

R. F. E. see Radio Free Europe.

**R. L. Banks & Associates, inc., Washington, D.
  C. see Banks (R. L.) & Associates, inc.,
  Washington, D. C.**

**R.L.G. military operations and activities in the
  Laotian Panhandle.** Vongsavanh, Soutchay.
RLG military operations and activities in the
Laotian panhandle /. Washington, D.C. , 1981.
p. cm. LC Card 81-10934 DDC 959.704/34 19
DS557.8.L3 V66

**R. O. T. C. see United States. Army. Reserve
  Officers' Training Corps.**

**R. P. A. see Regional Plan Association, New
  York.**

**R. P. D. B. see Central New York Regional
  Planning and Development Board.**

Raat, W. Dirk (William Dirk), 1939- Mexico,
from independence to revolution, 1810-1910 /.
Lincoln , c1982. p. cm. ISBN 0-8032-3858-4 LC
Card 81-10503 DDC 972 19
F1231.5 .M66

Rabb, R. L. Movement of highly mobile insects .
Raleigh, N.C. [1979] xii, 456 p. : LC Card
80-624277 DDC 595.78/04525 19
QL551.S85 M68

RABBIS - UNITED STATES - BIOGRAPHY.
Urofsky, Melvin I. A voice that spoke for
justice . Albany , 1981. p. cm. ISBN
0-87395-538-2 LC Card 81-5676 DDC
296.8/346/0924 B 19
BM755.W53 U76

Rabe, Fred W. Aquatic natural areas in Idaho /
by F.W. Rabe and N.L. Savage ; submitted to
Office of Water Research and Technology,
United States Dept. of the Interior. Moscow,
Idaho : Idaho Water Resources Research
Institute, University of Idaho, [1977] 103 p., [7]
leaves of plates : ill. ; 28 cm. At head of title:
Research technical completion report, project
A-046-IDA. "June 1977." Bibliography: p. 65-70. LC
Card 80-621482 DDC 333.95/2/09796 19
*1. Natural areas - Idaho. 2. Aquatic resources - Idaho.
I. Savage, N. L., joint author. II. United States. Dept.*

of the Interior. Office of Water Research and
Technology. III. Title.
QH76.5.I2 R33

Rabey, Daniel F. Leifer, Lewis. Soil survey of
Los Angeles County, California, west San
Fernando Valley area /. [Washington , 1980]
viii, 107 p., [2] fold. leaves of plates : LC Card
80-602305 DDC 631.4/7/79493 19
S599.C2 L44

Rabinowitz, Howard N., 1942- Southern Black
leaders of the Reconstruction era /. Urbana ,
c1982. p. cm. ISBN 0-252-00929-0 LC Card
81-11372 DDC 975/.004960730922 B 19
E185.92 .S68

Rabkin, Judith G. Attitudes toward the mentally
ill . Rockville, Md. (5600 Fisher Lane,
Rockville, Md., 20857) , Washington, D.C. ,
1980. ix, 76 p. ; LC Card 80-600135 DDC
362.2/042 19
RC455.2.P85 A85

Rabockai, Tibor. Físico-química de superfícies /
por Tibor Rabockai. Washington, D.C. :
Secretaria-Geral da Organização dos Estados
Americanos, Programa Regional de
Desenvolvimento Científico e Tecnológico,
1979. vii, 128 p. : ill. ; 23 cm. (Série de química .
monografia no. 20) "79-XXII-B-021-S"--p. 4 of cover.
Includes bibliographical references. LC Card
80-103037 DDC 540 s 541.3/453 19
*1. Surfaces (Physics). 2. Surface chemistry. I. Title. II.
Series.*
QD1 .S303 no. 20 QC173.4.S94

Raburn, Don R. Texas. Industrial Commission.
Financing industrial facilities in Texas. Austin,
Tex. [1980] 35 leaves ; LC Card 80-623086
DDC 658.1/52 19
HG4070.T4 T49 1980

RACE.
King, James C., 1904- The biology of race /.
Berkeley , c1981. p. cm. ISBN 0-520-04223-9
LC Card 81-1345 DDC 572 19
QH401 .K55 1981

RACE DISCRIMINATION.
United Nations. General Assembly. Committee
on the Elimination of Racial Discrimination.
Committee on the Elimination of Racial
Discrimination and the progress made towards
the achievement of the objectives of the
International Convention on the Elimination of
All Forms of Racial Discrimination . New
York , 1979. vi, 35 p. : LC Card 80-115627
DDC 300 s 341.4/81 19
JX1977 .A2 CERD/1 HT1521

RACE HORSES - DISEASES.
Boyd, Joseph H. New York State Racing and
Wagering Board drug medication study .
[Albany] , 1976. 69 leaves ; LC Card 78-621360
DDC 636.1/089558 19
SF951 .B79

**RACE PREJUDICE. see RACE
  DISCRIMINATION.**

Race relations in Oklahoma /. Phillips, Glenn S.
Oklahoma City, Okla. , 1979. 81 p. ; LC Card
80-621086 DDC 305.8/009766 19
F705.A1 P48

Race track messenger services . Illinois. General
Assembly. Legislative Investigating Commission.
Chicago , 1977. vi, 62 p. ; LC Card 77-623003
HV6721.I3 I43 1977   **NYPL [*XME-9550]**

Rachal, J. Valley. (joint author) Rufener, Brent L.
Management effectiveness measures for NIDA
drug abuse treatment programs /. Rockville,
Md. , Washington, D.C. , 1977. 2 v. ; LC Card
80-603129 DDC 362.2/9386/0973 19
RC564 .R83

**RACIAL DISCRIMINATION. see RACE
  DISCRIMINATION.**

The racing and breeding industry views itself .
New York (State). Legislature. Joint Legislative
Task Force to Study and Evaluate the
Pari-Mutuel Racing and Breeding Industry in
New York State. Advisory Council. Albany,
N.Y. [1979] vi, 187 p. ; LC Card 81-622047
DDC 338.4/7984/009747 19
SF335.U6 N697 1979

RACISM - UNITED STATES.
Dovidio, John F. The subtlety of white racism .
Newark , 1977. 85 leaves : LC Card 78-621433
DDC 305.8/96073 19
E185.615 .D67

**Racketeer Influenced and Corrupt Organizations
  Act.** New Jersey. State Legislature. General
Assembly. Judiciary, Law, Public Safety, and
Defense Committee. Committee meeting before
Assembly Judiciary, Law, Public Safety, and
Defense Committee on A-1079 (Racketeer
Influenced and Corrupt Organizations Act) .
[Trenton] [1980] 18, 22, 36 p. ; LC Card
81-621304 DDC 345.749 347.4905 19
KFN1811.4 .J78 1980a

RACKETEERING - NEW JERSEY.
New Jersey. State Legislature. General
Assembly. Judiciary, Law, Public Safety, and
Defense Committee. Committee meeting before
Assembly Judiciary, Law, Public Safety, and
Defense Committee on A-1079 (Racketeer
Influenced and Corrupt Organizations Act) .
[Trenton] [1980] 18, 22, 36 p. ; LC Card
81-621304 DDC 345.749 347.4905 19
KFN1811.4 .J78 1980a

Radan, George T. The Archaeology of Roman
Pannonia /. Lexington, Ky. , Budapest, c1980.
506 p., clxvii p. of plates : ISBN 963-05-1886-4
(Akadémiai Kiadó) LC Card 77-80463 DDC
939/.8 19
DG59.P2 A73

RADAR IN AERONAUTICS.
United States. Congress. House. Committee on
Armed Services. Subcommittee on
Investigations. Leaks of classified national
defense information--stealth aircraft .
Washington , 1980 [i.e. 1981] ii, 228 p. ; LC
Card 81-601135 DDC 353.0071/45 19
KF27 .A753 1980c

**RADAR IN SPEED LIMIT ENFORCEMENT -
  LAW AND LEGISLATION - NORTH
  CAROLINA.**
North Carolina. Legislative Research
Commission. Police traffic radar . [Raleigh]
[1980] 11, [36] p. : LC Card 80-623288 DDC
363.2/52 19
KFN7697.8 .A25 1980

Radatz, Clark G. Wisconsin. Legislative reference
bureau. Wisconsin's outlook on energy /.
Madison, Wis. [1980] 17 p. ; LC Card
80-624141 DDC 300/.9775 s 346.77504/679
300/.9775 s 347.75064679 19
KFW2415 .L4 80-4 KFW2686

Rader, Melvin Miller, 1903- The right to hope :
crisis and community / by Melvin Rader.
Seattle : University of Washington Press, c1981.
p. cm. Includes index. ISBN 0-295-95836-7 LC
Card 81-51284 DDC 909.82 19
*1. Civilization, Modern - 1950- - Addresses, essays,
lectures. 2. Hope - Addresses, essays, lectures. 3.
Community - Addresses, essays, lectures. I. Title.*
HM101 .R24

Radiation control act of Indiana . Indiana. Laws,
statutes, etc. Indianapolis [1959?] 8 p. ; LC
Card 80-125356 DDC 344.772/0472
347.7204472 19
KFI3380.A8 A32 1959

**Radiation control programs provide limited
  protection .** United States. General Accounting
Office. [Washington, D.C. , 1979] iv, 62 p. ;
LC Card 80-601720 DDC 363.1/79 19
RA569 .U4966 1979

**RADIATION DISEASE. see RADIATION -
  TOXICOLOGY.**

RADIATION - DOSAGE.
Cook, John R. (John Richard), 1950-
Occupational exposure to ionizing radiation in
the United States . Washington, D.C. , 1980
[i.e. 1981] x, 74, [68] p. : LC Card 81-601500
DDC 363.1/79 19
RC965.R25 C66

United States. Ad Hoc Interagency Population
Dos Assessement Group. Population dose and
health impact of the accident at the Three Mile
Island Nuclear Station . Washington , 1979. 77,
[16] p. : LC Card 79-602730
RA569 .U46 1979

United States. President's Commission on the
Accident at Three Mile Island. Public Health
and Safety Task Force. Reports of the Public
Health and Safety Task Force on public health
and safety summary, health physics and
dosimetry, radiation health effects, behavioral
effects, public health and epidemiology.
Washington, D.C. [1980] 423 p. : LC Card

80-601717   DDC 363.1/79 19
RA569 .U4977 1980

RADIATION - DOSAGE - CONGRESSES.
Known effects of low-level radiation exposure .
[Bethesda, Md.] [1980] 147 p. :   LC Card
80-601671   DDC 616.9/897 19
RA1231.R2 K59

Radioactivity in consumer products /.
Washington , Springfield, Va. , 1978. xi, 509
p. :   LC Card 79-602786
RA569 .R29

Radiation exposure compensation act of 1979 .
United States. Congress. Senate. Committee on
Labor and Human Resources. Subcommittee on
Health and Scientific Research. Washington ,
1980. iv, 132 p. :   LC Card 80-603432   DDC
346.7303/8 347.30638 19
KF26 .L274 1980d

**RADIATION INJURY. see RADIATION -
PHYSIOLOGICAL EFFECT;
RADIATION - TOXICOLOGY.**

**RADIATION, IONIZING. see IONIZING
RADIATION.**

**RADIATION - PHYSIOLOGICAL EFFECT -
CONGRESSES. .**
Known effects of low-level radiation exposure .
[Bethesda, Md.] [1980] 147 p. :   LC Card
80-601671   DDC 616.9/897 19
RA1231.R2 K59

**RADIATION PROTECTION. see
RADIATION - SAFETY MEASURES.**

RADIATION - SAFETY MEASURES.
(1978) United States. Congress. Senate.
Committee on Governmental Affairs. Federal
regulation of radiation health and safety .
Washington , 1978. v, 180 p. ;   LC Card
80-602517   DDC 363.1/79 19
RA569 .U4962 1978

(1979) United States. General Accounting
Office. Radiation control programs provide
limited protection . [Washington, D.C. , 1979]
iv, 62 p. ;   LC Card 80-601720   DDC 363.1/79 19
RA569 .U4966 1979

**RADIATION - SAFETY MEASURES -
GOVERNMENT POLICY - UNITED
STATES.**
United States. Congress. Senate. Committee on
Governmental Affairs. Federal regulation of
radiation health and safety . Washington , 1978.
v, 180 p. ;   LC Card 80-602517   DDC 363.1/79 19
RA569 .U4962 1978

United States. General Accounting Office.
Radiation control programs provide limited
protection . [Washington, D.C. , 1979] iv, 62
p. ;   LC Card 80-601720   DDC 363.1/79 19
RA569 .U4966 1979

United States Radiation Policy Council.
Progress report and preliminary 1981-83
agenda. Washington, D.C. (Room 3026, New
Executive Office Building, 726 Jackson Place,
N.W., Washington, D.C., 20503) , 1980. 177 p.
in various pagings ;   LC Card 81-600523   DDC
353.0075 19
RA569 .U17 1980

**RADIATION - SAFETY REGULATIONS -
ILLINOIS.**
Illinois. Dept. of Public Health. Rules and
regulations for protection against radiation.
[Springfield] [197-] ca. 210 p. in various
pagings ;   LC Card 80-621603   DDC 344.773/0472
19
KFI1580.A8 A3 1974

**RADIATION - SAFETY REGULATIONS -
INDIANA.**
Indiana. Laws, statutes, etc. Radiation control
act of Indiana . Indianapolis [1959?] 8 p. ;   LC
Card 80-125356   DDC 344.772/0472
347.7204472 19
KFI3380.A8 A32 1959

**RADIATION - SAFETY REGULATIONS -
UNITED STATES.**
Radiological health, March 1936-March 1978 .
[Rockville, Md.] [1979] xii, 232 p. ;   LC Card
80-602315   DDC 344.7/0472 19
KF3948 .A33 1979

United States. Bureau of Radiological Health.
Regulations for the administration and
enforcement of the Radiation control for health
and safety act of 1968. Rockville, Md. ,

Washington, D.C. , 1978. vi, 68 p. :   LC Card
79-603753   DDC 344.73/0472 19
KF3948.A355 A2 1978

United States. Congress. Senate. Committee on
Governmental Affairs. Federal regulation of
radiation health and safety . Washington , 1978.
v, 180 p. ;   LC Card 80-602517   DDC 363.1/79 19
RA569 .U4962 1978

United States. Congress. Senate. Committee on
Labor and Human Resources. Subcommittee on
Health and Scientific Research.
Consumer-patient radiation safety and health
act of 1979 . Washington , 1980. iv, 316 p. :
LC Card 80-603350   DDC 344.73/0472 19
KF26 .L274 1980c

United States. General Accounting Office.
Radiation control programs provide limited
protection . [Washington, D.C. , 1979] iv, 62
p. ;   LC Card 80-601720   DDC 363.1/79 19
RA569 .U4966 1979

**RADIATION SHIELDING. see SHIELDING
(RADIATION)**

RADIATION - TOXICOLOGY.
United States. Ad Hoc Interagency Population
Dos Assessement Group. Population dose and
health impact of the accident at the Three Mile
Island Nuclear Station . Washington , 1979. 77,
[16] p. :   LC Card 79-602730
RA569 .U46 1979

United States. President's Commission on the
Accident at Three Mile Island. Public Health
and Safety Task Force. Reports of the Public
Health and Safety Task Force on public health
and safety summary, health physics and
dosimetry, radiation health effects, behavioral
effects, public health and epidemiology.
Washington, D.C. [1980] 423 p. :   LC Card
80-601717   DDC 363.1/79 19
RA569 .U4977 1980

**RADIATION - TOXICOLOGY -
CONGRESSES.**
Known effects of low-level radiation exposure .
[Bethesda, Md.] [1980] 147 p. :   LC Card
80-601671   DDC 616.9/897 19
RA1231.R2 K59

**RADIATION WORKERS - DISEASES AND
HYGIENE - UNITED STATES.**
Cook, John R. (John Richard), 1950-
Occupational exposure to ionizing radiation in
the United States . Washington, D.C. , 1980
[i.e. 1981] x, 74, [68] p. :   LC Card 81-601500
DDC 363.1/79 19
RC965.R25 C66

RADICALS (CHEMISTRY) - SPECTRA.
(1981) Hug, Gordon L. Optical spectra of
nonmetallic inorganic transient species in
aqueous solution /. Washington [1981] vi, 159
p. :   LC Card 80-606826   DDC 602/.18 s 543/.0858
19
QC100 .U573 no. 69 QC454.A2

**RADIO AIR TRAFFIC CONTROL SYSTEMS -
CONGRESSES.**
OTA Seminar on the Discrete Address Beacon
System (DABS), Washington, D.C., 1980.
Proceedings of the OTA Seminar on the
Discrete Address Beacon System (DABS).
Washington, D.C. [1980] vii, 46 p. :   LC Card
80-600093   DDC 387.7/4042/0973 19
TL696.R25 O18 1980

**RADIO AUDIENCES - ILLINOIS -
STATISTICS.**
Elrick and Lavidge. Public library usage in
Illinois . Springfield , 1977. 31 p. :   LC Card
78-620783   DDC 302.2/3 19
HE8700.7.A8 E57 1977 suppl

RADIO BROADCASTING - ROMANIA.
United States. Congress. House. Committee on
Foreign Affairs. Subcommittee on International
Operations. Allegations concerning the
Romanian service of Radio Free Europe .
Washington , 1980. iii, 98 p. ;   LC Card
80-602459   DDC 384.54/43 19
KF27 .F647 1980

RADIO - CONGRESSES.
United States. Congress. House. Committee on
Foreign Affairs. Subcommittee on International
Operations. The World Administrative Radio
Conference and international communications
policy . Washington , 1980. iii, 135 p. :   LC

Card 80-603991   DDC 384.54 19
KF27 .F647 1979e

**RADIO-ELEMENTS. see RADIOACTIVE
SUBSTANCES.**

RADIO FREE EUROPE.
United States. Congress. House. Committee on
Foreign Affairs. Subcommittee on International
Operations. Allegations concerning the
Romanian service of Radio Free Europe .
Washington , 1980. iii, 98 p. ;   LC Card
80-602459   DDC 384.54/43 19
KF27 .F647 1980

**RADIO FREQUENCY - HANDBOOKS,
MANUALS, ETC.**
National Measurement Laboratory (U. S.). Time
and Frequency Division. Time and frequency
users' manual /. Washington, D.C. , 1979. xvi,
248 p. :   LC Card 79-600169   DDC 602/.18 s
529/.7 19
QC100 .U57 no. 559 QB209

RADIO IN AERONAUTICS.
(1979) United States. Advisory Committee on
Cable Signal Leakage. Final report of the
Advisory Committee on Cable Signal Leakage
to the Chief, Cable Television Bureau, Federal
Communications Commission. Washington,
D.C. [1979] 110, [132] p. :   LC Card 80-601686
DDC 629.135 19
TL694.I6 U45 1979

**RADIO INDUSTRY AND TRADE - LAW
AND LEGISLATION - UNITED STATES.**
United States. Congress. House. Committee on
Interstate and Foreign Commerce.
Subcommittee on Communications. Financial
disclosure . Washington , 1980. iii, 99 p. ;   LC
Card 80-602502   DDC 343.73/09945 19
KF27 .I5537 1980a

**RADIO - LAW AND LEGISLATION -
UNITED STATES.**
United States. Congress. House. Committee on
Interstate and Foreign Commerce.
Subcommittee on Communications. Prohibited
renewal considerations and crossownership
restrictions . Washington , 1980. iii, 98 p. ;   LC
Card 80-602804   DDC 343.73/09945 19
KF27 .I5537 1980b

**RADIO MODULATION. see MODULATION
(ELECTRONICS)**

**RADIO STATIONS - LICENSES - UNITED
STATES.**
United States. Congress. House. Committee on
Interstate and Foreign Commerce.
Subcommittee on Communications. Financial
disclosure . Washington , 1980. iii, 99 p. ;   LC
Card 80-602502   DDC 343.73/09945 19
KF27 .I5537 1980a

RADIO VISION. see TELEVISION.

**RADIOACTIVE CHROMIUM. see
CHROMIUM.**

RADIOACTIVE DATING.
Irradiation of samples for $^{40}Ar/^{39}Ar$ dating
using the Geological Survey TRIGA reactor /.
Washington , 1980. p. cm.   LC Card 80-607859
DDC 551.7/01 19
QE508 .I77

Mixon, Robert B. Uranium-series dating of
mollusks and corals and age of Pleistocene
deposits, Chesapeake Bay area, Virginia and
Maryland /. Washington , 1981. p. cm.   LC
Card 81-607014   DDC 551.7/92/097521 19
QE697 .M7

Radioactive decay data tables . Kocher, David C.
Oak Ridge, TN , 1981. p. cm.   ISBN
0-87079-124-9   LC Card 81-607800   DDC
539.7/5 19
QC795.8.D4 K62

RADIOACTIVE DECAY - TABLES.
Kocher, David C. Radioactive decay data
tables . Oak Ridge, TN , 1981. p. cm.   ISBN
0-87079-124-9   LC Card 81-607800   DDC
539.7/5 19
QC795.8.D4 K62

RADIOACTIVE DECONTAMINATION.
United States. Nuclear Regulatory Commission.
Three Mile Island Program Office. Final
environmental assessment for decontamination
of the Three Mile Island Unit 2 reactor building
atmosphere. Washington , 1980. 1 v. :

NYPL [JSK 80-129]

RADIOACTIVE DUST. see RADIOACTIVE FALLOUT.

RADIOACTIVE FALLOUT.
Spencer, L. V. (Lewis Van Clief), 1924-
Structure shielding against fallout gamma rays from nuclear detonations /. [Washington, D.C.?] , 1980. xvi, 967 p : LC Card 80-600120
DDC 602/.18 s 363.1/89 19
QC100 .U57 no. 570 UF787

RADIOACTIVE ISOTOPES. see RADIOISOTOPES.

Radioactive mineral occurrences of Colorado and bibliography /. Nelson-Moore, James L.
Denver, Colo. , 1978. ix, 1054 p. (2 fold.) : LC Card 80-621968   DDC 557.88 s 553.4/93/09788 19
QE91 .A4 no. 40 QE364.2.R3

RADIOACTIVE POLLUTION.
United Nations. Scientific Committee on the Effects of Atomic Radiation. Sources and effects of ionizing radiation . New York , 1977. 725 p. : LC Card 79-112082 DDC 616.9/897 19
QP82.2.I53 U54 1977

RADIOACTIVE POLLUTION - CONGRESSES.
Roundtable Discussion of Radon in Buildings, National Bureau of Standards, 1979. Radon in buildings . Washington, D.C. [1980] x, 77 p. : LC Card 80-600069   DDC 602/.18 s 628.5/35 19
QC100 .U57 no. 581 TD885.5.R33

RADIOACTIVE POLLUTION - PENNSYLVANIA - HARRISBURG REGION.
United States. President's Commission on the Accident at Three Mile Island. Public Health and Safety Task Force. Reports of the Public Health and Safety Task Force on public health and safety summary, health physics and dosimetry, radiation health effects, behavioral effects, public health and epidemiology. Washington, D.C. [1980] 423 p. : LC Card 80-601717   DDC 363.1/79 19
RA569 .U4977 1980

RADIOACTIVE POLLUTION - PENNSYLVANIA - HARRISBURG REGION - MEASUREMENT.
United States. Ad Hoc Interagency Population Dos Assessement Group. Population dose and health impact of the accident at the Three Mile Island Nuclear Station . Washington , 1979. 77, [16] p. : LC Card 79-602730
RA569 .U46 1979

RADIOACTIVE POLLUTION - PENNSYLVANIA - HARRISBURG REGION - MEASUREMENT - CONGRESSES.
Known effects of low-level radiation exposure . [Bethesda, Md.] [1980] 147 p. : LC Card 80-601671   DDC 616.9/897 19
RA1231.R2 K59

RADIOACTIVE POLLUTION - UNITED STATES.
United States. General Accounting Office. The Environmental Protection Agency needs congressional guidance and support to guard the public in a period of radiation proliferation . [Washington] 1978. vii, 81 p. : LC Card 78-602990
TD171 .U57 1978   **NYPL [JLF 81-156]**

RADIOACTIVE PROSPECTING - SOUTH CAROLINA - CHARLESTON REGION.
Aeroradioactivity maps in heavy-mineral exploration--Charleston, South Carolina area /. Washington [1981] p. cm. LC Card 80-607879
DDC 622/.18 19
TN269 .A28

RADIOACTIVE SUBSTANCES - COLORADO.
Nelson-Moore, James L. Radioactive mineral occurrences of Colorado and bibliography /. Denver, Colo. , 1978. ix, 1054 p. (2 fold.) : LC Card 80-621968   DDC 557.88 s 553.4/93/09788 19
QE91 .A4 no. 40 QE364.2.R3

RADIOACTIVE SUBSTANCES - COLORADO - BIBLIOGRAPHY.
Nelson-Moore, James L. Radioactive mineral occurrences of Colorado and bibliography /. Denver, Colo. , 1978. ix, 1054 p. (2 fold.) : LC Card 80-621968   DDC 557.88 s 553.4/93/09788

19
QE91 .A4 no. 40 QE364.2.R3

RADIOACTIVE SUBSTANCES - LAW AND LEGISLATION - ILLINOIS.
Illinois. Dept. of Public Health. Rules and regulations for protection against radiation. [Springfield] [197-] ca. 210 p. in various pagings ; LC Card 80-621603   DDC 344.773/0472 19
KFI1580.A8 A3 1974

RADIOACTIVE SUBSTANCES - LAW AND LEGISLATION - INDIANA.
Indiana. Laws, statutes, etc. Radiation control act of Indiana . Indianapolis [1959?] 8 p. ; LC Card 80-125356   DDC 344.772/0472 347.7204472 19
KFI3380.A8 A32 1959

RADIOACTIVE SUBSTANCES - LAW AND LEGISLATION - NORTH CAROLINA.
North Carolina. Radiation Protection Commission. North Carolina regulations for protection against radiation /. Raleigh, N.C. [1980] 170 p. ; LC Card 80-622690 DDC 344.756/0472 19
KFN7780.A8 A32 1980

RADIOACTIVE SUBSTANCES - NEW JERSEY - TRANSPORTATION.
New Jersey. Legislature. General Assembly. Transportation and Communications Committee. Public hearing before subcommittee of Assembly Transportation and Communications Committee to investigate the transportation of radioactive cargo on highways within New Jersey (created pursuant to Assembly Resolution 3003), held August 21, 1979, Freeholders' Chambers, Bergen County Administration Building, Hackensack, New Jersey. [Trenton] [1979?] 59, 10 p. ; LC Card 80-622508 DDC 343.749/093 19
KFN1811.4 .T7 1979

RADIOACTIVE SUBSTANCES - SAFETY MEASURES - CONGRESSES.
Radioactivity in consumer products /. Washington , Springfield, Va. , 1978. xi, 509 p. : LC Card 79-602786
RA569 .R29

RADIOACTIVE SUBSTANCES - SAFETY REGULATIONS - IOWA.
Iowa. State Dept. of Health. Rules governing Radiation Emitting Equipment, State Department of Health . Des Moines , 1980. vii, 45 p. ; LC Card 81-621270 DDC 344.777/0472 347.7704472 19
KFI4580.A8 A32 1980

RADIOACTIVE SUBSTANCES - SAFETY REGULATIONS - NEW JERSEY.
New Jersey. Legislature. General Assembly. Committee on Agriculture and Environment. Public hearing before Assembly Agriculture and Environment Committee, on A-966 (the Radiation emergency response act), held April 8, 1980, Assembly Chamber, State House, Trenton, New Jersey. [Trenton] [1980] 79 p. in various pagings ; LC Card 80-623636 DDC 344.749/0472 19
KFN1811.4 .A3 1980

RADIOACTIVE SUBSTANCES - SAFETY REGULATIONS - NORTH CAROLINA.
North Carolina. Radiation Protection Commission. North Carolina regulations for protection against radiation /. Raleigh, N.C. [1980] 170 p. ; LC Card 80-622690 DDC 344.756/0472 19
KFN7780.A8 A32 1980

RADIOACTIVE SUBSTANCES - SAFETY REGULATIONS - UNITED STATES - CONGRESSES.
Radioactivity in consumer products /. Washington , Springfield, Va. , 1978. xi, 509 p. : LC Card 79-602786
RA569 .R29

RADIOACTIVE SUBSTANCES - SAFETY REGULATIONS - UNITED STATES - STATES.
Federal-State Reports, inc. Compilation of state laws and regulations on transportation of radioactive materials /. Washington, D.C. , 1980. ca. 300 p. ; LC Card 80-601610 DDC 343.73/093 19
KF3948.Z95 F4

RADIOACTIVE SUBSTANCES - TOXICOLOGY.
National Council on Radiation Protection and Measurements. Management of persons accidentally contaminated with radionuclides . Washington, D.C. , 1980, c1979. vi, 205 . ISBN 0-913392-49-9 (pbk.) LC Card 79-91648 DDC 616.9/897 19
RA1231.R2 N26 1979

RADIOACTIVE SUBSTANCES - TRANSPORTATION - LAW AD LEGISLATION - UNITED STATES.
United States. Congress. House. Committee on Public Works and Transportation. Subcommittee on Surface Transportation. Transportation of hazardous materials through city streets . Washington , 1980. iv, 220 p. : LC Card 81-600847   DDC 343.73/0942 347.303942 19
KF27 .P8966 1980d

RADIOACTIVE SUBSTANCES - TRANSPORTATION - LAW AND LEGISLATION - NEW JERSEY.
New Jersey. Legislature. General Assembly. Transportation and Communications Committee. Public hearing before subcommittee of Assembly Transportation and Communications Committee to investigate the transportation of radioactive cargo on highways within New Jersey (created pursuant to Assembly Resolution 3003), held August 21, 1979, Freeholders' Chambers, Bergen County Administration Building, Hackensack, New Jersey. [Trenton] [1979?] 59, 10 p. ; LC Card 80-622508 DDC 343.749/093 19
KFN1811.4 .T7 1979

RADIOACTIVE SUBSTANCES - TRANSPORTATION - LAW AND LEGISLATION - UNITED STATES - STATES.
Federal-State Reports, inc. Compilation of state laws and regulations on transportation of radioactive materials /. Washington, D.C. , 1980. ca. 300 p. ; LC Card 80-601610 DDC 343.73/093 19
KF3948.Z95 F4

RADIOACTIVE WASTE DISPOSAL - CONGRESSES.
Symposium on Waste Management. Waste management; proceedings. Tucson, Ariz.
NYPL [JSP 80-332]

RADIOACTIVE WASTE DISPOSAL IN THE GROUND - RESEARCH - UNITED STATES.
U. S. Geological Survey research in radioactive waste disposal--fiscal year 1979 /. Reston, Va. , 1981. p. cm. LC Card 81-607990 DDC 557.3 s 621.48/38 19
QE75 .C5 no. 847 TD898

RADIOACTIVE WASTE DISPOSAL IN THE GROUND - UNITED STATES.
United States. Congress. House. Committee on Science and Technology. Subcommittee on Energy Research and Production. Low-level nuclear waste burial grounds . Washington , 1980. iii, 100 p. : LC Card 80-601955 DDC 363.7/28 19
KF27 .S3936 1979l

RADIOACTIVE WASTE DISPOSAL - KENTUCKY.
Kentucky. Interim Special Advisory Committee on Nuclear Waste Disposal. Report of the 1978-79 Interim Special Advisory Committee on Nuclear Waste Disposal. Frankfort, Ky. , 1980. viii, 95 p. : LC Card 80-621286 DDC 363.7/28 19
TD898 .K46 1980

RADIOACTIVE WASTE DISPOSAL - LAW AND LEGISLATION - NEW YORK (STATE) - WEST VALLEY.
United States. Congress. House. Committee on Interstate and Foreign Commerce. Subcommittee on Energy and Power. West Valley Demonstration Project Act . Washington , 1980. iv, 173 p. p. : LC Card 80-603899 DDC 344.73/04622 347.3044622 19
KF27 .I5542 1980m

RADIOACTIVE WASTE DISPOSAL - LAW AND LEGISLATION - UNITED STATES.
United States. Congress. House. Committee on Interstate and Foreign Commerce. Subcommittee on Energy and Power. Nuclear waste disposal . Washington , 1980. iii, 240 p. :

LC Card 80-603993   DDC 344.73/04622
347.3044622 19
KF27 .I5542 1980j

United States. Congress. House. Committee on
Interstate and Foreign Commerce.
Subcommittee on Energy and Power. Spent fuel
storage and disposal . Washington , 1980. iv,
342 p. :   LC Card 80-601371   DDC 344.73/04622
19
KF27 .I5542 1979p

United States. Congress. House. Committee on
Science and Technology. Subcommittee on
Energy Research and Production. H.R.
7418--Nuclear Waste Research, Development,
and Demonstration Act of 1980 . Washington ,
1980. iii, 118 p. :   LC Card 80-604068   DDC
344.73/04622 347.3044622 19
KF27 .S3936 1980a

United States. Congress. Senate. Committee on
Governmental Affairs. Subcommittee on
Energy, Nuclear Proliferation, and Federal
Services. Nuclear waste management
reorganization act of 1979 . Washington , 1980.
iv, 772 p. :   LC Card 80-602895   DDC
344.73/04622 19
KF26 .G6728 1979m

**RADIOACTIVE WASTE DISPOSAL - NEW
HAMPSHIRE.**
United States. Congress. Senate. Committee on
Appropriations. Subcommittee on
HUD-Independent Agencies. Nuclear and
hazardous waste problems in New Hampshire .
Washington , 1980 [i.e. 1981] iii, 122 p. ;   LC
Card 81-601754   DDC 363.7/28 19
KF26 .A6486 1980b

**RADIOACTIVE WASTE DISPOSAL -
UNITED STATES.**
United States. General Accounting Office.
Nuclear energy's dilemma . [Washington] ,
1977. xvii, 78 p. :   LC Card 77-603908
TD898 .U54 1977

United States. General Accounting Office. The
problem of disposing of nuclear low-level
waste . [Washington, D.C.] , 1980. vii, 30 p. ;
  LC Card 80-601696   DDC 363.7/28 19
TD898 .U54 1980

**RADIOACTIVE WASTE DISPOSAL -
UNITED STATES - FINANCE.**
United States. Congress. House. Committee on
Interior and Insular Affairs. Subcommittee on
Energy and the Environment. Department of
Energy authorizations for fiscal year 1981 .
Washington , 1980. iii, 116 p. :   LC Card
80-603650   DDC 353.0072/236823 19
KF27 .I518 1980a

United States. Congress. House. Committee on
Interstate and Foreign Commerce.
Subcommittee on Energy and Power. Spent fuel
storage and disposal . Washington , 1980. iv,
342 p. :   LC Card 80-601371   DDC 344.73/04622
19
KF27 .I5542 1979p

**Radioactive Waste Management Symposium. see
Symposium on Waste Management.**

**RADIOACTIVITY - GAMMA RAYS. see
GAMMA RAYS.**

Radioactivity in consumer products / edited by
A. Alan Moghissi ... [et al.]. Washington : U. S.
Nuclear Regulatory Commission ; Springfield,
Va. : can be obtained from National Technical
Information Service, 1978. xi, 509 p. : ill. ; 24
cm. "NUREG/CP-0001." Based on papers presented at
a symposium sponsored by the Bureau of Radiological
Health of the Food and Drug Administration, the
Office of Radiation Programs of the Environmental
Protection Agency, and the Office of Standards
Development of the Nuclear Regulatory Commission;
organized by the Office of Interdisciplinary Programs of
Georgia Institute of Technology and held in Atlanta
Feb. 2-4, 1977. Includes bibliographies and index. LC
Card 79-602786
*1. Radioactive substances - Safety measures -
Congresses. 2. Radiation - Dosage - Congresses. 3.
Commercial products - Congresses. 4. Radioactivity -
Physiological effect - Congresses. 5. Radioactive
substances - Safety regulations - United States -
Congresses. 6. Product safety - Law and legislation -
United States - Congresses. I. Moghissi, A. Alan. II.
United States. Bureau of Radiological Health. III.
United States. Environmental Protection Agency. Office
of Radiation Programs. IV. United States. Nuclear*

Regulatory Commission. Office of Standards
Development. V. Georgia. Institute of Technology,
Atlanta. Office of Interdisciplinary Programs.
RA569 .R29

**RADIOACTIVITY - PHYSIOLOGICAL
EFFECT - CONGRESSES.**
Radioactivity in consumer products /.
Washington , Springfield, Va. , 1978. xi, 509
p. :   LC Card 79-602786
RA569 .R29

**RADIOCHEMICAL ANALYSIS -
CONGRESSES.**
Conference on Analytical Chemistry in Energy
Technology, 23d, Gatlinburg, Tenn., 1979.
Radioelement analysis . Ann Arbor, Mich. ,
1980. xii, 424 p. :   ISBN 0-250-40343-9   LC Card
79-55145
QD605 .C66 1979   **NYPL *[JSE 80-1475]***

RADIOCHROMIUM. see CHROMIUM.

**RADIODIAGNOSIS. see DIAGNOSIS,
RADIOSCOPIC.**

Radioelement analysis . Conference on Analytical
Chemistry in Energy Technology, 23d,
Gatlinburg, Tenn., 1979. Ann Arbor, Mich. ,
1980. xii, 424 p. :   ISBN 0-250-40343-9   LC Card
79-55145
QD605 .C66 1979   **NYPL *[JSE 80-1475]***

**RADIOGRAPHY, MEDICAL - UNITED
STATES.**
United States. Congress. House. Committee on
Interstate and Foreign Commerce.
Subcommittee on Oversight and Investigations.
Unnecessary exposure to radiation from medical
and dental x-rays . Washington , 1980. v, 15
p. ;   LC Card 80-603049   DDC 363.1/89 19
RC78 .U534 1980

**RADIOISOTOPES IN MEDICINE. see
NUCLEAR MEDICINE.**

RADIOISOTOPES - TOXICOLOGY.
National Council on Radiation Protection and
Measurements. Management of persons
accidentally contaminated with radionuclides .
Washington, D.C. , 1980, c1979. vi, 205 ;
   ISBN 0-913392-49-9 (pbk.)   LC Card 79-91648
   DDC 616.9/897 19
RA1231.R2 N26 1979

**RADIOLOGIC TECHNOLOGISTS -
OREGON - DIRECTORIES.**
Oregon. State Board of Radiologic Technology.
1980 directory of licensees /. Portland, Or.
[1980] 77 p. :   LC Card 80-622693   DDC
616.07/57/025795 19
R895.A4 O73 1980

**RADIOLOGICAL DECONTAMINATION. see
RADIOACTIVE DECONTAMINATION.**

Radiological health, March 1936-March 1978 :
preamble compilation. [Rockville, Md.] : U. S.
Dept. of Health, Education, and Welfare, Public
Health Service, Food and Drug Administration,
[1979] xii, 232 p. ; 25 cm. Kept up to date by
pocket supplements. "All narrative preambles have been
compiled from published Federal register." LC Card
80-602315   DDC 344.73/0472 19
*1. Radiation - Safety regulations - United States. I.
United States. Food and Drug Administration. II.
Federal register.*
KF3948 .A33 1979

RADIOLOGY, MEDICAL - DIRECTORIES.
Directory of personnel responsible for
radiological health programs. Rockville, Md..
          NYPL *[JLL 80-243]*

**RADIOSCOPIC DIAGNOSIS. see
DIAGNOSIS, RADIOSCOPIC.**

**RADIOTHERAPY, HIGH ENERGY -
CONGRESSES.**
Conference on Neutrons from Electron Medical
Accelerators, National Bureau of Standards,
1979. Proceedings of a Conference on Neutrons
from Electron Medical Accelerators .
Washington , 1979. vii, 175 p. ;   LC Card
79-600133   DDC 602/.18 s 615.8/422 19
QC100 .U57 no. 554 RM849

Radner, Daniel. United States. Federal
Committee on Statistical Methodology.
Subcommittee on Matching Techniques. Report
on exact and statistical matching techniques /.
[Washington] , 1980] vii, 57 p. ;   LC Card
80-603147   DDC 001.4/224 19
HB849.49 .U53 1980

**RADON - ENVIRONMENTAL ASPECTS -
CONGRESSES.**
Roundtable Discussion of Radon in Buildings,
National Bureau of Standards, 1979. Radon in
buildings . Washington, D.C. [1980] x, 77 p. :
  LC Card 80-600069   DDC 602/.18 s 628.5/35
19
QC100 .U57 no. 581 TD885.5.R33

Radon in buildings . Roundtable Discussion of
Radon in Buildings, National Bureau of
Standards, 1979. Washington, D.C. [1980] x,
77 p. :   LC Card 80-600069   DDC 602/.18 s
628.5/35 19
QC100 .U57 no. 581 TD885.5.R33

Radwan, M. A., 1926- Impregnating and coating
with endrin to protect Douglas-fir seed from
rodents / M.A. Radwan, G.L. Crouch, and
W.D. Ellis. Portland, Or.: Pacific Northwest
Forest and Range Experiment Station, Forest
Service, U. S. Dept. of Agriculture, 1970. 17
p. : ill. ; 27 cm. (USDA Forest Service research
paper PNW - 94) Cover title. Bibliography: p. 17. LC
Card 77-608734   DDC 634.9/0979 s
634.9/75466 19
*1. Douglas fir - Diseases and pests. 2. Douglas fir -
Seed. 3. Endrin. 4. Peromyscus maniculatus. I. Crouch,
Glenn LeRoy, 1929- joint author. II. Ellis, Walter Dale,
joint author. III. Series: United States. Pacific
Northwest Forest and Range Experiment Station,
Portland, Or. USDA Forest Service research paper
PNW , 94. IV. Title.*
SD11 .A45614 no. 94 SB608.D6

Rae, James W. Trends in California transit labor
contract settlements / by James W. Rae,
Michael A. Grob. Sacramento : California Dept.
of Transportation, Division of Mass
Transportation, 1978. iii leaves, 48 p. : graphs ;
28 cm. "DMT-048." Includes bibliographical
references.   LC Card 79-625551   DDC
331.89/0413884/09794 19
*1. Collective bargaining - Transport workers -
California. I. Grob, Michael A., joint author. II.
California. Division of Mass Transportation. III. Title.*
HD6976.T72 U67

Ragan, James E. Water quality of selected North
Dakota lakes / Game and Fish Dept., Division
of Fisheries ; submitted by James E. Ragan.
[Bismarck, N.D.] : The Dept., 1978. [112] p. :
graphs ; 28 cm. (Report - North Dakota State Game
and Fish Department ; no. 1059A) "Dingell-Johnson
Division, Project F-2-R-25, Study II, Job II-A." LC
Card 79-626040   DDC 553.7/8/09784 19
*1. Water quality - North Dakota - Statistics. 2. Lakes -
North Dakota - Statistics. I. North Dakota. Division of
Fisheries. II. Series: North Dakota. Game and Fish
Dept. Report - North Dakota State Game and Fish
Department , no. 1059A. III. Title.*
TD224.N9 R33

Ragsdale, J. T.
(joint author) McJunkin, R. D. Compilation of
strong-motion records and preliminary data
from the Imperial Valley earthquake of 15
October 1979 /. Sacramento, CA , 1980. viii,
53 p. :   LC Card 80-622916   DDC 551.2/2/0979499
19
QE535.2.U6 M33

(joint author) Porter, Lawrence Delpino, 1932-
Processed data from the strong-motion records
of the Santa Barbara earthquake of 13 August
1978 . Sacramento, CA , 1979. 3 v. :   LC Card
80-622289   DDC 557.94 s 551.2/2/0979491 19
TN24.C2 A33 no. 144 QE535.2.U6

Rahenkamp, Sachs, Wells, and Associates.
Innovative zoning: a local officials guidebook /
prepared by Rahenkamp, Sachs, Wells and
Associates, inc. With the American Society of
Planning Officials and David Stoloff for the U.
S. Department of Housing and Urban
Development Office of Policy Development and
Research. [Washington] : The Office, 1977. 28
p.: ill. ; 28 cm. Microfiche (neg.) 1 sheet. 11 x 15
cm. (NYPL FSN 34,081) "Contract number H-2333R."
*1. Zoning - United States. I. American Society of
Planning Officials. II. Stoloff, David. III. United States.
Dept. of Housing and Urban Development. Office of
Policy Development and Research. IV. Title.*
         NYPL *[*XME-8967]*

Rahim, Enayetur. Scholars' guide to Washington,
D.C., for South Asian studies : Afghanistan,
Bangladesh, Bhutan, India, Maldive Islands,
Nepal, Pakistan, Sri Lanka / Enayetur Rahim ;
consultants, Purnima M. Bhatt, Louis A. Jacob.
Washington, D.C. : Smithsonian Institution

Raikes, Ralph, 1907-   *BIBLIOGRAPHIC GUIDE*   *182*

Press, 1981. p. cm. (Scholar's guide to Washington, D. C. no. 8) Bibliography: p. Includes indexes.   ISBN 0-87474-778-3 :   LC Card 81-607847   DDC 016.954/0720753 19

1. South Asia - Library resources - Washington, D.C. 2. South Asia - Archival resources - Washington, D.C. 3. South Asia - Societies, etc. - Directories. I. Title.
Z3185 .R34 DS335

RAIKES, RALPH, 1907-
United States. Congress. Senate. Committee on Agriculture, Nutrition, and Forestry. Nominations of Ralph Raikes and William D. Wampler . Washington , 1980. iii, 31 p. :   LC Card 80-604017   DDC 353.0082/33045 19
KF26 .A35 1980c

Rail Act of 1980 . United States. Congress. House. Committee on Interstate and Foreign Commerce. Subcommittee on Transportation and Commerce. Washington , 1980. vi, 653 p. ;   LC Card 80-603811   DDC 343.73/095/0262 347.303950262 19
KF27 .I5589 1980i

The Rail act of 1980 . United States. Congress. House. Committee on Interstate and Foreign Commerce. Subcommittee on Transportation and Commerce. Washington , 1980. vii, 91 p. :   LC Card 80-602213   DDC 343.73/095 19
KF2275.5 .I58

Rail deregulation study. Arizona. Transportation Planning Division. [Phoenix] [1980] 56 p. ;   LC Card 80-622666   DDC 385/.068 19
HE2757 .A73 1980

Rail-line abandonment in the North Central region /. Anderson, Dale G. Manhattan , 1979. 36 p. ;   LC Card 80-622127   DDC 385/.2042 19
HE2757 .A53

Rail restructuring assistance act of 1979 . United States. Congress. Senate. Committee on Commerce, Science, and Transportation. Subcommittee on Surface Transportation. Washington , 1980. iii, 59 p. :   LC Card 80-602440   DDC 343.73/095/0262 19
KF26 .C698 1980a

Rail service commuter problems on the Northeast Corridor. United States. Congress. House. Committee on Interstate and Foreign Commerce. Subcommittee on Transportation and Commerce. Washington , 1981. iv, 222 p. :   LC Card 81-600979   DDC 385/.22/0974 19
KF27 .I5589 1980m

Rail system investment analysis. Ernst and Ernst. Washington, 1977. 66 p. in various pagings   *NYPL [*XME-9311]*

Railpax. see Amtrak.

RAILROAD COMMISSION OF TEXAS.
Prindle, David F. (David Forrest), 1948- Petroleum politics and the Texas Railroad Commission /. Austin , 1981. p. cm.   ISBN 0-292-76474-X   LC Card 81-7535   DDC 353.97640087/5/06 19
HD9567.T3 P74

Railroad deregulation act of 1979 . United States. Congress. House. Committee on Interstate and Foreign Commerce. Subcommittee on Transportation and Commerce. Washington , 1979 i.e. 1980. viii, 1292 p. :   LC Card 80-603016   DDC 343.73/095 19
KF27 .I5589 1979o

RAILROAD LAW - GEORGIA.
Georgia. Public Service Commission. Transportation rules of the Georgia Public Service Commission . Atlanta, Ga. [1979?] 194 p. ;   LC Card 80-621174   DDC 343.758/093/02636 19
KFG296.A435 A2 1979

RAILROAD LAW - NORTHEASTERN STATES.
United States. Congress. House. Committee on Interstate and Foreign Commerce. Subcommittee on Transportation and Commerce. Northeast corridor improvement project . Washington , 1980. iii, 161 p. ;   LC Card 80-603407   DDC 343.73/0958 347.303958 19
KF27 .I5589 1980g

United States. Congress. Senate. Committee on Commerce, Science, and Transportation. Subcommittee on Surface Transportation. Northeast corridor completion act of 1979 . Washington , 1980. iii, 89 p. ;   LC Card

80-602086   DDC 343.73/095 347.30395 19
KF26 .C698 1980

RAILROAD LAW - UNITED STATES.
United States. Congress. House. Committee on Interstate and Foreign Commerce. Subcommittee on Transportation and Commerce. Amtrak fiscal year 1980 authorization and Amtrak route restructuring . Washington , 1980. viii, 725 p. :   LC Card 80-601471   DDC 353.0087/51 19
KF27 .I5589 1979l

United States. Congress. House. Committee on Interstate and Foreign Commerce. Subcommittee on Transportation and Commerce. Rail Act of 1980 . Washington , 1980. vi, 653 p. ;   LC Card 80-603811   DDC 343.73/095/0262 347.303950262 19
KF27 .I5589 1980i

United States. Congress. House. Committee on Interstate and Foreign Commerce. Subcommittee on Transportation and Commerce. The Rail act of 1980 . Washington , 1980. vii, 91 p. :   LC Card 80-602213   DDC 343.73/095 19
KF2275.5 .I58

United States. Congress. House. Committee on Interstate and Foreign Commerce. Subcommittee on Transportation and Commerce. Railroad deregulation act of 1979 . Washington , 1979 i.e. 1980. viii, 1292 p. :   LC Card 80-603016   DDC 343.73/095 19
KF27 .I5589 1979o

United States. Congress. House. Committee on the Judiciary. Subcommittee on Civil and Constitutional Rights. Milwaukee road's freight-carrying capacity . Washington , 1980. iii, 31 p. ;   LC Card 80-602526   DDC 343.73/0958 19
KF27 .J847 1979d

United States. Congress. Senate. Committee on Commerce, Science, and Transportation. Subcommittee on Surface Transportation. Northeast corridor completion act of 1979 . Washington , 1980. iii, 89 p. ;   LC Card 80-602086   DDC 343.73/095 347.30395 19
KF26 .C698 1980

United States. Congress. Senate. Committee on Commerce, Science, and Transportation. Subcommittee on Surface Transportation. Rail restructuring assistance act of 1979 . Washington , 1980. iii, 59 p. :   LC Card 80-602440   DDC 343.73/095/0262 19
KF26 .C698 1980a

United States. Congress. Senate. Committee on Commerce, Science, and Transportation. Subcommittee on Surface Transportation. Rock Island transition act . Washington , 1980. iv, 146 p. :   LC Card 80-602527   DDC 343.73/095 19
KF26 .C698 1980b

United States. Congress. Senate. Committee on Commerce, Science, and Transportation. Subcommittee on Surface Transportation. USRA--nomination, authorization, Conrail plant rationalization, and employee protection program . Washington , 1980. iv, 125 p. ;   LC Card 80-602781   DDC 343.73/095 19
KF26 .C698 1980c

Railroad retirement annuity increase--1980 . United States. Congress. Senate. Committee on Labor and Human Resources. Washington , 1980. iii, 78 p. ;   LC Card 81-600578   DDC 344.73/012529 347.30412529 19
KF26 .L27 1980o

Railroad Retirement Board. see United States. Railroad Retirement Board.

Railroad retirement system . United States. Congress. House. Committee on Interstate and Foreign Commerce. Subcommittee on Transportation and Commerce. Washington , 1980. iii, 80 p. ;   LC Card 81-600853   DDC 344.73/012529 347.30412529 19
KF27 .I5589 1980k

Railroad safety . United States. Congress. House. Committee on Interstate and Foreign Commerce. Subcommittee on Transportation and Commerce. Washington , 1980. iii, 213 p. :   LC Card 80-603701   DDC 363.1/22/0973 19
KF27 .I5589 1980h

The Railroad situation : a perspective on the present, past, and future of the railroad

industry : final report : prepared for U. S. Department of Transportation, Federal Railroad Administration, Office of Policy and Program Development. Washington : The Office : for sale by the Supt. of Docs., U. S. Govt. Print. Off., 1979. 487 p. : ill. ; 28 cm. (United States. Federal Railroad Administration. Office of Policy and Program Development. Report. no. FRA-OPPD-79-7) Cover title. Bibliography: p. 468-487.   LC Card 79-602934
1. Railroads - United States. I. United States. Federal Railroad Administration. Office of Policy and Program Development.
HE2751 .R13   *NYPL [JLF 81-372]*

RAILROADS AND STATE - ARIZONA.
Arizona. Transportation Planning Division. Rail deregulation study. [Phoenix] [1980] 56 p. ;   LC Card 80-622666   DDC 385/.068 19
HE2757 .A73 1980

RAILROADS AND STATE - MIDDLE WEST.
Anderson, Dale G. Rail-line abandonment in the North Central region /. Manhattan , 1979. 36 p. ;   LC Card 80-622127   DDC 385/.2042 19
HE2757 .A53

RAILROADS AND STATE - UNITED STATES.
Arizona. Transportation Planning Division. Rail deregulation study. [Phoenix] [1980] 56 p. ;   LC Card 80-622666   DDC 385/.068 19
HE2757 .A73 1980

Ernst and Ernst. Rail system investment analysis. Washington, 1977. 66 p. in various pagings   *NYPL [*XME-9311]*

United States. Congress. House. Committee on Interstate and Foreign Commerce. Subcommittee on Transportation and Commerce. Future funding for Conrail . Washington , 1980. iii, 84 p. :   LC Card 80-603456   DDC 385/.1 19
KF27 .I5589 1980f

RAILROADS - CROSSINGS - ADDRESSES, ESSAYS, LECTURES.
Grade crossings, devices, visibility, and freeway operations /. Washington, D.C. , 1980. iv, 49 p. :   ISBN 0-309-03117-6   LC Card 81-4730   DDC 380.5 s 625.7/94 19
TE7 .H5 no. 773 TE228

RAILROADS - ECONOMIC ASPECTS - UNITED STATES.
United States. Congress. Joint Economic Committee. Subcommittee on Economic Growth and Stabilization. The impact of the Soviet grain embargo on rail and barge transportation . Washington , 1980. iii, 47 p. ;   LC Card 80-602769   DDC 385/.1/0973 19
KF25 .E232 1980

RAILROADS - MIDDLE WEST - ABANDONMENT.
Anderson, Dale G. Rail-line abandonment in the North Central region /. Manhattan , 1979. 36 p. ;   LC Card 80-622127   DDC 385/.2042 19
HE2757 .A53

RAILROADS - MIDDLE WEST - FINANCE - HISTORY.
Kaitz, Gary M. An economic history of five midwestern railroads /. Washington , Springfield, Va. [1977] viii, 79 p. :   LC Card 78-600991
HE2231 .K27   *NYPL [*XME-9388]*

RAILROADS - NEW JERSEY.
New Jersey. Dept. of Transportation. New Jersey State rail plan for rail transportation and local rail services . [Trenton] , 1979. vii, 153, 135 p. :   LC Card 80-620740   DDC 385/.068 19
HE2771.N5 N48 1979

RAILROADS - NEW JERSEY - PASSENGER TRAFFIC.
New Jersey. Dept. of Transportation. New Jersey State rail plan for rail transportation and local rail services . [Trenton] , 1979. vii, 153, 135 p. :   LC Card 80-620740   DDC 385/.068 19
HE2771.N5 N48 1979

RAILROADS - NORTH CAROLINA.
Smith (Wilbur) and Associates. North Carolina rail plan, 1979 /. [Raleigh] [1979] 300 p. in various pagings, [2] leaves of plates :   LC Card 80-621028   DDC 385/.09756 19
TF24.N8 S64 1979

RAILROADS - NORTHEASTERN STATES - COMMUTING TRAFFIC.

United States. Congress. House. Committee on Interstate and Foreign Commerce. Subcommittee on Transportation and Commerce. Rail service commuter problems on the Northeast Corridor . Washington , 1981. iv, 222 p. :   LC Card 81-600979   DDC 385/.22/0974 19
KF27 .I5589 1980m

RAILROADS - NORTHEASTERN STATES - FINANCE.
United States. Congress. House. Committee on Interstate and Foreign Commerce. Subcommittee on Transportation and Commerce. Northeast corridor improvement project . Washington , 1980. iii, 161 p. ;   LC Card 80-603407   DDC 343.73/0958 347.303958 19
KF27 .I5589 1980g

United States. Congress. Senate. Committee on Commerce, Science, and Transportation. Subcommittee on Surface Transportation. Northeast corridor completion act of 1979 . Washington , 1980. iii, 89 p. ;   LC Card 80-602086   DDC 343.73/095 347.30395 19
KF26 .C698 1980

RAILROADS - NORTHEASTERN STATES - FREIGHT.
United States. Congress. House. Committee on Interstate and Foreign Commerce. Subcommittee on Transportation and Commerce. Future funding for Conrail . Washington , 1980. iii, 84 p. :   LC Card 80-603456   DDC 385/.1 19
KF27 .I5589 1980f

RAILROADS - NORTHEASTERN STATES - MAINTENANCE AND REPAIR.
United States. Congress. House. Committee on Interstate and Foreign Commerce. Subcommittee on Transportation and Commerce. Rail service commuter problems on the Northeast Corridor . Washington , 1981. iv, 222 p. :   LC Card 81-600979   DDC 385/.22/0974 19
KF27 .I5589 1980m

RAILROADS - SAFETY REGULATIONS - UNITED STATES.
United States. Congress. Senate. Committee on Commerce, Science, and Transportation. Subcommittee on Surface Transportation. Amendments to the Federal railway safety act of 1970 . Washington , 1980. iii, 156 p. :   LC Card 80-602782   DDC 343.73/095 19
KF26 .C698 1980d

RAILROADS - TEXAS - EL PASO - HISTORY.
Leonard, Edward A. (Edward Almand) Rails at the Pass of the North /. [El Paso] , c1981. 60 p., [4] p. of plates :   ISBN 0-87404-122-8 (pbk.) :   LC Card 81-144980   DDC 385/.09764/96 19
HE2781.E4 L46

RAILROADS - TEXAS - FREIGHT.
Texas. Railroad Commission. The Texas rail freight system . Austin, Tex. [1979] xvi, 276 p. :   LC Card 80-622071   DDC 385/.24/09764 19
HE2771.T4 T49 1979

RAILROADS - THE WEST - RATES.
Lyndon B. Johnson School of Public Affairs. Western Coal Transportation Policy Research Project. The economic regulation of western coal transportation . [Austin, Tex.] , 1980. xiii, 405 p. :   ISBN 0-89940-638-6 (pbk.)   LC Card 80-82502   DDC 343.78/07752 19
KF2355.C6 L96

RAILROADS, UNDERGROUND. see SUBWAYS.

RAILROADS - UNITED STATES.
The Railroad situation . Washington , 1979. 487 p. :   LC Card 79-602934
HE2751 .R13   **NYPL [JLF 81-372]**

United States. Dept. of Transportation. Guidelines for the railroad industry in a national emergency. [Washington] 1974. 54 p. :
                              NYPL [JLF 80-736]

RAILROADS - UNITED STATES - ACCOUNTS, BOOKKEEPING, ETC.
United States. Interstate Commerce Commission. Supplement to the third revised issue of the Classification of operating expenses as prescribed by the Interstate Commerce Commission for steam roads in accordance with section 20 of the Act to regulate commerce.

Washington , 1908-1913. 2 v. ;   LC Card 81-459319   DDC 657/.8 19
HE2241 .U5 1908d Suppl

United States. Interstate Commerce Commission. Uniform system of accounts for railroad companies /. Washington, D. C., 1974. 117 p.;   **NYPL [JLE 81-288]**

RAILROADS - UNITED STATES - EMPLOYEES - DISCIPLINE.
Lazar, Joseph, 1916- Due process in disciplinary hearings . Los Angeles , c1980. 459 p. ;   LC Card 80-135569   DDC 344.73/012598 19
KF3580.R2 L38 1980

RAILROADS - UNITED STATES - EQUIPMENT AND SUPPLIES.
United States. Interstate Commerce Commission. Supplement to the third revised issue of the Classification of operating expenses as prescribed by the Interstate Commerce Commission for steam roads in accordance with section 20 of the Act to regulate commerce. Washington , 1908-1913. 2 v. ;   LC Card 81-459319   DDC 657/.8 19
HE2241 .U5 1908d Suppl

RAILROADS - UNITED STATES - FINANCE.
Ernst and Ernst. Rail system investment analysis. Washington, 1977. 66 p. in various pagings   **NYPL [*XME-9311]**

United States. Congress. House. Committee on Interstate and Foreign Commerce. Subcommittee on Transportation and Commerce. The Rail act of 1980 . Washington , 1980. vii, 91 p. :   LC Card 80-602213   DDC 343.73/095 19
KF2275.5 .I58

United States. Congress. Senate. Committee on Commerce, Science, and Transportation. Subcommittee on Surface Transportation. Rail restructuring assistance act of 1979 . Washington , 1980. iii, 59 p. :   LC Card 80-602440   DDC 343.73/095/0262 19
KF26 .C698 1980a

RAILROADS - UNITED STATES - FREIGHT.
United States. Congress. House. Committee on Agriculture. Subcommittee on Family Farms, Rural Development, and Special Studies. Agricultural subterminal facilities act of 1979 and Rural Transportation Advisory Task Force report . Washington , 1980. iii, 89 p. :   LC Card 80-603304   DDC 343.73/0851 19
KF27 .A344 1980

United States. Congress. House. Committee on the Judiciary. Subcommittee on Civil and Constitutional Rights. Milwaukee road's freight-carrying capacity . Washington , 1980. iii, 31 p. ;   LC Card 80-602526   DDC 343.73/0958 19
KF27 .J847 1979d

RAILROADS - UNITED STATES - MAPS.
United States. Geological Survey. Transportation map of ... [Washington] 1975-76. 41 col. maps on sheets 43 x 56 cm. and 56 x 43 cm. Scales vary. Each sheet separately titled. "Transportation zone edition." Shows lines that may be subject to abandonment, those operating under rail service continuation provisions, and other operating lines. Includes "Index to railroads." Accompanied by text. [2] p.   **NYPL [Map Div. 80-3426]**

RAILROADS - UNITED STATES - NOISE CONTROL.
United States. Environmental Protection Agency. Office of Noise Abatement and Control. Official docket for proposed revision to rail carrier noise emission regulation /. Washington, 1980. 1 v.;   **NYPL [JLM 81-95]**

RAILROADS - UNITED STATES - PASSENGER TRAFFIC.
United States. Congress. House. Committee on Interstate and Foreign Commerce. Subcommittee on Transportation and Commerce. Amtrak fiscal year 1980 authorization and Amtrak route restructuring . Washington , 1980. viii, 725 p. :   LC Card 80-601471   DDC 353.0087/51 19
KF27 .I5589 1979l

RAILROADS - UNITED STATES - PENSIONS.
United States. Congress. House. Committee on Interstate and Foreign Commerce. Subcommittee on Transportation and Commerce. Railroad retirement system .

Washington , 1980. iii, 80 p. ;   LC Card 81-600853   DDC 344.73/012529 347.30412529 19
KF27 .I5589 1980k

United States. Congress. House. Committee on Ways and Means. Subcommittee on Oversight. Employer liability for taxes under the Railroad retirement tax act . Washington , 1980. iii, 128 p. ;   LC Card 80-602012   DDC 353.0087/5068 19
KF27 .W345 1979j

United States. Congress. Senate. Committee on Labor and Human Resources. Railroad retirement annuity increase--1980 . Washington , 1980. iii, 78 p. ;   LC Card 81-600578   DDC 344.73/012529 347.30412529 19
KF26 .L27 1980o

United States. Railroad Retirement Board. Handbook on railroad retirement and unemployment insurance systems. [Chicago?] 1974. 1 v. (various pagings)   LC Card 78-3501
                              NYPL [JLF 80-1047]

RAILROADS - UNITED STATES - PENSIONS - STATISTICS - PERIODICALS.
United States. Railroad Retirement Board. Monthly benefit statistics. Mar. 1968- Chicago [etc.]   LC Card 76-646293   **NYPL [JLN 80-91]**

RAILROADS - UNITED STATES - RATES.
United States. Congress. House. Committee on Interstate and Foreign Commerce. Subcommittee on Oversight and Investigations. Coal rates and Federal railroad regulation . Washington , 1980. ii, 111 p. ;   LC Card 80-602961   DDC 353.0087/512 19
KF27 .I5547 1979t

United States. Congress. House. Committee on Interstate and Foreign Commerce. Subcommittee on Oversight and Investigations. ICC ratemaking in noncompetitive markets--oversight . Washington , 1980. iii, 87 p. ;   LC Card 80-603486   DDC 353.0087/512 19
KF27 .I5547 1980i

RAILROADS - UNITED STATES - SAFETY MEASURES.
United States. Congress. House. Committee on Interstate and Foreign Commerce. Subcommittee on Transportation and Commerce. Railroad safety . Washington , 1980. iii, 213 p. :   LC Card 80-603701   DDC 363.1/22/0973 19
KF27 .I5589 1980h

RAILROADS - UNITED STATES - STATIONS - REMODELING FOR OTHER USE.
Webber, Margo B. Reuse of historically and architecturally significant railroad stations for transportation and other community needs . Washington, D.C. , 1978. ii, 126 p. :   LC Card 79-603620   DDC 725/.31/0288 19
NA6311 .W4

RAILROADS - UNITED STATES - TRAIN DISCONTINUANCE.
United States. Congress. House. Committee on Interstate and Foreign Commerce. Subcommittee on Transportation and Commerce. Amtrak fiscal year 1980 authorization and Amtrak route restructuring . Washington , 1980. viii, 725 p. :   LC Card 80-601471   DDC 353.0087/51 19
KF27 .I5589 1979l

Rails at the Pass of the North /. Leonard, Edward A. (Edward Almand) [El Paso] , c1981. 60 p., [4] p. of plates :   ISBN 0-87404-122-8 (pbk.) :   LC Card 81-144980   DDC 385/.09764/96 19
HE2781.E4 L46

RAILWAYS. see RAILROADS.

RAIN AND RAINFALL - CALIFORNIA.
California. Dept. of Water Resources. Division of Planning. California rainfall summary . [Sacramento] [1980] vi, 55 p., [6] leaves of plates :   LC Card 80-622884   DDC 551.57/812794 19
QC925.1.U8 C23 1980

RAIN AND RAINFALL - CONGRESSES.
International Symposium on Urban Storm Runoff, University of Kentucky, 1980. International Symposium on Urban Storm Runoff, July 28-31, 1980 . Lexington , c1980.

319 p. : ISBN 0-89779-040-5 (pbk.) LC Card
   80-52482 DDC 551.48/8/091732 19
GB980 .I58 1980

RAIN AND RAINFALL - KANSAS.
Bark, Laurence Dean, 1926- Cloud seeding .
Manhattan [1979] 24 p. : LC Card 80-621773
   DDC 630/.2/516876 19
S600.7.R35 B37

**RAIN AND RAINFALL - WASHINGTON
   (STATE) - WHITMAN COUNTY - MAPS.**
United States. Soil Conservation Service.
Average annual rainfall, Whitman County,
Washington /. Portland, Or. , 1977. 1 map :
   LC Card 81-691519
G4283.W6C883 1977 .U5

United States. Soil Conservation Service.
Rainfall distribution, Whitman County,
Washington /. Portland, Or. , 1979. 1 map :
   LC Card 81-691526
G4283.W6C883 1978 .U5

**RAIN FOREST ECOLOGY - COSTA RICA -
   CORCOVADO NATIONAL PARK.**
Herwitz, Stanley Robert. The regeneration of
selected tropical wet forest tree species in
Corcovado National Park, Costa Rica /.
Berkeley, Calif. [1981] p. cm.   ISBN
   0-520-09631-2 LC Card 80-26413 DDC 910 s
   582.16/052642/0972867 19
G58 .C3 vol. 24 QK217

**RAIN-MAKING - ENVIRONMENTAL
   ASPECTS - WASHINGTON (STATE) -
   LEWIS RIVER WATERSHED.**
Washington (State). Dept. of Ecology. Final
environmental impact statement . [Olympia]
[1974] ca. 100 p. in various pagings ; LC Card
   76-624014 DDC 333.9/2 19
TD195.R34 W37 1974

RAIN-MAKING - KANSAS.
Bark, Laurence Dean, 1926- Cloud seeding .
Manhattan [1979] 24 p. : LC Card 80-621773
   DDC 630/.2/516876 19
S600.7.R35 B37

Rainbow snake. San Diego : Center for Women's
Studies and Services, San Diego State College
Foundation, 1971. 62 p. : ill. ; 28 cm. Poems and
drawings. LC Card 77-370047
   *1. American poetry - Women authors. 2. College
   verse - California. State College, San Diego. 3.
   American poetry - 20th century. I. California. State
   College, San Diego. Center for Women's Studies and
   Services.*
PS589 .R34   **NYPL [JFF 80-1089]**

RAINBOW TROUT.
Axon, James R. Evaluation of the "two story"
trout fishery in Lake Cumberland /.
[Frankfort] , 1974. 69 p. : LC Card 76-624539
   DDC 639/.2 s 333.95/6 19
SH222.K4 A3 no. 60 QL638.S2

Van Velson, Rodney C. The McConaughy
rainbow . Lincoln, Nebraska , 1978. 83 p. : LC
   Card 79-626007 DDC 639.3/755 19
QL638.S2 V36

**Rainfall distribution, Whitman County,
Washington /.** United States. Soil Conservation
Service. Portland, Or. , 1979. 1 map : LC Card
   81-691526
G4283.W6C883 1978 .U5

Rainof, Alexandre. A Drug terminology--general
glossary, English-Spanish/Spanish-English . [Los
Angeles] [1980] vi, 134 p. ; LC Card 80-135304
   DDC 616.86/3/00326 19
RC564 .D783

RAINSTORMS - HAWAII.
Schroeder, Thomas A. Mesoscale structure of
Hawaiian rainstorms /. Honolulu [1978] x, 69
p. : LC Card 79-626234 DDC 553.7/09969 s
   551.57/81/09969 19
TC1 .H36 no. 119 QC925.1.U8H3

RAINSTORMS - ILLINOIS.
Huff, Floyd A. Hydrometeorological
characteristics of severe rainstorms in Illinois /.
Urbana, 1979. 18 p. : LC Card 80-621484 DDC
   553.7/09773 s 551.57/81 19
GB705.I3 A3 no. 90 QC925.1.U8I3

RAISE DRILLING - SAFETY MEASURES.
Maksimovic, S. D. Control of methane by
ventilation of shafts during raise drilling /.
[Washington] , 1981. p. cm. LC Card 80-606851
   DDC 622 s 622/.8 19
TN295 .U4

Raleigh Lions Clinic for the Blind. Technology
and the handicapped: telecommunication
services in the rehabilitation of the blind .
Raleigh , 1977. v leaves, 163 p. : LC Card
   79-623503 DDC 362.4/183 19
HV1701 .T43

Raleigh, N. C. Agricultural Experiment Station.
see **North Carolina. Agricultural Experiment
Station, Raleigh.**

Raleigh, N. C. North Carolina State University.
see **North Carolina. State University,
Raleigh.**

Raleigh, N. C. State University. see **North
Carolina. State University, Raleigh.**

Ralph Waldo Emerson, a descriptive bibliography
/. Myerson, Joel. Pittsburgh, Pa. , 1982. p. cm.
   ISBN 0-8229-3452-3 LC Card 81-11502 DDC
   016.814/3 19
Z8265 .M94 PS1631

Ramberg, Bennett. Destruction of nuclear energy
facilities in war : the problem and the
implications / Bennett Ramberg. Lexington,
Mass. : Lexington Books, c1980. xvi, 203 p. :
ill. ; 24 cm. "Written under the auspices of the Center
for International and strategic Affairs, University of
California, Los Angeles, and the Center of International
Studies, Princeton University." Includes bibliographical
references and index. LC Card 80-7691
   *1. War damage, Industrial. 2. Nuclear facilities -
   Military aspects. 3. Nuclear facilities - Defense
   measures. I. California. University. University at Los
   Angeles. Center for International and Strategic Affairs.
   II. Princeton University. Center of International Studies.
   III. Title.*
UA929.95.A87 R35   **NYPL [JLE 81-179]**

Ramp, Lenin. Geology and mineral resources of
Josephine County, Oregon / by Len Ramp and
Norman V. Peterson. Portland, Or. : State of
Oregon, Dept. of Geology and Mineral
Industries, 1979. iv, 45 p. : ill., maps (3 fold. in
pocket) ; 28 cm. (Bulletin - State of Oregon,
Department of Geology and Mineral Industries ; 100)
Bibliography: p. 43-45. LC Card 80-622943 DDC
   553/.09795 s 557.95/25 19
   *1. Geology - Oregon - Josephine Co. 2. Mines and
   mineral resources - Oregon - Josephine Co. I. Peterson,
   Norman V., joint author. II. Series: Oregon. State Dept.
   of Geology and Mineral Industries. Bulletin , 100. III.
   Title.*
QE155 .A3 no. 100 QE156.J67

Ramsett, David E. A conceptual model for the
coal severance tax / David E. Ramsett. [Grand
Forks] : Bureau of Business and Economic
Research, University of North Dakota, [1979]
iii, 49 p. : ill. ; 28 cm. (North Dakota economic
studies. no. 24) "October 1979." Includes bibliographical
references. LC Card 80-622818 DDC
   336.2/78622334/0973 19
   *1. Coal - Taxation - United States. 2. Coal - Taxation -
   North Dakota. 3. Mines and mineral resources -
   Taxation - United States. I. North Dakota. University.
   Bureau of Business and Economic Research. II. Title.
   III. Series.*
HD9540.8.U5 R35   **NYPL [TAA no. 24]**

**RANCH LIFE - NEVADA - PARADISE
   VALLEY - EXHIBITIONS.**
Marshall, Howard W. Buckaroos in Paradise .
Washington , 1980. xvi, 95 p. : ISBN
   0-8444-0348-2 LC Card 80-23261 DDC
   979.3/54 19
F847.H8 M37

**RANCHES - ECONOMIC ASPECTS -
   COLORADO.**
Gee, C. Kerry. Economies of size for mountain
and plains cow-calf ranches /. Fort Collins ,
1979. ii, 28 p. ; LC Card 79-626243 DDC
   338.1/6 19
SF196.U5 G45

RANCHES - OREGON.
Holst, David. Effects of the 1977 drought on
eastern Oregon ranches /. [Corvallis] [1979] 25
p. : LC Card 79-625679 DDC 630/.9795 s 338.1/4
   19
S105 .E43 no. 555 S600.7.D76

Rand Corporation. Petersilia, Joan. The prison
experience of career criminals /. Washington,
D.C. , 1980. xviii, 87 p. : LC Card 81-601009
   DDC 365/.66 19
HV9304 .P44

Rand McNally and Company. Fagg, Ken. Explore
the Adirondacks . Elizabethtown, N.Y. [1980?]

1 view : LC Card 81-692877
G3802.A2E635 1980 .F3

Randazzo, Anthony F. Petrography and
stratigraphy of the Carolina Slate Belt, Union
County, North Carolina / by Anthony F.
Randazzo. Raleigh : North Carolina, Dept. of
Natural and Economic Resources, 1972. iii
leaves, 38 p., [1] fold leaf of plates : ill. ; 28
cm. (Special publication - Division of Mineral
Resources . 4) Bibliography: p. 35-38. LC Card
   80-623227 DDC 553/.09756 s 552.09756/755
   19
   *1. Petrology - North Carolina - Union County. 2.
   Geology - North Carolina - Union County. I. Series:
   North Carolina. Division of Mineral Resources. Special
   publication , 4. II. Title.*
QE147 .A32 no. 4 QE445.N8

Randich, Philip G., 1909- Ground-water resources
of Grant and Sioux Counties, North Dakota /
by P. G. Randich ; prepared by the U. S.
Geological Survey, in cooperation with the
North Dakota Geological Survey ... [et al.].
Bismarck, N.D. : [North Dakota Geological
Survey?], 1979. vi, 49 p. : ill. (5 fold. in
pocket) ; 23 cm. (County ground-water studies ; 24,
pt. 3) Bulletin - North Dakota Geological Survey ; 67,
pt. 3 Bibliography: p. 45-48. LC Card 80-621090
   DDC 553.7/9/09784 s 553.7/9/0978487 19
   *1. Water, Underground - North Dakota - Grant Co. 2.
   Water, Underground - North Dakota - Sioux Co. I.
   United States. Geological Survey. II. Series: County
   ground-water studies , 24, pt. 3. III. Title.*
GB705.N9 A25 no. 24, pt. 3 TD224.N9

**RANDOLPH (A. PHILIP) INSTITUTE -
   MEDALS.**
United States. Congress. House. Committee on
Banking, Finance and Urban Affairs.
Subcommittee on Consumer Affairs. To
authorize the President of the United States to
present on behalf of the Congress specially
struck gold medals to Bryan Lewis Allen and to
the A. Philip Randolph Institute . Washington ,
1980. iii, 15 p. : LC Card 80-601396 DDC
   344.73/091 19
KF27 .B535 1980b

**Random differential equations in water quality
modeling /.** Finney, Brad A. Logan, Utah
[1979] viii, 41 p. : LC Card 80-622173 DDC
   553.7/028 19
TD367 .F56

RANDOM PROCESSES. see **STOCHASTIC
PROCESSES.**

RANDOM VARIABLES.
Finney, Brad A. Random differential equations
in water quality modeling /. Logan, Utah
[1979] viii, 41 p. : LC Card 80-622173 DDC
   553.7/028 19
TD367 .F56

RANDOM WALKS (MATHEMATICS)
Turner, James Harold, 1942- Improvement of
the steady floating random walk Monte Carlo
method near straight line and circular
boundaries, with application to groundwater
flow . [Manhattan, Kan.] , 1978, cover 1977. iv,
96 p. : LC Card 79-624986 DDC 551.49/0724 19
GB1197.7 .T87

RANGE, ATHALIE, 1916-
United States. Congress. Senate. Committee on
Commerce, Science, and Transportation.
Nominations--Amtrak . Washington , 1980. iii,
24 p. ; LC Card 80-602501 DDC 353.0087/5 19
KF26 .C69 1980m

RANGE MANAGEMENT - KANSAS.
Launchbaugh, John L. Kansas rangelands, their
management based on a half century of
research /. Manhattan [1978?] 56 p. : LC Card
   80-621772 DDC 633.2/02/09781 19
SF85.35.K3 L38

**RANGE MANAGEMENT - SOUTH DAKOTA -
   MAPS.**
United States. Soil Conservation Service. South
Dakota range condition classes /. Lincoln,
Nebr. , 1976. 1 map : LC Card 81-691108
G4181.J1 1975 .U5

RANGE MANAGEMENT - THE WEST.
United States. Congress. Senate. Committee
on Energy and Natural Resources. Subcommittee
on Parks, Recreation, and Renewable
Resources. Bureau of Land Management
wilderness review and rangeland management
programs . Washington , 1980. iii, 189 p. ; LC

Card 80-602719   DDC 346.7304/6782/0262 19
KF26 .E5565 1980a

RANGE MANAGEMENT - UNITED STATES - CONGRESSES.
Symposium on Rangeland Policies for the Future, Tucson, Ariz., 1979. Rangeland policies for the future . [Washington, D.C.] , 1979. v, 114 p. ;   LC Card 80-600538   DDC 333.74/0973 19
HD241 .S95 1979

RANGE POLICY - UNITED STATES - CONGRESSES.
Symposium on Rangeland Policies for the Future, Tucson, Ariz., 1979. Rangeland policies for the future . [Washington, D.C.] , 1979. v, 114 p. ;   LC Card 80-600538   DDC 333.74/0973 19
HD241 .S95 1979

RANGE POLICY - WEST (U. S.)
United States. Congress. Senate. Committee on Appropriations. Subcommittee on Department of the Interior and Related Agencies. Rangeland management policy and wood energy development . Washington , 1980. iii, 883, vii p. :   LC Card 80-603996   DDC 353.0082/326 19
KF26 .A652 1979a

Rangeland management policy and wood energy development . United States. Congress. Senate. Committee on Appropriations. Subcommittee on Department of the Interior and Related Agencies. Washington , 1980. iii, 883, vii p. :   LC Card 80-603996   DDC 353.0082/326 19
KF26 .A652 1979a

Rangeland policies for the future . Symposium on Rangeland Policies for the Future, Tucson, Ariz., 1979. [Washington, D.C.] , 1979. v, 114 p. ;   LC Card 80-600538   DDC 333.74/0973 19
HD241 .S95 1979

RANGELANDS - GREAT BASIN.
Hubbard, Kenneth G. The Great Basin climate study for range fire management /. Logan , 1978. vi, 25 p. :   LC Card 80-620825   DDC 634.9/618/015516 19
SD421.37 .H8

Rango, Albert. Workshop on Operational Applications of Satellite Snowcover Observations, Sparks, Nev., 1979. Operational applications of satellite snowcover observations . Washington, D.C. , 1980. vi, 301 p. :   LC Card 80-602361   DDC 551.57/846 19
GB2601.72.A83 W67 1979

RANK. see SOCIAL CLASSES.

Rankin, Douglas W. Correlation chart for Precambrian rocks of the eastern United States /. Reston, Va. , 1981. p. cm.   LC Card 81-607917   DDC 551.7/1/0973 19
QE653 .C68

Rankin, Janna S. When is a stream a stream? : Some geomorphic, hydrologic, and legal considerations / by Janna S. Rankin, G. Thomas Foggin, School of Forestry, University of Montana. Bozeman, MT : Montana Water Resources Research Center, Montana State University, [1980] iv, 43 leaves : ill. ; 29 cm. (MWRRC research report ; no. 104) "Final report. Project no. A-115-MONT." Bibliography: leaves 39-43.   LC Card 80-623138   DDC 346.78604/69162/014 19
1. Rivers - Terminology. 2. Rivers - Law and legislation. I. Foggin, G. Thomas, joint author. II. Montana. University, Missoula. School of Forestry. III. Series: Montana University Joint Water Resources Research Center. Report , no. 104. IV. Title.
GB1201.5 .R36

Rankin, Sue B. Applying the Uniform child custody jurisdiction act / by Sue B. Rankin. Chapel Hill : Institute of Government, University of North Carolina at Chapel Hill, 1979, c1978. 7 p. ; 29 cm. (Administration of justice memoranda ; no. 79/06) Caption title. Includes bibliographical references.   LC Card 80-620669   DDC 347.756 s 346.75601/7 19
1. Custody of children - North Carolina. 2. Conflict of laws - Custody of children - North Carolina. I. Series: University of North Carolina at Chapel Hill. Institute of Government. Administration of justice memoranda , no. 79/06. II. Title.
KFN7908.A15 U6 No. 79/06 KFN7504

Ranuzzi collection. Zevelechi Wells, Maria Xenia. The Ranuzzi manuscripts /. [Austin] , c1980. 89 p. :   ISBN 0-87959-094-7   LC Card 80-622235

DDC 091 19
Z6621.T372 R358 Z881.A935

RANUZZI COSPI, FERDINANDO VINCENZO ANTONIO, 1658-1726 - LIBRARY - EXHIBITIONS.
Zevelechi Wells, Maria Xenia. The Ranuzzi manuscripts /. [Austin] , c1980. 89 p. :   ISBN 0-87959-094-7   LC Card 80-622235   DDC 091 19
Z6621.T372 R358 Z881.A935

RANUZZI FAMILY - LIBRARY - EXHIBITIONS.
Zevelechi Wells, Maria Xenia. The Ranuzzi manuscripts /. [Austin] , c1980. 89 p. :   ISBN 0-87959-094-7   LC Card 80-622235   DDC 091 19
Z6621.T372 R358 Z881.A935

The Ranuzzi manuscripts /. Zevelechi Wells, Maria Xenia. [Austin] , c1980. 89 p. :   ISBN 0-87959-094-7   LC Card 80-622235   DDC 091 19
Z6621.T372 R358 Z881.A935

Rao, K. R. International Conference on Thermoelectric Energy Conversion, 2d, University of Texas at Arlington, 1978. Proceedings of the second International Conference on Thermoelectric Energy Conversion . New York , c1978. vi, 137 p. :   LC Card 78-107945
TK2950 .I53 1978   NYPL [JSF 81-128]

Rao, Vaman. Evaluation of real income of welfare recipients in Missouri / Vaman Rao. [Columbia] : [Published by] University of Missouri--Columbia for the Division of Budget and Planning, Office of Administration, State of Missouri, 1978. 73 p. ; 29 cm. Bibliography: p. 73.   LC Card 79-623417   DDC 362.5/2/09778 19
1. Welfare recipients - Missouri - Statistics. 2. Income maintenance programs - Missouri - Statistics. I. Title.
HV98.M8 R36

Rape, guidelines for a community response /. Carrow, Deborah. [Washington, D.C.] [1980] iii, 296 p. ;   LC Card 80-601822   DDC 362.8/8 19
HV6561 .C37

Rape in Massachusetts . Roy, Marjorie Brown. Boston (206 New Court House, Boston 02108) [1980] 84 p. ;   LC Card 80-623646   DDC 364.1/532/09744 19
HV6565.M4 R68

RAPE - MASSACHUSETTS.
Roy, Marjorie Brown. Rape in Massachusetts . Boston (206 New Court House, Boston 02108) [1980] 84 p. ;   LC Card 80-623646   DDC 364.1/532/09744 19
HV6565.M4 R68

RAPE - MASSACHUSETTS - STATISTICS.
Roy, Marjorie Brown. Rape in Massachusetts . Boston (206 New Court House, Boston 02108) [1980] 84 p. ;   LC Card 80-623646   DDC 364.1/532/09744 19
HV6565.M4 R68

RAPE - NORTH CAROLINA.
North Carolina. Council on the Status of Women. Aftermath . Raleigh , 1978. xvii, 37 p. ;   LC Card 79-624323   DDC 364.1/532/09756 19
HV6565.N8 N67 1978

RAPE - UNITED STATES.
Carrow, Deborah. Rape, guidelines for a community response /. [Washington, D.C.] [1980] iii, 296 p. :   LC Card 80-601822   DDC 362.8/8 19
HV6561 .C37

RAPE - UNITED STATES - PREVENTION.
Carrow, Deborah. Rape, guidelines for a community response /. [Washington, D.C.] [1980] iii, 296 p. :   LC Card 80-601822   DDC 362.8/8 19
HV6561 .C37

RAPE VICTIMS - SERVICES FOR - NORTH CAROLINA.
North Carolina. Council on the Status of Women. Aftermath . Raleigh , 1978. xvii, 37 p. ;   LC Card 79-624323   DDC 364.1/532/09756 19
HV6565.N8 N67 1978

RAPE VICTIMS - SERVICES FOR - UNITED STATES.
Carrow, Deborah. Rape, guidelines for a community response /. [Washington, D.C.] [1980] iii, 296 p. :   LC Card 80-601822   DDC

362.8/8 19
HV6561 .C37

RAPID TRANSIT. see LOCAL TRANSIT.

Rapoport, Ronald. Abramowitz, Alan. Party activists in Virginia . Charlottesville , 1981. x, 106 p. ;   LC Card 81-142700   DDC 324.5/6/09755 19
JK2295.V83 A24

Rappaccini's children . Shurr, William. Lexington [1981] p. cm.   ISBN 0-8131-1427-6   LC Card 79-57573   DDC 810/.9/382 19
PS166 .S5

RARE BOOKS - CONSERVATION AND RESTORATION.
Brown, Margaret. Design and construction of boxes for the protection of rare books /. Washington , 1981. p. cm.   ISBN 0-8444-0365-2   LC Card 81-607965   DDC 676./32 19
Z1029 .B76

RARE PLANTS - ALABAMA.
Endangered, threatened, and special concern plants of Alabama /. Auburn, Ala. , 1979. 25 p. :   LC Card 80-620907   DDC 582.09761 19
QK86.U6 E5

RARE PLANTS - OREGON.
Siddall, Jean L. Rare, threatened, and endangered vascular plants in Oregon . Salem, Or. [1979] iv, 109 p. :   LC Card 80-621881   DDC 582.09795 19
QK86.U6 S52

Rare, threatened, and endangered vascular plants in Oregon . Siddall, Jean L. Salem, Or. [1979] iv, 109 p. :   LC Card 80-621881   DDC 582.09795 19
QK86.U6 S52

Rasin, V. James. Potomac River Basin water quality, 1978-1979 / prepared by V. James Rasin, Jr., Keith M. Brooks, and Kevin C. Flynn ; with an appendix by William J. McCaw III. Rockville, Md. (1055 1st St., Rockville 20850) : Interstate Commission on the Potomac River Basin, [1980] vii, 77, 22 p. : ill. ; 28 cm. (ICPRB technical publication . 80-1) "September 1980." One map inserted. Bibliography: p. 75-77.   LC Card 80-624161   DDC 363.7/3942/0972 19
1. Water quality - Potomac River watershed. I. Brooks, Keith M., 1952-. II. Flynn, Kevin C. III. Title. IV. Series.
TD225.P74 R373

Rasmussen, Marcy. Evaluation of the Minneapolis Community Crime Prevention demonstration : an evaluation report / produced by the Research and Evaluation Unit of the Crime Control Planning Board ; by Marcy Rasmussen, William Muggli, C. Michael Crabill, with the assistance of Barbara E. Davis. St. Paul, Minn. : The Board, [1979] xiii, 253 p. ; 28 cm. (Report - Research and Evaluation Unit, Minnesota Crime Control Planning Board) "December, 1979." Bibliography: p. 251-253.   LC Card 80-621231   DDC 364.4/09776/579 19
1. Crime prevention - Minnesota - Minneapolis - Evaluation. I. Muggli, William, joint author. II. Crabill, C. Michael, joint author. III. Minnesota. Crime Control Planning Board. Research and Evaluation Unit. IV. Series: Minnesota. Crime Control Planning Board. Research and Evaluation Unit. Report - Research and Evaluation Unit, Minnesota Crime Control Planning Board. V. Title.
HV6795.M55 R37

Rast, Walter. Phosphorus managemnt strategies or lakes . Ann Arbor, Mich. , 1980. vi, 490 p. :   ISBN 0-250-40332-3   LC Card 79-55150
TD223.3 .P48

Ratcliff, Angela.
Mississippi. Legislature. Audit Committee. A special follow-up report to the legislature detailing State agency compliance with selected bills passed during the 1978 and 1979 legislative sessions /. [Jackson, Miss.] [1980] x, 91 p. ;   LC Card 80-622027   DDC 353.976207/8 19
KFM7040 .A25 1980

Mississippi. Legislature. Audit Committee. Special investigation, political activities of MVC employees /. [Jackson, Miss.] [1980] xi, 76 p. ;   LC Card 80-623578   DDC 353.976201/6 19
HE5633.M7 M57 1980

Mississippi. Legislature. Audit Committee. A survey of State agency insurance coverage, March 24, 1980 /. [Jackson, Miss. , 1980] ix,

81 p. : LC Card 80-622528 DDC 368.4/2/009762 19
JK4660.H4 M57 1980

Ratcliff, Ann. Moon, Jay Charles. An evaluation of the Mississippi Council on Aging food service contracts for fiscal years 1978-1980 . [Jackson, Miss. , 1979?] x, 126 p. : LC Card 80-621642 DDC 362.6/3 19
HV1468.M65 M66

RATING OF EMPLOYEES. see EMPLOYEES, RATING OF.

Rational decision-making . Stein, Janice Gross. Columbus , c1980. xv, 399 p. : ISBN 0-8142-0312-4 LC Card 80-13589
DS119.2 .S73 **NYPL [JLE 81-169]**

Rational use of energy program pilot study. Gordian Associates. The plastics industry /. Oak Ridge, Tenn. , 1977. v, 31 p. ; ISBN 0-87079-202-4 : LC Card 77-12044 DDC 338.4/5 19
TP1120 .G59 1977

RATIONALIZATION OF INDUSTRY. see INDUSTRIAL MANAGEMENT.

RATIONING, CONSUMER - HAWAII.
An Analytical study of alternative gasoline rationing plans for Hawaii /. Honolulu , 1975. 32 p. ; LC Card 76-622980 DDC 333.8/232 19
HD9579.G45 H32

RATIONING, CONSUMER - UNITED STATES.
United States. Congress. House. Committee on Interstate and Foreign Commerce. Subcommittee on Energy and Power. 1980 standby gasoline rationing plan . Washington , 1980. iv, 236 p. : LC Card 80-603634 DDC 346.7304/68232 347.306468232 19
KF27 .I5542 1980h

United States. Dept. of Energy. Office of Regulations and Emergency Planning. Standby gasoline rationing plan. Washington, D.C. [Springfield, Va. , 1980] 114 p. ; LC Card 80-603194 DDC 333.8/232 19
HD9579.G5 U58 1980

RATIONING, CONSUMER - WASHINGTON METROPOLITAN AREA.
United States. General Accounting Office. Effects in Washington, D.C., area of 1979 gasoline shortage . Washington, D.C. [1980] viii, 47 p. ; LC Card 80-602653 DDC 338.4/766553827/09753 19
HD9579.G5 U595 1980

Ratner, Ronnie Steinberg, 1947- A modest Magna Carta : the rise and growth of wage and hour standards laws in the United States, 1900-1973 : a social indicators approach / by Ronnie Steinberg Ratner. [New York City, N. Y. : New York University], 1977 2 v. (xxxiv, 880 leaves) ; 22 cm. Microfiche (neg.) NTIS. 7 sheets. 11 x 15 cm. (PB-273 926) Thesis - New York University. "Prepared for the Employment and Training Administration, U. S. Department of Labor, under Research and Development Grant No. 91-36-74-42." Bibliography: leaves 579-597.
1. Wages - Minimum wage - United States - History. 2. Hours of labor - United States - History. 3. Labor laws and legislation - United States - History. I. United States. Employment and Training Administration. II. Title. **NYPL [*XME-9376]**

Rattlesnake roadless area . United States. Congress. Senate. Committee on Energy and Natural Resources. Subcommittee on Parks, Recreation, and Renewable Resources. Washington , 1980. iii, 119 p. : LC Card 80-602500 DDC 346.7304/6782 347.30646782 19
KF26 .E5565 1979k

Rau, Weldon W. Washington coastal geology between the Hoh and Quillayute Rivers / by Weldon W. Rau. Olympia, Wash. : State of Washington, Dept. of Natural Resources, Division of Geology and Earth Resources, 1980. xii, 57 p. : ill. ; 28 cm. (Bulletin - State of Washington, Division of Geology and Earth Resources . no. 72) Bibliography: p. 56-57. LC Card 80-623473 DDC 557.9794 19
1. Geology - Washington (State) - Olympic Peninsula - Guide-books. 2. Coasts - Washington (State) - Olympic Peninsula. I. Series: Washington (State). Division of Geology and Earth Resources. Bulletin - Division of Geology and Earth Resources , no. 72. II. Title.
QE176.O43 R38

Raub, R. A. Summary and critique of the literature pertaining to the effects of increased enforcement of traffic laws on improving traffic safety (reducing accidents) / prepared for the Illinois Department of Law Enforcement, Division of State Police, Field Operations Command by R.A. Raub. [Springfield] : The Dept., [1979] 58 leaves ; 28 cm. "December 1979." Bibliography: leaves 49-58. LC Card 81-621246 DDC 363.1/256/0973 19
1. Traffic safety - United States - Abstracts. 2. Traffic regulations - United States - Abstracts. I. Illinois State Police. Field Operations Command. II. Title.
HE5614.2 .R38

Rauch, Leo. The political animal : studies in political philosophy from Machiavelli to Marx / by Leo Rauch. Amherst, MA : University of Massachusetts Press, c1981. p. cm. Includes bibliographical references and index. ISBN 0-87023-338-6 : LC Card 81-3070 DDC 320/.01/09 19
1. Political science - History. I. Title.
JA83 .R34

Rautio, Sandra A. Annotated bibliography of the geothermal resources of Montana / compiled by Sandra A. Rautio and John L. Sonderegger. [Butte] : Montana Bureau of Mines and Geology, 1980. 25 p. ; 23 cm. (Bulletin - Montana Bureau of Mines and Geology . 110) Includes indexes. LC Card 80-623786 DDC 553.7 19
1. Geothermal resources - Montana - Abstracts. 2. Geothermal resources - Montana - Bibliography. I. Sonderegger, J. L., joint author. II. Series: Montana. State Bureau of Mines and Geology. Bulletin , 110. III. Title.
GB1199.7.M9 R38

Raw materials in the United States economy, 1900-1977 /. Spencer, Vivian Eberle, 1907- Washington, D.C. , 1980. 90 p. : LC Card 80-603173 DDC 333.7/0973 19
HF1052 .S63

RAW MATERIALS - UNITED STATES - STATISTICS.
Spencer, Vivian Eberle, 1907- Raw materials in the United States economy, 1900-1977 /. Washington, D.C. , 1980. 90 p. : LC Card 80-603173 DDC 333.7/0973 19
HF1052 .S63

Rawlings, Stephen, 1945- Families maintained by female householders, 1970 to 1979 / Stephen Rawlings. [Washington] : U. S. Dept. of Commerce, Bureau of the Census, 1980. p. cm. (Current population reports : Special studies : Series P-23 ; no. 107) LC Card 80-25731 DDC 312/.0973 s 306.8 19
1. Single-parent family - United States - Statistics. 2. Women heads of households - United States - Statistics. I. United States. Bureau of the Census. II. Series: United States. Bureau of the Census. Current population reports: Special studies: Series P-23, no. 107. III. Title.
HA203 .A218 no. 107 HQ536

Rawson, Jack. Water quality of Livingston Reservoir on the Trinity River, Southeastern Texas / by Jack Rawson. Austin, Tex. : Texas Dept. of Water Resources, 1979. v, 46 p. : ill. ; 28 cm. (Report - Texas Department of Water Resources ; 230) Bibliography: p. 17. LC Card 79-625432 DDC 553.7/8/0976416 19
1. Water quality - Texas - Livingston, Lake. I. Series: Texas. Dept. of Water Resources. Report - Texas Department of Water Resources , 230. II. Title.
TD224.T4 A333 no. 230

Ray, Daryll E. (joint author) Richardson, James W. An application of optimal control techniques to agricultural policy analysis /. [Stillwater, Okla.] , 1979. 41 p. ; LC Card 79-625383 DDC 338.1/873 19
HD1765 1979 .R52

Ray, Dorothy Jean. (joint author) Renner, Louis L., 1926- Pioneer missionary to the Bering Strait Eskimos . Portland, Ore. , 1979. xv, 207 p. : ISBN 0-8323-0343-7 : LC Card 79-53362
E99.E7 L257 **NYPL [JFE 80-4064]**

Rayfield, Robert E. McCarthy, James R. Linebacker II . [Montgomery] Ala. , Washington , 1979. xvi, 208 p. : LC Card 79-603001
DS558.8 .M32

REA and energy conservation . United States. Congress. Senate. Committee on Agriculture, Nutrition, and Foresty. Subcommittee on Agricultural Credit and Rural Electrification.

Washington , 1980. iii, 113 p. : LC Card 81-600598 DDC 334/.68136362 19
KF26 .A3533 1980a

Rea, Louis M. (joint author) Corso, Anthony. Job satisfaction among urban planners . [San Diego] , 1978. viii, 76 leaves ; LC Card 79-622099
HT167.5.C2 C67 **NYPL [JLF 80-1454]**

REACTION RATE (CHEMISTRY) see CHEMICAL REACTION, RATE OF.

Reactions to crime . DuBow, Fred. Washington, D.C. , 1980. viii, 90 p. ; LC Card 80-602129 DDC 364.1/01/9 19
HV6791 .D82

REACTOR FUELS. see NUCLEAR FUELS.

REACTORS (ATOMIC ENERGY) see NUCLEAR REACTORS.

REACTORS, BREEDER. see BREEDER REACTORS.

REACTORS (NUCLEAR PHYSICS) see NUCLEAR REACTORS.

Reader on nuclear nonproliferation / prepared for the Subcommittee on Energy, Nuclear Proliferation, and Federal Services of the Committee on Governmental Affairs, United States Senate, by the Congressional Research Service, Library of Congress. Washington : U. S. G.P.O. : For sale by the Supt. of Docs., U. S. G.P.O., 1980. x, 344 p. : ill. ; 24 cm. At head of title: 96th Congress, 2d session. Committee print. "Compiled by Donna S. Kramer"--P. v. "December 1980." S/N 052-070-05493-0 Item 1037-A Bibliography: p. 129. LC Card 81-600802 DDC 327.1/74 19
1. Nuclear nonproliferation - Addresses, essays, lectures. 2. Atomic power - International control - Addresses, essays, lectures. I. Kramer, Donna S. II. United States. Congress. Senate. Committee on Governmental Affairs. Subcommittee on Energy, Nuclear Proliferation, and Federal Services. III. Library of Congress. Congressional Research Service.
JX1974.73 .R4

A reader's guide for parents of children with mental, physical, or emotional disabilities /. Moore, Coralie B. Rockville, Md. , Washington, D.C. , 1979. viii, 144 : LC Card 79-601825 DDC 016.3624/088054 19
Z5814.C52 M66 1979 HV888

A reader's guide to William Gaddis's Recognitions /. Moore, Steven, 1951- Lincoln , c1982. p. cm. ISBN 0-8032-3072-9 LC Card 81-7572 DDC 813/.54 19
PS3557.A28 R435 1982

READERSHIP SURVEYS - UNITED STATES.
Government Studies & Systems, inc. Braille reader survey analysis /. Philadelphia , 1974. viii, 17 p., [45] p. of tables ;
NYPL [*Z-3211]

READING (ADULT EDUCATION)
Adult literacy program handbook . Washington, D.C. , 1980. viii, 179 p. : LC Card 80-602326 DDC 374/.012/0973 19
LC5225.R4 A29

Readings from the new book on nature . Nadeau, Robert L., 1944- Amherst , 1981. p. cm. ISBN 0-87023-331-9 : LC Card 81-2625 DDC 813/.54/09356 19
PS374.P45 N3

Readings in intercultural communication . (v. 1) The Intercultural communication workshop /. Pittsburgh , 1975. 143 p. ; LC Card 79-119932 DDC 370.19/6 19
LC1099 .I54

Readings on the protection and management of marine and submerged resources of the national parks : printed at the request of the Committee on Energy and Natural Resources, United States Senate. Washington : U. S. Govt. Print. Off., 1980. ix, 157 p. : maps ; 24 cm. At head of title: 96th Congress, 2d session. Committee print. "August 1980." "Publication no. 96-113." Includes bibliographies. LC Card 80-603550 DDC 333.91/0973 19
1. Marine parks and reserves - United States. 2. Marine resources conservation - United States. 3. National parks and reserves - United States. I. United States. Congress. Senate. Committee on Energy and Natural Resources.
QH91.75.U6 R4

Readle, Elmer L. Soil survey of Osceola County area, Florida / United States Department of Agriculture, Soil Conservation Service, in cooperation with University of Florida, Institute of Food and Agricultural Sciences and Agricultural Experiment Stations, Soil Science Department ; [by Elmer L. Readle ; fieldwork by Elmer L. Readle, Allen L. Moore, and William B. Warmack]. [Washington] : [National Cooperative Soil Survey], 1979. x, 151 p., [59] fold. leaves of plates : ill. ; 28 cm. Bibliography: p. 80. LC Card 79-602772 DDC 631.4/7/75925 19
1. Soils - Florida - Osceola Co. - Maps. I. Moore, Allen L. II. Warmack, William B. III. United States. Soil Conservation Service. IV. Florida. University, Gainesville. Institute of Food and Agricultural Sciences. V. Florida. Agricultural Experiment Station, Gainesville. Soil Science Dept. VI. Title.
S599.F6 R42

REAL ESTATE. see REAL PROPERTY.

REAL ESTATE AGENTS - LICENSES - NEBRASKA.
Nebraska. Nebraska real estate license laws and rules and regulations /. Lincoln, Neb. (301 Centennial Mall, South, P.O. Box 94667, Lincoln 68509) , 1980. 41 p. in various pagings ; LC Card 80-624276 DDC 346.78204/37 347.8206437 19
KFN282.R4 A3 1980

REAL ESTATE BROKERS. see REAL ESTATE AGENTS.

REAL ESTATE BUSINESS - HAWAII - EMPLOYEES - STATISTICS.
Hawaii. Labor Market and Employment Service Research Section. Occupational Information Unit. Hawaii's finance, insurance, and real estate industries, 1978 /. [Honolulu, Hawaii , 1978?] 40 p. : LC Card 80-623579 DDC 331.12/513321/09969 19
HD8039.B27 U547 1978

REAL ESTATE BUSINESS - LAW AND LEGISLATION - OKLAHOMA.
Oklahoma. Real Estate Commission. The Oklahoma manual for real estate brokers and sales associates /. Oklahoma City, Okla. , 1978. xiii, 77 p. : LC Card 80-623214 DDC 333.33/09766 19
HD266.O5 O37 1978

REAL ESTATE BUSINESS - LAW AND LEGISLATION - WYOMING.
Wyoming. Real Estate Commission. Real estate manual /. Cheyenne, Wyo. [1979] v, 320 p. : LC Card 79-625847 DDC 346.78704/37 19
KFW4482.R4 A87 1979

REAL ESTATE BUSINESS - LICENSES - INDIANA.
Indiana. Laws, statutes, etc. Real estate license laws. Indianapolis [1959] 15 p. ; LC Card 79-119386 DDC 346.77204/37 347.7206437 19
KFI3282.R4 A3 1959

Indiana. Laws, statutes, etc. Real estate license laws /. Indianapolis , 1972. 27 p. ; LC Card 79-119630 DDC 346.77204/37 19
KFI3282.R4 A3 1972

REAL ESTATE BUSINESS - NEW JERSEY - EMPLOYEES - SUPPLY AND DEMAND - STATISTICS.
New Jersey. Dept. of Labor and Industry. Division of Planning and Research. Occupational employment in selected finance-insurance-real estate industries in New Jersey. Trenton, N.J. , 1979. iii, 112 p. : LC Card 80-623798 DDC 331.12/513321/09749 19
HD5718.I482 U55 1979

REAL ESTATE BUSINESS - OKLAHOMA - HANDBOOKS, MANUALS, ETC.
Oklahoma. Real Estate Commission. The Oklahoma manual for real estate brokers and sales associates /. Oklahoma City, Okla. , 1978. xiii, 77 p. : LC Card 80-623214 DDC 333.33/09766 19
HD266.O5 O37 1978

REAL ESTATE BUSINESS - UNITED STATES.
United States Conference of Mayors. The private development process . [Washington] [1979] iii, 49 p. ; LC Card 79-601943
HD259 .U53 1979

REAL ESTATE BUSINESS - UNITED STATES - PERIODICALS.
United States. Dept. of Agriculture. Economic

Research Service. Farm real estate market developments. CD. 58-82; May 1961-Jan. 1978. Washington. 25 no. in 2 v.
NYPL [M-10 7260]

REAL ESTATE DEVELOPMENT - COSTS.
Burchell, Robert W. The fiscal impact guidebook . [Washington] , 1979. xxii, 617 p. ; LC Card 79-602895
HD4431 .B85 1979

REAL ESTATE DEVELOPMENT - ENVIRONMENTAL ASPECTS - NEW JERSEY.
Rutgers University, New Brunswick, N.J. Center for Coastal and Environmental Studies. Comparison of natural and altered estuarine systems . [New Brunswick, N.J.] [1979] xv, 247 p. : LC Card 80-623603 DDC 574.5/26365 19
QH105.N5 R87 1979

REAL ESTATE DEVELOPMENT - ENVIRONMENTAL ASPECTS - NEW JERSEY - MANAHAWKIN REGION.
Rutgers University, New Brunswick, N.J. Center for Coastal and Environmental Studies. Comparison of natural and altered estuarine systems . [New Brunswick, N.J.] [1979] 2 v. : LC Card 80-623604 DDC 574.5/26365 19
QH105.N5 R87 1979a

REAL ESTATE DEVELOPMENT - LAW AND LEGISLATION - UNITED STATES.
Wallace School of Community Service and Public Affairs. Bureau of Governmental Research and Service. The development standards document, with section-by-section explanation. [Eugene] [1979] 172 p. ; LC Card 80-624205 DDC 346.7304/5 347.30645 19
HD205 1979 .W34

REAL ESTATE DEVELOPMENT - NEW YORK (CITY)
New York (State). Division of Audits and Accounts. Report no. 7, the New York State Mitchell-Lama program . [Albany] , 1978. 65 leaves ; LC Card 79-622401 DDC 353.97470072/32 19
HD268.N5 N26 1978

REAL ESTATE DEVELOPMENT - STANDARDS - UNITED STATES.
Wallace School of Community Service and Public Affairs. Bureau of Governmental Research and Service. The development standards document, with section-by-section explanation. [Eugene] [1979] 172 p. ; LC Card 80-624205 DDC 346.7304/5 347.30645 19
HD205 1979 .W34

REAL ESTATE DEVELOPMENT - UNITED STATES - COSTS - CONGRESSES.
HUD National Conference on Housing Costs, Washington, D.C., 1979. Reducing the development costs of housing . [Washington, D.C.] , 1979. xv, 275 p. : LC Card 80-601844 DDC 338.4/36908/0973 19
HD7293 .H82 1979

REAL ESTATE DEVELOPMENT - UNITED STATES - STATES.
Alm, Robert A. A survey of states' efforts to improve land development review procedures /. Honolulu [1980] v, 68 p. ; LC Card 80-623819 DDC 333.73/15/0973 19
HT392 .A75

REAL ESTATE INVESTMENT - MATHEMATICAL MODELS.
Findlay, M. Chapman. FMRR simulation model and user manual /. Storrs, Conn. , Los Angeles, Calif. [1980] 51, 22 leaves ; ISBN 0-931176-76-X (pbk.) : LC Card 80-623842 DDC 333.33 s 332.63/24/0724 19
HD251 .R283 no. 30 HD1375

Real estate license laws. Indiana. Laws, statutes, etc. Indianapolis [1959] 15 p. ; LC Card 79-119386 DDC 346.77204/37 347.7206437 19
KFI3282.R4 A3 1959

Real estate license laws /. Indiana. Laws, statutes, etc. Indianapolis , 1972. 27 p. ; LC Card 79-119630 DDC 346.77204/37 19
KFI3282.R4 A3 1972

Real estate manual. Oklahoma. Real Estate Commission. The Oklahoma manual for real estate brokers and sales associates /. Oklahoma City, Okla. , 1978. xiii, 77 p. : LC Card 80-623214 DDC 333.33/09766 19
HD266.O5 O37 1978

Real estate manual /. Wyoming. Real Estate Commission. Cheyenne, Wyo. [1979] v, 320 p. : LC Card 79-625847 DDC 346.78704/37 19
KFW4482.R4 A87 1979

Real estate reports .
(no. 30) Findlay, M. Chapman. FMRR simulation model and user manual /. Storrs, Conn. , Los Angeles, Calif. [1980] 51, 22 leaves ; ISBN 0-931176-76-X (pbk.) : LC Card 80-623842 DDC 333.33 s 332.63/24/0724 19
HD251 .R283 no. 30 HD1375

(no. 32) McEachern, William A. An analysis of Connecticut's 1979 school finance formula /. Storrs, Conn., c1980. 91, 11 p. ; ISBN 0-931176-78-6 (pbk.) LC Card 80-623844 DDC 379.1/222/09746 19
HD251 .R283 no. 32 LB2826.C8

Real Estate Research Corporation.
Economics of revitalization . [Washington, D.C.?] , 1981 i.e. 1980. 94 p. : LC Card 81-601655 DDC 352.94/18/0973 19
HT175 .E27

Selling the solar home '80 : market findings for the housing industry / prepared for Solar Demonstration Program, Division of Energy, Building Technology, and Standards, Office of Policy Development and Research, U. S. Department of Housing and Urban Development, in cooperation with the U. S. Department of Energy ; prepared by Real Estate Research Corporation. [Washington, D.C.] : HUD : [for sale by the Supt. of Docs., U. S. Govt. Print. Off.], 1980. 26 p. (p. 26 blank) : ill. ; 28 cm. "HUD-PDR-514." LC Card 80-602366 DDC 690/.869/0688 19
1. Solar houses - United States. 2. House buying. 3. House selling. I. Solar Demonstration Program (U. S.). II. Title.
HD7293 .R36 1980

Urban infill : the literature / prepared by Real Estate Research Corporation under contract no. H-2982 for the Department of Housing and Urban Development, Office of Policy Development and Research. [Washington, D.C.] : The Office : for sale by the Supt. of Docs., U. S. Govt. Print. Off., [1980] 76 p. ; 28 cm. "January 1980." "HUD-PDR-557." LC Card 80-602851 DDC 016.33377/13/0973 19
1. Land use, Urban - United States - Bibliography. I. United States. Dept. of Housing and Urban Development. Office of Policy Development and Research. II. Title.
Z7164.L3 R4 1980 HD205

REAL ESTATE SALESMEN. see REAL ESTATE AGENTS.

Real estate settlement procedures act.
Washington, D.C. : Dept. of Housing and Urban Development, Office of Neighborhoods, Voluntary Associations, and Consumer Protection, [1979] 7, 39, [12] p. : forms ; 27 cm. Bibliography: p. 38-39. CONTENTS. - Statute.--Regulations.--Special information booklet. LC Card 80-601047 DDC 346.7304/373 19
1. Settlement costs - United States. I. United States. Dept. of Housing and Urban Development. Office of Neighborhoods, Voluntary Associations, and Consumer Protection. II. United States. Laws, statutes, etc. Real estate settlement procedures act of 1974. 1979. III. United States. Dept. of Housing and Urban Development. Regulation X. 1979. IV. United States. Dept. of Housing and Urban Development. Settlement costs. 1979.
KF681 .R4

REAL ESTATE TAX. see REAL PROPERTY TAX.

REAL PROPERTY AND TAXATION - UNITED STATES.
Moore, Mary. Income tax law changes affecting real estate /. College Station, Tex. [1980] 56 p. ; LC Card 81-621043 DDC 343.7305/4 347.30354 19
KF6535.Z9 M66

United States. Congress. House. Committee on Ways and Means. Subcommittee on Select Revenue Measures. Expiring historic structure tax provisions . Washington , 1981. viii, 578 p. : LC Card 81-601397 DDC 343.7305/4 347.30354 19
KF27 .W3468 1980e

REAL PROPERTY, EXCHANGE OF - MICHIGAN.

United States. Congress. House. Committee on Armed Services. Subcommittee on Military Installations and Facilities. Hearing on H.R. 6312 (H.R. 6464), to authorize the Secretary of the Army to convey to the Michigan Job Development Authority the lands and improvements comprising the Michigan Army Missile Plant in Sterling Heights, Macomb County, Mich., before the Military Installations and Facilities Subcommittee of the Committee on Armed Services, House of Representatives, Ninety-sixth Congress, second session, February 7, 1980. Washington , 1980. ii, 32 p. : LC Card 80-601382 DDC 343.73/0253/0262 19
KF27 .A76397 1980

REAL PROPERTY, EXCHANGE OF - UNITED STATES.
United States. Congress. House. Committee on Armed Services. Subcommittee on Military Installations and Facilities. Hearing on H.R. 6312 (H.R. 6464), to authorize the Secretary of the Army to convey to the Michigan Job Development Authority the lands and improvements comprising the Michigan Army Missile Plant in Sterling Heights, Macomb County, Mich., before the Military Installations and Facilities Subcommittee of the Committee on Armed Services, House of Representatives, Ninety-sixth Congress, second session, February 7, 1980. Washington , 1980. ii, 32 p. : LC Card 80-601382 DDC 343.73/0253/0262 19
KF27 .A76397 1980

REAL PROPERTY INVESTMENT. see REAL ESTATE INVESTMENT.

REAL PROPERTY - MICHIGAN - GOGEBIC COUNTY - MAPS.
Rockford Map Publishers, Rockford, Ill. Land plat book, with index to land owners, Gogebic County, Michigan. Rockford, 1965. 55 p. LC Card Map68-420
NYPL [Map Div. 80-375]

REAL PROPERTY - MINNESOTA.
Minnesota. Real Estate Section. Minnesota real estate manual /. St. Paul, Minn. [1975] 249 p. : LC Card 79-118936 DDC 346.77604/3 19
KFM5512 .A873 1975

REAL PROPERTY - MINNESOTA - AITKIN CO. - MAPS.
Minnesota. Dept. of Iron Range Resources and Rehabilitation. Land ownership, Aitkin County /. Hibbing, Minn. [1974] 2 leaves : LC Card 80-675190 DDC 912/.77672
G1428.A3G46 M5 1974

REAL PROPERTY - MINNESOTA - BECKER CO. - MAPS.
Minnesota. Dept. of Iron Range Resources and Rehabilitation. Land ownership, Becker County /. Hibbing, Minn. [1974] 2 leaves : LC Card 80-675191 DDC 912/.77684
G1428.B2G46 M5 1974

REAL PROPERTY - MINNESOTA - CARLTON CO. - MAPS.
Minnesota. Dept. of Iron Range Resources and Rehabilitation. Land ownership, Carlton County /. Hibbing, Minn. [1975] 1 leaf : LC Card 80-675193 DDC 912/.77673
G1428.C2G46 M5 1975

REAL PROPERTY - MINNESOTA - CASS CO. - MAPS.
Minnesota. Dept. of Iron Range Resources and Rehabilitation. Land ownership, Cass County /. Eveleth, Minn. [1977] 4 leaves : LC Card 80-675194 DDC 912/.77686
G1428.C3G46 M5 1977

REAL PROPERTY - MINNESOTA - CLEARWATER CO. - MAPS.
Minnesota. Dept. of Iron Range Resources and Rehabilitation. Land ownership, Clearwater County /. Hibbing, Minn. [1974] 1 leaf : LC Card 80-675195 DDC 912/.77683
G1428.C55G46 M5 1974

REAL PROPERTY - MINNESOTA - COOK CO. - MAPS.
Minnesota. Dept. of Iron Range Resources and Rehabilitation. Land ownership, Cook County /. Eveleth, Minn. [1976] 3 leaves : LC Card 80-675201 DDC 912/.77675
G1428.C6G46 M5 1976

REAL PROPERTY - MINNESOTA - HUBBARD CO. - MAPS.
Minnesota. Dept. of Iron Range Resources and

Rehabilitation. Land ownership, Hubbard County /. Hibbing, Minn. [1974] 1 leaf : LC Card 80-675197 DDC 912/.77685
G1428.H8G46 M5 1974

REAL PROPERTY - MINNESOTA - ITASCA CO. - MAPS.
Minnesota. Dept. of Iron Range Resources and Rehabilitation. Land ownership, Itasca County /. Hibbing, Minn. [1973] 3 leaves : LC Card 80-675198 DDC 912/.77678
G1428.I8G46 M5 1973

REAL PROPERTY - MINNESOTA - KOOCHICHING CO. - MAPS.
Minnesota. Dept. of Iron Range Resources and Rehabilitation. Land ownership, Koochiching County /. Hibbing, Minn. [1973] 4 leaves : LC Card 80-675199 DDC 912/.77679
G1428.K6G46 M5 1973

REAL PROPERTY - MINNESOTA - LAKE CO. - MAPS.
Minnesota. Dept. of Iron Range Resources and Rehabilitation. Land ownership, Lake County /. Hibbing, Minn. [1973] 3 leaves : LC Card 80-675202 DDC 912/.77676
G1428.L3G46 M5 1973

REAL PROPERTY - MINNESOTA - LAKE OF THE WOODS CO. - MAPS.
Minnesota. Dept. of Iron Range Resources and Rehabilitation. Land ownership, Lake of the Woods County /. Eveleth, Minn. [1977] 4 leaves : LC Card 80-675203 DDC 912/.77681
G1428.L4G46 M5 1977

REAL PROPERTY - MINNESOTA - MILLE LACS CO. - MAPS.
Minnesota. Dept. of Iron Range Resources and Rehabilitation. Land ownership, Mille Lacs County /. Hibbing, Minn. [1972] 1 leaf : LC Card 80-675205 DDC 912/.77668
G1428.M5G46 M5 1972

REAL PROPERTY - MINNESOTA - ST. LOUIS CO. - MAPS.
Minnesota. Dept. of Iron Range Resources and Rehabilitation. Land ownership, St. Louis County /. Hibbing, Minn. [1973] 7 leaves : LC Card 80-675210 DDC 912/.77677
G1428.S2G46 M5 1973

REAL PROPERTY - MINNESOTA - WADENA CO. - MAPS.
Minnesota. Dept. of Iron Range Resources and Rehabilitation. Land ownership, Wadena County /. [Hibbing? Minn.] [1976] 1 leaf : LC Card 80-675212 DDC 912/.77687
G1428.W3G46 M5 1976

REAL PROPERTY - NORTH CAROLINA - FOREIGN OWNERSHIP.
North Carolina. Legislative Research Commission. Alien landholding . Raleigh, N.C. (Room 2126, 2226, State Legislative Bldg., Raleigh, N.C. 27611) [1981] 42 p. in various pagings : LC Card 81-621648 DDC 346.75604/32 347.5606432 19
KFN7512.5 .A25 1981

REAL PROPERTY - RESTRICTIONS. see ZONING.

REAL PROPERTY TAX - CALIFORNIA.
California. Legislature. Assembly. Committee on Housing and Community Development. Property taxation (ACA 55-Mori), housing program incentives . Sacramento, CA [1979] ii, 95, [21] p. : LC Card 80-621896 DDC 338.4/33335/09794 19
KFC10.4 .H67 1979a

California. Legislature. Assembly. Committee on Judiciary. Legal position of the tenant in the post Proposition 13 era . Sacramento, CA [1980] iv, 143 p. : LC Card 80-621956 DDC 346.79404/34 19
KFC10.4 .J8 1979c

California. Property Tax Dept. Assessment practices survey, a special study of agricultural properties under California land conservation act contracts. [Sacramento] [1980] v leaves, 98 p. : LC Card 80-622948 DDC 353.97940072/42 19
HJ4191 .C35 1980

Doerr, David R. Proposition 13 assessment issues . [Sacramento CA] , 1980] 1 v. (various pagings) : LC Card 81-620793 DDC 333.33/2/09794 19
HJ4121.C22 D63

REAL PROPERTY TAX - ILLINOIS - STATISTICS.
Illinois. State Board of Education (Founded 1973). Dept. of Finance and Reimbursements. Equalized assessed valuations and tax rates, 1978 . [Springfield, Ill.] [1980] 81 p., [1] leaf of plates : LC Card 80-622959 DDC 336.22/2 19
HJ9228 .I39 1980

REAL PROPERTY TAX - IOWA.
Iowa. Division of Municipal Affairs. Handbook for urban revitalization /. [Des Moines, Iowa] [1979] 48 p. ; LC Card 80-622540 DDC 346.77704/5 19
KFI4660 .A853

REAL PROPERTY TAX - KENTUCKY.
Neuhaus, William B. Urban abandonment and property tax delinquency /. Frankfort, Ky. , 1978. iii, 22 p. ; LC Card 79-621078 DDC 343.76905/4 347.690354 19
KFK1679 .N48

REAL PROPERTY TAX - LAW AND LEGISLATION - CALIFORNIA.
Doerr, David R. Proposition 13 assessment issues . [Sacramento CA] , 1980] 1 v. (various pagings) : LC Card 81-620793 DDC 333.33/2/09794 19
HJ4121.C22 D63

REAL PROPERTY TAX - MAINE - STATISTICS.
Halperin, Raymond L. Summary 1980 State valuation as filed with the Secretary of State, January 25, 1980 /. Augusta, Me. [1980] 41 leaves ; LC Card 80-621327 DDC 336.22/2 19
HJ4223 .H35

Municipal valuation return . [Augusta, Me. , 1979?] ca. 150 leaves in various pagings ; LC Card 80-623459 DDC 336.22/2/09741 19
HJ9249 .M86

REAL PROPERTY TAX - NEW JERSEY - DEDUCTIONS.
New Jersey. Legislature. General Assembly. Revenue, Finance, and Appropriations Committee. Public hearing before Assembly Revenue, Finance, and Appropriations Committee on ACR-29 . [Trenton] [1980] 3, 9, 23 p. ; LC Card 80-623639 DDC 343.74905/4 347.490354 19
KFN1811.4 .R45 1980a

New Jersey. Legislature. Senate. Revenue, Finance and Appropriations Committee. Public hearing before Senate Revenue, Finance, and Appropriations Committee on SCR 90, held May 28, 1980, Assembly Chamber, State House, Trenton, New Jersey. [Trenton] [1980] 13 p. ; LC Card 80-623722 DDC 343.749/054 347.490354 19
KFN1811.3 .R48 1980

REAL PROPERTY TAX - NEW YORK (N.Y.)
New York (State). Legislature. Senate. Standing Committee on Cities and City of New York. Certiorari . [Albany, N.Y.] , 1980. 119 p. ; LC Card 80-624086 DDC 353.7470072/421 19
KFN5010.72 .C57 1980

REAL PROPERTY TAX - NEW YORK (STATE)
Adams, Sylvia. The classified real property tax . Albany, NY [1980] 41 p. ; LC Card 80-622879 DDC 336.22/09747 19
HJ4181 .A67

Boyd, Donald, 1955- New York State real property tax circuit breaker relief /. Albany, NY [1979] iii, 38 p. ; LC Card 80-622832 DDC 336.22 19
HJ4249 .B69

McCord, Thomas. Business property taxes and exemptions in New York State . Albany, NY [1980] xi, 101 p. : LC Card 80-622828 DDC 336.22/5 19
HJ4249 .M3

McCord, Thomas. The quality of assessment practices in New York State . Albany, N.Y. [1980] 20 p. : LC Card 80-622878 DDC 336.22/2 19
HJ4249 .M33

New York (State). Legislature. Assembly. Task Force on School Finance and Real Property Taxation. The legislative response to the property tax crisis . Albany, N.Y. (The Capitol, Albany 12248) [1979] 66 p. : LC Card

81-621126 DDC 336.22/2 19
HJ4249 .N444 1979

New York (State). Legislature. Senate. Standing
Committee on Cities and City of New York.
Certiorari . [Albany, N.Y.] , 1980. 119 p. ; LC
   Card 80-624086 DDC 353.7470072/421 19
KFN5010.72 .C57 1980

New York (State). State Board of Equalization
and Assessment. Educational finance and the
New York State real property tax . Albany,
NY , 1979. 56 p. ; LC Card 80-621873 DDC
   379.1/3 19
HJ4249 .N45 1979

Patenaude, John J. Report on proposed State
assessments of all public utility real property in
New York State /. Albany, N.Y. [1980] 10 p. ;
   LC Card 80-621854 DDC 336.22/2 19
HD2767.N74 P37

**REAL PROPERTY TAX - NEW YORK (STATE)
   - STATISTICS.**
New York (State). Division of Equalization and
Assessment. Full value programs during the
1970's. Albany, NY [1979] 14 p. ; LC Card
   80-621877 DDC 336.22/2 19
HJ4249 .N44 1979a

REAL PROPERTY TAX - SOUTH DAKOTA.
Favero, Philip. The Dakota proposition .
Brookings, S.D. [1979] 12 leaves : LC Card
   80-624255 DDC 336.22/2/09783 19
HJ4267 .F38

REAL PROPERTY TAX - UNITED STATES.
Adams, Sylvia. The classified real property tax .
Albany, NY [1980] 41 p. ; LC Card 80-622879
   DDC 336.22/09747 19
HJ4181 .A67

Kupferman, Michael E. Classified real property
tax systems in the United States /. Albany,
N.Y. [1980] 65, xv p. ; LC Card 80-622877
   DDC 336.22/2 19
HJ4181 .K86

**REAL PROPERTY TAX - UNITED STATES -
   STATES.**
Massachusetts. Legislative Research Council.
Report relative to voter approval of borrowing
and property taxes /. [Boston] , 1979. 57 p. ;
   LC Card 79-625031 DDC 353.97440072 19
HJ4181 .M37 1979

REAL PROPERTY TAX - VIRGINIA.
Virginia. General Assembly. Joint Subcommittee
to Study Real Property Tax Exemptions. Report
of the Joint Subcommittee to Study Real
Property Tax Exemptions to the Governor and
the General Assembly of Virginia. Richmond ,
1980. 73 p. ; LC Card 80-622737 DDC 300/.9755
   s 343.75505/43 19
J87 .V9 1980c no. 35 KFV2411.62

**REAL PROPERTY - TAXATION. see REAL
   PROPERTY TAX.**

REAL PROPERTY - UNITED STATES.
Wallace School of Community Service and
Public Affairs. Bureau of Governmental
Research and Service. The development
standards document, with section-by-section
explanation. [Eugene] [1979] 172 p. ; LC Card
   80-624205 DDC 346.7304/5 347.30645 19
HD205 1979 .W34

**REAL PROPERTY - UNITED STATES -
   CLASSIFICATION.**
Adams, Sylvia. The classified real property tax .
Albany, NY [1980] 41 p. ; LC Card 80-622879
   DDC 336.22/09747 19
HJ4181 .A67

Kupferman, Michael E. Classified real property
tax systems in the United States /. Albany,
N.Y. [1980] 65, xv p. ; LC Card 80-622877
   DDC 336.22/2 19
HJ4181 .K86

**REAL PROPERTY - UNITED STATES -
   FOREIGN OWNERSHIP.**
Krause, Kenneth R., 1934- Foreign investment
in the U. S. food and agricultural system .
[Washington, D.C.] , 1980] vii, 84 p. ; LC Card
   80-602345 DDC 338.1 s 332.6/73/0973 19
HD1751 .A91854 no. 456 HD9005

United States. Treasury Dept. Taxation of
foreign investment in U. S. real estate.
[Washington] , 1979. 68 p. ; LC Card 79-602968
KF6441 .A85   *NYPL [JLF 81-449]*

**REAL PROPERTY - VALUATION -
   MASSACHUSETTS - LEE -
   MATHEMATICAL MODELS.**
Rich, Peter, 1955- Measuring certain intangible
benefits of water pollution abatement by use of
changes of impacted real estate values /.
Amherst, Mass. [1979] 52 leaves : LC Card
   80-621812 DDC 333.33/22 19
HD268.L44 R5

**REAL PROPERTY - VALUATION -
   VIRGINIA.**
Bertelsen, Michael K. Landowner
supply-response behavior and the land
conversion process in the rural urban fringe /.
Blacksburg [1980] vi, 69 p. : LC Card
   80-623705 DDC 081 s 333.76/13/09755 19
AS36 .V512 no. 155 HD211.V8

**REAL PROPERTY - VALUATION -
   WASHINGTON (STATE) -
   MATHEMATICAL MODELS.**
Palmquist, Raymond B. Impact of highway
improvements on property values in
Washington /. Olympia, WA [1980] 247 p. ;
   LC Card 80-622759 DDC 333.33/2/09797 19
HD266.W2 P34

REAL-TIME DATA PROCESSING.
(1980) Liestman, Arthur L. A fault-tolerant
scheduling problem /. Urbana, Ill. [1980] 23
p. : LC Card 80-622970 DDC 001.64 s 001.64/404
   19
QA76 .I4 no. 1010 QA76.54

REALITY.
Brumbaugh, Robert Sherrick, 1918- Process
metaphysics and educational theory /. Albany ,
1981. p. cm. ISBN 0-87395-574-9 LC Card
   81-14329 DDC 370/.1 19
LB85.P7 B78

REALTORS. see REAL ESTATE AGENTS.

REALTY. see REAL PROPERTY.

Ream, H. W. Plant juice protein and moisture
expression from organic materials . Madison
[1978] 17 p. ; LC Card 79-625898 DDC
   016.664/6 19
Z5524.P83 P53 TP453.P7

**Reauthorization for the U. S. Railway
Association for fiscal year 1981 .** United States.
Congress. House. Committee on Interstate and
Foreign Commerce. Subcommittee on
Transportation and Commerce. Washington ,
1980. iii, 73 p. ; LC Card 80-603452 DDC
   353.0072/236875 19
KF27 .I5589 1980d

**Reauthorization of appropriation for the National
Historical Publications and Records
Commission .** United States. Congress. House.
Committee on Government Operations.
Subcommittee on Government Information and
Individual Rights. Washington , 1980. iii, 66
p. : LC Card 80-603008 DDC 344.73/092 19
KF27 .G6628 1979b

**Reauthorization of National climate program
act .** United States. Congress. Senate.
Committee on Commerce, Science, and
Transportation. Subcommittee on Science,
Technology, and Space. Washington , 1980. iii,
28 p. ; LC Card 80-602777 DDC
   353.0072/23682324 19
KF26 .C697 1980b

**Reauthorization of National earthquake hazards
reduction act .** United States. Congress. Senate.
Committee on Commerce, Science, and
Transportation. Subcommittee on Science,
Technology, and Space. Washington , 1980. iii,
84 p. : LC Card 80-602466 DDC 353.0075/4 19
KF26 .C697 1980a

**Reauthorization of the Federal fire prevention
and control act .** United States. Congress.
Senate. Committee on Commerce, Science, and
Transportation. Subcommittee for Consumers.
Washington , 1980. iii, 77 p. ; LC Card
   80-602434 DDC 353.0078/2 19
KF26 .C693 1980

**Reauthorization of the Juvenile Justice and
Delinquency Prevention Act of 1974 .** United
States. Congress. Senate. Committee on the
Judiciary. Washington , 1980. viii, 555 p. : LC
   Card 81-602037 DDC 344.73/03274
   347.3043274 19
KF26 .J8 1980i

**Reauthorization of the National Foundation for
the Arts and the Humanities act and the
Museum services act .** United States. Congress.
House. Committee on Education and Labor.
Subcomittee on Postsecondary Education.
Washington , 1980. xii, 1105 p. : LC Card
   80-603480 DDC 353.0072/236854 19
KF27 .E369 1980a

**Reauthorization of the national sea grant college
program .** United States. Congress. Senate.
Committee on Labor and Human Resources.
Subcommittee on Education, Arts, and
Humanities. Washington , 1980. iii, 204 p. ;
   LC Card 80-603079 DDC 346.7304/695 19
KF26 .L2735 1980a

**Reauthorization of the Older Americans Act,
1981 .** United States. Congress. House. Select
Committee on Aging. Subcommittee on Human
Services. Washington , 1980- v. <1> ; LC
   Card 80-603785 DDC 353.0084/6 19
KF27.5 .A36 1980c

REBELLIONS. see REVOLUTIONS.

RECALL - CALIFORNIA.
California. Legislature. Assembly. Committee on
Elections and Reapportionment. Assembly
Elections and Reapportionment Committee .
[Sacramento, Calif.] [1979] 101 p. ; LC Card
   80-622284 DDC 324.6/8/09794 19
KFC10.4 .E4 1979

**Receipt of Social Security benefits by persons
incarcerated in penal institutions .** United
States. Congress. House. Committee on Ways
and Means. Subcommittee on Social Security.
Washington , 1980. iv, 96 p. ; LC Card
   80-603715 DDC 368.4/00880692 19
KF27 .W347 1980b

**Recency and character of faulting offshore from
Metropolitan San Diego, California /** final
technical report, fiscal year, 1978-1979 / M. P.
Kennedy ... [et al.]. [Sacramento?] : California
Division of Mines & Geology, [1979 or 1980]
ii, 37 leaves : ill., maps (1 fold. in pocket) ; 28
cm. "Date submitted: October 15, 1979." "U. S.
Geological Survey contract 14-08-0001-17699."
Bibliography: leaves 33-37. LC Card 80-622874
   DDC 551.8/7/0979498 19
1. Faults (Geology) - California - San Diego region. I.
Kennedy, Michael P. II. California. Division of Mines
and Geology.
QE606.5.U6 R42

**Recensement de la circulation motorisée sur les
grandes routes de circulation internationale
(1975)** United Nations. Economic Commission
for Europe. Census of motor traffic on main
international traffic arteries (1975) =. New
York , 1979. 1 portfolio (96 p. in various
pagings : LC Card 80-675269 DDC
   912/.138831/094
G1797.21.P21 U55 1979

**Recent and pending federal activities affecting
motor vehicles.** The Automobile calendar .
[Washington, D.C.] , 1981. ii, 392 p. ; LC Card
   81-601095 DDC 343.73/078629222/02636
   347.037862922202636 19
KF2204.6 1981

**Recent developments in gravitation, Cargèse,
1978 /.** Cargèse Summer Institute on Recent
Developments in Gravitation, 1978. New
York , c1979. viii, 596 p. : ISBN 0-306-40198-3
   LC Card 79-9174
QC178 .C18 1978

Recent developments in ocean thermal energy.
United States. Congress. Office of Technology
Assessment. Washington, D.C. , 1980. 32 p. :
   LC Card 80-600074 DDC 621.31/243 19
TK1056 .U52 1980

**Recent developments, new opportunities in civil
rights and women's rights .** Western Regional
Civil Rights and Women's Rights Conference,
4th, San Francisco, 1977. - Washington [1977].
vi, 178 p. ;   *NYPL [JLE 80-2420]*

**Recent developments pertaining to grain
embargo .** United States. Congress. House.
Committee on Agriculture. Washington , 1980.
iii, 44 p. ; LC Card 80-603662 DDC
   382/.4131/0973 19
KF27 .A3 1980b

**RECENT EPOCH (PALEOBOTANY) see
   PALEOBOTANY - RECENT.**

Recent fluctuations in meteorological and oceanographic parameters in Alaska waters /. Niebauer, H. J. Fairbanks, Alaska [1980] iv, 34 p. : LC Card 80-623130 DDC 551.46 551.46/634 19
GC1 .A497 no. 79-2 QC994.6

Recent gifts and acquisitions, 1976-1980. Vermont. University. Robert Hull Fleming Museum. Burlington [1980] 60 p. : LC Card 80-622800 DDC 708.143/17 19
N525.7 .A66

The recent history and current status of abortion law. Solomon, Jodee. Madison, Wis. [1980] 12 p. ; LC Card 80-624142 DDC 344.775/0419 347.7504419 19
KFW2415 .L4 80-5 KFW2753

The recent history of productivity in selected Berkshire lakes /. Ludlam, Stuart D. Amherst , 1977. ii, 66 p. : LC Card 79-624503 DDC 333.91/009744 s 581.5/26322/097441 19
TD224.M4 M37 no. 90 QH105.M4

Recent monetary policy developments . United States. Congress. House. Committee on Banking, Finance, and Urban Affairs. Subcommittee on Domestic Monetary Policy. Washington , 1981. iii, 73 p. : LC Card 81-600807 DDC 331.4/973 19
KF27 .B537 1980c

Recent population change in the United States. Borchert, David J. Minneapolis [1978]. [32] p. : LC Card 80-223350
NYPL [Map Div. 81-43]

Recent Soviet gains and possible targets, 1978. United States. Central Intelligence Agency. [Washington , 1978] 1 map : LC Card 81-690525
G7001.F35 1978 .U5

Recent suburbanization of Blacks, how much, who, and where /. Nelson, Kathryn P. [Washington] , 1979. 34 p. : LC Card 79-602959
HD7288.72.U5 N44

Recidivism of adult offenders . Oregon. Law Enforcement Council. [Salem, Ore.] [1980] ii, 22 p. : LC Card 80-622692 DDC 364.3/09795 19
HV6793.O7 O73 1980

RECIDIVISTS - CALIFORNIA. Petersilia, Joan. Criminal careers of habitual felons /. [Washington] , 1978. xxvi, 161 p. : LC Card 79-602505 DDC 364.3/09794 19
HV6793.C2 P47 1978

RECIDIVISTS - CONNECTICUT. Francisconi, Frank T. Evaluation of Connecticut's Department of Motor Vehicles program for alcohol-involved drivers . [Hartford] [1979] i, 119 p. : LC Card 80-622671 DDC 364.6/8 19
HE5620.D7 F67

RECIDIVISTS - MARYLAND - BALTIMORE. Lenihan, Kenneth J. Unlocking the second gate . [Washington] , 1977. iv, 71 p. : LC Card 77-600960
HD5701 .U53 no. 45 HV9306.B2
*NYPL [*XME-9551]*

RECIDIVISTS - OREGON. Oregon. Law Enforcement Council. Recidivism of adult offenders . [Salem, Ore.] [1980] ii, 22 p. : LC Card 80-622692 DDC 364.3/09795 19
HV6793.O7 O73 1980

RECIDIVISTS - PENNSYLVANIA. Pennsylvania. Division of Planning and Program Evaluation. Community service center recidivism evaluation /. [Harrisburg, Pa.] [1976] 44 p. ; LC Card 80-622329 DDC 364.3 19
HV9305.P3 P43 1976

RECIDIVISTS - RESEARCH - MASSACHUSETTS. LeClair, Daniel P. Development of base expectancy prediction tables for treatment and control groups in correctional research /. [Boston] , 1977. 35 p. ; LC Card 79-621662 DDC 364.6/0720744 19
HV6024.5 .L43

RECIDIVISTS - UNITED STATES. Petersilia, Joan. The prison experience of career criminals /. Washington, D.C. , 1980. xviii, 87 p. : LC Card 81-601009 DDC 365/.66 19
HV9304 .P44

RECIDIVISTS - VIRGINIA. Virginia. Dept. of Corrections. Bureau of Research, Reporting and Evaluation. A study of

recidivism. [Richmond] , 1977. i, 16 leaves ; LC Card 78-621733 DDC 364.3 19
HV7296 .A6 1977b

Reciprocity in investment . United States. Congress. House. Committee on Interstate and Foreign Commerce. Subcommittee on Consumer Protection and Finance. Washington , 1981. iii, 225 p. ; LC Card 81-601378 DDC 346.73/07 347.3067 19
KF27 .I554 1980k

Reclamation authorizations . United States. Congress. Senate. Committee on Energy and Natural Resources. Subcommittee on Energy Research and Development. Washington , 1980. iii, 200 p. : LC Card 80-603810 DDC 353.0082/326 19
KF26 .E554 1980a

RECLAMATION OF LAND - CONGRESSES. International Hill Lands Symposium, West Virginia University, 1976. Hill lands . [Morgantown, WV] [1976?] xiv, 770 p. : LC Card 80-100503 DDC 333.76/09143 19
S604.3 .I57 1976

Seminar on the Role of Overburden Analysis in Surface Mining (1980 : Wheeling, W. VA.) Proceedings of Seminar on the Role of Overburden Analysis in Surface Mining, Wheeling, W. Va., May 6-7, 1980 /. Washington , 1981. p. cm. LC Card 81-607049 DDC 622 s 622/.31 19
TN295 .U4 TD195.S75

RECLAMATION OF LAND - ILLINOIS. D'Antuono, James R. Some aspects of natural vegetation establishment on abandoned underground coal mine refuse areas in Illinois /. Chicago, IL , 1979. xii, 83 p. : LC Card 79-626016 DDC 631.6/4 19
S621.5.S65 D36

RECLAMATION OF LAND - LAW AND LEGISLATION - UNITED STATES. United States. Congress. House. Committee on Interior and Insular Affairs. Subcommittee on Energy and the Environment. Reclamation practices and environmental problems of surface mining . Washington , 1977. 4 v. : LC Card 77-603316 DDC 346.7304/68 347.306468 19
KF27 .I518 1977j

United States. Congress. Senate. Committee on Energy and Natural Resources. Subcommittee on Energy Research and Development. Reclamation authorizations . Washington , 1980. iii, 200 p. : LC Card 80-603810 DDC 353.0082/326 19
KF26 .E554 1980a

RECLAMATION OF LAND - NEW MEXICO. Severson, R. C. (Ronald Charles), 1945- Geochemical variability of natural soils and reclaimed mine-spoil soils in the San Juan Basin, New Mexico /. Washington , 1981. p. cm. LC Card 81-607985 DDC 631.6/4 19
S599.N6 S46

RECLAMATION OF LAND - RESEARCH - UNITED STATES. United States. Bureau of Reclamation. Reclamation research . [Washington] , 1979. vi, 121 p. : LC Card 80-602385 DDC 333.91/0072073 19
TC423 .U48 1979

RECLAMATION OF LAND - THE WEST - COSTS. Leathers, Kenneth L. Costs of strip mine reclamation in the West /. [Washington, D.C.] , 1980. iv, 82 p. : LC Card 80-601672 DDC 338.2/3 19
TD195.C58 L4

RECLAMATION OF LAND - UNITED STATES. Johnson, Wilton. Land utilization and reclamation in the mining industry, 1930-80 /. [Avondale, MD] [1981] p. cm. LC Card 81-38489 DDC 622 s 333.73 19
TN295 .U4 TN23

United States. Congress. House. Committee on Interior and Insular Affairs. Subcommittee on Energy and the Environment. Oversight on the Surface Mining Control and Reclamation Act of 1977 . Washington , 1981. vi, 621 p. ; LC Card 81-601889 DDC 353.0082/382 19
KF27 .I518 1980d

RECLAMATION OF LAND - UNITED STATES - FINANCE. United States. Congress. Senate. Committee on Energy and Natural Resources. Subcommittee on Energy Research and Development. Reclamation authorizations . Washington , 1980. iii, 200 p. : LC Card 80-603810 DDC 353.0082/326 19
KF26 .E554 1980a

RECLAMATION OF LAND - UNITED STATES - HISTORY - SOURCES - BIBLIOGRAPHY - CATALOGS. United States. National Archives and Records Service. Preliminary inventory of the records of the Civilian Conservation Corps . Washington , 1980. vii, 23 p. ; LC Card 80-28921 DDC 016.973 s 016.3337/2/0973 19
CD3026 .A32 no. 11, 1980 CD3035

RECLAMATION OF WATER. see WATER REUSE.

Reclamation practices and environmental problems of surface mining . United States. Congress. House. Committee on Interior and Insular Affairs. Subcommittee on Energy and the Environment. Washington , 1977. 4 v. : LC Card 77-603316 DDC 346.7304/68 347.306468 19
KF27 .I518 1977j

Reclamation research . United States. Bureau of Reclamation. [Washington] , 1979. vi, 121 p. : LC Card 80-602385 DDC 333.91/0072073 19
TC423 .U48 1979

A reclassification of the Polia complex for North America (Lepidoptera: Noctuidae) /. McCabe, Timothy Lee. Albany, N.Y. [1980] vi, 141 p. : LC Card 80-623061 DDC 595.78/1 19
QL561.N7 M27

RECOMBINANT DNA - INDUSTRIAL APPLICATIONS. United States. Congress. Senate. Committee on Commerce, Science, and Transportation. Subcommittee on Science, Technology, and Space. Industrial applications of recombinant DNA techniques . Washington , 1980. iii, 90 p. : LC Card 80-603025 DDC 338.4/766062 19
KF26 .C697 1980c

Recommendations for child care centers /. Community Design Center (Milwaukee, Wis.) Milwaukee , 1979. 453 leaves in various foliations : LC Card 80-153764 DDC 362.7/12 19
HV851 .C65 1979

Recommendations for child play areas / Uriel Cohen ... [et al.]. [Milwaukee] : School of Architecture & Urban Planning, University of Wisconsin-Milwaukee, [1980?] vi, 808 leaves : ill. ; 28 cm. Cover title. LC Card 80-153214 DDC 711/.558 19
1. Playgrounds - Planning. 2. Recreation areas - Planning. 3. Play. I. Cohen, Uriel.
GV423 .R33

Recommendations for database management system standards /. Fips Task Group on Database Management System Standards. Washington , 1979. x, 88 p. ; LC Card 79-600087 DDC 001.64/0218 19
QC100 .U57 no. 500-51 QA76.9.D3

Recommendations for ground water use regulation . Hawaii. Hydrologic Advisory Committee. Honolulu, Hawaii [1980] x, 33 p. : LC Card 80-622659 DDC 333.7/09969 s 346.96904/69104 333.7/09969 s 349.6906469104 19
GB832.H4 A43 no. C80 KFH446

Recommendations for legislative and administrative change to the public sector collective bargaining laws of Pennsylvania /. Pennsylvania. Governor's Study Commission on Public Employe Relations. [Harrisburg] , 1978. ii, 76 p. : LC Card 78-623470 DDC 344.748/01890413539 19
KFP332.8.P77 A84

Recommendations for national action . United Nations Conference on Human Settlements, Vancouver, B.C., 1976. [New York?] 1976. 75 p. ; LC Card 81-453323 DDC 300 s 361.6 19
JX1977 .A2 A/CONF.70/5

Recommendations to presession caucuses /. Montana. Legislature. Interim Committee on Legislative Improvement. Helena, Mont. (Room 138, State Capitol, Helena 59601) [1980] iv,

42, [37] p. ;   LC Card 81-621341   DDC 328.786 19
JK7371 .M65 1980

Recommended Illinois designations attainment/non-attainment pursuant to Sec. 107(D)(1) of the Clean air act, as amended, December 5, 1977. Illinois. Environmental Protection Agency. Springfield, Ill. [1977?] 9, [26] p. ;   LC Card 79-621589   DDC 363.7/39263/09773 19
TD883.5.I45 I43 1977

Recommended standards for courthouses in Missouri /. SRT Architects/Planners. [Jefferson City, Mo.] [1979] 70 leaves :   LC Card 80-623576   DDC 725/.15 19
KFM8259.C67 S16

Recommended technical provisions for construction practice in shoring and sloping of trenches and excavations /. Yokel, Felix Y. Washington, DC [1980] xvi, 68 p. :   LC Card 80-600068   DDC 690/.02/18 s 624.1/52 19
TA435 .U58 no. 127 TA770

Reconciliation (S. 2885) and special rules for its consideration together with the reports to the Budget Committee of the instructed committees /. United States. Congress. Senate. Committee on the Budget. Washington , 1980. vii, 390 p. ;   LC Card 80-603544   DDC 343.73/034 19
KF6221.A55 C666

Reconnaissance assessment of erosion and sedimentation in the Cañada de los Alamos basin, Los Angeles and Ventura Counties, California /. Knott, J. M. Washington, D.C. , 1980. iv, 26 p. :   LC Card 80-600012   DDC 551.3/009794/93 19
QE571 .K54

A reconnaissance of streamflow and fluvial sediment transport, Incline Village area, Lake Tahoe, Nevada . Glancy, Patrick A. Carson City , 1976. v, 42 p. ;   LC Card 80-623612   DDC 551.48/09793/57 19
GB1225.N3 G56

Reconstructing reality in the courtroom . Bennett, W. Lance. New Brunswick, N.J. , c1981. p. cm.   ISBN 0-8135-0922-X :   LC Card 81-5125   DDC 345.73/05 347.3055 19
KF9656 .B46

RECONSTRUCTION.
Gambill, Edward L. (Edward Lee), 1936- Conservative ordeal, northern Democrats and Reconstruction, 1865-1868 /. Ames , 1981. viii, 188 p. ;   ISBN 0-8138-1385-9   LC Card 81-1560   DDC 973.8/1 19
E668 .G18

RECONSTRUCTION - ADDRESSES, ESSAYS, LECTURES.
Southern Black leaders of the Reconstruction era /. Urbana , c1982. p. cm.   ISBN 0-252-00929-0   LC Card 81-11372   DDC 975/.004960730922 B 19
E185.92 .S68

RECONSTRUCTION - LOUISIANA.
Dawson, Joseph G., 1945- Army generals and Reconstruction . Baton Rouge , c1982. p. cm.   ISBN 0-8071-0896-0 :   LC Card 81-11735   DDC 976.3/061 19
F375 .D27

Reconstruction of thinking /. Neville, Robert C. Albany , 1981. p. cm.   ISBN 0-87395-494-7   LC Card 81-5347   DDC 128/.3 19
B105.T54 N48

RECONSTRUCTION (1939-1951) - EUROPE.
Rostow, W. W. (Walt Whitman), 1916- The division of Europe after World War II, 1946 /. Austin , 1981. p. cm.   ISBN 0-292-70358-9   LC Card 81-11640   DDC 940.55/4 19
D816 .R67

Record of an early cretaceous marine transgression--Longford Member, Kiowa Formation. Franks, Paul C. Paralic to fluvial record of an early Cretaceous marine transgression--Longford Member, Kiowa Formation, north-central Kansas /. [Lawrence, Kan.] [1979] 55 p. :   LC Card 80-621776   DDC 557.81 s 551.7/7 19
QE113 .A2 no. 219 QE686

RECORD SYSTEMS, DUAL. see DUAL RECORD SYSTEMS.

Recording studio in the District of Columbia. Checchi and Company, Washington, D. C.

Final report : feasibility of establishing a recording studio in the District of Columbia . Washington , 1973. 124 p. :
*NYPL [*LE 80-1766]*

RECORDS, BUSINESS. see BUSINESS RECORDS.

Records management in Federal agencies . United States. Commission on Federal Paperwork. Washington , 1977. 66 p. :   LC Card 78-601367
JK468.P76 U5 1977b   *NYPL [JLE 81-453]*

Records of Black and Mulatto persons [in Ohio]. [1804-57] 1 reel. Microfilm by Wright State University. Title from microfilm header. Photoreproduction of ms. records. CONTENTS. - Greene County, 1805-41. - Logan County, 1831-57. - Miami County, 1833-47. - Montgomery County, 1804-5.
1. Afro-Americans - Ohio. 2. Ohio - Genealogy. I. Wright State University. II. Title: Black and Mulatto persons in Ohio. III. Title: Mulatto persons in Ohio.
*NYPL [*ZI-276]*

Records of Pennsylvania's revolutionary governments, 1775-1790. Pennsylvania. Historical and Museum Commission. Guide to the microfilm of the records of Pennsylvania's revolutionary governments, 1775-1790 (record group 27) in the Pennsylvania State Archives, 54 rolls . Harrisburg , 1978 [c1979] vii, 351 p. ;   LC Card 79-624725
E263.P4 P37 1979   *NYPL [ISC 80-2758]*

Records relating to Tennessee in the North Carolina State archives /. North Carolina. Division of Archives and History. Raleigh, N.C. , 1980. 7 p. :   LC Card 80-623026   DDC 975.6 s 016.9768 19
F251 .N67a no. 3, 1980 CD3424

Recovery of aluminum hydroxy sulfate from aluminum sulfate solution by high-temperature hydrolysis /. Shanks, D. E. (Donald E.) [Washington] [1981] p. cm.   LC Card 80-606902   DDC 622 s 622/.34926 19
TN23 .U43 TP152.H82

Recovery of byproduct heavy minerals from Oregon and Washington sand and gravel operations /. Martinez, G. M. (George M.) Washington , 1981. p. cm.   LC Card 81-6080   DDC 622 s 622/.751 19
TN23 .U43 TN939

Recovery of coliforms by the MPN and MF techniques using a 2n - factorial experimental design /. Janardan, K. G. Chicago , 1977. iii, 39 p. :   LC Card 77-624164   DDC 628.1/682/0287 19
QR48 .J36

Recovery of copper and associated precious metals from electronic scrap /. Salisbury, H. B. Washington [1981] p. cm.   LC Card 80-607807   DDC 622 s 699/.3 19
TN23 .U43 no. 8500 TD812.5.C66

Recovery of lithium from clay by selective chlorination /. Davidson, Charles F. Washington [1981] p. cm.   LC Card 80-607822   DDC 622 s 669/.725 19
TN23 .U43 TN799.L57

RECOVERY OF NATURAL RESOURCES. see RECYCLING (WASTE, ETC.)

Recovery of principal metal values from electrolytic zinc waste /. Hebble, T. L. (Terry L.) Avondale, MD [1981] p. cm.   LC Card 81-10044   DDC 622 s 669/.52 19
TN23 .U43 TN796

Recovery of sanitary-indicator bacteria from streams containing acid mine water /. Double, Mark L. Morgantown , 1978. v, 30 p. :   LC Card 78-622769   DDC 333.91/009754 s 628.1/6832/0287 19
QC986.W4 W46 no. 11 QR48

RECOVERY OF WASTE HEAT. see HEAT RECOVERY.

RECOVERY OF WASTE MATERIALS. see RECYCLING (WASTE, ETC.)

RECOVERY OF WASTE PRODUCTS. see SALVAGE (WASTE, ETC.)

RECREATION AREAS - ABSTRACTS.
Hill, Ann B. Abstracts on child play areas and child support facilities /. Milwaukee [Wis.] , Milwaukee, WI (P.O. Box 413, Milwaukee, Wis. 53201) , c1978. v, 102 leaves :   LC Card

81-106795   DDC 790/.06/8 19
GV423 .H54

RECREATION AREAS - CALIFORNIA - GUIDE-BOOKS.
California coastal access guide /. Berkeley , c1981. p. cm.   ISBN 0-520-04576-9   LC Card 81-14667   DDC 917.94/0453 19
F859.3 .C26

RECREATION AREAS - COLORADO - PIKE NATIONAL FOREST - MAPS.
United States. Forest Service. Rocky Mountain Region. Pike National Forest, Colorado; west-[east] half. [Denver] 1970. 2 col. maps on sheet 106 x 65 cm. Scale 1:126,720; 1/2" = 1 mile. Printed on both sides of sheet. "Reprinted 1977." "Polyconic projection, 1927 North American datum." Relief shown by hachures and spot heights. Forest Service map. Includes text, col. illus., index to recreation sites, and location map.   LC Card GM72-1927
G4312.P48 1970 .U5
NYPL [Map Div. 80-3344]

RECREATION AREAS - LAW AND LEGISLATION - OKLAHOMA.
Oklahoma. Division of State Parks. Rules & regulations /. [Oklahoma City, Okla.] [1979] 19 p. ;   LC Card 80-622622   DDC 346.766/046783 19
KFO1652.5.A435 A2 1979

Oklahoma. Division of State Parks. Rules & regulations /. [Oklahoma City, Okla.] , 1980. 19 p. :   LC Card 80-623108   DDC 346.766/046783 19
KFO1652.5.A439 A2 1980

RECREATION AREAS - MIDDLE ATLANTIC STATES - COSTS.
Public acquisition costs of recreation land to the year 2000 /. New York , 1968. 23 p. ;
*NYPL [*ZT-1244]*

RECREATION AREAS - MONTANA.
United States. Congress. Senate. Committee on Energy and Natural Resources. Subcommittee on Parks, Recreation, and Renewable Resources. Rattlesnake roadless area . Washington , 1980. iii, 119 p. :   LC Card 80-602500   DDC 346.7304/6782 347.30646782 19
KF26 .E5565 1979k

RECREATION AREAS - NEW JERSEY.
Foresta, Ronald A., 1944- Open space policy . New Brunswick, N.J. , c1981. p. cm.   ISBN 0-8135-0923-8 :   LC Card 81-2513   DDC 333.78/4 19
HT393.N5 F67

RECREATION AREAS - NEW YORK (STATE) - MONROE COUNTY.
Monroe County, N. Y. Dept. of Parks. Program compare. Rochester, N. Y., 1966. 118 p. :
NYPL [JLF 81-3]

RECREATION AREAS - PLANNING.
Recommendations for child play areas /. [Milwaukee] [1980?] vi, 808 leaves :   LC Card 80-153214   DDC 711/.558 19
GV423 .R33

RECREATION AREAS - PLANNING - MIDDLE ATLANTIC STATES.
Public acquisition costs of recreation land to the year 2000 /. New York , 1968. 23 p. ;
*NYPL [*ZT-1244]*

RECREATION AREAS - UNITED STATES.
How effective are your community recreation services? [Washington] , 1973. 189 p. in various pagings /.   *NYPL [JFF 80-1149]*

Urban waterfront revitalization . Washington [1980]. 2 v.   *NYPL [JLM 80-739]*

RECREATION AREAS - UNITED STATES - SECURITY MEASURES.
United States. Congress. House. Committee on Government Operations. Environment, Energy, and Natural Resources Subcommittee. Crime in Federal recreation areas . Washington , 1978. iii, 60 p. ;   LC Card 80-603630   DDC 364.1/0973 19
KF27 .G655 1978d

RECREATION AREAS - UNITED STATES - VANDALISM.
United States. Congress. House. Committee on Government Operations. Environment, Energy, and Natural Resources Subcommittee. Crime in Federal recreation areas . Washington , 1978.

iii, 60 p. ;   LC Card 80-603630   DDC 364.1/0973
19
KF27 .G655 1978d

RECREATION AREAS - WISCONSIN - WOOD COUNTY - MAPS.
United States. Soil Conservation Service. Public
and private parks and recreation areas, Wood
County, Wisconsin /. Lincoln, Nebr. , 1978. 1
map : LC Card 81-691238
G4123.W9G52 1978 .U5

RECREATION - ECONOMIC ASPECTS - MONTANA.
Haroldsen, Ancel D. The economic impact of a
recreational development at Big Sky, Montana
/. Bozeman , 1975. 24, [3] leaves ; LC Card
75-623213
HC107.M9 H37   **NYPL [*XME-9520]**

RECREATION - FLORIDA - PLANNING.
Florida. Dept. of Administration.
Recreation/leisure element of the State
comprehensive plan . [Tallahassee] , 1977?] iii,
10 p. ; LC Card 79-625479   DDC 790/.09759 19
GV54.F6 F54 1977

Recreation in Nevada.
Eckbo, Dean, Austin & Williams. Nevada
state-wide trails study . [Carson City] [1978]
48, [16] leaves ; LC Card 80-620874 DDC
790/.09793 19
GV191.42.N27 E24

**Recreation/leisure element of the State
comprehensive plan .** Florida. Dept. of
Administration. [Tallahassee] , 1977?] iii, 10 p. ;
    LC Card 79-625479   DDC 790/.09759 19
GV54.F6 F54 1977

**Recreation site planning and improvement in
national forests, 1891-1942 /.** Tweed, William
C. Washington, D.C. , 1980 [i.e. 1981] vi, 29
p. ; LC Card 81-601100   DDC 333.78/3/0973 19
GV191.4 .T83

RECREATION - UNITED STATES.
United States. Heritage Conservation and
Recreation Service. National urban recreation
study . [Washington , 1978] 184 p. ; LC Card
78-602420
GV53 .U54 1978

**Recreation '76 Conference, University of
Washington, 1976.** Recreation '76 Conference
proceedings, February 23 and 24, 1976,
University of Washington / co-chairmen,
Robert F. Goodwin, Leonard R. Askham ;
editor, Robert F. Goodwin. Seattle : Coastal
Resources Program, Washington Sea Grant
Marine Advisory Program, Institute for Marine
Studies, University of Washington ; Pullman :
Cooperative Extension Service, Washington
State University, [1976] iv, 114 p. : ill. ; 28 cm.
"A Washington Sea Grant/Cooperative Extension
Service report." "WSG-WO 76-1." Includes
bibliographies. LC Card 77-623136   DDC 333.78/4
19
*1. Coasts - Washington (State) - Recreational use -
Congresses. 2. Coasts - Recreational use - Law and
legislation - Washington (State) - Congresses. 3.
Outdoor recreation - Washington (State) - Congresses.
I. Goodwin, Robert F. II. Askham, Leonard R. III.
Washington (State). University. Institute for Marine
Studies. Coastal Resources Program. IV. Washington
(State). State University, Pullman. Extension Service.*
GV191.42.W2 R42 1976

**Recreational and commercial finfish catch
statistics for Texas bay systems, September
1978-August 1979 /.** McEachron, L. W.
[Austin] [1980] iv, 76 p. ; LC Card 80-623181
    DDC 333.95/611/097641 19
SH222.T4 M32

**Recreational boating in the Continental United
States in 1973 and 1976 .** United States. Coast
Guard. Office of Boating Safety. Washington,
D.C. [1979] vii, 121, [131] p. ; LC Card
79-602077
GV776.A2 U54 1979

**Recreational Boating Safety and Facilities
Improvement Act of 1979 .** United States.
Congress. Senate. Committee on Commerce,
Science, and Transportation. Washington ,
1980. iii, 70 p. ; LC Card 81-600592 DDC
344.73/0476 347.304476 19
KF26 .C69 1980v

**Recreational fishing use of artificial reefs on the
Texas Coast /.** Ditton, Robert B., 1943-
[Austin] 1978. x, 155 p. : LC Card 79-624070

DDC 799.1/6634 19
SH551 .D57

RECREATIONAL SURVEYS - IDAHO - STATISTICS.
Idaho. University. Wildland Recreation
Management Dept. Idaho ski study, winter
1977-1978 /. [Moscow, Idaho] [1979] iv, 72
p. : LC Card 80-621844   DDC 338.4/779693/09796
19
GV854.5.I2 I3 1979

RECREATIONAL SURVEYS - NORTHEASTERN STATES.
Kottke, Marvin Walter. Projected changes in
Northeastern skiing participation and supply
capacity as influenced by a changing economy
/. Storrs, Conn. [1980] 38 p. ; LC Card
80-624079   DDC 796.93/0974 19
GV854.5.N58 K67

RECREATIONAL SURVEYS - SOUTH DAKOTA.
Nordstrom, Paul E. South Dakota recreational
trails plan, January 1, 1980 /. [Pierre, S.D.]
[1979?] 178 p. : LC Card 80-622746   DDC
790/.09783 19
GV191.42.S8 N67

RECREATIONAL SURVEYS - UNITED STATES.
How effective are your community recreation
services? [Washington] , 1973. 189 p. in various
pagings :   **NYPL [JFF 80-1149]**
United States. Coast Guard. Office of Boating
Safety. Recreational boating in the Continental
United States in 1973 and 1976 . Washington,
D.C. [1979] vii, 121, [131] p. : LC Card
79-602077
GV776.A2 U54 1979

United States. Heritage Conservation and
Recreation Service. National urban recreation
study . [Washington , 1978] 184 p. : LC Card
78-602420
GV53 .U54 1978

RECREATIONAL SURVEYS - WASHINGTON (STATE)
Nash, A. E. Keir. Understanding and planning
for ORV recreation . Tumwater, Wash. , 19. v,
159 p. ; LC Card 79-625837   DDC 338.3/4 19
GV191.42.W2 N37

RECREATIONS. see PLAY.

RECRUITING OF EMPLOYEES - UNITED STATES.
Glover, Robert W. Placing minority women in
professional jobs . Washington , 1978. vii, 75
p. ; LC Card 78-600751
HD5701 .U53 no. 55 HD6053.6.U5
          NYPL [Sc F 81-49]

**RECURRENT EDUCATION. see
CONTINUING EDUCATION.**

Recycling historic railroad stations. Webber,
Margo B. Reuse of historically and
architecturally significant railroad stations for
transportation and other community needs .
Washington, D.C. , 1978. ii, 126 p. : LC Card
79-603620   DDC 725/.31/0288 19
NA6311 .W4

Recycling neighborhoods . Texas. Dept. of
Community Affairs. [Austin] [1978] 2 v. : LC
Card 79-622456   DDC 363.5/8 19
HD7293 .T46 1978

**Recycling of sewage effluent by sugarcane
irrigation .** Lau, Leung-Ku Stephen. Honolulu,
Hawaii [1978?] x, 59 p. : LC Card 79-625336
    DDC 628.3/62 19
TC1 .H36 no. 121 TD760

Recycling of used oil . United States. Congress.
Senate. Committee on Environment and Public
Works. Washington , 1980. iii, 111 p. ; LC
Card 80-603011   DDC 346.73/04622 19
KF26 .E6 1980d

**Recycling of waste magnesite-chrome refractories
from copper smelting furnaces /.** Petty, A. V.
Avondale, MD [1981] p. cm. LC Card
81-607818   DDC 622 s 669/.734 19
TN23 .U43 TN799.C5

RECYCLING OF WASTE PRODUCTS. see SALVAGE (WASTE, ETC.)

RECYCLING (WASTE, ETC.) - ECONOMIC ASPECTS - ALASKA - ANCHORAGE.
Nebesky, William E. An economic evaluation
of the potential for recycling waste materials in

Anchorage, Alaska . Fairbanks [1980] xiv, 156
p. ; LC Card 80-623358   DDC 363.7/28 19
TD794.5 .N43

RECYCLING (WASTE, ETC.) - ILLINOIS - DIRECTORIES.
Illinois Institute of Natural Resources. Illinois
directory of environmental information /.
Chicago, IL [1980] iv, 217 p. ; LC Card
80-622763   DDC 363.7/0025/773 19
TD169.6 .I46 1980

RECYCLING (WASTE, ETC.) - LAW AND LEGISLATION - UNITED STATES.
United States. Congress. Senate. Committee on
Commerce, Science and Transportation.
Beverage container reuse and recycling act of
1979 . Washington , 1980. iii, 69 p. ; LC Card
80-602792   DDC 344.73/04622 19
KF26 .C69 1980j

RECYCLING (WASTE, ETC.) - UNITED STATES - ABSTRACTS.
United States. Dept. of Commerce. Office of
Environmental Affairs. Marketing and financing
aspects of resource recovery /. [Washington,
D.C.] , 1980. 63 p. ; LC Card 80-601647 DDC
338.4/36046/0973 19
HD9975.U52 U54 1980

RECYCLING (WASTE, ETC.) - WASHINGTON (STATE)
Price, Eleonore B. From waste to energy--the
recycling connection . [Olympia, Wash.] [1980]
v leaves, 112 p. ; LC Card 81-621765 DDC
363.7/28 19
TD794.5 .P73

Red Basin. Texas. Dept. of Water Resources.
Projected land use maps year 2000, Red Basin.
Austin, Tex. , 1978. [11] leaves : LC Card
80-675296   DDC 912/.133373/3097642 19
G1372.R4G4 T4 1978

Red Corn, Jim. Subject report, American Indians
of Oklahoma by county : report / by Jim Red
Corn and Helen John Tonemah. Oklahoma
City, Okla. : Oklahoma Indian Affairs
Commission, [1980] v, 30 leaves ; 28 cm. Tables.
    LC Card 80-622934   DDC 312/.93 19
*1. Indians of North America - Oklahoma - Statistics. I.
Tonemah, Helen John, joint author. II. Title.*
E78.O45 R43

Red harvest . Dyson, Lowell K., 1929- Lincoln ,
c1982. p. cm. ISBN 0-8032-1659-9 LC Card
81-8200   DDC 324.273/75 19
HX550.A37 D97

**RED LINING. see DISCRIMINATION IN
MORTGAGE LOANS.**

RED RICE - BIBLIOGRAPHY.
Eastin, E. F. Selected bibliography of red rice
and other wild rices (Oryza spp.) /. College
Station , 1979. 59 p. ; LC Card 79-625846 DDC
016.6331/87 19
Z5356.R43 E25 SB615.R4

Red River . Hanft, Robert M. Chico, Calif.
[1980] 304 p. : ISBN 0-9602894-5-3 LC Card
79-53190   DDC 385/.54/0979426 19
TF24.C3 H36

RED RIVER LUMBER COMPANY.
Hanft, Robert M. Red River . Chico, Calif.
[1980] 304 p. : ISBN 0-9602894-5-3 LC Card
79-53190   DDC 385/.54/0979426 19
TF24.C3 H36

RED RIVER VALLEY, TEX.-LA. - ANTIQUITIES.
Davis, Hester A., 1930- Archeological and
historical resources of the Red River Basin.
[Fayetteville] 1970. ix, 194 p. LC Card
77-633171   DDC 976.6/6 19
E99.C12 D4   **NYPL [ITV 74-585]**

Red River Valley tornadoes of April 10, 1979 .
United States. National Oceanic and
Atmospheric Administration. Rockville, Md.
[1980] v, 60 p., [2] leaves of plates : LC Card
80-601568   DDC 363.3/492 19
QC955.5.T4 U54 1980

RED SALMON. see SOCKEYE SALMON.

RED WILLOW COUNTY (NEB.) - MAPS.
United States. Soil Conservation Service. Red
Willow County, Nebraska /. Lincoln, Nebr. ,
1978. 1 map : LC Card 81-691004
G4193.R4 1978 .U5

RED WILLOW VALLEY, NEB. - ANTIQUITIES.

Grange, Roger T. Salvage archeology in the Red Willow Reservoir, Nebraska /. Lincoln, Neb. , 1980. xi, 236 p., [1] leaf of plates : LC Card 80-624104 DDC 978.2 s 978.2/83 19
F661 .N32 no. 9 E78.N3
NYPL [HBA no. 9]

Reddel, Carl W., 1937- Mitchell, William A., 1940- The Republic of Turkey . United States Air Force Academy, Colo. [1981] p. cm. LC Card 81-607896 DDC 956.1/0007/1178881 19
DR438.95.U6 M57

Redden, James A. Oregon. Dept. of Justice. The Attorney General's model rules of procedure under the Administrative procedure act, effective December 3, 1979 /. Salem, Or. [1979?] iii, 143 p. : LC Card 80-622995 DDC 342.795/066 19
KFO2840 .A825 1979

Reddy, Sigrid R. Hodges, Maud deLeigh, 1888-1972. Crossroads on the Charles . Canaan, N.H. , c1980. vii, 243 p. : ISBN 0-914016-68-7 : LC Card 80-13753
F74.W33 H76 1980
NYPL [IQH+ (Watertown) 81-74]

REDEVELOPMENT, URBAN. see CITY PLANNING.

Redfield, Kent. Special districts in Illinois / Kent Redfield, Dawn Brown (House Democratic Staff). [Springfield?] Ill. : House of Representatives, 1979- v. ; 28 cm. Five hundred copies printed. Includes bibliographical references. CONTENTS. - v. 1. Inventory of special districts, powers and numbers in existence. LC Card 80-622899 DDC 352/.0095 19
1. Special districts - Illinois. I. Brown, Dawn, joint author. II. Illinois. General Assembly. House of Representatives. Democratic Staff. III. Title.
JS451.I35 R42

Redford, Lawrence H. The Occupation of Japan . Norfolk, Va. , 1980. x, 382 p. ; LC Card 80-144161 DDC 338.952 19
HC462.9 .O23

Rediscoveries, literature and place in Illinois /. Bray, Robert C. Urbana , c1982. p. cm. ISBN 0-252-00911-8 LC Card 81-3353 DDC 810/.9/9773 19
PS283.I3 B7

REDLINING. see DISCRIMINATION IN MORTGAGE LOANS.

Redmond, Charles Edward, 1932- Soil survey of Ashland County, Ohio / [by C. E. Redmond and D. L. Brown] ; United States Department of Agriculture, Soil Conservation Service, in cooperation with Ohio Department of Natural Resources, Division of Lands and Soil, and Ohio Agricultural Research and Development Center. [Washington] : The Service, [1980] vii, 179 p., [31] fold. leaves of plates : ill. ; 28 cm. Cover title. "Issued January 1980." Bibliography: p. 112-113. LC Card 80-602507 DDC 631.4/7/77129 19
1. Soils - Ohio - Ashland Co. - Maps. I. Brown, Dennis L., joint author. II. United States. Soil Conservation Service. III. Ohio. Division of Lands and Soil. IV. Ohio Agricultural Research and Development Center. V. Title.
S599.O3 R39

Reduced recruitment in Utah mule deer relative to winter condition /. Zwank, Phillip J., 1944- [Salt Lake City] [1979] ix, 80 p. : LC Card 80-621214 DDC 333.95/5 s 599.73/57 19
SK453 .A25 no. 79-11 QL737.U55

Reducing residential crime and fear . Fowler, Floyd J. Washington, D.C. , 1979. xxiii, 309 p. : LC Card 80-601262 DDC 364.4/0458/097463 19
HV6795.H3 F68

Reducing the development costs of housing . HUD National Conference on Housing Costs, Washington, D.C., 1979. [Washington, D.C.] , 1979. xv, 275 p. : LC Card 80-601844 DDC 338.4/36908/0973 19
HD7293 .H82 1979

Reducing the Federal budget : strategies and examples, fiscal years 1982-1986 / the Congress of the United States, Congressional Budget Office. Washington, D.C. : The Office : For sale by the Supt. of Docs., U. S. G.P.O., [1981] xi, 187 p. ; 26 cm. (A CBO study) "February 1981." LC Card 81-601803 DDC 353.0072/22 19

1. United States - Appropriations and expenditures. 2. Government spending policy - United States. 3. Tax and expenditure limitations - United States. I. United States. Congressional Budget Office. II. Series.
HJ2051 .R42

Reducing worker absenteeism : proceedings of a University of Michigan workshop / conducted by Dallas L. Jones, Edwin L. Miller, and John A. Fossum ; sponsored by Graduate School of Business Administration and the Industrial Development Division, Institute of Science and Technology, The University of Michigan. Ann Arbor, Mich. : The Division, 1979. 72 p. ; 23 cm. LC Card 80-622258 DDC 658.3/14 19
1. Absenteeism (Labor) - United States - Congresses. I. Jones, Dallas Lee. II. Miller, Edwin Leroy, 1929-. III. Fossum, John A. IV. Michigan. University. Graduate School of Business Administration. V. Michigan. University. Institute of Science and Technology. Industrial Development Division.
HD5115.2.U5 R43

Reduction of airborne contaminants from welding exhaust at surface mines /. Derby, George K. Avondale, MD , 1981. p. cm. LC Card 81-607864 DDC 622 s 671.5/2 19
TN295 .U4

Reduction roasting and beneficiation of a hematitic-geothitic taconite /. Peterson, R. E. (Roy Ernest), 1926- [Washington, D.C.] [1981] p. cm. LC Card 80-606877 DDC 622 s 669/.141 19
TN23 .U43 TN538.I7

Redwood tanks. Seidler, Ramon J. Health significance of Klebsiella pneumoniae in drinking water emanating from redwood tanks /. Corvallis, Or. , 1977. 81 p. : LC Card 78-624331 DDC 333.91/009795 s 628.1/3 19
HD1694.O7 A13 no. 54 QR48

Ree, William Oscar, 1913- National Research Council. Transportation Research Board. Design of sedimentation basins. Washington, D.C. , 1980. 53 p. : ISBN 0-309-03027-7 (pbk.) : LC Card 80-52843 DDC 625.7/34 19
TD439 .N37 1980

Reed, Alan D. The Archeology and stabilization of the Dominguez and Escalante ruins. Denver , 1979. ix, 496 p. : LC Card 79-603760
E99.P9 A72 **NYPL [HBC 81-508]**

Reed, Edith I. The Stratosphere . Washington, D.C. [Springfield, Va.] 1979. xiv, 432 p. : LC Card 81-600765 DDC 551.5/142 19
QC881.2.S8 S85

Reed, Jeffrey A. North Dakota farm labor market : wage standards, wages, and employment / by Jeffrey A. Reed. [Grand Forks] : Bureau of Business and Economic Research, University of North Dakota, [1979] iii, 54 p. ; 28 cm. (North Dakota economic studies. no. 25) "December 1979." Includes bibliographical references. LC Card 80-622819 DDC 331.12/53/09784 19
1. Agricultural laborers - North Dakota - Supply and demand. 2. Agricultural wages - North Dakota. I. North Dakota. University. Bureau of Business and Economic Research. II. Title. III. Series.
HD1527.N85 R43 **NYPL [TAA no. 25]**

Reed, John Calvin, 1930- The river and the rocks : the geologic story of Great Falls and Potomac River Gorge / by John C. Reed, Jr., Robert S. Sigafoos, and George W. Fisher.[2d ed.]. Washington : U. S. Govt. Print. Off. : for sale by the Supt. of Docs., U. S. Govt. Print. Off., 1980. vii, 75 p. : ill. ; 23 cm. (U. S. Geological Survey bulletin ; 1471) Edition of 1970 by United States Geological Survey and National Park Service. Bibliography: p. 76. LC Card 80-600023 DDC 557.3 s 557.52 19
1. Geology - Great Falls, Potomac River - Guide-books. 2. Natural history - Great Falls, Potomac River - Guide-books. 3. Great Falls, Potomac River. I. Sigafoos, Robert Sumner, 1920- joint author. II. Fisher, George Wescott, 1937- joint author. III. United States. Geological Survey. The river and the rocks. IV. Series: United States. Geological Survey. Bulletin , 1471. V. Title.
QE75 .B9 no. 1471 QE122.G7

Reed, John Robert, 1938- The natural history of H.G. Wells / by John R. Reed. Athens : Ohio University Press, c1981. p. cm. Includes bibliographical references and index. ISBN 0-8214-0628-0 LC Card 81-11261 DDC 823/.912 19

1. Wells, H. G. (Herbert George), 1866-1946 - Philosophy. 2. Wells, H.G. (Herbert George), 1866-1946 - Criticism and interpretation. 3. Philosophy in literature. I. Title.
PR5778.P5 R4 1981

Reeder, Richard J. United States. Advisory Commission on Intergovernmental Relations. Countercyclical aid and economic stabilization . Washington , 1978. viii, 50 p. : LC Card 79-601504
HJ275 .U52 1978b **NYPL [JLF 81-317]**

REEF BAY ESTATE, V.I.
Hatch, Charles E. "Par Force" (Reef Bay) Estate Great House and Reef Bay Sugar Factory in Virgin Islands National Park. [Washington] 1969. iii, 18 l. LC Card 80-503016 DDC 972.97/22 19
F2136.9.R43 H37 1969

Reese, Lymon C. (joint author) Yokel, Felix Y. Soil classification for construction practice in shallow trenching /. Washington, D.C. [1980] xiv, 76 p. : LC Card 80-600014 DDC 690/.02/18 s 624.1/51/012 19
TA435 .U58 no. 121 TA710

REFERENCE BOOKS - BIBLIOGRAPHY.
Nichols, Margaret Irby. Handbook of reference sources /. Austin, Tex. , 1981. ix, 429 p. ; LC Card 81-149285 DDC 011/.02 19
Z711 .N53 1981

REFERENCE BOOKS - MEXICAN AMERICANS - CATALOGS.
University of California, Los Angeles. Chicano Studies Research Center. Quien sabe? . Los Angeles, Calif. , 1981. p. cm. ISBN 0-89551-000-6 LC Card 81-10156 DDC 016.973/046872 19
Z1361.M4 U55 1981 E184.M5

Reference data on halfway houses for the mentally ill and alcoholics, United States, 1973 /. United States. National Institute of Mental Health. Division of Biometry. Survey and Reports Branch. Rockville, Md. , 1974. 28 p. : **NYPL [*ZT-1264]**

Reference information paper .
(no. 75) United States. National Archives and Records Service. Agricultural maps in the National Archives of the United States, ca. 1860-1930 /. Washington , 1976. vii, 25 p. : LC Card 79-124956 DDC 015.73 s 912/.163/0973 19
CD3023 .A35 no. 75 S494.5.C3

A reference method for the determination of lithium in serum. National Measurement Laboratory (U. S.) Standard reference materials . Washington, D.C. , 1980. xiv, 99 p. : LC Card 80-600091 DDC 602/.18 s 616.07/56 19
QC100 .U57 no. 260-69 RB46

REFERENDUM - NEW JERSEY.
New Jersey. Legislature. Senate. Judiciary Committee. Public hearing before Senate Judiciary Committee ... held June 30, 1980, room 223, State House, Trenton, New Jersey. Trenton, N.J. [1980] [40], 40, 58 p. ; LC Card 80-623800 DDC 328/.2 19
KFN1811.3 .J8 1980

REFERENDUM - NEW YORK (STATE)
New York (State). Legislature. Senate. Task Force on Critical Problems. The popular interest versus the public interest ... . Albany, N.Y. [1979] iv, 83 p. ; LC Card 80-622244 DDC 328/.2 19
JF495 .N582 1979

Referendum : proposed Charter change /. Bureau of Governmental Research, New Orleans. New Orleans , 1964. 16 l. ; **NYPL [*ZT-1245]**

REFERENDUM - UNITED STATES.
Abt Associates. Factors affecting pollution referenda. Washington, 1971. v, 331 p. LC Card 73-614491
HG4952 .A6

New York (State). Legislature. Senate. Task Force on Critical Problems. The popular interest versus the public interest ... . Albany, N.Y. [1979] iv, 83 p. ; LC Card 80-622244 DDC 328/.2 19
JF495 .N582 1979

Referral strategies for polydrug abusers /. National Institute on Drug Abuse. Rockville, Md. [1977] viii, 60 p. ; LC Card 78-602531

DDC 362.2/938 19
HV5825 .N35 1977

**REFLECTION (PSYCHOLOGY) see
THOUGHT AND THINKING.**

Reflections of America : commemorating the
statistical abstract centennial / Norman
Cousins, honorary editor. Washington, D.C. : U.
S. Dept. of Commerce, Bureau of the Census,
[1981] p. cm. "Issued January 1981." Bibliography: p.
LC Card 80-607843   DDC 317.3 19
*1. United States - Economic conditions - Addresses,
essays, lectures. 2. United States - Social conditions -
Addresses, essays, lectures. 3. United States. Bureau of
the Census. Statistical abstract of the United States -
Addresses, essays, lectures. I. Cousins, Norman.*
HC103 .R43

REFORESTATION - CALIFORNIA.
Adams, Ronald S. California reforestation, 1977
and 1978 /. [Sacramento, CA , 1979?] 46 p. :
LC Card 80-621409   DDC 634.9/56/09794 19
SD409 .A38

Reform and renewal in higher education .
Conference on Library Orientation for
Academic Libraries, 9th, Eastern Michigan
University, 1979. Ann Arbor, Mich. , 1980. ix,
126 p. ;   ISBN 0-87650-124-2 LC Card 80-81485
Z675.U5 C748 1979
NYPL [JFL 75-159 no. 10]

REFORM OF CRIMINALS. see PROBATION.

**REFRACTORIES. see REFRACTORY
MATERIALS.**

REFRACTORY MATERIALS - RECYCLING.
Petty, A. V. Recycling of waste
magnesite-chrome refractories from copper
smelting furnaces /. Avondale, MD [1981] p.
cm. LC Card 81-607818   DDC 622 s 669/.734 19
TN23 .U43 TN799.C5

**REFRIGERATION INDUSTRY - LICENSES -
NORTH CAROLINA.**
North Carolina. State Board of Refrigeration
Examiners. North Carolina State Board of
Refrigeration Examiners register, as of February
28, 1979 . Raleigh, N.C. [1979] 33 p. ; LC
Card 79-625627   DDC 353.97560082/42 19
HD9999.A53 U554 1979

Refugee consultation . United States. Congress.
Senate. Committee on the Judiciary.
Washington , 1980. iii, 22 p. ; LC Card
80-603491   DDC 342.73/082 347.30282 19
KF26 .J8 1979u

REFUGEES.
United States. Congress. Senate. Committee on
the Judiciary, United States Senate,
Ninety-sixth Congress, second session,
September 19, 1980. U. S. refugee programs,
1981 . Washington , 1980. iii, 288 p. : LC Card
80-604094   DDC 362.8/7/0973 19
KF26 .J8 1980f

REFUGEES - ASIA, SOUTHEASTERN.
United States. Congress. Senate. Committee on
Foreign Relations. Subcommittee on East Asian
and Pacific Affairs. Southeast Asia .
Washington , 1980. iii, 92 p. ; LC Card
80-602433   DDC 959/.053 19
KF26 .F6354 1980

REFUGEES - CAMBODIA.
United States. Congress. House. Committee on
Foreign Affairs. Subcommittee on Asian and
Pacific Affairs. 1980--the tragedy in Indochina
continues . Washington , 1980. v, 148 p. : LC
Card 80-604058   DDC 362.8/7/09596 19
KF27 .F638 1980c

**REFUGEES - GOVERNMENT POLICY -
UNITED STATES.**
United States. Congress. House. Committee on
Foreign Affairs. Subcommittee on International
Operations. U. S. refugee policy . Washington ,
1980. iii, 18 p. ; LC Card 81-600867 DDC
325/.21/0973 19
KF27 .F647 1979f

REFUGEES - INDOCHINA.
United States. Congress. House. Committee on
Foreign Affairs. Subcommittee on Asian and
Pacific Affairs. 1979--tragedy in Indochina .
Washington , 1980. viii, 233 p. ; LC Card
80-601996   DDC 959/.053 19
KF27 .F638 1979h

**REFUGEES - LEGAL STATUS, LAWS, ETC. -
UNITED STATES.**
Moore, Charlotte J. Review of U. S. refugee

resettlement programs and policies .
Washington , 1980. viii, 342 p. : LC Card
80-603884   DDC 362.8/7/0973 19
HV640.4.U54 M66

United States. Congress. Senate. Committee on
Agriculture, Nutrition, and Forestry.
Subcommittee on Foreign Agricultural Policy.
Public law 480 aid for refugees . Washington ,
1980. iii, 29 p. ; LC Card 80-602524   DDC
344.73/03287 19
KF26 .A3549 1980

United States. Congress. Senate. Committee on
the Judiciary. Refugee consultation .
Washington , 1980. iii, 22 p. ; LC Card
80-603491   DDC 342.73/082 347.30282 19
KF26 .J8 1979u

REFUGEES, POLITICAL - CUBA.
United States. Congress. House. Committee on
the Judiciary. Subcommittee on Immigration,
Refugees, and International Law. Caribbean
migration . Washington , 1980 [i.e. 1981] iv,
313 p. ; LC Card 81-601637 DDC 325/.21/09729
19
KF27 .J8645 1980c

United States. Congress. Senate. Committee on
the Judiciary. Caribbean refugee crisis, Cubans
and Haitians . Washington , 1980. iii, 288 p. ;
LC Card 80-602964   DDC 325/.21/09729 19
KF26 .J8 1980c

REFUGEES, POLITICAL - HAITI.
United States. Congress. House. Committee on
the Judiciary. Subcommittee on Immigration,
Refugees, and International Law. Caribbean
migration . Washington , 1980 [i.e. 1981] iv,
313 p. ; LC Card 81-601637 DDC 325/.21/09729
19
KF27 .J8645 1980c

United States. Congress. Senate. Committee on
the Judiciary. Caribbean refugee crisis, Cubans
and Haitians . Washington , 1980. iii, 288 p. ;
LC Card 80-602964   DDC 325/.21/09729 19
KF26 .J8 1980c

**REFUGEES, POLITICAL - LEGAL STATUS,
LAWS, ETC. - UNITED STATES.**
United States. Congress. Senate. Committee on
Finance. Subcommittee on International Trade.
Extension of the president's authority to waive
section 402 (freedom of emigration
requirements) of the Trade Act of 1974 .
Washington , 1980. v, 515 p. : LC Card
81-600640   DDC 342.73/082 347.3028202646 19
KF26 .F554 1980d

REFUGEES, POLITICAL - LIBERIA.
United States. Congress. House. Committee on
Foreign Affairs. Subcommittee on Africa. The
situation in Liberia, spring 1980--update .
Washington , 1980. iii, 25 p. ; LC Card
80-603661   DDC 325/.21/096662 19
KF27 .F625 1980c

REFUGEES, POLITICAL - UNITED STATES.
United States. Congress. House. Committee on
Foreign Affairs. Subcommittee on Africa. The
situation in Liberia, spring 1980--update .
Washington , 1980. iii, 25 p. ; LC Card
80-603661   DDC 325/.21/096662 19
KF27 .F625 1980c

United States. Congress. House. Committee on
the Judiciary. Subcommittee on Immigration,
Refugees, and International Law. Caribbean
migration . Washington , 1980 [i.e. 1981] iv,
313 p. ; LC Card 81-601637 DDC 325/.21/09729
19
KF27 .J8645 1980c

United States. Congress. Senate. Committee on
the Judiciary. Caribbean refugee crisis, Cubans
and Haitians . Washington , 1980. iii, 288 p. ;
LC Card 80-602964   DDC 325/.21/09729 19
KF26 .J8 1980c

REFUGEES - SOMALIA.
Rousseau, Rudolph. An assessment of the
refugee situation in Somalia . Washington ,
1980. v, 19 p. : LC Card 80-603863   DDC
362.8/7/096773 19
HV640.4.S58 R68

REFUGEES - UNITED STATES.
Moore, Charlotte J. Review of U. S. refugee
resettlement programs and policies .
Washington , 1980. viii, 342 p. : LC Card
80-603884   DDC 362.8/7/0973 19
HV640.4.U54 M66

United States. Congress. Senate. Committee on
the Judiciary. U. S. refugee programs .
Washington , 1980. iii, 412 p. (p. 412 blank) :
LC Card 80-602735   DDC 362.8/7/0973 19
KF26 .J8 1980a

United States. Congress. Senate. Committee on
the Judiciary, United States Senate,
Ninety-sixth Congress, second session,
September 19, 1980. U. S. refugee programs,
1981 . Washington , 1980. iii, 288 p. : LC Card
80-604094   DDC 362.8/7/0973 19
KF26 .J8 1980f

United States. Select Commission on
Immigration and Refugee Policy. Semiannual
report to Congress /. Washington , 1980. v, 74
p. ; LC Card 80-603270   DDC 353.0081/7 19
JV6481 1980 .S44

**REFUSE AND REFUSE DISPOSAL -
ECONOMIC ASPECTS - NEW YORK
(STATE)**
New York (State). Division of Land Resources
and Forest Management. Resources Program
Development. The environmental control
industry in New York State . [Albany] [1979]
iv, 73 p. ; LC Card 80-622827   DDC
338.4/7628/09747 19
TD24.N7 N47 1979

**REFUSE AND REFUSE DISPOSAL -
INDEXES.**
United States. Environmental Protection
Agency. Available information materials on
solid waste management . [Washington] , 1979.
v, 240 p. ; LC Card 80-601846   DDC 016.3637/28
19
Z5853.S22 U4285 1979a TD791

**REFUSE AND REFUSE DISPOSAL - LAW
AND LEGISLATION - UNITED STATES.**
United States. Congress. Senate. Committee on
Commerce, Science, and Transportation.
Beverage container reuse and recycling act of
1979 . Washington , 1980. iii, 69 p. ; LC Card
80-602792   DDC 344.73/04622 19
KF26 .C69 1980j

United States. Congress. Senate. Committee on
Energy and Natural Resources. Subcommittee
on Energy Conservation and Supply. Municipal
solid waste to energy act of 1979 .
Washington , 1980. iii, 217 p. : LC Card
80-602495   DDC 344.73/04622 19
KF26 .E553 1980

**REFUSE AND REFUSE DISPOSAL - LAW
AND LEGISLATION - WASHINGTON
(STATE)**
Washington (State). Laws, statutes, etc.
Compendium of State laws and regulations
concerning solid waste management in
Washington State. [Olympia] , 1974. 1 v. ; LC
Card 74-622943
KFW359.R3 A2 1974   **NYPL [JLF 81-89]**

**REFUSE AND REFUSE DISPOSAL -
MAINE - PLANNING.**
Maine. Division of Water Quality Evaluation
and Planning. Detailed work plan for the fiscal
year 1978, Maine Statewide 208 Waste
Treatment Management Planning Program /.
[Augusta] [1980] 77 p. in various pagings :
LC Card 80-621395   DDC 363.7/28 19
TD788.4.M2 M32 1980

**REFUSE AND REFUSE DISPOSAL - NEW
JERSEY - LAKEHURST.**
United States. Congress. House. Committee on
Interstate and Foreign Commerce.
Subcommittee on Transportation and
Commerce. Hazardous waste disposal problems
at federal facilities . Washington , 1981. iii, 78
p. : LC Card 81-601166   DDC 082 363.7/28 19
KF27 .I5589 1980l

**REFUSE AND REFUSE DISPOSAL, RURAL -
ECONOMIC ASPECTS - LOUISIANA.**
Guedry, Leo J. An economic analysis of rural
parish wide solid waste collection and disposal
systems in Louisiana /. [Baton Rouge] [1980]
ii, 85 p. : LC Card 80-624066   DDC 338.1/09763 s
363.7/28 19
HD1775.L8 L7 no. 569 TD788.4.L8

**REFUSE AND REFUSE DISPOSAL -
UNITED STATES.**
United States. Congress. House. Committee on
Interstate and Foreign Commerce.
Subcommittee on Oversight and Investigations.
Hazardous waste matters . Washington , 1980.

iii, 117 p. ; LC Card 80-603987 DDC 353.0077/2 19
KF27 .I5547 1980k

United States. Congress. House. Committee on Interstate and Foreign Commerce. Subcommittee on Transportation and Commerce. Hazardous waste disposal problems at federal facilities . Washington , 1981. iii, 78 p. : LC Card 81-601166 DDC 082 363.7/28 19
KF27 .I5589 1980l

REFUSE AND REFUSE DISPOSAL - VIRGINIA.
Virginia. Solid Waste Commission. Report of the Solid Waste Commission to the Governor and the General Assembly of Virginia. Richmond, Va. , 1980. 16 p. ; LC Card 80-621794 DDC 300/.9755 s 363.7/2 19
J87 .V9 1980b, no. 25 TD788.4.V8

REFUSE AND REFUSE DISPOSAL - WASHINGTON (STATE) - JEFFERSON COUNTY.
Kramer, Chin & Mayo. Jefferson County solid waste management plan. Seattle, 1973. 1 v. (various pagings): **NYPL [JSF 80-734]**

REFUSE AS FUEL.
Demonstration of solar energy conversion of agricultural or industrial wastes to fuels . [Austin] , 1979. xiii, 103 p. : LC Card 80-620768 DDC 662/.8 19
TP360 .D45

REFUSE AS FUEL - CONGRESSES.
Conference on Wood Chips for Fuel and Energy, Clarkson College, 1978. Conference on Wood Chips for Fuel and Energy, Clarkson College, Potsdam, New York, January 11, 1978 /. [Albany, N.Y.] [1978] 181 p. : LC Card 80-621929 DDC 662/.65 19
TP324 .C66 1978

REFUSE AS FUEL - LAW AND LEGISLATION - UNITED STATES.
United States. Congress. House. Committee on Interstate and Foreign Commerce. Subcommittee on Energy and Power. Municipal waste-to-energy act of 1980 . Washington , 1980. iii, 160 p. ; LC Card 80-602960 DDC 346.7304/67938/0262 19
KF27 .I5542 1980b

United States. Congress. House. Committee on Interstate and Foreign Commerce. Subcommittee on Transportation and Commerce. Municipal waste-to-energy act of 1980 . Washington , 1980. iii, 111 p. ; LC Card 80-603438 DDC 346.7304/67938 19
KF27 .I5589 1980c

United States. Congress. House. Committee on Science and Technology. Subcommittee on Energy Development and Applications. Municipal waste-to-energy act . Washington , 1980. iii, 218 p. : LC Card 80-603352 DDC 344.73/04622 19
KF27 .S3934 1980a

United States. Congress. Senate. Committee on Energy and Natural Resources. Subcommittee on Energy Conservation and Supply. Municipal solid waste to energy act of 1979 . Washington , 1980. iii, 217 p. : LC Card 80-602495 DDC 344.73/04622 19
KF26 .E553 1980

REFUSE AS FUEL - UNITED STATES - FINANCE.
United States. Congress. Senate. Committee on Energy and Natural Resources. Subcommittee on Energy Conservation and Supply. Municipal solid waste to energy act of 1979 . Washington , 1980. iii, 217 p. : LC Card 80-602495 DDC 344.73/04622 19
KF26 .E553 1980

Regan, Dennis C. Wreck diving in North Carolina : a directory of shipwrecks along the North Carolina coast / by Dennis C. Regan and Virginia Worthington. Raleigh, N.C. : UNC Sea Grant, North Carolina State University, [1978] 16 p. : maps ; 23 cm. (UNC sea grant publication ; UNC-SG-78-13) "November 1978." Bibliography: p. 16. LC Card 79-623528 DDC 910/.0916348 19
1. Shipwrecks - North Carolina. I. Worthington, Virginia, joint author. II. Series: Sea grant publication (Raleigh) ; UNC-SG-78-13. III. Title.
G525 .R375

Regan, Mary, 1930- (joint author) Paltridge, James Gilbert. Mid-career education and training . Davis, Calif. , 1979. v, 93 leaves : LC Card 80-623848 DDC 374 19
LC1037.5 .P33 **NYPL [JLM 77-672 no. 6]**

REGENERATION (BIOLOGY)
(1979) Sullivan, James Richard, 1947- The stone crab, Menippe mercenaria, in the southwest Florida fishery /. St. Petersburg, Fla. , 1979. 37 p. : LC Card 80-622656 DDC 333.95/5 19
QL444.M33 S93

REGENERATION (FORESTRY) see FOREST REPRODUCTION.

The regeneration of selected tropical wet forest tree species in Corcovado National Park, Costa Rica /. Herwitz, Stanley Robert. Berkeley, Calif. [1981] p. cm. ISBN 0-520-09631-2 LC Card 80-26413 DDC 910 s 582.16/052642/0972867 19
G58 .C3 vol. 24 QK217

Regional assessment of the saline-seep problem and a water-quality inventory of the Montana Plains . Montana. State Bureau of Mines and Geology. Bozeman, Mont. [1980] 24 p. : LC Card 80-623140 DDC 363.7/3942/09786 19
TD224.M9 M64 1980

Regional development in the USSR : trends and prospects : colloquium, 25-27 April, 1979, Brussels = Le developpement regional en URSS : tendances et perspectives : colloque, 25-27, Avril, 1979, Bruxelles / NATO Economics Directorate, Information Directorate, eds. ; [designed & illustrated, Mary Jane Medved]. Newtonville, Mass. : Oriental Research Partners, 1979. 294 p. (p. 294 blank) : ill. ; 23 cm. Includes bibliographical references. ISBN 0-89250-115-4 LC Card 79-91195
1. Regional planning - Russia - Congresses. I. North Atlantic Treaty Organization. Economics Directorate. II. North Atlantic Treaty Organization. Information Directorate. III. Title: Developpement regional en URSS.
HT395.R8 R43 **NYPL [JLE 80-2914]**

Regional development in the USSR : trends and prospects : colloquium, 25-27 April, 1979, Brussels = Le developpement regional en URSS : tendances et perspectives : colloque, 25-27, Avril, 1979, Bruxelles / NATO Economics Directorate, Information Directorate, eds. ; [designed & illustrated, Mary Jane Medved]. Newtonville, Mass. : Oriental Research Partners, 1979. 294 p. (p. 294 blank) : ill. ; 23 cm. Includes bibliographical references. ISBN 0-89250-115-4 LC Card 79-91195
1. Regional planning - Russia - Congresses. I. North Atlantic Treaty Organization. Economics Directorate. II. North Atlantic Treaty Organization. Information Directorate. III. Title: Developpement regional en URSS.
HT395.R8 R43

REGIONAL ECONOMICS - COLLECTED WORKS.
United States. Advisory Commission on Intergovernmental Relations. Regional growth. Washington, D.C. [1980- v. <1- > : LC Card 80-603208 DDC 361.6/0973 19
HT392 .U5 1980

Regional efficiency in the organization of agricultural processing facilities . Stollsteimer, John F. [Berkeley] , 1975. 148 p. : LC Card 76-622988 DDC 338.1 s 664/.80413 19
HD1407 .C27 no. 35 SB373

Regional growth. United States. Advisory Commission on Intergovernmental Relations. Washington, D.C. [1980- v. <1- > : LC Card 80-603208 DDC 361.6/0973 19
HT392 .U5 1980

Regional housing study, phase II. Birmingham Regional Planning Commission. [Birmingham, Ala.] 1972. 63 l. LC Card 81-468368 DDC 361.5/1/097617 19
HD7303.A2 B57 1972

Regional Irrigation Practices Leadership Seminar : NESA Region, 1st, Izmir, 1956. First Regional Irrigation Practices Leadership Seminar, Izmir, Turkey. [Washington] : International Cooperation Administration, [195-] 91 p. : ill. ; 28 cm. Cover title. Includes bibliographical references. LC Card 80-500427 DDC 631.7/0956 19

1. Irrigation - Near East - Congresses. 2. Irrigation - South Asia - Congresses. I. United States. International Cooperation Administration.
S616.N34 R33 1956

Regional Legislative Workshop on Higher Education, 3d, San Francisco, 1961. The role of the universities in the economic development of the West / edited by Kevin P. Bunnell, Roma K. McNickle. Boulder, Colo. : Western Interstate Commission for Higher Education, 1962. x, 28 p. : ill. ; 29 cm. LC Card 79-124780 DDC 378.78 19
1. Education, Higher - Economic aspects - The West - Congresses. I. Bunnell, Kevin P. II. McNickle, Roma K. III. Western Interstate Commission for Higher Education. IV. Title.
LC67.65.W47 R43 1961

REGIONAL MEDICAL PROGRAMS - CONNECTICUT.
Connecticut. Office of Policy & Management. Division of Management and Evaluation. Emergency medical services . [Hartford] , 1980. 65 p. ; LC Card 80-621532 DDC 362.1/8/09746 19
RA645.6.C8 C66 1980

Regional Plan Association, New York.
Transportation and economic opportunity: a report to the Transportation Administration of the City of New York. [New York, 1973] 206 p. illus., maps (part col.) 28 cm. Bibliography: p. 204-206.
1. Urban transportation - New York (City). I. New York (City). Transportation Administration. II. Title. **NYPL [JLF 81-23]**

REGIONAL PLANNING - ALABAMA.
Alabama. Office of State Planning and Federal Programs. Alabama state plan for economic growth and development. Montgomery, Ala. [1979] ix, 185 p. : LC Card 80-623529 DDC 361.6/09761 19
HT393.A2 A28 1979

Alabama. Office of State Planning and Federal Programs. Supplement to Alabama Appalachian development plan . Montgomery, Ala. [1980] 84 p. : LC Card 80-623530 DDC 361.6/09761 19
HT393.A2 A28 1980

REGIONAL PLANNING - ALABAMA - BIBLIOGRAPHY.
Alabama. Development Office. A selected bibliography of Alabama county and regional planning and development documents /. Montgomery , 1974. xiii, 254 p. : LC Card 74-623967
Z7165.U6 A416 1974 HC107.A4

REGIONAL PLANNING - ALABAMA - PERIODICALS.
Guiding growth in Alabama. Montgomery. LC Card 78-622552 **NYPL [JLM 80-1091]**

Regional planning and development councils.
West Virginia. Community Development Division. Directory of regional planning and development councils /. [Charleston], W. Va. , 1979. 89 p. ; LC Card 80-621499 DDC 353.97540081/8/025 19
HT393.W4 W47 1979

REGIONAL PLANNING - CALIFORNIA.
Waldhorn, Steven A. Picket fence planning in California. Sacramento , 1976-77. NUL, 62 p.
JS451.C25 W34 **NYPL [*XME-9440]**

REGIONAL PLANNING - CITIZEN PARTICIPATION - CONGRESSES.
United Nations Conference on Human Settlements, Vancouver, B.C., 1976. Physical elements and mobilization of human resources . [New York?] 1976. 92 p. ; LC Card 80-514948 DDC 300 s 361.6 19
JX1977 .A2 A/CONF.70/A/3

REGIONAL PLANNING - CONGRESSES.
United Nations Conference on Human Settlements, Vancouver, B.C., 1976. Physical elements and mobilization of human resources . [New York?] 1976. 92 p. ; LC Card 80-514948 DDC 300 s 361.6 19
JX1977 .A2 A/CONF.70/A/3

United Nations Conference on Human Settlements, Vancouver, B.C., 1976. Recommendations for national action . [New York?] 1976. 75 p. ; LC Card 81-453323 DDC 300 s 361.6 19
JX1977 .A2 A/CONF.70/5

Regional Planning Council, Baltimore.
Comprehensive correctional services study :
Baltimore County / produced by the Regional
Planning Council, Region V criminal justice
planning staff. Baltimore : The Council, 1978.
43 leaves ; 28 cm. Microfiche (neg.) 1 sheet. 11 x
15 cm. (NYPL FSN 35,135) Cover title.
*1. Corrections - Maryland - Baltimore County. 2.
Baltimore, County, Md. - History. I. Title.*
NYPL [*XME-9198]

**REGIONAL PLANNING - DATA
    PROCESSING - BIBLIOGRAPHY.**
South Florida Regional Planning Council.
Developing geographic-based information files .
[Miami] , 1976. 19 p.   **NYPL [*XMQ-2197]**

**REGIONAL PLANNING DISTRICTS -
    MARYLAND - MONTGOMERY
    COUNTY - MAPS.**
Maryland-National Capital Park and Planning
Commission. Second draft, selected
transportation elements including the master
plan of highways . [Silver Spring? Md.] [1980]
1 map :   LC Card 81-692907
G3843.M6P1 1980 .M3

REGIONAL PLANNING - FLORIDA.
Florida. Bureau of Comprehensive Planning.
Growth policy element of the State
comprehensive plan . [Tallahassee] , 1976. iii,
52 p. ;   LC Card 77-621538   DDC 361.6/09759 19
HT393.F5 F53 1976

REGIONAL PLANNING - GEORGIA.
United States. Bureau of the Census. Guide to
county census data. Washington , 1979. 123 p.;
                          NYPL [*R-Econ. 80-2970]

REGIONAL PLANNING - GREAT PLAINS.
Twomey, James P. Governmental programs,
resources and regulatory powers available to
assist localities during coal development . -
Denver , 1974. i, 29, [65] p. ;
                          NYPL [JLF 80-707]

REGIONAL PLANNING - HAWAII.
Hawaii. Dept. of Planning and Economic
Development. The Hawaii State plan.
[Honolulu?] , 1978. 48 p. :   LC Card 78-624130
HT393.H3 H36 1978   **NYPL [JLF 80-1349]**

Hawaii. Dept. of Planning and Economic
Development. Urban design primer, Hawaii.
[Honolulu] , 1975. vi, 101 p. :   LC Card
76-624060
HT167.5.H3 H34 1975   **NYPL [JLF 80-1338]**

**REGIONAL PLANNING - HAWAII -
    COLLECTED WORKS.**
Hawaii. Dept. of Planning and Economic
Development. The Hawaii state plan .
[Honolulu] , 1977. [5] v. :   LC Card 78-620900
HC107.H3 H38 1977

**REGIONAL PLANNING - HAWAII -
    HAWAII CO.**
Hawaii Co., Hawaii. Planning Dept. The general
plan: County of Hawaii. [Hilo] 1971. 101 p.
    LC Card 81-474003   DDC 711/.3/099691 19
HT393.H32 H383 1971

REGIONAL PLANNING - ILLINOIS.
Henke, Joseph T. A case study of Greater
Egypt Regional Planning and Development
Commission /. Eugene, 1971. 48 l.   LC Card
76-106858   **NYPL [JLF 80-1283]**

Meyer, Douglas K. East central Illinois .
Normal, Ill. , 1980. vi, 31 p. (p. 31 publisher's
list) ;   LC Card 80-622845   DDC 361.6/1/097736
19
HT393.I4 M49

Regional planning in Missouri . Missouri.
Division of Budget and Planning. [Jefferson
City, Mo. , 1980] 68 p. :   LC Card 80-622356
    DDC 353.977807/2/025 19
HT393.M8 M54 1980

**REGIONAL PLANNING - LAW AND
    LEGISLATION - ALABAMA -
    PERIODICALS.**
Guiding growth in Alabama. Montgomery.   LC
    Card 78-622552   **NYPL [JLM 80-1091]**

**REGIONAL PLANNING - LAW AND
    LEGISLATION - MONTANA.**
Montana. Dept. of Community Affairs.
Montana's local planning legislation. [Helena]
[1979] 54 p. ;   LC Card 80-622221   DDC
    346.78604/5 19
KFM9458 .A833

**REGIONAL PLANNING - LAW AND
    LEGISLATION - NEW JERSEY.**
New Jersey. Laws, statutes, etc. Planning,
environmental and related enabling legislation.
[Trenton] , 1980. 66 p. ;   LC Card 80-622986
    DDC 344.749/046 19
KFN2154 .A3 1980

**REGIONAL PLANNING - MISSOURI -
    DIRECTORIES.**
Missouri. Division of Budget and Planning.
Regional planning in Missouri . [Jefferson City,
Mo. , 1980] 68 p. :   LC Card 80-622356   DDC
    353.977807/2/025 19
HT393.M8 M54 1980

**REGIONAL PLANNING - NEW JERSEY -
    BERGEN COUNTY - COLLECTED
    WORKS.**
Planner's data book for Bergen County.
Hackensack, N. J..   **NYPL [JLM 81-199]**

**REGIONAL PLANNING - NEW JERSEY -
    HUNTERDON COUNTY.**
Hunterdon County, N. J. Parks and Open Land
Advisory Committee. The Hunterdon County
Park and Open Space Plan /. [Flemington, N.
J.] 1972. 83, [4] p.:   **NYPL [JLF 79-1725]**

**REGIONAL PLANNING - NEW YORK
    (STATE)**
Danielson, Michael N. New York, the politics
of urban regional development / . Berkeley ,
c1981. p. cm.   ISBN 0-520-04371-5   LC Card
    81-7480   DDC 307.7/6 19
HT393.N7 D3

REGIONAL PLANNING - NORTH DAKOTA.
North Dakota. State University of Agriculture
and Applied Science, Fargo. Center for
Economic Development. A program of
management and technical assistance in EDA
designated areas in North Dakota . Fargo, N.
D. , 1974. 70 p. :   **NYPL [JLF 80-1351]**

REGIONAL PLANNING - PENNSYLVANIA.
Intergovernmental Organization for Planning. A
case study of the northern tier region of
northeastern Pennsylvania. Eugene, Or., 1971.
58 l.   **NYPL [JLF 80-1285]**

**REGIONAL PLANNING - RUSSIA -
    CONGRESSES.**
Regional development in the USSR .
Newtonville, Mass. , 1979. 294 p. (p. 294
blank) ;   ISBN 0-89250-115-4   LC Card 79-91195
HT395.R8 R43   **NYPL [JLE 80-2914]**

Regional development in the USSR .
Newtonville, Mass. , 1979. 294 p. (p. 294
blank) ;   ISBN 0-89250-115-4   LC Card 79-91195
HT395.R8 R43

**REGIONAL PLANNING - STUDY AND
    TEACHING - UNITED STATES.**
Urban gaming/simulation '77 . Ann Arbor ,
c1977. x, 57, 376 p. ;   LC Card 77-151140   DDC
    307.7/6/0724 19
HT165.52 .U7

REGIONAL PLANNING - UNITED STATES.
Pennsylvania. Dept. of Community Affairs.
Reversing regional decline . [Harrisburg]
[1976] 13, [8] leaves :   LC Card 76-624629
HJ275 .P45 1976   **NYPL [*XME-9553]**

**REGIONAL PLANNING - UNITED STATES -
    COLLECTED WORKS.**
United States. Advisory Commission on
Intergovernmental Relations. Regional growth.
Washington, D.C. [1980- v. <1- > :   LC Card
    80-603208   DDC 361.6/0973 19
HT392 .U5 1980

**REGIONAL PLANNING - VERMONT -
    WINDHAM COUNTY.**
Henke, Joseph T. A case study of Windham
Regional Planning and Development
Commission /. Eugene, Or., 1970. 69
l.   LC Card 73-101271   **NYPL [JLF 80-1288]**

**REGIONAL PLANNING - WASHINGTON
    (STATE) - DIRECTORIES.**
Washington (State). Planning and Community
Affairs Agency. Directory of city, county,
regional, state & federal planning agencies.
Olympia , 1978. 47 p. ;   LC Card 79-621293
    DDC 350.007/2/025797 19
HT393.W3 W34 1978

**REGIONAL PLANNING - WEST VIRGINIA -
    DIRECTORIES.**
West Virginia. Community Development
Division. Directory of regional planning and

development councils /. [Charleston], W. Va. ,
1979. 89 p. ;   LC Card 80-621499   DDC
    353.97540081/8/025 19
HT393.W4 W47 1979

**Regional Scientific and Technological
    Development Program. see Programa
    Regional de Desarrollo Científico y
    Tecnológico.**

**Regional solar energy centers and the Solar
    Energy Research Institute .** United States.
Congress. House. Committee on Science and
Technology. Subcommittee on Energy
Development and Applications. Washington ,
1980. v, 23 p. ;   LC Card 80-603269   DDC
    333.79/23/072073 19
TJ810 .U57 1980

Regional stability in northern Africa . United
States. Congress. House. Washington , 1980. v,
29 p. ;   LC Card 80-603274   DDC 327/.096 19
DT204 .U48 1980

Regional surface drainage plan and program.
Central New York Regional Planning and
Development Board. Syracuse , 1974. 195 p. :
                          NYPL [JSF 81-285]

**Regional Symposium on Industrial Development,
    Cairo, 1966.** Engineering industries in Africa.
[New York] : United Nations, Economic and
Social Council, 1965- v. <2> : ill. ; 28 cm.
([Document] - United Nations.
E/CN.14/INR/AS/II/2.i) At head of title: Economic
Commission for Africa, Regional Symposium on
Industrial Development. CONTENTS. --pt. 2. Map,
graphs, tables, and annexes.   LC Card 79-117715
    DDC 300 s 338.4/76218/096 19
*1. Engineering - Africa. 2. Machinery - Trade and
manufacture - Africa. I. United Nations. Economic
Commission for Africa. II. Series: United Nations.
[Document] E/CN.14/INR/AS/II/2.i. III. Title.*
JX1977 .A2 E/CN.14/INR/AS/II/2.i

Regionalism and the United Nations / edited by
Berhanykun Andemicael. Dobbs Ferry, N.Y. :
Published for the United Nations Institute for
Training and Research [by] Oceana
Publications, 1979. xx, 603 p. ; 25 cm. Includes
bibliographical references and index.   ISBN
    0-379-00591-3 :   LC Card 79-14018
*1. Regionalism (International organization) - Addresses,
essays, lectures. 2. United Nations - Addresses, essays,
lectures. I. Andemicael, Berhanykun. II. United Nations
Institute for Training and Research.*
JX1979 .R43   **NYPL [JLE 80-3132]**

**REGIONALISM (INTERNATIONAL
    ORGANIZATION) - ADDRESSES,
    ESSAYS, LECTURES.**
Regionalism and the United Nations /. Dobbs
Ferry, N.Y. , 1979. xx, 603 p. ;   ISBN
    0-379-00591-3 :   LC Card 79-14018
JX1979 .R43   **NYPL [JLE 80-3132]**

**REGIONALISM - UNITED STATES -
    COLLECTED WORKS.**
United States. Advisory Commission on
Intergovernmental Relations. Regional growth.
Washington, D.C. [1980- v. <1- > :   LC Card
    80-603208   DDC 361.6/0973 19
HT392 .U5 1980

**Register of foreign consulates and associated
    government offices in New York.** New York
(City). City Commission for the United Nations
and for the Consular Corps. New York.
    NYPL [*R-Econ. 80-806 & JLL 80-238]

Registered lobbyists in Illinois . Illinois.
Legislative Council. Springfield, Ill. [197-] iv,
60 p. ;   LC Card 80-621673   DDC 328/.38/025773
    19
JK5774 .A3 no. 152 JK5774.5

**REGISTERS OF BIRTHS, ETC. -
    MISSISSIPPI - COLUMBUS.**
Friendship Cemetery, Columbus, Mississippi :
tombstone inscriptions and burial records /.
Columbus , 1979. 2 v. (xii, 358 p.) :
                          NYPL [APR (Columbus, Miss.) 81-100]

**REGISTERS OF BIRTHS, ETC. - NORTH
    CAROLINA - CLEVELAND COUNTY.**
DePriest, Virginia Greene. 1870 census of
Cleveland County, North Carolina /. Shelby, N.
C. , c1979. 175 p. ;   LC Card 80-105685
F262.C5 D46   **NYPL [APR (Cleveland Co.,
                          N.C.) 80-3069]**

REGISTERS OF BIRTHS, ETC. - UTAH.
Utah. State Archives. Veterans with Federal

service buried in the State of Utah, Territorial
period to 1965. [Salt Lake City] , 1965- v. ;
     LC Card 80-53986   DDC 929/.3792 19
F825 .U85 1965

**REGISTERS OF BIRTHS, ETC. - VIRGINIA -
NORTHAMPTON COUNTY.**
Mihalyka, Jean Merritt. Gravestone inscriptions
in Northampton County, Virginia /. Richmond,
Va. , 1980. xxxiii, 99 p. :   ISBN 0-88490-092-4
(pbk.)   LC Card 81-621014   DDC
929.5/09755/15 19
F232.N85 M53

Registers of planned emergency producers.
United States. Defense Logistics Agency.
Washington , 1980. 290 p. in various pagings ;
                    NYPL [JLF 80-1284]

**REGISTRATION OF TRADE-MARKS. see
TRADE-MARKS.**

Reglamento de la Asamblea General .
Organization of American States. General
Assembly. Washington, D.C. , 1978. v, 30 p. ;
     LC Card 80-142828   DDC 341.24/5 s 341.24/5
19
F1402 .A169 OEA/Ser. P/I.1 rev. 5 F1402.A4

**REGULATED INDUSTRIES. see PUBLIC
UTILITIES.**

**Regulating occupations in California ; the role of
public members on State boards /.** Schutz,
Howard G. [Berkeley] , 1980. ix, 22 p. ;   ISBN
0-87772-276-5   LC Card 80-15719
HD3630.U7 S38

**Regulation and construction of nuclear
powerplants--South Texas nuclear project .**
United States. Congress. House. Committee on
Interstate and Foreign Commerce.
Subcommittee on Oversight and Investigations.
Washington , c1981. iii, 198 p. ;   LC Card
81-601168   DDC 343.73/0925 347.303925 19
KF27 .I5547 1980u

The regulation of natural gas . Sanders, M.
Elizabeth, 1943- Philadelphia , 1981. p. cm.
     ISBN 0-87722-221-5 :   LC Card 81-9239   DDC
333.8/23317/0973 19
HD9581.U5 S26

**REGULATION OF PRICES. see PRICE
REGULATION.**

**REGULATION OF TRADE. see TRADE
REGULATION.**

Regulation Q and related measures . United
States. Congress. House. Committee on
Banking, Finance and Urban Affairs.
Subcommittee on Financial Institutions
Supervision, Regulation and Insurance.
Washington , 1980. v, 1013 p. :   LC Card
80-602494   DDC 346.73/082 19
KF27 .B544 1980a

Regulation reform act of 1979 . United States.
Congress. House. Committee on the Judiciary.
Subcommittee on Administrative Law and
Governmental Relations. Washington , 1980-
v. ;   LC Card 80-603418   DDC 342.73/066 19
KF27 .J832 1980a

Regulations and standards for hospitals.
Nebraska. Dept. of Health. Rule 30, regulations
and standards for hospitals . Lincoln, Neb.
[1979] 51 p. :   LC Card 81-621038   DDC
344.782/03211 347.82043211 19
KFN361.A433 A2 1979

**Regulations concerning abatement of air
pollution /.** Connecticut. Dept. of
Environmental Protection. [Hartford] [1980] 42
p. ;   LC Card 81-621086   DDC 344.746/046342
347.460446342 19
KFC3958.A435 A2 1980

**Regulations concerning compensation of civil
service employees.** West Virginia. Civil Service
System. [Charleston] [1976] 43 p. ;   LC Card
80-623167   DDC 353.9755001/23 19
JK4057 .W47 1976

**Regulations for the administration and
enforcement of the Radiation control for health
and safety act of 1968.** United States. Bureau
of Radiological Health. Rockville, Md. ,
Washington, D.C. , 1978. vi, 68 p. :   LC Card
79-603753   DDC 344.73/0472 19
KF3948.A355 A2 1978

**Regulations governing pier construction, deposit
of fill, dredging, or alteration of Lake Tahoe
shoreline, adopted September 24, 1979 /.**

Nevada. State Dept. of Conservation and
Natural Resources. [Carson City, Nev.] [1979]
8 p. ;   LC Card 80-622985   DDC 346.793/57046917
19
KFN1051.8.A434 A2 1979

Regulations of the Boards : adopted August 29,
1977, effective October 19, 1977, statutes,
chapter 1.1, title 54, chapter 24, title 54 /
Commonwealth of Virginia, the State Board of
Behavioral Science [and] the State Board of
Professional Counselors. Richmond, Va. (2
South Ninth St., P.O. Box 1-X, Richmond, Va.
23202) : Dept. of Professional and Occupational
Regulation, [1977?] 36 p. ; 26 cm.   Cover title.
     LC Card 80-623907   DDC 344.755/0176115
347.5504176115 19
1. Psychologists - Legal status, laws, etc. - Virginia. 2.
Counselors - Legal status, laws, etc. - Virginia. I.
Virginia. Board of Behavioral Science. II. Virginia. State
Board of Professional Counselors.
KFV2726.5.P73 A3 1977

**Regulations of the Virginia Alcoholic Beverage
Control Commission, in force and effect as of
January 15, 1980, including rules of practice
before hearing officers and the Commission.**
Virginia. Alcoholic Beverage Control
Commission. [Richmond] [1980] 36 p. ;   LC
Card 80-622997   DDC 344.755/0541 19
KFV2775.A439 A2 1980

**Regulations to implement the Comprehensive
older Americans act amendments of 1978 .**
United States. Congress. Senate. Special
Committee on Aging. Washington , 1980- v. ;
     LC Card 80-603040   DDC 353.0084/6 19
KF26.5 .A3 1979i

Regulatory reform highlights . United States.
Regulatory Council. [Washington, D.C.] [1980]
xi, 172 p. ;   LC Card 80-602350   DDC 353.09/3 19
KF1600 .A877

**Regulatory requirements for business,
construction, land development.** Oregon.
Executive Dept. Salem, Or. [1980] 30, 2, 14
p. ;   LC Card 80-623339   DDC 342.795/0664 19
KFO2630 .A46 1980

Rehabilitation and maintenance program plan .
Maine. Bureau of Health Planning and
Development. [Augusta, Me.] [1980] iii, 156
p. :   LC Card 80-622394   DDC 362.1/9897/009741
19
RA564.8 .M34 1980

REHABILITATION - BIBLIOGRAPHY.
Schwab, Lois. Rehabilitation for independent
living . Washington, D.C. , 1980. 47 p. ;   LC
Card 80-601692   DDC 016.3624/048 19
Z7254 .S37 HV3000

Rehabilitation, Claremont 1978 . Historic
American Engineering Record. Washington,
D.C. [1979] 89 p. :   LC Card 80-601586   DDC
711/.5524 19
NA2793 .H57 1979a

**Rehabilitation, comprehensive services, and
developmental disabilities legislation ... .**
United States. [Rehabilitation Act of 1973.]
Washington [1979] viii, 94 p. ;   LC Card
80-603984   DDC 344.73/0159 347.304159 19
KF3738 .A3 1979

Rehabilitation for independent living . Schwab,
Lois. Washington, D.C. , 1980. 47 p. ;   LC Card
80-601692   DDC 016.3624/048 19
Z7254 .S37 HV3000

**REHABILITATION OF CRIMINALS -
MARYLAND.**
Maryland. Division of Correction. Community
Reintegration Project. The Community
Reintegration Project. [Baltimore, 1973] xxiv,
135 p.   *NYPL [*XME-9301]*

**REHABILITATION OF CRIMINALS -
MARYLAND - BALTIMORE.**
Lenihan, Kenneth J. Unlocking the second
gate . [Washington] , 1977. iv, 71 p. :   LC Card
77-600960
HD5701 .U53 no. 45 HV9306.B2
                 *NYPL [*XME-9551]*

**REHABILITATION OF CRIMINALS -
MASSACHUSETTS - STATISTICS.**
Williams, Lawrence T. A profile of
characteristics distinguishing between program
completers and program non-completers.
[Boston] , 1980. 20 leaves ;
                *NYPL [*ZT-1263]*

**REHABILITATION OF CRIMINALS -
UNITED STATES.**
Petersilia, Joan. The prison experience of career
criminals /. Washington, D.C. , 1980. xviii, 87
p. :   LC Card 81-601009   DDC 365/.66 19
HV9304 .P44

United States. National Institute of Mental
Health. Center for Studies of Crime and
Delinquency. Graduated release /. Rockville,
Md. , 1971. 30 p. ;   *NYPL [*XME-9048]*

**REHABILITATION OF CRIMINALS -
UNITED STATES - CONGRESSES.**
Rehabilitation, what part of corrections? .
Arlington, Tex. [1977?] vi, 152 p. :   LC Card
80-621842   DDC 364.6/01 19
HV9303 .R43

**REHABILITATION OF CRIMINALS -
WASHINGTON (STATE)**
Sykes, Thomas M. An analysis of program
needs of prison inmates in Washington State /.
Olympia, Wash. [1980] xxi, 139 p. ;   LC Card
80-620028   DDC 365/.66/09797 19
HV9475.W2 S93

**REHABILITATION OF JUVENILE
DELINQUENTS - CALIFORNIA.**
Lewis, Roy V. The Squires of San Quentin .
[Sacramento, Calif.] , 1979. iii, 136 p. ;   LC
Card 80-621637   DDC 364.4/8 19
HV9105.C2 L483

**REHABILITATION OF JUVENILE
DELINQUENTS - UNITED STATES.**
United States. Congress. Senate. Committee on
the Judiciary. Reauthorization of the Juvenile
Justice and Delinquency Prevention Act of
1974 . Washington , 1981. viii, 555 p. :   LC
Card 81-602037   DDC 344.73/03274
347.3043274 19
KF26 .J8 1980i

**REHABILITATION OF JUVENILE
DELINQUENTS - VIRGINIA.**
Virginia. State Crime Commission. Children and
youth in trouble in Virginia . Richmond, Va.
[1977] xvi, 188 p. ;   LC Card 80-622757   DDC
364.3/6/09755 19
HV9105.V7 V53 1977

**REHABILITATION OF JUVENILE
DELINQUENTS - VIRGINIA -
EVALUATION.**
Virginia. Dept. of Corrections. Bureau of
Research, Reporting and Evaluation. NYPUM
program evaluation. [Richmond] , 1977. 171
p. ;   LC Card 79-621982   DDC 365/.9755462 19
HV9105.V7 V5 1977

**REHABILITATION OF PRISONERS -
UNITED STATES - ABSTRACTS.**
Levine, Mark. Jail-based inmate programs .
[Washington, D.C.] , 1979. vii, 24 p. ;   LC Card
80-601763   DDC 016.365/66 19
HV9304 .L43

**REHABILITATION RESEARCH - UNITED
STATES.**
Muthard, John E., 1917- Putting rehabilitation
knowledge to use . Gainesville, Fla. , 1980. vii,
80 p. ;   LC Card 80-622447   DDC 362/.0425 s
362/.0425 19
RM930.A1 F55 no. 11 HD7256.U5

**REHABILITATION, RURAL. see RURAL
DEVELOPMENT.**

Rehabilitation service series. United States.
Rehabilitation Services Administration.
63/32-69/13 (incomplete) Washington
[1968-69] 27 cm.   *NYPL [JLM 81-302]*

**REHABILITATION - UNITED STATES -
EFFECT OF INFLATION ON.**
United States. Congress. House. Committee on
Education and Labor. Subcommittee on Select
Education. Oversight hearing on the impact of
inflation on rehabilitation services .
Washington , 1980. iii, 50 p. :   LC Card
80-603046   DDC 362/.0425 19
KF27 .E373 1980a

**REHABILITATION - UNITED STATES -
PERIODICALS.**
American rehabilitation. v. 1- ; Sept./Oct. 1975-
[Washington]   LC Card 75-648421
                  NYPL [JLM 80-958]

**REHABILITATION, VOCATIONAL. see
VOCATIONAL REHABILITATION.**

Rehabilitation, what part of corrections? :
Division of Public Administration, University of

New Mexico, May 2-4, 1977 / conference convener, Leonard Stitleman ; editors, Brenda Bradshaw, Peter J. Eck ; [co-sponsored by the Division of Public Administration, University of New Mexico, and the Institute of Urban Studies, Research and Service Programs Division, University of Texas at Arlington]. Arlington, Tex. : The Institute, [1977?] vi, 152 p. : ill. ; 21 cm. (New directions for corrections . v. 5) Bibliography: p. 71-74. LC Card 80-621842 DDC 364.6/01 19
1. Rehabilitation of criminals - United States - Congresses. 2. Corrections - United States - Congresses. I. Bradshaw, Brenda. II. Eck, Peter. III. New Mexico. University. Division of Public Administration. IV. Texas. University at Arlington. Institute of Urban Studies. Research and Service Programs Division. V. Series.
HV9303 .R43

Rehfeldt, Kenneth R. (joint author) Gross, Gerardo Wolfgang. Paul Spring, an investigation of recharge in the Roswell (N.M.) artesian basin /. Las Cruces, N.M. [1979] 135 p. : LC Card 80-622504 DDC 551.49//09789/43 19
GB705.N6 N64 no. 113 GB1199.3.N6

Reichardt, Paul B. (joint author) Nevé, Richard A. Development of a chemical assay for saxitoxin or paralytic shellfish poison (PSP) . Fairbanks , 1978. iv, 23 leaves : LC Card 78-623526 DDC 634/.9 19
QP632.S27 N48

Reid, Clarice D. Prenatal approaches to the diagnosis of fetal hemoglobinopathies . [Bethesda, Md.] , 1980. xiii, 259 p. : LC Card 80-602909 DDC 618.3/2 19
RG629.H45 P73

Reid, George Willard, 1917- Final report on the Governor's Conference on Research and Development Priorities for the State of Oklahoma / prepared by George W. Reid ; submitted to Office of Intergovernmental Science Programs, National Science Foundation, from Office of Research Administration, University of Oklahoma. [Norman, Okla. : Office of Research Administration, University of Oklahoma, 1973] 293 p. in various pagings : ill. ; 29 cm. "August, 1973." LC Card 80-621267 DDC 338.9766 19
1. Research, Industrial - Oklahoma. 2. Technology and state - Oklahoma. I. United States. National Science Foundation. Office of Intergovernmental Science Programs. II. Oklahoma. University. Office of Research Administration. III. Title.
T176 .R4

Reid, Judith Krause. North Carolina. County Court (Gates Co.) Gates County, North Carolina, court minutes /. [Calumet Park, Il.] [1979?- v. : LC Card 80-100182
KFN7916.G38 A7 1779

Reigh, Robert C. Fishes of the western tributaries of the Missouri River in North Dakota : final draft report to the Regional Environmental Assessment Program under agreement for services number 6-01-1 / by Robert C. Reigh and John B. Owen. [Bismarck, N.D.] : The Program, [1979] xi, 207 p. : maps ; 29 cm. (REAP reports ; no. 79-2) Bibliography: p. 205-207. LC Card 80-622780 DDC 597.092/9784/7 19
1. Fishes - North Dakota - Geographical distribution. 2. Fishes - Missouri River - Geographical distribution. 3. Fishes - Geographical distribution. I. Owen, John B., joint author. II. Series: North Dakota. Regional Environmental Assessment Program. REAP reports , no. 79-2. III. Title.
QL628.N9 R44

REIGN OF TERROR. see FRANCE - HISTORY - REVOLUTION, 1789-1799.

Reiling, Stephen D. Louisiana agriculture, 1940-1977 : economic trends and current status / Stephen D. Reiling, Fred H. Wiegmann. [Baton Rouge] : Louisiana State University and Agricultural and Mechanical College, Center for Agricultural Sciences and Rural Development, Agricultural Experiment Station, 1979. 74 p. (p. 74 blank) : ill. ; 22 cm. (Bulletin - Agricultural Experiment Station ; no. 718) Includes bibliographical references. LC Card 79-624475 DDC 338.1/09763 19
1. Agriculture - Economic aspects - Louisiana. I. Wiegmann, Fred, joint author. II. Series: Louisiana. Agricultural Experiment Station, Baton Rouge. Bulletin - Agricultural Experiment Station , no. 718. III.

Title.
HD1775.L8 R44

Reilly, James R. (joint author) Casey, Timothy J. Chemical and biological investigations of mice and deer in the vicinity of two coal-fired power plants near Stanton, North Dakota / . Grand Forks , 1976. viii, 58 p. : LC Card 77-621848 DDC 599.02/4 19
QH545.C57 C37

Reimann, Buechner, Crandall Partnership. Hudson-Mohwak Industrial Gateway, inc. Some interesting buildings, sites, and natural features in the Hudson-Mohawk Urban Cultural Park /. [Troy? N.Y.] [1979] 1 map : LC Card 81-692835
G3802.H87E635 1979 .H8

Reimbursement alternatives for long-term nursing care in Missouri. Missouri. Division of Budget and Planning. [Jefferson City] [1979] 130 p. ; LC Card 80-620611 DDC 362.1/6/0681 19
RA997.5.M8 M55 1979

Reimers, G. W. (George W.) Khalafalla, S. E. Beneficiation with magnetic fluids /. Washington, D.C. [1981] p. cm. LC Card 81-607043 DDC 622 s 622/.77 19
TN23 .U43 TN530

Reinbold, Keturah A. (joint author) Ewing, Ben B. Economic impact of a proposed change in lead effluent standards /. Chicago, IL [1980] vi, 83 p. ; LC Card 80-623378 DDC 363.7/394 19
TD427.H45 E92

Reineback, L. M. Soil survey of Grundy County, Illinois / [by L. M. Reineback] ; United States Department of Agriculture, Soil Conservation Service, in cooperation with Illinois Agricultural Experiment Station. [Washington] : The Service, [1980] vii, 131 p., [35] fold. leaves of plates : ill. ; 28 cm. (Illinois Agricultural Experiment Station soil report ; no. 142) Cover title. Bibliography: p. 73. LC Card 80-602552 DDC 631.4/9773 s 631.4/7/773265 19
1. Soils - Illinois - Grundy Co. - Maps. I. United States. Soil Conservation Service. II. Illinois. Agricultural Experiment Station, Urbana. III. Series: Illinois. Agricultural Experiment Station, Urbana. Soil report , no. 142. IV. Title.
S599.I5 A3 no. 142

REINFORCED CONCRETE CONSTRUCTION - TESTING.
Moehle, Jack P. Experiments to study earthquake response of R/C structures with stiffness interruptions . Urbana, Ill. [1980] xiii, 421 p. : LC Card 80-624330 DDC 693.8/52 19
TA683 .M66

Reinhard, Christine. Fond du Lac County, Wisconsin, cartographic catalog /. Madison, WI (University of Wisconsin, 1555 Science Hall, Madison 53706) [1979] 1 v. (various pagings) : LC Card 80-624194 DDC 016.912/775/68 19
Z6027.U5 F65 GA458

Reinhold, Ruth M. Sky pioneering : Arizona in aviation history / Ruth M. Reinhold. Tucson : University of Arizona Press, 1982. p. cm. ISBN 0-8165-0737-6 : LC Card 81-11514 DDC 387.7/09791 19
1. Aeronautics - Arizona - History. I. Title.
TL522.A6 R44

Reinstatement of oil and gas lease, New Mexico 33955 . United States. Congress. Senate. Committee on Energy and Natural Resources. Subcommittee on Energy Resources and Materials Production. Washington , 1980. iii, 32 p. ; LC Card 80-603814 DDC 346.78904/6823 347.890646823 19
KF26 .E5543 1980d

The rejected . Evoy, John J. University Park [1981] p. cm. ISBN 0-271-00285-9 : LC Card 81-47172 DDC 155.9/24 19
RC455.4.F3 E96

The relation of geology to mine roof conditions in the Pocahontas No. 3 coalbed /. Moebs, Noel N. Avondale, MD [1981] p. cm. LC Card 81-607819 DDC 622 s 622/.334/09754873 19
TN295 .U4

The relationship between women's studies, career development, and vocational choice /. Bose, Christine E. Washington, D.C. , 1980. xi, 59 p. ; LC Card 80-602291 DDC 305.4/2/072073 19
HQ1181.U5 B67

Relationship of costs and water use efficiency for irrigation projects in Idaho /. Allen, Rick G. Moscow, Idaho [1979] xvi, 288 p. : LC Card 80-622427 DDC 333.91/3/09796 19
HD1739.I2 A6

Relationship of highway development and city development for non-metropolitan places in Indiana . Yamin, Hadi. West Lafayette, Ind. , 1979. xii, 175 leaves : LC Card 80-620933 DDC 388.1/1 19
TE24.I6 Y35

Relationships between growth need strength and other individual differences measures employed in job design research /. Stone, Eugene F. West Lafayette, Ind. , 1977. 17 leaves ; LC Card 78-101255 DDC 658/.001/9 s 658.3/1422 19
HD6483 .P8 no. 644 HF5549.5.J63

The relationships of the Pedionomidae (Aves, Charadriiformes) /. Olson, Storrs L. Washington , 1981. p. cm. LC Card 81-412 DDC 591 s 598/.33 19
QL1 .S54 no. 337 QL696.C465

Relative attractiveness of different foods at wild bird feeders /. Geis, Aelred D., 1929- Washington, D.C. , 1980. p. cm. LC Card 80-607831 DDC 639.9/79/0973 s 664/.764 19
SK361 .A256 no. 233 QL676.5

Relative cost of shipbuilding. United States. Maritime Administration. Washington .
NYPL [JLM 80-1114]

Relative costs of U. S. and foreign nodule transport ships /. Andrews, Benjamin V. Rockville, Md. , 1978. vi, 70 p. : LC Card 78-602299
HE746 .A75

Relative economic status and fertility . MacDonald, Maurice, 1947- [Madison] [1976?] 25 p. ; LC Card 78-624376 DDC 304.6/3 19
HQ760 .M32

Relative validity of two item formats for obtaining length of service data from job inventories/. Carpenter, James B. Brooks Air Force Base, Tex., 1973. 4 leaves.
*NYPL [*XME-9684]*

Reliability Analysis Center. Nicholls, David B. Digital evaluation and failure analysis data /. Griffiss Air Force Base, NY , 1980. 2 v. ; LC Card 80-144504 DDC 621.381/73/0278 19
TK7874 .N48

Reliability of national hospital discharge survey data . Institute of Medicine. Washington, D.C. , 1980. viii, 105, [51] p. : ISBN 0-309-03079-X LC Card 80-81950 DDC 362.1/1/0212 19
RA971.6 .I57 1980

Reliability of stochastic models generating hydrologic series /. Gan, Thian-Yew. Austin, Tex. [1980] 64 leaves ; LC Card 80-622521 DDC 551.48/072 19
GB656.2.S7 G36

RELIGION AND LAW - SOCIETIES, ETC. - DIRECTORIES.
Christensen, Carol W. Guide to religion-based organizations of attorneys /. [Austin] , 1979. v, 33 leaves ; ISBN 0-935630-01-5 (pbk.) LC Card 80-621543 DDC 340/.06/073 19
KF195.R44 C48

Religion and mental health . Summerlin, Florence A. Rockville, Md. (5600 Fishers Lane, Rockville, Md. 20857) , Washington, D.C. , 1980. 401 p. in various pagings ; LC Card 81-601117 DDC 016.3622 19
Z6664.N5 S94 RA790

RELIGION AND PSYCHOANALYSIS.
Van Herik, Judith. Freud on femininity and faith /. Berkeley , c1981. p. cm. ISBN 0-520-04368-5 LC Card 81-3413 DDC 155.3/33/0924 19
BF173.F85 V26

RELIGION IN LITERATURE - ADDRESSES, ESSAYS, LECTURES.
Shaw and religion /. University Park , 1981. vi, 258 p. ; ISBN 0-271-00280-8 : LC Card 81-956 DDC 822/.912 19
PR5368.R4 S5

Religion in Tennessee, 1777-1945 /. Norton, Herman Albert. Knoxville , c1981. p. cm. ISBN 0-87049-317-5 : LC Card 81-1562 DDC

280/.09768 19
BR555.T2 N67

RELIGION IN THE PUBLIC SCHOOLS - LAW AND LEGISLATION - UNITED STATES.
United States. Congress. House. Committee on the Judiciary. Subcommittee on Courts, Civil Liberties, and the Administration of Justice. Prayer in public schools and buildings--federal court jurisdiction . Washington , 1981. iv, 976 p. ; LC Card 81-601626   DDC 344.73/0796 347.304796 19
KF27 .J857 1980a

RELIGION, INDIAN-AMERICAN. see INDIANS OF NORTH AMERICA - RELIGION AND MYTHOLOGY.

RELIGION - PHILOSOPHY - ADDRESSES, ESSAYS, LECTURES.
Anscombe, G. E. M. (Gertrude Elizabeth Margaret) Ethics, religion, and politics /. Minneapolis , c1981. p. cm.   ISBN 0-8166-1082-7 : LC Card 81-4315   DDC 192 s 170 19
B1618 .A571 1981, vol. 3 BJ1012

Religious discrimination : a neglected issue : a consultation / sponsored by the United States Commission on Civil Rights, Washington, D.C., April 9-10, 1979. [Washington, D.C.] : The Commission, [1980] viii, 541 p. ; ill. ; 23 cm. Bibliography: p. 535-541. LC Card 80-602570 DDC 261.7/2/0973 19
1. Religious liberty - United States - Congresses. 2. Discrimination - United States - Congresses. 3. Civil rights - United States - Congresses. I. United States. Commission on Civil Rights.
BR516 .R37

RELIGIOUS LIBERTY - UNITED STATES - CONGRESSES.
Religious discrimination . [Washington, D.C.] [1980] viii, 541 p. : LC Card 80-602570   DDC 261.7/2/0973 19
BR516 .R37

Religious requirements and practices of certain selected groups . Kirschner Associates. [Washington] , 1980. vi, 200 p. in various pagings ; LC Card 80-602248   DDC 291/.0973 19
BL2530.U6 K57 1980

The religious revolution in the Ivory Coast .
Walker, Sheila S. Chapel Hill , c1982. p. cm. ISBN 0-8078-1503-9 LC Card 81-13010 DDC 289/.9 19
BV3785.H348 W34

RELIGIOUS TOLERANCE - UNITED STATES.
United States. Equal Employment Opportunity Commission. Hearings before the United States Equal Employment Opportunity Commission on religious accommodation . [Washington] , 1979. x, 649 p. ; LC Card 80-601627   DDC 331.13/3 19
HD4903.5.U58 U536 1979

RELOCATION (HOUSING) - LAW AND LEGISLATION - UNITED STATES.
United States. Congress. Senate. Committee on Governmental Affairs. Subcommittee on Intergovernmental Relations. Amendments to the uniform relocation assistance and property acquisitions policies act of 1970 . Washington , 1980. vi, 813 p. ; LC Card 80-601495   DDC 343.73/025 19
KF26 .G6738 1979g

RELOCATION (HOUSING) - NEW YORK (CITY)
New York (State). Division of Audits and Accounts. Client relocation and related payments, New York City Human Resources Administration. [Albany] , 1979. 4, 27 leaves ; LC Card 79-624387   DDC 352.7/5/097471 19
HV87.N5 N46 1979

RELOCATION (HOUSING) - NEW YORK (STATE) - NIAGARA FALLS.
United States. Congress. House. Committee on Interstate and Foreign Commerce. Subcommittee on Oversight and Investigations. Love Canal, health studies and relocation . Washington , 1980. v, 71 p. : LC Card 80-604042 DDC 363.7/28 19
KF27 .I5547 1980o

REMOTE CONTROL.
Hardesty & Hanover, firm, engineers, New York. Capital project TD-4 : remote control of

movable bridges/. [New York] , 1974. iii, 114 p., 17 leaves of plates :   *NYPL [JSF 80-410]*

Remote control of movable bridges. Hardesty & Hanover, firm, engineers, New York. Capital project TD-4 : remote control of movable bridges/. [New York] , 1974. iii, 114 p., 17 leaves of plates :   *NYPL [JSF 80-410]*

Remote sensing and non-destructive archeology /. Symposium on Cultural Resources Management and Remote Sensing, Tucson, Ariz. 1978. Washington, DC , 1978. vii, 71 p. : LC Card 80-602610   DDC 930.1/028 19
CC76.4 .S9 1978

Remote sensing and problems of the hydrosphere : proceedings of a workshop / sponsored by NASA Langley Research Center Environmental Quality Projects Office and NASA headquarters Office of Space and Terrestrial Applications and held at Warner Springs, California, January 29-31, 1979 ; Eedward D. Goldberg, editor. Washington, D.C. : National Aeronautics and Space Administration, Scientific and Technical Information Branch ; [Springfield, Va. : For sale by the National Technical Information Service], 1979. v, 56 p. : ill. ; 28 cm. (NASA conference publication . 2109) Item 830-H-10 (microfiche) Includes bibliographical references.   LC Card 81-601298   DDC 551.4/028/7 19
1. Water quality - Remote sensing - Congresses. 2. Freshwater ecology - Congresses. 3. Marine ecology - Congresses. I. Goldberg, Edward G. II. United States. National Aeronautics and Space Administration. Scientific and Technical Information Branch. III. United States. Office of Space and Terrestrial Applications. IV. Langley Research Center. Environmental Quality Projects Office. V. Workshop on "Remote sensing and Problems of the Hydrosphere" 1979 : Warner Springs, Calif.)
TD370 .R45

Remote sensing and problems of the hydrosphere : a focus for future research : proceedings of a working group meeting / sponsored by NASA Langley Research Center Environmental Quality Projects Office and NASA Headquarters Office of Space and Terrestrial Applications and held at New Orleans, Louisiana, May 9-11, 1979 ; Edward D. Goldberg, editor. Washington, D.C. : National Aeronautics and Space Administration, Scientific and Technical Information Office, 1980. iv, 30 p. ; 27 cm. (NASA conference publication . 2132) Includes bibliographies. LC Card 80-603169   DDC 553.7/028/7 19
1. Water - Pollution - Remote sensing - Congresses. 2. Environmental monitoring - Congresses. I. Goldberg, Edward D. II. United States. Langley Research Center, Hampton, Va. Environmental Quality Projects Office. III. United States. Office of Space and Terrestrial Applications. IV. Series: United States. National Aeronautics and Space Administration. NASA conference publication , 2132.
TD419.5 .R45

REMOTE SENSING - CONGRESSES.
Remote Sensing Symposium, Reston, Va., 1979. Remote Sensing Symposium, 29-31 October 1979, Sheraton International Conference Center, Reston, Virginia /. [Washington] [1980] xi, 383, 27 p. : LC Card 80-602920   DDC 621.36/78 19
G70.4 .R468 1979

REMOTE SENSING - GOVERNMENT POLICY - UNITED STATES.
United States. Congress. House. Committee on Science and Technology. Subcommittee on Space Science and Applications. Operational civil remote sensing systems . Washington , 1980. iii, 315 p. : LC Card 80-603708   DDC 338.4/76213678 19
KF27 .S3995 1980a

United States. Congress. Senate. Committee on Commerce, Science, and Transportation. Subcommittee on Science, Technology, and Space. Civil remote sensing satellite system . Washington , 1980. iv, 237 p. : LC Card 80-603670   DDC 338.4/76213678 19
KF26 .C697 1980e

REMOTE SENSING - ILLINOIS.
Illinois. Environmental Protection Agency. A land cover inventory from space . Springfield, Ill. , 1978. x, 73, [23] p. : LC Card 79-621007 DDC 333.73/13/028 19
HD211.I3 I33 1978

REMOTE SENSING - STUDY AND TEACHING - CONGRESSES.
Conference of Remote Sensing Educators, Stanford University, 1978. Conference of Remote Sensing Educators (CORSE-78) . [Washington, D.C.] [Springfield, Va.] 1980. xviii, 645 p. : LC Card 80-602394   DDC 621.36/78/0711 19
G70.4 .C64 1978

Remote sensing supplement .
(no. 3) Lyons, Thomas R. Aerial anthropological perspectives . Washington, D.C. , 1980. p. cm. LC Card 80-25967 DDC 930.1/028 s 016.9301/028 19
CC76.4 .L96 Suppl., no. 3 Z5133.A34

Remote Sensing Symposium, Reston, Va., 1979.
Remote Sensing Symposium, 29-31 October 1979, Sheraton International Conference Center, Reston, Virginia / organized by the U. S. Army Engineer Topographic Laboratories ; sponsored by the Civil Works Directorate Office, Chief of Engineers. [Washington] : U. S. Army Corps of Engineers, [1980] xi, 383, 27 p. : ill. ; 27 cm. Includes bibliographical references. LC Card 80-602920   DDC 621.36/78 19
1. Remote sensing - Congresses. I. United States. Army Engineer Topographic Laboratories. II. United States. Army. Corps of Engineers. Directorate of Civil Works. III. United States. Army. Corps of Engineers.
G70.4 .R468 1979

REMOTE SENSING - TEXAS.
Texas. Natural Resources Information System Task Force. Landsat in Texas State agencies, April 1979. [Austin] [1979] 18 leaves ; LC Card 80-621072   DDC 333.7/09764 19
G70.5.U6 T49 1979

Removal of organic contaminants from aluminum chloride solutions /. White, J. C. (Jack C.) Avondale, Md. , 1981. p. cm. LC Card 81-607812   DDC 622 s 622/.34926 19
TN23 .U43 TP245.A4

Removing children from adult jails . Illinois. University at Urbana-Champaign. Community Research Forum. Champaign, Ill. , c1980. 89, [17] p. : LC Card 80-622234   DDC 365 19
HV9104 .I43 1980

Renaissance eloquence : studies in the theory and practice of Renaissance rhetoric / edited by James J. Murphy. Berkeley : University of California Press, 1981, c1982. p. cm. Bibliography: p. Includes index. ISBN 0-520-04543-2 LC Card 81-13128   DDC 808/.009/03 19
1. Rhetoric - 1500-1800 - Congresses. I. Murphy, James Jerome.
PN171.6 .R4 1982

RENAISSANCE - SOURCES - BIBLIOGRAPHY - CATALOGS.
Illinois. University at Urbana-Champaign. Library. Rare Book Room. The Renaissance at Illinois . [Urbana Ill.] , c1980. 58 p. : LC Card 80-622396   DDC 011/.44/0977366 19
Z6207.R4 I43 1980 CB361

RENAL INSUFFICIENCY - MISCELLANEA.
Schwitters, Sylvia Yuen, 1942- About kidney failure, dialysis, and transplantation /. Honolulu, Hawaii [1982] p. cm. LC Card 81-2538   DDC 617/.461 19
RC918.R4 S45

Renaud, Bertrand M. (joint author) Pham, Tu Duc. Labor force growth and employment expansion in Hawaii /. [Honolulu, Hawaii] [1979] 38, [1] p. : LC Card 80-623585 DDC 331.12/09969 19
HD5725.H3 P45

Renault, Pierre, 1936- Satellite Conference on Naltrexone, Richmond, 1976. Narcotic antagonists, naltrexone . Rockville, Md. , Springfield, Va.] 1976. x, 181 p. : LC Card 76-40692 DDC 615/.7822 19
RC568.H4 S27 1976

Rendall, Marian K. A guide to some research collections in the University Library / by Marian K. Rendall and others; edited by Kenneth J. Carpenter. Reno: University of Nevada, University Library, 1971. ca. 140 p.; 28 cm.
1. Nevada. University. Library. 2. Library resources - Nevada - Reno. I. Carpenter, Kenneth J. II. Nevada. University. Library. III. Title.
NYPL [JFF 80-473]

RENDERING WORKS.
Osag, T. R. Control of odors from

inedibles-rendering plants /. Research Triangle
Park, N. C., 1974. vi, 51 p. in various pagings.
NYPL [JSF 80-793]

**"Renegotiable rate" mortgage proposals of
Federal Home Loan Bank Board** . United
States. Congress. House. Committee on
Government Operations. Commerce, Consumer,
and Monetary Affairs Subcommittee.
Washington , 1980. v, 776 p. ; LC Card
80-602892 DDC 332.7/22 19
KF27 .G634 1980b

RENEWABLE ENERGY SOURCES.
Parker, Harry W. Alternative energy sources for
agricultural applications including gasification of
fibrous residues . [Austin] [1979] xi, 101 p. :
LC Card 80-620767 DDC 333.79/38 19
TJ163.2 .P362

**RENEWABLE ENERGY SOURCES -
ALASKA - TANANA LOOP.**
Skaggs, Samuel. A design for agriculture in the
Tanana Loop . [Juneau] , 1978. ii, 61 p. : LC
Card 79-620899 DDC 338.1/09798/6 19
S451.A3 S58

**RENEWABLE ENERGY SOURCES -
FLORIDA.**
United States. Congress. House. Committee on
Science and Technology. Subcommittee on
Energy Development and Applications.
Florida's renewable energy potential .
Washington , 1980 [i.e. 1981] iii, 226 p. : LC
Card 81-600971 DDC 333.7/09759 19
KF27 .S3934 1980f

**RENEWABLE ENERGY SOURCES -
HANDBOOKS, MANUALS, ETC.**
Energy education guidebook. [Washington,
D.C.] , 1980. xi, 209 p. : LC Card 80-603568
DDC 333.79/07/1 19
TJ163.3 .E544

**RENEWABLE ENERGY SOURCES - LAW
AND LEGISLATION - UNITED STATES.**
United States. Congress. Senate. Committee on
Energy and Natural Resources. Pacific basin
energy . Washington , 1980. iv, 546 p. : LC
Card 81-600636 DDC 346.7304/679
347.3064679 19
KF26 .E55 1980i

**RENEWABLE ENERGY SOURCES -
MONTANA.**
Montana. Energy Division. Montana renewable
energy viability project . Helena, Mont. , 1980.
v, 103 p. : LC Card 80-622559 DDC 333.79 19
TJ163.25.U6 M653 1980

**RENEWABLE ENERGY SOURCES - NEW
YORK (STATE)**
Cline, James G. The status of alternative energy
technologies, March 1980 /. Albany, N.Y.
(Assembly P.O. Box 167, Albany 12248)
[1980] 23 p. ; LC Card 81-621009 DDC
333.79/09747 19
TJ163.25.U6 C59

**RENEWABLE ENERGY SOURCES - UNITED
STATES.**
Quammen, David, 1948- Appropriate jobs .
Butte, Mont. , c1980. 14 p. : LC Card 80-138213
DDC 331.12/0973 19
HC103.7 .Q35

United States. Congress. Senate. Committee on
Agriculture, Nutrition, and Forestry.
Subcommittee on Agricultural Research and
General Legislation. Agricultural waste products
as alternative energy sources . Washington ,
1980. iii, 74 p. ; LC Card 80-602751 DDC
333.79/38 19
KF26 .A3534 1980

United States. Congress. Senate. Committee on
Energy and Natural Resources. Subcommittee
on Energy Conservation and Supply.
International applications of renewable energy
resources . Washington , 1980. iii, 240 p. : LC
Card 81-600634 DDC 333.79 19
KF26 .E553 1980d

**RENEWABLE NATURAL RESOURCES -
GOVERNMENT POLICY - UNITED
STATES.**
United States. Congress. House. Committee on
Agriculture. Subcommittee on Forests. 1980
RPA program and policy statement .
Washington , 1980 [i.e. 1981] iv, 234 p. : LC
Card 81-601149 DDC 333.75/0973 19
KF27 .A348 1980c

**RENEWABLE NATURAL RESOURCES -
UNITED STATES.**
United States. Forest Service. The 1980 report
to Congress on the nation's renewable resources
/. [Washington, D.C.] [1980] xvii, 155 p. : LC
Card 80-602939 DDC 333.7/0973 19
HC103.7 .U52 1980

Renewable ocean energy sources /. Baham
Corporation. Washington, D.C. , 1978- v. : LC
Card 80-502142 DDC 333.91/64 19
TK1056 .B33 1978

Renewable ocean energy sources. United States.
Congress. Office of Technology Assessment.
Washington , 1978- v. : LC Card 78-600053
DDC 333.91/64 19
TJ163.2 .U48 1978

Renner, Louis L., 1926- Pioneer missionary to the
Bering Strait Eskimos : Bellarmine Lafortune,
S.J. / by Louis L. Renner, in collaboration with
Dorothy Jean Ray. 1st ed. Portland, Ore. :
published by Binford & Mort for the Alaska
Historical Commission, 1979. xv, 207 p. : ill. ;
24 cm. Bibliography: p. 183-191. Includes index.
ISBN 0-8323-0343-7 : LC Card 79-53362
1. Lafortune, Bellarmine, 1869-1947. 2. Eskimos -
Alaska - Bering Strait region - Missions. 3.
Missionaries - Alaska - Biography. 4. Eskimos -
Alaska - Seward Peninsula - Missions. I. Ray, Dorothy
Jean, joint author. II. Alaska Historical Commission.
III. Title.
E99.E7 L257 **NYPL [JFE 80-4064]**

Reno Research Center. Shanks, D. E. (Donald
E.) Recovery of aluminum hydroxy sulfate from
aluminum sulfate solution by high-temperature
hydrolysis /. [Washington] [1981] p. cm. LC
Card 80-606902 DDC 622 s 622/.34926 19
TN23 .U43 TP152.H82

Rensselaer County, N. Y. Bureau of Planning.
Capital improvement program / Rensselaer
County Bureau of Planning. Troy, N. Y.: The
Bureau, 1974. 30 leaves; 28 cm. Microfilm.
"NYP-1038"
1. Capital budget - New York (State) - Rensselaer
County. I. Title. **NYPL [*ZT-1264]**

**Rensselaer County, N. Y. Planning Bureau of.
see Rensselaer County, N. Y. Bureau of
Planning.**

RENT SUBSIDIES - UNITED STATES.
United States. Dept. of Housing and Urban
Development. Office of Policy Development
and Research. Lower Income Housing
Assistance Program (Section 8) . [Washington] ,
Washington , 1978 i.e. 1979. xx, 101 p. : LC
Card 79-602087
HD7293 .A5 1979b **NYPL [JLF 81-553]**

**RENT SUBSIDIES - UNITED STATES -
STATISTICS.**
Yap, Lorene. Lower Income Housing Assistance
Program (Section 8) . Washington , 1978 i.e.
1979. ix, 232 p. ; LC Card 79-602558
HD7293 .A5 1979b Suppl.
NYPL [JLF 81-460]

Rental housing . United States. Congress. Senate.
Committee on Banking, Housing and Urban
Affairs. Subcommittee on Housing and Urban
Affairs. Washington , 1980. 3 v. : LC Card
80-602974 DDC 338.4/73635/0973 19
KF26 .B3945 1980b

**RENTAL HOUSING - CALIFORNIA -
FINANCE.**
California. Legislature. Assembly. Committee on
Housing and Community Development.
Property taxation (ACA 55-Mori), housing
program incentives . Sacramento, CA [1979] ii,
95, [21] p. : LC Card 80-621896 DDC
338.4/33335/09794 19
KFC10.4 .H67 1979a

**Rental housing conversion and sale (Council Act
3-204)** . United States. Congress. House.
Committee on the District of Columbia.
Washington , 1980. iv, 170 p. : LC Card
81-601407 DDC 346.7304/33 347.306433 19
KF27 .D5 1980a

**RENTAL HOUSING - LAW AND
LEGISLATION - UNITED STATES.**
United States. Congress. Senate. Committee on
Banking, Housing and Urban Affairs.
Subcommittee on Housing and Urban Affairs.
Rental housing . Washington , 1980. 3 v. : LC
Card 80-602974 DDC 338.4/73635/0973 19
KF26 .B3945 1980b

**RENTAL HOUSING - LAW AND
LEGISLATION - WASHINGTON (D.C.)**
United States. Congress. House. Committee on
the District of Columbia. Rental housing
conversion and sale (Council Act 3-204) .
Washington , 1980. iv, 170 p. : LC Card
81-601407 DDC 346.7304/33 347.306433 19
KF27 .D5 1980a

RENTAL HOUSING - NEW JERSEY.
United States. Congress. Senate. Committee on
Banking, Housing and Urban Affairs.
Subcommittee on Housing and Urban Affairs.
Rental housing . Washington , 1980. 3 v. : LC
Card 80-602974 DDC 338.4/73635/0973 19
KF26 .B3945 1980b

**RENTAL HOUSING - NEW YORK (CITY) -
FINANCE.**
New York (State). Division of Audits and
Accounts. The financial viability of Starrett City
under the New York State Mitchell-Lama
Program. Albany [1980] 32 p., [15] leaves p. ;
LC Card 80-622788 DDC 363.5/8 19
HD7288.85.U62 N75 1980

RENTAL HOUSING - UNITED STATES.
United States. Congress. House. Committee on
Banking, Finance, and Urban Affairs.
Subcommittee on Housing and Community
Development. Task Force on Rental Housing.
Task Force on Rental Housing . Washington ,
1980. vii, 1072 p. : LC Card 80-603282 DDC
363.5/8 19
KF27 .B5467 1980

United States. Congress. Senate. Committee on
Banking, Housing and Urban Affairs.
Subcommittee on Housing and Urban Affairs.
Rental housing . Washington , 1980. 3 v. : LC
Card 80-602974 DDC 338.4/73635/0973 19
KF26 .B3945 1980b

Rentoul, J. N., 1909- Growing orchids :
cymbidiums and slippers / J.N. Rentoul.
Seattle : University of Washington Press, [1981]
c1980. p. cm. Bibliography: p. Includes index. ISBN
0-295-95839-1 LC Card 81-3023 DDC
635.9/3415 19
1. Orchid culture. 2. Cymbidium. 3. Paphiopedilum. I.
Title.
SB409 .R4 1981

RENUNCIATION (PHILOSOPHY)
Van Herik, Judith. Freud on femininity and
faith /. Berkeley , c1981. p. cm. ISBN
0-520-04368-5 LC Card 81-3413 DDC
155.3/33/0924 19
BF173.F85 V26

Renwick Gallery. Folk art of the Oregon country
/. [Salem?] , c1980. 128 p. : LC Card 80-622779
DDC 745/.09795/074013 19
NK805.O7 F64

Reorganization plan no. 1 of 1980 . United
States. Congress. Senate. Committee on
Governmental Affairs. Washington , 1980. iv,
402 p. ; LC Card 80-603288 DDC 353.0087/22 19
KF26 .G67 1980g

**Reorganization plan no. 1 of 1980 (Nuclear
Regulatory Commission)** . United States.
Congress. House. Committee on Government
Operations. Legislation and National Security
Subcommittee. Washington , 1980. iii, 100 p. ;
LC Card 80-602817 DDC 353.0087/22 19
KF27 .G6676 1980b

**Reorganization study of federal community and
economic development programs.** President's
Reorganization Project (U. S.) Organizing for
development . Washington, D.C. , 1979. viii,
66, [36] p. : LC Card 81-601244 DDC 338.973 19
HC110.P63 P73 1979

Reorganizing for pacification support /. Scoville,
Thomas W. Washington, D.C. [1981] p. cm.
LC Card 81-10204 DDC 959.704/3373 19
DS558.2 .S27

REPARATION - ABSTRACTS.
Cain, Anthony A. Restitution . [Washington,
D.C.] [1979 i.e. 1980] vii, 61 p. ; LC Card
80-601596 DDC 364.6/8 19
HV8608 .C34

REPARATION - LOUISIANA.
Louisiana. Criminal Justice Information System
Division. Crime victim reparation legislation.
Baton Rouge , 1978. 36 p. ; DDC 344.73/03288 19
KF1328 .A833

REPARATION - NORTH DAKOTA.
North Dakota. Laws, statutes, etc. [Workmen's compensation act.] North Dakota Workmen's compensation act and Crime victims reparations act and rules of procedure, effective July 1, 1979 /. [Bismarck] [1979] 105 p. ; LC Card 80-621922 DDC 344.784/021/02632 19
KFN8942.A335 A2 1979

REPARATION - UNITED STATES.
Carrow, Deborah. Crime victim compensation /. [Washington, D.C.] [1980] i, 235 p. : LC Card 80-602243 DDC 362.8/8 19
HV6250.3.U5 C37

United States. Congress. House. Committee on the Judiciary. Subcommittee on Criminal Justice. Compensating crime victims . Washington , 1980 [i.e. 1981] iii, 228 p. ; LC Card 81-600967 DDC 344.73/03288 347.3043288 19
KF27 .J859 1979

REPARATION - UNITED STATES - ABSTRACTS.
Cain, Anthony A. Restitution . [Washington, D.C.] [1979 i.e. 1980] vii, 61 p. ; LC Card 80-601596 DDC 364.6/8 19
HV8688 .C34

REPARATION - UNITED STATES - STATES.
Louisiana. Criminal Justice Information System Division. Crime victim reparation legislation. Baton Rouge , 1978. 36 p. ; LC Card 79-621106 DDC 344.73/03288 19
KF1328 .A833

REPARATIONS.
United States. Congress. House. Committee on the Judiciary. Subcommittee on Administrative Law and Governmental Relations. Compensation of military personnel and government employees for loss of personal property incident to their foreign service . Washington , 1980. iii, 110 p. : LC Card 80-602775 DDC 346.7304/7 19
KF27 .J832 1980

Repayment of loans made to state unemployment compensation programs . United States. Congress. Senate. Committee on Finance. Subcommittee on Unemployment and Related Problems. Washington , 1980. iii, 188 p. : LC Card 80-603704 DDC 344.73/024 347.30424 19
KF26 .F58 1980

Repeal of "equal time" requirements . United States. Congress. House. Committee on Interstate and Foreign Commerce. Subcommittee on Communications. Washington , 1980. ii, 106 p. ; LC Card 80-602171 DDC 343.73/09945 19
KF27 .I5537 1980

Replacement of earnings of the disabled under social security . Muller, L. Scott. Washington, D.C. , 1980] vi, 45 p. : LC Card 80-600107 DDC 368.4/3/00973 s 368.4/3/00973 19
HD7123 .A39 no. 53 HD7106.U5

Replication of habitat profiles for birds /. Johnston, Richard F. Lawrence , 1979. 11 p. : LC Card 79-624990 DDC 598.2/5 19
QL677.5 .J63

Report. United States. Congress. House. Select Committee on Emancipation and Colonization. Washington , 1862. 83 p. ;
NYPL [Sc Micro R-3657]

Report, "America's small business economy agenda for action" . United States. Congress. House. Committee on Small Business. Washington , 1980. iii, 111 p. ; LC Card 80-602911 DDC 338.6/42/0973 19
KF27 .S6 1980

Report and recommendations /. Oregon. Legislative Assembly. Legislative Task Force on Hospice. [Salem, Or.] [1980] v, 59 p. ; LC Card 81-620893 DDC 362.1/9 19
R726.8 .O73 1980

Report and recommendations of the Interim Committee on Corrections Policy and Facility Needs . Montana. Legislature. Study Committee on Corrections. Helena, Mont. (Room 138, State Capitol, Helena 59601) [1980] 119 p. in various pagings ; LC Card 81-621005 DDC 344.786/035 347.860435 19
KFM9587 .A25 1980

Report and recommendations of the State of New Jersey, Commission of Investigation on questionable practices and procedures by local, county, and other public bodies in the purchase and administration of public insurance programs. New Jersey. Commission of Investigation. [Trenton, N.J.] [1980?] 367 p. : LC Card 80-623824 DDC 350.82/56/09749 19
HG8215.N5 N48 1980

Report and recommendations on the misuse of public funds in the operation of non-public schools for handicapped children /. New Jersey. Commission of Investigation. [Trenton] [1978] 211 p. ; LC Card 78-623079 *LB2827.5.N5 N48 1978*
NYPL [JLF 80-1650]

Report and recommendations to the Governor from the Oklahoma Delegation to the White House Conference on Balanced National Growth and Economic Development. Oklahoma. Delegation to the White House Conference on Balanced National Growth and Economic Development, Washington, D.C., 1978. [Oklahoma City] , 1978. 12, 2 [i.e. 3] leaves ; LC Card 79-620770 DDC 338.9766 19
HC107.O5 O44 1978

Report and recommendations to the 1980 session, Sixty-eighth General Assembley [sic] from the State Board of Public Instruction. Iowa. State Board of Public Instruction. [Des Moines, Iowa] [1980] 38 p. ; LC Card 80-622984 DDC 370/.9777 19
LA286 .A495 1980

Report and tentative recommendations of the Committee to Consider Standards for Admission to Practice in the Federal Courts to the Judicial Conference of the United States, September 21, 22, 1978. Judicial Conference of the UnitedStates. Committee to consider Standards for Admission to Practice in the Federal Courts. [Washington, D.C.] [1978] 167 p. in various pagings ; LC Card 79-601448 DDC 347.73/504 19
KF302 .J8

Report availability notice : Summer 1974 . United States. Office of Naval Research. Ocean Science and Technology Division. Arlington, VA. , 1974. ii, 308 p. ; *NYPL [JSF 80-767]*

Report by deputy mayor Edward F. Cavanagh, jr. to Mayor Robert F. Wagner regarding the Women's House of Detention. New York (City). Office of the Mayor. [New York] 1965. 9 p. ; *NYPL [*ZT-1247]*

Report of agent of the Passamaquoddy tribe of Indians. Maine. Agent Passamaquody Indians. Augusta. *NYPL [*ZAN-H394]*

Report of congressional study group visit by the Committee on Education and Labor to the Department of Defense overseas schools, April 1979 /. United States. Congress. House. Committee on Education and Labor. Washington , 1979. ii, 7 p. ; LC Card 80-601733 DDC 355.3/4 19
LC5081 .U54 1979

Report of Governor Brendan Byrne's Hazardous Waste Advisory Commission. New Jersey. Hazardous Waste Advisory Commission. Trenton, N.J. [1980] 70, [36] p. : LC Card 80-621669 DDC 363.7/28 19
TD811.5 .N48 1980

Report of nurse population in Oklahoma, 1979 /. Oklahoma. Board of Nurse Registration and Nursing Education. Oklahoma City, Okla. [1980] [11] p. : LC Card 80-623277 DDC 331.12/5161073/09766 19
RT5.O5 O32 1980

Report of papers presented at the spring conference, April 19, 20, 21, 1979 . Spring Conference "Relationships Between People and the Land," University of South Dakota, 1979. [Vermillion, S.D.] [1979?] 211 p. ; LC Card 80-621621 DDC 970.004/97 19
E98.R3 S724 1979

Report of results of Standards and Goals Conference held at Civic Center, December 6, 7, and 8, 1973 /. Maine. Law Enforcement Planning & Assistance Agency. Augusta, Me. [1974] ca. 150 p. ; LC Card 80-623219 DDC 363.2/09741 19
HV7571 .M22 1974

Report of Seminar Bankruptcy Law (New), August 24-25, 1979. Kentucky. University. Office of Continuing Legal Education. Seminar on Bankruptcy Law (New) . Lexington, Ky. , c1980. 100 p. ; LC Card 80-131695 DDC 346.73/078 19
KF1524.A2 K46

Report of seminar, Kentucky civil procedure. Seminar on Kentucky Civil Procedure, University of Kentucky, 1979. Seminar on Kentucky Civil Procedure, held at the College of Law, University of Kentucky, Lexington, Kentucky, June 15-16, 1979 /. Lexington, Ky. , c1980. 113 p. ; LC Card 80-131042 DDC 347.769/05 19
KFK1730.A2 S44 1979

Report of Statewide Task Force on School Counseling /. California. Statewide Task Force on School Counseling. [Sacramento] [1979] iii, 41 p. ; LC Card 80-621961 DDC 371.4/09794 19
LB1027.5 .C347 1979

Report of Task Force on Epidemiology of Respiratory Diseases . National Heart, Lung, and Blood Institute. Division of Lung Diseases. Task Force on Epidemiology of Respiratory Diseases. [Bethesda, Md.?] , 1980. vii, 244 p. : LC Card 81-600681 DDC 614.5/92/00973 19
RA645.R4 N37 1980

Report of the Assembly Judiciary, Law, Public Safety, and Defense Committee, Juvenile Justice Subcommittee, on juvenile violence, vandalism, and the juvenile justice system / State of New Jersey, Assembly Judiciary, Law, Public Safety, and Defense Committee. Trenton, N.J. : The Committee, [1980] ii, 30 p. ; 28 cm. "May 8, 1980." LC Card 80-624394 DDC 364.3/6/09749 19
1. Juvenile delinquency - New Jersey. 2. Violence - New Jersey. 3. Vandalism - New Jersey. 4. Juvenile courts - New Jersey. I. New Jersey. Legislature. General Assembly. Judiciary, Law, Public Safety, and Defense Committee. Subcommittee on Juvenile Justice.
HV9105.N5 R46

Report of the Attorney General on the February 2 and 3, 1980 riot at the Penitentiary of New Mexico. New Mexico. Attorney General's Office. [Santa Fe] , 1980- v. : LC Card 80-623176 DDC 365/.641 19
HV9475.N62 N46 1980

Report of the Blue Ribbon Commission on the State Personnel Act to the eleventh Alaska State Legislature, second session /. Alaska. Blue Ribbon Commission on the State Personnel Act. Juneau, Alaska , 1980. viii, 49, [32] p. ; LC Card 80-622121 DDC 353.9798001 19
JK9555 .A52 1980

Report of the Chief of the Forest Service. United States. Forest Service. 1882/83- [Washington]
NYPL [VQO (U. S. Forest Service. Report of the Chief of the Forest Service)]

Report of the Commission on Presidential Press Conferences. Commission on Presidential Press Conference (U. S.) [Charlottesville] [Washington, D.C. , c1981] 9 p. ; ISBN 0-8191-1461-8 (pbk.) : LC Card 81-140872 DDC 353.03/5 19
JK518 .C62 1981

Report of the Commodity Futures Trading Commission on recent developments in the silver futures markets [prepared for the] Committee on Agriculture, Nutrition, and Forestry, United States Senate. United States. Commodity Futures Trading Commission. Washington , 1980. viii, 123 p. : LC Card 80-602270 DDC 332.63/28 19
HG307.U5 U54 1980

Report of the delegation to Africa . United States. Congress. House. Committee on Armed Services. Delegation to Africa. Washington , 1980. iii, 29 p. ; LC Card 80-601793 DDC 355/.03306 19
DT30 .U58 1980

Report of the Federal Labor Relations Council, January 1, 1970-December 31, 1976. United States. Federal Labor Relations Council. Washington , 1977. 90 p. ; LC Card 78-600833 DDC 344.73/0189041353 19
KF5365 .A837

Report of the Floodplain Management Subcommittee to the Alaska Land Managers Cooperative Task Force. Alaska Land Managers Cooperative Task Force. Floodplain Management Subcommittee. [Juneau] , 1979. 27, [41] p. ;   LC Card 79-625492   DDC 363.3/493/09761 19
GB565.A4 A42 1979

Report of the Forest Service, highlights. United States. Forest Service. 1976/77- [Washington]   LC Card 80-648919   *NYPL [JLM 81-47]*

Report of the Governor's Jail and Detention Standards Review Committee /. Illinois. Governor's Jail and Detention Standards Review Committee. [Springfield, Ill.] [1979] ca. 200 p. in various pagings ;   LC Card 80-623376   DDC 353.97730084/95 19
HV8332 .I32 1979

Report of the Governor's Primary Care Task Force /. North Carolina. Governor's Primary Care Task Force. [Raleigh , 1979] ii, 23 p. ;   LC Card 80-622769   DDC 362.1/09756 19
RA412.5.U6 N8 1979

Report of the Group of Governmental Experts on Reverse Transfer of Technology, held at the Palais des Nations, Geneva, from 27 February to 7 March, 1978. United Nations. Conference on Trade and Development. Group of Governmental Experts on Reverse Transfer of Technology. [New York] , 1978. 30, 7, 4 p. ;   LC Card 78-111923   DDC 300 s 331.12/791 19
JX1977 .A2 TD/B/C.6/28 TD/B/C.6/AC.4/10 HD8038.A1

Report of the House State Planning and Community Affairs Committee and the Senate Industry, Labor, and Tourism Committee on sunset legislation. Georgia. General Assembly. House of Representatives. State Planning and Community Affairs Committee. Atlanta [1979] 42 p. ;   LC Card 80-623191   DDC 342.758/06 19
KFG11.82 .P55 1979

Report of the Illinois Citizens Task Force on Homeowners' Insurance Availability. Illinois. Citizens Task Force on Homeowners' Insurance Availability. [Chicago] [1979?] 43, [45] p. :   LC Card 80-622570   DDC 368.1 19
HG9986.35.I3 I44 1979

The report of the intensive survey of the Richard B. Russell Dam and Lake, Savannah River, Georgia and South Carolina /. Taylor, Richard Lee, 1946- Columbia, S.C. [1978] xvii, 531 p. :   LC Card 79-623568   DDC 975.7/35 19
F292.R49 T39

The report of the Interagency Task Force on Thrift Institutions . United States. Interagency Task force on Thrift Institutions. Washington , 1980. viii, 267 p. ;   LC Card 80-603280   DDC 332.2/0973 19
HG2151 .U53 1980

Report of the Joint Advisory Committee on State Prison Facilities and Incarceration Alternatives. California. Legislature. Joint Advisory Committee on State Prison Facilities and Incarceration Alternatives. [Sacramento, Calif. (Rm. 6001, State Capitol, Sacramento 95812)] [1978] 41 p. ;   LC Card 81-620647   DDC 365/.9794 19
HV9475.C2 C35 1978

Report of the Joint Committee for the Courts of Justice of the House and Senate studying sentencing in criminal cases to the General Assembly of Virginia. Virginia. General Assembly. Joint Committee for the Courts of Justice. Richmond, Va. , 1980. 19 p. ;   LC Card 80-623756   DDC 300/.9755 s 345.755/0772 300/.9755 s 347.5505772 19
J87 .V9 1979c no. 26 KFV2411.62

Report of the Joint Legislative audit and Review Commission on federal funds in Virginia to the Governor and the General Assembly of Virginia. Virginia. General Assembly. Joint Legislative Audit and Review Commission. Richmond, Va. , 1981. vii, 122 p. ;   LC Card 81-621744   DDC 300/9755 s 353.97550072/52 19
J87 .V9 1981c no. 6 HJ745

Report of the Joint Legislative/Executive Task Force on Prison Overcrowding. Michigan. Joint Legislative/Executive Task Force on Prison Overcrowding. [Lansing, Mich. , 1980] iii leaves, 24, [85] p. :   LC Card 80-624338   DDC

365/.646 19
HV8342 .M53 1980

Report of the Joint Standing Committee on Aging, Retirement, and Veterans of the statutory review of the rules of the Bureau of Veterans' Services. Maine. Legislature. Joint Standing Committee on Aging, Retirement, and Veterans. [Augusta, Me.] [1980?] 27 leaves ;   LC Card 80-623270   DDC 343.741/011 347.410311 19
KFM11.62 .A34 1980

Report of the Joint Subcommittee of the Courts of Justice Committees of the Senate and House of Delegates Studying Virginia's Mechanic's Lien Laws Under House Joint Resolution No. 229 to the Governor and the General Assembly of Virginia. Virginia. General Assembly. Joint Subcommittee of the Courts of Justice Committees of the Senate and House of Delegates Studying Virginia's Mechanic's Lien Laws Under House Joint Resolution No. 229. Richmond , 1980. 10 p. ;   LC Card 80-623941   DDC 346.755/024 19
J87 .V9 1980c, no. 32 KFV2411.62.M

Report of the Joint Subcommittee of the House and Senate Transportation Committees on Hazardous Materials /. Tennessee. General Assembly. Joint Subcommittee on Hazardous Materials. [Nashville] [1980] 77 p. ;   LC Card 80-623841   DDC 343.768/093 347.680393 19
KFT11.62 .H39 1980

Report of the Joint Subcommittee Studying the Virginia Resource Information System (VARIS) to the Governor and the General Assembly of Virginia. Virginia. General Assembly. Joint Subcommittee Studying the Virginia Resource Information System. Richmond , 1980. 134 p. ;   LC Card 80-622729   DDC 300/.9755 s 025/.063337/09755 19
J87 .V9 1980c no. 20 HC107.V8

Report of the Joint Subcommittee to Study the Care of the Impaired Elderly to the Governor and the General Assembly of Virginia. Virginia. General Assembly. Joint Subcommittee to Study the Care of the Impaired Elderly. Richmond , 1980. 43, 7, [8] p. ;   LC Card 81-621718   DDC 300/.9755 s 362.6/09755 19
J87 .V9 1980c, no. 20a HV1468.V8

Report of the Joint Subcommittee to Study the Virginia Individual Income Tax Structure to the Governor and the General Assembly of Virginia. Virginia. General Assembly. Joint Subcommittee to Study the Virginia Industrial Income Tax Structure. Richmond, Va. , 1980. 133 p. ;   LC Card 80-623141   DDC 300/.9755 s 343.75505/2 19
J87 .V9 1980b no. 16 KFV2411.62.S75

Report of the Liquor Price Fixing Investigation Commission to the 1978 session of the Connecticut General Assembly, State of Connecticut pursuant to Special act 77-97 . Connecticut. General Assembly. Liquor Price Fixing Investigation Commission. [Hartford, Conn.] , 1978. iii, 138 p. ;   LC Card 80-621801   DDC 343.746/08556635 347.46038556635 19
KFC3611.62 .L56 1978

Report of the Long-range Planning Committee, Michigan Council for the Arts. Michigan Council for the Arts. Long-range Planning Committee. Detroit , 1977. 75 p. :   LC Card 79-128232   DDC 353.97740085/4 19
NX24.M5 M5326

Report of the Motor Vehicle Service Delivery Task Force. New Jersey. Motor Vehicle Service Delivery Task Force. [Trenton, N.J.] , 1979. iii, 58, 67 p. ;   LC Card 80-623765   DDC 353.97490087/834 19
HE5633.N5 N47 1979

Report of the Panel on Communicative Disorders to the National Advisory Neurological and Communicative Disorders and Stroke Council, National Institute of Neurological and Communicative Disorders and Stroke. Panel on Communicative Disorders (U. S.) [Bethesda, Md.] [1979] xvii, 351 p. ;   LC Card 80-601219   DDC 616.85/5/0072073 19
RC423 .P24 1979

Report of the Panel on Convulsive and Neuromuscular Disorders to the National Advisory Neurological and Communicative Disorders and Stroke Council, National Institute of Neurological and Communicative Disorders and Stroke. Panel on Convulsive and Neuromuscular Disorders (U. S.) [Bethesda, Md.] [1979] xiii, 124 p. :   LC Card 80-601220   DDC 616.7/4/0072073 19
RC925.5 .P26 1979

Report of the Preparatory Committee on its first-[second] session /. United Nations Conference on Human Settlements, Vancouver, B.C., 1976. Preparatory Committee. [New York?] 1975-1976. 3 v. in 1 ;   LC Card 81-452275   DDC 300 s 307.7/6 19
JX1977 .A2 A/CONF.70/PC/11, etc.

Report of the presiding officer on proposed trade regulation rule . United States. Federal Trade Commission. [Washington, D.C.] [1978] vii, 373 p. ;   LC Card 79-602495   DDC 346.73/073 19
KF1040 .A68

Report of the presiding officer on proposed trade regulation rule . United States. Federal Trade Commission. [Washington] , 1979. ii, 213 p. ;   LC Card 79-602972   DDC 344.73/099 19
KF2042.P49 A877

Report of the Securities and Exchange Commission on beneficial ownership reporting requirements pursuant to section 13(h) of the Securities exchange act of 1934. United States. Securities and Exchange Commission. Washington , 1980. viii, 242 p. ;   LC Card 80-602870   DDC 346.73/0666 19
KF1448 .A88

Report of the Senate Interim Task Force on Intergovernmental Coordination. Oregon. Legislative Assembly. Senate. Interim Task Force on Intergovernmental Coordination. [Salem, Or. (447 State Capitol, Salem, Or. 97310)] [1979] xiv, 103 p. ;   LC Card 81-620891   DDC 352.0795 19
JS451 .O7 1979

Report of the Southwest Consultation on the Educational Needs of Rural Girls and Women, convened by the Information Resources Committee, Advisory Council on Women's Educational Programs in Santa Fe, New Mexico, September 10 and 11, 1976 /. Young, Tasia. Albuquerque [1976?] 25 leaves ;   LC Card 79-623319   DDC 376/.9789 19
LC1758.N6 Y68

Report of the Special Commission Relative to Evaluating the Extent of the Use of Asbestos as Fireproofing in the Schools and Public Buildings of the Commonwealth and its Containment and Removal . Massachusetts. Special Commission Relative to Evaluating the Extent of the Use of Asbestos as Fireproofing in the Schools and Public Buildings of the Commonwealth and its Containment and Removal. [Boston?] 1976 [i.e. 1977]. 34 p. ;   LC Card 77-623289   DDC 300/.9744 s 363.1/79 19
J87 .M4 1977g no. 5344 RA1231.A8

Report of the State Auditor, General Assembly and supporting functions, House of Representatives, three years ended June 30, 1979. Missouri. Auditor's Office. [Jefferson City] , 1980. i, 28 p. ;   LC Card 80-623051   DDC 328.778/0068/1 19
JK5478 .M82 1980

Report of the Steel Tripartite Committee . United States. Congress. Senate. Committee on Environment and Public Works. Washington , 1981. iii, 124 p. ;   LC Card 81-601353   DDC 338.4/7669142/0973 19
KF26 .E6 1980k

Report of the subcommittee of the Committee for Courts of Justice studying the jurisdictional limits of general district courts and juvenile and domestic relations district courts to the General Assembly of Virginia. Virginia. General Assmebly. House of Delegates. Committee for Courts of Justice. Richmond, Va. , 1980. 27 p. ;   LC Card 80-623901   DDC 300/.9755 s 347.755/012 300/.9755 s 347.550712 19
J87 .V9 1980c, no. 27 KFV2411.82.C

Report of the U. S. S. New Jersey Battleship Commission (created by JR-6 of 1975). United States S. New Jersey Battleship Commission

(N.J.) [Trenton, N.J.? , 1977?] 28, 4 p. ; LC Card 80-620534 DDC 359.3/252 19
VA65.N5 U22 1977

Report of the United Nations Conference on Science and Technology for Development, Vienna 20-31 August 1979. United Nations Conference on Science and Technology for Development, Vienna, 1979. New York , 1979. iv, 133 p. ; LC Card 80-100608 DDC 303.4/83 19
JX1977 .A2 A/CONF.81/16

Report of the unveiling and dedication of Indiana monument at Andersonville, Georgia. Indiana. Andersonville Monument Commission. Indianapolis, 1909. 128 p. LC Card 10-33016
NYPL [ITK (Andersonville) 80-3015]

Report of the 1978-79 Interim Special Advisory Committee on Nuclear Waste Disposal. Kentucky. Interim Special Advisory Committee on Nuclear Waste Disposal. Frankfort, Ky. , 1980. viii, 95 p. : LC Card 80-621286 DDC 363.7/28 19
TD898 .K46 1980

Report on assessment, equalization, and revaluation /. New Jersey. Legislature. General Assembly. Committee on Taxation. [Trenton] [1977?] 41 p. ; LC Card 78-621479
HJ4121.N5 N46 1977   **NYPL [*ZT-1263]**

Report on business expansion in the Commonwealth of Massachusetts, 1979 / Department of Commerce and Development. [Boston] : The Dept., [1980] 34 leaves ; 28 cm. Cover title. LC Card 80-623432 DDC 338.09744 19
1. Massachusetts - Industries. 2. Business enterprises - Massachusetts. I. Massachusetts. Dept. of Commerce and Development.
HC107.M4 R46

Report on C.E.T.A., the Comprehensive employment and training act program in Maine /. Maine. Legislature. Joint Standing Committee on Audit and Program Review. [Augusta, Me.] [1980] [62] leaves : LC Card 80-622815 DDC 331.11/09741 19
HD5725.M3 M335 1980

Report on compensation paid to consulting firms under selected support-service contracts /. United States. Dept. of Energy. Office of Inspector General. [Washington, D.C.] [1979] 29, [29] p. ; LC Card 80-601687 DDC 353.09/3 19
JK468.C7 U534 1979

Report on Connecticut Resources Recovery Authority, fiscal years ended June 30, 1977 and 1978. Connecticut. Auditors of Public Accounts. [Hartford] [1979?] 23 p. [20] p. ; LC Card 80-621025 DDC 353.97460077/2 19
TD794.5 .C6615 1979

Report on Department of Agriculture, fiscal years ended June 30, 1977 and 1978. Connecticut. Auditors of Public Accounts. [Hartford] [1980] 35, [25] p. ; LC Card 80-621306 DDC 353.97460072/32 19
HD1775.C8 C55 1980

Report on Department of Motor Vehicles, fiscal years ended June 30, 1977 and 1978. Connecticut. Auditors of Public Accounts. [Hartford] [1980] 25, [12] p. ; LC Card 80-621305 DDC 353.97460087/834 19
HE5633.C7 C67 1980

Report on Department of Planning and Energy Policy, fiscal years ended June 30, 1976 and 1977. Connecticut. Auditors of Public Accounts. [Hartford] [1979] 20, [6] p. ; LC Card 79-624175 DDC 353.97460072/32 19
HD9502.U53 C82 1979

Report on economic conditions in New York City. Jan./June, 1980- New York. Issued jointly by the Office of Management and Budget, and the Office of Economic Development of the City of New York.
I. New York (City). Office of Management and Budget. II. New York (City). Office of Economic Development.
NYPL [Econ. Div.]

Report on exact and statistical matching techniques /. United States. Federal Committee on Statistical Methodology. Subcommittee on Matching Techniques. [Washington] , 1980] vii, 57 p. ; LC Card 80-603147 DDC 001.4/224 19
HB849.49 .U53 1980

Report on executive agency compliance with legislative intent--1st session, 9th Legislature .

Fowler, Susi L. [Juneau, Alaska , 1976] 62, 4 p. ; LC Card 80-622554 DDC 353.979804 19
JK9538 1976 .F68

Report on Federal Government programs that relate to children, 1979 /. United States. Federal Interagency Committee for the International Year of the Child. [Washington, D.C.] , 1979. vi, 125 p. ; LC Card 79-603379
HV741 .U5245 1979   **NYPL [JLF 81-458]**

Report on health personnel in the United States. United States. Health Resources Administration. [Washington, D.C.] [1979] 38 p. ; LC Card 80-601525 DDC 331.12/3161/0973 19
RA410.7 .U555 1979

Report on my third year in office /. Washington (State). Governor, 1977- (Ray) [Olympia, Wash. , 1980] iv, 31 p. ; LC Card 80-622791 DDC 353.979703/5 19
J87 .W222 1980

Report on Office of the Medical Examiner for the fiscal years ended June 30, 1975, 1976, and 1977. Connecticut. Auditors of Public Accounts. [Hartford] [1979] 11, [7] p. ; LC Card 79-622283 DDC 353.97460072/23677 19
RA1063.4 .C66 1979

A report on pesticide use and regulatory programs in Illinois /. Enviromental Health Resource Center. Chicago, IL [1979] x, 169 p. : LC Card 80-621689 DDC 363.1/79 19
SB970.4.U5 E57 1979

Report on physical count and accountability of state investments in securities /. Montana. Office of the Legislative Auditor. Helena , 1971. iii, 25 l. ;   **NYPL [*ZT-1250]**

Report on proceedings of the 5th Annual Indian Town Hall on the the [sic] topic of tribal water rights, today's concern . Indian Town Hall, 5th, White Mountain Apache Reservation, 1977. [Phoenix] [1978] v leaves, 78 p. : LC Card 78-622727 DDC 333.33/9 19
KFA2905.6.W38 I5 1977

Report on proposed State assessments of all public utility real property in New York State /. Patenaude, John J. Albany, N.Y. [1980] 10 p. ; LC Card 80-621854 DDC 336.22/2 19
HD2767.N74 P37

A report on public and community health personnel . United States. Health Resources Administration. Bureau of Health Manpower. Washington, D.C. , 1980. viii, 220 p. ; LC Card 80-602370 DDC 331.12/913621 19
RA440.9 .U47 1980

Report on reconnaissance studies of irrigation projects . Wyoming. State Water Planning Program. [Cheyenne, Wyo,] 1977. 41 leaves in various foliations, [7] leaves of plates : LC Card 79-622405 DDC 333.91/315/0978733 19
TC824.W8 W96 1977

Report on SPEDY conferences . United States. Employment and Training Administration. Office of Youth Programs. [Washington] [1979] viii, 297 p. ; LC Card 79-603023
HD6273 .U514 1979a

Report on State Insurance Purchasing Board, fiscal year ended June 30, 1977. Connecticut. Auditors of Public Accounts. [Hartford] [1978?] 18 p. ; LC Card 78-623818 DDC 353.97460072/32 19
HG8215.C8 C62 1978

Report on statistical uses of administrative records /. United States. Federal Committee on Statistical Methodology. Subcommittee on Statistical Uses of Administrative Records. [Washington, D.C.?] , 1980 [i.e. 1981] xii, 106 p. : LC Card 81-601438 DDC 353.0081/9 19
HA37.U55 U55 1981

Report on the count and balance of cash of the trial Court of Massachusetts, the Massachusetts Appeals Court, and the Supreme Judicial Court for Suffolk County as of June 30, 1979. Massachusetts. Dept. of the State Auditor. [Boston , 1979?] 94 p. ; LC Card 80-621646 DDC 347.744/01 347.44071 19
KFM2910.5.A3 A82

Report on the environment . Indiana. Environmental Management Board. Indianapolis, Ind. , 1977. xii, 96 p. : LC Card 80-622166 DDC 363.7/009772 19
TD171.3.I6 I52 1977

Report on the examination of the accounts of the child support enforcement program as of July 1, 1976. Massachusetts. Dept. of the State Auditor. [Boston] [1977] 39 leaves ; LC Card 78-623287 DDC 353.97440084/7 19
HV742.M4 M34 1977

Report on the examination of the accounts of the Commissioner of Probation, March 8, 1976 to January 31, 1977. Massachusetts. Dept. of the State Auditor. [Boston] [1977] 11 leaves ; LC Card 78-623006 DDC 353.97440072/32 19
HV9305.M4 M26 1977

Report on the examination of the accounts of the Department of Corporations and Taxation, April 21, 1976 to February 10, 1977. Massachusetts. Dept. of the State Auditor. [Boston] [1977] 66 leaves ; LC Card 78-623288 DDC 353.97440072/32 19
HJ3303.2 .M37 1977

Report on the examination of the accounts of the Department of Correction, January 21, 1977 to February 6, 1978. Massachusetts. Dept. of the State Auditor. [Boston] [1978] 18 leaves ; LC Card 78-624160 DDC 353.97440072/32 19
HV7271 .A6 1978b

Report on the examination of the accounts of the Energy Facilities Siting Council, September 1, 1976 to July 29, 1977. Massachusetts. Dept. of the State Auditor. [Boston , 1978] 7 leaves ; LC Card 78-623293 DDC 353.97440072/32 19
HD2767.M44 M37 1978

Report on the examination of the accounts of the Government Land Bank, May 15, 1975 to October 8, 1976. Massachusetts. Dept. of the State Auditor. [Boston] [1976] 15 leaves ; LC Card 78-623296 DDC 353.97440072/32 19
HD211.M4 M37 1976

Report on the examination of the accounts of the Massachusetts Historical Commission, July 1, 1976 to June 30, 1977. Massachusetts. Dept. of the State Auditor. [Boston] [1977] 12 leaves ; LC Card 78-623294 DDC 974.4/006/0744 19
F61 .M23 1977

Report on the examination of the accounts of the Massachusetts State Lottery Commission, January 1, 1976 to December 31, 1976. Massachusetts. Dept. of the State Auditor. [Boston] [1977?] 39 leaves ; LC Card 78-623005 DDC 353.97440072/32 19
HG6133.M35 M33 1977

Report on the examination of the accounts of the Massachusetts State Lottery Commission, January 1, 1978 to June 30, 1979. Massachusetts. Dept. of the State Auditor. [Boston] [1979] 2, 54 leaves : LC Card 80-623712 DDC 353.97440072/32 19
HG6133.M35 M33 1979

Report on the examination of the accounts of the Office of the Commissioner of the Department of Food and Agriculture, July 29, 1975 to July 1, 1976. Massachusetts. Dept. of the State Auditor. [Boston , 1976] 15 leaves ; LC Card 78-623295 DDC 353.97440072/32 19
HD1775.M4 M36 1976

Report on the examination of the accounts of the Office of the Commissioner of the Massachusetts Commission for the Blind, April 12, 1976 to April 12, 1977. Massachusetts. Dept. of the State Auditor. [Boston] [1977] 21 leaves ; LC Card 78-623298 DDC 353.97440072/32 19
HV1796.M39 M34 1977

Report on the examination of the accounts of the State Board of Retirement, January 1, 1975 to December 31, 1975. Massachusetts. Dept. of the State Auditor. [Boston] [1977?] 14 leaves ; LC Card 78-623299 DDC 353.9744601/82/06 19
JK3160.P4 M3 1977

Report on the failure of hospitals to take action on adverse determinations issued by the New York County Health Services Review Organization/. New York (City). Bureau of Audit and Control. New York, 1978. ix, 13 l. ;
NYPL [*ZT-1265]

Report on the fall, 1978, investigations at the George C. Davis Site, Caddoan Mounds State Historic Site, Cherokee County, Texas /. Thurmond, J. Peter. [Austin] [1979] ix, 103 leaves, [14] leaves of plates : LC Card 80-620782

DDC 976.4/183 19
E99.C13 T48

A report on the feasibility of telecommunications for instruction in the State of Alaska /. Alaska. Instructional Television. [Juneau] [1980] 225 p. in various pagings ; LC Card 80-622196 DDC 371.3/358/09798 19
LB1044.8 .A43 1980

Report on the inspection of U. S. military bases in Puerto Rico, Cuba, and the Panama Canal Zone of the Committee on Armed Services, House of Representatives, Ninety-sixth Congress, second session. United States. Congress. House. Committee on Armed Services. Washington , 1980. v, 24 p. : LC Card 80-603272 DDC 355.7/0973 19
UA23 .U4735 1980

A report on the institutional student financial aid resources survey, academic years 1971-72 to 1977-78 /. California. Student Aid Commission. Sacramento, Calif. [1980] 245 p. : LC Card 80-623193 DDC 378.3/09794 19
LB2337.5.C2 C35 1980

Report on the opinions and experiences of Oregon youth. Oregon. Governor's Commission on Youth. Salem , 1976. 51, 10 p. ; LC Card 77-621410
HQ796 .O647 1976 *NYPL [*XME-9430]*

Report on the sale of Carson City silver dollars by General Services Administration : staff report of the Subcommittee on Consumer affairs of the Committee on Banking, Finance, and Urban Affairs, House of Representatives, 96th Congress, second session. Washington : U. S. G.P.O., 1981. v, 20 p. ; 24 cm. At head of title: Committee print 96-23. "December 1980." Item 1013 LC Card 81-601279 DDC 737.4973 19
1. Dollar, American (Coin). 2. United States. General Services Administration. I. United States. Congress. House. Committee on Banking, Finance and Urban Affairs. Subcommittee on Consumer Affairs. II. Title: Carson City silver dollars.
CJ1835 .R46

Report on the situation of human rights in Argentina /. Inter-American Commission on Human Rights. Washington, D.C. [1980] iii, 266 p. ; ISBN 0-8270-1099-0 (pbk.) : LC Card 80-128497 DDC 341.24/5 s 323.4/0983 19
F1405.5 1959 .O7 OEA/Ser.L ; V/II.49, doc. 19, corr. 1 JC599.A7

Report on the situation of human rights in Nicaragua . Inter-American Commission on Human Rights. [Informe sobre la situación de los derechos humanos en Nicaragua. English.] Washington, D.C. , 1978. 78 p. ; LC Card 81-161420 DDC 323.4/9/097285 19
JC599.N5 I5413 1978

Report on the strategic implications of the Omnibus maritime bill, H.R. 6899 . United States. Congress. House. Committee on Merchant Marine and Fisheries. Washington , 1980. ii, 35 p. : LC Card 80-602266 DDC 359.2/7/0973 19
VA77 .U56 1980

A report on the U. S. semiconductor industry. United States. Industry and Trade Administration. Office of Producer Goods. Washington, D.C. , 1979. ix, 132 p. ; LC Card 79-604001
HD9696.S43 U54 1979 *NYPL [JLF 81-168]*

Report on youth in the Utah labor force /. Coverston, G. Scott. [Salt Lake City] , 1979. vii, 50 p. ; LC Card 80-620745 DDC 331.3/4125/09792 19
HD6274.U8 C66

Report relative to voter approval of borrowing and property taxes /. Massachusetts. Legislative Research Council. [Boston] , 1979. 57 p. ; LC Card 79-625031 DDC 353.97440072 19
HJ4181 .M37 1979

Report SE .
(v. 25) Poppe, Barbara B. Directory of world seismograph stations. Boulder, Colo. , 1980- v. <1, pt. 1 > : LC Card 80-603927 DDC 551 s 551.2/2/2025 19
QE500 .W67a no. 25 QE540.U6

Report series on mental health statistics; series A: mental health facility reports. Mental health statistics; Series A: mental health facilities

report. Rockville, Md..
NYPL [JLM 80-1073]

Report series on mental health statistics; series C: methodology reports. Mental health statistics; series C: methodology reports. Rockville, Md. [etc.] *NYPL [JLM 80-1069]*

Report to Congress on firefighter safety and health /. United States. Fire Administration. [Washington, D.C.] [1980] ii, 56 p. : LC Card 80-603745 DDC 363.1/19628925/0973 19
TH9182 .U54 1980

A report to Congress on migration /. Appalachian Regional Commission. Washington, D.C. [1979] 188 p. : LC Card 80-603526 DDC 304.8/2/0974 19
HB1971 .A67 1979

Report to Governor Edward J. King, June 15, 1980 /. Special Commission Established to Study the Laws and Regulations Governing the Alcoholic Beverage Industry in the Commonwealth of Massachusetts. Boston (Leverett Saltonstall Building, Government Center, 100 Cambridge St., Boston 02202) , 19. [13] leaves ; LC Card 81-621083 DDC 343.744/0786631 347.4403786631 19
KFM2775 .A847

Report to the Board of Higher Education on the results of the New Jersey college basic skills placement testing, May 1, 1978-September 28, 1978 /. New Jersey Basic Skills Council. [Trenton, N.J.] [1978] 54 p. : LC Card 80-622754 DDC 379.1/54/09749 19
LC1032.5.N5 N48 1978

Report to the Board of Higher Education on the results of the New Jersey college basic skills placement testing, May 1, 1978-September 28, 1978, aggregated according to sending high schools /. New Jersey Basic Skills Council. [Trenton? N.J.] [1978] [76] p. in various pagings : LC Card 80-622753 DDC 370/.9749 19
LC1035.7.N5 N48 1978

Report to the Congress on ocean pollution and offshore development. United States. National Oceanic and Atmospheric Administration. Oct. 1977/Sept. 1978- [Washington]
NYPL [JSP 81-88]

Report to the Coordinating Board for Higher Education of the Computer Policy Task Force. Missouri. Computer Policy Task Force. Jefferson City, Mo. [1979] 214 p. in various pagings ; LC Card 80-621798 DDC 378.778 19
LB2341 .M54 1979

Report to the Governor and General Assembly on the feasibility of adopting a uniform fuel and purchased gas adjustment clause /. Illinois. Commerce Commission. [Springfield] [1979] i, 302 p. ; LC Card 79-622711 DDC 338.4/336362 19
HD9685.U6 I26 1979

Report to the Governor in the matter of Sacco and Vanzetti. Massachusetts. [Boston] [1977] 2, 38 p. ; LC Card 80-620508 DDC 345.73/02523 19
KF224.S2 M32

Report to the House of Representatives /. Becker, Reynold E. [Springfield] [1980] 20 p. ; LC Card 80-623320 DDC 365/.65/09773 19
HV8929.I42 B43

Report to the Illinois General Assembly on code revision /. Illinois. Commission to Revise and Rewrite the Public Aid Code. [Springfield, Ill.] (612 South Second St., Springfield 62706) [1980] 1v. (various pagings) ; LC Card 81-621938 DDC 344.773/03 347.73043 19
KFI1549 .A25 1980

Report to the legislature on the Open meetings law /. New York (State). Dept. of State. Committee on Public Access to Records. Albany, N.Y. [1977] 12 p. ; LC Card 80-622378 DDC 342.747/0664 347.4702664 19
KFN5747.P83 A86 1977

Report to the mayor of the poisonings from the consumption of alcohol or the denatured alcohol. New York (City). Office of Chief Medical Examiner. 1925/26. New York. 1 v.
*NYPL [*ZAN-T5201]*

Report to the Michigan State Legislature /. Michigan. Legislature. Joint Special Committee on Developmental Disabilities. [Lansing, Mich.] [1978?] 16 p. ; LC Card 79-624617 DDC

362.1/968/009774 19
HV3006.M5 M55 1978

Report to the New Mexico Energy and Minerals Department of storage and alternative options for increasing the availability of natural gas. Zinder (H.) and Associates, inc. Socorro, N.M. [1979] 61, [61] p. : LC Card 80-622030 DDC 333.8/23311/09789 19
TN881.N6 Z52 1979

Report to the President /. United States. National Commission on the International Year of the Child. Washington, D.C. [1980] xi, 227 p. : LC Card 80-602206 DDC 353.0084/7 19
HQ767.9 .I57 1979z

Report to the President /. United States. National Historical Publications and Records Commission. Washington , 1978 i.e. 1979. 59 p. ; LC Card 80-601723 DDC 027.5 19
E175.4 .U55 1978

Report to the Secretary of Defense on the national military command structure. Steadman, Richard C. The national military command structure . Washington , 1978. iii, 79 p. ; LC Card 79-602790
UA23.3 .S73

Report to the Sunset Advisory Commission /. Texas. State Board of Library Examiners. [Austin] [1979] 67 leaves ; LC Card 80-620788 DDC 021.8/2 19
Z682.2.U5 T49 1979

Report to the 109th Maine Legislature and summary of the Commission's study and recommendations concerning Maine probate law /. Maine. Probate Law Revision Commission. [Augusta, Me.] [1978] 2, 51 p. ; LC Card 80-622558 DDC 346.74105/2 19
KFM144 .A868

Report to the 1979 General Aasembly of North Carolina, second session, 1980 /. North Carolina. General Assembly. Committee on Retirement Benefits in Addition to Salary. [Raleigh , 1980] 74 p. in various pagings ; LC Card 80-624247 DDC 353.9756005 19
JK4160 .N666 1980

Report to Utah State Legislature .
(no. 76-7A) Utah. Office of the Legislative Auditor General. A performance audit of mental health programs funded by the State of Utah. [Salt Lake City] , 1976. 177 p. : LC Card 77-621216 DDC 353.97920084/2045 19
RA790.65.U8 U86 1976

(no. 78-7) Welsh, Wayne. A performance audit of the WICHE student exchange program . [Salt Lake City] , 1978. iii, 45 leaves ; LC Card 78-622932 DDC 370.19/62 19
R847.6.U8 W44

(no. 79-11) Utah. Office of the Legislative Auditor General. A performance audit of the Utah Schools for the Deaf and Blind /. [Salt Lake City, Utah] , 1979. iii, 41, 10 leaves ; LC Card 79-626146 DDC 371.91/1/09792 19
HV2561.U82 U857 1979

(no. 79-14) Utah. Office of the Legislative Auditor General. A performance audit of electronic repair dealer registration in Utah . [Salt Lake City] [1979] ii, 14, 3 leaves ; LC Card 79-626149 DDC 353.97920082/42 19
HC107.U83 C637 1979

(no. 79-4) Utah. Office of the Legislative Auditor General. A program audit of equal employment opportunity in Utah State Government /. [Salt Lake City] , 1979. ii, 58 p. : LC Card 79-624189 DDC 353.9792001/04 19
JK8460.A33 U82 1979

(no. 80-10) Utah. Office of the Legislative Auditor General. A performance audit of the Division of Purchasing in the Department of Finance /. [Salt Lake City] (412 State Capitol, Salt Lake City, 84114) [1980] ii, 62, 4 p. ; LC Card 80-623434 DDC 353.97920071/2 19
JK8488.A1 U86 1980

(no. 80-5) Utah. Office of the Legislative Auditor General. A performance audit of the Division of Fine Arts /. [Salt Lake City] , 1980. 39, 8 p. ; LC Card 80-621609 DDC 353.97920085/4 19
NX24.U8 U7938 1980

(report no. 80-1) Utah. Office of the Legislative Auditor General. A performance audit of the Motor Vehicle Business Administration /. [Salt

Lake City] [1980] 48, 13 p. ; LC Card
80-621605 DDC 353.97920087/834 19
HD9710.U53 U88 1980

(report no. 80-6) Utah. Office of the Legislative
Auditor General. A performance audit of the
State Department of Insurance /. [Salt Lake
City] [1980] iii, 42 p. : LC Card 80-622523
DDC 353.97920082/55 19
HG8538.U8 U85 1980

Reported induced abortions, Minnesota, 1978.
Minnesota. Center for Health Statistics.
Minneapolis, Minn. [1979] viii, 30 p. ; LC
Card 80-621950 DDC 363.4/6/09776 19
HQ767.5.U5 M55 1979

**Reported mortality, together with the actual
mortality.** New York (City) Dept. of Health
Bureau of Records and Statistics. 1877-80,
1883. [New York] **NYPL** [*ZAN-T5209]

**Reported occupational injuries and illnesses,
South Dakota, 1972 and 1973 .** South Dakota.
State Dept. of Health. Division of Public Health
Statistics. Pierre , 1974. 37 p. ; LC Card
81-472623 DDC 312/.39803/09783 19
RC964 .S667 1974

**REPORTS, CORPORATION. see
CORPORATION REPORTS.**

Reports of the Chaco Center .
(no. 4) Brusse, David M. A history of the
Chaco Navajos /. Albuquerque, N.M. ,
Washington, D.C. , 1980. viii, 542 p. : LC Card
81-601717 DDC 978.9/8200497 19
E99.N3 B76

**Reports of the national juvenile justice
assessment centers.**
National Juvenile Justice System Assessment
Center (U. S.) A preliminary national
assessment of the status offender and the
juvenile justice system . [Washington, D.C.]
[1980] c1979. xv, 221 p. : LC Card 80-600044
DDC 364.3/6/0973 19
HV9104 .N23 1980a

National Juvenile Justice System Assessment
Center (United States) A national assessment of
serious juvenile crime and the juvenile justice
system . [Washington, D.C.] [1980] 4 v. : LC
Card 80-602691 DDC 364.3/6/0973 19
HV9104 .N23 1980

Smith, Charles P., 1931- A preliminary national
assessment of child abuse and neglect and the
juvenile justice system . [Washington, D.C.]
[1980] c1979. xiv, 154 p. ; LC Card 80-600045
DDC 362.7/044 19
HV741 .S55 1980

Weis, Joseph G. Jurisdiction and the elusive
status offender . Washington, D.C. [1980]
c1979. ix, 135 p. : LC Card 80-602845 DDC
364.3/6/0973 19
HV9104 .W447

**Reports of the Public Health and Safety Task
Force on public health and safety summary,
health physics and dosimetry, radiation health
effects, behavioral effects, public health and
epidemiology.** United States. President's
Commission on the Accident at Three Mile
Island. Public Health and Safety Task Force.
Washington, D.C. [1980] 423 p. : LC Card
80-601717 DDC 363.1/79 19
RA569 .U4977 1980

**Reports of the Subcommittees on National Needs
and Problems; Data Collection, Storage, and
Distribution; Monitoring; Research and
Development:** Working papers 2-5 for the
Federal Plan for Ocean Pollution Research,
Development and Monitoring, fiscal years
1979-83 / Interagency Committee on Ocean
Pollution Research, Development, and
Monitoring, Federal Coordinating Council for
Science, Engineering, and Technology.
Springfield, Va. : sold by the National
Technical Information Center, 1979. v, 177 p. :
ill. ; 28 cm. Working papers 1, 6-7 are published
separately.
*1. Marine pollution - United States - Addresses, essays,
lectures. I. United States. Interagency Committee on
Ocean Pollution Research, Development, and
Monitoring. II. United States. Federal Coordinating
Council for Science, Engineering, and Technology.*
NYPL [JSF 80-409]

**Reports of the Subcommittees on National Needs
and Problems, Data Collection, Storage, and
Distribution, Monitoring, Research and
Development .** United States. Interagency
Committee on Ocean Pollution Research,
Development, and Monitoring. [Washington,
D.C.] , Springfield, VA , 1979. v, 177 p. : LC
Card 80-601835 DDC 363.7/394 19
GC511 .U625 1979

**Reports on data recovery operations at two sites
in the Papago Indian Reservation, Arizona .**
Vogler, Lawrence. [Tucson, Ariz.] [1978] v, 45,
v, 44, leaves : LC Card 80-622637 DDC 979.1/77
19
E99.H68 V63

Reports on the fauna and flora of Wisconsin .
(no. 16) Bowers, Frank D. Atlas of Wisconsin
bryophytes /. Stevens Point, Wis. [1979] 2 v.
(135 [i.e. 230] p.) : LC Card 80-623149 DDC
574.9775 s 912/.1588/09775 19
QH105.W6 R43 no. 16 G1416.D2

Representable compensation plan . Oregon.
Executive Dept. Personnel Division.
Compensation and Classification Services Unit.
[Salem, Or.] [1980] 97 p. ; LC Card 80-622740
DDC 353.9795001/23 19
JK9057 .O73 1980

**Reproduction of smallmouth bass, Micropterus
dolomieui, in Bull Shoals Lake, Arkansas /.**
Vogele, Louis E. Washington, D.C. , 1981. p.
cm. LC Card 81-607977 DDC 639 s 597/.58 19
SH11 .A313 no. 106 QL638.C3

**Reproductive biology of lizards on the American
Samoan Islands /.** Schwaner, Terry D.
[Lawrence, Kan.] 1980. 53 p. : LC Card
80-624051 DDC 597.95/0416 19
QL666.L2 S37

Reprograming action--Trident submarine . United
States. Congress. House. Committee on Armed
Services. Subcommittee on Seapower and
Strategic and Critical Materials. Washington ,
1980. ii, 48 p. ; LC Card 80-603992 DDC
359.3/257/0973 19
KF27 .A769 1980

Reprograming of military aid to Somalia . United
States. Congress. House. Committee on Foreign
Affairs. Subcommittee on Africa. Washington ,
1980. iii, 35 p. : LC Card 80-603684 DDC
355/.032/6773 19
KF27 .F625 1980b

Reps, John William. The forgotten frontier :
urban planning in the American West before
1890 / John W. Reps. Columbia : University of
Missouri Press, 1982, c1981. p. cm. Based on the
author's paper delivered at the International Conference
on the History of Urban and Regional Planning held in
London, Sept. 1977. Bibliography: p. Includes index.
ISBN 0-8262-0351-5 LC Card 81-10322 DDC
307.7/6/0978 19
*1. City planning - West (U. S.) - History - 19th
century. 2. Urbanization - West (U. S.) - History - 19th
century. I. Title.*
HT123 .R44 1982

**REPTILES - AMERICAN SAMOA -
REPRODUCTION.**
Schwaner, Terry D. Reproductive biology of
lizards on the American Samoan Islands /.
[Lawrence, Kan.] 1980. 53 p. : LC Card
80-624051 DDC 597.95/0416 19
QL666.L2 S37

REPTILES - ANDES - CLASSIFICATION.
Cei, José Miguel, 1918- A new species of
Liolaemus (Sauria: Iguanidae) from the Andean
Mountains of the southern Mendoza volcanic
region of Argentina /. Lawrence , 1978. 6 p. :
LC Card 79-621682 DDC 597.95 19
QL666.L25 C44

**REPTILES - ARGENTINE REPUBLIC -
MENDOZA (PROVINCE) -
CLASSIFICATION.**
Cei, José Miguel, 1918- A new species of
Liolaemus (Sauria: Iguanidae) from the Andean
Mountains of the southern Mendoza volcanic
region of Argentina /. Lawrence , 1978. 6 p. :
LC Card 79-621682 DDC 597.95 19
QL666.L25 C44

REPTILES - AUSTRALIA - QUEENSLAND.
Legler, John M. A new genus and species of
Chelid turtle from Queensland, Australia /. Los
Angeles, Calif. , 1980. 18 p. : LC Card

80-138331 DDC 574 s 597.92 19
Q11 .L52 no. 324 QL666.C535

**REPTILES - AUSTRALIA - QUEENSLAND -
CLASSIFICATION.**
Greer, Allen E. A new species of Lampropholis
(Lacertilia, Scincidae) from the rainforests of
northeastern Queensland /. Ann Arbor, Mich.
[1980] 12 p. : LC Card 80-622058 DDC 597.95
19
QL666.L28 G73

REPTILES - BRAZIL - CLASSIFICATION.
Thomas, Robert A. A new systematic
arrangement for Philodryas serra (Schlegel) and
Philodryas pseudoserra Amaral (Serpentes :
Colubridae) /. Austin , 1977. 20 p. : LC Card
78-621007 DDC 574 s 597.96 19
AM101 .T474 no. 27 QL666.O636

REPTILES - CLASSIFICATION.
Cei, José Miguel, 1918- New species of
Liolaemus (Sauria: Iguanidae) from the Andean
Mountains of the southern Mendoza volcanic
region of Argentina /. Lawrence, 1978. 6 p. :
LC Card 79-621682 DDC 597.95 19
QL666.L25 C44

Greer, Allen E. A new species of Lampropholis
(Lacertilia, Scincidae) from the rainforests of
northeastern Queensland /. Ann Arbor, Mich.
[1980] 12 p. : LC Card 80-622058 DDC 597.95
19
QL666.L28 G73

Lawson, Robin. Biochemical genetics and
systematics of garter snakes of the Thamnophis
elegans-couchii-ordinoides complex /. Baton
Rouge, La. , 1979. 24 p. : LC Card 80-620693
DDC 591 s 597.96 19
QL3 .L67 no. 56 QL666.O636

Rossman, Douglas Athon, 1936- Morphological
evidence for taxonomic partitioning of the
Thamnophis elegans complex (Serpentes,
Colubridae) /. Baton Rouge, La. , 1979. 12 p. :
LC Card 80-620692 DDC 591 s 597.96 19
QL3 .L67 no. 55 QL666.O636

Thomas, Robert A. A new systematic
arrangement for Philodryas serra (Schlegel) and
Philodryas pseudoserra Amaral (Serpentes :
Colubridae) /. Austin , 1977. 20 p. : LC Card
78-621007 DDC 574 s 597.96 19
AM101 .T474 no. 27 QL666.O636

REPTILES - FLORIDA.
Christman, Steven P. Patterns of geographic
variation in Florida snakes /. Gainesville ,
1980. p. 158-256 : LC Card 81-621400 DDC 574
s 597.95/09759 19
QH1 .F6 vol. 25, no. 3 QL666.O6

REPTILES - GENETICS.
Lawson, Robin. Biochemical genetics and
systematics of garter snakes of the Thamnophis
elegans-couchii-ordinoides complex /. Baton
Rouge, La. , 1979. 24 p. : LC Card 80-620693
DDC 591 s 597.96 19
QL3 .L67 no. 56 QL666.O636

**REPTILES - GEOGRAPHICAL
DISTRIBUTION.**
Christman, Steven P. Patterns of geographic
variation in Florida snakes /. Gainesville ,
1980. p. 158-256 : LC Card 81-621400 DDC 574
s 597.95/09759 19
QH1 .F6 vol. 25, no. 3 QL666.O6

REPTILES - IDENTIFICATION.
Linzey, Donald W. Snakes of Virginia /.
Charlottesville , 1981. p. cm. ISBN
0-8139-0826-4 LC Card 81-12951 DDC
597.96/09755 19
QL666.O6 L74

REPTILES - LOUISIANA.
Louisiana. Wild Life and Fisheries Commission.
The fur animals, the alligator, and the fur
industry in Louisiana. [Baton Rouge] [1975?]
v, 66 p. : LC Card 76-621305 DDC 574 s 599.06
19
SK401 .A3 no. 106 QL719.L8

REPTILES - NORTH AMERICA.
North American tortoises . Washington, D.C. ,
1981. p. cm. LC Card 81-607867 DDC 597.92 19
QL666.C584 N67

REPTILES - REPRODUCTION.
Schwaner, Terry D. Reproductive biology of
lizards on the American Samoan Islands /.
[Lawrence, Kan.] 1980. 53 p. : LC Card

80-624051 DDC 597.95/0416 19
QL666.L2 S37

REPTILES - VARIATION.
Christman, Steven P. Patterns of geographic
variation in Florida snakes /. Gainesville ,
1980. p. 158-256 : LC Card 81-621400 DDC 574
s 597.95/09759 19
QH1 .F6 vol. 25, no. 3 QL666.O6

REPTILES - VIRGINIA - IDENTIFICATION.
Linzey, Donald W. Snakes of Virginia /.
Charlottesville , 1981. p. cm. ISBN
0-8139-0826-4 LC Card 81-12951 DDC
597.96/09755 19
QL666.O6 L74

REPTILES - YUCATAN PENINSULA - ECOLOGY.
Lee, Julian C. An ecogeographic analysis of the
herpetofauna of the Yucatán Peninsula /.
Lawrence , 1980. 75 p. : LC Card 80-621460
DDC 597.6/045/09726 19
QL655 .L43

REPTILES - YUCATAN PENINSULA - GEOGRAPHICAL DISTRIBUTION.
Lee, Julian C. An ecogeographic analysis of the
herpetofauna of the Yucatán Peninsula /.
Lawrence , 1980. 75 p. : LC Card 80-621460
DDC 597.6/045/09726 19
QL655 .L43

The Republic of Chad. France. Ambassade.
United States. Service de presse et
d'information. New York, 1961. 32 p.: LC Card
62-3950   *NYPL [Sc Micro R-3644]*

Republic of Indonesia. see **Indonesia.**

The Republic of Niger . France. Ambassade.
United States. Service de presse et
d'information. New York , 1960. 32 p. : LC
Card 62-37711   *NYPL [Sc Micro R-3644]*

The Republic of Senegal. France. Ambassade.
United States. Service de presse et
d'information. New York, 1960. 32 p.: LC Card
62-37710   *NYPL [Sc Micro R-3644]*

Republic of the United States of Indonesia. see
Indonesia.

The Republic of Turkey . Mitchell, William A.,
1940- United States Air Force Academy, Colo.
[1981] p. cm. LC Card 81-607896 DDC
956.1/0007/1178881 19
DR438.95.U6 M57

Republik Indonesia Serikat. see **Indonesia.**

République du Niger. see **Niger.**

République gabonaise. see **Gabon.**

République islamique de Mauritanie. see
Mauritania.

**Requirements and guidelines for high school
graduation.** Washington (State). State Board of
Education. [Olympia , 1980] iv, 20 p. ; LC
Card 80-623898 DDC 373.12/912/09797 19
LB1627.7 .W37 1980

**Requirements for recurring reports to the
Congress.** 1976- Washington. 28 cm.
(Congressional sourcebook series) "PAD." Issued by the
U. S. General Accounting Office, Office of Program
Analysis, 1976; by the Comptroller General, 1977-
*1. Administrative agencies - United States -
Bibliographies. 2. United States - Executive
departments - Bibliography. 3. United States -
Government publications - Bibliography. I. United
States. General Accounting Office. Office of Program
Analysis. II. United States. General Accounting Office.
III. Series.*
*NYPL [*R-Econ. 77-323 & JLM 77-313]*

**Requirements of laws and regulations enforced by
the U. S. Food and Drug Administration.**
United States. Food and Drug Administration.
Rockville, Md. , Washington, D.C. , 1979] vi,
72 p. ; LC Card 79-601809
KF3869 .A32 1979   NYPL [JLE 81-479]

**Research and development, a 16-year
compendium (1963-78) /.** United States.
Employment and Training Administration.
Washington, D.C. , 1979. xiv, 608 p. ; LC Card
80-601625 DDC 331.11/0973 19
HD5724 .U6285 1979

RESEARCH AND DEVELOPMENT CONTRACTS, GOVERNMENT - UNITED STATES.
Communications research and development /.
Washington , 1980 [i.e. 1981] viii, 34 p. ; LC

Card 81-601506 DDC 621.38/072073 19
TK5102.8.U6 C65

United States. Congress. House. Committee on
Science and Technology. H.R. 7178 (superseded
by H.R. 7689), the Research and development
authorization estimates act . Washington , 1980.
iii, 321 p. : LC Card 80-603641 DDC 346.73/023
347.30623 19
KF27 .S39 1980c

United States. Congress. House. Committee on
Science and Technology. Subcommittee on
Investigation and Oversight. Small, high
technology firms and innovation . Washington ,
1980 [i.e. 1981] xviii, 791 p. : LC Card
81-600956 DDC 338.6/42/0973 19
KF27 .S3975 1979b

United States. Congress. House. Committee on
Science and Technology. Subcommittee on
Science, Research, and Technology.
Government patent policy . Washington , 1979.
iii, 221 p. ; LC Card 80-602808 DDC 353.0082/4
19
KF27 .S399 1979r

United States. Congress. House. Committee on
Science and Technology. Subcommittee on
Science, Research, and Technology. The
Government-university accountability
relationship in the field of scientific research .
Washington , 1980. iii, 251 p. ; LC Card
80-602710 DDC 001.4/4 19
KF27 .S399 1980b

United States. Congress. House. Committee on
Science and Technology. Subcommittee on
Transportation, Aviation, and Communications.
Communications research and development .
Washington , 1980. iii, 481 p. : LC Card
80-603502 DDC 384/.072073 19
KF27 .S3997 1980d

United States. Congress. Senate. Select
Committee on Small Business. Small business
and Department of Energy research and
development programs . Washington , 1980. iii,
77 p. : LC Card 80-602727 DDC 353.0082/048045
19
KF26.5 .S6 1980e

RESEARCH AND DEVELOPMENT CONTRACTS - UNITED STATES.
United States. Dept. of Health, Education, and
Welfare. A guide for colleges and universities .
Washington, D. C., 1974. 97 p. ;
NYPL [JLF 80-937]

United States. General Accounting Office.
Agency for International Development needs to
strengthen its management of study, research,
and evaluation activities . [Washington] 1979.
iii, 30 p. ; LC Card 79-601658 DDC 353.0089 19
HC60.U6 G4 1979

RESEARCH AND DEVELOPMENT CONTRACTS - UNITED STATES - PERIODICALS.
United States. National Institutes of Health.
Research and development contracts. [Bethesda,
Md.] LC Card 76-646048   *NYPL [JLL 80-227]*

**Research and development programs of the
National Oceanic and Atmospheric
Adminstration** . United States. Congress.
House. Committee on Science and Technology.
Subcommittee on Natural Resources and
Environment. Washington , 1979, [i.e. 1980] iii,
229 p. ; LC Card 80-602771 DDC 353.0082/32 19
KF27 .S398 1979i

**Research and innovation in the building
regulatory process** . NBS/NCSBCS Joint
Conference on Research and Innovation in the
Building Regulatory Process, 3d, Annapolis,
1978. Washington , 1979. x, 360 p. : LC Card
79-600090 DDC 602/.18 s 343.73/07869 19
QC100 .U57 no. 552 KF5701

**Research bulletin / Hawaii Agricultural
Experiment Station, College of Tropical
Agriculture and Human Resources,
University of Hawaii** .
(173) Green, Richard E. (Richard Ervin), 1931-
Soil-water relations and physical properties of
irrigated soils in the Kula area, Island of Maui,
Hawaii /. Honolulu , 1981. p. cm. LC Card
81-93 DDC 631.4/32/09969 19
S599.H4 G73

RESEARCH - CONGRESSES.
The Joys of research /. Washington, D.C. ,

1981. p. cm. ISBN 0-87474-858-5 LC Card
81-9347 DDC 001.4 19
Q179.9 .J69

Research extension series, 0271-9916 .
Leonhardt, Kenneth W. (Kenneth William),
1950- Investment analysis of dendrobiums /.
Honolulu, Hawaii [1981] p. cm. LC Card
81-7033 DDC 635.9/3415 19
SB409 .L45

Research Frontiers in Aging and Cancer . United
States. Congress. House. Select Committee on
Aging. Washington , 1981. iii, 48 p. ; LC Card
81-601752 DDC 362.1/9699400973 19
KF27.5 .A3 1980n

RESEARCH FRONTIERS IN AGING AND CANCER: INTERNATIONAL SYMPOSIUM FOR THE 1980S (1980 : WASHINGTON, D.C.)
United States. Congress. House. Select
Committee on Aging. Research Frontiers in
Aging and Cancer . Washington , 1981. iii, 48
p. ; LC Card 81-601752 DDC 362.1/9699400973
19
KF27.5 .A3 1980n

RESEARCH GRANTS - UNITED STATES.
United States. Congress. House. Committee on
Science and Technology. Subcommittee on
Science, Research, and Technology. The
Government-university accountability
relationship in the field of scientific research .
Washington , 1980. iii, 251 p. ; LC Card
80-602710 DDC 001.4/4 19
KF27 .S399 1980b

**Research guide to the Godoi-Díaz Pérez
Collection in the Library of the University of
California, Riverside /.** California. University,
Riverside. Library. Godoi-Díaz Pérez
Collection. Riverside , 1973. 60 p. ;
NYPL [HLM 81-769]

RESEARCH - ILLINOIS.
Science staff services in the Illinois Legislative
Council . [Springfield, Ill.] [1979] x, 74 p. :
LC Card 80-622583 DDC 328.773/0761 19
Q180.U5 S364

**Research in nonlinear structural and solid
mechanics** : research-in-progress papers
presented at a symposium / sponsored by
NASA Langley Research Center, Hampton,
Virginia, and the George Washington
University, Washington, D.C., in cooperation
with the National Science Foundation, the
American Society of Civil Engineers, and the
American Society of Mechanical Engineers, and
held at Washington, D.C., October 6-8, 1980 ;
compiled by Harvey G. McComb, Jr., Ahmed
K. Noor. Washington, D.C. : National
Aeronautics and Space Administration,
Scientific and Technical Information Branch ;
[Springfield, Va. : For sale by the National
Technical Information Service], 1980. viii, 289
p. : ill. ; 27 cm. (NASA conference publication .
2147) "The George Washington University, Joint
Institute for Advancement of Flight Sciences, NASA
Langley Research Center." Includes bibliographical
references. LC Card 81-601087 DDC
624.1/71/0724 19
*1. Structures, Theory of - Mathematical models -
Congresses. 2. Finite element method - Congresses. 3.
Nonlinear mechanics - Mathematical models -
Congresses. I. Noor, Ahmed Khairy, 1938-. II.
McComb, Harvey G. III. United States. National
Aeronautics and Space Administration. Scientific and
Technical Information Branch. IV. Langley Research
Center. V. George Washington University. VI. Joint
Institute for Advancement of Flight Sciences. VII.
American Society of Civil Engineers. VIII. American
Society of Mechanical Engineers. IX. Symposium on
the Computational Methods in Nonlinear Structural and
Solid Mechanics (1980 : Washington, D.C.).*
TA646 .R38

Research in sociology in South Dakota. Wagner,
Robert T. Characteristics and needs of the aged
in South Dakota, 1980-1990 /. Brookings,
S.D. , 1978. ix, 238 leaves : LC Card 80-622161
DDC 305.2/6/09783 19
HQ1064.U6 S7

**Research in the Geysers-Clear Lake geothermal
area, northern California /** Robert J.
McLaughlin and Julie M. Donnelly-Nolan,
editors ; contributions from Cascadia
Exploration Corporation, consulting
geologists ... [et al.]. Washington : U. S. Govt.

Print. Off. : for sale by the Supt. of Docs.,
GPO, 1981. viii, 259 p. : ill. ; 29 cm. (Geological
Survey professional paper ; 1141) Includes
bibliographies.   LC Card 80-607169   DDC 557.94 19
1. Geology - California - The Geysers region. 2.
Geothermal resources - California - The Geysers region.
I. McLaughlin, Robert J. II. Donnelly-Nolan, Julie M.
III. Cascadia Exploration Corporation. IV. Series:
United States. Geological Survey. Professional paper,
1141.
QE90.G45 R45

Research in Washington higher education /.
Fischer, Norman M. [Olympia] , 1978. 112 p. :
LC Card 79-623622
LB1028 .F484   ***NYPL [JFF 80-1521]***

RESEARCH, INDUSTRIAL -
MANAGEMENT.
Lane, Henry W., 1942- Managing large research
and development programs /. Albany , c1981.
x, 166 p. :   ISBN 0-87395-473-4   LC Card 81-849
DDC 607/.2/68 19
T175 .L28

RESEARCH, INDUSTRIAL - OKLAHOMA.
Reid, George Willard, 1917- Final report on the
Governor's Conference on Research and
Development Priorities for the State of
Oklahoma /. [Norman, Okla. , 1973] 293 p. in
various pagings :   LC Card 80-621267   DDC
338.9766 19
T176 .R4

RESEARCH, INDUSTRIAL - UNITED
STATES.
Mogee, Mary Ellen. Technology and trade .
Washington , 1980. viii, 36 p. ;   LC Card
80-602065   DDC 338/.06 19
HC110.T4 M64

Seminar on Research, Productivity, and the
National Economy, U. S. House of
Representatives, 1980. Seminar on Research,
Productivity, and the National Economy .
Washington , 1980. v, 111 p. :   LC Card
80-603648   DDC 338/.06 19
KF27 .S39 1980d

RESEARCH INSTITUTES - RUSSIA -
DIRECTORIES.
United States. Central Intelligence Agency.
National Foreign Assessment Center. Directory
of Soviet research organization[s] /. Seattle ,
Forest Grove, OR , 1979. v, 290 p. ;   ISBN
0-89875-006-7   LC Card 79-121624
Q180.R9 U32 1979
             NYPL [Desk-Slav. Div. 80-626]

RESEARCH - INTERNATIONAL
COOPERATION.
Programa Regional de Desarrollo Científico y
Tecnológico. Aspectos organizacionales de la
política científica y tecnológica en América
Latina . Washington, D.C. [1979?] iii, 66 p. ;
LC Card 79-119687
Q127.L38 P76 1979

Research issues - National Institute on Drug
Abuse .
(18) Drug users and the criminal justice system
/. Rockville, Md. , Washington , 1977. xv, 150
p. ;   LC Card 77-604248   DDC 362.2/93/0973 19
HV5825 .D7775

(27) Austin, Gregory A. Guide to the drug
research literature /. Rockville, Md. ,
Washington, D.C. , 1979. xx, 397 p. ;   LC Card
80-601861   DDC 016.61686/3 19
RC564 .A96

Research issues update, 1978 /. Documentation
Associates Information Services Incorporated.
Rockville, Md. , Washington , 1979. xvii, 308
p. :   LC Card 79-601820   DDC 362.2/93/072 19
HV5809 .D62 1979a

RESEARCH - LATIN AMERICA -
MANAGEMENT.
Programa Regional de Desarrollo Científico y
Tecnológico. Aspectos organizacionales de la
política científica y tecnológica en América
Latina . Washington, D.C. [1979?] iii, 66 p. ;
LC Card 79-119687
Q127.L38 P76 1979

RESEARCH - LAW AND LEGISLATION -
ILLINOIS.
Science staff services in the Illinois Legislative
Council . [Springfield, Ill.] [1979] x, 74 p. :
LC Card 80-622583   DDC 328.773/0761 19
Q180.U5 S364

RESEARCH LIBRARIES -
ADMINISTRATION.
Johnson, Edward R. An assessment of the
impact of the management review and analysis
program (MRAP) /. University Park, Pa.
[1977] 202 leaves :   LC Card 80-622450   DDC
026 19
Z675.R45 J63

Research manuscript series .
(no. 147) Brooks, Mark J. An intensive
archeological survey of Amoco realty property
in Berkeley County, South Carolina . Columbia,
S.C. , 1978. xi, 79 p. :   LC Card 79-625384
DDC 975.7/93 19
E78.S6 B73

(no. 148) Lewis, Kenneth E. Middleton Place .
Columbia, S.C. [1979] vii, 92 p. :   LC Card
79-625656   DDC 975.7/94 19
F279.M46 L48

(no. 153) Goodyear, Albert C. Archeological
reconnaissance and testing along the Broad
River, Richland County, South Carolina /.
[Columbia, S.C.] [1979] 22 p. :   LC Card
80-621581   DDC 975.7/71 19
F277.B73 G66

(no. 154) Michie, James L. The Bass Pond dam
site, intensive archaeological testing at a
formative period base camp on Kiawah Island,
South Carolina /. Columbia, S.C. , 1979. vi,
106 p. :   LC Card 80-621582   DDC 975.7/91 19
E78.S6 M54

(no. 156) Goodyear, Albert C. A hypothesis for
the use of cryptocrystalline raw materials
among Paleo-Indian groups of North America
/. Columbia, S.C. [1979] 15 leaves ;   LC Card
80-621585   DDC 970.01/1 19
E98.I4 G66

(134) Hanson, Glen T. The preliminary
archeological inventory of the Savannah River
Plant, Aiken and Barnwell Counties, South
Carolina /. Columbia , 1978. viii, 166 p. :   LC
Card 79-620819   DDC 975.7/75 19
E78.S6 H38

(141) Hanson, Glen T. The intensive
archeological survey of the independent spent
fuel storage facility, Savannah River plant,
Aiken and Barnwell Counties, South Carolina /.
Columbia , 1978. viii, 68 p. :   LC Card 79-623910
DDC 975.7/76 19
F277.B25 H36

(142) Taylor, Richard Lee, 1946- The report of
the intensive survey of the Richard B. Russell
Dam and Lake, Savannah River, Georgia and
South Carolina /. Columbia, S.C. [1978] xvii,
531 p. :   LC Card 79-623568   DDC 975.7/35 19
F292.R49 T39

RESEARCH, MEDICAL. see MEDICAL
RESEARCH.

RESEARCH NATURAL AREAS - ALASKA.
Underwood, Larry S. An ecological reserves
report /. Anchorage, Alaska , 1979- v. :   LC
Card 80-620900   DDC 304.2/0720798 19
QH76.5.A4 U52 1979

RESEARCH NATURAL AREAS - ALASKA -
MANAGEMENT.
United States. Dept. of the Interior. Final
environmental supplement . Washington
[1978?] ca. 600 p. in various pagings :   LC Card
79-601643
QH76.5.A4 U54 1978   ***NYPL [JLF 81-375]***

Research on the effects of television advertising
on children : a review of the literature and
recommendations for future research : report
prepared for National Science Foundation,
Research Applications Directorate,
RANN--Research applied to National Needs,
Division of Advanced Productivity Research
and Technology. [Washington] : NSF : [for sale
by the Supt. of Docs., U. S. Govt. Print. Off.,
1977] viii, 229 p. : graphs ; 27 cm. Microfiche
(neg.) NTIS. 3 sheets. 11 x 15 cm. (PB 273 074) Cover
title. "Principal investigator: Richard P. Adler."
"NSF/RA 770115." Bibliography: p. 207-229.   LC
Card 77-604793
1. Television advertising and children - United States.
2. Television advertising and children - Research -
United States. I. Adler, Richard. II. United States.
National Science Foundation. Division of Advanced
Productivity Research and Technology.
HQ784.T4 R47   ***NYPL [*XME-9373]***

Research on the fetus . United States. National
Commission for the Protection of Human
Subjects of Biomedical and Behavioral
Research. [Bethesda, Md.] , 1975. 88 p. ;   LC
Card 76-603269
RG600 .U53 1975   ***NYPL [JFF 80-1527]***

Research paper PNW .
(276) Ueda, Michihiko. The outlook for housing
in Japan to the year 2000 /. [Portland, Or.?] ,
c1980. 25 p. :   LC Card 81-600898   DDC
634.9/09795 s 363.5/0952 19
SD11 .A45614 no. 276 HD7367.A3

Research papers and policy studies .
(no. 1) U. S.-Japan economic relations .
[Berkeley] , 1980. x, 57 p. ;   ISBN 0-912966-25-4
(pbk.) :   LC Card 80-620017   DDC 337.52073
19
HF1456.5.J3 U554

Research report of the Interdepartmental
Workers' Compensation Task Force.
Washington: U. S. Dept. of Labor, Employment
and Training Administration, 1979. 1 v.; 28 cm.
1. Workmen's compensation - United States. I. United
States. Interdepartmental Workers' Compensation Task
Force.   ***NYPL [JLM 80-745]***

Research Resources Information Center. Freiherr,
Gregory. The seeds of artificial intelligence .
Bethesda, Md. , Washington, D.C. [1980] 74
p. :   LC Card 80-602247   DDC 001.64 19
R858 .F73

RESEARCH - SOVIET UNION.
Science policy . [Washington, D.C.?] , 1980. 2
v. ;   LC Card 80-604130   DDC 507/.2073 19
Q127.U6 S319

RESEARCH SUPPORT - DIRECTORIES.
United States. National Institutes of Health.
Research and development contracts. [Bethesda,
Md.]   LC Card 76-646048   ***NYPL [JLL 80-227]***

Research Triangle Institute. Center for
Educational Research and Evaluation.
Tabular summary of the third follow-up
questionnaire data / Samuel S. Peng ... [et al.] ;
Elmer F. Collins, project officer ; prepared for
the National Center for Education Statistics,
Office of the Assistant Secretary for Education,
Department of Health, Education, and Welfare.
[Washington] : The Dept. : for sale by the Supt.
of Docs., U. S. Govt. Print. Off., 1978. 4 v. ;
26 cm. (Sponsored reports series) "NCES 79-228."
Includes bibliographical references.   LC Card
79-602292
1. High school graduates - United States - Longitudinal
studies. I. Peng, Samuel S. II. National Center for
Education Statistics. III. Title.
LA229 .R46 1978a

Research Triangle Institute. Educational
Research and Evaluation, Center for. see
Research Triangle Institute. Center for
Educational Research and Evaluation.

Research Triangle Park, N. C. Air Pollution
Training Institute. see Air Pollution Training
Institute.

RESEARCH - UNITED STATES.
Science policy . [Washington, D.C.?] , 1980. 2
v. ;   LC Card 80-604130   DDC 507/.2073 19
Q127.U6 S319

United States. Congress. House. Committee on
Science and Technology. Outlooks from Nobel
Prize winners . Washington , 1981. iii, 66 p. :
LC Card 81-601401   DDC 607/.2/73 19
KF27 .S39 1980i

United States. Dept. of Defense. Basic research
program /. [Washington, D.C.?] [1980] 71 p. :
LC Card 80-603588   DDC 355/.07/0973 19
.U393 .U524 1980

RESEARCH - UNITED STATES - FINANCE.
United States. National Science Foundation. An
analysis of Federal R & D funding by function.
- Washington [1974] x, 69 p. :   LC Card
74-601163   ***NYPL [JLF 80-1457]***

RESERVATIONS, INDIANS. see INDIANS
OF NORTH AMERICA -
RESERVATIONS.

Reserve forces (U. S.) see United States - Armed
Forces - Reserves.

RESERVOIR ECOLOGY - GHANA - VOLTA
LAKE.
Freeman, Peter H. The environmental impact of
a large tropical reservoir . Washington , 1974.

86 p., [1] fold. leaf of plates : LC Card
81-450719 DDC 333.78/46 19
QH195.G53 F73

**RESERVOIR ECOLOGY - MISSOURI RIVER
BASIN.**
Benson, Norman Gustaf, 1928- Effects of
post-impoundment shore modifications on fish
populations in Missouri River reservoirs /.
Washington, D.C. , 1980. p. cm. LC Card
80-21800 DDC 639.9/0973 s 639.9/77 19
SH11 .A3 no. 80 SH173.5

**RESERVOIR SEDIMENTATION -
WISCONSIN - COON CREEK
WATERSHED (MONROE COUNTY-
VERNON COUNTY)**
Trimble, Stanley Wayne. Soil conservation,
erosion, and sedimentation, Coon Creek Basin,
Wisconsin /. Reston, Va. [1981] p. cm. LC
Card 81-607057 DDC 631.4/5/0977554 19
S624.W5 T74

**RESERVOIRS - ENVIRONMENTAL
ASPECTS - COLORADO - WILLOW
CREEK.**
Nolting, Donald H. Electric fish screen
efficiency, Willow Creek Reservoir /. Denver /,
1962. iv, 24 p. : LC Card 81-464857 DDC
639.9/7755 19
SH157.85.F54 N64

RESERVOIRS - MASSACHUSETTS.
Massachusetts. Water Quality and Research
Section. Compilation of lakes, ponds, and
reservoirs relative to the Massachusetts Lake
Classification Program /. Westborough, Mass. ,
1976. 124 p. ; LC Card 79-623986 DDC
551.48/2/09744 19
GB1625.M3 M37 1976

**RESERVOIRS - REGULATION -
ENVIRONMENTAL ASPECTS -
MISSOURI RIVER BASIN.**
Benson, Norman Gustaf, 1928- Effects of
post-impoundment shore modifications on fish
populations in Missouri River reservoirs /.
Washington, D.C. , 1980. p. cm. LC Card
80-21800 DDC 639.9/0973 s 639.9/77 19
SH11 .A3 no. 80 SH173.5

RESERVOIRS - SHORELINES.
Benson, Norman Gustaf, 1928- Effects of
post-impoundment shore modifications on fish
populations in Missouri River reservoirs /.
Washington, D.C. , 1980. p. cm. LC Card
80-21800 DDC 639.9/0973 s 639.9/77 19
SH11 .A3 no. 80 SH173.5

**RESERVOIRS - TEMPERATURE -
ENVIRONMENTAL ASPECTS - TEXAS.**
Thompson, Kenneth W. Analysis of potential
environmental factors, especially thermal, which
would influence the survivorship of exotic Nile
perch if introduced into artificially heated
reservoirs in Texas /. [Austin] , 1977. 37 p. :
LC Card 78-620720 DDC 639.9/7758 19
QL638.C34 T48

**Residence location, geographic mobility, and the
attainments of women in academia /.** Marwell,
Gerald, 1937- Madison , 1976. 31 p. ; LC Card
78-623190 DDC 378/.12/0973 19
LB2331.72 .M37

**RESIDENCES. see ARCHITECTURE,
DOMESTIC; DWELLINGS.**

**Resident and nonresident, undergraduate and
graduate tuition and/or required fees .**
Washington (State). Council for Postsecondary
Education. [Olympia, Wash.] [1980] 21 p. :
LC Card 80-621762 DDC 379.1/3/09797 19
LB2342 .W316 1980

**RESIDENT PHYSICIANS. see HOSPITALS -
STAFF.**

Residential and commercial energy conservation .
United States. Congress. Senate. Committee on
Energy and Natural Resources. Washington ,
1980. iii, 296 p. : LC Card 80-601488 DDC
346.7304/67916/0262 19
KF26 .E55 1979aa

**Residential energy conservation outreach
activities .** United States. General Accounting
Office. Washington, D.C. , 1981. iv, 31 p. ; LC
Card 81-601119 DDC 333.79/16/0973 19
HD7287.5 .U49 1981

**RESIDENTIAL MOBILITY - OHIO -
COLUMBUS.**
Choice mechanisms in the migration decision.

Columbus] 1974. vii, 129 p.
NYPL [JLF 80-1365]

**RESIDENTIAL MOBILITY - UNITED
STATES.**
Chi, Peter S. K. Population redistribution and
changes in housing tenure status in the United
States /. [Washington, D.C.] [1980] 27 p. :
LC Card 80-601677 DDC 304.8/2/0973 19
HD7287.82.U6 C45

Nelson, Kathryn P. Recent suburbanization of
Blacks, how much, who, and where /.
[Washington] , 1979. 34 p. : LC Card 79-602959
HD7288.72.U5 N44

**RESIDENTIAL MOBILITY - UNITED
STATES - CASE STUDIES.**
Joint Center for Urban Studies. The behavioral
foundations of neighborhood change /.
Washington [1979] 205 p. ; LC Card 79-601949
HT123 .J63 1979 *NYPL [JLF 81-252]*

**Residential programs for court-involved youth in
Massachusetts /.** Fay, Juliette E. Boston
[1979] 61 p. ; LC Card 79-625507 DDC
365/.42/09744 19
HV9105.M4 F38

Residential solar design review . Jaffe, Martin S.
[Washington, D.C.] [1980] 86 p. : LC Card
80-603400 DDC 728/.047 19
NA7208 .J3

**RESIDENTIAL SUBDIVISIONS. see REAL
ESTATE DEVELOPMENT.**

Residents' satisfaction in HUD-assisted housing :
design and management factors : prepared for
the Office of Policy Development and
Research, U. S. Department of Housing and
Urban Development / Guido Francescato ... [et
al.] ; prepared by the University of Illinois,
Housing Research and Development Program,
under contract H-2653. Washington : The
Office : for sale by the Supt. of Docs., U. S.
Govt. Print. Off., [1979] ca. 200 p. in various
pagings : ill. ; 28 cm. "HUD-PDR-390." Includes
bibliography. LC Card 79-601946
*1. Public housing - United States. 2. Housing - Resident
satisfaction - United States. I. Francescato, Guido. II.
Illinois. University at Urbana-Champaign. Housing
Research and Development Program. III. United States.
Dept. of Housing and Urban Development. Office of
Policy Development and Research.*
HD7293 .R372 *NYPL [JLF 81-344]*

**Resolution of inquiry concerning human rights
policies .** United States. Congress. House.
Committee on Foreign Affairs. Washington ,
19. iii, 29 p. ; LC Card 81-600587 DDC
323.4/0973 19
KF27 .F6 1980m

**Resolution to disapprove Location of chanceries
amendment act of 1979 .** United States.
Congress. Senate. Committee on Governmental
Affairs. Subcommittee on Governmental
Efficiency and the District of Columbia.
Washington , 1980. iv, 98 p. ; LC Card
80-602103 DDC 346.75304/5 19
KF26 .G6735 1979i

**Resolutions of disapproval pertaining to the
shipment of nuclear fuel to India .** United
States. Congress. House. Committee on Foreign
Affairs. Washington , 1980. iii, 170 p. ; LC
Card 80-603439 DDC 353.0089 19
KF27 .F6 1980g

**Resource Analysis & Management Group,
Oklahoma City.** The effects of the crude oil
windfall profits tax on recoverable crude oil
resources and production therefrom / prepared
for the Interstate Oil Compact Commission [by]
Resource Analysis & Management Group.
Oklahoma City, Okla. : The Commission, 1980.
v, 46 leaves : ill. ; 28 cm. LC Card 80-82957
DDC 338.2/7282/0973 19
*1. Petroleum - Taxation - United States. 2. Excess
profits tax - United States. I. Interstate Oil Compact
Commission. II. Title.*
HD9560.8.U5 R47 1980

Resource bulletin SO .
(75) Bertelson, Daniel F. Arkansas forest
industries, 1977 /. New Orleans, La. , 1980. 18
p. : LC Card 81-600548 DDC 333.75/0976 s
338.1/7498/09767 19
SD11 .A45793 no. 75 HD9757.A9

Resource Conservation and Development Act .
United States. Congress. Senate. Committee on

Agriculture, Nutrition, and Forestry.
Subcommittee on Environment, Soil
Conservation, and Forestry. Washington , 1980.
iv, 206 p. : LC Card 80-603906 DDC 346.7304/4
347.30644 19
KF26 .A3543 1980d

The resource file . JRB Associates. [Washington,
D.C.] [Springfield, Va. , 1980] 189 p. in
various pagings ; LC Card 80-602300 DDC
016.33379/16/0973 19
Z5853.P83 J16 1980 TJ163.3

**A Resource guide for interpreter training for the
deaf programs** / editors, Anna
Witter-Merithew ... [et al.]. 1980 ed.
[Washington, D.C. : U. S. Dept. of Health,
Education, and Welfare, Office of Human
Development Services, Office for Handicapped
Individuals, 1980] 62 p. ; 23 cm. "January, 1980."
LC Card 80-602341 DDC 419 19
*1. Deaf - Translating - Study and teaching - United
States - Directories. I. Witter-Merithew, Anne.*
HV2395 .R45 1980

Resource management journal. 1st.- ed.; [1980?]-
[Washington, U. S. Comptroller of the Army]
I. United States. Office of the Comptroller of the Army.
NYPL [Econ. Div.]

Resource manual for gifted/talented programs : a
procedural manual designed to accompany
Administrative rules & regulations for special
education, July 15, 1979. Rev. 1980. Boise,
Idaho : State of Idaho, Dept. of Education,
[1980] vi, 68 p. : forms ; 28 cm. Cover title.
Bibliography: p. 67-68. "November 1980." LC Card
81-621268 DDC 371.95/09796 19
*1. Gifted children - Education - Idaho. I. Idaho. State
Superintendent of Public Instruction. II. Idaho. State
Superintendent of Public Instruction. Administrative
rules and regulations for special education, July 15,
1979.*
LC3994.I2 R47 1980

Resource publication. United States. Bureau of
Sport Fisheries and Wildlife. 1-122
(incomplete). Washington, 1965-74.
NYPL [M-11 3071]

**RESOURCE RECOVERY. see RECYCLING
(WASTE, ETC.)**

Resources and development . Wisconsin Seminar
on Natural Resource Policies in Relation to
Economic Development and International
Cooperation, University of Wisconsin--Madison,
1977-1978. Madison , London , c1980. xv, 500
p. ; ISBN 0-299-08250-4 : LC Card 80-10577
HC55 .W57 1977a *NYPL [JLE 80-3198]*

**Resources for biomedical research and education :
Report .**
(no. 18) Brown, Carol M. Trends in graduate
enrollment and Ph.D. output in scientific fields,
1960-61 through 1967-68. [Washington] , 1969
[i.e. 1970] vii, 204 p. ; LC Card 73-606834
DDC 610/.7 s 610/.7/073 19
RA440.6 .R4 no. 18 R854.U5

**Resources for the vocational preparation of
disabled youth.** United States. President's
Committee on Employment of the
Handicapped. Washington, D.C. , 1980] iii, 44
p. ; LC Card 80-602690 DDC 016.3624/088055 19
Z7164.L1 U873 1980 HD7256.U5

Resources information series .
(no. 2) Nault, Michael J. Bibliography and
index of theses and dissertations on the geology
of Louisiana /. Baton Rouge, La. [1980] iv, 36
leaves : LC Card 80-623624 DDC 016.55763 19
Z6034.U5 L86 QE117

**RESOURCES, NATURAL. see NATURAL
RESOURCES.**

Resources planning act . United States. Congress.
Senate. Committee on Agriculture, Nutrition,
and Forestry. Subcommittee on Environment,
Soil Conservation, and Forestry. Washington ,
1980. iii, 67 p. ; LC Card 80-603686 DDC
346.7304/675/0262 347.30646750262 19
KF26 .A3543 1980a

**Resources planning act assessment and Domestic
timber supply act .** United States. Congress.
House. Committee on Agriculture.
Subcommittee on Forests. Washington , 1980.
iv, 210 p. : LC Card 80-603793 DDC
346.7304/675 347.3064675 19
KF27 .A348 1980a

RESOURCES, RENEWABLE NATURAL. see RENEWABLE NATURAL RESOURCES.

Respirable particulate matter characteristics in Chicago, 1954 to the present /. Scheff, Peter A. Chicago, IL [1979] iv, 21 p. : LC Card 80-621152 DDC 628.5/3 19
RA576 .S3

RESPIRATORY ORGANS - DISEASES - DIAGNOSIS - ABSTRACTS.
Torchia, Marion. Chest X-ray screening practices . Rockville, Md. , Washington, D.C. [1980] v, 57 p. ; LC Card 80-602827 DDC 363.1/79 19
RA645.R4 T67

RESPIRATORY ORGANS - DISEASES - RESEARCH - UNITED STATES.
National Heart, Lung, and Blood Institute. Division of Lung Diseases. Task Force on Epidemiology of Respiratory Diseases. Report of Task Force on Epidemiology of Respiratory Diseases . [Bethesda, Md.?] , 1980. vii, 244 p. : LC Card 81-600681 DDC 614.5/92/00973 19
RA645.R4 N37 1980

RESPIRATORY ORGANS - DISEASES - UNITED STATES.
National Heart, Lung, and Blood Institute. Division of Lung Diseases. Task Force on Epidemiology of Respiratory Diseases. Report of Task Force on Epidemiology of Respiratory Diseases . [Bethesda, Md.?] , 1980. vii, 244 p. : LC Card 81-600681 DDC 614.5/92/00973 19
RA645.R4 N37 1980

RESPONDEAT SUPERIOR - NORTH CAROLINA.
Cannaday, Kenneth S. Conspiracy and vicarious liability--North Carolina Supreme Court "disapproves" existing caselaw /. Chapel Hill, N.C. , 1980, c1978. 5 p. ; LC Card 81-621376 DDC 345.756/02 347.56052 19
KFN7908.A15 U6 no. 80/07 KFN7974

Response Analysis Corporation. Fishburne, Patricia M. National survey on drug abuse : main findings 1979 /. Rockville, Md. , 1980. 279 p. in various pagings, [9] leaves of plates :
NYPL [JLF 81-136]

Response of phytoplankton to water quality in the Chowan River system /. North Carolina. State University, Raleigh. Dept. of Botany. [Raleigh, N.C.] [1979] xv, 204 p. : LC Card 79-626203 DDC 589.4 19
HD1694.N8 N6 no. 129 QK571.5.N8

Response time analysis /. Kansas City, Mo. Police Dept. Washington , 1978. 2 v. : LC Card 79-603050
HV8148.K22 K34 1978

A response to the report of the Governor's Committee on Unification of the Public Mental Health System /. Michigan. Dept. of Mental Health. [Lansing] [1980] v, 45 p. ; LC Card 80-623048 DDC 353.97740084/2 19
RA790.65.M5 M45 1980

Responses of submersed vascular plant communities to environmental change . Davis, Graham J. Washington, D.C. , 1980. x, 70 p. : LC Card 80-607178 DDC 581.5/2623 19
QK930 .D38

Ressel, Dennis. (joint author) Coffee, Daniel R., 1919- Soil survey of Dallas County, Texas /. [Washington] [1980] vii, 153 p., [38] fold. leaves of plates : LC Card 80-601832 DDC 631.4/7/7642811 19
S599.T4 C63

Ressources en eau, leur planification, et leur gestion. United Nations. Dag Hammarskjold Library. Water resources, planning, and management . New York , 1977. vi, 117 p. ; LC Card 81-478046 DDC 300 s 016.33391 19
JX1977 .A2 ST/LIB/SER.B/23 TC405

REST HOMES - LAW AND LEGISLATION - ILLINOIS.
Illinois. Dept. of Public Health. Minimum standards, rules, and regulations for classification and licensure of sheltered care facilities. [Springfield] [1980] x, 242, [3] p. ; LC Card 80-622598 DDC 344.773/03216 19
KFI1482.R45 A32 1980

REST HOMES - LAW AND LEGISLATION - OHIO.
Ohio. Laws, statutes, etc. [Nursing home and rest home licensure law.] Nursing and rest

home law and rules. [Columbus] [1978?] 18 p. ; LC Card 80-622700 DDC 344.771/03216 19
KFO363.N8 A3 1978

REST HOMES - NEW JERSEY - FIRES AND FIRE PREVENTION.
New Jersey. State Legislature. Senate. Institutions, Health, and Welfare Committee. Public hearing before Senate Institutions, Health, and Welfare Committee and Assembly Institutions, Health, and Welfare Committee on rooming house fire in Bradley Beach . [Trenton? , 1980?] 40, 35, 6 p. ; LC Card 80-623979 DDC 362.1/6 19
KFN1811.3 .I47 1980b

REST HOMES - NEW YORK (STATE)
Close, Beatrice A. Private proprietary homes for adults . [Albany] [1979] 132 p. ; LC Card 79-625315 DDC 362.6/1/09747 19
HV1468.N7 C55

REST HOMES - WASHINGTON (STATE)
Washington (State). Center for Health Statistics. Boarding homes in Washington State, 1978 /. Olympia, Wash. [1979] iv, 23 p. ; LC Card 80-621771 DDC 362.6/1/09797 19
HV1468.W2 W35 1979

RESTAURANTS, LUNCH ROOMS, ETC. - LAW AND LEGISLATION - FLORIDA.
Florida. Legislature. Senate. Committee on Commerce. A review of the Advisory Council to the Division of Hotels and Restaurants in the Department of Business Regulation /. [Tallahassee] [1980] i, 24 p. ; LC Card 81-621206 DDC 353.97590082/43 19
KFF282.H6 A25 1980

RESTAURANTS, LUNCH ROOMS, ETC. - LAW AND LEGISLATION - TENNESSEE.
Tennessee. Laws, statutes, etc. Tennessee laws, rules, and regulations for restaurants. Nashville, Tenn. [1952] 33 p. ; LC Card 79-119875 DDC 344.768/0464 347.6804464 19
KFT282.H6 A3 1952

Restitution . Cain, Anthony A. [Washington, D.C.] [1979 i.e. 1980] vii, 61 p. ; LC Card 80-601596 DDC 364.6/8 19
HV8688 .C34

RESTITUTION - ABSTRACTS.
Cain, Anthony A. Restitution . [Washington, D.C.] [1979 i.e. 1980] vii, 61 p. ; LC Card 80-601596 DDC 364.6/8 19
HV8688 .C34

Restitution and victims of crime : Louisiana State University, Baton Rouge, Louisiana, February 23-25, 1977 / conference convener, Fred Wrighton ; editing, Brenda Bradshaw, Georgann [sic] English ; [co-sponsored by Governmental Services Institute, Division of Continuing Education, Louisiana State University, and the Institute of Urban Studies, Research and Service Programs Division, the University of Texas at Arlington]. Arlington, Tex. : The Institute, [1977?] iv, 86 p. : ill. ; 22 cm. (New directions for corrections . v. 2) LC Card 80-621838 DDC 364.6/8 19
1. Victims of crimes - United States - Congresses. 2. Restitution - United States - Congresses. I. Bradshaw, Brenda. II. English, Georgeann. III. Louisiana State University, Baton Rouge. Governmental Services Institute. IV. Texas. University at Arlington. Institute of Urban Studies. Research and Service Programs Division. V. Series.
HV6250.2 .R47

RESTITUTION - NEW YORK (STATE)
New York (State). Legislature. Senate. Minority Task Force on Criminal Justice. The criminal must pay! . [Albany] [1980] 51 p. ; LC Card 80-622773 DDC 344.747/03288 19
KFN5010.72 .C73 1980

RESTITUTION - UNITED STATES - ABSTRACTS.
Cain, Anthony A. Restitution . [Washington, D.C.] [1979 i.e. 1980] vii, 61 p. ; LC Card 80-601596 DDC 364.6/8 19
HV8688 .C34

RESTITUTION - UNITED STATES - CONGRESSES.
Restitution and victims of crime . Arlington, Tex. [1977?] iv, 86 p. : LC Card 80-621838 DDC 364.6/8 19
HV6250.2 .R47

Restle, James. Leipsic, Ohio . [Leipsic, Ohio] , 1980. 180 p. : LC Card 81-126527 DDC

977.1/18 19
F499.L44 L44

Restoring effective enforcement of the anti-trust laws . United States. Congress. House. Committee on the Judiciary. Subcommittee on Monopolies and Commercial Law. Washington , 1979. v, 504 p. ; LC Card 80-603813 DDC 343.73/072/0262 347.303720262 19
KF27 .J8663 1979a

RESTRAINT OF TRADE - UNITED STATES - MATHEMATICAL MODELS - CASE STUDIES.
Morkre, Morris E. The effects of restrictions on United States imports . [Washington, D.C.] [1980] xv, 212 p. : LC Card 80-603259 DDC 382/.5/0973 19
HF1731 .M67

A restudy of the Ostracode genus Pleoschisma Brady, 1890 (Myodocopina) /. Kornicker, Louis S., 1919- Washington, D.C. , 1981. iii, 16 p. : LC Card 80-607813 DDC 591 s 595.3/3 19
QL1 .S54 no. 332 QL444.O85

Results of areawide water quality monitoring program for the Raymond Basin, July 1, 1978 - June 30, 1979 . California. Dept. of Water Resources. Southern District. [Los Angeles] [1980] v, 29 p., 1 fold. leaf of plates : LC Card 80-621916 DDC 363.6/1 19
TD224.C3 C24 1980

Results of national alcohol safety action projects /. United States. National Highway Traffic Safety Administration. Washington, D.C. , 1979. 118 p. : LC Card 80-601080
HE5620.D7 U56 1979a NYPL [JLF 81-157]

Results of the general election held November 4, 1975, for the office of 80 members of the General Assembly and six public questions /. New Jersey. [Trenton] [1975?] 10 p. ; LC Card 78-613094 DDC 324.9749/043 19
JK3593 1975 .N48 1975

Results of the national ASAP program. United States. National Highway Traffic Safety Administration. Results of national alcohol safety action projects /. Washington, D.C. , 1979. 118 p. : LC Card 80-601080
HE5620.D7 U56 1979a NYPL [JLF 81-157]

Results of the recent elections in Zimbabwe . United States. Congress. House. Committee on Foreign Affairs. Subcommittee on Africa. Washington , 1980. iii, 101 p. ; LC Card 80-602533 DDC 324.96891/04 19
KF27 .F625 1980

RÉSUMÉS (EMPLOYMENT)
Ultrasystems, inc. Evaluation and analysis of the Cleff job matching system: final report /. - Irvine, Calif. , 1975. 2 v. in 1 :
*NYPL [*XME-9380]*

Resurge '79 . United States. Office of Education. Division of Vocational and Technical Education. Washington, D. C. , 1980. 81 p. ;
NYPL [JLF 81-624]

Resurrection Bay and Aialik Bay, Alaska. Feder, Howard M. A preliminary survey of the benthos of Resurrection Bay and Aialik Bay, Alaska /. Fairbanks, Alaska , 1979. iii, 53 p. : LC Card 80-623129 DDC 551.46 s 591.9798/3 19
GC1 .A497 R78-7 QL161

RETAIL ADVERTISING. see ADVERTISING.

Retail location theory /. Huff, David Lynch, 1931- Austin, Tex. , 1980. [15] leaves : LC Card 80-624130 DDC 381/.1 19
HF5429.275 .H83

RETAIL TRADE - DELAWARE - WILMINGTON METROPOLITAN AREA - EMPLOYEES - STATISTICS.
Delaware. Dept. of Labor. Office of Planning, Research & Evaluation. Wilmington SMSA occupational employment statistics . Newark, DE , 1978. i, 80 leaves ; LC Card 78-624189 DDC
HD5725.D3 D33 1978a NYPL [JLF 81-109]

RETAIL TRADE - INDIANA - EMPLOYEES - STATISTICS.
Indiana. Employment Security Division. Research and Statistics Section. Staffing patterns in wholesale and retail trade industries in Indiana . [Indianapolis, Ind.] , 1978. viii, 67 p. : LC Card 79-625864 DDC 331.12/51381/09772 19
HD5725.I6 I53 1978a

RETAIL TRADE - LAW AND LEGISLATION - MISSISSIPPI.
Gotthelf, Harold, 1916- Major government regulations affecting small retail businesses in Mississippi /. Jackson, Miss. [1979] v, 115 p. :
LC Card 80-620872   DDC 346.762/0652 19
KFM6881.A1 G67 1979

RETAIL TRADE - UNITED STATES - SECURITY MEASURES.
United States. Congress. Senate. Select Committee on Small Business. Crime and its impact on small business . Washington , 1980. iii, 115 p. ;   LC Card 80-603285   DDC 338.6/42/0973 19
KF26.5 .S6 1980k

RETAIL TRADING AREAS. see MARKET SURVEYS.

RETAINING WALLS.
(1980) Yokel, Felix Y. Recommended technical provisions for construction practice in shoring and sloping of trenches and excavations /. Washington, DC [1980] xvi, 68 p. :   LC Card 80-600068   DDC 690/.02/18 s 624.1/52 19
TA435 .U58 no. 127 TA770

RETAINING WALLS - MATERIALS.
A Study of lumber used for bracing trenches in the United States . Washington, D.C. [1980] 218 p. in various pagings :   LC Card 80-600015   DDC 690/.02/18 s 624.1/52 19
TA435 .U58 no. 122 TA770

RETALIATION (ECONOMICS) see TARIFF.

Retardation, corrections, and retarded offenders . Santamour, Miles. Washington [1979] i, 156 p. ;   LC Card 79-604176   DDC 016.3646 19
Z5703.4.M46 S26 1979 HV6791

RETIRED MILITARY PERSONNEL - EMPLOYMENT - UNITED STATES.
United States. Congress. House. Committee on Post Office and Civil Service. Subcommittee on Compensation and Employee Benefits. Minimum benefit provision of the disability retirement program . Washington , 1980. iii, 35 p. ;   LC Card 80-602789   DDC 353.005 19
KF27 .P638 1980a

RETIREMENT AGE - UNITED STATES.
Shipp, P. Royal. Background material on work, retirement, and social security /. Washington , 1980. v, 24 p. :   LC Card 80-603060   DDC 368.4/3/00973 19
HD7125 .S527

United States. Congress. House. Subcommittee on Post Office and Civil Service. Subcommittee on Compensation and Employee Benefits. Voluntary retirements under the civil service retirement system . Washington , 1980. iii, 72 p. ;   LC Card 80-603099   DDC 353.005 19
KF27 .P638 1980g

United States. Congress. House. Committee on Ways and Means. Subcommittee on Oversight. Strategies to encourage older workers to voluntarily extend their worklives . Washington , 1980. iii, 264 p. :   LC Card 80-604060   DDC 368.4/3/00973 19
KF27 .W345 1980k

United States. Congress. House. Select Committee on Aging. Subcommittee on Retirement Income and Employment. Oversight on recommendations of 1979 Social Security Advisory Council . Washington , 1980. iv, 208 p. :   LC Card 80-603006   DDC 368.4/00973 19
KF27.5 .A374 1980

United States. Congress. House. Select Committee on Aging. Subcommittee on Retirement Income and Employment. Social security . Washington , 1980. v, 39 p. :   LC Card 80-603864   DDC 353.0082/56 19
HD7125 .U537 1980a

Retirement and migration in the North Central States . Honnen, James S. Madison , 1969. 57 p. ;   LC Card 76-632644   DDC 317.75 s 364.8/09775 19
HB3525.W6 W5 no. 19 HQ1064.U6W55

Retirement appeals, military leave, and quadrennial pay commission . United States. Congress. House. Committee on Post Office and Civil Service. Subcommittee on Compensation and Employee Benefits. Washington , 1980. iii, 20 p. ;   LC Card 80-602189   DDC 343.73/011 19
KF27 .P638 1980

Retirement benefits, are they fair and are they enough? . United States. Congress. Senate. Special Committee on Aging. Washington , 1981. iii, 74 p. ;   LC Card 81-602039   DDC 331.25/2/0973 19
KF26.5 .A3 1980j

RETIREMENT - FLORIDA.
Honnen, James S. Retirement and migration in the North Central States . Madison , 1969. 57 p. ;   LC Card 76-632644   DDC 317.75 s 364.8/09775 19
HB3525.W6 W5 no. 19 HQ1064.U6W55

Retirement income goals /. Meier, Elizabeth L. Washington, D.C. [1980] v, 60 p. ;   LC Card 80-602550   DDC 331.25/2/0973 19
HD7106.U5 M37

RETIREMENT INCOME - KANSAS.
United States. Congress. Senate. Special Committee on Aging. Retirement benefits, are they fair and are they enough? . Washington , 1981. iii, 74 p. ;   LC Card 81-602039   DDC 331.25/2/0973 19
KF26.5 .A3 1980j

RETIREMENT INCOME - NEW YORK (CITY) - EFFECT OF INFLATION ON.
United States. Congress. House. Select Committee on Aging. Subcommittee on Retirement Income and Employment. Inflation and New York's elderly . Washington , 1980. iv, 201 p. ;   LC Card 80-603004   DDC 330.9747/1043/0880565 19
KF27.5 .A374 1980a

RETIREMENT INCOME - NORTH CAROLINA.
North Carolina. General Assembly. Committee on Retirement Benefits in Addition to Salary. Report to the 1979 General Aasembly of North Carolina, second session, 1980 /. [Raleigh , 1980] 74 p. in various pagings ;   LC Card 80-624247   DDC 353.9756005 19
JK4160 .N666 1980

United States. Congress. House. Select Committee on Aging. Subcommittee on Retirement Income and Employment. Income status of the rural elderly . Washington , 1980. iii, 74 p. ;   LC Card 81-601192   DDC 362.6/042 19
KF27.5 .A374 1980b

RETIREMENT INCOME - UNITED STATES.
Meier, Elizabeth L. Retirement income goals /. Washington, D.C. [1980] v, 60 p. ;   LC Card 80-602550   DDC 331.25/2/0973 19
HD7106.U5 M37

United States. Congress. House. Select Committee on Aging. Retirement, the broken promise . Washington , 1981. iii, 91 p. ;   LC Card 81-601334   DDC 331.25/2/0973 19
KF27.5 .A3 1980j

United States. Congress. Senate. Special Committee on Aging. Retirement benefits, are they fair and are they enough? . Washington , 1981. iii, 74 p. ;   LC Card 81-602039   DDC 331.25/2/0973 19
KF26.5 .A3 1980j

United States. President's Commission on Pension Policy. An interim report /. Chicago, Ill. , 1980. 51, [13] p. :   LC Card 80-132555   DDC 331.25/2/0973 19
HD7106.U5 U644 1980a

United States. President's Commission on Pension Policy. An interim report /. Washington, D.C. (736 Jackson Place, N.W., Washington, D.C. 20006) , 1980. 66 p. in various pagings :   LC Card 81-600721   DDC 331.25/2/0973 19
HD7106.U5 U644 1981

United States. Social Security Administration. Office of Research and Statistics. Income & resources of the aged /. [Washington, D.C.] [1980] 35 p. :   LC Card 80-600019
HD7106.U5 U65 1980

Urban Institute. Emerging options for work and retirement policy (an analysis of major income and employment issues with an agenda for research priorities) . Washington , 1980. vi, 186 p. 23 cm.   LC Card 80-603277   DDC 331.25/2/0973 19
HD7106.U5 U7 1980

RETIREMENT - IOWA - CASE STUDIES.
Goudy, Willis J. Older workers in small towns . Ames, Iowa [1977] viii, 205 p. :   LC Card

80-623924   DDC 331.3/98/09777 19
HD6281.I8 G68

RETIREMENT, MANDATORY - UNITED STATES.
United States. Congress. House. Select Committee on Aging. EEOC enforcement of the Age Discrimination in Employment Act . Washington , 1980. iii, 110 p. :   LC Card 81-600653   DDC 331.3/98 19
KF27.5 .A3 1980h

RETIREMENT PENSIONS. see OLD AGE PENSIONS.

Retirement, the broken promise . United States. Congress. House. Select Committee on Aging. Washington , 1981. iii, 91 p. ;   LC Card 81-601334   DDC 331.25/2/0973 19
KF27.5 .A3 1980j

RETIREMENT - WISCONSIN.
Honnen, James S. Retirement and migration in the North Central States . Madison , 1969. 57 p. ;   LC Card 76-632644   DDC 317.75 s 364.8/09775 19
HB3525.W6 W5 no. 19 HQ1064.U6W55

Retterath, Quentin. North Dakota. Laws, statutes, etc. [Workmen's compensation act.] North Dakota Workmen's compensation act and Crime victims reparations act and rules of procedure, effective July 1, 1979 /. [Bismarck] [1979] 105 p. ;   LC Card 80-621922   DDC 344.784/021/02632 19
KFN8942.A335 A2 1979

Return engagement . Gambee, Budd Leslie. [Urbana] , 1977. 26 p. ;   LC Card 79-620558   DDC 020 19
Z672.5 .G35

Returning the mentally disabled to the community . United States. General Accounting Office. [Washington] 1977. x, 254 p. ;   LC Card 77-601175
RA790.6 .U55 1977

REUSABLE SPACE VEHICLES.
United States. Congress. Senate. Committee on Appropriations. Subcommittee on HUD-Independent Agencies. Space shuttle and Galileo mission . Washington , 1980. iv, 132 p. ;   LC Card 80-601987   DDC 353.0072/2368778 19
KF26 .A6486 1979c

Reuse of historically and architecturally significant railroad stations for transportation and other community needs . Webber, Margo B. Washington, D.C. , 1978. ii, 126 p. :   LC Card 79-603620   DDC 725/.31/0288 19
NA6311 .W4

REUSE OF WATER. see WATER REUSE.

Revealed preferences, functional form, and labor supply /. Dickinson, Jonathan, 1943- [Madison] , 1979. 50 p. :   LC Card 80-622900   DDC 331.2/973 19
HD5724 .D52 1979

REVEGETATION - ILLINOIS.
D'Antuono, James R. Some aspects of natural vegetation establishment on abandoned underground coal mine refuse areas in Illinois /. Chicago, Ill. , 1979. xii, 83 p. :   LC Card 79-626016   DDC 631.6/4 19
S621.5.S65 D36

REVEGETATION - UNITED STATES.
Establishment of seeded grasslands for wildlife habitat in the prairie pothole region /. Washington, D.C. , 1981. p. cm.   LC Card 81-607001   DDC 639.9/79/0973 s 639.9/79 19
SK361 .A256 no. 234

REVENUE ESTIMATING. see TAX REVENUE ESTIMATING.

Revenue from state sources by administrative unit, 1976-77 /. Lauver, Paul H. [Harrisburg, PA] , 1978. 20 leaves ;   LC Card 80-620574   DDC 379.1/22/09748 19
LB2826.P4 L38

REVENUE - GEORGIA.
Coe, Charles K. Maximizing revenue, minimizing expenditures /. Athens , 1981. p. cm.   ISBN 0-89854-070-4 LC Card 80-29269   DDC 352.1/09758 19
HJ9221 .C63

Revenue laws . North Carolina. Legislative Research Commission. [Raleigh] [1980] ix, 31,

[51] p. ; LC Card 80-623283 DDC 343.75604 19
KFN7870 .A25 1980

REVENUE SHARING - ILLINOIS.
Walzer, Norman. Revenue sharing in Illinois
municipalities /. Springfield, IL [1979] 6, 47,
[67] p. : LC Card 80-623316 DDC 336.1/85 19
HJ9227 .W345

Revenue sharing in Illinois municipalities /.
Walzer, Norman. Springfield, IL [1979] 6, 47,
[67] p. : LC Card 80-623316 DDC 336.1/85 19
HJ9227 .W345

Revenue sharing, Iowa. Campana, Joyce. A study
of Federal revenue sharing in Iowa /. Iowa
City, Iowa [1980] vi, 67 p. : LC Card 80-623091
DDC 336.1/85 19
HJ9236 .C35

REVENUE SHARING - IOWA.
Campana, Joyce. A study of Federal revenue
sharing in Iowa /. Iowa City, Iowa [1980] vi,
67 p. : LC Card 80-623091 DDC 336.1/85 19
HJ9236 .C35

**REVENUE SHARING - LAW AND
LEGISLATION - UNITED STATES.**
United States. Congress. House. Committee on
Government Operations. Intergovernmental
Relations and Human Resources Subcommittee.
State and Local Fiscal Assistance Act of 1972 .
Washington , 1980. vi, 909 p. ; LC Card
80-603812 DDC 343.73/034 347.30334 19
KF27 .G664 1980

United States. Congress. Senate. Committee on
Finance. Subcommittee on Revenue Sharing,
Intergovernmental Revenue Impact, and
Economic Problems. Proposed general revenue
sharing extension . Washington , 1980. iv, 650
p. : LC Card 80-603507 DDC 343.73/034 19
KF26 .F567 1980

REVENUE SHARING - NEW YORK (STATE)
New York (State). State University at
Binghamton. Social Policy Institute. Local
planning and special revenue sharing .
[Albany?] , 1975. i, 37 leaves ; LC Card
76-623363 DDC 331.11/09747 19
HD5725.N7 N47 1975

United States. General Accounting Office. How
revenue sharing formulas distribute aid .
[Washington, D.C.] [1980] iii, 61 p. : LC Card
80-602651 DDC 353.0072/5 19
HJ275 .U54 1980

REVENUE SHARING - NORTH CAROLINA.
North Carolina. Legislative Research
Commission. State revenue sharing . [Raleigh]
[1980] 17, [148] p. ; LC Card 80-623285 DDC
336.1/85 19
HJ615 .N67 1980

REVENUE SHARING - UNITED STATES.
United States. Congress. Senate. Committee on
Governmental Affairs. Subcommittee on
Intergovernmental Relations. Scope of the
general revenue sharing program . Washington ,
1980. iii, 227 p. ; LC Card 80-602990 DDC
336.1/85 19
KF26 .G6738 1980a

United States. General Accounting Office.
Antirecession assistance--an evaluation .
[Washington] 1977. v, 128 p. ; LC Card
77-604896
HD5724 .U629 1977   **NYPL [JLF 81-298]**

United States. General Accounting Office. How
revenue sharing formulas distribute aid .
[Washington, D.C.] [1980] iii, 61 p. : LC Card
80-602651 DDC 353.0072/5 19
HJ275 .U54 1980

**REVENUE SHARING - UNITED STATES -
STATES.**
United States. General Accounting Office.
Impact of eliminating the States from the
general revenue sharing program--a nine-state
assessment . Washington, D.C. [1980] iv, 39
p. : LC Card 80-603192 DDC 353.0072/5 19
HJ275 .U54 1980a

REVENUE - UNITED STATES.
Coe, Charles K. Maximizing revenue,
minimizing expenditures /. Athens , 1981. p.
cm. ISBN 0-89854-070-4 LC Card 80-29269
DDC 352.1/09758 19
HJ9221 .C63

United States. Congress. House. Committee on
Ways and Means. President's cash management
initiatives in the fiscal year 1981 budget .

Washington , 1980. iv, 197 p. : LC Card
80-602770 DDC 353.0072/6 19
KF27 .W3 1980f

Reversing regional decline . Pennsylvania. Dept.
of Community Affairs. [Harrisburg] [1976] 13,
[8] leaves : LC Card 76-624629
HJ275 .P45 1976   **NYPL [*XME-9553]**

**Review and briefing on legislative analyst report
on the State Bar .** California. Legislature.
Special Legislative Investigating Committee on
the State Bar. Sacramento, Calif. [1980] i, 42
p. ; LC Card 80-622945 DDC 340/.06/0794 19
KFC10 .S73 1980

**Review and comparative analysis of oilseed raw
materials and processes ...** Mattil, K. F. Review
and comparative analysis of oilseed raw
materials and processes suitable for the
production of protein products for human
consumption. New York , 1974. viii, 36 p. :
LC Card 81-465132 DDC 300 s 664/.64 19
JX1977 .A2 ID/126 (ID/WG.120/10/Rev. 1)

**Review and response to the final report of the
National Black Health Providers Task Force
on High Blood Pressure Education and
Control.** [Bethesda, Md.?] : U. S. Dept of
Health and Human Services, Public Health
Service, National Institutes of Health, National
Heart, Lung, and Blood Institute, 1980. vii, 57
p. : ill. ; 28 cm. (NIH publication. no. 80-2187) Oct.
1980. Item 507-E-1 LC Card 80-604145 DDC
362.1/9613205/08996073 19
*1. Hypertension - United States - Prevention. 2.
Afro-Americans - Health and hygiene - United States. I.
National Black Health Providers Task Force on High
Blood Pressure Education and Control (U. S.). II.
National Heart, Lung, and Blood Institute. III. Series:
DHHS publication, no. (NIH) 80-2187.*
RC685.H8 R43

**Review of activities of the Overseas Private
Investment Corporation .** United States.
Congress. House. Committee on Foreign
Affairs. Subcommittee on International
Economic Policy and Trade. Washington ,
1980. iii, 111 p. ; LC Card 80-602111 DDC
353.0082 19
KF27 .F6465 1979d

Review of Agricultural trade act of 1978 . United
States. Congress. House. Committee on
Agriculture. Washington , 1980. iii, 42 p. ; LC
Card 80-602236 DDC 343.73/0851/0262 19
KF27 .A3 1979b

Review of child nutrition programs . United
States. Congress. Senate. Committee on
Agriculture, Nutrition, and Forestry.
Subcommittee on Nutrition. Washington , 1980.
iv, 130 p. ; LC Card 80-603080 DDC
363.8/0880544 19
KF26 .A3559 1980a

Review of compensation and DIC programs .
United States. Congress. House. Committee on
Veterans' Affairs. Subcommittee on
Compensation, Pension, Insurance, and
Memorial Affairs. Washington , 1980. iii, 93
p. ; LC Card 80-603330 DDC 343.73/0112 19
KF27 .V43 1980a

Review of Davis-Dolwig allocation methodology .
California. Dept. of Finance. Program
Evaluation Unit. [Sacramento] [1979] xviii, 85
p. : LC Card 80-620662 DDC 333.78/09794 19
GV191.42.C2 C33 1979

**A review of Division of Veterans' Affairs,
Department of Commerce and Economic
Development, July 1, 1976-June 30, 1977.**
Alaska. Division of Legislative Audit. Juneau,
Alaska [1978] 29 leaves ; LC Card 78-624010
DDC 353.97980081/2 19
UB358.A4 A29 1978

**Review of education, training, and employment
programs administered by the Veterans'
Administration .** United States. Congress.
House. Committee on Veterans' Affairs.
Subcommittee on Education, Training, and
Employment. Washington , 1980. iv, 275 p. ;
LC Card 80-602986 DDC 355.1/152/0973 19
KF27 .V436 1980

**A review of electric power demand forecasts and
suggestions for improving future forecasts /.**
Tuck, Bradford H. [Juneau, Alaska] [1980] 73
p. ; LC Card 81-621101 DDC 333.79/3213 19
HD9685.U6 A477

**Review of energy situation pertaining to
agriculture .** United States. Congress. House.
Committee on Agriculture. Subcommittee on
Department Investigations, Oversight, and
Research. Washington , 1980. iii, 36 p. ; LC
Card 80-603351 DDC 333.79 19
KF27 .A33265 1979f

A review of forest taxation in Washington /.
Conklin, John B. [Olympia, Wash.] [1980] vi,
116 p. : LC Card 80-623470 DDC 336.22/5 19
HJ4280.A3 C65

Review of GAO preliminary study of parity .
United States. Congress. House. Committee on
Agriculture. Subcommittee on Family Farms,
Rural Development, and Special Studies.
Washington , 1980. iii, 119 p. : LC Card
80-603990 DDC 338.1/8 19
KF27 .A344 1980c

Review of harmful substances /.
IMCO/FAO/UNESCO/WMO/WHO/IAEA/U
N Joint Group of Experts on the Scientific
Aspects of Marine Pollution. New York [1976]
iv, 80 p. ; LC Card 80-508634 DDC 628.1/68 19
GC1085 .I15 1976a

**Review of Illinois summer precipitation
conditions /.** Changnon, Stanley Alcide.
Urbana , 1980. 160 p. : LC Card 80-623561
DDC 551.57/72/773 19
QC925.1.U8 I325

**Review of implementation of Basket II of the
Helsinki Final Act .** United States. Congress.
House. Committee on Foreign Affairs.
Subcommittee on International Economic Policy
and Trade. Washington , 1980. iii, 82 p. ; LC
Card 80-604051 DDC 337.73047 19
KF27 .F6465 1980d

**Review of military clubs and package beverage
stores .** United States. Congress. House.
Committee on Armed Services. Subcommittee
on Investigations. Nonappropriated Fund Panel.
Washington , 1980. iii, 21 p. ; LC Card
80-601774 DDC 355.3/46/0973 19
U56 .U56 1980

**Review of New York City audits of supplemental
welfare funds.** New York (State). Division of
Audits and Accounts. Albany [1980] 4, 20
leaves ; LC Card 80-622251 DDC
352.94/4/097471 19
HV86 .N77 1980

**Review of progress on Teamsters' Central States
pension fund reform .** United States. Congress.
House. Committee on Ways and Means.
Subcommittee on Oversight. Washington ,
1980. iii, 236 p. ; LC Card 80-602733 DDC
331.25/22 19
KF27 .W345 1980b

**Review of readiness considerations in the
development of the defense budget .** United
States. Congress. House. Committee on Armed
Services. Procurement and Military Nuclear
Systems Subcommittee. Readiness Panel.
Washington , 1980 [i.e. 1981] ii, 161 p. : LC
Card 81-600960 DDC 355/.033073 19
KF27 .A7657 1980d

**A review of section 288.39(6), Florida statutes,
Small Business Advisory Council /.** Florida.
Legislature. Senate. Economic, Community, and
Consumer Affairs Committee. [Tallahassee, Fla.]
[1980] i, 22 p. ; LC Card 81-621214 DDC
346.759/0652 347.5906652 19
KFF234 .A25 1980

**A review of section 570.543, Florida statutes,
Florida Consumers' Council /.** Florida.
Legislature. Senate. Economic, Community, and
Consumer Affairs Committee. [Tallahassee]
[1980] i, 25 p. ; LC Card 81-621212 DDC
353.97590082/042 19
KFF230 .A25 1980

**A review of section 719.501(2), Florida statutes
Cooperative Advisory Board (part I) and
section 718.501(2), Florida statutes
Condominium Advisory Board (part II) /.**
Florida. Legislature. Senate. Economic,
Community, and Consumer Affairs Committee.
[Tallahassee] [1980] i, 12, 28 p. ; LC Card
81-621215 DDC 346.75904/33 347.5906433 19
KFF114.C6 A25 1980

**A review of selected Federal vaccine and
immunization policies .** United States.
Congress. Office of Technology Assessment.

Washington , 1979. xvi, 208 p. : LC Card 79-600165 DDC 614.4/7/0973 19
RA638 .U48 1979

Review of taxpayer privacy issues . United States. Congress. House. Committee on Ways and Means. Subcommittee on Oversight. Washington , 1980. iii, 185 p. ; LC Card 80-603900 DDC 323.44/83/0973 19
KF27 .W345 1980g

A review of the accuracy of treasury revenue forecasts, 1963-1978 /. Saunders, Hyman. [Washington, D.C.] , 1981. xi, 42 p. ; LC Card 81-601118 DDC 353.0072/2252 19
HJ2051 .S26

A review of the Advisory Council to the Division of Hotels and Restaurants in the Department of Business Regulation /. Florida. Legislature. Senate. Committee on Commerce. [Tallahassee] [1980] i, 24 p. ; LC Card 81-621206 DDC 353.97590082/43 19
KFF282.H6 A25 1980

A review of the authority of the Secretary of State to appoint advisory councils in the Department of State /. Florida. Legislature. Senate. Governmental Operations Committee. [Tallahassee] [1980] ii leaves, 28 p. ; LC Card 81-621198 DDC 353.9759063 19
KFF427.5.S4 A25 1980

A review of the Cal-Vet program, Department of Veterans Affairs /. California. Dept. of Finance. Program Evaluation Unit. [Sacramento] [1980] xiii, 105 p. : LC Card 80-623745 DDC 353.97940081/2 19
UB358.C2 C27 1980

A review of the Capitol Center Planning Commission in the Department of General Services /. Florida. Legislature. Senate. Governmental Operations Committee. [Tallahassee] [1980] i, 110 p. : LC Card 81-621189 DDC 353.97590081/9 19
KFF410.C3 A25 1980

A review of the Council for the Purchase of Products and Services of the Blind or Other Severely Handicapped in the Department of General Services /. Florida. Legislature. Senate. Governmental Operations Committee. [Tallahassee] [1980] i, 36 p. ; LC Card 81-621188 DDC 353.97590084/4 19
HV1652 .F574 1980

A review of the Cyphophthalmi of the United States and Mexico, with a proposed reclassification of the suborder (Arachnida, Opiliones) /. Shear, William A. New York, N.Y. , 1980. 34 p. : LC Card 80-147274 DDC 591 s 595.4/3 19
QL1 .A436 no. 2705 QL458.4

Review of the deep-sea genus Argyropeza (Gastropoda, Prosobranchia, Cerithiidae) /. Houbrick, Richard S. Washington , 1980. iii, 30 p. : LC Card 80-607017 DDC 591 s 594/.32 19
QL1 .S54 no. 321 QL430.5.C4

A review of the extinct wolverine, Plesiogulo (Carnivora, Mustelidae) from North America /. Harrison, Jessica A. City of Washington , 1981. p. cm. LC Card 81-607075 DDC 560 s 569/.74 19
QE701 .S56 no. 46 QE882.C15

A review of the Fertilizer Technical Council in the Department of Agriculture and Consumer Services /. Florida. Legislature. Senate. Committee on Agriculture. [Tallahassee] [1980] 1, 20, [11] p. ; LC Card 81-621221 DDC 353.97590082/42 19
KFF267.F4 A25 1980

A Review of the Florida Fire Safety Board in the Department of Insurance / prepared pursuant to the Sundown Act by staff of the Florida Senate Committee on Commerce. [Tallahassee] : The Committee, [1980] i, 16 p. ; 28 cm. "November, 1980." LC Card 81-621731 DDC 344.759/0537 347.5904537 19
1. Florida Fire Safety Board. 2. Fire prevention - Law and legislation - Florida. I. Florida. Legislature. Senate. Committee on Commerce.
KFF381 .A25 1980

A review of the Florida Student Financial Aid Advisory Council in the Department of Education /. Florida. Legislature. Senate. Committee on Education. [Tallahassee, Fla.] [1980] i, 22 p. ; LC Card 81-621729 DDC

344.759/0795 347.5904795 19
KFF396 .A25 1980

A review of the Florida Tourism Commission in the Department of Commerce . Florida. Legislature. Senate. Committee on Commerce. [Tallahassee? Fla.] [1980] i, 20 p. ; LC Card 81-621209 DDC 353.97590082/7 19
KFF282.T7 A25 1980

Review of the Hamilton Test Systems motor vehicle inspection program in the south coast air basin /. California. Legislature. Assembly. Select Committee on Regulatory Oversight. Sacramento, Calif. [1980] iv, 307 p. ; LC Card 80-623736 DDC 353.97940087/834 19
KFC10.4 .R43 1980a

A review of the historic preservation boards of trustees in the Department of State / prepared pursuant to the Sundown Act by staff of the Florida Senate Committee on Governmental Operations. [Tallahassee] : The Committee, [1980] iii, 112 p. : forms ; 28 cm. "September, 1980." LC Card 81-621200 DDC 353.97590085/9 19
1. Historic sites - Law and legislation - Florida. I. Florida. Legislature. Senate. Governmental Operations Committee.
KFF398.9 .A25 1980a

A review of the Historic Preservation Project Review Council in the Department of State /. Florida. Legislature. Senate. Governmental Operations Committee. [Tallahassee] [1980] i, 18 p. ; LC Card 81-621190 DDC 344.759/094 347.590494 19
KFF398.9 .A25 1980

Review of the implementation of recommendations relating to the death of Representative Leo J. Ryan . United States. Congress. House. Committee on Foreign Affairs. Subcommittee on International Operations. Washington , 1980. iii, 78 p. ; LC Card 80-603637 DDC 364.1/524/098811 19
KF27 .F647 1980a

A review of the Medical Advisory Board in the Department of Highway Safety and Motor Vehicles /. Florida. Legislature. Senate. Committee on Transportation. [Tallahassee, Fla.] [1980] 50 p. : LC Card 81-621728 DDC 353.97590087/83/0289 19
TL152.35 .F58 1980

A review of the Monte Carlo method for radiation transport calculations. Monte Carlo Seminar-Workshop, Oak Ridge National Laboratory, 1970. Oak Ridge, Tenn. [1971] vii, 144 p.:   ***NYPL [JSF 80-645]***

Review of the national cemetery system administered by the Veterans' Administration, also H.R. 6146 . United States. Congress. House. Committee on Veterans' Affairs. Subcommittee on Compensation, Pension, Insurance, and Memorial Affairs. Washington , 1980. iii, 36 p. ; LC Card 80-603344 DDC 353.0086 19
KF27 .V43 1980c

Review of the operation of the overseas cemeteries and memorials administered by the American Battle Monuments Commission and Arlington National Cemetery, also H.R 6355 and H.R. 6356 . United States. Congress. House. Committee on Veterans' Affairs. Subcommittee on Compensation, Pension, Insurance, and Memorial Affairs. Washington , 1980. iii, 52 p. ; LC Card 80-603070 DDC 343.73/0256 19
KF27 .V43 1980

A review of the Pesticide Technical Council in the Department of Agriculture and Consumer Services /. Florida. Legislature. Senate. Committee on Agriculture. [Tallahassee] [1980] i, 21, [7] p. ; LC Card 81-621222 DDC 344.759/04633 347.59044633 19
KFF380.P4 A25 1980

Review of the Presidential certification of Nicaragua's connection to terrorism . United States. Congress. House. Committee on Foreign Affairs. Subcommittee on Inter-American Affairs. Washington , 1980. iii, 50, p. ; LC Card 80-603450 DDC 353.0089/097285 19
KF27 .F646 1980d

A review of the Private Security Advisory Council in the Department of State /. Florida. Legislature. Senate. Governmental Operations

Committee. [Tallahassee] [1980] i, 28 p. ; LC Card 81-621187 DDC 353.97590074 19
KFF282.D47 A25 1980

A review of the property acquisition program conducted by the Division of Real Estate Services /. California. Dept. of Finance. Program Evaluation Unit. [Sacramento] [1979] xvi, 50 p. : LC Card 80-621383 DDC 353.97940082/326 19
HD243.C2 C34 1979

A review of the Proteutheria and Insectivora of the Willwood Formation (Lower Eocene), Bighorn Basin, Wyoming /. Bown, Thomas M. Washington , 1981. p. cm. LC Card 81-607068 DDC 557.3 s 569/.12 19
QE75 .B9 no. 1523 QE882.I5

A review of the Soybean Advisory Council in the Department of Agriculture and Consumer Services /. Florida. Legislature. Senate. Committee on Agriculture. [Tallahassee] [1980] i, 14, [9] p. ; LC Card 81-621220 DDC 353.97590082/61334 19
KFF244.S66 A25 1980

A review of the State Apprenticeship Council in the Department of Labor and Employment Security /. Florida. Legislature. Senate. Committee on Commerce. [Tallahassee, Fla.] [1980] i, 29 p. ; LC Card 81-620797 DDC 353.97590083/4 19
HD4885.U5 F56 1980

A review of the Thoroughbred Racing Advisory Committee in the Department of Business Regulation /. Florida. Legislature. Senate. Committee on Commerce. [Tallahassee] [1980] i, 18 p. ; LC Card 81-621207 DDC 344.759/099 347.590499 19
KFF384 .A25 1980

A review of the Tourism Advisory Council in the Department of Commerce /. Florida. Legislature. Senate. Committee on Commerce. [Tallahassee] [1980] i, 29 p. ; LC Card 81-621210 DDC 353.7590082/6591 19
G155.U6 F53 1980

Review of the U. S. generalized system of preferences . United States. Congress. Senate. Committee on Finance. Subcommittee on International Trade. Washington , 1981. iv, 300 p. : LC Card 81-601603 DDC 382.7/53/0973 19
KF26 .F554 1980g

Review of the 32d International Whaling Commission meeting . United States. Congress. House. Committee on Foreign Affairs. Subcommittee on International Organizations. Washington , 1980. iii, 97 p. ; LC Card 80-603893 DDC 341.7/622 19
KF27 .F648 1980c

Review of the 36th session of the United Nations Commission on Human Rights . United States. Congress. House. Committee on Foreign Affairs. Subcommittee on International Organizations. Washington , 1980. iii, 41 p. ; LC Card 80-602983 DDC 341.4/81 19
KF27 .F648 1980b

Review of Title V of the National energy conservation policy act . United States. Congress. House. Committee on Public Works and Transportation. Subcommittee on Public Buildings and Grounds. Washington , 1980. iv, 240 p. : LC Card 80-601868 DDC 346.7304/67916/0262 19
KF27 .P8964 1979b

Review of treatment records documenting Medicaid billings at Office of Mental Health outpatient facilities in New York City. New York (State). Division of Audits and Accounts. [Albany] , 1979. 2, 8, [6] leaves ; LC Card 79-625695 DDC 353.97470082/56 19
HD7102.U5 N66 1979

Review of U. S. refugee resettlement programs and policies . Moore, Charlotte J. Washington , 1980. viii, 342 p. : LC Card 80-603884 DDC 362.8/7/0973 19
HV640.4.U54 M66

Revised bibliography of the Hawaiian monk seal . Balazs, George H. [Manoa] , 1979. iv, 27 p. ; LC Card 79-625332 DDC 016.59974/8 19
Z7996.P5 B27 QL737.P64

A revised estimate of the cost of completing the national system of interstate and defense highways . United States. Dept. of

Transportation. Washington , 1981. iii, 27 p. :
LC Card 81-601266   DDC 338.1/12/0973 19
HE355.3.E3 U54 1981

**The revised State plan for the identification and
diagnosis of children who are handicapped .**
Virginia. Office of the Secretary of Human
Resources. Richmond , 1979. [73] p. ;   LC Card
79-624128   DDC 300/.9755 s 362.4/048 19
J87 .V9 1979c no. 37 RJ102.5.V8

**Revision of Indo-West Pacific lizardfishes of the
genus Synodus (Pisces: Synodontidae) /.**
Cressey, Roger F., 1930- City of Washington ,
1981. p. cm.   LC Card 81-14389   DDC 591 s
597/.53 19
QL1 .S54 no. 342 QL638.S96

**A revision of the tribal and subtribal limits of
the Heliantheae (Asteraceae) /.** Robinson,
Harold Ernest, 1932- City of Washington ,
1981. p. cm.   LC Card 81-607993   DDC 581 s
583/.55 19
QK1 .S2747 no. 51 QK495.C74

Revista internacional de política criminal.
International review of criminal policy. NO. 1- ;
1952- New York.   *NYPL [*ZAN-4630]*

Revitalizing North American neighborhoods .
United States. Dept. of Housing and Urban
Development. [Washington] [1978] 28 p. ;   LC
Card 79-602727   DDC 307.7/6/0973 19
HN90.C6 U6 1978

Révolution automobile. English. The automobile
revolution / by J.-P. Bardou ... [et al.] ;
translated from the French by James M. Laux.
Chapel Hill, N.C. : University of North
Carolina Press, c1982. p. cm.   Translation of: La
Révolution automobile. Bibliography: p. Includes index.
ISBN 0-8078-1496-2   LC Card 81-11571   DDC
303.4/83 19
*1. Automobiles - Social aspects - History - Addresses,
essays, lectures. 2. Automobile industry and trade -
History - Addresses, essays, lectures. I. Bardou, Jean
Pierre, 1935-. II. Title.*
HE5613 .R4213

**REVOLUTION, FRENCH. see FRANCE -
HISTORY - REVOLUTION, 1789-1799.**

Revolutionary America, 1763-1789. Gephart,
Ronald M. Washington , 1982. p. cm.   ISBN
0-8444-0359-8   LC Card 80-606802   DDC
016.9733 19
Z1238 .G43 E208

**REVOLUTIONISTS - IRELAND -
BIOGRAPHY.**
Touhill, Blanche M. (Blanche Marie), 1931-
William Smith O'Brien and his Irish
revolutionary companions in penal exile /.
Columbia , 1981. p. cm.   ISBN 0-8262-0339-6
LC Card 81-1899   DDC 941.5081/092/4 19
DA952.O22 T68

**REVOLUTIONS AND THE ARTS. see ARTS
AND REVOLUTIONS.**

REVOLUTIONS - EL SALVADOR.
Communist interference in El Salvador .
[Washington, D.C.?] , 1981. 1 v. (various
pagings), [3] leaves of plates (1 folded) :   LC
Card 81-601684   DDC 322.4/2/097284 19
HX148.5 C65

Revue internationale de politique criminelle.
International review of criminal policy. NO. 1- ;
1952- New York.   *NYPL [*ZAN-4630]*

Reyes, Teofilo. (joint author) Steffy, Wilbert.
Productivity and cost control for the small and
medium-sized firm /. Ann Arbor , 1980. vii,
170 p. :   LC Card 80-622255   DDC 338.1/6 19
HD56 .S75

Reynolds, Andrew W. Nikodem, Zdenek D.
Nuclear power regulation /. Washington, D.C. ,
1980. xxvi, 230 p. :   LC Card 80-603213   DDC
343.73/0925 347.303925 19
KF2138 .N54

Reynolds, Charles Arthur, 1937- Soil survey of
Middlesex County, Connecticut / [by Charles
A. Reynolds] ; United States Department of
Agriculture, Soil Conservation Service, in
cooperation with Connecticut Agricultural
Experiment Station, Storrs Agricultural
Experiment Station. [Washington] : The
Service, [1979] ix, 155 p., [28] fold. leaves of
plates : ill., maps ; 28 cm.   Cover title. "Issued
February 1979." Bibliography: p. 73.   LC Card
80-601842   DDC 631.4/7/7444 19
1. Soils - Connecticut - Middlesex County - Maps. I.

United States. Soil Conservation Service. II.
Connecticut. Agricultural Experiment Station, Storrs.
III. Title.
S599.C76 R5

Reynolds, Don R. Foliicolous Ascomycetes 1 :
the Capnodiaceous genus Scorias reproduction /
by Don R. Reynolds. Los Angeles : Natural
History Museum of Los Angeles County, 1978.
16 p. : ill. ; 23 cm. (Contributions in science . no.
288) Bibliography: p. 15-16.   LC Card 78-104483
DDC 574 s 589.2/3 19
*1. Scorias spongiosa. 2. Scorias. 3. Fungi -
Reproduction. I. Title. II. Series.*
Q11 .L52 no. 288 QK623.C36

Reznik, Gerd. Clinical anatomy of the European
hamster : Cricetus cricetus, L. / [by Gerd
Reznik, Hildegard Reznik-Schüller, Ulrich
Mohr ; edited by Paul C. Walter, Peter
Dodson, assistant editor, Ronald B. Levine].
Washington : For sale by the Supt. of Docs., U.
S. Govt. Print. Off., [1978] xi, 247 p. : ill. ; 27
cm. Bibliography: p. 207-210. Includes index.   LC
Card 79-602139   DDC 619/.93 19
*1. Hamsters - Anatomy. 2. Hamsters as laboratory
animals. I. Reznik-Schüller, Hildegard, joint author. II.
Mohr, Ulrich, joint author. III. Walter, Paul C. IV.
Dodson, Peter. V. Levine, Ronald B. VI. Title. VII.
Title: Cricetus cricetus, L.*
QL813.H35 R49

Reznik-Schüller, Hildegard. (joint author) Reznik,
Gerd. Clinical anatomy of the European
hamster . Washington [1978] xi, 247 p. :   LC
Card 79-602139   DDC 619/.93 19
QL813.H35 R49

Rhee, Chu S.
District of Columbia. Dept. of Human
Resources. Research and Statistics Division. VD
facts in the District of Columbia /.
[Washington] , 1976. ii, 17 p. ;   LC Card
78-620889   DDC 312/.3951/09753 19
RA644.V4 D57 1976

District of Columbia. Dept. of Human
Resources. Research and Statistics Division. VD
facts in the District of Columbia.
[Washington] , 1977. iii leaves, [19] p. ;   LC
Card 79-624170   DDC 312/.3951/09753 19
RA644.V4 D57 1977

Rhee, Sang-Woo. Themes of North Korea's
unification messages : a study on pattern shifts,
1948-68 / Sang-Woo Rhee. [Honolulu] :
Dimensionality of Nations Project, Dept. of
Political Science, University of Hawaii, 1973.
iv, 39 leaves : graphs ; 28 cm. (Research report -
Dept. of Political Science, University of Hawaii . no.
66) "Prepared for presentation at the 25th annual
meeting of the Association for Asian Studies, Chicago,
March 30-April 1, 1973." "Contract no.
N00014-67-A-0387-0003, contract authority
identification number NR 177-915." Bibliography: leaves
35-39.   LC Card 77-623945   DDC 951.9/04 19
*1. Korea reunification question (1945-). 2. Korea
(Democratic People's Republic) - Foreign relations. I.
Hawaii. University, Honolulu. Dimensionality of
Nations Project. II. Series: Hawaii. University,
Honolulu. Dept. of Political Science. Research report ,
no. 66. III. Title.*
DS917.25 .R53

RHEODYTES LEUKOPS.
Legler, John M. A new genus and species of
Chelid turtle from Queensland, Australia /. Los
Angeles, Calif. , 1980. 18 p. :   LC Card
80-138331   DDC 574 s 597.92 19
Q11 .L52 no. 324 QL666.C535

RHETORIC - 1500-1800.
Trousdale, Marion, 1929- Shakespeare and the
rhetoricians /. Chapel Hill , c1981. p. cm.
ISBN 0-8078-1482-2   LC Card 81-40703   DDC
822.3/3 19
PR2976 .T77

RHETORIC - 1500-1800 - CONGRESSES.
Renaissance eloquence . Berkeley , 1981,
c1982. p. cm.   ISBN 0-520-04543-2   LC Card
81-13128   DDC 808/.009/03 19
PN171.6 .R4 1982

**RHEUMATISM - RESEARCH - UNITED
STATES.**
National Institute of Arthritis, Metabolism, and
Digestive Diseases. Office of the Associate
Director for Arthritis, Bone, and Skin Diseases.
Progress against the rheumatic diseases
(1967-1977) . [Bethesda, Md.] , 1978. vii, 39
p. ;   LC Card 79-602034   DDC 616.7/23/0072073

19
RC927 .N38 1978

Rhoades, Stephen A. Impact of bank holding
companies on competition and performance in
banking markets / Stephen A. Rhoades and
Roger D. Rutz. [Washington] : Board of
Governors of the Federal Reserve System,
[1979] 30 p. ; 28 cm. (Staff studies . 107) "August
1979." Includes bibliographical references.   LC Card
80-602134   DDC 332.1/6 19
*1. Bank holding companies - United States. 2. Banks
and banking - United States. I. Rutz, Roger D., joint
author. II. United States. Board of Governors of the
Federal Reserve System. III. Title. IV. Series.*
HG2491 .R46

Rhoads, James Berton. United States. National
Archives and Records Service. The National
Archives and Records Service in 1978 /.
[Washington, D.C.] [1979?] 20 p. :   LC Card
80-601808   DDC 027.5753 19
CD3023 .U54 1979a

Rhoads, S. C. Nilsen, D. N. Solvent extraction of
nickel and copper from laterite-ammoniacal
leach liquors /. Avondale, MD , 1981. p. cm.
LC Card 81-38488   DDC 622 s 669/.7332 19
TN23 .U43 TN799.N6

Rhode, Grant F. China (People's Republic of
China, 1949-). Treaties, etc. Treaties of the
People's Republic of China, 1949-1978 /.
Boulder, Colo. , 1980. ix, 207 p. :   ISBN
0-89158-761-6 :   LC Card 79-27904
JX926 1980 .C47   *NYPL [JFE 80-3747]*

Rhode Island. Board of Education. The status of
public school support in Rhode Island /.
Providence : Rhode Island State Board of
Education, 1955. 31 p. : ill. ; 23 cm. (State
Department of Education studies of State and local
responsibilities for public school finance and control :
Staff study ; no. 1) Includes bibliographical references.
LC Card 80-510733   DDC 379.1/2209745 s
379.1/2209745 19
*1. Education - Rhode Island - Finance. I. Series: Rhode
Island. Dept. of Education. Studies of State and local
responsibilities of public school finance and control :
Staff study , no. 1. II. Title.*
LA358 .R43a no. 1 LB2826.R4

**Rhode Island. Dept. of Administration. Statewide
Planning Program. see Rhode Island.
Statewide Planning Program.**

Rhode Island. Dept. of Education.
**Studies of State and local responsibilities of
public school finance and control : Staff
study /.**
(no. 1) Rhode Island. Board of Education.
The status of public school support in Rhode
Island. Providence , 1955. 31 p. :   LC Card
80-510733   DDC 379.1/2209745 s
379.1/2209745 19
LA358 .R43a no. 1 LB2826.R4

**Rhode Island. Health Planning & Resources
Development.**
The story of private hospitals in Rhode Island /
Health Planning and Resources Development.
[Providence] : Rhode Island Dept. of Health,
1979. 69 p. : ill. ; 28 cm. (Technical report -
Health Planning & Resources Development ; no. 18)
Bibliography: p. 59-64.   LC Card 80-620722   DDC
362.1/1/09745 19
*1. Hospitals, Proprietary - Rhode Island - History. 2.
Sanatoriums - Rhode Island - History. I. Series: Rhode
Island. Health Planning & Resources Development.
Technical report - Health Planning & Resources
Development , no. 18. II. Title.*
RA981.R4 R5 1979

**Technical report - Health Planning &
Resources Development .**
(no. 18) Rhode Island. Health Planning &
Resources Development. The story of private
hospitals in Rhode Island /. [Providence] ,
1979. 69 p. :   LC Card 80-620722   DDC
362.1/1/09745 19
RA981.R4 R5 1979

**Rhode Island. Historical Preservation
Commission.** Nebiker, Walter. State of Rhode
Island and Providence Plantations, preliminary
survey report, Town of Glocester /. Providence,
R. I. , 1980. iv, 62 leaves, [14] leaves of plates :
NYPL [IQK (Glocester) 81-780]

Rhode Island. Office of State Planning. 1977
mobile source air pollutant emission inventory.
Providence, R.I. : Office of State Planning,

Rhode Island Statewide Planning Program,
1979. xi, 91, [42] p. : ill. ; 28 cm. (Technical
paper - Rhode Island Statewide Planning Program ; no.
85) Written by J. E. Brownell.   LC Card 79-625664
DDC 363.7/3922 19
1. Air - Pollution - Rhode Island. 2. Transportation -
Environmental aspects - Rhode Island. I. Brownell,
John E. II. Series: Rhode Island. Statewide Planning
Program. Technical paper , no. 85. III. Title.
TD883.5.R4 R46 1979

Rhode Island. Statewide Planning Program.
Land use and eocnomic development
perspectives of Rhode Island property taxes.
Providence, R.I. : Rhode Island Statewide
Planning Program, [1980] xviii, 165 p. ; 28 cm.
(Technical paper - Rhode Island Statewide Planning
Program ; no. 78) Cover title. "March 1980."
Bibliography: p. 164-165.   LC Card 80-622771 DDC
336.22/09745 19
1. Property tax - Rhode Island. 2. Land use - Rhode
Island - Planning. I. Series: Rhode Island. Statewide
Planning Program. Technical paper , no. 78. II. Title.
HJ4121.R42 R46 1980

The property tax and economic development.
Providence, R.I. : Rhode Island Statewide
Planning Program, [1980] x, 132 p. ; 28 cm.
(Report - Rhode Island Statewide Planning Program ;
no. 36D) At head of title: Target industries. Includes
bibliographical references.   LC Card 80-622770 DDC
361.6/09745 s 336.22/09745 19
1. Property tax - Rhode Island. 2. Industrial
promotion - Rhode Island. I. Series: Rhode Island.
Statewide Planning Program. Report - Rhode Island
Statewide Planning Program , no. 36D. II. Title.
HT393.R5 R45b no. 36D HJ4121.R42

Report - Rhode Island Statewide Planning
Program .
(no. 36D) Rhode Island. Statewide Planning
Program. The property tax and economic
development. Providence, R.I. [1980] x, 132
p. ;   LC Card 80-622770 DDC 361.6/09745 s
336.22/09745 19
HT393.R5 R45b no. 36D HJ4121.R42

Technical paper .
(no. 78) Rhode Island. Statewide Planning
Program. Land use and eocnomic
development perspectives of Rhode Island
property taxes. Providence, R.I. [1980] xviii,
165 p. ;   LC Card 80-622771 DDC
336.22/09745 19
HJ4121.R42 R46 1980

(no. 85) Rhode Island. Office of State
Planning. 1977 mobile source air pollutant
emission inventory. Providence, R.I., 1979.
xi, 91, [42] p. ;   LC Card 79-625664 DDC
363.7/3922 19
TD883.5.R4 R46 1979

Rhode Island. University. Conference on the
Physics of Fiber Optics, University of Rhode
Island, 1978. Fiber optics, advances in research
and development /. New York , c1979. x, 693
p. :   ISBN 0-306-40167-3 LC Card 79-10554
TA1800 .C66 1978   **NYPL** *[JSF 80-1085]*

Rhode Island. Water Resources Board.
Dickerman, David C. Geohydrologic data for
the Beaver-Pasquiset ground-water reservoir,
Rhode Island . [Providence, R.I.] , 1977. 128
p. :   LC Card 80-622751 DDC 553.7/9/09745 19
GB1025.R4 D53

Rhodes, Harold, 1951- California. Dept. of Water
Resources. Division of Planning. Windstorms in
California /. [Sacramento] , 1979. v, 34 p. :
LC Card 80-620557 DDC 551.5/5 19
QC943.5.U6 C34 1979

Rhodes, Harold L. An apparatus and procedure
for calibrating a water vapor analyzer in the
0.1- to 15-ppm range / by Harold L. Rhodes.
Washington, D.C. : U. S. Dept. of the Interior,
1980. p. cm. (Report of investigations / Bureau of
Mines) Bibliography: p.   LC Card 80-606926 DDC
622 s 665.8/22 19
1. Helium - Moisture - Measurement. 2. Moisture
meters - Calibration. I. Series: United States Bureau of
Mines. Report of investigations ,. II. Title.
TN23 .U43 TP245.H4

Rhodesia . United States. Congress. Senate.
Committee on Foreign Relations. Washington ,
1980. iii, 59 p. :   LC Card 80-601055 DDC
968.91/04 19
KF26 .F6 1979ab

Rhodesian sanctions, should the United States
lift them? . United States. Congress. House.
Committee on Foreign Affairs. Washington ,
1980. iii, 80 p. ;   LC Card 80-601130 DDC
327.7306891 19
KF27 .F6 1979j

RHODOTORULA MUCILAGINOSA.
Thompson, Frederick C. Tolerance and
synthetic ability of sewage microorganisms in
acid mine water /. Morgantown , 1975. ix, 60
p. :   LC Card 76-622086 DDC 628.1/6832 19
QR88 .T48

RIBONUCLEIC ACID, TRANSFER -
CONGRESSES.
Transfer RNA and transfer RNA modification
in differentiation and neoplasia . [Washington]
1971 [i.e. 1974] p. 591-724 :   LC Card 78-601843
DDC 616.99/4 s 616.99/2071 19
RC261 .A274 vol. 31 QP623

Riccolo, Robert L. (joint author) Sykes, Thomas M.
An analysis of program needs of prison inmates
in Washington State /. Olympia, Wash. [1980]
xxi, 139 p. ;   LC Card 80-620028 DDC
365/.66/09797 19
HV9475.W2 S93

Rice, Dorothy P. United States. National Center
for Health Statistics. Social and economic
implications of cancer in the United States .
Hyattsville, Md. , Washington [1981]. iv, 43
p. :   ISBN 0-8406-0203-0 LC Card 80-607176
DDC 362.1/96994 19
RC276 .U56 1981

Rice, Dudley R. Mudge, Melville Rhodes, 1921-
Lower Cretaceous Mount Pablo formation,
northwestern Montana /. Washington [1981] p.
cm.   LC Card 81-607900 DDC 557.3 s
551.7/7/097868 19
QE75 .B9 no. 1502-D QE686

RICE - LOSSES.
Rice postharvest losses in developing countries.
[Oakland, Calif. , 1980] vi, 227 p. ;   LC Card
80-602131 DDC 664/.725 19
TS2159.R5 R49

Rice, Philip A. Wayne County, New York,
highway system. Lyons, N. Y, 1976. col. map
43 x 45 cm. Scale ca. *:125,000. Includes index.
1. Wayne County, N. Y. - Maps. 2. Wayne County, N.
Y. - Road maps. 3. Wayne County, N. Y. -
Administrative and political divisions - Maps. I. Wayne
County, N. Y. Superintendent of Highways.
NYPL *[Map Div. 80-3337]*

RICE - PHILIPPINE ISLANDS - COST
EFFECTIVENESS - MATHEMATICAL
MODELS.
Antiporta, Donato B. Consumer benefits from
new rice varieties in the Philippines /. St. Paul ,
1974. iv, 27 leaves :   LC Card 81-452417 DDC
338.1/3318/09599 19
HD9066.P62 A7

Rice postharvest losses in developing countries.
[Oakland, Calif. : Agricultural Research
(Western Region), Science and Education
Administration, U. S. Dept. of Agriculture,
1980] vi, 227 p. ; 26 cm. (Science and Education
Administration, Agricultural reviews and manuals :
Western series ; no. 12 0193-3760) "April/1980."
"ARM-W-12." Includes bibliographical references and
index. Selected bibliography of rice postharvest
publications. CONTENTS. - Saunders, R. M., et al. A
1978 survey of rice postharvest losses during threshing,
drying, parboiling, milling, and the potential for
reducing such losses in developing countries.--Mossman,
A. P. LC Card 80-602131 DDC 664/.725 19
1. Rice processing. 2. Rice - Losses. I. Series:
Agricultural reviews and manuals : Western series , no.
12.
TS2159.R5 R49

RICE PROCESSING.
Rice postharvest losses in developing countries.
[Oakland, Calif. , 1980] vi, 227 p. ;   LC Card
80-602131 DDC 664/.725 19
TS2159.R5 R49

Rice, Roy Warren, 1934- Symposium on the
Science of Ceramic Machining and Surface
Finishing, 2d, National Bureau of Standards,
1978. The science of ceramic machining and
surface finishing II . Gaithersburg, Md. ,
Washington, D.C. , 1979. xii, 532 p. :   LC Card
79-600149 DDC 602/.18 s 666 19
QC100 .U57 no. 562 TP814

RICE TRADE - PHILIPPINE ISLANDS -
MATHEMATICAL MODELS.
Antiporta, Donato B. Consumer benefits from
new rice varieties in the Philippines /. St. Paul ,
1974. iv, 27 leaves :   LC Card 81-452417 DDC
338.1/3318/09599 19
HD9066.P62 A7

RICE TRADE - UNITED STATES -
MATHEMATICAL MODELS.
Grant, Warren R. Factors affecting supply,
demand, and prices of U. S. rice /.
Washington , 1979. iv, 57 p. :   LC Card
79-602178 DDC 338.1/0973 s 338.1/7318/0973
19
HD1759 .U56a no. 47 HD9066.U45

RICE TRADE - UNITED STATES -
STATISTICS.
Holder, Shelby Herbert, 1931- U. S. rice
distribution update /. Washington, D.C. [1980]
ii, 50 p. ;   LC Card 80-603201 DDC 338.1/0973 s
381/.41318/0973 19
HD1751 .A5 no. 640 HD9066.U45

RICE - UNITED STATES - VARIETIES.
Dalrymple, Dana G. Development and spread
of semi-dwarf varieties of wheat and rice in the
United States . Washington, D.C. [1980] xiv,
150 p. :   LC Card 80-602635 DDC 338.1 s
633.1/17/0973 19
HD1751 .A91854 no. 455 SB191.W5

Rich, Peter, 1955- Measuring certain intangible
benefits of water pollution abatement by use of
changes of impacted real estate values / by
Peter Rich and John H. Foster. Amherst,
Mass. : Water Resources Research Center,
University of Massachusetts at Amherst, [1979]
52 leaves : graph ; 28 cm. (Completion report -
Water Resources Research Center, University of
Massachusetts at Amherst) "November 1979."
Bibliography: leaves 49-52.   LC Card 80-621812
DDC 333.33/22 19
1. Real property - Valuation - Massachusetts - Lee -
Mathematical models. 2. Water - Pollution -
Massachusetts - Lee - Mathematical models. I. Foster,
John Henry, 1926- joint author. II. Series: University of
Massachusetts at Amherst. Water Resources Research
Center. Completion report - Water Resources Research
Center, University of Massachusetts at Amherst. III.
Title.
HD268.L44 R5

RICHARD B. RUSSELL LAKE, GA. AND S.C.
- ANTIQUITIES.
Taylor, Richard Lee, 1946- The report of the
intensive survey of the Richard B. Russell Dam
and Lake, Savannah River, Georgia and South
Carolina /. Columbia, S.C. [1978] xvii, 531 p. :
LC Card 79-623568 DDC 975.7/35 19
F292.R49 T39

Richard T. Greener : his life and work / Ruth
Ann Stewart, David M. Kahn ; an exhibit and
tribute sponsored by the National Park Service
and the National Park Foundation [at] the
General Grant National Memorial ... June 4,
1980-October 31, 1980. [Washington, D. C.] :
National Park Service, 1980. 16 p. : ill., ports. ;
23 cm. CONTENTS. - Richard T. Greener:
biography/R. A. Stewart. - Greener and Grant's
Tomb/David M. Kahn. - Selected bibliography (p. 16).
1. Greener, Richard Theodore, 1844-1922. 2. General
Grant National Memorial. I. Stewart, Ruth Ann. II.
Kahn, David M. III. National Park Foundation. IV.
United States. National Park Service.
NYPL *[Sc F 80-218]*

Richard, Valliere T., 1952- Norman McLaren,
manipulator of movement : the National Film
Board years, 1947-1967 / Valliere T. Richard.
Newark [N.J.] : University of Delaware Press,
c1981. p. cm. Filmography: p. Bibliography: p.
Includes index.   ISBN 0-87413-192-8 LC Card
80-53998 DDC 791.43/023/0924
1. McLaren, Norman, 1914-. 2. National Film Board of
Canada. 3. Moving-picture cartoons - Canada. I. Title.
NC1766.C32 M357 1981

Richardson, Edmund Arlo, 1914- (joint author)
Hubbard, Kenneth G. Tabulation and
application of pan evaporation data for Utah
through 1976. Logan, Utah , 1979. vi, 76 p. :
LC Card 80-622271 DDC 551.57/2/09792 19
QC915.7.U5 H82

Richardson, Elmo. BLM's billion-dollar
checkerboard : managing the O and C lands /
by Elmo Richardson. Santa Cruz, Calif. : Forest
History Society ; Washington, D.C. : For sale

by the Supt. of Docs., U. S.G.P.O., c1980. x, 200 p. : ill., maps ; 24 cm. Includes index. "Contract YA-512-CT7-121"--verso of t.p. Includes bibliographical references. S/N 024-011-001247 Item 631　LC Card 81-600781　DDC 333.75/09795 19
1. Forest policy - Oregon - History. 2. Forest management - Oregon - History. 3. Douglas fir - History. 4. Lumber trade - Oregon - History. I. United States. Bureau of Land Management. Oregon State Office. II. Forest History Society. III. Title. IV. Title: O and C lands.
SD566.O7 R5

Richardson, James W. An application of optimal control techniques to agricultural policy analysis / [James W. Richardson and Daryll E. Ray]. [Stillwater, Okla.] : Agricultural Experiment Station, Oklahoma State University, 1979. 41 p. ; 23 cm. (Technical bulletin - Agricultural Experiment Station, Oklahoma State University . T-154) Cover title. "Research reported herein was conducted under Oklahoma Station project no. 1612." Bibliography: p. 39-41.　LC Card 79-625383　DDC 338.1/873 19
1. Agriculture and state - United States. 2. Control theory. 3. Mathematical optimization. I. Ray, Daryll E., joint author. II. Oklahoma. Agricultural Experiment Station, Stillwater. III. Series: Oklahoma. Agricultural Experiment Station, Stillwater. Technical bulletin , T-154. IV. Title.
HD1765 1979 .R52

Richardson, Samuel, 1689-1761.
　　PAMELA.
　　　Fortuna, James Louis, 1943- "The unsearchable wisdom of God . Gainesville , c1980. vii, 130 p. ;　ISBN 0-8130-0676-7 :　LC Card 80-14919
PR3664.P4 F6　　　***NYPL [L-10 3842 no. 49]***

Richardson, Selma K. An analytical survey of Illinois Public Library services to children / Selma K. Richardson. [Springfield] : Illinois State Library, 1978. xiv, 345 p. : forms ; 28 cm. "LSCA project I-77-III-B." Bibliography: p. 336-240.　LC Card 80-620891　DDC 027.62/5/09773 19
1. Libraries, Children's - Illinois. 2. Library surveys - Illinois. I. Illinois. State Library, Springfield. II. Title.
Z718.1 .R48

Richland and Lexington Counties Joint Planning Commission. Columbia, S. C. Dept. of City Planning. Population. Columbia, S. C., 1964. iv, 47 p.　　　　　***NYPL [JLF 78-1628]***

RICHLAND COUNTY (ILL.) - MAPS.
United States. Soil Conservation Service. Richland County, Illinois /. Lincoln, Nebr. , 1980. 1 map :　LC Card 81-691426
G4103.R5 1980 .U5

RICHLAND COUNTY, S. C. - POPULATION.
Columbia, S. C. Dept. of City Planning. Population. Columbia, S. C., 1964. iv, 47 p.
　　　　　NYPL [JLF 78-1628]

Richland, Wash. Pacific Northwest Laboratory. see Battelle Memorial Institute, Columbus, Ohio. Pacific Northwest Laboratory, Richland, Wash.

Richmond, Chester R. Oak Ridge National Laboratory Life Sciences Symposium, 1st, Oak Ridge, Tenn., 1978. Synthetic fossil fuel teachnology. Ann Arbor, Mich. , c1980. xiii, 288 p. :　LC Card 80-68338
　　　　　NYPL [JSF 81-116]

Richmond, Davie L. General soil map, Greenlee County, Arizona. Portland, Or., U. S. Soil Conservation Service, 1973. 49 p. map (in pocket) 27 cm.
1. Soils - Arizona - Maps. 2. Soils - Arizona - Greenlee County. I. United States. Soil Conservation Service. II. Title.　　***NYPL [JSF 80-721]***

Richmond. Virginia Museum of Fine Arts. see Virginia Museum of Fine Arts, Richmond.

Richter, Kenneth. Fagg, Ken. Explore the Adirondacks . Elizabethtown, N.Y. [1980?] 1 view :　LC Card 81-692877
G3802.A2E635 1980 .F3

Rickert, David A., 1940- United States. Geological Survey. Synthetic fuels development . Washington, D.C. , 1979. 45 p. :　LC Card 79-600206　DDC 662/.66/0973 19
TP360 .U584 1979

Rickert-Ziebold Trust award art exhibition. [Carbondale : Southern Illinois University, School of Art, 1977] [28] p. : chiefly ill. ; 29

cm. Cover title. Exhibition held in the Mitchell Gallery of Southern Illinois University, April 25-29, 1977.　LC Card 80-496137　DDC 709/.773/994 19
1. Rickert-Ziebold Trust - Awards - Exhibitions. 2. Art, American - Exhibitions. 3. Art, Modern - 20th century - United States - Exhibitions. 4. Art in universities and colleges - Illinois - Exhibitions. I. Illinois. Southern Illinois University, Carbondale. School of Art. II. Mitchell Gallery.
N394 .R52

RICKERT-ZIEBOLD TRUST - AWARDS - EXHIBITIONS.
Rickert-Ziebold Trust award art exhibition. [Carbondale , 1977] [28] p. :　LC Card 80-496137　DDC 709/.773/994 19
N394 .R52

Rico, Susan.
　(joint author) Meisner, Charlotte. Variety and distribution of occupations in Massachusetts . Boston, MA. [1980] ii, 61 p. ;　LC Card 80-623644　DDC 331.12/5/09744 19
HB2615.M4 M44

Winer, Elliot A. Employment requirements for Massachusetts by occupation, by industry, 1976-1985 /. Boston, MA [1979] 58 leaves :　LC Card 80-623635　DDC 331.12/3/09744 19
HD5725.M4 W56

Riddle, Theodate Pope, 1868-1946.
　Paine, Judith. Theodate Pope Riddle, her life and work. [Washington?] , 1979. [26] p. :　LC Card 79-52952
NA737.R53 A4 1979
　　　　NYPL [3-MQZ (Riddle) 81-627]

RIDDLE, THEODATE POPE, 1868-1946 - EXHIBITIONS.
Paine, Judith. Theodate Pope Riddle, her life and work. [Washington?] , 1979. [26] p. :　LC Card 79-52952
NA737.R53 A4 1979
　　　　NYPL [3-MQZ (Riddle) 81-627]

Ridzon, David. United States. Employment Standards Administration. Motion picture theaters /. [Washington] , 1979. 93 p. in various pagings ;　LC Card 79-602947
HD4966.M79 U58 1979
　　　　　NYPL [JLF 81-423]

Riedel, John T. (joint author) Ho, Francis P. Seasonal variation of 10-square-mile probable maximum precipitation estimates, United States, east of the 105th meridian /. Silver Spring, Md. , 1980. vi, 89 p. :　LC Card 80-602668　DDC 551.57/0973 s 551.57/813/0973 19
QC925.1 .U586 no. 53 QC925.1.U8A14

Riemann, Hans, 1920- (joint author) Torres-Anjel, Manuel J. Enterotoxigenic Clostridium perfringens type A in selected humans . Washington , 1977. 32 p. ;　LC Card 78-102859　DDC 362.1/09181/2 s 615.9/52995 19
RA10 .P252 no. 350 QR201.C54

Ries, Peter W. Jack, Susan S. Current estimates from the health interview survey, United States, 1979 . Hyattsville, Md. , 1981. p. cm.　ISBN 0-8406-0219-7　LC Card 81-607002　DDC 312/.3/0973 19
RA407.3 .J32

Riesenberg, Peter N., 1925- The Humanist as citizen /. Chapel Hill , c1981. p. cm.　ISBN 0-8078-1450-4　LC Card 81-4021　DDC 001.3 19
AZ103 .H84

Riess, Suzanne B. California. University. Regional Oral History Office. Catalogue of the Regional Oral History Office, 1954-1979 /. Berkeley , 1980. xiii, 119 p., [4] leaves of plates :　ISBN 0-9604164-0-4 (pbk.) :　LC Card 80-65525　DDC 016.9794 19
Z1261 .C117 1980 F861

Riffe, Don A. Hedging strategies to protect the financial position of cattle feeders and lenders / [Don A. Riffe and Wayne D. Purcell]. [Stillwater] : Agricultural Experiment Station, Oklahoma State University, 1979. 39 p. : graphs ; 23 cm. (Bulletin - Agricultural Experiment Station, Oklahoma State University . B-743) Cover title. Page 39 is p. [3] of cover. Bibliography: p. 39.　LC Card 79-625381　DDC 338.4/36213/0724 19
1. Beef cattle - United States - Prices - Mathematical models. 2. Beef cattle - Feeding and feeds - Economic aspects - United States - Mathematical models. I. Purcell, Wayne D., joint author. II. Series: Oklahoma. Agricultural Experiment Station, Stillwater. Bulletin ,

B-743. III. Title.
HD9433.U4 R54

Rigby, Phillip. Alaska groundfish fishery review, 1978 / Alaska Department of Fish and Game, Commercial Fisheries Division ; by Phillip Rigby. [Juneau] : The Division, [1978] [34] leaves : ill. ; 28 cm. Cover title. "June 14, 1978." Includes bibliography.　LC Card 80-622126　DDC 338.3/72758/09798 19
1. Fisheries - Alaska - Statistics. I. Alaska. Division of Commercial Fisheries. II. Title.
SH222.A4 R54

Riggan, William, 1946- Pícaros, madmen, naïfs, and clowns : the unreliable first-person narrator / by William Riggan.1st ed. Norman : University of Oklahoma Press, c1981. p. cm. Bibliography: p. Includes index.　ISBN 0-8061-1714-1 :　LC Card 81-2791　DDC 809.3/923 19
1. First person narrative. I. Title.
PN3383.P64 R5

RIGHT OF PRIVACY. see PRIVACY, RIGHT OF.

RIGHT OF PRIVATE PROPERTY. see RIGHT OF PROPERTY.

RIGHT OF PROPERTY - ECONOMIC ASPECTS.
Umbeck, John R., 1945- A theory of property rights . Ames , 1981. p. cm.　ISBN 0-8138-1675-0　LC Card 81-1141　DDC 323.4/6 19
HB711 .U52

RIGHT OF WAY - ALASKA.
Joint Federal-State Land Use Planning Commission for Alaska. Public easements under the Alaska native claims settlement act . Anchorage, Alaska , 1979. 181 p. ;　LC Card 79-624668　DDC 346.79804/32/08997 19
KFA1650 .J64

RIGHT OF WAY - UNITED STATES.
United States. Congress. House. Committee on Public Works and Transportation. Subcommittee on Surface Transportation. Coal pipeline carriers . Washington , 1980. iv, 393 p. :　LC Card 80-602973　DDC 343.73/093 19
KF27 .P8966 1979d

RIGHT TO COUNSEL - NORTH CAROLINA.
Farb, Robert L. The impact of Baldasar v. Illinois on uncounseled misdemeanor convictions in North Carolina /. Chapel Hill , N.C. , 1980, c1978. 4 p. ;　LC Card 80-622793　DDC 347.756 s 345.756/056 19
KFN7908.A15 U6 no. 80/04 KFN7978

The right to hope . Rader, Melvin Miller, 1903- Seattle , c1981. p. cm.　ISBN 0-295-95836-7　LC Card 81-51284　DDC 909.82 19
HM101 .R24

RIGHT TO PRIVACY. see PRIVACY, RIGHT OF.

RIGHT TO PROPERTY. see RIGHT OF PROPERTY.

The rights & responsibilities of women . United States. Dept. of Health, Education, and Welfare. Secretary's Advisory Committee on the Rights and Responsibilities of Women. [Washington] [1976?] ii, 103 p. ;　LC Card 77-603753　DDC 362.8/3/0973 19
HQ1426 .U52 1976

RIGHTS, CIVIL. see CIVIL RIGHTS.

Rights handbook for the handicapped /. Nevada. Governor's Committee on Employment of the Handicapped. [Carson City] , 1977. iv, 80 p. ;　LC Card 79-621844　DDC 346.79301/3 19
KFN691.H3 A837

Rights of adopted children . North Carolina. Legislative Research Commission. Raleigh (State Legislative Building, Raleigh 27611) [1981] 19, [23] p. ;　LC Card 81-621509　DDC 346.75601/78 347.5606178 19
KFN7504.5 .A25 1981

RIGHTS OF CHILDREN. see CHILDREN'S RIGHTS.

Rights of Recipients of Mental Health Services, Symposium on Safeguarding the. see Symposium on Safeguarding the Rights of Recipients of Mental Health Services, East Lansing, Mich., 1977.

RIGHTS OF WOMEN. see WOMEN'S RIGHTS.

Riley, Peter, 1950- Food and agricultural marketing in developing countries : an annotated bibliography of doctoral research in the social sciences, 1969-79 / by Peter Riley and Michael T. Weber. East Lansing, Mich. : Dept. of Agricultural Economics, Michigan State University, 1979. 49 p. ; 27 cm. (MSU rural development series : Working paper ; no. 5) "Part of a broader project entitled Alternative rural development strategies." "Based on the abstracts published in DAI [Dissertation abstracts international]" Includes index. LC Card 80-622267 DDC 016.381/41/091724 19
1. Underdeveloped areas - Produce trade - Bibliography. I. Weber, Michael T., joint author. II. Alternative rural development strategies. III. Dissertation abstracts international. IV. Series: MSU rural development papers : Working paper , no. 5. V. Title.
Z7164.F7 R54 HD9000.5

Riley, W. D. (William D.)
Covino, B. S. (Bernard S.) Corrosion resistance of materials in the aqueous hydrochloric acid environments associated with the recovery of alumina from kaolinitic clays /. Washington , 1981. p. cm. LC Card 80-606916 DDC 622 s 661/.0673/028 19
TN23 .U43 TA462

Effect of ferric ion on corrosion resistance of zirconium in HCl-AlCl₃ environment / by William D. Riley and Bernard S. Covino, Jr. Avondale, Md. : U. S. Dept. of the Interior, Bureau of Mines, 1981. p. cm. (Report of investigations / Bureau of Mines) Bibliography: p. LC Card 81-607817 DDC 622 s 620.1/8935223 19
1. Zirconium - Corrosion. 2. Iron ions. 3. Chlorides. I. Covino, B. S. (Bernard S.). II. Series: Report of investigations (United States. Bureau of Mines). III. Title.
TN23 .U43 TA480.Z65

Rindfuss, Ronald R., 1946- (joint author) MacDonald, Maurice, 1947- Relative economic status and fertility . [Madison] [1976?] 25 p. ; LC Card 78-624376 DDC 304.6/3 19
HQ760 .M32

Rinzler, Ralph. The Meaders family, north Georgia potters / Ralph Rinzler and Robert Sayers. Washington, D.C. : Smithsonian Institution Press, 1981. p. cm. (Smithsonian folklife studies . no. 1) Bibliography: p. LC Card 81-607995 DDC 738/.092/2 B 19
1. Meador family. 2. Pottery, American - Georgia. 3. Folk art - Georgia. I. Sayers, Robert. II. Title. III. Series.
NK4210.M35 R56

Rio de Janeiro. Pan American Foot and Mouth Disease Center.
Manual de procedimientos para la atención de un predio donde ocurre fiebre aftosa / Centro Panamericano de Fiebre Aftosa. Washington : Organización Panamericana de la Salud, Oficina Sanitaria Panamericana, Oficina Regional de la Organización Mundial de la Salud, 1974. 45 p. ; 21 cm. (Serie de manuales técnicos - Centro Panamericano de Fiebre Aftosa . no. 1) LC Card 79-123524
1. Foot-and-mouth disease - Prevention - Handbooks, manuals, etc. 2. Veterinary public heatlh - Handbooks, manuals, etc. I. Series: Rio de Janeiro. Pan American Foot and Mouth Disease Center. Serie de manuales técnicos - Centro Panamericano de Fiebre Aftosa , no. 1. II. Title.
SF793 .R55 1974

Manual de procedimientos para la prevención y erradicación de las enfermedades vesiculares de los animales / Centro Panamericano de Fiebre Aftosa. Washington : Organización Panamericana de la Salud, Oficina Sanitaria Panamericana, Oficina Regional de la Organización Mundial de la Salud, 1975. 77 p. ; 22 cm. (Serie de manuales técnicos - Centro Panamericano de Fiebre Aftosa . no. 3) LC Card 79-123539
1. Foot-and-mouth disease - Prevention. 2. Vesicular stomatitis - Prevention. 3. Veterinary public health. I. Series: Rio de Janeiro. Pan American Foot and Mouth Disease Center. Serie de manuales técnicos - Centro Panamericano de Fiebre Aftosa , no. 3. II. Title.
SF793 .R55 1975

Serie de manuales técnicos - Centro Panamericano de Fiebre Aftosa .
(no. 1) Rio de Janeiro. Pan American Foot and Mouth Disease Center. Manual de

procedimientos para la atención de un predio donde ocurre fiebre aftosa /. Washington , 1974. 45 p. ; LC Card 79-123524
SF793 .R55 1974

(no. 3) Rio de Janeiro. Pan American Foot and Mouth Disease Center. Manual de procedimientos para la prevención y erradicación de las enfermedades vesiculares de los animales /. Washington , 1975. 77 p. ; LC Card 79-123539
SF793 .R55 1975

Rio Grande Basin. Texas. Dept. of Water Resources. Projected land use maps year 2000, Rio Grande Basin. Austin, Tex. , 1978. [18] leaves : LC Card 80-675297 DDC 912/.133373/3097644 19
G1372.R5G4 T4 1978

RIO GRANDE NATIONAL FOREST - MAPS.
(1975) United States. Forest Service. Rocky Mountain Region. Rio Grande National Forest, Colorado, 1975. [Denver] 1975] col. map on sheet 142 x 67 cm. Scale 1:126,720; 1/2″ = 1 mile. Folded title: Rio Grande National Forest, Colorado. Printed on both sides of sheet. "Polyconic projection. New Mexico and sixth principal meridians." Relief shown by hachures and spot heights. "Forest visitors map." Includes key maps, "Vicinity map", recreation indexes, text, and col. illus. LC Card 76-690740
G4312.R5 1975 .U5
       NYPL [Map Div. 80-3418]

RIOS, RICHARD JOHN, 1942-
United States. Congress. Senate. Committee on Labor and Human Resources. Nomination . Washington , 1980. ii, 46 p. ; LC Card 80-602975 DDC 353.0084 19
KF26 .L27 1980d

RIPARIAN ECOLOGY - CALIFORNIA - CONGRESSES.
Riparian forests in California . [Berkeley, Ca.] , c1980. vi, 122 p. : ISBN 0-931876-41-9 (pbk.) : LC Card 80-624097 DDC 574.5/2642 19
QH105.C2 R56

RIPARIAN ECOLOGY - IOWA.
Effects of habitat alterations on riparian plant and animal communities in Iowa /. Kearneyville, WV [1981] p. cm. LC Card 81-607834 DDC 574.5/264 19
QH545.S8 E37

RIPARIAN ECOLOGY - KANKAKEE RIVER WATERSHED.
Illinois Institute of Technology. Pritzker Dept. of Environmental Engineering. Environmental observations of a riparian ecosystem during flood season . Urbana, Ill. [1979] iv, 64 p. : LC Card 80-623373 DDC 333.91/009773 s 574.5/26323/0977363 19
HD1644 .A136 no. 142 QH105.I3

Riparian ecosystem during flood season: final report. Illinois Institute of Technology. Pritzker Dept. of Environmental Engineering. Environmental observations of a riparian ecosystem during flood season . Urbana, Ill. [1979] iv, 64 p. : LC Card 80-623373 DDC 333.91/009773 s 574.5/26323/0977363 19
HD1644 .A136 no. 142 QH105.I3

Riparian forests in California : their ecology and conservation : a symposium / sponsored by Institute of Ecology, University of California, Davis, California and Davis Audubon Society, May 14, 1977 ; edited by Anne Sands. [Berkeley, Ca.] : Division of Agricultural Sciences, University of California, c1980. vi, 122 p. : ill. ; 28 cm. "Originally published as Institute of Ecology publication no. 15." Includes bibliographies. ISBN 0-931876-41-9 (pbk.) : LC Card 80-624097 DDC 574.5/2642 19
1. Riparian ecology - California - Congresses. 2. Forest ecology - California - Congresses. 3. Forest conservation - California - Congresses. I. Sands, Anne. II. California. University, Davis. Institute of Ecology. III. Davis Audubon Society.
QH105.C2 R56

RIPARIAN RIGHTS - MAINE.
Freeman, Martha. The Mill act, the Abandoned dams act, and the Neglected dams act . [Augusta, Me.] , 1979. ii, 54 p. ; LC Card 80-623039 DDC 346.74104/6914 19
KFM447.8 .F73

RIPARIAN RIGHTS - UNITED STATES.
Althaus, Helen F. Public trust rights /. [Washington] , 1978. xxxix, 421 p. ; LC Card

80-602390 DDC 346.7304/691 19
KF5571 .A94

The rise and fall of the political press in Britain . Koss, Stephen E. Chapel Hill [1981] p. cm. ISBN 0-8078-1483-0 LC Card 81-1707 DDC 072 19
PN5124.P6 K6 1981

The rise of literacy and the common school in the United States . Soltow, Lee. Chicago , 1981. p. cm. ISBN 0-226-76812-0 LC Card 81-7464 DDC 428.4 19
LC151 .S64

Rising hospital costs can be restrained by regulating payments and improving management . United States. General Accounting Office. Washington, D.C. , 1980. vi, 210 p. ; LC Card 81-600511 DDC 362.1/1/0681 19
RA981.A2 U53 1980a

Rising infant mortality in the U. S.S.R. in the 1970's /. Davis, Christopher, 1948- Washington, D.C. , 1980. 33 p. ; LC Card 81-600791 DDC 304.6 s 304.6/4 19
HC331 .U52 no. 74 HB1323.I4

Rising sugar costs and their effect on retail bakers . United States. Congress. House. Committee on Small Business. Subcommittee on Special Small Business Problems. Washington , 1980 [i.e. 1981] iii, 40 p. ; LC Card 81-600856 DDC 381/.45664752/0973 19
KF27 .S686 1980a

RISK.
Meier, Richard L. Risk-taking considered in a community ecology framework /. Berkeley , 1978. vii, 29 p. : LC Card 79-622123 DDC 363.7/05 19
HC79.E5 M44

Risk/benefit analysis in the legislative process . Congress/Science Forum, Washington, D.C., 1979. Washington , 1980. vi, 228 p. : LC Card 80-601466 DDC 328.73/077 19
KF27 .S399 1979n

Risk/benefit analysis in the legislative process . United States. Library of Congress. Congressional Research Service. Washington , 1980. ix, 36 p. ; LC Card 80-602214 DDC 363.1/056/0973 19
T174.5 .U57 1980

RISK CAPITAL. see VENTURE CAPITAL.

RISK - CONGRESSES.
United States. Library of Congress. Congressional Research Service. Risk/benefit analysis in the legislative process . Washington , 1980. ix, 36 p. ; LC Card 80-602214 DDC 363.1/056/0973 19
T174.5 .U57 1980

RISK MANAGEMENT.
Bilder, Richard B., 1927- Managing the risks of international agreement /. Madison , 1981. xi, 302 p. ; ISBN 0-299-08360-8 : LC Card 80-52288 DDC 341.3/7 19
JX4165 .B47

RISK MANAGEMENT - UNITED STATES.
United States. Congress. House. Committee on Science and Technology. Subcommittee on Science, Research, and Technology. Comparative risk assessment . Washington, , 1980. iv, 571 p. : LC Card 80-603895 DDC 342.73/066 347.30266 19
KF27 .S399 1980g

RISK - MATHEMATICAL MODELS.
Findlay, M. Chapman. FMRR simulation model and user manual /. Storrs, Conn. , Los Angeles, Calif. [1980] 51, 22 leaves ; ISBN 0-931176-76-X (pbk.) : LC Card 80-623842 DDC 333.33 s 332.63/24/0724 19
HD251 .R283 no. 30 HD1375

Risk-taking considered in a community ecology framework /. Meier, Richard L. Berkeley , 1978. vii, 29 p. : LC Card 79-622123 DDC 363.7/05 19
HC79.E5 M44

Ritchie, Albert Cabell, 1876-1936. Maryland. Laws, statutes, etc. Laws relating to State banks, trust companies, and savings institutions in force in the State of Maryland /. [Baltimore] 1916. 42 p. ; LC Card 78-109967 DDC 346.752/082/02632 19
KFM1365 .A3 1916

Ritchie, Theodore P. A comprehensive review of the commercial clam industries in the United States / conducted in cooperation with, and under contract to, the National Marine Fisheries Service, Washington, D.C., by Theodore P. Ritchie. Washington : The Service : for sale by the Supt. of Docs., U. S. Govt. Print. Off., 1977. ix, 106 p. : graphs ; 28 cm. Microfiche (neg.) NTIS. 2 sheets. 11 x 15 cm. (PB 273 615) "Stock number 003-020-00132-7." Includes bibliographies.　LC Card 77-602000
1. Clams. 2. Shellfish trade - United States. I. United States. National Marine Fisheries Service. II. Title.
HD9472.C53 U57　　　　*NYPL [*XME-9426]*

Rittenhouse, Joan Dunne. SRI International. Consequences of alcohol & marijuana use . Rockville, Md. , Washington, D.C. , 1980. xii, 227 p. :　LC Card 80-601619　DDC 616.86/1 19
RC564 .S18 1980

Ritter, Eric W.
Lyneis, Margaret M. Impacts, damage to cultural resources in the California desert /. Riverside, Calif. , 1980. viii, 171 p. :　LC Card 81-600782　DDC 979.4/9 19
F863 .L95

Norwood, Richard H. A cultural resource overview of the Eureka, Saline, Panamint, and Darwin region, east central California /. Riverside, Calif. , 1980. 219, [26] p. :　LC Card 81-601926　DDC 979.4/87 19
F863 .N67

Ritter, Lawrence S. Sproul, Allan, 1896- Selected papers of Allan Sproul /. [New York] [1980] xi, 233 p., [8] p. of plates :　LC Card 80-67915　DDC 332 19
HG2563 .S64

Rituals and ceremonies in popular culture / edited by Ray B. Browne. Bowling Green, Ohio : Bowling Green University Popular Press, c1980. 349 p. : ill. ; 24 cm. Includes bibliographical references.　ISBN 0-87972-160-X　LC Card 80-83188　DDC 306/.4 19
1. United States - Popular culture - Addresses, essays, lectures. 2. United States - Social life and customs - 20th century - Addresses, essays, lectures. I. Browne, Ray Broadus.
E169.12 .R55

Rituals of manhood : male initiation in Papua New Guinea / edited by Gilbert H. Herdt ; with an introduction by Roger M. Keesing. Berkeley : University of California Press, c1981. p. cm. Includes index.　ISBN 0-520-04448-7　LC Card 81-1807　DDC 392/.14 19
1. Puberty rites - Papua New Guinea - Addresses, essays, lectures. 2. Papua New Guinea - Social life and customs - Addresses, essays, lectures. I. Herdt, Gilbert H., 1949-.
GN671.N5 R55

The river and the rocks . Reed, John Calvin, 1930- Washington , 1980. vii, 75 p. :　LC Card 80-600023　DDC 557.3 s 557.52 19
QE75 .B9 no. 1471 QE122.G7

River Associates. see Charles River Associates.

River basin and watershed progress, Colorado /. United States. Soil Conservation Service. Portland, Or. , 1979. 1 map :　LC Card 81-691540
G4311.C315 1979 .U5

River basin monetary authorizations. United States. Congress. House. Committee on Public Works. Subcommittee on Flood Control and Internal Development. Washington , 1972. iii, 50 p.　LC Card 72-600616
NYPL [JLE 81-118]

River basins study areas. United States. Soil Conservation Service. South Dakota river basins study areas /. Lincoln, Nebr. , 1980. 1 map :　LC Card 81-691105
G4181.C315 1980 .U5

RIVER BOATS - ECONOMIC ASPECTS - UNITED STATES.
United States. Congress. Joint Economic Committee. Subcommittee on Economic Growth and Stabilization. The impact of the Soviet grain embargo on rail and barge transportation . Washington , 1980. iii, 47 p. ;　LC Card 80-602769　DDC 385/.1/0973 19
KF25 .E232 1980

RIVER CHANNELS - IOWA.
Hallberg, George R. Changes in the channel

area of the Missouri River in Iowa, 1879-1976 /. Iowa City, Iowa , 1979. iv, 32 p. :　LC Card 80-622112　DDC 551.48/3/097777 19
GB565.I8 H34

RIVER CHANNELS - MISSISSIPPI.
Hydrologic and biologic characteristics of natural channels in coastal marsh of Mississippi /. Mississippi State, Miss. , 1977. iii, 22 leaves :　LC Card 79-625357　DDC 551.46/09 19
QH105.M7 H9

RIVER CHANNELS - MISSOURI VALLEY.
Osterkamp, W. R. Perennial-streamflow characteristics related to channel geometry and sediment in the Missouri River basin /. [Reston, Va.?] [1981] p. cm.　LC Card 81-607905　DDC 551.48/3/0978 19
GB1227.M7 O84

River (Charles) Associates. see Charles River Associates.

RIVER CONSERVATIONS. see STREAM CONSERVATION.

RIVER FLOOD PLAINS. see FLOODPLAINS.

RIVER LIFE - ALASKA.
Gudgel-Holmes, Dianne. Ethnohistory of four interior Alaskan waterbodies /. [Anchorage, Alaska] [1979] 148 p. :　LC Card 80-623266　DDC 979.8/4 19
F910 .G78

River survey report of North Fork Crow River and Crow River /. Kucera, Thomas. [St. Paul] , 1977. 79 p. :　LC Card 78-620652　DDC 597.092/9776/5 19
QL628.M6 K83

RIVERS - GAUGING. see STREAM MEASUREMENTS.

Rivers, Larry, 1923-
Hirshhorn Museum and Sculpture Garden. Larry Rivers . Washington, D.C. , 1981. p. cm.　LC Card 81-607310　DDC 709/.2/4 19
N6537.R57 A4 1981

RIVERS, LARRY, 1923- - EXHIBITIONS.
Hirshhorn Museum and Sculpture Garden. Larry Rivers . Washington, D.C. , 1981. p. cm.　LC Card 81-607310　DDC 709/.2/4 19
N6537.R57 A4 1981

RIVERS - LAW AND LEGISLATION.
Rankin, Janna S. When is a stream a stream? . Bozeman, MT [1980] iv, 43 leaves :　LC Card 80-623138　DDC 346.78604/69162/014 19
GB1201.5 .R36

RIVERS - MONTANA.
Foggin, G. Thomas. Completion report, using topographic characteristics to predict total solute concentrations in streams draining small forested watersheds in Western Montana /. Bozeman, Mont. , 1977. 42 leaves :　LC Card 79-624615　DDC 551.48/3/09786 19
GB855 .F63

RIVERS - POLLUTION. see WATER - POLLUTION.

RIVERS - POWER UTILIZATION.
Kariyawasam, Hettigamage. Evaluation of hydropower potential in a river basin /. Austin, Tex. [1980] ix, 141 p. :　LC Card 80-624120　DDC 333.91/4 19
TC147 .K37

RIVERS - TERMINOLOGY.
Rankin, Janna S. When is a stream a stream? . Bozeman, MT [1980] iv, 43 leaves :　LC Card 80-623138　DDC 346.78604/69162/014 19
GB1201.5 .R36

RIVERS - UNITED STATES.
United States. Congress. House. Committee on Public Works. Subcommittee on Flood Control and Internal Development. River basin monetary authorizations. Washington , 1972. iii, 50 p.　LC Card 72-600616
NYPL [JLE 81-118]

RIVERS - WASHINGTON (STATE) - WHITMAN COUNTY - MAPS.
United States. Soil Conservation Service. Major streams and drainages, Whitman County, Washington /. Portland, Or. , 1977. 1 map :　LC Card 81-691522
G4283.W6C3 1977 .U5

RIVERS - WISCONSIN - MAPS.
United States. Soil Conservation Service. [Major rivers of Wisconsin] /. Lincoln, Nebr. , 1981. 1

map :　LC Card 81-691249
G4121.C3 1981 .U5

The Riverton culture . Winters, Howard D. Springfield , 1969. xiii, 164 p., 48 [i.e. 24] leaves of plates :　LC Card 79-629858　DDC 977.3 s 977.2/401 19
AM101 .I374 no. 13 E78.I3

Rives, Jerry L. Soil survey of Pecos County, Texas / [by Jerry L. Rives] ; United States Department of Agriculture, Soil Conservation Service, in cooperation with Texas Agricultural Experiment Station. [Washington] : The Service, [1980] vii, 97 p., [77] fold. leaves of plates : ill. ; 28 cm. Cover title. "Issued May 1980." Bibliography: p. 48.　LC Card 80-602640　DDC 631.4/7/764923 19
1. Soils - Texas - Pecos Co. - Maps. I. United States. Soil Conservation Service. II. Texas. Agricultural Experiment Station, College Station. III. Title.
S599.T4 R59

Rivet, Philip G. (joint author) Weinstein, Richard A. Beau Mire, a late Tchula period site of the Tchefuncte culture, Ascension Parish, Louisiana /. Baton Rouge, La. , 1978. vii, 125, [9] p. :　LC Card 80-137100　DDC 976.3/19 19
E78.T4 W44

RLG military operations and activities in the Laotian panhandle /. Vongsavanh, Southchay. Washington, D.C. , 1981. p. cm.　LC Card 81-10934　DDC 959.704/34 19
DS557.8.L3 V66

Roach, Michael. Montana. Bureau of Air Quality. Scientific and Engineering Advisory Panel on Poplar River Air Quality. Issue paper /. Helena, Mont. [1979] 32 p. ;　LC Card 80-621735　DDC 363.7/392 19
TD883.5.M6 M66 1979

ROAD ACCESSORIES. see ROADS - ACCESSORIES.

ROAD BUILDING. see ROAD CONSTRUCTION.

ROAD CONSTRUCTION - CONTRACTS AND SPECIFICATIONS - DELAWARE.
Delaware. Division of Highways. Supplemental specifications to Standard specifications for road and bridge construction (dated January 1, 1974) /. Dover, Del. [1980] v, 142 p. ;　LC Card 80-622254　DDC 625.7/0212 19
TE180 .D42 1980

ROAD CONSTRUCTION - CONTRACTS AND SPECIFICATIONS - NEBRASKA.
Nebraska. Dept. of Roads. Supplemental specifications to standard specifications for highway construction, series 1973 /. [Lincoln] [1978?] 104 p. :　LC Card 79-625491　DDC 625.7/0218 19
TE24.N2 N43 1978

ROAD CONSTRUCTION - CONTRACTS AND SPECIFICATIONS - NEW YORK (STATE) - PHILIPSTOWN.
Bryan & Panico, Inc. Road construction specifications . Philipstown, N. Y. , 1974. 35 leaves in various pagings :
NYPL [JSF 81-54]

ROAD CONSTRUCTION - CONTRACTS AND SPECIFICATIONS - UNITED STATES.
United States. Forest Service. Forest service standard specifications for construction of roads and bridges. Washington , 1979. vii, 461 p. :　LC Card 79-603953　DDC 625.7/0212 19
TE180 .U66 1979

ROAD CONSTRUCTION - ENVIRONMENTAL ASPECTS.
National Research Council. Transportation Research Board. Design of sedimentation basins. Washington, D.C. , 1980. 53 p. :　ISBN 0-309-03027-7 (pbk.) :　LC Card 80-52843　DDC 625.7/34 19
TD439 .N37 1980

ROAD CONSTRUCTION - IOWA - SAFETY MEASURES.
Carstens, Robert Lowell. Safer construction and maintenance practices to minimize potential liability by counties from highway accidents . Ames, Iowa [1979] xiv, 113 p. ;　LC Card 80-623075　DDC 363.1/251 19
HE5614.3.I8 C37

Road construction specifications . Bryan & Panico, Inc. Philipstown, N. Y. , 1974. 35

leaves in various pagings :
NYPL [JSF 81-54]

ROAD CONSTRUCTION WORKERS.
Roy Jorgenson Associates. Construction
engineering manpower management : system
design manual /. [Gaithersburg, Md.], 1978. 1
v. (loose-leaf); **NYPL [JSF 80-656]**

ROAD DESIGN. see ROADS - DESIGN.

**ROAD ENGINEERING. see HIGHWAY
ENGINEERING.**

**ROAD RESEARCH. see HIGHWAY
RESEARCH.**

**ROAD SIGNS. see SIGNS AND SIGN-
BOARDS.**

**ROAD TRAFFIC. see TRAFFIC
ENGINEERING.**

ROADS - ACCESSORIES.
United States. Federal Highway Administration.
A handbook of highway safety design and
operating practices. Washington [1973] 1 v.
(loose-leaf). **NYPL [JLF 80-1456]**

ROADS - ALASKA.
Alaska. Legislature. House of Representatives.
Special Committee on Roads and Highways.
Interim report /. [Juneau, Alaska] , 1979. 56,
[214] p. : LC Card 80-622414 DDC
388.1/14/09798 19
KFA1211.4 .R6 1979

ROADS - ALASKA - FINANCE.
Alaska. Legislature. House of Representatives.
Special Committee on Roads and Highways.
Interim report /. [Juneau, Alaska] , 1979. 56,
[214] p. : LC Card 80-622414 DDC
388.1/14/09798 19
KFA1211.4 .R6 1979

ROADS - ARKANSAS - FINANCE.
Arkansas. State Highway Commission. Ten-year
highway program . [Little Rock, Ark.] [1979]
vi, 50 p. : LC Card 80-622650 DDC 338.1/09767
19
HE356.A8 A5184 1979

**ROADS - CONSTRUCTION. see ROAD
CONSTRUCTION.**

**ROADS - DESIGN - STANDARDS -
NEBRASKA.**
Nebraska. Dept. of Roads. Supplemental
specifications to standard specifications for
highway construction, series 1973 /. [Lincoln]
[1978?] 104 p. : LC Card 79-625491 DDC
625.7/0218 19
TE24.N2 N43 1978

**ROADS - ENVIRONMENTAL ASPECTS -
IOWA.**
Iowa. Dept. of Transportation. Planning and
Research Division. Office of Project Planning.
Deicing practices in Iowa . [Des Moines, Iowa]
[1980] iii, 37, 90 p. : LC Card 80-622580 DDC
625.7/63/09777 19
TE220.5 .I68 1980

ROADS, FOREST. see FOREST ROADS.

ROADS - INDIANA.
Yamin, Hadi. Relationship of highway
development and city development for
non-metropolitan places in Indiana . West
Lafayette, Ind. , 1979. xii, 175 leaves : LC
Card 80-620933 DDC 388.1/1 19
TE24.I6 Y35

**ROADS - IOWA - MAINTENANCE AND
REPAIR.**
Carstens, Robert Lowell. Safer construction and
maintenance practices to minimize potential
liability by counties from highway accidents .
Ames, Iowa [1979] xiv, 113 p. ; LC Card
80-623075 DDC 363.1/251 19
HE5614.3.I8 C37

**ROADS - IOWA - SNOW AND ICE
CONTROL.**
Iowa. Dept. of Transportation. Planning and
Research Division. Office of Project Planning.
Deicing practices in Iowa . [Des Moines, Iowa]
[1980] iii, 37, 90 p. : LC Card 80-622580 DDC
625.7/63/09777 19
TE220.5 .I68 1980

ROADS - NEBRASKA.
Focus on Nebraska highways. [Lincoln, 1974?]
36 p.: **NYPL [JLF 80-597]**

ROADS - NEVADA.
Nevada. Dept. of Highways. Planning Survey

Division. Transportation systems . [Carson
City] , 1978. iii, 31 leaves, [1] leaf of plates :
LC Card 80-620633 DDC 380.5/068 19
HE213.N3 N48 1978

ROADS - NEW JERSEY - STATISTICS.
New Jersey. Dept. of Transportation. Four
years of highway accomplishments. [Trenton]
[1974?] 75 p. ; **NYPL [JLF 80-998]**

Roads of rural America / [compiled by] Arvin R.
Bunker, T. Q. Hutchinson. Washington, D.C. :
U. S. Dept. of Agriculture, Economics,
Statistics, and Cooperatives Service ;
Springfield, Va. : available from National
Technical Information Service, 1979. iii, 57 p. :
graphs ; 26 cm. (ESCS ; 74) Cover title. Includes
bibliographies. LC Card 80-602646 DDC
388.1/0973 19
*1. Roads - United States - Addresses, essays, lectures.
2. Transportation planning - United States - Addresses,
essays, lectures. I. Bunker, Arvin R. II. Hutchinson,
Thurlow Quinton, 1935-. III. United States. Dept. of
Agriculture. Economics, Statistics, and Cooperatives
Service. IV. Series: United States. Dept. of Agriculture.
Economics, Statistics, and Cooperatives Service. ESCS ,
74.*
HE355 .R57

**ROADS - RESEARCH. see HIGHWAY
RESEARCH.**

ROADS - RIGHT OF WAY - MULTIPLE USE.
United States. Federal Highway Administration.
Highway joint development and multiple use.
[Washington , Washington , 1979] 132 p. : LC
Card 79-602134
HE355.8 .U54 1979

ROADS - SAFETY MEASURES.
United States. Federal Highway Administration.
A handbook of highway safety design and
operating practices. Washington [1973] 1 v.
(loose-leaf). **NYPL [JLF 80-1456]**

**ROADS - SIGNS. see SIGNS AND SIGN-
BOARDS.**

**ROADS - SNOW AND ICE CONTROL -
ADDRESSES, ESSAYS, LECTURES.**
Guideway snow and ice control and roadside
maintenance /. Washington, D.C. [1981] p.
cm. ISBN 0-309-03121-4 LC Card 81-3965 DDC
380.5 s 625.7/63 19
TE7 .H5 no. 776 TE220.5

ROADS - STANDARDS - NEBRASKA.
Nebraska. Dept. of Roads. Supplemental
specifications to standard specifications for
highway construction, series 1973 /. [Lincoln]
[1978?] 104 p. : LC Card 79-625491 DDC
625.7/0218 19
TE24.N2 N43 1978

ROADS - UNITED STATES.
United States. Federal Highway Administration.
Highway functional classification . [Washington]
1974. [34] p. in various pagings :
NYPL [*ZT-1259]

**ROADS - UNITED STATES - ADDRESSES,
ESSAYS, LECTURES.**
Roads of rural America /. Washington, D.C. ,
Springfield, Va. , 1979. iii, 57 p. : LC Card
80-602646 DDC 388.1/0973 19
HE355 .R57

ROADS - UNITED STATES - FINANCE.
United States. Congress. Senate. Committee on
Environment and Public Works. Subcommittee
on Transportation. Funding for the Federal-aid
highway program . Washington , 1980. iv, 552
p. : LC Card 80-603903 DDC 343.73/0942
347.303942 19
KF26 .E679 1980a

**ROADS - UNITED STATES - FINANCE -
HISTORY - ADDRESSES, ESSAYS,
LECTURES.**
Martin, James Walter, 1893- State tax systems
under changing technology . Lexington, Ky. ,
c1980. x, 322 p. : LC Card 80-131133 DDC
353.9/3878 19
HE355 .M37

**ROADS - UNITED STATES - STATES -
FINANCE.**
Cooper, Thomas W. The State highway finance
outlook /. [Washington] , 1978. viii, 101 p. :
LC Card 79-601548
HE355 .C66

ROADS - UNITED STATES - SURVEYING.
United States. Federal Highway Administration.

Office of Environmental Policy. The
consideration of archeology and paleontology in
the Federal-aid highway program.
[Washington] , 1979. 79 p. : LC Card 79-602652
E159.5 .U54 1978 **NYPL [HBC 81-515]**

ROADS - VIRGINIA.
Pawlett, Nathaniel Mason. The route of the
Three Notch'd Road . Charlottesville, Va.
[1980] vi, 26 p. : LC Card 80-620018 DDC
388.1/09755/4 19
HE356.V8 P39

Young, Douglas, 1953- A brief history of the
Staunton and James River Turnpike /.
Charlottesville, Va. [1980] vii, 22 p. : LC Card
80-620005 DDC 388.1/22/0975548 19
HE356.V8 Y68 1980

**ROADSIDE IMPROVEMENT - ADDRESSES,
ESSAYS, LECTURES.**
Guideway snow and ice control and roadside
maintenance /. Washington, D.C. [1981] p.
cm. ISBN 0-309-03121-4 LC Card 81-3965 DDC
380.5 s 625.7/63 19
TE7 .H5 no. 776 TE220.5

**ROADSIDE IMPROVEMENT - LAW AND
LEGISLATION - UNITED STATES.**
United States. Congress. Senate. Committee on
Environment and Public Works. S. 344, the
Highway beautification assistance act of 1979 .
Washington , 1980. iii, 9 p. ; LC Card 80-601737
DDC 346.7304/5 19
KF5532 .A25 1980

**ROADSIDE IMPROVEMENT - UNITED
STATES - FINANCE.**
United States. Congress. Senate. Committee on
Environment and Public Works. S. 344, the
Highway beautification assistance act of 1979 .
Washington , 1980. iii, 9 p. ; LC Card 80-601737
DDC 346.7304/5 19
KF5532 .A25 1980

Roanhouse, Michael. (joint author. 0700) Jones,
Ronald, 1945- Problems affecting low-rent
public housing projects . [Washington, D.C.]
[1979] x, 317 p. : LC Card 80-600612
HD7293 .J66

ROASTING (METALLURGY)
Behavior of cadmium during roasting of zinc
concentrate /. Washington, D.C. [1981] p. cm.
LC Card 80-607819 DDC 622 s 669/.5 19
TN23 .U43 TN796

Robards, F. Stuart. (joint author) Schmidt, Artwin.
Annual performance report for inventory and
cataloging special management problems /.
Juneau , 1976. 70 p. : LC Card 77-621096 DDC
597/.05/028 19
QL628.A4 S33

**ROBBERY - WASHINGTON (STATE) -
SEATTLE.**
Whitcomb, Debra. Focus on robbery .
[Washington] , 1979. iii, 76 p. : LC Card
79-602932 DDC 363.2/52 19
HV8145.W2 W45

**ROBBINS, TOM - CRITICISM AND
INTERPRETATION.**
Siegel, Mark Richard. Tom Robbins /. Boise,
Idaho , c1980. 52 p. : ISBN 0-88430-066-8
(pbk.) : LC Card 80-69013 DDC 813/.54 19
PS3568.O233 Z87

Robeck, Bruce W. Texas A & M Research
Foundation. Ballot access /. - [Washington]
1978. 4 v. in 1 ; **NYPL [*XME-9374]**

**Robert Hull Fleming Museum. see Vermont.
University. Robert Hull Fleming Museum.**

Robert Penn Warren . Grimshaw, James A.
Charlottesville , 1981. p. cm. ISBN
0-8139-0891-4 LC Card 81-3003 DDC
016.813/52 19
Z8949.73 .G75 PS3545.A748

**Robert S. Kerr Environmental Research
Laboratory.** Sammis, Theodore W.
Demonstration of irrigation return flow water
quality in the Mesilla Valley, New Mexico /.
Las Cruces, N.M. [1980] ix, 149 p. : LC Card
80-623166 DDC 333.91/009789 s 631.7 19
GB705.N6 N64 no. 117 TC824.N6

Robert W. Retherford Associates. International
Engineering Company, inc., San Francisco.
Anchorage-Fairbanks transmission intertie
economic feasibility study report /. [Juneau,
Alaska] [1979] ca. 350 p. in various pagings :
LC Card 80-622633 DDC 338.4/3621319/09798

19
HD9685.U6 A475 1979

Roberts, Jay T. (joint author) Glass, Gary B. Coals and coal-bearing rocks of the Hanna Coal Field, Wyoming /. Laramie, Wyo. , 1980. iv, 43 p. (3 fold.) : LC Card 80-622620 DDC 557.87 s 553.2/4/0978786 19
QE181 .A26 no. 22 TN805.W8

Roberts, Jean, 1918- Hypertension in adults 25-74 years of age, United States, 1971-1975 / [Jean Roberts and Michael Rowland]. Hyattsville, Md. : National Center for Health Statistics, 1980. p. cm. (Vital and health statistics : Series 11, Data from the National health Survey ; no. 221) DHHS publication ; no. (PHS) 81-1671 Includes bibliographical references. ISBN 0-8406-0207-3 LC Card 80-607834 DDC 312/.0973 s 614.5/9132/0973 19
1. Hypertension - United States. 2. Hypertension - Social aspects - United States. 3. Hypertension - United States - Statistics. 4. Health surveys - United States. I. Rowland, Michael, joint author. II. Series: United States. National Center for Health Statistics. Vital and health statistics : Series 11, Data from the National Health Survey, Data from the health examination survey , no. 221. III. Title.
RA407.3 .A347 no. 221 RC685.H8

Roberts, Matt, 1929- Bookbinding and the conservation of books : a dictionary of descriptive terminology / Matt T. Roberts and Don Etherington ; drawings by Margaret R. Brown. Washington : Library of Congress, 1981. p. cm. Bibliography: p. ISBN 0-8444-0366-0 LC Card 81-607974 DDC 686.3/03 19
1. Bookbinding - Dictionaries. 2. Books - Conservation and restoration - Dictionaries. I. Etherington, Don. II. Title.
Z266.7 .R62

Roberts, Nigel Keith. (joint author) Cretin, Shan. Surgical care for cardiovascular disease in California . Berkeley, Calif. , 1981. x, 37 p. ; ISBN 0-87772-277-3 LC Card 80-39873 DDC 617/.41 19
RD597 .C73

ROBERTS, PAUL CRAIG, 1939-
United States. Congress. Senate. Committee on Finance. Nominations of John E. Chapoton, Roscoe L. Egger, Jr., and Paul C. Roberts . Washington , 1981. iii, 40 p. ; LC Card 81-601602 DDC 353.2 19
KF26 .F5 1981d

Roberts, W. Lewis (William Lewis), 1877-1960.
Legal tidbits for women / by W. Lewis Roberts. Lexington [Ky.] : University of Kentucky, Dept. of University Extension, [1936] 97 p. ; 23 cm. (Bulletin / University of Kentucky. University Extension series : v. 15, no. 3) "March 1936." Includes bibliographical references. LC Card 80-144806 DDC 349.769 347.69 19
1. Law - Kentucky - Popular works. 2. Women - Legal status, laws, etc. - Kentucky - Popular works. I. Series: Bulletin / University of Kentucky. University Extension series ; v. 15, no. 3. II. Title.
KFK1281 .R6

Robertson, Cheryl. Milwaukee Art Museum. "China that's ancient and blue" . [Milwaukee, Wis.] (750 N. Lincoln Memorial Dr., Milwaukee) , c1980. [32] p. : LC Card 80-84056 DDC 738.2/074/017595 19
NK4565.5 .M54 1980

Robertson, James I. Civil War sites in Virginia : a tour guide / James I. Robertson, Jr. Charlottesville : University Press of Virginia, 1981. p. cm. Includes index. ISBN 0-8139-0907-4 LC Card 81-7426 DDC 917.55/0443 19
1. Historic sites - Virginia - Guide-books. 2. Virginia - Description and travel - 1951- - Guide-books. 3. Virginia - History - Civil War, 1861-1865. I. Title.
F227 .R59

Robertson, Nat Clinton. Science policy . [Washington, D.C.?] , 1980. 2 v. ; LC Card 80-604130 DDC 507/.2073 19
Q127.U6 S319

Robertson, Richard Neal, 1940- Impact of removal of tolls on travel in Tidewater Virginia / by R. N. Robertson and Gary R. Allen. Charlottesville, Va. : Virginia Highway & Transportation Research Council, [1977?] 3 v. : ill. ; 28 cm. In cooperation with the U. S. Federal Highway Administration. "VHTRC 78-R4, [R11, R12]" July 1977." Includes bibliographical references. CONTENTS. - v. 1. Hampton Roads Bridge-Tunnel.--v.

2. James River Bridge.--v. 3. Coleman Bridge. LC Card 79-625466 DDC 388.1/14 19
1. Toll bridges - Virginia. I. Allen, Gary R., joint author. II. Virginia Highway & Transportation Research Council. III. United States. Federal Highway Administration. IV. Title.
HE376.A2 V87

Robichaux, Jim. (joint author) Shaw, Bill, 1940- Council on Environmental Quality /. Austin, Tex. , 1979. [13] leaves ; LC Card 79-626084 DDC 363.7/05/0973 19
HC110.E5 S48

Robinette, Michael. State of Washington Water Research Center. An assessment of potential hydroelectric power and energy for the State of Washington /. [Olympia] [1979] 5 v. : LC Card 80-622476 DDC 553.7/09797 s 333.91/4 19
TD224.W2 S8 no. 34 TK1424.W2

Robinove, Charles Joseph, 1931- Walker, A. S. (Alta Sharon), 1942- Annotated bibliography of remote sensing methods for monitoring desertification /. Washington , 1981. p. cm. LC Card 81-607078 DDC 557.3 s 016.508315/4 19
QE75 .C5 no. 851 Z6004.D4 GB612

Robinson, Anna T. Nikki Giovanni : from revolution to revelation / Anna T. Robinson. Columbus : State Library of Ohio, 1979. 25 p. ; 23 cm. (Ohio authors) Bibliography: p. 25. LC Card 80-137505 DDC 811/.54 19
1. Giovanni, Nikki - Criticism and interpretation - Addresses, essays, lectures. I. Series.
PS3557.I55 Z87

Robinson, Arthur Howard, 1915- Early thematic mapping in the history of cartography / Arthur H. Robinson. Chicago : University of Chicago Press, 1982. p. cm. Bibliography: p. Includes index. ISBN 0-226-72285-6 : LC Card 81-11516 DDC 912 19
1. Cartography - History. I. Title.
GA201 .R63

Robinson, Charles Sherwood, 1920- (joint author) Warner, Lawrence Allen, 1914- Geology of the eastern part of the Harold D. Roberts Tunnel, Colorado (Stations 690+00 to 1238+58) /. Washington , 1980. p. cm. LC Card 80-607839 DDC 624.1/92 19
QE92.H37 W37

Robinson, Colan Michael, 1952- On-line image recognition using radial profiles / by Colan Michael Robinson. Urbana, Ill. : Dept. of Computer Science, University of Illinois at Urbana-Champaign, [1980] vii leaves, 104 p. : ill. ; 28 cm. ([Report] - Department of Computer Science, University of Illinois at Urbana-Champaign . UIUCDCS-R-80-1023) "May 1980." Originally presented as the author's thesis, University of Illinois at Urbana-Champaign, 1980. Bibliography: p. 76-78. LC Card 80-623656 DDC 001.6/4 s 621.3819/598 19
1. Optical pattern recognition. 2. Robots, Industrial. I. Illinois. University at Urbana-Champaign. Dept. of Computer Science. II. Series: Illinois. University at Urbana-Champaign. Dept. of Computer Science. Report, UIUCDCS-R-80-1023. III. Title.
QA76 .I4 no. 1023 TA1650

Robinson, E. Thomas. Accounting for Alaska nonprofit salmon enhancement facilities, including a chart of accounts / by E. Thomas Robinson. Fairbanks : Alaska Sea Grant Program, University of Alaska, 1978. xii, 67 p. : ill. ; 28 cm. (Sea grant report. 77-13) LC Card 79-623795 DDC 639.3/755 19
1. Fish-culture - Economic aspects - Alaska. 2. Pacific salmon. 3. Fish-culture - Accounting. I. Series: Alaska sea grant report, 77-13. II. Title.
SH35.A62 R62

Robinson, George William, 1926- Combs, Bert T., 1911- The public papers of Governor Bert T. Combs, 1959-1963 /. Lexington , c1979. xxvi, 539 p., [1] leaf of plates : ISBN 0-8131-0604-4 : LC Card 78-58103
J87 .K417 1959   NYPL [ITY 80-2687]

Robinson, Harold Ernest, 1932-
Chromosome numbers in Compositae, XII. Washington , 1981. p. cm. LC Card 81-607855 DDC 581 s 5831.55 19
QK1 .S2747 no. 52 QK495.C74

A revision of the tribal and subtribal limits of the Heliantheae (Asteraceae) / Harold

Robinson. City of Washington : Smithsonian Institution Press, 1981. p. cm. (Smithsonian contributions to botany . no. 51) Bibliography: p. Includes index. LC Card 81-607993 DDC 581 s 583/.55 19
1. Compositae - Classification. 2. Botany - Classification. I. Title. II. Title: Heliantheae (Asteraceae). III. Series.
QK1 .S2747 no. 51 QK495.C74

Robinson, Linda J. Louisiana. Criminal Justice Information System Division. Arrests in Louisiana, 1975-1977. Baton Rouge, La. [197-?] iii, 120 p. : LC Card 80-621813 DDC 364.1/09763 19
HV7268 .A6 1970

Robinson, Robert, 1920- United States. Social Security Administration. Office of Research and Statistics. Income & resources of the aged /. [Washington, D.C.] [1980] 35 p. : LC Card 80-600019
HD7106.U5 U65 1980

Robinton, Elizabeth Dorothy. The Mill River and its floodplain in Northampton and Williamsburg, Massachusetts : a study of the vascular plant flora, vegetation, and the presence of the bacterial family Pseudomonadaceae in relation to patterns of land use / Elizabeth D. Robinton and C. John Burk, principal investigators. Amherst : Water Resources Research Center, University of Massachusetts at Amherst, [1972?] vii leaves, 72 p. : maps ; 28 cm. (Completion report - Water Resources Research Center, University of Massachusetts at Amherst ; 72-4) Includes bibliographies. LC Card 80-497906 DDC 581.5/26323 19
1. Botany - Massachusetts - Mill River watershed. 2. Land use - Massachusetts - Mill River watershed. 3. Mill River watershed, Mass. 4. Pseudomonadaceae. I. Bark, Carl John, 1935- joint author. II. Series: University of Massachusetts at Amherst. Water Resources Research Center. Completion report - Water Resources Research Center, University of Massachusetts at Amherst, 72-4. III. Title.
QK166 .R67

ROBOTS, INDUSTRIAL.
Robinson, Colan Michael, 1952- On-line image recognition using radial profiles /. Urbana, Ill. [1980] vii leaves, 104 p. : LC Card 80-623656 DDC 001.6/4 s 621.3819/598 19
QA76 .I4 no. 1023 TA1650

ROCK BURSTS.
Moebs, Noel N. Geologic structures in coal mine roof /. Avondale, Md. [1981] p. cm. LC Card 81-607308 DDC 622 s 622/.8 19
TN23 .U43 TN295

Moebs, Noel N. The relation of geology to mine roof conditions in the Pocahontas No. 3 coalbed /. Avondale, MD [1981] p. cm. LC Card 81-607819 DDC 622 s 622/.334/09754873 19
TN295 .U4

ROCK-CRYSTAL. see QUARTZ.

ROCK DEFORMATION - CALIFORNIA - TRANSVERSE RANGES.
Rodgers, Donald A. Vertical deformation, stress accumulation, and secondary faulting in the vicinity of the transverse ranges of southern California /. Sacramento, Calif. , 1979. v, 74 p. : LC Card 79-625539 DDC 557.94 s 551.8 19
TN24.C2 A3 no. 203 QE604

A rock in a weary land . Walker, Clarence Earl. Baton Rouge , c1981. p. cm. ISBN 0-8071-0883-9 : LC Card 81-11731 DDC 287/.83 19
BX8443 .W27 1981

ROCK ISLAND COUNTY, ILL. - MAPS.
(1980) United States. Soil Conservation Service. Rock Island County, Illinois /. Lincoln, Nebr. , 1980. 1 map : LC Card 81-691427
G4103.R6 1980 .U5

Rock Island transition act . United States. Congress. Senate. Committee on Commerce, Science, and Transportation. Subcommittee on Surface Transportation. Washington , 1980. iv, 146 p. : LC Card 80-602527 DDC 343.73/095 19
KF26 .C698 1980b

ROCK MECHANICS.
(1981) Peng, Syd S., 1939- Stress distribution and pillar design in oil shale retorts /. Avondale, Md. , 1981. p. cm. LC Card

81-607827   DDC 622 s 622/.3382 19
TN23 .U43 TN858

ROCK PAINTINGS - UTAH.
Castleton, Kenneth Bitner, 1903- Petroglyphs
and pictographs of Utah /. Salt Lake City ,
1978-1979. 2 v. : LC Card 78-53941   DDC
709/.01/1309792 19
E78.U55 C37

**ROCK PHOSPHATES. see PHOSPHATE
ROCK.**

**ROCKEFELLER, NELSON ALDRICH, 1908- -
ADDRESSES, ESSAYS, LECTURES.**
United States. 96th Congress, 1st session, 1979.
Memorial addresses and other tributes in the
Congress of the United States on the life and
contributions of Nelson A. Rockefeller /.
Washington , 1979. xi, 279 p., [1] leaf of
plates : LC Card 80-603613   DDC 973.925/092/4
B 19
E748.R673 U56 1979

Rockford Map Publishers, Rockford, Ill. Land
plat book, with index to land owners, Gogebic
County, Michigan. Edited by County Extension
Service of Michigan State University. Rockford,
1965. 55 p. maps. 29 cm. Cover title. Scale of
township maps 1:50,688; 1 1/4 inch equals 1 mile. LC
Card Map68-420
*1. Gogebic County, Mich. - Maps. 2. Real property -
Michigan - Gogebic County - Maps. I. Michigan. State
University, East Lansing. Cooperative Extension
Service. II. Title.*   **NYPL [Map Div. 80-375]**

The Rockies /. Lavender, David Sievert, 1910-
Lincoln , 1981, c1968. p. cm.   ISBN
0-8032-2857-0   LC Card 81-3427   DDC 978 19
F721 .L3 1981

ROCKINGHAM COUNTY, N. H. - MAPS.
(1980) United States. Soil Conservation Service.
Rockingham County, New Hampshire /.
Lanham, Md. , 1980. 1 map ; LC Card
81-690125
G3743.R6 1980 .U5

Rockland County, N. Y. Planning Board.
Development plan : town of Stony Point, N.
Y. : background studies, proposed plan and
effectuation / Town Planning Board. Stony
Point, N. Y. : The Board, 1973. iv, 118 p. : ill.,
maps (some col., part fold., 2 in pocket) ; 28
cm. Bibliography: p. 117-118.
*1. City planning - New York (State). 2. Stony Point, N.
Y. (Township) - City planning. I. Title.*
NYPL [JLF 80-571]

**ROCKS - AGE. see GEOLOGY,
STRATIGRAPHIC.**

ROCKS, CARBONATE.
Clark, John H. Geology of the carbonate rocks
in western Franklin County, Pennsylvania /.
[Harrisburg] , 1970. 1 portfolio ([1] fold. leaf :
col. map) ; LC Card 74-621156   DDC 557.48 s
557.48/44 19
QE157 .A293 no. 180 QE656

Okuma, Angelo. Geology of the carbonate
rocks of Path Valley, Franklin County,
Pennsylvania /. [Harrisburg] , 1970. 1 portfolio
([1] fold. leaf : col. map) ; LC Card 74-621157
DDC 557.48 s 557.48/44 19
QE157 .A293 no. 179 QE660

Schultze, L. E. (Lawrence E.) Extracting
uranium from carbonaceous ores /.
[Washington, D.C.] , [1981] p. cm. LC Card
81-10150   DDC 622 s 669/.2931 19
TN23 .U43 TN799.U7

ROCKS, ERUPTIVE. see ROCKS, IGNEOUS.

ROCKS, IGNEOUS.
(1981) Pavlides, Louis, 1921- The central
Virginia volcanic-plutonic belt . Washington ,
1981. p. cm. LC Card 81-607018   DDC 552/.1 19
QE461 .P328

ROCKS, SEDIMENTARY.
(1979) Baird, Gordon C. Sedimentary
relationships of Portland Point and associated
Middle Devonian rocks in central and western
New York /. Albany, N.Y. [1979] iv, 24 p. :
LC Card 79-625700   DDC 551.7/4 19
QE665 .B23

ROCKS, SILICEOUS.
Goodyear, Albert C. A hypothesis for the use
of cryptocrystalline raw materials among
Paleo-Indian groups of North America /.
Columbia, S.C. [1979] 15 leaves ; LC Card

80-621583   DDC 970.01/1 19
E98.I4 G66

ROCKS - TESTING.
(1970) Sokolowski, Thomas J. Elastic
parameters computed for materials subjected to
modest pressures or temperatures. [Honolulu]
1970. vii, 159 p. LC Card 74-634032   DDC 551 s
624.1/5132 19
QE500 .H35 no. 70-20. TA706.5

**Rockville, Md. National Institute on Drug
Abuse. see National Institute on Drug
Abuse.**

ROCKY MOUNTAINS REGION - HISTORY.
Lavender, David Sievert, 1910- The Rockies /.
Lincoln , 1981, c1968. p. cm.   ISBN
0-8032-2857-0   LC Card 81-3427   DDC 978 19
F721 .L3 1981

Roczey, Patricia A. (joint author) Brown, Carol M.
Trends in graduate enrollment and Ph.D. output
in scientific fields, 1960-61 through 1967-68.
[Washington] , 1969 [i.e. 1970] vii, 204 p. ;
LC Card 73-606834   DDC 610/.7 s 610/.7/073
19
RA440.6 .R4 no. 18 R854.U5

Rodee, Marian E. Maxwell Museum of
Anthropology. Southwestern weaving .
Albuquerque , 1981. p. cm.   ISBN 0-8263-0587-3
LC Card 81-8143   DDC
746.1/4/08997079074018961 19
E78.S7 M35 1981

RODENTIA - REPRODUCTION.
Voss, Robert. Male accessory glands and the
evolution of copulatory plugs in rodents /. Ann
Arbor, Mich. , 1979. 27 p. ; LC Card 79-624538
DDC 599.32/32 19
QP257 .V67

**Rodeo an anthropologist looks at the wild and
the tame /.** Lawrence, Elizabeth Atwood, 1929-
Knoxville , c1982. p. cm.   ISBN 0-87049-328-0 :
LC Card 81-3330   DDC 791/.8 19
GV1834.5 .L38

RODEOS - SOCIAL ASPECTS - CANADA.
Lawrence, Elizabeth Atwood, 1929- Rodeo an
anthropologist looks at the wild and the tame /.
Knoxville , c1982. p. cm.   ISBN 0-87049-328-0 :
LC Card 81-3330   DDC 791/.8 19
GV1834.5 .L38

**RODEOS - SOCIAL ASPECTS - UNITED
STATES.**
Lawrence, Elizabeth Atwood, 1929- Rodeo an
anthropologist looks at the wild and the tame /.
Knoxville , c1982. p. cm.   ISBN 0-87049-328-0 :
LC Card 81-3330   DDC 791/.8 19
GV1834.5 .L38

Roder, H. M. Survey of properties of the hydrgen
isotopes below their critical temperatures /.
Washington , 1973. vii, 113 p. :
NYPL [JSF 81-57]

Rodgers, Barbara G. Environmental Design
Conference on City Centers in Transition,
University of North Carolina at Chapel Hill,
1976. City centers in transition . Chapel Hill ,
1976. xii, 90 leaves ; LC Card 76-29226
NYPL [JLF 80-1605]

Rodgers, Donald A. Vertical deformation, stress
accumulation, and secondary faulting in the
vicinity of the transverse ranges of southern
California / by Donald A. Rodgers.
Sacramento, Calif. : California Division of
Mines and Geology, 1979. v, 74 p. : ill. ; 28
cm. (Bulletin - California Division of Mines and
Geology ; 203) Bibliography: p. 49-52. LC Card
79-625539   DDC 557.94 s 551.8 19
*1. Rock deformation - California - Transverse Ranges.
2. Faults (Geology) - California - Transverse Ranges. I.
Series: California. Division of Mines and Geology.
Bulletin , 203. II. Title.*
TN24.C2 A3 no. 203 QE604

Rodríguez-Alcalá, Hugo. Nine essays on Rómulo
Gallegos /. Riverside, CA [1979] ii, 215 p. :
LC Card 80-621557   DDC 863 19
PQ8549.G24 D6296

Rodríguez, Celso. Hanke, Lewis. Guía de las
fuentes en hispanoamérica para el estudio de la
administración virreinal española en México y
en el Perú, 1535-1700 /. Washington, D.C. ,
1980. x, 523 p. ;   ISBN 0-8270-1091-5 : LC Card
81-115511   DDC 972 19
Z1426 .H36 F1231

Roeming, Robert F. Wisconsin. University,
Madison. Library. Catalog of little magazines .
Madison , Ann Arbor , 1979. xv, 137 p. ; LC
Card 79-5414
Z6944.L5 W57 1979 PN4836
NYPL [*R-*D 80-3900]

**ROENTGENOLOGY, DIAGNOSTIC. see
DIAGNOSIS, RADIOSCOPIC.**

Roering, Kenneth J. Marketing profile of efforts
expended by states to promote commercial and
industrial development / by Kenneth J. Roering
and Ben M. Enis. [Columbia] : Dept. of
Marketing, College of Business and Public
Administration, University of
Missouri-Columbia, for the Division of Budget
and Planning, Office of Administration, State of
Missouri, 1979. 136 p. ; 28 cm. Cover title:
Marketing environment review. "Contract
(05-25-01581-01/EDA-7808)." Bibliography: p. 123-136.
LC Card 79-625260   DDC 332.6/7322778 19
*1. Industrial promotion - Missouri. 2. Missouri -
Commercial policy. I. Enis, Ben M., joint author. II.
Title. III. Title: Marketing environment review.*
HC107.M83 I538

**Roger Zelazny and Andre Norton, proponents of
individualism /.** Yoke, Carl B. Columbus ,
1979. 26 p. ;   LC Card 80-137489   DDC 813/.54
19
PS374.S35 Y6

Rogers & Golden. Macpherson, George S. Outer
Continental Shelf oil and gas activities in the
mid-Atlantic and their onshore impacts .
Reston, VA [1980] viii, 63 p. : LC Card
80-129968   DDC 338.2/728/0974 19
TN872.A5 M32

Rogers, Brian, 1950- Final report /. [Juneau]
[1980] 27 p. : LC Card 81-621099   DDC
333.79/3212/097983 19
TK1424.A4 F56

Rogers, Charlie Ellic, 1938- Selected bibliography
of insect pests of sunflower / [C. E. Rogers].
College Station, Tex. : Texas Agricultural
Experiment Station, Texas A & M University
System ; [Beltsville, Md.] : Federal
Research--Science and Education
Administration, U. S. Dept. of Agriculture,
[1979] 41 p. ; 28 cm. Cover title. "December 1979."
"MP-1439." LC Card 80-621131   DDC 016.6338/5
19
*1. Sunflowers - Diseases and pests - Bibliography. 2.
Insects, Injurious and beneficial - Bibliography. I. Texas.
Agricultural Experiment Station, College Station. II.
United States. Science and Education Administration.
Federal Research. III. Title.*
Z5354.P3 S867 SB608.S92

Rogers, David, 1953- Alaska. Legislature. House
of Representatives. Committee on Natural
Resources. Lands Subcommittee. Interim report
of Lands Subcommittee. Juneau, Alaska [1980]
25 p. ; LC Card 80-622468   DDC 346.79804/4 19
KFA1211.82 .N374 1980

Rogers, Donald E. (joint author) Harris, Colin K.
Forecast of the sockeye salmon run to Bristol
Bay in 1979 /. Seattle , 1979. 50 p. : LC Card
79-624864   DDC 639/.2 s 597/.55 19
SH1 .W3352 no. 79-2 QL638.S2

Rogers, Earl M. A bibliography of the history of
the University of Iowa, 1847-1978 / Earl M.
Rogers. Prelim. ed. Iowa City : University of
Iowa Libraries, 1979. iv, 52 p. ; 29 cm. Includes
index. LC Card 80-621225   DDC 016.378777/655
19
1. Iowa. University - History - Bibliography. I. Title.
Z5816.I63 R63 LD2569

Rogers, J. Daniel. (joint author) Powell, Mary
Lucas. Bioarchaeology of the
McCutchan-McLaughlin site (34Lt-11) .
Norman, Okla. , 1980. vi, 98 p. : LC Card
80-622411   DDC 976.6/76 19
E78.O45 P66   **NYPL [HBA no. 5]**

Rogers, Melvin D. South Carolina Crop and
Livestock Reporting Service. South Carolina
cash receipts, 1972 and 1973 /. Columbia,
South Carolina , 1974. 18 p. ;
NYPL [*ZT-1259]

Rogers, Rebecca M. The dependencies of the
Nelson, Smith, and Ballard houses, Colonial
National Historical Park, Yorktown, Virginia :
historic structure report, architectural data
section / by Rebecca M. Rogers.
[Washington] : Denver Service Center,

Mid-Atlantic/North Atlantic Team, Branch of Historic Preservation, National Park Service, U. S. Dept. of the Interior, 1979. vii, 25 p., [27] leaves of plates : ill. ; 27 cm. Includes bibliographical references. LC Card 79-603752 DDC 975.5/423 19
1. Yorktown, Va. Nelson House. 2. Yorktown, Va. Smith House. 3. Yorktown, Va. Ballard House. I. United States. National Park Service. Denver Service Center. Mid-Atlantic/North Atlantic Team. Branch of Historic Preservation. II. Title.
F234.Y6 R63

Rogge, A. E. (joint author) Brown, Patricia Eyring. Archaeological investigations at AZ U:6:61 (ASU), a prehistoric limited activity site in south-central Arizona /. [Tempe, Ariz.] 1980. vi, 84 p. : LC Card 80-620023 DDC 979.1/73 19
E78.A7 B73

The Rogovin report. United States. Congress. House. Committee on Government Operations. Environment, Energy, and Natural Resources Subcommittee. Nuclear Regulatory Commission--the Rogovin report . Washington , 1980. iii, 90 p. ; LC Card 80-602901 DDC 363.1/79 19
KF27 .G655 1980b

ROGUE RIVER, OR. - GUIDE-BOOKS.
Purdom, William B. Guide to the geology and lore of the wild reach of the Rogue River, Oregon /. Eugene , 1977. 67 p. : LC Card 77-622970 DDC 917.95/2 19
QH1 .O7 no. 22 QH105.O7

Roizen, Judith. Medrich, Elliott A. The serious business of growing up . Berkeley , c1981. p. cm. ISBN 0-520-04296-4 LC Card 81-7630 DDC 305.2/3/0979466 19
HQ792.U5 M42

ROLAND, a case for or against NATO standardization? /. Malone, Daniel K. Washington, DC , 1980. ix, 120 p. ; LC Card 80-602358 DDC 358/.175/091821 19
UF530 .M26

ROLAND (MISSILE)
Malone, Daniel K. ROLAND, a case for or against NATO standardization? /. Washington, DC , 1980. ix, 120 p. ; LC Card 80-602358 DDC 358/.175/091821 19
UF530 .M26

Role and scope of the Montana University System /. Montana University System. Board of Regents. Helena [1979] 60 p. ; LC Card 79-624776 DDC 378.786 19
LB2341.6.M9 M658 1979

ROLE EXPECTATION.
Dovidio, John F. The subtlety of white racism . Newark , 1977. 85 leaves : LC Card 78-621433 DDC 305.8/96073 19
E185.615 .D67

Role of commercial banks in the financing of the debt of the city of Cleveland . United States. Congress. House. Committee on Banking, Finance and Urban Affairs. Subcommittee on Financial Institutions Supervision, Regulation and Insurance. Washington , 1980. iv, 988 p. : LC Card 80-603313 DDC 352.1/09771/32 19
KF27 .B544 1979f

Role of government funding and its impact on small business in the solar energy industry . United States. Congress. House. Committee on Small Business. Washington , 1980. vi, 68 p. : LC Card 80-603851 DDC 338.6/42 19
HD9681.U62 U526 1980

Role of government funding and its impact on small business in the solar energy industry . United States. Congress. House. Committee on Small Business. Subcommittee on Energy, Environment, Safety and Research. Washington , 1979 i.e. 1980- v. : LC Card 80-603085 DDC 338.4/362147/0973 19
KF27 .S639 1979b

The role of language characteristics in the socioeconomic attainment process of Hispanic origin men and women /. Veltman, Calvin J. [Washington, D.C.?] , 1980. iv, 103 p. ; LC Card 81-601023 DDC 305.8/68073 19
E184.S75 V44

The role of scientific and technical information in critical period management. /. Gellman Research Associates. Jenkintown, Pa. , 1977. 2

v. (various pagings) LC Card 77-604051
HD30.3 .G45 1977   NYPL [*XME-9434]

The role of small business in the nation's economic recovery . United States. Congress. Senate. Select Committee on Small Business. Washington , 1981. iii, 207 p. : LC Card 81-601882 DDC 338.6/42/0973 19
KF26.5 .S6 1981a

The role of the coach in public service employment. Burleson, Erica. [Montpelier, Vt.] 1973. ix, 43 p.   NYPL [*XME-9294]

Role of the federal government in state and local law enforcement . United States. Congress. Senate. Committee on the Judiciary. Subcommittee on Jurisprudence and Governmental Relations. Washington , 1981. iv, 388 p. : LC Card 81-601785 DDC 364/.973 19
KF26 .J8556 1980b

The role of the North Atlantic Assembly /. United States. Library of Congress. Foreign Affairs and National Defense Division. Washington , 1979. vii, 55 p. ; LC Card 80-601029 DDC 341.24/3 19
JX1393.N67 U519 1979

The role of the replacement rate in the design of the social security benefit structure /. Leimer, Dean R. Washington, D.C. , 1979. iv, 15 p. : LC Card 79-600182 DDC 368.4/3/00973 s 368.4/3/00973 19
HD7123 .A395 no. 36 HD7125

The role of the States in energy /. United States. Dept. of Energy. Office of the Assistant Secretary for Policy and Evaluation. Washington [Springfield, Va.] 1978. iii, 39 p. ; LC Card 79-601823
HD9502.U52 U5125 1978

The role of the universities in the economic development of the West /. Regional Legislative Workshop on Higher Education, 3d, San Francisco, 1961. Boulder, Colo. , 1962. x, 28 p. : LC Card 79-124780 DDC 378.78 19
LC67.65.W47 R43 1961

Rolling, R. E. Soil survey of Cottonwood County, Minnesota / [by R. E. Rolling] ; United States Department of Agriculture, Soil Conservation Service, in cooperation with Minnesota Agricultural Experiment Station. [Washington] : The Service, [1979] viii, 142 p., [28] fold. leaves of plates : ill. ; 28 cm. Cover title. LC Card 80-602397 DDC 631.4/7/77622 19
1. Soils - Minnesota - Cottonwood County - Maps. I. United States. Soil Conservation Service. II. Minnesota. Agricultural Experiment Station, St. Anthony Park. III. Title.
S599.M45 R64

ROLLING-STOCK. see LOCOMOTIVES.

Rollins, Alden M., 1946- The Anchorage documents file, 1970- / by Alden M. Rollins. Anchorage, Alaska : University of Alaska, Anchorage, Library, 1978. 47, 1, 9 leaves ; 22 x 36 cm. (Publications - University of Alaska, Anchorage, Library ; no. 1) Includes index. LC Card 80-622423 DDC 016.9798 19
1. Anchorage, Alaska - Bibliography. 2. Anchorage, Alaska - Government publications - Bibliography. I. University of Alaska, Anchorage. Library. II. Title.
Z1256.A52 R64 F914.A5

Roloff, Richard Roy, 1952- Iterative solution of matrix equations for symmetric matrices possessing positive and negative eigenvalues / by Richard Roy Roloff. Urbana, Ill. : Dept. of Computer Science, University of Illinois at Urbana--Champaign, [1979] iv leaves, 47 p. : ill. ; 28 cm. ([Report] - UIUCDCS-R-79 ; 1018) "UILU-ENG 79 1749." Originally presented as the author's thesis, University of Illinois at Urbana--Champaign. Bibliography: p. 34-35. LC Card 80-622971 DDC 001.64 s 512.9/434 19
1. Matrices. 2. Symmetric matrices. 3. Eigenvalues. 4. Iterative methods (Mathematics). I. Series: Illinois. University at Urbana-Champaign. Dept. of Computer Science. Report, 1018. II. Title.
QA76 .I4 no. 1018 QA188

Romalis, Shelly, 1939- Childbirth, alternatives to medical control /. Austin , 1981. p. cm. ISBN 0-292-71072-0 ; LC Card 81-11644 DDC 362.1/982 19
RG940 .C47

The Roman Catholic Church in colonial Latin America /. Greenleaf, Richard E. (comp)

Tempe, Ariz. , c1977. xi, 272 p. ; LC Card 79-66416 DDC 282/.8 19
BX1426.2 .G73 1977

ROMAN PHILOSOPHY. see PHILOSOPHY, ANCIENT.

Romantic love, a philosophical inquiry /. Van de Vate, Dwight, 1929- University Park [Pa.] , c1981. 150 p. ; ISBN 0-271-00288-3 : LC Card 81-47171 DDC 306.7 19
BD436 .V36

Rome Air Development Center, Rome, N. Y. see United States. Air Development Center, Rome, N. Y.

ROME. ARMY - MEDALS, BADGES, DECORATIONS, ETC.
Maxfield, Valerie A. Dona militaria . Berkeley, Calif. , 1981. p. cm. ISBN 0-520-04499-1 LC Card 81-7406 DDC 355.1/342/0937 19
UB435.R65 M39 1981

Rome - Government. see Rome - Politics and government.

ROME - HISTORY - REPUBLIC, 265-30 B.C.
Greenhalgh, P. A. L. Pompey, the Roman Alexander /. Columbia , 1981, c1980. xix, 267 p., [4] p. of plates : ISBN 0-8262-0335-3 LC Card 80-54460 DDC 937/.05/0924 B 19
DG258 .G73 1981

ROME (ITALY) - DESCRIPTION - ADDRESSES, ESSAYS, LECTURES.
Krautheimer, Richard, 1897- Three Christian capitals . Berkeley , 1981, c1982. p. cm. ISBN 0-520-04541-6 LC Card 81-13148 DDC 937/.08 19
DG63 .K7

Rome, N. Y. Air Development Center. see United States. Air Development Center, Rome, N. Y.

ROME - POLITICS AND GOVERNMENT - 510-30 B.C.
Nicolet, Claude, 1930- [Métier de citoyen dans la Rome républicaine. English.] The world of the citizen in republican Rome /. Berkeley , 1980. 435 p. ; ISBN 0-520-03545-3 LC Card 77-80474 DDC 323.6/0937 19
DG83.1 .N513 1980b

Rompkey, Ronald. Salusbury, John, 1707-1762. Expeditions of honour . Newark , London , c1981. p. cm. ISBN 0-87413-169-3 LC Card 81-11537 DDC 971.6/01 19
F1038 .S2 1981

Ronfeldt, David F. (joint author) Gonzalez, Edward. Post-revolutionary Cuba in a changing world . Santa Monica, CA , 1975. ix, 78 p. ; LC Card 80-468852
AS36.R3 R-1844 F1788

NYPL [HOF 80-3135]

Rony, A. Kohar, 1933- Library of Congress. Vietnamese holdings in the Library of Congress . Washington , 1981. p. cm. ISBN 0-8444-0362-8 LC Card 81-2847 DDC 016.9597 19
Z3228.V5 L52 1981 DS556.3

ROOF PENDANTS (GEOLOGY)
Nokleberg, Warren J. Stratigraphy and structure of the Strawberry mine roof pendant, central Sierra Nevada, California /. Washington , 1980. p. cm. LC Card 80-607173 DDC 551.7/6/097944 19
QE675 .N64

ROOF-TRUSSES. see ROOFS.

ROOFS - MAINTENANCE AND REPAIR.
White, Richard, 1924- Olmsted Park System, Jamaica Pond boathouse, Jamaica Plain, Massachusetts . Washington, D.C. , 1979. 51 p. : LC Card 80-601622 DDC 690/.587/0288 19
TH2401 .W47

ROOFS - MOISTURE.
Knab, Lawrence I. The effect of moisture on the thermal conductance of roofing systems /. [Washington] , 1980. x, 46 p. : LC Card 80-600031 DDC 690/.0218 s 690/.15 19
TA435 .U58 no. 123 TH2401

ROOFS - THERMAL PROPERTIES.
Knab, Lawrence I. The effect of moisture on the thermal conductance of roofing systems /. [Washington] , 1980. x, 46 p. : LC Card 80-600031 DDC 690/.0218 s 690/.15 19
TA435 .U58 no. 123 TH2401

Roomet, Louise. Hewitt, Karen. Educational toys in America, 1800 to the present /. Burlington, Vt. , c1979. 141 p. : LC Card 80-131686 DDC 688.7/25 19
LB1029.T6 H48

ROOSEVELT ISLAND, N. Y. - MAPS.
(1978) Urban Development Corporation. Roosvelt Island Development Plan. New York, 1978. map 32 x 76 cm. Scale ca. 1:4,700. Blue line print. North oriented toward upper right corner.
NYPL [Map Div. 80-3265]

ROOSEVELT NATIONAL FOREST, COLO. - MAPS.
(1974) United States. Forest Service. Rocky Mountain Region. Roosevelt National Forest, Colorado. [Denver] 1974. col. map on sheet 66 x 92 cm. Scale 1:126,720; 1/2˝ = 1 mile. Printed on both sides of sheet. "Polyconic projection. Sixth principal meridian." Relief shown by hachures and spot heights. "Forest Service map class A." "Forest visitors map." Includes text, 2 recreation directories, "Vicinity map," 2 key maps, and col. illus. LC Card 76-690738
G4312.R66 1974 .U5
NYPL [Map Div 80-3346]

Root, Forrest K. Lane, Donald W. Geologic map atlas and summary of economic mineral resources of Converse County, Wyoming /. Laramie , 1972. 22 p. : LC Card 74-623237 DDC 912/.1553/0978716
G1478.C6C5 L3 1972

Root, Kenneth. Perspectives for communities and organizations on plant closings and job dislocations / by Kenneth A. Root. Ames, Iowa : North Central Regional Center for Rural Development, Iowa State University, [1979] iv, 32 leaves ; 28 cm. "October 1979." Bibliography: leaves 29-32. LC Card 80-623164 DDC 338.6/042 19
1. Plant shutdowns - United States. 2. Unemployed - United States. I. Title.
HD5708.55.U6 R66

Rosario Strait region of Northern Puget Sound, ... Smith, Gary Frederick. A quantitative sampling program of benthic communities in nearshore subtidal areas within the Rosario Strait region of Northern Puget Sound, Washington State (1976) /. [Olympia] [1979] vi, 105 p. : LC Card 80-622612 DDC 591.9797/7 19
QH105.W2 S65

Rose, Tim H. United States. Agency for International Development. Southern Africa Task Force. A framework for U. S. assistance in southern Africa . [Washington] [1977- v. : LC Card 80-503603 DDC 338.91/73/068 19
HC900 .U54 1977

Rosen, Murray. Covino, B. S. (Bernard S.) Corrosion resistance of materials in the aqueous hydrochloric acid environments associated with the recovery of alumina from kaolinitic clays /. Washington , 1981. p. cm. LC Card 80-606916 DDC 622 s 661/.0673/028 19
TN23 .U43 TA462

Rosen, Robert C., 1947- John Dos Passos, politics and the writer / by Robert C. Rosen. Lincoln : University of Nebraska Press, c1981. p. cm. Bibliography: p. Includes index. ISBN 0-8032-3860-6 LC Card 81-1928 DDC 813/.52 19
1. Dos Passos, John, 1896-1970 - Political and social views. 2. Politics in literature. 3. Politics and United States. 4. Authors, American - 20th century - Biography. I. Title.
PS3507.O743 Z79

Rosen, Seymour Michael, 1924- Education in the U. S. S. R., current status of higher education / by Seymour M. Rosen. Washington : U. S. Govt. Print. Off. : for sale by the Supt. of Docs., U. S. Govt. Print. Office, 1980. vi, 64 p. ; 24 cm. (DHEW publication. no. (OE) 79-19140) Bibliography: p. 64. LC Card 80-603405 DDC 378.47 19
1. Education, Higher - Russia. I. Series: United States. Dept. of Health, Education and Welfare. DHEW publication, no. (OE) 79-19140. II. Title.
LA838 .R58

Rosenberg, William G. Thurston, Robert W. Russian history and politics . [Ann Arbor] , c1978. 57 p. ; LC Card 81-621451 DDC 016.947 19
Z2506 .T47 DK40

Rosenfeld, Rachel. (joint author) Marwell, Gerald, 1937- Residence location, geographic mobility, and the attainments of women in academia /. Madison , 1976. 31 p. ; LC Card 78-623190 DDC 378/.12/0973 19
LB2331.72 .M37

Rosenmeyer, Thomas G. The art of Aeschylus / Thomas G. Rosenmeyer. Berkeley : University of California Press, c1981. p. cm. Bibliography: p. Includes indexes. ISBN 0-520-04440-1 LC Card 81-1291 DDC 882/.01 19
1. Aeschylus - Criticism and interpretation. I. Title.
PA3829 .R63

Rosenstein, Marilyn. The characteristics of persons served by the federally funded community mental health centers program, 1974 / Marilyn Rosenstein, Rosalyn D. Bass. Rockville, Md. : U. S. Dept. of Health, Education, and Welfare, Public Health Service, Alcohol, Drug Abuse, and Mental Health Administration, National Institute of Mental Health ; Washington, D.C. : for sale by the Supt. of Docs., U. S. Govt. Print. Off., [1979] iv, 19, [33] p. ; 27 cm. (Report series on mental health statistics : Series A, Mental health facility reports ; no. 20) DHEW publication ; no. (ADM) 79-771 LC Card 80-602392 DDC 312/.389/00973 19
1. Community mental health services - United States - Utilization - Statistics. 2. Federal aid to community mental health services - United States. 3. Mental health - United States - Statistics. 4. United States - Statistics, Medical. I. Bass, Rosalyn D., joint author. II. Series: Mental health statistics : Series A, Mental health facility reports , no. 20. III. Title.
RA790.6 .R67

Rosenthal, Karen. Cantor, Marjorie H. The elderly in the inner city of New York. New York [1973] 29 leaves ;
*NYPL [*XME-9046]*

Rosenthal, Samuel. United States. Health Resources Administration. Bureau of Health Manpower. Program Management Information Systems Section. Health professions schools . [Rockville, Md.] , 1978. vi, 268, 72 p. : LC Card 78-601985
R745 .U485 1978   *NYPL [JLF 81-386]*

Rosenzweig, Phyllis D. Hirshhorn Museum and Sculpture Garden. Larry Rivers . Washington, D.C. , 1981. p. cm. LC Card 81-607310 DDC 709/.2/4 19
N6537.R57 A4 1981

Rosoff, Jeannie I. Alan Guttmacher Institute. Family planning, contraception, voluntary sterilization, and abortion . Rockville, Md. , Washington, D.C. , 1978. xix, 380 p. ; LC Card 80-601267 DDC 344.73/048 19
KF3771.Z95 A37

Ross, B. B. A Model for evaluating the effect of land uses on flood flows . Blacksburg , 1978. x, 137 p. : LC Card 79-621996 DDC [551.48/9/0724] 19
TD201 .V57 no. 85 GB1399

Ross, John P., 1943- United States. Advisory Commission on Intergovernmental Relations. Countercyclical aid and economic stabilization . Washington , 1978. viii, 50 p. : LC Card 79-601504
HJ275 .U52 1978b   *NYPL [JLF 81-317]*

Ross, Judith, 1947- Wisconsin public library building survey for handicapped accessibility / prepared by Judith Ross, Alan Zimmerman. Madison, WI : Wisconsin Dept. of Public Instruction, Division for Library Services, Bureau of Public and Cooperative Library Services, [1979] 16, 2 p. ; 28 cm. "November 1979." LC Card 80-621510 DDC 727/.8/04209775 19
1. Library architecture and the physically handicapped - Wisconsin. 2. Public libraries - Wisconsin. 3. Library surveys - Wisconsin. I. Zimmerman, Alan, joint author. II. Title.
Z711.92.P5 R67

Ross, Stanley Robert, 1921- Weintraub, Sidney, 1922- The illegal alien from Mexico . [Austin] , c1980. ix, 65 p. ; ISBN 0-292-73822-6 (pbk). LC Card 80-80323 DDC 325/.272/0973 19
E184.M5 W46

Rossabi, Morris. China among equals . Berkeley , c1982. p. cm. ISBN 0-520-04383-9 LC Card

81-11486 DDC 951/.02 19
DS750.82 .C46

Rossiĭskaia Kommunisticheskaia Partiia (Bol'shevikov) see **Kommunisticheskaia partiia Sovetskogo Soiuza.**

Rossiĭskaia Sotsial-demokraticheskaia Rabochaia Partiia (Bol'shevikov) see **Kommunisticheskaia partiia Sovetskogo Soiuza.**

Rossman, Douglas Athon, 1936- Morphological evidence for taxonomic partitioning of the Thamnophis elegans complex (Serpentes, Colubridae) / by Douglas A. Rossman. Baton Rouge, La. : Louisiana State University, 1979. 12 p. : ill. ; 23 cm. (Occasional papers of the Museum of Zoology, Louisiana State University . no. 55) Caption title. Bibliography: p. 12. LC Card 80-620692 DDC 591 s 597.96 19
1. Thamnophis elegans - Classification. 2. Garter snakes - Classification. 3. Reptiles - Classification. I. Series: Louisiana State University, Baton Rouge. Museum of Zoology. Occasional papers of the Museum of Zoology , no. 55. II. Title.
QL3 .L67 no. 55 QL666.O636

Roster of registered veterinarians as of April 1, 1980. Connecticut. State Board of Veterinary Registration and Examination. Hartford, Conn. [1980] [17] leaves ; LC Card 80-621971 DDC 636.089/025/746 19
SF611 .C66 1980

Rostkowycz, Christina S. Wayne State University, Detroit. Folklore Archive. German and German-American folklore collections /. Detroit , 1980. 20 p. ; LC Card 80-621843 DDC 016.39/000943 19
Z5984.U6 W39 1980 GR111.G47

Rostow, W. W. (Walt Whitman), 1916- The division of Europe after World War II, 1946 / by W.W. Rostow. 1st ed. Austin : University of Texas Press, 1981. p. cm. (Ideas and action series . no. 2) ISBN 0-292-70358-9 LC Card 81-11640 DDC 940.55/4 19
1. World War, 1939-1945 - Peace. 2. Europe - Politics and government - 1945-. 3. Reconstruction (1939-1951) - Europe. 4. United States - Foreign relations - 1945-1953. I. Title. II. Series.
D816 .R67

Rotar, Peter P. A Selected bibliography of Centrosema, Desmodium, Stylosanthes and other tropical and subtropical pasture legumes [microform] /. Honolulu , 1981. p. cm. LC Card 81-2533 DDC 016.6333 19
Z5074 .L3 SB203.3.T76

Rothberg, Abraham. The four corners of the house : stories / by Abraham Rothberg. Urbana : University of Illinois Press, [1982] c1981. p. cm. (Illinois short fiction) CONTENTS. - The red dress -- The animal trainer -- The pearl fishers -- Roman portrait -- The Dürer hands -- Pluto is the furthest planet -- The sand dunes -- Polonaise. ISBN 0-252-00922-3 LC Card 81-10464 DDC 813/.54 19
I. Title.
PS3568.O857 F6 1982

Rothberg, Paul F. Synfuels from coal and the national synfuels production program . Washington , 1981. x, 304 p. : LC Card 81-601287 DDC 338.4/76626622/0973 19
TP360 .S939

Rothe, Thomas C. Derksen, Dirk V. Use of wetland habitats by birds in the National Petroleum Reserve--Alaska /. Washington, D.C. , 1981. p. cm. LC Card 81-607937 DDC 639.9/784109798 19
S914 .A3 no.141 QL684A4

Rothenberg, Morris Jerome, 1934- Public transportation : an element of the urban transportation system / prepared by Morris J. Rothenberg. [Washington, D.C.] : U. S. Dept. of Transportation, Federal Highway Administration, Urban Mass Transportation Administration, [1980] viii, 200, [160] p. : ill. ; 28 cm. (Technology sharing report . FHWA-TS-80-211) Includes bibliographical references and index. LC Card 80-602279 DDC 388.4/0973 19
1. Urban transportation - United States. 2. Local transit - United States. 3. Transportation planning - United States. I. Title. II. Series.
HE308 .R67

Rothenberger, Dale M. Shepherd, Jack R. Police-juvenile diversion . Washington, D.C. ,

1980. x, 77, [91] p. : LC Card 81-601094 DDC 364.6/8 19
HV9105.M5 S5 1980

Rothman, David J. Incarceration and its alternatives in 20th century America / by David J. Rothman. Washington, D.C. : U. S. Dept. of Justice, Law Enforcement Assistance Administration, National Institute of Law Enforcement and Criminal Justice : for sale by the Supt. of Docs., U. S. Govt. Print. Off., 1979. iii, 76 p. ; 28 cm. LC Card 80-601544 DDC 364.6/0973 19
1. Corrections - United States. 2. Criminal justice, Administration of - United States. 3. Juvenile justice, Administration of - United States. I. Title.
HV9304 .R67

Rothrock, Gail. Sugarloaf Regional Trails (Project) Circling historic landscapes . Silver Spring, Md. , c1980. 99 p. : LC Card 80-117883 DDC 917.52/87 19
GV191.42.M3 S93 1980

Rotifer sensitivity to combinations of inorganic water pollutants /. Buikema, Arthur L. Blacksburg , 1977. vi, 42 p. : LC Card 78-621510 DDC 333.91/09755 s 595.1/81 19
TD201 .V57 no. 92 QL391.R8

ROTIFERA - EFFECT OF WATER POLLUTION ON.
Buikema, Arthur L. Rotifer sensitivity to combinations of inorganic water pollutants /. Blacksburg , 1977. vi, 42 p. : LC Card 78-621510 DDC 333.91/09755 s 595.1/81 19
TD201 .V57 no. 92 QL391.R8

Rough in brutal print . Siegchrist, Mark, 1944- Columbus [1981] p. cm. ISBN 0-8142-0327-2 LC Card 81-3993 DDC 821/.8 19
PR4222.R353 S55

ROUGH RIVER LAKE, KY.
Hoyt, Robert D. Population dynamics and catch susceptibility of smallmouth buffalo in Rough River Reservoir /. [Frankfort, Ky.] , 1976. vii, 67 p. : LC Card 79-624983 DDC 639/.2 s 597/.52 19
SH222.K4 A3 no. 62 QL638.C27

Rouin, Carole. Basic assessment and intervention techniques for deaf-blind and multihandicapped children . Sacramento , 1977. v, 34 p. ; LC Card 78-621790 DDC 362.4/12/088054 19
HV1597 .B37

Round Table Conference on Capacity Utilization, Washington, D.C., 1978. Measures of capacity utilization, problems and tasks / Frank de Leeuw ... [et al.]. [Washington, D.C.] : Board of Governors of the Federal Reserve System, [1979] 259 p. : graphs ; 28 cm. (Staff studies . 105) Includes bibliographical references. LC Card 79-603771 DDC 338.0973 19
1. Industrial capacity - United States - Congresses. I. De Leeuw, Frank, 1930-. II. Title. III. Series.
HD69.C3 R68 1978

ROUND VALLEY, CALIF. - HISTORY.
Carranco, Lynwood. Genocide and vendetta . Norman , c1981. p. cm. ISBN 0-8061-1549-1 LC Card 81-7469 DDC 979.4/1504 19
F868.M5 C3

Roundtable Discussion of Radon in Buildings, National Bureau of Standards, 1979. Radon in buildings : proceedings of a Roundtable Discussion of Radon in Buildings held at the National Bureau of Standards, Gaithersburg, Maryland, June 15, 1979 / edited by R. Collé , Preston E. McNall, Jr. ; organized by National Bureau of Standards. Washington, D.C. : The Bureau : for sale by the Supt. of Docs., U. S. Govt. Print. Off., [1980] x, 77 p. : graphs ; 27 cm. (NBS special publication . 581) "Issued June 1980." Includes bibliographical references. LC Card 80-600069 DDC 602/.18 s 628.5/35 19
1. Radon - Environmental aspects - Congresses. 2. Radioactive pollution - Congresses. I. Collé, R. II. McNall, Preston. III. United States. National Bureau of Standards. IV. Series. V. Series: United States. National Bureau of Standards Special publication, 581. VI. Title.
QC100 .U57 no. 581 TD885.5.R33

Rouse, W. Victor. Crime in public housing : a review of major issues and selected crime reduction strategies / W. Victor Rouse, Herb Rubenstein ; prepared for the Department of Housing and Urban Development, Office of Policy Development and Research. Washington, D.C. : The Office : for sale by the Supt. of

Docs., U. S. Govt. Print. Off., 1978 [i.e. 1979- v. ; 28 cm. "HUD-PDR-468-1." CONTENTS. - v. 1. A report. LC Card 79-603818
1. Crime and criminals - United States - Collected works. 2. Public housing - United States - Collected works. 3. Crime prevention - United States - Collected works. I. Rubenstein, Herb, joint author. 0700. II. United States. Dept. of Housing and Urban Development. Office of Policy Development and Research. III. Title.
HV6791 .R67

Rousseau, Rudolph. An assessment of the refugee situation in Somalia : a staff report / prepared for the Committee on Foreign Relations, United States Senate. Washington : U. S. G.P.O., 1980. v, 19 p. : ill. ; 24 cm. At head of title: 96th Congress, 2d session. Committee print. Prepared by: R. Rousseau and J. Fox. LC Card 80-603863 DDC 362.8/7/096773 19
1. Refugees - Somalia. I. Fox, James, 1941-. II. United States. Congress. Senate. Committee on Foreign Relations. III. Title.
HV640.4.S58 R68

The route of the Three Notch'd Road . Pawlett, Nathaniel Mason. Charlottesville, Va. [1980] vi, 26 p. : LC Card 80-620018 DDC 388.1/09755/4 19
HE356.V8 P39

ROUTES OF TRADE. see TRADE ROUTES.

ROUTES OF TRAVEL. see OCEAN TRAVEL.

Rowan Group. National Survey Research Group, New York. Survey report on the economic impact of D2 lands restrictions and the public view of alternative uses of State capital expenditures to offset such effects /. Juneau, Alaska [1980] i, 49 p. : LC Card 80-622486 DDC 333.1/09798 19
HD243.A3 N37 1980

Rowe, Gene A. The hired farm working force of 1977 / Gene Rowe. Washington, D.C. : U. S. Dept. of Agriculture, Economics, Statistics, and Cooperatives Service, 1979. 53 p. : ill. ; 26 cm. (Agricultural economic report . no. 437) Cover title. Includes bibliographical references. LC Card 79-604210 DDC 338.1 s 331.7/63/0973 19
1. Agricultural laborers - United States - Statistics. I. United States. Dept. of Agriculture. Economics, Statistics, and Cooperatives Service. II. Title. III. Series.
HD1751 .A91854 no. 437 HD1525

Rowell, A. J. Inarticulate brachiopods of the Lower and Middle Cambrian Pioche shale of the Ploche District, Nevada / A. J. Rowell. Lawrence, Kan. : University of Kansas Paleontological Institute, 1980. 26 p., [4] leaves of plates : ill. ; 25 cm. (The University of Kansas paleontological contributions : Paper ; 98 0075-5052) Cover title. Bibliography: p. 21-22. LC Card 80-621789 DDC 560 s 564/.8 19
1. Inarticulata, Fossil. 2. Paleontology - Cambrian. 3. Paleontology - Nevada - Pioche region. I. Series: Kansas. University. University of Kansas paleontological contributions : paper , 98. II. Title.
QE701 .K33 no. 98 QE797.I5

Rowland, Michael. (joint author) Roberts, Jean, 1918- Hypertension in adults 25-74 years of age, United States, 1971-1975 /. Hyattsville, Md. , 1980. p. cm. ISBN 0-8406-0207-3 LC Card 80-607834 DDC 312/.0973 19 614.5/9132/0973 19
RA407.3 .A347 no. 221 RC685.H8

Rowlett, Richard A. Observations of marine birds and mammals in the northern Chesapeake Bight / prepared for National Coastal Ecosystems Team, Office of Biological Services, Fish and Wildlife Service, U. S. Department of the Interior by Richard A. Rowlett. [Washington, D.C.] : Fish and Wildlife Service, U. S. Dept. of Interior, 1980. xii, 87 p. : ill. ; 28 cm. On cover: Biological services program. "FWS/OBS-80/04." "February 1980." "Contract no. 14-16-0005-77-021." Bibliography: p. 68-74. LC Card 80-602344 DDC 598.2975 19
1. Sea birds - North Atlantic Ocean. 2. Sea birds - Atlantic coast (United States). 3. Marine mammals - North Atlantic Ocean. 4. Marine mammals - Atlantic coast (United States). I. National Coastal Ecosystems Team. II. Title. III. Title: Chesapeake Bight. IV. Title: Biological services program.
QL683.A87 R68

Roy, Delwin A. Southeast exporting : profiles, typology, and the role of technology in selected U. S. firms / by Delwin A. Roy, Claude L.

Simpson, Jr., Cedric L. Suzman ; sponsored by Georgia World Congress Institute, Georgia State University. Atlanta, Ga. : College of Business Administration, Georgia State University, 1981. p. cm. (Research monograph . no. 90) ISBN 0-88406-146-9 : LC Card 81-6287 DDC 382/.0975 19
1. Southern States - Commerce. 2. Southern States - Manufactures. 3. Export marketing. I. Simpson, Claude L. II. Suzman, Cedric L. III. Series: Research monograph (Georgia State University. College of Business Administration) , no. 90. IV. Title.
HF3153 .R69

Roy, Ewell Paul. Economic feasibility of liquid feed supplement operations in Louisiana / by Ewell P. Roy. [Baton Rouge] : Dept. of Agricultural Economics and Agribusiness, Louisiana State University, 1979. ii, 40 p. ; 28 cm. (D.A.E. research report . no. 556) Bibliography: p. 38-40. LC Card 79-625588 DDC 338.1/09763 s 338.4/76646 19
1. Flour and feed trade - Louisiana. 2. Feed additives - Louisiana. 3. Cattle - Louisiana - Feeding and feeds. I. Louisiana. Agricultural Experiment Station, Baton Rouge. Dept. of Agricultural Economics and Agribusiness. II. Title. III. Title: Liquid feed supplement. IV. Series: Louisiana. Agricultural Experiment Station, Baton Rouge. Dept. of Agricultural Economics and Agribusiness. D.A.E. research report , no. 556.
HD1775.L8 L7 no. 556 HD9056.U5.L8

Roy, John. University of Nebraska-Lincoln. Remote Sensing Center. General land use in Nebraska--summer 1973. [Lincoln] 1974. col. map 43 x 76 cm. Scale ca. 1:1,000,000. Relief shown by spot heights. Includes text. LC Card 78-691032
G4191.G4 1973 .U5
NYPL [Map Div. 81-3033]

Roy Jorgenson Associates. Construction engineering manpower management : system design manual / prepared for U. S. Department of Transportation, Federal Highway Administration [and] sponsoring state highway agencies by Roy Jorgenson Associates. [Gaithersburg, Md.]: Roy Jorgenson Associates, 1978. 1 v. (loose-leaf); 29 cm. At head of title: National pooled fund study.
1. Highway engineering - Management. 2. Road construction workers. I. United States. Federal Highway Administration. II. Title. *NYPL [JSF 80-656]*

Roy, Marjorie Brown.
Drug defendants in Massachusetts, 1978 / prepared by Marjorie Brown Roy, Anne Derrane. Boston : Commonwealth of Massachusetts, Office of Commissioner of Probation, 1979. 31 leaves ; 28 cm. LC Card 79-623946 DDC 364.1/77/09744 19
1. Narcotics and crime - Massachusetts - Statistics. 2. Narcotic addicts - Massachusetts - Statistics. 3. Narcotics, Control of - Massachusetts - Statistics. I. Derrane, Anne, joint author. II. Massachusetts. Officer of the Commissioner of Probation. III. Title.
HV5831.M4 A5 1979

Patterns of crime and delinquency in Massachusetts, 1979-1978 / prepared by Marjorie Brown Roy, Elaine Greenblatt. Boston : Commonwealth of Massachusetts, Commissioner of Probation, [1980] 18 leaves ; 28 cm. "February 3, 1980." LC Card 80-623647 DDC 364.1/09744 19
1. Criminal statistics - Massachusetts. 2. Juvenile delinquency - Massachusetts - Statistics. 3. Crime and criminals - Massachusetts. I. Greenblatt, Elaine, joint author. II. Massachusetts. Office of the Commissioner of Probation. III. Title.
HV6793.M4 R69

Rape in Massachusetts : convictions and sentences, 1974-1978 / prepared by Marjorie Brown Roy, Lauren Herbert, Michelle Strout. Boston (206 New Court House, Boston 02108) : Commonwealth of Massachusetts, Commissioner of Probation, [1980] 84 p. ; 28 cm. "February 13, 1980." Bibliography: p. 74-76. LC Card 80-623646 DDC 364.1/532/09744 19
1. Rape - Massachusetts. 2. Rape - Massachusetts - Statistics. I. Herbert, Lauren. II. Strout, Michelle. III. Title.
HV6565.M4 R68

ROYAL CHITWAN NATIONAL PARK (NEPAL)
Sunquist, Melvin E. The social organization of tigers (Panthera tigris) in Royal Chitwan National Park, Nepal /. Washington [D.C.] ,

1981. p. cm. LC Card 81-607928 DDC 591 s
599.74/428 19
QL1 .S54 no. 336 QL737.C23

Royce, Anya Peterson. Ethnic identity : strategies
of diversity / Anya Peterson Royce.
Bloomington : Indiana University Press, c1982.
p. cm. Bibliography: p. Includes index. ISBN
0-253-31035-0 LC Card 81-47168 DDC 305.8
19
1. Ethnicity. I. Title.
GN495.6 .R68

Roycraft, Philip R. Shiawassee River study :
Linden to Byron, August 15-16, 1978 / by
Philip R. Roycraft, Stephen G. Buda.
[Lansing] : State of Michigan, Dept. of Natural
Resources, Environmental Services Division,
1979. 55 p. : ill. ; 28 cm. "Publication number
4833-9260." LC Card 80-620626 DDC
363.7/3942/09774 19
1. Water quality - Michigan - Shiawassee River. I.
Buda, Stephen G., joint author. II. Michigan.
Environmental Protection Bureau. Environmental
Services Division. III. Title.
TD224.M5 R694

Rozier, John. Black boss : political revolution in a
Georgia county / John Rozier. Athens :
University of Georgia Press, c1981. p. cm.
Bibliography: p. Includes index. ISBN 0-8203-0568-5
LC Card 81-1298 DDC 305.8/96073/0758623
19
1. Afro-Americans - Georgia - Hancock County -
Politics and suffrage. 2. McCown, John. 3. Hancock
County (Ga.) - Politics and government. I. Title.
F292.H3 R69

RUBBER GOODS INDUSTRY. see RUBBER
INDUSTRY AND TRADE.

RUBBER INDUSTRY AND TRADE -
ENVIRONMENTAL ASPECTS.
Howarth, John T. Economic analysis of
proposed effluent guidelines, the rubber
processing industry (phase II) /. Washington ,
1974. 60, 5 p. : *NYPL [JLF 80-559]*

RUBBER - LAW AND LEGISLATION.
United States. Congress. House. Committee on
Foreign Affairs. International Natural Rubber
Agreement . Washington , 1980 [i.e. 1981] iii,
113 p. : LC Card 81-601156 DDC
341.7/547138952/0973 19
KF27 .F6 1980j

United States. Congress. Senate. Committee on
Foreign Relations. International natural rubber
agreement of 1979 . Washington , 1980. iii, 52
p. : LC Card 80-603353 DDC
341.7/547/1389520265 19
KF26 .F6 1980o

RUBBER - LAW AND LEGISLATION -
UNITED STATES.
United States. Congress. House. Committee on
Foreign Affairs. International Natural Rubber
Agreement . Washington , 1980 [i.e. 1981] iii,
113 p. : LC Card 81-601156 DDC
341.7/547138952/0973 19
KF27 .F6 1980j

RUBBER - PRICES.
United States. Congress. House. Committee on
Foreign Affairs. International Natural Rubber
Agreement . Washington , 1980 [i.e. 1981] iii,
113 p. : LC Card 81-601156 DDC
341.7/547138952/0973 19
KF27 .F6 1980j

RUBBER - TRADE AND STATISTICS. see
RUBBER INDUSTRY AND TRADE.

Rubel, Robert J. National Institute of Law
Enforcement and Criminal Justice. Crime and
disruption in schools . Washington, D.C. , 1979.
vii, 104 p. : LC Card 80-601518 DDC
371.5/8/0973 19
LB3013.3 .N375 1979

Rubenstein, Daryl R. Max Weber, prints and
color variations : July 11-October 5, 1980,
National Collection of Fine Arts, Smithsonian
Institution, Washington, D.C. / Daryl R.
Rubenstein. [Washington, D.C.] : The
Institution, c1980. 15 p. : ill. ; 27 cm. Includes
bibliographical references. LC Card 80-51701 DDC
769.92/4 19
1. Weber, Max, 1881-1961 - Exhibitions. I. Weber,
Max, 1881-1961. II. Smithsonian Institution. National
Collection of Fine Arts. III. Title.
NE539.W38 A4 1980a

Rubenstein, Herb. (joint author. 0700) Rouse, W.
Victor. Crime in public housing . Washington,
D.C. , 1978 [i.e. 1979- v. ; LC Card 79-603818
HV6791 .R67

Rubenstein, James M. (joint author) Underhill,
Jack A. French national urban policy and the
Paris region new towns . [Washington] [1980]
131 p. : LC Card 80-602925 DDC 307.7/6/0944
19
HT165.P37 U52

Rubin, David Lee. The knot of artifice : a poetic
of the French lyric in the early 17th century /
David Lee Rubin. Columbus : Ohio State
University Press, c1981. x, 109 p. ; 24 cm.
Bibliography: p. 103-106. Includes index. ISBN
0-8142-0322-1 : LC Card 80-26260 DDC
841/.0409 19
1. French poetry - 17th century - History and criticism.
I. Title.
PQ421 .R8

Rubin, David M. United States. President's
Commission on the Accident at Three Mile
Island. Public's Right to Information Task
Force. Report of the Public's Right to
Information Task Force /. Washington, D.C.
[1980] 262 p. ; LC Card 80-601569 DDC
363.1/79 19
HD9698.U54 M478 1980

Rubin, Irene. Running in the red : the political
dynamics of urban fiscal stress / by Irene
Rubin. Albany : State University of New York
Press, 1982. p. cm. (SUNY series on urban public
policy) Bibliography: p. Includes index. ISBN
0-87395-564-1 LC Card 81-9329 DDC
352.1/0973 19
1. Municipal finance - United States. 2. Municipal
government - United States. I. Title. II. Series.
HJ9145 .R8

Rubin, Victor. Medrich, Elliott A. The serious
business of growing up . Berkeley , c1981. p.
cm. ISBN 0-520-04296-4 LC Card 81-7630 DDC
305.2/3/0979466 19
HQ792.U5 M42

Rubinstein, Alberto, 1944- (joint author) Gregersen,
H. M. Economics of public forestry incentive
programs . [St. Paul] 1979. 65 p. : LC Card
79-625488 DDC 333.75/158/09776 19
SD144.M6 G73

Rubinstein, Michael L. Alaska bans plea
bargaining / by Michael L. Rubinstein, Stevens
H. Clarke, Teresa J. White. Washington, D.C. :
U. S. Dept. of Justice, National Institute of
Justice : For sale by the Supt. of Docs., U. S.
G.P.O., 1980. viii, 312 p. : 9 charts ; 28 cm.
"July 1980." "Grant No. 76-NI-10-0001, awarded to the
Alaska Judicial Council"-T.p. verso. S/N
027-000-00976-0 Item 718-A LC Card 81-601045
DDC 345.798/072 347.980572 19
I. Clarke, Stevens H. II. White, Teresa J. III. Alaska.
Judicial Council. IV. National Institute of Justice (U.
S.). V. Title.
KFA1778.5 .R8

Rublee, Parke A. Bacteria in a North Carolina
salt marsh : standing crop and importance in
the decomposition of Spartina alterniflora / by
Parke A. Rublee, Leon M. Cammen, and John
E. Hobbie. [Raleigh : North Carolina State
University : available from UNC sea grant],
1978. 80 p. : ill. ; 28 cm. (UNC sea grant
publication ; UNC-SG-78-11) Bibliography: p. 79-80.
LC Card 79-621361 DDC 574.5/2636 19
1. Marine microbiology. 2. Spartina alterniflora. 3.
Tidemarsh ecology - North Carolina. I. Cammen, Leon
M., joint author. II. Hobbie, John E., joint author. III.
Series: Sea grant publication (Raleigh) , UNC-SG-78-11.
IV. Title.
QR106 .R82

Ruby, Mike. (joint author) Otis, Ted. Some
economic aspects of air pollution in Montana /.
Helena, Mont. [1979] ii, 94 p. ; LC Card
80-622032 DDC 338.4/73637392/09786 19
HC107.M93 A45

Ruby, Robert H. Indians of the Pacific
Northwest : a history / by Robert H. Ruby and
John A. Brown ; with a foreword by Alvin M.
Josephy, Jr.1st ed. Norman : University of
Oklahoma Press, c1981 p. cm. (The Civilization of
the American Indian series. v. 158) Bibliography: p.
Includes index. ISBN 0-8061-1731-1 LC Card
80-5946 DDC 979/.00497 19
1. Indians of North America - Northwest, Pacific -
History. I. Brown, John Arthur. II. Series: Civilization

of the American Indian series, v. 158. III. Title.
E78.N77 R8

Rucker Agee Map Collection. Birmingham, Ala.
Public Library. A list of 16th, 17th & 18th
century material in the Rucker Agee Map
Collection, Birmingham Public Library.
[Birmingham, Ala. , 1978?] 100 p. ; LC Card
80-126180
Z6028 .B56 1978 GA197.A34
NYPL [Mappp Div. 81-139]

Rudd, Robert R.
[Papers] [1875-1906] 2 boxes. Black soldier. In
Schomburg Center for Research in Black Culture.
Personal papers: 1875-1901. Correspondence:
1900-1906. Rosters: 1899-1900. Ledgers: 1899-1901.
1. Rudd, Robert R. - Correspondence. 2.
Afro-American soldiers - Biography - Sources. 3.
Mountain Province, Philippines - Sources. 4. United
States - History - War of 1898 - Sources. I. Schomburg
Center for Research in Black Culture.
NYPL [Sc Rare Mss-51]

RUDD, ROBERT R. - CORRESPONDENCE.
Rudd, Robert R. [Papers] [1875-1906] 2 boxes.
NYPL [Sc Rare Mss-51]

Rudins, George. U. S. and USSR MHD electrode
materials development. - Santa Monica : Rand,
1974. vii, 71 p. : ill. ; 28 cm. (Rand Corporation.
Rand report. R-1656-ARPA) Prepared for Defense
Advanced Research Projects Agency. Bibliography: p.
65-71.
1. Magnetohydrodynamic generators. I. United States.
Defense Advanced Research Projects Agency. II. Title.
NYPL [JSF 81-299]

Ruegg, Rosalie T.
(joint author) Marshall, Harold E. Efficient
allocation of research funds . Washington, D.C.
[1979] viii, 47 p. : LC Card 79-600210 DDC
602/.18 s 338.4/569/0072073 19
QC100 .U57 no. 558 TH23

(joint author) Marshall, Harold E. Energy
conservation in buildings . Washington, D.C.
[1980] xii, 144 p. : LC Card 80-600056 DDC
333.79 19
TJ163.5.B84 M36

The police patrol car : economic efficiency in
acquisition, operation, and disposition :
prepared for National Institute of Law
Enforcement and Criminal Justice, Law
Enforcement Assistance Administration, U. S.
Department of Justice / by Rosalie T. Ruegg ;
prepared by Law Enforcement Standards
Laboratory, Center for Consumer Product
Technology, National Bureau of Standards.
Washington : The Bureau : for sale by the Supt.
of Docs., U. S. Govt. Print. Off., 1978. xvii,
117 p. ; 26 cm. (Law enforcement equipment
technology) Microfiche (neg.) NTIS. 2 sheets. 11 x 15
cm. (PB 281 805) NBS special publication ; 480-15
Bibliography: p. 112-117. LC Card 77-13244
1. Police vehicles - Eonomic aspects. 2. Police
vehicles - Cost effectiveness. 3. Police vehicles - Cost of
operation. I. National Institute of Law Enforcement and
Criminal Justice. II. Law Enforcement Standards
Laboratory. III. Title.
QC100 .U57 no. 480-15 HV7936.V4
*NYPL [*XME-9526]*

Rühl, Werner. Nato Advanced Study Institute on
Field Theoretical Methods in Particle Physics,
University of Kaiserslautern, 1979. Field
theoretical methods in particle physics /. New
York , c1980. ix, 598 p. : ISBN 0-306-40444-3
LC Card 80-11773
QC793.3.F5 N37 1979 NYPL [JSF 80-1051]

Rufener, Brent L. Management effectiveness
measures for NIDA drug abuse treatment
programs / by Brent L. Rufener, J. Valley
Rachal, Alvin M. Cruze. Rockville, Md. :
National Institute on Drug Abuse, Office of
Program Development and Analysis ;
Washington, D.C. : for sale by the Supt. of
Docs., U. S. Govt. Print. Off., 1977. 2 v. ; 26
cm. (Technical paper - National Institute on Drug
Abuse) DHEW publication ; no. (ADM)
77-423-(ADM) 77-424 Includes bibliographies.
CONTENTS. - v. 1. Cost benefit analysis.--v. 2. Costs
to society of drug abuse. LC Card 80-603129 DDC
362.2/9386/0973 19
1. Drug abuse - Treatment - United States - Evaluation.
2. National Institute on Drug Abuse. I. Rachal, J.
Valley, joint author. II. Cruze, Alvin M., joint author.
III. Series: National Institute on Drug Abuse. Technical

paper - National Institute on Drug Abuse. IV. Title.
RC564 .R83

RUFFED GROUSE - EGGS AND NESTS.
Kubisiak, John F. Brood characteristics and
summer habitats of ruffed grouse in central
Wisconsin /. Madison, Wis. , 1978. 10, [1] p. :
LC Card 79-624430   DDC 639.9/09775 s
598/.616 19
SK463 .A27 no. 108 QL696.G285

RUFFED GROUSE - HABITAT.
Kubisiak, John F. Brood characteristics and
summer habitats of ruffed grouse in central
Wisconsin /. Madison, Wis. , 1978. 10, [1] p. :
LC Card 79-624430   DDC 639.9/09775 s
598/.616 19
SK463 .A27 no. 108 QL696.G285

Rugh, John. Oral motor behavior . [Bethesda,
Md.] , 1979. vi, 261 p. : LC Card 79-604290
DDC 617/.522 19
RK480 .O7

**RUGS - UNITED STATES - HISTORY - 18TH
CENTURY.**
Anderson, Susan H. The most splendid carpet
/. Philadelphia , Washington , 1978. x, 93 [3]
p. : LC Card 79-602679
NK3012.S46 A52   NYPL [3-MOP 81-683]

Ruiz, Pablo. see Picasso, Pablo, 1881-1973.

**Ruiz Picasso, Pablo. see Picasso, Pablo, 1881-
1973.**

**Ruiz y Picasso, Pablo. see Picasso, Pablo, 1881-
1973.**

Rule, A. R. (Albert R.) Dahlin, D. C. (David
Clifford), 1951- Beneficiation of potential
platinum resources from southeastern Alaska /.
Washington, D.C. [1981] p. cm.   LC Card
81-607026   DDC 622 s 622/.3424 19
TN23 .U43 TN538.P53

**Rule on development of reimbursable local
special education programs for handicapped
children.** Nebraska. State Dept. of Education.
Rule 51, the State Department of Education
rule on development of reimbursable local
special education programs for handicapped
children. Lincoln, Neb. [1978?] iii, 48, a-d p. ;
LC Card 80-622035   DDC 371.9/09782 19
LC4032.N4 N43 1978

Rule 30, regulations and standards for hospitals .
Nebraska. Dept. of Health. Lincoln, Neb.
[1979] 51 p. ; LC Card 81-621038   DDC
344.782/03211 347.82043211 19
KFN361.A433 A2 1979

Rules & regulations /. Nevada. State Board of
Architecture. Las Vegas, Nev. (800 E. Sahara
Ave., Suite 2, Las Vegas 89104) , 1980. [30]
p. ; LC Card 81-621037   DDC 344.793/0176172
347.9304176172 19
KFN929.A7 A32 1980

Rules and regulations. Nevada. State Board of
Architecture. Rules & regulations /. Las Vegas,
Nev. (800 E. Sahara Ave., Suite 2, Las Vegas
89104) , 1980. [30] p. ; LC Card 81-621037
DDC 344.793/0176172 347.9304176172 19
KFN929.A7 A32 1980

Rules and regulations. New Mexico. Motor
Transportation Division. [Santa Fe, N.M.
(P.E.R.A. Bldg., P.O. Box 1028, Santa Fe
87503)] [1980] ii, 57 p. : LC Card 81-621088
DDC 343.789/0944/02636 347.890394402636 19
KFN3897.A433 A2 1980

Rules & regulations /. Oklahoma. Division of
State Parks. [Oklahoma City, Okla.] [1979] 19
p. ; LC Card 80-622622 DDC 346.766/046783 19
KFO1652.5.A435 A2 1979

Rules & regulations /. Oklahoma. Division of
State Parks. [Oklahoma City, Okla.] , 1980. 19
p. : LC Card 80-623108 DDC 346.766/046783 19
KFO1652.5.A439 A2 1980

Rules and regulations /. Vermont Criminal
Justice Training Council. [Montpelier?] [1979?]
24 p. ; LC Card 80-623937   DDC 345.743/052
347.430552 19
KFV435.8.S7 A32 1979

**Rules and regulations, adopted May 30, 1975,
amended December 17, 1976, March 10, 1977,
March 2, 1979, published June 1, 1979,
effective July 1, 1979 ; Statutes, March 2,
1979, chapter 1.1, title 54, Chapter 3, title 54,
chapter 24, title 54, chapter 7, title 13.1 /.**
Virginia. State Board of Architects, Professional

Engineers, and Land Surveyors. Richmond, Va.
[1979] 39 p. ; LC Card 80-621955   DDC
344.755/01762 19
KFV2729.A7 A32 1979

**Rules and regulations concerning practice and
procedure, effective February 10, 1947 /.**
Indiana. Public Service Commission.
[Indianapolis] [1947] 27 p. ; LC Card 80-126275
DDC 342.772/068/0269 347.7202680269 19
KFI3285.1.A4315 A2 1947

**Rules and regulations for conducting a drivers'
school and private service bureau.** New York
(State). Dept. of Motor Vehicles. [Albany]
[1977?] 18, 3, 3 p. ; LC Card 80-622375   DDC
353.97470087/832 19
KFN5475 .A4 1977

**Rules and regulations for protection against
radiation.** Illinois. Dept. of Public Health.
[Springfield] [197-] ca. 210 p. in various
pagings ; LC Card 80-621603   DDC 344.773/0472
19
KFI1580.A8 A3 1974

**Rules and regulations for public water systems,
adopted 1978.** Texas. Water Hygiene Division.
[Austin] , 1980. 47 p. ; LC Card 80-623755
DDC 343.764/0924 19
KFT1556.5.A434 A2 1980

**Rules and regulations for the licensing of home
health agencies.** North Carolina. Dept. of
Human Resources. Division of Facility Services.
Licensure and Certification Section. Raleigh,
N.C. [1980] 14 p. ; LC Card 81-621294   DDC
344.756/03214 347.56043214 19
KFN7763.H65 A32 1980

**Rules and regulations for the licensing of nursing
homes and home for the aged beds when
licensed as a part of a nursing home.** North
Carolina. Dept. of Human Resources. Division
of Facility Services. Licensure and Certification
Section. Raleigh, N.C. (P.O. Box 12200,
Raleigh 27605) [1980] 34 p. ; LC Card
81-621297   DDC 344.756/03216 347.56043216
19
KFN7763.N8 A32 1980

**Rules and regulations for the Transportation of
natural and other gas by pipeline.** Texas.
Railroad Commission. Gas Utilities Division.
[Austin] [1980] 110 p. ; LC Card 80-622926
DDC 363.1/79 19
TN880.5 .T49 1980

**Rules and regulations governing service and
safety of operations of taxicabs under the
jurisdiction of the Taxicab Authority of Nevada
/.** Nevada. Taxicab Authority. Carson City
[197-] 16 p. ; LC Card 79-625366   DDC
343.793/0982 19
KFN900.T3 A32 1979

**Rules and regulations governing the renewal and
reinstatement of nurses' licenses, 1979.**
Nebraska. State Board of Nursing. Lincoln,
Neb. [1980] 9 p. : LC Card 80-622055   DDC
344.782/0414 347.8204414 19
KFN326.5.N81 A32 1980

**Rules & regulations, Nebraska state personnel
system.** Nebraska. Dept. of Personnel. [Lincoln,
Neb. (P.O. Box 94905, 301 Centennial Mall
South, Lincoln, Neb. 68509)] [1980] [56] p. ;
LC Card 80-624216   DDC 342.782/068
347.820268 19
KFN435.A435 A2 1980

**Rules and regulations of the North Dakota State
Engineer governing the drainage of water.**
North Dakota. State Engineer. [Bismarck,
N.D. , 1979] iii, 15, [7] p. : LC Card 80-622991
DDC 343.784/07862754/02636 19
KFN9051.A434 A2 1979

**Rules & regulations of the State Board of Health
for environmental sanitation, primary &
secondary schools.** Washington (State). State
Board of Health. Olympia, Wash. [1980] 10
p. ; LC Card 80-623897   DDC 344.797/07
347.94047 19
KFW459.S3 A32 1980

**Rules and regulations on licensing of
superintendents or operators of public water
supply systems, public water treatment plants,
and public sewage treatment plants.** New
Jersey. Dept. of Environmental Protection.
[Trenton] , 1973. 19 p. ; LC Card 79-624793

DDC 344.749/0176281 19
KFN2129.E61 A32 1973

**Rules and regulations pertaining to compost
sites, effective date, October 30, 1978 /.**
Nebraska. Dept. of Environmental Control.
[Lincoln] [1978] 16 p. in various pagings ;   LC
Card 79-625022   DDC 344.782/04626
347.82044626 19
KFN359.R3 A32 1978

**Rules and regulations prescribing general
standards for the construction and maintenance
of water wells in Oregon.** Oregon. Water
Resources Dept. [Salem, Or.] [1979] 27 p.,
[17] leaves of plates : LC Card 80-623342   DDC
353.97950087/1 19
KFO2849.A435 A2 1979

**Rules and regulations setting minimum standards
for health care facilities.** Iowa. Health Facilities
Division. Des Moines, Iowa [1979] 314 p. ;
LC Card 80-622536   DDC 344.777/03211 19
KFI4561 .A4 1979

**Rules and regulations to govern the
administration and operation of special
education.** Illinois. Office of Education.
[Springfield, Ill.] [197-] i, 21 p. ; LC Card
80-620914   DDC 344.773/0791 19
KFI1595.9.H3 A32 1976

**Rules, chapter 1, home heating crisis assistance
program as amended 1/28/80 by amendment
number 1 ... /.** Maine. Division of Community
Services. [Augusta, Me.] [1980] ii, 25 leaves ;
LC Card 80-623905   DDC 344.741/03263
347.41043263 19
KFM351.E53 A32 1980

Rules for family day care . Nebraska. Division of
Social Services. [Lincoln] [1978] 15 p. ; LC
Card 80-620953   DDC 344.782/032712
347.820432712 19
KFN282.D3 A32 1978a

Rules for licensing . Michigan. Dept. of Social
Services. Lansing, Mich. [1980] ii, 5 p. ; LC
Card 80-622838   DDC 361.9/774 s
344.774/032733 19
HV86 .M536 no. 10 KFM4550.C4

**Rules for regulating family day care homes in
Michigan.** Michigan. Dept. of Social Services.
Lansing, MI [1980] 8 p. ; LC Card 80-622370
DDC 361/.9774 s 362.7/12/09774 19
HV86 .M536 no. 246 (rev. 3-80) HV857

**Rules for state personnel administration, effective
January 1980.** Nevada. Carson City, Nev.
(Capitol Complex, Room 200, Blasdel Building,
Carson City 89710) [1980] p. 309-442 : LC
Card 81-621067   DDC 353.9793001 19
KFN1035.A434 A2 1980

**Rules governing Radiation Emitting Equipment,
State Department of Health .** Iowa. State
Dept. of Health. Des Moines , 1980. vii, 45 p. ;
LC Card 81-621270   DDC 344.777/0472
347.7704472 19
KFI4580.A8 A32 1980

**RULES OF ORDER. see PARLIAMENTARY
PRACTICE.**

**Rules of practice ; and, Law directory of the
Appellate Court of Illinois, Fourth District.**
Illinois. Appellate Court (4th District) [Rules of
practice.] Mt. Vernon [Ill.] [1939?] 78 p. : LC
Card 80-139424   DDC 347.773/03 347.73073 19
KFI1757 4th.A436 A2 1939

**Rules of practice and procedure before the Texas
Aeronautics Commission.** Texas Aeronautics
Commission. [Austin] [1979?] iii, 42 p. ; LC
Card 80-624269   DDC 343.764/097/02636
347.64039702636 19
KFT1505 .A4 1979

Rules of procedure /. United Nations. Conference
on Trade and Development. New York , 1968.
v, 23 p. ; LC Card 81-469003   DDC 341.7/54 19
HF1410 .U57 1968b

**Rules of procedure of the main committees of the
Trade and Development Board.** United
Nations. Conference on Trade and
Development. Trade and Development Board.
New York , 1979. v, 38 p. ; LC Card 79-121793
DDC 300 s 341.7/54 19
JX1977 .A2 TD/B/740 HF1410

**Rules of procedure of the Nebraska Workmen's
Compensation Court.** Nebraska. Court Rules.
Workmen's Compensation Court. Lincoln, Neb.

[1978] 23 p. ; LC Card 78-111321 DDC
344.782/021/0269 19
KFN342.A435 A2 1978

**Rules of professional conduct of certified public
accountants, licensed public accountants, and
public accountants** /. Washington (State). Board
of Accountancy. [Olympia, WA] [1978?] [5]
p. ; LC Card 80-620938 DDC 346.797/06648 19
KFW329.A252 A32 1978

**Rules of the Department of Human Services
relating to boys, girls, boys and girls, day
camps, and primitive and trip camping.** Maine.
Dept. of Human Services. [Augusta] [1979] 11
p. ; LC Card 80-621356 DDC 344.741/099 19
KFM282.C35 A32 1979

**Rules of the Department of Human Services
relating to mobile home parks.** Maine. Division
of Health Engineering. State of Maine, rules of
the Department of Human Services relating to
mobile home parks. [Augusta, Me.] [1977?] 20
p. ; LC Card 80-622535 DDC 346.74104/3 19
KFM282.T68 A32 1977

**Rules of the Minnesota Senate, 71st Legislature,
1979-1980** /. Minnesota. Legislature. Senate. St.
Paul, Minn. [1979] 29 p. ; LC Card 80-623524
DDC 328.776/05 19
KFM5822 .A25 1979

**Rules of the Supreme Court of the United
States, adopted April 14, 1980, effective June
30, 1980.** United States. Supreme Court.
[Washington] , 1980. ii, 78 p. ; LC Card
80-602260 DDC 347.73/265 19
KF9056.A315 A2 1980

**Rules of the Supreme Court of Virginia governing
practice and procedure in courts and the
admission of foreign attorneys, with
amendments adopted through February 1,
1980.** Virginia. Supreme Court. [Richmond] ,
c1979. 178 p. : LC Card 80-624098 DDC
347.755/0355 347.5507355 19
KFV2958.A445 A2 1980

Rules, Regular Division /. Oregon. Tax Court.
Research Division. Salem, Or. [1980] iv, 61
p. ; LC Card 80-623341 DDC 343.79504/0269 19
KFO2871.5.A437 A2 1980

Rules, regulations, and modes of procedure /.
Oklahoma. Water Resources Board. [Oklahoma
City] [1979] iii, 73 p. ; LC Card 80-621865
DDC 333.91/009766 s 333.91/00766 s
346.76604/691/002636 347.66064691002636 19
TD224.O5 A3 no. 90 KFO1646

**Rules relating to catering establishments
preparing foods for vending machines,
dispensing foods other than in original sealed
packages, eating and lodging places, and
lodging places** . Maine. Dept. of Human
Services. [Augusta, Me. , 1979] 49 p. ; LC
Card 80-622537 DDC 343.741/0786424 19
KFM282.C37 A32 1979

Rules relating to siting energy facilities .
Washington (State). Energy Facility Site
Evaluation Council. Olympia, Wash. , 1978.
133 p. ; LC Card 79-624605
KFW286 .A4 1978

**Rules 60-66, rules of procedure of Occupational
Safety and Health Review Board ; Rule 67,
rules of occupational safety and health
recordkeeping requirements ; Rule 68, rules for
inspections, citations, and proposed penalties ;
Rule 69, rules of practice for variances,
limitations, variations, tolerances, and
exemptions** /. Nevada. Dept. of Occupational
Safety and Health. Carson City, Nev. [1980]
vi, 50 p. ; LC Card 80-622837 DDC 344.793/0465
19
KFN935.A443 A2 1980

**Rules 60-66, rules of procedure of Occupational
Safety and Health Review Board ; Rule 67,
rules of occupational safety and health
recordkeeping requirements ; Rule 68, rules for
inspections, citations, and proposed penalties ;
Rule 69, rules of practice for variances** /.
Nevada. Dept. of Occupational Safety and
Health. Carson City, Nev. (515 East Musser
St., Carson City 89714) [1981] vi, 50 p. ; LC
Card 81-622215 DDC 344.793/0465/02636
347.930446502636 19
KFN935.A444 A2 1981

Rum River. Kucera, Thomas. A biological
reconnaissance of the Rum River /. [St. Paul] ,

1978. vii, 107 p. 18 leaves of plates : LC Card
78-622616 DDC 574.92/9/7766 19
QH105.M55 K83

Rumble, J. R. (joint author) Gallagher, J. W.
Bibliography of low energy electron and photon
cross section data, (January 1975 through
December 1977) /. Washington , 1979. vi, 106
p. ; LC Card 78-600156 DDC 602/.18 s 539.7/54
19
*QC100 .U57 no. 426, suppl. 1 Z7144.N8
QC794.6.C7*

Rumford and Three Mile Rivers . Massachusetts.
Divison of Water Pollution Control. Boston
[1971] 63 p. : LC Card 80-118665 DDC
363.7/3942/0974485 19
TD224.M4 M36 1971b

Runaway youth program directory /. National
Youth Workers Alliance, Washington, D.C.
[Washington, D.C.] [1979] 109 p. : LC Card
79-604199
HV1431 .N37 1979   **NYPL [JLD 81-606]**

**RUNAWAY YOUTH - SERVICES FOR -
UNITED STATES - DIRECTORIES.**
National Youth Workers Alliance, Washington,
D.C. Runaway youth program directory /.
[Washington, D.C.] [1979] 109 p. : LC Card
79-604199
HV1431 .N37 1979   **NYPL [JLD 81-606]**

RUNAWAY YOUTH - UNITED STATES.
United States. Congress. Senate. Committee on
the Judiciary. Subcommittee on the
Constitution. Homeless youth . Washington ,
1980. vii, 256 p. : LC Card 81-600668 DDC
362.7/4 19
HV881 .U54 1980

Runck, Bette. Biofeedback : issues in treatment
assessment / by Bette Runck. Rockville, Md.
(5600 Fishers Lane, Rockville, Md. 20857) : U.
S. Dept. of Health and Human Services, Public
Health Service, Alcohol, Drug Abuse, and
Mental Health Administration, National
Institute of Mental Health, [Division of
Scientific and Public Information], 1980. xi, 99
p. ; 21 cm. (Science reports / National Institute of
Mental Health) DHHS publication ; no. (ADM)
80-1032 Bibliography: p. 81-99. LC Card 80-600134
DDC 615.8/51 19
1. Biofeedback training. 2. Therapeutics, Physiological.
I. National Institute of Mental Health (U. S.). Division
of Scientific and Public Information. II. Series: Science
reports (National Institute of Mental Health (U. S.)).
III. Title.
RC489.B53 R86

RUNNELS, HAROLD LOWELL, 1924-1980.
United States. Congress. House. Committee on
Armed Services. Full committee consideration
of committee resolution in honor of the late
Hon. Harold Runnels ... /. Washington , 1980.
ii, 30 p. ; LC Card 80-603490 DDC 328.73/092/4
19
KF27 .A7 1980d

Running in the red . Rubin, Irene. Albany , 1982.
p. cm. ISBN 0-87395-564-1 LC Card 81-9329
DDC 352.1/0973 19
HJ9145 .R8

RUNOFF - CONGRESSES.
Workshop on Operational Applications of
Satellite Snowcover Observations, Sparks, Nev.,
1979. Operational applications of satellite
snowcover observations . Washington, D.C. ,
1980. vi, 301 p. : LC Card 80-602361 DDC
551.57/846 19
GB2601.72.A83 W67 1979

**RUNOFF - ENVIRONMENTAL ASPECTS -
TEXAS - TRINITY RIVER WATERSHED.**
Trinity River Authority of Texas. Planning and
Environmental Management Division. Low flow
nutrient loss in the mid-Trinity River ;
Runoff-related pollutant loadings in the
mid-Trinity River /. [Austin] , 1978. iii, 72, iv,
73 p. : LC Card 80-622543 DDC
363.7/3942/097642 19
TD224.T4 T74 1978

**RUNOFF - MICROBIOLOGY - ADDRESSES,
ESSAYS, LECTURES.**
Microbiology of the aquatic environment /.
Reston, Va. , 1981. p. cm. LC Card 81-607912
DDC 557.3 s 576.1/51/09169 19
QE75 .C5 no. 848-E QR105.5

RUNOFF - NEVADA - CARSON VALLEY.
Nevada. Agricultural Experiment Station, Reno.

Quality monitoring of flows from irrigation
water and surface runoff in Carson Valley,
Nevada, 1976 irrigation season /. Reno [1979]
ix, 130 p. (p. 129-130 blank) : LC Card
79-625751 DDC 363.7/3942/0979359 19
TC824.N3 N48 1979

**Runoff-related pollutant loadings in the
mid-Trinity River.** Trinity River Authority of
Texas. Planning and Environmental
Management Division. Low flow nutrient loss
in the mid-Trinity River ; Runoff-related
pollutant loadings in the mid-Trinity River /.
[Austin] , 1978. iii, 72, iv, 73 p. : LC Card
80-622543 DDC 363.7/3942/097642 19
TD224.T4 T74 1978

RUNOFF - VIRGINIA.
Smolen, M. D. Agricultural land use .
Blacksburg, Va. , 1980. vii, 82 p. : LC Card
80-622278 DDC 333.91/009755 s 363.7/3941
19
TD201 .V57 no. 125 TD428.A37

**RUNOFF - WASHINGTON (STATE) -
ENTIAT RIVER WATERSHED - MAPS.**
United States. Soil Conservation Service.
Precipitation and runoff, Entiat River Basin,
Chelan County, Washington /. Portland, Or. ,
1979. 1 map : LC Card 81-691528
G4282.E5C88 1978 .U5

Ruopp, Richard. Children at the center .
Cambridge, MA , 1979. xli, 298 p. : ISBN
0-89011-532-X LC Card 79-87500
HV854 .C53   **NYPL [JLE 80-2984]**

Rupp, R. W. (joint author) Paffenbarger, George
Corbly, 1902- Organizations engaged in
preparing standards for dental materials and
therapeutic agents with a list of standards /.
[Washington, D.C.] [1980] iii, 51 p. ; LC Card
80-600041 DDC 602/.18 s 362.1/7 19
QC100 .U57 no. 571 RK681

Ruppel, Edward Thompson, 1925- Cenozoic block
uplifts in east-central Idaho and southeast
Montana / by Edward T. Ruppel. Washington :
U. S. Govt. Print. Off., 1981. p. cm.
(Contributions to stratigraphy) Geological Survey
professional paper ; 1224 Bibliography: p. LC Card
80-607875 DDC 551.7/8/09796 19
1. Geology, Stratigraphic - Cenozoic. 2. Geology -
Idaho. 3. Geology - Montana. I. Series. II. Series:
United States. Geological Survey. Professional paper,
1224. III. Title.
QE691 .R85

Ruppert, David E. Lake Mead national recreation
area : an ethnographic overview / by David E.
Ruppert. Tucson, Ariz. : Western Archeological
Center, National Park Service, 1976. ix, 90 p. :
ill. ; 27 cm. Includes bibliographies. LC Card
80-601435 DDC 979.3/12 19
1. Indians of North America - Arizona. 2. Indians of
North America - Nevada. 3. Lake Mead National
Recreation Area. I. Western Archeological Center. II.
Title.
E78.A7 R86

**RURAL AGED - GOVERNMENT POLICY -
MAINE.**
United States. Congress. Senate. Special
Committee on Aging. Maine's rural elderly .
Washington , 1980. iv, 125 p. ; LC Card
80-604071 DDC 362.6/09741 19
KF26.5 .A3 1980c

**RURAL AGED - GOVERNMENT POLICY -
NEW MEXICO.**
United States. Congress. Senate. Special
Committee on Aging. Rural elderly--the isolated
population . Washington , 1980. iv, 94 p. : LC
Card 81-600599 DDC 362.6/09789 19
KF26.5 .A3 1980f

RURAL AGED - KENTUCKY - POWELL CO.
Larson, Donald Keith, 1932- Problems of rural
elderly households in Powell County, Kentucky
/. [Washington] [Springfield, Va. , 1978] iii, 25
p. ; LC Card 81-451882 DDC 362.6/09769/585 19
HV1468.K4 L37

RURAL AGED - MAINE.
United States. Congress. Senate. Special
Committee on Aging. Maine's rural elderly .
Washington , 1980. iv, 125 p. ; LC Card
80-604071 DDC 362.6/09741 19
KF26.5 .A3 1980c

**RURAL AGED - NORTH CAROLINA -
ECONOMIC CONDITIONS.**
United States. Congress. House. Select

Committee on Aging. Subcommittee on Retirement Income and Employment. Income status of the rural elderly . Washington , 1980. iii, 74 p. ; LC Card 81-601192   DDC 362.6/042 19
KF27.5 .A374 1980b

RURAL AGED - SERVICES FOR - UNITED STATES - CONGRESSES.
National Strategy Conference on Improving Service Delivery to the Rural Elderly (1979 : Des Moines, Iowa) Improving services for the rural elderly . Washington, D.C. [1980] ix, 62 p. ; LC Card 80-69618   DDC 362.6/0973 19
HV1465 .N36 1979

RURAL ARCHITECTURE. see ARCHITECTURE, DOMESTIC.

RURAL COMMUNITY DEVELOPMENT. see RURAL DEVELOPMENT.

RURAL CONDITIONS.
Chuta, Enyinna. Rural non-farm employment . East Lansing, Mich. , 1979. vi, 96 p. ; LC Card 80-621248   DDC 331.12/09173/4 19
HD5852 .C56

Rural courts and highway safety /. United States. National Highway Safety Advisory Committee. Subcommittee on Alcohol and Adjudication. Washington , 1977. viii, 52 p. : LC Card 77-604399
KF2231 .A86

RURAL CREDIT. see AGRICULTURAL CREDIT.

RURAL DEVELOPMENT - AFRICA - BIBLIOGRAPHY.
Schatzberg, Michael G. Bibliography of small urban centers in rural development in Africa /. [Madison] , 1979. ix, 246 p. ; LC Card 80-623484   DDC 016.3077/6/096 19
Z7164.U7 S25 HT148.A2

RURAL DEVELOPMENT - AFRICA - DIRECTORIES.
United Nations. Economic Commission for Africa. Directory of activities of international voluntary agencies in rural development in Africa /. New York , 1977. iii, 173 p. ; LC Card 79-109825   DDC 300 s 361.7/7/0256 19
JX1977 .A2 E/CN.14/SWCD/68

RURAL DEVELOPMENT - AFRICA, EAST.
Moris, Jon R. Managing induced rural development /. Bloomington, Ind. , c1981. p. cm.   ISBN 0-89249-033-0   LC Card 81-6938   DDC 352.94/2/0976 19
HD1417 .M69

RURAL DEVELOPMENT - ALABAMA.
Molnar, Joseph J. Development characteristics in non-metropolitan Alabama . Auburn, Ala. , 1979. 31 p. : LC Card 79-622432   DDC 307.7/2/09761 19
HN25 .M64

RURAL DEVELOPMENT - CONGRESSES.
Expert Group Meeting on Industrialization in Relation to Integrated Rural Development, Vienna, 1977. Industrialization and rural development. New York , 1978. vii, 104 p. : LC Card 79-109252   DDC 300 s 338.09173/4 19
JX1977 .A2 ID/215(ID/WG.257/23) HD1405

RURAL DEVELOPMENT - HAITI.
Zuvekas, Clarence. Agricultural development in Haiti . Washington, D.C. [1978] xiv, 355 p. : LC Card 80-601532   DDC 338.1/097294 19
HD1841 .Z69

RURAL DEVELOPMENT - LAW AND LEGISLATION - KENTUCKY.
Kentucky. Professional Schools Admissions Committee. A plan to provide professional education and services to underserved areas of the State . Frankfort, Ky. , 1979. x, 48 p. ; LC Card 80-620638   DDC 344.769/011231 347.690411231 19
KFK1325 .A25 1979

RURAL DEVELOPMENT - LAW AND LEGISLATION - UNITED STATES.
United States. Congress. Senate. Committee on Agriculture, Nutrition, and Forestry. Subcommittee on Environment, Soil Conservation, and Forestry. Resource Conservation and Development Act . Washington , 1980. iv, 206 p. : LC Card 80-603906   DDC 346.7304/4 347.30644 19
KF26 .A3543 1980d

RURAL DEVELOPMENT - MANAGEMENT.
Moris, Jon R. Managing induced rural

development /. Bloomington, Ind. , c1981. p. cm.   ISBN 0-89249-033-0   LC Card 81-6938   DDC 352.94/2/0976 19
HD1417 .M69

Rural development research report .
(no. 19) Leathers, Kenneth L. Costs of strip mine reclamation in the West /. [Washington, D.C.] , 1980. iv, 82 p. : LC Card 80-601672   DDC 338.2/3 19
TD195.C58 L4

RURAL DEVELOPMENT - SOUTHERN STATES - ADDRESSES, ESSAYS, LECTURES.
Human resource dimensions of rural development /. Austin , c1977. 258 p. ;   ISBN 0-87755-211-8   LC Card 78-102278
HD5725.S85 H85   **NYPL [JLF 80-1421]**

RURAL DEVELOPMENT - UNITED STATES.
New directions in rural preservation. Washington, D.C. [1980?] xi, 115 p. : LC Card 81-601043   DDC 307.7/2/0973 19
HN59 .N398

United States. Congress. Senate. Committee on Agriculture, Nutrition, and Forestry. Subcommittee on Rural Development. Accuracy of census taking in small communities and rural areas . Washington , 1980. iii, 32 p. ; LC Card 80-603442   DDC 001.4/33 19
KF26 .A3574 1980a

United States. Congress. Senate. Committee on Agriculture, Nutrition, and Forestry. Subcommittee on Rural Development. Administration's rural development policy . Washington , 1980. iii, 80 p. ; LC Card 80-603035   DDC 338.973 19
KF26 .A3574 1980

RURAL ECONOMIC DEVELOPMENT. see RURAL DEVELOPMENT.

Rural elderly--the isolated population . United States. Congress. Senate. Special Committee on Aging. Washington , 1980. iv, 94 p. : LC Card 81-600599   DDC 362.6/09789 19
KF26.5 .A3 1980f

RURAL ELECTRIFICATION - UNITED STATES.
United States. Congress. House. Committee on Agriculture. Subcommittee on Conservation and Credit. Increases in electric rates in rural areas . Washington , 1980. iii, 222 p. : LC Card 80-603462   DDC 338.4/336362 19
KF27 .A3226 1980

United States. Congress. House. Committee on Agriculture. Subcommittee on Conservation and Credit. Rural home weatherization and energy conservation . Washington , 1980. iii, 181 p. ; LC Card 80-602803   DDC 696 19
KF27 .A3226 1980a

United States. Congress. Senate. Committee on Agriculture, Nutrition, and Forestry. Subcommittee on Agricultural Credit and Rural Electrification. REA and energy conservation . Washington , 1980. iii, 113 p. : LC Card 81-600598   DDC 334/.68136362 19
KF26 .A3533 1980a

RURAL EXODUS. see RURAL-URBAN MIGRATION.

Rural health and rural health care, U. S. and Idaho /. Sargent, Merle J. Moscow , 1980. 43, [11] p. : LC Card 80-622141   DDC 362.1/0425 19
RA771.5 .S27

Rural health delivery systems, Haiti . United States. Agency for International Development. Washington, D.C. [1979?] ca. 500 p. in various pagings : LC Card 80-602874   DDC 362.1/0425 19
RA771.7.H2 U54 1979a

RURAL HEALTH - IDAHO.
Sargent, Merle J. Rural health and rural health care, U. S. and Idaho /. Moscow , 1980. 43, [11] p. : LC Card 80-622141   DDC 362.1/0425 19
RA771.5 .S27

Rural health in the People's Republic of China : report of a visit by the Rural Health Systems Delegation, June 1978 / Committee on Scholarly Communication with the People's Republic of China. [Bethesda, Md.] : U. S. Dept. of Health and Human Services, Public Health Service, National Institutes of Health ; Washington, D.C. : For sale by the Supt. of Docs., U. S. G.P.O., 1980 [i.e. 1981] ix, 207 p. : charts, forms, 1 map ; 23 cm. (HIH

publication . no. 81-2124) Nov. 1980. S/N 017-053-00076-1 Item 507-C-1 Includes bibliographical references and index.   LC Card 81-601104   DDC 362.1/0425 19
1. Rural health services - China. I. National Academy of Sciences (U. S.). Committee on Scholarly Communication with the People's Republic of China. II. National Institutes of Health (U. S.). III. Series: DHHS publication, no. (NIH) 81-2124.
RA771.7.C6 R87

Rural health services . Seymour, Scott. [Lexington, Ky.] , c1980. 8 p. ; LC Card 80-140001   DDC 353.9 s 362.1/0425 19
JS308 .C6 no. 688 RA771.5

RURAL HEALTH SERVICES - CHINA.
Rural health in the People's Republic of China . [Bethesda, Md.] , Washington, D.C. , 1980 [i.e. 1981] ix, 207 p. : LC Card 81-601104   DDC 362.1/0425 19
RA771.7.C6 R87

RURAL HEALTH SERVICES - CONGRESSES.
Maternal and child health/family planning program . New York, N.Y. , 1980. v, 341 p. : LC Card 80-143941   DDC 362.1/982/0091724 19
RG940 .M368

RURAL HEALTH SERVICES - HAITI.
United States. Agency for International Development. Rural health delivery systems, Haiti . Washington, D.C. [1979?] ca. 500 p. in various pagings : LC Card 80-602874   DDC 362.1/0425 19
RA771.7.H2 U54 1979a

RURAL HEALTH SERVICES - IDAHO.
Sargent, Merle J. Rural health and rural health care, U. S. and Idaho /. Moscow , 1980. 43, [11] p. : LC Card 80-622141   DDC 362.1/0425 19
RA771.5 .S27

RURAL HEALTH SERVICES - UNITED STATES.
Sargent, Merle J. Rural health and rural health care, U. S. and Idaho /. Moscow , 1980. 43, [11] p. : LC Card 80-622141   DDC 362.1/0425 19
RA771.5 .S27

Seymour, Scott. Rural health services . [Lexington, Ky.] , c1980. 8 p. ; LC Card 80-140001   DDC 353.9 s 362.1/0425 19
JS308 .C6 no. 688 RA771.5

RURAL HEALTH SERVICES - UNITED STATES - DIRECTORIES.
Bureau of Social Science Research, Washington, D. C. Directory of rural health care programs, 1979 /. [Washington, D.C.] [1980] ix, 499 p. ; LC Card 80-602309   DDC 362.1/0425 19
RA771.5 .B87 1980

RURAL HEALTH - UNITED STATES.
Sargent, Merle J. Rural health and rural health care, U. S. and Idaho /. Moscow , 1980. 43, [11] p. : LC Card 80-622141   DDC 362.1/0425 19
RA771.5 .S27

Rural home weatherization and energy conservation . United States. Congress. House. Committee on Agriculture. Subcommittee on Conservation and Credit. Washington , 1980. iii, 181 p. ; LC Card 80-602803   DDC 696 19
KF27 .A3226 1980a

Rural housing oversight and reauthorizations . United States. Congress. Senate. Committee on Banking, Housing, and Urban Affairs. Subcommittee on Rural Housing and Development. Washington , 1980. iv, 234 p. : LC Card 80-602981   DDC 344.73/063635 19
KF26 .B3953 1980

RURAL LIFE. see COUNTRY LIFE.

Rural non-farm employment . Chuta, Enyinna. East Lansing, Mich. , 1979. vi, 96 p. ; LC Card 80-621248   DDC 331.12/09173/4 19
HD5852 .C56

RURAL POOR - KENTUCKY - POWELL CO.
Larson, Donald Keith, 1932- Problems of rural elderly households in Powell County, Kentucky /. [Washington] [Springfield, Va. , 1978] iii, 25 p. ; LC Card 81-451882   DDC 362.6/09769/585 19
HV1468.K4 L37

RURAL POOR - NORTH CAROLINA.
United States. Congress. House. Select Committee on Aging. Subcommittee on Retirement Income and Employment. Income status of the rural elderly . Washington , 1980.

iii, 74 p. ; LC Card 81-601192 DDC 362.6/042 19
KF27.5 .A374 1980b

RURAL POOR - WISCONSIN.
Saupe, William E. Changes in farm poverty in
Wisconsin /. [Madison] [1979] 24 p. ; LC
Card 80-622902 DDC 338.1/3/09775 19
HC107.W63 P6246

RURAL POPULATION.
United Nations. Dept. of International
Economic and Social Affairs. Patterns of urban
and rural population growth. New York , 1980.
ix, 175 p. : LC Card 80-138417 DDC 081 s
304.6/2 19
JX1977 .A2 ST/ESA/SER.A/68 HB1951

RURAL POPULATION - DRUG USE.
National Institute on Drug Abuse. Services
Research Branch. Nonurban drug abuse
programs . [Rockville, Md.] , Washington ,
1978. 27 p. ; LC Card 78-602308 DDC
362.2/93/0973 19
HV5825 .N35 1978b

RURAL POVERTY. see RURAL POOR.

**RURAL-URBAN MIGRATION - SOUTHERN
STATES - ADDRESSES, ESSAYS,
LECTURES.**
Human resource dimensions of rural
development /. Austin, c1977. 258 p. ; ISBN
0-87755-211-8 LC Card 78-102278
HD5725.S85 H85 **NYPL [JLF 80-1421]**

RURAL WOMEN - UNITED STATES.
United States. Congress. Senate. Special
Committee on Aging. Impact of federal estate
tax policies on rural women . Washington ,
1981. iii, 57 p. ; LC Card 81-601884 DDC
330.973/0927/088042 19
KF26.5 .A3 1981

RURAL YOUTH.
United States. Rural Development Service. How
USDA can help you involve youth in
community development. Washington, 1973. 15
p.: **NYPL [*XME-9362]**

Rush, F. Eugene. Geohydrology of Smith Valley,
Nevada, with special reference to the water-use
period, 1953-72 / by F.E. Rush and C.V.
Schroer ; prepared cooperatively by the United
States Department of the Interior Geological
Survey. [Carson City] : State of Nevada, Dept.
of Conservation and Natural Resources,
Division of Water Resources, 1976. 95 p. : ill.,
maps (1 fold. in pocket) ; 28 cm. (Water-resources
bulletin. no. 43) Bibliography: p. 83-84. LC Card
80-623615 DDC 553.7/09793/58 19
*1. Hydrology - Nevada - Smith Valley. 2.
Water-supply - Nevada - Smith Valley. I. Schroer, C.
V., joint author. II. United States. Geological Survey.
III. Nevada. Division of Water Resources. IV. Series:
Water resources bulletin (Carson City, Nev.) , no. 43.
V. Title.*
GB705.N3 R87

Rush, Thomas Vale. The prevalence and intensity
of alcohol and illicit drug use in Pennsylvania; a
household survey; report prepared in the Office
of Research and Evaluation, the Governor's
Council on Drug and Alcohol Abuse [by]
Thomas Vale Rush [and] Alden Small.
[Harrisburg] 1977 2 v. 28 cm. Includes
bibliography. CONTENTS: - v. 1. Highlights. - v. 2.
Main report.
*1. Alcoholism - Pennsylvania. 2. Drug abuse -
Pennsylvania. I. Small, Alden, joint auhtor. II.
Pennsylvania. Governor's Council on Drug and Alcohol
Abuse. Office of Research and Evaluation. III. Title.*
NYPL [JLF 79-928]

Russek, Frank. Iden, George. The productivity
problem . [Washington, D.C.] , 1981. xvii, 137
p. ; LC Card 81-600899 DDC 331.11/8/0973 19
HC110.C3 I32

Russell, D. A. (Donald Andrew) Criticism in
antiquity / D.A. Russell. Berkeley : University
of California Press, c1981. p. cm. Bibliography: p.
Includes index. ISBN 0-520-04466-5 : LC Card
81-3348 DDC 801/.95/0938 19
*1. Classical literature - History and criticism. 2.
Criticism. I. Title.*
PA3013 .R82

Russell, Kenneth R. (joint author) Currier, Mary
Jean P. Mountain lion population and harvest
near Canon City, Colorado, 1974-1977 /.
[Denver] , 1977. vi, 12 p. : LC Card 78-621470
DDC 639.9/7974428 19
QL737.C23 C83

Russell, Marian Sloan, 1845-1937. Land of
enchantment : memoirs of Marian Russell along
the Santa Fé TRail / as dictated to Mrs. Hal
Russell.Illustrated facsim. ed. with new photos.,
a new map, and a new afterword / by Marc
Simmons. Albuquerque : University of New
Mexico Press, [1981] c1954. xiv, 163 p. : ill. ;
24 cm. Reprint. Originally published: Evanston, Ill. :
Branding Iron Press, 1954. Includes index. ISBN
0-8263-0571-7 : LC Card 80-54564 DDC
917.8 19
*1. Santa Fe Trail. 2. Frontier and pioneer life -
Southwest, New. 3. Overland journeys to the Pacific. 4.
Russell, Marian Sloan, 1845-1937. 5. Pioneers -
Southwest, New - Biography. 6. Southwest, New -
Biography. I. Title.*
F786 .R96 1981

RUSSELL, MARIAN SLOAN, 1845-1937.
Russell, Marian Sloan, 1845-1937. Land .of
enchantment . Albuquerque [1981] c1954. xiv,
163 p. : ISBN 0-8263-0571-7 : LC Card 80-54564
DDC 917.8 19
F786 .R96 1981

Russell, Robert Cone, 1917- Soil survey of
Marion County, Iowa / [by Robert C. Russell
and L. Dale Lockridge ; fieldwork by Robert C.
Russell ... et al.] ; United States Department of
Agriculture, Soil Conservation Service, in
cooperation with the Iowa Agriculture and
Home Economics Experiment Station,
Cooperative Extension Service, Iowa State
University, and the Department of Soil
Conservation, State of Iowa. [Washington,
D.C.] : U. S. Dept. of Agriculture, [1980] ix,
183 p., [72] fold. leaves of plates : ill. ; 28 cm.
Bibliography: p. 99-100. Includes index. LC Card
80-602332 DDC 631.4/7/77783 19
*1. Soils - Iowa - Marion Co. - Maps. I. Lockridge, L.
Dale, joint author. II. United States. Soil Conservation
Service. III. Title.*
S599.I8 R88

Russell, Thomas W. (joint author) Taylor, Robert
Gay, 1940- Effects of bacteria on nitrate and
nitrite concentrations in groundwater of the
Ogallala aquifer /. Las Cruces, N.M. [1979]
vii, 20 leaves : LC Card 80-622275 DDC
333.91/09789 s 628.1/68 19
GB705.N6 N64 no. 114 TD224.N6

RUSSIA - COMMERCE - UNITED STATES.
United States. Congress. Senate. Committee on
Governmental Affairs. Permanent Subcommittee
on Investigations. Transfer of technology to the
Soviet bloc . Washington , 1980. iii, 156 p. ;
LC Card 80-602191 DDC 338.91/73/047 19
KF26 .G674 1980

RUSSIA - ECONOMIC CONDITIONS - 1976-
United States. Central Intelligence Agency.
National Foreign Assessment Center. The
Soviet economy in 1978-79 and prospects for
1980 /. Washington, D.C. [1980] vi, 25 p. :
LC Card 80-602919 DDC 330.947/0853 19
HC336.25 .U54 1980

United States. Congress. House. Permanent
Select Committee on Intelligence.
Subcommittee on Program and Budget
Authorization. Soviet internal developments .
Washington , 1980. iii, 134 p. ; LC Card
80-602084 DDC 947.085/3 19
KF27.5 .I56 1980

**RUSSIA - FOREIGN ECONOMIC
RELATIONS - UNITED STATES.**
United States. Central Intelligence Agency.
National Foreign Assessment Center. Soviet
strategy and tactics in economic and
commercial negotiations with the United States
/. Washington , 1979. v, 11 p. ; LC Card
79-602793
HF1456.5.R9 U54 1979 **NYPL [*XME-9336]**

**RUSSIA - FOREIGN RELATIONS -
AFGHANISTAN.**
United States. Congress. Senate. Committee on
Banking, Housing and Urban Affairs.
Subcommittee on International Finance. U. S.
embargo of food and technology to the Soviet
Union . Washington , 1980. v, 250 p. ; LC
Card 80-602113 DDC 382/.64/0973 19
KF26 .B3946 1980a

RUSSIA - FOREIGN RELATIONS - CUBA.
United States. Congress. House. Committee on
Foreign Affairs. Subcommittee on
Inter-American Affairs. Impact of Cuban-Soviet
ties in the Western Hemisphere, spring 1980 .

Washington , 1980. iii, 122 p. ; LC Card
80-602979 DDC 355/.03308 19
KF27 .F646 1980a

**RUSSIA - FOREIGN RELATIONS - UNITED
STATES.**
United States. Congress. Committee on Foreign
Affairs. Subcommittee on Europe and the
Middle East. East-West relations in the
aftermath of Soviet invasion of Afghanistan.
Washington , 1980. iii, 125 p. ; LC Card
80-602490 DDC 327.73047 19
KF27 .F64214 1980

United States. Congress. House. Committee on
Agriculture. Recent developments pertaining to
grain embargo . Washington , 1980. iii, 44 p. ;
LC Card 80-603662 DDC 382/.4131/0973 19
KF27 .A3 1980b

United States. Congress. House. Committee on
Foreign Affairs. U. S. participation in the 1980
summer Olympic games . Washington , 1980.
iii, 88 p. ; LC Card 80-602748 DDC
796.4/8/0947431 19
KF27 .F6 1980d

United States. Congress. House. Committee on
Interstate and Foreign Commerce.
Subcommittee on Transportation and
Commerce. Alternatives to the Moscow
Olympics . Washington , 1980. iii, 83 p. ; LC
Card 80-602442 DDC 353.0085/8 19
KF27 .I5589 1980a

United States. Congress. Senate. Committee on
Banking, Housing and Urban Affairs.
Subcommittee on International Finance. U. S.
embargo of food and technology to the Soviet
Union . Washington , 1980. v, 250 p. ; LC
Card 80-602113 DDC 382/.64/0973 19
KF26 .B3946 1980a

United States. Congress. Senate. Committee on
Foreign Relations. 1980 summer Olympics
boycott . Washington , 1980. iii, 97 p. ; LC
Card 80-602014 DDC 796.4/8/094731 19
KF26 .F6 1980d

RUSSIA - MILITARY POLICY.
United States. Congress. House. Committee on
Foreign Affairs. Subcommittee on International
Security and Scientific Affairs. Strategic
implications of chemical and biological warfare .
Washington , 1980. iii, 69 p. ; LC Card
80-602441 DDC 358/.34 19
KF27 .F64825 1980b

**RUSSIA - POLITICS AND GOVERNMENT -
1953-**
United States. Congress. House. Permanent
Select Committee on Intelligence.
Subcommittee on Program and Budget
Authorization. Soviet internal developments .
Washington , 1980. iii, 134 p. ; LC Card
80-602084 DDC 947.085/3 19
KF27.5 .I56 1980

**RUSSIA - RELATIONS (GENERAL) WITH
THE UNITED STATES.**
United States. Congress. House. Committee on
Foreign Affairs. Subcommittee on International
Security and Scientific Affairs. United States
scientific and technical exchanges with the
Soviet Union . Washington , 1980. iii, 57 p. ;
LC Card 80-602821 DDC 327.73047 19
KF27 .F64825 1980c

**RUSSIA - STUDY AND TEACHING -
UNITED STATES.**
United States. General Accounting Office.
Federally-financed research and communication
on Soviet affairs . [Washington, D.C. , 1980] ii,
37 p. ; LC Card 80-602671 DDC 947/.007/073 19
DK38.8 .U54 1980

**Russia (1917- R. S. F. S. R.). Voenno-Morskoĭ
flot. see Russia (1923- U. S. S. R.). Voenno-
Morskoĭ flot.**

**Russia (1923- U. S. S. R.) Navy. see Russia
(1923- U. S. S. R.). Voenno-Morskoĭ flot.**

**Russia (1923- U. S. S. R.). State Committee of
Council of Ministers of the USSR on
Science and Engineering. see Russia (1923-
U. S.S.R.). Gosudarstvennyĭ komitet po
nauke i tekhnike.**

**RUSSIA (1923- U. S. S. R.). VOENNO-
MORSKOĬ FLOT.** (Old Catalog form:
Union of Soviet Socialist Republics. Voyenno-
morskoĭ flot)
United States. Congressional Budget Office.

Shaping the general purpose Navy of the eighties . Washington, D.C. , 1980. xxvii, 145 p. : LC Card 80-600968 DDC 359/.03/0973 19
VA53 .U52 1980

Russia (1923- U. S.S.R.). Gosudarstvennyĭ komitet po nauke i tekhnike. Conference on the Future of Enzyme Engineering Development, Tiflis, 1978. Enzyme engineering . New York , c1980. xiv, 521 p. : ISBN 0-306-40442-7 LC Card 80-12061
TP248.E5 C68 1978 NYPL [JSE 80-1231]

Russian. De La Cruz, Nina. Washington, 1973. xxix, 138 p. LC Card 73-602523
*PG2121 .D4 1973 NYPL [*QCI 81-322]*

Russian Communist Party (Bolshevik) see **Kommunisticheskaĭa partiĭa Sovetskogo Soĭuza.**

RUSSIAN ECONOMIC ASSISTANCE. see **ECONOMIC ASSISTANCE, RUSSIAN.**

RUSSIAN GERMANS - NORTHWEST, PACIFIC - HISTORY.
Scheuerman, Richard D. The Volga Germans . Moscow, Idaho , c1980. 245 p. : ISBN 0-89301-073-1 LC Card 80-52314 DDC 979.5 19
F855.2.R85 S33

Russian history and politics . Thurston, Robert W. [Ann Arbor] , c1978. 57 p. ; LC Card 81-621451 DDC 016.947 19
Z2506 .T47 DK40

RUSSIAN LANGUAGE - CONVERSATION AND PHRASE BOOKS.
De La Cruz, Nina. Russian. Washington, 1973. xxix, 138 p. LC Card 73-602523
*PG2121 .D4 1973 NYPL [*QCI 81-322]*

RUSSIAN PROPAGANDA. see **PROPAGANDA, RUSSIAN.**

Russian River red salmon studies. Nelson, David Charles, 1943- Annual performance report for Russian River red salmon study /. Juneau [1977?] 54 p. : LC Card 78-621575 DDC 597/.55 19
QL638.S2 N449

Russian satellites. see **Communist countries.**

RUST. see **CORROSION AND ANTI-CORROSIVES.**

Rust, Richard Dilworth. Cooper, James Fenimore, 1789-1851. The Pathfinder or, The inland sea /. Albany , c1981. xxvi, 569 p., [6] leaves of plates : ISBN 0-87395-365-7 LC Card 79-15598 DDC 813/.2 19
PS1410.A2 R8

RUSTLESS COATINGS. see **CORROSION AND ANTI-CORROSIVES.**

RUSTS (FUNGI)
Littlefield, Larry J. Biology of the plant rusts . Ames, Iowa , 1981. p. cm. ISBN 0-8138-1670-X LC Card 81-3734 DDC 632/.425 19
SB741.R8 L39

Rutgers College, New Brunswick, N. J. see **Rutgers University, New Brunswick, N. J.**

Rutgers University, New Brunswick, N. J. Governor's Conference on the Future of the New Jersey Shore, Point Pleasant, N.J., 1979. The future of the New Jersey shore . New Brunswick, N.J. , 1980. ix, 113 p. ; LC Card 80-623449 DDC 333.91/7/09749 19
HT393.N5 G68 1979

Rutgers University, New Brunswick, N. J. Agricultural Experiment Station. see **New Jersey. Agricultural Experiment Station, New Brunswick.**

Rutgers University, New Brunswick, N. J. Center for Urban Policy Research. Burchell, Robert W. The fiscal impact guidebook . [Washington] , 1979. xxii, 617 p. ; LC Card 79-602895
HD4431 .B85 1979

Rutgers University, New Brunswick, N. J. Urban Policy Research, Center for. see **Rutgers University, New Brunswick, N. J. Center for Urban Policy Research.**

Rutgers University, New Brunswick, N. J. Water Resources Research Institute. Whipple, William, 1909- Principles of water resources planning (phase II) /. [New Brunswick] [1978]

26 leaves ; LC Card 79-623366 DDC 333.91 19
TC409 .W48

Rutgers University, New Brunswick, N.J. Center for Coastal and Environmental Studies. The coastal geomorphology of New Jersey. New Brunswick : Center for Coastal and Environmental Studies, Rutgers--the State University of New Jersey, [1977] 2 v. : ill. ; 28 cm. (Technical report - Center for Coastal and Environmental Studies . 77-1) "Prepared by the Center for Coastal and Environmental Studies at Rutgers--the State University of New Jersey for the Office of Coastal Zone Management, Division of Marine Services, New Jersey Department of Environmental Protection." "December 1977." Includes bibliographies. CONTENTS. - v. 1. Nordstrom, K.F. Management techniques and management strategies.--v. 2. Nordstrom, K.F., et al. Basis and background for management techniques and management strategies. LC Card 80-623995 DDC 333.91/7/09749 19
1. Coasts - New Jersey. 2. Coastal zone management - New Jersey. I. Nordstrom, Karl F. II. New Jersey. Office of Coastal Zone Management. III. Series: Rutgers University, New Brunswick, N.J. Center for Coastal and Environmental Studies. Technical report - Center for Coastal and Environmental Studies , 77-1. IV. Title.
GB459.4 .R87 1977

Comparison of natural and altered estuarine systems : analysis. [New Brunswick, N.J.] : Center for Coastal and Environmental Studies, Rutgers--the State University of New Jersey, [1979] xv, 247 p. : ill. ; 28 cm. Cover title. Written by T. Sugihara, et al. Prepared in cooperation with the Division of Fish, Game, and Shellfisheries, and the Bureau of Coastal Planning and Development of the New Jersey Dept. of Environmental Protection. "September 1979." "Contract no. C29358." Bibliography: p. 201-219. LC Card 80-623603 DDC 574.5/26365 19
1. Tidemarsh ecology - New Jersey. 2. Real estate development - Environmental aspects - New Jersey. I. Sugihara, Teruo. II. New Jersey. Division of Fish, Game, and Shellfisheries. III. New Jersey. Bureau of Coastal Planning and Development. IV. Title.
QH105.N5 R87 1979

Comparison of natural and altered estuarine systems : the field data / [edited by Teruo Sugihara, Norbert P. Psuty, James B. Durand ; cartography by Janice Limb, Lesley Ogrosky]. [New Brunswick, N.J.] : Center for Coastal and Environmental Studies, Rutgers--the State University of New Jersey, [1979] 2 v. : ill. ; 28 cm. "Prepared by the Center for Coastal and Environmental Studies, Rutgers--the State University of New Jersey in cooperation with the Division of Fish, Game, and Shellfisheries, and the Bureau of Coastal Planning and Development of the New Jersey Department of Environmental Protection." "September 1979." "Contract no. C29358." "CCES pub. no. NJ/RU-DEP-11-9-79." Includes bibliographies. LC Card 80-623604 DDC 574.5/26365 19
1. Estuarine ecology - New Jersey - Manahawkin region. 2. Real estate development - Environmental aspects - New Jersey - Manahawkin region. 3. Estuarine area conservation - New Jersey - Manahawkin region. 4. Estuaries - New Jersey - Manahawkin region. I. Sugihara, Teruo. II. Psuty, Norbert P. III. Durand, James B. IV. New Jersey. Division of Fish, Game, and Shellfisheries. V. New Jersey. Bureau of Coastal Planning and Development. VI. Title.
QH105.N5 R87 1979a

Governor's Conference on the Future of the New Jersey Shore, Point Pleasant, N.J., 1979. The future of the New Jersey shore . New Brunswick, N.J. , 1980. ix, 113 p. ; LC Card 80-623449 DDC 333.91/7/09749 19
HT393.N5 G68 1979

Onshore support bases for OCS oil and gas development : implications for New Jersey / by Bruce H. Hoff ... [et al.] ; cartography, Charles Ogrosky ... [et al.]. New Brunswick, N.J. : Center for Coastal and Environmental Studies, Rutgers--The State University of New Jersey, [1977] xvi, 234 p. : ill. ; 27 cm. "September 1977." Prepared for the Office of Coastal Zone Management, Division of Marine Services, New Jersey Dept. of Environmental Protection. Bibliography: p. 207-214. LC Card 80-622533 DDC 338.2/7282/09749 19
1. Petroleum in submerged lands - New Jersey. 2. Gas, Natural, in submerged lands - New Jersey. 3. Energy facilities - New Jersey. I. Hoff, Bruce H. II. New

Jersey. Office of Coastal Zone Management. III. Title.
TN872.N5 R87 1977

Technical report - Center for Coastal and Environmental Studies . (77-1) Rutgers University, New Brunswick, N.J. Center for Coastal and Environmental Studies. The coastal geomorphology of New Jersey. New Brunswick [1977] 2 v. : LC Card 80-623995 DDC 333.91/7/09749 19
GB459.4 .R87 1977

Rutgers University, New Brunswick, N.J. Institute on Aging. Green, Vera. Cultural perspectives on aging . New Brunswick, N.J. , c1980. ii leaves, 88 p. ; LC Card 80-129770 DDC 016.3052/6 19
Z7164.O4 G67 HQ1060

Ruth, Robert H. Effect of shade on germination and growth of salmonberry / by Robert H. Ruth. Portland, Or. : Pacific Northwest Forest and Range Experiment Station, Forest Service, U. S. Dept. of Agriculture, 1970. 10 p. : ill. ; 27 cm. Cover title. Bibliography: p. 9-10. LC Card 70-608740 DDC 634.9/09795 s 634/.711 19
1. Salmonberry. 2. Plants, Effect of shade on. 3. Germination. 4. Forest ecology - Northwest, Pacific. I. Series: United States. Pacific Northwest Forest and Range Experiment Station, Portland, Or. USDA Forest Service research paper PNW , 96. II. Title.
SD11 .A45614 no. 96 QK495.R78

Ruthberg, Zella G. Audit and evaluation of computer security II . [Washington, D.C.] [1980] ca. 250 p. in various pagings : LC Card 80-600034 DDC 602/.18 s 684.4/78 19
QC100 .U57 no. 500-57 HF5548.2

RUTHENIAN AMERICANS - HISTORY - SOURCES.
[The Carpatho-Ruthenian microfilm project : newspapers and periodicals] [Minneapolis , 197-] - reels ;
*NYPL [*ZAN-*Q1169 - *ZAN-*Q1230]*

Rutherford, Shirley. Minnesota. Dept. of Agriculture (1929-) Division of Planning and Development. High voltage transmission lines . St. Paul, Minn. [1979] 119 p. ; LC Card 79-624098 DDC 363.6/2 19
TD195.E37 M56 1979

Rution, Joseph A. (joint author) Mattson, Robert E. Considerations in the selection of public service employers. [Montpelier, Vt.] 1973. xiii, 51 p.
*NYPL [*XME-9291]*

Rutkoff, Peter M., 1942- Staudinger, Hans, 1889- The inner Nazi . Baton Rouge , c1981. p. cm. ISBN 0-8071-0882-0 : LC Card 81-7277 DDC 943.085/092/4 19
DD247.H5 A3583

Rutter, Jeremy B. Ceramic change in the Aegean Early Bronze Age : the Kastri group, Lefkandi I, and Lerna IV : a theory concerning the origin of Early Helladic II ceramics / Jeremy B. Rutter. [Los Angeles] : Institute of Archaeology, University of California, Los Angeles, [c1979] 37 p. : ill. ; 28 cm. (Occasional paper - Institute of Archaeology, University of California, Los Angeles ; no. 5) Bibliography: p. 26-29. ISBN 0-917956-11-7 LC Card 80-620674 DDC 738.3/09391 19
1. Bronze age - Greece. 2. Pottery, Prehistoric - Greece. 3. Greece, Modern - Antiquities. 4. Bronze age - Aegean Sea region. 5. Pottery, Prehistoric - Aegean Sea region. 6. Aegean Sea region - Antiquities. I. Series: California. University. University at Los Angeles. Institute of Archaeology. Occasional paper - Institute of Archaeology, University of California, Los Angeles , no. 5. II. Title.
GN778.22.G8 R87

Rutz, D. A. Factors affecting production of the mosquito, Culex quinquefasciatus (=fatigans) from anaerobic animal waste lagoons / D.A. Rutz, R.C. Axtell. [Raleigh] : North Carolina Agricultural Experiment Station, 1978. 32 p. : ill. ; 23 cm. (Technical bulletin - North Carolina Agricultural Experiment Station . no. 256) Bibliography: p. 30-32. LC Card 80-622296 DDC 630 s 614.4/323 19
1. Mosquito control. 2. Mosquitoes - Larvae. 3. Culex quinquefasciatus. 4. Sewage lagoons. 5. Farm manure. I. Axtell, Richard C., joint author. II. Series: North Carolina. Agricultural Experiment Station. Technical bulletin , no. 256. III. Title.
S97 .E25 no. 256 RA640

Rutz, Roger D. (joint author) Rhoades, Stephen A. Impact of bank holding companies on competition and performance in banking markets /. [Washington] [1979] 30 p. ; LC Card 80-602134   DDC 332.1/6 19
HG2491 .R46

Rützler, Klaus. The Atlantic barrier reef ecosystem at Carrie Bow Cay, Belize /. Washington , 1981- p. cm. LC Card 81-607039 DDC 574.5/26367/097282 19
QH108.B43 A87

Ruys, Pablo. see Picasso, Pablo, 1881-1973.

Ruys Picasso, Pablo. see Picasso, Pablo, 1881-1973.

Ryan, Joseph D. (joint author) Maddox, Gary P. Assessment, impact, and future perspective of Missouri's criminalistics laboratories, 1975-1978. /. Jefferson City [1979] ix, 230 p. : LC Card 80-620536   DDC 363.2/56/09778 19
HV8073 .M22

RYAN, LEO J. - ADDRESSES, ESSAYS, LECTURES.
United States. 96th Congress, 1st session, 1979. Memorial services held in the House of Representatives and Senate of the United States, together with remarks presented in eulogy of Leo J. Ryan, a late Representative from California /. Washington , 1979. vii, 88 p., [1] leaf of plates : LC Card 79-603246
E840.8.R88 U5 1979   *NYPL [JFE 81-694]*

RYAN, LEO J. - ASSASSINATION.
United States. Congress. House. Committee on Foreign Affairs. Staff Investigative Group. The assassination of Representative Leo J. Ryan and the Jonestown, Guyana, tragedy . Washington , 1979. xv, 782 p. : LC Card 80-600543
E840.8.R88 U48 1979

United States. Congress. House. Committee on Foreign Affairs. Subcommittee on International Operations. Review of the implementation of recommendations relating to the death of Representative Leo J. Ryan . Washington , 1980. iii, 78 p. ; LC Card 80-603637   DDC 364.1/524/098811 19
KF27 .F647 1980a

Ryan, Marie Vida. California. Dept. of Corrections. Management Information Section. California prisoners, 1977 and 1978 . Sacramento, Calif. [1979?] vii, 157 p. : LC Card 80-623512   DDC 364.3/09794 19
HV7254 .A6 1979

Ryan, Paul, 1930- An analysis of petroleum company investments in non-petroleum energy sources / prepared by Paul Ryan, Jr., Thomas C. Ryan for U. S. Dept. of Energy, Energy Information Administration, Assistant Administrator for Applied Analysis, Office of Economic Analysis. Washington, D.C. : The Office ; [Springfield, VA : available from National Technical Information Service, U. S. Dept. of Commerce, 1979] 2 v. : ill. ; 28 cm. "October 1979." "DOE/EIA/8556-1." Includes bibliographical references. LC Card 80-601258 DDC 332.6/7254 19
1. Petroleum industry and trade - United States - Finance. 2. Power resources - United States - Finance. I. Ryan, Thomas C., joint author. II. United States. Energy Information Administration. Office of Economic Analysis. III. Title.
HD9565 .R9

Ryan, Thomas C. (joint author) Ryan, Paul, 1930- An analysis of petroleum company investments in non-petroleum energy sources /. Washington, D.C. [Springfield, VA , 1979] 2 v. : LC Card 80-601258   DDC 332.6/7254 19
HD9565 .R9

Rydell, Lars H. Maine's progress toward a free, appropriate, public education for handicapped children /. [Augusta, Me.] [1979] xix, 141 p. : LC Card 80-623621   DDC 371.9/09741 19
LC4032.M2 M36

Ryle, Patricia M. An economic profile of Bergen County, New Jersey / Patricia M. Ryle. [Trenton, N.J.] : Office of Economic Research, Division of Planning and Research, N.J. Dept. of Labor and Industry, [1980] xviii, 152 p., [1] fold. leaf of plates : ill. ; 28 cm. "March 1980." Bibliography: p. 149-151. LC Card 80-622725 DDC 330.9749/21043 19
1. Bergen Co., N.J. - Economic conditions. I. New Jersey. Dept. of Labor and Industry. Office of

Economic Research. II. Title.
HC107.N53 B477

S. A. E. see Society of Automotive Engineers.

S. A. L. T. see Strategic Arms Limitation Talks.

S. E. C. see United States. Securities and Exchange Commission.

SEC monthly statistical review. United States. Securities and Exchange Commission. v. 39, no. 8- ; Aug. 1980- [Washington]
NYPL [Econ. Div.]

SEG report. Alaska. University. Institute of Social, Economic, and Government Research. no. 13-22; 1967-69. College.
NYPL [JLM 71-123]

S. G. I. see Search Group.

SI. see METRIC SYSTEM.

S. I. D. see Society for Information Display.

SI-METRIC. see METRIC SYSTEM.

S. I. P. C. see Securities Investor Protection Corporation.

S. R. I. see Stanford Research Institute.

S. R. S. see United States. Social and Rehabilitation Service.

SWP versus PEP. Burleson, Richard A. [Montpelier, Vt.] 1973. xi, 77 p.
*NYPL [*XME-9290]*

S. 1860, Small Business Innovation Act of 1979 . United States. Congress. Senate. Select Committee on Small Business. Washington , 1980 [i.e. 1981] iv, 611 p. : LC Card 81-601186 DDC 346.73/0652 347.306652 19
KF26.5 .S6 1980x

S. 1916 . United States. Congress. Senate. Committee on Foreign Relations. Washington , 1980. iii, 32 p. ; LC Card 80-601997 DDC 346.51/07 19
KF26 .F6 1980a

S. 2224, small business energy loan program . United States. Congress. Senate. Select Committee on Small Business. Washington , 1980. iii, 148 p. : LC Card 80-602162 DDC 346.7304/679158/0262 19
KF26.5 .S6 1980a

S. 2635, the Small business energy conservation act . United States. Congress. Senate. Select Committee on Small Business. Washington , 1980. iii, 30 p. ; LC Card 80-603682 DDC 346.7304/67916/02632 347.30646791602632 19
KF26.5 .S6 1980l

S. 2873, to provide SBA loans to small businesses in the communications industry . United States. Congress. Senate. Select Committee on Small Business. Subcommittee on Government Procurement. Washington , 1980. iii, 52 p. ; LC Card 80-603716 DDC 346.73/0652 347.3016652 19
KF26.5 .S625 1980

S. 344, the Highway beautification assistance act of 1979 . United States. Congress. Senate. Committee on Environment and Public Works. Washington , 1980. iii, 9 p. ; LC Card 80-601737 DDC 346.7304/5 19
KF5532 .A25 1980

Saavedra, Mario Correa. see Correa Saavedra, Mario.

Sabine Basin. Texas. Dept. of Water Resources. Projected land use maps year 2000, Sabine Basin. Austin, Tex. , 1978. [10] leaves : LC Card 80-675298   DDC 912/.133373/309764179 19
G1372.S15G4 T4 1978

Sabloff, Jeremy A. Archaeology /. Austin , 1981. p. cm. ISBN 0-292-77556-3 LC Card 81-4353 DDC 972/.01 19
F1219 .A76

SACCO-VANZETTI CASE.
Massachusetts. Report to the Governor in the matter of Sacco and Vanzetti. [Boston] [1977] 2, 38 p. ; LC Card 80-620508 DDC 345.73/02523 19
KF224.S2 M32

SACCO-VANZETTI CASE - CONGRESSES.
Sacco-Vanzetti, developments and reconsiderations, 1979 . Boston , 1981. p. cm. ISBN 0-89073-067-9 LC Card 81-12986 DDC

345.73/02523 347.3052523 19
KF224.S2 S24

Sacco-Vanzetti, developments and reconsiderations, 1979 : selected conference proceedings. Boston : Trustees of the Public Library of the City of Boston, 1981. p. cm. Papers presented at a conference sponsored by and held at the Boston Public Library, Oct. 26-27, 1979. ISBN 0-89073-067-9 LC Card 81-12986 DDC 345.73/02523 347.3052523 19
1. Sacco-Vanzetti case - Congresses. 2. Trials (Murder) - Massachusetts - Dedham - Congresses. 3. Felicani, Aldino, 1891-1967 - Congresses. I. Boston. Public Library.
KF224.S2 S24

Sachs, Hans, 1494-1576.
DAS STANDEBUCH - ILLUSTRATIONS.
Lehmann-Haupt, Hellmut, 1903- The book of trades in the iconography of social typology /. Boston , 1976. vi, 12 p., [15] p. of plates : LC Card 76-8399
*NYPL [*KSD 80-202 no. 1]*

Sacramento, Calif. State Library. see California. State Library, Sacramento.

SACRAMENTO RIVER - CHANNEL.
California. Dept. of Water Resources. Northern District. Observations of Sacramento River bank erosion, 1977-1979. [Sacramento, Calif.] [1979] x, 58 p. : LC Card 80-621717 DDC 551.3/52/097945 19
GB565.C2 C34 1979

Sacramento Southern Railroad Company. (plaintiff) MacBride, Dexter D. Power and process: a commentary on eminent domain and condemnation. [Washington, 1979] x, 84 p. LC Card 70-77921
KF5599 .Z9M3   *NYPL [JLD 80-3601]*

Sadacca, Robert. (joint author) Yap, Lorene. Lower Income Housing Assistance Program (Section 8) . Washington , 1978 i.e. 1979. ix, 232 p. ; LC Card 79-602558
HD7293 .A5 1979b Suppl.
NYPL [JLF 81-460]

Sadka, Efraim. (joint author) Balcer, Yves. Family size, personal income tax credits, and horizontal equity /. [Madison] [1979] 30 p. : LC Card 80-622907   DDC 336.24/216 19
HJ4621 .B28

Safe, effective, and therapeutically equivalent prescription drugs . New York (State). Office of Public Health. Albany [1978?] xiv, 122 p. ; LC Card 79-621906 DDC 615/.1 19
RS51 .N484 1978

Safe streets, 1968-1980 . Utah. Council on Criminal Justice Administration. Salt Lake City, Utah [1980] 13 leaves ; LC Card 80-623598 DDC 364/.9792 19
HV7294 .A6 1980

Safeguarding the Rights of Recipients of Mental Health Services, Symposium on. see Symposium on Safeguarding the Rights of Recipients of Mental Health Services, East Lansing, Mich., 1977.

Safer, Arnold E. A strategy of oil proliferation : a study / prepared for the use of the Subcommittee on Energy of the Joint Economic Committee, Congress of the United States [by Arnold E. Safer]. Washington : U. S. Govt. Print. Off. : for sale by the Supt. of Docs., U. S. Govt. Print. Off., 1980. vii, 20 p. ; 24 cm. At head of title: 96th Congress, 2d session. Joint committee print. "June 30, 1980." Includes bibliographical references. LC Card 80-603267 DDC 333.8/23215 19
1. Petroleum. 2. Energy policy - United States. I. United States. Congress. Joint Economic Committee. Subcommittee on Energy. II. Title.
TN870 .S22

Safer construction and maintenance practices to minimize potential liability by counties from highway accidents . Carstens, Robert Lowell. Ames, Iowa [1979] xiv, 113 p. ; LC Card 80-623075   DDC 363.1/251 19
HE5614.3.I8 C37

Safety and health within U. S. Postal Service . United States. Congress. House Committee on Post Office and Civil Service. Subcommittee on Postal Personnel and Modernization. Washington , 1980. vi, 392 p. : LC Card

80-603078　DDC 363.1/193834973 19
KF27 .P6677 1980a

SAFETY EDUCATION - CONGRESSES.
Bike-ed '77 . Washington, D. C. , 1977. i, 105
p. : LC Card 77-604118
GV1055 .B54　　　　**NYPL [JFF 80-1530]**

**SAFETY ENGINEERING. see INDUSTRIAL
SAFETY.**

**SAFETY, INDUSTRIAL. see INDUSTRIAL
SAFETY.**

**SAFETY MEASURES. see COAL MINES AND
MINING - SAFETY MEASURES;
INDUSTRIAL SAFETY.**

Safety of the air traffic control systems . United
States. Congress. House. Committee on Public
Works and Transportation. Subcommittee on
Aviation. Washington , 1980. iv, 506 p. : LC
Card 80-602811　DDC 363.1/2472 19
KF27 .P89624 1979i

**SAFETY REGULATIONS - ECONOMIC
ASPECTS - UNITED STATES.**
Christiansen, Gregory. Environmental and
health/safety regulations, productivity growth,
and economic performance . Washington ,
1980. v, 94 p. : LC Card 80-603059 DDC
339/.0973 19
HC110.E5 C5

**SAFETY REGULATIONS - NEW YORK (CITY)
- PERIODICALS.**
New York (City). Dept. of Personnel. Annual
report under executive order 109 - employee
safety program. New York.
　　　　　　NYPL [JLM 80-702]

SAFETY REGULATIONS - UNITED STATES.
Massachusetts Institute of Technology. Center
for Policy Alternatives. Benefits of
environmental, health, and safety regulation /.
Washington , 1980. vii, 100 p. : LC Card
80-601784　DDC 363.7/00973 19
HC110.E5 M38 1980

The Sagebrush Rebellion . Chomski, Joseph M.
[Juneau? Alaska] , 1980. 130, lxxxiv p. : LC
Card 80-622635 DDC 343.78/025 19
KF5605.Z95 C48

Sagiv, Yehoshua.
(joint author) Maier, David, 1953- On the
complexity of inferring join dependencies /.
Urbana, Ill. [1979] 23 p. ; LC Card 80-622080
DDC 001.64 s 001.64/2 19
QA76 .I4 no. 985 QA76.9.D3

Quadratic algorithms for minimizing joins in
restricted relational expressions / Yehoshua
Sagiv. Urbana, Ill. : Dept. of Computer Science,
University of Illinois at Urbana-Champaign,
[1979] 38 p. ; 28 cm. ([Report] - UIUCDCS-R-79 :
992) "October 1979." "UILU-ENG 79 1740."
Bibliography: p. 36-38.　LC Card 80-622081 DDC
001.64 s 519.7 19
*1. Data base management. 2. Information storage and
retrieval systems. I. Series: Illinois. University at
Urbana-Champaign. Dept. of Computer Science. Report,
992. II. Title.*
QA76 .I4 no. 992 QA76.9.D3

Subset dependencies as an alternative to
embedded multivalued dependencies /
Yehoshua Sagiv, Scott Walecka. Urbana, Ill. :
Dept. of Computer Science, University of
Illinois at Urbana-Champaign, 1979. 25 p. : ill. ;
28 cm. ([Report] - UIUCDCS-R-79 ; 980)
"UILU-ENG 79-1732." Bibliography: p. 22-25. LC
Card 80-621695 DDC 001.64 s 519.7 19
*1. Data base management. I. Walecka, Scott, joint
author. II. Series: Illinois. University at
Urbana-Champaign. Dept. of Computer Science. Report,
980. III. Title.*
QA76 .I4 no. 980 QA76.9.D3

SAHARA - POLITICS AND GOVERNMENT.
United States. Congress. House. Study Mission
to Morocco, the Western Sahara, Mauritania,
Algeria, Liberia, Spain, and France. Arms for
Morocco? . Washington , 1979. viii, 26 p. : LC
Card 80-601042　DDC 355/.032/64 19
E183.8.M8 U54 1979

SAHEL - FAMINES.
Baumer, Michel. Towards a strategy for
development in the Sahelian and
Sudano-Sahelian zones /. [New York] , 1973.
17 p. ; LC Card 73-23298 DDC 300 s 338.966 19
JX1977 .A2 ST/SSO/1/Rev.1 HC1000.Z9F3

SAILFISH.
Jolley, John W. The biology and fishery of
Atlantic sailfish Istiophorus platypterus, from
Southeast Florida /. St. Petersburg , 1977. 31
p. : LC Card 78-620516　DDC 597/.58 19
QL638.I88 J64

SAILFISH FISHING - FLORIDA.
Jolley, John W. The biology and fishery of
Atlantic sailfish Istiophorus platypterus, from
Southeast Florida /. St. Petersburg , 1977. 31
p. : LC Card 78-620516　DDC 597/.58 19
QL638.I88 J64

SAILING.
Sailing and seamanship. Washington, D.C. ,
1980. 248 p. in various pagings : ISBN
0-930028-02-3 (pbk.) : LC Card 81-129619
DDC 797.1/24 19
GV811 .S253 1980

Sailing and seamanship. 3rd ed. Washington,
D.C. : U. S. Coast Guard Auxiliary, 1980. 248
p. in various pagings : ill. (some col.) ; 28 cm.
Bibliography: p. A-1. Includes index.　ISBN
0-930028-02-3 (pbk.) : LC Card 81-129619
DDC 797.1/24 19
*1. Sailing. 2. Seamanship. I. United States. Coast Guard
Auxiliary.*
GV811 .S253 1980

Sailing directions (enroute) for the Philippines.
Defense Mapping Agency.
Hydrographic/Topographic Center. Washington,
D.C. , 1979- 1 v. : LC Card 80-602879　DDC
623.89/29599 19
VK911 .D43 1979

**Sailing directions (enroute) for the South China
Sea and Gulf of Thailand.** Defense Mapping
Agency. Hydrographic/Topographic Center.
Washington, D.C. , 1979- 1 v. : LC Card
80-600971　DDC 623.89/29597 19
VK905 .D43 1979

**Sailing directions (enroute) for the Strait of
Malacca and Sumatera.** Defense Mapping
Agency. Hydrographic Center. [Washington] ,
1978- 1 v. : LC Card 78-603700
VK931 .D43 1978　　　　**NYPL [JFF 81-152]**

**St. Anthony Park, Minn. Agricultural
Experiment Station. see Minnesota.
Agricultural Experiment Station, St.
Anthony Park.**

ST. CLAIR CO., ILL. - ANTIQUITIES.
Kelly, John Edward. The archaeological
intensive survey of the FAI-270 alignment in
the American Bottom region of Southern
Illinois /. [Springfield] , 1979. iv, 121 p., [8]
leaves of plates : LC Card 80-623314　DDC
977.3/8 19
E78.I3 K44

ST. CLAIR COUNTY, ILL. - MAPS.
(1980) United States. Soil Conservation Service.
St. Clair County, Illinois /. Lincoln, Nebr. ,
1980. 1 map ; LC Card 81-691443
G4103.S2 1980 .U49

St. Elizabeths Hospital . United States. Congress.
House. Committee on the District of Columbia.
Subcommittee on Fiscal Affairs and Health.
Washington , 1980. iv, 206 p. : LC Card
80-601896　DDC 362.2/1/09753 19
KF27 .D5392 1979a

**SAINT ELIZABETHS HOSPITAL,
WASHINGTON, D. C.** (Old Catalog form:
United States. Saint Elizabeths Hospital,
Washington, D. C.)
United States. Congress. House. Committee on
the District of Columbia. Subcommittee on
Fiscal Affairs and Health. St. Elizabeths
Hospital . Washington , 1980. iv, 206 p. : LC
Card 80-601896　DDC 362.2/1/09753 19
KF27 .D5392 1979a

**SAINT HELENS, MOUNT, WASH. -
ERUPTION, 1980.**
Channel conditions in the lower Toutle and
Cowlitz rivers resulting from the mudflows of
May 18, 1980 /. [Reston, Va.?] , Alexandria,
Va. (604 S. Pickett Street, Alexandria, Va.
22304) , 1981. v, 16 p. : LC Card 81-600040
DDC 557.3 s 551.48/9/0979788 19
QE75 .C5 no. 850-c QE599.U5

United States. Congress. Senate. Committee on
Appropriations. Disaster assistance Pacific
Northwest--Mount Saint Helens eruption .
Washington , 1980. iv, 241 p. : LC Card

80-603023　DDC 363.3/495/0979788 19
KF26 .A6 1980

United States. Congress. Senate. Committee on
Commerce, Science, and Transportation. Mount
St. Helens impact . Washington , 1980. iv, 146
p. : LC Card 80-603517　DDC 363.3/495 19
KF26 .C69 1980r

St. Joseph, Mo. United States. Public Health
Service. Pollution of interstate waters.
[Washington] 1959. 2 v.　LC Card 75-80621
　　　　　　NYPL [JSF 81-65]

**St. Lawrence-Black River Regional Planning
Board. see Black River-St. Lawrence
Regional Planning Board.**

St. Lawrence Seaway Development Corporation.
New York (State). St. Lawrence-Eastern
Ontario Commission. Evaluation of shore
structures and shore erodibility . Massena,
N.Y. , Watertown, N.Y. , 1977. vi, 165 p. :
LC Card 80-621706　DDC 627/.12 19
TC225.S138 N48 1977

**ST. LAWRENCE VALLEY - ECONOMIC
CONDITIONS - STATISTICS.**
Parsons, Carl. Summary of housing and
socio-economic data : Black River-St. Lawrence
region /. Springfield, Va. , 1974. vi, 106 p. :
　　　　　　NYPL [JLF 81-31]

**ST. LOUIS CO., MINN. - PUBLIC LANDS -
MAPS.**
Minnesota. Dept. of Iron Range Resources and
Rehabilitation. Land ownership, St. Louis
County /. Hibbing, Minn. [1973] 7 leaves :
LC Card 80-675210　DDC 912/.77677
G1428.S2G46 M5 1973

Saints of sage and saddle . Fife, Austin E. Salt
Lake City , 1980. xviii, 367 p. : ISBN
0-87480-180-X (pbk.)　LC Card 81-137868
DDC 289.3/09 19
BX8611 .F5 1980

SAKHAROV, ANDREĬ DMITRIEVICH, 1921-
United States. Congress. House. Committee on
Foreign Affairs. Soviet detention of Andrei
Sakharov . Washington , 1980. iii, 31 p. ; LC
Card 80-602485　DDC 323.4/0947 19
KF26 .F6 1980b

United States. Congress. House. Committee on
Foreign Affairs. Subcommittee on International
Organizations. Human rights and the detention
of Andrei Sakharov, update . Washington ,
1980. iii, 35 p. ; LC Card 80-602958　DDC
323.4/0947 19
KF27 .F648 1980a

Sakowitz, Anita R. Indiana. Legislative Services
Agency. Digest of acts, 1979, first regular
session, 101st General Assembly /.
Indianapolis, Ind. [1979] 119 p. ; LC Card
80-622703　DDC 348.772/026 19
KFI3025 .5 1979

SALADS.
Woodman, Mary. Salads for all the year round
/. New York , 1981. p. cm. ISBN 0-8490-3210-5
LC Card 81-4204　DDC 641.8/3 19
TX740 .W6 1981

Salads for all the year round /. Woodman, Mary.
New York , 1981. p. cm. ISBN 0-8490-3210-5
LC Card 81-4204　DDC 641.8/3 19
TX740 .W6 1981

Salary plan of the State of Maryland. Maryland.
Dept. of Personnel. [Baltimore, Md. , 1980] x,
142 p. ; LC Card 80-623623　DDC
353.9752001/232 19
JK3857 .M34 1980

**Salary schedule and alpha listing of classes,
October 1, 1979.** Washington (State). Dept. of
Personnel. [Olympia] [1979] [57] p. ; LC Card
80-621509　DDC 331.2/813539797 19
JK9257 .W36 1979

**Salary schedule information on Utah school
districts.** Utah. Div. of Education Support
Services. State & Federal Data Support
Services. Salt Lake City, Utah [1979] 201 p.
28 cm.　LC Card 80-622337　DDC
331.2/813711/009792 19
LB2842.2 .U85 1979

Salazar-Carrillo, Jorge. Prices and purchasing
power parities in Latin America, 1960-1972 /
Jorge Salazar-Carrillo. Washington, D.C. :
Published for the ECIEL Program by the
Organization of American States, 1978. ca. 350

p. in various pagings ; 23 cm. "An ECIEL study."
Includes bibliographical references.   LC Card
  80-134989   DDC 338.5/2/098 19
*1. Prices - Latin America. 2. Purchasing power - Latin
America. I. Program de Estudios Conjuntos sobre
Integración Económica Latinoamericana. II. Title.*
HB235.L25 S34

SALCHA RIVER, ALASKA.
Dinneford, W. Bruce. Final report of the
commercial fish-technical evaluation study,
Salcha River /. [Anchorage, Alaska] , 1978. vii,
93, 2 p. :   LC Card 79-625785   DDC 597/.55 19
QL628.A4 D55

SALE OF BUSINESS ENTERPRISES. see
BUSINESS ENTERPRISES, SALE OF.

**Sale of Carson City silver dollars by the General
Services Administration** . United States.
Congress. House. Committee on Banking,
Finance and Urban Affairs. Subcommittee on
Consumer Affairs. Washington , 1980. iii, 65
p. ;   LC Card 80-603492   DDC 353.0082/2 19
KF27 .B535 1980d

SALE OF MILITARY EQUIPMENT. see
MILITARY ASSISTANCE.

**Sale of roe from subsistence-caught salmon in the
Artic-Yukon-Kuskokwim region, 1974-1977** .
Alaska. Dept. of Fish and Game. [Juneau] ,
1978. ii, 36 leaves :   LC Card 78-624006   DDC
  333.95/6 19
SH222.A4 A33 1978

Sales, Estella. Love songs and new spirituals .
[Iowa City] , c1980. [23] p. ;   LC Card 80-125470
  DDC 811/.008/0896073 19
PS591.N4 L63

SALES, EXPORT. see **EXPORT SALES.**

Sales finance companies . Sullivan, A. Charlene.
West Lafayette, Ind. , 1980. ii, 14, [12] leaves ;
  LC Card 81-620933   DDC 332.3/5/0973 19
HG3756.U54 S93

**SALES FORECASTING - MATHEMATICAL
  MODELS.**
Leone, Robert P. An approach to building
competitive sales response models . Austin ,
1978. 31 p. :   LC Card 79-623639   DDC
  658.8/18/0724 19
HF5438.2 .L46

SALES, INTERNATIONAL. see **EXPORT
  SALES.**

Sales management . Bellenger, Danny N., 1946-
Atlanta, Ga. , 1981. p. cm.   ISBN 0-88406-147-7 :
  LC Card 81-6559   DDC 016.6588/1 19
Z7164.M18 B39 HF5438.4

SALES MANAGEMENT - BIBLIOGRAPHY.
Bellenger, Danny N., 1946- Sales management .
Atlanta, Ga. , 1981. p. cm.   ISBN 0-88406-147-7 :
  LC Card 81-6559   DDC 016.6588/1 19
Z7164.M18 B39 HF5438.4

SALES TAX - MAINE.
Maine. Legislature. Committee on Taxation.
Report of the Joint Standing Committee on
Taxation of the statutory review of the sales
and use tax exemptions contained in Title 36
Section 1760, Sub-sections 15-23 and 25-29.
Augusta, Me. [1980] 43, [17] leaves ;   LC Card
  80-622574   DDC 343.74105/5 347.410355 19
KFM11.62 .T3 1980

**SALES TAX - OKLAHOMA - STATISTICS -
  PERIODICALS.**
Oklahoma Tax Commission. Monthly research
and statistical bulletin. Jan. 1970, Feb-July,
1971. Oklahoma City.   **NYPL [JLM 80-920]**

SALES TAX - UNITED STATES.
United States. Federal Council on the Aging.
The impact of the tax structure on the elderly.
Washington , 1975. iv, 119 p. ;   LC Card
  76-601234
HJ4653.A82 U55 1975 **NYPL [JLF 80-1411]**

SALESMANSHIP. see **SELLING.**

Salient factor scores . LeClair, Daniel P.
[Boston] , 1980. 48 leaves ;
                          NYPL [*ZT-1259]

**SALINAS, PEDRO, 1892-1951 - CRITICISM
  AND INTERPRETATION.**
Allen, Rupert C. Symbolic experience, a study
of poems by Pedro Salinas /. University, Ala ,
c1981. p. cm.   ISBN 0-8173-0081-3   LC Card
  81-10307   DDC 861/.62 19
PQ6635.A32 Z54

SALINE COUNTY, ILL. - GENEALOGY.
Public Library, Winnetka, Ill. Genealogy
Projects Committee. An index to the names of
persons appearing in The History of Gallatin,
Saline, Hamilton, Franklin and Williamson
Counties, Illinois. (Chicago, The Goodspeed
Pub. Co., 1887). Thomson, Ill. [c1973] 122 p. ;
  NYPL [APR (Gallatin Co., Ill.) 80-1987]

SALINE COUNTY, KAN. - MAPS.
(1979) United States. Soil Conservation Service.
Saline County, Kansas /. [Lincoln? Neb.]
[1979?] 1 map :   LC Card 81-691133
G4203.S2 1979 .U5

SALINE SOILS. see **SOILS, SALTS IN.**

SALINE WATER CONVERSION.
(1977) New Mexico Energy Institute at New
Mexico State University. An appraisal study of
the geothermal resources of Arizona and
adjacent areas in New Mexico and Utah and
their value for desalination and other uses /.
Las Cruces, N.M. [1977] vii, 76 leaves, [12]
leaves of plates :   LC Card 80-623249   DDC 553.7
  19
GB1199.5 .N48 1977

**SALINE WATERS - COLORADO RIVER
  WATERSHED.**
Narayanan, Rangesan. An economic evaluation
of the salinity impacts from energy
development . Logan, Utah , 1979. x, 71 p. :
  LC Card 80-622072   DDC 363.7/394 19
TD195.E5 N37

**SALINE WATERS - COLORADO RIVER
  WATERSHED - MATHEMATICAL
  MODELS.**
Stochastic analysis of water quality /. Logan
[1979] viii, 75 p. :   LC Card 80-621125   DDC
  628.1/61 19
TD367 .S8

SALINE WATERS - DEMINERALIZATION.
  see **SALINE WATER CONVERSION.**

SALINE WATERS - MONTANA.
Montana. State Bureau of Mines and Geology.
Regional assessment of the saline-seep problem
and a water-quality inventory of the Montana
Plains . Bozeman, Mont. [1980] 24 p. :   LC
  Card 80-623140   DDC 363.7/3942/09786 19
TD224.M9 M64 1980

SALINE WATERS - NEBRASKA.
McCarraher, D. Bruce. Nebraska's sandhills
lakes /. Lincoln , 1977. 67 p. :   LC Card
  77-623677   DDC 574.5/2636 19
QH105.N2 M32

Salisbury, H. B.
Beneficiation of low-grade California chromite
ores / by H.B. Salisbury, M.L. Wouden, and
M.B. Shirts. [Avondale, Md.] : U. S. Dept. of
the Interior, Bureau of Mines, 1981. p. cm.
(Report of investigations) Bibliography: p.   LC Card
  81-607307   DDC 622 s 622/.34643 19
*1. Chromite - California. 2. Ore-dressing. I. Wouden,
M. L. (Marinus L.). II. Shirts, M. B. III. Series: Report
of investigations (United States. Bureau of Mines). IV.
Title.*
TN23 .U43 TN538.C57

Recovery of copper and associated precious
metals from electronic scrap / by H. B.
Salisbury, L. J. Duchene, and J. H. Bilbrey, Jr.
Washington : U. S. Dept. of the Interior,
Bureau of Mines, [1981] p. cm. (Report of
investigations - [United States] Bureau of Mines ; 8500)
Bibliography: p.   LC Card 80-607807   DDC 622 s
  699/.3 19
*1. Copper - Recycling. 2. Precious metals - Recycling.
3. Electronics - Materials - Recycling. I. Duchene,
Leslie J., joint author. II. Bilbrey, Joseph H., joint
author. III. Series: United States. Bureau of Mines.
Report of investigations ; 8500. IV. Title.*
TN23 .U43 no. 8500 TD812.5.C66

Salley, E. Jean. Checklist of types in the U. S.
national parasite collection / researched and
compiled by E. Jean Salley, in collaboration
with J. Ralph Lichtenfels and Judith H. Shaw ;
prepared by Science and Education
Administration. [Washington] : U. S. Dept. of
Agriculture : for sale by the Supt. of Docs., U.
S. Govt. Print. Off., 1978. iv, 233 p. ; 26 cm.
(Index-catalogue of medical and veterinary zoology :
Special publication . no. 4) Includes index.   LC Card
  78-602796   DDC 591.52/49/0740153 19
*1. Parasites - Catalogs and collections. 2. Parasites -
United States - Catalogs and collections. 3. Type*

*specimens (Natural history). I. Lichtenfels, J. Ralph,
joint author. II. Shaw, Judith H., joint author. III.
United States. Science and Education Administration.
IV. Title. V. Series.*
QL757 .S23

Salm, Don. Wisconsin. Legislature. Legislative
Council. Case and opinion review. Madison,
Wis. [1980] 4 v. ;   LC Card 81-621133   DDC
  347.775/012 347.750712 19
KFW2807 .A25 1980

SALMON-FISHERIES - ALASKA.
United States. Congress. House. Committee on
Merchant Marine and Fisheries. Subcommittee
on Fisheries and Wildlife Conservation and the
Environment. Northwest salmon enhancement
program--salmon interception . Washington ,
1980. v, 512 p. :   LC Card 80-603908   DDC
  343.73/07692755 347.3037692755 19
KF27 .M447 1979h

**SALMON FISHERIES - ALASKA - BRISTOL
  BAY.**
Harris, Colin K. Forecast of the sockeye salmon
run to Bristol Bay in 1979 /. Seattle , 1979. 50
p. :   LC Card 79-624864   DDC 639/.2 s 597/.55 19
SH1 .W3352 no. 79-2 QL638.S2

**SALMON-FISHERIES - ALASKA -
  PHONOTAPE CATALOGS.**
Levey, Stephen B. The southeast Alaska salmon
fishery . Juneau , 1979. 48 p. :   LC Card
  79-625771   DDC 016.639/2755 19
SH348 .L48

**SALMON-FISHERIES - LAW AND
  LEGISLATION - ALASKA.**
United States. Congress. House. Committee on
Merchant Marine and Fisheries. Subcommittee
on Fisheries and Wildlife Conservation and the
Environment. Northwest salmon enhancement
program--salmon interception . Washington ,
1980. v, 512 p. :   LC Card 80-603908   DDC
  343.73/07692755 347.3037692755 19
KF27 .M447 1979h

**SALMON-FISHERIES - LAW AND
  LEGISLATION - WASHINGTON (STATE)**
United States. Congress. House. Committee on
Merchant Marine and Fisheries. Subcommittee
on Fisheries and Wildlife Conservation and the
Environment. Northwest salmon enhancement
program--salmon interception . Washington ,
1980. v, 512 p. :   LC Card 80-603908   DDC
  343.73/07692755 347.3037692755 19
KF27 .M447 1979h

United States. Congress. Senate. Committee on
Commerce, Science, and Transportation.
Washington State's salmon and steelhead
resources . Washington , 1980. iv, 208 p. ;   LC
  Card 80-603093   DDC 346.7304/6956 19
KF26 .C69 1980p

SALMONBERRY.
Ruth, Robert H. Effect of shade on germination
and growth of salmonberry /. Portland, Or. ,
1970. 10 p. :   LC Card 70-608740   DDC
  634.9/09795 s 634/.711 19
SD11 .A45614 no. 96 QK495.R78

Salo, John E. Taunton River study : background
data on water quality / John E. Salo and
William R. Jobin ; Water Quality Section,
Division of Water Pollution Control,
Massachusetts Water Resources Commission.
Boston : The Division, [1971] 31 leaves : ill. ;
28 cm. "May 1971." Chiefly tables.   LC Card
  80-118663   DDC 363.7/3942/097448 19
*1. Water quality - Massachusetts - Taunton River
watershed. 2. Water - Pollution - Massachusetts -
Taunton River watershed. 3. Sewage disposal in rivers,
lakes, etc. - Massachusetts - Taunton River watershed.
I. Jobin, William R., joint author. II. Massachusetts.
Division of Water Pollution Control. Water Quality
Section. III. Title.*
TD224.M4 S25

Saloutos, Theodore. The American farmer and the
New Deal / Theodore Saloutos. 1st ed. Ames :
Iowa State University Press, 1982, c1981. p.
cm. Bibliography: p. Includes index.   ISBN
0-8138-1076-0   LC Card 81-12396   DDC
  338.1/873 19
*1. Agriculture and state - United States. 2. Agriculture -
Economic aspects - United States. 3. Farmers - United
States. 4. United States - Economic policy - 1933-1945.
I. Title.*
HD1761 .S2 1982

The salt marsh of southern New Jersey /.

Carlson, Cathy. Pomona, N.J. , c1980. iv, 50 p. :   LC Card 80-121932   DDC 574.5/2636 19
QH105.N5 C37

SALT MINES AND MINING - DUST CONTROL.
Page, Steven J. Effectiveness of wet cutter bars in reducing salt mine dust /. Washington [1980] p. cm.   LC Card 80-607782   DDC 622 s 622/.3632 19
TN23 .U43 TN312

SALT Talks. see Strategic Arms Limitation Talks.

SALT WATER CONVERSION. see SALINE WATER CONVERSION.

SALTS, FUSED. see FUSED SALTS.

SALTS, SOLUBLE.
Foggin, G. Thomas. Completion report, using topographic characteristics to predict total solute concentrations in streams draining small forested watersheds in Western Montana /. Bozeman, Mont. , 1977. 42 leaves :   LC Card 79-624615   DDC 551.48/3/09786 19
GB855 .F63

SALTWATER ENCROACHMENT - ATLANTIC COAST (UNITED STATES)
United States. Geological Survey. Summary of hydrologic testing in Tertiary limestone aquifer, Tenneco offshore exploratory well-Atlantic OCS, lease-block 427 (Jacksonville NH 17-5) /. Washington , 1981. p. cm.   LC Card 80-606901   DDC 553/.79/09759 19
GB1199.2 .U54 1981

SALTWATER ENCROACHMENT - FLORIDA.
Wilson, William Edward, 1934- Estimated effects of projected ground-water withdrawals on movement of the saltwater front in the Floridan aquifer, 1976-2000, west-central Florida /. Washington , Arlington, VA , 1981. p. cm.   LC Card 81-607085   DDC 628.1/1 19
GB1197.83.F6 W54

Salusbury, John, 1707-1762. Expeditions of honour : the journal of John Salusbury in Halifax, Nova Scotia, 1749-53 / edited by Ronald Rompkey. Newark : University of Delaware Press ; London : Associated University Presses, c1981. p. cm. Bibliography: p.   ISBN 0-87413-169-3   LC Card 81-11537   DDC 971.6/01 19
1. Nova Scotia - History - 1713-1763. 2. Nova Scotia - Description and travel. 3. Halifax, N.S. - History. 4. Halifax, N. S. - Description. 5. Salusbury, John, 1707-1762. 6. British - Nova Scotia - Halifax - Biography. 7. Halifax (N.S.) - Biography. I. Rompkey, Ronald. II. Title.
F1038 .S2 1981

SALUSBURY, JOHN, 1707-1762.
Salusbury, John, 1707-1762. Expeditions of honour . Newark , London , c1981. p. cm.   ISBN 0-87413-169-3   LC Card 81-11537   DDC 971.6/01 19
F1038 .S2 1981

Salvage archeology in the Red Willow Reservoir, Nebraska /. Grange, Roger T. Lincoln, Neb. , 1980. xi, 236 p., [1] leaf of plates :   LC Card 80-624104   DDC 978.2 s 978.2/83 19
F661 .N32 no. 9 E78.N3
                                             NYPL [HBA no. 9]

SALVAGE (WASTE, ETC.)
Kittitas County, Wash. Solid Waste Management Planning Committee. A cooperative countywide solid waste management plan for Kittitas County and City of Ellensburg, City of Cle Elum, City of Roslyn, City of South Cle Elum, City of Kittitas. [Ellensburg, Wash.] , 1973. 1 v. (various pagings)   *NYPL [JSF 80-1026]*

SAMLL BUSINESS - TAXATION - UNITED STATES.
United States. Congress. Joint Committee on Taxation. Staff recommendations for simplification of tax rules relating to subchapter S corporations . Washington , 1980. iii, 27 p. ;   LC Card 80-602271   DDC 343.7306/8 19
KF6491 .A25 1980

Sammel, Edward A. The geothermal hydrology of Warner Valley, Oregon : a reconnaissance study / by Edward A. Sammel and Robert W. Craig. Washington : U. S. G.P.O., 1981. p. cm. (Geohydrology of geothermal systems) Geological Survey professional paper ; 1044-I. Bibliography: p.

LC Card 81-607830   DDC 553.7 19
1. Geothermal resources - Oregon - Warner Valley. 2. Water, Underground - Oregon - Warner Valley. I. Craig, Robert W. II. Title. III. Series.
GB1199.7.O7 S24

Sammet, Loy Luther. (joint author) Stollsteimer, John F. Regional efficiency in the organization of agricultural processing facilities . [Berkeley] , 1975. 148 p. :   LC Card 76-622988   DDC 338.1 s 664/.80413 19
HD1407 .C27 no. 35 SB373

Sammis, Theodore W.
Consumptive use and yields of crops in New Mexico /. Las Cruces, N.M. [1979] vi, 108 p. :   LC Card 80-622505   DDC 333.91/009789 s 631.7 19
GB705.N6 N64 no. 115 S600.7.E93

Demonstration of irrigation return flow water quality in the Mesilla Valley, New Mexico / by Theodore W. Sammis, in cooperation with Department of Agricultural Engineering and New Mexico Agricultural Experiment Station, New Mexico State University, for Robert S. Kerr Environmental Research Laboratory, Office of Research and Development, U. S. Environmental Protection Agency. Las Cruces, N.M. : WRRI, [1980] ix, 149 p. : ill. ; 28 cm. (WRRI report . no. 117) "EPA grant no. S803565-03-0." Bibliography: p. 75-76.   LC Card 80-623166   DDC 333.91/009789 s 631.7 19
1. Irrigation water - New Mexico - Mesilla Valley - Quality. 2. Irrigation - New Mexico - Mesilla Valley - Tailwater recovery systems. 3. Soils - New Mexico - Mesilla Valley - Leaching. 4. Soils, Salts in - New Mexico - Mesilla Valley. I. New Mexico State University. Dept. of Agricultural Engineering. II. New Mexico. Agricultural Experiment Station, University Park. III. Robert S. Kerr Environmental Research Laboratory. IV. Series: New Mexico State University. Water Resources Research Institute. WRRI report , no. 117. V. Title.
GB705.N6 N64 no. 117 TC824.N6

Sampair, James L. Buried oyster shell resource evaluation of the eastern region of the Albemarle Sound / by James L. Sampair ; in cooperation with the Division of Marine Fisheries. Raleigh : North Carolina, Dept. of Natural and Economic Resources, Division of Earth Resources, Geology and Mineral Resources Section, 1976. iii, 47 p. : ill., maps (3 fold. in pocket) ; 28 cm. (Bulletin - North Carolina, Geology and Mineral Resources Section ; 85)   LC Card 78-623214   DDC 553.5 19
1. Oyster shell. 2. Marine resources - North Carolina - Albemarle Sound. 3. Marine sediments - North Carolina - Albemarle Sound. 4. Seismic reflection method. 5. Core drilling. I. North Carolina. Division of Marine Fisheries. II. Series: North Carolina. Geology and Mineral Resources Section. Bulletin - North Carolina, Geology and Mineral Resources Section , 85. III. Title.
SH379.5 .S25

Sampling landings of halibut for age composition
/. Southward, G. Morris. Seattle , 1976. 31 p. :   LC Card 81-456583   DDC 639/.2758 s 597/.5 19
SH351.H2 I54 no. 58 QL638.P7

SAMPLING (STATISTICS)
Smith, Gary Frederick. A quantitative sampling program of benthic communities in nearshore subtidal areas within the Rosario Strait region of Northern Puget Sound, Washington State (1976) /. [Olympia] [1979] vi, 105 p. :   LC Card 80-622612   DDC 591.9797/7 19
QH105.W2 S65

Southward, G. Morris. Sampling landings of halibut for age composition /. Seattle , 1976. 31 p. :   LC Card 81-456583   DDC 639/.2758 s 597/.5 19
SH351.H2 I54 no. 58 QL638.P7

United Nations. Statistical Office. A short manual on sampling. New York , 1972- v. ;   LC Card 80-119414   DDC 300 s 519.5 19
JX1977 .A2 ST/STAT/SER.F/9/Rev.1, etc. QA276.6

Sampson, Frank W. Missouri fur harvests / by Frank W. Sampson ; illustrations by Charles W. Schwartz ; edited by Jim Auckley. Jefferson City, Mo. : Missouri Dept. of Conservation, 1980. 59 p. : ill. ; 28 cm. (Terrestrial series ; no. 7) Bibliography: p. 15.   LC Card 81-621615   DDC 381/.456753/09778 19

1. Fur trade - Missouri. 2. Fur-bearing animals - Missouri. 3. Mammal populations - Missouri. 4. Wildlife conservation - Missouri. I. Auckley, Jim. II. Series. III. Series: Terrestrial series , # 7. IV. Title.
HD9944.U46 M87

San Antonio Basin. Texas. Dept. of Water Resources. Projected land use maps year 2000, San Antonio Basin. Austin, Tex. , 1978. [5] leaves :   LC Card 80-675299   DDC 912/.133373/3097641 19
G1372.S22G4 T4 1978

San Antonio. Institute of Texan Cultures. see Institute of Texan Cultures.

SAN ANTONIO - OFFICIALS AND EMPLOYEES - SALARIES, ALLOWANCES, ETC.
United States. Bureau of Labor Statistics. Southwest Regional Office. Municipal government wage survey, San Antonio, Texas, November 1975 /. [Dallas] , 1976. v, 57 p. ;   LC Card 76-602063
JS1425.4 .A4 1975   *NYPL [JLF 80-1369]*

San Diego State University. Center on Aging.
Institute on Minority Aging, 3d, San Diego State University, 1975. Minority aging and the legislative process. - San Diego , c1977. xxi, 96 p. :   *NYPL [JLF 80-1458]*

San Diego State University. Institute of Public and Urban Affairs. Corso, Anthony. Job satisfaction among urban planners . [San Diego] , 1978. viii, 76 leaves ;   LC Card 79-622099
HT167.5.C2 C67   *NYPL [JLF 80-1454]*

San Diego State University. School of Public Administration and Urban Studies. Institute of Public and Urban Affairs. see San Diego State University. Institute of Public and Urban Affairs.

San Diego State University. School of Social Work. Center of Aging. see San Diego State University. Center on Aging.

SAN FRANCISCO BAY - BRIDGES - DUMBARTON BRIDGE.
California. Toll Bridge Administration. Final environmental impact statement. [Sacramento?] 1973. ca 458 p.:   *NYPL [JLF 80-591]*

San Francisco. Board of Supervisors. San Francisco. Citizens Charter Revision Committee. Final report of the San Francisco Citizens Charter Revision Committee, to the Mayor and Board of Supervisors. [San Francisco] , 1972. 75 p. :   LC Card 81-459949   DDC 342.794/6102 347.9461022 19
KFX2354 .A733

SAN FRANCISCO - BRIDGES - SAN FRANCISCO OAKLAND BAY BRIDGE.
MacCalden, M, Scott. Feasibility study of closed circuit television for traffic surveillance. [Sacramento] 1973. 74, 10 p.
                                             NYPL [JLF 80-556]

SAN FRANCISCO - CHARTERS.
San Francisco. Citizens Charter Revision Committee. Final report of the San Francisco Citizens Charter Revision Committee, to the Mayor and Board of Supervisors. [San Francisco] , 1972. 75 p. :   LC Card 81-459949   DDC 342.794/6102 347.9461022 19
KFX2354 .A733

San Francisco. Citizens Charter Revision Committee. Final report of the San Francisco Citizens Charter Revision Committee, to the Mayor and Board of Supervisors. [San Francisco] : The Committee, 1972. 75 p. : ill. ; 28 cm. Cover title.   LC Card 81-459949   DDC 342.794/6102 347.9461022 19
1. San Francisco - Charters. I. San Francisco. Mayor. II. San Francisco. Board of Supervisors.
KFX2354 .A733

SAN FRANCISCO - EARTHQUAKE, 1906.
Hansen, Gladys C., 1925- Who perished . San Francisco, CA , 1980. 4, [51] p. ;   LC Card 80-126237   DDC 929/.379461 19
F869.S353 A23

SAN FRANCISCO - FIRE, 1906.
Hansen, Gladys C., 1925- Who perished . San Francisco, CA , 1980. 4, [51] p. ;   LC Card 80-126237   DDC 929/.379461 19
F869.S353 A23

SAN FRANCISCO - GENEALOGY.
Hansen, Gladys C., 1925- Who perished . San

Francisco, CA , 1980. 4, [51] p. ;   LC Card
80-126237   DDC 929/.379461 19
F869.S353 A23

San Francisco. Mayor. San Francisco. Citizens
Charter Revision Committee. Final report of
the San Francisco Citizens Charter Revision
Committee, to the Mayor and Board of
Supervisors. [San Francisco] , 1972. 75 p. :   LC
Card 81-459949   DDC 342.794/6102
347.9461022 19
KFX2354 .A733

**San Francisco. University. see University of
California San Francisco.**

**SAN ISABEL NATIONAL FOREST, COLO. -
MAPS.**
(1972) United States. Forest Service. Rocky
Mountain Region. San Isabel National Forest,
Colorado. [Denver] 1972. col. map on sheet
115 x 66 cm. Scale 1:126,720; 1/2″ = 1 mile.
Printed on both sides of sheet. Relief shown by
hachures and spot heights. "Polyconic projection ... New
Mexico and sixth principal meridians." "Forest Service
map." "Forest visitors map." Includes col. illus., text,
map keys, listings of "Forest Service recreation sites,"
index to "Points of interest," and "Vicinity map."
"Reprinted 1978."   LC Card 74-696335
G4312.S2 1972 .U5
            NYPL   [Map Div. 80-3362]

San Jacinto Basin. Texas. Dept. of Water
Resources. Projected land use maps year 2000,
San Jacinto Basin. Austin, Tex. , 1978. [4]
leaves :   LC Card 80-675300   DDC
912/.133373/309764141 19
G1372.S24G4 T4 1978

SAN JOSE, CALIF. - CENSUS - MAPS.
United States. Bureau of the Census. Urban
atlas, tract data for standard metropolitan
statistical areas . Washington, D.C. , 1974 [i.e.
1975] [16] p. :   LC Card 80-600861   DDC
912/.1312/0979474
G1527.S33E25 U5 1975

**SAN JUAN NATIONAL FOREST, COLO. -
MAPS.**
(1974) United States. Forest Service. Rocky
Mountain Region. San Juan National Forest,
Colorado. [Denver] , 1974. col. map. on sheet
66 x 105 cm. Scale 1:126,720; 1/2″ = 1 mile.
Printed on both sides of sheet. Relief shown by
hachures and spot heights. "Polyconic projection." "New
Mexico principal meridian." "Reprinted 1976." "Forest
visitors map." "Forest Service map class A." Includes
inset of Mesa Verde National Park, 2 map keys,
"Vicinity map," "Recreation directory," text, and col.
illus.   *NYPL   [Map Div. 80-3365]*

**SAN JUAN RIVER WATERSHED (COLO.
=UTAH)**
Severson, R. C. (Ronald Charles), 1945-
Geochemical variability of natural soils and
reclaimed mine-spoil soils in the San Juan
Basin, New Mexico /. Washington , 1981. p.
cm.   LC Card 81-607985   DDC 631.6/4 19
S599.N6 S46

**SAN LUIS REY RIVER, CALIF. - WATER-
RIGHTS.**
United States. Congress. Senate. Select
Committee on Indian Affairs. Settlement of San
Luis Rey River water claims . Washington ,
1980. iii, 56 p. ;   LC Card 80-602905   DDC
346.7304/691 19
KF26.5 .I4 1980g

SAN MARTÍN, JOSÉ DE, 1778-1850.
Al libertador general San Martín . Washington,
D.C. [1978] vii, 51 p., [1] leaf of plates :   LC
Card 80-145557   DDC 980/.02/0924 B 19
F2235.4 .A677

**San Quentin, Calif. State Prison. see California.
State Prison, San Quentin.**

**SANATORIUMS - RHODE ISLAND -
HISTORY.**
Rhode Island. Health Planning & Resources
Development. The story of private hospitals in
Rhode Island . [Providence] , 1979. 69 p. :
LC Card 80-620722   DDC 362.1/1/09745 19
RA981.R4 R5 1979

SANCTIONS (INTERNATIONAL LAW)
United States. Congress. House. Committee on
Foreign Affairs. Rhodesian sanctions, should
the United States lift them? . Washington ,
1980. iii, 80 p. ;   LC Card 80-601130   DDC
327.7306891 19
KF27 .F6 1979j

**SAND AND GRAVEL INDUSTRY -
ENVIRONMENTAL ASPECTS - ALASKA.**
Burger, Carl. Environmental surveillance of
gravel removal on the Trans-Alaska Pipeline
System, with recommendations for future gravel
mining /. Anchorage, Alaska , 1977. 35 leaves :
LC Card 79-625780   DDC 333.95/4 19
TD195.S3 B87

**SAND-DUNES - LAW AND LEGISLATION -
NEW JERSEY.**
New Jersey. Legislature. General Assembly.
Energy and Natural Resources Committee.
Public hearing before Assembly Energy and
Natural Resources Committee on A-1825, Dune
and shorefront protection act. [Trenton] [1980]
2 v. ;   LC Card 80-623987   DDC 346.74904/6917
347.490646917 19
KFN1811.4 .E53 1980

**SAND-DUNES - MICHIGAN -
CLASSIFICATION.**
Buckler, William R. Dune type inventory and
barrier dune classification study of Michigan's
Lake Michigan shore /. Lansing, Mich. , 1979.
v, 20, [11] p. :   LC Card 80-622269   DDC 557.74
s 333.91/7 19
QE125 .A417 no. 23 GB635.M5

**SAND FILTERS. see SEWAGE -
PURIFICATION - FILTRATION;
WATER - PURIFICATION -
FILTRATION.**

**SAND - FLORIDA - BREVARD COUNTY -
MAPS.**
United States. Soil Conservation Service.
Brevard County, Florida . Fort Worth, Tex. ,
1980. 1 map :   LC Card 81-690350
G3933.B7H5 1980 .U5

The sandal and the cave . Cressman, Luther
Sheeleigh, 1897- Corvallis, Or. , c1981. xiii, 81
p. ;   ISBN 0-87071-078-8   LC Card 81-915   DDC
979.5/00497 19
E78.O6 C72 1981

Sande, Innis. (joint author) Burke, Mary.
Inter-American investigation of mortality in
childhood . Washington, D.C. , 1979. v, 145
p. :   ISBN 92-75-11386-6 (pbk.) :   LC Card
80-132481   DDC 362.1/09181/2 s 304.6/4 19
RA10 .P252 no. 386 HB1323.C5

Sanders, Charles Leonard, 1938- Hanford Life
Sciences Symposium, 19th, Richland, Wash.,
1979. Pulmonary toxicology of respirable
particles . Oak Ridge, Tenn. , 1980. xi, 676 p. :
ISBN 0-87079-121-4   LC Card 80-22907   DDC
616.2/44 19
RC756 .H3 1979

Sanders, Herman O. Abate - effects of the
organophosphate insecticide on bluegills and
invertebrates in ponds / by Herman O. Sanders,
David F. Walsh, Robert S. Campbell.
Washington, D.C. : United States Dept. of the
Interior, Fish and Wildlife Service, 1981. 6 p. :
ill. ; 26 cm. (Technical papers of the U. S. Fish and
Wildlife Service . 104)   LC Card 80-606806   DDC
639 s 628.9/657 19
*1. Temephos - Physiological effect. 2. Insecticides -
Environmental aspects. 3. Fishes, Effect of water
pollution on. 4. Bluegill - Physiology. I. Walsh, David
F., joint author. II. Campbell, Robert Seymour, 1913-
joint author. III. Series: United States. Fish and Wildlife
Service. Technical papers of the U. S. Fish and Wildlife
Service , 104. IV. Title.*
SH11 .A313 no. 104 SH177.P44

Sanders, Hyman.
Chaikind, Stephen. Paying for social security .
[Washington, D.C.], 1981. xix, 47 p. ;   LC Card
81-601225   DDC 353.0082/56 19
HD7125 .C47

United States. Congressional Budget Office.
Indexing the individual income tax for inflation
/. [Washington, D.C.] [1980] xv, 81 p. ;   LC
Card 80-603390   DDC 336.24/2/0973 19
HJ4637 .U53 1980

Sanders, M. Elizabeth, 1943- The regulation of
natural gas : policy and politics, 1938-1978 /
M. Elizabeth Sanders. Philadelphia : Temple
University Press, 1981. p. cm. Includes
bibiliographical references and index.   ISBN
0-87722-221-5 :   LC Card 81-9239   DDC
333.8/23317/0973 19
*1. Gas industry - Government policy - United States. 2.
Gas - Law and legislation - United States. 3. Trade*

regulation - Economic aspects - United States. I. Title.
HD9581.U5 S26

Sanders, Nell S. Programs of developmental
studies in Missouri State-supported institutions
of higher education / Nell S. Sanders.
[Jefferson City] : Missouri Dept. of Higher
Education, [1978] 65 leaves : forms ; 28 cm. "A
consultant report to the Missouri Department of Higher
Education."   LC Card 79-621793   DDC
379.1/54/09778 19
*1. Competency based education - Missouri. 2. State
universities and colleges - Missouri. I. Missouri. Dept.
of Higher Education. II. Title.*
LC1032.5.M8 S26

Sandhills lakes. McCarraher, D. Bruce.
Nebraska's sandhills lakes /. Lincoln , 1977. 67
p. :   LC Card 77-623677   DDC 574.5/2636 19
QH105.N2 M32

Sandier, S. Comparison of health expenditures in
France and the United States / S. Sandier.
Hyattsville, Md. : U. S. Dept. of Health and
Human Services, Public Health Service, Office
of the Assistant Secretary for Health, National
Center for Health Statistics, 1981. p. cm. (Vital
and health statistics : Series 3, analytical studies . no.
21) DHHS publications ; no. (PHS) 81-1405.
Bibliography: p.   ISBN 0-8406-0224-3   LC Card
81-11078   DDC 338.4/736210944 19
*1. Medical care, Cost of - United States. 2. Medical
care, Cost of - France. 3. Medical care - United States -
Finance. 4. Medical care - France - Finance. I. Series:
DHHS publication, no. (PHS) 81-1405. II. Title.*
RA410.53 .S26

Sands, Anne. Riparian forests in California .
[Berkeley, Ca.] , c1980. vi, 122 p. :   ISBN
0-931876-41-9 (pbk.) :   LC Card 80-624097
DDC 574.5/2642 19
QH105.C2 R56

**SANDSTONE - MONTANA - BEARPAW
MOUNTAINS REGION.**
Gautier, Donald L. Petrology of the Eagle
Sandstone, Bearpaw Mountains area,
north-central Montana /. Washington [1981] p.
cm.   LC Card 81-607963   DDC 557.3 s 552/.5 19
QE75 .B9 no. 1521 QE471.15.S25

Sandwich Islands. see Hawaii.

SANDY SOILS - FLORIDA.
Movement of fertilizer and herbicide through
irrigated sands /. [Gainesville] , 1976. iv, 50
p. :   LC Card 77-623198   DDC 631.5/87/09759 19
S616.U6 M68

**SANDY SOILS - FLORIDA - BREVARD
COUNTY - MAPS.**
United States. Soil Conservation Service.
Brevard County, Florida . Fort Worth, Tex. ,
1980. 1 map :   LC Card 81-690350
G3933.B7H5 1980 .U5

Sanford, John Elliot, 1830-1907. Massachusetts.
Laws, statutes, etc. Laws of the Commonwealth
of Massachusetts relating to insurance and
insurance companies . Boston , 1870. 99 p. :
LC Card 80-110113   DDC 346.755/086/02632
347.55068602632 19
KFM2585 .A3 1870

Sanghi, Ajay K. Illinois. Bureau of the Budget.
Office of Planning. The impact of the 1977-78
coal miners' strike on Illinois electric utilities.
[Springfield] [1979] 57 p. :   LC Card 80-621483
DDC 338.4/736362 19
HD9685.U6 I25 1979a

SANITARY AFFAIRS. see PUBLIC HEALTH.

**SANITARY BACTERIOLOGY. see SANITARY
MICROBIOLOGY.**

**SANITARY ENGINEERING - ECONOMIC
ASPECTS - NEW YORK (STATE)**
New York (State). Division of Land Resources
and Forest Management. Resources Program
Development. The environmental control
industry in New York State . [Albany] [1979]
iv, 73 p. ;   LC Card 80-622827   DDC
338.4/7628/09747 19
TD24.N7 N47 1979

**SANITARY FILLS. see SANITARY
LANDFILLS.**

SANITARY LANDFILLS - UNITED STATES.
United States. Office of Solid Waste
Management Programs. Hazardous Waste
Management Division. An environmental
assessment of potential gas and leachate

problems at land disposal sites /. -
[Washington] , 1973 [i. e. 1975] v, 33 p. ;
NYPL [*ZV-185 Reel 1]

SANITARY MICROBIOLOGY.
(1977) Seidler, Ramon J. Health significance of
Klebsiella pneumoniae in drinking water
emanating from redwood tanks /. Corvallis,
Or. , 1977. 81 p. :   LC Card 78-624331   DDC
333.91/009795 s 628.1/3 19
HD1694.O7 A13 no. 54 QR48

(1978) Stinebring, Warren R. Endotoxin in
waters of the State of Vermont /. [Montpelier]
[1978?] iv leaves, 25 p. ;   LC Card 79-624701
DDC 363.7/394 19
QR48 .S74

(1979) Hain, Kathleen E. The survival of
enteric viruses in septic tanks and septic tank
drain fields /. Las Cruces, N.M. [1979] x, 73
p. :   LC Card 80-621472   DDC 628/.742 19
GB705.N6 N64 no. 108 QR48

(1979) Utah Water Research Laboratory.
Studies on viruses in water /. Logan, Utah ,
1979. viii, 35 p. :   LC Card 80-621126   DDC
628.3 19
QR48 .U8 1979

**SANITARY MICROBIOLOGY - NORTH
DAKOTA - METIGOSHE LAKE.**
North Dakota. Agricultural Experiment Station,
Fargo. Bacteriological analyses of Lake
Metigoshe water and sediments /. Fargo , 1978.
ii, 14 p. :   LC Card 79-625005   DDC
363.7/3942/0978461 19
QR48 .N67 1978

SANITARY MICROBIOLOGY - TECHNIQUE.
Double, Mark L. Recovery of sanitary-indicator
bacteria from streams containing acid mine
water /. Morgantown , 1978. v, 30 p. :   LC
Card 78-622769   DDC 333.91/009754 s
628.1/6832/0287 19
QC986.W4 W46 no. 11 QR48

Janardan, K. G. Recovery of coliforms by the
MPN and MF techniques using a 2n - factorial
experimental design /. Chicago , 1977. iii, 39
p. :   LC Card 77-624164   DDC 628.1/682/0287 19
QR48 .J36

SANITARY MICROBIOLOGY - VIRGINIA.
Erkenbrecher, Carl W. Sediment bacteria as a
water quality indicator in the Lynnhaven
estuary /. Blacksburg, Va. [1980] x, 118 p. :
LC Card 80-622517   DDC 333.91/009755 s
628.168/028/7 19
TD201 .V57 no. 126 QR48

Sant, Donald. (joint author) Ippolito, Richard A.
Staff report on consumer responses to cigarette
health information /. [Washington] , 1979. 64
p. ;   LC Card 79-604242
HV5760 .I66   **NYPL [JLF 81-240]**

**SANTA ANA, CALIF. - BUILDINGS - GUIDE-
BOOKS.**
Weidman, Michael. Santa Ana's architectural
heritage . Santa Ana , c1980. 65 p. :   LC Card
80-137507   DDC 917.94/96 19
NA735.S4 W44

**SANTA ANA, CALIF. - DWELLINGS - GUIDE-
BOOKS.**
Weidman, Michael. Santa Ana's architectural
heritage . Santa Ana , c1980. 65 p. :   LC Card
80-137507   DDC 917.94/96 19
NA735.S4 W44

Santa Ana Historic Survey. Weidman, Michael.
Santa Ana's architectural heritage . Santa Ana ,
c1980. 65 p. :   LC Card 80-137507   DDC
917.94/96 19
NA735.S4 W44

Santa Ana's architectural heritage . Weidman,
Michael. Santa Ana , c1980. 65 p. :   LC Card
80-137507   DDC 917.94/96 19
NA735.S4 W44

The Santa Barbara bicentennial historical series.
(no. 5) Hageman, Fred C. An archeological and
restoration study of Mission La Purísima
Concepción . Santa Barbara, Calif. , Glendale,
Calif. , 1980. xxxi, 307 p. :   LC Card 79-64806
F869.P89 H33   **NYPL [IXH (Purísima
Concepción Mission) 81-684]**

**SANTA BARBARA, CALIF. - EARTHQUAKE,
1978 - CHARTS, DIAGRAMS, ETC.**
Porter, Lawrence Delpino, 1932- Processed data
from the strong-motion records of the Santa
Barbara earthquake of 13 August 1978 .

Sacramento, CA , 1979. 3 v. :   LC Card
80-622289   DDC 557.94 s 551.2/2/0979491 19
TN24.C2 A33 no. 144 QE535.2.U6

**Santa Barbara College, Santa Barbara, Calif.
(Founded 1943) see California. University,
Santa Barbara.**

Santa Barbara Museum of Art. Larson, Judy L.
Enchanted images . Santa Barbara, Calif. ,
1980. 68 p. :   ISBN 0-89951-038-8 (pbk.)   LC Card
80-53811   DDC 741.64/2/0973 19
NC975 .L37

Santa Barbara Trust for Historic Preservation.
Hageman, Fred C. An archeological and
restoration study of Mission La Purísima
Concepción . Santa Barbara, Calif. , Glendale,
Calif. , 1980. xxxi, 307 p. :   LC Card 79-64806
F869.P89 H33   **NYPL [IXH (Purísima
Concepción Mission) 81-684]**

**SANTA CLARA PUEBLO (N.M.) - SOCIAL
LIFE AND CUSTOMS.**
Hill, W. W. (Willard Williams), 1902-1974.
Ethnography of Santa Clara Pueblo, New
Mexico /. Albuquerque , c1981. p. cm.   ISBN
0-8263-0555-5   LC Card 80-52277   DDC
970.004/97 19
E99.T35 H5 1981

Santa Clara Valley Water District. California.
Dept. of Water Resources. Anderson Reservoir
limnologic investigation . [Sacramento] , 1978.
x, 240 p. :   LC Card 78-623877   DDC
574.92/9/79473 19
QH105.C2 C34 1978

**Santa Fe daily New Mexican. see Santa Fe New
Mexican.**

SANTA FE, N. M. - DESCRIPTION.
Kraft, James. John Sloan in Santa Fe .
Washington, D.C. , 1981. p. cm.   ISBN
0-86528-011-8   LC Card 81-607831   DDC
759.13 19
ND237.S476 A4 1981

Santa Fe, N. M. School of American Research.
(Old Catalog form: Schools of American
Research, Santa Fe, N. M.)
The New Mexico historical review. v. 1- ;
1926- Santa Fe, N. M.   **NYPL [IAA (New
Mexico historical review.)]**

Santa Fe New Mexican. New Mexico (Ter.).
Legislative Assembly. House of Representatives.
State of New Mexico: House [proceedings],
1907. [Santa Fe, 1907] 43 leaves;
NYPL [*ZT-1265]

**Santa Fe New Mexican and review. see Santa Fe
New Mexican.**

**Santa Fe New Mexican review. see Santa Fe
New Mexican.**

SANTA FE (N.M.) IN ART - EXHIBITIONS.
Kraft, James. John Sloan in Santa Fe .
Washington, D.C. , 1981. p. cm.   ISBN
0-86528-011-8   LC Card 81-607831   DDC
759.13 19
ND237.S476 A4 1981

SANTA FE TRAIL.
Russell, Marian Sloan, 1845-1937. Land of
enchantment . Albuquerque [1981] c1954. xiv,
163 p. :   ISBN 0-8263-0571-7 :   LC Card 80-54564
DDC 917.8 19
F786 .R96 1981

**Santa Momica Hospital Medical Center. Center
for the Partially Sighted. see Center for the
Partially Sighted.**

**Santa Monica, Calif. Center for the Partially
sighted. see Center for the Partially Sighted.**

Santamour, Miles. Retardation, corrections, and
retarded offenders : a bibliography of relevant
research, programs, and literature, with
annotations / by Miles Santamour and
Bernadette West. Washington : U. S. Dept. of
Health, Education, and Welfare, President's
Committee on Mental Retardation, [1979] i,
156 p. ;   28 cm. (DHEW publication ; no. (HDS)
79-21025)   LC Card 79-604176   DDC 016.3646 19
1. Mentally handicapped and crime - United States -
Bibliography. I. West, Bernadette, joint author. II.
Series: United States. Dept. of Health, Education and
Welfare. DHEW publication, no. (HDS) 79-21025. III.
Title.
Z5703.4.M46 S26 1979 HV6791

Santelli, James S. A brief history of the 7th
Marines / by James S. Santelli. Washington,

D.C. : History and Museums Division,
Headquarters, U. S. Marine Corps, 1980. vii, 83
p. :   ill., maps ;   27 cm. Includes bibliographical
references.   LC Card 81-600697   DDC 359.9/6/0973
19
1. United States. Marine Corps. Marines, 7th History. I.
United States. Marine Corps. History and Museums
Division. II. Title.
VE23.25 7th .S25

Santerre, Michael T. A computerized selected
bibliography on relevant aspects of the
aquaculture of unicellular and filamentous algae
/ edited by Michael T. Santerre, Gordon L.
Dugan, Patrick K. Takahashi. Honolulu :
Hawaii Natural Energy Institute, University of
Hawaii at Manoa : Dept. of Planning and
Economic Development, State of Hawaii,
[1978] ca. 400 p. ;   28 cm. "September 1978."   LC
Card 79-623030   DDC 016.639 19
1. Algae culture - Bibliography. I. Dugan, G. L., joint
author. II. Takahashi, Patrick K., joint author. III.
Hawaii Natural Energy Institute. IV. Hawaii. Dept. of
Planning and Economic Development. V. Title.
Z5973.A45 S26 SH389

SAP.
Gibbs, Carter B. The effect of xylem age on
volume yield & sugar content of sugar maple
sap /. Upper Darby, Pa. , 1969. 11 p. :ill.   LC
Card 75-605745   DDC 333.76/0974 s 633.3/4 19
SD11 .A455493 no. 141 SB239.M3

**SAPELO ISLAND (GA.) - ANTIQUITIES -
ADDRESSES, ESSAYS, LECTURES.**
Sapelo papers . Carrollton, Ga. , 1980. vii, 114
p. :   LC Card 81-620962   DDC 975.8/733 19
F292.M15 S26

**SAPELO ISLAND (GA.) - DESCRIPTION
AND TRAVEL.**
Teal, Mildred. Portrait of an island /. Athens,
Ga. [1981] p. cm.   ISBN 0-8203-0585-5   LC Card
81-7631   DDC 574.9758/737 19
QH105.G4 T4 1981

**SAPELO ISLAND (GA.) - HISTORY -
ADDRESSE, ESSAYS, LECTURES.**
Sapelo papers . Carrollton, Ga. , 1980. vii, 114
p. :   LC Card 81-620962   DDC 975.8/733 19
F292.M15 S26

Sapelo papers : researches in the history and
prehistory of Sapelo Island, Georgia / [Daniel
P. Juengst, volume editor]. Carrollton, Ga. :
West Georgia College, 1980. vii, 114 p. :   ill.,
maps ;   23 cm. (Studies in the social sciences. v. 19)
Cover title. Bibliography: p. 109-114.   LC Card
81-620962   DDC 975.8/733 19
1. Sapelo Island (Ga.) - History - Addresse, essays,
lectures. 2. Sapelo Island (Ga.) - Antiquities -
Addresses, essays, lectures. 3. Indians of North
America - Georgia - Sapelo Island - Antiquities -
Addresses, essays, lectures. 4. Excavations
(Archaeology) - Georgia - Sapelo Island - Addresses,
essays, lectures. 5. Georgia - Antiquities - Addresses,
essays, lectures. I. Juengst, Daniel P. II. Series: Studies
in the social sciences (West Georgia College) , v. 19.
F292.M15 S26

Sapienza, Diane. (joint author) Mubarak, Jill.
Gerontology and the law . Los Angeles, Calif. ,
1979. xiv, 102 p. ;   LC Card 79-123375   DDC
016.34473/0326 19
KF390.A4 M8

Saratoga Performing Arts Center. Fifteen under
forty. [Albany, N.Y., 1970] 1 v. (unpaged)   LC
Card 72-633963
ND238.N5 F5

Sargent, Merle J. Rural health and rural health
care, U. S. and Idaho / Merle J. Sargent.
Moscow : Agricultural Experiment Station,
University of Idaho, College of Agriculture,
1980. 43, [11] p. :   graphs ;   28 cm. (Progress
report - Agricultural Experiment Station, University of
Idaho ; no. 211) Cover title. Bibliography: p. [44]-[46]
LC Card 80-622141   DDC 362.1/0425 19
1. Rural health - United States. 2. Rural health
services - United States. 3. United States - Rural
conditions. 4. Rural health - Idaho. 5. Rural health
services - Idaho. I. Series: Idaho. Agricultural
Experiment Station, Moscow. Progress report -
Agricultural Experiment Station, University of Idaho ,
no. 211. II. Title.
RA771.5 .S27

SARPY COUNTY (NEB.) - MAPS.
United States. Soil Conservation Service. Sarpy
County, Nebraska /. Lincoln, Nebr. , 1978. 1

map :   LC Card 81-691003
G4193.S3 1978 .U5

Satellite Conference on Naltrexone, Richmond, 1976. Narcotic antagonists, naltrexone : progress report / editors, Demetrios Julius, Pierre Renault. Rockville, Md. : U. S. Dept. of Health, Education, and Welfare, Public Health Service, Alcohol, Drug Abuse and Mental Health Administration ; Springfield, Va. : for sale by National Technical Information Service], 1976. x, 181 p. : ill. ; 27 cm. (NIDA research monograph series ; 9) DHEW publication ; no. (ADM) 76-387 Papers presented at the Satellite Naltrexone Conference, held June 6 and 7, 1976, in Richmond, Va. Includes bibliographies.   LC Card 76-40692   DDC 615/.7822 19
1. Naloxone - Congresses. 2. Heroin habit - Treatment - Congresses. I. Julius, Demetrios. II. Renault, Pierre, 1936-. III. Series: National Institute on Drug Abuse. NIDA research monograph series, no. 9.
RC568.H4 S27 1976

SATELLITE VEHICLES. see SPACE STATIONS.

SATELLITES - JUPITER.
Satellites of Jupiter /. Tucson, Ariz. , c1981. p. cm.   ISBN 0-8165-0762-7 :   LC Card 81-13050   DDC 523.4/5 19
QB404 .S34

SATELLITES, LANDSAT. see LANDSAT SATELLITES.

Satellites of Jupiter / edited by David Morrison, with the assistance of Mildred Shapley Matthews ; with 47 collaborating authors. Tucson, Ariz. : University of Arizona Press, c1981. p. cm. (Space science series) Includes index.   ISBN 0-8165-0762-7 :   LC Card 81-13050   DDC 523.4/5 19
1. Satellites - Jupiter. I. Morrison, David, 1940-. II. Matthews, Mildred Shapley. III. Series.
QB404 .S34

Sather classical lectures .
(v. 48) Dihle, Albrecht. The theory of will in classical antiquity /. Berkeley , c1982. p. cm.   ISBN 0-520-04059-7   LC Card 81-7424   DDC 128/.3 19
B187.F7 D54

SATIRE - PERIODICALS.
Studies in contemporary satire. Clarion, Pa.
NYPL [JFK 80-293]

Satterfield, R. D. British Columbia. Ministry of Mines and Petroleum Resources. Pipelines of British Columbia /. [Victoria] [1978] 1 map ; 73 x 92 cm. Scale 1:1,900,800; 30 miles to 1 in. Photocopy. "May 1978." Inset: Fort St. John area.   LC Card 79-691292
G3511.P4 1978 .B7
NYPL [Map Div. 81-3030]

SAUCERS, FLYING. see UNIDENTIFIED FLYING OBJECTS.

SAUDI ARABIA - FOREIGN RELATIONS - UNITED STATES.
Gold, Fern R. Access to oil . [Washington , 1977. xiii, 113 p. ;   LC Card 78-600524
HD9566 .G64   **NYPL [JLE 81-460]**

Saul, Louella Rankin. The North Pacific cretaceous Trigoniid genus Yaadia / by Louella R. Saul. Berkeley : University of California Press, 1978. 65 p., 12 leaves of plates : ill. ; 26 cm. (University of California publications in geological sciences ; v. 119) Bibliography: p. 60-65.   ISBN 0-520-09582-0   LC Card 77-84990   DDC 564/.11 19
1. Trigoniidae. 2. Paleontology - Cretaceous. 3. Paleontology - California. 4. Paleontology - Oregon. I. Series: California. University. University of California publications in geological sciences , v. 119. II. Title.
QE812.T74 S28

SAUNDERS COUNTY (NEB.) - MAPS.
United States. Soil Conservation Service. Saunders County, Nebraska /. Lincoln, Nebr. , 1978. 1 map :   LC Card 81-691002
G4193.S35 1978 .U5

Saunders, Dorothy Chapman. Saunders, George Bradford, 1907- Waterfowl and their wintering grounds in Mexico, 1937-64 /. Washington, D.C. , 1981. p. cm.   LC Card 81-607010   DDC 333.95/4 s 598.4/1 19
S914 .A3 no. 138a QL696.A5

Saunders, George Bradford, 1907- Waterfowl and their wintering grounds in Mexico, 1937-64 /

by George B. Saunders, Dorothy Chapman Saunders. Washington, D.C. : U. S. Dept. of the Interior, Fish and Wildlife Service, 1981. p. cm. (Resource publication . no. 138) Includes bibliographical references.   LC Card 81-607010   DDC 333.95/4 s 598.4/1 19
1. Waterfowl - Mexico. 2. Waterfowl - Mexico - Wintering. 3. Birds - Mexico. 4. Birds - Wintering. I. Saunders, Dorothy Chapman. II. Series: Resource publication (U. S. Fish and Wildlife Service) , no. 138. III. Title.
S914 .A3 no. 138a QL696.A5

Saunders, Hyman. A review of the accuracy of treasury revenue forecasts, 1963-1978 / the Congress of the United States, Congressional Budget Office. [Washington, D.C.] : The Office, 1981. xi, 42 p. ; 26 cm. Staff working paper "February 1981"--Cover. Item 1005-C Includes bibliographical references.   LC Card 81-601118   DDC 353.0072/2252 19
1. Tax revenue estimating - United States. 2. United States. Treasury Dept. I. United States. Congressional Budget Office. II. Title.
HJ2051 .S26

Saupe, William E. Changes in farm poverty in Wisconsin / William E. Saupe, William R. Garland, Deborah Streeter. [Madison] : University of Wisconsin-Madison, Institute for Research on Poverty, [1979] 24 p. ; 28 cm. (Discussion papers - University of Wisconsin-Madison, Institute for Research on Poverty ; DP 583-79) "November 1979." Bibliography: p. 22-24.   LC Card 80-622902   DDC 338.1/3/09775 19
1. Rural poor - Wisconsin. 2. Agriculture - Economic aspects - Wisconsin. I. Garland, William R., joint author. II. Streeter, Deborah, joint author. III. Series: Wisconsin. University, Madison. Institute for Research on Poverty. Discussion papers, 583-79. IV. Title.
HC107.W63 P6246

Savage, Eldon P. National household pesticide usage study, 1976-1977 : final report / Eldon P. Savage, Thomas J. Keefe, H. William Wheeler. Washington, D.C. : U. S. Environmental Protection Agency, Office of Pesticide Programs, [1979] cover 1980. ix, 126 p. : ill. ; 28 cm. "EPA 540/9-80-002." "November 1979." Includes bibliographical references.   LC Card 80-603384   DDC 363.7/384 19
1. Household pests - Control - United States. 2. Garden pests - Control - United States. 3. Pesticides - United States. I. Keefe, Thomas J., joint author. II. Wheeler, H. William, joint author. III. United States. Environmental Protection Agency. Office of Pesticide Programs. IV. Title.
TX325 .S28

Savage, N. L. (joint author) Rabe, Fred W. Aquatic natural areas in Idaho /. Moscow, Idaho [1977] 103 p., [7] leaves of plates :   LC Card 80-621482   DDC 333.95/2/09796 19
QH76.5.I2 R33

Savanick, George A. Water jet perforation : a new method of completing and stimulating in situ leaching wells / by G. A. Savanick and W. G. Krawza. Washington, D.C. : U. S. Dept. of the Interior, Bureau of Mines, 1981. p. cm. (Report of investigations / Bureau of Mines ; Bibliography: p.   LC Card 80-607781   DDC 622 s 622/.184932 19
1. In situ processing (Mining). 2. Jet cutting. 3. Uranium mines and mining. I. Krawza, Walter G., joint author. II. Series: United States Bureau of Mines. Report of investigations , . III. Title.
TN23 .U43 TN278.3

Savannah River Plant, Aiken and Barnwell Counties, South Carolina. Hanson, Glen T. The preliminary archeological inventory of the Savannah River Plant, Aiken and Barnwell Counties, South Carolina /. Columbia , 1978. viii, 166 p. :   LC Card 79-620819   DDC 975.7/75 19
E78.S6 H38

Save the Children Day, 1980 . United States. Congress. Senate. Committee on Labor and Human Resources. Subcommittee on Child and Human Development. Washington , 1980. iii, 18 p. ;   LC Card 80-603311   DDC 362.7/95/0973 19
KF26 .L273 1980

SAVING AND INVESTMENT - UNITED STATES.
United States. Congress. House. Committee on Small Business. Subcommittee on Access to Equity Capital and Business Opportunities. Inventory accounting as a burden on the capital

formation process . Washington , 1980- v. ;   LC Card 80-601994   DDC 346.73/0652 19
KF27 .S63 1980

United States. Congress. House. Committee on Ways and Means. Tax incentives for savings . Washington , 1980. vii, 774 p. :   LC Card 80-602478   DDC 343.7305/23 19
KF27 .W3 1980c

United States. Congress. Joint Economic Committee. Savings and economic growth . Washington , 1981. iii, 54 p. ;   LC Card 81-601400   DDC 332/.0415/0973 19
KF25 .E2 1980l

United States. General Accounting Office. An analytical framework for federal policies and programs influencing capital formation in the United States . Washington, D.C. , 1980. v, 80 p. :   LC Card 80-603955   DDC 332/.0415/0973 19
HC110.S3 U63 1980

SAVING AND INVESTMENT - UNITED STATES - EFFECT OF INFLATION ON.
United States. Congress. Joint Economic Committee. Capital formation and inflation . Washington , 1980. iii, 108 p. :   LC Card 80-604035   DDC 332/.0415/0973 19
KF25 .E2 1980g

SAVING AND THRIFT.
United States. Congress. House. Committee on Ways and Means. Tax incentives for savings . Washington , 1980. vii, 774 p. :   LC Card 80-602478   DDC 343.7305/23 19
KF27 .W3 1980c

SAVING-BANKS - LAW AND LEGISLATION - UNITED STATES.
United States. Congress. Senate. Committee on Banking, Housing and Urban Affairs. Cross-industry takeovers between commercial banks and thrift institutions . Washington , 1980 [i.e. 1981] iv, 148 p. ;   LC Card 81-601367   DDC 346.73/082 347.30682 19
KF26 .B39 1980aa

SAVINGS ACCOUNTS - UNITED STATES - STATISTICS.
United States. Federal Home Loan Bank Board. Summary of savings accounts by geographic area . Washington, D.C. [1979] 2, 141 p. ;   LC Card 80-602040   DDC 332.3/2/0973 19
HG2151 .U52 1979

Savings and economic growth . United States. Congress. Joint Economic Committee. Washington , 1981. iii, 54 p. ;   LC Card 81-601400   DDC 332/.0415/0973 19
KF25 .E2 1980l

SAVINGS-BANKS - MARYLAND.
Maryland. Laws, statutes, etc. Laws relating to State banks, trust companies, and savings institutions in force in the State of Maryland /. [Baltimore] 1916. 42 p. :   LC Card 78-109967   DDC 346.752/082/02632 19
KFM1365 .A3 1916

SAVINGS-BANKS - UNITED STATES.
United States. Interagency Task force on Thrift Institutions. The report of the Interagency Task Force on Thrift Institutions . Washington , 1980. viii, 267 p. ;   LC Card 80-603280   DDC 332.2/0973 19
HG2151 .U53 1980

Savio, John A. (joint author) Double, Mark L. Recovery of sanitary-indicator bacteria from streams containing acid mine water /. Morgantown , 1978. v, 30 p. :   LC Card 78-622769   DDC 333.91/009754 s 628.1/6832/0287 19
QC986.W4 W46 no. 11 QR48

Savitt, Mark, 1953- 112 Workshop, 112 Greene Street, 1970-1978 . New York , 1981. p. cm.   ISBN 0-8147-1037-9 :   LC Card 78-71391   DDC 700/.6/07471 19
NX511.N4 A16

SAWDUST. see WOOD WASTE.

SAWHILL, JOHN C., 1936-
United States. Congress. Senate. Committee on Energy and Natural Resources. Synthetic Fuels Corporation nominations . Washington , 1980. iii, 185 p. ;   LC Card 80-603446   DDC 353.09/2 19
KF26 .E55 1980h

SAWMILL WORKERS - DISEASES AND HYGIENE - CALIFORNIA - STATISTICS.
California. Dept. of Industrial Relations. Division of Labor Statistics and Research.

California sawmills and planing mills industry . San Francisco , 1978. v, 26 p. ; LC Card 79-623207 DDC 312/.43/09794 19
RC965.W6 C28 1978

SAWMILLS - CALIFORNIA - ACCIDENTS - STATISTICS.
California. Dept. of Industrial Relations. Division of Labor Statistics and Research. California sawmills and planing mills industry . San Francisco , 1978. v, 26 p. ; LC Card 79-623207 DDC 312/.43/09794 19
RC965.W6 C28 1978

Sawtooth Mountain. Mount Livermore and Sawtooth Mountain /. [Austin] , 1973. 84 p., [1] leaf of plates : LC Card 80-623871 DDC 508.764/934 19
QH105.T4 M68

Sawyer, Ann L. Procedures to be followed for the placement of children with special needs in educational programs : a comparison between the Administrative Procedure Act and regulations of the Department of Public Instruction, the Department of Human Resources, and the United States Department of Health, Education, and Welfare / compiled by Ann L. Sawyer and H. Rutherford Turnbull III. Chapel Hill : Institute of Government, University of North Carolina at Chapel Hill, [1979] 58 p. ; 28 cm. LC Card 81-621674 DDC 344.756/0791 347.5604791 19
1. Handicapped children - Education - Law and legislation - North Carolina. 2. Handicapped children - Education - Law and legislation - United States. I. Turnbull, H. Rutherford. II. University of North Carolina at Chapel Hill. Institute of Government. III. Title.
KFN7795.9.H3 S28

Sawyer, Dwight L. Maysilles, J. H. (James H.) Aluminum chloride hexahydrate crystallization by HCl gas sparging /. Avondale, MD , 1981. p. cm. LC Card 81-607822 DDC 622 s 622/.34926 19
TN23 .U43 TP245.A4

Sawyer, John C. (joint author) Kreplick, Ruth. Effectiveness of information transfer through water resources researcher/user group interaction /. Amherst , 1976. xvii, 144 p. ; LC Card 78-622292 DDC 333.91/009744 s 333.91/0072 19
TD224.M4 M37 no. 73

SAXITOXIN - ANALYSIS.
Nevé, Richard A. Development of a chemical assay for saxitoxin or paralytic shellfish poison (PSP) . Fairbanks , 1978. iv, 23 leaves : LC Card 78-623526 DDC 634/.9 19
QP632.S27 N48

Sayers, Mollie. Theories on drug abuse . Rockville, Md. . xli, 488 p. : LC Card 80-600058 DDC 616.86/3 19
RC564 .T5

Sayers, Robert. Rinzler, Ralph. The Meaders family, north Georgia potters /. Washington, D.C. , 1981. p. cm. LC Card 81-607995 DDC 738/.092/2 B 19
NK4210.M35 R56

SBA legislative request . United States. Congress. House. Committee on Small Business. Subcommittee on SBA and SBIC Authority and General Small Business Problems. Washington , 1980. iii, 46 p. ; LC Card 80-603112 DDC 346.73/0652 19
KF27 .S6814 1980

SBA' paperwork measurement and reduction program . United States. Congress. Senate. Select Committee on Small Business. Washington , 1980. iii, 153 p. : LC Card 80-603688 DDC 353.0082/048 19
KF26.5 .S6 1980n

SBA proposed size standards . United States. Congress. House. Committee on Small Business. Subcommittee on General Oversight and Minority Enterprise. Washington , 1980- v. ; LC Card 80-603083 DDC 338.6/42/0973 19
KF27 .S64 1980b

SBA surety bond guarantee program . United States. Congress. Senate. Select Committee on Small Business. Washington , 1980 [i.e. 1981] iv, 320 p. : LC Card 81-601160 DDC 353.0082/048045 19
KF26.5 .S6 1980w

SCALES (FISHES)
Kissner, Paul D. Annual performance report for a study of chinook salmon in southeast Alaska /. Juneau [1974] 30 p. ; LC Card 81-454187 DDC 597/.55 19
QL638.S2 K56 1974

SCALING, PSYCHOLOGICAL. see PSYCHOMETRICS.

SCALING (SOCIAL SCIENCES)
Cox, Eli Peace. The optimal number of response alternatives for a scale . Austin, Tex. [1980] 43, [8] p. ; LC Card 80-624133 DDC 300/.1/5195 19
H61 .C68

Scammell, Geoffrey Vaughn. The world encompassed : the first European maritime empires, c. 800-1650 / G.V. Scammell. Berkeley : University of California Press, 1981. p. cm. Includes bibliographical references and index. ISBN 0-520-04422-3 LC Card 81-4302 DDC 940.1 19
1. Europe - History - 476-1492. 2. Europe - History - 1492-1648. 3. Discoveries (in geography). I. Title.
D104 .S35

Scarlata, Leslie. (joint author) O'Connor, Linda. Enrollments of students in N.J. colleges and universities by age category, fall 1977 and fall 1978 /. [Trenton] [1979] [47] p. ; LC Card 80-621679 DDC 378/.1059/749 19
LC144.N5 O26

SCENERY. see LANDSCAPE.

SCEPTICISM. see SKEPTICISM.

Schaal, Herbert R. (joint author) Viets, Victor F. Minnesota coal transport evaluations /. St. Paul, Minn. [1979] 126 p. in various pagings : LC Card 79-625704 DDC 380.5/24 19
HE2321.C6 V53

Schacht, John N., 1943- Three faces of Midwestern isolationism /. Iowa City, Iowa , 1981. p. cm. ISBN 0-87414-019-6 (pbk.) : LC Card 82-2741 DDC 327.73 19
E806 .T58

Schaefer, Seth C. Electrochemical determination of Gibbs energies of formation of cobalt and nickel sulfides / by Seth C. Schaefer. Washington, D.C. : U. S. Dept. of the Interior, Bureau of Mines, [1981] p. cm. (Report of investigations / United States Department of the Interior, Bureau of Mines) Bibliography: p. LC Card 81-10082 DDC 622 s 546/.62357 19
1. Electrochemistry. 2. Gibbs' free energy. 3. Cobalt sulphide. 4. Nickel sulphide. I. Series: Report of investigations (United States. Bureau of Mines). II. Title.
TN23 .U43 QD555.5

Schafer, Robert.
Equal credit opportunity : accessibility to mortgage funds by women and by minorities : final technical report / by Robert Schafer, Helen F. Ladd (Joint Center for Urban Studies of the Massachusetts Institute of Technology and Harvard University). [Washington, D.C.] : U. S. Dept. of Housing and Urban Development, Office of Policy Development and Research : for sale by the Supt. of Docs., U. S. Govt. Print. Off., 1980. 2 v. : ill. ; 28 cm. Includes bibliographical references. LC Card 80-602636 DDC 332.7/22 19
1. Discrimination in mortgage loans - California. 2. Discrimination in mortgage loans - New York (State). I. Ladd, Helen F., joint author. II. Joint Center for Urban Studies. III. United States. Dept. of Housing and Urban Development. Office of Policy Development and Research. IV. Title.
HG2040.2 .S3

Equal credit opportunity, accessibility to mortgage funds by women and minorities : final technical report / by Robert Schafer, Helen F. Ladd. Washington : U. S. Dept. of Housing and Urban Development, Office of Policy Development and Research, 1980. 2 v. ; 28 cm. On title page: Joint Center for Urban Studies of the Massachusetts Institute of Technology and Harvard University. "H-2879."
1. Discrimination in mortgage loans. 2. Mortgages. 3. Consumer credit. I. Ladd, Helen F. II. United States. Dept. of Housing and Urban Development. III. Joint Center for Urban Studies. IV. Title.
NYPL [JLM 80-1138]

Schankler, David M. Bown, Thomas M. A review of the Proteutheria and Insectivora of the

Willwood Formation (Lower Eocene), Bighorn Basin, Wyoming /. Washington , 1981. p. cm. LC Card 81-607068 DDC 557.3 s 569/.12 19
QE75 .B9 no. 1523 QE882.I5

Schatzberg, Michael G. Bibliography of small urban centers in rural development in Africa / compiled by Michael G. Schatzberg ; [cover photo. by Jean Tabachnick ; edited by Aidan Southall]. [Madison] : African Studies Program, University of Wisconsin-Madison, 1979. ix, 246 p. ; 28 cm. On spine: Small urban centers in rural development in Africa. Includes indexes. LC Card 80-623484 DDC 016.3077/6/096 19
1. Cities and towns - Africa - Bibliography. 2. Urbanization - Africa - Bibliography. 3. Rural development - Africa - Bibliography. I. Southall, Aidan. II. Title. III. Title: Small urban centers in rural development in Africa.
Z7164.U7 S25 HT148.A2

Schechter, Evan S. United States. Social Security Administration. Office of Research and Statistics. 1974 followup of disabled & nondisabled adults /. Washington , 1979. 2 v. in 1 ; *NYPL [JLF 80-1201]*

Schechter, William I. United States. International Trade Commission. Pipes and tubes of iron or steel from Japan . Washington, D.C. [1980] ii, 29, 37 p. ; LC Card 80-602337 DDC 382/.4567283/0973 19
HF2651.S76 U54 1980a

SCHEDULING (MANAGEMENT)
Liestman, Arthur L. A fault-tolerant scheduling problem /. Urbana, Ill. [1980] 23 p. : LC Card 80-622970 DDC 001.64 s 001.64/404 19
QA76 .I4 no. 1010 QA76.54

SCHEDULING OF OPERATIONS. see SCHEDULING (MANAGEMENT)

Scheff, Peter A. Respirable particulate matter characteristics in Chicago, 1954 to the present / by Peter A. Scheff, Mary Jo Cooke, and Samuel S. Epstein. Chicago, IL : State of Illinois, Institute of Natural Resources, [1979] iv, 21 p. : graphs ; 28 cm. (Document - Illinois Institute of Natural Resources ; no. 79/37) "November 1979." "Project no. 90.002." "Quantity printed: 200." Bibliography: p. 19-21. LC Card 80-621152 DDC 628.5/3 19
1. Air - Pollution - Toxicology. 2. Aerosols - Toxicology. 3. Air - Pollution - Illinois - Chicago. I. Cooke, Mary Jo, joint author. II. Epstein, Samuel S., joint author. III. Series: Illinois Institute of Natural Resources. Document - Illinois Institute of Natural Resources , no. 79/37. IV. Title.
RA576 .S3

Schefter, John E. An economic analysis of selected strategies for dissolved-oxygen management, Chattahoochee River, Georgia / by John E. Schefter and Robert M. Hirsch. Washington : U. S. Govt. Print. Off. ; for sale by the Supt. of Docs., U. S. Govt. Print. Off., 1980. iv, 26 p. : graphs ; 29 cm. (Geological Survey professional paper . 1140) LC Card 80-600113 DDC 363.7/394 19
1. Water quality management - Chattahoochee River watershed - Costs. 2. Water quality management - Georgia - Costs. 3. Water - Dissolved oxygen. I. Hirsch, Robert M., joint author. II. Series. III. Series: United States. Geological Survey. Professional paper , 1140. IV. Title.
TD225.C35 S33

Schein, Fred. (joint author) Huddleston, Jack R. Economic change and the urban poor . Madison, Wis. , 1976. 53 p. : LC Card 77-621328 DDC 330.9775/95043/0880624 19
HD5726.M5 H82

Scheiner, Bernard J. (joint author) Stanley, Donald A. Treatment of Florida surface waters for use in phosphate beneficiation /. [Washington, D.C.] [1981] p. cm. LC Card 80-606882 DDC 622 s 661/.43 19
TN23 .U43

Schell, L. C. Conwell, Cleland N. Energy resource map of Alaska /. College, AK , 1977. 1 map : 82 x 118 cm. Scale 1:2,500,000. "Base by U. S. Geological Survey: Alaska, Map E, 1954." Insets: [Cook Inlet area]--[Aleutian Islands]--Oil and gas regions and provinces. LC Card 79-692512
G4371.H1 1977 .C6
NYPL [Map Div. 81-3049]

Schell, Richard Marion, 1949- (joint author) Mickunas, M. Dennis. Parallel compilation in a

multiprocessor environment /. Urbana, Ill. [1979] 29 p. : LC Card 80-621699 DDC 001.64 s 001.64/2 19
QA76 .I4 no. 991 QA76.6

Schenck, George K. SIC-based demand information system for nonfuel minerals / by George K. Schenck and Balakrishnan K. Nair. Washington : U. S. Dept. of the Interior, Bureau of Mines, 1981. p. cm. (Information circular) Bibliography: p. LC Card 81-607810 DDC 622 s 025/.06553 19
1. Mineral industries - Data processing. 2. Mines and mineral resources - Data processing. I. Nair, Balakrishnan K. II. Series: Information circular (United States. Bureau of Mines) . III. Title.
TN295 .U4 HD9506.A2

Schenectady County : a guide to the municipal records /. New York (State). State University, Albany. School of Library and Information Science. Albany , 1977. [136] p. ;
NYPL [JLF 80-1434]

Schenker, Eric, 1931- The Great Lakes transportation system / by Eric Schenker, Harold M. Mayer, Harry C. Brockel, with the collaboration of Margaret S. Balfe ... [et al.]. [Madison, Wis.] : University of Wisconsin Sea Grant College Program, 1976. xvii, 292 p. : maps ; 23 cm. (Technical report - University of Wisconsin Sea Grant College Program ; 230) Includes bibliographies. LC Card 75-42825 DDC 386/.544/0977 19
1. Shipping - Great Lakes. I. Mayer, Harold Melvin, 1916- joint author. II. Brockel, H. C., joint author. III. Series: Sea grant college technical report , 230. IV. Title.
HE398 .S33

Scherzinger, R. J. Ohio. Division of Lands and Soil. An inventory of Ohio soils, Madison County. [Columbus, Ohio] , 1979. 48 p. (p. 46-48 blank) : LC Card 80-621013 DDC 631.4/9771 s 631.4/977155 19
S599.O3 A25 no. 57

Scheuerman, Richard D. The Volga Germans : pioneers of the Northwest / by Richard D. Scheuerman and Clifford E. Trafzer. Moscow, Idaho : University Press of Idaho, c1980. 245 p. : ill. ; 23 cm. (Gem books) Bibliography: p. 232-240. Includes index. ISBN 0-89301-073-1 LC Card 80-52314 DDC 979.5 19
1. Russian Germans - Northwest, Pacific - History. 2. Northwest, Pacific - History. I. Trafzer, Clifford E. II. Title.
F855.2.R85 S33

Schexnaydre, Linda. Index to the Emporia State research studies, volumes I-XXVIII (1952-1980) /. Emporia, Kan. , 1980. 55 p. ; LC Card 80-623416 DDC 370/.7/8078162 19
AI3 .I675

Schiff, Arthur. The impact of food stamp reform on the Northeast / [prepared for the legislative leadership of the Northeastern States by Arthur Schiff, program and committee staff, New York State Assembly. [Albany : The Assembly], 1977. 17 p. : diagrs. ; 28 cm. LC Card 79-624025 DDC 363.8 19
1. Food stamp program - Law and legislation - Northeastern States. I. New York (State). Legislature. Assembly. II. Title.
KF3745.F62 S34

Schild, Alfred, 1921- Spacetime and geometry . Austin , c1982. p. cm. ISBN 0-292-77567-9 LC Card 81-11488 DDC 530.1/1 19
QC173.6 .S67

Schilling, John Harold, 1927- (joint author) Garside, Larry J. Thermal waters of Nevada /. Reno , 1979. 163 p. : LC Card 80-621826 DDC 553.7 19
GB1199.7.N3 G37

Schinzinger, Roland. Emergencies in water delivery / by Roland Schinzinger and Henry Fagin, with the assistance of Richard Chee, Jr., ... [et al.]. Davis, Calif. : California Water Resources Center, University of California, 1979. v, 131 p. : ill. ; 28 cm. (Contribution - California Water Resources Center, University of California ; no. 177 0575-4941) "Technical completion report." Bibliography: p. 124-131. LC Card 80-621183 DDC 333.91/009794 s 363.6/1 19
1. Emergency water supply - California. 2. Emergency water supply - California - San Diego Co. I. Fagin, Henry, 1913- joint author. II. Series: California. University. Water Resources Center. Contribution, no.

177. III. Title.
GB705.C2 C27 no. 177 TD224.C3

SCHIZOPHRENIA.
Special report . Rockville, Md. , Washington, D.C. , 1981. 160 p. : LC Card 81-601423 DDC 616.89/82 19
RC514 .S68

Schizophrenia, 1980. Special report . Rockville, Md. , Washington, D.C. , 1981. 160 p. : LC Card 81-601423 DDC 616.89/82 19
RC514 .S68

Schlepp, Richard L. Soil survey of Aurora County, South Dakota. [Washington, D.C.?] : U. S. Dept. of Agriculture, Soil Conservation Service, c1980. vii, 148 p., 58 folded p. of plates : ill., maps (1 col.) ; 28 cm. "In cooperation with South Dakota Agricultural Experiment Station." "Issued September 1981"--p. iii. Item 102-B-42 Bibliography: p. 83. LC Card 81-600698 DDC 631.4/7/783375 19
1. Soils - South Dakota - Aurora County - Maps. 2. United States. Soil Conservation Service. 3. South Dakota Agricultural Experiment Station. I. Title.
S599.S6 S34

Schluter, Gerald E. Projected 1980 overall agricultural employment by regions, commodities, and related sectors / by Gerald E. Schluter and Earl O. Heady. Ames, Iowa : Center for Agricultural and Rural Development, Iowa State University, [1975] v leaves, 85 p. : map ; 24 cm. (CARD report. 59) "August 1975." Bibliography: p. 83-85. LC Card 80-623869 DDC 331.12/33/0973 19
1. Agricultural industries - United States - Employees - Supply and demand. 2. Agricultural laborers - United States - Supply and demand. I. Heady, Earl Orel, 1916- joint author. II. Series: Iowa. State University of Science and Technology, Ames. Center for Agricultural and Rural Development. CARD report, 59. III. Title.
HD5718.A272 U67

Schluter, R. B. (Robert B.) Haas, L. A. (Larry A.) Low pressure leaching of Duluth complex matte /. Avondale, Md. , 1981. p. cm. LC Card 80-606897 DDC 622 s 669/.7332 19
TN23 .U43 TN799.N6

Schmid, William D. Phillips, Gary L. Fishes of the Minnesota region /. Minneapolis , 1982. p. cm. ISBN 0-8166-0979-9 : LC Card 81-14693 DDC 597.092/9776 19
QL628.M6 P47

Schmidly, David J. (joint author) Honeycutt, Rodney L. Chromosomal and morphological variation in the plains pocket gopher, Geomys bursarius, in Texas and adjacent states /. [Lubbock] , 1979. 54 p. : LC Card 79-623970 DDC 599.32/32 19
QL737.R654 H66

Schmidt, Artwin.
Annual performance report for inventory and cataloging special management problems / by Artwin Schmidt and Stuart F. Robards. Juneau : Alaska Dept. of Fish and Game, Sport Fish Division, 1976. 70 p. : ill. ; 28 cm. At head of title: Volume 17, study G-I-S. On cover: Federal aid in fish restoration. Bibliography: p. 66-68. LC Card 77-621096 DDC 597/.05/028 19
1. Fishes - Alaska - Statistics. 2. Echo sounding in fishing - Alaska. I. Robards, F. Stuart, joint author. II. Title. III. Title: Inventory and cataloging special management problems.
QL628.A4 S33

Inventory and cataloging / by Artwin Schmidt. Juneau : Alaska Dept. of Fish and Game, Sport Fish Division, [1978?] 124 p. : ill. ; 28 cm. Cover title. At head of title: Federal aid in fish restoration, volume 19, July 1, 1977-June 30, 1978. Includes bibliographies. CONTENTS. - G-I-R, High quality fishing waters in southeast.--G-I-S, Special management problems. LC Card 78-624206 DDC 639/.2/09798 19
1. Fishes - Alaska - Statistics. 2. Limnology - Alaska - Statistics. I. Alaska. Division of Sport Fish. II. Title.
QL628.A4 S34

Schmidt, James J.
Ground-water resources of Knox County / by James J. Schmidt ; cartography, VK. Columbus : Ohio Dept. of Natural Resources, Division of Water, 1980. 1 map : col. ; 71 x 88 cm. Relief shown by contours and spot heights. Includes location map. LC Card 81-691460 19
1. Water, Underground - Ohio - Knox County - Maps.

I. Ohio. Division of Water.
G4083.K6C34 1980 .S3

Ground-water resources of Pickaway County / by James J. Schmidt ; cartography, VK. Columbus : Ohio Dept. of Natural Resources, Division of Water, 1980. 1 map : col. ; 69 x 85 cm. Relief shown by contours and spot heights. Includes location map. LC Card 81-691459
1. Water, Underground - Ohio - Pickaway County - Maps. I. Ohio. Division of Water.
G4083.P5C34 1980 .S3

Ground-water resources of Ross County / by James J. Schmidt ; cartography, VK. Columbus : Ohio Dept. of Natural Resources, Division of Water, 1980. 1 map : col. ; 81 x 95 cm. Relief shown by contours and spot heights. Includes location map. LC Card 81-691461
1. Water, Underground - Ohio - Ross County - Maps. I. Ohio. Division of Water.
G4083.R6C34 1980 .S3

Schmidt, Richard A. A study of surface coal mining in West Virginia; final report. Compiled by R. A. Schmidt and W. C. Stoneman. Menlo Park, Calif. : Stanford Research Institute, 1972. xiii, 180 p. illus. 28 cm. "SRI project 1293." "Prepared for West Virginia Legislature, Joint Committee on Government and Finance." Includes bibliographical references. LC Card 72-611225
1. Coal mines and mining - West Virginia. 2. Strip mining - West Virginia. I. Stoneman, W. C., joint author. II. Stanford Research Institute. III. West Virginia. Legislature. Joint Committee on Government and Finance. IV. Title.
TN805.W4 S28   *NYPL [JLF 81-203]*

Schmidt, S. C. (Stephen C.) London, Alan C. Coarse grain consumption and import relationships in the European Community /. [Urbana, Ill.] [1979] 36 p. : LC Card 80-623669 DDC 338.1 s 382/.4131/094 19
HD1401 .I42 no. 177 HD9045.E82

Schmidt, Walter, 1950- Florida. Bureau of Geology. The limestone, dolomite, and coquina resources of Florida /. Tallahassee , 1979. vi, 54 p. (p. 54 blank) : LC Card 80-621937 DDC 557.59 s 553.5/16/09759 19
QE99 .A32 no. 88 TN967

Schmisseur, Ed. (joint author) Holst, David. Effects of the 1977 drought on eastern Oregon ranches /. [Corvallis] [1979] 25 p. : LC Card 79-625679 DDC 630/.9795 s 338.1/4 19
S105 .E43 no. 555 S600.7.D76

Schmuhl, Robert. The Classroom and the newsroom /. Bloomington, Ind. , 1979. 140 p. ; LC Card 80-140151 DDC 070/.07 19
PN4888.S6 C58

SCHMULTS, EDWARD C., 1931-
United States. Congress. Senate. Committee on the Judiciary. Confirmation hearing on Edward C. Schmults, nominee, to be deputy attorney general . Washington , 1981. iii, 62 p. ; LC Card 81-601773 DDC 353.5 19
KF26 .J8 1981a

Schneider, Mary Jo. (joint author) Fryar, Michelle Davis. The impact of nutrition programs on the health status of elderly Arkansans /. Fayetteville , 1979. 24 p. : LC Card 80-620832 DDC 362.1/9897/009767 19
RA564.8 .F78

Schneider, Robert. U. S. Geological Survey research in radioactive waste disposal--fiscal year 1979 /. Reston, Va. , 1981. p. cm. LC Card 81-607990 DDC 557.3 s 621.48/38 19
QE75 .C5 no. 847 TD898

Schoellhamer, J. E. Geology of the eastern Los Angeles basin, southern California /. Washington , 1980. p. cm. LC Card 81-607011 DDC 551.7/09794/96 19
QE90.S15 G46

Schoen, John W. Evaluation of deer range and habitat utilization in various successional stages / by John W. Schoen. Juneau : State of Alaska, Dept. of Fish and Game, Division of Game, [1978] i, 28 p. : ill. ; 28 cm. Cover title. "Final report, Federal aid in wildlife restoration, project W-17-10, job 2.5 R." Bibliography: p. 25-28. LC Card 79-620862 DDC 599.73/57 19
1. Deer - Habitat. 2. Deer - Food. 3. Forest ecology - Alaska. 4. Mammals - Habitat. 5. Mammals - Food. 6. Mammals - Alaska. I. Title.
QL737.U55 S35

Schoenborn, Charlotte A. Basic data from Wave I of the National survey of personal health practices and consequences : United States, 1979 / [Charlotte A. Schoenborn, Kthleen M. Danchik, Jack Elinson]. Hyattsville, Md. : U. S. Dept. of Health and Human Services, Public Health Services, Office of the Assistant Secretary for Health, National Center for Health Statistics, 1981. p. cm. (Vital and health statistics. Series 15 . no. 2) DHHS publication ; no. (PHS) 81-1163 Includes bibliographical references.
   ISBN 0-8406-0230-8   LC Card 81-11274   DDC 614.4/273 19
1. Health status indicators - United States. 2. Health behavior - United States - Statistics. 3. Health surveys - United States. I. Danchik, Kathleen M. II. Elinson, Jack. III. National Center for Health Statistics (U. S.). IV. Title.
RA407.3 .S36

Schoening, Niles. (joint author) Quindry, Kenneth E. The Tennessee constitutional spending limitation . Knoxville , 1979. vii, 69 p. :   LC Card 80-621169   DDC 336.3/9/09768 19
HJ2434 .Q56

SCHOHARIE CREEK WATERSHED (N.Y.) - MAPS.
United States. Soil Conservation Service. Upper Schoharie Creek watershed, Delaware, Greene, and Schoharie Counties, New York. Lanham, MD , 1980. 1 map :   LC Card 81-690285
G3802.S42 1980 .U5

Scholars as contractors : report of a workshop on the contract archeology process / edited by William J. Mayer-Oakes and Alice W. Portnoy ; participants, Lawrence E. Aten ... [et al.]. Washington : U. S. Dept. of the Interior, Heritage Conservation and Recreation Service, Interagency Archeological Services Division : for sale by the Supt. of Docs., U. S. Govt. Print. Off., 1979. 265 p. in various pagings : ill. ; 29 cm. (Cultural resource management studies) HCRS publication ; no. 14 Prepared under contract to Interagency Archeological Services Division, Heritage Conservation and Recreation Service by the Cultural Resources Institute, Dept. of Anthropology, Texas Tech University. Includes bibliographies.   LC Card 79-603005
1. Archaeology and state - United States - Congresses. 2. Archaeological surveying - United States - Congresses. 3. Public contracts - United States - Congresses. 4. United States - Antiquities - Congresses. I. Mayer-Oakes, William J., 1923-. II. Portnoy, Alice W. III. Aten, Lawrence E. IV. United States. Interagency Archeological Services Division. V. Texas Tech University. Cultural Resources Institute.
CC136 .S36   ***NYPL [JLF 81-76]***

Scholars as managers, or how can the managers do it better . Workshop on Management Techniques Applied to Archeology, Texas Tech University, 1977. Washington , 1978. vii, 21 p., [2] leaves of plates :   LC Card 79-602641
CC51 .W67 1977

Scholars' guide to Washington, D.C., for Middle Eastern studies /. Dorr, Steven R. Washington, D.C. , 1981. p. cm.   ISBN 0-87474-372-9   LC Card 81-607073   DDC 956/.00720753 19
Z3013.6 .D67 DS61.9.U6

Scholars' guide to Washington, D.C., for South Asian studies . Rahim, Enayetur. Washington, D.C. , 1981. p. cm.   ISBN 0-87474-778-3 :   LC Card 81-607847   DDC 016.954/0720753 19
Z3185 .R34 DS335

Scholarship program; report to Congress. United States. National Health Service Corps. [Hyattsville, Md.]   ***NYPL [JLM 81-63]***

SCHOLASTIC APITITUDE TEST.
Nochumson, Bayla S. New Mexico ACT and SAT results, 1978-79 /. Santa Fe, N.M. [1980] v, 35 p. :   LC Card 80-623171   DDC 378/.1664 19
LB2353.42 .N6

SCHOLASTIC APTITUDE TESTS.
Nochumson, Bayla S. New Mexico's standardized test results. Santa Fe, N.M. , 1979. ii, 38 p. :   LC Card 80-621725   DDC 371.2/6/09789 19
LB3052.N6 N6

Schomburg Center for Research in Black Culture. (Old Catalog form: New York Public Library. Schomberg Collection of Negro Literature)

Cosme, Eusebia Adriana, 1911- [Papers] [1927-1973] 3 boxes.   ***NYPL [Sc Rare Mss-46 & Sc Micro R-3619]***

Dafora, Asadata, 1890-1965. [Papers] [1933-1963] 1 box.   ***NYPL [Sc Rare Mss-48]***

Records. 1924-1979. 53 boxes. In Schomburg Center for Research in Black Culture. Correspondence: general (1924-1979); reference (1933-1979); memoranda (1947-1978); subject files (1921-1979); v); visitor's register (1952-1979). Includes partial index to significant correspondents.
1. Schomburg Center for Research in Black Culture - Records and correspondence. 2. Ira Aldridge Society - History - Source. 3. Martin Luther King, Jr. Center for Social Change - History - Sources. 4. National Urban League - History - Sources. 5. North Manhattan Project - History - Sources. I. Title: Curator's file.
   NYPL [Sc Rare MSS-44]

Rudd, Robert R. [Papers] [1875-1906] 2 boxes.
   NYPL [Sc Rare Mss-51]

Whipper, Leigh Rollin, 1876-1975. [Papers] [1861-1963, n. d.]. 1 box.   ***NYPL [Sc Rare Mss-47 & Sc Micro R-3807]***

SCHOMBURG CENTER FOR RESEARCH IN BLACK CULTURE - RECORDS AND CORRESPONDENCE.
Schomburg Center for Research in Black Culture. Records. 1924-1979. 53 boxes.
   NYPL [Sc Rare MSS-44]

Schomburg Collection of Negro Literature and History. see **Schomburg Center for Research in Black Culture.**

Schomer, Karine. Mahadevi Varma and the chhayavad age of modern Hindi poetry / Karine Schomer. Berkeley : University of California Press, 1981, c1982. p. cm. Bibliography: p. Includes index.   ISBN 0-520-04255-7   LC Card 81-13002   DDC 891/.4316 19
1. Varma, Maha Devi, 1907- - Criticism and interpretation. 2. Chayavada. I. Title.
PK2098.V3 Z878 1982

SCHOOL ADMINISTRATORS - MAINE - SALARIES, PENSIONS, ETC. - STATISTICS.
Maine. Dept. of Educational and Cultural Services. Division of Planning and Management Information. Local Administrative Unit. State of Maine public full-time professional staff average salaries for the 1978-79 school year /. [Augusta] [1979?] iv, 47 p. ;   LC Card 79-622302   DDC 331.2/813711/009741 19
LB2842.2 .M338 1979

SCHOOL ADMINISTRATORS - UTAH - SALARIES, PENSIONS, ETC.
Utah. Div. of Education Support Services. State & Federal Data Support Services. Salary schedule information on Utah school districts. Salt Lake City, Utah [1979] 201 p. 28 cm.   LC Card 80-622337   DDC 331.2/813711/009792 19
LB2842.2 .U85 1979

SCHOOL ATTENDANCE - HIGH SCHOOL - UNITED STATES - LONGITUDINAL STUDIES.
Crain, Robert L. The influence of high school racial composition on Black college attendance and test performance /. [Washington] , 1978, c1979 printing. xix, 143 p. ;   LC Card 79-601911
LC146 .C72 1978   ***NYPL [JLF 81-370]***

SCHOOL ATTENDANCE - LAW AND LEGISLATION - MAINE.
Maine. Dept. of Educational and Cultural Services. Guidelines for implementation of an act relating to habitual truants and dropouts /. Augusta, Me. , 1978. i, 8 p. ;   LC Card 80-620682   DDC 344.741/0792 347.4104792 19
KFM392 .A83 1978

SCHOOL ATTENDANCE - MISSOURI - PLANNING - STATISTICS.
Enrollment projections for elementary and secondary public schools in Missouri, 1979-1984 /. [Jefferson City] [1979] 5, 1, 10 p. :   LC Card 80-623486   DDC 371.2/19/778 19
LC144.M8 E57

SCHOOL ATTENDANCE - NEW YORK (STATE) - WESTCHESTER COUNTY.
Westchester County, N. Y. Dept. of Planning. Selected enrollment and financial data for school districts in Westchester. White Plains, N. Y., 1964. 29 p.   ***NYPL [*Z-3176]***

SCHOOL ATTENDANCE - VERMONT - STATISTICS.
Vermont. Dept. of Education. 1978-1979 Vermont school enrollment . [Montpelier, Vt.] [1979?] [6], 27 p. ;   LC Card 80-621761   DDC 371.2/19/743 19
LC144.V4 V47 1979

SCHOOL BREAKFAST PROGRAMS - UNITED STATES.
United States. Food and Nutrition Service. Office of Policy, Planning, and Evaluation. Factors influencing school and student participation in the school breakfast program, 1977-78. [Washington] , 1980. x, 54 p. ;   LC Card 80-602327   DDC 371.7/16/0973 19
LB3479 .U55 1980

United States. General Accounting Office. Major factors inhibit expansion of the school breakfast program . [Washington, D.C. , 1980] vi, 65 p. ;   LC Card 80-602650   DDC 371.7/16/0973 19
LB3479 .U55 1980a

SCHOOL BUILDINGS - LAW AND LEGISLATION - UNITED STATES.
United States. Congress. Senate. Committee on Labor and Human Resources. Subcommittee on Education, Arts, and Humanities. Asbestos school hazard detection and control act of 1979 . Washington, D.C. , 1980. iv, 277 p. :   LC Card 80-602756   DDC 344.73/07 19
KF26 .L2735 1980

SCHOOL BUILDINGS - LAW AND LEGISLATION - WASHINGTON (STATE)
Washington (State). State Board of Health. Rules & regulations of the State Board of Health for environmental sanitation, primary & secondary schools. Olympia, Wash. [1980] 10 p. ;   LC Card 80-623897   DDC 344.797/07 347.94047 19
KFW459.S3 A32 1980

SCHOOL BUILDINGS - MASSACHUSETTS - FIRES AND FIRE PREVENTION.
Massachusetts. Special Commission Relative to Evaluating the Extent of the Use of Asbestos as Fireproofing in the Schools and Public Buildings of the Commonwealth and its Containment and Removal. Report of the Special Commission Relative to Evaluating the Extent of the Use of Asbestos as Fireproofing in the Schools and Public Buildings of the Commonwealth and its Containment and Removal . [Boston?] 1976 [i.e. 1977]. 34 p. ;   LC Card 77-623289   DDC 300/.9744 s 363.1/79 19
J87 .M4 1977g no. 5344 RA1231.A8

SCHOOL BUILDINGS - UNITED STATES - STATISTICS.
United States. Public Works Administration. Projects Division. Research Section. Allotments for educational building construction . [Washington] , 1936. 158 leaves ;   LC Card 81-456134
LB3218.A1 U55 1963

SCHOOL BUSES - IOWA - DESIGN AND CONSTRUCTION.
Iowa. Dept. of Public Instruction. Minimum standards for construction of school transportation equipment (legal requirements and regulations). [Des Moines, Iowa] , 1979. xiv, 45 p. ;   LC Card 80-623088   DDC 343.777/07862922233 19
KFI4497.94.A435 A2 1979

SCHOOL BUSES - LAW AND LEGISLATION - COLORADO.
Colorado. Dept of Education. Office of Field Services. Colorado rules and regulations governing operation of school transportation vehicles /. Denver , 1980. 9 p. ;   LC Card 81-621994   DDC 344.788/0794 347.8804794 19
KFC2097.94.A434 A2 1980

SCHOOL BUSES - LAW AND LEGISLATION - IOWA.
Iowa. Dept. of Public Instruction. Minimum standards for construction of school transportation equipment (legal requirements and regulations). [Des Moines, Iowa] , 1979. xiv, 45 p. ;   LC Card 80-623088   DDC 343.777/07862922233 19
KFI4497.94.A435 A2 1979

SCHOOL CENSUS - SOUTH CAROLINA.
South Carolina. Dept. of Education. Office of Research. Management Information Section.

Births, projected first grade enrollment, high school graduates, and number entering college for the state and the counties /. Columbia, S.C. [1979] v leaves, 48 p. ; LC Card 80-620567 DDC 371.2/19/757 19
LC132.S6 S68 1979

SCHOOL CHILDREN - FOOD.
Barr, Phyllis. School lunch recipe book /. Harrisburg, PA (333 Market St., Harrisburg PA 17126) [1980] c1979. 340 p. : LC Card 80-624454 DDC 641.5/71 19
TX820 .B34 1980

SCHOOL CHILDREN - FOOD - ALASKA.
Hippler, Arthur E. A study to determine causes of decline in the national school lunch program in Alaska /. Anchorage [1979] 119, 15, 28 leaves : LC Card 80-623189 DDC 371.7/16/09798 19
LB3479.U6 H56

SCHOOL CHILDREN - FOOD - BIBLIOGRAPHY.
United States. National Agricultural Library. Food and Nutrition Information and Educational Materials Center. Index to the proceedings of 10 USDA-Land-Grant university seminars. [Washington, 1974] xiii, 27 p.
NYPL [*Z-3211]

SCHOOL CHILDREN - FOOD - KANSAS - PLANNING.
Kansas. State Dept. of Education. School food service . Topeka, Kan. [1979?] ii, 83 p., [1] leaf of plates : LC Card 80-622953 DDC 371.7/16/09781 19
LB3479.U6 K36 1979

SCHOOL CHILDREN - FOOD - NEW YORK (STATE)
New York (State). Legislative Commission on Expenditure Review. School food programs . Albany , 1978. 5, ii, 50 p. : LC Card 79-621326 DDC 371.7/16/09747 19
LB3479 .U55 1978

SCHOOL CHILDREN - FOOD - UNITED STATES.
United States. Congress. Senate. Committee on Agriculture, Nutrition, and Forestry. Subcommittee on Nutrition. Review of child nutrition programs . Washington , 1980. iv, 130 p. ; LC Card 80-603080 DDC 363.8/0880544 19
KF26 .A3559 1980a

United States. Congressional Budget Office. Feeding children . [Washington] [1980] xxiii, 149 p. : LC Card 80-603241 DDC 362.7/1 19
HV696.F6 U6146 1980

SCHOOL CHILDREN - TEXAS - TRANSPORTATION.
Texas. School Transportation Section. Public school transportation. Austin, Tex. , 1980. vi, 57 p. : LC Card 80-622617 DDC 371.8/72/09764 19
LB2864 .T42 1980

SCHOOL CHILDREN - UNITED STATES - STATISTICS.
Williams, Jeffrey W. Students and schools /. [Washington] , 1979. viii, 85 p. : LC Card 79-602036
LC69 .W54   *NYPL [JLF 81-365]*

School crime and disruption : prevention models. Washington : U. S. Dept. of Health, Education and Welfare, National Institute of Education : for sale by the Supt. of Docs., U. S. Govt. Print. Off., 1978. v, 195 p. ; 26 cm. "June 1978." Includes bibliographical references. LC Card 79-602563
1. School vandalism - Addresses, essays, lectures. 2. School violence - Addresses, essays, lectures. I. National Institute of Education.
LB3249 .S37   *NYPL [JLF 81-295]*

School desegregation in Tacoma, Washington .
United States. Commission on Civil Rights. Washington, D.C. [1979] vii, 18 p. ; LC Card 79-602709 DDC 370.19/342/09797 19
LC214.23.T3 U54 1979

SCHOOL DISCIPLINE - OHIO.
Ohio. Governor's Task Force on School Discipline. Report /. [Columbus, Ohio] [1980] 16 p. ; LC Card 80-622226 DDC 371.5/09771 19
LB3012 .O33 1980

School district profiles for the State of Idaho /.
Idaho. Office of Management Information. Boise, Idaho [1980] 116 p. ; LC Card 80-622810

DDC 331.2/813711009796 19
LB2842.2 .I3 1980

SCHOOL DISTRICTS - ALASKA.
University of Alaska, Fairbanks. Center for Northern Educational Research. New school districts in rural Alaska . Fairbanks , 1978. v, 247 p., [1] fold. leaf of plates : LC Card 78-622541 DDC 370.19/346 19
LC5147.A4 U54 1978

SCHOOL DISTRICTS - ILLINOIS - FINANCE.
Illinois. State Aid Equalization Study. Selected expenditures in Illinois school districts /. [Springfield] [1980] 48 p. : LC Card 80-623952 DDC 379.1/535 19
LB2826.I3 I4768 1980

SCHOOL DISTRICTS - KANSAS - FINANCE - STATISTICS.
Kansas. State Dept. of Education. LEA Finance Section. 1978-79 unified school district wealth /. Topeka, Kan. [1979] iv, 36 p. ; LC Card 80-622259 DDC 379.1/3/09781 19
LB2826.K2 K38 1979c

SCHOOL DISTRICTS - KANSAS - NESS COUNTY - MAPS.
United States. Soil Conservation Service. Township, school, and hospital district map, Ness County, Kansas /. Lincoln, Nebr. , 1979. 1 map : LC Card 81-691149
G4203.N5F7 1979 .U5

SCHOOL DISTRICTS - KANSAS - STATISTICS.
Kansas. State Dept. of Education. 1979 mill levies of the 306 unified school districts of Kansas. Topeka [1979] 40 p. ; LC Card 80-622607 DDC 379.1/22/09781 19
LB2826.K2 K38 1979b

SCHOOL DISTRICTS - NEW JERSEY - FINANCE.
New Jersey. Legislature. Senate. Committee on Education. Public hearing before Senate Education Committee on the impact of spending limitations on local school districts . [Trenton , 1979?] 134 p. in various pagings ; LC Card 80-621237 DDC 379.1/222/09749 19
KFN1811.3 .E3 1979a

School districts of South Carolina . Stuckey, Dale C. Columbia, S.C. [1979] iii, 51 p. ; LC Card 80-622553 DDC 379.15/35 19
LB2817 .S75

SCHOOL DISTRICTS - SOUTH CAROLINA.
Stuckey, Dale C. School districts of South Carolina . Columbia, S.C. [1979] iii, 51 p. ; LC Card 80-622553 DDC 379.15/35 19
LB2817 .S75

SCHOOL DISTRICTS - UNITED STATES - DIRECTORIES.
Directory of elementary and secondary school districts, and schools in selected school districts . Washington, D.C. , 1980. 2 v. (xlvii, 1605 p.) ; LC Card 81-601659 DDC 379.1/535 19
L901 .D5116

SCHOOL EMPLOYEES - SALARIES, PENSIONS, ETC. - LAW AND LEGISLATION - KANSAS.
Kansas. Laws, statutes, etc. State school retirement law of Kansas. [Topeka] , 1960. 15 p. ; LC Card 81-453498 DDC 344.781/012529 19
KFK393.5.A333 A2 1960

SCHOOL EMPLOYEES - UTAH - SALARIES, PENSIONS, ETC.
Utah. Div. of Education Support Services. State & Federal Data Support Services. Salary schedule information on Utah school districts. Salt Lake City, Utah [1979] 201 p. 28 cm. LC Card 80-622337 DDC 331.2/813711/009792 19
LB2842.2 .U85 1979

SCHOOL FACILITIES - NORTH CAROLINA - PLANNING.
North Carolina. Legislative Research Commission. Public school facility needs . Raleigh, N.C. [1980] i, 26, [96] p. ; LC Card 80-622592 DDC 371.6/2/09756 19
LB3241.3.N8 N67 1980

SCHOOL FACILITIES - UNITED STATES - STATISTICS.
United States. Public Works Administration. Projects Division. Research Section. Allotments for educational building construction . [Washington] , 1936. 158 leaves ; LC Card

81-456134
LB3218.A1 U55 1963

School finance studies . North Carolina. Legislative Research Commission. Raleigh, N.C. (State Legislative Building, Raleigh 27611) [1981] v, 10, [21] p. ; LC Card 81-621656 DDC 379.1/22/09756 19
LB2826.N8 N67 1981

School food programs . New York (State). Legislative Commission on Expenditure Review. Albany , 1978. 5, ii, 50 p. : LC Card 79-621326 DDC 371.7/16/09747 19
LB3479 .U55 1978

School food service . Kansas. State Dept. of Education. Topeka, Kan. [1979?] ii, 83 p., [1] leaf of plates : LC Card 80-622953 DDC 371.7/16/09781 19
LB3479.U6 K36 1979

SCHOOL HYGIENE - CONNECTICUT.
Connecticut. School Health Task Force. Connecticut's school health policy . [Hartford, CT.] [1980] vi, 82 p. ; LC Card 80-621534 DDC 371.7/09746 19
LB3409.U6 C83 1980

SCHOOL HYGIENE - LAW AND LEGISLATION - WASHINGTON (STATE)
Washington (State). Office of Community Health Services. Child Health Section. Washington State school immunization manual. Olympia, Wash. [1980] 146 p. : LC Card 80-622798 DDC 344.797/043 19
KFW357.9.I44 A836 1980

Washington (State). State Board of Health. Rules & regulations of the State Board of Health for environmental sanitation, primary & secondary schools. Olympia, Wash. [1980] 10 p. ; LC Card 80-623897 DDC 344.797/07 347.94047 19
KFW459.S3 A32 1980

SCHOOL INTEGRATION - INDIANA - HISTORY.
Indiana. Division of Equal Educational Opportunity. Indiana school desegregation . [Indianapolis] , 1979. ix, 17 p. ; LC Card 79-625868 DDC 370.19/342/09772 19
LC214.22.I6 I52 1979

SCHOOL INTEGRATION - WASHINGTON (STATE) - TACOMA.
United States. Commission on Civil Rights. School desegregation in Tacoma, Washington . Washington, D.C. [1979] vii, 18 p. ; LC Card 79-602709 DDC 370.19/342/09797 19
LC214.23.T3 U54 1979

The school laws of Indiana . Indiana. Laws, statutes, etc. Indianapolis , 1903. 12 p. ; LC Card 80-135034 DDC 344.772/07/02632 19
KFI3390 .A3 1903

SCHOOL LIBRARIES - ADMINISTRATION.
Bundy, Mary Lee, 1927- The school library supervisor and her situation : final report. [Washington?] 1970. viii, 95, 25 p.
NYPL [*XM-7267]

SCHOOL LIBRARIES - MARYLAND - STATISTICS.
Maryland. School Library Media Services Branch. Facts about Maryland's school library media programs, 1977-78. [Baltimore, Md.] [1979] [26] leaves ; LC Card 80-621218 DDC 027.8/09752 19
Z675.S3 M276 1979

SCHOOL LIBRARIES - NEW YORK (STATE)
New York (State). University. Office of the President of the University and Commissioner of Education. Report of the Commissioner of Education, Gordon M. Ambach, to the New York State Legislature on library pilot projects, organized under chapter 787, Laws of 1978, New York State, covering the period December 15, 1978 - August 31, 1979. Albany, NY [1977?] iii, 44, [19] p. ; LC Card 80-622745 DDC 027.8/09747 19
Z675.S3 N53 1977

The school library supervisor and her situation : final report. Bundy, Mary Lee, 1927- [Washington?] 1970. viii, 95, 25 p.
NYPL [*XM-7267]

School lunch recipe book /. Barr, Phyllis. Harrisburg, PA (333 Market St., Harrisburg PA 17126) [1980] c1979. 340 p. : LC Card

80-624454 DDC 641.5/71 19
TX820 .B34 1980

SCHOOL LUNCHES. see **SCHOOL CHILDREN - FOOD.**

SCHOOL MANAGEMENT AND ORGANIZATION - LOUISIANA - JEFFERSON PARISH - HISTORY.
Daul, George Cecil, 1916- The administration of the public schools of Jefferson Parish since the Civil War (1860-1940) . Metairie, La. (3330 N. Causeway Blvd., Metairie, La. 70002) , 1981. p. cm. LC Card 81-8468 DDC 371.2/009763/38 19
LB2819 .D2 1981

SCHOOL MANAGEMENT AND ORGANIZATION - MARYLAND.
Maryland. Governor's Study Commission on Structure and Governance of Education. Final report of the Governor's Commission on Education /. [Baltimore] , 1975. ix, 53 p. ; LC Card 77-620950
LB2809.M38 M35 1975
                        *NYPL [*XME-9436]*

SCHOOL MANAGEMENT AND ORGANIZATION - OREGON.
Oregon. Dept. of Education. Oregon administrative rules /. Salem, Or. [1979- 1 v. : LC Card 80-621418 DDC 371.2/009795 19
LB2809.O7 O73 1979

SCHOOL MANAGEMENT AND ORGANIZATION - SWITZERLAND.
Bodenman, Paul S., 1912- The educational system of Switzerland /. Washington, D.C. , 1979 i.e. 1980. 35 p. ; LC Card 80-602306 DDC 371.2/009485 19
LB2936 .B6

SCHOOL MANAGEMENT AND ORGANIZATION - UNITED STATES - ADDRESSES, ESSAYS, LECTURES.
New concerns in educational administration. Bloomington, Ind. , 1980. iii, 117 p. : LC Card 80-128415 DDC 371.2/00973 19
LB2805 .N487

School of American Research, Santa Fe, N. M. see **Santa Fe, N. M. School of American Research.**

SCHOOL TEACHING. see **TEACHING.**

SCHOOL VANDALISM - ADDRESSES, ESSAYS, LECTURES.
School crime and disruption . Washington , 1978. v, 195 p. ; LC Card 79-602563
LB3249 .S37   *NYPL [JLF 81-295]*

SCHOOL VANDALISM - UNITED STATES.
National Institute of Law Enforcement and Criminal Justice. Crime and disruption in schools . Washington, D.C. , 1979. vii, 104 p. : LC Card 80-601518 DDC 371.5/8/0973 19
LB3013.3 .N375 1979

SCHOOL VIOLENCE - ADDRESSES, ESSAYS, LECTURES.
School crime and disruption . Washington , 1978. v, 195 p. ; LC Card 79-602563
LB3249 .S37   *NYPL [JLF 81-295]*

SCHOOL VIOLENCE - UNITED STATES.
National Institute of Law Enforcement and Criminal Justice. Crime and disruption in schools . Washington, D.C. , 1979. vii, 104 p. : LC Card 80-601518 DDC 371.5/8/0973 19
LB3013.3 .N375 1979

The schooling of the horse /. Young, John Richard. Norman , 1982. p. cm. ISBN 0-8061-1787-7 LC Card 81-11539 DDC 636.1/0888 19
SF287 .Y6 1982

SCHOOLS, COMMERCIAL. see **BUSINESS EDUCATION.**

Schools of public health . Association of Schools of Public Health. [Washington] , 1980. x, 149 p. ; LC Card 80-602404 DDC 614/.07/1173 19
RA440.7.U6 A87 1980

Schools of public health . Hall, Thomas L. [Washington] [1980] vi, 58 p. ; LC Card 80-602405 DDC 614/.07/1173 19
RA440.7.U6 H34

SCHOOLS OF PUBLIC HEALTH - UNITED STATES - STATISTICAL SERVICES.
Association of Schools of Public Health. Schools of public health . [Washington] , 1980. x, 149 p. ; LC Card 80-602404 DDC

614/.07/1173 19
RA440.7.U6 A87 1980

SCHOOLS OF PUBLIC HEALTH - UNITED STATES - STATISTICS.
Association of Schools of Public Health. Schools of public health . [Washington] , 1980. x, 149 p. ; LC Card 80-602404 DDC 614/.07/1173 19
RA440.7.U6 A87 1980

Hall, Thomas L. Schools of public health . [Washington] [1980] vi, 58 p. ; LC Card 80-602405 DDC 614/.07/1173 19
RA440.7.U6 H34

SCHOOLS - SAFETY REGULATIONS - PENNSYLVANIA.
Pennsylvania. Dept. of Education. Pennsylvania regulations and guidelines concerning safety in the school science laboratory. Harrisburg , 1978. [67] p. ; LC Card 80-621291 DDC 344.748/075 347.480475 19
KFP380.A1 A3 1978

SCHOOLS - VIRGINIA - PUBLIC RELATIONS.
Virginia. Secretary of Education. Report of the Secretary of Education and the Secretary of Public Safety on Senate joint resolution 159 to the General Assembly of Virginia. Richmond, Va. , 1980. iii, 10 p. ; LC Card 80-621140 DDC 300/.9755 s 362.7/4/09755 19
J87 .V9 1980c, no. 4 HV9105.V7

SCHOOLTEACHING. see **TEACHING.**

Schorr, Alan Edward. Alaska place names / edited by Alan Edward Schorr. 2d ed. Juneau : University Library, University of Alaska, 1980. 77 p. ; 29 cm. (Library occasional papers . no. 1) LC Card 80-622301 DDC 917.98/00321 19
1. Alaska - Gazetteers. I. Title. II. Series.
F902 .S36 1980

Schramm, Wayne F.
Perinatal mortality and prematurity in Missouri / by Wayne F. Schramm. Jefferson City : Missouri Dept. of Social Services, Division of Health, Missouri Center for Health Statistics, Bureau of Health Data Analysis, [1979] ix, 68 p. : ill. ; 28 cm. "November 1979." "Missouri Center for Health Statistics publication no. 4.14." LC Card 80-621734 DDC 362.1/9832 19
1. Perinatal mortality - Missouri - Statistics. 2. Infants - Missouri - Mortality - Statistics. 3. Childbirth - Missouri - Statistics. 4. Infants (Premature) - Missouri - Statistics. 5. Prenatal care - Missouri - Statistics. 6. Missouri - Statistics, Medical. 7. Missouri - Statistics, Vital. I. Title.
RG632.U62 M57

Trends in nonmarital fertility and spacing between marriage and first birth in Missouri / [by Wayne F. Schramm]. Jefferson City : Missouri Dept. of Social Services, Division of Health, Missouri Center for Health Statistics, [1980] vi, 17 p. : graph ; 28 cm. "Missouri Center for Health Statistics publication no. 4.19." Includes bibliographical references. LC Card 80-623989 DDC 304.6/3 19
1. Fertility, Human - Missouri - Statistics. 2. Birth interval - Missouri - Statistics. 3. Illegitimacy - Missouri - Statistics. I. Missouri Center for Health Statistics. II. Title.
HB935.M8 S37

Schraufnagel, Stanley A. Supply control and U. S. agriculture : an analysis of national and regional impacts under land and fertilizer restrictions / by Stanley A. Schraufnagel, Earl O. Heady. Ames, Iowa : Center for Agricultural and Rural Development, Iowa State University, [1980] xiii leaves, 84 p. : ill. ; 28 cm. (CARD report. 94) "July 1980." Bibliography: p. 73-74. LC Card 80-623951 DDC 338.1/873 19
1. Agriculture and state - United States. 2. Agriculture - Economic aspects - United States. I. Heady, Earl Orel, 1916- joint author. II. Series: Iowa. State University of Science and Technology, Ames. Center for Agricultural and Rural Development. CARD report, 94. III. Title.
HD1761 .S258

Schreiner, Price J. California. Dept. of Water Resources. Division of Planning. California Central Valley natural flow data /. [Sacramento] [1980] v, 77 p. : LC Card 80-623071 DDC 551.48/3/097945 19
GB1225.C3 C34 1980

Schriesheim, Chester. Leadership, beyond establishment views /. Carbondale , c1981. p.

cm. ISBN 0-8093-1026-0 LC Card 81-8739 DDC 303.3/4 19
HM141 .L393

Schroeder, David C. Phosphorus export from rural Maine watersheds / by David C. Schroeder. [Orono, Me.] : Land and Water Resources Center, University of Maine at Orono, [1979] iv, 42 leaves : ill. ; 28 cm. (Completion report / Land and Water Resources Center, University of Maine at Orono) "December, 1979." Bibliography: leaves 40-41. "Project A-042-ME." LC Card 80-623370 DDC 363.7/394 19
1. Water - Phosphorus content. 2. Water quality - Maine. I. Series: Completion report (University of Maine at Orono. Land and Water Resources Center. II. Title.
TD427.P56 S37

Schroeder, Roy A. Peters, Norman E. Temporal trends in the acidity of precipitation and surface waters of New York /. Reston, Va. , 1981. p. cm. LC Card 81-607082 DDC 551.57/09747 19
GB2825.N7 P47

Schroeder, Thomas A. Mesoscale structure of Hawaiian rainstorms / Thomas A. Schroeder. Honolulu : Water Resources Research Center, University of Hawaii, [1978] x, 69 p. : ill. ; 28 cm. (Technical report - Water Resources Research Center, University of Hawaii ; no. 119) "September 1978." "UHMET 78-03." "OWRT project no.: A-072-HI. Project period: 1 October 1877 to 30 September 1978." Bibliography: p. 55-57. LC Card 79-626234 DDC 553.7/09969 s 551.57/81/09969 19
1. Rainstorms - Hawaii. 2. Mesometeorology - Hawaii. 3. Floods - Hawaii. I. Series: Hawaii. University, Honolulu. Water Resources Research Center. Technical report , no. 119. II. Title.
TC1 .H36 no. 119 QC925.1.U8H3

Schroer, C. V.
Nevada streamflow characteristics / by C.V. Schroer and Otto Moosburner ; prepared cooperatively by the Geological Survey, U. S. Department of the Interior. Carson City : State of Nevada, Dept. of Conservation and Natural Resources, Division of Water Resources, [1978] 478 p. : map (fold. in pocket) ; 28 cm. (Water resources-information series . report 28) "October 1978." Chiefly tables. Includes bibliographical references and index. LC Card 80-623614 DDC 551.48/3/09793 19
1. Stream measurements - Nevada. I. Moosburner, Otto, joint author. II. United States. Geological Survey. III. Nevada. Division of Water Resources. IV. Title. V. Series.
GB1225.N3 S37

(joint author) Rush, F. Eugene. Geohydrology of Smith Valley, Nevada, with special reference to the water-use period, 1953-72 /. [Carson City] , 1976. 95 p. : LC Card 80-623615 DDC 553.7/09793/58 19
GB705.N3 R87

Schroyer, Helen Q. A guide to a course in government documents / by Helen Q. Schroyer. [Champaign, Ill.] : University of Illinois, Graduate School of Library Science, 1978. 51 p. ; 28 cm. (Occasional papers - University of Illinois, Graduate School of Library Science ; no. 135 0073-5310) Caption title. Bibliography: p. 34-35. LC Card 79-625738 DDC 026/.01573 19
1. Libraries - Special collections - Government publications. 2. United States - Government publications. 3. Government publications. I. Series: Illinois. University at Urbana-Champaign. Graduate School of Library Science. Occasional papers , no. 135. II. Title.
Z688.G6 S36

Schubert, Frank N. Vanguard of expansion : Army Engineers in the trans-Mississippi West, 1819-1879 / by Frank. N. Schubert. Washington, D.C. : Historical Division, Office of Administrative Services, Office of the Chief of Engineers : for sale by the Supt. of Docs., U. S. Govt. Print. Off., [1980] xii, 160 p. : ill. ; 23 cm. Includes bibliographical references and index. LC Card 80-144567 DDC 358/.22/0973 19
1. United States. Army. Corps of Engineers - History - 19th century. 2. The West - History - To 1848. 3. The West - History - 1848-1950. I. United States. Army. Corps of Engineers. Historical Division. II. Title.
UG23 .S38

Schuenemeyer, J. H. Drew, Lawrence J. Estimation of the future rates of oil and gas discoveries in the western Gulf of Mexico /. Washington , 1981. p. cm. LC Card 81-6768

DDC 553.2/8/09726 19
TN872.A5 D73

Schulman, Mark A. A survey of spousal violence against women in Kentucky / by Mark A. Schulman. Washington, D.C. : U. S. Dept. of Justice, Law Enforcement Assistance Administration : for sale by the Supt. of Docs., U. S. Govt. Print. Off., 1980 printing. 67, 13 p., p. a-b : ill. ; 28 cm. "July 1979." "Study no. 792701 conducted for Kentucky Commission on Women." LC Card 80-602365 DDC 362.8/2 19
1. Wife abuse - Kentucky. I. Kentucky Commission on Women. II. Title.
HV6626 .S38

Schultz, Charles R. Bibliography of maritime and naval history periodical articles published 1976-1977 / compiled by Charles R. Schultz. College Station : Sea Grant College Program, Texas A&M University, 1979. 90 p. ; 28 cm. "TAMU-SG-79-607." Includes indexes. LC Card 79-624012 DDC 016.3875/09 19
1. Navigation - History - Bibliography. 2. Merchant marine - History - Bibliography. 3. Naval history - Bibliography. 4. Naval art and science - History - Bibliography. I. Title.
Z6837 .S38 VK15

Schultz, Ronald R. The social and economic effects of the Florida tourist industry / by Ronald R. Schultz, William B. Stronge ; prepared for the Office of Manpower Planning, Florida Department of Community Affairs. Boca Raton : Florida Atlantic University, 1978. x, 123 p. : ill. ; 29 cm. Bibliography: p. 121-123. LC Card 79-622949
1. Tourist trade - Florida. I. Stronge, William B., joint author. 0700. II. Florida. Office of Manpower Planning. III. Title.
G155.U6 S37

Schultze, L. E. (Lawrence E.) Extracting uranium from carbonaceous ores / by L.E. Schultze, D.J. Bauer, and M.T. Morimoto. [Washington, D.C.] : U. S. Dept. of the Interior, Bureau of Mines, [1981] p. cm. (Report of investigations) Bibliography: p. LC Card 81-10150 DDC 622 s 669/.2931 19
1. Uranium - Metallurgy. 2. Uranium ores - United States. 3. Rocks, Carbonate. I. Bauer, D. J. (Donald J.). II. Morimoto, M. T. (Michael T.). III. Series: Report of investigations (United States. Bureau of Mines). IV. Title.
TN23 .U43 TN799.U7

Schumacher, Thomas M. Soil survey of Campbell County, South Dakota / [by Thomas M. Schumacher and Kenneth J. Heil] ; United States Department of Agriculture, Soil Conservation Service, in cooperation with South Dakota Agricultural Experiment Station. [Washington] : The Service, [1979] vii, 175 p., [32] fold. leaves of plates : ill. ; 29 cm. Cover title. LC Card 80-602616 DDC 631.4/7/78317 19
1. Soils - South Dakota - Campbell Co. - Maps. I. Heil, Kenneth J., joint author. II. United States. Soil Conservation Service. III. South Dakota. Agricultural Experiment Station, Brookings.
S599.S6 S4

Schuman, Richard. From landfill to park. New York, 1974. 45 p.: *NYPL [*ZI-281]*

SCHURZ, CARL, 1829-1906.
Trefousse, Hans Louis. Carl Schurz, a biography /. Knoxville , c1981. p. cm. ISBN 0-87049-326-4 : LC Card 81-3370 DDC 973.8/092/4 B 19
E664.S39 T7

Schuster, Allan D. Motor common carrier corporate strategy in an uncertain regulatory environment / Allan D. Schuster. Austin : Graduate School of Business, University of Texas at Austin : distributed by Bureau of Business Research, University of Texas at Austin, [1979] 20 p. ; 28 cm. (Working paper - Graduate School of Business, University of Texas at Austin ; 79-17) "July 1979." Includes bibliographical references. LC Card 79-625407 DDC 388.3/24/0973 19
1. Transportation, Automotive - United States - Freight. I. Series: Texas. University at Austin. Graduate School of Business. Working paper - Graduate School of Business, University of Texas at Austin , 79-17. II. Title.
HE5623 .S375

Schwab, Eleanor A. South Dakota. Board of Examiners of Psychologists. Directory of

licensed psychologists and associate psychologists /. [Pierre?] , 1979. [7] p. ; LC Card 79-625660 DDC 150/.25/783 19
BF30 .S68 1979

Schwab, Lois. Rehabilitation for independent living : a selected bibliography / prepared by Lois O. Schwab. Washington, D.C. : Women's Committee, President's Committee on Employment of the Handicapped, 1980. 47 p. ; 28 cm. "Janurary 1980." LC Card 80-601692 DDC 016.3624/048 19
1. Rehabilitation - Bibliography. I. United States. President's Committee on Employment of the Handicapped. Women's Committee. II. Title.
Z7254 .S37 HV3000

Schwalbe, Rosanne M. Health insurance coverage of disabled persons under Medicaid and private insurance / Rosanne M. Schwalbe and Maurice MacDonald. [Madison] : University of Wisconsin-Madison, Institute for Research on Poverty, [1980] 55 p. ; 28 cm. (Discussion papers - University of Wisconsin-Madison, Institute for Research on Poverty ; DP # 585-79) "January 1980." Bibliography: p. 50. LC Card 80-622904 DDC 368.3/8/00880816 19
1. Insurance, Health - United States. 2. Medicaid. 3. Handicapped - United States. I. MacDonald, Maurice, 1947- joint author. II. Series: Wisconsin. University. Madison. Institute for Research on Poverty. Discussion papers, 585-79. III. Title.
HG9396 .S28

Schwaner, Terry D. Reproductive biology of lizards on the American Samoan Islands / by Terry D. Schwaner. [Lawrence, Kan. : Museum of Natural History, University of Kansas], 1980. 53 p. : graphs ; 23 cm. (Occasional papers of the Museum of Natural History, the University of Kansas . no. 86) Caption title. Bibliography: p. 51-53. LC Card 80-624051 DDC 597.95/0416 19
1. Lizards - American Samoa - Reproduction. 2. Reptiles - Reproduction. 3. Reptiles - American Samoa - Reproduction. I. Series: Kansas. University. Museum of Natural History. Occasional papers , no. 86. II. Title.
QL666.L2 S37

Schwartz, Charles Walsh. Wildlife drawings / Charles W. Schwartz ; Michael McIntosh, editor. 1st ed. Jefferson City, Mo. : Missouri Dept. of Conservation, c1980. 122 p. : ill. ; 31 x 39 cm. LC Card 81-621407 DDC 599 19
1. Animals - Pictorial works. 2. Zoology - Missouri - Pictorial works. I. McIntosh, Michael. II. Title.
QL46 .S395

Schwartz, Jerome L. California. County Health Care Costs Study. Health care costs and services in California counties . Sacramento, Calif. , 1978. xx, 136 p. : LC Card 78-623918
RA412.5.U6 C29 1978 ***NYPL [JLF 81-148]***

SCHWARTZ, ROSALIND MERL.
Conference on Occupational Stress, Los Angeles, 1978. New developments in occupational stress . Los Angeles, Calif. [1979] v, 120 p. ; LC Card 80-621405 DDC 158.7 19
HF5548.85 .C65 1978

Schwartz, Victor E. United States. Dept. of Commerce. Task Force on Product Liability and Accident Compensation. Uniform product liability act . [Washington] , 1979. 44 p. ; LC Card 80-601839 DDC 346.7303/82 19
KF1296 .A8168

Schwarz, Harry E. University of Massachusetts at Amherst. Water Resources Research Center. Urbanization and water quality planning . Amherst, Mass. [1979] viii, 121 [14] p. ; LC Card 80-623703 DDC 333.91/009744 s 363.7/39456/068 19
TD224.M4 M37 no. 104

Schwarz, Leroy B. (joint author) Deuermeyer, Bryan L. A model for the analysis of system service level in warehouse-retailer distribution systems . West Lafayette, Ind. [1979] 33, [16], 9 leaves : LC Card 80-621782 DDC 658/.001/9 s 658.7/81 19
HD6483 .P8 no. 716 HF5429

SCHWEIKER, RICHARD SCHULTZ, 1926-
United States. Congress. Senate. Committee on Finance. Nomination of Richard S. Schweiker . Washington , c1981. iii, 39 p. ; LC Card 81-600829 DDC 353.842 19
KF26 .F5 1981

Schweizerische Kreditanstalt. see Crédit suisse.

Schwitzgebel, Ralph K., 1934- Legal aspects of the enforced treatment of offenders / by R. Kirkland Schwitzgebel. Rockville, Md. : U. S. Dept. of Health, Education, and Welfare, Public Health Service, Alcohol, Drug Abuse, and Mental Health Administration, National Institute of Mental Health, Center for Studies of Crime and Delinquency ; Washington, D.C. : for sale by the Supt. of Docs., U. S. Govt. Print. Off., [1979] vii, 133 p. : forms ; 23 cm. (Crime and delinquency issues) DHEW publication ; no. (ADM) 79-831 Includes bibliographical references. LC Card 80-600988 DDC 344.73/044 347.30444 19
1. Insane, Criminal and dangerous - United States. 2. Mental health laws - United States. I. Series: United States. Dept. of Health, Education and Welfare. DHEW publication, no. (ADM) 79-831. II. Title.
KF3828 .S38

Science and cancer /. Shimkin, Michael Boris, 1912- [Bethesda? Md.] , 1980. viii, 109 p. : LC Card 80-603983 DDC 616.99/4 19
RC263 .S48 1980

SCIENCE AND LITERATURE. see LITERATURE AND SCIENCE.

SCIENCE AND POETRY. see LITERATURE AND SCIENCE.

SCIENCE AND STATE - CHINA.
Background readings on science, technology, and energy R. & D. in Japan and China /. Washington , 1981. xii, 499 p. : LC Card 81-600676 DDC 609.52 19
Q127.J3 B3

SCIENCE AND STATE - EGYPT.
Planning for trilateral scientific and technological cooperation by Egypt, Israel, and the United States . Washington , 1980. vii, 49 p. ; LC Card 80-603873 DDC 327.1/7 19
Q127.U6 P53

SCIENCE AND STATE - ISRAEL.
Planning for trilateral scientific and technological cooperation by Egypt, Israel, and the United States . Washington , 1980. vii, 49 p. ; LC Card 80-603873 DDC 327.1/7 19
Q127.U6 P53

SCIENCE AND STATE - JAPAN.
Background readings on science, technology, and energy R. & D. in Japan and China /. Washington , 1981. xii, 499 p. : LC Card 81-600676 DDC 609.52 19
Q127.J3 B3

SCIENCE AND STATE - LATIN AMERICA.
Programa Regional de Desarrollo Científico y Tecnológico. Aspectos organizacionales de la política científica y tecnológica en América Latina . Washington, D.C. [1979?] iii, 66 p. ; LC Card 79-119687
Q127.L38 P76 1979

SCIENCE AND STATE - MAINE.
Maine. State Science, Engineering, and Technology Study Group. Science in the Statehouse . Orono , 1979. iii leaves, 57, cxxvi p. ; LC Card 79-624434 DDC 353.97410085/5 19
Q127.U6 M27 1979

SCIENCE AND STATE - SOVIET UNION.
Science policy . [Washington, D.C.?] , 1980. 2 v. ; LC Card 80-604130 DDC 507/.2073 19
Q127.U6 S319

SCIENCE AND STATE - UNITED STATES.
Linking science and technology to public policy . [Albany] [1979] viii, 156 p. (p. 155-156 blank) : ISBN 0-915194-03-1 LC Card 78-22608 DDC 353.9/172 19
Q127.U6 L56

Planning for trilateral scientific and technological cooperation by Egypt, Israel, and the United States . Washington , 1980. vii, 49 p. ; LC Card 80-603873 DDC 327.1/7 19
Q127.U6 P53

Science policy . [Washington, D.C.?] , 1980. 2 v. ; LC Card 80-604130 DDC 507/.2073 19
Q127.U6 S319

United States. Congress. House. Committee on Science and Technology. H.R. 7178 (superseded by H.R. 7689), the Research and development authorization estimates act . Washington , 1980. iii, 321 p. : LC Card 80-603641 DDC 346.73/023 347.30623 19
KF27 .S39 1980c

United States. Congress. House. Committee on

Science and Technology. Subcommittee on Science, Research, and Technology. The Helsinki forum and East-West scientific exchange . Washington , 1980. v, 323 p. ; LC Card 80-602155　DDC 327.1/7 19
KF27 .S399 1980

United States. Congress. Senate. Committee on Commerce, Science, and Transportation. Subcommittee on Science, Technology, and Space. Office of Science and Technology Policy . Washington , 1980. iii, 72 p. ; LC Card 80-603897　DDC 353.0085/5 19
KF26 .C697 1980g

United States. General Accounting Office. Increasing costs, competition may hinder U. S. position of leadership in high energy physics . Washington, D.C. , 1980. v, 222 p. : LC Card 80-603949　DDC 539.7/6/072073 19
QC793.4 .U54 1980

United States. National Science Foundation. The five-year outlook . [Washington, D.C.] [1980?- v. ; LC Card 80-603198　DDC 509/.73 19
Q127.U6 U489 1980

United States. President's Commission for a National Agenda for the Eighties. Panel on Science and Technology. Science and technology . Washington , 1981. p. cm.　LC Card 80-28290　DDC 306/.4 19
T21 .U56 1981

SCIENCE AND STATE - UNITED STATES - PERIODICALS.
United States. National Science Foundation. The Five-year outlook: problems, opportunities and constraints in science and technology. 1980- [Washington].　　*NYPL [JSP 81-1]*

Science and technology . United States. President's Commission for a National Agenda for the Eighties. Panel on Science and Technology. Washington , 1981. p. cm.　LC Card 80-28290　DDC 306/.4 19
T21 .U56 1981

Science and Technology for Development, United Nations Conference on. see United Nations Conference on Science and Technology for Development, Vienna, 1979.

Science and technology intern program . Wisconsin. Legislative Council. Madison, Wis. , 1979. iv, 152 p. ; LC Card 79-624457　DDC 328.775/0761 19
Q127.U6 W57 1979

SCIENCE AND TECHNOLOGY INTERN PROGRAM.
Wisconsin. Legislative Council. Science and technology intern program . Madison, Wis. , 1979. iv, 152 p. ; LC Card 79-624457　DDC 328.775/0761 19
Q127.U6 W57 1979

Science Applications, inc.
Environmental assessment of the Alaskan continental shelf . [Rockville, Md.?] , 1980. xv, 313 p. : LC Card 81-600735　DDC 574.5/2636/09798 19
QH105.A4 E586

A study of postulated accidents at California nuclear power plants / prepared for the State of California Office of Emergency Services by Science Applications, Inc. [Sacramento] : The Office, [1980] ca. 700 p. in various pagings : ill. ; 28 cm. & appendices (ca. 400 p. in various pagings : ill.) Cover title. "July 1980." Includes bibliographical references. LC Card 80-623073　DDC 363.1/79 19
1. Atomic power-plants - California - Accidents - Mathematical models. 2. Atomic power-plants - California - Accidents - Data processing. I. California. Office of Emergency Services. II. Title.
TK1344.C2 S28 1980

SCIENCE, APPLIED. see TECHNOLOGY.

SCIENCE - CONGRESSES.
The Joys of research /. Washington, D.C. , 1981. p. cm.　ISBN 0-87474-858-5 LC Card 81-9347　DDC 001.4 19
Q179.9 .J69

United Nations Conference on Science and Technology for Development, Vienna, 1979. Report of the United Nations Conference on Science and Technology for Development, Vienna 20-31 August 1979. New York , 1979. iv, 133 p. ; LC Card 80-100608　DDC 303.4/83 19
JX1977 .A2 A/CONF.81/16

Science education databook/. United States. National Science Foundation. Directorate for Science Education. Office of Program Integration. [Washington, D.C.] [1980] ix, 154 p. : LC Card 80-602336　DDC 507/.1073 19
Q183.3.A1 U55 1980

SCIENCE FICTION, AMERICAN - HISTORY AND CRITICISM - ADDRESSES, ESSAYS, LECTURES.
Yoke, Carl B. Roger Zelazny and Andre Norton, proponents of individualism /. Columbus , 1979. 26 p. ; LC Card 80-137489　DDC 813/.54 19
PS374.S35 Y6

Science in the Statehouse . Maine. State Science, Engineering, and Technology Study Group. Orono , 1979. iii leaves, 57, cxxvi p. ; LC Card 79-624434　DDC 353.97410085/5 19
Q127.U6 M27 1979

SCIENCE - INDEXES.
United States. Defense Documentation Center. Directorate of Technical Service. Delimited AD document index /. - Alexandria, Va. , 1977. 116 p. ;　　　*NYPL [*XMQ-2162]*

SCIENCE - INFORMATION SERVICES.
North Atlantic Treaty Organization. Advisory Group for Aerospace Research and Development. How to obtain information in different fields of science and technology. Langley Field, Va., 1974. 1 v. of various pagings;　　　*NYPL [JSG 80-127]*

SCIENCE - INFORMATION SERVICES - UNITED STATES - DIRECTORIES.
Directory of federally supported information analysis centers, 1979 /. Washington , 1979. ix, 87 p. ; LC Card 80-601664　DDC 507/.2 19
Q223.5 .D57 1979

SCIENCE - INTERNATIONAL COOPERATION.
Planning for trilateral scientific and technological cooperation by Egypt, Israel, and the United States . Washington , 1980. vii, 49 p. ; LC Card 80-603873　DDC 327.1/7 19
Q127.U6 P53

United States. Congress. House. Committee on Science and Technology. Subcommittee on Science, Research, and Technology. United States-Mexico scientific and technological cooperation . Washington , 1979. iii, 289 p. : LC Card 80-602192　DDC 338.9 19
KF27 .S399 1979k

SCIENCE - LATIN AMERICA - CONGRESSES.
Inter-American Council for Education, Science, and Culture. Anexos al Informe final de la novena reunión de la CEPCIECC. Washington , 1974. iii, 363 p. ;　　*NYPL [JFF 80-1286]*

Science, medicine, and technology in East Asia . (v. 1) Sung, Tz'u, 1186-1249. [Hsi yüan chi lu. English.] The washing away of wrongs . Ann Arbor , 1981. p. cm.　ISBN 0-89264-801-5 : LC Card 81-6195　DDC 614/.1 19
RA1063 .S9613

SCIENCE, MENTAL. see PSYCHOLOGY.

SCIENCE - METHODOLOGY.
(1981) Simon, Michael A. Understanding human action . Albany , c1981. p. cm.　ISBN 0-87395-498-X　LC Card 81-5280　DDC 302 19
HM251 .S622

SCIENCE - METHODS. see SCIENCE - METHODOLOGY.

SCIENCE, MORAL. see ETHICS.

The science of ceramic machining and surface finishing II . Symposium on the Science of Ceramic Machining and Surface Finishing, 2d, National Bureau of Standards, 1978. Gaithersburg, Md. , Washington, D.C. , 1979. xii, 532 p. : LC Card 79-600149　DDC 602/.18 s 666 19
QC100 .U57 no. 562 TP814

The science of fingerprints . United States. Federal Bureau of Investigation. [Washington] , Washington, D.C. [1979] v, 209 p. : LC Card 80-602568　DDC 363.2/58 19
HV6074 .U6 1979

SCIENCE OF LANGUAGE. see LINGUISTICS.

Science of organization and organization of science /. Malinovskiĭ, Aleksandr

Aleksandrovich, 1909- [Washington] 1972. 18 p.　　　　*NYPL [*XMQ-2148]*

SCIENCE - PERIODICALS - BIBLIOGRAPHY - CATALOGS.
Tucker, Jane C. New serial holdings, 1977 /. [Washington] [Springfield, Va.] 1977. vi, 232 p. ; LC Card 77-602720
Z7403 .T79 Q158.5　　*NYPL [JSF 81-153]*

SCIENCE - PHILOSOPHY.
(1981) Philosophy of science and the occult /. Albany , 1981. p. cm.　ISBN 0-87395-572-2 LC Card 81-13552　DDC 001.9/01 19
BF1411 .P49

SCIENCE - PHILOSOPHY - ADDRESSES, ESSAYS, LECTURES.
(1972) Malinovskiĭ, Aleksandr Aleksandrovich, 1909- Science of organization and organization of science /. [Washington] 1972. 18 p.
　　　　*NYPL [*XMQ-2148]*

Science policy : USA/USSR / [report prepared for National Science Foundation, Directorate for Scientific, Technological and International Affairs, Division of International Programs]. [Washington, D.C.?] : The Foundation : For sale by the Supt. of Docs., U. S. G.P.O., 1980. 2 v. ; 23 cm. S/N 038-000-00456-5 (v. 1) 038-000-00457-3 (v. 2) Item 834-C Includes bibliographical references. CONTENTS. - v. 1. Science policy in the United States / Nat C. Robertson -- v. 2. Science policy in the Soviet Union / Paul M. Cooks. LC Card 80-604130　DDC 507/.2073 19
1. Science and state - United States. 2. Science and state - Soviet Union. 3. Research - United States. 4. Research - Soviet Union. I. Robertson, Nat Clinton. II. Cooks, Paul, 1941-. III. National Science Foundation (U. S.). Division of International Programs.
Q127.U6 S319

SCIENCE, POLITICAL. see POLITICAL SCIENCE.

SCIENCE - RESEARCH. see RESEARCH.

SCIENCE, SOCIAL. see SOCIOLOGY.

Science staff services in the Illinois Legislative Council : report to the General Assembly : catalog of services, identification of needs, improvement plan / prepared by Margaret M. Cetera ... [et al.] for the Illinois Legislative Council. [Springfield, Ill.] : The Council, [1979] x, 74 p. : ill. ; 28 cm. On cover: State science, engineering & technology project. "April 1979." Includes bibliographical references.　LC Card 80-622583　DDC 328.773/0761 19
1. Research - Illinois. 2. Illinois. Legislative Council - Officials and employees. 3. Research - Law and legislation - Illinois. I. Cetera, Margaret M. II. Illinois. Legislative Council. III. Illinois. General Assembly. IV. Title: State science, engineering & technology project.
Q180.U5 S364

SCIENCE - STUDY AND TEACHING - CHINA - HISTORY.
United States. Library of Congress. Research Services. Manpower for science and engineering in China /. Washington , 1980. v, 36 p. ; LC Card 80-603062　DDC 331.12/9150951 19
Q149.C5 U56 1980

SCIENCE - STUDY AND TEACHING (GRADUATE) - UNITED STATES - STATISTICS.
Brown, Carol M. Trends in graduate enrollment and Ph.D. output in scientific fields, 1960-61 through 1967-68. [Washington] , 1969 [i.e. 1970] vii, 204 p. ; LC Card 73-606834　DDC 610/.7 s 610/.7/073 19
RA440.6 .R4 no. 18 R854.U5

SCIENCE - STUDY AND TEACHING (HIGHER) - UNITED STATES.
United States. National Science Foundation. Office of Experimental Projects and Programs. College science improvement programs. Washington, D. C [1974] v, 191 p.
　　　　NYPL [JSF 80-775]

SCIENCE - STUDY AND TEACHING - UNITED STATES - STATISTICS.
United States. National Science Foundation. Directorate for Science Education. Office of Program Integration. Science education databook/. [Washington, D.C.] [1980] ix, 154 p. : LC Card 80-602336　DDC 507/.1073 19
Q183.3.A1 U55 1980

SCIENCE - SUBJECT HEADINGS. see SUBJECT HEADINGS - SCIENCE.

SCIENCE - UNITED STATES.
United States. National Science Foundation.
The five-year outlook . [Washington, D.C.]
[1980?- v. ; LC Card 80-603198 DDC 509/.73 19
Q127.U6 U489 1980

SCIENCES, OCCULT. see OCCULT SCIENCES.

SCIENCES, SOCIAL. see SOCIAL SCIENCES.

SCIENTIFIC APPARATUS AND INSTRUMENTS - STANDARDS - UNITED STATES - EXHIBITIONS.
United States. National Bureau of Standards.
Museum. Catalog of artifacts on display in the
NBS Museum /. Washington, D.C. , 1977. ca.
200 p. : LC Card 79-603912
Q185.7 .U54 1977

SCIENTIFIC EXCHANGES. see EXCHANGES, LITERARY AND SCIENTIFIC.

SCIENTIFIC ILLUSTRATION - CATALOGS.
Smithsonian Institution. Finders' guide to prints
and drawings in the Smithsonian Institution /.
Washington, D.C. , 1981. p. cm. ISBN
0-87474-317-6 LC Card 81-607070 DDC
760/.074/0153 19
N855.8 .A56

SCIENTIFIC MANAGEMENT. see INDUSTRIAL MANAGEMENT.

SCIENTIFIC METHOD. see SCIENCE - METHODOLOGY.

SCIENTIFIC PROGRAMMING. see SCHEDULING (MANAGEMENT)

SCIENTIFIC RESEARCH. see RESEARCH.

Scientific research with the space telescope :
International Astronomical Union colloquium
number 54, held at the Institute for Advanced
Study, Princeton, N.J., August 8-11, 1979 /
co-sponsored by COSPAR ; [editors], M. S.
Longair, J. W. Warner. [Huntsville, Ala.] :
[National Aeronautics and Space
Administration, George C. Marshall Space
Flight Center] ; Washington, D.C. : for sale by
the Supt. of Docs., U. S. Govt. Print. Off.,
[1979] xii, 327 p. : ill. ; 23 cm. (NASA ;
CP-2111) Includes bibliographies. LC Card 80-601618
DDC 520 19
*1. Astronomical research - United States - Congresses.
2. Orbiting astronomical observatories - Congresses. I.
Longair, M. S., 1941-. II. Warner, John Ward, 1944-.
III. International Astronomical Union. IV. International
Council of Scientific Unions. Committee on Space
Research. V. Title: International Astronomical Union
colloquium no. 54. VI. Title: Space telescope. VII.
Series: United States. National Aeronautics and Space
Administration. NASA conference proceedings ,
CP2111.*
QB61 .S33

SCIENTIST - UNITED STATES - STATISTICS - PERIODICALS.
United States. National Science Foundation.
Scientists and engineers from abroad.
Washington, D. C. ***NYPL [M-11 4663]***

Scientists and engineers from abroad. United
States. National Science Foundation.
Washington, D. C. ***NYPL [M-11 4663]***

SCIENTISTS - CHINA.
United States. Library of Congress. Research
Services. Manpower for science and engineering
in China /. Washington , 1980. v, 36 p. ; LC
Card 80-603062 DDC 331.12/9150951 19
Q149.C5 U56 1980

SCIENTISTS - EMPLOYMENT - UNITED STATES.
Berry, Richard M. Employment patterns of
academic scientists and engineers, 1973-78.
[Washington, D.C.] , 1980. v, 15 p. : LC Card
80-603833 DDC 331.12/515/0973 19
Q149.U5 B47

SCIENTISTS IN GOVERNMENT - WISCONSIN.
Wisconsin. Legislative Council. Science and
technology intern program . Madison, Wis. ,
1979. iv, 152 p. ; LC Card 79-624457 DDC
328.775/0761 19
Q127.U6 W57 1979

SCIENTISTS - UNITED STATES - STATISTICS.
United States. Bureau of the Census. Selected
characteristics of persons in physical science,
1978. Washington, D.C. , U. S. Dept. of

Commerce, Bureau of the Census. iv, 30 p. :
LC Card 80-607850 DDC 312/.0973 s
509/.02/2 19
HA203 .A218 no. 108 Q149.U5

Scoggins, James R. Knight, Keith Shelburne.
Atmospheric structure determined from satellite
data /. Washington, D.C. [Springfield, Va.]
1981. x, 95 p. : LC Card 81-601075 DDC
551.5/14 19
QC879.59.A .K58

Scope of the general revenue sharing program .
United States. Congress. Senate. Committee on
Governmental Affairs. Subcommittee on
Intergovernmental Relations. Washington ,
1980. iii, 227 p. ; LC Card 80-602990 DDC
336.1/85 19
KF26 .G6738 1980a

SCOPE 80's. Illinois. SCOPE 80's Task Force.
Strategies for computer-oriented productivity
and effectiveness in the 80's . [Springfield, Ill.]
[1980] ca. 300 p. in various pagings : LC Card
80-623318 DDC 353.977304//02854 19
JK5749.A8 I46 1980

SCORIAS.
Reynolds, Don R. Foliicolous Ascomycetes 1 .
Los Angeles , 1978. 16 p. : LC Card 78-104483
DDC 574 s 589.2/3 19
Q11 .L52 no. 288 QK623.C36

SCORIAS SPONGIOSA.
Reynolds, Don R. Foliicolous Ascomycetes 1 .
Los Angeles , 1978. 16 p. : LC Card 78-104483
DDC 574 s 589.2/3 19
Q11 .L52 no. 288 QK623.C36

SCORP 1978. Vermont. Agency of
Environmental Conservation. Division of
Planning. Vermont State comprehensive outdoor
recreation plan . [Montpelier] , 1978. ca. 500 p.
in various pagings, [17] fold. leaves of plates (8
fold. in pocket) : LC Card 80-622420 DDC
790/.09743 19
GV191.42.V5 V48 1978

SCORPIONS - BRITISH VIRGIN ISLANDS - CLASSIFICATION.
Francke, Oscar F. Scorpions from the Virgin
Islands (Arachnida, Scorpiones) /. [Lubbock,
Tex.] , 1980. 19 p. : LC Card 80-623501 DDC
595.4/6097297/2 19
QL458.7 .F73

Scorpions from the Virgin Islands (Arachnida, Scorpiones) /. Francke, Oscar F. [Lubbock,
Tex.] , 1980. 19 p. : LC Card 80-623501 DDC
595.4/6097297/2 19
QL458.7 .F73

SCORPIONS - VIRGIN ISLANDS OF THE UNITED STATES - CLASSIFICATION.
Francke, Oscar F. Scorpions from the Virgin
Islands (Arachnida, Scorpiones) /. [Lubbock,
Tex.] , 1980. 19 p. : LC Card 80-623501 DDC
595.4/6097297/2 19
QL458.7 .F73

SCOTIA MINE DISASTER, OVEN FORK, KY., 1976.
United States. Congress. Senate. Committee on
Labor and Public Welfare. Subcommittee on
Labor. Scotia Mine disaster, 1976 .
Washington , 1976. vi, 279 p. ; LC Card
76-602873
KF26 .L363 1976f ***NYPL [JLE 81-466]***

Scotia Mine disaster, 1976 . United States.
Congress. Senate. Committee on Labor and
Public Welfare. Subcommittee on Labor.
Washington , 1976. vi, 279 p. ; LC Card
76-602873
KF26 .L363 1976f ***NYPL [JLE 81-466]***

SCOTLAND IN ART.
Finley, Gerald. Landscapes of memory .
Berkeley , c1980. 272 p. : ISBN 0-520-04436-3
LC Card 80-5956 DDC 741.64/092/4 19
NC978.5.T87 F56 1982

Scott, Charles D. Symposium on Biotechnology
in Energy Production and Conservation, 1st,
Gatlinburg, Tenn., 1978. Biotechnology in
energy production and conservation . New
York , c1979. vi, 513 p. : ISBN 0-471-05745-2
(pbk.) LC Card 80-128733
TJ163.7 .S97 1978 ***NYPL [JSE 80-1362]***

Scott, Frank S. (Frank Sanford), 1921-
Economic viability of small macadamia nut
farms in Kona / by Frank S. Scott, Jr. and
Herbert K. Marutani. Honolulu, Hawaii :

Hawaii Institute of Tropical Agriculture and
Human Resources, College of Tropical
Agriculture and Human Resources, University
of Hawaii at Manoa, 1981. p. cm. (Research
series / Hawaii Institute of Tropical Agriculture and
Human Resources, 0197-9310) Bibliography: p. LC
Card 81-6946 DDC 338.1/745 19
*1. Macadamia nut industry - Hawaii - Kona (Hawaii
Island). 2. Farms, Small - Hawaii - Kona (Hawaii
Island). I. Marutani, Herbert K. (Herbert Katsuyuki),
1931-. II. Series: Research series (Hawaii Institute of
Tropical Agriculture and Human Resources) . III. Title.*
HD9259.M233 U67

Scott, John H. Evaluation of REO model BT 300
C-D blasting machine tester / by John H.
Scott, Karl R. Becker, and J. Edmund Hay.
[Avondale, Md.] : U. S. Dept of the Interior,
Bureau of Mines, [1981] p. cm. (Report of
investigations) LC Card 81-607976 DDC 622 s
622/.23 19
*1. Blasting machines - Testing. 2. Testing-machines -
Testing. I. Becker, Karl R. II. Hay, J. Edmund. III.
Series: Report of investigations (United States. Bureau
of Mines). IV. Title.*
TN23 .U43 TN279

Scott, Kevin M., 1935- Erosion and sedimentation
in the Kenai River, Alaska / by Kevin M.
Scott ; prepared in cooperation with the U. S.
Fish and Wildlife Service. Washington : U. S.
G.P.O., 1981. p. cm. (Geological Survey
professional paper . 1235) Bibliography: p. LC Card
81-6755 DDC 553.7/8/097983 19
*1. Sediments (Geology) - Alaska - Kenai River
watershed. 2. Erosion - Alaska - Kenai River watershed.
I. United States. Fish and Wildlife Service. II. Title. III.
Series.*
QE571 .S412

Scott, Lilabeth. TVA/EPRI Workshop on Factors
Affecting Power Plant Waste Heat Utilization,
Atlanta, 1978. Factors affecting power plant
waste heat utilization /. New York , c1980.
xvii, 230 p. : ISBN 0-08-025548-5 LC Card
79-29656
TJ260 .T17 1978 ***NYPL [JSE 81-98]***

Scott, Michael James, 1948- Standards for
determining child support obligations in Alaska
/ by Michael J. Scott and Paul Stout.
Anchorage : Institute of Social and Economic
Research, University of Alaska : Child Support
Enforcement Agency, Dept. of Revenue,
Alaska, [1978] 156 p. in various pagings :
graphs ; 28 cm. "June 1978." "Revenue" (12 p.)
inserted. Includes bibliography. LC Card 79-622825
DDC 362.7/95 19
*1. Child welfare - Alaska. 2. Support (Domestic
relations) - Alaska. I. Stout, Paul, joint author. II.
University of Alaska, Fairbanks. Institute of Social and
Economic Research. III. Alaska. Child Support
Enforcement Agency. IV. Title.*
HV742.A4 S37

Scott, Robert Bruce, 1916- (joint author) Harding,
Roger A. Forest inventory with Landsat .
Olympia , 1978. ix, 221 p. : LC Card 79-621899
DDC 634.9/285 19
SD387.R4 H37

SCOTT, WALTER, SIR, 1771-1832 - ILLUSTRATIONS.
Finley, Gerald. Landscapes of memory .
Berkeley , c1980. 272 p. : ISBN 0-520-04436-3
LC Card 80-5956 DDC 741.64/092/4 19
NC978.5.T87 F56 1982

Scott, William B., 1945- Staudinger, Hans, 1889-
The inner Nazi . Baton Rouge , c1981. p. cm.
ISBN 0-8071-0882-0 : LC Card 81-7277 DDC
943.085/092/4 19
DD247.H5 A3583

SCOTTS BLUFF COUNTY (NEB.) - MAPS.
United States. Soil Conservation Service. Scotts
Bluff County, Nebraska /. Lincoln, Neb. , 1980.
1 map : LC Card 81-691078
G4193.S4 1980 .U5

Scoville, Thomas W. Reorganizing for pacification
support / Thomas W. Scoville. Washington,
D.C. : Center of Military History, United States
Army, [1981] p. cm. Bibliography: p. LC Card
81-10204 DDC 959.704/3373 19
*1. United States. Military Assistance Command,
Vietnam. Civil Operations and Rural Development
Support. 2. Vietnamese Conflict, 1961-1975 - United
States. 3. Vietnamese Conflict, 1961-1975 -
Underground movements. I. Title.*
DS558.2 .S27

SCRAP METALS - RECYCLING.
DeBarbadillo, John J., 1942- Process for recovering chromium and other metals from superalloy scrap /. Avondale, Md. [1981] p. cm. LC Card 81-6102 DDC 622 s 669/.734 19
TN23 .U43 TN799.C5

Pyrometallurgical recovery of chromium from scrap metals . [Avondale, Md.] [1981] p. cm. LC Card 81-10147 DDC 622 s 669/.734 19
TN23 .U43 TN799.C5

SCRAP METALS - UNITED STATES - RECYCLING.
United States. Congress. Office of Technology Assessment. Technical options for conservation of metals . Washington, D.C. [1979] x, 125 p. : LC Card 79-600172
TA459 .U615 1979 **NYPL [JSF 81-158]**

Screening of selected fluoroaromatic compounds for use as agrichemicals, I / R. H. Shiley ... [et al.]. Urbana, Ill. : Illinois State Geological Survey, [1979] 17 p. : ill. ; 28 cm. (Circular - Illinois State Geological Survey ; 508) On cover: Illinois Institute of Natural Resources. Bibliography: p. 11. LC Card 80-622082 DDC 557.73 s 632/.952 19
1. Organofluorine compounds. 2. Aromatic compounds. 3. Herbicides - Testing. 4. Fungicides - Testing. I. Shiley, R. H. II. Illinois Institute of Natural Resources. III. Series: Illinois. State Geological Survey. Circular , 508.
QE105 .A45 no. 508 SB952.F55

Screpetis, Arthur J.
(joint author) Chesebrough, Eben W. Baseline water quality studies of selected lakes and ponds in the Blackstone River Basin, 1977 /. Westborough, Mass. , 19. 172 p. : LC Card 80-620852 DDC 363.7/3942/097443 19
TD225.B65 C43

(joint author) Chesebrough, Eben W. Baseline water quality surveys of selected lakes and ponds in the Housatonic River basin, Berkshire County, 1976 /. Westborough, Mass. , 1976. 91 p. : LC Card 79-620583 DDC 363.7/3942/097441 19
TD225.H75 C45

(joint author) Chesebrough, Eben W. Baseline water quality surveys of selected lakes and ponds in the Nashua River basin, 1977 /. Westborough, Mass. [1978] 141 p. : LC Card 79-620602 DDC 363.7/3942/097443 19
TD225.N2 C47

(joint author) Chesebrough, Eben W. Indian Lake . Westborough, Mass. [1978] 44, A-M p. : LC Card 79-623988 DDC 363.7/3942/097443 19
TD224.M4 C477

(joint author) Chesebrough, Eben W. Lake Mattawa . Westborough, Mass. [1978] 49, A-O p. : LC Card 79-620592 DDC 363.7/3942/0974422 19
TD224.M4 C479

(joint author) Chesebrough, Eben W. South Watuppa Pond . Westborough, Mass. [1977] 69 p. : LC Card 79-621235 DDC 363.7/3942/0974485 19
TD224.M4 C485

(joint author) Chesebrough, Eben W. Upper Mystic Lake . Westborough, Mass. [1975] 75 p. : LC Card 79-620591 DDC 363.7/3942/097444 19
TD224.M4 C488

SCRIP. see SECURITIES.

Scripps Institution for Biological Research. see California. University. Scripps Institution of Oceanography, La Jolla.

Scripps Institution of Oceanography, La Jolla, Calif. see California. University. Scripps Institution of Oceanography, La Jolla.

Script Ohio, 1878-79--1978-79 / [Eric W. Aho, editor-in-chief]. Centennial ed. Columbus, Ohio : Ohio State University Marching Band, c1979. 223 p. : ill. ; 31 cm. Bibliography: p. 221. Includes index. LC Card 80-153680 DDC 785/.06/277157 19
1. Ohio State University. Marching Band. I. Aho, Eric W. II. Ohio State University. Marching Band.
ML1311 .S4

Scruggs, Frank P. Coal in Alabama / Frank P. Scruggs, Jr. Montgomery : Alabama Energy Management Board, 1974. v, 36 p. : ill. ; 28 cm. Microfiche (neg.) 1 sheet. 11 x 15 cm. (NYPL

FSN 34,972) "Selected bibliography": p. 35-36.
1. Coal - Alabama. I. Alabama. Energy Management Board. II. Title. **NYPL [*XMQ-2142]**

Scully, Robert E. Tumors of the ovary and maldeveloped gonads / by Robert E. Scully. Washington, D.C. : Armed Forces Institute of Pathology, 1979. 413 p. : ill. ; 26 cm. (Atlas of tumor pathology : Second series . fasc. 16 0160-6344) Includes bibliographies and index. LC Card 80-602599 DDC 616.99/2 s 616.99/465 19
1. Ovaries - Tumors. 2. Generative organs, Female - Tumors. 3. Generative organs, Female - Abnormalities. 4. Generative organs, Female - Tumors - Atlases. I. Title. II. Series.
RD651 .A8 fasc. 16 RC280.O8

The sculpted word /. Frischer, Bernard. Berkeley , c1982. p. cm. ISBN 0-520-04190-9 LC Card 81-13143 DDC 187 19
B573 .F74

SCULPTURE - AFRICA, WEST.
Armstrong, Robert Plant. Forms and processes of African sculpture. Austin [1970] 23 p., LC Card 72-634368
NB1098 .A75 **NYPL [Sc 730.96-A]**

SCULPTURE, BAKONGO (AFRICAN PEOPLE) - EXHIBITIONS.
Thompson, Robert Farris. The four moments of the sun . Washington , 1981. p. cm. ISBN 0-89468-003-X LC Card 81-14033 DDC 730/.09675/10740153 19
NB1099.C6 T5

SCULPTURE, CLASSICAL - UNITED STATES.
Vermeule, Cornelius Clarkson, 1925- Greek and Roman sculpture in America /. Berkeley, Calif. , c1981. p. cm. ISBN 0-520-04324-3 LC Card 81-3057 DDC 733/.074/013 19
NB86 .V47

The sculpture of Richard Stankiewicz .
Stankiewicz, Richard, 1922- [Albany, N.Y. , 1979] [28] p. : LC Card 80-621808 DDC 730/.92/4 19
NB237.S5793 A4 1979

SCULPTURE, PRIMITIVE - AFRICA, WEST.
Armstrong, Robert Plant. Forms and processes of African sculpture. Austin [1970] 23 p., LC Card 72-634368
NB1098 .A75 **NYPL [Sc 730.96-A]**

SCULPTURE, PRIMITIVE - ZAIRE - EXHIBITIONS.
Thompson, Robert Farris. The four moments of the sun . Washington , 1981. p. cm. ISBN 0-89468-003-X LC Card 81-14033 DDC 730/.09675/10740153 19
NB1099.C6 T5

Scurry, James D. (joint author) Brooks, Mark J. An intensive archeological survey of Amoco realty property in Berkeley County, South Carolina . Columbia, S.C. , 1978. xi, 79 p. : LC Card 79-625384 DDC 975.7/93 19
E78.S6 B73

SEA BIRDS - ATLANTIC COAST (UNITED STATES)
Rowlett, Richard A. Observations of marine birds and mammals in the northern Chesapeake Bight /. [Washington, D.C.] , 1980. xii, 87 p. : LC Card 80-602344 DDC 598.2975 19
QL683.A87 R68

SEA BIRDS - NORTH ATLANTIC OCEAN.
Rowlett, Richard A. Observations of marine birds and mammals in the northern Chesapeake Bight /. [Washington, D.C.] , 1980. xii, 87 p. : LC Card 80-602344 DDC 598.2975 19
QL683.A87 R68

SEA, DOMINION OF THE. see MARITIME LAW; SEA-POWER.

Sea, earth, sky : the art of Walter Anderson : an exhibition at the Mississippi State Historical Museum, Jackson, Mississippi. [Jackson] : Mississippi Dept. of Archives and History, c1980. [32] p. : ill. (some col.) ; 26 cm. LC Card 80-620021 DDC 709/.2/4 19
1. Anderson, Walter Inglis, 1903-1965 - Exhibitions. I. Anderson, Walter Inglis, 1903-1965. II. Mississippi State Historical Museum.
N6537.A48 A4 1980

SEA-FISHERIES. see FISHERIES.

Sea grant college technical report .
(230) Schenker, Eric, 1931- The Great Lakes transportation system /. [Madison, Wis.] , 1976.

xvii, 292 p. : LC Card 75-42825 DDC 386/.544/0977 19
HE398 .S33

Sea grant cooperative report .
(UNIHI-SEAGRANT-CR-80-01) Environmental survey techniques for coastal water assessment . [Honolulu, Hawaii] [1980] iv, 229 p. : LC Card 80-621111 DDC 628.1/686162/0287 19
TD763 .E58

Sea grant programs . United States. Congress. House. Committee on Merchant Marine and Fisheries. Subcommittee on Oceanography. Washington , 1976. 2 v. ; LC Card 76-602454
KF27 .M473 1976
NYPL [JLE 77-2823 & JLL 81-82]

Sea grant publication (Raleigh) .
(UNC-SG-75-02) Hester, Joseph M. Nekton population dynamics in the Albemarle Sound and Neuse River estuaries /. Raleigh , 1975. 129 p. : LC Card 75-622760 DDC 592 19
QH105.N8 H47

(UNC-SG-76-10) Ustach, Joseph F. Effects of sub-lethal oil levels on the reproduction of a copepod, Nitocra affinis /. [Raleigh] 1977. 16 leaves : LC Card 79-623524 DDC 595.3/4 19
QL444.C74 U87

(UNC-SG-76-13) Blankinship, Paul R. A flow study of Drum Inlet, North Carolina /. Raleigh , 1976. 56 p. : LC Card 77-624531 DDC 551.46/09 19
GC512.N8 B55

(UNC-SG-77-07) Onslow Bay physical/dynamical experiments, summer-fall, 1975 . [Raleigh] 1978. xxiv, 170 p. : LC Card 78-623321 DDC 551.46/148 19
GC512.N8 O56

(UNC-SG-77-11) Machemehl, Jerry L. Flow dynamics and sediment movement in Lockwoods Folly Inlet, North Carolina /. [Raleigh] , 1977. viii, 139 p. : LC Card 78-622678 DDC 551.46/148 19
GC299 .M33

(UNC-SG-78-11) Rublee, Parke A. Bacteria in a North Carolina salt marsh . [Raleigh , 1978. 80 p. : LC Card 79-621361 DDC 574.5/2636 19
QR106 .R82

(UNC-SG-78-13) Regan, Dennis C. Wreck diving in North Carolina . Raleigh, N.C. [1978] 16 p. : LC Card 79-623528 DDC 910/.0916348 19
G525 .R375

(UNC-SG-78-17) Galloway, G. E. Assessing man's impact on wetlands /. [Raleigh, N.C. , 1978] iv, 115 p. : LC Card 79-625636 DDC 333.91/81 19
QH76 .G34

SEA (IN RELIGION, FOLKLORE, ETC.) - UNITED STATES - INFORMATION SERVICES.
Bartis, Peter. Maritime folklife resources . Washington, D.C. , 1980. iii, 129 p. ; LC Card 80-602335 DDC 390/.4/6238 19
GR105 .B37

Sea Island coastal region of South Carolina and Georgia. Miglarese, John V. Ecological characterization of the sea island coastal region of South Carolina and Georgia . [Washington, D.C.] [1979] x, 35 p. : LC Card 80-601523 DDC 574.5/267/09757 19
QH105.S6 M53

SEA LAWS. see MARITIME LAW.

SEA POLLUTION. see MARINE POLLUTION.

SEA-POWER.
United States. Congressional Budget Office. Shaping the general purpose Navy of the eighties . Washington, D.C. , 1980. xxvii, 145 p. : LC Card 80-600968 DDC 359/.03/0973 19
VA53 .U52 1980

SEA POWER - UNITED STATES.
United States. Congress. House. Committee on Armed Services. Subcommittee on Seapower and Strategic and Critical Materials. National policy objectives and the adequacy of our current navy forces . Washington , 1980 [i.e. 1981] ii, 137 p. : LC Card 81-601761 DDC 359/.03/0973 19
KF27 .A769 1979e

SEA ROUTES. see TRADE ROUTES.

SEA THERMAL POWER PLANTS. see OCEAN THERMAL POWER PLANTS.

Sea training at maritime academies oversight .
United States. Congress. House. Committee on
Merchant Marine and Fisheries. Ad Hoc Select
Subcommittee on Maritime Education and
Training. Washington , 1980 [i.e. 1981] iv, 246
p. : LC Card 81-600941 DDC 623.88/07073 19
KF27 .M458 1980

SEA TRAVEL. see OCEAN TRAVEL.

SEA-WATER - BACTERIOLOGY. see MARINE MICROBIOLOGY.

SEA-WATER CORROSION - CONGRESSES.
International Conference on Performance of
Concrete in Marine Environment, St. Andrew's,
N. B., 1980. Performance of concrete in marine
environment. Detroit , c1980. vii, 627 p. : LC
Card 80-67890
TA440 .I525 1980

SEA-WATER - DENSITY.
National Ocean Survey. Surface water
temperature and density, Atlantic Coast .
Rockville, Md. , Washington, D. C. , 1973. 109
p. ;   *NYPL [JSF 81-4]*

SEA-WATER - POLLUTION. see MARINE POLLUTION.

**Seafaring guide & directory of labor management
affiliations.** United States. Maritime
Administration. Washington, D.C. [1980] v, 49
p. ; LC Card 80-602281 DDC 331.88/113875/0973
19
HD6515.S42 U46 1980

**SEAFOOD PROCESSING - UNITED
STATES - WASTE DISPOSAL.**
Overcash, Michael R. Characterization and land
application of seafood industry wastewaters /.
Raleigh [1980] ix, 34 leaves : LC Card
80-623929 DDC 664/.94996 19
TD774 .O92

SEALING - ALASKA - PRIBILOF ISLANDS.
United States. National Oceanic and
Atmospheric Administration. The story of the
Pribilof fur seals. [Washington] [1976] 34 p. :
LC Card 77-601364 DDC 333.95/9 19
SH361 .U75 1976

SEALS (NUMISMATICS) - EXHIBITIONS.
Los Angeles County Museum of Art. Ancient
bronzes, ceramics, and seals . Los Angeles,
Calif. , c1981. p. cm. ISBN 0-87587-100-3 LC
Card 81-1270 DDC 730/.093 19
NK7907 .L67 1981

SEAMANSHIP.
(1980) Sailing and seamanship. Washington,
D.C. , 1980. 248 p. in various pagings : ISBN
0-930028-02-3 (pbk.) : LC Card 81-129619
DDC 797.1/24 19
GV811 .S253 1980

**SEAMANSHIP - STUDY AND TEACHING -
UNITED STATES.**
United States. Congress. House. Committee on
Merchant Marine and Fisheries. Ad Hoc Select
Subcommittee on Maritime Education and
Training. Sea training at maritime academies
oversight . Washington , 1980 [i.e. 1981] iv,
246 p. : LC Card 81-600941 DDC 623.88/07073
19
KF27 .M458 1980

**SEAMEN, AFRO-AMERICAN. see AFRO-
AMERICAN SEAMEN.**

**SEAMEN, MERCHANT. see MERCHANT
SEAMEN.**

SEAPOWER. see SEA-POWER.

Search Group. Privacy and security of criminal
history information . Washington, D.C. , c1979.
xi, 545 p. ; LC Card 80-601565 DDC
342.73/0858 19
KF9751.Z95 N37 Suppl

SEARCHES AND SEIZURES - CALIFORNIA.
California. Legislature. Assembly. Committee on
Criminal Justice. The Exclusionary rule .
Sacramento, CA (Box 90, Sacramento 95814)
[1980?] iii, 119, [26] p. ; LC Card 81-621372
DDC 345.794/062 347.940562 19
KFC10.4 .C68 1980

**SEARCHES AND SEIZURES - UNITED
STATES.**
United States. Congress. Senate. Committee on

the Judiciary. Privacy protection act .
Washington , 1980. iv, 233 p. ; LC Card
80-602900 DDC 342.73/0853 19
KF26 .J8 1980b

**SEARCHES AND SEIZURES - UNITED
STATES - CASES.**
Cannaday, Kenneth S. Persons who may object
to unlawful searches seizures . Chapel Hill,
N.C. (P.O. Box 990, Chapel Hill 27514)
[1981], c1978. 10 p. ; LC Card 81-621675 DDC
347.756 s 345.73/0552 347.5607 s 347.5605552
19
KFN7908.A15 U6 no. 81/01 KF9662

Searcy, Seth S. Privacy and public records :
statement of the Texas Advisory Commission
on Intergovernmental Relations : background
paper / by Seth S. Searcy III. Austin : The
Commission, 1977. xv, 82 p. ; 28 cm. Microfiche
(neg.) NTIS. 1 sheet. 11 x 15 cm. (PB 273
985)Includes bibliographical references. LC Card
77-623845
*1. Public records - Law and legislation - Texas. 2.
Privacy, Right of - Texas. 3. Public records - Law and
legislation - United States. 4. Privacy, Right of - United
States. I. Texas. Advisory Commission on
Intergovernmental Relations. II. Title.*
*KFT1662.5.P8 S4   NYPL [*XME-9391]*

**Seasonal patterns of monthly prices and
production for Louisiana farm products,
1975-1979, with projections for 1980 /.** Fielder,
Lonnie L. [Baton Rouge] [1980] v, 27 p. ; LC
Card 80-623328 DDC 338.1/09763 s
338.1/3/09763 19
HD1775.L8 L7 no. 567 HD9417.L8

**Seasonal variation of 10-square-mile probable
maximum precipitation estimates, United
States, east of the 105th meridian /.** Ho,
Francis P. Silver Spring, Md. , 1980. vi, 89 p. :
LC Card 80-602668 DDC 551.57/0973 s
551.57/813/0973 19
QC925.1 .U586 no. 53 QC925.1.U8A14

**The Seattle-Denver income maintenance
experiment .** Setzer, Florence. [[Washington] ,
1978. xv, 54 p. ; LC Card 78-603699
HC110.I5 S4   NYPL [JLF 81-429]

Seattle. Dept of Transportation. Voorhees (Alan
M.) and Associates. Blue Streak bus rapid
transit demonstration project . Seattle, 1973. 6,
11 p. LC Card 74-132895   *NYPL [*ZT-1265]*

**SEATTLE - OFFICIALS AND EMPLOYEES -
SALARIES, ALLOWANCES, ETC.**
United States. Bureau of Labor Statistics.
Pacific Regional Office. Municipal Government
wage survey, Seattle, Washington, January 1979
/. San Francisco, Calif. [1979] ii, 78 p. ; LC
Card 80-601650 DDC 331.2/813520797/77 19
JS1455.4 .A4 1979

SEATTLE - TRANSIT SYSTEMS.
Voorhees (Alan M.) and Associates. Blue
Streak bus rapid transit demonstration project .
Seattle, 1973. 6, 11 p. LC Card 74-132895
*NYPL [*ZT-1265]*

**Seattle. Transportation, Dept. of. see Seattle.
Dept of Transportation.**

SEATTLE (WASH.) - HISTORY.
Morgan, Murray Cromwell, 1916- Skid road .
Seattle , 1981 [c1960] p. cm. ISBN
0-295-95846-4 (pbk.) : LC Card 81-11701
DDC 979.7/77 19
F899.S457 M67 1981

Seay, Edmond E. Analysis of electric
generation & energy use in the Susq[u]ehanna
River Basin, 1978 / [prepared by Edmond E.
Seay]. Harrisburg, Pa. : Susquehanna River
Basin Commission, [1980] ii, 25 p. ; 29 cm.
(Publication - Susquehanna River Basin Commission ;
no. 65) Cover title. LC Card 80-622024 DDC
363.6/2 19
*1. Electric power production - Susquehanna River
watershed. 2. Electric utilities - Susquehanna River
watershed - Statistics. I. Series: Susquehanna River
Basin Commission. Publication - Susquehanna River
Basin Commission , no. 65. II. Title.*
TK1193.U5 S45

Sebeok, Thomas Albert, 1920- The play of
musement / Thomas A. Sebeok. Bloomington :
Indiana University Press, c1981. p. cm.
(Advances in semiotics) Includes bibliographical
references and index. ISBN 0-253-39994-7 LC Card
80-8846 DDC 001.51 19

1. Semiotics - Addresses, essays, lectures. I. Title.
P99 .S33

**Second concurrent resolution on the
budget--fiscal year, 1981 .** United States.
Congress. Senate. Committee on the Budget.
Washington , 1980. iv, 412 p. : LC Card
80-603471 DDC 353.0072/2 19
KF26 .B8 1980b

**Second draft, selected transportation elements
including the master plan of highways .**
Maryland-National Capital Park and Planning
Commission. [Silver Spring? Md.] [1980] 1
map : LC Card 81-692907
G3843.M6P1 1980 .M3

**A second exploratory analysis of the relations
among institutional variables .** Sherman,
Charles Roger, 1944- Washington , 1977. vi, 34
p. ; LC Card 77-153938
*R745 .S493   NYPL [*XME-9427]*

**SECOND HOMES - NORTHEASTERN
STATES.**
Sim, Robert, 1949- Demand, supply, and spatial
distribution of second homes in the Northeast
/. Storrs, Conn. [1979] 57 p. ; LC Card
80-621316 DDC 333.33/8 19
HD7293 .S54

Secondary area vocational system, spring 1980.
Indiana. State Board of Vocational and
Technical Education. Bloomington, IN , c1980.
v, 114 p. : LC Card 80-623920 DDC
373/.01/1309772 19
LC1046.I4 I55 1980

**SECONDARY BATTERIES. see STORAGE
BATTERIES.**

SECRECY (LAW) - UNITED STATES.
United States. Congress. House. Committee on
the Judiciary. Subcommittee on Civil and
Constitutional Rights. Prepublication review and
secrecy requirements imposed upon federal
employees . Washington , 1981. iii, 100 p. ;
LC Card 81-601753 DDC 353.0071/45 19
KF27 .J847 1980g

The secret cause . Berlin, Normand. Amherst ,
1981. 127 p. ; ISBN 0-87023-336-X : LC Card
81-4089 DDC 809.2/512 19
PN1892 .B43

**SECRETARIAL PRACTICE. see OFFICE
PRACTICE.**

**The Secretary of the Interior's standards for
historic preservation projects .** Morton, W.
Brown. Washington, D.C. , 1979. vi, 46 p. ;
LC Card 80-603172 DDC 720/.28/8 19
NA106 .M67

**The Secretary of the Interior's standards for
historic preservation projects .** United States.
Dept. of the Interior. Washington, D. C. , 1973.
vi, 46 p. ;   *NYPL [*ZM-150]*

**Section index to bills introduced, LB 598
through LB 986 and carried-over bills.**
Nebraska. Legislature. Nebraska unicameral,
eighty-sixth legislature, second session .
[[Lincoln , 1980] 14 p. ; LC Card 80-623547
DDC 348.782/01 347.82081 19
KFN10 .L43

**A section 147 rural public transportation
demonstration manual.** Washington : U. S.
Dept. of Transportation, Federal Highway
Administration, Urban Mass Transportation
Administration, Office of the Secretary, 1979. 5
v. in 1 ; 28 cm. "Final report." Cover title.
CONTENTS: - no. 1. Rural public transportation
services and performance. - no. 2. Planning rural public
transportation systems. - no. 3. Rural public
transportation coordination efforts. - no. 4. Rural public
transportation vehicles. - no. 5. Marketing rural public
transportation.
*1. Transportation planning - United States. I. United
States. Urban Mass Transportation Administration.*
NYPL [JLF 80-1345]

Securities Acts Amendments of 1975--oversight .
United States. Congress. House. Committee on
Interstate and Foreign Commerce.
Subcommittee on Oversight and Investigations.
Washington , 1978. viii, 1187 p. : LC Card
81-601238 DDC 353.0082/58 19
KF27 .I5547 1977q

**Securities and Exchange Commission
authorizations for fiscal years 1981, 1982, and
1983 .** United States. Congress. House.
Committee on Interstate and Foreign

Commerce. Subcommittee on Consumer Protection and Finance. Washington , 1980. iii, 158 p. : LC Card 80-603892 DDC 353.0072/2368258 19
KF27 .I554 1980b

SECURITIES EXCHANGE. see STOCK-EXCHANGE.

Securities Investor Protection Act Amendment . United States. Congress. House. Committee on Interstate and Foreign Commerce. Subcommittee on Consumer Protection and Finance. Washington , 1980. iii, 34 p. ; LC Card 80-604115 DDC 346.73/0666 347.306666 19
KF27 .I554 1980d

SECURITIES INVESTOR PROTECTION CORPORATION.
United States. Congress. House. Committee on Interstate and Foreign Commerce. Subcommittee on Consumer Protection and Finance. Securities Investor Protection Act Amendment . Washington , 1980. iii, 34 p. ; LC Card 80-604115 DDC 346.73/0666 347.306666 19
KF27 .I554 1980d

SECURITIES - MICHIGAN.
Michigan. Securities Bureau. Securities rules, 1968 /. Lansing [1968] 32 p. : LC Card 80-623215 DDC 346.774/0666 19
KFM4379.A434 A2 1968

Securities rules, 1968 /. Michigan. Securities Bureau. Lansing [1968] 32 p. : LC Card 80-623215 DDC 346.774/0666 19
KFM4379.A434 A2 1968

SECURITIES, TAX-EXEMPT - UNITED STATES.
United States. Congress. House. Committee on Ways and Means. Subcommittee on Oversight. Guaranteed student loan tax-exempt financing . Washington , 1980. iii, 96 p. : LC Card 80-603435 DDC 379.1/3 19
KF27 .W345 1980h

SECURITIES - UNITED STATES.
Barth, James R. Evaluating the impact of securities regulation on venture capital markets /. Washington, D.C. , 1980. iv, 38 p. : LC Card 80-600036 DDC 602.18 s 332/.0414 19
QC100 .U556 no. 166 HG4963

United States. Congress. House. Committee on Government Operations. Commerce, Consumer, and Monetary Affairs Subcommittee. Silver prices and the adequacy of Federal actions in the marketplace, 1979-80 . Washington , 1980. v, 1203 p. : LC Card 80-603499 DDC 332.63/28 19
KF27 .G634 1980c

United States. Congress. House. Committee on Interstate and Foreign Commerce. Subcommittee on Oversight and Investigations. National market system, five year status report . Washington , 1980. vii, 105 p. ; LC Card 80-603861 DDC 332.64/273 19
HG4910 .U54 1980

United States. Congress. House. Committee on Interstate and Foreign Commerce. Subcommittee on Oversight and Investigations. Securities Acts Amendments of 1975--oversight . Washington , 1978. viii, 1187 p. : LC Card 81-601238 DDC 353.0082/58 19
KF27 .I5547 1977q

United States. Congress. Senate. Committee on Banking, Housing and Urban Affairs. Subcommittee on Securities. Federal securities laws and small business legislation . Washington , 1980. ix, 812 p. : LC Card 80-603327 DDC 346.73/0666 19
KF26 .B3954 1980a

United States. Securities and Exchange Commission. Directorate of Economic and Policy Research. Staff report on the securities industry in 1977 /. [Washington] [1978] 21, [30] leaves : LC Card 80-602626 DDC 332.6/2/0973 19
HG4910 .U55 1978

SECURITY ASSISTANCE PROGRAM - AUDITING AND INSPECTION.
United States. General Accounting Office. Correct balance of Defense's foreign military sales trust fund unknown . Washington, DC [1980] iii, 23 p. ; LC Card 80-602832 DDC

355/.032/0973 19
UA12 .U527 1980

SECURITY CLASSIFICATION (GOVERNMENT DOCUMENTS) - UNITED STATES.
United States. Congress. House. Committee on the Judiciary. Subcommittee on Civil and Constitutional Rights. Use of classified information in federal criminal cases . Washington , 1980 [i.e. 1981] iii, 103 p. ; LC Card 81-600944 DDC 347.73/64 347.30764 19
KF27 .J847 1980f

United States. Congress. Senate. Committee on the Judiciary. Subcommittee on Criminal Justice. Graymail, S. 1482 . Washington , 1980. iii, 189 p. ; LC Card 80-603342 DDC 345.73/064 19
KF26 .J8377 1980d

SECURITY, INTERNATIONAL.
Commission on Security and Cooperation in Europe. Implementation of the final act of the Conference on Security and Cooperation in Europe . Washington , 1980. ix, 341 p. ; LC Card 80-603557 DDC 327.1/7/094 19
JX1393.C65 C66 1980

Defense Institute of Security Assistance Management (U. S.) The management of security assistance. [Dayton] Ohio [1980] ca. 900 p. in various pagings : LC Card 80-602381 DDC 355/.032/0973 19
UA12 .D43 1980

SECURITY INVESTIGATIONS. see LOYALTY-SECURITY PROGRAM, 1947-

Security procedures at U. S. embassies . United States. Congress. House. Committee on Foreign Affairs. Subcommittee on International Operations. Washington . 1980. iii, 240 p. ; LC Card 80-604070 DDC 353.008/92 19
KF27 .F647 1980b

SECURITY PROGRAM. see LOYALTY-SECURITY PROGRAM, 1947-

SECURITY TESTS. see LOYALTY-SECURITY PROGRAM, 1947-

SEDGWICK COUNTY, KANSAS - POLICE - COMPLAINTS AGAINST.
United States. Commission on Civil Rights. Kansas Advisory Committee. Police-community relations in the city of Wichita and Sedgwick County . Washington, D.C. [1980] xi, 95 p. : LC Card 80-603162 DDC 363.2/2/0978186 19
HV7936.P8 U53 1980

Sediment bacteria as a water quality indicator in the Lynnhaven estuary /. Erkenbrecher, Carl W. Blacksburg, Va. [1980] x, 118 p. : LC Card 80-622517 DDC 333.91/009755 s 628.168/028/7 19
TD201 .V57 no. 126 QR48

SEDIMENT CONTROL - ECONOMIC ASPECTS - UNITED STATES.
Campbell, Joseph C. Potential economic and environmental impacts of alternative sediment control policies /. Ames, Iowa [1979] viii leaves, 91 p. : LC Card 80-623102 DDC 333.76/16/0973 19
TD427.S33 C35

SEDIMENT CONTROL - IOWA - IOWA RIVER WATERSHED - LINEAR PROGRAMMING.
Alt, Klaus F. Economics and the environment . Ames Iowa [1977] iv, 54 leaves ; LC Card 80-623678 DDC 338.1/09777/6 19
S624.I6 A47

SEDIMENT LOAD. see SEDIMENT, SUSPENDED.

SEDIMENT LOAD OF STREAMS. see SEDIMENT TRANSPORT.

SEDIMENT, SUSPENDED.
Wooldridge, David D. Suspended sediment from truck traffic on forest roads, Meadow and Coal Creeks /. Seattle [1978] 33 p. :
*NYPL [*ZV-185 Reel 1]*

SEDIMENT, SUSPENDED - ENVIRONMENTAL ASPECTS - ALASKA - SALCHA RIVER.
Dinneford, W. Bruce. Third interim report of the commercial fish-technical evaluation study, Salcha River /. Anchorage, Alaska , 1977. vi, 88 p. : LC Card 79-625783 DDC 597/.55 19
QL638.S2 D56

SEDIMENT, SUSPENDED - KANSAS - MAPS.
United States. Soil Conservation Service. Sediment sources map, Kansas /. Lincoln, Nebr. , 1979. 1 map : LC Card 81-691121
G4201.J4 1980 .U5

SEDIMENT TRANSPORT - LONG ISLAND SOUND.
United States. Congress. House. Committee on Science and Technology. Subcommittee on Natural Resources and Environment. Long Island Sound dredge-spoil dumping . Washington , 1980. iii, 180 p. ; LC Card 80-602186 DDC 333.91/64/0916346 19
KF27 .S398 1979j

SEDIMENT TRANSPORT - MAINE.
Maine. Land Use Regulation Commission. A survey of erosion and sedimentation problems associated with logging in Maine /. [Augusta, Me.] [1979] 56 p. : LC Card 80-620932 DDC 333.75/16/09741 19
TD428.F67 M34 1979

SEDIMENT TRANSPORT - MISSOURI VALLEY.
Osterkamp, W. R. Perennial-streamflow characteristics related to channel geometry and sediment in the Missouri River basin /. [Reston, Va.?] [1981] p. cm. LC Card 81-607905 DDC 551.48/3/0978 19
GB1227.M7 O84

Sedimentary relationships of Portland Point and associated Middle Devonian rocks in central and western New York /. Baird, Gordon C. Albany, N.Y. [1979] iv, 24 p. : LC Card 79-625700 DDC 551.7/4 19
QE665 .B23

SEDIMENTARY ROCKS. see ROCKS, SEDIMENTARY.

SEDIMENTATION AND DEPOSITION.
Knott, J. M. Reconnaissance assessment of erosion and sedimentation in the Cañada de los Alamos basin, Los Angeles and Ventura Counties, California /. Washington, D.C. , 1980. iv, 26 p. : LC Card 80-600012 DDC 551.3/009794/93 19
QE571 .K54

Spicer, Robert A., 1950- The sorting and deposition of allochthonous plant material in a modern environment at Silwood Lake, Silwood Park, Berkshire, England /. Washington , 1981. v, 77 p. : LC Card 80-607854 DDC 560/.1/78 19
QE931.3 .S64

SEDIMENTATION AND DEPOSITION - ENVIRONMENTAL ASPECTS.
National Research Council. Transportation Research Board. Design of sedimentation basins. Washington, D.C. , 1980. 53 p. : ISBN 0-309-03027-7 (pbk.) : LC Card 80-52843 DDC 625.7/34 19
TD439 .N37 1980

SEDIMENTATION AND DEPOSITION - ENVIRONMENTAL ASPECTS - UNITED STATES.
Campbell, Joseph C. Potential economic and environmental impacts of alternative sediment control policies /. Ames, Iowa [1979] viii leaves, 91 p. : LC Card 80-623102 DDC 333.76/16/0973 19
TD427.S33 C35

SEDIMENTS (GEOLOGY) - ALASKA - KENAI RIVER WATERSHED.
Scott, Kevin M., 1935- Erosion and sedimentation in the Kenai River, Alaska /. Washington , 1981. p. cm. LC Card 81-6755 DDC 553.7/8/097983 19
QE571 .S412

SEDIMENTS (GEOLOGY) - COLORADO - DENVER REGION - TESTING.
Hansen, Wallace R., 1920- Environmental geology of the Front Range Urban Corridor and vicinity, Colorado /. Washington , 1981. p. cm. LC Card 81-4280 DDC 624.1/51/097883 19
QE92.F7 H36

SEDIMENTS (GEOLOGY) - MISSOURI - ANALYSIS.
Ebens, Richard J. Geochemistry of loess and carbonate residuum /. Washington , 1980. iii, 32 p. : LC Card 80-607796 DDC 553.6 19
QE499 .E23

SEDIMENTS (GEOLOGY) - NEVADA - INCLINE VILLAGE REGION.

Glancy, Patrick A. A reconnaissance of streamflow and fluvial sediment transport, Incline Village area, Lake Tahoe, Nevada . Carson City , 1976. v, 42 p. ; LC Card 80-623612 DDC 551.48/09793/57 19
GB1225.N3 G56

SEDIMENTS, SUSPENDED - TEXAS - TABLES.

Dougherty, John Philip, 1923- Suspended-sediment load of Texas streams . Austin [1979] v, 82 p., [1] leaf of plates : LC Card 79-625851 DDC 333.91/009764 s 551.3/54 19
TD224.T4 A333 no. 233 GB1225.T4

See, Carolyn L. (joint author) Buikema, Arthur L. Rotifer sensitivity to combinations of inorganic water pollutants /. Blacksburg , 1977. vi, 42 p. : LC Card 78-621510 DDC 333.91/09755 s 595.1/81 19
TD201 .V57 no. 92 QL391.R8

Seed certification in Montana : a report to the Forty-seventh Legislature / Study Committee on Seed Certification. Helena, Mont. (Rm. 138, State Capitol, Helena 59601) : Montana Legislative Council, [1980] 17 p. ; 28 cm. Cover title: Certification of agricultural seeds in Montana. "November 15, 1980." Bibliography: p. 11. LC Card 81-621002 DDC 353.97860082/333 19
1. Seeds - Montana - Certification. 2. Seed industry and trade - Law and legislation - Montana. I. Montana. Legislature. Study Committee on Seed Certification. II. Montana. Legislative Council. III. Title: Certification of agricultural seeds in Montana.
KFM9244.S4 A25 1980

SEED INDUSTRY AND TRADE - LAW AND LEGISLATION - MISSOURI.

Missouri. [Missouri Seed Law.] Missouri Seed Law and regulations. Jefferson City, Mo. (P.O. Box 630, Jefferson City, Mo. 65102) [1979 or 1980] 20 p. ; LC Card 81-621036 DDC 343.778/076 347.780376 19
KFM8044.S4 A32 1980

SEED INDUSTRY AND TRADE - LAW AND LEGISLATION - MONTANA.

Seed certification in Montana . Helena, Mont. (Rm. 138, State Capitol, Helena 59601) [1980] 17 p. ; LC Card 81-621002 DDC 353.97860082/333 19
KFM9244.S4 A25 1980

SEED INDUSTRY AND TRADE - OREGON - WILLAMETTE VALLEY.

Conklin, Frank S. An evaluation of expected private losses from selected public policies for reducing open field burning, Willamette Valley, Oregon /. Corvallis [1979] 78 p. ; LC Card 80-620510 DDC 363.7/392 19
TD884 .C74

Seeded grasslands for wildlife habitat in the prairie pothole region. Establishment of seeded grasslands for wildlife habitat in the prairie pothole region /. Washington, D.C. , 1981. p. cm. LC Card 81-607001 DDC 639.9/79/0973 s 639.9/79 19
SK361 .A256 no. 234

SEEDS - MONTANA - CERTIFICATION.

Seed certification in Montana . Helena, Mont. (Rm. 138, State Capitol, Helena 59601) [1980] 17 p. ; LC Card 81-621002 DDC 353.97860082/333 19
KFM9244.S4 A25 1980

The seeds of artificial intelligence . Freiherr, Gregory. Bethesda, Md. , Washington, D.C. [1980] 74 p. ; LC Card 80-602247 DDC 001.64 19
R858 .F73

Seelig, Sharon Cadman. The shadow of eternity : belief and structure in Herbert, Vaughn, and Traherne / Sharon Cadman Seelig. Lexington, Ky : University Press of Kentucky, 1981. p. cm. Includes index. ISBN 0-8131-1444-6 : LC Card 80-51018 DDC 821/.3/09 19
1. English poetry - Early modern, 1500-1700 - History and criticism. 2. Herbert, George, 1593-1633 - Criticism and interpretation. 3. Vaughn, Henry, 1622-1695 - Criticism and interpretation. 4. Traherne, Thomas, d. 1674 - Criticism and interpretation. I. Title.
PR545.M4 S4

Segelquist, Charles.
Davis, Graham J. Responses of submersed

vascular plant communities to environmental change . Washington, D.C. , 1980. x, 70 p. : LC Card 80-607178 DDC 581.5/2623 19
QK930 .D38

Effects of habitat alterations on riparian plant and animal communities in Iowa /. Kearneysville, WV [1981] p. cm. LC Card 81-607834 DDC 574.5/264 19
QH545.S8 E37

SEGREGATION IN EDUCATION.

Blaustein, Albert P., 1921- Civil rights U. S. A.. [Washington, D. C., 1964] v, 55 p.: LC Card 64-60745 *NYPL [Sc D 80-371]*

SEGREGATION IN EDUCATION - NEW YORK (CITY)

New York (City). Board of Education. Chancellor's report on programs and problems affecting integration of the New York City public schools. New York, 1974. 36 p. LC Card 77-27109 *NYPL [*Z-3211]*

Segye Unhaeng. see International Bank for Reconstruction and Development.

Seidel, Laurence H. The veteran in New Jersey, 1978 : a labor market information publication of the N.J. Department of Labor & Industry, Division of Planning and Research / [researched and prepared by Laurence H. Seidel]. Trenton, N.J. : The Division, 1979. 16, [7] leaves : graph ; 29 cm. Includes bibliographical references. LC Card 80-620973 DDC 355.1/154/09749 19
1. Veterans - Employment - New Jersey. 2. Labor supply - New Jersey. I. New Jersey. Dept. of Labor and Industry. Division of Planning and Research. II. Title.
UB358.N5 S4

Seidler, Ramon J. Health significance of Klebsiella pneumoniae in drinking water emanating from redwood tanks / by Ramon J. Seidler. Corvallis, Or. : Water Resources Research Institute, Oregon State University, 1977. 81 p. : ill. ; 28 cm. (WRRI . 54) Includes bibliographical references. LC Card 78-624331 DDC 333.91/009795 s 628.1/3 19
1. Sanitary microbiology. 2. Klebsiella pneumoniae. 3. Drinking water - Contamination. I. Title. II. Title: Redwood tanks. III. Series: Oregon. State University, Corvallis. Water Resources Research Institute. WRRI , 54.
HD1694.O7 A13 no. 54 QR48

SEIDMAN, HERTA LANDE, 1939-

United States. Congress. Senate. Committee on Banking, Housing and Urban Affairs. Nominations of Herta Lande Seidman and Stephen J. Friedman . Washington , 1980. iii, 53 p. : LC Card 80-602446 DDC 353.82 19
KF26 .B39 1980c

Seiling, Virginia.
Health characteristics of veterans and nonveterans : health interview surveys, 1971-1974 / by Virginia Seiling, William Frank Page. Washington, D.C. : Reports and Statistics Service, Office of Controller, Veterans Administration, [1980] v, 75 p. : graphs ; 28 cm. (Controller monograph ; no. 11) "April 1980." Includes bibliographical references. LC Card 80-602055 DDC 362.1/9 19
1. Men - Diseases - United States - Statistics. 2. Men - Medical care - United States - Statistics. 3. Veterans - Diseases - United States - Statistics. 4. Veterans - Medical care - United States - Statistics. 5. Health surveys - United States. 6. United States - Statistics, Medical. I. Page, William Frank, 1948- joint author. II. United States. Veterans Administration. Reports and Statistics Service. III. Series: United States. Veterans Administration. Office of the Controller. Controller monograph , no. 11. IV. Title.
RA408.M4 S44

United States. Veterans Administration. Office of the Controller. The most frequently occurring diagnoses in VA hospitals, 1971-1976 . Washington , 1977. viii, 75 p. : LC Card 77-601849 DDC 362.1/0973 19
UB369 .U57 1977a

SEISMIC PROSPECTING - HANDBOOKS, MANUALS, ETC.

Lepper, C. Melvin. Guidelines for selecting seismic detectors for high resolution applications /. [Washington, D.C.] , 1981. p. cm. LC Card 80-607789 DDC 622 s 622/.159 19
TN23 .U43 TN269

SEISMIC REFLECTION METHOD.

Sampair, James L. Buried oyster shell resource evaluation of the eastern region of the Albemarle Sound /. Raleigh , 1976. iii, 47 p. : LC Card 78-623214 DDC 553.5 19
SH379.5 .S25

SEISMOGRAPH. see SEISMOMETERS.

SEISMOLOGICAL RESEARCH - LAW AND LEGISLATION - UNITED STATES.

United States. Congress. Senate. Committee on Commerce, Science, and Transportation. Subcommittee on Science, Technology, and Space. Reauthorization of National earthquake hazards reduction act . Washington , 1980. iii, 84 p. : LC Card 80-602466 DDC 353.0075/4 19
KF26 .C697 1980a

SEISMOLOGICAL RESEARCH - UNITED STATES - FINANCE.

United States. Congress. Senate. Committee on Commerce, Science, and Transportation. Subcommittee on Science, Technology, and Space. Reauthorization of National earthquake hazards reduction act . Washington , 1980. iii, 84 p. : LC Card 80-602466 DDC 353.0075/4 19
KF26 .C697 1980a

SEISMOLOGICAL STATIONS - BERMUDA ISLANDS - DIRECTORIES.

Poppe, Barbara B. Directory of world seismograph stations. Boulder, Colo. , 1980- v. <1, pt. 1 > : LC Card 80-603927 DDC 551 s 551.2/2/2025 19
QE500 .W67a no. 25 QE540.U6

SEISMOLOGICAL STATIONS - CANADA - DIRECTORIES.

Poppe, Barbara B. Directory of world seismograph stations. Boulder, Colo. , 1980- v. <1, pt. 1 > : LC Card 80-603927 DDC 551 s 551.2/2/2025 19
QE500 .W67a no. 25 QE540.U6

SEISMOLOGICAL STATIONS - UNITED STATES - DIRECTORIES.

Poppe, Barbara B. Directory of world seismograph stations. Boulder, Colo. , 1980- v. <1, pt. 1 > : LC Card 80-603927 DDC 551 s 551.2/2/2025 19
QE500 .W67a no. 25 QE540.U6

SEISMOLOGY - STATISTICAL METHODS - BIBLIOGRAPHY.

International Association of Seismology and the Physics of the Earth's Interior. European Seismological Commission. Working Group on Statistical Methods. Bibliography of statistical aspects of seismicity /. Boulder, Colo. , 1978. iv, 74 p. ; LC Card 79-603198 DDC 551 s 551.2/2/072 19
QE500 .W67a no. 13 Z6033.E1 QE539

SEISMOLOGY - UNITED STATES - INFORMATION SERVICES.

Hays, Walter W. Program and plans of the U. S. Geological Survey for producing information needed in national seismic hazards and risk assessment, fiscal years 1980-84 /. [Arlington, Va.] , 1979. iv, 40 p. : LC Card 80-602831 DDC 557.3 s 363.3/495 19
QE75 .C5 no. 816 QE535.2.U6

SEISMOMETERS.

Durkin, John. Evaluation of the seismic system for location of trapped miners /. [Washington] , 1981. p. cm. LC Card 81-2170 DDC 622 s 622/.8 19
TN23 .U43 TN297

SEISMOMETERS - HANDBOOKS, MANUALS, ETC.

Lepper, C. Melvin. Guidelines for selecting seismic detectors for high resolution applications /. [Washington, D.C.] , 1981. p. cm. LC Card 80-607789 DDC 622 s 622/.159 19
TN23 .U43 TN269

Seitz, Charles A. Automatic and continuous transducer drift compensator for end point detection systems / by Charles A. Seitz and George M. Lucich. Washington : U. S. Dept. of the Interior, Bureau of Mines, 1981. p. cm. (Report of investigations / United States Department of the Interior, Bureau of Mines) Bibliography: p. LC Card 80-606887 DDC 622 s 621.5/19 19
1. Transducers - Drift. 2. Equalizers (Electronics). 3. Low temperature engineering. I. Lucich, George M., joint author. II. Series: United States Bureau of Mines. Report of investigations . III. Title.
TN23 .U43

Sekai Ginkō. see **International Bank for Reconstruction and Development.**

Sekaran, Uma. Leadership, beyond establishment views /. Carbondale , c1981. p. cm. ISBN 0-8093-1026-0 LC Card 81-8739 DDC 303.3/4 19
HM141 .L393

Selden, Samuel, 1899- First principles of play direction, by Samuel Selden ... issued by the Bureau of community drama. Chapel Hill, N. C., The University of North Carolina press [1937] 57 p. front., plates. diagrs. 23 cm. "University of North Carolina extension bulletin, v. 17, no. 4." Bibliography: p. [56]-57. LC Card 38-28085
1. Theater. 2. Acting. I. North Carolina. University. Bureau of Community Drama.
NYPL [MWEO 81-10]

A select bibliography for genealogical research in North Carolina /. Stevenson, George, 1936- Raleigh, N.C. , c1980. 18 p. ; LC Card 80-623027 DDC 975.6 s 016.929/1/09756 19
F251 .N67a no. 10, 1980 Z1319 F253

Select list of recent purchases in certain departments of literature, 1901-1903 /. United States. Library of Congress. Washington , 1904. vi, 326 p. ; LC Card 80-495444 DDC 018/.1/09753 19
Z881 .U5 1904

Selected, annotated bibliography on health maintenance organizations, 1974-1978. Group Health Foundation Library (U. S.) Comprehensive bibliography on health maintenance organizations, 1974-1978 /. Washington, D.C. , 1980. 2 v. ; LC Card 80-602118 DDC 016.3621/0425 19
Z6675.H4 G76 1980 RA413

A selected bibliography of Alabama county and regional planning and development documents /. Alabama. Development Office. Montgomery , 1974. xiii, 254 p. : LC Card 74-623967
Z7165.U6 A416 1974 HC107.A4

A Selected bibliography of Centrosema, Desmodium, Stylosanthes and other tropical and subtropical pasture legumes [microform] / Peter P. Rotar ... [et al.]. Honolulu : Hawaii Institute of Tropical Agriculture and Human Resources, University of Hawaii, 1981. p. cm. (Research series, 0197-9310) Includes indexes. LC Card 81-2533 DDC 016.6333 19
1. Legumes - Tropics - Bibliography. 2. Centrosema - Bibliography. 3. Desmodium - Bibliography. 4. Stylosanthes - Bibliography. 5. Pastures - Tropics - Bibliography. 6. Tropical crops - Bibliography. I. Rotar, Peter P. II. Hawaii Institute of Tropical Agriculture and Human Resources. III. Series: Research series (Hawaii Institute of Tropical Agriculture and Human Resources) .
Z5074 .L3 SB203.3.T76

Selected bibliography of essential hypertension / U. S. Dept. of Health and Human Services, Public Health Service, National Institutes of Health, National Heart, Lung, and Blood Institute, High Blood Pressure Information Center (HBPIC). Bethesda, Md. : N.I.H., 1980. 24 p. ; 28 cm. (NIH publication. v no. 81-2190) Nov. 1980. Item 507-E-8 LC Card 81-600700 DDC 016.6161/32 19
1. Hypertension - Bibliography. I. High Blood Pressure Information Center (U. S.). II. National Institutes of Health (U. S.). III. Series: DHHS publication, v no. (NIH) 81-2190.
Z6664.H9 S44 RC685.H8

Selected bibliography of insect pests of sunflower /. Rogers, Charlie Ellic, 1938- College Station, Tex. [Beltsville, Md.] [1979] 41 p. ; LC Card 80-621131 DDC 016.6338/5 19
Z5354.P3 S867 SB608.S92

Selected bibliography of red rice and other wild rices (Oryza spp.) /. Eastin, E. F. College Station , 1979. 59 p. ; LC Card 79-625846 DDC 016.6331/87 19
Z5356.R43 E25 SB615.R4

Selected bibliography on ethnic and racial factors in hypertension / U. S. Dept. of Health and Human Services, Public Health Service, National Institutes of Health, National Heart, Lung, and Blood Institute, High Blood Pressure Information Center. Bethesda, Md. : N.I.H., 1980. 10 p. ; 28 cm. (NIH publiocation. no. 81-2201) Nov. 1980. Item 507-E-8 LC Card 81-600730 DDC 016.6161/32071 19

1. Hypertension - Bibliography. 2. Health and race - Bibliography. I. National Institutes of Health (U. S.). II. Series: DHHS publication, no. (NIH) 81-2201.
Z6664.H9 S45 RC685.H8

Selected business indicators and market data for Northeastern Minnesota 1967 and 1968. Meyers, Cecil H. Duluth, 1970. 30 p. LC Card 74-77177
NYPL [*XME-9350]

Selected characteristics of persons in physical science, 1978. United States. Bureau of the Census. Washington, D.C. , U. S. Dept. of Commerce, Bureau of the Census, 1980, 30 p. : LC Card 80-607850 DDC 312/.0973 s 509/.02/2 19
HA203 .A218 no. 108 Q149.U5

Selected characteristics of the living arrangements and institutionalization of the elderly in the States, HEW regions, and the United States . United States. Health Care Financing Administration. Office of Policy, Planning, and Research. Washington , 1978. vii, 501 p. : LC Card 79-603338
HD7287.8 .U5 1978   **NYPL [JLF 81-290]**

Selected characteristics of travel to work in 20 metropolitan areas, 1977. United States. Bureau of the Census. Washington , 1981. p. cm. LC Card 80-606807 DDC 312/.0973 s 388.4/0973 19
HA203 .A218 no. 105 HE308

Selected documents pertaining to black workers among the records of the Department of Labor ... United States. National Archives and Records Service. Selected documents pertaining to black workers among the records of the Department of Labor and its component bureaus, 1902-1969 /. Washington , 1977. viii, 55 p. ; LC Card 77-12904
Z1361.N39 U63 1977 E185.8
NYPL [Sc F 81-48]

Selected enrollment and financial data for school districts in Westchester. Westchester County, N. Y. Dept. of Planning. White Plains, N. Y., 1964. 29 p.   **NYPL [*Z-3176]**

Selected expenditures in Illinois school districts /. Illinois. State Aid Equalization Study. [Springfield] [1980] 48 p. : LC Card 80-623952 DDC 379.1/535 19
LB2826.I3 I4768 1980

Selected findings on the black elderly from The elderly in the inner city. New York (City). Office for the Aging. Research Dept. New York [1974] 15 p.;   **NYPL [*ZT-1250]**

A selected guide to audio-visual materials on alcohol and alocholism /. National Institute on Alcohol Abuse and Alcoholism. Rockville, Md. , 1975. viii, 34 p. : LC Card 79-42259
NYPL [*XME-8890]

Selected list of postsecondary education opportunities for minorities and women. United States. Office of Education. [Washington] , 1978. 87 p. ; LC Card 78-603500
LC3731 .U58 1978   **NYPL [JFF 81-168]**

Selected municipal cost-cutting measures. Knoxville : University of Tennessee's Municipal Technical Advisory Service in cooperation with the Tennessee Municipal League, 1979. 39 p. ; 28 cm. Microfilm. Includes bibliographical references.
1. Municipal services - United States - Costs. 2. Municipal officials and employees - United States - Labor productivity. I. Tennessee. University. Municipal Technical Advisory Service. II. Tennessee Municipal League. III. Title: Municipal cost-cutting measures.
NYPL [*ZT-1263]

Selected natality characteristics for single live births, United States, 1974. United States. Health Services Administration. Bureau of Community Health Services. Rockville, Md. , Washington , 1979. 34, [130] p. : LC Card 79-602931
HB915 .U48 1979

Selected 1970 census statistics for New York State minor civil divisions. New York (State). Office of Planning Services. Data and Systems Bureau. [Albany?, 1973] 1 v. (loose-leaf)
NYPL [*R-Econ. 78 4041]

Selected papers of Allan Sproul /. Sproul, Allan, 1896- [New York] [1980] xi, 233 p., [8] p. of plates : LC Card 80-67915 DDC 332 19
HG2563 .S64

Selected readings on mother-infant bonding.

[Washington, D.C. : U. S. Dept. of Health, Education, and Welfare, Office of Human Development Services, Administration for Children, Youth, and Families [and] Children's Bureau, National Center on Child Abuse and Neglect : for sale by the Supt. of Docs., U. S. Govt. Print. Off., 1979] 115 p. : ill. ; 28 cm. (DHEW publication. no. (OHDS) 79-30225) Cover title. Compiled by K.M. Yost. Includes bibliographical references. LC Card 79-604305 DDC 306.8/7 19
1. Mother and child - Addresses, essays, lectures. I. Yost, Kathleen M. II. United States. Administration for Children, Youth and Families. III. National Center on Child Abuse and Neglect. IV. Series: United States. Dept. of Health, Education and Welfare. DHEW publication, no. (OHDS) 79-30225.
HQ759 .S44

Selected topics in the study of Markov operators /. Foguel, Shaul R., 1931- [Chapel Hill, NC] , 1980. 116 p. ; LC Card 81-111770 DDC 515.4/2 19
QA313 .F63

Selected transportation elements including the master plan of highways. Maryland-National Capital Park and Planning Commission. Second draft, selected transportation elements including the master plan of highways . [Silver Spring? Md.] [1980] 1 map : LC Card 81-692907
G3843.M6P1 1980 .M3

Selected venereal disease statistics, Idaho, 1974. Idaho. Bureau of Preventive Medicine. [Boise] [1975] 19 leaves : LC Card 75-622999 DDC 312.39/51/009796 19
RA644.V4 I3 1975

Selected wage information 1980 for Montana and 14 labor market areas /. Montana. Division of Employment Security. Research and Analysis Section. Helena, MT [1980] ii, 209 p. : LC Card 80-623620 DDC 331.2/9786 19
HD4976.M84 M63 1980

Selected world shipping lanes and straits. United States. Central Intelligence Agency. [Washington , 1980] 1 map : LC Card 81-690686
G3201.P54 1980 .U5

Selection and oversight of administrative law judges . United States. Congress. House. Committee on Post Office and Civil Service. Washington , 1980. iii, 131 p. ; LC Card 80-603065 DDC 342.73/0664 19
KF27 .P6 1980a

Selection bibliography . Buckingham, Betty Jo. Des Moines, Iowa , 1979. 35 p. ; LC Card 80-623364 DDC 016/.01162 19
Z1037.A1 B83 1979 PN1009.A1

Selection of lixiviants for in situ uranium leaching /. Tweeton, Daryl R. Avondale, MD [1981] p. cm. LC Card 81-6103 DDC 622 s 622/.34932 19
TN295 .U4 TN490.U7

Selections from the N. Y. U. Art Collection. A Handbook of twentieth century art. - Storrs, Conn. , 1973. 71, iv p. :
NYPL [3-MAVZ (New York) 80-2266]

SELECTIVE ABSORPTION. see ABSORPTION SPECTRA.

Selective extraction of metals from Pacific sea nodules with dissolved sulfur dioxide /. Khalafalla, S. E. Avondale, Md. , 1980. p. cm. LC Card 80-606861 DDC 622 s 669/.028/3 19
TN23 .U43 TN291.5

Selective guide to climatic data sources /. Butson, Keith D. Washington [1979] xvi, 142 p. : LC Card 80-602294 DDC 551.5 s 016.5516 19
Z6685 .U64 no. 4.11 1979 Z6683.C5 QC981

Selective Service reform . United States. President, 1977- (Carter) Washington , 1980. ix, 62 p. ; LC Card 80-601724 DDC 343.73/0122 19
KF7263 .A25 1980

Selective service registration . United States. Congress. House. Committee on the Budget. Task Force on Defense and International Affairs. Washington , 1980. iii, 77 p. ; LC Card 80-602430 DDC 355.2/2363/0973 19
KF27 .B8438 1980a

Self-administration of abused substances : methods for study / editor Norman A. Krasnegor. Rockville, Md. : Dept. of Health, Education, and Welfare, Public Health Service, Alcohol, Drug Abuse, and Mental Health Administration, National Institute on Drug

Abuse, Division of Research, 1978. ix, 246 p. :
ill. ; 23 cm. (National Institute on Drug Abuse.
NIDA research monograph series. [no.] 20) DHEW
publication ; (ADM) 78-727 "Based on papers presented
at a technical review conducted by Plog Research, inc.,
Reseda, California, under NIDA contract no.
271-77-3413 ... on February 14 and 15, 1978, in
Reston, Virginia." Includes bibliographies.   LC Card
78-63094
1. Drug abuse - Congresses. 2. Obesity - Congresses. 3.
Cigarette habit - Congresses. I. Krasnegor, Norman A.
II. Plog Research, inc. III. National Institute on Drug
Abuse. IV. Series.
RC564 .S44   NYPL [JLM 76-1439 [no.] 20]

**SELF-EMPLOYED - TAXATION - UNITED
   STATES.**
United States. Congress. House. Committee on
Ways and Means. Subcommittee on Oversight.
Underground economy . Washington , 1980. iv,
501 p. ;   LC Card 80-602166   DDC 353.0072/44 19
KF27 .W345 1979i

United States. Congress. Joint Economic
Committee. The underground economy .
Washington , 1980. iii, 76 p. :   LC Card
80-602483   DDC 353.0072/442 19
KF25 .E2 1979m

SELF-HELP DEVICES FOR THE DISABLED.
Bell, Trudy. Technologies for the handicapped
and the aged . [Washington] , 1979. iii, 43 p. :
   LC Card 80-601228   DDC 617 19
R856 .B4

**SELF-INTEREST - ADDRESSES, ESSAYS,
   LECTURES.**
Bureaucracy vs. environment . Ann Arbor ,
c1981. p. cm.   ISBN 0-472-10010-6 :   LC Card
81-10382   DDC 363.7/00973 19
HC110.E5 B88 1981

**Self-mutilation at the penitentiary and
   Powhatan** . Virginia. Dept. of Corrections.
Research and Reporting Unit. [Richmond]
[1978] 10 leaves :   LC Card 79-622551   DDC
365/.641 19
HV9475.V82 R57 1978

SELF-MUTILATION - STATISTICS.
Virginia. Dept. of Corrections. Research and
Reporting Unit. Self-mutilation at the
penitentiary and Powhatan . [Richmond]
[1978] 10 leaves :   LC Card 79-622551   DDC
365/.641 19
HV9475.V82 R57 1978

SELF-REALIZATION.
Van Herik, Judith. Freud on femininity and
faith /. Berkeley , c1981. p. cm.   ISBN
0-520-04368-5   LC Card 81-3413   DDC
155.3/33/0924 19
BF173.F85 V26

**Self service gasoline marketing practices in
   Illinois** . Illinois. General Assembly. Legislative
Investigating Commission. Chicago, Ill. [1980]
ix, 94 p. ;   LC Card 80-622131   DDC
381/.4566553827/09773 19
HD9567.I3 I34 1980

Selkregg, Lidia L.
Report on cooperative institutions. 1979.
   Federal-State institutions for cooperative
   planning and management : publication /
   compiled and edited by Thelma J. Thrasher.
   Anchorage, Alaska [1979] iv, 47, 109 p. ;
   LC Card 80-620899   DDC 353.0082/326/09798
   19
HD211.A4 F43

SELLERS, DOROTHY ANN, 1943-
United States. Congress. Senate. Committee on
Governmental Affairs. Nominations of Dorothy
Sellers and Ricardo M. Urbina . Washington ,
1980. iii, 34 p. ;   LC Card 81-600816   DDC
353.008/8/09753 19
KF26 .G67 1980m

**SELLING - AUTOMOBILES - TAXATION -
   HAWAII.**
Ishado, Lester. A study of Hawaii's general
excise tax on warranty parts and labor /.
Honolulu, Hawaii , 1976. 31 leaves ;
                                *NYPL [*ZT-1259]*
SELLING, DIRECT. see DIRECT SELLING.

Selling the solar home '80 . Real Estate Research
Corporation. [Washington, D.C.] , 1980. 26 p.
(p. 26 blank) :   LC Card 80-602366   DDC
690/.869/0688 19
HD7293 .R36 1980

SEMANTICS.
Altieri, Charles, 1942- Act & quality .
Amherst , c1981. vi, 343 p. ;   ISBN
0-87023-327-0 :   LC Card 81-2147   DDC
808/.00141 19
PN81 .A453

SEMASIOLOGY. see SEMANTICS.

SEMEIOTICS. see SEMIOTICS.

**SEMI-CONDUCTOR DEVICES. see
   SEMICONDUCTORS.**

**SEMI-CONDUCTORS. see
   SEMICONDUCTORS.**

**Semi-dwarf varieties of wheat and rice in the
   United States.** Dalrymple, Dana G.
Development and spread of semi-dwarf varieties
of wheat and rice in the United States .
Washington, D.C. [1980] xiv, 150 p. :   LC
   Card 80-602635   DDC 338.1 s 633.1/17/0973 19
HD1751 .A91854 no. 455 SB191.W5

**Semiannual report to Congress on the
   effectiveness of the Civil Aviation Security
   Program.** United States. Civil Aviation Security
Service. July 1/Dec. 31, 1978- [Washington]
           LC Card 79-644552   *NYPL [Econ. Div.]*

Semick, Georgette. Lockard, James L. Directory
of community crime prevention programs,
national and State levels /. Washington , 1978.
xiii, 129 p. ;   LC Card 79-603996
HV6789 .L62

**SEMICONDUCTING MATERIALS. see
   SEMICONDUCTORS.**

**SEMICONDUCTOR DIODES. see DIODES,
   SEMICONDUCTOR.**

SEMICONDUCTOR INDUSTRY.
United States. Congress. House. Committee on
Ways and Means. Subcommittee on Trade.
Market conditions and international trade in
semiconductors . Washington , 1980. iii, 107
p. :   LC Card 80-602967   DDC
380.1/4562/38152/0973 19
KF27 .W348 1980b

**SEMICONDUCTOR INDUSTRY -
   GOVERNMENT POLICY - JAPAN.**
Gresser, Julian. High technology and Japanese
industrial policy . Washington , 1980. xiii, 73
p. :   LC Card 80-603865   DDC
338.4/5621381958/0952 19
HD9696.S43 J33

**SEMICONDUCTOR INDUSTRY - UNITED
   STATES.**
United States. Congress. House. Committee on
Ways and Means. Subcommittee on Trade.
Market conditions and international trade in
semiconductors . Washington , 1980. iii, 107
p. :   LC Card 80-602967   DDC
380.1/4562/38152/0973 19
KF27 .W348 1980b

United States. Industry and Trade
Administration. Office of Producer Goods. A
report on the U. S. semiconductor industry.
Washington, D.C. , 1979. ix, 132 p. ;   LC Card
79-604001
HD9696.S43 U54 1979   NYPL [JLF 81-168]

Semiconductor measurement technology.
Bullis, W. Murray, 1930- Metrology for
submicrometer devices and circuits /.
Washington, D.C. , 1980. vi, 34 p. :   LC Card
   80-600054   DDC 602/.18 s 621.381/73/0287 19
QC100 .U57 no. 400-61 TK7874

Kenney, James M. Modulation measurements
for microwave mixers /. [Washington, D.C.] ,
1980. v, 80 p. :   LC Card 79-600161   DDC
602/.18 s 621.381/33 19
QC100 .U57 no. 400-16 TK7872.M5

SEMICONDUCTORS - MEASUREMENT.
Bullis, W. Murray, 1930- Metrology for
submicrometer devices and circuits /.
Washington, D.C. , 1980. vi, 34 p. :   LC Card
   80-600054   DDC 602/.18 s 621.381/73/0287 19
QC100 .U57 no. 400-61 TK7874

SEMICONDUCTORS - TESTING.
Bullis, W. Murray, 1930- Metrology for
submicrometer devices and circuits /.
Washington, D.C. , 1980. vi, 34 p. :   LC Card
   80-600054   DDC 602/.18 s 621.381/73/0287 19
QC100 .U57 no. 400-61 TK7874

**SEMICONDUCTORS - TESTING -
   CONGRESSES.**

Nato Advanced Study Institute on
Nondestructive Evaluation of Semiconductor
Materials and Devices, Villa Tuscolano, Italy,
1978. Nondestructive evaluation of
semiconductor materials and devices . New
York , c1979. xi, 782 p. :   ISBN 0-306-40293-9
   LC Card 79-16499
TK7871.85 .N376 1978   NYPL [JSF 80-961]

**Seminar on Bankruptcy Law (New), University
   of Kentucky, 1979.** Kentucky. University.
Office of Continuing Legal Education. Seminar
on Bankruptcy Law (New) . Lexington, Ky. ,
c1980. 100 p. ;   LC Card 80-131695   DDC
346.73/078 19
KF1524.A2 K46

**Seminar on Industrial Pretreatment, Federal,
   State, and Local Government Perspectives
   and Industry's Interests, New Jersey
   Institute of Technology, 1979.** Proceedings :
Seminar on Industrial Pretreatment, Federal,
State, and Local Government Perspectives and
Industry's Interests / edited by Theresa C. Van
Rixport. [Trenton] : State of New Jersey, Dept.
of Environmental Protection, [1980] vii, 73 p. ;
28 cm.   LC Card 80-620966   DDC 628.1/683 19
1. Factory and trade waste - Congresses. 2. Sewage -
Purification - Congresses. I. Van Rixport, Theresa C. II.
New Jersey. Dept. of Environmental Protection.
TD896 .S45 1979

**Seminar on Investing in America, New York,
   1973.** Investing in America ; speeches. [New
York] De Hellerman, Co. 1973. 1 v. (various
pagings) ; 25 cm. Sponsored by Yamaichi
International (America), Inc., with the cooperation of
the Department of Commerce, State of New York, held
October 29-30, 1973 in New York City.
1. Investments - Congresses. I. Yamaichi International
(America). II. New York (State). Dept. of Commerce.
III. Title.   NYPL [JLE 80-1704]

**Seminar on Kentucky Civil Procedure, University
   of Kentucky, 1979.** Seminar on Kentucky
Civil Procedure, held at the College of Law,
University of Kentucky, Lexington, Kentucky,
June 15-16, 1979 / prepared by the Office of
Continuing Legal Education. Lexington, Ky. :
The Office, c1980. 113 p. ; 28 cm. Title on cover:
Report of seminar, Kentucky civil procedure.   LC Card
80-131042   DDC 347.769/05 19
1. Civil procedure - Kentucky - Congresses. I.
Kentucky. Office of Continuing Legal Education. II.
Title: Report of seminar, Kentucky civil procedure.
KFK1730.A2 S44 1979

**Seminar on Law Office Management, University
   of Kentucky, 1978.** Report of Seminar on
Law Office Management, held at the College of
Law, University of Kentucky, Lexington,
Kentucky, November 17-18, 1978 / John K.
Hickey, presiding ; prepared by the Office of
Continuing Legal Education. Lexington, Ky. :
The Office, c1979. 111 p. ; 28 cm. "Presented by
the Office of Continuing Legal Education, University of
Kentucky College of Law, in cooperation with the
Kentucky Bar Association."   LC Card 80-113276
   DDC 651/.934 19
1. Law offices - Kentucky - Congresses. I. Hickey, John
K. II. Kentucky. University. Office of Continuing Legal
Education. III. Kentucky State Bar Association.
KFK1277 .S45 1978

**Seminar on National and Local Institutions for
   the Promotion and Protection of Human
   Rights, Geneva, 1978.** Seminar on National
and Local Institutions for the Promotion and
Protection of Human Rights, Geneva, 18-29
September, 1978 / organized by the United
Nations Division of Human Rights. New York :
United Nations, 1978. iv, 49 p. ; 30 cm.
([Document] - United Nations. ST/HR/SER.A/2)   LC
   Card 79-111295   DDC 300 s 342/.085 300 s
342.85 19
1. Civil rights - Congresses. 2. Civil rights (International
law) - Congresses. I. United Nations. Division of
Human Rights. II. Series: United Nations. [Document]
ST/HR/SER.A/2.
JX1977 .A2 ST/HR/SER.A/2

**Seminar on Natural Resource Policies in
   Relation to Economic Development and
   International Cooperation, Wisconsin. see
   Wisconsin Seminar on Natural Resource
   Policies in Relation to Economic
   Development and International Cooperation,
   University of Wisconsin--Madison, 1977-
   1978.**

Seminar on Research, Productivity, and the National Economy, U. S. House of Representatives, 1980. Seminar on Research, Productivity, and the National Economy : seminar before the Committee on Science and Technology, U. S. House of Representatives, Ninety-sixth Congress, second session, June 18, 1890. Washington : U. S. Govt. Print. Off., 1980. v, 111 p. : ill. ; 24 cm. "No. 127." Includes bibliographical references. LC Card 80-603648 DDC 338/.06 19
1. Research, Industrial - United States. 2. Technological innovations - United States. 3. Industrial productivity - United States. I. United States. Congress. House. Committee on Science and Technology.
KF27 .S39 1980d

Seminar on the Role of Overburden Analysis in Surface Mining (1980 : Wheeling, W. VA.) Proceedings of Seminar on the Role of Overburden Analysis in Surface Mining, Wheeling, W. Va., May 6-7, 1980 / compiled by D.G. Simpson and W.T. Plass ; sponsored by the American Council for Reclamation Research and Bureau of Mines. Washington : United States Dept. of the Interior, Bureau of Mines, 1981. p. cm. (Information circular ;v) Bibliography: p. LC Card 81-607049 DDC 622 s 622/.31 19
1. Strip mining - Environmental aspects - Congresses. 2. Reclamation of land - Congresses. 3. Soils - Analysis - Congresses. I. Simpson, D. G. (David G.) II. Plass, W. T. III. American Council for Reclamation Research. IV. United States. Bureau of Mines. V. Series: Information circular (United States. Bureau of Mines) . VI. Title.
TN295 .U4 TD195.S75

Seminar on the Social and Cultural Impacts of Tourism, Joint Unesco-World Bank. see Joint Unesco-World Bank Seminar on the Social and Cultural Impacts of Tourism, Washington, D.C., 1976.

Seminar series (Washington, D.C.) . (1979-1980) Evolving strategic realities . Washington, DC , 1980. xi, 222 p. ; LC Card 80-602927 DDC 355/.033073 19
UA23 .E97

Seminario sobre Organización de Servicios para el Retrasado Mental, Cartagena, Colombia, 1973. Seminario sobre Organización de Servicios para el Retrasado Mental : Cartagena, Colombia, 17-21 de diciembre de 1973. Washington : Organización Panamericana de la Salud, Oficina Sanitaria Panamericana, 1974. iii, 100 p. ; 26 cm. (Publicación científica - Organización Panamericana de la Salud . no. 293) Includes bibliographies. LC Card 80-513008
1. Mental retardation services - Congresses. 2. Mental retardation services - South America - Congresses. I. Series: Pan American Health Organization. Publicaciones científicas , no. 293.
RA10 .P252 no. 293 RC569.9

SEMIOLOGY (LINGUISTICS) see SEMIOTICS.

SEMIOLOGY (SEMANTICS) see SEMANTICS.

SEMIOTICS - ADDRESSES, ESSAYS, LECTURES.
Sebeok, Thomas Albert, 1920- The play of musement /. Bloomington , c1981. p. cm. ISBN 0-253-39994-7 LC Card 80-8846 DDC 001.51 19
P99 .S33

SEMIPROFESSIONALS IN SOCIAL SERVICE. see PARAPROFESSIONALS IN SOCIAL SERVICE.

Senate delegation report. Perspectives on NATO's southern flank . Washington , 1980. v, 46 p. ; LC Card 80-603559 DDC 355/.0330182/2 19
UA646.55 .P47

Senate (U. S.) see United States. Congress. Senate.

SENEGAL.
France. Ambassade. United States. Service de presse et d'information. The Republic of Senegal. New York, 1960. 32 p.: LC Card 62-37710 *NYPL [Sc Micro R-3644]*

SENESCENCE. see AGING; OLD AGE.

Seni, S. J. (joint author) McGowen, J. H. Depositional framework of the Lower Dockum Group (Triassic), Texas Panhandle /. Austin,

Tex. , 1979. 60 p. : LC Card 80-621656 DDC 553/.09764 s 551.7/62 19
QE167 .T42 no. 97 QE677

Senier, John K. S. Annual occupational withdrawal rates for Pennsylvania and the major labor market areas / by John Senier (Division of Research, Bureau of Information Systems, Pennsylvania Department of Education). Harrisburg, Pa. : Pennsylvania Dept. of Education, 1974. iv, 51 p. ; 28 cm. Chiefly tables. Includes bibliographical references. LC Card 80-621271 DDC 331.12/09748 19
1. Labor supply - Pennsylvania - Statistics. 2. Pennsylvania - Occupations - Statistics. I. Pennsylvania. Dept. of Education. Bureau of Information Systems. Division of Research. II. Title.
HD5725.P4 S46

The sense of well-being in America . Campbell, Angus, 1910- New York , c1981. xiii, 263 p. ; ISBN 0-07-009683-X LC Card 80-14379
HN59 .C29 NYPL [JLE 81-367]

Sensitivity of vertebrate embryos to heavy metals as a criterion of water quality, phase II . Birge, Wesley J. Lexington , 1975. iii, 36 p. : LC Card 76-624547 DDC 628.1/6836 19
QH90.57.B5 B6

SENSITIVITY TRAINING. see GROUP RELATIONS TRAINING.

SENSORY DISCRIMINATION - EXHIBITIONS.
Goldberg, Joshua. Hands-on, Japan . Tucson, Ariz. , c1980. 24 p., [6] leaves of plates : LC Card 80-53235 DDC 709/.52/074019177 19
N7352 .G64

SENTENCES (CRIMINAL PROCEDURE) - GREAT BRITAIN.
Shroff, Kersi B. Individualized sentencing and the use of social inquiry (presentence) reports in England /. Washington , 1978. 20 p. ; LC Card 78-600143 DDC 345.42/0772 19
KD8406 .S55

SENTENCES (CRIMINAL PROCEDURE) - MINNESOTA.
Thomssen, Carol. Sentencing in Minnesota district courts . St. Paul , 1978. viii, 80 p. : LC Card 78-622567 DDC 345.776/0772 19
KFM5983.2 .T56

SENTENCES (CRIMINAL PROCEDURE) - NEW YORK (STATE)
New York (State). Executive Advisory Committee on Sentencing. Crime and punish in New York. [Albany] , 1979. 2 v. ; *NYPL [JLE 80-2963]*
New York (State). Executive Advisory Committee on Sentencing. Crime and punishment in New York . [Albany] [1979] xvii, 214 p. ; LC Card 80-622706 DDC 345.747/0772 19
KFN6172 .A873

SENTENCES (CRIMINAL PROCEDURE) - NORTH CAROLINA.
Drennan, James C. Punishment chart for crimes of general interest in the Superior Courts of North Carolina /. [Chapel Hill] , 1978. ix, 40 p. ; LC Card 78-624325 DDC 345.756/077 19
KFN7983.2.Z9 D73

SENTENCES (CRIMINAL PROCEDURE) - VIRGINIA.
Virginia. General Assembly. Joint Committee for the Courts of Justice. Report of the Joint Committee for the Courts of Justice of the House and Senate studying sentencing in criminal cases to the General Assembly of Virginia. Richmond, Va. , 1980. 19 p. ; LC Card 80-623756 DDC 300/.9755 s 345.755/0772 300/.9755 s 347.5505772 19
J87 .V9 1979c no. 26 KFV2411.62

SENTENCES (CRIMINAL PROCEDURE) - WASHINGTON (STATE) - SEATTLE - STATISTICAL METHODS.
Lichtenstein, Karen. Assessment of variables used in presentence recommendations and court decisions /. Olympia, Wash. [1980] vii, 29 p. : LC Card 80-623909 DDC 345.797/77077/0723 347.977705770723 19
KFX2379.89 .L52

Sentencing in Minnesota district courts . Thomssen, Carol. St. Paul , 1978. viii, 80 p. : LC Card 78-622567 DDC 345.776/0772 19
KFM5983.2 .T56

SEPARATE MAINTENANCE - UNITED STATES.
United States. Congress. House. Committee on Armed Services. Subcommittee on Military Compensation. Hearing on H.R. 2817, H.R. 3677, and H.R. 6270, legislation related to benefits for former spouse of a military retiree, before the Military Compensation Subcommittee of the Committee on Armed Services, House of Representatives, Ninety-sixth Congress, second session, May 28, 1980. Washington , 1980 [i.e. 1981] ii, 126 p. : LC Card 81-600974 DDC 343.73/0112 347.303112 19
KF27 .A76392 1980c

SEPTIC TANKS.
Hain, Kathleen E. The survival of enteric viruses in septic tanks and septic tank drain fields /. Las Cruces, N.M. [1979] x, 73 p. : LC Card 80-622272 DDC 628/.742 19
GB705.N6 N64 no. 108 QR48

SEPTIC TANKS - ENVIRONMENTAL ASPECTS - MONTANA.
Peavy, Howard S. The effects of non-sewered subdivisions on ground water quality /. Bozeman, MT [1980?] iv, 65, 22 p. : LC Card 80-623175 DDC 363.7/394 19
TD224.M9 P33

SEPTIC TANKS - GEORGIA - BALDWIN COUNTY - MAPS.
United States. Soil Conservation Service. Baldwin County, Georgia . Fort Worth, Tex. , 1979. 1 map : LC Card 81-690364
G3923.B26N46 1978 .U5

SEPTIC TANKS - GEORGIA - TOOMBS COUNTY - MAPS.
United States. Soil Conservation Service. Toombs County, Georgia . Fort Worth, Tex. , 1979. 1 map : LC Card 81-690349
G3923.T6N46 1978 .U5

SEPTIC TANKS - MAINE.
White, Gregory K. Institutional structures affecting on-site waste disposal in Maine /. [Orono, Me.] , 1979. 46 p. : LC Card 80-622060 DDC 363.7/28 19
TD778 .W49

Sequences in writing, grades K-13 / by Gail Siegel ... [et al. ; cover design, Gene Izuno]. Berkeley, Calif. : University of California, Berkeley, Bay Area Writing Project, c1980. v, 55 p. : ill. ; 23 cm. (Curriculum publication . no. 13) Bibliography: p. 52-55. LC Card 80-155709 DDC 808/.042 19
1. English language - Rhetoric. 2. Creative writing. I. Siegel, Gail. II. Series.
PE1408 .S458

Serials holdings list . Hawaii State Library. [Honolulu] , 1979. vi, 184 p. ; LC Card 79-624871 DDC 011/.34 19
Z6945 .H4 1979 PN4801

Série de química .
(monografia no. 20) Rabockai, Tibor. Físico-química de superfícies /. Washington, D.C. , 1979. vii, 128 p. : LC Card 80-103037 DDC 540 s 541.3/453 19
QD1 .S303 no. 20 QC173.4.S94
(monografiá no. 22) Posadas, Dionisio. Introducción a la electroquímica /. Washington, D.C. , 1980. vii, 136 p. : ISBN 0-08-270122-0 (pbk.) : LC Card 81-119707 DDC 540 s 541.3/7 19
QD1 .S303 no. 22 QD553

Serie sobre tratados .
(no. 41) Inter-American convention on conflict of laws concerning checks. Convención interamericana sobre conflictos de leyes en materia de cheques =. Washington , 1975. iii, 8 p. ; LC Card 81-463811 DDC 341.24/5 s 341.7/51 19
F1402 .A169 OEA/Ser. A/19 (SEPF)
(no. 42) Inter-American convention on international commercial arbitration. Convención interamericana sobre arbitraje comercial internacional =. Washington , 1975. iii, 12 p. ; LC Card 81-463810 DDC 341.24/5 s 341.5/22/0265 19
F1402 .A169 OEA/Ser. A/20 (SEPF)
(no. 43) Inter-American convention on letters rogatory. Convención interamericana sobre exhortos o cartas rogatorias =. Washington , 1975. iii, 20 p. ; LC Card 81-463813 DDC

341.24/5 s 341.7/8/0265 19
F1402 .A169 OEA/Ser. A/21 (SEPF)

(no. 44) Inter-American convention on the taking of evidence abroad. Convención interamericana sobre recepción de pruebas en el extranjero =. Washington , 1975. iii, 20 p. ;
LC Card 81-463809   DDC 341.24/5 s
341.7/8/0265 19
F1402 .A169 OEA/Ser. A/22 (SEPF)

(no. 45) Inter-American convention on the legal regime of powers of attorney to be used abroad. Convención interamericana sobre régimen legal de poderes para ser utilizados en el extranjero =. Washington , 1975. iii, 16 p. ;   LC Card 81-463812   DDC 341.24/5 s 341.7/8/0265 19
F1402 .A169 OEA/Ser. A/23 (SEPF)

(53) Inter-American convention on proof of and information on foreign law. Convención interamericana sobre prueba e información acerca del derecho extranjero . Washington, D.C. , 1979. iii, 27 p. ;   LC Card 80-113645   DDC 341.24/5 s 341.7/8/0265 19
F1402 .A169 OEA/Ser. A/30 (SEPF)

(57-57A) United States. Treaties, etc. Panama, Sept. 7, 1977. Tratados sobre el Canal de Panamá suscritos entre la República de Panamá y los Estados Unidos de América =. Washington, D.C. , 1979. 2 v. :   LC Card 80-121836   DDC 341.4/46/02667307287 19
JX1398.72 1979 .U54 1977

The serious business of growing up . Medrich, Elliott A. Berkeley , c1981. p. cm.   ISBN 0-520-04296-4   LC Card 81-7630   DDC 305.2/3/0979466 19
HQ792.U5 M42

SERUM - ANALYSIS - STANDARDS.
National Measurement Laboratory (U. S.) Standard reference materials . Washington, D.C. , 1980. xiv, 99 p. :   LC Card 80-600091   DDC 602/.18 s 616.07/56 19
QC100 .U57 no. 260-69 RB46

SERVICE INDUSTRIES.
United States. Congress. Senate. Committee on Commerce, Science, and Transportation. Service Industries Development Act . Washington , 1981. iii, 137 p. :   LC Card 81-600931   DDC 343.73/078 347.30378 19
KF26 .C69 1980 w

Service Industries Development Act . United States. Congress. Senate. Committee on Commerce, Science, and Transportation. Washington , 1981. iii, 137 p. :   LC Card 81-600931   DDC 343.73/078 347.30378 19
KF26 .C69 1980 w

SERVICE INDUSTRIES - LAW AND LEGISLATION - UNITED STATES.
United States. Congress. Senate. Committee on Commerce, Science, and Transportation. Service Industries Development Act . Washington , 1981. iii, 137 p. :   LC Card 81-600931   DDC 343.73/078 347.30378 19
KF26 .C69 1980 w

SERVICE INDUSTRIES WORKERS - HAWAII - SUPPLY AND DEMAND.
Hawaii. Labor Market and Employment Service Research Section. Occupational Information Unit. Hawaii's services industry, 1978 . [Honolulu, Hawaii] [1979?] 100 p. (p. 100 blank) :   LC Card 80-623582   DDC 331.12/51/0009969 19
HD5718.S452 U54 1979

SERVICE INDUSTRIES WORKERS - NEW JERSEY - STATISTICS.
Charpentier, Thomas. Occupational employment in selected service industries in New Jersey. Trenton, N.J. , 1980. v, 230 p. :   LC Card 80-624024   DDC 331.12/51/0009749 19
HD5718.S452 U53

SERVICE RATING. see EMPLOYEES, RATING OF.

SERVICE STATIONS, AUTOMOBILE. see AUTOMOBILES - SERVICE STATIONS.

Services, facilities, and costs of medical care and hospitalization for township relief cases /. Indiana. Unemployment Relief Commission. Indianapolis , 1941. 11, [19] leaves ;   LC Card 80-500265   DDC 362.1/9 19
RA418.5.P6 I54 1941

Services for the elderly in Albuquerque, N. Mex. . United States. Congress. House. Select Committee on Aging. Subcommittee on Housing and Consumer Interests. Washington , 1980 [i.e. 1981] iv, 56 p. ;   LC Card 81-601154   DDC 362.6/3/0978961 19
KF27.5 .A358 1980a

SERVITUDES - UNITED STATES.
Daugherty, Arthur Berry, 1936- Open space preservation . Washington , Springfield, Va. , 1978. v, 32 p. ;   LC Card 79-601799   DDC 338.1/0973 s 336.24/216 19
HD1759 .U56a no. 32 HJ4653.C73

Seton-Watson, Christopher. Seton-Watson, Hugh. The making of a new Europe . Seattle , c1981. x, 458 p. :   ISBN 0-295-95792-1   LC Card 80-8795   DDC 940/.072024 B 19
D15.S57 S47

Seton-Watson, Hugh. The making of a new Europe : R.W. Seton-Watson and the last years of Austria-Hungary / Hugh and Christopher Seton-Watson. Seattle : University of Washington Press, c1981. x, 458 p. : port. ; 24 cm. Maps on lining papers. Bibliography: p. [443]-445. Includes indexes.   ISBN 0-295-95792-1   LC Card 80-8795   DDC 940/.072024 B 19
1. Seton-Watson, Robert William, 1879-1951. 2. Historians - Great Britain - Biography. 3. Austria - History - 1867-1918. 4. Europe, Eastern - History. I. Seton-Watson, Christopher. II. Title.
D15.S57 S47

SETON-WATSON, ROBERT WILLIAM, 1879-1951.
Seton-Watson, Hugh. The making of a new Europe . Seattle , c1981. x, 458 p. :   ISBN 0-295-95792-1   LC Card 80-8795   DDC 940/.072024 B 19
D15.S57 S47

Setting public management research agendas . Public Management Research Conference, Brookings Institution, 1979. [Washington, D.C.] [1980] iv, 95 p. :   LC Card 80-602841   DDC 350/.00072/073 19
JF1338.A2 P85 1979

SETTLEMENT COSTS - UNITED STATES.
Real estate settlement procedures act. Washington, D.C. [1979] 7, 39, [12] p. :   LC Card 80-601047   DDC 346.7304/373 19
KF681 .R4

Settlement of claims against Czechoslavakia . United States. Congress. House. Committee on Foreign Affairs. Subcommittee on Europe and the Middle East. Washington , 1981. iv, 225 p. ;   LC Card 81-600940   DDC 346.7304/3 347.30643 19
KF27 .F64214 1980e

Settlement of Indian land claims in the state of Maine . United States. Congress. House. Committee on Interior and Insular Affairs. Washington , 1980 [i.e. 1981] iv, 287 p. ;   LC Card 81-600935   DDC 346.7304/3/08997 347.3064308997 19
KF27 .I5 1980c

Settlement of San Luis Rey River water claims . United States. Congress. Senate. Select Committee on Indian Affairs. Washington , 1980. iii, 56 p. ;   LC Card 80-602905   DDC 346.7304/691 19
KF26.5 .I4 1980g

Settlement of the Cayuga Indian Nation land claims in the state of New York . United States. Congress. House. Committee on Interior and Insular Affairs. Washington , 1980. v, 404 p. :   LC Card 81-600597   DDC 346.7304/32/08997 347.30643208997 19
KF27 .I5 1980

Settlement patterns of the Western Hueco Bolson /. Whalen, Michael E. [El Paso] , 1978. xv, 260 p., [1] leaf of plates :   LC Card 79-624053   DDC 976.4/96 19
F392.H82 W45

SETTLING BASINS.
Neher, Michael A. Heavy metal accumulation and its effect on the biota of an industrial settling pond . Bozeman , 1977. viii, 96, 2 p., [1] leaf of plates :   LC Card 79-624616   DDC 574.5/26322 19
QH545.H42 N44

SETTLING BASINS - DESIGN AND CONSTRUCTION.
National Research Council. Transportation Research Board. Design of sedimentation basins. Washington, D.C. , 1980. 53 p. :   ISBN 0-309-03027-7 (pbk.) :   LC Card 80-52843   DDC 625.7/34 19
TD439 .N37 1980

Setzer, Florence. The Seattle-Denver income maintenance experiment : midexperimental labor supply results and a generalization to the national population : summary report / [written by Florence Setzer, Richard Kasten, and David Betson ; conducted by Stanford Research Institute and Mathematica Policy Research for the Department of Health, Education, and Welfare. [Washington] : The Dept., 1978. xv, 54 p. ; 27 cm. Bibliography: p. [51]-54.   LC Card 78-603699
1. Income maintenance programs - United States - Case studies. 2. Income maintenance programs - Washington (State) - Seattle. 3. Income maintenance programs - Colorado - Denver. 4. Labor supply - United States - Case studies. 5. Welfare recipients - Employment - United States - Case studies. I. Kasten, Richard, joint author. II. Betson, David, joint author. III. Stanford Research Institute. IV. Mathematica Policy Research, Inc. V. United States. Dept. of Health, Education, and Welfare. VI. Title.
HC110.I5 S4   **NYPL [JLF 81-429]**

The seven ages of a medical scientist . Corner, George Washington, 1889- Philadelphia , 1981. p. cm.   ISBN 0-8122-7811-9   LC Card 81-51143   DDC 610/.92/4 B 19
QM16.C66 A37

Seven years later, the experiences of the 1970 cohort of immigrants in the United States. United States. Employment and Training Administration. [Washington, D.C.] , 1979. v, 172 p. :   LC Card 80-601560   DDC 331.11/0973 s 331.6/2/0973 19
HD5701 .U53 no. 71 HD8081.A5

Seventeen eighty-nine, the emblems of reason. Starobinski, Jean. [1789, les emblèmes de la raison. English.] 1789, the emblems of reason /. Charlottesville , 1981. p. cm.   ISBN 0-8139-0915-5   LC Card 81-13135   DDC 709/.44 19
NX452.5.N4 S7

Severo-Amerikanskie Shtaty. see United States.

Severson, R. C. (Ronald Charles), 1945-
Geochemical variability of natural soils and reclaimed mine-spoil soils in the San Juan Basin, New Mexico / by R.C. Severson and L.P. Gough. Washington : U. S.G.P.O., 1981. p. cm. (Geochemical survey of the western energy regions) Geological Survey professional paper ; 1134-C   Bibliography: p.   LC Card 81-607985   DDC 631.6/4 19
1. Soils - New Mexico - Composition. 2. Soils - San Juan River watershed (Colo.=Utah) - Composition. 3. Coal mine waste - New Mexico - Farmington region - Composition. 4. Reclamation of land - New Mexico. 5. San Juan River watershed (Colo.=Utah). I. Gough, L. P. II. Title. III. Title: Mine-spoil soils in San Juan Basin, New Mexico. IV. Series.
S599.N6 S46

SEWAGE AS FERTILIZER - UNITED STATES.
Overcash, Michael R. Characterization and land application of seafood industry wastewaters /. Raleigh [1980] ix, 34 leaves :   LC Card 80-623929   DDC 664/.94996 19
TD774 .O92

SEWAGE DISPOSAL.
United States. Environmental Protection Agency. Office of Water Program Operations. Estimating laboratory needs for municipal wastewater treatment facilities. Washington, 1973. i, 23, [104] p. :   **NYPL [JSF 80-271]**

SEWAGE DISPOSAL - ECONOMIC ASPECTS - ILLINOIS.
Huff, Linda L. Economic impact analysis of proposed change in Illinois deoxygenating regulations, R77-12, docket C /. Chicago , 1979. xvii, 78 p. :   LC Card 80-620894   DDC 363.7/394 19
TD224.I3 H833

SEWAGE DISPOSAL - EMPLOYEES - CERTIFICATION - ILLINOIS.
Illinois. Environmental Protection Agency. Procedures for the certification of operators of wastewater treatment works. [Springfield, Ill. , 1980] 29 p. :   LC Card 80-623066   DDC 353.97730087/1 19
TD524.I3 I44 1980

SEWAGE DISPOSAL - FILTRATION. see SEWAGE - PURIFICATION - FILTRATION.

SEWAGE DISPOSAL IN RIVERS, LAKES, ETC. - BLACKSTONE RIVER WATERSHED.
Massachusetts. Division of Water Pollution Control. Water Quality Section. Blackstone River basin . Westborough [1974] 36 p. : LC Card 80-120648 DDC 363.7/3942/097443 19
TD225.B65 M37 1974

Massachusetts. Water Quality and Research Section. Blackstone River basin . Westborough , 1976. 33 p. : LC Card 79-620584 DDC 363.7/3942/097443 19
TD225.B65 M38 1976

Massachusetts. Water Quality and Research Section. Blackstone River basin . Westborough [1978] 34 p. : LC Card 79-620585 DDC 363.7/3942/097443 19
TD225.B65 M38 1978

SEWAGE DISPOSAL IN RIVERS, LAKES, ETC. - CONNECTICUT RIVER WATERSHED.
Massachusetts. Division of Water Pollution Control. Water Quality Section. Connecticut River . Westborough, Mass. [1976] 52 p. : LC Card 77-622207 DDC 363.7/3942/097442 19
TD225.C74 M37 1976

Massachusetts. Water Quality and Research Section. Connecticut River . Westborough, Mass. , 1977. 35 p. : LC Card 79-620576 DDC 363.7/3942/097442 19
TD225.C74 M38 1977

Massachusetts. Water Quality and Research Section. Connecticut River . Westborough, Mass. , 1978. 58 p. : LC Card 79-623996 DDC 363.7/3942/097442 19
TD225.C74 M38 1978

SEWAGE DISPOSAL IN RIVERS, LAKES, ETC. - DEERFIELD RIVER WATERSHED.
Massachusetts. Division of Water Pollution Control. Water Quality Section. Deerfield River basin . Westborough , 1976. 22 p. : LC Card 79-620577 DDC 363.7/3942/0974422 19
TD225.D24 M36 1976a

Massachusetts. Division of Water Pollution Control. Water Quality Section. Deerfield River basin . Westborough , 1976. 18 p. : LC Card 77-622638 DDC 363.7/3942/0974422 19
TD225.D24 M36 1976

Massachusetts. Division of Water Pollution Control. Water Quality Section. Deerfield River basin /. Westborough , 1977- v. : LC Card 79-620578 DDC 363.7/3942/0974422 19
TD225.D24 M36 1977

Massachusetts. Water Quality and Research Section. Deerfield River basin . Westborough, Mass. , 1978. 16 p. : LC Card 79-623991 DDC 363.7/3942/0974422 19
TD225.D24 M38 1978

SEWAGE DISPOSAL IN RIVERS, LAKES, ETC. - GREAT LAKES - CONGRESSES.
Phosphorus managemnt strategies or lakes . Ann Arbor, Mich. , 1980. vi, 490 p. : ISBN 0-250-40332-3 LC Card 79-55150
TD223.3 .P48

SEWAGE DISPOSAL IN RIVERS, LAKES, ETC. - ILLINOIS.
Muchmore, C. B. Economic impact of the proposed averaging rule, R76-21 /. Chicago, IL , 1978. xi, 43 p. : LC Card 80-622962 DDC 363.7/39462 19
TD224.I3 M84

SEWAGE DISPOSAL IN RIVERS, LAKES, ETC. - MASSACHUSETTS - ASSABET RIVER WATERSHED.
Massachusetts. Division of Water Pollution Control. Water Quality Section. SUASCO River basin . Westborough, Mass. [1976] 36 p. : LC Card 77-622200 DDC 363.7/3942/097444 19
TD224.M4 M36 1976l

Massachusetts. Water Quality and Research Section. SUASCO River basin . Westborough, Mass. , 1977. 33 p. : LC Card 79-622377 DDC 363.7/3942/097444 19
TD224.M4 M368 1977

SEWAGE DISPOSAL IN RIVERS, LAKES, ETC. - MASSACHUSETTS - BOSTON

BAY WATERSHED.
Massachusetts. Water Quality and Research Section. Boston Harbor . Westborough, Mass. , 1977. iv, 48 p. : LC Card 79-620587 DDC 363.7/3942/097446 19
TD225.B7 M39 1977

SEWAGE DISPOSAL IN RIVERS, LAKES, ETC. - MASSACHUSETTS - BUZZARDS BAY WATERSHED - STATISTICS.
Massachusetts. Water Quality and Research Section. Buzzards Bay . Westborough, Mass. [1978] 62 p. : LC Card 79-620588 DDC 363.7/3942/097448 19
TD224.M4 M39 1978g

SEWAGE DISPOSAL IN RIVERS, LAKES, ETC. - MASSACHUSETTS - CHARLES RIVER WATERSHED.
Massachusetts. Division of Water Pollution Control. Water Quality Section. Charles River . Westborough [1974] 33 p. : LC Card 77-622229 DDC 363.7/3942/097447 19
TD224.M4 M36 1974d

Massachusetts. Division of Water Pollution Control. Water Quality Section. Charles River . Westborough, Mass. [1976] 55 p. : LC Card 80-120642 DDC 363.7/3942/097447 19
TD224.M4 M36 1976f

Massachusetts. Water Quality and Research Section. Charles River /. Westborough, Mass. , 1978- v. : LC Card 79-623994 DDC 363.7/3942/097447 19
TD224.M4 M39 1978e

SEWAGE DISPOSAL IN RIVERS, LAKES, ETC. - MASSACHUSETTS - CHICOPEE RIVER WATERSHED.
Massachusetts. Water Quality Research Section. Chicopee River basin . Westborough , 1976. 40 p. : LC Card 77-622227 DDC 363.7/3942/0974426 19
TD224.M4 M39 1976

SEWAGE DISPOSAL IN RIVERS, LAKES, ETC. - MASSACHUSETTS - CONCORD RIVER WATERSHED.
Massachusetts. Division of Water Pollution Control. Water Quality Section. SUASCO River basin . Westborough, Mass. [1976] 36 p. : LC Card 77-622200 DDC 363.7/3942/097444 19
TD224.M4 M36 1976l

Massachusetts. Water Quality and Research Section. SUASCO River basin . Westborough, Mass. , 1977. 33 p. : LC Card 79-622377 DDC 363.7/3942/097444 19
TD224.M4 M368 1977

SEWAGE DISPOSAL IN RIVERS, LAKES, ETC. - MASSACHUSETTS - FRENCH RIVER WATERSHED.
Massachusetts. Water Quality and Research Section. French and Quinebaug Rivers . Westborough [1978] 43 p. : LC Card 79-620581 DDC 363.7/3942/097443 19
TD224.M4 M39 1978d

SEWAGE DISPOSAL IN RIVERS, LAKES, ETC. - MASSACHUSETTS - IPSWICH RIVER WATERSHED.
Massachusetts. Water Quality and Research Section. Parker and Ipswich Rivers . Westborough, Mass. [1977] 13 p. : LC Card 79-620594 DDC 363.7/3942/097445 19
TD224.M4 M368 1977a

SEWAGE DISPOSAL IN RIVERS, LAKES, ETC. - MASSACHUSETTS - MILLERS RIVER WATERSHED.
Massachusetts. Water Quality and Research Section. Millers River . Westborough, Mass. [1979] 39 p. : LC Card 79-623981 DDC 363.7/3942/0974422 19
TD224.M4 M39 1979

SEWAGE DISPOSAL IN RIVERS, LAKES, ETC. - MASSACHUSETTS - MYSTIC RIVER WATERSHED.
Massachusetts. Division of Water Pollution Control. Water Quality Section. Mystic River . Westborough, Mass. [1976] 37 p. : LC Card 77-622204 DDC 363.7/3942/097444 19
TD224.M4 M36 1976a

SEWAGE DISPOSAL IN RIVERS, LAKES, ETC. - MASSACHUSETTS - NEPONSET RIVER WATERSHED.
Massachusetts. Division of Water Pollution Control. Water Quality Section. Neponset River . Westborough [1976] 38, A-U p. : LC

Card 77-622675 DDC 363.7/3942/097447 19
TD224.M4 M36 1976h

SEWAGE DISPOSAL IN RIVERS, LAKES, ETC. - MASSACHUSETTS - NORTH RIVER WATERSHED.
Massachusetts. Division of Water Pollution Control. Water Quality Section. North River basin . Westborough , 1975. 16 p. : LC Card 78-621331 DDC 363.7/3942/0974482 19
TD224.M4 M36 1975i

Massachusetts. Division of Water Pollution Control. Water Quality Section. North River basin . Westborough [1976] 22 p. : LC Card 79-620607 DDC 363.7/3942/0974482 19
TD224.M4 M36 1976i

Massachusetts. Water Quality and Research Section. North River . Westborough , 1977. 53 p. : LC Card 79-622379 DDC 363.7/3942/0974482 19
TD224.M4 M39 1977i

SEWAGE DISPOSAL IN RIVERS, LAKES, ETC. - MASSACHUSETTS - PARKER RIVER WATERSHED.
Massachusetts. Water Quality and Research Section. Parker and Ipswich Rivers . Westborough, Mass. [1977] 13 p. : LC Card 79-620594 DDC 363.7/3942/097445 19
TD224.M4 M368 1977a

SEWAGE DISPOSAL IN RIVERS, LAKES, ETC. - MASSACHUSETTS - SUDBURY RIVER WATERSHED.
Massachusetts. Division of Water Pollution Control. Water Quality Section. SUASCO River basin . Westborough, Mass. [1976] 36 p. : LC Card 77-622200 DDC 363.7/3942/097444 19
TD224.M4 M36 1976l

Massachusetts. Water Quality and Research Section. SUASCO River basin . Westborough, Mass. , 1977. 33 p. : LC Card 79-622377 DDC 363.7/3942/097444 19
TD224.M4 M368 1977

SEWAGE DISPOSAL IN RIVERS, LAKES, ETC. - MASSACHUSETTS - TAUNTON RIVER WATERSHED.
Massachusetts. Water Quality and Research Section. Taunton River Basin wastewater discharge survey, 1975, 1976, 1978, 1979 /. Westborough [Mass.] [1979] 133 p. : LC Card 80-621549 DDC 363.7/3942/097448 19
TD224.M4 M368 1979

Salo, John E. Taunton River study . Boston [1971] 31 leaves : LC Card 80-118663 DDC 363.7/3942/097448 19
TD224.M4 S25

SEWAGE DISPOSAL IN RIVERS, LAKES, ETC. - MASSACHUSETTS - TEN MILE RIVER WATERSHED.
Lord, Sabin M. Ten Mile River study, 1968 /. [Boston] [1970]- v. : LC Card 80-120118 DDC 363.7/3942/0974485 19
TD224.M4 L67

Massachusetts. Division of Water Pollution Control. Water Quality Section. Ten Mile River basin . Westborough, Mass. , 1976. 46 p. ; LC Card 77-622202 DDC 363.7/39456/0974485 19
TD224.M4 M36 1976b

Massachusetts. Water Quality and Research Section. Ten Mile River basin . Westborough [1978] 42 p. : LC Card 79-620593 DDC 363.7/3942/0974485 19
TD224.M4 M39 1978b

SEWAGE DISPOSAL IN RIVERS, LAKES, ETC. - MASSACHUSETTS - WESTFIELD RIVER WATERSHED.
Massachusetts. Water Quality and Research Section. Westfield River basin /. Westborough , 1975. 2 v. : LC Card 77-622217 DDC 363.7/394/0974426 19
TD224.M4 M39 1975

SEWAGE DISPOSAL IN RIVERS, LAKES, ETC. - MASSACHUSETTS - WESTFIELD RIVER WATERSHED - STATISTICS.
Massachusetts. Water Quality and Research Section. Westfield River basin . Westborough, Mass. , 1978. 113 p. : LC Card 79-623982 DDC 363.7/3942/0974426 19
TD224.M4 M39 1978f

SEWAGE DISPOSAL IN RIVERS, LAKES, ETC. - MASSACHUSETTS - WEYMOUTH BACK RIVER WATERSHED.

Massachusetts. Water Quality and Research Section. Weymouth Fore and Back River survey, 1975 /. Westborough [1976] 58 p. : LC Card 79-620589 DDC 363.7/3942/097447 19
TD224.M4 M39 1976a

SEWAGE DISPOSAL IN RIVERS, LAKES, ETC. - MASSACHUSETTS - WEYMOUTH FORE RIVER WATERSHED.
Massachusetts. Water Quality and Research Section. Weymouth Fore and Back River survey, 1975 /. Westborough [1976] 58 p. : LC Card 79-620589 DDC 363.7/3942/097447 19
TD224.M4 M39 1976a

SEWAGE DISPOSAL IN RIVERS, LAKES, ETC. - MERRIMACK RIVER WATERSHED, N.H. AND MASS.
Massachusetts. Water Quality and Research Section. Merrimack River basin . Westborough , 1977. 15 p. : LC Card 79-620606 DDC 363.7/3942/097445 19
TD225.M514 M37 1977

Massachusetts. Water Quality and Research Section. Merrimack River basin . Westborough [1978] 30 p. : LC Card 79-624447 DDC 363.7/3942/097445 19
TD225.M514 M37 1978

SEWAGE DISPOSAL IN RIVERS, LAKES, ETC. - NASHUA RIVER WATERSHED, MASS. AND N.H. - STATISTICS.
Massachusetts. Division of Water Pollution Control. Water Quality Section. Nashua River basin . Westborough [1975] 38 p. : LC Card 79-620604 DDC 363.7/3942/097443 19
TD225.N2 M37 1975

Massachusetts. Water Quality and Research Section. Nashua River basin . Westborough, Mass. [1978] 31 p. : LC Card 79-620603 DDC 363.7/3942/097444 19
TD225.N2 M38 1978

SEWAGE DISPOSAL IN RIVERS, LAKES, ETC. - QUINEBAUG RIVER WATERSHED, CONN. AND MASS.
Massachusetts. Water Quality and Research Section. French and Quinebaug Rivers . Westborough [1978] 43 p. : LC Card 79-620581 DDC 363.7/3942/097443 19
TD224.M4 M39 1978d

SEWAGE DISPOSAL IN THE GROUND - ENVIRONMENTAL ASPECTS - HAWAII.
Petty, Susan. Hawaiian waste injection practices and problems /. Honolulu, Hawaii [1979] viii, 104 p. : LC Card 80-621493 DDC 553.7/09969 s 627/.56 19
TC1 .H36 no. 123 TD760

SEWAGE DISPOSAL IN THE GROUND - GEORGIA - BALDWIN COUNTY - MAPS.
United States. Soil Conservation Service. Baldwin County, Georgia . Fort Worth, Tex. , 1979. 1 map : LC Card 81-690364
G3923.B26N46 1978 .U5

SEWAGE DISPOSAL IN THE GROUND - GEORGIA - TOOMBS COUNTY - MAPS.
United States. Soil Conservation Service. Toombs County, Georgia . Fort Worth, Tex. , 1979. 1 map : LC Card 81-690349
G3923.T6N46 1978 .U5

SEWAGE DISPOSAL IN THE GROUND - HAWAII.
Petty, Susan. Hawaiian waste injection practices and problems /. Honolulu, Hawaii [1979] viii, 104 p. : LC Card 80-621493 DDC 553.7/09969 s 627/.56 19
TC1 .H36 no. 123 TD760

SEWAGE DISPOSAL IN THE GROUND - ILLINOIS.
Fehr, Graham, and Associates. Economic impact of proposed regulation R77-12 (Rule 950) on wastewater sludge disposal in the State of Illinois /. Chicago , 1979. ix, 108 p. ; LC Card 80-621691 DDC 363.7/3946 19
TD774 .F44 1979

SEWAGE DISPOSAL IN THE GROUND - LAW AND LEGISLATION - ECONOMIC ASPECTS - ILLINOIS.
Fehr, Graham, and Associates. Economic impact of proposed regulation R77-12 (Rule 950) on wastewater sludge disposal in the State of Illinois /. Chicago , 1979. ix, 108 p. ; LC

Card 80-621691 DDC 363.7/3946 19
TD774 .F44 1979

SEWAGE DISPOSAL IN THE OCEAN - HAWAII - CONGRESSES.
Environmental survey techniques for coastal water assessment . [Honolulu, Hawaii] [1980] iv, 229 p. : LC Card 80-621111 DDC 628.1/686162/0287 19
TD763 .E58

SEWAGE DISPOSAL IN THE OCEAN - MASSACHUSETTS - BOSTON.
Massachusetts. Division of Water Pollution Control. Water Quality Section. Boston Harbor . Westborough, Mass. [1976] 18 p. : LC Card 77-622213 DDC 363.7/3942/097446 19
TD225.B7 M37 1976

Massachusetts. Division of Water Pollution Control. Water Quality Section. Boston Harbor . Westborough, Mass. , 1977. 20 p. : LC Card 79-620586 DDC 363.7/3942/097446 19
TD225.B7 M37 1977

Massachusetts. Water Quality and Research Section. Boston Harbor . Westborough, Mass. , 1977. iv, 48 p. : LC Card 79-620587 DDC 363.7/3942/097446 19
TD225.B7 M39 1977

SEWAGE DISPOSAL IN THE OCEAN - MASSACHUSETTS - STATISTICS.
Massachusetts. Water Quality and Research Section. North Coastal water quality survey, 1976 /. Westborough, Mass. [1978] v, 53 p. : LC Card 79-620601 DDC 363.7/3942/097445 19
TD224.M4 M39 1978c

Massachusetts. Water Quality and Research Section. South Coastal . Westborough [1977] 72 p. : LC Card 79-620597 DDC 363.7/3942/0974482 19
TD224.M4 M39 1977h

SEWAGE DISPOSAL - MICHIGAN - GRAND RAPIDS - PERIODICALS.
Grand Rapids. Wastewater Treatment Plant. Annual report. 38- ; 1967/68- Grand Rapids.
NYPL [JSP 80-408]

SEWAGE DISPOSAL - MISSOURI RIVER WATERSHED.
United States. Public Health Service. Pollution of interstate waters. [Washington] 1959. 2 v. LC Card 75-80621   *NYPL [JSF 81-65]*

SEWAGE DISPOSAL PLANTS.
(1980) Operation of wastewater treatment plants . Sacramento , <1980-. v. <3 > : LC Card 81-114782 DDC 628.3 19
TD746 .O64 1980

SEWAGE DISPOSAL PLANTS - ILLINOIS.
Illinois. Environmental Protection Agency. Procedures for the certification of operators of wastewater treatment works. [Springfield, Ill. , 1980] 29 p. : LC Card 80-623066 DDC 353.97730087/1 19
TD524.I3 I44 1980

SEWAGE DISPOSAL PLANTS - UNITED STATES - FINANCE.
United States. Congress. House. Committee on Public Works and Transportation. Subcommittee on Oversight and Review. Implementation of the Federal water pollution control act (the Municipal Construction Grants Program and the State Management Assistance Program) . Washington , 1980. v, 1458 p. : LC Card 80-603421 DDC 353.0082/325 19
KF27 .P89636 1979d

SEWAGE DISPOSAL PLANTS - WISCONSIN - MILWAUKEE METROPOLITAN AREA - COSTS.
United States. Congress. Senate. Select Committee on Small Business. Impact of funding EPA sewer treatment construction program on small business contractors . Washington , 1980. iii, 180 p. : LC Card 80-603692 DDC 338.4/36283/0977595 19
KF26.5 .S6 1980p

SEWAGE DISPOSAL PLANTS - WISCONSIN - MILWAUKEE METROPOLITAN AREA - FINANCE.
United States. Congress. Senate. Select Committee on Small Business. Impact of funding EPA sewer treatment construction

program on small business contractors . Washington , 1980. iii, 180 p. : LC Card 80-603692 DDC 338.4/36283/0977595 19
KF26.5 .S6 1980p

SEWAGE DISPOSAL, RURAL - LAW AND LEGISLATION - MAINE.
White, Gregory K. Institutional structures affecting on-site waste disposal in Maine /. [Orono, Me.] , 1979. 46 p. : LC Card 80-622060 DDC 363.7/28 19
TD778 .W49

SEWAGE DISPOSAL - UNITED STATES - COSTS.
United States. Congress. Senate. Committee on Environment and Public Works. Subcommittee on Environmental Pollution. Industrial cost recovery . Washington , 1980. iii, 342 p. ; LC Card 80-602810 DDC 353.0082/325 19
KF26 .E645 1980a

SEWAGE DISPOSAL - UNITED STATES - FINANCE.
Abt Associates. Factors affecting pollution referenda. Washington, 1971. v, 331 p. LC Card 73-614491
HG4952 .A6

United States. Congress. Senate. Committee on Environment and Public Works. Subcommittee on Environmental Pollution. Industrial cost recovery . Washington , 1980. iii, 342 p. ; LC Card 80-602810 DDC 353.0082/325 19
KF26 .E645 1980a

SEWAGE-FARMS. see SEWAGE IRRIGATION.

SEWAGE - FILTRATION. see SEWAGE - PURIFICATION - FILTRATION.

SEWAGE IRRIGATION.
(1978) Collins, Edmond R. Swine lagoon effluent on a soil-plant environment . Blacksburg , 1978. v, 38 p. ; LC Card 78-624385 DDC 333.91/009755 s 636.4/0831 19
TD201 .V57 no. 110 TD930

(1978) Lau, Leung-Ku Stephen. Recycling of sewage effluent by sugarcane irrigation . Honolulu, Hawaii [1978?] x, 59 p. : LC Card 79-625336 DDC 628.3/62 19
TC1 .H36 no. 121 TD760

SEWAGE IRRIGATION - HAWAII.
Lau, Leung-Ku Stephen. Recycling of sewage effluent by sugarcane irrigation . Honolulu, Hawaii [1978?] x, 59 p. : LC Card 79-625336 DDC 628.3/62 19
TC1 .H36 no. 121 TD760

SEWAGE IRRIGATION - MICHIGAN - MUSKEGON CO.
McDonald, M. G. Hydraulic characteristics of an underdrained irrigation circle, Muskegon County wastewater disposal system, Michigan /. Reston, VA , 1981. p. cm. LC Card 80-607871 DDC 628.3/623 19
TD760 .M32

SEWAGE IRRIGATION - NEVADA.
URS Company/Las Vegas. Land application of wastewater in Nevada . Carson City, Nev. [1979] xv, 267 p. : LC Card 80-623617 DDC 628.3/62 19
TD760 .U17 1979

SEWAGE LAGOONS.
Rutz, D. A. Factors affecting production of the mosquito, Culex quinquefasciatus (=fatigans) from anaerobic animal waste lagoons /. [Raleigh] , 1978. 32 p. : LC Card 80-622296 DDC 630 s 614.4/323 19
S97 .E25 no. 256 RA640

SEWAGE - MICROBIOLOGY.
Hain, Kathleen E. The survival of enteric viruses in septic tanks and septic tank drain fields /. Las Cruces, N.M. [1979] x, 73 p. : LC Card 80-622272 DDC 628/.742 19
GB705.N6 N64 no. 108 QR48

Lin, S. D. Development and evaluation of a two-step membrane filter method for fecal coliform recovery in chlorinated sewage effluents /. Urbana , 1978. 14 p. ; LC Card 79-622684 DDC 628.3/2/0287 19
GB705.I3 A3 no. 87 QR48

Thompson, Frederick C. Tolerance and synthetic ability of sewage microorganisms in acid mine water /. Morgantown , 1975. ix, 60 p. : LC Card 76-622086 DDC 628.1/6832 19
QR88 .T48

SEWAGE - PURIFICATION - AERATION - HYGIENIC ASPECTS - CONGRESSES.
Symposium on Wastewater Aerosols and Disease (1979 : Cincinnati, Ohio) Wastewater aerosols and disease . Cincinnati, Ohio , Springfield, Va. , 1980 [i.e. 1981] xv, 367 p. :
LC Card 81-601460   DDC 363.7/28 19
RA567 .S94 1979

SEWAGE - PURIFICATION - CONGRESSES.
Seminar on Industrial Pretreatment, Federal, State, and Local Government Perspectives and Industry's Interests, New Jersey Institute of Technology, 1979. Proceedings . [Trenton] [1980] vii, 73 p. ; LC Card 80-620966 DDC 628.1/683 19
TD896 .S45 1979

SEWAGE - PURIFICATION - FILTRATION.
(1978) Lin, S. D. Development and evaluation of a two-step membrane filter method for fecal coliform recovery in chlorinated sewage effluents /. Urbana , 1978. 14 p. ; LC Card 79-622684   DDC 628.3/2/0287 19
GB705.I3 A3 no. 87 QR48

SEWAGE - PURIFICATION - FILTRATION - TESTING.
Cowan, Peter A. Modeling the performance of the intermittent sand filter /. Logan, Utah [1979] xii, 115 p. : LC Card 80-622170 DDC 628.3/52/0724 19
TD753 .C68

SEWAGE - PURIFICATION - ORGANIC COMPOUNDS REMOVAL.
Bonner, William P. Effects of wastewater process operation on organics in potable water supplies /. Knoxville , 1978. ix, 109 leaves :
LC Card 79-624195   DDC 628.1/62 19
TD758.5.O75 B66

SEWAGE SLUDGE - ILLINOIS.
Fehr, Graham, and Associates. Economic impact of proposed regulation R77-12 (Rule 950) on wastewater sludge disposal in the State of Illinois . Chicago , 1979. ix, 108 p. ; LC Card 80-621691   DDC 363.7/3946 19
TD774 .F44 1979

SEWAGE TREATMENT PLANTS. see SEWAGE DISPOSAL PLANTS.

SEWAGE WORKS. see SEWAGE DISPOSAL PLANTS.

SEWARD COUNTY (NEB.) - MAPS.
United States. Soil Conservation Service. Seward County, Nebraska /. Lincoln, Nebr. , 1979. 1 map : LC Card 81-691001
G4193.S5 1979 .U5

SEWERAGE.
(1973) United States. Environmental Protection Agency. Office of Water Program Operations. Estimating laboratory needs for municipal wastewater treatment facilities. Washington, 1973. i, 23, [104] p. :   *NYPL [JSF 80-271]*

SEWERAGE - KOREA.
United States. Army. Corps of Engineers. Water supply and sewerage of Korea. [Washington] 1945. iii, 36, A-6 p. LC Card 59-27970   *NYPL [JSF 80-676]*

SEWERAGE - LAW AND LEGISLATION - MAINE.
Maine. Bureau of Water Quality Control. Division of Municipal Services. Suggested sewer use ordinance for the cities and towns of the state of Maine /. Augusta, Me (State Office Building, Station 17, Augusta 04333) [1980] 23, [24] p. : LC Card 81-621085   DDC 344.741/04622 347.41044622 19
KFM359.S4 A887

SEWERAGE - MANCHURIA.
United States. Army. Corps of Engineers. Water supply and sewerage of Manchuria (in one volume) Washington, 1945. iii, 55, A 1-A 6 p. LC Card 72-614996
TA7 .U53 no. 160 TD310.M3

SEWERS. see SEWERAGE.

SEWERS, STORM. see STORM SEWERS.

SEX CUSTOMS - AFRICA - BIBLIOGRAPHY.
Beck, Roger B. A bibliography of Africana in the Institute for Sex Research, Indiana University /. [Bloomington] , 1979. ii, 134 p. ; LC Card 80-624457   DDC 016.3046/096 19
Z7164.S42 B43 HQ18.A35

SEX DIFFERENCES.
Johnson, Gordon C. Metropolitan professional sexual differentiation . [Madison] [1979] 27 p. ; LC Card 80-622903   DDC 331.11/4 19
HD8038.U5 J6

SEX DIFFERENCES IN EDUCATION - UNITED STATES - COLLECTED WORKS.
Butler, Matilda. Education, the critical filter . [Washington] , San Francisco, Calif. , 1979- v. :
LC Card 80-131869   DDC 376/.973 19
LC1752 .B93

SEX DISCRIMINATION AGAINST WOMEN - LAW AND LEGISLATION - NEW JERSEY.
New Jersey. Commission on Sex Discrimination in the Statutes. Public hearing before Commission on Sex Discrimination in the Statutes held June 2, 1979, Senate Conference Room, State House, Trenton, New Jersey. [Trenton, N.J.] [1979] 2, 74, 84 p. ; LC Card 79-625604   DDC 344.749/014133 19
KFN2134.5.D5 A876

SEX DISCRIMINATION AGAINST WOMEN - PENNSYLVANIA - CONGRESSES.
Conference on Women and Health, Philadelphia, 1974. Proceedings of the Conference on Women and Health, June 27, 28, 29, 1974, Philadelphia, Pa. [Philadelphia] [1976?] 28 p. : LC Card 76-623061   DDC 362.1/088042 19
RA564.85 .C66 1974

SEX DISCRIMINATION AGAINST WOMEN - TEXAS.
United States. Congress. House Committee on Post Office and Civil Service. Subcommittee on Postal Personnel and Modernization. Equal employment opportunity and sexual harassment in the Postal Service . Washington , 1981. iii, 85 p. : LC Card 81-602045   DDC 353.001/04 19
KF27 .P6677 1980d

SEX DISCRIMINATION AGAINST WOMEN - UNITED STATES.
United States. Congress. House. Committee on Small Business. Subcommittee on General Oversight and Minority Enterprise. Women in business . Washington , 1980 [i.e. 1981] iv, 178 p. : LC Card 81-600836   DDC 331.4/8165/00973 19
KF27 .S64 1980k

United States. General Accounting Office. Women in prison . Washington, D.C. , 1980. v, 50 p. ; LC Card 81-600746   DDC 365/.43/0973 19
HV9471 .U53 1980

United States. Women's Bureau. The earnings gap between women and men /. [Washington, D.C.] , 1979. 22 p. ; LC Card 80-602542   DDC 331.2/1 19
HD6061.2.U6 U53 1979

SEX DISCRIMINATION IN EDUCATION - CONNECTICUT - STATISTICS.
Connecticut. Bureau of Vocational Program Planning & Development. Summary of selected statistics . [Hartford] [1979] 29 p. : LC Card 79-624847   DDC 379.1/552/09746 19
LC1046.C8 C663 1979

SEX DISCRIMINATION IN EDUCATION - UNITED STATES.
Marwell, Gerald, 1937- Residence location, geographic mobility, and the attainments of women in academia /. Madison , 1976. 31 p. ; LC Card 78-623190   DDC 378/.12/0973 19
LB2331.72 .M37

SEX DISCRIMINATION IN EMPLOYMENT - LAW AND LEGISLATION - MONTANA.
Uda, Joan A. Montana working woman . [Helena, Mont.] [1979?] xi, 55 p. : LC Card 80-623400 DDC 344.786/014 19
KFM9334.5.D5 U3

SEX DISCRIMINATION IN EMPLOYMENT - LAW AND LEGISLATION - NEW JERSEY.
New Jersey. Commission on Sex Discrimination in the Statutes. Public hearing before Commission on Sex Discrimination in the Statutes held June 2, 1979, Senate Conference Room, State House, Trenton, New Jersey. [Trenton, N.J.] [1979] 2, 74, 84 p. ; LC Card 79-625604   DDC 344.749/014133 19
KFN2134.5.D5 A876

SEX DISCRIMINATION IN EMPLOYMENT - UNITED STATES.
Johnston, Jerome. An evaluation of Freestyle . Ann Arbor, Mich. , 1980. x, 297 p. : ISBN 0-87944-256-5 (pbk.) LC Card 80-81676
HQ784.T4 J63   *NYPL [JLF 81-164]*

United States. Women's Bureau. Employment goals of the world . Washington, D.C. [1980] vi, 54, [22] p. : LC Card 80-602858 DDC 331.4/133/0973 19
HD6095 .U54 1980

SEX DISCRIMINATION IN INSURANCE - LAW AND LEGISLATION - UNITED STATES.
United States. Congress. House. Committee on Interstate and Foreign Commerce. Subcommittee on Consumer Protection and Finance. Nondiscrimination in insurance . Washington , 1981. iv, 425 p. : LC Card 81-601385   DDC 346.73/086 347.30686 19
KF27 .I554 1980j

SEX DISCRIMINATION IN MEDICINE - PENNSYLVANIA - CONGRESSES.
Conference on Women and Health, Philadelphia, 1974. Proceedings of the Conference on Women and Health, June 27, 28, 29, 1974, Philadelphia, Pa. [Philadelphia] [1976?] 28 p. : LC Card 76-623061   DDC 362.1/088042 19
RA564.85 .C66 1974

SEX DISCRIMINATION IN VOCATIONAL INTERESTS TESTING - UNITED STATES - ADDRESSES, ESSAYS, LECTURES.
Sex-fair interest measurement . Washington , 1978, 1979 printing. xvii, 169 p. : LC Card 79-602075   DDC 153.9/4 19
HF5381.5 .S4

SEX DISCRIMINATION - LAW AND LEGISLATION - IOWA.
1980 Iowa constitutional issues. Iowa City [1980] 23 p. ; LC Card 80-624270 DDC 342.777/087 347.770287 19
KFI4611.7.Z9 A15

SEX DISCRIMINATION - LAW AND LEGISLATION - NEW JERSEY.
New Jersey. Commission on Sex Discrimination in the Statutes. Public hearing before Commission on Sex Discrimination in the Statutes on marriage and family law . [Trenton] [1980] 37, 15, 134 p. : LC Card 80-622456   DDC 346.74901/5 19
KFN1894 .A83

New Jersey. Commission on Sex Discrimination in the Statutes. Public hearing before Commission on Sex Discrimination in the Statutes on sex discrimination in marriage and family law . [Trenton] [1980] 39, 19, 43 p. : LC Card 80-622457   DDC 346.74901/5 19
KFN1894 .A84

SEX DISCRIMINATION - LAW AND LEGISLATION - UNITED STATES.
Kanowitz, Leo. Equal rights, the male stake /. Albuquerque , c1981. p. cm. ISBN 0-8263-0594-6 : LC Card 81-52056 DDC 342.73/0878 347.302878 19
KF4758 .K36

Sex-fair interest measurement : research and implications / edited by Carol Kehr Tittle and Donald G. Zytowski. Washington : Dept. of Health, Education, and Welfare, National Institute of Education, 1978, 1979 printing. xvii, 169 p. : graphs ; 27 cm. Includes bibliographies. LC Card 79-602075 DDC 153.9/4 19
1. Sex discrimination in vocational interests testing - United States - Addresses, essays, lectures. I. Tittle, Carol K., 1933- . II. Zytowski, Donald G.
HF5381.5 .S4

SEX IN LITERATURE.
Thurin, Erik Ingvar. Emerson as priest of Pan . Lawrence , c1981. p. cm. ISBN 0-7006-0216-X : LC Card 81-4818 DDC 814/.3 19
PS1642.S47 T5

SEX OFFENDERS - LEGAL STATUS, LAWS, ETC. - MASSACHUSETTS.
Massachusetts. Post Audit and Oversight Bureau. Department of Mental Health, Bridgewater Treatment Center /. [Boston] [1979] 3, viii, 37 leaves ; LC Card 80-620614   DDC 364.1/53/09744 19
HQ72.U53 M28 1979

SEX OFFENDERS - LEGAL STATUS, LAWS, ETC. - NEBRASKA.
Nebraska. Legislature. Judiciary Committee. Deviant sexual behavior . [Lincoln] [1978?] 291 leaves : LC Card 80-624459 DDC 363.4/8/09782 19
KFN11.72 .J8 1978

SEX OFFENDERS - MASSACHUSETTS.
Massachusetts. Post Audit and Oversight Bureau. Department of Mental Health, Bridgewater Treatment Center /. [Boston] [1979] 3, viii, 37 leaves ; LC Card 80-620614 DDC 364.1/53/09744 19
HQ72.U53 M28 1979

SEX OFFENDERS - NEBRASKA.
Nebraska. Legislature. Judiciary Committee. Deviant sexual behavior . [Lincoln] [1978?] 291 leaves : LC Card 80-624459 DDC 363.4/8/09782 19
KFN11.72 .J8 1978

SEX RATIO.
Downs, Floyd Leslie. Unisexual Ambystoma for the Bass Islands of Lake Erie /. Ann Arbor , 1978. 36 p. : LC Card 78-622915 DDC 597.6/5 19
QL668.C23 D68

SEX ROLE.
Johnston, Jerome. An evaluation of Freestyle . Ann Arbor, Mich. , 1980. x, 297 p. : ISBN 0-87944-256-5 (pbk.) LC Card 80-81676
HQ784.T4 J63   *NYPL [JLF 81-164]*

SEX ROLE - BIBLIOGRAPHY.
Grady, Kathleen E. The male sex role . Rockville, Md. , Washington, D.C. , 1979. x, 196 p. ; LC Card 79-604183 DDC 016.3053 19
Z7164.S42 G7 HQ1075

Sexton, James D. Bizarro Ujpán, Ignacio. Son of Tecún Umán . Tucson , 1981. p. cm. ISBN 0-8165-0736-8 : LC Card 81-11702 DDC 972.81/004970924 B 19
F1465.2.T9 B59

The sexual abuse of children in Massachusetts . Blose, James. [Boston] , 1979. xvi, 113 p. ; LC Card 80-621665 DDC 362.7/044 19
HV6626 .B56

SEXUAL DEVIATION - NEBRASKA.
Nebraska. Legislature. Judiciary Committee. Deviant sexual behavior . [Lincoln] [1978?] 291 leaves : LC Card 80-624459 DDC 363.4/8/09782 19
KFN11.72 .J8 1978

SEXUAL DIMORPHISM IN HUMANS. see SEX DIFFERENCES.

Sexual exploitation of children . Illinois. General Assembly. Legislative Investigating Commission. Chicago, Ill. (300 W. Washington St., Chicago 60606) [1980] ix, 317 p. : LC Card 80-624398 DDC 362.7/1 19
HQ72.U53 I34 1980

Sexual harassment in the Federal Government /. United States. Congress. House. Committee on Post Office and Civil Service. Subcommittee on Investigations. Washington , 1980. iii, 32 p. ; LC Card 80-602591 DDC 353-001/04 19
JK721 .U554 1980

SEXUAL HARASSMENT OF WOMEN - TEXAS.
United States. Congress. House Committee on Post Office and Civil Service. Subcommittee on Postal Personnel and Modernization. Equal employment opportunity and sexual harassment in the Postal Service . Washington , 1981. iii, 85 p. : LC Card 81-602045 DDC 353.001/04 19
KF27 .P6677 1980d

SEXUAL HARASSMENT OF WOMEN - UNITED STATES.
United States. Congress. House. Committee on Post Office and Civil Service. Subcommittee on Investigations. Sexual harassment in the Federal Government /. Washington , 1980. iii, 32 p. ; LC Card 80-602591 DDC 353-001/04 19
JK721 .U554 1980

SEXUAL INVERSION. see HOMOSEXUALITY.

Sexual preference, its development in men and women /. Bell, Alan P., 1932- Bloomington , c1981. p. cm. ISBN 0-253-16673-X LC Card 81-47006 DDC 306.7/6 19
HQ76 .B438

Sexuality/textuality . Cottrell, Robert D. Columbus , 1981. p. cm. ISBN 0-8142-0326-4 LC Card 81-2085 DDC 844/.3 19
PQ1643 .C67

Seymour, Scott. Rural health services : a sample of state efforts / by Scott Seymour. [Lexington, Ky.] : Council of State Governments, c1980. 8 p. ; 29 cm. (Innovations) RM ; 688 Caption title. Includes bibliographical references. LC Card 80-140001 DDC 353.9 s 362.1/0425 19
1. Rural health services - United States. 2. Medicine, Rural - Practice - United States. 3. Medically underserved areas - United States. 4. State aid to medical education - United States. I. Series: Council of State Governments. RM publications, 688. II. Title.
JS308 .C6 no. 688 RA771.5

SF₆ tracer gas tests of bagging-machine hood enclosures /. Vinson, Robert P. [Avondale, Md.] , 1981. p. cm. LC Card 80-606907 DDC 661/.06832 19
TN23 .U43 TH7697.C54

Shacklette, Hansford T. Ebens, Richard J. Geochemistry of some rocks, mine spoils, stream sediments, soils, plants, and waters in the western energy region of the conterminous United States /. Washington [D.C.] , 1981. p. cm. LC Card 81-607846 DDC 551.9/0978 19
QE515 .E23

SHAD, JOHN S. R., 1923-
United States. Congress. Senate. Committee on Banking, Housing and Urban Affairs. Nomination of John S. R. Shad . Washington , 1981. ii, 34 p. ; LC Card 81-601937 DDC 353.0082/58 19
KF26 .B39 1981h

Shadoan, Arlene Theuer. Kentucky. University. Bureau of Business Research. Organization, role, and staffing of State budget offices /. Lexington, Ky. , 1961, 1965 printing. vi, 122 p. ; LC Card 80-506084 DDC 353.9/3722 19
HJ2053.A1 K46 1961

The shadow of eternity . Seelig, Sharon Cadman. Lexington, Ky , 1981. p. cm. ISBN 0-8131-1444-6 : LC Card 80-51018 DDC 821/.3/09 19
PR545.M4 S4

Shafer, Bernard A. (joint author) Washichek, Jack N. Summary of snow survey measurements for Colorado and New Mexico, 1971-1977 . Denver, Colo. [1978] xxiii, 128 p. : LC Card 79-601670 DDC 551.57/9/788 19
GB2625.C6 W37

Shafer, Carl E. (joint author) Jackson, David M. U. S. sorghum industry /. [Washington, D.C.] [1980] iii, 84 p. : LC Card 80-602638 DDC 338.1 s 338.1/73174/0973 19
HD1751 .A91854 no. 457 HD9049.S6U5

Shaffer, Douglas Howerth. Clocks / Douglas H. Shaffer. [New York] : Cooper-Hewitt Museum, c1980. 127 p. : ill. (some col.) ; 29 cm. (The Smithsonian illustrated library of antiques) Bibliography: p. 129. Includes index. LC Card 78-62729 DDC 681.1/13 19
1. Clocks and watches - History. I. Cooper-Hewitt Museum. II. Title. III. Series.
TS542 .S5

Shafie, Mahmoud A. Wisconsin Seminar on Natural Resource Policies in Relation to Economic Development and International Cooperation, University of Wisconsin--Madison, 1977-1978. Resources and development . Madison , London , c1980. xv, 500 p. ; ISBN 0-299-08250-4 : LC Card 80-10577
HC55 .W57 1977a   *NYPL [JLE 80-3198]*

Shafritz, Jay M. Symposium on Productivity and Managerial Assessment, Albany, 1975. Public utility productivity . Albany [1975?] xv, 256 p. : LC Card 75-41898
HD2766 .S95 1975   *NYPL [*XME-9419]*

Shakespeare and the rhetoricians /. Trousdale, Marion, 1929- Chapel Hill , c1981. p. cm. ISBN 0-8078-1482-2 LC Card 81-40703 DDC 822.3/3 19
PR2976 .T77

Shakespeare, William, 1564-1616.
ALL'S WELL THAT ENDS WELL.
Cole, Howard C. The All's well story from Boccaccio to Shakespeare /. Urbana , c1981. p. cm. ISBN 0-252-00883-9 LC Card 81-2474

DDC 822.3/3 19
PR2801 .C6

ALL'S WELL THAT ENDS WELL - SOURCES.
Cole, Howard C. The All's well story from Boccaccio to Shakespeare /. Urbana , c1981. p. cm. ISBN 0-252-00883-9 LC Card 81-2474 DDC 822.3/3 19
PR2801 .C6

HAMLET.
King, Walter N. Hamlet's search for meaning /. Athens, Ga. , 1982. p. cm. ISBN 0-8203-0597-9 LC Card 81-12979 DDC 822.3/3 19
PR2807 .K48

Plays. For individual plays see individual titles, e.g.: **Shakespeare, William, 1564-1616. Hamlet.**

Tragedy of Hamlet Prince of Denmark. see Shakespeare, William, 1564-1616. Hamlet.

SHAKESPEARE, WILLIAM, 1564-1616 - AESTHETICS.
Trousdale, Marion, 1929- Shakespeare and the rhetoricians /. Chapel Hill , c1981. p. cm. ISBN 0-8078-1482-2 LC Card 81-40703 DDC 822.3/3 19
PR2976 .T77

Shakespeare, William, 1564-1616 - Commentaries. see Shakespeare, William, 1564-1616 - Criticism and interpretation.

SHAKESPEARE, WILLIAM, 1564-1616 - CRITICISM AND INTERPRETATION.
Trousdale, Marion, 1929- Shakespeare and the rhetoricians /. Chapel Hill , c1981. p. cm. ISBN 0-8078-1482-2 LC Card 81-40703 DDC 822.3/3 19
PR2976 .T77

Shakespeare, William, 1564-1616 - Ethical ideas. see Shakespeare, William, 1564-1616 - Religion and ethics.

Shakespeare, William, 1564-1616 - Knowledge - Bible. see Shakespeare, William, 1564-1616 - Religion and ethics.

Shakespeare, William, 1564-1616 - Knowledge - Catholic Church. see Shakespeare, William, 1564-1616 - Religion and ethics.

Shakespeare, William, 1564-1616 - Knowledge - Ethics. see Shakespeare, William, 1564-1616 - Religion and ethics.

Shakespeare, William, 1564-1616 - Knowledge - Honor. see Shakespeare, William, 1564-1616 - Religion and ethics.

Shakespeare, William, 1564-1616 - Knowledge - Religion. see Shakespeare, William, 1564-1616 - Religion and ethics.

Shakespeare, William, 1564-1616 - Moral ideas. see Shakespeare, William, 1564-1616 - Religion and ethics.

Shakespeare, William, 1564-1616 - Mysticism. see Shakespeare, William, 1564-1616 - Religion and ethics.

SHAKESPEARE, WILLIAM, 1564-1616 - RELIGION AND ETHICS.
King, Walter N. Hamlet's search for meaning /. Athens, Ga. , 1982. p. cm. ISBN 0-8203-0597-9 LC Card 81-12979 DDC 822.3/3 19
PR2807 .K48

Shakespeare, William, 1564-1616 - Theology. see Shakespeare, William, 1564-1616 - Religion and ethics.

SHAKESPEARE, WILLIAM, 1564-1616 - TRAGICOMEDIES.
Uphaus, Robert W. Beyond tragedy . Lexington , 1981. p. cm. ISBN 0-8131-1441-1 : LC Card 80-5184 DDC 822.3/3 19
PR2981.5 .U6

SHALE - KANSAS.
Cubitt, John M. The geochemistry, mineralogy, and petrology of upper Paleozoic shales of Kansas /. Lawrence [1979] vi, 117 p. : LC Card 80-622956 DDC 557.81 s 552/.5 19
QE113 .A2 no. 217 QE471.15.S5

SHALE - UNITED STATES.
Conkin, James Elvin. Devonian black shale in the Eastern United States /. Louisville, Ky. , c1980- v. <1 > : LC Card 80-54589 DDC

552/.5 19
QE471.15.S5 C66

SHAME.
Wurmser, Leon. The mask of shame /.
Baltimore , c1981. p. cm.   ISBN 0-8018-2527-X
   LC Card 81-964   DDC 152.4 19
BF575.S45 W87

Shane, Richard C. (joint author) Brown, Ralph J.
Simulating the impact of irrigation development
in the Third Planning District . [Vermillion,
S.D. , 1979] i, 90 p. :   LC Card 80-621868   DDC
330 s 330.9783/3/00724 19
HF5006 .S6 no. 127 HD1739.S8

Shanholtz, Vernon O., 1935- (joint author) Smolen,
M. D. Agricultural land use . Blacksburg, Va. ,
1980. vii, 82 p. :   LC Card 80-622278   DDC
333.91/009755 s 363.7/3941 19
TD201 .V57 no. 125 TD428.A37

Shanks, D. E. (Donald E.)
Hydrogen chloride sparging crystallization of
aluminum chloride hexahydrate / by D.E.
Shanks, J.A. Eisele, and D.J. Bauer. Avondale,
MD : U. S. Dept. of the Interior, Bureau of
Mines, 1981. p. cm. (Report of investigations)
Bibliography: p.   LC Card 81-607311   DDC 622 s
669/.722 19
*1. Aluminum chloride hexahydrate. 2. Hydrochloric
acid. 3. Crystallization. I. Eisele, J. A. (Judith A.). II.
Bauer, D. J. (Donald J.). III. Series: Report of
investigations (United States. Bureau of Mines). IV.
Title.*
TN23 .U43 TP245.A4

Recovery of aluminum hydroxy sulfate from
aluminum sulfate solution by high-temperature
hydrolysis / by D.E. Shanks, J.A. Eisele, and
D.J. Bauer (Reno Research Center, Reno,
Nevada). [Washington] : U. S. Dept. of the
Interior, Bureau of Mines, [1981] p. cm. (Report
of investigations) Bibliography: p.   LC Card 80-606902
DDC 622 s 622/.34926 19
*1. Hydrolysis. 2. Aluminum hydroxide sulphate. 3.
Aluminum sulphate. I. Eisele, J. A. (Judith A.). II.
Bauer, D. J. (Donald J.). III. Reno Research Center. IV.
Series: Report of investigations (United States. Bureau
of Mines). V. Title.*
TN23 .U43 TP152.H82

Shanley, Mark. International policing : a selected
bibliography / by Mark Shanley, Marjorie
Kravitz. [Washington] : National Institute of
Law Enforcement and Criminal Justice, Law
Enforcement Assistance Administration, United
States Department of Justice, 1978. vii, 97 p. ;
27 cm. "Prepared for the National Institute of Law
Enforcement and Criminal Justice, Law Enforcement
Assistance Administration, U. S. Department of
Justice ... under contract number J-LEAA-023-77."
   LC Card 78-602822
*1. Police - Bibliography. 2. Police training -
Bibliography. 3. International police - Bibliography. I.
Kravitz, Marjorie, joint author. II. National Institute of
Law Enforcement and Criminal Justice. III. Title.*
Z7164.P76 S5 HV7921   **NYPL   [JLF 80-1418]**

Shannon, Joe. R.B. Kitaj /. Washington, D.C. ,
1981. p. cm.   LC Card 81-607809   DDC 759.13 19
N6537.K53 A4 1981

Shapard, John. (joint author) Bermant, Gordon.
The voir dire examination, juror challenges, and
adversary advocacy /. [Washington] , 1978. v,
50 p. :   LC Card 79-602041   DDC 347.73/752 19
KF8979 .B48

Shapero, Albert.
Exit, a high communicator of long standing
leaves : studies of the effective use of scientific
and technical information / Albert Shapero, D.
Maitland Huffman, Albert M. Chammah ;
prepared for the Office of Science Information
Service, National Science Foundation. Austin :
Graduate School of Business, University of
Texas at Austin : distributed by Bureau of
Business Research, University of Texas at
Austin, 1978. 31 p. : ill. ; 28 cm. (Working
paper - Graduate School of Business, University of
Texas at Austin ; 78-59) Bibliography: p. 31.   LC Card
79-621448   DDC 302.3/5 19
*1. Communication in organizations. I. Huffman,
Devereaux Maitland, joint author. II. Chammah, Albert
M., joint author. III. United States. National Science
Foundation. Office of Science Information Service. IV.
Series: Texas. University at Austin. Graduate School of
Business. Working paper - Graduate School of Business,
University of Texas at Austin , 78-59. V. Title.*
HM131 .S446

Spatial rearragement of people : a department's
geography is rearranged--studies in the effective
use of scientific and technical information /
Albert Shapero, D. Maitland Huffman, Albert
M. Chammah. Austin : Graduate School of
Business, University of Texas at Austin :
distributed by Bureau of Business Research,
University of Texas at Austin, 1978. 37 p. ; 28
cm. (Working paper - Graduate School of Business, the
University of Texas at Austin ; 78-58) Bibliography: p.
37.   LC Card 79-621447   DDC 658.3/128 19
*1. Communication in organizations. 2. Employees,
Relocation of. I. Huffman, Devereaux Maitland, joint
author. II. Chammah, Albert M., joint author. III.
Series: Texas. University at Austin. Graduate School of
Business. Working paper - Graduate School of Business,
University of Texas at Austin , 78-58. IV. Title.*
HD30.3 .S5

**Shaping accelerated development and
international changes .** United Nations.
Economic and Social Council. Committee for
Development Planning. New York , 1980. vi,
45 p. :   LC Card 80-132246   DDC 300 s 338.91 19
JX1977 .A2 ST/ESA/105

Shaping the future of Lake Champlain . Lake
Champlain Basin Study (United States.)
[Boston, Mass.] [1979] x, 124, 45 p. ;   LC Card
80-622025   DDC 333.91/6316/097454 19
TD225.L252 L34 1979

**Shaping the general purpose Navy of the
eighties .** United States. Congressional Budget
Office. Washington, D.C. , 1980. xxvii, 145 p. :
   LC Card 80-600968   DDC 359/.03/0973 19
VA53 .U52 1980

Shaping the world's finest freshwater fishery /.
Tanner, Howard A. Lansing, Mich. [1980] 86
p. :   LC Card 80-622892   DDC 333.95/6/09744 19
SH464.G7 T36

Shapley, Fern Rusk. United States. National
Gallery of Art. Catalogue of the Italian
paintings /. Washington , c1979. 2 v. :   LC
Card 79-4410
ND611 .U54 1979
   NYPL   [MAVY (Washinton, D. C.) 81-62]

Share, Marjorie L., 1950- (joint author) Stapp,
William F., 1945- Picture it! /. Washington,
D.C. , 1981. 95 p. :   ISBN 0-86528-004-5   LC
Card 80-28867   DDC 770 19
TR149 .S68

**SHAREHOLDERS - LEGAL STATUS, LAWS,
ETC. - UNITED STATES.**
United States. Securities and Exchange
Commission. Report of the Securities and
Exchange Commission on beneficial ownership
reporting requirements pursuant to section
13(h) of the Securities exchange act of 1934.
Washington , 1980. viii, 242 p. ;   LC Card
80-602870   DDC 346.73/0666 19
KF1448 .A88

Sharp, Bobby H. Books consumerists (and others)
should know about : an annotated bibliography
/ by Bobby H. Sharp, E. Thomas Garman,
Glen H. Mitchell. Blacksburg, Va. : Dept. of
Management, Housing, and Family
Development, College of Home Economics,
Virginia Polytechnic Institute and State
University, [1980] iii, 30 p. ; 28 cm. "March
1980." "MW-36." On cover: Extension Division, Virginia
Polytechnic Institute and State University.   LC Card
80-622383   DDC 016.64073 19
*1. Consumer education - Bibliography. I. Garman, E.
Thomas, joint author. II. Mitchell, Glen H., joint
author. III. Virginia Polytechnic Institute and State
University. Dept. of Management, Housing, and Family
Development. IV. Virginia Polytechnic Institute and
State University. Extension Division. V. Title.*
Z5776.C65 S5 TX335

Sharp, Frederick A. Freedman, Robert W.
Further development of a filter for removing
particulates from diesel engine exhaust /.
Avondale, Md. , 1981. p. cm.   LC Card
81-607804   DDC 622 s 622.6 19
TN23 .U43

Sharp, John Malcolm, 1944- (joint author) Davis,
Peter N. Missouri instream flow requirements .
Jefferson City, Mo. [1980] xviii, 415 p., [1]
fold. leaf of plates :   LC Card 80-623733   DDC
346.77804/691 347.78064691 19
KFM8246 .D36

Shaughnessy, Marlene. Bickner, Mei Liang.
Women at work . [Los Angeles] , 1977. 1 v. ;

LC Card 77-622630
Z7963.E7 B52 HD6095
   NYPL   [JLM 80-1110]

SHAW .
(v. 1) Shaw and religion /. University Park ,
1981. vi, 258 p. ;   ISBN 0-271-00280-8 :   LC Card
81-956   DDC 822/.912 19
PR5368.R4 S5

Shaw and religion / Charles A. Berst, editor.
University Park : Pennsylvania State University
Press, 1981. vi, 258 p. ; 24 cm. (SHAW . v. 1)
Bibliography: p. [225]-246. CONTENTS: - Shaydullah
sees Shaw / R.F. Bosworth -- In the beginning : the
poetic genesis of Shaw's God / Charles A. Berst --
Shaw and Ra : religion and some historic plays / J.L.
Wisenthal -- Lady Cicely, I presume : converting the
heathen, Shavian style / Ina Rae Hark -- "Some
necessary repairs to religion" : resurrecting an early
Shavian "sermon" / Charles A. Berst -- Superman and
Jew : Mr. Bernard Shaw and Herr Brainin--a notable
conversation / Israel Cohen -- The Lord's Prayer and
Major Barbara / Sidney P. Albert -- Shaw's The
shewing-up of Blanco Posnet and Tolstoy's The power
of darkness / David Matual -- Back to Methuselah : a
Blakean interpretation / Valli Rao -- Too true to be
good and Shaw's romantic synthesis / Daniel Leary --
The adventures of Shaw, the nun, and the Black girl /
Warren Sylvester Smith.   ISBN 0-271-00280-8 :   LC
Card 81-956   DDC 822/.912 19
*1. Shaw, Bernard, 1856-1950 - Religion and ethics -
Addresses, essays, lectures. 2. Religion in literature -
Addresses, essays, lectures. I. Berst, Charles A. II.
Series.*
PR5368.R4 S5

**SHAW, BERNARD, 1856-1950 - RELIGION
AND ETHICS - ADDRESSES, ESSAYS,
LECTURES.**
Shaw and religion /. University Park , 1981. vi,
258 p. ;   ISBN 0-271-00280-8 :   LC Card 81-956
DDC 822/.912 19
PR5368.R4 S5

Shaw, Bill, 1940-
Council on Environmental Quality / Bill Shaw,
Jim Robichaux. Austin, Tex. : College of
Business Administration, University of Texas at
Austin : distributed by Bureau of Business
Research, University of Texas at Austin, 1979.
[13] leaves ; 28 cm. (Working paper - The
University of Texas at Austin, College of Business
Administration ; 79-22) Includes bibliographical
references.   LC Card 79-626084   DDC
363.7/05/0973 19
*1. Environmental policy - United States. 2.
Environmental law - United States. 3. Environmental
impact statements - United States. I. Robichaux, Jim,
joint author. II. Series: Texas. University at Austin.
College of Business Administration. Working paper -
College of Business Administration, University of Texas
at Austin , 79-22. III. Title.*
HC110.E5 S48

Current environmental issues / Bill Shaw.
Austin : College of Business Administration,
University of Texas at Austin : distributed by
Bureau of Business Research, University of
Texas at Austin, 1979. 31 p. ; 28 cm. (Working
paper - College of Business Administration, University
of Texas at Austin ; 79-7) Includes bibliographical
references.   LC Card 79-624831   DDC 344.73/046 19
*1. Environmental law - United States. I. Series: Texas.
University at Austin. College of Business
Administration. Working paper - College of Business
Administration, University of Texas at Austin , 79-7. II.
Title.*
KF3775.Z9 S5

Shaw, Bryant P., 1945- Mitchell, William A.,
1940- The Republic of Turkey . United States
Air Force Academy, Colo. [1981] p. cm.   LC
Card 81-607896   DDC 956.1/0007/1178881 19
DR438.95.U6 M57

Shaw, Judith H. (joint author) Salley, E. Jean.
Checklist of types in the U. S. national parasite
collection /. [Washington] , 1978. iv, 233 p. ;
   LC Card 78-602796   DDC 591.52/49/0740153
19
QL757 .S23

Shaw, William, 1944- Chŏn, Pong-dŏk, 1910-
Traditional Korean legal attitudes /. Berkeley,
Calif. , c1980. vii, 101 p. ;   ISBN 0-912966-30-0
(pbk.) :   LC Card 80-620036   DDC 349.519/09
345.1909 19
LAW

Shawsheen River . Massachusetts. Division of

Water Pollution Control. Water Quality Section. Westborough [1975] 59 p. : LC Card 79-620598 DDC 363.7/3942/09444 19
TD224.M4 M36 1975f

Shawsheen River study, 1968 /. Cooperman, Alan N. Boston , 1970. 16 leaves : LC Card 80-118847 DDC 363.7/3942/097444 19
TD224.M4 C67

Shea, M. A. Tables of vertical cutoff rigidities for epochs 1955 and 1960 /. Hanscom AFB, Mass. , 1974. 91 p. :   *NYPL [JSF 81-117]*

Shealy, M. H. (joint author) Bishop, J. M. Biological observations on commercial penaeid shrimps caught by bottom trawl in South Carolina estuaries, February 1973-January 1975 /. [Charleston] [197-] xi, 97 p. : LC Card 80-621322 DDC 595.3/843 19
QL444.M33 B57

Shear, William A. A review of the Cyphophthalmi of the United States and Mexico, with a proposed reclassification of the suborder (Arachnida, Opiliones) / William A. Shear. New York, N.Y. : American Museum of Natural History, 1980. 34 p. : ill. ; 26 cm. (American Museum novitates : no. 2705 0003-0082) Cover title. Bibliography: p. 32-34. LC Card 80-147274 DDC 591 s 595.4/3 19
1. Opiliones - Classification. 2. Arachnida - Classification. 3. Arachnida - United States - Classification. 4. Arachnida - Mexico - Classification. I. Title. II. Title: Cyphophthalmi of the United States and Mexico, with a proposed reclassification of the suborder (Arachnida, Opiliones). III. Series.
QL1 .A436 no. 2705 QL458.4

Sheatsley, David W. Fairfax Co., Va. Office of Research and Statistics. Community Development Branch. Fairfax County profile /. Fairfax, Va. , 1977. 130 p. : LC Card 79-123912 DDC 317.55/291 19
HA687.F3 F34 1977

SHEDDING OF FRUIT. see ABSCISSION (BOTANY)

Shee, Mary-Venner, 1951- Jacques Hurtubise, recent works/oeuvres récentes : the Art Museum and Galleries, California State University, Long Beach, February 9 - March 15, 1981 / by Mary-Venner Shee. Long Beach, Calif. : The Museum and Galleries, c1981. p. cm. Catalog of an exhibition. Bibliography: p. ISBN 0-936270-16-0 : LC Card 81-33 DDC 759.11 19
1. Hurtubise, Jacques 1939- - Exhibitions. I. California State University, Long Beach. Art Museum and Galleries. II. Title.
ND249.H88 A4 1981

Sheehan, David M. The children's puzzle : a study of services to children in Massachusetts : a report in memorandum form / David M. Sheehan. Boston : Institute for Governmental Services, University of Massachusetts, 1977. 41, [18] leaves ; 28 cm. Report of an investigation conducted by the Children's Services Task Force under the auspices of the Institute for Governmental Services, University of Massachusetts. LC Card 79-621668 DDC 362.7/95/09744 19
1. Child welfare - Massachusetts. I. Children's Services Task Force. II. University of Massachusetts (System). Institute for Governmental Services. III. Title.
HV742.M4 S53

Sheehan, Regis P. World economic trends . Atlanta, Ga. [1979 or 1980] iii leaves, 33 p. ; LC Card 80-132705 DDC 337./09/04 19
HF1410.5 .W67

SHEEP - HAWAII - MAUNA KEA GAME MANAGEMENT AREA - ECOLOGY.
Hawaii. Division of Fish and Game. Ecology of the feral sheep on Mauna Kea . [Honolulu] [1975] 90 leaves : LC Card 76-622866 DDC 639.9/797358 19
QL737.U53 H38 1975

Sheet erosion for all lands, Missouri /. United States. Soil Conservation Service. Lincoln, Nebr. , 1978. 1 map : LC Card 81-691219
G4161.J4 1977 .U5

Sheet erosion for cropland, hay, and pasture, Missouri /. United States. Soil Conservation Service. Lincoln, Nebr. , 1978. 1 map : LC Card 81-691218
G4161.J4 1977 .U51

Sheet erosion for grazed forest land, Missouri /.

United States. Soil Conservation Service. Lincoln, Nebr. , 1978. 1 map : LC Card 81-691217
G4161.J4 1977 .U52

Sheet erosion for non-grazed forest, Missouri /. United States. Soil Conservation Service. Lincoln, Nebr. , 1978. 1 map : LC Card 81-691216
G4161.J4 1977 .U53

Sheet erosion for permanent pasture, Missouri /. United States. Soil Conservation Service. Lincoln, Nebr. , 1978. 1 map : LC Card 81-691215
G4161.J4 1977 .U54

Sheet erosion for tilled land, Missouri /. United States. Soil Conservation Service. Lincoln, Nebr. , 1978. 1 map : LC Card 81-691214
G4161.J4 1977 .U55

Sheff, Rosalyn L. Environmental benefits assessment in economic impact studies : a review / by Rosalyn L. Sheff. Chicago, Il : State of Illinois, Institute of Natural Resources, 1979. iv, 51 p. ; 28 cm. (Document - Illinois Institute of Natural Resources . no. 79/19) Bibliography: p. 51. LC Card 79-626017 DDC 363.7/009773 19
1. Environmental policy - Illinois - Cost effectiveness. 2. Environmental protection - Economic aspects - Illinois. 3. Environmental law - Economic aspects - Illinois. I. Series: Illinois Institute of Natural Resources. Document - Illinois Institute of Natural Resources , no. 79/19. II. Title.
HC107.I33 E56

SHELBY COUNTY (IOWA) - MAPS.
United States. Soil Conservation Service. Shelby County, Iowa /. [Lincoln, Neb.] [1979?] 1 map : LC Card 81-691184
G4153.S5 1979 .U5

Sheldon, Charles S. United States. Library of Congress. Congressional Research Service. United States and Soviet progress in space . Washington , 1980. xiii, 91 p. ; LC Card 80-602269 DDC 387.8 19
TL789.8.U5 U54 1980

Sheldon, Henry Davidson, 1874-1948. Henry Davidson Sheldon and the University of Oregon, 1874-1948 : a biographical essay with selected letters / edited by James H. Hitchman. Bellingham, Wash. : Center for Pacific Northwest Studies, Western Washington University, 1979. xvi, 192 p. : ill., ports. ; 23 cm. (Occasional paper / Center for Pacific Northwest Studies, Western Washington University . no. 13) Includes bibliographical references and index. LC Card 81-110768 DDC 378/.111 19
1. Sheldon, Henry Davidson, 1874-1948. 2. College administrators - Oregon - Biography. 3. College teachers - Oregon - Biography. 4. University of Oregon. I. Hitchman, James H. II. Series: Occasional paper (Western Washington University. Center for Pacific Northwest Studies) , no. 13. III. Title.
LD4362.8.S53 A34

SHELDON, HENRY DAVIDSON, 1874-1948.
Sheldon, Henry Davidson, 1874-1948. Henry Davidson Sheldon and the University of Oregon, 1874-1948 . Bellingham, Wash. , 1979. xvi, 192 p. : LC Card 81-110768 DDC 378/.111 19
LD4362.8.S53 A34

SHELLFISH - MEXICO, GULF OF - DISEASES.
Overstreet, Robin M. Marine maladies? . [Ocean Springs, Miss.] , c1978. 140 p. : LC Card 78-112833 DDC 591.52/49 19
SH175 .O94

SHELLFISH TAGGING - FLORIDA.
Sullivan, James Richard, 1947- The stone crab, Menippe mercenaria, in the southwest Florida fishery /. St. Petersburg, Fla. , 1979. 37 p. : LC Card 80-622656 DDC 333.95/5 19
QL444.M33 S93

SHELLFISH TRADE.
Earl R. Combs Inc. A study to determine the export and domestic markets for currently underutilized fish and shellfish /. [Washington] 1978 [i. e. 1979] xxxv, 416 p. : LC Card 79-603273   *NYPL [JLF 81-419]*

SHELLFISH TRADE - HAWAII.
Lee, Steven R. The Hawaiian prawn industry . [Honolulu, Hawaii] [1979] ix, 32 p. : LC Card

80-621980 DDC 338.3/71543/09969 19
HD9472.S63 U54

SHELLFISH TRADE - UNITED STATES.
Earl R. Combs Inc. A study to determine the export and domestic markets for currently underutilized fish and shellfish /. [Washington] 1978 [i. e. 1979] xxxv, 416 p. : LC Card 79-603273   *NYPL [JLF 81-419]*

Ritchie, Theodore P. A comprehensive review of the commercial clam industries in the United States /. Washington , 1977. ix, 106 p. : LC Card 77-602000
HD9472.C53 U57   *NYPL [*XME-9426]*

United States. Office of Fisheries Development. A comprehensive review of the commercial oyster industries in the United States /. Washington , 1977. vi, 63 p. ; LC Card 77-602004
HD9472.O83 U56   *NYPL [*XME-9429]*

Shelter project for battered women . Connecticut. Office of Policy & Management. Division of Management and Evaluation. [Hartford] , 1979. 55 leaves ; LC Card 79-624247 DDC 362.8/3 19
HV699 .C63 1979

SHELTERED WORKSHOPS - UNITED STATES.
United States. Congress. House. Committee on Education and Labor. Subcommittee on Labor Standards. Oversight hearings on section 14(C) of the Fair Labor Standards Act . Washington , 1980. v, 540 p. : LC Card 80-603995 DDC 353.0083/6 19
KF27 .E348 1980d

SHELTERED WORKSHOPS - UNITED STATES - CONGRESSES.
Stimulating government utilization of sheltered workshops /. Memphis [1977] xiv, 319 p. : LC Card 78-622547
HD7256.U5 S83   *NYPL [JLE 81-488]*

SHELTERS, ATOMIC BOMB. see ATOMIC BOMB SHELTERS.

Shelton, John W. Geology and mineral resources of Noble County, Oklahoma / John W. Shelton, with a chapter on petroleum by John W. Shelton and William A. Jenkins and a chapter on water resources by Roy H. Bingham. Norman : University of Oklahoma, 1979. v, 66 p. : ill., maps (2 fold. in pocket) ; 25 cm. (Bulletin - Oklahoma Geological Survey ; 128 0078-4389) Cover title: Geology of Noble County, Oklahoma. Bibliography: p. 50-52. Includes index. LC Card 80-621935 DDC 557.66 s 557.66/27 19
1. Geology - Oklahoma - Noble Co. 2. Mines and mineral resources - Oklahoma - Noble Co. I. Jenkins, William A., joint author. II. Bingham, Roy H., 1930- joint author. III. Title. IV. Title: Geology of Noble County, Oklahoma. V. Series: Oklahoma. Geological Survey. Bulletin , 128.
QE153 .A2 no. 128 QE154.N58

SHELTON LAUREL VALLEY (N.C.) - MASSACRE, 1863.
Paludan, Phillip S., 1938- Victims . Knoxville , c1981. p. cm. ISBN 0-87049-316-7 LC Card 81-2578 DDC 973.7/33 19
F262.M25 P34

Shenk, Lynette O. Excavations at the Tubac Presidio / by Lynette O. Shenk and George A. Teague ; with appendix by James M. Hewitt ; prepared for the Arizona State Parks Board. [Tucson] : Cultural Resource Management Section, Arizona State Museum, University of Arizona, 1975. xii, 234 p. : ill. ; 28 cm. (Archaeological series ; no. 85) Includes bibliographies. LC Card 80-621272 DDC 979.1/79 19
1. Tubac, Ariz. Presidio. 2. Spaniards in Tubac, Ariz. - History. I. Teague, George A., joint author. II. Hewitt, George A., joint author. III. Arizona. State Parks Board. IV. Arizona. State Museum, Tucson. Cultural Resource Management Section. V. Series: Archaeological series (Tucson) , no. 85. VI. Title.
F819.T88 S5

Shepard, Lawrence. (joint author. 0700) Schutz, Howard G. Regulating occupations in California ; the role of public members on State boards /. [Berkeley] , 1980. ix, 22 p. ; ISBN 0-87772-276-5 LC Card 80-15719
HD3630.U7 S38

Shepard, Marietta Daniels, 1913- ... A solicitud de los países ... : asistencia que la OEA brinda a Latinoamérica en el campo de la información / por Marietta Daniels Shepard. Washington,

D.C. : Secretaría General, Organización de los Estados Americanos, 1974. 27 p. ; 28 cm. (Cuadernos bibliotecológicos . no. 62) "Preparado ... para servir como documento de base de XIII Asamblea General Regional de la Federación Internacional de Documentación, Bogotá, 16-19 de octubre de 1973." LC Card 80-121848 DDC 020 s 021.6/4 19
1. Library cooperation - Latin America - Addresses, essays, lectures. 2. Documentation - International cooperation - Addresses, essays, lectures. 3. Technology - International cooperation - Addresses, essays, lectures. I. Series: Organization of American States. Library Development Program. Cuadernos bibliotecológicos , no. 62. II. Title.
Z674 .P182 no. 62 Z738

Shepherd, Jack R. Police-juvenile diversion : an alternative to prosecution / by Jack R. Shepherd, Dale M. Rothenberger. Washington, D.C. : U. S. Dept. of Justice, Law Enforcement Assistance Administration, Office of Juvenile and Delinquency Prevention, 1980. x, 77, [91] p. : ill., forms ; 28 cm. Originally issued Dec. 1977. "Supported by grant number 22951-1A77, awarded to the Michigan Department of State Police by the Michigan Office of Criminal Justice Programs and the Law Enforcement Assistance Administration, United States Department of Justice." Item 968-H-1 Includes bibliography. LC Card 81-601094 DDC 364.6/8 19
1. Juvenile corrections - Michigan. 2. Police services for juveniles - Michigan. 3. Pre-trial intervention - Michigan. I. Rothenberger, Dale M. II. United States. Law Enforcement Assistance Administration. Office of Juvenile Justice and Delinquency Prevention. III. Michigan. Office of Criminal Justice Programs. IV. Michigan. Dept. of State Police. Community Services Section. Juvenile Unit. V. Title.
HV9105.M5 S5 1980

Shepley, Lawrence C., 1939- Spacetime and geometry . Austin , c1982. p. cm. ISBN 0-292-77567-9 LC Card 81-11488 DDC 530.1/1 19
QC173.6 .S67

Sherald, Margaret A. UJNR Panel on Fire Research and Safety. Fire research and safety . Washington, D.C. , 1979. x, 718 p. : LC Card 79-600054 DDC 602/.18 s 628.9/22 19
QC100 .U57 no. 540 TH9112

Shergold, Peter R., 1946- Working-class life : the "American standard" in comparative perspective, 1899-1913 / Peter R. Shergold. Pittsburgh, Pa. : University of Pittsburgh Press, c1981. p. cm. Includes bibliographical references. ISBN 0-8229-3802-2 LC Card 81-50921 DDC 339.4/7/0973 19
1. Cost and standard of living - United States - History. 2. Cost and standard of living - Great Britain - History. I. Title.
HD6983 .S45

Sheriff, Steven L. (joint author) Currier, Mary Jean P. Mountain lion population and harvest near Canon City, Colorado, 1974-1977 /. [Denver] , 1977. vi, 12 p. : LC Card 78-621470 DDC 639.9/7974428 19
QL737.C23 C83

Sherman, Charles Roger, 1944- A second exploratory analysis of the relations among institutional variables : final report / Charles R. Sherman. Washington : Division of Operational Studies, Association of American Medical Colleges, 1977. vi, 34 p. ; 28 cm. Microfiche (neg.) NTIS. 1 sheet. 11 x 15 cm. (PB 266 715) On cover: U. S. Department of Health, Education and Welfare, Public Health Service, Health Resources Administration, Bureau of Health Manpower, contract no. 231-76-0011. Bibliography: p. 21. LC Card 77-153938
1. Medical colleges - United States - Classification - Statistical methods. 2. Factor analysis. I. Association of American Medical Colleges. Division of Operational Studies. II. United States. Health Resources Administration. Bureau of Health Manpower. III. Title.
R745 .S493 **NYPL [*XME-9427]**

SHERMAN, WILLIAM T. (WILLIAM TECUMESH), 1820-1891 - RELATIONS WITH JOURNALISTS.
Marszalek, John F., 1939- Sherman's other war . Memphis, TN , c1981. p. cm. ISBN 0-87870-203-2 : LC Card 81-9483 DDC 973.7 19
E609 .M37

Sherman's other war . Marszalek, John F., 1939- Memphis, TN , c1981. p. cm. ISBN 0-87870-203-2 : LC Card 81-9483 DDC 973.7

19
E609 .M37

Sherwani, Jabbar K. Public policy for the management of groundwater in the coastal plain of North Carolina / by Jabbar K. Sherwani. [Raleigh, N.C.] : Water Resources Research Institute of the University of North Carolina, [1980] xv, 63 p. : ill. ; 28 cm. (Report - Water Resources Research Institute of the University of North Carolina . no. 158) "July 1980." Bibliography: p. 62-63. LC Card 80-623572 DDC 333.91/009756 s 333.91/04/09756 19
1. Water, Underground - North Carolina - Management. I. Series: University of North Carolina (System). Water Resources Research Institute. Report , no. 158. II. Title.
HD1694.N8 N6 no. 158 TD224.N8

Sherwood, Roger. Polyzoides, Stephanos. Courtyard housing in Los Angeles . Berkeley , c1982. p. cm. ISBN 0-520-04251-4 LC Card 80-6057 DDC 728/.09794/94 19
NA7238.L6 P6

SHI, XIAOQING.
Lao, She, 1898-1966. [Lo t'o Hsiang-tzu. English.] Camel Xiangzi /. Bloomington , Beijing , c1981. p. cm. ISBN 0-253-31296-5 LC Card 81-47584 DDC 895.1/35 19
PL2804.C5 L613 1981

Shiawassee River study . Roycraft, Philip R. [Lansing] , 1979. 55 p. : LC Card 80-620626 DDC 363.7/3942/09774 19
TD224.M5 R694

SHIELDING (RADIATION)
Spencer, L. V. (Lewis Van Clief), 1924- Structure shielding against fallout gamma rays from nuclear detonations /. [Washington, D.C.?] , 1980. xvi, 967 p : LC Card 80-600120 DDC 602/.18 s 363.1/89 19
QC100 .U57 no. 570 UF787

Shields, Elizabeth A. Center of Military History. Highlights in the history of the Army Nurse Corps / . Washington, D.C. , 1981. 88 p. : LC Card 81-601493 DDC 355.3/45/0973 19
UH493 .C46 1981

Shifrine, Moshe. The Canine as a biomedical research model . [Oak Ridge, TN] , Springfield, Va. , 1980. x, 425 p. : ISBN 0-87079-122-2 (pbk.) : LC Card 80-24174 DDC 619/.7 19
RB125 .C36

Shigeta, Daniel, 1928- Yee, Warren, 1921- Plum culture in Hawaii /. Honolulu , 1981. p. cm. LC Card 81-6824 DDC 634/.22/09969 19
SB377 .Y43

Shigo, Alex L., 1930- Some effects of paraformaldehyde on wood surrounding tapholes in sugar maple trees / by Alex L. Shigo and Frederick M. Laing. Upper Darby, Pa. : Northeastern Forest Experiment Station, Forest Service, U. S. Dept. of Agriculture, 1970. 11 p. : ill. ; 24 cm. (U. S.D.A. Forest Service research paper . NE-161) Cover title. "University of Vermont Agricultural Experiment Station journal article 229." Bibliography: p. 11. LC Card 81-460882 DDC 634.9/0974 s 633.6/49 19
1. Sugar-maple - Wounds and injuries. 2. Sugar-maple - Tapping. 3. Plants, Effect of polyoxymethylene on. 4. Polyoxymethylene - Physiological effect. 5. Micro-organisms - Physiology. I. Laing, Frederick M., joint author. II. Series: United States. Northeastern Forest Experiment Station, Upper Darby, Pa. United States D.A. Forest Service research paper , NE-161. III. Title.
SD11 .A455493 no. 161 SB608.S913

Shih, Jason. Earth covered buildings . [Washington, D.C.] [Springfield, Va. , foreword 1979] vi, 272 p. : LC Card 79-600114 DDC 690 19
TH4819.E27 E38

Shiley, R. H. Screening of selected fluoroaromatic compounds for use as agrichemicals, I /. Urbana, Ill. [1979] 17 p. : LC Card 80-622082 DDC 557.73 s 632/.952 19
QE105 .A45 no. 508 SB952.F55

Shimane, Robert. (joint author) Mubarak, Jill. Gerontology and the law . Los Angeles, Calif. , 1979. xiv, 102 p. ; LC Card 79-123375 DDC 016.34473/0326 19
KF390.A4 M8

Shimkin, Michael Boris, 1912- Science and cancer / by Michael B. Shimkin. 3rd revision

1980. [Bethesda? Md.] : U. S. Dept. of Health and Human Services, Public Health Service, National Institutes of Health, National Cancer Institute, 1980. viii, 109 p. : ill., charts ; 23 cm. (NIH publication. no. 80-568) Bibliography: p. 103-104. LC Card 80-603983 DDC 616.99/4 19
1. Cancer. I. National Cancer Institute (U. S.). II. National Institutes of Health (U. S.). III. Series: DHHS publication, no. (NIH) 80-568. IV. Title.
RC263 .S48 1980

Shinn, Rinn-Sup. China, a country study /. Washington, D.C. , 1981. p. cm. LC Card 81-12878 DDC 951 19
DS706 .C489 1981

SHIP-BUILDING - COSTS - YEARBOOKS.
United States. Maritime Administration. Relative cost of shipbuilding. Washington.
NYPL [JLM 80-1114]

SHIP-BUILDING - FINANCE.
United States. Maritime Administration. Office of Policy and Plans. The maritime aids of the six major maritime nations, /. [Washington] , 1977. ca. 500 p. in various pagings : LC Card 78-600514
HE741 .U55 1977 **NYPL [*XME-9415]**

SHIP-BUILDING - UNITED STATES.
Cole, Brady M. Procurement of Naval ships . Washington, D.C. , 1979. vi, 52 p. (p. 52 advertisements) : LC Card 79-604212 DDC 338.7/6238/200973 19
VM299.6 .C64

United States. General Accounting Office. Better Navy management of shipbuilding contracts could save millions of dollars . [Washington] [1980] v, 40 p. ; LC Card 80-602619 DDC 359.6/211/0973 19
VM299.6 .U55 1980

SHIP-BUILDING - UNITED STATES - MATHEMATICAL MODELS.
Port Authority of New York and New Jersey. Planning and Development Dept. Economic impact of the U. S. merchant marine and shipbuilding industries . New York, 1977. viii, 272 p.;
HE746 .C48 **NYPL [*XME-9407]**

SHIP SUBSIDIES. see SHIPPING BOUNTIES AND SUBSIDIES.

SHIP TERMINALS. see MARINE TERMINALS.

Shipp, P. Royal. Background material on work, retirement, and social security / prepared by the Congressional Research Service ; [by P. Royal Shipp]. Washington : U. S. Govt. Print. Off., 1980. v, 24 p. : ill. ; 24 cm. At head of title: 96th Congress, 2d session. Committee print. WMCP: 96-69. Excerpted from the report prepared for the Subcommittee on Oversight of the Committee on Ways and Means. "August 1980." Bibliography: p. 23-24. LC Card 80-603060 DDC 368.4/3/00973 19
1. Social security - United States. 2. Retirement age - United States. I. United States. Congress. House. Committee on Ways and Means. Subcommittee on Oversight. II. United States. Library of Congress. Congressional Research Service. III. Title.
HD7125 .S527

Shipper's export declarations . United States. Congress. Senate. Committee on Governmental Affairs. Washington , 1980. iii, 149 p. ; LC Card 80-603643 DDC 343.73/0878 347.303878 19
KF26 .G67 1980i

SHIPPING AGREEMENTS. see SHIPPING CONFERENCES.

SHIPPING BOUNTIES AND SUBSIDIES.
United States. Maritime Administration. Office of Policy and Plans. The maritime aids of the six major maritime nations, /. [Washington] , 1977. ca. 500 p. in various pagings : LC Card 78-600514
HE741 .U55 1977 **NYPL [*XME-9415]**

SHIPPING COMBINES. see SHIPPING CONFERENCES.

SHIPPING CONFERENCES.
United States. Congress. House. Committee on the Judiciary. Subcommittee on Monopolies and Commercial Law. Omnibus Maritime Regulatory Reform Revitalization and Reorganization Act of 1980 . Washington , 1980 [i.e. 1981] iii, 160 p. ; LC Card 81-601640

DDC 343.73/096 347.30396 19
KF27 .J8663 1980a

SHIPPING - DATA PROCESSING.
Computer Sciences Corporation. Shipping
operations information system /. Falls Church,
Va., 1973. 2 v.   **NYPL [*XMQ-2149]**

SHIPPING - GREAT LAKES.
Schenker, Eric, 1931- The Great Lakes
transportation system /. [Madison, Wis.] , 1976.
xvii, 292 p. :   LC Card 75-42825   DDC
386/.544/0977 19
HE398 .S33

SHIPPING - LAW. see MARITIME LAW.

SHIPPING - MAPS.
United States. Central Intelligence Agency.
Selected world shipping lanes and straits.
[Washington , 1980] 1 map :   LC Card 81-690686
G3201.P54 1980 .U5

United States. Hydrographic Office. Division of
Chart Construction. Tracks for full powered
steam vessels with the shortest navigable
distances in nautical miles /. Washington ,
1900. 1 map :   LC Card 81-690532
G3201.P54 1900 .U5

Shipping operations information system /.
Computer Sciences Corporation. Falls Church,
Va., 1973. 2 v.   **NYPL [*XMQ-2149]**

**SHIPPING - SUBSIDIES. see SHIPPING
BOUNTIES AND SUBSIDIES.**

SHIPPING - TAXATION - UNITED STATES.
United States. Congress. House. Committee on
Ways and Means. Omnibus maritime regulatory
reform, revitalization, and reorganization act .
Washington , 1980. iii, 144 p. :   LC Card
80-602429   DDC 343.73/096 19
KF27 .W3 1980b

**SHIPPING TRUSTS. see SHIPPING
CONFERENCES.**

**SHIPPING - UNITED STATES - COST OF
OPERATION.**
Andrews, Benjamin V. Relative costs of U. S.
and foreign nodule transport ships /. Rockville,
Md. , 1978. vi, 70 p. :   LC Card 78-602299
HE746 .A75

**SHIPPING - UNITED STATES - DATA
PROCESSING.**
Computer Sciences Corporation. Shipping
operations information system /. Falls Church,
Va., 1973. 2 v.   **NYPL [*XMQ-2149]**

**SHIPPING - UNITED STATES -
PERIODICALS.**
United States. Maritime Administration. Report.
Washington.   **NYPL [JLM 80-989]**

**SHIPPING - VIRGIN ISLANDS OF THE
UNITED STATES.**
United States. Federal Maritime Commission.
Office of Economic Analysis. Virgin Islands
trade study . Washington, D.C. [1979] ca. 500
p. in various pagings :   LC Card 80-601213   DDC
387/.0097297/22 19
HE796.3 .U54 1979

**Ships, aircraft, and weapons of the United States
Navy.** United States. Navy Dept. Office of
Information. [Washington, D.C. , 1980] 51 p. :
  LC Card 80-603251   DDC 359.3/2/0973 19
VF347 .U57 1980

**SHIPS - FIRES AND FIRE PREVENTION -
COST EFFECTIVENESS.**
Stanford Research Institute. SRI International.
Cost effectiveness of marine fire protection
programs . [Washington] , 1978. xvii, 212 p. :
  LC Card 79-602278
VK1258 .S18 1979   **NYPL [JLF 81-262]**

SHIPS - INSPECTION - UNITED STATES.
United States. Congress. House. Committee on
Merchant Marine and Fisheries. Subcommitee
on Coast Guard and Navigation. Small
commercial vessel inspection and manning .
Washington , 1980. iv, 301 p. :   LC Card
80-601442   DDC 343.73/0965 19
KF27 .M434 1979d

United States. Congress. Senate. Committee on
Commerce, Science, and Transportation. Coast
Guard authority . Washington , 1980. iii, 104
p. ;   LC Card 81-600824   DDC 343.73/0965
347.303965 19
KF26 .C69 1980x

**SHIPS - MANNING - LAW AND
LEGISLATION - UNITED STATES.**
United States. Congress. House. Committee on
Merchant Marine and Fisheries. Subcommitee
on Coast Guard and Navigation. Small
commercial vessel inspection and manning .
Washington , 1980. iv, 301 p. :   LC Card
80-601442   DDC 343.73/0965 19
KF27 .M434 1979d

United States. Congress. Senate. Committee on
Commerce, Science, and Transportation. Coast
Guard authority . Washington , 1980. iii, 104
p. ;   LC Card 81-600824   DDC 343.73/0965
347.303965 19
KF26 .C69 1980x

SHIPS - NATIONALITY - DIRECTORIES.
United States. Maritime Administration.
Division of Trade Studies and Statistics.
Foreign flag mechant ships owned by U. S.
parent companies as of June 30, 1974 /.
Washington [1975?] 54 p. ;
       NYPL [JLF 79-1500]

SHIPWRECKS - NORTH CAROLINA.
Regan, Dennis C. Wreck diving in North
Carolina . Raleigh, N.C. [1978] 16 p. :   LC
Card 79-623528   DDC 910/.0916348 19
G525 .R375

Shireman, Joan F. Brown, H. Frederick. Policies
and practices of the child protective services
system in Cook County /. [Chicago, Ill.]
[1978] 30, 16 p. :   LC Card 80-623540   DDC
344.773/10327044 347.73104327044 19
KFI1799.C62 C7215

Shirk, Susan L. Competitive comrades : career
incentives and student strategies in China /
Susan L. Shirk. Berkeley : University of
California Press, c1981. p. cm. Bibliography: p.
Includes index.   ISBN 0-520-04299-9   LC Card
81-2772   DDC 371.8/1/091 19
1. Students - China - Political activity. 2. Socialism and
youth - China. I. Title.
LA1133.7 .S553

Shirley, Glenn. Heck Thomas, frontier marshal /
by Glenn Shirley. Norman : University of
Oklahoma Press, 1981, c1962. p. cm. Originally
published: Philadelphia : Chilton Co., Book Division,
1962. Bibliography: p. Includes index.   ISBN
0-8061-1664-1   LC Card 81-40293   DDC
976.6/04/0924 B 19
1. Thomas, Heck, 1850-1912. 2. Crime and criminials -
Oklahoma - History. 3. Oklahoma - History. 4. Peace
officers - Oklahoma - Biography. I. Title.
F698.T48 S48 1981

Shirts, M. B. Salisbury, H. B. Beneficiation of
low-grade California chromite ores /.
[Avondale, Md.] , 1981. p. cm.   LC Card
81-607307   DDC 622 s 622/.34643 19
TN23 .U43 TN538.C57

Shives, T. R. Mechanical Failures Prevention
Group. Detection, diagnosis, and prognosis .
[Washington] , 1979. vi, 370 p. :   LC Card
79-600078   DDC 602/.18 s 620.1/126 19
QC100 .U57 no. 547 TA409

Shmelzer, June L. (ed) Interdisciplinary Workshop
on Transportation and Aging, Washington, D.
C., 1970. Transportation and aging; selected
issues. Washington [1971] 208 p.   LC Card
79-619017
HQ1063.5 .I5 1970   **NYPL [JLF 81-91]**

Shoemaker, Eugene Merle, 1928- Guidebook to
the geology of Meteor Crater, Arizona /
prepared by Eugene M. Shoemaker and Susan
W. Kieffer for the 37th annual meeting of the
Meteoritical Society, August 7, 1974. Rev.
1979. Tempe, Ariz. : Center for Meteorite
Studies, Arizona State University, [1979] i, 66
p., [1] fold. leaf of plates : ill. ; 28 cm.
(Publication - Center for Meteorite Studies, Arizona
State University ; no. 17) Bibliography: p. 63-66.   LC
Card 80-622424   DDC 523.5 s 557.91/33 19
1. Geology - Arizona - Meteor Crater - Guide-books. 2.
Meteor Crater, Ariz. I. Kieffer, Susan W., joint author.
II. Meteoritical Society. III. Series: Arizona. State
University, Tempe. Center for Meteorite Studies.
Publication, no. 17. IV. Title.
QB755 .A75 no. 17 QE86.M5

Sholton, Erwin J. A kenaf development program
for Benue Plateau State / by Erwin J. Sholton.
New York : Agri-Business Consultants, 1973.
16, 112 leaves, [1] leaf of plates : map ; 33 cm.
"Under contract with Ministry of Natural Resources,

Jos, Benue Plateau State, Nigeria."   LC Card
81-458472   DDC 338.1/7356 19
1. Kenaf - Nigeria - Benue-Plateau. 2. Agriculture and
state - Nigeria - Benue-Plateau. I. Agri-Business
Consultants. II. Title.
SB261.A5 S56

Shomo, Elwood Warren. Nathan (Robert R.)
Associates, Washington, D. C. Assessment and
evaluation of the impact of archetypal national
health insurance plans on U. S. health
manpower requirements /. [Bethesda, Md.] ,
1974. xviii, 117 p. :   **NYPL [JLF 80-904]**

Shonka, D. B. United States. National
Laboratory, Oak Ridge, Tenn. Transportation
energy conservation data book /. Oak Ridge,
Tenn. , 1977. xxv, 536 p. :
HE18 1977 .N37 1977   **NYPL [JLF 81-192]**

SHOOTING - SAFETY MEASURES.
United States. Dept. of the Army. Firearm and
archery safety /. [Washington], 1974. 22 p.:
       NYPL [*XM-13354]

**SHOPPERS' GUIDES. see CONSUMER
EDUCATION.**

**SHOPPING CENTERS - GEORGIA -
ATLANTA METROPOLITAN AREA.**
Dent, Borden D. Trade area analysis of
Atlanta's regional shopping centers /. Atlanta,
Ga. , 1978, c1980. vi, 66 leaves (1 folded) :
  LC Card 80-624405   DDC 381/.1/097582 19
HF5430.5.A7 D46

**SHOPPING CENTERS - UNITED STATES -
ADDRESSES, ESSAYS, LECTURES.**
Shopping centers, USA /. New Brunswick, N.J.
[1981] p. cm.   ISBN 0-88285-068-7 :   LC Card
80-21702   DDC 381.1/0973 19
HF5430.3 .S47

Shopping centers, USA / edited by George
Sternlieb, James W. Hughes. New Brunswick,
N.J. : Rutgers University, Center for Urban
Policy Research, [1981] p. cm. Bibliography: p.
Includes index.   ISBN 0-88285-068-7 :   LC Card
80-21702   DDC 381.1/0973 19
1. Shopping centers - United States - Addresses, essays,
lectures. I. Sternlieb, George. II. Hughes, James W.
HF5430.3 .S47

Shopping in New York. The ultimate guide to
shopping in New York /. [New York] , c1979.
48 p. :   **NYPL [IRGV 80-2533]**

**SHOPPING - NEW YORK (CITY) -
DIRECTORIES.**
The ultimate guide to shopping in New York /.
[New York] , c1979. 48 p. :
       NYPL [IRGV 80-2533]

Shore erosion a bibliography, 1976. Wisconsin.
Shore Erosion Study. Annotated bibliography of
shore erosion and related physical materials
concerning Wisconsin's Great Lakes coastal
areas /. [Madison, Wis.] , 1976. 116 p. :   LC
Card 79-623658   DDC 016.5513/52 19
Z6004.C6 W57 1976 GB459.5.M5

**SHORE-LINES - LAW AND LEGISLATION -
WASHINGTON (STATE)**
Washington (State). Dept. of Ecology. Lakes
constituting shorelines of the State Shoreline
Management Act of 1971. [n. p., 1973] 27 p.
       NYPL [*ZT-1250]

**SHORE-LINES - MICHIGAN, LAKE -
BIBLIOGRAPHY.**
Wisconsin. Shore Erosion Study. Annotated
bibliography of shore erosion and related
physical materials concerning Wisconsin's Great
Lakes coastal areas /. [Madison, Wis.] , 1976.
116 p. :   LC Card 79-623658   DDC 016.5513/52 19
Z6004.C6 W57 1976 GB459.5.M5

**SHORE-LINES - SUPERIOR, LAKE -
BIBLIOGRAPHY.**
Wisconsin. Shore Erosion Study. Annotated
bibliography of shore erosion and related
physical materials concerning Wisconsin's Great
Lakes coastal areas /. [Madison, Wis.] , 1976.
116 p. :   LC Card 79-623658   DDC 016.5513/52 19
Z6004.C6 W57 1976 GB459.5.M5

SHORE PORTERS. see STEVEDORES.

SHORE PROTECTION - FENWICK ISLAND.
Dolan, Robert. Geographical analysis of
Fenwick Island, Maryland, a Middle Atlantic
coast barrier island /. Washington, D.C. , 1980.
24 p. :   LC Card 79-600212   DDC 333.7 19
GB126.M3 D64

SHORE PROTECTION - LAW AND LEGISLATION - MASSACHUSETTS.
Massachusetts. Dept. of Environmental Quality Engineering. Division of Wetlands. A guide to the coastal wetlands regulations of the Massachusetts wetlands protection act (G.L. 131,s.40). Boston [1979] 158 p. : LC Card 79-623454
KFM2851.8 .A83

SHORE PROTECTION - LAW AND LEGISLATION - NEW JERSEY.
New Jersey. Legislature. General Assembly. Energy and Natural Resources Committee. Public hearing before Assembly Energy and Natural Resources Committee on A-1825, Dune and shorefront protection act. [Trenton] [1980] 2 v. ; LC Card 80-623987 DDC 346.74904/6917 347.490646917 19
KFN1811.4 .E53 1980

SHORE PROTECTION - LAW AND LEGISLATION - TAHOE, LAKE.
Nevada. State Dept. of Conservation and Natural Resources. Regulations governing pier construction, deposit of fill, dredging, or alteration of Lake Tahoe shoreline, adopted September 24, 1979 /. [Carson City, Nev.] [1979] 8 p. ; LC Card 80-622985 DDC 346.793/57046917 19
KFN1051.8.A434 A2 1979

SHORE PROTECTION - LAW AND LEGISLATION - TEXAS.
Texas. Laws, Statutes, etc. Texas coastal legislation /. [Austin] , 1979. iv, 219 p. ; LC Card 80-621294 DDC 346.76404/6917 19
KFT1651.8 .A3 1979

Texas. Legislature. Senate. Committee to Study Texas Beaches. Interim report of the Senate Committee to Study Texas Beaches, 65th Legislature /. [Austin] , 1979. ii leaves, 48 p. ; LC Card 79-625806 DDC 346.76404/6917 19
LAW

SHORE PROTECTION - LAW AND LEGISLATION - UNITED STATES.
Althaus, Helen F. Public trust rights /. [Washington] , 1978. xxxix, 421 p. ; LC Card 80-602390 DDC 346.7304/691 19
KF5571 .A94

SHORE PROTECTION - ST. LAWRENCE RIVER.
New York (State). St. Lawrence-Eastern Ontario Commission. Evaluation of shore structures and shore erodibility. Massena, N.Y. , Watertown, N.Y. , 1977. vi, 165 p. : LC Card 80-621706 DDC 627/.12 19
TC225.S138 N48 1977

SHORE PROTECTION - VIRGINIA.
Virginia. Coastal Erosion Abatement Commission. Interim report of the Coastal Erosion Abatement Commission to the Governor and the General Assembly of Virginia. Richmond , 1979. 17 p. ; LC Card 79-623624 DDC 300/.9755 s 627/.58/09755 19
J87 .V9 1979b, no. 23 TC224.V8

Virginia. Coastal Erosion Abatement Commission. Report of the Coastal Erosion Abatement Commission to the Governor and the General Assembly of Virginia. Richmond , 1979. 52 p. : LC Card 80-621165 DDC 300/.9755 s 333.91/716/09755 19
J87 .V9 1979b, no. 4a TC224.V8

Shorelines changes on Mustang Island and North Padre Island (Aransas Pass to Yarborough Pass) . Morton, Robert A. Austin , 1977. 45 p. : LC Card 78-621044 DDC 553/.09764 s 551.3/6/09764113 19
TN24.T4 T38 no. 77-1 GB459.4

Shorelines management '77 : performance and prospects : a conference and workshop for practitioners and users : proceedings, September 22-23, 1977 / Robert F. Goodwin, editor. Seattle : [Washington Sea Grant Program, Division of Marine Resources], University of Washington, [1978?] ix, 163 p. : graphs ; 23 cm. (A Washington sea grant publication) Conference sponsors, Coastal Resources Program, Institute for Marine Studies, University of Washington and Washington State Department of Ecology, Shorelands Division. Includes bibliographical references. LC Card 79-624199 DDC 333.91/7/0973 19
1. Coastal zone management - United States - Congresses. I. Goodwin, Robert F. II. Washington (State). University. Institute for Marine Studies. Coastal

Resources Program. III. Washington (State). Dept. of Ecology. Shorelands Division. IV. Series: Washington sea grant publication (unnumb.).
HT392 .S54

Short- and long-term health effects on the surviving population of a nuclear war . United States. Congress. Senate. Committee on Labor and Human Resources. Subcommittee on Health and Scientific Research. Washington , 1980 [i.e. 1981] iv, 133 p. ; LC Card 81-601151 DDC 363.1/79 19
KF26 .L274 1980m

SHORT BALLOT. see BALLOT.

A short manual on sampling. United Nations. Statistical Office. New York , 1972- v. ; LC Card 80-119414 DDC 300 s 519.5 19
JX1977 .A2 ST/STAT/SER.F/9/Rev.1, etc.
QA276.6

SHORT STORIES, AMERICAN - MEXICAN AMERICAN AUTHORS.
Cuentos Chicanos /. Albuquerque, N.M. , c1980. 109 p. : LC Card 81-110854 DDC 813/.01/08868 19
PS647.M49 C8

SHORT TAKE-OFF AND LANDING AIRCRAFT.
(1981) Kohlman, David L., 1937- Introduction to V/STOL airplanes /. Ames , 1981. xii, 231 p. : ISBN 0-8138-0660-7 LC Card 81-3776 DDC 629.133/35 19
TL685 .K64

Shorter contributions to stratigraphy and structural geology, 1979. Washington : U. S. Govt. Print. Off., 1980. ca. 150 p. in various pagings : ill., maps (1 fold. in pocket) ; 29 cm. (Geological Survey professional paper ; 1126-A-J) Includes bibliographies. LC Card 80-600016 DDC 557.3 19
1. Geology - United States - Addresses, essays, lectures. 2. Geology - Brazil - Minas Gerais - Addresses, essays, lectures. I. Series: United States. Geological Survey. Professional paper, 1126-A-J.
QE77 .S47

SHOSHONE NATIONAL FOREST, WYO. - MAPS.
(1969) United States. Forest Service. Rocky Mountain Region. Shoshone National Forest, Wyoming. [Denver] 1969. col. map on sheet 66 x 92 cm. Scale 1:126,720; 1/2˝ = 1 mile. Folded title: North half Shoshone National Forest, Wyoming. Printed on both sides of sheet. Relief shown by hachures and spot heights. "Polyconic projection ... Sixth principal meridian, Wind River meridian." "Forest visitors map." "Forest Service map, class A." Includes col. illus., text, index to "Forest Service recreation sites," 2 key maps, and "Vicinity map." LC Card 74-696308
G4262.S5 1969 .U5
NYPL [Map Div. 80-3348]

(1971) United States. Forest Service. Rocky Mountain Region. Shoshone National Forest, Wyoming. [Denver] 1971. col. map on sheet 67 x 92 cm. Scale 1:126,720; 1/2˝ = 1 mile. Folded title: Shoshone National Forest, Wyoming, south half. Printed on both sides of sheet. Relief shown by hachures and spot heights. "Polyconic projection ... Sixth principal meridian, Wind River meridian." "Forest visitors map." "Forest Service map, class A." Includes col. illus., text, indexes to "Forest Service recreation sites," and "State recreation sites," 2 key maps, and "Vicinity map." LC Card 74-696307
G4262.S5 1971 .U5
NYPL [Map Div. 80-3347]

Shoshone National Forest, Wyoming, south half. United States. Forest Service. Rocky Mountain Region. Shoshone National Forest, Wyoming. [Denver] 1971. col. map on sheet 67 x 92 cm. Scale 1:126,720; 1/2˝ = 1 mile. Folded title: Shoshone National Forest, Wyoming, south half. Printed on both sides of sheet. Relief shown by hachures and spot heights. "Polyconic projection ... Sixth principal meridian, Wind River meridian." "Forest visitors map." "Forest Service map, class A." Includes col. illus., text, indexes to "Forest Service recreation sites," and "State recreation sites," 2 key maps, and "Vicinity map." LC Card 74-696307
G4262.S5 1971 .U5
NYPL [Map Div. 80-3347]

SHOSHONI INDIANS.
Iroquois Research Institute. A land use history of Coso Hot Springs, Inyo County, California /. China Lake, Calif. , 1979. xiv, 232 p., [2] leaves

of plates (1 fold.) : LC Card 79-602009 DDC 979.4/87 19
E99.P2 I7 1979

Should the Federal government significantly strengthen the regulation of mass media communication in the United States? : Intercollegiate debate topic, 1979-1980, pursuant to Public law 88-246 / compiled by the Congressional Research Service, Library of Congress. Washington : U. S. Govt. Print. Off. : for sale by the Supt. of Docs., U. S. Govt. Print. Off., 1979. ix, 425 p. : ill. ; 24 cm. (Document - 96th Congress, 1st session, House of Representatives ; 96-167) Includes bibliographical references. LC Card 80-602647 DDC 343.73/099 19
1. Mass media - Law and legislation - United States - Addresses, essays, lectures. 2. Mass media - Law and legislation - United States - Bibliography. I. United States. Library of Congress. Congressional Research Service. II. Series: United States. 96th Congress, 1st session, 1979. House. Document ; no. 96-167.
KF2750.A75 S48

Should the United States significantly increase its foreign military commitments? : Intercollegiate debate topic, 1980-1981, persuant to Public Law 88-246 / compiled by the Congressional Research Service, Library of Congress. Washington : U. S. G.P.O. : For sale by the Supt. of Docs., U. S. G.P.O., 1980. v, 484 p. : ill., maps ; 24 cm. (Document / House of Representatives, 96th Congress, 2d session . v. 96-366) Bibliography: p. 427-476. LC Card 80-603968 DDC 355/.031/0973 19
1. United States - Military policy - Addresses, essays, lectures. 2. United States - Foreign relations - 1977- - Addresses, essays, lectures. I. Library of Congress. Congressional Research Service. II. Title: Intercollegiate debate topic, 1980-1981. III. Series: House document (United States. Congress (96th, 2nd session : 1980). House) , no. 96-366.
UA23 .S485

Shpilberg, David. De Neufville, Richard, 1939- Investment strategies for developing areas : models of transport. Cambridge, 1973. 83 p.
NYPL [JLF 80-1121]

Shreve, Cathy. (joint author) Silver, Jennifer. Condominium conversion controls . Washington, D.C. , 1979 [i.e.] 1980. 61 p. ; LC Card 80-601762 DDC 346.7304/33 19
KF581 .S54

SHRIMP FISHERIES - HAWAII.
Lee, Steven R. The Hawaiian prawn industry . [Honolulu, Hawaii] [1979] ix, 32 p. : LC Card 80-621980 DDC 338.3/71543/09969 19
HD9472.S63 U54

SHRIMP FISHERIES - SOUTH ATLANTIC STATES.
The Shrimp fishery of the South Atlantic United States . Charleston , 1975. vi, 66 leaves ; LC Card 75-623488 DDC 333.95/5 19
SH380.62.U6 S52

The Shrimp fishery of the Southeastern United States . Charleston , 1974. vi, 229 p. : LC Card 75-621474 DDC 338.3/7253843/0974 19
SH380.62.U6 S53

SHRIMP FISHERIES - SOUTH CAROLINA.
Bishop, J. M. Biological observations on commercial penaeid shrimps caught by bottom trawl in South Carolina estuaries, February 1973-January 1975 /. [Charleston] [197-] xi, 97 p. : LC Card 80-621322 DDC 595.3/843 19
QL444.M33 B57

The Shrimp fishery of the South Atlantic United States : a regional management plan / edited by Peter J. Eldridge, Steven A. Goldstein. Charleston : South Carolina Marine Resources Center, South Carolina Wildlife and Marine Resources Dept., 1975. xi, 66 leaves ; 28 cm. (Technical report - South Carolina Wildlife and Marine Resources Department ; no. 8) Bibliography: leaves [65]-66. LC Card 75-623488 DDC 333.95/5 19
1. Shrimp fisheries - South Atlantic States. 2. Fishery management - South Atlantic States. I. Eldridge, Peter J. II. Goldstein, Steven A. III. Series: South Carolina. Marine Resources Division. Technical report - Marine Resources Division, South Carolina Wildlife and Marine Resources Department , no. 8.
SH380.62.U6 S52

The Shrimp fishery of the Southeastern United States : a management planning profile / edited by Dale R. Calder, Peter J. Eldridge, Edwin B. Joseph. Charleston : South Carolina Marine

Resources Center, South Carolina Wildlife and Marine Resources Department, 1974. vi, 229 p. : ill. ; 28 cm. (Technical report - South Carolina Wildlife and Marine Resources Department ; no. 5) Includes bibliographies. LC Card 75-621474 DDC 338.3/7253843/0974 19
1. Shrimp fisheries - South Atlantic States. 2. Fishery management - South Atlantic States. I. Calder, Dale R. II. Eldridge, Peter J. III. Joseph, Edwin Bibb. IV. Series: South Carolina. Marine Resources Division. Technical report - Marine Resources Division, South Carolina Wildlife and Marine Resources Department , no. 5.
SH380.62.U6 S53

SHRIMPS - FLORIDA.
Huff, James Alan, 1949- Penaeoid and Sergestoid shrimps (Crustacea. St. Petersburg, Fla. , 1979. 102 p. : LC Card 80-622670 DDC 574.92/34 s 595.3/843/09759 19
QH92.3 .M45 vol. 5, pt. 4 QL444.M33

SHRIMPS - MEXICO, GULF OF.
Huff, James Alan, 1949- Penaeoid and Sergestoid shrimps (Crustacea. St. Petersburg, Fla. , 1979. 102 p. : LC Card 80-622670 DDC 574.92/34 s 595.3/843/09759 19
QH92.3 .M45 vol. 5, pt. 4 QL444.M33

Shrivastava, Prakash K. Known effects of low-level radiation exposure . [Bethesda, Md.] [1980] 147 p. : LC Card 80-601671 DDC 616.9/897 19
RA1231.R2 K59

Shroba, R. R. Hansen, Wallace R., 1920- Environmental geology of the Front Range Urban Corridor and vicinity, Colorado /. Washington , 1981. p. cm. LC Card 81-4280 DDC 624.1/51/097883 19
QE92.F7 H36

Shroff, Kersi B. Individualized sentencing and the use of social inquiry (presentence) reports in England / prepared by Kersi B. Shroff. Washington : Library of Congress, Law Library, 1978. 20 p. ; 27 cm. (Law Library publications) LC Card 78-600143 DDC 345.42/0772 19
1. Sentences (Criminal procedure) - Great Britain. 2. Pre-sentence investigation reports - Great Britain. I. Series: United States. Library of Congress. Law Library. Law Library publications. II. Title.
KD8406 .S55

Shropshire, Walter. The Joys of research /. Washington, D.C. , 1981. p. cm. ISBN 0-87474-858-5 LC Card 81-9347 DDC 001.4 19
Q179.9 .J69

SHRUBS - SOUTHWEST, NEW - IDENTIFICATION.
Benson, Lyman David, 1909- Trees and shrubs of the southwestern deserts /. Tucson , c1981. p. cm. ISBN 0-8165-0591-8 : LC Card 81-7617 DDC 582.160979 19
QK484.S89 B46 1981

Shryock, Henry S. The methods and materials of demography / by Henry S. Shryock, Jacob S. Siegel, and associates ; Elizabeth A. Larmon, editorial associate ; [associate authors, Francisco Bayo ... et al.]. 3rd print., rev. [Washington] : U. S. Dept. of Commerce, Bureau of the Census : for sale by the Supt. of Docs. U. S. Govt. Print. Off., 1975. 2 v. (xvi, 888, 20 p.) : ill. ; 29 cm. "A United States Department of Commerce publication." Errata slip inserted. Includes bibliographies and indexes. LC Card 75-600077
1. Demography. I. Siegel, Jacob S., joint author. 0700. II. Larmon, Elizabeth A. III. United States. Bureau of the Census. IV. Title.
HB881 .S526 1975

Shubow, Midge. United States. Office of Consumer Affairs. Consumer Information Division. Consumer's resource handbook /. [Washington] , Pueblo, Colo. [1979] iv, 76 p. : LC Card 80-603215 DDC 381./33/0973 19
HC110.C63 U5 1979

Shull, Ralph B. (joint author) Adams, Jack E. The potential impact of negotiable order of withdrawal accounts on the banking industry in Arkansas . Fayetteville, Ark. [1979] iv, 55 leaves ; LC Card 80-622482 DDC 332.1/09769 19
HG1660.U5 A28

Shulman, Julius. Polyzoides, Stephanos. Courtyard housing in Los Angeles . Berkeley , c1982. p. cm. ISBN 0-520-04251-4 LC Card

80-6057 DDC 728/.09794/94 19
NA7238.L6 P6

Shum, John. Illinois Institute of Natural Resources. Illinois State plan, energy conservation in institutions . [Springfield, Ill.] [Springfield, Va. , 1979 or 1980] ii, 76 p. : LC Card 80-622576 DDC 333.79 19
TJ163.5.B84 I43 1979

Shumway, C. Richard. (joint author) Ospina, Enrique. Disaggregated econometric analysis of U. S. slaughter beef supply /. College Station, Tex. [1980] 57 p. ; LC Card 80-621501 DDC 338.1/76213/0973 19
HD9433.U4 O84

Shurr, William. Rappaccini's children : American writers in a Calvinist world / William H. Shurr. Lexington : University Press of Kentucky, [1981] p. cm. Includes index. ISBN 0-8131-1427-6 LC Card 79-57573 DDC 810/.9/382 19
1. American literature - History and criticism. 2. Calvinism in literature. 3. Calvinism - United States. I. Title.
PS166 .S5

SIC-based demand information system for nonfuel minerals /. Schenck, George K. Washington , 1981. p. cm. LC Card 81-607810 DDC 622 s 025/.06553 19
TN295 .U4 HD9506.A2

Sichel, Werner. Applications of economic principles in public utility industries /. [Ann Arbor] , c1981. ix, 155 p. ; ISBN 0-87712-211-3 LC Card 81-936 DDC 338.4/33636/0973 19
HD2763 .A66

SICK - HEALTH EDUCATION. see PATIENT EDUCATION.

SICK LEAVE - NEW JERSEY.
New Jersey. Commission of Investigation. Interim report and recommendations of the State of New Jersey Commission of Investigation on incorrect injury leave practices in the counties. [Trenton, N.J. , 1979?] 64 p. ; LC Card 79-623334 DDC 352/.005164/09749 19
HD5115.6.U52 N56 1979

SICK - MISSOURI - SOCIOECONOMIC STATUS - STATISTICS.
United States. Ozarks Regional Commission. Missouri, socioeconomic strata health analysis . [Washington] , 1975. xi, 432 p. : LC Card 78-622054 DDC 362.1/09778 19
RA407.4.M8 U54 1975

SICK - OZARK MOUNTAIN REGION - SOCIOECONOMIC STATUS - STATISTICS.
United States. Ozarks Regional Commission. Missouri, socioeconomic strata health analysis . [Washington] , 1975. xi, 432 p. : LC Card 78-622054 DDC 362.1/09778 19
RA407.4.M8 U54 1975

SICKLE CELL ANEMIA - HOSPITALS - UNITED STATES - DIRECTORIES.
National Sickle Cell Disease Program. Directory of national, Federal, and local sickle cell disease programs /. Bethesda, Md. [1978] 30 p. ; LC Card 79-601535 DDC 362.1/96152700973 19
RC641.7/S5 N36 1978

SICKLE CELL ANEMIA - UNITED STATES - SOCIETIES, ETC. - DIRECTORIES.
National Sickle Cell Disease Program. Directory of national, Federal, and local sickle cell disease programs /. Bethesda, Md. [1978] 30 p. ; LC Card 79-601535 DDC 362.1/96152700973 19
RC641.7/S5 N36 1978

SICKNESS INSURANCE. see INSURANCE, HEALTH.

Siddall, Jean L. Rare, threatened, and endangered vascular plants in Oregon : an interim report / by Jean L. Siddall, Kenton L. Chambers, David H. Wagner. Salem, Or. : Oregon Natural Area Preserves Advisory Committee, Oregon State Land Board, Division of State Lands, [1979] iv, 109 p. : map ; 28 cm. "October 1979." Bibliography: p. 99-100. Includes index. LC Card 80-621881 DDC 582.09795 19
1. Rare plants - Oregon. 2. Endangered species - Oregon. I. Chambers, Kenton Lee, 1929- joint author. II. Wagner, David H., 1945- joint author. III. Title.
QK86.U6 S52

Sidman, Kenneth R. Howarth, John T. Economic analysis of proposed effluent guidelines, the rubber processing industry (phase II) /. Washington , 1974. 60, 5 p. :
      NYPL [JLF 80-559]

Siegchrist, Mark, 1944- Rough in brutal print : the legal sources of Browning's Red cotton night-cap country / Mark Siegchrist. Columbus : Ohio State University Press, [1981] p. cm. Includes bibliographical references and index. ISBN 0-8142-0327-2 LC Card 81-3993 DDC 821/.8 19
1. Browning, Robert, 1812-1889. Red cotton night-cap country - Sources. 2. Law in literature. 3. Caen (France) - Biography. 4. Mellerio family. 5. Mellerio, Antonio, 1827-1870. 6. Debacker, Anna Sophie Trayer, 1830-1887. I. Title.
PR4222.R353 S55

Siegel, Gail. Sequences in writing, grades K-13 /. Berkeley, Calif. , c1980. v, 55 p. : LC Card 80-155709 DDC 808/.042 19
PE1408 .S458

Siegel, Jacob S. (joint author. 0700) Shryock, Henry S. The methods and materials of demography /. [Washington] , 1975. 2 v. (xvi, 888, 20 p.) : LC Card 75-600077
HB881 .S526 1975

Siegel, Mark Richard. Tom Robbins / by Mark Siegel. Boise, Idaho : Boise State University, c1980. 52 p. ; 21 cm. (Boise State University Western writers series. no.42) Bibliography: p. 52. ISBN 0-88430-066-8 (pbk.) : LC Card 80-69013 DDC 813/.54 19
1. Robbins, Tom - Criticism and interpretation. I. Title.
PS3568.O233 Z87

Siegfried, John J. The Economics of firm size, market structure, and social performance . [Washington, D.C.?] , 1980. viii, 388 p. ; LC Card 81-600757 DDC 338.6/4/0973 19
HD60.5.U5 E26

Siemens, R. E. (Richard E.) Mussler, R. E. (Ralph E.) Electrowinning of nickel and cobalt from domestic laterite processing . [Avondale, MD] [1981] p. cm. LC Card 81-607807 DDC 622 s 669/.733 19
TN23 .U43 TN799.N6

Nilsen, D. N. Solvent extraction of nickel and copper from laterite-ammoniacal leach liquors /. Avondale, MD , 1981. p. cm. LC Card 81-38488 DDC 622 s 669/.7332 19
TN23 .U43 TN799.N6

Sierra Madre elk-deer ecology study /. Compton, Thomas. [Cheyenne] , 1975. ix, 125 p. : LC Card 76-622419 DDC 599.73/57 19
QL737.U55 C63

Sigafoos, Robert Sumner, 1920- (joint author) Reed, John Calvin, 1930- The river and the rocks . Washington , 1980. vii, 75 p. : LC Card 80-600023 DDC 557.3 s 557.52 19
QE75 .B9 no. 1471 QE122.G7

SIGILLOGRAPHY. see SEALS (NUMISMATICS)

SIGN-BOARDS. see SIGNS AND SIGN-BOARDS.

SIGNBOARDS. see SIGNS AND SIGN-BOARDS.

SIGNETS. see SEALS (NUMISMATICS)

Significance of pesticides from irrigated agriculture in California /. California. State Water Resources Control Board. [Sacramento, CA] , 1977, 1979 printing. vi, 152, [98] leaves of plates : LC Card 80-621350 DDC 628.1/68/09794 s 632/.95/09794 19
TD224.C3 A47 no. 62 SB950.2.C2

Significant decisions of the Supreme Court, 1976-1977 term /. Fein, Bruce E. - Washington , c1978. 168 p. :
      NYPL [JLE 80-1347]

SIGNS. see SIGNS AND SIGN-BOARDS.

SIGNS (ADVERTISING) see SIGNS AND SIGN-BOARDS.

SIGNS AND SIGN-BOARDS - UNITED STATES.
Anderson, Warren H. Vanishing roadside America /. Tucson , c1981. p. cm. ISBN 0-8165-0746-5 : LC Card 81-11529 DDC 741.973 19
NC998.5.A1 A5

Sikkim and western Bhutan, selected ethnic groups. United States. Central Intelligence Agency. [Washington , 1970] 1 map : LC Card 81-692567
G7653.S5E1 1970 .U5

SIKKIM (INDIA) - MAPS.
United States. Central Intelligence Agency. Sikkim. [Washington , 1965] 1 map : LC Card 81-692565
G7653.S5 1965 .U5

Silber, Stanley C. Handbook : foundation support for mental health and related services / edited by Stanley Silber. Rockville, Md. : National Institute of Mental Health, 1974. v, 89 p. ; 24 cm. (United States. Dept. of Health, Education and Welfare. DHEW publication (NIH) no. 74-658.) Bibliography: p. 89 LC Card NUC75-137492
1. Mental health - United States - Finance - Handbooks, manuals, etc. I. United States. National Institute of Mental Health. II. Title.
NYPL [JLE 80-2424]

Silence Dogood, pseud. see Franklin, Benjamin, 1706-1790.

SILENT FILMS - CATALOGS.
United States. Library of Congress. Motion Picture, Broadcasting, and Recorded Sound Division. The George Kleine collection of early motion pictures in the Library of Congress . Washington , 1980. xxxvi, 270 p. : ISBN 0-8444-0331-8 LC Card 79-607073
PN1998.A1 U57 1980
NYPL [MFLE 81-199]

SILETZ INDIANS - LEGAL STATUS, LAWS, ETC.
United States. Congress. Senate. Select Committee on Indian Affairs. Establishment of a Siletz Indian reservation . Washington , 1980. iii, 183 p. : LC Card 80-601313 DDC 346.7304/32/08997 19
KF26.5 .I4 1980

SILETZ INDIANS - RESERVATIONS.
United States. Congress. Senate. Select Committee on Indian Affairs. Establishment of a Siletz Indian reservation . Washington , 1980. iii, 183 p. : LC Card 80-601313 DDC 346.7304/32/08997 19
KF26.5 .I4 1980

SILICA.
Vinson, Robert P. SF_4 tracer gas tests of bagging-machine hood enclosures /. [Avondale, Md.] , 1981. p. cm. LC Card 80-606907 DDC 661/.06832 19
TN23 .U43 TH7697.C54

SILICON NITRIDE - ADDITIVES.
Jong, B. W. Effect of additives on sintering of silicon nitride-alumina-aluminum nitride compositions /. Washington , 1981. p. cm. LC Card 80-606862
TN23 .U43

Sill, Webster H., 1916- Plant protection : an integrated interdisciplinary approach / Webster H. Sill, Jr. Ames, Iowa : Iowa State University Press, [1981] p. cm. Bibliography: p. Includes index. ISBN 0-8138-1665-3 LC Card 81-12323 DDC 632 19
1. Plants, Protection of. 2. Pest control, Integrated. I. Title.
SB950 .S54

SILT - CALIFORNIA - COLMA CREEK.
Brown, David Wayne, 1949- Development of a model to predict the adsorption of lead from solution on a natural streambed sediment /. Washington [1981] p. cm. LC Card 81-607984 DDC 628.1/6836 19
QD547 .B76

SILURIAN PERIOD, LOWER. see GEOLOGY, STRATIGRAPHIC - ORDOVICIAN; PALEONTOLOGY - ORDOVICIAN.

Silva, Mauricio, Ing. Informe sobre el estudio "Análisis del proceso evolutivo y de las soluciones autónomas en el Proyecto San José del Pino" / preparado por equipo de investigación O.E.A., Mauricio Silva, coordinador, Carlos Armando Linares, Renaldo Lara, en coordinación con la Unidad de Evaluación de la F.S.D.V.M. : entidad ejecutora, Fundación Salvadoreña de Desarrollo y Vivienda Mínima. [Washington] : Programa Regional de Desarrollo Científico y Tecnológico, 1977. v, 39, [73] p. : ill. ; 27 cm.
At head of title: Proyectos especiales, Proyecto

Programa de Investigación de Vivienda Popular. LC Card 80-117186
1. Housing - Salvador - San José del Pino. 2. Labor and laboring classes - Dwellings - Salvador - San José del Pino. I. Linares, Carlos Armando, joint author. II. Lara, Renaldo, joint author. III. Fundación Salvadoreña de Desarrollo y Vivienda Mínima. IV. Programa Regional de Desarrollo Científico y Tecnológico. V. Title. VI. Title: Análisis del proceso evolutivo y de las soluciones autónomas en el Proyecto San José del Pino.
HD7313.S3 S54

SILVER IODIDE - ENVIRONMENTAL ASPECTS - WASHINGTON (STATE) - LEWIS RIVER WATERSHED.
Washington (State). Dept. of Ecology. Final environmental impact statement . [Olympia] [1974] ca. 100 p. in various pagings ; LC Card 76-624014 DDC 333.9/2 19
TD195.R34 W37 1974

Silver, Jennifer. Condominium conversion controls : an information bulletin of the Community and Economic Development Task Force of the Urban Consortium / prepared by Jennifer Silver and Cathy Shreve ; supported by U. S. Department of Housing and Urban Development, Office of Policy Development and Research. Washington, D.C. : The Office : for sale by the Supt. of Docs., U. S. Govt. Print. Off., 1979 [i.e.] 1980. 61 p. ; 28 cm. (Information Bulletin - Urban Consortium) "February 1980." "HUD-PDR-516." Includes bibliographical references. LC Card 80-601762 DDC 346.7304/33 19
1. Condominium (Housing) - United States. I. Shreve, Cathy, joint author. II. Urban Consortium for Technology Initiatives. Community and Economic Development Task Force. III. United States. Dept. of Housing and Urban Development. Office of Policy Development and Research. IV. Series: Urban Consortium for Technology Initiatives. Information bulletin - Urban Consortium. V. Title.
KF581 .S54

SILVER LAKE, WASH.
Washington (State). State University, Pullman. Dept. of Civil and Environmental Engineering. Study of Silver Lake eutrophication . Pullman, Wash. [1975] xviii, 298 p. : LC Card 79-625419 DDC 553.7/09797 s 363.7/3942/0979788 19
TD224.W2 S8 no. 9a QH105.W2

Silver, Larry. Directory of State building codes & regulations / compiled by Larry Silver ; edited by Cathy Americus. Mclean, Va. : National Conference of States on Building Codes & Standards, c1980. ca. 100 p. in various pagings : ports. ; 28 cm. LC Card 80-124004 DDC 016.3467304/5 016.34730645 19
1. Building laws - United States - States - Bibliography. 2. Building inspectors - United States - States - Directories. I. Americus, Cathy. II. National Conference of States on Building Codes & Standards. III. Title.
KF5701.Z95 S5

SILVER - PRICES.
United States. Congress. Senate. Committee on Agriculture, Nutrition, and Forestry. Subcommittee on Agricultural Research and General Legislation. Price volatility in the silver futures market . Washington , 1980. iv, 619 p. ; LC Card 80-602947 DDC 332.63/28 19
KF26 .A3534 1980a

Silver prices and the adequacy of Federal actions in the marketplace, 1979-80 . United States. Congress. House. Committee on Government Operations. Commerce, Consumer, and Monetary Affairs Subcommittee. Washington , 1980. v, 1203 p. : LC Card 80-603499 DDC 332.63/28 19
KF27 .G634 1980c

SILVER - PRICES - UNITED STATES.
United States. Congress. House. Committee on Government Operations. Commerce, Consumer, and Monetary Affairs Subcommittee. Silver prices and the adequacy of Federal actions in the marketplace, 1979-80 . Washington , 1980. v, 1203 p. : LC Card 80-603499 DDC 332.63/28 19
KF27 .G634 1980c

United States. Congress. Senate. Committee on Agriculture, Nutrition, and Forestry. Subcommittee on Agricultural Research and General Legislation. Price volatility in the silver futures market . Washington , 1980. iv, 619 p. ; LC Card 80-602947 DDC 332.63/28 19
KF26 .A3534 1980a

SILVER SALMON.
Alaska. Division of Commercial Fisheries. Coho salmon (Oncorhynchus kisutch) fluorescent pigment mark-recovery program for the Taku, Berners, and Chilkat Rivers in southeastern Alaska, 1972-1974 /. Juneau , 1978. vi, 75 p. : LC Card 79-620864 DDC 639/.2/09798 s 597/.55 19
SH11 .A724 no. 176 QL638.S2

Francisco, Kim. Fourth interim report of the commercial fish-technical evaluation study . [Anchorage, Alaska] , 1977. v, 50 p. : LC Card 79-625958 DDC 597.092/9798 19
QL628.A4 F73

SILVER - UNITED STATES.
United States. Commodity Futures Trading Commission. Report of the Commodity Futures Trading Commission on recent developments in the silver futures markets [prepared for the] Committee on Agriculture, Nutrition, and Forestry, United States Senate. Washington , 1980. viii, 123 p. : LC Card 80-602270 DDC 332.63/28 19
HG307.U5 U54 1980

Sim, Robert, 1949- Demand, supply, and spatial distribution of second homes in the Northeast / by Robert Sim and Marvin Kottke. Storrs, Conn. : Storrs Agricultural Experiment Station, College of Agriculture and Natural Resources, University of Connecticut, [1979] 57 p. ; 28 cm. (Research report - Storrs Agricultural Experiment Station, University of Connecticut ; 51) Cover title. "February 1979." Bibliography: p. 53-55. LC Card 80-621316 DDC 333.33/8 19
1. Second homes - Northeastern States. I. Kottke, Marvin Walter, joint author. II. Series: Connecticut. Agriculture Experiment Station, Storrs. Research report ; 51. III. Title.
HD7293 .S54

Simmons, Jack.
(joint author) Lopp, Thomas G. Fish, fresh, chilled, or frozen, whether or not whole, but not otherwise prepared or preserved, from Canada . Washington, D.C. [1980] vi, 32, 121 p. : LC Card 80-602376 DDC 382/.4566494 19
HF2651.F5 U44

Stahmer, C. B. Butter cookies from Denmark . Washington, D.C. [1980] ii, 15, 50 p. ; LC Card 80-602669 DDC 382/.456647525 19
HD9057.D42 S7

Simmons, John Barry, 1937- Conference on the Functions of Living Plant Collections in Conservation and Conservation-Orientated Research and Public Education, Kew, Eng., 1975. Conservation of threatened plants . New York , c1976. xvi, 336 p. : ISBN 0-306-32801-1 LC Card 76-20762
QK86.A1 C66 1975 NYPL [JSK 77-181 v.1]

Simmons, M. L. National Cancer Institute Symposium on Biohazards and Zoonotic Problems of Primate Procurement, Quarantine, and Research, Frederick Cancer Research Center, 1975. Biohazards and zoonotic problems of primate procurement, quarantine, and research . [Bethesda, Md.] 1975. 137 p. : LC Card 76-600529 DDC 614.4/3 19
RA641.P7 N37 1975

Simmons, Patricia M. (joint author) Hillery, Mable A. The guide to the use of street/folk/musical games in the classroom /. New York , c1976- v. <1> : LC Card 79-115771 DDC 371.3/07/8 19
LB1583.8 .H54

Simon, Edward. Delaware. Dept. of Labor. Office of Planning, Research & Evaluation. Wilmington SMSA occupational employment statistics . Newark, DE , 1978. i, 80 leaves ; LC Card 78-624189
HD5725.D3 D33 1978a NYPL [JLF 81-109]

Simon, Edward, 1946-
Delaware. Dept. of Labor. Office of Planning, Research & Evaluation. Delaware occupational employment statistics. Wilmington , 1977. 26 l. : *NYPL [*XME-8711]*

Delaware occupational employment statistics : selected manufacturing industries, 1977 / prepared by Edward Simon, George Pribula, Vinnie Sorden. Newark, DE : State of Delaware, Dept. of Labor, Office of Planning, Research & Evaluation, [1979?] iii, 76 p. ; 28 cm. "December 1979." LC Card 80-621965 DDC

331.12/57/09751 19
1. Labor supply - Delaware - Statistics. 2. Delaware - Occupations - Statistics. I. Pribula, George, joint author. II. Sorden, Vinnie, joint author. III. Delaware. Dept. of Labor. Office of Planning, Research & Evaluation. IV. Title.
HD5725.D3 S53

Delaware occupational employment statistics : selected non-manufacturing industries, 1978 / prepared by Edward Simon, George Pribula, Vinnie Sorden ; supervised by David Goland. Newark, DE : State of Delaware, Dept. of Labor, Office of Planning, Research & Evaluation, [1980] iv, 65 p. ; 28 cm. "March 1980." LC Card 80-622179 DDC 331.12/51/0009751 19
1. Labor supply - Delaware - Statistics. 2. Delaware - Occupations - Statistics. I. Pribula, George, joint author. II. Sorden, Vinnie, joint author. III. Delaware. Dept. of Labor. Office of Planning, Research & Evaluation. IV. Title.
HD5725.D3 S54

Simon, Michael A. Understanding human action : social explanation and the vision of social science / Michael A. Simon. Albany : State University of New York Press, c1981. p. cm. (SUNY series in philosophy) Bibliography: p. Includes index. ISBN 0-87395-498-X LC Card 81-5280 DDC 302 19
1. Social psychology. 2. Human behavior. 3. Social sciences - Methodology. 4. Science - Methodology. I. Title. II. Series.
HM251 .S622

Simone Weil, interpretations of a life / edited by George Abbott White. Amherst : Univerity of Massachusetts Press, 1981. p. Bibliography: p. Includes index.
CONTENTS. - Introduction / George Abbott White -- The jagged edge / Michele Murray -- Simone Weil's mind / Robert Coles -- The life and death of Simone Weil / J.M. Cameron -- Simone Weil, last things / Michele Murray -- Simone Weil's Iliad / Michael K. Feber -- Notes on Simone Weil's Iliad / Joseph H. Summers -- Simone Weil as political theorist / Sheldon S. Wolin -- Patroitism and The need for roots / Conor Cruise O'Brien -- Marxism-Leninism and the language of Politics magazine / Staughton Lynd -- Simone Weil's work experiences / George Abbott White. ISBN 0-87023-343-2 : LC Card 81-7460 DDC 194 19
1. Weil, Simone, 1909-1943 - Addresses, essays, lectures. 2. Philosophers - France - Biography - Addresses, essays, lectures. I. White, George Abbott.
B2430.W474 S617

Simonett, David S. Marine Sciences and Ocean Policy Symposium, University of California, Santa Barbara, 1979. Marine Sciences and Ocean Policy Symposium . [Santa Barbara] , 1979. xviii, 318 p. : ISBN 0-937202-00-2 LC Card 80-51564 DDC 333.91/64 19
GC64 .M37 1979

Simonetti, Martha L.
Pennsylvania. Division of Archives and Manuscripts. Descriptive list of the map collection in the Pennsylvania State Archives . Harrisburg , 1976. 178 p. ; LC Card 77-623410
Z6027.U5 P46 1976 GA447
         NYPL [Map Div. 81-152]

Pennsylvania. Historical and Museum Commission. Guide to the microfilm of the records of Pennsylvania's revolutionary governments, 1775-1790 (record group 27) in the Pennsylvania State Archives, 54 rolls . Harrisburg , 1978 [c1979] vii, 351 p. ; LC Card 79-624725
E263.P4 P37 1979   **NYPL [ISC 80-2758]**

Pennsylvania. Historical and Museum Commission. Guide to the published archives of Pennsylvania, covering the 138 volumes of Colonial records and Pennsylvania archives, series I-IX /. Harrisburg , 1976. v, 91 p. ; LC Card 79-623725 DDC 016.9748 19
F146.C622 P46 1976

Simonov, Anatoliĭ Il'ich. American-Soviet Symposium on Chemical Pollution of the Marine Environment, 1st, Odessa, 1977. First American-Soviet Symposium on Chemical Pollution of the Marine Environment, Odessa, USSR, May 24 to 28, 1977 /. Gulf Breeze, Fla. , Springfield, Va. , 1978. vi, 199 p. : LC Card 79-603026 DDC 628.1/686162 19
GC1081 .A63 1977

Simopoulos, Artemis P. The Biomedical and behavioral basis of clinical nutrition . [Bethesda, Md.] , Washington, D.C. , 1979. xii, 217 p. ;
LC Card 80-601711 DDC 616.3/9 19
RC620.5 .B52

Simpson, Bruce. Information and advocacy : needs of disabled Kentuckians / prepared by Bruce Simpson. Frankfort, Ky. : Legislative Research Commission, 1979. viii, 76 p. ; 28 cm. (Research report - Legislative Research Commission ; no. 165) Bibliography: p. 61-64. LC Card 80-621284 DDC 362.4/09769 19
1. Handicapped services - Kentucky. 2. Handicapped - Law and legislation - Kentucky. I. Kentucky. Legislative Research Commission. II. Series: Kentucky. Legislative Research Commission. Research report , no. 165. III. Title.
HV1555.K4 S55

Simpson, C. David. Effects of elephant and other wildlife on vegetation along the Chobe River, Botswana / C. David Simpson. [Lubbock] : Museum, Texas Tech University, 1978. 15 p. : ill. ; 23 cm. (Occasional papers - the Museum, Texas Tech University . no. 48) Caption title. Bibliography: p. 15. LC Card 78-621508 DDC 639.9/5 19
1. Wildlife management - Botswana. 2. Wildlife depredation - Botswana. 3. Chobe National Park, Botswana. 4. Elephants - Food. I. Series: Texas Tech University. Museum. Occasional papers , no. 48. II. Title.
SK575.B6 S54

Simpson, Claude L. Roy, Delwin A. Southeast exporting . Atlanta, Ga. , 1981. p. cm. ISBN 0-88406-146-9 : LC Card 81-6287 DDC 382/.0975 19
HF3153 .R69

Simpson, Clinton H. The development of a methodology for transportation safety planning in Virginia / by Clinton H. Simpson, Jr., and Amy J. Plevin. Charlottesville, Va. : Virginia Dept. of Transportation Safety, [1980] 37, [24] p. ; 28 cm. "A report prepared by the Virginia Highway and Transportation Research Council under the sponsorship of the Virginia Department of Transportation Safety." "February 1980." "VHTRC 80-R35." Includes bibliographical references. LC Card 80-622408 DDC 363.1/206/09755 19
1. Traffic safety - Virginia. I. Plevin, Amy J., joint author. II. Virginia Highway & Transportation Research Council. III. Virginia. Dept. of Transportation Safety. IV. Title.
HE5614.3.V8 S57

Simpson, D. G. (David G.) Seminar on the Role of Overburden Analysis in Surface Mining (1980 : Wheeling, W. VA.) Proceedings of Seminar on the Role of Overburden Analysis in Surface Mining, Wheeling, W. Va., May 6-7, 1980 /. Washington , 1981. p. cm. LC Card 81-607049 DDC 622 s 622/.31 19
TN295 .U4 TD195.S75

Simpson, Dennis Dwayne, 1943- Alcohol and illicit drug use : national followup study of admissions to drug abuse treatments in the DARP during 1969-1971 / [D. Dwayne Simpson and Michael R. Lloyd]. [Rockville, Md.] : U. S. Dept. of Health, Education, and Welfare, Public Health Service, Alcohol, Drug Abuse, and Mental Health Administration ; Washington : for sale by the Supt. of Docs., U. S. Govt. Print. Off., 1977. iv, 21 p. ; 26 cm. (Services research report - National Institute on Drug Abuse) DHEW publication ; no. (ADM)77-496 Bibliography: p. 20-21. LC Card 77-603897 DDC 362.2/922/0973 19
1. Alcoholism - United States - Longitudinal studies. 2. Drug abuse - United States - Longitudinal studies. I. Lloyd, Michael R., joint author. II. Series: National Institute on Drug Abuse. Services research report - National Institute on Drug Abuse. III. Title.
HV5292 .S53

Simpson, Edwin L. Lasker, Harry. Adult development and approaches to learning /. Washington, D.C. , 1980. viii, 74 p. : LC Card 81-601198 DDC 374/.973 19
LC5251 .L35

Simpson, James R.
Economic considerations of United States canned beef imports / James R. Simpson. Gainesville : Food and Resource Economics Dept., Agricultural Experiment Stations, Institute of Food and Agricultural Sciences, University of Florida, [1980] iii, 25 p. : ill. ; 28 cm. (Economic information report . 125) Cover title.

"January 1980." Bibliography: p. 25. LC Card 80-622178 DDC 382/.45664922/0973 19
1. Beef, Canned - Economic aspects - United States. 2. Beef, Canned - Economic aspects. I. Florida. University, Gainesville. Food and Resource Economics Dept. II. Title. III. Series.
HD9330.B343 U547

Legal and ethical implications of the U. S. agricultural structure controversy / by James R. Simpson and James S. Wershow. Gainesville, Fla. : Food and Resource Economics Dept., Institute of Food and Agricultural Sciences, University of Florida, [1980] 16 p. ; 28 cm. (Staff paper - Food and Resource Economics Department, University of Florida ; 141) "Paper presented at the 1980 Southern Agricultural Economics Association meetings in Hot Springs, Arkansas, February 4-5." Bibliography: p. 15-16. LC Card 80-622541 DDC 343.73/076 19
1. Family farms - Law and legislation - United States. 2. Irrigation laws - United States. I. Wershow, James S., joint author. II. Series: Florida. University, Gainesville. Food and Resource Economics Dept. Staff paper - Food and Resource Economics Department, University of Florida , 141. III. Title.
KF1686.Z9 S55

Simpson, Karl W. Common larvae of Chironomidae (Diptera) from New York State streams and rivers : with particular reference to the fauna of artificial substrates / Karl W. Simpson and Robert W. Bode ; New York State Department of Health, Division of Laboratories and Research, in conjunction with New York State Department of Environmental Conservation and New England Interstate Water Pollution Control Commission. Albany, N.Y. : New York State Museum, University of the State of New York, State Education Dept., 1980, c1979. v, 105 p. : ill. ; 28 cm. (Bulletin / New York State Museum . no. 439) Spine title: Common larvae of Chironomidae from New York State. Addenda slip inserted. Bibliography: p. 95-99. LC Card 80-624096 DDC 595.77/1 19
1. Chironomidae - Larvae. 2. Insects, Aquatic - New York - Larvae. 3. Insects - Larvae. 4. Insects - New York (State) - Larvae. I. Bode, Robert W. II. New York (State). Dept. of Health. Division of Laboratories and Research. III. Title. IV. Title: Common larvae of Chironomidae from New York State. V. Series: Bulletin / New York State Museum , no. 439.
QL537.C456 S55

Simpson, Kay. (joint author) Gunn, Joel. Hop Hill . San Antonio , 1977. x, 295 p. : LC Card 78-621351 DDC 976.4/65 19
E78.T4 G86

Simpson, Kimball T.
Connecticut River : 1973 water quality analysis / Kimball T. Simpson ; Water Quality Section, Division of Water Pollution Control, Massachusetts Water Resources Commission. Westborough, Mass. : The Division, 1975. 67 p. : ill. ; 28 cm. "January 1975." "Part c." Bibliography: p. 65-67. LC Card 77-622233 DDC 363.7/3942/097442 19
1. Water quality - Connecticut River watershed. I. Massachusetts. Division of Water Pollution Control. Water Quality Section. II. Title.
TD225.C74 S55

Massachusetts. Division of Water Pollution Control. Water Quality Section. Deerfield River /. Westborough , 1973- v. : LC Card 77-622223 DDC 362.7/3942/0974422 19
TD225.D24 M36 1973

Massachusetts. Division of Water Pollution Control. Water Quality Section. Deerfield River basin /. Westborough , 1977- v. : LC Card 79-620578 DDC 363.7/3942/0974422 19
TD225.D24 M36 1977

Simulated changes in water level in the Piney Point aquifer in Maryland /. Williams, James Frank, 1944- [Baltimore, Md.] , 1979. v, 50 p. : LC Card 80-621643 DDC 557.52 s 551.49/09752/4 19
QE121 .A23 no. 31 GB1199.3.M3

SIMULATED TRAINING DEVICES. see SYNTHETIC TRAINING DEVICES.

Simulating the impact of irrigation development in the Third Planning District . Brown, Ralph J. [Vermillion, S.D. , 1979] i, 90 p. : LC Card 80-621868 DDC 330 s 330.9783/3/00724 19
HF5006 .S6 no. 127 HD1739.S8

SIMULATION GAMES IN EDUCATION.
Urban gaming/simulation '77 . Ann Arbor ,
c1977. x, 57, 376 p. ; LC Card 77-151140 DDC
307.7/6/0724 19
HT165.52 .U7

SIMULATORS, TRAINING OF. see
SYNTHETIC TRAINING DEVICES.

Sinai Peninsula, Israeli settlements. United
States. Central Intelligence Agency.
[Washington , 1980] 1 map : LC Card 81-692568
G8302.S5G4 1980 .U5

Singer, Burton. Some methodological issues in
the analysis of longitudinal surveys / Burton
Singer, Seymour Spilerman. [Madison] :
University of Wisconsin-Madison, 1976. 56 p. ;
28 cm. (Discussion papers - Institute for Research on
Poverty. 331-76) Bibliography: p. 51-56. LC Card
78-624379 DDC 330/.723 19
*1. Social science research. 2. Longitudinal method. I.
Spilerman, Seymour, joint author. II. Series: Wisconsin.
University, Madison. Institute for Research on Poverty.
Discussion papers, 331-76. III. Title.*
H62 .S4775

Singer, Rexford D. Ground water quality in
southeastern Minnesota / by Rexford D. Singer,
Michael T. Osterholm, Conrad P. Straub.
Minneapolis, Minn. : Water Resources Research
Center, Graduate School, University of
Minnesota, [1980] vi, 79, 64 leaves : ill. ; 28
cm. Includes bibliographical references. LC Card
80-622728 DDC 553.7/9/097761 19
*1. Water, Underground - Minnesota. 2. Water quality -
Minnesota. I. Osterholm, Michael T., joint author. II.
Straub, Conrad P., joint author. III. Minnesota.
University. Water Resources Research Center. IV. Title.*
TD224.M6 S56

Singh, Gurbhag.
Household-income distribution, 1970-2000 / by
Gurbhag Singh. [Frankfort, Ky.] :
Commonwealth of Kentucky, Dept. of
Transportation, 1979. iv, 58 leaves ; 28 cm.
(Report - Kentucky Department of Transportation ; no.
4) Cover title: Kentucky household-income distribution,
1970-2000. Chiefly tables. LC Card 80-621282 DDC
339.2/2 19
*1. Income distribution - Kentucky. 2. Households -
Kentucky. I. Title. II. Title: Kentucky household-income
distribution, 1970-2000. III. Series: Kentucky. Dept. of
Transportation. Report - Kentucky Department of
Transportation , no. 4.*
HC107.K43 I517

Kentucky Department of Transportation income
projections / by Gurbhag Singh. [Frankfort,
Ky.] : The Dept., [1979] v, 57, [21] leaves :
ill. ; 28 cm. (Report - Commonwealth of Kentucky,
Department of Transportation ; no. 3) "September
1979." Chiefly tables. LC Card 80-622391 DDC
339.2/2/09769 19
*1. Income - Kentucky. 2. Economic forecasting -
Kentucky. I. Kentucky. Dept. of Transportation. II.
Series: Kentucky. Dept. of Transportation. Report -
Kentucky Department of Transportation , no. 3. III.
Title.*
HC107.K43 I518

**A single agency needed to manage port-of-entry
inspections--particularly at U. S. airports,
Department of Justice, Department of the
Treasury, Department of Agriculture,
Department of Health, Education, and Welfare.**
United States. General Accounting Office.
[Washington] 1973. 33 p. LC Card 73-602073
DDC 353.007 19
HE9797.5.U5 U52 1973

**SINGLE-PARENT FAMILY - SERVICES
FOR - CALIFORNIA.**
Iseri, Joyce. Low-income single mothers and
public assistance programs /. [Sacramento,
Calif.] [1980] iii, 53 leaves ; LC Card 81-621365
DDC 362.8/282/09794 19
HV699 .I75

**SINGLE-PARENT FAMILY - UNITED
STATES - STATISTICS.**
Rawlings, Stephen, 1945- Families maintained
by female householders, 1970 to 1979 /.
[Washington] , 1980. p. cm. LC Card 80-25731
DDC 312/.0973 s 306.8 19
HA203 .A218 no. 107 HQ536

**SINGLE PEOPLE - TAXATION - UNITED
STATES.**
United States. Congress. House. Committee on
Ways and Means. Tax treatment of married,
head of household, and single taxpayers .

Washington , 1980. vi, 415 p. : LC Card
80-603314 DDC 343.7305/2042 19
KF27 .W3 1980h

United States. Congress. Joint Committee on
Taxation. The income tax treatment of married
couples and single persons . Washington , 1980.
iii, 68 p. ; LC Card 80-601745 DDC
343.7305/2/024065 19
KF6355.5 .T38

**Single variable tabulations for 1973-1976 North
Carolina accidents /.** Clark, Verneta J. Chapel
Hill, N.C. [1977] xiii, 20, ca. 200 p. : LC Card
80-622768 DDC 312/.44/09756 19
HE5614.3.N6 C52

**SINGLE WOMEN - SERVICES FOR -
CALIFORNIA.**
Iseri, Joyce. Low-income single mothers and
public assistance programs /. [Sacramento,
Calif.] [1980] iii, 53 leaves ; LC Card 81-621365
DDC 362.8/282/09794 19
HV699 .I75

Singleton, Francis Dail, 1943- Solid fuels
conversion costs for Texas-coal and lignite
utilization in electric power generation and
other industries . [Austin] , 1979. v, 101 p. :
LC Card 80-620773 DDC 338.4/3662625 19
TP326.U5 S67

The singular life story of heedless Hopalong /.
Grimmelshausen, Hans Jakob Christoph von,
1625-1676. [Seltzame Springinsfeld. English.]
Detroit , 1981. p. cm. ISBN 0-8143-1688-3 LC
Card 81-10446 DDC 833/.5 19
PT1731.S7 E5 1981

Sinhala . MacDougall, Bonnie G. [Washington,
D.C.] , 1979. 3 v. : LC Card 80-601818 DDC
491/.4883421 19
PK2812 .M25

SINHALESE LANGUAGE - GRAMMAR.
MacDougall, Bonnie G. Sinhala . [Washington,
D.C.] , 1979. 3 v. : LC Card 80-601818 DDC
491/.4883421 19
PK2812 .M25

**SINHALESE LITERATURE - 20TH
CENTURY - TRANSLATIONS INTO
ENGLISH.**
An Anthology of modern writing from Sri
Lanka /. Tucson, Ariz. [1981], c1979. p. cm.
ISBN 0-8165-0702-3 : LC Card 81-1140 DDC
891/.487/08 19
PK2871.E1 A5

**Sinkhole collapse in Montgomery County,
Tennessee .** Kemmerly, Phillip R. [Nashville] ,
1980. iv, 42 p. : LC Card 80-622526 DDC
551.4/4 19
GB609.2 .K45

**SINKHOLES - TENNESSEE -
MONTGOMERY CO.**
Kemmerly, Phillip R. Sinkhole collapse in
Montgomery County, Tennessee . [Nashville] ,
1980. iv, 42 p. : LC Card 80-622526 DDC
551.4/4 19
GB609.2 .K45

SINKLER, LOUISE E. - ART COLLECTIONS.
Philadelphia. Library Company. A flock of
beautiful birds . Philadelphia , 1977. 43 p. : LC
Card 77-155254
QL674 .P34 1977   **NYPL [JFE 80-3586]**

Sinnock, Mary. Counts, I. Wilmer. A
photographic legacy /. Bloomington, Ind. ,
c1979. 72 p. :   **NYPL [IT 80-2223]**

Sinnott, Allen, 1917- Summary appraisals of the
nation's ground-water resources--New England
region / by Allen Sinnott. Washington : U. S.
G.P.O., 1981. p. cm. (Geological Survey
professional paper . 813-T) LC Card 81-607880
DDC 553.7/9/0974 19
*1. Water, Underground - New England. I. Title. II.
Series.*
GB1016.3 .S57

Sino-American relations . United States. Library
of Congress. Foreign Affairs and National
Defense Division. Washington , 1980. iii, 12
p. ; LC Card 80-603273 DDC 327.73051 19
E183.8.C5 U58 1980

The Sino-Soviet conflict : a global perspective /
edited by Herbert J. Ellison. Seattle : University
of Washington Press, c1981. p. cm. Papers
presented at a conference sponsored by the Center for
Contemporary Chinese and Soviet Studies of the
University of Washington and held at the Battelle

Research Center, Seattle, Oct. 30-Nov. 1, 1980.
Includes index. ISBN 0-295-95854-5 : LC Card
81-51279 DDC 327.51047 19
*1. China - Foreign relations - Soviet Union -
Congresses. 2. Soviet Union - Foreign relations -
China - Congresses. 3. World politics - 1975-1985 -
Congresses. I. Ellison, Herbert J. II. University of
Washington. Center for Contemporary Chinese and
Soviet Studies.*
DS740.5.S65 S56

SINTERING.
Jong, B. W. Effect of additives on sintering of
silicon nitride-alumina-aluminum nitride
compositions /. Washington , 1981. p. cm. LC
Card 80-606862
TN23 .U43

Sioux City, Iowa. United States. Public Health
Service. Pollution of interstate waters.
[Washington] 1959. 2 v. LC Card 75-80621
NYPL [JSF 81-65]

**SIPIROK REGION (INDONESIA) - SOCIAL
LIFE AND CUSTOMS.**
Siregar, Susan Rodgers. Adat, Islam, and
Christianity in a Batak homeland /. Athens,
Ohio , 1981. p. cm. ISBN 0-89680-110-1 LC
Card 81-11073 DDC 959.8/1 19
DS632.B3 S57

Sir Thomas Malory and the Morte Darthur .
Life, Page West. Charlottesville , 1980. xiii, 297
p. ; ISBN 0-8139-0868-X LC Card 80-16180
Z8545.5 .L53 PR2045   **NYPL [JFE 80-3924]**

Siregar, Susan Rodgers. Adat, Islam, and
Christianity in a Batak homeland / by Susan
Rodgers Siregar. Athens, Ohio : Ohio
University, Center for International Studies,
1981. p. cm. (Papers in international studies.
Southeast Asia series . no. 57) Bibliography: p. ISBN
0-89680-110-1 LC Card 81-11073 DDC
959.8/1 19
*1. Batak - Social life and customs. 2. Batak - Religion.
3. Sipirok region (Indonesia) - Social life and customs.
4. Christianity - Indonesia - Sipirok region. 5. Islam -
Indonesia - Sipirok region. I. Title. II. Series.*
DS632.B3 S57

Siskind, D. E.
(joint author) Stachura, Virgil J. Airblast
instrumentation and measurement techniques
for surface mine blasting /. [Washington, D.C.]
[1981] p. cm. LC Card 80-607860 DDC 622 s
622/.31 19
TN23 .U43 TN291

United States. Bureau of Mines. Structure
response and damage produced by ground
vibration from surface mine blasting /.
Washington, D.C. [1981] p. cm. LC Card
80-607825 DDC 622 s 690/.21 19
TN23 .U43 TA654.7

Sissom, W. David. (joint author) Francke, Oscar F.
Scorpions from the Virgin Islands (Arachnida,
Scorpiones) /. [Lubbock, Tex.] , 1980. 19 p. :
LC Card 80-623501 DDC 595.4/6097297/2 19
QL458.7 .F73

Sisson, Charles Adair, 1946- Tax burdens in
American agriculture : an intersectoral
comparison / Charles Adair Sisson.1st ed.
Ames : Iowa State University Press, 1981. p.
cm. Bibliography: p. ISBN 0-8138-1680-7 LC Card
81-8206 DDC 336.2/7863/0973 19
*1. Agriculture - Taxation - United States. 2. Taxation -
United States. I. Title.*
HD1295.U5 S58

Site characterization & exploration : proceedings,
specialty workshop, Northwestern University,
Evanston, Illinois, June 12-14, 1978 / C. H.
Dowding, editor ; sponsored by National
Science Foundation ; hosted by Northwestern
University ; approved for publication by the
Geotechnical Engineering Division of the
American Society of Civil Engineers. New
York : American Society of Civil Engineers,
c1979. vi, 395 p. : ill. ; 22 cm. Includes
bibliographies. LC Card 79-115992
*1. Engineering geology - Congresses. 2. Building sites -
Congresses. I. Dowding, C. H. II. United States.
National Science Foundation.*
TA705 .S537   **NYPL [JSd 81-100]**

SITE CLASSIFICATION (FORESTRY) see
FOREST SITE QUALITY.

SITE EVALUATION (FORESTRY) see
FOREST SITE QUALITY.

Site planning for solar access . Erley, Duncan. [Washington] [1979] 149 p. : LC Card 80-600615
TH7414 .E74   ***NYPL [JSF 81-159]***

SITE QUALITY (FORESTRY) see FOREST SITE QUALITY.

Sitterley, John H. Ohio. Dept. of Agriculture. Agricultural land use in Ohio. [Columbus [1979] 97 p. : LC Card 80-621589 DDC 333.76/13/09771 19
HD211.O3 O37 1979

Sitterly, Preston D. Miller, Robert A. Geologic hazards map of Tennessee /. [Nashville] , 1977. 1 map : 34 x 127 cm. Scale ca. 1:633,600. Shows earthquake, landslide, karst, and flooding areas. Published jointly with the State Planning Office, Natural Resources Section. Includes text. Bibliography. LC Card 79-691501
G3961.C5 1977 .M5
          NYPL [Map Div. 81-3060]

The situation in Iran . United States. Congress. Senate. Committee on Foreign Relations. Washington , 1980 [i.e. 1981] v, 48 p. ; LC Card 81-601146 DDC 353.03/22 19
KF26 .F6 1980t

The situation in Liberia, spring 1980--update . United States. Congress. House. Committee on Foreign Affairs. Subcommittee on Africa. Washington , 1980. iii, 25 p. ; LC Card 80-603661 DDC 325/.21/096662 19
KF27 .F625 1980c

Situation 79 . TVA Fertilizer Conference, St. Louis, 1979. [Muscle Shoals, Ala. , 1979] 76 p. ; LC Card 80-602627 DDC 631.8/1 s 338.4/766862/0973 19
S631 .U48 no. 145 HD9483.U52

SIVA (HINDU DEITY) - CULT.
Dye, Joseph M., 1944- Ways to Shiva . Philadelphia, PA , 1980. p. cm. ISBN 0-87633-038-3 : LC Card 80-25113 DDC 294.5 19
BL2001.2 .D93

Six year Idaho transportation improvement program . Idaho. Transportation Dept. [Boise] [1979] vii, 210 p. : LC Card 79-626024 DDC 380.5/068 19
HE213.I2 I3 1979

Sixty years of aeronautical research, 1917-1977 /. Anderton, David A. Washington , 1978. 89 p. : LC Card 79-601508
TL521.312 .A65   ***NYPL [JSF 81-171]***

SIZE OF INDUSTRIES. see INDUSTRIES, SIZE OF.

SIZE OF PARTICLES. see PARTICLES.

Sizing distributed systems . Mamrak, Sandra A., 1944- Washington, D.C. [1980] iv, 16 p. : LC Card 80-600061 DDC 001.64 s 001.64 19
QC100 .U57 no. 500-60 QA76.9.D5

Sjedinjene Američke Države. see United States.

Skaadel, J. United Nations. Industrial Development Organization. A fertilizer bulk blending and bagging plant /. New York , 1976. vii, 31 p. : LC Card 81-465178 DDC 300 s 668/.62 19
JX1977 .A2 ID/SER.F/8 TP963

Skaggs, Samuel. A design for agriculture in the Tanana Loop : appropriate technology and small-scale farming / prepared for State of Alaska, Office of Northern Technology, by Fairbanks Environmental Center, Samuel Skaggs, Wendy Warnick. [Juneau] : The Office, 1978. ii, 61 p. : ill. ; 28 cm. Includes bibliographical references. LC Card 79-620899 DDC 338.1/09798/6 19
1. Agriculture - Alaska - Tanana Loop. 2. Agriculture - Alaska - Tanana Loop - Energy consumption. 3. Renewable energy sources - Alaska - Tanana Loop. 4. Agriculture and state - Alaska - Tanana Loop. 5. Soil conservation - Alaska - Tanana Loop. 6. Cottage industries - Alaska - Tanana Loop. 7. Tanana Loop, Alaska - Industries. I. Warnick, Wendy, joint author. II. Fairbanks Environmental Center. III. Alaska. Office of Northern Technology. IV. Title.
S451.A3 S58

SKATEBOARDING - ACCIDENTS AND INJURIES.
United States. Consumer Product Safety Commission. Directorate for Hazard Identification and Analysis. Division of

Program Analysis. Hazard analysis injuries associated with skateboards (product code 1333) /. [Washington] , 1978. 130, [1] p. : LC Card 78-602300
GV859.8 .U54 1978   ***NYPL [JLF 81-381]***

SKATEBOARDING - UNITED STATES - ACCIDENTS AND INJURIES - STATISTICS.
United States. Consumer Product Safety Commission. Directorate for Hazard Identification and Analysis. Division of Program Analysis. Hazard analysis injuries associated with skateboards (product code 1333) /. [Washington] , 1978. 130, [1] p. : LC Card 78-602300
GV859.8 .U54 1978   ***NYPL [JLF 81-381]***

Skeen, David. Disclosure of criminal and traffic records : a law enforcement perspective / by David Skeen. Grand Forks, N.D. : Bureau of Governmental Affairs, University of North Dakota, [1980] i, 22, 3 p. ; 28 cm. (Special report / Bureau of Governmental Affairs, University of North Dakota . no. 58) Cover title. "September 1980." LC Card 81-620708 DDC 320.9784 s 345.73/056 320.9784 s 347.30556 19
1. Criminal registers - North Dakota. 2. Traffic violations - North Dakota. 3. Privacy, Right of - North Dakota. I. Series: Special report (University of North Dakota, Bureau of Governmental Affairs) , no. 58. II. Title.
JK6401 .N65 no. 58 KFN9192.5

SKELETAL REMAINS. see MAN, PREHISTORIC.

SKEPTICISM.
Klein, Peter D. (Peter David), 1940- Certainty, a refutation of scepticism /. Minneapolis , 1981. p. cm. ISBN 0-8166-0995-0 : LC Card 81-13040 DDC 121/.63 19
BD171 .K55

SKI LIFTS - LAW AND LEGISLATION - MAINE.
Maine. Board of Elevator and Tramway Safety. State of Maine elevator and tramway rules . Augusta, Me. [1979?] 91 p. ; LC Card 80-624243 DDC 343.741/07872183 347.41037872183 19
KFM459.7 .A4 1979

Skid road . Morgan, Murray Cromwell, 1916- Seattle , 1981 [c1960] p. cm. ISBN 0-295-95846-4 (pbk.) : LC Card 81-11701 DDC 979.7/77 19
F899.S457 M67 1981

SKIN.
Sokolov, Vladimir Evgen'evich. Mammal skin /. Berkeley , c1981. p. cm. ISBN 0-520-03198-9 LC Card 81-3037 DDC 599.04/7 19
QL739 .S68

SKIN - CANCER - ETIOLOGY.
Cutchis, Pythagoras. On the linkage of solar ultraviolet radiation to skin cancer . Washington, D.C. , 1978. xiv, 146, [13] p. : LC Card 79-602135 DDC 616.99/477071 19
RC280.S5 C83

SKIN - CANCER - STATISTICS.
Cutchis, Pythagoras. On the linkage of solar ultraviolet radiation to skin cancer . Washington, D.C. , 1978. xiv, 146, [13] p. : LC Card 79-602135 DDC 616.99/477071 19
RC280.S5 C83

SKIN - PAPILLARY RIDGES. see FINGERPRINTS.

SKIS AND SKIING - ECONOMIC ASPECTS - UNITED STATES.
United States. Forest Service. Planning considerations for winter sports resort development /. [Washington] , 1973. iii, 53 p. :
          NYPL [JLF 79-1344]

SKIS AND SKIING - IDAHO - STATISTICS.
Idaho. University. Wildland Recreation Management Dept. Idaho ski study, winter 1977-1978 /. [Moscow, Idaho] [1979] iv, 72 p. : LC Card 80-621844 DDC 338.4/779693/09796 19
GV854.5.I2 I3 1979

SKIS AND SKIING - NORTHEASTERN STATES.
Kottke, Marvin Walter. Projected changes in Northeastern skiing participation and supply capacity as influenced by a changing economy /. Storrs, Conn. [1980] 38 p. ; LC Card

80-624079 DDC 796.93/0974 19
GV854.5.N58 K67

SKOOKUMCHUCK RIVER - FLOODS.
United States. Army. Corps of Engineers. Seattle, Washington, District. Flood plain information: Skookumchuck River, Bucoda, Washington. [Seattle] 1968. ii, 31 p. LC Card 80-510638 DDC 363.3/493/0979779 19
GB1399.4.W2 U54 1968

Skow, Milford L. Creating a safer environment in U. S. coal mines : the Bureau of Mines methane control program, 1964-79 / by Milford L. Skow, Ann G. Kim, and Maurice Deul. [Washington, D.C. : U. S. Dept. of the Interior, Bureau of Mines] : for sale by the Supt. of Docs., U. S. Govt. Print. Off., 1980. 50 p. : ill. ; 28 cm. (A Bureau of Mines impact report) Bibliography: p. 46-50. LC Card 80-602933 DDC 622/.8 19
1. Coal mines and mining - United States - Safety measures. I. Kim, Ann G., joint author. II. Deul, Maurice, joint author. III. United States. Bureau of Mines. IV. Series: United States. Bureau of Mines. Bureau of Mines impact report. V. Title.
TN295 .S55

Skvarla, John J. (joint author) Nowicke, Joan W. Pollen morphology and phylogenetic relationships of the Berberidaceae /. Washington , 1981. p. cm. LC Card 80-21960 DDC 581 s 583/.117 19
QK1 .S2747 no. 50 QK495.B45

Sky pioneering . Reinhold, Ruth M. Tucson , 1982. p. cm. ISBN 0-8165-0737-6 : LC Card 81-11514 DDC 387.7/09791 19
TL522.A6 R44

Slack, James Richard, 1944- Smith, Richard A. A study of trends in total phosphorus measurements at NASQAN stations /. Reston, Va. [1981] p. cm. LC Card 81-607899 DDC 363.7/394 19
TD427.P56 S64

Slack, John F. Mineral resources of the Big Frog wilderness study area and additions, Polk County, Tennessee and Fannin County, Georgia / by John F. Slack and Gertrude C. Gazdik and Maynard L. Dunn, Jr. Washington : U. S. G.P.O., 1981. p. cm. (Studies related to wilderness--study areas) Geological Survey bulletin ; 1531 Bibliography: p. LC Card 81-607907 DDC 557.3 s 557.68/875 19
1. Mines and mineral resources - Tennessee - Polk County. 2. Mines and mineral resources - Georgia - Fannin County. I. Gazdik, Gertrude C. II. Dunn, Maynard L. III. Title. IV. Series.
QE75 .B9 no. 1531 TN24.T

SLACK, JOHN MARK, 1915-1980 - ADDRESSES, ESSAYS, LECTURES.
United States. 96th Congress, 2d session, 1980. Memorial services held in the House of Representatives and Senate of the United States, together with remarks presented in eulogy of John M. Slack, late a Representative from West Virginia /. Washington , 1980. vii, 69 p., [1] leaf of plates : LC Card 80-603140 DDC 328.73/092/4 19
E840.8.S55 U54 1980

Slackman, Joel N. Costs of the National Service Act (H.R. 2206) : a technical analysis / the Congress of the United States, Congressional Budget Office. [Washington, D.C.] : The Office, c1980. xii, 42 p. ; 27 cm. "December 1980." Item 1005-C Includes bibliographical references. LC Card 81-600733 DDC 355.2/236/0973 19
1. Youth - Employment - United States. 2. Military service, Voluntary - United States. 3. National service - United States. I. United States. Congressional Budget Office. II. Title.
HD6273 .S57

SLAG.
Evaluation of synthetic fluorspar in BOF slags /. Washington, D.C. [1981] p. cm. LC Card 81-607971 DDC 622 s 669/.142 19
TN23 .U43 TN747

Paige, J. I. (Jack I.) Introduction of sulfur into copper converter slags to produce copper matte /. Washington, D.C. , 1981. p. cm. LC Card 81-607890 DDC 622 s 669/.3 19
TN23 .U43 TN780

Slajchert, Margaret. Vermont. State Planning Office. The people book. Montpelier, Vt. , 1978. v, 70 p. : LC Card 79-623073 DDC

312/.8/09743 19
HA673 .S72 1978

Slater, Charles C. Macro-marketing Seminar, 2d, University of Colorado, 1977. Macro-marketing . Boulder , c1978. vii, 477 p. ; *HF5415.125 .M32 1976*
NYPL [JLF 80-1496]

Slatick, Eugene R. Coal data, a reference / prepared by Eugene R. Slatick. [2nd ed.]. Washington, D.C. : U. S. Dept. of Energy, Energy Information Administration, Assistant Administrator for Energy Data Operations : For sale by the Supt. of Docs., U. S. G.P.O., 1980. vii, 53 p. : ill. ; 28 cm. "July 1980." "DOE/EIA-0064 (80). UC-90." Bibliography: p. 51-52. LC Card 80-603221 DDC 553.2/4/0973 19 *1. Coal trade - United States. I. United States. Energy Information Administration. Office of Energy Data Operations. II. Title.* *HD9545 .S5 1980*

Slatkin, Nora. Hillier, Pat. U. S. ground forces . [Washington, D.C.] , 1980. xxiii, 87 p. : LC Card 81-600683 DDC 355/.033073 19 *UA23 .H513*

SLAUGHTER, JOHN BROOKS, 1934- United States. Congress. Senate. Committee on Labor and Human Resources. Nomination . Washington , 19. ii 28 p. ; LC Card 80-604090 DDC 353.0085/5 19 *KF26 .L27 1980m*

SLAVE-TRADE. United States. 14th Congress, 2d session, 1816-1817. Joint resolution for abolishing the traffick in slaves. [Washington? D. C.] 1817. 2 p. ; ***NYPL [Sc Micro F-8079]***

SLAVE-TRADE - AFRICA - CONGRESSES. The Abolition of the Atlantic slave trade . Madison , 1981. p. cm. ISBN 0-299-08490-6 : LC Card 80-52290 DDC 382/.44 19 *HT855 .A26*

SLAVE-TRADE - AFRICA - HISTORY - 18TH CENTURY. Palmer, Colin A., 1942- Human cargoes . Urbana , c1981. xv, 183 p. : ISBN 0-252-00846-4 : LC Card 81-3326 DDC 3-82/.44/0941 19 *HT1161 .P34*

SLAVE-TRADE - AMERICA - CONGRESSES. The Abolition of the Atlantic slave trade . Madison , 1981. p. cm. ISBN 0-299-08490-6 : LC Card 80-52290 DDC 382/.44 19 *HT855 .A26*

SLAVE-TRADE - EUROPE - CONGRESSES. The Abolition of the Atlantic slave trade . Madison , 1981. p. cm. ISBN 0-299-08490-6 : LC Card 80-52290 DDC 382/.44 19 *HT855 .A26*

SLAVE-TRADE - GREAT BRITAIN - HISTORY - 18TH CENTURY. Palmer, Colin A., 1942- Human cargoes . Urbana , c1981. xv, 183 p. : ISBN 0-252-00846-4 : LC Card 81-3326 DDC 3-82/.44/0941 19 *HT1161 .P34*

SLAVE-TRADE - LATIN AMERICA - HISTORY - 18TH CENTURY. Palmer, Colin A., 1942- Human cargoes . Urbana , c1981. xv, 183 p. : ISBN 0-252-00846-4 : LC Card 81-3326 DDC 3-82/.44/0941 19 *HT1161 .P34*

SLAVERY IN THE U. S. see SLAVERY IN THE UNITED STATES.

SLAVERY IN THE UNITED STATES. New York (State). Legislature. Joint Committee on So Much of the Governor's Message as Relates to Domestic Slavery. Report. [Albany? 1836]. 5 p. ; LC Card CA26-298 ***NYPL [Sc Micro F-9174]***

Slavic-American imprints . Lovejoy Library. [Edwardsville, Ill.] , 1979- v. ; LC Card 80-622920 DDC 016.947 19 *Z2483 .L68 1972 Suppl.*

SLAVIC IMPRINTS - UNITED STATES - CATALOGS. Lovejoy Library. Slavic-American imprints . [Edwardsville, Ill.] , 1979- v. ; LC Card 80-622920 DDC 016.947 19 *Z2483 .L68 1972 Suppl.*

SLIMES (MINING) Thompson, Philip, 1950- Development of a continuous flotation process for removal of insoluble slimes from potash ore /. Washington [1980] p. cm. LC Card 80-607785 DDC 622/.3636 19 *TN23 .U43*

Sloan, Helen Farr, 1911- Kraft, James. John Sloan in Santa Fe . Washington, D.C. , 1981. p. cm. ISBN 0-86528-011-8 LC Card 81-607831 DDC 759.13 19 *ND237.S476 A4 1981*

SLOAN, JOHN, 1871-1951 - EXHIBITIONS. Kraft, James. John Sloan in Santa Fe . Washington, D.C. , 1981. p. cm. ISBN 0-86528-011-8 LC Card 81-607831 DDC 759.13 19 *ND237.S476 A4 1981*

Slocum, Alfred A. Bakke, Allan Paul, petitioner. Allan Bakke versus Regents of the University of California /. Dobbs Ferry, N.Y. , 1978- v. ; ISBN 0-379-20297-2 : LC Card 78-3573 *KF228.B34 A3* ***NYPL [Sc E 80-286]***

Slone, John. Duncan, J. T. Skip. Citizen crime prevention tactics . Washington, D.C. [1980] v, 116 p. ; LC Card 80-602862 DDC 016.3628/8 19 *HV6791 .D86*

Slope class map, Chickies Creek watershed, Lancaster and Lebanon Counties, Pennsylvania /. United States. Soil Conservation Service. Hyattsville, Md. [1978] 1 map : LC Card 81-690268 *G3822.C45C28 1978 .U5*

SLOPES (PHYSICAL GEOGRAPHY) - CALIFORNIA - COAST RANGE. Bedrossian, Trinda L. Geology and slope stability in selected parts of the Geysers Geothermal Resources Area . Sacramento, CA , 1980. vi, 65 p. : LC Card 80-622288 DDC 557.94 s 624.1/51/097941 19 *TN24.C2 A33 no. 142 QE90.C58*

SLOPES (PHYSICAL GEOGRAPHY) - PENNSYLVANIA - CHICKIES CREEK WATERSHED - MAPS. United States. Soil Conservation Service. Slope class map, Chickies Creek watershed, Lancaster and Lebanon Counties, Pennsylvania /. Hyattsville, Md. [1978] 1 map : LC Card 81-690268 *G3822.C45C28 1978 .U5*

SLOPES (SOIL MECHANICS) Yokel, Felix Y. Recommended technical provisions for construction practice in shoring and sloping of trenches and excavations /. Washington, DC [1980] xvi, 68 p. : LC Card 80-600068 DDC 690/.02/18 s 624.1/52 19 *TA435 .U58 no. 127 TA770*

Slovak, Jeffrey S. (joint author) Greisinger, George W. Civil service systems . Washington, D.C. [1979] xxii, 141, [64] p. : LC Card 80-601604 DDC 352.2/0973 19 *HV7935 .G73*

Slowick, Judith. Defense dependency in Connecticut / prepared by Judith Slowick. [Hartford, Conn.] : Economic Development Planning, Connecticut Department of Economic Development, [1980] 99 p. : maps ; 28 cm. "February 1, 1980." Bibliography: p. 98. LC Card 80-621533 DDC 330.9746/043 19 *1. Economic assistance, Domestic - Connecticut. 2. Disarmament - Economic aspects - Connecticut. 3. Industry and state - Connecticut. 4. Defense contracts - Connecticut. I. Connecticut. Dept. of Economic Development. Economic Development Planning. II. Title.* *HC107.C83 P635*

SLUM CLEARANCE. see CITY PLANNING; HOUSING.

SLURRY. Colaizzi, Gary J. Pumped-slurry backfilling of abandoned coal mine workings for subsidence control at Rock Springs, Wyoming /. Washington , 1981. p. cm. LC Card 80-39876 DDC 622 s 622/.334 19 *TN295 .U4 TN319*

SLURRY - DEWATERING. Backer, R. R. (Ronald R.) Fine coal refuse dewatering /. Washington [1981] p. cm. LC Card 81-607041 DDC 622 s 662.6/23 19 *TN23 .U43 TN816*

Small, Alden. (joint auhtor) Rush, Thomas Vale. The prevalence and intensity of alcohol and illicit drug use in Pennsylvania. [Harrisburg] 1977 2 v. ***NYPL [JLF 79-928]***

Small and medium-sized family farms and Presidential Commission on World Hunger report . United States. Congress. House. Committee on Agriculture. Subcommittee on Family Farms, Rural Development, and Special Studies. Washington , 1980. iii, 167 p. ; LC Card 80-603660 DDC 338.1/9 19 *KF27 .A344 1980b*

SMALL ARMS. see FIREARMS.

SMALL BUSINESS. United States. Occupational Safety and Health Administration. Policy Analysis and Integration Staff. Occupational Safety and Health Administration's impact on small business . [Washington] , 1976. v, 55, [71] p. : LC Card 77-602353 *HD7654 .U55 1976* ***NYPL [*XME-9522]***

University of Georgia. International Trade and Development Center. A small business export development program /. Athens, Ga. , c1980. 24 p. : LC Card 80-624106 DDC 658.8/48 19 *HF1009.5 .U55 1980*

SMALL BUSINESS - ACCOUNTING. see ACCOUNTING.

Small Business Administration loans to veterans . United States. Congress. House. Committee on Veterans' Affairs. Subcommittee on Special Investigations. Washington , 1981. iii, 223 p. ; LC Card 81-600813 DDC 353.0082/048045 19 *KF27 .V458 1980c*

Small Business Administration 8(a) pilot program . United States. Congress. Senate. Select Committee on Small Business. Washington , 1981. iii, 84 p. ; LC Card 81-601381 DDC 353.0071/2 19 *KF26.5 .S6 1981b*

Small Business Administration's veterans' assistance programs . United States. Congress. Senate. Select Committee on Small Business. Washington , 1980. iii, 97 p. ; LC Card 80-603678 DDC 355.1/15 19 *KF26.5 .S6 1980m*

Small business and Department of Energy research and development programs . United States. Congress. Senate. Select Committee on Small Business. Washington , 1980. iii, 77 p. : LC Card 80-602727 DDC 353.0082/048045 19 *KF26.5 .S6 1980e*

Small business & innovation . United States. Small Business Administration. Office of the Chief Counsel for Advocacy. [Washington] , 1979. 130 p. in various pagings : LC Card 79-603309 *HD2346.U5 U57 1979* ***NYPL [JLF 81-384]***

Small business automobile dealers . United States. Congress. Senate. Select Committee on Small Business. Washington , 1980. iii, 294 p. : LC Card 80-602971 DDC 381/.456292/0973 19 *KF26.5 .S6 1980f*

Small business energy loan program. United States. Congress. Senate. Select Committee on Small Business. S. 2224, small business energy loan program . Washington , 1980. iii, 148 p. : LC Card 80-602162 DDC 346.7304/679158/0262 19 *KF26.5 .S6 1980a*

Small business export assistance . United States. Congress. Senate. Committee on Banking, Housing and Urban Affairs. Subcommittee on International Finance. Washington , 1980. iv, 143 p. ; LC Card 80-603092 DDC 343.73/0878 19 *KF26 .B3946 1980d*

A small business export development program /. University of Georgia. International Trade and Development Center. Athens, Ga. , c1980. 24 p. : LC Card 80-624106 DDC 658.8/48 19 *HF1009.5 .U55 1980*

SMALL BUSINESS - FINANCE. Sullivan, A. Charlene. Credit and collections for small stores /. Washington, D.C. , 1980. v, 67 p. : LC Card 81-600882 DDC 658.8/8 19 *HD30 .U5 no. 43 HG3751*

SMALL BUSINESS - GOVERNMENT POLICY - NEW YORK (STATE) New York (State). Legislature. Assembly.

Office of the Speaker. Small business, New York's forgotten majority. [Albany, N.Y.] [1980] 103 p. : LC Card 81-621131 DDC 338.6/42/09747 19
HD2346.U52 N556 1980

SMALL BUSINESS - GOVERNMENT POLICY - UNITED STATES.

United States. Congress. Senate. Select Committee on Small Business. The role of small business in the nation's economic recovery . Washington , 1981. iii, 207 p. : LC Card 81-601882 DDC 338.6/42/0973 19
KF26.5 .S6 1981a

Small Business Innovation Act of 1979. United States. Congress. Senate. Select Committee on Small Business. S. 1860, Small Business Innovation Act of 1979 . Washington , 1980 [i.e. 1981] iv, 611 p. : LC Card 81-601186 DDC 346.73/0652 347.306652 19
KF26.5 .S6 1980x

Small business innovation act of 1980. United States. Congress. House. Committee on Small Business. H.R. 5607--Small business innovation act of 1980 . Washington , 1980. v, 459 p. ; LC Card 80-603308 DDC 346.73/0652 19
KF27 .S6 1980a

SMALL BUSINESS INVESTMENT COMPANIES.

United States. Congress. Senate. Committee on Banking, Housing and Urban Affairs. Subcommittee on Securities. Federal securities laws and small business legislation . Washington , 1980. ix, 812 p. : LC Card 80-603327 DDC 346.73/0666 19
KF26 .B3954 1980a

SMALL BUSINESS INVESTMENT COMPANIES - UNITED STATES.

United States. Congress. House. Committee on Interstate and Foreign Commerce. Subcommittee on Consumer Protection and Finance. Venture Capital Improvements Acts of 1980 . Washington , 1980. iii, 244 p. : LC Card 81-600877 DDC 346.73/0922 347.306922 19
KF27 .I554 1980e

SMALL BUSINESS - KOREA.

Ho, Sam P. S. Small-scale enterprises in Korea and Taiwan /. Washington, D.C. , 1980. vi, 151 p. ; LC Card 80-134204 DDC 338.6/42/0951249 19
HD2346.K6 H6

SMALL BUSINESS - LAW AND LEGISLATION - FLORIDA.

Florida. Legislature. Senate. Economic, Community, and Consumer Affairs Committee. A review of section 288.39(6), Florida statutes, Small Business Advisory Council /. [Tallahassee, Fla.] [1980] i, 22 p. ; LC Card 81-621214 DDC 346.759/0652 347.5906652 19
KFF234 .A25 1980

SMALL BUSINESS - LAW AND LEGISLATION - MISSISSIPPI.

Gotthelf, Harold, 1916- Government regulations affecting small retail businesses in Mississippi /. Jackson, Miss. [1979] v, 115 p. : LC Card 80-620872 DDC 346.762/0652 19
KFM6881.A1 G67 1979

SMALL BUSINESS - LAW AND LEGISLATION - UNITED STATES.

United States. Congress. House. Committee on Small Business. Government procurement from small and small disadvantaged businesses (Public Law 95-507 and accompanying reports) /. Washington , 1980. v, 165 p. ; LC Card 80-602069 DDC 346.73/0652 19
KF843.5 .S42

United States. Congress. House. Committee on Small Business. H.R. 5607--Small business innovation act of 1980 . Washington , 1980. v, 459 p. ; LC Card 80-603308 DDC 346.73/0652 19
KF27 .S6 1980a

United States. Congress. House. Committee on Small Business. Subcommittee on Antitrust and Restraint of Trade Activities Affecting Small Business. Small Business Motor Fuel Marketer Preservation Act-H.R. 6722 . Washington , 1980. vii, 835 p. : LC Card 80-604087 DDC 343.73/078629287 347.30378629287 19
KF27 .S6335 1980b

United States. Congress. House. Committee on Small Business. Subcommittee on Minority Enterprise and General Oversight. H.R. 2377,

H.R. 2379, and Small Business Administration activities . Washington , 1977. iv, 188 p. ; LC Card 77-604012
KF27 .S65 1977c

United States. Congress. House. Committee on Small Business. Subcommittee on SBA and SBIC Authority and General Small Business Problems. Judicial access/court costs--H.R. 5103 and H.R. 6429 . Washington , 1980. iv, 335 p. : LC Card 80-603019 DDC 346.73/0652/0269 19
KF27 .S6814 1980a

United States. Congress. House. Committee on Small Business. Subcommittee on SBA and SBIC Authority and General Small Business Problems. SBA legislative request . Washington , 1980. iii, 46 p. ; LC Card 80-603112 DDC 346.73/0652 19
KF27 .S6814 1980

United States. Congress. Senate. Committee on Banking, Housing and Urban Affairs. Subcommittee on International Finance. Small business export assistance . Washington , 1980. iv, 143 p. ; LC Card 80-603092 DDC 343.73/0878 19
KF26 .B3946 1980d

United States. Congress. Senate. Committee on Banking, Housing and Urban Affairs. Subcommittee on Securities. Federal securities laws and small business legislation . Washington , 1980. ix, 812 p. : LC Card 80-603327 DDC 346.73/0666 19
KF26 .B3954 1980a

United States. Congress. Senate. Select Committee on Small Business. Customer pickup proposals and their impact on small business and the Robinson-Patman act . Washington , 1980. iii, 266 p. : LC Card 80-602985 DDC 338.5/2 19
KF26.5 .S6 1980d

United States. Congress. Senate. Select Committee on Small Business. H.R. 5612, to amend the Small Business Act to extend the current SBA 8(a) pilot program . Washington , 1980. iii, 211 p. : LC Card 80-604024 DDC 346.73/0652 347.306652 19
KF26.5 S6 1980u

United States. Congress. Senate. Select Committee on Small Business. S. 1860, Small Business Innovation Act of 1979 . Washington , 1980 [i.e. 1981] iv, 611 p. : LC Card 81-601186 DDC 346.73/0652 347.306652 19
KF26.5 .S6 1980x

United States. Congress. Senate. Select Committee on Small Business. S. 2040, the Small business export expansion act, S. 2104, the Small business export development act . Washington , 1980. iii, 178 p. ; LC Card 80-602190 DDC 343.73/0878 19
KF26.5 .S6 1980c

United States. Congress. Senate. Select Committee on Small Business. S. 2224, small business energy loan program . Washington , 1980. iii, 148 p. ; LC Card 80-602162 DDC 346.7304/679158/0262 19
KF26.5 .S6 1980a

United States. Congress. Senate. Select Committee on Small Business. S. 2635, the Small business energy conservation act . Washington , 1980. iii, 30 p. ; LC Card 80-603682 DDC 346.7304/67916/02632 347.30646791602632 19
KF26.5 .S6 1980l

United States. Congress. Senate. Select Committee on Small Business. Subcommittee on Government Procurement. S. 2873, to provide SBA loans to small businesses in the communications industry . Washington , 1980. iii, 52 p. ; LC Card 80-603716 DDC 346.73/0652 347.30165252 19
KF26.5 .S625 1980

SMALL BUSINESS - MANAGEMENT.

Haas, Raymond M. Long-range planning for small businesses. [Bloomington] 1964. ix, 133 p. LC Card 64-8438 *NYPL [JLD 78-3496]*

Small Business Motor Fuel Marketer Preservation Act-H.R. 6722 . United States. Congress. House. Committee on Small Business. Subcommittee on Antitrust and Restraint of Trade Activities Affecting Small Business.

Washington , 1980. vii, 835 p. : LC Card 80-604087 DDC 343.73/078629287 347.30378629287 19
KF27 .S6335 1980b

Small Business Motor Fuel Marketer Preservation Act of 1980 . United States. Congress. Senate. Committee on the Judiciary. Subcommittee on Antitrust, Monopoly, and Business Rights. Washington , 1981. v, 491 p. : LC Card 81-601869 DDC 343.73/088566553827 347.30388566553827 19
KF26 .J835 1980d

Small business, New York's forgotten majority. New York (State). Legislature. Assembly. Office of the Speaker. [Albany, N.Y.] [1980] 103 p. : LC Card 81-621131 DDC 338.6/42/09747 19
HD2346.U52 N556 1980

Small business preferential procurement programs . United States. Congress. House. Committee on Small Business. Subcommittee on General Oversight and Minority Enterprise. Washington , 1980 [i.e. 1981] iv, 640 p. : LC Card 81-600845 DDC 353.0071/2 19
KF27 .S64 1980l

Small business reports. Washington : U. S. Dept. of Commerce, Bureau of the Census, [1981] p. cm. (1977 enterprise statistics . ES77-3) LC Card 81-607797 DDC 338.0973 s 338.6/42/0973 19
1. Small business - United States - Statistics. I. United States. Bureau of the Census. II. Series.
HC106.7 .A14 ES77-3 HD2346.U5

SMALL BUSINESS - TAIWAN.

Ho, Sam P. S. Small-scale enterprises in Korea and Taiwan /. Washington, D.C. , 1980. vi, 151 p. ; LC Card 80-134204 DDC 338.6/42/0951249 19
HD2346.K6 H6

SMALL BUSINESS - TAXATION - UNITED STATES.

United States. Congress. Senate. Committee on Governmental Affairs. Subcommittee on Oversight of Government Management. Internal Revenue Service collection practices . Washington , 1980. v, 29 p. ; LC Card 80-603867 DDC 353.0072/4 19
HD2346.U5 U515 1980a

United States. Congress. Senate. Committee on Governmental Affairs. Subcommittee on Oversight of Government Management. IRS summary collection policy impact on small business . Washington , 1980. iv, 415 p. ; LC Card 80-603735 DDC 338.6/42/0973 19
KF26 .G676 1980a

United States. Congress. Senate. Select Committee on Small Business. Subcommittee on Taxation, Financing, and Investment. Procedural difficulties encountered by smaller business in dealing with the IRS . Washington , 1980. iii, 172 p. ; LC Card 80-603483 DDC 353.0072/4 19
KF26.5 .S686 1980

SMALL BUSINESS - UNITED STATES.

Bunn, Verne A. Buying and selling a small business /. Washington, D.C. , 1979. v, 122 p. ; LC Card 80-600978 DDC 658/.022 19
HD2346.U5 B8 1979

United States. Congress. House. Committee on Science and Technology. Innovation . Washington , 1980. v, 228 p. ; LC Card 80-602110 DDC 338/.06 19
KF27 .S39 1979f

United States. Congress. House. Committee on Science and Technology. Subcommittee on Investigation and Oversight. Small, high technology firms and innovation . Washington , 1980 [i.e. 1981] xviii, 791 p. : LC Card 81-600956 DDC 338.6/42/0973 19
KF27 .S3975 1979b

United States. Congress. House. Committee on Science and Technology. Subcommittee on Investigations and Oversight. Small, high technology firms and innovation . Washington , 1980. v, 65 p. ; LC Card 80-602579 DDC 338.4/76/0973 19
T173.8 .U5 1980

United States. Congress. House. Committee on Small Business. Report, "America's small business economy agenda for action" . Washington , 1980. iii, 111 p. ; LC Card

80-602911   DDC 338.6/42/0973 19
KF27 .S6 1980

United States. Congress. House. Committee on
Small Business. Subcommittee on Antitrust and
Restraint of Trade Activities Affecting Small
Business. Conglomerate mergers--their effects
on small business and local communities .
Washington , 1980. vi, 1217 p. :   LC Card
    80-603730   DDC 338.8/3/0973 19
KF27 .S6335 1980

United States. Congress. House. Committee on
Small Business. Subcommittee on Energy,
Environment, Safety and Research. Role of
government funding and its impact on small
business in the solar energy industry .
Washington , 1979 i.e. 1980- v. :   LC Card
    80-603085   DDC 338.4/362147/0973 19
KF27 .S639 1979b

United States. Congress. House. Committee on
Small Business. Subcommittee on General
Oversight and Minority Enterprise. Contracting
out/government competition . Washington ,
1980. iv, 276 p. :   LC Card 81-600619   DDC
    353.0071/1 19
KF27 .S64 1980i

United States. Congress. House. Committee on
Small Business. Subcommittee on General
Oversight and Minority Enterprise. Impact of
inflation on small business . Washington , 1980.
iv, 343 p. :   LC Card 80-603791   DDC
    338.6/42/0973 19
KF27 .S64 1980f

United States. Congress. House. Committee on
Small Business. Subcommittee on General
Oversight and Minority Enterprise. SBA
proposed size standards . Washington , 1980-
v. ;   LC Card 80-603083   DDC 338.6/42/0973 19
KF27 .S64 1980b

United States. Congress. House. Committee on
Small Business. Subcommittee on General
Oversight and Minority Enterprise. Small
business preferential procurement programs .
Washington , 1980 [i.e. 1981] iii, 640 p. :   LC
    Card 81-600845   DDC 353.0071/2 19
KF27 .S64 1980l

United States. Congress. House. Committee on
Small Business. Subcommittee on SBA and
SBIC Authority and General Small Business
Problems. Timber purchase set-aside program .
Washington , 1980. iii, 128 p. ;   LC Card
    80-603666   DDC 339.6/42/0973 19
KF27 .S6814 1980b

United States. Congress. Senate. Select
Committee on Small Business. Business
economic outlook . Washington , 1980. iii, 145
p. :   LC Card 80-602443   DDC 338.5/443/0973 19
KF26.5 .S6 1979w

United States. Congress. Senate. Select
Committee on Small Business. Economic
growth . Washington , 1980- v. :   LC Card
    80-603331   DDC 338.973 19
KF26.5 .S6 1980j

United States. Congress. Senate. Select
Committee on Small Business. Impact of
non-tariff barriers on the ability of small
business to export to Japan . Washington ,
1980. iii, 424 p. :   LC Card 80-603719   DDC
    382/.64 19
KF26.5 .S6 1980r

United States. Congress. Senate. Select
Committee on Small Business. Report by the
White House Commission on Small Business .
Washington , 1980. iii, 44 p. ;   LC Card
    80-603047   DDC 338.6/42/0973 19
KF26.5 .S6 1980i

United States. Congress. Senate. Select
Committee on Small Business. The role of small
business in the nation's economic recovery .
Washington , 1981. iii, 207 p. :   LC Card
    81-601882   DDC 338.6/42/0973 19
KF26.5 .S6 1981a

United States. Congress. Senate. Select
Committee on Small Business. SBA surety bond
guarantee program . Washington , 1980 [i.e.
1981] iv, 320 p. :   LC Card 81-601160   DDC
    353.0082/048045 19
KF26.5 .S6 1980w

United States. Congress. Senate. Select
Committee on Small Business. Small business
and Department of Energy research and

development programs . Washington , 1980. iii,
77 p. :   LC Card 80-602727   DDC 353.0082/048045
    19
KF26.5 .S6 1980e

United States. Congress. Senate. Select
Committee on Small Business. Small business
automobile dealers . Washington , 1980. iii, 294
p. :   LC Card 80-602971   DDC 381/.456292/0973
    19
KF26.5 .S6 1980f

United States. Congress. Senate. Select
Committee on Small Business.
Women-in-business programs in the Federal
government . Washington , 1980. iii, 207 p. ;
    LC Card 80-603041   DDC 353.0082/048 19
KF26.5 .S6 1980h

United States. Small Business Administration.
Office of the Chief Counsel for Advocacy.
Small business & innovation . [Washington] ,
1979. 130 p. in various pagings :   LC Card
    79-603309
HD2346.U5 U57 1979   **NYPL   [JLF 81-384]**

United States. Small Business Administration.
Paperwork Measurement and Reduction
Program. Government paperwork and small
business . [Washington] [1980?] iv, 86 p. :   LC
    Card 80-601425   DDC 353.0082/048 19
HD2346.U5 U57 1980

SMALL BUSINESS - UNITED STATES - CONGRESSES.

White House Conference on Small Business,
Washington, D.C., 1980. Delegate
recommendations /. Washington , 1980. v, 77
p. ;   LC Card 80-602062   DDC 338.6/42/0973 19
HD2346.U5 W54 1980

SMALL BUSINESS - UNITED STATES - FINANCE.

Klaasen, Thomas A. Venture capital and the
New Orleans economy /. [New Orleans] ,
1980. 30 leaves ;   LC Card 80-622446   DDC 330 s
    332/.04154 19
HC107.L8 L58 no. 34 HG3729.U5

United States. Congress. House. Committee on
Science and Technology. Subcommittee on
Investigation and Oversight. Small, high
technology firms and innovation . Washington ,
1980 [i.e. 1981] xviii, 791 p. :   LC Card
    81-600956   DDC 338.6/42/0973 19
KF27 .S3975 1979b

United States. Congress. House. Committee on
Small Business. Role of government funding
and its impact on small business in the solar
energy industry . Washington , 1980. vi, 68 p. :
    LC Card 80-603851   DDC 338.6/42 19
HD9681.U62 U526 1980

United States. Congress. House. Committee on
Small Business. Subcommittee on SBA and
SBIC Authority and General Small Business
Problems. SBA legislative request .
Washington , 1980. iii, 46 p. ;   LC Card
    80-603112   DDC 346.73/0652 19
KF27 .S6814 1980

United States. Congress. Senate. Select
Committee on Small Business. S. 2635, the
Small business energy conservation act .
Washington , 1980. iii, 30 p. ;   LC Card
    80-603682   DDC 346.7304/67916/02632
    347.30646791602632 19
KF26.5 .S6 1980l

United States. Congress. Senate. Select
Committee on Small Business. Subcommittee on
Government Procurement. S. 2873, to provide
SBA loans to small businesses in the
communications industry . Washington , 1980.
iii, 52 p. ;   LC Card 80-603716   DDC 346.73/0652
    347.3016652 19
KF26.5 .S625 1980

SMALL BUSINESS - UNITED STATES - MANAGEMENT.

United States. Congress. Senate. Select
Committee on Small Business. Subcommittee on
Government Regulation and Paperwork.
Oversight of SBA's management assistance
programs . Washington , 1980. iii, 201 p. :   LC
    Card 80-602431   DDC 353.0082/048 19
KF26.5 .S629 1979b

SMALL BUSINESS - UNITED STATES - SECURITY MEASURES.

United States. Congress. Senate. Select
Committee on Small Business. Crime and its

impact on small business . Washington , 1980.
iii, 115 p. ;   LC Card 80-603285   DDC
    338.6/42/0973 19
KF26.5 .S6 1980k

SMALL BUSINESS - UNITED STATES - STATES - FINANCE.

United States. Congress. House. Committee on
Small Business. Subcommittee on General
Oversight and Minority Enterprise. State usury
ceilings and their impact on small businesses .
Washington , 1980. iii, 294 p :   LC Card
    81-600855   DDC 338.6/42/0973 19
KF27 .S64 1980g

SMALL BUSINESS - UNITED STATES - STATES - INFORMATION SERVICES - DIRECTORIES.

Directory of state small business programs.
Washington.
    NYPL   [*R-Econ. 81-178 & JLM 81-180]

SMALL BUSINESS - UNITED STATES - STATISTICS.

Small business reports. Washington [1981] p.
cm.   LC Card 81-607797   DDC 338.0973 s
    338.6/42/0973 19
HC106.7 .A14 ES77-3 HD2346.U5

SMALL BUSINESS - UNITED STATES - TAXATION.

United States. Congress. Senate. Select
Committee on Small Business. Economic
growth . Washington , 1980- v. :   LC Card
    80-603331   DDC 338.973 19
KF26.5 .S6 1980j

The Small Claims Court Experimental Project :
a report to the legislature on the monetary
jurisdiction experiment, final / Roger
Dickinson, project coordinator. Sacramento, CA
(1020 N. St., Sacramento, 95814) : State of
California Dept. of Consumer Affairs, Division
of Consumer Services, [1980] [11], v, 118 p. :
ill., forms ; 28 cm. "October 1980."   LC Card
    81-621863   DDC 347.794/04 347.94074 19
1. Small claims courts - California. I. Dickinson, Roger,
1950-. II. California. Division of Consumer Services.
KFC976 .S42

SMALL CLAIMS COURTS - CALIFORNIA.

California. Legislature. Assembly. Committee on
Judiciary. Court improvement . [Sacramento ,
1979] v, 124 p. ;   LC Card 80-622833   DDC
    347.794/01 19
KFC10.4 .J8 1979d

The Small Claims Court Experimental Project .
Sacramento, CA (1020 N. St., Sacramento,
95814) [1980] [11], v, 118 p. :   LC Card
    81-621863   DDC 347.794/04 347.94074 19
KFC976 .S42

Small commercial vessel inspection and
manning . United States. Congress. House.
Committee on Merchant Marine and Fisheries.
Subcommitee on Coast Guard and Navigation.
Washington , 1980. iv, 301 p. :   LC Card
    80-601442   DDC 343.73/0965 19
KF27 .M434 1979d

SMALL COMPUTERS. see MINICOMPUTERS.

Small farm development . Dayao, Benefa M.
College, Laguna, Philippines , 1977. iv, 160
leaves ;   LC Card 80-122267   DDC 016.3381/6 19
Z5075.A76 D39 HD1476.A78

Small-farm issues . ESCS Small-Farm Workshop,
Alexandria, Va., 1978. Washington , Springfield,
Va. , 1979. v, 73 p. :   LC Card 79-602951   DDC
    338.1/0973 s 338.1/6 19
HD1759 .U56a no. 60 HD1476.U5

Small farm programs . Orden, David.
Blacksburg , 1978. xvi, 200 p. :   LC Card
    79-623060   DDC 081 s 338.1/8755 19
AS36 .V512 no. 135 HD1476.U5

SMALL FARMS. see FARMS, SMALL.

SMALL GROUPS - MEMBERSHIP.

Brown, Keith Cates, 1933- Modeling the group
admissions process . West Lafayette, Ind. ,
1978. 17, 7 p. ;   LC Card 78-623489   DDC
    658/.001/9 s 302.3/4 19
HD6483 .P8 no. 668 HM133

Small, high technology firms and innovation .
United States. Congress. House. Committee on
Science and Technology. Subcommittee on
Investigation and Oversight. Washington , 1980
[i.e. 1981] xviii, 791 p. :   LC Card 81-600956

DDC 338.6/42/0973 19
KF27 .S3975 1979b

Small, high technology firms and innovation .
United States. Congress. House. Committee on
Science and Technology. Subcommittee on
Investigations and Oversight. Washington ,
1980. v, 65 p. ;   LC Card 80-602579   DDC
338.4/76/0973 19
T173.8 .U5 1980

Small police agency consolidation . Koepsell,
Terry W. [Washington] , 1979. xii, 102 p. ;   LC
Card 79-603014   DDC 352.2/0973 19
HV7921 .K63

**Small royalty owners exemption from the
windfall profit tax .** United States. Congress.
Senate. Committee on Finance. Subcommittee
on Taxation and Debt Management Generally.
Washington , 1980. vii, 442 p. ;   LC Card
81-600593   DDC 343.7305/244 347.3035244 19
KF26 .F5695 1980d

Small-scale enterprises in Korea and Taiwan /.
Ho, Sam P. S. Washington, D.C. , 1980. vi, 151
p. ;   LC Card 80-134204   DDC 338.6/42/0951249
19
HD2346.K6 H6

Small-scale farming in the Westlands . Ely,
George. Davis, Calif. [197-] viii, 64 leaves ;
LC Card 79-626029   DDC 338.1/6 19
HD1476.U5 E49

Small-scale fuel alcohol production /. United
States. Dept. of Agriculture. Washington, D.C.
[1980] 221 p. in various pagings :   LC Card
80-601860   DDC 662/.669 19
TP358 .U7 1980

**Small urban centers in rural development in
Africa.** Schatzberg, Michael G. Bibliography of
small urban centers in rural development in
Africa /. [Madison] , 1979. ix, 246 p. ;   LC
Card 80-623484   DDC 016.3077/6/096 19
Z7164.U7 S25 HT148.A2

Smalley, Shirley F. A local school
implementation plan for performance based
vocational education : a project report / written
by Shirley F. Smalley. Bloomington : Vocational
Education Information Services, Indiana
University, 1980. ix, 70 p. : ill., forms ; 23 cm.
(Information series / Vocational Education Information
Services, Indiana University . no. 11) Bibliography: p.
69-70.   LC Card 81-622007   DDC 373.2/46/09772
19
*1. Vocational education - Indiana. I. Indiana University,
Bloomington. Vocational Education Information
Services. II. Series: Information series (Indiana
University, Bloomington. Vocational Education
Information Services) , no. 11. III. Title.*
LC1046.I4 S55

SMALLMOUTH BASS - REPRODUCTION.
Vogele, Louis E. Reproduction of smallmouth
bass, Micropterus dolomieui, in Bull Shoals
Lake, Arkansas /. Washington, D.C. , 1981. p.
cm.   LC Card 81-607977   DDC 639 s 597/.58 19
SH11 .A313 no. 106 QL638.C3

SMALLMOUTH BUFFALO.
Hoyt, Robert D. Population dynamics and
catch susceptibility of smallmouth buffalo in
Rough River Reservoir /. [Frankfort, Ky.] ,
1976. vii, 67 p. :   LC Card 79-624983   DDC
639/.2 s 597/.52 19
SH222.K4 A3 no. 62 QL638.C27

Smallwood, Benjamin F. Soil survey of Marshall
County, Indiana. [Washington, D.C.?] : U. S.
Dept. of Agriculture, Soil Conservation Service,
1980. vii, 136 p., 63 folded p. of plates : ill.,
maps (1 col.) ; 28 cm. Cover title. "In cooperation
with Purdue University Agricultural Experiment Station,
and Indiana Department of Natural Resources, Soil and
Water Conservation Committee." "Issued October
1980"--P. iii. Item 102-B-14 Bibliography: p. 81.   LC
Card 81-601062   DDC 631.4/7/77288 19
*1. Soils - Indiana - Marshall County - Maps. I. United
States. Soil Conservation Service. II. Purdue University.
Agricultural Experiment Station. III. Indiana. Soil and
Water Conservation Committee. IV. Title.*
S599.I63 S6

Smathers, W. M. (joint author) Clifton, Ivery D.
Alien investment in Georgia's agricultural lands
/. [Athens, Ga.] , 1980. 26 p. :   LC Card
80-623104   DDC 332.63/242 19
HD266.G4 C56

Smathers, Webb M. (joint author) Broder, Josef M.
An economic analysis of rural court
consolidation in Georgia /. [Athens, Ga.]
[1980] 21 p. :   LC Card 80-623190   DDC
347.758/012 19
KFG516.C55 B76

Smith, Alan P. Growth and population dynamics
of Espeletia (Compositae) in the Venezuelan
Andes / Alan P. Smith. Washington :
Smithsonian Institution Press, 1981. p. cm.
(Smithsonian contributions to botany . no. 48)
Bibliography: p.   LC Card 81-607061   DDC 581 s
583/.55 19
*1. Espeletia. 2. Growth (Plants). 3. Plant populations -
Andes. 4. Plant populations - Venezuela. 5. Alpine
flora - Andes. 6. Alpine Flora - Venezuela. 7. Botany -
Andes - Ecology. 8. Botany - Venezuela - Ecology. I.
Title. II. Series.*
QK1 .S2747 no. 48 QK495.C74

**Smith Associates. see Herbert H. Smith
Associates.**

Smith, B. Othanel (Bunnie Othanel) A design
for a school of pedagogy / by B. Othanel Smith
in collaboration with Stuart H. Silverman, Jean
M. Bors, and Betty V. Fry. Washington, D.C. :
U. S. Dept. of Education : For sale by the Supt.
of Docs., U. S. G.P.O., 1980. ix, 118 p. : ill. ;
26 cm. (Publication . no. E-80-42000) S/N
017-080-02098-0 Item 455-B-2 Includes indexes.
Includes bibliographical references.   LC Card
80-603928   DDC 370/.7/30973 19
*1. Teachers, Training of - United States. 2. Education -
Study and teaching (Higher) - United States. I. United
States. Dept. of Education. II. Series: Publication
(United States. Dept. of Education) , no. E-80-42000.
III. Title.*
LB1715 .S47

Smith, Baird M. Dampness in historic buildings :
methods of diagnosis and treatment :
preliminary report / Baird M. Smith.
Washington, DC : US Dept. of the Interior,
Heritage Conservation and Recreation Service,
Technical Preservation Services Division, 1980.
p. cm. (Heritage Conservation and Recreation Service
publication ; no. 52) TPS reports Bibliography: p.   LC
Card 80-607172   DDC 690/.24 19
*1. Dampness in buildings. 2. Historic buildings -
Maintenance and repair. I. Series: United States.
Heritage Conservation and Recreation Service. HCRS
publication, no. 52. II. Title.*
TH9031 .S64

Smith, Bryant D. The impact of trade policy on
exports in oil rich countries : the cases of
Ecuador and Trinidad & Tobago / [Bryant D.
Smith]. Washington : International Trade Unit,
Dept. of External Cooperation, Organization of
American States, 1975. ix, 136 p. : graphs ; 28
cm.   LC Card 80-469796
*1. Ecuador - Commerce. 2. Ecuador - Commercial
policy. 3. Trinidad and Tobago - Commerce. 4.
Trinidad and Tobago - Commercial policy. I.
Organization of American States. International Trade
Unit. II. Title.*
HF3436.5 .S63

Smith, C. W. (Carl W.) Crushing techniques for
pneumatic concentration of mica / by C.W.
Smith, C.E. Jordan, and G.V. Sullivan.
[Avondale, Md.] : U. S. Dept. of the Interior,
Bureau of Mines, 1981. p. cm. (Report of
investigations) Includes bibliographical references.   LC
Card 81-607301   DDC 622 s 622/.3674 19
*1. Mica. 2. Crushing machinery - Testing. 3. Air
classifiers. I. Jordan, C. E. II. Sullivan, G. V. III. Series:
Report of investigations (United States. Bureau of
Mines). IV. Title.*
TN23 .U43 TN933

Smith, Charles P., 1931-
A national assessment of case disposition and
classification in the juvenile justice system:
inconsistent labeling / by Charles P. Smith, T.
Edwin Black, Fred R. Campbell ; [prepared by
the National Juvenile Justice System
Assessment Center of the American Justice
Institute]. Washington, D.C. : U. S. Dept. of
Justice, Law Enforcement Assistance
Administration, Office of Juvenile Justice and
Delinquency Prevention, National Institute for
Juvenile Justice and Delinquency Prevention :
For sale by the Supt. of Docs., U. S. G.P.O.,
1979-80. 3 v. : ill., charts, maps ; 28 cm. Reports
of the national juvenile justice assessment centers. S/N
027-000-00936 (v. 1) S/N 027-000-00944-1 (v. 2) S/N
027-000-00945-0 (v. 3) Item 717-N-5 Includes

bibliographies. CONTENTS. - v. 1. Process description
and summary -- v. 2. Results of a literature search / by
Charles P. Smith, T. Edwin Black, Adrianne W. Weir --
v. 3 Results of a survey.   LC Card 80-600043   DDC
364.3/6/0973 19
*1. Juvenile justice, Administration of - United States -
Collected works. 2. Juvenile courts - United States -
Collected works. I. Black, T. Edwin. II. Campbell, Fred
R. III. Weir, Adrianne W. IV. National Juvenile Justice
System Assessment Center (U. S.). V. National Institute
for Juvenile Justice and Delinquency Prevention. VI.
Title.*
HV9104 .S6

**National Juvenile Justice System Assessment
Center (U. S.)** A preliminary national
assessment of the status offender and the
juvenile justice system . [Washington, D.C.]
[1980] c1979. xv, 221 p. :   LC Card 80-600044
DDC 364.3/6/0973 19
HV9104 .N23 1980a

**National Juvenile Justice System Assessment
Center (United States)** A national assessment of
serious juvenile crime and the juvenile justice
system . [Washington, D.C.] [1980] 4 v. :   LC
Card 80-602691   DDC 364.3/6/0973 19
HV9104 .N23 1980

A preliminary national assessment of child
abuse and neglect and the juvenile justice
system : the shadows of distress / by Charles P.
Smith, David J. Berkman, Warren M. Fraser.
[Washington, D.C.] : U. S. Dept. of Justice,
Law Enforcement Assistance Administration,
Office of Juvenile Justice and Delinquency
Prevention, National Institute for Juvenile
Justice and Delinquency Prevention, [1980]
c1979. xiv, 154 p. ; 28 cm. (Reports of the national
juvenile justice assessment centers) "April 1980." Title
on spine: Child abuse and neglect. Includes
bibliographies.   LC Card 80-600045   DDC 362.7/044
19
*1. Child abuse - United States - Prevention. 2. Child
abuse - Services - United States. 3. Juvenile justice,
Administration of - United States. I. Berkman, David J.,
joint author. II. Fraser, Warren M., joint author. III.
National Institute for Juvenile Justice and Delinquency
Prevention. IV. Title. V. Title: Child abuse and neglect.
VI. Series.*
HV741 .S55 1980

Smith, Clyde Fuhriman, 1913- An annotated list
of Aphidinae (Homoptera) of the Caribbean
islands and South and Central America / Clyde
F. Smith, Mario M. Cermeli. [Raleigh] : North
Carolina Agricultural Research Service, 1979.
131 p. ; 23 cm. (Tech. bul. - North Carolina
Agricultural Research Service . no. 259) Bibliography:
p. 82-118. Includes index.   LC Card 80-621377   DDC
595.7/52 19
*1. Aphididae - Latin America. 2. Insects - Latin
America. I. Cermeli, Mario M., joint author. II. Series:
North Carolina. Agricultural Research Service.
Technical bulletin - Agricultural Research Service , no.
259. III. Title.*
QL527.A64 S64

Smith, Dave, 1942- Homage to Edgar Allan Poe :
poems / by Dave Smith. Baton Rouge :
Louisiana State University Press, 1981. p. cm.
ISBN 0-8071-0873-1 :   LC Card 81-4767   DDC
811/.54 19
I. Title.
PS3569.M5173 H6

Smith, Dennis K. (joint author) Orden, David.
Small farm programs . Blacksburg , 1978. xvi,
200 p. :   LC Card 79-623060   DDC 081 s
338.1/8755 19
AS36 .V512 no. 135 HD1476.U5

SMITH, DOROTHY I.
United States. Congress. Senate. Committee on
Energy and Natural Resources. Subcommittee
on Energy Resources and Material Production.
Amending the Mineral leasing act of 1920 and
for the relief of Keith C. Hayes and Dorothy
Smith . Washington , 1980. iii, 66 p. :   LC Card
80-602537   DDC 346.7304/6822 19
KF26 .E5543 1980b

Smith, Ed R. The effect of several configuration
interaction target states on the elastic scattering
of low-energy electrons by complex atoms / Ed
R. Smith. Hanscomb AFB, Mass. : Aeronomy
Laboratory, Air Force Cambridge Research
Laboratorie, Air Force Systems Command,
USAF, 1975. 25 p. ; 28 cm. (United States. Air
Force. Cambridge Research Laboratories. Physical
sciences research papers. no. 625) Microfiche (neg.) 1

sheet. 11 x 15 cm. (NYPL FSN 34,974) Cover title. "Project 8627." Bibliography: p. 25.
1. Electrons - Scattering. 2. Collisions (Nuclear physics). 3. Atoms. I. United States. Air Force. Cambridge Research Laboratories. Aeronomy Laboratory. II. Title.   **NYPL [*XMQ-2123]**

Smith, Frank Avery, 1925- (joint author) Souders, Vernon L. Geology and groundwater supplies of Box Butte County, Nebraska /. [Lincoln] [1980] vii, 205 p. : LC Card 80-623050 DDC 553/.7/09782 s 551.7/9/0978294 19
GB1025.N2 N42 no. 47 QE136.B67

Smith, Gary Frederick. A quantitative sampling program of benthic communities in nearshore subtidal areas within the Rosario Strait region of Northern Puget Sound, Washington State (1976) / conducted for the Washington State Department of Ecology, Oil baseline program by Gary Frederick Smith. [Olympia] : State of Washington, Dept. of Ecology, [1979] vi, 105 p. : ill. ; 28 cm. Cover title: W.W.U. subtidal study, Huxley College. Appendix L to North Puget Sound baseline program, 1974-1977, edited by F. Gardner. LC Card 80-622612 DDC 591.9797/7 19
1. Marine biology - Washington (State) - Puget Sound. 2. Benthos - Washington (State) - Puget Sound. 3. Sampling (Statistics). I. Gardner, Fred. North Puget Sound baseline program, 1974-1977. II. Washington (State). Dept. of Ecology. III. Western Washington University. IV. Huxley College of Environmental Studies. V. Title. VI. Title: W.W.U. subtidal study, Huxley College. VII. Title: Rosario Strait region of Northern Puget Sound, ...
QH105.W2 S65

Smith, Gilbert D. International Association of Auto Theft Investigators. Proceedings of the International Association of Auto Theft Investigators twenty-first annual seminar, Arlington, Texas, August 19-24, 1973. [Arlington] [1973?] 126 p. : LC Card 80-623391 DDC 363.2/5 19
HV8079.A97 I57 1973

Smith, Glenn L. Mississippi. Legislature. Audit Committee. Special investigation, political activities of MVC employees /. [Jackson, Miss.] [1980] xi, 76 p. ; LC Card 80-623578 DDC 353.9762001/6 19
HE5633.M7 M57 1980

Smith, Gregory Bennett, 1947- Comparative efficacy of artificial and natural Gulf of Mexico reefs as fish attractants / Gregory B. Smith, Dannie A. Hensley, and Heyward H. Mathews. St. Petersburg, Fla. : Florida Dept. of Natural Resources, Marine Research Laboratory, 1979. 7 p. : ill. ; 28 cm. (Florida marine research publications . no. 35 0095-0157) "June 1979." Bibliography: p. 6-7. LC Card 80-620715 DDC 639.9/77 19
1. Artificial reefs. 2. Fishes - Florida - Clearwater region. I. Hensley, Dannie A., joint author. II. Mathews, Heyward H., joint author. III. Marine Research Laboratory, St. Petersburg, Fla. IV. Title. V. Series.
SH157.85.A7 S58

Smith (Herbert H.) Associates. see Herbert H. Smith Associates.

Smith, Herbert McKelden, 1951- Architectural resources : an inventory of historic architecture, High Point, Jamestown, Gibsonville, Guilford County / directed and edited by H. McKelden Smith. Raleigh, N.C. : North Carolina Department of Cultural Resources, Division of Archives and History, 1979. 177 p. : ill. ; 21 cm. Includes bibliographical references and index. LC Card 80-622823 DDC 720/.9756/62 19
1. Architecture - North Carolina - Guilford County. 2. Historic buildings - North Carolina - Guilford County. I. North Carolina. Division of Archives and History. II. Title.
NA730.N82 G847

Smith, Howard Christopher, 1948- (joint author) Hole, Thornton J. F. Soil survey of Ocean County, New Jersey /. [Washington] [1980] vii, 102 p., [35] fold. leaves of plates : LC Card 80-602312 DDC 631.4/7/74948 19
S599.N5 H64

Smith, Jay A. (joint author) Jennings, Kenneth M. Study of unions, management rights, and the public interest in mass transit. Washington , 1977. 276 p. : LC Card 77-604540
HD6976.T72 U55   **NYPL [*XME-9441]**

Smith, Jeffrey B. French and Quinebaug Rivers : 1974 & 1976 water quality analysis / Jeffrey B. Smith ; Water Quality and Research Section, Division of Water Pollution Control, Massachusetts Water Resources Commission. Westborough, Mass. : The Division, [1978] 94 p. : ill. ; 28 cm. "September 1978." "Part C." Bibliography: p. 92-94. LC Card 79-622381 DDC 363.7/3942/097443 19
1. Water quality - Massachusetts - French River watershed. 2. Water quality - Quinebaug River watershed, Conn. and Mass. I. Massachusetts. Water Quality and Research Section. II. Title.
TD224.M4 S64

Smith, John, 1580-1631.
[Works. 1983]
The complete works of Captain John Smith (1580-1631) / edited by Philip L. Barbour. Chapel Hill : Published for the Institute of Early American History and Culture, Williamsburg, Va. by the University of North Carolina Press, c1983. p. cm. Bibliography: p. Includes index. ISBN 0-8078-1525-X LC Card 81-10364 DDC 975.5/02 19
1. Virginia - History - Colonial period, ca. 1600-1775 - Collected works. 2. New England - History - Colonial period, ca. 1600-1775 - Collected works. 3. America - Discovery and exploration - English - Collected works. I. Barbour, Philip L. II. Institute of Early American History and Culture, Williamsburg, Va. III. Title.
F229 .S59 1983

Smith, John Melvin, 1937- (joint author) Peacock, Richard D. SPEED2, a computer program for the reduction of data from automatic data acquisition systems /. [Washington, D.C.] [1979] 58, 68, 22, [7] p. ; LC Card 79-603987 DDC 602/.18 s 001.6 19
QC100 .U5753 no. 1108 QA276

Smith, Libby, 1954- Mississippi. Legislature. Audit Committee. A special follow-up report to the legislature detailing State agency compliance with selected bills passed during the 1978 and 1979 legislative sessions /. [Jackson, Miss.] [1980] x, 91 p. ; LC Card 80-622027 DDC 353.976207/8 19
KFM7040 .A25 1980

Smith, Marcia S.
United States civilian space programs, 1958-1978 . Washington , 1981- v. <1 > : LC Card 81-602024 DDC 629.4 19
TL789.8.U5 U58

United States. Library of Congress. Congressional Research Service. Alternative breeding cycles for nuclear power . Washington , 1980. xx, 124 p. : LC Card 80-603560 DDC 333.79/24/0973 19
TK9203.B7 U53 1980

Smith, Marion F. (joint author) Taylor, Richard Lee, 1946- The report of the intensive survey of the Richard B. Russell Dam and Lake, Savannah River, Georgia and South Carolina /. Columbia, S.C. [1978] xvii, 531 p. : LC Card 79-623568 DDC 975.7/35 19
F292.R49 T39

Smith, Michael, 1953- Liability of local governments in federal court for the violation of federal rights--Monell, Owen, and Thiboutot / Michael R. Smith. Chapel Hill : Institute of Government, University of North Carolina at Chapel Hill, 1980, c1979. 24 p. ; 28 cm. (Local government law bulletin . no. 21) Caption title. Includes bibliographical references. LC Card 81-621377 DDC 342.756/09 s 347.56029 s 342.73/09 347.3029 19
1. Government liability - United States. 2. Tort liability of municipal corporations - United States. I. Title. II. Series.
KFN7830.A15 L6 no. 21 KF1321

Smith, Nancy Brite. Lynn, Warren M. Cultural resource survey of Choke Canyon Reservoir, Live Oak and McMullen Counties, Texas /. Austin , 1979. xiv, 273 p. : LC Card 78-622852 DDC 976.4/447 19
F392.F92 L96

Smith, Ollie L. National Institute of Law Enforcement and Criminal Justice. Publications of the National Institute of Law Enforcement and Criminal Justice . [Washington] , 1978. vii, 230 p. ; LC Card 79-601977 DDC 016.364/973 19
Z7164.P76 N37 HV8138

Smith, R. Marlin. A Guide for municipal zoning administration with forms / R. Marlin Smith,

Clyde W. Forrest, Jr., Eric C. Freund. Urbana-Champaign, Ill. : Bureau of Urban and Regional Planning Research, Dept. of Urban and Regional Planning, University of Illinois at Urbana-Champaign, 1972. 136 p. ; 26 cm. Bibliography: p. 133-136.
1. Zoning - Illinois. I. Forrest, Clyde W. II. Freund, Eric C. III. Illinois. University at Urbana-Champaign. Bureau of Urban and Regional Planning Research. IV. Title.   **NYPL [JLF 81-263]**

Smith, Richard A. The Oilspill risk analysis model of the U. S. Geological Survey /. Washington [1981] p. cm. LC Card 80-606812 DDC 363.7/394
GC1085 .O44

Smith, Robert J., 1935- The Ecole normale superieure and the Third Republic / Robert J. Smith. Albany : State University of New York Press, [1981] p. cm. Based on the author's thesis, University of Pennsylvania. Bibliography: p. ISBN 0-87395-540-4 LC Card 81-8810 DDC 370/.944 19
1. Ecole normale supérieure (Paris, France) - History - 19th century. I. Title.
LB2077.P3 S65

Smith, Robert James, 1956- (joint author) Easom, William Davison. Electrical logs of water wells and test holes on file at the Bureau of Geology and Energy Resources /. Jackson, Miss. , 1979. 306 p. : LC Card 80-620873 DDC 551.49/09762 19
GB1025.M7 E27

Smith, Roland, 1943- (joint author) Fuller, Stephen. Economics of grain sorghum production and marketing /. College Station, Tex. , 1979. iii, 43 p. ; LC Card 80-620821 DDC 338.1/73174/09764 19
HD9049.S6 U53

Smith, Samuel D. Historical background and archaeological testing of the Davy Crockett Birthplace State Historical Area, Greene County, Tennessee / Samuel D. Smith. [Nashville, Tenn. : Division of Archaeology, Tennessee Dept. of Conservation], 1980. v, 67 p. : ill. ; 28 cm. (Research series - Division of Archaeology, Tennessee Department of Conservation . no. 6) Bibliography: p. 64-67. LC Card 80-623481 DDC 976.8/91 19
1. Davy Crockett Birthplace State Historic Area, Tenn. 2. Excavations (Archaeology) - Tennessee - Greene Co. 3. Greene Co., Tenn. - Antiquities. 4. Tennessee - Antiquities. 5. Indians of North America - Tennessee - Greene Co. - Antiquities. I. Series: Tennessee. Division of Archaeology. Research series - Division of Archaeology, Tennessee Department of Conservation , no. 6. II. Title.
F444.D28 S64

Smith, Verne E. (joint author) Hampe, Gary D. Water-related aesthetic preferences of Wyoming residents /. Laramie [1974] 111 p. : LC Card 74-623922 DDC 553.7/09787 s 719 19
TD201 .W9 no. 46 BH301.L3

Smith, Vernon K. (joint author) Swanson, Robert William. Income and benefit receipt among Michigan AFDC families /. [Lansing] [1979] xix, 150 p. : LC Card 80-621648 DDC 361/.9774 s 362.7/13/09774 19
HV86 .M536 no. 31 (11-79)
          NYPL [JLM 75-1607 no. 13]

Smith, Victor E. Michigan. State University, East Lansing. Dept. of Agricultural Economics. Household food consumption in rural Sierra Leone /. East Lansing, Mich. , 1979. x, 111 p. : LC Card 80-621811 DDC 362.1/9639 19
TX360.S5 M52 1979

Smith, Virginia, 1932- (joint author) Molnar, Joseph J. Development characteristics in non-metropolitan Alabama . Auburn, Ala. , 1979. 31 p. : LC Card 79-622432 DDC 307.7/2/09761 19
HN25 .M64

Smith (Wilbur) and Associates. North Carolina rail plan, 1979 / prepared by Wilbur Smith and Associates. [Raleigh] : North Carolina Dept. of Transportation, Office of the Assistant Secretary for Planning, [1979] 300 p. in various pagings, [2] leaves of plates : maps ; 22 x 30 cm. Includes bibliographical references. LC Card 80-621028 DDC 385/.09756 19
1. Railroads - North Carolina. I. North Carolina. Dept. of Transportation. Office of the Assistant Secretary for

Planning. II. Title.
TF24.N8 S64 1979

SMITH, WILLIAM FRENCH, 1917-
United States. Congress. Senate. Committee on the Judiciary. Confirmation hearing on William French Smith, nominee, to be attorney general . Washington , 1981. iv, 179 p. ; LC Card 81-601872 DDC 353.5 19
KF26 .J8 1981

SMITH, WILLIAM LEE, 1929-
United States. Congress. Senate. Committee on Labor and Human Resources. Nomination . Washington , 1980. ii, 29 p. : LC Card 80-602538 DDC 353.842 19
KF26 .L27 1980b

Smith, William T., 1916- New York (State). State Temporary Commission to Revise the Social Services Law. Children in need . Albany, N.Y. , 1978. iii, 55 p. ; LC Card 79-623521 DDC 362.7/33/09747 19
KFN5600.A73 S7 no. 7 HV875

Smitherman, Geneva. National Invitational Symposium on the King Decision (1980 : Wayne State University) Black English and the education of Black children and youth . Detroit, Mich. , c1981. 441 p. : LC Card 80-85071 DDC 371.97/96073 19
LC2771 .N37 1981

Smithers, W. D. (Wilfred Dudley), 1895- Circuit riders of the Big Bend / by W.D. Smithers. [El Paso] : Texas Western Press, c1981. 39 p., [8] p. of plates : ill., map, ports. ; 23 cm. (Southwestern studies / University of Texas at El Paso . monograph no. 64) ISBN 0-87407-124-4 (pbk.) : LC Card 81-159927 DDC 280/.092/2 B 19
1. Clergy - Texas - Biography. 2. Itinerancy (Church polity). 3. Texas - Biography. I. Series: Southwestern studies / University of Texas at El Paso , monograph no. 64. II. Title.
BR555.T4 S64

A Smithsonian book of comic-book comics / Michael Barrier and Martin Williams, editors. [Washington, D.C.] : Smithsonian Institution ; [New York] : H.N. Abrams, 1981. p. cm. Bibliography: p. ISBN 0-87474-228-5 : LC Card 81-607842 DDC 741.5/973 19
1. Comic books, strips, etc.- United States. I. Barrier, J. Michael. II. Williams, Martin T. III. Smithsonian Institution.
PN6726 .S58

Smithsonian contributions to botany .
(no. 48) Smith, Alan P. Growth and population dynamics of Espeletia (Compositae) in the Venezuelan Andes / . Washington , 1981. p. cm. LC Card 81-607061 DDC 581 s 583/.55 19
QK1 .S2747 no. 48 QK495.C74

(no. 51) Robinson, Harold Ernest, 1932- A revision of the tribal and subtribal limits of the Heliantheae (Asteraceae) / . City of Washington , 1981. p. cm. LC Card 81-607993 DDC 581 s 583/.55 19
QK1 .S2747 no. 51 QK495.C74

(no. 52) Chromosome numbers in Compositae, XII. Washington , 1981. p. cm. LC Card 81-607855 DDC 581 s 583.55 19
QK1 .S2747 no. 52 QK495.C74

Smithsonian contributions to paleobiology .
(no. 43) Cooper, G. Arthur (Gustav Arthur), 1902- Brachiopoda from the southern Indian Ocean (recent) / . Washington, D.C. [1981] p. cm. LC Card 81-607935 DDC 560 s 564/.8/09165 19
QE701 .S56 no. 43 QL395.75

(no. 44) Cooper, G. Arthur (Gustav Arthur), 1902- Brachiopoda from the Gulf of Gascogne, France (recent) / . City of Washington , 1981. p. cm. LC Card 81-607040 DDC 560 s 595.3/20944 19
QE701 .S56 no. 44 QL395.3.B58

(no. 45) Cifelli, Richard. Textural observations on some living species of planktonic foraminifera / . Washington , 1982. p. cm. LC Card 81-607840 DDC 560 s 592.1/304471 19
QE701 .S56 no. 45 QL368.F6

(no. 46) Harrison, Jessica A. A review of the extinct wolverine, Plesiogulo (Carnivora, Mustelidae) from North America / . City of Washington , 1981. p. cm. LC Card 81-607075 DDC 560 s 569/.74 19
QE701 .S56 no. 46 QE882.C15

(no. 48) Fossil vertebrates from the Bahamas . Washington , 1982. p. cm. LC Card 81-13543 DDC 560 s 566/.097296 19
QE701 .S56 no. 48 QE841

(no. 49) Hueber, Francis M. Megaspores and a palynomorph from the lower Potomac Group in Virginia / . Washington , 1982. p. cm. LC Card 81-607852 DDC 560 s 561/.13 19
QE701 .S56 no. 49 QE996

Smithsonian contributions to the marine sciences .
(no. 10) Menez, Ernani G. The marine algae of Tunisia / . City of Washington , 1981. p. cm. LC Card 81-607084 DDC 589.3961/1 19
QK576.T8 M46

(no. 11) Sohm Abyssal Plain . Washington , 1981. p. cm. LC Card 81-607056 DDC 551.46/4 19
GC383 .S64

(no. 12) The Atlantic barrier reef ecosystem at Carrie Bow Cay, Belize / . Washington , 1981- p. cm. LC Card 81-607039 DDC 574.5/26367/097282 19
QH108.B43 A87

(no. 13) Blanpied, Christian. Uniform mud (unifite) deposition in the Hellenic trench, eastern Mediterranean / . City of Washington , 1981. p. cm. LC Card 81-607825 DDC 551.46/083/384 19
GC389 .B57

(no. 7) Norris, James N. Articulated coralline algae of the Gulf of California, Mexico / . Washington , 1981- p. cm. LC Card 81-607063 DDC 589.4/1 19
QK569.C8 N67

Smithsonian contributions to zoology .
(no. 321) Houbrick, Richard S. Review of the deep-sea genus Argyropeza (Gastropoda, Prosobranchia, Cerithiidae) / . Washington , 1980. iii, 30 p. : LC Card 80-607017 DDC 591 s 594/.32 19
QL1 .S54 no. 321 QL430.5.C4

(no. 327) Litte, Marcia. Social biology of the polistine wasp Mischocyttarus labiatus . Washington , 1981. p. cm. LC Card 81-607071 DDC 591 s 595.79/8 19
QL1 .S54 no. 327 QL568.V5

(no. 336) Sunquist, Melvin E. The social organization of tigers (Panthera tigris) in Royal Chitawan National Park, Nepal /. Washington [D.C.] , 1981. p. cm. LC Card 81-607928 DDC 591 s 599.74/428 19
QL1 .S54 no. 336 QL737.C23

(no. 337) Olson, Storrs L. The relationships of the Pedionomidae (Aves, Charadriiformes) / . Washington , 1981. p. cm. LC Card 81-412 DDC 591 s 598/.33 19
QL1 .S54 no. 337 QL696.C465

(no. 339) Cressey, Roger F., 1930- Parasitic copepods from the Gulf of Mexico and Caribbean Sea, I . Washington , 1981. p. cm. LC Card 81-9055 DDC 591 s 595.3/4 19
QL1 .S54 no. 339 QL444.C73

(no. 340) Kornicker, Louis S., 1919- Angulorostrum, a new genus of myodocopid Ostracoda (Philomedidae, Pseudophilomedinae) / . Washington, D.C. , 1981. p. cm. LC Card 81-607892 DDC 591 s 595.3/3 19
QL1 .S54 no. 340 QL444.O85

(no. 342) Cressey, Roger F., 1930- Revision of Indo-West Pacific lizardfishes of the genus Synodus (Pisces: Synodontidae) / . City of Washington , 1981. p. cm. LC Card 81-14389 DDC 591 s 597/.53 19
QL1 .S54 no. 342 QL638.S96

(no. 343) Krombein, Karl V. Biosystematic studies of Ceylonese wasps, VIII . Washington , 1981. p. cm. LC Card 81-607805 DDC 591 s 595.79/8 19
QL1 .S54 no. 343 QL568.P5

(no. 344) Mead, James G. Biological observations on Mesoplodon carlhubbsi (Cetacea:Ziphiidae) / . Washington, D.C. , 1981. p. cm. LC Card 81-9311 DDC 591 s 599.5/3 19
QL1 .S54 no. 344 QL237.C438

Smithsonian folklife studies .
(no. 1) Rinzler, Ralph. The Meaders family, north Georgia potters /. Washington, D.C. , 1981. p. cm. LC Card 81-607995 DDC

738/.092/2 B 19
NK4210.M35 R56

The Smithsonian illustrated library of antiques.
Shaffer, Douglas Howerth. Clocks /. [New York] , c1980. 127 p. : LC Card 78-62729 DDC 681.1/13 19
TS542 .S5

Smithsonian Institution.
Finders' guide to prints and drawings in the Smithsonian Institution / Lynda Corey Claassen. Washington, D.C. : Smithsonian Institution Press, 1981. p. cm. (Finders' guides to works in the Smithsonian Institution) Includes bibliographies and index. ISBN 0-87474-317-6 LC Card 81-607070 DDC 760/.074/0153 19
1. Art - Catalogs. 2. Scientific illustration - Catalogs. 3. Medical illustration - Catalogs. 4. Smithsonian Institution - Catalogs. I. Claassen, Lynda C. II. Series: Smithsonian Institution. Finders' guides to works in the Smithsonian Institution. III. Title.
N855.8 .A56

Finders' guides to works in the Smithsonian Institution.
Smithsonian Institution. Finders' guide to prints and drawings in the Smithsonian Institution /. Washington, D.C. , 1981. p. cm. ISBN 0-87474-317-6 LC Card 81-607070 DDC 760/.074/0153 19
N855.8 .A56

The Joys of research /. Washington, D.C. , 1981. p. cm. ISBN 0-87474-858-5 LC Card 81-9347 DDC 001.4 19
Q179.9 .J69

Official guide to the Smithsonian. Washington, D.C. : Smithsonian Institution Press, 1981. p. cm. LC Card 80-607800 DDC 069/.09753 19
1. Smithsonian Institution - Guide-books. I. Title.
Q11 .S79 1981

A Smithsonian book of comic-book comics /. [Washington, D.C.] [New York] , 1981. p. cm. ISBN 0-87474-228-5 : LC Card 81-607842 DDC 741.5/973 19
PN6726 .S58

Smithsonian contributions to botany .
(no. 50) Nowicke, Joan W. Pollen morphology and phylogenetic relationships of the Berberidaceae /. Washington , 1981. p. cm. LC Card 80-21960 DDC 581 s 583/.117 19
QK1 .S2747 no. 50 QK495.B45

Smithsonian contributions to the marine sciences .
(no. 11) Sohm Abyssal Plain . Washington , 1981. p. cm. LC Card 81-607056 DDC 551.46/4 19
GC383 .S64

Smithsonian contributions to zoology .
(no. 321) Houbrick, Richard S. Review of the deep-sea genus Argyropeza (Gastropoda, Prosobranchia, Cerithiidae) /. Washington , 1980. iii, 30 p. : LC Card 80-607017 DDC 591 s 594/.32 19
QL1 .S54 no. 321 QL430.5.C4

(no. 328) Waller, Thomas R. Functional morphology and development of veliger larvae of the European oyster, Ostrea edulis Linné /. Washington , 1981. iii, 70 p. : LC Card 80-23129 DDC 591 s 594/.11 19
QL1 .S54 no. 328 QL430.7.O9

(no. 330) Flint, Oliver S. Studies of neotropical caddisflies, XXVIII . Washington , 1981. p. cm. LC Card 80-607182 DDC 591 s 595.7/450987 19
QL1 .S54 no. 330 QL517.3.V4

(no. 331) Kornicker, Louis S., 1919- Benthic marine Cypridinoidea from Bermuda (Ostracoda) /. Washington , 1981. p. cm. LC Card 80-607812 DDC 591 s 595.3/4 19
QL1 .S54 no. 331 QL444.O85

(no. 332) Kornicker, Louis S., 1919- A restudy of the Ostracode genus Pleoschisma Brady, 1890 (Myodocopina) / . Washington, D.C. , 1981. iii, 16 p. : LC Card 80-607813 DDC 591 s 595.3/3 19
QL1 .S54 no. 332 QL444.O85

(no. 333) Opler, Paul A. The leafmining moths of the genus Cameraria associated with Fagaceae in California (Lepidoptera, Gracillariidae) /. Washington , 1981. p. cm. LC Card 80-26743 DDC 591 s 595.78/1 19
QL1 .S54 no. 333 QL561.G7

(no. 337) Olson, Storrs L. The relationships of the Pedionomidae (Aves, Charadriiformes) /. Washington , 1981. p. cm.   LC Card 81-412   DDC 591 s 598/.33 19
QL1 .S54 no. 337 QL696.C465

SMITHSONIAN INSTITUTION - CATALOGS.
Smithsonian Institution. Finders' guide to prints and drawings in the Smithsonian Institution /. Washington, D.C. , 1981. p. cm.   ISBN 0-87474-317-6   LC Card 81-607070   DDC 760/.074/0153 19
N855.8 .A56

Smithsonian Institution. Cooper-Hewitt Museum of Decorative Arts and Design. see Cooper-Hewitt Museum of Decorative Arts and Design.

SMITHSONIAN INSTITUTION - GUIDE-BOOKS.
Smithsonian Institution. Official guide to the Smithsonian. Washington, D.C. , 1981. p. cm.   LC Card 80-607800   DDC 069/.09753 19
Q11 .S79 1981

Smithsonian Institution. Hirshhorn Museum and Sculpture Garden. see Hirshhorn Museum and Sculpture Garden.

Smithsonian Institution. National Air Museum. see National Air and Space Museum.

Smithsonian Institution. National Collection of Fine Arts.
Across the nation : fine art for Federal buildings, 1972-1979. Washington, D.C. : National Collection of Fine Arts, Smithsonian Institution, c1980. 35 p. : ill. ; 26 cm. Catalogue of an exhibition prepared by V. M. Mecklenburg, and held at the National Collection of Fine Arts, Smithsonian Institution, June 4-Sept. 1, 1980 and at Hunter Museum of Art, Jan. 11-Mar. 1, 1981.   LC Card 80-51702   DDC 709/.73/0740153 19
1. Art, American - Exhibitions. 2. Art, Modern - 20th century - United States - Exhibitions. 3. Art and state - United States - Exhibitions. 4. United States - Public buildings - Exhibitions. I. Mecklenburg, Virginia, 1946-. II. Hunter Museum of Art. III. Title.
N6512 .S6 1980

Flint, Janet A. Supplement to "Checklist of prints," Jacob Kainen, prints, a retrospective /. Washington , 1980. p. cm.   LC Card 80-26344   DDC 769.92/4 19
NE539.K25 A4 1980

Rubenstein, Daryl R. Max Weber, prints and color variations . [Washington, D.C.] , c1980. 15 p. :   LC Card 80-51701   DDC 769.92/4 19
NE539.W38 A4 1980a

Smithsonian Institution. National Collection of Fine Arts. Renwick Gallery. see Renwick Gallery.

Smithsonian Institution. National Gallery of Art (Mellon Gallery) see United States. National Gallery of Art.

Smithsonian Institution. National Gallery of Art (now National Collection of Fine Arts) see Smithsonian Institution. National Collection of Fine Arts.

Smithsonian Institution. National Museum of History and Technology. see National Museum of History and Technology.

SMITHSONIAN INSTITUTION. NATIONAL PORTRAIT GALLERY.
Voss, Frederick. We never sleep . Washington, D.C. , 1981. p. cm.   LC Card 81-607851   DDC 363.2/89/0973 19
HV8087.P75 V67

Smithsonian Institution. Office of International and Environmental Programs. Freeman, Peter H. The environmental impact of a large tropical reservoir . Washington , 1974. 86 p., [1] fold. leaf of plates :   LC Card 81-450719   DDC 333.78/46 19
QH195.G53 F73

Smithsonian Institution. Renwick Gallery. see Renwick Gallery.

Smithsonian Institution. Traveling Exhibition Service.
Corcoran Gallery of Art. Of time and place . Washington, D.C. , 1981. p. cm.   ISBN 0-86528-010-X   LC Card 81-607836   DDC 704.9/42/0973074013 19
N6510 .C69 1981

Kraft, James. John Sloan in Santa Fe . Washington, D.C. , 1981. p. cm.   ISBN 0-86528-011-8   LC Card 81-607831   DDC 759.13 19
ND237.S476 A4 1981

Muratorio, Ricardo. A feast of color, Corpus Christi dance costumes of Ecuador . Washington, D.C. , 1981. p. cm.   ISBN 0-86528-008-8   LC Card 80-29379   DDC 793.3/19866 19
GT4995.C6 M87

Ostroff, Eugene. Western views and Eastern visions /. Washington , 1981. 118 p. :   ISBN 0-86528-005-3 (pbk.)   LC Card 81-70   DDC 779/.9978 19
TR23.6 .O87

The Photographer's hand /. Washington, D.C. , c1980. p. cm.   LC Card 80-27845   DDC 779/.09/047074013 19
TR646.U5 P45

Pottery, a notebook for new potters /. Washington, D.C. [1981] p. cm.   ISBN 0-86528-009-6   LC Card 81-5828   DDC 738.1 19
TT920 .P6

Venini glass /. [Washington, D.C.] , 1981. p. cm.   ISBN 0-86528-012-6   LC Card 81-14395   DDC 748.295/31 19
NK5198.V38 A4 1981

Witteborg, Lothar P., 1927- Good show, a practical guide for temporary exhibitions /. Washington, D.C. , 1981. 172 p. :   ISBN 0-86528-007-X   LC Card 80-39543   DDC 069.5 19
N4396 .W57

SMOKE - ECONOMIC ASPECTS - OREGON - WILLAMETTE VALLEY.
Conklin, Frank S. An evaluation of expected private losses from selected public policies for reducing open field burning, Willamette Valley, Oregon /. Corvallis [1979] 78 p. ;   LC Card 80-620510   DDC 363.7/392 19
TD884 .C74

SMOKE - ENVIRONMENTAL ASPECTS - OREGON - WILLAMETTE VALLEY.
Conklin, Frank S. An evaluation of expected private losses from selected public policies for reducing open field burning, Willamette Valley, Oregon /. Corvallis [1979] 78 p. ;   LC Card 80-620510   DDC 363.7/392 19
TD884 .C74

SMOKING AND YOUTH - UNITED STATES.
Green, Dorothy E. Teenage smoking . Washington, D.C. [1979] ix, 259 p. ;   LC Card 80-601231   DDC 362.2/9 19
HV5745 .G74

SMOKING AND YOUTH - UNITED STATES - ADDRESSES, ESSAYS, LECTURES.
The Behavioral aspects of smoking /. Rockville, Md. , Washington, D.C. , 1979. vii, 192 p. ;   LC Card 79-600141   DDC 362.2/9 19
HV5740 .B43

SMOKING AND YOUTH - UNITED STATES - LONGITUDINAL STUDIES.
Green, Dorothy E. Teenage smoking . Washington, D.C. [1979] ix, 259 p. ;   LC Card 80-601231   DDC 362.2/9 19
HV5745 .G74

SMOKING - UNITED STATES.
Ippolito, Richard A. Staff report on consumer responses to cigarette health information /. [Washington] , 1979. 64 p. ;   LC Card 79-604242
HV5760 .I66   **NYPL [JLF 81-240]**

Smolen, M. D. Agricultural land use : effects on the chemical quality of runoff / M. D. Smolen, V. O. Shanholtz. Blacksburg, Va. : Virginia Water Resources Research Center, Virginia Polytechnic Institute and State University, 1980. vii, 82 p. : ill. ; 23 cm. (Bulletin - Virginia Water Resources Research Center ; 125) Bibliography: p. 29-30.   LC Card 80-622278   DDC 333.91/009755 s 363.7/3941 19
1. Agricultural pollution - Virginia. 2. Water - Pollution - Virginia. 3. Runoff - Virginia. I. Shanholtz, Vernon O., 1935- joint author. II. Series: Virginia Polytechnic Institute and State University. Water Resources Research Center. Bulletin, 125. III. Title.
TD201 .V57 no. 125 TD428.A37

Smolka, Richard G. Handbook of state election agencies and election officials / prepared for

Federal Election Commission by Richard G. Smolka. [Springfield, Va.] : U. S. Dept. of Commerce, National Technical Information Service, 1976. 176, 23, 56 p. ; 28 cm. Microfiche (neg.) NTIS. 3 sheets. 11 x 15 cm. (PB-257 816) "PB-257-816."   LC Card 76-603434
1. Elections - United States - Handbooks, manuals, etc. I. United States. Federal Election Commission. II. Title.
JK2021 .S58   **NYPL [*XME-9548]**

SMS Associates. A directory of Federal Government business assistance programs for women business owners : a small business guide. [Washington, D.C.] : U. S. Dept. of Commerce, U. S. Small Business Administration, [1980] iv, 71 p. ; 28 cm. "April 1980." Prepared for the Economic Development Administration, U. S. Dept. of Commerce, and the Small Business Administration. Includes indexes.   LC Card 80-602878   DDC 353.0082/048 19
1. Federal aid to minority business enterprises - United States. 2. Federal aid to minority business enterprises - United States - Directories. 3. Women-owned business enterprises - United States. I. United States. Economic Development Administration. II. United States. Small Business Administration. III. Title.
HD2346.U5 S17 1980

Smyres, G. A. (joint author) Hill, S. D. Electrowinning of zinc from zinc chloride in monopolar and bipolar fused-salt cells /. Washington [1981] p. cm.   LC Card 80-607820   DDC 622 s 669/.52 19
TN23 .U43 TN796

SNAKE INDIANS. see SHOSHONI INDIANS.

Snake River . United States. National Park Service. [Washington] [1980] viii, 302 p. :   LC Card 80-602290   DDC 333.78/45/097961 19
QH76.5.S62 U54 1980

SNAKE RIVER.
United States. National Park Service. Snake River . [Washington] [1980] viii, 302 p. :   LC Card 80-602290   DDC 333.78/45/097961 19
QH76.5.S62 U54 1980

SNAKES - FLORIDA - GEOGRAPHICAL DISTRIBUTION.
Christman, Steven P. Patterns of geographic variation in Florida snakes /. Gainesville , 1980. p. 158-256 :   LC Card 81-621400   DDC 574 s 597.95/09759 19
QH1 .F6 vol. 25, no. 3 QL666.O6

SNAKES - FLORIDA - VARIATION.
Christman, Steven P. Patterns of geographic variation in Florida snakes /. Gainesville , 1980. p. 158-256 :   LC Card 81-621400   DDC 574 s 597.95/09759 19
QH1 .F6 vol. 25, no. 3 QL666.O6

Snakes of Virginia /. Linzey, Donald W. Charlottesville , 1981. p. cm.   ISBN 0-8139-0826-4   LC Card 81-12951   DDC 597.96/09755 19
QL666.O6 L74

SNAKES - VIRGINIA - IDENTIFICATION.
Linzey, Donald W. Snakes of Virginia /. Charlottesville , 1981. p. cm.   ISBN 0-8139-0826-4   LC Card 81-12951   DDC 597.96/09755 19
QL666.O6 L74

Snearley, K. E. Environmental inventory of the Chain of Lakes and Fox River region of Illinois / K. E. Snearley. [Antioch] : State of Illinois, Chain of Lakes-Fox River Commission, 1977. ix, 185 p., [5] leaves of plates (4 fold.) : maps ; 28 cm. Bibliography: p. 177-183.   LC Card 78-620605   DDC 574.9773/2 19
1. Natural history - Illinois - Chain O'Lakes region. 2. Natural history - Fox River, Wis. and Ill. 3. Chain O'Lakes region, Ill. 4. Fox River, Wis. and Ill. I. Illinois. Chain of Lakes-Fox River Commission. II. Title.
QH105.I3 S65

SNODGRASS, CHARLES WILLIAM, 1940-
United States. Congress. Senate. Committee on Armed Services. Nomination of Charles W. Snodgrass . Washington , 1980. ii, 7 p. ;   LC Card 80-602952   DDC 353.63 19
KF26 .A7 1980b

Snow and Quemado Lakes. Brandvold, D. K. Chemical and biological survey of the Upper Gila River system in New Mexico . Las Cruces, N.M. [1979] iii, 48 p. ;   LC Card 80-622273

DDC 333.91/009789 s 628.1/686789/692 19
GB705.N6 N64 no. 110 QH105.N6

SNOW - CONGRESSES.
Workshop on Operational Applications of
Satellite Snowcover Observations, Sparks, Nev.,
1979. Operational applications of satellite
snowcover observations . Washington, D.C. ,
1980. vi, 301 p. : LC Card 80-602361 DDC
551.57/846 19
GB2601.72.A83 W67 1979

Snow, David E. Paradise Inn, Mount Rainier
National Park, Washington / by David E.
Snow. [Denver] : Denver Service Center,
Historic Preservation Division, National Park
Service, U. S. Dept. of the Interior, [1979?] vii,
153 p. : ill. ; 28 cm. "Historic structure report."
Bibliography: p. 104-105. LC Card 79-603743 DDC
728/.5/0288 19
1. Mount Rainier National Park. Paradise Inn. I. Title.
TX941.P37 S64

SNOW SURVEYS - COLORADO.
Washichek, Jack N. Summary of snow survey
measurements for Colorado and New Mexico,
1971-1977 . Denver, Colo. [1978] xxiii, 128
p. : LC Card 79-601670 DDC 551.57/9/788 19
GB2625.C6 W37

SNOW SURVEYS - NEW MEXICO.
Washichek, Jack N. Summary of snow survey
measurements for Colorado and New Mexico,
1971-1977 . Denver, Colo. [1978] xxiii, 128
p. : LC Card 79-601670 DDC 551.57/9/788 19
GB2625.C6 W37

Snowbarger, Marvin. A general model for the
study of union membership / by Marvin
Snowbarger. San Jose : Institute for Business
and Economic Research, School of Business,
California State University, 1973. 38 p. ; 28 cm.
Microfilm.
1. Trade-unions. I. California State University, San Jose.
Institute for Business and Economic Research. II. Title.
NYPL [*ZT-1259]

Snyder, John Parr, 1926- Space oblique mercator
projection mathematical development / by John
P. Snyder. Reston, VA : U. S. Geological
Survey, [1981] p. cm. (Geological Survey bulletin .
1518) Bibliography: p. LC Card 81-607029 DDC
557.3 s 526.8 19
1. Space oblique Mercator projection (Cartography). I.
Title.
QE75 .B9 no. 1518 GA115

So proudly we hail . Furlong, William Rea, 1881-
Washington, D.C. , 1981. p. cm. ISBN
0-87474-448-2 LC Card 81-607808 DDC
929.9/2/0973 19
CR113 .F93

SOAP - WASTE DISPOSAL.
United States. Environmental Protection
Agency. Office of Water and Hazardous
Materials. Effluent Guidelines Division.
Development document for effluent limitations
guidelines and new source performance
standards . - Washington , 1974. xiii, 202 p. :
NYPL [JSF 80-270]

**Social and Cultural Impacts of Tourism, Joint
Unesco-World Bank Seminar on the.** see
**Joint Unesco-World Bank Seminar on the
Social and Cultural Impacts of Tourism,
Washington, D.C., 1976.**

**The social and economic effects of the Florida
tourist industry /.** Schultz, Ronald R. Boca
Raton , 1978. x, 123 p. : LC Card 79-622949
G155.U6 S37

**Social and economic implications of cancer in the
United States .** United States. National Center
for Health Statistics. Hyattsville, Md. ,
Washington [1981]. iv, 43 p. : ISBN
0-8406-0203-0 LC Card 80-607176 DDC
362.1/96994 19
RC276 .U56 1981

**The social and economic status of the Black
population in the United States, 1790-1978 .**
United States. Bureau of the Census.
Washington [1979] x, 271 p. ; LC Card
79-607000 DDC 312/.0973 s 301.45/19/6073 19
HA203 .A218 no. 80 E185.8

**Social and medical services in housing for the
aged /.** Lawton, Mortimer Powell. Rockville,
Md. , Washington, D.C. , 1980. vii, 112 p. ;
LC Card 80-603249 DDC 363.5/9 19
HD7287.92.U54 L383

SOCIAL BEHAVIOR IN ANIMALS.
Escherich, Peter C. Social biology of the
bushy-tailed woodrat, Neotoma cinerea /.
Berkeley , 1981. p. cm. ISBN 0-520-09647-9 LC
Card 81-11492 DDC 599.32/33 19
QL737.R638 E79

Litte, Marcia. Social biology of the polistine
wasp Mischocyttarus labiatus . Washington ,
1981. p. cm. LC Card 81-607071 DDC 591 s
595.79/8 19
QL1 .S54 no. 327 QL568.V5

Sunquist, Melvin E. The social organization of
tigers (Panthera tigris) in Royal Chitawan
National Park, Nepal /. Washington [D.C.] ,
1981. p. cm. LC Card 81-607928 DDC 591 s
599.74/428 19
QL1 .S54 no. 336 QL737.C23

**Social biology of the bushy-tailed woodrat,
Neotoma cinerea /.** Escherich, Peter C.
Berkeley , 1981. p. cm. ISBN 0-520-09647-9 LC
Card 81-11492 DDC 599.32/33 19
QL737.R638 E79

**Social biology of the polistine wasp
Mischocyttarus labiatus .** Litte, Marcia.
Washington , 1981. p. cm. LC Card 81-607071
DDC 591 s 595.79/8 19
QL1 .S54 no. 327 QL568.V5

SOCIAL CHANGE.
Hedebro, Göran, 1945- Communication and
social change in developing nations . Ames ,
1981. p. cm. ISBN 0-8138-0326-8 LC Card
81-8191 DDC 302.2/09172/4 19
HN980 .H4 1981

SOCIAL CHANGE - CASE STUDIES.
Joint Center for Urban Studies. The behavioral
foundations of neighborhood change /.
Washington [1979] 205 p. ; LC Card 79-601949
HT123 .J63 1979 **NYPL [JLF 81-252]**

**Social characteristics of neighborhoods as
indicators of the effects of highway
improvements.** Marshall Kaplan, Gans, and
Kahn. Washington, 1972. vii, 81, A88 p. LC
Card 73-601292 DDC 388.1/22/0973 19
HE355.3.E3 M37 1972

**SOCIAL CLASSES - ADDRESSES, ESSAYS,
LECTURES.**
Classes, power, and conflict . Berkeley , 1981,
c1982. p. cm. ISBN 0-520-04535-1 LC Card
81-43382 DDC 305.5 19
HT611 .C55

**SOCIAL CLASSES - FRANCE - TOULOUSE -
HISTORY.**
Aminzade, Ronald, 1949- Class, politics, and
early industrial capitalism . Albany, N.Y. ,
1981. p. cm. LC Card 80-28284 DDC 330.944/86
19
HD8437.T68 A46 1981

**SOCIAL CONFLICT - ADDRESSES, ESSAYS,
LECTURES.**
Classes, power, and conflict . Berkeley , 1981,
c1982. p. cm. ISBN 0-520-04535-1 LC Card
81-43382 DDC 305.5 19
HT611 .C55

The social context of helping . Taber, Merlin.
Rockville, Md. , Washington , 1980. v, 259 p. ;
LC Card 80-602564 DDC 362.4/048 19
HV1568 .T33

SOCIAL DEMOCRACY. see SOCIALISM.

**SOCIAL DEVIANCE. see DEVIANT
BEHAVIOR.**

SOCIAL ECOLOGY. see HUMAN ECOLOGY.

**Social effects of changes in uses of Bear Lake, an
interstate body of water /.** Andrews, Wade H.
Logan , 1975. x, 119 p. : LC Card 77-623439
DDC 333.91/63/0979213 19
HD1695.B38 A52

SOCIAL ETHICS.
Tipton, Steven M. Getting saved from the
sixties . Berkeley , c1981. p. cm. ISBN
0-520-03868-1 LC Card 81-3033 DDC 973.92
19
HN59 .T58

SOCIAL ETHICS - CONGRESSES.
Extending the human life span . [Chicago] ,
Washington [1977] v, 70 p. : LC Card
77-604795
HQ1064.U5 E9 **NYPL [*XME-9403]**

SOCIAL HYGIENE. see PUBLIC HEALTH.

Social indicator series .
(SIS-4) Maine. State Planning Office. Indicators
of poverty. [Augusta, Me. , 1980] [22] p. ; LC
Card 80-621545 DDC 339.4/6/09741 19
HC107.M23 P625 1980

SOCIAL INDICATORS - ALABAMA.
Molnar, Joseph J. Development characteristics
in non-metropolitan Alabama . Auburn, Ala. ,
1979. 31 p. : LC Card 79-622432 DDC
307.7/2/09761 19
HN25 .M64

**SOCIAL INDICATORS - NEW HAMPSHIRE -
HILL.**
Adler, Steven P. Hill reestablishment . Fort
Belvoir, Va. , Springfield, Va. , 1978. viii, 229
p. : LC Card 79-601444
HN80.H54 A34

SOCIAL INDICATORS - SOUTH DAKOTA.
Wagner, Robert T. Characteristics and needs of
the aged in South Dakota, 1980-1990 /.
Brookings, S.D. , 1978. ix, 238 leaves : LC
Card 80-622161 DDC 305.2/6/09783 19
HQ1064.U6 S7

SOCIAL INDICATORS - UNITED STATES.
Campbell, Angus, 1910- The sense of well-being
in America . New York , c1981. xiii, 263 p. ;
ISBN 0-07-009683-X LC Card 80-14379
HN59 .C29 **NYPL [JLE 81-367]**

**SOCIAL INDICATORS - UNITED STATES -
CONGRESSES.**
A Numerator and denominator for measuring
change . Washington , 1975. 195 p. : LC Card
75-619192 DDC 001.4/33 19
HA37 .U52 1975

**SOCIAL INSURANCE. see SOCIAL
SECURITY.**

SOCIAL JUSTICE.
Winslow, Gerald R. Triage and justice /.
Berkeley , c1982. p. cm. ISBN 0-520-04328-6
LC Card 81-10434 DDC 174/.2 19
R725.5 .W56

SOCIAL LEGISLATION - UNITED STATES.
United States. Panel on Government and the
Regulation of Corporate and Individual
Decisions. Government and the regulation of
corporate and individual decisions in the
eighties . Washington , 1980. 113 p. ; LC Card
80-29251 DDC 343.73/08 19
KF1600 .A843

**SOCIAL MEDICINE - UNITED STATES -
HISTORY - 19TH CENTURY.**
Fellman, Anita Clair. Making sense of self .
Philadelphia , 1981. p. cm. ISBN 0-8122-7810-0
LC Card 81-51141 DDC 613/.07/073 19
RA440.3.U5 F43

**SOCIAL ORGANIZATION. see SOCIAL
STRUCTURE.**

**The social organization of tigers (Panthera tigris)
in Royal Chitawan National Park, Nepal /.**
Sunquist, Melvin E. Washington [D.C.] , 1981.
p. cm. LC Card 81-607928 DDC 591 s 599.74/428
19
QL1 .S54 no. 336 QL737.C23

SOCIAL PROGRESS. see PROGRESS.

SOCIAL PSYCHIATRY - CONGRESSES.
Conference on Mental Health and the
Economy, Hunt Valley, Md., 1978. Mental
health and the economy . Kalamazoo, Mich.
[1979] viii, 423 p. : ISBN 0-911558-69-1 LC
Card 79-25809
RC455 .C625 1978 **NYPL [JLE 80-2456]**

SOCIAL PSYCHOLOGY.
Simon, Michael A. Understanding human
action . Albany , c1981. p. cm. ISBN
0-87395-498-X LC Card 81-5280 DDC 302 19
HM251 .S622

**SOCIAL RESEARCH. see SOCIAL SCIENCE
RESEARCH.**

**SOCIAL SCIENCE. see SOCIAL SCIENCES;
SOCIOLOGY.**

SOCIAL SCIENCE RESEARCH.
Singer, Burton. Some methodological issues in
the analysis of longitudinal surveys /.
[Madison] , 1976. 56 p. ; LC Card 78-624379
DDC 330/.723 19
H62 .S4775

SOCIAL SCIENCES. Here and with local
subdivisions are entered works on the

discipline of social sciences.

SOCIAL SCIENCES - BIBLIOGRAPHY.
Coal and the social sciences . [Lexington, Ky.]
[1979] 41 leaves ;   LC Card 80-624324   DDC
016.622/334 19
Z6738.C6 C62 TN800

Social sciences, economics. United States. Library
of Congress. Subject Cataloging Division.
Classification, Class H, Subclasses H-HJ, social
sciences, economics /. Washington , 1981. xiii,
400 p. ;   ISBN 0-8444-0353-9 (pbk.)   LC Card
80-607827   DDC 025.4/63 19
Z696.U5 H-HJ 1981

**SOCIAL SCIENCES - MATHEMATICAL
      MODELS.**
Hirshfeld, Stephen F. Algebraic systems ;
applications in the behavioral and social
sciences /. Alexandria, Va. , 1978. 119 p. ;
                    NYPL [JLF 80-1630]

SOCIAL SCIENCES - METHODOLOGY.
Simon, Michael A. Understanding human
action . Albany , c1981. p. cm.   ISBN
0-87395-498-X   LC Card 81-5280   DDC 302 19
HM251 .S622

**SOCIAL SCIENCES - PERIODICALS -
      BIBLIOGRAPHY - UNION LISTS.**
Indiana University, Bloomington. Libraries.
Current Japanese serials in the humanities and
social sciences received in American libraries /.
Bloomington, Ind. , 1980. vii, 337 p. ;   LC Card
80-127108
Z6958.J3 I5 1980 PN5407.P4
                    *NYPL [*OSB 80-3783]*

**SOCIAL SCIENTISTS IN GOVERNMENT -
      UNITED STATES.**
United States. General Accounting Office.
Federally-financed research and communication
on Soviet affairs . [Washington, D.C. , 1980] ii,
37 p. ;   LC Card 80-602671   DDC 947/.007/073 19
DK38.8 .U54 1980

Social security . United States. Congress. House.
Select Committee on Aging. Subcommittee on
Retirement Income and Employment.
Washington , 1980. v, 39 p. ;   LC Card
80-603864   DDC 353.0082/56 19
HD7125 .U537 1980a

The Social Security Act and related laws /.
United States. [Social Security Act.]
Washington , 1980. viii, 856, xxx p. ;   LC Card
81-601049   DDC 344.73/02 347.3042 19
KF3644 1980

**Social Security Administration office space
      problems .** United States. Congress. House.
Committee on Ways and Means. Subcommittee
on Social Security. Washington , 1980. iii, 137
p. :   LC Card 80-603328   DDC 353.0082/56/0682
19
KF27 .W347 1980a

Social Security and economic cycles /. Koitz,
David. Washington , 1980. vii, 21 p. ;   LC Card
80-604122   DDC 338.4/336843/00973 19
HD7125 .K588

Social security dependents' benefits . United
States. Congress. House. Committee on Ways
and Means. Subcommittee on Social Security.
Washington , 1980. iii, 73 p. ;   LC Card
80-604069   DDC 368.4/3/00973 19
KF27 .W347 1980c

Social security financing . United States.
Congress. Senate. Committee on Finance.
Subcommittee on Social Security. Washington ,
1980. iii, 169 p. ;   LC Card 80-602164   DDC
353.0072 19
KF26 .F568 1980

**SOCIAL SECURITY - LAW AND
      LEGISLATION - UNITED STATES.**
United States. [Social Security Act.] The Social
Security Act and related laws /. Washington ,
1980. viii, 856, xxx p. ;   LC Card 81-601049
DDC 344.73/02 347.3042 19
KF3644 1980

United States. Congress. House. Committee on
Post Office and Civil Service. Subcommittee on
Compensation and Employee Benefits.
Withholding state income tax for annuitants
and amending student survivor annuity
provisions . Washington , 1981. iii, 31 p. ;   LC
Card 81-601887   DDC 343.7305/242
347.3035242 19
KF27 .P638 1981

United States. Congress. House. Committee on
Ways and Means. Subcommittee on Social
Security. Receipt of Social Security benefits by
persons incarcerated in penal institutions .
Washington , 1980. iv, 96 p. ;   LC Card
80-603715   DDC 368.4/00880692 19
KF27 .W347 1980b

United States. Congress. Senate. Committee on
Finance. Subcommittee on Social Security.
Social security retirement test . Washington ,
1980. iv, 305 p. ;   LC Card 80-603289   DDC
344.73/023 19
KF26 .F568 1980a

**Social security programs in the President's fiscal
      year 1981 budget .** United States. Congress.
House. Committee on Ways and Means.
Subcommittee on Social Security. Washington ,
1980. iii, 225 p. ;   LC Card 80-602523   DDC
353.0072 19
KF27 .W347 1980

Social security retirement test . United States.
Congress. Senate. Committee on Finance.
Subcommittee on Social Security. Washington ,
1980. iv, 305 p. ;   LC Card 80-603289   DDC
344.73/023 19
KF26 .F568 1980a

**SOCIAL SECURITY TAXES - ECONOMIC
      ASPECTS - UNITED STATES.**
United States. Congress. Senate. Committee on
Banking, Housing, and Urban Affairs.
Subcommittee on Economic Stabilization.
Economic impact of payroll taxes .
Washington , 1980. iv, 65 p. :   LC Card
80-602496   DDC 330.973/0926 19
KF26 .B39425 1980a

SOCIAL SECURITY TAXES - TEXAS.
Jarrett, James E. Texas assumes the social
security obligation. [Lexington, Ky.] [1979] 12
p. ;   LC Card 80-140046   DDC 353.9 s
353.9764001/234 19
JS308 .C6 no. 680 JK4857

**SOCIAL SECURITY TAXES - UNITED
      STATES.**
Chaikind, Stephen. Paying for social security .
[Washington, D.C.], 1981. xix, 47 p. ;   LC Card
81-601225   DDC 353.0082/56 19
HD7125 .C47

United States. Congress. Senate. Committee on
Finance. Subcommittee on Social Security.
Social security financing . Washington , 1980.
iii, 169 p. ;   LC Card 80-602164   DDC 353.0072
19
KF26 .F568 1980

United States. Federal Council on the Aging.
The impact of the tax structure on the elderly.
Washington , 1975. iv, 119 p. ;   LC Card
76-601234
HJ4653.A82 U55 1975 NYPL [JLF 80-1411]

SOCIAL SECURITY - UNITED STATES.
Burkhauser, Richard V. Disentangling the
annuity from the redistributive aspects of social
security /. [Madison] , 1979. 30 p. ;   LC Card
80-622901   DDC 368.4/4 19
HD7125 .B84

Koitz, David. Summary of recommendations
and surveys on social security and pension
policies . Washington , 1980. vii, 48 p. ;   LC
Card 80-603856   DDC 368.4/3/00973 19
HD7125 .K59

Legislative history, titles I-XX of the Social
security act . - Washington , 1980. ca. 1060 p. ;
                    NYPL [JLE 81-598]

Leimer, Dean R. The role of the replacement
rate in the design of the social security benefit
structure /. Washington, D.C. , 1979. iv, 15 p. ;
      LC Card 79-600182   DDC 368.4/00973 s
368.4/3/00973 19
HD7123 .A395 no. 36 HD7125

Shipp, P. Royal. Background material on work,
retirement, and social security /. Washington ,
1980. v, 24 p. :   LC Card 80-603060   DDC
368.4/3/00973 19
HD7125 .S527

United States. Congress. House. Committee on
Post Office and Civil Service. Subcommittee on
Compensation and Employee Benefits.
Desirability and feasibility of universal social
security coverage . Washington , 1980. iii, 89
p. ;   LC Card 80-603299   DDC 353.0082/56 19
KF27 .P638 1980i

United States. Congress. House. Committee on
Ways and Means. Subcommittee on Oversight.
Strategies to encourage older workers to
voluntarily extend their worklives .
Washington , 1980. iii, 264 p. ;   LC Card
80-604060   DDC 368.4/3/00973 19
KF27 .W345 1980k

United States. Congress. House. Committee on
Ways and Means. Subcommittee on Social
Security. Social security dependents' benefits .
Washington , 1980. iii, 73 p. ;   LC Card
80-604069   DDC 368.4/3/00973 19
KF27 .W347 1980c

United States. Congress. House. Select
Committee on Aging. Subcommittee on
Retirement Income and Employment. Oversight
on recommendations of 1979 Social Security
Advisory Council . Washington , 1980. iv, 208
p. :   LC Card 80-603006   DDC 368.4/00973 19
KF27.5 .A374 1980

United States. Congress. House. Select
Committee on Aging. Subcommittee on
Retirement Income and Employment. Social
security . Washington , 1980. v, 39 p. :   LC
Card 80-603864   DDC 353.0082/56 19
HD7125 .U537 1980a

United States. Congress. Senate. Special
Committee on Aging. Adapting social security
to a changing work force . Washington , 1980.
iii, 102 p. :   LC Card 80-602460   DDC
368.4/3/00973 19
KF26.5 .A3 1979d

United States. Congress. Senate. Special
Committee on Aging. Social security, what
changes are necessary? . Washington , 1981. 4
v. :   LC Card 81-600970   DDC 368.4/3/00973 19
KF26.5 .A3 1980e

United States. Social Security Administration.
Office of Research and Statistics. 1974 followup
of disabled & nondisabled adults /.
Washington , 1979. 2 v. in 1 ;
                    NYPL [JLF 80-1201]

**SOCIAL SECURITY - UNITED STATES -
      FINANCE.**
Chaikind, Stephen. Paying for social security .
[Washington, D.C.], 1981. xix, 47 p. ;   LC Card
81-601225   DDC 353.0082/56 19
HD7125 .C47

Koitz, David. Social Security and economic
cycles /. Washington , 1980. vii, 21 p. ;   LC
Card 80-604122   DDC 338.4/336843/00973 19
HD7125 .K588

United States. Congress. House. Committee on
Ways and Means. Subcommittee on Social
Security. Social security programs in the
President's fiscal year 1981 budget .
Washington , 1980. iii, 225 p. ;   LC Card
80-602523   DDC 353.0072 19
KF27 .W347 1980

**SOCIAL SECURITY - UNITED STATES -
      MANAGEMENT.**
United States. Congress. Senate. Committee on
Finance. Subcommittee on Social Security.
Social security financing . Washington , 1980.
iii, 169 p. ;   LC Card 80-602164   DDC 353.0072
19
KF26 .F568 1980

Social security, what changes are necessary? .
United States. Congress. Senate. Special
Committee on Aging. Washington , 1981. 4 v. :
LC Card 81-600970   DDC 368.4/3/00973 19
KF26.5 .A3 1980e

**SOCIAL SERVICE - ADMINISTRATION. see
      SOCIAL WORK ADMINISTRATION.**

**SOCIAL SERVICE - CALIFORNIA -
      DIRECTORIES.**
California. Community Care Licensing Division.
Directory of community care facilities .
[Sacramento, Ca.] [1980?] vii, 572 p. ;   LC
Card 80-621902   DDC 362/.025/794 19
HV89 .C34 1980

SOCIAL SERVICE - CONGRESSES.
United Nations Conference on Human
Settlements, Vancouver, B.C., 1976. Analysis of
programmes of the organizations in the United
Nations system in the field of human
settlements . [New York?] 1976. 133 p. (6
fold)   LC Card 80-515449
JX1977 .A2 A/CONF.70/A/4

SOCIAL SERVICE - HAWAII.
Nishimura, Charles H. The feasibility of
integrating human services in Hawaii .
Honolulu , 1978. xiii, 262 p. : LC Card
78-624136 DDC 027.6/5 s 361/.9969 19
KFH20 .H38 1978, no. 1 HV98.H3

SOCIAL SERVICE - ILLINOIS - FINANCE.
Illinois. Bureau of Title XX Administration.
Title XX Donated Funds Initiative . Springfield,
Ill. , 1979. 53 p. : LC Card 79-624230 DDC
361.7 19
HV41 .I29 1979

SOCIAL SERVICE - ILLINOIS - PLANNING.
Testa, Mark. Human services in Illinois .
[Chicago] , 1978 [i.e. 1979] vi, 172 p. : LC
Card 80-623960 DDC 361.6/09773 19
HV98.I15 T48

**SOCIAL SERVICE - INDIANA -
DIRECTORIES.**
Indiana. Commission for Higher Education.
Directory of educational information and
counseling services. Indianapolis , 1979. iv, 108
p. : LC Card 79-625886 DDC 370/.25/772 19
L903.I6 I53 1979

**SOCIAL SERVICE - INFORMATION
SERVICES - OREGON - DIRECTORIES.**
Oregon. Information and Referral Task Force.
Oregon Information and Referral Task Force
report. Salem , 1978. ca. 300 p. in various
pagings ; LC Card 79-620753 DDC 361/.007 19
HV86 .O84 1978

**SOCIAL SERVICE - KANSAS -
DIRECTORIES.**
Kansas. Dept. of Economic Development.
Kansas directory of State associations. Topeka,
Kan. [1979] 44 p. in various pagings ; LC
Card 79-625232 DDC 361.7/025/781 19
HV86 .K27 1979

SOCIAL SERVICE - MINNESOTA.
Minnesota. Office of Human Services.
Consumer access study /. [St. Paul] , 1976. 23,
[16] p. ; LC Card 77-623076 DDC 361/.9776 19
HV86 .M675 1976c

**SOCIAL SERVICE - MINNESOTA -
EXAMINATIONS.**
Nelson, David D. Validation of selection
procedures for welfare specialists /. [St. Paul] ,
1976. 46 p. ; LC Card 77-622755 DDC 361/.0076
19
HV98.M65 N44

SOCIAL SERVICE - MONTANA.
Montana. Dept. of Community Affairs. Human
Resources Division. Community action for
Montana /. [Helena] [1978?] A, 73 p. : LC
Card 79-620736 DDC 361/.9786 19
HV86 .M95 1978

Social service needs of elder minorities . United
States. Congress. House. Select Committee on
Aging. Subcommittee on Housing and
Consumer Interests. Washington , 1981. iii, 39
p. ; LC Card 81-601324 DDC 362.6/089 19
KF27.5 .A358 1980c

**SOCIAL SERVICE - NEW YORK (CITY) -
DIRECTORIES.**
HRA basic facts. New York.
NYPL [JLM 80-980]

SOCIAL SERVICE - PUBLIC RELATIONS.
see PUBLIC RELATIONS - SOCIAL
SERVICE.

SOCIAL SERVICE - TEAM WORK.
MacNair, Ray H. Case coordination . Athens,
Ga. (300 Old College, Athens 30602) , c1980.
xi, 46, [1] p. : LC Card 81-621677 DDC
361.3/068 19
HV41 .M273

SOCIAL SERVICE - TEXAS.
Texas. Joint Advisory Committee on
Government Operations. Subcommittee on
Health and Welfare. Initial report with
recommendations to the Joint Advisory
Committee on Government Operations as
modifed by the Structure and Policy
Subcommittee /. [Austin?] [1976] iii leaves,
124 p. ; LC Card 80-622733 DDC 362/.9764 19
HV86 .T548 1976

SOCIAL SERVICE - UNITED STATES.
Nishimura, Charles H. The feasibility of
integrating human services in Hawaii .
Honolulu , 1978. xiii, 262 p. : LC Card

78-624136 DDC 027.6/5 s 361/.9969 19
KFH20 .H38 1978, no. 1 HV98.H3

SOCIAL SERVICE - VIRGINIA - PLANNING.
Virginia. Office of the Secretary of Human
Resources. The effects of services integration in
Virginia at the local and state level /.
Richmond [1978] 58 p. ; LC Card 79-624121
DDC 361.6/09755 19
HV86 .V86 1978

**SOCIAL SERVICE - WASHINGTON (STATE)
- DIRECTORIES.**
Washington (State). Office of Community
Development. A brief survey of CSA-related
anti-poverty organizations in Washington State.
[Olympia] , 1978. 64 p. ; LC Card 79-621288
DDC 361/.007 19
HV86 .W365 1978a *NYPL [JLF 81-121]*

Social services law bulletin
(no. 1) Davis, Bonnie E. Disclosure of adoption
records /. [Chapel Hill] , 1980. 10 p. ; LC Card
81-621375 DDC 346.75601/78 347.5606178 19
KFN7504.5.Z9 D38

**SOCIAL STRATIFICATION. see SOCIAL
CLASSES.**

SOCIAL STRUCTURE.
Adams, Richard Newbold, 1924- Observations
on the use of energy in social structure analysis
/. [Austin] , 1979. ii, 76 leaves ; LC Card
79-624609 DDC 303.4/83 19
TJ163.2 .A3

Jones, Lynne McCallister. Studying egocentric
networks by mass survey /. [Berkeley] , 1978.
v, 77 p. : LC Card 78-622144 DDC 301/.0723 19
HN29 .J63

SOCIAL STUDIES. see SOCIAL SCIENCES.

SOCIAL SURVEYS.
Jones, Lynne McCallister. Studying egocentric
networks by mass survey /. [Berkeley] , 1978.
v, 77 p. : LC Card 78-622144 DDC 301/.0723 19
HN29 .J63

**SOCIAL SURVEYS - ENGLAND -
BIRMINGHAM - COLLECTED WORKS.**
City of Birmingham structure plan .
[Birmingham] , 1973- v.<1-5> : ISBN
0-905122-05-4 : LC Card 80-515869 DDC
307.7/6/0942496 19
HT169.G72 B54639

SOCIAL SURVEYS - OREGON.
Oregon. Dept. of Economic Development.
[Oregon community profiles /. Portland, Or.]
[1978?- <75 > pamphlet ; LC Card 78-623103
DDC 979.5 19
HN79.O7 O73 1978

SOCIAL SURVEYS - UNITED STATES.
Michigan. University. Survey Research Center.
A panel study of income dynamics. Wave 1- ;
1968- Ann Arbor. *NYPL [M-11 5247]*

United States. Dept. of Housing and Urban
Development. Developmental needs of small
cities . [Washington] , 1979. vii, 294 p. : LC
Card 79-602073
HT123 .U43 1979

**SOCIAL SURVEYS - UNITED STATES -
LONGITUDINAL STUDIES -
CONGRESSES.**
Conference on the National Longitudinal
Surveys of Mature Women, United States
Department of Labor, 1978. Women's changing
roles at home and on the job . Washington ,
1978. iii, 331 p. : LC Card 79-601912
HQ1403 .C53 1978 *NYPL [JLF 81-250]*

SOCIAL SURVEYS - WASHINGTON (STATE)
An In-depth analysis of the needs assessment of
the elderly, 1976, Washington State . [Salem] ,
1978. 117 xvii p. ; LC Card 79-621901 DDC
362.6/09797 19
HQ1064.U6 W295

SOCIAL WELFARE. see SOCIAL SERVICE.

Social welfare services in Africa.
United Nations. Economic Commission for
Africa. Directory of activities of international
voluntary agencies in rural development in
Africa /. New York , 1977. iii, 173 p. ; LC
Card 79-109825 DDC 300 s 361.7/7/0256 19
JX1977 .A2 E/CN.14/SWCD/68

SOCIAL WORK. see SOCIAL SERVICE.

SOCIAL WORK ADMINISTRATION.
MacNair, Ray H. Case coordination . Athens,
Ga. (300 Old College, Athens 30602) , c1980.

xi, 46, [1] p. : LC Card 81-621677 DDC
361.3/068 19
HV41 .M273

**SOCIAL WORK ADMINISTRATION -
UNITED STATES - ABSTRACTS.**
Project SHARE. The Project Share collection,
1976-1979. Rockville, Md. [1979] vii, 891 p.,
28 cm. LC Card 80-601833 DDC 361.3/068 19
HV91 .P763 1979

**SOCIAL WORK EDUCATION -
MASSACHUSETTS.**
Massachusetts. Dept. of Public Welfare. Title
XX/FY 1979 . [Boston , 1978] 66 p. in various
pagings, [2] fold. leaves of plates : LC Card
80-620540 DDC 361/.007/15 19
HV11 .M365 1978

**Social work in a state-based system of child
health care .** Tri-Regional Workshop for Social
Workers in Maternal and Child Health Services
(1980 : Raleigh, N.C.) Chapel Hill [1981?] v,
156 p. : LC Card 81-50559 DDC
362.1/9892/000973 19
RJ102 .T74 1980

**SOCIAL WORK WITH CHILDREN -
UNITED STATES.**
Borgman, Robert D. Crisis intervention .
[Washington, D.C.] , 1979. ix, 33, [2] p. ; LC
Card 79-603994 DDC 362.7/1 19
HV873 .B65

**SOCIAL WORK WITH CHILDREN -
UNITED STATES - CONGRESSES.**
Tri-Regional Workshop for Social Workers in
Maternal and Child Health Services (1980 :
Raleigh, N.C.) Social work in a state-based
system of child health care . Chapel Hill
[1981?] v, 156 p. : LC Card 81-50559 DDC
362.1/9892/000973 19
RJ102 .T74 1980

**SOCIAL WORK WITH DELINQUENTS AND
CRIMINALS - VIRGINIA.**
Virginia. State Crime Commission. Children and
youth in trouble in Virginia . Richmond, Va.
[1977] xvi, 188 p. ; LC Card 80-622757 DDC
364.3/6/09755 19
HV9105.V7 V53 1977

**SOCIAL WORKERS - IN-SERVICE
TRAINING - UNITED STATES - CASE
STUDIES.**
Krantz, Steven. The effects of in-service
training on client progress and staff attitudes in
community residential facilities for the
developmentally disabled /. [Jefferson City,
Mo.] , 1979. v leaves, 46 p. ; LC Card
80-622405 DDC 362.1/968 19
HV91 .K67

**SOCIAL WORKERS - TRAINING OF -
ILLINOIS.**
Illinois. Bureau of Title XX Administration.
Handbook for Title XX training /. [Chicago ,
1977 or 1978] 46, [44] p. : LC Card 79-621587
DDC 361.3/07/15 19
HV11 .I39 1977

SOCIALISM AND YOUTH - CHINA.
Shirk, Susan L. Competitive comrades .
Berkeley , c1981. p. cm. ISBN 0-520-04299-9
LC Card 81-2772 DDC 371.8/1/091 19
LA1133.7 .S553

SOCIALISM IN FRANCE - HISTORY.
Hutton, Patrick H. The cult of the
revolutionary tradition . Berkeley , c1981. p.
cm. ISBN 0-520-04114-3 LC Card 80-28850
DDC 322.4/2/0944 19
HX263.B56 H87

SOCIALISM - UNITED STATES - HISTORY.
Lipow, Arthur. Authoritarian socialism in
America . Berkeley , c1981. p. cm. ISBN
0-520-04005-8 LC Card 79-65763 DDC
320.5/31/0973 19
HX86 .L73

**SOCIALIZATION, POLITICAL. see
POLITICAL SOCIALIZATION.**

**SOCIALIZED MEDICINE. see INSURANCE,
HEALTH.**

**SOCIALLY HANDICAPPED CHILDREN -
EDUCATION - CARIBBEAN AREA.**
Organization of American States. Dept. of
Educational Affairs. Educational deficits in the
Caribbean =. [Washington, D.C.] [1979] viii,
128 p. : LC Card 80-132005 DDC 371.9/67/09729

19
LC4095.C37 O73 1979

SOCIALLY HANDICAPPED CHILDREN - EDUCATION - CONGRESSES.
Achievement testing of disadvantaged and minority students for educational program evaluation /. [Monterey, CA] [1979] viii, 464 p. : LC Card 78-4519
LB3051 .A528   **NYPL [Sc D 80-645]**

SOCIALLY HANDICAPPED CHILDREN - EDUCATION - MISSOURI.
Missouri. Dept. of Elementary and Secondary Education. Title I, ESEA, manual of operational policies and guidelines. [Jefferson City, Mo.] [1980] ii, 80 p. ; LC Card 80-623988 DDC 371.96/7/09778 19
LC4092.M5 M57 1980

SOCIALLY HANDICAPPED CHILDREN - EDUCATION - WISCONSIN - STATISTICS.
Wisconsin. Division for Instructional Services. Title I Unit. Educational programs for disadvantaged children, funded through Title I of the Elementary and secondary education act in Wisconsin school districts during 1972-73 /. [Madison] , 1973. iii, 411 p. ; LC Card 75-624181 DDC 370/.9775 s 371.96/7/09775 19
L216 .B36 no. 3540 LC4092.W6

SOCIALLY HANDICAPPED - EDUCATION - UNITED STATES.
United States. Office of Education. Division of Vocational and Technical Education. Resurge '79 . Washington, D. C. , 1980. 81 p. ;
     NYPL [JLF 81-624]

Walther, Regis H. The measurement of work-relevant attitudes . - Washington , 1975. 19, 2. [4] p. ;   **NYPL [*XM-13884]**

SOCIALLY HANDICAPPED - UNITED STATES.
Walther, Regis H. The measurement of work-relevant attitudes . - Washington , 1975. 19, 2. [4] p. ;   **NYPL [*XM-13884]**

Sociedad Americana de Proyectistas. see American Society of Planning Officials.

Societal aspects of hydrogen energy systems / prepared for the Subcommittee on Advanced Energy Technologies and Energy Conservation Research, Development, and Demonstration of the Committee on Science and Technology, U. S. House of Representatives, Ninety-fifth Congress, second session, by the National Bureau of Standards and the Science Policy Research Division of the Library of Congress. Washington : U. S. Govt. Print. Off. : for sale by the Supt. of Docs., U. S. Govt. Print. Off., 1979. vii, 161 p. : diagrs. ; 24 cm. (Foresight . v. 1) At head of title: Committee print. "Serial YYY." "December 1978." Includes bibliographies.
     CONTENTS. - pt. A. Hydrogen, a workshop on societal aspects of hydrogen energy systems, prepared by National Bureau of Standards.--pt. B. Retrospective forecasting and the space program, prepared by the Library of Congress, Science Policy Research Division.
     LC Card 80-602232 DDC 338.4/766581/0973 19
     1. Hydrogen as fuel - Congresses. I. United States. National Bureau of Standards. II. United States. Library of Congress. Science Policy Research Division. III. United States. Congress. House. Committee on Science and Technology. Subcommittee on Advanced Energy Technologies and Energy Conservation Research, Development, and Demonstration. IV. Series.
TP359.H8 S58

Société de crédit suisse. see Crédit suisse.

SOCIETY AND ART. see ART AND SOCIETY.

SOCIETY AND ATOMIC WARFARE. see ATOMIC WARFARE AND SOCIETY.

SOCIETY AND DRUG ABUSE. see DRUG ABUSE - SOCIAL ASPECTS.

SOCIETY AND ENERGY POLICY. see ENERGY POLICY - SOCIAL ASPECTS.

SOCIETY AND LITERATURE. see LITERATURE AND SOCIETY.

Society and religion in Elizabethan England /. Greaves, Richard L. Minneapolis , c1981. ix, 925 p. ; ISBN 0-8166-1030-4 : LC Card 81-2530 DDC 942.05/5 19
HN460.M6 G7

SOCIETY AND THE ARTS. see ARTS AND SOCIETY.

Society for Information Display. Display Research Conference, 5th, Cherry Hill, N.J., 1978. Conference record of 1978 Biennial Display Research Conference . New York , Piscataway, N.J. , c1978. 87 p. : LC Card 78-113235
TK7882.I6 D567 1978   **NYPL [JSF 81-137]**

Society for the Study of Midwestern Literature. Midamerica; the yearbook of the Society for the Study of Midwestern Literature. 1- ; 1974- East Lansing, Mich..   **NYPL [JFL 80-267]**

Society of Automotive Engineers. Highway Tire Committee. R & D Planning Workshop, Transportation Systems Center, 1977. Tire rolling losses and fuel economy . Troy, MI , c1977. iii, 202 p. : LC Card 78-51861
TL151.6 .R18 1977

Society of Naval Architects and Marine Engineers, New York. Panel M-16 Modernization of Propulsion Shaft System) United States. Office of Noise Abatement and Control. Information on levels of environmental noise requisite to protect public health and welfare with an adequate margin of safety. Washington, 1974. ca 159 p. in various pagings: LC Card 76-11078   **NYPL [JSF 80-574]**

Society of Naval Architects and Marine Engineers New York. Ship's Machinery Committee. Panel M-16 (Modermzation of Propulsion Shaft System) see Society of Naval Architects and Marine Engineers, New York. Panel M-16 Modernization of Propulsion Shaft System)

Socio-economic and community factors in planning urban freeways. Bishop, A. Bruce. [Washington] 1970. xiii, 216 p. LC Card 73-610102
HE356.C2 B5   **NYPL [JLF 81-276]**

Socio-economic characteristics for Maine's counties and regions. Maine. Economic Planning and Statistical Services Division. [Augusta, Me. , 1979] 73 p. : LC Card 80-621816 DDC 330.9741/043 19
HC107.M2 M315 1979

The socio-economic impact of the Three Mile Island accident . Pennsylvania. Governor's Office of Policy and Planning. Harrisburg, Pa. [1980] iii, 162, [43] p., [1] folded leaf of plates : LC Card 81-621645 DDC 330.9748/18 19
HD9698.U54 M476 1980

SOCIOBIOLOGY - BIBLIOGRAPHY.
Brantley, James R. The etiology of criminality . Washington, D.C. , 1979. vii, 45 p. ; LC Card 80-601563 DDC 016.3643 19
Z5703 .B72 HV6115

The socioeconomic status of households headed by women . Mott, Frank. Washington, D.C. , 1979, 1980 printing. xiii, 68 p. : LC Card 80-601212 DDC 331.11/0973 s 305.4/8 19
HD5701 .U53 no. 72 HQ536

Sociological studies in aging. Goudy, Willis J. Older workers in small towns . Ames, Iowa [1977] viii, 205 p. : LC Card 80-623924 DDC 331.3/98/09777 19
HD6281.I8 G68

SOCIOLOGY. Here and with local subdivision are entered works on the discipline of sociology. Works on the social conditions of particular regions, countries, cities, etc., are entered under the name of the place subdivided by Social conditions.

SOCIOLOGY AND ART. see ART AND SOCIETY.

SOCIOLOGY AND LITERATURE. see LITERATURE AND SOCIETY.

SOCIOLOGY AND MEDICINE. see SOCIAL MEDICINE.

SOCIOLOGY AND THE ARTS. see ARTS AND SOCIETY.

SOCIOLOGY, CHRISTIAN - GREAT BRITAIN - HISTORY - SOURCES.
Greaves, Richard L. Society and religion in Elizabethan England /. Minneapolis , c1981. ix, 925 p. ; ISBN 0-8166-1030-4 : LC Card 81-2530 DDC 942.05/5 19
HN460.M6 G7

SOCIOLOGY - COLLECTED WORKS.
Alexander, Jeffrey C. Theoretical logic in sociology /. Berkeley , c1981- p. cm. ISBN 0-520-03062-1 (set) LC Card 75-17305 DDC 301 19
HM24 .A465

SOCIOLOGY, MEDICAL. see SOCIAL MEDICINE.

SOCIOLOGY, MILITARY - ASIA.
Ethnicity and the military in Asia /. Buffalo , 1978. ii, 169 p. : LC Card 80-623011 DDC 950 s 306/.2 19
DS1 .J637 vol. 3, no. 2 UB416

SOCIOLOGY, RURAL - CONGRESSES.
International Hill Lands Symposium, West Virginia University, 1976. Hill lands . [Morgantown, WV] [1976?] xiv, 770 p. : LC Card 80-100503 DDC 333.76/09143 19
S604.3 .I57 1976

SOCKEY SALMON.
Harris, Colin K. Forecast of the sockeye salmon run to Bristol Bay in 1979 /. Seattle , 1979. 50 p. : LC Card 79-624864 DDC 639/.2 s 597/.55 19
SH1 .W3352 no. 79-2 QL638.S2

SOCKEYE SALMON.
Nelson, David Charles, 1943- Annual performance report for Russian River red salmon study /. Juneau [1977?] 54 p. : LC Card 78-621575 DDC 597/.55 19
QL638.S2 N449

SOCORRO REGION, N.M. - ANTIQUITIES.
Berman, Mary Jane. Cultural resources overview of Socorro, New Mexico /. Albuquerque, N.M. : Santa Fe, N.M. : v, 128 p. : LC Card 80-602245 DDC 978.9/62 19
E78.N65 B36

Software and related technical reports. United States. National Technical Information Service. A directory of computer software & related technical reports, 1980. [Springfield, VA] , c1980. vii, 202, [108] p. ; LC Card 80-602222 DDC 001.64/25/029473 19
Z5644 .U54 1980 QA76.6

SOFTWARE, COMPUTER. see COMPUTER PROGRAMS; PROGRAMMING LANGUAGES (ELECTRONIC COMPUTERS)

Sohm Abyssal Plain : evaluating proximal sediment provenance / D.J. Stanley ... [et al.]. Washington : Smithsonian Institution Press, 1981. p. cm. (Smithsonian contributions to the marine sciences . no. 11) Bibliography: p. LC Card 81-607056 DDC 551.46/4 19
     1. Marine sediments - Sohm Plain. I. Stanley, Daniel J. II. Series. III. Series: Smithsonian Institution. Smithsonian contributions to the marine sciences , no. 11.
GC383 .S64

SOIL AND PLANTS. see PLANT-SOIL RELATIONSHIPS.

Soil and rock anchors for mobile homes . Kovacs, William D. Washington, D.C. , 1979. xvi, 147 p. : LC Card 79-600143 DDC 690/.02/18 s 690/.79 19
TA435 .U58 no. 107 TH4819.M6

Soil association map, Franklin County Conservation District, Franklin County, Washington /. United States. Soil Conservation Service. Portland, Or. , 1980. 1 map : LC Card 81-691509
G4283.F7J3 1980 .U51

SOIL CLASSIFICATION. see SOILS - CLASSIFICATION.

Soil classification for construction practice in shallow trenching /. Yokel, Felix Y. Washington, D.C. [1980] xiv, 76 p. : LC Card 80-600014 DDC 690/.02/18 s 624.1/51/012 19
TA435 .U58 no. 121 TA710

Soil conservation . United States. Congress. Senate. Committee on Agriculture, Nutrition, and Forestry. Subcommittee on Environment, Soil Conservation, and Forestry. Washington , 1980. v. 332 p. : LC Card 80-603997 DDC 333.76/16/09777 19
KF26 .A3543 1980c

SOIL CONSERVATION - ALASKA - TANANA LOOP.
Skaggs, Samuel. A design for agriculture in the Tanana Loop . [Juneau] , 1978. ii, 61 p. : LC

Card 79-620899   DDC 338.1/09798/6 19
S451.A3 S58

SOIL CONSERVATION DISTRICTS - VIRGINIA - DIRECTORIES.
Virginia. Soil and Water Conservation Commission. Directory of the Virginia soil & water conservation districts, 1979 /. Richmond , 1979. 40 p. :   LC Card 79-624120   DDC 631.4/025/755 19
S624.V8 V57 1979

Soil conservation, erosion, and sedimentation, Coon Creek Basin, Wisconsin /. Trimble, Stanley Wayne. Reston, Va. [1981] p. cm.   LC Card 81-607057   DDC 631.4/5/0977554 19
S624.W5 T74

SOIL CONSERVATION - IOWA.
United States. Congress. House. Committee on Agriculture. Subcommittee on Conservation and Credit. Special Areas Soil Conservation Act of 1980 . Washington , 1980. iv, 105 p. :   LC Card 81-600625   DDC 346.7304/67316/0262 347.3064673160262 19
KF27 .A3226 1980d

United States. Congress. Senate. Committee on Agriculture, Nutrition, and Forestry. Subcommittee on Environment, Soil Conservation, and Forestry. Soil conservation . Washington , 1980. v. 332 p. :   LC Card 80-603997   DDC 333.76/16/09777 19
KF26 .A3543 1980c

SOIL CONSERVATION - IOWA - IOWA RIVER WATERSHED - LINEAR PROGRAMMING.
Alt, Klaus F. Economics and the environment . Ames Iowa [1977] iv, 54 leaves ;   LC Card 80-623678   DDC 338.1/09777/6 19
S624.I6 A47

SOIL CONSERVATION - LAW AND LEGISLATION - UNITED STATES.
United States. Congress. House. Committee on Agriculture. Subcommittee on Conservation and Credit. Special Areas Soil Conservation Act of 1980 . Washington , 1980. iv, 105 p. :   LC Card 81-600625   DDC 346.7304/67316/0262 347.3064673160262 19
KF27 .A3226 1980d

SOIL CONSERVATION - WISCONSIN - COON CREEK WATERSHED (MONROE COUNTY-VERNON COUNTY)
Trimble, Stanley Wayne. Soil conservation, erosion, and sedimentation, Coon Creek Basin, Wisconsin /. Reston, Va. [1981] p. cm.   LC Card 81-607057   DDC 631.4/5/0977554 19
S624.W5 T74

SOIL ENGINEERING. see SOIL MECHANICS.

SOIL EROSION - KANSAS - MAPS.
United States. Soil Conservation Service. Erosion areas map, Kansas /. Lincoln, Nebr. , 1979. 1 map :   LC Card 81-691126
G4201.J4 1979 .U5

SOIL EROSION - MAINE.
Maine. Land Use Regulation Commission. A survey of erosion and sedimentation problems associated with logging in Maine /. [Augusta, Me.] [1979] 56 p. :   LC Card 80-620932   DDC 333.75/16/09741 19
TD428.F67 M34 1979

SOIL EROSION - MISSOURI - MAPS.
United States. Soil Conservation Service. Gully erosion problem areas, Missouri /. Lincoln, Nebr. , 1978. 1 map :   LC Card 81-691213
G4161.J4 1978 .U51

United States. Soil Conservation Service. Sheet erosion for all lands, Missouri /. Lincoln, Nebr. , 1978. 1 map :   LC Card 81-691219
G4161.J4 1977 .U5

United States. Soil Conservation Service. Sheet erosion for cropland, hay, and pasture, Missouri /. Lincoln, Nebr. , 1978. 1 map :   LC Card 81-691218
G4161.J4 1977 .U51

United States. Soil Conservation Service. Sheet erosion for grazed forest land, Missouri /. Lincoln, Nebr. , 1978. 1 map :   LC Card 81-691217
G4161.J4 1977 .U52

United States. Soil Conservation Service. Sheet erosion for non-grazed forest, Missouri /. Lincoln, Nebr. , 1978. 1 map :   LC Card

81-691216
G4161.J4 1977 .U53

United States. Soil Conservation Service. Sheet erosion for permanent pasture, Missouri /. Lincoln, Nebr. , 1978. 1 map :   LC Card 81-691215
G4161.J4 1977 .U54

United States. Soil Conservation Service. Sheet erosion for tilled land, Missouri /. Lincoln, Nebr. , 1978. 1 map :   LC Card 81-691214
G4161.J4 1977 .U55

SOIL EROSION - NEBRASKA - MAPS.
United States. Soil Conservation Service. Soil erosion hazard map, Nebraska /. Lincoln, Nebr. , 1980. 1 map :   LC Card 81-691020
G4191.J4 1980 .U5

SOIL EROSION - SOUTH DAKOTA - MAPS.
United States. Soil Conservation Service. Pasture production and soil loss areas, western South Dakota river basins /. Lincoln, Nebr. , 1979. 1 map :   LC Card 81-691116
G4181.J67 1979 .U5

SOIL EROSION - TENNESSEE - CROCKETT COUNTY - MAPS.
United States. Soil Conservation Service. Crockett County, Tennessee . Fort Worth, Tex. , 1980. 1 map :   LC Card 81-692293
G3963.C7N22 1977 .U5

SOIL EROSION - TENNESSEE - OBION COUNTY - MAPS.
United States. Soil Conservation Service. Obion County, Tennessee /. Fort Worth, Tex. , 1980. 1 map :   LC Card 81-692275
G3963.O2J4 1980 .U5

SOIL EROSION - WISCONSIN - COON CREEK WATERSHED (MONROE COUNTY-VERNON COUNTY)
Trimble, Stanley Wayne. Soil conservation, erosion, and sedimentation, Coon Creek Basin, Wisconsin /. Reston, Va. [1981] p. cm.   LC Card 81-607057   DDC 631.4/5/0977554 19
S624.W5 T74

SOIL EROSION - WISCONSIN - MAPS.
United States. Soil Conservation Service. Erosion potential of Wisconsin soils /. Lincoln, Nebr. , 1979. 1 map :   LC Card 81-691253
G4121.J4 1979 .U5

SOIL FAUNA - NORTH DAKOTA.
Kannowski, Paul Bruno, 1927- Invertebrates of southwestern North Dakota . Grand Forks, N.D. [1978] x, 255 p. :   LC Card 80-622687   DDC 592/.0526404/097848 19
QL197 .K36 1978

SOIL MECHANICS.
(1980) Yokel, Felix Y. Soil classification for construction practice in shallow trenching /. Washington, D.C. [1980] xiv, 76 p. :   LC Card 80-600014   DDC 690/.02/18 s 624.1/51/012 19
TA435 .U58 no. 121 TA710

SOIL MICRO-ORGANISMS.
Ko, Wen-hsiung, 1939- Effects of nutritional factors on chemical and soil microbiostasis /. Honolulu [1981] p. cm.   LC Card 81-6708   DDC 632/.952 19
QR111 .K58

SOIL MICROBIOLOGY. see SOIL MICRO-ORGANISMS.

Soil microbiostasis. Ko, Wen-hsiung, 1939- Effects of nutritional factors on chemical and soil microbiostasis /. Honolulu [1981] p. cm.   LC Card 81-6708   DDC 632/.952 19
QR111 .K58

SOIL MOISTURE - HAWAII - KULA.
Green, Richard E. (Richard Ervin), 1931- Soil-water relations and physical properties of irrigated soils in the Kula area, Island of Maui, Hawaii /. Honolulu , 1981. p. cm.   LC Card 81-93   DDC 631.4/32/09969 19
S599.H4 G73

SOIL MOISTURE - PENNSYLVANIA - CHICKIES CREEK WATERSHED - MAPS.
United States. Soil Conservation Service. Wet soils, Chickies Creek watershed, Lancaster and Lebanon Counties, Pennsylvania /. Hyattsville, Md. , 1977. 1 map :   LC Card 81-690274
G3822.C45J3 1977 .U51

SOIL PERCOLATION - FLORIDA - HOLMES COUNTY - MAPS.

United States. Soil Conservation Service. Holmes County, Florida . Fort Worth, Tex. , 1980. 1 map :   LC Card 81-690356
G3933.H8C34 1979 .U5

SOIL-PLANT RELATIONSHIPS. see PLANT-SOIL RELATIONSHIPS.

SOIL POLLUTION.
Griffin, Robert A. Attenuation of water--soluble polychlorinated biphenyls by earth materials /. Urbana, Ill. [1980] iii, 98 p. :   LC Card 80-622556   DDC 557.73 s 628.5/5 19
QE105 .A32 no. 86 TD879.P64

SOIL PRODUCTIVITY - MINNESOTA.
Minnesota. State Planning Agency. Environmental Planning Division. Minnesota cropland resources. St. Paul, Minn. [1979] v, 36 p. :   LC Card 79-625364   DDC 631.4/9776 19
S599.M45 M56 1979

SOIL SALINITY. see SOILS, SALTS IN.

Soil salinity and cotton yields as affected by surface and trickle irrigation . Wierenga, Petrus Johannes. Las Cruces, N.M. [1979] vi, 212 p. :   LC Card 80-622502   DDC 333.91/009789 s 631.4/16 19
GB705.N6 N64 no. 106 S616.U6

Soil survey area status map, as of December 31, 1980, New Hampshire /. United States. Soil Conservation Service. Lanham, MD , 1981. 1 map :   LC Card 81-692784
G3741.J3 1980 .U5

Soil survey Burt County, Nebraska. Da Moude, Dean W. [Washington, D.C.?] , 1980. vii, 165 p., 44 folded p. of plates :   LC Card 81-601021   DDC 631.4/7/782243 19
S599.N2 D34

Soil survey of Abbeville County, South Carolina /. Herren, Edward C. [Washington] [1980] viii, 82 p., [25] fold. leaves of plates :   LC Card 80-602551   DDC 631.4/7/75735 19
S599.S58 H46

Soil survey of Ada County area, Idaho /. Collett, Russell A. [Washington] , 1980. ix, 327 p., [39] fold. leaves of plates :   LC Card 80-603366   DDC 631.4/7/79628 19
S599.I2 C64

Soil survey of Adams County, Illinois /. Bushue, Lester J., 1930- [Washington] , 1979. i, 143, [66] leaves of plates :   LC Card 80-601805   DDC 631.4/9773 s 631.4/7/77344 19
S599.I5 A3 no. 101

Soil survey of Adams County, Wisconsin. Jakel, Dale L. [Washington, D.C.?] , 1980. vii, 142 p., 57 folded p. of plates :   LC Card 81-600526   DDC 631.4/7/77556 19
S599.W5 J34

Soil survey of Anderson County, South Carolina /. Herren, Edward C. [Washington , 1979] viii, 79 p., [34] leaves of plates :   LC Card 79-604161   DDC 631.4/7/75725 19
S599.S58 H47

Soil survey of Ashland County, Ohio /. Redmond, Charles Edward, 1932- [Washington] [1980] vii, 179 p., [31] fold. leaves of plates :   LC Card 80-602507   DDC 631.4/7/77129 19
S599.O3 R39

Soil survey of Ashley County, Arkansas /. United States. Soil Conservation Service. [Washington, D.C. , 1979] vii, 92 p., [40] fold. leaves of plates :   LC Card 80-601804   DDC 631.4/7/76783 19
S599.A75 U54 1979

Soil survey of Aurora County, South Dakota. Schlepp, Richard L. [Washington, D.C.?] , c1980. vii, 148 p., 58 folded p. of plates :   LC Card 81-600698   DDC 631.4/7/783375 19
S599.S6 S34

Soil survey of Bay County, Michigan /. Weesies, Glenn A. [Washington, D.C.] , 1980. vii, 105 p., [23] fold. leaves of plates :   LC Card 80-602508   DDC 631.4/7/77447 19
S599.M4 W43

Soil survey of Beadle County, South Dakota /. Heil, Dennis M. [Washington] , 1979. viii, 169 p., [98] fold. leaves of plates :   LC Card 80-602070   DDC 631.4/7/783274 19
S599.S6 H43

Soil survey of Benewah County area, Idaho /. Weisel, Charles J. [Washington] [1980] x, 188

p., [25] fold. leaves of plates : LC Card
80-602396 DDC 631.4/7/79693 19
S599.I2 W44

Soil survey of Berkeley County, South Carolina
/. Long, Bobby M. [Washington, D.C.] 1980.
viii, 94 p., [51] fold. leaves of plates : LC Card
80-601634 DDC 631.4/7/75793 19
S599.S58 L66

Soil survey of Berrien County, Michigan. Larson,
Jerry D. [Washington, D.C.?] , 1980. vii, 192 p.
90 folded p. of plates : LC Card 81-600705
DDC 631.4/7/77411 19
S599.M4 L363

Soil survey of Blount County, Alabama /. United
States. Soil Conservation Service. [Washington]
[1979] iii, 73 p., [2] fold. leaves of plates : LC
Card 80-601827 DDC 631.4/7/76172 19
S599.A4 U54 1979

Soil survey of Bosque County, Texas /. Stringer,
Billy R. [Washington, D.C.] [1980] vii, 102 p.,
[31] fold. leaves of plates : LC Card 80-602639
DDC 631.4/7/764518 19
S599.T4 S75

Soil survey of Bowie County, Texas. Fox,
Richard W. [Washington, D.C.?] , 1980. vii,
128 p., 76 fold. p. of plates : LC Card 81-601439
DDC 631.4/7/764197 19
S599.T4 F678

Soil survey of Brown and Mills Counties, Texas.
Clower, Dennis F. [Washington, D.C.?] , 1980.
vii, 170 p., 92 fold. p. of plates : LC Card
81-601467 DDC 631.4/7/764512 19
S599.T4 C57

Soil survey of Butler County, Ohio /. Lerch,
Norbert K. [Washington] [1980] vii, 175 p.,
[38] fold. leaves of plates : LC Card 80-602516
DDC 631.4/7/77175 19
S599.O3 L36

Soil survey of Caddo Parish, Louisiana /. United
States. Soil Conservation Service. [Washington]
[1980] vii, 137 p., [43] fold. leaves of plates :
LC Card 80-603369 DDC 631.4/7/76399 19
S599.L6 U54 1980a

**Soil survey of Calhoun and Dallas Counties,
Arkansas /.** United States. Soil Conservation
Service. [Washington] [1980] viii, 80 p., [59]
fold. leaves of plates : LC Card 80-601636 DDC
631.4/7/76764 19
S599.A75 U54 1980

**Soil survey of Calumet and Maitowoc Counties,
Wisconsin /.** Otter, Augustine J. [Washington,
D.C.] 1980. vii, 176 p., [64] fold. leaves of
plates : LC Card 80-602383 DDC 631.4/7/77566
19
S599.W5 O86

**Soil survey of Candler, Evans, and Tattnall
Counties, Georgia /.** Paulk, Herschel Leverne,
1934- [Washington] [1980] viii, 96 p., [42]
fold. leaves of plates : LC Card 80-601838 DDC
631.4/7/75877 19
S599.G4 P315

**Soil survey of Chaves County, New Mexico,
southern part /.** United States. Soil
Conservation Service. [Washington] [1980] iv,
143 p., [90] fold. leaves of plates : LC Card
80-602510 DDC 631.4/7/78943 19
S599.N6 U54 1980

Soil survey of Clark County, Illinois /. Awalt, F.
L. [Washington, D.C. , 1980] iii, 104 p., [38]
fold. leaves of plates : LC Card 80-602050 DDC
631.4/7/77371 19
S599.I5 A92

**Soil survey of Clayton, Fayette, and Henry
Counties, Georgia/.** Murphy, James O.
[Washington] [1979] viii, 74 p., [32] fold.
leaves of plates : LC Card 80-602614 DDC
631.4/7/75843 19
S599.G4 M87

Soil survey of Conejos County area, Colorado.
[Washington, D.C.?]: U. S. Dept. of Agriculture,
Soil Conservation Service, 1980. vii, 144 p. :
ill., maps (1 col.) ; 28 cm. + 17 folded maps.
Cover title. Authors: James M. Yenter and others. "In
cooperation with the Colorado Agricultural Experiment
Station." Issued September 1980"--P. iii. Issued in case
(31 x 26 cm.). Item 102-B-6 Bibliography: p. 70. LC
Card 81-600706 DDC 631.4/7/78833 19
*1. Soils - Colorado - Conejos County - Maps. I. Yenter,
James M. II. United States. Soil Conservation Service.*

III. Colorado Agricultural Experiment Station.
S599.C6 S66

Soil survey of Conway County, Arkansas /.
Townsend, William R. [Washington] [1980] vii,
91 p., [27] fold. leaves of plates : LC Card
80-603205 DDC 631.4/7/76731 19
S599.A75 T67

Soil survey of Cottonwood County, Minnesota /.
Rolling, R. E. [Washington] [1979] viii, 142 p.,
[28] fold. leaves of plates : LC Card 80-602397
DDC 631.4/7/77622 19
S599.M45 R64

Soil survey of Cowley County, Kansas /. Horsch,
Marcellus L. [Washington] [1980] viii, 123 p.,
[47] fold. leaves of plates : LC Card 80-601849
DDC 631.4/7/78189 19
S599.K2 H578

Soil survey of Crawford County, Arkansas /.
Garner, Billy A. [Washington] , 1979. viii, 91,
[22] fold. leaves of plates : LC Card 80-601639
DDC 631.4/7/76735 19
S599.A75 G37

Soil survey of Dallas County, Texas /. Coffee,
Daniel R., 1919- [Washington] [1980] vii, 153
p., [38] fold. leaves of plates : LC Card
80-601832 DDC 631.4/7/7642811 19
S599.T4 C63

Soil survey of Dodge County, Wisconsin /. Fox,
Robert E. [Washington] [1980] ix, 201 p., [71]
fold. leaves of plates : LC Card 80-602249 DDC
631.4/7/776153 19
S599.W5 F69

Soil survey of Dubois County, Indiana /.
Wingard, Robert C. [Washington, D.C. , 1980]
vii, 117 p., [36] fold. leaves of plates : LC Card
80-602049 DDC 631.4/7/77237 19
S599.I63 W57

**Soil survey of Elbert County, Colorado, western
part /.** Larsen, Lynn Seymour, 1913-
[Washington, D.C.] [1980] viii, 135 p., [2] fold.
leaves of plates : LC Card 80-603150 DDC
631.4/7/78887 19
S599.C6 L382

Soil survey of Franklin County, Iowa /. Voy,
Kermit D. [Washington, D.C.] [1980] ix, 183
p., [37] fold. leaves of plates : LC Card
80-602539 DDC 631.4/7/77728 19
S599.I8 V68

Soil survey of Franklin County, Ohio /. McLoda,
N. A. [Washington] [1980] viii, 188 p., [37]
fold. leaves of plates : LC Card 80-602372 DDC
631.4/7/77156 19
S599.O3 M32

Soil survey of Freeborn County, Minnesota /.
Carlson, Carroll Richard, 1928- [Washington,
D.C.] [1979] ix, 228 p., [56] fold. leaves of
plates : LC Card 80-601843 DDC 631.4/7/77618
19
S599.M45 C37

**Soil survey of Glacier County area and part of
Pondera County, Montana /.** United States.
Soil Conservation Service. [Washington, D.C.]
[1980] v, 161 p., [92] leaves of plates : LC
Card 80-602512 DDC 631.4/7/78652 19
S599.M57 U54 1980

Soil survey of Gloucester County, Virginia.
[Washington, D.C.?] : U. S. Dept. of
Agriculture, Soil Conservation Service, 1980.
vii, 88 p., 35 folded p. of plates : ill., maps (1
col.) ; 28 cm. Cover title. Authors: Michael E.
Newhouse and others. "In cooperation with Virginia
Polytechnic Institute and State University." "Issued
September 1980"--p. iii. Item 102-B-47 Bibliography: p.
49. LC Card 80-604149 DDC 631.4/7/75532 19
*1. Soils - Virginia - Gloucester County - Maps. I.
United States. Soil Conservation Service. II. Virginia
Polytechnic Institute and State University.*
S599.V8 S64

Soil survey of Goochland County, Virginia /.
Nicholson, John C. [Washington] , 1980. ix,
137 p., [22] fold. leaves of plates : LC Card
80-601854 DDC 631.4/7/755455 19
S599.V8 N52

**Soil survey of Grant and Pendleton Counties,
Kentucky /.** Froedge, Ronald D. [Washington] ,
1980. vii, 85 p., [40] fold. leaves of plates : LC
Card 80-602321 DDC 631.4/7/76933 19
S599.K4 F76

Soil survey of Grayson County, Texas /. Cochran,

Rex. [Washington? , 1980] vii, 141 p., [41]
leaves of plates : LC Card 80-602304 DDC
631.4/7/764557 19
S599.T4 C593

Soil survey of Greene County, North Carolina /.
Barnhill, William L. [Washington] [1980] vii,
83 p., [2] fold. leaves of plates : LC Card
80-602829 DDC 631.4/7/756393 19
S599.N6 B37

**Soil survey of Greenwood and McCormick
Counties, South Carolina /.** Camp, Wallace
Jefferson, 1906- [Washington, D.C. , 1980] iv,
68 p., [42] fold. leaves of plates : LC Card
80-602310 DDC 631.4/7/75733 19
S599.S58 C36

Soil survey of Grundy County, Illinois /.
Reineback, L. M. [Washington] [1980] vii, 131
p., [35] fold. leaves of plates : LC Card
80-602552 DDC 631.4/9773 s 631.4/7/773265
19
S599.I5 A3 no. 142

Soil survey of Hanover County, Virginia /.
Virginia Polytechnic Institute and State
University. [Washington, D.C. , 1980] ix, 218
p., [35] fold. leaves of plates : LC Card
80-602048 DDC 631.4/7/755462 19
S599.V8 V57 1980

**Soil survey of Henderson County, North Carolina
/.** King, John M. [Washington, D.C. , 1980]
viii, 89 p., [15] fold. leaves of plates : LC Card
80-602311 DDC 631.4/7/75692 19
S599.N8 K55

Soil survey of Huron County, Michigan /.
Linsemier, Lyle H. [Washington] , 1979. vii,
145 p., [37] fold. leaves of plates : LC Card
80-602145 DDC 631.4/7/77444 19
S599.M4 L56

Soil survey of Itawamba County, Mississippi /.
Murphree, Leland C., 1912- [Washington]
[1979] viii, 86 p., [25] fold. leaves of plates :
LC Card 80-602033 DDC 631.4/7/762982 19
S599.M5 M89

Soil survey of Keya Paha County, Nebraska.
[Washington, D.C.?] : U. S. Dept. of
Agriculture, Soil Conservation Service, 1980. ix,
224 p., 62 folded p. of plates : ill., maps (1
col.) ; 28 cm. Cover title. Authors: Merritt Plantz
and Richard Zink. "In cooperation with University of
Nebraska Conservation and Survey Division." "Issued
October 1980"--P. iii. Item 102-B-27 Bibliography: p.
129. LC Card 81-600561 DDC 631.4/7/782725 19
*1. Soils - Nebraska - Keya Faha County - Maps. I.
Plantz, Merritt A. (Merritt Alexander), 1921-. II. Zink,
Richard. III. United States. Soil Conservation Service.
IV. University of Nebraska--Lincoln. Conservation and
Survey Division.*
S599.N2 S63

Soil survey of Lagrange County, Indiana /. Hillis,
John H. [Washington] [1980] vii, 135 p., [19]
fold. leaves of plates : LC Card 80-602561 DDC
631.4/7/77279 19
S599.I63 H54

Soil survey of Lawrence County, South Dakota /.
Meland, Arvid C. [Washington, D.C. , 1979]
viii, 173 p., [25] fold. leaves of plates : LC
Card 80-601071 DDC 631.4/7/78391 19
S599.S6 M44

Soil survey of Logan County, Arkansas.
[Washington, D.C.?] : U. S. Dept. of
Agriculture, Soil Conservation Service, 1980.
vii, 100 p., 42 folded p. of plates : ill., maps (1
col.) ; 28 cm. Cover title. Authors: Bill A. Garner
and others. "In cooperation with Arkansas Agricultural
Experiment Station." "Issued November 1980"--P. iii.
Item 102-B-4 Bibliography: p. 59. LC Card 81-600695
DDC 631.4/7/76737 19
*1. Soils - Arkansas - Logan County - Maps. I. Garner,
Billy A. II. United States. Soil Conservation Service.
III. University of Arkansas. Agricultural Experiment
Station.*
S599.A75 S66

**Soil survey of Los Angeles County, California,
west San Fernando Valley area /.** Leifer,
Lewis. [Washington , 1980] viii, 107 p., [2]
fold. leaves of plates : LC Card 80-602305 DDC
631.4/7/79493 19
S599.C2 L44

Soil survey of Lowndes County, Mississippi /.
Brent, Floyd V. [Washington] [1979] viii, 137
p., [24] fold. leaves of plates : LC Card

80-602618   DDC 631.4/7/762973 19
S599.M5 B7

Soil survey of Luna County, New Mexico /.
Neher, R. E. [Washington, D.C.] 1980. iii, 80
p., [81] folded leaves of plates :   LC Card
    80-603368   DDC 631.4/7/78968 19
S599.N6 N4

**Soil survey of Malheur County, Oregon,
northeastern part /.** Lovell, Burrell B.
[Washington, D.C.] 1980. viii, 94 p., [22]
folded leaves of plates :   LC Card 80-603621
    DDC 631.4/7/79597 19
S599.O7 L68

Soil survey of Marion County, Iowa /. Russell,
Robert Cone, 1917- [Washington, D.C.] [1980]
ix, 183 p., [72] fold. leaves of plates :   LC Card
    80-602332   DDC 631.4/7/77783 19
S599.I8 R88

Soil survey of Marion County, South Carolina /.
Pitts, J. J. [Washington] , 1980. vii, 99 p., [27]
fold. leaves of plates :   LC Card 80-603206   DDC
    631.4/7/75786 19
S599.S58 P58

Soil survey of Marshall County, Indiana /.
Smallwood, Benjamin F. [Washington, D.C.?]
1980. vii, 136 p., 63 folded p. of plates :   LC
    Card 81-601062   DDC 631.4/7/77288 19
S599.I63 S6

Soil survey of Marshall County, Oklahoma /.
Burgess, Dent Louis, 1913- [Washington, D.
C. , 1980] vii, 92 p., [20] fold. leaves of plates :
    LC Card 80-602509   DDC 631.4/7/76661 19
S599.O4 B88

Soil survey of McCook County, South Dakota /.
Heil, Dennis M. [Washington] , 1980. vii, 123
p., [25] fold. leaves of plates :   LC Card
    80-601638   DDC 631.4/7/783372 19
S599.S6 H44

**Soil survey of McLean and Muhlenberg Counties,
Kentucky /.** Cox, Frank R., 1918- [Washington]
[1980] viii, 124 p., 61 fold p. of plates :   LC
    Card 80-604148   DDC 631.4/7/769826 19
S599.K4 C68

Soil survey of Middlesex County, Connecticut /.
Reynolds, Charles Arthur, 1937- [Washington]
[1979] ix, 155 p., [28] fold. leaves of plates :
    LC Card 80-601842   DDC 631.4/7/7444 19
S599.C76 R5

Soil survey of Mitchell County, Kansas /.
Hamilton, Vernon Leroy, 1932- [Washington] ,
1980. vii, 94 p., [30] fold. leaves of plates :   LC
    Card 80-602876   DDC 631.4/7/78123 19
S599.K2 H315

Soil survey of Mobile County, Alabama /.
Hickman, Glenn L. [Washington] , 19. vii, 134
p., [60] fold. leaves of plates :   LC Card
    80-603367   DDC 631.4/7/76122 19
S599.A4 H53

Soil survey of Nacogdoches County, Texas /.
Dolezel, Raymond. [Washington] , 1980. vii,
146 p., [30] fold. leaves of plates :   LC Card
    80-602411   DDC 631.4/7/764182 19
S599.T4 D63

**Soil survey of Navajo Indian Reservation, San
Juan County, Utah /.** Nielson, Woodrow.
[Washington] [1980] viii, 119 p., [12] fold.
leaves of plates :   LC Card 80-602348   DDC
    631.4/7/79259 19
S599.U8 N53

Soil survey of Ocean County, New Jersey /.
Hole, Thornton J. F. [Washington] [1980] vii,
102 p., [35] fold. leaves of plates :   LC Card
    80-602312   DDC 631.4/7/74948 19
S599.N5 H64

Soil survey of Ogle County, Illinois /. United
States. Soil Conservation Service. [Washington]
[1980] ix, 242 p., [58] fold. leaves of plates :
    LC Card 80-602563   DDC 631.4/7/77332 19
S599.I5 U54 1980

Soil survey of Olmsted County, Minnesota /.
Poch, George A. [Washington, D.C.] [1980] ix,
202 p., [53] fold. leaves of plates :   LC Card
    80-602323   DDC 631.4/7/776155 19
S599.M45 P62

Soil survey of Osceola County area, Florida /.
Readle, Elmer L. [Washington] , 1979. x, 151
p., [59] fold. leaves of plates :   LC Card
    79-602772   DDC 631.4/7/75925 19
S599.F6 R42

Soil survey of Pecos County, Texas /. Rives,
Jerry L. [Washington] [1980] vii, 97 p., [77]
fold. leaves of plates :   LC Card 80-602640   DDC
    631.4/7/764923 19
S599.T4 R59

Soil survey of Pickaway County, Ohio /. Kerr,
James W. [Washington, D.C.] [1980] vii, 172
p., [36] fold. leaves of plates :   LC Card
    80-602251   DDC 631.4/7/771815 19
S599.O3 K47

**Soil survey of Ponce area of southern Puerto
Rico /.** Gierbolini, Roberto E. [Washington]
[1979] iii, 80 p., [22] fold. leaves of plates :
    LC Card 80-602349   DDC 631.4/7/72957 19
S599.25.P832 P663

Soil survey of Randolph County, Arkansas /.
Brown, James Henry, 1946- [Washington]
[1980] viii, 103 p., [30] fold. leaves of plates :
    LC Card 80-602554   DDC 631.4/7/76724 19
S599.A75 B76

Soil survey of Rapides Parish, Louisiana /.
United States. Soil Conservation Service.
[Washington] , 1980. iii, 86 p., [59] fold. leaves
of plates :   LC Card 80-602333   DDC
    631.4/7/76369 19
S599.L6 U54 1980

Soil survey of Richland County, Montana.
Pesoado, Pedro. [Washington, D.C.?] , C1980.
iv, 71 p., 142 folded p. of plates :   LC Card
    80-604152   DDC 631.4/7/78623 19
S599.M57 P47

Soil survey of Rio Grande County area, Colorado
/. Pannell, James P., 1926- [Washington] ,
1980. iv, 89 p., [2] fold. leaves of plates :   LC
    Card 80-602320   DDC 631.4/7/78837 19
S599.C6 P36

Soil survey of Rush County, Kansas /. United
States. Soil Conservation Service. [Washington,
D.C.] [1980] vi, 62 p., [31] fold. leaves of
plates :   LC Card 80-603364   DDC 631.4/7/78148
    19
S599.K2 U54 1980

**Soil survey of San Bernardino County,
southwestern part, California /.** Woodruff,
George A. [Washington] [1980] ii, 64 p., [2]
fold. leaves of plates :   LC Card 80-601256   DDC
    631.4/7/79495 19
S599.C2 W66

Soil survey of Sangamon County, Illinois /.
Steinkamp, James F. [Washington, D.C.]
[1980] vii, 139 p., [71] fold. leaves of plates :
    LC Card 80-602641   DDC 631.4/7/77356 19
S599.I5 S73

Soil survey of Santa Cruz County, California /.
Bowman, Roy H. [[Washington] [1980] vii,
148 p., [2] fold. leaves of plates :   LC Card
    80-603187   DDC 631.4/7/79471 19
S599.C2 B68

Soil survey of Santa Rosa County, Florida /.
United States. Soil Conservation Service.
[Washington] [1980] vii, 150 p., [47] fold.
leaves of plates :   LC Card 80-602511   DDC
    631.4/7/759985 19
S599.F6 U54 1980a

Soil survey of Sauk County, Wisconsin /.
Gundlach, Howard F. [Washington] [1980] ix,
248 p., [67] fold. leaves of plates :   LC Card
    80-602384   DDC 631.4/7/77576 19
S599.W5 G86

Soil survey of Sedgwick County, Kansas /.
Penner, Harold L. [Washington , 1979] vii, 126
p., [41] fold. leaves of plates :   LC Card
    79-603621   DDC 631.4/7/78186 19
S599.K2 P44

Soil survey of Seneca County, Ohio. Ernst, James
Edgar. [Washington, D.C.?] , 1980. vii, 143 p.,
81 folded p. of plates :   LC Card 80-604150
    DDC 631.4/7/77124 19
S599.O3 E77

Soil survey of Shelby County, Kentucky /.
United States. Soil Conservation Service.
[Washington, D.C. , 1980] vii, 84 p., [20] leaves
of plates :   LC Card 80-602322   DDC
    631.4/7/769435 19
S599.K4 U54 1980

Soil survey of St. Lucie County area, Florida /.
Watts, Frank C. [Washington] [1980] vii, 183
p., [26] fold. leaves of plates :   LC Card

80-602562   DDC 631.4/7/75929 19
S599.F6 W37

Soil survey of Stillwater County area, Montana
/. Parker, John Leon, 1912- [Washington,
D.C.]. [1980] vii, 131, 98, [4] p., [1] fold. leaf
of plates :   LC Card 80-603196   DDC
    631.4/7/786651 19
S599.M9 P37

Soil survey of Summit County area, Colorado /.
Miles, Ray L. [Washington] [1980] vii, 74 p.,
[2] fold. leaves of plates :   LC Card 80-602603
    DDC 631.4/7/78845 19
S599.C6 M54

Soil survey of Thomas County, Kansas /. United
States. Soil Conservation Service. [Washington]
[1980] vii, 57 p., [43] fold. leaves of plates :
    LC Card 80-603122   DDC 631.4/7/781132 19
S599.K2 U54 1980a

Soil survey of Volusia County, Florida /. United
States. Soil Conservation Service. [Washington,
D.C.] [1980] ix, 207 p., [55] fold. leaves of
plates :   LC Card 80-602334   DDC 631.4/7/75921
    19
S599.F6 U54 1980

**Soil survey of Washington and Ramsey Counties,
Minnesota /.** Vinar, Kenneth R. [Washington]
[1980] ix, 246 p., [56] fold. leaves of plates :
    LC Card 80-602943   DDC 631.4/7/77658 19
S599.M52 V56

Soil survey of Whitman County, Washington /
United States Department of Agriculture, Soil
Conservation Service, in cooperation with
Washington State University, Agricultural
Research Center. [Washington?] : The Service,
[1980] v, 185 p., [75] folded leaves of plates :
ill. ; 29 cm. Cover title. Prepared by Norman C.
Donaldson. Includes bibliographical references and
index.   LC Card 80-602555   DDC 631.4/7797/39 19
    1. Soils - Washington (State) - Whitman County -
Maps. I. Donaldson, Norman C. II. United States. Soil
Conservation Service. III. Washington State University.
Agricultural Research Center. IV. Title.
S599.W32 S63

**Soil survey of Winnebago and Boone Counties,
Illinois /.** Grantham, Dana R., 1936-
[Washington] , 1980. ix, 279 p., [53] leaves of
plates :   LC Card 80-602556   DDC 631.4/9773 s
    631.4/7/77329 19
S599.I5 A3 no. 107

Soil survey of Winnebago County, Wisconsin /.
Mitchell, Michael J. [Washington] [1980] vii,
182 p., [23] fold. leaves of plates :   LC Card
    80-602659   DDC 631.4/7/77564 19
S599.W5 M58

Soil survey status, Washington /. United States.
Soil Conservation Service. Portland, Or. , 1979.
1 map :   LC Card 81-691502
G4281.J3 1979 .U5

SOIL-SURVEYS - INDIANA - MAPS.
United States. Soil Conservation Service. Status
of soil surveys, State of Indiana, October 1979
/. Lincoln, Nebr. , 1979. 1 map :   LC Card
    81-691255
G4091.J3 1979 .U5

United States. Soil Conservation Service. Status
of soil surveys, State of Indiana, October 1980
/. Lincoln, Nebr. , 1980. 1 map :   LC Card
    81-691256
G4091.J3 1980 .U5

SOIL-SURVEYS - KANSAS - MAPS.
United States. Soil Conservation Service. Status
of soil surveys in Kansas, October 1, 1978 /.
Lincoln, Nebr. , 1978. 1 map :   LC Card
    81-691130
G4201.J3 1978 .U5

United States. Soil Conservation Service. Status
of soil surveys in Kansas, October 1, 1979 /.
Lincoln, Nebr. , 1979. 1 map :   LC Card
    81-691129
G4201.J3 1979 .U51

United States. Soil Conservation Service. Status
of soil surveys in Kansas, October 1, 1980 /.
Lincoln, Nebr. , 1980. 1 map :   LC Card
    81-691128
G4201.J3 1980 .U51

SOIL-SURVEYS - MICHIGAN - MAPS.
United States. Soil Conservation Service. Status
of soil surveys, Michigan, August 1979 /.
Lincoln, Nebr. , 1979. 1 map :   LC Card

81-691406
G4111.J3 1979 .U5

United States. Soil Conservation Service. Status of soil surveys, Michigan, August 1980 /. Lincoln, Nebr. , 1980. 1 map : LC Card 81-691409
G4111.J3 1980 .U5

SOIL-SURVEYS - MISSOURI - MAPS.
United States. Soil Conservation Service. Status of the national cooperative soil survey in Missouri /. Lincoln, Nebr. , 1979. 1 map : LC Card 81-691211
G4161.J3 1979 .U5

United States. Soil Conservation Service. Status of the national cooperative soil survey in Missouri, July 1, 1980 /. Lincoln, Nebr. , 1980. 1 map : LC Card 81-691210
G4161.J3 1980 .U5

SOIL-SURVEYS - NEBRASKA - MAPS.
United States. Soil Conservation Service. Status of recent soil surveys in Nebraska, Oct. 1, 1978 /. Lincoln, Nebr. , 1978. 1 map : LC Card 81-691095
G4191.J3 1978 .U5

United States. Soil Conservation Service. Status of recent soil surveys in Nebraska, Oct. 1, 1979 /. Lincoln, Nebr. , 1979. 1 map : LC Card 81-691096
G4191.J3 1979 .U52

United States. Soil Conservation Service. Status of recent soil surveys in Nebraska, Oct. 1, 1980 /. Lincoln, Nebr. , 1980. 1 map : LC Card 81-691097
G4191.J3 1980 .U51

SOIL-SURVEYS - NEW HAMPSHIRE - MAPS.
United States. Soil Conservation Service. Soil survey area status map, as of December 31, 1980, New Hampshire /. Lanham, MD , 1981. 1 map : LC Card 81-692784
G3741.J3 1980 .U5

SOIL-SURVEYS - NEW YORK (STATE) - MAPS.
United States. Soil Conservation Service. Status of New York soil surveys . Lanham, MD , 1980. 1 map : LC Card 81-690084
G3801.J3 1980 .U5

SOIL-SURVEYS - NORTH DAKOTA - MAPS.
United States. Soil Conservation Service. Status of soil surveys in North Dakota, FY-1979 /. Lincoln, Nebr. , 1978. 1 map : LC Card 81-691263
G4171.J3 1979 .U5

United States. Soil Conservation Service. Status of soil surveys in North Dakota, FY 1980 /. Lincoln, Nebr. , 1979. 1 map : LC Card 81-691262
G4171.J3 1980 .U5

United States. Soil Conservation Service. Status of soil surveys in North Dakota, FY 1981 /. Lincoln, Nebr. , 1980. 1 map : LC Card 81-691261
G4171.J3 1981 .U5

SOIL-SURVEYS - OHIO - MAPS.
United States. Soil Conservation Service. Ohio status of soil surveys, October 1980 /. Lincoln, Nebr. , 1980. 1 map : LC Card 81-691033
G4081.J3 1980 .U5

United States. Soil Conservation Service. Ohio status of soil survyes, October 1979 /. Lincoln, Nebr. , 1979. 1 map : LC Card 81-691035
G4081.J3 1979 .U5

SOIL-SURVEYS - SOUTH DAKOTA - MAPS.
United States. Soil Conservation Service. Progress of soil surveys, January 1, 1979, state of South Dakota /. Lincoln, Nebr. , 1979. 1 map : LC Card 81-691098
G4181.J3 1979 .U5

United States. Soil Conservation Service. Status of soil surveys South Dakota, January 1, 1980 /. Lincoln, Nebr. , 1980. 1 map : LC Card 81-691112
G4181.J3 1980 .U5

SOIL-SURVEYS - UNITED STATES - BIBLIOGRAPHY - CATALOGS.
United States. National Archives and Records Service. Preliminary inventory of the cartographic records of the Soil Conservation Service /. Washington , 1981. p. cm. LC Card

81-3988   DDC 016.3530082/326 19
CD3026 .A32 no. 195 CD3038

SOIL-SURVEYS - VERMONT - MAPS.
United States. Soil Conservation Service. Status of detailed soil surveys, Vermont. Lanham, MD , 1980. 1 map : LC Card 81-690085
G3751.J3 1980 .U5

SOIL-SURVEYS - VIRGINIA - MAPS.
United States. Soil Conservation Service. Status of soil surveys, Virginia. Lanham, Md. , 1979. 1 map : LC Card 81-690106
G3881.J3 1979 .U51

United States. Soil Conservation Service. Status of soil surveys, Virginia. Lanham, Md. , 1981. 1 map : LC Card 81-692880
G3881.J3 1981 .U5

SOIL-SURVEYS - WASHINGTON(STATE) - MAPS.
United States. Soil Conservation Service. Soil survey status, Washington /. Portland, Or. , 1979. 1 map : LC Card 81-691502
G4281.J3 1979 .U5

SOIL-SURVEYS - WISCONSIN - MAPS.
United States. Soil Conservation Service. Status of soil surveys, Wisconsin, October 1, 1980 /. Lincoln, Nebr. , 1980. 1 map : LC Card 81-691247
G4121.J3 1980 .U51

United States. Soil Conservation Service. Status of soil surveys, Wisconsin, September 30, 1979 /. Lincoln, Nebr. , 1979. 1 map : LC Card 81-691245
G1421.J3 1979 .U51

SOIL TEXTURE - WASHINGTON (STATE) - FRANKLIN COUNTY - MAPS.
United States. Soil Conservation Service. Soil texture, Franklin County Conservation District, Franklin County, Washington /. Portland, Or. , 1980. 1 map : LC Card 81-691508
G4283.F7J3 1980 .U5

SOIL TYPES. see SOILS - CLASSIFICATION.

Soil-water relations and physical properties of irrigated soils in the Kula area, Island of Maui, Hawaii /. Green, Richard E. (Richard Ervin), 1931- Honolulu , 1981. p. cm. LC Card 81-93   DDC 631.4/32/09969 19
S599.H4 G73

SOILLESS AGRICULTURE. see HYDROPONICS.

SOILS - ALABAMA - BLOUNT CO. - MAPS.
United States. Soil Conservation Service. Soil survey of Blount County, Alabama /. [Washington] [1979] iii, 73 p., [2] fold. leaves of plates : LC Card 80-601827 DDC 631.4/7/76172 19
S599.A4 U54 1979

SOILS - ALABAMA - MOBILE CO. - MAPS.
Hickman, Glenn L. Soil survey of Mobile County, Alabama /. [Washington] , 19. vii, 134 p., [60] fold. leaves of plates : LC Card 80-603367 DDC 631.4/7/76122 19
S599.A4 H53

SOILS - ANALYSIS - CONGRESSES.
Seminar on the Role of Overburden Analysis in Surface Mining (1980 : Wheeling, W. VA.) Proceedings of Seminar on the Role of Overburden Analysis in Surface Mining, Wheeling, W. Va., May 6-7, 1980 /. Washington , 1981. p. cm. LC Card 81-607049 DDC 622 s 622/.31 19
TN295 .U4 TD195.S75

SOILS AND ANIMAL NUTRITION.
Hannaway, D. B. Plant nutrition, magnesium and hypomagnesemia in animals /. Lexington, Ky [1980] 90 p. ; LC Card 80-623110 DDC 581.1/3354 19
QK753.M27 H36

SOILS - ARIZONA - GREENLEE COUNTY.
Richmond, Davie L. General soil map, Greenlee County, Arizona. Portland, Or., 1973. 49 p.   ***NYPL [JSF 80-721]***

SOILS - ARIZONA - MAPS.
Richmond, Davie L. General soil map, Greenlee County, Arizona. Portland, Or., 1973. 49 p.   ***NYPL [JSF 80-721]***

SOILS - ARIZONA - MARICOPA COUNTY.
Hartman, George William, 1935- General soil map with soil interpretations for land use planning: [Maricopa County, Arizona] /.

Portland, Or., 1973. 49 p.:
     NYPL [Map Div. 80-258]

SOILS - ARIZONA - MARICOPA COUNTY - MAPS.
Hartman, George William, 1935- General soil map with soil interpretations for land use planning: [Maricopa County, Arizona] /. Portland, Or., 1973. 49 p.:
     NYPL [Map Div. 80-258]

SOILS - ARKANSAS - ASHLEY CO. - MAPS.
United States. Soil Conservation Service. Soil survey of Ashley County, Arkansas /. [Washington, D.C. , 1979] vii, 92 p., [40] fold. leaves of plates : LC Card 80-601804 DDC 631.4/7/76783 19
S599.A75 U54 1979

SOILS - ARKANSAS - CALHOUN CO. - MAPS.
United States. Soil Conservation Service. Soil survey of Calhoun and Dallas Counties, Arkansas /. [Washington] [1980] vii, 80 p., [59] fold. leaves of plates : LC Card 80-601636 DDC 631.4/7/76764 19
S599.A75 U54 1980

SOILS - ARKANSAS - CONWAY COUNTY - MAPS.
Townsend, William R. Soil survey of Conway County, Arkansas /. [Washington] [1980] vii, 91 p., [27] fold. leaves of plates : LC Card 80-603205 DDC 631.4/7/76731 19
S599.A75 T67

SOILS - ARKANSAS - CRAWFORD CO. - MAPS.
Garner, Billy A. Soil survey of Crawford County, Arkansas /. [Washington] , 19. viii, 91, [22] fold. leaves of plates : LC Card 80-601639 DDC 631.4/7/76735 19
S599.A75 G37

SOILS - ARKANSAS - DALLAS CO. - MAPS.
United States. Soil Conservation Service. Soil survey of Calhoun and Dallas Counties, Arkansas /. [Washington] [1980] vii, 80 p., [59] fold. leaves of plates : LC Card 80-601636 DDC 631.4/7/76764 19
S599.A75 U54 1980

SOILS - ARKANSAS - LOGAN COUNTY - MAPS.
Soil survey of Logan County, Arkansas. [Washington, D.C.?] , 1980. vii, 100 p., 42 folded p. of plates : LC Card 81-600695 DDC 631.4/7/76737 19
S599.A75 S66

SOILS - ARKANSAS - RANDOLPH CO. - MAPS.
Brown, James Henry, 1946- Soil survey of Randolph County, Arkansas /. [Washington] [1980] viii, 103 p., [30] fold. leaves of plates : LC Card 80-602554 DDC 631.4/7/76724 19
S599.A75 B76

SOILS - CALIFORNIA - LOS ANGELES CO. - MAPS.
Leifer, Lewis. Soil survey of Los Angeles County, California, west San Fernando Valley area /. [Washington , 1980] viii, 107 p., [2] fold. leaves of plates : LC Card 80-602305 DDC 631.4/7/79493 19
S599.C2 L44

SOILS - CALIFORNIA - SAN BERNARDINO CO. - MAPS.
Woodruff, George A. Soil survey of San Bernardino County, southwestern part, California /. [Washington] [1980] ii, 64 p., [2] fold. leaves of plates : LC Card 80-601256 DDC 631.4/7/79495 19
S599.C2 W66

SOILS - CALIFORNIA - SAN FERNANDO VALLEY - MAPS.
Leifer, Lewis. Soil survey of Los Angeles County, California, west San Fernando Valley area /. [Washington , 1980] viii, 107 p., [2] fold. leaves of plates : LC Card 80-602305 DDC 631.4/7/79493 19
S599.C2 L44

SOILS - CALIFORNIA - SANTA CRUZ CO. - MAPS.
Bowman, Roy H. Soil survey of Santa Cruz County, California /. [[Washington] [1980] vii, 148 p., [2] fold. leaves of plates : LC Card 80-603187 DDC 631.4/7/79471 19
S599.C2 B68

Soils, Chickies Creek watershed, Lancaster and Lebanon Counties, Pennsylvania /. United States. Soil Conservation Service. Hyattsville, Md. [1978] 1 map ; LC Card 81-690272
G3822.C45J3 1978 .U5

SOILS - CLASSIFICATION.
Yokel, Felix Y. Soil classification for construction practice in shallow trenching /. Washington, D.C. [1980] xiv, 76 p. : LC Card 80-600014 DDC 690/.02/18 s 624.1/51/012 19
TA435 .U58 no. 121 TA710

SOILS - COLORADO - CONEJOS COUNTY - MAPS.
Soil survey of Conejos County area, Colorado. [Washington, D.C.?], 1980. vii, 144 p. : LC Card 81-600706 DDC 631.4/7/78833 19
S599.C6 S66

SOILS - COLORADO - ELBERT COUNTY - MAPS.
Larsen, Lynn Seymour, 1913- Soil survey of Elbert County, Colorado, western part /. [Washington, D.C.] [1980] viii, 135 p., [2] fold. leaves of plates : LC Card 80-603150 DDC 631.4/7/78887 19
S599.C6 L382

SOILS - COLORADO - RIO GRANDE COUNTY - MAPS.
Pannell, James P., 1926- Soil survey of Rio Grande County area, Colorado /. [Washington] , 1980. iv, 89 p., [2] fold. leaves of plates : LC Card 80-602320 DDC 631.4/7/78837 19
S599.C6 P36

SOILS - COLORADO - SUMMIT CO. - MAPS.
Miles, Ray L. Soil survey of Summit County area, Colorado /. [Washington] [1980] vii, 74 p., [2] fold. leaves of plates : LC Card 80-602603 DDC 631.4/7/78845 19
S599.C6 M54

SOILS - CONNECTICUT - MAPS.
Gonick, Walter N. General soil map of Connecticut /. Hyattsville, Md. , 1978. 1 map : LC Card 81-690080
G3781.J3 1978 .G6

SOILS - CONNECTICUT - MIDDLESEX COUNTY - MAPS.
Reynolds, Charles Arthur, 1937- Soil survey of Middlesex County, Connecticut /. [Washington] [1979] ix, 155 p., [28] fold. leaves of plates : LC Card 80-601842 DDC 631.4/7/7444 19
S599.C76 R5

SOILS (ENGINEERING) see SOIL MECHANICS.

SOILS - FERTILIZER MOVEMENT.
Movement of fertilizer and herbicide through irrigated sands /. [Gainesville] , 1976. iv, 50 p. : LC Card 77-623198 DDC 631.5/87/09759 19
S616.U6 M68

SOILS - FLORIDA - OSCEOLA CO. - MAPS.
Readle, Elmer L. Soil survey of Osceola County area, Florida /. [Washington] , 1979. x, 151 p., [59] fold. leaves of plates : LC Card 79-602772 DDC 631.4/7/75925 19
S599.F6 R42

SOILS - FLORIDA - ST. LUCIE CO. - MAPS.
Watts, Frank C. Soil survey of St. Lucie County area, Florida /. [Washington] [1980] vii, 183 p., [26] fold. leaves of plates : LC Card 80-602562 DDC 631.4/7/75929 19
S599.F6 W37

SOILS - FLORIDA - SANTA ROSA CO. - MAPS.
United States. Soil Conservation Service. Soil survey of Santa Rosa County, Florida /. [Washington] [1980] vii, 150 p., [47] fold. leaves of plates : LC Card 80-602511 DDC 631.4/7/759985 19
S599.F6 U54 1980a

SOILS - FLORIDA - VOLUSIA CO. - MAPS.
United States. Soil Conservation Service. Soil survey of Volusia County, Florida /. [Washington, D.C.] [1980] ix, 207 p., [55] fold. leaves of plates : LC Card 80-602334 DDC 631.4/7/75921 19
S599.F6 U54 1980

SOILS, FROZEN. see FROZEN GROUND.

SOILS - GEORGIA - CANDLER CO. - MAPS.
Paulk, Herschel Leverne, 1934- Soil survey of Candler, Evans, and Tattnall Counties, Georgia

/. [Washington] [1980] viii, 96 p., [42] fold. leaves of plates : LC Card 80-601838 DDC 631.4/7/75877 19
S599.G4 P315

SOILS - GEORGIA - CLAYTON CO. - MAPS.
Murphy, James O. Soil survey of Clayton, Fayette, and Henry Counties, Georgia/. [Washington] [1979] viii, 74 p., [32] fold. leaves of plates : LC Card 80-602614 DDC 631.4/7/75843 19
S599.G4 M87

SOILS - GEORGIA - EVANS CO. - MAPS.
Paulk, Herschel Leverne, 1934- Soil survey of Candler, Evans, and Tattnall Counties, Georgia /. [Washington] [1980] viii, 96 p., [42] fold. leaves of plates : LC Card 80-601838 DDC 631.4/7/75877 19
S599.G4 P315

SOILS - GEORGIA - FAYETTE CO. - MAPS.
Murphy, James O. Soil survey of Clayton, Fayette, and Henry Counties, Georgia/. [Washington] [1979] viii, 74 p., [32] fold. leaves of plates : LC Card 80-602614 DDC 631.4/7/75843 19
S599.G4 M87

SOILS - GEORGIA - HENRY CO. - MAPS.
Murphy, James O. Soil survey of Clayton, Fayette, and Henry Counties, Georgia/. [Washington] [1979] viii, 74 p., [32] fold. leaves of plates : LC Card 80-602614 DDC 631.4/7/75843 19
S599.G4 M87

SOILS - GEORGIA - TATTNALL CO. - MAPS.
Paulk, Herschel Leverne, 1934- Soil survey of Candler, Evans, and Tattnall Counties, Georgia /. [Washington] [1980] viii, 96 p., [42] fold. leaves of plates : LC Card 80-601838 DDC 631.4/7/75877 19
S599.G4 P315

SOILS - GREAT PLAINS.
Aandahl, Andrew Russell, 1912- Soils of the Great Plains . Lincoln , c1982. p. cm. ISBN 0-8032-1011-6 LC Card 81-7435 DDC 631.4/978 19
S599.A1 A17

SOILS - HAWAII - KULA.
Green, Richard E. (Richard Ervin), 1931- Soil-water relations and physical properties of irrigated soils in the Kula area, Island of Maui, Hawaii /. Honolulu , 1981. p. cm. LC Card 81-93 DDC 631.4/32/09969 19
S599.H4 G73

SOILS - HAWAII - MOLOKAI.
Dissipation of phytotoxic diuron residues in Hawaii pineapple soils /. Honolulu [1981] p. cm. LC Card 81-6945 DDC 632/.954 19
S592.6.H47 D57

SOILS - HERBICIDE CONTENT.
Dissipation of phytotoxic diuron residues in Hawaii pineapple soils /. Honolulu [1981] p. cm. LC Card 81-6945 DDC 632/.954 19
S592.6.H47 D57

SOILS - HERBICIDE MOVEMENT.
Movement of fertilizer and herbicide through irrigated sands /. [Gainesville] , 1976. iv, 50 p. : LC Card 77-623198 DDC 631.5/87/09759 19
S616.U6 M68

SOILS - HERBICIDE MOVEMENT - MATHEMATICAL MODELS.
Johnson, Howard P. Movement of herbicides in soil by mass flow . Ames , 1975. iii, 35 leaves : LC Card 76-622340 DDC 632/.954 19
S592.6.H47 J64

SOILS - IDAHO - ADA CO. - MAPS.
Collett, Russell A. Soil survey of Ada County area, Idaho /. [Washington] , 1980. ix, 327 p., [39] fold. leaves of plates : LC Card 80-603366 DDC 631.4/7/79628 19
S599.I2 C64

SOILS - IDAHO - BENEWAH CO. - MAPS.
Weisel, Charles J. Soil survey of Benewah County area, Idaho /. [Washington] [1980] x, 188 p., [25] fold. leaves of plates : LC Card 80-602396 DDC 631.4/7/79693 19
S599.I2 W44

SOILS - ILLINOIS - ADAMS CO. - MAPS.
Bushue, Lester J., 1930- Soil survey of Adams County, Illinois /. [Washington] , 1979. i, 143, [66] fold. leaves of plates : LC Card 80-601805

DDC 631.4/9773 s 631.4/7/77344 19
S599.I5 A3 no. 101

SOILS - ILLINOIS - BOONE CO. - MAPS.
Grantham, Dana R., 1936- Soil survey of Winnebago and Boone Counties, Illinois /. [Washington] , 1980. ix, 279 p., [53] leaves of plates : LC Card 80-602556 DDC 631.4/9773 s 631.4/7/77329 19
S599.I5 A3 no. 107

SOILS - ILLINOIS - CLARK CO. - MAPS.
Awalt, F. L. Soil survey of Clark County, Illinois /. [Washington, D.C.] , 1980. i, 104 p., [38] fold. leaves of plates : LC Card 80-602050 DDC 631.4/7/77371 19
S599.I5 A92

SOILS - ILLINOIS - GRUNDY CO. - MAPS.
Reineback, L. M. Soil survey of Grundy County, Illinois /. [Washington] [1980] vii, 131 p., [35] fold. leaves of plates : LC Card 80-602552 DDC 631.4/9773 s 631.4/7/773265 19
S599.I5 A3 no. 142

SOILS - ILLINOIS - OGLE CO. - MAPS.
United States. Soil Conservation Service. Soil survey of Ogle County, Illinois /. [Washington] [1980] ix, 242 p., [58] fold. leaves of plates : LC Card 80-602563 DDC 631.4/7/77332 19
S599.I5 U54 1980

SOILS - ILLINOIS - SANGAMON CO. - MAPS.
Steinkamp, James F. Soil survey of Sangamon County, Illinois /. [Washington, D.C.] [1980] vii, 139 p., [71] fold. leaves of plates : LC Card 80-602641 DDC 631.4/7/77356 19
S599.I5 S73

SOILS - ILLINOIS - WHITE COUNTY - MAPS.
United States. Soil Conservation Service. General soil map, White County, Illinois /. Lincoln, Nebr. , 1978. 1 map : LC Card 81-691445
G4103.W5J3 1978 .U51

SOILS - ILLINOIS - WINNEBAGO CO. - MAPS.
Grantham, Dana R., 1936- Soil survey of Winnebago and Boone Counties, Illinois /. [Washington] , 1980. ix, 279 p., [53] leaves of plates : LC Card 80-602556 DDC 631.4/9773 s 631.4/7/77329 19
S599.I5 A3 no. 107

SOILS - INDIANA - DUBOIS CO. - MAPS.
Wingard, Robert C. Soil survey of Dubois County, Indiana /. [Washington, D.C. , 1980] vii, 117 p., [36] fold. leaves of plates : LC Card 80-602049 DDC 631.4/7/77237 19
S599.I63 W57

SOILS - INDIANA - FAYETTE COUNTY - MAPS.
United States. Soil Conservation Service. General soil map, Fayette and Union Counties, Indiana. [Lincoln, Neb. , 1980?] 1 map : LC Card 81-691259
G4093.F3J3 1980 .U5

SOILS - INDIANA - LAGRANGE CO. - MAPS.
Hillis, John H. Soil survey of Lagrange County, Indiana /. [Washington] [1980] vii, 135 p., [19] fold. leaves of plates : LC Card 80-602561 DDC 631.4/7/77279 19
S599.I63 H54

SOILS - INDIANA - MARSHALL COUNTY - MAPS.
Smallwood, Benjamin F. Soil survey of Marshall County, Indiana. [Washington, D.C.?] , 1980. vii, 136 p., 63 folded p. of plates : LC Card 81-601062 DDC 631.4/7/77288 19
S599.I63 S6

SOILS - INDIANA - UNION COUNTY - MAPS.
United States. Soil Conservation Service. General soil map, Fayette and Union Counties, Indiana. [Lincoln, Neb. , 1980?] 1 map : LC Card 81-691259
G4093.F3J3 1980 .U5

SOILS - IOWA - BUTLER COUNTY - MAPS.
United States. Soil Conservation Service. General soil map, Butler County, Iowa /. Lincoln, Nebr. , 1978. 1 map : LC Card 81-691196
G4153.B9J3 1978 .U5

SOILS - IOWA - DALLAS COUNTY - MAPS.
United States. Soil Conservation Service.
General soil map, Dallas County, Iowa /.
Lincoln, Nebr. , 1980. 1 map ; LC Card
    81-691197
G4153.D2J3 1980 .U5

SOILS - IOWA - DICKINSON COUNTY - MAPS.
United States. Soil Conservation Service.
General soil map, Dickinson County, Iowa /.
Lincoln, Nebr. , 1979. 1 map ; LC Card
    81-691199
G4153.D7J3 1979 .U5

SOILS - IOWA - FRANKLIN CO. - MAPS.
Voy, Kermit D. Soil survey of Franklin County,
Iowa /. [Washington, D.C.] [1980] ix, 183 p.,
[37] fold. leaves of plates : LC Card 80-602539
    DDC 631.4/7/77728 19
S599.I8 V68

SOILS - IOWA - JOHNSON COUNTY - MAPS.
United States. Soil Conservation Service.
General soil map, Johnson County, Iowa /.
Lincoln, Nebr. , 1979. 1 map ; LC Card
    81-691404
G4153.J5J3 1979 .U5

SOILS - IOWA - KOSSUTH COUNTY - MAPS.
United States. Soil Conservation Service.
General soil map, Kossuth County, Iowa /.
Lincoln, Nebr. , 1980. 1 map ; LC Card
    81-691200
G4153.K6J3 1980 .U5

SOILS - IOWA - MARION CO. - MAPS.
Russell, Robert Cone, 1917- Soil survey of
Marion County, Iowa /. [Washington, D.C.]
[1980] ix, 183 p., [72] fold. leaves of plates :
    LC Card 80-602332 DDC 631.4/7/77783 19
S599.I8 R88

SOILS, IRRIGATED - FLORIDA.
Movement of fertilizer and herbicide through
irrigated sands /. [Gainesville] , 1976. iv, 50
p. : LC Card 77-623198 DDC 631.5/87/09759 19
S616.U6 M68

SOILS, IRRIGATED - HAWAII - KULA.
Green, Richard E. (Richard Ervin), 1931-
Soil-water relations and physical properties of
irrigated soils in the Kula area, Island of Maui,
Hawaii /. Honolulu , 1981. p. cm. LC Card
    81-93 DDC 631.4/32/09969 19
S599.H4 G73

SOILS, IRRIGATED - NEW MEXICO - MESILLA VALLEY.
Wierenga, Petrus Johannes. Soil salinity and
cotton yields as affected by surface and trickle
irrigation . Las Cruces, N.M. [1979] vi, 212
p. : LC Card 80-622502 DDC 333.91/009789 s
    631.4/16 19
GB705.N6 N64 no. 106 S616.U6

SOILS - KANSAS - COWLEY CO. - MAPS.
Horsch, Marcellus L. Soil survey of Cowley
County, Kansas /. [Washington] [1980] viii,
123 p., [47] fold. leaves of plates : LC Card
    80-601849 DDC 631.4/7/78189 19
S599.K2 H578

SOILS - KANSAS - MAPS.
United States. Soil Conservation Service. Soils
map, Kansas /. Lincoln, Nebr. , 1979. 1 map :
    LC Card 81-691120
G4201.J3 1979 .U5

United States. Soil Conservation Service. Soils
map, Kansas /. Lincoln, Nebr. , 1980. 1 map :
    LC Card 81-691119
G4201.J3 1980 .U5

SOILS - KANSAS - MITCHELL CO. - MAPS.
Hamilton, Vernon Leroy, 1932- Soil survey of
Mitchell County, Kansas /. [Washington] ,
1980. vii, 94 p., [30] fold. leaves of plates : LC
    Card 80-602876 DDC 631.4/7/78123 19
S599.K2 H315

SOILS - KANSAS - RUSH CO. - MAPS.
United States. Soil Conservation Service. Soil
survey of Rush County, Kansas /. [Washington,
D.C.] [1980] vi, 62 p., [31] fold. leaves of
plates : LC Card 80-603364 DDC 631.4/7/78148
    19
S599.K2 U54 1980

SOILS - KANSAS - SEDGWICK CO. - MAPS.
Penner, Harold L. Soil survey of Sedgwick
County, Kansas /. [Washington , 1979] vii, 126

p., [41] fold. leaves of plates : LC Card
    79-603621 DDC 631.4/7/78186 19
S599.K2 P44

SOILS - KANSAS - SEWARD COUNTY - MAPS.
United States. Soil Conservation Service.
General soil map, Seward County, Kansas /.
Lincoln, Nebr. , 1979. 1 map : LC Card
    81-691144
G4203.S45J3 1979 .U5

SOILS - KANSAS - STAFFORD COUNTY - MAPS.
United States. Soil Conservation Service.
General soil map, Stafford County, Kansas /.
[Lincoln, Neb.] [1977?] 1 map : LC Card
    81-691171
G4203.S7J3 1977 .U5

SOILS - KANSAS - THOMAS CO. - MAPS.
United States. Soil Conservation Service. Soil
survey of Thomas County, Kansas /.
[Washington] [1980] vii, 57 p., [43] fold. leaves
of plates : LC Card 80-603122 DDC
    631.4/7/781132 19
S599.K2 U54 1980a

SOILS - KENTUCKY - GRANT COUNTY - MAPS.
Froedge, Ronald D. Soil survey of Grant and
Pendleton Counties, Kentucky /. [Washington] ,
1980. vii, 85 p., [40] fold. leaves of plates : LC
    Card 80-602321 DDC 631.4/7/76933 19
S599.K4 F76

SOILS - KENTUCKY - MCLEAN COUNTY - MAPS.
Cox, Frank R., 1918- Soil survey of McLean
and Muhlenberg Counties, Kentucky /.
[Washington] [1980] viii, 124 p., 61 fold p. of
plates : LC Card 80-604148 DDC 631.4/7/769826
    19
S599.K4 C68

SOILS - KENTUCKY - MUHLENBERG COUNTY - MAPS.
Cox, Frank R., 1918- Soil survey of McLean
and Muhlenberg Counties, Kentucky /.
[Washington] [1980] viii, 124 p., 61 fold p. of
plates : LC Card 80-604148 DDC 631.4/7/769826
    19
S599.K4 C68

SOILS - KENTUCKY - PENDLETON COUNTY - MAPS.
Froedge, Ronald D. Soil survey of Grant and
Pendleton Counties, Kentucky /. [Washington] ,
1980. vii, 85 p., [40] fold. leaves of plates : LC
    Card 80-602321 DDC 631.4/7/76933 19
S599.K4 F76

SOILS - KENTUCKY - SHELBY CO. - MAPS.
United States. Soil Conservation Service. Soil
survey of Shelby County, Kentucky /.
[Washington, D.C. , 1980] vii, 84 p., [20] leaves
of plates : LC Card 80-602322 DDC
    631.4/7/769435 19
S599.K4 U54 1980

SOILS - LEACHING.
United States. Office of Solid Waste
Management Programs. Hazardous Waste
Management Division. An environmental
assessment of potential gas and leachate
problems at land disposal sites /. -
[Washington] , 1973 [i. e. 1975] v, 33 p. ;
    *NYPL [*ZV-185 Reel 1]*

SOILS - LOUISIANA - CADDO PARISH - MAPS.
United States. Soil Conservation Service. Soil
survey of Caddo Parish, Louisiana /.
[Washington] [1980] vii, 137 p., [43] fold.
leaves of plates : LC Card 80-603369 DDC
    631.4/7/76399 19
S599.L6 U54 1980a

SOILS - LOUISIANA - RAPIDES PARISH - MAPS.
United States. Soil Conservation Service. Soil
survey of Rapides Parish, Louisiana /.
[Washington] , 1980. iii, 86 p., [59] fold. leaves
of plates : LC Card 80-602333 DDC
    631.4/7/76369 19
S599.L6 U54 1980

SOILS - MARYLAND - ST. MARYS COUNTY - MAPS.
United States. Soil Conservation Service.
Natural soil groups, St. Marys County,
Maryland /. [Lanham? Md.] [1981] 1 map :

LC Card 81-693031
G3843.S3J3 1981 .U5

SOILS - MARYLAND - TALBOT COUNTY - MAPS.
United States. Soil Conservation Service. Talbot
County, Maryland /. [Lanham, MD] [1980] 1
map : LC Card 81-690094
G3843.T3J3 1980 .U5

SOILS - MARYLAND - WORCESTER COUNTY - MAPS.
United States. Soil Conservation Service.
Natural soil groups, Worcester County,
Maryland /. [Lanham? Md.] [1980?] 1 map :
    LC Card 81-693029
G3843.W6J3 1980 .U5

SOILS - MECHANICS. see SOIL MECHANICS.

SOILS - MICHIGAN - BAY CO. - MAPS.
Weesies, Glenn A. Soil survey of Bay County,
Michigan /. [Washington, D.C.] , 1980. vii, 105
p., [23] fold. leaves of plates : LC Card
    80-602508 DDC 631.4/7/77447 19
S599.M4 W43

SOILS - MICHIGAN - BERRIEN COUNTY - MAPS.
Larson, Jerry D. Soil survey of Berrien County,
Michigan. [Washington, D.C.?] , 1980. vii, 192
p. 90 folded p. of plates : LC Card 81-600705
    DDC 631.4/7/77411 19
S599.M4 L363

SOILS - MICHIGAN - HURON CO. - MAPS.
Linsemier, Lyle H. Soil survey of Huron
County, Michigan /. [Washington] , 1979. vii,
145 p., [39] fold. leaves of plates : LC Card
    80-602145 DDC 631.4/7/77444 19
S599.M4 L56

SOILS - MICHIGAN - ROSCOMMON COUNTY - MAPS.
United States. Soil Conservation Service.
General soil map, Roscommon County,
Michigan /. Lincoln, Nebr. , 1979. 1 map ; LC
    Card 81-691401
G4113.R6J3 1979 .U5

SOILS - MINNESOTA - CHISAGO COUNTY - MAPS.
United States. Soil Conservation Service.
General soil map, Chisago County, Minnesota
/. Lincoln, Nebr. , 1979. 1 map : LC Card
    81-691228
G4143.C45J3 1979 .U5

SOILS - MINNESOTA - COTTONWOOD COUNTY - MAPS.
Rolling, R. E. Soil survey of Cottonwood
County, Minnesota /. [Washington] [1979] viii,
142 p., [28] fold. leaves of plates : LC Card
    80-602397 DDC 631.4/7/77622 19
S599.M45 R64

SOILS - MINNESOTA - FREEBORN CO. - MAPS.
Carlson, Carroll Richard, 1928- Soil survey of
Freeborn County, Minnesota /. [Washington,
D.C.] [1979] ix, 228 p., [56] fold. leaves of
plates : LC Card 80-601843 DDC 631.4/7/77618
    19
S599.M45 C37

SOILS - MINNESOTA - KANABEC COUNTY - MAPS.
United States. Soil Conservation Service.
General soil map, Kanabec County, Minnesota
/. Lincoln, Nebr. , 1979. 1 map : LC Card
    81-691229
G4143.K3J3 1979 .U5

SOILS - MINNESOTA - MILLE LACS COUNTY - MAPS.
United States. Soil Conservation Service.
General soil map, Mille Lacs County,
Minnesota /. Lincoln, Nebr. , 1979. 1 map :
    LC Card 81-691230
G4143.M5J3 1979 .U5

SOILS - MINNESOTA - OLMSTED CO. - MAPS.
Poch, George A. Soil survey of Olmsted
County, Minnesota /. [Washington, D.C.]
[1980] ix, 202 p., [53] fold. leaves of plates :
    LC Card 80-602323 DDC 631.4/7/776155 19
S599.M45 P62

SOILS - MINNESOTA - PINE COUNTY - MAPS.
United States. Soil Conservation Service.
General soil map, Pine County, Minnesota /.

Lincoln, Nebr. , 1979. 1 map :　LC Card
81-691231
G4143.P4J3 1979 .U5

**SOILS - MINNESOTA - RAMSEY CO. -
MAPS.**
Vinar, Kenneth R. Soil survey of Washington
and Ramsey Counties, Minnesota /.
[Washington] [1980] ix, 246 p., [56] fold.
leaves of plates :　LC Card 80-602943　DDC
631.4/7/77658 19
S599.M52 V56

**SOILS - MINNESOTA - SCOTT COUNTY -
MAPS.**
United States. Soil Conservation Service.
General soil map of Scott County, Minnesota /.
Lincoln, Nebr. , 1980. 1 map :　LC Card
81-691232
G4143.S3J3 1980 .U5

**SOILS - MINNESOTA - WASHINGTON CO. -
MAPS.**
Vinar, Kenneth R. Soil survey of Washington
and Ramsey Counties, Minnesota /.
[Washington] [1980] ix, 246 p., [56] fold.
leaves of plates :　LC Card 80-602943　DDC
631.4/7/77658 19
S599.M52 V56

**SOILS - MISSISSIPPI - ITAWAMBA CO. -
MAPS.**
Murphree, Leland C., 1912- Soil survey of
Itawamba County, Mississippi /. [Washington]
[1979] viii, 86 p., [25] fold. leaves of plates :
LC Card 80-602033　DDC 631.4/7/762982 19
S599.M5 M89

**SOILS - MISSISSIPPI - LOWNDES CO. -
MAPS.**
Brent, Floyd V. Soil survey of Lowndes
County, Mississippi /. [Washington] [1979]
viii, 137 p., [24] fold. leaves of plates :　LC
Card 80-602618　DDC 631.4/7/762973 19
S599.M5 B7

**SOILS - MONTANA - GLACIER COUNTY -
MAPS.**
United States. Soil Conservation Service. Soil
survey of Glacier County area and part of
Pondera County, Montana /. [Washington,
D.C.] [1980] v, 161 p., [92] leaves of plates :
LC Card 80-602512　DDC 631.4/7/78652 19
S599.M57 U54 1980

**SOILS - MONTANA - PONDERA COUNTY -
MAPS.**
United States. Soil Conservation Service. Soil
survey of Glacier County area and part of
Pondera County, Montana /. [Washington,
D.C.] [1980] v, 161 p., [92] leaves of plates :
LC Card 80-602512　DDC 631.4/7/78652 19
S599.M57 U54 1980

**SOILS - MONTANA - RICHLAND COUNTY -
MAPS.**
Pesoado, Pedro. Soil survey of Richland
County, Montana. [Washington, D.C.?] , C1980.
iv, 71 p., 142 folded p. of plates :　LC Card
80-604152　DDC 631.4/7/78623 19
S599.M57 P47

**SOILS - MONTANA - STILLWATER CO. -
MAPS.**
Parker, John Leon, 1912- Soil survey of
Stillwater County area, Montana /.
[Washington, D.C.]. [1980] vii, 131, 98, [4] p.,
[1] fold. leaf of plates :　LC Card 80-603196
DDC 631.4/7/786651 19
S599.M9 P37

**SOILS - NAVAHO INDIAN RESERVATION -
MAPS.**
Nielson, Woodrow. Soil survey of Navajo
Indian Reservation, San Juan County, Utah /.
[Washington] [1980] viii, 119 p., [12] fold.
leaves of plates :　LC Card 80-602348　DDC
631.4/7/79259 19
S599.U8 N53

**SOILS - NEBRASKA - BURT COUNTY -
MAPS.**
Da Moude, Dean W. Soil survey Burt County,
Nebraska. [Washington, D.C.?] , 1980. vii, 165
p., 44 folded p. of plates :　LC Card 81-601021
DDC 631.4/7/782243 19
S599.N2 D34

United States. Soil Conservation Service.
General soil map, Burt County, Nebraska /.
Lincoln, Nebr. , 1979. 1 map ;　LC Card
81-691073
G4193.B85J3 1979 .U5

**SOILS - NEBRASKA - GOSPER COUNTY -
MAPS.**
United States. Soil Conservation Service.
General Soil map, Gosper County, Nebraska /.
Lincoln, Nebr. , 1979. 1 map ;　LC Card
81-691075
G4193.G6J3 1979 .U51

**SOILS - NEBRASKA - KEYA FAHA
COUNTY - MAPS.**
Soil survey of Keya Paha County, Nebraska.
[Washington, D.C.?] , 1980. ix, 224 p., 62
folded p. of plates :　LC Card 81-600561　DDC
631.4/7/782725 19
S599.N2 S63

SOILS - NEBRASKA - MAPS.
United States. Soil Conservation Service. Soil
areas of Nebraska /. Lincoln, Nebr. , 1979. 1
map :　LC Card 81-691022
G4191.J3 1979 .U5

**SOILS - NEVADA - BIG SMOKY VALLEY -
MAPS.**
Candland, David M. Soil survey of Big Smoky
Valley Area, Nevada, part of Nye County /.
[Washington] 1980. iii, 140 p. [2] fold. leaves
of plates :　LC Card 80-601637　DDC
631.4/7/79334 19
S599.N425 C36

**SOILS - NEW JERSEY - OCEAN CO. -
MAPS.**
Hole, Thornton J. F. Soil survey of Ocean
County, New Jersey /. [Washington] [1980]
vii, 102 p., [35] fold. leaves of plates :　LC
Card 80-602312　DDC 631.4/7/74948 19
S599.N5 H64

**SOILS - NEW MEXICO - CHAVES CO. -
MAPS.**
United States. Soil Conservation Service. Soil
survey of Chaves County, New Mexico,
southern part /. [Washington] [1980] iv, 143
p., [90] fold. leaves of plates :　LC Card
80-602510　DDC 631.4/7/78943 19
S599.N6 U54 1980

SOILS - NEW MEXICO - COMPOSITION.
Severson, R. C. (Ronald Charles), 1945-
Geochemical variability of natural soils and
reclaimed mine-spoil soils in the San Juan
Basin, New Mexico /. Washington , 1981. p.
cm.　LC Card 81-607985　DDC 631.6/4 19
S599.N6 S46

**SOILS - NEW MEXICO - LAS CRUCES
REGION.**
Gile, Leland H. The desert project soil
monograph . [Washington] , 1979. x, 984 p. :
LC Card 80-600512　DDC 631.4/978966 19
S599.N6 G54

**SOILS - NEW MEXICO - LUNA COUNTY -
MAPS.**
Neher, R. E. Soil survey of Luna County, New
Mexico /. [Washington, D.C.] 1980. iii, 80 p.,
[81] folded leaves of plates :　LC Card 80-603368
DDC 631.4/7/78968 19
S599.N6 N4

**SOILS - NEW MEXICO - MESILLA VALLEY -
LEACHING.**
Sammis, Theodore W. Demonstration of
irrigation return flow water quality in the
Mesilla Valley, New Mexico /. Las Cruces,
N.M. [1980] ix, 149 p. :　LC Card 80-623166
DDC 333.91/009789 s 631.7 19
GB705.N6 N64 no. 117 TC824.N6

SOILS - NEW YORK (STATE) - MAPS.
United States. Soil Conservation Service.
Important farmland of New York /. [Lanham?
Md.] , 1979. 1 map :　LC Card 81-693111
G3801.J15 1977 .U5

**SOILS - NORTH CAROLINA - GREENE CO. -
MAPS.**
Barnhill, William L. Soil survey of Greene
County, North Carolina /. [Washington]
[1980] vii, 83 p., [2] fold. leaves of plates :　LC
Card 80-602829　DDC 631.4/7/756393 19
S599.N6 B37

**SOILS - NORTH CAROLINA - HENDERSON
CO. - MAPS.**
King, John M. Soil survey of Henderson
County, North Carolina /. [Washington, D.C. ,
1980] viii, 89 p., [15] fold. leaves of plates :
LC Card 80-602311　DDC 631.4/7/75692 19
S599.N8 K55

Soils of the Great Plains . Aandahl, Andrew

Russell, 1912- Lincoln, c1982. p. cm.　ISBN
0-8032-1011-6　LC Card 81-7435　DDC
631.4/978 19
S599.A1 A17

SOILS - OHIO - ASHLAND CO. - MAPS.
Redmond, Charles Edward, 1932- Soil survey
of Ashland County, Ohio /. [Washington]
[1980] vii, 179 p., [31] fold. leaves of plates :
LC Card 80-602507　DDC 631.4/7/77129 19
S599.O3 R39

SOILS - OHIO - BUTLER CO. - MAPS.
Lerch, Norbert K. Soil survey of Butler County,
Ohio /. [Washington] [1980] vii, 175 p., [38]
fold. leaves of plates :　LC Card 80-602516　DDC
631.4/7/77175 19
S599.O3 L36

SOILS - OHIO - FRANKLIN CO. - MAPS.
McLoda, N. A. Soil survey of Franklin County,
Ohio /. [Washington] [1980] viii, 188 p., [37]
fold. leaves of plates :　LC Card 80-602372　DDC
631.4/7/77156 19
S599.O3 M32

SOILS - OHIO - MADISON CO.
Ohio. Division of Lands and Soil. An inventory
of Ohio soils, Madison County. [Columbus,
Ohio] , 1979. 48 p. (p. 46-48 blank) :　LC Card
80-621013　DDC 631.4/9771 s 631.4/977155 19
S599.O3 A25 no. 57

SOILS - OHIO - PICKAWAY CO. - MAPS.
Kerr, James W. Soil survey of Pickaway
County, Ohio /. [Washington, D.C.] [1980] vii,
172 p., [36] fold. leaves of plates :　LC Card
80-602251　DDC 631.4/7/771815 19
S599.O3 K47

SOILS - OHIO - SENECA COUNTY - MAPS.
Ernst, James Edgar. Soil survey of Seneca
County, Ohio. [Washington, D.C.?] , 1980. vii,
143 p., 81 folded p. of plates :　LC Card
80-604150　DDC 631.4/7/77124 19
S599.O3 E77

**SOILS - OKLAHOMA - MARSHALL
COUNTY - MAPS.**
Burgess, Dent Louis, 1913- Soil survey of
Marshall County, Oklahoma /. [Washington, D.
C. , 1980] vii, 92 p., [20] fold. leaves of plates :
LC Card 80-602509　DDC 631.4/7/76661 19
S599.O4 B88

**SOILS - OREGON - MALHEUR COUNTY -
MAPS.**
Lovell, Burrell B. Soil survey of Malheur
County, Oregon, northeastern part /.
[Washington, D.C.] 1980. viii, 94 p., [22]
folded leaves of plates :　LC Card 80-603621
DDC 631.4/7/79597 19
S599.O7 L68

SOILS - OREGON - MAPS.
United States. Soil Conservation Service. Soil
survey status, Oregon /. Portland, Or. , 1980. 1
map :　LC Card 81-691564
G4291.J3 1979 .U5

**SOILS - PENNSYLVANIA - ARMSTRONG
COUNTY - MAPS.**
United States. Soil Conservation Service.
General soil map, Armstrong County,
Pennsylvania /. [Lanham, Md.] [1980?] 1
map :　LC Card 81-690078
G3823.A6J3 1974 .U5

**SOILS - PENNSYLVANIA - CHICKIES
CREEK WATERSHED - MAPS.**
United States. Soil Conservation Service.
Hydrologic soil groups, Chickies Creek
watershed, Lancaster and Lebanon Counties,
Pennsylvania /. Hyattsville, Md. , 1977. 1
map :　LC Card 81-690273
G3822.C45J3 1977 .U5

United States. Soil Conservation Service. Soils,
Chickies Creek watershed, Lancaster and
Lebanon Counties, Pennsylvania /. Hyattsville,
Md. [1978] 1 map ;　LC Card 81-690272
G3822.C45J3 1978 .U5

**SOILS - PUERTO RICO - PONCE REGION -
MAPS.**
Gierbolini, Roberto E. Soil survey of Ponce
area of southern Puerto Rico /. [Washington]
[1979] iii, 80 p., [22] fold. leaves of plates :
LC Card 80-602349　DDC 631.4/7/72957 19
S599.25.P832 P663

SOILS - RIO GRANDE VALLEY.
Gile, Leland H. The desert project soil
monograph . [Washington] , 1979. x, 984 p. :

LC Card 80-600512   DDC 631.4/978966 19
S599.N6 G54

**SOILS, SALTS IN - NEW MEXICO -
MESILLA VALLEY.**
Sammis, Theodore W. Demonstration of
irrigation return flow water quality in the
Mesilla Valley, New Mexico /. Las Cruces,
N.M. [1980] ix, 149 p. :   LC Card 80-623166
DDC 333.91/009789 s 631.7 19
GB705.N6 N64 no. 117 TC824.N6

Wierenga, Petrus Johannes. Soil salinity and
cotton yields as affected by surface and trickle
irrigation . Las Cruces, N.M. [1979] vi, 212
p. :   LC Card 80-622502   DDC 333.91/009789 s
631.4/16 19
GB705.N6 N64 no. 106 S616.U6

**SOILS - SAN JUAN RIVER WATERSHED
(COLO.=UTAH) - COMPOSITION.**
Severson, R. C. (Ronald Charles), 1945-
Geochemical variability of natural soils and
reclaimed mine-spoil soils in the San Juan
Basin, New Mexico /. Washington , 1981. p.
cm. LC Card 81-607985   DDC 631.6/4 19
S599.N6 S46

**SOILS - SOUTH CAROLINA - ABBEVILLE
COUNTY - MAPS.**
Herren, Edward C. Soil survey of Abbeville
County, South Carolina /. [Washington] [1980]
viii, 82 p., [25]. fold. leaves of plates :   LC Card
80-602551   DDC 631.4/7/75735 19
S599.S58 H46

**SOILS - SOUTH CAROLINA - ANDERSON
CO. - MAPS.**
Herren, Edward C. Soil survey of Anderson
County, South Carolina /. [Washington , 1979]
viii, 79 p., [34] leaves of plates :   LC Card
79-604161   DDC 631.4/7/75725 19
S599.S58 H47

**SOILS - SOUTH CAROLINA - BERKELEY
CO. - MAPS.**
Long, Bobby M. Soil survey of Berkeley
County, South Carolina /. [Washington, D.C.]
1980. viii, 94 p., [51] fold. leaves of plates :
LC Card 80-601634   DDC 631.4/7/75793 19
S599.S58 L66

**SOILS - SOUTH CAROLINA - GREENWOOD
COUNTY - MAPS.**
Camp, Wallace Jefferson, 1906- Soil survey of
Greenwood and McCormick Counties, South
Carolina /. [Washington, D.C. , 1980] iv, 68 p.,
[42] fold. leaves of plates :   LC Card 80-602310
DDC 631.4/7/75733 19
S599.S58 C36

**SOILS - SOUTH CAROLINA - MARION CO. -
MAPS.**
Pitts, J. J. Soil survey of Marion County, South
Carolina /. [Washington] , 1980. vii, 99 p., [27]
fold. leaves of plates :   LC Card 80-603206   DDC
631.4/7/75786 19
S599.S58 P58

**SOILS - SOUTH CAROLINA - MCCORMICK
COUNTY - MAPS.**
Camp, Wallace Jefferson, 1906- Soil survey of
Greenwood and McCormick Counties, South
Carolina /. [Washington, D.C. , 1980] iv, 68 p.,
[42] fold. leaves of plates :   LC Card 80-602310
DDC 631.4/7/75733 19
S599.S58 C36

**SOILS - SOUTH DAKOTA - AURORA
COUNTY - MAPS.**
Schlepp, Richard L. Soil survey of Aurora
County, South Dakota. [Washington, D.C.?] ,
c1980. vii, 148 p., 58 folded p. of plates :   LC
Card 81-600698   DDC 631.4/7/783375 19
S599.S6 S34

**SOILS - SOUTH DAKOTA - BEADLE CO. -
MAPS.**
Heil, Dennis M. Soil survey of Beadle County,
South Dakota /. [Washington] , 1979. viii, 169
p., [98] fold. leaves of plates :   LC Card
80-602070   DDC 631.4/7/783274 19
S599.S6 H43

**SOILS - SOUTH DAKOTA - CAMPBELL CO. -
MAPS.**
Schumacher, Thomas M. Soil survey of
Campbell County, South Dakota /.
[Washington] [1979] vii, 175 p., [32] fold.
leaves of plates :   LC Card 80-602616   DDC
631.4/7/78317 19
S599.S6 S4

**SOILS - SOUTH DAKOTA - CUSTER
COUNTY - MAPS.**
United States. Soil Conservation Service.
General soil map, Custer County, South Dakota
/. Lincoln, Nebr. , 1979. 1 map :   LC Card
81-691164
G4183.C8J3 1979 .U5

**SOILS - SOUTH DAKOTA - LAWRENCE CO.
- MAPS.**
Meland, Arvid C. Soil survey of Lawrence
County, South Dakota /. [Washington, D.C. ,
1979] viii, 173 p., [25] fold. leaves of plates :
LC Card 80-601071   DDC 631.4/7/78391 19
S599.S6 M44

SOILS - SOUTH DAKOTA - MAPS.
United States. Soil Conservation Service. Soils
of South Dakota /. Lincoln, Nebr. , 1976. 1
map :   LC Card 81-691113
G4181.J3 1976 .U5

**SOILS - SOUTH DAKOTA - MCCOOK CO. -
MAPS.**
Heil, Dennis M. Soil survey of McCook
County, South Dakota /. [Washington] , 1980.
vii, 123 p., [25] fold. leaves of plates :   LC Card
80-601638   DDC 631.4/7/783372 19
S599.S6 H44

**SOILS - SOUTH DAKOTA - MELLETTE
COUNTY - MAPS.**
United States. Soil Conservation Service.
General soil map, Mellette County, South
Dakota /. [Lincoln, Neb.] [1978?] 1 map :   LC
Card 81-691165
G4183.M6J3 1973 .U5

SOILS - TEXAS - BOSQUE CO. - MAPS.
Stringer, Billy R. Soil survey of Bosque County,
Texas /. [Washington, D.C.] [1980] vii, 102 p.,
[31] fold. leaves of plates :   LC Card 80-602639
DDC 631.4/7/764518 19
S599.T4 S75

SOILS - TEXAS - BOWIE COUNTY - MAPS.
Fox, Richard W. Soil survey of Bowie County,
Texas. [Washington, D.C.?] , 1980. vii, 128 p.,
76 fold. p. of plates :   LC Card 81-601439   DDC
631.4/7/764197 19
S599.T4 F678

SOILS - TEXAS - BROWN COUNTY - MAPS.
Clower, Dennis F. Soil survey of Brown and
Mills Counties, Texas. [Washington, D.C.?] ,
1980. vii, 170 p., 92 fold. p. of plates :   LC
Card 81-601467   DDC 631.4/7/764512 19
S599.T4 C57

SOILS - TEXAS - DALLAS CO. - MAPS.
Coffee, Daniel R., 1919- Soil survey of Dallas
County, Texas /. [Washington] [1980] vii, 153
p., [38] fold. leaves of plates :   LC Card
80-601832   DDC 631.4/7/7642811 19
S599.T4 C63

**SOILS - TEXAS - GALVESTON COUNTY -
MAPS.**
United States. Soil Conservation Service.
General soil map, Galveston County, Texas /.
[Fort Worth, Tex.] [1980] 1 map :   LC Card
81-692258
G4033.G25J3 1980 .U5

SOILS - TEXAS - GRAYSON CO. - MAPS.
Cochran, Rex. Soil survey of Grayson County,
Texas /. [Washington? , 1980] vii, 141 p., [41]
leaves of plates :   LC Card 80-602304   DDC
631.4/7/764557 19
S599.T4 C593

SOILS - TEXAS - MILLS COUNTY - MAPS.
Clower, Dennis F. Soil survey of Brown and
Mills Counties, Texas. [Washington, D.C.?] ,
1980. vii, 170 p., 92 fold. p. of plates :   LC
Card 81-601467   DDC 631.4/7/764512 19
S599.T4 C57

**SOILS - TEXAS - NACOGDOCHES CO. -
MAPS.**
Dolezel, Raymond. Soil survey of Nacogdoches
County, Texas /. [Washington] , 1980. vii, 146
p., [30] fold. leaves of plates :   LC Card
80-602411   DDC 631.4/7/764182 19
S599.T4 D63

SOILS - TEXAS - PECOS CO. - MAPS.
Rives, Jerry L. Soil survey of Pecos County,
Texas /. [Washington] [1980] vii, 97 p., [77]
fold. leaves of plates :   LC Card 80-602640   DDC
631.4/7/764923 19
S599.T4 R59

SOILS - UTAH - SAN JUAN CO. - MAPS.
Nielson, Woodrow. Soil survey of Navajo
Indian Reservation, San Juan County, Utah /.
[Washington] [1980] viii, 119 p., [12] fold.
leaves of plates :   LC Card 80-602348   DDC
631.4/7/79259 19
S599.U8 N53

SOILS - VIBRATIONS.
United States. Bureau of Mines. Structure
response and damage produced by ground
vibration from surface mine blasting /.
Washington, D.C. [1981] p. cm.   LC Card
80-607825   DDC 622 s 690/.21 19
TN23 .U43 TA654.7

**SOILS - VIRGINIA - GLOUCESTER
COUNTY - MAPS.**
Soil survey of Gloucester County, Virginia.
[Washington, D.C.?] , 1980. vii, 88 p., 35
folded p. of plates :   LC Card 80-604149   DDC
631.4/7/75532 19
S599.V8 S64

**SOILS - VIRGINIA - GOOCHLAND CO. -
MAPS.**
Nicholson, John C. Soil survey of Goochland
County, Virginia /. [Washington] , 1980. ix,
137 p., [22] fold. leaves of plates :   LC Card
80-601854   DDC 631.4/7/755455 19
S599.V8 N52

**SOILS - VIRGINIA - HANOVER CO. -
MAPS.**
Virginia Polytechnic Institute and State
University. Soil survey of Hanover County,
Virginia /. [Washington, D.C. , 1980] ix, 218
p., [35] fold. leaves of plates :   LC Card
80-602048   DDC 631.4/7/755462 19
S599.V8 V57 1980

SOILS - VIRGINIA - MAPS.
United States. Soil Conservation Service.
General soil map, Virginia /. Lanham, MD ,
1979. 1 map :   LC Card 81-690105
G3881.J3 1979 .U5

**SOILS - WASHINGTON (STATE) -
FRANKLIN COUNTY - MAPS.**
United States. Soil Conservation Service. Soil
association map, Franklin County Conservation
District, Franklin County, Washington /.
Portland, Or. , 1980. 1 map :   LC Card
81-691509
G4283.F7J3 1980 .U51

**SOILS - WASHINGTON (STATE) - WALLA
WALLA COUNTY - MAPS.**
United States. Soil Conservation Service.
General soil map, Walla Walla County Soil
Conservation District, Walla Walla County,
Washington /. Portland, Or. , 1979. 1 map :
LC Card 81-691504
G4283.W3J3 1979 .U5

**SOILS - WASHINGTON (STATE) -
WHITMAN COUNTY - MAPS.**
Soil survey of Whitman County, Washington /.
[Washington?] [1980] v, 185 p., [75] folded
leaves of plates :   LC Card 80-602555   DDC
631.4/7797/39 19
S599.W32 S63

United States. Soil Conservation Service.
General soil map, Whitman County,
Washington /. Portland, Or. , 1977. 1 map :
LC Card 81-691518
G4283.W6J3 1977 .U5

SOILS - WEST VIRGINIA - MAPS.
United States. Soil Conservation Service.
General soil map, West Virginia /. Lanham,
MD , 1980. 1 map :   LC Card 81-690096
G3891.J3 1979 .U5

**SOILS - WISCONSIN - ADAMS COUNTY -
MAPS.**
Jakel, Dale E. Soil survey of Adams County,
Wisconsin. [Washington, D.C.?] , 1980. vii, 142
p., 57 folded p. of plates :   LC Card 81-600526
DDC 631.4/7/77556 19
S599.W5 J34

United States. Soil Conservation Service.
General soil map, Adams County, Wisconsin /.
Lincoln, Nebr. , 1980. 1 map :   LC Card
81-691244
G4123.A2J3 1979 .U5

**SOILS - WISCONSIN - CALUMET CO. -
MAPS.**
Otter, Augustine J. Soil survey of Calumet and
Maitowoc Counties, Wisconsin /. [Washington,

D.C.] 1980. vii, 176 p., [64] fold. leaves of plates : LC Card 80-602383 DDC 631.4/7/77566 19
S599.W5 O86

SOILS - WISCONSIN - DODGE CO. - MAPS.
Fox, Robert E. Soil survey of Dodge County, Wisconsin /. [Washington] [1980] ix, 201 p., [71] fold. leaves of plates : LC Card 80-602249 DDC 631.4/7/776153 19
S599.W5 F69

SOILS - WISCONSIN - KEWAUNEE COUNTY - MAPS.
United States. Soil Conservation Service. General soil map, Kewaunee County, Wisconsin /. Lincoln, Nebr. , 1979. 1 map : LC Card 81-691242
G4123.K5J3 1979 .U5

SOILS - WISCONSIN - MANITOWOC COUNTY - MAPS.
Otter, Augustine J. Soil survey of Calumet and Manitowoc Counties, Wisconsin /. [Washington, D.C.] 1980. vii, 176 p., [64] fold. leaves of plates : LC Card 80-602383 DDC 631.4/7/77566 19
S599.W5 O86

SOILS - WISCONSIN - MAPS.
United States. Soil Conservation Service. Soil areas of Wisconsin /. Lincoln, Nebr. , 1980. 1 map : LC Card 81-691248
G4121.J3 1980 .U5

SOILS - WISCONSIN - ONEIDA COUNTY - MAPS.
United States. Soil Conservation Service. General soil map, Oneida County, Wisconsin /. Lincoln, Nebr. , 1980. 1 map : LC Card 81-691233
G4123.O5J3 1979 .U5

SOILS - WISCONSIN - OUTAGAMIE COUNTY - MAPS.
United States. Soil Conservation Service. General soil map, Outagamie County, Wisconsin /. Lincoln, Nebr. , 1980. 1 map : LC Card 81-691241
G4123.O8J3 1977 .U5

SOILS - WISCONSIN - SAUK CO. - MAPS.
Gundlach, Howard F. Soil survey of Sauk County, Wisconsin /. [Washington] [1980] ix, 248 p., [67] fold. leaves of plates : LC Card 80-602384 DDC 631.4/7/77576 19
S599.W5 G86

SOILS - WISCONSIN - WINNEBAGO CO. - MAPS.
Mitchell, Michael J. Soil survey of Winnebago County, Wisconsin /. [Washington] [1980] vii, 182 p., [23] fold. leaves of plates : LC Card 80-602659 DDC 631.4/7/77564 19
S599.W5 M58

SOILS - WISCONSIN - WOOD COUNTY - MAPS.
United States. Soil Conservation Service. General soil map, Wood County, Wisconsin /. Lincoln, Nebr. , 1978. 1 map : LC Card 81-691237
G4123.W9J3 1978 .U5

SOIS final report.
Computer Sciences Corporation. Shipping operations information system /. Falls Church, Va., 1973. 2 v.
*NYPL [*XMQ-2149]*

Sokolik, Stanley Lewis, 1928-
Computer crime : its setting and the need for deterrent legislation / Stanley L. Sokolik. Springfield, Ill. : Data Information Systems Commission, Illinois General Assembly, 1979. vii, 72 p. ; 28 cm. Bibliography: p. 46. LC Card 79-625195 DDC 345.773/0263 19
1. Computer crimes - Illinois. 2. Computer crimes - United States. I. Illinois. Data Information Systems Commission. II. Title.
KFI1768.C65 S64

Protecting the privacy of Illinois citizens : responding to Federal initiatives / Stanley L. Sokolik. Springfield, Ill. : Data Information Systems Commission, Illinois General Assembly, [1979] vii, 88 p. ; 28 cm. Cover title. Bibliography: p. 63-65. LC Card 80-623377 DDC 323.44/8/09773 19
1. Privacy, Right of - Illinois. I. Illinois. Data Information Systems Commission. II. Title.
JC596.2.U5 S65

Sokolov, Vladimir Evgen'evich. Mammal skin / V.E. Sokolov. Berkeley : University of California Press, c1981. p. cm. Includes bibliographical references and index. ISBN 0-520-03198-9 LC Card 81-3037 DDC 599.04/7 19
1. Mammals - Anatomy. 2. Mammals - Physiology. 3. Skin. I. Title.
QL739 .S68

Sokolowski, Thomas J. Elastic parameters computed for materials subjected to modest pressures or temperatures, by T.J. Sokolowski. [Honolulu, Hawaii Institute of Geophysics, University of Hawaii] 1970. vii, 159 p. illus. 28 cm. (Hawaii Institute of Geophysics. HIG-70-20) Bibliography: p. 157-159. LC Card 74-634032 DDC 551 s 624.1/5132 19
1. Rocks - Testing. 2. Elasticity. I. Title.
QE500 .H35 no. 70-20. TA706.5

SOLAR ACTIVITY - CONGRESSES.
International Solar-Terrestrial Predictions Proceedings and Workshop Program. Solar-terrestrial predictions proceedings . - [Washington] , 1979-80. 2 v. :
NYPL [JSK 80-93]

International Solar-Terrestrial Predictions Proceedings, and Workshop Program, Boulder, Colo., 1979. Solar-terrestrial predictions proceedings /. - [Washington] , 1979. 2 v. :
NYPL [JSK 80-80]

SOLAR ACTIVITY - FORECASTING - CONGRESSES.
International Solar-Terrestrial Predictions Proceedings, and Workshop Program, Boulder, Colo., 1979. Solar-terrestrial predictions proceedings /. [Washington] [1979- v. : LC Card 80-601689 DDC 523.7 19
QC883.2.S6 I57 1979

SOLAR AIR CONDITIONING - STUDY AND TEACHING - UNITED STATES.
Colorado. State University, Fort Collins. Solar Energy Applications Laboratory. Solar heating and cooling of residential buildings . [Washington] , 1980. ca. 700 p. LC Card 77-604564
TH7413 .C64 1977   *NYPL [JSF 81-155]*

SOLAR AIR CONDITIONING - UNITED STATES.
United States. General Accounting Office. Federal demonstrations of solar heating and cooling on commercial buildings have not been very effective . [Washington, D.C. , 1980] v, 36 p. : LC Card 80-601697 DDC 697/.78 19
TH7413 .U53 1980

Solar Collector Conference, Flat-plate. see **Flat-plate Solar Collector Conference, Orlando, Fla., 1977.**

SOLAR COLLECTORS - CONGRESSES.
Flat-plate Solar Collector Conference, Orlando, Fla., 1977. Proceedings /. [Washington] , 1978. x, 662 p. : LC Card 78-601524
TJ810 .F56 1977   *NYPL [JSF 81-189]*

Solar Demonstration Program (U. S.) Real Estate Research Corporation. Selling the solar home '80 . [Washington, D.C.] , 1980. 26 p. (p. 26 blank) : LC Card 80-602366 DDC 690/.869/0688 19
HD7293 .R36 1980

Solar energy. United States. Patent and Trademark Office. Office of Technology Assessment and Forecast. [Washington, D.C.] [1980] iii, 190 p. : LC Card 80-601594 DDC 621.47/0272 19
TJ810 .U63 1980

SOLAR ENERGY.
Blake, Floyd. Development and demonstration of low cost heliostats . [Austin] [1979] xv, 74 p. : LC Card 80-620769 DDC 621.47 19
TJ810 .B5

Demonstration of solar energy conversion of agricultural or industrial wastes to fuels . [Austin] , 1979. xiii, 103 p. : LC Card 80-620768 DDC 662/.8 19
TP360 .D45

Solar energy, active and passive systems for space and water heating /. Toledo Metropolitan Area Council of Governments. Toledo, Ohio , c1980. ii, 41 p. : LC Card 80-150114 DDC 697/.78 19
TH7413 .T64 1980

SOLAR ENERGY - AFRICA.
PRC Energy Analysis Company. Solar energy commercialization for African countries /. [Washington] , Springfield, Va. [1978] ix, 103 p. : LC Card 79-602118 DDC 333.79/23/0967 19
TJ810 .P27 1978

Solar energy, an economic analysis . Hill, Lewis E. [Austin, Tex.] [1979] xii, 200 p. : LC Card 80-620775 DDC 333.79/23/09764 19
TJ810 .H55

SOLAR ENERGY - CALIFORNIA.
Hollon, Jennifer K. Solar energy for California's residential sector . Berkeley, Calif. , 1980. p. cm. ISBN 0-87772-279-X LC Card 80-29096 DDC 333.79/23 19
TJ810 .H64

Solar energy commercialization for African countries /. PRC Energy Analysis Company. [Washington] , Springfield, Va. [1978] ix, 103 p. : LC Card 79-602118 DDC 333.79/23/0967 19
TJ810 .P27 1978

SOLAR ENERGY - CONGRESSES.
National Passive Solar Conference. Proceedings. Newark, Del..   *NYPL [JSP 80-342]*

SOLAR ENERGY - ECONOMIC ASPECTS.
Hill, Lewis E. Solar energy, an economic analysis . [Austin, Tex.] [1979] xii, 200 p. : LC Card 80-620775 DDC 333.79/23/09764 19
TJ810 .H55

Solar energy for California's residential sector /. Hollon, Jennifer K. Berkeley, Calif. , 1980. p. cm. ISBN 0-87772-279-X LC Card 80-29096 DDC 333.79/23 19
TJ810 .H64

SOLAR ENERGY - GOVERNMENT POLICY - UNITED STATES.
United States. Congress. House. Committee on Science and Technology. Subcommittee on Energy Development and Applications. Oversight, DOE solar and conservation programs . Washington , 1980. iii, 210 p. : LC Card 81-600834 DDC 353.0082/3 19
KF27 .S3934 1980e

SOLAR ENERGY INDUSTRIES - GOVERNMENT POLICY - UNITED STATES.
United States. Congress. Senate. Committee on the Judiciary. Subcommittee on Antitrust, Monopoly, and Business Rights. DOE's role in the solar energy industry, and possible anticompetitive trends . Washington , 1981. iii, 105 p. : LC Card 81-601624 DDC 338.4/76147/0973 19
KF26 .J835 1980f

SOLAR ENERGY INDUSTRIES - OREGON.
Isaak, David. Solar system economics . Salem, Or. , 1980. 119, [24] p. : LC Card 80-623275 DDC 338.4/362147/09795 19
HD9681.U63 O75

SOLAR ENERGY INDUSTRIES - UNITED STATES - CONGRESSES.
Symposium on Competition in the Solar Energy Industry, Washington, D.C., 1977. The solar market . Washington , 1978. xi, 299 p. : LC Card 79-602870
HD9681.U62 S95 1977   *NYPL [JLF 81-299]*

SOLAR ENERGY INDUSTRIES - UNITED STATES - FINANCE.
United States. Congress. House. Committee on Small Business. Role of government funding and its impact on small business in the solar energy industry . Washington , 1980. vi, 68 p. : LC Card 80-603851 DDC 338.6/42 19
HD9681.U62 U526 1980

United States. Congress. House. Committee on Small Business. Subcommittee on Energy, Environment, Safety and Research. Role of government funding and its impact on small business in the solar energy industry . Washington , 1979 i.e. 1980- v. : LC Card 80-603085 DDC 338.4/362147/0973 19
KF27 .S639 1979b

Solar Energy Industry, Symposium on Competition in the. see **Symposium on Competition in the Solar Energy Industry, Washington, D.C., 1977.**

SOLAR ENERGY - LAW AND LEGISLATION - UNITED STATES.
United States. Congress. House. Committee on Public Works and Transportation. Subcommittee

on Public Buildings and Grounds. Review of
Title V of the National energy conservation
policy act . Washington , 1980. iv, 240 p. : LC
Card 80-601868   DDC 346.7304/67916/0262 19
KF27 .P8964 1979b

SOLAR ENERGY - MEXICO.
Hawkins, Donna. Energy in Mexico . Golden,
Colo. , Washington, D.C. [1980] 35 p. ; LC
Card 80-602377   DDC 333.79/23/0972 19
TJ810 .H363

**SOLAR ENERGY - NEW YORK (STATE) -
PASSIVE SYSTEMS.**
New York State Energy Research and
Development Authority. 1979 NYSERDA
passive solar design awards /. Albany, N.Y.
[c1980] vii, 72 p. : LC Card 80-128412 DDC
728/.68 19
TH7414 .N48 1980

Solar energy objectives, calendar year 1980 /.
United States. Dept. of Energy. Washington,
D.C. , 1980. iii, 354, 73 p. ; LC Card 80-602116
DDC 333.79/23/0973 19
HD9681.U62 U53 1980

SOLAR ENERGY - PASSIVE SYSTEMS.
California Energy Commission. Solar gain .
[Sacramento] , 1980. 119 p. : LC Card
80-623072   DDC 690/.869 19
TH7414 .C34 1980

Franklin Research Center. The first passive
solar home awards, January 1979 /.
[Washington] , 1979. 226 p. : LC Card
79-603049
TH7414 .F73 1979   *NYPL [JSF 81-210]*

**SOLAR ENERGY - PASSIVE SYSTEMS -
LAW AND LEGISLATION - UNITED
STATES.**
United States. Congress. House. Committee on
Ways and Means. Tax credits to homebuilders
using passive solar design and building
techniques . Washington , 1980. iv, 147 p. :
LC Card 81-600616   DDC 343.73/0523
347.303523 19
KF27 .W3 1980l

SOLAR ENERGY - PATENTS.
United States. Patent and Trademark Office.
Office of Technology Assessment and Forecast.
Solar energy. [Washington, D.C.] [1980] iii,
190 p. : LC Card 80-601594 DDC 621.47/0272 19
TJ810 .U63 1980

**SOLAR ENERGY POLICY - UNITED
STATES.**
United States. Dept. of Energy. Solar energy
objectives, calendar year 1980 /. Washington,
D.C. , 1980. iii, 354, 73 p. ; LC Card 80-602116
DDC 333.79/23/0973 19
HD9681.U62 U53 1980

United States. General Accounting Office.
Commercializing solar heating . [Washington]
1979. xii, 66 p. ; LC Card 79-603062 DDC
338.4/769778/0973 19
HD9681.U62 U54 1979

United States. General Accounting Office.
Federal demonstrations of solar heating and
cooling on commercial buildings have not been
very effective . [Washington, D.C. , 1980] v, 36
p. : LC Card 80-601697 DDC 697/.78 19
TH7413 .U53 1980

**SOLAR ENERGY POLICY - UNITED
STATES - CONGRESSES.**
Transcript from the National Hearings on the
Federal nonnuclear energy R&D program.
Washington, D.C. , 1980 i.e. 1981. xix, 207 p. :
LC Card 81-601492 DDC 333.79/23/0973 19
HD9502.U52 T7

Solar energy, progress and promise /. United
States. Council on Environmental Quality.
Washington , 1978. vii, 52 p. ; LC Card
78-601990
TJ810 .U58 1978

**SOLAR ENERGY RESEARCH -
GOVERNMENT POLICY - UNITED
STATES.**
United States. Congress. House. Committee on
Science and Technology. Subcommittee on
Energy Development and Applications. Solar
photovoltaic program . Washington , 1980. iii,
161 p. : LC Card 80-603425 DDC
338.4/762131244/0973 19
KF27 .S3934 1980c

Solar Energy Research Institute. Hawkins,
Donna. Energy in Mexico . Golden, Colo. ,
Washington, D.C. [1980] 35 p. ; LC Card
80-602377 DDC 333.79/23/0972 19
TJ810 .H363

SOLAR ENERGY RESEARCH INSTITUTE.
United States. Congress. House. Committee on
Science and Technology. Subcommittee on
Energy Development and Applications.
Regional solar energy centers and the Solar
Energy Research Institute . Washington , 1980.
v, 23 p. ; LC Card 80-603269   DDC
333.79/23/072073 19
TJ810 .U57 1980

**SOLAR ENERGY RESEARCH - UNITED
STATES.**
United States. Congress. House. Committee on
Science and Technology. Subcommittee on
Energy Development and Applications.
Regional solar energy centers and the Solar
Energy Research Institute . Washington , 1980.
v, 23 p. ; LC Card 80-603269   DDC
333.79/23/072073 19
TJ810 .U57 1980

**SOLAR ENERGY - TEXAS - ECONOMIC
ASPECTS.**
Hill, Lewis E. Solar energy, an economic
analysis . [Austin, Tex.] [1979] xii, 200 p. :
LC Card 80-620775 DDC 333.79/23/09764 19
TJ810 .H55

SOLAR ENERGY - THE WEST.
United States. Congress. House. Committee on
Science and Technology. Subcommittee on
Energy Development and Applications.
Oversight, Western solar energy activities .
Washington , 1980. iii, 127 p. ; LC Card
80-603333 DDC 333.79/23/0978 19
KF27 .S3934 1980b

SOLAR ENERGY - UNITED STATES.
United States. Congress. Office of Technology
Assessment. Conservation and solar energy
programs of the Department of Energy .
Washington, D.C. [1980] viii, 80 p. : LC Card
80-600092
TJ163.4.U6 U5445 1980

                    NYPL [JSF 80-1097]

United States. Council on Environmental
Quality. Solar energy, progress and promise /.
Washington , 1978. vii, 52 p. ; LC Card
78-601990
TJ810 .U58 1978

Solar gain . California Energy Commission.
[Sacramento] , 1980. 119 p. : LC Card
80-623072 DDC 690/.869 19
TH7414 .C34 1980

SOLAR HEAT. see SOLAR HEATING.

**SOLAR-HEATED HOUSES. see SOLAR
HOUSES.**

SOLAR HEATING.
Toledo Metropolitan Area Council of
Governments. Solar energy, active and passive
systems for space and water heating /. Toledo,
Ohio , c1980. ii, 41 p. : LC Card 80-150114
DDC 697/.78 19
TH7413 .T64 1980

**Solar heating and cooling of residential
buildings .** Colorado. State University, Fort
Collins. Solar Energy Applications Laboratory.
[Washington] , 1980. ca. 700 p. LC Card
77-604564
TH7413 .C64 1977   *NYPL [JSF 81-155]*

**SOLAR HEATING - ECONOMIC ASPECTS -
OREGON.**
Isaak, David. Solar system economics /. Salem,
Or. , 1980. 119, [24] p. : LC Card 80-623275
DDC 338.4/362147/09795 19
HD9681.U63 O75

**SOLAR HEATING - ECONOMIC ASPECTS -
UNITED STATES.**
United States. General Accounting Office.
Commercializing solar heating . [Washington]
1979. xii, 66 p. ; LC Card 79-603062 DDC
338.4/769778/0973 19
HD9681.U62 U54 1979

**SOLAR HEATING - PASSIVE SYSTEMS -
LAW AND LEGISLATION - UNITED
STATES.**
United States. Congress. House. Committee on
Ways and Means. Tax credits to homebuilders
using passive solar design and building

techniques . Washington , 1980. iv, 147 p. :
LC Card 81-600616   DDC 343.73/0523
347.303523 19
KF27 .W3 1980l

**SOLAR HEATING - STUDY AND
TEACHING - UNITED STATES.**
Colorado. State University, Fort Collins. Solar
Energy Applications Laboratory. Solar heating
and cooling of residential buildings .
[Washington] , 1980. ca. 700 p. LC Card
77-604564
TH7413 .C64 1977   *NYPL [JSF 81-155]*

SOLAR HEATING - UNITED STATES.
United States. General Accounting Office.
Federal demonstrations of solar heating and
cooling on commercial buildings have not been
very effective . [Washington, D.C. , 1980] v, 36
p. : LC Card 80-601697 DDC 697/.78 19
TH7413 .U53 1980

SOLAR HOUSES.
Franklin Research Center. The first passive
solar home awards, January 1979 /.
[Washington] , 1979. 226 p. : LC Card
79-603049
TH7414 .F73 1979   *NYPL [JSF 81-210]*

**SOLAR HOUSES - DESIGN AND
CONSTRUCTION.**
California Energy Commission. Solar gain .
[Sacramento] , 1980. 119 p. : LC Card
80-623072 DDC 690/.869 19
TH7414 .C34 1980

SOLAR HOUSES - ILLINOIS.
Pogany, D. Z. The potential economic impact
of solar heated residences in Illinois, 1976-2000
/. [Springfield] , 1976. viii, 101 p. : LC Card
77-622518
HD7303.I3 P64   *NYPL [*XME-9620]*

SOLAR HOUSES - LOCATION.
Erley, Duncan. Site planning for solar access .
[Washington] [1979] 149 p. : LC Card
80-600615
TH7414 .E74   *NYPL [JSF 81-159]*

**SOLAR HOUSES - NEW YORK (STATE) -
DESIGN AND CONSTRUCTION.**
New York State Energy Research and
Development Authority. 1979 NYSERDA
passive solar design awards /. Albany, N.Y.
[c1980] vii, 72 p. : LC Card 80-128412 DDC
728/.68 19
TH7414 .N48 1980

**SOLAR HOUSES - STUDY AND TEACHING -
UNITED STATES.**
Colorado. State University, Fort Collins. Solar
Energy Applications Laboratory. Solar heating
and cooling of residential buildings .
[Washington] , 1980. ca. 700 p. LC Card
77-604564
TH7413 .C64 1977   *NYPL [JSF 81-155]*

SOLAR HOUSES - UNITED STATES.
Real Estate Research Corporation. Selling the
solar home '80 . [Washington, D.C.] , 1980. 26
p. (p. 26 blank) : LC Card 80-602366 DDC
690/.869/0688 19
HD7293 .R36 1980

**SOLAR HOUSES - UNITED STATES -
FINANCE.**
United States. Congress. House. Committee on
Veterans' Affairs. Subcommittee on Housing.
VA direct loans for residential solar energy
systems . Washington , 1980. iii, 20 p. ; LC
Card 80-603113 DDC 343.73/011 19
KF27 .V446 1980

The solar market . Symposium on Competition in
the Solar Energy Industry, Washington, D.C.,
1977. Washington , 1978. xi, 299 p. : LC Card
79-602870
HD9681.U62 S95 1977 *NYPL [JLF 81-299]*

Solar photovoltaic program . United States.
Congress. House. Committee on Science and
Technology. Subcommittee on Energy
Development and Applications. Washington ,
1980. iii, 161 p. : LC Card 80-603425 DDC
338.4/762131244/0973 19
KF27 .S3934 1980c

SOLAR POWER. see SOLAR ENERGY.

SOLAR RADIATION - CONGRESSES.
Workshop on Earth Radiation Budget Science,
Williamsburg, Va., 1978. Earth radiation budget
science, 1978 . [Washington, D.C.] , Springfield,
Va. , 1979. vi, 72 p. : LC Card 80-601801 DDC

551.5/272 19
QC809.E6 W67 1978

SOLAR RADIATION - PHYSIOLOGICAL EFFECT.
Cutchis, Pythagoras. On the linkage of solar ultraviolet radiation to skin cancer . Washington, D.C. , 1978. xiv, 146, [13] p. : LC Card 79-602135   DDC 616.99/477071 19
RC280.S5 C83

SOLAR SEA POWER PLANTS. see OCEAN THERMAL POWER PLANTS.

Solar system economics /. Isaak, David. Salem, Or. , 1980. 119, [24] p. :   LC Card 80-623275   DDC 338.4/362147/09795 19
HD9681.U63 O75

Solar-terrestrial predictions proceedings . International Solar-Terrestrial Predictions Proceedings and Workshop Program. - [Washington] , 1979-80. 2 v. :
                                NYPL [JSK 80-93]

Solar-terrestrial predictions proceedings /. International Solar-Terrestrial Predictions Proceedings, and Workshop Program, Boulder, Colo., 1979. - [Washington] , 1979. 2 v. :
                                NYPL [JSK 80-80]

Solar-terrestrial predictions proceedings /. International Solar-Terrestrial Predictions Proceedings, and Workshop Program, Boulder, Colo., 1979. [Washington] [1979- v. :   LC Card 80-601689   DDC 523.7 19
QC883.2.S6 I57 1979

Solar-Terrestrial Predictions Proceedings and Workshop Program, International. see International Solar-Terrestrial Predictions Proceedings and Workshop Program; International Solar-Terrestrial Predictions Proceedings, and Workshop Program, Boulder, Colo., 1979.

Solarz, Stephen J. United States. Congress. House. Study Mission to Morocco, the Western Sahara, Mauritania, Algeria, Liberia, Spain, and France. Arms for Morocco? . Washington , 1979. viii, 26 p. :   LC Card 80-601042   DDC 355/.032/64 19
E183.8.M8 U54 1979

Solberg, Patrice. North Carolina. Laws, statutes, etc. 1979 supplement to North Carolina dog law manual /. [Chapel Hill] [1979?] 47 p. ;   LC Card 80-623111   DDC 346.75604/7 19
KFN7484.5.D63 A3 1979 Suppl

Solbrig, Otto Thomas. Demography and evolution in plant populations /. Berkeley , 1980. xiv, 222 p. :   ISBN 0-520-03931-9   LC Card 79-64486   DDC 581.5/248 19
QK910 .D45

Soldiers' dependents, Medical care of. see United States - Armed Forces - Medical care.

SOLDIERS - EDUCATION, NON-MILITARY - COLORADO.
Mitchell, William A., 1940- The Republic of Turkey . United States Air Force Academy, Colo. [1981] p. cm.   LC Card 81-607896   DDC 956.1/0007/1178881 19
DR438.95.U6 M57

SOLDIERS - EDUCATION, NON-MILITARY - UNITED STATES - DIRECTORIES.
United States. Dept. of the Air Force. Educational opportunities on Air Force bases /. [Washington, D.C.] [1980] ca. 150 p. in various pagings :   LC Card 80-603210   DDC 378.73 19
U716 .A533 1980

Soldiers - Medical benefits. see United States - Armed Forces - Medical care.

SOLDIERS - UNIFORMS. see UNIFORMS, MILITARY.

SOLDIERS - UNITED STATES - DRUG USE.
United States. Congress. House. Select Committee on Narcotics Abuse and Control. Drug abuse in the Armed Forces of the United States . Washington , 1980. iii, 66 p. ;   LC Card 80-603858   DDC 362.2/936 19
UH630 .U62 1980

United States. Congress. House. Select Committee on Narcotics Abuse and Control. Drug abuse in the Armed Forces of the United States . Washington , 1980. iii, 144 p. :   LC Card 80-601999   DDC 353.0084/29 19
KF27.5 .N3 1979g

Soldo, Beth J. (joint author) Struyk, Raymond J. Improving the elderly's housing . Cambridge, Mass. , c1980. xxii, 325 p. :   ISBN 0-88410-495-8   LC Card 79-3008
HD7287.92.U55 S77   NYPL [JLE 80-2769]

Solem, Robert A. Community-based care systems for the functionally disabled . Olympia, Wash. , 1979. xiv, 339 p. :   LC Card 79-620045   DDC 362.1/4/09797 19
RA645.36.W2 C65

Solid fuels conversion costs for Texas-coal and lignite utilization in electric power generation and other industries : final report : prepared for Texas Energy Advisory Council, Energy Development Fund / F.D. Singleton, Jr. ... [et al.]. [Austin] : The Council, 1979. v, 101 p. : ill. ; 28 cm. (Report - Texas Energy Advisory Council, Energy Development Fund . #EDF-008) "January 31, 1979." Includes bibliographies.   LC Card 80-620773   DDC 338.4/3662625 19
1. Coal - Texas. 2. Lignite - Texas. 3. Coal liquefaction. 4. Coal gasification. I. Singleton, Francis Dail, 1943-. II. Texas. Energy Development Fund. III. Series: Texas. Energy Development Fund. Report - Texas Energy Advisory Council, Energy Development Fund , #EDF-008.
TP326.U5 S67

SOLID WASTE MANAGEMENT. see SALVAGE (WASTE, ETC.)

SOLIDS - FRACTURE. see FRACTURE MECHANICS.

Solomon, Jack, 1927- Ghosts and goosebumps . University, Ala. , c1982. p. cm.   ISBN 0-8173-0075-9   LC Card 81-7461   DDC 398.2/09761 19
GR110.A2 B56

Solomon, Jodee. The recent history and current status of abortion law. Madison, Wis. : State of Wisconsin, Legislative Reference Bureau, [1980] 12 p. ; 28 cm. (Informational bulletin / The State of Wisconsin, Legislative Reference Bureau . 80-IB-5) Cover title. "September 1980." Bibliography: p. 12.   LC Card 80-624142   DDC 344.775/0419   347.7504419 19
1. Abortion - Law and legislation - Wisconsin. 2. Abortion - Law and legislation - United States. I. Wisconsin. Legislative reference bureau. II. Series: Informational bulletin (Wisconsin. Legislative Reference Bureau) , 80-IB-5. III. Title.
KFW2415 .L4 80-5 KFW2753

Solomon, Olivia, 1937- Ghosts and goosebumps . University, Ala. , c1982. p. cm.   ISBN 0-8173-0075-9   LC Card 81-7461   DDC 398.2/09761 19
GR110.A2 B56

Solomon, Samuel R. The governors of the American states, commonwealths, and territories, 1900-1980 / compiled by Samuel R. Solomon. Lexington, Ky. (Iron Works Pike, P.O. Box 11910, Lexington, Ky. 40578) : Council of State Governments, c1980. 79, [1] p. ; 28 cm. (RM-684) Previously published as: The Governors of the States, 1900-1974. Bibliography: p. 80.   LC Card 80-624452   DDC 353.9/131 19
1. Governors - United States. I. Council of State Governments. II. Series: RM, 684. III. Title.
JK2447 .S6

Soltero, Raymond A. Further investigation as to the cause and effect of eutrophication in Long Lake, Washington; project completion report. Principal investigator, Raymond A. Soltero; co-investigators: Anthony F. Gasperino [and] William G. Graham. Cheney, Wash., Eastern Washington State College, Dept. of Biology, 1974. x, 85 p.: ill.; 28 cm. Bibliography: p. 80-85. "D. O. E. Project number: 74-025A. D. O. E. Accounting note: 001-01. Allotment period; July 1, 1973 to June 30, 1974."   LC Card 76-9604
1. Eutrophication - Washington (State) - Long Lake. I. Gasperino, Anthony F., joint author. II. Graham, William G., joint author. III. Washington (State). Eastern Washington State College, Cheney. Dept. of Biology. IV. Washington (State). Dept. of Ecology. V. Title.   NYPL [JSF 80-397]

Soltow, Lee. The rise of literacy and the common school in the United States : a socioeconomic analysis to 1870 / Lee Soltow and Edward Stevens. Chicago : University of Chicago Press, 1981. p. cm. Bibliography: p. Includes index.   ISBN 0-226-76812-0   LC Card 81-7464   DDC 428.4 19
1. Illiteracy - United States - History - 19th century. 2.

Public school - United States - History - 19th century. I. Title.
LC151 .S64

Soltow, Martha Jane. Michigan. State University, East Lansing. Library. American labor history . East Lansing, Mich. , 1980. 88 p. ;   LC Card 80-119371
HD8066 .M52 1980   NYPL [JLD 81-144]

SOLUBLE FERMENTS. see ENZYMES.

SOLVENT ABUSE.
Mason, Terry. Inhalant use and treatment /. Rockville, Md. , Washington , 1979. vii, 62 p. ;   LC Card 79-603028   DDC 362.2/93 19
RC568.S64 M37

SOLVENT ABUSE - TREATMENT.
Mason, Terry. Inhalant use and treatment /. Rockville, Md. , Washington , 1979. vii, 62 p. ;   LC Card 79-603028   DDC 362.2/93 19
RC568.S64 M37

SOLVENT EXTRACTION.
Nilsen, D. N. Solvent extraction of nickel and copper from laterite-ammoniacal leach liquors /. Avondale, MD , 1981. p. cm.   LC Card 81-38488   DDC 622 s 669/.7332 19
TN23 .U43 TN799.N6

Solvent extraction of nickel and copper from laterite-ammoniacal leach liquors /. Nilsen, D. N. Avondale, MD , 1981. p. cm.   LC Card 81-38488   DDC 622 s 669/.7332 19
TN23 .U43 TN799.N6

SOLVENTS.
Tweeton, Daryl R. Selection of lixiviants for in situ uranium leaching /. Avondale, MD [1981] p. cm.   LC Card 81-6103   DDC 622 s 622/.34932 19
TN295 .U4 TN490.U7

SOLVENTS - THERMAL PROPERTIES.
Christos, Theodore. Thermal degradation products of solvents and hydraulic fluids used in mining /. Washington [1980] p. cm.   LC Card 80-607783   DDC 622 s 622/.3 19
TN23 .U43 QD544

Soma Shekar, M. (joint author) Muchmore, C. B. Economic impact of the proposed averaging rule, R76-21 /. Chicago, IL , 1978. xi, 43 p. :   LC Card 80-622962   DDC 363.7/39462 19
TD224.I3 M84

Some aspects of natural vegetation establishment on abandoned underground coal mine refuse areas in Illinois /. D'Antuono, James R. Chicago, IL , 1979. xii, 32 p. :   LC Card 79-626016   DDC 631.6/4 19
S621.5.S65 D36

Some aspects of the carrying capacity of Prince William Sound, Alaska, for hatchery released pink and chum salmon fry /. University of Alaska, Fairbanks. Institute of Marine Science. Fairbanks , 1978. ix, 98 p. :   LC Card 78-624148   DDC 551.46 s 639.3/755 19
GC1 .A497 no. 78-3 SH167.S17

Some aspects of the ghetto labor market in New York. United States. Bureau of Labor Statistics. New York, 1971. 21 p.   LC Card 72-601109
*HD5726.N5 A54 1971b   NYPL [*ZT-1264]*

Some economic aspects of air pollution in Montana /. Otis, Ted. Helena, Mont. [1979] ii, 94 p. ;   LC Card 80-622032   DDC 338.4/73637392/09786 19
HC107.M93 A45

Some economic consequences of technological advance in medical care . Geweke, John. [Madison, Wis.] [1980] 52 p. :   LC Card 80-622910   DDC 338.4/33621963433061 19
RA645.P46 G48 1980

Some effects of paraformaldehyde on wood surrounding tapholes in sugar maple trees /. Shigo, Alex L., 1930- Upper Darby, Pa. , 1970. 11 p. :   LC Card 81-460882   DDC 634.9/0974 s 633.6/49 19
SD11 .A455493 no. 161 SB608.S913

Some interesting buildings, sites, and natural features in the Hudson-Mohawk Urban Cultural Park /. Hudson-Mohawk Industrial Gateway, inc. [Troy? N.Y.] [1979] 1 map :   LC Card 81-692835
G3802.H87E635 1979 .H8

Some methodological issues in the analysis of longitudinal surveys /. Singer, Burton. [Madison] , 1976. 56 p. ;   LC Card 78-624379

DDC 330/.723 19
H62 .S4775

Some perspectives on oil availability for the non-OPEC LDCs : a research paper / National Foreign Assessment Center. Washington, D.C. : Central Intelligence Agency : Document Expeditions (DOCEX) Project, Exchange and Gift Division, Library of Congress [distributor], 1980. viii, 48 p. : ill., charts, 3 maps ; 27 cm. "Research for this report was completed on 20 July 1980." "September 1980." "ER 80-10493." LC Card 80-603931 DDC 333.8/23211/091724 19
1. Underdeveloped areas - Petroleum industry and trade. I. United States. Central Intelligence Agency. II. National Foreign Assessment Center (U. S.).
HD9560.5 .S62

Some tropical landforms of Puerto Rico .
Monroe, Watson Hiner, 1907- Washington , 1980. iv, 39 p. : LC Card 80-600071 DDC 551.4/097295 19
GB428.5.P9 M66

Someone special : how Mike learns to live with kidney disease / editors, Glenn H. Bock, Marshall G. Hoff ; writer, Phyllis Czaia Haensel ; illustrator, Pam Belding. Minneapolis, Minn. : University of Minnesota, Division of Pediatric Nephrology : Minnesota Medical Foundation, 1981. p. cm. Recounts how Mike's kidney disease was detected and how it is treated. Also tells how kidneys function. ISBN 0-940210-00-2 LC Card 81-51347 DDC 618.92/61 19
1. Pediatric nephrology - Juvenile literature. 2. Kidneys - Diseases - Juvenile literature. I. Bock, Glenn H. II. Hoff, Marshall G. III. Haensel, Phyllis Czaia. IV. Belding, Pamela S., ill. V. University of Minnesota. Division of Pediatric Nephrology.
RJ476.K5 S65

Sommer, Frederick, 1905- Frederick Sommer at seventy-five : a retrospective / edited by Constance W. Glenn and Jane K. Bledsoe ; published on the occasion of an exhibition organized by Leland Rice for the Art Museum and Galleries, California State University, Long Beach, February 11-March 9, 1980. Long Beach : Art Museum and Galleries, California State University, Long Beach, 1980. [72] p. : ill. ; 27 cm. Includes bibliography. LC Card 80-310
1. Photography, Artistic - Exhibitions. 2. Sommer, Frederick, 1905-. I. Glenn, Constance. II. Bledsoe, Jane K., 1937-. III. California State University, Long Beach. Art Museum and Galleries. IV. Title.
TR647 .S62 1980
NYPL [MFX (Sommer) 81-836]

SOMMER, FREDERICK, 1905-
Sommer, Frederick, 1905- Frederick Sommer at seventy-five . Long Beach , 1980. [72] p. : LC Card 80-310
TR647 .S62 1980
NYPL [MFX (Sommer) 81-836]

Somoshegyi-Szokol, Gaston. California. University. Library. Contemporary Chilean literature in the University Library at Berkeley . Berkeley , 1975. iv, 161 leaves ; LC Card 76-367520
Z1713 .C25 1975 PQ7953
*NYPL [*XM-13759]*

Son of Tecún Umán . Bizarro Ujpán, Ignacio. Tucson , 1981. p. cm. ISBN 0-8165-0736-8 : LC Card 81-11702 DDC 972.81/004970924 B 19
F1465.2.T9 B59

SONAR IN FISHING - ALASKA.
Blankenbeckler, Dennis. Pacific herring (Clupea pallasi) harvest statistics and a summary of hydroacoustical surveys conducted in Southeastern Alaska during the fall, winter, and spring of 1975-1976 /. Juneau [1976] 95 p. : LC Card 77-620582 DDC 639/.09798 s 333.95/6 19
SH11 .A7252a no. 28 SH351.H5

Sonderegger, J. L. (joint author) Rautio, Sandra A. Annotated bibliography of the geothermal resources of Montana /. [Butte] , 1980. 25 p. ; LC Card 80-623786 DDC 553.7 19
GB1199.7.M9 R38

SONNETS, ENGLISH - HISTORY AND CRITICISM.
Harris, Daniel A., 1942- Inspirations unbidden, Hopkins's poetics in the "terrible sonnets" /. Berkeley , c1982. p. cm. ISBN 0-520-04539-4 LC Card 81-11497 DDC 821/.8 19
PR4803.H44 Z6467

Sonnichsen, C. L. (Charles Leland), 1901- The ambidextrous historian : historical writers and writing in the American West / by C.L. Sonnichsen.1st ed. Norman : University of Oklahoma Press, c1981. p. cm. Bibliography: p. Includes index. ISBN 0-8061-1690-0 LC Card 81-2786 DDC 978/.0072 19
1. West (U. S.) - Historiography - Addresses, essays, lectures. 2. Historiography - United States - Addresses, essays, lectures. I. Title.
F591 .S67

SONOMA CO., CALIF. - ANTIQUITIES.
Baumhoff, Martin A. An archaeological assay on Dry Creek, Sonoma County, California /. Berkeley , 1979. xi, 244 p. : LC Card 80-620631 DDC 979.4/18 19
E51 .C2 no. 40 E78.C15

The Sonoran Desert . Caldwell, Mary. Tucson, Ariz. [1976] ca. 400 p. : LC Card 79-625338 DDC 016.9172/170954 19
Z7408.S59 C34 QH104.5.S58

SONORAN DESERT - BIBLIOGRAPHY.
Caldwell, Mary. The Sonoran Desert . Tucson, Ariz. [1976] ca. 400 p. : LC Card 79-625338 DDC 016.9172/170954 19
Z7408.S59 C34 QH104.5.S58

Sooy, Diana. National Symposium on Job-Task Analysis in Criminal Justice, Dallas, 1978. National Symposium on Job-Task Analysis in Criminal Justice . Washington, D.C. , 1979. ix, 465 p. ; LC Card 79-603983 DDC 363.2/2 19
HV8143 .N39 1978

SOPORIFICS. see NARCOTICS.

Sorden, Vinnie.
(joint author) Simon, Edward, 1946- Delaware occupational employment statistics . Newark, DE [1979?] iii, 76 p. ; LC Card 80-621965 DDC 331.12/57/09751 19
HD5725.D3 S53

(joint author) Simon, Edward, 1946- Delaware occupational employment statistics . Newark, DE [1980] iv, 65 p. ; LC Card 80-622179 DDC 331.12/51/0009751 19
HD5725.D3 S54

Sørensen, Aage Bøttger. Experimental matching of people to jobs / Aage B. Sørensen. [Madison] : University of Wisconsin-Madison, Institute for Research on Poverty, 1980. 17 p. ; 29 cm. (Discussion papers - University of Wisconsin-Madison, Institute for Research on Poverty . 594-80) Bibliography: p. 17. LC Card 80-622909 DDC 658.3/128 19
1. Job satisfaction - United States. I. Series: Wisconsin. University, Madison. Institute for Research on Poverty. Discussion papers, 594-80. II. Title.
HF5549.5.J63 S57

Sorensen, Harry, 1922- (joint author) Johnson, Allan Michael, 1935- Drill core investigation of the Fiborn Limestone member in Schoolcraft County, Mackinac and Chippewa Counties, Michigan /. Lansing , 1978. v, 51 p. : LC Card 79-623935 DDC 557.74 s 553.5/16/097749 19
QE125 .A417 no. 18 QE471.15.L5

Sorensen, Martin L. Crittenden, Max D. The Facer Formation, a new early Proterozoic unit in northern Utah /. [Reston, Va.?] , Washington, D.C. , 1980. iv, F28 p. : LC Card 80-600144 DDC 557.3 s 551.7/15/09792 19
QE75 .B9 no. 1482-F QE653

Sorenson, L. Orlo. (joint author) Anderson, Dale G. Rail-line abandonment in the North Central region /. Manhattan , 1979. 36 p. ; LC Card 80-622127 DDC 385/.2042 19
HE2757 .A53

SORGHUM INDUSTRY - TEXAS.
Fuller, Stephen. Economics of grain sorghum production and marketing /. College Station, Tex. , 1979. iii, 43 p. ; LC Card 80-620821 DDC 338.1/73174/09764 19
HD9049.S6 U53

SORGHUM INDUSTRY - UNITED STATES.
Jackson, David M. U. S. sorghum industry /. [Washington, D.C.] [1980] iii, 84 p. : LC Card 80-602638 DDC 338.1 s 338.1/73174/0973 19
HD1751 .A91854 no. 457 HD9049.S6U5

SORPTION. see ADSORPTION.

Sorrels, Charles A. United States. Congressional Budget Office. Planning U. S. general purpose forces . Washington , 1977. xxiii, 95 p. ; LC

Card 77-603153
UA26.E27 U54 1977

Sorrentino, Constance. Youth unemployment, an international perspective. Washington, D.C. : U. S. Dept. of Labor, Bureau of Labor Statistics, [1981] p. cm. (Bulletin . 2098) "July 1981." Bibliography: p. LC Card 81-607979 DDC 331.3/4137 19
1. Youth - Employment. 2. Unemployed. I. Series: Bulletin (United States. Bureau of Labor Statistics) , 2098. II. Title.
HD6270 .S66

The sorting and deposition of allochthonous plant material in a modern environment at Silwood Lake, Silwood Park, Berkshire, England /. Spicer, Robert A., 1950- Washington , 1981. v, 77 p. : LC Card 80-607854 DDC 560/.1/78 19
QE931.3 .S64

Souders, Vernon L. Geology and groundwater supplies of Box Butte County, Nebraska / Vernon L. Souders, Frank A. Smith, and James B. Swinehart ; prepared in cooperation with the Upper Niobrara-White Natural Resources District. [Lincoln] : Conservation and Survey Division, Institute of Agriculture and Natural Resources, University of Nebraska--Lincoln, [1980] vii, 205 p. : ill. ; 28 cm. (Nebraska water survey paper . no. 47) Bibliography: p. 161-166. LC Card 80-623050 DDC 553/.7/09782 s 551.7/9/0978294 19
1. Geology - Nebraska - Box Butte County. 2. Water, Underground - Nebraska - Box Butte County. I. Smith, Frank Avery, 1925- joint author. II. Swinehart, James B., joint author. III. Upper Niobrara-White Natural Resources District. IV. University of Nebraska--Lincoln. Conservation and Survey Division. V. Title. VI. Series.
GB1025.N2 N42 no. 47 QE136.B67

Sound propagation in the sea /. Urick, Robert J. [Arlington, Va.] , Washington, D.C. , 1979. ca. 300 p. in various pagings : LC Card 80-601623 DDC 534/.23 19
QC233 .U76

SOUND RECORDING INDUSTRY - WASHINGTON, D. C.
Checchi and Company, Washington, D. C. Final report : feasibility of establishing a recording studio in the District of Columbia . Washington , 1973. 124 p. :
*NYPL [*LE 80-1766]*

SOUND - TRANSMISSION - MEASUREMENT.
Urick, Robert J. Sound propagation in the sea /. [Arlington, Va.] , Washington, D.C. , 1979. ca. 300 p. in various pagings : LC Card 80-601623 DDC 534/.23 19
QC233 .U76

SOUND-WAVES - SCATTERING - CONGRESSES.
Oceanic sound scattering prediction /. New York , c1979, xii, 859 p. : ISBN 0-306-35505-1 LC Card 77-3445
QC242 .O25 *NYPL [JSF 81-96]*

Sourcebook of hydrologic and ecological features . United States. National Laboratory, Oak Ridge, Tenn. Environmental Sciences Division. Ann Arbor, Mich. , c1980. x, 126 p. : ISBN 0-250-40355-2 LC Card 79-56108
GB701 .U54 1980 *NYPL [JSE 80-1263]*

Sources and effects of ionizing radiation . United Nations. Scientific Committee on the Effects of Atomic Radiation. New York , 1977. 725 p. : LC Card 79-112082 DDC 616.9/897 19
QP82.2.I53 U54 1977

South Africa . Study Commission on U. S. Policy toward Southern Africa (U. S.) Berkeley , c1981. xxvii, 517 p., [26] p. of plates : ISBN 0-520-04504-1 LC Card 81-2742 DDC 327.73068 19
E183.8.S6 S78 1981

SOUTH AFRICA - FOREIGN RELATIONS - UNITED STATES.
Study Commission on U. S. Policy toward Southern Africa (U. S.) South Africa . Berkeley , c1981. xxvii, 517 p., [26] p. of plates : ISBN 0-520-04504-1 LC Card 81-2742 DDC 327.73068 19
E183.8.S6 S78 1981

United States. Congress. House. Committee on Foreign Affairs. Subcommittee on International Economic Policy and Trade. U. S. policy toward South Africa . Washington , 1980. iv,

912 p. :   LC Card 80-603998   DDC 327.73068 19
KF27 .F6465 1980b

South Africa, homelands. United States. Central
Intelligence Agency. [Washington , 1980] 1
map :   LC Card 81-692033
G8501.G6 1980 .U5

**SOUTH AFRICA - POLITICS AND
GOVERNMENT - 1961-**
United States. Congress. House. Committee on
Foreign Affairs. Subcommittee on International
Economic Policy and Trade. U. S. policy
toward South Africa . Washington , 1980. iv,
912 p. :   LC Card 80-603998   DDC 327.73068 19
KF27 .F6465 1980b

**South African Homelands, South Africa. see
Homelands, South Africa.**

**SOUTH AMERICA - HISTORY - TO 1806 -
ARCHIVAL RESOURCES - LATIN
AMERICA.**
Hanke, Lewis. Guía de las fuentes en
hispanoamérica para el estudio de la
administración virreinal española en México y
en el Perú, 1535-1700 /. Washington, D.C. ,
1980. x, 523 p. ;   ISBN 0-8270-1091-5 :   LC Card
81-115511   DDC 972 19
Z1426 .H36 F1231

**SOUTH AMERICA - HISTORY - WARS OF
INDEPENDENCE, 1806-1830.**
Al libertador general San Martín . Washington,
D.C. [1978] vii, 51 p., [1] leaf of plates :   LC
Card 80-145557   DDC 980/.02/0924 B 19
F2235.4 .A677

**SOUTH ASIA - ARCHIVAL RESOURCES -
WASHINGTON, D.C.**
Rahim, Enayetur. Scholars' guide to
Washington, D.C., for South Asian studies .
Washington, D.C. , 1981. p. cm.   ISBN
0-87474-778-3 :   LC Card 81-607847   DDC
016.954/0720753 19
Z3185 .R34 DS335

**SOUTH ASIA - LIBRARY RESOURCES -
WASHINGTON, D.C.**
Rahim, Enayetur. Scholars' guide to
Washington, D.C., for South Asian studies .
Washington, D.C. , 1981. p. cm.   ISBN
0-87474-778-3 :   LC Card 81-607847   DDC
016.954/0720753 19
Z3185 .R34 DS335

**SOUTH ASIA - SOCIETIES, ETC. -
DIRECTORIES.**
Rahim, Enayetur. Scholars' guide to
Washington, D.C., for South Asian studies .
Washington, D.C. , 1981. p. cm.   ISBN
0-87474-778-3 :   LC Card 81-607847   DDC
016.954/0720753 19
Z3185 .R34 DS335

South Carolina. Agricultural Experiment Station.
Herren, Edward C. Soil survey of Anderson
County, South Carolina /. [Washington , 1979]
viii, 79 p., [34] leaves of plates :   LC Card
79-604161   DDC 631.4/7/75725 19
S599.S58 H47

**South Carolina. Agricultural Experiment Station,
Clemson.**
Camp, Wallace Jefferson, 1906- Soil survey of
Greenwood and McCormick Counties, South
Carolina /. [Washington, D.C. , 1980] iv, 68 p.,
[42] fold. leaves of plates :   LC Card 80-602310
DDC 631.4/7/75733 19
S599.S58 C36

Long, Bobby M. Soil survey of Berkeley
County, South Carolina /. [Washington, D.C.]
1980. viii, 94 p., [51] fold. leaves of plates :
LC Card 80-601634   DDC 631.4/7/75793 19
S599.S58 L66

Pitts, J. J. Soil survey of Marion County, South
Carolina /. [Washington] , 1980. vii, 99 p., [27]
fold. leaves of plates :   LC Card 80-603206   DDC
631.4/7/75786 19
S599.S58 P58

**South Carolina. Agricultural Experiment Station,
Clemson. Agricultural Economics and Rural
Sociology, Dept. of. see South Carolina.
Agricultural Experiment Station, Clemson.
Dept. of Agricultural Economics and Rural
Sociology.**

**South Carolina. Agricultural Experiment Station,
Clemson. Dept. of Agricultural Economics
and Rural Sociology.**

AE.
(404) South Carolina Crop and Livestock
Reporting Service. South Carolina fruit tree
survey, 1978 . [Clemson, S.C.] [Washington]
[1979] 26 p. :   LC Card 80-621005   DDC 338.1
s 338.1/7411/09757 19
HD1775.S6 S6 no. 404 SB320.7.S6

SOUTH CAROLINA - ANTIQUITIES.
Brooks, Mark J. An intensive archeological
survey of Amoco realty property in Berkeley
County, South Carolina . Columbia, S.C. , 1978.
xi, 79 p. :   LC Card 79-625384   DDC 975.7/93 19
E78.S6 B73

Goodyear, Albert C. Archeological
reconnaissance and testing along the Broad
River, Richland County, South Carolina /.
[Columbia, S.C.] [1979] 22 p. :   LC Card
80-621581   DDC 975.7/71 19
F277.B73 G66

Hanson, Glen T. The intensive archeological
survey of the independent spent fuel storage
facility, Savannah River plant, Aiken and
Barnwell Counties, South Carolina /.
Columbia , 1978. viii, 68 p. :   LC Card 79-623910
DDC 975.7/76 19
F277.B25 H36

Hanson, Glen T. The preliminary archeological
inventory of the Savannah River Plant, Aiken
and Barnwell Counties, South Carolina /.
Columbia , 1978. viii, 166 p. :   LC Card
79-620819   DDC 975.7/75 19
E78.S6 H38

Jackson, Susan, 1950- A survey and evaluation
of the archeological resources of the Little
Lynches Creek watershed in Lancaster County,
South Carolina /. Columbia , 1975. 17 leaves,
[1] leaf of plates :   LC Card 76-622781   DDC
975.7/45 19
F277.L2 J32

Taylor, Richard Lee, 1946- The report of the
intensive survey of the Richard B. Russell Dam
and Lake, Savannah River, Georgia and South
Carolina /. Columbia, S.C. [1978] xvii, 531 p. :
LC Card 79-623568   DDC 975.7/35 19
F292.R49 T39

**South Carolina - Archaeology. see South
Carolina - Antiquities.**

**SOUTH CAROLINA - BOUNDARIES -
GEORGIA.**
De Vorsey, Louis. The Georgia-South Carolina
boundary . Athens, Ga. , c1982. p. cm.   ISBN
0-8203-0591-X   LC Card 81-10441   DDC
911/.758 19
F292.B7 D45

South Carolina cash receipts, 1972 and 1973 /.
South Carolina Crop and Livestock Reporting
Service. Columbia, South Carolina , 1974. 18
p. :   *NYPL [*ZT-1259]*

**SOUTH CAROLINA - CENSUS, 1820 -
INDEXES.**
United States. Census Office. South Carolina
index to the United States census of 1820.
Tustin, Calif., 1972. 426 p. :
NYPL [APR (South Carolina) 80-2338]

**South Carolina. Commission on Higher
Education.** South Carolina master plan for
higher education. Columbia : South Carolina
Commission on Higher Education, 1979. xiii
leaves, 375 p. : ill. ; 28 cm.   LC Card 80-621324
DDC 379.1/54/09757 19
*1. Education, Higher - South Carolina - Planning. I.
Title.*
LA361.5 .S66 1979

South Carolina. County Court (Union County)
Union County, South Carolina, minutes of the
County Court, 1785-1799 / [edited] by Brent
H. Holcomb. Easley, S.C. : Southern Historical
Press, c1979. 523 p. ; 24 cm. Includes also
minutes of the Intermediate Court. Includes index.
ISBN 0-89308-159-0   LC Card 79-66945
*1. Court records - South Carolina - Union County. 2.
Union County, S. C. - Genealogy. I. Holcomb, Brent.
II. South Carolina. Intermediate Court (Union County).
III. Title.*
KFS2316.U54 A7 1785
NYPL [APR (Union Co., S. C.) 80-3258]

**South Carolina. Courts. County Court (Union
County) see South Carolina. County Court
(Union County)**

**South Carolina. Courts. Intermediate Court
(Union County) see South Carolina.
Intermediate Court (Union County)**

**South Carolina Crop and Livestock Reporting
Service.** South Carolina fruit tree survey,
1978 : peaches-apples-grapes / compiled by
South Carolina Crop and Livestock Reporting
Service. [Clemson, S.C.] : Dept. of Agricultural
Economics and Rural Sociology, South Carolina
Agricultural Experiment Station, Clemson
University ; [Washington] : United States Dept.
of Agriculture, Economics, Statistics &
Cooperatives Service, [1979] 26 p. : ill. ; 29 cm.
(AE ; 404) Cover title: South Carolina--1978 fruit tree
survey. "May 1979." LC Card 80-621005 DDC
338.1 s 338.1/7411/09757 19
*1. Peaches - South Carolina - Statistics. 2. Apples -
South Carolina - Statistics. 3. Viticulture - South
Carolina - Statistics. I. Title. II. Title: South
Carolina--1978 fruit tree survey. III. Series: South
Carolina. Agricultural Experiment Station, Clemson.
Dept. of Agricultural Economics and Rural Sociology.
AE, 404.*
HD1775.S6 S6 no. 404 SB320.7.S6

South Carolina. Dept. of Education.
Assessment of vocational and technical
education needs in South Carolina. [Columbia,
S.C.] : Dept. of Education, South Carolina,
[1978] 497 p. in various pagings : ill. ; 28 cm.
Cover title.   LC Card 80-621836   DDC 379/.155 19
*1. Vocational education - South Carolina - Education.
2. Technical education - South Carolina - Evaluation. 3.
Federal aid to education - South Carolina. I. Title.*
LC1046.S7 S68 1978

**South Carolina. Dept. of Education. Office of
Planning.** Stuckey, Dale C. School districts of
South Carolina . Columbia, S.C. [1979] iii, 51
p. ;   LC Card 80-622553   DDC 379.15/35 19
LB2817 .S75

**South Carolina. Dept. of Education. Office of
Research.**
Office of Research report series .
(v. 1, no. 46) South Carolina. Dept. of
Education. Office of Research. Management
Information Section. Births, projected first
grade enrollment, high school graduates, and
number entering college for the state and the
counties /. Columbia, S.C. [1979] v leaves,
48 p. ;   LC Card 80-620567   DDC 371.2/19/757
19
LC132.S6 S68 1979

(v. 1, no. 47) South Carolina. Dept. of
Education. Office of Research. South
Carolina statewide testing program 1978-79 .
Columbia, S.C. [1979] ix, 25 p. ;   LC Card
80-620568   DDC 371.2/6/09757 19
LB3052.S6 S67 1979

(v. 1, no. 48) South Carolina. Dept. of
Education. Office of Research. Management
Information Section. 1979-80 teacher salary
study /. Columbia, S.C. [1980] iv, 95 p. ;
LC Card 80-621884   DDC 331.2/813711/009757
19
LB2842.2 .S64 1980

South Carolina statewide testing program
1978-79 : summary report / Division of
Administration and Planning, Office of
Research, South Carolina Department of
Education. Columbia, S.C. : The Dept., [1979]
ix, 25 p. ; 28 cm. (Office of Research report series ;
v. 1, no. 47) "September, 1979." LC Card 80-620568
DDC 371.2/6/09757 19
*1. Educational tests and measurements - South
Carolina. 2. Ability - Testing. I. Series: South Carolina.
Dept. of Education. Office of Research. Office of
Research report series , v. 1, no. 47. II. Title.*
LB3052.S6 S67 1979

**South Carolina. Dept. of Education. Office of
Research. Management Information Section.**
Births, projected first grade enrollment, high
school graduates, and number entering college
for the state and the counties / Division of
Administration and Planning, Office of
Research, Management Information Section,
South Carolina Department of Education.
Columbia, S.C. : The Section, [1979] v leaves,
48 p. ; 22 x 28 cm. (Office of Research report
series ; v. 1, no. 46) On cover: 1979 through 1985.
Prepared by James R. Felker and Cynthia A. Hearn.
"September 1979." Bibliography: p. 48. LC Card
80-620567 DDC 371.2/19/757 19
*1. School census - South Carolina. I. Felker, James R.
II. Hearn, Cynthia A. III. Series: South Carolina. Dept.*

of Education. Office of Research. Office of Research
report series , v. 1, no. 46. IV. Title.
LC132.S6 S68 1979

1979-80 teacher salary study / Division of
Administration and Planning, Office of
Research, Management Information Section.
Columbia, S.C. : South Carolina Dept. of
Education, [1980] iv, 95 p. ; 28 cm. (Office of
Research report series : v. 1, no. 48) On cover: Teacher
salary study, 1979-80. Chiefly tables. "March 1980."
Bibliography: p. 95.   LC Card 80-621884   DDC
331.2/813711/009757 19
*1. Teachers - South Carolina - Salaries, pensions, etc. -
Statistics. I. Title. II. Title: Teacher salary study,
1979-80. III. Series: South Carolina. Dept. of
Education. Office of Research. Office of Research
report series , v. 1, no. 48.*
LB2842.2 .S64 1980

**South Carolina. Dept. of Soils and Resource
Development. Land Resources Conservation
Commission. see South Carolina. Land
Resources Conservation Commission.**

South Carolina fruit tree survey, 1978 . South
Carolina Crop and Livestock Reporting Service.
[Clemson, S.C.] [Washington] [1979] 26 p. :
LC Card 80-621005   DDC 338.1 s
338.1/7411/09757 19
HD1775.S6 S6 no. 404 SB320.7.S6

SOUTH CAROLINA - GENEALOGY.
United States. Census Office. South Carolina
index to the United States census of 1820.
Tustin, Calif., 1972. 426 p.;
NYPL [APR (South Carolina) 80-2338]

**SOUTH CAROLINA - HISTORICAL
GEOGRAPHY.**
De Vorsey, Louis. The Georgia-South Carolina
boundary . Athens, Ga. , c1982. p. cm.   ISBN
0-8203-0591-X   LC Card 81-10441   DDC
911/.758 19
F292.B7 D45

**South Carolina index to the United States census
of 1820.** United States. Census Office. Tustin,
Calif., 1972. 426 p.;
NYPL [APR (South Carolina) 80-2338]

**South Carolina. Intermediate Court (Union
County)** South Carolina. County Court
(Union County) Union County, South Carolina,
minutes of the County Court, 1785-1799 /.
Easley, S.C. , c1979. 523 p. ;   ISBN
0-89308-159-0   LC Card 79-66945
KFS2316.U54 A7 1785
NYPL [APR (Union Co., S. C.) 80-3258]

**South Carolina. Land Resources Conservation
Commission.**
Herren, Edward C. Soil survey of Anderson
County, South Carolina /. [Washington , 1979]
viii, 79 p., [34] leaves of plates :   LC Card
79-604161   DDC 631.4/7/75725 19
S599.S58 H47

Long, Bobby M. Soil survey of Berkeley
County, South Carolina /. [Washington, D.C.]
1980. viii, 94 p., [51] fold. leaves of plates :
LC Card 80-601634   DDC 631.4/7/75793 19
S599.S58 L66

Pitts, J. J. Soil survey of Marion County, South
Carolina /. [Washington] , 1980. vii, 99 p., [27]
fold. leaves of plates :   LC Card 80-603206   DDC
631.4/7/75786 19
S599.S58 P58

**South Carolina. Marine Resources Division.
Technical report - Marine Resources Division,
South Carolina Wildlife and Marine
Resources Department .**
(no. 25) Bishop, J. M. Biological observations
on commercial penaeid shrimps caught by
bottom trawl in South Carolina estuaries,
February 1973-January 1975 /. [Charleston]
[197-] xi, 97 p. :   LC Card 80-621322   DDC
595.3/843 19
QL444.M33 B57

(no. 5) The Shrimp fishery of the
Southeastern United States . Charleston ,
1974. vi, 229 p. :   LC Card 75-621474   DDC
338.3/7253843/0974 19
SH380.62.U6 S53

(no. 8) The Shrimp fishery of the South
Atlantic United States . Charleston , 1975. vi,
66 leaves ;   LC Card 75-623488   DDC 333.95/5
19
SH380.62.U6 S52

South Carolina master plan for higher education.
South Carolina. Commission on Higher
Education. Columbia , 1979. xiii leaves, 375 p. :
LC Card 80-621324   DDC 379.1/54/09757 19
LA361.5 .S66 1979

**South Carolina statewide testing program
1978-79** . South Carolina. Dept. of Education.
Office of Research. Columbia, S.C. [1979] ix,
25 p. ;   LC Card 80-620568   DDC 371.2/6/09757
19
LB3052.S6 S67 1979

**South Carolina. University. College of Business
Administration. Division of Research.
Occasional studies - Division of Research,
College of Business Administration, the
University of South Carolina .**
(no. 13) Pugh, Olin S. Commercial banking
trends, 1950-1979 . [Columbia] , 1980. viii,
86 p. ;   LC Card 80-622707   DDC 332.1/2/0973
19
HG2491 .P79

**South Carolina. University. Dept. of Foreign
Languages and Literature.** French Literature
Conference, University of South Carolina, 1980.
Manifestoes and movements. Columbia, S.C. ,
1980. 132 p. ;   LC Card 80-623035   DDC 840/.9
19
PQ31 .F7 1980   *NYPL [JFL 77-274 v. 7]*

**South Carolina. University. Institute of
Archaeology and Anthropology.**
Brooks, Mark J. An intensive archeological
survey of Amoco realty property in Berkeley
County, South Carolina . Columbia, S.C. , 1978.
xi, 79 p. :   LC Card 79-625384   DDC 975.7/93 19
E78.S6 B73

Michie, James L. The Bass Pond dam site,
intensive archaeological testing at a formative
period base camp on Kiawah Island, South
Carolina /. Columbia, S.C. , 1979. vi, 106 p. :
LC Card 80-621582   DDC 975.7/91 19
E78.S6 M54

**South Carolina. University. Institute of
Archeology and Anthropology.
Anthropological studies.**
([no.] 3) House, John H. Windy Ridge, a
prehistoric site in the inter-riverine Piedmont
in South Carolina /. [Columbia] , 1978. xv,
158 p. :   LC Card 78-624313
E78.S6 H69   *NYPL [HBC 81-156]*

House, John H. Windy Ridge, a prehistoric
site in the inter-riverine Piedmont in South
Carolina /. [Columbia] , 1978. xv, 158 p. :
LC Card 78-624313
E78.S6 H69   *NYPL [HBC 81-156]*

Goodyear, Albert C. Archeological
reconnaissance and testing along the Broad
River, Richland County, South Carolina /.
[Columbia, S.C.] [1979] 22 p. :   LC Card
80-621581   DDC 975.7/71 19
F277.B73 G66

Goodyear, Albert C. A hypothesis for the use of
cryptocrystalline raw materials among
Paleo-Indian groups of North America /.
Columbia, S.C. [1979] 15 leaves ;   LC Card
80-621583   DDC 970.01/1 19
E98.I4 G66

Hanson, Glen T. The intensive archeological
survey of the independent spent fuel storage
facility, Savannah River plant, Aiken and
Barnwell Counties, South Carolina /.
Columbia , 1978. viii, 68 p. :   LC Card 79-623910
DDC 975.7/76 19
F277.B25 H36

House, John H. Windy Ridge, a prehistoric site
in the inter-riverine Piedmont in South Carolina
/. [Columbia] , 1978. xv, 158 p. :   LC Card
78-624313
E78.S6 H69   *NYPL [HBC 81-156]*

Jackson, Susan, 1950- A survey and evaluation
of the archeological resources of the Little
Lynches Creek watershed in Lancaster County,
South Carolina /. Columbia , 1975. 17 leaves,
[1] leaf of plates :   LC Card 76-622781   DDC
975.7/45 19
F277.L2 J32

Lewis, Kenneth E. Middleton Place . Columbia,
S.C. [1979] vii, 92 p. :   LC Card 79-625656
DDC 975.7/94 19
F279.M46 L48

Notebook. Columbia, S. C. illus. 28 cm.

Bimonthly. Began with Jan. 1969 issue.   LC Card
75-617003
*1. Indians of North America - South Carolina -
Antiquities - Periodicals.*   **NYPL [HBA 80-939]**

**Occasional papers. see South Carolina.
University. Institute of Archeology and
Anthropology. Anthropological studies.**

**Reseach manuscript series - Institute of
Archeology and Anthropology, University
of South Carolina .**
(no. 75) Jackson, Susan, 1950- A survey and
evaluation of the archeological resources of
the Little Lynches Creek watershed in
Lancaster County, South Carolina /.
Columbia , 1975. 17 leaves, [1] leaf of
plates :   LC Card 76-622781   DDC 975.7/45 19
F277.L2 J32

Taylor, Richard Lee, 1946- The report of the
intensive survey of the Richard B. Russell Dam
and Lake, Savannah River, Georgia and South
Carolina /. Columbia, S.C. [1978] xvii, 531 p. :
LC Card 79-623568   DDC 975.7/35 19
F292.R49 T39

**South Carolina. University. Institute of
International Studies.
Occasional paper - Institute of International
Studies, University of South Carolina .**
(no. 2) Strausz-Hupé, Robert, 1903- NATO,
task of adaptation /. [Columbia] , 1978. 18
p. ;   LC Card 79-622644   DDC 341.7/2 19
JX1393.N67 S77

South Carolina--1978 fruit tree survey. South
Carolina Crop and Livestock Reporting Service.
South Carolina fruit tree survey, 1978 .
[Clemson, S.C.] [Washington] [1979] 26 p. :
LC Card 80-621005   DDC 338.1 s
338.1/7411/09757 19
HD1775.S6 S6 no. 404 SB320.7.S6

**South Central New York Resource Conservation
and Development Project /.** United States. Soil
Conservation Service. [Lanham? Md.] [1967?]
1 map ;   LC Card 81-692937
G3804.B6A1 1967 .U5

South Coastal . Massachusetts. Water Quality and
Research Section. Westborough [1977] 72 p. :
LC Card 79-620597   DDC 363.7/3942/0974482
19
TD224.M4 M39 1977h

South Dakota Agricultural Experiment Station.
United States. Soil Conservation Service.
General soil map, Custer County, South Dakota
/. Lincoln, Nebr. , 1979. 1 map :   LC Card
81-691164
G4183.C8J3 1979 .U5

United States. Soil Conservation Service.
General soil map, Mellette County, South
Dakota /. [Lincoln, Neb.] [1978?] 1 map :   LC
Card 81-691165
G4183.M6J3 1973 .U5

**SOUTH DAKOTA AGRICULTURAL
EXPERIMENT STATION.**
Schlepp, Richard L. Soil survey of Aurora
County, South Dakota. [Washington, D.C.?] ,
c1980. vii, 148 p., 58 folded p. of plates :   LC
Card 81-600698   DDC 631.4/7/783375 19
S599.S6 S34

**South Dakota. Agricultural Experiment Station,
Brookings.**
Heil, Dennis M. Soil survey of Beadle County,
South Dakota /. [Washington] , 1979. viii, 169
p., [98] fold. leaves of plates :   LC Card
80-602070   DDC 631.4/7/783274 19
S599.S6 H43

Heil, Dennis M. Soil survey of McCook
County, South Dakota /. [Washington] , 1980.
vii, 123 p., [25] fold. leaves of plates :   LC Card
80-601638   DDC 631.4/7/783372 19
S599.S6 H44

Meland, Arvid C. Soil survey of Lawrence
County, South Dakota /. [Washington, D.C. ,
1979] viii, 173 p., [25] fold. leaves of plates :
LC Card 80-601071   DDC 631.4/7/78391 19
S599.S6 M44

Schumacher, Thomas M. Soil survey of
Campbell County, South Dakota /.
[Washington] [1979] vii, 175 p., [32] fold.
leaves of plates :   LC Card 80-602616   DDC
631.4/7/78317 19
S599.S6 S4

South Dakota. Agricultural Experiment Station, Brookings. Dept. of Rural Sociology. see South Dakota. Agricultural Experiment Station, Brookings. Rural Sociology Dept.

South Dakota. Agricultural Experiment Station, Brookings. Rural Sociology Dept. Wagner, Robert T. Characteristics and needs of the aged in South Dakota, 1980-1990 /. Brookings, S.D. , 1978. ix, 238 leaves : LC Card 80-622161 DDC 305.2/6/09783 19
HQ1064.U6 S7

SOUTH DAKOTA - ANTIQUITIES - ADDRESSES, ESSAYS, LECTURES.
The Future of South Dakota's past /. Vermillion, S.D. , 1981. p. cm. LC Card 81-14812 DDC 978.3/01 19
E78.S63 F87

SOUTH DAKOTA - BIOGRAPHY.
Pressler, Larry, 1942- U. S. senators from the prairie /. Washington, D.C. [1980] p. cm. ISBN 0-88249-033-8 : LC Card 80-25220 DDC 328.73/092/2 B 920 19
E747 .P83

South Dakota. Board of Examiners of Psychologists. Directory of licensed psychologists and associate psychologists / South Dakota Board of Examiners of Psychologists ; Eleanor A. Schwab ... [et al.]. [Pierre?] : The Board, 1979. [7] p. ; 28 cm. LC Card 79-625660 DDC 150/.25/783 19
1. Psychologists - South Dakota - Directories. I. Schwab, Eleanor A. II. Title.
BF30 .S68 1979

SOUTH DAKOTA - CIVILIZATION - SOURCES.
South Dakota. Office of Cultural Preservation. Policy and procedures manual /. [Pierre] †1980] 48 leaves ; LC Card 80-152347 DDC 353.97830085/9 19
F652 .S68 1980

South Dakota. Code Commission (Created 1970)
1974 administrative rules of South Dakota, Title 67, Department of Social Services . [Pierre] [1976?] 396 p. ; LC Card 80-126719 DDC 344.783/03 19
KFS3349.A434 A2 1976

1974 administrative rules of South Dakota, Title 70, Department of Transportation . [Pierre] [1976?] 110 p. ; LC Card 80-126722 DDC 343.783/093/02636 19
KFS3295.A434 A2 1976

South Dakota. Dept. of Labor. Research and Statistics.
Job outlook : vocational/technical occupations / prepared by Research and Statistics. Aberdeen, S.D. : South Dakota Dept. of Labor, Office of Administrative Services, 1980. 54 p. : graphs ; 29 cm. Chiefly tables. LC Card 80-621867 DDC 331.12/09783 19
1. Labor supply - South Dakota - Statistics. 2. South Dakota - Occupations - Statistics. I. Title.
HD5725.S8 S63 1980

Occupational employment in nonmanufacturing industries : South Dakota, 1978 / South Dakota Department of Labor, Research and Statistics. Aberdeen, S.D. : South Dakota Dept. of Labor, Research and Statistics, 1979. i, 38 leaves ; 28 cm. Cover title: South Dakota occupational employment statistics, 1979. Chiefly tables. LC Card 80-621189 DDC 331.12/5/09783 19
1. Labor supply - South Dakota - Statistics. 2. Employment forecasting - South Dakota - Statistics. 3. South Dakota - Occupations - Statistics. I. Title. II. Title: South Dakota occupational employment statistics, 1979.
HD5725.S8 S63 1979a

Report - Research and Statistics, South Dakota Department of Labor.
(no. 4) South Dakota. Dept. of Labor. Research and Statistics. South Dakota employment projections to 1985 /. Aberdeen, S.D. [1979] 72 p. : LC Card 80-621909 DDC 331.12/3/09783 19
HD5725.S8 S63 1979

South Dakota employment projections to 1985 / prepared by Research and Statistics. Aberdeen, S.D. : South Dakota Dept. of Labor, Office of Administrative Services, [1979] 72 p. : graphs ; 28 cm. (Report - South Dakota Department of Labor, Research and Statistics ; no. 4) "June 1979." Includes bibliographical references. LC Card

80-621909 DDC 331.12/3/09783 19
1. Labor supply - South Dakota. 2. South Dakota - Occupations. 3. Employment forecasting - South Dakota. I. Series: Report - Research and Statistics, South Dakota Department of Labor , no. 4. II. Title.
HD5725.S8 S63 1979

Veterans characteristics as related to employment activities : fiscal year 1978 / [prepared by South Dakota Department of Labor, Research and Statistics]. Aberdeen : The Department, 1979. ii, 37 p. : graphs ; 29 cm. Microfiche (neg.) 1 sheet. 11 x 15 cm. (NYPL FSN 35,559) Cover title: Veterans characteristics related to employment activities. LC Card 79-623547
1. Veterans - Employment - South Dakota - Statistics. I. Title.
UB358.S8 S68 1979   **NYPL [*XME-9453]**

South Dakota. Dept. of Natural Resource Development. Brown, Ralph J. Simulating the impact of irrigation development in the Third Planning District . [Vermillion, S.D. , 1979] i, 90 p. : LC Card 80-621868 DDC 330 s 330.9783/3/00724 19
HF5006 .S6 no. 127 HD1739.S8

South Dakota. Dept. of Social Services.
1974 administrative rules of South Dakota, Title 67, Department of Social Services . [Pierre] [1976?] 396 p. ; LC Card 80-126719 DDC 344.783/03 19
KFS3349.A434 A2 1976

South Dakota. Dept. of Social Services.
Statistical Analysis and Reports. Statistical analysis report. v. 10, no. 10- ; Oct. 1979-Pierre. For earlier file, whose numbering it continues, see: South Dakota. Dept. of Social Services. Program Analysis Unit. Program analysis report.
I. Title.   **NYPL [Econ. Div.]**

South Dakota. Dept. of Transportation.
1974 administrative rules of South Dakota, Title 70, Department of Transportation . [Pierre] [1976?] 110 p. ; LC Card 80-126722 DDC 343.783/093/02636 19
KFS3295.A434 A2 1976

South Dakota. Dept. of Transportation. Office of System Analysis. Highway traffic report, 1979 / prepared by the South Dakota Department of Transportation, Division of Policy Development and Evaluation, Office of System Analysis in cooperation with US Department of Transportation, Federal Highway Administration. [Pierre] : The Division, [1980] 146 p. : ill. ; 28 cm. Cover title. LC Card 80-622944 DDC 388.3/142/09783 19
1. Traffic surveys - South Dakota - Statistics. I. United States. Federal Highway Administration. II. Title.
HE371.S8 S68 1980

South Dakota. Dept. of Transportation. System Analysis, Office of. see South Dakota. Dept. of Transportation. Office of System Analysis.

SOUTH DAKOTA - DESCRIPTION AND TRAVEL - 1951- - GUIDE-BOOKS.
Historic sites of South Dakota . [Vermillion, S.D.] , 1980. x, 126 p. : LC Card 80-623927 DDC 917.83/0433 19
F652 .H57

South Dakota. Division of Drugs and Substances Control. NIDA State plan for drug abuse prevention for the State of South Dakota : FY 1980 / Division of Drugs and Substances Control. [Pierre] : The Division, [1979] 223 p. : ill. ; 28 cm. Cover title. LC Card 80-621620 DDC 362.2/937/09783 19
1. South Dakota. Division of Drugs and Substances Control. 2. Drug abuse - South Dakota - Prevention. I. National Institute on Drug Abuse. II. Title.
HV5831.S66 A5 1979a

SOUTH DAKOTA. DIVISION OF DRUGS AND SUBSTANCES CONTROL.
South Dakota. Division of Drugs and Substances Control. NIDA State plan for drug abuse prevention for the State of South Dakota . [Pierre] [1979] 223 p. ; LC Card 80-621620 DDC 362.2/937/09783 19
HV5831.S66 A5 1979a

South Dakota. Division of Highway Safety. State & Community Programs. South Dakota highway safety plan, fiscal year 1980 / prepared by Department of Public Safety, Division of Highway Safety, State and Community

Programs, in cooperation with Region VIII NHTSA-FHWA, Department of Transportation. [Pierre, S.D.] : The Division, [1980?] 237 p. : ill. ; 28 cm. Cover title. LC Card 80-621619 DDC 363.1/256/09783 19
1. Traffic safety - South Dakota. I. United States. National Highway Traffic Safety Administration. Region VIII. II. United States. Federal Highway Administration. III. Title.
HE5614.3.S8 S68 1980

South Dakota. Division of Parks & Recreation. Nordstrom, Paul E. South Dakota recreational trails plan, January 1, 1980 /. [Pierre, S.D.] [1979?] 178 p. : LC Card 80-622746 DDC 790/.09783 19
GV191.42.S8 N67

South Dakota. Division of Public Health Statistics. see South Dakota. State Dept. of Health. Division of Public Health Statistics.

SOUTH DAKOTA - ECONOMIC CONDITIONS - MATHEMATICAL MODELS.
Brown, Ralph J. Simulating the impact of irrigation development in the Third Planning District . [Vermillion, S.D. , 1979] i, 90 p. : LC Card 80-621868 DDC 330 s 330.9783/3/00724 19
HF5006 .S6 no. 127 HD1739.S8

SOUTH DAKOTA - ECONOMIC POLICY - CITIZEN PARTICIPATION.
Bergman, W. H. Evaluation report . [Vermillion , 1977] 135 p. : LC Card 78-623244 DDC 338.9783 19
HC107.S8 B47

South Dakota employment projections to 1985 /. South Dakota. Dept. of Labor. Research and Statistics. Aberdeen, S.D. [1979] 72 p. : LC Card 80-621909 DDC 331.12/3/09783 19
HD5725.S8 S63 1979

South Dakota. Free Library Commission. see South Dakota. State Library Commission.

South Dakota health facility survey, 1978 /. South Dakota. State Center for Health Statistics. Pierre, S.D. [1979] iv, 94 p. : LC Card 80-621908 DDC 362.1/1/09783 19
RA981.S62 S7 1979

South Dakota highway safety plan, fiscal year 1980 /. South Dakota. Division of Highway Safety. State & Community Programs. [Pierre, S.D.] [1980?] 237 p. : LC Card 80-621619 DDC 363.1/256/09783 19
HE5614.3.S8 S68 1980

South Dakota. Historical Preservation Center. Historic sites of South Dakota . [Vermillion, S.D.] , 1980. x, 126 p. : LC Card 80-623927 DDC 917.83/0433 19
F652 .H57

SOUTH DAKOTA - HISTORY, LOCAL.
Historic sites of South Dakota . [Vermillion, S.D.] 1980. x, 126 p. : LC Card 80-623927 DDC 917.83/0433 19
F652 .H57

SOUTH DAKOTA HOUSING DEVELOPMENT AUTHORITY.
Brown, Ralph J. A study of certain aspects of the South Dakota Housing Development Authority program /. Pierre, S.D. , 1979. 32 p. ; LC Card 80-622224 DDC 353.97830086/5045 19
HD7303.S8 B76

South Dakota. Legislative Research Council, State. see South Dakota. State Legislative Research Council.

South Dakota. Legislature. Health Rules Sunset Committee. Final report of the Health Rules Sunset Committee / presented to the South Dakota Legislative Research Council. Pierre, S.D. : The Council, [1980] iii, 26 p. ; 28 cm. LC Card 80-622825 DDC 344.783/04 19
1. Public health laws - South Dakota. I. South Dakota. State Legislative Research Council.
KFS3011.62 .H43 1980

South Dakota. Legislature. State Legislative Research Council. see South Dakota. State Legislative Research Council.

South Dakota. Natural Resource Development, Dept. of. see South Dakota. Dept. of Natural Resource Development.

GOVERNMENT PUBLICATIONS - U.S.: 1981

293   South Dakota. University. Institute of Indian Studies.

South Dakota occupational employment statistics, 1979. South Dakota. Dept. of Labor. Research and Statistics. Occupational employment in nonmanufacturing industries . Aberdeen, S.D. , 1979. i, 38 leaves ;   LC Card 80-621189   DDC 331.12/5/09783 19
HD5725.S8 S63 1979a

South Dakota occupational injuries and illnesses, 1972 and 1973. South Dakota. State Dept. of Health. Division of Public Health Statistics. Reported occupational injuries and illnesses, South Dakota, 1972 and 1973 . Pierre , 1974. 37 p. ;   LC Card 81-472623   DDC 312/.39803/09783 19
RC964 .S667 1974

SOUTH DAKOTA - OCCUPATIONS.
South Dakota. Dept. of Labor. Research and Statistics. South Dakota employment projections to 1985 /. Aberdeen, S.D.   [1979] 72 p. :   LC Card 80-621909   DDC 331.12/3/09783 19
HD5725.S8 S63 1979

SOUTH DAKOTA - OCCUPATIONS - STATISTICS.
South Dakota. Dept. of Labor. Research and Statistics. Job outlook . Aberdeen, S.D. , 1980. 54 p. :   LC Card 80-621867   DDC 331.12/09783 19
HD5725.S8 S63 1980

South Dakota. Dept. of Labor. Research and Statistics. Occupational employment in nonmanufacturing industries . Aberdeen, S.D. , 1979. i, 38 leaves ;   LC Card 80-621189   DDC 331.12/5/09783 19
HD5725.S8 S63 1979a

South Dakota. Office of Cultural Preservation.
Policy and procedures manual / Office of Cultural Preservation. [Pierre] : South Dakota Dept. of Education and Cultural Affairs, [1980] 48 leaves ; 28 cm. Cover title.   LC Card 80-152347   DDC 353.97830085/9 19
1. South Dakota. Office of Cultural Preservation. 2. Cultural property, Protection of - South Dakota. 3. Historic sites - South Dakota - Conservation and restoration. 4. South Dakota - Civilization - Sources. I. Title.
F652 .S68 1980

SOUTH DAKOTA. OFFICE OF CULTURAL PRESERVATION.
South Dakota. Office of Cultural Preservation. Policy and procedures manual /. [Pierre] [1980] 48 leaves ;   LC Card 80-152347   DDC 353.97830085/9 19
F652 .S68 1980

South Dakota. Office of State Health Planning and Development. South Dakota. Statewide Health Coordinating Council. South Dakota state plan for health, 1980-1985. [Pierre, S.D.] , 1980. 334 p. in various pagings :   LC Card 80-623024   DDC 362.1/09783 19
RA395.A4 S68 1980

SOUTH DAKOTA - POPULATION - MAPS.
United States. Soil Conservation Service. Population density, 1975, persons per square mile, South Dakota /. Lincoln, Nebr. , 1977. 1 map :   LC Card 81-691168
G4181.E2 1975 .U5

South Dakota. Recreational Trails Committee.
Nordstrom, Paul E. South Dakota recreational trails plan, January 1, 1980 /. [Pierre, S.D.] [1979?] 178 p. :   LC Card 80-622746   DDC 790/.09783 19
GV191.42.S8 N67

South Dakota recreational trails plan, January 1, 1980 /. Nordstrom, Paul E. [Pierre, S.D.] [1979?] 178 p. :   LC Card 80-622746   DDC 790/.09783 19
GV191.42.S8 N67

South Dakota Retirement System. South Dakota Retirement System financial report, July 1974-June 1978. [Pierre] : The System, [197-] 26 p. : graphs ; 23 x 36 cm. Cover title.   LC Card 80-623014   DDC 353.9783001/82 19
1. South Dakota Retirement System. 2. Civil service pensions - South Dakota - Finance.
JK6560.P4 S68 1970

SOUTH DAKOTA RETIREMENT SYSTEM.
South Dakota Retirement System. South Dakota Retirement System financial report, July 1974-June 1978. [Pierre] [197-] 26 p. :   LC Card 80-623014   DDC 353.9783001/82 19
JK6560.P4 S68 1970

SOUTH DAKOTA - SOCIAL POLICY - CITIZEN PARTICIPATION.
Bergman, W. H. Evaluation report . [Vermillion , 1977] 135 p. :   LC Card 78-623244   DDC 338.9783 19
HC107.S8 B47

South Dakota. Social Services, Dept. of. see South Dakota. Dept. of Social Services.

South Dakota. State Center for Health Statistics. South Dakota health facility survey, 1978 / South Dakota Department of Health, State Center for Health Statistics. Pierre, S.D. : The Dept., [1979] iv, 94 p. : ill. ; 28 cm. "August 27, 1979."   LC Card 80-621908   DDC 362.1/1/09783 19
1. Health facilities - South Dakota - Statistics. 2. Health facilities - South Dakota - Utilization - Statistics. I. Title.
RA981.S62 S7 1979

South Dakota. State Dept. of Health. Division of Public Health Statistics. Reported occupational injuries and illnesses, South Dakota, 1972 and 1973 : a summary of work related injuries and illnesses compiled from employees' first reports of injuries / South Dakota Department of Health, Public Health Statistics. Pierre : The Division, 1974. 37 p. ; 22 x 29 cm. Cover title: South Dakota occupational injuries and illnesses, 1972 and 1973.   LC Card 81-472623   DDC 312/.39803/09783 19
1. Occupational diseases - South Dakota - Statistics. 2. Industrial accidents - South Dakota - Statistics. I. Title. II. Title: South Dakota occupational injuries and illnesses, 1972 and 1973.
RC964 .S667 1974

South Dakota. State Dept. of Health. Public Health Statistics,Division of. see South Dakota. State Dept. of Health. Division of Public Health Statistics.

South Dakota. State Dept. of Social Services. see South Dakota. Dept. of Social Services.

South Dakota. State Legislative Research Council. (Old Catalog form: South Dakota. Legislative Research Council.)
Brown, Ralph J. Simulating the impact of irrigation development in the Third Planning District . [Vermillion, S.D. , 1979] i, 90 p. :   LC Card 80-621868   DDC 330 s   330.9783/3/00724 19
HF5006 .S6 no. 127 HD1739.S8

Brown, Ralph J. A study of certain aspects of the South Dakota Housing Development Authority program /. Pierre, S.D. , 1979. 32 p. ;   LC Card 80-622224   DDC 353.97830086/5045 19
HD7303.S8 B76

South Dakota. Legislature. Health Rules Sunset Committee. Final report of the Health Rules Sunset Committee /. Pierre, S.D. [1980] iii, 26 p. ;   LC Card 80-622825   DDC 344.783/04 19
KFS3011.62 .H43 1980

South Dakota State Library . South Dakota. State Library Commission. Pierre, S.D. , 1979. 50 p. :   LC Card 80-621618   DDC 027.0783 19
Z678.4.S8 S68 1979

South Dakota State Library. South Dakota union list of serials, including colleges of mid-America /. Brookings, S.D. , 1979. viii, 728 p. :   LC Card 79-626200   DDC 011/.34 19
Z6945 .S612 1979 PN4832

SOUTH DAKOTA STATE LIBRARY.
South Dakota. State Library Commission. South Dakota State Library . Pierre, S.D. , 1979. 50 p. :   LC Card 80-621618   DDC 027.0783 19
Z678.4.S8 S68 1979

South Dakota. State Library Commission. (Old Catalog form: South Dakota. Free Library Commission.)
South Dakota State Library : planning for the future, 1979-1983. Pierre, S.D. : South Dakota State Library, 1979. 50 p. : maps ; 28 cm. Bibliography: p. 49-50.   LC Card 80-621618   DDC 027.0783 19
1. Libraries - South Dakota. 2. South Dakota State Library. I. Title. II. Title: Planning for the future.
Z678.4.S8 S68 1979

South Dakota state plan for health, 1980-1985.
South Dakota. Statewide Health Coordinating Council. [Pierre, S.D.] , 1980. 334 p. in various pagings :   LC Card 80-623024   DDC 362.1/09783

19
RA395.A4 S68 1980

South Dakota, State University. Agricultural Experiment Station, Brookings. see South Dakota. Agricultural Experiment Station, Brookings.

South Dakota State University. Agricultural Extension Service.
Extension circular .
(no. 566) Collins, Paul E. Trees of South Dakota /. Brookings [1979?] xvi, 51 p. :   LC Card 80-622715   DDC 582.1609783 19
QK484.S8 C64

South Dakota State University. Library. South Dakota union list of serials, including colleges of mid-America /. Brookings, S.D. , 1979. viii, 728 p. :   LC Card 79-626200   DDC 011/.34 19
Z6945 .S612 1979 PN4832

South Dakota. Statewide Health Coordinating Council.
Medical facilities supplement to the South Dakota state plan for health / South Dakota Statewide Health Coordinating Council, Office of State Health Planning and Development, South Dakota State Department of Health. [Pierre, S.D.] : The Council, [1980] iii, 209 p. : ill. ; 29 cm. "May 1980."   LC Card 80-623023   DDC 362.1/1/09783 19
1. Hospitals - South Dakota - Planning. 2. Hospitals - South Dakota - Statistics. 3. Hospital utilization - South Dakota - Statistics. I. Title.
RA395.A4 S68 1980 Suppl

South Dakota state plan for health, 1980-1985. [Pierre, S.D.] : South Dakota Statewide Health Coordinating Council, Office of State Health Planning and Development, South Dakota State Department of Health, 1980. 334 p. in various pagings : ill. ; 29 cm. Includes bibliographical references.   LC Card 80-623024   DDC 362.1/09783 19
1. Health planning - South Dakota. 2. Medical policy - South Dakota. 3. Public health - South Dakota. 4. Medical care - South Dakota. I. South Dakota. Office of State Health Planning and Development. II. Title.
RA395.A4 S68 1980

South Dakota. Transportation, Dept. of. see South Dakota. Dept. of Transportation.

South Dakota union list of serials, including colleges of mid-America / produced by the Minnesota Interlibrary Telecommunication Exchange (MINITEX), as a joint project with the South Dakota State Library and South Dakota State University Library. 4th ed. Brookings, S.D. : South Dakota State Library, 1979. viii, 728 p. : ill. ; 28 cm.   LC Card 79-626200   DDC 011/.34 19
1. Periodicals - Bibliography - Union lists. 2. Catalogs, Union - South Dakota. I. Minnesota Interlibrary Telecommunication Exchange. II. South Dakota State Library. III. South Dakota State University. Library.
Z6945 .S612 1979 PN4832

South Dakota. University. Business Administration School. Business Research Bureau. see South Dakota. University. Business Research Bureau.

South Dakota. University. Business Research Bureau. (Old Catalog form: South Dakota. University. Business Administration School. Business Research Bureau).
Brown, Ralph J. Simulating the impact of irrigation development in the Third Planning District . [Vermillion, S.D. , 1979] i, 90 p. :   LC Card 80-621868   DDC 330 s   330.9783/3/00724 19
HF5006 .S6 no. 127 HD1739.S8

Bulletin .
(no. 126) Poth, Leonard A. The economic impact of the mineral industry of South Dakota /. Vermillion, S.D. [1978] 135 p. :   LC Card 80-622563   DDC 330 s 338.2/09783 19
HF5006 .S6 no. 126 HD9506.U63S5

(127) Brown, Ralph J. Simulating the impact of irrigation development in the Third Planning District . [Vermillion, S.D. , 1979] i, 90 p. :   LC Card 80-621868   DDC 330 s   330.9783/3/00724 19
HF5006 .S6 no. 127 HD1739.S8

South Dakota. University. Institute of Indian Studies. Spring Conference "Relationships Between People and the Land," University of South Dakota, 1979. Report of papers presented

at the spring conference, April 19, 20, 21, 1979 . [Vermillion, S.D.] [1979?] 211 p. ; LC Card 80-621621 DDC 970.004/97 19
E98.R3 S724 1979

South Dakota. University. School of Business, Business Research Bureau. see South Dakota. University. Business Research Bureau.

South Dakota. University. Weeks (I. D.) Library. see Weeks (I. D.) Library.

South Florida Regional Planning Council. Developing geographic-based information files : a bibliographic essay / by South Florida Regional Planning Council. [Miami] : The Council, 1976. 19 p. Microfiche (neg.) NTIS. 1 sheet. 11x15 cm. (PB-257 668)
1. Information storage and retrieval systems - Regional planning - Bibliography. 2. Regional planning - Data processing - Bibliography. I. Title.
NYPL [*XMQ-2197]

South Fork Trinity River . California. Dept. of Water Resources. Northern District. [Sacramento] [1979] x, 83, 8 p. : LC Card 80-621406 DDC 551.3/02 19
QE581 .C29 1979

SOUTH SEA COMPANY - HISTORY - 18TH CENTURY. Palmer, Colin A., 1942- Human cargoes . Urbana , c1981. xv, 183 p. : ISBN 0-252-00846-4 : LC Card 81-3326 DDC 3-82/.44/0941 19
HT1161 .P34

South Vietnam, provincial maps. United States. Central Intelligence Agency. Office of Basic and Geographical Intelligence. [Washington] , 1967. [52] leaves : LC Card 80-675252 DDC 912/.597
G2371.F7 U54 1967

South Watuppa Pond . Chesebrough, Eben W. Westborough, Mass. [1977] 69 p. : LC Card 79-621235 DDC 363.7/3942/0974485 19
TD224.M4 C485

Southall, Aidan. Schatzberg, Michael G. Bibliography of small urban centers in rural development in Africa /. [Madison] , 1979. ix, 246 p. ; LC Card 80-623484 DDC 016.3077/6/096 19
Z7164.U7 S25 HT148.A2

SOUTHCOTT, JOANNA, 1750-1814. Hopkins, James K., 1941- A woman to deliver her people . Austin , c1981. p. cm. ISBN 0-292-79017-1 : LC Card 81-10462 DDC 303.4/84 19
BF1815.S7 H66

The southeast Alaska salmon fishery . Levey, Stephen B. Juneau , 1979. 48 p. : LC Card 79-625771 DDC 016.639/2755 19
SH348 .L48

Southeast Asia . United States. Congress. Senate. Committee on Foreign Relations. Subcommittee on East Asian and Pacific Affairs. Washington , 1980. iii, 92 p. ; LC Card 80-602433 DDC 959/.053 19
KF26 .F6354 1980

Southeast Conference on Urban Stormwater Management, North Carolina State University, 1979. Urban stormwater management : proceedings of a Southeast Regional Conference, April 10-11, 1979, at North Carolina State University / sponsored by water research institutes and water resource agencies of the southeast States ; edited by David H. Howells ; conference chairman, Neil S. Grigg. [Raleigh, N.C.] : Water Resources Research Institute of the University of North Carolina, [1980] vi, 252 p. : ill. ; 28 cm. LC Card 80-623271 DDC 363.6/1 19
1. Urban runoff - Southern States - Congresses. 2. Storm sewers - Southern States - Congresses. 3. Flood damage prevention - Southern States - Congresses. 4. Watershed management - Southern States - Congresses. I. Howells, David H. II. North Carolina. State University, Raleigh. III. Title.
TD657 .S68 1979

Southeast exporting . Roy, Delwin A. Atlanta, Ga. , 1981. p. cm. ISBN 0-88406-146-9 : LC Card 81-6287 DDC 382/.0975 19
HF3153 .R69

Southern Africa pamphlets . (no. 2) Gervasi, Sean. The United States and the arms embargo against South Africa .

[Binghamton] , c1978. 49 p. ; LC Card 78-112749 DDC 382/.456234/0968 19
HD9743.S62 G47

Southern Black leaders of the Reconstruction era / edited by Howard N. Rabinowitz. Urbana : University of Illinois Press, c1982. p. cm. (Blacks in the new world) Includes bibliographical references and index. ISBN 0-252-00929-0 LC Card 81-11372 DDC 975/.004960730922 B 19
1. Afro-American leadership - Southern States - History - 19th century - Addresses, essays, lectures. 2. Afro-Americans - Southern States - History - 19th century - Addresses, essays, lectures. 3. Afro-Americans - Southern States - Biography - Addresses, essays, lectures. 4. Reconstruction - Addresses, essays, lectures. 5. Southern States - History - 1865-1877 - Addresses, essays, lectures. 6. Southern States - Race relations - Addresses, essays, lectures. 7. Southern States - Biography - Addresses, essays, lectures. I. Rabinowitz, Howard N., 1942- II. Series.
E185.92 .S68

Southern Forest Experiment Station (New Orleans, La.) Bertelson, Daniel F. Arkansas forest industries, 1977 /. New Orleans, La. , 1980. 18 p. : LC Card 81-600548 DDC 333.75/0976 s 338.1/7498/09767 19
SD11 .A45793 no. 75 HD9757.A9

Southern Illinois University. Coal Extraction and Utilization Research Center. Coal & Illinois industry . Chicago, IL [1979] vi, 53 p. : LC Card 80-620896 DDC 333.79/13/09773 19
HC107.I3 C56

Southern Illinois University, Edwardsville. Center for Urban and Environmental Research and Services. CUERS report.
(no. 11) Community harmony . Edwardsville, Ill. , 1980. 126 p. : ISBN 0-936272-09-0 LC Card 80-80232 DDC 720/.28/8 19
NA2793 .C65

Southern Illinois University, Edwardsville. Lovejoy Library. see Lovejoy Library.

Southern Illinois University. University Libraries. Bibliographic contributions. For other vols. in this series, see entry in Old Catalog: Illinois. Southern Illinois University, Carbondale. Library. Bibliographic Contributions.
(no. 9) Lovejoy Library. Slavic-American imprints . [Edwardsville, Ill.] , 1979- v. ; LC Card 80-622920 DDC 016.947 19
Z2483 .L68 1972 Suppl.

The Southern Journal of philosophy. v. 1- ; spring, 1963- Memphis, Philosophy Dept., Memphis State University. 23 cm. Microfilm. Quarterly. Includes book reviews. LC Card 68-7760
1. Philosophy - Periodicals. I. Tennessee. State University, Memphis. Dept. of Philosophy.
NYPL [*ZAN-3214]

SOUTHERN OYSTER DRILL. Breithaupt, Rob L. A study of the southern oyster drill (Thais haemastoma) distribution and density on the oyster seed grounds /. New Orleans, La. [1979] vii, 20 p. : LC Card 80-621329 DDC 639/.411/09763 19
QL430.5.M9 B73

The Southern quarterly. v. 1- ; Oct. 1962- [Hattiesburg, Miss., University of Southern Mississippi] illus. 23 cm. Microfilm. LC Card 64-5999
1. American periodicals (General). I. Mississippi. University of Southern Mississippi, Hattiesburg.
NYPL [*ZAN-4513]

SOUTHERN STATES - AMUSEMENTS. National Endowment for the Arts. Research Division. Audience development . Washington, D.C. , 1981. 47 p. ; ISBN 0-89062-097-0 (pbk.) LC Card 80-600125 DDC 790.2/068/8 19
PN1590.A9 N3 1981

SOUTHERN STATES - BIOGRAPHY - ADDRESSES, ESSAYS, LECTURES. Southern Black leaders of the Reconstruction era /. Urbana , c1982. p. cm. ISBN 0-252-00929-0 LC Card 81-11372 DDC 975/.004960730922 B 19
E185.92 .S68

SOUTHERN STATES - CIVILIZATION. Young, Thomas Daniel, 1919- Waking their neighbors up . Athens , c1982. p. cm. ISBN

0-8203-0600-2 LC Card 81-14736 DDC 810/.9/975 19
PS261 .Y63

SOUTHERN STATES - COMMERCE. Roy, Delwin A. Southeast exporting . Atlanta, Ga. , 1981. p. cm. ISBN 0-88406-146-9 : LC Card 81-6287 DDC 382/.0975 19
HF3153 .R69

SOUTHERN STATES - ECONOMIC CONDITIONS - 1945- - PERIODICALS. Studies in human resource development. no. 1- Austin, 1974- **NYPL [JLL 80-248]**

SOUTHERN STATES - GENEALOGY. Baker, Jack D. Cherokee emigration rolls, 1817-1835 /. Oklahoma City , c1977. 67 leaves : LC Card 77-156017
E99.C5 B27

SOUTHERN STATES - HISTORY - 1865-1877 - ADDRESSES, ESSAYS, LECTURES. Southern Black leaders of the Reconstruction era /. Urbana , c1982. p. cm. ISBN 0-252-00929-0 LC Card 81-11372 DDC 975/.004960730922 B 19
E185.92 .S68

SOUTHERN STATES - MANUFACTURES. Roy, Delwin A. Southeast exporting . Atlanta, Ga. , 1981. p. cm. ISBN 0-88406-146-9 : LC Card 81-6287 DDC 382/.0975 19
HF3153 .R69

SOUTHERN STATES - RACE RELATIONS - ADDRESSES, ESSAYS, LECTURES. Southern Black leaders of the Reconstruction era /. Urbana , c1982. p. cm. ISBN 0-252-00929-0 LC Card 81-11372 DDC 975/.004960730922 B 19
E185.92 .S68

Southern Tier East Regional Planning Board. Housing related census data: Broome-Tioga counties / prepared by Southern Tier East Regional Planning Board. Binghamton, N. Y.: The Board, 1974. 97 p.; 28 cm. "December, 1974." Bibliography: p. 97.
1. Broome County, N. Y. - Census, 1970. 2. Tioga County, N. Y. - Census, 1970. 3. Housing - New York (State) - Broome County - Statistics. 4. Housing - New York (State) - Tioga County - Statistics. I. Title.
NYPL [JLF 80-1377]

Southward, G. Morris. Sampling landings of halibut for age composition / by G. Morris Southward. Seattle : International Pacific Halibut Commission, 1976. 31 p. : ill. ; 28 cm. (Scientific report . no. 58) Bibliography: p. 25-26. LC Card 81-456583 DDC 639/.2758 s 597/.5 19
1. Pacific halibut - Age. 2. Fishes - Age - Statistical methods. 3. Sampling (Statistics). I. Series: International Pacific Halibut Commission (U. S. and Canada). Scientific report , no. 58. II. Title.
SH351.H2 I54 no. 58 QL638.P7

Southwest Africa. see Namibia.

Southwest Asia. United States. Central Intelligence Agency. [Washington , 1980] 1 map : LC Card 81-692534
G7420 1980 .U5

Southwest Consultation on the Educational Needs of Rural Girls and Women, Santa Fe, N.M., 1976. Young, Tasia. Report of the Southwest Consultation on the Educational Needs of Rural Girls and Women, convened by the Information Resources Committee, Advisory Council on Women's Educational Programs in Santa Fe, New Mexico, September 10 and 11, 1976 /. Albuquerque [1976?] 25 leaves ; LC Card 79-623319 DDC 376/.9789 19
LC1758.N6 Y68

Southwest Cultural Resources Center. Remote Sensing Division. Symposium on Cultural Resources Management and Remote Sensing, Tucson, Ariz. 1978. Remote sensing and non-destructive archeology /. Washington, DC , 1978. vii, 71 p. : LC Card 80-602610 DDC 930.1/028 19
CC76.4 .S9 1978

Southwest Florida Water Management District. Wilson, William Edward, 1934- Estimated effects of projected ground-water withdrawals on movement of the saltwater front in the Floridan aquifer, 1976-2000, west-central Florida /. Washington , Arlington, VA , 1981. p. cm. LC Card 81-607085 DDC 628.1/1 19
GB1197.83.F6 W54

Southwest Missouri State University. Center for Archaeological Research. Cooley, Robert E. An archaeological and historical survey of areas to be affected by the construction of the Missouri River L-246 levee, Chariton County, Missouri, 1976, project CAR-31 . Springfield, Mo. , 1976. 122 p. :   LC Card 77-623633   DDC 977.8/25 19
F472.C44 C66

SOUTHWEST, NEW - ANTIQUITIES - PERIODICALS.
Southwestern lore. V. 1- ; JUNE, 1935- [Denver, etc.]   LC Card 40-2540
      NYPL [HBA (Southwestern lore)]

SOUTHWEST, NEW - BIOGRAPHY.
Russell, Marian Sloan, 1845-1937. Land of enchantment . Albuquerque [1981] c1954. xiv, 163 p. :   ISBN 0-8263-0571-7 :   LC Card 80-54564   DDC 917.8 19
F786 .R96 1981

SOUTHWEST, NEW - HISTORY - TO 1848.
John, Elizabeth Ann Harper, 1928- Storms brewed in other men's worlds . Lincoln , 1981, c1975. p. cm.   ISBN 0-8032-7554-4 (pbk.)   LC Card 81-3401   DDC 978/.00497 19
E78.S7 J64 1981

Southwest Ohio River basin study area, Ohio.
United States. Soil Conservation Service. Average annual precipitation in inches, 1931-60, southwest Ohio River basin study area, Ohio /. Lincoln, Nebr. , 1978. 1 map :   LC Card 81-691036
G4081.C88 1960 .U5

Southwest Ohio River basin study area, Ohio.
United States. Soil Conservation Service. P.L. 566 watershed status, southwest Ohio River basin study area, Ohio /. Lincoln, Nebr. , 1978. 1 map :   LC Card 81-691040
G4081.C315 1978 .U5

SOUTHWEST, OLD - BIOGRAPHY.
Penick, James L. The great western land pirate . Columbia , 1981. p. cm.   ISBN 0-8262-0342-6   LC Card 81-1779   DDC 364.1/5/0924 B 19
F396.M95 P46

SOUTHWEST, OLD - HISTORY.
Penick, James L. The great western land pirate . Columbia , 1981. p. cm.   ISBN 0-8262-0342-6   LC Card 81-1779   DDC 364.1/5/0924 B 19
F396.M95 P46

Southwestern lore. V. 1- ; JUNE, 1935- [Denver, etc.] illus. 23 cm. Quarterly. Vol. 1, no. 1-4 issued as Western State College bulletin, v. 24, no. 7-9, v. 25, no. 4. Official publication of the Southwestern Colorado Archaeological Society and the Museum of Western State College, June, 1935-Mar. 1936; of the Colorado Archaeological Society, June, 1936- . INDEXES: Vols. 1-20, 1935-55 (issued as v. 21, no. 1, pt. 2) with v. 20.   LC Card 40-2540
1. Colorado - Antiquities - Periodicals. 2. Southwest, New - Antiquities - Periodicals. I. Colorado Archaeological Society. II. Colorado. Western State College, Gunnison.
      NYPL [HBA (Southwestern lore)]

SOUTHWESTERN STATES - ECONOMIC CONDITIONS - PERIODICALS.
Studies in human resource development. no. 1- Austin, 1974-   *NYPL [JLL 80-248]*

Southwestern weaving . Maxwell Museum of Anthropology. Albuquerque , 1981. p. cm.   ISBN 0-8263-0587-3   LC Card 81-8143   DDC 746.1/4/08997079074018961 19
E78.S7 M35 1981

Souza, Al, 1944- Davies, Hugh Marlais. 1948- Al Souza /. [Amherst] , c1979. [24] p. :   LC Card 79-4894
TR647 .S69 1979
      NYPL [MFX (Souza) 80-2495]

SOUZA, AL, 1944-
Davies, Hugh Marlais. 1948- Al Souza /. [Amherst] , c1979. [24] p. :   LC Card 79-4894
TR647 .S69 1979
      NYPL [MFX (Souza) 80-2495]

Soviet-American relations in Asia, 1945-1954 /. Buhite, Russell D. Norman , 1981. p. cm.   ISBN 0-8061-1729-X   LC Card 81-40285   DDC 327.47073 19
E183.8.S65 B83

Soviet biological warfare activities . United

States. Congress. House. Permanent Select Committee on Intelligence. Subcommittee on Oversight. Washington , 1980. ii, 5 p. ;   LC Card 80-603268   DDC 358/.38/0947 19
UG447.8 .U45 1980

Soviet bloc. see **Communist countries.**

Soviet covert action (the forgery offensive) .
United States. Congress. House. Permanent Select Committee on Intelligence. Subcommittee on Oversight. Washington , 1980. iii, 245 p. :   LC Card 80-603647   DDC 327.1/2/0947 19
KF27.5 .I55 1980b

Soviet defense expenditures and related programs . United States. Congress. Senate. Committee on Armed Services. Subcommittee on General Procurement. Washington , 1980. iv, 215 p. :   LC Card 81-600583   DDC 355.6/212/0947 19
KF26 .A7543 1979a

Soviet detention of Andrei Sakharov . United States. Congress. House. Committee on Foreign Affairs. Washington , 1980. iii, 31 p. ;   LC Card 80-602485   DDC 323.4/0947 19
KF26 .F6 1980b

The Soviet economy in 1978-79 and prospects for 1980 /. United States. Central Intelligence Agency. National Foreign Assessment Center. Washington, D.C. [1980] vi, 25 p. :   LC Card 80-602919   DDC 330.947/0853 19
HC336.25 .U54 1980

Soviet gains and possible targets, 1978. United States. Central Intelligence Agency. Recent Soviet gains and possible targets, 1978. [Washington , 1978] 1 map :   LC Card 81-690525
G7001.F35 1978 .U5

Soviet housing and urban design / Steven A. Grant, editor. [Washington, D.C.] : U. S. Dept. of Housing and Urban Development, [1980] v, 68 p. : ill. ; 27 cm. "Papers ... prepared for a conference ... held December 19, 1979, co-sponsored by the Office of International Affairs at HUD and the Kennan Institute for Advanced Russian Studies of the Wilson Center." "HUD-IA-595." "September 1980." Includes bibliographical references.   LC Card 80-603575   DDC 363.7/0947 19
1. Housing - Russia - Addresses, essays, lectures. 2. Construction industry - Russia - Addresses, essays, lectures. I. Grant, Steven A. II. United States. Dept. of Housing and Urban Development. Office of International Affairs. III. Kennan Institute for Advanced Russian Studies.
HD7345.A3 S64

Soviet internal developments . United States. Congress. House. Permanent Select Committee on Intelligence. Subcommittee on Program and Budget Authorization. Washington , 1980. iii, 134 p. ;   LC Card 80-602084   DDC 947.085/3 19
KF27.5 .I56 1980

Soviet pressure, 1946-53. United States. Central Intelligence Agency. Application of Soviet pressure, 1946-53. [Washington , 1978] 1 map :   LC Card 81-690523
G5701.F33 1953 .U5

Soviet strategic forces . United States. Congress. House. Permanent Select Committee on Intelligence. Subcommittee on Oversight. Washington , 1980. iii, 76 p. ;   LC Card 80-602765   DDC 358/.17/0947 19
KF27.5 .I55 1980

Soviet strategy and tactics in economic and commercial negotiations with the United States /. United States. Central Intelligence Agency. National Foreign Assessment Center. Washington , 1979. v, 11 p. ;   LC Card 79-602793
*HF1456.5.R9 U54 1979   NYPL   [*XME-9336]*

SOVIET UNION - ADMINISTRATIVE AND POLITICAL DIVISIONS - MAPS.
United States. Central Intelligence Agency. USSR administrative divisions, 1979. [Washington , 1980] 1 map :   LC Card 81-692775
G7001.F7 1979 .U5

SOVIET UNION - ARMED FORCES - PROCUREMENT.
United States. Congress. House. Permanent Select Committee on Intelligence. Subcommittee on Oversight. CIA estimates of Soviet defense spending . Washington , 1980 [i.e. 1981] iii, 95 p. :   LC Card 81-600837   DDC

355/.033047 19
KF27.5 .I55 1980c

United States. Congress. Senate. Committee on Armed Services. Subcommittee on General Procurement. Soviet defense expenditures and related programs . Washington , 1980. iv, 215 p. :   LC Card 81-600583   DDC 355.6/212/0947 19
KF26 .A7543 1979a

SOVIET UNION - ECONOMIC CONDITIONS - 1976-
Update--impact of agricultural trade restrictions on the Soviet Union. [Washington, D.C.] [1980] 9 p. ;   LC Card 80-603822   DDC 338.1 s 330.947/0853 19
HD1411 .F59 no. 160 HD9036

SOVIET UNION - FOREIGN ECONOMIC RELATIONS - UNITED STATES.
United States. Congress. House. Committee on Foreign Affairs. Subcommittee on International Economic Policy and Trade. Review of implementation of Basket II of the Helsinki Final Act . Washington , 1980. iii, 82 p. ;   LC Card 80-604051   DDC 337.73047 19
KF27 .F6465 1980d

United States. Congress. Senate. Committee on Banking, Housing and Urban Affairs. Suspension of United States exports of high technology and grain to the Soviet Union . Washington , 1980. v, 156 p. :   LC Card 80-604066   DDC 382/.4131/0973 19
KF26 .B39 1980x

Update--impact of agricultural trade restrictions on the Soviet Union. [Washington, D.C.] [1980] 9 p. ;   LC Card 80-603822   DDC 338.1 s 330.947/0853 19
HD1411 .F59 no. 160 HD9036

SOVIET UNION - FOREIGN RELATION - UNITED STATES.
Update--impact of agricultural trade restrictions on the Soviet Union. [Washington, D.C.] [1980] 9 p. ;   LC Card 80-603822   DDC 338.1 s 330.947/0853 19
HD1411 .F59 no. 160 HD9036

SOVIET UNION - FOREIGN RELATIONS - 1945-
Buhite, Russell D. Soviet-American relations in Asia, 1945-1954 /. Norman , 1981. p. cm.   ISBN 0-8061-1729-X   LC Card 81-40285   DDC 327.47073 19
E183.8.S65 B83

SOVIET UNION - FOREIGN RELATIONS - ASIA.
Buhite, Russell D. Soviet-American relations in Asia, 1945-1954 /. Norman , 1981. p. cm.   ISBN 0-8061-1729-X   LC Card 81-40285   DDC 327.47073 19
E183.8.S65 B83

SOVIET UNION - FOREIGN RELATIONS - CHINA.
Ewing, Thomas E. Between the hammer and the anvil? . Bloomington , 1980. vi, 300 p. ;   ISBN 0-933070-07-063   LC Card 80-52924   DDC 951/.704 19
DS798.75 .E95

SOVIET UNION - FOREIGN RELATIONS - CHINA - CONGRESSES.
The Sino-Soviet conflict . Seattle , c1981. p. cm.   ISBN 0-295-95854-5 :   LC Card 81-51279   DDC 327.51047 19
DS740.5.S65 S56

SOVIET UNION - FOREIGN RELATIONS - NORWAY.
Amundsen, Kirsten. Norway, NATO, and the forgotten Soviet challenge /. Berkeley , c1981. vi, 50 p. :   ISBN 0-87725-514-8 (pbk.) :   LC Card 81-80337   DDC 355/.0330481 19
UA750 .A56

SOVIET UNION - FOREIGN RELATIONS - UNITED STATES.
Buhite, Russell D. Soviet-American relations in Asia, 1945-1954 /. Norman , 1981. p. cm.   ISBN 0-8061-1729-X   LC Card 81-40285   DDC 327.47073 19
E183.8.S65 B83

SOVIET UNION. GOSUDARSTVENNYĬ KOMITET PO NAUKE I TEKHNIKE.
Nolting, Louvan E. The structure and functions of the U. S.S.R. State Committee for Science and Technology /. [Washington, D.C.] [1979] iv, 53 p. ;   LC Card 80-602662   DDC 354.470085/5

19
Q127.S696 N64   **NYPL   [JLM 78-229 19]**

**SOVIET UNION - HISTORY -
BIBLIOGRAPHY - CATALOGS.**
Thurston, Robert W. Russian history and
politics . [Ann Arbor] , c1978. 57 p. ;   LC Card
81-621451   DDC 016.947 19
Z2506 .T47 DK40

**SOVIET UNION - HISTORY - SOURCES -
BIBLIOGRAPHY - CATALOGS.**
Thurston, Robert W. Russian history and
politics . [Ann Arbor] , c1978. 57 p. ;   LC Card
81-621451   DDC 016.947 19
Z2506 .T47 DK40

SOVIET UNION - MILITARY POLICY.
United States. Congress. House. Permanent
Select Committee on Intelligence.
Subcommittee on Oversight. CIA estimates of
Soviet defense spending . Washington , 1980
[i.e. 1981] iii, 95 p. :   LC Card 81-600837   DDC
355/.033047 19
KF27.5 .I55 1980c

**SOVIET UNION - POLITICS AND
GOVERNMENT - 1689-1800.**
Meehan-Waters, Brenda, 1942- Autocracy and
aristocracy, the Russian service elite of 1730 /.
New Brunswick, N.J. [1982] p. cm.   ISBN
0-8135-0938-6 :   LC Card 81-13960   DDC
947/.061 19
DK150 .M43

**SOVIET UNION - POLITICS AND
GOVERNMENT - 1894-1917 -
ADDRESSES, ESSAYS, LECTURES.**
Latin American populism in comparative
perspective /. Albuquerque , c1981. p. cm.
ISBN 0-8263-0580-6 :   LC Card 80-54572
DDC 320.98 19
JL966 .L36

SOYBEAN AS FOOD.
Soybeans as human food . [Washington] , 1979.
iv, 54 p. :   LC Card 79-603033   DDC 641.3/5655
19
TX558.S7 S69 1979b

Soybean crop losses to natural disasters . United
States. Congress. House. Committee on
Agriculture. Subcommittee on Oilseeds and
Rice. Washington , 1980 [i.e. 1981] iii, 29 p. ;
LC Card 81-600857   DDC 343.73/07633491
347.3037633491 19
KF27 .A367 1980b

**SOYBEAN - LAW AND LEGISLATION -
UNITED STATES.**
United States. Congress. House. Committee on
Agriculture. Subcommittee on Oilseeds and
Rice. Soybean crop losses to natural disasters .
Washington , 1980 [i.e. 1981] iii, 29 p. ;   LC
Card 81-600857   DDC 343.73/07633491
347.3037633491 19
KF27 .A367 1980b

SOYBEAN - LOSSES - MISSOURI.
United States. Congress. House. Committee on
Agriculture. Subcommittee on Oilseeds and
Rice. Soybean crop losses to natural disasters .
Washington , 1980 [i.e. 1981] iii, 29 p. ;   LC
Card 81-600857   DDC 343.73/07633491
347.3037633491 19
KF27 .A367 1980b

**SOYBEAN - MARKETING - LAW AND
LEGISLATION - FLORIDA.**
Florida. Legislature. Senate. Committee on
Agriculture. A review of the Soybean Advisory
Council in the Department of Agriculture and
Consumer Services /. [Tallahassee] [1980] i,
14, [9] p. ;   LC Card 81-621220   DDC
353.97590082/61334 19
KFF244.S66 A25 1980

SOYBEAN - TROPICS - CONGRESSES.
Workshop on Soybeans for Tropical and
Subtropical Conditions, University of Puerto
Rico Mayagüez Campus, 1974. Proceedings of
the Workshop on Soybeans for Tropical and
Subtropical Conditions, February 4-6, 1974,
University of Puerto Rico Mayagüez campus.
[Urbana] , 1974, 1978 printing. 184 p. :   LC
Card 80-620583   DDC 635/.655/0913 19
SB205.S7 W65 1974

SOYBEAN - UNITED STATES.
United States. Congress. House. Committee on
Agriculture. Subcommittee on Oilseeds and
Rice. Loan eligibility for 1979 soybean crop .
Washington , 1980. iii, 26 p. ;   LC Card

80-603101   DDC 343.73/076334 19
KF27 .A367 1980a

Soybeans as human food : unprocessed and
simply processed / H.L. Wang ... [et al.] ;
compiled for the Agency for International
Development, U. S. Department of State [by]
Science and Education Administration, U. S.
Department of Agriculture.Slightly rev. July
1979. [Washington] : The Administration : [for
sale by the Supt. of Docs., U. S. Govt. Print.
Off.], 1979. iv, 54 p. : ill. ; 26 cm. (Utilization
research report . no. 5) Includes bibliographies.   LC
Card 79-603033   DDC 641.3/5655 19
*1. Soybean as food. I. Wang, Hwa Lih, 1921-. II.
United States. Agency for International Development.
III. United States. Science and Education
Administration. IV. Series: United States. Department
of Agriculture. Utilization research report , no. 5.*
TX558.S7 S69 1979b

Sozen, Mete Avni, 1930- Moehle, Jack P.
Experiments to study earthquake response of
R/C structures with stiffness interruptions .
Urbana, Ill. [1980] xiii, 421 p. :   LC Card
80-624330   DDC 693.8/52 19
TA683 .M66

**SPACE AND TIME - ADDRESSES, ESSAYS,
LECTURES.**
Spacetime and geometry . Austin , c1982. p.
cm.   ISBN 0-292-77567-9   LC Card 81-11488
DDC 530.1/1 19
QC173.6 .S67

SPACE CARS. see SPACE STATIONS.

SPACE COLONIES - CONGRESSES.
Ames Summer Study on Space Settlements and
Industrialization Using Nonterrestrial Materials,
Ames Research Center, 1977. Space resources
and space settlements . Washington, D.C. ,
1979. x, 288 p. :   LC Card 79-603821   DDC
629.44/2 19
TL795.7 .A45 1977

**SPACE COLONIES - ECONOMIC ASPECTS -
UNITED STATES.**
Wolken, Lawrence C. The exploration and
colonization of space . College Station, Tex. ,
c1980. 28 p. ;   LC Card 81-621410   DDC 919.9/04
19
HC110.O93 W64

**SPACE COLONIES - POLITICAL ASPECTS -
UNITED STATES.**
Wolken, Lawrence C. The exploration and
colonization of space . College Station, Tex. ,
c1980. 28 p. ;   LC Card 81-621410   DDC 919.9/04
19
HC110.O93 W64

**SPACE COMMUNITIES. see SPACE
COLONIES.**

**SPACE EXPLORATION (ASTRONAUTICS)
see OUTER SPACE - EXPLORATION.**

**SPACE FLIGHT - LAW AND LEGISLATION.
see SPACE LAW.**

**SPACE FLIGHT - PHYSIOLOGICAL
EFFECT.**
Ahn, Chung-Hae. NASA's biomedical research
program /. Washington, D.C. , 1981. p. cm.
LC Card 81-607969   DDC 616.9/80214 19
RC1150 .A35

Walisora, J. M. The physiological basis for
spacecraft environmental limits /. Washington,
D.C. [Springfield, Va.] c1979. xvii, 217 p. :
LC Card 81-600766   DDC 612/.0145 19
RC1150 .W34

**SPACE FLIGHT TRAINING FACILITIES -
TEXAS - HOUSTON - ACCIDENTS.**
United States. Congress. House. Committee on
Science and Technology. Subcommittee on
Space Science and Applications. Water
immersion facility, Johnson Space Center .
Washington , 1979. iii, 44 p. :   LC Card
80-601329   DDC 629.45/82/028 19
KF27 .S3995 1979h

SPACE HABITATS. see SPACE COLONIES.

SPACE IN ECONOMICS - BIBLIOGRAPHY.
Muller, Peter O. Locational analysis and
economic geography . [Philadelphia] [197-] iii,
94 p. ;   LC Card 78-109442   DDC 016.3309 19
Z6004.C7 M84 HF1025

**SPACE IN ECONOMICS - MATHEMATICAL
MODELS.**
Huff, David Lynch, 1931- Retail location

theory /. Austin, Tex. , 1980. [15] leaves :   LC
Card 80-624130   DDC 381/.1 19
HF5429.275 .H83

Space industrialization act of 1980. United
States. Congress. House. Committee on Science
and Technology. Subcommittee on Space
Science and Applications. H.R. 7412, the Space
industrialization act of 1980 . Washington ,
1980. iii, 88 p. ;   LC Card 80-603674   DDC
344.73/095 347.30495 19
KF27 .S3995 1980

**SPACE INDUSTRIALIZATION
CORPORATION.**
United States. Congress. House. Committee on
Science and Technology. Subcommittee on
Space Science and Applications. H.R. 7412, the
Space industrialization act of 1980 .
Washington , 1980. iii, 88 p. ;   LC Card
80-603674   DDC 344.73/095 347.30495 19
KF27 .S3995 1980

SPACE LAW.
(1980) Agreement governing the activities of
states on the moon and other celestial bodies /.
Washington , 1980. ix, 264 p. ;   LC Card
80-602580   DDC 341.4/6 19
JX5810 .A37

(1980) United States. Congress. House.
Committee on Science and Technology.
Subcommittee on Space Science and
Applications. H.R. 7412, the Space
industrialization act of 1980 . Washington ,
1980. iii, 88 p. ;   LC Card 80-603674   DDC
344.73/095 347.30495 19
KF27 .S3995 1980

(1980) United States. Congress. Senate.
Committee on Commerce, Science, and
Transportation. Subcommittee on Science,
Technology, and Space. The Moon treaty .
Washington , 1980. iv, 267 p. ;   LC Card
80-603774   DDC 341.4/7 19
KF26 .C697 1980f

**SPACE MEDICINE - RESEARCH - UNITED
STATES.**
Ahn, Chung-Hae. NASA's biomedical research
program /. Washington, D.C. , 1981. p. cm.
LC Card 81-607969   DDC 616.9/80214 19
RC1150 .A35

Space missions to comets . Symposium on Space
Missions to Comets, Goddard Space Flight
Center, 1977. [Washington] , 1979. v, 226 p. :
LC Card 79-604295   DDC 523.6 19
QB721 .S97 1977

**SPACE OBLIQUE MERCATOR
PROJECTION (CARTOGRAPHY)**
Snyder, John Parr, 1926- Space oblique
mercator projection mathematical development
/. Reston, VA [1981] p. cm.   LC Card
81-607029   DDC 557.3 s 526.8 19
QE75 .B9 no. 1518 GA115

**Space oblique mercator projection mathematical
development** /. Snyder, John Parr, 1926-
Reston, VA [1981] p. cm.   LC Card 81-607029
DDC 557.3 s 526.8 19
QE75 .B9 no. 1518 GA115

Space photography index. United States. National
Aeronautics and Space Administration.
Washington.   **NYPL   [JSP 81-22]**

**SPACE PHOTOGRAPHY - INDEXES -
PERIODICALS.**
United States. National Aeronautics and Space
Administration. Space photography index.
Washington.   **NYPL   [JSP 81-22]**

**SPACE RESEARCH. see OUTER SPACE -
EXPLORATION.**

Space resources and space settlements . Ames
Summer Study on Space Settlements and
Industrialization Using Nonterrestrial Materials,
Ames Research Center, 1977. Washington,
D.C. , 1979. x, 288 p. :   LC Card 79-603821
DDC 629.44/2 19
TL795.7 .A45 1977

Space science comes of age : perspectives in the
history of the space sciences / edited by Paul
A. Hanle and Von Del Chamberlain ; with
contributions by Stephen G. Brush ... [et al.].
Washington : National Air and Space Museum,
Smithsonian Institution ; distributed by the
Smithsonian Institution Press, 1981. xiii, 194
p. : ill. ; 27 cm. Papers presented at a symposium
held at and sponsored by the National Air and Space

Museum, Washington, D.C., Mar. 23-24, 1981. Includes bibliographical references and index. ISBN 0-87474-508-X : LC Card 80-28966 DDC 500.5/09 19

1. Space sciences - History - Congresses. I. Hanle, Paul A. II. Chamberlain, Von Del. III. Brush, Stephen G. IV. National Air and Space Museum.

QB500 .S62

Space science series.
Satellites of Jupiter /. Tucson, Ariz. , c1981. p. cm. ISBN 0-8165-0762-7 : LC Card 81-13050 DDC 523.4/5 19

QB404 .S34

SPACE SCIENCES - HISTORY - CONGRESSES.
Space science comes of age . Washington , 1981. xiii, 194 p. : ISBN 0-87474-508-X : LC Card 80-28966 DDC 500.5/09 19

QB500 .S62

SPACE SCIENCES - UNITED STATES.
Bell, Trudy. Technologies for the handicapped and the aged . [Washington] , 1979. iii, 43 p. : LC Card 80-601228 DDC 617 19

R856 .B4

Space shuttle and Galileo mission . United States. Congress. Senate. Committee on Appropriations. Subcommittee on HUD-Independent Agencies. Washington , 1980. iv, 132 p. ; LC Card 80-601987 DDC 353.0072/2368778 19

KF26 .A6486 1979c

SPACE SHUTTLES. see REUSABLE SPACE VEHICLES.

SPACE STATIONS - INDUSTRIAL APPLICATIONS - CONGRESSES.
Ames Summer Study on Space Settlements and Industrialization Using Nonterrestrial Materials, Ames Research Center, 1977. Space resources and space settlements . Washington, D.C. , 1979. x, 288 p. : LC Card 79-603821 DDC 629.44/2 19

TL795.7 .A45 1977

SPACE STATIONS - INDUSTRIAL APPLICATIONS - FINANCE.
United States. Congress. House. Committee on Science and Technology. Subcommittee on Space Science and Applications. H.R. 7412, the Space industrialization act of 1980 . Washington , 1980. iii, 88 p. ; LC Card 80-603674 DDC 344.73/095 347.30495 19

KF27 .S3995 1980

SPACE STATIONS - LAW AND LEGISLATION. see SPACE LAW.

Space telescope. Scientific research with the space telescope . [Huntsville, Ala.] , Washington, D.C. [1979] xii, 327 p. : LC Card 80-601618 DDC 520 19

QB61 .S33

SPACE-TIMES. see SPACE AND TIME.

SPACEBORNE PHOTOGRAPHY. see SPACE PHOTOGRAPHY.

Spacetime and geometry : the Alfred Schild lectures / edited by L.C. Shepley and Richard A. Matzner. Austin : University of Texas Press, c1982. p. cm. Includes index. Why is the universe so symmetrical? / Dennis Sciama -- Null congruences and Plebanski-Schild spaces / Ivor Robinson -- Linearization stability / Dieter Brill -- Nonlinear model field theories based on harmonic mappings / Charles W. Misner -- Gravitational fields in general relativity / Roy F. Kerr -- On the potential barriers surrounding the Schwarzschild black hole / S. Chandrasekhar -- The initial value problem and beyond / James W. York, Jr. and Tsvi Piran. ISBN 0-292-77567-9 LC Card 81-11488 DDC 530.1/1 19

1. General relativity (Physics) - Addresses, essays, lectures. 2. Gravitation - Addresses, essays, lectures. 3. Space and time - Addresses, essays, lectures. 4. Geometry - Addresses, essays, lectures. I. Schild, Alfred, 1921-. II. Shepley, Lawrence C., 1939-. III. Matzner, Richard A. (Richard Alfred), 1942-.

QC173.6 .S67

Spain and NATO. Dreisonstok, Thomas F. Carlisle Barracks, Pa., 1971. iii, 52 leaves. *NYPL [*XME-9305]*

SPAIN - COLONIES - AMERICA.
Crawford, Leslie. Las Casas, hombre de los siglos . Washington , 1978. 205 p. : LC Card 79-105297 DDC 980/.004/98 19

F1411 .C84

Spain - History - Revolution of American colonies, 1806-1830. see South America - History - Wars of Independence, 1806-1830.

Spain - History - War of 1898. see United States - History - War of 1898.

SPAIN - HISTORY - CIVIL WAR, 1936-1939 - FOREIGN PUBLIC OPINION - ADDRESSES, ESSAYS, LECTURES.
The Spanish Civil War, 1936-39 . Lincoln , c1982. p. cm. ISBN 0-8032-1961-X LC Card 81-14644 DDC 946.081 19

DP269.8.P8 S6

SPAIN - HISTORY - CIVIL WAR, 1936-1939 - INFLUENCE AND RESULTS - ADDRESSES, ESSAYS, LECTURES.
The Spanish Civil War, 1936-39 . Lincoln , c1982. p. cm. ISBN 0-8032-1961-X LC Card 81-14644 DDC 946.081 19

DP269.8.P8 S6

SPAIN - HISTORY - SOURCES - BIBLIOGRAPHY.
California. University, Riverside. Library. Godoi-Díaz Pérez Collection. Research guide to the Godoi-Díaz Pérez Collection in the Library of the University of California, Riverside /. Riverside , 1973. 60 p. ;

NYPL [HLM 81-769]

SPAIN - MILITARY POLICY.
Dreisonstok, Thomas F. Spain and NATO. Carlisle Barracks, Pa., 1971. iii, 52 leaves.

*NYPL [*XME-9305]*

SPANIARDS IN TUBAC, ARIZ. - HISTORY.
Shenk, Lynette O. Excavations at the Tubac Presidio /. [Tucson] , 1975. xii, 234 p. : LC Card 80-621272 DDC 979.1/79 19

F819.T88 S5

SPANISH AMERICAN LITERATURE - HISTORY AND CRITICISM - ADDRESSES, ESSAYS, LECTURES.
Icons and fallen idols . Berkeley , c1982. p. cm. ISBN 0-520-04291-3 LC Card 81-14663 DDC 860/.9 19

PQ6048.W6 I26

SPANISH AMERICAN LITERATURE - WOMEN AUTHORS - HISTORY AND CRITICISM - ADDRESSES, ESSAYS, LECTURES.
Icons and fallen idols . Berkeley , c1982. p. cm. ISBN 0-520-04291-3 LC Card 81-14663 DDC 860/.9 19

PQ6048.W6 I26

SPANISH-AMERICAN WAR, 1898. see UNITED STATES - HISTORY - WAR OF 1898.

The Spanish Civil War, 1936-39 : American hemispheric perspectives / edited by Mark Falcoff and Fredrick B. Pike. Lincoln : University of Nebraska Press, c1982. p. cm. Includes index. CONTENTS. - Annotated chronology / by Fredrick B. Pike -- Introduction: the background to the Civil War in Spain ... / by Fredrick B. Pike -- Mexico / by T.G. Powell -- Cuba / by Alistair Hennessy -- Colombia / by David Bushnell -- Peru / by Thomas N. Davies, Jr. -- Chile / by Paul W. Drake -- Argentina / by Mark Falcoff. ISBN 0-8032-1961-X LC Card 81-14644 DDC 946.081 19

1. Spain - History - Civil War, 1936-1939 - Foreign public opinion - Addresses, essays, lectures. 2. Spain - History - Civil War, 1936-1939 - Influence and results - Addresses, essays, lectures. 3. Latin America - History - 20th century - Addresses, essays, lectures. I. Falcoff, Mark, 1941-. II. Pike, Fredrick B.

DP269.8.P8 S6

Spanish in the courtrooms of Puerto Rico, H.R. 5563 . United States. Congress. Senate. Committee on the Judiciary. Subcommittee on Improvements in Judicial Machinery. Washington , 1980. iii, 86 p. ; LC Card 80-603690 DDC 347.73/222 347.30722 19

KF26 .J855 1980b

SPANISH LANGUAGE - DICTIONARIES - ENGLISH.
A Drug terminology--general glossary, English-Spanish/Spanish-English . [Los Angeles] [1980] vi, 134 p. ; LC Card 80-135304 DDC 616.86/3/00326 19

RC564 .D783

SPANISH LANGUAGE - EXAMINATIONS, QUESTIONS, ETC.
United States. Foreign Service Institute. Testing

kit, French and Spanish /. [Washington, D.C.] [1979] x, 140 p. (p. 140 blank) : LC Card 80-602389 DDC 440[.76 19

PB36 .U54 1979

SPANISH LANGUAGE - POLITICAL ASPECTS.
United States. Congress. Senate. Committee on the Judiciary. Subcommittee on Improvements in Judicial Machinery. Spanish in the courtrooms of Puerto Rico, H.R. 5563 . Washington , 1980. iii, 86 p. ; LC Card 80-603690 DDC 347.73/222 347.30722 19

KF26 .J855 1980b

SPANISH LITERATURE - HISTORY AND CRITICISM - ADDRESSES, ESSAYS, LECTURES.
Icons and fallen idols . Berkeley , c1982. p. cm. ISBN 0-520-04291-3 LC Card 81-14663 DDC 860/.9 19

PQ6048.W6 I26

SPANISH LITERATURE - WOMEN AUTHORS - HISTORY AND CRITICISM - ADDRESSES, ESSAYS, LECTURES.
Icons and fallen idols . Berkeley , c1982. p. cm. ISBN 0-520-04291-3 LC Card 81-14663 DDC 860/.9 19

PQ6048.W6 I26

SPANISH LITERATURE - WOMEN AUTHORS - HISTORY AND CRITICISM - BIBLIOGRAPHY.
Alarcón, Norma. Bibliography of Hispanic women writers /. Bloomington, IN. , c1980. iv, 86 p. ; LC Card 80-138062 DDC 016.86/09/9287 19

Z1609.L7 A45 PQ6055

SPANISH MISSIONS OF NEW MEXICO.
Kessell, John L. The missions of New Mexico since 1776 /. Albuquerque , 1980. xii, 276 p., [6] leaves of plates : ISBN 0-8263-0514-8 : LC Card 79-4934

F797 .K47 *NYPL [IWSB 80-3227]*

Spanish Sahara - Government. see Spanish Sahara - Politics and government.

SPANISH SAHARA - POLITICS AND GOVERNMENT.
United States. Congress. House. Committee on Foreign Affairs. Subcommittee on Africa. Current situationin the western Sahara, 1980 . Washington , 1981. iii, 24 p. ; LC Card 81-600927 DDC 327.73061 19

KF27 .F625 1980f

Spann, Barbara T. Carlby / by Barbara T. Spann. Fairfax, Va. : Fairfax County Office of Comprehensive Planning, in cooperation with Fairfax County History Commission, 1976. vii, 168 p. : ill. ; 28 cm. Bibliography: p. 161-168. LC Card 80-53974 DDC 975.5/291 19

1. Carlby, Va. I. Fairfax Co., Va. Office of Comprehensive Planning. II. Fairfax Co., Va. History Commission. III. Title.

F232.F2 S66

Sparkman, Betty D. (joint author) Ward, Keith J. Property tax administration . Auburn, Ala. [1980] xiv, 167 p. : LC Card 80-622123 DDC 353.97610072/42 19

HJ4121.A22 W37

SPARTINA ALTERNIFLORA.
Rublee, Parke A. Bacteria in a North Carolina salt marsh . [Raleigh] , 1978. 80 p. : LC Card 79-621361 DDC 574.5/2636 19

QR106 .R82

SPATIAL ANALYSIS (STATISTICS)
Batsell, Richard R. Deriving areal extent boundaries from two-dimensional point distributions /. Austin , 1979. 15 p. : LC Card 79-623643 DDC 519.5 19

QA278.2 .B38

Spatial rearragement of people . Shapero, Albert. Austin , 1978. 37 p. : LC Card 79-621447 DDC 658.3/128 19

HD30.3 .S5

A spatial simulation model of lake-edge wetland formation /. Kratz, Timothy K. Madison , 1979. 59 p. : LC Card 80-621224 DDC 574.5/26325/0724 19

QH541.5.M3 K7

Speakers and clerks of the Virginia House of Burgesses, 1643-1776 /. Kukla, Jon, 1948- Richmond , 1981. x, 163 p. : ISBN

0-88490-075-4   LC Card 81-5051   DDC
328.755/0762/0922 B 19
JK83.V8 K84

**Speaker's Symposium on Language Disabilities,
Austin, Tex., 1966.** Proceedings. [Austin?
1966?] 48 p. ports. 27 cm. Cover title.   LC Card
81-471024   DDC 618.92/8552 19
*1. Language disorders in children - Congresses. 2.
Dyslexia - Congresses. 3. Learning disabilities -
Congresses.*
RJ496.L35 S63 1966

Spears, James R. H. Indiana's citizen soldiers .
Indianapolis , 1980. vi, 232 p. :   LC Card
80-620014   DDC 355.3/7/09772 19
UA180 .I53

Special Areas Soil Conservation Act of 1980 .
United States. Congress. House. Committee on
Agriculture. Subcommittee on Conservation and
Credit. Washington , 1980. iv, 105 p. :   LC
Card 81-600625   DDC 346.7304/67316/0262
347.3064673160262 19
KF27 .A3226 1980d

**Special Central America economic assistance ;
Compensation for hostages in Iran ;
International conference on Cambodia** . United
States. Congress. House. Committee on Foreign
Affairs. Washington , 1980. iii, 130 p. ;   LC
Card 80-601146   DDC 338.91/730596 19
KF27 .F6 1979k

**Special Commission Established to Study the
Laws and Regulations Governing the
Alcoholic Beverage Industry in the
Commonwealth of Massachusetts.** Report to
Governor Edward J. King, June 15, 1980 /
Special Commission Established to Study the
Laws and Regulations Governing the Alcoholic
Beverage Industry in the Commonwealth of
Massachusetts. Boston (Leverett Saltonstall
Building, Government Center, 100 Cambridge
St., Boston 02202) : Commonwealth of
Massachusetts, Alcoholic Beverages Control
Commission, 1980 [13] leaves ; 28 cm.   LC
Card 81-621083   DDC 343.744/0786631
347.4403786631 19
*1. Liquor laws - Massachusetts. 2. Brewing industry -
Law and legislation - Massachusetts. I. Title.*
KFM2775 .A847

**Special Committee on Developing NATO
Countries. Greek-Turkish Economic
Cooperation Project.** see Greek-Turkish
Economic Cooperation Project.

Special demographic analyses .
(CDS-80-2) Long, Larry H. Migration to
nonmetropolitan areas . Washington , 1980. p.
cm.   LC Card 80-607185   DDC 304.8/2/0973 19
HB1965 .L58

SPECIAL DISTRICTS - FLORIDA.
Florida. Legislature. House of Representatives.
Committee on Community Affairs. Independent
special districts in Florida . [Tallahassee]
[1980] vi, 35, [24] p. ;   LC Card 80-621966
DDC 352/.0073/09759 19
KFF11.82 .C65 1980

SPECIAL DISTRICTS - ILLINOIS.
Illinois. General Assembly. House of
Representatives. Counties and Townships
Committee. Special Districts Subcommittee. A
presentation of oral testimony received at
hearings of the Special District[s]
Subcommittee . [Springfield] [1980] xiv, 134
p. ;   LC Card 80-623558   DDC 352/.0073 19
KFI1211.4 .C686 1979

Redfield, Kent. Special districts in Illinois /.
[Springfield? Ill. , 1979- v. ;   LC Card 80-622899
DDC 352/.0095 19
JS451.I35 R42

Special districts in Illinois /. Redfield, Kent.
[Springfield? Ill. , 1979- v. ;   LC Card 80-622899
DDC 352/.0095 19
JS451.I35 R42

SPECIAL DISTRICTS - OREGON.
Oregon. Legislative Assembly. Senate. Interim
Task Force on Intergovernmental Coordination.
Report of the Senate Interim Task Force on
Intergovernmental Coordination. [Salem, Or.
(447 State Capitol, Salem, Or. 97310)] [1979]
xiv, 103 p. ;   LC Card 81-620891   DDC 352.0795
19
JS451 .O7 1979

**Special education and "related services" for
handicapped children /.** Turnbull, H.
Rutherford. [Chapel Hill] , 1980. 25 p. ;   LC
Card 80-624006   DDC 371.9/09756 19
LC4031 .T88

**A special follow-up report to the legislature
detailing State agency compliance with
selected bills passed during the 1978 and 1979
legislative sessions /.** Mississippi. Legislature.
Audit Committee. [Jackson, Miss.] [1980] x,
91 p. ;   LC Card 80-622027   DDC 353.976207/8 19
KFM7040 .A25 1980

Special Greenwich Street Development District
/. New York (City). Office of Lower
Manhattan Development. New York [1971] 55
p.:   **NYPL [JLF 80-1634]**

**SPECIAL GREENWICH STREET
DEVELOPMENT DISTRICT, NEW YORK
(CITY)**
New York (City). Office of Lower Manhattan
Development. Special Greenwich Street
Development District /. New York [1971] 55
p.:   **NYPL [JLF 80-1634]**

**Special investigation, political activities of MVC
employees /.** Mississippi. Legislature. Audit
Committee. [Jackson, Miss.] [1980] xi, 76 p. ;
LC Card 80-623578   DDC 353.9762001/6 19
HE5633.M7 M57 1980

Special oil taxes . United States. Congress.
Senate. Committee on Finance. Subcommittee
on Taxation and Debt Management Generally.
Washington , 1980 [i.e. 1981] iii, 222 p. :   LC
Card 81-601139   DDC 336.2/783338232/0973
19
KF26 .F5695 1980j

SPECIAL OLYMPICS - CONGRESSES.
Train-a-champ . Albany, N.Y. , c1979. vii, 95
p. :   LC Card 81-119267   DDC 371.9/044 19
GV445 .T73

Special pay for military veterinary officers .
United States. Congress. House. Committee on
Armed Services. Subcommittee on Military
Compensation. Washington , 1980 [i.e. 1981] ii,
59 p. :   LC Card 81-600607   DDC
331.2/81636089/0973 19
KF27 .A76392 1980

**Special publication of the South Dakota
Archaeological Society** .
(no. 2) The Future of South Dakota's past /.
Vermillion, S.D. , 1981. p. cm.   LC Card
81-14812   DDC 978.3/01 19
E78.S63 F87

Special report : schizophrenia, 1980 / National
Institute of Mental Health ; [editors-in-chief,
Samuel J. Keith, Loren R. Mosher]. Rockville,
Md. : U. S. Dept. of Health and Human
Services, Public Health Service, Alcohol, Drug
Abuse, and Mental Health Administration ;
Washington, D.C. : For sale by the Supt. of
Docs., U. S. G.P.O., 1981. 160 p. : form ; 27
cm. (DHHS publication. no. (ADM) 81-1064) Cover
title. "Reprinted from Schizophrenia Bulletin, vol. 5, no.
4, 1979 and vol. 6, no. 3, 1980"--P. 1. S/N
017-024-01048-1 Item 507-B-7 Includes bibliographies.
LC Card 81-601423   DDC 616.89/82 19
*1. Schizophrenia. I. Keith, Samuel J. II. Mosher, Loren
R., 1933-. III. United States. Alcohol, Drug Abuse, and
Mental Health Administration. IV. National Institute of
Mental Health (U. S.). V. Title: Schizophrenia, 1980.*
RC514 .S68

Special report on rural education. United States.
National Advisory Council on the Education of
Disadvantaged Children. Washington, D.C.
[1979] 82 p. ;   LC Card 80-602041   DDC
370.19/346/0973 19
LC5146 .U54 1979

Special report on veterans. West Virginia. Dept.
of Employment Security. Labor and Economic
Research. Charleston, 1978. 29 p. ;
NYPL [*ZT-1245]

Special reports in urban affairs series .
(no. 1) Griffin, Burt W. Cities within a city .
Cleveland, Ohio , c1981. viii, 133 p. :   LC Card
81-135043   DDC 352/.000473/0977132 19
JS773 .G74

**Special rules of practice and procedure and
substantive rules /.** Texas. Railroad
Commission. Gas Utilities Division. [Austin,
Tex.] [1980] 67 leaves ;   LC Card 80-622927

DDC 343.764/0926 19
KFT1488.A447 A2 1980

Special scientific report--wildlife .
(no. 230) Blus, Lawrence J. Breeding biology
and relation of pollutants to black skimmers
and gull-billed terns in South Carolina /.
Washington, D.C. , 1980. p. cm.   LC Card
80-607954   DDC 639.9/79/0973 s 598/.338 19
SK361 .A256 no. 230 QL696.C479

(no. 231) Craven, Scott R. The Canada goose
(Branta Canadensis) . Washington, D.C. , 1981.
66 p. :   LC Card 80-607166   DDC 639.9/79/0973 s
016.5984/1 19
SK361 .A256 no. 231 Z5333.O8 QL696.A52

(no. 233) Geis, Aelred D., 1929- Relative
attractiveness of different foods at wild bird
feeders /. Washington, D.C. , 1980. p. cm.   LC
Card 80-607831   DDC 639.9/79/0973 s 664/.764
19
SK361 .A256 no. 233 QL676.5

(no. 234) Establishment of seeded grasslands for
wildlife habitat in the prairie pothole region /.
Washington, D.C. , 1981. p. cm.   LC Card
81-607001   DDC 639.9/79/0973 s 639.9/79 19
SK361 .A256 no. 234

Special study on economic change .
(v. 10) Productivity, the foundation of growth .
Washington , 1980. v, 128 p.   LC Card
81-601972   DDC 338/.06/0973 19
HC110.I52 P77

**SPECIAL SUPPLEMENTAL FOOD
PROGRAM FOR WOMEN, INFANTS,
AND CHILDREN - ILLINOIS.**
Illinois. General Assembly. Legislative
Investigating Commission. The WIC program in
Illinois . Chicago, Ill. [1979] vii, 169 p. :   LC
Card 80-622568   DDC 362.8/283 19
HV696.F6 I35 1979

Special youth report, State of Virginia /.
Virginia. Employment Commission. Manpower
Research Division. Labor Market Analysis Unit.
Richmond, Va. [1979] 24 p. :   LC Card
79-625797   DDC 331.3/4/09755 19
HD6274.V8 V57 1979

Special Zoning District. New York (City). Office
of Downtown Brooklyn Development. Atlantic
Avenue, Special Zoning District /. Brooklyn, N.
Y. , 1974. 47 p. :   **NYPL [IRH 80-2879]**

**Specialists' Session on Chemical Kinetics
Calculations, University of California, 1968.**
[Papers] Berkeley, Calif. 1968. 1 v. (various
pagings) illus. 29 cm. Sponsored by Western States
Section, Combustion Institute and College of
Engineering, University of California at Berkeley.
Includes bibliographies.
*1. Chemical reaction, Rate of. I. Combustion Institute.
Western States Section. II. California. University.
College of Engineering. III. Title.*
NYPL [JSF 75-122]

SPECIE. see GOLD; MONEY; SILVER.

Specific problem analysis summary report . Utah.
Division of Water Resources. [Salt Lake City] ,
1977. 87 p., [1] leaf of plates :   LC Card
80-620890   DDC 333.9/1/09792 19
TC423.6 .U82 1977

SPECTOGRAPHY, MASS. see MASS
SPECTROMETRY.

SPECTRA, ABSORPTION. see ABSORPTION
SPECTRA.

SPECTROPHOTOMETERS - STANDARDS.
Mavrodineanu, Radu, 1910- Metal-on-quartz
filters as a standard reference material for
spectrophotometry--SRM 2031 /. [Washington,
D.C.] [1980] xiii, 110 p. :   LC Card 79-600192
DDC 602/.18 s 681/.414 19
QC100 .U57 no. 260-68 QC465

Spectrum anthology, 1957 to 1978. Santa
Barbara : University of California, Santa
Barbara, c1980. 236 p. : ill. ; 23 cm. Includes
bibliographical references. LC Card 80-623034   DDC
820/.8/00914 19
*1. American literature - 20th century. 2. English
literature - 20th century. I. Spectrum (Goleta, Calif.).*
PS535.5 .S6

Spectrum (Goleta, Calif.) Spectrum anthology,
1957 to 1978. Santa Barbara , c1980. 236 p. :
LC Card 80-623034   DDC 820/.8/00914 19
PS535.5 .S6

SPECULATION.
United States. Congress. House. Committee on Government Operations. Commerce, Consumer, and Monetary Affairs Subcommittee. Silver prices and the adequacy of Federal actions in the marketplace, 1979-80 . Washington , 1980. v, 1203 p. : LC Card 80-603499 DDC 332.63/28 19
KF27 .G634 1980c

United States. Congress. Senate. Committee on Banking, Housing and Urban Affairs. Margin requirements for transactions in financial instruments . Washington , 1980. vii, 850 p. : LC Card 80-603509 DDC 346.73/0922 19
KF26 .B39 1980r

SPEDY conferences. United States. Employment and Training Administration. Office of Youth Programs. Report on SPEDY conferences . [Washington] [1979] viii, 297 p. ; LC Card 79-603023
HD6273 .U514 1979a

SPEECH AND SOCIAL STATUS - MARYLAND - BALTIMORE.
Milller, Peggy J. (Peggy Jo), 1950- Amy, Wendy, and Beth . Austin , 1982. p. cm. ISBN 0-292-70357-0 LC Card 81-11656 DDC 401/.9 19
P118 .M54

SPEED LIMITS - LAW AND LEGISLATION - UNITED STATES.
United States. Congress. Senate. Committee on Environment and Public Works. Subcommittee on Transportation. To provide compliance with the national maximum speed limit . Washington , 1980. iii, 141 p. : LC Card 80-603026 DDC 343.73/0946 19
KF26 .E679 1980

SPEED2, a computer program for the reduction of data from automatic data acquisition systems /. Peacock, Richard D. [Washington, D.C.] [1979] 58, 68, 22, [7] p. ; LC Card 79-603987 DDC 602/.18 s 001.6 19
QC100 .U5753 no. 1108 QA276

SPEED2 (COMPUTER PROGRAM)
Peacock, Richard D. SPEED2, a computer program for the reduction of data from automatic data acquisition systems /. [Washington, D.C.] [1979] 58, 68, 22, [7] p. ; LC Card 79-603987 DDC 602/.18 s 001.6 19
QC100 .U5753 no. 1108 QA276

Speelpenning, B. Compiling fast partial derivatives of functions given by algorithms / by Bert Speelpenning. Urbana, Ill. : Dept. of Computer Science, University of Illinois at Urbana-Champaign, [1980] v, 75 p. : ill. ; 28 cm. ([Report] - UIUCDCSD-R-80 . 1002) "UILU-ENG-80 1702." "January 1980." Bibliography: p. 74. LC Card 80-623652 DDC 001.64 s 519.4 19
1. Numerical differentiation - Data processing. 2. Jacobians - Data processing. I. Series: Illinois. University of Urbana-Champaign. Dept. of Computer Science. Report , 1002. II. Title.
QA76 .I4 no. 1002 QA299

Speer, Roberta D. (joint author) Etchieson, Gerald Meeks. An archeological survey of certain tracts in and near Caprock Canyons State Park in eastern Briscoe County, Texas /. Canyon, Tex. , 1977. ii, 84, [66] p. : LC Card 78-623263 DDC 976.4/839 19
E78.T4 E83

Spencer, Elizabeth. Marilee : three stories / by Elizabeth Spencer. Jackson : University Press of Mississippi, 1981. 63 p. ; 20 cm. Originally published as part of: the author's The stories of Elizabeth Spencer. Garden City, N.Y. : Doubleday, 1981. CONTENTS. - Contents: A Southern landscape -- Sharon -- Indian summer. ISBN 0-87805-140-6 (lim ed.) LC Card 81-7444 DDC 813/.54 19
I. Title.
PS3537.P4454 M3 1981

Spencer, L. V. (Lewis Van Clief), 1924- Structure shielding against fallout gamma rays from nuclear detonations / L. V. Spencer, A. B. Chilton, C. M. Eisenhauer. [Washington, D.C.?] : U. S. Dept. of Commerce, National Bureau of Standards : For sale by the Supt. of Docs., U. S. G.P.O., 1980. xvi, 967 p : ill. ; 29 cm. (NBS special publication . 570) "Center for Radiation Research, National Measurement Laboratory." "University of Illinois." "Issued September 1980." S/N 003-003-02246-2 Includes bibliographical references and

indexes. LC Card 80-600120 DDC 602/.18 s 363.1/89 19
1. Atomic warfare. 2. United States - Civil defense. 3. Shielding (Radiation). 4. Gamma rays. 5. Radioactive fallout. 6. Atomic bomb shelters. I. Chilton, Arthur B. II. Eisenhauer, Charles. III. National Measurement Laboratory (U. S.). Center for Radiation Research. IV. United States. National Bureau of Standards. V. University of Illinois at Urbana-Champaign. VI. Title. VII. Series.
QC100 .U57 no. 570 UF787

Spencer Museum of Art, Lawrence, Kans. see **Helen Foresman Spencer Museum of Art.**

Spencer, Susan. Lobbying in Florida . [Tallahassee] [1981] 118, 62 columns ; LC Card 81-621917 DDC 328.759/078/025 19
JK4474.5 .L6

Spencer, Vivian Eberle, 1907- Raw materials in the United States economy, 1900-1977 / prepared under contract by Vivian Eberle Spencer ; U. S. Department of Commerce, Bureau of the Census, U. S. Department of Interior, Bureau of Mines. Washington, D.C. : U. S. Dept. of Commerce, Bureau of the Census : for sale by the Supt. of Docs., U. S. Govt. Print. Off., 1980. 90 p. : ill. ; 28 cm. (Technical paper - Bureau of the Census ; 47) LC Card 80-603173 DDC 333.7/0973 19
1. Raw materials - United States - Statistics. 2. United States - Industries - Statistics. I. United States. Bureau of the Census. II. United States. Bureau of Mines. III. Series: United States. Bureau of the Census. Technical paper , 47. IV. Title.
HF1052 .S63

Spencer, Wallace H. Environmental management of Puget Sound : certain problems of political organization and alternative approaches / Wallace H. Spencer. Seattle : University of Washington, [1971] 50 p. ; 28 cm. (A Washington sea grant publication ; WSG-MP 71-2) On cover: Washington Sea Grant Program. "November 1971." Bibliography: p. 43-44. LC Card 80-505800 DDC 333.91/009797/7 19
1. Water resources development - Puget Sound area. 2. Land use - Puget Sound area. 3. Water resources development - Washington (State). 4. Land use - Washington (State). I. Washington Sea Grant Program. II. Series: Washington sea grant publication, WSG-MP 71-2. III. Title.
HD1695.P83 S67

Spending reductions . United States. Congress. House. Committee on Interstate and Foreign Commerce. Washington , 1980. v, 217 p. ; LC Card 81-601122 DDC 353.0072/232 19
KF6231.A55 I557

Spendlove, Rex S. Utah Water Research Laboratory. Studies on viruses in water /. Logan, Utah , 1979. viii, 35 p. : LC Card 80-621126 DDC 628.3 19
QR48 .U8 1979

Spent fuel storage and disposal . United States. Congress. House. Committee on Interstate and Foreign Commerce. Subcommittee on Energy and Power. Washington , 1980. iv, 342 p. : LC Card 80-601371 DDC 344.73/04622 19
KF27 .I5542 1979p

SPENT REACTOR FUELS - STORAGE - LAW AND LEGISLATION - UNITED STATES.
United States. Congress. House. Committee on Interior and Insular Affairs. Subcommittee on National Parks and Insular Affairs. Nuclear spent fuel storage in the Pacific . Washington , 1980. iv, 233 p. : LC Card 80-602767 DDC 344.73/04622 19
KF27 .I5365 1979b

United States. Congress. Senate. Committee on Governmental Affairs. Subcommittee on Energy, Nuclear Proliferation, and Federal Services. Nuclear waste management reorganization act of 1979 . Washington , 1980. iv, 772 p. : LC Card 80-602895 DDC 344.73/04622 19
KF26 .G6728 1979m

SPHALERITE - NEW YORK (STATE) - ADIRONDACK MOUNTAINS.
Foose, M. P. Geology, geochemistry, and regional resource implications of a stratabound sphalerite occurrence in the northwest Adirondacks, New York /. Washington , 1981. p. cm. LC Card 81-607033 DDC 557.3 s 549/.32 19
QE75 .B9 no. 1519 QE391.S65

SPHRAGISTICS. see **SEALS (NUMISMATICS)**

Spicer, Robert A., 1950- The sorting and deposition of allochthonous plant material in a modern environment at Silwood Lake, Silwood Park, Berkshire, England / by Robert A. Spicer. Washington : U. S. Govt. Print. Off. : for sale by the Supt. of Docs., 1981. v, 77 p. : ill. ; 29 cm. (Geological Survey professional paper ; 1143) Bibliography: p. 66-69. LC Card 80-607854 DDC 560/.1/78 19
1. Paleobotany - Recent. 2. Paleobotany - England - Silwood Lake. 3. Paleolimnology - England - Silwood Lake. 4. Sedimentation and deposition. I. Series: United States. Geological Survey. Professional paper, 1143. II. Title.
QE931.3 .S64

Spielmann, Heinz, 1919- Structure, conduct, and performance of agricultural cooperative associations in Hawaii, 1977 / Heinz Spielmann and Jack T. Ishida. Honolulu : Hawaii Institute of Tropical Agriculture and Human Resources, College of Tropical Agriculture and Human Resources, University of Hawaii at Manoa, [1981] p. cm. (Research bulletin, 0073-098X . 193) LC Card 81-6275 DDC 334/.683/09969 19
1. Agriculture, Cooperative - Hawaii. I. Ishida, Jack T. II. Series: Research bulletin (Hawaii Institute of Tropical Agriculture and Human Resources) , 193. III. Title.
HD1484 .S67

Spiess, Arthur E. Willoughby, Charles Clark, 1857-1943. Indian antiquities of the Kennebec Valley /. Augusta, Me. , c1980. 128 p., [22] leaves of plates : ISBN 0-913764-13-2 LC Card 81-119254 DDC 974.1/22 19
E78.M2 W54 1980

SPIESS, GERALD F. - MEDALS.
United States. Congress. House. Committee on Banking, Finance and Urban Affairs. Subcommittee on Consumer Affairs. Legislation authorizing issuance of gold medals to Canadian Ambassador Kenneth Taylor, Simon Wiesenthal, Gerald F. Spiess, and commemorative medals for the United States Capitol Historical Society . Washington , 1980. iii, 73 p. ; LC Card 80-601297 DDC 344.73/091 347.30491 19
KF27 .B535 1980c

Spilerman, Seymour.
(joint author) Marwell, Gerald, 1937- Residence location, geographic mobility, and the attainments of women in academia /. Madison , 1976. 31 p. ; LC Card 78-623190 DDC 378/.12/0973 19
LB2331.72 .M37

(joint author) Singer, Burton. Some methodological issues in the analysis of longitudinal surveys /. [Madison] , 1976. 56 p. ; LC Card 78-624379 DDC 330/.723 19
H62 .S4775

SPIN (AERODYNAMICS)
United States. Congress. House. Committee on Science and Technology. Subcommittee on Investigations and Oversight. Spin recovery training . Washington , 1980 [i.e. 1981] iii, 239 p. : LC Card 81-601185 DDC 363.1/2492 19
KF27 .S3975 1980

Spin recovery training . United States. Congress. House. Committee on Science and Technology. Subcommittee on Investigations and Oversight. Washington , 1980 [i.e. 1981] iii, 239 p. : LC Card 81-601185 DDC 363.1/2492 19
KF27 .S3975 1980

Spinal cord regeneration . United States. Congress. House. Committee on Interstate and Foreign Commerce. Subcommittee on Health and the Environment. Washington , 1980. iv, 272 p. : LC Card 80-603794 DDC 344.73/0419 347.304419 19
KF27 .I5543 1980o

SPINAL CORD - REGENERATION - RESEARCH - LAW AND LEGISLATION - UNITED STATES.
United States. Congress. House. Committee on Interstate and Foreign Commerce. Subcommittee on Health and the Environment. Spinal cord regeneration . Washington , 1980. iv, 272 p. : LC Card 80-603794 DDC 344.73/0419 347.304419 19
KF27 .I5543 1980o

SPINAL CORD - WOUNDS AND INJURIES - RESEARCH GRANTS - UNITED STATES.
United States. Congress. House. Committee on Interstate and Foreign Commerce. Subcommittee on Health and the Environment. Spinal cord regeneration . Washington , 1980. iv, 272 p. :   LC Card 80-603794   DDC 344.73/0419 347.304419 19
KF27 .I5543 1980o

SPIRITS, ALCOHOLIC. see LIQUORS.

SPIRITUAL LIFE - MIDDLE AGES, 600-1500 - ADDRESSES, ESSAYS, LECTURES.
Bynum, Caroline Walker. Jesus as mother . Berkeley , c1982. p.cm.   ISBN 0-520-04194-1 LC Card 81-13137   DDC 255 19
BV4490 .B96

SPIRITUOUS LIQUORS. see LIQUORS.

Spiro Mounds, Okla. see Spiro site, Okla.

SPIRO SITE, OKLA.
Gardner, Joan S. The conservation of fragile specimens from the Spiro Mound, LeFlore County, Oklahoma . Norman, Okla. , 1980. iv, 75 leaves :   LC Card 80-623068   DDC 976.6/79 19
E78.O45 G34

SPIROMETRY.
O'Brien, Richard J. Basic data on spirometry in adults 25-74 years of age, United States, 1971-75 /. Hyattsville, Md. , 1980. p. cm.   LC Card 80-607829   DDC 312/.0973 s 312/.6 19
RA407.3 .A347 no. 222 RC734.S65

Spironello, Victor R. An evaluation of used aluminum shelter potlining as a substitute for fluorspan in cupola ironmelting / by V. R. Spironello and R. H. Nafziger. [Avondale, Md.] : U. S. Dept. of the Interior, Bureau of Mines, [1981] p. cm. (Report of investigations / United States Department of the Interior, Bureau of Mines) Bibliography: p.   LC Card 80-606836   DDC 622 s 672.2/4 19
1. Iron - Metallurgy. 2. Cupola-furnaces. 3. Fluorspar. 4. Aluminum - Recycling. I. Nafziger, Ralph H., joint author. II. United States. Bureau of Mines. III. Series: United States Bureau of Mines. Report of investigations ,. IV. Title.
TN23 .U43 TN707

Spisak, James W. Malory, Thomas, Sir, 15th cent. [Morte d'Arthur.] Caxton's Malory /. Berkeley , c1982. p. cm.   ISBN 0-520-03825-8 LC Card 81-7434   DDC 823/.2 19
PR2040 1982

Spitler, James F. International Demographic Data Center (U. S.) International population dynamics, 1950-79 . Washington, D.C. [1980] iv, 258 p. ;   LC Card 80-602932   DDC 312/.8 19
HA155 .I57 1980

SPITS (GEOMORPHOLOGY) - CALIFORNIA - MORRO BAY REGION.
California. Dept. of Water Resources. Southern District. Morro Bay sandspit investigation . [Sacramento, Calif.] [1979] viii, 64 p., [1] leaf of plates :   LC Card 79-626228   DDC 553.7/9/0979478 19
GB1025.C2 C14 1979c

Spitzer, Cary R. Viking orbiter views of Mars /. Washington, D.C. , 1980. vii, 182 p. :   LC Card 80-600167   DDC 356/.00634 19
QB641 .V55

SPOILS SYSTEM. see CIVIL SERVICE REFORM.

Spojené staty americké. see United States.

SPORES (BOTANY), FOSSIL.
Hueber, Francis M. Megaspores and a palynomorph from the lower Potomac Group in Virginia /. Washington , 1982. p. cm.   LC Card 81-607852   DDC 560 s 561/.13 19
QE701 .S56 no. 49 QE996

SPOROMORPHS. see PALYNOLOGY.

Sport fish investigations of Alaska : annual performance report for study no. G-III, Lake and stream investigations. Juneau : Alaska Dept. of Fish and Game, Sport Fish Division, [1977] 115 p. : ill. ; 28 cm. -- "Volume 18, July 1, 1976-June 30, 1977. Federal aid in fish restoration." Includes bibliographies. CONTENTS. - Chlupach, R. S. Population studies of game fish and evaluation of managed lakes in the Upper Cook Inlet drainage.--Peckham, R. D. A study of a typical spring-fed stream of interior Alaska.--Kramer, M. J. Evaluation of interior Alaska waters and sport fish with

emphasis on managed lakes, Fairbanks District.--Peckham, R. D. Evaluation of interior Alaska waters and sport fish with emphasis on managed waters.--Kramer, M. J. Enhancement of silver salmon stocks in interior Alaska waters through transplants of smolts from nursery lakes.   LC Card 78-621554   DDC 333.95/6/09798 19
1. Fishes - Alaska. 2. Fishery management - Alaska. I. Chlupach, Robert S. Population studies of game fish and evaluation of managed lakes in the Upper Cook Inlet drainage. 1977. II. Peckham, Richard D. III. Kramer, Michael, 1944-. IV. Alaska. Division of Sport Fish. V. Title: Lake and stream investigations.
QL628.A4 S67

Sport fish investigations of Alaska.
Alaska. Division of Sport Fish. Annual performance report for study no. G-I . Juneau [1977?] 93 p. :   LC Card 79-625181   DDC 333.95/611/09798 19
QL628.A4 A4 1977

Elliott, Steven T. A study of land use activities and their relationship to the sport fish resources in Alaska . Juneau [1977] 36 p. ;   LC Card 78-621567   DDC 333.95/6 19
SK367 .E44

Hubartt, Dennis. A study of land use activities and their relationship of [i.e. to] sport fish resources in Alaska . Juneau , 1978. 52 p. ;   LC Card 78-624204   DDC 333.95/6/09798 19
SK367 .H83

Pearse, Gary A. Inventory and cataloging . Juneau [1978] 76 p. :   LC Card 79-621586   DDC 333.95/6/09798 19
QL628.A4 P42

Sport fish resources in Alaska. Elliott, Steven T. A study of land use activities and their relationship to the sport fish resources in Alaska . Juneau [1977] 36 p. ;   LC Card 78-621567   DDC 333.95/6 19
SK367 .E44

Sport fish resources in Alaska. Hubartt, Dennis. A study of land use activities and their relationship of [i.e. to] sport fish resources in Alaska . Juneau , 1978. 52 p. ;   LC Card 78-624204   DDC 333.95/6/09798 19
SK367 .H83

Sporting magazine. Hounds in the morning . Lexington, KY , 1981. p. cm.   ISBN 0-8131-1411-X :   LC Card 81-51017   DDC 796/.0942 19
GV605 .H68

SPORTS AND STATE - RUSSIA.
United States. Congress. House. Committee on Interstate and Foreign Commerce. Subcommittee on Transportation and Commerce. Alternatives to the Moscow Olympics . Washington , 1980. iii, 83 p. ;   LC Card 80-602442   DDC 353.0085/8 19
KF27 .I5589 1980a

SPORTS AND STATE - UNITED STATES.
United States. Congress. House. Committee on Foreign Affairs. U. S. participation in the 1980 summer Olympic games . Washington , 1980. iii, 88 p. ;   LC Card 80-602748   DDC 796.4/8/0947431 19
KF27 .F6 1980d

United States. Congress. House. Committee on Interstate and Foreign Commerce. Subcommittee on Transportation and Commerce. Alternatives to the Moscow Olympics . Washington , 1980. iii, 83 p. ;   LC Card 80-602442   DDC 353.0085/8 19
KF27 .I5589 1980a

SPORTS - CONGRESSES.
National Conference of Senior Officials to Consider Unesco Recommendations on Physical Education and Sport, Washington, D.C., 1977. Report of the National Conference of Senior Officials to Consider Unesco Recommendations on Physical Education and Sport, held in Washington, D.C., November 16-18, 1977. [Washington] , 1979. vii, 143 p. ;   LC Card 80-601246   DDC 613.7 19
GV205 .N234 1977

SPORTS - ENGLAND - HISTORY - 19TH CENTURY - ADDRESSES, ESSAYS, LECTURES.
Hounds in the morning . Lexington, KY , 1981. p. cm.   ISBN 0-8131-1411-X :   LC Card 81-51017 DDC 796/.0942 19
GV605 .H68

SPORTS FOR WOMEN - LAW AND LEGISLATION - UNITED STATES.
More hurdles to clear . [Washington, D.C.] [1980] vii, 87 p. :   LC Card 80-602854   DDC 796/.01/94 19
KF4755 .A83 no. 63 GV709

SPORTS FOR WOMEN - UNITED STATES.
More hurdles to clear . [Washington, D.C.] [1980] vii, 87 p. :   LC Card 80-602854   DDC 796/.01/94 19
KF4755 .A83 no. 63 GV709

SPORTS - MEDALS - LAW AND LEGISLATION - UNITED STATES.
United States. Congress. House. Committee on Banking, Finance and Urban Affairs. Subcommittee on Consumer Affairs. Medals for the 1980 U. S. summer Olympic team . Washington , 1980. iii, 15 p. ;   LC Card 80-602976   DDC 344.73/099 347.30499 19
KF27 .B535 1980e

SPORTS STORIES - HISTORY AND CRITICISM.
Higgs, Robert J., 1932- Laurel & thorn . Lexington, Ky. , c1980. p. cm.   ISBN 0-8131-1412-8 :   LC Card 80-51014   DDC 810/.9/355 19
PS173.A85 H5

Spotts, Carol A. (joint author) Spotts, James V. Use and abuse of amphetamine and its substitutes /. Rockville, Md. , Washington, D.C. , 1980. xvi, 560 p. ;   LC Card 80-601718   DDC 362.2/9 19
RC568.A45 S68

Spotts, James V. Use and abuse of amphetamine and its substitutes / James V. Spotts, Carol A. Spotts. Rockville, Md. : National Institute on Drug Abuse ; Washington, D.C. : for sale by the Supt. of Docs., U. S. Govt. Print. Off., 1980. xvi, 560 p. ; 27 cm. (Research issues - National Institute on Drug Abuse ; 25) DHEW publication ; no. (ADM) 80-941 Bibliography: p. 511-549. Includes indexes.   LC Card 80-601718 DDC 362.2/9 19
1. Amphetamine abuse - Abstracts. 2. Amphetamine - Abstracts. I. Spotts, Carol A., joint author. II. Series: National Institute on Drug Abuse. Research issues - National Institute on Drug Abuse , 25. III. Title.
RC568.A45 S68

Spragens, Thomas A. The irony of liberal reason / Thomas A. Spragens, Jr. Chicago : University of Chicago Press, 1981. p. cm. Includes bibliographical references and index.   ISBN 0-226-76975-5 :   LC Card 81-3027   DDC 320.5/1 19
1. Liberalism. I. Title.
HM276 .S67

Sprague Library. see New Jersey. State College, Montclair. Sprague Library.

SPRAY NOZZLES.
High-pressure shrouded water sprays for dust control /. Avondale, Md. , 1981. p. cm.   LC Card 80-606801   DDC 622 s 622/.8 19
TN23 .U43 TN312

The spread of violent crime from city to countryside, 1955-1975 /. Fischer, Claude S., 1948- Berkeley , 1978. 37 p. :   LC Card 79-622125   DDC 364.1/5/0973 19
HV6783 .F57

Spreckelmeyer, Kent F., 1950- Marans, Robert W. Evaluating built environments . [Ann Arbor] , 1981. p. cm.   ISBN 0-87944-272-7 :   LC Card 81-6709   DDC 725/.1 19
TH6025 .M37

Spring characteristics of the western Roswell artesian basin . Davis, Paul, 1950- Las Cruces, N.M. [1980] viii, 93 p. :   LC Card 80-623165 DDC 333.91/009789 s 551.49/8 19
GB705.N6 N64 no. 116 GB1198.3.N6

Spring Conference "Relationships Between People and the Land," University of South Dakota, 1979. Report of papers presented at the spring conference, April 19, 20, 21, 1979 : theme, relationships between people & the land / Institute of Indian Studies, the University of South Dakota, Vermillion, South Dakota. [Vermillion, S.D.] : The Institute, [1979?] 211 p. ; 28 cm. Cover title. Includes bibliographies.   LC Card 80-621621   DDC 970.004/97 19
1. Indians of North America - Religion and mythology - Congresses. 2. Indians of North America - Education - Congresses. 3. Indians of North America - Art - Congresses. 4. Indians of North America -

Economic conditions - Congresses. I. South Dakota. University. Institute of Indian Studies. II. Title.
E98.R3 S724 1979

Springfield, Ill. State Library. see Illinois. State Library, Springfield.

Springfield, Ill. State Museum. see Illinois. State Museum, Springfield.

SPRINGS - NEW MEXICO - ROSWELL REGION.
Davis, Paul, 1950- Spring characteristics of the western Roswell artesian basin . Las Cruces, N.M. [1980] viii, 93 p. : LC Card 80-623165 DDC 333.91/009789 s 551.49/8 19
GB705.N6 N64 no. 116 GB1198.3.N6

Gross, Gerardo Wolfgang. Paul Spring, an investigation of recharge in the Roswell (N.M.) artesian basin /. Las Cruces, N.M. [1979] 135 p. : LC Card 80-622504 DDC 551.49/09789/43 19
GB705.N6 N64 no. 113 GB1199.3.N6

SPRINKEL, BERYL WAYNE, 1923-
United States. Congress. Senate. Committee on Finance. Nominations of Norman B. Ture and Beryl Wayne Sprinkel . Washington , 1981. iii, 17 p. ; LC Card 81-601959 DDC 353.2 19
KF26 .F5 1981e

SPRINKLER IRRIGATION - MICHIGAN - MUSKEGON CO.
McDonald, M. G. Hydraulic characteristics of an underdrained irrigation circle, Muskegon County wastewater disposal system, Michigan /. Reston, VA , 1981. p. cm. LC Card 80-607871 DDC 628.3/623 19
TD760 .M32

Spritzer, Allan David, 1941- (ed) Public sector labor relations. 1972- University, Ala..
NYPL [JLM 80-1034]

Sproul, Allan, 1896- Selected papers of Allan Sproul / edited by Lawrence S. Ritter. [New York] : Federal Reserve Bank of New York, [1980] xi, 233 p., [8] p. of plates : facsims., ports. ; 24 cm. "December 1980." Includes bibliographical references. LC Card 80-67915 DDC 332 19
1. Federal Reserve banks - Addresses, essays, lectures. 2. Monetary policy - United States - Addresses, essays, lectures. 3. Economic assistance, American - Addresses, essays, lectures. 4. International finance - Addresses, essays, lectures. I. Ritter, Lawrence S. II. Federal Reserve Bank of New York. III. Title.
HG2563 .S64

Squatter settlements and housing policy . Popko, Edward. [Washington, D.C.?] , Cambridge, Mass. , 1980. vi, 200 p. : LC Card 81-600768 DDC 363.5/8/09861 19
HD7325.A3 P658

SQUATTER SETTLEMENTS - COLOMBIA.
Popko, Edward. Squatter settlements and housing policy . [Washington, D.C.?] , Cambridge, Mass. , 1980. vi, 200 p. : LC Card 81-600768 DDC 363.5/8/09861 19
HD7325.A3 P658

Squid, Project. see Project Squid.

The Squires of San Quentin . Lewis, Roy V. [Sacramento, Calif.] , 1979. iii, 136 p. ; LC Card 80-621637 DDC 364.4/8 19
HV9105.C2 L483

SRI International. Consequences of alcohol & marijuana use : survey items for perceived assessment / editor, Joan Dunne Rittenhouse. Rockville, Md. : U. S. Dept. of Health, Education, and Welfare, Public Health Service, Alcohol, Drug Abuse, and Mental Health Administration, National Institute on Drug Abuse, Office of Medical and Professional Affairs ; Washington, D.C. : for sale by the Supt. of Docs., U. S. Govt. Print. Off., 1980. xii, 227 p. : port. ; 23 cm. (DHEW publication ; no. (ADM) 80-920) On cover: National Institute on Drug Abuse. "Developed by the SRI International and the Institute for Research in Social Behavior for the Office of Medical and Professional Affairs, National Institute on Drug Abuse." Includes bibliographies. LC Card 80-601619 DDC 616.86/1 19
1. Drug abuse - Complications and sequelae. 2. Marihuana - Physiological effect. 3. Alcohol - Physiological effect. 4. Mental health surveys. I. Rittenhouse, Joan Dunne. II. National Institute on Drug Abuse. III. National Institute on Drug Abuse. Office of Medical and Professional Affairs. IV. Institute for Research in Social Behavior (Oakland, Calif.). V.

Series: United States. Dept. of Health, Education and Welfare. DHEW publication, no. (ADM) 80-920. VI. Title.
RC564 .S18 1980

Sri Lanka. Perera, Lakshmi. [New York, N.Y. (485 Lexington Ave., New York 10017)] [1980] 30 p. ; ISBN 0-89714-011-7 (pbk.) : LC Card 80-138983 DDC 304.6/09549/3 19
HB3636.8.A3 P47

SRI LANKA - ECONOMIC POLICY.
Meier, Richard L. Gateway development . [Berkeley] [1980] 15 p. ; LC Card 80-623099 DDC 338.9549/3 19
HC424 .M35

SRI LANKA - POPULATION.
Perera, Lakshmi. Sri Lanka. [New York, N.Y. (485 Lexington Ave., New York 10017)] [1980] 30 p. ; ISBN 0-89714-011-7 (pbk.) : LC Card 80-138983 DDC 304.6/09549/3 19
HB3636.8.A3 P47

SRI LANKA - SOCIAL POLICY.
Meier, Richard L. Gateway development . [Berkeley] [1980] 15 p. ; LC Card 80-623099 DDC 338.9549/3 19
HC424 .M35

SRI LANKAN LITERATURE (ENGLISH) - 20TH CENTURY.
An Anthology of modern writing from Sri Lanka /. Tucson, Ariz. [1981], c1979. p. cm. ISBN 0-8165-0702-3 : LC Card 81-1140 DDC 891/.487/08 19
PK2871.E1 A5

SRT Architects/Planners. Recommended standards for courthouses in Missouri / [SRT Architects/Planners]. [Jefferson City, Mo.] : Missouri Supreme Court, [1979] 70 leaves : map ; 30 cm. Cover title. "November 1979." Based on a pilot study conducted for the Facilities Subcommittee of the Judicial Planning Committee, Missouri Supreme Court. LC Card 80-623576 DDC 725/.15 19
1. Court-houses - Missouri. 2. Court-houses - Missouri - Designs and plans. I. Missouri. Supreme Court. II. Missouri. Judicial Planning Committee. Facilities Subcommittee. III. Title.
KFM8259.C67 S16

STABILIZATION, ECONOMIC. see ECONOMIC STABILIZATION.

Stachura, Virgil J. Airblast instrumentation and measurement techniques for surface mine blasting / by Virgil J. Stachura, David E. Siskind, and Alvin J. Engler. [Washington, D.C.] : U. S. Dept. of the Interior, Bureau of Mines, [1981] p. cm. (Report of investigations) Bibliography: p. LC Card 80-607860 DDC 622 s 622/.31 19
1. Strip mining. 2. Blasting. 3. Blast effect - Measurement. I. Siskind, D. E., joint author. II. Engler, Alvin J., joint author. III. Series: United States Bureau of Mines. Report of investigations . IV. Title.
TN23 .U43 TN291

STACK GASES. see FLUE GASES.

Städtische Kunsthalle Düsseldorf. (Old Catalog form: Düsseldorf (City). Kunsthalle.) R.B. Kitaj /. Washington, D.C. , 1981. p. cm. LC Card 81-607809 DDC 759.13 19
N6537.K53 A4 1981

Staff data and materials relating to social and child welfare services /. United States. Congress. Senate. Committee on Finance. Washington , 1979. iv, 65 p. ; LC Card 79-603783 DDC 362.7 19
HV741 .U523 1979a

Staff data and materials relating to the International sugar stabilization act of 1979 /. United States. Congress. Senate. Committee on Finance. Washington , 1979. iii, 70 p. ; LC Card 79-601697 DDC 343.73/08756641 347.3038756641 19
KF1996.S8 A25 1979

Staff evaluation of the Legal Services Corporation's responses to the recommendations made by the U. S. General Accounting Office in three reports issued in 1978 and 1979 /. United States. Congress. Senate. Committee on Labor and Human Resources. Subcommittee on Employment, Poverty, and Migratory Labor. Washington , 1980. ii, 15 p. ; LC Card 80-602593 DDC

353.0084/5 19
KF336 .A717

Staff paper .
(no. 1) Archibald, Marybelle. Appropriative water rights in California . [Sacramento] , 1977. 63 p. ; LC Card 79-624937 DDC 346.79404/691 19
KFC790 .A97

Staff recommendations for simplication of tax rules relating to subchapter S corporations . United States. Congress. Joint Committee on Taxation. Washington , 1980. iii, 27 p. ; LC Card 80-602271 DDC 343.7306/8 19
KF6491 .A25 1980

Staff report, county officers' salaries /. Florida. Legislature. House of Representatives. Committee on Community Affairs. [Tallahassee] [1980] viii, 62, [51] p. ; LC Card 80-622644 DDC 352/.0051232/09759 19
JS451 .F6 1980

Staff report on consumer responses to cigarette health information /. Ippolito, Richard A. [Washington] , 1979. 64 p. ; LC Card 79-604242
HV5760 .I66   **NYPL [JLF 81-240]**

Staff report on corporate accountability . United States. Securities and Exchange Commission. Division of Corporation Finance. Washington , 1980. 782 p. ; LC Card 80-603877 DDC 346.73/0666 347.306666 19
KF1448 .A8837

Staff report on effects of restrictions on advertising and commercial practice in the professions. United States. Federal Trade Commission. Bureau of Economics. Economic report [on] effects of restrictions on advertising and commercial practice in the professions . Washington, D.C. [1980] viii, 120 p. : LC Card 80-602861 DDC 338.4/761775/0973 19
RE959.3 .U53 1980

Staff report on physician control of Blue Shield plans. Kass, David I. Physician control of Blue Shield plans . [Washington, D.C.] [1979] v, 139 p. ; LC Card 80-601542 DDC 368.3/8 19
RA413.3.B49 K37

A staff report on the oversight of the Occupational Safety and Health Administration with respect to grain elevator fires and explosions /. United States. Congress. House. Committee on Education and Labor. Subcommittee on Health and Safety. Washington , 1980. v, 151 p. : LC Card 80-601779 DDC 363.3/79 19
TH9445.G7 U53 1980

Staff report on the securities industry in 1977 /. United States. Securities and Exchange Commission. Directorate of Economic and Policy Research. [Washington] [1978] 21, [30] leaves : LC Card 80-602626 DDC 332.6/2/0973 19
HG4910 .U55 1978

Staff research report.
Gaylord, Kathleen A. History of taxation in Minnesota /. St. Paul, Minn. [1979] 93 p. : LC Card 80-621230 DDC 336.2/009776 19
HJ2415.A2 G39 1979

Staff studies .
(105) Round Table Conference on Capacity Utilization, Washington, D.C., 1978. Measures of capacity utilization, problems and tasks /. [Washington, D.C.] [1979] 259 p. : LC Card 79-603771 DDC 338.0973 19
HD69.C3 R68 1978

(107) Rhoades, Stephen A. Impact of bank holding companies on competition and performance in banking markets /. [Washington] [1979] 30 p. ; LC Card 80-602134 DDC 332.1/6 19
HG2491 .R46

Staff study of computer security in Federal programs /. United States. Congress. Senate. Committee on Government Operations. Washington , 1977. v, 2,8 p. : LC Card 79-602721
JK468.A8 U47 1977   **NYPL [JLE 81-477]**

Staff study of the emergency building temperature regulations / Permanent Subcommittee on Investigations of the Committee on Governmental Affairs, United States Senate. Washington : U. S. G.P.O., 1980 [i.e. 1981] v, 36 p. ; 24 cm. At head of title: 96th

Congress, 2d session. Committee print. "December 1980." Item 1037-A Includes bibliographical references. LC Card 81-600667 DDC 333.79 19
1. Buildings - United States - Energy conservation. 2. Energy policy - United States. 3. Temperature control. I. United States. Congress. Senate. Committee on Governmental Affairs. Permanent Subcommittee on Investigations.
TJ163.5.B84 S7

Staff study on management and cost issues associated with construction of the CRESAP coal liquefaction facility . United States. Congress. House. Committee on Science and Technology. Washington , 1978. vii, 348 p. : LC Card 79-601594 DDC 333.79/0973 s 338.4/76626622/0975416 19
KF27 .S397 1978 vol. 4 TP352

Staff technical report .
(STR 79-12) Virginia. State Council of Higher Education. Enrollment projections, Virginia's state-supported institutions, 1980-82 biennium. [Richmond, Va.] [1980] 70 p. ; LC Card 80-622506 DDC 378/.1059755 19
LC148 .V52 1980

(79-13) Virginia. State Council of Higher Education. Out-of-state institutions operating in Virginia, 1978-79. [Richmond] [1979] 42 p. ; LC Card 80-622044 DDC 378.73 19
LA227.3 .V57 1979

Staff working paper.
An Analysis of President Carter's budgetary proposals for fiscal year 1982 /. [Washington, D.C.] , 1981. xix, 167 p. ; LC Card 81-601303 DDC 353.0072/225 19
HJ2051 .A778

Federal credit activities . [Washington, D.C.] , 1981. xix, 106 p. ; LC Card 81-601827 DDC 353.0072/6 19
HJ8119 .F39

Ginsburg, Paul B. The CBO hospital cost containment model . [Washington, D.C.] , 1981. xiv, 36 p. ; LC Card 81-601120 DDC 362.1/1 19
RA981.A2 G49

Staffing patterns in the manufacturing industries in Indiana . Indiana. Employment Security Division. [Indianapolis] , 1976. xv, 85 p. : LC Card 77-621779
HD5725.I6 I53 1976 **NYPL [*XME-9536]**

Staffing patterns in wholesale and retail trade industries in Indiana . Indiana. Employment Security Division. Research and Statistics Section. [Indianapolis, Ind.] , 1978. viii, 67 p. : LC Card 79-625864 DDC 331.12/51381/09772 19
HD5725.I6 I53 1978a

Stafford, Charles J. (joint author) Blus, Lawrence J. Breeding biology and relation of pollutants to black skimmers and gull-billed terns in South Carolina /. Washington, D.C. , 1980. p. cm. LC Card 80-607954 DDC 639.9/79/0973 s 598/.338 19
SK361 .A256 no. 230 QL696.C479

STAGE. see ACTING; THEATER.

Stahmer, C. B. Butter cookies from Denmark : determination of no material injury or threat thereof in investigation no. 701-TA-51 (final) under section 104(a) of the Trade agreements act of 1979, together with the information obtained in the investigation / [prepared by C.B. Stahmer, assisted by Gerry Benedick, Jack Simmons]. Washington, D.C. : U. S. International Trade Commission, [1980] ii, 15, 50 p. ; 28 cm. (USITC publication. 1077) Cover title. LC Card 80-602669 DDC 382/.456647525 19
1. Bakers and bakeries - Denmark. 2. Cookies. I. Benedick, Gerald R. II. Simmons, Jack. III. United States. International Trade Commission. IV. Series: United States. International Trade Commission USITC publication, 1077. V. Title.
HD9057.D42 S7

Staiger, Roger. United States. Congress. House. Committee on Interstate and Foreign Commerce. LNG facility accident at Cove Point, Maryland . Washington , 1980. iii, 60 p. : LC Card 80-602216 DDC 363.1/79 19
TP761.L5 U54 1980

Stallings, Wayne. Confidentially and public access policy for local government / Wayne Stallings. Chapel Hill: North Carolina University, Dept. of City and Regional Planning, 1972. v, 32, 17

p. Microfiche (neg.) by NTIS. 1 sheet. 11 x 15 cm. (SHR-0000567) "Prepared for Charlotte Municipal Information System, N. C." Bibliography: p. 17 (3rd group)
1. Public records - Access control. 2. Privacy, Right of. 3. Freedom of information. I. Charlotte Municipal Information System. II. Title.
NYPL [*XME-9237]

Stamas, Brian. Virginia. Dept. of Corrections. Bureau of Research, Reporting and Evaluation. A study of recidivism. [Richmond] , 1977. i, 16 leaves ; LC Card 78-621733 DDC 364.3 19
HV7296 .A6 1977b

Stammerjohan, George R. California. Dept. of Parks and Recreation. Los Encinos State Historic Park . Sacramento , 1978. iv, 22 p. : LC Card 79-622127 DDC 979.4/93 19
F869.E53 C34 1978

STANDARD ATMOSPHERE.
United States Committee on Extension to the Standard Atmosphere. U. S. standard atmosphere, 1976 /. Washington , 1976. xv, 227 p. : LC Card 77-601158
TL557.A8 U55 1976 **NYPL [JSF 81-142]**

Standard international trade classification . United Nations. Statistical Office. New York , 1975. viii, 102, 15 p. ;
NYPL [*R-Econ 80-4009]

STANDARD OF VALUE. see MONEY.

Standard reference material. Velapoldi, R. A. A Fluorescence standard reference material, quinine sulfate dihydrate /. Washington, D.C. , 1980. xvi, 122 p. : LC Card 79-600119 DDC 602/.18 s 535/.35 19
QC100 .U57 no. 260-64 QC477

Standard reference materials . National Measurement Laboratory (U. S.) Washington, D.C. , 1980. xiv, 99 p. : LC Card 80-600091 DDC 602/.18 s 616.07/56 19
QC100 .U57 no. 260-69 RB46

Standard time zones of the world. United States. Central Intelligence Agency. [Washington , 1980] 1 map : LC Card 81-690683
G3201.B2 1980 .U5

STANDARDIZATION - INFORMATION SERVICES - CONGRESSES.
Symposium on International Standards Information and Isonet, National Bureau of Standards, 1979. Symposium on International Standards Information and ISONET . Washington, D.C. [1980] vii, 59 p. : LC Card 80-600073 DDC 602/.18 s 389/.6/0601 19
QC100 .U57 no. 579 T59.A1

STANDARDIZATION - INTERNATIONAL COOPERATION - CONGRESSES.
Symposium on International Standards Information and Isonet, National Bureau of Standards, 1979. Symposium on International Standards Information and ISONET . Washington, D.C. [1980] vii, 59 p. : LC Card 80-600073 DDC 602/.18 s 389/.6/0601 19
QC100 .U57 no. 579 T59.A1

Standards and Goals Conference, Augusta, Me., 1973. Maine. Law Enforcement Planning & Assistance Agency. Report of results of Standards and Goals Conference held at Civic Center, December 6, 7, and 8, 1973 /. Augusta, Me. [1974] ca. 150 p. ; LC Card 80-623219 DDC 363.2/09741 19
HV7571 .M22 1974

Standards and procedures for the administration of elementary and secondary adult education programs under the provisions of Education and training of welfare recipients, section 10:22.20, of the School Code of Illinois, and/or Federal adult education, section 304 of the Federal adult education act (public law 91-230, as amended) /. Illinois. Office of Education. Adult and Continuing Education Section. [Springfield, Ill.] [1977] 24 leaves ; LC Card 80-622539 DDC 374/.9773 19
LC5252.I5 I43 1977

STANDARDS, ENGINEERING - UNITED STATES.
Development of a probability based load criterion for American national standard A58 . [Washington, D.C.] , 1980. v, 222 p. : LC Card 80-600067 DDC 602/.18 s 690/.21 19
QC100 .U57 no. 577 TH845

Steiner, Bruce W. An institutional plan for

developing national standards . [Washington, D.C.] , 1979. vi, 17 p., [7] leaves of plates (2 fold.) : LC Card 79-600116 DDC 602/.18 s 620/.00218 19
QC100 .U556 no. 165 TA368

Standards for adult probation services in Texas. Texas Adult Probation Commission. [Austin, Tex.] [1980] iii leaves, 20 p. ; LC Card 80-623900 DDC 364.6/3/09764 19
HV9305.T4 T5 1980

Standards for determining child support obligations in Alaska /. Scott, Michael James, 1948- Anchorage [1978] 156 p. in various pagings : LC Card 79-622825 DDC 362.7/95 19
HV742.A4 S37

Standards for historic preservation projects. Morton, W. Brown. The Secretary of the Interior's standards for historic preservation projects . Washington, D.C. , 1979. vi, 46 p. ; LC Card 80-603172 DDC 720/.28/8 19
NA106 .M67

Standards for the education of exceptional children /. West Virginia. Division of Special Education and Student Support Systems. [Charleston] , 1979. iii, 109 p., [8] leaves of plates : LC Card 80-621051 DDC 371.9/09754 19
LC3982.W4 W47 1979

Standards of care in adult and juvenile correctional institutions . Levine, Mark. Washington, D.C. , 1980. vii, 40 p. ; LC Card 80-602119 DDC 016.365/973/0218 19
HV9304 .L44

Standby gasoline rationing plan. United States. Dept. of Energy. Office of Regulations and Emergency Planning. Washington, D.C. [Springfield, Va. , 1980] 114 p. ; LC Card 80-603194 DDC 333.8/232 19
HD9579.G5 U58 1980

STANDING ROCK INDIAN RESERVATION, S.D. AND N.D.
United States. Congress. Senate. Select Committee on Indian Affairs. Inheritance of trust or restricted land on the Standing Rock Sioux Reservation . Washington , 1980. iii, 14 p. ; LC Card 80-603114 DDC 346.7305/2/08997 19
KF26.5 .I4 1980l

Standing rules for conducting business in the United States Senate /. United States. Congress. Senate. Washington , 1979. iv, 77 p. ; LC Card 80-602241 DDC 328.73/05 19
KF4982 .S74

Standing rules of the Senate (pursuant to the adoption of S. Res. 274 and S. Res. 389, 96th Cong., Nov. 14, 1979, and Mar. 25, 1980, respectively). United States. Congress. Senate. Washington , 1980. iv, 69 p. ; LC Card 80-603245 DDC 328.73/05 19
KF4982 .S75

Stanfield, Robert E. The uses of paraprofessionals in the delivery of manpower and social services through public service employment: the Vermont experience / Robert E. Stanfield, principal author. [Montpelier, Vt.: Dept. of Employment Security], 1973. xiii, 64 p. Microfiche (neg.) by NTIS. 1 sheet. 11 x 15 cm. (PB-231 897) "Prepared for the Manpower Administration, U. S. Department of Labor." Bibliography: p. 63-64.
1. Paraprofessionals in social service - Vermont. 2. Public service employment - Vermont. I. Vermont. Dept. of Employment Security. II. Title.
NYPL [*XME-9293]

Stanford, E. Percil. Institute on Minority Aging, 3d, San Diego State University, 1975. Minority aging and the legislative process. - San Diego , c1977. xxi, 96 p. : **NYPL [JLF 81-1458]**

Stanford Research Institute. (Old Catalog form: Stanford Research Institute, Stanford University.)
Schmidt, Richard A. A study of surface coal mining in West Virginia. Menlo Park, Calif., 1972. xiii, 180 p. LC Card 72-611225
TN805.W4 S28 **NYPL [JLF 81-203]**

Setzer, Florence. The Seattle-Denver income maintenance experiment . [[Washington] , 1978. xv, 54 p. ; LC Card 78-603699
HC110.I5 S4 **NYPL [JLF 81-429]**

Stanford Research Institute. SRI International. Cost effectiveness of marine fire protection

programs : final report / by Stanford Research Institute International, Kenneth R. Oppenheimer, project leader ... [et al.]. ; prepared for U. S. Department of Commerce, Maritime Administration, National Fire Protection [i.e. Prevention] and Control Administration, National Bureau of Standards. [Washington] : The Department, 1978. xvii, 212 p. : ill. ; 27 cm. Bibliography: p. 208-212.   LC Card 79-602278
1. Ships - Fires and fire prevention - Cost effectiveness. I. Oppenheimer, Kenneth R. II. United States. Maritime Administration. III. United States. Maritime Fire Prevention and Control Administration. IV. United States. National Bureau of Standards. V. Title.
VK1258 .S18 1979   NYPL [JLF 81-262]

Lyman, Theodore R. Prevention, detection, and correction of corruption in local government . Washington , 1978. vi, 83 p. ;   LC Card 79-603441
JS401 .L95   NYPL [JLF 81-328]

Stanford University. Stanford Research Institute. see Stanford Research Institute.

Stankey, Daniel L. (joint author) Watts, Frank C. Soil survey of St. Lucie County area, Florida /. [Washington] [1980] vii, 183 p., [26] fold. leaves of plates :   LC Card 80-602562   DDC 631.4/7/75929 19
S599.F6 W37

Stankiewicz, Richard, 1922-
The sculpture of Richard Stankiewicz : a selection of works from the years, 1953-1979. [Albany, N.Y. : University Art Gallery, State University of New York at Albany, 1979] [28] p. : ill. ; 24 cm. "Organized by the University Art Gallery, State University of New York at Albany." Catalog of the exhibition held during 1979 and 1980 at the University Art Gallery and other institutions. Bibliography: p. [22]-[23]   LC Card 80-621808   DDC 730/.92/4 19
1. Stankiewicz, Richard, 1922- - Exhibitions. I. New York (State). State University, Albany. Art Gallery. II. Title.
NB237.S5793 A4 1979

STANKIEWICZ, RICHARD, 1922- - EXHIBITIONS.
Stankiewicz, Richard, 1922- The sculpture of Richard Stankiewicz . [Albany, N.Y. , 1979] [28] p. :   LC Card 80-621808   DDC 730/.92/4 19
NB237.S5793 A4 1979

Stanley, Daniel J.
Blanpied, Christian. Uniform mud (unifite) deposition in the Hellenic trench, eastern Mediterranean /. City of Washington , 1981. p. cm.   LC Card 81-607825   DDC 551.46/083/384 19
GC389 .B57

Sohm Abyssal Plain . Washington , 1981. p. cm.   LC Card 81-607056   DDC 551.46/4 19
GC383 .S64

Stanley, Donald A. Treatment of Florida surface waters for use in phosphate beneficiation / by D.A. Stanley, B.J. Scheiner, and P. Brown. [Washington, D.C.] : U. S. Dept. of the Interior, Bureau of Mines, [1981] p. cm. (Report of investigations) Bibliography: p.   LC Card 80-606882   DDC 622 s 661/.43 19
1. Water - Purification - Flocculation. 2. Water - Purification - Filtration. 3. Phosphate industry - Florida - Equipment and supplies. I. Scheiner, Bernard J., joint author. II. Brown, Pat M., joint author. III. Series: United States Bureau of Mines. Report of investigations . IV. Title.
TN23 .U43

Stanley, Donald W. (joint author) Kuenzler, Edward J. Nutrient kinetics of phytoplankton in the Pamlico River, North Carolina /. [Raleigh] [1979] xxii, 163 p. :   LC Card 79-626205   DDC 333.91/009756 s 589.4 19
HD1694.N8 N6 no. 139 QK571.5.N8

Stanley, Glenn M. Interim report [on the development of telecommunications for the State of Alaska] / Glenn M. Stanley. Juneau, Alaska : Alaska State Legislature, House of Representative, Committee on Commerce, [1980] 52 p. ; 28 cm.   LC Card 80-623344   DDC 384/.09798 19
1. Telecommunications - Alaska. I. Alaska. Legislature. House of Representatives. Committee on Commerce.
HE7791.A4 S72

Stanley, William J. (joint author) Petto, Anthony C. Environmental regulations and other factors

influencing industrial plant migrations /. Chicago, Ill. [1979] xxi, 106 p. ;   LC Card 79-626019   DDC 338.6/042/0977 19
HC107.A14 P47

Stapp, William F., 1945- Picture it! / William F. Stapp, Marjorie L. Share. Washington, D.C. : Smithsonian Institution Trraveling Exhibition Service, 1981. 95 p. : ill. ; 27 cm. "Originally conceived to accompany the exhibition, Photographs from the National Portrait Gallery." Bibliography: p. 94-95. Presents the development of photography accompanied by portraits illustrating various photographic techniques. Includes suggestions for organizing and maintaining a collection of prints.
    ISBN 0-86528-004-5   LC Card 80-28867   DDC 770 19
1. Photography. 2. Photography - History. I. Share, Marjorie L., 1950- joint author. II. Title.
TR149 .S68

Star, Deborah. Summary parole : a six and twelve month follow-up evaluation / Deborah Star. [Sacramento] : Research Unit, California Dept. of Corrections, [1979] x, 193 p. : ill. ; 29 cm. (Research report - California Department of Corrections ; no. 60) Bibliography: p. 181-183. "June 1979."   LC Card 80-620661   DDC 364.6/09794 s 364.6/2/09794 19
1. Parole - California - Evaluation. I. Series: California. Dept. of Corrections. Research report , no. 60. II. Title.
HV9305.C3 A32 no. 60

The Star lake archaeological project : anthropology of a headwaters area of Chaco Wash, New Mexico / edited by Walter K. Wait and Ben A. Nelson. Carbondale : Southern Illinois University Press, c1982. p. cm. (Publications in archaeology . 1) Bibliography: p. Includes index.   ISBN 0-8093-0949-1   LC Card 81-13596   DDC 978.9/83 19
1. Indians of North America - New Mexico - Star Lake region (McKinley County) - Antiquities. 2. Star Lake region (McKinlay County, N.M.) - Antiquities. 3. New Mexico - Antiquities. I. Wait, Walter K. II. Nelson, Ben A. III. Series: Publications in archaeology (Southern Illinois University at Carbondale. Center for Archaeological Investigations , 1.
E78.N65 S75

STAR LAKE REGION (MCKINLAY COUNTY, N.M.) - ANTIQUITIES.
The Star lake archaeological project . Carbondale , c1982. p. cm.   ISBN 0-8093-0949-1   LC Card 81-13596   DDC 978.9/83 19
E78.N65 S75

Starch INRA Hooper. Italy : a study of the international travel market : results of a sampling survey among residents of the seven largest cities in Italy, indicating their international travel habits and patterns, attitudes and preferences for foreign travel, and their demographic and trip characteristics / conducted by Starch INRA Hooper for United States Department of Commerce, United States Travel Service, Research & Analysis Division. [Washington] : The Division, 1978. vi, 65 p. : ill. ; 27 cm.   LC Card 78-601739
1. Tourist trade - United States. 2. Travelers - Italy. I. United States. Travel Service. Research and Analysis Division. II. Title.
G155.U6 S65 1978a

Stark, Phillip E. (joint author) Peavy, Howard S. The effects of non-sewered subdivisions on ground water quality /. Bozeman, MT [1980?] iv, 65, 22 p. :   LC Card 80-623175   DDC 363.7/394 19
TD224.M9 P33

Starobinski, Jean.
[1789, les emblèmes de la raison. English]
    1789, the emblems of reason / Jean Starobinski ; translated by Barbara Bray. Charlottesville : University Press of Virginia, 1981. p. cm. Translation of: 1789, les emblèmes de la raison. Bibliography: p. Includes index.   ISBN 0-8139-0915-5   LC Card 81-13135   DDC 709/.44 19
1. Neoclassicism (Art). 2. Arts and revolutions. 3. France - History - Revolution, 1789 - Influence. I. Title. II. Title: Seventeen eighty-nine, the emblems of reason.
NX452.5.N4 S7

Starting a labor-management committee in your organization . National Center for Productivity and Quality of Working Life. Washington , 1978. 55 p. ;   LC Card 78-603560
HD6490.L33 N37 1978

Starzyk, Patricia M.
Pharmacists in Washington State, 1977 / written by Patricia M. Starzyk. Olympia, Wash. : Center for Health Statistics, MS LL-15, Health Services Division, Dept. of Social and Health Services, [1979] 39 p. : map ; 28 cm. (Report - State of Washington, Center for Health Statistics)   LC Card 80-621514   DDC 331.11/916151/09797 19
1. Pharmacists - Washington (State) - Statistics. I. Series: Washington (State). Center for Health Statistics. Report - Washington State, Center for Health Statistics. II. Title.
RS67.U7 W37

Physical therapists in Washington State, 1978 / Center for Health Statistics, Health Services Division, Department of Social and Health Services ; Patricia M. Starzyk. Olympia, Wash. : The Center, [1978?] 35 p. : ill. ; 28 cm. "MS 11-15." Includes bibliographical references.   LC Card 80-621085   DDC 331.1/2916158/09797 19
1. Physical therapists - Washington (State) - Statistics. I. Center for Health Statistics (Washington). II. Title.
RM699.3.U6 S8

Staski, Edward. Wilson, Rex L. Bottles on the western frontier /. Tucson, Ariz. , c1981. p. cm.   ISBN 0-8165-0414-8 :   LC Card 81-11703   DDC 748.8/2/0973 19
NK5440.B6 W57

State activities to implement priority directions of the Hawaii state plan. Hawaii. Planning Division. [Honolulu] [1980] xx, 98 p. ;   LC Card 80-623120   DDC 338.9969 19
HC107.H3 H389 1980

State advisory committee handbook. United States. Commission on Civil Rights. Washington, D.C. , 1980. v, 26 p. :   LC Card 80-604132   DDC 353.0081/1 19
JC599.U5 U6 1980

State Agency Libraries of Texas. Guide to Texas State agency libraries / by State Agency Libraries of Texas and Texas Natural Resources Information System. Austin, Tex. : Texas Natural Resources Information System Task Force, 1980. vi, 65 p. : ill. ; 22 cm. "TNRIS-020."   LC Card 80-623699   DDC 027.5/025/764 19
1. Libraries, Governmental, administrative, etc. - Texas - Directories. I. Texas Natural Resources Information System. II. Title.
Z675.G7 S73 1980

The State agency resource compendium . Wohlford, Laura. Richmond, Va. [1979] 242 p. in various pagings ;   LC Card 80-622046   DDC 364/.07 19
HV8145.V8 W63

State agency rules mandated by or related to Federal statutes or regulations /. North Dakota. Legislative Council. [Bismarck] [1979] 5, [12] p. ;   LC Card 80-623546   DDC 342.784/0664 19
KFN9040 .A25 1979

State agricultural preservation programs . McCord, Thomas. Albany, NY [1979] iii, 49, 5 p. :   LC Card 80-622880   DDC 353.9/372421 19
HJ4181 .M32

STATE AID HIGHER EDUCATION - MISSOURI - STATISTICS.
Missouri. Coordinating Board for Higher Education. Missouri higher education budget recommendations, FY 1981 /. Jefferson City, Mo. [1980?] 102 p. ;   LC Card 80-623455   DDC 379.1/214/09778 19
LB2329.5 .M57 1980

STATE AID TO EDUCATION - FLORIDA.
Florida. Dept. of Education. Minimum student performance standards for Florida schools, 1980-81, 1981-82, 1982-83, 1983-84, 1984-85 . [Tallahassee, Fla.] c1979. iii, 128 p. ;   LC Card 80-621914   DDC 371.9/09759 19
LC4632.F6 F56 1979

STATE AID TO EDUCATION - ILLINOIS.
Illinois. State Aid Equalization Study. Selected expenditures in Illinois school districts /. [Springfield] [1980] 48 p. ;   LC Card 80-623952   DDC 379.1/535 19
LB2826.I3 I4768 1980

STATE AID TO EDUCATION - KANSAS - STATISTICS.
Kansas. State Dept. of Education. General State equalization aid for Kansas U. S.D.--1978-79. Topeka, Kan. [1979] iv leaves, 36 p. ;   LC Card

80-621760   DDC 379.1/22/09781 19
LB2828.5.K2 K36 1979

STATE AID TO EDUCATION - MAINE.
Maine. Interim Education Finance Commission.
The evolution of school finance in Maine .
[Augusta] , 1979. 22, [14] leaves ;   LC Card
79-623332   DDC 379.1/22/09741 19
KFM390 .A83

**STATE AID TO EDUCATION -
PENNSYLVANIA - STATISTICS.**
Pennsylvania. Dept. of Education. Estimates of
school district subsidies payable 1979-80 .
[Harrisburg] , 1979. v, 20 leaves ;   LC Card
80-621560   DDC 379.1/3/09748 19
LB2466.P4 P373 1979

**STATE AID TO EDUCATION - UNITED
STATES.**
Munse, Albert Ralph, 1923- State programs for
public school support /. Washington , 1965. vii,
113 p. ;   LC Card 80-502015   DDC 370/.973 s
379.1/22/0973 19
L111 .A614 no. 52 LB2828

**STATE AID TO MEDICAL EDUCATION -
UNITED STATES.**
Seymour, Scott. Rural health services .
[Lexington, Ky.], c1980. 8 p. ;   LC Card
80-140001   DDC 353.9 s 362.1/0425 19
JS308 .C6 no. 688 RA771.5

State support for health professions education /.
Washington , 1981. xiii, 109 p. ;   LC Card
81-601289   DDC 610/.7/1173 19
R745 .S74

**STATE AID TO PARAMEDICAL
EDUCATION - UTAH.**
Welsh, Wayne. A performance audit of the
WICHE student exchange program . [Salt Lake
City] , 1978. iii, 45 leaves ;   LC Card 78-622932
DDC 370.19/62 19
R847.6.U8 W44

**STATE AID TO PRIVATE SCHOOLS -
MARYLAND.**
Maryland. Committee to Study Private Higher
Education in Maryland. Private higher
education in Maryland . Annapolis , 1973. 159
p. in various pagings :   LC Card 77-621589
LB2342 .M344 1973   *NYPL [*XME-9542]*

**STATE AND AGRICULTURE. see
AGRICULTURE AND STATE.**

**STATE AND CHURCH. see CHURCH AND
STATE.**

State and county population forecasts by age and
sex, 1980-2000. Washington (State). Office of
Financial Management. Forecasting and Support
Services Division. [Olympia] [1980] [31] p. ;
LC Card 80-622047   DDC 312/.8/09797 19
HA693 .W36 1980

**STATE AND EDUCATION. see EDUCATION
AND STATE.**

STATE AND ENERGY. see ENERGY POLICY.

**STATE AND ENVIRONMENT. see
ENVIRONMENTAL POLICY.**

**STATE AND HOUSING. see HOUSING
POLICY.**

**STATE AND INDUSTRY. see INDUSTRY
AND STATE.**

**STATE AND INSURANCE. see SOCIAL
SECURITY.**

State and Local Fiscal Assistance Act of 1972 .
United States. Congress. House. Committee on
Government Operations. Intergovernmental
Relations and Human Resources Subcommittee.
Washington , 1980. vi, 909 p. ;   LC Card
80-603812   DDC 343.73/034 347.30334 19
KF27 .G664 1980

State and local government finances and the
changing national economy . United States.
Congress. Joint Economic Committee. Special
Study on Economic Change. Washington ,
1980. iii, 71 p. :   LC Card 80-603784   DDC
336.73 19
KF25 .E23 1980

State and national water use trends to the year
2000 . United States. Library of Congress.
Congressional Research Service. Washington ,
1980. x, 297 p. :   LC Card 80-602584   DDC
333.91/13/0973 19
TD223 .U53 1980a

**STATE AND NUTRITION. see NUTRITION
POLICY.**

**STATE AND TECHNOLOGY. see
TECHNOLOGY AND STATE.**

**STATE AND TRANSPORTATION. see
TRANSPORTATION AND STATE.**

**STATE AND URBAN TRANSPORTATION.
see URBAN TRANSPORTATION
POLICY.**

State/area plan on aging for the State of North
Dakota for fiscal year 1978 /. North Dakota.
Administration on Aging. [Bismark] [1977] ii,
118 p. :   LC Card 79-623544   DDC 362.6/09784 19
HV1468.N9 N67 1977

STATE BAR OF CALIFORNIA.
California. Legislature. Special Legislative
Investigating Committee on the State Bar.
Election of board of governors and the
president and state bar's legislative program .
Sacramento, CA (Box 90, Sacramento 95814]
[1980] iii, 174 p. :   LC Card 81-621668   DDC
340/.06794 19
KFC10 .S73 1980a

California. Legislature. Special Legislative
Investigating Committee on the State Bar.
Review and briefing on legislative analyst report
on the State Bar . Sacramento, Calif. [1980] i,
42 p. ;   LC Card 80-622945   DDC 340/.06/0794 19
KFC10 .S73 1980

State Bar of Texas. Legal Assistants Committee.
Legal Assistants Seminar on Civil Litigation,
Houston, Tex., 1979. Legal Assistants Seminar
on Civil Litigation, Houston, November
30-December 1, 1979 /. [Austin] [1979] ca.
250 p. in various pagings :   LC Card 80-621743
DDC 347.764/07 19
KFT1738.A2 L43 1979

State Bar of Texas. Peer Committee. Legal
Assistants Seminar on Civil Litigation, Houston,
Tex., 1979. Legal Assistants Seminar on Civil
Litigation, Houston, November 30-December 1,
1979 /. [Austin] [1979] ca. 250 p. in various
pagings :   LC Card 80-621743   DDC 347.764/07 19
KFT1738.A2 L43 1979

The State board test pool examination for
registered nurse licensure / prepared by the
Examination Committee of the National
Council of State Boards of Nursing ; by Eileen
A. McQuaid and Michael Kane. 1st ed.
Chicago, Ill. : Chicago Review Press, 1981. 122
p. ; 28 cm.   ISBN 0-914091-02-6 (pbk.) :   LC Card
81-6107   DDC 610.73/076 19
*1. Nursing - Examinations, questions, etc. 2. National
Council of State Boards of Nursing (U. S.) -
Examinations - Study guides. I. McQuaid, Eileen A. II.
Kane, Michael T. III. National Council of State Boards
of Nursing (U. S.) Examination Committee.*
RT55 .S73

STATE BONDS - NEW JERSEY.
New Jersey. Legislature. General Assembly.
Committee on Agriculture and Environment.
Public hearing before Assembly Agriculture and
Environment Committee, on Assembly no. 1818
(Natural resources bond issue) . [Trenton]
[1980] 24, 6 p. ;   LC Card 80-623796   DDC
344.749/046 347.490446 19
KFN1811.4 .A3 1980a

New Jersey. Legislature. General Assembly.
Committee on Institutions, Health & Welfare.
Public hearing before Assembly Institutions,
Health, and Welfare Committee on A-1823
(Institutional bond issue) . [Trenton] [1980] 3
v. ;   LC Card 80-623827   DDC 336.3/1 19
KFN1811.4 .I58 1980

**STATE BONDS - TAXATION - UNITED
STATES - STATES.**
United States. Congressional Budget Office.
State profits on tax-exempt student loan bonds .
[Washington] [1980] xvi, 57 p. ;   LC Card
80-601571   DDC 379.1/214/0973 19
HG4946 .U52 1980

STATE BONDS - UNITED STATES - STATES.
United States. Congressional Budget Office.
State profits on tax-exempt student loan bonds .
[Washington] [1980] xvi, 57 p. ;   LC Card
80-601571   DDC 379.1/214/0973 19
HG4946 .U52 1980

State-building in modern China . Bedeski, Robert
E. [Berkeley] , c1981. x, 181 p. ;   ISBN

0-912966-28-9 (pbk.) :   LC Card 80-85389
JQ1509 1928 .B42

State Capitol Historical Association of
Washington. see Washington (State). State
Capitol Historical Association.

**STATE, COMMUNIST. see COMMUNIST
STATE.**

State delegation on Tennessee Veterans'
Administration medical services . United States.
Congress. House. Committee on Veterans'
Affairs. Subcommittee on Medical Facilities and
Benefits. Washington , 1980. iii, 57 p. ;   LC
Card 80-603034   DDC 355.1/156/09768 19
KF27 .V459 1980b

State directory of higher education institutions
and agencies in Maryland. Annapolis,
Maryland Council for Higher Education. 23 cm.
Annual.   LC Card 75-643681
*1. Universities and colleges - Maryland - Directories. 2.
Educational associations - Maryland - Directories. I.
Maryland. Council for Higher Education.*
NYPL [JLL 80-277]

**STATE ENCOURAGEMENT OF SCIENCE,
LITERATURE AND ART - ALASKA.**
Alaska. Division of Arts and Crafts (Proposed)
Final report. [Juneau] 1973. ii, 116 p. :
NYPL [JLF 80-995]

State financial assistance due New York City for
City University community colleges, fiscal year
ended June 30, 1975. New York (State).
Division of Audits and Accounts. [Albany]
[1979] 3, 27 leaves ;   LC Card 80-620516   DDC
379.1/22/097471 19
LB2826.5.N5 N46 1979

State forest practice laws and regulations .
Ellefson, Paul V. [St. Paul] , 1980. 42 p. ;   LC
Card 80-623522   DDC 346.77604/675 19
KFM5649 .E4

State forms management program /. Washington
(State). Legislature. Budget Committee.
Olympia [1979] v, 57 p. ;   LC Card 79-626055
DDC 353.97970072/32 s 353.97970071/4 19
HJ11 .W2453 no. 79-4 JK9249.P36

State functional plan for health . Hawaii. Dept.
of Health. [Honolulu] [1980] xiv, 280, [110]
p. :   LC Card 80-623119   DDC 362.1/09969 19
RA395.A4 H32 1980

**State Geological Survey of Kansas.
Bulletin .**
(219) . Franks, Paul C. Paralic to fluvial record
of an early Cretaceous marine
transgression--Longford Member, Kiowa
Formation, north-central Kansas /.
[Lawrence, Kan.] [1979] 55 p. :   LC Card
80-621776   DDC 557.81 s 551.7/7 19
QE113 .A2 no. 219 QE686

STATE GOVERNMENT.
United States. Civil Service Commission.
Bureau of Intergovernmental Personnel
Programs. Guidelines for qualitative evaluations
of personnel operations in state and local
governments. [Washington] 1974. 21 p.
NYPL [*XME-9074]

State Government Energy Conservation (Wis.)
Energy use in state-owned facilities for fiscal
year 1978-79 . [Madison, Wis.] [1980] 15 p. :
LC Card 80-623506   DDC 333.79 19
HD9502.U53 W584

State government in Georgia /. Hepburn,
Lawrence R., 1940- Athens, GA [1981] p. cm.
LC Card 80-24403   DDC 320.4758 19
JK4325 1981 .H46

State Government Productivity Research Center
(U. S.) Berry, Frances Stokes. New Jersey's
productivity improvement investment account.
Lexington, Ky. (P.O. Box 11910, Lexington
40578) , 1980. 12 p. ;   LC Card 81-144027   DDC
353.9749001/47 19
JK3560.L3 B47

STATE GOVERNMENTS.
Mabbutt, Richard. Federal and State mandates .
[Boise? Idaho] , 1977. iii, 40 leaves ;   LC Card
78-621711   DDC 352.073 19
JS348 .M23

Montana. Legislature. Study Committee on
Energy Forecasting. Energy forecasting--a role
for state government? . Helena, Mont. (Room
138, State Capitol, Helena 59620) , 1980. vii,
55, [28] p. ;   LC Card 81-621337   DDC 333.79/13

19
HD9502.U53 M942 1980

STATE GOVERNMENTS - OFFICIALS AND EMPLOYEES.
Vause, W. Gary. Labor arbitration in state and local government /. Tallahassee, Fla. , 1981. viii, 214 p. : LC Card 81-622006 DDC 344.73/0189143 347.304189143 19
KF3450.P8 V38

STATE GOVERNMENTS - OFFICIALS AND EMPLOYEES - PENSIONS.
United States. Congress. House. Committee on Education and Labor. Subcommittee on Labor-Management Relations. Welfare and Pension Plans Task Force. Hearings on the Public Employee Retirement Income Security Act of 1980 . Washington , 1980 [i.e. 1981] vii, 1726 p. : LC Card 81-601635 DDC 342.73/0686 347.302686 19
KF27 .E347 1980g

State health plan. Hawaii. Dept. of Health. State functional plan for health . [Honolulu] [1980] xiv, 280, [110] p. : LC Card 80-623119 DDC 362.1/09969 19
RA395.A4 H32 1980

State health plan, Commonwealth of Virginia /. Virginia. Statewide Health Coordinating Council. [Richmond, Va.] [1979] 2 v. : LC Card 80-620762 DDC 362.1/09755 19
RA395.A4 V88 1979

State health plan for Alaska. Alaska. Statewide Health Coordinating Council. Approved State health plan for Alaksa₂ /. Juneau, Alaska , 1980. 455 p. in various pagings : LC Card 80-622664 DDC 362.1/09798 19
RA395.A4 A45 1980

State Highway Department, year ended June 30, 1979. Missouri. State Auditor. Jefferson City [1980] ii, 53 p. ; LC Card 80-623985 DDC 353.97780072/32 19
HE356.M8 M45 1980

The State highway finance outlook /. Cooper, Thomas W. [Washington] , 1978. viii, 101 p. : LC Card 79-601548
HE355 .C66

State Historical Society, Boise, Idaho. see Idaho. State Historical Society.

State Historical Society of Iowa. see Iowa. State Historical Society.

State Historical Society of Michigan. see Michigan State Historical Society.

State housing plan . Hawaii. Housing Authority. [Honolulu] [1980] 393 p. in various pagings : LC Card 80-622668 DDC 363.5/8/09969 19
HD7303.H3 H37 1980

State implementation plan for air quality . Maine. Dept. of Environmental Protection. [Augusta] [1980- 1 v. : LC Card 80-623534 DDC 363.7/39256/09741 19
TD883.5.M2 M33 1980

State implementation plan under section III of the Federal Clean air act for control of total fluoride emmissions from existing phosphate fertilizer plants. Louisiana. Dept. of Natural Resources. Baton Rouge, LA [1980] 21 p. ; LC Card 80-621676 DDC 363.7/392 19
TD888.F45 L68 1980

State Justice Institute act of 1979 . United States. Congress. Senate. Committee on the Judiciary. Subcommittee on Jurisprudence and Governmental Relations. Washington , 1980. iv, 229 p. ; LC Card 80-602173 DDC 347.73 19
KF26 .J8556 1979

State Justice Institute/annual message of chief justice--1980 . United States. Congress. House. Committee on the Judiciary. Subcommittee on Courts, Civil Liberties, and the Administration of Justice. Washington , 1981. iii, 276 p. ; LC Card 81-601790 DDC 347.73 347.307 19
KF27 .J857 1980c

STATE JUSTICE INSTITUTE (U. S.)
United States. Congress. House. Committee on the Judiciary. Subcommittee on Courts, Civil Liberties, and the Administration of Justice. State Justice Institute/annual message of chief justice--1980 . Washington , 1981. iii, 276 p. ; LC Card 81-601790 DDC 347.73 347.307 19
KF27 .J857 1980c

United States. Congress. Senate. Committee on

the Judiciary. Subcommittee on Jurisprudence and Governmental Relations. State Justice Institute act of 1979 . Washington , 1980. iv, 229 p. ; LC Card 80-602173 DDC 347.73 19
KF26 .J8556 1979

State land disposal policy study /. Northern Resource Management. [Juneau, Alaska] [1980] 90, [38] p. : LC Card 80-623199 DDC 333.1/6/09798 19
HD243.A3 N67 1980

State lands inventory; ownership, control and use summary. Washington (State). Office of Program Planning and Fiscal Management. 1970- [Olympia]. LC Card 73-649668
NYPL [JLM 80-900]

State law and rules and regulations applicable to the dry cleaning industry . New Mexico. Laws, statutes, etc. Santa Fe, N.M. [1952] 35 p. ; LC Card 79-119739 DDC 343.789/07866712/02632 347.8903786671202632 19
KFN3882.L38 A32 1952

State legal standards for the provision of public education . Lawyers' Committee for Civil Rights Under Law. Washington , 1978. 153 p. ; LC Card 79-600821
KF4120 .L37 **NYPL [JLF 81-35]**

State legislatures . Holt, Dorothy. Albany, N.Y. [1980] 9 p. ; LC Card 80-622699 DDC 016.32873 19
Z7164.R4 H6 JK2488

STATE LIABILITY. see GOVERNMENT LIABILITY.

State-local finances in recession and inflation . United States. Advisory Commission on Intergovernmental Relations. Washington , 1979. viii, 82 p. : LC Card 79-602933
HJ275 .U52 1979a **NYPL [JLF 81-450]**

STATE-LOCAL FISCAL RELATIONS. see INTERGOVERNMENTAL FISCAL RELATIONS.

STATE-LOCAL RELATIONS - MONTANA.
The Effects of state-owned property on local governments . Helena, Mont. (Room 138, State Capitol, Helena 59601) [1980] i, 18, 36, [31] p. ; LC Card 81-621004 DDC 336.2/014/786 19
HJ545 .E33

State manufacturing enterprise in a mixed economy . Wålstedt, Bertil. Baltimore , c1980. xxii, 354 p. : ISBN 0-8018-2226-2 : LC Card 78-21398
HD4276.7 .W34 **NYPL [JLE 81-426]**

State of Alaska coal haul road system report /. Alaska. Dept. of Transportation and Public Facilities. Transportation Planning Division. [Juneau] [1978?] 27, [13] leaves : LC Card 79-622823 DDC 333.8/22152/09798 19
HE199.5.C6 A44 1978

The State of Alaska comprehensive plan . Alaska. Division of Policy Development and Planning. [Juneau] [1978?] 66 leaves ; LC Card 80-622385 DDC 363.5/09798 19
HD7303.A4 A55 1978

State of Alaska proposed revisions to air quality control plan. Alaska. Dept. of Environmental Conservation. [Juneau] [1977-1979] 2 v. : LC Card 80-622386 DDC 363.7/39256/09798 19
TD883.5.A4 A43 1979

The State of Arizona affirmative action plan /. Arizona. Office of Affirmative Action. [Phoenix, Ariz.] [1979?] 35 p. : LC Card 80-622646 DDC 353.9791001/04 19
HF5549.5.A34 A74 1979

State of Colorado. United States. Geological Survey. Colorado, base map with highways /. Reston, Va. , 1980. 1 map :. LC Card 81-691605
G4310 1980 .U5

The state of competition in gasoline marketing . Delaney, James B. Washington, D.C. [Springfield, Va.] 1980- v. : LC Card 80-602541 DDC 338.6/048 19
HD9565 .D44

State of Connecticut licensure of coordination, assessment, and monitoring agency regulations, effective September 20, 1978. Connecticut. Community Nursing and Home Health Division. Hartford [1978?] 15 p. ; LC Card 79-622645 DDC 344.746/03214 19
KFC3963.H65 A32 1978

State of Florida air implementation plan. Florida. Dept. of Pollution Control. Tallahassee [1972] 592 p. in various pagings : LC Card 80-623778 DDC 363.7/379456/09759 19
TD883.5.F6 F55 1972

State of Georgia supplemental budget for the fiscal year ending June 30, 1974. Georgia. Office of Planning and Budget. [Atlanta , 1974] 13 p. ; LC Card 80-623221 DDC 353.97580072/254 19
HJ2053.G4 G47 1974

State of Hawaii airport statistics /. Tamanaha, Myra. [Honolulu] [1978] 59 leaves : LC Card 78-622125 DDC 387.7/36/09969 19
HE9813.H4 T35

State of judiciary address, S. 2483 . United States. Congress. Senate. Committee on the Judiciary. Subcommittee on Jurisprudence and Governmental Relations. Washington , 1980. iii, 35 p. ; LC Card 81-600615 DDC 347.73/00262 347.30700262 19
KF26 .J8556 1980

A state of knowledge on Indian water rights in Kansas . Collins, D. Cheryl. Manhattan, Kan. , 1980. 44 p. : LC Card 80-623437 DDC 346.78104/32 347.8106432 19
KFK505.6.W38 C64

State of Louisiana primary and general election returns, October 27, 1979, and December 8, 1979 /. Louisiana. Dept. of State. [Baton Rouge] [1980?] ca 600 p. ; LC Card 80-622571 DDC 324.9763/063 19
JK4793 1979 .L68

State of Louisiana supplemental energy conservation plan. Louisiana. Dept. of Natural Resources. State supplemental energy conservation plan . Baton Rouge, La. , 1979. 50 p. in various pagings : LC Card 80-620853 DDC 333.79/16/09763 19
TJ163.4.U6 L67 1979

State of Maine elevator and tramway rules . Maine. Board of Elevator and Tramway Safety. Augusta, Me. [1979?] 91 p. ; LC Card 80-624243 DDC 343.741/07872183 347.41037872183 19
KFM459.7 .A4 1979

State of Maine elevators and tramways, revised law and rules. Maine. Board of Elevator and Tramway Safety. State of Maine elevator and tramway rules . Augusta, Me. [1979?] 91 p. ; LC Card 80-624243 DDC 343.741/07872183 347.41037872183 19
KFM459.7 .A4 1979

State of Maine highway safety plan for fiscal year 1980 /. Maine. Dept. of Transportation. Bureau of Safety. [Augusta] [1979] 141, [38] leaves : LC Card 80-622557 DDC 363.1/256/09741 19
HE5614.3.M2 M34 1979

State of Maine public full-time professional staff average salaries for the 1978-79 school year /. Maine. Dept. of Educational and Cultural Services. Division of Planning and Management Information. Local Administrative Unit. [Augusta] [1979?] iv, 47 p. ; LC Card 79-622302 DDC 331.2/813711/009741 19
LB2842.2 .M338 1979

State of Maine, rules of the Department of Human Services relating to mobile home parks. Maine. Division of Health Engineering. [Augusta, Me.] [1977?] 20 p. : LC Card 80-622535 DDC 346.74104/3 19
KFM282.T68 A32 1977

State of Mississippi income tax law and regulations . Mississippi. Laws, statutes, etc. Jackson, Miss. [1980] 367 p. ; LC Card 80-622993 DDC 343.76205/2/02632 19
KFM7075.A334 A2 1980

State of Nevada air quality regulations adopted by Nevada State Environmental Commission ; administered by Department of Conservation and Natural Resources, Division of Environmental Protection. Nevada. State Environmental Commission. [Carson City, Nev.] [1980] ca. 100 p. in various pagings ; LC Card 80-622609 DDC 344.793/046342 19
KFN958.A436 A2 1980

State of Nevada allied health manpower inventory and planning estimates for 1975 and 1980. Nevada. State Comprehensive Health

Planning. [Carson City] [1975] 133 p. ; LC Card 80-623229 DDC 331.12/9161/09793 19
RA410.8.N3 N48 1975

State of Nevada, Department of Administration, Budget Division, audit report, fiscal year ended June 30, 1977. Nevada. Legislative Auditor. Carson City, Nev. [197-] 18 leaves ; LC Card 78-623421 DDC 353.97930072/32 19
HJ2053.N4 N44 1970z

State of Nevada, Department of Conservation and Natural Resources, Division of State Lands audit report, fiscal year ended June 30, 1977. Nevada. Legislative Auditor. Carson City, Nev. [1977?] 21 leaves ; LC Card 78-623424 DDC 353.97930072/32 19
HD243.N4 N47 1977

State of Nevada, Department of Energy audit report, fiscal year ended June 30, 1979. Nevada. Legislative Auditor. Carson City, Nev. [1980] 23 leaves ; LC Card 80-621823 DDC 353.97930072/32 19
HD9502.U53 N464 1980

State of Nevada Public Service Commission audit report, fiscal year ended June 30, 1977. Nevada. Legislative Auditor. Carson City, Nev. [1978] 33 leaves ; LC Card 78-623423 DDC 353.97930072/32 19
HD2767.N29 N47 1978

State of Nevada Public Works Board audit report, fiscal year ended June 30, 1978. Nevada. Legislative Auditor. Carson City, Nev. [1979?] 26 leaves ; LC Card 80-621821 DDC 353.97930072/32 19
TA24.N3 N48 1979

State of New Hampshire general highway maps /. New Hampshire. Dept. of Public Works and Highways. Planning and Economics Division. [Concord] [1977?] [78] leaves of plates : LC Card 79-625810 DDC 912/.742
G1221.P2 N4 1977

State of New Jersey financial report year ended June 30, 1979. New Jersey. Division of Budget and Accounting. [Trenton, N.J.] , 1979?] 53 p. ; LC Card 80-621346 DDC 353.97490072/31 19
HJ585 .N36 1979

State of New Mexico surface coal mining regulations, Rule 80-1 /. New Mexico. Mining and Minerals Division. Santa Fe, N.M. [1980] xvi, 262 p. ; LC Card 80-624203 DDC 346.78904/68 347.8906468 19
KFN3855.5.A435 A2 1980

State of New York legislative document. New York (State). Legislature. Senate. Standing Committee on Cities and City of New York. Certiorari . [Albany, N.Y.] , 1980. 119 p. ; LC Card 80-624086 DDC 353.7470072/421 19
KFN5010.72 .C57 1980

State of Ohio unified correctional master plan. Prototype Incorporated. [Columbus, Ohio] [1979] 241 p. in various pagings ; LC Card 80-621188 DDC 364.6/09771 19
HV9305.O2 P76 1979

State of Oregon. United States. Geological Survey. Oregon, base map with highways and contours /. Reston, Va. , 1979. 1 map : LC Card 81-691602
G4290 1979 .U5

State of Rhode Island and Providence Plantations, preliminary survey report, Town of Glocester /. Nebiker, Walter. Providence, R. I. , 1980. iv, 62 leaves, [14] leaves of plates :
NYPL [IQK (Glocester) 81-780]

The State of Texas water quality inventory /. Texas. Dept. of Water Resources. Construction Grants and Water Quality Planning Division. [Austin] , 1980. 540 p., 1 fold. leaf of plates : LC Card 80-622419 DDC 363.7/3942/09764 19
TD224.T4 T36 1980a

The state of the city, 1975 /. Los Angeles. Community Analysis Bureau. [Los Angeles] , 1975- v. : LC Card 80-498669 DDC 979.4/94/053 19
HN80.L7 L66 1975

The state of the economy . United States. Congress. Joint Economic Committee. Washington , 1980. iii, 77 p. ; LC Card 80-603429 DDC 330.973/0926 19
KF25 .E2 1980c

State of the health message . New York (State).

Governor, 1975- (Carey) [Albany] [1980] 25 p. ; LC Card 80-623008 DDC 362.1/09747 19
RA395.A4 N76213 1980

State of the Union address and State of the Union message. United States. President, 1977- (Carter) [Washington? D.C.] 1980. 96 p. ; LC Card 80-602059 DDC 353.03/52 19
J82 .E44 1980

State of Vermont Electricians' Licensing Board rules. Vermont. Electricians' Licensing Board. [Montpelier] [1978?] 8 leaves ; LC Card 80-623527 DDC 344.743/01762131924 19
KFV282.E4 A32 1980

State of Vermont program and financial plan for vocational rehabilitation agencies. Vermont. [Montpelier , 1979] 56 leaves ; LC Card 80-621209 DDC 353.97430083 19
HD7256.U6 V42 1979

State of Washington Water Research Center. An assessment of potential hydroelectric power and energy for the State of Washington / by Claud C. Lomax, principle investigator ; Michael Robinette, research associate ; John J. Cassidy, director ; conducted by the State of Washington Water Research Center. [Olympia] : State of Washington Dept. of Ecology, [1979] 5 v. : ill. ; 28 cm. (Report - State of Washington Water Research Center ; no. 34) "September 1979." CONTENTS. - v. 1. General information.--v. 2. Detailed information, WRIA's 1-9.--v. 3. Detailed information, WRIA's 10-23.--v. 4. Detailed information, WRIA's 24-28.--v. 5. Detailed information, WRIA's 29-62. LC Card 80-622476 DDC 553.7/09797 s 333.91/4 19
1. Hydroelectric power plants - Washington (State). 2. Water-power - Washington (State). I. Lomax, Claud C. II. Robinette, Michael. III. Series: State of Washington Water Research Center. Report , no. 34. IV. Title.
TD224.W2 S8 no. 34 TK1424.W2

Non-Federal financing of water resources development . Corvallis, 1978. 80 p. ; LC Card 79-621887
HD1695.N74 N66   ***NYPL [JLF 80-1601]***

Report .
(no. 13) A summary of quantity, quality, and economic methodology for establishing minimum flows . Pullman , 1973- v. <1> : LC Card 75-620707 DDC 553.7/09797 s 333.9/0217/09797 19
TD224.W2 S8 no. 13 GB1225.W3

(no. 26) Investigation to determine extent and nature of nonpoint source enrichment and hydrology of several recreational lakes of eastern Washington . Pullman , 1976. xvi, 309 p. : LC Card 79-623617 DDC 553.7/09797 s 333.91/631/09797 19
TD224.W2 S8 no. 26 GB1625.W2

(no. 34) State of Washington Water Research Center. An assessment of potential hydroelectric power and energy for the State of Washington /. [Olympia] [1979] 5 v. : LC Card 80-622476 DDC 553.7/09797 s 333.91/4 19
TD224.W2 S8 no. 34 TK1424.W2

(no. 9) Washington (State). State University, Pullman. Dept. of Civil and Environmental Engineering. Study of Silver Lake eutrophication . Pullman, Wash. [1975] xviii, 298 p. : LC Card 79-625419 DDC 553.7/09797 s 363.7/3942/0979788 19
TD224.W2 S8 no. 9a QH105.W2

State of Wyoming. United States. Geological Survey. Wyoming, base map /. Reston, Va. , 1980. 1 map ; LC Card 81-691604
G4260 1980 .U5

State of Wyoming. United States. Geological Survey. Wyoming, base map with highways /. Reston, Va. , 1980. 1 map : LC Card 81-691607
G4260 1980 .U51

State offices on aging : history and statutory authority : an information paper / prepared for use by the Special Committee on Aging, United States Senate. Washington : U. S. G.P.O. : For sale by the Supt. of Docs., U. S. G.P.O., 1980. vii, 37 p. ; 24 cm. At head of title: 96th Congress, 2d session. Committee print. "December 1980." Item 1009 LC Card 81-600673 DDC 362.6/0973 19
1. Old age assistance - United States - States. 2. Aged - Legal status, laws, etc. - United States - States. 3. Aged - Government policy - United States - States. I. United States. Congress. Senate. Special Committee on

Aging.
KF3737.Z95 S73

State payroll by election district, last half of 1978. Alaska. Legislative Finance Division. State salaries by location, 01/14/79. [Juneau , 1979] ca. 300 p. in various pagings ; LC Card 79-625250 DDC 331.2/813539798 19
JK9557 .A58 1979

A State plan for educational television in Illinois /. Illinois. Educational Television Commission. [Springfield] [1977?] iv, 16 leaves, [2] leaves of plates : LC Card 80-620585 DDC 371.3/358/09773 19
LB1044.7 .I39 1977

State plan for part B of the Education of the handicapped act as amended by P.L. 94-142 . Montana. Office of Public Instruction. Special Education Unit. Helena, Mont. [1980] 60, 16 p. ; LC Card 80-622031 DDC 371.9/046/09786 19
LC4032.M9 M67 1980

State plan on aging for the State of Indiana for fiscal year 1980. Indiana. State Commission on the Aging and Aged. [Indianapolis, Ind.] [1979] ca. 50 p. in various pagings ; LC Card 80-621779 DDC 362.6/09772 19
HV1468.I6 I47 1979

State plan on aging under Title III of the Older Americans Act for New Mexico, fiscal years 1981-83. [Santa Fe, N.M. (440 Saint Michael's Dr., Santa Fe 87503) : State Agency on Aging, 1980] 126 p. in various pagings ; 28 cm. Cover title: New Mexico state plan on aging, fiscal years 1981-83. LC Card 81-620578 DDC 362.6/09789 19
1. Aged Government policy - New Mexico. I. New Mexico. State Agency on Aging. II. Title: New Mexico state plan on aging, fiscal years 1981-83.
HQ1064.U6 N283

State plan profiles, 1979-1980. National Institute on Alcohol Abuse and Alcoholism. State Assistance Branch. [Rockville, Md.] [1980] iv, 232 p. ; LC Card 80-602308 DDC 362.29/18/0973 19
HV5035 .N37 1980

STATE PLANNING. see ECONOMIC POLICY; REGIONAL PLANNING.

State planning and policy analysis. Hawaii. Planning Division. State activities to implement priority directions of the Hawaii state plan. [Honolulu] [1980] xx, 98 p. ; LC Card 80-623120 DDC 338.9969 19
HC107.H3 H389 1980

State prison facilities and incarceration alternatives. California. Legislature. Joint Advisory Committee on State Prison Facilities and Incarceration Alternatives. Report of the Joint Advisory Committee on State Prison Facilities and Incarceration Alternatives. [Sacramento, Calif. (Rm. 6001, State Capitol, Sacramento 95812)] [1978] 41 p. ; LC Card 81-620647 DDC 365/.9794 19
HV9475.C2 C35 1978

State profits on tax-exempt student loan bonds . United States. Congressional Budget Office. [Washington] [1980] xvi, 57 p. ; LC Card 80-601571 DDC 379.1/214/0973 19
HG4946 .U52 1980

A state program of funded self-insurance for public schools (S.P. 627) . Maine. Legislature. Committee on Business Legislation. [Augusta? Me. , 1980] 15, [12] leaves ; LC Card 80-622974 DDC 368/.06 19
KFM11.62 .B8 1980a

A state program of funded self-insurance for public schools (S.P. 627) . Maine. Legislature. Committee on Business Legislation. [Augusta? Me. , 1980] 11 leaves ; LC Card 80-622975 DDC 368/.06 19
KFM11.62 .B8 1980b

State programs and services in food and drug control /. United States. Food and Drug Administration. Division of Federal-State Relations. State Services Branch. Rockville, Md. , 1978. xiv, 68 p. ; LC Card 79-600638 DDC 353.0077/82 19
TX531 .U536 1978

State programs for public school support /. Munse, Albert Ralph, 1923- Washington , 1965. vii, 113 p. ; LC Card 80-502015 DDC 370/.973 s 379.1/22/0973 19
L111 .A614 no. 52 LB2828

State publications . Lane, Margaret T. Austin,

TX , 1980. iii, 178, 4 p. ; LC Card 80-622732
DDC 027.5 19
Z1223.5.A1 L36

State rankings per capita of Federal aid to States. Florida. Bureau of Intergovernmental Relations. Tallahassee, LC Card 78-641567
NYPL [JLM 80-993]

The State register . New York (State). Legislature. Administrative Regulations Review Committee. [Albany] 1978. 58 leaves ; LC Card 79-625699 DDC 342.747/06 347.47026 19
KFN5010.62 .A35 1978c

State regulations pertaining to the use of internal-combustion engines underground /. Waytulonis, Robert W. [Avondale, Md.] [1981] p. cm. LC Card 81-607000 DDC 622 s 363.1/89 19
TN295 .U4

STATE RESPONSIBILITY. see GOVERNMENT LIABILITY.

State restrictions on vision care providers : the effects on consumers ("Eyeglasses II") : report of the staff to the Federal Trade Commission / by Gary Hailey ... [et al.]. [Washington, D.C.?] : Bureau of Consumer Protection, 1980. xix, 289 p. ; 28 cm. "July 1980"--Cover. Item 535 Includes bibliographical references. LC Card 81-600519 DDC 343.73/078681411 347.30378681411 19
1. Eyeglasses - Law and legislation - United States - States. 2. Contact lenses - Law and legislation - United States - States. 3. Optical trade - Law and legislation - United States - States. I. Hailey, Gary. II. United States. Bureau of Consumer Protection. III. United States. Federal Trade Commission.
KF2036.E93 Z957

State revenue sharing . North Carolina. Legislative Research Commission. [Raleigh] [1980] 17, [148] p. ; LC Card 80-623285 DDC 336.1/85 19
HJ615 .N67 1980

State salaries by location, 01/14/79. Alaska. Legislative Finance Division. [Juneau , 1979] ca. 300 p. in various pagings ; LC Card 79-625250 DDC 331.2/813593798 19
JK9557 .A58 1979

State school retirement law of Kansas. Kansas. Laws, statutes, etc. [Topeka] , 1960. 15 p. ; LC Card 81-453498 DDC 344.781/012529 19
KFK393.5.A333 A2 1960

State science, engineering & technology project. Science staff services in the Illinois Legislative Council . [Springfield, Ill.] [1979] x, 74 p. : LC Card 80-622583 DDC 328.773/0761 19
Q180.U5 S364

State subsidized low rent public housing : program audit / Legislative Commission on Expenditure Review. Albany, N.Y. (111 Washington Ave., Albany 12210) : The Commission, [1980] 10, iii, 92 p. : ill. ; 28 cm. Cover title. "December 1980." Includes bibliographical references. LC Card 81-621642 DDC 363.5/8 19
1. Public housing - New York (State) - Finance. 2. Housing subsidies - New York (State). I. New York (State). Legislature. Legislative Commission on Expenditure Review.
HD7288.78.U52 N77

STATE SUCCESSION - CONGRESSES.
United Nations Conference on Succession of States in Respect of Treaties, Vienna, 1977-1978. Official records /. New York , 1979- v. ; LC Card 80-121295 DDC 300 s 341.3/7 19
JX1977 .A2 A/CONF.80/16/Add.1, etc.

State supplemental energy conservation plan . Louisiana. Dept. of Natural Resources. Baton Rouge, La. , 1979. 50 p. in various pagings : LC Card 80-620853 DDC 333.79/16/09763 19
TJ163.4.U6 L67 1979

State support for health professions education / prepared for the Committee on Labor and Human Resources, United States Senate ; by the Congressional Research Service, Library of Congress, Ninety-sixth Congress, second session. Washington : U. S. G.P.O., 1981. xiii, 109 p. ; 24 cm. At head of title: 96th Congress, 2d session. Committee print. "Prepared for the Congressional Research Service by Lewin and Associates, Inc."--P. ix. "December 1980." Item 1043 LC Card 81-601289 DDC 610/.7/1173 19

1. State aid to medical education - United States. I. United States. Congress. Senate. Committee on Labor and Human Resources. II. Lewin and Associates. III. Library of Congress. Congressional Research Service.
R745 .S74

State tax systems under changing technology . Martin, James Walter, 1893- Lexington, Ky. , c1980. x, 322 p. : LC Card 80-131133 DDC 353.9/3878 19
HE355 .M37

State taxation of interstate commerce and worldwide corporate income . United States. Congress. Senate. Committee on Finance. Subcommittee on Taxation and Debt Management Generally. Washington , 1980. 2 v. (v, 983 p.) ; LC Card 80-604089 DDC 343.7305/267 347.3035267 19
KF26 .F5695 1980e

STATE, THE - HISTORY OF THEORIES. see POLITICAL SCIENCE - HISTORY.

STATE, THE - RESPONSIBILITY. see GOVERNMENT LIABILITY.

STATE, THE - SUABILITY. see GOVERNMENT LIABILITY.

The state uniform construction code . New Jersey. Legislature. General Assembly. Municipal Government Committee. [Trenton] [1980] ii, 34 p. ; LC Card 80-624085 DDC 343.749/07869 347.49037869 19
KFN1811.82 .M86 1980

STATE UNIVERSITIES AND COLLEGES - LAW AND LEGISLATION - UNITED STATES.
United States. Congress. House. Committee on Agriculture. Subcommittee on Department Investigations, Oversight, and Research. Grants for certain purposes to 1890 land-grant colleges . Washington , 1980. iii, 40 p. ; LC Card 80-604033 DDC 344.73/076 347.30476 19
KF27 .A33265 1980d

STATE UNIVERSITIES AND COLLEGES - MISSOURI.
Sanders, Nell S. Programs of developmental studies in Missouri State-supported institutions of higher education /. [Jefferson City] [1978] 65 leaves : LC Card 79-621793 DDC 379.1/54/09778 19
LC1032.5.M8 S26

STATE UNIVERSITIES AND COLLEGES - MISSOURI - STATISTICS.
Missouri. Coordinating Board for Higher Education. Missouri higher education budget recommendations, FY 1981 /. Jefferson City, Mo. [1980?] 102 p. : LC Card 80-623455 DDC 379.1/214/09778 19
LB2329.5 .M57 1980

STATE UNIVERSITIES AND COLLEGES - TEXAS - CONGRESSES.
Proceedings of the Texas postsecondary education outlook, 1980-1985 . [Austin] , c1979. xv, 166 p. : LC Card 80-623590 DDC 378.764 19
LB2329.5 .P76

STATE UNIVERSITIES AND COLLEGES - UNITED STATES.
Outreach programs of the land grant university, which publics should they serve? . [Manhattan , 1979] 246 p. ; LC Card 80-622898 DDC 378/.054/0973 19
LB2329.5 .O9

State University College (Brockport, N.Y.) Train-a-champ . Albany, N.Y. , c1979. vii, 95 p. : LC Card 81-119267 DDC 371.9/044 19
GV445 .T73

State University of Agriculture and Applied Science, Fargo, N. D. see North Dakota. State University of Agriculture and Applied Science, Fargo.

State University of New York at Albany. see New York (State). State University, Albany.

State University of New York College at Plattsburgh. Dept. of Sociology. Veltman, Calvin J. The role of language characteristics in the socioeconomic attainment process of Hispanic origin men and women /. [Washington, D.C.?] , 1980. iv, 103 p. ; LC Card 81-601023 DDC 305.8/68073 19
E184.S75 V44

State usury ceilings and their impact on small businesses . United States. Congress. House. Committee on Small Business. Subcommittee on General Oversight and Minority Enterprise. Washington , 1980. iii, 294 p : LC Card 81-600855 DDC 338.6/42/0973 19
KF27 .S64 1980g

STATEN ISLAND, N. Y. - MAPS.
(1977) New York City Transit Authority. Staten Island bus map. New York, c1977. col. map, 46 x 46 cm. Scale not given. Oriented with north toward upper left. Text, guides to hours and frequency of service, route digram of Staten Island rapid transit, and Staten Island ferry schedule on verso. Text, guides to hours and frequency of service, route diagramof Staten Island rapid transit, and Staten Island ferry schedule on verso.
NYPL [Map Div. 80-3371]

States are funding juvenile justice projects that conform to legislative objectives . United States. General Accounting Office. [Washington, D.C.] , 1980. iii, 129 p. ; LC Card 80-601282 DDC 353.9/38492 19
HV9104 .U52 1980

STATES, CREATION OF. see STATE SUCCESSION.

The States report on children and youth. National Council of State Committees for Children and Youth. [Washington? 1960] 232 p. LC Card 60-61000 *NYPL [JLD 80-3271]*

STATES, SUCCESSION OF. see STATE SUCCESSION.

STATESMEN - IRAN - BIOGRAPHY.
Nashat, Guity, 1937- The origins of modern reform in Iran /. Urbana , c1981. p. cm. ISBN 0-252-00822-7 LC Card 81-3343 DDC 955/.04 19
DS307 .N26

STATESMEN - SOUTH AMERICA - BIOGRAPHY.
Al libertador general San Martín . Washington, D.C. [1978] vii, 51 p., [1] leaf of plates : LC Card 80-145557 DDC 980/.02/0924 B 19
F2235.4 .A677

STATESMEN - UNITED STATES - BIOGRAPHY.
Lopez, Claude Anne. Benjamin Franklin's "good house" /. Washington, D.C. , 1981. p. cm. LC Card 81-607929 DDC 974.8/11 19
E302.6.F8 L78

Trefousse, Hans Louis. Carl Schurz, a biography /. Knoxville , c1981. p. cm. ISBN 0-87049-326-4 : LC Card 81-3370 DDC 973.8/092/4 B 19
E664.S39 T7

A statewide comprehensive plan for fish and wildlife on the national forests in the State of Oregon . Oregon. Dept. of Fish and Wildlife. [Portland] [1979?] 84 p. : LC Card 80-621380
SK439 .O75 1979 *NYPL [JLF 81047]*

Statewide master plan for fire protection. Nevada. Legislative Commission. [Carson City] [1980] ix, 65 p. ; LC Card 81-621360 DDC 363.3/77/09793 19
TH9504 .N34 1980

Statewide plan for fire education and training in Connecticut /. Connecticut. Commission on Fire Prevention and Control. [Meriden, Conn.] , 1980. ix, 156, [32] p. : LC Card 80-621538 DDC 628.9/2/0710746 19
TH9124.C8 C66 1980

Statewide postsecondary planning for 1980-1985 . Conference on Postsecondary Statewide Planning for 1980-1985, Montgomery, Ala., 1978. Montgomery, Ala. [1979?] 109 p. ; LC Card 79-623281 DDC 378/.107/09761 19
LA231.5 .C66 1978

Statistical abstract of Arizona, 1976 /. Arizona. University. Division of Economic and Business Research. Tucson, Ariz. [1976] 519 p. : LC Card 80-622590 DDC 317.91 19
HA246 .A74 1976

STATISTICAL ANALYSIS, MULTIVARIATE. see MULTIVARIATE ANALYSIS.

A statistical analysis of the quality of surface water in Nebraska /. Engberg, R. A. Washington , 1981. p. cm. LC Card 81-2161 DDC 553.7/9/09782 19
TD224.N18 E5

Statistical analysis report. South Dakota. Dept. of Social Services. Statistical Analysis and Reports. v. 10, no. 10- ; Oct. 1979- Pierre.
NYPL [Econ. Div.]

Statistical and expenditure data for intermediate unit operated programs and services for exceptional children, 1976-77 /. Stewart, Gerald. Harrisburg, Pa. , 1978. 28 p. ; LC Card 80-623258 DDC 371.9/09748 19
LC4032.P4 S73

Statistical and financial information of Kansas community junior colleges. Kansas. State Dept. of Education. LEA Finance Section. Topeka [1980] 37 leaves ; LC Card 80-622606 DDC 379.1/18/09781 19
LB2328 .K32 1980

Statistical data on Department of Defense training of foreign military personnel . United States. General Accounting Office. [Washington, D.C.] , 1980. 2, 107 p. ; LC Card 80-602018 DDC 355/.032/0973 19
U408.3 .U54 1980

Statistical data on the Oklahoma Legislature . Oklahoma. State Legislative Council. Oklahoma City, Okla. (305 State Capitol, Oklahoma City, Okla.) [1980] 16 leaves ; LC Card 80-624227 DDC 328.766/077 19
KFO1215.2 1980

Statistical data on the Oklahoma Legislature . Oklahoma. State Legislative Council. Division of Fiscal Services. Oklahoma City, Okla. [1979] 12 leaves ; LC Card 80-623058 DDC 328.766/077 19
KFO1215.2 1979a

STATISTICAL DESIGN. see EXPERIMENTAL DESIGN.

STATISTICAL INFERENCE. see PROBABILITIES.

Statistical matching techniques. United States. Federal Committee on Statistical Methodology. Subcommittee on Matching Techniques. Report on exact and statistical matching techniques /. [Washington] , 1980] vii, 57 p. ; LC Card 80-603147 DDC 001.4/224 19
HB849.49 .U53 1980

Statistical policy working paper .
(v. 6) United States. Federal Committee on Statistical Methodology. Subcommittee on Statistical Uses of Administrative Records. Report on statistical uses of administrative records /. [Washington, D.C.?] , 1980 [i.e. 1981] xii, 106 p. ; LC Card 81-601438 DDC 353.0081/9 19
HA37.U55 U55 1981

(5) United States. Federal Committee on Statistical Methodology. Subcommittee on Matching Techniques. Report on exact and statistical matching techniques /. [Washington] , 1980] vii, 57 p. ; LC Card 80-603147 DDC 001.4/224 19
HB849.49 .U53 1980

Statistical profile of handicapped Federal civilian employees. United States. Office of Personnel Management. Selective Placement Programs Office. [Washington, D.C.] [1980] 41 p. : LC Card 80-602254 DDC 353.001/04 19
JK723.H3 U56 1980

Statistical profile. Ser. SP. United States. Bureau of the Census. no. 1-136; Feb. 1962-Aug. 1962. Washington. 136 no. in 3 v. LC Card A62-9234
NYPL [TAA (United States. Census Bureau. Statistical profile. Ser. SP.)]

Statistical-research bulletin. Pennsylvania. Office of Administration. Bureau of Management Services. v. 1, issue 1, v. 2-4 ; [Mar. 1972?], Mar. 1973-1974. Harrisburg, Pa.
NYPL [JLM 80-57]

Statistical studies in field geochemistry. Ebens, Richard J. Geochemistry of some rocks, mine spoils, stream sediments, soils, plants, and waters in the western energy region of the conterminous United States /. Washington [D.C.] , 1981. p. cm. LC Card 81-607846 DDC 551.9/0978 19
QE515 .E23

Statistics of Louisiana adult education programs /. Meno, Marie A. [Baton Rouge] , 1979. 14 leaves : LC Card 80-621815 DDC 374/.9763 19
L154 .B32 no. 1468, 1979 LC5252.L8

STATISTICS OF SAMPLING. see SAMPLING (STATISTICS)

Statue of Liberty, Ellis Island National Monument, New York. Building Conservation Technology/The Ehrenkrantz Group. Mechanical and electrical rehabilitation, Main Building, Ellis Island, Statue of Liberty National Monument, New York . Denver, Colo. , 1980. 97 leaves, ca. 500 leaves of plates : LC Card 80-601419 DDC 725/.1 19
NA4510.I6 B84 1980a

STATURE - UNITED STATES - STATISTICS. Fulwood, Robinson. Height and weight of adults, ages 18-74 years, by socioeconomic and geographic variables, United States, 1971-74 /. Hyattsville, Md. , 1981. p. cm. ISBN 0-8406-0221-9 LC Card 81-607970 DDC 312/.6 19
RA407.3 .A347 no. 224 GN66

The status, mortality, and response to management of the bighorn sheep of Whiskey Mountain /. Wyoming. Game and Fish Dept. Cheyenne [1979] 213 p. : LC Card 80-622756 DDC 639.9/797358 19
QL737.U53 W96 1979

The status of alternative energy technologies, March 1980 /. Cline, James G. Albany, N.Y. (Assembly P.O. Box 167, Albany 12248) [1980] 23 p. ; LC Card 81-621009 DDC 333.79/09747 19
TJ163.25.U6 C59

Status of army air defense planning . United States. Congress. House. Committee on Armed Services. Special Subcommittee on Nato Standardization, Interoperability, and Readiness. Washington , 1980. ii, 52 p. : LC Card 80-604007 DDC 358.4/145/0973 19
KF27 .A7642 1980

Status of Army manpower . United States. Congress. House. Committee on Armed Services. Washington , 1981. ii, 130 p. ; LC Card 81-601854 DDC 355.2/2/0973 19
KF27 .A7 1980l

The status of basic skills attainment in Michigan public schools, 1979 /. Michigan. Dept. of Education. [Lansing] [1979] 22 p. : LC Card 79-625999 DDC 371.2/6/09774 19
LB3052.M5 M53 1979

Status of civil rights in Michigan, 1973-1978. Michigan. Dept. of Civil Rights. Detroit [1979?] 27, [1] p. : LC Card 79-623308 DDC 323.4/09774 19
LAW

Status of detailed soil surveys, Vermont. United States. Soil Conservation Service. Lanham, MD , 1980. 1 map : LC Card 81-690085
G3751.J3 1980 .U5

Status of ... high blood pressure control programs in Illinois . Illinois. Dept. of Public Health. [Springfield] [1979?] 111 leaves in various foliations : LC Card 80-621704 DDC 362.1/96132 19
RA645.H9 I45 1979

The status of hospital discharge data in Denmark, Scotland, West Germany, and the United States /. Kozak, Lola Jean. Hyattsville, Md. , 1981. p. cm. ISBN 0-8406-0211-1 LC Card 80-607865 DDC 312/.07/23 s 362.1/1/0684 19
RA409 .U45 no. 88 RA971.6

Status of implementation of the Part-Time Career Employment Act of 1978 . United States. Congress. Senate. Committee on Governmental Affairs. Subcommittee on Governmental Efficiency and the District of Columbia. Washington , 1980 [i.e. 1981] iv, 77 p. : LC Card 81-601317 DDC 353.001/4 19
KF26 .G6735 1980d

Status of local planning in Virginia, 1979 /. Virginia. Dept. of Housing and Community Development. Richmond, Va. [1979] 55 p. : LC Card 80-622615 DDC 352.9/6/025755 19
HT167.5.V8 V53 1979

Status of New York soil surveys . United States. Soil Conservation Service. Lanham, MD , 1980. 1 map : LC Card 81-690084
G3801.J3 1980 .U5

The status of public school support in Rhode Island. Rhode Island. Board of Education. Providence , 1955. 31 p. : LC Card 80-510733

DDC 379.1/2209745 s 379.1/2209745 19
LA358 .R43a no. 1 LB2826.R4

Status of soil surveys, Virginia. United States. Soil Conservation Service. Lanham, Md. , 1979. 1 map : LC Card 81-690106
G3881.J3 1979 .U51

Status of soil surveys, Virginia. United States. Soil Conservation Service. Lanham, Md. , 1981. 1 map : LC Card 81-692880
G3881.J3 1981 .U5

Status of the Airport and Airway Trust Fund . United States. Congress. House. Committee on Ways and Means. Washington , 1980. iv, 242 p. : LC Card 80-603519 DDC 343.73/0977 347.303977 19
KF27 .W3 1980j

Status of the MX missile system . United States. Congress. House. Committee on Armed Services. Washington , 1980. ii, 46 p. : LC Card 80-604003 DDC 358/.174/0973 19
KF27 .A7 1980j

The status of the Third United Nations Conference on the Law of the Sea, spring 1980 . United States. Congress. House. Committee on Foreign Affairs. Washington , 1980. iii, 84 p. ; LC Card 80-602730 DDC 341.4/5 19
KF27 .F6 1980c

Status of Vietnam veterans in the bay area . United States. Congress. House. Committee on Veterans' Affairs. Washington , 1980. iii, 64 p. ; LC Card 80-604108 DDC 355.1/15/097946 19
KF27 .V4 1980a

Status of watershed assistance under P.L.566, Oregon /. United States. Soil Conservation Service. Portland, Or. , 1979. 1 map : LC Card 81-691561
G4291.C315 1979 .U5

Status of women in Kentucky State agencies . Kentucky. Commission on Human Rights. Frankfort, Ky. [1979] ii. 21 p. : LC Card 80-622262 DDC 353.9769001/04 19
JK5360.5.W6 K46 1979

Status offender. National Juvenile Justice System Assessment Center (U. S.) A preliminary national assessment of the status offender and the juvenile justice system . [Washington, D.C.] [1980] c1979. xv, 221 p. : LC Card 80-600044 DDC 364.3/6/0973 19
HV9104 .N23 1980a

STATUS OFFENDERS - CALIFORNIA. Johns, Dennis. AB 3121 impact evaluation . [Sacramento] [1980] vii, 188 p. : LC Card 80-621711 DDC 364.3/6/09794 19
HV9105.C2 J63

STATUS OFFENDERS - LEGAL STATUS, LAWS, ETC. - NEW JERSEY. Dannefer, Dale. Juvenile justice in New Jersey . Trenton, N.J. , 1979. xxxv, 270 p. ; LC Card 80-623797 DDC 345.749/08 19
KFN2397.5 .D36

STATUS OFFENDERS - LEGAL STATUS, LAWS, ETC. - VIRGINIA. Virginia. Dept. of Corrections. Evaluation and Monitoring Unit. Impacts of the first year of the 1977 Juvenile code revision /. [Richmond] , 1978. 13, x p. : LC Card 79-622561 DDC 345.755/08 19
KFV2995 .A83

STATUS OFFENDERS - UNITED STATES. National Juvenile Justice System Assessment Center (U. S.) A preliminary national assessment of the status offender and the juvenile justice system . [Washington, D.C.] [1980] c1979. xv, 221 p. : LC Card 80-600044 DDC 364.3/6/0973 19
HV9104 .N23 1980a

Weis, Joseph G. Jurisdiction and the elusive status offender . Washington, D.C. [1980] c1979. ix, 135 p. : LC Card 80-602845 DDC 364.3/6/0973 19
HV9104 .W447

Status report of the Assembly Judiciary, Law, Public Safety, and Defense Committee, Task Force on Juvenile Justice. New Jersey. State Legislature. General Assembly. Judiciary, Law, Public Safety, and Defense Committee. Trenton, N.J. [1980] ii, 12 p. : LC Card 80-624424 DDC 345.749/08 347.49058 19
KFN1811.82 .J83 1980

Statute of limitations for certain claims by the United States on behalf of Indians . United States. Congress. House. Committee on the Judiciary. Subcommittee on Administrative Law and Governmental Relations. Washington , 1980. iii, 61 p. ;   LC Card 80-603453   DDC 346.7304/32/08897 347.30643208897 19
KF27 .J832 1980b

The statutes of California . California. Laws, statutes, etc. San José [Calif.] , 1850. ix, 482 p. ;   LC Card 79-121477   DDC 348.794/022 19
KFC25.2 1849

Statutes of Georgia passed by the General Assembly of 1890. Georgia. Laws, statutes, etc. Atlanta, Ga. , 1891. 90 p. ;   LC Card 79-116429   DDC 348.758/022 19
KFG25.2 1890

Statutory requirements for all schools (K-12). North Dakota. Dept. of Public Instruction. Bismarck, N.D. [1979?] 8 p. ;   LC Card 80-623544   DDC 344.784/071 19
KFN8990 .A868

Staudinger, Hans, 1889- The inner Nazi : a critical analysis of Mein Kampf / Hans Staudinger ; edited with an introduction and a biographical afterword by Peter M. Rutkoff and William B. Scott. Baton Rouge : Louisiana State University Press, c1981. p. cm.   ISBN 0-8071-0882-0 :   LC Card 81-7277   DDC 943.085/092/4 19
1. Hitler, Adolf, 1889-1945. Mein Kampf. 2. National socialism. I. Rutkoff, Peter M., 1942-. II. Scott, William B., 1945-. III. Title.
DD247.H5 A3583

Stauffer, Truman. Underground utilization . Kansas City , 1978. 8 v. :   LC Card 79-625497   DDC 333.8 19
HD268.K2 U53

Steadman, David W. (joint author) Olson, Storrs L. The relationships of the Pedionomidae (Aves, Charadriiformes) /. Washington , 1981. p. cm.   LC Card 81-412   DDC 591 s 598/.33 19
QL1 .S54 no. 337 QL696.C465

Steadman, Richard C. The national military command structure : report of a study requested by the President and conducted in the Department of Defense. Washington : The Dept. : for sale by the Supt. of Docs., U. S. Govt. Print. Off., 1978. iii, 79 p. ; 27 cm. Cover title: Report to the Secretary of Defense on the national military command structure.   LC Card 79-602790
1. United States. Dept. of Defense. 2. United States - Armed Forces - Organization. 3. United States - Armed Forces - Management. I. United States. Dept. of Defense. II. Title. III. Title: Report to the Secretary of Defense on the national military command structure.
UA23.3 .S73

Steahr, Thomas E. Cause of death and socioeconomic structures of towns in Connecticut / by Thomas E. Steahr and Ronald Pitruzzello. Storrs : Storrs Agricultural Experiment Station, College of Agriculture and Natural Resources, University of Connecticut, 1976. 43 p. : ill. ; 28 cm. (Bulletin - Storrs Agricultural Experiment Station . 443) Cover title. Bibliography: p. 42-43.   LC Card 76-624113   DDC 304.6/4/09746 19
1. Mortality - Connecticut. 2. Death - Causes - Statistics. 3. Mortality - Social aspects - Connecticut. 4. Diseases - Social aspects - Connecticut. 5. Connecticut - Statistics, Medical. 6. Connecticut - Statistics, Vital. I. Pitruzzello, Ronald, joint author. II. Series: Connecticut. Agricultural Experiment Station, Storrs. Bulletin , 443. III. Title.
RA407.4.C6 S73

Stealth aircraft. United States. Congress. House. Committee on Armed Services. Subcommittee on Investigations. Leaks of classified national defense information--stealth aircraft . Washington , 1980 [i.e. 1981] iii, 9 p. ;   LC Card 81-601284   DDC 353.0071/45 19
UB247 .U53 1981

STEAM POWER-PLANTS - ENVIRONMENTAL ASPECTS - UNITED STATES.
United States. Congress. House. Committee on Public Works and Transportation. Subcommittee on Investigations and Review. Implementation of the Federal Water Pollution Control Act, 1977 . Washington , 1977. viii, 594 p. :   LC Card 81-601587   DDC 353.0082/325 19
KF27 .P89634 1977b

STEAM ROAD-WAGONS. see MOTOR-TRUCKS.

Steel imports and the administration of the antidumping laws . United States. Congress. House. Committee on Government Operations. Commerce, Consumer, and Monetary Affairs Subcommitte. Washington , 1980. iii, 109 p. :   LC Card 81-600594   DDC 353.0082/42 19
KF27 .G634 1979h

STEEL INDUSTRY AND TRADE.
National Foreign Assessment Center (U. S.) The OECD steel industries . Washington, D.C. [1980] v, 15 p. :   LC Card 80-603610   DDC 338.4/7669142 19
HD9510.5 .N26 1980

STEEL INDUSTRY AND TRADE - ADDRESSES, ESSAYS, LECTURES.
United Nations. Industrial Development Organization. Technological profiles on the iron and steel industry /. New York , 1978. x, 44 p. :   LC Card 79-109235   DDC 300 s 338.4/76691 19
JX1977 .A2 ID/218 TS307

STEEL INDUSTRY AND TRADE - UNITED STATES.
United States. Congress. House. Committee on Government Operations. Commerce, Consumer, and Monetary Affairs Subcommitte. Steel imports and the administration of the antidumping laws . Washington , 1980. iii, 109 p. :   LC Card 81-600594   DDC 353.0082/42 19
KF27 .G634 1979h

United States. Congress. Office of Technology Assessment. Technology and steel industry competitiveness. Washington, D.C. , 1980. vii, 374 p. :   LC Card 80-600111
TS303 .U54 1980   **NYPL [JLF 80-1648]**

United States. Congress. Senate. Committee on Environment and Public Works. Report of the Steel Tripartite Committee . Washington , 1981. iii, 124 p. ;   LC Card 81-601353   DDC 338.4/7669142/0973 19
KF26 .E6 1980k

STEEL - MANUFACTURE. see STEEL INDUSTRY AND TRADE; STEEL - METALLURGY.

STEEL - METALLURGY - OXYGEN PROCESSES.
Evaluation of synthetic fluorspar in BOF slags /. Washington, D.C. [1981] p. cm.   LC Card 81-607971   DDC 622 s 669/.142 19
TN23 .U43 TN747

STEEL - TRADE AND STATISTICS. see STEEL INDUSTRY AND TRADE.

Steele, Frederic L. Hodgdon, A. R. (Albion R.), d. 1976. Grasses of New Hampshire /. Durham, N.H. , <1979-. v. <1> :   LC Card 80-623173   DDC 584/.909742 19
QK495.G74 H625

Steele, John.
(joint author) Bright, Richard. Early hardening of asphalt in hot bituminous paving mixtures . [Raleigh] , 1966. vi, 70 p. :   LC Card 80-508397   DDC 625.8/5 s 625.8/5 19
TE270 .B67 pt. 2

(joint author) Bright, Richard. The effect of viscosity of asphalt on the properties of bituminous paving mixtures /. [Raleigh] , 1966. 2 v. :   LC Card 80-508426   DDC 625.8/5 19
TE270 .B67

(joint author) Bright, Richard. Hardening of asphalt in hot bituminous base, binder, and sand mixtures . [Raleigh] , 1966. vi, 83 p. :   LC Card 80-508398   DDC 625.8/5 s 625.8/5 19
TE270 .B67 pt. 1

STEELHEAD FISHING - LAW AND LEGISLATION - WASHINGTON (STATE)
United States. Congress. Senate. Committee on Commerce, Science, and Transportation. Washington State's salmon and steelhead resources . Washington , 1980. iv, 208 p. ;   LC Card 80-603093   DDC 346.7304/6956 19
KF26 .C69 1980p

Steffy, Wilbert. Productivity and cost control for the small and medium-sized firm / by Wilbert Steffy, Naveed Ahmad, Teofilo Reyes. Ann Arbor : Industrial Development Division, Institute of Science and Technology, University of Michigan, 1980. vii, 170 p. : ill. ; 23 cm. Includes bibliographical references.   LC Card 80-622255   DDC 338.1/6 19
1. Industrial productivity. 2. Cost control. I. Ahmad, Naveed, joint author. II. Reyes, Teofilo, joint author. III. Title.
HD56 .S75

Stegner, Wallace Earle, 1909- Mormon country / by Wallace Stegner. 1st Bison book printing. Lincoln : University of Nebraska Press, 1981, c1970. p. cm. "A Bison book." Reprint. Originally published: New York : Duell, Sloan and Pearce, 1942. Includes index.   ISBN 0-8032-4129-1   LC Card 81-3410   DDC 979.2 19
1. Utah - History. 2. Mormons - Utah - History. I. Title.
F826 .S75 1981

Stein, Janice Gross. Rational decision-making : Israel's security choices, 1967 / Janice Gross Stein and Raymond Tanter. Columbus : Ohio State University Press, c1980. xv, 399 p. : ill. ; 24 cm. "A publication of the Mershon Center for Education in National Security." Includes bibligraphies and index.   ISBN 0-8142-0312-4   LC Card 80-13589
1. Israel - Defenses - Decision making. 2. Israel-Arab War, 1967 - Causes. I. Tanter, Raymond, joint author. II. Ohio. State University, Columbus. Mershon Center for Education in National Security. III. Title.
DS119.2 .S73   **NYPL [JLE 81-169]**

Stein, Joan Z.
Dietary management in gastrointestinal diseases / Joan Z. Stein, Charlette R. Gallagher-Allred. Columbus, Ohio (456 Clinic Dr., Columbus 43210) : Dept. of Family Medicine, College of Medicine, Ohio State University, c1980. 28 p. ; 27 cm. (Nutrition in primary care . 13) Bibliography: p. 22.   LC Card 81-620948   DDC 616.3/30654 19
1. Gastrointestinal system - Diseases - Diet therapy. I. Gallagher-Allred, Charlette R. II. Title. III. Series.
RC802 .S69

Gallagher-Allred, Charlette R. Nutrient content of foods, nutritional supplements, and food fallacies /. Columbus, Ohio (456 Clinic Dr., Columbus 43210) , c1980. 40 p. :   LC Card 81-620936   DDC 641.1 19
TX551 .G26

Steinberg, Joseph. Workshop on Synthetic Estimates, Princeton, N. J., 1978. Synthetic estimates for small areas . Rockville, Md. , Washington , 1979. viii, 282 p. :   LC Card 79-600067
RC563.2 .W67 1978

Steiner, Bruce W. An institutional plan for developing national standards : with special reference to environment, safety, and health / Bruce W. Steiner. [Washington, D.C.] : U. S. Dept. of Commerce, National Bureau of Standards : for sale by the Supt. of Docs., U. S. Govt. Print. Off., 1979. vi, 17 p., [7] leaves of plates (2 fold.) : ill. ; 26 cm. (National Bureau of Standards monograph. 165) "Issued September 1979."   LC Card 79-600116   DDC 602/.18 s 620/.00218 19
1. Standards, Engineering - United States. I. Series: United States. National Bureau of Standards. Monograph , 165. II. Title.
QC100 .U556 no. 165 TA368

Steinhauer, Marcia B. Family home care program : a study of geriatric foster care services as an alternative housing environment in Illinois / by Marcia B. Steinhauer. [Springfield] : Illinois Dept. on Aging, [1978] 25 p. : ill. ; 29 cm. Bibliography: p. 22-25.   LC Card 79-623260   DDC 362.6/3 19
1. Aged - Home care - Illinois. 2. Foster home care - Illinois. 3. Aged - Home care - United States. 4. Foster home care - United States. I. Illinois. Dept. on Aging. II. Title.
HV1468.I3 S73

Steinhaus, Virginia S.
A list of vertebrates of northcentral North Dakota / Virginia S. Steinhaus. Grand Forks, N.D. : Institute for Ecological Studies, University of North Dakota, [1979] 29 p. ; 28 cm. (Special publication - Institute for Ecological Studies, University of North Dakota ; no. 7) "August 1979." Includes bibliographies.   LC Card 80-622454   DDC 596.09784 19
1. Vertebrates - North Dakota. 2. Zoology - North Dakota. I. Series: North Dakota. University. Institute for Ecological Studies. Special publication - Institute for Ecological Studies, University of North Dakota , no. 7. II. Title.
QL197 .S85

A list of vertebrates of northwestern North Dakota / Virginia S. Steinhaus. Grand Forks, N.D. : Institute for Ecological Studies, University of North Dakota, [1979] 28 p. ; 28 cm. (Special publication - Institute for Ecological Studies, University of North Dakota . no. 6) Includes bibliographies.   LC Card 80-622453   DDC 596.09784/7 19
1. Vertebrates - North Dakota. 2. Zoology - North Dakota. I. Series: North Dakota. University. Institute for Ecological Studies. Special publication - Institute for Ecological Studies, University of North Dakota , no. 6. II. Title.
QL197 .S86

A list of vertebrates of southcentral North Dakota / Virginia S. Steinhaus. Grand Forks, N.D. : Institute for Ecological Studies, University of North Dakota, [1979] 30 p. ; 28 cm. (Special publication - Institute for Ecological Studies, University of North Dakota ; no. 5) "June 1979." Includes bibliographies.   LC Card 80-622452   DDC 596.09784 19
1. Vertebrates - North Dakota. 2. Zoology - North Dakota. I. Series: North Dakota. University. Institute for Ecological Studies. Special publication - Institute for Ecological Studies, University of North Dakota , no. 5. II. Title.
QL197 .S87

A list of vertebrates of southeastern North Dakota / Virginia S. Steinhaus. Grand Forks, N.D. : Institute for Ecological Studies, University of North Dakota, [1979] 29 p. ; map ; 28 cm. (Special publication - Institute for Ecological Studies, University of North Dakota ; no. 4) "May 1979." Bibliography: p. 29.   LC Card 80-622451   DDC 596.09784 19
1. Vertebrates - North Dakota. 2. Zoology - North Dakota. I. Series: North Dakota. University. Institute for Ecological Studies. Special publication - Institute for Ecological Studies, University of North Dakota , no. 4. II. Title.
QL197 .S88

Steinkamp, James F. Soil survey of Sangamon County, Illinois / [by James F. Steinkamp] ; United States Department of Agriculture, Soil Conservation Service, in cooperation with Illinois Agricultural Experiment Station. [Washington, D.C.] : The Service, [1980] vii, 139 p., [71] fold. leaves of plates : ill. ; 28 cm. Cover title. Bibliography: p. 79-80.   LC Card 80-602641   DDC 631.4/7/77356 19
1. Soils - Illinois - Sangamon Co. - Maps. I. United States. Soil Conservation Service. II. Illinois. Agricultural Experiment Station, Urbana. III. Title.
S599.I5 S73

STELIDOTA - BIBLIOGRAPHY.
Weiss, Michael J. An annotated bibliography of the genus Stelidota Erichson (Coleoptera: Nitidulidae, Nitidulinae) /. Wooster, Ohio [1980] 37 p. ;   LC Card 80-623557   DDC 016.59576/43 19
Z5858.S74 W44 QL596.N58

Steller, Mary-Ellen. Population and labor force projections for Massachusetts / prepared by Mary-Ellen Steller, Peter Maloy. Boston : Job Market Research, Massachusetts Division of Employment Security, 1980. 45 leaves : graphs ; 28 cm. (Labor area research publication) At head of title: The Commonwealth of Massachusetts, Department of Employment Security.   LC Card 80-623457   DDC 312/.8/09744 19
1. Population forecasting - Massachusetts. 2. Employment forecasting - Massachusetts. I. Maloy, Joseph Peter, joint author. II. Massachusetts. Division of Employment Security. Job Market Research Service. III. Massachusetts. Division of Employment Security. IV. Title.
HB3525.M4 S77

Stenzel, William John. A class of compact high speed parallel multiplication schemes / by William John Stenzel. Urbana : Dept. of Computer Science, University of Illinois at Urbana-Champaign, 1975. vi, 72 p. : ill. ; 28 cm. ([Report] - UIUCDCS-R-75 . 756) Originally presented as the author's thesis (M.S.), University of Illinois. Bibliography: p. 71-72.   LC Card 76-620849   DDC 001.64 s 621.3819/5835 19
1. Computer arithmetic and logic units. 2. Multiplication. I. Series: Illinois. University at Urbana-Champaign. Dept. of Computer Science. Report, 756. II. Title.
QA76 .I4 no. 756 TK7888.4

A step-by-step guide to resources for economic development /. Urban Development Corporation. New York, N.Y., c1980. 208 p. ;   LC Card 80-620009   DDC 353.0082/09747 19
HC107.N73 P6385 1980

Stephens, Richard H. Human resources / Richard H. Stephens. Washington : National Defense University, 1978. v, 150 p. : graphs ; 24 cm. (National security management series) At head of title: National security management. Edition of 1972, by Eston T. White, published under title: Human resources for national strength. Bibliography: p. 139-143. Includes index.   LC Card 78-602425   DDC 331.11/0973 19
1. Manpower policy - United States. 2. Human capital - United States. 3. Manpower - United States. I. White, Eston T. Human resources for national strength. II. Title.
HD5724 .S68

STEPHENSON COUNTY, ILL. - MAPS.
(1980) United States. Soil Conservation Service. Stephenson County, Illinois /. Lincoln, Nebr., 1980. 1 map :   LC Card 81-691429
G4103.S9 1980 .U5

Stepp, Robert. Learning without negative examples via variable-valued logic characterizations : the uniclass inductive program AQ7UNI / by Robert Stepp. Urbana : Dept. of Computer Science, University of Illinois at Urbana-Champaign, [1979] 57 p. : ill. ; 28 cm. (Report - UIUCDCS-R-79 ; 982) "July 1979." "UILU-ENG 79-1730." Bibliography: p. 56-57.   LC Card 80-621697   DDC 001.64 s 001.64/25 19
1. AQ7UNI (Computer program). 2. Many-valued logic. I. Series: Illinois. University at Urbana-Champaign. Dept. of Computer Science. Report, 982. II. Title.
QA76 .I4 no. 982 QA9.45

STEREOTYPE (PSYCHOLOGY)
Dovidio, John F. The subtlety of white racism . Newark , 1977. 85 leaves :   LC Card 78-621433   DDC 305.8/96073 19
E185.615 .D67

STEREOTYPED BEHAVIOR. see STEREOTYPE (PSYCHOLOGY)

STERILIZATION (BIRTH CONTROL) - LAW AND LEGISLATION - UNITED STATES - STATES.
Alan Guttmacher Institute. Family planning, contraception, voluntary sterilization, and abortion . Rockville, Md. , Washington, D.C. , 1978. xix, 380 p. ;   LC Card 80-601267   DDC 344.73/048 19
KF3771.Z95 A37

Sterling and Francine Clark Art Institute, Williamstown, Mass. Hewitt, Karen. Educational toys in America, 1800 to the present /. Burlington, Vt., c1979. 141 p. :   LC Card 80-131686   DDC 688.7/25 19
LB1029.T6 H48

Stern, James L. The legal framework for collective bargaining in the urban transit industry /. Madison, Wisc., 1976. iv, 188 p. ;   *NYPL [*XME-9332]*

Stern, Loren.
(joint author) Campo, Joe. 1978 summary of commercial salmon fishing regulations in the Boldt case area /. [Olympia], 1979. 174 p. :   LC Card 79-625420   DDC 343.979/07692755 19
KFW505.6.H85 C35

1977 summary of Department of Fisheries and treaty Indian commercial salmon fishing regulations in the Boldt case area / by Loren Stern, A. Dennis Austin. [Olympia] : State of Washington, Dept. of Fisheries, 1978. i, 44 p. ; 28 cm. (Technical report - State of Washington, Department of Fisheries ; no. 40) Chiefly tables.   LC Card 79-624606   DDC 343.979/07692755 19
1. Indians of North America - Washington (State) - Legal status, laws, etc. 2. Indians of North America - Washington (State) - Fishing. I. Austin, Albert Dennis, 1944- joint author. II. Title. III. Title: Boldt case area. IV. Series: Washington (State). Dept. of Fisheries. Technical report , no. 40.
KFW505.6.H85 S73

Stern, Richard G., 1928- The invention of the real / Richard Stern. Athens : University of Georgia Press, 1982. p. cm.   ISBN 0-8203-0589-8   LC Card 81-10466   DDC 818/.5403 19
I. Title.
PS3569.T39 A16 1982

Sternlieb, George. Shopping centers, USA /. New Brunswick, N.J. [1981] p. cm.   ISBN 0-88285-068-7 :   LC Card 80-21702   DDC 381.1/0973 19
HF5430.3 .S47

STEVEDORES - LEGAL STATUS, LAWS, ETC. - UNITED STATES.
United States. Congress. House. Committee on Education and Labor. Subcommittee on Labor Standards. Oversight hearings on the Longshoremen's and harbor workers' compensation act . Washington , 1980. viii, 1231 p. :   LC Card 80-603416   DDC 353.0082/56 19
KF27 .E348 1979d

United States. Congress. House. Committee on Education and Labor. Subcommittee on Labor Standards. Oversight hearings on the Longshoremen's and Harbor Workers' Compensation Act. Supplement . Washington , 1980. v, 57 p. ;   LC Card 80-604153   DDC 344.73/0217 347.304217 19
KF27 .E348 1979d Suppl

United States. Congress. Senate. Committee on Labor and Human Resources. Oversight on the Longshoremen's and Harbor Workers' Compensation Act, 1980 . Washington , 1981. v, 472 p. :   LC Card 81-601328   DDC 353.0082/56 19
KF26 .L27 1980t

STEVEDORES - THE WEST - HISTORY.
Fairley, Lincoln. Facing mechanization . Los Angeles [c1979] xiii, 447 p. :   LC Card 80-621453
HD6331.18.L82 U543   NYPL [TB no. 23]

STEVEDORES - UNITED STATES.
United States. Congress. House. Committee on Education and Labor. Subcommittee on Labor Standards. Oversight hearings on the Longshoremen's and harbor workers' compensation act . Washington , 1980. viii, 1231 p. :   LC Card 80-603416   DDC 353.0082/56 19
KF27 .E348 1979d

United States. Congress. House. Committee on Education and Labor. Subcommittee on Labor Standards. Oversight hearings on the Longshoremen's and Harbor Workers' Compensation Act. Supplement . Washington , 1980. v, 57 p. ;   LC Card 80-604153   DDC 344.73/0217 347.304217 19
KF27 .E348 1979d Suppl

United States. Congress. Senate. Committee on Labor and Human Resources. Oversight on the Longshoremen's and Harbor Workers' Compensation Act, 1980 . Washington , 1981. v, 472 p. :   LC Card 81-601328   DDC 353.0082/56 19
KF26 .L27 1980t

Stevens, Andrea. Witteborg, Lothar P., 1927- Good show, a practical guide for temporary exhibitions /. Washington, D.C. , 1981. 172 p. :   ISBN 0-86528-007-X   LC Card 80-39543   DDC 069.5 19
N4396 .W57

Stevens County Conservation District, Stevens County, Washington. United States. Soil Conservation Service. Land ownership, Stevens County Conservation District, Stevens County, Washington /. Portland, Or. , 1980. 1 map :   LC Card 81-691516
G4283.S8G5 1979 .U5

STEVENS COUNTY (WASH.) - PUBLIC LANDS - MAPS.
United States. Soil Conservation Service. Land ownership, Stevens County Conservation District, Stevens County, Washington /. Portland, Or. , 1980. 1 map :   LC Card 81-691516
G4283.S8G5 1979 .U5

Stevens, Dean. (joint author) Stinebring, Warren R. Endotoxin in waters of the State of Vermont /. [Montpelier] [1978?] iv leaves, 25 p. ;   LC Card 79-624701   DDC 363.7/394 19
QR48 .S74

Stevens, James William. International Association of Auto Theft Investigators. Proceedings of the International Association of Auto Theft Investigators twenty-first annual seminar, Arlington, Texas, August 19-24, 1973. [Arlington] [1973?] 126 p. :   LC Card 80-623391

DDC 363.2/5 19
HV8079.A97 I57 1973

**STEVENS, WALLACE, 1879-1955 -
CRITICISM AND INTERPRETATION.**
Litz, A. Walton. Wallace Stevens .
Washington , 1981. p. cm.   ISBN 0-8444-0370-9
LC Card 81-607906   DDC 811/.52 19
PS3537.T4753 Z676

Stevenson, George, 1936-
North Carolina. Division of Archives and
History. Records relating to Tennessee in the
North Carolina State archives /. Raleigh, N.C. ,
1980. 7 p. :   LC Card 80-623026   DDC 975.6 s
016.9768 19
F251 .N67a no. 3, 1980 CD3424

A select bibliography for genealogical research
in North Carolina / by George Stevenson.
Raleigh, N.C. : State of North Carolina, Dept.
of Cultural Resources, Division of Archives and
History, c1980. 18 p. ; 28 cm. (Archives
information circular . no. 10) Caption title.   LC Card
80-623027   DDC 975.6 s 016.929/1/09756 19
*1. North Carolina - Genealogy - Bibliography. I. North
Carolina. Division of Archives and History. II. Title.
III. Series.*
F251 .N67a no. 10, 1980 Z1319 F253

Stewart, Gerald. Statistical and expenditure data
for intermediate unit operated programs and
services for exceptional children, 1976-77 /
prepared by Gerald Stewart for the Bureau of
Special Education, Pennsylvania Department of
Education. Harrisburg, Pa. : The Dept., 1978.
28 p. ; 28 x 22 cm. Tables.   LC Card 80-623258
DDC 371.9/09748 19
*1. Handicapped children - Education - Pennsylvania -
Costs - Statistics. I. Pennsylvania. Bureau of Special
Education. II. Title.*
LC4032.P4 S73

Stewart, James M. Floods in western North
Carolina, November 1977 : a lesson for the
future / by James M. Stewart, Ralph C. Heath,
John N. Morris. [Raleigh : Water Resources
Research Institute of the University of North
Carolina, 1978] 21, [3] p. : ill. ; 28 cm.   LC
Card 79-621805   DDC 363.3/493/09756 19
*1. Floods - North Carolina. I. Heath, Ralph C., joint
author. II. Morris, John Neal, joint author. III. Title.*
GB1399.4.N8 S74

Stewart, John, 1943- (joint author) Dolan, Robert.
Geographical analysis of Fenwick Island,
Maryland, a Middle Atlantic coast barrier
island /. Washington, D.C. , 1980. 24 p. :   LC
Card 79-600212   DDC 333.7 19
GB126.M3 D64

Stewart, Lucille C. The Future of South Dakota's
past /. Vermillion, S.D. , 1981. p. cm.   LC Card
81-14812   DDC 978.3/01 19
E78.S63 F87

Stewart, Robert E. Conference on Mining and
Power Production, Dickinson State College,
1973. Conference on Mining and Power
Production /. Fargo, N.D. , 1973. v, 130 p., [8]
leaves of plates :   LC Card 80-621258   DDC
333.8/2215/097848 19
TN805.N9 C66 1973

Stewart, Ruth Ann. Richard T. Greener .
[Washington, D. C.] , 1980. 16 p. :
NYPL [Sc F 80-218]

Sticht, Thomas G. The Textbook in American
society . Washington , 1981. x, 55 p. ;   ISBN
0-8444-0355-5 (pbk.)   LC Card 80-27657
DDC 371.3/2/0973 19
LB3047 .T48

Stick, David, 1919-
North Carolina lighthouses / by David Stick.
Raleigh : North Carolina Dept. of Cultural
Resources, Division of Archives and History,
1980. xi, 85 p. : ill. ; 23 cm. Bibliography: p.
77-78. Includes index.   ISBN 0-86526-144-X (pbk.) :
LC Card 80-622599   DDC 387.1/55 19
1. Lighthouses - North Carolina - History. I. Title.
VK1024.N8 S74

Stick, Frank. An artist's catch . Chapel Hill ,
c1981. p. cm.   ISBN 0-8078-1485-7   LC Card
81-2965   DDC 759.13 19
ND1839.S78 A4 1981

Stick, Frank. An artist's catch : watercolors / by
Frank Stick ; edited by David Stick. Chapel
Hill : University of North Carolina Press,
c1981. p. cm. Includes index.   ISBN 0-8078-1485-7

LC Card 81-2965   DDC 759.13 19
*1. Stick, Frank. 2. Fishes in art. I. Stick, David, 1919-.
II. Title.*
ND1839.S78 A4 1981

STICK, FRANK.
Stick, Frank. An artist's catch . Chapel Hill ,
c1981. p. cm.   ISBN 0-8078-1485-7   LC Card
81-2965   DDC 759.13 19
ND1839.S78 A4 1981

Stifle, J. M. (joint author) Haskins, James, 1941-
He will lift up his head . [Washington] [1978?]
55 p. :   LC Card 79-602502
E99.N3 H33   **NYPL [HBC 81-604]**

**Stillwater, Okla. Agricultural Experiment
Station.** see **Oklahoma. Agricultural
Experiment Station, Stillwater.**

**Stimulating government utilization of sheltered
workshops** / compiled and edited by William
M. Jenkins, Robert M. Anderson, Sara J. Odle ;
with a foreword by Stephen J. Cornett.
Memphis : Bureau of Educational Research and
Services, Memphis State University, [1977] xiv,
319 p. : ill. ; 24 cm. Includes proceedings of a
conference held Aug. 12-13, 1975 in Orlando, Fla.
Includes bibliographies.   LC Card 78-622547
*1. Sheltered workshops - United States - Congresses. 2.
Public contracts - United States - Congresses. I.
Jenkins, William Mell, 1937-. II. Anderson, Robert
Meredith. III. Odle, Sara J.*
HD7256.U5 S83   **NYPL [JLE 81-488]**

Stinebring, Warren R. Endotoxin in waters of the
State of Vermont / Warren Stinebring,
[principal investigator ; coinvestigators, David
Boraker, Dean Stevens]. [Montpelier] : Vermont
Water Resources Research Center, [1978?] iv
leaves, 25 p. ; 28 cm. Cover title. Includes
bibliographical references.   LC Card 79-624701   DDC
363.7/394 19
*1. Sanitary microbiology. 2. Endotoxin - Analysis. 3.
Water - Pollution - Vermont. 4. Water - Analysis. I.
Boraker, David, joint author. II. Stevens, Dean, joint
author. III. Vermont. University. Vermont Resources
Research Center. IV. Title.*
QR48 .S74

Stinson, Robert L. Current and projected output
of the Massachusetts livestock industry and its
marketing structure / Robert L. Stinson, P.
Geoffrey Allen, Robert L. Christensen.
[Amherst] : Massachusetts Agricultural
Experiment Station, University of
Massachusetts at Amherst, College of Food and
Natural Resources, [1978?] iv, 60 p. : ill. ; 23
cm. (Research bulletin - Massachusetts Agricultural
Experiment Station ; no. 659) "December 1978."
Bibliography: p. 59-60.   LC Card 79-624550   DDC
338.1/76/009744 19
*1. Animal industry - Massachusetts. I. Allen, Philip
Geoffrey, 1942- joint author. II. Christensen, Robert
Lawrence, 1935- joint author. III. Series: Massachusetts.
Agricultural Experiment Station, Amherst (1888-).
Research bulletin - Massachusetts Agricultural
Experiment Station , no. 659. IV. Title.*
HD9417.M4 S8

Stith, David A. Chemical composition,
stratigraphy, and depositional environments of
the Black River Group (Middle Ordovician),
southwestern Ohio / by David A. Stith.
Columbus : State of Ohio, Dept. of Natural
Resources, Division of Geological Survey, 1979.
iv, 36 p. : ill., graphs (3 fold. in pocket) ; 28
cm. (Report of investigations - State of Ohio, Division
of Geological Survey ; no. 113) Bibliography: p. 16.
LC Card 80-622410   DDC 557.71 s 551.7/31 19
*1. Geology, Stratigraphic - Ordovician. 2. Geology -
Ohio. I. Series: Ohio. Division of Geological Survey.
Report of investigations , no. 113. II. Title.*
QE151 .A186 no. 113 QE660

STOCHASTIC ANALYSIS.
Gan, Thian-Yew. Reliability of stochastic
models generating hydrologic series /. Austin,
Tex. [1980] 64 leaves ;   LC Card 80-622521
DDC 551.48/072 19
GB656.2.S7 G36

Stochastic analysis of water quality / by Ronald
F. Malone ... [et al.]. Logan : Utah Water
Research Laboratory, College of Engineering,
Utah State University, [1979] viii, 75 p. :
graphs ; 28 cm. (Water quality series .)
UWRL/Q-79/01) "March 1979." Bibliography: p. 39-40.
LC Card 80-621125   DDC 628.1/61 19
*1. Water quality - Measurement - Statistical methods. 2.
Stochastic processes. 3. Phosphorus - Environmental*

aspects - Washington (State) - Washington, Lake -
Mathematical models. 4. Saline waters - Colorado River
watershed - Mathematical models. I. Malone, Ronald F.
II. Series.
TD367 .S8

STOCHASTIC PROCESSES.
(1979) Stochastic analysis of water quality /.
Logan [1979] viii, 75 p. :   LC Card 80-621125
DDC 628.1/61 19
TD367 .S8

STOCHASTIC SAMPLING. see **MONTE
CARLO METHOD.**

STOCHASTIC VARIABLES. see **RANDOM
VARIABLES.**

STOCK BROKERS. see **BROKERS.**

STOCK CONTROL. see **INVENTORY
CONTROL.**

STOCK CORPORATIONS. see
CORPORATIONS.

**STOCK-EXCHANGE - LAW AND
LEGISLATION - UNITED STATES.**
United States. Congress. House. Committee on
Interstate and Foreign Commerce.
Subcommittee on Oversight and Investigations.
Securities Acts Amendments of
1975--oversight . Washington , 1978. viii, 1187
p. :   LC Card 81-601238   DDC 353.0082/58 19
KF27 .I5547 1977q

STOCK-EXCHANGE - UNITED STATES.
United States. Congress. House. Committee on
Interstate and Foreign Commerce.
Subcommittee on Oversight and Investigations.
National market system, five year status
report . Washington , 1980. vii, 105 p. ;   LC
Card 80-603861   DDC 332.64/273 19
HG4910 .U54 1980

United States. Securities and Exchange
Commission. Directorate of Economic and
Policy Research. Staff report on the securities
industry in 1977 /. [Washington] [1978] 21,
[30] leaves   LC Card 80-602626   DDC
332.6/2/0973 19
HG4910 .U55 1978

STOCK MARKET. see **STOCK-EXCHANGE.**

STOCK OWNERSHIP FOR EMPLOYEES. see
EMPLOYEE OWNERSHIP.

STOCK OWNERSHIP - UNITED STATES.
United States. Securities and Exchange
Commission. Report of the Securities and
Exchange Commission on beneficial ownership
reporting requirements pursuant to section
13(h) of the Securities exchange act of 1934.
Washington , 1980. viii, 242 p. ;   LC Card
80-602870   DDC 346.73/0666 19
KF1448 .A88

STOCKBROKERS. see **BROKERS.**

**STOCKHOLDERS - LEGAL STATUS, LAWS,
ETC. - UNITED STATES.**
United States. Congress. Senate. Committee on
Banking, Housing and Urban Affairs.
Subcommittee on Securities. Protection of
Shareholders' Rights Act of 1980 .
Washington , 1981. iv, 479 p. :   LC Card
81-601417   DDC 346.73/0666 347.306666 19
KF26 .B3954 1980b

United States. Securities and Exchange
Commission. Division of Corporation Finance.
Staff report on corporate accountability .
Washington , 1980. 782 p. ;   LC Card 80-603877
DDC 346.73/0666 347.306666 19
KF1448 .A8837

**STOCKHOLDERS' VOTING - UNITED
STATES.**
United States. Securities and Exchange
Commission. Division of Corporation Finance.
Staff report on corporate accountability .
Washington , 1980. 782 p. ;   LC Card 80-603877
DDC 346.73/0666 347.306666 19
KF1448 .A8837

STOCKKEEPING. see **INVENTORY
CONTROL.**

STOCKMAN, DAVID ALAN, 1946-
United States. Senate. Committee on
Governmental Affairs. Nomination of David A.
Stockman . Washington , 1981. iii, 169 p. ;   LC
Card 81-601411   DDC 353.0071 19
KF26 .G67 1981a

Stockpile report to the Congress. United States.

Federal Emergency Management Agency. Apr./Sept. 1979- Washington.

Stocks of grains, oilseeds, and hay : final estimates by states, 1974-79 / United States Department of Agriculture, Economics and Statistics Service, Crop Reporting Board. Washington, D.C. : The Board, 1981. 71 p. ; 28 cm. (Statistical bulletin . no. 649) Cover title. Chiefly tables. Jan. 1981. LC Card 81-601041 DDC 338.1/0973 s 338.1/731/0973 19
1. Grain trade - United States - Statistics. 2. Oil industries - United States - Statistics. 3. Hay - United States - Statistics. I. United States. Crop Reporting Board. II. Series: Statistical bulletin (United States. Dept. of Agriculture) , no. 649.
HD1751 .A5 no. 649 HD9034

Stockton State College. Center for Environmental Research. Carlson, Cathy. The salt marsh of southern New Jersey /. Pomona, N.J. , c1980. iv, 50 p. : LC Card 80-121932 DDC 574.5/2636 19
QH105.N5 C37

STOICHIOMETRY. see CHEMISTRY, PHYSICAL AND THEORETICAL.

Stokes, Billy Ray. Physical education for the handicapped : Louisiana needs assessment / [directed and compiled by Billy Ray Stokes]. [Baton Rouge] : State of Louisiana, Dept. of Education, 1978. vi, 152 p. ; 28 cm. (Bulletin - State of Louisiana, Department of Education ; 1506) Bibliography: p. 79-82. LC Card 80-620856 DDC 371.9/044 19
1. Physical education for handicapped children - Louisiana. I. Series: Louisiana. Dept. of Education. Bulletin, 1506. II. Title.
L154 .B32 no. 1506 GV445

Stokker, Kathleen, 1946- Norsk : nordmenn og Norge / av Kathleen Stokker og Odd Haddal ; illustrasjoner av Caroline Beckett. Madison, Wis. : University of Wisconsin Press, 1981. p. cm. English and Norwegian. Includes index. ISBN 0-299-08690-9 : LC Card 81-50827 DDC 439.8/282/421 19
1. Norwegian language - Grammar. I. Haddal, Odd. II. Title.
PD2623 .S86

STOL AIRCRAFT. see SHORT TAKE-OFF AND LANDING AIRCRAFT.

Stollsteimer, John F. Regional efficiency in the organization of agricultural processing facilities : an application to pear packing in the Lake County Pear District, California / John F. Stollsteimer, Richard H. Courtney, and L.L. Sammet. [Berkeley] : California Agricultural Experiment Station, 1975. 148 p. : ill. ; 26 cm. (Giannini Foundation monograph . no. 35) Cover title. At head of title: University of California Division of Agricultural Sciences, Giannini Foundation of Agricultural Economics. Based on J.F. Stollsteimer's thesis, University of California, Berkeley, 1961. Bibliography: p. 145-148. LC Card 76-622988 DDC 338.1 s 664/.80413 19
1. Pear - Packing - Economic aspects - California - Lake Co. 2. Industries, Location of - California - Lake Co. I. Courtney, Richard H., joint author. II. Sammet, Loy Luther, joint author. III. Series: California. University. Giannini Foundation of Agricultural Economics. Monograph, no. 35. IV. Title.
HD1407 .C27 no. 35 SB373

Stoloff, Carolyn. Swiftly now / Carolyn Stoloff. Athens : Ohio University Press, 1982. p. cm. ISBN 0-8214-0646-9 LC Card 81-11150 DDC 811/.54 19
1. Title.
PS3569.T623 S9

Stoloff, David. Rahenkamp, Sachs, Wells, and Associates. Innovative zoning: a local officials guidebook /. [Washington] , 1977. 28 p.:

STOLYPIN, PETR ARKAD'EVICH, 1862-1911. Yaney, George L. The urge to mobilize . Urbana , c1982. p. cm. ISBN 0-252-00910-X LC Card 81-11527 DDC 333.3/1/47 19
HD1333.S65 Y36

The stone crab, Menippe mercenaria, in the southwest Florida fishery /. Sullivan, James Richard, 1947- St. Petersburg, Fla. , 1979. 37 p. : LC Card 80-622656 DDC 333.95/5 19
QL444.M33 S93

Stone, Eugene F. Relationships between growth need strength and other individual differences measures employed in job design research / by Eugene F. Stone, Daniel C. Ganster, and Richard W. Woodman. West Lafayette, Ind. : Institute for Research in the Behavioral, Economic, and Management Sciences, Krannert Graduate School of Management, Purdue University, 1977. 17 leaves ; 28 cm. (Paper - Institute for Research in the Behavioral, Economic, and Management Sciences, Krannert Graduate School of Management . no. 644) Bibliography: leaves 14-15.
    LC Card 78-101255 DDC 658/.001/9 s 658.3/1422 19
1. Job satisfaction. I. Ganster, Daniel C., joint author. II. Woodman, Richard W., joint author. III. Series: Krannert Graduate School of Management. Institute for Research in the Behavioral, Economic, and Management Sciences. Paper - Institute for Research in the Behavioral, Economic, and Management Sciences, Krannert Graduate School of Management , no. 644. IV. Title.
HD6483 .P8 no. 644 HF5549.5.J63

STONE IMPLEMENTS. Dreiman, Richard N. Methods in artifact analysis . Berkeley [1979] 79 p. : LC Card 80-623478 DDC 930.1 s 930.1/2 19
E51 .C2 no. 42 GN772.A1

Stone, Julius, 1907- Hathaway, Barbara Drexler. Julius Stone . Austin , 1980. i, 51 leaves ; ISBN 0-935630-20-3 (pbk.) LC Card 80-114099 DDC 340/.1 19
K235 .H37

STONE, JULIUS, 1907- Hathaway, Barbara Drexler. Julius Stone . Austin , 1980. i, 51 leaves ; ISBN 0-935630-20-3 (pbk.) LC Card 80-114099 DDC 340/.1 19
K235 .H37

STONE, JULIUS, 1907- - BIBLIOGRAPHY. Hathaway, Barbara Drexler. Julius Stone . Austin , 1980. i, 51 leaves ; ISBN 0-935630-20-3 (pbk.) LC Card 80-114099 DDC 340/.1 19
K235 .H37

Stone, Paul S. (joint author) Fearn, Robert M. Employment and wage changes in North Carolina /. Raleigh, N.C. [1980] 38 p. ; LC Card 80-624073 DDC 338.1 s 331.12/5/09756 19
S97 .Z4 no. 60 HD5725.N8

Stone, Sean Murphy. (joint author) Poore, Richard Z. Biostratigraphy and paleoecology of the upper Miocene (Messinian) and lower Pliocene (?) Cerro de Almendral section, Alermía Basin, southern Spain /. Washington , 1981. iii, 11 p., [2] leaves of plates : LC Card 80-607164 DDC 551.7/86/094681 19
QE694 .P67

Stoneman, W. C. (joint author) Schmidt, Richard A. A study of surface coal mining in West Virginia. Menlo Park, Calif., 1972. xiii, 180 p. LC Card 72-611225
TN805.W4 S28

Stony Brook . Massachusetts. Division of Water Pollution Control. Water Quality Section. Westborough [1975] 51 p. : LC Card 79-620595 DDC 363.7/3942/097444 19
TD224.M4 M36 1975a

Stony Creek, Dauphin and Lebanon Counties, Pennsylvania. Brezina, Edward R. An aquatic biological investigation of Stony Creek, Dauphin and Lebanon Counties, Pennsylvania /. Harrisburg , 1974. 27 p. ; LC Card 75-623487 DDC 363.6/1 s 574.92/9/74818 19
TD224.P4 P45A no. 36 QH105.P4

STONY POINT, N. Y. (TOWNSHIP) - CITY PLANNING. Rockland County, N. Y. Planning Board. Development plan : town of Stony Point, N. Y. . Stony Point, N. Y. , 1973. iv, 118 p. :

STOPPARD, TOM - CRITICISM AND INTERPRETATION. Dean, Joan Fitzpatrick, 1949- Tom Stoppard . Columbia , 1981. 109 p. ; ISBN 0-8262-0332-9 (pbk.) LC Card 80-26400 DDC 822/.914 19
PR6069.T6 Z63

Stoppard, Tom - Interpretation and criticism. see Stoppard, Tom - Criticism and interpretation.

STORAGE. see WAREHOUSES.

Storage and alternative options for increasing the availability of natural gas. Zinder (H.) and Associates, inc. Report to the New Mexico Energy and Minerals Department of storage and alternative options for increasing the availability of natural gas. Socorro, N.M. [1979] 61, [61] p. : LC Card 80-622030 DDC 333.8/23311/09789 19
TN881.N6 Z52 1979

STORAGE AND MOVING TRADE - LAW AND LEGISLATION - UNITED STATES. United States. Congress. Senate. Committee on Commerce, Science, and Transportation. Household goods transportation act of 1979 . Washington , 1979 [i.e. 1980] iv, 413 p. ; LC Card 80-601172 DDC 343.73/08856489 19
KF26 .C69 1979ac

STORAGE AND MOVING TRADE - PRICES - UNITED STATES. United States. Congress. Senate. Committee on Commerce, Science, and Transportation. Household goods transportation act of 1979 . Washington , 1979 [i.e. 1980] iv, 413 p. ; LC Card 80-601172 DDC 343.73/08856489 19
KF26 .C69 1979ac

STORAGE BATTERIES. United States. Congress. House. Committee on Science and Technology. Subcommittee on Energy Research and Production. Storage batteries for electric vehicle applications . Washington , 1980. iii, 199 p. : LC Card 80-602013 DDC 629.2/593 19
KF27 .S3936 1979m

Storage batteries for electric vehicle applications . United States. Congress. House. Committee on Science and Technology. Subcommittee on Energy Research and Production. Washington , 1980. iii, 199 p. : LC Card 80-602013 DDC 629.2/593 19
KF27 .S3936 1979m

STORAGE WAREHOUSES. see WAREHOUSES.

Store image and positioning /. Pessemier, Edgar A., 1922- West Lafayette, Ind. [1979] 16, [2], 7 p. (p. [1]-7, 3d group, advertisements) : LC Card 80-621467 DDC 658/.001/9 s 658.8/374 19
HD6483 .P8 no. 709 HF5415.3

STORE LOCATION - MATHEMATICAL MODELS. Huff, David Lynch, 1931- Retail location theory /. Austin, Tex. , 1980. [15] leaves : LC Card 80-624130 DDC 381/.1 19
HF5429.275 .H83

STORE LOCATION - NEW YORK (STATE) - WESTCHESTER COUNTY - MAPS. Westchester County (N.Y.). Office of Economic Development. Westchester County, New York, vacant land zoned commercial or industrial . White Plains, N.Y. [1978] 1 map : LC Card 81-692859
G3803.W5Q46 1978 .W4

Storey, James R. Urban Institute. Emerging options for work and retirement policy (an analysis of major income and employment issues with an agenda for research priorities) . Washington , 1980. vi, 186 p. 23 cm. LC Card 80-603277 DDC 331.25/2/0973 19
HD7106.U5 U7 1980

STORM DRAINAGE SYSTEMS. see STORM SEWERS.

STORM SEWERS - LAW AND LEGISLATION - NEW JERSEY. New Jersey. Legislature. General Assembly. Municipal Government Committee. Public hearing before Assembly Municipal Government Committee on Assembly bill 1819 (storm water management) . [Trenton] [1979?] 3,60 p. ; LC Card 80-621670 DDC 346.74904/691 347.49064691 19
KFN1811.4 .M8 1979c

STORM SEWERS - SOUTHERN STATES - CONGRESSES. Southeast Conference on Urban Stormwater Management, North Carolina State University, 1979. Urban stormwater management . [Raleigh, N.C.] [1980] vi, 252 p. : LC Card 80-623271 DDC 363.6/1 19
TD657 .S68 1979

STORM WATER RETENTION BASINS - LAW AND LEGISLATION - NEW JERSEY.
New Jersey. Legislature. General Assembly. Municipal Government Committee. Public hearing before Assembly Municipal Government Committee on Assembly bill 1819 (storm water management) . [Trenton] [1979?] 3,60 p. ; LC Card 80-621670 DDC 346.74904/691 347.49064691 19
KFN1811.4 .M8 1979c

Storms brewed in other men's worlds . John, Elizabeth Ann Harper, 1928- Lincoln , 1981, c1975. p. cm. ISBN 0-8032-7554-4 (pbk.) LC Card 81-3401 DDC 978/.00497 19
E78.S7 J64 1981

Storper, Michael. Systems and marxist theories of industrial location : a review / Michael Storper and Richard Walker. Berkeley : Institute of Urban and Regional Development, University of California, 1979. viii, 92, [6] p. ; 28 cm. (Working paper - Institute of Urban and Regional Development, University of California ; no. 312) Bibliography: p. 86-[98] LC Card 80-623098 DDC 338.6/042/01 19
1. Industries, Location of. 2. System theory. . 3. Marxian economics. I. Walker, Richard, 1947- joint author. II. Series: California. University. Institute of Urban and Regional Development. Working paper - Institute of Urban & Regional Development, University of California , no. 312. III. Title.
HD58 .S679

Storrs Agricultural Experiment Station. Gonick, Walter N. General soil map of Connecticut /. Hyattsville, Md. , 1978. 1 map : LC Card 81-690080
G3781.J3 1978 .G6

Storrs, Conn. Agricultural Experiment Station. see Connecticut. Agricultural Experiment Station, Storrs.

Story, Dale, 1950- Entrepreneurs and the state in Mexico : examining the authoritarian thesis / Dale Story. Austin : Office for Public Sector Studies, Institute of Latin American Studies, University of Texas at Austin, 1980. 14 p. ; 27 cm. (Technical papers series . no. 30) Bibliography: p. 13-14. LC Card 81-621756 DDC 338.972 19
1. Industry and state - Mexico. 2. Mexico - Industries. 3. Businessmen - Mexico. I. Title. II. Series.
HD3616.M42 S76

The story of private hospitals in Rhode Island /. Rhode Island. Health Planning & Resources Development. [Providence] , 1979. 69 p. : LC Card 80-620722 DDC 362.1/1/09745 19
RA981.R4 R5 1979

The story of the Columbia Basin project. United States. Bureau of Reclamation. Denver , Washington , 1978. 45 p. : LC Card 79-601522 DDC 333.91/3/0979731 19
TC425.C7 U54 1978

The story of the Pribilof fur seals. United States. National Oceanic and Atmospheric Administration. [Washington] [1976] 34 p. : LC Card 77-601364 DDC 333.95/9 19
SH361 .U75 1976

Stosberg, Don. Kentucky's Black teacher gap : an analysis of teacher employment, 1954-1974 / [prepared by Don Stosberg, D. Patricia Wagner, and Douglas Hamilton]. Frankfort : Kentucky Commission on Human Rights, Commonwealth of Kentucky, 1975. 20 p. ; 28 cm. Microfiche (neg.) NTIS. 1 sheet. 11 x 15 cm. (PB 269 039) Cover title. LC Card 77-621256
1. Afro-American teachers - Kentucky - Statistics. I. Wagner, D. Patricia, joint author. II. Hamilton, Douglas, 1950- joint author. III. Kentucky. Commission on Human Rights. IV. Title.
LC214.32.K4 S76   **NYPL [*XME]**

Stose, George Willis, 1869-1960. United States. Geological Survey. Geologic map of Colorado /. Denver [1975] 1 map : 93 x 127 cm. Scale 1:500,000. "Modified polyconic projection." Reprinted in 1975 from the 1935 ed. Includes "Index map of Colorado, showing principal sources of geologic data." Bibliography. LC Card 78-695857
G4311.C5 1935 .U51
       NYPL [Map Div. 81-3090]

Stout, Paul. (joint author) Scott, Michael James, 1948- Standards for determining child support obligations in Alaska /. Anchorage [1978] 156 p. in various pagings : LC Card 79-622825 DDC

362.7/95 19
HV742.A4 S37

STOWAGE, MINE. see MINE FILLING.

STRAFFORD COUNTY (N.H.) - MAPS.
United States. Soil Conservation Service. Strafford County, New Hampshire /. Lanham, MD , 1980. 1 map : LC Card 81-690023
G3743.S7 1975 .U5

Strahan, Genevieve W. Inpatient health facilities statistics, United States, 1978 / Genevieve W. Strahan. Hyattsville, Md. : U. S. Dept. of Health and Human Services, Public Health Service, Office of Health Research, Statistics, and Technology, National Center for Health Statistics, 1980. p. cm. (Vital and health statistics : Series 14, Data from the National Health Survey ; no. 24) DHHS publication ; no. (PHS) 81-1819 Includes bibliographical references. ISBN 0-8406-0204-9 LC Card 80-607845 DDC 362.1/1/0973 19
1. Hospitals - United States - Statistics. 2. Nursing homes - United States - Statistics. I. Series: United States. National Center for Health Statistics. Vital and health statistics : Series 14, Data from the National Health Survey, Data on health resources, manpower, and facilities , no. 24. II. Title.
RA981.A2 S78

STRAITS - MAPS.
United States. Central Intelligence Agency. Selected world shipping lanes and straits. [Washington , 1980] 1 map : LC Card 81-690686
G3201.P54 1980 .U5

Strand, M. R. (joint author) Gold, J. R. Chromosome formulae of North American fishes /. College Station , 1979. 24 p. ; LC Card 79-624059 DDC 597/.015 19
QL638.99 .G64

STRAND, PAUL, 1890-1976 - ARCHIVES.
Arizona. University. Center for Creative Photography. Paul Strand archive /. Tucson, Ariz. , c1980. 25 p. ; LC Card 80-144141 DDC 770/.92/4 19
TR140.S7345 A73 1980

Strange, Heather. (joint author) Green, Vera. Cultural perspectives on aging . New Brunswick, N.J. , c1980. ii leaves, 88 p. ; LC Card 80-129770 DDC 016.3052/6 19
Z7164.O4 G67 HQ1060

STRATEGIC ARMS LIMITATION TALKS.
United States. Congress. Senate. Committee on Foreign Relations. Nuclear war strategy . Washington , 1981. iii, 40 p. ; LC Card 81-601145 DDC 355/.0217/0973 19
KF26 .F6 1980s

STRATEGIC FORCES - RUSSIA.
United States. Congress. House. Permanent Select Committee on Intelligence. Subcommittee on Oversight. Soviet strategic forces . Washington , 1980. iii, 76 p. ; LC Card 80-602765 DDC 358/.17/0947 19
KF27.5 .I55 1980

STRATEGIC FORCES - UNITED STATES.
United States. Congress. House. Committee on Armed Services. Hearings on H.R. 8390 . Washington , 1977. ii, 471 p. : LC Card 78-601218
KF27 .A7 1977q

United States. General Accounting Office. The Air Force can reduce its stated requirements for strategic airlift crews . [Washington] 1979. v, 23 p. ; LC Card 79-603765 DDC 358.4/161/0973 19
UG773 .U54 1979

Strategic implications of chemical and biological warfare . United States. Congress. House. Committee on Foreign Affairs. Subcommittee on International Security and Scientific Affairs. Washington , 1980. iii, 69 p. ; LC Card 80-602441 DDC 358/.34 19
KF27 .F64825 1980b

Strategic implications of the Omnibus maritime bill, H.R. 6899. United States. Congress. House. Committee on Merchant Marine and Fisheries. Report on the strategic implications of the Omnibus maritime bill, H.R. 6899 . Washington , 1980. ii, 35 p. : LC Card 80-602266 DDC 359.2/7/0973 19
VA77 .U56 1980

STRATEGIC MATERIALS - LAW AND LEGISLATION - UNITED STATES.
Compilation of the Energy Security Act of

1980, and 1980 amendments to the Defense Production Act of 1950 /. Washington , 1980. 3 v. (v. 2252 p.) ; LC Card 80-603878 DDC 346.7304/679 347.3064679 19
KF2120.A32 A15 1980

STRATEGIC MATERIALS - UNITED STATES.
United States. Congress. House. Committee on Interior and Insular Affairs. Subcommittee on Mines and Mining. Sub-Sahara Africa, its role in critical mineral needs of the Western World . Washington , 1980. viii, 29 p. : LC Card 80-603266 DDC 338.2/0967 19
TN119.Z3 U55 1980

STRATEGIC MATERIALS - UNITED STATES - FINANCE.
Holt, Barry J. Financing options for the strategic petroleum reserve /. [Washington, D.C.] , 1981. xv, 40 p. ; LC Card 81-601992 DDC 353.0072/22538 19
HD9565 .H6

STRATEGIC MATERIALS - UNITED STATES - STORAGE.
United States. General Accounting Office. U. S. strategic petroleum reserve at a turning point . Washington, D.C. , 1980. iv p., 28 leaves : LC Card 80-601078 DDC 333.8/23211/0973 19
TP692.5 .U624 1980

STRATEGIC MATERIALS - UNITED STATES - STORAGE - PERIODICALS.
United States. Strategic Petroleum Reserve Office. Annual strategic petroleum reserve report. [Washington]. LC Card 78-645585
      NYPL [JSP 80-382]

Strategic petroleum reserve . United States. Strategic Petroleum Reserve Office. [Washington] , 1976- v. : LC Card 77-602345
TP692.5 .U627 1976a

Strategic petroleum reserve and the naval petroleum reserve . United States. Congress. Senate. Committee on Energy and Natural Resources. Subcommittee on Energy Resources and Materials Production. Washington , 1980. iii, 65 p. ; LC Card 80-602779 DDC 333.8/23211/0973 19
KF26 .E5543 1980a

Strategic petroleum reserve annual report. United States. Strategic Petroleum Reserve Office. Annual strategic petroleum reserve report. [Washington]. LC Card 78-645585
      NYPL [JSP 80-382]

Strategic planning study, Canteen Creek watershed, Madison & St. Clair Counties /. Booker Associates. St. Louis, Mo. [1978] iiii, 46, [17] leaves, 19 fold. leaves of plates : LC Card 79-623263 DDC 627/.12/0977386 19
TC424.I3 B66 1978

Strategic warning system false alerts . United States. Congress. House. Committee on Armed Services. Washington , 1980. ii, 30 p. ; LC Card 80-603048 DDC 358/.17/0973 19
KF27 .A7 1980c

Strategies for computer-oriented productivity and effectiveness in the 80's . Illinois. SCOPE 80's Task Force. [Springfield, Ill.] [1980] ca. 300 p. in various pagings : LC Card 80-623318 DDC 353.977304/02854 19
JK5749.A8 I46 1980

Strategies to encourage older workers to voluntarily extend their worklives . United States. Congress. House. Committee on Ways and Means. Subcommittee on Oversight. Washington , 1980. iii, 264 p. : LC Card 80-604060 DDC 368.4/3/00973 19
KF27 .W345 1980k

A strategy of oil proliferation . Safer, Arnold E. Washington , 1980. vii, 20 p. ; LC Card 80-603267 DDC 333.8/23215 19
TN870 .S22

Stratiform zinc-lead deposits in the Drenchwater Creek area, Howard Pass quadrangle, northwestern Brooks Range, Alaska /. Nokleberg, Warren J. Menlo Park, CA , 1981. p. cm. LC Card 81-607994 DDC 553.4/4/097987 19
TN483.A64 N64

STRATIGRAPHIC CORRELATION - UNITED STATES.
Correlation chart for Precambrian rocks of the eastern United States /. Reston, Va. , 1981. p.

cm.   LC Card 81-607917   DDC 551.7/1/0973 19
QE653 .C68

STRATIGRAPHIC GEOLOGY. see GEOLOGY, STRATIGRAPHIC.

Stratigraphy and diagenetic history of the lower part of the Triassic Chitistone Limestone /. Armstrong, Augustus K. Washington , 1981. p. cm.   LC Card 81-6608   DDC 552/.5 19
QE471.15.L5 A75

Stratigraphy and structure of the Strawberry mine roof pendant, central Sierra Nevada, California /. Nokleberg, Warren J. Washington , 1980. p. cm.   LC Card 80-607173   DDC 551.7/6/097944 19
QE675 .N64

Stratigraphy and structure of the western Kentucky fluorspar district /. Trace, Robert Denny, 1917- Washington , 1981. p. cm.   LC Card 80-607000   DDC 551.7/009769 19
QE672 .T7

Stratigraphy, paleontology, and geology of the central Santa Cruz Mountains, California Coast Ranges /. Clark, Joseph C. Washington , 1981. p. cm.   LC Card 81-607048   DDC 551.7/8/097947 19
QE691 .C42

STRATOPAUSE. see STRATOSPHERE.

The Stratosphere : present and future / edited by Robert D. Hudson and Edith I. Reed. Washington, D.C. : National Aeronautics and Space Administration, Scientific and Technical Information Branch ; [Springfield, Va. : For sale by the National Technical Information Service], '1979. xiv, 432 p. : ill., maps ; 27 cm. (NASA reference publication. 1049) "NASA Goddard Space Flight Center." Dec. 1979. Bibliography: p. 363-428.   LC Card 81-600765   DDC 551.5/142 19
1. Stratosphere. I. Hudson, Robert D., 1931-. II. Reed, Edith I. III. United States. National Aeronautics and Space Administration. Scientific and Technical Information Office. IV. Goddard Space Flight Center.
QC881.2.S8 S85

STRATOSPHERE.
Garvin, David, 1923- Chemicl kinetics data survey VII. Washington, 1974. 101 p.
                                        NYPL [JSF 80-995]

National Research Council. Committee on Impacts of Stratospheric Change. Protection against depletion of stratospheric ozone by chlorofluorocarbons /. Washington, D.C. , 1979. xvii, 392 p. :   ISBN 0-309-02947-3 LC Card 79-57247
TD887.C47 N37 1979   **NYPL [JSE 81-221]**

The Stratosphere . Washington, D.C. [Springfield, Va.] 1979. xiv, 432 p. :   LC Card 81-600765   DDC 551.5/142 19
QC881.2.S8 S85

Stratton, Peter J. (joint author) Walzer, Norman. Financing township services /. [Macomb] [Urbana-Champaign] [1979?] 84 p. :   LC Card 80-621226   DDC 352.1/09773 19
HJ9227 .W32

Straub, Conrad P. (joint author) Singer, Rexford D. Ground water quality in southeastern Minnesota /. Minneapolis, Minn. [1980] vi, 79, 64 leaves :   LC Card 80-622728   DDC 553.7/9/097761 19
TD224.M6 S56

Strausz-Hupé, Robert, 1903- NATO, task of adaptation / by Robert Strausz-Hupé. [Columbia] : University of South Carolina, Institute of International Studies, 1978. 18 p. ; 23 cm. (Occasional paper - University of South Carolina, Institute of International Studies . no. 2) Cover title.   LC Card 79-622644   DDC 341.7/2 19
1. North Atlantic Treaty Organization. I. Series: South Carolina. University. Institute of International Studies. Occasional paper - Institute of International Studies, University of South Carolina , no. 2. II. Title.
JX1393.N67 S77

STRAW.
Chi, Chia-hsiung, 1943- Inhibition of Cellulomonas sp. by heat-treated sugarcane bagasse and rice straw /. Honolulu , 1981. p. cm.   LC Card 81-4120   DDC 632/.32 19
QR160 .C47

STRAWBERRIES - HARVESTING - LAW AND LEGISLATION - UNITED STATES.
United States. Congress. House. Committee on Education and Labor. Subcommittee on Labor

Standards. Oversight hearing on the child labor provisions of the Fair labor standards act . Washington , 1980. iv, 196 p. :   LC Card 80-603516   DDC 353.0083/82 19
KF27 .E348 1980b

Strawn, Keith. Barfield, Rodney. The Bechtlers and their coinage . Raleigh, N.C. , c1980. xi, 65 p. :   ISBN 0-86526-175-X   LC Card 80-66204   DDC 737.49756 19
CJ1848.N8 B37

STREAM CHANNELIZATION - ENVIRONMENTAL ASPECTS.
Nunnally, Nelson R. Use of fluvial processes to minimize adverse effects of stream channelization /. [Raleigh, N.C.] , 1979. viii, 115 p. :   LC Card 80-620990   DDC 333.91/009756 s 627/.12 19
HD1694.N8 N6 no. 144 TC424.N8

STREAM CHANNELIZATION - ENVIRONMENTAL ASPECTS - IOWA.
Effects of habitat alterations on riparian plant and animal communities in Iowa /. Kearneysville, WV [1981] p. cm.   LC Card 81-607834   DDC 574.5/264 19
QH545.S8 E37

STREAM CHANNELIZATION - ENVIRONMENTAL ASPECTS - NORTH CAROLINA - MECKLENBURG CO.
Nunnally, Nelson R. Use of fluvial processes to minimize adverse effects of stream channelization /. [Raleigh, N.C.] , 1979. viii, 115 p. :   LC Card 80-620990   DDC 333.91/009756 s 627/.12 19
HD1694.N8 N6 no. 144 TC424.N8

STREAM CONSERVATION.
Nunnally, Nelson R. Use of fluvial processes to minimize adverse effects of stream channelization /. [Raleigh, N.C.] , 1979. viii, 115 p. :   LC Card 80-620990   DDC 333.91/009756 s 627/.12 19
HD1694.N8 N6 no. 144 TC424.N8

STREAM CONSERVATION - NORTH CAROLINA - MECKLENBURG CO.
Nunnally, Nelson R. Use of fluvial processes to minimize adverse effects of stream channelization /. [Raleigh, N.C.] , 1979. viii, 115 p. :   LC Card 80-620990   DDC 333.91/009756 s 627/.12 19
HD1694.N8 N6 no. 144 TC424.N8

STREAM ECOLOGY - KANSAS - KANSAS RIVER.
Marzolf, G. Richard. Kansas River limnology . Manhattan , 1979. 56 p. :   LC Card 79-625208   DDC 574.5/26323/09781 19
QH105.K3 M37

STREAM ECOLOGY - MINNESOTA - CANNON RIVER.
Minnesota. Dept. of Natural Resources. Cannon River resource analysis. [St. Paul] [1979] 48 p. :   LC Card 79-623707   DDC 333.91/62/09776 19
QH76.5.M6 M54 1979

STREAM ECOLOGY - MINNESOTA - MINNESOTA RIVER.
Minnesota. Wild and Scenic Rivers Program. Minnesota River resource analysis. [St. Paul] , 1979. 55 p. :   LC Card 79-625703   DDC 333.91/621/097763 19
QH105.M55 M56 1979

STREAM ECOLOGY - MINNESOTA - ST. LOUIS RIVER.
Peterson, Arthur R. Fish and wildlife survey of the St. Louis River /. [St. Paul] [1979] vii, 103 p., [25] leaves of plates :   LC Card 80-621233   DDC 574.5/26323/09776 19
QH105.M55 P48

STREAM ECOLOGY - PENNSYLVANIA - DAUPHIN CO.
Brezina, Edward R. An aquatic biological investigation of Stony Creek, Dauphin and Lebanon Counties, Pennsylvania /. Harrisburg , 1974. 27 p. ;   LC Card 75-623487   DDC 363.6/1 s 574.92/9/74818 19
TD224.P4 P45A no. 36 QH105.P4

STREAM ECOLOGY - PENNSYLVANIA - LEBANON CO.
Brezina, Edward R. An aquatic biological investigation of Stony Creek, Dauphin and Lebanon Counties, Pennsylvania /. Harrisburg , 1974. 27 p. ;   LC Card 75-623487   DDC 363.6/1 s 574.92/9/74818 19
TD224.P4 P45A no. 36 QH105.P4

STREAM ECOLOGY - WISCONSIN.
Avery, Eddie L. The influence of chemical reclamation on a small brown trout stream in southwestern Wisconsin /. Madison, Wis. , 1978. 35 p. :   LC Card 79-624431   DDC 639.9/09775 s 597/.55 19
SK463 .A27 no. 110 QL638.S2

Hilsenhoff, William LeRoy, 1929- Use of arthropods to evaluate water quality of streams /. Madison, WI , 1977. 15 p. :   LC Card 78-623368   DDC 639.9/09775 s 628.1/68/028/7 19
SK463 .A27 no. 100 QH105.W6

STREAM IMPROVEMENT (ECOLOGY) see STREAM CONSERVATION.

STREAM MEASUREMENTS - ALABAMA.
Bingham, Roy H., 1930- Low-flow characteristics of Alabama streams /. Washington , 1981. p. cm.   LC Card 80-607849   DDC 551.48/3/09761 19
GB1225.A2 B56 1981

STREAM MEASUREMENTS - CALIFORNIA - CENTRAL VALLEY.
California. Dept. of Water Resources. Division of Planning. California Central Valley natural flow data /. [Sacramento] [1980] v, 77 p. :   LC Card 80-623071   DDC 551.48/3/097945 19
GB1225.C3 C34 1980

STREAM MEASUREMENTS - CHOWAN RIVER WATERSHED.
Contractor, D. N. Streamflow and water quality modeling of the Chowan River /. Blacksburg, Va. [1980] vii, 71 p. :   LC Card 80-623862   DDC 333.91/009755 s 363.7/3942/0724 19
TD201 .V57 no. 119 TD225.C53

STREAM MEASUREMENTS - ILLINOIS - KASKASKIA RIVER.
Bhowmik, Nani G. Hydraulics of flow in the Kaskaskia River, Illinois /. Urbana , 1979. 116 p. :   LC Card 80-621692   DDC 553.7/09773 s 551.48/3/09773 19
GB705.I3 A3 no. 91 GB1225.I27

STREAM MEASUREMENTS - LOUISIANA.
Forbes, Max J., 1930- Low-flow characteristics of Louisiana streams /. Baton Rouge, La. , 1980. iv, 95 p., [1] fold. leaf of plates :   LC Card 80-623625   DDC 551.48/3/09763 19
GB1225.L6 F67

STREAM MEASUREMENTS - MISSOURI VALLEY.
Osterkamp, W. R. Perennial-streamflow characteristics related to channel geometry and sediment in the Missouri River basin /. [Reston, Va.?] [1981] p. cm.   LC Card 81-607905   DDC 551.48/3/0978 19
GB1227.M7 O84

STREAM MEASUREMENTS - NEVADA.
Schroer, C. V. Nevada streamflow characteristics /. Carson City [1978] 478 p. :   LC Card 80-623614   DDC 551.48/3/09793 19
GB1225.N3 S37

STREAM MEASUREMENTS - NEVADA - INCLINE VILLAGE REGION.
Glancy, Patrick A. A reconnaissance of streamflow and fluvial sediment transport, Incline Village area, Lake Tahoe, Nevada . Carson City , 1976. v, 42 p. :   LC Card 80-623612   DDC 551.48/09793/57 19
GB1225.N3 G56

STREAM MEASUREMENTS - NEW YORK (STATE)
Eissler, Benjamin B. Low-flow data and frequency analysis of streams in New York, excluding New York City and Long Island /. Albany, N.Y. , 1979. v, 176 p. :   LC Card 80-622145   DDC 551.48/3/09747 19
GB1225.N7 E37

STREAM MEASUREMENTS - OHIO RIVER WATERSHED - TABLES.
Virginia. Bureau of Water Control Management. Flow characteristics of Virginia streams, Ohio River basin. Richmond, Va. [1979] xxv, 197 p. :   LC Card 80-622497   DDC 551.48/3/09755 19
GB1225.V8 V57 1979a

STREAM MEASUREMENTS - OREGON - OCHOCO CREEK WATERSHED.
Berndt, H. W. Forest land use and streamflow in central Oregon /. Portland, Or. , 1970. 15 p. :   LC Card 71-608738   DDC 634.9/09795 s

553.7/09795/83 19
SD11 .A45614 no. 93 SD387.M8

**STREAM MEASUREMENTS - TEXAS -
TRINITY RIVER WATERSHED.**
Trinity River Authority of Texas. Planning and
Environmental Management Division. Low flow
nutrient loss in the mid-Trinity River ;
Runoff-related pollutant loadings in the
mid-Trinity River /. [Austin] , 1978. iii, 72, iv,
73 p. :　LC Card 80-622543　DDC
363.7/3942/097642 19
TD224.T4 T74 1978

STREAM MEASUREMENTS - VIRGINIA.
Flow characteristics of Virginia streams, South
Atlantic slope basin. Richmond, Va. [1979]
xvi, 421 p. :　LC Card 80-622496　DDC
551.48/3/09755 19
GB1225.V8 F58

**STREAM MEASUREMENTS - VIRGINIA -
TABLES.**
Virginia. Bureau of Water Control Management.
Flow characteristics of Virginia streams, North
Atlantic slope basin. Richmond, Va. [1979] xv,
254 p. :　LC Card 80-622495　DDC 551.48/3/09755
19
GB1225.V8 V57 1979

Virginia. Bureau of Water Control Management.
Flow characteristics of Virginia streams, Ohio
River basin. Richmond, Va. [1979] xxv, 197
p. :　LC Card 80-622497　DDC 551.48/3/09755 19
GB1225.V8 V57 1979a

**STREAM MEASUREMENTS -
WASHINGTON (STATE)**
A summary of quantity, quality, and economic
methodology for establishing minimum flows .
Pullman , 1973- v. <1> :　LC Card 75-620707
DDC 553.7/09797 s 333.9/0217/09797 19
TD224.W2 S8 no. 13 GB1225.W3

**STREAM POLLUTION. see WATER -
POLLUTION.**

**STREAM PRESERVATION. see STREAM
CONSERVATION.**

**STREAM SEDIMENT TRANSPORT. see
SEDIMENT TRANSPORT.**

**Streamflow and water quality modeling of the
Chowan River /.** Contractor, D. N. Blacksburg,
Va. [1980] vii, 71 p. :　LC Card 80-623862
DDC 333.91/009755 s 363.7/3942/0724 19
TD201 .V57 no. 119 TD225.C53

STREAMLING. see AERODYNAMICS.

**STREET-RAILROADS - WASHINGTON
(STATE)**
Turbeville, Daniel E. The electric railway era in
Northwest Washington, 1890-1930 /.
Bellingham, WA , 1978, c1979. xi, 199 p. :　LC
Card 81-621749　DDC 388.4/6/097977 19
TF724.W2 T87 1979

Street, Susan L. McGinn, Noel F., 1934- Higher
education policies in Mexico /. Austin , 1980.
11 p. ;　LC Card 81-621755　DDC 370/.972 19
LC177.M6 M23

**STREET TRAFFIC. see TRAFFIC
ENGINEERING.**

Streeter, Deborah. (joint author) Saupe, William E.
Changes in farm poverty in Wisconsin /.
[Madison] [1979] 24 p. ;　LC Card 80-622902
DDC 338.1/3/09775 19
HC107.W63 P6246

Streib, Gordon Franklin, 1918- Programs for
older Americans . Gainesville , 1981. p. cm.
ISBN 0-8130-0705-4　LC Card 81-11645　DDC
305.2/6/0973 19
HQ1064.U5 P73

Strengthening environmental programs /. United
States. National Science Foundation. National
Science Board. Subcommittee on Environmental
Programs. [Washington] , 1976. 27 p. ;　LC
Card 78-601436　DDC 551.48/072073 19
GB658.7 .U57 1976

Strengthening the legislative process . National
Conference of State Legislatures. Denver, Colo.
(1124 17th St., Suite 1500, Denver 80202)
[1980?] 32 p. ;　LC Card 81-621044　DDC 328.73
19
JK2495 .N37 1980

**Stress distribution and pillar design in oil shale
retorts /.** Peng, Syd S., 1939- Avondale, Md. ,
1981. p. cm.　LC Card 81-607827　DDC 622 s

622/.3382 19
TN23 .U43 TN858

**STRESS (PSYCHOLOGY) - ADDRESSES,
ESSAYS, LECTURES.**
Family medicine and supportive interventions .
Chapel Hill , 1981. vi, 71 p. ;　ISBN
0-89143-076-8　LC Card 80-39948　DDC 610
19
RA418.5.F3 F36

STRESS (PSYCHOLOGY) - CONGRESSES.
Conference on Mental Health and the
Economy, Hunt Valley, Md., 1978. Mental
health and the economy . Kalamazoo, Mich.
[1979] viii, 423 p. :　ISBN 0-911558-69-1　LC
Card 79-25809
RC455 .C625 1978　　　**NYPL [JLE 80-2456]**

Strickland, Bonnie B. Turnbull, H. Rutherford.
Special education and "related services" for
handicapped children /. [Chapel Hill] , 1980.
25 p. ;　LC Card 80-624006　DDC 371.9/09756 19
LC4031 .T88

Strickland, Lucy. The law and the elderly in
North Carolina / Lucy Strickland, Mason P.
Thomas, Jr. Rev. ed. [Chapel Hill]: Institute of
Government, University of North Carolina at
Chapel Hill, 1980. x, 154 p. ; 23 cm. Includes
bibliographical references.　LC Card 81-620519　DDC
344.765/0326 347.6504326 19
*1. Aged - Legal status, laws, etc. - North Carolina. 2.
Old age assistance - North Carolina. I. Thomas, Mason
P. II. Institute of Government (Chapel Hill, N.C.). III.
Title.*
KFN7491.A3 S75 1980

Strickland, Rennard. Oklahoma memories /.
Norman , 1981. p. cm.　ISBN 0-8061-1689-7　LC
Card 81-2777　DDC 976.6 19
F693 .O37

Strickler, Paul T. United States population data
methodology /. Alexandria, Va. , 1973. v, 258
p. ;　　　　　　　　　　　　**NYPL [JLF 81-353]**

**STRIKES AND LOCKOUTS -
AGRICULTURAL LABORERS -
CALIFORNIA.**
California. Legislature. Assembly. Selected
Committee on Farm Labor. Chairman's report
/. Sacramento, CA [1980] 2 v. :　LC Card
80-621898　DDC 331.89/043/09794 19
KFC10.4 .F35 1980

**STRIKES AND LOCKOUTS - LOCAL
TRANSIT - CALIFORNIA.**
California. Legislature. Assembly. Committee on
Transportation. Transit labor law . [Sacramento]
[1979] 151 p. ;　LC Card 80-621411　DDC
344.794/01890413884 19
KFC10.4 .T7 1979

**STRIKES AND LOCKOUTS - TEACHERS -
PENNSYLVANIA.**
Pennsylvania. Dept. of Education. Teacher
strike report, 1977-78, Pennsylvania public
schools. [Harrisburg, PA] [1978] 23 [7],
leaves ;　LC Card 80-622147　DDC
331.89/2813711/009748 19
LB2844.47.U62 P466

Pennsylvania. Dept. of Education. Teacher
strike report, 1978-79, Pennsylvania public
schools. [Harrisburg, PA] [1979] 27, [15]
leaves :　LC Card 80-622148　DDC
331.89/2813711/009748 19
LB2844.47.U62 P4662

**STRIKES AND LOCKOUTS - UNITED
STATES.**
Kaufman, Bruce E. Wage-price expectations and
cyclical strike activity /. Washington , 1979. vi,
257 leaves :　　　　　　　**NYPL [JLF 80-1484]**

Stringer, Billy R. Soil survey of Bosque County,
Texas / [by Billy R. Stringer] ; United States
Department of Agriculture, Soil Conservation
Service, in cooperation with Texas Agricultural
Experiment Station. [Washington, D.C.] : The
Service, [1980] vii, 102 p., [31] fold. leaves of
plates : ill. ; 28 cm. Cover title. Includes
bibliographical references and index.　LC Card
80-602639　DDC 631.4/7/764518 19
*1. Soils - Texas - Bosque Co. - Maps. I. United States.
Soil Conservation Service. II. Texas. Agricultural
Experiment Station, College Station. III. Title.*
S599.T4 S75

STRIP MINING.
(1981) Stachura, Virgil J. Airblast
instrumentation and measurement techniques

for surface mine blasting /. [Washington, D.C.]
[1981] p. cm.　LC Card 80-607860　DDC 622 s
622/.31 19
TN23 .U43 TN291

**STRIP MINING - ENVIRONMENTAL
ASPECTS.**
United States. Bureau of Mines. Structure
response and damage produced by ground
vibration from surface mine blasting /.
Washington, D.C. [1981] p. cm.　LC Card
80-607825　DDC 622 s 690/.21 19
TN23 .U43 TA654.7

**STRIP MINING - ENVIRONMENTAL
ASPECTS - CONGRESSES.**
Seminar on the Role of Overburden Analysis in
Surface Mining (1980 : Wheeling, W. VA.)
Proceedings of Seminar on the Role of
Overburden Analysis in Surface Mining,
Wheeling, W. Va., May 6-7, 1980 /.
Washington , 1981. p. cm.　LC Card 81-607049
DDC 622 s 622/.31 19
TN295 .U4 TD195.S75

**STRIP MINING - ENVIRONMENTAL
ASPECTS - UNITED STATES.**
United States. Congress. House. Committee on
Interior and Insular Affairs. Subcommittee on
Energy and the Environment. Oversight on the
Surface Mining Control and Reclamation Act of
1977 . Washington , 1981. vi, 621 p. ;　LC Card
81-601889　DDC 353.0082/382 19
KF27 .I518 1980d

**STRIP MINING - GOVERNMENT POLICY -
UNITED STATES.**
United States. Congress. House. Committee on
Interior and Insular Affairs. Subcommittee on
Energy and the Environment. Oversight on the
Surface Mining Control and Reclamation Act of
1977 . Washington , 1981. vi, 621 p. ;　LC Card
81-601889　DDC 353.0082/382 19
KF27 .I518 1980d

**STRIP MINING - LAW AND LEGISLATION -
NEW MEXICO.**
New Mexico. Mining and Minerals Division.
State of New Mexico surface coal mining
regulations, Rule 80-1 /. Santa Fe, N.M.
[1980] xvi, 262 p. ;　LC Card 80-624203　DDC
346.78904/68 347.8906468 19
KFN3855.5.A435 A2 1980

**STRIP MINING - LAW AND LEGISLATION -
UNITED STATES.**
United States. Congress. House. Committee on
Interior and Insular Affairs. Subcommittee on
Energy and the Environment. Reclamation
practices and environmental problems of surface
mining . Washington , 1977. 4 v. :　LC Card
77-603316　DDC 346.7304/68 347.306468 19
KF27 .I518 1977j

**STRIP MINING - LAW AND LEGISLATION -
UNITED STATES - STATES.**
United States. General Accounting Office.
Issues surrounding the Surface mining control
and reclamation act . [Washington, D.C.] ,
1979. v, 45 p. :　LC Card 79-603742　DDC
353.0082/382 19
KF1823.Z95 U53

**STRIP MINING - LAW AND LEGISLATION -
WEST (U. S.)**
Dyer, Barbara, 1951- The Surface Mining Act
in the West . Lexington, Ky. (Iron Works Pike,
Lexington 40578) , c1980. vii, 31 p. :　LC Card
81-133232　DDC 346.7304/68 347.306468 19
KF1823 .D94

STRIP MINING - SAFETY MEASURES.
Derby, George K. Reduction of airborne
contaminants from welding exhaust at surface
mines /. Avondale, MD , 1981. p. cm.　LC
Card 81-607864　DDC 622 s 671.5/2 19
TN295 .U4

STRIP MINING - WEST VIRGINIA.
Schmidt, Richard A. A study of surface coal
mining in West Virginia. Menlo Park, Calif. ,
1972. xiii, 180 p.　LC Card 72-611225
TN805.W4 S28　　　　**NYPL [JLF 81-203]**

STRIP MINING - WYOMING - STATISTICS.
Wyoming. Dept. of Labor and Statistics.
Wyoming coal strip mining . Cheyenne, Wyo. ,
1979] iii, 40 p. ;　LC Card 79-625469　DDC
331.12/522334/09787 19
HD4966.M63 U59 1979

Stripper oil miscertification . United States.
Congress. House. Committee on Interstate and

Foreign Commerce. Subcommittee on Oversight and Investigations. Washington , 1980. iii, 63 p. :   LC Card 80-604004   DDC 338.2/3 19
KF27 .I5547 1980j

Stronge, William B. (joint author. 0700) Schultz, Ronald R. The social and economic effects of the Florida tourist industry /. Boca Raton , 1978. x, 123 p. :   LC Card 79-622949
G155.U6 S37

Stroup, Richard. Bureaucracy vs. environment . Ann Arbor , c1981. p. cm.   ISBN 0-472-10010-6 :   LC Card 81-10382   DDC 363.7/00973 19
HC110.E5 B88 1981

Strout, Michelle. Roy, Marjorie Brown. Rape in Massachusetts . Boston (206 New Court House, Boston 02108) [1980] 84 p. ;   LC Card 80-623646   DDC 364.1/532/09744 19
HV6565.M4 R68

STRUCTURAL ANALYSIS (ENGINEERING)
see **STRUCTURES, THEORY OF.**

Structural change in trade in manufactured goods between industrial and developing countries /. Balassa, Bela A. Washington, D.C. , c1980. 46 leaves ;   LC Card 80-141926   DDC 382/.45 19
HD9720.5 .B34

Structural changes in industry /. International Centre for Industrial Studies. Global and Conceptual Studies Section. [New York?] , 1979. iv, 152 p. ;   LC Card 80-121831   DDC 300 s 338.09172/4 19
JX1977 .A2 UNIDO/ICIS.136

Structural characteristics of beef cattle raising in the United States /. Boykin, Calvin Clay, 1924- Washington, D.C. [1980] ii, 111 p. :   LC Card 80-602144   DDC 338.1 s 636.2/13/0973 19
HD1751 .A91854 no. 450 SF196.U5

STRUCTURAL ENGINEERING.
(1980) Development of a probability based load criterion for American national standard A58 . [Washington, D.C.] , 1980. v, 222 p. :   LC Card 80-600067   DDC 602/.18 s 690/.21 19
QC100 .U57 no. 577 TH845

Structural framework, stratigraphy, and petroleum geology of the area of oil and gas lease Sale no. 49 on the U. S. Atlantic Continental Shelf and slope / Robert E. Mattick and Jacqueline L. Hennessy, editors. Arlington, Va. : Branch of Distribution, U. S. Geological Survey, 1980. v, 101 p. : ill. ; 26 cm. (Geological survey circular ; 812) "Free on application." Bibliography: p. 97-101.   LC Card 80-600090   DDC 557.3 s 553.2/82/0974 19
1. *Geology - Atlantic coast (United States).* 2. *Petroleum - Geology - Atlantic coast (United States).* 3. *Continental margins - United States.* I. *Mattick, Robert E.* II. *Hennessy, Jacqueline L.* III. *Series: United States. Geological Survey. Circular ; 812.*
QE75 .C5 no. 812 QE78.3

Structural Pest Control Act, with Rules and regulations . California. Sacramento, Calif. , 1980. 60 p. ;   LC Card 81-621018   DDC 344.794/04633 347.94044633 19
KFC641.5.P63 A3 1980

STRUCTURAL UNEMPLOYMENT. see UNEMPLOYMENT, TECHNOLOGICAL.

STRUCTURALISM (LITERARY ANALYSIS)
Todorov, Tzvetan, 1939- [Poétique. English.] Introduction to poetics /. Minneapolis , 1981. p. cm.   ISBN 0-8166-1008-8 :   LC Card 81-3073   DDC 808.1 19
PN1043 .T613

The structure and functions of the U. S. S. R. State Committee for Science and Technology /. Nolting, Louvan E. [Washington, D.C.] [1979] iv, 53 p. ;   LC Card 80-602662   DDC 354.470085/5 19
Q127.S696 N64   **NYPL [JLM 78-229 19]**

Structure, conduct, and performance of agricultural cooperative associations in Hawaii, 1977 /. Spielmann, Heinz, 1919- Honolulu [1981] p. cm.   LC Card 81-6275   DDC 334/.683/09969 19
HD1484 .S67

Structure of corporate concentration . United States. Congress. Senate. Committee on Governmental Affairs. Washington , 1980 [i.e. 1981] 2 v. :   LC Card 81-601004   DDC 338.8/0973 19
HG4910 .U54 1981

The Structure of North Dakota state government : a compendium of North Dakota state agencies, boards, commissions & institutions : 1979-80 supplement. Bismarck, ND : State Library Commission, [1979] 76 leaves in various foliations ; 28 cm. Cover title. Pref. signed: Boyd L. Wright, Bureau of Governmental Affairs. "December 1979." Includes index.   LC Card 80-622720   DDC 353.978404 19
1. *Administrative agencies - North Dakota - Directories.* 2. *North Dakota - Executive department - Directories.* I. *Wright, Boyd L.* II. *North Dakota. State Library Commission.* III. *University of North Dakota. Bureau of Governmental Affairs.*
JK6431 1979 .S77

Structure response and damage produced by ground vibration from surface mine blasting /. United States. Bureau of Mines. Washington, D.C. [1981] p. cm.   LC Card 80-607825   DDC 622 s 690/.21 19
TN23 .U43 TA654.7

Structure shielding against fallout gamma rays from nuclear detonations /. Spencer, L. V. (Lewis Van Clief), 1924- [Washington, D.C.?] , 1980. xvi, 967 p :   LC Card 80-600120   DDC 602/.18 s 363.1/89 19
QC100 .U57 no. 570 UF787

Structure study of a CF_2Br_2-inhibited methane flame--the effect of CF_2Br_2 on composition, net reaction rates, and rate coefficients /. Papp, John F. [Washington] , 1981. p. cm.   LC Card 80-606846   DDC 622 s 628.9/223 19
TN23 .U43 QD516

STRUCTURES, DATA (COMPUTER SCIENCE) see DATA STRUCTURES (COMPUTER SCIENCE)

STRUCTURES, ENGINEERING OF. see STRUCTURAL ENGINEERING.

STRUCTURES, INFORMATION (COMPUTER SCIENCE) see DATA STRUCTURES (COMPUTER SCIENCE)

STRUCTURES, THEORY OF - MATHEMATICAL MODELS - CONGRESSES.
Research in nonlinear structural and solid mechanics . Washington, D.C. [Springfield, Va.] 1980. viii, 289 p. :   LC Card 81-601087   DDC 624.1/71/0724 19
TA646 .R38

Struyk, Raymond J. Improving the elderly's housing : a key to preserving the nation's housing stock and neighborhoods / Raymond J. Struyk and Beth J. Soldo. Cambridge, Mass. : Ballinger Pub. Co., c1980. xxii, 325 p. : ill. ; 24 cm. Includes bibliographies and index. "Written to provide the Department of Housing and Urban Development with set of carefully documented alternatives to its current programs."   ISBN 0-88410-495-8   LC Card 79-3008
1. *Aged - United States - Dwellings.* 2. *Housing policy - United States.* I. *Soldo, Beth J., joint author.* II. *United States. Dept. of Housing and Urban Development.* III. *Title.*
HD7287.92.U55 S77   **NYPL [JLE 80-2769]**

Stuart, Patricia, 1927- Forms of town and city government in Connecticut / by Patricia Stuart. Storrs : Institute of Public Service, University of Connecticut, 1978. v, 34 p. : diagrs. ; 23 cm. Includes bibliographical references.   LC Card 79-624577   DDC 352/.0072/09746 19
1. *Municipal government - Connecticut.* I. *Title.*
JS451.C85 S76 1978

Stubbs, Robert S. Georgia. Dept. of Law. The attorney general of Georgia. [Atlanta] [1979?] vi, 33 p. :   LC Card 80-622300   DDC 353.97585/092/2 B 19
KFG427.5.A8 A8384

Stuckey, Dale C. School districts of South Carolina : organization and administration / [prepared by Dale C. Stuckey and Preston B. Haines (legal researchers, Office of Planning)]. Columbia, S.C. : South Carolina Dept. of Education, Division of Administration and Planning, [1979] iii, 51 p. ; 22 x 29 cm. "January, 1979."   LC Card 80-622553   DDC 379.15/35 19
1. *School districts - South Carolina.* I. *Haines, Preston B., joint author.* II. *South Carolina. Dept. of Education. Office of Planning.* III. *Title.*
LB2817 .S75

Studds, Gerry E. Central America, 1981 : report to the Committee on Foreign Affairs, U. S. House of Representatives. Washington : U. S. G.P.O., 1981. vii, 33 p. ; 24 cm. At head of title: 97th Congress, 1st session. Committee print. Authors: Gerry E. Studds and William Woodward. "March 1981." Item 1017-A, 1017-B (microfiche)   LC Card 81-601664   DDC 320.9728 19
1. *Central America - Politics and government - 1951-.*
2. *Central America - Economic conditions.* 3. *Military assistance, American - Central America.* I. *Woodward, William, 1951-.* II. *United States. Congress. House. Committee on Foreign Affairs.* III. *Title.*
F1439 .S88

STUDENT AID - CALIFORNIA.
California. Student Aid Commission. A report on the institutional student financial aid resources survey, academic years 1971-72 to 1977-78 /. Sacramento, Calif. [1980] 245 p. :   LC Card 80-623193   DDC 378.3/09794 19
LB2337.5.C2 C35 1980

STUDENT AID - LAW AND LEGISLATION - FLORIDA.
Florida. Legislature. Senate. Committee on Education. A review of the Florida Student Financial Aid Advisory Council in the Department of Education /. [Tallahassee, Fla.] [1980] i, 22 p. ;   LC Card 81-621729   DDC 344.759//0795 347.5904795 19
KFF396 .A25 1980

STUDENT AID - LAW AND LEGISLATION - UNITED STATES.
Barkin, Tom. Legal implications of the Office [of] Education criteria for the self-supporting student /. [Madison] , 1974. 38 p. ;   LC Card 77-621624
KF4235 .B47   **NYPL [*XME-9435]**

United States. Congress. House. Committee on Post Office and Civil Service. Subcommittee on Compensation and Employee Benefits. Withholding state income tax for annuitants and amending student survivor annuity provisions . Washington , 1981. iii, 31 p. ;   LC Card 81-601887   DDC 343.7305/242 347.3035242 19
KF27 .P638 1981

STUDENT AID - NEBRASKA.
Nebraska Coordinating Commission for Postsecondary Education. Analysis of the State student incentive grant programs for 1977-78 /. Lincoln , 1979. 17 leaves ;   LC Card 79-623374   DDC 378/.3/09782 19
LB2337.5.N2 N4 1979

STUDENT AID - NEW YORK (CITY)
New York (State). Division of Audits and Accounts. Tuition assistance program receivables and payables of the City University of New York, fiscal year ended June 30, 1978 /. Albany [1980] 3, 24 leaves ;   LC Card 80-622250   DDC 379.1/22/097471 19
LD3835 .N49 1980

STUDENT AID - NEW YORK (STATE)
New York (State). Division of Audits and Accounts. Implementation of the New York State tuition assistance program at community colleges of the City University of New York, July 1, 1976--December 31, 1978. Albany [1980] 4, 29 leaves ;   LC Card 80-621893   DDC 378.3/09747/1 19
LD3853 .N48 1980

STUDENT AID - OHIO.
Financial aid for the non-traditional, part-time student . [Bowling Green, Ohio] , c1980. vii, 56 leaves ;   LC Card 80-129745   DDC 378.3/0973 19
LB2337.5.O3 F56

STUDENT AID - UNITED STATES.
United States. Congress. Senate. Committee on Labor and Human Resources. Subcommittee on Education, Arts, and Humanities. Family contribution schedule for the Basic educational opportunity grant program, 1980 . Washington , 1980. iii, 49 p. :   LC Card 80-602447   DDC 378/.3/0973 19
KF26 .L2735 1979c

United States. Congressional Budget Office. Federal student assistance . Washington, D.C. [1980] xvii, 73 p. ;   LC Card 80-602039   DDC 379.1/214/0973 19
LB2337.4 .U515 1980

United States. Office of Education. Bureau of Student Financial Assistance. Student financial

aid . [Washington] [1979] ca. 300 p. in various pagings : LC Card 80-601252 DDC 378/.3/0973 19
LB2337.4 .U55 1979

STUDENT AID - UNITED STATES - STATISTICS - PERIODICALS.
United States. Office of Education. Bureau of Student Financial Assistance. End of year report, basic grants. [Washington] LC Card 79-644063 *NYPL [JLM 80-975]*

Student financial aid . United States. Office of Education. Bureau of Student Financial Assistance. [Washington] [1979] ca. 300 p. in various pagings : LC Card 80-601252 DDC 378/.3/0973 19
LB2337.4 .U55 1979

STUDENT LOAN FUNDS - UNITED STATES.
United States. Congress. House. Committee on Ways and Means. Subcommittee on Oversight. Guaranteed student loan tax-exempt financing . Washington , 1980. iii, 96 p. : LC Card 80-603435 DDC 379.1/3 19
KF27 .W345 1980h

STUDENT LOAN FUNDS - UNITED STATES - STATES.
United States. Congressional Budget Office. State profits on tax-exempt student loan bonds . [Washington] [1980] xvi, 57 p. ; LC Card 80-601571 DDC 379.1/214/0973 19
HG4946 .U52 1980

Student migration . Frankel, Doreen. Hartford , 1979. 20 p. : LC Card 79-623189 DDC 378/.198/09746 19
LB2377.6.C8 F7

STUDENT MOBILITY.
Frankel, Doreen. Student migration . Hartford , 1979. 20 p. : LC Card 79-623189 DDC 378/.198/09746 19
LB2377.6.C8 F7

STUDENT MOVEMENTS - UNITED STATES - BIBLIOGRAPHY - CATALOGS.
DeVergie, Adrienne, 1936- Bibliography on student activism, 1963-1970 /. [Austin, Tex.] 1970. 84 leaves ; LC Card 80-622264 DDC 016.378/1981 19
KF4150.A1 D48

STUDENT PROTEST. see STUDENT MOVEMENTS.

STUDENT UNREST. see STUDENT MOVEMENTS.

Students and schools /. Williams, Jeffrey W. [Washington] , 1979. viii, 85 p. : LC Card 79-602036
LC69 .W54 *NYPL [JLF 81-365]*

STUDENTS - CHINA - POLITICAL ACTIVITY.
Shirk, Susan L. Competitive comrades . Berkeley , c1981. p. cm. ISBN 0-520-04299-9 LC Card 81-2772 DDC 371.8/1/091 19
LA1133.7 .S553

STUDENTS - GRADING AND MARKING. see GRADING AND MARKING (STUDENTS)

STUDENTS, INTERCHANGE OF - THE WEST.
Welsh, Wayne. A performance audit of the WICHE student exchange program . [Salt Lake City] , 1978. iii, 45 leaves ; LC Card 78-622932 DDC 370.19/62 19
R847.6.U8 W44

STUDENTS, INTERCHANGE OF - UTAH.
Welsh, Wayne. A performance audit of the WICHE student exchange program . [Salt Lake City] , 1978. iii, 45 leaves ; LC Card 78-622932 DDC 370.19/62 19
R847.6.U8 W44

STUDENTS - LEGAL STATUS, LAWS, ETC. - UNITED STATES.
Barkin, Tom. Legal implications of the Office [of] Education criteria for the self-supporting student /. [Madison] , 1974. 38 p. ; LC Card 77-621624
KF4235 .B47 *NYPL [*XME-9435]*

STUDENTS - LEGAL STATUS, LAWS, ETC. - UNITED STATES - BIBLIOGRAPHY - CATALOGS.
DeVergie, Adrienne, 1936- Bibliography on student activism, 1963-1970 /. [Austin, Tex.] 1970. 84 leaves ; LC Card 80-622264 DDC

016.378/1981 19
KF4150.A1 D48

STUDENTS - NEW YORK (CITY) - ATTITUDES.
Ginzberg, Eli, 1911- Tell me about your school . Washington, D.C. [1979] 79 p. ; LC Card 80-602363 DDC 371.8/1 19
LA339.N5 G48

STUDENTS, PART-TIME - OHIO.
Financial aid for the non-traditional, part-time student . [Bowling Green, Ohio] , c1980. vii, 56 leaves ; LC Card 80-129745 DDC 378.3/0973 19
LB2337.5.O3 F56

STUDENTS, RATING OF - CONGRESSES.
Achievement testing of disadvantaged and minority students for educational program evaluation /. [Monterey, CA] [1979] viii, 464 p. : LC Card 78-4519
LB3051 .A528 *NYPL [Sc D 80-645]*

STUDENTS - TENNESSEE - MEMPHIS - DRUG USE.
United States. Congress. House. Select Committee on Narcotics Abuse and Control. Drug use and abuse in the Memphis-Shelby County school system . Washington , 1980. iii, 184 p. ; LC Card 80-602786 DDC 362.2/932/088375 19
KF27.5 .N3 1980a

STUDENTS - TENNESSEE - SHELBY CO. - DRUG USE.
United States. Congress. House. Select Committee on Narcotics Abuse and Control. Drug use and abuse in the Memphis-Shelby County school system . Washington , 1980. iii, 184 p. ; LC Card 80-602786 DDC 362.2/932/088375 19
KF27.5 .N3 1980a

STUDENTS - UNITED STATES - HEALTH AND HYGIENE.
United States. Congress. Senate. Committee on Labor and Human Resources. Subcommittee on Education, Arts, and Humanities. Asbestos school hazard detection and control act of 1979 . Washington, D.C. , 1980. iv, 277 p. : LC Card 80-602756 DDC 344.73/07 19
KF26 .L2735 1980

Studies from interagency data links. Report.
United States. Social Security Administration. Office of Research and Statistics. no. 9- ; Nov. 1979- Washington. *NYPL [Econ. Div.]*

Studies in advertising (AEI) see American Enterprise Institute for Public Policy Research. AEI studies.

Studies in contemporary language .
(2) Linguistics, stylistics, and the teaching of composition /. Akron, Ohio , c1979. xii, 221 p. : LC Card 79-63524 DDC 808/.042/071173 19
PE1404 .L56

Studies in contemporary satire. Clarion, Pa. Dept. of English, Clarion State College. illus. 21 cm. Annual.
1. Satire - Periodicals. I. Clarion State College. Dept. of English. *NYPL [JFK 80-293]*

Studies in East European and Soviet planning, development, and trade .
(no. 22) US financing of East-West trade ; the political economy of government credits and the national interest /. Bloomington , 1975. xiv, 442 p. ; LC Card 79-129495 DDC 382/.63 19
HG3754.U5 U17

Studies in economic policy (AEI) see American Enterprise Institute for Public Policy Research. AEI studies.

Studies in energy and environment.
Illinois. Bureau of the Budget. Office of Planning. A handbook of sources of electric utility data (with specific reference to Illinois). [Springfield] , 1979. iii, 76 p. ; LC Card 79-625211 DDC 338.4/736362 19
HD9685.U6 I25 1979

Illinois. Bureau of the Budget. Office of Planning. The impact of the 1977-78 coal miners' strike on Illinois electric utilities. [Springfield] [1979] 57 p. ; LC Card 80-621483 DDC 338.4/736362 19
HD9685.U6 I25 1979a

Studies in energy policy (AEI) see American Enterprise Institute for Public Policy Research. AEI studies.

Studies in government regulation (AEI) see American Enterprise Institute for Public Policy Research. AEI studies.

Studies in human resource development. no. 1- Austin, 1974- 23 cm. Irregular. Vols. for 1974- issued by Bureau of Business Research of the University of Texas at Austin (1974-75 with the university's Center for the Study of Human Resources).
1. Manpower - Southern States - Periodicals. 2. Manpower - Southwestern States - Periodicals. 3. Southern States - Economic conditions - 1945- - Periodicals. 4. Southwestern States - Economic conditions - Periodicals. I. Texas. University at Austin. Bureau of Business Research. II. Texas. University at Austin. Center for the study of Human Resources.
NYPL [JLL 80-248]

Studies in Oklahoma's past. For additional listing of contents, see Old Catalog.
(no. 5) Powell, Mary Lucas. Bioarchaeology of the McCutchan-McLaughlin site (34Lt-11) . Norman, Okla. , 1980. vi, 98 p. : LC Card 80-622411 DDC 976.6/76 19
E78.O45 P66 *NYPL [HBA no. 5]*

Studies in political and social processes (AEI) see American Enterprise Institute for Public Policy Research. AEI studies.

Studies in welfare policy.
(no. 13) Swanson, Robert William. Income and benefit receipt among Michigan AFDC families /. [Lansing] [1979] xix, 150 p. : LC Card 80-621648 DDC 361/.9774 s 362.7/13/09774 19
HV86 .M536 no. 31 (11-79)
NYPL [JLM 75-1607 no. 13]

Studies of neotropical caddisflies, XXVIII . Flint, Oliver S. Washington , 1981. p. cm. LC Card 80-607182 DDC 591 s 595.7/450987 19
QL1 .S54 no. 330 QL517.3.V4

Studies of the Permian Phosphoria formation and related rocks, Great Basin-Rocky Mountain region / Bruce R. Wardlaw, editor.
Washington : U. S. Govt. Print. Off. : for sale by the Supt. of Docs., U. S. Govt. Print. Off., 1979. iii, 22 p. : ill. ; 29 cm. (Geological Survey professional paper ; 1163-A-D) Includes bibliographies. CONTENTS. - Wardlaw, B. R. Transgression of the retort phosphatic shale member of the Phosphoria formation (Permian) in Idaho, Montana, Utah, and Wyoming.--Wardlaw, B. R., Collinson, J. W., and Maughan, E. K. The Murdock Mountain formation.--Wardlaw, B. R. Collinson, J. W., and Maughan, E. K. Stratigraphy of Park City group equivalents in southern Idaho, northeastern Nevada, and northwestern Utah.--Wardlaw, B. R. and Collinson, J. W. Biostratigraphic zonation of the Park City group.
LC Card 79-607907 DDC 551.7/5 19
1. Geology, Stratigraphic - Permian. 2. Geology - Great Basin. 3. Geology - Rocky Mountain region. I. Wardlaw, Bruce R. II. Collinson, James W. III. Maughan, Edwin K., 1926-. IV. Series: United States. Geological Survey. Professional paper, 1163-A-D.
QE674 .S78

Studies on the morphology and systematics of scale insects .
(no. 11) Hamon, Avas B. Morphology and systematics of the first instars of the genus Cerococcus (Homoptera:Coccoidea:Cerococcidae) /. Blacksburg, Va. [1979] v, 122 p. : LC Card 80-622297 DDC 595.7/52 19
AS36 .V512 no. 146 QL527.C43

Studies on viruses in water /. Utah Water Research Laboratory. Logan, Utah , 1979. viii, 35 p. : LC Card 80-621126 DDC 628.3 19
QR48 .U8 1979

Studies related to wilderness.
Lesure, Frank Gardner, 1927- Mineral resources of the Mill Creek, Mountain Lake, and Peters Mountain wilderness study areas, Craig and Giles Counties, Virginia, and Monroe County, West Virginia /. Washington , 1981. p. cm. LC Card 80-607815 DDC 557.3 s 553/.09755/795 19
QE75 .B9 no. 1510 TN24.V8

Mineral-resource evaluation of the Round Lake Wilderness study, area, Price and Vilas Counties, Wisconsin . Washington , 1980. p. cm. LC Card 80-607793 DDC 557.3 s 553/.09715/23 19
QE75 .B9 no. 1512 TN24.W6

Studies related to wilderness-primitive areas.
Caliuro Wilderness and further planning areas,

Arizona . Washington , 1981. p. cm. LC Card
81-607019 DDC 557.3 s 553/.09791/54 19
QE75 .B9 no. 1490 TN24.A6

Mineral resources of proposed additions to the
Salmon-Trinity Alps Primitive Area, California
/. Washington , 1981. p. cm. LC Card 81-607910
DDC 622 s 553/.09794/14 19
QE75 .B9 no. 1514 TN24.C2

Studies related to wilderness--study areas.
Mineral resources of the Chama-southern San
Juan Mountains wilderness study area--Mineral,
Rio Grande, Archuleta, and Conejos Counties,
Colorado. Washington [1981] p. cm. LC Card
81-607047 DDC 557.3 s 553/.09788/3 19
QE75 .B9 no. 1524 TN24.C6

Slack, John F. Mineral resources of the Big
Frog wilderness study area and additions, Polk
County, Tennessee and Fannin County, Georgia
/. Washington , 1981. p. cm. LC Card 81-607907
DDC 557.3 s 557.68/875 19
QE75 .B9 no. 1531 TN24.T

Studies related to wilderness--wilderness areas.
Mineral resources of the Snow Mountain
Wilderness study area, California /.
Washington , 1981. p. cm. LC Card 80-606866
DDC 557.3 s 553/.09794/3 19
QE75 .B9 no. 1495 TN24.C2

Study and teaching opportunities abroad .
McIntyre, Pat Kern. Washington, D.C. , 1980.
v, 68 p. ; LC Card 80-602357 DDC 370.19/6 19
LB2376 .M25 1980

Study Commission on U. S. Policy toward
Southern Africa (U. S.) South Africa : time
running out : the report of the Study
Commission on U. S. Policy Toward Southern
Africa. Berkeley : University of California Press,
c1981. xxvii, 517 p., [26] p. of plates : ill., col.
map ; 24 cm. Map on lining papers. Bibliography: p.
479-490. Includes index. ISBN 0-520-04504-1 LC
Card 81-2742 DDC 327.73068 19
1. United States - Foreign relations - South Africa. 2.
South Africa - Foreign relations - United States. I.
Title.
E183.8.S6 S78 1981

A study in American pluralism through oral
histories of holocaust survivors /. Epstein,
Helen, 1947- [New York] [1977?] 157, xciv
leaves ; LC Card 77-153163
E184.J5 E613   **NYPL [*PXY 80-4926]**

A study of airport system financing, Department
of Transportation . Hawaii. Office of the
Legislative Auditor. [Honolulu] 1977. 76 p. :
LC Card 77-623574 DDC 387.7/1 19
HE9797.5.U52 H337 1977

Study of California driving performance by zip
code (phase I) . California. Dept. of Insurance.
Rate Regulation Division. [Sacramento?]
[1978] 320 p. in various pagings ; LC Card
80-623737 DDC 368.5/72/009794 19
HG9970.35.C2 C23 1978

A study of certain aspects of the South Dakota
Housing Development Authority program /.
Brown, Ralph J. Pierre, S.D. , 1979. 32 p. ;
LC Card 80-622224 DDC 353.97830086/5045
19
HD7303.S8 B76

A study of chinook salmon in southeast Alaska.
Kissner, Paul D. Annual performance report for
a study of chinook salmon in southeast Alaska
/. Juneau [1974] 30 p. ; LC Card 81-454187
DDC 597/.55 19
QL638.S2 K56 1974

A study of detention in urban stormwater
management /. Malcom, H. Rooney. [Raleigh,
N.C.] [1980] xvi, 78 p. : LC Card 80-623571
DDC 333.91/009756 s 628/.212 19
HD1694.N8 N6 no. 156 TD657

A study of factors related to the implementation
and use of water conservation technology in
Mississippi /. Cartee, Charles P. Mississippi
State, Miss. , 1979. vi, 49 leaves : LC Card
80-622039 DDC 333.91/22 19
TD224.M65 C38

A study of federal and state legislation
concerning the construction of proposed oil
refineries /. Grant, Cy. Raleigh, NC (105 1911
Bldg. North Carolina State University, Raleigh
27650) , 1980. 23, 4 p. : LC Card 80-624348
DDC 343.756/0772 347.5603772 19
KFN7658.R43 G72

A study of Federal immigration policies and
practices in Southern California . United
States. Commission on Civil Rights. California
Advisory Committee. Washington, D.C. [1980]
ix, 61 p. : LC Card 80-602885 DDC
353.0081/7/097949 19
JV6920 .U54 1980

A study of Federal revenue sharing in Iowa /.
Campana, Joyce. Iowa City, Iowa [1980] vi, 67
p. : LC Card 80-623091 DDC 336.1/85 19
HJ9236 .C35

Study of former prisoners of war . United States.
Veterans Administration. Washington , 1980. v,
181 p. ; LC Card 80-602576 DDC 35.1/156/0973
19
UB369 .U57 1980

Study of former prisoners of war /. United
States. Veterans Administration. Office of
Planning and Program Evaluation. Washington,
D.C. , 1980. iii, 181 p. ; LC Card 80-602667
DDC 355.1/15 19
UB369 .U57 1980a

A study of Hawaii's general excise tax on
warranty parts and labor /. Ishado, Lester.
Honolulu, Hawaii , 1976. 31 leaves ;
                          NYPL [*ZT-1259]

Study of highway transportation of hazardous
materials in Illinois. Illinois. Division of Traffic
Safety. Illinois traffic safety programs report of
evaluation or assessment . [Springfield] [1977]
ca. 250 p. in various pagings : LC Card
79-623261 DDC 343.773/093 19
KFI1580.A1 A884

A study of land use activities and their
relationship to the sport fish resources in
Alaska . Elliott, Steven T. Juneau [1977] 36
p. ; LC Card 78-621567 DDC 333.95/6 19
SK367 .E44

A study of land use activities and their
relationship to the sport fish resources in
Alaska. Elliott, Steven T. Annual performance
report for a study of land use activities and
their relationship to the sport fish resources in
Alaska /. [Juneau] [1976] 44 p. : LC Card
77-620584 DDC 333.95/6/09798 19
QL628.A4 E42

A study of library cooperatives, networks, and
demonstration projects . Patrick, Ruth J. New
York , 1980. p. cm. ISBN 0-89664-313-1 : LC
Card 79-20231
Z731 .P34

A Study of lumber used for bracing trenches in
the United States : report to Occupational
Safety and Health Administration, Department
of Labor, Washington, D.C. 20210 / Lawrence
I. Knab ... [et al.]. Washington, D.C. : U. S.
Dept. of Commerce, National Bureau of
Standards : for sale by the Supt. of Docs., U. S.
Govt. Print. Off., [1980] 218 p. in various
pagings : ill. ; 26 cm. (NBS building science series ;
122) "Issued March 1980." Includes bibliographies. LC
Card 80-600015 DDC 690/.02/18 s 624.1/52 19
1. Retaining walls - Materials. 2. Excavation. 3.
Lumber. I. Knab, Lawrence I. II. United States.
Occupational Safety and Health Administration. III.
Series: United States. National Bureau of Standards.
Building science series , 122.
TA435 .U58 no. 122 TA770

A study of maritime public coast station
operations, services, and industry . United
States. Federal Communications Commission.
[Washington, D.C.] [1979] 48, 31, [15] p. ;
LC Card 80-602044 DDC 353.0087/45453 19
VK397 .U47 1979

Study of methods for increasing safety belt use .
National Research Council. Transportation
Research Board. Steering Committee for the
Study of Methods to Increase Use of Safety
Belts. Washington , 1980. ix, 22 p. ; LC Card
80-602588 DDC 363.1/2572 19
TL159 .N34 1980

A study of neonatal deaths from linked records,
Arizona, 1978 /. Arizona. Bureau of Vital
Records and Information Services. Research
and Statistical Analysis. Phoenix, Ariz. [1980]
10 p. : LC Card 80-623695 DDC 618.92/01 19
RJ60.U52 A62 1980

Study of physician reimbursement under
medicare and medicaid /. Muller, Charlotte
Feldman, 1921- [Washington] 1979- v. : LC

Card 80-601289 DDC 338.4/33621/0973 19
R728.5 .M84

The study of politics and education . Hastings,
Anne H. [Eugene, Or.] , 1980. ix, 291 p. ; LC
Card 80-129023 DDC 016.37973 19
Z5815.U5 H37 LC89

A study of postulated accidents at California
nuclear power plants /. Science Applications,
inc. [Sacramento] [1980] ca. 700 p. in various
pagings : LC Card 80-623073 DDC 363.1/79 19
TK1344.C2 S28 1980

A study of public works investment in the United
States /. Consad Research Corporation.
[Washington] , 1980. 826 p. in various pagings :
LC Card 80-603199 DDC 336.3/9/0973 19
HD3885 .C66 1980

A study of recidivism. Virginia. Dept. of
Corrections. Bureau of Research, Reporting and
Evaluation. [Richmond] , 1977. i, 16 leaves ;
LC Card 78-621733 DDC 364.3 19
HV7296 .A6 1977b

Study of Silver Lake eutrophication . Washington
(State). State University, Pullman. Dept. of
Civil and Environmental Engineering. Pullman,
Wash. [1975] xviii, 298 p. : LC Card 79-625419
DDC 553.7/09797 s 363.7/3942/0979788 19
TD224.W2 S8 no. 9a QH105.W2

A study of spouse battering in Montana /.
Adrian, Martha. Helena, MT [1978] 117 p. ;
LC Card 80-622328 DDC 362.8/3 19
HV6626 .A37

Study of State fees . Pennsylvania. General
Assembly. Legislative Budget and Finance
Committee. Harrisburg, PA. , 1978. iv, 33 p. ;
LC Card 79-621202 DDC 353.97480085/8 19
KFP11.62 .B8 1978

Study of State fees . Pennsylvania. General
Assembly. Legislative Budget and Finance
Committee. Harrisburg, Pa. [1979] vi, 89 p. ;
LC Card 80-622146 DDC 353.97480072/6 19
HT167.5.P4 P46 1979

A study of surface coal mining in West Virginia.
Schmidt, Richard A. Menlo Park, Calif., 1972.
xiii, 180 p. LC Card 72-611225
TN805.W4 S28   **NYPL [JLF 81-203]**

A study of the commercial finfish in coastal
Louisiana /. Louisiana. Seafood Division. New
Orleans, La. , 1979. viii, 87 p. : LC Card
80-621328 DDC 333.95/6/09763 19
SH222.L8 L68 1979

A study of the conflict of interest statutes .
Maine. Legislature. Joint Select Committee on
Government Ethics. [Augusta] [1980] 20
leaves in various foliations ; LC Card 80-621401
DDC 342.741/0684 19
KFM11.62 .G68 1980

A study of the Cretaceous-Tertiary unconformity
in the Piceance Creek Basin, Colorado .
Johnson, Ronald Carl, 1950- Washington ,
1980. iii, 27 p. : LC Card 80-607774 DDC
551.7/7 19
QE688 .J63

A study of the New Mexico liquor control act /.
Parker, Alfred L. [Albuquerque, N.M.] , 1980.
173, 39 p. : LC Card 80-624137 DDC
363.4/1/09789 19
HV5086.N6 P37

A study of the southern oyster drill (Thais
haemastoma) distribution and density on the
oyster seed grounds /. Breithaupt, Rob L. New
Orleans, La. [1979] vii, 20 p. : LC Card
80-621329 DDC 639/.411/09763 19
QL430.5.M9 B73

A study of trends in total phosphorus
measurements at NASQAN stations /. Smith,
Richard A. Reston, Va. [1981] p. cm. LC Card
81-607899 DDC 363.7/394 19
TD427.P56 S64

Study of unions, management rights, and the
public interest in mass transit . Jennings,
Kenneth M. Washington, 1977. 276 p. : LC
Card 77-604540
HD6976.T72 U55   **NYPL [*XME-9441]**

A study to determine causes of decline in the
national school lunch program in Alaska /.
Hippler, Arthur E. Anchorage [1979] 119, 15,
28 leaves : LC Card 80-623189 DDC
371.7/16/09798 19
LB3479.U6 H56

A study to determine the export and domestic markets for currently underutilized fish and shellfish /. Earl R. Combs Inc. [Washington] 1978 [i. e. 1979] xxxv, 416 p. : LC Card 79-603273   *NYPL [JLF 81-419]*

Studying egocentric networks by mass survey /. Jones, Lynne McCallister. [Berkeley] , 1978. v, 77 p. : LC Card 78-622144 DDC 301/.0723 19
HN29 .J63

Stullken, Lloyd E. (joint author) Fader, Stuart Wesley, 1919- Geohydrology of the Great Bend Prairie, southcentral Kansas /. Lawrence , 1978. 19 p. : LC Card 78-624087 DDC 553.7/9/097818 19
GB1025.K2 F3

Stupak, Ronald J. The President's program directors the Assistant Secretaries . Charlottesville, Va. [1977]. iii, 112 p. : LC Card 77-603586
JK518 .P75

Sturgeon, James I. Illinois. Office of Consumer Services. A consumer's guide to the economics of electric utility ratemaking /. Washington, D.C. , Springfield, Va. , 1980. ix, 233 p. : LC Card 80-602857 DDC 338.4/336362 19
HD9685.U5 I44 1980

Stutts, Jane C. (joint author) Hunter, William W. Mopeds, an analysis of 1976-1978 North Carolina accidents /. Chapel Hill, N.C. [1979] 194 p. in various pagings : LC Card 80-622241 DDC 363.1/259 19
HE5614.3.N6 H86

STYLOSANTHES - BIBLIOGRAPHY.
A Selected bibliography of Centrosema, Desmodium, Stylosanthes and other tropical and subtropical pasture legumes [microform] /. Honolulu , 1981. p. cm. LC Card 81-2533 DDC 016.6333 19
Z5074 .L3 SB203.3.T76

SUASCO River basin . Massachusetts. Division of Water Pollution Control. Water Quality Section. Westborough [1976] 106, [37] p. : LC Card 79-620596 DDC 363.7/39456/097444 19
TD224.M4 M36 1976k

SUASCO River basin . Massachusetts. Division of Water Pollution Control. Water Quality Section. Westborough, Mass. [1976] 36 p. : LC Card 77-622200 DDC 363.7/3942/097444 19
TD224.M4 M36 1976l

SUASCO River basin . Massachusetts. Water Quality and Research Section. Westborough, Mass. , 1977. 33 p. : LC Card 79-622377 DDC 363.7/3942/097444 19
TD224.M4 M368 1977

SUBAQUEOUS WELL-BORING (PETROLEUM) see OIL WELL DRILLING, SUBMARINE.

Subcommittee on Mandated Programs before the House Committee on Elementary & Secondary Education, Illinois House of Representatives, 80th General Assembly . Illinois. General Assembly. House of Representatives. Elementary and Secondary Education Committee. Subcommittee on Mandated Programs. [Springfield] [1978] 67, 13 p. ; LC Card 79-623273 DDC 344.773/074 19
KFI1211.4 .E435 1978

SUBJECT HEADINGS.
Library of Congress. Subject Cataloging Division. Library of Congress subject headings . Washington , 1981. p. cm. LC Card 81-4444 DDC 025.4/9 19
Z695 .L695 1981

United States. Library of Congress. Subject Cataloging Division. Library of Congress subject headings /. Washington , 1980. 2 v. (xxiii, 2591 p.) ; ISBN 0-8444-0299-0 LC Card 79-22742
Z695 .U4749 1980
    NYPL [Perf. Arts Ref. 81-651]

SUBJECT HEADINGS, ENGLISH. see SUBJECT HEADINGS.

SUBJECT HEADINGS - LATIN AMERICA.
Valk, Barbara G. HAPI thesaurus and name authority, 1975-1977 /. Los Angeles , c1979. 113 p. ; ISBN 0-87903-403-3 LC Card 79-620062 DDC 980/.005 19
Z1605.H162 V34 F1408

SUBJECT HEADINGS - SCIENCE.
United States. Defense Documentation Center. ASTIA subject headings. - Arlington, Va., 1959. v, 758 p.; LC Card 59-61320
    NYPL [JSF 80-818]

SUBJECT HEADINGS - TECHNOLOGY.
United States. Defense Documentation Center. ASTIA subject headings. - Arlington, Va., 1959. v, 758 p.; LC Card 59-61320
    NYPL [JSF 80-818]

Subject report, American Indians of Oklahoma by county . Red Corn, Jim. Oklahoma City, Okla. [1980] v, 30 leaves ; LC Card 80-622934 DDC 312/.93 19
E78.O45 R43

Sublett, Michael D. (joint author) Meyer, Douglas K. East central Illinois . Normal, Ill. , 1980. vi, 31 p. (p. 31 publisher's list) ; LC Card 80-622845 DDC 361.6/1/097736 19
HT393.I4 M49

Submarine alternatives study . United States. Congress. House. Committee on Armed Services. Subcommittee on Seapower and Strategic and Critical Materials. Washington , 1980. ii, 182 p. ; LC Card 80-603515 DDC 623.8/2574 19
KF27 .A769 1979d

SUBMARINE DIVING. see DIVING, SUBMARINE.

SUBMARINE TOPOGRAPHY - ARCTIC REGIONS.
Vigdorchik, Michael E. Arctic Pleistocene history and the development of submarine permafrost /. Boulder, Colo. , 1980. xviii, 286 p. : ISBN 0-89158-658-X LC Card 79-17321
QE697 .V48   *NYPL [JSF 80-1146]*

SUBMERGED LANDS - NEW JERSEY - INDEXES.
New Jersey. Office of Environmental Analysis. Index, lands subject to investigation for areas now or formerly below mean high water /. [Trenton, N.J.] [1979] [150] leaves : LC Card 79-625373 DDC 912/.1333918/09749 19
G1256.G4 N4 1979

SUBMERGED LANDS - NEW JERSEY - MAPS.
New Jersey. Office of Environmental Analysis. Index, lands subject to investigation for areas now or formerly below mean high water /. [Trenton, N.J.] [1979] [150] leaves : LC Card 79-625373 DDC 912/.1333918/09749 19
G1256.G4 N4 1979

SUBMERGED LANDS - UNITED STATES.
Althaus, Helen F. Public trust rights /. [Washington] , 1978. xxxix, 421 p. ; LC Card 80-602390 DDC 346.7304/691 19
KF5571 .A94

SUBMERSIBLES, OCEANOGRAPHIC. see OCEANOGRAPHIC SUBMERSIBLES.

Submittal of the Senate Committee on Energy and Natural Resources to the Senate Budget Committee pursuant to Section 301(c) of the Congressional Budget Act /. United States. Congress. Senate. Committee on Energy and Natural Resources. Washingon , 1977. vii, 45 p. ; LC Card 80-601121 DDC 328.73/07652 19
JK1240.E53 U54 1977

Sub-Sahara Africa, its role in critical mineral needs of the Western World . United States. Congress. House. Committee on Interior and Insular Affairs. Subcommittee on Mines and Mining. Washington , 1980. viii, 29 p. : LC Card 80-603266 DDC 338.2/0967 19
TN119.Z3 U55 1980

Sub-Saharan Africa and the United States . Clark, G. Edward (Gilbert Edward), 1917- [Washington, D.C.] , 1980. 46 p., [1] leaf of plates : LC Card 80-603396 DDC 967 19
DT353.5.U6 C55 1980

Subset dependencies as an alternative to embedded multivalued dependencies /. Sagiv, Yehoshua. Urbana, Ill. , 1979. 25 p. : LC Card 80-621695 DDC 001.64 s 519.7 19
QA76 .I4 no. 980 QA76.9.D3

Subsidence over four room and pillar sections in southwestern Pennsylvania /. Moebs, Noel N. Washington, D.C. , 1981. p. cm. LC Card 81-607835 DDC 622 s 622/.8 19
TN23 .U43 TN319

SUBSIDENCES AND BUILDING. see EARTH MOVEMENTS AND BUILDING.

SUBSIDENCES (EARTH MOVEMENTS) - LOUISIANA - BATON ROUGE REGION.
Whiteman, C. D. Measuring local subsidence with extensometers in the Baton Rouge area, Louisiana, 1975-1979 /. Baton Rouge, La. , 1980. iv, 18 p. : LC Card 80-621814 DDC 551.4/4 19
QE600.3.U6 W48

SUBSIDENCES (EARTH MOVEMENTS) - TENNESSEE - MONTGOMERY CO.
Kemmerly, Phillip R. Sinkhole collapse in Montgomery County, Tennessee . [Nashville] , 1980. iv, 42 p. : LC Card 80-622526 DDC 551.4/4 19
GB609.2 .K45

SUBSIDENCES (EARTH MOVEMENTS) - UNITED STATES.
HRB-Singer, inc., State College, Pa. Energy and Natural Resources Program Dept. The nature and distribution of subsidence problems affecting HUD and urban areas (task A) /. [Washington, D.C.] , 1979. x, 113 p. ; LC Card 79-603258
TH1094 .H17 1979   *NYPL [JSF 81-154]*

SUBSIDIES - MINNESOTA.
Gregersen, H. M. Economics of public forestry incentive programs . [St. Paul] 1979. 65 p. : LC Card 79-625488 DDC 333.75/158/09776 19
SD144.M6 G73

SUBSIDIES - NEW JERSEY.
New Jersey. Dept. of Transportation. New Jersey motor bus contract assistance . [Trenton] [1979] viii leaves, 61 p. : LC Card 79-623830 DDC 388.4/1322 19
HE5633.N5 N45 1979

SUBSIDIES - UNITED STATES.
United States. Congress. House. Committee on the Judiciary. Subcommittee on Civil and Constitutional Rights. Oversight on GAO report . Washington , 1980. iii, 131 p. ; LC Card 81-600610 DDC 353.0081/1 19
KF27 .J847 1980b

SUBSISTENCE ECONOMY - ALASKA - CONGRESSES.
The Subsistence lifestyle in Alaska . Fairbanks [1979] iii, 180 p. : LC Card 79-623800 DDC 330.9798/05/08997 19
E78.A3 S9

The Subsistence lifestyle in Alaska : now and in the future : the proceedings of a seminar series held by the School of Agriculture and Land Resources Management, University of Alaska, Fairbanks, Alaska, January 19 through April 27, 1978 / edited by Mayo Murray ; Carol E. Lewis, seminar leader. Fairbanks : The School, [1979] iii, 180 p. : ill. ; 28 cm. (Special publication - School of Agriculture and Land Resources Management, University of Alaska. 1) "March 1979." Includes bibliographical references. LC Card 79-623800 DDC 330.9798/05/08997 19
1. Indians of North America - Alaska - Economic conditions - Congresses. 2. Eskimos - Alaska - Economic conditions - Congresses. 3. Subsistence economy - Alaska - Congresses. 4. Alaska - Economic conditions - Congresses. I. Murray, Mayo. II. University of Alaska, Fairbanks. School of Agriculture and Land Resources Management. III. Series: University of Alaska, Fairbanks. School of Agriculture and Land Resources Management. Special publication - School of Agriculture and Land Resources Management, University of Alaska, Fairbanks , 1.
E78.A3 S9

SUBSISTENCE STORES. see MILITARY SUPPLIES.

SUBSONIC AERODYNAMICS. see AERODYNAMICS.

SUBSTITUTION (TECHNOLOGY)
Evaluation of synthetic fluorspar in BOF slags /. Washington, D.C. [1981] p. cm. LC Card 81-607971 DDC 622 s 669/.142 19
TN23 .U43 TN747

SUBTERRANEAN CONSTRUCTION. see UNDERGROUND CONSTRUCTION.

SUBTERRANEAN WATER. see WATER, UNDERGROUND.

The subtlety of white racism . Dovidio, John F. Newark , 1977. 85 leaves : LC Card 78-621433

DDC 305.8/96073 19
E185.615 .D67

SUBURBS - UNITED STATES.
Nelson, Kathryn P. Recent suburbanization of
Blacks, how much, who, and where /.
[Washington] , 1979. 34 p. : LC Card 79-602959
HD7288.72.U5 N44

SUBVENTIONS. see SUBSIDIES.

**SUBVERSIVE ACTIVITIES - UNITED
STATES.**
United States. Congress. Senate. Committee on
the Judiciary. Subcommittee to Investigate the
Administration of the Internal Security Act and
Other Internal Security Laws. The Puerto Rican
Revolutionary Workers Organization .
Washington , 1976. v, 47, viii p. ; LC Card
76-601803 DDC 322.4/2/0973 19
HV6432 .U54 1976

**SUBWAYS - ENVIRONMENTAL ASPECTS -
CALIFORNIA - SAN FRANCISCO BAY
REGION.**
Graff, Donald Louis, 1935- Environmental
impacts of BART . Washington [Springfield,
Va.] 1980. ca. 150 p. in various pagings : LC
Card 80-603252 DDC 388.4/2/097946 19
TD195.S9 G7

**SUBWAYS - ENVIRONMENTAL ASPECTS -
WASHINGTON METROPOLITAN AREA.**
United States. Urban Mass Transportation
Administration. Draft environmental impact
statement . [Washington] , 1979. 204 p. in
various pagings, [17] fold. leaves of plates : LC
Card 79-602769 DDC 388.4/2/09753 19
TD195.S9 U54 1979

SUBWAYS - WASHINGTON, D. C. - MAPS.
Washington Metropolitan Area Transit
Authority. Inauguration Day . [Washington ,
1981] 1 map ; LC Card 81-690316
G3851.P33 1981 .W3

Washington Metropolitan Area Transit
Authority. Metro service . Washington [1980]
1 map : LC Card 81-690217
G3851.P33 1980 .W31

**SUBWAYS - WASHINGTON
METROPOLITAN AREA - FIRES AND
FIRE PREVENTION.**
United States. Congress. House. Committee on
the District of Columbia. Subcommittee on
Metropolitan Affairs. Washington Metropolitan
Area Transit Authority . Washington , 1980. iv,
92 p. : LC Card 80-603077 DDC 363.3/79 19
KF27 .D563 1980

**SUBWAYS - WASHINGTON
METROPOLITAN AREA - MAPS.**
Washington Metropolitan Area Transit
Authority. Metro service . Washington [1980]
1 map : LC Card 81-690217
G3851.P33 1980 .W31

Success of Asian Americans : fact or fiction?
Washington, D.C. : The Commission on Civil
Rights, 1980. vii, 28 p. : ill. ; 26 cm.
(Clearinghouse publication . 64) Authors: Ki-Taek Chun
and others. Sept. 1980. Item 288-A Includes
bibliographical references. LC Card 80-604177 DDC
305.8/95/073 19
*1. Asian Americans - Economic conditions. I. Chun,
Ki-Taek. II. United States. Commission on Civil Rights.
III. Series.*
E184.O6 S78

**SUCCESSION OF STATES. see STATE
SUCCESSION.**

**Sudan - Government. see Sudan - Politics and
government.**

**Sudan in U. S. press, from June 1977 to June
1978** / compiled by Embassy of the Democratic
Republic of the Sudan. Washington : The
Embassy, [1979] 33 p. : ill. ; 27 cm. LC Card
79-108357 DDC 962.4/04 19
*1. Sudan - Politics and government - Addresses, essays,
lectures. I. Sudan. Safārah (U. S.).*
DT157.5 .S825

**SUDAN - POLITICS AND GOVERNMENT -
ADDRESSES, ESSAYS, LECTURES.**
Sudan in U. S. press, from June 1977 to June
1978 /. Washington [1979] 33 p. : LC Card
79-108357 DDC 962.4/04 19
DT157.5 .S825

Sudan. Safārah (U. S.) Sudan in U. S. press, from
June 1977 to June 1978 /. Washington [1979]

33 p. : LC Card 79-108357 DDC 962.4/04 19
DT157.5 .S825

**SUDDEN DEATH IN INFANTS -
ABSTRACTS.**
Sudden infant death syndrome research and
grief counseling . [Washington, D.C.?] [1981]
p. cm. LC Card 81-607992 DDC 618.72 19
RJ59 .S83

**SUDDEN DEATH IN INFANTS - HAWAII -
STATISTICS.**
Burch, Thomas Adams, 1918- Sudden infant
deaths in Hawaii, 1974-1977 /. [Honolulu]
[1979] 10 p. ; LC Card 79-626235 DDC
304.6/09969 s 618.92 19
HB3525.H3 H33a no. 27 RJ60.U52H3

**SUDDEN DEATH IN INFANTS -
PSYCHOLOGICAL ASPECTS -
ABSTRACTS.**
Sudden infant death syndrome research and
grief counseling . [Washington, D.C.?] [1981]
p. cm. LC Card 81-607992 DDC 618.72 19
RJ59 .S83

**SUDDEN DEATH IN INFANTS -
PSYCHOLOGICAL ASPECTS -
CONGRESSES.**
National Conference on Mental Health Issues
Related to Sudden Infant Death Syndrome,
Baltimore, Md., 1977. Mental health issues in
grief counseling . Rockville, Md. , Washington,
D.C. , 1979 i.e. 1980. 133 p. ; LC Card
80-602299 DDC 362.8/286 19
RJ59 .N37 1977

**SUDDEN DEATH - NEW JERSEY - CASE
STUDIES.**
New Jersey. Commission of Investigation.
Report and recommendations of the State of
New Jersey Commission of Investigation on the
investigation of sudden death cases. [Trenton,
N.J.] [1979?] 169, 2, 6 p. ; LC Card 80-620967
DDC 363.2/5 19
HV6533.N23 N48 1979

Sudden Infant Death Syndrome Clearinghouse.
Sudden infant death syndrome research and
grief counseling . [Washington, D.C.?] [1981]
p. cm. LC Card 81-607992 DDC 618.72 19
RJ59 .S83

**Sudden infant death syndrome research and grief
counseling :** a selected bibliography / prepared
by Sudden Infant Death Syndrome
Clearinghouse. [Washington, D.C.?] : U. S.
Dept. of Health and Human Services, Public
Health Service, Health Services Administration,
Bureau of Community Health Services, Sudden
Infant Death Syndrome Program, [1981] p. cm.
(HSA publication . no. 81-) "April 1981." Includes
index. LC Card 81-607992 DDC 618.72 19
*1. Sudden death in infants - Abstracts. 2. Sudden death
in infants - Psychological aspects - Abstracts. 3. Grief -
Abstracts. I. Sudden Infant Death Syndrome
Clearinghouse. II. Series: DHHS publication, no. 81-.*
RJ59 .S83

Sudden infant deaths in Hawaii, 1974-1977 /.
Burch, Thomas Adams, 1918- [Honolulu]
[1979] 10 p. ; LC Card 79-626235 DDC
304.6/09969 s 618.92 19
HB3525.H3 H33a no. 27 RJ60.U52H3

Sudman, Seymour. Health care surveys using
diaries / Seymour Sudman, Linda Bean
Lannom. Hyattsville, Md. : U. S. Dept. of
Health and Human Services, Public Health
Service, Office of Health Research, Statistics,
and Technology, National Center for Health
Services Research, [1980] vii, 123, [173] p. :
forms ; 27 cm. (NCHSR research report series)
DHHS publication ; no. (PHS) 80-3279 "July 1980."
Bibliography: p. 120-123 (2d group) LC Card
80-600121 DDC 362.1/0723 19
*1. Health surveys. 2. Medical history taking. 3. Diaries.
4. Health surveys - Illinois. I. Lannom, Linda Bean,
joint author. II. Series: National Center for Health
Services Research. NCHSR research report series. III.
Title.*
RA408.5 .S9

Sudy of the laws concerning annexation, 1980 .
Tennessee. General Assembly. Special Joint
Committee Created Pursuant to House Joint
Resolution No. 308. Nashville, Tenn. (Suite
G-10, War Memorial Bldg., Nashville, Tenn.
37219) [1980] 105 p. : LC Card 80-624151
DDC 352/.006/09768 19
KFT431.9.A5 A25 1980

Suffolk County, N. Y. Planning Commission.
Suffolk County office study, prepared by the
Suffolk County Planning Commission.
Hauppauge, N. Y., 1974. 33 p. map. 28 cm. On
cover: Suffolk County office building Study.
*1. Office layout. 2. Offices - Location - New York
(State) - Suffolk County. I. Title.*
NYPL [JLF 81-19]

SUFFOLK COUNTY (N.Y.) - LIBRARIES.
Feinberg, Richard P. A union list of microform
collections in Nassau and Suffolk County
libraries /. Stony Brook, N.Y. , Bellport, N.Y. ,
1980. viii, 220 p. ; LC Card 81-111481 DDC
011/.36 19
Z1033.M5 F43

Suffolk County office study. Suffolk County, N.
Y. Planning Commission. Hauppauge, N. Y.,
1974. 33 p.   *NYPL [JLF 81-19]*

**SUGAR BOUNTIES. see SUGAR LAWS AND
LEGISLATION; SUGAR TRADE.**

SUGAR-CANE - HAWAII - IRRIGATION.
Lau, Leung-Ku Stephen. Recycling of sewage
effluent by sugarcane irrigation . Honolulu,
Hawaii [1978?] x, 59 p. : LC Card 79-625336
DDC 628.3/62 19
TC1 .H36 no. 121 TD760

SUGAR-CANE - IRRIGATION.
Lau, Leung-Ku Stephen. Recycling of sewage
effluent by sugarcane irrigation . Honolulu,
Hawaii [1978?] x, 59 p. : LC Card 79-625336
DDC 628.3/62 19
TC1 .H36 no. 121 TD760

**Sugar from Belgium, France, and West
Germany .** Greer, T. Vernon. Washington ,
1979. 21, 62 p. ; LC Card 79-602639 DDC
382/.4136/0973 19
HF2651.S8 U54

**SUGAR - LAW AND LEGISLATION. see
SUGAR LAWS AND LEGISLATION.**

SUGAR LAWS AND LEGISLATION.
United States. Congress. House. Committee on
Ways and Means. Subcommittee on Trade.
International sugar agreement . Washington ,
1980. iii, 46 p. ; LC Card 80-601959 DDC
341.7/547/136 19
KF27 .W348 1979n

United States. Congress. Senate. Committee on
Finance. Staff data and materials relating to the
International sugar stabilization act of 1979 /.
Washington , 1979. iii, 70 p. ; LC Card
79-601697 DDC 343.73/08756641
347.3038756641 19
KF1996.S8 A25 1979

**SUGAR LAWS AND LEGISLATION -
UNITED STATES.**
United States. Congress. House. Committee on
Ways and Means. Subcommittee on Trade.
International sugar agreement . Washington ,
1980. iii, 46 p. ; LC Card 80-601959 DDC
341.7/547/136 19
KF27 .W348 1979n

United States. Congress. Senate. Committee on
Finance. Staff data and materials relating to the
International sugar stabilization act of 1979 /.
Washington , 1979. iii, 70 p. ; LC Card
79-601697 DDC 343.73/08756641
347.3038756641 19
KF1996.S8 A25 1979

**SUGAR LOAF MOUNTAIN, MD. -
DESCRIPTION AND TRAVEL - GUIDE-
BOOKS.**
Sugarloaf Regional Trails (Project) Circling
historic landscapes . Silver Spring, Md. , c1980.
99 p. : LC Card 80-117883 DDC 917.52/87 19
GV191.42.M3 S93 1980

SUGAR-MAPLE.
Gibbs, Carter B. The effect of xylem age on
volume yield & sugar content of sugar maple
sap /. Upper Darby, Pa. , 1969. 11 p. :ill. LC
Card 75-605745 DDC 333.76/0974 s 633.3/4 19
SD11 .A455493 no. 141 SB239.M3

Sugar maple sap. Gibbs, Carter B. The effect of
xylem age on volume yield & sugar content of
sugar maple sap /. Upper Darby, Pa. , 1969. 11
p. :ill. LC Card 75-605745 DDC 333.76/0974 s
633.3/4 19
SD11 .A455493 no. 141 SB239.M3

SUGAR-MAPLE - TAPPING.
Shigo, Alex L., 1930- Some effects of
paraformaldehyde on wood surrounding

tapholes in sugar maple trees /. Upper Darby,
Pa. , 1970. 11 p. : LC Card 81-460882 DDC
634.9/0974 s 633.6/49 19
SD11 .A455493 no. 161 SB608.S913

SUGAR-MAPLE - WOUNDS AND INJURIES.
Shigo, Alex L., 1930- Some effects of
paraformaldehyde on wood surrounding
tapholes in sugar maple trees /. Upper Darby,
Pa. , 1970. 11 p. : LC Card 81-460882 DDC
634.9/0974 s 633.6/49 19
SD11 .A455493 no. 161 SB608.S913

SUGAR - PRICES - UNITED STATES.
United States. Congress. House. Committee on
Small Business. Subcommittee on Special Small
Business Problems. Rising sugar costs and their
effect on retail bakers . Washington , 1980 [i.e.
1981] iii, 40 p. ; LC Card 81-600856 DDC
381/.45664752/0973 19
KF27 .S686 1980a

SUGAR SUBSTITUTES - ECONOMIC ASPECTS - UNITED STATES.
Carman, Hoy Fred, 1938- High fructose corn
sweeteners . Davis , 1979. vi, 63 p. : LC Card
79-625537 DDC 338.1/09794 s 338.4/76645 19
HD9000.1 .C3 no. 79-2 HD9119.C6

SUGAR TRADE - LAW AND LEGISLATION. see SUGAR LAWS AND LEGISLATION.

SUGAR TRADE - UNITED STATES.
Carman, Hoy Fred, 1938- High fructose corn
sweeteners . Davis , 1979. vi, 63 p. : LC Card
79-625537 DDC 338.1/09794 s 338.4/76645 19
HD9000.1 .C3 no. 79-2 HD9119.C6

Sugarloaf Regional Trails (Project) Circling
historic landscapes : bicycling, canoeing &
walking trails near Sugarloaf Mountain, Md. /
Sugarloaf Regional Trails ; directed and edited
by Gail Rothrock ; graphic design by Tom
Riley, ill. by Harry Jaecks. Silver Spring, Md. :
Montgomery County Planning Board,
Maryland-National Capital Park and Planning
Commission, c1980. 99 p. : ill. ; 22 x 28 cm.
"Sponsored by the Maryland-National Capital Park and
Planning Commission." LC Card 80-117883 DDC
917.52/87 19
*1. Outdoor recreation - Maryland - Sugar Loaf
Mountain - Guide-books. 2. Sugar Loaf Mountain,
Md. - Description and travel - Guide-books. I.
Rothrock, Gail. II. Maryland. Maryland-National
Capital Park and Planning Commission. III. Title.
GV191.42.M3 S93 1980*

Sugars and sirups from Canada . Greer, T.
Vernon. Washington, D.C. [1980] ii, 17, 66 p. ;
LC Card 80-602338 DDC 382/.4136/0973 19
HF2651.S8 U55

**Suggested guidelines for local education agency
compliance with Section 504 of the
Rehabilitation Act of 1973** / Oklahoma State
Department of Education. [Oklahoma City,
Okla.] : The Dept., [ca. 1979] 83 p. : ill. ; 28
cm. Bibliography: p. 78-80. LC Card 80-624295
DDC 362.4/0483 19
*1. Architecture and physically handicapped students -
Oklahoma. I. Oklahoma. State Dept. of Education.
NA2545.P5 S8*

**Suggested sewer use ordinance for the cities and
towns of the state of Maine** /. Maine. Bureau
of Water Quality Control. Division of
Municipal Services. Augusta, Me (State Office
Building, Station 17, Augusta 04333) [1980]
23, [24] p. : LC Card 81-621085 DDC
344.741/04622 347.41044622 19
KFM359.S4 A887

**Suggested State auditing acts and constitutional
amendments** /. United States. General
Accounting Office. [Washington, D. C.] , 1974.
73 p. ; LC Card 77-33784
NYPL [JLE 80-3204]

SUGGESTION SYSTEMS - UNITED STATES.
United States. Congress. House. Committee on
Post Office and Civil Service. Subcommittee on
Compensation and Employee Benefits. Incentive
and performance awards program .
Washington , 1980. iii, 138 p. ; LC Card
81-600582 DDC 353.001/47 19
KF27 .P638 1980m

SUGGESTION SYSTEMS - UNITED STATES - PERIODICALS.
United States. Civil Service Commission. Office
of Incentive Systems. Progress through
achievements. 1976/77- Washington. LC Card
79-643386
NYPL [JLM 80-1092]

Sugihara, Teruo.
Rutgers University, New Brunswick, N.J.
Center for Coastal and Environmental Studies.
Comparison of natural and altered estuarine
systems . [New Brunswick, N.J.] [1979] 2 v. :
LC Card 80-623604 DDC 574.5/26365 19
QH105.N5 R87 1979a

Rutgers University, New Brunswick, N.J.
Center for Coastal and Environmental Studies.
Comparison of natural and altered estuarine
systems . [New Brunswick, N.J.] [1979] xv,
247 p. : LC Card 80-623603 DDC 574.5/26365 19
QH105.N5 R87 1979

Suko, Randy. Washington (State). Planning and
Community Affairs Agency. Local Government
Services Division. Housing, the problems in
Washington State. Olympia, Wash. [1980?] v,
29, [10] p. : LC Card 80-622049 DDC
363.5/09797 19
HD7303.W2 W38 1980

SULFUR. see SULPHUR.

Sullenberger, Martha. Dogholes and donkey
engines : a historical resources study of six state
park system units on the Mendocino Coast.
Sacramento, CA : State of California, Resources
Agency, Dept. of Parks and Recreation, [1980]
iv, 133 p. : ill. ; 28 cm. "April 1980." Bibliography:
p. 126-133. LC Card 80-623070 DDC
363.6/9/0979415 19
*1. Mendocino Co., Calif. - History. 2. Lumber trade -
California - Mendocino Co. - History. 3. Parks -
California - Mendocino Co. I. California. Dept. of Parks
and Recreation. II. Title.
F868.M5 S94*

Sullivan, A. Charlene.
Credit and collections for small stores / by A.
Charlene Sullivan and Robert W. Johnson.
Washington, D.C. : U. S. Small Business
Administration : For sale by the Supt. of Docs.,
U. S. G.P.O., 1980. v, 67 p. : ill. ; 24 cm. (Small
business management series. no. 43) S/N
045-000-00169-5 Bibliography: p. 65-66. LC Card
81-600882 DDC 658.8/8 19
*1. Credit management. 2. Collecting of accounts. 3.
Small business - Finance. I. Johnson, Robert Willard. II.
United States. Small Business Administration. III.
Series: Small business management series (United
States. Small Business Administration) , no. 43. IV.
Title.
HD30 .U5 no. 43 HG3751*

Sales finance companies : CRC 1979 creditors
survey / [A. Charlene Sullivan and Debra A.
Drecnik]. West Lafayette, Ind : Credit
Research Center, Krannert Graduate School of
Management, Purdue University, 1980. ii, 14,
[12] leaves ; 28 cm. (Monograph / Credit Research
Center . no. 20) Cover title. LC Card 81-620933
DDC 332.3/5/0973 19
*1. Consumer credit - United States. 2. Commercial
finance companies - United States. I. Drecnik, Debra A.
II. Series: Monograph (Krannert Graduate School of
Management. Credit Research Center) , no. 20. III.
Title.
HG3756.U54 S93*

Sullivan, Daniel E. Minerals and the Tokyo
Round of the MTN / by Daniel Ed. Sullivan.
Washington : U. S. Dept of the Interior, Bureau
of Mines, [1981] p. cm. (Information circular /
Bureau of Mines) Bibliography: p. LC Card
81-607909 DDC 622 s 382/.42 19
*1. Mineral industries. 2. Tariff on minerals. 3. Nontariff
trade barriers. 4. Mineral industries - United States. 5.
Tokyo Round, 1973-1977. I. Series: Information circular
(United States. Bureau of Mines) . II. Title.
TN295 .U4 HD9506.A2*

Sullivan, G. V. Smith, C. W. (Carl W.) Crushing
techniques for pneumatic concentration of mica
/. [Avondale, Md.] , 1981. p. cm. LC Card
81-607301 DDC 622 s 622/.3674 19
TN23 .U43 TN933

Sullivan, James Richard, 1947- The stone crab,
Menippe mercenaria, in the southwest Florida
fishery / James R. Sullivan. St. Petersburg,
Fla. : Florida Dept. of Natural Resources,
Marine Research Laboratory, 1979. 37 p. : ill. ;
28 cm. (Florida marine research publications . no. 36
0095-0157) "December 1979." Bibliography: p. 23. LC
Card 80-622656 DDC 333.95/5 19
*1. Menippe mercenaria. 2. Shellfish tagging - Florida. 3.
Crab fisheries - Florida. 4. Chelae. 5. Regeneration
(Biology). I. Florida. Marine Research Laboratory, St.*

*Petersburg, Fla. II. Title. III. Series.
QL444.M33 S93*

Sullivan, Mark, 1932- Pflieger, William L. The
fishes of Missouri /. [Jefferson City] , 1975.
viii, 343 p., [2] leaves of plates : LC Card
81-620611 DDC 597.092/9778 19
QL628.M8 P47

Sullivan, Thomas A. McBee, William C.
Modified-sulfur cements for use in concretes,
flexible pavings, coatings, and grouts /.
Washington, D.C. , 1981. p. cm. LC Card
81-607031 DDC 622 s 666/.95 19
TN23 .U43 TP884.S85

SULPHATES - TOXICOLOGY.
Carnow, Bertram W. Health effects of SO₂ and
sulfates /. Chicago, IL [1979] vi, 83 p. : LC
Card 80-621687 DDC 615.9/257232 19
RA577.S9 C36

SULPHIDES.
Bennetts, J. (John) Preparation of platinum
flotation concentrate from stillwater complex
ore /. Avondale, Md. [1981] p. cm. LC Card
80-606913 DDC 622 s 622/.3424 19
TN23 .U43 TN523

SULPHUR.
Paige, J. I. (Jack I.) Introduction of sulfur into
copper converter slags to produce copper matte
/. Washington, D.C. , 1981. p. cm. LC Card
81-607890 DDC 622 s 669/.3 19
TN23 .U43 TN780

Sulphur Basin. Texas. Dept. of Water Resources.
Projected land use maps year 2000, Sulphur
Basin. Austin, Tex. , 1978. [4] leaves LC Card
80-675301 DDC 912/.133373/3097642 19
G1372.S8G4 T4 1978

SULPHUR CEMENT.
McBee, William C. Modified-sulfur cements for
use in concretes, flexible pavings, coatings, and
grouts /. Washington, D.C. , 1981. p. cm. LC
Card 81-607031 DDC 622 s 666/.95 19
TN23 .U43 TP884.S85

SULPHUR COMPOUNDS - ENVIRONMENTAL ASPECTS - UNITED STATES.
United States. Congress. Senate. Committee on
Energy and Natural Resources. Effects of acid
rain . Washington , 1980- v. <1-> : LC Card
80-603417 DDC 363.7/394 19
KF26 .E55 1980f

SULPHUR DIOXIDE.
(1980) Khalafalla, S. E. Selective extraction of
metals from Pacific sea nodules with dissolved
sulfur dioxide /. Avondale, Md. , 1980. p. cm.
LC Card 80-606861 DDC 622 s 669/.028/3 19
TN23 .U43 TN291.5

SULPHUR DIOXIDE - ENVIRONMENTAL ASPECTS - ILLINOIS.
Cohen, Alan S., 1944- Economic impact of
sulfur dioxide and particulate matter regulations
in Illinois, R77-15 /. Chicago, IL , 1979. xii,
123 p. : LC Card 80-620893 DDC 363.7/387 19
TD885.5.S8 C63

SULPHUR DIOXIDE - TOXICOLOGY.
Carnow, Bertram W. Health effects of SO₂ and
sulfates /. Chicago, IL [1979] vi, 83 p. : LC
Card 80-621687 DDC 615.9/257232 19
RA577.S9 C36

SULPHURETTED HYDROGEN. see HYDROGEN SULPHIDE.

Sultz, Harry A. Longitudinal study of nurse
practitioners . Hyattsville, Md. , Washington,
D.C. , 1980. xv, 221 p. : LC Card 80-602207
DDC 610.73/0692 19
RT82.8 .L67

SUMEX-AIM (COMPUTER SYSTEM)
Freiherr, Gregory. The seeds of artificial
intelligence . Bethesda, Md. , Washington, D.C.
[1980] 74 p. : LC Card 80-602247 DDC 001.64
19
R858 .F73

Summaries of research in the chemical sciences.
United States. Dept. of Energy. Division of
Chemical Sciences. Washington. LC Card
79-644349
NYPL [JSP 80-279]

**Summary: an evaluation of the options of the U.
S. Government in its relationship to U. S.
firms in international petroleum affairs.**
Nossman, Waters, Krueger, Marsh & Riordan.

Los Angeles, 1975. 122 p.;
NYPL [JLF 80-599]

Summary and analysis, heavy truck-hazardous material accidents. Washington (State) Utilities and Transportation Commission. Olympia, Wash. [1979] [13], 34 p. ; LC Card 80-621084 DDC 363.1/259 19
HE5614.3.W2 W394 1979

A Summary and analysis of President Reagan's fiscal year 1982 budget revisions / Committee on the Budget, U. S. House of Representatives. Washington : U. S. G.P.O., 1981. iii, 70 p. ; 26 cm. At head of title: 97th Congress, 1st session. Committee print. "CP-5." March 1981. Item 1035-B-1, 1035-B-2 (microfiche) LC Card 81-601828 DDC 353.0072/24 19
1. Budget - United States. I. United States. Congress. House. Committee on the Budget.
HJ2051 .S93

Summary and critique of the literature pertaining to the effects of increased enforcement of traffic laws on improving traffic safety (reducing accidents) /. Raub, R. A. [Springfield] [1979] 58 leaves ; LC Card 81-621246 DDC 363.1/256/0973 19
HE5614.2 .R38

Summary and evaluation of crest-stage-gage data in New York. Eissler, Benjamin B. Albany, N. Y., 1974. 24 p. **NYPL [JSF 81-23]**

Summary appraisals of the nation's ground-water resources--New England region /. Sinnott, Allen, 1917- Washington , 1981. p. cm. LC Card 81-607880 DDC 553.7/9/0974 19
GB1016.3 .S57

Summary characteristics for governmental units. 1980 census of population and housing. Washington [1981]- p. cm. LC Card 81-607959 DDC 312/.0973 19
HA201 1980 .A147

A Summary digest of laws enacted by the second regular session and the first extraordinary session of the Thirty-seventh Oklahoma Legislature, 1980 / prepared for members of the State Legislative Council by the Division of Research and Reference Services and Division of Fiscal Services. Oklahoma City, Okla. (305 State Capitol, Oklahoma City, Okla.) : TheCouncil, 1980. vi leaves, 221 p. ; 28 cm. LC Card 80-624215 DDC 348.766/026 347.660826 19
1. Legislation - Oklahoma. I. Oklahoma. State Legislative Council. II. Oklahoma. State Legislative Council. Division of Research and Reference Services. III. Oklahoma. State Legislative Council. Division of Fiscal Services.
KFO1225.5 1980

Summary digest of statutes enacted and resolutions adopted, including proposed constitutional amendments, and table of sections affected. California. Laws, statutes, etc. [Sacramento] **NYPL [XWZ (California. Legislative Counsel Bureau. Summary digest of statutes enacted ...)]**

Summary digest of statutes enacted and resolutions (including proposed constitutional amendments) adopted, and Statutory record. California. Laws, statutes, etc. 1970- [Sacramento] **NYPL [JLL 81-13]**

Summary inventory, 1979 /. Detroit. Institute of Arts. Museum Archives and Records Center. [Detroit] [c1979] ii, 17 leaves, [3] leaves of plates : LC Card 80-126808 DDC 069/.97/0074017434 19
N560 .A87

Summary of geologic and hydrologic information pertinent to tunneling in selected urban areas/. United States. Geological Survey. Washington, 1974. [370] p.: **NYPL [JSF 81-3]**

Summary of government housing activities in New York City /. New York (City). Housing and Development Administration. Office of Programs and Policies. [New York] [1974?] ca. 160 leaves in various pagings;
NYPL [JLF 80-1475]

Summary of H.R. 5741, and Mortgage subsidy bond tax act of 1979 /. United States. Congress. Joint Committee on Taxation. Washington , 1979. iii, 8 p. ; LC Card 80-602686 DDC 343.7305/23 19
KF6383 .A25 1979

Summary of housing and socio-economic data : Black River-St. Lawrence region /. Parsons, Carl. Springfield, Va. , 1974. vi, 106 p. :
NYPL [JLF 81-31]

Summary of hydrologic testing in Tertiary limestone aquifer, Tenneco offshore exploratory well-Atlantic OCS, lease-block 427 (Jacksonville NH 17-5) /. United States. Geological Survey. Washington , 1981. p. cm. LC Card 80-606901 DDC 553/.79/09759 19
GB1199.2 .U54 1981

Summary of legislation approved by the second regular session of the Sixty-eighth Iowa General Assembly meeting in the year 1980 /. Iowa. Legislative Service Bureau. [Des Moines] [1980] 107 p. ; LC Card 80-623021 DDC 348.777/026 19
KFI4215.2 1980

A summary of legislation truly agreed to and finally passed by the 80th General Assembly, second regular session /. Missouri. General Assembly. Senate. Division of Research. [Jefferson City] 1980. 27 p. ; LC Card 80-623526 DDC 348.778/026 347.780826 19
KFM7825.5 1978

Summary of MARC format specifications for technical reports. Library of Congress. Washington, D.C. [1981] 42 p. ; LC Card 81-607066 DDC 025/.04 19
Z699.4.M2 L5 1981

Summary of national hearings of the White House Conference on Families /. National Institute for Advance Studies (U. S.) Washington, D.C. [1980] ca. 150 p. in various pagings ; LC Card 80-602558 DDC 362.8/2/0973 19
HQ536 .N39 1980

Summary of progress through 1980 /. National Cooperative Highway Research Program. Washington, D.C. (2101 Constitution Avenue, N.W., Washington 20418) , 1980. 168 p. ; LC Card 81-123734 DDC 625.7/072073 19
TE23 .N24 1980

A summary of quantity, quality, and economic methodology for establishing minimum flows : establishment of low-flow criteria for conservation, recreation, and aesthetic purposes / by James A. Crutchfield ... [et al.]. Pullman : State of Washington Water Research Center, Washington State University and University of Washington, 1973- v. <1> : ill. ; 28 cm. (Report - State of Washington Water Research Center . no. 13) "Project completion report, OWRR project number: B-037-WASH, OWRR agreement number: 14-31-0001-3349." Includes bibliographies. CONTENTS. - v. 1. Summary. LC Card 75-620707 DDC 553.7/09797 s 333.9/0217/09797 19
1. Stream measurements - Washington (State). 2. Lakes - Washington (State). 3. Water-supply - Washington (State). I. Crutchfield, James Arthur. II. Title: Minimum flows. III. Series: State of Washington Water Research Center. Report , no. 13.
TD224.W2 S8 no. 13 GB1225.W3

Summary of recommendations and surveys on social security and pension policies . Koitz, David. Washington , 1980. vii, 48 p. ; LC Card 80-603856 DDC 368.4/3/00973 19
HD7125 .K59

Summary of recommendations in the "Analysis of the 1980-81 budget bill". California. Legislature. Joint Budget Committee. Legislative Analyst. Sacramento, Calif. , 1980. 150 p. ; LC Card 80-621714 DDC 343.794/034 347.940334 19
KFC10.62 .B834 1980

Summary of recommended legislative changes contained in the "Analysis of the 1980-81 budget bill". California. Legislature. Joint Budget Committee. Legislative Analyst. Sacramento, Calif. [1980] 63 p. ; LC Card 80-621715 DDC 343.794/03 19
KFC842 .A25 1980

Summary of savings accounts by geographic area . United States. Federal Home Loan Bank Board. Washington, D.C. [1979] 2, 141 p. ; LC Card 80-602040 DDC 332.3/2/0973 19
HG2151 .U52 1979

Summary of selected statistics . Connecticut. Bureau of Vocational Program Planning & Development. [Hartford] [1979] 29 p. ; LC Card 79-624847 DDC 379.1/552/09746 19
LC1046.C8 C663 1979

Summary of the Missouri campaign finance disclosure law of 1978 . Missouri. Campaign Reporting Division. Jefferson City [1980] 61 p. ; LC Card 80-623311 DDC 342.778/07 19
KFM8220.85.C2 A837

Summary of the new Indiana juvenile code, including the 1980 General Assembly amendments. Bloomington, Ind. : Distributed by the Center for the Study of Legal Policy Relating to Children, Indiana University, School of Law, 1980, c1979. iv, 21 p. ; 28 cm. LC Card 80-622110 DDC 345.772/08 347.72058 19
1. Juvenile justice, Administration of - Indiana. 2. Juvenile courts - Indiana. 3. Children - Legal status, laws, etc. - Indiana. I. Indiana University, Bloomington. Center for the Study of Legal Policy Relating to Children.
KFI3595 .S95 1980

Summary of the regular 1980 legislative session of the Virginia General Assembly /. Virginia. Division of Legislative Services. [Richmond, Va.] [1980] 53 p. ; LC Card 80-622921 DDC 348.755/01 19
KFV2415.2 1980

Summary parole . Star, Deborah. [Sacramento] [1979] x, 193 p. ; LC Card 80-620661 DDC 364.6/09794 s 364.6/2/09794 19
HV9305.C3 A32 no. 60

Summary uniform demographic and economic data. Illinois. Bureau of the Budget. Uniform demographic and economic data, 1970-2000 : summary /. [Springfield] , 1973. 68 p. :
NYPL [JLF 81-5]

Summary 1980 State valuation as filed with the Secretary of State, January 25, 1980 /. Halperin, Raymond L. Augusta, Me. [1980] 41 leaves ; LC Card 80-621327 DDC 336.22/2 19
HJ4223 .H35

SUMMER CAMPS. see CAMPS.

Summer crane flies of Lake Itasca vicinity, Minnesota /. Byers, George William, 1923- [Lawrence] , 1979. p. 604-613 ; LC Card 79-622728 DDC 500 s 595.77/1 19
Q1 .K17 vol. 51, no. 20 QL537.T5

SUMMER - ILLINOIS.
Changnon, Stanley Alcide. Review of Illinois summer precipitation conditions /. Urbana , 1980. 160 p. : LC Card 80-623561 DDC 551.57/72/773 19
QC925.1.U8 I325

Summer Institute on Recent Developments in Gravitation, Cargèse. see Cargèse Summer Institute on Recent Developments in Gravitation, 1978.

The summer of 1962 . New York (City). Youth Board. New York , 1962. iv, 64 p. ;
NYPL [JLF 80-1632]

Summer Program for Economically Disadvantaged Youth. United States. Employment and Training Administration. Office of Youth Programs. Report on SPEDY conferences . [Washington] [1979] viii, 297 p. ; LC Card 79-603023
HD6273 .U514 1979a

Summerlin, Florence A. Religion and mental health : a bibliography / compiled by Florence A. Summerlin. Rockville, Md. (5600 Fishers Lane, Rockville, Md. 20857) : U. S. Dept. of Health and Human Services, Public Health Service, Alcohol, Drug Abuse, and Mental Health Administration, National Institute of Mental Health ; Washington, D.C. : For sale by the Supt. of Docs., U. S. G.P.O., 1980. 401 p. in various pagings ; 26 cm. (DHHS publication. no. (ADM) 80-964) Includes indexes. S/N 017-024-01023-5 Item 507-B-9 LC Card 81-601117 DDC 016.3622 19
1. Mental health - Bibliography. 2. Pastoral psychology - Bibliography. 3. Psychiatry and religion - Bibliography. 4. Psychology and religion - Bibliography. I. National Institute of Mental Health (U. S.). II. Title.
Z6664.N5 S94 RA790

Summers, Max. Viral pesticides . Research Triangle Park, N.C. , 1978. xix, 312 p. : LC Card 79-601644 DDC 632/.96 19
SB942 .V57

SUMMONS - WISCONSIN.
Wisconsin. Legislative Council. Issues relating to pretrial release pursuant to the issuance of a citation or summons /. Madison, Wis. [1980]

54 p. ; LC Card 80-624139 DDC 347.775/072
347.750772 19
KFW2976.6 .A25 1980

Sumner, James. (joint author) Black, David R.
Historic architectural resources of downtown
Asheville, North Carolina /. Asheville, N.C. ,
Raleigh, N.C. , 1979. 60 p., [1] fold. leaf of
plates : LC Card 80-623846 DDC 720/.9756/88
19
NA735.A74 B57

Sumner, Stephen M. Tennessee domestic
relations law for attorneys and legal assistants
/. Knoxville, Tenn. (1505 W. Cumberland Ave.,
Knoxville 37916) , c1980. 1 v. (various
pagings) : LC Card 81-132962 DDC 346.76801/5
347.680615 19
KFT94 .T45

Sumsion, C. T. (joint author) Bolke, E. L.
Hydrologic reconnaissance of the Fish Springs
Flat area, Tooele, Juab, and Millard counties,
Utah /. [Salt Lake City] , 1978. iv, 30 p. : LC
Card 79-621928 DDC 553/.09792 s
553.7/9/097924 19
TA7 .U77 no. 64 GB705.U8

**SUN-HEATED HOUSES. see SOLAR
HOUSES.**

**SUN PROTECTION IN ARCHITECTURE. see
ARCHITECTURE AND SOLAR
RADIATION.**

**SUNDRY CIVIL APPROPRIATIONS BILLS.
see UNITED STATES -
APPROPRIATIONS AND
EXPENDITURES.**

**SUNFLOWERS - DISEASES AND PESTS -
BIBLIOGRAPHY.**
Rogers, Charlie Ellic, 1938- Selected
bibliography of insect pests of sunflower /.
College Station, Tex. [Beltsville, Md.] [1979]
41 p. ; LC Card 80-621131 DDC 016.6338/5 19
Z5354.P3 S867 SB608.S92

Sung, Tz'u, 1186-1249.
[Hsi yüan chi lu. English]
The washing away of wrongs : forensic
medicine in thirteenth-century China /
translated by Brian E. McKnight. Ann
Arbor : Center for Chinese Studies,
University of Michigan, 1981. p. cm. (Science,
medicine, and technology in East Asia . v. 1)
Translation of: Hsi yüan chi lu. Bibliography: p.
Includes index. ISBN 0-89264-801-5 : LC Card
81-6195 DDC 614/.1 19
*1. Forensic pathology - Early works to 1800. 2.
Coroners - China - Early works to 1800. 3. Coroners -
China - History. I. McKnight, Brian E. II. Title. III.
Series.*
RA1063 .S9613

Sunquist, Melvin E. The social organization of
tigers (Panthera tigris) in Royal Chitawan
National Park, Nepal / Melvin E. Sunquist.
Washington [D.C.] : Smithsonian Institution
Press, 1981. p. cm. (Smithsonian contributions to
zoology . no. 336) Bibliography: p. LC Card
81-607928 DDC 591 s 599.74/428 19
*1. Tigers - Behavior. 2. Social behavior in animals. 3.
Mammals - Behavior. 4. Mammals - Nepal - Royal
Chitwan National Park. 5. Royal Chitwan National
Park (Nepal). I. Title. II. Series.*
QL1 .S54 no. 336 QL737.C23

Sunset in Alaska. Alaska. Legislature. House of
Representatives. Committee on Commerce.
Interim report, sunset in Alaska, 1979-1980 /.
[Juneau, Alaska] [1980] 233 p. ; LC Card
80-622465 DDC 353.979807/5 19
KFA1211.82 .C65 1980

Sunset report .
(no. 8) Phillips, Diana Buder. Sunset 1979.
Austin, Tex. , 1979. 5, [15] p. ; LC Card
80-620628 DDC 328.764/07456 19
JK4838 1979 .P48

Sunset review. Nevada. Legislative Commission.
[Carson City, Nev.] [1980] 238 p. in various
pagings : LC Card 81-621606 DDC 353.979307/6
19
JK8538 1980 .N486

**SUNSET REVIEW OF GOVERNMENT
PROGRAMS - TEXAS.**
Texas. Legislative Budget Board. Program
Evaluation. Civil Air Patrol Commission .
Austin, Tex. , 1979. 23 leaves ; LC Card

80-622077 DDC 353.97640075/4 19
UA928.T4 T49 1979

"Sunset" review of instructional television (ITV) .
Timar, Thomas. [Sacramento] [1981] 33
leaves ; LC Card 81-621873 DDC
371.3/358/09794 19
LB1044.7 .T53

**SUNSET REVIEWS OF GOVERNMENT
PROGRAMS - ALASKA.**
Alaska. Legislature. House of Representatives.
Committee on Commerce. Interim report,
sunset in Alaska, 1979-1980 /. [Juneau, Alaska]
[1980] 233 p. ; LC Card 80-622465 DDC
353.979807/5 19
KFA1211.82 .C65 1980

**SUNSET REVIEWS OF GOVERNMENT
PROGRAMS - LAW AND LEGISLATION -
ALASKA.**
Alaska. Legislature. House of Representatives.
Committee on Commerce. Interim report,
sunset in Alaska, 1979-1980 /. [Juneau, Alaska]
[1980] 233 p. ; LC Card 80-622465 DDC
353.979807/5 19
KFA1211.82 .C65 1980

**SUNSET REVIEWS OF GOVERNMENT
PROGRAMS - LAW AND LEGISLATION -
GEORGIA.**
Georgia. General Assembly. House of
Representatives. State Planning and Community
Affairs Committee. Report of the House State
Planning and Community Affairs Committee
and the Senate Industry, Labor, and Tourism
Committee on sunset legislation. Atlanta
[1979] 42 p. ; LC Card 80-623191 DDC
342.758/06 19
KFG11.82 .P55 1979

**SUNSET REVIEWS OF GOVERNMENT
PROGRAMS - LAW AND LEGISLATION -
HAWAII.**
Azama, Calvin. Sunset, the concept and its
experience /. [Honolulu] , 1978. iii, 107 p. ;
LC Card 78-622651 DDC 342.969/066 19
KFH421.5.S95 A98

**SUNSET REVIEWS OF GOVERNMENT
PROGRAMS - LAW AND LEGISLATION -
UNITED STATES - STATES.**
Azama, Calvin. Sunset, the concept and its
experience /. [Honolulu] , 1978. iii, 107 p. ;
LC Card 78-622651 DDC 342.969/066 19
KFH421.5.S95 A98

**SUNSET REVIEWS OF GOVERNMENT
PROGRAMS - MAINE.**
Maine. Legislature. Joint Standing Committee
on Audit and Program Review. A report of the
Joint Standing Committee on Audit and
Program Review . [Augusta, Me.] [1979] 53,
[54] p. ; LC Card 80-623307 DDC 353.974107/2
19
KFM11.62 .A8 1979

**SUNSET REVIEWS OF GOVERNMENT
PROGRAMS - NEVADA.**
Nevada. Legislative Commission. Sunset review.
[Carson City, Nev.] [1980] 238 p. in various
pagings : LC Card 81-621606 DDC 353.979307/6
19
JK8538 1980 .N486

**SUNSET REVIEWS OF GOVERNMENT
PROGRAMS - TEXAS.**
Phillips, Diana Buder. Sunset 1979. Austin,
Tex. , 1979. 5, [15] p. ; LC Card 80-620628
DDC 328.764/07456 19
JK4838 1979 .P48

Sunset, the concept and its experience /. Azama,
Calvin. [Honolulu] , 1978. iii, 107 p. ; LC Card
78-622651 DDC 342.969/066 19
KFH421.5.S95 A98

Sunset 1979. Phillips, Diana Buder. Austin, Tex. ,
1979. 5, [15] p. ; LC Card 80-620628 DDC
328.764/07456 19
JK4838 1979 .P48

SUNY Press series on administrative systems.
Zammuto, Raymond F. Assessing organizational
effectiveness . Albany , 1982. p. cm. ISBN
0-87395-552-8 LC Card 81-9130 DDC
658.4/01 19
HD58.9 .Z35

SUNY series in administrative systems.
Lane, Henry W., 1942- Managing large research
and development programs /. Albany , c1981.
x, 166 p. : ISBN 0-87395-473-4 LC Card 81-849

DDC 607/.2/68 19
T175 .L28

SUNY series in modern Jewish history.
Urofsky, Melvin I. A voice that spoke for
justice . Albany , 1981. p. cm. ISBN
0-87395-538-2 LC Card 81-5676 DDC
296.8/346/0924 B 19
BM755.W53 U76

SUNY series in philosophy.
Brumbaugh, Robert Sherrick, 1918- Process
metaphysics and educational theory /. Albany ,
1981. p. cm. ISBN 0-87395-574-9 LC Card
81-14329 DDC 370/.1 19
LB85.P7 B78

Philosophy of science and the occult /.
Albany , 1981. p. cm. ISBN 0-87395-572-2 LC
Card 81-13552 DDC 001.9/01 19
BF1411 .P49

Simon, Michael A. Understanding human
action . Albany , c1981. p. cm. ISBN
0-87395-498-X LC Card 81-5280 DDC 302 19
HM251 .S622

SUNY series on American social history.
Cumbler, John T. Factory reform and response
to industrialism . Albany , 1982. p. cm. ISBN
0-87395-558-7 LC Card 81-9338 DDC 974.4/5
19
HN80.L97 C85

SUNY series on urban public policy.
Rubin, Irene. Running in the red . Albany ,
1982. p. cm. ISBN 0-87395-564-1 LC Card
81-9329 DDC 352.1/0973 19
HJ9145 .R8

The superfund concept . United States.
Interagency Task Force on Compensation and
Liability for Releases of Hazardous Substances.
[Washington] , 1979. 315 p. in various pagings :
LC Card 79-603356 DDC 344.73/04632 19
KF1298 .A83

**Superintendent of Public Instruction, special
education for the handicapped program.**
Washington (State). Legislature. Budget
Committee. Olympia , 1979. iv, 35 p. ; LC
Card 80-621134 DDC 371.9/042 19
HJ11 .W2453 no. 79-6 LC4032.W2

SUPERSTITION - ALABAMA.
Ghosts and goosebumps . University, Ala. ,
c1982. p. cm. ISBN 0-8173-0075-9 LC Card
81-7461 DDC 398.2/09761 19
GR110.A2 B56

SUPERTANKERS. see TANKERS.

**Supplement to Alabama Appalachian
development plan .** Alabama. Office of State
Planning and Federal Programs. Montgomery,
Ala. [1980] 84 p. : LC Card 80-623530 DDC
361.6/09761 19
HT393.A2 A28 1980

**Supplement to "Checklist of prints," Jacob
Kainen, prints, a retrospective /.** Flint, Janet
A. Washington , 1980. p. cm. LC Card 80-26344
DDC 769.92/4 19
NE539.K25 A4 1980

**Supplement to Laws of the State of Louisiana
relating to banks and trust companies, and
building and loan or homestead associations /.**
Louisiana. Laws, statutes, etc. New Orleans ,
1927. 56 p. ; LC Card 81-452406 DDC
346.763/082/02632 19
KFL165 .A3 1917 Suppl.

**Supplement to the Handbook of Middle
American Indians .**
(v. 1) Archaeology /. Austin , 1981. p. cm.
ISBN 0-292-77556-3 LC Card 81-4353 DDC
972/.01 19
F1219 .A76

**Supplement to the State 1202 Commission
March 1978 report .** Texas. State 1202
Commission. Austin, Tex. [1980] 210 p. ; LC
Card 80-622866 DDC 331.12/09764 19
HD5725.T5 T38 1978 Suppl.

**Supplemental appropriation and rescission bill,
1981 .** United States. Congress. House.
Committee on Appropriations. Washington ,
1981- v. <1, 3-4 > : LC Card 81-601881 DDC
353.0072/236 19
KF27 .A6 1981a

**SUPPLEMENTAL SECURITY INCOME -
UNITED STATES - STATISTICS.**
Urban Systems Research & Engineering. Survey

of blind and disabled children receiving supplemental security income benefits /. [Washington, D.C.] , 1980. xii, 94, [178] p. :
LC Card 80-602123   DDC 362.4/0482/088054 19
HV1791 .U7 1980

Supplemental specifications to standard specifications for highway construction, series 1973 /. Nebraska. Dept. of Roads. [Lincoln] [1978?] 104 p. : LC Card 79-625491   DDC 625.7/0218 19
TE24.N2 N43 1978

Supplemental specifications to Standard specifications for road and bridge construction (dated January 1, 1974) /. Delaware. Division of Highways. Dover, Del. [1980] v, 142 p. ;
LC Card 80-622254   DDC 625.7/0212 19
TE180 .D42 1980

SUPPLEMENTAL UNEMPLOYMENT BENEFITS - UNITED STATES.
United States. Congress. House. Committee on Ways and Means. Subcommittee on Oversight. Examination of special jobless benefit programs . Washington , 1980. iii, 91 p. ; LC Card 80-602951   DDC 368.4/4/00973 19
KF27 .W345 1980c

SUPPLIES, MILITARY. see MILITARY SUPPLIES.

Supply and input choice response by multiple product firms : new approaches : proceedings of a symposium presented at joint meetings of the American Agricultural Economics Association and Canadian Agricultural Economics Society at Virginia Polytechnic Institute and State University, August 8, 1978. University Park, PA : Pennsylvania State University, [1978] 50 leaves ; 28 cm. Cover title. "A.E. & R.S. 137." Incluces bibliographies. LC Card 79-626266   DDC 658.4/033 19
1. Decision-making - Mathematical models - Congresses. I. American Agricultural Economics Association. II. Canadian Agricultural Economics Society.
HD30.23 .S88

Supply control and U. S. agriculture .
Schraufnagel, Stanley A. Ames, Iowa [1980] xiii leaves, 84 p. : LC Card 80-623951   DDC 338.1/873 19
HD1761 .S258

Supply, demand, and economics of fuelwood markets in selected population centers of Arizona / [Peter F. Ffolliott ... et al.]. [Phoenix] : Arizona State Land Dept., 1979. ii, 74 p. : graphs ; 29 cm. (Arizona land marks . v. 9, book 2) Cover title. Bibliography: p. 42-43. LC Card 80-621038   DDC 338.4/766265/09791 19
1. Fuelwood industry - Arizona. I. Ffolliott, Peter F. II. Series.
HD9769.F843 U67

SUPPLY OF MONEY. see MONEY SUPPLY.

Supply of optometrists in the United States .
United States. Health Resources Administration. Bureau of Health Manpower. [Bethesda? Md.] , 1978. iii, 23 p. ; LC Card 79-603959   DDC 331.12/916177/00973 19
RE959 .U54 1978

SUPPORT (DOMESTIC RELATIONS) - ALASKA.
Scott, Michael James, 1948- Standards for determining child support obligations in Alaska /. Anchorage [1978] 156 p. in various pagings : LC Card 79-622825   DDC 362.7/95 19
HV742.A4 S37

Supreme Court (U. S.) see United States. Supreme Court.

SURFACE CHEMISTRY.
(1979) Rabockai, Tibor. Físico-química de superfícies /. Washington, D.C. , 1979. vii, 128 p. : LC Card 80-103037   DDC 540 s 541.3/453 19
QD1 .S303 no. 20 QC173.4.S94

Surface design for fabric /. Proctor, Richard M. Seattle , c1982. p. cm.   ISBN 0-295-95874-X   LC Card 81-7420   DDC 677/.022 19
TS1475 .P76

SURFACE MINING. see STRIP MINING.

The Surface Mining Act in the West . Dyer, Barbara, 1951- Lexington, Ky. (Iron Works Pike, Lexington 40578) , c1980. vii, 31 p. ; LC Card 81-133232   DDC 346.7304/68 347.306468

19
KF1823 .D94

Surface Mining Control and Reclamation Act of 1977. United States. Congress. House. Committee on Interior and Insular Affairs. Subcommittee on Energy and the Environment. Reclamation practices and environmental problems of surface mining . Washington , 1977. 4 v. : LC Card 77-603316   DDC 346.7304/68 347.306468 19
KF27 .I518 1977j

SURFACE PHENOMENA. see SURFACE CHEMISTRY.

Surface transportation act of 1980 . United States. Congress. House. Committee on Public Works and Transportation. Subcommittee on Surface Transportation. Washington , 1980. v, 464 p. : LC Card 80-603733   DDC 343.73/0982 347.303982 19
KF27 .P8966 1980a

SURFACE WATER SEWERS. see STORM SEWERS.

Surface water temperature and density, Atlantic Coast . National Ocean Survey. Rockville, Md. , Washington, D. C. , 1973. 109 p. :
NYPL [JSF 81-4]

SURFACES (CHEMISTRY) see SURFACE CHEMISTRY.

SURFACES (PHYSICS)
Rabockai, Tibor. Físico-química de superfícies /. Washington, D.C. , 1979. vii, 128 p. : LC Card 80-103037   DDC 540 s 541.3/453 19
QD1 .S303 no. 20 QC173.4.S94

Surficial geology and processes . Updike, Randall G. Anchorage, Alaska , 1979. iii, 6 p., 17 leaves (14 fold.) of plates : LC Card 79-626004   DDC 912/.1551/097987 19
G1532.P7C5 U6 1979

Surficial geology handbook for coastal Maine /. Thompson, Woodrow B. Augusta, Me. , 1978. vii, 66 p., [41] leaves of plates : LC Card 79-622304   DDC 553/.09741 19
QE119 .T48 1978

Surficial geology handbook for coastal Maine /. Thompson, Woodrow B. Augusta, Me. , 1979. vii, 68 p., [39] leaves of plates : LC Card 80-620848   DDC 553/.09741 19
QE119 .T48 1979

Surficial sediments and seagrasses of eastern Great South Bay, N.Y. / G. T. Greene ... [et al.]. Stony Brook, N.Y. : Marine Sciences Research Center, State University of New York, 1978. ii, 30 p. : ill. ; 28 cm. (Special report - Marine Sciences Research Center, State University of New York . 12) "Reference 77-9." Bibliography: p. 29-30. LC Card 80-620917   DDC 551.46/146 19
1. Marine sediments - New York (State) - Great South Bay. 2. Zostera marina. 3. Marine ecology - New York (State) - Great South Bay. I. Greene, G. T. II. Series: New York (State). State University at Stony Brook. Marine Sciences Research Center. Special report , 12.
GC383 .S87

SURGEONS - LEGAL STATUS, LAWS, ETC. see MEDICAL LAWS AND LEGISLATION.

SURGEONS - UNITED STATES - FEES.
United States. Congress. House. Committee on Interstate and Foreign Commerce. Subcommittee on Oversight and Investigations. Wasted surgical dollars . Washington , 1981. ii, 38 p. ; LC Card 81-601159   DDC 362.1/97/0973 19
KF27 .I5547 1980q

SURGERY - CALIFORNIA.
Cretin, Shan. Surgical care for cardiovascular disease in California . Berkeley, Calif. , 1981. x, 37 p. ;   ISBN 0-87772-277-3   LC Card 80-39873   DDC 617/.41 19
RD597 .C73

SURGERY, EXPERIMENTAL.
Dougherty, R. W. (Robert Watson), 1904- Experimental surgery in farm animals /. Ames , 1981. p. cm.   ISBN 0-8138-1540-1   LC Card 81-3693   DDC 636.089/79/0724 19
RD29 .D68

SURGERY, UNNECESSARY - UNITED STATES.
United States. Congress. House. Committee on Interstate and Foreign Commerce. Subcommittee on Oversight and Investigations. Wasted surgical dollars . Washington , 1981. ii, 38 p. ; LC Card 81-601159   DDC 362.1/97/0973 19
KF27 .I5547 1980q

Surgical care for cardiovascular disease in California . Cretin, Shan. Berkeley, Calif. , 1981. x, 37 p. ;   ISBN 0-87772-277-3   LC Card 80-39873   DDC 617/.41 19
RD597 .C73

Surgical sterilization surveillance . Center for Disease Control. Family Planning Evaluation Division. Atlanta, Ga. [1979] 22 p. ; LC Card 79-600096   DDC 363.9/7/0973 19
RG138 .C46 1979

SURPLUS GOVERNMENT PROPERTY - OKLAHOMA.
Oklahoma. State Legislative Council. Post-Audit Section. Performance audit, State Agency for Surplus Property, a division of the State Board of Public Affairs /. [Oklahoma City] [1980] 35 p. ; LC Card 80-622935   DDC 353.97660071/3045 19
JK1669.O5 O34 1980

A survey and evaluation of the archeological resources ... Jackson, Susan, 1950- A survey and evaluation of the archeological resources of the Little Lynches Creek watershed in Lancaster County, South Carolina /. Columbia , 1975. 17 leaves, [1] leaf of plates : LC Card 76-622781   DDC 975.7/45 19
F277.L2 J32

A survey and evaluation of the archeological resources of the Little Lynches Creek watershed in Lancaster County, South Carolina /. Jackson, Susan, 1950- Columbia , 1975. 17 leaves, [1] leaf of plates : LC Card 76-622781   DDC 975.7/45 19
F277.L2 J32

Survey-guided development. Pecorella, Patricia A. [Washington?] , 1974. 1 v. (various pagings) ;
NYPL [JLF 81-585]

A survey of adult and continuing educaton programs in Nevada. Nevada. State Dept. of Education. Vocational-Technical and Adult Education Branch. Carson City.
NYPL [JLM 80-726]

A survey of arson and arson response capabilities in selected jurisdictions /. Webster, Stephen H. [Washington] , 1979. 41 p. : LC Card 79-601901   DDC 364.1/64 19
HV8079.A7 W4

Survey of blind and disabled children receiving supplemental security income benefits /. Urban Systems Research & Engineering. [Washington, D.C.] , 1980. xii, 94, [178] p. : LC Card 80-602123   DDC 362.4/0482/088054 19
HV1791 .U7 1980

A survey of continuing education programs in Nevada. Nevada. State Dept. of Education. Vocational-Technical and Adult Education Branch. A survey of adult and continuing educaton programs in Nevada. Carson City.
NYPL [JLM 80-726]

Survey of cultural resources at Malakoff Diggins State Historic Park. California. Dept. of Parks and Recreation. Sacramento, CA , 1979. v, 182 p. : LC Card 79-625567   DDC 979.4/37 19
F868.N5 C34 1979

Survey of current business. United States. Bureau of Economic Analysis. The detailed input-output structure of the U. S. economy, 1972. [Washington, D.C.] , 1979- v. ; LC Card 80-601759   DDC 339.2/3/0973 19
HC106.7 .U537 1979

A survey of EDP performance measurement for local government /. Matthews, Joseph R. - Irvine, Calif. , 1975. iii, 31 p. :
*NYPL [*XME-9422]*

Survey of election boards . Analytic Systems, inc. Washington, D.C. [1974] ii, 111 p. ; LC Card 74-602978   DDC 353.008 19
JK1980 .A55 1974

Survey of election boards . United States. Office of Federal Elections. Washington , 1974. 229 p. ;
NYPL [JLF 80-1622]

A survey of erosion and sedimentation problems associated with logging in Maine /. Maine.

Land Use Regulation Commission. [Augusta, Me.] [1979] 56 p. : LC Card 80-620932 DDC 333.75/16/09741 19
TD428.F67 M34 1979

Survey of factors relating to job satisfaction among VA nurses . United States. Veterans Administration. [Washington] , 1973. 20, [45] p. : *NYPL [JLF 80-1691]*

Survey of fish species in Ohio waters of Lake Erie, July 1, 1973 to June 30, 1974 . VanVooren, Allan R. [Columbus] , 1974. 68 leaves : LC Card 75-622209 DDC 597.092/9771/2 19
QL625.5 .V36

Survey of Japanese collections in the United States, 1979-1980 /. Fukuda, Naomi. Ann Arbor , 1981. p. cm. ISBN 0-939512-09-2 : LC Card 81-4481 DDC 026/.952 19
Z3306 .F84 DS806

Survey of museums and historical societies in New York State. New York (State) State Museum, Albany. Albany , 1979. vii, 67 p. ; LC Card 80-621017 DDC 974.7/006/0747 19
F116 .N273 1979

A survey of national geocoding systems. Werner, Pamela A. [Cambridge, Mass.], 1974. xi, 344 p. LC Card 76-51887 *NYPL [JFF 80-1538]*

Survey of Nebraska women's employment participation, attitudes, and needs /. Frost, Murray. Omaha, Neb. , 1979. vi, 97 p. ; LC Card 80-621228 DDC 331.4/09782 19
HD6096.N3 F76

Survey of Negro life in New Jersey . New Jersey Conference of Social Work. Interracial Committee. Trenton, N. J. , 1932. 18 v. ; *NYPL [Sc Micro R-3667]*

A survey of non-resident lending and borrowing activity in Massachusetts /. Piggford, Roland R. Boston, MA [1979] i, 150, 7 p. : LC Card 80-622848 DDC 025.6/09744 19
Z732.M41 P53

Survey of properties of the hydrgen isotopes below their critical temperatures / H. M. Roder ... [et al.] Washington : U. S. Dept. of Commerce, National Bureau of Standards, 1973. vii, 113 p. : ill. ; 28 cm. (NBS technical note. 641) Bibliography: p. 98-113.
1. Hydrogen - Isotopes. 2. Low temperatures. I. Roder, H. M. II. United States. National Bureau of Standards. *NYPL [JSF 81-57]*

A survey of recreational lodging and outdoor recreation by northeastern households /. Kottke, Marvin Walter. Storrs, Conn. [1979] 48 p. ; LC Card 80-621317 DDC 338.4/76479474 19
TX909 .K67

Survey of research on transnational corporations /. United Nations. Centre on Transnational Corporations. New York , 1977. iii, 533 p. ; LC Card 80-491957 DDC 300 s 338.8/8/072 19
JX1977 .A2 ST/CTC/3

A survey of small hydroelectric potential at existing sites in California. California. Dept. of Water Resources. [Sacramento] , 1979. viii, 28 p. : LC Card 80-620653 DDC 621.31/2134/09794 19
TK1424.C2 C34 1979

A survey of spousal violence against women in Kentucky /. Schulman, Mark A. Washington, D.C. , 1980 printing. 67, 13 p., p. a-b : LC Card 80-602365 DDC 362.8/2 19
HV6626 .S38

A survey of State agency insurance coverage, March 24, 1980 /. Mississippi. Legislature. Audit Committee. [Jackson, Miss. , 1980] ix, 81 p. : LC Card 80-622528 DDC 368.4/2/009762 19
JK4660.H4 M57 1980

A survey of state laws to remove barriers. United States. President's Committee on Employment of the Handicapped. - Washington , 1973. 31 p. ; *NYPL [*XME-9572]*

A survey of states' efforts to improve land development review procedures /. Alm, Robert A. Honolulu [1980] v, 68 p. ; LC Card 80-623819 DDC 333.73/15/0973 19
HT392 .A75

Survey of the epifaunal invertebrates of Norton Sound, southeastern Chukchi Sea, and Kotzebue Sound /. Feder, Howard M.

Fairbanks , 1978. vii, 124 p. : LC Card 79-622468 DDC 551.46 s 592.09798 19
GC1.A497 R78-1 QL161

A Survey of the town forest resources in New Hampshire / by T.G. Gregoire ... [et al.]. Durham, N.H. : New Hampshire Agricultural Experiment Station, University of New Hampshire, [1980] ii, 18 p. : ill. ; 28 cm. (Research report - New Hampshire Agricultural Experiment Station, University of New Hampshire . no. 81) Caption title. Bibliography: p. 10. LC Card 80-622912 DDC 333.75/09742 19
1. Community forests - New Hampshire. 2. Forests and forestry - New Hampshire. I. Gregoire, T. G. II. Title: Town forest resources in New Hampshire. III. Series: New Hampshire. Agricultural Experiment Station, Durham. Research report , no. 81.
SD566.N4 S87

Survey report on the economic impact of D2 lands restrictions and the public view of alternative uses of State capital expenditures to offset such effects /. National Survey Research Group, New York. Juneau, Alaska [1980] i, 49 p. : LC Card 80-622486 DDC 333.1/09798 19
HD243.A3 N37 1980

SURVEYORS - LEGAL STATUS, LAWS, ETC. - VIRGINIA.
Virginia. State Board of Architects, Professional Engineers, and Land Surveyors. Rules and regulations, adopted May 30, 1975, amended December 17, 1976, March 10, 1977, March 2, 1979, published June 1, 1979, effective July 1, 1979 ; Statutes, March 2, 1979, chapter 1.1, title 54, Chapter 3, title 54, chapter 24, title 54, chapter 7, title 13.1 /. Richmond, Va. [1979] 39 p. ; LC Card 80-621955 DDC 344.755/01762 19
KFV2729.A7 A32 1979

SURVEYS, DEMOGRAPHIC. see DEMOGRAPHIC SURVEYS.

SURVEYS, ECONOMIC. see ECONOMIC SURVEYS.

SURVEYS, SOCIAL. see SOCIAL SURVEYS.

SURVIVAL (HUMAN ECOLOGY) see HUMAN ECOLOGY.

Survival in Antarctica. United States. National Science Foundation. Division of Polar Programs. Washington, D.C. , 1979. v, 99 p. : LC Card 80-601811 DDC 613.6/9/09989 19
GV200.5 .U54 1979

The survival of enteric viruses in septic tanks and septic tank drain fields /. Hain, Kathleen E. Las Cruces, N.M. [1979] x, 73 p. : LC Card 80-622272 DDC 628/.742 19
GB705.N6 N64 no. 108 QR48

Survivals of pastoral / edited by Richard F. Hardin. Lawrence : University of Kansas Publications, 1979. x, 150 p. ; 23 cm. (University of Kansas publications : Humanistic studies ; 52) Includes bibliographical references. CONTENTS. - Hardin, R. F. The pastoral moment.--Eversole, R. William Collins and the end of the shepherd pastoral.--Sutton, M. K. Truth and the pastor's vision in George Crabbe, William Barnes, and R. S. Thomas.--Girdley, R. E. Some versions of the primitive and the pastoral on the Great Plains of America.--O'Donnell, T. J. "Une exploration des déserts de ma mémoire": pastoral aspects of Lévi-Strauss's Tristes tropiques.--Ruhe, E. L. Pastoral paradigms and displacements, with some proposals. LC Card 80-621786 DDC 809/.9145 19
1. Pastoral literature - History and criticism - Addresses, essays, lectures. I. Hardin, Richard F. II. Series: Kansas. University. Humanistic studies, 52.
PN56.P3 S9

SURVIVORS' BENEFITS (OLD AGE PENSIONS) see OLD AGE PENSIONS.

SURVIVORS' BENEFITS - UNITED STATES.
United States. Congress. House. Committee on Armed Services. Subcommittee on Military Compensation. Benefits for survivors of retired military personnel, S. 91 . Washington , 1981 [i.e. 1981] ii, 130 p. : LC Card 81-600805 DDC 343.73/0112 347.303112 19
KF27 .A76392 1980b

United States. Congress. House. Committee on Armed Services. Subcommittee on Military Compensation. Hearing on H.R. 2817, H.R. 3677, and H.R. 6270, legislation related to

benefits for former spouse of a military retiree, before the Military Compensation Subcommittee of the Committee on Armed Services, House of Representatives, Ninety-sixth Congress, second session, May 28, 1980. Washington , 1980 [i.e. 1981] ii, 126 p. : LC Card 81-600974 DDC 343.73/0112 347.303112 19
KF27 .A76392 1980c

United States. Congress. House. Committee on Education and Labor. Subcommittee on Labor Standards. Hearings on a death benefit for Federal law enforcement officers and firefighters . Washington , 1980. iv, 161 p. ; LC Card 80-602763 DDC 344.73/023 19
KF27 .E348 1980

United States. Congress. House. Committee on Veterans' Affairs. Subcommittee on Compensation, Pension, Insurance, and Memorial Affairs. Review of compensation and DIC programs . Washington , 1980. iii, 93 p. ; LC Card 80-603330 DDC 343.73/0112 19
KF27 .V43 1980a

United States. Congress. Senate. Committee on Veterans' Affairs. Veterans' disability compensation and survivors' benefits amendments of 1980 . Washington , 1980, [i.e. 1981] iv, 601 p. : LC Card 81-601405 DDC 343.73/0116 347.303116 19
KF26 .V4 1981h

Susan River water quality study /. California. Dept. of Water Resources. Northern District. [Sacramento] , 1979. vii, 63 p. : LC Card 80-621635 DDC 363.7/3942/0979426 19
TD224.C3 C24 1979e

SUSITUA HYDROELECTRIC PROJECT (ALASKA)
Final report /. [Juneau] [1980] 27 p. : LC Card 81-621099 DDC 333.79/3212/097983 19
TK1424.A4 F56

Suski, Nancy. (joint author) Eating hints . [Bethesda, Md.] [1980] iii, 86 p. : LC Card 80-602402 DDC 641.5/631 19
RC271.D52 M67 1980

SUSPENDED LOAD. see SEDIMENT, SUSPENDED.

SUSPENDED LOAD OF STREAMS. see SEDIMENT TRANSPORT.

Suspended sediment from truck traffic on forest roads, Meadow and Coal Creeks /. Wooldridge, David D. Seattle [1978] 33 p.: *NYPL [*ZV-185 Reel 1]*

Suspended-sediment load of Texas streams /. Dougherty, John Philip, 1923- Austin [1979] v, 82 p., [1] leaf of plates : LC Card 79-625851 DDC 333.91/009764 s 551.3/54 19
TD224.T4 A333 no. 233 GB1225.T4

SUSPENDED SENTENCE. see PROBATION.

Suspension of grain shipments to the Soviet Union . United States. Congress. House. Committee on Agriculture. Washington , 1980. iii, 127 p. : LC Card 80-602450 DDC 382/.4131/0973 19
KF27 .A3 1980

Suspension of United States exports of high technology and grain to the Soviet Union . United States. Congress. Senate. Committee on Banking, Housing and Urban Affairs. Washington , 1980. v, 156 p. : LC Card 80-604066 DDC 382/.4131/0973 19
KF26 .B39 1980x

Susquehanna River Basin Commission. Publication - Susquehanna River Basin Commission .
(no. 65) Seay, Edmond E. Analysis of electric generation & energy use in the Susq[u]ehanna River Basin, 1978 /. Harrisburg, Pa. [1980] ii, 25 p. ; LC Card 80-622024 DDC 363.6/2 19
TK1193.U5 S45

SUSSEX COUNTY (DEL.) - MAPS.
United States. Soil Conservation Service. Sussex County, Delaware /. Lanham, MD , 1980. 1 map : LC Card 81-690014
G3833.S8 1980 .U5

Suta, Benjamin E. Human population exposures to Mirex and Kepone / prepared for U. S. Environmental Protection Agency, Office of Research and Development. ... by Benjamin E.

Suta. Washington : U. S. Environmental Protection Agency, Office of Research and Development, 1978. ix, 139 p. ; 28 cm. (Environmental health effects research ; EPA-600/1-78-045) Bibliography: p. 133-139. LC Card 78-602606 DDC 363.7/384 19
1. Chlordecone - Toxicology - United States. 2. Mirex - Toxicology - United States. 3. Chlordecone - Environmental aspects - United States. I. Series: Environmental health effects research series , EPA-600/1-78-045. II. Title.
RA1242.C43 S93

Suter, Glenn W. Effects of geothermal energy development on fish and wildlife / Glenn W. Suter Ii ; Power Plant Project/Geothermal Project, Office of Biological Services, Fish and Wildlife Service, U. S. Department of the Interior. [Washington, D.C.] : Fish and Wildlife Service, U. S. Dept. of the Interior, 1978. 20 p. : ill. ; 27 cm. (Topical briefs--fish and wildlife resources and electric power generation . no. 6) "Biological services program." "FWS/OBS-76/20.6." Bibliography: p. 16-18. LC Card 79-603793 DDC 333.8/81 19
1. Geothermal power plants - Environmental aspects. I. United States. Fish and Wildlife Service. Power Plant Project. II. United States. Fish and Wildlife Service. Geothermal Project. III. Title. IV. Title: Biological services program. V. Series.
QH545.G46 S87

Sutter, Robert G. Executive-legislative consultations on China policy, 1978-79 / [prepared by Robert G. Sutter]. Washington : U. S. Govt. Print. Off. : for sale by the Supt. of Docs. , U. S. Govt. Print. Off., 1980. vii, 42 p. ; 24 cm. (Congress and foreign policy series . no. 1) At head of title: Foreign Affairs Committee print. Prepared by the Congressional Research Service for the Subcommittee on Europe and the Middle East of the House Committee on Foreign Affairs. LC Card 80-602678 DDC 327.73051 19
1. United States - Foreign relations - China. 2. China - Foreign relations - United States. 3. United States - Foreign relations - Taiwan. 4. Taiwan - Foreign relations - United States. I. United States. Library of Congress. Congressional Research Service. II. United States. Congress. House. Committee on Foreign Affairs. Subcommittee on Europe and the Middle East. III. Title. IV. Series.
JX1428.C6 S97

Suwojo Wojowasito. see Wojowasito, Suwojo.

Suzman, Cedric L. Roy, Delwin A. Southeast exporting . Atlanta, Ga. , 1981. p. cm. ISBN 0-88406-146-9 : LC Card 81-6287 DDC 382/.0975 19
HF3153 .R69

Svenningsen, Robert, 1941- United States. National Archives and Records Service. Preliminary inventory of the Pueblo records created by field offices of the Bureau of Indian Affairs . Washington , 1980. vii, 34 p. ; LC Card 80-607174 DDC 016.973 s 016.3231/197/073 19
CD3026 .A32 no. 192 Z1210.P8 E99.P9

The Sverdlovsk incident . United States. Congress. House. Permanent Select Committee on Intelligence. Subcommittee on Oversight. Washington , 1980. iii, 18 p. ; LC Card 80-603451 DDC 358/.38/0947 19
KF27.5 .I55 1980a

SWAHILI-SPEAKING PEOPLES - SOCIAL LIFE AND CUSTOMS.
Mtoro bin Mwinyi Bakari. [Desturi za Waswahili. English.] The customs of the Swahili people . Berkeley , c1981. p. cm. ISBN 0-520-04122-4 LC Card 81-3387 DDC 305.8/963 19
DT433.542 .M7813

SWAMP ECOLOGY - FLORIDA.
Forested wetlands of Florida . Tallahassee , 1977. v, 348 p. : LC Card 78-621426 DDC 333.91/8/09759 19
QH105.F6 F67 1977

Swanberg, Chandler A. New Mexico Energy Institute at New Mexico State University. An appraisal study of the geothermal resources of Arizona and adjacent areas in New Mexico and Utah and their value for desalination and other uses /. Las Cruces, N.M. [1977] vii, 76 leaves, [12] leaves of plates : LC Card 80-623249 DDC 553.7 19
GB1199.5 .N48 1977

Swank, G. W. (joint author) Berndt, H. W. Forest land use and streamflow in central Oregon /. Portland, Or. , 1970. 15 p. : LC Card 71-608738 DDC 634.9/09795 s 553.7/09795/83 19
SD11 .A45614 no. 93 SD387.M8

Swanson, Gustav Adolph, 1910- Mitigation Symposium, Colorado State University, 1979. The Mitigation Symposium . Fort Collins, Colo , 1979. xi, 684 p. : LC Card 80-602560 DDC 639.9/2/0973 19
SK361 .M57 1979

Swanson, Robert William. Income and benefit receipt among Michigan AFDC families / principal authors, Robert W. Swanson, Vernon K. Smith, Gary A. Howitt. [Lansing] : Michigan Dept. of Social Services, Office of Planning, Budget, and Evaluation, Income Maintenance Analysis Division, [1979] xix, 150 p. : ill. ; 28 cm. (Studies in welfare policy. no. 13) DSS publication ; 31 (11-79 "September 1979." LC Card 80-621648 DDC 361/.9774 s 362.7/13/09774 19
1. Welfare recipients - Michigan - Statistics. I. Smith, Vernon K., joint author. II. Howitt, Gary A., joint author. III. Michigan. Dept. of Social Services. Income Maintenance Analysis Division. IV. Series. V. Series: Michigan. Dept. of Social Services. DSS publication, 31 (11-79).
HV86 .M536 no. 31 (11-79)
NYPL [JLM 75-1607 no. 13]

SWAPO.
United States. Congress. House. Committee on Foreign Affairs. Subcommittee on Africa. Namibia update . Washington , 1981. iv, 35 p. : LC Card 81-600962 DDC 968.8/03 19
KF27 .F625 1980h

Sweeney, Dwight P. Double jeopardy . Ann Arbor , c1979. 332 p. ; LC Card 80-621753 DDC 362.3/0880565 19
HV3006.M54 D68

Sweeney, Gerard M. Sherwood Anderson, wanderer and myth-maker / Gerard M. Sweeney. Columbus : State Library of Ohio, 1979. 23 p. ; 23 cm. (Ohio authors) Bibliography: p. 23. LC Card 80-137471 DDC 813/.52 B 19
1. Anderson, Sherwood, 1876-1941 - Addresses, essays, lectures. 2. Authors, American - 20th century - Biography - Addresses, essays, lectures. I. Series.
PS3501.N4 Z855

Sweet, Richard N. Wisconsin. Legislative Council. Legislation and case law relating to the definition of death /. Madison , 1978. i, 54 p. ; LC Card 79-621977 DDC 346.77501/2 19
KFW2767.D4 A25 1978

Swenson, Lou. (joint author) Burger, Carl. Environmental surveillance of gravel removal on the Trans-Alaska Pipeline System, with recommendations for future gravel mining /. Anchorage, Alaska , 1977. 35 leaves : LC Card 79-625780 DDC 333.95/4 19
TD195.S3 B87

Swift and the Ciceronian tradition /. Thornburg, Thomas R. Muncie, Ind. , 1980. 28 p. ; LC Card 80-67735 DDC 828/.5/09 19
PR3728.T4 T47

SWIFT, JONATHAN, 1667-1745 - POETIC WORKS.
Barnett, Louise K. Swift's poetic worlds /. Newark , c1981. p. cm. ISBN 0-87413-187-1 LC Card 80-54538 DDC 821/.5 19
PR3728.P58 B35

SWIFT, JONATHAN, 1667-1745 - TECHNIQUE - ADDRESSES, ESSAYS, LECTURES.
Thornburg, Thomas R. Swift and the Ciceronian tradition /. Muncie, Ind. , 1980. 28 p. ; LC Card 80-67735 DDC 828/.5/09 19
PR3728.T4 T47

Swiftly now /. Stoloff, Carolyn. Athens , 1982. p. cm. ISBN 0-8214-0646-9 LC Card 81-11150 DDC 811/.54 19
PS3569.T623 S9

Swift's poetic worlds /. Barnett, Louise K. Newark , c1981. p. cm. ISBN 0-87413-187-1 LC Card 80-54538 DDC 821/.5 19
PR3728.P58 B35

SWIMMING POOLS - SANITATION.
Koertge, Henry Herman. The turbidity of public swimming pool waters /. Urbana , 1967. iv, 75

leaves : LC Card 79-627486 DDC 363.7/292 19
RA606 .K57

SWINE.
Hugh, Williams Inglis, 1928- Feeding and management of growing-finishing pigs /. Honolulu , 1981. p. cm. LC Card 81-13055 DDC 636.4 19
SF395 .H74

SWINE - FEEDING AND FEEDS.
Hugh, Williams Inglis, 1928- Feeding and management of growing-finishing pigs /. Honolulu , 1981. p. cm. LC Card 81-13055 DDC 636.4 19
SF395 .H74

SWINE - FEEDING AND FEEDS - LAW AND LEGISLATION - UNITED STATES.
United States. Congress. House. Committee on Agriculture. Subcommittee on Department Investigations, Oversight, and Research. Swine health protection act . Washington , 1980. iii, 59 p. ; LC Card 80-603521 DDC 344.73/043 347.30443 19
KF27 .A33265 1980b

Swine health protection act . United States. Congress. House. Committee on Agriculture. Subcommittee on Department Investigations, Oversight, and Research. Washington , 1980. iii, 59 p. ; LC Card 80-603521 DDC 344.73/043 347.30443 19
KF27 .A33265 1980b

SWINE - HOUSING - WASTE DISPOSAL.
Collins, Edmond R. Swine lagoon effluent on a soil-plant environment . Blacksburg , 1978. v, 38 p. ; LC Card 78-624385 DDC 333.91/009755 s 636.4/0831 19
TD201 .V57 no. 110 TD930

Swine lagoon effluent on a soil-plant environment . Collins, Edmond R. Blacksburg , 1978. v, 38 p. ; LC Card 78-624385 DDC 333.91/009755 s 636.4/0831 19
TD201 .V57 no. 110 TD930

Swinehart, James B. (joint author) Souders, Vernon L. Geology and groundwater supplies of Box Butte County, Nebraska /. [Lincoln] [1980] vii, 205 p. : LC Card 80-623050 DDC 553/.7/09782 s 551.7/9/0978294 19
GB1025.N2 N42 no. 47 QE136.B67

Swing bed experiments to provide long-term care in rural hospitals. An Evaluation of swing bed experiments to provide long-term care in rural hospitals. Denver, Colo. (4200 East Ninth Ave., Denver 80262) [1980] 2 v. ; LC Card 80-65248 DDC 362.1/1/091734 19
RA975.R87 E9

SWISS AMERICANS - MINNESOTA - BIOGRAPHY.
Bost, Théodore, 1834-1920. A frontier family in Minnesota . Minneapolis , c1981. p. cm. ISBN 0-8166-1032-0 : LC Card 81-10401 DDC 977.6/5 B 19
F606 .B75313

Swiss Kredit Bank. see Crédit suisse.

Switching Requirements and R & D for Fusion Reactors, Workshop on. see Workshop on Switching Requirements and R & D for Fusion Reactors, Palo Alto, Calif., 1976.

SWITCHING THEORY.
(1979) Cutler, Robert Brian. Exposition of Tison's method to derive all prime implicants and all irredundant disjunctive forms for a given switching function /. Urbana, Ill. [1979] 125 p. ; LC Card 80-622397 DDC 001.64 s 621.3815/37 19
QA76 .I4 no. 993 QA268.5

SWORD GUARDS - JAPAN.
Cooper-Hewitt Museum of Decorative Arts and Design. Tsuba, and Japanese sword fittings in the collection of the Cooper-Hewitt Museum, the Smithsonian Institution's National Museum of Design. [New York, NY] , c1980. [36] p. : LC Card 80-67169 DDC 739.7/22 19
NK6784.A1 C66 1980

SWORD MOUNTINGS - JAPAN.
Cooper-Hewitt Museum of Decorative Arts and Design. Tsuba, and Japanese sword fittings in the collection of the Cooper-Hewitt Museum, the Smithsonian Institution's National Museum of Design. [New York, NY] , c1980. [36] p. : LC Card 80-67169 DDC 739.7/22 19
NK6784.A1 C66 1980

Sykes, Gresham M. The future of crime / Gresham M. Sykes. Rockville, Md. (5600 Fishers Lane, Rockville, Md., 20857) : U. S. Dept. of Health and Human Services, Public Health Service, Alcohol, Drug Abuse, and Mental Health Administration, National Institute of Mental Health, Center for Studies of Crime and Delinquency ; Washington, D.C. : For sale by the Supt. of Docs., U. S. G.P.O., 1980. vi, 85 p. : ill. ; 23 cm. (Crime and delinquency issues) DHHS publication ; no. (ADM) 80-912 Includes bibliographical references. Contract no. 282-76-0409. LC Card 80-603932 DDC 364/.973 19

1. Crime and criminals - United States. I. Center for Studies of Crime and Delinquency (U. S.). II. Title.
HV6789 .S96

Sykes, Thomas M.
An analysis of program needs of prison inmates in Washington State / Thomas M. Sykes, Robert L. Riccolo, Joann K. Thompson. Olympia, Wash. : Washington State Dept. of Social & Health Services, Analysis and Information Services Division, [1980] xxi, 139 p. ; 28 cm. (Report - Washington State Dept. of Social & Health Services . 01-24) Title on spine: Program needs of prison inmates. "April 1980." Includes bibliographical references. LC Card 80-620028 DDC 365/.66/09797 19

1. Prisoners - Washington (State). 2. Prisoners - Services for - Washington (State). 3. Rehabilitation of criminals - Washington (State). I. Riccolo, Robert L., joint author. II. Thompson, Joann K., joint author. III. Title. IV. Title: Program needs of prison inmates. V. Series: Washington (State). Dept. of Social and Health Services. Report - Washington State Dept. of Social & Health Services , 01-24.
HV9475.W2 S93

(joint author) Dennen, Taylor. An analysis and evaluation of information and assistance programs for the elderly in the State of Washington /. Olympia, Wash. , 1979. xxv, 182 p. : LC Card 79-620026 DDC 362.6/09797 19
HV1468.W2 D46

Symbolic experience, a study of poems by Pedro Salinas /. Allen, Rupert C. University, Ala , c1981. p. cm. ISBN 0-8173-0081-3 LC Card 81-10307 DDC 861/.62 19
PQ6635.A32 Z54

SYMBOLISM IN LITERATURE.
Allen, Rupert C. Symbolic experience, a study of poems by Pedro Salinas /. University, Ala , c1981. p. cm. ISBN 0-8173-0081-3 LC Card 81-10307 DDC 861/.62 19
PQ6635.A32 Z54

SYMMETRIC MATRICES.
Roloff, Richard Roy, 1952- Iterative solution of matrix equations for symmetric matrices possessing positive and negative eigenvalues /. Urbana, Ill. [1979] iv leaves, 47 p. : LC Card 80-622971 DDC 001.64 s 512.9/434 19
QA76 .I4 no. 1018 QA188

Symons, Van Jay. Ch'ing ginseng management : Ch'ing monopolies in microcosm / by Van Jay Symons. Tempe, Ariz. : Center for Asian Studies, Arizona State University, 1981. vi, 121 p. ; 23 cm. (Occasional paper / Center for Asian Studies, Arizona State University . no. 13) Bibliography: p. 114-120. ISBN 0-939252-09-0 (pbk.) . LC Card 80-71096

1. Ginseng industry - China - History. 2. China - History - Ch'ing dynasty, 1644-1912. 3. Government monopolies - China - History. I. Series: Occasional paper (Arizona State University. Center for Asian Studies) , no. 13. II. Title.
HD9019.G552 C67

Symposia on the American Revolution, Library of Congress. see **Library of Congress Symposia on the American Revolution, 1st, 1972.**

Symposium : the changing mission of the United States Employment Service : increasing productivity and improving the operation of the labor market : report of symposium presentations, discussions, and recommendations on occasion of the 40th anniversary observance of the United States Employment Service, June 6, 1973 / edited by Peter G. Petro ; sponsored by the United States Department of Labor, Employment and Training Administration. Washington : U. S. Dept. of Labor, Employment and Training Administration, 1977. ix, 141 p. ; 26 cm. Microfiche (neg.) NTIS. 2 sheets. 11 x 15 cm. (PB-265 811) Cover title: A

symposium commemorating the fortieth anniversary observance of the United States Employment Service. Includes bibliographical references. LC Card 77-601861

1. United States. Employment Service - Congresses. 2. Manpower policy - United States - Congresses. I. Petro, Peter G. II. United States. Employment and Training Administration. III. Title: The changing mission of the United States Employment Service. IV. Title: A symposium commemorating the fortieth anniversary observance ...
HD5875 .S95   **NYPL [*XME-9409]**

A symposium commemorating the fortieth anniversary observance ... Washington , 1977. ix, 141 p. ; LC Card 77-601861
HD5875 .S95   **NYPL [*XME-9409]**

Symposium on a Review and Critique of Cost Accounting for Pharmaceutical Services, New York, 1977. Cost accounting for pharmaceutical services : held in New York, N.Y., May 16, 1977 / edited by Jean Paul Gagnon ; sponsored by Economic and Administrative Sciences Section, Academy of Pharmaceutical Sciences. Hyattsville, Md. : U. S. Dept. of Health, Education, and Welfare, Public Health Service, Office of Health Research, Statistics, and Technology, National Center for Health Services Research, [1980] v, 70 p. : ill. ; 28 cm. (NCHSR research proceedings series) DHEW publication ; no. (PHS) 80-3215 "February 1980." Includes bibliographical references. LC Card 80-602830 DDC 362.1/7 19

1. Pharmaceutical services - Accounting. I. Gagnon, Jean Paul, 1941-. II. Academy of Pharmaceutical Sciences. Economic and Administrative Sciences Section. III. Series: National Center for Health Services Research. NCHSR research proceedings series. IV. Title.
RS92 .S96 1977

Symposium on Accuracy in Powder Diffraction, National Bureau of Standards, 1979. Accuracy in powder diffraction : proceedings of a Symposium on Accuracy in Powder Diffraction held at the National Bureau of Standards, Gaithersburg, Maryland, June, 11-15, 1979 / edited by S. Block, C. R. Hubbard ; sponsored by International Union of Crystallography [and] Chemistry Division, National Research Council of Canada [and] National Measurement Laboratory, National Bureau of Standards. [Washington, D.C.] : U. S. Dept. of Commerce, National Bureau of Standards : for sale by the Supt. of Docs., U. S. Govt. Print. Off., [1980] x, 572 p. : ill. ; 27 cm. (NBS special publication ; 567) "February 1980." Includes bibliographical references. LC Card 80-600010 DDC 602/.18 s 548/.83 19

1. X-rays - Diffraction - Measurement - Congresses. 2. Powders - Optical properties - Measurement - Congresses. 3. Chemistry, Physical and theoretical - Congresses. I. Block, Stanley, 1926-. II. Hubbard, C. R. III. International Union of Crystallography. IV. National Research Council of Canada. Division of Chemistry (1969/70-). V. National Measurement Laboratory (U. S.). VI. Series: United States. National Bureau of Standards Special publication, 567. VII. Title.
QC100 .U57 no. 567 QC482.D5

Symposium on Biotechnology in Energy Production and Conservation, 1st, Gatlinburg, Tenn., 1978. Biotechnology in energy production and conservation : proceedings of the First Symposium on Biotechnology in Energy Production and Conservation, held at Gatlinburg, Tennessee, May 10-12, 1978 / sponsored by the Department of Energy and the Oak Ridge National Laboratory ; editor, Charles D. Scott. New York : Wiley, c1979. vi, 513 p. : ill. ; 23 cm. (Biotechnology and bioengineering symposium. no. 8) "An Interscience publication." Includes bibliographical references and index. ISBN 0-471-05745-2 (pbk.) LC Card 80-128733

1. Power (Mechanics) - Congresses. 2. Energy conservation - Congresses. 3. Bioengineering - Congresses. I. Scott, Charles D. II. United States. Dept. of Energy. III. United States. National Laboratory, Oak Ridge, Tenn. IV. Title.
TJ163.7 .S97 1978   **NYPL [JSE 80-1362]**

Symposium on channel stabilization problems. Vicksburg, Miss. : Committee on Channel Stabilization, Corps of Engineers, U. S. Army, 1964-66. 3 v. : ill., maps ; 28 cm. "Committee on Channel Stabilization technical report no. 1." Papers

from the second and Fourth meetings of the committee held in October 1962 and June 1963.

1. Channels (Hydraulic engineering) - Congresses. I. United States. Army. Corps of Engineers. Committee on Channel Stabilization. II. Title: Channel stabilization problems.   **NYPL [JSK 81-44]**

Symposium on Competition in the Solar Energy Industry, Washington, D.C., 1977. The solar market : proceedings of the Symposium on Competition in the Solar Energy Industry. Washington : Bureau of Competition, Federal Trade Commission : for sale by the Supt. of Docs., U. S. Govt. Print. Off., 1978. xi, 299 p. : ill. ; 28 cm. Includes bibliographical references. LC Card 79-602870

1. Solar energy industries - United States - Congresses. 2. Competition - United States - Congresses. I. United States. Bureau of Competition. II. Title.
HD9681.U62 S95 1977   **NYPL [JLF 81-299]**

Symposium on Comprehensive Health Care for Addicted Families and Their Children, New York, N.Y., 1976. Symposium on Comprehensive Health Care for Addicted Families and Their Children, May 20 & 21, 1976, New York, New York / [sponsored by] Services Research Branch, Division of Resource Development, National Institute on Drug Abuse and Center for Comprehensive Health Practice, New York Medical College ; compiled and edited by George Beschner, Richard Brotman. Rockville, Md. : National Institute on Drug Abuse, Alcohol, Drug Abuse and Mental Health Administration, Public Health Service, Dept. of Health, Education, and Welfare, [1977] ix, 122 p. ; 27 cm. (National Institute on Drug Abuse. Services research report) DHEW publication ; no. (ADM) 77-480 Includes bibliographical references. LC Card 77-603390

1. Drug abuse in pregnancy - Congresses. 2. Prenatal care - Congresses. 3. Methadone maintenance - Congresses. 4. Infants (Newborn) - Drug effects - Congresses. 5. Infants (Newborn) - Diseases - Congresses. I. Beschner, George M. II. Brotman, Richard Emanuel. III. National Institute on Drug Abuse. Services Research Branch. IV. New York Medical College, Flower and Fifth Avenue Hospitals. Center for Comprehensive Health Practice.
RG580.D76 S93 1976   **NYPL [JLF 81-175]**

Symposium on Cultural Resources Management and Remote Sensing, Tucson, Ariz. 1978. Remote sensing and non-destructive archeology / edited by Thomas R. Lyons and James I. Ebert ; Remote Sensing Division, Southwest Cultural Resources Center, National Park Service, and University of New Mexico. Washington, DC : Cultural Resources Management Division, National Park Service, 1978. vii, 71 p. : ill. ; 27 cm. Includes bibliographies. LC Card 80-602610 DDC 930.1/028 19

1. Archaeology - Remote sensing - Congresses. 2. United States - Antiquities - Congresses. I. Lyons, Thomas R. II. Ebert, James I. III. Southwest Cultural Resources Center. Remote Sensing Division. IV. New Mexico. University. V. Title.
CC76.4 .S9 1978

Symposium on Economic Growth--Problems, Prospects, and Policies, Washington, D.C., 1980. Blewer, Cecilia. Economic growth . Washington , 1980. v, 56 p. ; LC Card 80-603061 DDC 338.973 19
HC106.7 .B59

Symposium on HVDC Power Transmission. Proceedings. [1]- ; 1976- [Portland, Or.], Bonneville Power Administration. illus. 28 cm. "Held by the US-USSR Joint Committee on Cooperation in the Field of Energy".

1. Electric power distribution - Direct current - Congresses. 2. High voltages - Congresses. I. United States. Bonneville Power Administration. II. US-USSR Joint Committee on Cooperation in the Field of Energy.   **NYPL [JSP 80-272]**

Symposium on International Standards Information and ISONET . Symposium on International Standards Information and Isonet, National Bureau of Standards, 1979. Washington, D.C. [1980] vii, 59 p. : LC Card 80-600073 DDC 602/.18 s 389/.6/0601 19
QC100 .U57 no. 579 T59.A1

Symposium on International Standards Information and Isonet, National Bureau of Standards, 1979. Symposium on International Standards Information and ISONET :

proceedings of a symposium held at the National Bureau of Standards, Gaithersburg, Maryland, October 11-12, 1979 / edited by Charles B. Phucas ; sponsored in part by American National Standards Institute. Washington, D.C. : U. S. Dept. of Commerce, National Bureau of Standards : for sale by the Supt. of Docs., U. S. Govt. Print. Off., [1980] vii, 59 p. : ill. ; 28 cm. (NBS Special publication ; 579) "June 1980." LC Card 80-600073 DDC 602/.18 s 389/.6/0601 19
1. Standardization - Information services - Congresses. 2. Standardization - International cooperation - Congresses. I. Phucas, Charles B. II. American National Standards Institute. III. United States. National Bureau of Standards. IV. Series: United States. National Bureau of Standards Special publication, 579. V. Title.
QC100 .U57 no. 579 T59.A1

Symposium on Job-Task Analysis in Criminal Justice, National. see National Symposium on Job-Task Analysis in Criminal Justice, Dallas, 1978.

Symposium on Media Concentration, Washington, D.C., 1978. Proceedings of the Symposium on Media Concentration, December 14 an 15, 1978. [Washington] : Bureau of Competition, Federal Trade Commission : for sale by the Supt. of Docs., U. S. Govt. Print. Off., [1979] 2 v. (xi, 761 p.) : ill. ; 28 cm. Includes bibliographical references. LC Card 79-603944
1. Mass media - Economic aspects - United States - Congresses. 2. Mass media - Laws and legislation - United States - Congresses. I. United States. Bureau of Competition.
P96.E25 S95 1978

Symposium on Nuclear Waste Management. see Symposium on Waste Management.

Symposium on Piloting and VTS Systems, Washington, D.C., 1979. Proceedings / Symposium on Piloting and VTS Systems ; Maritime Transportation Research Board, Commission on Sociotechnical Systems, National Research Council. Washington, D.C. : National Academy of Sciences, 1980. ix, 233 p. ; 28 cm. LC Card 80-126646 DDC 387.1/66 19
1. Pilots and pilotage - Congresses. 2. Harbors - Traffic control - Congresses. I. National Research Council. Maritime Transportation Research Board.
VK1645 .S95 1979

Symposium on Problems Related to the Redefinition of North American Geodetic Networks, International. see International Symposium on Problems Related to the Redefinition of North American Geodetic Networks, 2d, Arlington, Va., 1978.

Symposium on Productivity and Managerial Assessment, Albany, 1975. Public utility productivity : management and measurement : Proceedings of a symposium sponsored by the New York State Department of Public Service and the State University of New York at Albany, August 1975 ; edited by Walter L. Balk, Jay M. Shafritz. Albany : New York State Dept. of Public Service, [1975?] xv, 256 p. : ill. ; 23 cm. Microfiche (neg.) NTIS. 3 sheets. 11 x 15 cm. (PB 258 432) On spine: Public utilities productivity. Includes bibliographical references. LC Card 75-41898
1. Public utilities - United States - Congresses. 2. Industrial productivity - United States - Congresses. I. Balk, Walter L. II. Shafritz, Jay M. III. New York (State). Dept. of Public Service. IV. New York (State). State University, Albany. V. Title.
HD2766 .S95 1975   *NYPL [*XME-9419]*

Symposium on Psychology in the Dept. of Defense (7th : 1980 : Colorado Springs, Colo.) Proceedings of the seventh symposium, psychology in the Department of Defense, 16 April-18 April 1980. Colorado Springs, Colo. [Springfield, Va. (5285 Port Royal Rd., Springfield 22151)] 1980. xxiv, 635 p. : LC Card 80-604141 DDC 355/.001/9 19
U22.3 .P712

Symposium on Rangeland Policies for the Future, Tucson, Ariz., 1979. Rangeland policies for the future : proceedings of a symposium, January 28-31, 1979, Tucson, Arizona / United States Department of Agriculture, United States Department of the Interior, [and] Council on Environmental Quality in cooperation with School of Renewable Natural Resources, College of Agriculture, University of Arizona, and private organizations and citizens' groups.

[Washington, D.C.] : Forest Service : for sale by the Supt. of Docs., U. S. Govt. Print. Off., 1979. v, 114 p. ; 28 cm. (GTR-WO-17) Includes bibliographical references. LC Card 80-600538 DDC 333.74/0973 19
1. Range policy - United States - Congresses. 2. Range management - United States - Congresses. 3. United States - Public lands - Congresses. I. United States. Dept. of Agriculture. II. Arizona. University. School of Renewable Resources. III. Series: United States. Forest Service. USDA Forest Service general technical report WO , 17. IV. Title.
HD241 .S95 1979

Symposium on Safeguarding the Rights of Recipients of Mental Health Services, East Lansing, Mich., 1977. Proceedings / Symposium on Safeguarding the Rights of Recipients of Mental Health Services, October 17-19, 1977, East Lansing, Michigan ; co-sponsors, National Institute of Mental Health, Division of Mental Health Service Programs, Mental Health Care & Service Financing Branch, Patient Rights and Advocacy Program [and] Michigan Department of Mental Health, Office of Recipient Rights. [Rockville, Md.] : U. S. Dept. of Health, Education, and Welfare, Public Health Service, Alcohol, Drug Abuse, and Mental Health Administration, [1978] x, 59 p. : ill. ; 26 cm. LC Card 79-602277 DDC 344.73/044 19
1. Mental health laws - United States - Congresses. I. United States. National Institute of Mental Health. Patient Rights and Advocacy Program. II. Michigan. Dept. of Mental Health. Office of Recipient Rights.
KF3828.A75 S95 1977

Symposium on Space Missions to Comets, Goddard Space Flight Center, 1977. Space missions to comets : a conference / sponsored by NASA Office of Space Science and held at the Goddard Space Flight Center, Greenbelt, Maryland, October 1977 ; editors, M. Neugebauer ... [et al.]. [Washington] : National Aeronautics and Space Administration, Scientific and Technical Information Branch, 1979. v, 226 p. : ill. ; 27 cm. (NASA conference publication ; 2089) Includes bibliographies. LC Card 79-604295 DDC 523.6 19
1. Comets - Congresses. 2. Halley's comet - Congresses. 3. Outer space - Exploration - Congresses. I. Neugebauer, Marcia. II. United States. Office of Space Science. III. Series: United States. National Aeronautics and Space Administration. NASA conference publication , 2089. IV. Title.
QB721 .S97 1977

Symposium on Terrestrial Microcosms and Environmental Chemistry, Oregon State University, 1977. Terrestrial microcosms and environmental chemistry . [Washington] [1978?] xv, 147 p. : LC Card 79-601829 DDC 574.5/264 19
QH541.2 .T45

Workshop on Terrestrial Microcosms, Newport, Or., 1977. Terrestrial microcosms . [Washington] [1978?] xii, 35 p. : LC Card 79-602306 DDC 574.5/264 19
QH541.28 .W67 1977

Symposium on the Analysis of the Hydrocarbons and Halogenated Hydrocarbons in the Aquatic Environment, International. see International Symposium on the Analysis of Hydorcarbons and Halogenated Hydrocarbons in the Aquatic Environment, McMaster University, 1978.

Symposium on the Computational Methods in Nonlinear Structural and Solid Mechanics (1980 : Washington, D.C.) Research in nonlinear structural and solid mechanics . Washington, D.C. [Springfield, Va.] 1980. viii, 289 p. : LC Card 81-601087 DDC 624.1/71/0724 19
TA646 .R38

Symposium on the Science of Ceramic Machining and Surface Finishing, 2d, National Bureau of Standards, 1978. The science of ceramic machining and surface finishing II : proceedings of a symposium held at the National Bureau of Standards, Gaithersburg, Maryland, November 13-15, 1978 / edited by B. J. Hockey and R. W. Rice ; sponsored in part by Air Force Office of Scientific Research, American Ceramic Society, Office of Naval Research. Gaithersburg, Md. : U. S. Dept. of Commerce, National Bureau of Standards ; Washington,

D.C. : for sale by the Supt. of Docs, U. S. Govt. Print. Off., 1979. xii, 532 p. : ill. ; 27 cm. (NBS special publication ; 562) "Issued October 1979." Includes bibliographical references and index. LC Card 79-600149 DDC 602/.18 s 666 19
1. Ceramics - Finishing - Congresses. 2. Ceramics cutting - Congresses. I. Hockey, B. J. II. Rice, Roy Warren, 1934-. III. United States. National Bureau of Standards. IV. Series: United States. National Bureau of Standards Special publication, 562. V. Title.
QC100 .U57 no. 562 TP814

Symposium on Waste Management. Waste management; proceedings. Tucson, Ariz. illus. 23 cm. Sponsored by the University of Arizona, the Arizona Atomic Energy Commission and the Western Interstate Nuclear Board. Title varies: 1978, Waste management and fuel cycles.
1. Radioactive waste disposal - Congresses. I. Arizona. University. II. Arizona. Atomic Energy Commission. III. Western Interstate Nuclear Board. IV. Title. V. Title: Waste management and fuel cycles.
NYPL [JSP 80-332]

Symposium on Wastewater Aerosols and Disease (1979 : Cincinnati, Ohio) Wastewater aerosols and disease : proceedings of a Symposium, September 19-21, 1979 / sponsored by the Health Effects Research Laboratory ; edited by H. Pahren and W. Jakubowski. Cincinnati, Ohio : Office of Research and Development, U. S. Environmental Protection Agency ; Springfield, Va. : Available to the public through the National Technical Information Service, 1980 [i.e. 1981] xv, 367 p. : ill., maps ; 23 cm. "December 1980." "EPA-600/9-80-028." Item 431-J Includes bibliographical references. LC Card 81-601460 DDC 363.7/28 19
1. Sewage - Purification - Aeration - Hygienic aspects - Congresses. 2. Airborne infection - Congresses. 3. Aerosols - Microbiology - Congresses. 4. Aerosols - Toxicology - Congresses. I. Title.
RA567 .S94 1979

Synectics Corporation. The Expanded Food and Nutrition Education Program : historical and statistical profile / [prepared for SEA-Extension, United States Department of Agriculture, by Synectics Corporation]. [Washington] : SEA-Extention, [1979] xi, 131 p. : graphs ; 27 cm. "Program aid no. 1230." Bibliography: p. 117-118. LC Card 79-601895 DDC 641.1/07/073 19
1. Nutrition - Study and teaching - United States. 2. Expanded Food and Nutrition Education Program. I. United States. Science and Education Administration. II. Title.
TX364 .S96 1979

Synergy, inc. Booz, Allen and Hamilton, inc. Transportation Consulting Division. Planning for the phase-in of fixed-route accessible buses : interim report /. Washington , 1980. 1 v. :
NYPL [JLM 80-1153]

SYNESIUS, OF CYRENE, BISHOP OF PTOLEMAIS.
Bregman, Jay. Synesius of Cyrene, philosopher-bishop /. Berkeley , c1981. p. cm. ISBN 0-520-04192-5 LC Card 81-10293 DDC 186/.4 19
BR1720.S9 B72

Synesius of Cyrene, philosopher-bishop /. Bregman, Jay. Berkeley , c1981. p. cm. ISBN 0-520-04192-5 LC Card 81-10293 DDC 186/.4 19
BR1720.S9 B72

Synfuels from coal and the national synfuels production program : technical, environmental, and economic aspects / printed at the request of the Committee on Energy and Natural Resources, United States Senate. Washington : U. S. G.P.O., 1981. x, 304 p. : ill. ; 23 cm. At head of title: 97th Congress, 1st session. Committee print. "Publication no. 97-3." Authors: Paul F. Rothberg and others. "January 1981." S/N 052-070-05527-8 Item 1040-A, 1040-B (microfiche) LC Card 81-601287 DDC 338.4/76626622/0973 19
1. Synthetic fuels - United States. 2. Coal liquefaction - United States. 3. Coal gasification - United States. I. Rothberg, Paul F. II. United States. Congress. Senate. Committee on Energy and Natural Resources.
TP360 .S939

SYNODUS - CLASSIFICATION.
Cressey, Roger F., 1930- Revision of Indo-West Pacific lizardfishes of the genus Synodus (Pisces: Synodontidae) /. City of Washington ,

1981. p. cm.   LC Card 81-14389   DDC 591 s
597/.53 19
QL1 .S54 no. 342 QL638.S96

Synthesis of economic performance in Latin America. 1978- Washington, General Secretariat, Organization of American States. charts. 28 cm. Supersedes América en Cifras.
1. Latin America - Economic conditions - Yearbooks. I. Organization of American States. General Secretariat.
     NYPL [JLM 80-785]

Synthesis of highway practice .
(68 0547-5570) National Research Council. Transportation Research Board. Motor vehicle size and weight regulations, enforcement, and permit operations. Washington, D.C. [1980] 45 p. ISBN 0-390-03019-6 (pbk.) :   LC Card 80-66742
DDC 629.2/24 19
TL230 .N27 1980

(70 0547-5570) National Research Council. Transportation Research Board. Design of sedimentation basins. Washington, D.C. , 1980. 53 p. :   ISBN 0-309-03027-7 (pbk.) :   LC Card 80-52843   DDC 625.7/34 19
TD439 .N37 1980

(73) Alternative work schedules . Washington, D.C. , 1980. 54 p. :   ISBN 0-309-03153-2 (pbk.) :   LC Card 80-54556   DDC 388.4/13143/0973 19
HE308 .A62

Synthesis of highway practice, 0547-5570 .
(71) National Research Council (U. S.) Transportation Research Board. Direction finding from arterials to destinations . Washington, D.C. , 1980. 50 p. :   ISBN 0-309-03031-5 (pbk.) :   LC Card 80-54090 DDC 388.3/122 19
TE228 .N32 1980

Synthetic estimates for small areas . Workshop on Synthetic Estimates, Princeton, N. J., 1978. Rockville, Md. , Washington , 1979. viii, 282 p. :   LC Card 79-600067
RC563.2 .W67 1978

Synthetic fossil fuel teachnology. Oak Ridge National Laboratory Life Sciences Symposium, 1st, Oak Ridge, Tenn., 1978. Ann Arbor, Mich. , c1980. xiii, 288 p. :   LC Card 80-68338
     NYPL [JSF 81-116]

Synthetic fuel oversight hearing . United States. Congress. House. Committee on Banking, Finance and Urban Affairs. Subcommittee on Economic Stabilization. Washington , 1981. iii, 96 p. ;   LC Card 81-601770   DDC 353.0082/38 19
KF27 .B542 1981

Synthetic fuels. United States. Patent and Trademark Office. Office of Technology Assessment and Forecast. Washington, D.C. [1979] iii, 230 p. :   LC Card 80-601527   DDC 662/.66/0272 19
TP360 .U63 1979

SYNTHETIC FUELS - CONGRESSES.
Oak Ridge National Laboratory Life Sciences Symposium, 1st, Oak Ridge, Tenn., 1978. Synthetic fossil fuel teachnology. Ann Arbor, Mich. , c1980. xiii, 288 p. :   LC Card 80-68338
     NYPL [JSF 81-116]

Synthetic Fuels Corporation nominations .
United States. Congress. Senate. Committee on Energy and Natural Resources. Washington , 1980. iii, 185 p. ;   LC Card 80-603446   DDC 353.09/2 19
KF26 .E55 1980h

Synthetic Fuels Corporation oversight . United States. Congress. House. Committee on Government Operations. Environment, Energy, and Natural Resources Subcommittee. Washington , 1981. iii, 169 p. :   LC Card 81-601955   DDC 353.09/2 19
KF27 .G655 1981

SYNTHETIC FUELS CORPORATION (U. S.)
United States. Congress. House. Committee on Banking, Finance and Urban Affairs. Subcommittee on Economic Stabilization. Synthetic fuel oversight hearing . Washington , 1981. iii, 96 p. ;   LC Card 81-601770   DDC 353.0082/38 19
KF27 .B542 1981

United States. Congress. House. Committee on Government Operations. Environment, Energy, and Natural Resources Subcommittee. Synthetic Fuels Corporation oversight . Washington , 1981. iii, 169 p. :   LC Card 81-601955   DDC

353.09/2 19
KF27 .G655 1981

SYNTHETIC FUELS CORPORATION (U. S.) - EMPLOYEES.
United States. Congress. Senate. Committee on Energy and Natural Resources. Synthetic Fuels Corporation nominations . Washington , 1980. iii, 185 p. ;   LC Card 80-603446   DDC 353.09/2 19
KF26 .E55 1980h

Synthetic fuels development . United States. Geological Survey. Washington, D.C. , 1979. 45 p. :   LC Card 79-600206   DDC 662/.66/0973 19
TP360 .U584 1979

SYNTHETIC FUELS INDUSTRY - ENVIRONMENTAL ASPECTS - UNITED STATES.
United States. Congress. House. Committee on Science and Technology. Subcommittee on Energy Development and Applications. Oversight . Washington , 1980 [i.e. 1981] iii, 234 p. :   LC Card 81-600865   DDC 338.1/7665772 19
KF27 .S3934 1980g

SYNTHETIC FUELS INDUSTRY - UNITED STATES.
United States. Congress. House. Committee on Banking, Finance and Urban Affairs. Subcommittee on Economic Stabilization. Synthetic fuel oversight hearing . Washington , 1981. iii, 96 p. ;   LC Card 81-601770   DDC 353.0082/38 19
KF27 .B542 1981

SYNTHETIC FUELS - LAW AND LEGISLATION - UNITED STATES.
Compilation of the Energy Security Act of 1980, and 1980 amendments to the Defense Production Act of 1950 /. Washington , 1980. 3 v. (v. 2252 p.) ;   LC Card 80-603878   DDC 346.7304/679 347.3064679 19
KF2120.A32 A15 1980

United States. Congress. House. Committee on Banking, Finance and Urban Affairs. Subcommittee on Economic Stabilization. Defense Production Act Amendments of the Energy Security Act of 1980 . Washington , 1980. iii, 114 p. :   LC Card 80-604041   DDC 343.73/07866266/0262 347.30378662660262 19
KF27 .B542 1980b

United States. Congress. House. Committee on Interstate and Foreign Commerce. Subcommittee on Energy and Power. Commercialization of alternative fuels . Washington , 1980. iii, 53 p. ;   LC Card 80-601864   DDC 343.73/0786626 19
KF27 .I5542 1979ac

United States. Congress. Senate. Committee on Energy and Natural Resources. Synthetic fuels legislation . Washington , 1980. iii. 407 p. ;   LC Card 80-601946   DDC 343.73/07866266/0262 19
KF26 .E55 1979ad

United States. Congress. Senate. Committee on Energy and Natural Resources. Subcommittee on Energy Research and Development. Department of Energy fiscal years 1981-82 authorization (civilian applications) . Washington , 1980. iv, 1037 p. :   LC Card 80-604097   DDC 353.0072/236823 19
KF26 .E554 1980

Synthetic fuels legislation . United States. Congress. Senate. Committee on Energy and Natural Resources. Washington , 1980. iii. 407 p. ;   LC Card 80-601946   DDC 343.73/07866266/0262 19
KF26 .E55 1979ad

SYNTHETIC FUELS - PATENTS.
United States. Patent and Trademark Office. Office of Technology Assessment and Forecast. Synthetic fuels. Washington, D.C. [1979] iii, 230 p. :   LC Card 80-601527   DDC 662/.66/0272 19
TP360 .U63 1979

SYNTHETIC FUELS - PRICES - UNITED STATES.
Jelinek, Robert Vincent, 1926- Costs of synthetic fuels in relation to oil prices . Washington , 1981. xiii, 129 p. :   LC Card 81-601665   DDC 338.4/366266/0973 19
HD9564 .J44

SYNTHETIC FUELS - THE WEST.
United States. Congress. Joint Economic Committee. Subcommittee on Economic Growth and Stabilization. The impact of an accelerated coal-based synfuels program on western water resources . Washington, D.C. , 1980. iii, 105 p. :   LC Card 80-602753   DDC 333.91/00978 19
KF25 .E232 1979c

SYNTHETIC FUELS - UNITED STATES.
Synfuels from coal and the national synfuels production program . Washington , 1981. x, 304 p. :   LC Card 81-601287   DDC 338.4/76626622/0973 19
TP360 .S939

United States. Geological Survey. Synthetic fuels development . Washington, D.C. , 1979. 45 p. :   LC Card 79-600206   DDC 662/.66/0973 19
TP360 .U584 1979

SYNTHETIC TRAINING DEVICES.
United States. Congress. House. Committee on Merchant Marine and Fisheries. Ad Hoc Select Subcommittee on Maritime Education and Training. Sea training at maritime academies oversight . Washington , 1980 [i.e. 1981] iv, 246 p. :   LC Card 81-600941   DDC 623.88/07073 19
KF27 .M458 1980

SYRIA - ECONOMIC CONDITIONS - MAPS.
United States. Central Intelligence Agency. Syria. [Washington, 1979] col. map 40 x 49 cm. on sheet 44 x 85 cm. Scale 1:1,500,000. "503966 10-79 (544276)." Inset: Golan Heights. Maps in margin: Economic activity. - Land Utilization.--Population.--[Location].--[Size comparison] Relief shown by shading and spot heights.
G7460 1972 .U5   *NYPL [Map Div. 80-3386]*

SYRIA - MAPS.
(1979) United States. Central Intelligence Agency. Syria. [Washington, 1979] col. map 40 x 49 cm. on sheet 44 x 85 cm. Scale 1:1,500,000. "503966 10-79 (544276)." Inset: Golan Heights. Maps in margin: Economic activity. - Land Utilization.--Population.--[Location].--[Size comparison] Relief shown by shading and spot heights.
G7460 1972 .U5   *NYPL [Map Div. 80-3386]*

SYRIA - POPULATION - MAPS.
United States. Central Intelligence Agency. Syria. [Washington, 1979] col. map 40 x 49 cm. on sheet 44 x 85 cm. Scale 1:1,500,000. "503966 10-79 (544276)." Inset: Golan Heights. Maps in margin: Economic activity. - Land Utilization.--Population.--[Location].--[Size comparison] Relief shown by shading and spot heights.
G7460 1972 .U5   *NYPL [Map Div. 80-3386]*

Syrian agricultural sector assessment. College Station, Tex. : Texas Agricultural Experiment Station, Texas A&M University System, [1979]- v. <1, 3 > : ill. ; 28 cm. (Staff paper series. SP-10-<SP-12>) Departmental information report ; 79-1 Includes bibliographies. CONTENTS. - v. 1. Production/consumption trends, commodity demand projections, and price policy appraisal / Carl E. Shafer and Vito J. Blomo -- v. 3. Assessment and recommendations for the marketing systems of livestock, meat, poultry, eggs, and dairy products / Gregory M. Sullivan, Donald E. Farris   LC Card 80-623539   DDC 338.1/095691 19
1. Agriculture - Economic aspects - Syria. 2. Food supply - Syria. I. Texas Agricultural Experiment Station. Dept. of Agricultural Economics. II. Series: Staff paper series (Texas Agricultural Experiment Station. Dept. of Agricultural Economics) , SP-10-<12 >.
HD9016.S92 S93

Syrian Region, United Arab Republic. see Syria.

Syska & Hennesy. Building Conservation Technology/The Ehrenkrantz Group. Mechanical and electrical rehabilitation, Main Building, Ellis Island, Statue of Liberty National Monument, New York . Denver, Colo. , 1980. 97 leaves, ca. 500 leaves of plates :   LC Card 80-601419   DDC 725/.1 19
NA4510.I6 B84 1980a

SYSTEM ANALYSIS.
(1979) Zinn, Clyde Dale. Systems analysis of the Texas gulf coast geopressured resources . [Austin] , 1979. v, 33 p. ;   LC Card 80-620765 DDC 333.8/8/097641 19
TJ280.7 .Z58

SYSTEM ANALYSIS - CONGRESSES.
Lawrence Symposium on Systems and Decision

Sciences. Proceedings. 1- ; 1977- North Hollywood , Calif..   **NYPL** *[JSP 80-446]*

SYSTEM INTERCONNECTION, ELECTRIC POWER. see INTERCONNECTED ELECTRIC UTILITY SYSTEMS.

SYSTEM MANAGEMENT FACILITIES (COMPUTER PROGRAM)
Guideline on major job accounting systems . [Gaithersburg, Md.] , Washington , 1978. ix, 162 p. :   LC Card 78-600113   DDC 602/.18 s 001.64/25 19
QC100 .U57 no. 500-40 QA76.9.E94

System Sciences, inc. Evaluation of treatment alternatives to street crime : phase II report. [Washington] : National Institute of Law Enforcement and Criminal Justice, Law Enforcement Assistance Administration, U. S. Dept. of Justice : for sale by the Supt. of Docs., U. S. Govt. Print. Off., 1979. xii, 150 p. ; 29 cm. (National evaluation program : Series B . no. 1)   LC Card 79-602081   DDC 362.2/937/0973 19
1. Drug abuse - United States - Prevention. 2. Narcotic addicts - Rehabilitation - United States. 3. Crime prevention - United States. I. National Institute of Law Enforcement and Criminal Justice. II. Title. III. Series.
HV5825 .S94 1979

SYSTEM THEORY.
(1979) Storper, Michael. Systems and marxist theories of industrial location . Berkeley , 1979. viii, 92, [6] p. ;   LC Card 80-623098   DDC 338.6/042/01 19
HD58 .S679

SYSTEM THEORY - ADDRESSES, ESSAYS, LECTURES.
Malinovskiĭ, Aleksandr Aleksandrovich, 1909- Science of organization and organization of science /. [Washington] 1972. 18 p.
   NYPL *[*XMQ-2148]*

SYSTEMATIC BOTANY. see BOTANY - CLASSIFICATION.

Systematic monitoring and evaluation of integrated development programmes . United Nations. Dept. of Economic and Social Affairs. New York , 1978. vii, 150 p. :   LC Card 78-111938   DDC 300 s 338.9 19
JX1977 .A2 ST/ESA/78

Systematic nursing assessment. Taylor, Deane B. Bethesda, U. S [1974] viii, 164 p.
   NYPL *[JSF 80-1012]*

A systematic study of larvae in the tribes Pterostichini, Morionini, and Amarini (Coleoptera, Carabidae) /. Thompson, Raymond G. Fayetteville [1979]. 105 p. :   LC Card 80-621426   DDC 595.76/2 19
QL596.C2 T49

SYSTEMATICS (BOTANY) see BOTANY - CLASSIFICATION.

Systematics of bees of the genus Eufriesia (Hymenoptera, Apidae) /. Kimsey, Lynn Siri. Berkeley, CA , 1981. p. cm.   ISBN 0-520-09643-6   LC Card 81-7400   DDC 595.79/9 19
QL568.A6 K465

SYSTEMS ANALYSIS. see SYSTEM ANALYSIS.

Systems analysis of the Texas gulf coast geopressured resources . Zinn, Clyde Dale. [Austin] , 1979. v, 33 p. ;   LC Card 80-620765   DDC 333.8/8/097641 19
TJ280.7 .Z58

Systems and Decision Sciences, Lawrence Symposium on. see Lawrence Symposium on Systems and Decision Sciences.

Systems and marxist theories of industrial location . Storper, Michael. Berkeley , 1979. viii, 92, [6] p. ;   LC Card 80-623098   DDC 338.6/042/01 19
HD58 .S679

SYSTEMS OPTIMIZATION. see MATHEMATICAL OPTIMIZATION.

SYSTEMS, THEORY OF. see SYSTEM THEORY.

Szabad Európa Rádió. see Radio Free Europe.

Szabo, B. J. Mixon, Robert B. Uranium-series dating of mollusks and corals and age of Pleistocene deposits, Chesapeake Bay area, Virginia and Maryland /. Washington , 1981. p. cm.   LC Card 81-607014   DDC 551.7/92/097521 19
QE697 .M7

Szokol, Gaston Somoshegyi- see Somoshegyi-Szokol, Gaston.

T-GROUPS. see GROUP RELATIONS TRAINING.

T. U. A. see Tennessee Valley Authority.

TVA bibliography. Tennessee Valley Authority. Library. Muscle Shoals, Ala.
   NYPL *[JLM 80-973]*

TVA/EPRI Workshop on Factors Affecting Power Plant Waste Heat Utilization, Atlanta, 1978. Factors affecting power plant waste heat utilization / edited by L. Barry Goss, Lilabeth Scott. New York : Pergamon Press, c1980. xvii, 230 p. : ill. ; 24 cm. Includes bibliographical references and index.   ISBN 0-08-025548-5   LC Card 79-29656
1. Heat recovery - Congresses. 2. Electric power-plants - Congresses. I. Goss, L. Barry. II. Scott, Lilabeth. III. Tennessee Valley Authority. IV. Electric Power Research Institute. V. Title.
TJ260 .T17 1978   **NYPL** *[JSE 81-98]*

TVA Fertilizer Bulk Blending Conference, Louisville, Ky., 1973. TVA Fertilizer Bulk Blending Conference, August 1-2, 1973. [Muscle Shoals, Ala., National Fertilizer Development Center, Tennessee Valley Authority, 1973] 126 p. illus. 28 cm. Includes bibliographical references.
1. Fertilizer industry. 2. Fertilizers and manures - Addresses, essays, lectures. I. United States. National Fertilizer Development Center, Muscle Shoals, Ala.
   NYPL *[JLF 80-1485]*

Taber, Merlin. The social context of helping : a review of the literature on alternative care for the physically and mentally handicapped / by Merlin A. Taber. Rockville, Md. : U. S. Dept. of Health and Human Services, Public Health Service, Alcohol, Drug Abuse, and Mental Health Administration, National Institute of Mental Health ; Washington : for sale by the Supt. of Docs., U. S. Govt. Print. Off., 1980. v, 259 p. ; 23 cm. (Studies in social change) DHHS publication ; no. (ADM) 80-842 Bibliography: p. 107-259. Includes index.   LC Card 80-602564   DDC 362.4/048 19
1. Handicapped services - Abstracts. I. Series: United States. Dept. of Health and Human Services. DHHS publication, no. (ADM) 80-842. II. Title.
HV1568 .T33

Table of circumferences and areas. United States. Bureau of Ordnance (Navy Dept.) Washington, 1947. 101 p.   LC Card 51-61291
   NYPL *[JSF 81-40]*

Tables of vertical cutoff rigidities for epochs 1955 and 1960 / M. A. Shea ... [and others] Hanscom AFB, Mass. : Space Physics Laboratory, Air Force Cambridge Research Laboratory, Air Force Systems Command, USAF, 1974. 91 p. : maps ; 28 cm. (United States. Air Force. Cambridge Research Laboratories Environmental research papers. no. 493) Cover title. "Project 8600 AFCRL-TR-74-0550." Includes bibliographies.
1. Cosmic rays - Tables. I. Shea, M. A. II. United States. Air Force. Cambridge Research Laboratories. Space Physics Laboratory.   **NYPL** *[JSF 81-117]*

Tabular summary of the third follow-up questionnaire data /. Research Triangle Institute. Center for Educational Research and Evaluation. [Washington] , 1978. 4 v. ;   LC Card 79-602292
LA229 .R46 1978a

A tabular summation of 1977-78 higher education equal opportunity program survey findings /. Brehman, George E. Harrisburg, PA , 1979. iv, 41 p. ;   LC Card 80-621911   DDC 378.748 19
LA355.5 .B73

Tabulation and application of pan evaporation data for Utah through 1976 . Hubbard, Kenneth G. Logan, Utah , 1979. vi, 76 p. :   LC Card 80-622271   DDC 551.57/2/09792 19
QC915.7.U5 H82

Tacha, Athena. Athena Tacha: Tape sculptures: a series of eight installations: Wright State University Art Gallery, October 21-November 3, 1978. [Dayton] : The Gallery, 1978. 20 p. : chiefly ill. ; 21 cm.
1. Tacha, Athena. I. Wright State University. Fine Arts Gallery. II. Title: Tape sculptures.
   NYPL *[3-MGO (Tacha) 81-880]*

TACHA, ATHENA.
Tacha, Athena. Athena Tacha. [Dayton] , 1978. 20 p. :   **NYPL** *[3-MGO (Tacha) 81-880]*

TACOMA METROPOLITAN AREA, WASH. - OFFICIALS AND EMPLOYEES.
United States. Commission on Civil Rights. Washington State Advisory Committee. Equal employment opportunity in Tacoma area local government . [Washington] [1980] vii, 48 p. ;   LC Card 80-603135   DDC 352/.005104/0979778 19
JS1481.4 .A4 1980

Tacoma. Washington State Historical Society. see Washington State Historical Society.

TACONITE.
Peterson, R. E. (Roy Ernest), 1926- Benefication of a hemaititic taconite by reduction roasting, magnetic separation, and flotation /. Washington [1981] p. cm.   LC Card 81-3883   DDC 622 s 622/.341 19
TN23 .U43 TN538.I7

TACONITE - MINNESOTA - MESABA RANGE.
Peterson, R. E. (Roy Ernest), 1926- Reduction roasting and beneficiation of a hematitic-geothitic taconite /. [Washington, D.C.] [1981] p. cm.   LC Card 80-606877   DDC 622 s 669/.141 19
TN23 .U43 TN538.I7

TACTICS.
Doughty, Robert A. The evolution of US Army tactical doctrine, 1946-76 /. Fort Leavenworth, Kan. , 1979. 57 p. ;   LC Card 79-604167   DDC 355.4/2/0973 19
U165 .D58

Taft, Lisa Factor.
Refugee resettlement in the U. S. 1980. Moore, Charlotte J. Review of U. S. refugee resettlement programs and policies : a report / prepared at the request of Senator Edward M. Kennedy, chairman, Committee on the Judiciary, United States Senate, by the Congressional Research Service, Library of Congress, Ninety-sixth Congress, second session. Washington , 1980. viii, 342 p. :   LC Card 80-603884   DDC 362.8/7/0973 19
HV640.4.U54 M66

Taft, Lisa Factor. Herman Carl Mueller : architectural ceramics and the arts and crafts movement, New Jersey State Museum, Trenton, January 13 through March 18, 1979 / Lisa Factor Taft ; edited by Suzanne Corlette, Ed Grusheski. Trenton, N.J. : The Museum, c1979. 48 p. : ill. ; 22 cm.   LC Card 79-622661
1. Mueller, Herman Carl 1854-1941 - Exhibitions. 2. Tiles - United States - History - 19th century - Exhibitions. 3. Tiles - United States - History - 20th century - Exhibitions. 4. Decoration and ornament, Architectural - United States - Exhibitions. 5. Arts and crafts movement - Exhibitions. I. Mueller, Herman Carl, 1854-1941. II. Corlette, Suzanne. III. Grusheski, Ed. IV. New Jersey. State Museum, Trenton.
NK4670.7.M833 A4 1979

TAFT, WILLIAM HOWARD, 1945-
United States. Congress. Senate. Committee on Armed Services. Nominations of Fred C. Ikle, to be under secretary of defense for policy, and William H. Taft, IV, to be general counsel of the Department of Defense . Washington , 1981. ii, 24 p. ;   LC Card 81-602261   DDC 353.6 19
KF26 .A7 1981f

Tailings dams. Design and constructaion of tailings dams . Golden, Colo. , 1981. p. cm.   ISBN 0-918062-45-4 :   LC Card 81-10273   DDC 622/.7 19
TN292 .D46

TAILINGS DAMS - DESIGN AND CONSTRUCTION - CONGRESSES.
Design and constructaion of tailings dams . Golden, Colo. , 1981. p. cm.   ISBN 0-918062-45-4 :   LC Card 81-10273   DDC 622/.7 19
TN292 .D46

TAILINGS (METALLURGY)
Tesarik, D. R. (Douglas R.) Factor of safety charts for estimating the stability of saturated and unsaturated tailings pond embankments /. Avondale, Md. , 1981. p. cm.   LC Card 81-607986   DDC 622 s 622/.8 19
TN23 .U43 TA760

TAILINGS (METALLURGY) - ENVIRONMENTAL ASPECTS.
United States. Congress. House. Committee on Interior and Insular Affairs. Subcommittee on Energy and the Environment. Mill tailings dam break at Church Rock, New Mexico . Washington , 1980. iv, 232 p. :   LC Card 80-601962   DDC 622/.8 19
KF27 .I518 1979i

TAIWAN - CONGRESSES.
Taiwan, one year after United States-China normalization . Washington , 1980. v, 170 p. :   LC Card 80-603279   DDC 327.73051/249 19
E183.8.T3 T34

TAIWAN - FOREIGN RELATIONS - UNITED STATES.
Sutter, Robert G. Executive-legislative consultations on China policy, 1978-79 /. Washington , 1980. vii, 42 p. :   LC Card 80-602678   DDC 327.73051 19
JX1428.C6 S97

United States. Congress. House. Committee on Foreign Affairs. Subcommittee on Asian and Pacific Affairs. Implementation of the Taiwan Relations Act . Washington , 1981. v, 107 p. ;   LC Card 81-600827   DDC 327.73051/249 19
KF27 .F638 1980e

United States. Congress. Senate. Committee on Foreign Relations. Implementation of the Taiwan relations act . Washington , 1980. v, 61 p. ;   LC Card 80-603554   DDC 327.73051/249 19
E183.8.T3 U54 1980

United States. Congress. Senate. Committee on Foreign Relations. Subcommittee on East Asian and Pacific Affairs. Oversight of the Taiwan relations act . Washington , 1980. iii, 44 p. ;   LC Card 80-602822   DDC 327.73051/249 19
KF26 .F6354 1980a

TAIWAN - FOREIGN RELATIONS - UNITED STATES - CONGRESSES.
Taiwan, one year after United States-China normalization . Washington , 1980. v, 170 p. :   LC Card 80-603279   DDC 327.73051/249 19
E183.8.T3 T34

Taiwan, one year after United States-China normalization : a workshop / sponsored by the Committee on Foreign Relations, United States Senate and Congressional Research Service, Library of Congress. Washington : U. S. Govt. Print. Off., 1980. v, 170 p. : graphs ; 23 cm. At head of title: 96th Congress, 2d session. Committee print. Held in Washington, D.C., March 6-7, 1980. Includes bibliographical references.   LC Card 80-603279   DDC 327.73051/249 19
1. United States - Foreign relations - Taiwan - Congresses. 2. Taiwan - Foreign relations - United States - Congresses. 3. Taiwan - Congresses. I. United States. Congress. Senate. Committee on Foreign Relations. II. United States. Library of Congress. Congressional Research Service.
E183.8.T3 T34

Takacs, Dan. An evaluation of the adequacy of the State of Maryland demonstration bikeway projects / [Dan Takacs and Thomas Mulinazzi] ; Transportation Studies Center and the Department of Civil Engineering, University of Maryland. Rev. [Baltimore, Md.] : Maryland Dept. of Transportation, 1979. iv leaves, 67 p., [6] leaves of plates : ill. ; 28 cm. (Research project - State Highway Administration) "Prepared for Maryland State Highway Administration ... in cooperation with U. S. Department of Transportation, Federal Highway Administration." Bibliography: p. 62-66.   LC Card 80-621990   DDC 388.1/2 19
1. Cycling paths - Maryland - Design and construction. I. Mulinazzi, Thomas, joint author. II. Maryland. University. Transportation Studies Center. III. Maryland. University. Dept. of Civil Engineering. IV. Series: Maryland. State Highway Administration. Research report - State Highway Administration. V. Title.
TE301 .T34 1979

Takahashi, Patrick K. (joint author) Santerre, Michael T. A computerized selected bibliography on relevant aspects of the aquaculture of unicellular and filamentous algae /. Honolulu [1978] ca. 400 p. :   LC Card 79-623030   DDC 016.639 19
Z5973.A45 S26 SH389

Talamine, Jeanne Rabbitt. Winnetka Public Library. Genealogy Projects Committee. An index to the names of persons appearing in A

history of Lake County, Illinois. Thomson, Ill. , c1973. 77 p. ;   *NYPL [IVF (Lake Co.)*
(Halsey, J. Hist. of Lake Co. Index)]

Talc and chlorite depostis in Montana /. Berg, Richard B., 1937- [Butte] , 1979. vi, 66 p. :   LC Card 80-622034   DDC 553.6/76/097866 19
TN948.T2 B45

TALC - MONTANA.
Berg, Richard B., 1937- Talc and chlorite depostis in Montana /. [Butte] , 1979. vi, 66 p. :   LC Card 80-622034   DDC 553.6/76/097866 19
TN948.T2 B45

TALC - TOXICOLOGY.
Occupational exposure to talc containing asbestos . Cincinnati, Ohio , Washington, D.C. , 1980. xiii, 106 p. :   LC Card 80-602295   DDC 363.1/79 19
RC965.A7 O22

A tale of 51 Pennsylvania cities /. Pennsylvania. Municipal Statistics and Records Division. [Harrisburg] [1975?] 16 p. ;
*NYPL [*ZT-1263]*

TALES, AMERICAN - ALABAMA.
Ghosts and goosebumps . University, Ala. , c1982. p. cm.   ISBN 0-8173-0075-9   LC Card 81-7461   DDC 398.2/09761 19
GR110.A2 B56

TALKING BOOKS - BIBLIOGRAPHY - CATALOGS.
National Library Service for the Blind and Physically Handicapped. Libros parlantes, 1980. Washington , 1980. p. cm.   ISBN 0-8444-0345-8   LC Card 80-23606   DDC 011/.63 19
Z5347 .U59 1980

Talking to the moon /. Mathews, John Joseph, 1895- Norman [Okla.] [1981] c1945. viii, 243 p. :   ISBN 0-8061-1611-0   LC Card 81-137822   DDC 976.6/2505/0924 19
E99.O8 M298 1981

Tallahassee. University. see **Florida. State University, Tallahassee.**

Tamanaha, Myra. State of Hawaii airport statistics / Myra Tamanaha. [Honolulu] : State of Hawaii, Dept. of Transportation, Air Transportation Facilities Division, [1978] 59 leaves : ill. ; 29 cm.   LC Card 78-622125   DDC 387.7/36/09969 19
1. Aeronautics, Commercial - Hawaii - Statistics. 2. Airports - Hawaii - Statistics. I. Hawaii. Air Transportation Facilities Division. II. Title.
HE9813.H4 T35

Tamimi, Niniv. (joint author) French, Ben C. Marketing order program alternatives . [Davis] , 1978. v, 110 p. :   LC Card 78-623151   DDC 338.1/09794 s 381/.41/09794 19
HD9000.1 .C3 no. 78-2 HD9007.C2

TAMPA BAY REGION, FLA. - MAPS.
Tampa Bay Regional Planning Council. Tampa Bay region preliminary environmental assessment of development atlas /. [Tampa Bay? Fla.] , 1972. 1 portfolio (21 fold. leaves of plates :   LC Card 80-675325   DDC 912/.133373/0975965 19
G1317.T3 T34 1972

Tampa Bay region preliminary environmental assessment of development atlas /. Tampa Bay Regional Planning Council. [Tampa Bay? Fla.] , 1972. 1 portfolio (21 fold. leaves of plates :   LC Card 80-675325   DDC 912/.133373/0975965 19
G1317.T3 T34 1972

Tampa Bay Regional Planning Council. Tampa Bay region preliminary environmental assessment of development atlas / prepared for Coastal Coordinating Council [by the Tampa Bay Regional Planning Council]. [Tampa Bay? Fla.] : The Planning Council, 1972. 1 portfolio (21 fold. leaves of plates : 21 fold. maps) ; 54 cm. Cover title. CONTENTS. Preservation zoning.--Conservation zoning.--Composite development.--Wildlife habitat.   LC Card 80-675325   DDC 912/.133373/0975965 19
1. Tampa Bay region, Fla. - Maps. 2. Urbanization - Environmental aspects - Florida - Tampa Bay region - Maps. I. Title.
G1317.T3 T34 1972

TAN-ZAM RAILWAY.
Curran, James C. Communist China in Black Africa. Carlisle Barracks, Pa., 1971. iv, 83 leaves: *NYPL [*XM-13704]*

TANANA LOOP, ALASKA - INDUSTRIES.
Skaggs, Samuel. A design for agriculture in the Tanana Loop . [Juneau] , 1978. ii, 61 p. :   LC Card 79-620899   DDC 338.1/09798/6 19
S451.A3 S58

TANANA RIVER.
Francisco, Kim. Fourth interim report of the commercial fish-technical evaluation study . [Anchorage, Alaska] , 1977. v, 50 p. :   LC Card 79-625958   DDC 597.092/9798 19
QL628.A4 F73

Tangut (Hsi Hsia) studies . Kwanten, Luc. Bloomington , 1980. 125 p. ;   ISBN 0-933070-05-5 (pbk.)   LC Card 80-51975   DDC 016.951/024 19
DS751.82 .K85

Tangut studies. Kwanten, Luc. Tangut (Hsi Hsia) studies . Bloomington , 1980. 125 p. ;   ISBN 0-933070-05-5 (pbk.)   LC Card 80-51975   DDC 016.951/024 19
DS751.82 .K85

Tanimoto, Helene S. Najita, Joyce M. Guide to statutory provisions in public sector collective bargaining . Honolulu, Hawaii (2425 Campus Rd., Honolulu 96822) , c1981. v, 237 p. ;   LC Card 81-138923   DDC 344.73/0189041353 347.304189041353 19
KF3409.P77 Z9536

TANK - VESSELS. see **TANKERS.**

TANKER SHIPS. see **TANKERS.**

TANKERS - ENVIRONMENTAL ASPECTS - UNITED STATES.
United States. Maritime Administration. United States Department of Commerce final environmental impact statement . [Washington] [1979] ca. 350 p. in various pagings :   LC Card 79-602128   DDC 333.91/1/0973 19
TD427.P4 U58 1979

Tannenbaum, Arnold Sherwood, 1925- Conte, Michael. Employee ownership /. Ann Arbor, Mich. , 1981. vi, 65 p. ;   ISBN 0-87944-255-7 (pbk.)   LC Card 81-150054   DDC 331.2/164 19
HD5660.U5 C66

Tannenbaum, Kenneth A. Workers' compensation : a blueprint for cost containment / Kenneth A. Tannenbaum, hearing officer. [Springfield, Ill.] : Illinois Dept. of Insurance, Illinois Industrial Commission, [1980] 51 p. ; 28 cm. Cover title. Report of hearings held Nov. 26-Dec. 18, 1979.   LC Card 80-623567   DDC 338.4/336841/009773 19
1. Workmen's compensation - Illinois - Cost control. I. Illinois. Industrial Commission (1917-). II. Title.
HD7103.65.U6 T35

Tanner, Howard A. Shaping the world's finest freshwater fishery / by Howard A. Tanner, Mercer H. Patriarche, William J. Mullendore. Lansing, Mich. : Michigan Dept. of Natural Resources, [1980] 86 p. : ill. ; 28 cm. "April 1980."   LC Card 80-622892   DDC 333.95/6/09744 19
1. Fishery management - Michigan. 2. Fishery management - Great Lakes. 3. Animal introduction - Great Lakes. 4. Fisheries - Great Lakes. 5. Fishing - Great Lakes. I. Patriarche, Mercer H., joint author. II. Mullendore, William J., joint author. III. Michigan. Dept. of Natural Resources. IV. Title.
SH464.G7 T36

Tanner, Lucretia Dewey. United States. Federal Mediation and Conciliation Service. Office of Research. Impact of the 1974 health care amendments to the NLRA on collective bargaining in the health care industry /. [Washington] , 1979. x, 473 p. :   LC Card 79-603053
RA971.35 .U54 1979

Tanter, Raymond. (joint author) Stein, Janice Gross. Rational decision-making . Columbus , c1980. xv, 399 p. :   ISBN 0-8142-0312-4   LC Card 80-13589
DS119.2 .S73   *NYPL [JLE 81-169]*

Tantillo, Leonard F. New York State Energy Research and Development Authority. 1979 NYSERDA passive solar design awards /. Albany, N.Y. [c1980] vii, 72 p. :   LC Card 80-128412   DDC 728/.68 19
TH7414 .N48 1980

TANZANIA - ECONOMIC CONDITIONS - MAPS.
United States. Central Intelligence Agency.

Tanzania. [Washington, 1970] col. map 42 x 43 cm. on sheet 44 x 80 cm. Scale 1:3,220,000. Relief shown by shading and spot heights. "76839." Includes location map, comparative area map, and maps of "Population," "Economic activity," "Ethnic groups," and "Vegetation." LC Card GM70-4480
G8440 1970 .U51
        NYPL [Map Div. 80-3387]

Tanzania, land use and agricultural diversification / Anders J. Passey ... [et al.]. [Washington] : U. S. Dept. of Agriculture, [1968?] 90 p. : ill. ; 26 cm. Bibliography: p. 46-48. LC Card 81-462748 DDC 338.1/09678 19
1. Agriculture - Tanzania. 2. Land use, Rural - Tanzania. I. Passey, Anders J.
S473.T35 T36

TANZANIA - MAPS.
(1970) United States. Central Intelligence Agency. Tanzania. [Washington, 1970] col. map 42 x 43 cm. on sheet 44 x 80 cm. Scale 1:3,220,000. Relief shown by shading and spot heights. "76839." Includes location map, comparative area map, and maps of "Population," "Economic activity," "Ethnic groups," and "Vegetation." LC Card GM70-4480
G8440 1970 .U51
        NYPL [Map Div. 80-3387]

TANZANIA - POPULATION - MAPS.
United States. Central Intelligence Agency. Tanzania. [Washington, 1970] col. map 42 x 43 cm. on sheet 44 x 80 cm. Relief shown by shading and spot heights. "76839." Includes location map, comparative area map, and maps of "Population," "Economic activity," "Ethnic groups," and "Vegetation." LC Card GM70-4480
G8440 1970 .U51
        NYPL [Map Div. 80-3387]

Tanzania-Zambia Railway. see Tan-Zam Railway.

TAPE FILES. see DATA TAPES.

TAPE RECORDINGS (DATA STORAGE) see DATA TAPES.

Tape sculptures. Tacha, Athena. Athena Tacha. [Dayton] , 1978. 20 p. :
        NYPL [3-MGO (Tacha) 81-880]

Tarantello, R. (joint author) Findlay, M. Chapman. FMRR simulation model and user manual /. Storrs, Conn. , Los Angeles, Calif. [1980] 51, 22 leaves ; ISBN 0-931176-76-X (pbk.) : LC Card 80-623842 DDC 333.33 s 332.63/24/0724 19
HD251 .R283 no. 30 HD1375

The Tarapur nuclear fuel export issue . United States. Congress. Senate. Committee on Foreign Relations. Washington , 1980. iii, 134 p. : LC Card 80-602987 DDC 382/.4562148335/0973 19
KF26 .F6 1980l

Tarbell, Edmund Charles, 1862-1938.
Olney, Susan Faxon. Two American impressionists . Durham, N.H. , c1980. 22 p. : LC Card 80-80237 DDC 759.13 19
ND237.B4595 A4 1980

TARBELL, EDMUND CHARLES, 1862-1938 - EXHIBITIONS.
Olney, Susan Faxon. Two American impressionists . Durham, N.H. , c1980. 22 p. : LC Card 80-80237 DDC 759.13 19
ND237.B4595 A4 1980

Targan, Barry, 1932- Kingdoms : a novel / by Barry Targan. Albany : State University of New York Press, c1980. 252 p. ; 23 cm. LC Card 80-154403 DDC 813/.54 19
I. Title.
PS3570.A59 K5

Target system . United States. Congress. House. Committee on Veterans' Affairs. Subcommittee on Special Investigations. Washington , 1980. iii, 40 p. : LC Card 80-602467 DDC 353.0081/2 19
KF27 .V458 1980

Targeting community development : third report on the Brookings Institution monitoring study of the Community Development Block Grant Program : prepared under contract H-2323R / by Paul R. Dommel ... [et al.]. Washington, D.C. : U. S. Dept. of Housing and Urban Development : for sale by the Supt. of Docs., U. S. Govt. Print. Off., [1980] xvii, 212, [154] p. ; 28 cm. "January 1980." Includes bibliographical references. LC Card 80-602935 DDC 307 19
1. Community development - United States - Evaluation. 2. Federal aid to community development -

United States. 3. United States. Dept. of Housing and Urban Development. I. Dommel, Paul R., 1933-. II. Brookings Institution, Washington, D. C.
HN90.C6 T37

TARICHA GRANULOSA - PHYSIOLOGY.
Briggs, Jeffrey L. Control of the circadian rhythm of locomotion in the rough-skinned newt, Taricha granulosa /. Milwaukee , 1975. v, 25 p. : LC Card 81-461582 DDC 597.6/5 19
QL668.C28 B74 1975

TARIFF.
United Nations. Conference on Trade and Development. Operation and effects of the generalized system of preferences . New York , 1979. vi, 146 p. ; LC Card 80-121468 DDC 300 s 382.7/53 19
JX1977 .A2 TD/B/C.5/61

TARIFF - JURISPRUDENCE. see TARIFF - LAW AND LEGISLATION.

TARIFF - LAW AND LEGISLATION.
United States. International Trade Commission. Agreements being negotiated at the mutilateral trade negotiations in Geneva--U. S. International Trade Commission investigation no. 332-101 . Washington , 1979- v. ; LC Card 79-603800 DDC 341.7/54/0265 19
K4603 1973 .U54

TARIFF - LAW AND LEGISLATION - UNITED STATES.
United States. Congress. House. Committee on Ways and Means. Subcommittee on Trade. Certain tariff and trade bills . Washington , 1980. xi, 933 p. : LC Card 80-603420 DDC 343.73/087 19
KF27 .W348 1980e

United States. Congress. House. Committee on Ways and Means. Subcommittee on Trade. Leather apparel and miscellaneous bills . Washington , 1981. iv, 148 p. : LC Card 81-600942 DDC 343.7305/6 347.30356 19
KF27 .W348 1980l

United States. Congress. Senate. Committee on Finance. Subcommittee on International Trade. Miscellaneous tariff bills . Washington , 1980. v, 322 p. : LC Card 80-601975 DDC 343.7305/6/0262 19
KF26 .F554 1980

United States. Congress. Senate. Committee on Finance. Subcommittee on International Trade. Miscellaneous tariff bills . Washington , 1980 [i.e. 1981] iii, 158 p. : LC Card 81-601217 DDC 343.7305/6/0262 347.303560262 19
KF26 .F554 1980f

United States. International Trade Commission. Agreements being negotiated at the mutilateral trade negotiations in Geneva--U. S. International Trade Commission investigation no. 332-101 . Washington , 1979- v. ; LC Card 79-603800 DDC 341.7/54/0265 19
K4603 1973 .U54

TARIFF LISTS. see TARIFF - LAW AND LEGISLATION.

TARIFF ON AUTOMOBILE - UNITED STATES.
United States. Congress. Joint Economic Committee. U. S. trade and investment policy . Washington , 1980. iii, 148 p. : LC Card 80-603497 DDC 338.4/76292/0973 19
KF25 .E2 1980d

TARIFF ON BICYCLE INNER TUBES - UNITED STATES.
United States. International Trade Commission. Bicycle tires and tubes . Washington, D.C. , 1978. iv, 21, 131 p. ; LC Card 79-601748 DDC 382/.4567832 19
HF2651.B49 U58 1978

TARIFF ON BICYCLE TIRES - UNITED STATES.
United States. International Trade Commission. Bicycle tires and tubes . Washington, D.C. , 1978. iv, 21, 131 p. ; LC Card 79-601748 DDC 382/.4567832 19
HF2651.B49 U58 1978

TARIFF ON CUT ROSES - UNITED STATES.
Burket, Stephen D. Fresh cut roses . Washington, D.C. , 1980. iii, 9, 44 p. : LC Card 80-602339 DDC 382/.415933372/0973 19
HF2651.R85 U63

TARIFF ON FISHES - UNITED STATES.
Lopp, Thomas G. Fish, fresh, chilled, or frozen,

whether or not whole, but not otherwise prepared or preserved, from Canada . Washington, D.C. [1980] vi, 32, 121 p. : LC Card 80-602376 DDC 382/.4566494 19
HF2651.F5 U44

TARIFF ON GASOLINE - UNITED STATES.
United States. Congress. House. Committee on Government Operations. Environment, Energy, and Natural Resources Subcommittee. The petroleum import fee, Department of Energy Oversight . Washington , 1980. iii, 271 p. : LC Card 80-602747 DDC 382/.42282/0973 19
KF27 .G655 1980a

TARIFF ON IRON PIPE - UNITED STATES.
United States. International Trade Commission. Pipes and tubes of iron or steel from Japan . Washington, D.C. [1980] ii, 29, 37 p. ; LC Card 80-602337 DDC 382/.4567283/0973 19
HF2651.S76 U54 1980a

TARIFF ON LEATHER GARMENTS - LAW AND LEGISLATION - UNITED STATES.
United States. Congress. House. Committee on Ways and Means. Subcommittee on Trade. Leather apparel and miscellaneous bills . Washington , 1981. iv, 148 p. : LC Card 81-600942 DDC 343.7305/6 347.30356 19
KF27 .W348 1980l

United States. Congress. Senate. Committee on Finance. Subcommittee on International Trade. Import relief to the domestic industry producing certain leather coats and jackets . Washington , 1980. iii, 192 p. ; LC Card 81-600635 DDC 382/.4568522/0973 19
KF26 .F554 1980h

TARIFF ON LEATHER GARMENTS - UNITED STATES.
Magrath, Patrick J. Leather wearing apparel . Washington, D.C. [1980] iii, 15, 51 p. : LC Card 80-602342 DDC 382/.456852/0973 19
HF2651.L45 U496

United States. International Trade Commission. Leather wearing apparel from Uruguay . Washington, D.C. , 1980. ii, 9, 47 p. ; LC Card 81-600775 DDC 382/.4568522/0973 19
HF2651.L45 U64 1980

TARIFF ON MARINE RADAR SYSTEMS - UNITED STATES.
United States. International Trade Commission. Certain marine radar systems from the United Kingdom . Washington, D.C. [1979] ii, 8, 50 p. ; LC Card 80-602625 DDC 382/.45623863 19
HF2651.M385 U58 1979

TARIFF ON MINERALS.
Sullivan, Daniel E. Minerals and the Tokyo Round of the MTN /. Washington [1981] p. cm. LC Card 81-607909 DDC 622 s 382/.42 19
TN295 .U4 HD9506.A2

TARIFF ON MUSHROOMS - UNITED STATES.
United States. International Trade Commission. Mushrooms, report to the President on investigation no. TA-201-43, under section 201 of the Trade act of 1974. Washington, D.C. [1980] iv, 27, 78 p. : LC Card 80-603136 DDC 382/.4158/0973 19
HF2651.M83 U53 1980

TARIFF ON PEANUTS - UNITED STATES.
United States. Tariff Commission. Peanuts . Washington, 1955. 42 l. LC Card 55-60610
        NYPL [JLF 75-1381]

TARIFF ON PETROLEUM - UNITED STATES.
United States. Congress. House. Committee on Government Operations. Environment, Energy, and Natural Resources Subcommittee. The petroleum import fee, Department of Energy Oversight . Washington , 1980. iii, 271 p. : LC Card 80-602747 DDC 382/.42282/0973 19
KF27 .G655 1980a

United States. Congress. House. Committee on Ways and Means. Subcommittee on Trade. Oil import fees . Washington , 1980. iv, 443 p. : LC Card 80-603505 DDC 353.0082/75 19
KF27 .W348 1980d

United States. Congress. Senate. Committee on Finance. Subcommittee on Taxation and Debt Management Generally. Special oil taxes . Washington , 1980 [i.e. 1981] iii, 222 p. : LC Card 81-601139 DDC 336.2/783338232/0973

19
KF26 .F5695 1980j

TARIFF ON RAW MATERIALS. see TARIFF.

TARIFF ON STEEL PIPE - UNITED STATES.
United States. International Trade Commission.
Pipes and tubes of iron or steel from Japan .
Washington, D.C. [1980] ii, 29, 37 p. ; LC
Card 80-602337 DDC 382/.4567283/0973 19
HF2651.S76 U54 1980a

**TARIFF ON STEEL TUBES - UNITED
STATES.**
United States. International Trade Commission.
Pipes and tubes of iron or steel from Japan .
Washington, D.C. [1980] ii, 29, 37 p. ; LC
Card 80-602337 DDC 382/.4567283/0973 19
HF2651.S76 U54 1980a

TARIFF ON STEEL - UNITED STATES.
United States. International Trade Commission.
Certain carbon steel products from Belgium, the
Federal Republic of Germany, France, Italy,
Luxembourg, the Netherlands, and the United
Kingdom . Washington, D.C. [1980] vii, 71,
180 p. ; LC Card 80-602282 DDC 382/.45672 19
HF2651.S76 U54 1980

TARIFF ON SUGAR - UNITED STATES.
Greer, T. Vernon. Sugar from Belgium, France,
and West Germany . Washington , 1979. 21, 62
p. ; LC Card 79-602639 DDC 382/.4136/0973 19
HF2651.S8 U54

Greer, T. Vernon. Sugars and sirups from
Canada . Washington, D.C. [1980] ii, 17, 66
p. ; LC Card 80-602338 DDC 382/.4136/0973 19
HF2651.S8 U55

TARIFF ON SYRUPS - UNITED STATES.
Greer, T. Vernon. Sugars and sirups from
Canada . Washington, D.C. [1980] ii, 17, 66
p. ; LC Card 80-602338 DDC 382/.4136/0973 19
HF2651.S8 U55

**TARIFF ON TEXTILE FABRICS - UNITED
STATES.**
Cook, C. Lee. Textiles and textile products of
cotton from Pakistan . Washington, D.C.
[1980] vi, 56, 105 p. ; LC Card 80-602856 DDC
382/.4567721/0973 19
HD9856 .C66

TARIFF ON TOBACCO - UNITED STATES.
Cannon, Joseph Gurney, 1836-1926. $1,050,000
into the pockets of the American tobacco trust.
[Washington? D. C. , 1900] 16 p. ;
                    NYPL [Arents S 1607]

TARIFF PREFERENCES - UNITED STATES.
United States. Congress. House. Committee on
Ways and Means. Subcommittee on Trade.
Operation of the generalized system of
preferences . Washington , 1980. iii, 111 p. ;
   LC Card 80-603343 DDC 353.0082/7 19
KF27 .W348 1980c

United States. Congress. Senate. Committee on
Finance. Subcommittee on International Trade.
Review of the U. S. generalized system of
preferences . Washington , 1981. iv, 300 p. :
   LC Card 81-601603 DDC 382.7/53/0973 19
KF26 .F554 1980g

**TARIFF SCHEDULES. see TARIFF - LAW
AND LEGISLATION.**

TARIFF - UNITED STATES.
Bayard, Thomas O. Trade and employment
effects of tariff reductions agreed to in the
MTN /. [Washington, D.C.] [Springfield, Va.]
1980. 11, [31] p. ; LC Card 80-602631 DDC
382.7 19
HF1757 .B39

**TARIFF - UNITED STATES -
MATHEMATICAL MODELS - CASE
STUDIES.**
Morkre, Morris E. The effects of restrictions on
United States imports . [Washington, D.C.]
[1980] xv, 212 p. : LC Card 80-603259 DDC
382/.5/0973 19
HF1731 .M67

Tarlton Law Library.
   Tarlton Law Library legal bibliography series .
   (no. 19) Christensen, Carol W. Guide to
   religion-based organizations of attorneys /.
   [Austin] , 1979. v, 33 leaves ; ISBN
   0-935630-01-5 (pbk.) LC Card 80-621543
   DDC 340/.06/073 19
   KF195.R44 C48

   (no. 2) DeVergie, Adrienne, 1936-

Bibliography on student activism, 1963-1970
/. [Austin, Tex.] 1970. 84 leaves ; LC Card
80-622264 DDC 016.378/1981 19
KF4150.A1 D48

(no. 20) Hathaway, Barbara Drexler. Julius
Stone . Austin , 1980. i, 51 leaves ; ISBN
0-935630-20-3 (pbk.) LC Card 80-114099
DDC 340/.1 19
K235 .H37

(no. 21) O'Brien, David M. Theright of
privacy--its constitutional & social
dimensions . Austin , 1980. vi, 55 p. ; ISBN
0-935630-04-X (pbk.) LC Card 80-622796
DDC 016.34273/0858 19
KF1262.A1 O25

(no. 3) Olm, Jane. Bibliography on juvenile
delinquency in Texas /. [Austin] [1970] 34
leaves ; LC Card 80-622265 DDC
016.345764/08 016.34764058 19
KFT1795.A1 O4

The tarnished golden door . Dimas, Nicasio.
Washington, D.C. , 1980. ix, 158 p. : LC Card
80-604159 DDC 342.73/082 347.30282 19
KF4819 .D55

Tarquinio, Anthony. (joint author) Zaltzman, Raul.
Biological decomposition of cellulose.
Morgantown, 1969. iii, 107 p. LC Card
72-628129 DDC 620 s 581.19/2482 19
TA1 .W393 no. 6 QR160

Tarr, David G. (joint author) Morkre, Morris E.
The effects of restrictions on United States
imports . [Washington, D.C.] [1980] xv, 212
p. : LC Card 80-603259 DDC 382/.5/0973 19
HF1731 .M67

**TASC, an approach for dealing with the
substance abusing offender .** National
Association of State Drug Abuse Program
Coordinators. Washington , 1978 [i.e. 1979] iv,
77, [83] p. : LC Card 79-602048
HV5825 .N32 1979

**Task Force on Design, Art and Architecture in
Transportation. see United States. Task
Force on Design, Art and Architecture in
Transportation.**

**Task Force on Housing Costs. see United States.
Task Force on Housing Costs.**

Task Force on Rental Housing . United States.
Congress. House. Committee on Banking,
Finance, and Urban Affairs. Subcommittee on
Housing and Community Development. Task
Force on Rental Housing. Washington , 1980.
vii, 1072 p. : LC Card 80-603282 DDC 363.5/8
19
KF27 .B5467 1980

Task Force on the Future of Illinois. Testa,
Mark. Human services in Illinois . [Chicago] ,
1978 [i.e. 1979] vi, 172 p. : LC Card 80-623960
DDC 361.6/09773 19
HV98.I15 T48

**Task force report on epidemiology of respiratory
diseases.** National Heart, Lung, and Blood
Institute. Division of Lung Diseases. Task Force
on Epidemiology of Respiratory Diseases.
Report of Task Force on Epidemiology of
Respiratory Diseases . [Bethesda, Md.?] , 1980.
vii, 244 p. : LC Card 81-600681 DDC
614.5/92/00973 19
RA645.R4 N37 1980

TASMANIA - EXILES - BIOGRAPHY.
Touhill, Blanche M. (Blanche Marie), 1931-
William Smith O'Brien and his Irish
revolutionary companions in penal exile /.
Columbia , 1981. p. cm. ISBN 0-8262-0339-6
LC Card 81-1899 DDC 941.5081/092/4 19
DA952.O22 T68

Tassey, Gregory. Barth, James R. Evaluating the
impact of securities regulation on venture
capital markets /. Washington, D.C. , 1980. iv,
38 p. : LC Card 80-600036 DDC 602.18 s
332/.0414 19
QC100 .U556 no. 166 HG4963

Tasso, Torquato, 1544-1595.
[Selections. English. 1982]
Tasso's dialogues : a selection with the
Discourse on the art of the dialogue /
translated with introduction and notes by
Carnes Lord and Dain A. Trafton. Berkeley :
University of California Press, c1982. p. cm.
(Biblioteca italiana) Bibliography: p. ISBN
0-520-04464-X LC Card 81-12937 DDC 195

19
I. Lord, Carnes. II. Trafton, Dain A. III. Title. IV.
Series.
PQ4642 .E2 1982

Tasso's dialogues . Tasso, Torquato, 1544-1595.
[Selections. English. 1982.] Berkeley , c1982. p.
cm. ISBN 0-520-04464-9 LC Card 81-12937
DDC 195 19
PQ4642 .E2 1982

Taube, Carl A. United States. National Institute
of Mental Health. Biometry Branch. Survey and
Reports Section. Patients in public institutions
for the mentally retarded, 1967. Chevy Chase,
Md. , Washington , 1969. ii, 79 p. ; LC Card
81-452003 DDC 362.3/850973 19
RC570.5.U6 U65 1969

**TAULIPANG INDIANS. see ARECUNA
INDIANS.**

**Taunton River Basin wastewater discharge
survey, 1975, 1976, 1978, 1979 /.**
Massachusetts. Water Quality and Research
Section. Westborough [Mass.] [1979] 133 p. :
   LC Card 80-621549 DDC 363.7/3942/097448
19
TD224.M4 M368 1979

Taunton River study . Salo, John E. Boston
[1971] 31 leaves : LC Card 80-118663 DDC
363.7/3942/097448 19
TD224.M4 S25

**TAUREPAN INDIANS. see ARECUNA
INDIANS.**

Taweel, Michael. California. Dept. of Water
Resources. Southern District. Potential waste
disposal areas, northern Los Angeles County /.
[Sacramento] [1979] vii, 58 p. : LC Card
80-621404 DDC 363.7/28 19
TD811.5 .C34 1979

TAX ACCOUNTING - UNITED STATES.
United States. Congress. House. Committee on
Small Business. Subcommittee on Access to
Equity Capital and Business Opportunities.
Inventory accounting as a burden on the capital
formation process . Washington , 1980- v. ; LC
Card 80-601994 DDC 346.73/0652 19
KF27 .S63 1980

United States. Congress. House. Committee on
Ways and Means. Accounting treatment of the
investment tax credit and accelerated
depreciation for public utility ratemaking
purposes . Washington , 1980. iv, 136 p. ; LC
Card 80-603022 DDC 343.7305/267 19
KF27 .W3 1980g

TAX ADMINISTRATION AND PROCEDURE.
United States. Congress. Office of Technology
Assessment. A preliminary analysis of the IRS
tax administration system. - Washington ,
Springfield, Va. , 1977. x, 206 p. ;
                    *NYPL [*XME-9377]*

**TAX ADMINISTRATION AND
PROCEDURE - ALABAMA.**
Ward, Keith J. Property tax administration .
Auburn, Ala. [1980] xiv, 167 p. : LC Card
80-622123 DDC 353.97610072/42 19
HJ4121.A22 W37

**TAX ADMINISTRATION AND
PROCEDURE - NEW MEXICO.**
New Mexico. Taxation and Revenue Dept. A
checklist of New Mexico State and local taxes,
permits, and licenses. Santa Fe, N.M. [1979]
39 p. ; LC Card 80-623253 DDC
353.97890072/4/0025 19
HJ2423 .A7 1979

**TAX ADMINISTRATION AND
PROCEDURE - NEW YORK (STATE)**
New York (State). Division of Audits and
Accounts. Financial and operating practices,
Department of Taxation and Finance, Audit
Division, miscellaneous taxes, Albany, New
York, as of March 31, 1979 /. Albany [1980]
5, 31, 8 leaves ; LC Card 80-622160 DDC
353.97470072/4 19
HJ3325.3 .N48 1980

**TAX ADMINISTRATION AND
PROCEDURE - UNITED STATES.**
United States. Congress. House. Commitee on
Government Operations. Commerce, Consumer,
and Monetary Affairs Subcommittee. IRS'
administration of the tax laws (income
information document matching) . Washington ,
1980. iii, 178 p. : LC Card 81-600661 DDC

353.00072/4 19
KF27 .G634 1980f

United States. Congress. House. Committee on Ways and Means. Subcommittee on Oversight. Federal noncompliance with tax law reporting requirements . Washington , 1981. iii, 37 p. ; LC Card 81-601371 DDC 353.0072/4 19
KF27 .W345 1980l

United States. Congress. Joint Committee on Internal Revenue Taxation. Jeopardy and termination assessments, administrative summons, comprehensive administrative package, state conducted lotteries, and miscellaneous /. Washington , 1975. iii, 7 p. ; LC Card 80-600755 DDC 353.0072/4 19
KF6300 .A25 1975

United States. Congress. Senate. Select Committee on Small Business. Subcommittee on Taxation, Financing, and Investment. Procedural difficulties encountered by smaller business in dealing with the IRS . Washington , 1980. iii, 172 p. ; LC Card 80-603483 DDC 353.0072/4 19
KF26.5 .S686 1980

United States. Treasury Dept. President's cash management initiatives /. Washington , 1980. vi, 94 p. ; LC Card 80-601795 DDC 353.0072/4 19
HJ3252 .U58 1980

TAX AND EXPENDITURE LIMITATIONS - UNITED STATES.
Reducing the Federal budget . Washington, D.C. [1981] xi, 187 p. ; LC Card 81-601803 DDC 353.0072/22 19
HJ2051 .R42

TAX AND EXPENDITURE LIMITATIONS - UNITED STATES - CONGRESSES.
Managing revenue reductions . Davis, Calif. , 1981. 94 leaves ; LC Card 81-156255 DDC 350.72/6/0973 19
HJ2051 .M36

TAX AUDITING - NEW YORK (STATE)
New York (State). Division of Audits and Accounts. Financial and operating practices, Department of Taxation and Finance, Audit Division, miscellaneous taxes, Albany, New York, as of March 31, 1979 /. Albany [1980] 5, 31, 8 leaves ; LC Card 80-622160 DDC 353.97470072/4 19
HJ3325.3 .N48 1980

TAX BURDEN. see TAX INCIDENCE.

Tax burdens in American agriculture . Sisson, Charles Adair, 1946- Ames , 1981. p. cm. ISBN 0-8138-1680-7 LC Card 81-8206 DDC 336.2/7863/0973 19
HD1295.U5 S58

TAX COLLECTION - MONTANA.
Montana. Legislature. Revenue Oversight Committee. Payment of taxes under protest . Helena, Mont. (Room 138, State Capitol, Helena 59620) [1980] i, 27 p. ; LC Card 81-621340 DDC 353.97860072/4 19
KFM9471.5 .A25 1980

TAX COLLECTION - NEW YORK (STATE)
New York (State). Division of Audits and Accounts. Financial and operating practices, Department of Taxation and Finance, Audit Division, miscellaneous taxes, Albany, New York, as of March 31, 1979 /. Albany [1980] 5, 31, 8 leaves ; LC Card 80-622160 DDC 353.97470072/4 19
HJ3325.3 .N48 1980

TAX COLLECTION - PENNSYLVANIA - COSTS - STATISTICS.
Pennsylvania. Dept. of Education. Methods and costs of tax collection in school districts in Pennsylvania. [Harrisburg, Pa. , 1977?] 70 p. in various pagings ; LC Card 80-621623 DDC 352.1/3/09748 19
HJ9306 .P42 1977

TAX COLLECTION - UNITED STATES.
United States. Congress. House. Commitee on Government Operations. Commerce, Consumer, and Monetary Affairs Subcommittee. IRS' administration of the tax laws (income information document matching) . Washington , 1980. iii, 178 p. ; LC Card 81-600661 DDC 353.00072/4 19
KF27 .G634 1980f

United States. Congress. House. Committee on

Ways and Means. President's cash management initiatives in the fiscal year 1981 budget . Washington , 1980. iv, 197 p. : LC Card 80-602770 DDC 353.0072/6 19
KF27 .W3 1980f

United States. Congress. House. Committee on Ways and Means. Subcommittee on Oversight. Taxpayer complaints . Washington , 1980. iii, 178 p. ; LC Card 80-604065 DDC 353.0072/4 19
KF27 .W345 1980i

United States. Congress. House. Committee on Ways and Means. Subcommittee on Oversight. Underground economy . Washington , 1980. iv, 501 p. ; LC Card 80-602166 DDC 353.0072/44 19
KF27 .W345 1979i

United States. Congress. Joint Economic Committee. The underground economy . Washington , 1980. iii, 76 p. ; LC Card 80-602483 DDC 353.0072/442 19
KF25 .E2 1979m

United States. Congress. Senate. Committee on Governmental Affairs. Subcommittee on Oversight of Government Management. IRS summary collection policy impact on small business . Washington , 1980. iv, 415 p. ; LC Card 80-603735 DDC 338.6/42/0973 19
KF26 .G676 1980a

United States. Treasury Dept. President's cash management initiatives /. Washington , 1980. vi, 94 p. ; LC Card 80-601795 DDC 353.0072/4 19
HJ3252 .U58 1980

TAX COURTS - OREGON.
Oregon. Tax Court. Research Division. Rules, Regular Division /. Salem, Or. [1980] iv, 61 p. ; LC Card 80-623341 DDC 343.79504/0269 19
KFO2871.5.A437 A2 1980

TAX CREDITS - ALASKA.
Lasher, Deborah A. Fuel, conservation & individual credits relative to the individual income tax /. [Juneau] [1980] ii leaves, 21 p. : LC Card 80-622014 DDC 336.24/216 19
HJ4655.A33 L37

Tax credits to homebuilders using passive solar design and building techniques . United States. Congress. House. Committee on Ways and Means. Washington , 1980. iv, 147 p. : LC Card 81-600616 DDC 343.73/0523 347.303523 19
KF27 .W3 1980l

TAX CREDITS - UNITED STATES.
Daugherty, Arthur Berry, 1936- Open space preservation . Washington , Springfield, Va. , 1978. v, 32 p. ; LC Card 79-601799 DDC 338.1/0973 s 336.24/216 19
HD1759 .U56a no. 32 HJ4653.C73

United States. Congress. House. Committee on Small Business. Role of government funding and its impact on small business in the solar energy industry . Washington , 1980. vi, 68 p. : LC Card 80-603851 DDC 338.6/42 19
HD9681.U62 U526 1980

United States. Congress. House. Committee on Small Business. Subcommittee on Energy, Environment, Safety and Research. Role of government funding and its impact on small business in the solar energy industry . Washington , 1979 i.e. 1980- v. : LC Card 80-603085 DDC 338.4/362147/0973 19
KF27 .S639 1979b

Tax cut proposals . United States. Congress. Senate. Committee on Finance. Washington , 1980- v. : LC Card 80-603089 DDC 343.7304/0262 19
KF26 .F5 1980d

TAX DELINQUENCY. see TAX EVASION.

TAX-DODGING. see TAX EVASION.

TAX ESTIMATION. see TAX REVENUE ESTIMATING.

TAX EVASION - UNITED STATES.
United States. Congress. House. Committee on Ways and Means. Subcommittee on Oversight. Underground economy . Washington , 1980. iv, 501 p. ; LC Card 80-602166 DDC 353.0072/44 19
KF27 .W345 1979i

United States. Congress. Joint Economic Committee. The underground economy . Washington , 1980. iii, 76 p. ; LC Card

80-602483 DDC 353.0072/442 19
KF25 .E2 1979m

TAX EXPENDITURES - UNITED STATES.
United States. Congress. Joint Committee on Taxation. Estimates of federal tax expenditures for fiscal years, 1980-1985 /. Washington , 1980. ii, 21 p. ; LC Card 81-600720 DDC 336.2 19
HJ4652 .U627 1980

Tax incentives for savings . United States. Congress. House. Committee on Ways and Means. Washington , 1980. vii, 774 p. : LC Card 80-602478 DDC 343.7305/23 19
KF27 .W3 1980c

TAX INCIDENCE.
Balcer, Yves. Family size, personal income tax credits, and horizontal equity /. [Madison] [1979] 30 p. : LC Card 80-622907 DDC 336.24/216 19
HJ4621 .B28

Tax map, Galloway Township, Atlantic County, N.J. /. Galloway Township (N.J.). Township Engineer. [Mays Landing] [1933] 2 maps on 2 sheets : LC Card 81-690328
G3814.G17 s24 .G3

TAX PENALTIES - UNITED STATES.
United States. Congress. Senate. Committee on Governmental Affairs. Subcommittee on Oversight of Government Management. IRS summary collection policy impact on small business . Washington , 1980. iv, 415 p. ; LC Card 80-603735 DDC 338.6/42/0973 19
KF26 .G676 1980a

TAX PRACTICE. see TAX ADMINISTRATION AND PROCEDURE.

TAX PROCEDURE. see TAX ADMINISTRATION AND PROCEDURE.

TAX PROTESTS AND APPEALS - MONTANA.
Montana. Legislature. Revenue Oversight Committee. Payment of taxes under protest . Helena, Mont. (Room 138, State Capitol, Helena 59620) [1980] i, 27 p. ; LC Card 81-621340 DDC 353.97860072/4 19
KFM9471.5 .A25 1980

TAX PROTESTS AND APPEALS - NEW YORK (STATE)
New York (State). Legislature. Senate. Standing Committee on Cities and City of New York. Certiorari . [Albany, N.Y.] , 1980. 119 p. ; LC Card 80-624086 DDC 353.7470072/421 19
KFN5010.72 .C57 1980

TAX PROTESTS AND APPEALS - UNITED STATES.
United States. Congress. House. Committee on Ways and Means. Subcommittee on Select Revenue Measures. Payment of attorneys' fees in tax litigation . Washington , 1980 [i.e. 1981] iii, 111 p. ; LC Card 81-600811 DDC 343.7304/0269 347.30340269 19
KF27 .W3468 1980d

Tax rates and tables for prior years. United States. Internal Revenue Service. [Washington, D.C.?] , 1980. ii leaves, 89 p. : LC Card 80-603934 DDC 343.7305/2 347.30352 19
HJ2381 .U55 1980

TAX RETURNS - UNITED STATES.
United States. Congress. House. Commitee on Government Operations. Commerce, Consumer, and Monetary Affairs Subcommittee. IRS' administration of the tax laws (income information document matching) . Washington , 1980. iii, 178 p. : LC Card 81-600661 DDC 353.00072/4 19
KF27 .G634 1980f

United States. Congress. Joint Committee on Taxation. Description of bills (S. 2402, S. 2403, S. 2404, and S. 2405) relating to disclosure of tax returns and return information listed for a hearing before the Subcommittee on Oversight of the Internal Revenue Service of the Committee on Finance, on June 20, 1980 /. Washington , 1980. iii, 18 p. ; LC Card 80-602679 DDC 343.7305/2 19
KF6328 .A25 1980

TAX REVENUE ESTIMATING.
Burchell, Robert W. The fiscal impact guidebook . [Washington] , 1979. xxii, 617 p. ; LC Card 79-602895
HD4431 .B85 1979

TAX REVENUE ESTIMATING - UNITED STATES.
Saunders, Hyman. A review of the accuracy of treasury revenue forecasts, 1963-1978 /. [Washington, D.C.] , 1981. xi, 42 p. ; LC Card 81-601118 DDC 353.0072/2252 19
HJ2051 .S26

TAX-SALES - KENTUCKY.
Neuhaus, William B. Urban abandonment and property tax delinquency /. Frankfort, Ky. , 1978. iii, 22 p. ; LC Card 79-621078 DDC 343.76905/4 347.690354 19
KFK1679 .N48

TAX-SALES - MISSOURI - ST. LOUIS.
Neuhaus, William B. Urban abandonment and property tax delinquency /. Frankfort, Ky. , 1978. iii, 22 p. ; LC Card 79-621078 DDC 343.76905/4 347.690354 19
KFK1679 .N48

TAX SHARING. see REVENUE SHARING.

Tax treaties between developed and developing countries . United Nations. Dept. of Economic and Social Affairs. New York , 1973. v, 205 p. ;
JX1977 .A2 ST/ESA/18
                          NYPL [JLF 80-1510]

Tax treatment of married, head of household, and single taxpayers . United States. Congress. House. Committee on Ways and Means. Washington , 1980. vi, 415 p. ; LC Card 80-603314 DDC 343.7305/2042 19
KF27 .W3 1980h

TAXATION - ADMINISTRATION. see TAX ADMINISTRATION AND PROCEDURE.

The taxation and financing of transportation in Wisconsin . Wisconsin. Legislative reference bureau. Madison, Wis. [1980] 101 p. ; LC Card 80-621759 DDC 300/.9775 s 336.2/78 19
KFW2420 .L4 no. 80-2 HE213

TAXATION AND GOVERNMENT PROPERTY - UNITED STATES.
United States. Advisory Commission on Intergovernmental Relations. The adequacy of federal compensation to local governments for tax exempt federal lands . Washington , 1978. x, 203 p. : LC Card 79-601477
HJ4182.A3 U54 1978   NYPL [JLF 81-314]

Taxation and land use planning /. Henoch, Susan. Anchorage, Alaska [1979] 19 p. ; LC Card 79-625096 DDC 336.22/09798 19
HD211.A4 H46

TAXATION, DOUBLE - FLORIDA.
Florida. Advisory Council on Intergovernmental Relations. The double taxation issue . Tallahassee, Fla. [1978] 471 columns ; LC Card 79-622440 DDC 336.2/94 19
HJ2342.F6 F57 1978a

TAXATION, DOUBLE - TREATIES.
United Nations. Dept. of Economic and Social Affairs. Tax treaties between developed and developing countries . New York , 1973. v, 205 p. ;
JX1977 .A2 ST/ESA/18
                          NYPL [JLF 80-1510]

TAXATION, DOUBLE - UNITED STATES - TREATIES.
United States. Congress. House. Committee on Ways and Means. Subcommittee on Oversight. Income tax treaties . Washington , 1980. iii, 161 p. ; LC Card 80-603644 DDC 341.4/84 19
KF27 .W345 1980f

TAXATION - EVASION. see TAX EVASION.

TAXATION, EXEMPTION FROM - MAINE.
Maine. Legislature. Committee on Taxation. Report of the Joint Standing Committee on Taxation of the statutory review of the sales and use tax exemptions contained in Title 36 Section 1760, Sub-sections 15-23 and 25-29. Augusta, Me. [1980] 43, [17] leaves ; LC Card 80-622574 DDC 343.74105/5 347.410355 19
KFM11.62 .T3 1980

TAXATION, EXEMPTION FROM - NEW YORK (STATE)
McCord, Thomas. Business property taxes and exemptions in New York State . Albany, NY [1980] xi, 101 p. : LC Card 80-622828 DDC 336.22/5 19
HJ4249 .M3

TAXATION, EXEMPTION FROM - UNITED STATES.
United States. Congress. House. Committee on Ways and Means. Tax incentives for savings . Washington , 1980. vii, 774 p. : LC Card 80-602478 DDC 343.7305/23 19
KF27 .W3 1980c

United States. Congress. House. Committee on Ways and Means. Subcommittee on Select Revenue Measures. Expiring historic structure tax provisions . Washington , 1981. viii, 578 p. : LC Card 81-601397 DDC 343.7305/4 347.30354 19
KF27 .W3468 1980e

United States. Congress. Joint Committee on Taxation. Description of bills to provide tax incentives for savings . Washington , 1980. iii, 14 p. ; LC Card 81-600503 DDC 343.7305/23 347.303523 19
KF6417 .A25 1980

TAXATION, EXEMPTION FROM - UNITED STATES - STATES.
United States. Congressional Budget Office. State profits on tax-exempt student loan bonds . [Washington] [1980] xvi, 57 p. ; LC Card 80-601571 DDC 379.1/214/0973 19
HG4946 .U52 1980

TAXATION, EXEMPTION FROM - VIRGINIA.
Virginia. General Assembly. Joint Subcommittee to Study Real Property Tax Exemptions. Report of the Joint Subcommittee to Study Real Property Tax Exemptions to the Governor and the General Assembly of Virginia. Richmond , 1980. 73 p. ; LC Card 80-622737 DDC 300/.9755 s 343.75505/43 19
J87 .V9 1980c no. 35 KFV2411.62

TAXATION - HAWAII.
Ishado, Lester. A study of Hawaii's general excise tax on warranty parts and labor /. Honolulu, Hawaii , 1976. 31 leaves ;
                          *NYPL [*ZT-1259]*

TAXATION, INCIDENCE OF. see TAXATION.

TAXATION - KENTUCKY.
Patterson, Terry. Kentucky business and personal taxes /. [Frankfort] [1978] 24 p. ;
        LC Card 80-620588 DDC 353.97690072/4 19
HJ2408 .P37

TAXATION - LAW AND LEGISLATION - CRIMINAL PROVISIONS. see TAX EVASION.

TAXATION - LAW AND LEGISLATION - IOWA.
Iowa. Development Commission. Doing business in Iowa. Des Moines, Iowa [1978] 29 p. : LC Card 79-625983 DDC 344.777/01 347.77041 19
KFI4430 .A833 1978

TAXATION - LAW AND LEGISLATION - NEVADA.
Nevada. Legislative Commission. Effects of tax relief measures. [Carson City] [1980] vii, 42 p. ; LC Card 81-621361 DDC 343.79304 347.93034 19
KFN1070 .A25 1980

TAXATION - LAW AND LEGISLATION - NORTH CAROLINA.
North Carolina. Legislative Research Commission. Revenue laws . [Raleigh] [1980] ix, 31, [51] p. ; LC Card 80-623283 DDC 343.75604 19
KFN7870 .A25 1980

TAXATION - LAW AND LEGISLATION - UNITED STATES.
United States. Congress. House. Committee on Ways and Means. Hearing announcement on the "Tax restructuring act of 1979", H.R. 5665 . Washington , 1979. iii, 44 p. ; LC Card 80-602685 DDC 343.7304 19
KF6275.5 .W245

United States. Congress. House. Committee on Ways and Means. Subcommittee on Select Revenue Measures. Foreign convention tax rules and minor tax bills . Washington , 1980 [i.e. 1981] vi, 283 p. ; LC Card 81-600932 DDC 343.7305/2 347.30352 19
KF27 .W3468 1980c

United States. Congress. House. Committee on Ways and Means. Subcommittee on Select Revenue Measures. Minor tax bills .

Washington , 1980. vii, 521 p. : LC Card 80-604098 DDC 343.7304/0262 347.30340262 19
KF27 .W3468 1980b

United States. Congress. House. Committee on Ways and Means. Subcommittee on Select Revenue Measures. Minor tax bills . Washington , 1980. iii, 72 p. ; LC Card 80-602528 DDC 343.7304/0262 19
KF27 .W3468 1980

United States. Congress. Senate. Committee on Finance. Tax cut proposals . Washington , 1980- v. : LC Card 80-603089 DDC 343.7304/0262 19
KF26 .F5 1980d

United States. Congress. Senate. Committee on Finance. Subcommittee on Taxation and Debt Management Generally. Family Enterprise Estate and Gift Tax Equity Act and miscellaneous tax bills . Washington , 1980. v, 514 p. : LC Card 81-600624 DDC 343.7306/7 347.30367 19
KF26 .F5695 1980f

TAXATION - LAW AND LEGISLATION - VIRGINIA - OUTLINES, SYLLABI, ETC.
Virginia. Dept. of Taxation. Virginia tax facts. [Richmond, Va.] [1979] 57 p. ; LC Card 79-625802 DDC 343.75504 19
KFV2870 .A87

Taxation manual /. Pennsylvania. Dept. of Community Affairs. Information Services Center. Harrisburg, Pa. , c1979. iv, 88 p. ; LC Card 80-622479 DDC 343.74804/3 19
KFP490 .A855

TAXATION - MINNESOTA - HISTORY.
Gaylord, Kathleen A. History of taxation in Minnesota /. St. Paul, Minn. [1979] 93 p. : LC Card 80-621230 DDC 336.2/009776 19
HJ2415.A2 G39 1979

TAXATION - MONTANA.
Montana. Legislature. Revenue Oversight Committee. Miscellaneous studies, a report to the Forty-seventh Legislature /. Helena (Room 138, State Capitol, Helena 59620) [1980] ii, 80, [14] p. : LC Card 81-621344 DDC 336.2/009786 19
HJ2418 .A7 1980

TAXATION - NEW MEXICO.
New Mexico. Taxation and Revenue Dept. A checklist of New Mexico State and local taxes, permits, and licenses. Santa Fe, N.M. [1979] 39 p. ; LC Card 80-623253 DDC 353.97890072/4/0025 19
HJ2423 .A7 1979

Taxation of foreign earned income . United States. Congress. Senate. Committee on Finance. Subcommittee on Taxation and Debt Management Generally. Washington , 1980. iv, 777 p. : LC Card 80-604096 DDC 343.7305/24 347.3035248 19
KF26 .F5695 1980c

Taxation of foreign investment in U. S. real estate. United States. Treasury Dept. [Washington] , 1979. 68 p. ; LC Card 79-602968
KF6441 .A85   *NYPL [JLF 81-449]*

TAXATION OF FOREIGN INVESTMENTS. see INVESTMENTS, FOREIGN - LAW AND LEGISLATION; INVESTMENTS, FOREIGN - TAXATION.

TAXATION OF FRANCHISES. see CORPORATIONS - TAXATION.

TAXATION OF INCOME. see INCOME TAX.

Taxation of New York State owned lands /. Dorn, Alan D. Albany, N.Y. [1980] 36 p. : LC Card 80-622831 DDC 336.22/5 19
HJ9288 .D67

TAXATION OF PERSONAL PROPERTY - OKLAHOMA - STATISTICS.
Oklahoma. Ad Valorem Tax Division. 1980 Oklahoma personal property valuation schedule /. [Oklahoma City] [1980] 98 p. ; LC Card 80-621907 DDC 343.76605/42 19
HJ4591.O5 O37 1980

TAXATION OF PERSONAL PROPERTY - VIRGINIA.
Inflation and the Virginia income tax ; Personal property taxation in Virginia localities ; Transportation taxation in Virginia. Richmond, Va. , 1979. x, 210 p. ; LC Card 80-623840 DDC

336.2/009755 19
HJ4655.V88 I64

TAXATION OF REAL PROPERTY. see REAL PROPERTY TAX.

TAXATION - TENNESSEE.
Quindry, Kenneth E. The Tennessee constitutional spending limitation . Knoxville , 1979. vii, 69 p. : LC Card 80-621169 DDC 336.3/9/09768 19
HJ2434 .Q56

TAXATION - UNITED STATES.
Sisson, Charles Adair, 1946- Tax burdens in American agriculture . Ames , 1981. p. cm. ISBN 0-8138-1680-7 LC Card 81-8206 DDC 336.2/7863/0973 19
HD1295.U5 S58

TAXATION - UNITED STATES - PERIODICALS.
Compendium of tax research. Washington.
NYPL [JLL 81-3]

TAXATION - UNITED STATES - RATES AND TABLES.
United States. Internal Revenue Service. Tax rates and tables for prior years. [Washington, D.C.?] , 1980. ii leaves, 89 p. : LC Card 80-603934 DDC 343.7305/2 347.30352 19
HJ2381 .U55 1980

TAXATION - VIRGINIA.
Virginia. Division of Industrial Development. An outline of state and local taxes in Virginia. Richmond, Va. [1977] iii leaves, 18 p. ; LC Card 80-621940 DDC 336.2/009755 19
HF2438 .A7 1977

TAXATION - WASHINGTON (STATE) - HANDBOOKS, MANUALS, ETC.
Washington state taxes . [Olympia] [1980] 46 p. : LC Card 81-621438 DDC 343.79704 347.97034 19
HJ2439 .W27

TAXES. see TAXATION.

TAXICABS - NEVADA.
Nevada. Taxicab Authority. Rules and regulations governing service and safety of operations of taxicabs under the jurisdiction of the Taxicab Authority of Nevada /. Carson City [197-] 16 p. ; LC Card 79-625366 DDC 343.793/0982 19
KFN900.T3 A32 1979

Taxonomic revisions of some Upper Cambrian and Lower Ordovician conodonts with comments on their evolution /. Miller, James Frederick, 1943- Lawrence, Kan. , 1980. 39 p., [2] leaves of plates : LC Card 80-623003 DDC 560 s 562/.2 19
QE701 .K33 no. 99 QE899

Taxonomic studies of the Encyrtidae with the descriptions of new species and a new genus (Hymenoptera, Chalcicoidea) /. Gordh, Gordon. Berkeley , 1981. p. cm. ISBN 0-520-09629-0 LC Card 81-1327 DDC 595.79 19
QL568.E6 G67

TAXONOMY (BOTANY) see BOTANY - CLASSIFICATION.

Taxpayer complaints . United States. Congress. House. Committee on Ways and Means. Subcommittee on Oversight. Washington , 1980. iii, 178 p. ; LC Card 80-604065 DDC 353.0072/4 19
KF27 .W345 1980i

TAYLOR, DANIEL B., 1933-
United States. Congress. Senate. Committee on Labor and Human Resources. Nominations . Washington , 1980. ii, 54 p. ; LC Card 80-603437 DDC 353.844 19
KF26 .L27 1980g

Taylor, Deane B. Systematic nursing assessment; a step toward automation. [By] Deane B. Taylor [and] Onalee H. Johnson. Bethesda, U. S. Division of Nursing [for sale by the Supt. of Docs., U. S. Govt. Print. Off., 1974] viii, 164 p. illus. 29 cm. (DHEW publication no. (HRA) 74-17)
1. Information storage and retrieval systems - Nursing. I. Johnson, Onalee H., joint author. II. United States. Public Health Service. Division of Nursing. III. Title.
NYPL [JSF 80-1012]

Taylor, Karen Ann. (joint author) Berman, Susan Folsom. Municipal publications in the public library. Westerly, R. I. [197-] 28 p.;
*NYPL [*XM-13140]*

Taylor, Keith Weller. The birth of Vietnam / Keith Weller Taylor. Berkeley : University of California Press, c1982. p. cm. Revision of thesis (Ph.D.)--University of Michigan, 1976. Bibliography: p. Includes index. ISBN 0-520-04428-2 LC Card 81-11590 DDC 959.7/03 19
1. Vietnam - History - To 939. I. Title.
DS556.6 .T39 1982

TAYLOR, KENNETH, 1934- - MEDALS.
United States. Congress. House. Committee on Banking, Finance and Urban Affairs. Subcommittee on Consumer Affairs. Legislation authorizing issuance of gold medals to Canadian Ambassador Kenneth Taylor, Simon Wiesenthal, Gerald F. Spiess, and commemorative medals for the United States Capitol Historical Society . Washington , 1980. iii, 73 p. ; LC Card 80-601297 DDC 344.73/091 347.30491 19
KF27 .B535 1980c

Taylor, Kenneth A. (joint author) Luloff, A. E. New Hampshire's population . Durham, N.H. [1978?] iv, 37 : LC Card 79-622912 DDC 312/.8/09742 19
HA516 .L84

Taylor, Lynne. Pflieger, William L. The fishes of Missouri /. [Jefferson City] , 1975. viii, 343 p., [2] leaves of plates : LC Card 81-620611 DDC 597.092/9778 19
QL628.M8 P47

Taylor, Richard Lee, 1946- The report of the intensive survey of the Richard B. Russell Dam and Lake, Savannah River, Georgia and South Carolina / assembled by Richard L. Taylor, Marion F. Smith ; prepared by the Institute of Archeology and Anthropology, University of South Carolina. Columbia, S.C. : The Institute, [1978] xvii, 531 p. : ill. ; 27 cm. (Research manuscript series . 142) "December 1978." Bibliography: p. 494-531. LC Card 79-623568 DDC 975.7/35 19
1. Richard B. Russell Lake, Ga. and S.C. - Antiquities. 2. Indians of North America - Richard B. Russell Lake region, Ga. and S.C. - Antiquities. 3. Excavations (Archeology) - Richard B. Russell Lake region, Ga. and S.C. 4. Georgia - Antiquities. 5. South Carolina - Antiquities. I. Smith, Marion F., joint author. II. South Carolina. University. Institute of Archeology and Anthropology. III. Title. IV. Series.
F292.R49 T39

Taylor, Robert Gay, 1940- Effects of bacteria on nitrate and nitrite concentrations in groundwater of the Ogallala aquifer / by Robert G. Taylor, Thomas W. Hassett, Mathew Foster. Las Cruces, N.M. : New Mexico Water Resources Research Institute, [1979] vii, 20 leaves : ill. ; 28 cm. (WRRI report ; no. 114) "December 1979." "Technical completion report project no. 1345630." Bibliography: leaves 19-20. LC Card 80-622275 DDC 333.91/09789 s 628.1/68 19
1. Water, Underground - Pollution - New Mexico. 2. Water - Purification - Nitrogen removal. 3. Water - Bacteriology. 4. Bacteria, Denitrifying. 5. Ogallala Formation. I. Russell, Thomas W., joint author. II. Foster, Mathew, joint author. III. Series: New Mexico State University. Water Resources Research Institute. WRRI report , no. 114. IV. Title.
GB705.N6 N64 no. 114 TD224.N6

Tchad. see Chad.

TEA ROOMS. see RESTAURANTS, LUNCH ROOMS, ETC.

Teacher salary study, 1979-80. South Carolina. Dept. of Education. Office of Research. Management Information Section. 1979-80 teacher salary study /. Columbia, S.C. [1980] iv, 95 p. ; LC Card 80-621884 DDC 331.2/813711/009757 19
LB2842.2 .S64 1980

Teacher strike report, 1977-78, Pennsylvania public schools. Pennsylvania. Dept. of Education. [Harrisburg, PA] [1978] 23 [7], leaves ; LC Card 80-622147 DDC 331.89/2813711/009748 19
LB2844.47.U62 P466

Teacher strike report, 1978-79, Pennsylvania public schools. Pennsylvania. Dept. of Education. [Harrisburg, PA] [1979] 27, [15]

leaves : LC Card 80-622148 DDC 331.89/2813711/009748 19
LB2844.47.U62 P4662

TEACHERS - CERTIFICATION - MICHIGAN.
Michigan. State Board of Education. Administrative rules governing the certification of Michigan teachers /. [Lansing] [1977] iv, 13 p. ; LC Card 80-622894 DDC 379.1/57 19
LB1775 .M55 1977

TEACHERS - CERTIFICATION - NEW MEXICO.
New Mexico. Dept. of Education. New Mexico certification requirements /. Santa Fe, N.M. [1978] vi, 64 p. ; LC Card 79-625368 DDC 379.1/57/09789 19
LB1772.N6 N48 1978

TEACHERS - EMPLOYMENT - HAWAII.
Hawaii. Office of the Legislative Auditor. Evaluation of the job sharing pilot project in the Department of Education. [Honolulu] [1980] 39 p. ; LC Card 80-622012 DDC 353.9969 s 331.25/72 19
HJ9840.5 .A26a no. 80-10 LB2832.3.H3

TEACHERS - IDAHO - SALARIES, PENSIONS, ETC. - STATISTICS.
Idaho. Office of Management Information. School district profiles for the State of Idaho /. Boise, Idaho [1980] 116 p. : LC Card 80-622810 DDC 331.2/813711009796 19
LB2842.2 .I3 1980

TEACHERS - KANSAS - SALARIES, PENSIONS, ETC.
Kansas. State Board of Education. Certificate regulations for school personnel . Topeka, Kan. [1980] ii, 47 p. ; LC Card 80-624208 DDC 379.1/57
LB2842.2 .K34 1980

TEACHERS - MAINE - SALARIES, PENSIONS, ETC. - STATISTICS.
Maine. Dept. of Educational and Cultural Services. Division of Planning and Management Information. Local Administrative Unit. State of Maine public full-time professional staff average salaries for the 1978-79 school year /. [Augusta] [1979?] iv, 47 p. ; LC Card 79-622302 DDC 331.2/813711/009741 19
LB2842.2 .M338 1979

TEACHERS - MISSISSIPPI - SALARIES, PENSIONS, ETC. - PERIODICALS.
Mississippi. Dept. of Education. Division of Administration and Finance. Average salaries of instructional personnel by position assignment and average salaries of instructional personnel and classroom teachers by training levels. Jackson.
NYPL [JLM 80-889]

TEACHERS - MONTANA - SALARIES, PENSIONS, ETC.
Montana. Legislature. Interim Study Committee on Public Systems. Coping with inflation . Helena, Mont. (Room 138, State Capitol, Helena 59620) , 1980. i, 28, [38] p. ; LC Card 81-621342 DDC 353.9786005 19
HD7106.U5 M59 1980

TEACHERS OF SOCIALLY HANDICAPPED CHILDREN, TRAINING OF - UNITED STATES.
Bridge Project. The preparation of teachers for schools in culturally deprived neighborhoods /. Flushing, N. Y. , 1965. xviii, 400 p. ; LC Card 67-61064
NYPL [Sc F 80-191]

TEACHERS - RATING OF - NORTH DAKOTA - CASE STUDIES.
Olson, Ruth Anne. Evaluation as interaction in support of change /. Grand Forks, N.D. , 1980. 33 p. ; LC Card 80-85357 DDC 371.1/44/09784 19
LB2838 .O47

Teachers' seminars on children's thinking . Hull, Bill. Grand Forks, N.D. , 1978. 56 p. ; LC Card 78-52231 DDC 370.15/2 19
LB1117 .H95

TEACHERS - SOUTH CAROLINA - SALARIES, PENSIONS, ETC. - STATISTICS.
South Carolina. Dept. of Education. Office of Research. Management Information Section. 1979-80 teacher salary study /. Columbia, S.C. [1980] iv, 95 p. ; LC Card 80-621884 DDC 331.2/813711/009757 19
LB2842.2 .S64 1980

TEACHERS - TEXAS - SALARIES, PENSIONS, ETC. - STATISTICS.
Texas. Education Agency. Division of State Funding. Texas State public education compensation plan . Austin, Tex. [1980] [22] p. ;   LC Card 80-622335   DDC 331.2/813711/009764 19
LB2842.2 .T47 1980

TEACHERS, TRAINING OF - PENNSYLVANIA - STATISTICS.
Pennsylvania. Dept. of Education. Programs approved for teacher education in Pennsylvania colleges and universities. Harrisburg, PA , 1979. ii, 102 leaves ;   LC Card 80-621835   DDC 370/.7/309748 19
LB2167.P4 P46 1979

TEACHERS, TRAINING OF - UNITED STATES.
Smith, B. Othanel (Bunnie Othanel) A design for a school of pedagogy /. Washington, D.C. , 1980. ix, 118 p. :   LC Card 80-603928   DDC 370/.7/30973 19
LB1715 .S47

TEACHERS' UNIONS - UNITED STATES - BIBLIOGRAPHY.
Wayne State University, Detroit. Archives of Labor and Urban Affairs. An American Federation of Teachers bibliography /. Detroit , 1980. 222 p. ;   ISBN 0-8143-1659-X   LC Card 80-13142
Z5815.U5 W38 1980 LB2844.53.U6
NYPL [JLE 81-27]

TEACHERS - UTAH - SALARIES PENSIONS, ETC.
Utah. Div. of Education Support Services. State & Federal Data Support Services. Salary schedule information on Utah school districts. Salt Lake City, Utah [1979] 201 p. 28 cm.   LC Card 80-622337   DDC 331.2/813711/009792 19
LB2842.2 .U85 1979

TEACHERS - WASHINGTON (D.C.) - BIOGRAPHY.
Hutchinson, Louise Daniel. Anna J. Cooper, a voice from the South /. Washington (A&I Building-2280, Washington, D.C. 20560) , 1981. p. cm.   LC Card 81-5323   DDC 370/.92/4 B 19
F205.N4 C664

TEACHING - ADDRESSES, ESSAYS, LECTURES.
On teaching philosophy /. Bloomington, Ind. , 1980. v. 93 p. ;   LC Card 81-620733   DDC 371.1/02 19
LB41 .O576

TEACHING - AIDS AND DEVICES - CATALOGS - BIBLIOGRAPHY.
Buckingham, Betty Jo. Selection bibliography . Des Moines, Iowa , 1979. 35 p. ;   LC Card 80-623364   DDC 016/.01162 19
Z1037.A1 B83 1979 PN1009.A1

TEACHING MATERIALS. see TEACHING - AIDS AND DEVICES.

TEACHING TOYS. see EDUCATIONAL TOYS.

Teague, George A. (joint author) Shenk, Lynette O. Excavations at the Tubac Presidio /. [Tucson] , 1975. xii, 234 p. :   LC Card 80-621272   DDC 979.1/79 19
F819.T88 S5

Teal, David. Alaska. Unemployment Insurance Research Unit. Unemployment insurance actuarial study and financial handbook /. [Juneau, Alaska] [1979] 68 p. :   LC Card 80-622467   DDC 368.4/4/009798 19
HD7096.U6 A433 1979

Teal, John. Teal, Mildred. Portrait of an island /. Athens, Ga. [1981] p. cm.   ISBN 0-8203-0585-5   LC Card 81-7631   DDC 574.9758/737 19
QH105.G4 T4 1981

Teal, Mildred. Portrait of an island / Mildred Teal and John Teal ; with a new afterword by the authors ; sketches by Richard Rice. Athens, Ga. : University of Georgia Press, [1981] p. cm. Reprint. Originally published: New York : Atheneum, 1964. "Brown Thrasher books." Includes index.   ISBN 0-8203-0585-5   LC Card 81-7631   DDC 574.9758/737 19
1. Natural history - Georgia - Sapelo Island. 2. Sapelo Island (Ga.) - Description and travel. I. Teal, John. II. Title.
QH105.G4 T4 1981

Teamsters, Chauffeurs, Warehousemen and Helpers of America, International Brotherhood of. see International Brotherhood of Teamsters, Chauffeurs, Warehousemen and Helpers of America.

Teamsters Union. see International Brotherhood of Teamsters, Chauffeurs, Warehousemen and Helpers of America.

Teamwork in the delivery of Federal programs to the elderly . United States. Congress. House. Select Committee on Aging. Washington , 1980. v, 18 p. ;   LC Card 80-602675   DDC 362.6/0973 19
HV1461 .U63 1980a

TEAROOMS. see RESTAURANTS, LUNCH ROOMS, ETC.

Tebiwa .
(no. 11) Aikens, C. Melvin. Obsidian hydration dates for Klamath prehistory /. [Pocatello] , 1978. 17 p. :   LC Card 78-623053   DDC 500 s 979.5/2 19
E78.I18 T43 no. 11 E99.K7

(no. 13) Lyman, R. Lee. Prehistoric butchering techniques in the lower granite reservoir, southeastern Washington /. [Pocatello] , 1978. 25 p. :   LC Card 79-620641   DDC 979.7/4 19
E78.I18 T43 no. 13 E78.W3

(no. 17) Nichols, Ralph. Additional early Miocene mammals from the Lemhi Valley of Idaho /. [Pocatello] , 1979. 12 p. :   LC Card 79-624993   DDC 500 s 569 19
E78.I18 T43 no. 17 QE881

Technical advisory panel on the digital data communications network . United States. Congress. House. Committee on House Administration. Policy Group on Information and Computers. Washington , 1981. iv, 163 p. :   LC Card 81-601775   DDC 328.73/072/0684 19
KF27 .H652 1981

Technical analysis of the adequacy of the State implementation plan for the attainment and maintenance of the suspended particulate ambient air quality standards in the Chicago air quality maintenance area . Illinois. Division of Air Pollution Control. [Springfield] [1979- v. ;   LC Card 80-622605   DDC 363.7/39256/097731 19
TD883.5.I46 C44

Technical and economic review of control methods for total dissolved solids, sulfates, chlorides, iron, and manganese /. Huff, Linda L. Chicago, Ill. [1980] ix, 214 p. :   LC Card 80-622964   DDC 628.1/6832 19
TD899.M47 H83

TECHNICAL ASSISTANCE AGREEMENTS. see FOREIGN LICENSING AGREEMENTS.

TECHNICAL ASSISTANCE, AMERICAN.
United States. Congress. House. Committee on Foreign Affairs. Subcommittee on International Economic Policy and Trade. International energy development assistance programs . Washington , 1981. v, 120 p. ;   LC Card 81-601471   DDC 333.79/15/091724 19
KF27 .F6465 1980f

United States. Congress. House. Committee on Foreign Affairs. Subcommittee on International Economic Policy and Trade. Nuclear exports, international safety and environmental issues . Washington , 1980. iii, 226 p. ;   LC Card 80-603801   DDC 363.1/79 19
KF27 .F6465 1979f

United States. Congress. Senate. Committee on Energy and Natural Resources. Subcommittee on Energy Conservation and Supply. International applications of renewable energy resources . Washington , 1980. iii, 240 p. :   LC Card 81-600634   DDC 333.79 19
KF26 .E553 1980d

TECHNICAL ASSISTANCE, AMERICAN - CHINA.
United States. Congress. House. Committee on Science and Technology. Subcommittee on Science, Research, and Technology. Technology transfer to China . Washington , 1980. iii, 236 p. ;   LC Card 80-602094   DDC 338.91/73/051 19
KF27 .S399 1979o

TECHNICAL ASSISTANCE, AMERICAN - EUROPE. see TECHNICAL ASSISTANCE, AMERICAN.

TECHNICAL ASSISTANCE, AMERICAN - INDIA.
United States. Congress. Senate. Committee on Foreign Relations. The Tarapur nuclear fuel export issue . Washington , 1980. iii, 134 p. :   LC Card 80-602987   DDC 382/.4562148335/0973 19
KF26 .F6 1980l

TECHNICAL ASSISTANCE - CONGRESSES.
United Nations Conference on Technical Co-operation Among Developing Countries, Buenos Aires, 1978. The Buenos Aires plan of action for promoting and implementing technical co-operation among developing countries. [New York, N.Y. , 1979?] 23 p. ;   LC Card 79-123512   DDC 338.9172/4 19
HC59.7 .U4816 1978

TECHNICAL COLLEGE, IBADAN, NIGERIA.
Work plan, Western Michigan University-Technical College, Ibadan Project in cooperation with the United States Agency for International Development. [Kalamazoo] , 1966. vii, 53 leaves :   LC Card 81-450648   DDC 607/.116692 19
T173.I27 W67

TECHNICAL EDUCATION - SOUTH CAROLINA - EVALUATION.
South Carolina. Dept. of Education. Assessment of vocational and technical education in South Carolina. [Columbia, S.C.] [1978] 497 p. in various pagings :   LC Card 80-621836   DDC 379/.155 19
LC1046.S7 S68 1978

TECHNICAL EDUCATION - UNITED STATES - DIRECTORIES.
New York (State). University. Office on Noncollegiate Sponsored Instruction. A guide to educational programs in noncollegiate organizations. Albany , 1974. iv, 54 p. ;
NYPL [JFF 80-552]

Technical errors in and clarity of Public Law 95-598 . United States. Congress. House. Committee on the Judiciary. Subcommittee on Civil and Constitutional Rights. Washington , 1980. iii, 162 p. ;   LC Card 80-602797   DDC 346.73/078 19
KF27 .J847 1980

Technical highlights, health and safety research, 1970-1980 /. United States. Bureau of Mines. Avondale, Md. , 1981. p. cm.   LC Card 80-606917   DDC 622/.8 19
TN295 .U5 1981

TECHNICAL INNOVATIONS. see TECHNOLOGICAL INNOVATIONS.

TECHNICAL INSTITUTES. see TECHNICAL EDUCATION.

Technical issue paper series .
(1) Allen, Harry E. Critical Issues in Adult Probation . Washington, D.C. , 1979. vii, 289 p. ;   LC Card 79-604144   DDC 364.6/3/0973 19
HV9304 .A64

Technical options for conservation of metals .
United States. Congress. Office of Technology Assessment. Washington, D.C. [1979] x, 125 p. :   LC Card 79-600172
TA459 .U615 1979   *NYPL [JSF 81-158]*

Technical papers, June 1980. United States. Presidential Commission on World Hunger. [Washington, D.C.] [1980] ii, 201 p. ;   LC Card 80-603138   DDC 338.1/9 19
HD9000.5 .U55 1980b

Technical papers series .
(no. 29) McGinn, Noel F., 1934- Higher education policies in Mexico /. Austin , 1980. 11 p. ;   LC Card 81-621755   DDC 370/.972 19
LC177.M6 M23

(no. 30) Story, Dale, 1950- Entrepreneurs and the state in Mexico . Austin , 1980. 14 p. ;   LC Card 81-621756   DDC 338.972 19
HD3616.M42 S76

TECHNICAL SCHOOLS. see TECHNICAL EDUCATION.

Techniques for project evaluation . Boston, Guy D. [Washington] , 1977. vii, 70 p. ;   LC Card 79-602173   DDC 364/.973/072 19
HV8138 .B587

TECHNOLOGICAL INNOVATIONS - CONGRESSES.
Communication philosophy and the

technological age /. University , c1982. p. cm.
ISBN 0-8173-0077-5 LC Card 81-3420 DDC
001.51/01 19
P96.T42 C6

**TECHNOLOGICAL INNOVATIONS - LAW
AND LEGISLATION - UNITED STATES.**
United States. Congress. House. Committee on
Science and Technology. Subcommittee on
Science, Research, and Technology. H.R. 6910 .
Washington , 1981. iii, 887 p. : LC Card
81-601618 DDC 344.73/095 347.30495 19
KF27 .S399 1980i

United States. Congress. House. Committee on
Small Business. H.R. 5607--Small business
innovation act of 1980 . Washington , 1980. v,
459 p. ; LC Card 80-603308 DDC 346.73/0652 19
KF27 .S6 1980a

United States. Congress. Senate. Select
Committee on Small Business. S. 1860, Small
Business Innovation Act of 1979 . Washington ,
1980 [i.e. 1981] iv, 611 p. : LC Card 81-601186
DDC 346.73/0652 347.306652 19
KF26.5 .S6 1980x

**TECHNOLOGICAL INNOVATIONS -
UNITED STATES.**
Mogee, Mary Ellen. Technology and trade .
Washington , 1980. viii, 36 p. ; LC Card
80-602065 DDC 338/.06 19
HC110.T4 M64

Seminar on Research, Productivity, and the
National Economy, U. S. House of
Representatives, 1980. Seminar on Research,
Productivity, and the National Economy .
Washington , 1980. v, 111 p. : LC Card
80-603648 DDC 338/.06 19
KF27 .S39 1980d

United States. Congress. House. Committee on
Science and Technology. Innovation .
Washington , 1980. v, 228 p. ; LC Card
80-602110 DDC 338/.06 19
KF27 .S39 1979f

United States. Congress. House. Committee on
Science and Technology. Technology trade .
Washington , 1980. vii, 687 p. : LC Card
80-604020 DDC 338.973 19
KF27 .S39 1980g

United States. Congress. House. Committee on
Science and Technology. Subcommittee on
Investigation and Oversight. Small, high
technology firms and innovation . Washington ,
1980 [i.e. 1981] xviii, 791 p. : LC Card
81-600956 DDC 338.6/42/0973 19
KF27 .S3975 1979b

United States. Congress. House. Committee on
Science and Technology. Subcommittee on
Investigations and Oversight. Small, high
technology firms and innovation . Washington ,
1980. v, 65 p. ; LC Card 80-602579 DDC
338.4/76/0973 19
T173.8 .U5 1980

United States. Small Business Administration.
Office of the Chief Counsel for Advocacy.
Small business & innovation . [Washington] ,
1979. 130 p. in various pagings : LC Card
79-603309
HD2346.U5 U57 1979 **NYPL [JLF 81-384]**

**Technological profiles on the iron and steel
industry /.** United Nations. Industrial
Development Organization. New York , 1978.
x, 44 p. : LC Card 79-109235 DDC 300 s
338.4/76691 19
JX1977 .A2 ID/218 TS307

TECHNOLOGICAL TRANSFER. see
TECHNOLOGY TRANSFER.

TECHNOLOGICAL UNEMPLOYMENT. see
UNEMPLOYMENT, TECHNOLOGICAL.

Technologies for the handicapped and the aged .
Bell, Trudy. [Washington] , 1979. iii, 43 p. :
LC Card 80-601228 DDC 617 19
R856 .B4

**TECHNOLOGY - ABSTRACTS -
BIBLIOGRAPHY.**
United States. National Bureau of Standards.
Library. Abstract and index collection, National
Bureau of Standards Library /. Springfield, Va. ,
1980. 59 p. ; **NYPL [JSF 80-657]**

**TECHNOLOGY AND CIVILIZATION -
PERIODICALS.**
Texas. University at Austin. Bureau of Business

Research. Transference of technology series.
NO. 1-3. Austin, 1967-69. 3 v. **NYPL [VA
(Texas. University at Austin. Bureau
Business Research. Transference of
technology series.)]**

Technology and East-West trade. United States.
Congress. Office of Technology Assessment.
Washington, D.C. , 1979. viii, 303 p. : LC Card
79-600203
HF1411 .U615 1979 **NYPL [JLF 81-165]**

TECHNOLOGY AND STATE - CHINA.
Background readings on science, technology,
and energy R. & D. in Japan and China /.
Washington , 1981. xii, 499 p. : LC Card
81-600676 DDC 609.52 19
Q127.J3 B3

TECHNOLOGY AND STATE - JAPAN.
Background readings on science, technology,
and energy R. & D. in Japan and China /.
Washington , 1981. xii, 499 p. : LC Card
81-600676 DDC 609.52 19
Q127.J3 B3

**TECHNOLOGY AND STATE - LATIN
AMERICA.**
Programa Regional de Desarrollo Científico y
Tecnológico. Aspectos organizacionales de la
política científica y tecnológica en América
Latina . Washington, D.C. [1979?] iii, 66 p. ;
LC Card 79-119687
Q127.L38 P76 1979

Programa Regional de Desarrollo Científico y
Tecnológico. Determinación de prioridades de
desarrollo cientificotecnológico a nivel nacional.
Washington, D.C. , 1974. iii, 94 p. : LC Card
80-123437
T24.A1 P76 1974

TECHNOLOGY AND STATE - MAINE.
Maine. State Science, Engineering, and
Technology Study Group. Science in the
Statehouse . Orono , 1979. iii leaves, 57, cxxvi
p. ; LC Card 79-624434 DDC 353.97410085/5 19
Q127.U6 M27 1979

TECHNOLOGY AND STATE - OKLAHOMA.
Reid, George Willard, 1917- Final report on the
Governor's Conference on Research and
Development Priorities for the State of
Oklahoma /. [Norman, Okla. , 1973] 293 p. in
various pagings : LC Card 80-621267 DDC
338.9766 19
T176 .R4

**TECHNOLOGY AND STATE - UNITED
STATES.**
Linking science and technology to public
policy . [Albany] [1979] viii, 156 p. (p.
155-156 blank) : ISBN 0-915194-03-1 LC Card
78-22608 DDC 353.9/172 19
Q127.U6 L56

Planning for trilateral scientific and
technological cooperation by Egypt, Israel, and
the United States . Washington , 1980. vii, 49
p. ; LC Card 80-603873 DDC 327.1/7 19
Q127.U6 P53

United States. Congress. House. Committee on
Science and Technology. Subcommittee on
Science, Research, and Technology. H.R. 6910 .
Washington , 1981. iii, 887 p. : LC Card
81-601618 DDC 344.73/095 347.30495 19
KF27 .S399 1980i

United States. Congress. Senate. Committee on
Commerce, Science, and Transportation.
Subcommittee on Science, Technology, and
Space. Office of Science and Technology
Policy . Washington , 1980. iii, 72 p. ; LC Card
80-603897 DDC 353.0085/5 19
KF26 .C697 1980g

United States. National Science Foundation.
The five-year outlook . [Washington, D.C.]
[1980?- v. ; LC Card 80-603198 DDC 509/.73 19
Q127.U6 U489 1980

United States. President's Commission for a
National Agenda for the Eighties. Panel on
Science and Technology. Science and
technology . Washington , 1981. p. cm. LC
Card 80-28290 DDC 306/.4 19
T21 .U56 1981

**TECHNOLOGY AND STATE - UNITED
STATES - PERIODICALS.**
United States. National Science Foundation.
The Five-year outlook: problems, opportunities

and constraints in science and technology.
1980- [Washington]. **NYPL [JSP 81-1]**

Technology and steel industry competitiveness.
United States. Congress. Office of Technology
Assessment. Washington, D.C. , 1980. vii, 374
p. : LC Card 80-600111
TS303 .U54 1980 **NYPL [JLF 80-1648]**

Technology and the cost of health care . United
States. Congress. House. Committee on Science
and Technology. Subcommittee on Science,
Research, and Technology. Washington , 1980.
v. 16 p. ; LC Card 80-603866 DDC
338.4/33621/0973 19
RA410.53 .U53 1980

**Technology and the handicapped:
telecommunication services in the
rehabilitation of the blind :** conference :
Blockade Runner Motel, Wrightsville Beach,
North Carolina, October 26-29, 1976 / edited
by Nathaniel N. Fullwood ; [sponsored by
Raleigh Lions Clinic for the Blind for the
Division of Services for the Blind, North
Carolina Department of Human Resources].
Raleigh : Office of Publications, School of
Education, North Carolina State University,
1977. v leaves, 163 p. : ill. ; 28 cm. Includes
bibliographical references. LC Card 79-623503 DDC
362.4/183 19
*1. Blind - Rehabilitation - Congresses. 2.
Telecommunication - Apparatus and supplies -
Congresses. 3. Communication devices for the
disabled - Congresses. 4. Blind, Apparatus for the -
Congresses. I. Fullwood, Nathaniel N. II. Raleigh Lions
Clinic for the Blind. III. North Carolina. Division of
Services for the Blind.*
HV1701 .T43

Technology and trade . Mogee, Mary Ellen.
Washington , 1980. viii, 36 p. ; LC Card
80-602065 DDC 338/.06 19
HC110.T4 M64

Technology assessment . Wilson, Carol B.
Washington, D.C. [1979] iv, 32 p. ; LC Card
79-600154 DDC 602/.18 s 001.64 19
QC100 .U57 no. 500-53 QA76.9E95

TECHNOLOGY ASSESSMENT.
United States. Congress. Office of Technology
Assessment. Technology assessment in business
and government . - [Washington] , 1977. xii, 32
[i. e. 33] p. : **NYPL [*XME-9383]**

**TECHNOLOGY ASSESSMENT -
CONGRESSES.**
United Nations Seminar on Technology
Assessment for Development, Bangalore, India,
1978. Technology assessment for development .
New York , 1979. v, 165 p. : LC Card
80-121462 DDC 300 s 338.9/009172/4 19
JX1977 .A2 ST/ESA/95

United States. Library of Congress.
Congressional Research Service. Risk/benefit
analysis in the legislative process . Washington ,
1980. ix, 36 p. ; LC Card 80-602214 DDC
363.1/056/0973 19
T174.5 .U57 1980

Technology assessment for development . United
Nations Seminar on Technology Assessment for
Development, Bangalore, India, 1978. New
York , 1979. v, 165 p. : LC Card 80-121462
DDC 300 s 338.9/009172/4 19
JX1977 .A2 ST/ESA/95

**Technology assessment in business and
government .** United States. Congress. Office of
Technology Assessment. - [Washington] , 1977.
xii, 32 [i. e. 33] p. : **NYPL [*XME-9383]**

**Technology assessment of changes in the future
use and characteristics of the automobile
transportation system.** United States. Congress.
Office of Technology Assessment. Washington
[1979] 2 v. : LC Card 79-600030
HE5623 .U53 1979 **NYPL [JLM 81-210]**

**TECHNOLOGY ASSESSMENT - UNITED
STATES.**
United States. Congress. Office of Technology
Assessment. Technology assessment of changes
in the future use and characteristics of the
automobile transportation system. Washington
[1979] 2 v. : LC Card 79-600030
HE5623 .U53 1979 **NYPL [JLM 81-210]**

United States. Congress. Technology
Assessment Board. Technology assessment
activities in the industrial, academic, and

governmental communities . Washington , 1976.
v, 391 p. : LC Card 77-600690
T174.5 .U56 1976a   *NYPL [*XME-9524]*

TECHNOLOGY - CONGRESSES.
United Nations Conference on Science and
Technology for Development, Vienna, 1979.
Report of the United Nations Conference on
Science and Technology for Development,
Vienna 20-31 August 1979. New York , 1979.
iv, 133 p. ; LC Card 80-100608 DDC 303.4/83 19
JX1977 .A2 A/CONF.81/16

TECHNOLOGY - INDEXES.
United States. Defense Documentation Center.
Directorate of Technical Service. Delimited AD
document index /. - Alexandria, Va. , 1977.
116 p. ;   *NYPL [*XMQ-2162]*

**TECHNOLOGY - INDEXES -
    BIBLIOGRAPHY.**
United States. National Bureau of Standards.
Library. Abstract and index collection, National
Bureau of Standards Library /. Springfield, Va. ,
1980. 59 p. ;   *NYPL [JSF 80-657]*

**TECHNOLOGY - INFORMATION
    SERVICES.**
(1974) North Atlantic Treaty Organization.
Advisory Group for Aerospace Research and
Development. How to obtain information in
different fields of science and technology.
Langley Field, Va., 1974. 1 v. of various
pagings;   *NYPL [JSG 80-127]*

**TECHNOLOGY - INFORMATION
    SERVICES - UNITED STATES -
    DIRECTORIES.**
Directory of federally supported information
analysis centers, 1979 /. Washington , 1979. ix,
87 p. ; LC Card 80-601664 DDC 507/.2 19
Q223.5 .D57 1979

**TECHNOLOGY - INTERNATIONAL
    COOPERATION.**
Planning for trilateral scientific and
technological cooperation by Egypt, Israel, and
the United States . Washington , 1980. vii, 49
p. ; LC Card 80-603873 DDC 327.1/7 19
Q127.U6 P53

United States. Congress. House. Committee on
Science and Technology. Subcommittee on
Science, Research, and Technology. United
States-Mexico scientific and technological
cooperation . Washington , 1979. iii, 289 p. :
    LC Card 80-602192 DDC 338.9 19
KF27 .S399 1979k

**TECHNOLOGY - INTERNATIONAL
    COOPERATION - ADDRESSES, ESSAYS,
    LECTURES.**
Shepard, Marietta Daniels, 1913- ... A solicitud
de los países ... . Washington, D.C. , 1974. 27
p. ; LC Card 80-121848 DDC 020 s 021.6/4 19
Z674 .P182 no. 62 Z738

**The technology of closed system culture of
salmonids** /. Meade, Thomas L. [Narragansett ,
1974] i, 30 p. : LC Card 76-623379 DDC
639.3/755 19
SH154 .M4

**TECHNOLOGY - PERIODICALS -
    BIBLIOGRAPHY - CATALOGS.**
Tucker, Jane C. New serial holdings, 1977 /.
[Washington] [Springfield, Va.] 1977. vi, 232
p. ; LC Card 77-602720
Z7403 .T79 Q158.5   *NYPL [JSF 81-153]*

**Technology, productivity, and labor in the
bituminous coal industry, 1950-79.** United
States. Bureau of Labor Statistics. Washington ,
1980. p. cm. LC Card 80-607858 DDC
331.7/622334/0973 19
HD9545 .U54 1980

Technology sharing report .
(FHWA-TS-80-211) Rothenberg, Morris
Jerome, 1934- Public transportation .
[Washington, D.C.] [1980] viii, 200, [160] p. :
    LC Card 80-602279 DDC 388.4/0973 19
HE308 .R67

TECHNOLOGY - SOCIAL ASPECTS.
United Nations Seminar on Technology
Assessment for Development, Bangalore, India,
1978. Technology assessment for development .
New York , 1979. v, 165 p. : LC Card
80-121462 DDC 300 s 338.9/009172/4 19
JX1977 .A2 ST/ESA/95

TECHNOLOGY - SUBJECT HEADINGS. see
SUBJECT HEADINGS - TECHNOLOGY.

Technology trade . United States. Congress.
House. Committee on Science and Technology.
Washington , 1980. vii, 687 p. : LC Card
80-604020 DDC 338.973 19
KF27 .S39 1980g

TECHNOLOGY TRANSFER.
(1977) Jawaharlal Nehru University. The
pharmaceutical industry in India . [New York]
[1977] iv, 49 p. ; LC Card 81-479945 DDC 300
s 338.4/76151/09543 19
JX1977 .A2 TD/B/C.6/20

(1979) Bell, Trudy. Technologies for the
handicapped and the aged . [Washington] ,
1979. iii, 43 p. : LC Card 80-601228 DDC 617
19
R856 .B4

(1979) Galtung, Johan. Development,
environment, and technology . New York ,
1979. ix, 51 p. : LC Card 80-121830 DDC 300 s
338.9 19
JX1977 .A2 TD/B/C.6/23/Rev.1

(1979) United States. Congress. Office of
Technology Assessment. Technology and
East-West trade. Washington, D.C. , 1979. viii,
303 p. : LC Card 79-600203
HF1411 .U615 1979   *NYPL [JLF 81-165]*

(1980) United States. Congress. House.
Committee on Science and Technology.
Subcommittee on Science, Research, and
Technology. Technology transfer conference .
Washington , 1980. iii, 212 p. : LC Card
80-602824 DDC 338.973 19
KF27 .S399 1979p

(1980) United States. Congress. House.
Committee on Science and Technology.
Subcommittee on Science, Research, and
Technology. Technology transfer to China .
Washington , 1980. iii, 236 p. ; LC Card
80-602094 DDC 338.91/73/051 19
KF27 .S399 1979o

(1980) United States. Congress. Senate.
Committee on Governmental Affairs.
Permanent Subcommittee on Investigations.
Transfer of technology to the Soviet bloc .
Washington , 1980. iii, 156 p. ; LC Card
80-602191 DDC 338.91/73/047 19
KF26 .G674 1980

TECHNOLOGY TRANSFER - CHINA.
United States. Congress. House. Committee on
Science and Technology. Subcommittee on
Science, Research, and Technology. Technology
transfer to China . Washington , 1980. v, 35
p. ; LC Card 80-603271 DDC 338.91/73/051 19
T174.3 .U55 1980

Technology transfer conference . United States.
Congress. House. Committee on Science and
Technology. Subcommittee on Science,
Research, and Technology. Washington , 1980.
iii, 212 p. ; LC Card 80-602824 DDC 338.973 19
KF27 .S399 1979p

Technology transfer to China . United States.
Congress. House. Committee on Science and
Technology. Subcommittee on Science,
Research, and Technology. Washington , 1980.
iii, 236 p. ; LC Card 80-602094 DDC
338.91/73/051 19
KF27 .S399 1979o

Technology transfer to China . United States.
Congress. House. Committee on Science and
Technology. Subcommittee on Science,
Research, and Technology. Washington , 1980.
v, 35 p. ; LC Card 80-603271 DDC
338.91/73/051 19
T174.3 .U55 1980

**TECHNOLOGY TRANSFER - UNITED
    STATES.**
United States. Congress. House. Committee on
Science and Technology. Subcommittee on
Science, Research, and Technology. Technology
transfer to China . Washington , 1980. v, 35
p. ; LC Card 80-603271 DDC 338.91/73/051 19
T174.3 .U55 1980

**TECHNOLOGY - UNDERDEVELOPMED
    AREAS.** see **UNDERDEVELOPED
    AREAS - TECHNOLOGY.**

TECHNOLOGY - UNITED STATES.
Quammen, David, 1948- Appropriate jobs .
Butte, Mont. , c1980. 14 p. : LC Card 80-138213
    DDC 331.12/0973 19
HC103.7 .Q35

United States. National Science Foundation.
The five-year outlook . [Washington, D.C.]
[1980?- v. ; LC Card 80-603198 DDC 509/.73 19
Q127.U6 U489 1980

TECTONOPHYSICS. see **GEODYNAMICS.**

TEEN-AGE. see **ADOLESCENCE.**

TEEN-AGERS. see **YOUTH.**

**Teenage patients of family planning clinics,
United States, 1978** /. Eckard, Eugenia.
Hyattsville, Md. , 1981. p. cm. LC Card
81-11113 DDC 362.1/1/0973 s 362.1/2 19
RA407.3 .A349 no. 57 HQ766.5.U5

Teenage smoking . Green, Dorothy E.
Washington, D.C. [1979] ix, 259 p. ; LC Card
80-601231 DDC 362.2/9 19
HV5745 .G74

Teeples, Gary Ronald.
Accelerated Indexing Systems. Massachusetts
1840 census index /. Bountiful, Utath , 1978.
[60], 344 p. :
                NYPL [APR (Massachusetts) 81-115]

Accelerated Indexing Systems. Michigan 1850
census index. /. Bountiful, Utah , 1978. [60],
299 p. :   *NYPL [APR (Michigan) 81-117]*

(joint author. 0700) Jackson, Ronald Vern.
Kentucky 1830 census index /. Bountiful,
Utah , c1976. [23], 206 p. : LC Card 78-112588
F450 .J316

Teilborg, Judy Raye. (joint author) Washichek, Jack
N. Summary of snow survey measurements for
Colorado and New Mexico, 1971-1977 .
Denver, Colo. [1978] xxiii, 128 p. : LC Card
79-601670 DDC 551.57/9/788 19
GB2625.C6 W37

The Tejano community, 1836-1900 /. De Leon,
Arnoldo, 1945- Albuquerque [1982] p. cm.
    ISBN 0-8263-0586-5 : LC Card 81-52053
    DDC 976.4/0046872 19
F395.M5 D4

TELECOMMUNICATION - ALASKA.
Alaska. Instructional Television. A report on
the feasibility of telecommunications for
instruction in the State of Alaska /. [Juneau]
[1980] 225 p. in various pagings ; LC Card
80-622196 DDC 371.3/358/09798 19
LB1044.8 .A43 1980

**TELECOMMUNICATION - APPARATUS
    AND SUPPLIES - CONGRESSES.**
Technology and the handicapped:
telecommunication services in the rehabilitation
of the blind . Raleigh , 1977. v leaves, 163 p. :
    LC Card 79-623503 DDC 362.4/183 19
HV1701 .T43

**TELECOMMUNICATION EQUIPMENT
    INDUSTRY - GOVERNMENT POLICY -
    JAPAN.**
Gresser, Julian. High technology and Japanese
industrial policy . Washington , 1980. xiii, 73
p. : LC Card 80-603865 DDC
338.4/5621381958/0952 19
HD9696.S43 J33

TELECOMMUNICATION IN MINING. see
MINE COMMUNICATION SYSTEMS.

**TELECOMMUNICATION -
    INTERNATIONAL COOPERATION -
    CONGRESSES.**
United States. Congress. House. Committee on
Foreign Affairs. Subcommittee on International
Operations. The World Administrative Radio
Conference and international communications
policy . Washington , 1980. iii, 135 p. : LC
    Card 80-603991 DDC 384.54 19
KF27 .F647 1979e

**TELECOMMUNICATION - LAW AND
    LEGISLATION - UNITED STATES.**
United States. Congress. House. Committee on
the Judiciary. Subcommittee on Monopolies and
Commercial Law. Telecommunications Act of
1980 . Washington , 1981. iii, 803 p. : LC Card
81-601614 DDC 343.73/0994/0262
347.3039940262 19
KF27. J8663 1980b

**TELECOMMUNICATION - NORTH
    CAROLINA.**
North Carolina. Task Force on Public
Telecommunications. Interconnections for
North Carolina and beyond . [Raleigh, 1979] vi,
114 p. : LC Card 80-620760
HE7791.N8 N67 1979

TELECOMMUNICATION - PACIFIC AREA - CONGRESSES.
Pacific Telecommunications Conference, Honolulu, 1979. Pacific Telecommunications Conference . Honolulu , 1979. ca. 500 p. in various pagings : LC Card 79-110059
TK5102.3.P32 P32 1979
NYPL [JLF 80-1628]

TELECOMMUNICATION POLICY - NEW YORK (STATE)
New York (State). Commission on Cable Television. Cable communications in New York State . Albany, N.Y. , 1979. xii, 222 p. : LC Card 80-622826 DDC 384.55/56/09747 19
HE7791.N7 N48 1979

TELECOMMUNICATION POLICY - NORTH CAROLINA.
North Carolina. Task Force on Public Telecommunications. Interconnections for North Carolina and beyond . [Raleigh, 1979] vi, 114 p. : LC Card 80-620760
HE7791.N8 N67 1979

TELECOMMUNICATION POLICY - UNITED STATES.
Communications research and development /. Washington , 1980 [i.e. 1981] viii, 34 p. : LC Card 81-601506 DDC 621.38/072073 19
TK5102.8.U6 C65

United States. Congress. House. Committee on Science and Technology. Subcommittee on Transportation, Aviation, and Communications. Communications research and development . Washington , 1980. iii, 481 p. : LC Card 80-603502 DDC 384/.072073 19
KF27 .S3997 1980d

TELECOMMUNICATION - RESEARCH - UNITED STATES.
Communications research and development /. Washington , 1980 [i.e. 1981] viii, 34 p. ; LC Card 81-601506 DDC 621.38/072073 19
TK5102.8.U6 C65

United States. Congress. House. Committee on Science and Technology. Subcommittee on Transportation, Aviation, and Communications. Communications research and development . Washington , 1980. iii, 481 p. : LC Card 80-603502 DDC 384/.072073 19
KF27 .S3997 1980d

United States. Congress. House. Committee on Science and Technology. Subcommittee on Transportation, Aviation, and Communications. Compendium of Federal government communications R. & D. planned for fiscal year 1980-81 funding (civil agencies) /. Washington , 1980. v, 188 p. : LC Card 80-602263 DDC 380.3/0724 19
TK5102.8.U6 U54 1980

TELECOMMUNICATION - TRAFFIC.
MacCalden, M, Scott. Feasibility study of closed circuit television for traffic surveillance. [Sacramento] 1973. 74, 10 p. :
NYPL [JLF 80-556]

TELECOMMUNICATION - VIRGINIA.
Virginia. Telecommunications Study Commission. Telecommunications, a new Virginia initiative . Richmond, Va. , 1980. 79 p. ; LC Card 80-621795 DDC 300/.9755 s 353.975504 19
J87 .V9 1980b, no. 22 JK3949.C65

Telecommunications, a new Virginia initiative .
Virginia. Telecommunications Study Commission. Richmond, Va. , 1980. 79 p. ; LC Card 80-621795 DDC 300/.9755 s 353.975504 19
J87 .V9 1980b, no. 22 JK3949.C65

Telecommunications Act of 1980 . United States. Congress. House. Committee on the Judiciary. Subcommittee on Monopolies and Commercial Law. Washington , 1981. iii, 803 p. : LC Card 81-601614 DDC 343.73/0994/0262 347.3039940262 19
KF27. J8663 1980b

TELECOMMUNICATIONS - ALASKA.
Stanley, Glenn M. Interim report [on the development of telecommunications for the State of Alaska] /. Juneau, Alaska [1980] 52 p. ; LC Card 80-623344 DDC 384/.09798 19
HE7791.A4 S72

TELECOMMUNICATIONS - LAW AND LEGISLATION - UNITED STATES.

United States. Federal Trade Commission. Media policy session . Washington, D.C. , 1980. vi, 167, [37] p. ; LC Card 80-602844 DDC 343.73/0994 19
KF2765 .A355

TELECONFERENCING - ALASKA.
Alaska. Instructional Television. A report on the feasibility of telecommunications for instruction in the State of Alaska /. [Juneau] [1980] 225 p. in various pagings ; LC Card 80-622196 DDC 371.3/358/09798 19
LB1044.8 .A43 1980

TELEPHONE - ILLINOIS.
Illinois. Commerce Commission. 911 emergency telephone systems . [Springfield, Ill.] [1979] 16 p. ; LC Card 79-625197 DDC 384.6/42 19
TK6024.I3 I44 1979

TELEPHONE - LAW AND LEGISLATION - UNITED STATES.
United States. Congress. House. Committee on Interstate and Foreign Commerce. Subcommittee on Communications. Hearing--impaired . Washington , 1980. iii, 140 p. : LC Card 80-603358 DDC 343.73/09943 19
KF27 .I5537 1980c

TELEPHONE - TEXAS - EMERGENCY REPORTING SYSTEMS.
Texas. Advisory Commission on Intergovernmental Relations. 911 and other emergency single-number access systems in Texas . Austin, Tex. [foreword 1979] ix, 226 p. : LC Card 80-621339 DDC 384.6/42 19
TK6024.T4 T49 1979

TELEPHONE - UNITED STATES - APPARATUS AND SUPPLIES.
United States. Congress. House. Committee on Interstate and Foreign Commerce. Subcommittee on Communications. Hearing--impaired . Washington , 1980. iii, 140 p. : LC Card 80-603358 DDC 343.73/09943 19
KF27 .I5537 1980c

TELEPHONE - UNITED STATES - RATES.
Alleman, James H. The pricing structure of local telephone service . [Boulder, Colo.] , 1977. 21 p. ; LC Card 77-602916 DDC 384.6/3 19
HE8825 .A6

TELEPROCESSING NETWORKS. see COMPUTER NETWORKS.

TELETRAFFIC. see TELECOMMUNICATION - TRAFFIC.

TELEVISION ADVERTISING AND CHILDREN - RESEARCH - UNITED STATES.
Research on the effects of television advertising on children . [Washington] [1977] viii, 229 p. : LC Card 77-604793
HQ784.T4 R47   **NYPL [*XME-9373]**

TELEVISION ADVERTISING AND CHILDREN - UNITED STATES.
Research on the effects of television advertising on children . [Washington] [1977] viii, 229 p. : LC Card 77-604793
HQ784.T4 R47   **NYPL [*XME-9373]**

United States. Federal Trade Commission. FTC staff report on television advertising to children. [Washington] 19. 394 p. in various pagings ; LC Card 79-601465
HF6146.T42 U55 1978 **NYPL [JLF 81-278]**

TELEVISION AND CHILDREN.
Johnston, Jerome. An evaluation of Freestyle . Ann Arbor, Mich. , 1980. x, 297 p. : ISBN 0-87944-256-5 (pbk.) LC Card 80-81676
HQ784.T4 J63   **NYPL [JLF 81-164]**

TELEVISION AUDIENCES - ILLINOIS - STATISTICS.
Elrick and Lavidge. Public library usage in Illinois . Springfield , 1977. 31 p. : LC Card 78-620783 DDC 302.2/3 19
HE8700.7.A8 E57 1977 suppl

TELEVISION BROADCASTING - NEW JERSEY - PERIODICALS.
New Jersey. Public Broadcasting Authority. Instructional television programming (secondary). Trenton. **NYPL [MWGB 81-12]**

TELEVISION BROADCASTING - UNITED STATES - HISTORY.
Udelson, Joseph H., 1943- The great television race . University, Ala. , c1982. p. cm. ISBN 0-8173-0082-1 LC Card 81-7562 DDC

384.55/0973 19
HD9696.T463 U67

TELEVISION IN EDUCATION - ALASKA.
Alaska. Instructional Television. A report on the feasibility of telecommunications for instruction in the State of Alaska /. [Juneau] [1980] 225 p. in various pagings ; LC Card 80-622196 DDC 371.3/358/09798 19
LB1044.8 .A43 1980

TELEVISION IN EDUCATION - CALIFORNIA - EVALUATION.
Timar, Thomas. "Sunset" review of instructional television (ITV) . [Sacramento] [1981] 33 leaves ; LC Card 81-621873 DDC 371.3/358/09794 19
LB1044.7 .T53

TELEVISION IN EDUCATION - ILLINOIS.
Illinois. Educational Television Commission. A State plan for educational television in Illinois /. [Springfield] [1977?] iv, 16 leaves, [2] leaves of plates : LC Card 80-620585 DDC 371.3/358/09773 19
LB1044.7 .I39 1977

TELEVISION IN EDUCATION - NEW JERSEY - PERIODICALS.
New Jersey. Public Broadcasting Authority. Instructional television programming (secondary). Trenton. **NYPL [MWGB 81-12]**

TELEVISION INDUSTRY - ASIA.
United States. International Trade Commission. Color television receivers and subassemblies thereof . Washington, D.C. [1980] 144 p. in various pagings : LC Card 80-602557 DDC 382/.4562138804/0973 19
HD9696.T463 U68 1980

TELEVISION INDUSTRY - UNITED STATES.
United States. International Trade Commission. Color television receivers and subassemblies thereof . Washington, D.C. [1980] 144 p. in various pagings : LC Card 80-602557 DDC 382/.4562138804/0973 19
HD9696.T463 U68 1980

TELEVISION INDUSTRY - UNITED STATES - HISTORY.
Udelson, Joseph H., 1943- The great television race . University, Ala. , c1982. p. cm. ISBN 0-8173-0082-1 LC Card 81-7562 DDC 384.55/0973 19
HD9696.T463 U67

TELEVISION - LAW AND LEGISLATION - UNITED STATES.
United States. Congress. House. Committee on Interstate and Foreign Commerce. Subcommittee on Communications. Financial disclosure . Washington , 1980. iii, 99 p. ; LC Card 80-602502 DDC 343.73/09945 19
KF27 .I5537 1980a

United States. Congress. House. Committee on Interstate and Foreign Commerce. Subcommittee on Communications. Prohibited renewal considerations and crossownership restrictions . Washington , 1980. iii, 98 p. ; LC Card 80-602804 DDC 343.73/09945 19
KF27 .I5537 1980b

TELEVISION STATIONS - LICENSES - UNITED STATES.
United States. Congress. House. Committee on Interstate and Foreign Commerce. Subcommittee on Communications. Financial disclosure . Washington , 1980. iii, 99 p. ; LC Card 80-602502 DDC 343.73/09945 19
KF27 .I5537 1980a

Tell me about your school . Ginzberg, Eli, 1911- Washington, D.C. [1979] 79 p. ; LC Card 80-602363 DDC 371.8/1 19
LA339.N5 G48

Tell me, child: poems by the children of District 6; a project of Community School District 6, The Arts in General Education Program. New York: Community School District 6, c1980. 134 p.: ill.; 21 cm. Cover title.
1. Children's poetry, American - New York (City). I. New York (City). Community School Board. District 6.
NYPL [JFD 81-25]

Teller, Charles H., 1941- Cuantos somos . Austin , 1977. xvi, 238 p. ; ISBN 0-292-71045-3 (pbk.) LC Card 77-93093 DDC 304.6/089687 19
E184.M5 C8

TEMEPHOS - PHYSIOLOGICAL EFFECT.
Sanders, Herman O. Abate - effects of the
organophosphate insecticide on bluegills and
invertebrates in ponds /. Washington, D.C. ,
1981. 6 p. : LC Card 80-606806 DDC 639 s
628.9/657 19
SH11 .A313 no. 104 SH177.P44

TEMPERANCE - STUDY AND TEACHING.
see ALCOHOLISM - STUDY AND
TEACHING.

TEMPERATURE, ANIMAL AND HUMAN.
see BODY TEMPERATURE.

TEMPERATURE CONTROL.
Staff study of the emergency building
temperature regulations /. Washington , 1980
[i.e. 1981] v, 36 p. ; LC Card 81-600667 DDC
333.79 19
TJ163.5.B84 S7

TEMPERATURE CURVE. see BODY
TEMPERATURE.

TEMPERATURES, LOW. see LOW
TEMPERATURES.

Temple, Barker & Sloane. United States.
Maritime Administration. Office of Policy and
Plans. The maritime aids of the six major
maritime nations, /. [Washington] , 1977. ca.
500 p. in various pagings : LC Card 78-600514
HE741 .U55 1977 **NYPL [*XME-9415]**

**Temple Christian Church of the Disciples of
Christ Denomination.** see Peoples Temple.

**Temporal trends in the acidity of precipitation
and surface waters of New York /.** Peters,
Norman E. Reston, Va. , 1981. p. cm. LC Card
81-607082 DDC 551.57/09747 19
GB2825.N7 P47

Temporary employees retirement . North
Carolina. Legislative Research Commission.
Raleigh (State Legislative Building, Raleigh
27611) [1981] viii, 7, [25] p. ; LC Card
81-621507 DDC 344.756/012529 347.560412529
19
KFN7835.5 .A25 1981

Temporary housing feasibility study . Boise State
University. Center for Research, Grants, and
Contracts. Boise, Idaho [1979] 95, [53] p. :
LC Card 80-621684 DDC 363.5/8 19
HV554.5 .B64 1979

Ten First Street, Southeast . Hilker, Helen-Anne.
Washington , 1980. iii, 102 p. : ISBN
0-8444-0351-2 LC Card 80-607808 DDC
027.5753 19
Z679.2.U54 H54

Ten First Street, Southeast . Hilker, Helen-Anne.
Washington , 1981. p. cm. ISBN 0-8444-0368-7
LC Card 81-607983 DDC 027.573/074/0153 19
Z679.2.U54 H54 1981

Ten Haaf, C. J. (joint author) Ames, Glenn C. W.
Analysis of domestic grain supply in the
European Community, 1960-1974 /. [Athens,
Ga.] [1979] 47 p. ; LC Card 79-625644 DDC
382/.4131/094 19
HD9045.E82 A43

Ten Mile River. Lord, Sabin M. Ten Mile River
study, 1968 /. [Boston] [1970]- v. ; LC Card
80-120118 DDC 363.7/3942/0974485 19
TD224.M4 L67

Ten Mile River. Massachusetts. Division of Water
Pollution Control. Water Quality Section. Ten
Mile River basin . Westborough , 1975. 77, [45]
p. : LC Card 77-622203 DDC
363.7/39456/0974485 19
TD224.M4 M36 1975c

Ten Mile River. Massachusetts. Division of Water
Pollution Control. Water Quality Section. Ten
Mile River basin . Westborough, Mass. , 1976.
46 p. ; LC Card 77-622202 DDC
363.7/39456/0974485 19
TD224.M4 M36 1976b

Ten Mile River. Massachusetts. Water Quality
and Research Section. Ten Mile River basin .
Westborough [1978] 42 p. : LC Card 79-620593
DDC 363.7/3942/0974485 19
TD224.M4 M39 1978b

Ten Mile River basin . Massachusetts. Division of
Water Pollution Control. Water Quality Section.
Westborough , 1975. 77, [45] p. : LC Card
77-622203 DDC 363.7/39456/0974485 19
TD224.M4 M36 1975c

Ten Mile River basin . Massachusetts. Division of
Water Pollution Control. Water Quality Section.
Westborough, Mass. , 1976. 46 p. ; LC Card
77-622202 DDC 363.7/39456/0974485 19
TD224.M4 M36 1976b

Ten Mile River basin . Massachusetts. Water
Quality and Research Section. Westborough
[1978] 42 p. : LC Card 79-620593 DDC
363.7/3942/0974485 19
TD224.M4 M39 1978b

Ten Mile River study, 1968 /. Lord, Sabin M.
[Boston] [1970]- v. : LC Card 80-120118 DDC
363.7/3942/0974485 19
TD224.M4 L67

Ten women of mystery. 10 women of mystery /.
Bowling Green, Ohio , c1981. 304 p. : ISBN
0-87972-172-3 LC Card 80-85393 DDC
823/.0872/099287 19
PS374.D4 A12

**Tendencias y estructuras de la economía de Chile
en el último decenio /.** United Nations.
Economic Commission for Latin America.
[Nueva York] , 1972. iv, 35 p. ; LC Card
80-106375
JX1977 .A213 E/CN.12/929 HC192

Teng, Mei Su. The Photographer's hand /.
Washington, D.C. , c1980. p. cm. LC Card
80-27845 DDC 779/.09/047074013 19
TR646.U5 P45

Tennant, Peter A.
Ipswich River study, 1968 / Peter A. Tennant.
Part A, data record on water quality. Boston :
Division of Water Pollution Control,
Massachusetts Water Resources Commission,
[1969] [16] p. : map ; 28 cm. No more published.
"December 1969." Tables. LC Card 80-118035 DDC
363.7/3942/097445 19
*1. Water quality - Massachusetts - Ipswich River
watershed. I. Massachusetts. Division of Water
Pollution Control. II. Title.*
TD224.M4 T462 1969

Mystic River study, 1967 / Peter A. Tennant
and William R. Jobin. Part A, data record on
water quality. Boston : Division of Water
Pollution Control, Massachusetts Water
Resources Commission, [1970] 11 leaves :
map ; 28 cm. No more published. "February 1970."
Chiefly tables. LC Card 80-118857 DDC
363.7/3942/097444 19
*1. Water quality - Massachusetts - Mystic River
watershed - Statistics. I. Jobin, William R., joint author.
II. Massachusetts. Division of Water Pollution Control.
III. Title.*
TD224.M4 T464

TENNECO INC.
United States. Geological Survey. Summary of
hydrologic testing in Tertiary limestone aquifer,
Tenneco offshore exploratory well-Atlantic
OCS, lease-block 427 (Jacksonville NH 17-5) /.
Washington , 1981. p. cm. LC Card 80-606901
DDC 553/.79/09759 19
GB1199.2 .U54 1981

Tennessee agribusiness /. McManus, Benny R.
Knoxville [1979] 38 p. (p. 38 blank for
"Notes") : LC Card 80-622069 DDC 338.1/09768
19
HD9007.T2 M32

**Tennessee. Agricultural Experiment Station,
Knoxville.**
Bulletin .
(592) McManus, Benny R. Tennessee
agribusiness /. Knoxville [1979] 38 p. (p. 38
blank for "Notes") : LC Card 80-622069 DDC
338.1/09768 19
HD9007.T2 M32

TENNESSEE - ANTIQUITIES.
Mainfort, Robert C., 1948- Archaeological
investigations at Fort Pillow State Historic
Area, 1976-1978 /. [Nashville] , 1980. ix, 198
p. : LC Card 80-623480 DDC 976.8/16 19
F443.L35 M34

Smith, Samuel D. Historical background and
archaeological testing of the Davy Crockett
Birthplace State Historical Area, Greene
County, Tennessee /. [Nashville, Tenn.] 1980.
v, 67 p. : LC Card 80-623481 DDC 976.8/91 19
F444.D28 S64

**TENNESSEE - APPROPRIATIONS AND
EXPENDITURES.**
Quindry, Kenneth E. The Tennessee

constitutional spending limitation . Knoxville ,
1979. vii, 69 p. : LC Card 80-621169 DDC
336.3/9/09768 19
HJ2434 .Q56

Tennessee - Archaeology. see Tennessee -
Antiquities.

TENNESSEE - BIOGRAPHY.
Williams, Frank Broyles, 1913- Tennessee's
presidents /. Knoxville , c1981. p. cm. ISBN
0-87049-321-3 : LC Card 81-3391 DDC
973/.09/92 B 19
E176.1 .W7225

TENNESSEE - CHURCH HISTORY.
Norton, Herman Albert. Religion in Tennessee,
1777-1945 /. Knoxville , c1981. p. cm. ISBN
0-87049-317-5 : LC Card 81-1562 DDC
280/.09768 19
BR555.T2 N67

Tennessee. Conservation, Dept. of. see Tennessee.
Dept. of Conservation.

**The Tennessee constitutional spending
limitation .** Quindry, Kenneth E. Knoxville ,
1979. vii, 69 p. : LC Card 80-621169 DDC
336.3/9/09768 19
HJ2434 .Q56

Tennessee county history series.
(6) Lillard, Roy G. Bradley County /.
Memphis, Tenn. , c1980. x, 133 p. : ISBN
0-87870-099-4 LC Card 80-152916 DDC
976.8/873 19
F443.B8 L54

Tennessee. Dept. of Conservation. (Old Catalog
form: Tennessee. Conservation Dept.)
Tennessee. Laws, statutes, etc. Tennessee laws,
rules, and regulations for restaurants. Nashville,
Tenn. [1952] 33 p. ; LC Card 79-119875 DDC
344.768/0464 347.6804464 19
KFT282.H6 A3 1952

**Tennessee. Dept. of Conservation. Division of
Geology.** see Tennessee. Division of Geology.

**Tennessee. Dept. of Employment Security.
Research and Statistics Section.**
Occupational employment of selected
nonmanufacturing industries in Tennessee, 1975
/ prepared by Research and Statistics Section.
[Nashville] : The Section, [1977] i, 61 leaves :
graphs ; 28 cm. LC Card 78-621484 DDC
331.12/09768 19
*1. Labor supply - Tennessee - Statistics. 2. Tennessee -
Occupations - Statistics. 3. Employment forecasting -
Tennessee - Statistics. I. Title.*
HD5725.T4 T413 1977c

Tennessee. Division of Archaeology.
**Research series - Division of Archaeology,
Tennessee Department of Conservation .**
(no. 4) Mainfort, Robert C., 1948-
Archaeological investigations at Fort Pillow
State Historic Area, 1976-1978 /.
[Nashville] , 1980. ix, 198 p. : LC Card
80-623480 DDC 976.8/16 19
F443.L35 M34

(no. 6) Smith, Samuel D. Historical
background and archaeological testing of the
Davy Crockett Birthplace State Historical
Area, Greene County, Tennessee /.
[Nashville, Tenn.] 1980. v, 67 p. : LC Card
80-623481 DDC 976.8/91 19
F444.D28 S64

Tennessee. Division of Geology.
Bulletin .
(79) Geology of Hamilton County,
Tennessee. [Nashville] , 1979. 128 p. : LC
Card 80-622067 DDC 557.68 s 557.68/82 19
QE165 .A2 no. 79 QE166.H29

(80) Corgan, James X. Natural bridges of
Tennessee /. Nashville , 1979. viii, 102 p. :
LC Card 79-626059 DDC 557.68 s 551.4 19
QE165 .A2 no. 80 GB565.T4

Miller, Robert A. Environmental geology
summary of the Bellevue quadrangle, Tennessee
/. [Nashville] , 1980. vi, 21 p. : LC Card
80-622527 DDC 557.68/55 19
QE166.D38 M54

Miller, Robert A. Geologic hazards map of
Tennessee /. [Nashville] , 1977. 1 map : 34 x
127 cm. Scale ca. 1:633,600. Shows earthquake,
landslide, karst, and flooding areas. Published jointly
with the State Planning Office, Natural Resources
Section. Includes text. Bibliography. LC Card

79-691501
G3961.C5 1977 .M5
NYPL [Map Div. 81-3060]

Tennessee domestic relations law for attorneys and legal assistants / text, Stephen M. Sumner, primary contributor and general editor ; forms, Susan D. Kovac, primary contributor and general editor. Knoxville, Tenn. (1505 W. Cumberland Ave., Knoxville 37916) : Public Law Institute, University of Tennessee, College of Law, c1980. 1 v. (various pagings) : forms ; 28 cm. LC Card 81-132962 DDC 346.76801/5 347.680615 19
1. Domestic relations - Tennessee. I. Sumner, Stephen M. II. Kovac, Susan D. III. University of Tennessee, Knoxville. Public Law Institute.
KFT94 .T45

TENNESSEE - ECONOMIC CONDITIONS.
University of Tennessee, Knoxville. Center for Business and Economic Research. An economic report to the Governor of the State of Tennessee on the State's economic outlook /. Nashville, Tenn. [1979] xiv, 246 p. ; LC Card 79-623072 DDC 338.5/443/09768 19
HC107.T3 U53 1979

Tennessee. General Assembly. Joint Subcommittee on Hazardous Materials.
Report of the Joint Subcommittee of the House and Senate Transportation Committees on Hazardous Materials / William B. (Bill) Nolan, chairman. [Nashville] : General Assembly of Tennessee, [1980] 77 p. ; 28 cm. Cover title. LC Card 80-623841 DDC 343.768/093 347.680393 19
1. Hazardous substances - Transportation - Law and legislation - Tennessee. 2. Hazardous substances - Tennessee - Transportation. I. Title.
KFT11.62 .H39 1980

Tennessee. General Assembly. Legislative Council Committee. Legislators' manual. Nashville. 22 cm.
1. Tennessee. General Assembly - Rules and practice.
NYPL [JLK 80-140 & D-14 2542]

TENNESSEE. GENERAL ASSEMBLY - RULES AND PRACTICE.
Tennessee. General Assembly. Legislative Council Committee. Legislators' manual. Nashville. **NYPL [JLK 80-140 & D-14 2542]**

Tennessee. General Assembly. Special Joint Committee Created Pursuant to House Joint Resolution No. 308. Sudy of the laws concerning annexation, 1980 : final report of the Special Joint Committee Created Pursuant to House Joint Resolution No. 308 / Joseph A. Barnes, Katy Varney. Nashville, Tenn. (Suite G-10, War Memorial Bldg., Nashville, Tenn. 37219) : Office of Legal Services for the General Assembly, [1980] 105 p. : maps ; 28 cm. Cover title. LC Card 80-624151 DDC 352/.006/09768 19
1. Annexation (Municipal government) - Tennessee. I. Barnes, Joseph A. II. Varney, Katy. III. Title.
KFT431.9.A5 A25 1980

Tennessee. Geology, Division of. see Tennessee. Division of Geology.

Tennessee Historical Commission. Williams, Frank Broyles, 1913- Tennessee's presidents /. Knoxville , c1981. p. cm. ISBN 0-87049-321-3 : LC Card 81-3391 DDC 973/.09/92 B 19
E176.1 .W7225

Tennessee historical quarterly. v. 1- ; 1942- Nashville. illus. 25 cm. Supersedes the Tennessee historical magazine (in Old Catalog). Published jointly by the Tennessee Historical Society and Tennessee Historical Commission.
1. Tennessee - History - Periodicals. I. Tennessee Historical Society. II. Tennessee State Historical Commission. **NYPL [IAA (Tennesse historical quarterly)]**

Tennessee Historical Society. Tennessee historical quarterly. v. 1- ; 1942- Nashville. **NYPL [IAA (Tennessee historical quarterly)]**

TENNESSEE - HISTORY.
Lamon, Lester C., 1942- Blacks in Tennessee /. Knoxville , c1981. p. cm. ISBN 0-87049-323-X : LC Card 81-3396 DDC 976.8/00496073 19
E185.93.T3 L36

TENNESSEE - HISTORY - PERIODICALS.
Tennessee historical quarterly. v. 1- ; 1942- Nashville. **NYPL [IAA (Tennessee historical quarterly)]**

TENNESSEE - HISTORY - SOURCES - BIBLIOGRAPHY - CATALOGS.
North Carolina. Division of Archives and History. Records relating to Tennessee in the North Carolina State archives /. Raleigh, N.C. , 1980. 7 p. : LC Card 80-623026 DDC 975.6 s 016.9768 19
F251 .N67a no. 3, 1980 CD3424

TENNESSEE - INTELLECTUAL LIFE.
Young, Thomas Daniel, 1919- Literary movements in Tennessee /. Knoxville , c1981. p. cm. ISBN 0-87049-319-1 : LC Card 81-2206 DDC 810/.9/9768 19
PS266.T2 Y6

Tennessee law of criminal procedure / Patricia J. Cottrell, primary contributor and general editor. Knoxville : Public Law Institute, University of Tennessee, College of Law, c1981. 1 v. (various pagings) : forms ; 28 cm. LC Card 81-135057 DDC 345.768/05 347.68055 19
1. Criminal procedure - Tennessee. I. Cottrell, Patricia J. II. University of Tennessee, Knoxville. Public Law Institute.
KFT575 .T46

Tennessee laws, rules, and regulations for restaurants. Tennessee. Laws, statutes, etc. Nashville, Tenn. [1952] 33 p. ; LC Card 79-119875 DDC 344.768/0464 347.6804464 19
KFT282.H6 A3 1952

Tennessee. Laws, statutes, etc. Tennessee laws, rules, and regulations for restaurants. Nashville, Tenn. : Dept. of Conservation, [1952] 33 p. ; 24 x 11 cm. LC Card 79-119875 DDC 344.768/0464 347.6804464 19
1. Restaurants, lunch rooms, etc. - Law and legislation - Tennessee. I. Tennessee. Dept. of Conservation. II. Title.
KFT282.H6 A3 1952

Tennessee. Legislative Council Committee. see Tennessee. General Assembly. Legislative Council Committee.

TENNESSEE - MAPS.
(1977) Miller, Robert A. Geologic hazards map of Tennessee /. [Nashville] , 1977. 1 map : 34 x 127 cm. Scale ca. 1:633,600. Shows earthquake, landslide, karst, and flooding areas. Published jointly with the State Planning Office, Natural Resources Section. Includes text. Bibliography. LC Card 79-691501
G3961.C5 1977 .M5
NYPL [Map Div. 81-3060]

Tennessee Municipal League. Selected municipal cost-cutting measures. Knoxville , 1979. 39 p. ;
NYPL [*ZT-1263]

TENNESSEE - OCCUPATIONS - STATISTICS.
Tennessee. Dept. of Employment Security. Research and Statistics Section. Occupational employment of selected nonmanufacturing industries in Tennessee, 1975 /. [Nashville] [1977] i, 61 leaves : LC Card 78-621484 DDC 331.12/5/09768 19
HD5725.T4 T413 1977c

Tennessee. Planning Office. see Tennessee. State Planning Office.

TENNESSEE - RACE RELATIONS.
Lamon, Lester C., 1942- Blacks in Tennessee /. Knoxville , c1981. p. cm. ISBN 0-87049-323-X : LC Card 81-3396 DDC 976.8/00496073 19
E185.93.T3 L36

Tennessee. State Historical Commission. (Old Catalog form: Tennessee. Historical Commission.)
Tennessee historical quarterly. v. 1- ; 1942- Nashville. **NYPL [IAA (Tennessee historical quarterly)]**

Tennessee. State Planning Office.
University of Tennessee, Knoxville. Center for Business and Economic Research. An economic report to the Governor of the State of Tennessee on the State's economic outlook /. Nashville, Tenn. [1979] xiv, 246 p. ; LC Card 79-623072 DDC 338.5/443/09768 19
HC107.T3 U53 1979

Tennessee. State Planning Office. Natural Resources Section. Miller, Robert A. Geologic hazards map of Tennessee /. [Nashville] , 1977. 1 map : 34 x 127 cm. Scale ca. 1:633,600. Shows earthquake, landslide, karst, and flooding areas. Published jointly with the State Planning Office, Natural Resources Section. Includes text. Bibliography. LC Card 79-691501
G3961.C5 1977 .M5
NYPL [Map Div. 81-3060]

Tennessee. State University, Memphis. Dept. of Philosophy. The Southern Journal of philosophy. v. 1- ; spring, 1963- Memphis. LC Card 68-7760 **NYPL [*ZAN-3214]**

Tennessee. State University, Memphis. Philosophy, Dept. of. see Tennessee. State University, Memphis. Dept. of Philosophy.

Tennessee-Tombigbee Waterway . United States. Congress. Senate. Committee on Appropriations. Subcommittee on Energy and Water Development. Washington , 1980. ii, 56 p. : LC Card 80-603362 DDC 353.0087/6/09768 19
KF26 .A6469 1980

TENNESSEE-TOMBIGBEE WATERWAY.
United States. Congress. Senate. Committee on Appropriations. Subcommittee on Energy and Water Development. Tennessee-Tombigbee Waterway . Washington , 1980. ii, 56 p. : LC Card 80-603362 DDC 353.0087/6/09768 19
KF26 .A6469 1980

United States. Congress. Senate. Committee on Environment and Public Works. Subcommittee on Water Resources. Transportation needs of increased coal production and completion of the Tennessee-Tombigbee Waterway . Washington , 1980. iv, 550 p. : LC Card 80-603720 DDC 386/.3/09761 19
KF26 .E683 1980

Tennessee. University. Institute for Public Service. Municipal Technical Advisory Service. see Tennessee. University. Municipal Technical Advisory Service.

Tennessee. University. Municipal Technical Advisory Service. Selected municipal cost-cutting measures. Knoxville , 1979. 39 p. ;
NYPL [*ZT-1263]

Tennessee Valley Authority. (Old Catalog form: United States. Tennessee. Valley Authority.)
TVA/EPRI Workshop on Factors Affecting Power Plant Waste Heat Utilization, Atlanta, 1978. Factors affecting power plant waste heat utilization /. New York , c1980. xvii, 230 p. : ISBN 0-08-025548-5 LC Card 79-29656
TJ260 .T17 1978 **NYPL [JSE 81-98]**
Tributary area development. Knoxville. 28 cm.
1. Tennessee Valley - Economic conditions - Periodicals. I. Title. **NYPL [JLM 80-931]**

TENNESSEE VALLEY AUTHORITY.
United States. Congress. House. Committee on Interstate and Foreign Commerce. Subcommittee on Oversight and Investigations. Clean air act amendments of 1977-oversight . Washington , 1980. ii, 52 p. ; LC Card 80-602530 DDC 353.0082/324 19
KF27 .I5547 1979q

United States. Congress. Senate. Committee on Appropriations. Subcommittee on Energy and Water Development. Power program of the Tennessee Valley Authority . Washington , 1981. iii, 192 p. : LC Card 81-601951 DDC 353.0082/3/09768 19
KF26 .A6469 1980b

Tennessee Valley Authority. Division of Forestry, Fisheries and Wildlife Development.
Directory of forest products industries in 125 Tennessee Valley counties. [Norris, Tenn.].
NYPL [JLM 80-908]

Technical note - Division of Forestry, Fisheries, and Wildlife Development, Tennessee Valley Authority .
(no. B24) Carter, Virginia. Wetland classification system for the Tennessee Valley region /. [Norris] 1978. v, 36 p. : LC Card 79-103835 DDC 333.7/5/09768 s 574.5/26325/012 19
SD11 .T416 no. B24 QH541.5.M3

Tennessee Valley Authority. Forestry, Fisheries and Wildlife Development, Division of. see Tennessee Valley Authority. Division of

Forestry, Fisheries and Wildlife Development.

Tennessee Valley Authority. Geologic Branch. Mineral resources of the Tennessee Valley region. Compiled by R. A. Miller and others. [Knoxville, Tenn.] 1970. col. map 69 x 119 cm. Scale ca. 1:633,600. "Compiled from published reports, maps, and file data of the State geological organizations, the U. S. Geological Survey, and the U. S. Bureau of Mines; and from information furnished by companies producing mineral commodities in the region." "Cartography by TVA Maps and Surveys Branch." LC Card 75-695672
1. Mines and mineral resources - Tennessee Valley - Maps. 2. Tennessee Valley - Maps. I. Miller, Robert A. II. Title.
G3942.T4H1 1970 .T4
                    NYPL [Map Div. 81-3061]

Tennessee Valley Authority. Library. (Old Catalog form: United States. Tennessee Valley Authority. Technical Library.) TVA bibliography. Muscle Shoals, Ala. 28 cm. Irregular. Some issues lack title. Each issue covers a distinctive subject area.
1. Fertilizers and manures - Bibliography - Periodicals. I. Title.   *NYPL [JLM 80-973]*

Tennessee Valley Authority. National Fertilizer Development Center. see United States. National Fertilizer Development Center, Muscle Shoals, Ala.

Tennessee Valley Authority Office of Tributary Area Development. The junk car: from field to foundry: a guide for solving a community problem / [Tennessee Valley Authority, Office of Tributary Area Development]. Knoxville: Tennessee Valley Authority, 1973. 30 p.: ill.; 21 cm. Microfilm. Cover title. Reprint of the 1972 ed.
1. Automobile wrecking and used car industry - Tennessee Valley. I. Title. II. Title: From field to foundry.   *NYPL [*ZV-179]*

Tennessee Valley Authority. Technical Library. see Tennessee Valley Authority. Library.

Tennessee Valley Authority. Tributary Area Development, Office of. see Tennessee Valley Authority Office of Tributary Area Development.

TENNESSEE VALLEY - ECONOMIC CONDITIONS - PERIODICALS. Tennessee Valley Authority. Tributary area development. Knoxville.
                    NYPL [JLM 80-931]

TENNESSEE VALLEY - MAPS. (1970) Tennessee Valley Authority. Geologic Branch. Mineral resources of the Tennessee Valley region. [Knoxville, Tenn.] 1970. col. map 69 x 119 cm. Scale ca. 1:633,600. "Compiled from published reports, maps, and file data of the State geological organizations, the U. S. Geological Survey, and the U. S. Bureau of Mines; and from information furnished by companies producing mineral commodities in the region." "Cartography by TVA Maps and Surveys Branch." LC Card 75-695672
G3942.T4H1 1970 .T4
                    NYPL [Map Div. 81-3061]

Tennessee's presidents /. Williams, Frank Broyles, 1913- Knoxville , c1981. p. cm. ISBN 0-87049-321-3 : LC Card 81-3391 DDC 973'.09/92 B 19
E176.1 .W7225

Tennyson, Elizabeth J. Tennyson, G. B. An index to Nineteenth-century fiction, volumes 1-30, summer 1945-March 1976 /. Berkeley , c1977. viii, 195 p. ; ISBN 0-520-03334-5 LC Card 77-71900 DDC 823/.8/09 19
PR873.T762 T4 1977

Tennyson, G. B. An index to Nineteenth-century fiction, volumes 1-30, summer 1945-March 1976 / compiled by G.B. and Elizabeth J. Tennyson ; incorporating An analytical index to "Nineteenth-century fiction" compiled by Bradford A. Booth. Berkeley : University of California Press, c1977. viii, 195 p. ; 24 cm. ISBN 0-520-03334-5 LC Card 77-71900 DDC 823/.8/09 19
1. Nineteenth-century fiction - Indexes. 2. English fiction - 19th century - History and criticism - Bibliography. 3. Fiction - History and criticism - Bibliography. I. Tennyson, Elizabeth J. II. Booth, Bradford Allen, 1909- Analytical index to Nineteenth-century fiction. III. Nineteenth-century

fiction. IV. Title.
PR873.T762 T4 1977

TENURE OF LAND. see LAND TENURE.

Teodoro, Luis V., 1941- Out of this struggle . Honolulu , c1981. p. cm. ISBN 0-8248-0747-2 LC Card 81-714 DDC 996.9/0049921 19
DU624.7.F4 O9

Terenzio, Stephanie. A Handbook of twentieth century art. - Storrs, Conn. , 1973. 71, iv p. :
NYPL [3-MAVZ (New York) 80-2266]

Terkla, Dawn G. (joint author) Paltridge, James Gilbert. Mid-career education and training . Davis, Calif. , 1979. v, 93 leaves : LC Card 80-623848 DDC 374 19
LC1037.5 .P33   NYPL [JLM 77-672 no. 6]

TERMINAL CARE - ABSTRACTS. Care of the terminally ill . Rockville, Md. (P.O. Box 2309, Rockville, Md., 20852) , 1980. v, 23 p. ; LC Card 81-601199 DDC 362.1/9 19
R726.8 .C373

TERMINAL CARE FACILITIES - ABSTRACTS. Care of the terminally ill . Rockville, Md. (P.O. Box 2309, Rockville, Md., 20852) , 1980. v, 23 p. ; LC Card 81-601199 DDC 362.1/9 19
R726.8 .C373

TERMINAL CARE FACILITIES - LAW AND LEGISLATION - OREGON. Oregon. Legislative Assembly. Legislative Task Force on Hospice. Report and recommendations /. [Salem, Or.] [1980] v, 59 p. ; LC Card 81-620893 DDC 362.1/9 19
R726.8 .O73 1980

TERMINAL CARE FACILITIES - OREGON. Oregon. Legislative Assembly. Legislative Task Force on Hospice. Report and recommendations /. [Salem, Or.] [1980] v, 59 p. ; LC Card 81-620893 DDC 362.1/9 19
R726.8 .O73 1980

TERMINAL CARE FACILITIES - UNITED STATES - ABSTRACTS. Care of the terminally ill . Rockville, Md. (P.O. Box 2309, Rockville, Md., 20852) , 1980. v, 23 p. ; LC Card 81-601199 DDC 362.1/9 19
R726.8 .C373

TERMINAL CARE - OREGON. Oregon. Legislative Assembly. Legislative Task Force on Hospice. Report and recommendations /. [Salem, Or.] [1980] v, 59 p. ; LC Card 81-620893 DDC 362.1/9 19
R726.8 .O73 1980

TERMITE CONTROL - LAW AND LEGISLATION - LOUISIANA. Louisiana. Laws, statutes, etc. Louisiana, Structural pest control law ; Rules and regulations. Baton Rouge, La. [1980?] 25 p. ; LC Card 80-623022 DDC 344.763/046 19
KFL282.I5 A3 1980

Terms used in the budgetary process. A Glossary of terms used in the Federal budget process and related accounting, economic, and tax terms. Washington, D.C. [1981] p. cm. LC Card 81-607987 DDC 353.0072/2/0321 19
HJ2052 .G6 1981

TERRACES (GEOLOGY) - ALABAMA - UPHAPEE CREEK WATERSHED. Markewich, Helaine W. Pleistocene and Holocene fluvial history of Uphapee Creek, Macon County, Alabama /. Reston, VA [1981] p. cm. LC Card 81-607035 DDC 557.3 s 551.7/9/0976/49 19
QE75 .B9 no. 1522 QE696

Terrell, Carroll Franklin. A companion to the Cantos of Ezra Pound / by Carroll F. Terrell. Orono : National Poetry Foundation, University of Maine at Orono ; Berkeley : University of California Press, c1988- v. <1> ; 27 cm. Bibliography: v. 1, p. 361-362. ISBN 0-520-03687-5 (University of Calif. Press) LC Card 78-54802 DDC 811/.52 19
1. Pound, Ezra, 1885-1972. Cantos. I. Pound, Ezra, 1885-1972. Cantos. II. Title.
PS3531.O82 C289

Terrestrial microcosms . Workshop on Terrestrial Microcosms, Newport, Or., 1977. [Washington] [1978?] xii, 35 p. : LC Card 79-602306 DDC 574.5/264 19
QH541.28 .W67 1977

Terrestrial microcosms and environmental chemistry : the proceedings of two colloquia, held June 13-14, 1977, at Oregon State University, Corvallis, Oregon, as a part of the Symposium on Terrestrial Microcosms and Environmental Chemistry / edited by James M. Witt and James W. Gillett, Jane Wyatt, technical editor ; prepared for the National Science Foundation, Directorate of Research Applications, RANN-Research Applied to National Needs, Division of Advanced Environmental Research and Technology ; sponsored by Environmental Health Sciences Center, Oregon State University, U. S. Environmental Protection Agency, Office of Research and Development, National Science Foundation-RANN, Division of Advanced Environmental Research and Technology. [Washington] : NSF, [1978?] xv, 147 p. : ill. ; 28 cm. On cover: Prepared for the National Science Foundation, Directorate for Applied Science and Research Applications, Division of Problem-Focused Research Applications. "NSF/RA 79-0026." Includes bibliographies. LC Card 79-601829 DDC 574.5/264 19
1. Ecology - Research - Congresses. 2. Environmental chemistry - Congresses. I. Witt, James M. II. Gillett, James W. III. Wyatt, Jane. IV. Symposium on Terrestrial Microcosms and Environmental Chemistry, Oregon State University, 1977. V. Oregon. State University, Corvallis. Environmental Health Sciences Center. VI. United States. Environmental Protection Agency. Office of Research and Development. VII. United States. National Science Foundation. Division of Problem-Focused Research Applications.
QH541.2 .T45

Terrestrial series . (# 7) Sampson, Frank W. Missouri fur harvests /. Jefferson City, Mo. , 1980. 59 p. : LC Card 81-621615 DDC 381/.456753/09778 19
HD9944.U46 M87

(#8) LaVal, Richard K. Ecological studies and management of Missouri bats, with emphasis on cave-dwelling species /. Jefferson City, Mo. , 1980. 53 p. : LC Card 80-623996 DDC 599.4/09778 19
QL737.C5 L32

(no. 7) Sampson, Frank W. Missouri fur harvests /. Jefferson City, Mo. , 1980. 59 p. : LC Card 81-621615 DDC 381/.456753/09778 19
HD9944.U46 M87

TERRITORIAL WATERS - CANADA. United States. Congress. Senate. Committee on Foreign Relations. Maritime boundary settlement treaty and East coast fishery resources agreement . Washington , 1980. iv, 223 p. : LC Card 80-603064 DDC 341.4/48/026673071 19
KF26 .F6 1980m

United States. Congress. Senate. Committee on Foreign Relations. The maritime boundary treaty with Canada . Washington , 1981. iii, 46 p. ; LC Card 81-601779 DDC 341.4/48/026673071 19
KF26 .F6 1981b

TERRITORIAL WATERS - MAPS. United States. Central Intelligence Agency. Selected world shipping lanes and straits. [Washington , 1980] 1 map : LC Card 81-690686
G3201.P54 1980 .U5

United States. Central Intelligence Agency. 200-nautical-mile claims, January 1980. [Washington , 1980] 1 map : LC Card 81-690684
G3201.F3 1980 .U5

TERRITORIAL WATERS - UNITED STATES. United States. Congress. Senate. Committee on Commerce, Science, and Transportation. Coast Guard authority . Washington , 1980. iii, 104 p. ; LC Card 81-600824 DDC 343.73/0965 347.303965 19
KF26 .C69 1980x

United States. Congress. Senate. Committee on Foreign Relations. Maritime boundary settlement treaty and East coast fishery resources agreement . Washington , 1980. iv, 223 p. : LC Card 80-603064 DDC 341.4/48/026673071 19
KF26 .F6 1980m

United States. Congress. Senate. Committee on Foreign Relations. The maritime boundary treaty with Canada . Washington , 1981. iii, 46

p. ; LC Card 81-601779 DDC 341.4/48/026673071
19
KF26 .F6 1981b

**TERROR, REIGN OF. see FRANCE -
HISTORY - REVOLUTION, 1789-1799.**

TERRORISM.
United States. Congress. House. Committee on
Foreign Affairs. Subcommittee on
Inter-American Affairs. Review of the
Presidential certification of Nicaragua's
connection to terrorism . Washington , 1980. iii,
50, p. ; LC Card 80-603450 DDC
353.0089/097285 19
KF27 .F646 1980d

TERRORISM - SOVIET UNION.
Pike, David, 1950- German writers in Soviet
exile, 1933-1945 /. Chapel Hill , c1981. p. cm.
ISBN 0-8078-1492-X LC Card 81-10394 DDC
830/.9/00912 B 19
PT405 .P46

TERRORISM - UNITED STATES.
United States. Congress. House. Committee on
the Judiciary. Subcommittee on Civil and
Constitutional Rights. Federal capabilities in
crisis management and terrorism . Washington ,
1980 [i.e. 1981] iii, 68 p. ; LC Card 81-600980
DDC 353.0075 19
KF27 .J847 1980c

United States. Congress. Senate. Committee on
Governmental Affairs. Omnibus antiterrorism
act of 1979 . Washington , 1979. iv, 448 p. ;
LC Card 80-602011 DDC 345.73/023 19
KF26 .G67 1979am

United States. Congress. Senate. Committee on
the Judiciary. Subcommittee to Investigate the
Administration of the Internal Security Act and
Other Internal Security Laws. The Puerto Rican
Revolutionary Workers Organization .
Washington , 1976. v, 47, viii p. ; LC Card
76-601803 DDC 322.4/2/0973 19
HV6432 .U54 1976

**TERRORISM - UNITED STATES. -
PREVENTION.**
United States. Congress. House. Committee on
the Judiciary. Subcommittee on Civil and
Constitutional Rights. Federal capabilities in
crisis management and terrorism . Washington ,
1980 [i.e. 1981] iii, 68 p. ; LC Card 81-600980
DDC 353.0075 19
KF27 .J847 1980c

**Tertiary formations and associated Mesozoic
rocks in the Alaska Peninsula area, Alaska,
and their petroleum-reservoir and source-rock
potential /.** Alaska. Division of Geological and
Geophysical Surveys. Anchorage, Alaska ,
1979. iv, 65 p. ; LC Card 80-622183 DDC
553/.09798 s 553.2/82/097984 19
QE83 .A25 no. 62 QE691

**TERTIARY PERIOD. see GEOLOGY,
STRATIGRAPHIC - TERTIARY.**

Tesarik, D. R. (Douglas R.) Factor of safety
charts for estimating the stability of saturated
and unsaturated tailings pond embankments /
by D.R. Tesarik and P.C. McWilliams.
Avondale, Md. : U. S. Dept. of the Interior,
Bureau of Mines, 1981. p. cm. (Report of
investigations) Bibliography: p. LC Card 81-607986
DDC 622 s 622/.8 19
*1. Embankments - Safety measures - Charts, diagrams,
etc. 2. Tailings (Metallurgy). I. McWilliams, P. C. (Paul
C). II. Series: Report of investigations (United States.
Bureau of Mines). III. Title.*
TN23 .U43 TA760

Teske, Clarence E. (joint author) Hill, Lewis E.
Solar energy, an economic analysis . [Austin,
Tex.] [1979] xii, 200 p. ; LC Card 80-620775
DDC 333.79/23/09764 19
TJ810 .H55

Testa, Mark. Human services in Illinois : trends
and projections to the year 2000 / by Mark
Testa ; contributing authors, Frank Farrow,
Suzanne Petersen, Steve Hagy ; prepared for
the Task Force on the Future of Illinois.
[Chicago] : Task Force on the Future of
Illinois, 1978 [i.e. 1979] vi, 172 p. : ill. ; 28 cm.
"Prepared for the Task Force on the Future of Illinois."
Includes bibliographical references. LC Card
80-623960 DDC 361.6/09773 19
*1. Social service - Illinois - Planning. I. Task Force on
the Future of Illinois. II. Title.*
HV98.I15 T48

**A testbed for providing uniformity to
user-computer interaction languages /.** Treu,
Siegfried. [Washington, D.C.] , 1980. 72 p. in
various pagings : LC Card 80-603146 DDC
602/.18 s 001.64/24 19
QC100 .U57 no. 500-63 QA76.7

Testimony of Andrew L. Lewis, Jr. . United
States. Congress. Senate. Committee on
Environment and Public Works. Washington ,
1981. iii, 34 p. ; LC Card 81-601349 DDC
353.0087/5 19
KF26 .E6 1981a

TESTING.
United States. National Bureau of Standards.
Office of Measurement Services. Calibration
and related measurement services of the
National Bureau of Standards /. Washington ,
1978. vii, 100 p. ; LC Card 79-603214 DDC
602/.8/7 19
T50 .U57 1978

Testing for effects of chemical on ecosystems .
Environmental Studies Board. Committee to
Review Methods for Ecotoxicology.
Washington, D.C. , 1981. xv, 103 p. : ISBN
0-309-03142-7 (pbk.) LC Card 81-38392 DDC
574.5/222 19
QH545.A1 E59 1981

Testing kit, French and Spanish /. United States.
Foreign Service Institute. [Washington, D.C.]
[1979] x, 140 p. (p. 140 blank) : LC Card
80-602389 DDC 440[.76 19
PB36 .U54 1979

TESTING-MACHINES - TESTING.
Scott, John H. Evaluation of REO model BT
300 C-D blasting machine tester /. [Avondale,
Md.] [1981] p. cm. LC Card 81-607976 DDC
622 s 622/.23 19
TN23 .U43 TN279

Testing, teaching, and learning : report of a
conference on research on testing, August
17-26, 1978 / Ralph W. Tyler and Sheldon H.
White, chairmen. Washington, D.C. : U. S.
Dept. of Health, Education, and Welfare,
National Institute of Education, 1979. vii, 391,
[43] p. : ill. ; 26 cm. Sponsored by National
Institute of Education. Includes bibliographies. LC
Card 80-601554 DDC 371.2/6/0973 19
*1. Educational tests and measurements - United States -
Congresses. I. Tyler, Ralph Winfred, 1902-. II. White,
Sheldon Harold, 1928-. III. National Institute of
Education.*
LB3051 .T443

**TESTING, TOXICITY. see TOXICITY
TESTING.**

**TESTS AND MEASUREMENTS IN
EDUCATION. see EDUCATIONAL TESTS
AND MEASUREMENTS.**

**TESTS, EDUCATIONAL. see EDUCATIONAL
TESTS AND MEASUREMENTS.**

TETON DAM, IDAHO.
United States. Teton Dam Failure Review
Group. Failure of Teton Dam . Washington,
D.C. , 1980. ca. 800 p. in various pagings, [1]
leaf of plates : LC Card 80-601802 DDC
627/.83/0979656 19
TC557.I22 T488 1980

TETRACHLORODIBENZODIOXIN.
United States. General Accounting Office. U. S.
ground troops in South Vietnam were in areas
sprayed with herbicide orange . [Washington,
D.C.] , 1979. 9, 12 p. : LC Card 79-604309
DDC 363.1/79 19
DS559.8.C5 U54 1979

**TETRACHLORODIBENZODIOXIN -
TOXICOLOGY.**
United States. Congress. House. Committee on
Interstate and Foreign Commerce.
Subcommittee on Oversight and Investigations.
Involuntary exposure to agent orange and other
toxic spraying . Washington , 1980. iv, 256 p. :
LC Card 80-602744 DDC 363.1/79 19
KF27 .I5547 1979r

United States. Congress. House. Committee on
Veterans' Affairs. Subcommittee on Medical
Facilities and Benefits. Oversight hearing to
receive testimony on Agent Orange .
Washington , 1980. iii, 121 p. ; LC Card
80-602984 DDC 363.7/384 19
KF27 .V459 1980

**TEWA INDIANS - SOCIAL LIFE AND
CUSTOMS.**
Hill, W. W. (Willard Williams), 1902-1974.
Ethnography of Santa Clara Pueblo, New
Mexico /. Albuquerque , c1981. p. cm. ISBN
0-8263-0555-5 LC Card 80-52277 DDC
970.004/97 19
E99.T35 H5 1981

Texas.
Parks and Wildlife Dept. PWD report .
(3000-54) Texas. Parks and Wildlife Dept.
Coastal fisheries plan, 1978-1979, 1980-1981
/. [Austin] [1978] i, 44 p. ; LC Card
79-623627 DDC 333.95/6/097641 19
SH222.T4 T48 1978

(4000-242) Kegley, George. Archeological
investigations at 41EP2, Hueco Tanks State
Park, El Paso County, Texas /. [Austin, Tex.]
[1980] 40, [56] p., [10] leaves of plates : LC
Card 80-623083 DDC 976.4/96 19
E78.T4 K38

Texas A & M Research Foundation. Ballot access
/ submitted by Texas A & M Research
Foundation ; prepared by Bruce W. Robeck,
James A. Dyer, Henry J. Woods. -
[Washington : Clearinghouse on Election
Administration, Federal Election Commission :
available from National Tech. Information
Service], 1978. 4 v. in 1 ; 28 cm. Microfiche
(neg.) NTIS. 1 sheet. 11 x 15 cm. (PB 288446) "For a
project entitled An analysis of laws and procedures
governing the qualification and certification of Federal
candidates in the United States, sponsored by
Clearinghouse on Election Administration, Federal
Election Commission." Bibliography: v. 1, p. 83-87.
CONTENTS: v. 1. Administrative issues, problems, and
recommendations. - v. 2. A summary of state
administrative procedures. - v. 3. Legal problems,
memoranda, and recommendations. - v. 4. A brief
summary.
*1. Election law - United States. I. Robeck, Bruce W. II.
Dyer, James A. III. Woods, Henry J. IV. United States.
Clearinghouse on Election Administration. V. Title.*
*NYPL [*XME-9374]*

Texas. A & M University, College Station.
Sea Grant College Program. Texas. Agricultural
Experiment Station, College Station.
Recreation and Parks. Barrier islands on the
Texas coast : existing and future recreational
use and development / by Robert B.
Ditton ... [et al.] ; Texas Agricultural
Experiment Station (Recreation and Parks),
Texas A&M University System. College
Station, Tex. [1979] vi, 129 p. : LC Card
80-621229 DDC 333.7/09764 19
GV54.T59 T47 1979

**Texas. A & M University, College Station.
Agricultural Experiment Station. see Texas.
Agricultural Experiment Station, College
Station.**

**Texas. A & M University, College Station.
Agricultural Extension Service. see Texas
Agricultural Extension Service.**

Texas A & M University. Dept. of Meteorology.
Knight, Keith Shelburne. Atmospheric structure
determined from satellite data /. Washington,
D.C. [Springfield, Va.] 1981. x, 95 p. : LC
Card 81-601075 DDC 551.5/14 19
QC879.59.A .K58

Texas Adult Probation Commission. Standards for
adult probation services in Texas. [Austin,
Tex.] : The Commission, [1980] iii leaves, 20
p. ; 28 cm. Cover title. LC Card 80-623900 DDC
364.6/3/09764 19
1. Probation - Standards - Texas. I. Title.
HV9305.T4 T5 1980

**Texas. Advisory Commission on
Intergovernmental Relations.**
An Introduction to Texas county government.
Austin, Tex. , c1980. iii, 34 p. ; LC Card
80-624183 DDC 352/.0073 19
JS451.T45 I57

Medically indigent costs affecting local
governments : background and issues. [Austin,
Tex.] : Texas Advisory Commission on
Intergovernmental Relations, [1980] 26 p. :
map ; 27 cm. (Intergovernmental report . no. VIII-1)
Caption title. "June 1980." Bibliography: p. 25. LC
Card 80-623837 DDC 362.1/9 19
*1. Poor - Hospital care - Texas - Finance. 2. Poor -
Medical care - Texas - Finance. 3. Hospitals, Public -*

345

GOVERNMENT PUBLICATIONS - U.S.: 1981

Texas. Bureau of State Health Planning & Resource Development.

Texas. I. Title. II. Series.
RA981.T4 T33 1980

Searcy, Seth S. Privacy and public records .
Austin , 1977. xv, 82 p. ; LC Card 77-623845
KFT1662.5.P8 S4   **NYPL [*XME-9391]**

911 and other emergency single-number access
systems in Texas : an informational report.
Austin, Tex. : Texas Advisory Commission on
Intergovernmental Relations, [foreword 1979]
ix, 226 p. : maps ; 28 cm. Cover title. Bibliography:
p. 215-226. LC Card 80-621339 DDC 384.6/42 19
1. Telephone - Texas - Emergency reporting systems. I.
Title.
TK6024.T4 T49 1979

Texas Aeronautics Commission. Rules of practice
and procedure before the Texas Aeronautics
Commission. [Austin] : The Commission,
[1979?] iii, 42 p. ; 22 cm. LC Card 80-624269
DDC 343.764/097/02636 347.64039702636 19
1. Texas Aeronautics Commission. 2. Aeronautics,
Commercial - Law and legislation - Texas. I. Title.
KFT1505 .A4 1979

TEXAS AERONAUTICS COMMISSION.
Texas Aeronautics Commission. Rules of
practice and procedure before the Texas
Aeronautics Commission. [Austin] [1979?] iii,
42 p. ; LC Card 80-624269 DDC
343.764/097/02636 347.64039702636 19
KFT1505 .A4 1979

**Texas. Agricultural and Mechanical College,
College Station. Agricultural Experiment
Station.** see **Texas. Agricultural Experiment
Station, College Station.**

**Texas. Agricultural and Mechanical College,
College Station. Extension Service.** see
Texas Agricultural Extension Service.

Texas Agricultural Experiment Station.
Clower, Dennis F. Soil survey of Brown and
Mills Counties, Texas. [Washington, D.C.?] ,
1980. vii, 170 p., 92 fold. p. of plates : LC
Card 81-601467 DDC 631.4/7/764512 19
S599.T4 C57

Fox, Richard W. Soil survey of Bowie County,
Texas. [Washington, D.C.?] , 1980. vii, 128 p.,
76 fold. p. of plates : LC Card 81-601439 DDC
631.4/7/764197 19
S599.T4 F678

United States. Soil Conservation Service.
General soil map, Galveston County, Texas /.
[Fort Worth, Tex.] [1980] 1 map : LC Card
81-692258
G4033.G25J3 1980 .U5

**Texas. Agricultural Experiment Station, College
Station.**
Cochran, Rex. Soil survey of Grayson County,
Texas /. [Washington? , 1980] vii, 141 p., [41]
leaves of plates : LC Card 80-602304 DDC
631.4/7/764557 19
S599.T4 C593

Coffee, Daniel R., 1919- Soil survey of Dallas
County, Texas /. [Washington] [1980] vii, 153
p., [38] fold. leaves of plates : LC Card
80-601832 DDC 631.4/7/7642811 19
S599.T4 C63

Dolezel, Raymond. Soil survey of Nacogdoches
County, Texas /. [Washington] , 1980. vii, 146
p., [30] fold. leaves of plates : LC Card
80-602411 DDC 631.4/7/764182 19
S599.T4 D63

Miscellaneous publication .
(1411) Gold, J. R. Chromosome formulae of
North American fishes /. College Station ,
1979. 24 p. ; LC Card 79-624059 DDC
597/.015 19
QL638.99 .G64

(1443) Chykaliuk, P. B. Bibliography of
glyphosate /. College Station, Tex. [1980] 87
p. ; LC Card 80-622516 DDC 016.632/954 19
Z5074.P4 C48 SB952.G58

Miscellaneous publications .
(1424) Eastin, E. F. Selected bibliography of
red rice and other wild rices (Oryza spp.) /.
College Station , 1979. 59 p. ; LC Card
79-625846 DDC 016.6331/87 19
Z5356.R43 E25 SB615.R4

Rives, Jerry L. Soil survey of Pecos County,
Texas /. [Washington] [1980] vii, 97 p., [77]
fold. leaves of plates : LC Card 80-602640 DDC

631.4/7/764923 19
S599.T4 R59

Rogers, Charlie Ellic, 1938- Selected
bibliography of insect pests of sunflower /.
College Station, Tex. [Beltsville, Md.] [1979]
41 p. ; LC Card 80-621131 DDC 016.6338/5 19
Z5354.P3 S867 SB608.S92

Stringer, Billy R. Soil survey of Bosque County,
Texas /. [Washington, D.C.] [1980] vii, 102 p.,
[31] fold. leaves of plates : LC Card 80-602639
DDC 631.4/7/764518 19
S599.T4 S75

**Technical monograph - The Texas Agricultural
Experiment Station .**
(9) Ospina, Enrique. Disaggregated
econometric analysis of U. S. slaughter beef
supply /. College Station, Tex. [1980] 57 p. ;
LC Card 80-621501 DDC 338.1/76213/0973 19
HD9433.U4 O84

Williams, Jimmy R. HYMO: Problem-oriented
computer language for hydrologic modeling.
Washington, 1973. 76 p. :
NYPL [JSF 80-689]

**Texas. Agricultural Experiment Station, College
Station. Recreation and Parks.** Barrier
islands on the Texas coast : existing and future
recreational use and development / by Robert
B. Ditton ... [et al.] ; Texas Agricultural
Experiment Station (Recreation and Parks),
Texas A&M University System. College Station,
Tex. : Texas A&M University, Sea Grant
College Program, [1979] vi, 129 p. : ill. ; 28
cm. "August 1979." "TAMU-SG-79-203." Includes
bibliographical references. LC Card 80-621229 DDC
333.7/09764 19
1. Barrier islands - Texas - Recreational use - Case
studies. 2. Coastal zone management - Texas - Case
studies. I. Ditton, Robert B., 1943-. II. Texas. A & M
University, College Station. Sea Grant College Program.
III. Title.
GV54.T59 T47 1979

**Texas Agricultural Experiment Station. Dept. of
Agricultural Economics.** Syrian agricultural
sector assessment. College Station, Tex.
[1979]- v. <1, 3> : LC Card 80-623539 DDC
338.1/095691 19
HD9016.S92 S93

Texas Agricultural Extension Service. (Old
Catalog form: Texas. Agricultural and
Mechanical College, College Station.
Extension Service).
Edwards, Richard A., 1927- Texas farm labor
handbook /. [College Station, Tex.] [1979?] 61
p. : LC Card 79-625934 DDC 344.764/01763 19
KFT1538.A4 E38

Texas. Agriculture, Dept. of. see **Texas. Dept. of
Agriculture.**

Texas. Air Control Board.
Proposed revisions, Texas State implementation
plan, regulations : regulation I, regulation V,
regulation VI, general rules, procedural rules /
Texas Air Control Board. [Austin?] : The
Board, [1980] 113 p. in various pagings ; 28
cm. "March 14, 1980." LC Card 80-622987 DDC
344.764/046342 19
1. Air - Pollution - Law and legislation - Texas. I.
Texas. Air Control Board. State of Texas
implementation plan for attaining national ambient air
quality standards. II. Title.
KFT1558 .A82

**State of Texas implementation plan for
attaining national ambient air quality
standards.** Texas. Air Control Board.
Proposed revisions, Texas State
implementation plan, regulations : regulation
I, regulation V, regulation VI, general rules,
procedural rules / Texas Air Control Board.
[Austin?] [1980] 113 p. in various pagings ;
LC Card 80-622987 DDC 344.764/046342 19
KFT1558 .A82

TEXAS. AIR CONTROL BOARD.
Keith, Gary. Air Pollution control in Texas.
Austin, Tex. (Room 315-B, Capitol Bldg.,
Austin 78769) [1981] xv, 60 p. : LC Card
81-621709 DDC 344.764/046342 347.640446342
19
KFT1558. A25 1981

TEXAS - ANTIQUITIES.
Etchieson, Gerald Meeks. An archeological
survey of certain tracts in and near Caprock
Canyons State Park in eastern Briscoe County,

Texas /. Canyon, Tex. , 1977. ii, 84, [66] p. :
LC Card 78-623263 DDC 976.4/839 19
E78.T4 E83

Kegley, George. Archeological investigations at
41EP2, Hueco Tanks State Park, El Paso
County, Texas /. [Austin, Tex.] [1980] 40, [56]
p., [10] leaves of plates : LC Card 80-623083
DDC 976.4/96 19
E78.T4 K38

Lynn, Warren M. Cultural resource survey of
Choke Canyon Reservoir, Live Oak and
McMullen Counties, Texas /. Austin , 1977.
xiv, 273 p. : LC Card 78-622852 DDC 976.4/447
19
F392.F92 L96

McGraw, A. Joachim. A preliminary
archaeological survey for the Conquista project
in Gonzales, Atascosa, and Live Oak Counties,
Texas /. [San Antonio] , 1979. iii, 31 leaves :
LC Card 80-620819 DDC 976.4/445 19
E78.T4 M317

Thurmond, J. Peter. Report on the fall, 1978,
investigations at the George C. Davis Site,
Caddoan Mounds State Historic Site, Cherokee
County, Texas /. [Austin] [1979] ix, 103
leaves, [14] leaves of plates : LC Card 80-620782
DDC 976.4/183 19
E99.C13 T48

Two sites in Uvalde County. [Austin, Tex.]
[1979] vi, 15, vi, 19 p., : LC Card 80-622621
DDC 976.4/432 19
E78.T4 T89

Whalen, Michael E. Settlement patterns of the
Western Hueco Bolson /. [El Paso] , 1978. xv,
260 p., [1] leaf of plates : LC Card 79-624053
DDC 976.4/96 19
F392.H82 W45

Texas - Archaeology. see **Texas - Antiquities.**

Texas Archeological Research Laboratory.
Thurmond, J. Peter. Report on the fall, 1978,
investigations at the George C. Davis Site,
Caddoan Mounds State Historic Site, Cherokee
County, Texas /. [Austin] [1979] ix, 103
leaves, [14] leaves of plates : LC Card 80-620782
DDC 976.4/183 19
E99.C13 T48

Texas assumes the social security obligation.
Jarrett, James E. [Lexington, Ky.] [1979] 12
p. ; LC Card 80-140046 DDC 353.9 s
353.9764001/234 19
JS308 .C6 no. 680 JK4857

**Texas barrier islands region ecological
characterization** : a socioeconomic study / by
Edward B. Liebow ... [et al.] ; prepared for
National Coastal ecosystems team, Office of
Biological Services, Fish and Wildlife Service,
U. S. Department of the Interior. Washington,
D.C.?] : The Office, 1980. 2 v. : ill., maps ; 28
cm. "Biological services program"--Cover. "This study
was co-sponsord by the Bureau of Land Management,
U. S. Dept. of the Interior." "August 1980." Vol. 1:
"FWS/OBS-80/19." Vol. 2: "FWS/OBS-80/20." Item
612 Includes bibliographies. CONTENTS. - v. 1.
Synthesis papers -- v. 2. Data appendix. LC Card
81-600915 DDC 333.91/09764/1 19
1. Coastal ecology - Texas. 2. Island ecology - Texas. 3.
Land use - Texas. 4. Barrier islands - Texas. I. Liebow,
Edward B. II. National Coastal Ecosystems Team (U.
S.). III. United States Fish and Wildlife Service. Office
of Biological Services. IV. United States. Bureau of
Land Management.
QH105.T4 T52

TEXAS - BIOGRAPHY.
Smithers, W. D. (Wilfred Dudley), 1895-
Circuit riders of the Big Bend /. [El Paso] ,
c1981. 39 p., [8] p. of plates : ISBN
0-87407-124-4 (pbk.) : LC Card 81-159927
DDC 280/.092/2 B 19
BR555.T4 S64

**Texas. Bureau of State Health Planning &
Resource Development.**
**Technical report - Bureau of State Health
Planning and Resource Development .**
(no. 5) Patterson, Harrold P. Development of
a health status index for Texas counties /.
Austin, Tex. [1978] iv, 69 p. : LC Card
79-623634 DDC 362.1/09764 19
RA407.4.T45 P37

**Texas. Bureau of State Health Planning &
Resource Development. Data Collection and**

Analysis Division.
Texas health manpower report : nursing home administrators / statistics compiled by Data Collection and Analysis Division, Bureau of State Health Planning and Resource Development, Texas Department of Health. Austin, Tex. : The Division, 1978. 101 p. : map ; 28 cm.   LC Card 80-623855   DDC 331.12/9136216068 19
1. Nursing home and administrators - Texas - Statistics. I. Title.
RA997.5.T4 T432 1978

Texas health manpower reports : podiatrists, 1978 / statistics compiled by Data Collection and Analysis Division, Bureau of State Health Planning and Resource Development, Texas Department of Health. Austin, Tex. : Texas Dept. of Health, [1979?] 47 p. : ill. ; 28 cm.   LC Card 80-622795   DDC 331.12/91617585009764 19
1. Podiatrists - Texas - Statistics. I. Title.
RD563 .T49 1979

Texas. Bureau of State Health Planning & Resource Development. Division of Data Collection and Analysis.
Premature mortality, Texas, 1978. Austin, Tex. : Texas Dept. of Health, Bureau of State Health Planning and Resource Development, Division of Data Collection and Analysis, [1980] ix, 21 p. : graphs ; 28 cm.   LC Card 80-622852   DDC 304.6/4/09764 19
1. Mortality - Texas. 2. Life span, Productive - Texas. I. Title.
HB1355.T4 T49 1980

Texas health manpower report : physical therapists, 1978 : statistics / compiled by Data Collection and Analysis Division, Bureau of State Health Planning and Resource Development, Texas Department of Health. Austin, Tex. : The Dept., 1979. 127 p. : ill. ; 28 cm. Tables.   LC Card 80-622320   DDC 331.12/9161582/09794 19
1. Physical therapists - Texas - Statistics. I. Title.
RM699.3.U6 T49 1979

Texas health manpower report, veterinarians, 1978 / statistics compiled by Data Collection and Analysis Division, Bureau of State Health Planning and Resource Development, Texas Department of Health. Austin, Tex. : The Dept., [1979?] 124 p. ; 28 cm.   LC Card 80-622856   DDC 331.12/91636089/09764 19
1. Veterinarians - Texas - Supply and demand - Statistics. I. Title.
SF611 .T49 1979

Texas business review. Economic and business issues of the 1980's /. [Austin], c1980. vii, 235 p. :   ISBN 0-87755-242-8 (pbk.)   LC Card 80-137600   DDC 330.9764/063 19
HC107.T4 E27

Texas Christian University, Fort Worth. Institute of Behavioral Research. Comparative effectiveness of drug abuse treatment modalities. [Washington, D.C.] : U. S. Dept. of Health, Education, and Welfare, Public Health Service, Alcohol, Drug Abuse, and Mental Health Administration, [1979] vi, 55 p. ; 26 cm. (Services Research administrative report- National Institute on Drug Abuse) Bibliography: p. 54-55.   LC Card 79-601884   DDC 362.2/93 19
1. Drug abuse - Treatment. 2. Drug abuse - Treatment - Tables. I. Series: National Institute on Drug Abuse. Services Research Branch. Services Research administrative report. II. Title.
RC564 .T49 1979

TEXAS. CIVIL AIR PATROL COMMISSION.
Texas. Legislative Budget Board. Program Evaluation. Civil Air Patrol Commission . Austin, Tex. , 1979. 23 leaves ;   LC Card 80-622077   DDC 353.97640075/4 19
UA928.T4 T49 1979

TEXAS - CLIMATE.
Bomar, George W. 1979, too much rain--then not enough /. Austin, Tex. [1980] vi, 48 p. :   LC Card 80-622794   DDC 551.69764 19
QC984.T4 B66

Texas. Coastal and Marine Council.
Ditton, Robert B., 1943- Recreational fishing use of artificial reefs on the Texas Coast /. [Austin] 1978. x, 155 p. :   LC Card 79-624070   DDC 799.1/6634 19
SH551 .D57

Texas. Laws, Statutes, etc. Texas coastal

legislation /. [Austin] , 1979. iv, 219 p. ;   LC Card 80-621294   DDC 346.76404/6917 19
KFT1651.8 .A3 1979

Texas coastal legislation /. Texas. Laws, Statutes, etc. [Austin] , 1979. iv, 219 p. ;   LC Card 80-621294   DDC 346.76404/6917 19
KFT1651.8 .A3 1979

Texas. Commission on Law Enforcement Officer Standards and Education. National Symposium on Job-Task Analysis in Criminal Justice, Dallas, 1978. National Symposium on Job-Task Analysis in Criminal Justice . Washington, D.C. , 1979. ix, 465 p. ;   LC Card 79-603983   DDC 363.2/2 19
HV8143 .N39 1978

TEXAS - CONSTITUTIONAL LAW.
Proposed Constitution of the State of Texas. [Austin , 1975?] 23 p. ;   LC Card 76-620741   DDC 342/.764/023 19
KFT1601 1876 .A25456

TEXAS - CONSTITUTIONAL LAW - AMENDMENTS.
Texas. Legislative Council. Proposed constitutional amendments analyzed . [Austin? Tex.] [1980?] 24 p. ;   LC Card 80-622923   DDC 342.764/035 19
KFT1601 1876.A88 A45

Texas. Legislature. House of Representatives. Study Group. Constitutional amendments, 1980. Austin, Tex. [1980] 35 p. ;   LC Card 80-622623   DDC 342.764/035 19
KFT1601 1876.A7 L433 1980

Texas. Coordinating Board, Texas College and University System. Office, Postsecondary Educational Planning. Texas. State 1202 Commission. Postsecondary educational supply and occupational demand in Texas for the period of 1977-1983 . Austin, Tex. [1978] 119 p. ;   LC Card 79-620962   DDC 331.12/09764 19
HD5725.T5 T38 1978

Texas. Criminal Justice Division. Attorney General of Texas, Criminal Task Force for Organized Crime / Office of the Governor, Criminal Justice Division. Austin, Tex. : The Division, 1978. 55 p. ; 28 cm. "Audit report number 78-33."   LC Card 79-621910   DDC 353.97640074 19
1. Texas. Criminal Task Force for Organized Crime - Auditing and inspection.
HV8145.T4 T49 1978

TEXAS. CRIMINAL TASK FORCE FOR ORGANIZED CRIME - AUDITING AND INSPECTION.
Texas. Criminal Justice Division. Attorney General of Texas, Criminal Task Force for Organized Crime / Austin, Tex. , 1978. 55 p. ;   LC Card 79-621910   DDC 353.97640074 19
HV8145.T4 T49 1978

Texas. Dept. of Agriculture. (Old Catalog form: Texas. Agriculture Dept.)
Predator Control Summit, Austin, Tex., 1980. Proceedings of the Predator Control Summit, January 15, 1980, Austin, Texas /. Austin, Tex. [1980] 45 p. ;   LC Card 80-622863   DDC 636.08/3 19
SF810.6.U6 P74 1980

Texas. Dept. of Community Affairs.
Recycling neighborhoods : a catalog of housing rehabilitation programs and neighborhood preservation activities in Texas / prepared by the Texas Department of Community Affairs.1st ed. [Austin] : The Dept., [1978] 2 v. : ill. ; 22 x 30 cm. "March 1978." Includes indexes. CONTENTS. - pt. 1. Program catalog.--pt. 2. Program documents.   LC Card 79-622456   DDC 363.5/8 19
1. Housing - Rehabilitation - Texas. 2. Housing - Rehabilitation - Texas - Finance. 3. Community development - Texas. 4. Urban renewal - Texas. I. Title.
HD7293 .T46 1978

Texas State housing plan / prepared by the Texas Department of Community Affairs, in cooperation with the Office of the Governor, Division of Budget and Planning. [Austin : The Dept., 1978] 137 p. : maps ; 22 x 29 cm. Bibliography: p. 135-137.   LC Card 80-622869   DDC 363.5/8 19
1. Public housing - Texas. I. Texas. Governor's Budget and Planning Office. II. Title.
HD7303.T4 T495 1978

Texas. Dept. of Corrections. Research, Planning, and Development Division.
Comparison analysis of escapes from State and Federal correctional institutions, 1972 through 1975. Huntsville : Texas Dept. of Corrections, Treatment Directorate, Research, Planning, and Development Division, 1978. vi, 29 leaves : graphs ; 29 cm. (Technical note - Texas Dept. of Corrections, Treatment Directorate, Research, Planning, and Development Division ; no. 55) Prepared by Sheri D. Touchstone.   LC Card 78-622828   DDC 365/.641 19
1. Escapes - United States. I. Touchstone, Sheri D. II. Series: Texas. Dept. of Corrections. Research, Planning, and Development Division. Technical note - Texas Department of Corrections, Research, Planning and Development Division , no. 55. III. Title.
HV9304 .T46 1978

Technical note - Texas Department of Corrections, Research, Planning and Development Division .
(no. 55) Texas. Dept. of Corrections. Research, Planning, and Development Division. Comparison analysis of escapes from State and Federal correctional institutions, 1972 through 1975. Huntsville , 1978. vi, 29 leaves :   LC Card 78-622828   DDC 365/.641 19
HV9304 .T46 1978

Texas. Dept. of Health.
Food & fitness . [Austin, Tex.] [1979?] vi, 105 p. ;   LC Card 80-621074   DDC 362.1/9639 19
RA645.N87 F66

Texas. Laws, Statutes, etc. Migrant labor camp laws . [Austin, Tex.] [1980?] iv, 23 p. :   LC Card 80-622400   DDC 344.764/01544/02632 19
KFT1538.A4 A32 1980

Texas. Dept. of Highways and Public Transportation. see **Texas. State Dept. of Highways and Public Transportation.**

Texas. Dept. of Mental Health and Mental Retardation. The forensic psychiatric patient in Texas : historical perspective and normative research on dangerousness / Texas Department of Mental Health and Mental Retardation. Austin, Tex. : The Dept., [1980] 367 p. in various pagings ; 28 cm. Cover title. "March 1980." Includes bibliographical references.   LC Card 80-622802   DDC 364.3/8/09764 19
1. Insane, Criminal and dangerous - Texas. 2. Violence research - Texas. 3. Insane, Criminal and dangerous - Mental health. I. Title.
HV6133 .T43 1980

Texas. Dept. of Public Welfare. see **Texas. State Dept. of Public Welfare.**

Texas. Dept. of Water Resources.
Ground-water resources and model applications for the Edwards (Balcones Fault Zone) aquifer in the San Antonio region, Texas / by William B. Klemt ... [et al.]. Austin, Tex. : Texas Dept. of Water Resources, [1979] vi, 88 p., 30 leaves of plates : ill. ; 28 cm. (Report - Texas Department of Water Resources ; 239) "October 1979." Bibliography: p. 86-88.   LC Card 80-622334   DDC 553.7/9/0976435 19
1. Aquifers - Texas - San Antonio region - Mathematical models. 2. Aquifers - Texas - San Antonio region - Data processing. 3. Water, Underground - Texas - San Antonio region - Mathematical models. 4. Water, Underground - Texas - San Antonio region - Data processing. I. Klemt, William B. II. Series: Texas. Dept. of Water Resources. Report - Texas Department of Water Resources , 239. III. Title.
TD224.T4 A333 no. 239 GB1199.3.T4

Ouzts, W. Glenn. Land use/land cover maps of Texas /. Austin , 1977, 1978 printing. 47 leaves :   LC Card 80-675250   DDC 912/.133373/09764
G1371.G4 O9 1978

Playa Lake monitoring for the Llano Estacado total water management study : Texas, Oklahoma, New Mexico, Colorado, and Kansas / prepared by Texas Department of Water Resources and Texas Natural Resources Information System in cooperation with U. S. Bureau of Reclamation. [Austin] : Texas Dept. of Water Resources, 1980. 18 leaves, [2] leaves of plates : ill. ; 28 cm. "LP-114." "January 1980." Bibliography: leaves 17-18.   LC Card 80-621333   DDC 553.7/8/0723 19
1. Playas - Texas - Lubbock Co. - Data processing. 2.

Water-supply - Texas - Lubbock Co. - Data processing.
3. Playas - Texas - Lubbock Co. - Mathematical
models. 4. Water-Supply - Texas - Lubbock Co. -
Mathematical models. I. Texas Natural Resources
Information System. II. United States. Bureau of
Reclamation. III. Title.
TD224.T4 T36 1980

Projected land use maps year 2000, Brazos
Basin. Austin, Tex. : Texas Dept. of Water
Resources, 1978. [19] leaves : col. maps ; 28 x
44 cm. Cover title. Scale of maps ca. 1:500,000. Each
map dated Feb., 1977. "LP-50." LC Card 80-675289
    DDC 912/.133373/3097641 19
1. Land use - Texas - Brazos River watershed - Maps.
I. Title. II. Title: Brazos Basin.
G1372.B7G4 T4 1978

Projected land use maps year 2000, Canadian
Basin. Austin, Tex. : Texas Dept. of Water
Resources, 1978. [7] leaves : col. maps ; 28 x
44 cm. Cover title. Scale of maps ca. 1:500,000. Each
map dated Feb., 1977. "LP-43." LC Card 80-675290
    DDC 912/.133373/3097661 19
1. Land use - Canadian River watershed - Maps. I.
Title. II. Title: Canadian Basin.
G1372.C3G4 T4 1978

Projected land use maps year 2000, Colorado
Basin. Austin, Tex. : Texas Dept. of Water
Resources, 1978. [15] leaves : col. maps ; 28 x
44 cm. Cover title. Scale of maps ca. 1:500,000. Each
map dated Feb., 1977. "LP-49." LC Card 80-675288
    DDC 912/.133373/3097641 19
1. Land use - Texas - Colorado River watershed -
Maps. I. Title. II. Title: Colorado Basin.
G1372.C55G4 T4 1978

Projected land use maps year 2000, Guadalupe
Basin. Austin, Tex. : Texas Dept. of Water
Resources, 1978. [7] leaves : col. maps ; 28 x
44 cm. Cover title. Scale of maps ca. 1:500,000. Each
map dated Feb., 1977. "LP-42." LC Card 80-675292
    DDC 912/.133373/3097641 19
1. Land use - Texas - Guadalupe River watershed -
Maps. I. Title. II. Title: Guadalupe Basin.
G1372.G8G4 T4 1978

Projected land use maps year 2000, Lavaca
Basin. Austin, Tex. : Texas Dept. of Water
Resources, 1978. [4] leaves : col. maps ; 28 x
44 cm. Cover title. Scale of maps ca. 1:500,000. Each
map dated Feb., 1977. "LP-53." LC Card 80-675293
    DDC 912/.133373/3097641 19
1. Land use - Texas - Lavaca River watershed - Maps.
I. Title. II. Title: Lavaca Basin.
G1372.L3G4 T4 1978

Projected land use maps year 2000, Neches
Basin. Austin, Tex. : Texas Dept. of Water
Resources, 1978. [9] leaves : col. maps ; 28 x
44 cm. Cover title. Scale of maps ca. 1:500,000. Each
map dated Feb., 1977. "LP-54." LC Card 80-675294
    DDC 912/.133373/30976415 19
1. Land use - Texas - Neches River watershed - Maps.
I. Title. II. Title: Neches Basin.
G1372.N4G4 T4 1978

Projected land use maps year 2000, Nueces
Basin. Austin, Tex. : Texas Dept. of Water
Resources, 1978. [13] leaves : col. maps ; 28 x
44 cm. Cover title. Scale of maps ca. 1:500,000. Each
map dated Feb., 1977. "LP-45." LC Card 80-675295
    DDC 912/.133373/3097641 19
1. Land use - Texas - Nueces River watershed - Maps.
I. Title. II. Title: Nueces Basin.
G1372.N8G4 T4 1978

Projected land use maps year 2000, Red Basin.
Austin, Tex. : Texas Dept. of Water Resources,
1978. [11] leaves : col. maps ; 28 x 44 cm.
Cover title. Scale of maps ca. 1:500,000. Each map
dated Feb., 1977. "LP-48." LC Card 80-675296
    DDC 912/.133373/3097642 19
1. Land use - Red River watershed, Tex. and La. -
Maps. I. Title. II. Title: Red Basin.
G1372.R4G4 T4 1978

Projected land use maps year 2000, Rio Grande
Basin. Austin, Tex. : Texas Dept. of Water
Resources, 1978. [18] leaves : col. maps ; 28 x
44 cm. Cover title. Scale of maps ca. 1:500,000. Each
map dated Feb., 1977. "LP-56." LC Card 80-675297
    DDC 912/.133373/3097644 19
1. Land use - Rio Grande watershed - Maps. I. Title.
II. Title: Rio Grande Basin.
G1372.R5G4 T4 1978

Projected land use maps year 2000, Sabine
Basin. Austin, Tex. : Texas Dept. of Water
Resources, 1978. [10] leaves : col. maps ; 28 x
44 cm. Cover title. Scale of maps ca. 1:500,000. Each

map dated Feb., 1977. "LP-51." LC Card 80-675298
    DDC 912/.133373/30976479 19
1. Land use - Sabine River watershed - Maps. I. Title.
II. Title: Sabine Basin.
G1372.S15G4 T4 1978

Projected land use maps year 2000, San
Antonio Basin. Austin, Tex. : Texas Dept. of
Water Resources, 1978. [5] leaves : col. maps ;
28 x 44 cm. Cover title. Scale of maps ca. 1:500,000.
Each map dated Feb., 1977. "LP-47." LC Card
    80-675299 DDC 912/.133373/3097641 19
1. Land use - Texas - San Antonio River watershed -
Maps. I. Title. II. Title: San Antonio Basin.
G1372.S22G4 T4 1978

Projected land use maps year 2000, San Jacinto
Basin. Austin, Tex. : Texas Dept. of Water
Resources, 1978. [4] leaves : col. maps ; 28 x
44 cm. Cover title. Scale of maps ca. 1:500,000. Each
map dated Feb., 1977. "LP-46." LC Card 80-675300
    DDC 912/.133373/3097642 19
1. Land use - Texas - San Jacinto River watershed -
Maps. I. Title. II. Title: San Jacinto Basin.
G1372.S24G4 T4 1978

Projected land use maps year 2000, Sulphur
Basin. Austin, Tex. : Texas Dept. of Water
Resources, 1978. [4] leaves : col. maps ; 28 x
44 cm. Cover title. Scale of maps ca. 1:500,000. Each
map dated Feb., 1977. "LP-44." LC Card 80-675301
    DDC 912/.133373/3097642 19
1. Land use - Sulphur River watershed, Tex. and Ark. -
Maps. I. Title. II. Title: Sulphur Basin.
G1372.S8G4 T4 1978

Projected land use maps year 2000, Trinity
Basin. Austin, Tex. : Texas Dept. of Water
Resources, 1978. [11] leaves : col. maps ; 28 x
44 cm. Cover title. Scale of maps ca. 1:500,000. Each
map dated Feb., 1977. "LP-52." LC Card 80-675302
    DDC 912/.133373/309764 19
1. Land use - Texas - Trinity River watershed - Maps.
I. Title. II. Title: Trinity Basin.
G1372.T8G4 T4 1978

Report - Texas Department of Water
Resources .
    (230) Rawson, Jack. Water quality of
Livingston Reservoir on the Trinity River,
Southeastern Texas /. Austin, Tex. , 1979. v,
46 p. : LC Card 79-625432 DDC
    553.7/8/0976416 19
TD224.T4 A333 no. 230

    (233) Dougherty, John Philip, 1923-
Suspended-sediment load of Texas streams .
Austin [1979] v, 82 p., [1] leaf of plates :
    LC Card 79-625851 DDC 333.91/009764 s
    551.3/54 19
TD224.T4 A333 no. 233 GB1225.T4

    (238) Muller, Daniel A. Ground-water
availability in Texas . Austin, Tex. [1979]
vii, 77 p. : LC Card 80-620811 DDC
    333.91/009764 s 553.7/9/09764 19
TD224.T4 A333 no. 238 GB1025.T4

    (239) Texas. Dept. of Water Resources.
Ground-water resources and model
applications for the Edwards (Balcones Fault
Zone) aquifer in the San Antonio region,
Texas /. Austin, Tex. [1979] vi, 88 p., 30
leaves of plates : LC Card 80-622334 DDC
    553.7/9/0976435 19
TD224.T4 A333 no. 239 GB1199.3.T4

    (240) Price, Robert Donald, 1926-
Occurrence, quality, and quantity of ground
water in Wilbarger County, Texas /. Austin,
Tex. , 1979. viii, 229 p., [4] leaf of plates (3
fold.) : LC Card 80-621331 DDC
    333.91/009764 s 553.7/9/09764746 19
TD224.T4 A333 no. 240 GB1025.T4

Texas. Dept. of Water Resources. Construction
Grants and Water Quality Planning Division.
The State of Texas water quality inventory /
prepared by Construction Grants and Water
Quality Planning Division. 5th ed. [Austin] :
Texas Dept. of Water Resources, 1980. 540 p.,
1 fold. leaf of plates : map ; 28 cm. "LP-59." LC
Card 80-622419 DDC 363.7/3942/09764 19
1. Water quality - Texas. I. Title.
TD224.T4 T36 1980a

Texas. Dept. of Water Resources. Enforcement
and Field Operations Division. District 7
Office. Houston Ship Channel monitoring
program data, 1973-1978. Deer Park, Tex. :
District 7 Office, Enforcement and Field
Operations Division, Texas Dept. of Water

Resources, [1980] iii leaves, 65 p. : ill. ; 28 cm.
"April 1980." "LP-122." LC Card 80-622407 DDC
    363.7/39463/09764141 19
1. Water - Pollution - Texas - Houston Ship Channel. I.
Title.
TD224.T4 T36 1980b

Texas. Dept. of Water Resources. Weather
Modification and Technology Section.
Bomar, George W. 1979, too much rain--then
not enough /. Austin, Tex. [1980] vi, 48 p. :
    LC Card 80-622794 DDC 551.69764 19
QC984.T4 B66

TEXAS - ECONOMIC CONDITIONS.
Plaut, Thomas R. The gross regional product of
Texas and its regions /. Austin, c1981. xi, 54
p. : ISBN 0-87755-244-4 (pbk.) LC Card 80-68661
    DDC 339.3764 19
HC107.T4 P58

TEXAS - ECONOMIC CONDITIONS -
ADDRESSES, ESSAYS, LECTURES.
Economic and business issues of the 1980's /.
[Austin] , c1980. vii, 235 p. : ISBN
0-87755-242-8 (pbk.) LC Card 80-137600
    DDC 330.9764/063 19
HC107.T4 E27

TEXAS - ECONOMIC POLICY.
Greater South Texas Cultural Basin
Commission. Accelerating development of
South Texas . [Austin, Tex.] [1979] xiv, 118,
[67] p. , LC Card 79-623609 DDC 338.9764 19
HC107.T4 G7 1979

Texas. Education Agency.
Career education : a statewide assessment in
Texas. Austin, Tex. : Texas Education Agency,
1979. viii, 86 p. : ill. ; 23 cm. "Texas Assessment
Project." LC Card 80-624108 DDC 378/.013/09764
    19
1. Career education - Texas. I. Title.
LC1037.6.T4 T48 1979

Texas. Education Agency. Dept. of Special
Education. Policies and administrative
procedures for the education of handicapped
students. Austin, Tex. : Dept. of Special
Education, Texas Education Agency, [1979] xii,
179 p. ; 28 cm. "November 1979." Bibliography: p.
147-149. LC Card 80-621337 DDC 371.9/09764 19
1. Handicapped children - Education - Texas. I. Title.
LC4032.T5 T49 1979

Texas. Education Agency. Division of State
Funding. Texas State public education
compensation plan : foundation school program
salaries, 1980-81 school year only, section
16.056, Texas Education Code. Austin, Tex. :
Division of State Funding, Texas Education
Agency, [1980] [22] p. ; 28 cm. Tables. LC Card
80-622335 DDC 331.2/813711/009764 19
1. Teachers - Texas - Salaries, pensions, etc. - Statistics.
I. Title.
LB2842.2 .T47 1980

Texas. Employment Commission. Economic
Research and Analysis Dept. Texas
occupational employment statistics : industry
staffing patterns for selected nonmanufacturing
industries, 2nd quarter 1978 / prepared by
Texas Employment Commission, Economic
Research and Analysis. Austin, Tex. : TEC,
[1979] viii, 117 p. ; 28 cm. Chiefly tables.
Bibliography: p. 117. LC Card 80-621502 DDC
    331.12/51/0009764 19
1. Labor supply - Texas - Statistics. 2. Texas -
Occupations - Statistics. I. Title.
HD5725.T5 T34 1979a

Texas. Energy Advisory Council. Blake, Floyd.
Development and demonstration of low cost
heliostats . [Austin] [1979] xv, 74 p. : LC Card
    80-620769 DDC 621.47 19
TJ810 .B5

Texas. Energy Development Fund.
Demonstration of solar energy conversion of
agricultural or industrial wastes to fuels .
[Austin] , 1979. xiii, 103 p. : LC Card 80-620768
    DDC 662/.8 19
TP360 .D45

Hill, Lewis E. Solar energy, an economic
analysis . [Austin, Tex.] [1979] xii, 200 p. :
    LC Card 80-620775 DDC 333.79/23/09764 19
TJ810 .H55

Report - Texas Energy Advisory Council,
Energy Development Fund .
    (# EDF-015) Blake, Floyd. Development
and demonstration of low cost heliostats .

[Austin] [1979] xv, 74 p. : LC Card
80-620769   DDC 621.47 19
TJ810 .B5

(# EDF-017) Demonstration of solar energy
conversion of agricultural or industrial wastes
to fuels . [Austin] , 1979. xiii, 103 p. : LC
Card 80-620768   DDC 662/.8 19
TP360 .D45

(# EDF-018) Parker, Harry W. Alternative
energy sources for agricultural applications
including gasification of fibrous residues .
[Austin] [1979] xi, 101 p. : LC Card
80-620767   DDC 333.79/38 19
TJ163.2 .P362

(#EDF-008) Solid fuels conversion costs for
Texas-coal and lignite utilization in electric
power generation and other industries .
[Austin] , 1979. v, 101 p. : LC Card
80-620773   DDC 338.4/3662625 19
TP326.U5 S67

(#EDF-020) Zinn, Clyde Dale. Systems
analysis of the Texas gulf coast geopressured
resources . [Austin] , 1979. v, 33 p. ; LC
Card 80-620765   DDC 333.8/8/097641 19
TJ280.7 .Z58

**Report - Texas Energy Development Advisory
    Council, Energy Development Fund .**
(EDF-006) Hill, Lewis E. Solar energy, an
economic analysis . [Austin, Tex.] [1979] xii,
200 p. : LC Card 80-620775   DDC
333.79/23/09764 19
TJ810 .H55

Solid fuels conversion costs for Texas-coal and
lignite utilization in electric power generation
and other industries . [Austin] , 1979. v, 101
p. : LC Card 80-620773   DDC 338.4/3662625 19
TP326.U5 S67

Zinn, Clyde Dale. Systems analysis of the
Texas gulf coast geopressured resources .
[Austin] , 1979. v, 33 p. ; LC Card 80-620765
DDC 333.8/8/097641 19
TJ280.7 .Z58

Texas. Environmental Management Program.
Pipelines and natural resources of the Texas
coast / John Batterton, project manager ;
Rebecca Green, cartographer. [Austin, Tex.] :
Environmental Management Program, General
Land Office, [1980] vi, 266 p. : ill., maps (2
fold. col. in pocket) ; 30 cm. Bibliography: p.
237-239. LC Card 80-622734   DDC 388.5 19
*1. Petroleum - Pipe lines - Environmental aspects -
Texas - Gulf region. 2. Gas, Natural - Pipe lines -
Environmental aspects - Texas - Gulf region. I.
Batterton, John. II. Title.*
TD195.P5 T49 1980

**TEXAS - EXECUTIVE DEPARTMENTS -
    HANDBOOKS, MANUALS, ETC.**
Guide to Texas state agencies. [1st]- ed.
[Austin] 1956-   LC Card 73-29679
NYPL [JLM 80-731]

Texas farm labor handbook /. Edwards, Richard
A., 1927- [College Station, Tex.] [1979?] 61
p. : LC Card 79-625934   DDC 344.764/01763 19
KFT1538.A4 E38

**TEXAS - GENEALOGY - BIBLIOGRAPHY -
    CATALOGS.**
Texas State Library. Archives Division. Guide
to genealogical resources in the Texas State
Archives /. [Austin, Tex. (Box 12927, Austin,
Texas 78711) [197-?] 31 p. ; LC Card
80-624264   DDC 026/.929/109764 19
Z1339 .T352 1970 F385

TEXAS - GENEALOGY - PERIODICALS.
Dallas Genealogical Society. The quarterly. v.
23- ; 1977- Dallas. LC Card 77-646898
NYPL [APR (Texas) 81-225]

Local History and Genealogical Society, Dallas.
The quarterly. v. 1-22; Feb. 1955-1976
(incomplete). Dallas.   *NYPL [APR (Texas)*
(Local History and Genealogical Society,
Dallas, Tex. Quarterly)]

Texas. Governor. Texas. State Board of
Education. Legislative recommendations on
public education in Texas . [Austin, Tex.] (201
E. Eleventh St., Austin 78701) [1981] 18,
xxxviii p. ; LC Card 81-621842   DDC
379.1/22/09764 19
LB2826.T4 T48 1981

Texas. Governor's Budget and Planning Office.
Texas. Dept. of Community Affairs. Texas State

housing plan /. [Austin , 1978] 137 p. : LC
Card 80-622869   DDC 363.5/8 19
HD7303.T4 T495 1978

Texas. Governor's Office of Energy Resources.
Keeran, Duane. The proposed plan of the State
of Texas for technical assistance and energy
conservation measures available to schools,
hospitals, units of local government, and public
care institutions /. [Austin] [1979] xv, 64 p. ;
LC Card 80-621353   DDC 333.79/09764 19
HD9502.U53 T43

Texas. Health Facilities Commission. Texas
Health Facilities Commission rules. [Austin] :
The Commission, [1979] x, 81, [30] p. ; 28 cm.
Cover title. "August 1979." "Texas health planning and
development act": p. [19]-[30] (3d group) Includes
index.   LC Card 80-622988   DDC 344.764/03211 19
*1. Health facilities - Law and legislation - Texas. I.
Title.*
KFT1561.A433 A2 1979

Texas Health Facilities Commission rules. Texas.
Health Facilities Commission. [Austin] [1979]
x, 81, [30] p. ;   LC Card 80-622988   DDC
344.764/03211 19
KFT1561.A433 A2 1979

Texas health manpower report . Texas. Bureau of
State Health Planning & Resource
Development. Data Collection and Analysis
Division. Austin, Tex. , 1978. 101 p. :   LC Card
80-623855   DDC 331.12/9136216068 19
RA997.5.T4 T432 1978

Texas health manpower report . Texas. Bureau of
State Health Planning & Resource
Development. Division of Data Collection and
Analysis. Austin, Tex. [1979?] 127 p. :   LC
Card 80-622320   DDC 331.12/9161582/09794
19
RM699.3.U6 T49 1979

**Texas health manpower report, veterinarians,
1978 /.** Texas. Bureau of State Health
Planning & Resource Development. Division of
Data Collection and Analysis. Austin, Tex.
[1979?] 124 p. ;   LC Card 80-622856   DDC
331.12/91636089/09764 19
SF611 .T49 1979

Texas health manpower reports . Texas. Bureau
of State Health Planning & Resource
Development. Data Collection and Analysis
Division. Austin, Tex. [1979?] 47 p. :   LC Card
80-622795   DDC 331.12/91617585009764 19
RD563 .T49 1979

**Texas. Highways and Public Transportation,
    State Dept. of. see Texas. State Dept. of
    Highways and Public Transportation.**

Texas. Historic Sites and Restoration Branch.
Preservation plan and program for Caddoan
Mounds State Historic Site, Cherokee County,
Texas / prepared by Texas Parks & Wildlife
Department, Historic Sites & Restoration
Branch. [Austin, Tex.] : The Branch, [1978] 73,
25 p. : ill. ; 28 cm. Cover title: Caddoan Mounds
State Historic Site. "November 1978." "PWD plan
4000-153." Includes bibliographies.   LC Card
79-622483   DDC 333.78/3 19
*1. Caddoan Mounds State Historic Site, Tex. I. Title. II.
Title: Caddoan Mounds State Historic Site.*
E99.C12 T48 1978

TEXAS - HISTORY.
Flannery, John B., 1918- The Irish Texans /.
[San Antonio, Tex.] , c1980. 173 p. :   ISBN
0-933164-33-5 (pbk.)   LC Card 79-89957   DDC
976.4/0049162 19
F395.I6 F55

TEXAS - HISTORY - PERIODICALS.
East Texas historical journal. v. 1- ; July, 1963-
Nacogdoches, Tex.   LC Card 68-35211
NYPL [IAA (Texas) (East Texas
historical journal)]

**Texas homeowners, farm and ranch owners, fire
and extended coverage insurance .** Texas. State
Board of Insurance. Property and Casualty
Actuarial Division. [Austin] [1980] 43 p. ;   LC
Card 80-622853   DDC 368.1/009764 19
HG9986.35.T4 T47 1980

**Texas. Hospital Licensure and Certification
    Division.** Hospital licensing standards,
effective date April 15, 1969. [Austin, Tex.] :
Texas Dept. of Health, Hospital Licensure and
Certification Division, [1969?] 170 p. in various
pagings ; 28 cm. Cover title. Includes the text of the

Texas hospital licensing law. Includes index.   LC Card
80-623218   DDC 344.764/03211 19
*1. Hospitals - Licenses - Texas. 2. Hospitals - Law and
legislation - Texas. I. Texas. Laws, statutes, etc. Texas
hospital licensing law. 1969. II. Title.*
KFT1561.A432 A2 1969

**Texas. House of Representatives. see Texas.
    Legislature. House of Representatives.**

TEXAS - HURRICANES.
Henry, Walter K. Hurricanes on the Texas
coast /. [College Station, Tex.] [1975] 48 p. :
LC Card 80-623396   DDC 363.3/492 19
QC945 .H55

Texas. Industrial Commission.
Financing industrial facilities in Texas. Austin,
Tex. : Texas Industrial Commission, [1980] 35
leaves ; 28 cm. Written by D. R. Raburn.
Bibliography: leaf 35.   LC Card 80-623086   DDC
658.1/52 19
*1. Business enterprises - Texas - Finance. 2.
Corporations - Texas - Finance. I. Raburn, Don R. II.
Title.*
HG4070.T4 T49 1980

**Texas. Industrial Commission. Energy Utilization
Dept.** Conference on Industrial Energy
Conservation Technology, 1st, Houston, Tex.,
1979. Industrial energy conservation
technology . [Austin] [1979] 2 v. (xiii, 1073
p.) :   LC Card 80-621335   DDC 621.042 19
TJ163.27 .C66 1979

**TEXAS - INDUSTRIES - ADDRESSES,
    ESSAYS, LECTURES.**
Economic and business issues of the 1980's /.
[Austin] , c1980. vii, 235 p. :   ISBN
0-87755-242-8 (pbk.)   LC Card 80-137600
DDC 330.9764/063 19
HC107.T4 E27

Texas Infant Mortality Task Force. Texas Infant
Mortality Task Force report / prepared for the
use of the Committee on Interstate and Foreign
Commerce, House of Representatives and its
Subcommittee on Health and the Environment,
Ninety-sixth Congress, second session.
Washington : U. S. Govt. Print. Off., 1980. iv,
77 p. : ill. ; 24 cm. At head of title: 96th Congress,
2d session. Committee print 96-IFC.   LC Card
80-602575   DDC 362.1/9832/009764141 19
*1. Infants - Texas - Mortality. 2. Infants - Texas -
Harris Co. - Mortality. 3. Perinatal mortality - Texas. 4.
Perinatal mortality - Texas - Harris Co. 5. Maternal
health services - Texas - Harris Co. 6. Texas -
Statistics, Vital. 7. Harris Co., Tex. - Statistics, Vital. I.
United States. Congress. House. Committee on
Interstate and Foreign Commerce. Subcommittee on
Health and the Environment. II. Title.*
RJ60.U52 T497

Texas Infant Mortality Task Force report /.
Texas Infant Mortality Task Force.
Washington , 1980. iv, 77 p. :   LC Card
80-602575   DDC 362.1/9832/009764141 19
RJ60.U52 T497

**Texas. Intergovernmental Relations, Advisory
    Commission on. see Texas. Advisory
    Commission on Intergovernmental Relations.**

**Texas. Joint Advisory Committee on Government
    Operations. Structure and Policy
    Subcommittee.** Texas. Joint Advisory
Committee on Government Operations.
Subcommittee on Health and Welfare. Initial
report with recommendations to the Joint
Advisory Committee on Government
Operations as modified by the Structure and
Policy Subcommittee /. [Austin?] [1976] iii
leaves, 124 p. ;   LC Card 80-622733   DDC
362/.9764 19
HV86 .T548 1976

**Texas. Joint Advisory Committee on Government
    Operations. Subcommittee on Health and
    Welfare.** Initial report with recommendations
to the Joint Advisory Committee on
Government Operations as modifed by the
Structure and Policy Subcommittee / prepared
under Subcommittee direction by Subcommittee
staff. [Austin?] : Subcommittee on Health and
Welfare, [1976] iii leaves, 124 p. ; 28 cm. "July
30, 1976."   LC Card 80-622733   DDC 362/.9764 19
*1. Social service - Texas. 2. Texas - Social policy. I.
Texas. Joint Advisory Committee on Government
Operations. Structure and Policy Subcommittee. II.
Title.*
HV86 .T548 1976

Texas. Joint Committee on Long-Term Care Alternatives.
Final report / Joint Committee on Long-Term Care Alternatives. [Austin, Tex.] : The Committee, [1980] iii, 40 p. : ill. ; 28 cm. LC Card 80-620752 DDC 362.1/6/09764 19
1. Long-term care of the sick - Texas. 2. Aged - Medical care - Texas. 3. Community health services for the aged - Texas.
RA644.7.T4 T49 1980

Technical report - Joint Committee on Long-Term Care Alternatives .
(4) Texas. Joint Committee on Long-Term Care Alternatives. Well-being in old age . Austin, Tex. , 1978. xiii, 91 p. : LC Card 80-620754 DDC 362.6/042/09764 19
HV1468.T4 T49 1978

Well-being in old age : essential services / presented by Joint Committee on Long-Term Care Alternatives. Austin, Tex. : The Committee, 1978. xiii, 91 p. : ill. ; 28 cm. (Technical report - Joint Committee on Long-Term Care Alternatives ; 4) "Prepared by Bonny Gardner." "Fall 1978." Bibliography: p. 87-91. LC Card 80-620754 DDC 362.6/042/09764 19
1. Aged - Services for - Texas. 2. Aged - Texas - Government policy. I. Gardner, Bonny. II. Series: Texas. Joint Committee on Long-Term Care Alternatives. Technical report - Joint Committee on Long-Term Care Alternatives , 4. III. Title.
HV1468.T4 T49 1978

Texas. Law Enforcement Officer Standards and Education, Commission on. see Texas. Commission on Law Enforcement Officer Standards and Education.

Texas. Laws, Statutes, etc. (Old Catalog form: Texas. Statutes.)
Migrant labor camp laws : rules and regulations. [Austin, Tex.] : Texas Dept. of Health, [1980?] iv, 23 p. : ill. ; 23 cm. LC Card 80-622400 DDC 344.764/01544/02632 19
1. Migrant agricultural laborers - Law and legislation - Texas. 2. Labor camps - Law and legislation - Texas. I. Texas. Dept. of Health. II. Title.
KFT1538.A4 A32 1980

Texas coastal legislation / prepared by the Texas Coastal and Marine Council. 4th ed. [Austin] : The Council, 1979. iv, 219 p. ; 28 cm. LC Card 80-621294 DDC 346.76404/6917 19
1. Coastal zone management - Law and legislation - Texas. 2. Shore protection - Law and legislation - Texas. I. Texas. Coastal and Marine Council. II. Title.
KFT1651.8 .A3 1979

Texas hospital licensing law. 1969. Texas. Hospital Licensure and Certification Division. Hospital licensing standards, effective date April 15, 1969. [Austin, Tex.] [1969?] 170 p. in various pagings ; LC Card 80-623218 DDC 344.764/03211 19
KFT1561.A432 A2 1969

Texas. Legislative Budget Board. Program Evaluation. Civil Air Patrol Commission : staff report to the Sunset Advisory Commission. Austin, Tex. : Legislative Budget Office, Program Evaluation, 1979. 23 leaves ; 28 cm. LC Card 80-622077 DDC 353.97640075/4 19
1. Texas. Civil Air Patrol Commission. 2. Sunset review of government programs - Texas. I. Texas. Sunset Advisory Commission. II. Title.
UA928.T4 T49 1979

Texas. Legislative Council.
Guide to Texas state agencies. [1st]- ed. [Austin] 1956- LC Card 73-29679
NYPL [JLM 80-731]

Proposed constitutional amendments analyzed : analysis of three proposed constitutional amendments for election November 6, 1979 / prepared by the staff of the Texas Legislative Council. [Austin? Tex.] : The Council, [1980?] 24 p. ; 22 cm. LC Card 80-622923 DDC 342.764/035 19
1. Texas - Constitutional law - Amendments. I. Title.
KFT1601 1876.A88 A45

Texas. Legislature.
Members of the Texas Legislature, 1846-1980. [Austin] : The Legislature, [1981?] 615 p. ; 23 cm. Members of the Texas Legislature, 1963-1974, was issued by the Texas Legislative Council. Includes index.
LC Card 81-620996 DDC 328.764/073 19
1. Texas. Legislature - Registers. I. Texas. Legislature. Legislative Council. Members of the Texas Legislature,

1963-1974. II. Title.
JK4831 1981 .T44 1981

Proposed Constitution of the State of Texas. 1975. Proposed Constitution of the State of Texas. [Austin , 1975?] 23 p. ; LC Card 76-620741 DDC 342/.764/023 19
KFT1601 1876 .A25456

Texas. State Board of Education. Legislative recommendations on public education in Texas . [Austin, Tex.] (201 E. Eleventh St., Austin 78701) [1981] 18, xxxviii p. ; LC Card 81-621842 DDC 379.1/22/09764 19
LB2826.T4 T48 1981

Texas. Legislature. House of Representatives. (Old Catalog form: Texas. House of Representatives).
A Compilation of interim reports to the sixty-fifth legislative session, Texas House of Representatives, December 1976. [Austin] [1976?] 4 v. : LC Card 80-623602 DDC 348.764/01 19
KFT1220 .C648

Texas. Legislature. House of Representatives. Study Group.
Banning the income tax. Austin, Tex. : House Study Group, Texas House of Representatives, 1980. 55 p. : graphs ; 28 cm. (House Study Group special legislative report ; no. 54) Bibliography: p. 53-55. LC Card 80-621661 DDC 343.76405/2 19
1. Income tax - Law and legislation - Texas. I. Series: Texas. Legislature. House of Representatives. Study Group. Special legislative report - House Study Group , no. 54. II. Title.
KFT1675 .A25 1980

Constitutional amendments, 1980. Austin, Tex. : House Study Group, Texas House of Representatives, [1980] 35 p. ; 29 cm. (Special legislative report - House Study Group ; no. 57) "April 30, 1980." LC Card 80-622623 DDC 342.764/035 19
1. Texas - Constitutional law - Amendments. I. Series: Texas. Legislature. House of Representatives. Study Group. Special legislative report - House Study Group , no. 57. II. Title.
KFT1601 1876.A7 L433 1980

Keith, Gary. Air Pollution control in Texas. Austin, Tex. (Room 315-B, Capitol Bldg., Austin 78769) [1981] xv, 60 p. : LC Card 81-621709 DDC 344.764/046342 347.640446342 19
KFT1558. A25 1981

Overcrowding in Texas prisons. Austin : House Study Group, Texas House of Representatives, 1979. 23 p. ; 28 cm. (Special legislative report - House Study Group ; no. 43) LC Card 79-624889 DDC 365/.6 19
1. Prisons - Texas - Overcrowding. I. Series: Texas. Legislature. House of Representatives. Study Group. Special legislative report - House Study Group , no. 43. II. Title.
HV8363 .T42 1979

Phillips, Diana Buder. Sunset 1979. Austin, Tex. , 1979. 5, [15] p. ; LC Card 80-620628 DDC 328.764/07456 19
JK4838 1979 .P48

Piltz, Rick. Energy conservation. Austin, Tex. (P.O. Box 2910, Austin 78769) [1981] vii, 58 p. ; LC Card 81-622292 DDC 333.79/16/09764 19
HD9502.U53 T455

Special legislative report - House Study Group .
(no. 43) Texas. Legislature. House of Representatives. Study Group. Overcrowding in Texas prisons. Austin , 1979. 23 p. ; LC Card 79-624889 DDC 365/.6 19
HV8363 .T42 1979

(no. 54) Texas. Legislature. House of Representatives. Study Group. Banning the income tax. Austin, Tex. , 1980. 55 p. : LC Card 80-621661 DDC 343.76405/2 19
KFT1675 .A25 1980

(no. 56) Texas. Legislature. House of Representatives. Study Group. Wiretapping /. Austin, Tex. [1980] 34 p. : LC Card 80-622368 DDC 347.764/064 19
KFT1780.5.W5 A25 1980

(no. 57) Texas. Legislature. House of Representatives. Study Group. Constitutional amendments, 1980. Austin, Tex. [1980] 35

p. ; LC Card 80-622623 DDC 342.764/035 19
KFT1601 1876.A7 L433 1980

Wiretapping / [by Betty Anne Duke]. Austin, Tex. : House Study Group, [1980] 34 p. : graphs ; 28 cm. (House Study Group special legislative report ; no. 56) Bibliography: p. 34. LC Card 80-622368 DDC 347.764/064 19
1. Wire-tapping - Texas. 2. Wire-tapping - United States. I. Duke, Betty Anne. II. Series: Texas. Legislature. House of Representatives. Study Group. Special legislative report - House Study Group , no. 56. III. Title.
KFT1780.5.W5 A25 1980

Texas. Legislature. Joint Advisory Committee on Educational Services to the Deaf.
Texas. Legislature. Joint Advisory Committee on Educational Services to the Deaf. Subcommittee on Educational Programs. Final report of the Subcommittees on Educational Programs and Governmental Structure to the members of the Sixty-sixth Texas Legislature. [Austin, Tex.] [1979] x, 199 p. ; LC Card 79-623607 DDC 371.91/2/09764 19
HV2561.T6 T493 1979

Texas. Legislature. Joint Advisory Committee on Educational Services to the Deaf. Subcommittee on Educational Programs.
Final report of the Subcommittees on Educational Programs and Governmental Structure to the members of the Sixty-sixth Texas Legislature. [Austin, Tex.] : Joint Advisory Committee on Educational Services to the Deaf, [1979] x, 199 p. ; 28 cm. At head of title: Joint Advisory Committee on Educational Services to the Deaf. "January 1979." LC Card 79-623607 DDC 371.91/2/09764 19
1. Deaf - Education - Texas. I. Texas. Legislature. Joint Advisory Committee on Educational Services to the Deaf. Subcommittee on Governmental Structure. II. Texas. Legislature. Joint Advisory Committee on Educational Services to the Deaf.
HV2561.T6 T493 1979

Texas. Legislature. Joint Advisory Committee on Educational Services to the Deaf. Subcommittee on Governmental Structure.
Texas. Legislature. Joint Advisory Committee on Educational Services to the Deaf. Subcommittee on Educational Programs. Final report of the Subcommittees on Educational Programs and Governmental Structure to the members of the Sixty-sixth Texas Legislature. [Austin, Tex.] [1979] x, 199 p. ; LC Card 79-623607 DDC 371.91/2/09764 19
HV2561.T6 T493 1979

Texas. Legislature. Legislative Council.
Legislator's guide to the Texas Legislative Council / prepared by the staff of the Texas Legislative Council. Austin, Tex. (P.O. Box 12128, Capitol Station, Austin 78711) : The Council, [1980] 24 p. ; 28 cm. (Information report / Texas Legislative Council . no. 80-3) "November, 1980." LC Card 81-621424 DDC 328.758/0761 19
1. Texas. Legislature. Legislative Council. 2. Legislative reference bureaus - Texas. I. Series: Information report (Texas. Legislature. Legislative Council) , no. 80-3. II. Title.
JK4874 .T49 1980

TEXAS. LEGISLATURE. LEGISLATIVE COUNCIL.
Texas. Legislature. Legislative Council. Legislator's guide to the Texas Legislative Council /. Austin, Tex. (P.O. Box 12128, Capitol Station, Austin 78711) [1980] 24 p. ; LC Card 81-621424 DDC 328.758/0761 19
JK4874 .T49 1980

Texas. Legislature. Legislative Council. Members of the Texas Legislature, 1963-1974. Texas. Legislature. Members of the Texas Legislature, 1846-1980. [Austin] [1981?] 615 p. LC Card 81-620996 DDC 328.764/073 19
JK4831 1981 .T44 1981

TEXAS. LEGISLATURE - REGISTERS.
Texas. Legislature. Members of the Texas Legislature, 1846-1980. [Austin] [1981?] 615 p. ; LC Card 81-620996 DDC 328.764/073 19
JK4831 1981 .T44 1981

Texas. Legislature. Senate. (Old Catalog form: Texas. Senate.)
Texas water administration : a summary of the governmental units in Texas with authority over water / compiled by the staff of the Senate regional councils on water resources. [Austin] :

BIBLIOGRAPHIC GUIDE

Texas. Legislature. Senate. Committee to Study Texas Beaches.

350

The Senate, [197-] v, 87 p. ; 28 cm. LC Card 80-622555 DDC 353.97640082/325 19
1. Water resources development - Texas. 2. Water districts - Texas. 3. Administrative agencies - Texas. I. Title.
HD1694.T4 T3 1970

Texas. Legislature. Senate. Committee to Study Texas Beaches. Interim report of the Senate Committee to Study Texas Beaches, 65th Legislature / Jack Ogg, chairman. [Austin] : The Committee, 1979. ii leaves, 48 p. ; 28 cm. LC Card 79-625806 DDC 346.76404/6917 19
1. Beaches - Law and legislation - Texas. 2. Shore protection - Law and legislation - Texas. I. Title.
LAW

Texas. Legislature. Senate. Subcommittee on Housing. Interim report of the Senate Subcommittee on Housing, Senate of the State of Texas, 65th Legislature, Carl A. Parker, chairman. Austin : The Senate, 1978. 65 p. : ill. ; 28 cm. Cover title. LC Card 80-622731 DDC 363.5/09764 19
1. Housing - Texas. 2. Housing - Texas - Finance.
KFT1211.72 .H68 1978

Texas. Memorial Museum, Austin.
Pearce-Sellards series .
The Pearce-Sellards series .
(no. 27) Thomas, Robert A. A new systematic arrangement for Philodryas serra (Schlegel) and Philodryas pseudoserra Amaral (Serpentes : Colubridae) /. Austin , 1977. 20 p. : LC Card 78-621007 DDC 574 s 597.96 19
AM101 .T474 no. 27 QL666.O636

(no. 32) Dalquest, Walter Woelber, 1917- Late Hemphillian mammals of the Ocote local fauna, Guanajuato, Mexico /. Austin, Tex. , 19. 25 p. : LC Card 80-622865 DDC 574 s 569 19
AM101 .T474 no. 32 QE881

Texas Natural Resources Information System. State Agency Libraries of Texas. Guide to Texas State agency libraries /. Austin, Tex. , 1980. vi, 65 p. : LC Card 80-623699 DDC 027.5/025/764 19
Z675.G7 S73 1980

Texas. Dept. of Water Resources. Playa Lake monitoring for the Llano Estacado total water management study . [Austin] , 1980. 18 leaves, [2] leaves of plates : LC Card 80-621333 DDC 553.7/8/0723 19
TD224.T4 T36 1980

Texas. Natural Resources Information System Task Force. Landsat in Texas State agencies, April 1979. [Austin] : Texas Natural Resources Informations System, [1979] 18 leaves ; 29 cm. "April 1979." "TNRIS-014." LC Card 80-621072 DDC 333.7/09764 19
1. Remote sensing - Texas. 2. Landsat satellites. I. Title.
G70.5.U6 T49 1979

Texas occupational employment statistics . Texas. Employment Commission. Economic Research and Analysis Dept. Austin, Tex. [1979] viii, 117 p. ; LC Card 80-621502 DDC 331.12/51/0009764 19
HD5725.T5 T34 1979a

TEXAS - OCCUPATIONS - STATISTICS.
Texas. Employment Commission. Economic Research and Analysis Dept. Texas occupational employment statistics . Austin, Tex. [1979] viii, 117 p. ; LC Card 80-621502 DDC 331.12/51/0009764 19
HD5725.T5 T34 1979a

Texas. Office of the State Archeologist. Lynn, Warren M. Cultural resource survey of Choke Canyon Reservoir, Live Oak and McMullen Counties, Texas /. Austin , 1977. xiv, 273 p. : LC Card 78-622852 DDC 976.4/447 19
F392.F92 L96

TEXAS - OFFICIALS AND EMPLOYEES - SALARIES, ALLOWANCES, ETC.
Jarrett, James E. Texas assumes the social security obligation. [Lexington, Ky.] [1979] 12 p. ; LC Card 80-140046 DDC 353.9 s 353.9764001/234 19
JS308 .C6 no. 680 JK4857

Texas. Parks and Wildlife Dept.
Coastal fisheries plan, 1978-1979, 1980-1981 / Texas Parks and Willife Department. [Austin] : The Dept., [1978] i, 44 p. ; 28 cm. (PWD report . 3000-54) Bibliography: p. 43-44. LC Card 79-623627 DDC 333.95/6/097641 19

1. Fishery management - Texas. 2. Fisheries - Texas - Planning. I. Series: Texas. Parks and Wildlife Dept. PWD report , 3000-54. II. Title.
SH222.T4 T48 1978

Etchieson, Gerald Meeks. An archeological survey of certain tracts in and near Caprock Canyons State Park in eastern Briscoe County, Texas /. Canyon, Tex. , 1977. ii, 84, [66] p. : LC Card 78-623263 DDC 976.4/839 19
E78.T4 E83

Mount Livermore and Sawtooth Mountain /. [Austin] , 1973. 84 p., [1] leaf of plates : LC Card 80-623871 DDC 508.764/934 19
QH105.T4 M68

Technical series .
(no. 14) Moffett, Alan W. The hydrography and macro-biota of the Chocolate Bayou estuary, Brazoria County, Texas, 1969-1971 /. [Austin] , 1975. 72 p. : LC Card 81-479509 DDC 574.9764/137 19
QH105.T4 M63

(no. 22) Thompson, Kenneth W. Analysis of potential environmental factors, especially thermal, which would influence the survivorship of exotic Nile perch if introduced into artificially heated reservoirs in Texas /. [Austin] , 1977. 37 p. : LC Card 78-620720 DDC 639.9/7758 19
QL638.C34 T48

(no. 23) Johnson, Roy B. Fishery survey of Cedar Lakes and the Brazos and San Bernard River estuaries /. [Austin] , 1977. 65 p. : LC Card 78-622882 DDC 333.95/09764 s 639/.2/09764137 19
SH11.T4 A3 no. 3000-34 QL628.T4

Texas postsecondary education outlook, 1980-1985. Proceedings of the Texas postsecondary education outlook, 1980-1985 . [Austin] , c1979. xv, 166 p. : LC Card 80-623590 DDC 378.764 19
LB2329.5 .P76

Texas Public Health Association. Food & fitness . [Austin, Tex.] [1979?] vi, 105 p. ; LC Card 80-621074 DDC 362.1/9639 19
RA645.N87 F66

Texas. Public Welfare, State Dept. of. see **Texas. State Dept. of Public Welfare.**

The Texas rail freight system . Texas. Railroad Commission. Austin, Tex. [1979] xvi, 276 p. : LC Card 80-622071 DDC 385/.24/09764 19
HE2771.T4 T49 1979

Texas. Railroad Commission.
The Texas rail freight system : an overview and outlook. Austin, Tex. : Railroad Commission of Texas, [1979] xvi, 276 p. : maps ; 28 cm. "December 1979." Includes bibliographical references. LC Card 80-622071 DDC 385/.24/09764 19
1. Railroads - Texas - Freight. I. Title.
HE2771.T4 T49 1979

Texas. Railroad Commission. Gas Utilities Division.
Rules and regulations for the Transportation of natural and other gas by pipeline. [Austin] : Railroad Commission of Texas, Gas Utilities Division, [1980] 110 p. ; 28 cm. Cover title. Includes bibliographical references and index. LC Card 80-622926 DDC 363.1/79 19
1. Gas, Natural - Texas - Pipe lines - Safety measures. 2. Gas - Pipe lines - Safety measures. I. Title.
TN880.5 .T49 1980

Special rules of practice and procedure and substantive rules / Railroad Commission of Texas, Gas Utilities Division. [Austin, Tex.] : The Division, [1980] 67 leaves ; 28 cm. Cover title. LC Card 80-622927 DDC 343.764/0926 19
1. Gas companies - Texas - Rates. 2. Gas, Natural - Law and legislation - Texas. I. Title.
KFT1488.A447 A2 1980

Texas. Railroad Commission. Transportation Division. Motor transportation regulations before the Transportation Division / Railroad Commission of Texas, Transportation Division. Rev. Nov. 30, 1979. [Austin] : The Division, [1979] 7, 209 p. ; 28 cm. Cover title. LC Card 80-622401 DDC 343.764/0944/02636 19
1. Transportation, Automotive - Law and legislation - Texas. I. Title.
KFT1499.A435 A2 1979

Texas Real Estate Research Center. Moore, Mary. Income tax law changes affecting real

estate /. College Station, Tex. [1980] 56 p. ; LC Card 81-621043 DDC 343.7305/4 347.30354 19
KF6535.Z9 M66

Texas. Regional Center for Services to Deaf-Blind. Improving services to deaf-blind/multihandicapped individuals in residential facilities . Austin [1978?] v, 189 p. : LC Card 78-623256 DDC 362.4/048 19
HV1597.2 .I46

Texas. Rehabilitation Commission.
Interim state plan for independent living rehabilitation services, under title VII of the Rehabilitation act of 1973, as amended through 1978 / Texas Rehabilitation Commission. [Austin] : The Commission, [1979] 40 leaves ; 28 cm. "October 1, 1979." LC Card 80-622344 DDC 362/.0425 19
1. Vocational rehabilitation - Texas - Planning. 2. Texas. Rehabilitation Commission - Planning. I. Title.
HV1555.T4 T49 1979

Texas Rehabilitation Commission State plan : vocational rehabilitation services, fiscal years 1980, 1981 & 1982, under title 1 of the Rehabilitation act of 1973, as amended. [Austin] : The Commission, [1979] v, 45, [20] leaves : diagrs. ; 28 cm. Cover title. LC Card 80-622857 DDC 362/.0425 19
1. Vocational rehabilitation - Texas. 2. Texas. Rehabilitation Commission. I. Title.
HD7256.U6 T437 1979

TEXAS. REHABILITATION COMMISSION.
Texas. Rehabilitation Commission. Texas Rehabilitation Commission State plan . [Austin] [1979] v, 45, [20] leaves : LC Card 80-622857 DDC 362/.0425 19
HD7256.U6 T437 1979

TEXAS. REHABILITATION COMMISSION - PLANNING.
Texas. Rehabilitation Commission. Interim state plan for independent living rehabilitation services, under title VII of the Rehabilitation act of 1973, as amended through 1978 /. [Austin] [1979] 40 leaves ; LC Card 80-622344 DDC 362/.0425 19
HV1555.T4 T49 1979

Texas Rehabilitation Commission State plan . Texas. Rehabilitation Commission. [Austin] [1979] v, 45, [20] leaves : LC Card 80-622857 DDC 362/.0425 19
HD7256.U6 T437 1979

Texas. School Transportation Section. Public school transportation. Austin, Tex. : Division of Administrative Services, School Transportation Section, Texas Education Agency, 1980. vi, 57 p. : forms ; 28 cm. "ADO 936 02." LC Card 80-622617 DDC 371.8/72/09764 19
1. School children - Texas - Transportation. I. Title.
LB2864 .T42 1980

The Texas Seminoles and their language /. Hancock, Ian F. [Austin] , 1980. iv, 29 leaves ; LC Card 80-622194 DDC 427/.9764 19
PM7874.T48 H36

Texas. Senate. see **Texas. Legislature. Senate.**

TEXAS - SOCIAL CONDITIONS.
De Leon, Arnoldo, 1945- The Tejano community, 1836-1900 /. Albuquerque [1982] p. cm. ISBN 0-8263-0586-5 : LC Card 81-52053 DDC 976.4/0046872 19
F395.M5 D4

TEXAS - SOCIAL LIFE AND CUSTOMS.
De Leon, Arnoldo, 1945- The Tejano community, 1836-1900 /. Albuquerque [1982] p. cm. ISBN 0-8263-0586-5 : LC Card 81-52053 DDC 976.4/0046872 19
F395.M5 D4

TEXAS - SOCIAL POLICY.
Texas. Joint Advisory Committee on Government Operations. Subcommittee on Health and Welfare. Initial report with recommendations to the Joint Advisory Committee on Government Operations as modifed by the Structure and Policy Subcommittee /. [Austin?] [1976] iii leaves, 124 p. ; LC Card 80-622733 DDC 362/.9764 19
HV86 .T548 1976

Texas. State Board of Education. Legislative recommendations on public education in Texas : submitted to the Governor and the Sixty-seventh Legislature / State Board of

Education. [Austin, Tex.] (201 E. Eleventh St., Austin 78701) : The Board, [1981] 18, xxxviii p. ; 28 cm. Cover title. "January 1981"--P. 1. LC Card 81-621842 DDC 379.1/22/09764 19
1. Education - Texas - Finance. I. Texas. Governor. II. Texas. Legislature. III. Title.
LB2826.T4 T48 1981

Texas. State Board of Insurance. Procedures for licensing insurance adjusters / State Board of Insurance, State of Texas. [Austin, Tex.] : The Board, [1980?] 16 leaves ; 28 cm. Cover title. Includes index. LC Card 80-622804 DDC 346.764/086014 19
1. Insurance - Agents - Licenses - Texas. 2. Insurance - Texas - Adjustment of claims. I. Title.
KFT1385 .A846

Texas. State Board of Insurance. Property and Casualty Actuarial Division. Texas homeowners, farm and ranch owners, fire and extended coverage insurance : 1980 actuarial and statistical exhibit / prepared by Property and Casualty Actuarial Division, Texas State Board of Insurance. [Austin] : The Division, [1980] 43 p. ; 28 cm. Tables. LC Card 80-622853 DDC 368.1/009764 19
1. Insurance, Homeowners - Texas - Statistics. 2. Insurance, Fire - Texas - Statistics. 3. Insurance, Property - Texas - Statistics. I. Title.
HG9986.35.T4 T47 1980

Texas. State Board of Library Examiners. Report to the Sunset Advisory Commission / by State Board of Library Examiners. [Austin] : The Board, [1979?] 67 leaves ; 22 x 36 cm. "September 30, 1979." LC Card 80-620788 DDC 021.8/2 19
1. Public librarians - Certification - Texas. 2. Texas. State Board of Library Examiners. I. Texas. Sunset Advisory Commission. II. Title.
Z682.2.U5 T49 1979

TEXAS. STATE BOARD OF LIBRARY EXAMINERS. Texas. State Board of Library Examiners. Report to the Sunset Advisory Commission /. [Austin] [1979] 67 leaves ; LC Card 80-620788 DDC 021.8/2 19
Z682.2.U5 T49 1979

Texas. State Board of Vocational Nurse Examiners. Minimum standards for Vocational nurse education. Austin, Tex. : Board of Vocational Nurse Examiners, 1979. iii, 26 p. ; 28 cm. LC Card 80-622928 DDC 344.764/0414 19
1. Practical nursing - Study and teaching - Law and legislation - Texas. I. Title.
KFT1526.5.P66 A32 1979

Texas. State Dept. of Highways and Public Transportation. Womack, Katie N. Costs of public transportation in Texas, 1973-1977 /. College Station, Tex. , 1979. viii, 81 p. : LC Card 80-621655 DDC 388.4/042 19
HE4487.T4 W65

Texas. State Dept. of Public Welfare. Annual report. [Austin] tables. 28 cm. Report year ends Aug. 31st. For later file, see: Texas. Dept. of Human Resources. Annual report.
1. Texas. State Dept. of Public Welfare.
   NYPL [SHG (Texas. Public Welfare, State Dept. of. Annual report.)]

Directory: child welfare resources. Austin. 28 cm. Title also as: Directory of child welfare resources.
1. Child welfare - Texas - Directories. I. Title. II. Title: Directory of child welfare resources.
   NYPL [JLM 80-696]

TEXAS. STATE DEPT. OF PUBLIC WELFARE. Texas. State Dept. of Public Welfare. Annual report. [Austin] *NYPL [SHG (Texas. Public Welfare, State Dept. of. Annual report.)]*

The Texas state health plan /. Texas. Statewide Health Coordinating Council. [Austin] [1980] ca. 300 p. in various pagings : LC Card 80-623084 DDC 362.1/09764 19
RA395.A4 T4886 1980

Texas State housing plan /. Texas. Dept. of Community Affairs. [Austin , 1978] 137 p. : LC Card 80-622869 DDC 363.5/8 19
HD7303.T4 T495 1978

Texas State Library. Archives Division. Guide to genealogical resources in the Texas State Archives / Archives Division, Texas State Library. [Rev. ed.] [Austin, Tex. (Box 12927, Austin, Texas 78711) : The Division, [197-?] 31

p. ; 23 cm. LC Card 80-624264 DDC 026/.929/109764 19
1. Texas - Genealogy - Bibliography - Catalogs. 2. Texas State Library. Archives Division - Catalogs. I. Title.
Z1339 .T352 1970 F385

TEXAS STATE LIBRARY. ARCHIVES DIVISION - CATALOGS. Texas State Library. Archives Division. Guide to genealogical resources in the Texas State Archives /. [Austin, Tex. (Box 12927, Austin, Texas 78711) [197-?] 31 p. ; LC Card 80-624264 DDC 026/.929/109764 19
Z1339 .T352 1970 F385

Texas. State Library, Austin. Planning and Management Dept. Library services and construction act : long range plan, 1981-1985, updates / Texas State Library, Planning and Management Department.Completely rev. [Austin] : The Dept., [1979] 211 p. in various pagings : map ; 29 cm. Includes bibliographical references. LC Card 80-622318 DDC 027.0764 19
1. Libraries - Texas. 2. Federal aid to libraries - Texas. I. Title.
Z678.4.T4 T48 1979

Texas. State Property Tax Board. General appraisal manual : legal requirements, operations, valuation procedures / State Property Tax Board. [Austin, Tex.] : The Board, [1980?] 1 v. ; 32 cm. Loose-leaf for updating. LC Card 80-622895 DDC 353.97640072/421 19
1. Property tax - Texas. 2. Assessment - Texas. I. Title.
KFT1691.P7 A85

Texas State public education compensation plan . Texas. Education Agency. Division of State Funding. Austin, Tex. [1980] [22] p. ; LC Card 80-622335 DDC 331.2/813711/009764 19
LB2842.2 .T47 1980

Texas. State 1202 Commission. Postsecondary educational supply and occupational demand in Texas for the period of 1977-1983 : a report / by the State 1202 Commission. Austin, Tex. : Coordinating Board, Texas College and University System, [1978] 119 p. ; 28 cm. "Prepared by Office, Postsecondary Educational Planning, Coordinating Board, Texas College and University System." "March 1978." Includes bibliographical references and index. LC Card 79-620962 DDC 331.12/09764 19
1. Job vacancies - Texas. 2. High school graduates - Employment - Texas. I. Texas. Coordinating Board, Texas College and University System. Office, Postsecondary Educational Planning. II. Title.
HD5725.T5 T38 1978

Postsecondary educational supply and occupational demand in Texas for the period of 1977-1983. Texas. State 1202 Commission. Supplement to the State 1202 Commission March 1978 report : postsecondary educational supply and occupational demand in Texas for the period of 1977-1983. Austin, Tex. , [1980] 210 p. ; LC Card 80-622866 DDC 331.12/09764 19
HD5725.T5 T38 1978 Suppl.

Supplement to the State 1202 Commission March 1978 report : postsecondary educational supply and occupational demand in Texas for the period of 1977-1983. Austin, Tex. : Coordinating Board, Texas College and University System, [1980] 210 p. ; 28 cm. "January 1980." LC Card 80-622866 DDC 331.12/09764 19
1. Job vacancies - Texas. 2. Employment forecasting - Texas. 3. Labor supply - Texas. I. Texas. State 1202 Commission. Postsecondary educational supply and occupational demand in Texas for the period of 1977-1983. II. Title.
HD5725.T5 T38 1978 Suppl.

Texas. Statewide Health Coordinating Council. Proposed medical facilities planning annex to the Texas state health plan / accepted by Texas Statewide Health Coordinating Council, May 23, 1980. [Austin] : Texas Dept. of Health, [1980] ca. 200 p. in various pagings : ill. ; 28 cm. LC Card 80-624127 DDC 362.1/1/09764 19
1. Health facilities - Texas - Planning. 2. Health facilities - Texas - Statistics. 3. Health service areas - Texas. I. Texas. Statewide Health Coordinating Council. Texas state health plan. II. Title.
RA395.A4 T4886 1980 Suppl

The Texas state health plan / adopted by Texas Statewide Health Coordinating Council, January

25, 1980 ; approved by the Governor, March 18, 1980. [Austin] : Texas Dept. of Health, [1980] ca. 300 p. in various pagings ; 28 cm. Includes bibliographical references and index. LC Card 80-623084 DDC 362.1/09764 19
1. Health planning - Texas. 2. Medical policy - Texas. 3. Public health - Texas. 4. Medical care - Texas. I. Title.
RA395.A4 T4886 1980

Texas state health plan. Texas. Statewide Health Coordinating Council. Proposed medical facilities planning annex to the Texas state health plan / accepted by Texas Statewide Health Coordinating Council, May 23, 1980. [Austin] [1980] ca. 200 p. in various pagings : LC Card 80-624127 DDC 362.1/1/09764 19
RA395.A4 T4886 1980 Suppl

TEXAS - STATISTICS, VITAL. Texas Infant Mortality Task Force. Texas Infant Mortality Task Force report /. Washington , 1980. iv, 77 p. : LC Card 80-602575 DDC 362.1/9832/009764141 19
RJ60.U52 T497

Texas. Statutes. see Texas. Laws, Statutes, etc.

Texas. Stephen F. Austin State College, Nacogdoches. East Texas historical journal. v. 1- ; July, 1963- Nacogdoches, Tex. LC Card 68-35211 *NYPL [IAA (Texas) (East Texas historical journal)]*

Texas. Sunset Advisory Commission. Texas. Legislative Budget Board. Program Evaluation. Civil Air Patrol Commission . Austin, Tex. , 1979. 23 leaves ; LC Card 80-622077 DDC 353.97640075/4 19
UA928.T4 T49 1979

Texas. State Board of Library Examiners. Report to the Sunset Advisory Commission /. [Austin] [1979] 67 leaves ; LC Card 80-620788 DDC 021.8/2 19
Z682.2.U5 T49 1979

Texas. Task Force on Juvenile Delinquency. Olm, Jane. Bibliography on juvenile delinquency in Texas /. [Austin] [1970] 34 leaves ; LC Card 80-622265 DDC 016.345764/08 016.34764058 19
KFT1795.A1 O4

Texas Tech University. College of Agricultural Sciences. Publication . (no. T-1-186) The Cotton industry in the United States . [Washington, D.C.] , Lubbock, Tex. , 1980. v, 76 p. : LC Card 80-622867 DDC 338.1/7351/0973 19
HD9875 .C74

Texas Tech University. Cultural Resources Institute. Scholars as contractors . Washington , 1979. 265 p. in various pagings : LC Card 79-603005
CC136 .S36 *NYPL [JLF 81-76]*

Workshop on Management Techniques Applied to Archeology, Texas Tech University, 1977. Scholars as managers, or how can the managers do it better . Washington , 1978. vii, 21 p., [2] leaves of plates : LC Card 79-602641
CC51 .W67 1977

Texas Tech University. Dept. of Agricultural Economics. The Cotton industry in the United States . [Washington, D.C.] , Lubbock, Tex. , 1980. v, 76 p. : LC Card 80-622867 DDC 338.1/7351/0973 19
HD9875 .C74

Texas Tech University. Dept. of Anthropology. Cultural Resources Institute. see Texas Tech University. Cultural Resources Institute.

Texas Tech University, Dept. of Electrical Engineering. Workshop on Switching Requirements and R & D for Fusion Reactors, Palo Alto, Calif., 1976. Proceedings. Palo Alto , 1977. 1 v. of various pagings : *NYPL [JSF 80-697]*

Texas Tech University. Electrical Engineering, Dept. of. see Texas Tech University. Dept. of Electrical Engineering.

Texas Tech University. Museum. Occasional papers . (no. 48) Simpson, C. David. Effects of elephant and other wildlife on vegetation along the Chobe River, Botswana /. [Lubbock] , 1978. 15 p. : LC Card 78-621508

DDC 639.9/5 19
SK575.B6 S54

(no. 58) Honeycutt, Rodney L. Chromosomal and morphological variation in the plains pocket gopher, Geomys bursarius, in Texas and adjacent states /. [Lubbock] , 1979. 54 p. : LC Card 79-623970 DDC 599.32/32 19
QL737.R654 H66

(no. 65) Francke, Oscar F. Scorpions from the Virgin Islands (Arachnida, Scorpiones) /. [Lubbock, Tex.] , 1980. 19 p. : LC Card 80-623501 DDC 595.4/6097297/2 19
QL458.7 .F73

Texas Transportation Institute, College Station.
Technical report - Texas Transportation Institute .
(1060-1) Womack, Katie N. Costs of public transportation in Texas, 1973-1977 /. College Station, Tex. , 1979. viii, 81 p. : LC Card 80-621655 DDC 388.4/042 19
HE4487.T4 W65

Texas. University at Arlington.
Earth covered buildings and settlements /. [Washington, D.C.] [Springfield, Va. , 1979?] iv, 355 p. : LC Card 79-600115 DDC 690 19
TH4819.E27 E37

International Conference on Thermoelectric Energy Conversion, 2d, University of Texas at Arlington, 1978. Proceedings of the second International Conference on Thermoelectric Energy Conversion . New York , c1978. vi, 137 p. : LC Card 78-107945
TK2950 .I53 1978   *NYPL [JSF 81-128]*

Texas. University at Arlington. Institute of Urban Studies.
International Association of Auto Theft Investigators. Proceedings of the International Association of Auto Theft Investigators twenty-first annual seminar, Arlington, Texas, August 19-24, 1973. [Arlington] [1973?] 126 p. : LC Card 80-623391 DDC 363.2/5 19
HV8079.A97 I57 1973

Texas. University at Arlington. Institute of Urban Studies. Research and Service Programs Division.
Punishment, perspectives in a civilized society . Arlington, Tex. [1977?] iv, 129 p. : LC Card 80-621841 DDC 364.6/0973 19
HV9471 .P86

Rehabilitation, what part of corrections? . Arlington, Tex. [1977?] vi, 152 p. : LC Card 80-621842 DDC 364.6/01 19
HV9303 .R43

Restitution and victims of crime . Arlington, Tex. [1977?] iv, 86 p. : LC Card 80-621838 DDC 364.6/8 19
HV6250.2 .R47

Texas. University at Austin.
Working paper - Graduate School of Business, University of Texas at Austin .
(80-8) Askari, Hossein. National and international energy stabilization policies /. Austin, Tex. [1980] 14, [8] p. : LC Card 80-622514 DDC 333.79/0973 19
HD9502.U52 A79

Texas. University at Austin. Academic Center.
Texas. University at Austin. Humanities Research Center. An exhibition of Judaica and Hebraica. Austin, Tex., 1973. 26 p. LC Card 76-21717   *NYPL [*ZP-646]*

Texas. University at Austin. African and Afro-American Research Institute.
Occasional publication [Schomburg]
(7) Harris, Wilson. Fossil and psyche /. Austin [1974] 12 p. : LC Card 74-622729
PR9619.3.W5 V634   *NYPL [Sc 823-H]*

(9) Dem-say . Austin , 1974. 79 p. : LC Card 75-310621
PR9387.15 .D45   *NYPL [Sc 809.96-D]*

(10) Brutus, Dennis, 1924- China poems /. Austin [1975] 36 p. : LC Card 75-316144
PR9369.3.B73 C5   *NYPL [Sc 821-B]*

(1) Armstrong, Robert Plant. Forms and processes of African sculpture. Austin [1970] 23 p., LC Card 72-634368
NB1098 .A75   *NYPL [Sc 730.96-A]*

Texas. University at Austin. African and Afro-American Studies and Research Center.

Papers - African and Afro-American Studies and Research Center : Series 2 .
(no. 1) Hancock, Ian F. The Texas Seminoles and their language /. [Austin] , 1980. iv, 29 leaves ; LC Card 80-622194 DDC 427/.9764 19
PM7874.T48 H36

Texas. University at Austin. Art Museum.
Indiana, Robert, 1928- Robert Indiana : [exhibition] Austin , c1977. 59 p. : LC Card 77-88425   *NYPL [3-MCX+ I39 80-1362]*

Texas. University at Austin. Atmospheric Science Group.
Report.
(no. 50) Hillaker, Harry J. Atlas of water balance computations for 48 Texas coastal zone stations, 1941-1970 /. Austin , 1978. iv, 92 p. : LC Card 79-624055 DDC 551.5 s 551.48/097641 19
QC851 .T45 no. 50 GB705.T4

Texas. University at Austin. Bureau of Business Research. (Old Catalog form: Texas. University. Business Administration School. Business Research Bureau)
Manners, Ian R. The coastal energy impact program in Texas /. [Austin] , c1980. xi, 70 p. ; ISBN 0-87755-241-X (pbk.) LC Card 80-80851 DDC 333.79/1/097641 19
TJ163.25.U6 M36

Studies in human resource development. no. 1- Austin, 1974-   *NYPL [JLL 80-248]*

Transference of technology series. NO. 1-3. Austin, 1967-69. 3 v. illus. 28 cm. No more published?
1. Technology and civilization - Periodicals. I. Title.
NYPL [VA (Texas. University at Austin. Bureau Business Research. Transference of technology series.)]

Texas. University at Austin. Bureau of Economic Geology.
Collins, Edward W. Quaternary faulting in East Texas /. Austin, Tex. , 1980. iii, 20 p. : LC Card 80-621660 DDC 553/.09764 s 551.8/7/09764 19
TN24.T4 T38 no. 80-1 QE606.5.U6

Environmental geological atlas of the Texas coastal zone-Kingsville area / by L. F. Brown, Jr. ... [et al.] ; cartography by J. W. Macon, D. F. Scranton, and Barbara Hartmann ; L. F. Brown, Jr., project coordinator ; pref. by Peter T. Flawn. Austin : Bureau of Economic Geology, University of Texas at Austin, 1977. v, 131 p. : ill., maps (9 fold. in pockets) ; 29 cm. Bibliography: p. [129]-131. LC Card 79-622025 DDC 557.64/473 19
1. Geology - Texas - Kingsville region. 2. Coasts - Texas - Kingsville region. 3. Land use - Texas - Kingsville region. I. Brown, Leonard Franklin, 1928-. II. Title.
QE168.K56 T49 1977

Geological circular .
(77-1) Morton, Robert A. Shorelines changes on Mustang Island and North Padre Island (Aransas Pass to Yarborough Pass) . Austin , 1977. 45 p. : LC Card 78-621044 DDC 553/.09764 s 551.3/6/09764113 19
TN24.T4 T38 no. 77-1 GB459.4

(80-1) Collins, Edward W. Quaternary faulting in East Texas /. Austin, Tex. , 1980. iii, 20 p. : LC Card 80-621660 DDC 553/.09764 s 551.8/7/09764 19
TN24.T4 T38 no. 80-1 QE606.5.U6

Report of investigations .
(no. 100) Galloway, William E. Catahoula formation of the Texas Coastal Plain. Austin, Tex. , 1980. vi, 81 p. : LC Card 80-623081 DDC 553/.09764 s 553.4/932/09764 19
QE167 .T42 no. 100 QE693

(no. 102) Handford, C. Robertson. Lower Permian facies of the Palo Duro Basin, Texas . [Austin] , 1980. iv, 31 p. : LC Card 80-623707 DDC 553/.09764 s 551.7/5609764/8 19
QE167 .T42 no. 102 QE674

(no. 92) Land and water resources, historical changes, and dune criticality . Austin, Tex. , 1978. v, 46 p. : LC Card 79-623595 DDC 553/.09764 s 551.4/57/0976447 19
QE167 .T42 no. 92 GB459.4

(no. 97) McGowen, J. H. Depositional framework of the Lower Dockum Group

(Triassic), Texas Panhandle /. Austin, Tex. , 1979. 60 p. : LC Card 80-621656 DDC 553/.09764 s 551.7/62 19
QE167 .T42 no. 97 QE677

(no. 99) Doyle, James David. Depositional patterns of Miocene facies, middle Texas coastal plain /. Austin, Tex. , 1979. iv, 28 p. : LC Card 80-621657 DDC 553/.09764 s 551.7/87/097641 19
QE167 .T42 no. 99 QE694

Texas. University at Austin. Business Research, Bureau of. see Texas. University at Austin. Bureau of Business Research.

Texas. University at Austin. Center for Energy Studies.
Working paper - the University of Texas at Austin, Center for Energy Studies.
Adams, Richard Newbold, 1924- Observations on the use of energy in social structure analysis /. [Austin] , 1979. ii, 76 leaves ; LC Card 79-624609 DDC 303.4/83 19
TJ163.2 .A3

Texas. University at Austin. Center for Research in Water Resources. (Old Catalog form: Texas. University. Center for Research in Water Resources)
Before and after studies on the effects of a power plant installation on Lake Lyndon B. Johnson : literature evaluation : progress report #1 to the Lower Colorado River Authority. Austin : University of Texas at Austin, Center for Research in Water Resources, [1971?] xiv, 145 p. : graphs ; 28 cm. (CRWR ; 70) "Contract IAC (70-71)-533." Includes bibliographical references. LC Card 79-624702 DDC 333.91/62/0976462 19
1. Water quality - Texas - Lyndon B. Johnson, Lake. 2. Electric power-plants - Environmental aspects - Texas - Lyndon B. Johnson, Lake. I. Lower Colorado River Authority. II. Series: Texas. University at Austin. Center for Research in Water Resources. CRWR , 70. III. Title.
TD224.T4 T42 1971

CRWR .
(153) Armstrong, Neal Earl. Exchange rates for carbon, nitrogen, and phosphorus in the Colorado River Delta marshes . Austin , 1977. 39 leaves in various foliations : LC Card 78-622595 DDC 574.5/26325 19
QK188 .A74

(165) Beard, Leo R. Flood control effects of headwater reservoirs, Trinity River, Texas /. Austin , 1979. iii, 50, [78] p. : LC Card 79-625849 DDC 627/.44/097645 19
TC557.T39 B4

(168) Gan, Thian-Yew. Reliability of stochastic models generating hydrologic series /. Austin, Tex. [1980] 64 leaves ; LC Card 80-622521 DDC 551.48/072 19
GB656.2.S7 G36

(70) Texas. University at Austin. Center for Research in Water Resources. Before and after studies on the effects of a power plant installation on Lake Lyndon B. Johnson . Austin [1971?] xiv, 145 p. : LC Card 79-624702 DDC 333.91/62/0976462 19
TD224.T4 T42 1971

Transferability of methodology to the Lower Rio Grande Valley . [Austin] [1978] ca. 400 leaves in various foliations : LC Card 79-622507 DDC 333.91/7/097644 19
HT393.T48 T7

Texas. University at Austin. Center for Social Work Research. Punishment, perspectives in a civilized society . Arlington, Tex. [1977?] iv, 129 p. : LC Card 80-621841 DDC 364.6/0973 19
HV9471 .P86

Texas. University at Austin. Center for the study of Human Resources.
Human resource dimensions of rural development /. Austin , c1977. 258 p. ; ISBN 0-87755-211-8 LC Card 78-102278
HD5725.S85 H85   *NYPL [JLF 80-1421]*

Studies in human resource development. no. 1- Austin, 1974-   *NYPL [JLL 80-248]*

Texas. University at Austin. College of Business Administration.
Working paper - College of Business Administration, University of Texas at Austin .

(79-22) Shaw, Bill, 1940- Council on Environmental Quality /. Austin, Tex. , 1979. [13] leaves ; LC Card 79-626084 DDC 363.7/05/0973 19
HC110.E5 S48

(79-7) Shaw, Bill, 1940- Current environmental issues /. Austin , 1979. 31 p. ; LC Card 79-624831 DDC 344.73/046 19
KF3775.Z9 S5

Texas. University at Austin. Criminal Justice Reference Library. Olm, Jane. Bibliography on juvenile delinquency in Texas /. [Austin] [1970] 34 leaves ; LC Card 80-622265 DDC 016.345764/08 016.34764058 19
KFT1795.A1 O4

Texas. University at Austin. Dept. of Accounting. Working paper - Department of Accounting, University of Texas at Austin.
(78-51) Fellingham, John C. Agency and monitoring costs in a general equilibrium setting /. [Austin] , 1978. 24, [4] p. ; LC Card 79-621441 DDC 657/.45/0724 19
HF5667 .F46

Alderman, C. Wayne. Audit performance and time budgets . [Austin] , 1978. 14 p. ; LC Card 79-623638 DDC 657/.068/5 19
HF5667 .A5

Texas. University at Austin. Dept. of Civil Engineering. Center for Research in Water Resources. see Texas. University at Austin. Center for Research in Water Resources.

Texas. University at Austin. Environmental Health Engineering Research Laboratory. Center for Research in Water Resources. see Texas. University at Austin. Center for Research in Water Resources.

TEXAS. UNIVERSITY AT AUSTIN. GENERAL LIBRARIES - CATALOGS. DeVergie, Adrienne, 1936- Bibliography on student activism, 1963-1970 /. [Austin, Tex.] 1970. 84 leaves ; LC Card 80-622264 DDC 016.378/1981 19
KF4150.A1 D48

Texas. University at Austin. Graduate School of Business. Working paper - Graduate School of Business, University of Texas at Austin .
(78-40) Huff, David Lynch, 1931- Ireland's urban system /. Austin , 1978. 49 p. : LC Card 79-621433 DDC 307.7/6/09417 19
HT145.I7 H83

(78-58) Shapero, Albert. Spatial rearragement of people . Austin , 1978. 37 p. ; LC Card 79-621447 DDC 658.3/128 19
HD30.3 .S5

(78-59) Shapero, Albert. Exit, a high communicator of long standing leaves . Austin , 1978. 31 p. ; LC Card 79-621448 DDC 302.3/5 19
HM131 .S446

(78-76) Leone, Robert P. An approach to building competitive sales response models . Austin , 1978. 31 p. : LC Card 79-623639 DDC 658.8/18/0724 19
HF5438.2 .L46

(79-17) Schuster, Allan D. Motor common carrier corporate strategy in an uncertain regulatory environment /. Austin [1979] 20 p. ; LC Card 79-625407 DDC 388.3/24/0973 19
HE5623 .S375

(79-5) Batsell, Richard R. Deriving areal extent boundaries from two-dimensional point distributions /. Austin , 1979. 15 p. : LC Card 79-623643 DDC 519.5 19
QA278.2 .B38

(80-10) Franckle, Charles T. The effectiveness of rolling the hedge forward in the interest rate futures market /. Austin, Tex. [1980] 23 p. ; LC Card 80-622515 DDC 332.8/2 19
HG6024.5 .F7

(80-13) Huff, David Lynch, 1931- Retail location theory /. Austin, Tex. , 1980. [15] leaves : LC Card 80-624130 DDC 381/.1 19
HF5429.275 .H83

(80-15) Pethia, Robert F. The case for a multivariate treatment of situational diversity, complexity, change, and relatedness in studies of organizational design /. Austin, Tex.

[1980] 19 p. : LC Card 80-623771 DDC 302.3/5 19
HM131 .P393

(80-5) Walker, Ernest Winfield. Evaluation of investment alternatives . Austin, Tex. [1980] 23 leaves : LC Card 80-622513 DDC 658.1/52 19
HG4028.C4 W34

Texas. University at Austin. Graduate School of Business. Bureau of Business Research. see Texas. University at Austin. Bureau of Business Research.

Texas. University at Austin. Humanities Research Center.
An exhibition of Judaica and Hebraica at the Humanities Research Center and Academic Center, the University of Texas at Austin, October-November, 1973. Austin, Tex., 1973. 26 p. illus. 18 x 23 cm. Microfilm. "

ומי יזו/נ כל /מ ייי נביי/מ

LC Card 76-21717
1. Hebrew literature - Bibliography - Catalogs. 2. Jewish literature - Bibliography - Catalogs. I. Texas. University at Austin. Academic Center. II. Title.
NYPL [*ZP-646]

Ory, Norma R. Bookbinding, a living art . Houston, Tex. , c1980. 48 p. : ISBN 0-89090-004-3 (pbk.) LC Card 80-83065 DDC 686.3/074064/1411 19
Z269 .O79

Victoria's world : an exhibition from the Gernsheim collection. [Austin] : Humanities Research Center, University of Texas at Austin, c1980. [36] p. : ill. ; 23 cm. "Replaces the 1970 catalogue and represents modifications made to the exhibition itself." ISBN 0-87959-008-4 (pbk.) LC Card 80-131516 DDC 779/.9941081 19
1. Great Britain - History - Victoria, 1837-1901 - Pictorial works - Exhibitions. 2. Gernsheim, Helmut, 1913- - Photograph collections. 3. Gernsheim, Alison - Photograph collections. I. Title. II. Title: Gernsheim collection.
DA551 .T483 1980

Zevelechi Wells, Maria Xenia. The Ranuzzi manuscripts /. [Austin] , c1980. 89 p. : ISBN 0-87959-094-7 LC Card 80-622235 DDC 091 19
Z6621.T372 R358 Z881.A935

TEXAS. UNIVERSITY AT AUSTIN. HUMANITIES RESEARCH CENTER - EXHIBITIONS.
Zevelechi Wells, Maria Xenia. The Ranuzzi manuscripts /. [Austin] , c1980. 89 p. : ISBN 0-87959-094-7 LC Card 80-622235 DDC 091 19
Z6621.T372 R358 Z881.A935

Texas. University at Austin. Institute of Latin American Studies. Office for Public Sector Studies. Technical papers series - Office for Public Sector Studies, Institute of Latin American Studies, University of Texas at Austin .
(no. 23) Grindle, Merilee Serrill. Whatever happened to agrarian reform? . Austin , 1980. 36 p. : LC Card 80-623135 DDC 338.1/88 19
HD1333.L29 G74

(no. 24) Trebat, Thomas. An evaluation of the economic performance of large public enterprises in Brazil, 1965-1975 /. Austin , 1980. 23 p. ; LC Card 80-623136 DDC 338.7/4/0981 19
HD4093 .T73

Texas. University at Austin. Lyndon B. Johnson School of Public Affairs. see Lyndon B. Johnson School of Public Affairs.

Texas. University at Austin. Lyndon Baines Johnson Library. see Lyndon Baines Johnson Library.

Texas. University at Austin. Mining and Mineral Resources Research Institute. Van Rensburg, W. C. J. The future utilization of Texas lignites . Austin, Tex. , 1979. iv, 57 p. : LC Card 80-621659 DDC 553.2/2/09764 19
TP329 .V36

Texas. University at Austin. Social Work Research, Center for. see Texas. University at Austin. Center for Social Work Research.

Texas. University at Austin. Study of Human Resources, Center for the. see Texas.

University at Austin. Center for the study of Human Resources.

Texas. University at San Antonio. Institute of Texan Cultures. see Institute of Texan Cultures.

Texas. University. Institute of Public Affairs. Guide to Texas state agencies. [1st]- ed. [Austin] 1956- LC Card 73-29679
NYPL [JLM 80-731]

Texas. University. Institute of Texan Cultures. see Institute of Texan Cultures.

Texas. University of Arlington. Earth covered buildings . [Washington, D.C.] [Springfield, Va. , foreword 1979] vi, 272 p. : LC Card 79-600114 DDC 690 19
TH4819.E27 E38

Texas. University of Austin. Center for Research in Water Resources. CRWR .
(167) Bofill, Jordi. Uptake and release of phenol by algal cells /. Austin, Tex. [1979] vii leaves, 49 p. : LC Card 80-622520 DDC 589.3/133 19
QK565 .B57

Texas - Vital statistics. see Texas - Statistics, Vital.

Texas water administration . Texas. Legislature. Senate. [Austin] [197-] v, 87 p. ; LC Card 80-622555 DDC 353.97640082/325 19
HD1694.T4 T3 1970

Texas. Water Development Board. Armstrong, Neal Earl. Exchange rates for carbon, nitrogen, and phosphorus in the Colorado River Delta marshes . Austin , 1977. 39 leaves in various foliations : LC Card 78-622595 DDC 574.5/26325 19
QK188 .A74

Texas. Water Hygiene Division. Rules and regulations for public water systems, adopted 1978. Rev. [Austin] : Texas Dept. of Health, Water Hygiene Division, 1980. 47 p. ; 28 cm. Cover title. LC Card 80-623755 DDC 343.764/0924 19
1. Drinking water - Law and legislation - Texas. I. Title.
KFT1556.5.A434 A2 1980

Texas. Water Quality Board. Trinity River Authority of Texas. Planning and Environmental Management Division. Low flow nutrient loss in the mid-Trinity River ; Runoff-related pollutant loadings in the mid-Trinity River /. [Austin] , 1978. iii, 72, iv, 73 p. : LC Card 80-622543 DDC 363.7/3942/097642 19
TD224.T4 T74 1978

Texians and the Texans.
The Texians and the Texans.
Flannery, John B., 1918- The Irish Texans /. [San Antonio, Tex.] , c1980. 173 p. : ISBN 0-933164-33-5 (pbk.) LC Card 79-89957 DDC 976.4/0049162 19
F395.I6 F55

Flannery, John B., 1918- The Irish Texans /. [San Antonio, Tex.] , c1980. 173 p. : ISBN 0-933164-33-5 (pbk.) LC Card 79-89957 DDC 976.4/0049162 19
F395.I6 F55

TEXT-BOOKS - MISSISSIPPI - ADMINISTRATION.
Mississippi. State Textbook Purchasing Board. Textbook administration handbook . Jackson, Miss. , 1980. 36 p. ; LC Card 80-622628 DDC 379/.156/09762 19
LB3047.5.M7 M57 1980

Textbook administration handbook . Mississippi. State Textbook Purchasing Board. Jackson, Miss. , 1980. 36 p. ; LC Card 80-622628 DDC 379/.156/09762 19
LB3047.5.M7 M57 1980

TEXTBOOK BIAS - UNITED STATES.
Wirtenberg, Jeana. Characters in textbooks . [Washington, D.C.] , 1980. iii, 19 p. ; LC Card 80-602697 DDC 323.4/0973 s 379.1/56 19
KF4755 .A83 no. 62 LB3045.6

The Textbook in American society : a volume based on a conference at the Library of Congress on May 2-3, 1979 / edited by John Y. Cole and Thomas G. Sticht. Washington : The Library, 1981. x, 55 p. ; 23 cm. Includes

bibliographical references.   ISBN 0-8444-0355-5
(pbk.) :   LC Card 80-27657   DDC 371.3/2/0973
19
1. Textbooks - United States - Congresses. 2.
Textbooks - Publication and distribution - United
States - Congresses. I. Cole, John Young, 1940-. II.
Sticht, Thomas G. III. United States. Library of
Congress.
LB3047 .T48

TEXTBOOKS - PUBLICATION AND
DISTRIBUTION - UNITED STATES -
CONGRESSES.
The Textbook in American society .
Washington , 1981. x, 55 p. ;   ISBN
0-8444-0355-5 (pbk.) :   LC Card 80-27657
DDC 371.3/2/0973 19
LB3047 .T48

TEXTBOOKS - UNITED STATES -
CONGRESSES.
The Textbook in American society .
Washington , 1981. x, 55 p. ;   ISBN
0-8444-0355-5 (pbk.) :   LC Card 80-27657
DDC 371.3/2/0973 19
LB3047 .T48

TEXTBOOKS - WEST VIRGINIA -
BIBLIOGRAPHY.
Perry, Gerald K. Official State multiple list for
elementary schools, K-8 . Charleston, W.Va.
[1980] iv, 42, 10 p. ;   LC Card 80-621060   DDC
016.3791/56/09754 19
Z5817 .P47 LB3047.5.W4

TEXTILE DESIGN.
Proctor, Richard M. Surface design for fabric /.
Seattle , c1982. p. cm.   ISBN 0-295-95874-X   LC
Card 81-7420   DDC 677/.022 19
TS1475 .P76

TEXTILE INDUSTRY - PAKISTAN.
Cook, C. Lee. Textiles and textile products of
cotton from Pakistan . Washington, D.C.
[1980] vi, 56, 105 p. ;   LC Card 80-602856   DDC
382/.4567721/0973 19
HD9856 .C66

TEXTILE INDUSTRY - UNITED STATES.
Cook, C. Lee. Textiles and textile products of
cotton from Pakistan . Washington, D.C.
[1980] vi, 56, 105 p. ;   LC Card 80-602856   DDC
382/.4567721/0973 19
HD9856 .C66

Hager, Christine J. Textiles, U. S. trade
agreements, imports, and consumption /.
Washington, D.C. [1979] iii, 17 p. ;   LC Card
80-601609   DDC 382/.45677/00973 19
HD9856 .H33

Trade and employment effects of granting
most-favored-nation status to the People's
Republic of China /. Washington, D.C. ,
Springfield, Va. , 1980. 32 p. in various
pagings ;   LC Card 81-600776   DDC 382/.0951/073
19
HD5710.75.U6 T73

TEXTILE INDUSTRY - UNITED STATES -
STATISTICS.
United States. International Trade
Administration. U. S. production, imports &
import/production ratios for cotton, wool &
man-made fiber textiles & apparel.
[Washington] [1980] 143 p. ;   LC Card
80-602836   DDC 338.4/7677/00973 19
HD9854 .U55 1980

TEXTILE TRADE AND STATISTICS. see
TEXTILE INDUSTRY.

Textiles and textile products of cotton from
Pakistan . Cook, C. Lee. Washington, D.C.
[1980] vi, 56, 105 p. ;   LC Card 80-602856   DDC
382/.4567721/0973 19
HD9856 .C66

Textiles, U. S. trade agreements, imports, and
consumption /. Hager, Christine J. Washington,
D.C. [1979] iii, 17 p. ;   LC Card 80-601609
DDC 382/.45677/00973 19
HD9856 .H33

Textural observations on some living species of
planktonic foraminifera /. Cifelli, Richard.
Washington , 1982. p. cm.   LC Card 81-607840
DDC 560 s 592.1/304471 19
QE701 .S56 no. 45 QL368.F6

THAILAND - ANTIQUITIES.
Van Esterik, Penny. Cognition and design
production in Ban Chiang painted pottery /.
[Athens, Ohio] , 1981. p. cm.   ISBN

0-89680-078-4   LC Card 81-11172   DDC
738.3/7 19
NK4156.6.B36 V37

Thailand - Archaeology. see Thailand -
Antiquities.

THAILAND - ECONOMIC CONDITIONS.
Thailand, toward a development strategy of full
participation. [Washington, D.C.] 1980. xiv,
232 p., [2] fold. leaves of plates :   LC Card
80-121832   DDC 338.9593 19
HC445 .T45

THAILAND - ECONOMIC POLICY.
Thailand, toward a development strategy of full
participation. [Washington, D.C.] 1980. xiv,
232 p., [2] fold. leaves of plates :   LC Card
80-121832   DDC 338.9593 19
HC445 .T45

Thailand, toward a development strategy of full
participation. [Washington, D.C. : East Asia
and Pacific Regional Office, World Bank], 1980.
xiv, 232 p., [2] fold. leaves of plates : ill. ; 28
cm. (A World Bank country study) Cover title.   LC
Card 80-121832   DDC 338.9593 19
1. Thailand - Economic conditions. 2. Thailand -
Economic policy. I. International Bank for
Reconstruction and Development. East Asia and Pacific
Regional Office. II. Series: World Bank country study.
HC445 .T45

THALASSOGRAPHY. see OCEANOGRAPHY.

THAMNOPHIS COUCHII -
CLASSIFICATION.
Lawson, Robin. Biochemical genetics and
systematics of garter snakes of the Thamnophis
elegans-couchii-ordinoides complex /. Baton
Rouge, La. , 1979. 24 p. :   LC Card 80-620693
DDC 591 s 597.96 19
QL3 .L67 no. 56 QL666.O636

THAMNOPHIS ELEGANS -
CLASSIFICATION.
Lawson, Robin. Biochemical genetics and
systematics of garter snakes of the Thamnophis
elegans-couchii-ordinoides complex /. Baton
Rouge, La. , 1979. 24 p. :   LC Card 80-620693
DDC 591 s 597.96 19
QL3 .L67 no. 56 QL666.O636

Rossman, Douglas Athon, 1936- Morphological
evidence for taxonomic partitioning of the
Thamnophis elegans complex (Serpentes,
Colubridae) /. Baton Rouge, La. , 1979. 12 p. :
LC Card 80-620692   DDC 591 s 597.96 19
QL3 .L67 no. 55 QL666.O636

THAMNOPHIS ORDINOIDES -
CLASSIFICATION.
Lawson, Robin. Biochemical genetics and
systematics of garter snakes of the Thamnophis
elegans-couchii-ordinoides complex /. Baton
Rouge, La. , 1979. 24 p. :   LC Card 80-620693
DDC 591 s 597.96 19
QL3 .L67 no. 56 QL666.O636

THE WEST - PUBLIC LANDS.
Chomski, Joseph M. The Sagebrush Rebellion .
[Juneau? Alaska] , 1980. 130, lxxxiv p. :   LC
Card 80-622635   DDC 343.78/025 19
KF5605.Z95 C48

United States. Congress. Senate. Committee on
Energy and Natural Resources. Subcommittee
on Parks, Recreation, and Renewable
Resources. Bureau of Land Management
wilderness review and rangeland management
programs . Washington , 1980. iii, 189 p. ;   LC
Card 80-602719   DDC 346.7304/6782/0262 19
KF26 .E5565 1980a

THE WEST - PUBLIC LANDS - HISTORY.
Chomski, Joseph M. The Sagebrush Rebellion .
[Juneau? Alaska] , 1980. 130, lxxxiv p. :   LC
Card 80-622635   DDC 343.78/025 19
KF5605.Z95 C48

THEATER.
Selden, Samuel, 1899- First principles of play
direction. Chapel Hill, N. C. [1937] 57 p.   LC
Card 38-28085   **NYPL** [*MWEO 81-10*]

THEATER AUDIENCES.
National Endowment for the Arts. Research
Division. Audience development . Washington,
D.C. , 1981. 47 p. ;   ISBN 0-89062-097-0 (pbk.)
LC Card 80-600125   DDC 790.2/068/8 19
PN1590.A9 N3 1981

THEATERS - GEORGIA - ATHENS -
REMODELING FOR OTHER USE.
The Morton Theatre, Athens, Georgia . Athens,

Ga. [1981] p. cm.   LC Card 81-2693   DDC
725/.822/0288 19
NA6835.A82 M675

THEISM.
Auer, J. A. C. Fagginger (Johannes Abraham
Christoffel Fagginger), 1882- Humanism versus
theism /. Ames [1981] c1951. p. cm.   ISBN
0-8138-1336-0 (pbk.)   LC Card 81-13675   DDC
211/.6 19
B821 .A83 1981

Themes of North Korea's unification messages .
Rhee, Sang-Woo. [Honolulu] , 1973. iv, 39
leaves :   LC Card 77-623945   DDC 951.9/04 19
DS917.25 .R53

Theodate Pope Riddle, her life and work. Paine,
Judith. [Washington?] , 1979. [26] p. :   LC Card
79-52952
NA737.R53 A4 1979
                NYPL [*3-MQZ (Riddle) 81-627*]

THEOREM PROVING, AUTOMATIC. see
AUTOMATIC THEOREM PROVING.

THEORETICAL CHEMISTRY. see
CHEMISTRY, PHYSICAL AND
THEORETICAL.

Theoretical logic in sociology /. Alexander,
Jeffrey C. Berkeley , c1981- p. cm.   ISBN
0-520-03062-1 (set)   LC Card 75-17305   DDC
301 19
HM24 .A465

Theories on drug abuse : selected contemporary
perspectives / editors, Dan J. Lettieri, Mollie
Sayers, Helen Wallenstein Pearson. Rockville,
Md. : Dept. of Health and Human Services,
Public Health Service, Alcohol, Drug Abuse,
and Mental Health Administration : National
Institute on Drug Abuse, Division of Research ;
xli, 488 p. : ill. ; 24 cm. (NIDA Research
monograph . 30) DHHS publication ; no. (ADM)
80-967 "March 1980." Bibliography: p. 421-484.   LC
Card 80-600058   DDC 616.86/3 19
1. Drug abuse - Etiology. 2. Drug abuse - Psychological
aspects. 3. Drug abuse - Social aspects. I. Lettieri, Dan
J. II. Sayers, Mollie. III. Pearson, Helen Wallenstein.
IV. Series.
RC564 .T5

Theory and history of literature .
(v. 1) Todorov, Tzvetan, 1939- [Poétique.
English.] Introduction to poetics /.
Minneapolis , 1981. p. cm.   ISBN 0-8166-1008-8 :
LC Card 81-3073   DDC 808.1 19
PN1043 .T613

The theory of flammability limits . Hertzberg,
Martin. Washington, D.C. [1981] p. cm.   LC
Card 81-607904   DDC 622 s 628.9/22 19
TN23 .U43 QD516

A theory of property rights . Umbeck, John R.,
1945- Ames , 1981. p. cm.   ISBN 0-8138-1675-0
LC Card 81-1141   DDC 323.4/6 19
HB711 .U52

THEORY OF STRUCTURES. see
STRUCTURES, THEORY OF.

The theory of will in classical antiquity /. Dihle,
Albrecht. Berkeley , c1982. p. cm.   ISBN
0-520-04059-7   LC Card 81-7424   DDC 128/.3
19
B187.F7 D54

Therapeutic uses of marihuana and schedule I
drugs . United States. Congress. House. Select
Committee on Narcotics Abuse and Control.
Washington , 1980. iii, 351 p. :   LC Card
80-603422   DDC 363.1/94 19
KF27.5 .N3 1980d

Therapeutically equivalent prescription drugs.
New York (State). Office of Public Health.
Safe, effective, and therapeutically equivalent
prescription drugs . Albany [1978?] xiv, 122
p. ;   LC Card 79-621906   DDC 615/.1 19
RS51 .N484 1978

THERAPEUTICS, PHYSIOLOGICAL.
(1980) Runck, Bette. Biofeedback . Rockville,
Md. (5600 Fishers Lane, Rockville, Md.
20857) , 1980. xi, 99 p. ;   LC Card 80-600134
DDC 615.8/51 19
RC489.B53 R86

Theright of privacy--its constitutional & social
dimensions . O'Brien, David M. Austin , 1980.
vi, 55 p. ;   ISBN 0-935630-04-X (pbk.)   LC Card
80-622796   DDC 016.34273/0858 19
KF1262.A1 O25

Thermal degradation products of solvents and hydraulic fluids used in mining /. Christos, Theodore. Washington [1980] p. cm. LC Card 80-607783 DDC 622 s 622/.3 19
TN23 .U43 QD544

THERMAL EQUILIBRIUM. see THERMODYNAMICS.

THERMAL POLLUTION OF RIVERS, LAKES, ETC. - UNITED STATES.
United States. Congress. House. Committee on Public Works and Transportation. Subcommittee on Investigations and Review. Implementation of the Federal Water Pollution Control Act, 1977 . Washington , 1977. viii, 594 p. : LC Card 81-601587 DDC 353.0082/325 19
KF27 .P89634 1977b

Thermal springs list for the United States /. Berry, George W. Boulder, Colo. , Boulder, Colo. (Code D64, 325 Broadway, Boulder, Colo. 80303) , 1980. 59 p. : LC Card 81-600521 DDC 553.7 19
GB1198.2 .B47

THERMAL TRANSFER. see HEAT - TRANSMISSION.

THERMAL WATERS. see GEOTHERMAL RESOURCES.

Thermal waters of Nevada /. Garside, Larry J. Reno , 1979. 163 p. : LC Card 80-621826 DDC 553.7 19
GB1199.7.N3 G37

THERMODYNAMICS - COMPUTER PROGRAMS.
Beyer, R. P. (Richard P.) An algorithm for determining Debye temperatures /. Avondale, Md. [1981] p. cm. LC Card 81-607998 DDC [541.3/69] 19
TN23 .U43 QD504

THERMOELECTRIC APPARATUS AND APPLIANCES - CONGRESSES.
International Conference on Thermoelectric Energy Conversion, 2d, University of Texas at Arlington, 1978. Proceedings of the second International Conference on Thermoelectric Energy Conversion . New York , c1978. vi, 137 p. : LC Card 78-107945
TK2950 .I53 1978   *NYPL [JSF 81-128]*

Thermoelectric Energy Conversion, International Conference on. see International Conference on Thermoelectric Energy Conversion, 2d, University of Texas at Arlington, 1978.

THERMOELECTRICITY - CONGRESSES.
International Conference on Thermoelectric Energy Conversion, 2d, University of Texas at Arlington, 1978. Proceedings of the second International Conference on Thermoelectric Energy Conversion . New York , c1978. vi, 137 p. : LC Card 78-107945
TK2950 .I53 1978   *NYPL [JSF 81-128]*

THERMOELEMENTS. see THERMOELECTRIC APPARATUS AND APPLIANCES.

THERMONUCLEAR REACTORS, CONTROLLED. see FUSION REACTORS.

THESES. see DISSERTATIONS, ACADEMIC.

Theses on Washington geology . Manson, Connie. [Olympia, Wash.] , 1980. iii, 212 p. : LC Card 80-623709 DDC 557.97 s 016.55797 19
TN24.W2 A33 no. 70 Z6034.U5 QE175

THESIS WRITING. see DISSERTATIONS, ACADEMIC.

THESSALI.
Miller, Stella G. Two groups of Thessalian gold /. Berkeley , c1979. xiii, 78 p., [16] leaves of plates : ISBN 0-520-09580-4 LC Card 77-80473
DF261.O57 M54   *NYPL [L-11 622 v. 188]*

THESSALIANS. see THESSALI.

Thian, Raphael Prosper. United States. Adjutant-General's Office. Notes illustrating the military geography of the United States, 1813-1880 /. Austin , c1979. xii, 203 p. : ISBN 0-292-75515-5 LC Card 79-63158
UA26 .A2 1979   *NYPL [IBM 81-609]*

Thiessen, Jerry. Big game aerial surveys and check stations job progress report, project W 138 R 7 : job no. 1, Big game aerial surveys, July 1, 1974 to June 30, 1975 / by Jerry Thiessen. Boise : Idaho Dept. of Fish & Game, 1975. 90 p. : maps ; 28 cm. Cover title. "Federal aid to Wildlife Restoration." LC Card 76-623304 DDC 599.09796 19
1. Big game animals - Idaho. 2. Mammal populations - Idaho. 3. Mammals - Idaho. I. Idaho. Fish and Game Dept. II. Title.
QL719.I15 T48

Thill, Richard E. Peng, Syd S., 1939- Stress distribution and pillar design in oil shale retorts /. Avondale, Md. , 1981. p. cm. LC Card 81-607827 DDC 622 s 622/.3382 19
TN23 .U43 TN858

Thimons, Edward D.
Vinson, Robert P. SF₆ tracer gas tests of bagging-machine hood enclosures /. [Avondale, Md.] , 1981. p. cm. LC Card 80-606907 DDC 661/.06832 19
TN23 .U43 TH7697.C54

Volkwein, Jon C. Canopy air curtain dust reductions on a gathering-arm loader /. [Avondale, Md.] [1981] p. cm. LC Card 81-10148 DDC 622 s 622/.2 19
TN23 .U43 TN312

Think/leap/re-think/fall /. Acconci, Vito 1940- Dayton , c1976. [54] p. :
NYPL [3-MCF A172 80-2907]

THINKING. see THOUGHT AND THINKING.

THINKING, ARTIFICIAL. see ARTIFICIAL INTELLIGENCE.

Third interim report of the commercial fish-technical evaluation study, Salcha River /. Dinneford, W. Bruce. Anchorage, Alaska , 1977. vi, 88 p. : LC Card 79-625783 DDC 597/.55 19
QL638.S2 D56

Third interim report to the California State Legislature on the Sacramento-San Joaquin Delta levees study . California. Dept. of Water Resources. [Sacramento] , 1980. ii, 42, [3] p. : LC Card 80-621387 DDC 627/.42/097945 19
TC424.C2 C28 1980

THIRD WORLD. see UNDERDEVELOPED AREAS.

13 Communists speak to the Court / Elizabeth Gurley Flynn ... [et al.]. New York : New Century Publishers, 1953. 95 p. ; 20 cm. Microfilm. CONTENTS: Elizabeth Gurley Flynn. - Pettis Perry. - Claudia Jones. - Alexander Bittelman. - Alexander Trachtenberg. - V. J. Jerome. - Albert F. Lannon. - Louis Weinstock. - Arnold Johnson. - Betty Gannett. - Jacob Mindel. - William Weinstone. - George Blake Charney. LC Card 54-43867
1. Trials (Sedition) - United States. 2. Communist trial, New York, 1949. I. Flynn, Elizabeth Gurley. II. United States. District Court. New York (Southern District).
NYPL [Sc Micro R-3647]

THIRTY YEARS' WAR, 1618-1648 - FICTION.
Grimmelshausen, Hans Jakob Christoph von, 1625-1676. [Seltzame Springinsfeld. English.] The singular life story of heedless Hopalong /. Detroit , 1981. p. cm. ISBN 0-8143-1688-3 LC Card 81-10446 DDC 833/.5 19
PT1731.S7 E5 1981

Thom, Stephen. Adult literacy program handbook . Washington, D.C. , 1980. viii, 179 p. : LC Card 80-602326 DDC 374/.012/0973 19
LC5225.R4 A29

Thomas, Annabel, 1929- The phototropic woman / Annabel Thomas. Iowa City : University of Iowa Press, c1981. p. cm. (The Iowa School of Letters award for short fiction) ISBN 0-87745-113-3 LC Card 81-10469 DDC 813/.54 19
I. Title.
PS3570.H557 P5

THOMAS, BARBARA S., 1946-
United States. Congress. Senate. Committee on Banking, Housing and Urban Affairs. Nomination of Barbara S. Thomas . Washington , 1980. ii, 61 p. ; LC Card 80-603679 DDC 353.0082/58 19
KF26 .B39 1980s

Thomas, Bill, 1934- The Brown County book / by Bill Thomas. Bloomington : Indiana University Press, c1981. p. cm. ISBN 0-253-10546-3 LC Card 81-47292 DDC 977.2/253 19
1. Brown County, Ind. I. Title.
F532.B76 T47

THOMAS, CHARLES.
United States. Congress. House. Committee on Armed Services. Full committee consideration of H. Res. 777 requesting the President to furnish certain information to the House of Representatives concerning the disclosure of classified information relating to the new so-called stealth technology for military aircraft, and resolution in honor of Charles Sparks Thomas, Secretary of the Navy, May 1954 to April 1957 /. Washington , 1980. ii, 27 p. ; LC Card 80-603683 DDC 355.6 19
KF27 .A7 1980g

Thomas, David John, 1945- Order without government : the society of the Pemon Indians of Venezuela / David John Thomas. Urbana : University of Illinois Press, c1981. p. cm. (Illinois studies in anthropology. no. 13) Bibliography: p. Includes index. ISBN 0-252-00888-X LC Card 81-1818 DDC 980/.004/98 19
1. Arecuna Indians. I. Title. II. Series.
F2380.1.A7 T48

THOMAS, HECK, 1850-1912.
Shirley, Glenn. Heck Thomas, frontier marshal /. Norman , 1981, c1962. p. cm. ISBN 0-8061-1664-1 LC Card 81-40293 DDC 976.6/04/0924 B 19
F698.T48 S48 1981

Thomas Hill, the grand view / Marjorie Dakin Arkelian ; pref. by George W. Neubert ; [catalogue compiled by Barbara Bowman ; photography by Joe Samberg]. Oakland, Calif. : Oakland Museum, Art Dept., 1980. 64 p. : ill. (some col.) ; 28 cm. "Exhibitions itinerary: The Oakland Museum, September 23-November 16, 1980; Tacoma Art Museum, Tacoma, Washington, March 4-April 13, 1981; Joslyn Art Museum, Omaha, Nebraska, May 9-June 21, 1981; Anchorage Historical and Fine Arts Museum, Anchorage, Alaska, July 15-August 31, 1981; the Midland Art Council of the Midland Center for the Arts, Inc., Midland, Michigan, September-October, 1981." Bibliography: p. 52-60. LC Card 80-82938 DDC 759.13 19
1. Hill, Thomas, 1829- - Exhibitions. 2. The West in art - Exhibitions. I. Hill, Thomas, 1829-. II. Arkelian, Marjorie Dakin. III. Oakland Museum. Art Dept. IV. Oakland Museum.
ND237.H615 A4 1980

THOMAS, JAMES BERT, 1935-
United States. Congress. Senate. Committee on Governmental Affairs. Nomination of James Bert Thomas, Jr. . Washington , 1980 [i.e. 1981] iii, 33 p. ; LC Card 81-601163 DDC 353.844 19
KF26 .G67 1980n

Thomas, Marilyn R. United States. Social Security Administration. Office of Research and Statistics. Income & resources of the aged /. [Washington, D.C.] [1980] 35 p. : LC Card 80-600019
HD7106.U5 U65 1980

Thomas, Mason P. Strickland, Lucy. The law and the elderly in North Carolina /. [Chapel Hill], 1980. x, 154 p. ; LC Card 81-620519 DDC 344.765/0326 347.6504326 19
KFN7491.A3 S75 1980

Thomas, Paul R. Peterson, Gary R., 1948- Cobalt availability--domestic . Washington, D.C. , 1981. p. cm. LC Card 81-607981 DDC 622 s 553.4/8
TN295 .U4 HD9539.C463U5

Thomas, Robert A. A new systematic arrangement for Philodryas serra (Schlegel) and Philodryas pseudoserra Amaral (Serpentes : Colubridae) / by Robert A. Thomas and James R. Dixon. Austin : Texas Memorial Museum, 1977. 20 p. : ill. ; 26 cm. (The Pearce-Sellards series . no. 27) Bibliography: p. 18-20. LC Card 78-621007 DDC 574 s 597.96 19
1. Tropidodryas serra - Classification. 2. Tropidodryas striaticeps - Classification. 3. Reptiles - Classification. 4. Reptiles - Brazil - Classification. I. Dixon, James Ray, joint author. II. Series: Texas. Memorial Museum, Austin. The Pearce-Sellards series , no. 27. III. Title.
AM101 .T474 no. 27 QL666.O636

Thomas, Rosemary H., 1939- It's good to tell you . Columbia , 1981. p. cm. ISBN 0-8262-0327-2 LC Card 81-50530 DDC 398.2/09778 19
GR111.F73 I86

Thomas S. Clarkson Memorial College of Technology, Potsdam, N.Y. Conference on Wood Chips for Fuel and Energy, Clarkson College, 1978. Conference on Wood Chips for

Fuel and Energy, Clarkson College, Potsdam, New York, January 11, 1978 /. [Albany, N.Y.] [1978] 181 p. : LC Card 80-621929 DDC 662/.65 19
TP324 .C66 1978

Thomas, Steven K. Illinois Institute of Natural Resources. Illinois State plan, energy conservation in institutions . [Springfield, Ill.] [Springfield, Va. , 1979 or 1980] ii, 76 p. : LC Card 80-622576 DDC 333.79 19
TJ163.5.B84 I43 1979

Thompson, Bronald. North Dakota. Laws, statutes, etc. [Workmen's compensation act.] North Dakota Workmen's compensation act and Crime victims reparations act and rules of procedure, effective July 1, 1979 /. [Bismarck] [1979] 105 p. ; LC Card 80-621922 DDC 344.784/021/02632 19
KFN8942.A335 A2 1979

Thompson, Carole J. (joint author) Torrey, Barbara Boyle. An international comparison of pension systems /. [Washington, D.C.] , 1980. v, 52, [46] p. ; LC Card 80-602549 DDC 331.25/2 19
HD7105.3 .T67

Thompson, Frederick C. Tolerance and synthetic ability of sewage microorganisms in acid mine water / by Frederick C. Thompson and Harold A. Wilson. Morgantown : Water Research Institute, Center for Extension and Continuing Education, West Virginia University, 1975. ix, 60 p. : ill. ; 23 cm. (Bulletin - West Virginia University . ser. 76, no. 5-1) "WRI-WVU-75-03." Bibliography: p. 58-60. LC Card 76-622086 DDC 628.1/6832 19
1. Microbial metabolism. 2. Escherichia coli. 3. Rhodotorula mucilaginosa. 4. Sewage - Microbiology. 5. Acid mine drainage. I. Wilson, Harold Albert, 1905- joint author. II. West Virginia. University. Water Research Institute. III. Title: Tolerance and synthetic ability of sewage microorganisms ...
QR88 .T48

Thompson, Joann K. (joint author) Sykes, Thomas M. An analysis of program needs of prison inmates in Washington State /. Olympia, Wash. [1980] xxi, 139 p. ; LC Card 80-620028 DDC 365/.66/09797 19
HV9475.W2 S93

Thompson, Kenneth W. Analysis of potential environmental factors, especially thermal, which would influence the survivorship of exotic Nile perch if introduced into artificially heated reservoirs in Texas / by Kenneth W. Thompson and Clark Hubbs, Barry W. Lyons. [Austin] : Texas Parks and Wildlife Dept., 1977. 37 p. : ill. ; 23 cm. (Technical series - Texas Parks and Wildlife Department . no. 22) Bibliography: p. 26-28. LC Card 78-620720 DDC 639.9/7758 19
1. Nile perch. 2. Fishes - Effect of water temperature on. 3. Animal introduction - Texas. 4. Reservoirs - Temperature - Environmental aspects - Texas. 5. Fishes - Tanganyika, Lake. 6. Fishes - Texas. I. Hubbs, Clark, joint author. II. Lyons, Barry W., joint author. III. Title. IV. Title: Artificially heated reservoirs in Texas. V. Series: Texas. Parks and Wildlife Dept. Technical series , no. 22.
QL638.C34 T48

Thompson, Kenneth W., 1921- Cold war theories / Kenneth W. Thompson. Baton Rouge : Louisiana State University Press, c1981- p. cm. Includes index. CONTENTS. - v. 1. World polarization, 1944-1953.   ISBN 0-8071-0876-6 (v. 1) : LC Card 81-6001 DDC 327.1/12 19
1. World politics - 1945-. 2. Balance of power. I. Title.
D843 .T423

Thompson, Larry S. The effects of large-diameter underground crude-oil pipelines on wildlife : with emphasis on the proposed Northern Tier pipeline in Montana / by Larry Thompson in consultation with Olson-Elliott and Associates ; Dave Janis, project manager ; Kathy Hanson, editor. Helena, Mont. : Dept. of Natural Resources and Conservation, Energy Division, [1979] vii, 55 p. : ill. ; 28 cm. (Northern Tier report . no. 2) "August 1979." Bibliography: p. 47-55. LC Card 80-622216 DDC 333.79/09786 s 333.95/9 19
1. Petroleum - Pipe lines - Environmental aspects - Montana. 2. Northern Tier pipeline, Wash.-Minn. 3. Animal ecology - Montana. I. Hanson, Kathy. II. Olson-Elliott and Associates. III. Series: Montana. Energy Division. Northern Tier report , no. 2. IV. Title.
TJ163.25.U6 M653 1979, no. 2 TD195.P5

Thompson, Philip, 1950- Development of a continuous flotation process for removal of insoluble slimes from potash ore / by Philip Thompson and J. L. Huiatt ; with an appendix containing an economic evaluation by John J. Henn. Washington : U. S. Dept. of the Interior, Bureau of Mines, [1980] p. cm. (Report of investigations / Bureau of Mines) Bibliography: p. LC Card 80-607785 DDC 622/.3636 19
1. Flotation. 2. Potash. 3. Slimes (Mining). I. Huiatt, J. L., joint author. II. Series: United States Bureau of Mines. Report of investigations . III. Title.
TN23 .U43

Thompson, Raymond G. A systematic study of larvae in the tribes Pterostichini, Morionini, and Amarini (Coleoptera, Carabidae) / [by Raymond G. Thompson]. Fayetteville : Agricultural Experiment Station, Division of Agriculture, University of Arkansas, [1979]. 105 p. : ill. ; 23 cm. (Bulletin - Agricultural Experiment Station, University of Arkansas . 837) "September 1979." Bibliography: p. 103-105. LC Card 80-621426 DDC 595.76/2 19
1. Carabidae - Classification. 2. Larvae - Insects. 3. Insects - Classification. I. Series: Arkansas. Agricultural Experiment Station, Fayetteville. Bulletin , 837. II. Title.
QL596.C2 T49

Thompson, Robert Farris. The four moments of the sun : Kongo art in two worlds / Robert Farris Thompson and Joseph Cornet. Washington : National Gallery of Art, 1981. p. cm. "Catalogue": p. Bibliography: p. ISBN 0-89468-003-X LC Card 81-14033 DDC 730/.09675/10740153 19
1. Sculpture, Bakongo (African people) - Exhibitions. 2. Sculpture, Primitive - Zaire - Exhibitions. 3. Funeral rites and ceremonies, Bakongo (African people) - Influence - Exhibitions. 4. Funeral rites and ceremonies, Black - North America - Exhibitions. I. Cornet, Joseph. II. National Gallery of Art (U. S.). III. Title.
NB1099.C6 T5

Thompson, T. Scott. Ginsburg, Paul B. The CBO hospital cost containment model . [Washington, D.C.] , 1981. xiv, 36 p. : LC Card 81-601120 DDC 362.1/1 19
RA981.A2 G49

Thompson, Woodrow B. Surficial geology handbook for coastal Maine / by Woodrow B. Thompson ; prepared for the Maine State Planning Office by the Physical Geology Division, Maine Geological Survey, Department of Conservation. Augusta, Me. : The Division, 1978. vii, 66 p., [41] leaves of plates : ill. ; 28 cm. Bibliography: p. 57-63. Includes index. LC Card 79-622304 DDC 553/.09741 19
1. Geology - Maine. 2. Coasts - Maine. 3. Environmental protection - Maine. I. Maine. State Planning Office. II. Maine. Geological Survey (1929-). Physical Geology Division. III. Title.
QE119 .T48 1978

Surficial geology handbook for coastal Maine / Woodrow B. Thompson ; prepared for the Maine State Planning Office by the Physical Geology Division, Maine Geological Survey, Department of Conservation, 1978. Rev. Augusta, Me. : Maine Geological Survey, 1979. vii, 68 p., [39] leaves of plates : ill. ; 28 cm. Bibliography: p. 59-65. Includes index. LC Card 80-620848 DDC 553/.09741 19
1. Geology - Maine. 2. Coasts - Maine. 3. Environmental protection - Maine. I. Maine. State Planning Office. II. Maine. Geological Survey (1929-). Physical Geology Division. III. Title.
QE119 .T48 1979

Thomssen, Carol. Sentencing in Minnesota district courts : a preliminary report of the plea negotiation study / produced by the Minnesota Statistical Analysis Center, by Carol Thomssen, Peter J. Falkowski. St. Paul : Crime Control Planning Board, 1978. viii, 80 p. : ill. ; 28 cm. (Minnesota Crime Control Planning Board research report) LC Card 78-622567 DDC 345.776/0772 19
1. Sentences (Criminal procedure) - Minnesota. 2. District courts - Minnesota. I. Falkowski, Peter J., joint author. II. Minnesota. Crime Control Planning Board. Statistical Analysis Center. III. Series: Minnesota. Crime Control Planning Board. Minnesota Crime Control Planning Board research report. IV. Title.
KFM5983.2 .T56

Thor, Peter K. (joint author) Carman, Hoy Fred, 1938- High fructose corn sweeteners . Davis , 1979. vi, 63 p. : LC Card 79-625537 DDC

338.1/09794 s 338.4/76645 19
HD9000.1 .C3 no. 79-2 HD9119.C6

THOREAU, HENRY DAVID, 1817-1862 - CRITICISM AND INTERPRETATION.
Bridgman, Richard. Dark Thoreau /. Lincoln , c1982. p. cm. ISBN 0-8032-1167-8 LC Card 81-4788 DDC 818/.309 19
PS3054 .B7

THORIUM ORES - COLORADO - GUNNISON CO.
Olson, Jerry Chipman, 1917- Alkalic rocks and resources of thorium and associated elements in the Powderhorn District, Gunnison County, Colorado /. Washington , 1980. p. cm. LC Card 80-607811 DDC 552/.1 19
QE462.A4 O44

Thornburg, Thomas R. Swift and the Ciceronian tradition / Thomas R. Thornburg. Muncie, Ind. : Ball State University, 1980. 28 p. ; 23 cm. (Ball State monograph ; no. 28) Publications in English ; no. 20 Includes bibliographical references. LC Card 80-67735 DDC 828/.5/09 19
1. Swift, Jonathan, 1667-1745 - Technique - Addresses, essays, lectures. 2. Cicero, Marcus Tullius - Influence - Addresses, essays, lectures. I. Series: Indiana. Ball State University, Muncie. Ball State monograph , no. 28. II. Title.
PR3728.T4 T47

Thornburgh, Nancy. (joint author) Van Houten, John. Occupational employment statistics, non-manufacturing industries, Alaska, 1978 /. [Juneau] , 1979. 68 p. ; LC Card 80-620795 DDC 331.12/51/0009798 19
HD5725.A4 V32

Thorne, Richard E. A portable hydroacoustic data acquisition system for fish stock assessment / by Richard E. Thorne, Edmund P. Nunnallee, and James H. Green. Seattle : Division of Marine Resources, University of Washington, [1972] ii, 14 leaves : ill. ; 28 cm. (A Washington sea grant publication. WSG 72-4) On cover: Washington Sea Grant Program. "December 1972." Bibliography: leaf 14. LC Card 81-462262 DDC 639/.2 19
1. Echo sounding in fishing. 2. Fish populations - Measurement. I. Nunnallee, Edmund Pierce, joint author. II. Green, James H., joint author. III. Washington Sea Grant Program. IV. Title. V. Title: Fish stock assessment.
SH344.23.E3 T48

Thorne, Tom. Wyoming. Game and Fish Dept. The status, mortality, and response to management of the bighorn sheep of Whiskey Mountain /. Cheyenne [1979] 213 p. : LC Card 80-622756 DDC 639.9/797358 19
QL737.U53 W96 1979

Thorp, Robbin W., 1933- Bumble bees and cuckoo bumble bees of California (Hyenoptera, Apidae) /. Berkeley, CA , 1981. p. cm. ISBN 0-520-09645-2 LC Card 81-10422 DDC 595.7/09794 s 595.79/909794 19
QL475.C3 C3 vol. 23 QL568.A6

Thorson, Connie Capers, 1940- A million stars . Albuquerque , 1981. p. cm. ISBN 0-913630-05-5 LC Card 81-7396 DDC 025.2/187789/81 19
Z675.U5 M54

THOUGHT AND THINKING.
Neville, Robert C. Reconstruction of thinking /. Albany , 1981. p. cm. ISBN 0-87395-494-7 LC Card 81-5347 DDC 128/.3 19
B105.T54 N48

THOUGHT AND THINKING - CONGRESSES.
Hull, Bill. Teachers' seminars on children's thinking . Grand Forks, N.D. , 1978. 56 p. ; LC Card 78-52231 DDC 370.15/2 19
LB1117 .H95

Thrasher, Thelma J. Federal-State institutions for cooperative planning and management . Anchorage, Alaska [1979] iv, 47, 109 p. ; LC Card 80-620899 DDC 353.0082/326/09798 19
HD211.A4 F43

Threat of inflation. United States. Congress. Senate. Committee on the Budget. The present state of the American economy . Washington , 1981- v. <1 > : LC Card 81-600968 DDC 338.973 19
KF26 .B8 1981

Threatt-Ellis, Vita. National Family and Reproductive Health Association. A directory

of national health, education, and social service
organizations concerned with youth /.
Rockville, Md. [1979] 56 p. ; LC Card
80-601714
HV741 .N316 1979 **NYPL [JLF 80-1557]**

Three Christian capitals . Krautheimer, Richard,
1897- Berkeley , 1981, c1982. p. cm. ISBN
0-520-04541-6 LC Card 81-13148 DDC
937/.08 19
DG63 .K7

Three faces of Midwestern isolationism / John
N. Schacht, editor. Iowa City, Iowa : University
of Iowa, 1981. p. cm. "Papers prensented ... at a
conference held on April 2, 1980, in Iowa City under
the sponsorship of the Center for the Study of the
Recent History of the United States"--Foreword.
Includes bibliographical references. CONTENTS. -
Foreword / Leslie W. Dunlap -- Gerald P. Nye and
agrarian bases for the rise and fall of American
isolationism / Wayne S. Cole -- The isolationism of
General Robert E. Wood / Justus D. Doenecke -- John
L. Lewis and American foreign policy / Melvyn
Dubofsky -- Three faces of Midwestern isolationism /
Fredrick Adams -- Between the wars / Norman A.
Graebner. ISBN 0-87414-019-6 (pbk.) . LC Card
81-2741 DDC 327.73 19
*1. United States - Foreign relations - 1933-1945 -
Congresses. 2. United States - Neutrality - Congresses.
I. Schacht, John N., 1943-. II. Center for the Study of
the Recent History of the United States (Iowa City,
Iowa).*
E806 .T58

Three Mile Island cleanup and rehabilitation .
United States. Congress. House. Committee on
Interior and Insular Affirs. Subcommittee on
Energy and the Environment. Washington ,
1980. iv, 236 p. : LC Card 80-604111 DDC
363.7/28 19
KF27 .I518 1980b

Three Mile Island Nuclear Plant accident .
United States. Congress. House. Committee on
Science and Technology. Subcommittee on
Natural Resources and Environment.
Washington , 1979. iii, 251 p. : LC Card
80-601132 DDC 363.1/79 19
KF27 .S398 1979c

**THREE MILE ISLAND NUCLEAR PLANT,
PA.**
Health-related behavioral impact of the Three
Mile Island nuclear incident . [Harrisburg]
[1980- v. : LC Card 80-622808 DDC 363.1/79 19
BF789.D5 H42

**THREE MILE ISLAND NUCLEAR POWER
PLANT, PA.**
Hu, Teh-wei. Health-related economic costs of
the Three-mile Island accident /. University
Park, PA , 1980. viii, 53 p. ; LC Card 80-622809
DDC 363.1/79 19
RA569 .H8

Impact abroad of the accident at the Three
Mile Island Nuclear Power Plant . Washington ,
1980. xii, 81 p. ; LC Card 80-603262 DDC
333.79/24 19
TK9055 .I44

Nuclear accident and recovery at Three Mile
Island . Washington , 1980. vii, 423 p. : LC
Card 81-600709 DDC 363.1/79 19
TK1344.P4 N82

Pennsylvania. Governor's Commission on Three
Mile Island. Legal Subcommittee. Legal aspects
of the Three Mile Island accident . Harrisburg,
Pa. [1980] ii leaves, 69 p. ; LC Card 80-621928
DDC 344.748/0472 19
KFP290 .A87

Pennsylvania. Governor's Office of Policy and
Planning. The socio-economic impact of the
Three Mile Island accident . Harrisburg, Pa.
[1980] iii, 162, [43] p., [1] folded leaf of plates :
LC Card 81-621645 DDC 330.9748/18 19
HD9698.U54 M476 1980

United States. Ad Hoc Interagency Population
Dos Assessement Group. Population dose and
health impact of the accident at the Three Mile
Island Nuclear Station . Washington , 1979. 77,
[16] p. : LC Card 79-602730
RA569 .U46 1979

United States. Congress. House. Committee on
Interior and Insular Affirs. Subcommittee on
Energy and the Environment. Three Mile Island
cleanup and rehabilitation . Washington ,
1980. iv, 236 p. : LC Card 80-604111 DDC

363.7/28 19
KF27 .I518 1980b

United States. Congress. House. Committee on
Science and Technology. Subcommittee on
Natural Resources and Environment. Three
Mile Island Nuclear Plant accident .
Washington , 1979. iii, 251 p. : LC Card
80-601132 DDC 363.1/79 19
KF27 .S398 1979c

United States. Congress. Senate. Committee on
Environment and Public Works. Subcommittee
on Nuclear Regulation. Nuclear accident and
recovery at Three Mile Island . Washington ,
1980. vii, 423 p. : LC Card 80-603139 DDC
363.1/79 19
TK1345.H37 U5 1980

United States. Nuclear Regulatory Commission.
Three Mile Island Program Office. Final
environmental assessment for decontamination
of the Three Mile Island Unit 2 reactor building
atmosphere. Washington , 1980. 1 v. :
NYPL [JSK 80-129]

United States. President's Commission on the
Accident at Three Mile Island. Public Health
and Safety Task Force. Reports of the Public
Health and Safety Task Force on public health
and safety summary, health physics and
dosimetry, radiation health effects, behavioral
effects, public health and epidemiology.
Washington, D.C. [1980] 423 p. : LC Card
80-601717 DDC 363.1/79 19
RA569 .U4977 1980

United States. President's Commission on the
Accident at Three Mile Island. Public's Right
to Information Task Force. Report of the
Public's Right to Information Task Force /.
Washington, D.C. [1980] 262 p. ; LC Card
80-601569 DDC 363.1/79 19
HD9698.U54 M478 1980

**THREE MILE ISLAND NUCLEAR POWER
PLANT, PA. - CONGRESSES.**
Known effects of low-level radiation exposure .
[Bethesda, Md.] [1980] 147 p. : LC Card
80-601671 DDC 616.9/897 19
RA1231.R2 K59

**THREE-MILE LIMIT. see TERRITORIAL
WATERS.**

Three Notch'd Road. Pawlett, Nathaniel Mason.
The route of the Three Notch'd Road .
Charlottesville, Va. [1980] vi, 26 p. : LC Card
80-620018 DDC 388.1/09755/4 19
HE356.V8 P39

**Three-year interim state plan for Nebraska
Rehabilitation Services, fiscal years
1980-81-82.** Nebraska. Division of
Rehabilitation Services. [Lincoln , 1979?] iv, 64
p. ; LC Card 80-622103 DDC 362/.0425 19
HD7256.U6 N34 1979

**Three year interim state plan for vocational
rehabilitation, fiscal years 1980, 1981 & 1982.**
Illinois. Dept. of Rehabilitation Services.
Springfield, Ill. [1979] iv, 51, [33] p. : LC Card
80-622136 DDC 353.97730083/3 19
HD7256.U6 I266 1979

THRIFT. see SAVING AND THRIFT.

Thrift institutions. United States. Interagency
Task force on Thrift Institutions. The report of
the Interagency Task Force on Thrift
Institutions . Washington , 1980. viii, 267 p. ;
LC Card 80-603280 DDC 332.2/0973 19
HG2151 .U53 1980

Throne, Marilyn. Walter Havighurst, novelist of
the heartland / Marilyn Throne. Columbus :
State University of Ohio, 1979. 20 p. ; 23 cm.
(Ohio authors) Bibliography: p. 20. LC Card
80-137524 DDC 813/.54 19
*1. Havighurst, Walter, 1901- - Criticism and
interpretation. I. Title. II. Series.*
PS3515.A8694 Z89

**THULE CULTURE - NORTHWEST
TERRITORIES - ADDRESSES, ESSAYS,
LECTURES.**
Archaeological whale bone--a northern
resource . Fayetteville, ARK , 1979. xx, 558
p. : LC Card 80-624409 DDC 971.9/5 19
E99.E7 A73

**THUNDER BASIN NATIONAL GRASSLAND,
WYO. - MAPS.**
(1973) United States. Forest Service. Rocky
Mountain Region. Thunder Basin National

Grassland, Wyoming. [Denver] 1973. col. map
117 x 105 cm. Scale 1:126,720; 1/2" = 1 mile.
Relief shown by hachures and spot heights. "Polyconic
projection." "Sixth principal meridian." "Forest Service
map class A." Includes inset, "Source diagram," and
"Key map." LC Card 76-690850
G4262.T55 1973 .U5
NYPL [Map Div. 80-3355]

**THUNDER-STORMS. see
THUNDERSTORMS.**

**Thunderstorm-environment interactions
determined with three-dimensional trajectories**
/. Wilson, Gregory Sims. [Washington] , 1980.
viii, 153 p. : LC Card 80-603200 DDC 551.5/54
19
QC968 .W54

THUNDERSTORMS.
Wilson, Gregory Sims.
Thunderstorm-environment interactions
determined with three-dimensional trajectories
/. [Washington] , 1980. viii, 153 p. : LC Card
80-603200 DDC 551.5/54 19
QC968 .W54

Thurin, Erik Ingvar. Emerson as priest of Pan : a
study in the metaphysics of sex / Erik Ingvar
Thurin. Lawrence : Regents Press of Kansas,
c1981. p. cm. Bibliography: p. Includes index. ISBN
0-7006-0216-X : LC Card 81-4818 DDC
814/.3 19
*1. Emerson, Ralph Waldo, 1803-1882 - Criticism and
interpretation. 2. Sex in literature. 3. Polarity in
literature. 4. Love in literature. I. Title.*
PS1642.S47 T5

Thurmond, J. Peter. Report on the fall, 1978,
investigations at the George C. Davis Site,
Caddoan Mounds State Historic Site, Cherokee
County, Texas / J. Peter Thurmond, Ulrich
Kleinschmidt ; with appendices by Kenneth A.
Lord and J. Peter Thurmond, Raymond W.
Neck. [Austin] : Texas Archaeological Research
Laboratory, [1979] ix, 103 leaves, [14] leaves of
plates : ill. ; 28 cm. "August 1979." Bibliography: p.
102. LC Card 80-620782 DDC 976.4/183 19
*1. Caddoan Mounds State Historic Site, Tex. 2.
Caddoan Indians - Antiquities. 3. Texas - Antiquities. I.
Kleinschmidt, Ulrich, joint author. II. Texas
Archeological Research Laboratory. III. Title.*
E99.C13 T48

Thurston Co., Wash. United States. Army. Corps
of Engineers. Seattle, Washington, District.
Flood plain information: Skookumchuck River,
Bucoda, Washington. [Seattle] 1968. ii, 31 p.
LC Card 80-510638 DDC 363.3/493/0979779
19
GB1399.4.W2 U54 1968

THURSTON COUNTY (NEB.) - MAPS.
United States. Soil Conservation Service.
Thurston County, Nebraska /. Lincoln, Nebr. ,
1980. 1 map : LC Card 81-691000
G4193.T6 1979 .U5

Thurston, Robert W. Russian history and
politics : selected reference works / by Robert
W. Thurston and William G. Rosenberg. [Ann
Arbor] : Harlan Hatcher Graduate Library,
University of Michigan, c1978. 57 p. ; 23 cm.
(Graduate library guide series) Errata slip inserted.
Includes index. LC Card 81-621451 DDC 016.947
19
*1. Soviet Union - History - Bibliography - Catalogs. 2.
Soviet Union - History - Sources - Bibliography -
Catalogs. I. Rosenberg, William G. II. Harlan Hatcher
Graduate Library. III. Title. IV. Series.*
Z2506 .T47 DK40

Tice, James. Polyzoides, Stephanos. Courtyard
housing in Los Angeles . Berkeley , c1982. p.
cm. ISBN 0-520-04251-4 LC Card 80-6057 DDC
728/.09794/94 19
NA7238.L6 P6

**TIDAL FLAT ECOLOGY - NORTH
CAROLINA.**
Peterson, Charles Henry. The ecology of
intertidal flats of North Carolina . Slidell, LA ,
1979 [i.e. 1980] vi, 73 p. : LC Card 80-601522
DDC 574.5/2636 19
QH105.N8 P45

**TIDELANDS OIL. see PETROLEUM IN
SUBMERGED LANDS.**

TIDEMARSH ECOLOGY - MISSISSIPPI.
Hydrologic and biologic characteristics of
natural channels in coastal marsh of Mississippi
/. Mississippi State, Miss. , 1977. iii, 22 leaves :

LC Card 79-625357   DDC 551.46/09 19
QH105.M7 H9

TIDEMARSH ECOLOGY - NEW JERSEY.
Carlson, Cathy. The salt marsh of southern
New Jersey /. Pomona, N.J. , c1980. iv, 50 p. :
   LC Card 80-121932   DDC 574.5/2636 19
QH105.N5 C37

Rutgers University, New Brunswick, N.J.
Center for Coastal and Environmental Studies.
Comparison of natural and altered estuarine
systems . [New Brunswick, N.J.] [1979] xv,
247 p. :   LC Card 80-623603   DDC 574.5/26365 19
QH105.N5 R87 1979

**TIDEMARSH ECOLOGY - NORTH
CAROLINA.**
Rublee, Parke A. Bacteria in a North Carolina
salt marsh . [Raleigh , 1978. 80 p. :   LC Card
79-621361   DDC 574.5/2636 19
QR106 .R82

**TIDES - ENVIRONMENTAL ASPECTS -
MISSISSIPPI.**
Hydrologic and biologic characteristics of
natural channels in coastal marsh of Mississippi
/. Mississippi State, Miss. , 1977. iii, 22 leaves :
   LC Card 79-625357   DDC 551.46/09 19
QH105.M7 H9

Tierney, Kathleen J. Crisis intervention programs
for disaster victims : a source book and manual
for smaller communities / Kathleen J. Tierney,
Barbara Baisden (Disaster Research Center,
Ohio State University) ; project directors, E. L.
Quarantelli, Russell R. Dynes ; project officer,
Calvin J. Frederick, chief (Disaster Assistance
and Emergency Mental Health). Rockville,
Md. : U. S. Dept. of Health, Education, and
Welfare, Public Health Service, Alcohol, Drug
Abuse, and Mental Health Administration,
National Institute of Mental Health ;
Washington : for sale by the Supt. of Docs., U.
S. Govt. Print. Off., [1979] xvi, 203 p. ; 23 cm.
(DHEW publication ; no. (ADM) 79-675) Bibliography:
p. 167-203.   LC Card 79-603002   DDC 362.2 19
*1. Disaster relief - Research - United States. 2. Crisis
intervention (Psychiatry). 3. Community mental health
services - Law and legislation - United States. I.
Baisden, Barbara, joint author. II. Ohio. State
University, Columbus. Disaster Research Center. III.
United States. National Institute of Mental Health.
Disaster Assistance and Emergency Mental Health
Section. IV. Series: United States. Dept. of Health,
Education and Welfare. DHEW publication, no. (ADM)
79-675. V. Title.*
HV555.U6 T53

Tietenberg, Thomas H. Electricity demand in the
central Maine marketing area : an econometric
forecast / by T. H. Tietenberg, Michael
Donihue, and Al Maxwell. [Augusta, Me.] :
Office of Energy Resources, [1980?] vi, 105 p. :
graphs ; 28 cm. (Technical report - Office of Energy
Resources) Cover title. Issued with Maxwell, A.
Intensive energy conservation scenario, Augusta, Me.,
1980? Includes bibliographical references.   LC Card
80-621400   DDC 338.4/736362 19
*1. Electric utilities - Maine - Mathematical models. I.
Donihue, Michael, joint author. II. Maxwell, Alfred,
joint author. III. Series: Maine. Office of Energy
Resources. Technical report, Office of Energy
Resources. IV. Title.*
HD9685.U6 M38

TIGERS - BEHAVIOR.
Sunquist, Melvin E. The social organization of
tigers (Panthera tigris) in Royal Chitawan
National Park, Nepal /. Washington [D.C.] ,
1981. p. cm.   LC Card 81-607928   DDC 591 s
599.74/428 19
QL1 .S54 no. 336 QL737.C23

**TIGRAY (AFRICAN PEOPLE) see TIGRINYA
(AFRICAN PEOPLE)**

**TIGRIÑA (AFRICAN PEOPLE) see
TIGRINYA (AFRICAN PEOPLE)**

TIGRINYA (AFRICAN PEOPLE)
Bauer, Dan Franz. Household and society in
Ethiopia . East Lansing , c1977. xxxi, 183 p. :
   LC Card 77-155151
DT380.4.T54 B38   *NYPL [Sc E 80-273]*

**TILES - UNITED STATES - HISTORY - 19TH
CENTURY - EXHIBITIONS.**
Taft, Lisa Factor. Herman Carl Mueller .
Trenton, N.J. , c1979. 48 p. :   LC Card
79-622661
NK4670.7.M833 A4 1979

**TILES - UNITED STATES - HISTORY - 20TH
CENTURY - EXHIBITIONS.**
Taft, Lisa Factor. Herman Carl Mueller .
Trenton, N.J. , c1979. 48 p. :   LC Card
79-622661
NK4670.7.M833 A4 1979

Tilley, Steve. Washington (State). Dept. of
Ecology. Shorelands Division. Overview, coastal
aquatic management policies of Washington
State and federal agencies /. Olympia, Wash.
[1980] 29 p. ;   LC Card 80-624143   DDC
333.91/7/09797 19
HT393.W3 W3 1980

**TILT-UP CONCRETE CONSTRUCTION. see
PRECAST CONCRETE CONSTRUCTION.**

Timar, Thomas. "Sunset" review of instructional
television (ITV) : staff report to the California
State Legislature / prepared by Thomas Timar.
[Sacramento] : Assembly Office of Research,
California State Legislature, [1981] 33 leaves ;
28 cm. Cover title: Instructional television in
California. "January 1981." Includes bibliographical
references.   LC Card 81-621873   DDC
371.3/358/09794 19
*1. Television in education - California - Evaluation. I.
California. Legislature. Assembly. Office of Research.
II. Title. III. Title: Instructional television in California.*
LB1044.7 .T53

TIMBER - ARKANSAS - STATISTICS.
Bertelson, Daniel F. Arkansas forest industries,
1971 /. New Orleans , 1973. 29 p. :   LC Card
80-505836   DDC 333.75/0976 s
338.4/7674/009767 19
SD11 .A45793 no. 38 HD9757.A9

Bertelson, Daniel F. Arkansas forest industries,
1977 /. New Orleans, La. , 1980. 18 p. :   LC
Card 81-600548   DDC 333.75/0976 s
338.1/7498/09767 19
SD11 .A45793 no. 75 HD9757.A9

TIMBER - MARYLAND.
Powell, Douglas S. The forest resources of
Maryland /. Broomall, Pa. , 1980. 103 p. :   LC
Card 80-601810   DDC 333.75/0974 s
333.75/11/09752 19
SD11 .A455494 no. 61 SD144.M3

TIMBER - NEW HAMPSHIRE.
New Hampshire. Agricultural Experiment
Station, Durham. Timber values of town forests
/. Durham, N.H. [1979] ii, 44 p. :   LC Card
80-622381   DDC 333.1/1 19
SD428.N45 N48 1979

Timber purchase set-aside program . United
States. Congress. House. Committee on Small
Business. Subcommittee on SBA and SBIC
Authority and General Small Business
Problems. Washington , 1980. iii, 128 p. ;   LC
Card 80-603666   DDC 339.6/42/0973 19
KF27 .S6814 1980b

TIMBER - TROPICS.
Chudnoff, Martin. Tropical timbers of the world
/. Madison, Wis. [1980] iv, 826 p. ;   LC Card
80-602127   DDC 674/.13/0913 19
SD434 .C48

Timber values of town forests /. New Hampshire.
Agricultural Experiment Station, Durham.
Durham, N.H. [1979] ii, 44 p. :   LC Card
80-622381   DDC 333.1/1 19
SD428.N45 N48 1979

Timber yield tax revenue allocation . Leland,
Bob. Sacramento, CA (Box 90, Sacramento
95814) [1980] iii, 89, x, 86 p. ;   LC Card
81-620799   DDC 343.79405/5814928
347.940355814928 19
KFC881.8.F67 A25 1980

TIME - ADDRESSES, ESSAYS, LECTURES.
The Voices of time . Amherst , 1981. lx, 710
p. :   ISBN 0-87023-337-8   LC Card 81-3025   DDC
115 19
BD638 .V59 1981

Time and frequency users' manual /. National
Measurement Laboratory (U. S.). Time and
Frequency Division. Washington, D.C. , 1979.
xvi, 248 p. :   LC Card 79-600169   DDC 602/.18 s
529/.7 19
QC100 .U57 no. 559 QB209

The time is now . Massachusetts. Office of the
White House Conference on Handicapped
Individuals. Boston , 1978. v, 44 p. ;   LC Card
79-622359   DDC 362.4/048/09744 19
HV1555.M4 M37 1978

Time like a furrow . Hearst, James, 1900- Iowa
City , 1981. p. cm.   ISBN 0-89033-004-2 :   LC
Card 81-13736   DDC 818/.5203 B 19
PS3515.E146 Z475

TIME MANAGEMENT.
Alderman, C. Wayne. Audit performance and
time budgets . [Austin] , 1978. 14 p. ;   LC Card
79-623638   DDC 657/.068/5 19
HF5667 .A5

**TIME MANAGEMENT SURVEYS -
CALIFORNIA - OAKLAND.**
Medrich, Elliott A. The serious business of
growing up . Berkeley , c1981. p. cm.   ISBN
0-520-04296-4   LC Card 81-7630   DDC
305.2/3/0979466 19
HQ792.U5 M42

**TIME MEASUREMENTS - HANDBOOKS,
MANUALS, ETC.**
National Measurement Laboratory (U. S.). Time
and Frequency Division. Time and frequency
users' manual /. Washington, D.C. , 1979. xvi,
248 p. :   LC Card 79-600169   DDC 602/.18 s
529/.7 19
QC100 .U57 no. 559 QB209

**TIME - SYSTEMS AND STANDARDS -
MAPS.**
United States. Central Intelligence Agency.
Standard time zones of the world.
[Washington , 1980] 1 map :   LC Card 81-690683
G3201.B2 1980 .U5

Timmerhaus, Klaus D. Energy resource recovery
in arid lands /. Albuquerque , c1981. p. cm.
   ISBN 0-8263-0564-4   LC Card 80-54573   DDC
333.79/0978 19
TJ163.25.U6 E54

TIN INDUSTRY.
Witzig, Thomas J. Operation of the
International Tin Agreement /. [Avondale,
Md.] , 1981. p. cm.   LC Card 81-607844   DDC
622 s 338.2/7453 19
TN295 .U4 HD9539.T5

**TIN - TRADE AND STATISTICS. see TIN
INDUSTRY.**

TIOGA COUNTY, N. Y. - CENSUS, 1970.
Southern Tier East Regional Planning Board.
Housing related census data: Broome-Tioga
counties /. Binghamton, N. Y., 1974. 97 p.;
NYPL [JLF 80-1377]

**Tips on the care and adjustment of Vietnamese
and other Asian children in the United States.**
[Washington] : U. S. Dept. of Health,
Education, and Welfare, Office of Human
Development/Office of Child Development,
Children's Bureau : for sale by the Supt. of
Docs., U. S. Govt. Print. Off., [1975] 11, 11,
[6] p. ; 24 cm. (DHEW publication. no. (OHD)
75-72)   LC Card 75-602431   DDC 649/.145 19
*1. Children, Adopted - Care and hygiene - United
States. 2. Children - Care and hygiene - Vietnam. 3.
Children - Care and hygiene - Korea. 4. Intercountry
adoption - United States. 5. Interracial adoption -
United States. I. Series: United States. Dept. of Health,
Education and Welfare. DHEW publication, no. (OHD)
75-72.*
RJ102 .T56

Tipton, Steven M. Getting saved from the
sixties : the transformation of moral meaning in
American culture / Steven M. Tipton ;
foreword by Robert N. Bellah. Berkeley :
University of California Press, c1981. p. cm.
Bibliography: p. Includes index.   ISBN 0-520-03868-1
   LC Card 81-3033   DDC 973.92 19
*1. United States - Moral conditions. 2. Youth - United
States - Conduct of life. 3. Social ethics. I. Title.*
HN59 .T58

**TIRE INDUSTRY - LAW AND
LEGISLATION - UNITED STATES.**
United States. Congress. House. Committee on
Interstate and Foreign Commerce.
Subcommittee on Consumer Protection and
Finance. Tire recall . Washington , 1979. iii, 36
p. ;   LC Card 80-600683   DDC 346.7303/82 19
KF27 .I554 1979e

Tire recall . United States. Congress. House.
Committee on Interstate and Foreign
Commerce. Subcommittee on Consumer
Protection and Finance. Washington , 1979. iii,
36 p. ;   LC Card 80-600683   DDC 346.7303/82 19
KF27 .I554 1979e

Tire rolling losses and fuel economy . R & D

Planning Workshop, Transportation Systems
Center, 1977. Troy, MI , c1977. iii, 202 p. :
   LC Card 78-51861
TL151.6 .R18 1977

TISSUES - ANALYSIS - CONGRESSES.
Ultrasonic tissue characterization II .
Washington , 1979. xi, 362 p. :   LC Card
79-600026   DDC 602/.18 s 616.07/543 19
QC100 .U57 no. 525 RC78.7.U4

TITANIUM CASTINGS.
Calvert, Eugene D. An investment mold for
titanium casting /. Washington [1981] p. cm.
   LC Card 80-607847   DDC 622 s 673/.7322255
   19
TN23 .U43 TS562

**Title I, ESEA, manual of operational policies and
guidelines.** Missouri. Dept. of Elementary and
Secondary Education. [Jefferson City, Mo.]
[1980] ii, 80 p. ;   LC Card 80-623988   DDC
   371.96/7/09778 19
LC4092.M5 M57 1980

Title III of the Higher education act of 1965 .
United States. Congress. Senate. Committee on
the Judiciary. Subcommittee on Limitations on
Contracted and Delegated Authority.
Washington , 1980. iv, 345 p. :   LC Card
   80-602424   DDC 353.0085/1 19
KF26 .J857 1979

Title I ESEA. United States. Office of Education.
Washington, D. C., 1973. vi, 67 p.:
                                 NYPL [JLF 81-40]

**Title V authorization under the Regional rail
reorganization act of 1973 .** United States.
Congress. House. Committee on Interstate and
Foreign Commerce. Subcommittee on
Transportation and Commerce. Washington ,
1980. iii, 38 p. ;   LC Card 80-603098   DDC
   331.25/5 19
KF27 .I5589 1980b

**Title XX comprehensive annual services program
plan.** Maine. Dept. of Human Services.
[Augusta] 28 cm.   LC Card 79-642723
                                 NYPL [JLM 80-1072]

Title XX Donated Funds Initiative . Illinois.
Bureau of Title XX Administration. Springfield,
Ill. , 1979. 53 p. :   LC Card 79-624230   DDC
   361.7 19
HV41 .I29 1979

Title XX donated funds initiative . Illinois.
Bureau of Title XX Administration. Springfield,
Ill. [1980] 51 p. :   LC Card 80-623382   DDC
   353.97730084 19
HV86 .I37 1980

Title XX/FY 1979 . Massachusetts. Dept. of
Public Welfare. [Boston , 1978] 66 p. in various
pagings, [2] fold. leaves of plates :   LC Card
   80-620540   DDC 361/.007/15 19
HV11 .M365 1978

Tittle, Carol K., 1933- Sex-fair interest
measurement . Washington , 1978, 1979
printing. xvii, 169 p. :   LC Card 79-602075   DDC
   153.9/4 19
HF5381.5 .S4

**To amend the Bretton Woods agreements act to
authorize consent to an increase in the United
States quota in the International Monetary
Fund .** United States. Congress. House.
Committee on Banking, Finance and Urban
Affairs. Subcommittee on International Trade,
Investment and Monetary Policy. Washington ,
1980. iv, 621 p. :   LC Card 80-602758   DDC
   343.73/032 19
KF27 .B577 1980

To amend The Copyright Act, S. 2082 . United
States. Congress. Senate. Committee on the
Judiciary. Subcommittee on Improvements in
Judicial Machinery. Washington , 1981. iv, 152
p. :   LC Card 81-601346   DDC 346.7304/82
   347.306482 19
KF26 .J855 1980c

To amend the Disaster Relief Act . United States.
Congress. House. Committee on Public Works
and Transportation. Subcommittee on Water
Resources. Washington , 1980. iii, 62 p. ;   LC
   Card 80-604102   DDC 344.73/0534 347.304534
   19
KF27 .P8968 1980b

To amend the Geothermal steam act of 1970 .
United States. Congress. House. Committee on
Interior and Insular Affairs. Subcommittee on

Mines and Mining. Washington , 1980. iv, 134
p. ;   LC Card 80-601989   DDC 346.7304/688/0262
   19
KF27 .I536 1979d

**To amend the Hazardous materials
transportation act and to amend the
Independent safety board act .** United States.
Congress. House. Committee on Public Works
and Transportation. Subcommittee on Aviation.
Washington , 1980. v, 97 p. ;   LC Card
   80-603697   DDC 343.73/093 347.30393 19
KF27 .P89624 1980j

**To amend the Indian Health Care Improvement
Act .** United States. Congress. House.
Committee on Interior and Insular Affairs.
Washington , 1980 [i.e. 1981] vii, 497 p. :   LC
   Card 81-600862   DDC 344.73/0328497
   347.304328497 19
KF27 .I5 1980a

**To amend the National Visitor Center Facilities
Act of 1968 .** United States. Congress. House.
Committee on Public Works and
Transportation. Subcommittee on Public
Buildings and Grounds. Washington , 1980. iii,
34 p. :   LC Card 81-600581   DDC 344.73/09
   347.3049 19
KF27 .P8964 1979e

**To amend the Rehabilitation act of 1973, relating
to State agency organization requirements .**
United States. Congress. House. Committee on
Education and Labor. Subcommittee on Select
Education. Washington , 1980. v, 560 p. :   LC
   Card 80-602471   DDC 344.73/0769 19
KF27 .E373 1979e

**To amend the Small Business Act to extend the
current SBA 8(a) pilot program.** United States.
Congress. Senate. Select Committee on Small
Business. H.R. 5612, to amend the Small
Business Act to extend the current SBA 8(a)
pilot program . Washington , 1980. iii, 211 p. :
   LC Card 80-604024   DDC 346.73/0652
   347.306652 19
KF26.5 S6 1980u

To amend the Wild and scenic rivers act . United
States. Congress. Senate. Committee on Interior
and Insular Affairs. Environment and Land
Resources Subcommittee. Washington , 1975-
v. :   LC Card 76-600555
KF26 .I526 1975d

**To authorize the extension of the Council on
Wage and Price Stability .** United States.
Congress. House. Committee on Banking,
Finance and Urban Affairs. Subcommittee on
Economic Stabilization. Washington , 1980. iv,
475 p. ;   LC Card 80-602791   DDC 343.73/034 19
KF27 .B542 1980

**To authorize the President of the United States
to present on behalf of the Congress specially
struck gold medals to Bryan Lewis Allen and
to the A. Philip Randolph Institute .** United
States. Congress. House. Committee on
Banking, Finance and Urban Affairs.
Subcommittee on Consumer Affairs.
Washington , 1980. iii, 15 p. ;   LC Card
   80-601396   DDC 344.73/091 19
KF27 .B535 1980b

**To consider and report to the Senate Budget
Committee recommendations for Small
Business Administration programs .** United
States. Congress. Senate. Select Committee on
Small Business. Washington , 1981. iii, 53 p. ;
   LC Card 81-601795   DDC 353.0082/048 19
KF26.5 .S6 1981

**To create a Select Committee on Narcotics
Abuse and Control .** United States. Congress.
Senate. Committee on Rules and
Administration. Washington , 1980. iv, 224 p. :
   LC Card 80-602455   DDC 353.0076/5 19
KF26 .R8 1980

To enhance the safety mission of the FAA .
United States. Congress. House. Committee on
Public Works and Transportation. Subcommittee
on Aviation. Washington , 1980. iv, 560 p. :
   LC Card 80-604032   DDC 343.73/097 347.30397
   19
KF27 .P89624 1980m

**To enlarge the Indiana Dunes National
Lakeshore .** United States. Congress. House.
Committee on Interior and Insular Affairs.
Subcommittee on National Parks and Insular
Affairs. Washington , 1979. iv, 299 p. :   LC

Card 80-601516   DDC 346.7304/6784 19
KF27 .I5365 1978d

To establish a barrier islands protection system .
United States. Congress. House. Committee on
Interior and Insular Affairs. Subcommittee on
National Parks and Insular Affairs.
Washington , 1980. vii, 650 p. :   LC Card
   80-603095   DDC 346.7304/6784 19
KF27 .I5365 1980

**To establish a Commission on the International
Application of Antitrust Laws .** United States.
Congress. Senate. Committee on Governmental
Affairs. Washington , 1980. iii, 187 p. ;   LC
   Card 80-603105   DDC 343.73/072 19
KF26 .G67 1979ap

To establish a national water policy . United
States. Congress. Senate. Committee on
Environment and Public Works. Subcommittee
on Water Resources. Washington , 19<7. v.
<2> :   LC Card 81-461639   DDC 333.91/00973
   19
KF26 .E683 1978

**To extend the reorganization authority of the
President .** United States. Congress. Senate.
Committee on Governmental Affairs.
Washington , 1980. iii, 44 p. ;   LC Card
   80-603039   DDC 353/.073 19
KF26 .G67 1980f

**To make the Select Committee on Indian Affairs
a permanent committee of the Senate .** United
States. Congress. Senate. Committee on Rules
and Administration. Washington , 1980. v, 70
p. ;   LC Card 80-603072   DDC 328.73/07652 19
KF26 .R8 1980a

To modernize the Federal Reserve System .
United States. Congress. House. Committee on
Banking, Finance, and Urban Affairs.
Subcommittee on Domestic Monetary Policy.
Washington , 1980. iii, 96 p. ;   LC Card
   80-603677   DDC 346.73/08211 19
KF27 .B537 1980a

**To prohibit futures trading of potatoes on
commodity exchanges .** United States. Congress.
Senate. Committee on Agriculture, Nutrition,
and Forestry. Subcommittee on Agricultural
Research and General Legislation. Washington ,
1980. v, 257 p. :   LC Card 80-601327   DDC
   343.73/08513491/0262 19
KF26 .A3534 1979e

**To provide compliance with the national
maximum speed limit .** United States. Congress.
Senate. Committee on Environment and Public
Works. Subcommittee on Transportation.
Washington , 1980. iii, 141 p. :   LC Card
   80-603026   DDC 343.73/0946 19
KF26 .E679 1980

**A study of land use activities and their
relationship of [i.e. to] sport fish resources in
Alaska .** Hubartt, Dennis. Juneau , 1978. 52 p. ;
   LC Card 78-624204   DDC 333.95/6/09798 19
SK367 .H83

TOBACCO - BIBLIOGRAPHY.
Marin, Carmen M. Tobacco literature, a
bibliography /. Raleigh [1979] iii, 362 p. ;   LC
   Card 80-621376   DDC 016.6337/1 19
Z7882 .M37 SB273

Tobacco in the United States. United States.
Agricultural Marketing Service. [Washington]
[1979] 27 p. :   LC Card 79-601924   DDC
   633.7/1/0973 19
SB273 .U44 1979

**TOBACCO - LAW AND LEGISLATION -
PUERTO RICO.**
Cannon, Joseph Gurney, 1836-1926. $1,050,000
into the pockets of the American tobacco trust.
[Washington? D. C. , 1900] 16 p. ;
                              NYPL [Arents S 1607]

Tobacco literature, a bibliography /. Marin,
Carmen M. Raleigh [1979] iii, 362 p. ;   LC
   Card 80-621376   DDC 016.6337/1 19
Z7882 .M37 SB273

**TOBACCO MANUFACTURE AND TRADE -
UNITED STATES.**
United States. Agricultural Marketing Service.
Tobacco in the United States. [Washington]
[1979] 27 p. :   LC Card 79-601924   DDC
   633.7/1/0973 19
SB273 .U44 1979

**TOBACCO - TOXICOLOGY - UNITED
STATES - STATISTICS.**

Klebba, A. Joan. Mortality from diseases associated with smoking . Hyattsville, Md. , 1980. p. cm. ISBN 0-8406-0208-1 LC Card 80-607855 DDC 312/.2/0973 s 615.9/52379 19
HB1335 .A18 no. 17 RA1242.T6

TOBACCO - UNITED STATES.
United States. Agricultural Marketing Service. Tobacco in the United States. [Washington] [1979] 27 p. : LC Card 79-601924 DDC 633.7/1/0973 19
SB273 .U44 1979

Tobin, Wallace E. The mariner's pocket companion / Wallace E. Tobin III. Annapolis, Md. : Naval Institute Press, [1974. p. cm. Bibliography: p. ISBN 0-87021-381-4 : LC Card 79-84797 DDC 623.88/02/02 19
1. Navigation - Handbooks, manuals, etc. 2. Boats and boating - Handbooks, manuals, etc. I. Title.
VK155 .T6 1981

Todorov, Tzvetan, 1939-
[Poétique. English]
Introduction to poetics / Tzvetan Todorov ; translation from the French by Richard Howard ; introduction by Peter Brooks. Minneapolis : University of Minnesota Press, 1981. p. cm. (Theory and history of literature . v. 1) Translation of: Poétique. Includes bibliographical references and index. ISBN 0-8166-1008-8 : LC Card 81-3073 DDC 808.1 19
1. Poetics. 2. Structuralism (Literary analysis). I. Title. II. Series.
PN1043 .T613

Tōkaidō, adventures on the road in old Japan / catalogue essays by Marie Adams ... [et al.] ; edited by Stephen Addiss. Lawrence, Kan. : University of Kansas, Spencer Museum of Art, c1980. xv, 120 p. : ill. (some col.) ; 24 cm. "Published in conjunction with the exhibition at the Spencer Museum of Art, the University of Kansas, Lawrence, October 18-December 21, 1980."--p. vi. Bibliography: p. 117-120. LC Card 80-53851 DDC 769.92/4 19
1. Andō, Hiroshige, 1797-1858 - Addresses, essays, lectures. 2. Tōkaidō (Japan) in art - Addresses, essays, lectures. I. Adams, Marie Jeanne. II. Addiss, Stephen, 1935-. III. Helen Foreman Spencer Museum of Art.
NE1325.A5 T63

TŌKAIDŌ (JAPAN) IN ART - ADDRESSES, ESSAYS, LECTURES.
Tōkaidō, adventures on the road in old Japan /. Lawrence, Kan. , c1980. xv, 120 p. : LC Card 80-53851 DDC 769.92/4 19
NE1325.A5 T63

TOKYO ROUND, 1973-1977.
Sullivan, Daniel E. Minerals and the Tokyo Round of the MTN /. Washington [1981] p. cm. LC Card 81-607909 DDC 622 s 382/.42 19
TN295 .U4 HD9506.A2

Toledo Metropolitan Area Council of Governments.
Information paper - Toledo Metropolitan Area Council of Governments .
(no. 4) Toledo Metropolitan Area Council of Governments. Solar energy, active and passive systems for space and water heating /. Toledo, Ohio, c1980. ii, 41 p. : LC Card 80-150114 DDC 697/.78 19
TH7413 .T64 1980

Solar energy, active and passive systems for space and water heating / Toledo Metropolitan Area Council of Governments. Toledo, Ohio : TMACOG, c1980. ii, 41 p. : ill. ; 28 cm. (CCEMP series) Information paper - Toledo Metropolitan Area Council of Governments ; no. 4 "May, 1980." "Prepared under contract no. 31-109-38-4794, Argonne National Laboratory." Bibliography: p. 41. LC Card 80-150114 DDC 697/.78 19
1. Solar heating. I. United States. Argonne National Laboratory, Lemont, Ill. II. Series. III. Series: Toledo Metropolitan Area Council of Governments. Information paper - Toledo Metropolitan Area Council of Governments , no. 4. IV. Title.
TH7413 .T64 1980

Tolerance and synthetic ability of sewage microorganisms ... Thompson, Frederick C. Tolerance and synthetic ability of sewage microorganisms in acid mine water /. Morgantown , 1981. ix, 60 p. : LC Card 76-622086 DDC 628.1/6832 19
QR88 .T48

TOLL BRIDGES - VIRGINIA.
Robertson, Richard Neal, 1940- Impact of removal of tolls on travel in Tidewater Virginia /. Charlottesville, Va. [1977?] 3 v. : LC Card 79-625466 DDC 388.1/14 19
HE376.A2 V87

Tollenaar, Kenneth C. Oregon. University. Bureau of Governmental Research and Service. Local government boundary commissions . [Eugene] , 1978. iii, 112 p. ; LC Card 78-622792
JS451 .O7 1978a **NYPL [JLF 80-1445]**

Tolson, Melvin Beaunorus. Caviar and cabbage / by Melvin B. Tolson ; edited, with and introduction, by Robert M. Farnsworth. Columbia : University of Missouri Press, 1982. p. cm. Essays, originally published Nov. 1937-June 1944 as a column in the Washington Tribune. ISBN 0-8262-0348-5 LC Card 81-10480 DDC 814/.52 19
I. Farnsworth, Robert M. II. Title.
PS3539.O334 C3

Tom Robbins /. Siegel, Mark Richard. Boise, Idaho , c1980. 52 p. ; ISBN 0-88430-066-8 (pbk.) : LC Card 80-69013 DDC 813/.54 19
PS3568.O233 Z87

Tom Stoppard . Dean, Joan Fitzpatrick, 1949- Columbia , 1981. 109 p. ; ISBN 0-8262-0332-9 (pbk.) LC Card 80-26400 DDC 822/.914 19
PR6069.T6 Z63

Toman, Norman E. North Dakota. Agricultural Experiment Station, Fargo. Water as a parameter for development of energy resources in the Upper Great Plains . Fargo, N.D. [1978] ii, 144 p. : LC Card 79-625649 DDC 630 s 333.8/22/0978 19
S99 .A5a no. 71 HD9502.U53N683

Tomáš G. Masaryk, 1850-1937 . Kovtun, George J. Washington, D.C. , 1981. 26 p. : LC Card 80-600139 DDC 016.9437/03/0924 19
Z8552.7 .K68 DB2191.M38

TOMATO PRODUCTS - UNITED STATES.
King, Gordon A., 1924- Economic trends in the processing tomato industry. [Berkeley, 1973] ix, 130 p. LC Card 74-621129 DDC 338.1 s 338.4/7664805642/0973 19
HD9000.1 .C3 no. 73-4 HD9330.T73U6

TOMATOES, CANNED - UNITED STATES.
King, Gordon A., 1924- Economic trends in the processing tomato industry. [Berkeley, 1973] ix, 130 p. LC Card 74-621129 DDC 338.1 s 338.4/7664805642/0973 19
HD9000.1 .C3 no. 73-4 HD9330.T73U6

Tomimatsu, T. T.
The U. S. copper mining industry : a perspective on financial health / by T. T. Tomimatsu. [Washington, D.C.] ; Avondale, MD. : U. S. Bureau of Mines, [1981] p. cm. (Information circular - U. S. Bureau of mines) "June 10, 1980: DAS-A1." Bibliography: p. LC Card 80-607792 DDC 338.2/3 19
1. Copper industry and trade - United States - Finance. 2. Copper mines and mining - United States - Finance. I. Series: United States Bureau of Mines. Report of investigations . II. Title.
HD9539.C7 U576

The U. S. copper mining industry : a perspective on financial health / by T. T. Tomimatsu. [Washington, D.C.] : U. S. Bureau of Mines, [1981] p. cm. (Information circular - U. S. Bureau of mines) "June 10, 1980: DAS-A1." Bibliography: p. LC Card 80-609992 DDC 338.2/3 19
1. Copper industry and trade - United States - Finance. 2. Copper mines and mining - United States - Finance. I. Series: United States Bureau of Mines. Report of investigations . II. Title.
HD9539.C7 U576

Tomlinson, Roy E. (joint author) Birkenstein, Lillian R. Native names of Mexican birds . Washington , 1981. p. cm. LC Card 80-606886 DDC 333.95/4 s 598.2972/014 19
S914 .A3 no. 138 QL686

Tompkins, Evelyn H. California. Dept. of Water Resources. Southern District. Potential waste disposal areas, northern Los Angeles County /. [Sacramento] [1979] vii, 58 p. : LC Card 80-621404 DDC 363.7/28 19
TD811.5 .C34 1979

Tompkins, Joseph B. National priorities for the investigation and prosecution of white collar

crime : report of the Attorney General, Benjamin R. Civiletti / prepared by the Criminal Division ; principal author, Joseph B. Thomkins, Jr. Washington, D.C. ; U. S. Dept. of Justice : [Supt. of Docs., U. S. G.P.O., distributor], 1980. x, 50, 21-a p. ; 26 cm. "August 1980." S/N 027-000-00997-2 Item 717 LC Card 80-603918 DDC 364.1/68/0973 19
1. White collar crime - United States. 2. White collar crime investigation - United States. I. Civiletti, Benjamin R. II. United States. Dept. of Justice. III. United States. Dept. of Justice. Criminal Division. IV. Title.
HV8079.W47 T65

TONAWANDA, N. Y. - CITY PLANNING.
Candeub, Fleissig & Associates. Comprehensive policy plan for the city of Tonawanda, N. Y. /. Albany, N. Y. , 1975. v, 158 p. :
NYPL [JLF 80-1232]

Tonemah, Helen John. (joint author) Red Corn, Jim. Subject report, American Indians of Oklahoma by county . Oklahoma City, Okla. [1980] v, 30 leaves ; LC Card 80-622934 DDC 312/.93 19
E78.O45 R43

Tonklin, Leroy F. Alabama communities in perspective. Montgomery, Ala., Alabama Development Office, 1973. xi, 99 p. ; illus., tables. 22 x 28 cm. Sponsored by U. S. Dept. of Housing and Urban Development. Contract / grant no. CPA-AL-64-09-1020. Bibliography: p. 95-99. LC Card 74-192424
1. Alabama - Economic conditions. I. Alabama. Development Office. II. Title.
NYPL [JLF 80-177]

Tools and rules . Association of New Jersey Environmental Commissions. [Washington] , 1978 printing. 69, xii p. ; LC Card 79-602335
KF3775 .A97 1978 **NYPL [JLF 81-387]**

TOOTH LOSS - UNITED STATES - STATISTICS.
Harvey, Clair R. Decayed, missing, and filled teeth among persons 1-74 years, United States, 1971-74 . Hyattsville, Md. , 1980. p. cm. ISBN 0-8406-0209-X LC Card 80-607837 DDC 312/.0973 s 312/.30476 19
RA407.3 .A347 no. 223 RK52.2

Topical briefs--fish and wildlife resources and electric power generation .
(no. 6) Suter, Glenn W. Effects of geothermal energy development on fish and wildlife /. [Washington, D.C.] , 1978. 20 p. : LC Card 79-603793 DDC 333.8/81 19
QH545.G46 S87

Topical Conference on Basic Optical Properties of Materials, Gaithersburg, Md., 1980. Basic optical properties of materials : summaries of papers presented at the Topical Conference on Basic Optical Properties of Materials, held at the National Bureau of Standards, Gaithersburg, Maryland, May 5-7, 1980 / edited by Albert Feldman, in cooperation with the Optical Society of America. Washington, D.C. : U. S. Dept. of Commerce, National Bureau of Standards : for sale by the Supt. of Docs., U. S. Govt. Print. Off., [1980] x, 241 p. : ill., graphs ; 26 cm. (National Bureau of Standards special publication ; 574) Includes bibliographical references and index. LC Card 80-600038 DDC 602/.18 s 620.1/1295 19
1. Optical materials - Congresses. I. Feldman, Albert. II. United States. National Bureau of Standards. III. Optical Society of America. IV. Series: United States. National Bureau of Standards Special publication, 574. V. Title.
QC100 .U57 no. 574 QC374

Torchia, Marion. Chest X-ray screening practices : an annotated bibliography / compiled by Marion Torchia, JoAnne DuChez ; project officer, Jay A. Rachlin. Rockville, Md. : U. S. Dept. of Health, Education, and Welfare, Public Health Service, Food and Drug Administration, Bureau of Radiological Health ; Washington, D.C. : for sale by the Supt. of Docs., U. S. Govt. Print. Off., [1980] v, 57 p. ; 27 cm. (HEW publication ; (FDA) 80-8116) Includes index. LC Card 80-602827 DDC 363.1/79 19
1. Chest - Radiography - Abstracts. 2. Respiratory organs - Diseases - Diagnosis - Abstracts. 3. Medical screening - Abstracts. I. DuChez, JoAnne, joint author. II. Series: United States. Dept. of Health, Education and Welfare. DHEW publication, (FDA) 80-8116. III.

Title.
RA645.R4 T67

Torgerson, David. Energy and U. S. agriculture, 1974 and 1978 / [David Torgerson and Harold Cooper]. [Washington, D.C.] : U. S. Dept. of Agriculture, Economics, Statistics, and Cooperatives Service, [1980] ii, 115 p. ; 27 cm. (Statistical bulletin - U. S. Dept. of Agriculture ; no. 632) Cover title. Page 115 is p. [3] of cover. Chiefly tables. LC Card 80-602126 DDC 338.1/0973 s 333.79 19
1. Agriculture - United States - Energy consumption - Statistics. I. Cooper, Harold W., 1914- joint author. II. United States. Dept. of Agriculture. Economics, Statistics, and Cooperatives Service. III. Series: United States. Dept. of Agriculture. Statistical bulletin , no. 632. IV. Title.
HD1751 .A5 no. 632 S494.5.E5

TORNADO WARNING SYSTEMS - OKLAHOMA.
United States. National Oceanic and Atmospheric Administration. Red River Valley tornadoes of April 10, 1979 . Rockville, Md. [1980] v, 60 p., [2] leaves of plates : LC Card 80-601568 DDC 363.3/492 19
QC955.5.T4 U54 1980

TORNADO WARNING SYSTEMS - TEXAS.
United States. National Oceanic and Atmospheric Administration. Red River Valley tornadoes of April 10, 1979 . Rockville, Md. [1980] v, 60 p., [2] leaves of plates : LC Card 80-601568 DDC 363.3/492 19
QC955.5.T4 U54 1980

TORNADO WARNING SYSTEMS - UNITED STATES - DATA PROCESSING.
United States. Congress. House. Committee on Science and Technology. Subcommittee on Space Science and Applications. Centralized storm information system . Washington , 1980 [i.e. 1981] iii, 19 p. ; LC Card 81-600858 DDC 363.3/492 19
KF27 .S3995 1980c

Toronto, Ont. University. see University of Toronto.

Torres-Anjel, Manuel J. Enterotoxigenic Clostridium perfringens type A in selected humans : a prevalence study / Manuel J. Torres-Anjel, Hans P. Riemann, and Che C. Tsai. Washington : Pan American Health Organization, Pan American Sanitary Bureau, Regional Office of the World Health Organization, 1977. 32 p. ; 26 cm. (Scientific publication - Pan American Health Organization, World Health Organization . no. 350) Bibliography: p. 28-31. LC Card 78-102859 DDC 362.1/09181/2 s 615.9/52995 19
1. Clostridium diseases. 2. Clostridium perfringens. 3. Epidemiology. I. Riemann, Hans, 1920- joint author. II. Tsai, Che C., joint author. III. Series: Pan American Health Organization. Publicaciones científicas , no. 350. IV. Title.
RA10 .P252 no. 350 QR201.C54

Torrey, Barbara Boyle.
An international comparison of pension systems / prepared by Barbara Boyle Torrey and Carole J. Thompson, with the help of Karen Orlansky and Robert Firestine. [Washington, D.C.] : President's Commission on Pension Policy : [for sale by the Supt. of Docs., U. S. Govt. Print. Off.], 1980. v, 52, [46] p. ; 28 cm. (Working papers - President's Commission on Pension Policy) Bibliography: p. [41]-[46] (3d group) LC Card 80-602549 DDC 331.25/2 19
1. Old age pensions. I. Thompson, Carole J., joint author. II. United States. President's Commission on Pension Policy. III. Series: United States. President's Commission on Pension Policy. Working papers - President's Commission on Pension Policy. IV. Title.
HD7105.3 .T67

(joint author) Meier, Elizabeth L. Retirement income goals /. Washington, D.C. [1980] v, 60 p. ; LC Card 80-602550 DDC 331.25/2/0973 19
HD7106.U5 M37

TORT LIABILITY OF MANUFACTURERS. see PRODUCTS LIABILITY.

TORT LIABILITY OF MUNICIPAL CORPORATIONS - UNITED STATES.
Smith, Michael, 1953- Liability of local governments in federal court for the violation of federal rights--Monell, Owen, and Thiboutot /. Chapel Hill , 1980, c1979. 24 p. : LC Card 81-621377 DDC 342.756/09 s 347.56029 s

342.73/09 347.3029 19
KFN7830.A15 L6 no. 21 KF1321

TORT LIABILITY OF THE GOVERNMENT. see GOVERNMENT LIABILITY.

TORT LIABILITY OF THE STATE. see GOVERNMENT LIABILITY.

TORTURE.
United States. Congress. House. Committee on Foreign Affairs. Subcommittee on International Organizations. Human rights and the phenomenon of disappearances . Washington , 1980. viii, 636 p. ; LC Card 80-603094 DDC 323.4/3 19
KF27 .F648 1979g

Total solar eclipse of 16 February 1980 /. Fiala, Alan D. Washington, D.C. [1978] 42 p. : LC Card 80-601567 DDC 520 s 523.7/8 19
QB4 .W34 no. 158 QB544.80

Totten, Stanley M. (joint author) White, George Willard, 1903- Glacial geology of Ashtabula County, Ohio /. Columbus , 1979. iv, 48 p. : LC Card 80-622748 DDC 557.71 s 551.7/92/0977134 19
QE151 .A186 no. 112 QE697

Touchstone, Sheri D. Texas. Dept. of Corrections. Research, Planning, and Development Division. Comparison analysis of escapes from State and Federal correctional institutions, 1972 through 1975. Huntsville , 1978. vi, 29 leaves : LC Card 78-622828 DDC 365/.641 19
HV9304 .T46 1978

Touhill, Blanche M. (Blanche Marie), 1931- William Smith O'Brien and his Irish revolutionary companions in penal exile / Blanche M. Touhill. Columbia : University of Missouri Press, 1981. p. cm. Bibliography: p. Includes index. ISBN 0-8262-0339-6 LC Card 81-1899 DDC 941.5081/092/4 19
1. O'Brien, William Smith, 1803-1864. 2. Ireland - History - Rising of 1848. 3. Revolutionists - Ireland - Biography. 4. Tasmania - Exiles - Biography. I. Title.
DA952.O22 T68

Toulmin, Llewellyn. Conference on Local Financial Management, 1st, Detroit, 1979. Local financial management in the '80s . Washington, D.C. [1980] ix, 306 p. : LC Card 80-602329
HJ9141 .C66 1979 NYPL [JLF 80-1653]

Toulouse - Government. see Toulouse - Politics and government.

TOULOUSE - POLITICS AND GOVERNMENT.
Aminzade, Ronald, 1949- Class, politics, and early industrial capitalism . Albany, N.Y. , 1981. p. cm. LC Card 80-28284 DDC 330.944/86 19
HD8437.T68 A46 1981

TOURISM. see TOURIST TRADE.

Tourism and Hawaii's economy . Hawaii. Dept. of Planning and Economic Development. Research and Economic Analysis Division. [Honolulu] [1980] 29 p. : LC Card 80-622661 DDC 380.1/4591969044 19
G155.U6 H284 1980

Tourism--passport to development? . Joint Unesco-World Bank Seminar on the Social and Cultural Impacts of Tourism, Washington, D.C., 1976. [New York] , c1979. xviii, 360 p. : ISBN 0-19-520149-3 : LC Card 79-18116
G154.9 .J64 1976 NYPL [JLE 80-2592]

TOURIST CAMPS, HOTELS, ETC. - NORTHEASTERN STATES - STATISTICS.
Kottke, Marvin Walter. A survey of recreational lodging and outdoor recreation by northeastern households /. Storrs, Conn. [1979] 48 p. ; LC Card 80-621317 DDC 338.4/76479474 19
TX909 .K67

TOURIST INDUSTRY. see TOURIST TRADE.

TOURIST TRADE - CONGRESSES.
Joint Unesco-World Bank Seminar on the Social and Cultural Impacts of Tourism, Washington, D.C., 1976. Tourism--passport to development? . [New York] , c1979. xviii, 360 p. : ISBN 0-19-520149-3 : LC Card 79-18116
G154.9 .J64 1976 NYPL [JLE 80-2592]

Travel Research Association. The 80's, its impact on travel and tourism marketing . Salt Lake City, Utah , c1977. xv, 221 p. : LC Card

80-141505 DDC 380.1/459104 19
G154.9 .T72 1977

TOURIST TRADE - FLORIDA.
Schultz, Ronald R. The social and economic effects of the Florida tourist industry /. Boca Raton , 1978. x, 123 p. : LC Card 79-622949
G155.U6 S37

TOURIST TRADE - HAWAII.
Hawaii. Dept. of Planning and Economic Development. Research and Economic Analysis Division. Tourism and Hawaii's economy . [Honolulu] [1980] 29 p. : LC Card 80-622661 DDC 380.1/4591969044 19
G155.U6 H284 1980

TOURIST TRADE - HAWAII - CONGRESSES.
Canada--Hawaii, a look at the 1980's . Honolulu, Hawaii [1980] 58 p. ; LC Card 80-622006 DDC 382/.4591969044 19
G155.U6 C25 NYPL [M-10 9494 no. 15]

TOURIST TRADE - INFORMATION SERVICES - VERMONT.
Vermont. Agency of Transportation. Planning Division. Vermont travel information study . [Montpelier] , 1978. v, 77 p. : LC Card 78-623822 DDC 388.3/124 19
G155.U6 V37 1978

TOURIST TRADE - LAW AND LEGISLATION - FLORIDA.
Florida. Legislature. Senate. Committee on Commerce. A review of the Florida Tourism Commission in the Department of Commerce . [Tallahassee? Fla.] [1980] i, 20 p. ; LC Card 81-621209 DDC 353.97590082/7 19
KFF282.T7 A25 1980

TOURIST TRADE - UNITED STATES.
Analysis of the North American cruise industry /. [Washington, D.C.?] [1980] v, 145 p. : LC Card 80-604175 DDC 387.5/42 19
G550 .A56

Starch INRA Hooper. Italy . [Washington] , 1978. vi, 65 p. : LC Card 78-601739
G155.U6 S65 1978a

United States. General Accounting Office. More can be done to speed the entry of international travelers . [Washington, D.C. , 1979] vi, 59 p. : LC Card 80-601083 DDC 353.0082/6591 19
G155.U6 U54 1979

TOURIST TRADE - VIRGINIA - STATISTICS.
United States Travel Data Center. Travel in Virginia, 1978 . [Richmond, Va. , 1978] 12 p. : LC Card 80-622616 DDC 381/.45917550443 19
G155.U6 U58 1978

TOURIST TRAFFIC. see TOURIST TRADE.

TOURISTS. see TOURIST TRADE.

Toussoun, T. A., 1925- Fusarium . University Park, PA [1981] p. cm. ISBN 0-271-00293-X : LC Card 81-47174 DDC 632/.34 19
SB741.F9 F87

TOUTLE RIVER (WASH.)
Channel conditions in the lower Toutle and Cowlitz rivers resulting from the mudflows of May 18, 1980 /. [Reston, Va.?] , Alexandria, Va. (604 S. Pickett Street, Alexandria, Va. 22304) , 1981. v, 16 p. : LC Card 81-600040 DDC 557.3 s 551.48/9/0979788 19
QE75 .C5 no. 850-c QE599.U5

Toward a comprehensive energy research and development program for Florida /. Florida. Governor's Energy Office. [Tallahassee, Fla.] [1979] 21, 8, 221 p. ; LC Card 80-621492 DDC 333.79/0720759 19
TJ163.25.U6 F55 1979

Toward a national library and information service network . Library of Congress Network Advisory Group. Washington [1977] vii, 54 p. ; LC Card 80-601614 DDC 021.6/5 19
Z674.8 .L52 1977

Toward a Utah growth management strategy . (1) Utah. Office of the Utah State Planning Coordinator. Utah:2000 . Salt Lake City, Utah , 1980. iii, 65 leaves : LC Card 80-622474 DDC 338.5/443/09792 19
HC107.U8 U55 1980

'Towards a national spirit' . Bell, Whitfield Jenks. Boston , 1979. ix, 37 p. : LC Card 78-10486
*NYPL [*KSD 80-202 no. 6]*

Towards a strategy for development in the Sahelian and Sudano-Sahelian zones /. Baumer, Michel. [New York] , 1973. 17 p. ; LC Card 73-23298 DDC 300 s 338.966 19
JX1977 .A2 ST/SSO/1/Rev.1 HC1000.Z9F3

Toweill, Dale E. Bobcat populations : a review of available literature : special report / Dale E. Toweill. [Portland, Or.] : Oregon Dept. of Fish and Wildlife, Research and Development Section, [1979] i, 28 leaves ; 28 cm. (Information report series - Wildlife . no. 79-2) "November 1979." Bibliography: leaves 23-28. LC Card 80-622940 DDC 599.74/428 19
1. Bobcat. 2. Mammal populations - United States. 3. Mammals - United States. I. Title. II. Series.
QL737.C23 T68

Town forest resources in New Hampshire. A Survey of the town forest resources in New Hampshire /. Durham, N.H. [1980] ii, 18 p. : LC Card 80-622912 DDC 333.75/09742 19
SD566.N4 S87

Town forests. New Hampshire. Agricultural Experiment Station, Durham. Timber values of town forests /. Durham, N.H. [1979] ii, 44 p. : LC Card 80-622381 DDC 333.1/1 19
SD428.N45 N48 1979

TOWN MEETING. see LOCAL GOVERNMENT.

The Town of Colonie : a pictorial history / [compiler, Jean S. Olton ; editor, Warren F. Broderick ; contributing authors, David C. Barnet ... et al. ; illustrations, Elizabeth Lee ; introduction, Richard S. Allen]. Colonie, N.Y. : The Town, 1980. 190 p. : ill. ; 29 cm. Bibliography: p. 188-189. LC Card 81-141419 DDC 974.7/42 19
1. Colonie (N.Y. : Town) - History. 2. Colonie (N.Y. : Town) - Description. I. Olton, Jean S. II. Broderick, Warren F. III. Barnet, David C.
F129.C692 T68

TOWN PLANNING. see CITY PLANNING.

Townley, Nancy A. Gallagher-Allred, Charlette R. Dietary management in hyperlipidemia /. Columbus, Ohio (456 Clinic Dr., Columbus 43210) , c1980. 20 p. ; LC Card 81-620947 DDC 616.3/9970654 19
RC632.H87 G34

TOWNS. see CITIES AND TOWNS.

Townsend, William R. Soil survey of Conway County, Arkansas / [by William R. Townsend and Curtis R. Wilson] ; United States Department of Agriculture, Soil Conservation Service and Forest Service, in cooperation with Arkansas Agricultural Experiment Station. [Washington] : Soil Conservation Service, [1980] vii, 91 p., [27] fold. leaves of plates : ill. ; 28 cm. Cover title. Bibliography: p. 48-49. LC Card 80-603205 DDC 631.4/7/76731 19
1. Soils - Arkansas - Conway County - Maps. I. Wilson, Curtis R., joint author. II. United States. Soil Conservation Service. III. United States. Forest Service. IV. Arkansas. Agricultural Experiment Station, Fayetteville. V. Title.
S599.A75 T67

TOWNSHIP FINANCE. see LOCAL FINANCE.

TOWNSHIP GOVERNMENT. see LOCAL GOVERNMENT.

Township, school, and hospital district map, Ness County, Kansas /. United States. Soil Conservation Service. Lincoln, Nebr. , 1979. 1 map : LC Card 81-691149
G4203.N5F7 1979 .U5

Township supervisors handbook /. Pennsylvania. Dept. of Community Affairs. Information Services Center. Harrisburg [1980] v, 52 p. : LC Card 80-622716 DDC 352/.0072/09748 19
JS451 .P1 1980a

TOXIC AND INFLAMMABLE GOODS. see HAZARDOUS SUBSTANCES.

TOXIC SHOCK SYNDROME - UNITED STATES.
United States. Congress. Senate. Committee on Labor and Human Resources. Subcommittee on Health and Scientific Research. Toxic shock syndrome, 1980 . Washington , 1980. iii, 12 p. ; LC Card 80-603321 DDC 616.9 19
KF26 .L274 1980g

Toxic shock syndrome, 1980 . United States.

Congress. Senate. Committee on Labor and Human Resources. Subcommittee on Health and Scientific Research. Washington , 1980. iii, 12 p. ; LC Card 80-603321 DDC 616.9 19
KF26 .L274 1980g

TOXICITY TESTING.
Environmental Studies Board. Committee to Review Methods for Ecotoxicology. Testing for effects of chemical on ecosystems . Washington, D.C. , 1981. xv, 103 p. : ISBN 0-309-03142-7 (pbk.) LC Card 81-38392 DDC 574.5/222 19
QH545.A1 E59 1981

TOXICOLOGY - CONGRESSES.
Workshop on Behavioral Toxicology, National Institutes of Health, 1975. Proceedings /. [Bethesda, Md.] [1976?] v, 109 p. : LC Card 77-601979
RA1191 .W67 1975   **NYPL [JSF 81-141]**

TOXICOLOGY, EXPERIMENTAL - CONGRESSES.
Workshop on Behavioral Toxicology, National Institutes of Health, 1975. Proceedings /. [Bethesda, Md.] [1976?] v, 109 p. : LC Card 77-601979
RA1191 .W67 1975   **NYPL [JSF 81-141]**

TOXICOLOGY LABORATORIES - HYGIENIC ASPECTS - UNITED STATES.
United States. General Accounting Office. Health monitoring needed for laboratory employees, Environmental Protection Agency . Washington , 1976. iv, 26 p. ; LC Card 76-603278 DDC 363.1/79 19
RA566.26 .U47 1976

Trace, Robert Denny, 1917- Stratigraphy and structure of the western Kentucky fluorspar district / by Robert D. Trace and Dewey H. Amos ; prepared in cooperation with the Kentucky Geological Survey. Washington : U. S. Govt. Print. Off., 1981. p. cm. (Contributions to the geology of Kentucky) Geological Survey professional paper ; 1151-D Bibliography: p. LC Card 80-607000 DDC 551.7/009769 19
1. Geology, Stratigraphic - Mississippian. 2. Geology, Stratigraphic - Pennsylvanian. 3. Geology - Kentucky. I. Amos, Dewey Harold, 1925- joint author. II. Kentucky. Geological Survey. III. Series. IV. Series: United States. Geological Survey. Professional paper, 1151-D. V. Title.
QE672 .T7

TRACERS (CHEMISTRY)
Vinson, Robert P. SF₆ tracer gas tests of bagging-machine hood enclosures /. [Avondale, Md.] , 1981. p. cm. LC Card 80-606907 DDC 661/.06832 19
TN23 .U43 TH7697.C54

Tracks for full powered steam vessels with the shortest navigable distances in nautical miles /. United States. Hydrographic Office. Division of Chart Construction. Washington , 1900. 1 map : LC Card 81-690532
G3201.P54 1900 .U5

TRADE. see BUSINESS; COMMERCE.

TRADE ADJUSTMENT ASSISTANCE - CANADA.
Glenday, Graham. Worker adjustment to liberalized trade . Washington, D.C. (1818 H St., N.W., Washington) , 1980. 86 p. : LC Card 80-154970 DDC 362.8/5 19
HD5710.75.C2 G57

TRADE ADJUSTMENT ASSISTANCE - UNITED STATES - CONGRESSES.
Trade and employment . Washington, D.C. , 1979. 336 p. : LC Card 80-601562 DDC 331.12/0973 19
HD5710.75.U6 T7

TRADE AGREEMENTS (COMMERCE) see COMMERCIAL TREATIES.

Trade and employment : a conference report. Washington, D.C. : National Commission for Manpower Policy : for sale by the Supt. of Docs., U. S. Govt. Print. Off., 1979. 336 p. : graphs ; 28 cm. (A Special report of the National Commission for Manpower Policy ; no. 30) Cosponsored by the Bureau of International Labor Affairs and the National Commission for Manpower Policy. "November 1978." Includes bibliographical references. LC Card 80-601562 DDC 331.12/0973 19
1. Foreign trade and employment - United States - Congresses. 2. Trade adjustment assistance - United States - Congresses. I. United States. Bureau of International Labor Affairs. II. United States. National

Commission for Manpower Policy. III. Series: United States. National Commission for Manpower Policy. Special report - National Commission for Manpower Policy , no. 30.
HD5710.75.U6 T7

Trade and employment effects of granting most-favored-nation status to the People's Republic of China / by Thomas Bayard ... [et al.]. Washington, D.C. : Office of Foreign Economic Research, Bureau of International Labor Affairs ; Springfield, Va. : For sale by the National Technical Information Service, 1980. 32 p. in various pagings ; 27 cm. (Economic discussion paper . 4) "Prepared by the Office of Foreign Economic Research." "August 1980." LC Card 81-600776 DDC 382/.0951/073 19
1. Foreign trade and employment - United States. 2. United States - Commerce - China. 3. China - Commerce - United States. 4. Textile industry - United States. I. Bayard, Thomas. II. United States. Bureau of International Labor Affairs. Office of Foreign Economic Research. III. Series.
HD5710.75.U6 T73

Trade and employment effects of tariff reductions agreed to in the MTN /. Bayard, Thomas O. [Washington, D.C.] [Springfield, Va.] 1980. 11, [31] p. ; LC Card 80-602631 DDC 382.7 19
HF1757 .B39

Trade area analysis of Atlanta's regional shopping centers /. Dent, Borden D. Atlanta, Ga. , 1978, c1980. vi, 66 leaves (1 folded) : LC Card 80-624405 DDC 381/.1/097582 19
HF5430.5.A7 D46

TRADE BARRIERS. see COMMERCIAL POLICY.

Trade between Indians and Federal employees . United States. Congress. Senate. Select Committee on Indian Affairs. Washington , 1980. iii, 21 p. ; LC Card 80-601960 DDC 343.73/088/08997 19
KF26.5 .I4 1980e

Trade functions authorizations for fiscal year 1981 . United States. Congress. House. Committee on Ways and Means. Subcommittee on Trade. Washington , 1980. iii, 177 p. ; LC Card 80-602818 DDC 353.0082/7 19
KF27 .W348 1980

TRADE-MARKS - ALABAMA.
Hansford, Nathaniel. Alabama trademark act with commentary /. [University, Ala.] [1977?] 33 p. ; LC Card 80-622653 DDC 346.76104/88 19
KFA330 .H36

TRADE-MARKS - UNITED STATES.
United States. Congress. House. Committee on Government Operations. Legislation and National Security Subcommittee. Patent and Trademark Law Amendments of 1980 . Washington , 1980. iii, 218 p. ; LC Card 80-604009 DDC 346.7304/86 347.306486 19
KF27 .G6676 1980i

United States. Congress. House. Committee on the Judiciary. Subcommittee on Courts, Civil Liberties, and the Administration of Justice. Trademarks and the Federal Trade Commission . Washington , 1980. iii, 199 p. ; LC Card 80-602813 DDC 346.7304/88 19
KF27 .J857 1979j

TRADE-MARKS - UNITED STATES - FORMS.
United States. Patent and Trademark Office. Patent and trademark forms booklet /. Washington , 1979 [i. e. 1980] 1 v. :
*NYPL [*VBE 81-231]*

TRADE NAMES. see TRADE-MARKS.

TRADE PREFERENCES. see TARIFF PREFERENCES.

TRADE REGULATION - ECONOMIC ASPECTS - UNITED STATES.
Sanders, M. Elizabeth, 1943- The regulation of natural gas . Philadelphia , 1981. p. cm. ISBN 0-87722-221-5 : LC Card 81-9239 DDC 333.8/23317/0973 19
HD9581.U5 S26

TRADE REGULATION - OREGON - INDEXES.
Oregon. Executive Dept. Regulatory requirements for business, construction, land development. Salem, Or. [1980] 30, 2, 14 p. ; LC Card 80-623339 DDC 342.795/0664 19
KFO2630 .A46 1980

TRADE REGULATION - UNITED STATES.
United States. Congress. House. Committee on
the Judiciary. Subcommittee on Administrative
Law and Governmental Relations. Regulation
reform act of 1979 . Washington , 1980- v. ;
LC Card 80-603418   DDC 342.73/066 19
KF27 .J832 1980a

United States. Library of Congress.
Congressional Research Service. An inquiry into
conflicting and duplicative regulatory
requirements affecting selected industries and
sectors . Washington , 1980. v, 40 p. ;   LC Card
80-603057   DDC 343.73/08 347.3038 19
KF1600 .A25 1980

United States. Panel on Government and the
Regulation of Corporate and Individual
Decisions. Government and the regulation of
corporate and individual decisions in the
eighties . Washington , 1980. 113 p. ;   LC Card
80-29251   DDC 343.73/08 19
KF1600 .A843

United States. Regulatory Council. Regulatory
reform highlights . [Washington, D.C.] [1980]
xi, 172 p. ;   LC Card 80-602350   DDC 353.09/3 19
KF1600 .A877

TRADE REGULATION - UNITED STATES -
COST EFFECTIVENESS.
United States. Congress. House. Committee on
Interstate and Foreign Commerce.
Subcommittee on Oversight and Investigations.
Cost-benefit analysis . Washington , 1980 [i.e.
1981] vii, 49 p. ;   LC Card 81-600645   DDC
353.07/5 19
HD47.4 .U54 1981

United States. Congress. House. Committee on
Interstate and Foreign Commerce.
Subcommittee on Oversight and Investigations.
Use of cost-benefit analysis by regulatory
agencies . Washington , 1980. v, 482 p. ;   LC
Card 80-603329   DDC 353.09/1 19
KF27 .I5547 1979v

TRADE REGULATION - UTAH - AUDITING
AND INSPECTION.
Utah. Office of the Legislative Auditor General.
A performance audit of electronic repair dealer
registration in Utah . [Salt Lake City] [1979]
ii, 14, 3 leaves ;   LC Card 79-626149   DDC
353.97920082/42 19
HC107.U83 C637 1979

TRADE, RESTRAINT OF. see RESTRAINT
OF TRADE.

TRADE ROUTES - MAPS.
United States. Central Intelligence Agency.
Selected world shipping lanes and straits.
[Washington , 1980] 1 map :   LC Card 81-690686
G3201.P54 1980 .U5

TRADE SCHOOLS - NEW YORK (STATE)
New York (State). State Consumer Protection
Board. The profits of failure . Albany, N.Y.
[1978] 114 p. ;   LC Card 80-621030
LC1046.N5 N48 1978   **NYPL** *[JLF 80-1578]*

TRADE SCHOOLS - WEST VIRGINIA.
Van Dyke, John B. West Virginia private
proprietary schools . Charleston, W. Va. [1978]
50 p. ;   LC Card 79-124128   DDC 607/.11754 19
T74.W4 V36

TRADE-UNIONS.
Snowbarger, Marvin. A general model for the
study of union membership /. San Jose , 1973.
38 p. ;   **NYPL** *[*ZT-1259]*

TRADE-UNIONS - AGRICULTURAL
LABORERS - CALIFORNIA -
PERIODICALS.
California. Agricultural Labor Relations Board.
Annual report. Sacramento.   LC Card 79-644068
                                            NYPL *[JLL 81-34]*

TRADE-UNIONS - GOVERNMENT
EMPLOYEES - UNITED STATES -
PERIODICALS.
Union recognition in the federal government.
Washington.   **NYPL** *[M-11 4907]*

TRADE UNIONS - HAWAII -
DIRECTORIES.
Hawaii. Dept. of Labor and Industrial
Relations. Directory of Labor organizations and
affiliates. Honolulu.   **NYPL** *[M-10 4927]*

TRADE-UNIONS - MERCHANT SEAMEN -
UNITED STATES - DIRECTORIES.
United States. Maritime Administration.
Seafaring guide & directory of labor

management affiliations. Washington, D.C.
[1980] v, 49 p. ;   LC Card 80-602281   DDC
331.88/113875/0973 19
HD6515.S42 U46 1980

TRADE-UNIONS - POLICE - UNITED
STATES.
Burpo, John H. Police unions in the civil
service setting /. Washington D.C. , 1979. v, 38
p. ;   LC Card 80-601834   DDC 352/.005173/0973
19
HV7936.P47 B87

TRADE-UNIONS - SOCIAL ASPECTS -
UNITED STATES.
United States. Office of Education. Examining
the role of the workplace in citizen education /.
Washington [1978] viii, 102 p. ;   LC Card
79-602660
LC5051 .U54 1978   **NYPL** *[JFE 81736]*

TRADE-UNIONS - SOUTH AFRICA.
United States. Congress. House. Committee on
Foreign Affairs. Subcommittee on Africa. Labor
situation in South Africa--fall 1980 .
Washington , 1981. iii, 21 p. ;   LC Card
81-600943   DDC 331/.0968 19
KF27 .F625 1980g

TRADE-UNIONS - UNITED STATES -
ADDRESSES, ESSAYS, LECTURES.
Career education and organized labor /.
[Washington, D.C.] , 1979] iii, 98 p. ;   LC Card
79-602090   DDC 370.11/3/0973 19
LC1037.5 .C385

TRADE-UNIONS - UNITED STATES -
CHRONOLOGY.
United States. Dept. of Labor. Important events
in American labor history, 1778-1978 /.
[Washington, D.C.] [1979?] [36] p. :   LC Card
80-602346   DDC 331.88/0973 19
HD8066 .U54 1979

TRADE-UNIONS - UNITED STATES -
CONGRESSES.
Labor's views on employment policy .
Washington , 1978. 132 p. ;   LC Card 78-603516
HD5724 .L23   **NYPL** *[JLF 81-279]*

Trade with Japan . United States. Congress.
House. Committee on Ways and Means.
Subcommittee on Trade. Washington , 1980. iv,
230 p. :   LC Card 81-600633   DDC 382/.0973/052
KF27 .W348 1980h

TRADEMARKS. see TRADE-MARKS.

Trademarks and the Federal Trade Commission .
United States. Congress. House. Committee on
the Judiciary. Subcommittee on Courts, Civil
Liberties, and the Administration of Justice.
Washington , 1980. iii, 199 p. ;   LC Card
80-602813   DDC 346.7304/88 19
KF27 .J857 1979j

Trader waiver authority extension . United States.
Congress. House. Committee on Ways and
Means. Subcommittee on Trade. Washington ,
1980 [i.e. 1981] v, 310 p. ;   LC Card 81-600854
DDC 382/.0973/01717 19
KF27 .W348 1980j

TRADES. see INDUSTRIAL ARTS;
OCCUPATIONS.

TRADES-WASTE. see FACTORY AND TRADE
WASTE; WASTE PRODUCTS.

Traditional graduate admission standards and the
supply of Black professionals in agriculture .
Davis, Carlton G. Gainesville , 1973. iii, 59
leaves ;   LC Card 77-622478   DDC 630/.7/1175979
19
LC2780.2 .D38

Traditional Korean legal attitudes /. Chŏn,
Pong-dŏk, 1910- Berkeley, Calif. , c1980. vii,
101 p. ;   ISBN 0-912966-30-0 (pbk.) :   LC Card
80-620036   DDC 349.519/09 345.1909 19
LAW

The traditional land use inventory for the
mid-Beaufort Sea. North Slope Borough,
Alaska. Commission on History and Culture.
Qiñiqtuagaksrat utuqqanaat iñuuniağninisiqun .
Barrow, Alaska , c1980- v. :   ISBN 0-936052-00-7
(v. 1)   LC Card 80-80683   DDC 970.004/97 19
E99.E7 N64 1980

TRADITIONS. see FOLK-LORE.

TRAFFIC ACCIDENTS AND ALCOHOLISM.
see DRINKING AND TRAFFIC
ACCIDENTS.

TRAFFIC ACCIDENTS - CALIFORNIA.
California. Dept. of Insurance. Rate Regulation
Division. Study of California driving
performance by zip code (phase I) .
[Sacramento?] [1978] 320 p. in various
pagings ;   LC Card 80-623737   DDC
368.5/72/009794 19
HG9970.35.C2 C23 1978

TRAFFIC ACCIDENTS - IOWA -
STATISTICS.
Iowa. Motor Vehicle Division. Office of Safety
Programs. Iowa motorcycle accidents,
1974-1976. Des Moines, Iowa [1978] 11, 11
p. :   LC Card 80-622106   DDC 312/.44/09777 19
HE5614.3.I8 I58 1978

TRAFFIC ACCIDENTS - NEVADA -
STATISTICS.
Nevada. Dept. of Transportation. Safety
Section. 1978 Nevada fatal traffic accident
report /. [Carson City?] [1979?] 34, 44 leaves,
[6] leaves of plates (1 fold.) :   LC Card
80-623180   DDC 312/.274/09793 19
HE5614.3.N42 N47 1979

TRAFFIC ACCIDENTS - NORTH CAROLINA.
Hunter, William W. Mopeds, an analysis of
1976-1978 North Carolina accidents /. Chapel
Hill, N.C. [1979] 194 p. in various pagings :
LC Card 80-622241   DDC 363.1/259 19
HE5614.3.N6 H86

TRAFFIC ACCIDENTS - NORTH
CAROLINA - STATISTICS.
Clark, Verneta J. Single variable tabulations for
1973-1976 North Carolina accidents /. Chapel
Hill, N.C. [1977] xiii, 20, ca. 200 p. :   LC Card
80-622768   DDC 312/.44/09756 19
HE5614.3.N6 C52

TRAFFIC ACCIDENTS - PREVENTION. see
TRAFFIC SAFETY.

TRAFFIC ACCIDENTS - WASHINGTON
(STATE)
Washington (State) Utilities and Transportation
Commission. Summary and analysis, heavy
truck-hazardous material accidents. Olympia,
Wash. [1979] [13], 34 p. ;   LC Card 80-621084
DDC 363.1/259 19
HE5614.3.W2 W394 1979

Traffic assignment . Comsis Corporation.
Washington, 1973. 205 p.
                                            NYPL *[JLF 81-601]*

TRAFFIC, CITY. see TRAFFIC
ENGINEERING.

TRAFFIC CONTROL. see TRAFFIC
ENGINEERING.

TRAFFIC ENGINEERING - CONGRESSES.
Human factors and motorist information needs
/. Washington, D.C. , 1980. p. cm.   ISBN
0-309-03172-9   LC Card 81-9482   DDC 380.5 s
388.3/12 19
TE7 .H5 no. 782 HE332

TRAFFIC ENGINEERING
(TELECOMMUNICATION) see
TELECOMMUNICATION - TRAFFIC.

TRAFFIC ENGINEERING - UNITED
STATES.
Abrams, Charles M. Measures of effectiveness
for multimodal urban traffic management . -
Washington , Springfield, Va. , 1979. 1 v. :
                                            NYPL *[JLM 80-740]*

United States. Federal Highway Administration.
Urban origin-destination surveys. Washington,
1973. viii, 309 p.:   **NYPL** *[JLF 81-455]*

TRAFFIC FLOW - EUROPE - MAPS.
United Nations. Economic Commission for
Europe. Census of motor traffic on main
international traffic arteries (1975) =. New
York , 1979. 1 portfolio (96 p. in various
pagings :   LC Card 80-675269   DDC
912/.138831/094
G1797.21.P21 U55 1979

TRAFFIC FLOW - PENNSYLVANIA - MAPS.
Pennsylvania. Bureau of Transportation
Planning Statistics. Pennsylvania traffic volume
map /. [Harrisburg] , 1979. 1 map :   LC Card
81-692949
G3821.P21 1979 .P4

TRAFFIC FLOW - UNITED STATES.
Alternative work schedules . Washington,
D.C. , 1980. 54 p. :   ISBN 0-309-03153-2 (pbk.)

LC Card 80-54556   DDC 388.4/13143/0973 19
HE308 .A62

Traffic on the county federal-aid highway system.
Arizona. Transportation Planning Division.
[Phoenix, Ariz.] , 1976. 53 p., [21] leaves of
plates :   LC Card 80-620909   DDC
388.3/142/09791 19
HE371.A6 A55 1976

**TRAFFIC REGULATION. see TRAFFIC
ENGINEERING.**

TRAFFIC REGULATIONS - GEORGIA.
Georgia. Prosecuting Attorneys' Council.
Georgia traffic law. [Atlanta] , 1979. ca. 550 p.
in various pagings ;   LC Card 80-621978   DDC
343.758/0946 19
KFG297.8 .A86 1979

**TRAFFIC REGULATIONS - UNITED
STATES.**
United States. National Highway Safety
Advisory Committee. Subcommittee on Alcohol
and Adjudication. Rural courts and highway
safety /. Washington , 1977. viii, 52 p. :   LC
Card 77-604399
KF2231 .A86

**TRAFFIC REGULATIONS - UNITED
STATES - ABSTRACTS.**
Raub, R. A. Summary and critique of the
literature pertaining to the effects of increased
enforcement of traffic laws on improving traffic
safety (reducing accidents) /. [Springfield]
[1979] 58 leaves ;   LC Card 81-621246   DDC
363.1/256/0973 19
HE5614.2 .R38

TRAFFIC REGULATIONS - WISCONSIN.
Wisconsin. Laws, statutes, etc. Wisconsin motor
vehicle laws, 1973-1974. [Madison] [1974?]
239 p. in various pagings ;   LC Card 81-479063
DDC 343.775/0944/02632 347.750394402632 19
KFW2697 .A3 1974

**TRAFFIC SAFETY - CALIFORNIA - SAN
FRANCISCO METROPOLITAN AREA.**
MacCalden, M, Scott. Feasibility study of
closed circuit television for traffic surveillance.
[Sacramento] 1973. 74, 10 p.
NYPL [JLF 80-556]

TRAFFIC SAFETY - IOWA.
Carstens, Robert Lowell. Safer construction and
maintenance practices to minimize potential
liability by counties from highway accidents .
Ames, Iowa [1979] xiv, 113 p. ;   LC Card
80-623075   DDC 363.1/251 19
HE5614.3.I8 C37

TRAFFIC SAFETY - MAINE.
Maine. Dept. of Transportation. Bureau of
Safety. State of Maine highway safety plan for
fiscal year 1980 /. [Augusta] [1979] 141, [38]
leaves :   LC Card 80-622557   DDC
363.1/256/09741 19
HE5614.3.M2 M34 1979

TRAFFIC SAFETY - MASSACHUSETTS.
Massachusetts. Governor's Highway Safety
Bureau. Highway safety plan, fiscal year 1980 /.
[Boston] [1979] 132 p. in various pagings :
LC Card 80-622261   DDC 363.1/256/09744 19
HE5614.3.M3 M36 1979

TRAFFIC SAFETY - NEW YORK (STATE)
New York (State). Legislature. Senate.
Committee on Transportation. Public
transportation safety . [Albany] [1979] 16 p. ;
LC Card 80-622830   DDC 363.1/25 19
HE5614.3.N5 N48 1979

TRAFFIC SAFETY - SOUTH DAKOTA.
South Dakota. Division of Highway Safety.
State & Community Programs. South Dakota
highway safety plan, fiscal year 1980 /. [Pierre,
S.D.] [1980?] 237 p. :   LC Card 80-621619
DDC 363.1/256/09783 19
HE5614.3.S8 S68 1980

TRAFFIC SAFETY - UNITED STATES.
United States. Dept. of Transportation. The
national highway safety needs report .
Washington , 1976. 148 p. in various pagings :
LC Card 76-601953
HE5614.2 .U56 1976   ***NYPL [JLF 80-1698]***

**TRAFFIC SAFETY - UNITED STATES -
ABSTRACTS.**
Raub, R. A. Summary and critique of the
literature pertaining to the effects of increased
enforcement of traffic laws on improving traffic
safety (reducing accidents) /. [Springfield]

[1979] 58 leaves ;   LC Card 81-621246   DDC
363.1/256/0973 19
HE5614.2 .R38

TRAFFIC SAFETY - VIRGINIA.
Simpson, Clinton H. The development of a
methodology for transportation safety planning
in Virginia /. Charlottesville, Va. [1980] 37,
[24] p. ;   LC Card 80-622408   DDC
363.1/206/09755 19
HE5614.3.V8 S57

**TRAFFIC SIGNS AND SIGNALS -
ADDRESSES, ESSAYS, LECTURES.**
Grade crossings, devices, visibility, and freeway
operations /. Washington, D.C. , 1980. iv, 49
p. :   ISBN 0-309-03117-6   LC Card 81-4730   DDC
380.5 s 625.7/94 19
TE7 .H5 no. 773 TE228

**TRAFFIC SIGNS AND SIGNALS -
CONGRESSES.**
Human factors and motorist information needs
/. Washington, D.C. , 1980. p. cm.   ISBN
0-309-03172-9   LC Card 81-9482   DDC 380.5 s
388.3/12 19
TE7 .H5 no. 782 HE332

TRAFFIC SIGNS AND SIGNALS - IOWA.
Carstens, Robert Lowell. Safer construction and
maintenance practices to minimize potential
liability by counties from highway accidents .
Ames, Iowa [1979] xiv, 113 p. ;   LC Card
80-623075   DDC 363.1/251 19
HE5614.3.I8 C37

**TRAFFIC SIGNS AND SIGNALS - UNITED
STATES.**
National Research Council (U. S.)
Transportation Research Board. Direction
finding from arterials to destinations .
Washington, D.C. , 1980. 50 p. :   ISBN
0-309-03031-5 (pbk.) :   LC Card 80-54090
DDC 388.3/122 19
TE228 .N32 1980

TRAFFIC SURVEYS - ARIZONA.
Arizona. Transportation Planning Division.
Traffic on the county federal-aid highway
system. [Phoenix, Ariz.] , 1976. 53 p., [21]
leaves of plates :   LC Card 80-620909   DDC
388.3/142/09791 19
HE371.A6 A55 1976

TRAFFIC SURVEYS - EUROPE - MAPS.
United Nations. Economic Commission for
Europe. Census of motor traffic on main
international traffic arteries (1975) =. New
York , 1979. 1 portfolio (96 p. in various
pagings :   LC Card 80-675269   DDC
912/.138831/094
G1797.21.P21 U55 1979

**TRAFFIC SURVEYS - SOUTH DAKOTA -
STATISTICS.**
South Dakota. Dept. of Transportation. Office
of System Analysis. Highway traffic report,
1979 /. [Pierre] [1980] 146 p. :   LC Card
80-622944   DDC 388.3/142/09783 19
HE371.S8 S68 1980

TRAFFIC SURVEYS - UNITED STATES.
United States. Federal Highway Administration.
Urban origin-destination surveys. Washington,
1973. viii, 309 p.:   ***NYPL [JLF 81-455]***

**TRAFFIC SURVEYS - WASHINGTON
(STATE) - STATISTICS - PERIODICALS.**
Washington (State). Division of Public
Transportation and Planning. Annual traffic
report. [Olympia]   ***NYPL [JLM 80-967]***

Washington (State). State Highway
Commission. Annual traffic report. [Olympia]
NYPL [N-10 2121]

**TRAFFIC THEORY
(TELECOMMUNICATION) see
TELECOMMUNICATION - TRAFFIC.**

TRAFFIC VIOLATIONS - CALIFORNIA.
California. Dept. of Motor Vehicles. Abstract
reporting manual for courts. [Sacramento,
Calif.] [1980] [66] p. :   LC Card 80-623019
DDC 345.794/0247 19
KFC477 .A863

TRAFFIC VIOLATIONS - GEORGIA.
Georgia. Prosecuting Attorneys' Council.
Georgia traffic law. [Atlanta] , 1979. ca. 550 p.
in various pagings ;   LC Card 80-621978   DDC
343.758/0946 19
KFG297.8 .A86 1979

TRAFFIC VIOLATIONS - NORTH DAKOTA.
Skeen, David. Disclosure of criminal and traffic
records . Grand Forks, N.D. [1980] i, 22, 3
p. ;   LC Card 81-620708   DDC 320.9784 s
345.73/056 320.9784 s 347.30556 19
JK6401 .N65 no. 58 KFN9192.5

Trafton, Dain A. Tasso, Torquato, 1544-1595.
[Selections. English. 1982.] Tasso's dialogues .
Berkeley , c1982. p. cm.   ISBN 0-520-04464-9
LC Card 81-12937   DDC 195 19
PQ4642 .E2 1982

Trafzer, Clifford E. Scheuerman, Richard D. The
Volga Germans . Moscow, Idaho , c1980. 245
p. :   ISBN 0-89301-073-1   LC Card 80-52314   DDC
979.5 19
F855.2.R85 S33

TRAGEDY.
Berlin, Normand. The secret cause . Amherst ,
1981. 127 p. ;   ISBN 0-87023-336-X :   LC Card
81-4089   DDC 809.2/512 19
PN1892 .B43

Tragedy in Indochina continues. United States.
Congress. House. Committee on Foreign
Affairs. Subcommittee on Asian and Pacific
Affairs. 1980--the tragedy in Indochina
continues . Washington , 1980. v, 148 p. :   LC
Card 80-604058   DDC 362.8/7/09596 19
KF27 .F638 1980c

The tragic art of Ernest Hemingway /. Williams,
Wirt. Baton Rouge , c1981. p. cm.   ISBN
0-8071-0884-7 :   LC Card 81-4740   DDC
813/.52 19
PS3515.E37 Z952

TRAGIC, THE.
Williams, Wirt. The tragic art of Ernest
Hemingway /. Baton Rouge , c1981. p. cm.
ISBN 0-8071-0884-7 :   LC Card 81-4740   DDC
813/.52 19
PS3515.E37 Z952

**TRAHERNE, THOMAS, D. 1674 -
CRITICISM AND INTERPRETATION.**
Seelig, Sharon Cadman. The shadow of
eternity . Lexington, Ky , 1981. p. cm.   ISBN
0-8131-1444-6 :   LC Card 80-51018   DDC
821/.3/09 19
PR545.M4 S4

**TRAILER CAMPS - NORTHEASTERN
STATES - STATISTICS.**
Kottke, Marvin Walter. A survey of recreational
lodging and outdoor recreation by northeastern
households /. Storrs, Conn. [1979] 48 p. ;   LC
Card 80-621317   DDC 338.4/76479474 19
TX909 .K67

**TRAILERS, TRUCK. see MOTOR-TRUCKS -
TRAILERS.**

**TRAILS - NEBRASKA - LITTLE NEMAHA
RIVER WATERSHED - MAPS.**
United States. Soil Conservation Service.
Historical trails and sites, upper Little Nemaha
watershed, Lancaster, Cass, and Otoe Counties,
Nebraska /. Lincoln, Nebr. , 1979. 1 map :   LC
Card 81-691090
G4192.L5P25 1978 .U5

TRAILS - NEVADA - PLANNING.
Eckbo, Dean, Austin & Williams. Nevada
state-wide trails study . [Carson City] [1978]
48, [16] leaves :   LC Card 80-620874   DDC
790/.09793 19
GV191.42.N27 E24

TRAILS - SOUTH DAKOTA - PLANNING.
Nordstrom, Paul E. South Dakota recreational
trails plan, January 1, 1980 /. [Pierre, S.D.]
[1979?] 178 p. :   LC Card 80-622746   DDC
790/.09783 19
GV191.42.S8 N67

Train-a-champ : proceedings of a series of
workshops on the development of sports skills
of Special Olympic participants / edited by
Joseph P. Winnick ; state project consultant,
Dorothy Phillips ; sponsored by the Office for
Children with Handicapping Conditions, New
York State Education Department and the State
University College, Brockport, N.Y. Albany,
N.Y. : The Office, c1979. vii, 95 p. : ill. ; 28
cm. Includes bibliographies. LC Card 81-119267
DDC 371.9/044 19
*1. Physical education for mentally handicapped
children - Congresses. 2. Special Olympics - Congresses.
I. Winnick, Joseph P. II. Phillips, Dorothy. III. New
York (State). Office for Education of Children with*

Handicapping Conditions. IV. State University College (Brockport, N.Y.).
GV445 .T73

TRAINERS, SYNTHETIC. see SYNTHETIC TRAINING DEVICES.

Training curriculum on freeing children for adoption /. New York (State). Temporary State Commission on Child Welfare. [New York , 1979] 139 p. ;   LC Card 80-622702   DDC 346.74701/78 19
KFN5130 .A837

TRAINING DEVICES, SYNTHETIC. see SYNTHETIC TRAINING DEVICES.

Training for federal quality control review /. United States. Social and Rehabilitation Service. Office of Quality Control Management. Washington D. C. , 1974. 167 p. ;
NYPL [JLF 81-28]

Training grants directory. National Institute on Drug Abuse training grants directory. Rockville, Md..   *NYPL [JLM 81-16]*

TRAINING, OCCUPATIONAL. see OCCUPATIONAL TRAINING.

TRAINING OF EMPLOYEES. see EMPLOYEES, TRAINING OF.

Training/retraining plan for social services in the Commonwealth of Massachusetts. Massachusetts. Dept. of Public Welfare. Title XX/FY 1979 . [Boston , 1978] 66 p. in various pagings, [2] fold. leaves of plates :   LC Card 80-620540   DDC 361/.007/15 19
HV11 .M365 1978

TRAINING, VOCATIONAL. see OCCUPATIONAL TRAINING.

TRAINING WITHIN INDUSTRY. see EMPLOYEES, TRAINING OF.

TRANS ALASKA PIPELINE SYSTEM. Burger, Carl. Environmental surveillance of gravel removal on the Trans-Alaska Pipeline System, with recommendations for future gravel mining /. Anchorage, Alaska , 1977. 35 leaves :   LC Card 79-625780   DDC 333.95/4 19
TD195.S3 B87

TRANSCENDENTALISM. Harris, Wendell V. The omnipresent debate . DeKalb , c1981. p. cm.   LC Card 80-8663   DDC 828/.8/08 19
PR778.P55 H3

TRANSCONTINENTAL JOURNEYS (U. S.) see OVERLAND JOURNEYS TO THE PACIFIC.

Transcript from the national hearing on the Federal nonnuclear energy RD&D program : conducted on October 3, 4 and 5, 1979, Office of Personnel Management Auditorium, Washington, D.C. / sponsored by the Office of Environmental Engineering and Technology, within the Office of Research and Development, United States Environmental Protection Agency. Washington, D.C. : The Office, 1980. xv, 161 p. ; 28 cm. Cover title: Energy alternatives and the environment, 1979, the public reviews the Federal nonnuclear energy RD&D program. "July 1980"--Cover. "EPA-600/9-80-009"--Cover.   LC Card 81-600788   DDC 333.79/15/0973 19
1. United States. Dept. of Energy. 2. Energy development - Environmental aspects - United States - Congresses. 3. Power resources - Environmental aspects - United States - Congresses. I. United States. Environmental Protection Agency. Office of Environmental Engineering and Technology. II. Title: Energy alternatives and the environment, 1979.
TD195.E49 T7

Transcript from the National Hearings on the Federal nonnuclear energy R&D program : conducted on September 24 and 25, 1980, Office of Personnel Management Auditorium, Washington, D.C. / sponsored by the Office of Environmental Engineering and Technology within the Office of Research and Development, Washington, D.C. : U. S. Environmental Protection Agency, Office of Environmental Engineering and Technology, 1980 i.e. 1981. xix, 207 p. : ill. ; 28 cm. "A review of the Department of Energy's conservation & solar energy programs, national hearing transcript"--Cover. "December 1980"--Cover. "EPA-600/9-060"--Cover.   LC Card 81-601492   DDC

333.79/23/0973 19
1. Energy policy - United States - Congresses. 2. Energy conservation - United States - Congresses. 3. Solar energy policy - United States - Congresses. 4. United States. Dept. of Energy - Congresses. I. United States. Environmental Protection Agency. Office of Environmental Engineering and Technology. II. United States. Dept. of Energy. III. Title: The Federal nonnuclear energy R&D program.
HD9502.U52 T7

Transcript (investigation into DBCP) . California. Legislature. Assembly. Ad Hoc Committee on Water Contamination. Sacramento, CA , 1980. 140 p. :   LC Card 80-623739   DDC 363.7/394 19
KFC10.4 .W35 1980

Transcript (investigation into TCE) . California. Legislature. Assembly. Ad Hoc Committee on Water Contamination. Sacramento, CA [1980] 2, 188 p. :   LC Card 80-623094   DDC 363.7/394 19
TD427.T75 C34 1980

Transcript of hearing, Sacramento, California, April 18, 1980 /. California. Legislature. Assembly. Select Committee on Landslide Prevention. Sacramento, CA (Box 90, State Capitol, Sacramento 95814) , 1980] 106 p. ;   LC Card 81-620834   DDC 346.79404/4 347.940644 19
KFC10.4 .L36 1980

Transcript of proceedings . California. Legislature. Senate. Committee on Governmental Organization. Sacramento, Calif. [1980] iiii, 154 p. ;   LC Card 80-622919   DDC 355.1/15/09794 19
KFC10.3 .G6 1980

Transcript of proceedings, hearing on veterans employment problems, California State Capitol, room 2117, Sacramento, California, October 21, 1980 /. California. Legislature. Assembly. Select Committee on Veterans Affairs. Sacramento, CA (Box 90, State Capitol, Sacramento, 95814) [1980] ii, 139 p. ;   LC Card 81-621312   DDC 331.5/2/09794 19
KFC10.4 .V47 1980

TRANSDUCERS - DRIFT. Seitz, Charles A. Automatic and continuous transducer drift compensator for end point detection systems /. Washington , 1981. p. cm.   LC Card 80-606887   DDC 622 s 621.5/9 19
TN23 .U43

Transfer of authorities for implementation of building energy performance standards . United States. Congress. Senate. Committee on Governmental Affairs. Washington , 1980. iii, 196 p. :   LC Card 80-601881   DDC 353.0082/32 19
KF26 .G67 1979aj

Transfer of certain land and facilities used by the Bureau of Mines to Carnegie-Mellon University . United States. Congress. Senate. Committee on Energy and Natural Resources. Subcommittee on Energy Resources and Materials Production. Washington , 1980. iii, 35 p. :   LC Card 80-603896   DDC 343.73/025 347.30325 19
KF26 .E5543 1980f

Transfer of Cost Accounting Standards Board . United States. Congress. Senate. Committee on Banking, Housing and Urban Affairs. Washington , 1980. iii, 67 p. ;   LC Card 80-604039   DDC 353.0071/2044 19
KF26 .B39 1980y

Transfer of Indian lands to heirs or lineal descendants . United States. Congress. Senate. Select Committee on Indian Affairs. Washington , 1980. iii, 17 p. ;   LC Card 80-602489   DDC 346.7304/32/08997 19
KF26.5 .I4 1980c

Transfer of municipal court jurisdiction in Oregon. Oregon. University. Bureau of Governmental Research and Service. [Eugene, Ore.] [1980] 77 p. ;   LC Card 80-622705   DDC 347.795/01 19
KFO2918 .O73

TRANSFER OF TECHNOLOGY. see TECHNOLOGY TRANSFER.

Transfer of technology to the Soviet bloc . United States. Congress. Senate. Committee on Governmental Affairs. Permanent Subcommittee on Investigations. Washington , 1980. iii, 156

p. ;   LC Card 80-602191   DDC 338.91/73/047 19
KF26 .G674 1980

Transfer patterns in Alaskan limited entry fisheries . Langdon, Steve, 1948- [Juneau] [1980] ii, 153 p. :   LC Card 80-622470   DDC 333.95/6 19
SH222.A4 L36

Transfer RNA and transfer RNA modification in differentiation and neoplasia : symposium, held at the National Institutes of Health, Bethesda, Maryland, October 5-7, 1970 / sponsored by the National Cancer Institute and the John E. Fogarty International Center for Advanced Study in the Health Sciences ; Ernest Borek, scientific editor. [Washington : U. S. Govt. Print. Off.], 1971 [i.e. 1974] p. 591-724 : ill. ; 29 cm. (Fogarty International Center proceedings ; no. 5) Cancer research ; v. 31 Includes bibliographies.   LC Card 78-601843   DDC 616.99/4 s 616.99/2071 19
1. Ribonucleic acid, Transfer - Congresses. 2. Cell differentiation - Congresses. 3. Carcinogenesis - Congresses. 4. Transmethylation - Congresses. I. Borek, Ernest, 1911-. II. United States. National Cancer Institute. III. John E. Fogarty International Center for Advanced Study in the Health Sciences. IV. Series: John E. Fogarty International Center for Advanced Study in the Health Sciences. Proceedings, no. 5.
RC261 .A274 vol. 31 QP623

Transferability of methodology to the Lower Rio Grande Valley : final report for Research Applied to National Needs Program, National Science Foundation, Grant no. AEN74-13590-A01, and Division of Budget and Planning, Office of the Governor of Texas, Interagency Agreement IAA / coordinated through Center for Research in Water Resources, Division of Natural Resources and Environment, the University of Texas at Austin. [Austin] : The Center, [1978] ca. 400 leaves in various foliations : ill. ; 28 cm. (Methodology to evaluate alternative coastal zone management policies--application in the Texas coastal zone : Example application . 4) Edited by R. S. Kier and E. G. Fruh. Includes bibliographies.   LC Card 79-622507   DDC 333.91/7/097644 19
1. Coastal zone management - Texas. 2. Coastal zone management - Rio Grande Valley. I. Kier, R. S. II. Fruh, E. Gus, 1939-. III. Texas. University at Austin. Center for Research in Water Resources. IV. Series.
HT393.T48 T7

Transferable development rights : Saddle Brook, New Jersey, September 30-October 1, 1977 : a seminar / co-sponsored by the National Conference of State Legislatures and the New Jersey Law Revision and Legislative Services Commission. [Trenton] : The Commission, [1979?] xi, 340 p. ; 28 cm. Bibliography: p. 183.   LC Card 80-622361   DDC 346.7304/5 19
1. Development rights transfer - Law and legislation - United States - Congresses. 2. Development rights transfer - Law and legislation - New Jersey - Congresses. 3. Development rights transfer - United States - Congresses. 4. Development rights transfer - New Jersey - Congresses. I. National Conference of State Legislatures. II. New Jersey. Law Revision and Legislative Services Commission.
KF5698.5.A75 T7

Transference of technology series. Texas. University at Austin. Bureau of Business Research. No. 1-3. Austin, 1967-69. 3 v.   *NYPL [VA (Texas. University at Austin. Bureau Business Research. Transference of technology series.)]*

TRANSFERS OF FUNDS, ELECTRONIC. see ELECTRONIC FUNDS TRANSFERS.

The transformation of the classical heritage . (3) Bregman, Jay. Synesius of Cyrene, philosopher-bishop /. Berkeley , c1981. p. cm.   ISBN 0-520-04192-5   LC Card 81-10293   DDC 186/.4 19
BR1720.S9 B72

Trans-Hudson vehicular origin and destination survey. [New York]. tables. 22-28 cm. Annual. Issued by the Port Authority of New York and New Jersey (1969-70 under the authority's earlier name: Port of New York Authority). Prepared by the authority's Central Research and Statistics Division.
1. Origin and destination Traffic Surveys - New York metropolitan area - Periodicals. I. Port Authority of New York and New Jersey. II. Port of New York Authority.   *NYPL [JLM 80-891]*

Transit labor law . California. Legislature. Assembly. Committee on Transportation. [Sacramento] [1979] 151 p. ; LC Card 80-621411   DDC 344.794/01890413884 19
KFC10.4 .T7 1979

TRANSIT SYSTEMS. see LOCAL TRANSIT.

Transition in Southern Africa. United States. Agency for International Development. Southern Africa Task Force. A framework for U. S. assistance in southern Africa . [Washington] [1977- v. : LC Card 80-503603   DDC 338.91/73/068 19
HC900 .U54 1977

Transitions of aging . West Virginia University Gerontology Conference, 1st, 1979. New York , 1980. xv, 221 p.; ISBN 0-12-203580-1
HQ1064.U5 W47 1979

NYPL [JLE 80-2946]

TRANSMETHYLATION - CONGRESSES.
Transfer RNA and transfer RNA modification in differentiation and neoplasia . [Washington] 1971 [i.e. 1974] p. 591-724 : LC Card 78-601843   DDC 616.99/4 s 616.99/2071 19
RC261 .A274 vol. 31 QP623

TRANSMISSION OF DATA. see DATA TRANSMISSION SYSTEMS.

TRANSMISSION OF HEAT. see HEAT - TRANSMISSION.

Transnational corporations and the pharmaceutical industry /. United Nations. Centre on Transnational Corporations. New York , 1979. vi, 165 p. ; LC Card 79-122316   DDC 300 s 338.8/87 19
JX1977 .A2 ST/CTC/9

Transport of dangerous goods . United Nations. Committee of Experts on the Transport of Dangerous Goods (1957-) New York , 1977. viii, 377 p. : LC Card 81-479997   DDC 300 s /341.7/56 19
JX1977 .A2 ST/SG/AC.10/1/Rev. 1

TRANSPORT PHENOMENA. see TRANSPORT THEORY.

TRANSPORT PLANES.
(1964) United States. Federal Aviation Agency. Air carrier operations inspector's handbook. Washington [1964] 1 v. (loose-leaf)
NYPL [JSF 78-777]

Transport regulation in Missouri, phase II / Richard G. Boehm ... [et al.]. [Jefferson City] : Public Service Commission of the State of Missouri, [1979- v. <1> ; 28 cm. CONTENTS. - pt. 1. Final report. LC Card 80-620878   DDC 353.97780087/5 19
1. Transportation, Automotive - Missouri. 2. Transportation, Automotive - Law and legislation - Missouri. I. Boehm, Richard G. II. Missouri. Public Service Commission.
HE5633.M8 T68

TRANSPORT, SEDIMENT. see SEDIMENT TRANSPORT.

TRANSPORT THEORY - CONGRESSES.
Monte Carlo Seminar-Workshop, Oak Ridge National Laboratory, 1970. A review of the Monte Carlo method for radiation transport calculations. Oak Ridge, Tenn. [1971] vii, 144 p.:   *NYPL [JSF 80-645]*

TRANSPORT WORKERS - OREGON - SUPPLY AND DEMAND.
Oregon. Employment Division. Research and Statistics Section. Occupational profiles of selected regulated industries in Oregon, 1976 /. [Salem] [1979?] 54 p. ; LC Card 80-622149   DDC 331.12/5138/009795 19
HD5718.T72 U58 1979

Transportation and aging; selected issues.
Interdisciplinary Workshop on Transportation and Aging, Washington, D. C., 1970. Washington [1971] 208 p. LC Card 79-619017
HQ1063.5 .I5 1970   *NYPL [JLF 81-91]*

Transportation and economic opportunity.
Regional Plan Association, New York. [New York, 1973] 206 p.   *NYPL [JLF 81-23]*

TRANSPORTATION AND STATE - ADDRESSES, ESSAYS, LECTURES.
National Research Council (U. S.) Transportation Research Board. Transportation energy--data, forecasting, policy, and models. Washington, D.C. , 1980. v, 108 p. : ISBN 0-309-03107-9 LC Card 81-1665 DDC 380.5 s

333.79 19
TE7 .H5 no. 764 HE152.6

TRANSPORTATION AND STATE - IDAHO.
Idaho. Transportation Dept. Six year Idaho transportation improvement program . [Boise] [1979] vii, 210 p. : LC Card 79-626024   DDC 380.5/068 19
HE213.I2 I3 1979

TRANSPORTATION AND STATE - MAINE.
Maine. Dept. of Transportation. Transportation improvement program, 1980-1981. [Augusta] [1979?] ii, 26 p. : LC Card 79-622303   DDC 380.5/068 19
HE213.M2 M34 1979

TRANSPORTATION AND STATE - NEVADA.
Nevada. Dept. of Highways. Planning Survey Division. Transportation systems . [Carson City] , 1978. iii, 31 leaves, [1] leaf of plates : LC Card 80-620633   DDC 380.5/068 19
HE213.N3 N48 1978

TRANSPORTATION AND STATE - UNITED STATES.
Institute of Public Administration, Washington, D. C. Financing transit . [Washington] [1979] v, 331 p. : LC Card 80-601587   DDC 388.4/042 19
HE206.2 .I57 1979

United States. Congress. Senate. Committee on Environment and Public Works. Testimony of Andrew L. Lewis, Jr. . Washington , 1981. iii, 34 p. ; LC Card 81-601349   DDC 353.0087/5 19
KF26 .E6 1981a

United States. Congress. Senate. Committee on Environment and Public Works. Subcommittee on Transportation. Automobile use management . Washington , 1980. iii, 133 p. : LC Card 80-603909   DDC 388.4/1321 19
KF26 .E679 1980b

TRANSPORTATION AND STATE - VIRGINIA.
Virginia. General Assembly. Joint Legislative Audit and Review Commission. Interim report of the Joint Legislative Audit and Review Commission and the SJR 50 Subcommittee on the organization and administration of the Department of Highways and Transportation to the Governor and the General Assembly of Virginia. Richmond, Va. (910 Capitol St., Richmond 23219) , 1981. 85 p. : LC Card 81-622025 DDC 300/.9755 s 353.97550087/8/06 19
J87 .V9 1981b, no. 14 HE28.V8

Transportation and the urban environment .
United States /U. S.S.R. Urban Transportation Team. Washington , 1978. xii, 173 p. : LC Card 79-600645
HE308 .U568 1978

TRANSPORTATION, AUTOMOTIVE - LAW AND LEGISLATION - GEORGIA.
Georgia. Public Service Commission. Transportation rules of the Georgia Public Service Commission . Atlanta, Ga. [1979?] 194 p. ; LC Card 80-621174   DDC 343.758/093/02636 19
KFG296.A435 A2 1979

TRANSPORTATION, AUTOMOTIVE - LAW AND LEGISLATION - ILLINOIS.
Illinois. Division of Traffic Safety. Illinois traffic safety programs report of evaluation or assessment . [Springfield] [1977] ca. 250 p. in various pagings : LC Card 79-623261 DDC 343.773/093 19
KFI1580.A1 A884

TRANSPORTATION, AUTOMOTIVE - LAW AND LEGISLATION - MISSOURI.
Transport regulation in Missouri, phase II /. [Jefferson City] [1979- v. <1> ; LC Card 80-620878 DDC 353.97780087/5 19
HE5633.M8 T68

TRANSPORTATION, AUTOMOTIVE - LAW AND LEGISLATION - NEW JERSEY.
New Jersey. Legislature. General Assembly. Transportation and Communications Committee. Public hearing before subcommittee of Assembly Transportation and Communications Committee to investigate the transportation of radioactive cargo on highways within New Jersey (created pursuant to Assembly Resolution 3003), held August 21, 1979, Freeholders' Chambers, Bergen County Administration Building, Hackensack, New

Jersey. [Trenton] [1979?] 59, 10 p. ; LC Card 80-622508 DDC 343.749/093 19
KFN1811.4 .T7 1979

TRANSPORTATION, AUTOMOTIVE - LAW AND LEGISLATION - NEW MEXICO.
New Mexico. Motor Transportation Division. Rules and regulations. [Santa Fe, N.M. (P.E.R.A. Bldg., P.O. Box 1028, Santa Fe 87503)] [1980] ii, 57 p. : LC Card 81-621088   DDC 343.789/0944/02636 347.890394402636 19
KFN3897.A433 A2 1980

TRANSPORTATION, AUTOMOTIVE - LAW AND LEGISLATION - OREGON.
Oregon. Legislative Assembly. Senate. Interim Task Force on Regulation of the Motor Carrier Industry. Report of the Senate Interim Task Force on Regulation of the Motor Carrier Industry . [Salem] [1980] xi, 135 p. : LC Card 80-623673 DDC 343.795/09483 19
KFO2411.72 .R33 1980

TRANSPORTATION, AUTOMOTIVE - LAW AND LEGISLATION - TEXAS.
Texas. Railroad Commission. Transportation Division. Motor transportation regulations before the Transportation Division /. [Austin] [1979] 7, 209 p. ; LC Card 80-622401   DDC 343.764/0944/02636 19
KFT1499.A435 A2 1979

TRANSPORTATION, AUTOMOTIVE - LAW AND LEGISLATION - UNITED STATES.
United States. Congress. Senate. Committee on the Judiciary. Federal restraints on competition in the trucking industry . Washington , 1980. xxxvii, 351 p. : LC Card 80-603054 DDC 343.73/09483 19
KF2265 .A25 1980

TRANSPORTATION, AUTOMOTIVE - MISSOURI.
Transport regulation in Missouri, phase II /. [Jefferson City] [1979- v. <1> ; LC Card 80-620878   DDC 353.97780087/5 19
HE5633.M8 T68

TRANSPORTATION, AUTOMOTIVE - NEW JERSEY - FREIGHT.
New Jersey. Legislature. General Assembly. Transportation and Communications Committee. Public hearing before subcommittee of Assembly Transportation and Communications Committee to investigate the transportation of radioactive cargo on highways within New Jersey (created pursuant to Assembly Resolution 3003), held August 21, 1979, Freeholders' Chambers, Bergen County Administration Building, Hackensack, New Jersey. [Trenton] [1979?] 59, 10 p. ; LC Card 80-622508 DDC 343.749/093 19
KFN1811.4 .T7 1979

TRANSPORTATION, AUTOMOTIVE - TAXATION - UNITED STATES - HISTORY - ADDRESSES, ESSAYS, LECTURES.
Martin, James Walter, 1893- State tax systems under changing technology . Lexington, Ky. , c1980. x, 322 p. : LC Card 80-131133 DDC 353.9/3878 19
HE355 .M37

TRANSPORTATION, AUTOMOTIVE - UNITED STATES.
United States. Congress. Office of Technology Assessment. Technology assessment of changes in the future use and characteristics of the automobile transportation system. Washington [1979] 2 v. : LC Card 79-600030
HE5623 .U53 1979   *NYPL [JLM 81-210]*

TRANSPORTATION, AUTOMOTIVE - UNITED STATES - CONGRESSES.
Federal State Workshop on Motor Carrier Regulation, 1st, Washington, D.C., 1979. Proceedings of the Federal State Workshop on Motor Carrier Regulation, October 22-24, 1979 /. [Washington, D.C. , 1980] 194 p. ; LC Card 80-602343 DDC 388.3/24/0973 19
HE5623 .F43 1979

TRANSPORTATION, AUTOMOTIVE - UNITED STATES - FREIGHT.
Executive Services, inc. A cooperative approach to cargo security in the trucking industry /] Washington , 1973. 89 p. in various pagings ;
NYPL [JLF 80-1486]

Schuster, Allan D. Motor common carrier corporate strategy in an uncertain regulatory

environment /. Austin [1979] 20 p. ; LC Card 79-625407 DDC 388.3/24/0973 19
HE5623 .S375

United States. Congress. House. Committee on Small Business. Subcommittee on General Oversight and Minority Enterprise. Task Force on Minority Enterprise. Minority truckers participation in Federal procurement contracts . Washington , 1980. iv, 107 p. ; LC Card 80-603017 DDC 346.73/023 19
KF27 .S64 1980c

United States. Interstate Commerce Commission. Motor Carrier Task Force. Initial report of the Motor Carrier Task Force . Washington , 1979. 146 p. ; LC Card 79-603515
HE5623 .A4 1979b

TRANSPORTATION, AUTOMOTIVE - UNITED STATES - RATES.
United States. Congress. Senate. Committee on the Judiciary. Federal restraints on competition in the trucking industry . Washington , 1980. xxxvii, 351 p. ; LC Card 80-603054 DDC 343.73/09483 19
KF2265 .A25 1980

TRANSPORTATION, AUTOMOTIVE - UNITED STATES - SAFETY MEASURES.
United States. Congress. House. Committee on Public Works and Transportation. Subcommittee on Surface Transportation. Commercial motor carrier safety . Washington , 1980. iv, 218 p. : LC Card 80-603819 DDC 343.73/093 347.30393 19
KF27 .P8966 1980c

TRANSPORTATION BUILDINGS - UNITED STATES - PERIODICALS.
Design, art & architecture in transportation 1st- ; 1978- [Washington]
NYPL [JLM 80-1118]

TRANSPORTATION - CHILE - BIBLIOGRAPHY.
Programa de Transporta Marítimo OEA/CEPAL. Bibliografía sobre transporte en Chile /. [New York] , 1977. 66 p. ; LC Card 80-119987
Z7164.T8 P76 1977 HE234.A1

TRANSPORTATION, CHOICE OF. see **CHOICE OF TRANSPORTATION.**

Transportation energy conservation data book /. United States. National Laboratory, Oak Ridge, Tenn. Oak Ridge, Tenn. , 1977. xxv, 536 p. : *HE18 1977 .N37 1977* *NYPL [JLF 81-192]*

TRANSPORTATION - ENERGY CONSUMPTION - ADDRESSES, ESSAYS, LECTURES.
National Research Council (U. S.) Transportation Research Board. Transportation energy--data, forecasting, policy, and models. Washington, D.C. , 1980. v, 108 p. : ISBN 0-309-03107-9 LC Card 81-1665 DDC 380.5 s 333.79 19
TE7 .H5 no. 764 HE152.6

Transportation energy--data, forecasting, policy, and models. National Research Council (U. S.) Transportation Research Board. Washington, D.C. , 1980. v, 108 p. : ISBN 0-309-03107-9 LC Card 81-1665 DDC 380.5 s 333.79 19
TE7 .H5 no. 764 HE152.6

TRANSPORTATION - ENVIRONMENTAL ASPECTS - RHODE ISLAND.
Rhode Island. Office of State Planning. 1977 mobile source air pollutant emission inventory. Providence, R.I. , 1979. xi, 91, [42] p. : LC Card 79-625664 DDC 363.7/3922 19
TD883.5.R4 R46 1979

TRANSPORTATION - ENVIRONMENTAL ASPECTS - UNITED STATES - PERIODICALS.
Design, art & architecture in transportation 1st- ; 1978- [Washington]
NYPL [JLM 80-1118]

Transportation for the handicapped . Krummes, Daniel. [Berkeley] , 1978. i. 26 p. ; LC Card 78-624140 DDC 016.3624/0483 19
Z7254 .K78 1978 HV3022

TRANSPORTATION - FREIGHT. see **FREIGHT AND FREIGHTAGE.**

TRANSPORTATION - ILLINOIS - MAPS.
Illinois. Dept. of Transportation. Illinois public transportation map/directory. [Springfield] 1978. col. map 88 x 49 cm. Scale ca. 1:750,000.

"This map shows scheduled bus and rail passenger routes and communities having scheduled airline service and local public transportation." Includes text and maps of "Commuter rail service" and "Air service." "Public transportation directory" and lists of bus, rail, and air lines on verso.
G4101.P1 1976 .I5
NYPL [Map Div. 81-3035]

Transportation improvement program, 1980-1981. Maine. Dept. of Transportation. [Augusta] [1979?] ii, 26 p. : LC Card 79-622303 DDC 380.5/068 19
HE213.M2 M34 1979

TRANSPORTATION - KANSAS - MAPS.
United States. Soil Conservation Service. Transportation network, Greater Southwest Regional Planning Commission, Kansas /. Lincoln, Nebr. , 1979. 1 map : LC Card 81-691161
G4201.P1 1975 .U52

TRANSPORTATION - LAW AND LEGISLATION - SOUTH DAKOTA.
1974 administrative rules of South Dakota, Title 70, Department of Transportation . [Pierre] [1976?] 110 p. ; LC Card 80-126722 DDC 343.783/093/02636 19
KFS3295.A434 A2 1976

TRANSPORTATION - LAW AND LEGISLATION - UNITED STATES.
United States. Congress. Senate. Committee on Commerce, Science, and Transportation. National Transportation Safety Board authorization . Washington , 1980. iii, 26 p. ; LC Card 80-602102 DDC 353.0072/236875 19
KF26 .C69 1980h

TRANSPORTATION - LAWS AND REGULATIONS - UNITED STATES.
Kilmer, Richard Lee, 1943- The impact of regulation on transportation efficiency /. Columbus , 1974. 13, 3, 5 p. ;
*NYPL [*XME-9249]*

TRANSPORTATION - MAINE - FINANCE.
Maine. Dept. of Transportation. Transportation improvement program, 1980-1981. [Augusta] [1979?] ii, 26 p. : LC Card 79-622303 DDC 380.5/068 19
HE213.M2 M34 1979

TRANSPORTATION - MATHEMATICAL MODELS.
De Neufville, Richard, 1939- Investment strategies for developing areas : models of transport. Cambridge, 1973. 83 p.
NYPL [JLF 80-1121]

TRANSPORTATION, MILITARY - CONGRESSES.
WorldWide Strategic Mobility Conference, National Defense University, 1977. The WorldWide Strategic Mobility Conference 1977, 2-4 May 1977 /. [Washington, D.C. , 1977] ca. 100 p. in various pagings ; LC Card 80-601611 DDC 355.2/7 19
UC273 .W67 1977

TRANSPORTATION, MILITARY - PERIODICALS.
Defense transportation journal. v. 23, no. 5- ; Sept./Oct. 1967- [Washington] *NYPL [JSP 81-117 & VWA (Defense transportation journal)]*

Naval research logistics quarterly. v. 1- ; Mar. 1954- [Washington] *NYPL [*ZAN-5064]*

Transportation needs of increased coal production and completion of the Tennessee-Tombigbee Waterway . United States. Congress. Senate. Committee on Environment and Public Works. Subcommittee on Water Resources. Washington , 1980. iv, 550 p. : LC Card 80-603720 DDC 386/.3/09761 19
KF26 .E683 1980

TRANSPORTATION - NEVADA.
Nevada. Dept. of Highways. Planning Survey Division. Transportation systems . [Carson City] , 1978. iii, 31 leaves, [1] leaf of plates : LC Card 80-620633 DDC 380.5/068 19
HE213.N3 N48 1978

TRANSPORTATION - NEW YORK (STATE) - NEW YORK METROPOLITAN AREA - MAPS.
Westchester County, N. Y. Dept. of Planning. Westchester and metropolitan area transportation . White Plains, N.Y. [1976] 1

map : LC Card 81-692860
G3803.W5P1 1976 .W4

TRANSPORTATION - NEW YORK (STATE) - WESTCHESTER COUNTY - MAPS.
Westchester County, N. Y. Dept. of Planning. Westchester and metropolitan area transportation . White Plains, N.Y. [1976] 1 map : LC Card 81-692860
G3803.W5P1 1976 .W4

Transportation of hazardous materials through city streets . United States. Congress. House. Committee on Public Works and Transportation. Subcommittee on Surface Transportation. Washington , 1980. iv, 220 p. : LC Card 81-600847 DDC 343.73/0942 347.303942 19
KF27 .P8966 1980d

TRANSPORTATION - PENNSYLVANIA - BLAIR COUNTY - HISTORY.
Kurtz, Paul. Blair, main line . [Bellwood, Pa.] , 1976. 298 p. : LC Card 77-150164
F157.B5 K87

TRANSPORTATION - PENNSYLVANIA - FINANCE - STATISTICS.
Pennsylvania. Dept. of Education. Estimates of school district subsidies payable 1979-80 . [Harrisburg] , 1979. v, 20 leaves ; LC Card 80-621560 DDC 379.1/3/09748 19
LB2826.P4 P373 1979

TRANSPORTATION - PLANNING - BIBLIOGRAPHY.
National Research Council. Transportation Research Board. Bibliography on project evaluation and priority programming criteria. Washington, D.C. , 1980. 35 p. ; LC Card 80-112146 DDC 016.62904 19
Z5853.T7 N37 1980 TA1145

TRANSPORTATION PLANNING - EVALUATION - ADDRESSES, ESSAYS, LECTURES.
National Research Council (U. S.) Transportation Research Board. Consumer perspectives in travel choice and interactive travel data collection. Washington, D.C. , 1980. iv, 33 p. : ISBN 0-309-03108-7 LC Card 81-1664 DDC 380.5 s 388.4 19
TE7 .H5 no. 765 HE336.C5

TRANSPORTATION PLANNING - IDAHO.
Idaho. Transportation Dept. Six year Idaho transportation improvement program . [Boise] [1979] vii, 210 p. : LC Card 79-626024 DDC 380.5/068 19
HE213.I2 I3 1979

TRANSPORTATION PLANNING - MARYLAND - MONTGOMERY COUNTY - MAPS.
Maryland-National Capital Park and Planning Commission. Second draft, selected transportation elements including the master plan of highways . [Silver Spring? Md.] [1980] 1 map : LC Card 81-692907
G3843.M6P1 1980 .M3

TRANSPORTATION PLANNING - NEW JERSEY.
New Jersey. Dept. of Transportation. New Jersey State rail plan for rail transportation and local rail services . [Trenton] , 1979. vii, 153, 135 p. : LC Card 80-620740 DDC 385/.068 19
HE2771.N5 N48 1979

TRANSPORTATION PLANNING - UNITED STATES.
Abrams, Charles M. Measures of effectiveness for multimodal urban traffic management . Washington , Springfield, Va. , 1979. 1 v. :
NYPL [JLM 80-740]

Rothenberg, Morris Jerome, 1934- Public transportation . [Washington, D.C.] [1980] viii, 200, [160] p. : LC Card 80-602279 DDC 388.4/0973 19
HE308 .R67

A section 147 rural public transportation demonstration manual. Washington , 1979. 5 v. in 1 ; *NYPL [JLF 80-1345]*

TRANSPORTATION PLANNING - UNITED STATES - ADDRESSES, ESSAYS, LECTURES.
Roads of rural America /. Washington, D.C. , Springfield, Va. , 1979. iii, 57 p. : LC Card 80-602646 DDC 388.1/0973 19
HE355 .R57

TRANSPORTATION PLANNING - WASHINGTON (STATE)
Washington (State). Planning and Public Transportation Division. Public transportation in Washington State. Olympia, Wash. [1980] iii, 126, [67] p., [1] leaf of plates : LC Card 80-623197 DDC 380.5/068 19
HE213.W2 W36 1980

TRANSPORTATION POLICY. see TRANSPORTATION AND STATE.

Transportation Research Board. see National Research Council. Transportation Research Board.

Transportation research circular .
(no. 213 0097-8515) National Research Council. Transportation Research Board. Bibliography on project evaluation and priority programming criteria. Washington, D.C. , 1980. 35 p. ; LC Card 80-112146 DDC 016.62904 19
Z5853.T7 N37 1980 TA1145

Transportation research record .
(756 0361-1981) National Research Council. Transportation Research Board. Concrete pavements and pavement overlays /. Washington, D.C. , 1980. iv, 48 p. : ISBN 0-309-03070-6 LC Card 80-607869 DDC 380.5 s 625.8/4 19
TE7 .H5 no. 756 TE278

(764) National Research Council (U. S.) Transportation Research Board. Transportation energy--data, forecasting, policy, and models. Washington, D.C. , 1980. v, 108 p. : ISBN 0-309-03107-9 LC Card 81-1665 DDC 380.5 s 333.79 19
TE7 .H5 no. 764 HE152.6

(765) National Research Council (U. S.) Transportation Research Board. Consumer perspectives in travel choice and interactive travel data collection. Washington, D.C. , 1980. iv, 33 p. : ISBN 0-309-03108-7 LC Card 81-1664 DDC 380.5 s 388.4 19
TE7 .H5 no. 765 HE336.C5

(766) National Research Council (U. S.) Transportation Research Board. Application of pavement design models. Washington, D.C. , 1980. p. cm. ISBN 0-309-03109-5 LC Card 81-1639 DDC 380.5 s 625.8 19
TE7 .H5 no. 766 TE251

(773) Grade crossings, devices, visibility, and freeway operations /. Washington, D.C. , 1980. iv, 49 p. : ISBN 0-309-03117-6 LC Card 81-4730 DDC 380.5 s 625.7/94 19
TE7 .H5 no. 773 TE228

(776) Guideway snow and ice control and roadside maintenance /. Washington, D.C. [1981] p. cm. ISBN 0-309-03121-4 LC Card 81-3965 DDC 380.5 s 625.7/63 19
TE7 .H5 no. 776 TE220.5

(777) Asphalt--materials, mixes, and construction /. Washington, D.C. , 1981. p. cm. ISBN 0-309-03122-2 LC Card 81-38324 DDC 380.5 s 625.8/5 19
TE7 .H5 no. 777 TE270

(778) Paratransit 1980 /. Washington, D.C. , 1981. p. cm. ISBN 0-309-03123-0 LC Card 81-38318 DDC 380.5 s 388.4/132 19
TE7 .H5 no. 778 HE308

(780) National Seminar on Asphalt Pavement Recycling (1980 : Dallas-Fort Worth Regional Airport) Proceedings of the National Seminar on Asphalt Pavement Recycling. Washington, D.C. , 1981. p. cm. ISBN 0-309-03101-X LC Card 81-607072 DDC 380.5 s 666/.893 19
TE7 .H5 no. 780 TE270

(782) Human factors and motorist information needs /. Washington, D.C. , 1980. p. cm. ISBN 0-309-03172-9 LC Card 81-9482 DDC 380.5 s 388.3/12 19
TE7 .H5 no. 782 HE332

Transportation research records.
(0361-1981 ; 771) Advances in urban transportation planning /. Washington, D.C. , 1980. iv, 22 p. : ISBN 0-309-03115-X (pbk.) LC Card 81-4761 DDC 380.5 s 388.4/068 19
TE7 .H5 no. 771 HE305

TRANSPORTATION - RESEARCH - UNITED STATES.
United States. Urban Mass Transportation Administration. Innovation in public transportation . Washington , 1974. ix, 147 p. :
NYPL [JLF 80-1675]

Transportation rules of the Georgia Public Service Commission . Georgia. Public Service Commission. Atlanta, Ga. [1979?] 194 p. ; LC Card 80-621174 DDC 343.758/093/02636 19
KFG296.A435 A2 1979

Transportation system management plan for northeastern Illinois. Chicago, Chicago Area Transportation Study. 28 cm. Annual.
1. Urban Transportation policy - Illinois - Chicago metropolitan area - Periodicals. I. Chicago Area Transportation Study.   NYPL [JLM 80-1096]

Transportation systems . Nevada. Dept. of Highways. Planning Survey Division. [Carson City] , 1978. iii, 31 leaves, [1] leaf of plates : LC Card 80-620633 DDC 380.5/068 19
HE213.N3 N48 1978

Transportation Systems Center. R & D Planning Workshop, Transportation Systems Center, 1977. Tire rolling losses and fuel economy . Troy, MI , c1977. iii, 202 p. : LC Card 78-51861
TL151.6 .R18 1977

Transportation taxation in Virginia. Inflation and the Virginia income tax ; Personal property taxation in Virginia localities ; Transportation taxation in Virginia. Richmond, Va. , 1979. x, 210 p. ; LC Card 80-623840 DDC 336.2/009755 19
HJ4655.V88 I64

TRANSPORTATION - TAXATION - VIRGINIA.
Inflation and the Virginia income tax ; Personal property taxation in Virginia localities ; Transportation taxation in Virginia. Richmond, Va. , 1979. x, 210 p. ; LC Card 80-623840 DDC 336.2/009755 19
HJ4655.V88 I64

TRANSPORTATION - TAXATION - WISCONSIN.
Wisconsin. Legislative reference bureau. The taxation and financing of transportation in Wisconsin . Madison, Wis. [1980] 101 p. ; LC Card 80-621759 DDC 300/.9775 s 336.2/78 19
KFW2420 .L4 no. 80-2 HE213

TRANSPORTATION - UNDERDEVELOPED AREAS. see UNDERDEVELOPED AREAS - TRANSPORTATION.

TRANSPORTATION - UNITED STATES - ENERGY CONSUMPTION - STATISTICS.
United States. National Laboratory, Oak Ridge, Tenn. Transportation energy conservation data book /. Oak Ridge, Tenn. , 1977. xxv, 536 p. :
HE18 1977 .N37 1977   NYPL [JLF 81-192]

TRANSPORTATION - UNITED STATES - FINANCE.
Institute of Public Administration, Washington, D. C. Financing transit . [Washington] [1979] v, 331 p. : LC Card 80-601587 DDC 388.4/042 19
HE206.2 .I57 1979

TRANSPORTATION - UNITED STATES - MAPS.
United States. Geological Survey. Transportation map of ... [Washington] 1975-76. 41 col. maps on sheets 43 x 56 cm. and 56 x 43 cm. Scales vary. Each sheet separately titled. "Transportation zone edition." Shows lines that may be subject to abandonment, those operating under rail service continuation provisions, and other operating lines. Includes "Index to railroads." Accompanied by text. [2] p.   NYPL [Map Div. 80-3426]

TRANSPORTATION - VIRGINIA - ENERGY CONSERVATION.
Halstead, Woodrow J. The outlook for transportation energy . Charlottesville, Va. [1978?] v, 21 p. : LC Card 79-625794 DDC 333.79 19
TJ163.5.T7 H34

TRANSPORTATION - WISCONSIN - FINANCE.
Wisconsin. Legislative reference bureau. The taxation and financing of transportation in Wisconsin . Madison, Wis. [1980] 101 p. ; LC Card 80-621759 DDC 300/.9775 s 336.2/78 19
KFW2420 .L4 no. 80-2 HE213

Trap-efficiency study, highland creek flood retarding reservoir near Kelseyville, California, water years 1966-77 /. Trujillo, L. F. Washington , 1980. p. cm. LC Card 80-606911 DDC 627/.44 19
TC424.C2 T78

TRASH. see REFUSE AND REFUSE DISPOSAL.

Tratados sobre el Canal de Panamá suscritos entre la República de Panamá y los Estados Unidos de América =. United States. Treaties, etc. Panama, Sept. 7, 1977. Washington, D.C. , 1979. 2 v. : LC Card 80-121836 DDC 341.4/46/02667307287 19
JX1398.72 1979 .U54 1977

Traut, D. E. (Davis E.) Maysilles, J. H. (James H.) Aluminum chloride hexahydrate crystallization by HCl gas sparging /. Avondale, MD , 1981. p. cm. LC Card 81-607822 DDC 622 s 622/.34926 19
TN23 .U43 TP245.A4

Trautman, Milton Bernhard, 1899- The fishes of Ohio : with illustrated keys / by Milton B. Trautman.Rev. ed. [Columbus] : Ohio State University Press : in collaboration with the Ohio Sea Grant Program Center for Lake Erie Area Research, 1980. p. cm. Bibliography: p. Includes index. ISBN 0-8142-0213-6 LC Card 80-29521 DDC 597.092/9771 19
1. Fishes - Ohio. 2. Fishes - Identification. 3. Fishes - Ohio - Identification. I. Title.
QL628.O3 T7 1980

Trautmann, Joanne. Healing arts in dialogue . Carbondale, c1981. p. cm. ISBN 0-8093-1028-7 LC Card 81-8964 DDC 801/.9 19
PN56.M38 H4

Travel in Virginia, 1978 . United States Travel Data Center. [Richmond, Va. , 1978] 12 p. : LC Card 80-622616 DDC 381/.45917550443 19
G155.U6 U58 1978

TRAVEL PHOTOGRAPHY.
Davis, Keith F., 1952- Désiré Charnay, expeditionary photographer /. Albuquerque , c1981. p. cm. ISBN 0-8263-0592-X : LC Card 81-52052 DDC 770/.92/4 B 19
TR140.C46 D38

Travel Research Association.
Journal of travel research. Boulder, Colo. LC Card 77-607048   NYPL [JFM 80-226]

The 80's, its impact on travel and tourism marketing : the Travel Research Association Eighth Annual Conference proceedings, Scottsdale, Arizona, June 12-15, 1977. Salt Lake City, Utah : Bureau of Economic and Business Research, College of Business, University of Utah, c1977. xv, 221 p. : ill. ; 28 cm. Includes bibliographical references. LC Card 80-141505 DDC 380.1/459104 19
1. Tourist trade - Congresses. I. Utah. University. Bureau of Economic and Business Research. II. Title.
G154.9 .T72 1977

TRAVEL RESEARCH - PERIODICALS.
Journal of travel research. Boulder, Colo. LC Card 77-607048   NYPL [JFM 80-226]

TRAVEL RESTRICTIONS - RUSSIAN S.F.S.R. - LENINGRAD REGION - MAPS.
United States. Central Intelligence Agency. Leningrad area. [Washington , 1980] 1 map : LC Card 81-692776
G7004.L4E272 1980 .U5

TRAVEL RESTRICTIONS - RUSSIAN S.F.S.R. - MOSCOW REGION - MAPS.
United States. Central Intelligence Agency. Moscow, areas closed to foreigners, 4 January 1978. [Washington , 1980] 1 map : LC Card 81-692777
G7004.M7E272 1978 .U53

TRAVEL RESTRICTIONS - RUSSIAN S.F.S.R. - MOSKOVSKAIĂ OBLAST' - MAPS.
United States. Central Intelligence Agency. Moscow, areas closed to foreigners, 4 January 1978. [Washington , 1980] 1 map : LC Card 81-692777
G7004.M7E272 1978 .U53

TRAVEL TIME (TRAFFIC ENGINEERING) - TEXAS - AUSTIN - TABLES.
Location techniques for emergency medical service vehicles . [Austin, Tex.] , 1979. 4 v. : ISBN 0-89940-631-9 (pbk. : v. 1) LC Card

79-90645   DDC 362.1/8 19
RA995.5.T42 A954

TRAVELERS - CANADA - CONGRESSES.
Canada--Hawaii, a look at the 1980's .
Honolulu, Hawaii [1980] 58 p. ;   LC Card
80-622006   DDC 382/.4591969044 19
G155.U6 C25   **NYPL   [M-10 9494 no. 15]**

TRAVELERS - ITALY.
Starch INRA Hooper. Italy . [Washington] ,
1978. vi, 65 p. :   LC Card 78-601739
G155.U6 S65 1978a

**TRAVELERS - MEDICAL CARE - LAW AND
LEGISLATION - UNITED STATES.**
United States. Congress. House. Committee on
the Judiciary. Subcommittee on Administrative
Law and Governmental Relations. Good
Samaritan act . Washington , 1980 [i.e. 1981]
iii, 116 p. ;   LC Card 81-600969   DDC
346.7303/32 347.306332 19
KF27 .J832 1980e

Traveler's Rest and the Tugaloo crossroads /.
Bouwman, Robert Eldridge. [Atlanta] , c1980.
xv, 306 p., [12] leaves of plates :   LC Card
80-622189   DDC 975.8/132 19
F294.T73 B68

TRAVELER'S REST HISTORIC SITE, GA.
Bouwman, Robert Eldridge. Traveler's Rest and
the Tugaloo crossroads /. [Atlanta] , c1980. xv,
306 p., [12] leaves of plates :   LC Card
80-622189   DDC 975.8/132 19
F294.T73 B68

**TRAVELS. see OVERLAND JOURNEYS TO
THE PACIFIC.**

Travis, Stephen C.
(joint author) Bilger, Michael D. Nashua River .
Westborough, Mass. [1978] iv leaves, 45 p. :
LC Card 79-624432   DDC 363.7/3942/097443
19
TD225.N2 B54

(joint author) Erdmann, John B. Charles River
and Charles Basin . Westborough, Mass. [1977]
174 p. :   LC Card 80-620705   DDC
363.7/3942/097447 19
TD224.M4 E72

Traylor, M. Denise. Bellenger, Danny N., 1946-
Sales management . Atlanta, Ga. , 1981. p. cm.
ISBN 0-88406-147-7 :   LC Card 81-6559   DDC
016.6588/1 19
Z7164.M18 B39 HF5438.4

Traynham, Earle C. (joint author) Jennings,
Kenneth M. Study of unions, management
rights, and the public interest in mass transit .
Washington , 1977. 276 p. :   LC Card 77-604540
HD6976.T72 U55   **NYPL   [*XME-9441]**

Treadway, Ralph S. An economic profile of
Cumberland County, New Jersey / Ralph S.
Treadway. [Trenton, N.J.] : Office of Economic
Research, Division of Planning and Research,
Dept. of Labor and Industry, [1980] x, 119 p. :
ill. ; 28 cm. "March 1980." Bibliography: p. 117-119.
LC Card 80-623638   DDC 330.9749/94043 19
1. Cumberland Co., N.J. - Economic conditions. I.
Title.
HC107.N52 C857

**Treasury, Postal Service, and general government
appropriations for fiscal year 1981 .** United
States. Congress. Senate. Committee on
Appropriations. Subcommittee on the Dept. of
the Treasury, U. S. Postal Service, and General
Government Appropriations. Washington ,
1980- v. <1> ;   LC Card 80-603729   DDC
353.0072/236 19
KF26 .A662 1980

TREATIES.
Bilder, Richard B., 1927- Managing the risks of
international agreement /. Madison , 1981. xi,
302 p. ;   ISBN 0-299-08360-8 :   LC Card 80-52288
DDC 341.3/7 19
JX4165 .B47

**Treaties and other international agreements on
fisheries, oceanographic resources, and wildlife
involving the United States /.** United States.
Treaties, etc. Washington , 1977. xv, 1201 p. ;
LC Card 81-601815   DDC 341.7/62/026 19
JX236 1977 .U54

TREATIES - CONGRESSES.
United Nations Conference on Succession of
States in Respect of Treaties, Vienna,
1977-1978. Official records /. New York ,
1979- v. ;   LC Card 80-121295   DDC 300 s

341.3/7 19
JX1977 .A2 A/CONF.80/16/Add.1, etc.

**Treaties of the People's Republic of China,
1949-1978 .** China (People's Republic of China,
1949-). Treaties, etc. Boulder, Colo. , 1980. ix,
207 p. :   ISBN 0-89158-761-6 :   LC Card 79-27904
JX926 1980 .C47   **NYPL   [JFE 80-3747]**

**Treaties on the Panama Canal signed between
the United States of America and the Republic
of Panama.** United States. Treaties, etc.
Panama, Sept. 7, 1977. Tratados sobre el Canal
de Panamá suscritos entre la República de
Panamá y los Estados Unidos de América =.
Washington, D.C. , 1979. 2 v. :   LC Card
80-121836   DDC 341.4/46/02667307287 19
JX1398.72 1979 .U54 1977

**Treatment of Florida surface waters for use in
phosphate beneficiation /.** Stanley, Donald A.
[Washington, D.C.] [1981] p. cm.   LC Card
80-606882   DDC 622 s 661/.43 19
TN23 .U43

Trebat, Thomas. An evaluation of the economic
performance of large public enterprises in
Brazil, 1965-1975 / Thomas J. Trebat. Austin :
Office for Public Sector Studies, Institute of
Latin American Studies, University of Texas at
Austin, 1980. 23 p. ; 28 cm. (Technical papers
series - Office for Public Sector Studies, the Institute of
Latin American Studies, the University of Texas at
Austin ; no. 24) Includes bibliographical references.
LC Card 80-623136   DDC 338.7/4/0981 19
1. Government business enterprises - Brazil - History.
2. Corporations, Government - Brazil - History. I.
Series: Texas. University at Austin. Institute of Latin
American Studies. Office for Public Sector Studies.
Technical papers series - Office for Public Sector
Studies, Institute of Latin American Studies, University
of Texas at Austin , no. 24. II. Title.
HD4093 .T73

**TREE CROPS - HAWAII - WAIMANALO
REGION - CATALOGS AND
COLLECTIONS.**
University of Hawaii at Manoa. Plant Science
Instructional Arboretum. A catalog of plants in
the Plant Science Instructional Arboretum,
College of Tropical Agriculture and Human
Resources, University of Hawaii /. [Honolulu] ,
1981. p. cm.   LC Card 81-2897   DDC
582.16/061/074099691 19
SB171.U6 U54 1981

**Tree Wardens, Arborists, and Utilities
Conference, Chicopee, Mass., 1979.**
Proceedings of the Tree Wardens, Arborists,
and Utilities Conference, March 13-15, 1979 /
sponsored by Cooperative Extension Service,
University of Massachusetts, United States
Department of Agriculture and county
extension services cooperating, in collaboration
with Massachusetts Tree Wardens' and
Foresters' Association ... [et al.]. [Amherst,
Mass.] : The Service, [1979] 94 p. : forms ; 29
cm. Includes bibliographies.   LC Card 80-622844
DDC 635.9/77 19
1. Trees in cities - Congresses. 2. Trees, Care of -
Congresses. I. University of Massachusetts at Amherst.
Cooperative Extension Service. II. United States. Dept.
of Agriculture.
SB436 .T756 1979

Treece, Randall D. (joint author) Troy, Richard E.
California State park system plan, 1980 .
Sacramento, Calif. [1980] viii, 239 p. :   LC
Card 80-622915   DDC 333.78/3/09794 19
GV191.42.C2 T76

Trees and shrubs of the southwestern deserts /.
Benson, Lyman David, 1909- Tucson , c1981.
p. cm.   ISBN 0-8165-0591-8 :   LC Card 81-7617
DDC 582.160979 19
QK484.S89 B46 1981

TREES, CARE OF - CONGRESSES.
Tree Wardens, Arborists, and Utilities
Conference, Chicopee, Mass., 1979. Proceedings
of the Tree Wardens, Arborists, and Utilities
Conference, March 13-15, 1979 /. [Amherst,
Mass.] [1979] 94 p. :   LC Card 80-622844   DDC
635.9/77 19
SB436 .T756 1979

**TREES - COSTA RICA - CORCOVADO
NATIONAL PARK.**
Herwitz, Stanley Robert. The regeneration of
selected tropical wet forest tree species in
Corcovado National Park, Costa Rica /.
Berkeley, Calif. [1981] p. cm.   ISBN

0-520-09631-2   LC Card 80-26413   DDC 910 s
582.16/052642/0972867 19
G58 .C3 vol. 24 QK217

**TREES - DISEASES AND PESTS -
NORTHEASTERN STATES -
IDENTIFICATION.**
United States. Forest Insect and Disease
Management. A guide to common insects and
diseases of forest trees in the Northeastern
United States /. Broomall, PA. , Washington,
D.C. , 1979. vi, 127 p. :   LC Card 80-601798
DDC 634.9/67/0974 19
SB763.N67 U54 1979

TREES, FOSSIL.
Janssen, Raymond Ellsworth, 1903- Leaves and
stems from fossil forests . Springfield, Ill. ,
1979. 190 p. :   ISBN 0-89792-077-5   LC Card
80-622162   DDC 561/.074/017356 19
QE937.I5 J29 1979

TREES (GRAPH THEORY)
Brown, Thomas C. Canonical simplification of
finite objects, well quasi-ordered by tree
embedding /. Urbana, Ill. [1979] 33 p. :   LC
Card 80-621696   DDC 001.64 s 511.3 19
QA76 .I4 no. 981 QA9.5

TREES - GROWTH.
Puckett, Larry J. Dendroclimatic estimates of a
drought index for northern Virginia /.
Washington, D.C. [1981] p. cm.   LC Card
80-607816   DDC 551.6/4 19
QC929.D8 P84

TREES IN CITIES - BIBLIOGRAPHY.
Albrecht, Jean. Urban forestry . St. Paul, Minn.
[1980] 100 p. ;   LC Card 80-622738   DDC
016.6349/09173/2 19
Z5996.T74 A4 SB436

TREES IN CITIES - CONGRESSES.
Tree Wardens, Arborists, and Utilities
Conference, Chicopee, Mass., 1979. Proceedings
of the Tree Wardens, Arborists, and Utilities
Conference, March 13-15, 1979 /. [Amherst,
Mass.] [1979] 94 p. :   LC Card 80-622844   DDC
635.9/77 19
SB436 .T756 1979

Trees of north Texas /. Vines, Robert A., 1907-
Austin , c1981. p. cm.   ISBN 0-292-78018-4 :   LC
Card 81-1644   DDC 582.1609764 19
QK484.T4 V53

Trees of South Dakota /. Collins, Paul E.
Brookings [1979?] xvi, 51 p. :   LC Card
80-622715   DDC 582.1609783 19
QK484.S8 C64

**TREES - SOUTH DAKOTA -
IDENTIFICATION.**
Collins, Paul E. Trees of South Dakota /.
Brookings [1979?] xvi, 51 p. :   LC Card
80-622715   DDC 582.1609783 19
QK484.S8 C64

**TREES - SOUTHWEST, NEW -
IDENTIFICATION.**
Benson, Lyman David, 1909- Trees and shrubs
of the southwestern deserts /. Tucson , c1981.
p. cm.   ISBN 0-8165-0591-8 :   LC Card 81-7617
DDC 582.160979 19
QK484.S89 B46 1981

TREES - TEXAS - IDENTIFICATION.
Vines, Robert A., 1907- Trees of north Texas /.
Austin , c1981. p. cm.   ISBN 0-292-78018-4 :   LC
Card 81-1644   DDC 582.1609764 19
QK484.T4 V53

TREES - TROPICS.
Chudnoff, Martin. Tropical timbers of the world
/. Madison, Wis. [1980] iv, 826 p. ;   LC Card
80-602127   DDC 674/.13/0913 19
SD434 .C48

Trefousse, Hans Louis. Carl Schurz, a biography /
by Hans L. Trefousse. 1st ed. Knoxville :
University of Tennessee Press, c1981. p. cm.
Bibliography: p. Includes index.   ISBN 0-87049-326-4 :
LC Card 81-3370   DDC 973.8/092/4 B 19
1. Schurz, Carl, 1829-1906. 2. Statesmen - United
States - Biography. 3. United States. Congress. Senate -
Biography. 4. Legislators - United States - Biography. I.
Title.
E664.S39 T7

Trelease, Frank J., 1913- Back to basics--taking
the politics out of water law : keynote address /
Frank J. Trelease. [Sacramento? Calif.] : F.J.
Trelease, [1979?] 29 leaves ; 28 cm. At head of
title: Conference on Water Perspectives in the "Old

West States", Rapid City, South Dakota, December 13 & 14, 1979, sponsored by South Dakota Department of Water and Natural Resources. Includes bibliographical references. LC Card 81-621163 DDC 346.7304/691 347.3064691 19
1. Water - Law and legislation - West (U. S.) - Addresses, essays, lectures. 2. Water-rights - West (U. S.) - Addresses, essays, lectures. I. Title.
KF5571 .T74

TREMATODA - IDENTIFICATION.
McDonald, Malcolm Edwin, 1915- Key to trematodes reported in waterfowl /. Washington, D.C., 1981. p. cm. LC Card 81-607044 DDC 333.95/4/0973 s 639.9/741 19
S914 .A3 no. 142 QL391.P7

Trementozzi, Miriam, 1947- Preservation, an ethic for planning / prepared by Miriam Trementozzi. Concord, N.H. : Published for the New Hampshire State Historic Preservation Office by the New Hampshire Charitable Fund, 1980. p. cm. LC Card 80-26731 DDC 363.6/9 19
1. Historic buildings - United States - Conservation and restoration. 2. Historic buildings - New Hampshire - Conservation and restoration. 3. United States - History, Local. 4. New Hampshire - History, Local. I. Title.
E159 .T795

Trends and characteristics of international migration since 1950. United Nations. Dept. of Economic and Social Affairs. New York, 1979. vi, 172 p. : LC Card 79-127707 DDC 325/.09045 19
JX1977 .A2 ST/ESA/SER.A/64

Trends in airline unit costs. United States. Civil Aeronautics Board. Financial Analysis and Cost Division. Trends in unit costs. Washington.
NYPL [JLN 81-8]

Trends in bus transit financial and operating characteristics, 1960-1975 /. Control Data Corporation. [Washington] [Springfield, Va.] 1978, cover 1977. ca. 300 p. in various pagings : LC Card 79-602177
*HE5623 .A4 1977d**NYPL [JLF 81-376]*

Trends in California transit labor contract settlements /. Rae, James W. Sacramento, 1978. iii leaves, 48 p. : LC Card 79-625551 DDC 331.89/0413884/09794 19
HD6976.T72 U67

Trends in catch timing and distribution of the Washington commercial troll salmon fishery, 1960-1975 /. Miller, Marc C. [Olympia, Wash.], 1979. iii, 56 p. : LC Card 80-620830 DDC 338.3/72755 19
SH222.W2 M54

Trends in commitments to correctional institutions . Metzler, Charles, 1951- [Boston] [1979] [24] leaves : LC Card 80-620620 DDC 365/.4/09744 19
HV9305.M4 M476

Trends in graduate enrollment and Ph.D. output in scientific fields, 1960-61 through 1967-68. Brown, Carol M. [Washington], 1969 [i.e. 1970] vii, 204 p. ; LC Card 73-606834 DDC 610/.7 s 610/.7/073 19
RA440.6 .R4 no. 18 R854.U5

Trends in nonmarital fertility and spacing between marriage and first birth in Missouri /. Schramm, Wayne F. Jefferson City [1980] vi, 17 p. : LC Card 80-623989 DDC 304.6/3 19
HB935.M8 S37

Trends in the American diet . United States. Congress. Senate. Committee on Agriculture, Nutrition, and Forestry. Subcommittee on Nutrition. Washington, 1980. iii, 66 p. ; LC Card 80-602728 DDC 362.1/9639/073 19
KF26 .A3559 1980

Trends in U. S. trade, 1960-1979 /. Bayard, Thomas O. Washington, D.C., Springfield, Va., 1980. 48 p. : LC Card 81-600712 DDC 382/.0973 19
HF3031 .B35

Trends in unit costs. United States. Civil Aeronautics Board. Financial Analysis and Cost Division. Washington.*NYPL [JLN 81-8]*

TRENT, DARRELL MELVIN, 1938-
United States. Congress. Senate. Committee on Commerce, Science, and Transportation. Nomination--deputy secretary of transportation . Washington, 1981. iii, 25 p. ;

LC Card 81-600981 DDC 353.86 19
KF26 .C69 1981

Trent, Virgil A. Chemical analyses and physical properties of 12 coal samples from the Pocahontas field, Tazewell County, Virginia, and McDowell County, West Virginia /. Washington, 1981. p. cm. LC Card 81-607871 DDC 557.3 s 662.6/224/09755763 19
QE75 .B9 no. 1528 TP326.U5

Trenton (Mich.). Bicentennial Book Committee. Truaxton, Truago, Trenton. [Trenton, Mich., 1976] vi, 194 p. : LC Card 81-144056 DDC 977.4/33 19
F574.T83 T78

TRENTON (MICH.) - DESCRIPTION - VIEWS.
Truaxton, Truago, Trenton. [Trenton, Mich., 1976] vi, 194 p. : LC Card 81-144056 DDC 977.4/33 19
F574.T83 T78

TRENTON (MICH.) - HISTORY - PICTORIAL WORKS.
Truaxton, Truago, Trenton. [Trenton, Mich., 1976] vi, 194 p. : LC Card 81-144056 DDC 977.4/33 19
F574.T83 T78

Trenton, N. J. New Jersey State Museum. see New Jersey. State Museum, Trenton.

Trenton. State Library. see New Jersey. State Library, Trenton.

Treu, Siegfried. A testbed for providing uniformity to user-computer interaction languages / Siegfried Treu. [Washington, D.C.] : U. S. Dept. of Commerce, National Bureau of Standards : for sale by the Supt. of Docs., U. S. Govt. Print. Off., 1980. 72 p. in various pagings : diagrs. ; 26 cm. (Computer science & technology) NBS special publication ; 500-63 "Issued August 1980." Includes bibliography. LC Card 80-603146 DDC 602/.18 s 001.64/24 19
1. Programming languages (Electronic computers). 2. Interactive computer systems. 3. Information storage and retrieval systems. I. Series. II. Series: United States. National Bureau of Standards Special publication, 500-63. III. Title.
QC100 .U57 no. 500-63 QA76.7

Treude, Mai. Windows to the past : a bibliography of Minnesota county atlases / by Mai Treude ; [edited by Pamela Espeland and Judith H. Weir]. Minneapolis, Minn. (311 Walter Library, 117 Pleasant St. S.E., University of Minnesota, Minneapolis, Minn. 55455) : Center for Urban and Regional Affairs, 1980. ix, 187 p. : ill. ; 28 cm. (Publication . no. CURA 80-3) Includes index. LC Card 80-154529 DDC 016.912/776 19
1. Minnesota - Maps - Bibliography. I. Espeland, Pamela, 1951-. II. Weir, Judith H. III. Series: Publication (University of Minnesota (Mineapolis-St. Paul campus). Center for Urban and Regional Affairs), no. CURA 80-3. IV. Title.
Z6027.M65 T73 GA432

Triage and justice /. Winslow, Gerald R. Berkeley, c1982. p. cm. ISBN 0-520-04328-6 LC Card 81-10434 DDC 174/.2 19
R725.5 .W56

TRIAGE (MEDICINE) - MORAL AND RELIGIOUS ASPECTS.
Winslow, Gerald R. Triage and justice /. Berkeley, c1982. p. cm. ISBN 0-520-04328-6 LC Card 81-10434 DDC 174/.2 19
R725.5 .W56

Trial court management series.
Cooper, Caroline S. Executive summary /. Washington, 1979. iv, 136 p. ; LC Card 79-601909 DDC 347.73/1/068 19
KF8732 .C66

TRIAL PRACTICE - TEXAS - CONGRESSES.
Legal Assistants Seminar on Civil Litigation, Houston, Tex., 1979. Legal Assistants Seminar on Civil Litigation, Houston, November 30-December 1, 1979 /. [Austin] [1979] ca. 250 p. in various pagings : LC Card 80-621743 DDC 347.764/07 19
KFT1738.A2 L43 1979

TRIAL PRACTICE - UNITED STATES.
Bennett, W. Lance. Reconstructing reality in the courtroom . New Brunswick, N.J., c1981. p. cm. ISBN 0-8135-0922-X : LC Card 81-5125

DDC 345.73/05 347.3055 19
KF9656 .B46

TRIALS (MILITARY OFFENSES) - UNITED STATES.
Allen, Julius J. (defendant) Record and proceedings of a general court martial. [San Francisco?, 1945?] 8 v. (1655 leaves);
NYPL [Sc Micro R-3912]

TRIALS (MURDER) - MASSACHUSETTS - DEDHAM.
Massachusetts. Report to the Governor in the matter of Sacco and Vanzetti. [Boston] [1977] 2, 38 p. ; LC Card 80-620508 DDC 345.73//02523 19
KF224.S2 M32

TRIALS (MURDER) - MASSACHUSETTS - DEDHAM - CONGRESSES.
Sacco-Vanzetti, developments and reconsiderations, 1979 . Boston, 1981. p. cm. ISBN 0-89073-067-9 LC Card 81-12986 DDC 345.73//02523 347.3052523 19
KF224.S2 S24

TRIALS (SEDITION) - UNITED STATES.
13 Communists speak to the Court /. New York, 1953. 95 p. ; LC Card 54-43867
NYPL [Sc Micro R-3647]

Triangle J Council of Governments. North Carolina Region J inventory and atlas / Triangle J Council of Governments. Research Triangle Park, N.C. : The Council, 1974. [272] p. : maps ; 28 x 36 cm. CONTENTS. - Regional history.--Population data.--Housing data.--Income data.--Educational data.--Health data.--Public utility data.--Transportation data.--Government financial data.--Zoning and subdivision survey.--Regional section maps. LC Card 80-675218 DDC 912/.756 19
1. North Carolina - Maps. 2. North Carolina - Statistics. I. Title.
G1300 .T7 1974

Triapttsyn, V. A. Gordh, Gordon. Taxonomic studies of the Encyrtidae with the descriptions of new species and a new genus (Hymenoptera, Chalcicoidea) /. Berkeley, 1981. p. cm. ISBN 0-520-09629-0 LC Card 81-1327 DDC 595.79 19
QL568.E6 G67

TRIASSIC PERIOD. see GEOLOGY, STRATIGRAPHIC - TRIASSIC.

Tribal water rights, today's concern. Indian Town Hall, 5th, White Mountain Apache Reservation, 1977. Report on proceedings of the 5th Annual Indian Town Hall on the the [sic] topic of tribal water rights, today's concern . [Phoenix] [1978] v leaves, 78 p. : LC Card 78-622727 DDC 333.33/9 19
KFA2905.6.W38 I5 1977

Tribelhorn, R. E. Low-cost extrusion cookers . [Fort Collins, Colo., 1979] vii, 288 p. : LC Card 80-601551 DDC 664/.02 19
TP373 .L68

TRIBES AND TRIBAL SYSTEM - MADAGASCAR - MAPS.
United States. Central Intelligence Agency. Madagascar. [Washington, 1973] col. map 48 x 33 cm. Scale 1:3,465,000. Relief shown by shading and spot heights. "501245." Includes location map, comparative area map, and maps of "Population," "Tribal groups," "Economic activity," and "Vegetation." LC Card 75-690371
G8460 1973 .U51

NYPL [Map Div. 81-3036]

TRIBES AND TRIBAL SYSTEM - OMAN - MAPS.
United States. Central Intelligence Agency. Oman tribes. [Washington, 1980] 1 map : LC Card 81-692532
G7561.E1 1980 .U5

TRIBES AND TRIBAL SYSTEM - PAKISTAN - MAPS.
United States. Central Intelligence Agency. Pakistan major ethnic groups. [Washington, 1980] 1 map : LC Card 81-692533
G7641.E1 1980 .U5

Triborough Bridge and Tunnel Authority. (Old Catalog form: New York (City). Triborough Bridge and Tunnel Authority.) Triborough Bridge and Tunnel Authority facilities. New York: The Authority, 1973. 25 p.: ill., maps; 23 cm. Cover title.

1. New York (City) - Bridges. 2. Tunnels - New York (City). I. Title. **NYPL [JSE 80-724]**

Triborough Bridge and Tunnel Authority facilities. Triborough Bridge and Tunnel Authority. New York, 1973. 25 p.:
NYPL [JSE 80-724]

Tributary area development. Tennessee Valley Authority. Knoxville. **NYPL [JLM 80-931]**

Tributary flooding map, Kansas /. United States. Soil Conservation Service. Lincoln, Nebr. , 1979. 1 map : LC Card 81-691131
G4201.C32 1979 .U5

Tribute to Picasso . Organization of American States. General Secretariat. [Washington , 1973] [33] p. : LC Card 75-328387
ND202 .O73 1973

TRICHLOROETHYLENE - ENVIRONMENTAL ASPECTS - CALIFORNIA.
California. Legislature. Assembly. Ad Hoc Committee on Water Contamination. Transcript (investigation into TCE) . Sacramento, CA [1980] 2, 188 p. : LC Card 80-623094 DDC 363.7/394 19
TD427.T75 C34 1980

TRICHLOROPHENOXYACETIC ACID.
(1979) United States. General Accounting Office. U. S. ground troops in South Vietnam were in areas sprayed with herbicide orange . [Washington, D.C.] , 1979. 9, 12 p. : LC Card 79-604309 DDC 363.1/79 19
DS559.8.C5 U54 1979

TRICHLOROPHENOXYACETIC ACID - TOXICOLOGY.
United States. Congress. House. Committee on Interstate and Foreign Commerce. Subcommittee on Oversight and Investigations. Involuntary exposure to agent orange and other toxic spraying . Washington , 1980. iv, 256 p. : LC Card 80-602744 DDC 363.1/79 19
KF27 .I5547 1979r

United States. Congress. House. Committee on Veterans' Affairs. Subcommittee on Medical Facilities and Benefits. Oversight hearing to receive testimony on Agent Orange . Washington , 1980. iii, 121 p. ; LC Card 80-602984 DDC 363.7/384 19
KF27 .V459 1980

TRICHOLOMATACEAE.
Weaver, Margaret G. Mushroom flora of Minnesota--a contribution /. Minneapolis, Minn. [1980] 89 p. : LC Card 80-623787 DDC 589.2/2209776 19
QK629.T73 W4

TRICKLE IRRIGATION - NEW MEXICO - MESILLA VALLEY.
Wierenga, Petrus Johannes. Soil salinity and cotton yields as affected by surface and trickle irrigation . Las Cruces, N.M. [1979] vi, 212 p. : LC Card 80-622502 DDC 333.91/009789 s 631.4/16 19
GB705.N6 N64 no. 106 S616.U6

TRIDENT (WEAPONS SYSTEMS)
Davison, Richard H. The U. S. sea-based strategic force . [Washington, D.C.] [1980] xx, 62 p. : LC Card 80-601190 DDC 359.8/3 19
V993 .D38

United States. Congress. House. Committee on Armed Services. Subcommittee on Seapower and Strategic and Critical Materials. Reprograming action--Trident submarine . Washington , 1980. ii, 48 p. ; LC Card 80-603992 DDC 359.3/257/0973 19
KF27 .A769 1980

TRIFA, VALERIEN D. BP., 1914-
United States. Congress. House. Committee on Foreign Affairs. Subcommittee on International Operations. Allegations concerning the Romanian service of Radio Free Europe . Washington , 1980. iii, 98 p. ; LC Card 80-602459 DDC 384.54/43 19
KF27 .F647 1980

TRIGONIIDAE.
Saul, Louella Rankin. The North Pacific cretaceous Trigoniid genus Yaadia /. Berkeley , 1978. 65 p., 12 leaves of plates : ISBN 0-520-09582-0 LC Card 77-84990 DDC 564/.11 19
QE812.T74 S28

Trimble, Stanley Wayne. Soil conservation, erosion, and sedimentation, Coon Creek Basin, Wisconsin / by Stanley W. Trimble and Steven W. Lund. Reston, Va. : U. S. Geological Survey, [1981] p. cm. (Geological Survey professional paper . 1234) Bibliography: p. LC Card 81-607057 DDC 631.4/5/0977554 19
1. Soil conservation - Wisconsin - Coon Creek watershed (Monroe County-Vernon County). 2. Soil erosion - Wisconsin - Coon Creek watershed (Monroe County-Vernon County). 3. Reservoir sedimentation - Wisconsin - Coon Creek watershed (Monroe County-Vernon County). 4. Coon Creek watershed (Monroe County-Vernon County, Wis.). I. Lund, Steven W. II. United States. Geological Survey. III. Title. IV. Series.
S624.W5 T74

TRINIDAD AND TOBAGO - COMMERCE.
Smith, Bryant D. The impact of trade policy on exports in oil rich countries . Washington , 1975. ix, 136 p. : LC Card 80-469796
HF3436.5 .S63

TRINIDAD AND TOBAGO - COMMERCIAL POLICY.
Smith, Bryant D. The impact of trade policy on exports in oil rich countries . Washington , 1975. ix, 136 p. : LC Card 80-469796
HF3436.5 .S63

Trinity Basin. Texas. Dept. of Water Resources. Projected land use maps year 2000, Trinity Basin. Austin, Tex. , 1978. [11] leaves : LC Card 80-675302 DDC 912/.133373/309764 19
G1372.T8G4 T4 1978

Trinity River Authority of Texas. Planning and Environmental Management Division. Low flow nutrient loss in the mid-Trinity River ; Runoff-related pollutant loadings in the mid-Trinity River / [prepared under contract no. PG 75-36 for the Texas Water Quality Board, Austin, Texas, by the Planning and Environmental Management Division of the Trinity River Authority of Texas]. [Austin] : Texas Dept. of Water Resources, 1978. iii, 72, iv, 73 p. : ill. ; 28 cm. Cover title. "LP-15." Includes bibliographies. LC Card 80-622543 DDC 363.7/3942/097642 19
1. Water quality - Texas - Trinity River watershed. 2. Stream measurements - Texas - Trinity River watershed. 3. Runoff - Environmental aspects - Texas - Trinity River watershed. 4. Phosphorus - Environmental aspects - Texas - Trinity River watershed. 5. Nitrogen - Environmental aspects - Texas - Trinity River watershed. I. Texas. Water Quality Board. II. Title. III. Title: Runoff-related pollutant loadings in the mid-Trinity River.
TD224.T4 T74 1978

Trinity River Basin Fish and Wildlife Task Force. California. Dept. of Water Resources. Northern District. Main stem Trinity River watershed erosion investigation /. [Sacramento] [1980] vii, 35, [12] p. : LC Card 80-623096 DDC 551.3/52/097942 19
QE581 .C29 1980

TRIPLETT, ARLENE A.
United States. Congress. Senate. Committee on Commerce, Science, and Transportation. Nominations--assistant secretaries of commerce . Washington , 1981. iii, 4 p. ; LC Card 81-602035 DDC 353.82 19
KF26 .C69 1981h

Tri-Regional Workshop for Social Workers in Maternal and Child Health Services (1980 : Raleigh, N.C.) Social work in a state-based system of child health care : based on the proceedings of the 1980 Tri-Regional Workshop for Social Workers in Maternal and Child Health Services / sponsored by the Department of Maternal and Child Health, School of Public Health, University of North Carolina at Chapel Hill and the Office for Maternal and Child Health, Bureau of Community Health Services, Department of Health and Human Services ; edited, Elizabeth L. Watkins. Chapel Hill : Dept. of Maternal and Child Health, School of Public Health, University of North Carolina at Chapel Hill, [1981?] v, 156 p. : ill., forms ; 23 cm. Includes bibliographical references. LC Card 81-50559 DDC 362.1/0892/000973 19
1. Community health services for children - United States - Congresses. 2. Medicine, State - United States - Congresses. 3. Social work with children - United States - Congresses. 4. Medical social work - Congresses. I. Watkins, Elizabeth L. II. University of

North Carolina at Chapel Hill. Dept. of Maternal and Child Health. III. United States. Office for Maternal and Child Health. IV. Title.
RJ102 .T74 1980

Tri-State Regional Planning Commission. People, dwellings & neighborhoods : the housing element of the regional comprehensive plan. New York : Tri-State Regional Planning Commission, 1978. x, 45 p. : ill. ; 28 cm. Edition for 1973 published under title: Dwellings and neighborhoods. LC Card 79-620473
1. Housing policy - New York metropolitan area. I. Title.
HD7304.N5 T73 1978 **NYPL [JLF 80-1583]**

Tri-State Transportation Commission. Planning Division. Public acquisition costs of recreation land to the year 2000 /. New York , 1968. 23 p. ; **NYPL [*ZT-1244]**

Triwedi, Mitchell D. Bermúdez, Jéronimo, 16th cent. Primeras tragedias españolas /. [Chapel Hill] , Madrid, España , 1975. 223 p. ; ISBN 84-7039-219-0 (Editorial Castalia) LC Card 80-123086 DDC 862/.3 19
PQ6279.B47 P7 1975

TROLLING (FISHING) - STATISTICS.
Miller, Marc C. Trends in catch timing and distribution of the Washington commercial troll salmon fishery, 1960-1975 /. [Olympia, Wash.] , 1979. iii, 56 p. : LC Card 80-620830 DDC 338.3/72755 19
SH222.W2 M54

TRONA INDUSTRY - WYOMING - EMPLOYEES - SUPPLY AND DEMAND.
Wyoming. Dept. of Labor and Statistics. Wyoming bentonite & trona industries . [Cheyenne, Wyo.] 1980. iii, 59 p. : LC Card 80-623151 DDC 338.2/761 19
HD4966.B452 U69 1980

TROPICAL AGRICULTURE. see TROPICAL CROPS.

TROPICAL CROPS - BIBLIOGRAPHY.
A Selected bibliography of Centrosema, Desmodium, Stylosanthes and other tropical and subtropical pasture legumes [microform] /. Honolulu , 1981. p. cm. LC Card 81-2533 DDC 016.6333 19
Z5074 .L3 SB203.3.T76

TROPICAL RAIN FOREST ECOLOGY. see RAIN FOREST ECOLOGY.

Tropical timbers of the world /. Chudnoff, Martin. Madison, Wis. [1980] iv, 826 p. ; LC Card 80-602127 DDC 674/.13/0913 19
SD434 .C48

TROPIDODRYAS SERRA - CLASSIFICATION.
Thomas, Robert A. A new systematic arrangement for Philodryas serra (Schlegel) and Philodryas pseudoserra Amaral (Serpentes : Colubridae) /. Austin , 1977. 20 p. : LC Card 78-621007 DDC 574 s 597.96 19
AM101 .T474 no. 27 QL666.O636

TROPIDODRYAS STRIATICEPS - CLASSIFICATION.
Thomas, Robert A. A new systematic arrangement for Philodryas serra (Schlegel) and Philodryas pseudoserra Amaral (Serpentes : Colubridae) /. Austin , 1977. 20 p. : LC Card 78-621007 DDC 574 s 597.96 19
AM101 .T474 no. 27 QL666.O636

Trotta, Lee C. (joint author) Harr, C. Albert. Ground-water resources and geology of Columbia County, Wisconsin /. Madison, Wis. , 1978. vii, 30 p. : LC Card 80-623464 DDC 557.75 s 553.7/9/0977581 19
QE179 .A33 no. 37 GB1025.W6

Trotter, Robert T. Curanderismo, Mexican American folk healing / Robert T. Trotter II and Juan Antonio Chavira. Athens : University of Georgia Press, c1981. p. cm. Includes index. ISBN 0-8203-0556-1 LC Card 81-602 DDC 398/.353 19
1. Mexican American folk medicine. 2. Healing (in religion, folk-lore, etc.) - United States. I. Chavira, Juan Antonio. II. Title.
GR111.M49 T76

Trousdale, Marion, 1929- Shakespeare and the rhetoricians / by Marion Trousdale. Chapel Hill : University of North Carolina Press, c1981. p. cm. Includes bibliographical references and index. ISBN 0-8078-1482-2 LC Card 81-40703

DDC 822.3/3 19
1. Shakespeare, William, 1564-1616 - Criticism and interpretation. 2. Shakespeare, William, 1564-1616 - Aesthetics. 3. Rhetoric - 1500-1800. I. Title.
PR2976 .T77

TROUT.
Willers, W. B., 1938- Trout biology, an angler's guide /. Madison , 1981. p. cm. ISBN
0-299-08720-4 : LC Card 81-50829 DDC
597/.55 19
QL638.S2 W55

Trout biology, an angler's guide /. Willers, W. B., 1938- Madison , 1981. p. cm. ISBN
0-299-08720-4 : LC Card 81-50829 DDC
597/.55 19
QL638.S2 W55

TROUT FISHING.
Willers, W. B., 1938- Trout biology, an angler's guide /. Madison , 1981. p. cm. ISBN
0-299-08720-4 : LC Card 81-50829 DDC
597/.55 19
QL638.S2 W55

TROUT FISHING - KENTUCKY - CUMBERLAND, LAKE.
Axon, James R. Evaluation of the "two story" trout fishery in Lake Cumberland /. [Frankfort] , 1974. 69 p. : LC Card 76-624539
DDC 639/.2 s 333.95/6 19
SH222.K4 A3 no. 60 QL638.S2

TROUT - MORTALITY.
Nolting, Donald H. Electric fish screen efficiency, Willow Creek Reservoir /. Denver , 1962. iv, 24 p. : LC Card 81-464857 DDC
639.9/7755 19
SH157.85.F54 N64

Troutman, David E. Peters, Norman E. Temporal trends in the acidity of precipitation and surface waters of New York /. Reston, Va. , 1981. p. cm. LC Card 81-607082 DDC 551.57/09747 19
GB2825.N7 P47

Troutman, Frank H. Arkansas gross state product, selected years 1960-77 / Frank H. Troutman and Sarah G. Breshears. Little Rock, Ark. : Industrial Research and Extension Center, University of Arkansas, 1979. vi, 12 p. ; 28 cm. (Publication - Industrial Research and Extension Center, University of Arkansas ; 1979) Chiefly tables. Includes bibliographical references. LC Card 80-622211 DDC 338.09767 s 339.3767 19
1. Gross national product - Arkansas. I. Breshears, Sarah G., joint author. II. Series: Arkansas. University. Industrial Research and Extension Center. Publication , 1979. III. Title.
HC107.A8 A66 1979 HC107.A83I5

Troy, Richard E. California State park system plan, 1980 : an element of the California outdoor recreation resources plan / [prepared by Richard E. Troy, Randall D. Treece, Harold E. Hallett, Jr. ; with contributions from W. James Barry ... et al.]. Sacramento, Calif. : State of California, Resources Agency, Dept. of Parks and Recreation, [1980] viii, 239 p. : ill. ; 28 cm. "March 1980." Bibliography: p. 223-225. LC Card 80-622915 DDC 333.78/3/09794 19
1. Outdoor recreation - California - Planning. 2. Parks - California - Planning. I. Treece, Randall D., joint author. II. Hallett, Harold E., joint author. III. California. Dept. of Parks and Recreation. IV. Title.
GV191.42.C2 T76

Truaxton, Truago, Trenton. [Trenton, Mich. : Bicentennial Book Committee, 1976] vi, 194 p. : ill., maps, ports. ; 26 cm. Maps on lining papers. Includes index. LC Card 81-144056 DDC 977.4/33 19
1. Trenton (Mich.) - History - Pictorial works. 2. Trenton (Mich.) - Description - Views. I. Trenton (Mich.). Bicentennial Book Committee.
F574.T83 T78

Trubow, George B. Privacy and security of criminal history information : an analysis of privacy issues / [prepared by George B. Trubow]. [Washington] : National Criminal Justice Information and Statistics Service, Law Enforcement Assistnace Administration, U. S. Dept. of Justice : for sale by the Supt. of Docs., U. S. Govt. Print. Off., 1978. 73 p. ; 28 cm. Includes bibliographical references. LC Card 79-602370 DDC 342.73/0858 347.302858 19
1. Criminal registers - United States. 2. Privacy, Right of - United States. I. Title.
KF9751 .T78

Truby, Roy. Murray, Charles Robert, 1932- The West Virginia dropout study, 1978-1979 /. Charleston, W. Va. [1979] ii leaves, 30 p. : LC Card 80-622735 DDC 371.2/913/09754 19
LC144.W4 M87

Truck drivers . Waller, Patricia F., 1932- Chapel Hill, N.C. , Springfield, Va. [1979] xxvi, 222 p. : LC Card 80-622449 DDC 353.0087/8324 19
HE5614.2 .W34

TRUCK DRIVERS - LICENSES - UNITED STATES.
Waller, Patricia F., 1932- Truck drivers . Chapel Hill, N.C. , Springfield, Va. [1979] xxvi, 222 p. : LC Card 80-622449 DDC 353.0087/8324 19
HE5614.2 .W34

Truck-top markings for visual identification.
United States. Dept. of Transportation. Office of the Secretary. Washington, 1973. v, 70 p.
NYPL [JSE 81-6]

TRUCK TRAILERS. see MOTOR-TRUCKS - TRAILERS.

TRUCKS, AUTOMOBILE. see MOTOR-TRUCKS.

TRUCKS - LAW AND LEGISLATION - UNITED STATES.
National Research Council. Transportation Research Board. Motor vehicle size and weight regulations, enforcement, and permit operations. Washington, D.C. [1980] 45 p. ISBN
0-390-03019-6 (pbk.) : LC Card 80-66742
DDC 629.2/24 19
TL230 .N27 1980

TRUCKS - UNITED STATES - WEIGHT.
National Research Council. Transportation Research Board. Motor vehicle size and weight regulations, enforcement, and permit operations. Washington, D.C. [1980] 45 p. ISBN
0-390-03019-6 (pbk.) : LC Card 80-66742
DDC 629.2/24 19
TL230 .N27 1980

TRUCKS - WASHINGTON (STATE) - ACCIDENTS.
Washington (State) Utilities and Transportation Commission. Summary and analysis, heavy truck-hazardous material accidents. Olympia, Wash. [1979] [13], 34 p. ; LC Card 80-621084
DDC 363.1/259 19
HE5614.3.W2 W394 1979

Truesdale, John C., 1921- The NLRB and arbitration : recent developments / by John C. Truesdale, before New England Regional Arbitration Conference, Murray D. Lincoln Campus Center, University of Massachusetts at Amherst, Thursday, April 19, 1979 ; sponsored by Labor Relations & Research Center, University of Massachusetts, Amherst, School of Business Administration, University of Massachusetts, Amherst, and American Arbitration Association. Amherst : Labor Relations & Research Center, 1979. 18 p. ; 23 cm. Includes bibliographical references. LC Card 80-624267 DDC 344.73/0189143 347.304189143 19
1. United States. National Labor Relations Board. 2. Arbitration, Industrial - United States. I. Title.
KF3372.Z9 T78

TRUESDALE, JOHN C., 1921-
United States. Congress. Senate. Committee on Labor and Human Resources. Nomination . Washington , 1980. iv, 452 p. ; LC Card 80-603891 DDC 353.0083/2 19
KF26 .L27 1980j

TRUST COMPANIES - LOUISIANA.
Louisiana. Laws, statutes, etc. Supplement to Laws of the State of Louisiana relating to banks and trust companies, and building and loan or homestead associations /. New Orleans , 1927. 56 p. ; LC Card 81-452406 DDC
346.763/082/02632 19
KFL165 .A3 1917 Suppl.

TRUST COMPANIES - MARYLAND.
Maryland. Laws, statutes, etc. Laws relating to State banks, trust companies, and savings institutions in force in the State of Maryland /. [Baltimore] 1916. 42 p. ; LC Card 78-109967
DDC 346.752/082/02632 19
KFM1365 .A3 1916

TRUST COMPANIES - MICHIGAN - STATISTICS - PERIODICALS.

Michigan. Financial Institutions Bureau Bank and Trust Division. Annual report. 1977- [Lansing] LC Card 79-640084
NYPL [JLM 80-762]

Trust Territory of the Pacific Islands. United States. Geological Survey. [Washington] 1975. col. map 64 x 128 cm. Scale 1:4,000,000. Depths shown by gradient tints. "Lambert conformal conic projection based on standard parallels 6° and 30°." "Compiled and edited for the Trust Territory of the Pacific Islands by the U. S. Geological Survey from charts compiled by the U. S. Air Force, U. S. Army, and various other sources to 1973." Includes location map. Insets: Yap Islands.--Rota.--Saipan and Tinian.--Truk Islands.--Palau Islands.--Kwajalein Atoll.--Ponape Islands.--Majuro and Arno Atolls. LC Card 78-691550
G9405 1973 .U5

Truth in testing act of 1979, the Educational testing act of 1979 . United States. Congress. House. Committee on Education and Labor. Subcommittee on Elementary, Secondary, and Vocational Education. Washington , 1980. viii, 1194 p. : LC Card 80-601862 DDC 344.73/07 19
KF27 .E3364 1979r

Tsai, Che C. (joint author) Torres-Anjel, Manuel J. Enterotoxigenic Clostridium perfringens type A in selected humans . Washington , 1977. 32 p. : LC Card 78-102859 DDC 362.1/09181/2 s 615.9/52995 19
RA10 .P252 no. 350 QR201.C54

Tsang, C. Steve. Procedure employed to determine use-vaue of agricultural land in Virginia with estimate use-values for 57 jurisdictions authorizing use-value taxation for the tax-year 1979 / prepared by C. Steve Tsang, David B. Hull, and J. Paxton Marshall. Richmond, Va. : State Land Evaluation Advisory Committee, [197-] vii, 53, [12] p. ; 28 cm. Cover title: Procedures for determining ranges of use-values for agriculture, horticulture, forest, and open space land in Virginia with 1979 suggested use-values. "September 1978." LC Card 80-621172 DDC 336.22/2 19
1. Land value taxation - Virginia. I. Hull, David B., joint author. II. Marshall, James Paxton, joint author. III. Title. IV. Title: Procedures for determining ranges of use-values for agriculture, horticulture, forest, and open space land in Virginia with 1979 suggested use-values.
HJ4277 .T75

Tsuba, and Japanese sword fittings in the collection of the Cooper-Hewitt Museum, the Smithsonian Institution's National Museum of Design. Cooper-Hewitt Museum of Decorative Arts and Design. [New York, NY] , c1980. [36] p. : LC Card 80-67169 DDC 739.7/22 19
NK6784.A1 C66 1980

TUBAC, ARIZ. PRESIDIO.
Shenk, Lynette O. Excavations at the Tubac Presidio /. [Tucson] , 1975. xii, 234 p. : LC Card 80-621272 DDC 979.1/79 19
F819.T88 S5

TUBAL STERILIZATION - UNITED STATES - STATISTICS.
Center for Disease Control. Family Planning Evaluation Division. Surgical sterilization surveillance . Atlanta, Ga. [1979] 22 p. ; LC Card 79-600096 DDC 363.9/7/0973 19
RG138 .C46 1979

Tubbs, Carl H. The influence of light, moisture, and seedbed on yellow birch regeneration / Carl H. Tubbs. St. Paul : North Central Forest Experiment Station, U. S. Dept. of Agriculture, Forest Service, 1969. 12 p. : ill. ; 27 cm. (Research paper NC ; 27) Cover title. Bibliography: p. 11-12. LC Card 71-603400 DDC 634.9/0977 s 634.9/726 19
1. Yellow birch. 2. Forest site quality. 3. Forest reproduction. I. Series: United States. North Central Forest Experiment Station, St. Paul. USDA Forest Service research paper NC , 27. II. Title.
SD11 .A45476 no. 27 SD397.Y44

TUBE WELL. see WELLS.

Tuberculosis control program. Massachusetts. Division of Sanatoria and Tuberculosis. Boston [1978?] ca. 100 leaves : LC Card 79-623478 DDC 362.1/96995009744 19
RC309.M4 M37 1978

TUBERCULOSIS - HOSPITALS - MASSACHUSETTS - DIRECTORIES.

Massachusetts. Division of Sanatoria and Tuberculosis. Tuberculosis control program. Boston [1978?] ca. 100 leaves : LC Card 79-623478 DDC 362.1/96995009744 19
RC309.M4 M37 1978

TUBERCULOSIS - MASSACHUSETTS - STATISTICS.

Massachusetts. Division of Sanatoria and Tuberculosis. Tuberculosis control program. Boston [1978?] ca. 100 leaves : LC Card 79-623478 DDC 362.1/96995009744 19
RC309.M4 M37 1978

TUBERCULOSIS - NEW YORK (CITY) - STATISTICS - PERIODICALS.

New York (City). Dept. of Health. Births and infant mortality, tuberculosis cases and deaths. 1932-33. New York. 2 v.
*NYPL [*ZAN-T5294]*

TUBERCULOSIS - UNITED STATES - PREVENTION - PERIODICALS.

Tuberculosis statistics; states & cities. Atlanta.
NYPL [JLM 80-839]

TUBERCULOSIS - UNITED STATES - STATISTICS - PERIODICALS.

Tuberculosis statistics; states & cities. Atlanta.
NYPL [JLM 80-839]

Tuck, Bradford H. (joint author) Henoch, Susan. Taxation and land use planning /. Anchorage, Alaska [1979] 19 p. ; LC Card 79-625096 DDC 336.22/09798 19
HD211.A4 H46

A review of electric power demand forecasts and suggestions for improving future forecasts / prepared by Bradford H. Tuck for the House Power Alternatives Study Committee, Alaska State Legislature. [Juneau, Alaska] : The Committee, [1980] 73 p. ; 28 cm. "May, 1980." Bibliography: p. 68. LC Card 81-621101 DDC 333.79/3213 19
1. Electric power consumption - Alaska - Forecasting. I. Alaska. Legislature. House of Representatives. Power Alternatives Study Committee. II. Title.
HD9685.U6 A477

Tucker, Cynthia Grant. Kate Freeman Clark : a painter rediscovered / by Cynthia Grant Tucker. Jackson, MS : University Press of Mississippi, [1981] p. cm. Published in conjunction with a travelling exhibition, held at the Brooks Memorial Art Gallery, Memphis, the Parrish Art Museum, Southampton, N.Y., and the Mississippi State Historical Museum, Jackson. Bibliography: p. ISBN 0-87805-136-8 LC Card 81-4516 DDC 759.13 B 19
1. Clark, Kate Freeman. 2. Painters - Mississippi - Biography.
ND237.C555 T8

Tucker, Jane C. New serial holdings, 1977 / Jane C. Tucker, chief editor. [Washington] : U. S. Dept. of Commerce, National Bureau of Standards ; [Springfield, Va. : order from National Technical Information Service], 1977. vi, 232 p. ; 28 cm. (United States. National Bureau of Standards. NBSIR. 77-1215) Cover title: NBS serial holdings, 1977. LC Card 77-602720
1. Science - Periodicals - Bibliography - Catalogs. 2. Technology - Periodicals - Bibliography - Catalogs. 3. United States. National Bureau of Standards. Library - Catalogs. I. United States. National Bureau of Standards. II. Title. III. Title: NBS serial holdings, 1977.
Z7403 .T79 Q158.5 **NYPL [JSF 81-153]**

Tucker, Mary Louise. Louisiana State Museum, New Orleans. The Louisiana Portrait Gallery /. New Orleans , c1979- v. <1> : LC Card 80-624103 DDC 704.9/42/074016335 19
N7593.8.L8 L68 1979

Tucker, Richard L. (joint author) Yokel, Felix Y. Soil classification for construction practice in shallow trenching /. Washington, D.C. [1980] xiv, 76 p. : LC Card 80-600014 DDC 690/.02/18 s 624.1/51/012 19
TA435 .U58 no. 121 TA710

Tucker, William Jacob, 1926- An intensive survey of Illinois River and its tributaries : a comparison study of 1967 and 1978 stream conditions / prepared by William J. Tucker,; in cooperation with Field Operations Section staff. [Springfield] : Illinois Environmental Protection Agency, Division of Water Pollution Control, State of Illinois, [1979?] v, 158 p., [6] leaves of plates : ill. ; 28 cm. Chiefly tables. Bibliography: p.

158. LC Card 80-622577 DDC 363.7/3942/097735 19
1. Water quality - Illinois - Illinois River watershed. I. Illinois. Division of Water Pollution Control. Field Operations Section. II. Title.
TD224.I3 T83

Tuckermanty, Elizabeth. Normal diet, adolescent / Elizabeth Tuckermanty, Charlette R. Gallagher-Allred. Columbus, Ohio (456 Clinic Dr., Columbus 43210) : Dept. of Family Medicine, College of Medicine, Ohio State University, c1980. 31 p. : ill. ; 27 cm. (Nutrition in primary care . 6) Bibliography: p. 20-21. LC Card 81-620941 DDC 613.2/088055 19
1. Youth - Nutrition. I. Gallagher-Allred, Charlette R. II. Title. III. Series.
RJ235 .T83

Normal diet, age of parental control / Elizabeth Tuckermanty, Charlette R. Gallagher-Allred. Columbus, Ohio (456 Clinic Dr., Columbus 43210) : Dept. of Family Medicine, College of Medicine, Ohio State University, c1980. 31 p. : ill. ; 27 cm. (Nutrition in primary care . 5) Bibliography: p. 19-20. LC Card 81-620940 DDC 613.2/6 19
1. Children - Nutrition. I. Gallagher-Allred, Charlette R. II. Title. III. Series.
RJ206 .T83

Tueller, Paul T., 1934- Food habits and nutrition of mule deer on Nevada ranges / Paul T. Tueller. Reno : Agricultural Experiment Station, Max C. Fleischmann College of Agriculture, University of Nevada, [1979] vi, 104 p. : graphs ; 28 cm. "Final report, Federal aid in wildlife restoration project W-48-5, study 1, job 2, July 1979." "R128." Bibliography: p. 84-88. LC Card 79-625750 DDC 599.73/57 19
1. Mule deer - Food. 2. Mammals - Food. 3. Mammals - Nevada - Food. I. Title.
QL737.U55 T83

Tufts, Henry H. The development and organization of the U. S. Army Criminal Investigation Command, 1969-1974 / by Henry H. Tufts. [Falls Church, Va.] : The Command, [1979?] 68 leaves ; 29 cm. LC Card 80-600759 DDC 355.1/3323/0973 19
1. United States. Army Criminal Investigation Command. I. Title.
UB783 .T83

TUGALOO VALLEY, GA. - HISTORY.

Bouwman, Robert Eldridge. Traveler's Rest and the Tugaloo crossroads /. [Atlanta] , c1980. xv, 306 p., [12] leaves of plates : LC Card 80-622189 DDC 975.8/132 19
F294.T73 B68

Tuislande, South Africa. see Homelands, South Africa.

Tuition assistance program receivables and payables of the City University of New York, fiscal year ended June 30, 1978 /. New York (State). Division of Audits and Accounts. Albany [1980] 3, 24 leaves ; LC Card 80-622250 DDC 379.1/22/097471 19
LD3835 .N49 1980

TULSA, OKLA. - HISTORY.

Council on Affirmative Marketing. Affirmative marketing plan for fair and open housing /. [Tulsa] [1978] 17 leaves ;
*NYPL [*XME-9204]*

Tulsa, Okla. Mayor. Council on Affirmative Marketing. Affirmative marketing plan for fair and open housing /. [Tulsa] [1978] 17 leaves ;
*NYPL [*XME-9204]*

TULSA (OKLA.) - RACE RELATIONS.

Ellsworth, Scott. Death in a promised land . Baton Rouge , c1981. p. cm. ISBN 0-8071-0878-2 : LC Card 81-6017 DDC 976.6/86 19
F704.T92 E44

TULSA, OKLA. - RIOT, 1921.

Ellsworth, Scott. Death in a promised land . Baton Rouge , c1981. p. cm. ISBN 0-8071-0878-2 : LC Card 81-6017 DDC 976.6/86 19
F704.T92 E44

Tulsa race riot of 1921. Ellsworth, Scott. Death in a promised land . Baton Rouge , c1981. p. cm. ISBN 0-8071-0878-2 : LC Card 81-6017 DDC 976.6/86 19
F704.T92 E44

Tuma, Steven L. Illinois Institute of Natural Resources. Illinois State plan, energy conservation in institutions . [Springfield, Ill.] [Springfield, Ill.] , 1979 or 1980] ii, 76 p. : LC Card 80-622576 DDC 333.79 19
TJ163.5.B84 I43 1979

TUMORIGENESIS. see CARCINOGENESIS.

Tumors of the ovary and maldeveloped gonads /. Scully, Robert E. Washington, D.C. , 1979. 413 p. : LC Card 80-602599 DDC 616.99/2 s 616.99/465 19
RD651 .A8 fasc. 16 RC280.O8

TUMORS, RADIATION-INDUCED.

United States. General Accounting Office. Problems in assessing the cancer risks of low-level ionizing radiation exposure . Washington, D.C. , 1981. 2 v. : LC Card 81-600890 DDC 616.99/4071 19
RC268.55 .U54 1981

TUNA FISHERIES - LAW AND LEGISLATION - ATLANTIC OCEAN.

United States. Congress. House. Committee on Merchant Marine and Fisheries. Subcommittee on Fisheries and Wildlife Conservation and the Environment. Atlantic tuna . Washington , 1980. iv, 184 p. : LC Card 80-603672 DDC 353.0072/236822362 19
KF27 .M447 1980

TUNA FISHERIES - LAW AND LEGISLATION - UNITED STATES.

United States. Congress. House. Committee on Merchant Marine and Fisheries. Subcommittee on Fisheries and Wildlife Conservation and the Environment. Atlantic tuna . Washington , 1980. iv, 184 p. : LC Card 80-603672 DDC 353.0072/236822362 19
KF27 .M447 1980

Tung, Yeou-Koung. Optimal risk-based design of hydraulic structures : final report / by Yeou-Koung Tung and Larry W. Mays. Austin, Tex. : Center for Research in Water Resources, Bureau of Engineering Research, Dept. of Civil Engineering, College of Engineering, University of Texas at Austin, [1980] xix, 396 p. : ill. ; 28 cm. (CRWR . 171) Cover title: Optimal risk-based design of water resource engineering projects. "August 1980." Bibliography: p. 250-255. "National Science Foundation research grant initiation grant ENG 78-05449." LC Card 80-624307 DDC 627 19
1. Hydraulic engineering. 2. Engineering economy. I. Mays, Larry W. II. Title. III. Title: Optimal risk-based design of water resource engineering projects. IV. Series.
TC153 .T86

Tunis, Edwin, 1897- An historical and literary map of the old line state of Maryland showing forth divers curious and notable facts relating to scenes, incidents and persons worthy to be recalled on the state's three hundredth anniversary. Baltimore, Enoch Pratt Free Library, 1931, c1975. col. map 46 x 62 cm. Scale ca. 1:750,000. Puzzle map. Title at margin: Maryland: A historical and literary map designed and drawn by Edwin Tunis, produced as a jigsaw puzzle for the bicentennial year by the Enoch Pratt Free Library of Baltimore. Includes inset of Annapolis, Portrait of Cecil Calvert and 13 col. illus. 551 pieces in box, 32 x 42 x 4 cm. Box title: A historical and literary map of Maryland.
1. Maryland - Maps. 2. Maryland - History - Maps. 3. Maryland - Maps, Pictorial. I. Enoch Pratt Free Library, Baltimore. II. Title.
NYPL [Map Div. 81-3042]

TUNNELING.

(1974) United States. Geological Survey. Summary of geologic and hydrologic information pertinent to tunneling in selected urban areas/. Washington, 1974. [370] p.:
NYPL [JSF 81-3]

Tunnell, Curtis D. Lynn, Warren M. Cultural resource survey of Choke Canyon Reservoir, Live Oak and McMullen Counties, Texas /. Austin , 1977. xiv, 273 p. : LC Card 78-622852 DDC 976.4/447 19
F392.F92 L96

TUNNELS - NEW YORK (CITY)

Triborough Bridge and Tunnel Authority. Triborough Bridge and Tunnel Authority facilities. New York, 1973. 25 p.:
NYPL [JSE 80-724]

Tuohy, Donald R. Price, John A., 1933- The Washo Indians . [Carson City, Nev.] , c1980. vi, 82 p., [2] leaves of plates :   LC Card 80-623850   DDC 970.004/97 19
E99.W38 P74

Turbeville, Daniel E. The electric railway era in Northwest Washington, 1890-1930 / by Daniel E. Turbeville III. Bellingham, WA : Center for Pacific Northwest Studies, Western Washington University, 1978, c1979. xi, 199 p. : ill., maps ; 23 cm. (Occasional paper. #12) Originally presented as the author's thesis (M.A.--Western Washington University, 1976) Bibliography: p. 187-198.   LC Card 81-621749   DDC 388.4/6/097977 19
1. Street-railroads - Washington (State). I. Series: Occasional paper (Western Washington University. Center for Pacific Northwest Studies) , no. 12. II. Title.
TF724.W2 T87 1979

TURBIDITY.
California. Dept. of Water Resources. Northern District. South Fork Trinity River . [Sacramento] [1979] x, 83, 8 p. :   LC Card 80-621406   DDC 551.3/02 19
QE581 .C29 1979

TURBIDITY - MEASUREMENT.
Koertge, Henry Herman. The turbidity of public swimming pool waters /. Urbana , 1967. iv, 75 leaves :   LC Card 79-627486   DDC 363.7/292 19
RA606 .K57

The turbidity of public swimming pool waters /. Koertge, Henry Herman. Urbana , 1967. iv, 75 leaves :   LC Card 79-627486   DDC 363.7/292 19
RA606 .K57

TURBINE-POWERED TRANSPORTS. see JET TRANSPORTS.

TURBOJET TRANSPORTS. see JET TRANSPORTS.

TURBOLINERS. see JET TRANSPORTS.

TURE, NORMAN B.
United States. Congress. Senate. Committee on Finance. Nominations of Norman B. Ture and Beryl Wayne Sprinkel . Washington , 1981. iii, 17 p. ;   LC Card 81-601959   DDC 353.2 19
KF26 .F5 1981e

Turekian, Karl K. American-Soviet Symposium on Chemical Pollution of the Marine Environment, 1st, Odessa, 1977. First American-Soviet Symposium on Chemical Pollution of the Marine Environment, Odessa, USSR, May 24 to 28, 1977 /. Gulf Breeze, Fla. , Springfield, Va. , 1978. vi, 199 p. :   LC Card 79-603026   DDC 628.1/686162 19
GC1081 .A63 1977

TURKEY - FOREIGN ECONOMIC RELATIONS - GREECE - PERIODICALS.
Greek-Turkish Economic Cooperation Project. Report of the Executive Director. Washington .
NYPL [JLN 80-72]

TURKEY - FOREIGN ECONOMIC RELATIONS - UNITED STATES.
United States. Congress. House. Committee on Foreign Affairs. Subcommittee on Europe and the Middle East. United States-Turkey defense and economic cooperation agreement, 1980 . Washington , 1980. iii, 69 p. ;   LC Card 80-603044   DDC 327.730561 19
KF27 .F64214 1980a

TURKEY - FOREIGN RELATIONS - UNITED STATES.
United States. Congress. House. Committee on Foreign Affairs. Subcommittee on Europe and the Middle East. United States-Turkey defense and economic cooperation agreement, 1980 . Washington , 1980. iii, 69 p. ;   LC Card 80-603044   DDC 327.730561 19
KF27 .F64214 1980a

TURKEY - MANUFACTURES.
Wålstedt, Bertil. State manufacturing enterprise in a mixed economy . Baltimore , c1980. xxii, 354 p. :   ISBN 0-8018-2226-2 :   LC Card 78-21398
HD4276.7 .W34   *NYPL [JLE 81-426]*

TURKEY - STUDY AND TEACHING - COLORADO.
Mitchell, William A., 1940- The Republic of Turkey . United States Air Force Academy, Colo. [1981] p. cm.   LC Card 81-607896   DDC 956.1/0007/1178881 19
DR438.95.U6 M57

Turnbull, H. Rutherford.
Sawyer, Ann L. Procedures to be followed for

the placement of children with special needs in educational programs . Chapel Hill [1979] 58 p. ;   LC Card 81-621674   DDC 344.756/0791 347.5604791 19
KFN7795.9.H3 S28

Special education and "related services" for handicapped children / H. Rutherford Turnbull, III, Nell Barnes, and Bonnie Strickland. [Chapel Hill] : Institute of Govt., University of North Carolina at Chapel Hill, 1980. 25 p. ; 28 cm. Cover title. Includes bibliographical references.   LC Card 80-624006   DDC 371.9/09756 19
1. Handicapped children - Education (Preschool) - North Carolina. 2. Federal aid to handicapped services - North Carolina. 3. Federal aid to education - North Carolina. 4. Handicapped children - Education - Law and legislation - North Carolina. I. Barnes, Nell. II. Strickland, Bonnie B. III. Title.
LC4031 .T88

Turner, David Charles. Cambridge, Eng. Dept. of Architecture and Planning. Offices in Cambridge . [Cambridge] , 1976. 29 leaves in various pagings :   ISBN 0-902696-04-1   LC Card 81-458609   DDC 338.6/042/0942659 19
HT169.G72 C2932 1976

Turner, Decherd. Ory, Norma R. Bookbinding, a living art . Houston, Tex. , c1980. 48 p. :   ISBN 0-89090-004-3 (pbk.)   LC Card 80-83065   DDC 686.3/074064/1411 19
Z269 .O79

Turner, E. Winslow. United States. Congress. Senate. Committee on Governmental Affairs. Structure of corporate concentration . Washington , 1980 [i.e. 1981] 2 v. :   LC Card 81-601004   DDC 338.8/0973 19
HG4910 .U54 1981

TURNER, J. M. W. (JOSEPH MALLORD WILLIAM), 1775-1851.
Finley, Gerald. Landscapes of memory . Berkeley , c1980. 272 p. :   ISBN 0-520-04436-3   LC Card 80-5956   DDC 741.64/092/4 19
NC978.5.T87 F56 1982

Turner, James Harold, 1942- Improvement of the steady floating random walk Monte Carlo method near straight line and circular boundaries, with application to groundwater flow : a research project conducted by the Kansas Water Resources Research Institute at the University of Kansas / by James H. Turner, Louis C. Burmeister, Don W. Green. [Manhattan, Kan.] : The Institute, 1978, cover 1977. iv, 96 p. : ill. ; 28 cm. (Contribution / Kansas Water Resources Research Institute . no. 198) "Prepared for Office of Water Research and Technology, U. S. Department of Interior, Washington, D.C." Includes bibliographical references.   LC Card 79-624986   DDC 551.49/0724 19
1. Groundwater flow - Mathematical models. 2. Groundwater flow - Data processing. 3. Monte Carlo method. 4. Random walks (Mathematics). I. Burmeister, Louis C., joint author. II. Green, Don W., joint author. III. Kansas Water Resources Research Institute. IV. United States. Dept. of the Interior. Office of Water Research and Technology. V. Series: Kansas Water Resources Research Institute. Contribution , no. 198. VI. Title.
GB1197.7 .T87

Turner, Paul R., 1929- Bilingualism in the Southwest /. Tucson, Ariz. , c1981. p. cm.   ISBN 0-8165-0729-5 :   LC Card 81-1598   DDC 371.97/0979 19
LC3732.S59 B54 1981

Turner, Thomas Reed, 1941- Beware the people weeping : public opinion and the assassination of Abraham Lincoln / Thomas Reed Turner. Baton Rouge : Louisiana State University Press, c1982. p. cm. Includes index.   ISBN 0-8071-0986-X :   LC Card 81-14252   DDC 973.7/092/4 19
1. Lincoln, Abraham, 1809-1865 - Assassination - Public opinion. 2. Public opinion - United States. I. Title.
E457.5 .T96

The tutor and the writing student . Herman, Jerry, 1938- Berkeley, Calif. , c1979. iii, 22 p. ;   LC Card 80-155347   DDC 808/.042/071143 19
PE1404 .H4

TUTORS AND TUTORING - ADDRESSES, ESSAYS, LECTURES.
Herman, Jerry, 1938- The tutor and the writing student . Berkeley, Calif. , c1979. iii, 22 p. ;

LC Card 80-155347   DDC 808/.042/071143 19
PE1404 .H4

Tuttle, William M., 1937- Plain folk . Urbana , c1981. p. cm.   ISBN 0-252-00884-7   LC Card 81-3026   DDC 973.91/1/0922 B 19
E168 .P7

TV. see TELEVISION.

TVA Fertilizer Conference, St. Louis, 1979.
Situation 79 : TVA Fertilizer Conference, August 23-24, 1979, St. Louis, Missouri. [Muscle Shoals, Ala. : National Fertilizer Development Center, Tennessee Valley Authority , 1979] 76 p. ; 28 cm. (Bulletin Y - National Fertilizer Development Center, Tennessee Valley Authority ; 145) Includes bibliographical references.   LC Card 80-602627   DDC 631.8/1 s 338.4/766862/0973 19
1. Fertilizer industry - United States - Congresses. 2. Fertilizer industry - Congresses. I. Series: United States. National Fertilizer Development Center, Muscle Shoals, Ala. Bulletin Y., 145. II. Title.
S631 .U48 no. 145 HD9483.U52

Tvrdik, Valerie. Minnesota pottery, a potter's view . Minneapolis [1981] 32 p. :   LC Card 81-50237   DDC 738/.09776/0740176579 19
NK4025.M6 M56

Twain, Mark, 1835-1910.
LIFE ON THE MISSISSIPPI.
Kruse, Horst Hermann. Mark Twain and "Life on the Mississippi" /. Amherst , 1981. p. cm.   ISBN 0-87023-330-0 :   LC Card 81-7570   DDC 977 19
PS1314 .K713 1981

Mark Twain library.
Twain, Mark, 1835-1910. No. 44, the mysterious stranger . Berkeley [1981] c1969. p. cm.   ISBN 0-520-04544-0   LC Card 81-40326   DDC 813/.4 19
PS1322 .M97 1981

Mysterious stranger. Twain, Mark, 1835-1910. No. 44, the mysterious stranger : being an ancient tale found in a jug and freely translated from the jug : a selection from Mark Twain's Mysterious stranger manuscripts / by Mark Twain ; with foreword and notes by John S. Tuckey. Berkeley [1981] c1969. p. cm.   ISBN 0-520-04544-0   LC Card 81-40326   DDC 813/.4 19
PS1322 .M97 1981

No. 44, the mysterious stranger : being an ancient tale found in a jug and freely translated from the jug : a selection from Mark Twain's Mysterious stranger manuscripts / by Mark Twain ; with foreword and notes by John S. Tuckey. Berkeley : University of California Press, [1981] c1969. p. cm. (The Mark Twain library) Reprint. Originally published as part of Mark Twain's Mysterious stranger manuscripts: Berkeley : University of California Press, 1969. Includes bibliographical references.   ISBN 0-520-04544-0   LC Card 81-40326   DDC 813/.4 19
I. Twain, Mark, 1835-1910. Mysterious stranger. II. Series: Twain, Mark, 1835-1910. Mark Twain library. III. Title.
PS1322 .M97 1981

Tweed, William C. Recreation site planning and improvement in national forests, 1891-1942 / William C. Tweed. Washington, D.C. : U. S. Dept. of Agriculture, Forest Service : For sale by the Supt. of Docs., U. S. G.P.O., 1980 [i.e. 1981] vi, 29 p. : ill. ; 28 cm. Nov. 1980. "FS-354." S/N 001-001-00557-6 Includes bibliographical references.   LC Card 81-601100   DDC 333.78/3/0973 19
1. Forest reserves - United States - Recreational use - History. 2. National parks and reserves - United States - History. 3. Forest resources - United States - Recreational use - History. I. United States. Forest Service. II. Title.
GV191.4 .T83

Tweeton, Daryl R.
Nigbor, M. T. (Michael T.) Case history of a pilot scale acidic in situ uranium leaching experiment /. Avondale, MD , 1981. p. cm.   LC Card 81-607873   DDC 622 s 622/.34932 19
TN23 .U43 TN799.U7

Selection of lixiviants for in situ uranium leaching / by Daryl R. Tweeton and Kent A. Peterson. Avondale, MD : U. S. Dept. of the Interior, Bureau of Mines, [1981] p. cm.

(Information circular / Bureau of Mines) Bibliography: p. LC Card 81-6103 DDC 622 s 622/.34932 19
1. Uranium mines and mining. 2. In situ processing (Mining). 3. Leaching. 4. Solvents. I. Peterson, Kent A. II. Series: Information circular (United States. Bureau of Mines) . III. Title.
TN295 .U4 TN490.U7

Twentieth-century American literary naturalism .
Pizer, Donald. Carbondale , c1982. p. cm.
ISBN 0-8093-1027-9 LC Card 81-5606 DDC 813/.5/0912 19
PS374.N29 P5

TWENTIETH CENTURY - FORECASTS.
Global 2000 Study (U. S.) The global 2000 report to the President--entering the twenty-first century . Washington, D.C. , 1980- v. <1-2> : LC Card 80-602859 DDC 333.7 19
HC79.E5 G59 1980b

Twenty censuses . United States. Bureau of the Census. Washington, D.C. , 1978. 91 p. : LC Card 79-600181 DDC 353.0081/9 19
HA37 .U52 1978

TWENTY-FIRST CENTURY - FORECASTS.
Global 2000 Study (U. S.) The global 2000 report to the President--entering the twenty-first century . Washington, D.C. , 1980- v. <1-2> : LC Card 80-602859 DDC 333.7 19
HC79.E5 G59 1980b

Two American impressionists . Olney, Susan Faxon. Durham, N.H. , c1980. 22 p. : LC Card 80-80237 DDC 759.13 19
ND237.B4595 A4 1980

Two contracts for nuclear attack submarines modified by Public law 85-804--status as of December 23, 1978 . United States. General Accounting Office. Washington, D.C. , 1979. ii, 16 p. ; LC Card 79-603739 DDC 359.6/212/0973 19
VC263 .U54 1979

2, 4, 5-T. see TRICHLOROPHENOXYACETIC ACID.

Two groups of Thessalian gold /. Miller, Stella G. Berkeley , c1979. xiii, 78 p., [16] leaves of plates : ISBN 0-520-09580-4 LC Card 77-80473
DF261.O57 M54   *NYPL [L-11 622 v. 188]*

Two keys for appraising forest fire fuels /. Fahnestock, George R. Portland, Or. , 1970. 26 p. : LC Card 70-609148 DDC 634.9/0979 s 634.9/618 19
SD11 .A45614 no. 99 SD421

Two sites in Uvalde County. [Austin, Tex.] : Texas State Dept. of Highways and Public Transportation, Highway Design Division, [1979] vi, 15, vi, 19 p., : ill. ; 28 cm. (Publications in archaeology ; report no. 14-15) Includes bibliographies. LC Card 80-622621 DDC 976.4/432 19
1. Indians of North America - Texas - Uvalde Co. - Antiquities. 2. Uvalde Co., Tex. - Antiquities. 3. Texas - Antiquities. I. Young, Wayne C. Elm Creek site. 1979. II. Luke, Clive J. Cook's Slough site. 1979. III. Series: Publications in archaeology (Austin, Tex.) , report no. 14-15.
E78.T4 T89

The two-state collaborative mental health outcome study, State of Washington / Gary B. Cox ... [et al.] Olympia : Dept. of Social and Health Services, 1980. 2 v.; 28 cm.
1. Mental health services - Washington (State). I. Cox, Gary B. II. Washington (State). Dept. of Social and Health Services.   *NYPL [JLF 81-132]*

Two story trout fishery in Lake Cumberland. Axon, James R. Evaluation of the "two story" trout fishery in Lake Cumberland /. [Frankfort] , 1974. 69 p. : LC Card 76-624539 DDC 639/.2 s 333.95/6 19
SH222.K4 A3 no. 60 QL638.S2

Twomey, James P. Governmental programs, resources and regulatory powers available to assist localities during coal development : a revised preliminary report to the Socio-Economic and Cultural Aspects Work Group, Northern Great Plains Resources Program / by James P. Twomey with the assistance of Peter G. Kuh. - Denver : Northern Great Plains Resources Program, 1974. i, 29, [65] p. ; 27 cm.
1. Coal - Great Plains. 2. Regional planning - Great Plains. 3. Economic assistance, Domestic - Great Plains. 4. Industry and state - Great Plains. I. Kuh, Peter G. II.

Northern Great Plains Resources Program. Socio-Economic and Cultural Aspects Work Group. III. Title.   *NYPL [JLF 80-707]*

Tyler, Ralph Winfred, 1902- Testing, teaching, and learning . Washington, D.C. , 1979. vii, 391, [43] p. : LC Card 80-601554 DDC 371.2/6/0973 19
LB3051 .T443

Tyler, Scott. (joint author) Iannicelli, Donald. Surface impoundment assessment . Hartford, Conn. [1979] x, 53 leaves : LC Card 80-623424 DDC 363.7/394 19
TD224.C8 I26

TYNDARICOPSIS - CLASSIFICATION.
Gordh, Gordon. Taxonomic studies of the Encyrtidae with the descriptions of new species and a new genus (Hymenoptera, Chalcicoidea) /. Berkeley , 1981. p. cm. ISBN 0-520-09629-0 LC Card 81-1327 DDC 595.79 19
QL568.E6 G67

TYPE SPECIMENS (NATURAL HISTORY)
(1978) Salley, E. Jean. Checklist of types in the U. S. national parasite collection /. [Washington] , 1978. iv, 233 p. ; LC Card 78-602796 DDC 591.52/49/0740153 19
QL757 .S23

(1979) Plenge, Manuel A. Type specimens of birds in the Museo de Historia Natural "Javier Prado," Lima, Peru /. Baton Rouge , 1979. 13 p. ; LC Card 79-623920 DDC 591 s 598/.074/098525 19
QL3 .L67 no. 53 QL677.2

Type specimens of birds in the Museo de Historia Natural "Javier Prado," Lima, Peru /. Plenge, Manuel A. Baton Rouge , 1979. 13 p. ; LC Card 79-623920 DDC 591 s 598/.074/098525 19
QL3 .L67 no. 53 QL677.2

TYPEWRITER INDUSTRY - JAPAN.
United States. International Trade Commission. Portable electric typewriters from Japan . Washington, D.C. [1980] ii, 15, A-41 p. ; LC Card 80-602317 DDC 382/.4568161 19
HD9802.J32 U5 1980

TYPHA - CONTROL - WISCONSIN.
Beule, John D. Control and management of cattails in southeastern Wisconsin wetlands /. Madison, Wis. , 1979. 39 p. : LC Card 80-621497 DDC 639.9/09775 s 632/.58 19
SK463 .A27 no. 112 SB615.T96

TZUTUHIL INDIANS - BIOGRAPHY.
Bizarro Ujpán, Ignacio. Son of Tecún Umán . Tucson , 1981. p. cm. ISBN 0-8165-0736-8 : LC Card 81-11702 DDC 972.81/004970924 B 19
F1465.2.T9 B59

TZUTUHIL INDIANS - SOCIAL CONDITIONS.
Bizarro Ujpán, Ignacio. Son of Tecún Umán . Tucson , 1981. p. cm. ISBN 0-8165-0736-8 : LC Card 81-11702 DDC 972.81/004970924 B 19
F1465.2.T9 B59

US ARMY MILITARY HISTORY INSTITUTE - CATALOGS.
US Army Military History Institute. God save the Queen . Carlisle Barracks, Pa. [1979?] xvi, 390 p. ; LC Card 79-602252
Z2021.M5 U54 1979 DA50
   NYPL [JFF 81-151]

U. C. L. A. see California. University. University at Los Angeles.

U. E. O. For corporate body referred to by these initials, see: **Western European Union.**

UFO'S. see UNIDENTIFIED FLYING OBJECTS.

U. G. P. T. I. see Upper Great Plains Transportation Institute.

U. L. I. see Urban Land Institute.

U. N. For corporate body represented by these initials see: **United Nations.**

U. N. C. T. A. D. see United Nations. Conference on Trade and Development.

U. N. C. T. A. D./G. A. T. T. International Trade Center. see International Trade Centre.

U. N. D. P. see United Nations. Development Programme.

U. N. E. P. see United Nations. Environment Programme.

U. N. E. S. C. O. For corporate body represented by these initials see: **United Nations Educational, Scientific and Cultural Organization.**

U. N. I. C. E. F. see United Nations. Children's Fund.

U. N. I. T. A. R. see United Nations Institute for Training and Research.

U. N. O. For corporate body represented by these initials see: **United Nations.**

U.N. special session on development . United States. Congress. House. Committee on Foreign Affairs. Subcommittee on International Economic Policy and Trade. Washington , 1981. iii, 95 p. ; LC Card 81-601370 DDC 327.1/11/0973 19
KF27 .F6465 1980e

U. R. S. A. see Urban and Rural Systems Associates.

USAF Southeast Asia monograph series. (v. 5, monograph 7) Gropman, Alan L., 1938- Airpower and the airlift evacuation of Kham Duc /. [Washington] , 1979. viii, 87 p. : LC Card 80-601630 DDC 959.704/348 19
DS558.8 .G76
   NYPL [JFL 77-126 v. 5, monograph 7]

U. S. A. I. D. see United States. Agency for International Development.

U. S. agricultural export development efforts /. United States. Dept. of Agriculture. Washington , 1980. v, 36 p. : LC Card 80-603056 DDC 382/.41/0973 19
HD9006 .U557 1980

U. S. and Africa in the 70's. United States. Dept. of State. [Washington, 1970] 9 p. LC Card 70-607203
HC502 .U573

U. S. and USSR MHD electrode materials development. Rudins, George. - Santa Monica , 1974. vii, 71 p. ;   *NYPL [JSF 81-299]*

U. S. Army Corps of Engineers civil environmental R. & D. budget . United States. Congress. House. Committee on Science and Technology. Subcommittee on Natural Resources and Environment. Washington , 1980. iii, 57 p. ; LC Card 80-602776 DDC 353.0082/32 19
KF27 .S398 1980

U. S. Army Engineer Topographic Laboratories. see United States. Army Engineer Topographic Laboratories.

US Army Military History Institute.
God save the Queen : a bibliography of the British and Commonwealth holdings / by Lawrence James-Alexander Lentz. Carlisle Barracks, Pa. : U. S. Army Military History Institute, [1979?] xvi, 390 p. ; 27 cm. (US Army Military History Institute. Special bibliography. no. 18) LC Card 79-602252
1. Great Britain - History, Military - Bibliography - Catalogs. 2. Commonwealth of Nations - History, Military - Bibliography - Catalogs. 3. US Army Military History Institute - Catalogs. I. Lentz, Lawrence James-Alexander. II. Title. III. Series.
Z2021.M5 U54 1979 DA50
   NYPL [JFF 81-151]

Special bibliographic series. see US Army Military History Institute. Special bibliography.

Special bibliography. For earlier file whose numbering it continues, see: U. S. Army Military History Research Collection. Special bibliography.
(no. 18) US Army Military History Institute. God save the Queen . Carlisle Barracks, Pa. [1979?] xvi, 390 p. ; LC Card 79-602252
Z2021.M5 U54 1979 DA50
   NYPL [JFF 81-151]

U. S. C.-G. A. R. P. see United States Committee for the Global Atmospheric Research Program.

U. S. coal development--promises, uncertainties . United States. General Accounting Office. [Washington] , 1977. ca. 350 p. in various pagings : LC Card 77-604230
TN805 .A353 1977   *NYPL [JSF 81-165]*

U. S. Commission on Civil Rights fiscal year 1981 authorization . United States. Congress. Senate. Committee on the Judiciary. Subcommittee on the Constitution. Washington , 1980. iii, 69 p. ; LC Card 80-603460 DDC 353.0072/236811 19
KF26 .J835 1980a

U. S. commuter airline industry . United States. Congress. Senate. Committee on Commerce, Science, and Transportation. Washington , 1981. iii, 91 p. : LC Card 81-601625 DDC 387.7/42/0973 19
KF26 .C69 1981d

U. S. conventional arms transfer policy . United States. Congress. Senate. Committee on Foreign Relations. Washington , 1980. v, 11 p. ; LC Card 80-604139 DDC 355/.032/0973 19
HD9743.U6 U57 1980

The U. S. copper mining industry . Tomimatsu, T. T. [Washington, D.C.] , Avondale, MD. [1981] p. cm. LC Card 80-607792 DDC 338.2/3 19
HD9539.C7 U576

The U. S. copper mining industry . Tomimatsu, T. T. [Washington, D.C.] [1981] p. cm. LC Card 80-609992 DDC 338.2/3 19
HD9539.C7 U576

U. S. Customs guide for private flyers. United States. Customs Service. [Washington, D.C. , 1978] 55 p. : LC Card 79-603485 DDC 343.7305/6/0243877 19
KF6694 .A32 1978

U. S. design patents. United States. Patent and Trademark Office. Nov. 9, 1842- Woodbridge, Conn. *NYPL [*XFR-10]*

U. S. directory of environmental sources /. United States International Environmental Referral Center. Washington , 1977. 193, 496, [49] p. ; LC Card 77-604804
TD171 .U58 1977 *NYPL [*XME-9521]*

U. S. economic assistance programs in Asia . Hyndman, Vance. Washington , 1980. vii, 29 p. ; LC Card 80-603977 DDC 338.91/73/05 19
HC412 .H93

U. S. embargo of food and technology to the Soviet Union . United States. Congress. Senate. Committee on Banking, Housing and Urban Affairs. Subcommittee on International Finance. Washington , 1980. v, 250 p. ; LC Card 80-602113 DDC 382/.64/0973 19
KF26 .B3946 1980a

U. S. export competitiveness . United States. Congress. Joint Economic Committee. Washington , 1981. iii, 66 p. : LC Card 81-601784 DDC 382/.6/0973 19
KF25 .E2 1980k

U. S. exports: Schedule B commodity by country. United States. Bureau of the Census. Washington. *NYPL [JLM 81-161]*

U. S. exports: schedule B commodity groupings, schedule B commodity by county. United States. Bureau of the Census. 1967-77 (incomplete). Washington. 11 v. *NYPL [TLG (U. S. Census Bureau. [Report] FT [no.] 410.)]*

U. S. exports: schedule E commodity groupings, schedule E commodity by country. United States. Bureau of the Census. 1978- [Washington] LC Card 79-640385
NYPL [JLM 80-677]

U. S. fast breeder reactor program needs direction . United States. General Accounting Office. Washington, D.C. , 1980. vii, 54 p. ; LC Card 80-603953 DDC 353.0087/22 19
TK9203.B7 U5 1980

U. S. fats and oils statistics, 1963-78. United States. Economics, Statistics, and Cooperatives Service. [Washington, D.C.] [1980] iv, 104 p. ; LC Card 80-601591 DDC 338.1/0973 s 338.1/7385/0973 19
HD1751 .A5 no. 631 HD9490.U6

U. S. fed-beef production costs, 1976-77, and industry structure /. Gee, C. Kerry. Washington , 1979. i, 29 p. ; LC Card 79-602695 DDC 338.1 s 338.1/36213/0973 19
HD1751 .A91854 no. 424 SF203

U. S. foreign aid in Africa /. United States. Agency for International Development.

[Washington?] [1965?] 28 p. : *NYPL [Sc Micro F-9183]*

U. S. Geological Survey research in radioactive waste disposal--fiscal year 1979 / by Robert Schneider ... [et al.]. Reston, Va. : The Survey, 1981. p. cm. (Geological survey circular . 847) Bibliography: p. LC Card 81-607990 DDC 557.3 s 621.48/38 19
1. Radioactive waste disposal in the ground - Research - United States. 2. United States. Geological Survey. I. Schneider, Robert.
QE75 .C5 no. 847 TD898

U. S. government policy and supporting positions. United States government policy and supporting positions /. Washington , 1980. vii, 161 p. ; LC Card 80-604162 DDC 353.001/03 19
JK661 .U54

U. S. government relief assistance following the Italian earthquake of November 23, 1980 . United States. Congress. House. Committee on Foreign Affairs. Washington , 1980 [i.e. 1981] iii, 38 p. : LC Card 81-600803 DDC 363.3/495 19
KF27 .F6 1980l

U. S. ground forces . Hillier, Pat. [Washington, D.C.] , 1980. xxiii, 87 p. : LC Card 81-600683 DDC 355/.033073 19
UA23 .H513

U. S. ground troops in South Vietnam were in areas sprayed with herbicide orange . United States. General Accounting Office. [Washington, D.C.] , 1979. 9, 12 p. : LC Card 79-604309 DDC 363.1/79 19
DS559.8.C5 U54 1979

U. S.-Hungarian trade relations : documents for doing business / [prepared by Mona Levine]. [Washington] : U. S. Dept. of Commerce, Industry and Trade Administration, Office of East-West Country Affairs : for sale by the Supt. of Docs., U. S. Govt. Print. Off., 1979. 64 p. ; 24 cm. LC Card 80-600608 DDC 341.7/54/0266439073 19
1. United States - Commerce - Hungary. 2. Hungary - Commerce - United States. I. Levine, Mona. II. United States. Industry and Trade Administration. Office of East-West Country Affairs.
HF3097.5 .U54

U. S. I. C. A. see United States. International Communication Agency.

U. S. I. E. R. C. see United States International Environmental Referral Center.

U. S. immigration policy regarding Iranian nationals . United States. Congress. House. Committee on the Judiciary. Subcommittee on Immigration, Refugees, and International Law. Washington , 1981. iii, 60 p. ; LC Card 81-601599 DDC 325/.255/0973 19
KF27 .J8645 1980d

U. S. import restrictions . United States. General Accounting Office. [Washington , 1976] v, 72 p. : LC Card 77-600705
HD9275.U6 U56 1976 *NYPL [JLF 81-320]*

U. S. interests in, and policies toward, the Persian Gulf, 1980 . United States. Congress. House. Committee on Foreign Affairs. Subcommittee on Europe and the Middle East. Washington , 1980. iv, 471 p. : LC Card 80-603806 DDC 355/.0330536 19
KF27 .F64214 1980c

U. S. international trade strategy . United States. Congress. Senate. Committee on Finance. Subcommittee on International Trade. Washington , 1980. iii, 494 p. : LC Card 80-603898 DDC 382/.3/0973 19
KF26 .F554 1980e

U. S.-Japan economic relations : a symposium on critical issues / James C. Abegglen ... [et al.]. [Berkeley] : Institute of East Asian Studies, University of California, Berkeley, 1980. x, 57 p. ; 23 cm. (Research papers and policy studies . no. 1) ISBN 0-912966-25-4 (pbk.) : LC Card 80-620017 DDC 337.52073 19
1. United States - Foreign economic relations - Japan - Addresses, essays, lectures. 2. Japan - Foreign economic relations - United States - Addresses, essays, lectures. I. Abegglen, James C. II. Series.
HF1456.5.J3 U554

U. S. market profiles, series III /. Organization of American States. International Trade and Export Development Program. Washington, D.C. [1980] 19 v. : ISBN 0-8270-1011-7 (pbk. : v.

1) : LC Card 80-498362 DDC 658.8/35/0973 19
HC110.C6 O73 1980

U. S. Middle East policy . United States. Congress. Senate. Committee on Foreign Relations. Washington , 1980. iii, 55 p. ; LC Card 80-602819 DDC 327.73056 19
KF26 .F6 1980g

U. S. minerals vulnerability . United States. Congress. House. Committee on Interior and Insular Affairs. Subcommittee on Mines and Mining. Washington , 1980. xvi, 83 p. : LC Card 80-604127 DDC 333.8/5/0973 19
TN23 .U75 1980

U. S. mission and office operations, East Africa . United States. Congress. House. Committee on Government Operations. Legislation and National Security Subcommittee. Washington , 1980. iii, 72 p. ; LC Card 80-603484 DDC 353.008/92/09676 19
KF27 .G6676 1980f

U. S. mission and office operations--Egypt . United States. Congress. House. Committee on Government Operations. Legislation and National Security Subcommittee. Washington , 1980. iii, 161 p. ; LC Card 80-603495 DDC 353.008/92/0962 19
KF27 .G6676 1980h

U. S. mission and office operations--West Africa . United States. Congress. House. Committee on Government Operations. Legislation and National Security Subcommittee. Washington , 1980. iii, 75 p. ; LC Card 80-603676 DDC 353.008/92/0966 19
KF27 .G6676 1980j

U. S. national interest in Latin America . United States. Congress. House. Committee on Foreign Affairs. Subcommittee on Inter-American Affairs. Washington , 1981. iii, 67 p. : LC Card 81-601864 DDC 327.7308 19
KF27 .F646 1981

U. S. naval history sources in the United States /. Allard, Dean C., 1933- Washington, D.C. , 1979. vii, 235 p. : LC Card 79-600070 DDC 026/.359/00973 19
Z1249.N3 A48 E182

U. S. Navy diving operations: handbook. United States. Naval Ship Systems Command. Supervisor of Diving. Washington, 1974. 198 p. LC Card 76-86691 *NYPL [JSG 80-103]*

U. S. nuclear non-proliferation policy: impact on exports and nuclear industry could not be determined . United States. General Accounting Office. Washington, D.C. , 1980. vi, 78 p. ; LC Card 80-603954 DDC 382/.4562345119/0973 19
HD9698.U52 U55 1980b

U. S. P. S. see United States Postal Service.

U. S. participation in the multilateral development institutions . United States. Congress. House. Committee on Banking, Finance and Urban Affairs. Subcommittee on International Development Institutions and Finance. Washington , 1981. iii, 258 p. ; LC Card 81-601948 DDC 332.1/53 19
KF27 .B547 1981

U. S. participation in the 1980 summer Olympic games . United States. Congress. House. Committee on Foreign Affairs. Washington , 1980. iii, 88 p. ; LC Card 80-602748 DDC 796.4/8/0947431 19
KF27 .F6 1980d

U. S. policy toward South Africa . United States. Congress. House. Committee on Foreign Affairs. Subcommittee on International Economic Policy and Trade. Washington , 1980. iv, 912 p. : LC Card 80-603998 DDC 327.73068 19
KF27 .F6465 1980b

U. S. Postal Service Plan for nine-digit zip code . United States. Congress. House. Committee on Government Operations. Subcommittee on Government Information and Individual Rights. Washington , 1980. v, 462 p. : LC Card 81-601386 DDC 383/.145 19
KF27 .G6628 1980a

U. S. production, imports & import/production ratios for cotton, wool & man-made fiber textiles & apparel. United States. International Trade Administration. [Washington] [1980]

143 p. ;   LC Card 80-602836   DDC
338.4/7677/00973 19
HD9854 .U55 1980

**U. S. R. A. see United States Railway
Association.**

U. S. refineries . United States. Library of
Congress. Congressional Research Service.
Washington , 1980. v, 169 p. :   LC Card
80-603551   DDC 665.5/3/0973 19
TP690.3 .U538 1980

U. S. refugee policy . United States. Congress.
House. Committee on Foreign Affairs.
Subcommittee on International Operations.
Washington , 1980. iii, 18 p. ;   LC Card
81-600867   DDC 325/.21/0973 19
KF27 .F647 1979f

U. S. refugee programs . United States. Congress.
Senate. Committee on the Judiciary.
Washington , 1980. iii, 412 p. (p. 412 blank) :
LC Card 80-602735   DDC 362.8/7/0973 19
KF26 .J8 1980a

U. S. refugee programs, 1981 . United States.
Congress. Senate. Committee on the Judiciary,
United States Senate, Ninety-sixth Congress,
second session, September 19, 1980.
Washington , 1980. iii, 288 p. :   LC Card
80-604094   DDC 362.8/7/0973 19
KF26 .J8 1980f

U. S. rice distribution update /. Holder, Shelby
Herbert, 1931- Washington, D.C. [1980] ii, 50
p. ;   LC Card 80-603201   DDC 338.1/0973 s
381/.41318/0973 19
HD1751 .A5 no. 640 HD9066.U45

The U. S. sea-based strategic force . Davison,
Richard H. [Washington, D.C.] [1980] xx, 62
p. :   LC Card 80-601190   DDC 359.8/3 19
V993 .D38

**U. S. security interests and policies in Southwest
Asia** . United States. Congress. Senate.
Committee on Foreign Relations. Washington ,
1980. iii, 368 p. :   LC Card 80-603283   DDC
355/.033056 19
KF26 .F6 1980p

U. S. semiconductor industry. United States.
Industry and Trade Administration. Office of
Producer Goods. A report on the U. S.
semiconductor industry. Washington, D.C. ,
1979. ix, 132 p. ;   LC Card 79-604001
HD9696.S43 U54 1979   **NYPL [JLF 81-168]**

U. S. senators from the prairie /. Pressler, Larry,
1942- Washington, D.C. [1980] p. cm.   ISBN
0-88249-033-8 :   LC Card 80-25220   DDC
328.73/092/2 B 920 19
E747 .P83

U. S. sorghum industry /. Jackson, David M.
[Washington, D.C.] [1980] iii, 84 p. :   LC Card
80-602638   DDC 338.1 s 338.1/73174/0973 19
HD1751 .A91854 no. 457 HD9049.S6U5

The U. S. stake in the global economy . United
States. Congress. Senate. Committee on Foreign
Relations. Subcommittee on International
Economic Policy. Washington , 1981. iv, 298
p. :   LC Card 81-602271   DDC 337.73 19
KF26 .F648 1981

U. S. standard atmosphere, 1976 /. United States
Committee on Extension to the Standard
Atmosphere. Washington , 1976. xv, 227 p. :
LC Card 77-601158
TL557.A8 U55 1976   **NYPL [JSF 81-142]**

**U. S. strategic petroleum reserve at a turning
point** . United States. General Accounting
Office. Washington, D.C. , 1980. iv p., 28
leaves :   LC Card 80-601078   DDC
333.8/23211/0973 19
TP692.5 .U624 1980

U. S. tactical air forces . United States.
Congressional Budget Office. Washington ,
1976. 35 p. :   LC Card 76-602204
UG633 .U52 1976

U. S. trade and investment policy . United States.
Congress. Joint Economic Committee.
Washington , 1980. iii, 148 p. :   LC Card
80-603497   DDC 338.4/76292/0973 19
KF25 .E2 1980d

**U. S. trade opportunities resulting from the
MTN agreement on tariff cuts** /. Maurer, Alan
O. Washington, D.C. , 1980. vi, 40 p. ;   LC
Card 81-600731   DDC 382/.0973/04 19
HF3092.8 .M38

U. S. trade policy . United States. Congress.
House. Committee on Ways and Means.
Subcommittee on Trade. Washington , 1980. v,
632 p. :   LC Card 81-600879   DDC 382/.3/0973 19
KF27 .W348 1980g

**US/USSR Environmental Economics
Symposium.** Proceedings. 1st- [Washington]
U. S. Dept. of Commerce, Office of
Environmental Affairs, 1978- 28 cm. "Project
02.11-21. Harmonization of Air and Water Pollution
Standards. US/USSR Environmental Agreement."
Issued also in Russian ed. (Library has English ed.
only).   LC Card 79-602348
  *1. Environmental policy - United States - Congresses. 2.
Environmental policy - Russia - Congresses. I. United
States. Dept. of Commerce. Office of Environmental
Affairs.*   **NYPL [JLM 80-1005]**

U. S.-U. S.S.R. health cooperation, 1972-77 /.
John E. Fogarty International Center for
Advanced Study in the Health Sciences.
International Cooperation and Geographic
Studies Branch. [Bethesda, Md.] , 1979. vi, 108
p. ;   LC Card 80-601277   DDC 610/.72 19
R853.I57 J63 1979

**US-USSR Joint Committee on Cooperation in
the Field of Energy.** Symposium on HVDC
Power Transmission. Proceedings. [1]- ; 1976-
[Portland, Or.].   **NYPL [JSP 80-272]**

U. S. v. crime in the streets /. Cronin, Thomas
E. Bloomington , c1981. p. cm.   ISBN
0-253-19017-7   LC Card 80-8842   DDC
364/.973 19
HV6791 .C76

U. S. 69 project, Oklahoma. Oklahoma Highway
Archaeological Survey. An archaeological
survey of U. S. 69, Pittsburg, Atoka, and Bryan
Counties, Oklahoma /. [Norman] , 1976. v, 158
p. :   LC Card 77-621832   DDC 976.6/6 19
E78.O45 O48 1976

Uda, Joan A. Montana working woman : your job
rights / written and compiled for publication by
Joan A. Uda. [Helena, Mont.] : Dept. of
Labor & Industry, Labor Standards Division,
Women's Bureau, [1979?] xi, 55 p. : forms ; 23
cm. Includes index.   LC Card 80-623400   DDC
344.786/014 19
  *1. Women - Employment - Montana. 2. Sex
discrimination in employment - Law and legislation -
Montana. I. Montana. Women's Bureau. II. Title.*
KFM9334.5.D5 U3

Udelson, Joseph H., 1943- The great television
race : a history of the American television
industry, 1925-1941 / by Joseph H. Udelson.
University, Ala. : University of Alabama Press,
c1982. p. cm. Bibliography: p. Includes index.   ISBN
0-8173-0082-1   LC Card 81-7562   DDC
384.55/0973 19
  *1. Television industry - United States - History. 2.
Television broadcasting - United States - History. I.
Title.*
HD9696.T463 U67

Ueda, Michihiko. The outlook for housing in
Japan to the year 2000 / Michihiko Ueda and
David R. Darr. [Portland, Or.?] : U. S. Dept. of
Agriculture, Forest Service, Pacific Northwest
Forest and Range Experiment Station, c1980.
25 p. : ill. ; 28 cm. (Research paper PNW ; 276)
Cover title. "August 1980." Item 83-B Bibliography: p.
25.   LC Card 81-600898   DDC 634.9/09795 s
363.5/0952 19
  *1. Housing - Japan. 2. Housing - Japan - Statistics. I.
Darr, David R. II. Pacific Northwest Forest and Range
Experiment Station (Portland, Or.). III. Title. IV. Series.*
SD11 .A45614 no. 276 HD7367.A3

**UHT Processing and Aseptic Packaging of Milk
and Milk Products.** International Conference
on UHT Processing and Aseptic Packaging of
Milk and Milk Products, North Carolina State
University, 1979. International Conference on
UHT Processing and Aseptic Packaging of Milk
and Milk Products, November 27-29, 1979 .
Raleigh, N.C. , c1980. iv, 230 p. :   LC Card
80-120778   DDC 637 19
SF250.5 .I56 1979

Uhuru Railway. see Tan-Zam Railway.

UJNR Panel on Fire Research and Safety. Fire
research and safety : proceedings of the third
joint panel conference of the U. S.-Japan
Cooperative Program in Natural Resources,
held March 13-17, 1978, at the National
Bureau of Standards, Gaithersburg, MD /

edited by Margaret A. Sherald. Washington,
D.C. : U. S. Dept. of Commerce, National
Bureau of Standards : for sale by the Supt. of
Docs., U. S. Govt. Print. Off., 1979. x, 718 p. :
ill. ; 26 cm. (NBS special publication ; 540) Includes
bibliographical references.   LC Card 79-600054   DDC
602/.18 s 628.9/22 19
  *1. Fire prevention - Congresses. 2. Fire - Congresses. I.
Sherald, Margaret A. II. Series: United States. National
Bureau of Standards Special publication, 540. III. Title.*
QC100 .U57 no. 540 TH9112

Ullery, Scott J. (joint author) Jamail, Milton H.
International water use relations along the
Sonoran Desert borderlands /. Tuscon, Ariz. ,
1979. iv leaves, 139 p., [1] leaf of plates :   LC
Card 80-622139   DDC 333.91/13/0979 19
TD223.9 .J35

Ullman, Al. United States. Congress. House.
Committee on Ways and Means. Hearing
announcement on the "Tax restructuring act of
1979", H.R. 5665 . Washington , 1979. iii, 44
p. ;   LC Card 80-602685   DDC 343.7304 19
KF6275.5 .W245

Ulman, W. J. United States. Geological Survey.
Synthetic fuels development . Washington,
D.C. , 1979. 45 p. :   LC Card 79-600206   DDC
662/.66/0973 19
TP360 .U584 1979

Ulrich, George E. Geology of the Apollo 16 area,
Central Lunar Highlands . Washington , 1980.
p. cm.   LC Card 80-607170   DDC 559.9/1 19
QB592 .G47

The ultimate guide to shopping in New York /
produced in cooperation with the New York
State Department of Commerce and New York
magazine. [New York] : New York Magazine
Company, c1979. 48 p. : ill. (some col.) ; 28
cm.
  *1. New York (City) - Description - 1951- -
Guide-books. 2. Shopping - New York (City) -
Directories. I. New York (State). Dept. of Commerce.
II. New York magazine. III. Title: Guide to shopping in
New York. IV. Title: Shopping in New York.*
                                    NYPL [IRGV 80-2533]

**ULTRASONIC DIAGNOSIS. see DIAGNOSIS,
ULTRASONIC.**

Ultrasonic tissue characterization II : a
collection of reviewed papers based on talks
presented at the Second International
Symposium on Ultrasonic Tissue
Characterization held at the National Bureau of
Standards, Gaithersburg, Maryland, June 13-15,
1977 / edited by Melvin Linzer ; cosponsors ...
National Bureau of Standards (National
Measurement Laboratory), National Science
Foundation (Research Applied to National
Needs, RANN), National Institutes of Health
(Diagnostic Radiology Department, Clinical
Center). Washington : U. S. Dept. of
Commerce, National Bureau of Standards : for
sale by the Supt. of Docs., U. S. Govt. Print.
Off., 1979. xi, 362 p. : ill. ; 27 cm. (NBS special
publication ; 525) "Issued April 1979." Includes
bibliographical references and index.   LC Card
79-600026   DDC 602/.18 s 616.07/543 19
  *1. Diagnosis, Ultrasonic - Congresses. 2. Ultrasonic
waves - Measurement - Congresses. 3. Tissues -
Analysis - Congresses. I. Linzer, Melvin. II.
International Symposium on Ultrasonic Tissue
Characterization, 2d, National Bureau of Standards,
1977. III. National Measurement Laboratory (U. S.).
IV. United States. National Science Foundation.
Research Applied to National Needs Program. V.
United States. National Institutes of Health. Clinical
Center. Diagnostic Radiology Dept. VI. Series: United
States. National Bureau of Standards Special
publication, 525.*
QC100 .U57 no. 525 RC78.7.U4

**ULTRASONIC WAVES - MEASUREMENT -
CONGRESSES.**
Ultrasonic tissue characterization II .
Washington , 1979. xi, 362 p. :   LC Card
79-600026   DDC 602/.18 s 616.07/543 19
QC100 .U57 no. 525 RC78.7.U4

**ULTRASONOGRAPHY. see DIAGNOSIS,
ULTRASONIC.**

ULTRASTRUCTURE (BIOLOGY)
Cifelli, Richard. Textural observations on some
living species of planktonic foraminifera /.
Washington , 1982. p. cm.   LC Card 81-607840
DDC 560 s 592.1/304471 19
QE701 .S56 no. 45 QL368.F6

ULTRASTRUCTURE (BIOLOGY) - ATLASES.
Brown, Merton F. Phytopathogenic fungi .
[Columbia, Mo.] , c1979. vii, 355 p., : LC Card
79-91283   DDC 589.2/044 19
QK601 .B84

Ultrasystems, inc. Evaluation and analysis of the
Cleff job matching system: final report /
prepared by Ultrasystems, inc. - Irvine, Calif. :
Ultrasystems, 1975. 2 v. in 1 : ill. ; 28 cm.
Microfiche (neg.) NTIS. 4 sheets. 11 x 15 cm. (PB-266
108) On "Bibliographic data sheet": Author, Stanley N.
Nathanson. "Prepared for U. S. Department of Labor,
Manpower Administration, Office of Policy, Evaluation
and Research." "Contract no. B2C 5415" On cover:
Ultrasystems, Newport Beach, Calif. CONTENTS: v. 1.
Introduction and summary. - v. 2. Technical dissertation
and appendices.
*1. Job descriptions. 2. Résumés (Employment). I.
Nathanson, Stanley N. II. United States. Dept. of
Labor. Office of Manpower Policy, Evaluation, and
Research. III. Title. IV. Title: Cleff job matching
system.*   ***NYPL [*XME-9380]***

**ULTRA-VIOLET RAYS - PHYSIOLOGICAL
EFFECT.**
Cutchis, Pythagoras. On the linkage of solar
ultraviolet radiation to skin cancer .
Washington, D.C. , 1978. xiv, 146, [13] p. :
LC Card 79-602135   DDC 616.99/477071 19
RC280.S5 C83

Umatilla Army Depot, Or. see **United States.
Umatilla Army Depot.**

Umbeck, John R., 1945- A theory of property
rights : with application to the California gold
rush / John R. Umbeck.1st ed. Ames : Iowa
State University Press, 1981. p. cm. Bibliography:
p.   ISBN 0-8138-1675-0   LC Card 81-1141   DDC
323.4/6 19
*1. Property. 2. Right of property - Economic aspects. 3.
Land tenure. 4. California - Gold discoveries. I. Title.*
HB711 .U52

**Un Folleto sobre la ley de relaciones del trabajo
agrícola de California.** California. Agricultural
Labor Relations Board. A handbook on the
California agricultural labor relations law =.
Sacramento , 1978. 67 p. ;   LC Card 79-621311
KFC589.A4 A82   ***NYPL [JLC 81-140]***

Unaccepted applicants to medical school. Johns
Hopkins University. Office of Health Manpower
Studies. Career patterns of unaccepted
applicants to medical school . [Bethesda? Md.] ,
1974. vi, 207 p. :   LC Card 76-600905
R838.4 .J63 1974   ***NYPL [*XME-9527]***

**Unanswered questions on educating handicapped
children in local public schools** . United States.
General Accounting Office. Washington, D.C. ,
1981. v, 122 p. :   LC Card 81-601129   DDC
371.9/0973 19
LC4031 .U5 1981

UNBELIEF. see **SKEPTICISM.**

UNBORN CHILD. see **FETUS.**

UNC sea grant working paper .
(80-2) Grant, Cy. A study of federal and state
legislation concerning the construction of
proposed oil refineries /. Raleigh, NC (105
1911 Bldg. North Carolina State University,
Raleigh 27650) , 1980. 23, 4 p. :   LC Card
80-624348   DDC 343.756/0772 347.5603772 19
KFN7658.R43 G72

Unclassified fields of research. United States.
Atomic Energy Commission. Division of
Classification. Guide to the unclassified fields of
research /. Washington, 1972. 14 p.
NYPL [*XMQ-2152]

**UNCOMPAHGRE NATIONAL FOREST,
COLO. - MAPS.**
(1972) United States. Forest Service. Rocky
Mountain Region. Uncompahgre National
Forest, Colorado. [Denver] 1972. col. map on
sheet 65 x 97 cm. Scale 1:126,720; 1/2″ = 1 mile.
Printed on both sides of sheet. Relief shown by
hachures and spot heights. "New Mexico, Sixth, Ute
principal meridians." Includes text, col. illus., "Vicinity
map", "Map key[s]", and "Recreation site directory."
"Reprinted 1976." "Polyconic projection."   LC Card
75-690673
G4312.U6 1972 .U5
NYPL [Map Div. 80-3364]

**UNCONFORMITIES (GEOLOGY) -
COLORADO - PICEANCE CREEK
WATERSHED.**

Johnson, Ronald Carl, 1950- A study of the
Cretaceous-Tertiary unconformity in the
Piceance Creek Basin, Colorado . Washington ,
1980. iii, 27 p. :   LC Card 80-607774   DDC
551.7/7 19
QE688 .J63

Unconventional gas sources. National Petroleum
Council. Committee on Unconventional Gas
Sources. Interim summary, unconventional gas
sources /. [Washington] , c1980. 20, 7, 11 p. :
LC Card 80-139029   DDC 553.2/85/0973 19
TN880 .N29 1980

Unconventional petroleum resources in California
/. Hallmark, Fred O. Sacramento , 1980. iv, 17
p. :   LC Card 80-621718   DDC 553.2/82 19
TN872.C2 H28

UNCTAD/GATT International Trade Centre. see
International Trade Centre.

UNDERDEVELOPED AREAS.
Providencia . [Washington, D.C.?] , 1980. xiii,
327 p. :   LC Card 80-603922   DDC 330.9861/8 19
HC28 .P83 1980

United Nations. Conference on Trade and
Development. Secretariat. Financial solidarity
for development . New York , 1979. 2 v. ;   LC
Card 80-125802   DDC 300 s 338.91 19
JX1977 .A2 TD/B/C.7/31

United States. Central Intelligence Agency.
National Foreign Assessment Center.
Communist aid activities in non-Communist less
developed countries, 1978 /. Washington, D.C.
[1979] vii, 40 p. :   LC Card 80-602379   DDC
338.91/47/01724 19
HC60.U6 C45 1979

United States. Congress. House. Committee on
Foreign Affairs. Subcommittee on International
Economic Policy and Trade. North-South
dialog . Washington , 1980. iii, 267 p. ;   LC
Card 80-603478   DDC 337/.09/048 19
KF27 .F6465 1980a

United States. Congress. Senate. Committee on
Foreign Relations. Subcommittee on
International Economic Policy. The U. S. stake
in the global economy . Washington , 1981. iv,
298 p. :   LC Card 81-602271   DDC 337.73 19
KF26 .F648 1981

**UNDERDEVELOPED AREAS -
AGRICULTURAL EXTENSION WORK.**
Stavis, Benedict. Agricultural extension for
small farmers /. East Lansing , 1979. 81 p. ;
LC Card 79-626003   DDC 630/.7/15 19
S544 .S7

**UNDERDEVELOPED AREAS - ARMED
FORCES - APPROPRIATIONS AND
EXPENDITURES.**
Economic development versus military
expenditures in countries receiving U. S. aid .
Washington , 1980 [i.e. 1981] x, 93 p. ;   LC
Card 81-601000   DDC 338.91/73/01724 19
HC60 .E25

**UNDERDEVELOPED AREAS - BIRTH
CONTROL - CONGRESSES.**
Maternal and child health/family planning
program . New York, N.Y. , 1980. v, 341 p. :
LC Card 80-143941   DDC 362.1/982/0091724
19
RG940 .M368

**UNDERDEVELOPED AREAS - BIRTH
CONTROL - MATHEMATICAL MODELS.**
McLaughlin, Curtis P. Applying models to the
family planning programs of developing
countries /. [Chapel Hill] , c1972. vii, 33 p. :
LC Card 78-622761
HQ766 .M218

**UNDERDEVELOPED AREAS - BIRTH
CONTROL - STATISTICS.**
O'Leary, William. Family planning statistics,
1965 to 1973 . Washington , 1975. 74 p., [1]
fold. leaf of plates ;   LC Card 75-600039   DDC
363.9/6/091724 19
HQ766.7 .O43

**UNDERDEVELOPED AREAS - BRAIN
DRAIN.**
United Nations. Conference on Trade and
Development. Group of Governmental Experts
on Reverse Transfer of Technology. Report of
the Group of Governmental Experts on Reverse
Transfer of Technology, held at the Palais des
Nations, Geneva, from 27 February to 7
March, 1978. [New York] , 1978. 30, 7, 4 p. ;

LC Card 78-111923   DDC 300 s 331.12/791 19
*JX1977 .A2 TD/B/C.6/28 TD/B/C.6/AC.4/10
HD8038.A1*

**UNDERDEVELOPED AREAS - CHILD
HEALTH SERVICES - CONGRESSES.**
Maternal and child health/family planning
program . New York, N.Y. , 1980. v, 341 p. :
LC Card 80-143941   DDC 362.1/982/0091724
19
RG940 .M368

UNDERDEVELOPED AREAS - COMMERCE.
United Nations. Conference on Trade and
Development. Operation and effects of the
generalized system of preferences . New York ,
1979. vi, 146 p. ;   LC Card 80-121468   DDC 300
s 382.7/53 19
JX1977 .A2 TD/B/C.5/61

United States. Congress. House. Committee on
Ways and Means. Subcommittee on Trade.
Operation of the generalized system of
preferences . Washington , 1980. iii, 111 p. ;
LC Card 80-603343   DDC 353.0082/7 19
KF27 .W348 1980c

United States. Congress. Senate. Committee on
Finance. Subcommittee on International Trade.
Review of the U. S. generalized system of
preferences . Washington , 1981. iv, 300 p. :
LC Card 81-601603   DDC 382.7/53/0973 19
KF26 .F554 1980g

**UNDERDEVELOPED AREAS -
COMMUNICATION.**
Hedebro, Göran, 1945- Communication and
social change in developing nations . Ames ,
1981. p. cm.   ISBN 0-8138-0326-8   LC Card
81-8191   DDC 302.2/09172/4 19
HN980 .H4 1981

**UNDERDEVELOPED AREAS -
CONGRESSES.**
United Nations Seminar on Technology
Assessment for Development, Bangalore, India,
1978. Technology assessment for development .
New York , 1979. v, 165 p. :   LC Card
80-121462   DDC 300 s 338.9/009172/4 19
JX1977 .A2 ST/ESA/95

**UNDERDEVELOPED AREAS -
COOPERATIVE SOCIETIES.**
United States. General Accounting Office. AID
must consider social factors in establishing
cooperatives in developing countries .
[Washington, D.C.] [1980] iv, 42 p. ;   LC Card
80-602922   DDC 334/.09172/4 19
HD3575 .U54 1980

**UNDERDEVELOPED AREAS - ECONOMIC
ASSISTANCE.** see **ECONOMIC
ASSISTANCE.**

**UNDERDEVELOPED AREAS - ECONOMIC
POLICY.**
United Nations. Dept. of Technical
Co-operation for Development. Organizational
systems for national planning /. New York ,
1979. vi, 177 p. :   LC Card 79-123608   DDC 300
s 338.9/009172/4 19
JX1977 .A2 ST/ESA/SER.E/18

United Nations. Economic and Social Council.
Committee for Development Planning.
Launching a third decade of development .
New York , 1979. viii, 37 p. ;   LC Card
80-108221   DDC 300 s 338.91/1724 19
JX1977 .A2 ST/ESA/97

UNDERDEVELOPED AREAS - EDUCATION.
Organization of American States. Dept. of
Educational Affairs. Educational deficits in the
Caribbean =. [Washington, D.C.] [1979] viii,
128 p. :   LC Card 80-132005   DDC 371.9/67/09729
19
LC4095.C37 O73 1979

**UNDERDEVELOPED AREAS - FINANCE -
CONGRESSES.**
Conference on the International Financial
System and Concerns of Developing Nations,
Washington, D. C., 1975. The international
monetary system and the developing nations /.
Washington , 1976. vi, 210 p. :
NYPL [JLE 80-2857]

**UNDERDEVELOPED AREAS - FOOD
SUPPLY - MATHEMATICAL MODELS.**
Reutlinger, Shlomo. Food security in food
deficit countries /. Washington, D.C. , 1980. 39
leaves :   LC Card 80-134211   DDC 338.1/9/1724

19
HD9000.5 .R39

UNDERDEVELOPED AREAS - FOREIGN ECONOMIC RELATIONS - CONGRESSES.
Gilman, Benjamin A. United Nations 11th special session on economic development and cooperation, New York City, August 25-September 15, 1980 . Washington , 1981. vii, 18 p. ; LC Card 81-601276 DDC 338.91 19
HF1410.5 .G54

UNDERDEVELOPED AREAS - GOVERNMENT. see UNDERDEVELOPED AREAS - POLITICS AND GOVERNMENT.

UNDERDEVELOPED AREAS - GOVERNMENT CONSULTANTS.
United Nations. Dept. of Technical Co-operation for Development. Handbook on the improvement of administrative management in public administration . New York , 1979. vii, 67 p. : LC Card 80-119207 DDC 300 s 350.007/5/091724 19
JX1977 .A2 ST/ESA/SER.E/19

UNDERDEVELOPED AREAS - HOUSING POLICY.
United Nations. Dept. of Economic and Social Affairs. An economic framework for investment planning in housing and urban infrastructure. New York, 1973. 47 p.   *NYPL [*ZT-1250]*

UNDERDEVELOPED AREAS - INDUSTRIAL PROMOTION.
International Centre for Industrial Studies. Global and Conceptual Studies Section. Structural changes in industry /. [New York?] , 1979. iv, 152 p. ; LC Card 80-121831 DDC 300 s 338.09172/4 19
JX1977 .A2 UNIDO/ICIS.136

UNDERDEVELOPED AREAS - INDUSTRIES.
International Centre for Industrial Studies. Global and Conceptual Studies Section. Structural changes in industry /. [New York?] , 1979. iv, 152 p. ; LC Card 80-121831 DDC 300 s 338.09172/4 19
JX1977 .A2 UNIDO/ICIS.136

Providencia . [Washington, D.C.?] , 1980. xiii, 327 p. : LC Card 80-603922 DDC 330.9861/8 19
HC28 .P83 1980

UNDERDEVELOPED AREAS - INFANTS' SUPPLIES.
United States. Congress. House. Committee on Foreign Affairs. Subcommittee on International Economic Policy and Trade. Marketing and promotion of infant formula in developing countries . Washington , 1980 [i.e. 1981] iv, 184 p. ; LC Card 81-601782 DDC 380.1/4566462 19
KF27 .F6465 1980g

UNDERDEVELOPED AREAS - IRRIGATION - BIBLIOGRAPHY.
Keith, Susan Jo. The impact of groundwater development in arid lands . Tucson, Ariz. , 1977. vii leaves, 139 p. : LC Card 80-622481 DDC 333.91/0415/097154 19
Z7935 .K44 TD403

UNDERDEVELOPED AREAS - LABOR SUPPLY.
Chuta, Enyinna. Rural non-farm employment . East Lansing, Mich. , 1979. vi, 96 p. ; LC Card 80-621248 DDC 331.12/09173/4 19
HD5852 .C56

UNDERDEVELOPED AREAS - MASS MEDIA.
Hedebro, Göran, 1945- Communication and social change in developing nations . Ames , 1981. p. cm. ISBN 0-8138-0326-8 LC Card 81-8191 DDC 302.2/09172/4 19
HN980 .H4 1981

UNDERDEVELOPED AREAS - MATERNAL HEALTH SERVICES - CONGRESSES.
Maternal and child health/family planning program . New York, N.Y. , 1980. v, 341 p. : LC Card 80-143941 DDC 362.1/982/0091724 19
RG940 .M368

UNDERDEVELOPED AREAS - MILITARY POLICY.
Economic development versus military expenditures in countries receiving U. S. aid . Washington , 1980 [i.e. 1981] x, 93 p. ; LC

Card 81-601000 DDC 338.91/73/01724 19
HC60 .E25

UNDERDEVELOPED AREAS - NUTRITION POLICY.
American Technical Assistance Corporation. Planification de programmes nationaux de nutrition . [Washington, D.C.] [1973] 2 v. : LC Card 80-136136 DDC 362.1/9639 19
TX359 .A43 1973

UNDERDEVELOPED AREAS - PETROLEUM INDUSTRY AND TRADE.
Some perspectives on oil availability for the non-OPEC LDCs . Washington, D.C. , 1980. viii, 48 p. : LC Card 80-603931 DDC 333.8/23211/091724 19
HD9560.5 .S62

UNDERDEVELOPED AREAS - POLITICS AND GOVERNMENT.
United Nations. Dept. of Technical Co-operation for Development. Handbook on the improvement of administrative management in public administration . New York , 1979. vii, 67 p. : LC Card 80-119207 DDC 300 s 350.007/5/091724 19
JX1977 .A2 ST/ESA/SER.E/19

UNDERDEVELOPED AREAS - POOR - ADDRESSES, ESSAYS, LECTURES.
Implementing programs of human development /. Washington, D.C. (1818 H St., N.W., Washington 20433) , c1980. iv, 372 p. : LC Card 80-138428 DDC 361.6/091724 19
HN980 .I47

UNDERDEVELOPED AREAS - PRODUCE TRADE - BIBLIOGRAPHY.
Riley, Peter, 1950- Food and agricultural marketing in developing countries . East Lansing, Mich. , 1979. 49 p. ; LC Card 80-622267 DDC 016.381/41/091724 19
Z7164.F7 R54 HD9000.5

UNDERDEVELOPED AREAS - RENEWABLE ENERGY SOURCES.
United States. Congress. House. Committee on Foreign Affairs. Subcommittee on International Economic Policy and Trade. International energy development assistance programs . Washingon , 1981. v, 120 p. ; LC Card 81-601471 DDC 333.79/15/091724 19
KF27 .F6465 1980f

United States. Congress. Senate. Committee on Energy and Natural Resources. Subcommittee on Energy Conservation and Supply. International applications of renewable energy resources . Washington , 1980. iii, 240 p. : LC Card 81-600634 DDC 333.79 19
KF26 .E553 1980d

UNDERDEVELOPED AREAS - RURAL DEVELOPMENT. see RURAL DEVELOPMENT.

UNDERDEVELOPED AREAS - SOCIAL POLICY - ADDRESSES, ESSAYS, LECTURES.
Implementing programs of human development /. Washington, D.C. (1818 H St., N.W., Washington 20433) , c1980. iv, 372 p. : LC Card 80-138428 DDC 361.6/091724 19
HN980 .I47

UNDERDEVELOPED AREAS - TARIFF.
United Nations. Conference on Trade and Development. Operation and effects of the generalized system of preferences . New York , 1979. vi, 146 p. ; LC Card 80-121468 DDC 300 s 382.7/53 19
JX1977 .A2 TD/B/C.5/61

UNDERDEVELOPED AREAS - TECHNOLOGICAL INNOVATIONS.
National Research Council. Board on Science and Technology for International Development. Panel on Microbial Processes. Microbial processes . Washington, D.C. , 1979. xii, 198 p. : LC Card 79-91534 DDC 660/.62 19
QR53 .N35 1979

UNDERDEVELOPED AREAS - TECHNOLOGY - ABSTRACTS.
United States. National Technical Information Service. Appropriate technology information for developing countries . [Washington, D.C.] [c1980] xxiv, 384 p. (p. 383-384 ordering instructions) ; LC Card 80-601640 DDC 600 19
T49.5 .U56 1980

UNDERDEVELOPED AREAS - TECHNOLOGY - ADDRESSES, ESSAYS, LECTURES.
Appropriate industrial technology for paper products and small pulp mills. New York , 1979. xiii, 149 p. : LC Card 80-108650 DDC 300 s 338.4/7676 19
JX1977 .A2 ID/232/3, no. 3

United Nations. Industrial Development Organization. Conceptual and policy framework for appropriate industrial technology. New York , 1979. xi, 144 p. : LC Card 79-129629 DDC 300 s 338.9/009172/4 19
JX1977 .A2 ID/232/1

UNDERDEVELOPED AREAS - TECHNOLOGY - CONGRESSES.
United Nations Conference on Technical Co-operation Among Developing Countries, Buenos Aires, 1978. The Buenos Aires plan of action for promoting and implementing technical co-operation among developing countries. [New York, N.Y. , 1979?] 23 p. ; LC Card 79-123512 DDC 338.9172/4 19
HC59.7 .U4816 1978

UNDERDEVELOPED AREAS - TECHNOLOGY - DIRECTORIES.
Integrative Design Associates. Appropriate technology . Washington [Springfield, Va.] 1977. iii, 66 p. ; LC Card 77-603848 DDC 338.91/73/0025 19
T49.5 .I554 1977

Mathur, Brij. International directory of appropriate technology resources /. [Washington] , 1980. ca. 500 p. ; LC Card 80-602130 DDC 333.91/0025 19
T49.5 .M37

UNDERDEVELOPED AREAS - TRANSPORTATION.
De Neufville, Richard, 1939- Investment strategies for developing areas : models of transport. Cambridge, 1973. 83 p.
   NYPL [JLF 80-1121]

UNDERDEVELOPED AREAS - TRANSPORTATION - FINANCE.
Moavenzadeh, Fred. Investment strategies for developing areas. [Washington] 1973. xvii, 224 p.   *NYPL [JLF 80-1167]*

UNDERDEVELOPED AREAS - WATER RESOURCES DEVELOPMENT - BIBLIOGRAPHY.
United Nations. Dag Hammarskjold Library. Water resources, planning, and management . New York , 1977. vi, 117 p. ; LC Card 81-478046 DDC 300 s 016.33391 19
JX1977 .A2 ST/LIB/SER.B/23 TC405

UNDERDEVELOPED AREAS - WATER, UNDERGROUND - BIBLIOGRAPHY.
Keith, Susan Jo. The impact of groundwater development in arid lands . Tucson, Ariz. , 1977. vii leaves, 139 p. : LC Card 80-622481 DDC 333.91/0415/097154 19
Z7935 .K44 TD403

UNDERGROUND AREAS - MISSOURI - KANSAS CITY METROPOLITAN AREA - COLLECTED WORKS.
Underground utilization . Kansas City , 1978. 8 v. : LC Card 79-625497 DDC 333.8 19
HD268.K2 U53

UNDERGROUND CONSTRUCTION - ADDRESSES, ESSAYS, LECTURES.
Earth covered buildings . [Washington, D.C.] [Springfield, Va. , foreword 1979] vi, 272 p. : LC Card 79-600114 DDC 690 19
TH4819.E27 E38

Earth covered buildings and settlements /. [Washington, D.C.] [Springfield, Va. , 1979?] iv, 355 p. : LC Card 79-600115 DDC 690 19
TH4819.E27 E37

UNDERGROUND CONSTRUCTION - COLLECTED WORKS.
Underground utilization . Kansas City , 1978. 8 v. : LC Card 79-625497 DDC 333.8 19
HD268.K2 U53

Underground economy . United States. Congress. House. Committee on Ways and Means. Subcommittee on Oversight. Washington , 1980. iv, 501 p. : LC Card 80-602166 DDC 353.0072/44 19
KF27 .W345 1979i

**UNDERGROUND HOUSES. see EARTH
SHELTERED HOUSES.**

**UNDERGROUND RADIOACTIVE WASTE
DISPOSAL. see RADIOACTIVE WASTE
DISPOSAL IN THE GROUND.**

**UNDERGROUND RAILROADS. see
SUBWAYS.**

Underground utilization : a reference manual of
selected works / Truman Stauffer, Sr., editor.
Kansas City : Dept. of Geosciences, University
of Missouri--Kansas City, 1978. 8 v. : ill. ; 28
cm. (A Geographic publication) Includes bibliographies.
CONTENTS. - v. 1. Historical perspective.--v. 2. Uses
for underground space.--v. 3. Space construction
underground.--v. 4. Human response and social
acceptance of underground space.--v. 5. Advantages in
underground space use.--v. 6. Regulations and policy in
the use of underground space.--v. 7. The future of
underground development.--v. 8. Index. LC Card
79-625497   DDC 333.8 19
*1. Land use - Missouri - Kansas City metropolitan
area - Collected works. 2. Underground areas -
Missouri - Kansas City metropolitan area - Collected
works. 3. Underground construction - Collected works.
I. Stauffer, Truman. II. Series: Geographic publication.*
HD268.K2 U53

**UNDERGROUND WATER. see WATER,
UNDERGROUND.**

Underhill, Jack A. French national urban policy
and the Paris region new towns : the search for
community / by Jack A. Underhill, with Paul
Brace and James Rubenstein. [Washington] : U.
S. Dept. of Housing and Urban Development,
Office of International Affairs, [1980] 131 p. :
ill. ; 28 cm. "HUD-513-IA." Bibliography: p. 107-115.
LC Card 80-602925   DDC 307.7/6/0944 19
*1. New towns - France - Paris region. 2. Urban policy -
France. I. Brace, Paul, joint author. II. Rubenstein,
James M., joint author. III. United States. Dept. of
Housing and Urban Development. Office of
International Affairs. IV. Title.*
HT165.P37 U52

Underhill, James Campbell. Phillips, Gary L.
Fishes of the Minnesota region /. Minneapolis ,
1982. p. cm.   ISBN 0-8166-0979-9 :   LC Card
81-14693   DDC 597.092/9776 19
QL628.M6 P47

UNDERSTANDING. see COMPREHENSION.

Understanding and planning for ORV recreation .
Nash, A. E. Keir. Tumwater, Wash. , 19. v, 159
p. :   LC Card 79-625837   DDC 338.3/4 19
GV191.42.W2 N37

Understanding climatic change . United States
Committee for the Global Atmospheric
Research Program. Detroit, Mich. , 1980. xvii,
239 p. :   ISBN 0-8103-1019-8   LC Card 79-22423
QC981.8.C5 U54 1980   **NYPL [JSD 81-49]**

**Understanding fact finding and arbitration in the
public sector.** Zack, Arnold. [Washington,
D.C.] , 1980. 105, 23 p. ;   LC Card 80-601261
DDC 331.89/041353 19
HD8005.6.U5 Z33 1980

**Understanding grievance arbitration in the public
sector.** Zack, Arnold. [Washington, D.C.] ,
1980. 111, 23 p. ;   LC Card 80-602268   DDC
353.001/76 19
JK768.8 .Z32 1980

Understanding human action . Simon, Michael A.
Albany , c1981. p. cm.   ISBN 0-87395-498-X   LC
Card 81-5280   DDC 302 19
HM251 .S622

Understanding the Missouri Constitution. Karsch,
Robert Frederick, 1909- St. Louis [1967] iii,
135 p.   LC Card 68-2186
                          NYPL [JLF 80-1423]

Understandings . Kwilecki, Paul, 1928- Chapel
Hill , c1981. p. cm.   ISBN 0-8078-1486-5   LC
Card 81-2958   DDC 975.8/993043 19
F292.D27 K85

**UNDERTAKERS AND UNDERTAKING -
CONNECTICUT - DIRECTORIES.**
Connecticut. State Dept. of Health Services.
Official list of embalmers, funeral directors, and
funeral homes . Hartford, Conn. [1979] 65 p. ;
LC Card 80-623116   DDC 363.7/5/025746 19
RA622.A7 C66 1979

**UNDERTAKERS AND UNDERTAKING -
INDIANA - DIRECTORIES.**
Indiana. Laws, statutes, etc. [Embalmers' and

funeral directors' law.] Laws, rules, regulations,
and establishments /. [Indianapolis?] [1946?]
40 p. ;   LC Card 80-110713   DDC 344.772/045
347.720445 19
KFI3282.U5 A32 1946

**UNDERTAKERS AND UNDERTAKING -
LAW AND LEGISLATION - INDIANA.**
Indiana. Laws, statutes, etc. [Embalmers' and
funeral directors' law.] Laws, rules, regulations,
and establishments /. [Indianapolis?] [1946?]
40 p. ;   LC Card 80-110713   DDC 344.772/045
347.720445 19
KFI3282.U5 A32 1946

**UNDERTAKERS AND UNDERTAKING -
LAW AND LEGISLATION - UNITED
STATES.**
United States. Bureau of Consumer Protection.
Funeral industry practices . [Washington] ,
1978. 526, [12] p. ;   LC Card 78-603684
KF2042.U5 A8137   **NYPL [JLF 81-308]**

United States. Congress. House. Committee on
Interstate and Foreign Commerce.
Subcommittee on Oversight and Investigations.
Funeral industry, FTC proposed rulemaking .
Washington , 1980. iv, 402 p. ;   LC Card
80-603506   DDC 343.73/0786146 19
KF27 .I5547 1980e

**UNDERTAKERS AND UNDERTAKING -
LAW AND LEGISLATION - VIRGINIA.**
Virginia. Board of Funeral Directors and
Embalmers. Rules, regulations, and by-laws and
Chapter 10.2, Code of Virginia. [Richmond]
[1979?] 24 p. ;   LC Card 80-621938   DDC
344.755/045 347.550445 19
KFV2682.U5 A32 1979a

**UNDERTAKERS AND UNDERTAKING -
UNITED STATES.**
United States. Bureau of Consumer Protection.
Funeral industry practices . [Washington] ,
1978. 526, [12] p. ;   LC Card 78-603684
KF2042.U5 A8137   **NYPL [JLF 81-308]**

UNDERWATER ACOUSTICS.
Urick, Robert J. Sound propagation in the sea
/. [Arlington, Va.] , Washington, D.C. , 1979.
ca. 300 p. in various pagings :   LC Card
80-601623   DDC 534/.23 19
QC233 .U76

**UNDERWATER ACOUSTICS -
CONGRESSES.**
Oceanic sound scattering prediction /. New
York , c1977. xii, 859 p. :   ISBN 0-306-35505-1
LC Card 77-3445
QC242 .O25   **NYPL [JSF 81-96]**

**UNDERWATER DRILLING (PETROLEUM)
see OIL WELL DRILLING, SUBMARINE.**

UNDERWATER EXPLOSIONS.
Young, George Anthony, 1919- Effects of the
explosion of 45 tons of TNT under water at a
depth scaled to test Baker /. White Oak, Md. ,
1954. ix, 154 p. :   LC Card 80-514235   DDC
662/.27 19
VF540 .Y68

**UNDERWATER SOUND. see UNDERWATER
ACOUSTICS.**

Underwood, Larry S. An ecological reserves
report / by Larry S. Underwood and Glenn
Patrick Juday ; prepared for Joint Federal-State
Land Use Planning Commission for Alaska and
Alaska Ecological Reserves Council. Rev.
Anchorage, Alaska : The Commission, 1979-
v. : map (fold. in pocket) ; 29 cm. (A Commission
report - Federal-State Land Use Planning Commission
for Alaska ; 38) CONTENTS. - v. 1. Establishing a
system for Alaska.   LC Card 80-620900   DDC
304.2/0720798 19
*1. Research natural areas - Alaska. I. Juday, Glenn
Patrick, joint author. II. Alaska Ecological Reserves
Council. III. Joint Federal-State Land Use Planning
Commission for Alaska. IV. Series: Joint Federal-State
Land Use Planning Commission for Alaska.
Commission study - Joint Federal-State Land Use
Planning Commission for Alaska , 38. V. Title.*
QH76.5.A4 U52 1979

**UNDERWRITING. see INSURANCE;
SECURITIES.**

UNEMPLOYED.
Sorrentino, Constance. Youth unemployment,
an international perspective. Washington, D.C.
[1981] p. cm.   LC Card 81-607979   DDC

331.3/4137 19
HD6270 .S66

UNEMPLOYED - HAWAII.
Hawaii. Program memorandum: employment/.
[Honolulu], 1977. 30, 7 p.
                          NYPL [*XME-9682]

UNEMPLOYED - LOUISIANA - STATISTICS.
Louisiana. Dept. of Labor. Office of
Management and Finance. Louisiana women in
the labor force, January 1980 /. Baton Rouge,
La. [1980] 33 leaves ;   LC Card 80-622130
DDC 331.4/12/09763 19
HD6096.L85 L68 1980

UNEMPLOYED - STATISTICS.
Mushkin, Selma J., 1913- Indicators of youth
unemployment and education in industrialized
nations /. [Washington] , 1978. v, 181 p. :   LC
Card 79-602354
HD6270 .M87   **NYPL [JLG 81-24]**

UNEMPLOYED - UNITED STATES.
Root, Kenneth. Perspectives for communities
and organizations on plant closings and job
dislocations /. Ames, Iowa [1979] iv, 32
leaves ;   LC Card 80-623164   DDC 338.6/042 19
HD5708.55.U6 R66

United States. Congress. House. Committee on
Education and Labor. Subcommittee on
Employment Opportunities. Oversight hearing
on employment impact of current and proposed
economic policies . Washington , c1980 [i.e.
1981] iii, 51 p. ;   LC Card 81-601627   DDC
339.5/0973 19
KF27 .E3366 1980c

United States. Congressional Budget Office.
Youth unemployment . Washington , 1978. xvii,
45 p. :   LC Card 78-601457
HD6273 .U5 1978

**UNEMPLOYED - UNITED STATES -
CONGRESSES.**
Unemployment, problems and policies . Los
Angeles [1976] 73 p. :   LC Card 77-621485
HD5724 .U614   **NYPL [*XME-9401]**

UNEMPLOYMENT.
OECD countries . Washington, D.C. [1980] iv,
56 p. ;   LC Card 80-604134   DDC 331.13/7 19
HD5707.5 .O43

**UNEMPLOYMENT COMPENSATION. see
INSURANCE, UNEMPLOYMENT.**

**Unemployment compensation benefits to
servicemen released for the good of the
service** . United States. Congress. House.
Committee on Ways and Means. Subcommittee
on Public Assistance and Unemployment
Compensation. Washington , 1979. iii, 28 p. ;
LC Card 80-600678   DDC 343.73/0116 19
KF27 .W3464 1979c

Unemployment compensation bills . United
States. Congress. House. Committee on Ways
and Means. Subcommittee on Public Assistance
and Unemployment Compensation.
Washington , 1980. iv, 243 p. :   LC Card
80-603901   DDC 344.73/024 347.30424 19
KF27 .W3464 1980a

**UNEMPLOYMENT INSURANCE. see
INSURANCE, UNEMPLOYMENT.**

**Unemployment insurance actuarial study and
financial handbook** /. Alaska. Unemployment
Insurance Research Unit. [Juneau, Alaska]
[1979] 68 p. :   LC Card 80-622467   DDC
368.4/4/009798 19
HD7096.U6 A433 1979

Unemployment insurance occasional paper .
(79-6) Kiefer, Nicholas M., 1951- The effect of
alternative partial benefits formulas on
beneficiary part-time work behavior.
Washington, D.C. , 1979. v, 70 p. :   LC Card
80-602692   DDC 368.4/4/00973 s 331.25/723 19
HD7096.U5 U637 no. 79-6

Unemployment, problems and policies : selected
papers / edited by Irving Bernstein. Los
Angeles : Institute of Industrial Relations,
University of California, [1976] 73 p. : graphs ;
28 cm. Microfiche (neg.) NTIS. 1 sheet. 11 x 15 cm.
(PB 268 750) Includes bibliographical references. LC
Card 77-621485
*1. Unemployed - United States - Congresses. 2. United
States - Full employment policies - Congresses. I.
Bernstein, Irving. II. California. University. University
at Los Angeles. Institute of Industrial Relations.*
HD5724 .U614   **NYPL [*XME-9401]**

UNEMPLOYMENT - SOCIAL ASPECTS - UNITED STATES.

United States. Congress. Senate. Committee on Labor and Human Resources. Health and other effects of unemployment . Washington , 1980 [i.e. 1981] iii, 84 p. :   LC Card 81-601598   DDC 362.1/042/0973 19
KF26 .L27 1980r

UNEMPLOYMENT, TECHNOLOGICAL - UNITED STATES - CASE STUDIES.

National Center for Productivity and Quality of Working Life. Productivity and job security . Washington , 1977. vii, 116 p. ;   LC Card 77-604826
HD6331.2.U5 N37 1977

UNEMPLOYMENT - UNITED STATES.

United States. Bureau of Labor Statistics. Estimating State and local area unemployment . [Washington, D.C.] [1980] iv, 95 p. ;   LC Card 80-602828   DDC 331.13/7973 19
HD5724 .U625 1980b

United States. Congress. House. Committee on Education and Labor. Subcommittee on Labor-Management Relations. Hearings on plant closing problems . Washington , 1980. vi, 500 p. :   LC Card 81-600603   DDC 344.73/0125 347.304125 19
KF27 .E347 1980f

UNEMPLOYMENT - UNITED STATES - EFFECT OF INFLATION ON.

United States. Congress. House. Committee on Banking, Finance and Urban Affairs. Conduct of monetary policy (pursuant to Full Employment and Balanced Growth Act of 1978, P.L. 95-523) . Washington , 1981. iii, 191 p. :   LC Card 81-601949   DDC 332.4/973 19
KF27 .B5 1981a

United States. Congress. House. Committee on Banking, Finance and Urban Affairs. Conduct of monetary policy, pursuant to the Full employment and balance growth act of 1978, P.L. 95-523 . Washington , 1980. iii, 325 p. :   LC Card 80-603705   DDC 332.4/973 19
KF27 .B5 1980b

UNEMPLOYMENT - UNITED STATES - STATISTICAL METHODS.

Goldfarb, Robert S. Measuring types of unemployment . Washington , 1978. ix, 52 p. ;   LC Card 79-602636   DDC 331.13/704/0973 19
HD5724 .G63

UNEP. see United Nations. Environment Programme.

UNESCO and the U. S. National Commission for UNESCO . United States. National Commission for the United Nations Educational, Scientific and Cultural Organization. Washington, D.C. , 1977. viii, 48 p. ;   LC Card 78-602328   DDC 341.7/67 19
AS4.U825 U6 1977

UNFAIR COMPETITION. see COMPETITION, UNFAIR.

Unfair Foreign Competition Act of 1979, S. 938 . United States. Congress. Senate. Committee on the Judiciary. Subcommittee on Antitrust, Monopoly, and Business Rights. Washington , 1980. iii, 42 p. :   LC Card 80-604014   DDC 343.73/072 347.30372 19
KF26 .J835 1979n

UNFAIR TRADE PRACTICES. see COMPETITION, UNFAIR.

Unfairness : views on unfair acts and practices in violation of the Federal Trade Commission act : prepared at the request of Howard W. Cannon, chairman, Committee on Commerce, Science, and Transportation, United States Senate. Washington : U. S. Govt. Print. Off., 1980. iii, 248 p. ; 24 cm. At head of title: 96th Congress, 2d session. Committee print. "April 1980." Bibliography: p. 229-230.   LC Card 80-602217   DDC 343.73/072 19
1. Competition, Unfair - United States. 2. Advertising laws - United States. 3. United States. Federal Trade Commission. I. United States. Congress. Senate. Committee on Commerce, Science, and Transportation.
KF1603.5 .U55

UNGER, SHERMAN E., 1927-

United States. Congress. Senate. Committee on Commerce, Science, and Transportation. Nominations--Departments of Commerce and Transportation . Washington , 1981. iii, 5 p. ;

LC Card 81-601952   DDC 353.82 19
KF26 .C69 1981g

UNICAMERAL LEGISLATURES. see LEGISLATIVE BODIES.

UNIDENTIFIED FLYING OBJECTS.

Philosophy of science and the occult /. Albany , 1981. p. cm.   ISBN 0-87395-572-2   LC Card 81-13552   DDC 001.9/01 19
BF1411 .P49

Unification of community corrections /. Nelson, Elmer K. Washington, D.C. , 1980. vi, 164 p. :   LC Card 80-602244   DDC 364.6/8 19
HV9304 .N45

Uniform demographic and economic data, 1970-2000 : summary /. Illinois. Bureau of the Budget. [Springfield] , 1973. 68 p. :
NYPL [JLF 81-5]

Uniform guidelines on employee selection procedures / with an analysis by Mary Green Miner and John B. Miner ; questions and answers on the guidelines prepared by a joint government committee, and a bibliography on testing. Washington, D.C. : Bureau of National Affairs, c1979. 80 p. ; 22 cm. Cover title. "Published in the August 25, 1978, Federal Register [43 FR 38290]" "The guidelines ... adopted by the U. S. Civil Service Commission, the Department of Justice, the Equal Employment Opportunity Commission, and the Department of Labor, became effective as of September 25, 1978." "These guidelines will be applied ... in the enforcement of Title VII of the Civil Rights Act of 1964, as amended by the Equal Employment Opportunity act of 1972."   LC Card 80-134889   DDC 344.73/01133 19
1. Employee selection - Law and legislation - United States. 2. Employment tests - United States - Bibliography. I. Code of federal regulations.
KF3457 .U5

Uniform mud (unifite) deposition in the Hellenic trench, eastern Mediterranean /. Blanpied, Christian. City of Washington , 1981. p. cm.   LC Card 81-607825   DDC 551.46/083/384 19
GC389 .B57

Uniform product liability act . United States. Dept. of Commerce. Task Force on Product Liability and Accident Compensation. [Washington] , 1979. 44 p. ;   LC Card 80-601839   DDC 346.7303/82 19
KF1296 .A8168

Uniform supervision of trustees for charitable purposes act and related rules and regulations. California. Laws, statutes, etc. Sacramento , 1974. 13 p. ;   LC Card 79-119115   DDC 346.794/064 347.940664 19
KFC188 .A3 1974

Uniform system of accounts for railroad companies /. United States. Interstate Commerce Commission. Washington, D. C., 1974. 117 p.;   *NYPL [JLE 81-288]*

UNIFORMS, MILITARY.

United States. Coast Guard. Auxiliary uniform, awards, and flag code manual /. [Washington] , 1974. 115 p. :   *NYPL [JFE 80-1602]*

UNIFORMS, NAVAL. see UNIFORMS, MILITARY.

Unilateral U. S. force reduction in Western Europe. Giddings, Edward N. Carlisle Barracks, Pa., 1972. iii, 45 leaves.   *NYPL [*XM-13703]*

Union astronomique internationale. see International Astronomical Union.

UNION CATALOGS. see CATALOGS, UNION.

UNION COUNTY, ILL. - HISTORY.

Public Library, Winnetka, Ill. Genealogy Projects Committee. An index to the names of persons appearing in History of Alexander. Thomson, Ill. [1973] 129 p.;   LC Card 75-116464
NYPL [IVF (Alexander) (Perrin, W. H. History of Alexander, Union ... counties, Ill. Index)]

Union County, S. C. County Court. see South Carolina. County Court (Union County)

UNION COUNTY, S. C. - GENEALOGY.

South Carolina. County Court (Union County) Union County, South Carolina, minutes of the County Court, 1785-1799 /. Easley, S.C. , c1979. 523 p. ;   ISBN 0-89308-159-0   LC Card 79-66945
KFS2316.U54 A7 1785
NYPL [APR (Union Co., S. C.) 80-3258]

Union County, S. C. Intermediate Court. see South Carolina. Intermediate Court (Union County)

Union County, South Carolina, minutes of the County Court, 1785-1799 /. South Carolina. County Court (Union County) Easley, S.C. , c1979. 523 p. ;   ISBN 0-89308-159-0   LC Card 79-66945
KFS2316.U54 A7 1785
NYPL [APR (Union Co., S. C.) 80-3258]

Union de l'Europe occidental. see Western European Union.

Unión Internacional de Cristalografía. see International Union of Crystallography.

Union internationale de cristallographie. see International Union of Crystallography.

Union internationale de physique pure et appliquée. see International Union of Pure and Applied Physics.

Union list of items received by South Dakota Federal document depositories /. Olsgaard, John N. Vermillion, S.D. , c1980. 107 leaves ;   LC Card 80-623201   DDC 015.73 19
Z1223.Z7 O55 J83

A union list of microform collections in Nassau and Suffolk County libraries /. Feinberg, Richard P. Stony Brook, N.Y. , Bellport, N.Y. , 1980. viii, 220 p. ;   LC Card 81-111481   DDC 011/.36 19
Z1033.M5 F43

UNION LISTS OF PERIODICALS. see PERIODICALS - BIBLIOGRAPHY - UNION LISTS.

Union recognition in the federal government. Washington. 20 x 27 cm. Annual. Report year ends Nov. 30. Published by the U. S. Civil Service Commission, Office of Labor-Management Relations, 1967-77; by the U. S. Office of Personnel Management, Office of Labor-Management Relations, 1978-
1. Employee-management relations in government - United States - Periodicals. 2. Trade-unions - Government employees - United States - Periodicals. I. United States. Civil Service Commission. Office of Labor-Management Relations. II. United States. Office of Personnel Management. Office of Labor-Management Relations.   *NYPL [M-11 4907]*

UNIONS, TRADE. see TRADE-UNIONS.

Unisexual Ambystoma for the Bass Islands of Lake Erie /. Downs, Floyd Leslie. Ann Arbor , 1978. 36 p. :   LC Card 78-622915   DDC 597.6/5 19
QL668.C23 D68

UNIT TRUSTS. see INVESTMENT TRUSTS.

Unitar. see United Nations Institute for Training and Research.

Unitas XX June 16, 1979-December 13, 1979. [Washington, D.C.? : U. S. Dept. of the Navy?, 1980?] 128 p. : ill. (some col.) ; 29 cm. Pictorial cruisebook. Spine title: USS Dewey DDG-45 Unitas XX. Editor: Richard S. Goodwin; contributing photographs, T. Fulkerson et al.; art work, A. Beck.   LC Card 80-603957   DDC 359.3/252/0973 19
1. Dewey (Ship). I. Goodwin, Richard S. II. Fulkerson, T. III. Beck, A. IV. Title: USS Dewey DDG-45 Unitas XX.
VA65.D45 U54

UNITED ARAB EMIRATES - MAPS.

United States. Central Intelligence Agency. United Arab Emirates. [Washington , 1979] 1 map :   LC Card 81-692501
G7570 1979 .U5

United Arab Republic (al-Iqlīm al Misrī) see Egypt.

United Arab Republic (Egyptian region) see Egypt.

United Arab Republic (Southern region) see Egypt.

United Arab Republic (Syrian Region) see Syria.

United Cerebral Palsy Associations. Child abuse and developmental disabilities essays . [Washington] [1980] iii, 45 p. :   LC Card 80-602267   DDC 362.7/044 19
HV713 .C3817

United Cerebral Palsy of Rhode Island. Child abuse and developmental disabilities essays . [Washington] [1980] iii, 45 p. :   LC Card

80-602267   DDC 362.7/044 19
HV713 .C3817

A united front against hegemonism . Heaton, William R. Washington, DC , 1980. vi, 55 p. ; LC Card 80-601629   DDC 327.51 19
DS779.27 .H4

United Nationa. Economic Commission for Europe. High-level Meeting within the Framework of the ECE on the Protection of the Environment, Geneva, 1979. Report of the High-level Meeting within the Framework of the ECE on the Protection of the Environment, Geneva, 13-15 November, 1979 =. New York , 1980. 2 v. in 1 ; LC Card 80-134026   DDC 300 s 363.7 19
JX1977 .A2 ECE/HLM.1/2 TD169

United Nations.
[Document]
(A/CONF.70/A/1) United Nations Conference on Human Settlements, Vancouver, B.C., 1976. Global review of human settlements . [New York?] 1976. 237 p. : LC Card 80-515666   DDC 330 s 307.7/6 19
JX1977 .A2 A/CONF.70/A/1

(A/CONF.70/A/3) United Nations Conference on Human Settlements, Vancouver, B.C., 1976. Physical elements and mobilization of human resources . [New York?] 1976. 92 p. ; LC Card 80-514948   DDC 300 s 361.6 19
JX1977 .A2 A/CONF.70/A/3

(A/CONF.70/A/4) United Nations Conference on Human Settlements, Vancouver, B.C., 1976. Analysis of programmes of the organizations in the United Nations system in the field of human settlements . [New York?] 1976. 133 p. (6 fold) : LC Card 80-515449
JX1977 .A2 A/CONF.70/A/4

(A/CONF.70/INF.2) United Nations Conference on Human Settlements, Vancouver, B.C., 1976. List of documents prepared under the aegis of the Habitat secretariat. [New York?] , 1976. 17 p. ; LC Card 80-514088   DDC 300 s 016.307 19
JX1977 .A2 A/CONF. 70/INF. 2 HT391

(A/CONF.70/Misc.1/Rev.2) United Nations Conference on Human Settlements, Vancouver, B.C., 1976. List of participants. [New York?] , 1976. 238 p. ; LC Card 80-514476   DDC 300 s 307 19
JX1977 .A2 A/CONF.70/Misc.1/Rev.2

(A/CONF.70/PC/11, [etc.]) United Nations Conference on Human Settlements, Vancouver, B.C., 1976. Preparatory Committee. Report of the Preparatory Committee on its first-[second] session /. [New York?] 1975-1976. 3 v. in 1 ; LC Card 81-452275   DDC 300 s 307.7/6 19
JX1977 .A2 A/CONF.70/PC/11, etc.

(A/CONF.70/5) United Nations Conference on Human Settlements, Vancouver, B.C., 1976. Recommendations for national action . [New York?] 1976. 75 p. ; LC Card 81-453323   DDC 300 s 361.6 19
JX1977 .A2 A/CONF.70/5

(A/CONF.80/16/Add.1, [etc.]) United Nations Conference on Succession of States in Respect of Treaties, Vienna, 1977-1978. Official records /. New York , 1979- v. ; LC Card 80-121295   DDC 300 s 341.3/7 19
JX1977 .A2 A/CONF.80/16/Add.1, etc.

(A/CONF.81/16) United Nations Conference on Science and Technology for Development, Vienna, 1979. Report of the United Nations Conference on Science and Technology for Development, Vienna 20-31 August 1979. New York , 1979. iv, 133 p. ; LC Card 80-100608   DDC 303.4/83 19
JX1977 .A2 A/CONF.81/16

(CERD/1) United Nations. General Assembly. Committee on the Elimination of Racial Discrimination. Committee on the Elimination of Racial Discrimination and the progress made towards the achievement of the objectives of the International Convention on the Elimination of All Forms of Racial Discrimination . New York , 1979. vi, 35 p. ; LC Card 80-115627   DDC 300 s 341.4/81 19
JX1977 .A2 CERD/1 HT1521

(E/CEPAL/L.170) Programa de Transporta Marítimo OEA/CEPAL. Bibliografía sobre transporte en Chile /. [New York] , 1977. 66 p. ; LC Card 80-119987
Z7164.T8 P76 1977 HE234.A1

(E/CEPAL/L.190-194) United Nations. Economic Commission for Latin America. The economic relations of Latin America with Europe /. [New York] , 1979. 5 v. ; LC Card 80-122041   DDC 300 s 337.804 19
JX1977 .A2 E/CEPAL/L.190-194
HF1480.55.E9

(E/CN.14/INR/AS/II/2.i) Regional Symposium on Industrial Development, Cairo, 1966. Engineering industries in Africa. [New York] , 1965- v. <2> : LC Card 79-117715   DDC 300 s 338.4/76218/096 19
JX1977 .A2 E/CN.14/INR/AS/II/2.i

(E/CN.14/SWCD/68) United Nations. Economic Commission for Africa. Directory of activities of international voluntary agencies in rural development in Africa /. New York , 1977. iii, 173 p. ; LC Card 79-109825   DDC 300 s 361.7/7/0256 19
JX1977 .A2 E/CN.14/SWCD/68

(E/CN.4/Sub.2/383/Rev. 2) Khalifa, Ahmed M. Assistance to racist regimes in southern Africa . New York , 1979. 41 p. ; LC Card 80-121376   DDC 300 s 323.4/0968 19
JX1977 .A2 E/CN.4/Sub.2/383/Rev.2

(E/ECE/642) United Nations. Economic Commission for Europe. Studies and other publications issued under the auspices of the Economic Commission for Europe, 1947-1966. New York , 1967. viii, 61 p. ; LC Card 80-516623   DDC 300 s 016.33094055 19
JX1977 .A2 E/ECE/642 HC240

(E/ECE/984) United Nations. Economic Commission for Europe. Energy reserves and supplies in the ECE region . New York , 1979. vi, 74 p. : LC Card 80-125171   DDC 333.79/11/094 19
JX1977 .A2 E/ECE/984

(E/ECE/985) United Nations. Economic Commission for Europe. The Economic Commission for Europe and energy conservation . New York , 1980. 76 p. : LC Card 80-135486   DDC 300 s 333.79/16/094 19
JX1977 .A2 E/ECE/985

(E/ICEF/663) United Nations. Children's Fund. Directory of national action for the International Year of the Child (DONA) /. New York , 1979. vii, 396 p. ; LC Card 80-107884   DDC 300 s 362.7 19
JX1977 .A2 E/ICEF/663

(E/5981 ST/ESA/68) United Nations. Centre for Development Planning, Projections, and Policies. Economic and social progress in the second development decade . New York , 1977. ix, 114 p. ; LC Card 80-495289   DDC 300 s 337/.09/047 19
JX1977 .A2 E/5981 ST/ESA/68

(ECE/HLM.1/2) High-level Meeting within the Framework of the ECE on the Protection of the Environment, Geneva, 1979. Report of the High-level Meeting within the Framework of the ECE on the Protection of the Environment, Geneva, 13-15 November, 1979 =. New York , 1980. 2 v. in 1 ; LC Card 80-134026   DDC 300 s 363.7 19
JX1977 .A2 ECE/HLM.1/2 TD169

(ECE/WATER/5) United Nations. Economic Commission for Europe. Manual for the compilation of balances of water resources and needs /. New York , 1974. viii, 80 p. : LC Card 80-513013   DDC 300 s 333.91/0094 19
JX1977 .A2 ECE/WATER/5

(ID/CONF.4/2(ID/229)) United Nations. Industrial Development Organization. World industry since 1960 . New York , 1979. xviii, 422 p. : LC Card 80-105073   DDC 300 s 338.09/046 19
JX1977 .A2 ID/CONF.4/2(ID/229)

(ID/SER.F/8) United Nations. Industrial Development Organization. A fertilizer bulk blending and bagging plant /. New York , 1976. vii, 31 p. : LC Card 81-465178   DDC 300 s 668/.62 19
JX1977 .A2 ID/SER.F/8 TP963

(ID/SER.H/3) Hansen, John R. Guide to practical project appraisal . New York , 1978. viii, 121 p. : LC Card 78-111887   DDC 300 s 658.4/04 19
JX1977 .A2 ID/SER.H/3

(ID/126 (ID/WG.120/10/Rev. 1)) Mattil, K. F. Review and comparative analysis of oilseed raw materials and processes suitable for the production of protein products for human consumption. New York , 1974. viii, 36 p. : LC Card 81-465132   DDC 300 s 664/.64 19
JX1977 .A2 ID/126 (ID/WG.120/10/Rev. 1)

(ID/215(ID/WG.257/23)) Expert Group Meeting on Industrialization in Relation to Integrated Rural Development, Vienna, 1977. Industrialization and rural development. New York , 1978. vii, 104 p. : LC Card 79-109252   DDC 300 s 338.09173/4 19
JX1977 .A2 ID/215(ID/WG.257/23) HD1405

(ID/218) United Nations. Industrial Development Organization. Technological profiles on the iron and steel industry /. New York , 1978. x, 44 p. : LC Card 79-109235   DDC 300 s 338.4/76691 19
JX1977 .A2 ID/218 TS307

(ID/232/1) United Nations. Industrial Development Organization. Conceptual and policy framework for appropriate industrial technology. New York , 1979. xi, 144 p. ; LC Card 79-129629   DDC 300 s 338.9/009172/4 19
JX1977 .A2 ID/232/1

(ID/232/3) Appropriate industrial technology for paper products and small pulp mills. New York , 1979. xiii, 149 p. : LC Card 80-108650   DDC 300 s 338.4/7676 19
JX1977 .A2 ID/232/3, no. 3

(ID/238 (ID/CONF.4/4) United Nations. Industrial Development Organization. Implementation of the Lima declaration and plan of action . New York , 1979. vii, 60 p. ; LC Card 80-114398   DDC 300 s 338.91 19
JX1977 .A2 ID/238/(ID/CONF.4/4) HC60

(ID226(UNIDO/LIB/SER.D/3/Rev.1)) United Nations. Industrial Development Organization. Information sources on leather and leather products industries /. New York , 1979. xii, 85 p. ; LC Card 79-123699   DDC 300 s 016.3384/7675 19
JX1977 .A2 ID/226(UNIDO/LIB/SER.D/3/REV.1)

(ST/CTC/12) United Nations. Centre on Transnational Corporations. The activities of transnational corporations in the industrial, mining, and military sectors of southern Africa /. New York , 1980. v, 79 p. ; LC Card 80-120186   DDC 300 s 338.8/8868 19
JX1977 .A2 ST/CTC/12

(ST/CTC/13) United Nations. Centre on Transnational Corporations. Users guide to the information system on transnational corporations . New York , 1980. iii, 30 p. ; LC Card 80-131497   DDC 300 s 025/.0633888 19
JX1977 .A2 ST/CTC/13 HD2755.5

(ST/CTC/3) United Nations. Centre on Transnational Corporations. Survey of research on transnational corporations /. New York , 1977. iii, 533 p. ; LC Card 80-491957   DDC 300 s 338.8/8/072 19
JX1977 .A2 ST/CTC/3

(ST/CTC/9) United Nations. Centre on Transnational Corporations. Transnational corporations and the pharmaceutical industry /. New York , 1979. vi, 165 p. ; LC Card 79-122316   DDC 300 s 338.8/87 19
JX1977 .A2 ST/CTC/9

(ST/ECLA/Conf.48/L.7/Rev.2) Latin American Preparatory Meeting for the World Population Conference, San José, Costa Rica, 1974. Informe de la reunión /. [New York] , 1974. v, 248 p. ; LC Card 80-119992
HB3530.5 .L37 1974

(ST/ESA/SER.E/18) United Nations. Dept. of Technical Co-operation for Development. Organizational systems for national planning /. New York , 1979. vi, 177 p. : LC Card 79-123608   DDC 300 s 338.9/009172/4 19
JX1977 .A2 ST/ESA/SER.E/18

(ST/ESA/SER.E/22) United Nations. Dept. of Technical Co-operation for Development. Demographic evaluation and analysis of population census data . New York , 1980. iv, 30 p. ; LC Card 80-130816 DDC 300 s 304.6/0723 19
JX1977 .A2 ST/ESA/SER.E/22

(ST/ESA/SER.R/19, [etc.]) United Nations. Dept. of Economic and Social Affairs. National experience in the formulation and implementation of population policy, 1960-1976 /. New York , 1978- v. ; LC Card 78-109255 DDC 300 s 304.6 19
JX1977 .A2 ST/ESA/SER.R/19, etc.

(ST/ESA/SER.R/32) United Nations. Dept. of International Economic and Social Affairs. National experience in the formulation and implementation of population policy, 1960-1976 . New York , 1979. iv, 43 p., [1] leaf of plates : LC Card 80-112443 DDC 300 s 304.6/09598 19
JX1977 .A2 ST/ESA/SER.R/32

(ST/ESA/105) United Nations. Economic and Social Council. Committee for Development Planning. Shaping accelerated development and international changes . New York , 1980. vi, 45 p. : LC Card 80-132246 DDC 300 s 338.91 19
JX1977 .A2 ST/ESA/105

(ST/ESA/78) United Nations. Dept. of Economic and Social Affairs. Systematic monitoring and evaluation of integrated development programmes . New York , 1978. vii, 150 p. : LC Card 78-111938 DDC 300 s 338.9 19
JX1977 .A2 ST/ESA/78

(ST/ESA/95) United Nations Seminar on Technology Assessment for Development, Bangalore, India, 1978. Technology assessment for development . New York , 1979. v, 165 p. : LC Card 80-121462 DDC 300 s 338.9/009172/4 19
JX1977 .A2 ST/ESA/95

(ST/ESA/97) United Nations. Economic and Social Council. Committee for Development Planning. Launching a third decade of development . New York , 1979. viii, 37 p. ; LC Card 80-108221 DDC 300 s 338.91/1724 19
JX1977 .A2 ST/ESA/97

(ST/HR/SER.A/2) Seminar on National and Local Institutions for the Promotion and Protection of Human Rights, Geneva, 1978. Seminar on National and Local Institutions for the Promotion and Protection of Human Rights, Geneva, 18-29 September, 1978 /. New York , 1978. iv, 49 p. ; LC Card 79-111295 DDC 300 s 342/.085 300 s 342.85 19
JX1977 .A2 ST/HR/SER.A/2

(ST/HR/1/rev.1) Human rights . New York , 1978. vii, 132 p. ; LC Card 79-104910 DDC 341.4/81 19
JX1977 .A2 ST/HR/1/rev. 1

(ST/SG/AC.10/1/Rev. 1) United Nations. Committee of Experts on the Transport of Dangerous Goods (1957-) Transport of dangerous goods . New York , 1977. viii, 377 p. : LC Card 81-479997 DDC 300 s /341.7/56 19
JX1977 .A2 ST/SG/AC.10/1/Rev. 1

(ST/SSO/1/Rev.1) Baumer, Michel. Towards a strategy for development in the Sahelian and Sudano-Sahelian zones /. [New York] , 1973. 17 p. ; LC Card 73-23298 DDC 300 s 338.966 19
JX1977 .A2 ST/SSO/1/Rev.1 HC1000.Z9F3

(Trade/INF.2) United Nations. Economic Commission for Europe. Committee on the Development of Trade. Licensing and leasing. [New York] , 1976. 79 p. ; LC Card 81-479680 DDC 300 s 341.7/54 19
JX1977 .A2 Trade/INF.2

(TD/B/C.5/61) United Nations. Conference on Trade and Development. Operation and effects of the generalized system of preferences . New York , 1979. vi, 146 p. ; LC Card 80-121468 DDC 300 s 382.7/53 19
JX1977 .A2 TD/B/C.5/61

(TD/B/C.6/Rev.1) Galtung, Johan. Development, environment, and technology .

New York , 1979. ix, 51 p. : LC Card 80-121830 DDC 300 s 338.9 19
JX1977 .A2 TD/B/C.6/23/Rev.1

(TD/B/C.6/28, TD/B/C.6/AC.4/10) United Nations. Conference on Trade and Development. Group of Governmental Experts on Reverse Transfer of Technology. Report of the Group of Governmental Experts on Reverse Transfer of Technology, held at the Palais des Nations, Geneva, from 27 February to 7 March, 1978. [New York] , 1978. 30, 7, 4 p. ; LC Card 78-111923 DDC 300 s 331.12/791 19
JX1977 .A2 TD/B/C.6/28 TD/B/C.6/AC.4/10 HD8038.A1

(TD/B/C.7/31) United Nations. Conference on Trade and Development. Secretariat. Financial solidarity for development . New York , 1979. 2 v. ; LC Card 80-125802 DDC 300 s 338.91 19
JX1977 .A2 TD/B/C.7/31

(TD/B/740) United Nations. Conference on Trade and Development. Trade and Development Board. Rules of procedure of the main committees of the Trade and Development Board. New York , 1979. v, 38 p. ; LC Card 79-121793 DDC 300 s 341.7/54 19
JX1977 .A2 TD/B/740 HF1410

(TD/OLIVE OIL.6/10) United Nations Conference on Olive Oil, Geneva, 1978. United Nations Conference on Olive Oil, 1978. New York , 1978. iii, 7 p. ; LC Card 79-110907 DDC 300 s 341.7/5475664362 19
JX1977 .A2 TD/OLIVE OIL.6/10 K3947.O43

(UNIDO/ICIS.136) International Centre for Industrial Studies. Global and Conceptual Studies Section. Structural changes in industry /. [New York?] , 1979. iv, 152 p. ; LC Card 80-121831 DDC 300 s 338.09172/4 19
JX1977 .A2 UNIDO/ICIS.136

Document - United Nations .
(ST/ESA/SER.E/19) United Nations. Dept. of Technical Co-operation for Development. Handbook on the improvement of administrative management in public administration . New York , 1979. vii, 67 p. : LC Card 80-119207 DDC 300 s 350.007/5/091724 19
JX1977 .A2 ST/ESA/SER.E/19

Document: ST/ECA.
(186) United Nations. Dept. of Economic and Social Affairs. An economic framework for investment planning in housing and urban infrastructure. New York, 1973. 47 p.
NYPL [*ZT-1250]

(188) United Nations. Dept. of Economic and Social Affairs. Tax treaties between developed and developing countries . New York , 1973. v, 205 p. ;
JX1977 .A2 ST/ESA/18
NYPL [JLF 80-1510]

Documento .
(E/CN.12/929) United Nations. Economic Commission for Latin America. Tendencias y estructuras de la economía de Chile en el último decenio /. [Nueva York] , 1972. iv, 35 p. ; LC Card 80-106375
JX1977 .A213 E/CN.12/929 HC192

Documents .
(ST/ESA/SER.E/20) United Nations/INTOSAI Seminar on Government Auditing, Vienna, 1979. Public auditing techniques for performance improvement . New York , 1980. iii, 108 p. ; LC Card 80-130822 DDC 300 s 351.72/32 19
JX1977 .A2 ST/ESA/SER.E/20

UNITED NATIONS.
International youth organizations and the United Nations /. New York , 1973. v, 95 p. ;
NYPL [JLM 74-1459 no. 17]

United Nations. Dept. of Public Information. Pope John Paul II at the United Nations. New York , 1980. 64 p. : LC Card 80-146375 DDC 282/.092/4 19
BX1378.5 .U54 1980

United Nations. Ad Hoc Group of Experts on Demographic Projections. Prospects of population, methodology, and assumptions : papers of the Ad Hoc Group of Experts on Demographic Projections, United Nations

headquarters, 7-11 November 1977. New York : United Nations, 1979. iv, 292 p. : graphs ; 29 cm. (Population studies ; no. 67) [Document] - United Nations ; ST/ESA/SER.A/67 At head of title: Department of International Economic and Social Affairs. "United Nations publication. Sales no. E.79.XII.3." Bibliography: p. 276-277. LC Card 79-127715 DDC 300 s 304.6 19
1. Population - Congresses. 2. Population forecasting - Congresses. I. United Nations. Dept. of International Economic and Social Affairs. II. Series: Population studies (New York) ; no. 67. III. Title.
JX1977 .A2 ST/ESA/SER.A/67

UNITED NATIONS - ADDRESSES, ESSAYS, LECTURES.
Regionalism and the United Nations /. Dobbs Ferry, N.Y. , 1979. xx, 603 p. ; ISBN 0-379-00591-3 : LC Card 79-14018
JX1979 .R43 ***NYPL [JLE 80-3132]***

United Nations. Africa, Economic commission for. see United Nations. Economic Commission for Africa.

The United Nations and decision-making : the role of women / edited by Davidson Nicol and Margaret Croke. New York : UNITAR, [c1978] 2 v. : ill. ; 23 cm. "Sales no. E.78.XV.CR/10." Bibliography: v. 1, p. 181-185. CONTENTS. - v. 1. A. report on the proceedings of a UNITAR colloquium at Schloss Hernstein, Austria, 13-16 July 1977.--v. 2. Papers presented to a UNITAR colloquium at Schloss Hernstein, Austria, 13-16 July 1977. LC Card 79-126238 DDC 354.1/03 19
1. United Nations - Congresses. 2. Women diplomats - Congresses. 3. United Nations - Officials and employees - Congresses. I. Nicol, Davidson. II. Croke, Margaret. III. United Nations Institute for Training and Research.
JX1977 .U4257

United Nations. Centre for Development Planning, Projections, and Policies. Economic and social progress in the second development decade : assessment of progress made in the implementation of the international development strategy for the second United Nations development decade, the programme of action on the establishment of a new international economic order, the Charter of Economic Rights and Duties of States, and development and international economic co-operation : report of the Secretary-General. New York : United Nations, 1977. ix, 114 p. ; 29 cm. ([Document] - United Nations ; E/5981 ST/ESA/68) United Nations publication : sales no. E.77.II.A11 Includes bibliographical references. LC Card 80-495289 DDC 300 s 337/.09/047 19
1. Economic history - 1945-. 2. International economic relations. I. Series: United Nations. [Document] E/5981 ST/ESA/68. II. Title.
JX1977 .A2 E/5981 ST/ESA/68

United Nations. Centre for Economic and Social Information. Elliott, Charles, 1939- Fair chance for all. New York, 1973. iii, 70 p.;
NYPL [JLD 80-2020]

United Nations. Centre on Transnational Corporations.
The activities of transnational corporations in the industrial, mining, and military sectors of southern Africa / United Nations Centre on Transnational Corporations. New York : United Nations, 1980. v, 79 p. ; 28 cm. ([Document] - United Nations ; ST/CTC/12) "United Nations publication. Sales no. E.80.II.A.3." Includes bibliographical references. LC Card 80-120186 DDC 300 s 338.8/8868 19
1. Investments, Foreign - Africa, Southern. 2. International business enterprises - Africa, Southern. 3. Mineral industries - Africa, Southern. 4. Munitions - Africa, Southern. I. Series: United Nations. [Document] ST/CTC/12. II. Title.
JX1977 .A2 ST/CTC/12

Survey of research on transnational corporations / Centre on Transnational Corporations. New York : United Nations, 1977. iii, 533 p. ; 28 cm. ([Document] - United Nations ; ST/CTC/3) "United Nations publication. Sales no. E.77.II.A.16." Bibliography: p. 433-473. Includes indexes. LC Card 80-491957 DDC 300 s 338.8/8/072 19
1. International business enterprises - Research. I. Series: United Nations. [Document] ST/CTC/3. II. Title.
JX1977 .A2 ST/CTC/3

Transnational corporations and the pharmaceutical industry / United Nations

Centre on Transnational Corporations. New York : United Nations, 1979. vi, 165 p. ; 28 cm. ([Document] - United Nations. ST/CTC/9) "United Nations publication. Sales no. E.79.II.A.3." Bibliography: p. 154-165. LC Card 79-122316 DDC 300 s 338.8/87 19
1. Drug trade. 2. International business enterprises. I. Series: United Nations. [Document] ST/CTC/9. II. Title.
JX1977 .A2 ST/CTC/9

Users guide to the information system on transnational corporations : a technical paper / United Nations Centre on Transnational Corporations. New York : United Nations, 1980. iii, 30 p. ; 29 cm. ([Document] - United Nations. ST/CTC/13) "United Nations publications. Sales no. E.80.II.A." Includes bibliographical references. LC Card 80-131497 DDC 300 s 025/.0633888 19
1. Information storage and retrieval systems - International business enterprises. I. Series: United Nations. [Document] ST/CTC/13. II. Title.
JX1977 .A2 ST/CTC/13 HD2755.5

United Nations. Children's Fund. (Old Catalog form: United Nations children's fund) Directory of national action for the International Year of the Child (DONA) / United Nations Children's Fund. New York : United Nations, 1979. vii, 396 p. ; 28 cm. ([Document] - United Nations. E/ICEF/663) Cover title. LC Card 80-107884 DDC 300 s 362.7 19
1. International Year of the Child, 1979. 2. International Year of the Child, 1979 - Directories. I. Series: United Nations. [Document] E/ICEF/663. II. Title.
JX1977 .A2 E/ICEF/663

United Nations. Comisión Económica para Europa. see United Nations. Economic Commission for Europe.

United Nations. Commission économique pour l'Europe. see United Nations. Economic Commission for Europe.

UNITED NATIONS. COMMISSION ON HUMAN RIGHTS. (Old Catalog form: United Nations. Human Rights Commission.) United States. Congress. House. Committee on Foreign Affairs. Subcommittee on International Organizations. Review of the 36th session of the United Nations Commission on Human Rights . Washington , 1980. iii, 41 p. ; LC Card 80-602983 DDC 341.4/81 19
KF27 .F648 1980b

United Nations. Committee of Experts on the Transport of Dangerous Goods (1957-) Transport of dangerous goods : recommendations / prepared by the Committee of Experts on the Transport of Dangerous Goods.Rev. ed. New York : United Nations, 1977. viii, 377 p. : ill. ; 23 cm. ([Document] - United Nations. ST/SG/AC.10/Rev.1) "United Nations publication :Sales no. E77.VIII.1" Includes index. LC Card 81-479997 DDC 300 s /341.7/56 19
1. Hazardous subtances - Transportation - Law and legislation. I. Series: United Nations. [Document] ST/SG/AC.10/1/Rev. 1. II. Title.
JX1977 .A2 ST/SG/AC.10/1/Rev. 1

United Nations Conference on Human Settlements, Vancouver, B.C., 1976. Analysis of programmes of the organizations in the United Nations system in the field of human settlements : item 11 of the provisional agenda / Habitat--United Nations Conference on Human Settlements, Vancouver, 31 May to 11 June 1976. [New York? : United Nations], 1976. 133 p. (6 fold) : 28 cm. ([Document] - United Nations. A/CONF.70/A/4) LC Card 80-515449
1. Social service - Congresses. I. Series: United Nations. [Document] A/CONF.70/A/4. II. Title.
JX1977 .A2 A/CONF.70/A/4

Global review of human settlements : item 10 of the provisional agenda / Habitat--United Nations Conference on Human Settlements, Vancouver, 31 May to 11 June 1976. [New York? : United Nations], 1976. 237 p. : ill. ; 28 cm. ([Document] - United Nations. A/CONF.70/A/1) Includes bibliographical references. LC Card 80-515666 DDC 330 s 307.7/6 19
1. Urbanization - Congresses. 2. Quality of life - Congresses. 3. Land use - Congresses. I. Series: United Nations. [Document] A/CONF.70/A/1. II. Title.
JX1977 .A2 A/CONF.70/A/1

List of documents prepared under the aegis of the Habitat secretariat. [New York?] : United Nations, 1976. 17 p. ; 28 cm. ([Document] - United Nations. A/CONF.70/INF.2) LC Card 80-514088 DDC 300 s 016.307 19
1. United Nations Conference on Human Settlements, Vancouver, B.C., 1976 - Bibliography - Catalogs. I. Series: United Nations. [Document] A/CONF.70/INF.2. II. Title.
JX1977 .A2 A/CONF. 70/INF. 2 HT391

List of participants. [New York?] : United Nations, 1976. 238 p. ; 28 cm. ([Document] - United Nations. A/CONF.70/Misc.1/Rev.2) LC Card 80-514476 DDC 300 s 307 19
1. United Nations Conference on Human Settlements, Vancouver, B.C., 1976 - Directories. I. Series: United Nations. [Document] A/CONF.70/Misc.1/Rev.2. II. Title.
JX1977 .A2 A/CONF.70/Misc.1/Rev.2

Physical elements and mobilization of human resources : item 10 of the provisional agenda / Habitat--United Nations Conference on Human Settlements, Vancouver, 31 May to 11 June 1976. [New York? : United Nations], 1976. 92 p. ; 28 cm. ([Document] - United Nations. A/CONF.70/A/3) Includes bibliographical references. LC Card 80-514948 DDC 300 s 361.6 19
1. Regional planning - Congresses. 2. Regional planning - Citizen participation - Congresses. 3. Community development - Congresses. 4. Housing - Congresses. I. Series: United Nations. [Document] A/CONF.70/A/3. II. Title.
JX1977 .A2 A/CONF.70/A/3

Recommendations for national action : item 10 of the provisional agenda / Habitat--United Nations Conference on Human Settlements, Vancouver, 31 May to 11 June 1976. [New York? : United Nations], 1976. 75 p. ; 28 cm. ([Document] - United Nations. A/CONF.70/5) LC Card 81-453323 DDC 300 s 361.6 19
1. Regional planning - Congresses. 2. Housing - Congresses. 3. Land use - Congresses. 4. Human ecology - Congresses. 5. Community organization - Congresses. I. Series: United Nations. [Document] A/CONF.70/5. II. Title.
JX1977 .A2 A/CONF.70/5

UNITED NATIONS CONFERENCE ON HUMAN SETTLEMENTS, VANCOUVER, B.C., 1976. United Nations Conference on Human Settlements, Vancouver, B.C., 1976. Preparatory Committee. Report of the Preparatory Committee on its first-[second] session /. [New York?] 1975-1976. 3 v. in 1 ; LC Card 81-452275 DDC 300 s 307.7/6 19
JX1977 .A2 A/CONF.70/PC/11, etc.

UNITED NATIONS CONFERENCE ON HUMAN SETTLEMENTS, VANCOUVER, B.C., 1976 - BIBLIOGRAPHY - CATALOGS. United Nations Conference on Human Settlements, Vancouver, B.C., 1976. List of documents prepared under the aegis of the Habitat secretariat. [New York?] , 1976. 17 p. ; LC Card 80-514088 DDC 300 s 016.307 19
JX1977 .A2 A/CONF. 70/INF. 2 HT391

UNITED NATIONS CONFERENCE ON HUMAN SETTLEMENTS, VANCOUVER, B.C., 1976 - DIRECTORIES. United Nations Conference on Human Settlements, Vancouver, B.C., 1976. List of participants. [New York?] , 1976. 238 p. ; LC Card 80-514476 DDC 300 s 307 19
JX1977 .A2 A/CONF.70/Misc.1/Rev.2

United Nations Conference on Human Settlements, Vancouver, B.C., 1976. Preparatory Committee. Report of the Preparatory Committee on its first-[second] session / Habitat--United Nations Conference on Human Settlements, Preparatory Committee .... [New York? : United Nations], 1975-1976. 3 v. in 1 ; 28 cm. ([Document] - United Nations. A/CONF.70/PC/11, A/CONF.70/PC/18, A/CONF.70/PC/28) At head of title: United Nations. General Assembly. Includes errata sheets. LC Card 81-452275 DDC 300 s 307.7/6 19
1. United Nations Conference on Human Settlements, Vancouver, B.C., 1976. I. Series: United Nations. [Document] A/CONF.70/PC/11, [etc.]. II. Title.
JX1977 .A2 A/CONF.70/PC/11, etc.

United Nations Conference on Olive Oil, Geneva, 1978. United Nations Conference on Olive Oil, 1978. New York : United Nations, 1978.

iii, 7 p. ; 30 cm. ([Document] - United Nations. TD/OLIVE OIL.6/10) United Nations publication. Sales no. E.78.II.D.16 Held 5-7 April 1978. LC Card 79-110907 DDC 300 s 341.7/5475664362 19
1. Olive-oil - Law and legislation. I. Series: United Nations. [Document] TD/OLIVE OIL.6/10.
JX1977 .A2 TD/OLIVE OIL.6/10 K3947.O43

UNITED NATIONS CONFERENCE ON SCIENCE AND TECHNOLOGY FOR DEVELOPMENT. United Nations Conference on Science and Technology for Development, Vienna, 1979. Report of the United Nations Conference on Science and Technology for Development, Vienna 20-31 August 1979. New York , 1979. iv, 133 p. ; LC Card 80-100608 DDC 303.4/83 19
JX1977 .A2 A/CONF.81/16

United Nations Conference on Science and Technology for Development, Vienna, 1979. Report of the United Nations Conference on Science and Technology for Development, Vienna 20-31 August 1979. New York : United Nations, 1979. iv, 133 p. ; 28 cm. ([Document] - United Nations ; A/CONF.81/16) LC Card 80-100608 DDC 303.4/83 19
1. United Nations Conference on Science and Technology for Development. 2. Science - Congresses. 3. Technology - Congresses. I. Series: United Nations. [Document] A/CONF.81/16. II. Title.
JX1977 .A2 A/CONF.81/16

United Nations Conference on Succession of States in Respect of Treaties, Vienna, 1977-1978. Official records / United Nations Conference on Succession of States in Respect of Treaties. New York : United Nations, 1979- v. ; 29 cm. ([Document] - United Nations ; A/CONF.80/16Add.1-Add.2) CONTENTS. - --v. 2. Summary records of the plenary meetings and of the meetings of the Committee of the Whole: resumed session, Vienna, 31 July-23 August 1978.--v. 3. Documents of the conference: 1977 session and resumed session 1978, Vienna, 4 April-6 May 1977 and 31 July-23 August 1978. LC Card 80-121295 DDC 300 s 341.3/7 19
1. Treaties - Congresses. 2. State succession - Congresses. I. Series: United Nations. [Document] A/CONF.80/16/Add.1, [etc.].
JX1977 .A2 A/CONF.80/16/Add.1, etc.

United Nations Conference on Technical Co-operation Among Developing Countries, Buenos Aires, 1978. The Buenos Aires plan of action for promoting and implementing technical co-operation among developing countries. [New York, N.Y. : United Nations Development Programme, Division of Information, 1979?] 23 p. ; 22 cm. Cover title. Includes bibliographical references. LC Card 79-123512 DDC 338.9172/4 19
1. Underdeveloped areas - Technology - Congresses. 2. Technical assistance - Congresses. 3. International cooperation - Congresses. I. Title.
HC59.7 .U4816 1978

UNITED NATIONS CONFERENCE ON THE LAW OF THE SEA, 3D, NEW YORK, ETC., 1973- United States. Congress. House. Committee on Foreign Affairs. The status of the Third United Nations Conference on the Law of the Sea, spring 1980 . Washington , 1980. iii, 84 p. ; LC Card 80-602730 DDC 341.4/5 19
KF27 .F6 1980c

UNITED NATIONS CONFERENCE ON THE LAW OF THE SEA (3RD : 1973- : NEW YORK, ETC.) United States. Congress. Senate. Committee on Foreign Relations. Subcommittee on Arms Control, Oceans, International Operations, and Environment. Law of the sea negotiations . Washington , 1981. iii, 301 p. ; LC Card 81-601946 DDC 341.4/5 19
KF26 .F6286 1981

UNITED NATIONS CONFERENCE ON THE LAW OF THE SEA (3RD : 1973- NEW YORK, N.Y., ETC.) United States. Congress. House. Committee on Foreign Affairs. The 1980 Geneva session and status of the negotiations on the Law of the Sea . Washington , 1980. iii, 69 p. ; LC Card 80-604064 DDC 341.4/5 19
KF27 .F6 1980f

United Nations. Conference on Trade and Development. (Old Catalog form: United Nations Conference on Trade and

GOVERNMENT PUBLICATIONS - U.S.: 1981

385

United Nations. Dept. of International Economic and Social

Development)
Operation and effects of the generalized system of preferences : fourth review : selected studies submitted to the Special Committee on Preferences at its eighth session, Geneva 27 June--1 July 1977 / United Nations Conference on Trade and Development. New York : United Nations, 1979. vi, 146 p. ; 30 cm. ([Document] - United Nations ; TD/B/C.5/61) "United Nations publicztion: Sales no. E.79.II.D.11." Includes bibliographical references.   LC Card 80-121468   DDC 300 s 382.7/53 19
1. Underdeveloped areas - Tariff. 2. Tariff. 3. Underdeveloped areas - Commerce. 4. Commercial policy. I. Series: United Nations. [Document] TD/B/C.5/61. II. Title.
JX1977 .A2 TD/B/C.5/61

Rules of procedure / United Nations Conference on Trade and Development. New York : United Nations, 1968. v, 23 p. ; 21 cm. "United Nations publication : sales no. E.68.I.17."   LC Card 81-469003   DDC 341.7/54 19
1. United Nations. Conference on Trade and Development - Rules and practice. I. Title.
HF1410 .U57 1968b

United Nations. Conference on Trade and Development. Group of Governmental Experts on Reverse Transfer of Technology. Report of the Group of Governmental Experts on Reverse Transfer of Technology, held at the Palais des Nations, Geneva, from 27 February to 7 March, 1978. [New York] : United Nations, 1978. 30, 7, 4 p. ; 28 cm. ([Document] - United Nations. TD/B/C.6/28, TD/B/C.6/AC.4/10)   LC Card 78-111923   DDC 300 s 331.12/791 19
1. Underdeveloped areas - Brain drain. I. Series: United Nations. [Document] TD/B/C.6/28, TD/B/C.6/AC.4/10. II. Title.
JX1977 .A2 TD/B/C.6/28 TD/B/C.6/AC.4/10
HD8038.A1

United Nations. Conference on Trade and Development. International Trade Centre. see **International Trade Centre.**

UNITED NATIONS. CONFERENCE ON TRADE AND DEVELOPMENT - RULES AND PRACTICE. United Nations. Conference on Trade and Development. Rules of procedure /. New York , 1968. v, 23 p. ;   LC Card 81-469003   DDC 341.7/54 19
HF1410 .U57 1968b

United Nations. Conference on Trade and Development. Secretariat. Financial solidarity for development : efforts and institutions of the members of OPEC, 1973-1976 review : report / by the Secretariat of UNCTAD. New York : United Nations, 1979. 2 v. ; 30 cm. ([Document] - United Nations ; TD/B/C.7/31) "United Nations publication. Sales no. E.79.II.D.9." Vol. 2 is a statistical annex. Includes bibliographical references.   LC Card 80-125802   DDC 300 s 338.91 19
1. Organization of Petroleum Exporting Countries - Economic assistance. 2. Underdeveloped areas. I. Series: United Nations. [Document] TD/B/C.7/31. II. Title.
JX1977 .A2 TD/B/C.7/31

Galtung, Johan. Development, environment, and technology . New York , 1979. ix, 51 p. :   LC Card 80-121830   DDC 300 s 338.9 19
JX1977 .A2 TD/B/C.6/23/Rev.1

United Nations. Conference on Trade and Development. Trade and Development Board. Rules of procedure of the main committees of the Trade and Development Board. New York : United Nations, 1979. v, 38 p. ; 21 cm. ([Document] - United Nations ; TD/B/740) At head of title: United Nations Conference on Trade and Development, Geneva. "United Nations publication: Sales no. E.79.II.D.3."   LC Card 79-121793   DDC 300 s 341.7/54 19
1. United Nations. Conference on Trade and Development. Trade and Development Board. I. Series: United Nations. [Document] TD/B/740. II. Title.
JX1977 .A2 TD/B/740 HF1410

UNITED NATIONS. CONFERENCE ON TRADE AND DEVELOPMENT. TRADE AND DEVELOPMENT BOARD. United Nations. Conference on Trade and Development. Trade and Development Board. Rules of procedure of the main committees of the Trade and Development Board. New York , 1979. v, 38 p. ;   LC Card 79-121793   DDC 300 s

341.7/54 19
JX1977 .A2 TD/B/740 HF1410

United Nations. Conférence sur le commerce et le développement. see **United Nations. Conference on Trade and Development.**

United Nations. Conferencia sobre Comercio y Desarrollo. see **United Nations. Conference on Trade and Development.**

United Nations. Conferentie inzake Handel en Ontwikkeling. see **United Nations. Conference on Trade and Development.**

United Nations Congress on the Prevention of Crime and Treatment of Offenders, 5th, Geneva, 1975. Meeting of the Working Group of Experts on Agenda Item 1, "Changes in Forms and Dimensions of Criminality--Transnational and National," University of Maryland, 1975. Changes in forms and dimensions of criminality--transnational and national . College Park [1975?] v, 17 p. ;   LC Card 80-620579   DDC 364 19
HV6010 .M43 1975

UNITED NATIONS - CONGRESSES. The United Nations and decision-making . New York [c1978] 2 v. :   LC Card 79-126238   DDC 354.1/03 19
JX1977 .U4257

United Nations. Crime Prevention and Criminal Justice Section. Meeting of the Working Group of Experts on Agenda Item 1, "Changes in Forms and Dimensions of Criminality--Transnational and National," University of Maryland, 1975. Changes in forms and dimensions of criminality--transnational and national . College Park [1975?] v, 17 p. ;   LC Card 80-620579   DDC 364 19
HV6010 .M43 1975

United Nations. Dag Hammarskjold Library. Bibliographical series . (no. 13) United Nations. Dag Hammarskjold Library. Disarmament, a select bibliography, 1967-1972 /. New York , 1973. xvi, 63 p. ;   LC Card 81-465151   DDC 300 s 327.1/74 19
JX1977 .A2 ST/LIB/SER.B/13 JX1974

(no. 23) United Nations. Dag Hammarskjold Library. Water resources, planning, and management . New York , 1977. vi, 117 p. ;   LC Card 81-478046   DDC 300 s 016.33391 19
JX1977 .A2 ST/LIB/SER.B/23 TC405

Disarmament, a select bibliography, 1967-1972 / Dag Hammarskjold Library. New York : United Nations, 1973. xvi, 63 p. ; 28 cm. (Bibliographical series. no. 13) [Document] - United Nations ; ST/LIB/SER.B/13 "United Nations publication. Sales no. E.73.I.14."   LC Card 81-465151   DDC 300 s 327.1/74 19
1. Disarmament - Bibliography. I. Series. II. Series: United Nations. Dag Hammarskjöld Library. Bibliographical series , no. 13. III. Title.
JX1977 .A2 ST/LIB/SER.B/13 JX1974

Water resources, planning, and management : a select bibliography = Les ressources en eau, leur planification, et leur gestion : bibliographie sélective / Dag Hammarskjöld Library. New York : United Nations, 1977. vi, 117 p. ; 29 cm. (Bibliographical series - Dag Hammarskjöld Library . no. 23) [Document] - United Nations ; ST/LIB/SER.B/23 "United Nations publication ; Sales no. E/F.77.I.4."   LC Card 81-478046   DDC 300 s 016.33391 19
1. Water resources development - Bibliography. 2. Underdeveloped areas - Water resources development - Bibliography. I. Title. II. Title: Ressources en eau, leur planification, et leur gestion. III. Series: United Nations. Dag Hammarskjöld Library. Bibliographical series , no. 23.
JX1977 .A2 ST/LIB/SER.B/23 TC405

United Nations. Dept. of Economic and Social Affairs. An economic framework for investment planning in housing and urban infrastructure. New York, United Nations, 1973. 47 p. illus. 28 cm. (United Nations. Document: ST/ECA. 186) Microfilm. Bibliographical footnotes.
1. Housing - Finance. 2. Underdeveloped areas - Housing policy. I. Title. II. Series.

NYPL [*ZT-1250]

National experience in the formulation and implementation of population policy, 1960-1976

/ Department of Economic and Social Affairs. New York : United Nations, 1978- v. ; 28 cm. ([Document] - United Nations ; ST/ESA/SER.R/19, 23, 25, 28) Includes bibliographies. CONTENTS. - [1] Panama.--[2] Chad.--[3] Oman.--[4] United Republic of Tanzania.   LC Card 78-109255   DDC 300 s 304.6 19
1. Population policy - Collected works. 2. Population - Collected works. I. Series: United Nations. [Document] ST/ESA/SER.R/19, [etc.]. II. Title.
JX1977 .A2 ST/ESA/SER.R/19, etc.

Population studies. (no. 64) United Nations. Dept. of Economic and Social Affairs. Trends and characteristics of international migration since 1950. New York , 1979. vi, 172 p. :   LC Card 79-127707   DDC 325/.09045 19
JX1977 .A2 ST/ESA/SER.A/64

Systematic monitoring and evaluation of integrated development programmes : a source-book / Department of Economic and Social Affairs. New York : United Nations, 1978. vii, 150 p. : ill. ; 28 cm. ([Document] - United Nations. ST/ESA/78) "United Nations publication. Sales no. E.78.IV.11." Includes bibliographical references.   LC Card 78-111938   DDC 300 s 338.9 19
1. Economic development - Evaluation. I. Series: United Nations. [Document] ST/ESA/78. II. Title.
JX1977 .A2 ST/ESA/78

Tax treaties between developed and developing countries : fourth report / Department of Economic and Social Affairs. New York : United Nations, 1973. v, 205 p. ; 28 cm. (United Nations. Document: ST/ECA. 188) "United Nations publication. Sales no. E.73.XVI.1."
1. Taxation, Double - Treaties. I. Title. II. Series.
JX1977 .A2 ST/ESA/18

NYPL [JLF 80-1510]

Trends and characteristics of international migration since 1950. New York : United Nations, 1979. vi, 172 p. : graphs ; 28 cm. (Demographic [i.e. Population] studies ; no. 64) [Document] - United Nations ; ST/ESA/SER.A/64 Includes bibliographical references. "United Nations publication. Sales no. E.78.XIII.5."   LC Card 79-127707   DDC 325/.09045 19
1. Emigration and immigration - Statistics. I. Series: United Nations. Dept. of Economic and Social Affairs. Population studies, no. 64. II. Title.
JX1977 .A2 ST/ESA/SER.A/64

United Nations. Dept. of Economic and Social Affairs. Division of Narcotic Drugs. see **United Nations. Division of Narcotic Drugs.**

United Nations. Dept. of Economic and Social Affairs. Population Division. see **United Nations. Population Division.**

United Nations. Dept. of Economic and Social Affairs. Statistical Office. see **United Nations. Statistical Office.**

United Nations. Dept. of International Economic and Social Affairs. National experience in the formulation and implementation of population policy, 1960-1976 : Indonesia / Department of International Economic and Social Affairs. New York : United Nations, 1979. iv, 43 p., [1] leaf of plates : map ; 28 cm. ([Document] - United Nations ; ST/ESA/SER.R/32) Includes bibliographical references.   LC Card 80-112443   DDC 300 s 304.6/09598 19
1. Indonesia - Population policy. I. Series: United Nations. [Document] ST/ESA/SER.R/32. II. Title.
JX1977 .A2 ST/ESA/SER.R/32

Patterns of urban and rural population growth. New York : United Nations, 1980. ix, 175 p. : ill. ; 28 cm. (Population studies . no. 68) [Document] - United Nations ; ST/ESA/SER.A/68 "United Nations publication. Sales no. E.79.XIII.9." Includes bibliographical references.   LC Card 80-138417   DDC 081 s 304.6/2 19
1. Population. 2. Rural population. 3. Urbanization. I. Series: Population studies (New York) , no. 68. II. Title.
JX1977 .A2 ST/ESA/SER.A/68 HB1951

United Nations. Ad Hoc Group of Experts on Demographic Projections. Prospects of population, methodology, and assumptions . New York , 1979. iv, 292 p. :   LC Card 79-127715   DDC 300 s 304.6 19
JX1977 .A2 ST/ESA/SER.A/67

United Nations. Economic and Social Council.

BIBLIOGRAPHIC GUIDE

United Nations. Dept. of International Economic and Social

386

Committee for Development Planning. Launching a third decade of development . New York , 1979. viii, 37 p. ; LC Card 80-108221 DDC 300 s 338.91/1724 19
JX1977 .A2 ST/ESA/97

United Nations. Economic and Social Council. Committee for Development Planning. Shaping accelerated development and international changes . New York , 1980. vi, 45 p. : LC Card 80-132246 DDC 300 s 338.91 19
JX1977 .A2 ST/ESA/105

United Nations Seminar on Technology Assessment for Development, Bangalore, India, 1978. Technology assessment for development . New York , 1979. v, 165 p. : LC Card 80-121462 DDC 300 s 338.9/009172/4 19
JX1977 .A2 ST/ESA/95

United Nations. Dept. of Public Information.
Pope John Paul II at the United Nations. New York : Dept. of Public Information, United Nations, 1980. 64 p. : col ill. ; 29 cm. "United Nations publications. Sales no. E.80.I.8." LC Card 80-146375 DDC 282/.092/4 19
1. John Paul II, Pope, 1920- - Journeys - New York (City). 2. United Nations. 3. Popes - Voyages and travels - New York (City). I. John Paul II, Pope, 1920-. II. Title.
BX1378.5 .U54 1980

United Nations. Dept. of Social Affairs. (Old Catalog form: United Nations. Secretariat. Social Affairs Dept.)
Bulletin on narcotics. v. 1- ; Oct. 1949- New York [etc.] LC Card 53-18079 *NYPL [VTYA (United Nations. Secretariat. Social Affairs Dept. Bulletin on narcotics)]*

International review of criminal policy. NO. 1- ; 1952- New York. *NYPL [*ZAN-4630]*

United Nations. Dept. of Technical Cooperation for Development.
United Nations. Dept. of Technical Co-operation for Development.
Demographic evaluation and analysis of population census data : aspects of technical co-operation / Department of Technical Co-operation for Development. New York : United Nations, 1980. iv, 30 p. ; 28 cm. ([Document] - United Nations. ST/ESA/SER.E/22) Includes bibliographies. LC Card 80-130816 DDC 300 s 304.6/0723 19
1. Census. 2. Population assistance. I. Series: United Nations. [Document] ST/ESA/SER.E/22. II. Title.
JX1977 .A2 ST/ESA/SER.E/22

Handbook on the improvement of administrative management in public administration : measures to enhance the effectiveness of organization and methods services in government / United Nations, Department of Technical Co-operation for Development. New York : The Dept., 1979. vii, 67 p. : ill. ; 28 cm. ([Document] - United Nations ; ST/ESA/SER.E/19) LC Card 80-119207 DDC 300 s 350.007/5/091724 19
1. Public administration. 2. Organizational effectiveness. 3. Underdeveloped areas - Government consultants. 4. Underdeveloped areas - Politics and government. I. Series: United Nations. Document - United Nations , ST/ESA/SER.E/19. II. Title.
JX1977 .A2 ST/ESA/SER.E/19

Organizational systems for national planning / Department of Technical Co-operation for Development. New York : United Nations, 1979. vi, 177 p. : ill. ; 28 cm. ([Document] - United Nations ; ST/ESA/SER.E/18) Prepared by C. Y. Wu, J. Pajestka, and A. Lukaszewicz. "United Nations publication. Sales no. E.79.II.H.2." Includes bibliographical references. LC Card 79-123608 DDC 300 s 338.9/009172/4 19
1. Economic policy. 2. Underdeveloped areas - Economic policy. I. Wu, Ch'i-yüan, 1912-. II. Pajestka, Jozef. III. Lukaszewicz, Aleksander. IV. Series: United Nations. [Document] ST/ESA/SER.E/18. V. Title.
JX1977 .A2 ST/ESA/SER.E/18

United Nations/INTOSAI Seminar on Government Auditing, Vienna, 1979. Public auditing techniques for performance improvement . New York , 1980. iii, 108 p. ; LC Card 80-130822 DDC 300 s 351.72/32 19
JX1977 .A2 ST/ESA/SER.E/20

The United Nations Development Programme .
United Nations. Development Programme. New York, 1974. 28 p. *NYPL [JLF 81-606]*

United Nations. Development Programme. The United Nations Development Programme : a graphic picture of its operations. New York, The Programme, 1974. 28 p. ill., maps. 28 cm. Cover title. At head of title: UNDP.
1. United Nations. Development Programme. I. Title.
NYPL [JLF 81-606]

UNITED NATIONS. DEVELOPMENT PROGRAMME.
United Nations. Development Programme. The United Nations Development Programme . New York, 1974. 28 p. *NYPL [JLF 81-606]*

United Nations. Division of Human Rights.
Human rights . New York , 1978. vii, 132 p. ; LC Card 79-104910 DDC 341.4/81 19
JX1977 .A2 ST/HR/1/rev. 1

Seminar on National and Local Institutions for the Promotion and Protection of Human Rights, Geneva, 1978. Seminar on National and Local Institutions for the Promotion and Protection of Human Rights, Geneva, 18-29 September, 1978 /. New York , 1978. iv, 49 p. ; LC Card 79-111295 DDC 300 s 342/.085 300 s 342.85 19
JX1977 .A2 ST/HR/SER.A/2

United Nations. Division of Narcotic Drugs.
Bulletin on narcotics. v. 1- ; Oct. 1949- New York [etc.] LC Card 53-18079 *NYPL [VTYA (United Nations. Secretariat. Social Affairs Dept. Bulletin on narcotics)]*

United Nations. Economic and Social Affairs, Dept. of. see **United Nations. Dept. of Economic and Social Affairs.**

United Nations. Economic and Social Council. Commission on Human Rights. see **United Nations. Commission on Human Rights.**

United Nations. Economic and Social Council. Committee for Development Planning.
Launching a third decade of development : comments and recommendations of the Committee for Development Planning. New York : United Nations, 1979. viii, 37 p. ; 23 cm. ([Document] - United Nations. ST/ESA/97) At head of title: Department of International Economic and Social Affairs. "United Nations publication. Sales no. E.79.II.A.7." Bibliography: p. 35-36. LC Card 80-108221 DDC 300 s 338.91/1724 19
1. Underdeveloped areas - Economic policy. 2. International economic relations. I. United Nations. Dept. of International Economic and Social Affairs. II. Series: United Nations. [Document] ST/ESA/97. III. Title.
JX1977 .A2 ST/ESA/97

Shaping accelerated development and international changes : views and recommendations of the Committee for Development Planning relating to the international development strategy for a third United Nations development decade. New York : United Nations, 1980. vi, 45 p. : graph ; 23 cm. ([Document] - United Nations. ST/ESA/105) At head of title: Department of International Economic and Social Affairs. United Nations publication. Sales no. E.80.II.A.4. LC Card 80-132246 DDC 300 s 338.91 19
1. Economic assistance. 2. United Nations - Economic assistance. I. United Nations. Dept. of International Economic and Social Affairs. II. Series: United Nations. [Document] ST/ESA/105. III. Title.
JX1977 .A2 ST/ESA/105

United Nations Economic and Social Council. Development Programme. see **United Nations. Development Programme.**

United Nations. Economic and Social Council. Economic commission for Africa. see **United Nations. Economic Commission for Africa.**

United Nations. Economic and Social Council. Economic Commission for Europe. see **United Nations. Economic Commission for Europe.**

United Nations. Economic and Social Council. Economic Commission for Latin America. see **United Nations. Economic Commission for Latin America.**

UNITED NATIONS - ECONOMIC ASSISTANCE.
United Nations. Economic and Social Council. Committee for Development Planning. Shaping accelerated development and international changes . New York , 1980. vi, 45 p. : LC

Card 80-132246 DDC 300 s 338.91 19
JX1977 .A2 ST/ESA/105

United States. Congress. House. Committee on Foreign Affairs. Subcommittee on International Economic Policy and Trade. U.N. special session on development . Washington , 1981. iii, 95 p. ; LC Card 81-601370 DDC 327.1/11/0973 19
KF27 .F6465 1980e

United Nations. Economic Commission for Africa.
Directory of activities of international voluntary agencies in rural development in Africa / Economic Commission for Africa (Addis Ababa). 3d ed. New York : United Nations, 1977. iii, 173 p. ; 28 cm. (Social welfare services in Africa) [Document] - United Nations ; E/CN.14/SWCD/68. LC Card 79-109825 DDC 300 s 361.7/7/0256 19
1. Rural development - Africa - Directories. 2. Voluntarism - Africa - Directories. I. Series. II. Series: United Nations. [Document] E/CN.14/SWCD/68. III. Title.
JX1977 .A2 E/CN.14/SWCD/68

Regional Symposium on Industrial Development, Cairo, 1966. Engineering industries in Africa. [New York] , 1965- v. <2> : LC Card 79-117715 DDC 300 s 338.4/76218/096 19
JX1977 .A2 E/CN.14/INR/AS/II/2.i

United Nations. Economic Commission for Africa and Near East. see **United Nations. Economic Commission for Africa.**

Social welfare services in Africa. see **Social welfare services in Africa.**

United Nations. Economic Commission for Europe.
Census of motor traffic on main international traffic arteries (1975) = Recensement de la circulation motorisée sur les grandes routes de circulation internationale (1975). New York : Economic Commission for Europe, 1979. 1 portfolio (96 p. in various pagings : 10 fold. col. maps) ; 31 cm. Cover title. English and French. Each map accompanied by indexed tables: 1975 motor traffic density data at counting posts on E roads. "United Nations publication. Numéro de vente: E/F.78.11.3." LC Card 80-675269 DDC 912/.138831/094
1. Traffic surveys - Europe - Maps. 2. Traffic flow - Europe - Maps. 3. Europe - Road maps. I. Title. II. Title: Recensement de la circulation motorisée sur les grandes routes de circulation internationale (1975).
G1797.21.P21 U55 1979

The Economic Commission for Europe and energy conservation : recent experience and prospects / Economic Commission for Europe. New York : United Nations, 1980. 76 p. : ill. ; 30 cm. ([Document] - United Nations. E/ECE/985) "United Nations publication. Sales no. E.80.II.E.4." Includes bibliographical references. LC Card 80-135486 DDC 300 s 333.79/16/094 19
1. Europe - Industries - Energy conservation. 2. Energy conservation - Europe. 3. Energy policy - Europe. I. Series: United Nations. [Document] E/ECE/985. II. Title.
JX1977 .A2 E/ECE/985

Energy reserves and supplies in the ECE region : present situation and perspectives / Economic Commission for Europe. New York : United Nations, 1979. vi, 74 p. : ill. ; 30 cm. ([Document] - United Nations ; E/ECE/984) Includes bibliographical references. LC Card 80-125171 DDC 333.79/11/094 19
1. Power resources. 2. Power resources - Europe. I. Series: United Nations. [Document] E/ECE/984. II. Title.
JX1977 .A2 E/ECE/984

Manual for the compilation of balances of water resources and needs / Economic Commission for Europe. New York : United Nations, 1974. viii, 80 p. : ill. ; 28 cm. ([Document] - United Nations ; ECE/WATER/5) "United Nations publication. Sales no. E.74.II.E.2." Bibliography: p. 65-77. LC Card 80-513013 DDC s 333.91/0094 19
1. Water resource development - Europe. I. Series: United Nations. [Document] ECE/WATER/5. II. Title.
JX1977 .A2 ECE/WATER/5

Studies and other publications issued under the auspices of the Economic Commission for Europe, 1947-1966. New York : United Nations, 1967. viii, 61 p. ; 23 cm. ([Document] -

United Nations. E/ECE/642) "United Nations publication. Sales no. 67.II.E.4." Includes index. LC Card 80-516623 DDC 300 s 016.33094055 19
1. *Europe - Economic conditions - 1945- - Bibliography. I. Series: United Nations. [Document] E/ECE/642.*
JX1977 .A2 E/ECE/642 HC240

United Nations. Economic Commission for Europe. Committee on the Development of Trade. Licensing and leasing. [New York] : Committee on the Development of Trade, United Nations Economic Commission for Europe, 1976. 79 p. ; 28 cm. ([Document] - United Nations. Trade/INF.2) United Nations publication : sales no. E.76.II.E.15 Cover title. Bibliography: p. 24-31. LC Card 81-479680 DDC 300 s 341.7/54 19
1. *Foreign licensing agreements. 2. Leases. I. Series: United Nations. [Document] Trade/INF.2. II. Title.*
JX1977 .A2 Trade/INF.2

United Nations. Economic Commission for Latin America.
The economic relations of Latin America with Europe / United Nations, Economic and Social Council, Economic Commission for Latin America. [New York] : The Commission, 1979. 5 v. ; 28 cm. ([Document] - United Nations ; E/CEPAL/L.190-194) "79-5-1192-1196." Includes bibliographical references. CONTENTS. - 1. Latin America, a case of contradictory development.--2. Latin American trade with Europe.--3. Direct private investment.--4. Financing.--5. The future of these relations. Notes for an analysis. LC Card 80-122041 DDC 300 s 337.804 19
1. *Latin America - Foreign economic relations - Europe. 2. Europe - Foreign economic relations - Latin America. 3. Latin America - Economic conditions - 1945-. I. Series: United Nations. [Document] E/CEPAL/L.190-194. II. Title.*
JX1977 .A2 E/CEPAL/L.190-194
  HF1480.55.E9

Latin American Preparatory Meeting for the World Population Conference, San José, Costa Rica, 1974. Informe de la reunión /. [New York] , 1974. v, 248 p. ; LC Card 80-119992
HB3530.5 .L37 1974

Programa de Transporta Marítimo OEA/CEPAL. Bibliografía sobre transporte en Chile /. [New York] , 1977. 66 p. ; LC Card 80-119987
Z7164.T8 P76 1977 HE234.A1

Tendencias y estructuras de la economía de Chile en el último decenio / Naciones Unidas, Consejo Económico y Social, Comisión Económica para América Latina. [Nueva York] : La Comisión, 1972. iv, 35 p. ; 28 cm. ([Documento] - Naciones Unidas . E/CN.12/929) LC Card 80-106375
1. *Chile - Economic conditions - 1918-1970. 2. Chile - Social conditions. I. Series: United Nations. Documento , E/CN.12/929. II. Title.*
JX1977 .A213 E/CN.12/929 HC192

United Nations Educational, Scientific and Cultural Organization.
International Conference on Magnetohydrodynamic Electrical Power Generation, 7th, Massachusetts Institute of Technology, 1980. Seventh International Conference on MHD Electrical Power Generation /. Cambridge, Mass. , 1980. 2 v. :
    NYPL [JSF 80-963]

Joint Unesco-World Bank Seminar on the Social and Cultural Impacts of Tourism, Washington, D.C., 1976. Tourism--passport to development? . [New York] , c1979. xviii, 360 p. : ISBN 0-19-520149-3 : LC Card 79-18116
G154.9 .J64 1976   NYPL [JLE 80-2592]

UNITED NATIONS EDUCATIONAL, SCIENTIFIC AND CULTURAL ORGANIZATION.
United States. National Commission for the United Nations Educational, Scientific and Cultural Organization. UNESCO and the U. S. National Commission for UNESCO . Washington, D.C. , 1977. viii, 48 p. ; LC Card 78-602328 DDC 341.7/67 19
AS4.U825 U6 1977

United Nations Educational, Scientific and Cultural Organization. International Geological Correlation Programme. see International Geological Correlation Programme.

United Nations Educational, Scientific and Cultural Organization. Programme international de correlation geologique. see International Geological Correlation Programme.

United Nations Environment Program. see United Nations. Environment Programme.

United Nations. Environment Programme. Compendium of legislative authority. v. 1, suppl. 1- ; 1978- [New York]
    NYPL [Econ. Div.]

United Nations. Europäische Wirtschaftskommission. see United Nations. Economic Commission for Europe.

United Nations. Europe, Economic Commission for. see United Nations. Economic Commission for Europe.

United Nations. European Economic Commission. see United Nations. Economic Commission for Europe.

United Nations. European Office. Division of Narcotic Drugs. see United Nations. Division of Narcotic Drugs.

United Nations. Evropeiskaya Ekonomicheskaya Komissiya. see United Nations. Economic Commission for Europe.

United Nations Fund for Population Activities.
Consultation on population assistance co-ordination, Geneva, 15-16 March 1979. [New York, N.Y.] [1979] 38 p. ; LC Card 80-106090
HB884.5 .C66

Perera, Lakshmi. Sri Lanka. [New York, N.Y. (485 Lexington Ave., New York 10017)] [1980] 30 p. ; ISBN 0-89714-011-7 (pbk.) : LC Card 80-138983 DDC 304.6/09549/3 19
HB3636.8.A3 P47

United Nations. General Assembly.
[Charter of economic rights and duties of States]
Meagher, Robert F. An international redistribution of wealth and power : a study of the Charter of economic rights and duties of States / Robert F. Meagher. New York , c1979. xvii, 303 p. ; ISBN 0-08-022478-4 LC Card 78-27906
K3823 .M3   NYPL [JLE 81-2]

CHARTER OF ECONOMIC RIGHTS AND DUTIES OF STATES
Meagher, Robert F. An international redistribution of wealth and power . New York , c1979. xvii, 303 p. ; ISBN 0-08-022478-4 LC Card 78-27906
K3823 .M3   NYPL [JLE 81-2]

The international bill of human rights. New York : United Nations, 1978. 42 p. ; 23 cm. At head of title: Office of Public Information. CONTENTS. - Universal declaration of human rights.--International covenant on economic, social, and cultural rights.--International covenant on civil and political rights, and optional protocol. LC Card 78-109249 DDC 341.4/81 19
1. *Civil rights (International law). I. United Nations. Office of Public Information. II. Title.*
K3238.A1 I53

United Nations. General Assembly. 32d session, 1977. Votes at the thirty-second regular session of the General Assembly, 20 September-21 December, 1977. [Washington, D.C.] : U. S. Dept. of State, Office of Multilateral Affairs, Reference and Documents Section, Bureau of International Organization Affairs : Information Systems Office, Bureau of Administration, [1978?] lix, 469 p. ; 22 x 28 cm. Cover title. LC Card 80-601606 DDC 341.23/22 19
1. *United Nations - Voting - Indexes. I. United States. Dept. of State. Office of Multilateral Affairs. Reference and Documents Section. II. United States. Dept. of State. Information Systems Office. III. Title.*
JX1977.8.V6 U54 1977

United Nations. General Assembly. 34th session, 1979. Delegation from the United States.
Congressional delegates at the 1979 United Nations General Assembly : report to the Committee on Foreign Affairs, U. S. House of Representatives / by the Congressional members of the United States delegation to the 34th session of the General Assembly of the United Nations, September 18 to December 18,

1979. Washington : U. S. Govt. Print. Off., 1980. vii, 265 p. ; 24 cm. At head of title: Committee print, 96th Congress, 2d session. "April 1980." LC Card 80-602273 DDC 341.23/73 19
1. *United Nations - United States. I. United States. Congress. House. Committee on Foreign Affairs. II. Title.*
JX1977.2.U5 U55 1979a

United Nations. General Assembly. Committee on the Elimination of Racial Discrimination.
Committee on the Elimination of Racial Discrimination and the progress made towards the achievement of the objectives of the International Convention on the Elimination of All Forms of Racial Discrimination : published on the occasion of the World Conference to Combat Racism and Racial Discrimination, Geneva, 14-25 August 1978. New York : United Nations, 1979. vi, 35 p. ; 30 cm. ([Document] - United Nations ; CERD/1) "United Nations publication. Sales no. E.79.XIV.4." LC Card 80-115627 DDC 300 s 341.4/81 19
1. *Race discrimination. I. World Conference to Combat Racism and Racial Discrimination, Geneva, 1978. II. Series: United Nations. [Document] CERD/1. III. Title.*
JX1977 .A2 CERD/1 HT1521

United Nations. General Assembly. Conference on Trade and Development. see United Nations. Conference on Trade and Development.

United Nations. General Assembly. Palestine, Special Committee on. see United Nations. General Assembly. Special Committee on Palestine.

United Nations. General Assembly. Special Committee on Palestine. (Old Catalog form: United Nations, Palestine, Special Committee on.)
Palestine Economic Corporation. Memorandum /. New York [1947] 16 p. ;
    *NYPL [*XMH-1601]*

United Nations. Human Rights Commission. see United Nations. Commission on Human Rights.

United Nations. Industrial Development Organization.
Appropriate industrial technology for paper products and small pulp mills. New York , 1979. xiii, 149 p. ; LC Card 80-108650 DDC 300 s 338.4/7676 19
JX1977 .A2 ID/232/3, no. 3

Conceptual and policy framework for appropriate industrial technology. New York : United Nations, 1979. xi, 144 p. ; 24 cm. (Monographs on appropriate industrial technology . no. 1) [Document] - United Nations ; ID/232/1 At head of title: United Nations Industrial Development Organization. LC Card 79-129629 DDC 300 s 338.9/009172/4 19
1. *Underdeveloped areas - Technology - Addresses, essays, lectures. I. Series. II. Series: United Nations. [Document] ID/232/1. III. Title.*
JX1977 .A2 ID/232/1

Expert Group Meeting on Industrialization in Relation to Integrated Rural Development, Vienna, 1977. Industrialization and rural development. New York , 1978. vii, 104 p. : LC Card 79-109252 DDC 300 s 338.09173/4 19
JX1977 .A2 ID/215(ID/WG.257/23) HD1405

A fertilizer bulk blending and bagging plant / United Nations Industrial Development Organization. New York : United Nations, 1976. vii, 31 p. : 11 ill. ; 24 cm. (Fertilizer industry series . monograph no. 8) [Document] - United Nations ; ID/SER.F/8 "Prepared by J. Skaadel ... and the secretariat of UNIDO." "United Nations publication. Sales no.: E.76.II.B.2." Bibliography: p. 31. LC Card 81-465178 DDC 300 s 668/.62 19
1. *Fertilizers and manures - Packing. I. Skaadel, J. II. Series. III. Series: United Nations. [Document] ID/SER.F/8. IV. Title.*
JX1977 .A2 ID/SER.F/8 TP963

Implementation of the Lima declaration and plan of action : the country situation and contribution of international organizations : report of the secretariat of UNIDO / United Nations Industrial Development Organization. New York : United Nations, 1979. vii, 60 p. ; 25 cm. ([Document] - United Nations - ID/238 (ID/CONF.4/4)) LC Card 80-114398 DDC 300 s 338.91 19

1. Economic assistance. 2. International economic relations. I. Series: United Nations. [Document] ID/238 (ID/CONF.4/4. II. Title.
JX1977 .A2 ID/238/(ID/CONF.4/4) HC60

Industrial Development Centre for Arab States. Economic and Technical Dept. Comparative study of development plans of Arab states. New York , 1976. 268 p. ;   LC Card 80-495288   DDC 338.9/009174927 19
HC498 .I57 1976

Information sources on leather and leather products industries / United Nations Industrial Development Organization. Rev. ed. New York : United Nations, 1979. xii, 85 p. ; 21 cm. ([Document] - United Nations ; ID/226(UNIDO/LIB/SER.D/3/Rev.1)) UNIDO guides to information sources ; no. 3 Published in 1972 under title: Information sources on the leather and leather goods industry. Bibliography: p. 83-85.   LC Card 79-123699   DDC 300 s 016.3384/7675 19
1. Leather industry and trade - Information services. 2. Leather industry and trade - Directories. 3. Leather industry and trade - Bibliography. I. Series: United Nations. [Document] ID226(UNIDO/LIB/SER.D/3/Rev.1). II. Title.
JX1977 .A2
ID/226(UNIDO/LIB/SER.D/3/REV.1)

Information sources on the foundry industry / United Nations Industrial Development Organization. Rev. ed. New York : United Nations, 1977. xii, 87 p. ; 21 cm. (UNIDO guides to information sources . no. 5) [Document] - United Nations ; ID/192(UNIDO/LIB/ser.D/5/rev. 1 Introductory material in English, French, Russian, and Spanish. Bibliography: p. 85-87.   LC Card 80-514461 DDC 300 s 016.3384/76712 19
1. Foundries - Information services - Directories. 2. Foundries - Bibliography. I. Series: United Nations. Industrial Development Organization. UNIDO guides to information sources , no. 5. II. Title.
JX1977 .A2
ID/192(UNIDO/LIB/SER.D/5/Rev.1)

Mattil, K. F. Review and comparative analysis of oilseed raw materials and processes suitable for the production of protein products for human consumption. New York , 1974. viii, 36 p. :   LC Card 81-465132   DDC 300 s 664/.64 19
JX1977 .A2 ID/126 (ID/WG.120/10/Rev. 1)

Technological profiles on the iron and steel industry / United Nations Industrial Development Organization. New York : United Nations, 1978. x, 44 p. : ill. ; 30 cm. (Development and transfer of technology series . no. 11) [Document - United Nations ; ID/218   LC Card 79-109235   DDC 300 s 338.4/76691 19
1. Iron industry and trade - Addresses, essays, lectures. 2. Steel industry and trade - Addresses, essays, lectures. I. Series. II. Series: United Nations. [Document] ID/218. III. Title.
JX1977 .A2 ID/218 TS307

UNIDO guides to information sources .
(no. 5) United Nations. Industrial Development Organization. Information sources on the foundry industry /. New York , 1977. xii, 87 p. ;   LC Card 80-514461 DDC 300 s 016.3384/76712 19
JX1977 .A2
ID/192(UNIDO/LIB/SER.D/5/Rev.1)

World industry since 1960 : progress and prospects : special issue of the Industrial Development Survey for the third General Conference of UNIDO, New Delhi, India, 21 January-8 February, 1980 / United Nations Industrial Development Organization. New York : United Nations, 1979. xviii, 422 p. : ill. ; 24 cm. ([Document] - United Nations. ID/CONF.4/2(ID/229) "United Nations publication, sales no.: E.79.II.B.3." Includes bibliographical references.   LC Card 80-105073   DDC 300 s 338.09/046 19
1. Industry. 2. Industrial promotion. 3. Economic history - 1945-. I. Series: United Nations. [Document] ID/CONF.4/2(ID/229). I. Title.
JX1977 .A2 ID/CONF.4/2(ID/229)

United Nations Institute for Training and Research.
Africa, the Middle East, and the new international economic order /. New York , 1980. xx, 162 p. ;   ISBN 0-08-025117-X   LC Card 80-14688
HF1611 .A55 1980   *NYPL [Sc E 81-32]*

Eastern Europe and the new international

economic order . New York , c1980. xv, 107 p. ;   ISBN 0-08-025115-3   LC Card 79-20028
HF1531 .E27 1980   *NYPL [JLE 81-175]*

The International civil service . New York , c1980. xii, 245 p. ;   ISBN 0-08-024643-5   LC Card 79-19471
JX1995 .I5168 1979   *NYPL [JLE 81-145]*

International Conference on the Future of Small-Scale Mining, 1st, Jurica, Mexico, 1978. The future of small scale mining . [New York] , c1980. xxiii, 501 p. :   ISBN 0-7060-6649-5   LC Card 80-81984   DDC 338.2 19
TN5 .I5234 1978

International youth organizations and the United Nations /. New York , 1973. v, 95 p. ;
NYPL [JLM 74-1459 no. 17]

Regionalism and the United Nations /. Dobbs Ferry, N.Y. , 1979. xx, 603 p. ;   ISBN 0-379-00591-3 :   LC Card 79-14018
JX1979 .R43   *NYPL [JLE 80-3132]*

UNITAR research report.
(no. 17) International youth organizations and the United Nations /. New York , 1973. v, 95 p. ;   *NYPL [JLM 74-1459 no. 17]*

The United Nations and decision-making . New York [c1978] 2 v. :   LC Card 79-126238   DDC 354.1/03 19
JX1977 .U4257

United Nations. Konferentsiia po torgovle i razvitiiu. see United Nations. Conference on Trade and Development.

United Nations. Latin America, Economic Commission for. see United Nations. Economic Commission for Latin America.

United Nations. Library. see United Nations. Dag Hammarskjold Library.

United Nations. Narcotic Drugs, Division of. see United Nations. Division of Narcotic Drugs.

United Nations. Office of Public Information. (Old Catalog form: United Nations. Secretariat. Public Information Dept.) United Nations. General Assembly. The international bill of human rights. New York , 1978. 42 p. ;   LC Card 78-109249   DDC 341.4/81 19
K3238.A1 I53

UNITED NATIONS - OFFICIALS AND EMPLOYEES.
The International civil service . New York , c1980. xii, 245 p. ;   ISBN 0-08-024643-5   LC Card 79-19471
JX1995 .I5168 1979   *NYPL [JLE 81-145]*

UNITED NATIONS - OFFICIALS AND EMPLOYEES - CONGRESSES.
The United Nations and decision-making . New York [c1978] 2 v. :   LC Card 79-126238   DDC 354.1/03 19
JX1977 .U4257

United Nations Organization. see United Nations.

United Nations. Palestine, Special Committee on. see United Nations. General Assembly. Special Committee on Palestine.

United Nations. Population Division. Latin American Preparatory Meeting for the World Population Conference, San José, Costa Rica, 1974. Informe de la reunión /. [New York] , 1974. v, 248 p. ;   LC Card 80-119992
HB3530.5 .L37 1974

United Nations. Public Information, Dept. of. see United Nations. Dept. of Public Information.

United Nations. Public Information, Office of. see United Nations. Office of Public Information.

United Nations. Scientific Committee on the Effects of Atomic Radiation. Sources and effects of ionizing radiation : 1977 report to the General Assembly, with annexes / United Nations Scientific Committee on the Effects of Atomic Radiation. New York : United Nations, 1977. 725 p. : graphs ; 30 cm. "United Nations publication. Sales no. E.77.IX.1." Includes bibliographies.   LC Card 79-112082   DDC 616.9/897 19
1. Ionizing radiation - Physiological effect. 2. Radioactive pollution. I. Title.
QP82.2.I53 U54 1977

United Nations. Secretariat. Dept. of Social Affairs. see United Nations. Dept. of Social Affairs.

United Nations. Secretariat. Office of Public Information. see United Nations. Office of Public Information.

United Nations. Secretariat. Statistical Office. see United Nations. Statistical Office.

United Nations Seminar on Technology Assessment for Development, Bangalore, India, 1978. Technology assessment for development : report of the United Nations Seminar on Technology Assessment for Development, Bangalore, India, 30 October-10 November 1978. New York : United Nations, 1979. v, 165 p. : ill. ; 28 cm. ([Document] - United Nations. ST/ESA/95) At head of title: Department of International Economic and Social Affairs. "United Nations publication. Sales no. E.80.II.A.1." Includes bibliographical references.   LC Card 80-121462   DDC 300 s 338.9/009172/4 19
1. Underdeveloped areas - Congresses. 2. Technology assessment - Congresses. 3. Technology - Social aspects. I. United Nations. Dept. of International Economic and Social Affairs. II. Series: United Nations. [Document] ST/ESA/95. III. Title.
JX1977 .A2 ST/ESA/95

United Nations. Social Affairs, Dept. of. see United Nations. Dept. of Social Affairs.

United Nations. Statistical Office. (Old Catalog form: United Nations. Secretariat. Statistical Office.)
Methods used in compiling the United Nations price indexes for basic commodities in international trade / Department of International Economic and Social Affairs, Statistical Office. New York : United Nations, 1979. vi, 115 p. ; 28 cm. (Statistical papers ; ser. M, no. 29, rev. 2) [Document] - United Nations ; ST/STAT/ser. M/29/rev. 2 "United Nations publication. Sales no. E.79.XVII.6."   LC Card 80-106353   DDC 300 s 338.5/28 19
1. Price indexes. I. Series: United Nations. Statistical Office. Statistical papers , ser. M, no. 29, rev. 2. II. Title.
JX1977 .A2 ST/STAT/Ser.M/29/rev. 2 HB225

A short manual on sampling. New York : United Nations, 1972- v. ; 28 cm. (Studies in methods : ser. F ; no. 9, rev. 1, : ser. F ; no. 9, v. 2-add. 1) [Document - United Nations] ; ST/STAT/SER.F/9/Rev.1, ; ST/STAT/SER.F/9-v.2/Add.1 "United Nations publication. Sales no. E.72.XVII.5, E.73.XVII.8" Includes bibliography. CONTENTS. - v. 1. Elements of sample survey theory. v. 2-Computer programmes for sample designs.   LC Card 80-119414   DDC 300 s 519.5 19
1. Sampling (Statistics). I. Series: United Nations. Statistical Office. Studies in methods : ser. F. ; no. 9, etc. II. Title.
JX1977 .A2 ST/STAT/SER.F/9/Rev.1, etc. QA276.6

Standard international trade classification : revision 2 / Department of Economic and Social Affairs, Statistical Office. New York : United Nations, 1975. viii, 102, 15 p. ; 28 cm. (Its: Statistical papers, ser. M. no. 34/rev. 2) "ST/ESA/STAT/SER. M/34/REV. 2."
1. Commercial products - Classification. 2. Industry - Classification. I. Title.   *NYPL [*R-Econ 80-4009]*

Statistical papers .
(ser. M, no. 29, rev. 2) United Nations. Statistical Office. Methods used in compiling the United Nations price indexes for basic commodities in international trade /. New York , 1979. vi, 115 p. ;   LC Card 80-106353 DDC 300 s 338.5/28 19
JX1977 .A2 ST/STAT/Ser.M/29/rev. 2 HB225

Studies in methods : ser. F. ; no. 9, etc.
United Nations. Statistical Office. A short manual on sampling. New York , 1972- v. ;   LC Card 80-119414   DDC 300 s 519.5 19
JX1977 .A2 ST/STAT/SER.F/9/Rev.1, etc. QA276.6

United Nations. Translation Division. French Service. Lexique général anglais-français . New York , 1980. xv, 870 p. ;   LC Card 81-123648   DDC 413 19
PB331 .L45 1980

United Nations. United Nations Educational, Scientific and Cultural Organization. see

United Nations Educational, Scientific and Cultural Organization.

UNITED NATIONS - UNITED STATES.
United Nations. General Assembly. 34th session, 1979. Delegation from the United States. Congressional delegates at the 1979 United Nations General Assembly . Washington , 1980. vii, 265 p. ; LC Card 80-602273 DDC 341.23/73 19
JX1977.2.U5 U55 1979a

United States. Congress. Senate. Committee on Foreign Relations. Nomination of Jeane J. Kirkpatrick . Washington , 1981. iii, 110 p. ; LC Card 81-601348 DDC 353.1 19
KF26 .F6 1981a

UNITED NATIONS - VOTING - INDEXES.
United Nations. General Assembly. 32d session, 1977. Votes at the thirty-second regular session of the General Assembly, 20 September-21 December, 1977. [Washington, D.C.] [1978?] lix, 469 p. ; LC Card 80-601606 DDC 341.23/22 19
JX1977.8.V6 U54 1977

United Nations. Welthandels- und Entwicklungskonferenz. see **United Nations. Conference on Trade and Development.**

United Nations. World Health Organization. see **World Health Organization.**

United Nations' World Population Conference. see **World Population Conference.**

United Nations World Security Organization. see **United Nations.**

United Nations 11th special session on economic development and cooperation, New York City, August 25-September 15, 1980 . Gilman, Benjamin A. Washington , 1981. vii, 18 p. ; LC Card 81-601276 DDC 338.91 19
HF1410.5 .G54

United Nations/INTOSAI Seminar on Government Auditing, Vienna, 1979. Public auditing techniques for performance improvement : report of the United Nations/INTOSAI Seminar on Government Auditing, Vienna, 14-25 May 1979 / Department of Technical Co-operation for Development. New York : United Nations, 1980. iii, 108 p. ; 28 cm. ([Document] - United Nations. ST/ESA/SER.E/20) Includes bibliographical references. LC Card 80-130822 DDC 300 s 351.72/32 19
1. Finance, Public - Accounting. 2. Auditing. I. United Nations. Dept. of Technical Cooperation for Development. II. International Organization of Supreme Audit Institutions. III. Series: United Nations. Documents , ST/ESA/SER.E/20. IV. Title.
JX1977 .A2 ST/ESA/SER.E/20

UNITED NUCLEAR CORPORATION.
United States. Congress. House. Committee on Interior and Insular Affairs. Subcommittee on Energy and the Environment. Mill tailings dam break at Church Rock, New Mexico . Washington , 1980. iv, 232 p. : LC Card 80-601962 DDC 622/.8 19
KF27 .I518 1979i

United Republic of Tanganyika and Zanzibar. see **Tanzania.**

[United State. Central Intelligence Agency]
Papua and New Guinea administrative divisions. [Washington : Central Intelligence Agency, 1970] 1 map : col. ; 17 x 24 cm. "500072 11-70." LC Card 81-692529
1. Papua New Guinea - Administrative and political divisions - Maps.
G8161.F7 1970 .U5

United States. Congress. House. Committee on Banking, Finance, and Urban Affairs. Subcommittee on Financial Institutions Supervision, Regulation and Insurance.
Oversight hearings on Depository Institutions Deregulation Committee : hearings before the Subcommittee on Financial Institutions Supervision, Regulation, and Insurance of the Committee on Banking, Finance, and Urban Affairs, House of Representatives, Ninety-sixth Congress, second session, July 2, August 26, 1980. Washington : U. S. G.P.O., 1980. vi, 582 p. : ill. ; 24 cm. "Serial 96-76." Bibliography: p. 535-536. LC Card 81-600873 DDC 353.0082/52 19
1. United States. Depository Institutions Deregulation

Committee. 2. Banking law - United States. I. Title.
KF27 .B544 1980c

United State. Congress. House. Select Committee on Aging. Older Americans Act : a staff summary : includes the Older Americans Act of 1965 as amended by the 95th Congress / by the Select Committee on Aging, U. S. House of Representatives, Ninety-sixth Congress, first session.Rev. Washington, D.C. : U. S. G.P.O. : for sale by the Supt. of Docs., U. S. G.P.O., 1979. v, 124 p. ; 24 cm. At head of title: Committee print. "Comm. pub. no. 96-185." Includes bibliographical references and index. LC Card 80-603981 DDC 344.73/0326 347.304326 19
1. Old age assistance - United States. 2. Aged - Legal status, laws, etc. - United States. I. United States. Older Americans Act of 1965, as amended. 1979. II. Title.
KF3737 .A25 1979

United States.
Compilation of selected acts within the jurisdiction of the Committee on Energy and Commerce / prepared for the use of the House Committee on Energy and Commerce. Washington : U. S. G.P.O. : For sale by the Supt. of Docs., U. S. G.P.O., 1981. 4 v. ; 24 cm. Vol. 1: At head of title, 97th Congress, 1st session. Committee print. Committee print 97-A. Vol. 2: At head of title, 97th Congress, 1st session. Committee print. Committee print 97-B. Vol. 3: At head of title, 97th Congress, 1st session. Committee print. Committee print 97-C. Vol. 4: At head of title, 97th Congress, 1st session. Committee print. Committee print 97-D. S/N 052-070-05549-9 (v. 1) S/N 052-070-05541-3 (v. 2) S/N 052-070-04883-2 (v. 3) S/N 052-070-05543-0 (v. 4) Item 1019-A, 1019-B (microfiche) CONTENTS. - v. 1. Health law ... -- v. 2. Food, drug, and related law ... -- v. 3. Environment law ... -- v. 4. Consumer protection law .... LC Card 81-601845 DDC 344.73/04/02632 347.304402632 19
1. Public health laws - United States. 2. Food law and legislation - United States. 3. Environmental law - United States. 4. Consumer protection - Law and legislation - United States. I. United States. Congress. House. Committee on Energy and Commerce. II. Title.
KF3775 .A3 1981

ETHICS IN GOVERNMENT ACT OF 1978. TITLE 4-5.
Office of Government Ethics and Federal post-employment restrictions . Washington , 1980. vi, 304 p. ; LC Card 80-603840 DDC 342.73/068 347.30268 19
KF4568.A315 A15 1980

Federal election campaign laws / compiled by the Federal Election Commission. Washington, D.C. (1325 K Street, N.W., Washington, D.C., 20463) : The Commission : For sale by the Supt. of Docs., U. S. G.P.O., 1980. xi, 140 p. ; 23 cm. "Including the 'Federal Election Campaign Act Amendments of 1979,' Pub. L. No. 96-187." "January 1980." "Second printing September 1980"--T.p. verso. Includes index. S/N 052-006-00004-0 LC Card 80-603772 DDC 342.73/078 347.30278 19
1. Election law - United States. I. United States. Federal Election Commission. II. Title.
KF4885 .A3 1980a

FEDERAL REGISTER.
United States. Office of the Federal Register. The Federal register . [Washington] [1980] iv, 132 p. : LC Card 80-602839 DDC 348.73/25 19
KF240 .F5 1980

Mental Retardation Facilities and Community Health Centers Construction Act of 1963. 1979. United States. [Rehabilitation Act of 1973.] Rehabilitation, comprehensive services, and developmental disabilities legislation ... : a compilation / prepared for the Subcommittee on the Handicapped of the Committee on Labor and Human Resources, United States . Washington [1979] viii, 94 p. ; LC Card 80-603984 DDC 344.73/0159 347.304159 19
KF3738 .A3 1979

Older Americans Act of 1965, as amended. 1979. United State. Congress. House. Select Committee on Aging. Older Americans Act : a staff summary : includes the Older Americans Act of 1965 as amended by the 95th Congress / by the Select Committee on Aging, U. S. House of Representatives, Ninety-sixth Congress, first session.Rev. Washington, D.C. , 1979. v, 124 p. ; LC Card 80-603981 DDC 344.73/0326 347.304326

19
KF3737 .A25 1979

[Rehabilitation Act of 1973]
Rehabilitation, comprehensive services, and developmental disabilities legislation ... : a compilation / prepared for the Subcommittee on the Handicapped of the Committee on Labor and Human Resources, United States . Washington : U. S. G.P.O., [1979] viii, 94 p. ; 24 cm. At head of title: 96th Congress, 1st session. Committee print. "August 1979." CONTENTS. - Rehabilitation Act of 1973 (as amended by Public Law 93-516, Public Law 94-230, and Public Law 95-602) -- Mental Retardation Facilities and Community Health Centers Construction Act of 1963 (as amended by Public Laws 90-170, 91-517, 94-103, and 95-602). LC Card 80-603984 DDC 344.73/0159 347.304159 19
1. Vocational rehabilitation - Law and legislation - United States. 2. Handicapped - Employment - United States. I. United States. Mental Retardation Facilities and Community Health Centers Construction Act of 1963. 1979. II. Title.
KF3738 .A3 1979

[Social Security Act]
The Social Security Act and related laws / Committee on Finance, United States Senate, Russell B. Long, chairman. Nov. 1980 ed. Washington : U. S. G.P.O. : For sale by the Supt. of Docs., U. S. G.P.O., 1980. viii, 856, xxx p. ; 24 cm. At head of title: 96th Congress, 2d session. Committee print. CP 96-39. "Intended to supplement and not to replace the Compilation of the social security laws which is prepared by the Social Security Administration." "November 1980." S/N 052-070-05457-3 Item 1038 LC Card 81-601049 DDC 344.73/02 347.3042 19
1. Social security - Law and legislation - United States. I. Long, Russell B. II. United States. Congress. Senate. Committee on Finance. III. Title.
KF3644 1980

Supplement to Basic laws and authorities on housing and community development, revised through January 3, 1980 / Committee on Banking, Finance, and Urban Affairs, House of Representatives, 96th Congress, second session. Washington : U. S. G.P.O. : For sale by the Supt. of Docs., U. S.G.P.O., 1980. vi, 838 p. ; 24 cm. At head of title: Committee print 96-18. S/N 052-070-05449-2 Item 1013 Includes bibliographical references and index. LC Card 80-603964 DDC 346.7304/5 347.30645 19
1. Housing - Law and legislation - United States. 2. Community development - Law and legislation - United States. I. United States. Congress. House. Committee on Banking, Finance and Urban Affairs. II. Basic laws and authorities on housing and community development.
KF5424 1979 Suppl

United States. Accreditation and Institutional Eligibility, Advisory Committee on. see **United States. Advisory Committee on Accreditation and Institutional Eligibility.**

United States. ACTION (Service Corps) see **ACTION (Service Corps)**

United States. Ad Hoc Interagency Population Dos Assessement Group. Population dose and health impact of the accident at the Three Mile Island Nuclear Station : preliminary estimates for the period March 28, 1979 through April 7, 1979 / Lewis Battist ... [et al.]. Washington : U. S. Nuclear Regulatory Commission, 1979. 77, [16] p. : ill. ; 28 cm. On cover: Preliminary estimates prepared by the Ad Hoc Interagency Dose Assessment Group. "NUREG-0558." LC Card 79-602730
1. Radiation - Dosage. 2. Radioactive pollution - Pennsylvania - Harrisburg region - Measurement. 3. Three Mile Island Nuclear Power Plant, Pa. 4. Atomic power-plants - Environmental aspects - Pennsylvania - Harrisburg region. 5. Radiation - Toxicology. I. Battist, Lewis. II. United States. Nuclear Regulatory Commission. III. Title.
RA569 .U46 1979

United States, Ad Hoc Population Dose Assessment Group. see **United States. Ad Hoc Interagency Population Dos Assessement Group.**

United States. Adjustment Board. see **United States. National Railroad Adjustment Board.**

United States. Adjutant-General's Office. Notes illustrating the military geography of the United

United States. Administración de cooperación internacional. **BIBLIOGRAPHIC GUIDE**

390

States, 1813-1880 / compiled by Raphael P.
Thian ; with addenda edited by John M.
Carroll ; foreword by Robert M. Utley. Austin :
University of Texas Press, c1979. xii, 203 p. :
graphs (4 fold. in pocket) ; 24 cm. Includes
indexes.   ISBN 0-292-75515-5   LC Card 79-63158
1. Military departments and divisions - United States. 2.
Military geography - United States. I. Thian, Raphael
Prosper. II. Carroll, John M. III. Title.
UA26 .A2 1979   **NYPL** *[IBM 81-609]*

United States. Administración de cooperación
internacional. see United States.
International Cooperation Administration.

United States. Administration for Children,
Youth and Families.
Selected readings on mother-infant bonding.
[Washington, D.C. , 1979] 115 p. :   LC Card
  79-604305   DDC 306.8/7 19
HQ759 .S44

United States. Administration for Children,
Youth, and Families. Day Care Division.
Children at the center . Cambridge, MA , 1979.
xli, 298 p. :   ISBN 0-89011-532-X   LC Card
  79-87500
HV854 .C53   **NYPL** *[JLE 80-2984]*

United States. Administration on Aging. (Old
Catalog form: United States. Aging,
Administration on)
AoA occasional papers in gerontology .
(no. 1) National Clearinghouse on Aging.
Human resource issues in the field of aging .
[Washington, D.C.] [1980] v, 20 p. :   LC
  Card 80-602117   DDC 331.12/913621/60973 19
RA997 .N375 1980

Directory of senior centers and clubs. 1974-
Washington.   LC Card 75-643610
              NYPL *[JLM 80-1123]*

Interdisciplinary Workshop on Transportation
and Aging, Washington, D. C., 1970.
Transportation and aging; selected issues.
Washington [1971] 208 p.   LC Card 79-619017
HQ1063.5 .I5 1970   **NYPL** *[JLF 81-91]*

Kirschner Associates. Longitudinal evaluation of
the National Nutrition Program for the
Elderly . [Washington, D.C.] 1980] xiv, 333
p. :   LC Card 80-601632   DDC 362.6/3 19
HV696.F6 K57 1980

United States. Laws, statutes, etc. Older
Americans act of 1965, as amended .
Washington, D.C. [1979] viii, 173 p. ;   LC
  Card 80-602137   DDC 344.73/0326/02632 19
KF3737 .A3 1979

United States. Administration on Aging. Federal
Council on the Aging. see United States.
Federal Council on the Aging.

United States. Advanced Research Projects
Agency. (Old Catalog form: United States.
Defense Dept. Advanced Research Projects
Agency)
Fischhoff, Baruch. The art of cost-benefit
analysis /. - Springfield, Va. [1978?] [30] p. :
              NYPL *[*XME-9379]*

United States. Advisory Commission on
Intergovernmental Relations. (Old Catalog
form: United States. Intergovernmental
Relations, Advisory Commission on)
ACIR index. 1961/79- Princeton, N. J..
              NYPL *[*R-Econ. 81-89]*

The adequacy of federal compensation to local
governments for tax exempt federal lands : a
commission report. Washington : Advisory
Commission on Intergovernmental Relations :
for sale by the Supt. of Docs., U. S.
Government Print. Off., 1978. x, 203 p. :
graphs ; 27 cm. "A-68." Bibliography: p. 197-203.
  LC Card 79-601477
1. Taxation and government property - United States. 2.
United States - Public lands. 3. Intergovernmental fiscal
relations - United States. I. Title.
HJ4182.A3 U54 1978   **NYPL** *[JLF 81-314]*

Citizen participation in the American Federal
system / Advisory Commission on
Intergovernmental Relations. Washington,
D.C. : ACIR : for sale by the Supt. of Docs.,
U. S. Govt. Print. Off., [1980] v, 357 p. ; 28
cm. "A-73." Includes bibliographical references.   LC
  Card 80-602148   DDC 323/.042/0973 19
1. Political participation - United States. 2.
Intergovernmental fiscal relations - United States. I.

Title.
JK1764 .U54 1980

Countercyclical aid and economic stabilization :
a commission report. Washington : Advisory
Commission on Intergovernmental Relations :
for sale by the Supt. of Docs., U. S. Govt.
Print. Off., 1978. viii, 50 p. : graphs ; 27 cm.
Prepared by J. P. Ross, with the assistance of S. E.
Calkins and R. J. Reeder. "A-69." Bibliography: p.
49-50.   LC Card 79-601504
1. Intergovernmental fiscal relations - United States. 2.
Government spending policy - United States. I. Ross,
John P., 1943-. II. Calkins, Susannah E. III. Reeder,
Richard J. IV. Title.
HJ275 .U52 1978b   **NYPL** *[JLF 81-317]*

The federal role in the federal system : the
dynamics of growth : public assistance : the
growth of a federal function : a commission
report. Washington, D.C. : Advisory
Commission on Intergovernmantal Relations :
for sale by the Supt. of Docs., U. S. Govt.
Print. Off., [1980] vii, 123 p. : ill. ; 27 cm.
"A-79." "July 1980." Includes bibliographical references.
  LC Card 80-603209   DDC 361.6/0973 19
1. Federal aid to public welfare. I. Title.
HV95 .U518 1980

Partnership within the states . Urbana , 1976.
vi, 311 p. ;   LC Card 77-622179
JS348 .P25   **NYPL** *[*XME-9431]*

Regional growth. Washington, D.C. : Advisory
Commission on Intergovernmental Relations,
[1980- v. <1- > : ill. ; 27 cm. At head of title: A
commission report. Prepared by Janet Rothenberg Pack
and others. "A-74." Bibliography: v. 1, p. 95-103.
CONTENTS. - [1] Historic perspective.   LC Card
  80-603208   DDC 361.6/0973 19
1. Regional planning - United States - Collected works.
2. Regional economics - Collected works. 3.
Regionalism - United States - Collected works. I. Pack,
Janet Rothenberg. II. Title.
HT392 .U5 1980

State-local finances in recession and inflation :
an economic analysis. Washington : Advisory
Commission on Intergovernmental Relations,
1979. viii, 82 p. : graphs ; 27 cm. "A-70." Includes
bibliographical references.   LC Card 79-602933
1. Intergovernmental fiscal relations - United States. 2.
Finance, Public - United States - States. 3. Local
finance - United States. I. Title.
HJ275 .U52 1979a   **NYPL** *[JLF 81-450]*

United States. Advisory Committee on
Accreditation and Institutional Eligibility.
Annual report. [Washington] 22 x 28 cm.
              NYPL *[JLM 80-685]*

United States. Advisory Committee on Cable
Signal Leakage. Final report of the Advisory
Committee on Cable Signal Leakage to the
Chief, Cable Television Bureau, Federal
Communications Commission. Washington,
D.C. : The Committee, [1979] 110, [132] p. :
ill. ; 28 cm. "November 1, 1979."   LC Card
  80-601686   DDC 629.135 19
1. Radio in aeronautics. 2. Electromagnetic interference.
I. United States. Cable Television Bureau. II. Title.
TL694.I6 U45 1979

United States. Advisory Committee on Gross
National Product Data Improvement. Gross
national product data improvement project
report : report of the Advisory Committee on
Gross National Product Data Improvement,
October 1977. Washington : Office of Federal
Statistical Policy and Standards, U. S. Dept. of
Commerce : for sale by the Supt. of Docs., U.
S. Govt. Print. Off., 1979. xii, 204 p. ; 26 cm.
Includes bibliographical references.   LC Card
  79-602253
1. Gross national product - United States - Statistical
methods. 2. National income - United States -
Accounting. I. United States. Office of Federal
Statistical Policy and Standards. II. Title.
HC110.I5 U48 1979   **NYPL** *[JLF 81-487]*

United States. Advisory Council of Equality of
Educational Opportunity, National. see
United States. National Advisory Council on
Equality of Educational Opportunity.

United States. Advisory Council on Historic
Preservation. The contribution of historic
preservation to urban revitalization / Advisory
Council on Historic Preservation. Washington :
The Council : for sale by the Supt. of Docs., U.
S. Govt. Print. Off., 1979. 176 p. in various
pagings : ill. ; 28 cm. "Prepared for the Advisory

Council on Historic Preservation by Booz, Allen &
Hamilton." LC Card 79-602153
1. Urban renewal - United States - Case studies. 2.
Historic buildings - United States - Conservation and
restoration - Case studies. I. Booz, Allen and Hamilton,
inc. II. Title.
HT175 .U58 1979   **NYPL** *[JLF 81-453]*

United States. Advisory Council on Social
Security (1978-1979) United States.
Congress. House. Select Committee on Aging.
Subcommittee on Retirement Income and
Employment. Oversight on recommendations of
1979 Social Security Advisory Council .
Washington , 1980. iv, 208 p. :   LC Card
  80-603006   DDC 368.4/00973 19
KF27.5 .A374 1980

United States. Advisory Group on Electron
Devices. Display Research Conference, 5th,
Cherry Hill, N.J., 1978. Conference record of
1978 Biennial Display Research Conference .
New York , Piscataway, N.J. , c1978. 87 p. :
  LC Card 78-113235
TK7882.I6 D567 1978   **NYPL** *[JSF 81-137]*

United States. Aeronautical Chart Service.
Isobars & prevailing winds chart, January :
northern hemisphere / prepared by the
Aeronautical Chart Service, U. S. Army Air
Forces, Aug. 1946.Advance ed. [Washington] :
The Service, [1946] 1 map : col. ; 87 cm. in
diam. on sheet 91 x 91 cm. (GH / Aeronautical
Chart Service . 10) At head of title: U. S. Army Air
Forces. Relief indicated by spot heights. "Source:
Goode's School atlas, Rand McNally." Includes text.
"Base no. 1." LC Card 81-690547
1. Atmospheric pressure - Northern hemisphere - Maps.
2. Winds - Northern Hemisphere - Maps. I. Series: GH
(United States. Aeronautical Chart Service) , 10. II.
Title.
G3211.C842 1946 .U5

United States. Aeronautics and Space
Administration. see United States. National
Aeronautics and Space Administration.

United States. Aeronautics and Space Technology,
Office of. see United States. Office of
Aeronautics and Space Technology.

United States. Agency for International
Development. (Old Catalog form: United
States. International Development, Agency
for)
Haiti-small farmer marketing. Washington,
D.C. : Dept. of State, Agency for International
Development, [1977?] 84, [40] p. : ill. ; 27 cm.
Cover title. At head of title: Project paper. "Project
number: 521-0083." "LA/DR:77-5." LC Card
  80-601536   DDC 334/.683/097294 19
1. Cooperative marketing of farm produce - Haiti. 2.
Coffee trade - Haiti. 3. Economic assistance,
American - Haiti. I. Title.
HD9014.H342 U54 1977

New York University. School of Commerce,
Accounts and Finance. Final report, New York
University-University of Lagos Project. [New
York , 1970] 45 leaves ;   LC Card 80-503704
  DDC 650/.07/106691 19
HF1176.N62 L334 1970

Rural health delivery systems, Haiti : project
paper / Department of State, Agency for
International Development. Washington, D.C. :
AID, [1979?] ca. 500 p. in various pagings :
ill. ; 29 cm. "AID/LAC/P-008." "Project number:
521-0091." Includes bibliographical references.   LC
  Card 80-602874   DDC 362.1/0425 19
1. Rural health services - Haiti. 2. Medical assistance,
American - Haiti. I. Title.
RA771.7.H2 U54 1979a

Soybeans as human food . [Washington] , 1979.
iv, 54 p. :   LC Card 79-603033   DDC 641.3/5655
  19
TX558.S7 S69 1979b

U. S. foreign aid in Africa / Agency for
International Development. [Washington?] : The
Agency, [1965?] 28 p. : ill., map ; 23 cm.
Microfiche (neg.) 1 sheet. 11 x 15 cm. (NYPL FSN
Sc,017,987) Cover title.
1. Economic assistance, American - Africa. I. Title.
              NYPL *[Sc Micro F-9183]*

United States. National Technical Information
Service. Appropriate technology information for
developing countries . [Washington, D.C.]
[c1980] xxiv, 384 p. (p. 383-384 ordering

instructions) ; LC Card 80-601640 DDC 600 19
T49.5 .U56 1980

Work plan, Western Michigan
University-Technical College, Ibadan Project in
cooperation with the United States Agency for
International Development. [Kalamazoo] , 1966.
vii, 53 leaves : LC Card 81-450648 DDC
607/.116692 19
T173.I27 W67

UNITED STATES. AGENCY FOR INTERNATIONAL DEVELOPMENT.

United States. General Accounting Office.
Agency for International Development needs to
strengthen its management of study, research,
and evaluation activities . [Washington] 1979.
iii, 30 p. ; LC Card 79-601658 DDC 353.0089 19
HC60.U6 G4 1979

United States. General Accounting Office. AID
must consider social factors in establishing
cooperatives in developing countries .
[Washington, D.C.] [1980] iv, 42 p. ; LC Card
80-602922 DDC 334/.09172/4 19
HD3575 .U54 1980

UNITED STATES. AGENCY FOR INTERNATIONAL DEVELOPMENT - ACCOUNTING.

United States. Congress. House. Committee on
Government Operations. Legislation and
National Security Subcommittee. Adequacy of
aid resources for auditing overseas assistance
programs . Washington , 1980. iii, 46 p. ; LC
Card 80-603461 DDC 353.008/96 19
KF27 .G6676 1980g

United States. Agency for International Development. Bureau for Program and Policy Coordination.
Conference on the International Financial
System and Concerns of Developing Nations,
Washington, D. C., 1975. The international
monetary system and the developing nations /.
Washington , 1976. vi, 210 p. ;
        NYPL [JLE 80-2857]

United States. Agency for International Development. Bureau for Program and Policy Coordination. Office of Statistics and Reports. East Asia : economic growth trends.
[Washington] : Office of Statistics and Reports,
Bureau for Program and Policy Coordination,
Agency for International Development, 1971.
41 p. : ill. ; 28 cm. Cover title. Chiefly tables. LC
Card 81-453703 DDC 330.95/0427 19
1. East Asia - Economic conditions. 2. East Asia - Statistics. I. Title.
HC460.5 .U54 1971

United States. Agency for International Development. Nutrition, Office of. see
United States. Agency for International Development. Office of Nutrition.

United States. Agency for International Development. Office of Financial Management. Statistics and Reports Division. East Asia : economic growth trends.
[Washington] : Statistics and Reports Division,
Office of Financial Management, Bureau for
Program and Management Services, Agency for
International Development, [1974] 42 p. :
graphs ; 29 cm. Cover title. "October 1974." Tables
and graphs. LC Card 80-512034 DDC 330.95/0428
19
1. East Asia - Economic conditions. I. Title.
HC460.5 .U54 1974

United States. Agency for International Development. Office of Housing.
Botswana shelter sector assessment.
Washington, D.C. : Office of Housing, Agency
for International Development, [1979] iii, 134,
[5] p., [14] leaves of plates : ill. ; 28 cm. "June
1979." LC Card 80-602020 DDC 363.5/09681/1 19
1. Housing - Botswana. I. Title.
HD7374.9.A3 U54 1979

Lesotho shelter sector assessment / Office of
Housing, Agency for International
Development. [Washington, D.C.] : The Office,
[1978] ii, 129 p. : ill. ; 28 cm. LC Card
80-602029 DDC 363.5/09681/6 19
1. Housing - Lesotho. I. Title.
HD7374.7.A3 U54 1978

Peru shelter sector assessment. [Washington,
D.C.] : Agency for International Development,
Office of Housing, 1979. xii, 60, 15, [23] p. :
ill. ; 28 cm. "Study ... conducted by the Foundation

for Cooperative Housing." Includes bibliographical
references. LC Card 80-602028 DDC 363.5/0985 19
1. Housing - Peru. I. Foundation for Cooperative Housing. II. Title.
HD7329.A3 U53 1979

Popko, Edward. Squatter settlements and
housing policy . [Washington, D.C.?] ,
Cambridge, Mass. , 1980. vi, 200 p. : LC Card
81-600768 DDC 363.5/8/09861 19
HD7325.A3 P658

United States. Agency for International Development. Office of International training. Providencia . [Washington, D.C.?] ,
1980. xiii, 327 p. : LC Card 80-603922 DDC
330.9861/8 19
HC28 .P83 1980

United States. Agency for International Development. Office of Nutrition. American
Technical Assistance Corporation. Planification
de programmes nationaux de nutrition .
[Washington, D.C.] [1973] 2 v. : LC Card
80-136136 DDC 362.1/9639 19
TX359 .A43 1973

United States. Agency for International Development. Office of Small Business.
Directory of combination export managers.
Washington, Dept. of State, Agency for
International Development, Office of Small
Business, 1962. 5 v. 27 cm. CONTENTS. - section
1. Food, feed and fertilizer. - section 2. Fuel. - section.
3. Raw materials and semi-finished products. - section
4. Machinery and vehicles. - section 5. Miscellaneous
and unclassified. LC Card 62-61061
1. United States - Commerce - Directories. I. Title.
        NYPL [JLM 80-890]

United States. Agency for International Development. Small Business, Office of. see
United States. Agency for International Development. Office of Small Business.

United States. Agency for International Development. Southern Africa Task Force. A
framework for U. S. assistance in southern
Africa : country resource paper[s] / submitted
by the Office of Eastern and Southern Africa
Affairs, Bureau for Program and Policy
Coordination, Agency for
International Development ; [prepared by
Southern Africa Task Force]. [Washington] :
The Office, [1977- v. : ill. ; 28 cm. Added t.p. has
title: Transition in Southern Africa. Prepared under
contract AID/afr-C-1142, etc., by Tim Rose and others.
CONTENTS. - [1] Lesotho.--[2] Swaziland.--[3]
Botswana. LC Card 80-503603 DDC 338.91/73/068
19
1. Africa, Southern - Economic conditions. 2. Africa, Southern - Social conditions. 3. Economic assistance, American - Africa, Southern. I. Rose, Tim H. II. Title. III. Title: Transition in Southern Africa.
HC900 .U54 1977

United States. Agency of International Development. Office of Nutrition. Low-cost
extrusion cookers . [Fort Collins, Colo. , 1979]
vii, 288 p. : LC Card 80-601551 DDC 664/.02 19
TP373 .L68

United States. Aging, Administration on. see
United States. Administration on Aging.

United States. Aging, Federal Council on the. see
United States. Federal Council on the Aging.

United States. Aging, Special Committee on (Senate) see **United States. Congress. Senate. Special Committee on Aging.**

United States. Agricultural Marketing Service.
Packaged fluid milk sales in federal milk order
markets. [Washington] United States Dept. of
Agriculture, Agricultural Marketing Service. 26
cm. "By size and type of containers, and distribution
method." Cover title. LC Card 77-643112
1. Milk trade - United States - Statistics - Periodicals.
2. Milk - Containers - Statistics - Periodicals. I. Title.
        NYPL [JLM 80-754]

Tobacco in the United States. [Rev.].
[Washington] : U. S. Dept. of Agriculture,
Agricultural Marketing Service : for sale by the
Supt. of Docs., U. S. Govt. Print. Off., [1979]
27 p. : ill. ; 27 cm. (Miscellaneous publication - U.
S. Department of Agriculture ; no. 867) Cover title.
Previous editions by A. Doub. Includes bibliographical
references. LC Card 79-601924 DDC 633.7/1/0973
19
1. Tobacco - United States. 2. Tobacco manufacture and trade - United States. I. Doub, Albert, 1917- Tobacco in the United States. II. Series: United States.

Dept. of Agriculture. Miscellaneous publication, no.
867. III. Title.
SB273 .U44 1979

United States. Agricultural Marketing Service. Packers and Stockyards. Beef pricing report.
[Washington] : U. S. Dept. of Agriculture,
Agricultural Marketing Service, Packers ad
Stockyards Program, 1978. 39 p. : ill. ; 26 cm.
LC Card 79-602620
1. Beef - Prices - United States. I. Title.
HD9433.U4 U6 1978   *NYPL [JLF 81-521]*

United States. Agricultural Research Service.
Williams, Jimmy R. HYMO: Problem-oriented
computer language for hydrologic modeling.
Washington, 1973. 76 p.:
        NYPL [JSF 80-689]

United States. Agricultural Research Service. Northern Regional Research Center.
Publications and patents. Peoria, Ill. 27 cm.
Semiannual, July 1972-1975; annual, 1976- . Issues for
July 1972-1975 published by the U. S. Agricultural
Research Service Northern Regional Research
Laboratory. Supersedes: United States. Agricultural
Research Service. Northern Marketing and Nutrition
Research Division. Publications and patents.
1. United States. Agricultural Research Service.
Northern Regional Research Center. - Bibliography -
Periodicals. I. United States. Agricultural Research
Service. Northern Regional Research Laboratory.
        NYPL [JLM 80-1094]

UNITED STATES. AGRICULTURAL RESEARCH SERVICE. NORTHERN REGIONAL RESEARCH CENTER. - BIBLIOGRAPHY - PERIODICALS.

United States. Agricultural Research Service.
Northern Regional Research Center.
Publications and patents. Peoria, Ill.
        NYPL [JLM 80-1094]

United States. Agricultural Research Service. Northern Regional Research Laboratory.
United States. Agricultural Research Service.
Northern Regional Research Center.
Publications and patents. Peoria, Ill.
        NYPL [JLM 80-1094]

United States. Agricultural Research Service. Southern Marketing and Nutrition Research Division. Publications and patents with
abstracts. July/Dec. 1970- [New Orleans, La.]
        NYPL [*VA 80-314]

United States. Agricultural Research Service. Southern Regional Research Center.
Publications and patents with abstracts.
July/Dec. 1970- [New Orleans, La.]
        NYPL [*VA 80-314]

United States. Agricultural Stabilization and Conservation Service.
Forestry incentives program. Washington. 28
cm. Annual Report year ends Sept. 30.
1. Forests and forestry - Economic aspects - United States - Periodicals. I. Title.
        NYPL [JLM 80-1015]

Michigan: annual report. East Lansing, Mich.
27 cm.
1. Agriculture - Michigan - Statistics - Periodicals. 2. Agriculture and state - Michigan - Statistics - Periodicals.   *NYPL [JLM 80-874]*

United States. Agriculture and Forestry, Committee on (Senate) see **United States. Congress. Senate. Committee on Agriculture and Forestry.**

United States. Agriculture, Committee on (House) see **United States. Congress. House. Committee on Agriculture.**

United States. Agriculture, Dept. of. see **United States. Dept. of Agriculture.**

United States. AID Mission to Haiti. Zuvekas,
Clarence. Agricultural development in Haiti .
Washington, D.C. [1978] xiv, 355 p. : LC
Card 80-601532 DDC 338.1/097294 19
HD1841 .Z69

UNITED STATES - AIR DEFENSES, MILITARY.

United States. Congress. House. Committee on
Armed Services. Special Subcommittee on Nato
Standardization, Interoperability, and Readiness.
Status of army air defense planning .
Washington , 1980. ii, 52 p. ; LC Card
80-604007 DDC 358.4/145/0973 19
KF27 .A7642 1980

United States. Air Development Center, Rome, N. Y.

BIBLIOGRAPHIC GUIDE

392

United States. Air Development Center, Rome, N. Y. Nicholls, David B. Digital evaluation and failure analysis data /. Griffiss Air Force Base, NY , 1980. 2 v. ; LC Card 80-144504 DDC 621.381/73/0278 19
TK7874 .N48

United States. Air Force.
USAF Southeast Asia monograph series .
(v. 5, monograph 7) Gropman, Alan L., 1938- Airpower and the airlift evacuation of Kham Duc /. [Washington] , 1979. viii, 87 p. : LC Card 80-601630 DDC 959.704/348 19
DS558.8 .G76
NYPL [JFL 77-126 v. 5, monograph 7]

UNITED STATES. AIR FORCE.
United States. Congress. House. Committee on Armed Services. Hearings on H.R. 2637 ... and the posture of the U. S. Military Airlift, before the Committee on Armed Services, House of Representatives, Ninety-fifth Congress, first session, September 19, 20, 1977. Washington , 1977. ii, 187, iii p. : LC Card 78-600628
KF27 .A7 1977n

United States. Air Force Academy. Dept. of Behavioral Sciences and Leadership.
Proceedings of the seventh symposium, psychology in the Department of Defense, 16 April-18 April 1980. Colorado Springs, Colo. [Springfield, Va. (5285 Port Royal Rd., Springfield 22151)] 1980. xxiv, 635 p. : LC Card 80-604141 DDC 355/.001/9 19
U22.3 .P712

United States. Air Force. Aeronomy Laboratory.
see **United States. Air Force. Cambridge Research Laboratories. Aeronomy Laboratory.**

United States. Air Force. Air Research and Development Command. Scientific Research, Office of. see **United States. Air Force. Office of Scientific Research.**

UNITED STATES. AIR FORCE - ARCHIVES - CATALOGS.
Albert F. Simpson Historical Research Center. Personal files in the U. S. Air Force historical collection. [Maxwell Air Force Base, Ala.] , 1975. 29 p. ; LC Card 79-602942 DDC 016.3584/00973 19
Z6725.U5 A59 1975 UG633

United States. Air Force. Cambridge Research Laboratories. Aeronomy Laboratory. Smith, Ed R. The effect of several configuration interaction target states on the elastic scattering of low-energy electrons by complex atoms /. Hanscomb AFB, Mass. , 1975. 25 p. ;
*NYPL [*XMQ-2123]*

United States. Air Force. Cambridge Research Laboratories. Space Physics Laboratory.
Tables of vertical cutoff rigidities for epochs 1955 and 1960 /. Hanscom AFB, Mass. , 1974. 91 p. : *NYPL [JSF 81-117]*

United States. Air Force, Dept. of the. see **United States. Dept. of the Air Force.**

UNITED STATES. AIR FORCE. FAR EAST AIR FORCES.
Futrell, Robert Frank. The United States Air Force in Korea, 1950-1953 /. Washington, D.C. , 1981. p. cm. LC Card 81-607076 DDC 951.9/042 19
DS920.2.U5 F8 1981

UNITED STATES. AIR FORCE - HISTORY - VIETNAMESE CONFLICT, 1961-1975.
Ballard, Jack S. The development and employment of fixed-wing gunships, 1962-1972 /. Washington, D.C. , 1981. p. cm. LC Card 80-25422 DDC 959.704/348 19
DS558.8 .B35

Buckingham, William A. Operation Ranch Hand . Washington, D.C. , 1981. p. cm. LC Card 81-11244 DDC 959.704/348 19
DS559.8.C5 B82

Futrell, Robert Frank. The advisory years in Southeast Asia, to 1965 /. Washington, D.C. , 1980. p. cm. LC Card 80-24547 DDC 959.704/348 19
DS558.8 .F87

McCarthy, James R. Linebacker II . [Montgomery] Ala. , Washington , 1979. xvi, 208 p. : LC Card 79-603001
DS558.8 .M32

The United States Air Force in Korea, 1950-1953 /. Futrell, Robert Frank. Washington, D.C. , 1981. p. cm. LC Card 81-607076 DDC 951.9/042 19
DS920.2.U5 F8 1981

United States Air Force in Southeast Asia series.
Ballard, Jack S. The development and employment of fixed-wing gunships, 1962-1972 /. Washington, D.C. , 1981. p. cm. LC Card 80-25422 DDC 959.704/348 19
DS558.8 .B35

Futrell, Robert Frank. The advisory years in Southeast Asia, to 1965 /. Washington, D.C. , 1980. p. cm. LC Card 80-24547 DDC 959.704/348 19
DS558.8 .F87

United States. Air Force. Office of Scientific Research. (Old Catalog form: United States. Air Research and Development Command. Scientific Research, Office of)
Project Squid Workshop on Gas Turbine Combustor Design Problems, Purdue University, 1978. Gas turbine combustor design problems /. Washington , c1980. xvi, 431 p. : ISBN 0-89116-177-5 LC Card 79-22350
TJ778 .P74 1978 *NYPL [JSE 81-58]*

UNITED STATES. AIR FORCE - PERSONNEL MANAGEMENT.
United States. General Accounting Office. The Air Force can reduce its stated requirements for strategic airlift crews . [Washington] 1979. v, 23 p. ; LC Card 79-603765 DDC 358.4/161/0973 19
UG773 .U54 1979

United States. Air Pollution Training Institute.
see **Air Pollution Training Institute.**

UNITED STATES. AIR SAFETY ADMINISTRATION.
United States. Congress. House. Committee on Public Works and Transportation. Subcommittee on Aviation. To enhance the safety mission of the FAA . Washington , 1980. iv, 560 p. : LC Card 80-604032 DDC 343.73/097 347.30397 19
KF27 .P89624 1980m

United States. Air War College. Airpower Research Institute. see **United States. Airpower Research Institute.**

United States. Airpower Research Institute.
McCarthy, James R. Linebacker II . [Montgomery] Ala. , Washington , 1979. xvi, 208 p. : LC Card 79-603001
DS558.8 .M32

United States. Alcohol, Drug Abuse, and Mental Health Administration.
ADAMHA news. v. b, no. 14, July 11, 1980-Rockville, Md.
I. Title. *NYPL [Econ. Div.]*

Friends Medical Science Research Center. Narcotic addiction over a quarter of a century in a major American city, 1950-1977 . [Rockville, Md.] , 1980. vi, 92 p. : LC Card 80-601276 DDC 362.2/93/097526 19
HV5833.B2 F74 1980

Special report . Rockville, Md. , Washington, D.C. , 1981. 160 p. : LC Card 81-601423 DDC 616.89/82 19
RC514 .S68

United States. Alcohol, Drug Abuse and Mental Health Administration. National Institute of Mental Health. see **United States. National Institute of Mental Health.**

United States. Alcohol, Drug Abuse, and Mental Health Administration. National Institute on Alcohol Abuse and Alcoholism. see **National Institute on Alcohol Abuse and Alcoholism.**

United States. Alcohol, Drug Abuse, and Mental Health Administration. National Institute on Drug Abuse. see **National Institute on Drug Abuse.**

United States - Aliens. see **Aliens - United States.**

UNITED STATES. AMERICAN BATTLE MONUMENTS COMMISSION.
United States. Congress. House. Committee on Veterans' Affairs. Subcommittee on Compensation, Pension, Insurance, and Memorial Affairs. Review of the operation of the overseas cemeteries and memorials administered by the American Battle

Monuments Commission and Arlington National Cemetery, also H.R 6355 and H.R. 6356 . Washington , 1980. iii, 52 p. ; LC Card 80-603070 DDC 343.73/0256 19
KF27 .V43 1980

United States. Ames Research Center, Moffett Field, Calif. (Old Catalog form: United States. Ames Aeronautical Laboratory, Moffett Field, Calif.)
Conference of Remote Sensing Educators, Stanford University, 1978. Conference of Remote Sensing Educators (CORSE-78) . [Washington, D.C.] [Springfield, Va.] 1980. xviii, 645 p. : LC Card 80-602394 DDC 621.36/78/0711 19
G70.4 .C64 1978

The United States and Korea : American-Korean relations, 1866-1976 / edited with introduction by Andrew C. Nahm. Kalamazoo : Center for Korean Studies, Western Michigan University, 1979. 262 p. ; 24 cm. (Korean studies series . 6) Papers presented at a conference sponsored by the Center for Korean Studies, held at Western Michigan University, Nov. 4-6, 1976. Bibliography: p. 260-262.
LC Card 78-65924 DDC 327.730519 19
1. United States - Foreign relations - Korea - Congresses. 2. Korea - Foreign relations - United States - Congresses. I. Nahm, Andrew C. II. Western Michigan University. Center for Korean Studies. III. Series.
E183.8.K6 U54

United States and Soviet progress in space .
United States. Library of Congress. Congressional Research Service. Washington , 1980. xiii, 91 p. ; LC Card 80-602269 DDC 387.8 19
TL789.8.U5 U54 1980

The United States and the arms embargo against South Africa . Gervasi, Sean. [Binghamton] , c1978. 49 p. ; LC Card 78-112749 DDC 382/.456234/0968 19
HD9743.S62 G47

The United States and the People's Republic of China . United States. Congress. House. Committee on Foreign Affairs. Subcommittee on Asian and Pacific Affairs. Washington , 1980 [i.e. 1981] v, 163 p. ; LC Card 81-600985 DDC 327.73051 19
KF27 .F638 1980d

The United States and the world community in the eighties . United States. President's Commission for a National Agenda for the Eighties. Panel on the United States and the World Community. Washington, D.C. , 1980. 109 p. ; LC Card 80-28709 DDC 327.73 19
E840 .U67 1980

UNITED STATES - ANTIQUITIES.
United States. Federal Highway Administration. Office of Environmental Policy. The consideration of archeology and paleontology in the Federal-aid highway program. [Washington] , 1979. 79 p. : LC Card 79-602652
E159.5 .U54 1978 *NYPL [HBC 81-515]*

UNITED STATES - ANTIQUITIES - CONGRESSES.
Scholars as contractors . Washington , 1979. 265 p. in various pagings : LC Card 79-603005
CC136 .S36 *NYPL [JLF 81-76]*

Symposium on Cultural Resources Management and Remote Sensing, Tucson, Ariz. 1978. Remote sensing and non-destructive archeology /. Washington, DC , 1978. vii, 71 p. : LC Card 80-602610 DDC 930.1/028 19
CC76.4 .S9 1978

Workshop on Management Techniques Applied to Archeology, Texas Tech University, 1977. Scholars as managers, or how can the managers do it better . Washington , 1978. vii, 21 p., [2] leaves of plates : LC Card 79-602641
CC51 .W67 1977

United States. Antitrust Laws, Division for Enforcement of. see **United States. Dept. of Justice. Antitrust Division.**

United States. Appalachian Regional Commission. see **Appalachian Regional Commission.**

UNITED STATES - APPROPRIATIONS AND EXPENDITURES.
Coe, Charles K. Maximizing revenue, minimizing expenditures /. Athens , 1981. p.

cm. ISBN 0-89854-070-4 LC Card 80-29269
DDC 352.1/09758 19
HJ9221 .C63

Reducing the Federal budget . Washington,
D.C. [1981] xi, 187 p. ; LC Card 81-601803
DDC 353.0072/22 19
HJ2051 .R42

United States. Congress. House. Committee on
Post Office and Civil Service. Subcommittee on
Compensation and Employee Benefits. Federal
pay continuity act . Washington , 1980. iii, 128
p. ; LC Card 80-602950 DDC 353.001/23 19
KF27 .P638 1980c

United States. Congress. Senate. Committee on
Governmental Affairs. Subcommittee on
Oversight of Government Management.
"Hurry-up" spending . Washington , 1980. v, 45
p. ; LC Card 81-601507 DDC 353.0072/232 19
HJ7539 .U535 1980

UNITED STATES - APPROPRIATIONS AND EXPENDITURES, 1975.
United States. Congress. House. Committee on
Appropriations. Subcommittee on Foreign
Operations and Related Agencies
Appropriations. Foreign assistance and related
agencies appropriations for 1975 . Washington ,
1974. 2 v. : LC Card 74-602734
KF27 .A646 1974

UNITED STATES - APPROPRIATIONS AND EXPENDITURES, 1980.
United States. Congress. House. Committee on
Foreign Affairs. Subcommittee on International
Operations. Authorizing additional
appropriations for the Department of State, the
Board for International Broadcasting, and grants
to Radio Free Europe/Radio Liberty for fiscal
years 1980 and 1981 . Washington , 1980. iv,
103 p. ; LC Card 80-603796 DDC
353.0072/23689 19
KF27 .F647 1980c

United States. Congress. Senate. Committee on
Appropriations. Subcommittee on Dept. of the
Interior and Related Agencies. Department of
the Interior and related agencies appropriations
for fiscal year 1980 . Washington , 1980- v.
<1-4> ; LC Card 80-603500 DDC 353.0072/236
19
KF26 .A652 1980

United States. Congress. Senate. Committee on
Appropriations. Subcommittee on
HUD-Independent Agencies. Space shuttle and
Galileo mission . Washington , 1980. iv, 132
p. ; LC Card 80-601987 DDC 353.0072/2368778
19
KF26 .A6486 1979c

UNITED STATES - APPROPRIATIONS AND EXPENDITURES, 1981.
United States. Congress. House. Committee on
Appropriations. Supplemental appropriation and
rescission bill, 1981 . Washington , 1981- v.
<1, 3-4 > : LC Card 81-601881 DDC
353.0072/236 19
KF27 .A6 1981a

United States. Congress. House. Committee on
Appropriations. Subcommittee on Energy and
Water Development. Energy and water
development supplemental appropriations for
1981 . Washington , 1980. ii, 60 p. : LC Card
80-603978 DDC 353.0072/23687 19
KF27 .A64 1980a

United States. Congress. House. Committee on
Interstate and Foreign Commerce. Spending
reductions . Washington , 1980. v, 217 p. ; LC
Card 81-601122 DDC 353.0072/232 19
KF6231.A55 I557

United States. Congress. Senate. Committee on
Appropriations. Subcommittee on Agriculture,
Rural Development, and Related Agencies.
Agriculture, rural development, and related
agencies appropriations for fiscal year 1981 .
Washington , 1980. 3 v. : LC Card 80-603090
DDC 353.0072/23682/33 19
KF26 .A643 1980

United States. Congress. Senate. Committee on
Appropriations. Subcommittee on Energy and
Water Development. Energy and water
development appropriations for fiscal year
1981 . Washington , 1980- v. ; LC Card
80-603292 DDC 353.0072/23682325 19
KF26 .A6469 1980a

United States. Congress. Senate. Committee on
Appropriations. Subcommittee on Foreign
Operations. Foreign assistance and related
programs appropriations for fiscal year 1981 .
Washington , c1980- v. : LC Card 89-2356
HC60 .U5912 1981b

United States. Congress. Senate. Committee on
Appropriations. Subcommittee on Foreign
Operations. Foreign assistance and related
programs appropriations for fiscal year 1981 .
Washington , 1980- v.<1>: LC Card 80-603464
DDC 353.0072/23689 19
KF26 .A647 1980

United States. Congress. Senate. Committee on
Appropriations. Subcommittee on
HUD-Independent Agencies. Department of
Housing and Urban Development, and certain
independent agencies appropriations for fiscal
year 1981 . Washington , 1980. 2 v. (iii, 2553,
xiii p.) : LC Card 80-604053 DDC
353.0072/236865 19
KF26 .A6486 1980a

United States. Congress. Senate. Committee on
Appropriations. Subcommittee on the Dept. of
the Treasury, U. S. Postal Service, and General
Government Appropriations. Treasury, Postal
Service, and general government appropriations
for fiscal year 1981 . Washington , 1980- v.
<1> ; LC Card 80-603729 DDC 353.0072/236
19
KF26 .A662 1980

United States. Congress. Senate. Committee on
Appropriations. Subcommittee on
Transportation and Related Agencies.
Department of Transportation and related
agencies appropriations for fiscal year 1981 .
Washington , 1980- v. <1> : LC Card
80-603482 DDC 353.0072/236875 19
KF26 .A66 1980

UNITED STATES - APPROPRIATIONS AND EXPENDITURES, 1982.
United States. Congress. House. Committee on
Appropriations. The federal budget for 1982 .
Washington , 1981. ii, 242, ii p. : LC Card
81-601891 DDC 353.0072/22 19
KF27 .A6 1981

United States. Congress. House. Committee on
Appropriations. Subcommittee on Dept. of the
Interior and Related Agencies. Department of
the Interior and related agencies appropriations
for 1982 . Washington , 1981. 4 v. : LC Card
81-601601 DDC 353.0072/2368232 19
KF27 .A6484 1981

United States. Congress. House. Committee on
Appropriations. Subcommittee on Dept. of
Transportation and Related Agencies
Appropriations. Department of transportation
and related agencies appropriations for 1982 .
Washington , 1981- v. <1-3> ; LC Card
81-601415 DDC 353.0072/236875 19
KF27 .A667 1981

United States. Congress. House. Committee on
Appropriations. Subcommittee on Energy and
Water Development. Energy and water
development appropriations for 1982 .
Washington , 1981. 2 v. (2710, xviii p.) ; LC
Card 81-601647 DDC 353.0072/236823 19
KF27 .A64 1981

United States. Congress. House. Committee on
Appropriations. Subcommittee on Military
Construction Appropriations. Military
construction appropriations for 1982 .
Washington , 1981. 2 v. : LC Card 81-601195
DDC 358/.22/0973 19
KF27 .A655 1981

United States. Congress. House. Committee on
Appropriations. Subcommittee on the
Departments of Commerce, Justice, and State,
the Judiciary, and Related Agencies.
Departments of Commerce, Justice, and State,
the judiciary, and related agencies
appropriations for 1982 . Washington , 1981- v.
<1-2, 4> ; LC Card 81-601662 DDC
353.0072/236 19
KF27 .A6327 1981

United States. Appropriations, Committee on
(House) see United States. Congress. House.
Committee on Appropriations.

United States. Appropriations, Committee on
(Senate) see United States. Congress. Senate.
Committee on Appropriations.

United States - Archaeology. see Indians of
North America - Antiquities; United States -
Antiquities.

United States. Architectural and Transportation
Barriers Compliance Board. see
Architectural and Transportation Barriers
Compliance Board.

United States. Area Redevelopment
Administration. United States. Bureau of the
Census. Statistical profile. Ser. SP. no. 1-136;
Feb. 1962-Aug. 1962. Washington, 136 no. in 3
v. LC Card A62-9234 *NYPL [TAA (United
States. Census Bureau. Statistical profile.
Ser. SP.)]*

United States. Argonne National Laboratory,
Lemont, Ill. (Old Catalog form: United States.
Argonne National Laboratory, Chicago)
Proceedings of the NEACRP meeting of a
Monte Carlo study group. Argonne, Ill. [1974]
363 l. *NYPL [*XMQ-2014]*

Toledo Metropolitan Area Council of
Governments. Solar energy, active and passive
systems for space and water heating /. Toledo,
Ohio , c1980. ii, 41 p. : LC Card 80-150114
DDC 697/.78 19
TH7413 .T64 1980

United States. Argonne National Laboratory,
Lemont, Ill. Division of Environmental
Impact Studies.
A Biologist's manual for the evaluation of
impacts of coal-fired power plants on fish,
wildlife, and their habitats /. [Washington] ,
1978. xix p., 146 leaves, p. 147-206 : LC Card
79-100195
QH76 .U54a 78/75 QH545.C57

Impacts of coal-fired power plants on fish,
wildlife, and their habitats /. [Washington] ,
1978. xii, 261 p. : LC Card 78-602648 DDC
574.5/222 19
QH545.C57 I47

United States. Argonne National Laboratory,
Lemont, Ill. Energy and Environmental
Systems Division. American Society of
Planning Officials. Legal issues of emission
density zoning /. Research Triangle Park,
N.C. , 1978. vi, 136 p. ; LC Card 79-601742
DDC 344.73/046342 19
KF3812.5.E55 A94

United States. Argonne National Laboratory,
Lemont, Ill. Environmental Impact Studies,
Division of. see United States. Argonne
National Laboratory, Lemont, Ill. Division
of Environmental Impact Studies.

UNITED STATES - ARMED FORCES.
Hillier, Pat. U. S. ground forces . [Washington,
D.C.] , 1980. xxiii, 87 p. : LC Card 81-600683
DDC 355/.033073 19
UA23 .H513

United States. Congress. House. Committee on
the Budget. Military readiness and the Rapid
Deployment Joint Task Force (RDJTF) .
Washington , 1980. iii, 70 p. ; LC Card
80-604107 DDC 355.3/5 19
KF27 .B8 1980d

United States. Congressional Budget Office. U.
S. tactical air forces . Washington , 1976. 35
p. : LC Card 76-602204
UG633 .U52 1976

UNITED STATES - ARMED FORCES - BIOGRAPHY.
United States. Congress. Senate. Committee on
Veterans' Affairs. Medal of Honor recipients,
1863-1978 . Washington , 1979. xix, 1113 p. :
LC Card 80-603561 DDC 355.1/34 19
UB433 .U55 1979

UNITED STATES - ARMED FORCES - COMMISSARIAT.
United States. General Accounting Office.
Military commissaries . [Washington, D.C.] ,
1980. 46 p. ; LC Card 80-600969 DDC 355.3/41
19
UC703 .U54 1980

UNITED STATES - ARMED FORCES - COST CONTROL.
United States. General Accounting Office.
Implications of highly sophisticated weapon
systems on military capabilities ; report to the
Congress /. [Washington, D.C.] [1980] iv, 24
p. : LC Card 80-603238 DDC 355.8/2/0973 19
UF503 .U56 1980

UNITED STATES - ARMED FORCES - EUROPE.

United States. Congress. Senate. Committee on Armed Services. Subcommittee on Procurement Policy and Reprograming. NATO support agreements . Washington , 1980. iii, 17 p. ; LC Card 80-603045　DDC 341.7/2 19
KF26 .A768 1980

UNITED STATES - ARMED FORCES - FACILITIES - MANAGEMENT.

United States. General Accounting Office. A central manager is needed to coordinate the military diagnostic and calibration program, Department of Defense /. [Washington] , 1977. 12, 4 leaves :　LC Card 77-603003　DDC 355.6/213 19
UG455 .U54 1977

UNITED STATES - ARMED FORCES - FINANCES.

United States. Congress. House. Committee on Armed Services. Full committee consideration of recommendation to Budget Committee on reconciliation in concurrence with the first concurrent resolution and H.R. 7682, H.R. 7694, and H.R. 5856 /. Washington , 1980. ii, 22 p. ;　LC Card 80-603649　DDC 355.6/22/0973 19
KF27 .A7 1980i

UNITED STATES - ARMED FORCES - FUEL.

Compilation of the Energy Security Act of 1980, and 1980 amendments to the Defense Production Act of 1950 /. Washington , 1980. 3 v. (v. 2252 p.) ;　LC Card 80-603878　DDC 346.7304/679 347.3064679 19
KF2120.A32 A15 1980

United States. Congress. House. Committee on Armed Services. Subcommittee on Investigations. Department of Defense petroleum requirements and supplies . Washington , 1980. iii, 17 p. ;　LC Card 80-603555　DDC 355.2/4/0973 19
UC263 .U517 1980

United States. Congress. House. Committee on Armed Services. Subcommittee on Investigations. Department of Defense petroleum requirements and supplies . Washington , 1980. iii, 651 p. ;　LC Card 80-602946　DDC 355.2/43/0973 19
KF27 .A753 1979c

United States. Congress. Senate. Committee on Energy and Natural Resources. Subcommittee on Energy Resources and Materials Production. Strategic petroleum reserve and the naval petroleum reserve . Washington , 1980. iii, 65 p. ;　LC Card 80-602779　DDC 333.8/23211/0973 19
KF26 .E5543 1980a

UNITED STATES - ARMED FORCES - LEAVES AND FURLOUGHS - LAW AND LEGISLATION.

United States. Congress. House. Committee on Post Office and Civil Service. Subcommittee on Compensation and Employee Benefits. Retirement appeals, military leave, and quadrennial pay commission . Washington , 1980. iii, 20 p. ;　LC Card 80-602189　DDC 343.73/011 19
KF27 .P638 1980

UNITED STATES - ARMED FORCES - MANAGEMENT.

Steadman, Richard C. The national military command structure . Washington , 1978. iii, 79 p. ;　LC Card 79-602790
UA23.3 .S73

UNITED STATES - ARMED FORCES - MEDICAL CARE.

United States. Congress. House. Committee on Armed Services. Subcommittee No. 1. Subcommittee No. 1 hearing on H. R. 8413. Washington, 1969. 5403-5413 p.

NYPL [JLE 81-563]

United States. Congress. House. Committee on Armed Services. Subcommittee on Military Personnel. Hearings on civilian health and medical program of the uniformed services before the Military Personnel Subcommittee of the Committee on Armed Services, House of Representatives, Ninety-sixth Congress, second session, June 18, and September 15, 1980. Washington , 1980. ii, 232 p. ;　LC Card 80-603448　DDC 362.1/0973 19
KF27 .A76398 1980b

United States. Congress. House. Committee on Armed Services. Subcommittee on Military Personnel. Military health care delivery including CHAMPUS and inquiry of U. S. Naval Hospital, Oak Knoll, Calif., with appendix . Washington , 1981. ii, 701, iv p. :　LC Card 80-601886　DDC 355.3/45 19
KF27 .A76398 1977c

UNITED STATES - ARMED FORCES - MEDICAL CARE - LAW AND LEGISLATION - UNITED STATES.

United States. Congress. Senate. Committee on Governmental Affairs. Federal Interagency Medical Resources Sharing and Coordination Act of 1980 . Washington , 1980. iv, 324 p. :　LC Card 80-604081　DDC 343.73/0115 347.303115 19
KF26 .G67 1980k

UNITED STATES - ARMED FORCES - MILITARY CONSTRUCTION OPERATIONS.

United States. Congress. House. Committee on Appropriations. Subcommittee on Military Construction Appropriations. Military construction appropriations for 1982 . Washingon , 1981. 2 v. :　LC Card 81-601195　DDC 358/.22/0973 19
KF27 .A655 1981

United States. Congress. House. Committee on Armed Services. Subcommittee on Military Installations and Facilities. Hearings on H.R. 6493 (H.R. 7301) ... and fiscal year 1980 supplemental request, and fiscal year 1981 Budget amendment for the Military construction program before the Military Istallations and Facilities Subcommittee of the Committee on Armed Services, House of Representatives, Ninety-sixth Congress, second session. Washington , 1980. iiii, 662, x p. :　LC Card 80-602757　DDC 355.6/22/0973 19
KF27 .A76397 1980a

United States. Congress. Senate. Committee on Armed Services. Subcommittee on Military Construction and Stockpiles. Military construction authorization, fiscal year 1981 . Washington , 1980. iv, 694, xv p. :　LC Card 80-603503　DDC 355.6/22/0973 19
KF26 .A756 1980

UNITED STATES - ARMED FORCES - MOBILIZATION.

United States. Congress. Senate. Committee on Armed Services. Subcommittee on Manpower and Personnel. Providing greater flexibility for the armed forces in ordering reserves to active duty . Washington , 1980 [i.e. 1981] iii, 32 p. ;　LC Card 81-600808　DDC 343.73/012 347.30312 19
KF26 .A7548 1980b

UNITED STATES - ARMED FORCES - OFFICERS.

United States. Congress. House. Committee on Armed Services. Full committee consideration of H.R. 5503, DOPMA (Defense officer personnel management act) . Washington , 1977. ii, 131 p. ;　LC Card 77-603628
KF27 .A7 1977j

UNITED STATES - ARMED FORCES - OFFICERS CLUBS.

United States. Congress. House. Committee on Armed Services. Subcommittee on Investigations. Nonappropriated Fund Panel. Review of military clubs and package beverage stores . Washington , 1980. iii, 21 p. ;　LC Card 80-601774　DDC 355.3/46/0973 19
U56 .U56 1980

UNITED STATES - ARMED FORCES - OFFICERS - LEGAL STATUS, LAWS, ETC.

United States. Congress. House. Committee on Armed Services. Subcommittee on Military Compensation. Hearings on S. 1918, Defense Officer Personnel Management Act, (DOPMA), before the Military Compensation Subcommittee of the Committee on Armed Services, House of Representatives, Ninety-sixth Congress, second session, April 29, May 7, 13, 14, and September 29, 1980. Washington , 1981. ii, 388 p. ;　LC Card 81-600806　DDC 343.73/013 347.30313 19
KF27 .A76392 1980a

UNITED STATES - ARMED FORCES - OFFICIALS AND EMPLOYEES.

United States. Congress. House. Committee on Armed Services. Full committee consideration of recommendation to Budget Committee on reconciliation in concurrence with the first concurrent resolution and H.R. 7682, H.R. 7694, and H.R. 5856 /. Washington , 1980. ii, 22 p. ;　LC Card 80-603649　DDC 355.6/22/0973 19
KF27 .A7 1980i

UNITED STATES - ARMED FORCES - ORGANIZATION.

Steadman, Richard C. The national military command structure . Washington , 1978. iii, 79 p. ;　LC Card 79-602790
UA23.3 .S73

UNITED STATES - ARMED FORCES - PACIFIC AREA.

United States. Congressional Budget Office. Planning U. S. general purpose forces . Washington , 1977. xxiii, 95 p. :　LC Card 77-603153
UA26.E27 U54 1977

UNITED STATES - ARMED FORCES - PAY, ALLOWANCES, ETC.

United States. Congress. House. Committee on Armed Services. Subcommittee on Military Compensation. Special pay for military veterinary officers . Washington , 1980 [i.e. 1981] ii, 59 p. :　LC Card 81-600607　DDC 331.2/81636089/0973 19
KF27 .A76392 1980

United States. Congress. Senate. Committee on Armed Services. Subcommittee on Manpower and Personnel. Military compensation . Washington , 1980. ii, 73 p. ;　LC Card 81-600589　DDC 355.6/4/0973 19
KF26 .A7548 1980a

United States. Congress. Senate. Committee on Armed Services. Subcommittee on Manpower and Personnel. Proposed changes to military compensation . Washington , 1980. iii, 101 p. ;　LC Card 80-602795　DDC 355.6/4/0973 19
KF26 .A7548 1980

United States. Congressional Budget Office. Costs of manning the active-duty military /. Washington, D.C. [1980] xiv, 44 p. ;　LC Card 80-603176　DDC 355.6/4/0973 19
UC74 .U54 1980

UNITED STATES - ARMED FORCES - PAY, ALLOWANCES, ETC. - LAW AND LEGISLATION.

United States. Congress. House. Committee on Armed Services. Full committee consideration of H.R. 7626 to amend title 37, United States code, to improve certain special pays and allowances for members of the uniformed services, and for other purposes /. Washington , 1980. ii, 24 p. ;　LC Card 80-603657　DDC 343.73/013 347.30313 19
KF27 .A7 1980e

United States. Congress. House. Committee on Armed Services. Subcommittee on Military Compensation. Hearings on H.R. 5168, H.R. 7626, and S. 1454, miscellaneous military personnel management and military compensation legislation, before the Military Compensation Subcommittee of the Committee on Armed Services, House of Representatives, Ninety-sixth Congress, second session, September 10, November 15, December 4, 1979, February 22, June 4, 11, and 19, 1980. Washington , 1980 [i.e. 1981] ii, 127 p. ;　LC Card 81-600976　DDC 343.73/013 347.30313 19
KF27 .A76392 1979b

United States. Congress. House. Committee on Post Office and Civil Service. Subcommittee on Compensation and Employee Benefits. Retirement appeals, military leave, and quadrennial pay commission . Washington , 1980. iii, 20 p. ;　LC Card 80-602189　DDC 343.73/011 19
KF27 .P638 1980

United States. Congress. Senate. Committee on Armed Services. Subcommittee on Manpower and Personnel. Military medical programs and proposed revisions of military medical pay . Washington , 1980. iii, 78 p. :　LC Card 80-601938　DDC 343.73/013 19
KF26 .A7548 1979e

UNITED STATES - ARMED FORCES - PERIODICALS.

United States. Joint Chiefs of Staff. United
States military posture. [Washington]   LC Card
79-642632   NYPL [JLM 80-756]

**UNITED STATES - ARMED FORCES -
PERSONNEL MANAGEMENT.**
United States. General Accounting Office.
Military commissaries . [Washington, D.C.] ,
1980. 46 p. ;   LC Card 80-600969   DDC 355.3/41
19
UC703 .U54 1980

**UNITED STATES - ARMED FORCES -
PERSONNEL MANAGEMENT -
CONGRESSES.**
Proceedings of the seventh symposium,
psychology in the Department of Defense, 16
April-18 April 1980. Colorado Springs, Colo.
[Springfield, Va. (5285 Port Royal Rd.,
Springfield 22151)] 1980. xxiv, 635 p. ;   LC
   Card 80-604141   DDC 355/.001/9 19
U22.3 .P712

**UNITED STATES - ARMED FORCES -
PERSONNEL MANAGEMENT - LAW
AND LEGISLATION.**
United States. Congress. House. Committee on
Armed Services. Subcommittee on Military
Compensation. Hearings on H.R. 5168, H.R.
7626, and S. 1454, miscellaneous military
personnel management and military
compensation legislation, before the Military
Compensation Subcommittee of the Committee
on Armed Services, House of Representatives,
Ninety-sixth Congress, second session,
September 10, November 15, December 4,
1979, February 22, June 4, 11, and 19, 1980.
Washington , 1980 [i.e. 1981] ii, 127 p. ;   LC
   Card 81-600976   DDC 343.73/013 347.30313 19
KF27 .A76392 1979b

United States. Congress. House. Committee on
Armed Services. Subcommittee on Military
Compensation. Hearings on S. 1918, Defense
Officer Personnel Management Act, (DOPMA),
before the Military Compensation
Subcommittee of the Committee on Armed
Services, House of Representatives, Ninety-sixth
Congress, second session, April 29, May 7, 13,
14, and September 29, 1980. Washington ,
1981. ii, 388 p. :   LC Card 81-600806   DDC
   343.73/013 347.30313 19
KF27 .A76392 1980a

**UNITED STATES - ARMED FORCES -
PROCUREMENT.**
United States. Congress. Senate. Committee on
Armed Services. Subcommittee on Procurement
Policy and Reprograming. Vinson-Trammell act
repeal or revision . Washington , 1980. iii, 171
p. ;   LC Card 80-603036   DDC 346.73/023 19
KF26 .A768 1980a

**UNITED STATES - ARMED FORCES -
RECRUITING, ENLISTMENT, ETC.**
United States. Congress. Senate. Committee on
Veterans' Affairs. Educational incentives and
the all-volunteer force . Washington , 1980. iv,
195 p. :   LC Card 81-600866   DDC 343.73/011
   347.30311 19
KF26 .V4 1980f

**UNITED STATES - ARMED FORCES -
REGISTERS OF DEAD.**
Utah. State Archives. Veterans with Federal
service buried in the State of Utah, Territorial
period to 1965. [Salt Lake City] , 1965- v. ;
   LC Card 80-53986   DDC 929/.3792 19
F825 .U85 1965

**UNITED STATES - ARMED FORCES -
RESERVES.**
United States. Congress. House. Committee on
Armed Services. Subcommittee on Military
Personnel. Hearing on H.R. 5822, H.R. 2224,
H.R. 7295, and H.R. 7294 (H.R. 7682), reserve
readiness legislation . Washington , 1980. ii, 25
p. ;   LC Card 80-602908   DDC 343.73/013 19
KF27 .A76398 1980a

United States. Congress. Senate. Committee on
Armed Services. Subcommittee on Manpower
and Personnel. Providing greater flexibility for
the armed forces in ordering reserves to active
duty . Washington , 1980 [i.e. 1981] iii, 32 p. ;
   LC Card 81-600808   DDC 343.73/012 347.30312
   19
KF26 .A7548 1980b

**UNITED STATES - ARMED FORCES -
RESERVES - PERSONNEL
MANAGEMENT.**

United States. Congress. House. Committee on
Post Office and Civil Service. Subcommittee on
Investigations. Civilian technician program .
Washington , 1980. iii, 131 p. ;   LC Card
   80-603291   DDC 355.3/7/0973 19
KF27 .P646 1980b

**UNITED STATES - ARMED FORCES -
SANITARY AFFAIRS.**
United States. Congress. House. Select
Committee on Narcotics Abuse and Control.
Drug abuse in the Armed Forces of the United
States . Washington , 1980. iii, 66 p. ;   LC Card
   80-603858   DDC 362.2/936 19
UH630 .U62 1980

**UNITED STATES - ARMED FORCES -
SERVICE CLUBS.**
United States. Congress. House. Committee on
Armed Services. Subcommittee on
Investigations. Nonappropriated Fund Panel.
Review of military clubs and package beverage
stores . Washington , 1980. iii, 21 p. ;   LC Card
   80-601774   DDC 355.3/46/0973 19
U56 .U56 1980

**UNITED STATES - ARMED FORCES -
SUPPLIES AND STORES -
DIRECTORIES.**
United States. Defense Logistics Agency.
Registers of planned emergency producers.
Washington , 1980. 290 p. in various pagings :
                          NYPL [JLF 80-1284]

**UNITED STATES - ARMED FORCES -
TRANSPORTATION.**
Daniel, Marshall E. Defense transportation
organization . Washington, DC , 1979. vi, 113
p. ;   LC Card 79-603727   DDC 355.2/7/0973 19
UC273 .D36

United States. Congress. House. Committee on
Merchant Marine and Fisheries. Defense sealift
capability . Washington , 1980. iv, 301 p. :   LC
   Card 80-604083   DDC 359.9/82/0973 19
KF27 .M4 1979c

**UNITED STATES - ARMED FORCES -
TRANSPORTATION - CONGRESSES.**
WorldWide Strategic Mobility Conference,
National Defense University, 1977. The
WorldWide Strategic Mobility Conference 1977,
2-4 May 1977 /. [Washington, D.C. , 1977] ca.
100 p. in various pagings ;   LC Card 80-601611
   DDC 355.2/7 19
UC273 .W67 1977

**UNITED STATES - ARMED FORCES -
VOCATIONAL GUIDANCE.**
United States. Office of the Assistant Secretary
of Defense (Manpower, Reserve Affairs, and
Logistics) Pathways to military service for men
and women. [Washington] , 1978. 68 p. ;   LC
   Card 78-603689
UB147 .U49 1978

**UNITED STATES - ARMED FORCES -
WEAPONS SYSTEMS.**
United States. General Accounting Office.
Implications of highly sophisticated weapon
systems on military capabilities ; report to the
Congress /. [Washington, D.C.] [1980] iv, 24
p. :   LC Card 80-603238   DDC 355.8/2/0973 19
UF503 .U56 1980

**UNITED STATES - ARMED FORCES -
WEAPONS SYSTEMS - FINANCE.**
United States. Congress. House. Committee on
Armed Services. Procurement and Military
Nuclear Systems Subcommittee. Coordination
of Department of Energy/Department of
Defense nuclear weapons materials
requirements . Washington , 1980. ii, 23 p. ;
   LC Card 80-602992   DDC 355.8/25119/0973 19
KF27 .A7657 1980c

**UNITED STATES - ARMED FORCES -
WOMEN.**
United States. Congress. House. Committee on
Armed Services. Subcommittee on Military
Personnel. Women in the military .
Washington , 1981. ii, 369 p. :   LC Card
81-601874   DDC 355/.0088/042 19
KF27 .A76398 1979d

United States. Armed Services, Committee on
   (House) see United States. Congress. House.
   Committee on Armed Services.

United States. Arms Control and Disarmament
   Agency.
Arms control and disarmament agreements .
Washington, D.C. , 1980. vii, 239 p. ;   LC Card

   80-604129   DDC 327.1/74 s 341.7/33/0265 19
JX1974.A1 U52 no. 105 JX1974.7

Japan's contribution to military stability in
Northeast Asia / prepared for the
Subcommittee on East Asian and Pacific Affairs
of the Committee on Foreign Relations, United
States Senate, by the U. S. Arms Control and
Disarmament Agency. Washinton : U. S. Govt.
Print. Off., 1980. xi, 77 p. : ill. ; 24 cm. At head
of tile: 96th Congress, 2d session. Committee print.
   LC Card 80-602578   DDC 355/.033052 19
*1. Japan - Defenses. 2. East Asia - National security. I.
Title.*
UA845 U44 1980

United States. Army. 7th Army. Eurarmy. v. 14,
no. 9- ; Jan. 1976- New York.
                          NYPL [JFM 80-250]

**UNITED STATES. ARMY - 20TH CENTURY -
HISTORY - MANUSCRIPTS -
MICROFORM CATALOGS.**
Zeidlik, Hannah M. Catalog and index to
historical manuscripts, 1940-1966 /.
Washington, DC , 1979. 2 v. ;   LC Card
   79-604297   DDC 016.355/00973 19
Z1249.M5 Z44 E745

**UNITED STATES. ARMY - 20TH CENTURY -
HISTORY - SOURCES - MICROFORM
CATALOGS.**
Zeidlik, Hannah M. Catalog and index to
historical manuscripts, 1940-1966 /.
Washington, DC , 1979. 2 v. ;   LC Card
   79-604297   DDC 016.355/00973 19
Z1249.M5 Z44 E745

**UNITED STATES. ARMY - ADDRESSES,
ESSAYS, LECTURES.**
United States. Dept. of the Army. General
Staff. A framework for molding the Army of
the 1980s into a disciplined, well-trained
fighting force . [Washington, D.C.] , 1980. 17
p. :   LC Card 80-602648   DDC 355.3/0973 19
UA24 .A7 1980

UNITED STATES. ARMY - AVIATION.
United States. Congress. House. Committee on
Armed Services. Special Subcommittee on Nato
Standardization, Interoperability, and Readiness.
Status of army air defense planning .
Washington , 1980. ii, 52 p. :   LC Card
80-604007   DDC 358.4/145/0973 19
KF27 .A7642 1980

**Indochina monographs. see Indochina
monographs.**

United States. Army Command and General Staff
   College, Fort Leavenworth, Kan. Combat
   Studies Institute. Doughty, Robert A. The
evolution of US Army tactical doctrine,
1946-76 /. Fort Leavenworth, Kan. , 1979. 57
p. ;   LC Card 79-604167   DDC 355.4/2/0973 19
U165 .D58

**UNITED STATES. ARMY COMMAND AND
GENERAL STAFF COLLEGE, FORT
LEAVENWORTH, KAN. LIBRARY
SERVICES - MICROFORM CATALOGS.**
Zeidlik, Hannah M. Catalog and index to
historical manuscripts, 1940-1966 /.
Washington, DC , 1979. 2 v. ;   LC Card
   79-604297   DDC 016.355/00973 19
Z1249.M5 Z44 E745

United States. Army. Corps of Engineers. (Old
   Catalog form: United States. Engineer
   Bureau.)
Beard, Leo R. Flood control effects of
headwater reservoirs, Trinity River, Texas /.
Austin , 1979. iii, 50, [78] p. :   LC Card
   79-625849   DDC 627/.44/097645 19
TC557.T39 B4

Remote Sensing Symposium, Reston, Va., 1979.
Remote Sensing Symposium, 29-31 October
1979, Sheraton International Conference
Center, Reston, Virginia /. [Washington]
[1980] xi, 383, 27 p. :   LC Card 80-602920   DDC
   621.36/78 19
G70.4 .R468 1979

United States. Congress. Senate. Committee on
Appropriations. Subcommittee on Energy and
Water Development. Tennessee-Tombigbee
Waterway . Washington , 1980. ii, 56 p. :   LC
   Card 80-603362   DDC 353.0087/6/09768 19
KF26 .A6469 1980

Water supply and sewerage of Korea, prepared
by Engineer Research Office, North Atlantic

United States. Army. Corps of Engineers. (cont.)   BIBLIOGRAPHIC GUIDE

396

Division. [Washington] Strategic Intelligence Branch, Military Intelligence Division, Office, Chief of Engineers, U. S. Army, 1945. iii, 36, A-6 p. illus., fold., maps, 28 cm. (United States. Army. Corps of Engineers. Military Intelligence Division. Strategic engineering study. S. E. S. 155)
Bibliography: p. A-4 - A.5.   LC Card 59-27970
1. Water-supply - Korea. 2. Sewerage - Korea. I. Title. II. Series.   ***NYPL [JSF 80-676]***

UNITED STATES. ARMY. CORPS OF ENGINEERS.
United States. Congress. House. Committee on Science and Technology. Subcommittee on Natural Resources and Environment. U. S. Army Corps of Engineers civil environmental R. & D. budget . Washington , 1980. iii, 57 p. ;
LC Card 80-602776   DDC 353.0082/32 19
KF27 .S398 1980

United States. Army. Corps of Engineers. Alaska District. Davis, T. Neil. Probability of earthquake occurrence in the vicinity of the Chena Flood Control Dam near Fairbanks, Alaska . Fairbanks , 1978. i, 18 leaves, [10] leaves of plates :   LC Card 79-622804   DDC 551.2/2/097986 19
QE535.2.U6 D38

United States. Army. Corps of Engineers. Baltimore District.
Survey report, Beaverdam Creek basin, Prince George's County, Maryland / prepared by the United States Army, Corps of Engineers, Baltimore District. [Baltimore, Md.] : The Corps, 1979. [36] p. in various pagings, [4] folded leaves of plates : maps ; 28 cm.   LC Card 79-602007
1. Flood control - Maryland - Beaverdam Creek watershed (Prince Georges County).
TC424.M3 U54 1979   NYPL [JLF 80-1680]

United States. Army. Corps of Engineers. Baltimore District. Planning Division.
Mid-Atlantic Archaeological Research, inc. Cultural resources reconnaissance investigations for the metropolitan Washington area water supply study early action report . Newark, Del. [1979] [92] leaves, [24] leaves of plates :   LC Card 80-601709   DDC 975.3 19
F195.5 .M53 1979

United States. Army. Corps of Engineers. Channel Stabilization, Committee on. see United States. Army. Corps of Engineers. Committee on Channel Stabilization.

UNITED STATES. ARMY. CORPS OF ENGINEERS - CIVIL FUNCTIONS.
Crist, Charles E. Public participation practices of the U. S. Army Corps of Engineers /. Fort Collins, Colo. , 1979. vi, 123 p. ;   LC Card 79-626247   DDC 333.91/15/0973 19
TC423 .C76

United States. Army. Corps of Engineers. Committee on Channel Stabilization.
Symposium on channel stabilization problems. Vicksburg, Miss. , 1964-66. 3 v. :
NYPL [JSK 81-44]

United States. Army. Corps of Engineers. Directorate of Civil Works. Remote Sensing Symposium, Reston, Va., 1979. Remote Sensing Symposium, 29-31 October 1979, Sheraton International Conference Center, Reston, Virginia /. [Washington] [1980] xi, 383, 27 p. :   LC Card 80-602920   DDC 621.36/78 19
G70.4 .R468 1979

United States. Army. Corps of Engineers. Fort Worth District. Whalen, Michael E. Settlement patterns of the Western Hueco Bolson /. [El Paso] , 1978. xv, 260 p., [1] leaf of plates :   LC Card 79-624053   DDC 976.4/96 19
F392.H82 W45

United States. Army. Corps of Engineers. Historical Division. Schubert, Frank N. Vanguard of expansion . Washington, D.C. [1980] xii, 160 p. :   LC Card 80-144567   DDC 358/.22/0973 19
UG23 .S38

UNITED STATES. ARMY. CORPS OF ENGINEERS - HISTORY - 19TH CENTURY.
Schubert, Frank N. Vanguard of expansion . Washington, D.C. [1980] xii, 160 p. :   LC Card 80-144567   DDC 358/.22/0973 19
UG23 .S38

UNITED STATES. ARMY. CORPS OF ENGINEERS. HUNTSVILLE DIVISION - HISTORY.
Kitchens, James H., 1942- A history of the Huntsville Division, U. S. Army Corps of Engineers, 1967-1976 /. Huntsville, Ala. , 1978. xvii, 180 p. :   LC Card 80-601275   DDC 358/.22/0976197 19
UG23 .K55

United States. Army. Corps of Engineers. Kansas City District. Cooley, Robert E. An archaeological and historical survey of areas to be affected by the construction of the Missouri River L-246 levee, Chariton County, Missouri, 1976, project CAR-31 . Springfield, Mo. , 1976. 122 p. :   LC Card 77-623633   DDC 977.8/25 19
F472.C44 C66

UNITED STATES. ARMY. CORPS OF ENGINEERS. LITTLE ROCK DISTRICT - HISTORY.
Clay, Floyd Martin. A history of the Little Rock District, U. S. Army Corps of Engineers, 1881-1979 /. [Washington, D.C.] [1979] 113 p. :   LC Card 80-114942   DDC 358/.22/0976773 19
UG23 .C45 1979

United States. Army. Corps of Engineers. Military Intelligence Division. Strategic engineering study.
(S. E. S. 155) United States. Army. Corps of Engineers. Water supply and sewerage of Korea. [Washington] 1945. iii, 36, A-6 p. LC Card 59-27970   ***NYPL [JSF 80-676]***

United States. Army. Corps of Engineers. New England Division. see United States. Army Engineer Division, New England.

United States. Army. Corps of Engineers. New York District. Disposal of dredged material within the New York District /. McLean, Va., 1979. 1 v.:   ***NYPL [JSK 80-128]***

United States. Army. Corps of Engineers. North Atlantic Division. Quirk, Lawler & Matusky Engineers. Hydraulic analysis of the New York City water supply system /. Tappan, N. Y. , 1974. xviii, 82, A1-A9 p. :
NYPL [JSF 80-751]

United States. Army. Corps of Engineers. Ohio River Division. Ohio River navigation : past-present-future. Cincinnati, Ohio : U. S. Army Corps of Engineers, Ohio River Division, [1979] 64 p. : ill. ; 28 cm. Cover title. "October 1979." LC Card 80-601829   DDC 386/.32/0977 19
1. Ohio River - Navigation - History. I. Title.
TC625.O3 U54 1979

UNITED STATES. ARMY. CORPS OF ENGINEERS. ST. PAUL DISTRICT - HISTORY.
Merritt, Raymond H., 1936- Creativity, conflict & controversy . [Washington, D.C. , 1979] 461 p. :   LC Card 80-601799   DDC 358/.22/09776581 19
UG23 .M47

United States. Army. Corps of Engineers. Seattle, Washington, District. Flood plain information: Skookumchuck River, Bucoda, Washington. Prepared for the city of Bucoda and Thurston County. [Seattle] 1968. ii, 31 p. illus. 27 cm. Cover title.   LC Card 80-510638   DDC 363.3/493/0979779 19
1. Bucoda, Wash. - Floods. 2. Skookumchuck River - Floods. I. Bucoda, Wash. II. Thurston Co., Wash. III. Title.
GB1399.4.W2 U54 1968

United States. Army. Corps of Engineers. Special Projects Branch. Community Design Center (Milwaukee, Wis.) Recommendations for child care centers /. Milwaukee , 1979. 453 leaves in various foliations :   LC Card 80-153764   DDC 362.7/12 19
HV851 .C65 1979

UNITED STATES. ARMY CRIMINAL INVESTIGATION COMMAND.
Tufts, Henry H. The development and organization of the U. S. Army Criminal Investigation Command, 1969-1974 /. [Falls Church, Va.] [1979?] 68 leaves ;   LC Card 80-600759   DDC 355.1/3323/0973 19
UB783 .T83

United States. Army, Dept. of. see United States. Dept. of the Army.

United States. Army. Engineer Bureau. see United States. Army. Corps of Engineers.

United States. Army Engineer Division, New England. Adler, Steven P. Hill reestablishment . Fort Belvoir, Va. , Springfield, Va. , 1978. viii, 229 p. :   LC Card 79-601444
HN80.H54 A34

United States. Army Engineer Institute for Water Resources.
Adler, Steven P. Hill reestablishment . Fort Belvoir, Va. , Springfield, Va. , 1978. viii, 229 p. :   LC Card 79-601444
HN80.H54 A34

Engineering Foundation Conference "Hydropower: a National Energy Resource," Easton, Md., 1979. Hydropower . Washington, D.C. [1980] vi, 364 p. :   LC Card 80-602219
TK1423 .E53 1979   NYPL [JSD 80-860]

United States. Army Engineer Topographic Laboratories. Remote Sensing Symposium, Reston, Va., 1979. Remote Sensing Symposium, 29-31 October 1979, Sheraton International Conference Center, Reston, Virginia /. [Washington] [1980] xi, 383, 27 p. :   LC Card 80-602920   DDC 621.36/78 19
G70.4 .R468 1979

United States. Army - Enlistment. see United States. Army - Recruiting, enlistment, etc.

United States. Army. European Command. Office of the Chief of Public Affairs. Eurarmy. v. 14, no. 9- ; Jan. 1976- New York.
NYPL [JFM 80-250]

UNITED STATES ARMY. EUROPEAN COMMAND - PERIODICALS.
Eurarmy. v. 14, no. 9- ; Jan. 1976- New York.
NYPL [JFM 80-250]

United States. Army. European Command. Public Affairs, Office of the Chief of. see United States. Army. European Command. Office of the Chief of Public Affairs.

UNITED STATES. ARMY - FACILITIES.
United States. Congress. House. Committee on Armed Services. Subcommittee on Military Installations and Facilities. Hearing on H.R. 6312 (H.R. 6464), to authorize the Secretary of the Army to convey to the Michigan Job Development Authority the lands and improvements comprising the Michigan Army Missile Plant in Sterling Heights, Macomb County, Mich., before the Military Installations and Facilities Subcommittee of the Committee on Armed Services, House of Representatives, Ninety-sixth Congress, second session, February 7, 1980. Washington , 1980. ii, 32 p. :   LC Card 80-601382   DDC 343.73/0253/0262 19
KF27 .A76397 1980

UNITED STATES. ARMY - HANDBOOKS, MANUALS, ETC.
United States. Dept. of the Army. Combat readiness . [Baltimore, Md.] 1973. [20] p. :
NYPL [*Z-3211]

United States. Dept. of the Army. Office of the Chief of Legislative Liaison. Fact book for the 96th Congress. [Washington, D.C.] [1979] ca. 150 p. in various pagings ;   LC Card 79-602107   DDC 355.2/024/328 19
UA24 .A7 1979

UNITED STATES. ARMY - HISTORY - 20TH CENTURY.
Doughty, Robert A. The evolution of US Army tactical doctrine, 1946-76 /. Fort Leavenworth, Kan. , 1979. 57 p. ;   LC Card 79-604167   DDC 355.4/2/0973 19
U165 .D58

United States. Army. Institute of Heraldry.
Organization manual [of] the Institute of Heraldry, U. S. Army: a class II installation under the jurisdiction of the Adjutant General. Alexandria, Va.: The Institute, 1962. 20 l.; 27 cm. Microfilm.
*1. United States. Army. Institute of Heraldry. 2. Heraldry - United States.   NYPL [*ZI-281]*

UNITED STATES. ARMY. INSTITUTE OF HERALDRY.
United States. Army. Institute of Heraldry. Organization manual [of] the Institute of Heraldry, U. S. Army. Alexandria, Va., 1962. 20 l.;
NYPL [*ZI-281]

United States. Army Materials and Mechanics Research Center. Army Materials Technology Conference, 5th, Newport, R. I., 1977. Ceramics for high-performance applications II . Chestnut Hill. , 1978. xxxvi, 1090 : *NYPL [JSE 80-1511]*

UNITED STATES. ARMY. MILITARY DISTRICT OF WASHINGTON. FINANCE AND ACCOUNTING OFFICE - AUDITING AND INSPECTION.
United States. General Accounting Office. Major deficiencies in Army's Washington, D.C. finance and accounting operation . Washington, D.C. [1980] iii, 47 p. ; LC Card 80-602702 DDC 355.6/22 19
UB194.D6 U54 1980

United States. Army Military History Institute. see **US Army Military History Institute.**

UNITED STATES. ARMY NURSE CORPS.
Center of Military History. Highlights in the history of the Army Nurse Corps /. Washington, D.C. , 1981. 88 p. : LC Card 81-601493 DDC 355.3/45/0973 19
UH493 .C46 1981

UNITED STATES. ARMY NURSE CORPS - HISTORY.
Center of Military History. Highlights in the history of the Army Nurse Corps /. Washington, D.C. , 1981. 88 p. : LC Card 81-601493 DDC 355.3/45/0973 19
UH493 .C46 1981

UNITED STATES. ARMY - RECRUITING, ENLISTMENT, ETC.
United States. Congress. House. Committee on Armed Services. Status of Army manpower . Washington , 1981. ii, 130 p. ; LC Card 81-601854 DDC 355.2/2/0973 19
KF27 .A7 1980l

United States. Army Research Institute for the Behavioral and Social Sciences. see **United States. Dept. of the Army. Research Institute for the Behavioral and Social Sciences.**

United States. Army Research Office. Knight, Keith Shelburne. Atmospheric structure determined from satellite data /. Washington, D.C. [Springfield, Va.] 1981. x, 95 p. : LC Card 81-601075 DDC 551.5/14 19
QC879.59.A .K58

United States. Army Research Office, Durham, N. C. Conference on the Design of Experiments in Army Research Development and Testing. Proceedings. Research Triangle Park, N. C.. *NYPL [JSP 81-79]*

United States. Army. Reserve Officers' Training Corps. Facts. Washington : U. S. Govt. Print. Off., 1973. [36] p. : ill. ; 10 x 22 cm.
1. Military education - United States.
NYPL [JFD 81-1758]

United States. Army - Soldiers' handbooks. see **United States. Army - Handbooks, manuals, etc.**

United States. Army Topographic Command. Engineer Topographic Laboratories. see **United States. Army Engineer Topographic Laboratories.**

United States. Army War College.
Curran, James C. Communist China in Black Africa. Carlisle Barracks, Pa., 1971. iv, 83 leaves: *NYPL [*XM-13704]*

Dreisonstok, Thomas F. Spain and NATO. Carlisle Barracks, Pa., 1971. iii, 52 leaves.
*NYPL [*XME-9305]*

France. Ministère de la guerre. Notes on the use of the Viven-Bessières rifle grenade /. Washington, 1918. 12 p. *NYPL [*ZV-179]*

Fulton, William S. Command authority in selected aspects of the court-martial process /. Carlisle Barracks, Pa., 1971. iii, 67 leaves.
*NYPL [*XME-9304]*

Giddings, Edward N. Unilateral U. S. force reduction in Western Europe. Carlisle Barracks, Pa., 1972. iii, 45 leaves. *NYPL [*XM-13703]*

United States. Assistant Attorney-General in Charge of Customs Matters. see **United States. Dept. of Justice.**

United States. Assistant Attorney-General in Charge of the Defense of Suits against the

United States in the Court of Claims and District and Circuit Courts. see **United States. Dept. of Justice.**

United States. Assistant Secretary for Health and Surgeon General, Office of the. see **United States. Office of the Assistant Secretary for Health and Surgeon General.**

United States. Assistant Secretary of Defense (International Security Affairs)
Gonzalez, Edward. Post-revolutionary Cuba in a changing world . Santa Monica, CA , 1975. ix, 78 p. ; LC Card 80-468852
AS36.R3 R-1844 F1788
NYPL [HOF 80-3135]

National Security Affairs Conference, 6th, National Defense University, 1979. Continuity and change in the eighties and beyond . [Washington, D.C.] , 1979. xiii, 222 p. ; LC Card 80-601820 DDC 355/.033073 19
UA23 .N248 1979

UNITED STATES. ATOMIC ENERGY COMMISSION. ADVISORY COMMITTEE ON ATOMIC SAFEGUARDS - HISTORY.
Okrent, David. Nuclear reactor safety . Madison , 1981. p. cm. ISBN 0-299-08350-0 : LC Card 80-53958 DDC 621.48/35 19
TK9152 .O35

United States. Atomic Energy Commission. Classification, Division of. see **United States. Atomic Energy Commission. Division of Classification.**

United States. Atomic Energy Commission. Division of Classification. Guide to the unclassified fields of research / U. S. Atomic Energy Commission, Division of Classification. Washington: The Commission, 1972. 14 p. Microfiche (neg.) by NTIS. 1 sheet. 11 x 15 cm. (CG-UF-3) "This guide supersedes CG-UF-2, Guide to the unclassified fields of research, dated February 1966."
1. Atomic energy research - United States. I. Title. II. Title: Unclassified fields of research.
*NYPL [*XMQ-2152]*

United States. Atomic Energy Commission. Scientific Laboratory, Los Alamos, N. M. see **United States. Scientific Laboratory, Los Alamos, N. M.**

United States. Atomic Energy, Special Committee on. see **United States. Congress. Senate. Special Committee on Atomic Energy.**

United States. Attorney-General. see **United States. Dept. of Justice.**

United States. Automated Data and Telecommunications Service. Automatic data processing equipment inventory in the United States government. Washington. 21 x 27 cm. Annual. Report year ends Sept. 30. Continues its: Inventory of automatic data processing equipment in the United States government (not in the library), which in turn superseded, in part, its: Inventory and summary of federal ADP activities.
1. United States - Politics and government - Data processing - Periodicals. I. Title.
NYPL [JLM 80-1067]

United States. Aviation Forecast Branch. Profiles of scheduled air carrier airport operations. [Washington] 28 cm. Semiannual. For later file, see its Profiles of scheduled air carrier departure and arrival operations for top 100 U. S. airports.
1. Aeronautics, Commercial - United States - Statistics - Periodicals. 2. Airports - United States - Statistics - Periodicals. I. Title. *NYPL [JLM 80-1140]*

Profiles of scheduled air carrier departure and arrival operations for top 100 U. S. airports. NOV. 1978- Washington. For earlier file, see its Profiles of scheduled air carrier airport operations.
I. Title. *NYPL [Econ. Div.]*

United States. Aviation Information, Office of. see **United States. Office of Aviation Information.**

United States. Banking, Housing and Urban Affairs, Committee on. (Senate) see **United States. Congress. Senate. Committee on Banking, Housing and Urban Affairs.**

United States. Battle Monuments Commission. see **United States. American Battle Monuments Commission.**

National Endowment for the Humanities. Bicentennial reading, viewing, listening . Chicago [1976] [12] p. ; *NYPL [*ZH-661]*

UNITED STATES - BIOGRAPHY.
First person America /. New York , 1980. xxv, 287 p. : ISBN 0-394-41397-0 : LC Card 80-7660
E169 .56 *NYPL [ILH 81-601]*

UNITED STATES - BIOGRAPHY - ADDRESSES, ESSAYS, LECTURES.
Plain folk . Urbana , c1981. p. cm. ISBN 0-252-00884-7 LC Card 81-3026 DDC 973.91/1/0922 B 19
E168 .P7

UNITED STATES. BOARD FOR INTERNATIONAL BROADCASTING - APPROPRIATIONS AND EXPENDITURES.
United States. Congress. House. Committee on Foreign Affairs. Subcommittee on International Operations. Authorizing appropriations for fiscal years 1980-81 for the Department of State, the International Communication Agency, and the Board for International Broadcasting . Washington , 1980. iii, 24 p. ; LC Card 80-603032 DDC 353.0072/23689 19
KF27 .F647 1979d

United States. Board of Contract Appeals. see **United States. Dept. of Energy. Board of Contract Appeals.**

United States. Board of Engineers for Rivers and Harbors. (Old Catalog form: United States. Rivers and Harbors, Board of Engineers for.)
The port of Buffalo, New York. Water Resources Support Center (U. S.) The port of Buffalo, New York / prepared by Water Resources Support Center. Washington , Fort Belvoir, VA , 1980. vi, 55 p. : LC Card 80-601613 DDC 386/.8/0974797 19
HE554.B8 W37 1980

Port series. [New series]. no. 1- Washington, 1946- illus., maps (fold. in pocket) 27 cm. Some issues are revised ed. For later file, see: Water Resources Support Center (U. S.) Port series.
1. Harbors - United States - Collected works. I. Title.
NYPL [VDNA (United States. Rivers and Harbors, Board of Engineers. Port series. [New series].]

The ports of Panama City & Pensacola, FL and Pascagoula & Gulfport, MS / prepared by the Board of Engineers for Rivers and Harbors. Washington : U. S. Govt. Print. Off. ; Fort Belvoir, VA : for sale by the Board of Engineers for Rivers and Harbors, 1979. vi, 130 p. : ill., maps (5 fold. in pocket) ; 26 cm. (Port series . no. 19, rev. 1979) LC Card 80-603371 DDC 387.1/09759/95 19
1. Panama City, Fla. - Harbor. 2. Pensacola, Fla. - Harbor. 3. Gulfport, Miss. - Harbor. 4. Pascagoula, Miss. - Harbor. I. Title.
HE554.A4 U53 1979

United States. Board of Governors of the Federal Reserve System. (Old Catalog form: United States. Federal Reserve Board.)
Annual report to Congress on truth in lending. [Washington] 27 cm.
1. Consumer credit - Law and legislation - United States - Periodicals. I. Title.
NYPL [JLM 81-297]

Federal Reserve chart book. 1979- Washington.
NYPL [JLK 80-199]

F/F Seas. adj. United States. Board of Governors of the Federal Reserve System. Flow of funds, seasonally adjusted. F/F Seas. adj. Washington. *NYPL [K-10 6520]*

F/F Unadj. United States. Board of Governors of the Federal Reserve System. Flow of funds, unadjusted. F/F Unadj. Washington.
NYPL [K-10 6521]

Flow of funds accounts: seasonally adjusted and unadjusted. 2d quarter, 1976- Washington. Formed by the union of its: Flow of funds, unadjusted. F/F Unadj., and its: Flow of funds, seasonally adjusted, F/F Seas. adj
I. Title. *NYPL [Econ. Div.]*

Flow of funds, seasonally adjusted. F/F Seas. adj. Washington. 27 cm. Prepared by its Division of Research and Statistics. United with its: Flow of funds, unadjusted, F/F Unadj., to form its: Flow of funds accounts: seasonally adjusted and unadjusted.

BIBLIOGRAPHIC GUIDE

United States. Board of Governors of the Federal Reserve System.

398

1. Capital - United States - Periodicals. 2. Finance - United States - Periodicals. I. United States. Board of Governors of the Federal Reserve System. F/F Seas. adj. II. Title.   **NYPL [K-10 6520]**

Flow of funds, unadjusted. F/F Unadj. Washington. 27 cm. Prepared by its Division of Research and Statistics. United with its: Flow of funds, seasonally adjusted. F/F Seas. adj., to form its: Flow of funds accounts: seasonally adjusted and unadjusted.
1. Capital - United States - Periodicals. 2. Finance - United States - Periodicals. I. United States. Board of Governors of the Federal Reserve System. F/F Unadj. II. Title.   **NYPL [K-10 6521]**

Rhoades, Stephen A. Impact of bank holding companies on competition and performance in banking markets /. [Washington] [1979] 30 p. ; LC Card 80-602134 DDC 332.1/6 19
HG2491 .R46

UNITED STATES. BOARD OF GOVERNORS OF THE FEDERAL RESERVE SYSTEM.
United States. Congress. House. Committee on Banking, Finance, and Urban Affairs. Subcommittee on Domestic Monetary Policy. To modernize the Federal Reserve System . Washington , 1980. iii, 96 p. ; LC Card 80-603677 DDC 346.73/08211 19
KF27 .B537 1980a

United States. Congress. House. Committee on Interstate and Foreign Commerce. Subcommittee on Oversight and Investigations. Federal Reserve Board . Washington , 1980. iii, 181 p. ; LC Card 80-603518 DDC 346.73/073 19
KF27 .I5547 1980g

United States. Congress. Joint Economic Committee. Subcommittee on International Economics. Domestic and international implications of the Federal Reserve's new policy actions . Washington , 1980. iii, 88 p. ; LC Card 80-602731 DDC 332.4/973 19
KF25 .E253 1979a

UNITED STATES. BOARD OF GOVERNORS OF THE FEDERAL RESERVE SYSTEM - APPROPRIATIONS AND EXPENDITURES.
United States. Congress. Senate. Committee on Banking, Housing and Urban Affairs. 1980 budgets of the Federal bank regulatory agencies . Washington , 1980. v, 1323 p. ; LC Card 80-601901 DDC 353.0072/236825 19
KF26 .B39 1980e

UNITED STATES. BOARD OF GOVERNORS OF THE FEDERAL RESERVE SYSTEM - OFFICIALS AND EMPLOYEES.
United States. Congress. Senate. Committee on Banking, Housing and Urban Affairs. Nomination of Lyle E. Gramley . Washington, D.C. , 1980. iii, 124 p. : LC Card 80-602772 DDC 353.0082/5 19
KF26 .B39 1980g

United States. Board of Governors of the Federal Reserve Systems. Foreign takeovers of United States banks . [Washington, D.C.] , Washington , 1980. vi, 75 p. ; LC Card 81-601509 DDC 332.1/6 19
HG2491 .F64

UNITED STATES. BOARD OF VETERANS' APPEALS.
United States. Congress. House. Committee on Veterans' Affairs. Subcommittee on Compensation, Pension, Insurance, and Memorial Affairs. Workloads in the Department of Veterans Benefits and the Board of Veterans Appeals . Washington , 1980. iii, 45 p. ; LC Card 80-603663 DDC 353.0081/2 19
KF27 .V43 1980d

United States. Bonneville Power Administration. Symposium on HVDC Power Transmission. Proceedings. [1]- ; 1976- [Portland, Or.].
NYPL [JSP 80-272]

UNITED STATES - BOUNDARIES - CANADA.
United States. Congress. House. Committee on Merchant Marine and Fisheries. Subcommittee on Fisheries and Wildlife Conservation and the Environment. Oversight report on the U. S.-Canada East Coast fishery agreement and boundary treaty /. Washington , 1980. ii, 23 p. ; LC Card 80-601727 DDC 342.73/0413 347.302413 19
LAW

United States. Congress. Senate. Committee on

Foreign Relations. Maritime boundary settlement treaty and East coast fishery resources agreement . Washington , 1980. iv, 223 p. : LC Card 80-603064 DDC 341.4/48/026673071 19
KF26 .F6 1980m

United States. Congress. Senate. Committee on Foreign Relations. The maritime boundary treaty with Canada . Washington , 1981. iii, 46 p. ; LC Card 81-601779 DDC 341.4/48/026673071 19
KF26 .F6 1981b

UNITED STATES - BOUNDARIES - MEXICO.
Jamail, Milton H. International water use relations along the Sonoran Desert borderlands /. Tucson, Ariz. , 1979. iv leaves, 139 p., [1] leaf of plates : LC Card 80-622139 DDC 333.91/13/0979 19
TD223.9 .J35

United States. Bureau of Census. see United States. Bureau of the Census.

United States. Bureau of Community Health Services. see United States. Health Services Administration. Bureau of Community Health Services.

United States. Bureau of Competition.
Symposium on Competition in the Solar Energy Industry, Washington, D.C., 1977. The solar market . Washington , 1978. xi, 299 p. : LC Card 79-602870
HD9681.U62 S95 1977   **NYPL [JLF 81-299]**

Symposium on Media Concentration, Washington, D.C., 1978. Proceedings of the Symposium on Media Concentration, December 14 an 15, 1978. [Washington] [1979] 2 v. (xi, 761 p.) : LC Card 79-603944
P96.E25 S95 1978

United States. Bureau of Consumer Protection.
Disclosure of energy cost and consumption information in labeling and advertising of consumer appliances : final staff report to the Federal Trade Commission and recommended rule (16 CFR part 305) / Bureau of Consumer Protection ; Andrew I. Wolf ... [et al.]. [Washington] : Federal Trade Commission, Bureau of Consumer Protection : [for sale by the Supt. of Docs., U. S. Govt. Print. Off.], 1979. 227 p. in various pagings ; 28 cm. Cover title: Labeling and advertising of consumer appliances. "February 1979." "Public record docket no. 209-18." LC Card 79-602022 DDC 343.73/085568383 19
1. Household appliances, Electric - Labelling - Law and legislation - United States. 2. Advertising - Household appliances, Electric - Law and legislation - United States. 3. Household appliances, Electric - United States - Energy consumption. I. Wolf, Andrew I. II. United States. Federal Trade Commission. III. Title. IV. Title: Labeling and advertising of consumer appliances.
KF1620.A6 A825

Funeral industry practices : final staff report to the Federal Trade Commission and proposed trade regulation rule (16 CFR Part 453). [Washington] : Bureau of Consumer Protection, 1978. 526, [12] p. ; 28 cm. Includes bibliographical references. LC Card 78-603684
1. Undertakers and undertaking - Law and legislation - United States. 2. Undertakers and undertaking - United States. I. United States. Federal Trade Commission. II. Title.
KF2042.U5 A8137   **NYPL [JLF 81-308]**

Life insurance cost disclosure : a staff report to the Federal Trade Commission / Bureau of Consumer Protection [and] Bureau of Economics. [Washington, D.C.] : FTC : for sale by the Supt. of Docs., U. S. Govt. Print. Off., [1979] ca. 500 p. in various pagings ; 28 cm. "July 1979." Includes bibliographical references. LC Card 79-603257
1. Insurance, Life - United States - Costs. 2. Insurance, Life - United States. I. United States. Federal Trade Commission. II. United States. Federal Trade Commission. Bureau of Economics. III. Title.
HG8951 .U54 1979   **NYPL [JLF 81-342]**

State restrictions on vision care providers . [Washington, D.C.?] , 1980. xix, 289 p. ; LC Card 81-600519 DDC 343.73/078681411 347.30378681411 19
KF2036.E93 Z957

United States. Bureau of Consumer Protection. Division of Special Projects.

MEMORANDUM OF APRIL 19, 1974.
Johnson, Robert Willard. Cost/benefit analysis of creditors' remedies . [Lafayette, Ind.] , 1978. vii, 102 p. ; LC Card 81-621403 DDC 346.73/077 347.30677 19
KF1501.Z9 J63

United States. Bureau of Economic Analysis. The detailed input-output structure of the U. S. economy, 1972. [Washington, D.C.] : U. S. Dept. of Commerce, Bureau of Economic Analysis : for sale by the Supt. of Docs., U. S. Govt. Print. Off., 1979- v. ; 29 cm. Supplement to the Survey of current business. Tables. CONTENTS. - v. 1. The use and make of commodities by industries. LC Card 80-601759 DDC 339.2/3/0973 19
1. United States - Industries. 2. Interindustry economics. I. Survey of current business. II. Title.
HC106.7 .U537 1979

United States. Bureau of Economics of the Federal Trade Commission. see United States. Federal Trade Commission. Bureau of Economics.

United States. Bureau of Education for the Handicapped. State Program Implementation Studies Branch. Progress toward a free appropriate public education; a report to Congress on the implementation of Public Law 94-142: The Education for all handicapped children act. 1979- [Washington] U. S. Dept. of Health, Education, and Welfare, U. S. Office of Education. illus. 27 cm. (HEW publication; no. (OE)) Annual. LC Card 79-643307
1. Handicapped children - Education - United States - Periodicals. 2. Handicapped children - Education - Law and legislation - United States - Periodicals. I. Title.
NYPL [JLM 80-747]

United States. Bureau of Educational and Cultural Affairs. (Old Catalog form: United States. Educational and Cultural Affairs, Bureau of.)
Los Angeles. University of Southern California. Center for International Education. An evaluation of the Volunteers to America program, 1967-1968 . Los Angeles , 1968. 133, [32] leaves : LC Card 79-111308 DDC 370.19/0973 19
LB2376 .L67 1968

United States. Bureau of Health Planning. Little (Arthur D.) inc. An evaluation of the operation of subarea advisory councils /. [Hyattsville, Md.] [Springfield, Va.] 1979. x, 299 p. ; LC Card 79-603995
RA395.A3 L57 1979   **NYPL [JLF 81-358]**

United States. Bureau of Health Planning and Resources Development. Division of Planning Methods and Technology. National Health Planning Information Center. see National Health Planning Information Center.

United States. Bureau of Health Resources Development.
Johns Hopkins University. Office of Health Manpower Studies. Career patterns of unaccepted applicants to medical school . [Bethesda? Md.] , 1974. vi, 207 p. : LC Card 76-600905
R838.4 .J63 1974   **NYPL [*XME-9527]**

United States. Bureau of Health Resources Development. Division of Manpower Intelligence. Nathan (Robert R.) Associates, Washington, D. C. Assessment and evaluation of the impact of archetypal national health insurance plans on U. S. health manpower requirements /. [Bethesda, Md.] , 1974. xviii, 117 p. :   **NYPL [JLF 80-904]**

United States. Bureau of Helath Manpower. see United States. Health Resources Administration. Bureau of Health Manpower.

United States. Bureau of Higher and Continuing Education.
Factbook. 1978- [Washington] 28 cm. Annual. Continues: United States. Bureau of Postsecondary Education. Factbook (not in the library).
1. Federal aid to higher education - United States - Periodicals. I. Title.   **NYPL [JLM 80-749]**

United States. Bureau of Higher and Continuing Education. Community College Unit. Guide to Federal grants and technical assistance for two-year colleges, July 1978 / prepared by

Community College Unit. [Washington] : U. S. Dept. of Health, Education, and Welfare, Office of Education, Bureau of Higher and Continuing Education, 1978. 80 p. ; 27 cm. LC Card 79-603439

1. Endowments - United States. 2. Federal aid to higher education - United States. I. Title.
LB2336 .U54 1978   *NYPL [JLF 81-339]*

United States. Bureau of Indian Affairs. (Old Catalog form: United States. Indian Affairs Office.)
Baker, Jack D. Cherokee emigration rolls, 1817-1835 /. Oklahoma City , c1977. 67 leaves : LC Card 77-156017
E99.C5 B27

Minimum essential goals for Indian schools, levels seven, eight, and nine. Rev. ed. [Washington] : U. S. Dept. of the Interior, Bureau of Indian Affairs, Branch of Education, 1955. xvi, 186 p. ; 27 cm. LC Card 80-502124 DDC 371.97/97 19

1. Indians of North America - Education. I. Title.
E97.5 .U593 1955

Nielson, Woodrow. Soil survey of Navajo Indian Reservation, San Juan County, Utah /. [Washington] [1980] viii, 119 p., [12] fold. leaves of plates : LC Card 80-602348 DDC 631.4/7/79259 19
S599.U8 N53

1970 safety progress report : zero in on safety / Bureau of Indian Affairs. Washington : [G. P. O.], 1970. 74 p. : ill. ; 21 x 27 cm. On cover: The Pacesetter for safety.

1. Accidents - United States - Prevention.
     NYPL [JLF 80-1586]

United States Indian population and land, 1960. Washington : United States, Dept. of the Interior, Bureau of Indian Affairs, 1960. v, 32 p. ; 27 cm. (Reports - United States, Bureau of Indian Affairs) LC Card 80-505734 DDC 929/.3/08997 19
1. Indians of North America - Census, 1960. 2. Indians of North America - Land tenure. I. Title.
E98.C3 U453 1960

United States. National Archives and Records Service. Preliminary inventory of the Pueblo records created by field offices of the Bureau of Indian Affairs . Washington , 1980. vii, 34 p. ; LC Card 80-607174 DDC 016.973 s 016.3231/197/073 19
CD3026 .A32 no. 192 Z1210.P8 E99.P9

United States. Soil Conservation Service. General soil map, Mellette County, South Dakota /. [Lincoln, Neb.] [1978?] 1 map : LC Card 81-691165
G4183.M6J3 1973 .U5

United States. Soil Conservation Service. Soil survey of Glacier County area and part of Pondera County, Montana /. [Washington, D.C.] [1980] v, 161 p., [92] leaves of plates : LC Card 80-602512 DDC 631.4/7/78652 19
S599.M57 U54 1980

Weisel, Charles J. Soil survey of Benewah County area, Idaho /. [Washington] [1980] x, 188 p., [25] fold. leaves of plates : LC Card 80-602396 DDC 631.4/7/79693 19
S599.I2 W44

UNITED STATES. BUREAU OF INDIAN AFFAIRS.
BIA profile . Washington, D.C. , 1981. 72 p. : LC Card 81-601834 DDC 323.1/197/073 19
E93 .B18

UNITED STATES. BUREAU OF INDIAN AFFAIRS - APPROPRIATIONS AND EXPENDITURES.
United States. Congress. House. Committee on Interior and Insular Affairs. Bureau of Indian Affairs and Indian Health Service budget request for fiscal year 1981 . Washington , 1980. iii, 102 p. ; LC Card 81-600586 DDC 353.0072/23671497 19
KF27 .I5 1980b

UNITED STATES. BUREAU OF INDIAN AFFAIRS - BIBLIOGRAPHY - CATALOGS.
United States. National Archives and Records Service. Preliminary inventory of the Pueblo records created by field offices of the Bureau of Indian Affairs . Washington , 1980. vii, 34 p. ; LC Card 80-607174 DDC 016.973 s 016.3231/197/073 19
CD3026 .A32 no. 192 Z1210.P8 E99.P9

UNITED STATES. BUREAU OF INDIAN AFFAIRS. PORTLAND AREA OFFICE.
United States. Congress. House. Committee on Education and Labor. Subcommittee on Elementary, Secondary, and Vocational Education. Oversight hearings on the implementation of title XI, Public Law 95-561 . Washington , 1980. iii, 47 p. : LC Card 80-604010 DDC 371.97/97/0795 19
KF27 .E3364 1980f

United States. Bureau of Internal Revenue. see United States. Internal Revenue Service.

United States. Bureau of International Commerce. (Old Catalog form: United States. International Commerce, Bureau of.)
Computers and related equipment / U. S. Department of Commerce, Domestic and International Business Administration, Bureau of International Commerce. Washington, D. C. : For sale by the Supt. of Docs, U. S. Govt. Print. Off., 1973. iii, 167 p. : ill. ; 28 cm. (Global market survey) Supersedes the Global market survey covering Electronic data processing equipment, peripheral devices and software, issued September 1970.
1. Computer industry. 2. Computer industry - United States. I. Title.   *NYPL [JLF 81-349]*

Iran : a survey of U. S. business opportunities. [Washington] : U. S. Dept. of Commerce, Domestic and International Business Administration, Bureau of International Commerce ; for sale by the Supt. of Docs., U. S. Govt. Print. Off., 1977. vii, 296 p. : ill. ; 26 cm. (Country market sectoral survey) International marketing information series Bibliography: p. 295. LC Card 78-600517
1. Market surveys - Iran. 2. Iran - Industries. 3. Iran - Economic conditions - 1945-. I. Title.
HC475 .U48 1977

Nigeria : a survey of U. S. business opportunities. [Washington] : U. S. Dept. of Commerce, Domestic and International Business Administration, Bureau of International Commerce : for sale by the Supt. of Docs., U. S. Govt. Print. Off., 1976. v, 190 p. : ill. ; 26 cm. (Country market sectoral survey) International marketing information series Bibliography: p. 177-178. LC Card 76-602544
1. Nigeria - Economic conditions. 2. Market surveys - Nigeria. 3. Marketing - Nigeria. I. Title.
HC517.N48 U53 1976   *NYPL [JLF 81-313]*

Venezuela : a survey of U. S. business opportunities. [Washington] : U. S. Dept. of Commerce, Domestic and International Business Administration, Bureau of International Commerce, Office of International Marketing : for sale by the Supt. of Docs., U. S. Govt. Print. Off., 1976. 154 p. ; 27 cm. (Country market sectoral survey) International marketing information series LC Card 77-600918
1. Venezuela - Economic conditions - 1918-. 2. Venezuela - Industries. 3. Market surveys - Venezuela. I. Title.
HC237 .U52 1976   *NYPL [JLF 81-312]*

United States. Bureau of International Labor Affairs. (Old Catalog form: United States. International Labor Affairs, Office of).
Trade and employment . Washington, D.C. , 1979. 336 p. : LC Card 80-601562 DDC 331.12/0973 19
HD5710.75.U6 T7

United States. Bureau of International Labor Affairs. Office of Foreign Economic Research.
Aho, C. Michael, 1949- Assessing the changing structure of world trade /. Washington, D.C. , Springfield, Va. , 1980. 34 [i.e. 82] p. ; LC Card 81-600792 DDC 382/.45/000973 19
HF3031 .A59

Aho, C. Michael, 1949- Demographic and occupational characteristics of workers in trade-sensitive industries /. [Washington, D.C.] [Springfield, Va.] 1980. 17, [15] p. ; LC Card 80-602632 DDC 331.11/4 19
HD5710.75.U6 A37

Bayard, Thomas O. Trade and employment effects of tariff reductions agreed to in the MTN /. [Washington, D.C.] [Springfield, Va.] 1980. 11, [31] p. ; LC Card 80-602631 DDC 382.7 19
HF1757 .B39

Bayard, Thomas O. Trends in U. S. trade, 1960-1979 /. Washington, D.C. , Springfield,

Va. , 1980. 48 p. : LC Card 81-600712 DDC 382/.0973 19
HF3031 .B35

Bowen, Harry. Changes in the international pattern of factor abundance and the composition of trade /. Washington, D.C. , Springfield, Va. , 1980. 64 p. : LC Card 81-601296 DDC 382 19
HF1411 .B6685

Trade and employment effects of granting most-favored-nation status to the People's Republic of China /. Washington, D.C. , Springfield, Va. , 1980. 32 p. in various pagings ; LC Card 81-600776 DDC 382/.0951/073 19
HD5710.75.U6 T73

United States. Bureau of International Narcotics Matters. United States. Dept. of State. The global legal framework for narcotics and prohibitive substances . Washington, D.C. , 1979. 86, 14 p. ; LC Card 79-603788
K5282 .U54   *NYPL [JLF 81-316]*

United States. Bureau of Justice Statistics. Bureau of Justice Statistics reports .
(NCJ-62319) United States. Bureau of Justice Statistics. Intimate victims . Washington, D.C. [1980] v, 52, 4 p. : LC Card 80-601656 DDC 362.8/8 19
HV6250 .U52 1980

Intimate victims : a study of violence among friends and relatives. Washington, D.C. : U. S. Dept. of Justice, Bureau of Justice Statistics : for sale by the Supt. of Docs., U. S. Govt. Print. Off., [1980] v, 52, 4 p. : graphs ; 28 cm. (A National crime survey report. SD-NCS-N-14) Bureau of Justice Statistics reports ; NCJ-62319 "Written by Harold R. Lentzner and Marshall M. DeBerry." LC Card 80-601656 DDC 362.8/8 19
1. Family violence - United States. 2. Victims of crime surveys - United States. I. Lentzner, Harold R. II. DeBerry, Marshall M. III. Series: United States. Bureau of Justice Statistics. Bureau of Justice Statistics reports , NCJ-62319. IV. Title.
HV6250 .U52 1980

United States. Bureau of Labor Statistics. (Old Catalog form: United States. Labor Statistics Bureau.)
Bulletin.
(2051) United States. Bureau of Labor Statistics. Productivity . Washington, D.C. , 1980. iv, 166 p. ; LC Card 80-603243 DDC 016.338/06 19
Z7164.L1 U6672 1980 HC110.I52

(2057) United States. Bureau of Labor Statistics. Occupational employment in manufacturing industries, 1977 /. Washington, D.C. [1980] vi, 91 p., [1] leaf of plates : LC Card 80-602314 DDC 331.12/57/0973 19
HD5724 .U625 1980a

(2058) United States. Bureau of Labor Statistics. Estimating State and local area unemployment . [Washington, D.C.] [1980] iv, 95 p. ; LC Card 80-602828 DDC 331.13/7973 19
HD5724 .U625 1980b

(2072) United States. Bureau of Labor Statistics. Technology, productivity, and labor in the bituminous coal industry, 1950-79. Washington , 1980. p. cm. LC Card 80-607858 DDC 331.7/622334/0973 19
HD9545 .U54 1980

California. Dept. of Industrial Relations. Division of Labor Statistics and Research. California sawmills and planing mills industry . San Francisco , 1978. v, 26 p. ; LC Card 79-623207 DDC 312/.43/09794 19
RC965.W6 C28 1978

DiPillo, Salvatore A. Connecticut occupational staffing patterns . [Hartford] [1980] 86 p. : LC Card 80-623517 DDC 331.12/5/09746 19
HD5725.C8 D553

Directory of occupational wage surveys, Jan. 1970-Dec. 1977. [Washington] : U. S. Dept. of Labor, Bureau of Labor Statistics, 1979. i, 94 p. ; 21 cm. (Report - U. S. Department of Labor, Bureau of Labor Statistics ; 53) Cover title. "March 1979." LC Card 79-602338 DDC 331.1/0973 s 016.3312/973 19
1. Wage surveys - Bibliography. 2. Wages - United States - Bibliography. I. Series: United States. Bureau of

United States. Bureau of Labor Statistics. (cont.)   BIBLIOGRAPHIC GUIDE

400

Labor Statistics. Report, 53. II. Title.
HD8051 .A7876 no. 53 Z7164.W1 HD4975

Estimating State and local area unemployment : a guide for data users. [Washington, D.C.] : U. S. Dept. of Labor, Bureau of Labor Statistics : for sale by the Supt. of Docs., U. S. Govt. Print. Off., [1980] iv, 95 p. ; 28 cm. (Bulletin - Bureau of Labor Statistics . 2058) "April 1980." Chiefly tables. LC Card 80-602828   DDC 331.13/7973 19
1. Unemployment - United States. I. Series: United States. Bureau of Labor Statistics. Bulletin, 2058. II. Title.
HD5724 .U625 1980b

Indiana. Employment Security Division. Staffing patterns in the manufacturing industries in Indiana . [Indianapolis] , 1976. xv, 85 p. : LC Card 77-621779
HD5725.I6 I53 1976   **NYPL [*XME-9536]**

Indiana. Employment Security Division. Research and Statistics Section. Staffing patterns in wholesale and retail trade industries in Indiana . [Indianapolis, Ind.] , 1978. viii, 67 p. : LC Card 79-625864   DDC 331.12/51381/09772 19
HD5725.I6 I53 1978a

Keitt, Barbara L. Occupational employment in selected nonmanufacturing industries. Washington, D.C. , 1981. vi, 78 p. ; LC Card 81-601842   DDC 331.12/5/0973 19
HD5724 .K42

Labor force statistics derived from the current population survey . Washington, D.C. [1981] p. cm. LC Card 81-607902   DDC 331.11/0973 19
HD5724 .L19

Maine. Bureau of Labor. Research and Statistics Division. Characteristics of work-related injuries and illnesses in Maine . Augusta, Me. [1979] 76 p. ;   LC Card 80-621340   DDC 363.1/1209741 19
RC964 .M25 1979

Massachusetts. Dept. of Labor and Industries. Division of Statistics. 1972-1975 occupational injury and illness survey /. Boston, Mass. [1979] 17 p. :   LC Card 80-621949   DDC 312/.39803/09744 19
RC964 .M39 1979

Monthly labor review. v. 1- ; July 1915- Washington. illus., maps (part fold). 24-27 cm. Microfilm. Title varies: 1915-June 1918, Monthly review. Includes supplemnts. INDEXES: Vols. 1-11, July 1915-1920, on microfilm (Reel 35). - Vols. 12-51, 1921-60, on microfilm (Reel 35). - vols. 52-71, 1941-60, on microfilm (Reel 35). LC Card 15-26485
1. Labor and laboring classes - United States - Periodicals. 2. Labor and laboring classes - Periodicals. 3. Labor laws and legislation - United States - Periodicals. 4. Labor laws and legislation - Periodicals. I. Title.   **NYPL [*ZAN-T4971]**

New Hampshire. Dept. of Employment Security. Economic Analysis and Reporting Section. New Hampshire staffing patterns in selected nonmanufacturing industries, 1978 . [Concord, N.H.] , 1979. i, 172 p. : LC Card 80-621986   DDC 331.12/5/09742 19
HD5725.N4 N45 1979

Occupational earnings in all metropolitan area. July 1979- [Washington]. **NYPL [Econ. Div.]**

Occupational employment in manufacturing industries, 1977 / U. S. Department of Labor, Bureau of Labor Statistics. Washington, D.C. : The Bureau : for sale by the Supt. of Docs., U. S. Govt. Print. Off., [1980] vi, 91 p., [1] leaf of plates : ill. ; 28 cm. (Bulletin - U. S. Bureau of Labor Statistics ; 2057) Prepared by B. L. Keitt. LC Card 80-602314   DDC 331.12/57/0973 19
1. Labor supply - United States - Statistics. 2. United States - Manufactures - Employees - Statistics. 3. United States - Occupations - Statistics. I. Keitt, Barbara L. II. Series: United States. Bureau of Labor Statistics. Bulletin, 2057. III. Title.
HD5724 .U625 1980a

Pennsylvania. Bureau of Employment Security. Research and Statistics Division. Occupational staffing patterns of selected regulated industries in Pennsylvania. [Harrisburg] , 1979. ii, 73 p. ; LC Card 79-624037
HD5725.P4 P45 1979   **NYPL [JLF 80-1646]**

Pennsylvania. Office of Employment Security. Research and Statistics Division. Occupational staffing patterns of selected nonmanufacturing

industries in Pennsylvania . Harrisburg, Pa. [1980] iii, 326 p. ; LC Card 80-622719   DDC 331.12/5/09748 19
HD5725.P4 P458 1980

Productivity : a selected, annotated bibliography, 1976-78. Washington, D.C. : U. S. Dept. of Labor, Bureau of Labor Statistics : for sale by the Supt. of Docs., U. S. Govt. Print. Off., 1980. iv, 166 p. ; 28 cm. (Bulletin - Bureau of Labor Statistics ; 2051) Compiled by H. Brand and H.A. Belitsky. "April 1980." Includes indexes. LC Card 80-603243   DDC 016.338/06 19
1. Industrial productivity - United States - Bibliography. 2. Industrial productivity - Bibliography. I. Brand, Horst. II. Belitsky, Abraham Harvey, 1929-. III. Series: United States. Bureau of Labor Statistics. Bulletin, 2051. IV. Title.
Z7164.L1 U6672 1980 HC110.I52

Productivity measures for selected industries, 1954-79. Washington, D.C. , 1981. v, 206 p. : LC Card 81-601923   DDC 338/.06/0973 19
HC110.I52 P75

Report.
(53) United States. Bureau of Labor Statistics. Directory of occupational wage surveys, Jan. 1970-Dec. 1977. [Washington] , 1979. i, 94 p. ;   LC Card 79-602338   DDC 331.1/0973 s 016.3312/973 19
HD8051 .A7876 no. 53 Z7164.W1 HD4975

(575) Norwood, Janet Lippe. Women in the labor force . [Washington, D.C.] , 1979. 9 p. : LC Card 80-601713   DDC 331.1/0973 s 331.4/12/0973 19
HD8051 .A7876 no. 575 HD6094

Some aspects of the ghetto labor market in New York. New York, 1971. 21 p. illus. 28 cm. Microfilm. LC Card 72-601109
1. Labor supply - New York (City) - Statistics. 2. Minorities - Employment - New York (City) - Statistics. I. Title. II. Title: Ghetto labor market in New York.
HD5726.N5 A54 1971b   **NYPL [*ZT-1264]**

Technology, productivity, and labor in the bituminous coal industry, 1950-79. Washington : U. S. Dept. of Labor, Bureau of Labor Statistics, 1980. p. cm. (Bulletin - Bureau of Labor Statistics ; 2072) Prepared by R. N. Zeisel with the assistance of M. Dymmel and G. E. Falwell. Updates the Bureau's Technological change and productivity in the bituminous coal industry, 1920-60. LC Card 80-607858   DDC 331.7/622334/0973 19
1. Coal mines and mining - United States - History. 2. Coal-miners - United States - History. I. Zeisel, Rose N. II. Dymmel, Michael. III. Falwell, Gary E. IV. Series: United States. Bureau of Labor Statistics. Bulletin, 2072. V. Title.
HD9545 .U54 1980

Wisconsin. Dept. of Industry, Labor and Human Relations. Bureau of Administration, Planning, and Analysis. Occupational employment estimates for selected nonmanufacturing industries, 1978 /. [Madison, Wis.] [1980] iv, 212 p. : LC Card 80-623196   DDC 331.12/51/0009775 19
HD5725.W5 W55 1980

UNITED STATES. BUREAU OF LABOR STATISTICS.
United States. Congress. Senate. Committee on Labor and Human Resources. Labor statistics respondent privacy protection act of 1980 . Washington , 1980. iii, 43 p. : LC Card 80-603782   DDC 342.73/0853 347.302853 19
KF26 .L27 1980k

United States. Bureau of Labor Statistics. Mideast Regional Office. Wald, Michael L. Municipal government wage surveys, Washington, D.C., October 1978. Philadelphia, Pa. (P.O. Box 13309, Philadelphia 19101) [1979] v, 70 p. ; LC Card 80-603374   DDC 352/.005123/09753 19
JK2757 .W34

United States. Bureau of Labor Statistics. New England Regional Office. Johnson, Linda S. Municipal government wage surveys . [Boston, Mass.?] , 1980. iii, 79 p. ; LC Card 80-604138   DDC 352/.005123/0974461 19
JS614 .A4 1980

United States. Bureau of Labor Statistics. Pacific Regional Office.
Gateley, Paul. Municipal government wage

survey, Los Angeles, California, October 1979 /. [San Francisco, Calif.] (450 Golden Gate Ave., Box 36017, San Francisco 94102) , 1980. iv, 78 p. ; LC Card 80-603885   DDC 331.2/81352079494 19
JS1004 .A4 1980

Municipal Government wage survey, Seattle, Washington, January 1979 / U. S. Department of Labor, Bureau of Labor Statistics, Pacific Region. San Francisco, Calif. : The Bureau, [1979] ii, 78 p. ; 27 cm. (Pacific regional report - no. 57) Prepared by P. Gateley. LC Card 80-601650   DDC 331.2/813520797/77 19
1. Seattle - Officials and employees - Salaries, allowances, etc. I. Gateley, Paul. II. Series: United States. Bureau of Labor Statistics. Pacific Regional Office. Regional report, no. 57. III. Title.
JS1455.4 .A4 1979

Pacific regional report. see United States. Bureau of Labor Statistics. Pacific Regional Office. Regional report.

Regional report.
(no. 57) United States. Bureau of Labor Statistics. Pacific Regional Office. Municipal Government wage survey, Seattle, Washington, January 1979 /. San Francisco, Calif. [1979] ii, 78 p. ; LC Card 80-601650   DDC 331.2/813520797/77 19
JS1455.4 .A4 1979

United States. Bureau of Labor Statistics. Southwest Regional Office. Municipal government wage survey, San Antonio, Texas, November 1975 / U. S. Department of Labor, Bureau of Labor Statistics, Southwest Region. [Dallas] : The Office, 1976. v, 57 p. ; 27 cm. Cover title: Municipal government wage surveys, San Antonio, Texas, November 1975. Prepared by Woodrow C. Linn. LC Card 76-602063
1. San Antonio - Officials and employees - Salaries, allowances, etc. I. Linn, Woodrow C. II. Title. III. Title: Municipal government wage surveys, San Antonio, Texas, November 1975.
JS1425.4 .A4 1975   **NYPL [JLF 80-1369]**

United States. Bureau of Land Management.
(Old Catalog form: United States. Land Management Bureau.)
Candland, David M. Soil survey of Big Smoky Valley Area, Nevada, part of Nye County /. [Washington] 1980. iii, 140 p. [2] fold. leaves of plates : LC Card 80-601637   DDC 631.4/7/79334 19
S599.N425 C36

Environmental assessment of the Alaskan continental shelf . [Rockville, Md.?] , 1980. xv, 313 p. : LC Card 81-600735   DDC 574.5/2636/09798 19
QH105.A4 E586

Final environmental statement : proposed five-year OCS oil and gas lease sale schedule, March 1980-February 1985 / [prepared by the Bureau of Land Management]. [Washington] : The Bureau, [1980] viii, 384, [257] p. : ill. ; 27 cm. Includes bibliographies and index. LC Card 80-601418   DDC 333.33/9 19
1. Oil and gas leases - United States. I. Title. II. Title: Proposed five-year OCS oil and gas lease sale schedule, March 1980-February 1985.
HD9566 .U52 1980

Hubbard, Kenneth G. The Great Basin climate study for range fire management /. Logan , 1978. vi, 25 p. : LC Card 80-620825   DDC 634.9/618/015516 19
SD421.37 .H8

Managing the Nation's public lands : a program report prepared pursuant to requirements of the Federal land policy and management act of 1976. [Washington] : Bureau of Land Management, U. S. Dept. of the Interior, [1980] 166 p. ; 28 cm. "January 31, 1980." LC Card 80-603164   DDC 333.1/0973 19
1. Public lands - Public lands - Management. I. Title.
HD216 .U54 1980

Oregon, proposed initial inventory, roadless areas and islands which do not have wilderness characteristics / United States Department of the Interior, Bureau of Land Management. [Portland] : The Bureau, 1979. 3 maps : col. ; 61 x 94 cm. and 94 x 61 cm. Scale 1:500,000. Relief shown by spot heights. Includes index map. LC Card 79-695513
1. Land use, Rural - Oregon - Maps. 2. Oregon - Maps.

I. Title.
G4291.G4 s500 .U5

NYPL *[Map Div. 81-3037]*

Proposed domestic livestock grazing program
for the Challis Planning Unit : final
environmental statement / prepared by Bureau
of Land Management, Department of the
Interior. [Washington] : The Bureau, 1977. 1 v.
(various pagings) : ill., maps (some col.) ; 27
cm. Title on spine: Challis Unit grazing program, final
environmental statement. One folded map in pocket.
Includes bibliography.
1. Grazing - Environmental aspects - Idaho - Custer
County. 2. Environmental impact statements. I. Title.
II. Title: Challis Unit grazing program. III. Title: Final
environmental statement: proposed domestic livestock
grazing program for the Challis Planning Unit.
NYPL *[JLF 80-1442]*

Technical note - Bureau of Land Management .
(297) Zarn, Mark. Wild, free-roaming burros .
[Washington] , Denver, Colo. , 1979. 29 p. ;
LC Card 80-601254 DDC 639.9 s 016.59972/5
19
QL84.2 .U54a vol. 297 Z7997.D76 QL737.U62

Texas barrier islands region ecological
characterization . Washington, D.C.?] , 1980. 2
v. : LC Card 81-600915 DDC 333.91/09764/1 19
QH105.T4 T52

United States. Congress. Senate. Committee on
Energy and Natural Resources. Subcommittee
on Parks, Recreation, and Renewable
Resources. Various parks and Bureau of Land
Management related legislation . Washington ,
1980. iii, 194 p. : LC Card 81-600804 DDC
346.7304/6783/0262 347.306467830262 19
KF26 .E5565 1980h

United States. Soil Conservation Service. Soil
survey of Chaves County, New Mexico,
southern part /. [Washington] [1980] iv, 143
p., [90] fold. leaves of plates : LC Card
80-602510 DDC 631.4/7/78943 19
S599.N6 U54 1980

Willdan Associates. Mississippi Deltaic Plain
Region ecological characterization .
[Washington] [1980- v. <1> : LC Card
80-603195 DDC 330.9763/3063 19
HC108.N42 W54 1980

UNITED STATES. BUREAU OF LAND
MANAGEMENT.
United States. Congress. Senate. Committee on
Energy and Natural Resources. Subcommittee
on Energy Resources and Materials Production.
Coal leases on BLM lands in New Mexico .
Washington , 1980. iii, 211 p. ; LC Card
80-601117 DDC 333.33/9 19
KF26 .E5543 1979d

United States. Congress. Senate. Committee on
Energy and Natural Resources. Subcommittee
on Parks, Recreation, and Renewable
Resources. Bureau of Land Management
wilderness review and rangeland management
programs . Washington , 1980. iii, 189 p. ; LC
Card 80-602719 DDC 346.7304/6782/0262 19
KF26 .E5565 1980a

United States. Bureau of Land Management.
Colorado State Office. The Archeology and
stabilization of the Dominguez and Escalante
ruins. Denver , 1979. ix, 496 p. : LC Card
79-603760
E99.P9 A72 **NYPL** *[HBC 81-508]*

Cultural Resources series. see Cultural
resources series.

United States. Bureau of Land Management.
Desert Planning Staff.
Lyneis, Margaret M. Impacts, damage to
cultural resources in the California desert /.
Riverside, Calif. , 1980. viii, 171 p. : LC Card
81-600782 DDC 979.4/9 19
F863 .L95

Norwood, Richard H. A cultural resource
overview of the Eureka, Saline, Panamint, and
Darwin region, east central California /.
Riverside, Calif. , 1980. 219, [26] p. : LC Card
81-601926 DDC 979.4/87 19
F863 .N67

UNITED STATES. BUREAU OF LAND
MANAGEMENT - DIRECTORIES.
United States. Geological Survey. Catalog of
selected offices of the Office of Surface Mining,
Bureau of Land Management, and Geological

Survey relating to coal, 1981. Reston, Va. ,
1980. p. cm. LC Card 80-607870 DDC 557.3 s
353.0082/382 19
QE75 .C5 no. 840 TN12

United States. Bureau of Land Management.
District Office, Rock Springs, Wyo. Final
environmental assessment: Whitney Canyon &
Carter Creek natural gas processing projects /
Bureau of Land Management, Rock Springs
District, Wyoming. Washington : U. S. Govt.
Print. Off., 1980. vii, 82, A1-A105 p. : ill.,
maps ; 28 cm. Cover title. Bibliography: p.
A104-A105.
1. Gas industry - Environmental aspects - Wyoming. 2.
Gas industry - Environmental aspects - Utah. I. Title.
II. Title: Whitney Canyon and Carter Creek natural gas
processing projects. **NYPL** *[JSF 81-67]*

United States. Bureau of Land Management.
New Mexico State Office. Berman, Mary
Jane. Cultural resources overview of Socorro,
New Mexico /. Albuquerque, N.M. : Santa Fe,
N.M. : v, 128 p. : LC Card 80-602245 DDC
978.9/62 19
E78.N65 B36

United States. Bureau of Land Management.
New Orleans Outer Continental Shelf
Office. Final environmental impact
statement . [Washington, D.C.?] : New Orleans,
La. (Hale Boggs Federal Building, New Orleans,
La. 70130) : xiiii [sic], 227 p. : LC Card
81-601099 DDC 333.8/231/0976 19
TD195.P4 F56

United States Bureau of Land Management. New
York Outer Continental Shelf Office. Draft
environmental impact statement : proposed
1981 outer continental shelf oil gas lease sale
offshore the Mid-Atlantic States /. [New
York] , 1980. 1 v. of various pagings :
NYPL *[JSG 81-43]*

United States. Bureau of Land Management.
Oregon State Office. Richardson, Elmo.
BLM's billion-dollar checkerboard . Santa Cruz,
Calif. , Washington, D.C. , c1980. x, 200 p. :
LC Card 81-600781 DDC 333.75/09795 19
SD566.O7 R5

United States. Bureau of Land Management.
Rock Springs, Wyoming, District Office. see
United States. Bureau of Land Management.
District Office, Rock Springs, Wyo.

United States. Bureau of Land Management.
Socorro District. Berman, Mary Jane.
Cultural resources overview of Socorro, New
Mexico /. Albuquerque, N.M. : Santa Fe,
N.M. : v, 128 p. : LC Card 80-602245 DDC
978.9/62 19
E78.N65 B36

United States. Bureau of Land Management.
Utah State Office. Fike, Richard E. The
pony express stations of Utah in historical
perspective /. [Salt Lake City] [Washington,
D.C.] 1979. iii, 113 p. : LC Card 79-602930
DDC 917.92/0433 19
HE6375.P65 F54

United States. Bureau of Mines. (Old Catalog
form: United States. Mines Bureau.)
Backer, R. R. (Ronald R.) Fine coal refuse
dewatering /. Washington [1981] p. cm. LC
Card 81-607041 DDC 622 s 662.6/23 19
TN23 .U43 TN816

Bureau of Mines impact report.
Skow, Milford L. Creating a safer
environment in U. S. coal mines .
[Washington, D.C.] 1980. 50 p. : LC Card
80-602933 DDC 622/.8 19
TN295 .S55

Bureau of Mines Technology Transfer
Workshop (1981 : Denver, Colo.) Mine waste
disposal technology proceedings . [Washington,
D.C.] [1981] p. cm. LC Card 81-607857 DDC
622 s 622/.2 19
TN295 .U4 TD899.M5

Calvert, Eugene D. An investment mold for
titanium casting /. Washington [1981] p. cm.
LC Card 80-607847 DDC 622 s 673/.7322255
19
TN23 .U43 TS562

Covino, B. S. (Bernard S.) Corrosion resistance
of materials in the aqueous hydrochloric acid
environments associated with the recovery of
alumina from kaolinitic clays /. Washington ,

1981. p. cm. LC Card 80-606916 DDC 622 s
661/.0673/028 19
TN23 .U43 TA462

Crane, Stanley R. Hydrogen sulfide generation
by reaction of natural gas, sulfur, and steam /.
[Avondale Md.] [1981] p. cm. LC Card
80-606831 DDC 622 s 628.5/32 19
TN23 .U43 TP245.S9

Ferrante, M. J. (Michael John), 1930-
High-temperature enthalpy and x-ray powder
diffraction data for aluminum sulfide (Al$_2$S$_3$) /.
Washington , 1981. p. cm. LC Card 80-606912
DDC 622 s 546/.6732 19
TN23 .U43 QD181.A4

Information circular .
( ) Noise control of diesel-powered
underground mining machines, 1979 /.
Washington, D.C. [1981] p. cm. LC Card
80-607181 DDC 622 s 622/.2 19
TN295 .U4 TN345

Clancy, Timothy A. High-temperature
corrosion resistance of ceramic materials /.
[Avondale, Md.] [1981] p. cm. LC Card
80-606922 DDC 622 s 620.1/404223 19
TN295 .U4 TA455.C43

Colaizzi, Gary J. Pumped-slurry backfilling of
abandoned coal mine workings for subsidence
control at Rock Springs, Wyoming /.
Washington , 1981. p. cm. LC Card 80-39876
DDC 622 s 622/.334 19
TN295 .U4 TN319

Maksimovic, S. D. Control of methane by
ventilation of shafts during raise drilling /.
[Washington] , 1981. p. cm. LC Card
80-606851 DDC 622 s 622/.8 19
TN295 .U4

Opyrchal, Anthony M. Economic significance
of the Florida phosphate industry .
[Washington, D.C.] [1981] p. cm. LC Card
80-606892 DDC 622 s 338.2/764 19
TN295 .U4 HD9484.P5U5

Polychlorinated biphenyls . [Washington,
D.C.] , 1981. p. cm. LC Card 80-607190
DDC 622 s 363.1/79 19
TN295 .U4 T55.3.H3

Maksimovic, S. D. Control of methane by
ventilation of shafts during raise drilling /.
[Washington] , 1981. p. cm. LC Card 80-606851
DDC 622 s 622/.8 19
TN295 .U4

Monthly report. United States. Bureau of
Mines. Report of investigations.
[Washington], 1919- LC Card 58-62123
NYPL *[VHCA (United States. Mines*
Bureau. Report of investigations)]

Poth, Leonard A. The economic impact of the
mineral industry of South Dakota /. Vermillion,
S.D. [1978] 135 p. : LC Card 80-622563 DDC
330 s 338.2/09783 19
HF5006 .S6 no. 126 HD9506.U63S5

Report investigations .
() Cole, Ernest R. Insoluble anodes for
electrowinning zinc and other metals /.
Washington [1981] p. cm. LC Card 80-607823
DDC 622 s 669/.52 19
TN23 .U43 TN796

Report of investigations. [Washington], 1919-
illus. 27-29 cm. Irregular. Some early issues are
unnumbered. Title varies: Oct. 1919-Apr. 1920,
Monthly report. LC Card 58-62123
1. Mineral industries - Collected works. 2. Mines and
mineral resources - Collected works. I. United States.
Bureau of Mines. Monthly report. **NYPL** *[VHCA*
(United States. Mines Bureau. Report of
investigations)]

Report of investigations .
( ) Behavior of cadmium during roasting of
zinc concentrate /. Washington, D.C. [1981]
p. cm. LC Card 80-607819 DDC 622 s 669/.5
19
TN23 .U43 TN796

( ) Savanick, George A. Water jet
perforation . Washington, D.C. , 1981. p. cm.
LC Card 80-607781 DDC 622 s 622/.184932 19
TN23 .U43 TN278.3

( ) Christos, Theodore. Thermal degradation
products of solvents and hydraulic fluids used
in mining /. Washington [1980] p. cm. LC

United States. Bureau of Mines. (cont.)   *BIBLIOGRAPHIC GUIDE*

402

Card 80-607783   DDC 622 s 622/.3 19
TN23 .U43 QD544

( ) Hill, S. D. Electrowinning of zinc from zinc chloride in monopolar and bipolar fused-salt cells /. Washington [1981] p. cm.
LC Card 80-607820   DDC 622 s 669/.52 19
TN23 .U43 TN796

Brandt, Luther Warren, 1920- Dewatering Florida phosphatic clay wastes by a moving screen method /. [Washington] [1981] p. cm.
LC Card 80-607788   DDC 622 s 622/.364 19
TN23 .U43 TD899.P45

Calvert, Eugene D. An investment mold for titanium casting /. Washington [1981] p. cm.
LC Card 80-607847   DDC 622 s 673/.7322255 19
TN23 .U43 TS562

Crane, Stanley R. Hydrogen sulfide generation by reaction of natural gas, sulfur, and steam /. [Avondale Md.] [1981] p. cm.
LC Card 80-606831   DDC 622 s 628.5/32 19
TN23 .U43 TP245.S9

Davidson, Charles F. Recovery of lithium from clay by selective chlorination /. Washington [1981] p. cm.   LC Card 80-607822   DDC 622 s 669/.725 19
TN23 .U43 TN799.L57

Feed grade versus extraction correlations on uranium ores from New Mexico /. Avondale, Md. , 1981. p. cm.   LC Card 80-607857   DDC 622 s 622/.34932 19
TN23 .U43 TN490.U7

Good, Philip C. Direct preparation of phosphoric acid from intermediate-grade western phosphate shale /. [Washington] , 1981. p. cm.   LC Card 80-606841   DDC 622 s 661/.25 19
TN23 .U43 TP217.P5

High-pressure shrouded water sprays for dust control /. Avondale, Md. , 1981. p. cm.   LC Card 80-606801   DDC 622 s 622/.8 19
TN23 .U43 TN312

Jong, B. W. Effect of additives on sintering of silicon nitride-alumina-aluminum nitride compositions /. Washington , 1981. p. cm.
LC Card 80-606862
TN23 .U43

Khalafalla, S. E. Selective extraction of metals from Pacific sea nodules with dissolved sulfur dioxide /. Avondale, Md. , 1980. p. cm.   LC Card 80-606861   DDC 622 s 669/.028/3 19
TN23 .U43 TN291.5

Kripakov, Nicholas P. Analysis of pillar stability on steeply pitching seam using the finite element method /. Washington, D.C. [1981] p. cm.   LC Card 80-606871   DDC 622 s 622/.28 19
TN23 .U43 TN292

LaScola, John. Assessing the methane hazard of gassy coals in storage silos /. Avondale, Md. [1981] p. cm.   LC Card 80-606936   DDC 622 s 662.6/24 19
TN23 .U43 TP325

Lepper, C. Melvin. Guidelines for selecting seismic detectors for high resolution applications /. [Washington, D.C.] , 1981. p. cm.   LC Card 80-607789   DDC 622 s 622/.159 19
TN23 .U43 TN269

McIlwain, J. F. Consolidation of an iron-base superalloy by powder metallurgy techniques /. Washington, D.C. [1981] p. cm.   LC Card 80-607851   DDC 622 s 672.3/7 19
TN23 .U43 TN697.I7

Madsen, Brent W. Alternative methods for copper recovery from dump leach liquors /. Washington , 1981. p. cm.   LC Card 80-607826   DDC 622 s 669/.3 19
TN23 .U43 TN780

Page, Steven J. Effectiveness of wet cutter bars in reducing salt mine dust /. Washington [1980] p. cm.   LC Card 80-607782   DDC 622 s 622/.3632 19
TN23 .U43 TN312

Papp, John F. Structure study of a CF_2Br_2-inhibited methane flame--the effect of CF_2Br_2 on composition, net reaction rates, and rate coefficients /. [Washington] , 1981.

p. cm.   LC Card 80-606846   DDC 622 s 628.9/223 19
TN23 .U43 QD516

Rhodes, Harold L. An apparatus and procedure for calibrating a water vapor analyzer in the 0.1- to 15-ppm range /. Washington, D.C. , 1980. p. cm.   LC Card 80-606926   DDC 622 s 665.8/22 19
TN23 .U43 TP245.H4

Seitz, Charles A. Automatic and continuous transducer drift compensator for end point detection systems /. Washington , 1981. p. cm.   LC Card 80-606887   DDC 622 s 621.5/9 19
TN23 .U43

Spironello, Victor R. An evaluation of used aluminum shelter potlining as a substitute for fluorspan in cupola ironmelting /. [Avondale, Md.] [1981] p. cm.   LC Card 80-606836   DDC 622 s 672.2/4 19
TN23 .U43 TN707

Stachura, Virgil J. Airblast instrumentation and measurement techniques for surface mine blasting /. [Washington, D.C.] [1981] p. cm.
LC Card 80-607860   DDC 622 s 622/.31 19
TN23 .U43 TN291

Stanley, Donald A. Treatment of Florida surface waters for use in phosphate beneficiation /. [Washington, D.C.] [1981] p. cm.   LC Card 80-606882   DDC 622 s 661/.43 19
TN23 .U43

Thompson, Philip, 1950- Development of a continuous flotation process for removal of insoluble slimes from potash ore /. Washington [1980] p. cm.   LC Card 80-607785   DDC 622/.3636 19
TN23 .U43

Tomimatsu, T. T. The U. S. copper mining industry . [Washington, D.C.] , Avondale, MD. [1981] p. cm.   LC Card 80-607792   DDC 338.2/3 19
HD9539.C7 U576

Tomimatsu, T. T. The U. S. copper mining industry . [Washington, D.C.] [1981] p. cm.
LC Card 80-609992   DDC 338.2/3 19
HD9539.C7 U576

United States. Bureau of Mines. Structure response and damage produced by ground vibration from surface mine blasting /. Washington, D.C. [1981] p. cm.   LC Card 80-607825   DDC 622 s 690/.21 19
TN23 .U43 TA654.7

Report of investigations ; 8500.
Salisbury, H. B. Recovery of copper and associated precious metals from electronic scrap /. Washington [1981] p. cm.   LC Card 80-607807   DDC 622 s 699/.3 19
TN23 .U43 no. 8500 TD812.5.C66

Seminar on the Role of Overburden Analysis in Surface Mining (1980 : Wheeling, W. VA.) Proceedings of Seminar on the Role of Overburden Analysis in Surface Mining, Wheeling, W. Va., May 6-7, 1980 /. Washington , 1981. p. cm.   LC Card 81-607049   DDC 622 s 622/.31 19
TN295 .U4 TD195.S75

Skow, Milford L. Creating a safer environment in U. S. coal mines . [Washington, D.C.] 1980. 50 p. :   LC Card 80-602933   DDC 622/.8 19
TN295 .S55

Spencer, Vivian Eberle, 1907- Raw materials in the United States economy, 1900-1977 /. Washington, D.C. , 1980. 90 p. :   LC Card 80-603173   DDC 333.7/0973 19
HF1052 .S63

Spironello, Victor R. An evaluation of used aluminum shelter potlining as a substitute for fluorspan in cupola ironmelting /. [Avondale, Md.] [1981] p. cm.   LC Card 80-606836   DDC 622 s 672.2/4 19
TN23 .U43 TN707

Technical highlights, health and safety research, 1970-1980 / by staff, U. S. Bureau of Mines. Avondale, Md. : The Bureau, 1981. p. cm. (Special publication)   LC Card 80-606917   DDC 622/.8 19
1. Mine safety - United States. I. Series: Special publication (United States. Bureau of Mines). II. Title.
TN295 .U5 1981

UNITED STATES. BUREAU OF MINES.
United States. Congress. Senate. Committee on Energy and Natural Resources. Subcommittee on Energy Resources and Materials Production. Transfer of certain land and facilities used by the Bureau of Mines to Carnegie-Mellon University . Washington , 1980. iii, 35 p. :   LC Card 80-603896   DDC 343.73/025 347.30325 19
KF26 .E5543 1980f

United States. Bureau of Mines. Division of Minerals Environmental Technology.
Minerals environmental in-house and contract research and development in fiscal year 1981 / by staff, Division of Minerals Environmental Technology. Avondale, Md. : United States Dept. of the Interior, Bureau of Mines, 1981. p. cm. (Information circular / United States Department of the Interior, Bureau of Mines) Bibliography: p.   LC Card 81-1572   DDC 622 s 338.2 19
1. Mineral industries - Environmental aspects - Research - United States. I. Series: Information circular (United States. Bureau of Mines). II. Title.
TN295 .U4 TD195.M5

United States. Bureau of Mines. Division of Minerals Health and Safety Technology.
Minerals health and safety contract research, development, and demonstration in fiscal year 1981 /. Avondale, Md. , 1981. p. cm.   LC Card 81-1579   DDC 622 s 622/.8/0973 19
TN295 .U4

Minerals health and safety in-house research, development, and demonstration in fiscal year 1981 / by staff, Division of Minerals Health and Safety Technology. Avondale, Md. : United States Dept. of the Interior, Bureau of Mines, 1981. p. cm. (Information circular / United States Department of the Interior, Bureau of Mines) Bibliography: p.   LC Card 81-1580   DDC 622 s 622/.8/0973 19
1. Mine safety - United States. I. Series: Information circular (United States. Bureau of Mines). II. Title.
TN295 .U4

UNITED STATES. BUREAU OF MINES - OFFICIALS AND EMPLOYEES.
United States. Congress. Senate. Committee on Energy and Natural Resources. Lindsay D. Norman, Jr., and John D. Hughes nominations . Washington , 1980. iii, 123 p. :   LC Card 80-603780   DDC 353.0082/327 19
KF26 .E55 1980g

United States. Bureau of Naval Personnel. (Old Catalog form: United States. Naval Personnel Bureau.)
Gunner's mate G 1 & C. Naval Education and Training Program Development Center. Gunner's mate G 1 & C. [Rev. 1980]. [Pensacola, Fla. , Washington, D.C. , 1980] ca. 500 p. in various pagings :   LC Card 80-603250   DDC 623/.553 19
VF160 .N38 1980

United States Navy uniform regulations, [by] Department of the Navy, [Bureau of Naval Personnel. Washington, 1978] 1 v. ill. 26 cm. (Its: NAVPERS. 15665C.) Loose-leaf for updating. "This regulations supersede U. S. Navy Uniform regulations, 1975."
1. United States. Navy - Uniforms. I. Title.
NYPL [JFF 78-1006]

United States. Bureau of Naval Personnel. Human Resources Management Division.
Pecorella, Patricia A. Survey-guided development. [Washington?] , 1974. 1 v. (various pagings) ;   **NYPL [JLF 81-585]**

United States. Bureau of Navigation (Navy Dept.) see United States. Bureau of Naval Personnel.

United States. Bureau of Oceans and International Environmental and Scientific Affairs. see United States. Dept. of State. Bureau of Oceans and International Environmental and Scientific Affairs.

United States. Bureau of Ordnance and Hydrography. see United States. Bureau of Ordnance (Navy Dept.)

United States. Bureau of Ordnance (Navy Dept.)
Table of circumferences and areas. Washington, 1947. 101 p. 28 cm. Navord OD. 5797.   LC Card 51-61291
1. Area measurement - Tables. I. Title.
NYPL [JSF 81-40]

United States. Bureau of Outdoor Recreation.
(Old Catalog form: United States. Outdoor Recreation, Bureau of.)
How effective are your community recreation services? [Washington] , 1973. 189 p. in various pagings :   *NYPL [JFF 80-1149]*

United States. Bureau of Public Roads. (Old Catalog form: United States. Public Roads Bureau.)
Bright, Richard. Early hardening of asphalt in hot bituminous paving mixtures . [Raleigh] , 1966. vi, 70 p. :   LC Card 80-508397   DDC 625.8/5 s 625.8/5 19
TE270 .B67 pt. 2

Bright, Richard. The effect of viscosity of asphalt on the properties of bituminous paving mixtures /. [Raleigh] , 1966. 2 v. :   LC Card 80-508426   DDC 625.8/5 19
TE270 .B67

Bright, Richard. Hardening of asphalt in hot bituminous base, binder, and sand mixtures . [Raleigh] , 1966. vi, 83 p. :   LC Card 80-508398   DDC 625.8/5 s 625.8/5 19
TE270 .B67 pt. 1

Washington (State). State Highway Commission. Annual traffic report. [Olympia]
NYPL [N-10 2121]

United States. Bureau of Radiological Health.
(Old Catalog form: United States. Radiological Health, Division of.)
Conference on Neutrons from Electron Medical Accelerators, National Bureau of Standards, 1979. Proceedings of a Conference on Neutrons from Electron Medical Accelerators .
Washington , 1979. vii, 175 p. ;   LC Card 79-600133   DDC 602/.18 s 615.8/422 19
QC100 .U57 no. 554 RM849

Directory of personnel responsible for radiological health programs. Rockville, Md..
NYPL [JLL 80-243]

National Conference on Measurements of Laser Emissions for Regulatory Purposes, Rockville, Md., 1974. National Conference on Measurements of Laser Emissions for Regulatory Purposes . [Rockville, Md.] , Washington , 1976 i.e. 1977. vii, 255 p. :   LC Card 77-602983   DDC 535.5/8 19
QC689.5.L37 N37 1974

Radioactivity in consumer products /. Washington , Springfield, Va. , 1978. xi, 509 p. :   LC Card 79-602786
RA569 .R29

Recent & future developments in medical imaging, August 28-29, 1978, San Diego, California /. Bellingham, Wash. , c1978. vi, 136 p. (p. 136 blank) :   ISBN 0-89252-179-1   LC Card 80-122161
RC78.A1 R43

Regulations for the administration and enforcement of the Radiation control for health and safety act of 1968. Rockville, Md. : U. S. Dept. of Health, Education, and Welfare, Public Health Service, Food and Drug Administration, Bureau of Radiological Health ; Washington, D.C. : for sale by the Supt. of Docs., U. S. Govt. Print. Off., 1978. vi, 68 p. : ill. ; 23 cm.
(HEW publication ; (FDA)79-8035)   LC Card 79-603753   DDC 344.73/0472 19
1. Radiation - Safety regulations - United States. I. Series: United States. Dept. of Health, Education and Welfare. Publication, no. (FDA) 79-8035. II. Title.
KF3948.A355 A2 1978

United States. Bureau of Reclamation. (Old Catalog form: United States. Reclamation Service.)
Metric manual / by Lawrence D. Pedde ... [et al.]. Denver : U. S. Dept. of the Interior, Bureau of Reclamation, 1978. xvii, 278 p. : ill. ; 23 cm. Bibliography: p. 251-253. Includes index.
ISBN 0-8103-1020-1
1. Metric system - United States - Handbooks, manuals, etc. I. Pedde, Lawrence D. II. Title.
QC92.U54 U53 1980   NYPL [JSE 81-281]

Reclamation research : a progress report of the Bureau of Reclamation, 1979. [Washington] : The Bureau, 1979. vi, 121 p. : ill. ; 27 cm. Includes bibliographical references.   LC Card 80-602385   DDC 333.91/0072073 19
1. Water resources development - Research - United States. 2. Watershed management - Research - United States. 3. Reclamation of land - Research - United

States. I. Title.
TC423 .U48 1979

The story of the Columbia Basin project. Denver : U. S. Dept. of the Interior, Bureau of Reclamation ; Washington : for sale by Supt. of Docs., U. S. Govt. Print. Off., 1978. 45 p. : ill. ; 24 cm.   LC Card 79-601522   DDC 333.91/3/0979731 19
1. Columbia Basin project. I. Title. II. Title: Columbia Basin project.
TC425.C7 U54 1978

Texas. Dept. of Water Resources. Playa Lake monitoring for the Llano Estacado total water management study . [Austin] , 1980. 18 leaves, [2] leaves of plates :   LC Card 80-621333   DDC 553.7/8/0723 19
TD224.T4 T36 1980

Utah's 1977 drought /. Logan , 1978. viii, 49 p. :   LC Card 79-624684   DDC 363.3/492 19
QC929.D8 U72

Wyoming. State Water Planning Program. Report on reconnaissance studies of irrigation projects . [Cheyenne, Wyo,] 1977. 41 leaves in various foliations, [7] leaves of plates :   LC Card 79-622603   DDC 333.91/315/0978733 19
TC824.W8 W96 1977

United States. Bureau of Sport Fisheries and Wildlife. (Old Catalog form: United States. Sport Fisheries and Wildlife, Bureau of.)
Investigations in fish control. United States. Bureau of Sport Fisheries and Wildlife. Resource publication. 1-122 (incomplete). Washington, 1965-74.   *NYPL [M-11 3071]*

Research report. no. 63-73. Washington, 1964-68. illus. 26 cm. Irregular. For earlier file, whose numbering it continues, see: United States. Fish and Wildlife Service. Research report (in Old Catalog). Ceased publication with no. 73?   LC Card 41-50960
1. Fisheries - United States - Periodicals. 2. Game protection - United States - Periodicals.
NYPL [M-10 9252]

Resource publication. 1-122 (incomplete). Washington, 1965-74. illus. 26-28 cm. Irregular. Issues 7-15, 18-22, 33, 35-38 form its: Investigations in fish control, 3-21. (Beginning with no. 22 issued and cataloged separately, see (in Old Catalog): United States. Sport Fisheries and Wildlife, Bureau of. Investigations in fish control.). For later file, which continues its numbering, see: United States. Fish and Wildlife Service. Resource publication.
1. Fisheries - United States - Periodicals. 2. Game and game-birds - United States - Periodicals. 3. Game protection - United States - Periodicals. I. United States. Bureau of Sport Fisheries and Wildlife. Investigations in fish control. II. Investigations in fish control. III. Title.   *NYPL [M-11 3071]*

United States. Bureau of Sport Fisheries and Wildlife. Region 4. see United States. Bureau of Sport Fisheries and Wildlife.

United States. Bureau of Standards. see United States. National Bureau of Standards.

United States. Bureau of the Census. (Old Catalog form: United States. Census Bureau)
Alphabetical index of industries and occupations: 1980 census of population. United States. Bureau of the Census. 1980 census of population: alphabetical index of industries and occupations. 1st- ed. Washington, 1980-
*NYPL [*R-Econ. 81-164 & JLM 81-159]*

Auto-Carto, 2d, Reston, Va., 1975. Proceedings of the International symposium on Computer-Assisted Cartography . [Suitland, Md.] [Falls Church, Va.] [1975?] 614 p. :   LC Card 79-117745
GA108.7 .A95 1975

NYPL [Map Div. 81-153]

Census descriptions of geographic subdivisions and enumeration districts, 1830-1950. Washington : National Archives of the United States, 1978. 6 microfilm reels ; 35 mm. Caption title. United States. National Archives and Records Service. Microfilm publications. United States Census, 5th - 11th, 1830-1890. Rolls 1-4: T1224; rolls 5-6: T1227. "Part of Record Group 29, Bureau of the Census."
1. United States - Census. 2. Census districts - United States. 3. United States - Genealogy. I. United States. National Archives and Records Service. II. Title.
*NYPL [*ZI-283]*

Classified index of industries and occupations: 1980 census of population. United States. Bureau of the Census. 1980 census of population: classified index of industries and occupations. 1st- ed. Washington, 1980-
*NYPL [*R-Econ. 81-163 & JLM 81-158]*

Current housing reports. Series H-170. Annual housing survey : housing characteristics for selected metropolitan areas. 1974- [Washington] 29 cm. Each year comprises separate reports on selected areas.   LC Card 76-646429
1. Housing - United States - Statistics - Periodicals. I. Title.   *NYPL [JLM 80-1002]*

Current population reports: Special studies: Series P-23.
(no. 105) United States. Bureau of the Census. Selected characteristics of travel to work in 20 metropolitan areas, 1977. Washington , 1981. p. cm.   LC Card 80-606807   DDC 312/.0973 s 388.4/0973 19
HA203 .A218 no. 105 HE308

(no. 107) Rawlings, Stephen, 1945- Families maintained by female householders, 1970 to 1979 /. [Washington] , 1980. p. cm.   LC Card 80-25731   DDC 312/.0973 s 306.8 19
HA203 .A218 no. 107 HQ536

(no. 108) United States. Bureau of the Census. Selected characteristics of persons in physical science, 1978. Washington, D.C. , U. S. Dept. of Commerce, Bureau of the Census. iv, 30 p. :   LC Card 80-607850   DDC 312/.0973 s 509/.02/2 19
HA203 .A218 no. 108 Q149.U5

(no. 80) United States. Bureau of the Census. The social and economic status of the Black population in the United States, 1790-1978 . Washington [1979] x, 271 p. ;   LC Card 79-607000   DDC 312/.0973 s 301.45/19/6073 19
HA203 .A218 no. 80 E185.8

Davis, Christopher, 1948- Rising infant mortality in the U. S. S. R. in the 1970's /. Washington, D.C. , 1980. 33 p. ;   LC Card 81-600791   DDC 304.6 s 304.6/4 19
HC331 .U52 no. 74 HB1323.I4

General imports of cotton, wool, and man-made fiber manufacturers. Washington. 28 cm. (Its: FT-130) Monthly. For earlier file, see its General imports of cotton manufactures.
1. Cotton trade - United States - Statistics - Periodicals. 2. Wool trade and industry - United States - Statistics - Periodicals. 3. Man-made fibers industry - United States - Statistics - Periodicals. I. Title.
NYPL [JLM 80-725]

General report on industrial organization. Washington , 1981. 468 p. in various pagings ;   LC Card 81-607798   DDC 338.0973 s 338.6/0973 19
HC106.7 .A14 ES77-1

Graphic summary of the 1977 economic censuses. Washington, D.C. , 1981. 128 p. :   LC Card 81-1210   DDC 330.973/0926 19
HC106.7 .G7

Guide to county census data for planning economic development/U. S. Bureau of the Census, [written by Mike Adams ... et al.]. Washington : U. S. Govt. Print. Off., 1979. 123 p.; 28 cm. Prepared for the Office of Economic Research, Economic Development Administration (EDA). Includes bibliographical references.
1. Georgia - Economic conditions - Statistics. 2. Regional planning - Georgia. I. Adams, Mike. II. United States. Economic Development Administration. Office of Economic Research. III. Title.
*NYPL [*R-Econ. 80-2970]*

History of the 1977 economic censuses. Washington, D.C. : U. S. Dept. of Commerce, Bureau of the Census : for sale by the Supt. of Docs., U. S. Govt. Print. Off., 1980. vii, 549 p. : ill. ; 29 cm. "Issued December 1980."   LC Card 80-607818   DDC 330.973/0926 19
1. United States - Commerce - Statistical services. 2. United States - Industries - Statistical services. I. Title.
HF3001 .U54 1980

International population reports. Series P-95. [Washington] 28 cm. Irregular.
1. Population research - Collected works. I. United States. Bureau of the Census. Series P-95. II. Title.
NYPL [SDG (U. S. Census Bureau. International population reports. Series P-95)]

Long, Larry H. Migration to nonmetropolitan areas . Washington , 1980. p. cm. LC Card 80-607185 DDC 304.8/2/0973 19
HB1965 .L58

1980 census of population: alphabetical index of industries and occupations. 1st- ed. Washington, 1980- 28 cm.
1. United States - Industries - Indexes - Periodicals. 2. United States - Occupations - Indexes - Periodicals. 3. United States - Census, 20th, 1980 - Periodicals. I. United States. Bureau of the Census. Alphabetical index of industries and occupations: 1980 census of population. II. Title.
NYPL [*R-Econ. 81-164 & JLM 81-159]

1980 census of population: classified index of industries and occupations. 1st- ed. Washington, 1980- 28 cm.
1. United States - Industries - Indexes - Periodicals. 2. United States - Occupations - Indexes - Periodicals. 3. United States - Census, 20th, 1980 - Periodicals. I. United States. Bureau of the Census. Classified index of industries and occupations: 1980 census of population. II. Title.
NYPL [*R-Econ. 81-163 & JLM 81-158]

The population of Hawaii, 1977 : a report of the Federal-State cooperative program for local population estimates / prepared jointly by the U. S. Bureau of the Census, Hawaii State Department of Health, and Hawaii State Department of Planning and Economic Development. [Honolulu] : Research and Economic Analysis Division, Dept. of Planning and Econommic Development, [1978] 12 p. ; 28 cm. (Statistical report ; 125) "September 13, 1978." Bibliography: p. 3-5. LC Card 80-623123 DDC 319.69 s 304.6/2/09969 19
1. Hawaii - Population. I. Hawaii. Dept. of Health. II. Hawaii. Dept. of Planning and Economic Development. III. Series: Hawaii. Dept. of Planning and Economic Development. Statistical report , 125. IV. Title.
HA329.1 .A25 no. 125 HB3525.H3

The population of Hawaii, 1979 : a report of the Federal-State cooperative program for local population estimates / prepared jointly by the U. S. Bureau of the Census, Hawaii State Department of Health, and Hawaii State Department of Planning and Economic Development. [Honolulu, Hawaii] : Research and Economic Analysis Division, Dept. of Planning and Economic Development, [1980] 4, [7] p. ; 28 cm. (Statistical report ; 136) "April 24, 1980." Bibliography: p. 2-4. LC Card 80-622660 DDC 319.69 s 312/.8/09969 19
1. Hawaii - Population - Statistics. I. Hawaii. Dept. of Health. II. Hawaii. Dept. of Planning and Economic Development. III. Series: Hawaii. Dept. of Planning and Economic Development. Statistical report , 136. IV. Title.
HA329.1 .A25 no. 136 HA329.2

A profile analysis of Minnesota counties. [Washington, D.C.] : U. S. Dept. of Commerce, Bureau of the Census, 1979. ix, 79 p. : ill. ; 28 cm. "This study was conducted and published under an interagency agreement between the U. S. Bureau of the Census and the Minnesota State Planning Agency." Bibliography: p. 78-79. LC Card 79-603984
1. Minnesota - Statistics. I. Minnesota. State Planning Agency. II. Title.
HA453 .U54 1979   **NYPL [JLF 81-266]**

Providencia . [Washington, D.C.?] , 1980. xiii, 327 p. : LC Card 80-603922 DDC 330.9861/8 19
HC28 .P83 1980

Rawlings, Stephen, 1945- Families maintained by female householders, 1970 to 1979 /. [Washington] , 1980. p. cm. LC Card 80-25731 DDC 312/.0973 s 306.8 19
HA203 .A218 no. 107 HQ536

Schedule B commodity by country. United States. Bureau of the Census. U. S. exports: Schedule B commodity by country. Washington.   **NYPL [JLM 81-161]**

Schedule B commodity groupings, schedule B commodity by country. United States. Bureau of the Census. U. S. exports: schedule B commodity groupings, schedule B commodity by county. 1967-77 (incomplete). Washington. 11 v.   **NYPL [TLG (U. S. Census Bureau. [Report] FT [no.] 410.)]**

Schedule E commodity groupings, schedule E commodity by country. United States. Bureau of the Census. U. S. exports: schedule E commodity groupings, schedule E

commodity by country. 1978- [Washington] LC Card 79-640385   **NYPL [JLM 80-677]**

Selected characteristics of persons in physical science, 1978. Washington, D.C. : U. S. Dept. of Commerce, Bureau of Census : for sale by the Supt. of Docs., U. S. Govt. Print. Off., U. S. Dept. of Commerce, Bureau of the Census, iv, 30 p. : ill. ; 28 cm. (Current population reports : Special studies ; Series P-23 ; no. 108) Includes bibliographical references.   LC Card 80-607850 DDC 312/.0973 s 509/.02/2 19
1. Scientists - United States - Statistics. 2. Engineers - United States - Statistics. 3. Demographic surveys - United States. 4. United States - Population. I. Series: United States. Bureau of the Census. Current population reports: Special studies: Series P-23, no. 108. II. Title.
HA203 .A218 no. 108 Q149.U5

Selected characteristics of travel to work in 20 metropolitan areas, 1977. Washington : U. S. Dept. of Commerce, Bureau of the Census, 1981. p. cm. (Current population reports : Special studies : Series P-23 . no. 105) LC Card 80-606807 DDC 312/.0973 s 388.4/0973 19
1. Urban transportation - United States. 2. Commuting - United States. I. Series: United States. Bureau of the Census. Current population reports: Special studies: Series P-23, no. 105. II. Title.
HA203 .A218 no. 105 HE308

Series P-95. United States. Bureau of the Census. International population reports. Series P-95.   **NYPL [SDG (U. S. Census Bureau. International population reports. Series P-95)]**

Shryock, Henry S. The methods and materials of demography /. [Washington] , 1975. 2 v. (xvi, 888, 20 p.) :   LC Card 75-600077
HB881 .S526 1975

Small business reports. Washington [1981] p. cm.   LC Card 81-607797 DDC 338.0973 s 338.6/42/0973 19
HC106.7 .A14 ES77-3 HD2346.U5

Social and economic characteristics of Americans during midlife. Washington [1981] p. cm.   LC Card 81-607850 DDC 312/.0973 s 305.2/4/0973 19
HA203 .A218 no. 111 HQ1059.5.U5

The social and economic status of the Black population in the United States, 1790-1978 : an historical view. Washington : U. S. Dept. of Commerce, Bureau of the Census : for sale by the Supt. of Docs., U. S. Govt. Print. Off, [1979] x, 271 p. ; 28 cm. (Current population reports : Special studies : Series P-23 . no. 80) LC Card 79-607000 DDC 312/.0973 s 301.45/19/6073 19
1. Afro-Americans - Economic conditions - Statistics. 2. Afro-Americans - Social conditions - Statistics. I. Series: United States. Bureau of the Census. Current population reports: Special studies: Series P-23, no. 80. II. Title.
HA203 .A218 no. 80 E185.8

Spencer, Vivian Eberle, 1907- Raw materials in the United States economy, 1900-1977 /. Washington, D.C. , 1980. 90 p. :   LC Card 80-603173 DDC 333.7/0973 19
HF1052 .S63

STATISTICAL ABSTRACT OF THE UNITED STATES - ADDRESSES, ESSAYS, LECTURES.
Reflections of America . Washington, D.C. [1981] p. cm.   LC Card 80-607843 DDC 317.3 19
HC103 .R43

Statistical profile. Ser. SP. no. 1-136; Feb. 1962-Aug. 1962. Washington. 136 no. in 3 v. illus. 27 cm. Irregular. Prepared for Area Redevelopment Administration. No more published?   LC Card A62-9234
1. United States - Economic conditions - 1945- - Periodicals. I. United States. Area Redevelopment Administration. II. Title.   **NYPL [TAA (United States. Census Bureau. Statistical profile. Ser. SP.)]**

Technical paper .
(37) A Numerator and denominator for measuring change . Washington , 1975. 195 p. :   LC Card 75-619192 DDC 001.4/33 19
HA37 .U52 1975

(47) Spencer, Vivian Eberle, 1907- Raw materials in the United States economy, 1900-1977 /. Washington, D.C. , 1980. 90

p. :   LC Card 80-603173 DDC 333.7/0973 19
HF1052 .S63

Twenty censuses : population and housing questions, 1790-1980. Washington, D.C. : U. S. Dept. of Commerce, Bureau of the Census : for sale by the Supt. of Docs., U. S. Govt. Print. Off., 1978. 91 p. : ill. ; 28 cm. "October 1979." Prepared by F. G. Bohme. Bibliography: p. 91.   LC Card 79-600181 DDC 353.0081/9 19
1. United States - Census - History. I. Bohme, Frederick G. II. Title.
HA37 .U52 1978

U. S. exports: Schedule B commodity by country. Washington. 28 cm. (Its: FT. 446) Annual.
1. United States - Commerce - Periodicals. 2. Commercial products - United States - Statistics - Periodicals. I. United States. Bureau of the Census. Schedule B commodity by country. II. Title.
NYPL [JLM 81-161]

U. S. exports: schedule B commodity groupings, schedule B commodity by county. 1967-77 (incomplete). Washington. 11 v. 29 cm. (Its: FT. 410) Monthly. For earlier file, see its: Report FT no. 410. United States exports of domestic and foreign merchandise. Commodity by country of destination. Title varies: 1967-Nov. 1970, U. S. exports: Schedule B commodity and country; July, 1972-Nov. 1973, U. S. foreign trade: exports, commodity by country. For later file, see its: U. S. exports: schedule E commodity groupings, schedule E commodity by country.
1. United States - Commerce - Periodicals. 2. Commercial products - United States - Statistics - Periodicals. I. United States. Bureau of the Census. Schedule B commodity groupings, schedule B commodity by country. II. United States. Bureau of the Census. U. S. exports: schedule B commodity and country. III. United States. Bureau of the Census. U. S. foreign trade: exports, commodity by country. IV. Title.
NYPL [TLG (U. S. Census Bureau. [Report] FT [no.] 410.)]

U. S. exports: schedule E commodity groupings, schedule E commodity by country. 1978- [Washington] 28 cm. (Its: FT. 410) Monthly. For earlier file, see its: U. S. exports: schedule B commodity groupings, schedule B commodity by country. Cover title, 1978- : U. S. exports: Schedule E commodity by country.   LC Card 79-640385
1. United States - Commerce - Periodicals. 2. Commercial products - United States - Statistics - Periodicals. I. United States. Bureau of the Census. Schedule E commodity groupings, schedule E commodity by country. II. United States. Bureau of the Census. U. S. exports: schedule E commodity by country. III. Title.   **NYPL [JLM 80-677]**

U. S. exports: schedule B commodity and country. United States. Bureau of the Census. U. S. exports: schedule B commodity groupings, schedule B commodity by county. 1967-77 (incomplete). Washington. 11 v.
NYPL [TLG (U. S. Census Bureau. [Report] FT [no.] 410.)]

U. S. exports: schedule E commodity by country. United States. Bureau of the Census. U. S. exports: schedule E commodity groupings, schedule E commodity by country. 1978- [Washington]   LC Card 79-640385
NYPL [JLM 80-677]

U. S. foreign trade: exports, commodity by country. United States. Bureau of the Census. U. S. exports: schedule B commodity groupings, schedule B commodity by county. 1967-77 (incomplete). Washington. 11 v.
NYPL [TLG (U. S. Census Bureau. [Report] FT [no.] 410.)]

Urban atlas, tract data for standard metropolitan areas : Memphis, Tennessee-Arkansas / U. S. Department of Commerce, Bureau of the Census [and] U. S. Department of Labor, Manpower Administraton. Washington, D.C. : The Bureau : for sale by the Supt. of Docs., U. S. Govt. Print. Off., 1974 [i.e. 1975] [15] l. : maps (some col.) ; 44 x 56 cm. Cover title. Scale of most maps ca. 1:187,500. Maps compiled in 1975 from 1970 census data.   LC Card 80-600869 DDC 912/.1312/0976819
1. Census districts - Tennessee - Memphis - Maps. 2. Census districts - Arkansas - Crittenden Co. - Maps. 3. Crittenden Co., Ark. - Census - Maps. 4. Memphis - Census - Maps. I. United States. Dept. of Labor. Manpower Administraiton. II. Title.
G1337.M4E25 U5 1975

GOVERNMENT PUBLICATIONS - U.S.: 1981

405
United States. Census Office. 7th census, 1850.

Urban atlas, tract data for standard metropolitan statistical areas : Baltimore, Maryland / U. S. Department of Commerce, Bureau of the Census [and] U. S. Department of Labor, Manpower Administration. Washington, D.C. : The Bureau : for sale by the Supt. of Docs., U. S. Govt. Print. Off., 1974 [i.e. 1975] [31] p. : maps (some col.) ; 44 x 56 cm. Cover title. Scale of most maps ca. 1:290,000 and 1:70,000. Maps compiled in 1975 from 1970 census data.   LC Card 80-600856   DDC 912/.1312/097526
1. Census districts - Maryland - Baltimore - Maps. 2. Baltimore - Census - Maps. I. United States. Dept. of Labor. Manpower Administration. II. Title.
G1272.B3E25 U5 1975

Urban atlas, tract data for standard metropolitan statistical areas : Chicago, Illinois / U. S. Department of Commerce, Bureau of the Census [and] U. S. Department of Labor, Manpower Administration. Washington, D.C. : The Bureau : for sale by the Supt. of Docs., U. S. Govt. Print. Off., 1974 [i.e. 1975] [43] p. : maps (some col.) ; 44 x 56 cm. Cover title. Scale of most maps ca. 1:330,000 and 1:85,000. Maps compiled in 1975 from 1970 census data.   LC Card 80-600845   DDC 912/.1312/0977311
1. Census districts - Illinois - Chicago - Maps. 2. Chicago - Census - Maps. I. United States. Dept. of Labor. Manpower Administration. II. Title.
G1407.C54E25 U5 1975

Urban atlas, tract data for standard metropolitan statistical areas : San Jose, California / U. S. Department of Commerce, Bureau of the Census [and] U. S. Dept. of Labor, Manpower Administration. Washington, D.C. : The Bureau : for sale by the Supt. of Docs., U. S. Govt. Print. Off., 1974 [i.e. 1975] [16] p. : maps (some col.) ; 44 x 56 cm. Cover title. Scale of most maps ca. 1:188,000. Maps compiled in 1975 from 1970 census data.   LC Card 80-600861   DDC 912/.1312/0979474
1. Census districts - California - San Jose - Maps. 2. San Jose, Calif. - Census - Maps. I. United States. Dept. of Labor. Manpower Administration. II. Title.
G1527.S33E25 U5 1975

Urban atlas, tract data for standard metropolitan statistical areas : Greensboro, Winston-Salem, High Point, N.C. / U. S. Department of Commerce, Bureau of the Census [and] U. S. Department of Labor, Manpower Administration. Washington, D.C. : The Bureau : for sale by the Supt. of Docs., U. S. Govt. Print. Off., 1974 [i.e. 1975] [15] p. : maps (some col.) ; 44 x 56 cm. Cover title. Scale of most maps ca. 1:260,000. Maps compiled in 1975 from 1970 census data.   LC Card 80-600872   DDC 912/.1312/0975662
1. Census districts - North Carolina - Greensboro - Maps. 2. Census districts - North Carolina - High Point - Maps. 3. Census districts - North Carolina - Winston-Salem - Maps. 4. High Point, N.C. - Census - Maps. 5. Greensboro, N.C. - Census - Maps. 6. Winston-Salem, N.C. - Census - Maps. I. United States. Dept. of Labor. Manpower Administration. II. Title.
G1302.G7E25 U5 1975

Urban atlas, tract data for standard metropolitan statistical areas : Kansas City, Missouri-Kansas / U. S. Department of Commerce, Bureau of the Census [and] U. S. Department of Labor, Manpower Administration. Washington, D.C. : The Bureau : for sale by the Supt. of Docs., U. S. Govt. Print. Off., 1974 [i.e. 1975] [29] p. : maps (some col.) ; 44 x 56 cm. Cover title. Scale of most maps ca. 1:290,000 and 1:74,000. Maps compiled in 1975 from 1970 census data.   LC Card 80-600871   DDC 912/.1312/09778411
1. Census districts - Missouri - Kansas City - Maps. 2. Census districts - Kansas - Kansas City - Maps. 3. Kansas City, Kan. - Census - Maps. 4. Kansas City, Mo. - Census - Maps. I. United States. Dept. of Labor. Manpower Administraton. II. Title.
G1437.K2E25 U5 1975

Urban atlas, tract data for standard metropolitan statistical areas : Newark, New Jersey / U. S. Department of Commerce, Bureau of the Census [and] U. S. Department of Labor, Manpower Administration. Washington, D.C. : The Bureau : for sale by the Supt. of Docs., U. S. Govt. Print. Off., 1974 [i.e. 1975] [30] p. : maps (some col.) ; 44 x 56 cm. Cover title. Scale of most maps ca. 1:149,000 and 1:100,000. Maps compiled in 1975 from 1970 census data.   DDC 912/.1312/0974932

1. Census districts - New Jersey - Newark - Maps. 2. Newark, N.J. - Census - Maps. I. United States. Dept. of Labor. Manpower Administration. II. Title.
G1257.N5E25 U5 1975

1977 enterprise statistics. Washington [1981] p. cm.   LC Card 81-607012   DDC 338.0973 19
HC106.7 .A14

1980 census of housing. Washington [1981]- p. cm.   LC Card 81-607953   DDC 312/.9/0973 19
HD7273 .A6116

1980 census of housing. Washington [1981]- p. cm.   LC Card 81-607957   DDC 312/.9/0973 19
HD7293 .A6114

1980 census of housing. Washington [1982]- p. cm.   LC Card 81-607958   DDC 312/.9/0973 19
HD7293 .A6113

1980 census of housing. Washington [1982]- p. cm.   LC Card 81-607940   DDC 312/.9/0973 19
HD7293 .A6115

1980 census of population : classified index of industries and occupations. 1st ed. Washington, D.C. : U. S. Dept. of Commerce, Bureau of the Census ; for sale by the Supt. of Docs., U. S. Govt. Print. Off., 1980. xviii, 111, 157 p. ; 30 cm. "Issued October 1980."   LC Card 80-24960   DDC 331.7/0016 19
1. United States - Industries - Classification - Indexes. 2. United States - Occupations - Classification - Indexes. 3. United States - Census, 20th, 1980. I. Classified index of industries and occupations. II. Title.
HC106.7 .U542 1980a

1980 census of population. Washington [1982]- p. cm.   LC Card 81-607939   DDC 312/.0973 19
HA201 1980 .A132

1980 census of population and housing. Washington [1981]- p. cm.   LC Card 81-607959   DDC 312/.0973 19
HA201 1980 .A147

1980 census of population and housing. Washington [1981]- p. cm.   LC Card 81-607960   DDC 312/.0973 19
HA201 1980 .A142

1980 census of population and housing. Washington [1981]- p. cm.   LC Card 81-607944   DDC 312/.0973 19
HA201 1980 .A143

UNITED STATES. BUREAU OF THE CENSUS.
A Numerator and denominator for measuring change . Washington , 1975. 195 p. :   LC Card 75-619192   DDC 001.4/33 19
HA37 .U52 1975

United States. Congress. House. Committee on Government Operations. Commerce, Consumer, and Monetary Affairs Subcommittee. Problems with the 1980 census . Washington , 1980. iii, 174 p. ;   LC Card 80-602783   DDC 353.0081/9 19
KF27 .G634 1980

United States. Congress. House. Committee on Government Operations. Commerce, Consumer, and Monetary Affairs Subcommittee. Problems with the 1980 census count . Washington , 1980. vi, 284 p. ;   LC Card 80-604022   DDC 001.43/3 19
KF27 .G634 1980e

United States. General Accounting Office. Procedures to adjust 1980 census counts have limitations . Washington, D.C. , 1980. v, 37 p. ;   LC Card 81-600763   DDC 353.0081/9 19
HA201 1980

United States. Bureau of the Census. Center for Applied User Research. Guide to county census data for planning economic development. [Washington, D.C.] : U. S. Dept. of Commerce, Bureau of the Census, 1979. iii, 123 p. ; 28 cm.   LC Card 80-601079   DDC 330.973 19
1. United States - Statistical services. 2. United States - Census. 3. United States - Economic conditions - 1971-. I. Title.
HA37.U55 U54 1979

United States. Bureau of the Census. Foreign Demographic Analysis Division. Davis, Christopher, 1948- Rising infant mortality in the U. S.S.R. in the 1970's /. Washington, D.C. , 1980. 33 p. ;   LC Card 81-600791   DDC 304.6 s 304.6/4 19
HC331 .U52 no. 74 HB1323.I4

United States. Bureau of the Census. Geography Division. For publications, see: **United States.**

Bureau of the Census.

United States. Cable Television Bureau. United States. Advisory Committee on Cable Signal Leakage. Final report of the Advisory Committee on Cable Signal Leakage to the Chief, Cable Television Bureau, Federal Communications Commission. Washington, D.C. [1979] 110, [132] p. :   LC Card 80-601686   DDC 629.135 19
TL694.I6 U45 1979

United States/Canada electricity exchanges /. United States. Dept. of Energy. [Oak Ridge, Tenn.] , Washington , 1979. iii, 103, [120] p., [2] leaves of plates :   LC Card 79-602608
HD9685.U5 U495 1979   NYPL [JLF 81-451]

United States-Canada Interparliamentary Group. see **Canada-United States Interparliamentary Group.**

UNITED STATES CAPITOL HISTORICAL SOCIETY, WASHINGTON, D.C. - MEDALS.
United States. Congress. House. Committee on Banking, Finance and Urban Affairs. Subcommittee on Consumer Affairs. Legislation authorizing issuance of gold medals to Canadian Ambassador Kenneth Taylor, Simon Wiesenthal, Gerald F. Spiess, and commemorative medals for the United States Capitol Historical Society . Washington , 1980. iii, 73 p. ;   LC Card 80-601297   DDC 344.73/091 347.30491 19
KF27 .B535 1980c

UNITED STATES - CENSUS.
The Decennial census . Washington , 1980. ix, 465 p. ;   LC Card 81-601006   DDC 001.4/33 19
HA37.U55 D42

United States. Bureau of the Census. Census descriptions of geographic subdivisions and enumeration districts, 1830-1950. Washington , 1978. 6 microfilm reels ;   *NYPL [*ZI-283]*

United States. Bureau of the Census. Center for Applied User Research. Guide to county census data for planning economic development. [Washington, D.C.] , 1979. iii, 123 p. ;   LC Card 80-601079   DDC 330.973 19
HA37.U55 U54 1979

UNITED STATES - CENSUS - BIBLIOGRAPHY.
Parmer, Coleen K. Census bibliography /. [Bowling Green, Ohio , 197-] 80, [1] p. ;   LC Card 80-108176   DDC 016.3173 19
Z7553.C3 P37 HA215

United States. Census Bureau. see **United States. Bureau of the Census.**

United States. Census, Bureau of the. see **United States. Bureau of the Census.**

UNITED STATES - CENSUS - HISTORY.
United States. Bureau of the Census. Twenty censuses . Washington, D.C. , 1978. 91 p. :   LC Card 79-600181   DDC 353.0081/9 19
HA37 .U52 1978

United States. Census Office.
South Carolina index to the United States census of 1820. Tustin, Calif.: G. A. M. Publications, 1972. 426 p. ; 28 cm.
1. South Carolina - Census, 1820 - Indexes. 2. South Carolina - Genealogy. I. United States. Census Office. 4th census, 1820. II. Title.
NYPL [APR (South Carolina) 80-2338]

United States. Census Office. 4th census, 1820.
United States. Census Office. South Carolina index to the United States census of 1820. Tustin, Calif., 1972. 426 p.;
NYPL [APR (South Carolina) 80-2338]

United States. Census Office. 5th census, 1830.
Jackson, Ronald Vern. Kentucky 1830 census index /. Bountiful, Utah , c1976. [23], 206 p. :   LC Card 78-112588
F450 .J316

United States. Census Office. 6th census, 1840.
Accelerated Indexing Systems. Massachusetts 1840 census index /. Bountiful, Utath , 1978. [60], 344 p. :
NYPL [APR (Massachusetts) 81-115]

United States. Census Office. 7th census, 1850.
Accelerated Indexing Systems. Michigan 1850 census index. /. Bountiful, Utah , 1978. [60], 299 p. :   *NYPL [APR (Michigan) 81-117]*

Carroll County Public Library. Index to 1850

census of Carroll County, Maryland.
Westminster, Md. , 1978. 74 leaves ; LC Card
80-129193 DDC 929/.375277 19
F187.C25 C37 1978

United States. Census Office. 9th census, 1870.
DePriest, Virginia Greene. 1870 census of
Cleveland County, North Carolina /. Shelby, N.
C. , c1979. 175 p. ; LC Card 80-105685
F262.C5 D46   *NYPL [APR (Cleveland Co.,
N.C.) 80-3069]*

Weld County Genealogical Society. 1870
Colorado Territory census index. Greeley,
Colo. , 1977. 13, 377 p. : LC Card 80-128759
F775 .W52 1977
        NYPL [APR (Colorado) 81-165]

United States. Census Office. 12th census, 1900.
Descriptions of the enumeration districts of
the ... Twelfth census, June 1, 1900: with the
names of persons employed as enumerators.
[Washington, D. C.: National Archives and
Records Service, 1977?] 2 reels. Microfilm.
Caption - title. Reel 6 contains districts in the states of
Nebraska, Nevada, New Hampshire, New Jersey, New
Mexico, New York; reel 7: New York, North Carolina,
North Dakota and others.
*1. United States - Census, 12th, 1900. 2. Census
districts - United States. I. United States. National
Archives and Records Service. II. Title. III. Title:
Enumeration districts of the Twelfth census, 1900.*
        *NYPL [*ZI-275]*

UNITED STATES - CENSUS, 12TH, 1900.
United States. Census Office. 12th census,
1900. Descriptions of the enumeration districts
of the ... Twelfth census, June 1, 1900.
[Washington, D. C., 1977?] 2 reels.
        *NYPL [*ZI-275]*

UNITED STATES - CENSUS, 20TH, 1980.
The Decennial census . Washington , 1980. ix,
465 p. ; LC Card 81-601006 DDC 001.4/33 19
HA37.U55 D42

United States. Bureau of the Census. 1980
census of population . Washington, D.C. , 1980.
xviii, 111, 157 p. ; LC Card 80-24960 DDC
331.7/0016 19
HC106.7 .U542 1980a

United States. Congress. House. Committee on
Government Operations. Commerce, Consumer,
and Monetary Affairs Subcommittee. Problems
with the 1980 census . Washington , 1980. iii,
174 p. ; LC Card 80-602783 DDC 353.0081/9 19
KF27 .G634 1980

United States. Congress. House. Committee on
Government Operations. Commerce, Consumer,
and Monetary Affairs Subcommittee. Problems
with the 1980 census count . Washington ,
1980. vi, 284 p. ; LC Card 80-604022 DDC
001.43/3 19
KF27 .G634 1980e

United States. Congress. House. Committee on
Post Office and Civil Service. Subcommittee on
Census and Population. Briefing on implications
of internal migration . Washington , 1980. iii,
42 p. : LC Card 80-603710 DDC 304.8/2 19
KF27 .P634 1980

United States. Congress. Senate. Committee on
Agriculture, Nutrition, and Forestry.
Subcommittee on Rural Development. Accuracy
of census taking in small communities and rural
areas . Washington , 1980. iii, 32 p. ; LC Card
80-603442 DDC 001.4/33 19
KF26 .A3574 1980a

United States. Congress. Senate. Committee on
Governmental Affairs. Subcommittee on
Energy, Nuclear Proliferation, and Federal
Services. 1980 census, counting illegal aliens .
Washington , 1980. iii, 254 p. ; LC Card
80-602802 DDC 342.73/08 19
KF26 .G6728 1980

United States. General Accounting Office.
Procedures to adjust 1980 census counts have
limitations . Washington, D.C. , 1980. v, 37 p. ;
LC Card 81-600763 DDC 353.0081/9 19
HA201 1980

1980 census of housing. Washington [1981]- p.
cm. LC Card 81-607953 DDC 312/.9/0973 19
HD7273 .A6116

1980 census of housing. Washington [1981]- p.
cm. LC Card 81-607957 DDC 312/.9/0973 19
HD7293 .A6114

1980 census of housing. Washington [1982]- p.

cm. LC Card 81-607940 DDC 312/.9/0973 19
HD7293 .A6115

1980 census of housing. Washington [1982]- p.
cm. LC Card 81-607958 DDC 312/.9/0973 19
HD7293 .A6113

1980 census of population. Washington [1982]-
p. cm. LC Card 81-607939 DDC 312/.0973 19
HA201 1980 .A132

1980 census of population and housing.
Washington [1981]- p. cm. LC Card 81-607960
DDC 312/.0973 19
HA201 1980 .A142

1980 census of population and housing.
Washington [1981]- p. cm. LC Card 81-607959
DDC 312/.0973 19
HA201 1980 .A147

1980 census of population and housing.
Washington [1981]- p. cm. LC Card 81-607944
HA201 1980 .A143

**UNITED STATES - CENSUS, 20TH, 1980 -
CONGRESSES.**
Local public meeting on the 1980 census of
population and housing, March 19, 1975 ...
Honolulu, Hawaii. [Honolulu , 1975] 19 p. :
LC Card 81-455018 DDC 001.4/33 19
HA201 1980 .L62

**UNITED STATES - CENSUS, 20TH, 1980 -
PERIODICALS.**
United States. Bureau of the Census. 1980
census of population: alphabetical index of
industries and occupations. 1st- ed. Washington,
1980-
        *NYPL [*R-Econ. 81-164 & JLM 81-159]*

United States. Bureau of the Census. 1980
census of population: classified index of
industries and occupations. 1st- ed. Washington,
1980-
        *NYPL [*R-Econ. 81-163 & JLM 81-158]*

United States. Center for Disease Control. see
Center for Disease Control.

United States. Center for Population Research.
see United States. National Institute of
Child Health and Human Development.
Center for Population Research.

United States. Center for Studies of Crime and
Delinquency. see United States. National
Institute of Mental Health. Center for
Studies of Crime and Delinquency.

United States. Center for Studies of
Metropolitan Problems. see United States.
National Institute of Mental Health. Center
for Studies of Metropolitan Problems.

United States. Center for the Book. see Center
for the Book.

United States. Center of Military History. see
Center of Military History.

United States. Central Intelligence Agency.
Afghanistan. [Washington, 1972] col. map 43 x
54 cm. on sheet 47 x 89 cm. Scale 1:2,690,000.
"Base 500546." Relief shown by shading and spot
heights. Maps in margin: [Location] -- [Size
comparison] -- Population. -- Ethnolinguistic groups. --
Land use and economic activity. LC Card 73-691574
*1. Afghanistan - Maps. 2. Afghanistan - Maps, Physical.
3. Afghanistan - Population - Maps. 4. Ethnology -
Afghanistan - Maps. 5. Land use - Afghanistan - Maps.*
G7630 1972 .U5   *NYPL [Map Div. 80-3382]*

Afghanistan / Central Intelligence Agency.
[Washington] : The Agency, [1980] 1 map :
col. ; 61 x 76 cm. Relief shown by shading and spot
heights. "504637 10-80 (544990)." LC Card 81-692539
1. Afghanistan - Maps.
G7630 1980 .U5

Application of Soviet pressure, 1946-53.
[Washington : Central Intelligence Agency,
1978] 1 map : col. ; 25 x 47 cm. Shows major
European colonies in 1953, Soviet-dominated countries,
countries with Soviet pressure, and former European
colonies achieving independence. "503741 4-78
(541369)." "Map 3." LC Card 81-690523
*1. Europe - Colonies - Maps. 2. Communist countries -
Maps. 3. World maps. I. Title. II. Title: Soviet pressure,
1946-53.*
G5701.F33 1953 .U5

Azimuthal equidistant projection centered on
Kābul, Afghanistan. [Washington : Central
Intelligence Agency, 1980] 1 map : col. ; 77 x
77 cm. "504449 4-80 (545034)." Shows radial

distances. LC Card 81-692768
*1. Azimuthal equidistant projection (Cartography) -
Maps. 2. Eastern Hemisphere - Maps. 3. Kabul
(Afghanistan) - Distances, etc. - Maps. I. Title.*
G5671.B72 1980 .U5

Bhutan. [Washington : Central Intelligence
Agency, 1966] 1 map : col. ; 18 x 24 cm.
"52895 2-66." Relief shown by spot heights. LC Card
81-692503
1. Bhutan - Maps.
G7780 1966 .U5

Burma, ethnic groups. [Washington : Central
Intelligence Agency, 1970] 1 map : col. ; on
sheet 27 x 21 cm. "78663 8-70." LC Card
81-692502
1. Ethnology - Burma - Maps. I. Title.
G7721.E1 1970 .U5

Changing face of Europe and colonial tension,
late 1945. [Washington : Central Intelligence
Agency, 1978] 1 map : col. ; 25 x 47 cm. Also
shows Soviet-dominated countries. "503740 4-78
(541369)." "Map 2." LC Card 81-690522
*1. Europe - Colonies - Maps. 2. Communist countries -
Maps. 3. World maps. I. Title. II. Title: Europe and
colonial tension, late 1945.*
G5701.F33 1945 .U5

China. [Washington : Central Intelligence
Agency, 1979] 1 map : col. ; on sheet 86 x 102
cm. Scale 1:5,000,000. "504292 8-79 (542557)." Relief
shown by shading and spot heights. Depths shown by
gradient tints and soundings. Place names in Pinyin.
Index in Pinyin and Wade-Giles on verso. LC Card
80-691676
1. China - Maps.
G7820 1979 .U5   *NYPL [Map Div. 80-3381]*

Chinese Communist Party provincial leaders.
[Washington?] 1973. iv, 117 p. 27 cm. (Its:
Reference aid) "A 73-2." Previous ed. is entered under
title. LC Card 73-600959
1. Chung-kuo kung ch'an tang - Registers. I. Title.
JQ1519.A5 U553   *NYPL [JFF 80-1254]*

Collapse of colonial system, 1953-68.
[Washington : Central Intelligence Agency,
1978] 1 map : col. ; 25 x 47 cm. Shows major
European colonies in 1968, former European colonies
achieving independence, Soviet-dominated countries,
countries in presence of Soviet political/military efforts,
and countries in presence of Cuban support for
insurrection. "5[03]742 4-78 (541369)." "Map 4." LC
Card 81-690524
*1. Europe - Colonies - Maps. 2. Communist countries -
Maps. 3. World maps. I. Title. II. Title: Colonial
system, 1953-68.*
G5701.F33 1968 .U5

Eastern Europe. [Washington : Central
Intelligence Agency, 1980] 1 map : col. ; 76 x
66 cm. Gazetteer on verso. "504559 7-80 (543674)."
LC Card 81-692766
1. Europe, Eastern - Maps. I. Title.
G6965 1980 .U5

The eastern Mediterranean. [Washington :
Central Intelligence Agency, 1980] 1 map :
col. ; 107 x 84 cm. "504557 7-80." LC Card
81-692535
1. Near East - Maps. I. Title.
G7420 1980 .U51

El Salvador / Central Intelligence Agency.
[Washington] : The Agency, [1980] 1 map :
col. ; 27 x 44 cm. "Base 504474 10-80 (545171)."
LC Card 81-690695
1. El Salvador - Maps.
G4840 1980 .U5

Fiji, administrative divisions. [Washington :
Central Intelligence Agency, 1970] 1 map :
col. ; 24 x 17 cm. "77440 11-70." LC Card
81-692500
1. Fiji - Administrative and political divisions - Maps.
G9381.F7 1970 .U5

Iraq-Iran central and southern border areas.
[Washington : Central Intelligence Agency,
1980] 1 map : col. ; on sheet 85 x 104 cm.
Shows oil fields, gas fields, pipelines, refineries, and
tanker terminals. Relief shown by shading and spot
heights. "504634 9-80." LC Card 81-692540
*1. Iraq - Boundaries - Iran - Maps. 2. Iran -
Boundaries - Iraq - Maps. 3. Oil fields - Iraq - Maps. 4.
Oil fields - Iran - Maps. 5. Petroleum refineries - Iraq -
Maps. 6. Petroleum refineries - Iran - Maps. 7.
Petroleum shipping terminals - Iraq - Maps. 8.
Petroleum shipping terminals - Iran - Maps. 9. Gas,
Natural - Iraq - Maps. 10. Gas, Natural - Iran - Maps.*

11. Petroleum - Iraq - Pipe lines - Maps. 12.
Petroleum - Iran - Pipe lines - Maps. I. Title. II. Title:
Iran central and southern border areas.
G7611.F2 1980 .U5

Jerusalem and vicinity. [Washington : Central
Intelligence Agency, 1980] 1 map : col. ; 89 x
61 cm. Shows Israeli occupied and settled areas of
Jerusalem region. Relief shown by spot heights. "504368
3-80." LC Card 81-692537
1. Land settlements - Jerusalem region - Maps. I. Title.
G7504.J4F3 1980 .U51

Kābul. [Washington : Central Intelligence
Agency, 1980] 1 map : col. ; 16 x 22 cm.
"504523 6-80." LC Card 81-692530
1. Kabul (Afghanistan) - Maps.
G7634.K2 1980 .U5

Leningrad area. [Washington : Central
Intelligence Agency, 1980] 1 map : col. ; 89 x
87 cm. Shows areas closed to travel by foreigners.
"Source: Ministry of Foreign Affairs of the USSR,
Diplomatic Note No. 2lb, dated 13 November 1973,
Leningrad." "Map base from Defense Mapping Agency
series 1501 ..." Relief shown by contours and spot
heights. Depths shown by contours. "504135 9-80."
LC Card 81-692776
1. Aliens - Russian S.F.S.R. - Leningrad region - Travel
restrictions - Maps. 2. Travel restrictions - Russian
S.F.S.R. - Leningrad region - Maps. I. Title.
G7004.L4E272 1980 .U5

Madagascar. 6-73. [Washington, 1973] col. map
48 x 33 cm. Scale 1:3,465,000. Relief shown by
shading and spot heights. "501245." Includes location
map, comparative area map, and maps of "Population,"
"Tribal groups," "Economic activity," and "Vegetation."
LC Card 75-690371
1. Madagascar - Maps. 2. Madagascar - Population -
Maps. 3. Madagascar - Economic conditions - Maps. 4.
Tribes and tribal system - Madagascar - Maps. 5.
Phytogeography - Madagascar - Maps.
G8460 1973 .U51
                        NYPL [Map Div. 81-3036]

Major European colonial empires on the eve of
World War II, 1938. [Washington : Central
Intelligence Agency, 1978] 1 map : col. ; 25 x
47 cm. "503739 4-78 (541369)." "Map 1." LC Card
81-690521
1. Europe - Colonies - Maps. 2. World maps. I. Title.
II. Title: European colonial empires on the eve of
World War II, 1938.
G5701.F33 1938 .U5

Mediterranean basin. [Washington : Central
Intelligence Agency, 1980] 1 map : col. ; 39 x
108 cm. "504549 7-80." LC Card 81-692764
1. Mediterranean region - Maps. I. Title.
G5672.M4 1980 .U5

Middle East area oilfields and facilities.
[Washington : Central Intelligence Agency,
1980] 1 map : col. ; 86 x 96 cm. Relief shown by
shading. "504295 1-80 (544807)." LC Card 81-692536
1. Oil fields - Near East - Maps. 2. Petroleum - Near
East - Pipe lines - Maps. 3. Petroleum refineries - Near
East - Maps. 4. Petroleum shipping terminals - Near
East - Maps. I. Title.
G7421.H8 1980 .U5

Moscow : guide to streets, metro stations,
public buildings, embassies, hotels, theaters.
[Washington? : Central Intelligence Agency],
1980. 203 p. : col. maps ; 21 cm. Cover title.
Scale of principal maps 1:35,000 or 1 inch equals
approx. 1/2 mile. Edition for 1975 published under
title: Moscow street guide. Includes indexes. LC Card
80-675326 DDC 912/.47312 19
1. Moscow - Maps. I. Title.
G2114.M6 U47 1980

Moscow, areas closed to foreigners, 4 January
1978. [Washington : Central Intelligence
Agency, 1980] 1 map : col. ; 58 x 72 cm.
"Source: Ministry of Foreign Affairs of the USSR, Note
No. 1/Pr, dated 4 January 1978, Moscow." Inset:
Moscow Oblast. "504134 9-80." LC Card 81-692777
1. Aliens - Russian S.F.S.R. - Moscow region - Travel
restrictions - Maps. 2. Aliens - Russian S.F.S.R. -
Moskovskaīa oblast´ - Travel restrictions - Maps. 3.
Travel restrictions - Russian S.F.S.R. - Moscow region -
Maps. 4. Travel restrictions - Russian S.F.S.R. -
Moskovskaīa oblast´ - Maps. I. Title.
G7004.M7E272 1980 .U53

OECD countries . Washington, D.C. [1980] iv,
56 p. ; LC Card 80-604134 DDC 331.13/7 19
HD5707.5 .O43

Oman regions. [Washington : Central

Intelligence Agency, 1980] 1 map : col. ; 21 x
17 cm. "504408 1-80 (544486)" "Unclassified." LC
Card 81-692531
1. Oman - Administrative and political divisions -
Maps. I. Title.
G7561.F7 1980 .U5

Oman tribes. [Washington : Central Intelligence
Agency, 1980] 1 map : col. ; 21 x 17 cm.
"504409 1-80 (544486)." "Unclassified." LC Card
81-692532
1. Tribes and tribal system - Oman - Maps. I. Title.
G7561.E1 1980 .U5

Pakistan major ethnic groups. [Washington :
Central Intelligence Agency, 1980] 1 map :
col. ; 16 x 17 cm. "504491 5-80 (545359)" LC
Card 81-692533
1. Tribes and tribal system - Pakistan - Maps. I. Title.
G7641.E1 1980 .U5

Political map of the world : 1 September 1980.
[Washington : Central Intelligence Agency,
1980] 1 map : col. ; 52 x 100 cm. "504541 9-80
(545537)." LC Card 81-690682
1. World maps.
G3200 1980 .U5

Recent Soviet gains and possible targets, 1978.
[Washington : Central Intelligence Agency,
1978] 1 map : col. ; 25 x 47 cm. Shows
Soviet-dominated countries, countries with Soviet
presence and/or influence, countries identifed as
probable Soviet target of influence, countries with treaty
of friendship and cooperation with USSR, countries
with possible communist participation in European
government, and countries of assertive radical state.
"503743 4-78 (541369)." "Map 5." LC Card 81-690525
1. Communist countries - Maps. 2. World maps. I.
Title. II. Title: Soviet gains and possible targets, 1978.
G7001.F35 1978 .U5

Selected world shipping lanes and straits.
[Washington : Central Intelligence Agency,
1980] 1 map : col. ; 25 x 48 cm. Also shows
200-nautical-mile maritime zones. "504444 2-80
(541369)." "Unclassified." Indexed for straits. LC Card
81-690686
1. Shipping - Maps. 2. Trade routes - Maps. 3. Straits -
Maps. 4. Territorial waters - Maps. 5. World maps. I.
Title. II. Title: World shipping lanes and straits.
G3201.P54 1980 .U5

Sikkim. [Washington : Central Intelligence
Agency, 1965] 1 map : col. ; 24 x 18 cm.
"52365 9-65." LC Card 81-692565
1. Sikkim (India) - Maps.
G7653.S5 1965 .U5

Sikkim and western Bhutan, selected ethnic
groups. [Washington : Central Intelligence
Agency, 1970] 1 map : col. ; 24 x 18 cm.
"77569 2-70." LC Card 81-692567
1. Ethnology - India - Sikkim - Maps. 2. Ethnology -
Bhutan - Maps. I. Title.
G7653.S5E1 1970 .U5

Sinai Peninsula, Israeli settlements.
[Washington : Central Intelligence Agency,
1980] 1 map : col. ; 21 x 17 cm. "504464 3-80
(544089)." LC Card 81-692568
1. Land settlement - Egypt - Sinai Peninsula - Maps. I.
Title.
G8302.S5G4 1980 .U5

Some perspectives on oil availability for the
non-OPEC LDCs . Washington, D.C. , 1980.
viii, 48 p. : LC Card 80-603931 DDC
333.8/23211/091724 19
HD9560.5 .S62

South Africa, homelands. [Washington : Central
Intelligence Agency, 1980] 1 map : col. ; 22 x
17 cm. "504631 10-80 (543001)." LC Card
81-692033
1. Homelands, South Africa - Maps. I. Title.
G8501.G6 1980 .U5

Southwest Asia. [Washington : Central
Intelligence Agency, 1980] 1 map : col. ; 107 x
84 cm. "504440 4-80 (545025)." LC Card 81-692534
1. Near East - Maps. I. Title.
G7420 1980 .U5

Standard time zones of the world.
[Washington : Central Intelligence Agency,
1980] 1 map : col. ; 25 x 48 cm. "504427 8-80
(545038)." Includes notes. LC Card 81-690683
1. Time - Systems and standards - Maps. 2. World
maps. I. Title.
G3201.B2 1980 .U5

Syria. [Washington, 1979] col. map 40 x 49 cm.

on sheet 44 x 85 cm. Scale 1:1,500,000. "503966
10-79 (544276)." Inset: Golan Heights. Maps in margin:
Economic activity. - Land
Utilization.--Population.--[Location].--[Size comparison]
Relief shown by shading and spot heights.
1. Syria - Maps. 2. Syria - Economic conditions - Maps.
3. Land use - Syria - Maps. 4. Syria - Population -
Maps.
G7460 1972 .U5   NYPL [Map Div. 80-3386]

Tanzania. 5-70. [Washington, 1970] col. map 42
x 43 cm. on sheet 44 x 80 cm. Scale 1:3,220,000.
Relief shown by shading and spot heights. "76839."
Includes location map, comparative area map, and maps
of "Population," "Economic activity," "Ethnic groups,"
and "Vegetation." LC Card GM70-4480
1. Tanzania - Maps. 2. Tanzania - Population - Maps.
3. Tanzania - Economic conditions - Maps. 4.
Ethnology - Tanzania - Maps. 5. Phytogeography -
Tanzania - Maps.
G8440 1970 .U51
                        NYPL [Map Div. 80-3387]

United Arab Emirates. [Washington : Central
Intelligence Agency, 1979] 1 map : col. ; 16 x
21 cm. "504116 6-79 (544579)." Includes index of
emirates. LC Card 81-692501
1. United Arab Emirates - Maps.
G7570 1979 .U5

USSR administrative divisions, 1979.
[Washington : Central Intelligence Agency,
1980] 1 map : col. ; 25 x 40 cm. Includes notes
and key to Caucasian administrative divisions. "504352
3-80." LC Card 81-692775
1. Soviet Union - Administrative and political
divisions - Maps. I. Title.
G7001.F7 1979 .U5

World plotting series / published jointly by the
Central Intelligence Agency and the Defense
Mapping Agency, Topographic Center. Ed. 1.
Washington : The Center, [1976] 7 maps : col. ;
77 x 59 cm. or smaller. Scale 1:18,000,000.
"Lambert conformal conic, standard parallels 37ºN and
65ºN." "This map is designed to be used in conjunction
with automated cartographic systems." 540931-540937.
Includes "Index to sheets." "Series 1147."
CONTENTS. - 1. Eurasia.--2. N. America.--3. S.
America.--4. Africa.--5. Oceania.--6. Anarctica.--7.
Arctic. LC Card 79-691244
1. Plotting charts. 2. World maps. I. Defense Mapping
Agency. Topographic Center. II. Title.
G3201.A1 s18000 .U6
                        NYPL [Map. Div. 80-3396]

Yugoslavia. [Washington : Central Intelligence
Agency, 1980] 1 map : col. ; 38 x 44 cm. Relief
shown by shading and spot heights. Includes "List of
republics." "504459 3-80." LC Card 81-693055
1. Yugoslavia - Maps.
G6840 1980 .U5

200-nautical-mile claims, January 1980.
[Washington : Central Intelligence Agency,
1980] 1 map : col. ; 25 x 48 cm. "504524 6-80
(541369)." "Unclassified." LC Card 81-690684
1. Territorial waters - Maps. 2. World maps. I. Title.
G3201.F3 1980 .U5

**UNITED STATES. CENTRAL
    INTELLIGENCE AGENCY.**
United States. Congress. House. Committee on
Government Operations. Subcommittee on
Government Information and Individual Rights.
The Freedom of Information Act .
Washington , 1981. iii, 205 p. ; LC Card
81-601868 DDC 342.73/0418 347.302418 19
KF27 .G6628 1980d

United States. Congress. House. Permanent
Select Committee on Intelligence.
Subcommittee on Oversight. CIA estimates of
Soviet defense spending . Washington , 1980
[i.e. 1981] iii, 95 p. : LC Card 81-600837 DDC
355/.033047 19
KF27.5 .I55 1980c

United States. Congress. House. Permanent
Select Committee on Intelligence.
Subcommittee on Oversight. Intelligence on the
world energy outlook and its policy
implications . Washington , 1980. iii, 235 p. :
LC Card 80-603479 DDC 333.79 19
KF27.5 .I55 1979a

**United States. Central Intelligence Agency.
    Economic Research, Office of. see United
    States. Central Intelligence Agency. Office
    of Economic Research.**

BIBLIOGRAPHIC GUIDE

United States. Central Intelligence Agency. National Foreign   *408*

United States. Central Intelligence Agency. National Foreign Assessment Center.
Chinese defense spending, 1965-79 / National Foreign Assessment Center. [Washington, D.C.] : The Center, [1980] v, 9 p. : graphs ; 27 cm. (A Research paper - Central Intelligence Agency, National Foreign Assessment Center) "July 1980." "SR 80-10091." LC Card 80-602848
1. China - Armed Forces - Appropriations and expenditures - Addresses, essays, lectures. I. Title.
UA835 .U48 1980

Communist aid activities in non-Communist less developed countries, 1978 / National Foreign Assessment Center. Washington, D.C. : The Center, [1979] vii, 40 p. : graphs ; 27 cm. (A Research paper - National Foreign Assessment Center) "ER 79-10412U." "September 1979." LC Card 80-602379 DDC 338.91/47/01724 19
1. Economic assistance, Russian. 2. Economic assistance, East European. 3. Underdeveloped areas. 4. Communist countries - Foreign economic relations. I. Series: United States. Central Intelligence Agency. National Foreign Assessment Center. Research paper - Central Intelligence Agency, National Foreign Assessment Center. II. Title.
HC60.U6 C45 1979

Directory of Chinese officials : national level organizations / National Foreign Assessment Center. [Washington, D.C.] : The Center ; [Springfield, Va. : purchase from National Technical Information Service, 1980] x, 213 p. ; 27 cm. (A Reference aid- National Foreign Assessment Center) "CR 80-12651 (Supersedes CR 78-16506)." "July 1980." Includes index. LC Card 80-602916 DDC 354.51002 19
1. China - Officials and employees - Directories. I. Title.
JQ1507 .U452 1980

Directory of Chinese officials: national level organizations. July 1980- [Washington]
NYPL [JLM 81-15]

Directory of officials of the Czechoslovak Socialist Republic / National Foreign Assessment Center. [Washington, D.C.] : The Center ; [Springfield, Va. : may be purchased from National Technical Information Service], 1978. xi, 169 p. ; 27 cm. (A Reference aid- National Foreign Assessment Center) CR 78-14528 (supersedes A 72-17.) "Information received as of 30 April 1978." Includes index.
1. Czechoslovakia - Registers. 2. Komunistická strana Československa - Membership - Directories. 3. Associations, institutions, etc. - Czechoslovakia - Directories. I. Title.
JN2217 .U55 1980   ***NYPL [JLF 81-246]***

Directory of officials of the Czechoslovak Socialist Republic / National Foreign Assessment Center. [Washington, D.C.] : The Center ; [Springfield, Va. : may be purchased from National Technical Information Service], 1980. xiv, 175 p. ; 27 cm. (A Reference aid- National Foreign Assessment Center) "CR 80-11926 (supersedes CR 78-14528)" "Information received as of 30 April 1980." Includes index. LC Card 80-602887 DDC 354.437002 19
1. Czechoslovakia - Registers. 2. Komunistická strano Československa - Membership - Directories. 3. Associations, institutions, etc. - Czechoslovakia - Directories. I. Title.
JN2217 .U55 1980

Directory of Soviet research organization[s] / compiled by National Assessment Center, Central Intelligence Agency. Seattle : University Press of the Pacific ; Forest Grove, OR : distributed by International Scholarly Book Service, 1979. v, 290 p. ; 24 cm. Reprint of the 1978 ed. published by the National Foreign Assessment Center, Central Intelligence Agency. Includes index.
ISBN 0-89575-006-7 LC Card 79-121624
1. Research institutes - Russia - Directories. I. Title.
Q180.R9 U32 1979
NYPL [Desk-Slav. Div. 80-626]

Estimating Soviet and East European hard currency debt / National Foreign Assessment Center. Washington, D.C. : The Center, [1980] v, 32 p. ; 27 cm. (A Research paper - Central Intelligence Agency, National Foreign Assessment Center) "ER 80-10327." "Research for this report was completed on 19 May 1980." "June 1980." Includes bibliographical references. LC Card 80-602917 DDC 336.3/435/0947 19
1. Foreign exchange problem - Europe, Eastern. I. Series: United States. Central Intelligence Agency.

National Foreign Assessment Center. Research paper - Central Intelligence Agency, National Foreign Assessment Center. II. Title.
HG3942 .U54 1980

International economic & energy statistical review. ERIEESR 80-001- ; May 1, 1980- Washington. Supersedes its: Economic indicators weekly review.   ***NYPL [Econ. Div.]***

The new global fishing regime : impact and response / National Foreign Assessment Center. Washington, D.C. : Central Intelligence Agency, [1980] iv, 7 p., 3 fold. leaves of plates : maps ; 27 cm. (A Research paper - Central Intelligence Agency, National Foreign Assessment Center) "GC 80-10029." "June 1980." LC Card 80-602918 DDC 338.3/727 19
1. Fisheries. 2. Economic zones (Maritime law). 3. Joint ventures. I. Series: United States. Central Intelligence Agency. National Foreign Assessment Center. Research paper - Central Intelligence Agency, National Foreign Assessment Center. II. Title.
SH331 .U48 1980

Research paper - Central Intelligence Agency, National Foreign Assessment Center.
United States. Central Intelligence Agency. National Foreign Assessment Center. Communist aid activities in non-Communist less developed countries, 1978 /. Washington, D.C. [1979] vii, 40 p. : LC Card 80-602379 DDC 338.91/47/01724 19
HC60.U6 C45 1979

United States. Central Intelligence Agency. National Foreign Assessment Center. Estimating Soviet and East European hard currency debt /. Washington, D.C. [1980] v, 32 p. ; LC Card 80-602917 DDC 336.3/435/0947 19
HG3942 .U54 1980

United States. Central Intelligence Agency. National Foreign Assessment Center. The new global fishing regime . Washington, D.C. [1980] iv, 7 p., 3 fold. leaves of plates : LC Card 80-602918 DDC 338.3/727 19
SH331 .U48 1980

United States. Central Intelligence Agency. National Foreign Assessment Center. The Soviet economy in 1978-79 and prospects for 1980 /. Washington, D.C. [1980] vi, 25 p. : LC Card 80-602919 DDC 330.947/0853 19
HC336.25 .U54 1980

United States. Central Intelligence Agency. National Foreign Assessment Center. USSR, coal industry problems and prospects. Washington, D.C. [1980] iv, 20 p. : LC Card 80-602025 DDC 338.2/724/0947 19
HD9555.R82 U54 1980

The Soviet economy in 1978-79 and prospects for 1980 / National Foreign Assessment Center. Washington, D.C. : Director of Public Affairs, Central Intelligence Agency, [1980] vi, 25 p. : ill. ; 27 cm. (A Research paper - Central Intelligence Agency, National Foreign Assessment Center) "ER 80-10328." "June 1980." Errata slip inserted. Includes bibliographical references. LC Card 80-602919 DDC 330.947/0853 19
1. Russia - Economic conditions - 1976-. I. Series: United States. Central Intelligence Agency. National Foreign Assessment Center. Research paper - Central Intelligence Agency, National Foreign Assessment Center. II. Title.
HC336.25 .U54 1980

Soviet strategy and tactics in economic and commercial negotiations with the United States / National Foreign Assessment Center. Washington : The Center, 1979. v, 11 p. ; 27 cm. (United States. Central Intelligence Agency. National Foreign Assessment Center. Research paper) Microfiche (neg.) 1 sheet. 11 x 15 cm. (NYPL FSN 35,317) "ER 79-10276." LC Card 79-602793
1. United States - Foreign economic relations - Russia. 2. Russia - Foreign economic relations - United States. 3. Negotiation. I. Title.
*HF1456.5.R9 U54 1979 NYPL [*XME-9336]*

USSR, coal industry problems and prospects. Washington, D.C. : Central Intelligence Agency, National Foreign Assessment Center : [purchase from Photoduplication Service, Library of Congress, 1980] iv, 20 p. : ill. ; 27 cm. (A Research paper - Central Intelligence Agency, National Foreign Assessment Center) "ER 80-10154." "March 1980." Includes bibliographical references. LC Card 80-602025 DDC 338.2/724/0947 19

1. Coal trade - Russia. I. Series: United States. Central Intelligence Agency. National Foreign Assessment Center. Research paper - Central Intelligence Agency, National Foreign Assessment Center. II. Title.
HD9555.R82 U54 1980

United States. Central Intelligence Agency. Office of Basic and Geographical Intelligence. South Vietnam, provincial maps. [Washington] : Central Intelligence Agency, Office of Basic and Geographic Intelligence, 1967. [52] leaves : chiefly col. maps ; 27 cm. LC Card 80-675252 DDC 912/.597
1. Vietnam - Administrative and political divisions - Maps. I. Title.
G2371.F7 U54 1967

United States. Central Intelligence Agency. Office of Economic Research. The world oil market in the years ahead : a research paper / [prepared by the Central Intelligence Agency's Office of Economic Research]. Washington : National Foreign Assessment Center, Central Intelligence Agency, 1979. ix, 80 p. : ill. ; 27 cm. Cover title. "ER 79-10327U, August 1979." Includes bibliographical references. LC Card 79-603266
1. Petroleum industry and trade. 2. Economic forecasting. I. Title.
HD9565.6 .U53 1979

UNITED STATES. CENTRAL INTELLIGENCE AGENCY - OFFICIALS AND EMPLOYEES.
United States. Congress. House. Committee on the Judiciary. Subcommittee on Civil and Constitutional Rights. Prepublication review and secrecy requirements imposed upon federal employees . Washington , 1981. iii, 100 p. ; LC Card 81-601753 DDC 353.0071/45 19
KF27 .J847 1980g

United States. Congress. Senate. Select Committee on Intelligence. Nomination of Admiral B.R. Inman . Washington , 1981. iii, 36 p. ; LC Card 81-601774 DDC 327.1/2/06073 19
KF26.5 .I5 1981

United States. Congress. Senate. Select Committee on Intelligence. Nomination of William J. Casey . Washington , 1981. iv, 51 p. ; LC Card 81-601604 DDC 327.1/2/06073 19
KF26.5 .I5 1981a

United States Chamber of Commerce. see Chamber of Commerce of the United States of America.

United States. Chief of Naval Education and Training.
Campus; the Navy education training monthly. Pensacola. LC Card 75-640835
NYPL [JLM 80-1068]

Naval Education and Training Program Development Center. Gunner's mate G 1 & C. [Pensacola, Fla. , Washington , 1980] ca. 500 p. in various pagings : LC Card 80-603250 DDC 623/.553 19
VF160 .N38 1980

Naval Education and Training Program Development Center. Human behavior and leadership /. [Washington?] [1977] i.e. 1978. iii, 163, [51] p. : LC Card 78-601716 DDC 158/.4/024359 19
VB203 .N38 1978

United States. Chief of Staff, Office of. see United States. Dept. of the Army. General Staff.

United States. Children, Youth and Families, Administration for. see United States. Administration for Children, Youth and Families.

United States. Children's Bureau. National Center on Child Abuse and Neglect. see National Center on Child Abuse and Neglect.

United States. Citizen Education Staff Office. see United States. Office of Education. Citizen Education Staff.

United States. Civil Aeronautics Administration. Office of Aviation Information. see United States. Office of Aviation Information.

United States. Civil Aeronautics Board.
Airport activity statistics of certificated route air carriers. Washington. 23-36 cm. Semiannual (reports cover twelve month periods ending June 30

and Dec. 31 of each year) June 1962-1978; annual, 1979- Began publication in 1955. Issued in cooperation with the Federal Aviation Administration (June 1962-June 1968, as Federal Aviation Agency) Absorbed: United States. Federal Aviation Agency. Airports Division. Air commerce traffic pattern (scheduled carriers) in June 1962. (See that entry in Old Catalog)   LC Card 63-4959
1. Aeronautics, Commercial - United States - Statistics - Periodicals. I. United States. Federal Aviation Agency. II. United States. Federal Aviation Administration. III. Title.   **NYPL [VDS (United States. Civil Aeronautics Board. Airport activity Statistics of certificated route air carriers)]**

Telephone directory. July 1980- Washington.
NYPL [Econ. Div.]

UNITED STATES. CIVIL AERONAUTICS BOARD.
United States. Congress. Senate. Committee on Commerce, Science, and Transportation. Subcommittee on Aviation. Oversight on Civil Aeronautics Board . Washington , 1980. iii, 57 p. :   LC Card 80-603444   DDC 353.0087/7712 19
KF26 .C692 1980

United States. Civil Aeronautics Board. Bureau of Accounts and Statistics. Financial Analysis and Cost Division. see United States. Civil Aeronautics Board. Financial Analysis and Cost Division.

United States. Civil Aeronautics Board. Financial Analysis and Cost Division. Trends in unit costs. Washington. illus. 22 x 34 cm. "Domestic operations of the domestic trunk carriers, domestic operations of the local service carriers, and international operations of the trunk carriers." Cover title, 1979- : Trends in airline unit costs.
1. Air lines - United States - Cost of operations - Statistics - Periodicals. I. Title. II. Title: Trends in airline unit costs.   **NYPL [JLN 81-8]**

United States. Civil Aviation Security Service. Semiannual report to Congress on the effectiveness of the Civil Aviation Security Program. July 1/Dec. 31, 1978- [Washington] LC Card 79-644552
I. Title.   **NYPL [Econ. Div.]**

UNITED STATES - CIVIL DEFENSE.
Spencer, L. V. (Lewis Van Clief), 1924- Structure shielding against fallout gamma rays from nuclear detonations /. [Washington, D.C.?] , 1980. xvi, 967 p :   LC Card 80-600120 DDC 602/.18 s 363.1/89 19
QC100 .U57 no. 570 UF787

United States. Congress. House. Committee on Government Operations. Emergency planning around U. S. nuclear powerplants . Washington , 1979. v, 105 p. ;   LC Card 79-604246 DDC 363.3/497 19
KF32 .G6 1979a

United States. Civil Rights, Commission on. see United States. Commission on Civil Rights.

United States - Civil service. see Civil service - United States.

United States. Civil Service Commission. Bureau of Intergovernmental Personnel Programs. Guidelines for qualitative evaluations of personnel operations in state and local governments. [Washington, For sale by the Supt. of Docs., U. S. Govt. Print. Off.] 1974. 21 p. 27 cm. (Its: BIPP. 152-36) Microfiche (neg.) 1 sheet. 11 x 15 cm. (NYPL FSN 34,063) Cover title. Bibliography: p. [21]
1. State government. 2. Local government. 3. Personnel management. I. Title.   **NYPL [*XME-9074]**

Guidelines for the development of an affirmative action plan. Revised [ed. Washington] The Commission, 1975. [80] p.; 28 cm. (Its: BIPP. 152-61) Cover title.   LC Card 77-70944
1. Affirmative action programs - United States. 2. Discrimination in employment - United States. I. Title.
NYPL [JLF 80-570]

United States. Civil Service Commission. Bureau of Recruiting and Examining. Guide for Federal agency coordinators in selective placement of the handicapped; identifying and eliminating architectural barriers. Washington, 1974. 7 p.; 28 cm. Microfiche (neg.) 1 sheet. 11 x 15 cm. (NYPL FSN 35,126) Cover title.
1. Handicapped - Employment. 2. Architecture and the handicapped. I. Title.   **NYPL [*XME-9176]**

United States. Civil Service Commission. Bureau of Training. Personnel Management Training Center. Instructors' guide for workshop in employee development / [prepared under an interagency agreement with the Department of Housing and Urban Development by the] Civil Service Commission, Bureau of Training, Personnel Management Training Center. [Washington?] : United States Civil Service Commission, Bureau of Training, Personnel Management Training Center, 1973. 305 p. in various pagings : ill. ; 27 cm. With, as issued, Instructors' guide for Advanced workshop in employee development. Cover title: Workshops in employee development for state and local training officers: instructor's guides. "Interagency Training Programs." "Attachment to CSC 410-146."
1. Civil service - Study and teaching - United States. 2. Personnel management - Study and teaching - United States. 3. Employees, Training of - Study and teaching - United States. I. United States. Dept. of Housing and Urban Development. II. Title. III. Title: Workshops in employee development for state and local training officers. IV. Title: Instructors' guide for advanced workshop in employee development.
NYPL [JLF 80-1341]

United States. Civil Service Commission. Federal Executive Institute. see Federal Executive Institute.

United States. Civil Service Commission. Incentive System, Office of. see United States. Civil Service Commission. Office of Incentive Systems.

United States. Civil Service Commission. Intergovernmental Personnel Programs, Bureau of. see United States. Civil Service Commission. Bureau of Intergovernmental Personnel Programs.

United States. Civil Service Commission. Labor-Management Relations, Office of. see United States. Civil Service Commission. Office of Labor-Management Relations.

United States. Civil Service Commission. Office of Incentive Systems. Progress through achievements. 1976/77- Washington. illus. 27 cm. Annual. Report year ends Sept. 30. For earlier file, see: United States. Civil Service Commission. Achievements. For later file, see Achievements.   LC Card 79-643386
1. Civil service - United States - Periodicals. 2. Performance awards - United States - Periodicals. 3. Suggestion systems - United States - Periodicals.
NYPL [JLM 80-1092]

United States. Civil Service Commission. Office of Labor-Management Relations. Managing under bilateralism : a supervisor's guide / U. S. Civil Service Commission, Office of Labor-Management Relations. [Washington] : The Office, 1976. 58 p. ; 27 cm. (OLMR management practices manual. 6) Cover title. "This manual is a direct result of a study conducted in 1974 by the Office of Labor-Management Relations ... entitled Elements of success in Federal labor-management relations ..."
1. Management - Handbooks, manuals, etc. 2. Employee-management relations in government - United States - Handbooks, manuals, etc. I. Title.
NYPL [JLF 80-690]

Union recognition in the federal government. Washington.   **NYPL [M-11 4907]**

United States. Civil Service Commission. Personnel Management Training Center. see United States. Civil Service Commission. Bureau of Training. Personnel Management Training Center.

United States. Civil Service Commission. Recruiting and Examining, Bureau of. see United States. Civil Service Commission. Bureau of Recruiting and Examining.

UNITED STATES. CIVILIAN CONSERVATION CORPS - ARCHIVES - CATALOGS.
United States. National Archives and Records Service. Preliminary inventory of the records of the Civilian Conservation Corps . Washington , 1980. vii, 23 p. ;   LC Card 80-28921 DDC 016.973 s 016.3337/2/0973 19
CD3026 .A32 no. 11, 1980 CD3035

United States civilian space policy . United States. Congress. House. Committee on Science and Technology. Subcommittee on Space

Science and Applications. Washington , 1980. iii, 246 p. :   LC Card 80-603989   DDC 629.4/0973 19
KF27 .S3995 1980b

United States civilian space programs, 1958-1978 : report / prepared for the Subcommittee on Space Science and Applications of the Committee on Science and Technology, U. S. House of Representatives, Ninety-seventh Congress, first session, by the Science Policy Research Division, Congressional Research Service, Library of Congress. Washington : U. S. G.P.O. : For sale by the Supt. of Docs., U. S. G.P.O., 1981- v. <1 > : ill. ; 24 cm. At head of title: Committee print. Authors: Marcia S. Smith and others. "Serial D." Vol. 1: "January 1981." S/N 052-070-05579-1 (v. 1) Item 1025-A-1, 1025-A-2 (microfiche) Includes bibliographical references.   LC Card 81-602024   DDC 629.4 19
1. United States. National Aeronautics and Space Administration. 2. Astronautics - United States. I. Smith, Marcia S. II. United States. Congress. House. Committee on Science and Technology. Subcommittee on Space Science and Applications. III. Library of Congress. Science Policy Research Division.
TL789.8.U5 U58

UNITED STATES - CIVILIZATION - 20TH CENTURY.
Hsu, Francis L. K., 1909- Americans and Chinese . Honolulu , c1981. p. cm.   ISBN 0-8248-0710-3 :   LC Card 81-10461   DDC 951 19
DS721 .H685 1981

UNITED STATES - CIVILIZATION - 1970-
Booz, Allen Public Administration Services, inc. The quality of life concept . [Washington] , 1973. 1 v. (various pagings).
NYPL [*XME-9624]

UNITED STATES - CIVILIZATION - ADDRESSES, ESSAYS, LECTURES.
Boorstin, Daniel Joseph, 1914- The fertile verge . Washington , 1980. 19 p. ;   ISBN 0-8444-0357-1 (pbk.)   LC Card 80-27815   DDC 973 19
E169.1 .B693

UNITED STATES - CIVILIZATION - PERIODICALS.
Journal of American culture. v. 1- Spring 1978- [Bowling Green, Ohio]   LC Card 79-642570
NYPL [JFL 80-314]

UNITED STATES - CLAIMS.
United States. Congress. House. Committee on the Judiciary. Subcommittee on Administrative Law and Governmental Relations. Compensation of military personnel and government employees for loss of personal property incident to their foreign service . Washington , 1980. iii, 110 p. :   LC Card 80-624071   DDC 346.7304/7 19
KF27 .J832 1980

UNITED STATES - CLAIMS VS. CHINA.
United States. Congress. House. Committee on Foreign Affairs. China claims reallocation . Washington , 1980. iii, 37 p. ;   LC Card 81-600644   DDC 343.7305/2 347.30352 19
KF27 .F6 1980p

United States. Congress. Senate. Committee on Foreign Relations. China claims . Washington , 1980. iii, 42 p. ;   LC Card 80-602966   DDC 341.5/5 19
KF26 .F6 1980i

UNITED STATES - CLAIMS VS. CUBA.
United States. Congress. House. Committee on Foreign Affairs. Subcommittee on International Economic Policy and Trade. Outstanding claims against Cuba . Washington , 1980. iii, 21 p. ;   LC Card 80-603106   DDC 327.7291073 19
KF27 .F6465 1979e

UNITED STATES - CLAIMS VS. CZECHOSLOVAKIA.
United States. Congress. House. Committee on Foreign Affairs. Subcommittee on Europe and the Middle East. Settlement of claims against Czechoslovakia . Washington , 1981. iv, 225 p. ;   LC Card 81-600940   DDC 346.7304/3 347.30643 19
KF27 .F64214 1980e

United States. Congress. Senate. Committee on Finance. Subcommittee on International Trade. Unpaid claims of U. S. citizens against

Czechoslovakia . Washington , c1980 [i.e. 1981]
iii, 217 p. ; LC Card 81-600978 DDC 342.73/082
  347.30282 19
KF26 .F554 1981

**United States. Clearinghouse on Election
  Administration.** Texas A & M Research
Foundation. Ballot access /. - [Washington]
1978. 4 v. in 1 ;   *NYPL [*XME-9374]*

UNITED STATES - CLIMATE - INDEXES.
United States. Naval Oceanography Command
Detachment, Asheville, N.C. Guide to standard
weather summaries and climatic services /.
[Asheville, N.C.] 1980. ix, 92, 102, [6] p. ;
  LC Card 80-601710 DDC 551.6 19
QC982.5.U6 U53 1980

UNITED STATES - CLIMATE - TABLES.
United States. Naval Oceanography Command
Detachment, Asheville, N.C. Guide to standard
weather summaries and climatic services /.
[Asheville, N.C.] 1980. ix, 92, 102, [6] p. ;
  LC Card 80-601710 DDC 551.6 19
QC982.5.U6 U53 1980

**United States. Climatic Impact Assessment
  Program Office. see United States. Dept. of
  Transportation. Climatic Impact Assessment
  Program Office.**

**United States. Coal, President's Commission on.
  see United States. President's Commission
  on Coal.**

**United States. Coast and Geodetic Survey. Office
  of Standard Weights and Measures. see
  United States. National Bureau of
  Standards.**

United States. Coast Guard.
Air search and rescue : 63 years of aerial
lifesaving : a pictorial history, 1915-1978.
[Washington] : Dept. of Transportation, Coast
Guard, [1978] 43 p. : chiefly ill. ; 22 x 28 cm.
"Prepared by U. S. Coast Guard Fifth District Reserve
Public Affairs Division ... in cooperation with Public
Affairs Division (G-APA) U. S. Coast Guard
Headquarters." "CG-522." LC Card 78-603517
*1. United States. Coast Guard - Search and rescue
operations - History. I. United States. Coast Guard
Reserve. Fifth District. Public Affairs Division. II.
United States. Coast Guard. Public Affairs Division. III.
Title.*
VG53 .U53 1978

Auxiliary uniform, awards, and flag code
manual / Department of Transportation, Coast
Guard. [Washington] : United States Coast
Guard, 1974. 115 p. : ill. ; 23 cm. "CG-404."
*1. United States. Coast Guard - Handbooks, manuals,
etc. 2. United States. Coast Guard - Medals, badges,
decorations, etc. 3. Uniforms, Military. I. Title.*
                     NYPL [JFE 80-1602]

CHRIS. [Washington] : Dept. of Transportation,
Coast Guard, 1974- v. ; 28 cm. Cover title.
Caption title: Chemical hazards response information
system (CG-446) (CHRIS) CONTENTS. - 1. A
condensed guide to chemical hazards.--2. Hazardous
chemical data. LC Card 74-603274
*1. Hazardous substances - Handbooks, manuals, etc. 2.
Chemicals - Safety measures - Handbooks, manuals, etc.
I. Title. II. Title: Chemical hazards response information
system.*
T55.3.H3 U52 1974

UNITED STATES. COAST GUARD.
United States. Congress. Senate. Committee on
Commerce, Science, and Transportation. Coast
Guard authority . Washington , 1980. iii, 104
p. ; LC Card 81-600824 DDC 343.73/0965
  347.303965 19
KF26 .C69 1980x

**UNITED STATES. COAST GUARD -
  APPROPRIATIONS AND
  EXPENDITURES.**
United States. Congress. House. Committee on
Merchant Marine and Fisheries. Subcommittee
on Coast Guard and Navigation. Coast Guard
authorization, reserve, and oversight .
Washington , 1980. v, 363 p. ; LC Card
  80-604079 DDC 353.0072/23674 19
KF27 .M434 1980

United States. Congress. Senate. Committee on
Commerce, Science, and Transportation. Coast
Guard authorizations . Washington , 1980. iii,
59 p. ; LC Card 80-602815 DDC 353.0072/23674
  19
KF26 .C69 1980l

United States. Coast Guard Auxiliary.
Auxiliary bibliography of publications.
[Washington] : Dept. of Transportation, Coast
Guard, 1979. ii, 95 p. ; 23 cm. Cover title. LC
  Card 79-602683
*1. Boats and boating - Bibliography - Catalogs. 2. Boats
and boating - Safety measures - Bibliography - Catalogs.
3. Navigation - Bibliography - Catalogs. I. Title.*
Z7514.B6 U54 1979 VM321

Sailing and seamanship. Washington, D.C. ,
1980. 248 p. in various pagings : ISBN
  0-930028-02-3 (pbk.) : LC Card 81-129619
  DDC 797.1/24 19
GV811 .S253 1980

**UNITED STATES. COAST GUARD -
  HANDBOOKS, MANUALS, ETC.**
United States. Coast Guard. Auxiliary uniform,
awards, and flag code manual /. [Washington] ,
1974. 115 p. :   *NYPL [JFE 80-1602]*

**UNITED STATES. COAST GUARD -
  MEDALS, BADGES, DECORATIONS,
  ETC.**
United States. Coast Guard. Auxiliary uniform,
awards, and flag code manual /. [Washington] ,
1974. 115 p. :   *NYPL [JFE 80-1602]*

**United States. Coast Guard. Public Affairs
  Division.** United States. Coast Guard. Air
search and rescue . [Washington] [1978] 43
p. ; LC Card 78-603517
VG53 .U53 1978

**United States. Coast Guard Reserve. Fifth
  District. Public Affairs Division.** United
States. Coast Guard. Air search and rescue .
[Washington] [1978] 43 p. ; LC Card 78-603517
VG53 .U53 1978

**UNITED STATES. COAST GUARD - SEARCH
  AND RESCUE OPERATIONS -
  HISTORY.**
United States. Coast Guard. Air search and
rescue . [Washington] [1978] 43 p. : LC Card
  78-603517
VG53 .U53 1978

United States code. 1976 ed., supplement III .
United States. Laws, statutes, etc. Washington ,
1980- - v. ;
                *NYPL [*R-Econ. 78-895 Suppl. 3]*

**United States - Coinage. see Coinage - United
  States.**

**United States - Colonies. see United States -
  Insular possessions.**

UNITED STATES - COMMERCE.
Aho, C. Michael, 1949- Assessing the changing
structure of world trade /. Washington, D.C. ,
Springfield, Va. , 1980. 34 [i.e. 82] p. ; LC
  Card 81-600792 DDC 382/.45/000973 19
HF3031 .A59

Aho, C. Michael, 1949- An empirical analysis
of the structure of U. S. manufacturing trade,
1964-1976 /. [Washington, D.C.] [Springfield,
Va. , 1980] 45 p. : LC Card 80-602633 DDC
  382/.0973 19
HD9725 .A63

Bayard, Thomas O. Trends in U. S. trade,
1960-1979 /. Washington, D.C. , Springfield,
Va. , 1980. 48 p. : LC Card 81-600712 DDC
  382/.0973 19
HF3031 .B35

Bowen, Harry. Changes in the international
pattern of factor abundance and the
composition of trade /. Washington, D.C. ,
Springfield, Va. , 1980. 64 p. : LC Card
  81-601296 DDC 382 19
HF1411 .B6685

Mogee, Mary Ellen. Technology and trade .
Washington , 1980. viii, 36 p. ; LC Card
  80-602065 DDC 338/.06 19
HC110.T4 M64

United States. Central Intelligence Agency.
National Foreign Assessment Center. The US
position in world markets. Washington , 1979.
iii, 13 p. : LC Card 79-602644
HF3031 .U54 1979   *NYPL [*XME-9339]*

United States. President's Export Council. The
export imperative . Washington, D.C. , 1980. 2
v. : LC Card 81-600767 DDC 382/.63/0973 19
HF1455 .U475 1980

UNITED STATES - COMMERCE - CHINA.
Trade and employment effects of granting
most-favored-nation status to the People's

Republic of China /. Washington, D.C. ,
Springfield, Va. , 1980. 32 p. in various
pagings ; LC Card 81-600776 DDC 382/.0951/073
  19
HD5710.75.U6 T73

**UNITED STATES - COMMERCE - CHINA -
  CONGRESSES.**
The People's Republic of China and the U. S. .
Atlanta, Ga. [1979] v, 118 p. ; LC Card
  80-622176 DDC 382/.0951/073 19
HF3128 .P46

**UNITED STATES - COMMERCE -
  COMMUNIST COUNTRIES.**
United States. Congress. House. Committee on
Ways and Means. Subcommittee on Trade.
Trader waiver authority extension .
Washington , 1980 [i.e. 1981] v, 310 p. : LC
  Card 81-600854 DDC 382/.0973/01717 19
KF27 .W348 1980j

United States. Congress. Office of Technology
Assessment. Technology and East-West trade.
Washington, D.C. , 1979. viii, 303 p. : LC Card
  79-600203
HF1411 .U615 1979   NYPL [JLF 81-165]

**UNITED STATES - COMMERCE -
  CZECHOSLOVAKIA.**
United States. Congress. Senate. Committee on
Finance. Subcommittee on International Trade.
Unpaid claims of U. S. citizens against
Czechoslovakia . Washington , c1980 [i.e. 1981]
iii, 217 p. : LC Card 81-600978 DDC 342.73/082
  347.30282 19
KF26 .F554 1981

**United States. Commerce, Dept. of. see United
  States. Dept. of Commerce.**

**UNITED STATES - COMMERCE -
  DIRECTORIES.**
United States. Agency for International
Development. Office of Small Business.
Directory of combination export managers.
Washington, 1962. 5 v. LC Card 62-61061
                     NYPL [JLM 80-890]

**UNITED STATES - COMMERCE - EUROPE,
  EASTERN.**
United States. Congress. Senate. Committee on
Governmental Affairs. Permanent Subcommittee
on Investigations. Transfer of technology to the
Soviet bloc . Washington , 1980. iii, 156 p. ;
  LC Card 80-602191 DDC 338.91/73/047 19
KF26 .G674 1980

**UNITED STATES - COMMERCE - EUROPE,
  EASTERN - CONGRESSES.**
US financing of East-West trade ; the political
economy of government credits and the
national interest /. Bloomington , 1975. xiv,
442 p. ; LC Card 79-129495 DDC 382/.63 19
HG3754.U5 U17

**UNITED STATES - COMMERCE -
  EUROPEAN ECONOMIC COMMUNITY
  COUNTRIES.**
Maurer, Alan O. U. S. trade opportunities
resulting from the MTN agreement on tariff
cuts /. Washington, D.C. , 1980. vi, 40 p. ; LC
  Card 81-600731 DDC 382/.0973/04 19
HF3092.8 .M38

**UNITED STATES - COMMERCE -
  HUNGARY.**
U. S.-Hungarian trade relations . [Washington] ,
1979. 64 p. ; LC Card 80-600608 DDC
  341.7/54/0266439073 19
HF3097.5 .U54

UNITED STATES - COMMERCE - JAPAN.
Maurer, Alan O. U. S. trade opportunities
resulting from the MTN agreement on tariff
cuts /. Washington, D.C. , 1980. vi, 40 p. ; LC
  Card 81-600731 DDC 382/.0973/04 19
HF3092.8 .M38

United States. Congress. House. Committee on
Ways and Means. Subcommittee on Trade.
Trade with Japan . Washington , 1980. iv, 230
p. : LC Card 81-600633 DDC 382/.0973/052
KF27 .W348 1980h

United States. Congress. House. Committee on
Ways and Means. Subcommittee on Trade.
United States-Japan Trade Task Force. United
States-Japan trade report /. Washington , 1980.
viii, 92 p. ; LC Card 80-603556 DDC
  382/.0952/073 19
HF3127 .U52 1980

United States. Congress. Senate. Select

411

GOVERNMENT PUBLICATIONS - U.S.: 1981

United States. Commission on Civil Rights - Appropriations and

Committee on Small Business. Impact of non-tariff barriers on the ability of small business to export to Japan . Washington , 1980. iii, 424 p. : LC Card 80-603719 DDC 382/.64 19
KF26.5 .S6 1980r

United States. International Trade Commission. Pipes and tubes of iron or steel from Japan . Washington, D.C. [1980] ii, 29, 37 p. ; LC Card 80-602337 DDC 382/.4567283/0973 19
HF2651.S76 U54 1980a

UNITED STATES - COMMERCE - PERIODICALS.
United States. Bureau of the Census. U. S. exports: Schedule B commodity by country. Washington. *NYPL [JLM 81-161]*

United States. Bureau of the Census. U. S. exports: schedule B commodity groupings, schedule B commodity by county. 1967-77 (incomplete). Washington. 11 v. *NYPL [TLG (U. S. Census Bureau. [Report] FT [no.] 410.)]*

United States. Bureau of the Census. U. S. exports: schedule E commodity groupings, schedule E commodity by country. 1978- [Washington] LC Card 79-640385 *NYPL [JLM 80-677]*

UNITED STATES - COMMERCE - RUSSIA.
United States. Congress. Senate. Committee on Governmental Affairs. Permanent Subcommittee on Investigations. Transfer of technology to the Soviet bloc . Washington , 1980. iii, 156 p. ; LC Card 80-602191 DDC 338.91/73/047 19
KF26 .G674 1980

UNITED STATES - COMMERCE - STATISTICAL SERVICES.
United States. Bureau of the Census. History of the 1977 economic censuses. Washington, D.C. , 1980. vii, 549 p. : LC Card 80-607818 DDC 330.973/0926 19
HF3001 .U54 1980

UNITED STATES - COMMERCE - STATISTICAL SERVICES - LAW AND LEGISLATION.
United States. Congress. Senate. Committee on Governmental Affairs. Shipper's export declarations . Washington , 1980. iii, 149 p. ; LC Card 80-603643 DDC 343.73/0878 347.303878 19
KF26 .G67 1980i

United States - Commerce - Statistics. see United States - Commerce.

UNITED STATES - COMMERCIAL POLICY.
Future developments in the food industry and their implications for the Federal Trade Commission /. [Washington, D.C.?] 1980. i, 163 p. : LC Card 80-604179 DDC 338.1/973 19
HD9006 .F88

United States. Congress. House. Committee on Science and Technology. Technology trade . Washington , 1980. vii, 687 p. : LC Card 80-604020 DDC 338.973 19
KF27 .S39 1980g

United States. Congress. House. Committee on Ways and Means. Subcommittee on Trade. Trade functions authorizations for fiscal year 1981 . Washington , 1980. iii, 177 p. ; LC Card 80-602818 DDC 353.0082/7 19
KF27 .W348 1980

United States. Congress. House. Committee on Ways and Means. Subcommittee on Trade. U. S. trade policy . Washington , 1980. v, 632 p. : LC Card 81-600879 DDC 382/.3/0973 19
KF27 .W348 1980g

United States. Congress. Senate. Committee on Commerce, Science, and Transportation. Service Industries Development Act . Washington , 1981. iii, 137 p. : LC Card 81-600931 DDC 343.73/078 347.30378 19
KF26 .C69 1980 w

United States. Congress. Senate. Committee on Finance. Subcommittee on International Trade. U. S. international trade strategy . Washington , 1980. iii, 494 p. : LC Card 80-603898 DDC 382/.3/0973 19
KF26 .F554 1980e

United States. Congressional Budget Office. Assisting the developing countries . Washington, D.C. [1980] xviii, 126 p. ; LC

Card 80-603389 DDC 338.91/73/01724 19
HC60.U6 C66 1980

United States. President's Export Council. The export imperative . Washington, D.C. , 1980. 2 v. : LC Card 81-600767 DDC 382/.63/0973 19
HF1455 .U475 1980

UNITED STATES - COMMERCIAL POLICY - MATHEMATICAL MODELS - CASE STUDIES.
Morkre, Morris E. The effects of restrictions on United States imports . [Washington, D.C.] [1980] xv, 212 p. : LC Card 80-603259 DDC 382/.5/0973 19
HF1731 .M67

UNITED STATES - COMMERCIAL TREATIES.
Hager, Christine J. Textiles, U. S. trade agreements, imports, and consumption /. Washington, D.C. [1979] iii, 17 p. ; LC Card 80-601609 DDC 382/.45677/00973 19
HD9856 .H33

United States. Commission on Administrative Review. see United States. Congress. House. Commission on Administrative Review.

United States. Commission on Civil Rights. (Old Catalog form: United States. Civil Rights, Commission on)
Age discrimination in federally-assisted programs: hearing before the United States Commission on Civil Rights: hearing held in Denver, Colorado, July 28-29, 1977. [Washington]: The Commission, [1978?] 1 v.; 23 cm. On spine: Hearing on age discrimination, Denver, 1977. Includes index. CONTENTS. - v. 1. Testimony.
1. Age discrimination - United States. 2. Civil rights - United States. I. Title. II. Title: Hearing on age discrimination, Denver, 1977.
NYPL [JLL 80-146]

The age discrimination study : a report of the United States Commission on Civil Rights. [Washington] : The Commission, 1977. v, 112 p. ; 26 cm. Cover title. Includes bibliographical references. LC Card 78-600823
1. Economic assistance, Domestic - United States. 2. Age discrimination - United States. I. Title.
HC110.P63 U47 1977 NYPL [JLF 81-209]

Blaustein, Albert P., 1921- Civil rights U. S. A.. [Washington, D. C., 1964] v, 595 p.: LC Card 64-60745 *NYPL [Sc D 80-371]*

Civil rights issues of Asian and Pacific Americans . [Washington, D.C.] , 1980. xiii, 834, 20 p. ; LC Card 80-602622 DDC 323.1/195/073 19
E184.O6 C58

Civil rights issues of Euro-ethnic Americans in the United States . Washington, D.C. , 1980. vii, 592 p. : LC Card 81-600724 DDC 305.8/4 19
E184.E95 C58

Clearinghouse publication .
(62) Wirtenberg, Jeana. Characters in textbooks . [Washington, D.C.] , 1980. iii, 19 p. ; LC Card 80-602697 DDC 323.4/0973 s 379.1/56 19
KF4755 .A83 no. 62 LB3045.6

Dimas, Nicasio. The tarnished golden door . Washington, D.C. , 1980. ix, 158 p. : LC Card 80-604159 DDC 342.73/082 347.30282 19
KF4819 .D55

Energy and civil rights . Washington, D.C. [1980] xi, 31 p. : LC Card 80-602941 DDC 333.79/0973 19
HD9502.U52 E4485

Federal Bureau of Investigation--Indian reservations police abuse : hearing before the United States Commission on Civil Rights, hearing held in Washington, D.C., May 14, 1979. Washington, D.C. : for sale by the Supt. of Docs., U. S. Govt. Print. Off., [1979] iii, 69 p. ; 23 cm. LC Card 80-601782 DDC 323.1/197/073 19
1. Indians of North America - Civil rights. 2. Indians of North America - Reservations. 3. Indians of North America - Legal status, laws, etc. 4. United States. Federal Bureau of Investigation. 5. Police - United States - Complaints against. I. Title.
E93 .U53 1979

Hearing before the United States Commission on Civil Rights : national Indian civil rights issues : hearing held in Washington, D.C.,

March 19-20, 1979. [Washington] : U. S. G[ovt.] P[rint.] O[ff.], [1979- v. ; 23 cm. Includes index. CONTENTS. - v. 1. Testimony. LC Card 79-604247 DDC 323.1/197/073 19
1. Indians of North America - Civil rights. 2. Indians of North America - Legal status, laws, etc. I. Title. II. Title: National Indian civil rights issues.
E93 .U53 1979a

More hurdles to clear . [Washington, D.C.] [1980] vii, 87 p. : LC Card 80-602854 DDC 796/.01/94 19
KF4755 .A83 no. 63 GV709

Perspectives; the civil rights quarterly. v. 12, no. 1- ; spring 1980- Washingotn.
NYPL [Econ. Div.]

Religious discrimination . [Washington, D.C.] [1980] viii, 541 p. : LC Card 80-602570 DDC 261.7/2/0973 19
BR516 .R37

School desegregation in Tacoma, Washington : a staff report of the U. S. Commission on Civil Rights. Washington, D.C. : The Commission : for sale by the Supt. of Docs., U. S. Govt. Print. Off., [1979] vii, 18 p. ; 26 cm. "May 1979." Includes bibliographical references. LC Card 79-602709 DDC 370.19/342/09797 19
1. School integration - Washington (State) - Tacoma. I. Title.
LC214.23.T3 U54 1979

State advisory committee handbook. Washington, D.C. : U. S. Commission on Civil Rights, 1980. v, 26 p. : ill., forms ; 23 cm. October 1980. Item 288-A LC Card 80-604132 DDC 353.0081/1 19
1. United States. Commission on Civil Rights. 2. Civil rights - United States. I. Title.
JC599.U5 U6 1980

Success of Asian Americans . Washington, D.C. , 1980. vii, 28 p. : LC Card 80-604177 DDC 305.8/95/073 19
E184.O6 S78

United States. Commission on Civil Rights. Alaska Advisory Committee. Changing commitment into action . [Washington] , 1980. ix, 105 p. : LC Card 80-603134 DDC 353.9798001/04 19
HD6096.A4 U54 1980

Western Regional Civil Rights and Women's Rights Conference, 4th, San Francisco, 1977. Recent developments, new opportunities in civil rights and women's rights . - Washington [1977]. vi, 178 p. ; *NYPL [JLE 80-2420]*

UNITED STATES. COMMISSION ON CIVIL RIGHTS.
United States. Commission on Civil Rights. State advisory committee handbook. Washington, D.C. , 1980. v, 26 p. : LC Card 80-604132 DDC 353.0081/1 19
JC599.U5 U6 1980

United States. Commission on Civil Rights. Alaska Advisory Committee. Changing commitment into action : a report of the Alaska Advisory committee to the United States Commission on Civil Rights. [Washington] : The Commission, 1980. ix, 105 p. : maps ; 26 cm. On cover: Employment of women and minorities in Alaska State government. "July 1980." Includes bibliographical references. LC Card 80-603134 DDC 353.9798001/04 19
1. Women - Employment - Alaska. 2. Minorities - Employment - Alaska. 3. Civil serivce - Alaska. I. United States. Commission on Civil Rights. II. Title. III. Title: Empl9yment of women and minorities in Alaska State government.
HD6096.A4 U54 1980

UNITED STATES. COMMISSION ON CIVIL RIGHTS - APPROPRIATIONS AND EXPENDITURES.
United States. Congress. House. Committee on the Judiciary. Subcommittee on Civil and Constitutional Rights. Authorization request of the U. S. Commission on Civil Rights . Washington , 1980. iii, 16 p. : LC Card 80-603033 DDC 353.0072/236811 19
KF27 .J847 1980a

United States. Congress. Senate. Committee on the Judiciary. Subcommittee on the Constitution. U. S. Commission on Civil Rights fiscal year 1981 authorization . Washington , 1980. iii, 69 p. ; LC Card 80-603460 DDC

353.0072/236811 19
KF26 .J835 1980a

United States. Commission on Civil Rights. Arkansas State Advisory Committee. The community development block grant program in Arkansas : a report / prepared by the Arkansas Advisory Committee to the United States Commission on Civil Rights. [Little Rock, Ark.] : The Committee ; [Washington, D.C. : for sale by the Supt. of Docs., U. S. Govt. Print. Off., 1979] v, 37 p. : ill. ; 26 cm. "December 1979." Includes bibliographical references. LC Card 80-601546 DDC 307.7/09767 19
1. Federal aid to community development - Arkansas. 2. Block grants - Arkansas. I. Title.
HN79.A83 C68 1979

United States. Commission on Civil Rights. California Advisory Committee. California State employment : a report / prepared by the California Advisory Committee to the U. S. Commission on Civil Rights. [Washington, D.C.] : The Commission, [1980] ix, 26 p. : graphs ; 27 cm. "July 1980." Includes bibliographical references. LC Card 80-144884 DDC 353.9794001 19
1. California - Officials and employees - Statistics. I. Title.
JK8755 .U54 1980

A study of Federal immigration policies and practices in Southern California : a report / prepared by the California Advisory Committee to the United States Commission on Civil Rights. Washington, D.C. : The Commission : for sale by the Supt. of Docs., U. S. Govt. Print. Off., [1980] ix, 61 p. : graphs ; 26 cm. "June 1980." Includes bibliographical references. LC Card 80-602885 DDC 353.0081/7/097949 19
1. California, Southern - Emigration and immigration. 2. United States - Emigration and immigration. 3. Hispanic Americans - California, Southern. I. Title.
JV6920 .U54 1980

United States. Commission on Civil Rights. Colorado Advisory Committee. Energy and civil rights . Washington, D.C. [1980] xi, 31 p. : LC Card 80-602941 DDC 333.79/0973 19
HD9502.U52 E4485

Energy resource development . Washington, D.C. [1979] xiii, 221 p. : LC Card 79-604168
HD9502.U53 A1713   *NYPL [JLF 81-331]*

United States. Commission on Civil Rights. Hawaii Advisory Committee. Immigration issues in Hawaii : a report of the proceedings of a consultation conducted by the Hawaii Advisory Committee to the United States Commission on Civil Rights in Honolulu, Hawaii, August 25, 1978. [Washington, D.C.] : The Commission : for sale by the Supt. of Docs., U. S. Govt. Print. Off., 1979. v, 113 p. : graphs ; 26 cm. LC Card 79-604007
1. Hawaii - Emigration and immigration. I. Title.
JV6950.5 .U54 1979   *NYPL [JLF 81-284]*

United States. Commission on Civil Rights. Kansas Advisory Committee. Police-community relations in the city of Wichita and Sedgwick County : a report / prepared by the Kansas Advisory Committee to the U. S. Commission on Civil Rights. Washington, D.C. : The Commission, [1980] xi, 95 p. : ill. ; 27 cm. Includes bibliographical references. LC Card 80-603162 DDC 363.2/2/0978186 19
1. Public relations - Police. 2. Police - Kansas - Complaints against. 3. Wichita, Kansas - Police - Complaints against. 4. Sedgwick County, Kansas - Police - Complaints against. 5. Police - Kansas - Recruiting. I. Title.
HV7936.P8 U53 1980

United States. Commission on Civil Rights. South Carolina Advisory Committee. Equality in municipal services in Mullins, South Carolina : a report / prepared by the South Carolina Advisory Committee to the U. S. Commission on Civil Rights. [Washington] : The Commission, 1979. vii, 28 p. : ill. ; 26 cm. Includes bibliographical references. LC Card 79-602150 DDC 363/.09757/86 19
1. Discrimination in municipal services - South Carolina - Mullins. I. Title.
HD4606.M77 U54 1979

United States. Commission on Civil Rights. Washington State Advisory Committee. Equal employment opportunity in Tacoma area local government : a report / prepared by the Washington Advisory Committee to the United States Commission on Civil Rights. [Washington] : The Commission, [1980] vii, 48 p. ; 26 cm. "Written by Fred Kaplan." Includes bibliographical references. LC Card 80-603135 DDC 352/.005104/0979778 19
1. Discrimination in employment - Washington (State) - Tacoma metropolitan area. 2. Tacoma metropolitan area, Wash. - Officials and employees. I. Kaplan, Fred, 1950-. II. Title.
JS1481.4 .A4 1980

United States. Commission on Civil Rights. Western Regional Office. Puerto Ricans in California : a staff report of the Western Regional Office, United States Commission on Civil Rights. [Washington, D.C.] : The Commission : [for sale by the Supt. of Docs., U. S. Govt. Print. Off.], 1980. vii, 19 p. ; 27 cm. Written by P. Montez, with assistance from T. V. Pilla. "January 1980." Includes bibliographical references. LC Card 80-601602 DDC 323.1/1687295/0794 19
1. Puerto Ricans in California - Civil rights. 2. California - Ethnic relations. I. Montez, Philip. II. Pilla, Thomas V. III. Title.
F870.P85 U54 1980

United States. Commission on Coal, President's. see **United States. President's Commission on Coal.**

United States. Commission on Federal Paperwork. Records management in Federal agencies : a report of the Commission on Federal Paperwork. Washington : The Commission : for sale by the Supt. of Docs., U. S. Govt. Print. Off., 1977. 66 p. : ill. ; 23 cm. "Y 3.P 19:2." Includes bibliographical references. LC Card 78-601367
1. Public records - United States. 2. Government paperwork - United States. I. Title.
JK468.P76 U5 1977b   *NYPL [JLE 81-453]*

United States. Commission on Neighborhoods, National. see **United States. National Commission on Neighborhoods.**

United States Commission on Proposals for the National Academy of Peace and Conflict Resolution. Interim report of the U. S. Commission on Proposals for the National Academy of Peace and Conflict Resolution : Public Law 95-561 / prepared for the Committee on Labor and Human Resources, United States Senate. Washington : U. S. G.P.O., 1980. iii, 16, vii p. ; 24 cm. At head of title: 96th Congress, 2d session. Committee print. "October 1980." Item 1043 LC Card 80-604123 DDC 327.1/72/071173 19
1. United States Commission on Proposals for the National Academy of Peace and Conflict Resoultion. 2. Peace. 3. Pacific settlement of international disputes. I. United States. Congress. Senate. Committee on Labor and Human Resources. II. Title.
JX1963 .U14 1980

UNITED STATES COMMISSION ON PROPOSALS FOR THE NATIONAL ACADEMY OF PEACE AND CONFLICT RESOULTION. United States Commission on Proposals for the National Academy of Peace and Conflict Resolution. Interim report of the U. S. Commission on Proposals for the National Academy of Peace and Conflict Resolution . Washington , 1980. iii, 16, vii p. ; LC Card 80-604123 DDC 327.1/72/071173 19
JX1963 .U14 1980

United States. Commission on Security and Cooperation in Europe. United States. Congress. House. Committee on Foreign Affairs. Subcommittee on International Economic Policy and Trade. Review of implementation of Basket II of the Helsinki Final Act . Washington , 1980. iii, 82 p. ; LC Card 80-604051 DDC 337.73047 19
KF27 .F6465 1980d

UNITED STATES. COMMISSION ON THE INTERNATIONAL APPLICATION OF THE UNITED STATES ANTITRUST LAWS. United States. Congress. Senate. Committee on Governmental Affairs. To establish a Commission on the International Application of

Antitrust Laws . Washington , 1980. iii, 187 p. ; LC Card 80-603105 DDC 343.73/072 19
KF26 .G67 1979ap

United States. Commission on the Review of the National Policy toward Gambling. Helsing, Patricia. Gambling, the issues and policy decisions involved in the trend toward legalization . Washington [1976?] 16 p. ; LC Card 77-357575
KF9440 .H44   *NYPL [*XME-9532]*

United States. Commission on Unemployment Compensation, National. see **United States. National Commission on Unemployment Compensation.**

UNITED STATES. COMMISSION ON WARTIME RELOCATION AND INTERNMENT OF CIVILIANS. United States. Congress. House. Committee on the Judiciary. Subcommittee on Administrative Law and Governmental Relations. Commission on Wartime Relocation and Internment of Civilians . Washington , 1980 [i.e. 1981] iii, 179 p. : LC Card 81-600929 DDC 342.73/088 347.30288 19
KF27 .J832 1980h

United States. Congress. Senate. Committee on Governmental Affairs. Commission on wartime relocation and internment of civilians act . Washington , 1980. iv, 365 p. : LC Card 80-602970 DDC 342.73/0873 19
KF26 .G67 1980e

United States. Commissioner of Education. see **United States. Office of Education.**

United States. Commissioner of Indian Affairs. see **United States. Bureau of Indian Affairs.**

United States Committee for the Global Atmospheric Research Program. Understanding climatic change : a program for action / United States Committee for the Global Atmospheric Research Program, National Research Council. Detroit, Mich. : Grand River Books, 1980. xvii, 239 p. : ill. ; 22 cm. Bibliography: p. 236-239. Reprint of the 1975 ed. published by the National Academy of Sciences, Washington. ISBN 0-8103-1019-8 LC Card 79-22423
1. Climatic changes - Research - United States. 2. Global Atmospheric Research Program. I. Title.
QC981.8.C5 U54 1980   *NYPL [JSD 81-49]*

United States Committee on Extension to the Standard Atmosphere. U. S. standard atmosphere, 1976 / [adopted by the United States Committee on Extension to the Standard Atmosphere]. Washington : National Oceanic and Amospheric [sic] Administration : for sale by the Supt. of Docs., U. S. Govt. Print. Off., 1976. xv, 227 p. : graphs ; 30 cm. "Revises and replaces COESA's first report, U. S. extension to the ICAO standard atmosphere, tables and data to 300 standard geopotential kilometers, 1958." Includes bibliographical references. LC Card 77-601158
1. Standard atmosphere. I. Title.
TL557.A8 U55 1976   *NYPL [JSF 81-142]*

United States. Committee on Fair Employment Practice (1941-1943) (Old Catalog form: United States. Fair Employment Practice, Committee on)
Guide to microfilm record of selected documents of records of the Committee on Fair Employment Practice in the custody of the National Archives / Bruce I. Friend. Glen Rock, N. J. : Microfilming Corp. of America, 1970. iii, 131 p. ; 28 cm. Microfilm. Includes bibliographical references.
1. United States. Committee on Fair Employment Practice (1941-1943) - Archives. 2. United States. Committee on Fair Employment Practice (1943-1946) - Archives. 3. United States. National Archives. 4. Discrimination in employment - United States - Bibliography. 5. Documents on microfilm - Catalogs. I. Friend, Bruce I. II. United States. Committee on Fair Employment Practice (1943-1946). III. United States. National Archives and Records Service. IV. Title.
      NYPL [Sc Micro R-3644]

UNITED STATES. COMMITTEE ON FAIR EMPLOYMENT PRACTICE (1941-1943) - ARCHIVES. United States. Committee on Fair Employment Practice (1941-1943) Guide to the microfilm record of selected documents of records of the Committee on Fair Employment Practice in the custody of the National Archives /. Glen Rock,

GOVERNMENT PUBLICATIONS - U.S.: 1981

413

United States. Congress. House. Budget, Committee on the.

N. J. , 1970. iii, 131 p. ;
NYPL [Sc Micro R-3644]

United States. Committee on Fair Employment Practice (1943-1946)
United States. Committee on Fair Employment Practice (1941-1943) Guide to the microfilm record of selected documents of records of the Committee on Fair Employment Practice in the custody of the National Archives /. Glen Rock, N. J. , 1970. iii, 131 p. ;
NYPL [Sc Micro R-3644]

UNITED STATES. COMMITTEE ON FAIR EMPLOYMENT PRACTICE (1943-1946) - ARCHIVES.
United States. Committee on Fair Employment Practice (1941-1943) Guide to the microfilm record of selected documents of records of the Committee on Fair Employment Practice in the custody of the National Archives /. Glen Rock, N. J. , 1970. iii, 131 p. ;
NYPL [Sc Micro R-3644]

United States. Committee on Gross National Product Improvement, Advisory. see United States. Advisory Committee on Gross National Product Data Improvement.

United States. Commodity Futures Trading Commission. Report of the Commodity Futures Trading Commission on recent developments in the silver futures markets [prepared for the] Committee on Agriculture, Nutrition, and Forestry, United States Senate. Washington : U. S. Govt. Print. Off., 1980. viii, 123 p. : ill. ; 24 cm. At head of title: 96th Congress, 2d session. Committee print. "May 1980." Includes bibliographical references. LC Card 80-602270 DDC 332.63/28 19
1. Silver - United States. I. United States. Congress. Senate. Committee on Agriculture, Nutrition, and Forestry. II. Title.
HG307.U5 U54 1980

UNITED STATES. COMMODITY FUTURES TRADING COMMISSION.
United States. Congress. House. Committee on Agriculture. Subcommittee on Conservation and Credit. CFTC regulatory authority review . Washington , 1980. iv, 468 p. : LC Card 80-603726 DDC 353.0082/6 19
KF27 .A3226 1980b

United States. Congress. House. Committee on Government Operations. Commerce, Consumer, and Monetary Affairs Subcommittee. Silver prices and the adequacy of Federal actions in the marketplace, 1979-80 . Washington , 1980. v, 1203 p. : LC Card 80-603499 DDC 332.63/28 19
KF27 .G634 1980c

United States. Congress. Senate. Committee on Agriculture, Nutrition, and Forestry. Subcommittee on Agricultural Research and General Legislation. Oversight on the Commodity Futures Trading Commission . Washington , 1980. iii, 135 p. ; LC Card 80-602999 DDC 332.63/28 19
KF26 .A3534 1980c

United States. Community Planning and Development, Office of. see United States. Office of Community Planning and Development.

UNITED STATES. COMMUNITY RELATIONS SERVICE - APPROPRIATIONS AND EXPENDITURES.
United States. Congress. House. Committee on the Judiciary. Subcommittee on Civil and Constitutional Rights. Authorization request of the Community Relations Service at the Department of Justice . Washington , 1980 [i.e. 1981] iii, 53 p. : LC Card 81-601641 DDC 353.0072/234 19
KF27 .J847 1980d

United States. Community Services Administration.
CSA pamphlet .
(6143-14) Design Alternatives, inc. Poor and without heat . [Washington] , 1979] vi, 55 p. : LC Card 80-601856 DDC 363.5/8 19
HD7293 .D45 1979

Design Alternatives, inc. Poor and without heat . [Washington] , 1979] vi, 55 p. : LC Card 80-601856 DDC 363.5/8 19
HD7293 .D45 1979

Energy education guidebook. [Washington, D.C.] , 1980. xi, 209 p. : LC Card 80-603568 DDC 333.79/07/1 19
TJ163.3 .E544

Virginia. Dept. of Intergovernmental Affairs. Office of Human Resources. An overview of nutrition programs in Virginia /. [Richmond] , 1978. 93, [2] p. ; LC Card 79-621946 DDC 363.8/8/09755 19
HV696.F6 V57 1978

UNITED STATES. COMMUNITY SERVICES ADMINISTRATION.
United States. Congress. House. Committee on Government Operations. Manpower and Housing Subcommittee. Performance of the Community Services Administration . Washington , 1981. iv, 354 p. : LC Card 81-601643 DDC 353.0084 19
KF27 .G6678 1979g

United States. Community Services Administration. Office of the Inspector General. Semi-annual report to the Congress. Oct. 1, 1979/Mar. 31, 1980- Washington. LC Card 80-645132 *NYPL [Econ. Div.]*

UNITED STATES. COMMUNITY SERVICES ADMINISTRATION - OFFICIALS AND EMPLOYEES.
United States. Congress. Senate. Committee on Labor and Human Resources. Nomination . Washington , 1980. ii, 46 p. ; LC Card 80-602975 DDC 353.0084 19
KF26 .L27 1980d

United States. Competition, Bureau of. see United States. Bureau of Competition.

United States. Comptroller General of the United States. see United States. General Accounting Office.

United States. Comptroller of the Army, Office of the. see United States. Office of the Comptroller of the Army.

UNITED STATES. COMPTROLLER OF THE CURRENCY - APPROPRIATIONS AND EXPENDITURES.
United States. Congress. Senate. Committee on Banking, Housing and Urban Affairs. 1980 budgets of the Federal bank regulatory agencies . Washington , 1980. v, 1323 p. ; LC Card 80-601901 DDC 353.0072/236825 19
KF26 .B39 1980e

United States Conference of Mayors. The private development process : a guidebook for local government / prepared for Office of Community Planning and Development and Office of Policy Development and Research, U. S. Department of Housing and Urban Development by U. S. Conference of Mayors, National Community Development Association, Urban Land Institute. [Washington] : The Office of Policy Development and Research, [1979] iii, 49 p. ; 27 cm. "HUD-PDR-352-2." Bibliography: p. 40. LC Card 79-601943
1. Land subdivision - United States. 2. Real estate business - United States. I. National Community Development Association. II. Urban Land Institute. III. United States. Office of Community Planning and Development. IV. United States. Dept. of Housing and Urban Development. Office of Policy Development and Research. V. Title.
HD259 .U53 1979

United States. Congesss. House. Select Committee on Aging. United States. Library of Congress. Congressional Research Service. Federal responsibility to the elderly . Washington , 1979. iii, 16 p. : LC Card 79-600867 DDC 362.6/3/0973 19
HV1461 .U645 1979

UNITED STATES. CONGRESS - APPROPRIATIONS AND EXPENDITURES.
United States. Congress. Senate. Committee on Appropriations. Legislative branch appropriations for fiscal year 1968. Washington., 1967. 281, x p.
NYPL [JLE 81-395]

United States. Congress. Arrangements for the Commemoration of the Bicentennial, Joitnt Committee on. see United States. Congress. Joint Committee on Arrangements for the Commemoration of the Bicentennial.

United States. Congress. Committee on Foreign Affairs. Subcommittee on Europe and the Middle East. East-West relations in the aftermath of Soviet invasion of Afghanistan : hearings before the Subcommittee on Europe and the Middle East of the Committee on Foreign Affairs, House of Representatives, Ninety-sixth Congress, second session ... January 24 and 30, 1980. Washington : U. S. Govt. Print. Off., 1980. iii, 125 p. ; 23 cm. LC Card 80-602490 DDC 327.73047 19
1. United States - Foreign relations - Russia. 2. Russia - Foreign relations - United States. 3. International relations. 4. Afghanistan - History. I. Title.
KF27 .F64214 1980

United States. Congress. Congressional Budget Office. see United States. Congressional Budget Office.

United States. Congress. House. (Old Catalog form: United States. House of Representatives)
Regional stability in northern Africa : report of a study mission to northern Africa, Spain, and Malta, April 4-14, 1980, to the Committee on Foreign Affairs, U. S. House of Representatives, July 8, 1980. Washington : U. S. Govt. Print. Off., 1980. v, 29 p. : map ; 24 cm. At head of title: 96th Congress, 2d session. Committee print. LC Card 80-603274 DDC 327/.096 19
1. Africa, North - Politics and government. I. United States. Congress. House. Committee on Foreign Affairs. II. Title.
DT204 .U48 1980

Report .
(no. 96-1387, v. 1-2) United States. Congress. House. Committee on Standards of Official Conduct. In the matter of Representative Michael J. Myers . [Washington, D.C. , 1980] 2 v. : LC Card 81-601430 DDC 328.73/0766 19
KF32 .S7 1980b

(no. 96-1451) United States. Congress. House. Committee on Small Business. Role of government funding and its impact on small business in the solar energy industry . Washington , 1980. vi, 68 p. : LC Card 80-603851 DDC 338.6/42 19
HD9681.U62 U526 1980

UNITED STATES. CONGRESS. HOUSE.
The House at work /. Austin , 1981. p. cm. ISBN 0-292-73017-9 LC Card 81-2987 DDC 328.73/072 19
JK1319 .H68

United States. Congress. House. Administrative Review, Commission on. see United States. Congress. House. Commission on Administrative Review.

United States. Congress. House. Aging, Select Committee on. see United States. Congress. House. Select Committee on Aging.

United States. Congress. House. Assassinations, Select Committee on. see United States. Congress. House. Select Committee on Assassinations.

United States. Congress. House. Banking, Finance and Urban Affairs, Committee on. see United States. Congress. House. Committee on Banking, Finance and Urban Affairs.

UNITED STATES. CONGRESS. HOUSE - BIOGRAPHY - ADDRESSES, ESSAYS, LECTURES.
United States. 96th Congress, 1st session, 1979. Memorial services held in the House of Representatives and Senate of the United States, together with remarks presented in eulogy of Leo J. Ryan, a late Representative from California /. Washington , 1979. vii, 88 p., [1] leaf of plates : LC Card 79-603246
E840.8.R88 U5 1979   *NYPL [JFE 81-694]*

United States. 96th Congress, 2d session, 1980. Memorial services held in the House of Representatives and Senate of the United States, together with remarks presented in eulogy of John M. Slack, late a Representative from West Virginia /. Washington , 1980. vii, 69 p., [1] leaf of plates : LC Card 80-603140 DDC 328.73/092/4 19
E840.8.S55 U54 1980

United States. Congress. House. Budget, Committee on the. see United States. Congress. House. Committee on the Budget.

United States. Congress. House. Commerce, Consumer, and Monetary Affairs Subcommittee. see United States. Congress. House. Committee on Government Operations. Commerce, Consumer, and Monetary Affairs Subcommittee.

United States. Congress. House. Commission on Administrative Review. Final report of the Commission on Administrative Review : communication from the chairman, Commission on Administrative Review, U. S. House of Representatives, transmitting a final report pursuant to section 5 of House Resolution 1368, 94th Congress. Washington : U. S.G.P.O. : For sale by the Supt. of Docs., U. S.G.P.O., 1977. 2 v. (iii, 1389 p.) : ill. ; 24 cm. (House report / 95th Congress, 1st session . no. 95-272) CONTENTS. - v. 1. Work of the commission--Survey materials. LC Card 81-600558 DDC 328.73/072/068 19
1. United States. Congress. House - Management. 2. United States. Congress. House - Officials and employees. I. Series: House document (United States. Congress. House) , no. 95-272. II. Title.
JK1433 .U54 1977

United States. Congress. House. Commitee on Government Operations. Commerce, Consumer, and Monetary Affairs Subcommittee. IRS' administration of the tax laws (income information document matching) : hearing before a subcommittee of the Committee on Government Operations, House of Representatives, Ninety-sixt Congress, second session, October 1, 1980. Washington : U. S. G.P.O., 1980. iii, 178 p. : ill. ; 24 cm. LC Card 81-600661 DDC 353.00072/4 19
1. United States. Internal Revenue Service. 2. Tax returns - United States. 3. Tax collection - United States. 4. Tax administration and procedure - United States. I. Title.
KF27 .G634 1980f

United States. Congress. House. Commitee on House Administration. National publications act of 1980 : report / by the Committee on House Administration of the U. S. House of Representatives, together with minority, additional, and supplemental views. Washington : U. S. Govt. Print. Off., 1980. iv, 179 p. ; 23 cm. At head of title: 96th Congress, 2d session. House report no. 96-836, pt. 1. "March 19, 1980." LC Card 80-601753 DDC 343.73/0998 19
1. Printing, Public - United States. 2. United States - Government publications. I. Title.
KF32 .H6 1980

United States. Congress. House. Commitee on the Judiciary. Subcommittee on Civil and Constitutional Rights. FBI oversight : hearings before the Subcommittee on Civil and Constitutional Rights of the Committee on the Judiciary, House of Representatives, Ninety-sixth Congress, first and second session .... Washington : U. S. G.P.O., 1980. iii, 256 p. : ill. ; 24 cm. Hearings held Mar. 8, 1979-Mar. 17, 1980. "Serial no. 46." LC Card 80-604016 DDC 353.0074 19
1. United States. Federal Bureau of Investigation. I. Title.
KF27 .J847 1979f

United States. Congress. House. Committee on Agriculture. (Old Catalog form: United States. Agriculture, Committee on (House)) // Hearings printed in 1978 and later are available only in microform. Please consult the librarians in the Economic and Public Affairs Division.
Business meetings on U. S. grain standards act of 1976, H.R. 12572 ... Public law 94-582 / Committee on Agriculture, U. S. House of Representatives, Ninety-fourth Congress, second session. Washington : U. S. Govt. Print. Off., 1976. iii, 482 p. ; 23 cm. At head of title: 94th Congress, 2d session. Committee print. On spine: U. S. grain standards act of 1976. Meetings held Oct. 30, 1975-Mar. 17, 1976. LC Card 77-604290
1. Grain trade - Law and legislation - United States. I. Title.
KF27 .A3 1975h **NYPL [JLE 81-482]**

Financial problems facing American agriculture : hearings before the Committee on Agriculture, House of Representatives, Ninety-sixth Congress, second session, April 29, 30, and May 1, 1980. Washington : U. S. Govt. Print. Off., 1980. iv, 309 p. : graphs ; 24 cm.

"Serial no. 96-DDD." LC Card 80-603027 DDC 338.1/0973 19
1. Agricultural credit - United States. 2. Agriculture - Economic aspects - United States. I. Title.
KF27 .A3 1980a

Miscellaneous : hearings before the Committee on Agriculture, House of Representatives, Ninety-sixth Congress .... Washington : U. S. G.P.O., 1980. v, 69 p. ; 24 cm. "Serial no. 96-YYY." Hearings held: Apr. 25, 1979-Sept. 10, 1980 on H.R. 998, 1573, 3015, 3575, 5528, and S. 41. LC Card 80-603820 DDC 343.73/076 347.30376 19
1. Agricultural laws and legislation - United States. I. Title.
KF27 .A3 1979c

Recent developments pertaining to grain embargo : hearing before the Committee on Agriculture, House of Representatives, Ninety-sixth Congress, second session, June 25, 1980. Washington : U. S. Govt. Print. Off., 1980. iii, 44 p. ; 23 cm. "Serial. no. 96-KKK." LC Card 80-603662 DDC 382/.4131/0973 19
1. Grain trade - United States. 2. Grain trade - Russia. 3. United States - Foreign relations - Russia. 4. Russia - Foreign relations - United States. I. Title.
KF27 .A3 1980b

Review of Agricultural trade act of 1978 : joint hearing before the Committee on Agriculture and the Committee on Foreign Affairs, House of Representatives, Ninety-sixth Congress, first session, November 15, 1979. Washington : U. S. Govt. Print. Off., 1980. iii, 42 p. ; 24 cm. "Serial no. 96-II." LC Card 80-602236 DDC 343.73/0851/0262 19
1. Farm produce - United States - Marketing. 2. Export sales - United States. I. United States. Congress. House. Committee on Foreign Affairs. II. Title.
KF27 .A3 1979b

Suspension of grain shipments to the Soviet Union : hearing before the Committee on Agriculture, House of Representatives, Ninety-sixth Congress, second session, January 29, 1980. Washington : U. S. Govt. Print. Off., 1980. iii, 127 p. : graphs ; 23 cm. "Serial no. 96-QQ." LC Card 80-602450 DDC 382/.4131/0973 19
1. Grain trade - United States. 2. Grain trade - Russia. I. Title.
KF27 .A3 1980

United States. Congress. House. Committee on Science and Technology. Alcohol fuels . Washington , 1980 [i.e. 1981] v, 105 p. : LC Card 81-601361 DDC 338.4/7662669 19
KF27 .S39 1980h

United States. Dept. of Agriculture. Foreign meat inspection. Washington. LC Card 79-640123 **NYPL [JLM 80-791]**

USDA/FDA announcement on nitrites and related issues : hearing before the Committee on Agriculture, House of Representatives, Ninety-sixth Congress, second session, September 16, 1980. Washington : U. S. G.P.O., 1980. iv, 221 p. : ill. ; 1980. "Serial no. 96-VVV." Item 1010 Includes bibliographical references. LC Card 81-600861 DDC 363.1/92 19
1. Nitrites - Toxicology. 2. Food adulteration and inspection - United States. I. Title.
KF27 .A3 1980c

United States. Congress. House. Committee on Agriculture. Department Investigations, Oversight, and Research, Subcommittee on. see United States. Congress. House. Committee on Agriculture. Subcommittee on Department Investigations, Oversight, and Research.

United States. Congress. House. Committee on Agriculture. Subcommittee on Conservation and Credit.
CFTC regulatory authority review : hearings before the Subcommittee on Conservation and Credit of the Committee on Agriculture, House of Representatives, Ninety-sixth Congress, second session, February 12, May 21, 22, and 29, 1980. Washington : U. S. Govt. Print. Off., 1980. iv, 468 p. : ill. ; 24 cm. "Serial no. 96-RR." LC Card 80-603726 DDC 353.0082/6 19
1. United States. Commodity Futures Trading Commission. 2. Commodity exchanges - Law and legislation - United States. I. Title.
KF27 .A3226 1980b

Increases in electric rates in rural areas : hearing before the Subcommittee on

Conservation and Credit of the Committee on Agriculture, House of Representatives, Ninety-sixth Congress, second session, June 4, 1980. Washington : U. S. Govt. Print. Off., 1980. iii, 222 p. : ill. ; 24 cm. "Serial no. 96-HHH." LC Card 80-603462 DDC 338.4/336362 19
1. Electric utilities - United States - Rates. 2. Rural electrification - United States. I. Title.
KF27 .A3226 1980

Rural home weatherization and energy conservation : hearing before the Subcommittee on Conservation and Credit of the Committee on Agriculture, House of Representatives, Ninety-sixth Congress, second session, March 19, 1980. Washington : U. S. Govt. Print. Off., 1980. iii, 181 p. ; 24 cm. "Serial no. 96-XX." LC Card 80-602803 DDC 696 19
1. Dwellings - United States - Energy conservation. 2. Housing, Rural - United States. 3. Energy conservation - United States. 4. Rural electrification - United States. I. Title.
KF27 .A3226 1980a

Special Areas Soil Conservation Act of 1980 : hearing before the Subcommittee on Conservation and Credit of the Committee on Agriculture, House of Representatives, Ninety-sixth Congress, second session, H.R. 6732, September 27, 1980, Crescent, Iowa. Washington : U. S. G.P.O., 1980. iv, 105 p. : ill. ; 24 cm. "Serial No. 96-AAAA." Includes bibliographical references. LC Card 81-600625 DDC 346.7304/67316/0262 347.3064673160262 19
1. Soil conservation - Law and legislation - United States. 2. Soil conservation - Iowa. I. Title.
KF27 .A3226 1980d

United States. Congress. House. Committee on Agriculture. Subcommittee on Cotton. Cotton research and promotion program : hearings before the Subcommittee on Cotton of the Committee on Agriculture, House of Representatives, Ninety-sixth Congress, second session, February 26 and 27, 1980. Washington : U. S. Govt. Print. Off., 1980. v, 519 p. : graphs ; 24 cm. "Serial no. 96-WW." Includes bibliographical references. LC Card 80-602949 DDC 338.1/7351/0973 19
1. Cotton trade - United States. 2. Cotton research - United States. I. Title.
KF27 .A3228 1980

United States. Congress. House. Committee on Agriculture. Subcommittee on Dairy and Poultry. Agriculture problems in Hawaii : hearing before the Subcommittee on Dairy and Poultry of the Committee on Agriculture, House of Representatives, Ninety-sixth Congress, second session, January 10, 1980, Honolulu, Hawaii. Washington : U. S. Govt. Print. Off., 1980. iii, 43 p. ; 24 cm. "Serial no. 96-ZZ." LC Card 80-602754 DDC 338.1/09969 19
1. Agriculture - Hawaii. 2. Agriculture and state - Hawaii. I. Title.
KF27 .A3326 1980

United States. Congress. House. Committee on Agriculture. Subcommittee on Department Investigations, Oversight, and Research. Animal Cancer Research Act : hearings before the Subcommittee on Department Investigations, Oversight, and Research of the Committee on Agriculture, House of Representatives, Ninety-sixth Congress, second session, on S. 2043, August 20 and September 4, 1980. Washington : U. S. G.P.O., 1980. iv, 101 p. ; 24 cm. "Serial no. 96-TTT." LC Card 80-604025 DDC 344.73/0436994 347.304436994 19
1. Cancer - Law and legislation - United States. 2. Veterinary oncology. 3. Cancer - Animal models. I. Title.
KF27 .A33265 1980c

Animal damage control act of 1980 : hearings before the Subcommittee on Department Investigations, Oversight, and Research of the Committee on Agriculture, House of Representatives, Ninety-sixth Congress, second session, on H.R. 6725 and similar bills, April 16 and 17, 1980. Washington : U. S. Govt. Print. Off., 1980. iv, 305 p. ; 24 cm. "Serial no 96-BBB." LC Card 80-602972 DDC 343.73/0766083 19
1. Predator control - Law and legislation - United States. I. Title.
KF27 .A33265 1980

Extension of Federal insecticide, fungicide, and

rodenticide act : hearings before the Subcommittee on Department Investigations, Oversight, and Research of the Committee on Agriculture, House of Representatives, Ninety-sixth Congress, second session, on H.R. 7018, April 15 and May 1, 1980. Washington : U. S. Govt. Print. Off., 1980. iii, 209 p. ; 24 cm. "Serial no. 96-EEE." LC Card 80-603325 DDC 344.73/04633 19

1. Pesticides - Law and legislation - United States. I. Title.

KF27 .A33265 1980a

Grants for certain purposes to 1890 land-grant colleges : hearing before the Subcommittee on Department Investigations, Oversight, and Research of the Committee on Agriculture, House of Representatives, Ninety-sixth Congress, second session, on H.R. 7557 and H.R. 7757, July 29, 1980. Washington : U. S. G.P.O., 1980. iii, 40 p. ; 24 cm. "Serial no. 96-SSS." LC Card 80-604033 DDC 344.73/076 347.30476 19

1. State universities and colleges - Law and legislation - United States. 2. Federal aid to higher education - United States. I. Title.

KF27 .A33265 1980d

Plant variety protection act amendments : hearings before the Subcommittee on Department Investigations Oversight, and Research of the Committee on Agriculture, House of Representatives, Ninety-sixth Congress, first and second sessions, on H.R. 999, July 19, 1979, and April 22, 1980. Washington : U. S. Govt. Print. Off., 1980. v, 330 p. ; 24 cm. "Serial no. 96-CCC." Includes bibliographical references. LC Card 80-603003 DDC 346.7304/86 19

1. Plants - Patents. 2. Plants, Cultivated - Varieties - Law and legislation - United States. I. Title.

KF27 .A33265 1979e

Review of energy situation pertaining to agriculture : hearing before the Subcommittee on Department Investigations, Oversight, and Research of the Committee on Agriculture, House of Representatives, Ninety-sixth Congress, first session, March 29, 1979. Washington : U. S. Govt. Print. Off., 1980. iii, 36 p. ; 24 cm. "Serial no. 96-NNN." LC Card 80-603351 DDC 333.79 19

1. Agriculture - United States - Energy consumption. I. Title.

KF27 .A33265 1979f

Swine health protection act : hearing before the Subcommittee on Department Investigations, Oversight, and Research of the Committee on Agriculture, House of Representatives, Ninety-sixth Congress, second session, on H.R. 6593, July 1, 1980. Washington : U. S. Govt. Print. Off., 1980. iii, 59 p. ; 24 cm. "Serial no. 96-000." LC Card 80-603521 DDC 344.73/043 347.30443 19

1. Swine - Feeding and feeds - Law and legislation - United States. 2. Garbage as feed - Law and legislation - United States. 3. African swine flu. I. Title.

KF27 .A33265 1980b

United States. Congress. House. Committee on Agriculture. Subcommittee on Domestic Marketing, Consumer Relations, and Nutrition.
United States. Congress. House. Committee on Agriculture. Subcommittee on Domestic Marketing, Consumer Relations, and Nutritions. Agricultural Bargaining Act : hearings before the Subcommittee on Domestic Marketing, Consumer Relations, and Nutrition of the Committee on Agriculture, House of Representatives, Ninety-sixth Congress, first and second sessions, on H.R. 3535, July 10 and 11, 1979, Washington, D.C., and April 18, 1980 Sacramento, Calif. Washington : U. S. G.P.O., 1980. vi, 464 p. ; 24 cm. "Serial no. 96-UUU." Includes bibliographical references. LC Card 80-604049 DDC 343.73/0851/0262 347.3038510262 19

1. Cooperative marketing of farm produce - Law and legislation - United States. 2. Produce trade - Law and legislation - United States. I. Title.

KF27 .A3336 1979c

Expanded food and nutrition education program (Los Angeles, Calif.) : hearing before the Subcommittee on Domestic Marketing, Consumer Relations, and Nutrition of the Committee on Agriculture, House of

Representatives, Ninety-sixth Congress, second session, April 21, 1980, Los Angeles, Calif. Washington : U. S. G.P.O., 1980. iii, 106 p. ; 24 cm. "Serial no. 96-RRR." LC Card 80-604023 DDC 362.1/9639 19

1. Expanded Food and Nutrition Program. 2. Nutrition - Study and teaching - California. I. Title.

KF27 .A3336 1980a

Marketing orders for walnuts and olives and Freestone Peach Research and Education Act : hearing before the Subcommittee on Domestic Marketing, Consumer Relations, and Nutrition of the Committee on Agriculture, House of Representatives, Ninety-sixth Congress, second session, on H.R. 3765, H.R. 4710, and H.R. 1916, July 30, 1980. Washington : U. S. G.P.O., 1980. iii, 74 p. ; 24 cm. "Serial no. 96-QQQ." LC Card 80-604106 DDC 343.73/08514/0262 347.30385140262 19

1. Peach - Law and legislation - United States. 2. Olive - Marketing - Law and legislation - United States. 3. Walnut - Marketing - Law and legislation - United States. I. Title.

KF27 .A3336 1980b

National Academy of Sciences report on healthful diets : hearings before the Subcommittee on Domestic Marketing, Consumer Relations, and Nutrition of the Committee on Agriculture, House of Representatives, Ninety-sixth Congress, second session, June 18 and 19, 1980. Washington : U. S. Govt. Print. Off., 1980. iii, 312 p. ; 23 cm. "Serial no. 96-JJJ." Includes bibliographical references. LC Card 80-603777 DDC 613.2 19

1. Diet - United States. 2. Diet in disease. 3. National Research Council. Food and Nutrition Board. I. Title.

KF27 .A3336 1980

United States. Congress. House. Committee on Agriculture. Subcommittee on Family Farms, Rural Development, and Special Studies.
Absentee ownership of farmland : hearing before the Subcommittee on Family Farms, Rural Development, and Special Studies of the Committee on Agriculture, House of Representatives, Ninety-sixth Congress, second session, September 22, 1980, Sioux City, Iowa. Washington : U. S. G.P.O., 1980. iii, 91 p. ; 24 cm. "Serial no. 96-XXX." LC Card 80-604113 DDC 338.1/0973 19

1. Farm corporations - United States. 2. Farms - United States - Foreign ownership. 3. Family farms - United States. I. Title.

KF27 .A344 1980d

Agricultural subterminal facilities act of 1979 and Rural Transportation Advisory Task Force report : hearing before the Subcommittee on Family Farms, Rural Development, and Special Studies of the Committee on Agriculture, House of Representatives, Ninety-sixth Congress, second session, on H.R. 2968, April 23, 1980. Washington : U. S. Govt. Print. Off., 1980. iii, 89 p. : ill. ; 24 cm. "Serial no. 96-GGG." LC Card 80-603304 DDC 343.73/0851 19

1. Farm produce - Storage - Law and legislation - United States. 2. Farm produce - Transportation - Law and legislation - United States. 3. United States. Rural Transportation Advisory Task Force. 4. Farm produce - United States - Transportation. 5. Railroads - United States - Freight. I. Title.

KF27 .A344 1980

Review of GAO preliminary study of parity : hearing before the Subcommittee on Family Farms, Rural Development, and Special Studies of the Committee on Agriculture, House of Representatives, Ninety-sixth Congress, second session, September 18, 1980. Washington : U. S. G.P.O., 1980. iii, 119 p. : ill. ; 24 cm. "Serial no. 96-WWW." Includes bibliographical references. LC Card 80-603990 DDC 338.1/8 19

1. Agricultural price supports - United States. 2. Agricultural prices - United States. 3. Farm income - United States. I. Title.

KF27 .A344 1980c

Small and medium-sized family farms and Presidential Commission on World Hunger report : hearing before the Subcommittee on Family Farms, Rural Development, and Special Studies of the Committee on Agriculture, House of Representatives, Ninety-sixth Congress, second session, June 25, 1980. Washington : U. S. Govt. Print. Off., 1980. iii, 167 p. ; 23 cm. "Serial no. 96-III." "Overcoming world hunger: the challenge ahead. Report of the

Presidential Commission on World Hunger, an abridged version": p. 113-167. LC Card 80-603660 DDC 338.1/9 19

1. Family farms - United States. 2. Food supply - United States. 3. Food supply. 4. Hunger. I. United States. Presidential Commission on World Hunger. Overcoming world hunger. 1980. II. Title.

KF27 .A344 1980b

United States. Congress. House. Committee on Agriculture. Subcommittee on Forests.
Miscellaneous forests : hearings before the Subcommittee on Forests of the Committee on Agriculture, House of Representatives, Ninety-sixth Congress, second session, on H.R. 3559 ... August 26, 1980, and H.R. 5236 ... September 10, 1980, H.R. 6257 ... September 10, 1980, H.R. 7838 ... September 10, 1980. Washington : U. S. G.P.O., 1980. iv, 91 p. : ill. ; 24 cm. "Serial no. 96-ZZZ." LC Card 81-600654 DDC 346.7304/675/0262 347.30646750262 19

1. Forest reserves - United States. I. Title.

KF27 .A348 1980b

Phenoxy herbicides in forest management : efficacy and environmental effects : hearing before the Subcommittee on Forests of the Committee on Agriculture, House of Representatives, Ninety-sixth Congress, second session, January 3, 1980, Eugene, Oreg. Washington : U. S. Govt. Print. Off., 1980. iii, 152 p. : ill. ; 23 cm. "Serial no. 96-AAA." LC Card 80-602796 DDC 333.75/16/0978 19

1. Forests and forestry - Weed control - United States. 2. Phenoxy groups. 3. Plants, Effect of herbicides on. 4. Forests and forestry - Weed control - Oregon. I. Title.

KF27 .A348 1980

Resources planning act assessment and Domestic timber supply act : hearings before the Subcommittee on Forests of the Committee on Agriculture, House of Representatives, Ninety-sixth Congress, second session, on H.R. 7255, May 6 and 7, 1980. Washington : U. S. Govt. Print. Off., 1980. iv, 210 p. : ill. ; 24 cm. "Serial no. 96-MMM." LC Card 80-603793 DDC 346.7304/675 347.3064675 19

1. Forestry law and legislation - United States. 2. Forest policy - United States. 3. Lumber trade - United States. I. Title.

KF27 .A348 1980a

Wood residue utilization act : hearings before the Subcommittee on Forests of the Committee on Agriculture, House of Representatives, Ninety-sixth Congress, first and second sessions ... Sept. 12 and Nov. 15, 1979, and Mar. 11, 1980. Washington : U. S. Govt. Print. Off., 1980. iv, 226 p. ; 24 cm. Hearings on H.R. 4313, 5220, 5397, 5428, and 6755. "Serial no. 96-YY." LC Card 80-602766 DDC 346.7304/67513 19

1. Wood waste - Law and legislation - United States. I. Title.

KF27 .A348 1979b

1980 RPA program and policy statement : hearing before the Subcommittee on Forests of the Committee on Agriculture, House of Representatives, Ninety-sixth Congress, second session, November 20, 1980. Washington : U. S. G.P.O., 1980 [i.e. 1981] iv, 234 p. : ill. ; 24 cm. "Serial no. 96-CCCC." Item 1010 LC Card 81-601149 DDC 333.75/0973 19

1. Forest policy - United States. 2. Renewable natural resources - Government policy - United States. I. Title.

KF27 .A348 1980c

United States. Congress. House. Committee on Agriculture. Subcommittee on Livestock and Grains. Imported meat inspection and labeling : hearing before the Subcommittee on Livestock and Grains of the Committee on Agriculture, House of Representatives, Ninety-sixth Congress, second session, on H.R. 5395 and H.R. 1998, June 24, 1980. Washington : U. S. Govt. Print. Off., 1980. iv, 178 p. : graphs ; 23 cm. "Serial no. 96-LLL." LC Card 80-603441 DDC 343.73/08756649 19

1. Meat inspection - United States. 2. Meat - Labeling - Law and legislation - United States. I. Title.

KF27 .A365 1980a

United States. Congress. House. Committee on Agriculture. Subcommittee on Oilseeds and Rice.
Loan eligibility for 1979 soybean crop : hearing before the Subcommittee on Oilseeds and Rice of the Committee on Agriculture, House of Representatives, Ninety-sixth Congress, second

session, on H.R. 7142, May 13, 1980.
Washington : U. S. Govt. Print. Off., 1980. iii,
26 p. ; 24 cm. "Serial no. 96-FFF." LC Card
80-603101   DDC 343.73/076334 19
*1. Agricultural price supports - United States. 2.
Soybean - United States. I. Title.*
KF27 .A367 1980a

Soybean crop losses to natural disasters :
hearing before the Subcommittee on Oilseeds
and Rice of the Committee on Agriculture,
House of Representatives, Ninety-sixth
Congress, second session, on H.R. 7796 and
H.R. 7813, October 8, 1980, Portaseville, Mo.
Washington : U. S. G.P.O., 1980 [i.e. 1981] iii,
29 p. ; 24 cm. "Serial no. 96-BBBB." Item 1010 LC
Card 81-600857   DDC 343.73/07633491
347.3037633491 19
*1. Soybean - Law and legislation - United States. 2.
Disaster relief - United States. 3. Soybean - Losses -
Missouri. I. Title.*
KF27 .A367 1980b

1980 support price for peanuts : hearing before
the Subcommittee on Oilseeds and Rice of the
Committee on Agriculture, House of
Representatives, Ninety-sixth Congress, second
session, January 30, 1980. Washington : U. S.
Govt. Print. Off., 1980. iii, 70 p. ; 24 cm. "Serial
no. 96-NN." LC Card 80-601929   DDC 338.1/8 19
*1. Peanuts - United States. 2. Agricultural price
supports - United States. I. Title.*
KF27 .A367 1980

**United States. Congress. House. Committee on
Appropriations.** (Old Catalog form: United
States. Appropriations, Committee on //
Hearings printed in 1978 and later are
available only in microform. Please consult
the librarians in the Economic and Public
Affairs Division.
An Analysis of President Carter's budgetary
proposals for fiscal year 1982 /. [Washington,
D.C.] , 1981. xix, 167 p ; LC Card 81-601303
DDC 353.0072/225 19
HJ2051 .A778

The federal budget for 1982 : hearings before
the Committee on Appropriations, House of
Representatives, Ninety-seventh Congress, first
session. Washington : U. S. G.P.O., 1981. ii,
242, ii p. : ill. ; 24 cm. Includes index. LC Card
81-601891   DDC 353.0072/22 19
*1. Budget - United States. 2. United States -
Appropriations and expenditures. I. Title.*
KF27 .A6 1981

Supplemental appropriation and rescission bill,
1981 : hearings before subcommittees of the
Committee on Appropriations, House of
Representatives, Ninety-seventh Congress, first
session. Washington : U. S. G.P.O., 1981- v.
<1, 3-4 > : ill. ; 24 cm. Includes indexes. Item
1011, 1011-A (microfiche) CONTENTS. - pt. 1.
Treasury, Postal Service, and general government ... --
pt. 3. Departments of Labor, Health and Human
Services, Education, and related agencies -- pt. 4.
Department of Defense ... LC Card 81-601881   DDC
353.0072/236 19
*1. United States - Appropriations and expenditures,
1981. I. Title.*
KF27 .A6 1981a

United States. General Accounting Office.
Correct balance of Defense's foreign military
sales trust fund unknown . Washington, DC
[1980] iii, 23 p. ; LC Card 80-602832   DDC
355/.032/0973 19
UA12 .U527 1980

**United States. Congress. House. Committee on
Appropriations. Subcommittee on
Departments of Labor, and Health,
Education, and Welfare, and Related
Agencies.**
Departments of Labor and Health, Education,
and Welfare, and Related Agencies
appropriations for 1981 : hearing before a
subcommittee of the Committee on
Appropriations, House of Representatives,
Ninety-sixth Congress, second session /
Subcommittee on the Departments of Labor,
Health, Education, and Welfare, and Related
Agencies. Washington : U. S. Govt. Print. Off.,
1979. ii, 55, i p. ; 24 cm. "Social Security
Administration. Home energy assistance program": p.
43-55. LC Card 80-602536   DDC
353.0072/23682/56 19
*1. United States. Social Security Administration -
Appropriations and expenditures. 2. Aged - United*

States - Energy assistance. 3. Poor - United States -
Energy assistance. I. Title.
KF27 .A652 1980a

Equal employment opportunity for hispanics
within the Federal Government, San Francisco,
Calif., November 3, 1979 : hearing before a
subcommittee of the Committee on
Appropriations, House of Representatives,
Ninety-sixth Congress, second session /
Subcommittee on the Departments of Labor
and Health, Education, and Welfare, and
Related Agencies. Washington : U. S. Govt.
Print. Off., 1980. ii, 185, i p ; 23 cm. LC Card
80-601974   DDC 331.6/3/68073 19
*1. Hispanic Americans - Employment - California. 2.
Civil service - United States. I. Title.*
KF27 .A652 1979c

United States. Congress. Senate. Committee on
Labor and Human Resources. Subcommittee on
Aging. Impact of Alzheimer's disease on the
nation's elderly . Washington , 1980 [i.e. 1981]
vi, 199 p. ; LC Card 81-601182   DDC
362.1/989768983 19
KF26 .L2716 1980

**United States. Congress. House. Committee on
Appropriations. Subcommittee on Dept. of
the Interior and Related Agencies.**
Department of the Interior and related agencies
appropriations for 1982 : hearings before a
subcommittee of the Committee on
Appropriations, House of Representatives,
Ninety-seventh Congress, first session /
Subcommittee on the Department of the
Interior and Related Agencies. Washington : U.
S. G.P.O., 1981. 4 v. : ill. ; 24 cm. Includes
index. Item 1011, 1011-A (microfiche) CONTENTS. -
pt. 1-3. Justification of the budget estimates -- pt. 4.
Testimony of public witnesses. LC Card 81-601601
DDC 353.0072/2368232 19
*1. United States. Dept. of the Interior - Appropriations
and expenditures. 2. United States - Appropriations and
expenditures, 1982. I. Title.*
KF27 .A6484 1981

**United States. Congress. House. Committee on
Appropriations. Subcommittee on Dept. of
Transportation and Related Agencies
Appropriations.** Department of transportation
and related agencies appropriations for 1982 :
hearings before a subcommittee of the
Committee on Appropriations, House of
Representatives, Ninety-seventh Cogress, first
session / Subcommittee on the Department of
transportation and Related Agencies
Appropriations. Washington : U. S. G.P.O.,
1981- v. <1-3> ; 24 cm. Item Y
4.Ap6/1:T68/4/982/pt. 1- CONTENTS. - pt. 1-2. 1982
Budget justifications. LC Card 81-601415   DDC
353.0072/236875 19
*1. United States. Dept. of Transportation -
Appropriations and expenditures. 2. United States -
Appropriations and expenditures, 1982. I. Title. II.
Title: 1982 Budget justifications.*
KF27 .A667 1981

**United States. Congress. House. Committee on
Appropriations. Subcommittee on Energy
and Water Development.**
Energy and water development appropriations
for 1982 : hearings before a subcommittee of
the Committee on Appropriations, House of
Representatives, Ninety-seventh Congress, first
session / Subcommittee on Energy and Water
Development. Washington : U. S. G.P.O., 1981.
2 v. (2710, xviii p.) ; 24 cm. Includes indexes.
Item 1011, 1011-A (microfiche)   LC Card 81-601647
DDC 353.0072/236823 19
*1. Water resources development - United States -
Finance. 2. Power resources - United States - Finance.
3. United States - Appropriations and expenditures,
1982. I. Title.*
KF27 .A64 1981

Energy and water development supplemental
appropriations for 1981 : hearings before a
subcommittee of the Committee on
Appropriations, House of Representatives,
Ninety-sixth Congress, second session :
Department of Energy, atomic energy defense
activities, nuclear materials production /
Subcommittee on Energy and Water
Development. Washington : U. S. G.P.O., 1980.
ii, 60 p. : ill. ; 24 cm. LC Card 80-603978   DDC
353.0072/23687 19
*1. Atomic energy - United States - Finance. 2. United
States. Dept. of Energy - Appropriations and*

expenditures. 3. United States - Appropriations and
expenditures, 1981. I. Title.
KF27 .A64 1980a

**United States. Congress. House. Committee on
Appropriations. Subcommittee on Foreign
Operations and Related Agencies
Appropriations.** Foreign assistance and
related agencies appropriations for 1975 :
hearings before a subcommittee of the
Committee on Appropriations, House of
Representatives, Ninety-third Congress, second
session / Subcommittee on Foreign Operations
and Related Agencies. Washington : U. S.
Govt. Print. Off., 1974. 2 v. : ill. ; 24 cm.
Includes index. LC Card 74-602734
*1. Economic assistance, American. 2. Military
assistance, American. 3. United States - Appropriations
and expenditures, 1975. I. Title.*
KF27 .A646 1974

**United States. Congress. House. Committee on
Appropriations. Subcommittee on Military
Construction Appropriations.** Military
construction appropriations for 1982 : hearings
before a subcommittee of the Committee on
Appropriations, House of Representatives,
Ninety-seventh Congress, first session /
Subcommittee on Military Constructions
Appropriations. Washingon : U. S. G.P.O.,
1981. 2 v. : ill. ; 24 cm. pt. 1. Justification of the
budget estimates: active forces -- pt. 2. Justification of
the budget estimates: defense agencies, reserve
components and family housing, fiscal year 1982
amendments, and fiscal year 1981 supplemental. Item
1011, 1011-A (microfiche) LC Card 81-601195
DDC 358/.22/0973 19
*1. United States. Dept. of Defense - Appropriations and
expenditures. 2. United States - Armed Forces -
Military construction operations. 3. United States -
Appropriations and expenditures, 1982. I. Title. II.
Title: Justification of the budget estimates.*
KF27 .A655 1981

**United States. Congress. House. Committee on
Appropriations. Subcommittee on the
Departments of Commerce, Justice, and
State, the Judiciary, and Related Agencies.**
Departments of Commerce, Justice, and State,
the judiciary, and related agencies
appropriations for 1982 : hearings before a
subcommittee of the Committee on
Appropriations, House of Representatives,
Ninety-seventh Congress, first session /
Subcommittee on the Departments of
Commerce, Justice, and State, the Judiciary,
and Related Agencies. Washington : U. S.
G.P.O., 1981- v. <1-2, 4> ; ill. ; 24 cm. Item
1011, 1011-A (microfiche) Includes bibliographical
references and index. LC Card 81-601662   DDC
353.0072/236 19
*1. United States - Appropriations and expenditures,
1982. I. Title.*
KF27 .A6327 1981

**United States. Congress. House. Committee on
Armed Services.** (Old Catalog form: United
States. Armed Services, Committee on //
Hearings printed in 1978 and later are
available only in microform. Please consult
the librarians in the Economic and Public
Affairs Division.
Capability of U. S. defense industrial base :
hearings before the Committee on Armed
Services, and the Panel on Defense Industrial
Base of the Committee on Armed Services,
House of Representatives, Ninety-sixth
Congress, second session, September 17, 18, 25,
October 21, 22, 24, November 12, 13, 14, 17,
18, 19, 20, and December 3, 1980.
Washington : U. S. G.P.O., 1980 [i.e. 1981] ii,
1796, ii p. : ill. ; 23 cm. "H.A.S.C. no. 96-69." Item
1012 Includes bibliographical references and index.
LC Card 81-600988   DDC 355.2/6/0973 19
*1. United States - Industries. 2. Industrial mobilization -
United States. 3. Priorities, Industrial - United States. 4.
United States - Defenses. I. United States. Congress.
House. Committee on Armed Services. Panel on
Defense Industrial Base. II. Title.*
KF27 .A7 1980K

Full committee consideration of committee
resolution in honor of the late Hon. Harold
Runnels ... / Committee on Armed Services,
House of Representatives, Ninety-sixth
Congress, second session, August 26, 1980.
Washington : U. S. Govt. Print. Off., 1980. ii,
30 p. ; 24 cm. Includes hearings on H.R. 7878, H.R.
4627, H.R. 5766, and S. 91. "H.A.S.C. no. 96-53." LC

417 GOVERNMENT PUBLICATIONS - U.S.: 1981

United States. Congress. House. Committee on Armed Services.

Card 80-603490 DDC 328.73/092/4 19
1. Runnels, Harold Lowell, 1924-1980.
KF27 .A7 1980d

Full committee consideration of H.R. 5503, DOPMA (Defense officer personnel management act) : also markup session of the Military Compensation Subcommittee of the Committee on Armed Services, House of Representatives, Ninety-fifth Congress, first session, July 29, August 2, 1977. Washington : U. S. Govt. Print. Off., 1977. ii, 131 p. ; 23 cm. "H.A.S.C. no. 95-30." LC Card 77-603628
1. United States - Armed Forces - Officers. I. United States. Congress. House. Committee on Armed Services. Subcommittee on Military Compensation. II. Title.
KF27 .A7 1977j

Full committee consideration of H.R. 6464 ... S.J. Res. 149 ... : annual report to the Budget Committee on national defense function, resolution honoring Hon. David C. Treen / Committee on Armed Services, House of Representatives, Ninety-sixth Congress, second session. Washington : U. S. Govt. Print. Off., 1980. ii, 31 p. ; 24 cm. "March 6, 1980." "H.A.S.C. 96-38." LC Card 80-602774 DDC 343.73/01 347.3031 19
1. Military law - United States. I. Title.
KF27 .A7 1980f

Full committee consideration of H.R. 7265 ... H.R. 7252 ... H.R. 7301 ... H.R. 7303 ... / Committee on Armed Services, House of Representatives, Ninety-sixth Congress, second session. Washington : U. S. Govt. Print. Off., 1980. ii, 123 p. ; 24 cm. "H.A.S.C. no. 96-36." LC Card 80-602465 DDC 343.73/01 19
1. Military law - United States. I. Title.
KF27 .A7 1980b

Full committee consideration of H.R. 7536 to amend title 10, United States Code ... and H.R. 3351 to amend chapter 55 of title 10, United States code ... / Committee on Armed Services, House of Representatives, Ninety-sixth Congress, second session, June 17, 1980. Washington : U. S. Govt. Print. Off., 1980. ii, 11 p. ; 24 cm. "H.A.S.C. no. 96-40." LC Card 80-602762 DDC 343.73/013 19
1. CHAMPUS. I. Title.
KF27 .A7 1980a

Full committee consideration of H.R. 7552 ... H.R. 8188 ... H.R. 8189 ... / Committee on Armed Services, House of Representatives, Ninety-sixth Congress, second session, September 25, 1980. Washington : U. S. G.P.O., 1980. ii, 41 p. ; 24 cm. "H.A.S.C. no. 96-52." LC Card 80-604114 DDC 343.73/01 347.3031 19
1. Military law - United States. I. Title.
KF27 .A7 1980h

Full committee consideration of H.R. 7626 to amend title 37, United States code, to improve certain special pays and allowances for members of the uniformed services, and for other purposes / Committee on Armed Services, House of Representatives, Ninety-sixth Congress, second session, June 24, 1980. Washington : U. S. Govt. Print. Off., 1980. ii, 24 p. ; 23 cm. "H.A.S.C. no. 96-49." LC Card 80-603657 DDC 343.73/013 347.30313 19
1. United States - Armed Forces - Pay, allowances, etc. - Law and legislation. I. Title.
KF27 .A7 1980e

Full committee consideration of H. Res. 777 requesting the President to furnish certain information to the House of Representatives concerning the disclosure of classified information relating to the new so-called stealth technology for military aircraft, and resolution in honor of Charles Sparks Thomas, Secretary of the Navy, May 1954 to April 1957 / Committee on Armed Services, House of Representatives, Ninety-sixth Congress, second session, September 9, 1980. Washington : U. S. Govt. Print. Off., 1980. ii, 27 p. ; 24 cm. At head of title: H.A.S.C. no. 96-51." LC Card 80-603683 DDC 355.6 19
1. Defense information, Classified - United States. 2. Thomas, Charles. I. Title.
KF27 .A7 1980g

Full committee consideration of recommendation to Budget Committee on reconciliation in concurrence with the first concurrent resolution and H.R. 7682, H.R. 7694, and H.R. 5856 / Committee on Armed

Services, House of Representatives, Ninety-sixth Congress, second session. Washington : U. S. G.P.O., 1980. ii, 22 p. ; 24 cm. "July 1, 1980." "H.A.S.C. no. 96-50." LC Card 80-603649 DDC 355.6/22/0973 19
1. United States - Armed Forces - Finances. 2. Budget - United States. 3. United States - Armed Forces - Officials and employees. I. Title.
KF27 .A7 1980i

Hearings on H.R. 2637 ... and the posture of the U. S. Military Airlift, before the Committee on Armed Services, House of Representatives, Ninety-fifth Congress, first session, September 19, 20, 1977. Washington : U. S. Govt. Print. Off., 1977. ii, 187, iii p. : ill. ; 23 cm. "H.A.S.C. no. 95-42." Includes index. LC Card 78-600628
1. Airlift, Military. 2. United States. Air Force. I. Title.
KF27 .A7 1977n

Hearings on H.R. 8390 : supplemental authorization for appropriations for fiscal year 1978 and review of the state of U. S. strategic forces : also reprograming action nos. FY 78-2 P/A, FY 78-3 P/A, and 78-4 P/A / Committee on Armed Services, House of Representatives, Ninety-fifth Congress, first session .... Washington : U. S. Govt. Print. Off., 1977. ii, 471 p. : ill. ; 24 cm. Hearings held July 21-Nov. 29, 1977. "H.A.S.C. no. 95-47." Includes index. LC Card 78-601218
1. United States. Dept. of Defense - Appropriations and expenditures. 2. Strategic forces - United States. I. Title.
KF27 .A7 1977q

Hearings on military posture and H.R. 6495 (H.R. 6974) Department of Defense authorization for appropriations for fiscal year 1981 before the Committee on Armed Services, House of Representatives, Ninety-sixth Congress, second session. Washington : U. S. Govt. Print. Off. : for sale by the Supt. of Docs., U. S. Govt. Print. Off., 1980- v. in : ill. ; 24 cm. At head of title: H.A.S.C. no. 96-37. Hearings held Jan. 25- 1980. Vols. : Hearings held before various subcommittees of the Committee on Armed Services. Includes indexes. CONTENTS. - pt. 1. Military posture.-- --pt. 3. Seapower and Strategic & Critical Materials Subcommittee.--pt. 4. Research and development, Title II. LC Card 80-602996 DDC 355.6/22/0973 19
1. United States. Dept. of Defense - Appropriations and expenditures. 2. United States - Military policy. I. Title.
KF27 .A7 1980

Report on the inspection of U. S. military bases in Puerto Rico, Cuba, and the Panama Canal Zone of the Committee on Armed Services, House of Representatives, Ninety-sixth Congress, second session. Washington : U. S. Govt. Print. Off., 1980. v, 24 p. : maps ; 24 cm. At head of title: Committee print. 96th Congress, 2d session, no. 25. Prepared by W. L. Dickinson. LC Card 80-603272 DDC 355.7/0973 19
1. Military bases, American - Puerto Rico. 2. Military bases, American - Cuba. 3. Military bases, American - Canal Zone. I. Dickinson, William L. II. Title.
UA23 .U4735 1980

Status of Army manpower : hearings before the Committee on Armed Services, House of Representatives, Ninety-sixth Congress, second session, June 11 and 12, 1980. Washington : U. S. G.P.O., 1981. ii, 130 p. ; 24 cm. "H.A.S.C. no. 96-73." Item 1012 LC Card 81-601854 DDC 355.2/2/0973 19
1. United States. Army - Recruiting, enlistment, etc. I. Title.
KF27 .A7 1980l

Status of the MX missile system : hearing before the Committee on Armed Services, House of Representatives, Ninety-sixth Congress, second session, May 1, 1980. Washington : U. S. G.P.O., 1980. ii, 46 p. : ill. ; 24 cm. "H.A.S.C. no. 96-56." LC Card 80-604003 DDC 358/.174/0973 19
1. MX (Weapons systems). I. Title.
KF27 .A7 1980j

Strategic warning system false alerts : hearing before the Committee on Armed Services, House of Representatives, Ninety-sixth Congress, second session, June 24, 1980. Washington : U. S. Govt. Print. Off., 1980. ii, 30 p. ; 24 cm. "H.A.S.C. no. 96-47." LC Card 80-603048 DDC 358/.17/0973 19
1. North American Air Defense Command. 2. Ballistic missile early warning system - United States. 3. Distant

early warning system - United States. I. Title.
KF27 .A7 1980c

United States. Congress. House. Committee on Armed Services. Delegation to Africa. Report of the delegation to Africa : report to the Committee on Armed Services, House of Representatives, Ninety-sixth Congress, first session, March 4, 1980. Washington : U. S. Govt. Print. Off., 1980. iii, 29 p. ; 24 cm. At head of title: 96th Congress, 1st session. Committee print. LC Card 80-601793 DDC 355/.03306 19
1. Africa - Politics and government - 1960-. 2. Africa - Strategic aspects. 3. Africa - Economic conditions - 1945-. 4. National liberation movements - Africa. 5. Africa -Military policy. 6. Africa - Relations (military) with the United States. 7. United States - Relations (military) with Africa. I. Title.
DT30 .U58 1980

United States. Congress. House. Committee on Armed Services. Panel on Defense Industrial Base. United States. Congress. House. Committee on Armed Services. Capability of U. S. defense industrial base . Washington , 1980 [i.e. 1981] ii, 1796, ii p. : LC Card 81-600988 DDC 355.2/6/0973 19
KF27 .A7 1980K

United States. Congress. House. Committee on Armed Services. Procurement and Military Nuclear Systems Subcommittee.
United States. Congress. House. Committee on Armed Services. Procurement and Military Nuclear Systems Subcommittee. Readiness Panel. Coordination of Department of Energy/Department of Defense nuclear weapons materials requirements : hearing before the Procurement and Military Nuclear Systems Subcommittee of the Committee on Armed Services, House of Representatives, Ninety-sixth Congress, second session, June 18, 1980. Washington : U. S. Govt. Print. Off., 1980. ii, 23 p. ; 24 cm. At head of title: H.A.S.C. no. 96-44. LC Card 80-602992 DDC 355.8/25119/0973 19
1. Atomic weapons. 2. United States - Armed Forces - Weapons systems - Finance. 3. United States. Dept. of Defense. 4. United States. Dept. of Energy. I. Title.
KF27 .A7657 1980c

Hearing on H.R. 6362 (H.R. 7552) to amend title 10, United States Code, to provide for the investigation of accidents involving aircraft of an armed force and to clarify the use of reports of such investigations, before the Procurement and Military Nuclear Systems Subcommittee of the Committee on Armed Services, House of Representatives, Ninety-sixth Congress, second session, February 7, 1980. Washington : U. S. Govt. Print. Off., 1980. ii, 29 p. : graphs ; 24 cm. "H.A.S.C. no. 96-43)" LC Card 80-602907 DDC 343.73/018414 19
1. Aeronautics, Military - Law and legislation - United States. 2. Aeronautics, Military - United States - Accidents - Investigations. I. Title.
KF27 .A7657 1980b

Hearings on H.R. 6621 (H.R. 7265), Department of Energy authorization legislation (national security programs) for fiscal year 1981, before the Procurement and Military Nuclear Systems Subcommittee of the Committee on Armed Services, House of Representatives, Ninety-sixth Congress, second session .... Washington : U. S. Govt. Print. Off., 1980. xiv, 1088, vi p. : ill. ; 24 cm. "H.A.S.C. no. 96-39." Hearings held March 18, April 16, 17, 29, 30, and June 4, 1980. Includes bibliographical references and index. LC Card 80-602721 DDC 353.0072/236823 19
1. United States. Dept. of Energy - Appropriations and expenditures. 2. United States - National security. I. Title.
KF27 .A7657 1980a

The Los Alamos National Laboratory protective guard force : hearing before the Procurement and Military Nuclear Systems Subcommittee of the Committee on Armed Services, House of Representatives, Ninety-seventh Congress, first session, January 9, 1981. Washington : U. S. G.P.O., 1981. 215 p. : ill. ; 24 cm. "H.A.S.C. no 97-1." Item 1012-A, 1012-B (microfiche) LC Card 81-601645 DDC 343.73/013 347.30313 19
1. Los Alamos Scientific Laboratory - Security measures. I. Title.
KF27 .A7657 1981

Naval nuclear propulsion program--1980 : hearing on H.R. 6621 (H.R. 7265) ... before the

Procurement and Military Nuclear Systems Subcommittee of the Committee on Armed Services, House of Representatives, Ninety-sixth Congress, second session, March 18, 1980. Washington : U. S. Govt. Print. Off., 1980. vi, 246, iv p. : ill. ; 24 cm. "H.A.S.C. no. 96-35." Includes bibliographical references and index. LC Card 80-602476 DDC 343.73/0194 19
1. United States. Navy. 2. Atomic ships. 3. United States. Dept. of Energy - Appropriations and expenditures. I. Title.
KF27 .A7657 1980

Review of readiness considerations in the development of the defense budget : hearings before the Readiness Panel of the Procurement and Military Nuclear Systems Subcommittee of the Committee on Armed Services, House of Representatives, Ninety-sixth Congress, second session, September 10, 18, 24, November 12, and 13, 1980. Washington : U. S. G.P.O., 1980 [i.e. 1981] ii, 161 p. : ill. ; 24 cm. "H.A.S.C. no. 96-74." Item 1012 LC Card 81-600960 DDC 355/.033073 19
1. United States - Defenses. 2. United States - National security. I. Title.
KF27 .A7657 1980d

United States. Congress. House. Committee on Armed Services. Special Subcommittee on Nato Standardization, Interoperability, and Readiness. Status of army air defense planning : hearing before the Special Subcommittee on NATO Standardization, Interoperability, and Readiness of the Committee on Armed Services, House of Representatives, Ninety-sixth Congress, second session, September 30, 1980. Washington : U. S. G.P.O., 1980. ii, 52 p. : ill. ; 24 cm. "H.A.S.C. no. 96-57." LC Card 80-604007 DDC 358.4/145/0973 19
1. United States - Air defenses, Military. 2. United States. Army - Aviation. 3. Aeronautics, Military - United States. I. Title.
KF27 .A7642 1980

United States. Congress. House. Committee on Armed Services. Subcommitee on Investigations. National defense funding levels for fiscal year 1981 : hearing before the Investigations Subcommittee of the Committee on Armed Services, House of Representatives, Ninety-sixth Congress, second session, May 29, 1980. Washington : U. S. Govt. Print. Off., 1980. ii, 27 p. ; 24 cm. "H.A.S.C. no. 96-41." LC Card 80-602709 DDC 355.6/22/0973 19
1. United States. Dept. of Defense - Appropriations and expenditures. 2. United States - Defenses. I. Title.
KF27 .A753 1980a

United States. Congress. House. Committee on Armed Services. Subcommittee No. 1. Subcommittee No. 1 hearing on H. R. 8413, to amend title 10, United States code, to perscribe health care cost-sharing arrangements for certain surviving dependents, and for other purposes. Washington, 1969. 5403-5413 p. 23 cm. "H. A. S. C. no 91-37." Hearing held December 17, 1969.
1. United States - Armed Forces - Medical care.
NYPL [JLE 81-563]

United States. Congress. House. Committee on Armed Services. Subcommittee on Investigations. Defense contract settlement procedures : report of the Investigations Subcommittee of the Committee on Armed Services, House of Representatives, Ninety-sixth Congress, second session. Washington : U. S. G.P.O., 1980. iii, 20 p. ; 24 cm. At head of title: 96th Congress, 2d session. Committee print. No. 27. LC Card 80-603874 DDC 346.73/023 347.30623 19
1. Defense contracts - United States. I. Title.
KF858 .A25 1980

Defense contract settlement procedures : hearings before the Investigations Subcommittee of the Committee on Armed Services, House of Representatives, Ninety-sixth Congress, second session .... Washington : U. S. Govt. Print. Off., 1980. iii, 277 p. ; 24 cm. "H.A.S.C. no. 96-31." Hearings held Nov. 14-Dec. 12, 1979. LC Card 80-603711 DDC 346.73/023 347.30623 19
1. Defense contracts - United States. I. Title.
KF27 .A753 1979d

Department of Defense petroleum requirements and supplies : hearings before the Investigations Subcommittee of the Committee on Armed

Services, House of Representatives, Ninety-sixth Congress, second session .... Washington : U. S. Govt. Print. Off., 1980. iii, 651 p. : graphs ; 23 cm. "[H.A.S.C. no. 96-331]." Hearings held Oct. 5-Nov. 8, 1979 and Feb. 25, 1980. LC Card 80-602946 DDC 355.2/43/0973 19
1. United States - Armed Forces - Fuel. 2. Petroleum - United States - Reserves. 3. Petroleum - United States - Storage. I. Title.
KF27 .A753 1979c

Department of Defense petroleum requirements and supplies : report of the Investigations Subcommittee of the Committee on Armed Services, House of Representatives, Ninety-sixth Congress, second session, June 10, 1980. Washington : U. S. Govt. Print. Off., 1980. iii, 17 p. ; 24 cm. At head of title: 96th Congress, 2d session. Committee print. No. 23. LC Card 80-603555 DDC 355.2/4/0973 19
1. United States - Armed Forces - Fuel. 2. United States. Dept. of Defense. 3. Petroleum - United States. I. Title.
UC263 .U517 1980

Hearing on H.R. 7247, to waive the applicability of sections 2382 and 7300 of title 19, United States Code, to contracts for the construction or manufacture of naval vessels or military aircraft with respect to which final payment is made before October 1, 1981, before the Investigations Subcommittee of the Committee on Armed Services, House of Representatives, Ninety-sixth Congress, second session, June 25, 1980. Washington : U. S. Govt. Print. Off., 1980. iii, 135 p. ; 23 cm. "H.A.S.C. no. 96-46." LC Card 80-603284 DDC 346.7/023 19
1. Defense contracts - Price policy - United States. I. Title.
KF27 .A753 1980b

Leaks of classified national defense information--stealth aircraft : report of the Investigations Subcommittee of the Committee on Armed Services, House of Representatives, Ninety-sixth Congress, second session. Washington : U. S. G.P.O., 1980 [i.e. 1981] iii, 9 p. ; 24 cm. At head of title: 96th Congress, 2d session. Committee print. No. 30. "February 3, 1981." Item 1012 LC Card 81-601284 DDC 353.0071/45 19
1. Defense information, Classified - United States. 2. Jet planes, Military. 3. United States - National security. I. Title. II. Title: Stealth aircraft.
UB247 .U53 1981

Leaks of classified national defense information--stealth aircraft : hearings before the Investigations Subcommittee of the Committee on Armed Services, House of Representatives, Ninety-sixth Congress, second session, August 27, September 4, 16, and October 1, 1980. Washington : U. S. G.P.O., 1980 [i.e. 1981] ii, 228 p. ; 24 cm. "H.A.S.C. no. 96-67." Item 1012 LC Card 81-601135 DDC 353.0071/45 19
1. Defense information, Classified - United States. 2. United States - National security. 3. Radar in aeronautics. 4. Electronic countermeasures. I. Title.
KF27 .A753 1980c

United States. Congress. House. Committee on Armed Services. Subcommittee on Investigations. Nonappropriated Fund Panel. Review of military clubs and package beverage stores : report of the Nonappropriated Fund Panel of the Investigations Subcommittee of the Committee on Armed Services, House of Representatives, Ninety-sixth Congress, first session. Washington : U. S. Govt. Print. Off., 1980. iii, 21 p. ; 24 cm. At head of title: 96th Congress, 1st session, committee print, no. 18. LC Card 80-601774 DDC 355.3/46/0973 19
1. United States - Armed Forces - Service clubs. 2. United States - Armed Forces - Officers clubs. 3. Liquor traffic - United States. 4. Liquor laws - United States. I. Title.
U56 .U56 1980

United States. Congress. House. Committee on Armed Services. Subcommittee on Military Compensation. Benefits for survivors of retired military personnel, S. 91 : hearings before the Military Compensation Subcommittee of the Committee on Armed Services, House of Representatives, Ninety-sixth Congress, second session, July 2 and August 21, 1980. Washington : U. S.

G.P.O., 1981 [i.e. 1981] ii, 130 p. : ill. ; 24 cm. "H.A.S.C. no. 96-62." Item 1012 LC Card 81-600805 DDC 343.73/0112 347.303112 19
1. Survivors' benefits - United States. 2. Pensions, Military - United States. I. Title.
KF27 .A76392 1980b

Hearing on H.R. 2817, H.R. 3677, and H.R. 6270, legislation related to benefits for former spouse of a military retiree, before the Military Compensation Subcommittee of the Committee on Armed Services, House of Representatives, Ninety-sixth Congress, second session, May 28, 1980. Washington : U. S. G.P.O., 1980 [i.e. 1981] ii, 126 p. : ill., 24 cm. "H.A.S.C. no. 96-65." Item 1012 Includes bibliographical references. LC Card 81-600974 DDC 343.73/0112 347.303112 19
1. Pensions, Military - United States. 2. Survivors' benefits - United States. 3. Separate maintenance - United States. I. Title.
KF27 .A76392 1980c

Hearings on H.R. 5168, H.R. 7626, and S. 1454, miscellaneous military personnel management and military compensation legislation, before the Military Compensation Subcommittee of the Committee on Armed Services, House of Representatives, Ninety-sixth Congress, second session, September 10, November 15, December 4, 1979, February 22, June 4, 11, and 19, 1980. Washington : U. S. G.P.O., 1980 [i.e. 1981] ii, 127 p. ; 24 cm. "H.A.S.C. no. 96-64." Item 1012 LC Card 81-600976 DDC 343.73/013 347.30313 19
1. United States - Armed Forces - Pay, allowances, etc. - Law and legislation. 2. United States - Armed Forces - Personnel management - Law and legislation. 3. Physicians - Salaries, pensions, etc. - United States. I. Title.
KF27 .A76392 1979b

Hearings on S. 1918, Defense Officer Personnel Management Act, (DOPMA), before the Military Compensation Subcommittee of the Committee on Armed Services, House of Representatives, Ninety-sixth Congress, second session, April 29, May 7, 13, 14, and September 29, 1980. Washington : U. S. G.P.O., 1981. ii, 388 p. : ill. ; 24 cm. "H.A.S.C. no. 96-61." Item 1012 LC Card 81-600806 DDC 343.73/013 347.30313 19
1. United States - Armed Forces - Personnel management - Law and legislation. 2. United States - Armed Forces - Officers - Legal status, laws, etc. I. Title.
KF27 .A76392 1980a

Special pay for military veterinary officers : hearing before the Military Compensation Subcommittee of the Committee on Armed Services, House of Representatives, Ninety-sixth Congress, second session, March 10, 1980. Washington : U. S. G.P.O., 1980 [i.e. 1981] ii, 59 p. : ill. ; 24 cm. "H.A.S.C. no. 96-60." Item 1012 LC Card 81-600607 DDC 331.2/81636089/0973 19
1. United States - Armed Forces - Pay, allowances, etc. 2. Veterinarians - Salaries, pensions, etc. - United States. I. Title.
KF27 .A76392 1980

United States. Congress. House. Committee on Armed Services. Full committee consideration of H.R. 5503, DOPMA (Defense officer personnel management act) . Washington , 1977. ii, 131 p. ; LC Card 77-603628
KF27 .A7 1977j

United States. Congress. House. Committee on Armed Services. Subcommittee on Military Installations and Facilities. Hearing on H.R. 6312 (H.R. 6464), to authorize the Secretary of the Army to convey to the Michigan Job Development Authority the lands and improvements comprising the Michigan Army Missile Plant in Sterling Heights, Macomb County, Mich., before the Military Installations and Facilities Subcommittee of the Committee on Armed Services, House of Representatives, Ninety-sixth Congress, second session, February 7, 1980. Washington : U. S. Govt. Print. Off., 1980. ii, 32 p. : ill. ; 24 cm. "H.A.S.C. no. 96-30." LC Card 80-601382 DDC 343.73/0253/0262 19
1. United States. Army - Facilities. 2. Michigan Job Development Authority. 3. Real property, Exchange of - United States. 4. Real property, Exchange of -

Michigan. I. Title.
KF27 .A76397 1980

Hearings on H.R. 6493 (H.R. 7301) ... and fiscal year 1980 supplemental request, and fiscal year 1981 Budget amendment for the Military construction program before the Military Istallations and Facilities Subcommittee of the Committee on Armed Services, House of Representatives, Ninety-sixth Congress, second session. Washington : U. S. Govt. Print. Off., 1980. liii, 662, x p. : ill. ; 24 cm. Hearings held Feb. 19-22, 25-27 and Apr. 29, 1980. "H.A.S.C. no. 96-34." Includes index.   LC Card 80-602757   DDC 355.6/22/0973 19

1. United States - Armed Forces - Military construction operations. 2. United States. Dept. of Defense - Appropriations and expenditures. I. Title.
KF27 .A76397 1980a

United States. Congress. House. Committee on Armed Services. Subcommittee on Military Personnel.
Hearing on H.R. 5822, H.R. 2224, H.R. 7295, and H.R. 7294 (H.R. 7682), reserve readiness legislation : before the Military Personnel Subcommittee of the Committee on Armed Services, House of Representatives, Ninety-sixth Congress, second session, June 25, 1980. Washington : U. S. Govt. Print. Off., 1980. ii, 25 p. ; 24 cm. "H.A.S.C. no 96-42."   LC Card 80-602908   DDC 343.73/013 19

1. United States - Armed Forces - Reserves. I. Title.
KF27 .A76398 1980a

Hearing on H.R. 8386, for the relief of Roy P. Benavidez, before the Military Personnel Subcommittee of the Committee on Armed Services, House of Representatives, Ninety-sixth Congress, second session, November 21, 1980. Washington : U. S. G.P.O., 1980. ii, 10 p. ; 24 cm. "H.A.S.C. no. 96-59."   LC Card 80-604006   DDC 343.73/014 347.30314 19

1. Benavidez, Roy P. - Medals. I. Title.
KF27 .A76398 1980d

Hearing on H.R. 846 ... H.R. 4553 ... H.R. 7607 ... H.R. 5856 ... before the Military Personnel Subcommittee of the Committee on Armed Services, House of Representatives, Ninety-sixth Congress, second session, June 26, 1980. Washington : U. S. Govt. Print. Off., 1980. ii, 15 p. ; 24 cm. "H.A.S.C. no. 96-45." LC Card 80-602963   DDC 343.73/01 19

1. Military law - United States - Territories and possessions. I. Title.
KF27 .A76398 1980

Hearings on civilian health and medical program of the uniformed services before the Military Personnel Subcommittee of the Committee on Armed Services, House of Representatives, Ninety-sixth Congress, second session, June 18, and September 15, 1980. Washington : U. S. Govt. Print. Off., 1980. ii, 232 p. ; 24 cm. "H.A.S.C. no. 96-54." LC Card 80-603448   DDC 362.1/0973 19

1. CHAMPUS. 2. United States - Armed Forces - Medical care. 3. Military dependents - Medical care - United States. I. Title.
KF27 .A76398 1980b

Hearings on H.R. 6406 and H.R. 6298 : revision of the laws governing the U. S. Court of Military Appeals and the appeals process before the Military Personnel Subcommittee of the Committee on Armed Services, House of Representatives, Ninety-sixth Congress, second session, February 7, March 6, and September 23, 1980. Washington : U. S. G.P.O., 1980. ii, 117 p. ; 24 cm. "H.A.S.C. no. 96-55." Includes bibliographical references. LC Card 80-604104   DDC 343.73/0143 347.303143 19

1. United States. Court of Military Appeals. 2. Courts-martial and courts of inquiry - United States. I. Title.
KF27 .A76398 1980c

Military health care delivery including CHAMPUS and inquiry of U. S. Naval Hospital, Oak Knoll, Calif., with appendix : hearings before the Military Personnel Subcommittee of the Committee on Armed Services, House of Representatives, Ninety-fifth and Ninety-sixth Congresses, hearings held May 17, 18, 24, 25, June 2, 29, October 12, 13, 26, 1977, June 5, and November 18, 1980. Washington : U. S. G.P.O., 1981. ii, 701, iv p. : ill. ; 24 cm. "H.A.S.C. no. 96-70" Item 1012 Includes bibliographical references and index. LC Card

81-601886   DDC 355.3/45 19

1. CHAMPUS. 2. Military dependents - Medical care - United States. 3. United States - Armed Forces - Medical care. I. Title.
KF27 .A76398 1977c

Women in the military : hearings before the Military Personnel Subcommittee of the Committee on Armed Services, House of Representatives, Ninety-sixth Congress, first and second sessions, November 13, 14, 15, 16, 1979 and February 11, 1980. Washington : U. S. G.P.O., 1981. ii, 369 p. : ill. ; 24 cm. "H.A.S.C. no. 96-72." Item 1012 Includes bibliographical references.   LC Card 81-601874   DDC 355/.0088/042 19

1. United States - Armed Forces - Women. I. Title.
KF27 .A76398 1979d

United States. Congress. House. Committee on Armed Services. Subcommittee on Seapower and Strategic and Critical Materials.
National policy objectives and the adequacy of our current navy forces : hearings before the Seapower and Strategic and Critical Materials Subcommittee of the Committee on Armed Services, House of Representatives, Ninety-sixth Congress, second session, November 13, December 3, and 20, 1979. Washington : U. S. G.P.O., 1980 [i.e. 1981] ii, 137 p. : ill. ; 24 cm. "H.A.S.C. no. 96-76." Item 1012   LC Card 81-601761 DDC 359/.03/0973 19

1. United States - Military policy. 2. United States - National security. 3. Sea power - United States. 4. United States. Navy. I. Title.
KF27 .A769 1979e

Reprograming action--Trident submarine : hearing before the Seapower and Strategic and Critical Materials Subcommittee of the Committee on Armed Services, House of Representatives, Ninety-sixth Congress, second session, September 23, 1980. Washington : U. S. G.P.O., 1980. ii, 48 p. ; 24 cm. "H.A.S.C. no. 96-58."   LC Card 80-603992   DDC 359.3/257/0973 19

1. Trident (Weapons systems). 2. General Dynamics Corporation. Electric Boat Division. I. Title.
KF27 .A769 1980

Submarine alternatives study : hearings before the Seapower and Strategic and Critical Materials Subcommittee of the Committee on Armed Services, House of Representatives, Ninety-sixth Congress, second session ... Washington : U. S. Govt. Print. Off., 1980. ii, 182 p. ; 24 cm. "H.A.S.C. no. 96-48." Hearings held Sept. 25-Oct. 29, 1979.   LC Card 80-603515   DDC 623.8/2574 19

1. Atomic submarines. 2. United States - Defense. 3. United States. Navy - Procurement. I. Title.
KF27 .A769 1979d

United States. Congress. House. Committee on Banking, Finance and Urban Affairs.
The administration's economic program : hearing before the Committee on Banking, Finance, and Urban Affairs, House of Representatives, Ninety-seventh Congress, first session, March 5, 1981. Washington : U. S. G.P.O., 1981. iii, 76 p. ; 24 cm. Item 1013-A, 1013-B (microfiche)   LC Card 81-601944   DDC 338.954 19

1. United States - Economic policy - 1971-. I. Title.
KF27 .B5 1981

Compilation of the Energy Security Act of 1980, and 1980 amendments to the Defense Production Act of 1950 /. Washington , 1980. 3 v. (v. 2252 p.) ;   LC Card 80-603878   DDC 346.7304/679 347.3064679 19
KF2120.A32 A15 1980

Conduct of monetary policy (pursuant to Full Employment and Balanced Growth Act of 1978, P.L. 95-523) : Hearing before the Committee on Banking, Finance, and Urban Affairs, House of Representatives, Ninety-seventh Congress, first session, February 26, 1981. Washington : U. S. G.P.O., 1981. iii, 191 p. : ill. ; 24 cm. Item 1013-A, 1013-B (microfiche) "Serial no. 97-6."   LC Card 81-601949 DDC 332.4/973 19

1. Monetary policy - United States. 2. Unemployment - United States - Effect of inflation on. I. Title.
KF27 .B5 1981a

Conduct of monetary policy, pursuant to the Full employment and balance growth act of 1978, P.L. 95-523 : hearing before the Committee on Banking, Finance, and Urban

Affairs, House of Representatives, Ninety-sixth Congress, second session, July 23, 1980. Washington : U. S. Govt. Print. Off., 1980. iii, 325 p. : graphs ; 24 cm. "Serial no. 96-63."   LC Card 80-603705   DDC 332.4/973 19

1. Monetary policy - United States. 2. Inflation (Finance) - United States. 3. Unemployment - United States - Effect of inflation on. I. Title.
KF27 .B5 1980b

United States. Supplement to Basic laws and authorities on housing and community development, revised through January 3, 1980 /. Washington , 1980. vi, 838 p. ;   LC Card 80-603964   DDC 346.7304/5 347.30645 19
KF5424 1979 Suppl

United States. Interagency Task force on Thrift Institutions. The report of the Interagency Task Force on Thrift Institutions . Washington , 1980. viii, 267 p. ;   LC Card 80-603280   DDC 332.2/0973 19
HG2151 .U53 1980

World War II and the problems of the eighties : hearing before the Committee on Banking, Finance, and Urban Affairs, House of Representatives, Ninety-sixth Congress, second session, September 23, 1980. Washington : U. S. Govt. Print. Off., 1980. iii, 70 p. ; 24 cm. "Serial no. 96-66."   LC Card 80-603655   DDC 338.973 19

1. World War, 1939-1945 - Economic aspects - United States. 2. Industrial mobilization - United States. 3. United States - Economic policy - 1971-. I. Title.
KF27 .B5 1980a

United States. Congress. House. Committee on Banking, Finance, and Urban Affairs. Subcommittee on Consumer Affairs and Coinage.
United States. Congress. House. Committee on Banking, Finance and Urban Affairs. Subcommittee on Consumer Affairs.
The Cash Discount Act : hearing before the Subcommittee on Consumer Affairs and Coinage of the Committee on Banking, Finance and Urban Affairs, House of Representatives, Ninety-seventh Congress, first session, on H.R. 31 ... February 5, 1981. Washington : U. S. G.P.O., 1981. iii, 45 p. ; 24 cm. "Serial no. 97-1." Item 1013-A, 1013-B (microfiche)   LC Card 81-601339   DDC 346.73/073 347.30673 19

1. Discount, Cash - Law and legislation - United States. 2. Consumer credit - Law and legislation - United States. I. Title.
KF27 .B5 1981b

The Cash discount act, The Fair credit practices act : hearing before the Subcommittee on Consumer Affairs of the Committee on Banking, Finance, and Urban Affairs, House of Representatives, Ninety-sixth Congress, second session, on H.R. 6928 ... H.R. 7038 ... April 23, 1980. Washington : U. S. Gvot. Print. Off., 1980. iii, 96 p. ; 24 cm. "Serial no. 96-52."   LC Card 80-602449   DDC 346.73/073 19

1. Consumer credit - Law and legislation - United States. 2. Discount, Cash - Law and legislation - United States. I. Title.
KF27 .B535 1980a

Credit controls . Washington , 1980 [i.e. 1981] v, 40 p. ;   LC Card 81-600674   DDC 332.7/43 19
HG3756.U54 C74

Legislation authorizing issuance of gold medals to Canadian Ambassador Kenneth Taylor, Simon Wiesenthal, Gerald F. Spiess, and commemorative medals for the United States Capitol Historical Society : hearing before the Subcommittee on Consumer Affairs of the Committee on Banking, Finance, and Urban Affairs, House of Representatives, Ninety-sixth Congress, second session ... February 8, 1980. Washington : U. S. Govt. Print. Off., 1980. iii, 73 p. ; 24 cm. "Serial no. 96-41." Hearing on H.R. 6374, 5548, 4960, and S. 1515.   LC Card 80-601297 DDC 344.73/091 347.30491 19

1. Taylor, Kenneth, 1934-- - Medals. 2. Wiesenthal, Simon - Medals. 3. Spiess, Gerald F. - Medals. 4. United States Capitol Historical Society, Washington, D.C. - Medals. I. Title.
KF27 .B535 1980c

Medals for the 1980 U. S. summer Olympic team : hearing before the Subcommittee on Consumer Affairs of the Committee on Banking, Finance, and Urban Affairs, House of Representatives, Ninety-sixth Congress, second session, on H.R. 7482 ... June 25, 1980.

Washington : U. S. Govt. Print. Off., 1980. iii, 15 p. ; 24 cm. "Serial no. 96-59." LC Card 80-602976   DDC 344.73/099 347.30499 19
1. Sports - Medals - Law and legislation - United States. 2. Olympic Games, Moscow, 1980. I. Title.
KF27 .B535 1980e

Report on the sale of Carson City silver dollars by General Services Administration .
Washington , 1981. v, 20 p. ; LC Card 81-601279   DDC 737.4973 19
CJ1835 .R46

Sale of Carson City silver dollars by the General Services Administration : hearing before the Subcommittee on Consumer Affairs of the Committee on Banking, Finance, and Urban Affairs, House of Representatives, Ninety-sixth Congress, second session, August 19, 1980. Washington : U. S. Govt. Print. Off., 1980. iii, 65 p. ; 24 cm. "Serial no. 96-67." LC Card 80-603492   DDC 353.0082/2 19
1. Coinage - United States. 2. Dollar, American (Coin). 3. United States. General Services Administration. I. Title. II. Title: Carson City silver dollars.
KF27 .B535 1980d

To authorize the President of the United States to present on behalf of the Congress specially struck gold medals to Bryan Lewis Allen and to the A. Philip Randolph Institute : hearing before the Subcommittee on Consumer Affairs of the Committee on Banking, Finance, and Urban Affairs, House of Representatives, Ninety-sixth Congress, second session, on H.R. 5800 ... H.R. 5625 ... February 26, 1980. Washington : U. S. Govt. Print. Off., 1980. iii, 15 p. ; 24 cm. "Serial 96-45." LC Card 80-601396   DDC 344.73/091 19
1. Allen, Bryan L. - Medals. 2. Randolph (A. Philip) Institute - Medals. I. Title.
KF27 .B535 1980b

United States. Congress. House. Committee on Banking, Finance, and Urban Affairs. Subcommittee on Domestic Monetary Policy.
Measurement and control of the money supply : hearings before the Subcommittee on Domestic Monetary Policy of the Committee on Banking, Finance, and Urban Affairs, House of Representatives, Ninety-sixth Congress, second session, March 20 and 25, 1980. Washington : U. S. Govt. Print. Off., 1980. iii, 154 p. : graphs ; 24 cm. "Serial no. 96-51." Includes bibliographical references. LC Card 80-602423 DDC 332.4/14 19
1. Money supply - United States. 2. Monetary policy - United States. I. Title.
KF27 .B537 1980

Meeting the credit needs of minority communities : hearing before the Subcommittee on Domestic Monetary Policy of the Committee on Banking, Finance, and Urban Affairs, House of Representatives, Ninety-sixth Congress, second session, May 29, 1980. Washington : U. S. Govt. Print. Off., 1980. iii, 15 p. ; 24 cm. "Serial no. 96-65." LC Card 80-603640   DDC 332.7/0973 19
1. Federal aid to minority business enterprises - United States. 2. Minority business enterprises - United States - Finance. 3. Consumer credit - United States. 4. Minorities as consumers - United States. I. Title.
KF27 .B537 1980b

Recent monetary policy developments : hearing before the Subcommittee on Domestic Monetary Policy of the Committee on Banking, Finance, and Urban Affairs, House of Representatives, Ninety-sixth Congress, second session, November 19, 1980. Washington : U. S. G.P.O., 1981. iii, 73 p. : ill. ; 24 cm. "Serial no. 96-75." LC Card 81-600807 DDC 331.4/973 19
1. Monetary policy - United States. 2. Money supply - United States. I. Title.
KF27 .B537 1980c

To modernize the Federal Reserve System : hearing before the Subcommittee on Domestic Monetary Policy of the Committee on Banking, Finance, and Urban Affairs, House of Representatives, Ninety-sixth Congress, second session, on H.R. 7001 ... May 15, 1980. Washington : U. S. Govt. Print. Off., 1980. iii, 96 p. ; 23 cm. "Serial no. 96-62." LC Card 80-603677   DDC 346.73/08211 19
1. United States. Board of Governors of the Federal Reserve System. 2. Federal Reserve banks. I. Title.
KF27 .B537 1980a

Weintraub, Robert E., 1925- The impact of the

Federal Reserve System's monetary policies on the nation's economy (second report) .
Washington , c1980 [i.e. 1981] xii, 51 p. : LC Card 81-601005   DDC 330.973/0926 19
HG2565 .W44

United States. Congress. House. Committee on Banking, Finance and Urban Affairs. Subcommittee on Economic Stabilization.
Amendments to the Council on Wage and Price Stability act : hearings before the Subcommittee on Economic Stabilization of the Committee on Banking, Finance and Urban Affairs, House of Representatives, Ninety-fifth Congress, first session .... Washington : U. S. Govt. Print. Off., 1977. iv, 415 p. : ill. ; 24 cm. Hearings held April 6-26, 1977, on H.R. 2094, 2100, 3184 and 3810. LC Card 77-602660
1. United States - Economic policy - 1971-. 2. Inflation (Finance) - United States. 3. United States. Council on Wage and Price Stability. I. Title.
KF27 .B542 1977b   NYPL [JLE 81-450]

The Chrysler Corporation financial situation : hearings before the Subcommittee on Economic Stabilization of the Committee on Banking, Finance, and Urban Affairs, House of Representatives, Ninety-sixth Congress, first session, on H.R. 5805, entitled "Chrysler Corporation Loan Guarantee Act of 1979". Washington, D.C. : U. S. G.P.O. : For sale by the Supt. of Docs., U. S. G.P.O., 1979. 2 v. in 3 : ill. ; 24 cm. "Serial no. 96-34." Hearings held Oct. 18-Nov. 13, 1979. Includes bibliographical references.
LC Card 81-600718   DDC 343.73/0786292222 347.303786292222 19
1. Chrysler Corporation - Finance. 2. Automobile industry and trade - Law and legislation - United States. 3. Loans - United States - Government guaranty. I. Title.
KF27 .B542 1979g

Chrysler Corporation Loan Guarantee Board (U. S.) Findings of the Chrysler Corporation Loan Guarantee Board /. Washington , 1980. ii, 888 p. ; LC Card 80-602582 DDC 338.7/6292/0973 19
HD9710.U54 C42 1980

Chrysler Corporation Loan Guarantee Board (U. S.) Findings of the Chrysler Corporation Loan Guarantee Board /. Washington , 1981. vii, 281 p. : LC Card 81-601269 DDC 338.7/6292/0973 19
HD9710.U54 C42 1981

Defense Production Act Amendments of the Energy Security Act of 1980 : hearings before the Subcommittee on Economic Stabilization of the Committee on Banking, Finance, and Urban Affairs, House of Representatives, Ninety-sixth Congress, second session, July 30, and October 1, 1980. Washington : U. S. G.P.O., 1980. iii, 114 p. : ill. ; 24 cm. "Serial no. 96-69." LC Card 80-604041   DDC 343.73/07866266/0262 347.30378662660262 19
1. Synthetic fuels - Law and legislation - United States. 2. United States. Dept. of Defense. 3. United States. Dept. of Energy. I. Title.
KF27 .B542 1980b

Productivity performance and the American economy : hearings before the Subcommittee on Economic Stabilization of the Committee on Banking, Finance, and Urban Affairs, House of Representatives, Ninety-sixth Congress, second session .... Washington : U. S. Govt. Print. Off., 1980. iv, 318 p. : ill. ; 24 cm. Hearings held June 24-Aug. 27, 1980. "Serial no. 96-68." Includes bibliographical references. LC Card 80-603669 DDC 338./06/0973 19
1. Industrial productivity - Law and legislation - United States. 2. Industrial productivity - United States. 3. National Productivity Council (United States). 4. United States - Economic policy - 1971-. I. Title.
KF27 .B542 1980c

Synthetic fuel oversight hearing : hearing before the Subcommittee on Economic Stabilization of the Committee on Banking, Finance, and Urban Affairs, House of Representatives, Ninety-seventh Congress, first session, March 3, 1981. Washington : U. S. G.P.O., 1981. iii, 96 p. ; 24 cm. "Serial no. 97-2." Item 1013-A, 1913-B (microfiche) LC Card 81-601770 DDC 353.0082/38 19
1. Synthetic fuels industry - United States. 2. Synthetic Fuels Corporation (U. S.). I. Title.
KF27 .B542 1981

To authorize the extension of the Council on

Wage and Price Stability : hearings before the Subcommittee on Economic Stabilization of the Committee on Banking, Finance, and Urban Affairs, House of Representatives, Ninety-sixth Congress, second session, on H.R. 6777 ... March 19, 26, and May 6, 1980. Washington : U. S. Govt. Print. Off., 1980. iv, 475 p. ; 24 cm. "Serial no. 96-56." Includes bibliographical references. LC Card 80-602791 DDC 343.73/034 19
1. United States. Council on Wage and Price Stability. 2. Inflation (Finance) - United States. I. Title.
KF27 .B542 1980

United States. Congress. House. Committee on Banking, Finance and Urban Affairs. Subcommittee on Financial Institutions Supervision, Regulation and Insurance.
Community credit needs : hearings before the Subcommittee on Financial Institutions Supervision, Regulation, and Insurance of the Committee on Banking, Finance, and Urban Affairs, House of Representatives, Ninety-fifth Congress, second session. Washington : U. S. G.P.O., 1978. 2 v. (viii, 1503 p.) : ill. ; 24 cm. CONTENTS. - pt. 1. July 20, 25, 26; August 1, 2, and 3, 1978 -- pt. 2. August 8, 9, 10; September 21, 1978; and appendix. LC Card 81-600502 DDC 332.7/0973 19
1. Mortgage loans - United States. 2. Banking law - United States. 3. Discrimination in mortgage loans - Law and legislation - United States. 4. Community development, Urban - United States - Finance. 5. Financial institutions - United States. I. Title.
KF27 .B544 1978

Export trading companies legislation : hearing before the Subcommittee on Financial Institutions Supervision, Regulation and Insurance on the Committee on Banking, Finance, and Urban Affairs, House of Representatives, Ninety-sixth Congress, second session, September 30, 1980. Washington : U. S. G.P.O., 1981. iii, 85 p. ; 23 cm. "Serial no. 96-78." Item 1013 LC Card 81-600958 DDC 343.73/0878 347.30878 19
1. Export associations - Law and legislation. 2. Foreign trade promotion - Law and legislation - United States. 3. Export associations - Finance. 4. Bank investments - United States. I. Title.
KF27 .B544 1980d

Foreign bank operations and acquisitions in the United States : hearings before the Subcommittee on Financial Institutions Supervision, Regulation, and Insurance of Committee on Banking, Finance, and Urban Affairs, House of Representatives, Ninety-sixth Congress, second session .... Washington : U. S. G.P.O., 1981- v. <1> : ill. ; 24 cm. "Serial no. 96-77." Pt. 1: "September 24 and 25, 1980, and Appendixes I and II." Pt. 2: "Appendixes III, IV, and V." Item 1013 Includes bibliographical references. LC Card 81-601173 DDC 332.1/5/0973 19
1. Banks and banking, Foreign - United States. 2. Corporations, Foreign - United States. I. Title.
KF27 .B544 1980e

Home mortgage disclosure act extension amendments : hearings before the Subcommittee on Financial Institutions Supervision, Regulation, and Insurance of the Committee on Banking, Finance, and Urban Affairs, House of Representatives, Ninety-sixth Congress, second session ... April 16, 17, and 23, 1980. Washington : U. S. Govt. Print. Off., 1980. vi, 804 p. : ill. ; 24 cm. "Serial 96-58." LC Card 80-602944 DDC 344.7304/364 19
1. Mortgage loans - United States. 2. Discrimination in mortgage loans - Law and legislation - United States. 3. Housing - United States - Finance. I. Title.
KF27 .B544 1980b

Regulation Q and related measures : hearings before the Subcommittee on Financial Institutions Supervision, Regulation, and Insurance of the Committee on Banking, Finance, and Urban Affairs, House of Representatives, Ninety-sixth Congress, second session, on H.R. 4986 .... Washington : U. S. Govt. Print. Off., 1980. v, 1013 p. : ill. ; 24 cm. "Serial 96-50." Hearings held Jan. 24-Feb. 21, 1980. Includes bibliographical references. LC Card 80-602494 DDC 346.73/082 19
1. Banking law - United States. 2. Electronic funds transfers - Law and legislation - United States. 3. NOW accounts - Law and legislation - United States. 4. Credit unions - Law and legislation - United States. I. Title.
KF27 .B544 1980a

GOVERNMENT PUBLICATIONS - U.S.: 1981

421
United States. Congress. House. Committee on Education and

Role of commercial banks in the financing of the debt of the city of Cleveland : hearing before the Subcommittee on Financial Institutions Supervision, Regulation, and Insurance of the Committee on Banking, Finance, and Urban Affairs, House of Representatives, Ninety-sixth Congress, first session, July 10, 1979. Washington : U. S. Govt. Print. Off., 1980. iv, 988 p. : ill. ; 24 cm. "Serial 96-61." LC Card 80-603313 DDC 352.1/09771/32 19

1. Debts, Public - Ohio - Cleveland. 2. Finance, Public - Ohio - Cleveland. 3. Banks and banking - Ohio - Cleveland. I. Title.
KF27 .B544 1979f

United States. Congress. House. Committee on Banking, Finance and Urban Affairs. Subcommittee on General Oversight and Renegotiation.
Oversight hearings on National Development Bank legislation : hearings before the Subcommittee on General Oversight and Renegotiation of the Committee on Banking, Finance, and Urban Affairs, House of Representatives, Ninety-sixth Congress, second session, on H.R. 7902 ... September 10, 18, and 24, 1980. Washington : U. S. G.P.O., 1980. iii, 220 p. : ill. ; 24 cm. "Serial no. 96-73." Includes bibliographical references. LC Card 81-600651 DDC 346.73/0822 347.306822 19

1. National Development Bank (U. S.). 2. Development banks - Law and legislation - United States. 3. Government lending - United States. I. Title.
KF27 .B563 1980

Oversight hearings on the Currency and Foreign Transactions Reporting Act : hearings before the Subcommittee on General Oversight and Renegotiation of the Committee on Banking, Finance, and Urban Affairs, House of Representatives, Ninety-sixth Congress, second session, October 1, December 3, 1980. Washington : U. S. G.P.O., 24 cm. iii, 130 p. : ill. ; 24 cm. "Serial no. 96-79." Item 1013 LC Card 81-600959 DDC 353.0082/52 19

1. Confidential communications - Banking - United States. 2. Banks and banking - United States - Records and correspondence. 3. Foreign exchange - Law and legislation - United States. I. Title.
KF27 .B563 1980a

United States. Congress. House. Committee on Banking, Finance, and Urban Affairs. Subcommittee on Housing and Community Development. Task Force on Rental Housing.
United States. Congress. House. Committee on Banking, Finance, and Urban Affairs. Subcommittee on Housing and Community Development.
Earthquake insurance availability : hearings before the Subcommittee on Housing and Community Development of the Committee on Banking, Finance, and Urban Affairs, House of Representatives, Ninety-sixth Congress, second session, July 17, 1980, Santa Ana, Calif., July 18, 1980, San Francisco, Calif. Washington : U. S. Govt. Print. Off., 1980. v, 729 p. : ill. ; 24 cm. "Serial 96-64." Includes bibliographical references. LC Card 80-603498 DDC 368.1/22 19

1. Insurance, Earthquake - California. 2. Disaster relief - California. 3. Earthquakes - California. 4. Earthquakes and building - California. I. Title.
KF27 .B546 1980b

Housing and community development amendments of 1980 : hearings before the Subcommittee on Housing and Community Development of the Committee on Banking, Finance, and Urban Affairs, House of Representatives, Ninety-sixth Congress, second session. Washington : U. S. Govt. Print. Off., 1980. 2 v. (ix, 1290 p.) : ill. ; 24 cm. Hearings held Mar. 3-7, 1980. "Serial 96-55." LC Card 80-602519 DDC 344.73/063635 19

1. Housing - Law and legislation - United States. 2. Community development - Law and legislation - United States. I. Title.
KF27 .B546 1980a

Task Force on Rental Housing : hearings before the Subcommittee on Housing and Community Development of the Committee on Banking, Finance, and Urban Affairs, House of Representatives, Ninety-sixth Congress, second session .... Washington : U. S. Govt. Print. Off., 1980. vii, 1072 p. : ill. ; 24 cm. Hearings held in various cities, Feb. 18-May 31, 1980. "Serial 96-60."

Includes bibliographical references. LC Card 80-603282 DDC 363.5/8 19
1. Rental housing - United States. I. Title.
KF27 .B5467 1980

United States. Congress. House. Committee on Banking, Finance and Urban Affairs. Subcommittee on International Development Institutions and Finance.
United States. Congress. House. Committee on Banking, Finance and Urban Affairs. Subcommittee on International Trade, Investment and Monetary Policy.
Export trading companies legislation : hearing before the Subcommittee on International Trade, Investment, and Monetary Policy of the Committee on Banking, Finance, and Urban Affairs, House of Representatives, Ninety-sixth Congress, second session, on H.R. 7310 ... H.R. 7364 ... H.R. 7436 ... H.R. 7463 ... July 1 and 2, 1980. Washington : U. S. G.P.O., 1980. iii, 225 p. : 24 cm. "Serial no. 96-74." Item 1013 Includes bibliographical references. LC Card 81-600600 DDC 343.73/0878 347.303878 19

1. Export associations - Law and legislation. 2. Foreign trade promotion - Law and legislation - United States. 3. Export sales - United States. I. Title.
KF27 .B577 1980b

International Development Association sixth replenishment and African Development Bank membership / hearings before the Subcommittee on International Development Institutions and Finance of the Committee on Banking, Finance, and Urban Affairs, House of Representatives, Ninety-sixth Congress, second session, on H.R. 6811 ... March 26, 27, and April 16, 1980. Washington : U. S. Govt. Print. Off., 1980. iii, 325 p. : ill. ; 24 cm. "Serial no. 96-54." LC Card 80-602436 DDC 346.73/082153/0262 19

1. International Development Association. 2. African Development Bank. 3. Economic assistance, American. I. Title.
KF27 .B573 1980

Oversight hearings on the Export-Import Bank : hearings before the Subcommittee on International Trade, Investment and Monetary Policy of the Committee on Banking, Finance, and Urban Affairs, House of Representatives, Ninety-sixth Congress, second session, June 12 and 19, 1980. Washington : U. S. G.P.O., 1980. iii. 143 p. : ill. ; 24 cm. "Serial no. 96-71." LC Card 81-600657 DDC 353.0082/52 19

1. Export-Import Bank of the United States. I. Title.
KF27 .B577 1980a

To amend the Bretton Woods agreements act to authorize consent to an increase in the United States quota in the International Monetary Fund : hearings before the Subcommittee on International Trade, Investment, and Monetary Policy of the Committee on Banking, Finance, and Urban Affairs, House of Representatives, Ninety-sixth Congress, second sesson, on H.R. 5970 .... Washington : U. S. Govt. Print. Off., 1980. iv, 621 p. : ill. ; 24 cm. "Serial no. 96-57." Hearings held Feb. 4-Apr. 21, 1980. LC Card 80-602758 DDC 343.73/032 19

1. International Monetary Fund. 2. United States - Foreign economic relations. I. Title.
KF27 .B577 1980

U. S. participation in the multilateral development institutions : hearing before the Subcommittee on International Development Institutions and Finance of the Committee on Banking, Finance, and Urban Affairs, House of Representatives, Ninety-seventh Congress, first session, March 11, 1981. Washington : U. S. G.P.O., 1981. iii, 258 p. ; 24 cm. "Serial no. 97-5." Item 1013-A, 1013-B (microfiche) LC Card 81-601948 DDC 332.1/53 19

1. Economic asssistance, American. 2. World Bank. 3. African Development Bank. I. Title.
KF27 .B547 1981

United States. Congress. House. Committee on Science and Technology. Technology trade . Washington , 1980. vii, 687 p. : LC Card 80-604020 DDC 338.973 19
KF27 .S39 1980g

United States. Congress. House. Committee on Banking, Finance and Urban Affairs. Subcommittee on the City.
Bridgeport, Conn.: how an old industrial city adapts to change : hearing before the Subcommittee on the City of the Committee on

Banking, Finance and Urban Affairs, House of Representatives, Ninety-fifth Congress, first session, December 12, 1977. Washington : U. S. G.P.O., 1978. iii, 156 p. : ill. ; 24 cm. LC Card 81-601517 DDC 338.9746/9 19

1. Bridgeport (Conn.) - Economic policy. 2. Federal-city relations - Connecticut - Bridgeport. I. Title.
KF27 .B52 1977d

Compact cities : energy saving strategies for the eighties : report together with dissenting views / by the Subcommittee on the City of the Committee on Banking, Finance, and Urban Affairs, House of Representatives, 96th Congress, second session. Washington : U. S. Govt. Print. Off., 1980. viii, 86 p. ; 24 cm. "July 1980." "Committee print 96-15." Includes bibliographical references. LC Card 80-602867 DDC 333.79/0973 19

1. Land use and energy conservation - United States. 2. Energy conservation - United States. 3. Urban policy - United States. 4. Energy policy - United States. I. Title.
HD108.2 .U54 1980

Urban revitalization and industrial policy : hearings before the Subcommittee on the City of the Committee on Banking, Finannce, and Urban Affairs, House of Representatives, Ninety-sixth Congress, second session, September 16 and 17, 1980. Washington : U. S. G.P.O., 1980. iv, 388 p. : ill. ; 24 cm. "Serial no. 96-72." Includes bibliographical references. LC Card 81-600638 DDC 338.973 19

1. Industry and state - United States. 2. Urban policy - United States. I. Title.
KF27 .B52 1980

United States. Congress. House. Committee on Education. (Old catalog form: United States. Education Committee, House)
Motion Picture Commission : hearings before the Committee on Education, House of Representatives, Sixty-third Congress, second session, on bills to establish a Federal Motion Picture Commission. New York : Arno Press, 1978. 234 p. ; 24 cm. (Aspects of film) Hearing held Mar. 20-May 19, 1914. Reprint of the 1914 ed. published by Govt. Print. Off., Washington. ISBN 0-405-11136-3 LC Card 77-11386

1. Moving-pictures - Law and legislation - United States. I. Title.
KF27 .E28 1914 **NYPL [JLE 80-2425]**

United States. Congress. House. Committee on Education and Labor. (Old Catalog form: United States. Education and Labor, Committee on // Hearings printed in 1978 and later are available only in microform. Please consult the librarians in the Economic and Public Affairs Division.
Report of congressional study group visit by the Committee on Education and Labor to the Department of Defense overseas schools, April 1979 / Committee on Education and Labor, House of Representatives, 96th Congress. Washington : U. S. Govt. Print. Off., 1979. ii, 7 p. ; 24 cm. At head of title: Committee print. "November 1979." LC Card 80-601733 DDC 355.3/4 19

1. Military post schools, American. I. Title.
LC5081 .U54 1979

United States. Congress. Senate. Committee on Labor and Public Welfare. Subcommittee on Labor. Scotia Mine disaster, 1976 . Washington , 1976. vi, 279 p. ; LC Card 76-602873
KF26 .L363 1976f **NYPL [JLE 81-466]**

United States. Congress. House. Committee on Education and Labor. Subcommittee on Postsecondary Education. Reauthorization of the National Foundation for the Arts and the Humanities act and the Museum services act : hearings before the Subcommittee on Postsecondary Education of the Committee on Education and Labor, House of Representatives, Ninety-sixth Congress, second session ... held in Washington, D.C. Washington : U. S. Govt. Print. Off., 1980. xii, 1105 p. : ill. ; 23 cm. Hearings held Feb. 6, 21; Mar. 5; and April 2, 1980. LC Card 80-603480 DDC 353.0072/236854 19

1. National Foundation for the Arts and the Humanities - Appropriations and expenditures. 2. Federal aid to the arts - United States. 3. Federal aid to museums - United States. I. Title.
KF27 .E369 1980a

United States. Congress. House. Committee on Education and Labor. Subcommittee on

BIBLIOGRAPHIC GUIDE

United States. Congress. House. Committee on Education and

422

Elementary, Secondary, and Vocational Education.
Bureau of Indian Affairs implementation of title XI of Public law 95-561 : hearing before the Subcommittee on Elementary, Secondary, and Vocational Education of the Committee on Education and Labor, House of Representatives, Ninety-sixth Congress, second session held in Washington, D.C., on April 28, 1980.
Washington : U. S. Govt. Print. Off., 1980. iii, 31 p. ; 24 cm. LC Card 80-603069 DDC 353.0085/1/08897 19
1. Indians of North America - Education. I. Title.
KF27 .E3364 1980a

Cuban and Haitian refugee education : hearings before the Subcommittee on Elementary, Secondary, and Vocational Education of the Committee on Education and Labor, House of Representatives, Ninety-sixth Congress, second session, on H.R. 7425 ... held in Miami, Fla., on June 23, Washington, D.C., on July 1, 1980. Washington : U. S. G.P.O., 1980. iv, 160 p. ; 24 cm. LC Card 80-603905 DDC 344.73/07917/687291073 347.3047917687291073 19
1. Cubans - Education - Law and legislation - United States. 2. Haitians - Education - Law and legislation - United States. I. Title.
KF27 .E3364 1980g

Current issues in vocational education : hearings before the Subcommittee on Elementary, Secondary, and Vocational Education of the Committee on Education and Labor, House of Representatives, Ninety-sixth Congress, second session, hearing held in Washington, D.C., on September 17, 24, 25, and 30, 1980. Washington : U. S. G.P.O., 1980 [i.e. 1981] iv, 1178 p. : ill. ; 24 cm. Item 1015 Includes bibliographies. LC Card 81-601613 DDC 370.11/3 19
1. Vocational education - United States. I. Title.
KF27 .E3364 1980i

The Educational testing act of 1979 : hearings before the Subcommittee on Elementary, Secondary, and Vocational Education of the Committee on Education and Labor, House of Representatives, Ninety-sixth Congress, second session, on H.R. 4949 ... held in Washington, D.C., on June 5, and 11, 1980. Washington : U. S. Govt. Print. Off., 1980. iv, 407 p. : ill. ; 23 cm. LC Card 80-603455 DDC 344.73/079 19
1. Educational tests and measurements - Law and legislation - United States. 2. Universities and colleges - Entrance examinations - Law and legislation - United States. I. Title.
KF27 .E3364 1980d

Hearings on dismissing certain cases pending before the Education Appeal Board : hearings before the Subcommittee on Elementary, Secondary, and Vocational Education of the Committee on Education and Labor, House of Representatives, Ninety-sixth Congress, second session, on H.R. 8145 ... hearings held in Washington, D.C., on November 18, 19, and 20, 1980. Washington : U. S. G.P.O., 1981. v, 568 p. : ill. ; 24 cm. Item 1015 Bibliography: p. 415. LC Card 81-601633 DDC 344.73/076 347.30476 19
1. United States. Education Appeal Board. 2. Federal aid to education - United States. 3. Educational law and legislation - United States. I. Title.
KF27 .E3364 1980h

Hearings on the President's youth education and employment initiative : hearings before the Subcommittee on Elementary, Secondary, and Vocational Education of the Committee on Education and Labor, House of Representatives, Ninety-sixth Congress, second session, on H.R. 6711 .... Washington : U. S. Govt. Print. Off., 1980. vi, 938 p. ; 23 cm. Hearings held Feb. 25-Mar. 13, 1980 in Washington, D.C. LC Card 80-603474 DDC 344.73/013411 19
1. Children - Legal status, laws, etc. - United States. 2. Educational law and legislation - United States. 3. Youth - Employment - United States. I. Title.
KF27 .E3364 1980e

Indian education act--Title IV, Public law 92-318 : hearing before the Subcommittee on Elementary, Secondary, and Vocational Education of the Committee on Education and Labor, House of Representatives, Ninety-sixth Congress, second session ... held in Washington, D.C., on May 2, 1980. Washington : U. S.

Govt. Print. Off., 1980. iii, 71 p. : ill. ; 24 cm. LC Card 80-603109 DDC 344.73/079197 19
1. Indians of North America - Education - Law and legislation. 2. Indians of North America - Education. I. Title.
KF27 .E3364 1980b

Oversight hearing on Federal library programs : hearing before the Subcommittee on Elementary, Secondary, and Vocational Education and the Subcommittee on Postsecondary Education of the Committee on Education and Labor, House of Representatives, Ninety-sixth Congress, second session ... held in Washington, D.C., on April 15, 1980. Washington : U. S. Govt. Print. Off., 1980. iii, 71 p. : ill. ; 24 cm. LC Card 80-603097 DDC 353.0085/2 19
1. Federal aid to libraries - United States. I. United States. Congress. House. Committee on Education and Labor. Subcommittee on Postsecondary Education. II. Title.
KF27 .E3364 1980c

Oversight hearings on Indian education : hearings before the subcommittee on Elementary, Secondary, and Vocational Education of the Committee on Education and Labor, House of Representatives, Ninety-sixth Congress, second session, hearings held in Washington, D.C., on September 3 and 5, 1980. Washington : U. S. G.P.O., 1980 [i.e. 1981] iv, 252 p. : ill. ; 24 cm. Item 1015 LC Card 81-601356 DDC 353.0085/1/08897 19
1. Indians of North America - Education. I. Title.
KF27 .E3364 1980j

Oversight hearings on the implementation of title XI, Public Law 95-561 : problems in the BIA Portland area ; hearings before the Subcommittee on Elementary, Secondary, and Vocational Education of the Committee on Education and Labor, House of Representatives, Ninety-sixth Congress, second session, hearings held in Washington, D.C., on July 28 and 29, 1980. Washington : U. S.G.P.O., 1980. iii, 47 p. : ill. ; 24 cm. LC Card 80-604010 DDC 371.97/97/0795 19
1. United States. Bureau of Indian Affairs. Portland Area Office. 2. Indians of North America - Northwest, Pacific - Education. 3. Indians of North America - Northwest, Pacific - Government relations. I. Title.
KF27 .E3364 1980f

Truth in testing act of 1979, the Educational testing act of 1979 : hearings before the Subcommittee on Elementary, Secondary, and Vocational Education of the Committee on Education and Labor, House of Representatives, Ninety-sixth Congress, first session, on H.R. 3564 ... and H.R. 4949. Washington : U. S. Govt. Print. Off., 1980. viii, 1194 p. : ill. ; 24 cm. Hearings held July 31-Oct. 11, 1979. LC Card 80-601862 DDC 344.73/07 19
1. Educational tests and measurements - Law and legislation - United States. 2. Universities and colleges - Admission - Law and legislation - United States. 3. Occupational training - Law and legislation - United States. I. Title.
KF27 .E3364 1979r

United States. Congress. House. Committee on Education and Labor. Subcommittee on Employment Opportunities.
Civil Rights Amendments Act of 1979 : Hearing before the Subcommittee on Employment Opportunities of the Committee on Education and Labor, House of Representatives, Ninety-sixth Congress, second session, H.R 2074 ... hearing held in San Francisco, Calif., October 10, 1980. Washington : U. S. G.P.O., 1980 [i.e. 1981] iv, 161 p. : ill. ; 24 cm. Item 1015 Bibliography: p. 128-130. LC Card 81-601336 DDC 342.73/085 347.30285 19
1. Homosexuality - Law and legislation - United States. 2. Homosexuals - Civil rights - United States. I. Title.
KF27 .E3366 1980b

Comparison of employment trends for women and minorities in forty-five selected Federal agencies, 1980 / prepared by the Subcommittee on Employment, Opportunities of the Committee on Education and Labor, United States House of Representatives. Washington : U. S. Govt. Print. Off., 1980. v, 192 p. : graphs ; 24 cm. At head of title: 96th Congress, 2d session. Committee print. "July 1980." LC Card 80-603058 DDC 331.12/51353 19

1. Civil service - United States - Minority employment - Statistics. 2. Women in the civil service - United States - Statistics. I. Title.
HD8008 .U56 1980

Oversight hearing on employment impact of current and proposed economic policies : hearing before the Subcommittee on Employment Opportunities of the Committee on Education and Labor, House of Representatives, Ninety-sixth Congress, second session, hearing held in Washington, D.C., April 18, 1980. Washington : U. S. G.P.O., c1980 [i.e. 1981] iii, 51 p. ; 24 cm. Item 1015 LC Card 81-601627 DDC 339.5/0973 19
1. Unemployed - United States. 2. United States - Economic policy - 1971-. 3. United States - Full employment policies. I. Title.
KF27 .E3366 1980c

Oversight hearing on the federal enforcement of equal employment opportunity laws : hearing before the Subcommittee on Employment Opportunities of the Committee on Education and Labor, House of Representatives, Ninety-sixth Congress, second session, hearing held in Washington, D.C., August 19, 1980. Washington : U. S. G.P.O., 1980. iv, 98 p. : ill. ; 24 cm. LC Card 80-604008 DDC 353.001/04 19
1. Discrimination in employment - United States. 2. Civil service - United States. I. Title.
KF27 .E3366 1980a

Oversight on the Full employment and balanced growth act : hearings before the Subcommittee on Employment Opportunities of the Committee on Education and Labor, House of Representatives, Ninety-sixth Congress, second session, hearings held in New York, N.Y., on May 19 and Los Angeles, Calif., May 30, 1980. Washington : U. S. Govt. Print. Off., 1979. v, 234 p. : ill. ; 24 cm. LC Card 80-603323 DDC 353.0083 19
1. United States - Full employment policies. 2. United States - Economic policy - 1971-. I. Title.
KF27 .E3366 1980

United States. Congress. House. Committee on Education and Labor. Subcommittee on Labor-Management Relations. Hearings on plant closing problems . Washington , 1981. iv, 152 p. ; LC Card 81-601623 DDC 343.73/0742 347.303742 19
KF27 .E347 1980h

United States. Congress. Senate. Committee on Labor and Human Resources. Health and other effects of unemployment . Washington , 1980 [i.e. 1981] iii, 84 p. : LC Card 81-601598 DDC 362.1/042/0973 19
KF26 .L27 1980r

United States. Congress. House. Committee on Education and Labor. Subcommittee on Health and Safety.
Oversight hearings on OSHA--occupational safety and health for Federal employees : hearings before the Subcommittee on Health and Safety of the Committee on Education and Labor, House of Representatives, Ninety-sixth Congress, first session .... Washington : U. S. Govt. Print. Off., 1980- v. : ill. ; 24 cm. Hearings held Mar. 14- , 1979. CONTENTS. - pt. 1. Federal sector. LC Card 80-602740 DDC 353.001/6 19
1. United States - Officials and employees - Accidents. 2. United States - Officials and employees - Health and hygiene. I. Title.
KF27 .E3394 1979a

Oversight hearings on the Federal mine safety and health amendments act of 1977 : hearings before the Subcommittee on Health and Safety of the Committee on Education and Labor, House of Representatives, Ninety-sixth Congress, first session .... Washington, D.C. : U. S. Govt. Print. Off., 1980. v. <1-3> : ill. ; 24 cm. Hearings held in Washington Mar. 20, 1979-<Sept. 30, 1980> CONTENTS. - pt. 1. Nonmetallic mines.--pt. 2. Nonmetallic mines.--pt. 3. Coal, metal, and surface mine construction. LC Card 80-602787 DDC 353.0082/382/0289 19
1. Mine safety - United States. 2. Mine sanitation - United States. I. Title.
KF27 .E3394 1979

A staff report on the oversight of the Occupational Safety and Health Administration with respect to grain elevator fires and explosions / Subcommittee on Health and Safety, Committee on Education and Labor,

GOVERNMENT PUBLICATIONS - U.S.: 1981

United States. Congress. House. Committee on Education and

423

House of Representatives. Washington : U. S.
Govt. Print. Off., 1980. v, 151 p. : ill. ; 24 cm.
At head of title: 96th Congress, 2d session. Committee
print. Bibliography: p. 38.   LC Card 80-601779   DDC
363.3/79 19
1. Grain elevators - United States - Fires and fire
prevention. I. Title.
TH9445.G7 U53 1980

United States. Congress. House Committee on
Post Office and Civil Service. Subcommittee on
Postal Personnel and Modernization. Safety and
health within U. S. Postal Service .
Washington , 1980. vi, 392 p. :   LC Card
80-603078   DDC 363.1/193834973 19
KF27 .P6677 1980a

United States. Congress. House. Committee on
Education and Labor. Subcommittee on
Human Resources.
Economic opportunity amendments of 1980 :
hearings before the Subcommittee on Human
Resources of the Committee on Education and
Labor, House of Representatives, Ninety-sixth
Congress, second session, on H.R. 6619 ... held
in Washingon, D.C. on March 6 and 26, 1980.
Washington : U. S. Govt. Print. Off., 1980. v,
441 p. ; 24 cm.   LC Card 80-603732   DDC
344.73/0636358 347.304636358 19
1. Poor - Energy assistance - Law and legislation -
United States. 2. Handicapped - Energy assistance -
Law and legislation - United States. 3. Energy
conservation - Law and legislation - United States. I.
Title.
KF27 .E34 1980a

Federal efforts to aid low-income and elderly
individuals affected by life-threatening heat
conditions : hearing before the Subcommittee
on Human Resources of the Committee on
Education and Labor, House of Representatives,
Ninety-sixth Congress, second session, hearing
held in Washington, D.C., on July 30, 1980.
Washington : U. S. G.P.O., 1980 [i.e. 1981] iii,
53 p. : ill. ; 24 cm. Item 1015   LC Card 81-601392
DDC 362.5/8 19
1. Aged - United States - Energy assistance. 2. Poor -
United States - Energy assistance. 3. Heat -
Physiological effect. I. Title.
KF27 .E34 1980c

Juvenile justice amendments of 1980 : hearing
before the Subcommittee on Human Resources
of the Committee on Education and Labor,
House of Representatives, Ninety-sixth
Congress, second session ... held in Washington,
D.C., on March 19, 1980. [Washington, D.C. :
U. S. G.P.O., 1980] vii, 404 p. : ill. ; 24 cm.
Includes bibliographies.   LC Card 80-604074   DDC
345.73/08 347.3058 19
1. Juvenile justice, Adminstration of - United States. I.
Title.
KF27 .E34 1980b

United States. Congress. House. Committee on
Education and Labor. Subcommittee on
Labor-Management Relations.
Hearings on plant closing problems : hearings
before the Subcommittee on Labor-Management
Relations of the Committee on Education and
Labor, House of Representatives, Ninety-sixth
Congress, second session, on H.R. 5040 ...
hearings held in Missoula, Mont., August 16,
Eugene, Oreg., August 18, 1980. Washington :
U. S. G.P.O., 1980. vi, 500 p. : ill. ; 24 cm.
Includes bibliographical references.   LC Card
81-600603   DDC 344.73/0125 347.304125 19
1. Plant shutdowns - Law and legislation - United
States. 2. Economic assistance, Domestic - Law and
legislation - United States. 3. Unemployment - United
States. I. Title.
KF27 .E347 1980f

Hearings on plant closing problems : joint
hearing before the Subcommittee on
Labor-Management Relations of the
Subcommittee on Employment Opportunities of
the Committee on Education and Labor, House
of Representatives, Ninety-sixth Congress,
second session, on H.R. 5040 ... hearings held
in Martinez, Calif., on October 15, 1980.
Washington : U. S. G.P.O., 1981. iv, 152 p. :
ill. ; 24 cm. Item 1015   LC Card 81-601623   DDC
343.73/0742 347.303742 19
1. Plant shutdowns - Law and legislation - United
States. 2. Economic assistance, Domestic - Law and
legislation - United States. I. Congress.
House. Committee on Education and Labor.

Subcommittee on Employment Opportunities. II. Title.
KF27 .E347 1980h

Hospital housestaff employees : hearing before
the Subcommittee on Labor-Management
Relations of the Committee on Education and
Labor, House of Representatives, Ninety-sixth
Congress, first session on H.R. 2222 ... held in
Washington, D.C., on July 17, 1979.
Washington : U. S. Govt. Print. Off., 1979. iv,
90 p. ; 23 cm.   LC Card 79-604325   DDC
344.73/018904136211 19
1. Hospitals - Staff - Legal status, laws, etc. - United
States. 2. Collective labor agreements - Hospitals -
United States. I. Title.
KF27 .E347 1979a

Pressures in today's workplace : report of the
Subcommittee on Labor-Management Relations
of the Committee on Education and Labor,
House of Representatives. Washington : U. S.
G.P.O., 1981. vii, 62 p. ; 24 cm. At head of title:
96th Congress, 2d session. Committee Print. "December
1980." Item 1015   LC Card 81-601273   DDC
658.3/00973 19
1. Industrial relations - United States. 2. Civil rights -
United States. 3. Personnel management - United
States. I. Title.
HD8072.5 .U54 1981

United States. Congress. House. Committee on
Education and Labor. Subcommittee on
Labor-Management Relations. Welfare and
Pension Plans Task Force. Hearings on the
Public Employee Retirement Income Security
Act of 1980 : hearings before the Task Force
on Welfare and Pension Plans of the
Subcommittee on Labor-Management Relations
of the Committee on Education and Labor,
House of Representatives, Ninety-sixth
Congress, second session, on H.R. 6525 ...
hearings held in Washington, D.C. on
September 30 and October 1, 1980.
Washington : U. S. G.P.O., 1980 [i.e. 1981] vii,
1726 p. : ill. ; 24 cm. Item 1015 Includes
bibliographical references.   LC Card 81-601635   DDC
342.73/0686 347.302686 19
1. Civil service pensions - United States. 2. Local
officials and employees - Pensions - United States. 3.
State governments - Officials and employees - Pensions.
I. Title.
KF27 .E347 1980g

United States. Congress. House. Committee on
Education and Labor. Subcommittee on
Labor Standards.
Hearings on a death benefit for Federal law
enforcement officers and firefighters : hearings
before the Subcommittee on Labor Standards of
the Committee on Education and Labor, House
of Representatives, Ninety-sixth Congress,
second session, on H.R. 5834 ... and H.R.
5888 ... held in Washington, D.C., on March 12
and 13, 1980. Washington : U. S. Govt. Print.
Off., 1980. iv, 161 p. ; 23 cm.   LC Card
80-602763   DDC 344.73/023 19
1. Police - Salaries, pensions, etc. - United States. 2.
Fire fighters - Salaries, pensions, etc. - United States. 3.
Survivors' benefits - United States. I. Title.
KF27 .E348 1980

National workers' compensation standards act
of 1979 : hearings before the Subcommittee on
Labor Standards of the Committee on
Education and Labor, House of Representatives,
Ninety-sixth Congress, second session, on H.R.
5482 .... Washington : U. S. Govt. Print. Off.,
1980. vi, 815 p. : ill. ; 24 cm. Hearings held Mar.
25-May 15, 1980.   LC Card 80-603427   DDC
344.73/021 19
1. Workmen's compensation - United States - States. I.
Title.
KF27 .E348 1980c

Oversight hearing on the child labor provisions
of the Fair labor standards act : hearing before
the Subcommittee on Labor Standards of the
Committee on Education and Labor, House of
Representatives, Ninety-sixth Congress, second
session, on H.R. 5463 ... and H.R. 6774 ... :
hearing held in Washington, D.C. on May 20,
1980. Washington : U. S. Govt. Print. Off.,
1980. iv, 196 p. : ill. ; 24 cm.   LC Card
80-603516   DDC 353.0083/82 19
1. Children - Employment - United States. 2.
Strawberries - Harvesting - Law and legislation - United
States. 3. Pesticides - Toxicology - United States. I.
Title.
KF27 .E348 1980b

Oversight hearings on section 14(C) of the Fair
Labor Standards Act : hearings before the
Subcommittee on Labor Standards of the
Committee on Education and Labor, House of
Representatives, Ninety-sixth Congress, second
session ... held in Washington, D.C., on May 14
and 15, 1980. Washington : U. S. G.P.O., 1980.
v, 540 p. : ill. ; 24 cm.   LC Card 80-603995
DDC 353.0083/6 19
1. Wages - Handicapped - United States. 2. Sheltered
workshops - United States. I. Title.
KF27 .E348 1980d

Oversight hearings on the Federal employees'
compensation act : hearings before the
Subcommittee on Labor Standards of the
Committee on Education and Labor, House of
Representatives, Ninety-sixth Congress, second
session ... Washington, D.C. : U. S. Govt. Print.
Off., 1980- v. : ill. ; 24 cm. Hearings held Mar. 4-
CONTENTS. - pt. 1. Washington hearings.   LC Card
80-603447   DDC 353.0082/56 19
1. United States - Officials and employees - Salaries,
allowances, etc. 2. Workmen's compensation - United
States. I. Title.
KF27 .E348 1980a

Oversight hearings on the Longshoremen's and
harbor workers' compensation act : hearings
before the Subcommittee on Labor Standards of
the Committee on Education and Labor, House
of Representatives, Ninety-sixth Congress, first
session, hearings held in Washington, D.C. ....
Washington : U. S. Govt. Print. Off., 1980. viii,
1231 p. : ill. ; 23 cm. Hearings held Nov. 13-Dec.
6, 1979. Includes bibliographical references.   LC Card
80-603416   DDC 353.0082/56 19
1. Stevedores - United States. 2. Workmen's
compensation - United States. 3. Stevedores - Legal
status, laws, etc. - United States. I. Title.
KF27 .E348 1979d

Oversight hearings on the Longshoremen's and
Harbor Workers' Compensation Act.
Supplement : hearings before the Subcommittee
on Labor Standards of the Committee on
Education and Labor, House of Representatives,
Ninety-sixth Congress, first session ... held in
Washington, D.C., on November 13, 14, 15,
and 27, and December 6, 1979. Washington :
U. S. G.P.O., 1980. v, 57 p. ; 24 cm.   LC Card
80-604153   DDC 344.73/0217 347.304217 19
1. Stevedores - United States. 2. Workers'
compensation - Law and legislation - United States. 3.
Stevedores - Legal status, laws, etc. - United States. I.
Title.
KF27 .E348 1979d Suppl

United States. Congress. House. Committee on
Education and Labor. Subcommittee on
Postsecondary Education.
Field hearings on the reauthorization of the
National Foundation for the Arts and the
Humanities act and the Museum services act :
hearings before the Subcommittee on
Postsecondary Education of the Committee on
Education and Labor, House of Representatives,
Ninety-sixth Congress, second session.
Washington : U. S. Govt. Print. Off., 1980. xi,
1151 p. : ill. ; 23 cm. Hearings held in various
cities, Feb. 16-Mar. 31, 1980.   LC Card 80-603320
DDC 353.0085/4 19
1. National Foundation on the Arts and the
Humanities. 2. Federal aid to the arts - United States.
3. Federal aid to museums - United States. I. Title.
KF27 .E369 1980

United States. Congress. House. Committee on
Education and Labor. Subcommittee on
Elementary, Secondary, and Vocational
Education. Oversight hearing on Federal library
programs . Washington , 1980. iii, 71 p. :   LC
Card 80-603097   DDC 353.0085/2 19
KF27 .E3364 1980c

United States. Congress. House. Committee on
Education and Labor. Subcommittee on
Select Education.
Hearings on foreign languages and international
studies : hearings before the Subcommittee on
Select Education of the Committee on
Education and Labor, House of Representatives,
Ninety-sixth Congress, second session, on H.
Con. Res. 301 ... hearings held in Washington,
D.C. on September 10 and 17, 1980.
Washington : U. S. G.P.O., 1980 [i.e. 1981] iv,
134 p. : ill ; 24 cm. Item 1015 Bibliography: p. 93.
LC Card 81-601755   DDC 344.73/09 347.3049
19

United States. Congress. House. Committee on Education and

BIBLIOGRAPHIC GUIDE

424

1. Language and languages - Study and teaching. 2. Language policy - United States. 3. International relations - Study and teaching - United States. I. Title.
KF27 .E373 1980e

Oversight and reauthorization of action agency, 1979 : hearings before the Subcommittee on Select Education of the Committee on Education and Labor, House of Representatives, Ninety-sixth Congress, first session, on H.R. 2859 ... held in Washington, D.C. Washington : U. S. Govt. Print. Off., 1980. vii, 1719 p. : ill. ; 24 cm. Hearing held Apr. 4-June 20, 1979.   LC Card 80-603281 DDC 353.0072/23684 19
1. Action (Service Corps) - Appropriations and expenditures. 2. ACTION (Service Corps). I. Title.
KF27 .E373 1979f

Oversight hearing on the Architectural and Transportation Barriers Compliance Board : hearing before the Subcommittee on Select Education of the Committee on Education and Labor, House of Representatives, Ninety-sixth Congress, second session, hearing held in Washington, D.C., on June 11, 1980. Washington : U. S. G.P.O., 1981. iii, 219 p. : ill. ; 24cm. Item 1015 Includes bibliographical references.   LC Card 81-601157 DDC 353.0086/2 19
1. Architectural and Transportation Barriers Compliance Board. 2. Architecture and the physically handicapped - United States. 3. Physically handicapped - United States - Transportation. I. Title.
KF27 .E373 1980d

Oversight hearing on the impact of inflation on rehabilitation services : hearing before the Subcommittee on Select Education of the Committee on Education and Labor, House of Representatives, Ninety-sixth Congress, second session ... held in Washington, D.C., on April 30, 1980. Washington : U. S. Govt Print. Off., 1980. iii, 50 p. : graphs ; 24 cm. LC Card 80-603046 DDC 362/.0425 19
1. Rehabilitation - United States - Effect of inflation on. I. Title.
KF27 .E373 1980a

Oversight hearings on Title I--Child Abuse Prevention and Treatment and Adoption Reform Act of 1978 : hearings before the Subcommittee on Select Education of the Committee on Education and Labor, House of Representatives, Ninety-sixth Congress, second session, hearings held in Washington, D.C., on December 2 and 4, 1980. Washington : U. S. G.P.O., c1981. iv, 376 p. : ill. ; 24 cm. Item 1015-A Bibliography: p. 291-292. LC Card 81-601885 DDC 353.0084/7 19
1. Child abuse - Services - United States. 2. Adoption - United States. I. Title.
KF27 .E373 1980f

Proposed Presidential Commission on National Service Act of 1980 : hearing before the Subcommittee on Select Education of the Committee on Education and Labor, House of Representatives, Ninety-sixth Congress, second session, on H.R. 6868 ... held in Washington, D.C., on June 4, 1980. Washington : U. S. G.P.O., 1980. iii, 69 p. ; 24 cm. LC Card 80-604048 DDC 344.73/03137 347.3043137 19
1. United States. Presidential Commission on National Service. 2. National service - Law and legislation - United States. I. Title.
KF27 .E373 1980c

To amend the Rehabilitation act of 1973, relating to State agency organization requirements : hearings before the Subcommittee on Select Education of the Committee on Education and Labor, House of Representatives, Ninety-sixth Congress, first session, on H.R. 5143 ... hearings held in Washington, D.C., on October 17, and Lauderdale Lakes, Fla., on November 12, 1979. Washington : U. S. Govt. Print. Off., 1980. v, 560 p. : ill. ; 24 cm. LC Card 80-602471 DDC 344.73/0769 19
1. Vocational rehabilitation - Law and legislation - United States. 2. Vocational rehabilitation - Law and legislation - Florida. I. Title.
KF27 .E373 1979e

United States. Congress. House. Committee on Energy and Commerce. United States. Compilation of selected acts within the jurisdiction of the Committee on Energy and Commerce /. Washington , 1981. 4 v. ; LC Card 81-601845 DDC 344.73/04/02632

347.304402632 19
KF3775 .A3 1981

United States. Congress. House. Committee on Expenditures in the Executive Departments. see United States. Congress. House. Committee on Government Operations.

United States. Congress. House. Committee on Foreign Affairs. (Old Catalog form: United States. Foreign Affairs, Committee on (House))
China claims reallocation : hearing and markup before the Committee on Foreign Affairs and its Subcommittees on Asian and Pacific Affairs and on International Economic Policy and Trade, House of Representatives, Ninety-sixth Congress, second session, on H.R. 6440, September 29 and 30, 1980. Washington : U. S. G.P.O., 1980. iii, 37 p. ; 24 cm. Item 1017 LC Card 81-600644 DDC 343.7305/2 347.30352 19
1. United States - Claims vs. China. I. United States. Congress. House. Committee on Foreign Affairs. Subcommittee on Asian and Pacific Affairs. II. United States. Congress. House. Committee on Foreign Affairs. Subcommittee on International Economic Policy and Trade. III. Title.
KF27 .F6 1980p

Export trading companies : hearings and markup before the Committee on Foreign Affairs and its Subcommittee on International Economic Policy and Trade, House of Representatives, Ninety-sixth Congress, second session .... Washington : U. S. G.P.O., 1980. iv, 379 p. ; 24 cm. Hearings held May 22-July 1, 1980. Includes bibliographical references. LC Card 80-603910 DDC 382/.6/06073 19
1. Export associations - Law and legislation - United States. 2. Foreign trade promotion - Law and legislation - United States. I. United States. Congress. House. Committee on Foreign Affairs. Subcommittee on International Economic Policy and Trade. II. Title.
KF27 .F6 1980e

Gilman, Benjamin A. United Nations 11th special session on economic development and cooperation, New York City, August 25-September 15, 1980 . Washington , 1981. vii, 18 p. ; LC Card 81-601276 DDC 338.91 19
HF1410.5 .G54

Gulick, Lewis. Economic support fund programs in the Middle East . Washington , 1979. vii, 79 p. ; LC Card 79-602515 DDC 338.91/73/0174927 19
HC498 .G84

Hostage Relief Act of 1980 : hearings and markup before the Committee on Foreign Affairs and its Subcommittee on International Operations, House of Representatives, Ninety-sixth Congress, second session, on H.R. 7085, July 24, September 3 and 10, 1980. Washington : U. S. G.P.O., 1980. iii, 57 p. ; 24 cm. LC Card 81-600840 DDC 342.73/0412 347.302412 19
1. United States - Diplomatic and consular service - Appointments, promotions, salaries, etc. 2. Hostages - Legal status, laws, etc. - United States. 3. Hostages - Iran. I. United States. Congress. House. Committee on Foreign Affairs. Subcommittee on International Operations. II. Title.
KF27 .F6 1980i

Human rights in Eastern Europe and the Soviet Union : hearing and markup before the Committee on Foreign Affairs and its Subcommittee on International Organizations, House of Representatives, Ninety-sixth Congress, second session, on H. Con. Res. 434, September 16 and 24, 1980. Washington : U. S. G.P.O., 1980 [i.e. 1981] iv, 248 p. ; 24 cm. Item 1017 Includes bibliographies. LC Card 81-600864 DDC 232.4/0947 19
1. Civil rights - Europe, Eastern. 2. Civil rights - Soviet Union. 3. Wallenberg, Raoul. I. United States. Congress. House. Committee on Foreign Affairs. Subcommittee on International Organizations. II. Title.
KF27 .F6 1980n

Hyndman, Vance. U. S. economic assistance programs in Asia . Washington , 1980. vii, 29 p. ; LC Card 80-603977 DDC 338.91/73/05 19
HC412 .H93

International Natural Rubber Agreement : hearings and markup before the Committee on Foreign Affairs and its Subcommittee on International Economic Policy and Trade, House of Representatives, Ninety-sixth

Congress, second session, April 16, 22 and 24, and May 8, 1980. Washington : U. S. G.P.O., 1980 [i.e. 1981] iii, 113 p. : ill. ; 23 cm. Item 1017 Includes bibliographical references. LC Card 81-601156 DDC 341.7/547138952/0973 19
1. Rubber - Law and legislation. 2. Rubber - Law and legislation - United States. 3. Rubber - Prices. I. United States. Congress. House. Committee on Foreign Affairs. Subcommittee on International Economic Policy and Trade. II. Title.
KF27 .F6 1980j

NATO and Western security in the 1980's--the European perception : report of a staff study mission to seven NATO countries and Austria, January 2-18, 1980, to the Committee on Foreign Affairs, U. S. House of Representatives. Washington : U. S. Govt. Print. Off., 1980. viii, 78 p. : maps ; 24 cm. At head of title: 96th Congress, 2d session. Committee print. LC Card 80-601730 DDC 355/.03304 19
1. Europe - National security. 2. North Atlantic Treaty Organization. I. Title.
UA646 .U48 1980

OPIC services for U. S. investors in China : hearing and markup before the Committee on Foreign Affairs and its Subcommittees on Asian and Pacific Affairs and on International Economic Policy and Trade, House of Representatives, Ninety-sixth Congress, second session, May 20, June 10, and July 3, 1980. Washington : U. S. G.P.O., 1981. iii, 68 p. ; 24 cm. Item 1017 LC Card 81-600814 DDC 332.6/7373/051 19
1. Overseas Private Investment Corporation. 2. Investments, American - China. I. United States. Congress. House. Committee on Foreign Affairs. Subcommittee on Asian and Pacific Affairs. II. United States. Congress. House. Committee on Foreign Affairs. Subcommittee on International Economic Policy and Trade. III. Title.
KF27 .F6 1980o

Orleans, Leo A. China's population policies and population data . Washington , 1981. v, 32 p. ; LC Card 81-601675 DDC 304.6/0951 19
HB3654.A3 O74

Planning for trilateral scientific and technological cooperation by Egypt, Israel, and the United States . Washington , 1980. vii, 49 p. ; LC Card 80-603873 DDC 327.1/7 19
Q127.U6 P53

Resolution of inquiry concerning human rights policies : hearing before the Committee on Foreign Affairs, House of Representatives, Ninety-sixth Congress, second session, on H. Res. 551, February 6, 1980. Washington : U. S. G.P.O., 1980 iii, 29 p. ; 24 cm. Item 1017 LC Card 80-600587 DDC 323.4/0973 19
1. Civil rights. 2. United States - Foreign relations - 1977-1981. 3. United States - Foreign economic relations. I. Title.
KF27 .F6 1980m

Resolutions of disapproval pertaining to the shipment of nuclear fuel to India : hearings and markup before the Committee on Foreign Affairs, House of Representatives, Ninety-sixth Congress, second session, June 26, July 23, and September 10, 1980. Washington : U. S. G.P.O., 1980. iii, 170 p. ; 24 cm. LC Card 80-603439 DDC 353.0089 19
1. Nuclear fuels - India. 2. Nuclear nonproliferation. 3. Export controls - United States. I. Title.
KF27 .F6 1980g

Rhodesian sanctions, should the United States lift them? : Hearing and markup before the Committee on Foreign Affairs and its Subcommittees on Africa and on International Organizations, House of Representatives, Ninety-sixth Congress, first session, on S. 2076, December 5 and 11, 1979. Washington : U. S. Govt. Print. Off., 1980. iii, 80 p. ; 24 cm. LC Card 80-601130 DDC 327.7306891 19
1. United States - Foreign relations - Zimbabwe. 2. Zimbabwe - Foreign relations - United States. 3. Zimbabwe - Politics and government - 1980-. 4. Sanctions (International law). I. United States. Congress. House. Committee on Foreign Affairs. Subcommittee on Africa. II. United States. Congress. House. Committee on Foreign Affairs. Subcommittee on International Organizations. III. Title.
KF27 .F6 1979j

Soviet detention of Andrei Sakharov : markup before the Committee on Foreign Affairs, House of Representatives, Ninety-sixth

GOVERNMENT PUBLICATIONS - U.S.: 1981

United States. Congress. House. Committee on Foreign Affairs.

425

Congress, second session ... February 4, 1980. Washington : U. S. Govt. Print. Off., 1980. iii, 31 p. ; 23 cm. Hearing on H. Con. Res. 251, 259, 265, 266, and 272.   LC Card 80-602485   DDC 323.4/0947 19

1. Sakharov, Andreĭ Dmitrievich, 1921-. 2. Civil rights - Russia. I. Title.

KF26 .F6 1980b

Special Central America economic assistance ; Compensation for hostages in Iran ; International conference on Cambodia : hearing and markup before the Committee on Foreign Affairs, House of Representatives, Ninety-sixth Congress, first session, on H.R. 5954, H. Con. Res. 219 and 221, November 27 and December 11, 1979. Washington : U. S. Govt. Print. Off., 1980. iii, 130 p. ; 23 cm.   LC Card 80-601146   DDC 338.91/730596 19

1. Economic assistance, American - Central America. 2. Hostages - Iran. 3. United States - Officials and employees - Salaries, allowances, etc. 4. Food relief - Cambodia. I. Title.

KF27 .F6 1979k

The status of the Third United Nations Conference on the Law of the Sea, spring 1980 : hearing before the Committee on Foreign Affairs, House of Representatives, Ninety-sixth Congress, second session, April 17, 1980. Washington : U. S. Govt. Print. Off., 1980. iii, 84 p. ; 24 cm.   LC Card 80-602730   DDC 341.4/5 19

1. United Nations Conference on the Law of the Sea, 3d, New York, etc., 1973-. 2. Maritime law. 3. Ocean mining - Law and legislation - United States. I. Title.

KF27 .F6 1980c

Studds, Gerry E. Central America, 1981 . Washington , 1981. vii, 33 p. ;   LC Card 81-601664   DDC 320.9728 19

F1439 .S88

U. S. government relief assistance following the Italian earthquake of November 23, 1980 : hearing before the Committee on Foreign Affairs, House of Representatives, Ninety-sixth Congress, second session, December 1, 1980. Washington : U.S G.P.O., 1980 [i.e. 1981] iii, 38 p. : map ; 24 cm. Item 1017   LC Card 81-600803   DDC 363.3/495 19

1. Earthquakes - Italy. 2. Economic assistance, American - Italy. 3. Disaster relief - Italy. I. Title.

KF27 .F6 1980l

U. S. participation in the 1980 summer Olympic games : hearings and markup before the Committee on Foreign Affairs, House of Representatives, Ninety-sixth Congress, second session, on H. Con. Res. 249 and H. Res. 547, January 23 and February 4, 1980. Washington : U. S. Govt. Print. Off., 1980. iii, 88 p. ; 24 cm.   LC Card 80-602748   DDC 796.4/8/0947431 19

1. Olympic Games, Moscow, 1980. 2. Sports and state - United States. 3. Afghanistan - Politics and government - 1973-. 4. United States - Foreign relations - Russia. 5. Russia - Foreign relations - United States. I. Title.

KF27 .F6 1980d

United Nations. General Assembly. 34th session, 1979. Delegation from the United States. Congressional delegates at the 1979 United Nations General Assembly . Washington , 1980. vii, 265 p. ;   LC Card 80-602273   DDC 341.23/73 19

JX1977.2.U5 U55 1979a

United States. Congress. House. Regional stability in northern Africa . Washington , 1980. v, 29 p. ;   LC Card 80-603274   DDC 327/.096 19

DT204 .U48 1980

United States. Congress. House. Committee on Agriculture. Review of Agricultural trade act of 1978 . Washington , 1980. iii, 42 p. ;   LC Card 80-602236   DDC 343.73/0851/0262 19

KF27 .A3 1979b

United States. Congress. House. Special Study Mission to Mexico City. United States--Mexican relations and the energy crisis . Washington , 1980. vii, 17 p. ;   LC Card 80-602869   DDC 327.73072 19

E183.8.M6 U36 1980

United States. Congress. House. Special Study Mission to Venezuela, Barbados, Brazil, and Costa Rica. Assessment of trends and conditions in the Inter-American region . Washington , 1980. vii, 33 p. ;   LC Card

80-602265   DDC 327.7308 19

F1418 .U44 1980

United States. Congress. House. Study Mission to Morocco, the Western Sahara, Mauritania, Algeria, Liberia, Spain, and France. Arms for Morocco? . Washington , 1979. viii, 26 p. :   LC Card 80-601042   DDC 355/.032/64 19

E183.8.M8 U54 1979

United States. Congress. Office of Technology Assessment. Technology and East-West trade. Washington, D.C. , 1979. viii, 303 p. :   LC Card 79-600203

HF1411 .U615 1979   **NYPL [JLF 81-165]**

United States-European communities relations . Washington [D.C.] , 1979. x, 44 p. ;   LC Card 80-603969   DDC 337/.09/047 19

HF1411 .U64

United States-Japan economic relations : hearings and markup before the Committee on Foreign Affairs and its Subcommittees on Asian and Pacific Affairs and on International Economic Policy and Trade, House of Representatives, Ninety-sixth Congress, second session, on H. Con. Res. 363, September 16, 17, 18, 29, October 1 and 16, 1980. Washington : U. S. G.P.O., 1981. vi, 337 p. : ill. ; 24 cm. Item 1017 Includes bibliographical references.   LC Card 81-601171   DDC 337.52073 19

1. United States - Foreign economic relations - Japan. 2. Japan - Foreign economic relations - United States. I. United States. Congress. House. Committee on Foreign Affairs. Subcommittee on Asian and Pacific Affairs. II. United States. Congress. House. Committee on Foreign Affairs. Subcommittee on International Economic Policy and Trade. III. Title.

KF27 .F6 1980K

The 1980 Geneva session and status of the negotiations on the Law of the Sea : hearing before the Committee on Foreign Affairs, House of Representatives, Ninety-sixth Congress, second session, October 1, 1980. Washington : U. S. G.P.O., 1980. iii, 69 p. ; 24 cm.   LC Card 80-604064   DDC 341.4/5 19

1. United Nations Conference on the Law of the Sea (3rd : 1973- New York, N.Y., etc.). 2. Maritime law. I. Title.

KF27 .F6 1980f

United States. Congress. House. Committee on Foreign Affairs. Subcommittee on Africa.
Aid to Zimbabwe : hearing before the Subcommittee on Africa of the Committee on Foreign Affairs, House of Representatives, Ninety-sixth Congress, second session, September 23, 1980. Washington : U. S. G.P.O., 1980. iii, 20 p. ; 24 cm.   LC Card 80-604080   DDC 338.91/73/06891 19

1. Economic assistance, American - Zimbabwe. I. Title.

KF27 .F625 1980d

Current situationin the western Sahara, 1980 : hearing before the Subcommittee on Africa of the Committee on Foreign Affairs, House of Representatives, Ninety-sixth Congress, second session, December 4, 1980. Washington : U. S. G.P.O., 1981. iii, 24 p. ; 24 cm.   LC Card 81-600927   DDC 327.73061 19

1. United States - Foreign relations - Africa, North. 2. Africa, North - Foreign relations - United States. 3. Spanish Sahara - Politics and government. I. Title.

KF27 .F625 1980f

Food needs in East Africa : hearing before the Subcommittee on Africa of the Committee on Foreign Affairs, House of Representatives, Ninety-sixth Congress, second session, June 19, 1980. Washington : U. S. Govt. Print. Off., 1980. iii, 51 p. : graphs ; 24 cm.   LC Card 80-603665   DDC 338.1/9/676 19

1. Food supply - Africa, Eastern. I. Title.

KF27 .F625 1980a

Labor situation in South Africa--fall 1980 : hearing before the Subcommittee on Africa of the Committee on foreign Affairs, House of Representatives, Ninety-sixth Congress, second session, November 13, 1980. Washington : U. S. G.P.O., 1981. iii, 21 p. ; 24 cm. Item 1017   LC Card 81-600943   DDC 331/.0968 19

1. Labor and laboring classes - South Africa. 2. Trade-unions - South Africa. I. Title.

KF27 .F625 1980g

Namibia update : hearing before the Subcommittee on Africa of the Committee on Foreign Affairs, House of Representatives, Ninety-sixth Congress, second session,

September 9, 1980. Washington : U. S. G.P.O., 1981. iv, 35 p. : 1 map ; 24 cm.   LC Card 81-600962   DDC 968.8//03 19

1. Namibia - Politics and government. 2. Namibia - Foreign relations. 3. SWAPO. I. Title.

KF27 .F625 1980h

Reprograming of military aid to Somalia : hearing before the Subcommittee on Africa of the Committee on Foreign Affairs, House of Representatives, Ninety-sixth Congress, second session, August 26, 1980. Washington : U. S. Govt. Print. Off., 1980. iii, 35 p. : maps ; 24 cm.   LC Card 80-603684   DDC 355/.032/6773 19

1. Military assistance, American - Somalia. I. Title.

KF27 .F625 1980b

Results of the recent elections in Zimbabwe : hearing before the Subcommittee on Africa of the Committee on Foreign Affairs, House of Representatives, Ninety-sixth Congress, second session, March 27, 1980. Washington : U. S. Govt. Print. Off., 1980. iii, 101 p. ; 23 cm.   LC Card 80-602533   DDC 324.96891/04 19

1. Elections - Zimbabwe. 2. Zimbabwe - Politics and government - 1980-. I. Title.

KF27 .F625 1980

The situation in Liberia, spring 1980--update : hearing before the Subcommittee on Africa of the Committee on Foreign Affairs, House of Representatives, Ninety-sixth Congress, second session, April 29, 1980. Washington : U. S. Govt. Print. Off., 1980. iii, 25 p. ; 24 cm.   LC Card 80-603661   DDC 325/.21/096662 19

1. Liberia - Politics and government - 1980-. 2. Refugees, Political - Liberia. 3. Refugees, Political - United States. I. Title.

KF27 .F625 1980c

United States. Congress. House. Committee on Foreign Affairs. Rhodesian sanctions, should the United States lift them? . Washington , 1980. iii, 80 p. ;   LC Card 80-601130   DDC 327.7306891 19

KF27 .F6 1979j

United States policy toward Angola--update : hearings before the Subcommittee on Africa of the Committee on Foreign Affairs, House of Representatives, Ninety-sixth Congress, second session, September 17 and 30, 1980. Washington : U. S. G.P.O., 1980. iii, 76 p. : map ; 24 cm.   LC Card 81-600629   DDC 327.73067/3 19

1. United States - Foreign relations - Angola. 2. Angola - Foreign relations - United States. I. Title.

KF27 .F625 1980e

United States. Congress. House. Committee on Foreign Affairs. Subcommittee on Asian and Pacific Affairs.
Human rights in Asia : noncommunist countries : hearings before the Subcommittees on Asian and Pacific Affairs and on International Organizations of the Committee on Foreign Affairs, House of Representatives, Ninety-sixth Congress, second session, February 4, 6, and 7, 1980. Washington : U. S. Govt. Print. Off. : for sale by the Supt. of Docs., U. S. Govt. Print. Off., 1980. iv, 335 p. ; 24 cm. Includes bibliographical references.   LC Card 80-602725   DDC 323.4/095 19

1. Civil rights - Asia. I. United States. Congress. House. Committee on Foreign Affairs. Subcommittee on International Organizations. II. Title.

KF27 .F638 1980

Human rights in Asia : communist countries : hearing before the Subcommittees on Asian and Pacific Affairs and on International Organizations of the Committee on Foreign Affairs, House of Representatives, Ninety-sixth Congress, second session, October 1, 1980. Washington : U. S. G.P.O., 1981. iv, 190 p. ; 24 cm. Item 1017 Includes bibliographical references.   LC Card 81-601383   DDC 323.4/095 19

1. Civil rights - Asia. 2. Civil rights - Communist countries. I. United States. Congress. House. Committee on Foreign Affairs. Subcommittee on International Organizations. II. Title.

KF27 .F638 1980f

Implementation of the Taiwan Relations Act : hearings before the Subcommittee on Asian and Pacific Affairs of the Committee on Foreign Affairs, House of Representatives, Ninety-sixth Congress, second session, June 11, 17 and July 30, 1980. Washington : U. S. G.P.O., 1981. v, 107 p. ; 24 cm. Item 1017   LC Card 81-600827   DDC 327.73051/249 19

BIBLIOGRAPHIC GUIDE

United States. Congress. House. Committee on Foreign Affairs.

426

1. United States - Foreign relations - Taiwan. 2. Taiwan - Foreign relations - United States. I. Title.
KF27 .F638 1980e

North Pacific Fur Seal Protection Act : hearing before the Subcommittees on Asian and Pacific Affairs and on International Organizations of the Committee on Foreign Affairs, House of Representatives, Ninety-sixth Congress, first session, on H.R. 5033, September 27, 1979. Washington : U. S. G.P.O., 1980 [i.e. 1981] v, 152 p. : ill. ; 24 cm. Item 1017 Bibliography: p. 148. LC Card 81-600859 DDC 346.7304/6959 347.30646959 19
1. Northern fur seal - Law and legislation - United States. 2. Northern fur seal. I. United States. Congress. House. Committee on Foreign Affairs. Subcommittee on International Organizations. II. Title.
KF27 .F638 1979i

Pike, Douglas Eugene, 1924- Vietnam's foreign relations, 1975-78 . Washington , 1979. vii, 21 p. ; LC Card 80-603974 DDC 327.597 19
DS559.912 P54

POW/MIA's : oversight : hearing before the Subcommittee on Asian and Pacific Affairs of the Committee on Foreign Affairs, House of Representatives, Ninety-sixth Congress, second session, June 27, 1980. Washington : U. S. Govt. Print. Off., 1980. v, 49 p. ; 24 cm. LC Card 80-603653 DDC 959.704/37 19
1. Vietnamese Conflict, 1961-1975 - Prisoners and prisons. 2. Vietnamese Conflict, 1961-1975 - Missing in action. 3. United States - Foreign relations - Asia, Southeastern. 4. Asia, Southeastern - Foreign relations - United States. I. Title.
KF27 .F638 1980a

The United States and the People's Republic of China : issues for the 1980's : hearings before the Subcommittee on Asian and Pacific Affairs of the Committee on Foreign Affairs, House of Representatives, Ninety-sixth Congress, second session, April 1, July 22, August 26, and September 23, 1980. Washington : U. S. G.P.O., 1980 [i.e. 1981] v, 163 p. ; 24 cm. Includes bibliographical references. Item 1017 LC Card 81-600985 DDC 327.73051 19
1. United States - Foreign relations - China. 2. China - Foreign relations - United States. 3. Military Assistance, American - China. I. Title.
KF27 .F638 1980d

United States. Congress. House. Committee on Foreign Affairs. China claims reallocation . Washington , 1980. iii, 37 p. ; LC Card 81-600644 DDC 343.7305/2 347.30352 19
KF27 .F6 1980p

United States. Congress. House. Committee on Foreign Affairs. OPIC services for U. S. investors in China . Washington , 1981. iii, 68 p. ; LC Card 81-600814 DDC 332.6/7373/051 19
KF27 .F6 1980o

United States. Congress. House. Committee on Foreign Affairs. United States-Japan economic relations . Washington , 1981. vi, 337 p. ; LC Card 81-601171 DDC 337.52073 19
KF27 .F6 1980K

United States. Congress. House. Committee on Foreign Affairs. Subcommittee on International Operations. Security procedures at U. S. embassies . Washington , 1980. iii, 240 p. ; LC Card 80-604070 DDC 353.008/92 19
KF27 .F647 1980b

United States. Congress. House. Committee on Foreign Affairs. Subcommittee on International Security and Scientific Affairs. Strategic implications of chemical and biological warfare . Washington , 1980. iii, 69 p. ; LC Card 80-602441 DDC 358/.34 19
KF27 .F64825 1980b

United States. Congress. House. Special Study Mission to Asia. Asian security environment, 1980 . Washington , 1980. vii, 96 p. ; LC Card 80-602264 DDC 355/.03305 19
DS33.4.U6 U5 1980

United States. Library of Congress. Foreign Affairs and National Defense Division. Sino-American relations . Washington , 1980. iii, 12 p. ; LC Card 80-603273 DDC 327.73051 19
E183.8.C5 U58 1980

United States-South Korean relations : hearings before the Subcommittee on Asian and Pacific Affairs of the Committee on Foreign Affairs, House of Representatives, Ninety-sixth

Congress, second session, June 25 and August 28, 1980. Washington : U. S. G.P.O., 1980. v, 60 p. ; 24 cm. LC Card 80-604073 DDC 327.730519/5 19
1. United States - Foreign relations - Korea (South). 2. Korea (South) - Foreign relations - United States. I. Title.
KF27 .F638 1980b

1979--tragedy in Indochina : war, refugees, and famine : hearings before the Subcommittee on Asian and Pacific Affairs of the Committee on Foreign Affairs, House of Representatives, Ninety-sixth Congress, first session .... Washington : U. S. Govt. Print. Off., 1980. viii, 233 p. ; 24 cm. Hearings held Feb. 28-Dec. 19, 1979. LC Card 80-601996 DDC 959/.053 19
1. Vietnam - Foreign relations - Cambodia. 2. Cambodia - Foreign relations - Vietnam. 3. Refugees - Indochina. 4. Cambodia - Famines. I. Title.
KF27 .F638 1979h

1980--the tragedy in Indochina continues : war, refugees, and famine : hearings before the Subcommittee on Asian and Pacific Affairs of the Committee on Foreign Affairs, House of Representatives, Ninety-sixth Congress, second session, February 11, May 1, 6, and July 29, 1980. Washington : U. S. G.P.O., 1980. v, 148 p. : ill. ; 24 cm. Includes bibliographical references. LC Card 80-604058 DDC 362.8/7/09596 19
1. Cambodian-Vietnamese Conflict, 1977-. 2. Refugees - Cambodia. I. Title. II. Title: Tragedy in Indochina continues.
KF27 .F638 1980c

United States. Congress. House. Committee on Foreign Affairs. Subcommittee on Europe and the Middle East.
Export of frigate engines to Iraq : hearing before the Subcommittees on Europe and the Middle East and on International Economic Policy and Trade of thhe Committee on Foreign Affairs, House of Representatives, Ninety-sixth Congress, second session, May 14, 1980. Washington : U. S. G.P.O., 1981. iii, 72 p. ; 24 cm. Item 1017 LC Card 81-600961 DDC 355/.032/567 19
1. Military assistance, American - Iraq. 2. Export controls - United States. 3. Marine gas-turbines. 4. Frigates. I. United States. Congress. House. Committee on Foreign Affairs. Subcommittee on International Economic Policy and Trade. II. Title.
KF27 .F64214 1980f

Lunn, Simon. NATO after Afghanistan . Washington , 1980. ix, 64 p. ; LC Card 80-603855 DDC 355/.031/091821 19
UA646.3 .L85

Settlement of claims against Czechoslovakia : hearing and markup before the Subcommittees on Europe and the Middle East and on International Ecomomic Policy and Trade of the Committee on Foreign Affairs, House of Representatives, Ninety-sixth Congress, second session, on H.R. 7338, August 19 and September 30, 1980. Washington : U. S. G.P.O., 1981. iv, 225 p. ; 24 cm. Includes bibliographical references. Item 1017 LC Card 81-600940 DDC 346.7304/3 347.30643 19
1. United States - Claims vs. Czechoslovakia. I. United States. Congress. House. Committee on Foreign Affairs. Subcommittee on International Economic Policy and Trade. II. Title.
KF27 .F64214 1980e

Sutter, Robert G. Executive-legislative consultations on China policy, 1978-79 /. Washington , 1980. vii, 42 p. ; LC Card 80-602678 DDC 327.73051 19
JX1428.C6 S97

U. S. interests in, and policies toward, the Persian Gulf, 1980 : hearings before the Subcommittee on Europe and the Middle East of the Committee on Foreign Affairs, House of Representatives, Ninety-sixth Congress, second session .... Washington : U. S. G.P.O., 1980. iv, 471 p. ; 23 cm. Hearings held Mar. 24-Sept. 3, 1980. LC Card 80-603806 DDC 355/.0330536 19
1. Persian Gulf region - Strategic aspects. 2. United States - Foreign relations - 1977-. I. Title.
KF27 .F64214 1980c

United States-Jordanian relations and arms supply issues : hearings before the Subcommittee on Europe and the Middle East of the Committee on Foreign Affairs, House of Representatives, Ninety-sixth Congress, second session, July 29 and August 27, 1980.

Washington : U. S. G.P.O., 1980. iii, 71 p. ; 24 cm. LC Card 80-604082 DDC 327.7305695 19
1. United States - Foreign relations - Jordan. 2. Jordan - Foreign relations - United States. 3. Military assistance, American - Jordan. I. Title.
KF27 .F64214 1980d

United States-Turkey defense and economic cooperation agreement, 1980 : hearing before the Subcommittee on Europe and the Middle East of the Committee on Foreign Affairs, House of Representatives, Ninety-sixth Congress, second session, May 7, 1980. Washington : U. S. Govt. Print. Off., 1980. iii, 69 p. ; 24 cm. LC Card 80-603044 DDC 327.730561 19
1. United States - Foreign relations - Turkey. 2. Turkey - Foreign relations - United States. 3. United States - Foreign economic relations - Turkey. 4. Turkey - Foreign economic relations - United States. I. Title.
KF27 .F64214 1980a

United States-Western European relations in 1980 : hearings before the Subcommittee on Europe and the Middle East of the Committee on Foreign Affairs, House of Representatives, Ninety-sixth Congress, second session .... Washington : U. S. G.P.O., 1980. xi, 320 p. : ill. ; 24 cm. Hearings held June 25-July 2, 1980. LC Card 80-603423 DDC 327.7304 19
1. United States - Foreign relations - Europe. 2. Europe - Foreign relations - United States. 3. North Atlantic Treaty Organization. I. Title.
KF27 .F64214 1980b

United States. Congress. House. Committee on Foreign Affairs. Subcommittee on Inter-American Affairs.
Assessment of conditions in Central America : hearings before the Subcommittee on Inter-American Affairs of the Committee on Foreign Affairs, House of Representatives, Ninety-sixth Congress, second session, April 29 and May 20, 1980. Washington : U. S. Govt. Print. Off., 1980. iii, 137 p. ; 24 cm. LC Card 80-602995 DDC 972.8/052 19
1. Central America - Economic conditions. 2. Central America - Politics and government - 1951-. 3. United States - Foreign relations - Central America. 4. Central America - Foreign relations - United States. I. Title.
KF27 .F646 1980

Future development assistance to transitional countries : hearings before the Subcommittee on Inter-American Affairs of the Committee on Foreign Affairs, House of Representatives, Ninety-sixth Congress, second session, February 21 and July 23, 1980. Washington : U. S. Govt. Print. Off., 1980. iii, 76 p. ; 24 cm. LC Card 80-603355 DDC 338.91/73/08 19
1. Economic assistance, American - Latin America. I. Title.
KF27 .F646 1980c

Impact of Cuban-Soviet ties in the Western Hemisphere, spring 1980 : hearings before the Subcommittee on Inter-American Affairs of the Committee on Foreign Affairs, House of Representatives, Ninety-sixth Congress, second session .... Washington : U. S. Govt. Print. Off., 1980. iii, 122 p. ; 24 cm. Hearings held March 26-May 14, 1980. LC Card 80-602979 DDC 355/.03308 19
1. Cuba - Foreign relations - Russia. 2. Russia - Foreign relations - Cuba. 3. Military assistance, Cuban. 4. Latin America - Politics and government. I. Title.
KF27 .F646 1980a

Review of the Presidential certification of Nicaragua's connection to terrorism : hearing before the Subcommittee on Inter-American Affairs of the Committee on Foreign Affairs, House of Representatives, Ninety-sixth Congress, September 30, 1980. Washington : U. S. G.P.O., 1980. iii, 50, p. ; 24 cm. LC Card 80-603450 DDC 353.0089/097285 19
1. Economic assistance, American - Nicaragua. 2. Nicaragua - Foreign relations. 3. Terrorism. I. Title.
KF27 .F646 1980d

U. S. national interest in Latin America : hearing before the Subcommittee on Inter-American Affairs of the Committee on Foreign Affairs, House of Representatives, Ninety-seventh Congress, first session, March 4, 1981. Washington : U. S. G.P.O., 1981. iii, 67 p. : ill. ; 24 cm. Includes bibliographical references. LC Card 81-601864 DDC 327.7308 19
1. United States - Foreign relations - Latin America. 2.

GOVERNMENT PUBLICATIONS - U.S.: 1981

427

United States. Congress. House. Committee on Foreign Affairs.

Latin America - Foreign relations - United States. I. Title.
KF27 .F646 1981

United States. Congress. House. Committee on Foreign Affairs. Subcommittee on International Economic Policy and Trade. International energy development assistance programs . Washington , 1981. v, 120 p. ;   LC Card 81-601471   DDC 333.79/15/091724 19
KF27 .F6465 1980f

United States. Congress. House. Committee on Foreign Affairs. Subcommittee on International Economic Policy and Trade. Outstanding claims against Cuba . Washington , 1980. iii, 21 p. ;   LC Card 80-603106   DDC 327.7291073 19
KF27 .F6465 1979e

United States. Congress. House. Committee on Interstate and Foreign Commerce. Subcommittee on Consumer Protection and Finance. Motor vehicle theft prevention act . Washington , 1980. vii, 536 p. :   LC Card 80-603731   DDC 343.73/078629222 347.30378629222 19
KF27 .I554 1980a

Update, United States-Canadian/Mexican relations : hearings before the Subcommittee on Inter-American Affairs of the Committee on Foreign Affairs, House of Representatives, Ninety-sixth Congress, second session, June 17 and 26, 1980. Washington : U. S. Govt. Print. Off., 1980. iii, 71 p. ; 24 cm.   LC Card 80-603028   DDC 327.73071 19
1. United States - Foreign relations - Canada. 2. Canada - Foreign relations - United States. 3. United States - Foreign relations - Mexico. 4. Mexico - Foreign relations - United States. I. Title.
KF27 .F646 1980b

United States. Congress. House. Committee on Foreign Affairs. Subcommittee on International Economic Policy and Trade.
Deep seabed hard mineral resources act : hearings and markup before the Subcommittees on International Economic Policy and Trade and on International Organizations of the Committee on Foreign Affairs, House of Representatives, Ninety-sixth Congress, on H.R. 2759 ... Washington : U. S. Govt. Print. Off., 1980. iv, 271 p. ; 24 cm. Hearings held July 11, 1979-April 30, 1980.   LC Card 80-602899   DDC 346.7304/685 19
1. Marine mineral resources - Law and legislation - United States. 2. Ocean mining - Law and legislation - United States. I. United States. Congress. House. Committee on Foreign Affairs. Subcommittee on International Organizations. II. Title.
KF27 .F6465 1980

Export of hazardous products : hearings before the Subcommittee on International Economic Policy and Trade of the Committee on Foreign Affairs, House of Representatives, Ninety-sixth Congress, second session, June 5, 12, and September 9, 1980. Washington : U. S. G.P.O. : for sale by the Supt. of Docs., U. S. G.P.O., 1980. iv, 421 p. ; 24 cm. Bibliography: p. 355-364.   LC Card 81-600568   DDC 347.73/08756047 347.3038756047 19
1. Hazardous substances - Law and legislation - United States. 2. Export controls - United States. I. Title.
KF27 .F6465 1980c

International energy development assistance programs : joint hearing before the Subcommittees on International Economic Policy and Trade and on Inter-American Affairs of the Committee on Foreign Affairs, and the Subcommittee on Energy Development and Applications of the Committee on Science and Technology, U. S. House of Representatives, Ninety-sixth Congress, second session, March 5, 1980. Washington : U. S. G.P.O., 1981. v, 120 p. ; 24 cm. "No. 169 (Committee on Science and Technology)" Item 1017   LC Card 81-601471   DDC 333.79/15/091724 19
1. Energy development - International cooperation. 2. Underdeveloped areas - Renewable energy sources. 3. Technical assistance, American. I. United States. Congress. House. Committee on Foreign Affairs. Subcommittee on Inter-American Affairs. II. United States. Congress. House. Committee on Science and Technology. Subcommittee on Energy Development and Applications. III. Title.
KF27 .F6465 1980f

Marketing and promotion of infant formula in developing countries : hearings before the

Subcommittee on International Economic Policy and Trade of the Committee on Foreign Affairs, House of Representatives, Ninety-sixth Congress, second session, January 30 and February 11, 1980. Washington : U. S. G.P.O., 1980 [i.e. 1981] iv, 184 p. ; 23 cm. Item 1017 Includes bibliographical references.   LC Card 81-601782   DDC 380.1/4566462 19
1. Underdeveloped areas - Infants' supplies. 2. Infant formulas. 3. Infants - Nutrition. I. Title.
KF27 .F6465 1980g

Multilateral energy and mineral investment insurance : hearing before the Subcommittee on International Economic Policy and Trade of the Committee on Foreign Affairs, House of Representatives, Ninety-sixth Congress, first session, September 11, 1979. Washington : U. S. G.P.O., 1980. iii, 53 p. ; 24 cm. Item 1017   LC Card 81-600848   DDC 368.8/53 19
1. Insurance, Investment guaranty - United States. 2. Inter-American Development Bank. 3. Investments, American - Latin America. 4. Energy development - Latin America - Finance. 5. Mining industry and finance - Latin America. I. Title.
KF27 .F6465 1979g

North-South dialog : progress and prospects : hearings before the Subcommittees on International Economic Policy and Trade and on International Organizations of the Committee on Foreign Affairs, House of Representatives, Ninety-sixth Congress, second session .... Washington : U. S. Govt. Print. Off., 1980. iii, 267 p. ; 24 cm. Hearings held May 1-June 19, 1980. Includes bibliographical references.   LC Card 80-603478   DDC 337/.09/048 19
1. International economic relations. 2. United States - Foreign economic relations. 3. Underdeveloped areas. I. United States. Congress. House. Committee on Foreign Affairs. Subcommittee on International Organizations. II. Title.
KF27 .F6465 1980a

Nuclear exports, international safety and environmental issues : hearings before the Subcommittee on International Economic Policy and Trade of the Committee on Foreign Affairs, House of Representatives, Ninety-sixth Congress, December 18, 1979, and May 7, 1980. Washington : U. S. Govt. Print. Off., 1980. iii, 226 p. ; 24 cm.   LC Card 80-603801   DDC 363.1/79 19
1. Nuclear reactors - Safety measures. 2. Nuclear reactors - Environmental aspects. 3. Atomic power - International cooperation. 4. Technical assistance, American. I. Title.
KF27 .F6465 1979f

Outstanding claims against Cuba : hearing before the Subcommittees on International Economic Policy and Trade and on Inter-American Affairs of the Committee on Foreign Affairs, House of Representatives, Ninety-sixth Congress, first session, September 25, 1979. Washington : U. S. Govt. Print. Off., 1980. iii, 21 p. ; 24 cm.   LC Card 80-603106 DDC 327.7291073 19
1. United States - Claims vs. Cuba. I. United States. Congress. House. Committee on Foreign Affairs. Subcommittee on Inter-American Affairs. II. Title.
KF27 .F6465 1979e

Review of activities of the Overseas Private Investment Corporation : hearings before the Subcommittee on International Economic Policy and Trade of the Committee on Foreign Affairs, House of Representatives, Ninety-sixth Congress, July 17, 1979, and February 7, 1980. Washington : U. S. Govt. Print. Off., 1980. iii, 111 p. ; 23 cm.   LC Card 80-602111   DDC 353.0082 19
1. Overseas Private Investment Corporation. I. Title.
KF27 .F6465 1979d

Review of implementation of Basket II of the Helsinki Final Act : hearing before the Subcommittee on International Economic Policy and Trade of the Committee on Foreign Affairs, House of Representatives, and the Commission on Security and Cooperation in Europe, Ninety-sixth Congress, second session, March 6, 1980. Washington : U. S. G.P.O., 1980. iii, 82 p. ; 24 cm. Includes bibliographical references.   LC Card 80-604051   DDC 337.73047 19
1. Soviet Union - Foreign economic relations - United States. 2. United States - Foreign economic relations - Europe, Eastern. 3. Europe, Eastern - Foreign economic relations - United States. 4. Conference on Security and

Cooperation in Europe (1975 : Helsinki, Finland). 5. World politics - 1975-1985. I. United States. Commission on Security and Cooperation in Europe. II. Title.
KF27 .F6465 1980d

U.N. special session on development : a review : hearing before the Subcommittees on International Economic Policy and Trade and on International Organizations of the Committee on Foreign Affairs, House of Representatives, Ninety-sixth Congress, second session, November 19, 1980. Washington : U. S. G.P.O., 1981. iii, 95 p. ; 24 cm. Item 1017   LC Card 81-601370   DDC 327.1/11/0973 19
1. International economic relations. 2. Economic development. 3. United Nations - Economic assistance. 4. Economic assistance, American. I. United States. Congress. House. Committee on Foreign Affairs. Subcommittee on International Organizations. II. Title.
KF27 .F6465 1980e

U. S. policy toward South Africa : hearings before the Subcommittees on International Economic Policy and Trade, on Africa, and on International Organizations of the Committee on Foreign Affairs, House of Representatives, Ninety-sixth Congress, second session .... Washington : U. S. G.P.O. : For sale by the Supt. of Docs., U. S. G.P.O., 1980. iv, 912 p. : ill. ; 24 cm. Hearings held Apr. 30-June 10, 1980. Includes bibliographical references. S/N 052-070-05467-1   LC Card 80-603998   DDC 327.73068 19
1. United States - Foreign relations - South Africa. 2. South Africa - Foreign relations - United States. 3. South Africa - Politics and government - 1961-. I. United States. Congress. House. Committee on Foreign Affairs. Succommittee on Africa. II. United States. Congress. House. Committee on Foreign Affairs. Subcommittee on International Organizations. III. Title.
KF27 .F6465 1980b

United States. Congress. House. Committee on Foreign Affairs. China claims reallocation . Washington , 1980. iii, 37 p. ;   LC Card 81-600644   DDC 343.7305/2 347.30352 19
KF27 .F6 1980p

United States. Congress. House. Committee on Foreign Affairs. Export trading companies . Washington , 1980. iv, 379 p. ;   LC Card 80-603910   DDC 382/.6/06073 19
KF27 .F6 1980e

United States. Congress. House. Committee on Foreign Affairs. International Natural Rubber Agreement . Washington , 1980 [i.e. 1981] iii, 113 p. :   LC Card 81-601156   DDC 341.7/547138952/0973 19
KF27 .F6 1980j

United States. Congress. House. Committee on Foreign Affairs. OPIC services for U. S. investors in China . Washington , 1981. iii, 68 p. ;   LC Card 81-600814   DDC 332.6/7373/051 19
KF27 .F6 1980o

United States. Congress. House. Committee on Foreign Affairs. United States-Japan economic relations . Washington , 1981. vi, 337 p. :   LC Card 81-601171   DDC 337.52073 19
KF27 .F6 1980K

United States. Congress. House. Committee on Foreign Affairs. Subcommittee on Europe and the Middle East. Export of frigate engines to Iraq . Washington , 1981. iii, 72 p. ;   LC Card 81-600961   DDC 355/.032/567 19
KF27 .F64214 1980f

United States. Congress. House. Committee on Foreign Affairs. Subcommittee on Europe and the Middle East. Settlement of claims against Czechoslavakia . Washington , 1981. iv, 225 p. ;   LC Card 81-600940   DDC 346.7304/3 347.30643 19
KF27 .F64214 1980e

United States. Congress. House. Committee on Foreign Affairs. Subcommittee on International Security and Scientific Affairs. Department of Energy fiscal year 1981 budget . Washington , 1980. iii, 46 p. ;   LC Card 80-603009   DDC 353.0082/236823 19
KF27 .F64825 1980d

United States. Library of Congress. Environment and Natural Resources Policy Division. Nuclear proliferation factbook /. Washington , 1980. xi, 531 p. :   LC Card

BIBLIOGRAPHIC GUIDE

United States. Congress. House. Committee on Foreign Affairs.

428

80-603879   DDC 327.1/74 19
JX1974.73 .U55 1980

United States. Congress. House. Committee on Foreign Affairs. Subcommittee on International Operations.
Allegations concerning the Romanian service of Radio Free Europe : hearing before the Subcommittee on International Operations of the Committee on Foreign Affairs, House of Representatives, Ninety-sixth Congress, second session, February 21, 1980. Washington : U. S. Govt. Print. Off., 1980. iii, 98 p. ; 23 cm. LC Card 80-602459   DDC 384.54/43 19
1. Radio Free Europe. 2. Radio broadcasting - Romania. 3. Trifa, Valerien D. Bp., 1914-. I. Title.
KF27 .F647 1980

Authorizing additional appropriations for the Department of State, the Board for International Broadcasting, and grants to Radio Free Europe/Radio Liberty for fiscal years 1980 and 1981 : hearings before the Subcommittee on International Operations of the Committee on Foreign Affairs, House of Representatives, Ninety-sixth Congress, second session, March 26 and April 16, 1980. Washington : U. S.G.P.O., 1980. iv, 103 p. ; 24 cm. LC Card 80-603796   DDC 353.0072/23689 19
1. United States - Appropriations and expenditures, 1980. I. Title.
KF27 .F647 1980c

Authorizing appropriations for fiscal years 1980-81 for the Department of State, the International Communication Agency, and the Board for International Broadcasting : markup before the Subcommittee on International Operations of the Committee on Foreign Affairs, House of Representatives, Ninety-sixth Congress, first session, on H.R. 3363, March 8, 1979. Washington : U. S. Govt. Print. Off., 1980. iii, 24 p. ; 24 cm.   LC Card 80-603032   DDC 353.0072/23689 19
1. United States. Dept. of State - Appropriations and expenditures. 2. United States. International Communication Agency - Appropriations and expenditures. 3. United States. Board for International Broadcasting - Appropriations and expenditures. I. Title.
KF27 .F647 1979d

Review of the implementation of recommendations relating to the death of Representative Leo J. Ryan : hearings before the Subcommittee on International Operations of the Committee on Foreign Affairs, House of Representatives, Ninety-sixth Congress, second session, February 20 and March 4, 1980. Washington : U. S. Govt. Print. Off., 1980. iii, 78 p. ; 24 cm.   LC Card 80-603637   DDC 364.1/524/098811 19
1. Ryan, Leo J. - Assassination. 2. Jones, Jim, 1931-1978. 3. Peoples Temple. I. Title.
KF27 .F647 1980a

Security procedures at U. S. embassies : hearings before the Subcommittees on International Operations and on Asian and Pacific Affairs of the Committee on Foreign Affairs, House of Representatives, Ninety-sixth Congress, February 26 and April 26, 1979, February 28 and June 19, 1980. Washington : U. S. G.P.O., 1980. iii, 240 p. ; 24 cm.   LC Card 80-604070   DDC 353.008/92 19
1. Embassy buildings - United States - Security measures. I. United States. Congress. House. Committee on Foreign Affairs. Subcommittee on Asian and Pacific Affairs. II. Title.
KF27 .F647 1980b

U. S. refugee policy : hearing before the Subcommittee on International Operations of the Committee on Foreign Affairs, House of Representatives, Ninety-sixth Congress, first session, April 9, 1979. Washington : U. S. G.P.O., 1980. iii, 18 p. ; 24 cm. Item 1017 LC Card 81-600867   DDC 325/.21/0973 19
1. Refugees - Government policy - United States. I. Title.
KF27 .F647 1979f

United States. Congress. House. Committee on Foreign Affairs. Hostage Relief Act of 1980 . Washington , 1980. iii, 57 p. ;   LC Card 81-600840   DDC 342.73/0412 347.302412 19
KF27 .F6 1980i

United States. Congress. House. Committee on Foreign Affairs. Subcommittee on International Security and Scientific Affairs. United States scientific and technical exchanges with the

Soviet Union . Washington , 1980. iii, 57 p. ;   LC Card 80-602821   DDC 327.73047 19
KF27 .F64825 1980c

The World Administrative Radio Conference and international communications policy : hearings before the Subcommittee on International Operations of the Committee on Foreign Affairs, House of Representatives, Ninety-sixth Congress, June 14, 1979, and July 31, 1980. Washington : U. S. G.P.O., 1980. iii, 135 p. : ill. ; 24 cm.   LC Card 80-603991   DDC 384.54 19
1. Administrative Radio Conference, (1979 : Geneva, Switzerland). 2. Radio - Congresses. 3. Telecommunication - International cooperation - Congresses. I. Title.
KF27 .F647 1979e

United States. Congress. House. Committee on Foreign Affairs. Subcommittee on International Organizations.
Human rights and the detention of Andrei Sakharov, update : hearing before the Subcommittee on International Organizations of the Committee on Foreign Affairs, House of Representatives, Ninety-sixth Congress, second session, April 24, 1980. Washington : U. S. Govt. Print. Off. : for sale by the Supt. of Docs., U. S. Govt. Print. Off., 1980. iii, 35 p. ; 24 cm.   LC Card 80-602958   DDC 323.4/0947 19
1. Civil rights - Russia. 2. Political prisoners - Russia. 3. Sakharov, Andreĭ Dmitrievich, 1921-. I. Title.
KF27 .F648 1980a

Human rights and the phenomenon of disappearances : hearings before the Subcommittee on International Organizations of the Committee on Foreign Affairs, House of Representatives, Ninety-sixth Congress, first session, September 20, 25, and October 18, 1979. Washington : U. S. Govt. Print. Off. : for sale by the Supt. of Docs., U. S. Govt. Print. Off., 1980. viii, 636 p. ; 24 cm. Includes bibliographical references.   LC Card 80-603094   DDC 323.4/3 19
1. Abduction. 2. Civil rights. 3. Political prisoners. 4. Torture. I. Title.
KF27 .F648 1979g

Preparations for the 32d International Whaling Commission meeting : hearings before the Subcommittee on International Organizations of the Committee on Foreign Affairs, House of Representatives, Ninety-sixth Congress, second session, April 30 and May 20, 1980. Washington : U. S. Govt. Print. Off., 1980. iii, 155 p. ; 24 cm.   LC Card 80-602734   DDC 333.95/6 19
1. Whaling - Law and legislation. 2. Whaling - Law and legislation - United States. 3. International Whaling Commission. I. Title.
KF27 .F648 1980

Review of the 32d International Whaling Commission meeting : hearing before the Subcommittee on International Organizations of the Committee on Foreign Affairs, House of Representatives, Ninety-sixth Congress, second session, September 10, 1980. Washington : U. S. G.P.O., 1980. iii, 97 p. ; 24 cm. LC Card 80-603893   DDC 341.7/622 19
1. International Whaling Commission. 2. Whaling - Law and legislation. I. Title.
KF27 .F648 1980c

Review of the 36th session of the United Nations Commission on Human Rights : hearing before the Subcommittee on International Organizations of the Committee on Foreign Affairs, House of Representatives, Ninety-sixth Congress, second session, April 29, 1980. Washington : U. S. Govt. Print. Off., 1980. iii, 41 p. ; 24 cm.   LC Card 80-602983   DDC 341.4/81 19
1. United Nations. Commission on Human Rights. 2. Civil rights. 3. Civil rights (International law). I. Title.
KF27 .F648 1980b

United States. Congress. House. Committee on Foreign Affairs. Human rights in Eastern Europe and the Soviet Union . Washington , 1980 [i.e. 1981] iv, 248 p. ;   LC Card 81-600864   DDC 232.4/0947 19
KF27 .F6 1980n

United States. Congress. House. Committee on Foreign Affairs. Rhodesian sanctions, should the United States lift them? . Washington , 1980. iii, 80 p. ;   LC Card 80-601130   DDC

327.7306891 19
KF27 .F6 1979j

United States. Congress. House. Committee on Foreign Affairs. Subcommittee on Asian and Pacific Affairs. Human rights in Asia . Washington , 1980. iv, 335 p. ;   LC Card 80-602725   DDC 323.4/095 19
KF27 .F638 1980

United States. Congress. House. Committee on Foreign Affairs. Subcommittee on Asian and Pacific Affairs. Human rights in Asia . Washington , 1981. iv, 190 p. ;   LC Card 81-601383   DDC 323.4/095 19
KF27 .F638 1980f

United States. Congress. House. Committee on Foreign Affairs. Subcommittee on Asian and Pacific Affairs. North Pacific Fur Seal Protection Act . Washington , 1980 [i.e. 1981] v, 152 p. ;   LC Card 81-600859   DDC 346.7304/6959 347.30646959 19
KF27 .F638 1979i

United States. Congress. House. Committee on Foreign Affairs. Subcommittee on International Economic Policy and Trade. Deep seabed hard mineral resources act . Washington , 1980. iv, 271 p. ;   LC Card 80-602899   DDC 346.7304/685 19
KF27 .F6465 1980

United States. Congress. House. Committee on Foreign Affairs. Subcommittee on International Economic Policy and Trade. North-South dialog . Washington , 1980. iii, 267 p. ;   LC Card 80-603478   DDC 337/.09/048 19
KF27 .F6465 1980a

United States. Congress. House. Committee on Foreign Affairs. Subcommittee on International Economic Policy and Trade. U.N. special session on development . Washington , 1981. iii, 95 p. ;   LC Card 81-601370   DDC 327.1/11/0973 19
KF27 .F6465 1980e

United States. Congress. House. Committee on Foreign Affairs. Subcommittee on International Economic Policy and Trade. U. S. policy toward South Africa . Washington , 1980. iv, 912 p. ;   LC Card 80-603998   DDC 327.73068 19
KF27 .F6465 1980b

United States. Congress. House. Committee on Foreign Affairs. Subcommittee on International Organizations and Movements.
Behavioral sciences and the national security : together with part IX of the hearings ... / by the Subcommittee on International Organizations and Movements of the Committee on Foreign Affairs, House of Representatives. Washington : U. S. Govt. Print. Off., 1965. vi, 1OR, iii, 203 p. : ill. ; 24 cm. (Report on winning the cold war, the U. S. ideological offensive ; no. 4) At head of title: 89th Congress, 1st session. Committee print. Hearings, with special t.p., called pt. 9 of Winning the cold war: the U. S. ideological offensive.   LC Card 80-503601   DDC 327.73 s 327.1/1 19
1. United States - Foreign relations - 1963-1969. 2. United States - National security. 3. Psychological warfare. 4. World politics - 1955-1965. I. United States. Congress. House. Committee on Foreign Affairs. Subcommittee on International Organizations and Movements. Winning the cold war; hearings, pt. 9. II. Series: United States. Congress. House. Committee on Foreign Affairs. Subcommittee on International Organizations and Movements. Report on winning the cold war: the U. S. ideological offensive, no. 4. III. Title.
E840.2 .A3 no. 4 E846

Report on winning the cold war: the U. S. ideological offensive.
(no. 4) United States. Congress. House. Committee on Foreign Affairs. Subcommittee on International Organizations and Movements. Behavioral sciences and the national security . Washington , 1965. vi, 1OR, iii, 203 p. :   LC Card 80-503601   DDC 327.73 s 327.1/1 19
E840.2 .A3 no. 4 E846

Winning the cold war; hearings, pt. 9. United States. Congress. House. Committee on Foreign Affairs. Subcommittee on International Organizations and Movements. Behavioral sciences and the national security : together with part IX of the hearings ... / by the Subcommittee on

International Organizations and Movements of the Committee on Foreign Affairs, House of Representatives. Washington , 1965. vi, 1OR, iii, 203 p. : LC Card 80-503601 DDC 327.73 s 327.1/1 19
E840.2 .A3 no. 4 E846

United States. Congress. House. Committee on Foreign Affairs. Subcommittee on International Security and Scientific Affairs. Department of Energy fiscal year 1981 budget : nuclear nonproliferation programs : hearing before the Subcommittees on International Security and Scientific Affairs and on International Economic Policy and Trade of the Committee on Foreign Affairs, House of Representatives, Ninety-sixth Congress, second session, April 16, 1980. Washington : U. S. Govt. Print. Off., 1980. iii, 46 p. ; 24 cm. LC Card 80-603009 DDC 353.0082/236823 19
1. United States. Dept. of Energy - Appropriations and expenditures. 2. Nuclear nonproliferation. I. United States. Congress. House. Committee on Foreign Affairs. Subcommittee on International Economic Policy and Trade. II. Title.
KF27 .F64825 1980d

Strategic implications of chemical and biological warfare : hearing before the Subcommittees on International Security and Scientific Affairs and on Asian and Pacific Affairs of the Committee on Foreign Affairs, Ninety-sixth Congress, second session, April 24, 1980. Washington : U. S. Govt. Print Off., 1980. iii, 69 p. : ill. ; 24 cm. LC Card 80-602441 DDC 358/.34 19
1. Biological warfare. 2. Chemical warfare. 3. Asia, Southeastern - Military policy. 4. Russia - Military policy. I. United States. Congress. House. Committee on Foreign Affairs. Subcommittee on Asian and Pacific Affairs. II. Title.
KF27 .F64825 1980b

United States. Congress. House. Committee on Science and Technology. Subcommittee on Science, Research, and Technology. The Helsinki forum and East-West scientific exchange . Washington , 1980. v, 323 p. ; LC Card 80-602155 DDC 327.1/7 19
KF27 .S399 1980

United States scientific and technical exchanges with the Soviet Union : hearing before the Subcommittees on International Security and Scientific Affairs and International Operations of the Committee on Foreign Affairs, U. S. House of Representatives, Ninety-sixth Congress, second session, on H.J. Res. 534, May 20, 1980. Washington : U. S. Govt. Print. Off., 1980. iii, 57 p. ; 24 cm. LC Card 80-602821 DDC 327.73047 19
1. United States - Relations (general) with Russia. 2. Russia - Relations (general) with the United States. 3. Exchanges, Literary and scientific. I. United States. Congress. House. Committee on Foreign Affairs. Subcommittee on International Operations. II. Title.
KF27 .F64825 1980c

United States. Congress. House. Committee on Foreign Affairs. Succcommittee on Africa. United States. Congress. House. Committee on Foreign Affairs. Subcommittee on International Economic Policy and Trade. U. S. policy toward South Africa . Washington , 1980. iv, 912 p. : LC Card 80-603998 DDC 327.73068 19
KF27 .F6465 1980b

United States. Congress. House. Committee on Government Operations. (Old Catalog form: United States. Government Operations, Committee on // Hearings printed in 1978 and later are available only in microform. Please consult the librarians in the Economic and Public Affairs Division.
Emergency planning around U. S. nuclear powerplants : Nuclear Regulatory Commission oversight : fourth report / by the Committee on Government Operations, together with additional and dissenting views. Washington : U. S. Govt. Print. Off. : for sale by the Supt. of Docs., U. S. Govt. Print. Off., 1979. v, 105 p. ; 23 cm. (House report - 96th Congress, 1st session ; no. 96-413) At head of title: Union calendar no. 234. Includes bibliographical references. LC Card 79-604214 DDC 363.3/497 19
1. Atomic power-plants - United States - Safety measures. 2. Atomic power-plants - United States - Accidents. 3. United States - Civil defense. 4. United States. Nuclear Regulatory Commission. I. Series: United States. 96th Congress. 1st session, 1979. House.

Report , no. 96-413. II. Title.
KF32 .G6 1979a

United States. Congress. House. Committee on Government Operations. Legislation and National Security Subcommittee. Adequacy of aid resources for auditing overseas assistance programs . Washington , 1980. iii, 46 p. ; LC Card 80-603461 DDC 353.008/96 19
KF27 .G6676 1980g

United States. Laws, statutes, etc. Compiled statutes--Committee on Government Operations . Washington , 1980. xiv, 1065 p. ; LC Card 80-603543 DDC 342.73/06/02632 347.302602632 19
KF5102 1980

United States. Congress. House. Committee on Government Operations. Commerce, Consumer, and Monetary Affairs Subcommittee.
United States. Congress. House. Committee on Government Operations. Commerce, Consumer, and Monetary Affairs Subcommitte. Adequacy of COWPS enforcement of price standards for petroleum products : hearing before a subcommittee of the Committee on Government Operations, House of Representatives, Ninety-sixth Congress, second session, March 11, 1980. Washington : U. S. Govt. Print. Off., 1980. iii, 280 p. : graphs ; 24 cm. LC Card 80-602969 DDC 353.0082/62282044 19
1. Petroleum products - Prices - United States. 2. United States. Council on Wage and Price Stability. I. Title.
KF27 .G634 1980a

Bank treatment of inactive checking and savings accounts : hearings before a subcommittee of the Committee on Government Operations, House of Representatives, Ninety-sixth Congress, second session, July 23 and 24, 1980. Washington : U. S. G.P.O., 1980 [i.e. 1981] vi, 1101 p. : ill. ; 24 cm. Item 1016 Includes bibliographical references. LC Card 81-600990 DDC 332.1/2 19
1. Bank accounts - United States. 2. Banks and banking - United States - Service charges. 3. Estates, Unclaimed - United States. I. Title. II. Title: Inactive checking and savings accounts.
KF27 .G634 1980g

Foreign acquisitions of U. S. banks and the nonbanking activities of foreign bank holding companies : hearings before a subcommittee of the Committee on Government Operations, House of Representatives, Ninety-sixth Congress, second session, May 15 and June 25, 1980. Washington : U. S. G.P.O., 1980. vi, 999 p. ; 24 cm. Includes bibliographies. LC Card 80-604057 DDC 332.1/6 19
1. Bank holding companies - United States. 2. Banks and banking - United States - Foreign ownership. 3. Banking law - United States. 4. Competition - United States. I. Title.
KF27 .G634 1980d

Problems with the 1980 census : hearing before a subcommittee of the Committee on Government Operations, House of Representatives, Ninety-sixth Congress, second session, March 18, 1980. Washington : U. S. Govt. Print. Off., 1980. iii, 174 p. ; 24 cm. LC Card 80-602783 DDC 353.0081/9 19
1. United States - Census, 20th, 1980. 2. United States. Bureau of the Census. I. Title.
KF27 .G634 1980

Problems with the 1980 census count : joint hearing before the Commerce, Consumer, and Monetary Affairs Subcommittee of the Committee on Government Operations and the Census and Population Subcommittee of the Committee on Post Office and Civil Service, House of Representatives, Ninety-sixth Congress, second session, July 31, 1980. Washington : U. S. G.P.O., 1980. vi, 284 p. ; 24 cm. Includes bibliographical references. LC Card 80-604022 DDC 001.43/3 19
1. United States - Census, 20th, 1980. 2. United States. Bureau of the Census. I. United States. Congress. House. Committee on Post Office and Civil Service. Subcommittee on Census and Population. II. Title.
KF27 .G634 1980e

"Renegotiable rate" mortgage proposals of Federal Home Loan Bank Board : hearings before a subcommittee of the Committee on Government Operations, House of

Representatives, Ninety-sixth Congress, second session, March 26 and 27, 1980. Washington : U. S. Govt. Print. Off., 1980. v, 776 p. ; 23 cm. LC Card 80-602892 DDC 332.7/22 19
1. Mortgage loans, Variable rate - United States. 2. United States. Federal Home Loan Bank Board. I. Title.
KF27 .G634 1980b

Silver prices and the adequacy of Federal actions in the marketplace, 1979-80 : hearings before a Subcommittee of the Committee on Government Operations, House of Representatives, Ninety-sixth Congress, second session ... Washington : U. S. Govt. Print. Off., 1980. v, 1203 p. : ill. ; 24 cm. Hearings held March 31-May 22, 1980. LC Card 80-603499 DDC 332.63/28 19
1. Silver - Prices - United States. 2. United States. Commodity Futures Trading Commission. 3. Commodity exchanges - United States. 4. United States. Securities and Exchange Commission. 5. Securities - United States. 6. Speculation. I. Title.
KF27 .G634 1980c

Steel imports and the administration of the antidumping laws : hearing before a subcommittee of the Committee on Government Operations, House of Representatives, Ninety-sixth Congress, first session, December 20, 1979. Washington : U. S. G.P.O., 1980. iii, 109 p. : ill. ; 24 cm. LC Card 81-600594 DDC 353.0082/42 19
1. Steel industry and trade - United States. 2. Antidumping duties - United States. I. Title.
KF27 .G634 1980h

United States. Congress. House. Committee on Government Operations. Environment, Energy, and National Resources Subcommittee. Department of Energy's emergency energy conservation programs : hearings before a subcommittee of the Committee on Government Operations, House of Representatives, Ninety-sixth Congress, second session, September 4, 1980. Washington : U. S. G.P.O., 1980 [i.e. 1981] iii, 200 p. : ill. ; 24 cm. Item 1016 Includes bibliographical references. LC Card 81-600860 DDC 333.79/17/0973 19
1. Energy conservation - United States. 2. Energy policy - United States. 3. United States. Dept. of Energy. 4. Petroleum industry and trade - United States. I. Title.
KF27 .G655 1980f

United States. Congress. House. Committee on Government Operations. Environment, Energy, and Natural Resources Subcommittee. Automobile fuel economy, EPA oversight : hearings before a subcommittee of the Committee on Government Operations, House of Representatives, Ninety-sixth Congress, second session, January 29 and February 1, 1980. Washington : U. S. Govt. Print. Off., 1980. iv, 572 p. : graphs ; 24 cm. Includes bibliographical references. LC Card 80-601926 DDC 339.4/866553827/0973 19
1. Automobiles - United States - Fuel consumption. 2. United States. Environmental Protection Agency. I. Title.
KF27 .G655 1980c

Construction problems at Marble Hill nuclear facility : Nuclear Regulatory Commission oversight : hearings before a subcommittee of the Committee on Government Operations, House of Representatives, Ninety-sixth Congress, first session, November 27 and 28, 1979. Washington : U. S. Govt. Print. Off., 1980. iv, 349 p. : ill. ; 24 cm. LC Card 80-601154 DDC 363.1/79 19
1. Atomic power-plants - Indiana - Madison - Construction and design. 2. United States. Nuclear Regulatory Commission. I. Title. II. Title: Marble Hill nuclear facility.
KF27 .G655 1979k

Crime in Federal recreation areas : hearing before a subcommittee of the Committee on Government Operations, House of Representatives, Ninety-fifth Congress, second session, February 9, 1978. Washington : U. S. Govt. Print. Off., 1978. iii, 60 p. ; 23 cm. LC Card 80-603630 DDC 364.1/0973 19
1. Crime and criminals - United States. 2. Recreation areas - United States - Security measures. 3. Recreation areas - United States - Vandalism. I. Title.
KF27 .G655 1978d

Department of Energy gasohol policy : hearing before a subcommittee of the Committee on Government Operations, House of Representatives, Ninety-sixth Congress, second session, July 28, 1980. Washington : U. S. Govt. Print. Off., 1980. iii, 175 p. : ill. ; 24 cm. Includes bibliographical references.   LC Card 80-603776   DDC 333.8/232 19
1. Gasohol. 2. United States. Dept. of Energy. I. Title.
KF27 .G655 1980d

Effect of Iraqi-Iranian conflict on U. S. energy policy : hearing before a subcommittee on the Committee on Government Operations, House of Representatives, Ninety-sixth Congress, second session, September 30, 1980. Washington : U. S. G.P.O., 1981. iii, 70 p. : ill. ; 24 cm.   LC Card 81-600850   DDC 333.79/0973 19
1. Energy policy - United States. 2. Petroleum industry and trade. 3. Iraq - Foreign relations - Iran. 4. Iran - Foreign relations - Iraq. I. Title.
KF27 .G655 1980e

Home heating oil price and supply issues, the Department of Energy's record : hearing before a Subcommittee of the Committee on Government Operations, House of Representatives, Ninety-sixth Congress, second session, February 12, 1980. Washington : U. S. Govt. Print. Off., 1980. iii, 216 p. ; 24 cm.   LC Card 80-603000   DDC 338.4/36655384 19
1. Petroleum as fuel - Prices - United States. 2. Dwellings - United States - Heating and ventilation. 3. United States. Dept. of Energy. I. Title.
KF27 .G655 1980

NRC oversight : limitations on intervenors in licensing proceedings : hearing before a subcommittee of the Committee on Government Operations, House of Representatives, Ninety-sixth Congress, second session, July 2, 1980. Washington : U. S. G.P.O., 1980 [i.e. 1981] iii, 152 p. ; 24 cm. Item 1016 Includes bibliographical references.   LC Card 81-601389   DDC 353.0087/22 19
1. Atomic power-plants - Licenses - United States. 2. Administrative procedure - United States - Citizen participation. 3. Atomic power-plants - United States - Safety measures. I. Title.
KF27 .G655 1980g

Nuclear Regulatory Commission--the Rogovin report : hearing before a Subcommittee of the Committee on Government Operations, House of Representatives, Ninety-sixth Congress, second session, February 13, 1980. Washington : U. S. Govt. Print. Off., 1980. iii, 90 p. ; 23 cm.   LC Card 80-602901   DDC 363.1/79 19
1. United States. Nuclear Regulatory Commission. 2. Atomic power-plants - United States - Safety measures. 3. Nuclear facilities - United States - Safety measures. 4. Atomic power-plants - United States - Accidents. I. Title. II. Title: The Rogovin report.
KF27 .G655 1980b

The petroleum import fee, Department of Energy Oversight : hearings before a Subcommittee of the Committee on Government Operations, House of Representatives, Ninety-sixth Congress, second session .... Washington : U. S. Govt. Print. Off., 1980. iii, 271 p. : ill. ; 23 cm. Hearings held April 16, 24, 29, and May 14, 1980. Includes bibliographical references.   LC Card 80-602747   DDC 382/.42282/0973 19
1. Tariff on gasoline - United States. 2. Tariff on petroleum - United States. 3. United States. Dept. of Energy. I. Title.
KF27 .G655 1980a

Synthetic Fuels Corporation oversight : hearing before a subcommittee of the Committee on Government Operations, House of Representatives, Ninety-seventh Congress, first session, February 19, 1981. Washington : U. S. G.P.O., 1981. iii, 169 p. : ill. ; 24 cm. Item 1016-A, 1016-B (microfiche)   LC Card 81-601955   DDC 353.09/2 19
1. Synthetic Fuels Corporation (U. S.). I. Title.
KF27 .G655 1981

United States. Congress. House. Committee on Interstate and Foreign Commerce. Subcommittee on Oversight and Investigations. Love Canal, health studies and relocation . Washington , 1980. v, 71 p. :   LC Card 80-604042   DDC 363.7/28 19
KF27 .I5547 1980o

United States. Congress. House. Committee on Government Operations. Government Activities and Tansportation Subcommittee.
FAA-OSHA jurisdiction over workplace safety in the aviation industry : hearing before a subcommittee of the Committee on Government Operations, House of Representatives, Ninety-sixth Congress, second session, August 16, 1980. Washington : U. S. G.P.O., 1980. iii, 192 p. : ill. ; 24 cm. Bibliography: p. 125.   LC Card 81-600596   DDC 353.0087/77/0289 19
1. Aeronautics - United States - Safety measures. 2. United States. Federal Aviation Administration. 3. United States. Occupational Safety and Health Administration. I. Title.
KF27 .G6626 1980c

United States. Congress. House. Committee on Government Operations. Government Activities and Transportation Subcommittee.
Air traffic control computer failures : hearings before a subcommittee of the Committee on Government Operations, House of Representatives, Ninety-sixth Congress, second session, June 30 and August 15, 1980. Washington : U. S. G.P.O., 1980 [i.e. 1981] iv, 512 p. : ill. ; 24 cm.   LC Card 81-600878   DDC 363.1/2418/0973 19
1. Air traffic control - United States - Electronic equipment. 2. Aeronautics - United States - Safety measures. I. Title.
KF27 .G6626 1980b

Alleged violations of U. S. aviation laws and regulations by LAN Chile Airlines : hearing before a subcommittee of the Committee on Government Operations, House of Representatives, Ninety-sixth Congress, second session, May 9, 1980. Washington : U. S. G.P.O., 1980 [i.e. 1981]. iii, 65 p. : 24 cm. Item 1016   LC Card 81-601859   DDC 345.73/0235 347.305235 19
1. LAN Chile Airlines. 2. Aeronautics, Commercial - Chile. 3. Aeronautics, Commercial - United States. 4. Explosives - Transportation. I. Title.
KF27 .G6626 1980e

Amending the Federal Property and Administrative Services Act of 1949 : hearing before a subcommittee of the Committee on Government Operations, House of Representatives, Ninety-sixth Congress, second session, on H.R. 5381 ... June 9, 1980. Washington : U. S. G.P.O., 1980. iii, 224 p. : ill. ; 24 cm.   LC Card 80-604062   DDC 346.73/023/0262 347.30230262 19
1. Public contracts - United States. I. Title.
KF27 .G6626 1980a

Aviation safety : hazardous materials handling : hearing before a subcommittee of the Committee on Government Operations, House of Representatives, Ninety-sixth Congress, second session, August 16, 1980. Washington : U. S. G.P.O., 1980. iii, 149 p. : ill. ; 24 cm. Item 1016   LC Card 81-600663   DDC 363.1/76 19
1. Hazardous substances - United States - Transportation. 2. Aeronautics - United States - Safety measures. 3. Aeronautics, Commercial - United States - Freight. I. Title.
KF27 .G6626 1980d

Government travel per diem reimbursement rate : hearings before a Subcommittee of the Committee on Government Operations, House of Representatives, Ninety-sixth Congress, second session, on H.R. 6082 and H.R. 7072 ... February 26 and April 17, 1980. Washington : U. S. Govt. Print. Off., 1980. iii, 141 p. ; 24 cm.   LC Card 80-602902   DDC 353.001/6 19
1. United States - Officials and employees - Travel regulations. 2. United States - Officials and employees - Salaries, allowances, etc. I. Title.
KF27 .G6626 1980

United States. Congress. House. Committee on Government Operations. Government Information and Individual Rights Subcommittee. see United States. Congress. House. Committee on Government Operations. Subcommittee on Government Information and Individual Rights.

United States. Congress. House. Committee on Government Operations. Intergovernmental Relations and Human Resources Subcommittee.
Joint Funding Simplification Act of 1974 : hearing before a subcommittee of the

Committee on Government Operations, House of Representatives, Ninety-sixth Congress, second session, on H.R. 5595 and S. 1835 ... November 20, 1980. Washington : U. S. G.P.O., 1980 [i.e. 1981] iii, 130 p. : ill. ; 24 cm. Item 1016   LC Card 81-600870   DDC 343.73/034 347.30334 19
1. Grants-in-aid - United States. 2. Intergovernmental fiscal relations - United States. I. Title.
KF27 .G664 1980a

State and Local Fiscal Assistance Act of 1972 : hearings before a subcommittee of the Committee on Government Operations, House of Representatives, Ninety-sixth Congress, second session on H.R. 1771 ... H.R. 2291 ... H.R. 2698 .... Washington : U. S. G.P.O., 1980. vi, 909 p. ; 24 cm. Hearings held Mar. 19-Apr. 17, 1980.   LC Card 80-603812   DDC 343.73/034 347.30334 19
1. Revenue sharing - Law and legislation - United States. 2. Intergovernmental fiscal relations - United States. I. Title.
KF27 .G664 1980

United States. Congress. House. Committee on Government Operations. Legislation and National Security Subcommittee.
Adequacy of aid resources for auditing overseas assistance programs : hearing before a subcommittee of the Committee on Government Operations, House of Representatives, Ninety-sixth Congress, second session, June 26, 1980. Washington : U. S. Govt. Print. Off., 1980. iii, 46 p. ; 24 cm.   LC Card 80-603461   DDC 353.008/96 19
1. United States. Agency for International Development - Accounting. I. United States. Congress. House. Committee on Government Operations. II. Title.
KF27 .G6676 1980g

The Congressional reports elimination act of 1980 : hearing before a subcommittee of the Committee on Government Operations, House of Representatives, Ninety-sixth Congress, second session, on H.R. 6686 ... July 24, 1980. Washington : U. S. Govt. Print. Off., 1980. iii, 66 p. ; 24 cm.   LC Card 80-603104   DDC 342.73/066 19
1. Government paperwork - Law and legislation - United States. 2. Public records - Law and legislation - United States. I. Title.
KF27 .G6676 1980d

Extend reorganization authority of the President : hearing before a Subcommittee of the Committee on Government Operation, House of Representatives, Ninety-sixth Congress, second session on H.R. 6585 ... February 26, 1980. Washington : U. S. Govt. Print. Off., 1980. iii, 47 p. ; 23 cm.   LC Card 80-602439   DDC 353/.073 19
1. Administrative agencies - United States - Reorganization. 2. Executive power - United States. I. Title.
KF27 .G6676 1980a

Inspector General Act Amendments of 1980 : hearings before a sucommmittee of the Committee on Government Operations, House of Representatives, Ninety-sixth Congress, second session, on H.R. 7893 ... August 27 and 28, 1980. Washington : U. S. G.P.O., 1980. iv, 261 p. ; 24 cm.   LC Card 80-604018   DDC 342.73/066 347.30266 19
1. Governmental investigations - United States. 2. Auditors - Legal status, laws, etc. - United States. 3. United States - Executive departments - Officials and employees. I. Title.
KF27 .G6676 1980k

Limitation on yearend obligations : hearing before a subcommittee of the Committee on Government Operations, House of Representatives, Ninety-sixth Congress, second session, on H.R. 4717 ... March 25, 1980. Washington : U. S. Govt. Print. Off., 1980. iv, 237 p. : ill. ; 24 cm.   LC Card 80-602718   DDC 342.73/068 19
1. Administrative agencies - United States - Management. 2. Public contracts - United States. I. Title.
KF27 .G6676 1980c

National publications act of 1980 : hearing before a subcommittee of the Committee on Government Operations, House of Representatives, Ninety-sixth Congress, second session, on H.R. 5424 ... June 4, 1980. Washington : U. S. Govt. Print. Off., 1980. iii,

GOVERNMENT PUBLICATIONS - U.S.: 1981

431

United States. Congress. House. Committee on Interior and

277 p. ; 24 cm.   LC Card 80-603037   DDC
343.73/0998 19
*1. Printing, Public - United States. 2. Public records -
Law and legislation - United States. 3. United States.
Government Printing Office. I. Title.*
KF27 .G6676 1980e

Patent and Trademark Law Amendments of
1980 : hearings before a subcommittee of the
Committee on Government Operations, House
of Representatives, Ninety-sixth Congress,
second session, on H.R. 6933 ... September 16
and 17, 1980. Washington : U. S. G.P.O., 1980.
iii, 218 p. ; 24 cm. Includes bibliographical
resources.   LC Card 80-604009   DDC 346.7304/86
347.306486 19
*1. Patent laws and legislation - United States. 2.
Trade-marks - United States. I. Title.*
KF27 .G6676 1980i

Reorganization plan no. 1 of 1980 (Nuclear
Regulatory Commission) : hearing before a
subcommittee of the Committee on
Government Operations, House of
Representatives, Ninety-sixth Congress, second
session, May 6, 1980. Washington : U. S. Govt.
Print. Off., 1980. iii, 100 p. ; 23 cm.   LC Card
80-602817   DDC 353.0087/22 19
*1. United States. Nuclear Regulatory Commission. I.
Title.*
KF27 .G6676 1980b

U. S. mission and office operations, East
Africa : hearing before a subcommittee of the
Committee on Government Operations, House
of Representatives, Ninety-sixth Congress,
second session, February 13, 1980.
Washington : U. S. Govt. Print. Off., 1980. iii,
72 p. ; 24 cm.   LC Card 80-603484   DDC
353.008/92/09676 19
*1. United States - Foreign relations - Africa, Eastern. 2.
Africa, Eastern - Foreign relations. 3. United States -
Foreign relations administration. I. Title.*
KF27 .G6676 1980f

U. S. mission and office operations--Egypt :
hearing before a subcommittee of the
Committee on Government Operations, House
of Representatives, Ninety-sixth Congress,
second session, February 11, 1980.
Washington : U. S. Govt. Print. Off., 1980. iii,
161 p. ; 24 cm.   LC Card 80-603495   DDC
353.008/92/0962 19
*1. United States - Diplomatic and consular service -
Egypt. 2. United States - Foreign relations - Egypt. 3.
Egypt - Foreign relations - United States. 4. United
States - Foreign relations administration. I. Title.*
KF27 .G6676 1980h

U. S. mission and office operations--West
Africa : hearing before a subcommittee of the
Committee on Government Operations, House
of Representatives, Ninety-sixth Congress,
second session, February 16, 1980.
Washington : U. S. G.P.O., 1980. iii, 75 p. ; 24
cm.   LC Card 80-603676   DDC 353.008/92/0966 19
*1. United States - Diplomatic and consular service -
Africa, West. 2. United States - Foreign relations -
Africa, West. 3. Africa, West - Foreign relations -
United States. I. Title.*
KF27 .G6676 1980j

**United States. Congress. House. Committee on
Government Operations. Manpower and
Housing Subcommittee.**
CETA's vulnerability to fraud and abuse :
hearings before a subcommittee of the
Committee on Government Operations, House
of Representatives, Ninety-sixth Congress,
second session, May 20, 21, and July 23, 1980.
Washington : U. S. G.P.O., 1980. iv, 251 p. ;
24 cm.   LC Card 80-604021   DDC 353.0083 19
*1. Manpower policy - United States - Corrupt practices.
2. Occupational training - United States - Corrupt
practices. 3. Public service employment - United
States - Corrupt practices. I. Title.*
KF27 .G6678 1980g

Department of Housing and Urban
Development's cooperative housing programs :
hearings before a subcommittee of the
Committee on Government Operations, House
of Representatives, Ninety-sixth Congress,
second session, June 19 and 24, 1980.
Washington : U. S. G.P.O., 1980 [i.e. 1981] iii,
130 p. ; 24 cm. Item 1016   LC Card 81-601644
DDC 363.5/8 19
*1. Housing, Cooperative - United States. 2. Housing
policy - United States. 3. United States. Dept. of*

Housing and Urban Development. I. Title.
KF27 .G6678 1980f

Fiscal and accounting systems of the
Department of Housing and Urban
Development :hearing before a subcommittee of
the Committee on Government Operations,
House of Representatives, Ninety-sixth
Congress, first session, November 8, 1979.
Washington : U. S. Govt. Print. Off., 1980. iii,
90 p. ; 24 cm.   LC Card 80-602076   DDC 353.85
19
*1. United States. Dept. of Housing and Urban
Development. I. Title.*
KF27 .G6678 1979e

Operation of the U. S. Employment Service :
hearings before a subcommittee of the
Committee on Government Operations, House
of Representatives, Ninety-fourth Congress,
second session .... Washington : U. S. Govt.
Print. Off., 1976. iv, 359 p. : ill. ; 23 cm.
Hearings held Apr. 14-May 25, 1976.   LC Card
76-603085
1. United States. Employment Service. I. Title.
KF27 .G6678 1976b

Performance of the Community Services
Administration : hearings before a
subcommittee of the Committee on
Government Operations, House of
Representatives, Ninety-sixth Congress, first
session, July 17, 19, 1979, March 25, May 6, 8,
and June 25, 1980. Washington : U. S. G.P.O.,
1981. iv, 354 p. : ill. ; 24 cm. Item 1016   LC
Card 81-601643   DDC 353.0084 19
*1. United States. Community Services Administration. I.
Title.*
KF27 .G6678 1979g

Performance of the Occupational Safety and
Health Administration : hearings before a
subcommittee of the Committee on
Government Operations, House of
Representatives, Ninety-fifth Congress, first
session, April 27 and 28, 1977. Washington : U.
S. Govt. Print. Off., 1977. iv, 163 p. ; 24 cm.
LC Card 80-603631   DDC 353.008/3/0289 19
*1. United States. Occupational Safety and Health
Administration. I. Title.*
KF27 .G6678 1977f

**United States. Congress. House. Committee on
Government Operations. Subcommittee on
Government Information and Individual
Rights.**
Department of Justice internal audit
operations : hearings before a subcommittee of
the Committee on Government Operations,
House of Representatives, Ninety-sixth
Congress, second session, March 24 and April
24, 1980. Washington : U. S. G.P.O., 1980 [i.e.
1981] iv, 263 p. : ill. ; 24 cm. Item 1016 Includes
bibliographical references.   LC Card 81-601331   DDC
353.5 19
1. United States. Dept. of Justice - Accounting. I. Title.
KF27 .G6628 1980b

The Freedom of Information Act : Central
Intelligence Agency exemptions : hearings
before a subcommittee of the Committee on
Government Operations, House of
Representatives, Ninety-sixth Congress, second
session, H.R. 5129, H.R. 7055, and H.R.
7056 ... February 20 and May 29, 1980.
Washington : U. S. G.P.O., 1981. iii, 205 p. ;
24 cm. Item 1016-A Includes bibliographical
references.   LC Card 81-601868   DDC 342.73/0418
347.302418 19
*1. United States. Central Intelligence Agency. 2.
Government information - United States. 3. Defense
information, Classified - United States. I. Title.*
KF27 .G6628 1980d

International data flow : hearings before a
subcommittee of the Committee on
Government Operations, House of
Representatives, Ninety-sixth Congress, second
session, March 10, 13, 27, and April 21, 1980.
Washington : U. S. G.P.O., 1980. iv, 843 p. :
ill. ; 24 cm. Item 1016 Bibliography: p. 803-806.   LC
Card 81-600810   DDC 658.4/72 19
*1. Data protection - International cooperation. 2. Data
transmission systems - International cooperation. 3.
Computer networks - International cooperation. I. Title.*
KF27 .G6628 1980

National Archives and Records Service
documents preservation program and trust fund
operation : hearings before a subcommittee of
the Committee on Government Operations,

House of Representatives, Ninety-sixth
Congress, first session .... Washington : U. S.
Govt. Print. Off., 1980. v, 913 p. ; 24 cm.
Hearings held June 25-Nov. 8, 1979.   LC Card
80-602891   DDC 353.0071/46 19
*1. United States. National Archives and Records
Service - Management. 2. Archives - United States -
Finance. I. Title.*
KF27 .G6628 1979a

Public reaction to privacy issues : hearing
before a subcommittee of the Committee on
Government Operations, House of
Representatives, Ninety-sixth Congress, first
session, June 6, 1979. Washington : U. S.
G.P.O., c1980 [i.e. 1981] iii, 153 p. ; 24 cm.
Item 1016   LC Card 81-600838   DDC 323.44/8/0973
19
*1. Privacy, Right of - United States - Public opinion. 2.
Public opinion - United States. I. Title.*
KF27 .G6628 1979c

Reauthorization of appropriation for the
National Historical Publications and Records
Commission : hearing before a subcommittee of
the Committee on Government Operations,
House of Representatives, Ninety-sixth
Congress, first session, on H.R. 3717 ... April
30, 1979. Washington : U. S. Govt. Print. Off.,
1980. iii, 66 p. : ill. ; 24 cm.   LC Card 80-603008
DDC 344.73/092 19
*1. United States. National Historical Publications and
Records Commission - Appropriations and expenditures.
I. Title.*
KF27 .G6628 1979b

U. S. Postal Service Plan for nine-digit zip
code : hearing before a subcommittee of the
Committee on Government Operations, House
of Representatives, Ninety-sixth Congress,
second session, September 17, 1980.
Washington : U. S. G.P.O., 1980. v, 462 p. :
ill. ; 23 cm. Item 1016. Includes bibliographical
references.   LC Card 81-601386   DDC 383/.145 19
*1. United States Postal Service. 2. Zip code - United
States. I. Title.*
KF27 .G6628 1980a

Veterans Administration planning for medical
automated data processing needs : hearing
before a subcommittee of the Committee on
Government Operations, House of
Representatives, Ninety-sixth Congress, second
session, September 4, 1980. Washington : U. S.
G.P.O., 1980 [i.e. 1981] iv, 334 p. ; 24 cm. Item
1016   LC Card 81-600933   DDC 353.0081/2 19
*1. United States. Veterans Administration -
Management - Data processing. 2. Veterans - Medical
care - United States - Data processing. I. Title.*
KF27 .G6628 1980c

**United States. Congress. House. Committee on
House Administration.** (Old Catalog form:
United States. House Administration,
Committee on // Hearings printed in 1978
and later are available only in microform.
Please consult the librarians in the Economic
and Public Affairs Division.
United States. Laws, statutes, etc. Federal
election campaign laws relating to the U. S.
House of Representatives, as amended through
January 8, 1980 /. Washington , 1980. xiv, 232
p. ;   LC Card 80-602296   DDC 342.73/07 19
KF4914 .A3 1980

**United States. Congress. House. Committee on
House Administration. Policy Group on
Information and Computers.** Technical
advisory panel on the digital data
communications network : hearings before the
Policy Group on Information and Computers of
the Committee on House Administration,
House of Representatives, Ninety-seventh
Congress, first session, January 28 and 29,
1981, Washington, D.C. Washington : U. S.
G.P.O., 1981. iv, 163 p. : ill. ; 24 cm. Item
1018-A, 1018-B (microfiche) Includes bibliographical
references.   LC Card 81-601775   DDC
328.73/072/0684 19
*1. United States. Congress. House - Information
services. 2. United States. Congress. House - Data
processing. I. Title.*
KF27 .H652 1981

**United States. Congress. House. Committee on
Interior and Insular Affairs.** (Old Catalog
form: United States. Interior and Insular
Affairs, // Hearings printed in 1978 and later
are available only in microform. Please
consult the librarians in the Economic and

BIBLIOGRAPHIC GUIDE

United States. Congress. House. Committee on Interior and

432

Public Affairs Division.
Briefing by the secretary of the Interior :
oversight hearing before the Committee on
Interior and Insular Affairs, House of
Representatives, Ninety-seventh Congress, first
session, on briefing by the secretary of the
Interior, hearing held in Washington, D.C.,
February 5, 1981. Washington : U. S. G.P.O.,
1981. iii, 79 p. ; 24 cm. "Serial no. 97-1." Item
1023-A, 1023-B (microfiche)   LC Card 81-601759
DDC 353.3 19
*1. United States. Dept. of the Interior. 2. Watt, James
G., 1938-. I. Title.*
KF27 .I5 1981

Bureau of Indian Affairs and Indian Health
Service budget request for fiscal year 1981 :
oversight hearing before the Committee on
Interior and Insular Affairs, House of
Representatives, Ninety-sixth Congress, second
session ... held in Washington, D.C., February
19, 1980. Washington : U. S. G.P.O., 1980. iii,
102 p. ; 24 cm. "Serial no. 96-37."   LC Card
81-600586   DDC 353.0072/23671497 19
*1. United States. Bureau of Indian Affairs -
Appropriations and expenditures. 2. United States.
Indian Health Service - Appropriations and
expenditures. I. Title.*
KF27 .I5 1980b

Institute of American Indian Arts : hearing
before the Committee on Interior and Insular
Affairs, House of Representatives, Ninety-sixth
Congress, second session, on H.R. 6850 ...
hearing held in Washington, D.C., July 1, 1980.
Washington : U. S. G.P.O., 1981. iii, 102 p. ;
23 cm. "Serial no. 96-45." Item 1023   LC Card
81-601320
1. Institute of American Indian Arts. I. Title.
KF27 .I5 1980d

Settlement of Indian land claims in the state of
Maine : hearing before the Committee on
Interior and Insular Affairs, House of
Representatives, Ninety-sixth Congress, second
session, on H.R. 7919 ... hearing held in
Washington, D.C., August 25, 1980.
Washington : U. S. G.P.O., 1980 [i.e. 1981] iv,
287 p. ; 24 cm. "Serial ;no. 96-41." Item 1023   LC
Card 81-600935   DDC 346.7304/3/08997
347.3064308997 19
*1. Indians of North America - Maine - Claims. 2.
Indians of North America - Maine - Land transfers. I.
Title.*
KF27 .I5 1980c

Settlement of the Cayuga Indian Nation land
claims in the state of New York : hearing
before the Committee on Interior and Insular
Affairs, House of Representatives, Ninety-sixth
Congress, second session, on H.R. 6631 ...
hearing held in Washington, D.C., March 3,
1980. Washington : U. S. G.P.O., 1980. v, 404
p. : maps ; 24 cm. "Serial no. 96-35." Includes
bibliographical references.   LC Card 81-600597   DDC
346.7304/32/08997 347.30643208997 19
*1. Cayuga Indians - Land tenure. 2. Cayuga Indians -
Claims. 3. Indians of North America - New York
(State) - Land tenure. 4. Indians of North America -
New York (State) - Claims. I. Title.*
KF27 .I5 1980

To amend the Indian Health Care Improvement
Act : hearings before the Committee on Interior
and Insular Affairs, House of Representatives,
Ninety-sixth Congress, second session, on H.R.
6629 ... hearings held in Washington, D.C.,
March 6 and 25, 1980. Washington : U. S.
G.P.O., 1980 [i.e. 1981] vii, 497 p. : ill. ; 24
cm. "Serial no. 96-36." Includes bibliographical
references.   LC Card 81-600862   DDC
344.73/0328497 347.304328497 19
*1. Indians of North America - Medical care - Law and
legislation. 2. Indians of North America - Medical
care - Finance. I. Title.*
KF27 .I5 1980a

**United States. Congress. House. Committee on
Interior and Insular Affairs. Subcommittee
on Energy and the Environment.**
Department of Energy authorizations for fiscal
year 1981 : hearing before the Subcommittee on
Energy and the Environment of the Committee
on Interior and Insular Affairs, House of
Representatives, Ninety-sixth Congress, second
session, on H.R. 6627 ... held in Washington,
D.C., February 25, 1980. Washington : U. S.
Govt. Print. Off., 1980. iii, 116 p. : ill. ; 24 cm.
"Serial no. 96-33."   LC Card 80-603650   DDC

353.0072/236823 19
*1. United States. Dept. of Energy - Appropriations and
expenditures. 2. Radioactive waste disposal - United
States - Finance. I. Title.*
KF27 .I518 1980a

Mill tailings dam break at Church Rock, New
Mexico : oversight hearing before the
Subcommittee on Energy and the Environment
of the Committee on Interior and Insular
Affairs, House of Representatives, Ninety-sixth
Congress, first session ... hearing held in
Washington, D.C., October 22, 1979.
Washington : U. S. Govt. Print. Off., 1980. iv,
232 p. : ill. ; 24 cm. "Serial no. 96-25."   LC Card
80-601962   DDC 622/.8 19
*1. Dam failures - New Mexico - Church Rock. 2.
Uranium industry - Waste disposal. 3. Tailings
(Metallurgy) - Environmental aspects. 4. United
Nuclear Corporation. 5. Navaho Indians - Government
relations. I. Title.*
KF27 .I518 1979i

Nuclear plant shutdowns : oversight hearing
before the Subcommittee on Energy and the
Environment of the Committee on Interior and
Insular Affairs, House of Representatives,
Ninety-sixth Congress, first session ... hearing
held in Washington, D.C., March 19, 1979.
Washington : U. S. Govt. Print. Off., 1980. v,
346 p. : ill. ; 24 cm. Serial no. 96-29. LC Card
80-603454   DDC 363.1/79 19
*1. Atomic power-plants - United States - Safety
measures. 2. United States. Nuclear Regulatory
Commission. I. Title.*
KF27 .I518 1979j

Nuclear Regulatory Commission authorizations
for fiscal year 1981 : hearing before the
Subcommittee on Energy and the Environment
of the Committee on Interior and Insular
Affairs, House of Representatives, Ninety-sixth
Congress, second session, on H.R. 6628 ... held
in Washington, D.C., March 7, 1980.
Washington : U. S. Govt. Print. Off., 1980. iv,
503 p. : ill. ; 24 cm. "Serial no. 96-31." Includes
bibliographical references.   LC Card 80-603512   DDC
353.0072/2368722 19
*1. United States. Nuclear Regulatory Commission -
Appropriations and expenditures. I. Title.*
KF27 .I518 1980

Nuclear siting and licensing process (Limerick
Atomic Power Station, Pa.) : oversight hearing
before the Subcommittee on Energy and the
Environment of the Committee on Interior and
Insular Affairs, House of Representatives,
Ninety-sixth Congress, second session, on
nuclear siting and licensing process (Limerick
Atomic Power Station, Pa.), hearing held in
Newton, Pennsylvania, May 27, 1980.
Washington : U. S. G.P.O., 1980. iv, 305 p. :
ill. ; 24 cm. "Serial no. 96-34." Includes
bibliographical references.   LC Card 81-600605   DDC
343.73/0925 347.303925 19
*1. Limerick Atomic Power Station (Pa.). 2. United
States. Nuclear Regulatory Commission. 3. Atomic
power-plants - Licenses - Pennsylvania. 4. Atomic
power-plants - Pennsylvania - Accidents. 5. Atomic
power-plants - Pennsylvania - Safety measures. I. Title.*
KF27 .I518 1980c

Oversight on the Surface Mining Control and
Reclamation Act of 1977 : oversight hearings
before the Subcommittee on Energy and the
Environment of the Committee on Interior and
Insular Affairs, House of Representatives,
Ninety-sixth Congress, second session, on the
Surface Mining Control and Reclamation Act of
1977 (Public Law 95-87), hearings held in
Washington, D.C., March 27, 28, and 31, 1980.
Washington : U. S. G.P.O., 1981. vi, 621 p. ;
24 cm. "Serial no. 96-43." Item 1023   LC Card
81-601889   DDC 353.0082/382 19
*1. Strip mining - Environmental aspects - United States.
2. Strip mining - Government policy - United States. 3.
Reclamation of land - United States. I. Title.*
KF27 .I518 1980d

Reclamation practices and environmental
problems of surface mining : hearings before the
Subcommittee on Energy and the Environment
of the Committee on Interior and Insular
Affairs, House of Representatives, Ninety-fifth
Congress, first session, on H.R. 2 ... hearings
held in Washington, D.C. .... Washington : U.
S. G.P.O., 1977. 4 v. : ill. ; 23 cm. Pts. 2-4 have
title: Surface Mining Control and Reclamation Act of
1977. "Serial no. 95-1." Hearings held Jan. 10-Mar. 4,

1977. Includes bibliographical references.   LC Card
77-603316   DDC 346.7304/68 347.306468 19
*1. Strip mining - Law and legislation - United States. 2.
Reclamation of land - Law and legislation - United
States. I. Title. II. Title: Surface Mining Control and
Reclamation Act of 1977.*
KF27 .I518 1977j

**United States. Congress. House. Committee on
Interior and Insular Affairs. Subcommittee
on Indian Affairs and Public Lands.** Hearings
printed in 1978 and later are available only in
microform. Please consult the librarians in the
Economic and Public Affairs Division.
Indian Child Welfare Act of 1978 : hearings
before the Subcommittee on Indian Affairs and
Public Lands of the Committee on Interior and
Insular Affairs, House of Representatives,
Ninety-fifth Congress, second session, on S.
1214 ... hearings held in Washington, D.C.,
February 9 and March 9, 1978. Washington :
U. S. G.P.O., 1981. v, 303 p. : ill. ; 23 cm.
"Serial no. 96-42." Item 1023   LC Card 81-601388
DDC 344.73/032733 347.30432733 19
*1. Indians of North America - Children - Legal status,
laws, etc. 2. Foster home care - Law and legislation -
United States. 3. Interracial adoption - United States. I.
Title.*
KF27 .I528 1981

**United States. Congress. House. Committee on
Interior and Insular Affairs. Subcommittee
on Mines and Mining.**
Feasibility of a return to the gold standard :
oversight hearing before the Subcommittee on
Mines and Mining of the Committee on
Interior and Insular Affairs, House of
Representatives, Ninety-sixth Congress, second
session, on feasibility of a return to the gold
standard, hearing held in Washington, D.C.,
October 2, 1980. Washington : U. S. G.P.O.,
1980 [i.e. 1981] iii, 160 p. : ill. ; 24 cm. "Serial
no. 96-40." Item 1023 Includes bibliographical
references.   LC Card 81-600844   DDC
332.4/222/0973 19
*1. Gold standard. 2. Money supply - United States. 3.
Monetary policy - United States. I. Title.*
KF27 .I536 1980

Increasing the use of geothermal energy :
hearing before the Subcommittee on Mines and
Mining of the Committee on Interior and
Insular Affairs, House of Representatives,
Ninety-sixth Congress, first session, on H.R.
4471 ... H.R. 5187 ... held in Washington, D.C.,
September 6, 1979. Washington, D.C. : U. S.
Govt. Print. Off., 1980. iii, 211 p. ; 23 cm.
"Serial no. 96-18."   LC Card 80-602759   DDC
346.7304/68813/0262 19
*1. Geothermal resources - Law and legislation - United
States. 2. Geothermal leases - United States. I. Title.*
KF27 .I536 1979e

Sub-Sahara Africa, its role in critical mineral
needs of the Western World : a report /
prepared by the Subcommittee on Mines and
Mining of the Committee on Interior and
Insular Affairs of the U. S. House of
Representatives, Ninety-sixth Congress, second
session. Washington : U. S. Govt. Print. Off.,
1980. viii, 29 p. : maps ; 24 cm. At head of title:
96th Congress, 2d session. Committtee print no. 8.
"July 1980."   LC Card 80-603266   DDC 338.2/0967
19
*1. Mines and mineral resources - Zaire. 2. Mines and
mineral resources - South Africa. 3. Mines and mineral
resources - Zimbabwe. 4. Strategic materials - United
States. I. Title.*
TN119.Z3 U55 1980

To amend the Geothermal steam act of 1970 :
hearing before the Subcommittee on Mines and
Mining of the Committee on Interior and
Insular Affairs, House of Representatives,
Ninety-sixth Congress, first session on H.R.
4471 ... H.R. 5187 ... hearing held in
Washington, D.C., November 15, 1979.
Washington : U. S. Govt. Print. Off., 1980. iv,
134 p. ; 23 cm. "Serial no. 96-24."   LC Card
80-601989   DDC 346.7304/688/0262 19
*1. Geothermal resources - Law and legislation - United
States. I. Title.*
KF27 .I536 1979d

U. S. minerals vulnerability : national policy
implications : a report / prepared by the
Subcommittee on Mines and Mining of the
Committee on Interior and Insular Affairs of
the U. S. House of Representatives,

GOVERNMENT PUBLICATIONS - U.S.: 1981

433   United States. Congress. House. Committee on Interstate and

Ninety-sixth Congress, second session. Washington : U. S. G.P.O. : For sale by the Supt. of Docs., U. S. G.P.O., 1980. xvi, 83 p. : ill. ; 24 cm. At head of title: 96th Congress, 2d session. Committee print no. 9. "November 1980." Includes bibliographical references. LC Card 80-604127 DDC 333.8/5/0973 19
1. Mines and mineral resources - United States. 2. Mineral industries - United States. I. Title.
TN23 .U75 1980

United States. Congress. House. Committee on Interior and Insular Affairs. Subcommittee on National Parks and Insular Affairs. Legislative history of the Omnibus insular areas act of 1979-1980, (H.R. 3756), (Public law 96-205) /. Washington , 1980. iv, 185 p. ; LC Card 80-602286 DDC 342.73/0413 19
KF4635.A315 A15 1980

Nuclear spent fuel storage in the Pacific : hearing before the Subcommittee on National Parks and Insular Affairs of the Committee on Interior and Insular Affairs, House of Representatives, Ninety-sixth Congress, first session, on S. 1119 ... held in Honolulu, Hawaii, December 27, 1979. Washington : U. S. Govt. Print. Off., 1980. iv, 233 p. : ill. ; 24 cm. "Serial no. 96-27." LC Card 80-602767 DDC 344.73/04622 19
1. Spent reactor fuels - Storage - Law and legislation - United States. 2. Law - United States - Territories and possessions. I. Title.
KF27 .I5365 1979b

To enlarge the Indiana Dunes National Lakeshore : hearing before the Subcommittee on National Parks and Insular Affairs of the Committee on Interior and Insular Affairs, House of Representatives, Ninety-fifth Congress, second session, on H.R. 11110 ... and H.R. 12821 ... hearing held in Washington, D.C., August 10, 1978. Washington : U. S. Govt. Print. Off., 1979. iv, 299 p. : ill. ; 24 cm. "Serial no. 95-37." LC Card 80-601516 DDC 346.7304/6784 19
1. Indiana Dunes National Lakeshore. I. Title.
KF27 .I5365 1978d

To establish a barrier islands protection system : hearings before the Subcommittee on National Parks and Insular Affairs of the Committee on Interior and Insular Affairs, House of Representatives, Ninety-sixth Congress, second session, on H.R. 5981 ... held in Washington, D.C., March 24 and 27, 1980. Washington : U. S. Govt. Print. Off., 1980. vii, 650 p. : ill. ; 24 cm. "Serial no. 96-32." Includes bibliographies. LC Card 80-603095 DDC 346.7304/6784 19
1. Barrier islands - Law and legislation - United States. 2. National parks and reserves - United States. 3. Coastal zone management - Law and legislation - United States. I. Title.
KF27 .I5365 1980

United States. Congress. House. Committee on Interior and Insular Affairs. Subcommittee on Pacific Affairs. Activities of the Subcommittee on Pacific Affairs, including a report of the oversight inspection trip of January 3 to 17, 1980 : a report / prepared by the Subcommittee on Pacific Affairs of the Committee on Interior and Insular Affairs of the U. S. House of Representatives, Ninety-sixth Congress, second session. Washington : U. S. G.P.O., 1981. v, 12 p. ; 24 cm. At head of title: 96th Congress, 2d session. Committee print no. 10. "January 1981." Item 1023 LC Card 81-601831 DDC 328.73/07652 19
1. United States - Insular possessions. 2. United States. Congress. House. Committee on Interior and Insular Affairs. Subcommittee on Pacific Affairs. I. Title.
F970 .U577 1981

UNITED STATES. CONGRESS. HOUSE. COMMITTEE ON INTERIOR AND INSULAR AFFAIRS. SUBCOMMITTEE ON PACIFIC AFFAIRS. United States. Congress. House. Committee on Interior and Insular Affairs. Subcommittee on Pacific Affairs. Activities of the Subcommittee on Pacific Affairs, including a report of the oversight inspection trip of January 3 to 17, 1980 . Washington , 1981. v, 12 p. ; LC Card 81-601831 DDC 328.73/07652 19
F970 .U577 1981

United States. Congress. House. Committee on Interior and Insular Affairs. Subcommittee

on Public Lands. The MX missile system : oversight hearings before the Subcommittee on Public Lands of the Committee on Interior and Insular Affairs, House of Representatives, Ninety-sixth Congress, first and second sessions .... Washington : U. S. Govt. Print. Off., 1980. vii, 906 p. : ill. ; 23 cm. Hearings held in various cities, Oct. 2, 1979-June 18, 1980. "Serial no. 96-30." LC Card 80-603306 DDC 358/.174/0973 19
1. MX (Weapons system). 2. Nevada - Public lands. 3. Utah - Public lands. I. Title.
KF27 .I544 1979a

United States. Congress. House. Committee on Interior and Insular Affirs. Subcommittee on Energy and the Environment. Three Mile Island cleanup and rehabilitation : oversight hearing before the Subcommittee on Energy and the Environment of the Committee on Interior and Insular Affairs, House of Representatives, Ninety-sixth Congress, second session ... held in Washington, D.C., May 22, 1980. Washington : U. S. G.P.O, 1980. iv, 236 p. : ill. ; 24 cm. "Serial no. 96-38." Includes bibliographical references. LC Card 80-604111 DDC 363.7/28 19
1. Three Mile Island Nuclear Power Plant, Pa. I. United States. Nuclear Regulatory Commission. II. Title.
KF27 .I518 1980b

United States. Congress. House. Committee on Interstate and Foreign Commerce. (Old Catalog form: United States. Interstate and Foreign Commerce, Committee on (House)) Hearings printed in 1978 and later are available only in microform. Please consult the librarians in the Economic and Public Affairs Division.
LNG facility accident at Cove Point, Maryland : report / prepared for the use of the Committee on Interstate and Foreign Commerce, United States House of Representatives, and its Subcommittee on Energy and Power. Washington : U. S. Govt. Print. Off., 1980. iii, 60 p. : ill. ; 23 cm. Prepared by R. Staiger. "May 1980." At head of title: 96th Congress, 2d session. Committee print. Committee print 96-IFC 46. Includes bibliographical references. LC Card 80-602216 DDC 363.1/79 19
1. Liquefied natural gas - Accidents. 2. Liquefied natural gas - Storage - Safety measures - Maryland - Cove Point. I. Staiger, Roger. II. United States. Congress. House. Committee on Interstate and Foreign Commerce. Subcommittee on Energy and Power. III. Title.
TP761.L5 U54 1980

Spending reductions : recommendations of the Committee on Interstate and Foreign Commerce required by the reconciliation process of H. Com Res. 307, the first budget resolution for fiscal year 1981, together with additional views / Committee on Interstate and Foreign Commerce, U. S. House of Representatives. Washington : U. S.G.P.O., 1980. v, 217 p. ; 24 cm. At head of title: 96th Congress, 2d session. Committee print. Committee print 96-IFC 51. July 2, 1980. Item DGPO/DLC LC Card 81-601122 DDC 353.0072/232 19
1. United States - Appropriations and expenditures, 1981. 2. Government spending policy - United States. I. Title.
KF6231.A55 I557

United States. Congress. House. Committee on Interstate and Foreign Commerce. Subcommittee on Oversight and Investigations. Unnecessary exposure to radiation from medical and dental x-rays . Washington , 1980. v, 15 p. ; LC Card 80-603049 DDC 363.1/89 19
RC78 .U534 1980

United States. Congress. House. Committee on Interstate and Foreign Commerce. Subcommittee on Transportation and Commerce. The Rail act of 1980 . Washington , 1980. vii, 91 p. ; LC Card 80-602213 DDC 343.73/095 19
KF2275.5 .I58

United States. Congress. House. Committee on Science and Technology. Technology trade . Washington , 1980. vii, 687 p. ; LC Card 80-604020 DDC 338.973 19
KF27 .S39 1980g

United States. Health Resources Administration. Bureau of Health Manpower. A report on public and community health personnel .

Washington, D.C. , 1980. viii, 220 p. ; LC Card 80-602370 DDC 331.12/913621 19
RA440.9 .U47 1980

United States. Laws, statutes, etc. Compilation of energy-related legislation /. Washington , 1979. 3 v. ; LC Card 79-603457
KF2120 .A3 1979

United States. Laws, statutes, etc. Compilation of selected acts within the jurisdiction of the Committee on Interstate and Foreign Commerce . Washington , 1980- v. ; LC Card 80-601741 DDC 344.73/04/02632 19
KF3775 .A3 1980

United States. Congress. House. Committee on Interstate and Foreign Commerce. Subcommittee on Communications. Financial disclosure : hearing before the Subcommittee on Communications of the Committee on Interstate and Foreign Commerce, House of Representatives, Ninety-sixth Congress, second session, on H.R. 5430 ... March 4, 1980. Washington : U. S. Govt. Print. Off., 1980. iii, 99 p. ; 24 cm. "Serial no. 96-118." LC Card 80-602502 DDC 343.73/09943 19
1. Radio industry and trade - Law and legislation - United States. 2. Television - Law and legislation - United States. 3. Radio stations - Licenses - United States. 4. Television stations - Licenses - United States. 5. Financial statements - United States. I. Title.
KF27 .I5537 1980a

Hearing--impaired : hearing before the Subcommittee on Communications of the Committee on Interstate and Foreign Commerce, House of Representatives, Ninety-sixth Congress, second session, on H.R. 5022 ... March 27, 1980. Washington : U. S. Govt. Print. Off., 1980. iii, 140 p. : ill. ; 23 cm. "Serial no. 96-154." LC Card 80-603358 DDC 343.73/09943 19
1. Telephone - Law and legislation - United States. 2. Hearing aids - Law and legislation - United States. 3. Telephone - United States - Apparatus and supplies. I. Title.
KF27 .I5537 1980c

Prohibited renewal considerations and crossownership restrictions : hearing before the Subcommittee on Communications of the Committee on Interstate and Foreign Commerce, House of Representatives, Ninety-sixth Congress, second session, on H.R. 6228, a bill to amend the Communications act of 1934 ... April 23, 1980. Washington : U. S. Govt. Print. Off., 1980. iii, 98 p. ; 23 cm. "Serial no. 96-141." LC Card 80-602804 DDC 343.73/09945 19
1. Radio - Law and legislation - United States. 2. Television - Law and legislation - United States. 3. Press law - United States. I. Title.
KF27 .I5537 1980b

Repeal of "equal time" requirements : hearing before the Subcommittee on Communications of the Committee on Interstate and Foreign Commerce, House of Representatives, Ninety-sixth Congress, second session, on H.R. 6103 ... February 7, 1980. Washington : U. S. Govt. Print. Off., 1980. ii, 106 p. ; 24 cm. "Serial no. 96-117." LC Card 80-602171 DDC 343.73/09945 19
1. Equal time rule (Broadcasting) - United States. I. Title.
KF27 .I5537 1980

United States. Congress. House. Committee on Interstate and Foreign Commerce. Subcommittee on Consumer Protection and Finance. Automobile warranty and repair act : hearings before the Subcommittee on Consumer Protection and Finance of the Committee on Interstate and Foreign Commerce, House of Representatives, Ninety-sixth Congress, first session, on H.R. 1005 .... Washington : U. S. Govt. Print. Off., 1980. vi, 720 p. : ill. ; 24 cm. Hearings held July 10-Oct. 5, 1979. "Serial no. 96-155." Includes bibliographical references. LC Card 80-603473 DDC 343.73/0944 19
1. Automobiles - Maintenance and repair - Law and legislation - United States. 2. Automobile industry and trade - Law and legislation - United States. 3. Warranty - United States. I. Title.
KF27 .I554 1979h

Automotive fuel economy : hearing before the Subcommittee on Consumer Protection and

BIBLIOGRAPHIC GUIDE

United States. Congress. House. Committee on Interstate and

434

Finance of the Committee on Interstate and Foreign Commerce, House of Representatives, Ninety-sixth Congress, second session, on H.R. 6943 ... H.R. 5140 ... May 5, 1980. Washington : U. S. G.P.O., 1980. iii, 119 p. : ill. ; 24 cm. "Serial no. 96-206." LC Card 81-600612 DDC 343.73/078629253 347.30378629253 19
1. Automobiles - Fuel consumption - Law and legislation - United States. 2. Automobile industry and trade - Law and legislation - United States. I. Title.
KF27 .I554 1980c

Chronic hazards labeling legislation : hearings before the Subcommittee on Consumer Protection and Finance of the Committee on Interstate and Foreign Commerce, House of Representatives, Ninety-sixth Congress, second session, on H.R. 6977 ... September 16 and 17, 1980. Washington : U. S. G.P.O., 1980 [i.e. 1981] iv, 291 p. : ill. ; 24 cm. "Serial no. 96-217." Item 1019 Includes bibliographical references. LC Card 81-600947 DDC 343.73/082 347.30382 19
1. Hazardous substances - Labeling - Law and legislation - United States. I. Title.
KF27 .I554 1980h

Consumer Product Safety Commission post-employment restrictions : hearing before the Subcommittee on Consumer Protection and Finance of the Committee on Interstate and Foreign Commerce, House of Representatives, Ninety-sixth Congress, second session, on H.R. 6395 ... February 12, 1980. Washington : U. S. Govt. Print. Off., 1980. iii, 8 p. ; 24 cm. "Serial no. 96-113." LC Card 80-602437 DDC 343.73/071 19
1. United States. Consumer Product Safety Commission - Officals and employees. 2. United States - Officials and employees, Retired - Employment. I. Title.
KF27 .I554 1980

Motor vehicle theft prevention act : joint hearings before the Subcommittee on Consumer Protection and Finance of the Committee on Interstate and Foreign Commerce and the Subcommittee on Inter-American Affairs of the Committee on Foreign Affairs, House of Representatives, Ninety-sixth Congress, second session on H.R. 4178 ... June 2, 10, and 12, 1980. Washington : U. S. Govt. Print. Off., 1980. vii, 536 p. : ill. ; 24 cm. "Serial no. 96-179." Includes bibliographical references. LC Card 80-603731 DDC 343.73/078629222 347.30378629222 19
1. Automobile theft - United States. I. United States. Congress. House. Committee on Foreign Affairs. Subcommittee on Inter-American Affairs. II. Title.
KF27 .I554 1980a

Nondiscrimination in insurance : hearings before the Subcommittee on Consumer Protection and Finance of the Committee on Interstate and Foreign Commerce, House of Representatives, Ninety-sixth Congress, second session, on H.R. 100 ... August 21 and 28, 1980. Washington : U. S. G.P.O., 1981. iv, 425 p. : ill. ; 1981. "Serial no. 96-232." Item 1019 Includes bibliographical references. LC Card 81-601385 DDC 346.73/086 347.30686 19
1. Discrimination in insurance - Law and legislation - United States. 2. Sex discrimination in insurance - Law and legislation - United States. I. Title.
KF27 .I554 1980j

Product liability : legislative hearings : hearings before the Subcommittee on Consumer Protection and Finance of the Committee on Interstate and Foreign Commerce, House of Representatives, Ninety-sixth Congress, first session, on H.R. 5571 and H.R. 5258 (identical bills) ... H.R. 1061, H.R. 2891 and H.R. 4204 (identical bills) ... H.R. 1675, H.R. 1676, H.R. 2964, and H.R. 5626 (similar bills) ... October 25, 26, November 14, 15, 26, and 27, 1979. Washington : U. S. G.P.O., 1980. v, 1019 p. : ill. ; 24 cm. "Serial no. 96-163." Item 1019 Includes bibliographical references. LC Card 81-600641 DDC 346.7303/82 347.306382 19
1. Insurance, Products liability - United States. 2. Products liability - United States. I. Title.
KF27 .I554 1980i

Product liability, legislative hearings : hearings before the Subcommittee on Consumer Protection and Finance of the Committee on Interstate and Foreign Commerce, House of Representatives, Ninety-sixth Congress, first session .... Washington : U. S. Govt. Print. Off.,

1980. v, 1019 p. : ill. ; 24 cm. "Serial no. 96-163." Hearings held Oct. 25-Nov. 27, 1979. Includes bibliographical references. LC Card 80-603466 DDC 346.7303/82 19
1. Insurance, Products liability - United States. 2. Product safety - Law and legislation - United States. 3. Products liability - United States. I. Title.
KF27 .I554 1979i

Reciprocity in investment : hearings before the Subcommittee on Consumer Protection and Finance of the Committee on Interstate and Foreign Commerce, House of Representatives, Ninety-sixth Congress, second session, on H.R. 7791 ... and H.R. 7750 ... August 19 and September 9, 1980. Washington : U. S. G.P.O., 1981. iii, 225 p. ; 24 cm. "Serial no. 96-234." Item 1019 Includes bibliographical references. LC Card 81-601378 DDC 346.73/07 347.3067 19
1. Investments, Foreign - Law and legislation - United States. I. Title.
KF27 .I554 1980k

Securities and Exchange Commission authorizations for fiscal years 1981, 1982, and 1983 : hearing before the Subcommittee on Consumer Protection and Finance of the Committee on Interstate and Foreign Commerce, House of Representatives, Ninety-sixth Congress, second session, on H.R. 6830 ... March 20, 1980. Washington : U. S. G.P.O., 1980. iii, 158 p. : ill. ; 24 cm. "Serial no. 185." LC Card 80-603892 DDC 353.0072/2368258 19
1. United States. Securities and Exchange Commission - Appropriations and expenditures. I. Title.
KF27 .I554 1980b

Securities Investor Protection Act Amendment : hearing before the Subcommittee on Consumer Protection and Finance of the Committee on Interstate and Foreign Commerce, House of Representatives, Ninety-sixth Congress, second session, on H.R. 6831 ... June 3, 1980. Washington : U. S. G.P.O., 1980. iii, 34 p. ; 23 cm. "Serial no. 96-202." LC Card 80-604115 DDC 346.73/0666 347.306666 19
1. Securities Investor Protection Corporation. I. Title.
KF27 .I554 1980d

Tire recall : hearing before the Subcommittee on Consumer Protection and Finance of the Committee on Interstate and Foreign Commerce, House of Representatives, Ninety-sixth Congress, first session on H.R. 3949 and H.R. 1744 ... May 24, 1979. Washington : U. S. Govt. Print. Off., 1979. iii, 36 p. ; 23 cm. "Serial no. 96-55." LC Card 80-600683 DDC 346.7303/82 19
1. Tire industry - Law and legislation - United States. 2. Product recall - Law and legislation - United States. 3. Consumer protection - Law and legislation - United States. 4. Automobiles - Tires - Defects. I. Title.
KF27 .I554 1979e

United States. Congress. House. Committee on Interstate and Foreign Commerce. Subcommittee on Energy and Power. National automotive research act . Washington , 1980. v, 136 p. ; LC Card 80-602959 DDC 343.73/078629222 19
KF27 .I5542 1980a

United States. Congress. House. Committee on Interstate and Foreign Commerce. Subcommittee on Oversight and Investigations. Securities Acts Amendments of 1975--oversight . Washington , 1978. viii, 1187 p. ; LC Card 81-601238 DDC 353.0082/58 19
KF27 .I5547 1977q

United States. Congress. House. Committee on Interstate and Foreign Commerce. Subcommittee on Oversight and Investigations. Use of cost-benefit analysis by regulatory agencies . Washington , 1980. v, 482 p. : LC Card 80-603329 DDC 353.09/1 19
KF27 .I5547 1979v

United States. Congress. House. Committee on Small Business. Subcommittee on Antitrust and Restraint of Trade Activities Affecting Small Business. Small Business Motor Fuel Marketer Preservation Act-H.R. 6722 . Washington , 1980. vii, 835 p. ; LC Card 80-604087 DDC 343.73/078629287 347.30378629287 19
KF27 .S6335 1980b

Venture Capital Improvements Acts of 1980 : hearing before the Subcommittee on Consumer Protection and Finance of the Committee on

Interstate and Foreign Commerce, House of Representatives, Ninety-sixth Congress, second session, on H.R. 7554 ... H.R. 7491 ... June 17, 1980. Washington : U. S. G.P.O., 1980. iii, 244 p. : ill. ; 24 cm. "Serial no. 96-208." Includes bibliographical references. LC Card 81-600877 DDC 346.73/0922 347.306922 19
1. Venture capital - Law and legislation - United States. 2. Small business investment companies - United States. 3. Investment trusts - United States. I. Title.
KF27 .I554 1980e

United States. Congress. House. Committee on Interstate and Foreign Commerce. Subcommittee on Energy and Power. Alaska Federal Civilian Energy Efficiency Swap Act : hearing before the Subcommittee on Energy and Power of the Committee on Interstate and Foreign Commerce, House of Representatives, Ninety-sixth Congress, second session, on H.R. 5393 and S. 1784 ... November 17, 1980. Washington : U. S. G.P.O., 1981. iii, 71 p. ; 24 cm. "Serial no. 96-220." Item 1019 LC Card 81-601193 DDC 343.798/0929 347.9803929 19
1. Electric utilities - Law and legislation - Alaska. I. Title.
KF27 .I5542 1980t

Alternative fuels and compatible engine designs : hearing before the Subcommittee on Energy and Power of the Committee on Interstate and Foreign Commerce, House of Representatives, Ninety-sixth Congress, second session, on cost and flexibility of methanol as a fuel, government initiatives to accelerate its use, and the potential impact it may have on domestic enterprises, December 18, 1980. Washington : U. S. G.P.O., 1981. iv, 335 p. : ill. ; 24 cm. "Serial no. 96-237." Item 1019 Includes bibliographical references. LC Card 81-601338 DDC 621.43 19
1. Methanol as fuel - United States. 2. Methanol as fuel - Government policy - United States. 3. Automobiles - United States - Fuel consumption. 4. Motor fuels. I. Title.
KF27 .I5542 1980p

Automotive average fuel economy standards : hearings before the Subcommittee on Energy and Power of the Committee on Interstate and Foreign Commerce, House of Representatives, Ninety-sixth Congress, second session ... March 28 and April 15, 1980. Washington : U. S. Govt. Print. Off., 1980. iv, 230 p. : graphs ; 23 cm. Hearings on H.R. 5140, 5260, 5944, 6908, and 6943. "Serial no. 96-162." LC Card 80-603687 DDC 343.73/078629253 347.30378629253 19
1. Automobiles - Fuel consumption - Law and legislation - United States. 2. Automobile industry and trade - Law and legislation - United States. I. Title.
KF27 .I5542 1980f

Commercialization of alternative fuels : hearing before the Subcommittee on Energy and Power of the Committee on Interstate and Foreign Commerce, House of Representatives, Ninety-sixth Congress, first session, on H.R. 4345 and H.R. 4401 ... October 10, 1979. Washington : U. S. Govt. Print. Off., 1980. iii, 53 p. ; 23 cm. "Serial no. 96-103." LC Card 80-601864 DDC 343.73/0786626 19
1. Synthetic fuels - Law and legislation - United States. I. Title.
KF27 .I5542 1979ac

Enforcement of major refiner cases : Getty Oil and other settlements : hearing before the Subcommittee on Energy and Power of the Committee on Interstate and Foreign Commerce, House of Representatives, Ninety-sixth Congress, second session, on settlements by the Department of Energy on overcharges within the petroleum industry, October 14, 1980. Washington : U. S. G.P.O., 1981. iii, 883 p. ; 24 cm. "Serial no. 96-225." Item 1019 Includes bibliographical references. LC Card 81-601792 DDC 346.7304/68232/0262 347.3064682320262 19
1. Petroleum law and legislation - United States. 2. Petroleum products - Prices - United States. 3. Price regulation - United States. I. Title.
KF27 .I5542 1980q

Eomestic refinery policy--oversight : hearing before the Subcommittee on Energy and Power of the Committee on Interstate and Foreign Commerce, House of Representatives, Ninety-sixth Congress, second session,

GOVERNMENT PUBLICATIONS - U.S.: 1981

435

United States. Congress. House. Committee on Interstate and

December 17, 1980. Washington : U. S. G.P.O., 1981. iii, 208 p. : ill. ; 24 cm. "Serial no. 96-235." Item 1019 Includes bibliographical references. LC Card 81-601359 DDC 338.4/766553/0973 19
1. Petroleum refineries - United States. 2. Petroleum refineries - Government policy - United States. I. Title.
KF27 .I5542 1980o

Filling the strategic petroleum reserve, oversight, and H.R. 7252, use of the naval petroleum reserves : hearings before the Subcommittee on Energy and Power of the Committee on Interstate and Foreign Commerce, House of Representatives, Ninety-sixth Congress, second session, on H.R. 7252 ... April 25, May 21, and September 15, 1980. Washington : U. S. G.P.O., 1980. iv, 410 p. : ill. ; 24 cm. "Serial no. 96-198." Includes bibliographical references. LC Card 81-600602 DDC 346.7304/6823216 347.30646823216 19
1. Petroleum - Reserves - Law and legislation - United States. 2. United States. Navy - Fuel. I. Title.
KF27 .I5542 1980l

Final report of the World Coal Study : "Coal--bridge to the future" : hearing before the Subcommittee on Energy and Power of the Committee on Interstate and Foreign Commerce, House of Representatives, Ninety-sixth Congress, second session, May 20, 1980. Washington : U. S. Govt. Print. Off., 1980. iii, 88 p. : ill. ; 24 cm. "Serial no. 96-149." LC Card 80-603074 DDC 333.8/22 19
1. World Coal Study. Coal--bridge to the future. 2. Coal. I. Title.
KF27 .I5542 1980c

Fiscal year 1981 authorization for the Department of Energy and the Federal Energy Regulatory Commission : hearings before the Subcommittee on Energy and Power of the Committee on Interstate and Foreign Commerce, House of Representatives, Ninety-sixth Congress, second session, on H.R. 6627 .... Washington : U. S. Govt. Print. Off., 1980. vi, 1012 p. : ill. ; 24 cm. Hearings held Feb. 8-29, 1980. "Serial no. 96-156." LC Card 80-603496 DDC 353.0072/236823 19
1. United States. Dept. of Energy - Appropriations and expenditures. 2. United States. Federal Energy Regulatory Commission - Appropriations and expenditures. I. Title.
KF27 .I5542 1980e

Gasoline marketing practices : hearings before the subcommittee on Energy and Power of the Committee on Interstate and Foreign Commerce, House of Representatives, Ninety-sixth Congress, second session, on H.R. 7034 ... June 11 and September 25, 1980. Washington : U. S. G.P.O., 1981. iv, 470 p. : ill. ; 24 cm. "Serial no. 96-222." Item 1019 Includes bibliographical references. LC Card 81-601363 DDC 343.73/088566553827 347.30388566553827 19
1. Automobiles - Service stations - Law and legislation - United States. 2. Loans - United States - Government guaranty. 3. Petroleum law and legislation - United States. I. Title.
KF27 .I5542 1980r

Jimison, John. Energy--is there a policy to fit the crisis? . Washington , 1980. iii, 13 p. ; LC Card 80-603870 DDC 333.79/0973 19
HD9502.U52 J55

Kaufman, Alvin. Will the lights go on in 1990? . Washington , 1980. vii, 15 p. : LC Card 80-603985 DDC 333.79/32/0973 19
TK1193.U5 K32

Morrison, Robert Eugene, 1930- Possible effects on the atmosphere of large-scale helium extraction from the atmosphere /. Washington , 1979. vii, 14 p. ; LC Card 79-603780 DDC 333.9/2 19
TD888.G37 M67

Municipal waste-to-energy act of 1980 : hearing before the Subcommittee on Energy and Power of the Committee on Interstate and Foreign Commerce, House of Representatives, Ninety-sixth Congress, second session, on H.R. 6638 ... March 31, 1980. Washington : U. S. Govt. Print. Off., 1980. iii, 160 p. ; 24 cm. "Serial no. 96-147." LC Card 80-602960 DDC 346.7304/67938/0262 19
1. Refuse as fuel - Law and legislation - United States. I. Title.
KF27 .I5542 1980b

National automotive research act : joint hearing

before the Subcommittee on Energy and Power and the Subcommittee on Consumer Protection and Finance and the Subcommittee on Health and the Environment of the Committee on Interstate and Foreign Commerce, U. S. House of Representatives, Ninety-sixth Congress, second session, on H.R. 4678 ... May 28, 1980. Washington : U. S. Govt. Print. Off., 1980. v, 136 p. ; 24 cm. "Serial no. 96-146." LC Card 80-602959 DDC 343.73/078629222 19
1. Automobile engineering research - Law and legislation - United States. I. United States. Congress. House. Committee on Interstate and Foreign Commerce. Subcommittee on Consumer Protection and Finance. II. United States. Congress. House. Committee on Interstate and Foreign Commerce. Subcommittee on Health and the Environment. III. Title.
KF27 .I5542 1980a

National Energy Security Corporation : hearings before the Subcommittee on Energy and Power of the Committee on Interstate and Foreign Commerce, House of Representatives, Ninety-sixth Congress, first session on H.R. 5045. ... Washington : U. S. Govt. Print. Off., 1980. iv, 559 p. ; 24 cm. Hearings held Sept. 21-Oct. 18, 1979. "Serial no. 96-112." LC Card 80-602005 DDC 346.7304/67915 19
1. National Energy Security Corporation (U. S.). 2. Energy development - Law and legislation - United States. 3. Energy development - United States - Finance. I. Title.
KF27 .I5542 1979y

Natural gas issues, 1979 : hearings before the Subcommittee on Energy and Power of the Committee on Interstate and Foreign Commerce, House of Representatives, Ninety-sixth Congress, first session ... June 5 and 6, 1979. Washington : U. S. Govt. Print. Off., 1980. iii, 289 p. : ill. ; 24 cm. "Serial no. 96-135." LC Card 80-602780 DDC 333.8/233/0973 19
1. Gas, Natural - United States. I. Title.
KF27 .I5542 1979ae

Nuclear waste disposal : hearing before the Subcommittee on Energy and Power of the Committee on Interstate and Foreign Commerce, House of Representatives, Ninety-sixth Congress, second session, on H.R. 5809, H.R. 6390, and H.R. 7418 ... July 25, 1980. Washington : U. S. G.P.O., 1980. iii, 240 p. : ill., maps ; 24 cm. "Serial no. 96-203." LC Card 80-603993 DDC 344.73/04622 347.3044622 19
1. Radioactive waste disposal - Law and legislation - United States. 2. Interstate agreements - United States. I. Title.
KF27 .I5542 1980j

Ohio's self-help natural gas program : hearing before the Subcommittee on Energy and Power of the Committee on Interstate and Foreign Commerce, House of Representatives, Ninety-sixth Congress, second session ... August 29, 1980. Washington : U. S. G.P.O., 1980. iii, 171 p. : ill. ; 24 cm. "Serial no. 96-182." LC Card 80-603775 DDC 333.8/23315/09771 19
1. Gas, Natural - Ohio - Transportation. 2. Gas companies - Ohio. I. Title.
KF27 .I5542 1980k

Phase II incremental pricing of natural gas : hearings before the Subcommittee on Energy and Power of the Committee on Interstate and Foreign Commerce, House of Representatives, Ninety-sixth Congress, second session, on H. Res. 655 ... April 3 and May 6, 1980. Washington : U. S. Govt. Print. Off., 1980. iv, 389 p. ; 23 cm. "Serial no. 96-171." Includes bibliographical references. LC Card 80-603476 DDC 343.73/08556673 19
1. Gas, Natural - Law and legislation - United States. 2. Gas, Natural - Prices - United States. I. Title.
KF27 .I5542 1980d

Powerplant Fuel Conservation Act of 1980 : hearings before the Subcommittee on Energy and Power of the Committee on Interstate and Foreign Commerce, House of Representatives, Ninety-sixth Congress, second session, on H.R. 6930, H.R. 5669, H.R. 6514, H.R. 6947, and H.R. 6999 ... April 2, 18, and 21, 1980. Washington : U. S. G.P.O., 1980. iv, 623 p. : ill. ; 24 cm. "Serial no. 96-184." Includes bibliographical references. LC Card 80-604038 DDC 346.7304/67916/0262 347.3064679160262 19
1. Electric power-plants - Conversion to coal - Law and

legislation - United States. 2. Electric power-plants - Fuel consumption - Law and legislation - United States. I. Title.*
KF27 .I5542 1980i

Spent fuel storage and disposal : hearings before the Subcommittee on Energy and Power of the Committee on Interstate and Foreign Commerce, House of Representatives, Ninety-sixth Congress, first session ... June 26 and 27, 1979. Washington : U. S. Govt. Print. Off., 1980. iv, 342 p. : ill. ; 24 cm. "Serial no. 96-97." Hearings on H.R. 1071, 1791, 2586, and 2762. LC Card 80-601371 DDC 344.73/04622 19
1. Radioactive waste disposal - Law and legislation - United States. 2. Radioactive waste disposal - United States - Finance. I. Title.
KF27 .I5542 1979p

United States. Congress. House. Committee on Interstate and Foreign Commerce. LNG facility accident at Cove Point, Maryland . Washington , 1980. iii, 60 p. : LC Card 80-602216 DDC 363.1/79 19
TP761.L5 U54 1980

United States. Congress. House. Committee on Science and Technology. Subcommittee on Energy Development and Applications. H.R. 4382--Energy Management Partnership Act . Washington , 1980- v. <1, 3> : LC Card 80-604116 DDC 346.7304/679 347.3064679 19
KF27 .S3934 1979n

United States. Congressional Budget Office. An evaluation of the strategic petroleum reserve . Washington , 1980. xv, 36 p. : LC Card 80-602590 DDC 333.8/2311/0973 19
HD9502.U52 U512 1980a

United States. General Accounting Office. U. S. strategic petroleum reserve at a turning point . Washington, D.C. , 1980. iv p., 28 leaves : LC Card 80-601078 DDC 333.8/23211/0973 19
TP692.5 .U624 1980

United States. Library of Congress. Congressional Research Service. U. S. refineries . Washington , 1980. v, 169 p. : LC Card 80-603551 DDC 665.5/3/0973 19
TP690.3 .U538 1980

Utilities and energy conservation . Washington , 1980 [i.e. 1981] vii, 78 p. ; LC Card 81-601265 DDC 333.79 19
HD9685.U5 U87

West Valley Demonstration Project Act : hearing before the Subcommittee on Energy and Power of the Committee on Interstate and Foreign Commerce, House of Representatives, Ninety-sixth Congress, second session on H.R. 3193 and H.R. 6865 ... July 28, 1980. Washington : U. S. G.P.O., 1980. iv, 173 p. p. : ill. ; 23 cm. "Serial no. 96-194." LC Card 80-603899 DDC 344.73/04622 347.3044622 19
1. Radioactive waste disposal - Law and legislation - New York (State) - West Valley. 2. United States. Dept. of Energy. I. Title.
KF27 .I5542 1980m

1980 standby gasoline rationing plan : hearings before the Subcommittee on Energy and Power of the Committee on Interstate and Foreign Commerce, House of Representatives, Ninety-sixth Congress, second session ... January 31, June 23 and 27, 1980. Washington : U. S. Govt. Print. Off., 1980. iv, 236 p. : ill. ; 24 cm. "Serial 96-167." Hearings on H.J. Res. 571, 574, 575, and 577. LC Card 80-603634 DDC 346.7304/68232 347.306468232 19
1. Gasoline supply - Law and legislation - United States. 2. Rationing, Consumer - United States. I. Title.
KF27 .I5542 1980h

United States. Congress. House. Committee on Interstate and Foreign Commerce. Subcommittee on Health and the Environment.
Clean air act oversight--1980 : hearing before the Subcommittee on Health and the Environment of the Committee on Interstate and Foreign Commerce, House of Representatives, Ninety-sixth Congress, second session ... June 16, 1980. Washington : U. S. Govt. Print. Off., 1980. iii, 218 p. ; 23 cm. "Serial no. 96-151." LC Card 80-603296 DDC 353.0082/324 19
1. Air - Pollution - Standards - United States. 2. Air quality management - Government policy - United States. I. Title.
KF27 .I5543 1980g

BIBLIOGRAPHIC GUIDE

United States. Congress. House. Committee on Interstate and

436

Drug regulation reform--oversight : new drug approval process : hearing before the Subcommittee on Health and the Environment of the Committee on Interstate and Foreign Commerce, House of Representatives, Ninety-sixth Congress, second session, on Food and Drug Administration regulation of research, development, and marketing of drugs. Washington : U. S. Govt. Print. Off., 1980- v. <1- > ; 23 cm. Hearings held June 25- Vol. 1. Serial no. 96-170. LC Card 80-603639 DDC 353.0077/84 19
1. Drugs - Laws and legislation - United States. 2. Pharmacy - Law and legislation - United States. 3. United States. Food and Drug Administration. I. Title.
KF27 .I5543 1980j

Hazardous waste and drinking water : joint hearing before the Subcommittee on Health and the Environment and the Subcommittee on Transportation and Commerce of the Committee on Interstate and Foreign Commerce, House of Representatives, Ninety-sixth Congress, second session, August 22, 1980. Washington : U. S. G.P.O., 1981. v, 195 p. : ill., maps ; 24 cm. "Serial 96-219." Item 1019 Includes bibliographical references. LC Card 81-601136 DDC 363.7/394 19
1. Hazardous wastes - United States. 2. Waste disposal in the ground - United States. 3. Water - Pollution - United States. I. United States. Congress. House. Committee on Interstate and Foreign Commerce. Subcommittee on Transportation and Commerce. II. Title.
KF27 .I5543 1980q

Health professions educational assistance and nurse training act of 1980 : hearings before the Subcommittee on Health and the Environment of the Committee on Interstate and Foreign Commerce, House of Representatives, Ninety-sixth Congress, second session, on H.R. 6802 ... H.R. 6800 .... Washington : U. S. Govt. Print. Off., 1980. ix, 1023 p. : ill. ; 24 cm. "Serial no. 96-148." Includes bibliographical references. LC Card 80-603014 DDC 344.73/07684 19
1. Medical education - Law and legislation - United States. 2. Federal aid to medical education - United States. 3. Federal aid to nursing education - United States. I. Title.
KF27 .I5543 1980e

Health research act of 1980 : hearings before the Subcommittee on Health and the Environment of the Committee on Interstate and Foreign Commerce, House of Representatives, Ninety-sixth Congress, second session, on H.R. 6522 .... Washington : U. S. Govt. Print. Off., 1980. viii, 596 p. : ill. ; 24 cm. Hearings held Feb. 21-Mar. 3, 1980. "Serial no. 96-138." LC Card 80-602806 DDC 344.73/04 19
1. United States. National Institutes of Health. 2. Medical research - Law and legislation - United States.
KF27 .I5543 1980d

Integrated environmental assistance act : hearing before the Subcommittee on Health and the Environment of the Committee on Interstate and Foreign Commerce, House of Representatives, Ninety-sixth Congress, second session, on H.R. 4213 ... May 19, 1980. Washington : U. S. Govt. Print. Off., 1980. iii, 165 p. ; 23 cm. "Serial no. 96-153." LC Card 80-603346 DDC 344.73/046 19
1. Environmental law - United States. 2. Environmental protection - United States - Finance. 3. Grants-in-aid - United States. I. Title.
KF27 .I5543 1980f

Medicaid community care act of 1980 : hearings before the Subcommittee on Health and the Environment of the Committee on Interstate and Foreign Commerce, House of Representatives, Ninety-sixth Congress, second session, on H.R. 6194 ... June 10 and 23, 1980. Washington : U. S. Govt. Print. Off., 1980. iv, 421 p. : ill. ; 24 cm. "Serial no. 96-165." LC Card 80-603725 DDC 344.73/032104252 19
1. Medicaid - Law and legislation. 2. Community health services for the aged - Law and legislation - United States. I. Title.
KF27 .I5543 1980i

Nutritional quality of infant formula : hearings before the Subcommittee on Health and the Environment of the Committee on Interstate and Foreign Commerce, House of Representatives, Ninety-sixth Congress, second session ... February 28 and March 6, 1980.

Washington : U. S. Govt. Print. Off., 1980. ii, 212 p. ; 24 cm. Hearings on H.R. 5836, 5839, 6590, and 6608. "Serial no. 96-132." Includes bibliographical references. LC Card 80-602521 DDC 344.73/04232 19
1. Infant formulas - Law and legislation - United States. 2. Infants - Nutrition. I. Title.
KF27 .I5543 1980c

Propoxyphene--oversight : hearing before the Subcommittee on Health and the Environment of the Committee on Interstate and Foreign Commerce, House of Representatives, Ninety-sixth Congress, second session, May, 21 1980. Washington : U. S. G.P.O., 1980. iii, 187 p. : ill. ; 24 cm. "Serial no. 96-180." Includes bibliographical references. LC Card 80-604112 DDC 362.2/93 19
1. Propoxyphene nepsylata. 2. Medication abuse - United States. I. Title.
KF27 .I5543 1980m

Quality of drinking water--1980 : hearings before the Subcommittee on Health and the Environment of the Committee on Interstate and Foreign Commerce, House of Representatives, Ninety-sixth Congress, second session ... June 6, 9, and August 18, 1980. Washington: U. S. G.P.O., 1980. vii, 714 p. : ill. ; 24 cm. "Serial no. 96-188." Includes bibliographical references. LC Card 80-604005 DDC 363.6/1 19
1. Drinking water - United States. 2. Water quality - United States. I. Title.
KF27 .I5543 1980n

Spinal cord regeneration : hearing before the Subcommittee on Health and the Environment of the Committee on Interstate and Foreign Commerce, House of Representatives, Ninety-sixth Congress, second session, on H.R. 4358 ... July 22, 1980. Washington : U. S. G.P.O., 1980. iv, 272 p. : ill. ; 24 cm. "Serial no. 96-181." LC Card 80-603794 DDC 344.73/0419 347.304419 19
1. Spinal cord - Regeneration - Research - Law and legislation - United States. 2. Spinal cord - Wounds and injuries - Research grants - United States. 3. Federal aid to medical research - United States. I. Title.
KF27 .I5543 1980o

Texas Infant Mortality Task Force. Texas Infant Mortality Task Force report /. Washington , 1980. iv, 77 p. : LC Card 80-602575 DDC 362.1/9832/009764141 19
RJ60.U52 T497

United States. Congress. House. Committee on Interstate and Foreign Commerce. Subcommittee on Energy and Power. National automotive research act . Washington , 1980. v, 136 p. ; 24 cm. LC Card 80-602959 DDC 343.73/078629222 19
KF27 .I5542 1980a

Various medicaid proposals : hearing before the Subcommittee on Health and the Environment of the Committee on Interstate and Foreign Commerce, House of Representatives, Ninety-sixth Congress, second session ... September 8, 1980. Washington : U. S. G.P.O., 1980. iv, 205 p. : ill. ; 24 cm. "Serial no. 96-195." Hearings on H.R. 7028, 7029, 7030, 7031, and 7468. Includes bibliographical references. LC Card 80-603816 DDC 344.73/032104252 347.30432104252 19
1. Medicaid - Law and legislation. I. Title.
KF27 .I5543 1980k

United States. Congress. House. Committee on Interstate and Foreign Commerce. Subcommittee on Oversight and Investigations.
Acid rain : hearings before the Subcommittee on Oversight and Investigations of the Committee on Interstate and Foreign Commerce, House of Representatives, Ninety-sixth Congress, second session, February 26 and 27, 1980. Washington : U. S. Govt. Print. Off., 1980. iv, 784 p. : ill. ; 24 cm. "Serial no. 96-150." Includes bibliographies. LC Card 80-603088 DDC 363.7/394 19
1. Acid rain - United States. 2. Acid rain - Canada. 3. Coal - Combustion - Environmental aspects - United States. 4. Coal - Combustion - Environmental aspects - Canada. I. Title.
KF27 .I5547 1980c

Air ambulances : hearing before the Subcommittee on Oversight and Investigations of the Committee on Interstate and Foreign

Commerce, House of Representatives, Ninety-sixth Congress, second session, April 29, 1980. Washington : U. S. Govt. Print. Off., 1980. iii, 109 p. ; 23 cm. "Serial no. 96-159." LC Card 80-603680 DDC 362.1/8 19
1. Airplane ambulances - United States. 2. Airplane ambulances - Standards - United States. I. Title.
KF27 .I5547 1980h

The Case of the billion dollar stripper . Washington , 1980. v, 29 p. : LC Card 80-603868 DDC 338.2/3 19
HD9564 .C38

Clean air act amendments of 1977-oversight : hearing before the Subcommittee on Oversight and Investigations of the Committee on Interstate and Foreign Commerce, House of Representatives, Ninety-sixth Congress, first session, April 9, 1979. Washington : U. S. Govt. Print. Off., 1980. ii, 24 cm. "Serial no. 96-136." LC Card 80-602530 DDC 353.0082/324 19
1. Air - Pollution - Law and legislation - United States. 2. United States. Environmental Protection Agency. 3. Tennessee Valley Authority. I. Title.
KF27 .I5547 1979q

Coal rates and Federal railroad regulation : oversight of the Railroad revitalization and regulatory reform act of 1976 : supplemental hearing before the Subcommittee on Oversight and Investigations of the Committee on Interstate and Foreign Commerce, House of Representatives, Ninety-sixth Congress, first session, November 16, 1979. Washington : U. S. Govt. Print. Off., 1980. ii, 111 p. ; 24 cm. "Serial no. 96-142." LC Card 80-602961 DDC 353.0087/512 19
1. Coal - United States - Transportation - Costs. 2. Railroads - United States - Rates. I. Title.
KF27 .I5547 1979t

Community-based cancer control programs : hearing before the Subcommittee on Oversight and Investigations of the Committee on Interstate and Foreign Commerce, House of Representatives, Ninety-sixth Congress, second sesssion, May 16, 1980. Washington : U. S. Govt. Print. Off., 1980. iii, 89 p. ; 24 cm. "Serial no. 96-158." LC Card 80-603286 DDC 362.1/96994009747 19
1. Cancer - New York (State) - Long Island - Prevention. 2. Community health services - New York (State) - Long Island. 3. United States. National Cancer Institute. I. Title.
KF27 .I5547 1980d

Corporate disclosure and filing practices : hearing before the Subcommittee on Oversight and Investigations of the Committee on Interstate and Foreign Commerce, House of Representatives, Ninety-sixth Congress, second session, May 5, 1980. Washington : U. S. G.P.O., c1980 [i.e. 1981] iv, 530 p. : ill. ; 24 cm. Item 1019 Includes bibliographical references. LC Card 81-600991 DDC 346.73/0666 347.306666 19
1. Corporation reports - Law and legislation - United States. 2. Disclosure of information (Securities law) - United States. 3. Administrative law - United States. 4. Industry and state - United States. I. Title.
KF27 .I5547 1980p

Cost-benefit analysis : wonder tool or mirage? : report together with minority views / by the Subcommittee on Oversight and Investigations of the Committee on Interstate and Foreign Commerce, United States House of Representatives. Washington : U. S. G.P.O., 1980 [i.e. 1981] vii, 49 p. ; 24 cm. At head of title: 96th Congress, 2d session. Committee print. Committee print 96-IFC 62. "December 1980." Item 1019 Includes bibliographical references. LC Card 81-600645 DDC 353.07/5 19
1. Cost effectiveness. 2. Trade regulation - United States - Cost effectiveness. I. Title.
HD47.4 .U54 1981

Cost to consumers of deregulation of crude oil : hearing before the Subcommittee on Oversight and Investigations of the Committee on Interstate and Foreign Commerce, House of Representatives, Ninety-sixth Congress, second session, July 30, 1980. Washington : U. S. G.P.O., 1980. iii, 72 p. : ill. ; 24 cm. "Serial no. 96-183." LC Card 80-604045 DDC 338.2/3 19
1. Petroleum - Prices - United States. 2. Price regulation - United States. I. Title.
KF27 .I5547 1980l

GOVERNMENT PUBLICATIONS - U.S.: 1981

437   *United States. Congress. House. Committee on Interstate and*

Data transfer restrictions impede epidemiological research : report / by the Subcommittee on Oversight and Investigations of the Committee on Interstate and Foreign Commerce, House of Representatives, Ninety-sixth Congress, second session. Washington : U. S. G.P.O., c1980 [i.e. 1981] v, 32 p. ; 24 cm. At head of title: 96th Congress, 2d session. Committee print. Committee print 96-IFC 63. Author: Debra Jacobson. "December 1980." Item 1019 Includes bibliographical references. LC Card
   81-600797   DDC 363.1/1/0723 19
1. Epidemiology - Research - United States. 2. Data protection - United States. 3. Occupational diseases - Research - United States. 4. National Institute for Occupational Safety and Health. 5. United States. Social Security Administration - Records and correspondence. I. Jacobson, Debra. II. Title.
RA652.4 .U54 1981

DOE gasoline allocation regulations and enforcement : hearing before the Subcommittee on Oversight and Investigations of the Committee on Interstate and Foreign Commerce, House of Representatives, Ninety-sixth Congress, second session, May 27, 1980. Washington : U. S. G.P.O., 1980. iii, 216 p. : ill. ; 24 cm. "Serial no. 96-193."   LC Card 80-604027   DDC 353.0082/6566553827 19
1. Petroleum law and legislation - United States. 2. United States. Dept. of Energy. 3. Gasoline supply - United States. I. Title.
KF27 .I5547 1980m

EPA's action concerning nitrilotriacetic acid (NTA) : hearing before the Subcommittee on Oversight and Investigations of the Committee on Interstate and Foreign Commerce, House of Representatives, Ninety-sixth Congress, second session, June 26, 1980. Washington : U. S.G.P.O., 1980. iv, 393 p. ; 24 cm. "Serial no. 96-192." Includes bibliographies.   LC Card 80-603817   DDC 363.1/79 19
1. Detergent pollution of rivers, lakes, etc. - United States. 2. Nitrilotriacetic acid. 3. United States. Environmental Protection Agency. I. Title.
KF27 .I5547 1980r

Federal Reserve Board : restrictions on availability of consumer credit : hearing before the Subcommittee on Oversight and Investigations of the Committee on Interstate and Foreign Commerce, House of Representatives, Ninety-sixth Congress, second session, April 1, 1980. Washington : U. S. Govt. Print. Off., 1980. iii, 181 p. ; 23 cm. "Serial no. 96-160."   LC Card 80-603518   DDC 346.73/073 19
1. Credit cards - Law and legislation - United States. 2. Consumer credit - Law and legislation - United States. 3. United States. Board of Governors of the Federal Reserve System. I. Title.
KF27 .I5547 1980g

Funeral industry, FTC proposed rulemaking : hearings before the Subcommittee on Oversight and Investigations of the Committee on Interstate and Foreign Commerce, House of Representatives, Ninety-sixth Congress, second session, February 13 and 21, 1980. Washington : U. S. Govt. Print. Off., 1980. iv, 402 p. ; 23 cm. "Serial no. 96-174."   LC Card 80-603506   DDC 343.73/0786146 19
1. Undertakers and undertaking - Law and legislation - United States. 2. Administrative procedure - United States. I. Title.
KF27 .I5547 1980e

Hazardous waste matters : hearing before the Subcommittee on Oversight and Investigations of the Committee on Interstate and Foreign Commerce, House of Representatives, Ninety-sixth Congress, second session, July 2, 1980. Washington : U. S. G.P.O., 1980. iii, 117 p. ; 24 cm. "Serial no. 96-200."   LC Card 80-603987 DDC 353.0077/2 19
1. Hazardous wastes - United States. 2. Refuse and refuse disposal - United States. 3. United States. Environmental Protection Agency. I. Title.
KF27 .I5547 1980k

Hazardous waste: Memphis, Tennessee area : hearing before the Subcommittee on Oversight and Investigations of the Committee on Interstate and Foreign Commerce, House of Representatives, Ninety-sixth Congress, second session, April 2, 1980. Washington : U. S. Govt. Print. Off., 1980. iv, 315 p. : ill. ; 23 cm. "Serial no. 96-144."   LC Card 80-602717   DDC

363.7/28 19
1. Hazardous wastes - Toxicology - Tennessee - Memphis. I. Title.
KF27 .I5547 1980b

ICC ratemaking in noncompetitive markets--oversight : hearing before the Subcommittee on Oversight and Investigations of the Committee on Interstate and Foreign Commerce, House of Representatives, Ninety-sixth Congress, second session, August 28, 1980. Washington : U. S. Govt. Print. Off., 1980. iii, 87 p. ; 23 cm. "Serial no. 96-176." Includes bibliographical references.   LC Card 80-603486   DDC 353.0087/512 19
1. Railroads - United States - Rates. 2. United States. Interstate Commerce Commission. I. Title.
KF27 .I5547 1980i

Impact of energy inflation : hearings before the Subcommittee on Oversight and Investigations of the Committee on Interstate and Foreign Commerce, House of Representatives, Ninety-sixth Congress, first session, December 13 and 20, 1979. Washington : U. S. Govt. Print. Off., 1980. iii, 315 p. : ill. ; 23 cm. "Serial no. 96-137."   LC Card 80-602823   DDC 332.4/1/0973 19
1. Inflation (Finance) - United States - Effect of energy costs on. 2. Power resources - United States - Costs. I. Title.
KF27 .I5547 1979u

Involuntary exposure to agent orange and other toxic spraying : hearings before the Subcommittee on Oversight and Investigations of the Committee on Interstate and Foreign Commerce, House of Representatives, Ninety-sixth Congress, first session, June 26 and 27, 1979. Washington : U. S. Govt. Print. Off., 1980. iv, 256 p. : ill. ; 24 cm. "Serial no. 96-139."   LC Card 80-602744   DDC 363.1/79 19
1. Pesticides - Toxicology - United States. 2. Herbicides - Toxicology - United States. 3. Dichlorophenoxyacetic acid - Toxicology. 4. Trichlorophenoxyacetic acid - Toxicology. 5. Tetrachlorodibenzodioxin - Toxicology. 6. Veterans - Diseases - United States.
KF27 .I5547 1979r

Love Canal, health studies and relocation : joint hearing before the Subcommittee on Oversight and Investigations of the Committee on Interstate and Foreign Commerce, U. S. House of Representatives and the Subcommittee on Environment, Energy, and Natural Resources of the Committee on Government Operations, Ninety-sixth Congress, second session, May 22, 1980. Washington : U. S. G.P.O., 1980. v, 71 p. : ill. ; 24 cm. "Serial no. 96-191."   LC Card 80-604042   DDC 363.7/28 19
1. Love Canal Chemical Waste Landfill (Niagara Falls, N.Y.). 2. Pollution - Toxicology - New York (State) - Niagara Falls. 3. Relocation (Housing) - New York (State) - Niagara Falls. 4. Liability for hazardous substances - hazardous damages - New York (State) - Niagara Falls. I. United States. Congress. House. Committee on Government Operations. Environment, Energy, and Natural Resources Subcommittee. II. Title.
KF27 .I5547 1980o

Lower, Milton D. The energy inflation crisis . Washington , c1980. vii, 78 p. :   LC Card 81-600799   DDC 332.4/1/0973 19
HD9502.U52 L69

"Man-in-the-plant" revisited--a deceptive drug labeling practice continues : hearing before the Subcommittee on Oversight and Investigations of the Committee on Interstate and Foreign Commerce, House of Representatives, Ninety-sixth Congress, second session, March 6, 1980. Washington : U. S. Govt. Print. Off., 1980. iii, 59 p. ; 24 cm. "Serial no. 96-140."   LC Card 80-602750   DDC 363.1/94/0973 19
1. Drugs - Labeling - United States. 2. Drugs - United States - Generic substitution. 3. Drug trade - United States. I. Title.
KF27 .I5547 1980

National market system, five year status report : report, together with separate views / by the Subcommittee on Oversight and Investigations of the Committee on Interstate and Foreign Commerce, United States House of Representatives. Washington : U. S. G.P.O. : For sale by the Supt. of Docs., U. S., 1980. vii, 105 p. ; 23 cm. At head of title: Committee print. 96th Congress, 2d session. Committee print 96-IFC 56. "August 1980." Includes bibliographical references. LC

Card 80-603861   DDC 332.64/273 19
1. Stock-exchange - United States. 2. Securities - United States. I. Title.
HG4910 .U54 1980

Natural gas supplies : hearings before the Subcommittee on Oversight and Investigations of the Committee on Interstate and Foreign Commerce, House of Representatives, Ninety-fourth Congress, first session-[second] .... Washington : U. S. Govt. Print. Off., 1975- v. : ill. ; 23 cm. Hearings held June 9- 1975. "Serial no. 94-24." Includes bibliographical references. LC Card 75-602828
1. Gas, Natural - United States. I. Title.
KF27 .I5547 1975

PCB's, dangers associated with their storage and use : hearings before the Subcommittee on Oversight and Investigations of the Committee on Interstate and Foreign Commerce, House of Representatives, Ninety-sixth Congress, first and second sessions, September 28, 1979, February 28, and March 12, 1980. Washington : U. S. Govt. Print. Off., 1980. iv, 704 p. : ill. ; 24 cm. "Serial no. 96-134."   LC Card 80-602788   DDC 363.1/79 19
1. Polychlorinated biphenyls - Toxicology. 2. Polychlorinated biphenyls - Environmental aspects - United States. 3. Polychlorinated biphenyls - Storage. I. Title.
KF27 .I5547 1979s

Potential displacement of oil by nuclear energy and coal in electric utilities : hearing before the Subcommittee on Oversight and Investigations of the Committee on Interstate and Foreign Commerce, House of Representatives, Ninety-sixth Congress, second session, December 9, 1980. Washington : U. S. G.P.O., 1981. iii, 394 p. : ill. ; 24 cm. "Serial no. 96-230." Item 1019 Includes bibliographical references. LC Card 81-601364   DDC 333.79/3215/0973 19
1. Atomic power-plants - United States. 2. Coal-fired power plants - United States. 3. Electric power-plants - United States - Conversion to coal. I. Title.
KF27 .I5547 1980s

Regulation and construction of nuclear powerplants--South Texas nuclear project : hearing before the Subcommittee on Oversight and Investigations of the Committee on Interstate and Foreign Commerce, House of Representatives, Ninety-sixth Congress, second session, September 23, 1980. Washington : U. S. G.P.O., c1981. iii, 198 p. ; 24 cm. "Serial no. 96-223." Item 1019   LC Card 81-601168   DDC 343.73/0925 347.303925 19
1. Atomic power-plants - Texas - Design and construction. 2. Atomic power-plants - Texas - Safety measures. 3. United States. Nuclear Regulatory Commission. I. Title.
KF27 .I5547 1980u

Securities Acts Amendments of 1975--oversight : hearings before the Subcommittee on Oversight and Investigations and the Subcommittee on Consumer Protection and Finance of the Committee on Interstate and Foreign Commerce, House of Representatives, Ninety-fifth Congress, first session .... Washington : U. S. G.P.O., 1978. viii, 1187 p. : ill. ; 24 cm. Hearings held June 21-July 28, 1977. "Serial 95-80." Includes bibliographical references.   LC Card 81-601238   DDC 353.0082/58 19
1. Securities - United States. 2. Stock-exchange - Law and legislation - United States. I. United States. Congress. House. Committee on Interstate and Foreign Commerce. Subcommittee on Consumer Protection and Finance. II. Title.
KF27 .I5547 1977q

Stripper oil miscertification : hearing before the Subcommittee on Oversight and Investigations of the Committee on Interstate and Foreign Commerce, House of Representatives, Ninety-sixth Congress, second session, April 18, 1980. Washington : U. S. G.P.O., 1980. iii, 63 p. : ill. ; 24 cm. "Serial no. 96-190."   LC Card 80-604004   DDC 338.2/3 19
1. Petroleum - Prices - United States. I. Title.
KF27 .I5547 1980j

Unnecessary exposure to radiation from medical and dental x-rays : report together with separate views, prepared for the use of the Committee on Interstate and Foreign Commerce, United States House of Representatives and its Subcommittee on

BIBLIOGRAPHIC GUIDE

United States. Congress. House. Committee on Interstate and

438

Oversight and Investigations. Washington : U.
S. Govt. Print. Off., 1980. v, 15 p. ; 24 cm. At
head of title: 96th Congress, 2d session. Committee
print. Committee print 96-52. "August 1980." Includes
bibliographical references.   LC Card 80-603049   DDC
363.1/89 19

*1. Radiography, Medical - United States. 2. X-rays -
Physiological effect. I. United States. Congress. House.
Committee on Interstate and Foreign Commerce. II.
Title.*

RC78 .U534 1980

Use of cost-benefit analysis by regulatory
agencies : joint hearings before the
Subcommittee on Oversight and Investigations
and the Subcommittee on Consumer Protection
and Finance of the Committee on Interstate
and Foreign Commerce, House of
Representatives, Ninety-sixth Congress, first
session, July 30, October 10, and 24, 1979.
Washington : U. S. Govt. Print. Off., 1980. v,
482 p. : ill. ; 24 cm. "Serial no. 96-157." Includes
bibliographical references.   LC Card 80-603329   DDC
353.09/1 19

*1. Independent regulatory commissions - United States -
Cost effectiveness. 2. Trade regulation - United States -
Cost effectiveness. I. United States. Congress. House.
Committee on Interstate and Foreign Commerce.
Subcommittee on Consumer Protection and Finance. II.
Title.*

KF27 .I5547 1979v

Wasted health dollars : evaluation of
professional standards review organizations :
hearing before the Subcommittee on Oversight
and Investigations of the Committee on
Interstate and Foreign Commerce, House of
Representatives, Ninety-sixth Congress, second
session, July 31, 1980. Washington : U. S.
Govt. Print. Off., 1980. iv, 155 p. : ill. ; 23 cm.
"Serial no. 96-178."   LC Card 80-603470   DDC
353.0077 19

*1. Professional standards review organizations
(Medicine) - United States. I. Title.*

KF27 .I5547 1980f

Wasted health dollars : hearing before the
Subcommittee on Oversight and Investigations
of the Committee on Interstate and Foreign
Commerce, House of Representatives,
Ninety-sixth Congress, second session, March
21, 1980. Washington : U. S. Govt. Print. Off.,
1980. iii, 144 p. ; 24 cm. "Serial no. 96-143." LC
Card 80-602716   DDC 338.4/336210973 19

*1. Medical policy - United States. 2. Medical care, Cost
of - United States. 3. Medicare. 4. Medicaid. I. Title.*

KF27 .I5547 1980a

Wasted surgical dollars : hearing before the
Subcommittee on Oversight and Investigations
of the Committee on Interstate and Foreign
Commerce, House of Representatives,
Ninety-sixth Congress, second session,
December 2, 1980. Washington : U. S. G.P.O.,
1981. ii, 38 p. ; 24 cm. "Serial no. 96-228."   LC
Card 81-601159   DDC 362.1/97/0973 19

*1. Surgery, Unnecessary - United States. 2. Surgeons -
United States - Fees. 3. Medical care, Cost of - United
States. I. Title.*

KF27 .I5547 1980q

**United States. Congress. House. Committee on
Interstate and Foreign Commerce.
Subcommittee on Transportation and
Commerce.**

Alternatives to the Moscow Olympics : hearing
before the Subcommittee on Transportation and
Commerce of the Committee on Interstate and
Foreign Commerce, House of Representatives,
Ninety-sixth Congress, second session, January
30, 1980. Washington : U. S. Govt. Print. Off.,
1980. iii, 83 p. ; 23 cm. "Serial no. 96-130."   LC
Card 80-602442   DDC 353.0085/8 19

*1. Sports and state - United States. 2. Sports and state -
Russia. 3. Olympic Games, Moscow, 1980. 4. United
States - Foreign relations - Russia. 5. Russia - Foreign
relations - United States. I. Title.*

KF27 .I5589 1980a

Amtrak fiscal year 1980 authorization and
Amtrak route restructuring : hearings before the
Subcommittee on Transportation and
Commerce of the Committee on Interstate and
Foreign Commerce, House of Representatives,
Ninety-sixth Congress, first session ... April 3
and 4, 1979. Washington : U. S. Govt. Print.
Off., 1980. viii, 725 p. : ill. ; 24 cm. Hearings on
H. res. 93, 97, 105, 107, 109-110, 152, 182, 190, and
200. "Serial no. 96-71."   LC Card 80-601471   DDC

353.0087/51 19

*1. Amtrak - Finance. 2. Railroad law - United States. 3.
Railroads - United States - Train discontinuance. 4.
Railroads - United States - Passenger traffic. I. Title.*

KF27 .I5589 1979l

Coal slurry pipelines : hearing before the
Subcommittee on Transportation and
Commerce of the Committee on Interstate and
Foreign Commerce, House of Representatives,
Ninety-sixth Congress, second session, on H.R.
6879 ... August 28, 1980. Washington : U. S.
G.P.O., 1980. iii, 187 p. ; 24 cm. "Serial no.
96-205."   LC Card 80-604095   DDC 343.73/093
347.30393 19

*1. Coal - Pipe lines - Law and legislation - United
States. I. Title.*

KF27 .I5589 1980j

Coal transportation problems in the Midwest :
hearing before the Subcommittee on
Transportation and Commerce of the
Committee on Interstate and Foreign
Commerce, House of Representatives,
Ninety-sixth Congress, second session,
December 17, 1980. Washington : U. S. G.P.O.,
1981. iii, 125 p. : ill. ; 24 cm. "Serial no. 96-238."
Item 1019   LC Card 81-601631   DDC 380.5/24 19

1. Coal - Middle West - Transportation. I. Title.

KF27 .I5589 1980n

Future funding for Conrail : hearing before the
Subcommittee on Transportation and
Commerce of the Committee on Interstate and
Foreign Commerce, House of Representatives,
Ninety-sixth Congress, second session ... April
1, 1980. Washington : U. S. Govt. Print. Off.,
1980. iii, 84 p. : ill. ; 24 cm. "Serial 96-177."   LC
Card 80-603456   DDC 385/.1 19

*1. ConRail - Appropriations and expenditures. 2.
ConRail - Finance. 3. Railroads - Northeastern States -
Freight. 4. Railroads and state - United States. I. Title.*

KF27 .I5589 1980f

Hazardous waste disposal : our number one
environmental problem : hearing before the
Subcommittee on Transportation and
Commerce of the Committee on Interstate and
Foreign Commerce, House of Representatives,
Ninety-sixth Congress, second session, June 9,
1980. Washington : U. S. G.P.O., 1980 [i.e.
1981] iii, 97 p. ; 24 cm. "Serial no. 96-207." Item
1019 Includes bibliographical references.   LC Card
81-600820   DDC 363.7/28 19

*1. Hazardous wastes - Environmental aspects - New
Jersey. 2. Waste disposal sites - New Jersey. 3. Water -
Pollution - New Jersey. I. Title.*

KF27 .I5589 1980o

Hazardous waste disposal problems at federal
facilities : hearing before the Subcommittee on
Transportation and Commerce of the
Committee on Interstate and Foreign
Commerce, House of Representatives,
Ninety-sixth Congress, second session,
November 20, 1980. Washington : U. S.
G.P.O., 1981. iii, 78 p. : ill. ; 24 cm. "Serial no.
96-227." Item 1019   LC Card 81-601166   DDC 082
363.7/28 19

*1. Hazardous wastes - New Jersey - Lakehurst. 2.
Refuse and refuse disposal - New Jersey - Lakehurst. 3.
Hazardous wastes - United States. 4. Refuse and refuse
disposal - United States. I. Title.*

KF27 .I5589 1980l

Municipal waste-to-energy act of 1980 : hearing
before the Subcommittee on Transportation and
Commerce of the Committee on Interstate and
Foreign Commerce, House of Representatives,
Ninety-sixth Congress, second session, on H.R.
6638 ... April 22, 1980. Washington : U. S.
Govt. Print. Off., 1980. iii, 111 p. ; 24 cm.
"Serial no. 96-166."   LC Card 80-603438   DDC
346.7304/67938 19

*1. Refuse as fuel - Law and legislation - United States.
I. Title.*

KF27 .I5589 1980c

Northeast corridor improvement project :
hearing before the Subcommittee on
Transportation and Commerce of the
Committee on Interstate and Foreign
Commerce, House of Representatives,
Ninety-sixth Congress, second session, on H.R.
6438 ... February 26, 1980. Washington : U. S.
Govt. Print. Off., 1980. iii, 161 p. ; 23 cm.
"Serial no. 96-164."   LC Card 80-603407   DDC
343.73/0958 347.303958 19

1. Railroad law - Northeastern States. 2. Railroads -

Northeastern States - Finance. I. Title.

KF27 .I5589 1980g

Rail Act of 1980 : hearings before the
Subcommittee on Transportation and
Commerce of the Committee on Interstate and
Foreign Commerce, House of Representatives,
Ninety-sixth Congress, second session, on
regulatory reform legislation for the rail
industry, March 31 and April 2, 1980.
Washington : U. S. G.P.O., 1980. vi, 653 p. ;
24 cm. "Serial 96-186."   LC Card 80-603811   DDC
343.73/095/0262 347.303950262 19

1. Railroad law - United States. I. Title.

KF27 .I5589 1980i

The Rail act of 1980 : background materials /
prepared for the use of the Committee on
Interstate and Foreign Commerce, House of
Representatives, and its Subcommittee on
Transportation and Commerce, Ninety-sixth
Congress, second session. Washington : U. S.
Govt. Print. Off., 1980. vii, 91 p. : graphs ; 24
cm. At head of title: 96th Congress, 2d session.
Committee print. Committee print 96-IFC 45.   LC
Card 80-602213   DDC 343.73/095 19

*1. Railroad law - United States. 2. Railroads - United
States - Finance. I. United States. Congress. House.
Committee on Interstate and Foreign Commerce. II.
Title.*

KF2275.5 .I58

Rail service commuter problems on the
Northeast Corridor : hearing before the
Subcommittee on Transportation and
Commerce of the Committee on Interstate and
Foreign Commerce, House of Representatives,
Ninety-sixth Congress, second session, on how
to best coordinate on going commuter service
with our most extensive capital improvements
program in the northeast, September 2, 1980.
Washington : U. S. G.P.O., 1981. iv, 222 p. :
ill. ; 24 cm. "Serial 96-215." Item 1019   LC Card
81-600979   DDC 385/.22/0974 19

*1. Railroads - Northeastern States - Commuting traffic.
2. Railroads - Northeastern States - Maintenance and
repair. 3. Conrail. 4. Amtrak. I. Title.*

KF27 .I5589 1980m

Railroad deregulation act of 1979 : hearings
before the Subcommittee on Transportation and
Commerce of the Committee on Interstate and
Foreign Commerce, House of Representatives,
Ninety-sixth Congress, first session, on H.R.
4570 .... Washington : U. S. Govt. Print. Off.,
1979 i.e. 1980. viii, 1292 p. : ill. ; 24 cm.
Hearings held Apr. 24-Nov. 1, 1979. "Serial 96-145."
Includes bibliographical references.   LC Card
80-603016   DDC 343.73/095 19

1. Railroad law - United States. I. Title.

KF27 .I5589 1979o

Railroad retirement system : hearing before the
Subcommittee on Transportation and
Commerce of the Committee on Interstate and
Foreign Commerce, House of Representatives,
Ninety-sixth Congress, second session, on H.R.
7793 ... H.R. 4855 ... September 4, 1980.
Washington : U. S. G.P.O., 1980. iii, 80 p. ; 24
cm. "Serial 96-213."   LC Card 81-600853   DDC
344.73/012529 347.30412529 19

1. Railroads - United States - Pensions. I. Title.

KF27 .I5589 1980k

Railroad safety : hearing before the
Subcommittee on Transportation and
Commerce of the Committee on Interstate and
Foreign Commerce, House of Representatives,
Ninety-sixth Congress, second session ... March
25, 1980. Washington : U. S. Govt. Print. Off.,
1980. iii, 213 p. : ill. ; 24 cm. "Serial 96-172."
Includes bibliographical references.   LC Card
80-603701   DDC 363.1/22/0973 19

1. Railroads - United States - Safety measures. I. Title.

KF27 .I5589 1980h

Reauthorization for the U. S. Railway
Association for fiscal year 1981 : hearing before
the Subcommittee on Transportation and
Commerce of the Committee on Interstate and
Foreign Commerce, House of Representatives,
Ninety-sixth Congress, second session, on H.R.
6697 ... March 11, 1980. Washington : U. S.
Govt. Print. Off., 1980. iii, 73 p. ; 24 cm. "Serial
96-175."   LC Card 80-603452   DDC
353.0072/236875 19

*1. United States Railway Association - Appropriations
and expenditures. I. Title.*

KF27 .I5589 1980d

Title V authorization under the Regional rail

GOVERNMENT PUBLICATIONS - U.S.: 1981

439   *United States. Congress. House. Committee on Merchant Marine*

reorganization act of 1973 : hearing before the
Subcommittee on Transportation and
Commerce of the Committee on Interstate and
Foreign Commerce, House of Representatives,
Ninety-sixth Congress, second session, February
21, 1980. Washington : U. S. Govt. Print. Off.,
1980. iii, 38 p. ; 24 cm. "Serial no. 96-152." LC
Card 80-603098   DDC 331.25/5 19
1. Wages - Railroads - United States. 2. ConRail -
Appropriations and expenditures. I. Title.
KF27 .I5589 1980b

United States. Congress. House. Committee on
Interstate and Foreign Commerce.
Subcommittee on Health and the Environment.
Hazardous waste and drinking water .
Washington , 1981. v, 195 p. :   LC Card
81-601136   DDC 363.7/394 19
KF27 .I5543 1980q

United States. Congress. House. Committee on
Merchant Marine and Fisheries. (Old
Catalog form: United States. Merchant
Marine and Fisheries, Committee on (House))
// Hearings printed in 1978 and later are
available only in microform. Please consult
the librarians in the Economic and Public
Affairs Division.
Defense sealift capability : hearings before the
Committee on Merchant Marine and Fisheries,
House of Representatives, Ninety-sixth
Congress, on the Capability of our nation's
merchant marine to supply our military and
naval forces in the event we are involved in
hostilities overseas, December 12, 13, 1979,
March 5, 1980. Washington : U. S. G.P.O.,
1980. iv, 301 p. : ill. ; 24 cm. "Serial no. 96-46."
Bibliography: p. 208-209.   LC Card 80-604083   DDC
359.9/82/0973 19
1. United States - Armed Forces - Transportation. 2.
United States. Military Sealift Command. I. Title.
KF27 .M4 1979c

Dredge spoil disposal and PCB contamination :
hearings before the Committee on Merchant
Marine and Fisheries, House of Representatives,
Ninety-sixth Congress, second session, on
exploring the various aspects related to the
dumping of dredged spoil material in the ocean
and the PCB contamination issue, March 14,
May 21, 1980. Washington : U. S. G.P.O.,
1980. v, 698 p. : ill. ; 24 cm. "Serial no. 96-43."
Includes bibliographies.   LC Card 81-600658   DDC
363.7/28 19
1. Waste disposal in the ocean - Environmental
aspects - United States. 2. Dredging - Environmental
aspects - United States. 3. Dredging spoil - United
States. 4. Polychlorinated biphenyls - Environmental
aspects - United States. 5. Polychlorinated biphenyls -
Toxicology - United States. I. Title.
KF27 .M4 1980

Port development and related maritime
matters : hearings before the Committee on
Merchant Marine and Fisheries, House of
Representatives, Ninety-sixth Congress, second
session, on effort to review and maintain
oversight of port development and related
maritime matters and to receive comments on
the omnibus maritime bill, April 7, 9, and 10,
1980. Washington : U. S. G.P.O., 1980 [i.e.
1981] iv, 585 p. : ill., maps ; 23 cm. "Serial no.
96-51." Item 1021 Includes bibliographical references.
LC Card 81-601880   DDC 353.0087/71 19
1. Harbors - United States. 2. Marine terminals -
Washington (State). 3. Marine terminals - California. I.
Title.
KF27 .M4 1980a

Report on the strategic implications of the
Omnibus maritime bill, H.R. 6899 : a white
paper / submitted by John M. Murphy,
chairman to the Committee on Merchant
Marine and Fisheries. Washington : U. S. Govt.
Print. Off., 1980. ii, 35 p. : ill. ; 24 cm. At head
of title: 96th Congress, 2d session. Committee print.
"Serial no. 96-E." LC Card 80-602266   DDC
359.2/7/0973 19
1. United States. Navy - Mobilization. 2. Merchant
marine - United States - Military aspects. 3. Maritime
law - United States. I. Murphy, John M. II. Title. III.
Title: Strategic implications of the Omnibus maritime
bill, H.R. 6899.
VA77 .U56 1980

United States. Congress. House. Committee on
Merchant Marine and Fisheries. Subcommittee
on Fisheries and Wildlife Conservation and the
Environment. Atlantic tuna . Washington ,

1980. iv, 184 p. :   LC Card 80-603672   DDC
353.0072/236822362 19
KF27 .M447 1980

United States Public Health Service hospitals
and clinics : hearings before the Committee on
Merchant Marine and Fisheries, House of
Representatives, Ninety-sixth Congress, on ...
June 18, 19, 1979, Washington, D.C., April 8,
1980, Seattle, Washington. Washington : U. S.
Govt. Print. Off., 1980. iv, 182 p. ; 24 cm.
"Serial no. 96-30." LC Card 80-603303   DDC
362.1/1/0973 19
1. Hospitals, Public - United States. 2. Merchant
seamen - Medical care - United States. 3. United States.
Public Health Service. Division of Hospitals and Clinics.
I. Title.
KF27 .M4 1979b

United States. Congress. House. Committee on
Merchant Marine and Fisheries. Ad Hoc
Select Subcommittee on Maritime Education
and Training. Sea training at maritime
academies oversight : hearings before the Ad
Hoc Select Committee on Maritime Education
and Training of the Committee on Merchant
Marine and Fisheries, House of Representatives,
Ninety-sixth Congress, second session, on sea
training of United States Merchant Marine
officers and different ways of satisfying this
requirement at various maritime academies,
September 9, 1980. Washington : U. S. G.P.O.,
1980 [i.e. 1981] iv, 246 p. : ill. ; 23 cm. "Serial
no. 96-52." Item 1021   LC Card 81-600941   DDC
623.88/07073 19
1. Merchant marine - United States - Officers. 2.
Seamanship - Study and teaching - United States. 3.
Naval education - United States. 4. Synthetic training
devices. I. Title.
KF27 .M458 1980

United States. Congress. House. Committee on
Merchant Marine and Fisheries.
Subcommitee on Coast Guard and
Navigation. Small commercial vessel
inspection and manning : hearings before the
Subcommittee on Coast Guard and Navigation
of the Committee on Merchant Marine and
Fisheries, House of Representatives,
Ninety-sixth Congress, first session, on H.R.
1645 ... H.R. 5164 ... July 11, September 12,
18, 1979. Washington : U. S. Govt. Print. Off.,
1980. iv, 301 p. : ill. ; 23 cm. "Serial no. 96-24."
LC Card 80-601442   DDC 343.73/0965 19
1. Ships - Inspection - United States. 2. Ships -
Manning - Law and legislation - United States. I. Title.
KF27 .M434 1979d

United States. Congress. House. Committee on
Merchant Marine and Fisheries.
Subcommittee on Coast Guard and
Navigation.
Coast Guard authorization, reserve, and
oversight : hearings before the Subcommittee on
Coast Guard and Navigation of the Committee
on Merchant Marine and Fisheries, House of
Representatives, Ninety-sixth Congress, second
session, on ... H.R. 6672, March 13, 1980 ...
H.R. 6666, April 30, 1980 ... July 30, 1980.
Washington : U. S. G.P.O., 1980. v, 363 p. :
ill. ; 24 cm. "Serial no. 96-42." LC Card 80-604079
DDC 353.0072/23674 19
1. United States. Coast Guard - Appropriations and
expenditures. I. Title.
KF27 .M434 1980

Port safety and liquefied gas safety and siting :
hearings before the Subcommittees on Coast
Guard and Navigation, Merchant Marine, and
Oceanography of the Committee on Merchant
Marine and Fisheries, House of Representatives,
Ninety-sixth Congress, first session, on H.R.
2994 ... H.R. 1414 and H.R. 3749.
Washington : U. S. Govt. Print. Office, 1979.
vii, 748 p. : ill. ; 24 cm. "Serial no. 96-15." Includes
bibliographical references. Hearings held April 26-July
19, 1979.   LC Card 80-601892   DDC 343.73/0967 19
1. Harbors - Law and legislation - United States. 2.
Liquefied gases - Storage - Law and legislation - United
States. I. United States. Congress. House. Committee on
Merchant Marine and Fisheries. Subcommittee on
Merchant Marine. II. United States. Congress. House.
Committee on Merchant Marine and Fisheries.
Subcommittee on Oceanography. III. Title.
KF27 .M434 1979e

United States. Congress. House. Committee on
Merchant Marine and Fisheries.
Subcommittee on Fisheries and Wildlife

Conservation and the Environment.
American fisheries promotion : hearings before
the Subcommittee on Fisheries and Wildlife
Conservation and the Environment of the
Committee on Merchant Marine and Fisheries,
House of Representatives, Ninety-sixth
Congress, second session, on H.R. 7039 ... May
6, 19, 20, 1980. Washington : U. S. G.P.O.,
1980. vi, 467 p. : ill. ; 24 cm. "Serial no. 96-44."
Includes bibliographical references.   LC Card
80-604011   DDC 343.73/07692 347.3037692 19
1. Fishery law and legislation - United States. I. Title.
KF27 .M447 1980a

Amfish : hearings before the Subcommittee on
Fisheries and Wildlife Conservation and the
Environment of the Committee on Merchant
Marine and Fisheries, House of Representatives,
Ninety-sixth Congress, first session, on H.R.
4360 ... September 11, 24, 1979. Washington :
U. S. Govt. Print. Off., 1980. iv, 237 p. : ill. ;
24 cm. "Serial no. 96-18." LC Card 80-601398
DDC 343.73/0786238248 19
1. Fishery law and legislation - United States. 2. Fishing
boats - United States - Finance. I. Title.
KF27 .M447 1979d

Atlantic tuna : hearings before the
Subcommittee on Fisheries and Wildlife
Conservation and the Environment and the
Committee on Merchant Marine and Fisheries,
House of Representatives, Ninety-sixth
Congress, second session ... March 6, 1980 ...
May 1, 1980. Washington : U. S. Govt. Print.
Off., 1980. iv, 184 p. : ill. ; 23 cm. "Serial no.
96-37." LC Card 80-603672   DDC
353.0072/236822362 19
1. Tuna fisheries - Law and legislation - Atlantic Ocean.
2. Tuna fisheries - Law and legislation - United States.
I. United States. Congress. House. Committee on
Merchant Marine and Fisheries. II. Title.
KF27 .M447 1980

Dinsell-Johnson fund--N. Pacific fur seal :
hearings before the Subcommittee on Fisheries
and Wildlife Conservation and the Environment
of the Committee on Merchant Marine and
Fisheries, House of Representatives,
Ninety-sixth Congress, second session, on
Dinsell-Johnson expansion fund--H.R. 6074,
March 18, 1980, management of the North
Pacific fur seal--H.R. 5033, April 28, 1980.
Washington : U. S. G.P.O., 1980. vii, 540 p. :
ill. ; 24 cm. "Serial no. 96-49." Item 1021 Includes
bibliographical references.   LC Card 81-600826   DDC
343.7305/585333954 347.3035585333954 19
1. Fishery law and legislation - United States. 2.
Northern fur seal - Law and legislation - United States.
I. Title.
KF27 .M447 1980c

Fisheries miscellaneous : hearings before the
Subcommittees on Fisheries and Wildlife
Conservation and the Environment, and
Oceanography of the Committee on Merchant
Marine and Fisheries, House of Representatives,
Ninety-sixth Congress, on National Aquaculture
Act--H.R. 20, April 5, 1979, Fisheries
Development Act oversight, December 10,
1979, Commercial fisheries authorization and
oversight--H.R. 4890, February 11, 1980, U.
S.-Soviet fishing agreement, March 3, 1980.
Washington : U. S. G.P.O., 1980. viii, 478 p. :
ill. ; 24 cm. "Serial no. 96-45." LC Card 81-600601
DDC 343.73/07692 347.3037692 19
1. Fishery law and legislation - United States. I. United
States. Congress. House. Committee on Merchant
Marine and Fisheries. Subcommittee on Oceanography.
II. Title.
KF27 .M447 1979g

Indian fishing rights--fishery management :
hearings before the Subcommittee on Fisheries
and Wildlife Conservation and the Environment
of the Committee on Merchant Marine and
Fisheries, House of Representatives,
Ninety-sixth Congress, second session, on Great
Lakes Indian fishing rights--H.R. 7232, H.R.
2738, H.J.Res. 246, June 6, 1980. Washington :
U. S. G.P.O., 1980 [i.e. 1981] v, 540 p. : ill. ;
24 cm. "Serial no. 96-54." Item 1021 Bibliography: p.
370-372.   LC Card 81-601167   DDC
346.7304/6956/08997 347.3064695608997 19
1. Indians of North America - Great Lakes region -
Fishing - Law and legislation. 2. Fishery management -
United States. I. Title.
KF27 .M447 1980b

National wildlife refuges : hearings before the

BIBLIOGRAPHIC GUIDE

United States. Congress. House. Committee on Merchant Marine 440

Subcommittee on Fisheries and Wildlife
Conservation and the Enviroment of the
Committee on Merchant Marine and Fisheries,
House of Representatives, Ninety-sixth
Congress .... Washington : U. S. Govt. Print
Off., 1980. vii, 584 p. : ill. ; 24 cm. Hearings held
Sept. 27, 1979 to Mar. 21, 1980. "Serial no. 96-27."
    LC Card 80-602809   DDC 346.7304/695 19
*1. Wildlife refuges - Law and legislation - United States.
I. Title.*
KF27 .M447 1979f

Northwest salmon enhancement
program--salmon interception : hearings before
the Subcommittee on Fisheries and Wildlife
Conservation and the Environment of the
Committee on Merchant Marine and Fisheries,
House of Representatives, Ninety-sixth
Congress on ... H.R. 6959, S. 2163 ....
Washington : U. S. G.P.O., 1980. v, 512 p. :
ill. ; 24 cm. Hearings held October 15,
1979-September 18, 1980. "Serial no. 96-50."   LC Card
80-603908   DDC 343.73/07692755
347.3037692755 19
*1. Salmon-fisheries - Law and legislation - Washington
(State). 2. Salmon-fisheries - Law and legislation -
Alaska. 3. Salmon-fisheries - Alaska. I. Title.*
KF27 .M447 1979h

Ocean dumping : joint hearings before the
Subcommittee on Fisheries and Wildlife
Conservation and the Environment and the
Subcommittee on Oceanography of the
Committee on Merchant Marine and Fisheries,
House of Representatives, Ninety-fourth
Congress, first - [second] session ....
Washington : U. S. Govt. Print. Off., 1975- v. :
ill. ; 23 cm. "Serial no. 94-10, 94-25 Hearings held in
Washington and New York Apr. 24, 1975-
Bibliography: [v. 1] p. 115-124. CONTENTS. - [pt. 1]
On H.R. 5710 ... H.R. 6282.--pt. 2 On oversight of the
Marine protection, research, and sanctuaries act of
1972. LC Card 75-603626
*1. Waste disposal in the ocean - Law and legislation -
United States. I. United States. Congress. House.
Committee on Merchant Marine and Fisheries.
Subcommittee on Oceanography. II. Title.*
KF27 .M447 1975e

Oversight report on the administration of the
Endangered species act and the Convention on
International Trade in Endangered Species of
Wild Fauna and Flora / submitted by John B.
Breaux, chairman, Subcommittee on Fisheries
and Wildlife Conservation and the
Environment, Committee on Merchant Marine
and Fisheries. Washington : U. S. Govt. Print.
Off., 1980. ii, 28 p. ; 24 cm. At head of title: 96th
Congress, 2d session. Committee print. "April 7, 1980."
"Serial no. 96-D." LC Card 80-602275   DDC
353.0082/328 19
*1. Endangered species - United States. 2. Endangered
species - Law and legislation - United States. 3.
Convention on international trade in endangered species
of wild fauna and flora. 4. Wild animal trade. I. Breaux,
John B. II. Title.*
QL84.2 .U55 1980

Oversight report on the U. S.-Canada East
Coast fishery agreement and boundary treaty /
submitted by John B. Breaux, chairman,
Subcommittee on Fisheries and Wildlife
Conservation and the Environment, Committee
on Merchant Marine and Fisheries.
Washington : U. S. Govt. Print. Off., 1980. ii,
23 p. ; 23 cm. At head of title: 96th Congress, 2d
session. Committee print. "Serial no. 96-C." LC Card
80-601727   DDC 342.73/0413 347.302413 19
*1. Fishery law and legislation - United States. 2.
Fishery law and legislation - Canada. 3. United States -
Boundaries - Canada. 4. Canada - Boundaries - United
States. I. Title.*
LAW

United States. Congress. House. Committee on
Merchant Marine and Fisheries. Subcommittee
on Oceanography. Ocean dumping.
Washington , 1980. viii, 404 p. :   LC Card
80-603809   DDC 344.73/04626 347.3044626 19
KF27 .M473 1980b

**United States. Congress. House. Committee on
Merchant Marine and Fisheries.
Subcommittee on Merchant Marine.**
United States. Congress. House. Committee on
Merchant Marine and Fisheries. Subcommittee
on Coast Guard and Navigation. Port safety
and liquefied gas safety and siting .
Washington , 1979. vii, 748 p. :   LC Card

80-601892   DDC 343.73/0967 19
KF27 .M434 1979e

United States. Congress. House. Committee on
Merchant Marine and Fisheries. Subcommittee
on Oceanography. Ocean thermal energy
conversion . Washington , 1980. vii, 495 p. :
    LC Card 80-602723   DDC 346.7304/68 19
KF27 .M473 1979a

**United States. Congress. House. Committee on
Merchant Marine and Fisheries.
Subcommittee on Oceanography.**
Coastal zone management : hearings before the
Subcommittee on Oceanography of the
Committee on Merchant Marine and Fisheries,
House of Representatives, Ninety-sixth
Congress ... April 1, 16, 1980. Washington : U.
S. Govt. Print. Off., 1980- v. <1> : ill. ; 23
cm. "Serial no. 96-31." Hearings held in various cities.
Includes bibliographies.   LC Card 80-603481   DDC
346.7304/6917 347.30646917 19
*1. Coastal zone management - Law and legislation -
United States. 2. Coastal zone management - United
States. I. Title.*
KF27 .M473 1980a

Ocean dumping : hearings before the
Subcommittee on Oceanography and the
Subcommittee on Fisheries and Wildlife
Conservation and the Environment of the
Committee on Merchant Marine and Fisheries,
House of Representatives, Ninety-sixth
Congress ... March 5, 1979 ... June 27, 1979 ...
February 20, 1980. Washington : U. S. Govt.
Print. Off., 1980. viii, 404 p. : ill. ; 24 cm.
"Serial no. 96-40." LC Card 80-603809   DDC
344.73/04626 347.3044626 19
*1. Waste disposal in the ocean - Law and legislation -
United States. I. United States. Congress. House.
Committee on Merchant Marine and Fisheries.
Subcommittee on Fisheries and Wildlife Conservation
and the Environment. II. Title.*
KF27 .M473 1980b

Ocean thermal energy conversion : hearings
before the Subcommittee on Oceanography and
the Subcommittee on Merchant Marine of the
Committee on Merchant Marine and Fisheries,
House of Representatives, Ninety-sixth
Congress, on ocean thermal energy conversion
oversight, June 21, September 20, 1979, Ocean
thermal energy conversion act of 1980, H.R.
6154, January 30, 31, February 27, 1980.
Washington : U. S. Govt. Print. Off., 1980. vii,
495 p. : ill. ; 24 cm. "Serial no. 96-29." LC Card
80-602723   DDC 346.7304/68 19
*1. Ocean thermal power plants - Law and legislation -
United States. 2. Ocean thermal power plants - Hawaii.
I. United States. Congress. House. Committee on
Merchant Marine and Fisheries. Subcommittee on
Merchant Marine. II. Title.*
KF27 .M473 1979a

Sea grant programs : hearings before the
Subcommittee on Oceanography of the
Committee on Merchant Marine and Fisheries,
House of Representatives, Ninety-fourth
Congress, second session, on H.R. 12108 ....
Washington : U. S. Govt. Print. Off., 1976. 2
v. ; 23 cm. Hearings held Mar. 1-June 24, 1976.
"Serial no. 94-26" and "Serial no. 94-36." LC Card
76-602454
*1. Oceanographic research - United States. 2. Federal
aid to higher education - United States. I. Title.*
KF27 .M473 1976
        NYPL [JLE 77-2823 & JLL 81-82]

United States. Congress. House. Committee on
Merchant Marine and Fisheries. Subcommittee
on Coast Guard and Navigation. Port safety
and liquefied gas safety and siting .
Washington , 1979. vii, 748 p. :   LC Card
80-601892   DDC 343.73/0967 19
KF27 .M434 1979e

United States. Congress. House. Committee on
Merchant Marine and Fisheries. Subcommittee
on Fisheries and Wildlife Conservation and the
Environment. Fisheries miscellaneous .
Washington , 1980. viii, 478 p. :   LC Card
81-600601   DDC 343.73/07692 347.3037692 19
KF27 .M447 1979g

United States. Congress. House. Committee on
Merchant Marine and Fisheries. Subcommittee
on Fisheries and Wildlife Conservation and the
Environment. Ocean dumping . Washington ,
1975- v. :   LC Card 75-603626
KF27 .M447 1975e

**United States. Congress. House. Committee on
Merchant Marine and Fisheries.
Subcommittee on Panama Canal.** Panama
Canal oversight : hearings before the
Subcommittee on the Panama Canal of the
Committee on Merchant Marine and Fisheries,
House of Representatives, Ninety-sixth
Congress, second session ... July 28, 1980 ...
March 17, 1980. Washington : U. S. Govt.
Print. Off., 1980. iii, 158 p. : forms ; 24 cm.
"Serial no. 96-38." LC Card 80-603322   DDC
353.0087/6444 19
*1. Panama Canal. 2. Panama Canal Treaties, 1977. 3.
Panama Canal - Environmental aspects. 4. United
States. Panama Canal Commission. I. Title.*
KF27 .M475 1980a

**United States. Congress. House. Committee on
Narcotics Abuse and Control, Select. see
United States. Congress. House. Select
Committee on Narcotics Abuse and Control.**

**United States. Congress. House. Committee on
Post Office and Civil Service.** (Old Catalog
form: United States. Post Office and Civil
Service, Committee on (House))Hearings
printed in 1978 and later are available only in
microform. Please consult the librarians in the
Economic and Public Affairs Division.
Implications of proposed reductions in Postal
Service appropriations : hearings before the
Committee on Post Office and Civil Service,
House of Representatives, Ninety-sixth
Congress, second session, March 26, April 17,
1980. Washington : U. S. Govt. Print. Off.,
1980. iii, 90 p. ; 24 cm. "Serial no. 96-80." LC
Card 80-602977   DDC 383/.4973 19
*1. United States. Postal Service - Appropriations and
expenditures. 2. Postal service - United States. I. Title.*
KF27 .P6 1980

Selection and oversight of administrative law
judges : hearings before the Committee on Post
Office and Civil Service, House of
Representatives, Ninety-sixth Congress, second
session, on H.R. 6768 ... April 24, May 6,
1980. Washington : U. S. Govt. Print. Off.,
1980. iii, 131 p. ; 24 cm. "Serial no. 96-79."
Includes bibliographical references.   LC Card
80-603065   DDC 342.73/0664 19
*1. Examiners (Administrative procedure) - United
States. I. Title.*
KF27 .P6 1980a

United States government policy and supporting
positions /. Washington , 1980. vii, 161 p. ;
    LC Card 80-604162   DDC 353.001/03 19
JK661 .U54

**United States. Congress House Committee on
Post Office and Civil Service. Postal
Personnel and Modernization, Subcommittee
on. see United States. Congress. House
Committee on Post Office and Civil Service.
Subcommittee on Postal Personnel and
Modernization.**

**United States. Congress. House. Committee on
Post Office and Civil Service. Subcommittee
on Census and Population.**
Briefing on implications of internal migration :
briefing before the Subcommittee on Census
and Population of the Committee on Post
Office and Civil Service, House of
Representatives, Ninety-sixth Congress, second
session, July 22, 1980. Washington : U. S.
Govt. Print. Off., 1980. iii, 42 p. : ill. ; 24 cm.
"Serial no. 96-100." LC Card 80-603710   DDC
304.8/2 19
*1. Migration, Internal - United States. 2. United States -
Census, 20th, 1980. I. Title.*
KF27 .P634 1980

Confidentiality of shippers' export declaration :
hearing before the Subcommittee on Census and
Population of the Committee on Post Office
and Civil Service, House of Representatives,
Ninety-sixth Congress, second session, on H.R.
6842 ... March 26, 1980. Washington : U. S.
Govt. Print. Off., 1980. iii, 62 p. ; 24 cm. "Serial
no. 96-75." LC Card 80-602741   DDC 343.73/0878
19
*1. Export controls - United States. 2. Customs
administration - United States. 3. Bills of lading -
United States. 4. Privacy, Right of - United States. I.
Title.*
KF27 .P632 1980

United States. Congress. House. Committee on
Government Operations. Commerce, Consumer,
and Monetary Affairs Subcommittee. Problems

441

GOVERNMENT PUBLICATIONS - U.S.: 1981

United States. Congress. House. Committee on Post Office and

with the 1980 census count . Washington , 1980. vi, 284 p. ; LC Card 80-604022 DDC 001.43/3 19
KF27 .G634 1980e

United States. Congress. House. Committee on Post Office and Civil Service. Subcommittee on Civil Service.
Civil service reform oversight--1980 : equal employment opportunity : hearing before the Subcommittee on the Civil Service of the Committee on Post Office and Civil Service, House of Representatives, Ninety-sixth Congress, second session, June 10, 1980. Washington : U. S. G.P.O., 1981. iv, 433 p. ; 24 cm. "Serial no. 96-104." Item 1022 LC Card 81-600955 DDC 353.001/04 19
1. Civil service reform - United States. 2. Civil serice - United States - Minority employment. 3. Women in the civil service - United States. 4. Affirmative action programs - United States. I. Title.
KF27 .P635 1980d

Civil service reform oversight, 1980--performance appraisal : hearings before the Subcommittee on the Civil Service of the Committee on Post Office and Civil Service, House of Representatives, Ninety-sixth Congress, second session, May 13, 15, 1980. Washington : U. S. Govt. Print. Off., 1980. iv, 335 p. : ill. ; 24 cm. "Serial no. 96-89." LC Card 80-603315 DDC 353.006 19
1. Civil service reform - United States. 2. United States - Officials and employees - Rating of. I. Title.
KF27 .P635 1980b

Civil service reform oversight, 1980--whistleblower : hearings before the Subcommittee on the Civil Service of the Committee on Post Office and Civil Service, House of Representatives, Ninety-sixth Congress, second session. ... Washington : U. S. Govt. Print. Off., 1980. iii, 330 p. ; 23 cm. Hearings held March 4-12, 1980. "Serial no. 96-74." LC Card 80-602092 DDC 353.001 19
1. Whistle blowing - United States. 2. Civil service - United States. I. Title.
KF27 .P635 1980

Energy Department violation of SES 120-day rule--the Tina Hobson case : hearing before the Subcommittee on Civil Service of the Committee on Post Office and Civil Service, House of Representatives, Ninety-seventh Congress, first session, March 9, 1981. Washington : U. S. G.P.O., 1981. iii, 90 p. ; 24 cm. "Serial no. 97-3." Item 1022-B, 1022-C (microfiche) LC Card 81-601878 DDC 353.87 19
1. Hobson, Tina. 2. United States. Dept. of Energy - Officials and employees. 3. Civil service - United States. I. Title.
KF27 .P635 1981

Personal assistants for handicapped federal employees : hearing before the Subcommittee on the Civil Service of the Committee on Post Office and Civil Service, House of Representatives, Ninety-sixth Congress, second session, on H.R. 7466 ... August 20, 1980. Washington : U. S. G.P.O., 1980. iii, 84 p. : ill. ; 24 cm. "Serial no. 96-102." LC Card 80-604075 DDC 342.73/068 347.30268
1. Physically handicapped - Services for - Law and legislation - United States. 2. United States - Officials and employees. 3. Physically handicapped - Employment - United States. I. Title.
KF27 .P635 1980c

United States. Congress. House. Committee on Post Office and Civil Service. Subcommittee on Compensation and Employee Benefits.
Conversion of nonappropriated fund employees to competitive service : hearing before the Subcommittee on Compensation and Employee Benefits of the Committee on Post Office and Civil Service, House of Representatives, Ninety-sixth Congress, second session, October 2, 1980. Washington : U. S. G.P.O., 1980. iii, 52 p. ; 24 cm. "Serial no. 96-110." LC Card 81-600627 DDC 353.001/23 19
1. United States - Officials and employees - Salaries, allowances, etc. I. Title.
KF27 .P638 1980l

Cost of living allowances (Virgin Islands and Puerto Rico) : hearings before the Subcommittee on Compensation and Employee Benefits of the Committee on Post Office and Civil Service, House of Representatives, Ninety-fifth Congress, second session, February

10 and 13, 1978. Washington : U. S. G.P.O., 1978. iii, 87 p. ; 24 cm. "Serial no. 95-71." LC Card 81-601487 DDC 353.001/232 19
1. United States - Officials and employees - Salaries, allowances, etc. - Cost of living adjustments - Puerto Rico. 2. United States - Officials and employees - Salaries, allowances, etc. - Cost of living adjustments - Virgin Islands of the United States. I. Title.
KF27 .P638 1978i

Delay in processing retirement claims : hearing before the Subcommittee on Compensation and Employee Benefits of the Committee on Post Office and Civil Service, House of Representatives, Ninety-sixth Congress, second session, April 22, 1980. Washington : U. S. Govt. Print. Off., 1980. iii, 88 p. : graphs ; 24 cm. "Serial no. 96-81." LC Card 80-602978 DDC 353.005 19
1. Civil service pensions - United States. I. Title.
KF27 .P638 1980d

Dental health care : hearing before the Subcommittee on Compensation and Employee Benefits of the Committee on Post Office and Civil Service, House of Representatives, Ninety-sixth Congress, second session, on H.R. 6077 ... June 26, 1980. Washington : U. S. Govt. Print. Off., 1980. iii, 175 p. : ill. ; 24 cm. "Serial no. 96-98." LC Card 80-603671 DDC 344.73/022 347.30422 19
1. Insurance, Government employees' dental - United States. I. Title.
KF27 .P638 1980j

Desirability and feasibility of universal social security coverage : hearing before the Subcommittee on Compensation and Employee Benefits of the Committee on Post Office and Civil Service, House of Representatives, Ninety-sixth Congress, second session, April 15, 1980. Washington : U. S. Govt. Print. Off., 1980. iii, 89 p. ; 24 cm. "Serial no. 96-86." LC Card 80-603299 DDC 353.0082/56 19
1. Social security - United States. 2. Civil service pensions - United States. I. Title.
KF27 .P638 1980i

Errors in health benefits enrollment : hearing before the Subcommittee on Compensation and Employee Benefits of the Committee on Post Office and Civil Service, House of Representatives, Ninety-sixth Congress, second session, May 15, 1980. Washington : U. S. Govt. Print. Off., 1980. iii, 95 p. ; ill. ; 24 cm. ("Serial no. 96-87.") LC Card 80-603020 DDC 353.001/234 19
1. Insurance, government employees' health - United States - Auditing and inspection. I. Title.
KF27 .P638 1980f

Executive level and congressional pay : hearing before the Subcommittee on Compensation and Employee Benefits of the Committee on Post Office and Civil Service, House of Representatives, Ninety-sixth Congress, second session, July 29, 1980. Washington : U. S. G.P.O., 1980. iii, 55 p. ; 24 cm. "Serial no. 96-97." LC Card 80-604034 DDC 353.001/23 19
1. Government executives - United States - Salaries, pensions, etc. 2. United States. Congress - Salaries, pensions, etc. I. Title.
KF27 .P638 1980k

Federal employee health benefits network program : hearing before the Subcommittee on Compensation and Employee Benefits of the Committee on Post Office and Civil Service, House of Representatives, Ninety-sixth Congress, second session, June 17, 1980. Washington : U. S. Govt. Print. Off., 1980. iii, 116 p. ; 23 cm. "Serial no. 96-95." LC Card 80-603334 DDC 353.001/234 19
1. Insurance, Government employees' health - United States. 2. Health maintenance organizations - United States. I. Title.
KF27 .P638 1980h

Federal pay continuity act : hearings before the Subcommittee on Compensation and Employee Benefits of the Committee on Post Office and Civil Service, House of Representatives, Ninety-sixth Congress, second session, on H.R. 5995 ... February 5, 7, April 30, 1980. Washington : U. S. Govt. Print. Off., 1980. iii, 128 p. ; 23 cm. "Serial no. 96-84." LC Card 80-602950 DDC 353.001/23 19
1. United States - Officials and employees - Salaries, allowances, etc. 2. United States - Appropriations and

expenditures. I. Title.
KF27 .P638 1980c

Incentive and performance awards program : hearing before the Subcommittee on Compensation and Employee Benefits of the Committee on Post Office and Civil Service, House of Representatives, Ninety-sixth Congress, second session, August 28, 1980. Washington : U. S. G.P.O., 1980. iii, 138 p. ; 24 cm. "Serial no. 96-108." Includes bibliographical references. LC Card 81-600582 DDC 353.001/47 19
1. Civil service - United States. 2. Performance awards - United States. 3. Suggestion systems - United States. I. Title.
KF27 .P638 1980m

Limit initial cost of living adjustments for certain annuitants : hearing before the Subcommittee on Compensation and Employee Benefits of the Committee on Post Office and Civil Service, House of Representatives, Ninety-sixth Congress, second session, on H.R. 6740 ... March 24, 1980. Washington : U. S. Govt. Print. Off., 1980. iii, 12 p. ; 24 cm. "Serial no. 96-82." LC Card 80-602737 DDC 342.73/0686/0262 19
1. Civil service pensions - Cost-of-living adjustments - United States. I. Title.
KF27 .P638 1980b

Minimum benefit provision of the disability retirement program : hearing before the Subcommittee on Compensation and Employee Benefits of the Committee on Post Office and Civil Service, House of Representatives, Ninety-sixth Congress, second session, February 26, 1980. Washington : U. S. Govt. Print. Off., 1980. iii, 35 p. ; 24 cm. "Serial no. 96-83." LC Card 80-602789 DDC 353.005 19
1. Civil service pensions - United States. 2. Insurance, Disability - United States. 3. Retired military personnel - Employment - United States. 4. Pensions, Military - United States. I. Title.
KF27 .P638 1980a

Retirement appeals, military leave, and quadrennial pay commission : hearing before the Subcommittee on Compensation and Employee Benefits of the Committee on Post Office and Civil Service, House of Representatives, Ninety-sixth Congress, second session, on H.R. 5837, H.R. 6065, H.R. 6373, March 4, 1980. Washington : U. S. Govt. Print. Off., 1980. iii, 20 p. ; 24 cm. "Serial no. 96-73." LC Card 80-602189 DDC 343.73/011 19
1. Pensions, Military - United States. 2. United States - Armed Forces - Leaves and furloughs - Law and legislation. 3. United States - Armed Forces - Pay, allowances, etc. - Law and legislation. I. Title.
KF27 .P638 1980

Voluntary retirements under the civil service retirement system : hearing before the Subcommittee on Compensation and Employee Benefits of the Committee on Post Office and Civil Service, House of Representatives, Ninety-sixth Congress, second session, June 19, 1980. Washington : U. S. Govt. Print. Off., 1980. iii, 72 p. ; 24 cm. "Serial no. 96-91." LC Card 80-603099 DDC 353.005 19
1. Civil service pensions - United States. 2. Civil service retirement - United States. 3. Retirement age - United States. I. Title.
KF27 .P638 1980g

Voluntary withholding of State income tax for civil service annuitants : hearing before the Subcommittee on Compensation and Employee Benefits of the Committee on Post Office and Civil Service, House of Representatives, Ninety-sixth Congress, second session, on H.R. 6372 ... June 5, 1980. Washington : U. S. Govt. Print. Off., 1980. iii, 24 p. ; 24 cm. "Serial no. 96-90." LC Card 80-603116 DDC 343.7305/242 19
1. Withholding tax - United States - States. 2. Civil service pensions - United States. I. Title.
KF27 .P638 1980e

Withholding state income tax for annuitants and amending student survivor annuity provisions : hearing before the Subcommittee on Compensation and Employee Benefits of the Committee on Post Office and Civil Service, House of Representatives, Ninety-seventh Congress, first session, on H.R. 2463 ... and H.R. 2465 ... March 24, 1981. Washington : U. S. G.P.O., 1981. iii, 31 p. ; 24 cm. "Serial no. 97-4." Item 1022-B, 1022-C (microfiche) LC Card 81-601887 DDC 343.7305/242 347.3035242 19

BIBLIOGRAPHIC GUIDE

United States. Congress. House. Committee on Post Office and

442

1. Civil service pensions - United States. 2. Withholding tax - United States - States. 3. Student aid - Law and legislation - United States. 4. Social security - Law and legislation - United States. I. Title.
KF27 .P638 1981

United States. Congress. House. Committee on Post Office and Civil Service. Subcommittee on Human Resources.
Basic workweek of federal firefighters : hearing before the Subcommittee on Human Resources of the Committee on Post Office and Civil Service, House of Representatives, Ninety-sixth Congress, first session, on H.R. 2748 ... September 14, 1979. Washington : U. S. G.P.O., 1980. iii, 60 p. : ill. ; 24 cm. "Serial no. 96-113." Includes bibliographical references. LC Card 80-604093 DDC 342.73/0686 347.32686 19
1. Fire fighters - Legal status, laws, etc. - United States. 2. Hours of labor - United States. 3. Civil service - United States. I. Title.
KF27 .P6456 1979f

Consultant Reform Act of 1980 : hearings before the Subcommittee on Human Resources of the Committee on Post Office and Civil Service, House of Representatives, Ninety-sixth Congress, second session, on H.R. 7674 ... August 25, 28, 1980. Washington : U. S. G.P.O., 1980. iii, 187 p. ; 24 cm. "Serial no. 96-106." LC Card 80-603792 DDC 346.73/023 347.30623 19
1. Government consultants - Legal status, laws, etc. - United States. I. Title.
KF27 .P6456 1980a

Department of Housing and Urban Development year-end spending : hearing before the Subcommittee on Human Resources of the Committee on Post Office and Civil Service, House of Representatives, Ninety-sixth Congress, second session, May 8, 1980. Washington : U. S. Govt. Print. Off., 1980. iii, 38 p. ; 24 cm. "Serial no. 96-92." LC Card 80-603115 DDC 353.0072/232 19
1. United States. Dept. of Housing and Urban Development - Appropriations and expenditures. I. Title.
KF27 .P6456 1980

United States. Congress. Senate. Committee on Governmental Affairs. Subcommittee on Civil Service and General Services. Federal consulting service contracts . Washington , 1980- v. ; LC Card 80-603411 DDC 353.09/3 19
KF26 .G6724 1980

United States. General Accounting Office. Government agencies need effective planning to curb unnecessary year-end spending . [Washington, D.C. , 1980] viii, 101 p. ; LC Card 80-603214 DDC 353.0072 19
HJ2051 .U55 1980

United States. Congress. House. Committee on Post Office and Civil Service. Subcommittee on Investigations.
Administrative law judge program of the Federal Trade Commission : hearing before the Subcommittee on Investigations of the Committee on Post Office and Civil Service, House of Representatives, Ninety-sixth Congress, second session, June 17, 1980. Washington : U. S. Govt. Print. Off., 1980. iii, 66 p. ; 24 cm. "Serial no. 96-94." LC Card 80-603347 DDC 342.73/0664 19
1. Examiners (Administrative procedure) - United States. 2. United States. Federal Trade Commission. I. Title.
KF27 .P646 1980a

Air traffic control : hearings before the Subcommittee on Investigations of the Committee on Post Office and Civil Service, House of Representatives, Ninety-sixth Congress, second session, September 30, 1980. Washington : U. S. G.P.O., 1980. iii, 60 p. ; 24 cm. "Serial 96-111." Item 1022 LC Card 81-600595 DDC 338.89/2813877364 19
1. Air traffic controllers - United States. I. Title.
KF27 .P646 1980c

Civilian technician program : hearings before the Subcommittee on Investigations of the Committee on Post Office and Civil Service, House of Representatives, Ninety-sixth Congress, second session, April 29, May 1, 1980. Washington : U. S. Govt. Print. Off., 1980. iii, 131 p. ; 24 cm. "Serial 96-85." LC Card 80-603291 DDC 355.3/7/0973 19
1. United States - Armed Forces - Reserves - Personnel

management. 2. United States - National Guard - Personnel management. I. Title.
KF27 .P646 1980b

Federal paperwork burden : hearing before the Subcommittee on Investigations of the Committee on Post Office and Civil Service, House of Representatives, Ninety-sixth Congress, first session, November 12, 1979. Washington : U. S. Govt. Print. Off., 1980. iii, 167 p. ; 24 cm. "Serial no. 96-70." LC Card 80-602093 DDC 353.0071/4 19
1. Government paperwork - United States. I. Title.
KF27 .P646 1979f

Federal personnel security background investigations : hearing before the Subcommittee on Investigations of the Committee on Post Office and Civil Service, House of Representatives, Ninety-sixth Congress, second session, March 25, 1980. Washington : U. S. Govt. Print. Off., 1980. iii, 42 p. ; 24 cm. "Serial no. 96-76." LC Card 80-602954 DDC 353.0013/242 19
1. Loyalty-security program, 1947-. I. Title.
KF27 .P646 1980

Sexual harassment in the Federal Government / Subcommittee on Investigations of the Committee on Post Office and Civil Service, House of Representatives, Ninety-sixth Congress, second session. Washington : U. S. Govt. Print. Off., 1980. iii, 32 p. ; 24 cm. "April 30, 1980." At head of title: 96th Congress, 2d session. Committee print, no. 96-11. LC Card 80-602591 DDC 353-001/04 19
1. Women in the civil service - United States. 2. Sexual harassment of women - United States. I. Title.
JK721 .U554 1980

United States. Congress. House. Committee on Post Office and Civil Service. Subcommittee on Postal Operations and Services.
Absentee ballot legislation : hearing before the Subcommittee on Postal Operations and Services of the Committee on Post Office and Civil Service, House of Representatives, Ninety-sixth Congress, second session ... March 13, 1980. Washington : U. S. Govt. Print. Off., 1980. iii, 94 p. ; 24 cm. Hearings held on H.R. 4759, 4773, 4843, and 5529. "Serial no. 96-77." LC Card 80-603110 DDC 324.6/5 19
1. Voting, Absent - United States. I. Title.
KF27 .P6674 1980

USPS role in registering male citizens : hearing before the Subcommittee on Postal Operations and Services of the Committee on Post Office and Civil Service, House of Representatives, Ninety-sixth Congress, second session, July 24, 1980. Washington : U. S. Govt. Print. Off., 1980. iii, 40 p. ; 23 cm. "Serial no. 96-101." LC Card 80-603591 DDC 355.2/2363/0973 19
1. Military service, Compulsory - United States. 2. United States Postal Service. I. Title.
KF27 .P6674 1980a

United States. Congress. House Committee on Post Office and Civil Service. Subcommittee on Postal Personnel and Modernization.
Electronic message service systems : hearings before the Subcommittee on Postal Personnel and Modernization of the Committee on Post Office and Civil Service, House of Representatives, Ninety-sixth Congress, second session .... Washington : U. S. Govt. Print. Off., 1980. iv, 317 p. : ill. ; 24 cm. Hearings held Jan. 29-Apr. 1, 1980. "Serial no. 96-78." LC Card 80-602988 DDC 384.1/4 19
1. Electronic mail systems - United States. 2. Postal service - United States - Equipment and supplies. 3. United States Postal Service. I. Title.
KF27 .P6677 1980

Equal employment opportunity and sexual harassment in the Postal Service : hearing before the Subcommittee on Postal Personnel and Modernization of the Committee on Post Office and Civil Service, House of Representatives, Ninety-sixth Congress, second session, October 27, 1980. Washington : U. S. G.P.O., 1981. iii, 85 p. : ill. ; 24 cm. "Serial no. 96-114." LC Card 81-602045 DDC 353.001/04 19
1. United States Postal Service - Employees. 2. Discrimination in employment - Texas. 3. Sex discrimination against women - Texas. 4. Sexual harassment of women - Texas. I. Title.
KF27 .P6677 1980d

Health and safety in the postal service : hearings before the Subcommittee on Postal

Personnel and Modernization of the Committee on Post Office and Civil Service, House of Representatives, Ninety-sixth Congress, second session, August 26 and September 30, 1980. Washington : U. S. G.P.O., 1981. iii, 132 p. ; 24 cm. "Serial no. 96-107." Item 1022 LC Card 81-601394 DDC 353.001/61 19
1. Postal service - United States - Safety measures. 2. Postal service - United States - Employees - Diseases and hygiene. I. Title.
KF27 .P6677 1980c

Improvement in administering false representation statute : hearing before the Subcommittee on Postal Personnel and Modernization of the Committee on Post Office and Civil Service, House of Representatives, second session, on H.R. 6307 ... May 7, 1980. Washington : U. S. Govt. Print. Off., 1980. iii, 18 p. ; 24 cm. "Serial no. 96-96." LC Card 80-603694 DDC 343.73/0992 347.303992 19
1. Fraud - United States. 2. Postal service - Law and legislation - United States. I. Title.
KF27 .P6677 1980b

Safety and health within U. S. Postal Service : joint hearings before the Subcommittee on Postal Personnel and Modernization of the Committee on Post Office and Civil Service and the Subcommittee on Health and Safety of the Committee on Education and Labor, House of Representatives, Ninety-sixth Congress, second session, January 7, 8, March 6, 1980. Washington : U. S. Govt. Print. Off., 1980. vi, 392 p. : ill. ; 24 cm. "Serial no. 96-71." LC Card 80-603078 DDC 363.1/193834973 19
1. Postal service - United States - Employees - Diseases and hygiene. 2. Postal service - United States - Safety measures. 3. United States Postal Service. I. United States. Congress. House. Committee on Education and Labor. Subcommittee on Health and Safety. II. Title.
KF27 .P6677 1980a

United States. Congress. House. Committee on Public Works and Transportation.
National Research Council. Transportation Research Board. Steering Committee for the Study of Methods to Increase Use of Safety Belts. Study of methods for increasing safety belt use . Washington , 1980. ix, 22 p. ; LC Card 80-602588 DDC 363.1/2572 19
TL159 .N34 1980

United States. Dept. of Transportation. A revised estimate of the cost of completing the national system of interstate and defense highways . Washington , 1981. iii, 27 p. : LC Card 81-601266 DDC 338.1/12/0973 19
HE355.3.E3 U54 1981

United States. Congress. House. Committee on Public Works and Transportation. Subcommittee on Aviation.
Adequacies of the air traffic control systems in the New York City area : hearing before the Subcommittee on Aviation of the Committee on Public Works and Transportation, House of Representatives, Ninety-sixth Congress, second session, August 8, 1980, at New York, N.Y. Washington : U. S. G.P.O., 1980. ii, 57 p. ; 1980. "96-66." Item 1024 LC Card 81-600821 DDC 363.1/2472 19
1. Air traffic control - New York metropolitan area. I. Title.
KF27 .P89624 1980p

Air cargo and passenger deregulation : hearings before the Subcommittee on Aviation of the Committee on Public Works and Transportation, House of Representatives, Ninety-sixth Congress, first session .... Washington : U. S. Govt. Print. Off., 1980. vi, 1154 p. : ill. ; 24 cm. "(96-38)" Hearings held July 25-Aug. 2, 1979. Includes bibliographical references. LC Card 80-602889 DDC 343.73/0978 19
1. Aeronautics, Commercial - United States - Passenger traffic. 2. Aeronautics, Commercial - United States - Freight. I. Title.
KF27 .P89624 1979h

Competition in international air cargo transportation : hearing before the Subcommittee on Aviation of the Committee on Public Works and Transportation, Ninety-sixth Congress, first session, on H.R. 5882 ... November 29, 1979. Washington : U. S. Govt. Print. Off., 1980. iii, 35 p. ; 24 cm. "96-28." LC Card 80-600920 DDC 343.73/0978 19
1. Aeronautics, Commercial - Law and legislation - United States. 2. Competition, International. 3.

GOVERNMENT PUBLICATIONS - U.S.: 1981

443   United States. Congress. House. Committee on Public Works and

Aeronautics, Commercial - United States - Freight. 4.
Air lines - United States - Rates. I. Title.
KF27 .P89624 1979f

DOT/FAA proposed new policy for airports in
the metropolitan Washington area : hearings
before the Subcommittee on Aviation of the
Committee on Public Works and
Transportation, House of Representatives,
Ninety-sixth Congress, second session, June 11,
12, and 19, 1980. Washington : U. S. G.P.O.,
1980. viii, 923 p. : ill. ; 24 cm. "96-53." Includes
bibliographical references.   LC Card 80-604030   DDC
387.7/4042/09753 19
1. Airports - Government policy - Washington
metropolitan area. 2. United States. Dept. of
Transportation. 3. United States. Federal Aviation
Administration. I. Title.
KF27 .P89624 1980n

Providing additional civil and criminal penalties
for aviation safety violations : hearings before
the Subcommittee on Aviation of the
Committee on Public Works and
Transportation, House of Representatives,
Ninety-sixth Congress, second session, on H.R.
7488 ... July 1 and 2, 1980. Washington : U. S.
G.P.O., 1980. iv, 314 p. ; 24 cm. "96-61." Item
1024   LC Card 81-600604   DDC 343.73/0975
347.303975 19
1. Aeronautics - Law and legislation - United States. 2.
Aeronautics - Law and legislation - United States -
Criminal provisions. I. Title.
KF27 .P89624 1980o

Safety of the air traffic control systems :
hearings before the Subcommittee on Aviation
of the Committee on Public Works and
Transportation, House of Representatives,
Ninety-sixth Congress, first session, December
6 and 11, 1979. Washington : U. S. Govt. Print.
Off., 1980. iv, 506 p. : ill. ; 23 cm. "96-39."   LC
Card 80-602811   DDC 363.1/2472 19
1. Air traffic control - United States. 2. Aeronautics -
United States - Safety measures. I. Title.
KF27 .P89624 1979i

To amend the Hazardous materials
transportation act and to amend the
Independent safety board act : joint hearing
before the Subcommittee on Aviation and the
Subcommittee on Surface Transportation of the
Committee on Public Works and
Transportation, House of Representatives,
Ninety-sixth Congress, second session, on H.R.
6937 ... H.R. 6938 ... April 22, 1980.
Washington : U. S. Govt. Print. Off., 1980. v,
97 p. ; 24 cm. "96-51."   LC Card 80-603697   DDC
343.73/093 347.30393 19
1. Hazardous substances - Transportation - Law and
legislation - United States. 2. United States. National
Transportation Safety Board - Appropriations and
expenditures. I. United States. Congress. House.
Committee on Public Works and Transportation.
Subcommittee on Surface Transportation. II. Title.
KF27 .P89624 1980j

To enhance the safety mission of the FAA :
hearings before the Subcommittee on Aviation
of the Committee on Public Works and
Transpotation, House of Representatives,
Ninety-sixth Congress, second session, on H.R.
6771 ... H.R. 351 ... H.R. 7850 ... August 20
and 21, 1980. Washington : U. S. G.P.O., 1980.
iv, 560 p. : ill. ; 24 cm. "96-62." Includes
bibliographical references.   LC Card 80-604032   DDC
343.73/097 347.30397 19
1. United States. Federal Aviation Administration. 2.
Aeronautics, Commercial - Law and legislation - United
States. 3. Air traffic rules - United States. 4. United
States. Air Safety Administration. I. Title.
KF27 .P89624 1980m

**United States. Congress. House. Committee on
Public Works and Transportation.
Subcommittee on Investigations and Review.**
Implementation of the Federal Water Pollution
Control Act, 1977 : (thermal pollution and
other water impacts from steam electric power
generation) : hearings before the Subcommittee
on Investigations and Review of the Committee
on Public Works and Transportation, U. S.
House of Representatives, Ninety-fifth
Congress, first session, April 19, 20, 21, 1977.
Washington : U. S. G.P.O., 1977. viii, 594 p. :
ill. ; 24 cm. "95-15."   LC Card 81-601587   DDC
353.0082/325 19
1. Steam power-plants - Environmental aspects - United
States. 2. Thermal pollution of rivers, lakes, etc. -

United States. I. Title.
KF27 .P89634 1977b

**United States. Congress. House. Committee on
Public Works and Transportation.
Subcommittee on Oversight and Review.**
Cabin safety : "SAFER Committee" update
(aircraft passenger seat structural design) :
hearings before the Subcommittee on Oversight
and Review of the Committee on Public Works
and Transportation, House of Representatives,
Ninety-sixth Congress, second session, June 3,
4, 5, and September 10, 1980. Washington : U.
S. G.P.O., 1980 [i.e. 1981] iv, 703 p. : ill. ; 24
cm. "96-60." Item 1024 Includes bibliographical
references.   LC Card 81-600989   DDC 629.134/45 19
1. Aeronautics - United States - Safety measures. 2.
Aircraft cabins. 3. Airplanes - Seats. I. Title.
KF27 .P89636 1980c

Commuter air safety : hearings before the
Subcommittee on Oversight and Review of the
Committee on Public Works and
Transportation, U. S. House of Representatives,
Ninety-sixth Congress, second session ....
Washington : U. S. Govt. Print. Off., 1980. iii,
202 p. ; 24 cm. "96-44." Hearings held Feb. 26-29,
1980.   LC Card 80-603469   DDC 363.1/2493/0973
19
1. Aeronautics - United States - Safety measures. 2. Air
lines, Local service - United States. I. Title.
KF27 .P89636 1980

Implementation of the Federal water pollution
control act (the Municipal Construction Grants
Program and the State Management Assistance
Program) : hearings before the Subcommittee
on Oversight and Review of the Committee on
Public Works and Transportation, U. S. House
of Representatives, Ninety-sixth Congress, first
session, October 30, 31, and November 1,
1979. Washington : U. S. Govt. Print. Off.,
1980. v, 1458 p. : ill. ; 23 cm. "96-41."   LC Card
80-603421   DDC 353.0082/325 19
1. Federal aid to water quality management - United
States. 2. Sewage disposal plants - United States -
Finance. I. Title.
KF27 .P89636 1979d

Mobility for Americans in an era of increasing
energy, environmental, and financial
constraints : hearings before the Subcommittee
on Oversight and Review of the Committee on
Public Works and Transportation, U. S. House
of Representatives, Ninety-sixth Congress,
second session .... Washington : U. S. Govt.
Print. Off., 1980. v, 578 p. : ill. ; 24 cm.
Hearings held in various cities Jan. 7-Feb. 21, 1980.
"96-48."   LC Card 80-603419   DDC 380.5/0973 19
1. Urban transportation - United States. 2. Urban
transportation policy - United States. I. Title.
KF27 .P89636 1980a

**United States. Congress. House. Committee on
Public Works and Transportation.
Subcommittee on Public Buildings and
Grounds.**
Federal Protective Service : hearing before the
Subcommittee on Public Buildings and Grounds
of the Committee on Public Works and
Transportation, House of Representatives,
Ninety-sixth Congress, first session, on H.R.
2308 ..., H.R. 3284 ... October 11, 1979.
Washington : U. S. G.P.O., 1980. iv, 174 p. :
ill. ; 24 cm.   LC Card 80-603638   DDC 344.73/052
347.30452 19
1. United States. Federal Protective Service. 2. United
States - Government property. I. Title.
KF27 .P8964 1979d

Public building needs : hearings before the
Subcommittee on Public Buildings and Grounds
of the Committee on Public Works and
Transportation, House of Representatives,
Ninety-sixth Congress, second session ....
Washington : U. S. G.P.O., 1980. vi, 430 p. :
ill. ; 24 cm. "96-64." Hearings held in various cities,
Feb. 15-July 24, 1980.   LC Card 81-600628   DDC
353.0086/2 19
1. United States - Public buildings. I. Title.
KF27 .P8964 1980

Review of Title V of the National energy
conservation policy act : hearings before the
Subcommittee on Public Buildings and Grounds
of the Committee on Public Works and
Transportation, House of Representatives,
Ninety-sixth Congress, first session, September
26, 27, 1979. Washington : U. S. Govt. Print.
Off., 1980. iv, 240 p. : ill. ; 24 cm. "(96-33)"   LC

Card 80-601868   DDC 346.7304/67916/0262 19
1. Energy conservation - Law and legislation - United
States. 2. Solar energy - Law and legislation - United
States. 3. United States - Public buildings - Heating and
ventilation. 4. United States - Public buildings - Energy
conservation. I. Title.
KF27 .P8964 1979b

To amend the National Visitor Center Facilities
Act of 1968 : hearing before the Subcommittee
on Public Buildings and Grounds of the
Committee on Public Works and
Transportation, House of Representatives,
Ninety-sixth Congress, first session, on H.R.
3927 ... May 8, 1979. Washington : U. S.
G.P.O., 1980. iii, 34 p. : ill. ; 23 cm. "96-69."
Item 1024   LC Card 81-600581   DDC 344.73/09
347.3049 19
1. National Visitor Center. I. Title.
KF27 .P8964 1979e

**United States. Congress. House. Committee on
Public Works and Transportation.
Subcommittee on Surface Transportation.**
Cargo security : hearing before the
Subcommittee on Surface Transportation of the
Committee on Public Works and
Transportation, House of Representatives,
Ninety-sixth Congress, second session, on
H.R.655 ... December 3, 1980. Washington : U.
S. G.P.O., 1981. iv, 221 p. : ill. ; 23 cm. "96-70."
Item 1024 Bibliography: p. 85-87.   LC Card 81-601342
DDC 343.73/0932 347.303932 19
1. Freight and freightage - Law and legislation - United
States. I. Title.
KF27 .P8966 1980e

Coal pipeline carriers : hearings before the
Subcommittee on Surface Transportation of the
Committee on Public Works and
Transportation, House of Representatives,
Ninety-sixth Congress, first session, November
8, 9, 27, 1979. Washington : U. S. Govt. Print.
Off., 1980. iv, 393 p. : ill. ; 23 cm. Includes
bibliographical references.   LC Card 80-602973   DDC
343.73/093 19
1. Coal - Pipe lines - Law and legislation - United
States. 2. Right of way - United States. I. Title.
KF27 .P8966 1979d

Commercial motor carrier safety : hearing
before the Subcommittee on Surface
Transportation of the Committee on Public
Works and Tranksportation, House of
Representatives, Ninety-sixth Congress, second
session, August 4,1980, at Pittsburgh, Pa.
Washington : U. S. G.P.O., 1980. iv, 218 p. :
ill. ; 24 cm. "(96-57)" Bibliography: p. 157.   LC Card
80-603819   DDC 343.73/093 347.30393 19
1. Transportation, Automotive - United States - Safety
measures. I. Title.
KF27 .P8966 1980c

Impact of the President's new budget
recommendation on transportation program
funding levels : hearing before the
Subcommittee on Surface Transportation of the
Committee on Public Works and
Transportation, Ninety-sixth Congress, second
session, April 1, 1980. Washington : U. S. Govt. Print. Off.,
1980. iii, 29 p. ; 24 cm. "(96-54)"   LC Card
80-603695   DDC 353.0072/236875 19
1. Federal aid to transportation - United States. 2.
Budget - United States. I. Title.
KF27 .P8966 1980b

Proposed third bridge crossing on the Columbia
River between Vancouver, Washington, and
Portland, Oregon : hearing before the
Subcommittee on Surface Transportation of the
Committee on Public Works and
Transportation, Ninety-sixth Congress, second
session, February 2, 1980. Washington : U. S.
Govt. Print. Off., 1980. iii, 89 p. : ill. ; 24 cm.
"96-55."   LC Card 80-603449   DDC
388.1/32/0979549 19
1. Vancouver, Wash. - Bridges. 2. Portland, Or. -
Bridges. 3. Columbia River - Bridges. I. Title.
KF27 .P8966 1980

Surface transportation act of 1980 : hearings
before the Subcommittee on Surface
Transportation of the Committee on Public
Works and Transportation, House of
Representatives, Ninety-sixth Congress, second
session, on H.R. 6417 ... H.R. 6890 ... H.R.
6964 ... March 26, April 16 and 21, 1980.
Washington : U. S. Govt. Print. Off., 1980. v,
464 p. : ill. ; 24 cm. "(96-52)"   LC Card 80-603733

BIBLIOGRAPHIC GUIDE

United States. Congress. House. Committee on Public Works and

444

DDC 343.73/0982 347.303982 19
1. Local transit - Law and legislation - United States. 2. Highway law - United States. 3. Car pools - Law and legislation - United States. I. Title.
KF27 .P8966 1980a

Transportation of hazardous materials through city streets : hearing before the Subcommittee on Surface Transportation of the Committee on Public Works and Transportation, House of Representatives, Ninety-sixth Congress, second session, on H.R. 792 ... May 27, 1980, at New York, N.Y. Washington : U. S. G.P.O., 1980. iv, 220 p. : ill. ; 24 cm. "96-68." Includes bibliographical references. LC Card 81-600847 DDC 343.73/0942 347.303942 19
1. Radioactive substances - Transportation - Law ad legislation - United States. 2. Highway law - United States. I. Title.
KF27 .P8966 1980d

United States. Congress. House. Committee on Public Works and Transportation. Subcommittee on Aviation. To amend the Hazardous materials transportation act and to amend the Independent safety board act . Washington , 1980. v, 97 p. ; LC Card 80-603697 DDC 343.73/093 347.30393 19
KF27 .P89624 1980j

United States. Congress. House. Committee on Public Works and Transportation. Subcommittee on Water Resources.
Hazardous chemicals under the Federal Water Pollution Control Act : hearings before the Subcommittee on Water Resources of the Committee on Public Works and Transportation, House of Representatives, Ninety-sixth Congress, second session, April 15, 16, and 17, 1980. Washington : U. S. G.P.O., 1980. iv, 385 p. : ill. ; 24 cm. "96-56." LC Card 80-603815 DDC 344.73/046343 347.30446343 19
1. Liability for hazardous substances pollution damages - United States. 2. Liability for water pollution damages - United States. 3. Hazardous substances - Law and legislation - United States. 4. Hazardous wastes - Law and legislation - United States. I. Title.
KF27 .P8968 1980a

Industrial cost recovery : hearing before the Subcommittee on Water Resources of the Committee on Public Works and Transportation, House of Representatives, Ninety-sixth Congress, second session, on H.R. 6667 ... March 12, 1980. Washington : U. S. Govt. Print. Off., 1980. iv, 447 p. : ill. ; 23 cm. "96-42." LC Card 80-603642 DDC 344.73/046343 19
1. Water treatment plants - Law and legislation - United States. 2. Water - Pollution - Law and legislation - United States. 3. Water treatment plants - United States - Finance. I. Title.
KF27 .P8968 1980

To amend the Disaster Relief Act : hearing before the Subcommittee on Water Resources of the Committee on Public Works and Transportation, House of Representatives, Ninety-sixth Congress, second session, on H.R. 6863 ... March 26, 1980. Washington : U. S. G.P.O., 1980. iii, 62 p. ; 24 cm. LC Card 80-604102 DDC 344.73/0534 347.304534 19
1. Disaster relief - United States. I. Title.
KF27 .P8968 1980b

United States. Congress. House. Committee on Public Works. Subcommittee on Flood Control and Internal Development. River basin monetary authorizations. Disaster relief act amendments. Hearing, Ninety-second Congress, first session. November 30, 1971. Washington , U. S. Govt. Print. Off., 1972. iii, 50 p. 24 cm. "(92-23)" Hearing on S. 2887; H. R. 6269; H. R. 6834 and S. 1237; H. J. Res. 893. Supt. of Docs. no.: Y 4.P96/11: 92-23 LC Card 72-600616
1. Water resources development - Law and legislation - United States. 2. Rivers - United States. 3. Disaster relief - United States. I. Title. II. Title: Disaster relief act amendments. **NYPL [JLE 81-118]**

United States. Congress. House. Committee on Rules. Subcommittee on Rules of the House.
The National Publications Act of 1980 : hearings before the Subcommittee on Rules of the House of the Committee on Rules, House of Representatives, Ninety-sixth Congress, second session, on H.R. 5424 ... Mar 14 and 21, 1980. Washington : U. S. G.P.O., 1980. iii, 126 p. ; 24 cm. Item 1025 Includes bibliographical

references. LC Card 81-600621 DDC 343.73/0998 347.303998 19
1. United States. Government Printing Office. 2. Printing, Public - United States. 3. United States - Government publications. 4. Government information - United States. I. Title.
KF27 .R8737 1980

United States. Congress. House. Committee on Rules. Subcommittee on the Rules and Organization of the House. Excerpts from hearings on congressional procedures : report of the Subcommittee on the Rules and Organization of the House, Committee on Rules, U. S. House of Representatives, 95th Congress, second session. Washington : U. S. G.P.O., 1979. iii, 89 p. ; 24 cm. At head of title: 95th Congress, 2d session. Committee print. Subcommittee print no. 96-01. Includes index. LC Card 79-601693 DDC 328.73/05 19
1. United States. Congress. House - Rules and practice. I. Title.
KF4992 .U55

United States. Congress. House. Committee on Science and Technology. Hearings printed in 1978 and later are available only in microform. Please consult the librarians in the Economic and Public Affairs Division.
Alcohol fuels : joint hearings before the Committee on Science and Technology and the Committee on Agriculture, U. S. House of Representatives, Ninety-sixth Congress, second session, October 2, 1980. Washington : U. S. G.P.O., 1980 [i.e. 1981] v, 105 p. : ill. ; 24 cm. "No. 176 (Committee on Science and Technology)." "Serial no. 96-DDDD (Committee on Agriculture)." Item 1025-A LC Card 81-601361 DDC 338.4/7662669 19
1. Alcohol as fuel - Government policy - United States. I. United States. Congress. House. Committee on Agriculture. II. Title.
KF27 .S39 1980h

Background readings on science, technology, and energy R. & D. in Japan and China /. Washington , 1981. xii, 499 p. : LC Card 81-600676 DDC 609.52 19
Q127.J3 B3

H.R. 7178 (superseded by H.R. 7689), the Research and development authorization estimates act : hearings before the Committee on Science and Technology, U. S. House of Representatives, Ninety-sixth Congress, second session, May 30, June 3, 4, 1980. Washington : U. S. Govt. Print. Off., 1980. iii, 321 p. : ill. ; 24 cm. "No. 124." LC Card 80-603641 DDC 346.73/023 347.30623 19
1. Federal aid to research - United States. 2. Research and development contracts, Government - United States. 3. Science and state - United States. I. Title.
KF27 .S39 1980c

Innovation : startup, growth, and survival of small, new technology firms : joint hearing before the Committee on Science and Technology and the Committee on Small Business, U. S. House of Representatives and the Select Committee on Small Business, United States Senate, Ninety-sixth Congress, first session, November 1, 1979. Washington : U. S. Govt. Print. Off., 1980. v, 228 p. ; 23 cm. "No. 93." LC Card 80-602110 DDC 338/.06 19
1. New business enterprises - United States. 2. Small business - United States. 3. Technological innovations - United States. 4. Industry and state - United States. I. United States. Congress. House. Committee on Small Business. II. United States. Congress. Senate. Select Committee on Small Business. III. Title.
KF27 .S39 1979f

National Academy of Sciences report : Energy in transition, 1985-2010 : hearing before the Committee on Science and Technology, U. S. House of Representatives, Ninety-sixth Congress, second session, January 25, 1980. Washington : U. S. Govt. Print. Off., 1980. iii, 147 p. : ill. ; 24 cm. "No. 119." Includes bibliographical references. LC Card 80-603067 DDC 333.79/0973 19
1. National Research Council. Committee on Nuclear and Alternative Energy Systems. Energy in transition, 1985-2010. 2. Energy policy - United States. 3. Power resources - United States. I. Title. II. Title: Energy in transition, 1985-2010.
KF27 .S39 1980b

Outlooks from Nobel Prize winners : hearing before the Committee on Science and

Technology, U. S. House of Representatives, Ninety-sixth Congress, second session, November 19, 1980. Washington : U. S. G.P.O., 1981. iii, 66 p. : ill. ; 24 cm. "No. 177." Item 1025-A LC Card 81-601401 DDC 607/.2/73 19
1. Research - United States. 2. Nobel prizes. I. Title.
KF27 .S39 1980i

Oversight of energy development in Africa and the Middle East : report to the Committee on Science and Technology, U. S. House of Representatives, Ninety-sixth Congress, second session. Washington : U. S. Govt. Print. Off. : for sale by the Supt. of Docs., U. S. Govt Print Off., 1980. v, 132 p. : ill. ; 24 cm. At head of title: Committee print. "Serial QQ." LC Card 80-602581 DDC 333.79/15/096 19
1. Energy development - Africa. 2. Energy development - Near East. I. Title.
TJ163.25.A4 U54 1980

Pilot aging study : hearing before the Subcommittee on Investigations and Oversight of the Committee on Science and Technology, U. S. House of Representatives, Ninety-sixth Congress, second session, September 23, 1980. Washington : U. S. G.P.O., 1980 [i.e. 1981] iii, 63 p. ; 24 cm. "No. 173." Item 1025-A LC Card 81-601375 DDC 331.25 19
1. Air pilots - United States. 2. Age and employment - United States. I. Title.
KF27 .S3975 1980a

Posture hearings (EPA and NOAA) : hearing before the Committee on Science and Technology, U. S. House of Representatives, Ninety-sixth Congress, second session, January 30, 1980. Washington : U. S. G.P.O., 1980. iii, 70 p. ; 24 cm. "No. 143." Includes bibliographical references. LC Card 80-604052 DDC 353.0082/321 19
1. United States. Environmental Protection Agency. 2. United States. National Oceanic and Atmospheric Administration. I. Title.
KF27 .S39 1980e

Posture hearings (NASA and FAA) : hearing before the Committee on Science and Technology, U. S. House of Representatives, Ninety-sixth Congress, second session, January 29, 1980. Washington : U. S. Govt. Print. Off., 1980. iii, 107 p. ; 24 cm. "No. 112." LC Card 80-602953 DDC 353.0085/6 19
1. United States. National Aeronautics and Space Administration. 2. United States. Federal Aviation Administration. I. Title.
KF27 .S39 1980

Posture hearings (NSF, NBS, and FEMA) : hearing before the Committee on Science and Technology, U. S. House of Representatives, Ninety-sixth Congress, second session, January 30, 1980. Washington : U. S. G.P.O., 1980. iii, 200 p. ; 24 cm. "No. 138." LC Card 80-604103 DDC 353.008 19
1. National Science Foundation (U. S.). 2. United States. National Bureau of Standards. 3. United States. Federal Emergency Management Agency. I. Title.
KF27 .S39 1980f

Seminar on Research, Productivity, and the National Economy, U. S. House of Representatives, 1980. Seminar on Research, Productivity, and the National Economy . Washington , 1980. v, 111 p. : LC Card 80-603648 DDC 338/.06 19
KF27 .S39 1980d

Staff study on management and cost issues associated with construction of the CRESAP coal liquefaction facility : prepared for the Committee on Science and Technology, U. S. House of Representatives, Ninety-fifth Congress, second session. Washington : U. S. Govt. Print. Off., 1978. vii, 348 p. : ill. ; 24 cm. (Oversight . v. 4) At head of title: Committee print. "Serial NN." LC Card 79-601594 DDC 333.79/0973 s 338.4/76626622/0975416 19
1. Coal liquefaction - West Virginia. I. Series: United States. Congress. House. Committee on Science and Technology. Subcommittee on Fossil and Nuclear Energy Research, Development and Demonstration. Oversight , v. 4. II. Title.
KF27 .S397 1978 vol. 4 TP352

Technology trade : joint hearings before the Committee on Science and Technology and the Committee on Interstate and Foreign Commerce and the Subcommittee on International Trade, Investment, and Monetary

GOVERNMENT PUBLICATIONS - U.S.: 1981

445   United States. Congress. House. Committee on Science and

Policy of the Committee on Banking, Finance, and Urban Affairs, U. S. House of Representatives, and the House Task Force on Industrial Innovation, Ninety-sixth Congress, second session, June 24, 25, 26, 1980. Washington : U. S. G.P.O., 1980. vii, 687 p. : ill. ; 24 cm. "No. 149." "Serial no. 96-197." "Serial no. 96-70." Bibliography: p. 669-687.   LC Card 80-604020   DDC 338.973 19
1. Technological innovations - United States. 2. United States - Commercial policy. 3. Competition, International. I. United States. Congress. House. Committee on Interstate and Foreign Commerce. II. United States. Congress. House. Committee on Banking, Finance and Urban Affairs. Subcommittee on International Trade, Investment and Monetary Policy. III. United States. Congress. House. Task Force on Industrial Innovation. IV. Title.
KF27 .S39 1980g

United States. Library of Congress. Congressional Research Service. Alternative breeding cycles for nuclear power . Washington , 1980. xx, 124 p. :   LC Card 80-603560   DDC 333.79/24/0973 19
TK9203.B7 U53 1980

Wydler, John W. Oversight of energy development in northern Europe . Washington , 1980. v, 45 p. :   LC Card 80-603051   DDC 333.79/24 19
TJ163.25.E853 W93

Wydler, John W. Oversight of energy development in South America . Washington , 1980. v, 167 p. :   LC Card 80-603265   DDC 333.79/098 19
TJ163.25.S65 W92

1981 DOE authorization : hearing before the Committee on Science and Technology, U. S. House of Representatives, Ninety-sixth Congress, second session, January 31, 1980. Washington : U. S. Govt. Print. Off., 1980- v. ; 24 cm. "No. 108." LC Card 80-602945   DDC 353.0072/236823 19
1. United States. Dept. of Energy - Appropriations and expenditures. I. Title.
KF27 .S39 1980a

United States. Congress. House. Committee on Science and Technology. Subcommittee on Advanced Energy Technologies and Energy Conservation Research, Development, and Demonstration.
The Economic impact of energy conservation /. Washington , 1979- v. <3 > :   LC Card 80-603982   DDC 333.79/16/0973 19
TJ163.4.U6 E26

Societal aspects of hydrogen energy systems /. Washington , 1979. vii, 161 p. :   LC Card 80-602232   DDC 338.4/766581/0973 19
TP359.H8 S58

Workshop on Energy Conservation in Cities, Library of Congress, 1978. Energy conservation in cities /. Washington , 1979. vii, 117 p. :   LC Card 80-602834   DDC 333.79/16/0973 19
TJ163.4.U6 W67 1978

United States. Congress. House. Committee on Science and Technology. Subcommittee on Energy Development and Applications.
Advanced coal combustion systems : hearings before the Subcommittee on Energy Development and Applications of the Committee on Science and Technology, U. S. House of Representatives, Ninety-sixth Congress, second session, September 16, 17, 1980. Washington : U. S. G.P.O., 1980 [i.e. 1981] iv, 334 p. : ill. ; 24 cm. "No. 162." Item 1025-A Bibliography: p. 317.   LC Card 81-600951   DDC 338.4/76214023 19
1. Coal - Combustion. 2. Coal - Combustion - Environmental aspects - United States. I. Title.
KF27 .S3934 1980k

Anthracite mining and utilization : hearings before the Subcommittee on Energy Development and Applications of the Committee on Science and Technology, U. S. House of Representatives, Ninety-sixth Congress, second session, June 9, September 4, October 2, 1980. Washington: U. S. G.P.O., c1981. iv, 518 p. : ill. ; 24 cm. "No. 160." Item 1025-A Bibliography: p. 499.   LC Card 81-600964   DDC 333.8/22 19
1. Anthracite coal - Pennsylvania. 2. Anthracite coal - Northeastern States. 3. Energy policy - United States. I.

Title.
KF27 .S3934 1980i

Energy conservation in buildings : hearing before the Subcommittee on Energy Development and Applications of the Committee on Science and Technology, U. S. House of Representatives, Ninety-sixth Congress, second session, September 25, 1980. Washington : U. S. G.P.O., 1980 [i.e. 1981] iii, 140 p. : ill. ; 24 cm. "No. 171." Item 1025-A   LC Card 81-601183   DDC 333.79 19
1. Buildings - United States - Energy conservation. 2. Energy conservation - United States. I. Title.
KF27 .S3934 1980l

Energy from municipal solid wastes : report / prepared for the Subcommittee on Energy Development and Applications of the Committee on Science and Technology, U. S. House of Representatives, Ninety-sixth Congress, second session. Washington : U. S. Govt. Print. Off. : for sale by the Supt. of Docs., U. S. Govt. Print. Off., 1980. v, 26 p. ; 24 cm. At head of title: Committee print. "Serial UU." Bibliography: p. 24-26.   LC Card 80-603276   DDC 662/.8 19
1. Waste products as fuel. I. Title.
TP360 .U55 1980

Florida's renewable energy potential : hearing before the Subcommittee on Energy Development and Applications of the Committee on Science and Technology, U. S. House of Representatives, Ninety-sixth Congress, second session, May 16, 1980. Washington : U. S. G.P.O., 1980 [i.e. 1981] iii, 226 p. : ill. ; 23 cm. "No. 166." Item 1025-A Includes bibliographical references.   LC Card 81-600971   DDC 333.7/09759 19
1. Renewable energy sources - Florida. 2. Energy development - Florida. I. Title.
KF27 .S3934 1980f

H.R. 4382--Energy Management Partnership Act : joint hearings before the Subcommittee on Energy Development and Applications of the Committee on Science and Technology and the Subcommittee on Energy and Power of the Committee on Interstate and Foreign Commerce, U. S. House of Representatives, Ninety-sixth Congress, first and second sessions .... Washington : U. S. G.P.O., 1980- v. <1, 3> : ill. ; 24 cm. Hearings held Oct. 31, 1979-<May 13, 1980> Vol. 3: "Hearing before the Subcommittee on Energy Research and Production of the Committee on Science and Technology ... May 13, 1980." "No. 151" (v. 1) "No. 133" (v. 3) "Serial no. 96-201." LC Card 80-604116   DDC 346.7304/679 347.3064679 19
1. Energy conservation - Law and legislation - United States. 2. Energy development - Law and legislation - United States. 3. Energy policy - United States. 4. Federal government - United States. I. United States. Congress. House. Committee on Interstate and Foreign Commerce. Subcommittee on Energy and Power. II. United States. Congress. House. Committee on Science and Technology. Subcommittee on Energy Research and Productions. III. Title. IV. Title: Energy Management Partnership Act.
KF27 .S3934 1979n

H.R. 5428, Biomass research and development act : hearing before the Subcommittee on Energy Development and Applications of the Committee on Science and Technology, U. S. House of Representatives, Ninety-sixth Congress, first session, November 15, 1979. Washington : U. S. Govt. Print. Off. ; for sale by the Supt. of Docs., U. S. Govt. Print. Off., 1980. iii, 194 p. : ill. ; 24 cm. "No. 63."   LC Card 80-601296   DDC 346.7304/6953 19
1. Biomass energy - Law and legislation - United States. I. Title.
KF27 .S3934 1979g

H.R. 7474 : ocean thermal energy conversion : hearing before the Subcommittee on Energy Development and Applications of the Committee on Science and Technology, U. S. House of Representatives, Ninety-sixth Congress, second session, June 5, 1980. Washington : U. S. G.P.O., 1980 [i.e. 1981] iii, 68 p. : ill. ; 24 cm. "No. 163." Item 1025-A   LC Card 81-600876   DDC 346.7304/68 347.306468 19
1. Ocean thermal power plants - Law and legislation - United States. I. Title. II. Title: Ocean thermal energy

conversion.
KF27 .S3934 1980j

Industrial energy conservation : hearing before the Subcommittee on Energy Development and Applications of the Committee on Science and Technology, U. S. House of Representatives, Ninety-sixth Congress, first session, September 11, 1979. Washington : U. S. Govt. Print. Off. : for sale by the Supt. of Docs., U. S. Govt. Print. Off., 1979 [i.e. 1980] iii, 323 p. : ill. ; 24 cm. (Its Oversight. v. 10) "No 49." Bibliography: p. 312-313.   LC Card 80-602230   DDC 333.79/16/0973 19
1. Energy conservation - United States. 2. United States - Industries - Energy conservation. I. Title. II. Series.
KF27 .S3934 1979l

Jelinek, Robert Vincent, 1926- Costs of synthetic fuels in relation to oil prices . Washington , 1981. xiii, 129 p. :   LC Card 81-601665   DDC 338.4/366266/0973 19
HD9564 .J44

Municipal waste-to-energy act : hearing before the Subcommittee on Energy Development and Applications of the Committee on Science and Technology, U. S. House of Representatives, Ninety-sixth Congress, second session, March 11, 1980. Washington : U. S. Govt. Print. Off., 1980. iii, 218 p. : ill. ; 24 cm. "No. 122."   LC Card 80-603352   DDC 344.73/04622 19
1. Refuse as fuel - Law and legislation - United States. I. Title.
KF27 .S3934 1980a

Oversight : environmental impact statement on solvent refined coal : hearing before the Subcommittee on Energy Development and Applications of the Committee on Science and Technology, U. S. House of Representatives, Ninety-sixth Congress, second session, September 19, 1980. Washington : U. S. G.P.O., 1980 [i.e. 1981] iii, 234 p. : ill. ; 24 cm. "No. 156." Item 1025-A Includes bibliographical references.   LC Card 81-600865   DDC 338.1/7665772 19
1. Coal liquefaction - Environmental aspects - United States. 2. Coal gasification - Environmental aspects - United States. 3. Synthetic fuels industry - Environmental aspects - United States. I. Title. II. Title: Environmental impact statement on solvent refined coal.
KF27 .S3934 1980g

Oversight, alcohol fuels : hearing before the Subcommittee on Energy Development and Applications of the Committee on Science and Technology, U. S. House of Representatives, Ninety-sixth Congress, second session, February 22, 1980. Washington : U. S. Govt. Print. Off., 1980. iii, 115 p. : ill. ; 23 cm. "[No. 125]" Includes bibliographical references.   LC Card 80-603693   DDC 338.4/7662669 19
1. Alcohol as fuel - Government policy - United States. 2. Gasohol - Government policy - United States. I. Title.
KF27 .S3934 1980d

Oversight--biomass : hearing before the Subcommittee on Energy Development and Applications of the Committee on Science and Technology, U. S. House of Representatives, Ninety-sixth Congress, second session, March 10, 1980. Washington : U. S. Govt. Print. Off., 1980. iii, 175 p. : ill. ; 24 cm. "No. 116." Includes bibliographical references.   LC Card 80-603030   DDC 338.4/76628 19
1. Biomass energy - United States. I. Title.
KF27 .S3934 1980

Oversight, DOE solar and conservation programs : hearings before the Subcommittee on Energy Development and Applications of the Committee on Science and Technology, U. S. House of Representatives, Ninety-sixth Congress, second session, June 12, 1980 (the President's solar goal), September 9, 1980 (energy conservation--GAO report). Washington : U. S. G.P.O., 1980. iii, 210 p. : ill. ; 24 cm. "No. 157."   LC Card 81-600834   DDC 353.0082/3 19
1. Solar energy - Government policy - United States. 2. Energy conservation - Government policy - United States. 3. United States. Dept. of Energy. I. Title.
KF27 .S3934 1980e

Oversight, Western solar energy activities : hearing before the Subcommittee on Energy Development and Applications of the

BIBLIOGRAPHIC GUIDE

United States. Congress. House. Committee on Science and

446

Committee on Science and Technology, U. S. House of Representatives, Ninety-sixth Congress, second session, January 3, 1980. Washington : U. S. Govt. Print. Off., 1980. iii, 127 p. ; 24 cm. "No. 123." LC Card 80-603333 DDC 333.79/23/0978 19
1. Solar energy - The West. I. Title.
KF27 .S3934 1980b

Regional solar energy centers and the Solar Energy Research Institute : staff report / prepared for the Subcommittee on Energy Development and Applications of the Committee on Science and Technology, U. S. House of Representatives, Ninety-sixth Congress, second session. Washington : U. S. Govt. Print. Off., 1980. v, 23 p. ; 24 cm. At head of title: Committee print. "Serial WW." "July 1980." LC Card 80-603269 DDC 333.79/23/072073 19
1. Solar energy research - United States. 2. Solar Energy Research Institute. I. Title.
TJ810 .U57 1980

Solar photovoltaic program : hearing before the Subcommittee on Energy Development and Applications of the Committee on Science and Technology, U. S. House of Representatives, Ninety-sixth Congress, second session, February 29, 1980. Washington : U. S. Govt. Print. Off., 1980. iii, 161 p. : ill. ; 24 cm. (Its Oversight) "No. 135." LC Card 80-603425 DDC 338.4/762131244/0973 19
1. Photovoltaic power generation - Government policy - United States. 2. Solar energy research - Government policy - United States. I. Title. II. Series.
KF27 .S3934 1980c

United States. Congress. House. Committee on Foreign Affairs. Subcommittee on International Economic Policy and Trade. International energy development assistance programs . Washingon , 1981. v, 120 p. ; LC Card 81-601471 DDC 333.79/15/091724 19
KF27 .F6465 1980f

United States. Congress. House. Committee on Science and Technology. Subcommittee on Energy Research and Production. H.R. 7336 . Washington , 1981. iii, 385 p. : LC Card 81-601148 DDC 343.73/0772 347.303772 19
KF27 .S3936 1980c

United States. Congress. House. Committee on Science and Technology. Subcommittee on Energy Research and Production. Hydrogen--its production and energy uses . Washington , 1981. iii, 148 p. : LC Card 81-601180 DDC 338.4/766108 19
KF27 .S3936 1980e

Utilities and energy conservation . Washington , 1980 [i.e. 1981] vii, 78 p. ; LC Card 81-601265 DDC 333.79 19
HD9685.U5 U87

Wind energy systems act of 1980 : hearings before the Subcommittee on Energy Development and Applications of the Committee on Science and Technology, U. S. House of Representatives, Ninety-sixth Congress, first session ... Washington : U. S. Govt. Print. Off., 1980. iv, 429 p. : ill. ; 25 cm. "No. 137." Hearings held Sept. 18, 24, 26, and Oct. 17, 1979. LC Card 80-603413 DDC 346.7304/6792 19
1. Wind power - Law and legislation - United States. I. Title.
KF27 .S3934 1979m

United States. Congress. House. Committee on Science and Technology. Subcommittee on Energy Research and Productions.
United States. Congress. House. Committee on Science and Technology. Subcommittee on Energy Research and Production.
The Department of Energy's public information programs : major changes needed : report / prepared by the Staff of the Subcommittee on Energy Research and Production of the Committee on Science and Technology, U. S. House of Representatives, Ninety-sixth Congress, second session. Washington : U. S. G.P.O., 1980 [i.e. 1981] vii, 34 p. ; 24 cm. At head of title: Committee print. "Serial LLL." Item 1025-A Includes bibliographical references. LC Card 81-601001 DDC 353.87 19
1. United States. Dept. of Energy. 2. Government publicity - United States. 3. Energy industries - Information services - United States. 4. Energy policy - Information services - United States. I. Title.
HD9502.U52 U5 1980a

Fusion energy, an overview of magnetic confinement approach, its objectives, and pace . Washington , 1980. xiv, 182 p. : LC Card 81-600666 DDC 621.48/4 19
TK9204 .F87

H.R. 7190, Nuclear safety research and development act of 1980 : hearing before the Subcommittee on Energy Research and Production of the Committee on Science and Technology, U. S. House of Representatives, Ninety-sixth Congress, second session, June 19, 1980. Washington : U. S. Govt. Print. Off., 1980. iii, 93 p. ; 24 cm. "No. 120." LC Card 80-603021 DDC 343.73/0925 19
1. Atomic power-plants - Law and legislation - United States. 2. Atomic power-plants - Safety regulations - United States. I. Title. II. Title: Nuclear safety research and development act of 1980.
KF27 .S3936 1980

H.R. 7336 : Helium-Energy Act of 1980 : hearing before the Subcommittee on Energy Research and Production and the Subcommittee on Energy Development and Applications of the Committee on Science and Technology, U. S. House of Representatives, Ninety-sixth Congress, second session, June 17, 1980. Washington : U. S. G.P.O., 1981. iii, 385 p. : ill. ; 23 cm. "No. 170." Item 1025-A Includes bibliographical references. LC Card 81-601148 DDC 343.73/0772 347.303772 19
1. Helium - Law and legislation - United States. I. United States. Congress. House. Committee on Science and Technology. Subcommittee on Energy Development and Applications. II. Title. III. Title: Helium-Energy Act of 1980.
KF27 .S3936 1980c

H.R. 7418--Nuclear Waste Research, Development, and Demonstration Act of 1980 : hearing before the Subcommittee on Energy Research and Production of the Committee on Science and Technology, U. S. House of Representatives, Ninety-sixth Congress, second session, May 29, 1980. Washington : U. S. G.P.O., 1980. iii, 118 p. : ill. ; 24 cm. "No. 145." LC Card 80-604068 DDC 344.73/04622 347.3044622 19
1. Radioactive waste disposal - Law and legislation - United States. I. Title. II. Title: Nuclear Waste Research, Development, and Demonstration Act of 1980.
KF27 .S3936 1980a

Hydrogen--its production and energy uses : hearing before the Subcommittee on Energy Research and Production and the Subcommittee on Energy Development and Applications of the Committee on Science and Technology, U. S. House of Representatives, Ninety-sixth Congress, second session, June 25, 1980. Washington : U. S. G.P.O., 1981. iii, 148 p. : ill. ; 24 cm. "No. 174." Item 1025-A LC Card 81-601180 DDC 338.4/766108 19
1. Hydrogen as fuel. I. United States. Congress. House. Committee on Science and Technology. Subcommittee on Energy Development and Applications. II. Title.
KF27 .S3936 1980e

Low-level nuclear waste burial grounds : hearing before the Subcommittee on Energy Research and Production of the Committee on Science and Technology, U. S. House of Representatives, Ninety-sixth Congress, first session, November 7, 1979. Washington : U. S. Govt. Print. Off. : for sale by the Supt. of Docs., U. S. Govt. Print. Off., 1980. iii, 100 p. : ill. ; 23 cm. "No. 80." LC Card 80-601955 DDC 363.7/28 19
1. Radioactive waste disposal in the ground - United States. 2. Nuclear medicine - United States. I. Title.
KF27 .S3936 19791

New directions for nuclear R.D. & D., post-INFCE : hearings before the Subcommittee on Energy Research and Production of the Committee on Science and Technology, U. S. House of Representatives, Ninety-sixth Congress, second session, June 4, 5, 1980. Washington : U. S. G.P.O., 1980. iii, 401 p. : ill. ; 24 cm. "No. 152." LC Card 80-604001 DDC 363.1/79 19
1. Nuclear fuels. 2. Nuclear engineering. 3. Nuclear nonproliferation. 4. Nuclear research - United States. I. Title.
KF27 .S3936 1980b

Quests with U. S. accelerators--50 years, the high energy physics and nuclear physics

research programs : hearing before the Subcommittee on Energy Research and Production of the Committee on Science and Technology, U. S. House of Representatives, Ninety-sixth Congress, second session, July 23, 1980. Washington : U. S. G.P.O., c1980 [i.e. 1981] iii, 463 p. : ill. ; 23 cm. "No. 165." Item 1025-A Includes bibliographical references. LC Card 81-601187 DDC 539.7/072073 19
1. Nuclear research - United States. 2. Particles (Nuclear physics) - Research - United States. 3. Particle accelerators - United States. I. Title.
KF27 .S3936 1980d

Storage batteries for electric vehicle applications : hearing before the Subcommittee on Energy Research and Production of the Committee on Science and Technology, U. S. House of Representatives, Ninety-sixth Congress, first session, November 26, 1979. Washington : U. S. Govt. Print. Off. : for sale by the Supt. of Docs., U. S. GOvt. Print. Off., 1980. iii, 199 p. : ill. ; 23 cm. "No. 84." LC Card 80-602013 DDC 629.2/593 19
1. Automobiles, Electric - Batteries. 2. Storage batteries. I. Title.
KF27 .S3936 1979m

United States. Congress. House. Committee on Science and Technology. Subcommittee on Energy Development and Applications. H.R. 4382--Energy Management Partnership Act . Washington , 1980- v. <1, 3> : LC Card 80-604116 DDC 346.7304/679 347.3064679 19
KF27 .S3934 1979n

United States. Library of Congress. Congressional Research Service. Nuclear safeguards . Washington , 1980. xi, 50 p. ; LC Card 80-602868 DDC 363.1/79 19
HD9698.U52 U57 1980a

United States. Congress. House. Committee on Science and Technology. Subcommittee on Fossil and Nuclear Energy Research, Development and Demonstration. Oversight .
(v. 4) United States. Congress. House. Committee on Science and Technology. Staff study on management and cost issues associated with construction of the CRESAP coal liquefaction facility . Washington , 1978. vii, 348 p. : LC Card 79-601594 DDC 333.79/0973 s 338.4/76626622/0975416 19
KF27 .S397 1978 vol. 4 TP352

United States. Congress. House. Committee on Science and Technology. Subcommittee on Investigation and Oversight. Small, high technology firms and innovation : hearings (including report) before the Subcommittee on Investigations and Oversight and the Subcommittee on Science, Research, and Technology of the Committee on Science and Technology, House of Representatives, Ninety-sixth Congress, first and second sessions, December 10, 1979, January 28, February 23, March 21, April 10, June 10, 12, 1980. Washington : U. S. G.P.O., 1980 [i.e. 1981] xviii, 791 p. : ill. ; 24 cm. "No. 167." Item 1025-S LC Card 81-600956 DDC 338.6/42/0973 19
1. Small business - United States. 2. Small business - United States - Finance. 3. Research and development contracts, Government - United States. 4. Technological innovations - United States. I. United States. Congress. House. Committee on Science and Technology. Subcommittee on Science, Research, and Technology. II. Title.
KF27 .S3975 1979b

United States. Congress. House. Committee on Science and Technology. Subcommittee on Investigations and Oversight.
Design analysis of wide-body aircraft : hearings before the Subcommittee on Investigations and Oversight of the Committee on Science and Technology, U. S. House of Representatives, ninety-sixth Congress, first session. ... Washington : U. S. Govt. Print. Off., 1980. iii, 558 p. : ill. ; 23 cm. Hearings held July 17-Oct. 4, 1979. "No. 98." LC Card 80-602457 DDC 363.1/2492 19
1. Jet transports - Design and construction. 2. McDonnell Douglas DC-10 (Jet transport). I. Title.
KF27 .S3975 1979a

Small, high technology firms and innovation : report / prepared by Subcommittee on Investigations and Oversight of the Committee on Science and Technology, U. S. House of

447 GOVERNMENT PUBLICATIONS - U.S.: 1981

United States. Congress. House. Committee on Science and

Representatives, Ninety-sixth Congress, second session. Washington : U. S. Govt. Print. Off., 1980. v, 65 p. ; 24 cm. At head of title: Committee print. Based on hearings held by the Subcommittee, Dec. 10, 1979-Apr. 10, 1980.   LC Card 80-602579 DDC 338.4/76/0973 19
1. Technological innovations - United States. 2. Small business - United States. I. Title.
T173.8 .U5 1980

Spin recovery training : hearings before the Subcommittee on Investigations and Oversight of the Committee on Science and Technology, U. S. House of Representatives, Ninety-sixth Congress, second session, June 17, 18, 19, 1980. Washington : U. S. G.P.O., 1980 [i.e. 1981] iii, 239 p. : ill. ; 24 cm. "No. 172." Item 1025-A Includes bibliographical references. LC Card 81-601185   DDC 363.1/2492 19
1. Flight training - United States. 2. Spin (Aerodynamics). I. Title.
KF27 .S3975 1980

United States. Congress. House. Committee on Science and Technology. Subcommittee on Science, Research, and Technology. Technology transfer to China . Washington , 1980. v, 35 p. ; LC Card 80-603271   DDC 338.91/73/051 19
T174.3 .U55 1980

United States. Congress. House. Committee on Science and Technology. Subcommittee on Science, Research, and Technology. Technology transfer to China . Washington , 1980. iii, 236 p. ; LC Card 80-602094   DDC 338.91/73/051 19
KF27 .S399 1979o

United States. Congress. House. Committee on Science and Technology. Subcommittee on Natural Resources and Environment.
Coordination of Federal research and monitoring programs for toxic and hazardous substances in the Great Lakes region : hearing before the Subcommittee on Natural Resources and Environment of the Committee on Science and Technology, U. S. House of Representatives, Ninety-sixth Congress, first session, November 19, 1979. Washington : U. S. Govt. Print. Off., 1980. iii, 451 p. : ill. ; 24 cm. "No. 99." Includes bibliographies. LC Card 80-602529   DDC 363.7/38 19
1. Water - Pollution - Great Lakes region. 2. Water - Pollution - Great Lakes. I. Title.
KF27 .S398 1979h

DOE coal-conversion orders to electric utilities, including the Long Island Lighting Company : hearing before the Subcommittee on Natural Resources and Environment of the Committee on Science and Technology, U. S. House of Representatives, Ninety-sixth Congress, second session, February 28, 1980. Washington : U. S. Govt. Print. Off., 1980. iii, 209 p. : ill. ; 24 cm. "No. 117." LC Card 80-603029   DDC 338.4/7621312132 19
1. Coal-fired power plants - United States. 2. Electric power-plants - United States - Conversion to coal. 3. Long Island Lighting Company. I. Title.
KF27 .S398 1980c

EPA diesel particulate standards : hearings before the Subcommittee on Natural Resources and Environment of the Committee on Science and Technology, U. S. House of Representatives, Ninety-sixth Congress, second session, October 1, 2, 1980. Washington : U. S. G.P.O., 1981. iii, 192 p. : ill. ; 24 cm. "No. 181." Item 1025-A Includes bibliographical references. LC Card 81-601856   DDC 363.7/392 19
1. Diesel motor exhaust gas. 2. Automobiles - Motors - Exhaust gas. 3. Air - Pollution - United States - Physiological effect. 4. Air - Pollution - Standards - United States. I. Title.
KF27 .S398 1980e

Long Island Sound dredge-spoil dumping : hearing before the Subcommittee on Natural Resources and Environment of the Committee on Science and Technology, U. S. House of Representatives, Ninety-sixth Congress, first session, October 13, 1979. Washington : U. S. Govt. Print. Off., 1980. iii, 180 p. ; 24 cm. "No. 97." LC Card 80-602186   DDC 333.91/64/0916346 19
1. Dredging - Environmental aspects - Long Island Sound. 2. Dredging spoil - Long Island Sound. 3. Sediment transport - Long Island Sound. I. Title.
KF27 .S398 1979j

Research and development programs of the National Oceanic and Atmospheric

Adminstration : hearings before the Subcommittee on National Resources and Environment of the Committee on Science and Technology, U. S. House of Representatives, Ninety-sixth Congress, first session, November 13, 14, 1979. Washington : U. S. Govt. Print. Off., 1979, [i.e. 1980] iii, 229 p. ; 24 cm. "No. 100." LC Card 80-602771   DDC 353.0082/32 19
1. Atmospheric research - United States. 2. Oceanographic research - United State. 3. United States. National Oceanic and Atmospheric Administration. I. Title.
KF27 .S398 1979i

Three Mile Island Nuclear Plant accident : hearing before the Subcommittee on Natural Resources and Environment of the Committee on Science and Technology, U. S. House of Representatives, Ninety-sixth Congress, first session, June 2, 1979. Washington : U. S. Govt. Print. Off., 1979. iii, 251 p. : ill. ; 24 cm. "No. 54." Includes bibliographical references.   LC Card 80-601132   DDC 363.1/79 19
1. Three Mile Island Nuclear Power Plant, Pa. 2. Atomic power-plants - Pennsylvania - Accidents. 3. Atomic power-plants - Environmental aspects - Pennsylvania. I. Title.
KF27 .S398 1979c

U. S. Army Corps of Engineers civil environmental R. & D. budget : hearing before the Subcommittee on Natural Resources and Environment of the Committee on Science and Technology, U. S. House Of Representatives, Ninety-sixth Congress, second session, January 29, 1980. Washington : U. S. Govt. Print. Off., 1980. iii, 57 p. ; 24 cm. "No. 104." LC Card 80-602776   DDC 353.0082/32 19
1. Environmental engineering - Research - United States. 2. United States. Army. Corps of Engineers. I. Title.
KF27 .S398 1980

United States. Congress. House. Committee on Science and Technology. Subcommittee on Science, Research, and Technology. Natural resources and environment in the Bureau of Oceans and International Environmental and Scientific Affairs . Washington , 1980. iii, 159 p. ; LC Card 80-603700   DDC 353.0085/5 19
KF27 .S399 1980e

United States. Congress. House. Committee on Science and Technology. Subcommittee on Space Science and Applications. Operational civil remote sensing systems . Washington , 1980. iii, 315 p. : LC Card 80-603708   DDC 338.4/76213678 19
KF27 .S3995 1980a

United States. Library of Congress. Science Policy Research Division. Energy from biomass and solid wastes . Washington , 1980. xix, 169 p. : LC Card 80-603278   DDC 333.79/38 19
TP360 .U59 1980

1981 authorization for the Office of Research and Development, Environmental Protection Agency : hearings before the Subcommittee on Natural Resources and Environment of the Committee on Science and Technology, U. S. House of Representatives, Ninety-sixth Congress, second session, February 19 and 20, 1980. Washington : U. S. G.P.O., 1980. iii, 267 p. : ill. ; 24 cm. "No. 144." Includes bibliographical references. LC Card 80-604013   DDC 353.0072/23682321 19
1. United States. Environmental Protection Agency. Office of Research and Development - Appropriations and expenditures. I. Title.
KF27 .S398 1980d

1981 DOE authorization : environment programs : hearings before the Subcommittee on Natural Resources and Environment of the Committee on Science and Technology, U. S. House of Representatives, Ninety-sixth Congress, second session, February 5, 6, 1980. Washington : U. S. Govt. Print. Off., 1980. iii, 600 p. : ill. ; 24 cm. "[No. 107]" LC Card 80-602948   DDC 353.0072/236823 19
1. United States. Dept. of Energy - Appropriations and expenditures. 2. Environmental engineering - Research - United States - Finance. I. Title.
KF27 .S398 1980a

1981 NOAA authorization : hearings before the Subcommittee on Natural Resources and Environment of the Committee on Science and Technology, U. S. House of Representatives, Ninety-sixth Congress, second session, February

25, 26, 27, 1980. Washington : U. S. Govt. Print. Off., 1980. iii, 279 p. ; 24 cm. "No. 105." LC Card 80-602732   DDC 353.0072/2368232 19
1. United States. National Oceanic and Atmospheric Administration - Appropriations and expenditures. I. Title.
KF27 .S398 1980b

United States. Congress. House. Committee on Science and Technology. Subcommittee on Science, Research, and Technology.
Communications research and development /. Washington , 1980 [i.e. 1981] viii, 34 p. ; LC Card 81-601506   DDC 621.38/072073 19
TK5102.8.U6 C65

Comparative risk assessment : hearings before the Subcommittee on Science, Research, and Technology of the Committee on Science and Technology, U. S. House of Representatives, Ninety-sixth Congress, second session, May 14, 15, 1980. Washington : U. S. G.P.O., 1980. iv, 571 p. : ill. ; 24 cm. "No. 129." Includes bibliographical references. LC Card 80-603895   DDC 342.73/066 347.30266 19
1. Administrative procedure - United States. 2. Risk management - United States. I. Title.
KF27 .S399 1980g

Congress/Science Forum, Washington, D.C., 1979. Risk/benefit analysis in the legislative process . Washington , 1980. vi, 228 p. : LC Card 80-601466   DDC 328.73/077 19
KF27 .S399 1979n

Earthquake and Fire Act authorization : hearings before the Subcommittee on Science, Research, and Technology of the Committee on Science and Technology, U. S. House of Representatives, Ninety-sixth Congress, second session, February 26, 27, and 28, 1980. Washington : U. S. G.P.O., 1980. iv, 720 p. : ill. ; 24 cm. "No. 140." Bibliography: p. 664. LC Card 80-604029   DDC 353.0072/23675 19
1. Earthquakes and building - Law and legislation - United States. 2. Fire prevention - Law and legislation - United States. 3. Disaster relief - United States. 4. United States. Federal Emergency Management Agency. I. Title.
KF27 .S399 1980f

Government patent policy : hearings before the Subcommittee on Science, Research, and Technology of the Committee on Science and Technology, U. S. House of Representatives, Ninety-sixth Congress, first session, October 16, 17, 1979. Washington : U. S. Govt. Print. Off., 1979. iii, 221 p. ; 24 cm. "No. 102." LC Card 80-602808   DDC 353.0082/4 19
1. Patents and government-developed inventions - United States. 2. Patents, Government-owned - United States. 3. Research and development contracts, Government - United States. I. Title.
KF27 .S399 1979r

The Government-university accountability relationship in the field of scientific research : hearing before the Subcommittee on Science, Research, and Technology of the Committee on Science and Technology, U. S. House of Representatives, Ninety-sixth Congress, second session, March 24, 1980. Washington : U. S. Govt. Print. Off., 1980. iii, 251 p. ; 23 cm. "[No. 110]." LC Card 80-602710   DDC 001.4/4 19
1. Research grants - United States. 2. Research and development contracts, Government - United States. 3. Universities and colleges - United States. I. Title.
KF27 .S399 1980b

H.R. 5715, Government Patent Policy Act of 1980 : hearing before the Subcommittee on Science, Research, and Technology of the Committee on Science and Technology, U. S. House of Representatives, Ninety-sixth Congress, second session, February 8, 1980. Washington : U. S. G.P.O., 1980. iii, 184 p. : graphs ; 23 cm. "[No. 139]" Includes bibliographical references. LC Card 80-603795   DDC 346.7304/86 347.306486 19
1. Patents and government-developed inventions - United States. I. Title. II. Title: Government Patent Policy Act of 1980.
KF27 .S399 1980h

H.R. 6910 : National Technology Foundation Act of 1980 : hearings before the Subcommittee on Science, Research and Technology of the Committee on Science and Technology, U. S. House of Representatives, Ninety-sixth Congress, second session, September 9, 10, 16, 17, 18, 1980. Washington : U. S. G.P.O., 1981.

BIBLIOGRAPHIC GUIDE

United States. Congress. House. Committee on Science and

448

iii, 887 p. : ill. ; 23 cm. "No. 179." Item 1025-A Includes bibliographical references. LC Card 81-601618 DDC 344.73/095 347.30495 19
1. Technological innovations - Law and legislation - United States. 2. National Technology Foundation (U. S.). 3. Technology and state - United States. I. National Technology Foundation Act of 1980. II. Title.
KF27 .S399 1980i

H.R. 7270 : to promote excellence in design : hearing before the Subcommittee on Science, Research, and Technology of the Committee on Science and Technology, U. S. House of Representatives, Ninety-sixth Congress, second session, September 19, 1980. Washington : U. S. G.P.O., 1981. iii, 109 p. : ill. ; 24 cm. "No. 178." Item 1025-A LC Card 81-601351 DDC 344.73/095 347.30495 19
1. Design, Industrial - Law and legislation - United States. 2. Engineering design - Law and legislation - United States. 3. Environmental engineering - Law and legislation - United States. I. Title.
KF27 .S399 1980j

The Helsinki forum and East-West scientific exchange : joint hearing before the Subcommittee on Science, Research, and Technology of the Committee on Science and Technology and the Subcommittee on International Security and Scientific Affairs of the Committee on Foreign Affairs, House of Representatives, and the Commission on Security and Cooperation in Europe, Ninety-sixth Congress, second session, January 31, 1980. Washington : U. S. Govt. Print. Off., 1980. v, 323 p. ; 24 cm. "No. 89." LC Card 80-602155 DDC 327.1/7 19
1. Exchanges, Literary and scientific. 2. Science and state - United States. I. United States. Congress. House. Committee on Foreign Affairs. Subcommittee on International Security and Scientific Affairs. II. Commission on Security and Cooperation in Europe. III. Title.
KF27 .S399 1980

Information technology in education : joint hearings before the Subcommittee on Science, Research, and Technology of the Committee on Science and Technology and the Subcommittee on Select Education of the Committee on Education Labor, House of Representatives, Ninety-sixth Congress, second session, April 2, 3, 1980. Washington : U. S. Govt. Print. Off., 1980. v, 250 p. : ill. ; 24 cm. "[No. 134]" Bibliography: p. 224-227. LC Card 80-603501 DDC 370/.28/5 19
1. Education - Data processing. 2. Education - United States - Data processing. I. Title.
KF27 .S399 1980d

Natural resources and environment in the Bureau of Oceans and International Environmental and Scientific Affairs : hearing before the Subcommittee on Science, Research, and Technology and the Subcommittee on Natural Resources and Environment of the Committee on Science and Technology, U. S. House of Representatives, Ninety-sixth Congress, second session, April 16, 1980. Washington : U. S. Govt. Print. Off., 1980. iii, 159 p. ; 23 cm. "No. 128." LC Card 80-603700 DDC 353.0085/5 19
1. United States. Dept. of State. Bureau of Oceans and International Environmental and Scientific Affairs. I. United States. Congress. House. Committee on Science and Technology. Subcommittee on Natural Resources and Environment. II. Title.
KF27 .S399 1980e

Nutrition research methods and technology : hearings before the Subcommittee on Science, Research and Technology of the Committee on Science and Technology, U. S. House of Representatives, Ninety-sixth Congress, first session, September 25, 26, 27, 1979. Washington : U. S. Govt. Print. Off., 1979. iv, 415 p. : ill. ; 24 cm. "No. 109." Bibliography: p. 65-66. LC Card 80-602711 DDC 613.2/072073 19
1. Nutrition - Research - United States. 2. Nutrition - United States. I. Title.
KF27 .S399 1979q

Oversight hearing, United States Metric Board : statements for the record of the hearing before the Subcommittee on Science, Research, and Technology of the Committee on Science and Technology, U. S. House of Representatives, Ninety-sixth Congress, first session, November 26, 1979. Washington : U. S. Govt. Print. Off.,

1980. iii, 34 ; 24 cm. "No. 92." LC Card 80-602077 DDC 353.0082/1 19
1. United States Metric Board. I. Title.
KF27 .S399 1979m

Technology and the cost of health care : report / prepared by the Subcommittee on Science, Research, and Technology of the Committee on Science and Technology, U. S. House of Representives, Ninety-sixth Congress, second session. Washington : U. S. G.P.O., 1980. v. 16 p. ; 23 cm. At head of title: Committee print. "Serial FFF." Includes bibliographical references. LC Card 80-603866 DDC 338.4/33621/0973 19
1. Medical care, Cost of - United States. 2. Medical innovations - Economic aspects - United States. 3. Hospitals - United States - Cost of operation. 4. Medical innovations - United States - Evaluation. 5. Medical care - United States - Cost control. I. Title.
RA410.53 .U53 1980

Technology transfer conference : hearing before the Subcommittee on Science, Research and Technology of the Committee on Science and Technology, U. S. House of Representatives, Ninety-sixth Congress, first session, March 30, 1979. Washington : U. S. Govt. Print. Off., 1980. iii, 212 p. ; 24 cm. "No. 101." LC Card 80-602824 DDC 338.973 19
1. Technology transfer. 2. Federal government - United States. I. Title.
KF27 .S399 1979p

Technology transfer to China : report / prepared by Subcommittee on Science, Research, and Technology and the Subcommittee on Investigations and Oversight of the Committee on Science and Technology, U. S. House of Representatives, Ninety-sixth Congress, second session, July 1980. Washington : U. S. Govt. Print. Off. : for sale by the Supt. of Docs., U. S. Govt. Print. Off., 1980. v, 35 p. ; 23 cm. "Serial TT." At head of title: Committee print. LC Card 80-603271 DDC 338.91/73/051 19
1. Technology transfer - China. 2. Technology transfer - United States. I. United States. Congress. House. Committee on Science and Technology. Subcommittee on Investigations and Oversight. II. Title.
T174.3 .U55 1980

Technology transfer to China : hearings before the Subcommittee on Science, Research, and Technology and the Subcommittee on Investigations and Oversight of the Committee on Science and Technology, U. S. House of Representatives, Ninety-sixth Congress, first session, November 13 and 15, 1979. Washington : U. S. Govt. Print. Off., 1980. iii, 236 p. ; 24 cm. "No. 88." LC Card 80-602094 DDC 338.91/73/051 19
1. Technical assistance, American - China. 2. Technology transfer. I. United States. Congress. House. Committee on Science and Technology. Subcommittee on Investigations and Oversight. II. Title.
KF27 .S399 1979o

United States. Congress. House. Committee on Science and Technology. Subcommittee on Investigation and Oversight. Small, high technology firms and innovation . Washington , 1980 [i.e. 1981] xviii, 791 p. : LC Card 81-600956 DDC 338.6/42/0973 19
KF27 .S3975 1979b

United States. Congress. House. Committee on Science and Technology. Subcommittee on Transportation, Aviation, and Communications. Communications research and development . Washington , 1980. iii, 481 p. : LC Card 80-603502 DDC 384/.072073 19
KF27 .S3997 1980d

United States. General Accounting Office. FDA drug approval--a lengthy process that delays the availability of important new drugs . Washington, DC [1980] vi, 83 p. ; LC Card 80-602514 DDC 363.1/946/0973 19
RS189 .U54 1980

United States. Library of Congress. Congressional Research Service. Risk/benefit analysis in the legislative process . Washington , 1980. ix, 36 p. ; LC Card 80-602214 DDC 363.1/056/0973 19
T174.5 .U57 1980

United States. Library of Congress. Research Services. Manpower for science and engineering in China /. Washington , 1980. v, 36 p. ; LC

Card 80-603062 DDC 331.12/9150951 19
Q149.C5 U56 1980

United States-Mexico scientific and technological cooperation : hearings before the Subcommittee on Science, Research, and Technology of the Committee on Science and Technology, U. S. House of Representatives, Ninety-sixth Congress, first session, June 4, July 16 and 18, 1979. Washington : U. S. Govt. Print. Off., 1979. iii, 289 p. : ill. ; 24 cm. "No. 90." LC Card 80-602192 DDC 338.9 19
1. Science - International cooperation. 2. Technology - International cooperation. 3. United States - Relations (general) with Mexico. 4. Mexico - Relations (general) with the United States. I. Title.
KF27 .S399 1979k

Workshop on Research Needed to Improve the Quality of Socioeconomic Data Used in Regulatory Decisionmaking, Library of Congress, 1979. Workshop on Research Needed to Improve the Quality of Socioeconomic Data Used in Regulatory Decisionmaking . Washington , 1980. xiii, 296 p. ; LC Card 80-602262 DDC 361.6/1/072073 19
H22 .W67 1979

1981 National Bureau of Standards authorization : hearings before the Subcommittee on Science, Research, and Technology of the Committee on Science and Technology, U. S. House of Representatives, Ninety-sixth Congress, second session .... Washington : U. S. Govt. Print. Off., 1980. iii, 424 p. : ill. ; 24 cm. Hearings held Feb. 1-13, 1980. "No. 106." LC Card 80-602738 DDC 353.0072/23682/1 19
1. United States. National Bureau of Standards - Appropriations and expenditures. I. Title. II. Title: National Bureau of Standards authorization.
KF27 .S399 1980a

1981 National Science Foundation authorization : hearings before the Subcommittee on Science, Research, and Technology of the Committee on Science and Technology, U. S. House of Representatives, Ninety-sixth Congress, second session, on H.R. 6728 (superseded by H.R. 7115) .... Washington : U. S. Govt. Print. Off., 1980. iv, 853 p. : ill. ; 23 cm. "No. 126." Hearings held Feb. 5-20, 1980. LC Card 80-603468 DDC 353.0072/236855 19
1. United States. National Science Foundation - Appropriations and expenditures. I. Title. II. Title: National Science Foundation authorization.
KF27 .S399 1980c

United States. Congress. House. Committee on Science and Technology. Subcommittee on Space Science and Applications.
Centralized storm information system : hearing before the Subcommittee on Space Science and Applications of the Committee on Science and Technology, U. S. House of Representatives, Ninety-sixth Congress, second session, October 14, 1980. Washington : U. S. G.P.O., 1980 [i.e. 1981] iii, 19 p. : ill. ; 24 cm. "No. 161." Item 1025-A LC Card 81-600858 DDC 363.3/492 19
1. Tornado warning systems - United States - Data processing. I. Title.
KF27 .S3995 1980c

H.R. 7412, the Space industrialization act of 1980 : hearings before the Subcommittee on Space Science and Applications of the Committee on Science and Technology, U. S. House of Representatives, Ninety-sixth Congress, second session, June 11, 12, 1980. Washington : U. S. Govt. Print. Off., 1980. iii, 88 p. ; 24 cm. "No. 132." LC Card 80-603674 DDC 344.73/095 347.30495 19
1. Space law. 2. Space stations - Industrial applications - Finance. 3. Space Industrialization Corporation. I. Title. II. Title: Space industrialization act of 1980.
KF27 .S3995 1980

Operational civil remote sensing systems : hearings before the Subcommittee on Space Science and Applications and the Subcommittee on Natural Resources and Environment of the Committee on Science and Technology, U. S. House of Representatives, Ninety-sixth Congress, second session, June 24, 25, July 29, 1980. Washington : U. S. Govt. Print. Off., 1980. iii, 315 p. : ill. ; 24 cm. "[No. 131]" LC Card 80-603708 DDC 338.4/76213678 19
1. Landsat satellites. 2. Remote sensing - Government

449

GOVERNMENT PUBLICATIONS - U.S.: 1981

United States. Congress. House. Committee on Small Business.

policy - United States. I. United States. Congress. House. Committee on Science and Technology. Subcommittee on Natural Resources and Environment. II. Title.
KF27 .S3995 1980a

United States civilian space policy : hearings before the Subcommittee on Space Science and Applications of the Committee on Science and Technology, U. S. House of Representatives, Ninety-sixth Congress, second session, July 23, 24, 1980. Washington : U. S. G.P.O., 1980. iii, 246 p. : ill. ; 24 cm. "No. 153." Includes bibliographical references. LC Card 80-603989 DDC 629.4/0973 19
1. Astronautics and state - United States. I. Title.
KF27 .S3995 1980b

United States civilian space programs, 1958-1978 . Washington , 1981- v. <1 > : LC Card 81-602024 DDC 629.4 19
TL789.8.U5 U58

United States. Library of Congress. Congressional Research Service. United States and Soviet progress in space . Washington , 1980. xiii, 91 p. ; LC Card 80-602269 DDC 387.8 19
TL789.8.U5 U54 1980

Water immersion facility, Johnson Space Center : hearing before the Subcommittee on Space Science and Applications of the Committee on Science and Technology, U. S. House of Representatives, Ninety-sixth Congress, first session, September 13, 1979. Washington : U. S. Govt. Print. Off., 1979. iii, 44 p. : ill. ; 24 cm. "No. 73." LC Card 80-601329 DDC 629.45/82/028 19
1. Lyndon B. Johnson Space Center - Buildings. 2. Space flight training facilities - Texas - Houston - Accidents.
KF27 .S3995 1979h

United States. Congress. House. Committee on Science and Technology. Subcommittee on the Environment and the Atmosphere. United States. Library of Congress. Congressional Research Service. Effects of chronic exposure to low-level pollutants in the environment . Washington , 1975. ii, 402 p. ; LC Card 75-603631
QH545.A1 U54 1975 **NYPL [JSE 81-285]**

United States. Congress. House. Committee on Science and Technology. Subcommittee on Transportation, Aviation, and Communications. Communications research and development : hearings before the Subcommittee on Transportation, Aviation, and Communications and the Subcommittee on Science, Research, and Technology of the Committee on Science and Technology, U. S. House of Representatives, Ninety-sixth Congress, second session .... Washington : U. S. Govt. Print. Off., 1980. iii, 481 p. : ill. ; 24 cm. Hearings held May 20-28, 1980. "No. 130." LC Card 80-603502 DDC 384/.072073 19
1. Telecommunication - Research - United States. 2. Telecommunication policy - United States. 3. Research and development contracts, Government - United States. I. United States. Congress. House. Committee on Science and Technology. Subcommittee on Science, Research, and Technology. II. Title.
KF27 .S3997 1980d

Compendium of Federal government communications R. & D. planned for fiscal year 1980-81 funding (civil agencies) / prepared by the Subcommittee on Transportation, Aviation, and Communications of the Committee on Science and Technology, U. S. House of Representatives, Ninety-sixth Congress, second session, 1980. Washington : U. S. Govt. Print. Off., 1980. v, 188 p. : forms ; 24 cm. At head of title: Committee print. "Serial MM." LC Card 80-602263 DDC 380.3/0724 19
1. Telecommunication - Research - United States. 2. Electronics - Research - United States. I. Title.
TK5102.8.U6 U54 1980

H.R. 4678, the Automotive research act of 1979 : hearings before the Subcommittee on Transportation, Aviation, and Communications of the Committee on Science and Technology, U. S. House of Representatives, Ninety-sixth Congress, first session .... Washington : U. S. Govt. Print. Off., 1979. iii, 228 p. ; 24 cm. Hearings held July 11-Oct. 15, 1979. [No. 72] LC Card 80-601491 DDC 343.73/0786292222/0262

19
1. Automobile engineering research - Law and legislation - United States. I. Title.
KF27 .S3997 1979e

Methane transportation research, development, and demonstration act : hearing before the Subcommittee on Transportation, Aviation, and Communications of the Committee on Science and Technology, U. S. House of Representatives, Ninety-sixth Congress, second session, on H.R. 6889, June 11, 1980. Washington : U. S. Govt. Print. Off., 1980. iii, 362 p. : ill. ; 24 cm. "No. 121." Includes bibliographical references. LC Card 80-603312 DDC 346.7304/6793 19
1. Methane - Law and legislation - United States. I. Title.
KF27 .S3997 1980c

Urban mass transit R. & D. : hearings before the Subcommittee on Transportation, Aviation, and Communications of the Committee on Science and Technology, U. S. House of Representatives, Ninety-sixth Congress, second session, April 1, 2, 1980. Washington : U. S. Govt. Print. Off., 1980. iii, 200 p. : ill. ; 24 cm. "No. 115." LC Card 80-603002 DDC 388.4/072073 19
1. Local transit - Research - United States. 2. United States. Urban Mass Transportation Administration. I. Title.
KF27 .S3997 1980b

1982 DOE authorization (program review) : hearing before the Subcommittee on Transportation, Aviation, and Communications of the Committee on Science and Technology, U. S. House of Representatives, Ninety-sixth Congress, second session, September 30, 1980. Washington : U. S. G.P.O., 1980. iii, 54 p. ; 24 cm. "No. 148." LC Card 80-604028 DDC 353.0072/234 19
1. United States. Dept. of Energy. Office of Transportation Programs - Appropriations and expenditures. I. Title.
KF27 .S3997 1980f

1982 NASA authorization (program review) : hearing before the Subcommittee on Transportation, Aviation, and Communications of the Committee on Science and Technology, U. S. House of Representatives, Ninety-sixth Congress, second session .... Washington : U. S. G.P.O., 1980- v. <1> : ill. ; 24 cm. "No. 147." Hearings held Sept. 9, 1980- LC Card 80-604026 DDC 353.0087/78 19
1. United States. National Aeronautics and Space Administration. 2. Astronautics and state - United States. I. Title.
KF27 .S3997 1980e

United States. Congress. House. Committee on Science and Technology. Transportation, Aviation, and Communications. Communications research and development /. Washington , 1980 [i.e. 1981] viii, 34 p. ; LC Card 81-601506 DDC 621.38/072073 19
TK5102.8.U6 C65

United States. Congress. House. Committee on Science and Tecnology. Subcommittee on Energy Development and Applications. United States. Library of Congress. Science Policy Research Division. Energy from biomass and solid wastes . Washington , 1980. xix, 169 p. : LC Card 80-603278 DDC 333.79/38 19
TP360 .U59 1980

United States. Congress. House. Committee on Science and Tecnology. Subcommittee on Energy Research and Production. Population and energy : implications for policymakers : hearing before the Subcommittee on Energy Research and Production of the Committee on Science and Technology, U. S. House of Representatives, Ninety-sixth Congress, second session, September 24, 1980. Washington : U. S. G.P.O., 1981. iii, 154 p. : ill., maps ; 24 cm. "No. 1025-A Bibliography: p. 68-70. LC Card 81-601357 DDC 333.79/13/0973 19
1. Energy consumption - United States. 2. Energy policy - United States. 3. United States - Population. I. Title.
KF27 .S3936 1980f

United States. Congress. House. Committee on Science and Tecnology. Subcommittee on Science, Research, and Technology. United States. Library of Congress. Science Policy Research Division. Energy from biomass and

solid wastes . Washington , 1980. xix, 169 p. : LC Card 80-603278 DDC 333.79/38 19
TP360 .U59 1980

United States. Congress. House. Committee on Small Business. Hearings printed in 1978 and later are available only in microform. Please consult the librarians in the Economic and Public Affairs Division.
Government procurement from small and small disadvantaged businesses (Public Law 95-507 and accompanying reports) / Committee on Small Business, House of Representatives, Ninety-sixth Congress, second session. Washington : U. S. Govt. Print. Off., 1980. v, 165 p. ; 24 cm. At head of title: Committee print. 96th Congress, 2d session. "April 1980." LC Card 80-602069 DDC 346.73/0652 19
1. Government purchasing - United States. 2. Small business - Law and legislation - United States. I. Title.
KF843.5 .S42

H.R. 5607--Small business innovation act of 1980 : hearings before the Committee on Small Business, House of Representatives, Ninety-sixth Congress, second session, Washington, D.C. Washington : U. S. Govt. Print. Off., 1980. v, 459 p. ; 24 cm. Hearings held Mar. 4-Apr. 1, 1980. Includes bibliographical references. LC Card 80-603308 DDC 346.73/0652 19
1. Small business - Law and legislation - United States. 2. Technological innovations - Law and legislation - United States. I. Title. II. Title: Small business innovation act of 1980.
KF27 .S6 1980a

Petroleum products : supply, price, and marketing problems : report of the Committee on Small Business, House of Representatives, Ninety-sixth Congress, second session. Washington : U. S. Govt. Print. Off., 1980. v, 99 p. : ill. ; 24 cm. (Report - 96th Congress, 2d session, House of Representatives ; no. 96-1068) At head of title: Union calendar no. 666. "June 3, 1980--Committed to the Committee of the Whole House on the State of the Union and ordered to be printed." Includes bibliographical references. LC Card 80-602595 DDC 338.4/766553/0973 19
1. Petroleum products - United States. 2. Petroleum industry and trade - United States. I. Series: United States. 96th Congress, 2d session, 1980. House. Report , no. 96-1068. II. Title.
KF32 .S6 1980

Report, "America's small business economy agenda for action" : hearing before the Committee on Small Business, House of Representatives, Ninety-sixth Congress, second session, Washington, D.C., June 3, 1980. Washington : U. S. Govt. Print. Off., 1980. iii, 111 p. ; 24 cm. LC Card 80-602911 DDC 338.6/42/0973 19
1. Small business - United States. 2. Industry and state - United States. I. Title.
KF27 .S6 1980

Role of government funding and its impact on small business in the solar energy industry : report of the Committee on Small Business, House of Representatives, Ninety-sixth Congress, second session. Washington : U. S. G.P.O., 1980. vi, 68 p. : ill. ; 24 cm. (Report / House of Representatives . no. 96-1451) "October 2, 1980." Item 1008-C, 1008-D (microfiche) Includes bibliographical references. LC Card 80-603851 DDC 338.6/42 19
1. Solar energy industries - United States - Finance. 2. Small business - United States - Finance. 3. Energy policy - United States. 4. Tax credits - United States. I. Series: United States. Congress. House. Report , no. 96-1451. II. Title.
HD9681.U62 U526 1980

United States. Congress. House. Committee on Science and Technology. Innovation . Washington , 1980. v, 228 p. ; LC Card 80-602110 DDC 338/.06 19
KF27 .S39 1979f

White House Conference on Small Business, Washington, D.C., 1980. Delegate recommendations /. Washington , 1980. v, 77 p. ; LC Card 80-602062 DDC 338.6/42/0973 19
HD2346.U5 W54 1980

United States. Congress. House. Committee on Small Business. Special Small Business Problems, Subcommittee on. see United States. Congress. House. Committee on Small Business. Subcommittee on Special

BIBLIOGRAPHIC GUIDE

United States. Congress. House. Committee on Small Business.

450

Small Business Problems.

United States. Congress. House. Committee on Small Business. Subcommittee on Access to Equity Capital and Business Opportunities.
Inventory accounting as a burden on the capital formation process : hearing before the Subcommittee on Access to Equity Capital and Business Opportunities of the Committee on Small Business, House of Representatives, Ninety-sixth Congress, second session, Washington, D.C., ... Washington : U. S. Govt. Print. Off., 1980- v. ; 24 cm. Hearings held Feb. 12, June 10 and 11, 1980. Includes bibliographical references. LC Card 80-601994 DDC 346.73/0652 19
1. Inventories - United States - Accounting. 2. Tax accounting - United States. 3. Saving and investment - United States. I. Title.
KF27 .S63 1980

United States. Congress. House. Committee on Small Business. Subcommittee on Antitrust and Restraint of Trade Activities Affecting Small Business.
Conglomerate mergers--their effects on small business and local communities : hearings before the Subcommittee on Antitrust and Restraint of Trade Activities Affecting Small Business of the Committee on Small Business, House of Representatives, Ninety-sixth Congress, second session .... Washington : U. S. Govt. Print. Off., 1980. vi, 1217 p. : ill. ; 24 cm. Hearings held Jan. 31-Feb. 28, 1980. LC Card 80-603730 DDC 338.8/3/0973 19
1. Conglomerate corporations - United States. 2. Consolidation and merger of corporations - United States. 3. Small business - United States. 4. Antitrust law - United States. I. Title.
KF27 .S6335 1980

Small Business Motor Fuel Marketer Preservation Act-H.R. 6722 : joint hearings before the Subcommittee on Antitrust and Restraint of Trade Activities Affecting Small Business of the Committee on Small Business and Subcommittee on Consumer Protection and Finance of the Committee on Interstate and Foreign Commerce, House of Respresentatives, Ninety-sixth Congress, second session, on H.R. 6722 ... Washington, D.C., May 20, 21, June 4, and 5, 1980. Washington : U. S. G.P.O., 1980. vii, 835 p. : ill. ; 24 cm. "Serial no. 96-196." Includes bibliographies. LC Card 80-604087 DDC 343.73/078629287 347.30378629287 19
1. Automobiles - Service stations - Law and legislation - United States. 2. Petroleum law and legislation - United States. 3. Small business - Law and legislation - United States. 4. Loans - United States - Government guaranty. I. United States. Congress. House. Committee on Interstate and Foreign Commerce. Subcommittee on Consumer Protection and Finance. II. Title.
KF27 .S6335 1980b

United States. Congress. House. Committee on Small Business. Subcommittee on Energy, Environment, Safety and Research.
DOE petroleum allocation regulations--new stations vs. allocation problems for existing stations : hearing before the Subcommittee on Energy, Environment, Safety, and Research of the Committee on Small Business, House of Representatives, Ninety-sixth Congress, second session, Washington, D.C., May 15, 1980. Washington : U. S. G.P.O., 1980 [i.e. 1981] iv, 233 p. : ill. ; 24 cm. Item 1031 Includes bibliographical references. LC Card 81-600975 DDC 346.7304/68232 347.306468232 19
1. Gasoline supply - Law and legislation - United States. 2. Automobiles - Service stations - Law and legislation - United States. 3. United States. Dept. of Energy. I. Title.
KF27 .S639 1980

Role of government funding and its impact on small business in the solar energy industry : hearing before the Subcommittee on Energy, Environment, Safety, and Research of the Committee on Small Business, House of Representatives, Ninety-sixth Congress, first session .... Washington : U. S. Govt. Print. Off., 1979 i.e. 1980- v. : ill. ; 24 cm. Hearings held in various cities, May 4, 1979- . LC Card 80-603085 DDC 338.4/362147/0973 19
1. Solar energy industries - United States - Finance. 2. Energy policy - United States. 3. Small business - United States. 4. Tax credits - United States. I. Title.
KF27 .S639 1979b

United States. Congress. House. Committee on Small Business. Subcommittee on General Oversight and Minority Enterprise. Task Force on Minority Enterprise.
United States. Congress. House. Committee on Small Business. Subcommittee on General Oversight and Minority Enterprise.
Contracting out/government competition : hearing before the Subcommittee on General Oversight and Minority Enterprise of the Committee on Small Business, House of Representatives, Ninety-sixth Congress, second session, Washington, D.C., April 21, 1980. Washington : U. S. G.P.O., 1980. iv, 276 p. : ill. ; 24 cm. Item 1031 Includes bibliographical references. LC Card 81-600619 DDC 353.0071/1 19
1. Public contracts - United States. 2. Small business - United States. 3. Government competition - United States. I. Title.
KF27 .S64 1980i

Establishment of a Minority Business Development Administration in the Department of Commerce : hearings before the Subcommittee on General Oversight and Minority Enterprise of the Committee on Small Business, House of Representatives, Ninety-sixth Congress, second session, Washington, D.C., June 9 and 16, 1980. Washington : U. S. G.P.O., 1980. iv, 203 p. : ill. ; 24 cm. Item 1031 LC Card 81-600618 DDC 353.0082/048 19
1. United States. Minority Business Development Agency. 2. Federal aid to minority business enterprises - United States. I. Title.
KF27 .S64 1980h

Examination of minority business participation in federal programs in Alaska : hearings before the Task Force on Minority Enterprise of the Subcommittee on General Oversight and Minority Enterprise of the Committee on Small Business, House of Representatives, Ninety-sixth Congress, second session, Anchorage Alaska, July 16 and 17, 1980. Washington : U. S. G.P.O., 1980. iv, 234 p. ; 24 cm. LC Card 80-604091 DDC 338.9798 19
1. Federal aid to minority business enterprises - Alaska. 2. Minority business enterprises - Alaska. I. Title.
KF27 .S64 1980d

Impact of inflation on small business : hearings before the Subcommittee on General Oversight and Minority Enterprise of the Committee on Small Business, House of Representatives, Ninety-sixth Congress, second session, Washington, D.C., April 16, 17, and May 13, 1980. Washington : U. S. G.P.O., 1980. iv, 343 p. : ill. ; 23 cm. Bibliography: p. 318-321. LC Card 80-603791 DDC 338.6/42/0973 19
1. Small business - United States. 2. Inflation (Finance) - United States. 3. United States - Economic policy - 1971-. I. Title.
KF27 .S64 1980f

Media concentration : hearing before the Subcommittee on General Oversight and Minority Enterprise of the Committee on Small Business, House of Representatives, Ninety-sixth Congress, second session .... Washington : U. S. Govt. Print. Off., 1980- v. : ill. ; 24 cm. Hearings held in Washington, D.C., Jan. 21, 1980- Includes bibliographical references. LC Card 80-603015 DDC 302.2/3 19
1. Mass media - Economic aspects - United States. 2. Press monopolies - United States. 3. Mass media - Law and legislation - United States. I. Title.
KF27 .S64 1980a

Minority truckers participation in Federal procurement contracts : hearing before the Task Force on Minority Enterprise of the Subcommittee on General Oversight and Minority Enterprise of the Committee on Small Business, House of Representatives, Ninety-sixth Congress, second session, Washington, D.C., March 31, 1980. Washington : U. S. Govt. Print. Off., 1980. iv, 107 p. ; 24 cm. LC Card 80-603017 DDC 346.73/023 19
1. Transportation, Automotive - United States - Freight. 2. Federal aid to minority business enterprises - United States. 3. Public contracts - United States. I. Title.
KF27 .S64 1980c

Product liability insurance ratemaking : hearing before the Subcommittee on General Oversight and Minority Enterprise of the Committee on Small Business, House of Representatives,

Ninety-sixth Congress, second session, Washington, D.C., October 1, 1980. Washington : U. S. G.P.O., 1980. iii, 45 p. ; 24 cm. LC Card 80-604047 DDC 368.5 19
1. Insurance, Products liability - United States. 2. Insurance, Products liability - United States - Rates and tables. I. Title.
KF27 .S64 1980e

SBA proposed size standards : hearings before the Subcommittee on General Oversight and Minority Enterprise of the Committee on Small Business, House of Representatives, Ninety-sixth Congress, second session, Washington, D.C., March 25 and April 30, 1980. Washington : U. S. Govt. Print. Off., 1980- v. ; 24 cm. Includes bibliographical references. LC Card 80-603083 DDC 338.6/42/0973 19
1. Small business - United States. 2. United States. Small Business Administration. 3. Industries, Size of. I. Title.
KF27 .S64 1980b

Small business preferential procurement programs : hearings before the Subcommittee on General Oversight and Minority Enterprise of the Committee on Small Business, House of Representatives, Ninety-sixth Congress, second session, Washington, D.C., August 18 and October 27, 1980. Washington : U. S. G.P.O., 1980 [i.e. 1981] iii, 640 p. : ill. ; 24 cm. Item 1031 LC Card 81-600845 DDC 353.0071/2 19
1. Public contracts - United States. 2. Small business - United States. I. Title.
KF27 .S64 1980l

State usury ceilings and their impact on small businesses : hearings before the Subcommittee on General Oversight and Minority Enterprise of the Committee on Small Business, House of Representatives, Ninety-sixth Congress, second session, Washington D.C., August 26 and September 23, 1980. Washington : U. S. G.P.O., 1980. iii, 294 p : ill. ; 24 cm. Item 1031 Bibliography: p. 39-40. LC Card 81-600855 DDC 338.6/42/0973 19
1. Usury laws - United States - States. 2. Small business - United States - States - Finance. 3. Consumer credit - Law and legislation - United States - States. I. Title.
KF27 .S64 1980g

Women in business : hearing before the Subcommittee on General Oversight and Minority Enterprise of the Committee on Small Business, House of Representatives, Ninety-sixth Congress, second session, Washington, D.C., September 18, 1980. Washington : U. S. G.P.O., 1980 [i.e. 1981] iv, 178 p. : ill. ; 24 cm. Item 1031 Includes bibliographical references. LC Card 81-600836 DDC 331.4/8165/00973 19
1. Women in business - United States. 2. Sex discrimination against women - United States. I. Title.
KF27 .S64 1980k

United States. Congress. House. Committee on Small Business. Subcommittee on Minority Enterprise and General Oversight. H.R. 2377, H.R. 2379, and Small Business Administration activities : hearings before the Subcommittee on Minority Enterprise and General Oversight of the Committee on Small Business, House of Representatives, Ninety-fifth Congress, first session, Washington, D.C., May 23, 25, and 26, 1977. Washington : U. S. Govt. Print. Off., 1977. iv, 188 p. ; 24 cm. LC Card 77-604012
1. Small business - Law and legislation - United States. 2. United States. Small Business Administration. I. Title.
KF27 .S65 1977c

United States. Congress. House. Committee on Small Business. Subcommittee on SBA and SBIC Authority and General Small Business Problems.
Judicial access/court costs--H.R. 5103 and H.R. 6429 : hearings before the Subcommittee on SBA and SBIC Authority and General Small Business Problems of the Committee on Small Business, House of Representatives, Ninety-sixth Congress, second session, Washington, D.C., April 17, 23, and May 1, 1980. Washington : U. S. Govt. Print. Off., 1980. iv, 335 p. : map ; 24 cm. Includes bibliographical references. LC Card 80-603019 DDC 346.73/0652/0269 19
1. Costs (Law) - United States. 2. Government

GOVERNMENT PUBLICATIONS - U.S.: 1981

451   United States. Congress. House. Committee on the Budget. Task

litigation - United States. 3. Administrative procedure - United States. 4. Judicial review of administrative acts - United States. 5. Small business - Law and legislation - United States. I. Title.
KF7 .S6814 1980a

SBA legislative request : hearing before the Subcommittee on SBA and SBIC Authority and General Small Business Problems of the Committee on Small Business, House of Representatives, Ninety-sixth Congress, second session, Washington, D.C., March 3, 1980. Washington : U. S. Govt. Print. Off., 1980. iii, 46 p. ; 24 cm.   LC Card 80-603112   DDC 346.73/0652 19
1. Small business - Law and legislation - United States. 2. Small business - United States - Finance. I. Title.
KF27 .S6814 1980

Timber purchase set-aside program : hearings before the Subcommittee on SBA and SBIC Authority and General Small Business Problems of the Committee on Small Business, House of Representatives, Ninety-sixth Congress, second session, Washington, D.C., May 21 and 22, 1980. Washington : U. S. Govt. Print. Off., 1980. iii, 128 p. ; 24 cm.   LC Card 80-603666   DDC 339.6/42/0973 19
1. Lumber trade - United States. 2. Small business - United States. 3. Forest policy - United States. I. Title.
KF27 .S6814 1980b

United States. Congress. House. Committee on Small Business. Subcommittee on Special Small Business Problems.
Problems of U. S. office machine dealers : hearing before the Subcommittee on Special Small Business Problems of the Committee on Small Business, House of Representatives, Ninety-sixth Congress, second session, Washington, D.C. : U. S. G.P.O., 1980. iii, 92 p. : forms ; 24 cm.   LC Card 80-603808   DDC 381/.4568 19
1. Office equipment and supplies industry - United States. I. Title.
KF27 .S686 1980

Rising sugar costs and their effect on retail bakers : hearing before the Subcommittee on Special Small Business Problems of the Committee on Small Business, House of Representatives, Ninety-sixth Congress, second session, Washington, D.C. September 22, 1980. Washington : U. S. G.P.O., 1980 [i.e. 1981] iii, 40 p. ; 24 cm.   Item 1031   LC Card 81-600856   DDC 381/.45664752/0973 19
1. Sugar - Prices - United States. 2. Bakers and bakeries - United States - Costs. I. Title.
KF27 .S686 1980a

United States. Congress. House. Committee on Standards of Official Conduct. In the matter of Representative Michael J. Myers : report of Committee on Standards of Official Conduct (to accompany H. Res. 794). [Washington, D.C. : U. S. G.P.O., 1980] 2 v. ; 24 cm. (Report / House of Representatives . no. 96-1387, v. 1-2) Vol. 1 has note: "Together with desenting views" handstamped on cover. Vol. 2 "Appendix 3 to report of special counsel upon completion of preliminary inquiry." "September 24, 1980." Item 1008-C, 1008-D (microfiche) Includes bibliographical references.   LC Card 81-601430   DDC 328.73/0766 19
1. Myers, Michael J. 2. United States. Congress. House - Expulsion. 3. Misconduct in office - United States. 4. Abscam Bribery Scandal, 1980-. I. Series: United States. Congress. House. Report , no. 96-1387, v. 1-2. II. Title.
KF32 .S7 1980b

United States. Congress. House. Committee on the Budget. Hearings printed in 1978 and later are available only in microform. Please consult the librarians in the Economic and Public Affairs Division.

Budget issues for fiscal year 1982 : hearings before the Committee on the Budget, House of Representatives, Ninety-seventh Congress, first session .... Washington : U. S. G.P.O., 1981- v. <1-2, 4 > : ill. ; 24 cm. Vol. 1: "January 29, February 3, 19, 24, 25, and 26, 1981." Vol. 2: "March 3, 4, 5, 9, and 11, 1981." Vol. 4: "March 25, 26, and 27, 1981." "97-1A." "97-1B." "97-1D." Item 1035-B-1, 1035-B-2 (microfiche) Includes bibliographical references.   LC Card 81-601797   DDC 353.0072/22 19
1. Budget - United States. I. Title.
KF27 .B8 1981

The Congressional budget process .

Washington , 1981. iii, 95 p. ;   LC Card 81-601830   DDC 353.0072/2 19
HJ2051 .C658

Economic issues for fiscal year 1981 : hearings before the Committee on the Budget, House of Representatives, Ninety-sixth Congress, second session. Washington : U. S. Govt. Print. Off., 1980. 2 v. (vi, 1355 p.) : ill. ; 24 cm. Hearings held Jan. 29-Mar. 6, 1980. Includes bibliographical references.   LC Card 80-602893   DDC 330.973/0926 19
1. Budget - United States. 2. United States - Economic conditions - 1971-. 3. United States - Economic policy - 1971-. I. Title.
KF27 .B8 1980

March 15 House Committee report request and supporting information. Washington, U. S. Govt. Print Off. 26 cm. Annual. At head of title, 1977- : 95th Congress, 1st session - Committee print. Title varies: 1977-78, March 15 House Committee report, request and instructions; 1979, March 15 House Committee report request, instructions, and supporting information.
1. Budget - United States - Periodicals. I. Title.
NYPL   [JLM 81-40]

Mid-year perspective on the economy : hearings before the Committee on the Budget, House of Representatives, Ninety-sixth Congress, second session, July 23 and 24, 1980. Washington : U. S. Govt. Print. Off., 1980. iii, 432 p. : graphs ; 24 cm. Includes bibliographical references.   LC Card 80-603475   DDC 338.5/443/0973 19
1. Budget - United States. 2. United States - Economic conditions - 1971-. I. Title.
KF27 .B8 1980b

Military readiness and the Rapid Deployment Joint Task Force (RDJTF) : hearings before the Committee on the Budget, House of Representatives, Ninety-sixth Congress, second session, September 30 and October 1, 1980. Washington : U. S. G.P.O., 1980. iii, 70 p. ; 24 cm.   LC Card 80-604107   DDC 355.3/5 19
1. United States. Rapid Deployment Force. 2. United States - Defenses. 3. United States - Armed Forces. I. Title.
KF27 .B8 1980d

President's economic revitalization program : hearings before the Committee on the Budget, House of Representatives, Ninety-sixth Congress, second session, September 8, 9, and 10, 1980. Washington : U. S. G.P.O., 1980. iii, 205 p. : ill. ; 24 cm.   LC Card 80-604100   DDC 338.973 19
1. United States - Economic policy - 1971-. 2. Budget - United States. I. Title.
KF27 .B8 1980c

Proposals to balance the budget : hearings before the Committee on the Budget, House of Representatives, Ninety-sixth Congress, second session, March 10 and 12, 1980. Washington : U. S. Govt. Print. Off., 1980. iv, 281 p. ; 24 cm.   LC Card 80-602724   DDC 353.0072/22 19
1. Budget - United States. I. Title.
KF27 .B8 1980a

A Summary and analysis of President Reagan's fiscal year 1982 budget revisions /. Washington , 1981. iii, 70 p. ;   LC Card 81-601828   DDC 353.0072/24 19
HJ2051 .S93

United States. Congressional Budget Office. Entering the 1980s . [Washington, D.C.] [1980] xxi, 101 p. :   LC Card 80-602038   DDC 336.73 19
HJ257.2 .U57 1980

United States. Congressional Budget Office. Index to the legislative history of the Congressional budget and impoundment control act of 1974 /. [Washington] [1980] xi, 481 p. ;   LC Card 80-603388   DDC 343.73/034 347.30334 19
KF6222.115 .A15 1980

United States. Congress. House. Committee on the Budget. Task Force on Budget Process.
Budget act review : hearings before the Task Force on Budget Process of the Committee on the Budget, House of Representatives, Ninety-sixth Congress, first session, December 11 and 12, 1979. Washington : U. S. Govt. Print. Off., 1980. iii, 297 p. ; 24 cm.   LC Card 80-602470   DDC 353.0072/22 19
1. Budget - United States. I. Title.
KF27 .B842 1979c

United States. Congress. House. Committee on the Budget. Task Force on Defense and International Affairs. Selective service registration : hearing before the Task Force on Defense and International Affairs of the Committee on the Budget, House of Representatives, Ninety-sixth Congress, second session, February 20, 1980. Washington : U. S. Govt. Print. Off., 1980. iii, 77 p. ; 24 cm.   LC Card 80-602430   DDC 355.2/2363/0973 19
1. Military service, Compulsory - United States. I. Title.
KF27 .B8438 1980a

United States. Congress. House. Committee on the Budget. Task Force on Entitlements, Uncontrollables, and Indexing. Indexing and the federal budget : hearings before the Task Force on Entitlements, Uncontrollables, and Indexing of the Committee on the Budget, House of Representatives, Ninety-seventh Congress, first session, March 10, 12, and 16, 1981. Washington : U. S. G.P.O., 1981. iv, 215 p. : ill. ; 24 cm. "TTF2" Item 1035-B-1, 1035-B-2 (microfiche) Includes bibliographical references.   LC Card 81-602178   DDC 353.0072/22 19
1. Indexation (Economics). 2. Budget - United States. I. Title.
KF27 .B846 1981

United States. Congress. House. Committee on the Budget. Task Force on Government Efficiency. Consultant and service contracts : hearing before the Task Force on Government Efficiency of the Committee on the Budget, House of Representatives, Ninety-sixth Congress, second session, November 17, 1980. Washington : U. S. G.P.O., 1980 [i.e. 1981] iii, 140 p. ; 24 cm. Includes bibliographical references.   LC Card 81-600948   DDC 353.0071/1 19
1. Government consultants - United States. 2. Public contracts - United States. I. Title.
KF27 .B847 1980

United States. Congress. House. Committee on the Budget. Task Force on Human and Community Resources. Prospects for human services programs in the economic and social climate of the eighties : hearing before the Task Force on Human and CommunityResources of the Committee on the Budget, House of Representatives, Ninety-sixth Congress, second session, April 25, 1980. Washington : U. S. Govt. Print. Off., 1980. iii, 103 p. : graphs ; 24 cm. Includes bibliographical references.   LC Card 80-603013   DDC 361/.973 19
1. Public welfare - United States. I. Title.
KF27 .B848 1980

United States. Congress. House. Committee on the Budget. Task Force on Human Resources and Block Grants. Human resources programs and block grants : hearings before the Task Force on Human Resources and Block Grants of the Committee on the Budget, House of Representatives, Ninety-seventh Congress, first session .... Washington : U. S. G.P.O., 1981. 2 v. : ill. ; 24 cm. Pt. 1: "March 10, 12, and 13, 1981." Pt. 2: "March 16 and 19, 1981." "TTF8." Item 1035-B-1, 1035-B-2 (microfiche) Includes bibliographical references.   LC Card 81-602053   DDC 361.6/1/0973 19
1. Block grants - United States. 2. United States - Social policy. I. Title.
KF27 .B85 1981

United States. Congress. House. Committee on the Budget. Task Force on State and Local Government.
Impact of the fiscal year 1981 budget on state and local governments : hearings before the Task Force on State and Local Government of the Committee on the Budget, House of Representatives, Ninety-sixth Congress, second session, February 26 and 27, 1980. Washington : U. S. Govt. Print. Off., 1980. iv, 586 p. ; 24 cm. Includes bibliographical references.   LC Card 80-602764   DDC 353.0072/5 19
1. Budget - United States. 2. Intergovernmental fiscal relations - United States. I. Title.
KF27 .B879 1980

The nuclear crisis and State and local governments : hearing before the Task Force on State and Local Government of the Committee on the Budget, House of Representatives, Ninety-sixth Congress, first session, June 4, 1979, New York, N.Y. Washington : U. S. Govt. Print. Off., 1980. iii, 34 p. ; 24 cm.   LC Card 80-601148   DDC

BIBLIOGRAPHIC GUIDE

United States. Congress. House. Committee on the District of

452

353.97470082/65621483/0289 19
1. Atomic power-plants - New York (State) - Safety measures. I. Title.
KF27 .B879 1979a

United States. Congress. House. Committee on the District of Columbia. (Old Catalog form: United States. District of Columbia, Committee on // Hearings printed in 1978 and later are available only in microform. Please consult the librarians in the Economic and Public Affairs Division.
Problems in urban centers : oversight hearings before the Committee on the District of Columbia, House of Representatives, Ninety-sixth Congress, second session, on problems in urban centers, Washington, D.C., and the federal government role, June 25, 26, 27, July 23, 24, 30, and September 30, 1980. Washington : U. S. G.P.O., 1980 [i.e. 1981] ix, 936, x p. : ill. ; 24 cm. "Serial No. 96-16" incorrect in publication. Includes index. Item 1014 Bibliography: p. 850-856. LC Card 81-601760 DDC 361.6/09753 19
1. Washington, D. C. - Economic conditions. 2. Washington, D. C. - Social conditions. 3. Cities and towns - United States. I. Title.
KF27 .D5 1980

Rental housing conversion and sale (Council Act 3-204) : oversight hearings and markup before the Committee on the District of Columbia, House of Representatives, Ninety-sixth Congress, second session, on H. Con. Res. 420 ... September 4, 1980. Washington : U. S. G.P.O., 1980. iv, 170 p. : ill., 1 map ; 23 cm. "Serial no. 96-18." Item 1014 Includes bibliographical references. LC Card 81-601407 DDC 346.7304/33 347.306433 19
1. Rental housing - Law and legislation - Washington (D.C.). 2. Condominium (Housing) - Washington (D.C.) - Conversion. I. Title.
KF27 .D5 1980a

United States. Congress. House. Committee on the District of Columbia. Subcommittee on Government Affairs and Budget. Home Rule Act amendments . Washington , 1980 [i.e. 1981] v, 243 p. ; LC Card 81-601402 DDC 342.753/02 347.53022 19
KF27 .D5396 1979c

United States. Congress. House. Committee on the District of Columbia. Subcommittee on Metropolitan Affairs. Washington Metropolitan Area Transit Authority . Washington , 1980. iv, 92 p. ; LC Card 80-603077 DDC 363.3/79 19
KF27 .D563 1980

United States. Congress. House. Committee on the District of Columbia. Ad Hoc Task Force on Utility Preparedness. Utility preparedness : oversight hearings before the ad hoc task force of the Committee on the District of Columbia, House of Representatives, Ninety-sixth Congress, first session, on the effect of nuclear plant closings on VA.-Wash.-MD. electric supply and avoiding service cutbacks through regional cooperation, April 19 and 20, 1979. Washington : U. S. Govt. Print. Off., 1980. v, 250 p. : ill. ; 23 cm. "Serial no. 96-13." LC Card 80-603354 DDC 363.6/2 19
1. Interconnected electric utility systems - Atlantic States. 2. Atomic power-plants - Atlantic States - Safety measures. 3. Electric power distribution - Washington metropolitan area. 4. Electric utilities - Washington metropolitan area. I. Title.
KF27 .D59 1979

United States. Congress. House. Committee on the District of Columbia. Subcommittee on Fiscal Affairs and Health.
Infant mortality : oversight hearings before the Subcommittee on Fiscal Affairs and Health of the Committee on the District of Columbia, House of Representatives, Ninety-sixth Congress, second session, on infant mortality as part of the committee's continuing study of health problems in the District of Columbia, May 7 and 8, 1980. Washington : U. S. G.P.O., 1980 [i.e. 1981] v, 366 p. : ill. ; 24 cm. "Serial no. 96-15." Item 1014 Includes bibliographical references. LC Card 81-601615 DDC 362.1/9892/0109753 19
1. Infants - Washington (D.C.) - Mortality. 2. Maternal health services - Washington (D.C.). 3. Infants - Care and hygiene - Washington (D.C.). I. Title.
KF27 .D5392 1980

St. Elizabeths Hospital : oversight hearings before the Subcommittee on Fiscal Affairs and Health of the Committee on the District of Columbia, House of Representatives, Ninety-sixth Congress, first session ... October 24 and 25, 1979. Washington : U. S. Govt. Print Off., 1980. iv, 206 p. : ill. ; 24 cm. "Serial No. 96-10." LC Card 80-601896 DDC 362.2/1/09753 19
1. Saint Elizabeths Hospital, Washington, D. C. I. Title.
KF27 .D5392 1979a

United States. Congress. House. Committee on the District of Columbia. Subcommittee on Government Affairs and Budget. Home Rule Act amendments : hearings before the Subcommittee on Government Affairs and Budget and the Committee on the District of Columbia, House of Representatives, Ninety-sixth Congress, first session, on H.R. 5927 ... H.R. 5928 ... H.R. 6147 ... December 5, 1979, and June 11, 1980. Washington : U. S. G.P.O., 1980 [i.e. 1981] v, 243 p. ; 23 cm. "Serial no. 96-12." Item 1014 Includes bibliographical references. LC Card 81-601402 DDC 342.753/02 347.53022 19
1. Home rule (District of Columbia). I. United States. Congress. House. Committee on the District of Columbia. II. Title.
KF27 .D5396 1979c

United States. Congress. House. Committee on the District of Columbia. Subcommittee on Judiciary, Manpower, and Education.
Criminal justice reforms : hearing before the Subcommittee on Judiciary, Manpower, and Education of the Committee on the District of Columbia, House of Representatives, Ninety-sixth Congress, second session, on H.R. 7988 ... September 23, 1980. Washington : U. S. G.P.O., 1981. iv, 125 p. ; 23 cm. "Serial no. 96-21." Item 1014 Includes bibliographical references. LC Card 81-601323 DDC 345.73/05 347.3055 19
1. Criminal justice, Administration of - Washington (D.C.). 2. Judges - Washington (D.C.). I. Title.
KF27 .D558 1980

United States. Congress. House. Committee on the District of Columbia. Subcommittee on Metropolitan Affairs. Washington Metropolitan Area Transit Authority : oversight hearing before the Subcommittee on Metropolitan Affairs and the Committee on the District of Columbia, House of Representatives, Ninety-sixth Congress, second session ... April 29, 1980. Washington : U. S. Govt. Print. Off., 1980. iv, 92 p. : ill. ; 24 cm. "Serial no. 96-14." LC Card 80-603077 DDC 363.3/79 19
1. Subways - Washington metropolitan area - Fires and fire prevention. 2. Washington Metropolitan Area Transit Authority. I. United States. Congress. House. Committee on the District of Columbia. II. Title.
KF27 .D563 1980

United States. Congress. House. Committee on the Judiciary. (Old Catalog form: United States. Judiciary, Committee on the (House)) // Hearings printed in 1978 and later are available only in microform. Please consult the librarians in the Economic and Public Affairs Division.
Columbia Broadcasting System, inc. CBS News. CBS News special report: "Impeachment, the Committee votes". [New York, 1974] 12 leaves;
*NYPL [*XMB-1400]*

Department of Justice authorization--fiscal year 1981 : oversight hearing before the Committee on the Judiciary, House of Representatives, Ninety-sixth Congress, second session, on Department of Justice authorization--fiscal year 1981, March 6, 1980. Washington : U. S. G.P.O., 1981. iii, 53 p. ; 24 cm. "Serial no. 93." Item 1020 LC Card 81-601368 DDC 353.0072/234 19
1. United States. Dept. of Justice - Appropriations and expenditures. I. Title.
KF27 .J8 1980

Impeachment; selected materials. Ninety-third Congress, first session. Washington, U. S. Govt. Print. Off., 1973. vi, 718 p. 24 cm. At head of title: 93d Congress, 1st session. House committee print. Includes bibliographical references. LC Card 73-602919
1. Impeachments - United States. I. Title.
KF4960 .A45

United States. Courts of Appeals. Federal rules

of appellate procedure, with forms, October 1, 1979. Washington , 1979. x, 33 p. : LC Card 80-601760 DDC 347.73/8 19
KF9052 .A4 1979

United States. Select Commission on Immigration and Refugee Policy. Semiannual report to Congress /. Washington , 1980. v, 74 p. ; LC Card 80-603270 DDC 353.0081/7 19
JV6481 1980 .S44

United States. Congress. House. Committee on the Judiciary. Subcommittee on Administrative Law and Governmental Relations.
Commission on Wartime Relocation and Internment of Civilians : hearing before the Subcommittee on the Judiciary, House of Representatives, Ninety-sixth Congress, second session, on H.R. 5499 ... June 2, 1980. Washington : U. S. G.P.O., 1980 [i.e. 1981] iii, 179 p. : ill. ; 24 cm. "Serial no. 55." Item 1020 Bibliography: p. 83-85. LC Card 81-600929 DDC 342.73/088 347.30288 19
1. United States. Commission on Wartime Relocation and Internment of Civilians. 2. Japanese Americans - Legal status, laws, etc. 3. Japanese Americans - Evacuation and relocation, 1942-1945. I. Title.
KF27 .J832 1980h

Compensation of military personnel and government employees for loss of personal property incident to their foreign service : hearing before the Subcommittee on Administrative Law and Governmental Relations of the Committee on the Judiciary, House of Representatives, Ninety-sixth Congress, second session, on H.R. 6086 and companion measures ... February 6, 1980. Washington : U. S. Govt. Print. Off., 1980. iii, 110 p. : forms ; 23 cm. "Serial no. 30." LC Card 80-602775 DDC 346.7304/7 19
1. United States - Officials and employees in foreign countries. 2. Reparations. 3. United States - Claims. I. Title.
KF27 .J832 1980

Former Members of Congress : hearing before the Subcommittee on Administrative Law and Governmental Relations of the Committee on the Judiciary, House of Representatives, Ninety-sixth Congress, second session ... September 19, 1980. Washington : U. S. G.P.O., 1980. iii, 12 p. ; 24 cm. "Serial no. 42." LC Card 80-604044 DDC 342.73/055 347.30255 19
1. Former Members of Congress (Organization). I. Title.
KF27 .J832 1980d

Gold Star Wives : hearing before the Subcommittee on Administrative Law and Governmental Relations of the Committee on the Judiciary, House of Representatives, Ninety-sixth Congress, second session, on H.R. 154 ... June 16, 1980. Washington : U. S. G.P.O., 1980. iii, 112 p. : ill. ; 24 cm. "Serial no. 50." Item 1020 LC Card 81-600835 DDC 343.73/011 347.30311 19
1. Gold Star Wives of America. I. Title.
KF27 .J832 1980f

Good Samaritan act : hearing before the Subcommittee on Administrative Law and Governmental Relations of the Committee on the Judiciary, House of Representatives, Ninety-sixth Congress, second session, on H.R. 3203 ... July 28, 1980. Washington : U. S. G.P.O., 1980 [i.e. 1981] iii, 116 p. ; 24 cm. "Serial no. 53." Item 1020 Bibliography: p. 108-111. LC Card 81-600969 DDC 346.7303/32 347.306332 19
1. Medical personnel - Malpractice - United States. 2. Assistance in emergencies - United States. 3. Air lines - Employees - Legal status, laws, etc. - United States. 4. Travelers - Medical care - Law and legislation - United States. I. Title.
KF27 .J832 1980e

National ski patrol system recognition act of 1979 : hearing before the Subcommittee on Administrative Law and Governmental Relations of the Committee on thhe Judiciary, House of Representatives, Ninety-sixth Congress, second session, on H.R. 2279 ... July 28, 1980. Washington : U. S. G.P.O., 1980. iii, 62 p. ; 24 cm. "Serial no. 49." Item 1020 LC Card 81-600585 DDC 344.73/0476 347.304476 19
1. National Ski Patrol System (U. S.). I. Title.
KF27 .J832 1980g

Regulation reform act of 1979 : hearings before

GOVERNMENT PUBLICATIONS - U.S.: 1981

453

United States. Congress. House. Committee on the Judiciary.

the Subcommittee on Administrative Law and Governmental Relations of the Committee on the Judiciary, House of Representatives, Ninety-sixth Congress, first and second sessions, on H.R. 3263 .... Washington : U. S. Govt. Print. Off., 1980- v. ; 24 cm. Hearings held Nov. 7, 1979 "Serial no. 41." LC Card 80-603418 DDC 342.73/066 19
1. Administrative procedure - United States. 2. Trade regulation - United States. I. Title.
KF27 .J832 1980a

Statute of limitations for certain claims by the United States on behalf of Indians : hearing before the Subcommittee on Administrative Law and Governmental Relations of the Committee on the Judiciary, House of Representatives, Ninety-sixth Congress, second session, on S. 2222 ... February 27, 1980. Washington : U. S. Govt. Print. Off., 1980. iii, 61 p. ; 24 cm. "Serial no. 40." LC Card 80-603453 DDC 346.7304/32/08897 347.30643208897 19
1. Indians of North America - Claims. 2. Indians of North America - Land tenure. 3. Limitations of actions - United States. I. Title.
KF27 .J832 1980b

United States. Congress. House. Committee on the Judiciary. Subcommittee on Civil and Constitutional Rights.
Authorization request of the Community Relations Service at the Department of Justice : hearing before the Subcommittee on Civil and Constitutional Rights of the Committee on the Judiciary, House of Representatives, Ninety-sixth Congress, second session, on oversight--authorization request of the Community Relations Service at the Department of Justice for fiscal year 1981, February 29, 1980. Washington : U. S. G.P.O., 1980 [i.e. 1981] iii, 53 p. ; 24 cm. "Serial no. 89." Item 1020 LC Card 81-601641 DDC 353.0072/234 19
1. United States. Community Relations Service - Appropriations and expenditures. I. Title.
KF27 .J847 1980d

Authorization request of the U. S. Commission on Civil Rights : hearing before the Subcommittee on Civil and Constitutional Rights of the Committee on the Judiciary, House of Representatives, Ninety-sixth Congress, second session ... March 28, 1980. Washington : U. S. Govt. Print. Off., 1980. iii, 16 p. ; 24 cm. "Serial no. 37." LC Card 80-603033 DDC 353.0072/236811 19
1. United States. Commission on Civil Rights - Appropriations and expenditures. I. Title.
KF27 .J847 1980a

Equal employment opportunities at the Department of Justice : oversight hearing before the Subcommittee on Civil and Constitutional Rights of the Committee on the Judiciary, House of Representatives, Ninety-sixth Congress, first session, on equal employment opportunities at the Department of Justice, March 28, 1979. Washington : U. S. G.P.O., 1981. iii, 147 p. : ill. ; 24 cm. "Serial no. 86." Item 1020 Includes bibliographical references. LC Card 81-601922 DDC 353.5 19
1. United States. Dept. of Justice -Officials and employees. 2. Affirmative action programs - United States. 3. Discrimination in employment - United States. I. Title.
KF27 .J847 1979h

Equal employment opportunity practices in the federal judiciary : hearings before the Subcommittee on Civil and Constitutional Rights of the Committee on the Judiciary, House of Representatives, Ninety-sixth Congress, first and second sessions, on equal employment opportunity practices in the federal judiciary, May 10, 1979, May 30, and November 19, 1980. Washington : U. S. G.P.O., 1981. iv, 578 p. : ill. ; 24 cm. "Serial no. 88." Includes bibliographical references. LC Card 81-601852 DDC 353.008/8 19
1. Courts - United States - Officials and employees. 2. Discrimination in employment - United States. I. Title.
KF27 .J847 1979g

Federal capabilities in crisis management and terrorism : oversight hearings before the Subcommittee on Civil and Constitutional Rights of th Committee on the Judiciary, House of Representatives, Ninety-sixth Congress, first and second sessions, on federal capabilities in

crisis management and terrorism, April 5, 1979, and May 19, 1980. Washington : U. S. G.P.O., 1980 [i.e. 1981] iii, 68 p. ; 24 cm. "Serial no. 87." Item 1020 LC Card 81-600980 DDC 353.0075 19
1. Terrorism - United States. 2. Terrorism - United States. - Prevention. I. Title.
KF27 .J847 1980c

Legislative charter for the FBI : hearings before the Subcommittee on Civil and Constitutional Rights of the Committee on the Judiciary, House of Representatives, Ninety-sixth Congress, first and second sessions, on H.R. 5030 ... September 6, 12, October 18, 19, November 8, 13, 15, December 6, 1979, and February 7, 1980. Washington : U. S. G.P.O., 1980 [i.e. 1981] iv, 560 p. ; 24 cm. "Serial no. 52." Item 1020 Includes bibliographical references. LC Card 81-600983 DDC 344.73/0525 347.304525 19
1. United States. Federal Bureau of Investigation. I. Title.
KF27 .J843 1979a

Milwaukee road's freight-carrying capacity : hearing before the Subcommittee on Civil and Constitutional Rights of the Committee on the Judiciary, House of Representatives, Ninety-sixth Congress, first session, on H.R. 4686 ... July 23, 1979. Washington : U. S. Govt. Print. Off., 1980. iii, 31 p. ; 24 cm. "Serial no. 32." LC Card 80-602526 DDC 343.73/0958 19
1. Chicago, Milwaukee, St. Paul and Pacific Railroad. 2. Railroad law - United States. 3. Railroads - United States - Freight. I. Title.
KF27 .J847 1979d

Minority language provisions of the Voting Rights Act : hearing before the Subcommittee on Civil and Constitutional Rights of the Committee on the Judiciary, House of Representatives, Ninety-sixth Congress, second session, on minority language provisions of the Voting Rights Act, July 30, 1980. Washington : U. S. G.P.O., 1980. iii, 29 p. ; 24 cm. "Serial no. 91." Item 1020 LC Card 81-601330 DDC 324.6/4/0973 19
1. Voters, Registration of - United States. 2. Election law - United States. 3. Language policy - United States. I. Title.
KF27 .J847 1980e

Oversight on GAO report : hearing before the Subcommittee on Civil and Constitutional Rights of the Committee on the Judiciary, House of Representatives, Ninety-sixth Congress, second session, on oversight on GAO report, April 15, 1980. Washington : U. S. G.P.O., 1980. iii, 131 p. ; 24 cm. "Serial no. 51." Includes bibliographical references. LC Card 81-600610 DDC 353.0081/1 19
1. Discrimination - United States. 2. Economic assistance, Domestic - United States. 3. Subsidies - United States. I. Title.
KF27 .J847 1980b

Prepublication review and secrecy requirements imposed upon federal employees : hearing before the Subcommittee on Civil and Constitutional Rights of the Committee on the Judiciary, House of Representatives, Ninety-sixth Congress, second session, on prepublication review and secrecy requirements imposed upon federal employees, July 29, 1980. Washington : U. S. G.P.O., 1981. iii, 100 p. ; 24 cm. "Serial no. 90." Item 1020 Includes bibliographical references. LC Card 81-601753 DDC 353.0071/45 19
1. United States. Central Intelligence Agency - Officials and employees. 2. Government information - United States. 3. Secrecy (Law) - United States. I. Title.
KF27 .J847 1980g

Technical errors in and clarity of Public Law 95-598 : hearings before the Subcommittee on Civil and Constitutional Rights of the Committee on the Judiciary, House of Representatives, Ninety-sixth Congress, first and second sessions ... November 28, 1979, and April 29, 1980. Washington : U. S. Govt. Print. Off., 1980. iii, 162 p. ; 23 cm. "Serial no. 34." LC Card 80-602797 DDC 346.73/078 19
1. Bankruptcy - United States. 2. Municipal bankruptcy - United States. I. Title.
KF27 .J847 1980

Use of classified information in federal criminal cases : hearings before the Subcommittee on Civil and Constitutional Rights of the Committee on the Judiciary, House of

Representatives, Ninety-sixth Congress, second session, on H.R. 4736 ... April 24 and May 13, 1980. Washington : U. S. G.P.O., 1980 [i.e. 1981] iii, 103 p. ; 23 cm. "Serial no. 54." Item 1020 LC Card 81-600944 DDC 347.73/64 347.30764 19
1. Evidence, Documentary - United States. 2. Security classification (Government documents) - United States. 3. Government litigation - United States. I. Title.
KF27 .J847 1980f

United States. Congress. House. Committee on the Judiciary. Subcommittee on Courts, Civil Liberties, and the Administration of Justice.
Federal court organization and fifth circuit division : hearings before the Subcommittee on Courts, Civil Liberties, and the Administration of Justice of the Committee on the Judiciary, House of Representatives, Ninety-sixth Congress, second session, on H.R. 6060, H.R. 7665, and related bills ... August 22, 1980. Washington : U. S. G.P.O., 1980 [i.e. 1981] v, 463 p. : ill. ; 24 cm. "Serial no. 64." Item 1020 Includes bibliographical references. LC Card 81-601347 DDC 347.73/242 347.307332 19
1. United States. Court of Appeals (5th Circuit). 2. District courts - United States. 3. Appellate courts - United States. I. Title.
KF27 .J857 1980b

Judicial tenure and discipline, 1979-80 : hearings before the Subcommittee on Courts, Civil Liberties, and the Administration of Justice of the Committee on the Judiciary, House of Representatives, Ninety-sixth Congress, first and second sessions .... Washington : U. S. Govt. Print. Off., 1980. iv, 838 p. : ill. ; 24 cm. "Serial no. 36." Includes bibliographical references. LC Card 80-603096 DDC 347.73/14 19
1. Judges - United States - Appointment, qualifications, tenure, etc. 2. Judges - United States - Discipline. I. Title.
KF27 .J857 1979k

Judiciary implications of draft registration--1980 : hearings before the Subcommittee on Courts, Civil Liberties, and the Administration of Justice of the Committee on the Judiciary, House of Representatives, Ninety-sixth Congress, second session ... April 14 and May 22, 1980. Washington : U. S. G.P.O., 1980. iv, 390 p. : ill. ; 24 cm. "Serial no. 45." Includes bibliographical references. LC Card 80-604063 DDC 343.73/0122 347.303122 19
1. Military service, Compulsory - United States. 2. Military service, Compulsory - United States - Draft resisters. 3. Civil rights - United States. I. Title.
KF27 .J857 1980

Legal Services Corporation reauthorization : hearings before the Subcommittee on Courts, Civil Liberties, and the Administration of Justice of the Committee on the Judiciary, House of Representatives, Ninety-sixth Congress, first session, on Legal Services Corporation reauthorization, September 21, 27, 1979. Washington : U. S. G.P.O., 1981. xii, 976 p. : ill. ; 24 cm. "Serial no. 60." Item 1020 Includes bibliographical references. LC Card 81-601609 DDC 353.0072/234 19
1. Legal Services Corporation - Appropriations and expenditures. I. Title.
KF27 .J857 1979m

Prayer in public schools and buildings--federal court jurisdiction : hearings before the Subcommittee on Courts, Civil Liberties, and the Administration of Justice of the Committee on the Judiciary, House of Representatives, Ninety-sixth Congress, second session, on S. 450 ... July 29, 30, August 19, 21, and September 9, 1980. Washington : U. S. G.P.O., 1981. iv, 976 p. ; 24 cm. "Serial no. 63." Item 1020 Includes bibliographies. LC Card 81-601626 DDC 344.73/0796 347.304796 19
1. United States. Supreme Court. 2. Jurisdiction - United States. 3. Religion in the public schools - Law and legislation - United States. I. Title.
KF27 .J857 1980a

State Justice Institute/annual message of chief justice--1980 : hearing before the Subcommittee on Courts, Civil Liberties, and the Administration of Justice of the Committee on the Judiciary, House of Representatives, Ninety-sixth Congress, second session, on H.R. 6709, S. 2387, S. 2483, and H.R. 6597 ... September 19, 1980. Washington : U. S.

BIBLIOGRAPHIC GUIDE

United States. Congress. House. Committee on the Judiciary.

454

G.P.O., 1981. iii, 276 p. ; 24 cm. "Serial no. 65."
Item 1020 Includes bibliographical references. LC
Card 81-601790   DDC 347.73 347.307 19
1. State Justice Institute (U. S.). 2. Courts - United
States. 3. Justice, Administration of - United States. 4.
Judges - United States. I. Title.
KF27 .J857 1980c

Trademarks and the Federal Trade
Commission : hearings before the Subcommittee
on Courts, Civil Liberties, and the
Administration of Justice of the Committee on
the Judiciary, House of Representatives,
Ninety-sixth Congress, first session, on H.R.
3685 ... October 17 and 18, 1979. Washington :
U. S. Govt. Print. Off., 1980. iii, 199 p. ; 23
cm. "Serial no. 33."   LC Card 80-602813   DDC
346.7304/88 19
1. Trade-marks - United States. 2. United States.
Federal Trade Commission. I. Title.
KF27 .J857 1979j

United States. Congress. House. Committee on
the Judiciary. Subcommittee on Crime.
United States. Library of Congress.
Congressional Research Service. Corporate
crime /. Washington , 1980. iii, 106 p. ; LC
Card 80-602274   DDC 364.1/68 19
HV6769 .U55 1980

United States. Congress. House. Committee on
the Judiciary. Subcommittee on Criminal
Justice. Compensating crime victims :
hearings before the Subcommittee on Criminal
Justice of the Committee on the Judiciary,
House of Representatives, Ninety-sixth
Congress, first session, on H.R. 1899 ...
February 28 and April 3, 1979. Washington :
U. S. Govt. Print. Off., 1980 [i.e. 1981] iii, 228 p. ; 24
cm. "Serial no. 79." Item 1020 Includes bibliographical
references. LC Card 81-600967   DDC 344.73/03288
347.3043288 19
1. Reparation - United States. I. Title.
KF27 .J859 1979

United States. Congress. House. Committee on
the Judiciary. Subcommittee on Immigration,
Refugees, and International Law.
Admission of alien physicians for graduate
medical education : hearing before the
Subcommittee on Immigration, Refugees, and
International Law of the Committee on the
Judiciary, House of Representatives,
Ninety-sixth Congress, second session, on H.R.
7118 ... May 14, 1980. Washington : U. S.
Govt. Print. Off., 1980. iii, 250 p. ; 24 cm.
"Serial no. 38." Includes bibliographical references. LC
Card 80-603068   DDC 344.73/07684 19
1. Physicians, Foreign - Licenses - United States. 2.
Medical education - Law and legislation - United
States. 3. Emigration and immigration law - United
States. I. Title.
KF27 .J8645 1980

Caribbean migration : oversight hearings before
the Subcommittee on Immigration, Refugees,
and International Law of the Committee on the
Judiciary, House of Representatives,
Ninety-sixth Congress, second session, on
Caribbean migration, May 13, June 4, 17, 1980.
Washington : U. S. G.P.O., 1980 [i.e. 1981] iv,
313 p. ; 24 cm. "Serial no. 84." Item 1020 Includes
bibliographical references. LC Card 81-601637   DDC
325/.21/09729 19
1. Refugees, Political - United States. 2. Refugees,
Political - Cuba. 3. Refugees, Political - Haiti. I. Title.
KF27 .J8645 1980c

Efficiency of the Immigration and
Naturalization Service : hearing before the
Subcommittee on Immigration, Refugees, and
International Law of the Committee on the
Judiciary, House of Representatives,
Ninety-sixth Congress, first session, on H.R.
5087 ... October 31, 1979. Washington : U. S.
Govt. Print. Off., 1980. iii, 88 p. ; 24 cm. "Serial
no. 29." LC Card 80-602462   DDC 353.0081/7 19
1. Emigration and immigration law - United States. 2.
United States. Immigration and Naturalization Service.
I. Title.
KF27 .J8645 1979d

Immigration and Naturalization Service
oversight : hearings before the Subcommittee on
Immigration, Refugees, and International Law
of the Committee on the Judiciary, House of
Representatives, Ninety-sixth Congress, second
session ... February 27, 28, March 12, 1980.
Washington : U. S. G.P.O., 1980. iii, 230 p. ;
24 cm. "Serial no. 47." LC Card 80-604019   DDC

353.0081/7 19
1. United States. Immigration and Naturalization
Service. I. Title.
KF27 .J8645 1980b

U. S. immigration policy regarding Iranian
nationals : hearing before the Subcommittee on
Immigration, Refugees, and International Law
of the Committee on the Judiciary, House of
Representatives, Ninety-sixth Congress, second
session, on U. S. immigration policy regarding
Iranian nationals, Aprial 17, 1980. Washington :
U. S. G.P.O., 1981. iii, 60 p. ; 24 cm. "Serial no.
83." Item 1020   LC Card 81-601599   DDC
325/.255/0973 19
1. Iranians - United States. 2. Iran Hostage Crisis,
1979-1981. 3. United States - Emigration and
immigration. I. Title.
KF27 .J8645 1980d

Waiver of nonimmigrant visa requirements :
hearing before the Subcommittee on
Immigration, Refugees, and International Law
of the Committee on the Judiciary, House of
Representatives, Ninty-sixth Congress, second
session, on H.R. 7125 ... April 28, 1980.
Washington : U. S. Govt. Print. Off., 1980. iv,
146 p. ; 24 cm. "Serial no. 39." LC Card 80-603043
DDC 342.73/082 19
1. Admission of nonimmigrants - United States. 2.
Passports - United States. I. Title.
KF27 .J8645 1980a

United States. Congress. House. Committee on
the Judiciary. Subcommittee on Monopolies
and Commercial Law.
Antitrust exemptions and immunities : hearing
before the Subcommittee on Monopolies and
Commercial Law of the Committee on the
Judiciary, House of Representatives,
Ninety-fifth Congress, first session ... March 29,
1977. Washington : U. S. Govt. Print. Off.,
1977. 2 v. (iii, 1907 p.) : ill. ; 23 cm. "Serial no.
6." LC Card 80-603699   DDC 343.73/072 347.30372
19
1. Antitrust law - United States. I. Title.
KF27 .J8663 1977d

Customs Courts act of 1980 : hearings before
the Subcommittee on Monopolies and
Commercial Law of the Committee on the
Judiciary, House of Representatives,
Ninety-sixth Congress, second session, on H.R.
6394 ... February 13 and 28, 1980.
Washington : U. S. Govt. Print. Off., 1980. iii,
405 p. ; 24 cm. "Serial no. 31." LC Card 80-602768
DDC 343.7305/6/0269 19
1. Customs courts - United States. I. Title.
KF27 .J8663 1980

Omnibus Maritime Regulatory Reform
Revitalization and Reorganization Act of 1980 :
hearing before the Subcommittee on
Monopolies and Commercial Law of the
Committee on the Judiciary, House of
Representatives, Ninety-sixth Congress, second
session, on H.R. 6899 ... June 5, 1980.
Washington : U. S. G.P.O., 1980 [i.e. 1981] iii,
160 p. ; 24 cm. "Serial no. 68." Item 1020 Includes
bibliographical references. LC Card 81-601640   DDC
343.73/096 347.30396 19
1. Maritime law - United States. 2. Shipping
conferences. I. Title.
KF27 .J8663 1980a

Restoring effective enforcement of the anti-trust
laws : hearings before the Subcommittee on
Monopolies and Commercial Law of the
Committee on the Judiciary, House of
Representatives, Ninety-sixth Congress, first
session, on H.R. 2060 and H.R 2204 and other
proposals ... February 27, March 7, and April
10, 1979. Washington : U. S. G.P.O., 1979. v,
504 p. ; 24 cm. "Serial no. 2." LC Card 80-603813
DDC 343.73/072/0262 347.303720262 19
1. Antitrust law - United States. I. Title.
KF27 .J8663 1979a

Telecommunications Act of 1980 : hearings
before the Subcommittee on Monopolies and
Commercial Law of the Committee on the
Judiciary, House of Representatives,
Ninety-sixth Congress, second session, on H.R.
6121 ... September 9 and 16, 1980.
Washington : U. S. G.P.O., 1981. iii, 803 p. :
ill. ; 24 cm. "Serial no. 69." Item 1020 Includes
bibliographical references. LC Card 81-601614   DDC
343.73/0994/0262 347.3039940262 19
1. Telecommunication - Law and legislation - United

States. I. Title.
KF27. J8663 1980b

United States. Congress. House. Committee on
Veterans' Affairs. (Old Catalog form: United
States. Veterans' Affairs, Committee on //
Hearings printed in 1978 and later are
available only in microform. Please consult
the librarians in the Economic and Public
Affairs Division.
The American Legion legislative goals : hearing
before the Committee on Veteran's Affairs,
House of Representatives, Ninety-sixth
Congress, second session, September 23, 1980.
Washington : U. S. G.P.O., 1980. iii, 38 p. ; 24
cm. "Serial no. 97-1." LC Card 81-601142   DDC
343.73/011 347.30311 19
1. Veterans - Legal status, laws, etc. - United States. 2.
American Legion. I. Title.
KF27 .V4 1980b

Legislative priorities of our national service
organizations : hearing before the Committee on
Veterans' Affairs, House of Representatives,
Ninety-seventh Congress, first session, February
26, 1981. Washington : U. S. G.P.O., 1981. iii,
97 ; 24 cm. "Serial no. 97-3." Item 1027-A, 1027-B
(microfiche) LC Card 81-601764   DDC 343.73/011
347.30311 19
1. Veterans - Legal status, laws, etc. - United States. I.
Title.
KF27 .V4 1981

Legislative recommendations of the American
Legion for fiscal year 1978 : hearings before the
Committee on Veterans' Affairs, House of
Representatives, Ninety-fifth Congress, first
session ... September 27, 1977. Washington : U.
S. G.P.O., 1977. iii, 26 p. ; 24 cm. LC Card
81-601481   DDC 343.73/011 347.30311 19
1. Veterans - Legal status, laws, etc. - United States.
American Legion. II. Title.
KF27 .V4 1977c

Oversight on admission policies to VA medical
care facilities : joint hearing before the
Committees on Veterans' Affairs of the House
of Representatives and United States Senate,
Ninety-sixth Congress, first session, ... October
25, 1979. Washington, D.C. : U. S. Govt. Print.
Off., 1980. vi, 373 p. : ill. ; 24 cm. Includes
bibliographical references. LC Card 80-601953   DDC
353.0081/2 19
1. Hospitals, Veterans' - United States. 2. Veterans -
Medical care - United States. I. United States.
Congress. Senate. Committee on Veterans' Affairs. II.
Title.
KF27 .V4 1979f

Proposed Veterans' Administration budget for
fiscal year 1982 : hearing before the Committee
on Veterans' Affairs, House of Representatives,
Ninety-seventh Congress, first session, February
18, 1981. Washington : U. S. G.P.O., 1981. iii
87 p. : ill. ; 24 cm. "Serial no. 97-1." Item 1027-A,
1027-B (microfiche) LC Card 81-601758   DDC
353.0072/236812 19
1. United States. Veterans Administration -
Appropriations and expenditures. I. Title.
KF27 .V4 1981a

Status of Vietnam veterans in the bay area :
hearing before an ad hoc subcommittee of the
Committee on Veterans' Affairs, House of
Representatives, Ninety-sixth Congress, second
session, April 10, 1980. Washington : U. S.
G.P.O., 1980. iii, 64 p. ; 24 cm. LC Card
80-604108   DDC 355.1/15/097946 19
1. Veterans - California - San Francisco Bay region. 2.
Vietnamese Conflict, 1961-1975 - United States. I.
Title.
KF27 .V4 1980a

Veterans organizations legislative
recommendations : hearings before the
Committee on Veteran's Affairs, House of
Representatives, Ninety-sixth Congress, second
session ... February 26, March 4, 26, and 27,
1980. Washington : U. S. Govt. Print. Off.,
1980. iii, 108 p. ; 24 cm. LC Card 80-602461
DDC 343.73/011 19
1. Veterans - Legal status, laws, etc. - United States. I.
Title.
KF27 .V4 1980

1981 legislative program of the Disabled
American Veterans : hearing before the
Committee on Veterans' Affairs, House of
Representatives, Ninety-seventh Congress, first
session, February 24, 1981. Washington : U. S.
G.P.O., 1981. iii, 27 p. ; 27 cm. "Serial no. 97-2."

GOVERNMENT PUBLICATIONS - U.S.: 1981

455

United States. Congress. House. Committee on Veterans' Affairs.

Item 1027-A, 1027-B (microfiche)   LC Card
81-601622   DDC 343.73/0115/0262
347.3031150262 19
1. Veterans, Disabled - Legal status, laws, etc. - United States. I. Title.
KF27 .V4 1981b

United States. Congress. House. Committee on Veterans' Affairs. Subcommittee on Compensation, Pension, Insurance, and Memorial Affairs.
Benefits and services for former prisoners of war : hearing before the Subcommittee on Compensation, Pension, Insurance, and Memorial Affairs of the Committee on Veterans' Affairs, House of Representatives, Ninety-sixth Congress, second session, June 25, 1980. Washington : U. S. Govt. Print. Off., 1980. iii, 71 p. : ill. ; 24 cm.   LC Card 80-603807
DDC 343.73/0115 347.303115 19
1. Ex-prisoners of war - Medical care - United States. 2. Veterans, Disabled - Medical care - United States. 3. Veterans - Medical care - United States. I. Title.
KF27 .V43 1980e

Hearings on H.R. 4367 and H.R. 6688 : hearings before the Subcommittee on Compensation, Pension, Insurance, and Memorial Affairs of the Committee on Veterans' Affairs, House of Representatives, Ninety-sixth Congress, second session, on measures which would limit veterans benefits and services, April 22 and 28, 1980. Washington : U. S. Govt. Print. Off., 1980. iv, 353 p. : ill. ; 24 cm.   LC Card 80-603310   DDC 343.73/011 19
1. Veterans - Legal status, laws, etc. - United States. 2. Pensions, Military - United States. I. Title.
KF27 .V43 1980b

Life insurance programs for veterans and service persons : hearings before the Subcommittee on Compensation, Pension, Insurance, and Memorial Affairs of the Committee on Veteran's Affairs, House of Representatives, Ninety-sixth Congress, second session, May 20 and June 9, 1980. Washington : U. S. G.P.O., 1980. v, 314 p. : ill. ; 24 cm. Item 1027 Includes bibliographical references.   LC Card 81-601337   DDC 353.001/234 19
1. Insurance, Government life - United States. 2. Veterans - Legal status, laws, etc. - United States. I. Title.
KF27 .V43 1980f

Review of compensation and DIC programs : hearings before the Subcommittee on Compensation, Pension, Insurance, and Memorial Affairs of the Committee on Veterans' Affairs, House of Representatives, Ninety-sixth Congress, second session, April 29 and 30, 1980. Washington : U. S. Govt. Print. Off., 1980. iii, 93 p. ; 24 cm.   LC Card 80-603330 DDC 343.73/0112 19
1. Pensions, Military - United States. 2. Veterans, Disabled - United States. 3. Survivors' benefits - United States. I. Title.
KF27 .V43 1980a

Review of the national cemetery system administered by the Veterans' Administration, also H.R. 6146 : hearing before the Subcommittee on Compensation, Pension, Insurance, and Memorial Affairs of the Committee on Veterans' Affairs, House of Representatives, Ninety-sixth Congress, second session, May 12, 1980. Washington : U. S. Govt. Print. Off., 1980. iii, 36 p. ; 24 cm.   LC Card 80-603344   DDC 353.0086 19
1. National cemeteries - United States. 2. National cemeteries - Law and legislation - United States. I. Title.
KF27 .V43 1980c

Review of the operation of the overseas cemeteries and memorials administered by the American Battle Monuments Commission and Arlington National Cemetery, also H.R 6355 and H.R. 6356 : hearing before the Subcommittee on Compensation, Pension, Insurance, and Memorial Affairs of the Committee on Veterans' Affairs, House of Representatives, Ninety-sixth Congress, second session, March 24, 1980. Washington : U. S. Govt. Print. Off., 1980. iii, 52 p. ; 24 cm.   LC Card 80-603070   DDC 343.73/0256 19
1. National cemeteries - Law and legislation - United States. 2. National cemeteries, American. 3. United

States. American Battle Monuments Commission. I. Title.
KF27 .V43 1980

Workloads in the Department of Veterans Benefits and the Board of Veterans Appeals : hearing before the Subcommittee on Compensation, Pension, Insurance, and Memorial Affairs of the Committee on Veterans' Affairs, House of Representatives, Ninety-sixth Congress, second session, May 7, 1980. Washington : U. S. Govt. Print. Off., 1980. iii, 45 p. ; 24 cm.   LC Card 80-603663 DDC 353.0081/2 19
1. United States. Dept. of Veterans Benefits. 2. United States. Board of Veterans' Appeals. I. Title.
KF27 .V43 1980d

United States. Congress. House. Committee on Veterans' Affairs. Subcommittee on Education, Training, and Employment.
Hearing on the rehabilitation, education, and training programs administered by the Veterans' Administration--Nashville, Tenn. : hearing before the Subcommittee on Education, Training, and Employment of the Committee on Veterans' Affairs, House of Representatives, Ninety-sixth Congress, second session, September 26, 1980. Washington : U. S. G.P.O., 1981. iii, 181 p. ; 24 cm. Item 1027   LC Card 81-601153   DDC 355.1/15/09768 19
1. Veterans, Disabled - Vocational rehabilitation - Tennessee. 2. Veterans - Education - Tennessee. 3. United States. Veterans Administration. I. Title.
KF27 .V436 1980a

Oversight hearings on employment programs for veterans and veterans' preference in federal employment : hearing before the Subcommittee in Education, Training, and Employment of the Committee on Veterans' Afairs, House of Representatives, Ninety-sixth Congress, second session, August 21 and 26, 1980. Washington : U. S. G.P.O., 1981. iii, 221 p. : ill. ; 24 cm. Item 1027 Includes bibliographical references.   LC Card 81-601161   DDC 354.1/154/0973 19
1. Veterans - Employment - United States. 2. Civil service - Veterans' preference - United States. I. Title.
KF27 .V436 1980b

Review of education, training, and employment programs administered by the Veterans' Administration : hearings before the Subcommittee on Education, Training, and Employment of the Committee on Veterans' Affairs, House of Representatives, Ninety-sixth Congress, second session, February 20 and March 6, 1980. Washington : U. S. Govt. Print. Off., 1980. iv, 275 p. ; 24 cm.   LC Card 80-602986   DDC 355.1/152/0973 19
1. Veterans - Education - United States. 2. Veterans - Employment - United States. I. Title.
KF27 .V436 1980

United States. Congress. House. Committee on Veterans' Affairs. Subcommittee on Housing.
Hearings regarding the VA home loan program : hearings before the Subcommittee on Housing of the Committee on Veterans' Affairs, House of Representatives, Ninety-sixth Congress, second session, March 12 and 25, 1980. Washington : U. S. Govt. Print. Off., 1980. iii, 54 p. ; 24 cm.   LC Card 80-603111 DDC 353.0081/2 19
1. Veterans - Loans - United States. 2. Insurance, Mortgage guaranty - United States. 3. United States. Veterans Administration. I. Title.
KF27 .V446 1980a

VA direct loans for residential solar energy systems : hearing before the Subcommittee on Housing of the Committee on Veterans' Affairs, House of Representatives, Ninety-sixth Congress, second session, H.R. 6408, May 21, 1980. Washington : U. S. Govt. Print. Off., 1980. iii, 20 p. ; 24 cm.   LC Card 80-603113 DDC 343.73/011 19
1. Veterans - Loans - United States. 2. Solar houses - United States - Finance. 3. Energy conservation - United States - Finance. I. Title.
KF27 .V446 1980

United States. Congress. House. Committee on Veterans' Affairs. Subcommittee on Medical Facilities and Benefits.
Oversight hearing to receive testimony on Agent Orange : hearing before the Subcommittee on Medical Facilities and Benefits of the Committee on Veterans' Affairs, House of Representatives, Ninety-sixth

Congress, second session, February 25, 1980. Washington : U. S. Govt. Print. Off., 1980. iii, 121 p. ; 24 cm.   LC Card 80-602984   DDC 363.7/384 19
1. Dichlorophenoxyacetic acid - Toxicology. 2. Trichlorophenoxyacetic acid - Toxicology. 3. Tetrachlorodibenzodioxin - Toxicology. 4. Herbicides - War use. 5. Veterans - Diseases - United States. I. Title.
KF27 .V459 1980

Oversight in the recruitment and retention of Veterans' Administration physicians and dentists, and H.R. 6153 : hearing before the Subcommittee on Medical Facilities and Benefits of the Committee on Veterans' Affairs, House of Representatives, Ninety-sixth Congress, second session, February 4, 1980. Washington : U. S. G.P.O., 1981. iv, 168 p. : ill. ; 24 cm. Item 1027   LC Card 81-601384   DDC 353.001/31 19
1. United States. Veterans Administration. Dept. of Medicine and Surgery - Officials and employees. 2. Physicians - Salaries, pensions, etc. - Law and legislation - United States. 3. Dentists - Salaries, pensions, etc. - Law and legislation - United States. 4. Medical personnel - United States - Supply and demand. I. Title.
KF27 .V459 1980c

Oversight of veterans' health care program in Florida : hearing before the Subcommittee on Medical Facilities and Benefits of the Committee on Veterans' Affairs, House of Representatives, Ninety-sixth Congress, first session, October 27, 1979. Washington : U. S. Govt. Print. Off., 1980. iii, 67 p. ; 24 cm.   LC Card 80-603075   DDC 355.1/156/0973 19
1. Veterans - Medical care - Florida. 2. United States. Veterans Administration. I. Title.
KF27 .V459 1979b

State delegation on Tennessee Veterans' Administration medical services : hearing before the Subcommittee on Medical Facilities and Benefits of the Committee on Veterans' Affairs, House of Representatives, Ninety-sixth Congress, second session, April 2, 1980. Washington : U. S. Govt. Print. Off., 1980. iii, 57 p. ; 24 cm.   LC Card 80-603034   DDC 355.1/156/09768 19
1. Veterans - Medical care - Tennessee. I. Title.
KF27 .V459 1980b

Veterans' Administration 5-year medical construction plan for fiscal years 1980-84 : hearing before the Subcommittee on Medical Facilities and Benefits of the Committee on Veterans' Affairs, House of Representatives, Ninety-sixth Congress, second session, January 29, 1980. Washington : U. S. Govt. Print. Off., 1980. iii, 54 p. : graphs ; 24 cm.   LC Card 80-602752   DDC 362.11/0973 19
1. Hospitals, Military - United States - Design and construction. I. Title.
KF27 .V459 1980a

Veterans' Administration 5-year medical construction plan for fiscal years 1981-85 : hearing before the Subcommittee on Medical Facilities and Benefits of the Committee on Veterans' Affairs, House of Representatives, Ninety-sixth Congress, second session, September 9, 1980. Washington : U. S. G.P.O., 1981. iii, 29 p. ; 24 cm. Item 1027   LC Card 81-601369   DDC 353.0086/2 19
1. Hospitals, Veterans' - United States - Design and construction. 2. United States. Veterans Administration. I. Title.
KF27 .V459 1980d

United States. Congress. House. Committee on Veterans' Affairs. Subcommittee on Special Investigations.
Computer systems for the Veterans' Administration and procurement practices : hearings before the Subcommittee on Special Investigations of the Committee on Veterans' Affairs, House of Representatives, Ninety-sixth Congress, second session, April 15, May 1, 29, and September 24, 1980. Washington : U. S. G.P.O., 1981. iv, 230 p. ; 23 cm. Item 1027   LC Card 81-601147   DDC 362.1/1/0687 19
1. United States. Veterans Administration - Procurement. 2. Veterans - Medical care - United States - Data processing. I. Title.
KF27 .V458 1980d

Hearing on the collection of debts owed the Veterans' Administration : hearing before the Subcommittee on Special Investigations of the

BIBLIOGRAPHIC GUIDE

United States. Congress. House. Committee on Veterans' Affairs.

456

Committee on Veterans' Affairs, House of Representatives, Ninety-sixth Congress, second session, April 1, 1980. Washington : U. S. Govt. Print. Off., 1980. iii, 180 p. : forms ; 23 cm. LC Card 80-602904 DDC 353.0081/2 19
1. United States. Veterans Administration. 2. Collecting of accounts - United States. I. Title.
KF27 .V458 1980a

Judicial review of veteran's claims : hearings before the Subcommittee on Special Investigations of the Committee on Veterans' Affairs, House of Representatives, Ninety-sixth Congress, second session, November 13 and November 19, 1980. Washington : U. S. G.P.O., 1981. v, 371 p. ; 24 cm. Item 1027 Includes bibliographical references. LC Card 81-601404 DDC 343.73/011 347.30311 19
1. Veterans - Legal status, laws, etc. - United States. 2. Judicial review of administrative acts - United States. I. Title.
KF27 .V458 1980g

Small Business Administration loans to veterans : hearings before the Subcommittee on Special Investigations of the Committee on Veterans' Affairs, House of Representatives, Ninety-sixth Congress, second session, June 18 and September 10, 1980. Washington : U. S. G.P.O, 1981. iii, 223 p.; 24 cm. Item 1027 LC Card 81-600813 DDC 353.0082/048045 19
1. Veterans - Loans - United States. 2. Small Business Administration. I. Title.
KF27 .V458 1980c

Target system : hearing before the Subcommittee on Special Investigations of the Committee on Veterans' Affairs, House of Representatives, Ninety-sixth Congress, second session, March 6, 1980. Washington : U. S. Govt. Print. Off., 1980. iii, 40 p. : graphs ; 23 cm. LC Card 80-602467 DDC 353.0081/2 19
1. Veterans - United States - Data processing. I. Title.
KF27 .V458 1980

VA beneficiary travel : hearing before the Subcommittee on Special Investigations of the Committee on Veterans' Affairs, House of Representatives, Ninety-sixth Congress, second session, May 21, 1980. Washington : U. S. Govt. Print. Off., 1980. iii, 37 p. ; 23 cm. LC Card 80-603717 DDC 355.1/156/0973 19
1. Veterans - Medical care - United States - Travel expense reimbursement. I. Title.
KF27 .V458 1980b

VA target system : hearing before the Subcommittee on Special Investigations of the Committee on Veterans' Affairs, House of Representatives, Ninety-sixth Congress, second session, July 23, 1980. Washington : U. S. G.P.O., 1980 [i.e. 1981] iii, 36 p. ; 24 cm. Item 1027 LC Card 81-600822 DDC 362.1/1/0687 19
1. United States. Veterans Administration - Management - Data processing. 2. United States. Veterans Administration - Records and correspondence - Data processing. I. Title.
KF27 .V458 1980e

United States. Congress. House. Committee on Ways and Means. (Old Catalog form: United States. Ways and Means, Committee on (House) Hearings printed in 1978 and later are available only in microform. Please consult the librarians in the Economic and Public Affairs Division.

Accounting treatment of the investment tax credit and accelerated depreciation for public utility ratemaking purposes : hearing before the Committee on Ways and Means, House of Representatives, Ninety-sixth Congress, second session, on H.R. 6806 and H.R. 3165, April 15, 1980. Washington : U. S. Govt. Print. Off., 1980. iv, 136 p. ; 24 cm. "Serial 96-87." Includes bibliographical references. LC Card 80-603022 DDC 343.7305/267 19
1. Public utilities - Taxation - United States. 2. Tax accounting - United States. 3. Investment tax credit - United States. 4. Depreciation allowances - United States. 5. Public utilities - Rates. I. Title.
KF27 .W3 1980g

Advisability of a tax reduction in 1980 effective for 1981 : hearings before the Committee on Ways and Means, House of Representatives, Ninety-sixth Congress, second session, on advisability of enactment in 1980 of a tax cut to be effective beginning January 1, 1981, July 22, 23, 24, 25, 28, 29, 30, 31, August 18, 19,

20, and September 9, 1980. Washington : U. S. G.P.O., 1980- [i.e. 1981- v. <1, 3> : ill. ; 24 cm. Pt. 1: "July 22, 23, 24, 25, 28, and 29, 1980." Pt. 3: "August 19, 20, September 9, 1980." "Serial 96-133." "Serial 96-135." Item 1028 Includes bibliographical references. LC Card 81-601409 DDC 343.7305/23/0262 347.3035230262 19
1. Income tax - Law and legislation - United States. I. Title.
KF27 .W3 1980m

Background material and data on major programs within the jurisdiction of the Committee on Ways and Means /. Washington , 1981. v,158 p. ; LC Card 81-601270 DDC 338.973 19
HC110.P63 B29

:Bankruptcy Tax Act of 1980 : report of the Committee on Ways and Means, U. S. House of Representatives on H.R. 5043. Washington : U. S. G.P.O., 1980. iii, 101 p. ; 24 cm. (Report / 96th Congress, 2d session, House of Representatives . no. 96-833) LC Card 81-601680 DDC 343.7305/236 347.3035236 19
1. Bankruptcy - Taxation - United States. I. Title.
KF32 .W3 1980

Carryover basis provisions : hearing before the Committee on Ways and Means, House of Representatives, Ninety-sixth Congress, first session ... November 13, 1979. Washington : U. S. Govt. Print. Off., 1980. v, 340 p. : graphs ; 24 cm. "Serial 96-69." Includes bibliographical references. LC Card 80-602112 DDC 343.7305/32 19
1. Inheritance and transfer tax - United States. I. Title.
KF27 .W3 1979i

The Comprehensive oil pollution liability and compensation act, and the Hazardous waste containment act : hearing before the Committee on Ways and Means, House of Representatives, Ninety-sixth Congress, second session, on H.R. 85 and H.R. 7020 ... June 2, 1980. Washington : U. S. Govt. Print. Off., 1980. iv, 276 p. : ill. ; 24 cm. "Serial 96-100." Includes bibliographical references. LC Card 80-603514 DDC 344.73/04632 19
1. Liability for oil pollution damages - United States. 2. Liability for hazardous substances pollution damages - United States. 3. Liability for environmental damages - United States. I. Title.
KF27 .W3 1980i

Explanation of the "Airport and airway revenue act of 1980" : (committee amendment to be offered as Title II to H.R. 7021) / Committee on Ways and Means, U. S. House of Representatives. Washington : U. S. Govt. Print. Off., 1980. iii, 34 p. ; 24 cm. "WMCP: 96-62." At head of title: 96th Congress, 2d session. Committee print. LC Card 80-602681 DDC 343.7305/5853877/02632 19
1. Aeronautics, Commercial - Taxation - United States. 2. Airports - Law and legislation - United States. I. Title.
KF6614.A9 A25 1980

Hearing announcement on the "Tax restructuring act of 1979", H.R. 5665 : including background data and explanation of H.R. 5665, introduced by the Honorable Al Ullman on October 22, 1979 / Committee on Ways and Means, U. S. House of Representatives. Washington : U. S. Govt. Print. Off., 1979. iii, 44 p. ; 24 cm. At head of title: 96th Congress, 1st session. Committee print. "WMCP: 96-38." LC Card 80-602685 DDC 343.7304 19
1. Taxation - Law and legislation - United States. 2. Income tax - Law and legislation - United States. 3. Value-added tax - United States. I. Ullman, Al. II. Title.
KF6275.5 .W245

Omnibus maritime regulatory reform, revitalization, and reorganization act : hearing before the Committee on Ways and Means, House of Representatives, Ninety-sixth Congress, second session, on H.R. 4769 ... March 19, 1980. Washington : U. S. Govt. Print. Off., 1980. iii, 144 p. : graphs ; 23 cm. "Serial 96-80." Includes bibliographical references. LC Card 80-602429 DDC 343.73/096 19
1. Maritime law - United States. 2. Shipping - Taxation - United States. I. Title.
KF27 .W3 1980b

Organization and administration of the United States Tax Court : hearing before the Committee on Ways and Means, House of

Representatives, Ninety-sixth Congress, second session, April 1, 1980. Washington : U. S. Govt. Print. Off., 1980. iii, 38 p. ; 24 cm. "Serial 96-76." LC Card 80-602486 DDC 343.7304/0269 19
1. United States. Tax Court. I. Title.
KF27 .W3 1980d

President's cash management initiatives in the fiscal year 1981 budget : hearings before the Committee on Ways and Means, House of Representatives, Ninety-sixth Congress, second session ... February 26, March 10, 1980. Washington : U. S. Govt. Print. Off., 1980. iv, 197 p. : ill. ; 23 cm. "Serial 96-82." Includes bibliographical references. LC Card 80-602770 DDC 353.0072/6 19
1. Revenue - United States. 2. Cash management - United States. 3. Tax collection - United States. 4. Budget - United States. I. Title.
KF27 .W3 1980f

President's proposal for withholding on interest and dividends : hearings before the Committee on Ways and Means, House of Representatives, Ninety-sixth Congress, second session, April 30 and May 1, 1980. Washington : U. S. Govt. Print. Off., 1980. v, 310 p. : ill. ; 23 cm. "Serial 96-92." LC Card 80-603348 DDC 353.0072/44 19
1. Withholding tax - United States. 2. Dividends - Taxation - United States. 3. Interest and usury - Taxation - United States. 4. Income tax - United States. I. Title.
KF27 .W3 1980k

Status of the Airport and Airway Trust Fund : hearing before the Committee on Ways and Means, House of Representatives, Ninety-sixth Congress, second session ... April 16, 1980. Washington : U. S. Govt. Print. Off., 1980. iv, 242 p. : ill. ; 23 cm. "Serial 96-97." LC Card 80-603519 DDC 343.73/0977 347.303977 19
1. Airports - Law and legislation - United States. 2. Aeronautics, Commercial - Taxation - United States. I. Title. II. Title: Airport and Airway Trust Fund.
KF27 .W3 1980j

Tax credits to homebuilders using passive solar design and building techniques : hearing before the Committee on Ways and Means, House of Representatives, Ninety-sixth Congress, second session, on H.R. 7688, H.R. 7690, and H.R. 8019 ... September 8, 1980. Washington : U. S. G.P.O., 1980. iv, 147 p. : ill. ; 24 cm. "Serial 96-118." LC Card 81-600616 DDC 343.73/0523 347.303523 19
1. Energy tax credits - United States. 2. Solar energy - Passive systems - Law and legislation - United States. 3. Solar heating - Passive systems - Law and legislation - United States. I. Title.
KF27 .W3 1980l

Tax incentives for savings : hearings before the Committee on Ways and Means, House of Representatives, Ninety-sixth Congress, second session ... January 29, 30, 31, 1980. Washington : U. S. Govt. Print. Off., 1980. vii, 774 p. : ill. ; 23 cm. "Serial 96-75." LC Card 80-602478 DDC 343.7305/23 19
1. Saving and thrift. 2. Saving and investment - United States. 3. Taxation, Exemption from - United States. I. Title.
KF27 .W3 1980c

Tax treatment of married, head of household, and single taxpayers : hearings before the Committee on Ways and Means, House of Representatives, Ninety-sixth Congress, second session, ... April 2 and 3, 1980. Washington : U. S. Govt. Print. Off., 1980. vi, 415 p. : ill. ; 24 cm. "Serial 96-93." LC Card 80-603314 DDC 343.7305/2042 19
1. Income tax - Law and legislation - United States. 2. Husband and wife - Taxation - United States. 3. Single people - Taxation - United States. I. Title.
KF27 .W3 1980h

United States. Congress. Joint Committee on Internal Revenue Taxation. Jeopardy and termination assessments, administrative summons, comprehensive administrative package, state conducted lotteries, and miscellaneous /. Washington , 1975. iii, 7 p. ; LC Card 80-600755 DDC 353.0072/4 19
KF6300 .A25 1975

United States. Congress. Joint Committee on Taxation. Description of bills to provide tax incentives for savings . Washington , 1980. iii, 14 p. ; LC Card 81-600503 DDC 343.7305/23

GOVERNMENT PUBLICATIONS - U.S.: 1981

457

United States. Congress. House. Committee on Ways and Means.

347.303523 19
KF6417 .A25 1980

United States. Congress. Joint Committee on Taxation. Description of proposals relating to the tax treatment of foreign investment in the United States, scheduled for a hearing before the Committee on Ways and Means on October 25, 1979 /. Washington , 1979. iii, 8 p. ; LC Card 80-602684 DDC 343.7305/248 19
KF6419 .A25 1979

United States. Congress. Joint Committee on Taxation. Estimates of federal tax expenditures for fiscal years, 1980-1985 /. Washington , 1980. ii, 21 p. ; LC Card 81-600720 DDC 336.2 19
HJ4652 .U627 1980

United States. Congress. Joint Committee on Taxation. The income tax treatment of married couples and single persons . Washington , 1980. iii, 68 p. ; LC Card 80-601745 DDC 343.7305/2/024065 19
KF6355.5 .T38

United States. Congress. Joint Committee on Taxation. Staff recommendations for simplication of tax rules relating to subchapter S corporations . Washington , 1980. iii, 27 p. ; LC Card 80-602271 DDC 343.7306/8 19
KF6491 .A25 1980

United States. Congress. Joint Committee on Taxation. Summary of H.R. 5741, and Mortgage subsidy bond tax act of 1979 . Washington , 1979. iii, 8 p. ; LC Card 80-602686 DDC 343.7305/23 19
KF6383 .A25 1979

United States savings bonds program . [Washington, D.C.] 1981. 2, iii,90 p. ; LC Card 81-601928 DDC 332.63/23 19
HG4936 .U54

United States. Treasury Dept. President's cash management initiatives /. Washington , 1980. vi, 94 p. ; LC Card 80-601795 DDC 353.0072/4 19
HJ3252 .U58 1980

United States. Congress. House. Committee on Ways and Means. Subcommittee on Health.
Background information for hearings on problems facing financially troubled hospitals /. Washington , 1980. ii, 9 p. ; LC Card 81-600741 DDC 338.4/336211/0973 19
RA981.A2 B3

Experimental medicare claims processing contract : field hearing before the Subcommittee on Health of the Committee on Ways and Means, House of Representatives, Ninety-sixth Congress, second session ... April 28, 1980, Chicago, Ill. Washington : U. S. Govt. Print. Off., 1980. iv, 253 p. ; 24 cm. "Serial 96-99." LC Card 80-603646 DDC 353.0082/56 19
1. Medicare - Illinois - Claims administration - Evaluation. 2. Electronic Data Systems Federal Corporation. I. Title.
KF27 .W344 1980d

Federal privacy of medical information act : hearing before the Subcommittee on Health of the Committee on Ways and Means, House of Representatives, Ninety-sixth Congress, second session, on H.R. 5935 ... April 17, 1980. Washington : U. S. Govt. Print. Off., 1980. iii, 110 p. ; 24 cm. "Serial 96-88." LC Card 80-602993 DDC 344.43/041 19
1. Medical records - Law and legislation - United States. 2. Medical records - United States - Access control. I. Title.
KF27 .W344 1980a

The hospital financing crisis : hearing before the Subcommittee on Health of the Committee on Ways and Means, House of Representatives, Ninety-sixth Congress, second session, February 29, 1980. Washington : U. S. Govt. Print. Off., 1980. v, 160 p. ; 23 cm. "Serial 96-107." LC Card 80-603696 DDC 338.4/336211/0973 19
1. Federal aid to hospitals - United States. 2. Hospitals - United States - Finance. 3. Poor - Hospital care - United States. I. Title.
KF27 .W344 1980c

Issues affecting the financing and operation of hospitals : field hearing before the Subcommittee on Health of the Committee on Ways and Means, House of Representatives, Ninety-sixth Congress, second session, October 16, 1980, Van Nuys, California. Washington :

U. S. G.P.O., c1980 [i.e. 1981] iv, 178 p. : ill. ; 24 cm. "Serial 96-128." Item 1028 Includes bibliographical references. LC Card 81-601137 DDC 362.1/09794 19
1. Hospitals - California - Finance. 2. Hospitals - California - Cost of operation. 3. Federal aid to hospitals - California. 4. Nurses - California - Supply and demand. I. Title.
KF27 .W344 1980f

Physician reimbursement under medicare . Washington , 1980 [i.e. 1981] vii, 58 p. ; LC Card 81-600995 DDC 338.4/33621/0973 19
HD7102.U4 P49

Problems facing financially troubled hospitals : field hearings before the Subcommittee on Health of the Committee on Ways and Means, House of Representatives, Ninety-sixth Congress, second session, March 14, 1980, New York City, April 18, 1980, Memphis, Tenn., May 27, 1980, Chicago, Ill. Washington : U. S. Govt. Print. Off., 1980. vi, 584 p. : ill. ; 24 cm. "Serial 96-98." LC Card 80-603721 DDC 338.4/336211/0973 19
1. Hospitals - New York (City) - Finance. 2. Poor - Hospital care - New York (City). 3. Hospitals - Tennessee - Memphis - Finance. 4. Poor - Hospital care - Tennessee - Memphis. 5. Hospitals - Illinois - Chicago - Finance. 6. Poor - Hospital care - Illinois - Chicago. I. Title.
KF27 .W344 1980b

Professional standards review organization program : hearing before the Subcommittee on Health of the Committee on Ways and Means, House of Representatives, Ninety-sixth Congress, second session, August 25, 1980. Washington : U. S. G.P.O., 1980. vii, 459 p. : ill. ; 24 cm. "Serial 96-117." Includes bibliographical references. LC Card 81-600622 DDC 362.1/068 19
1. Professional standards review organization (Medicine) - United States. I. Title.
KF27 .W344 1980e

Proposals to restructure the financing of private health insurance : hearing before the Subcommittee on Health of the Committee on Ways and Means, House of Representatives, Ninety-sixth Congress, second session, on H.R. 5740 ... February 25, 1980. Washington : U. S. Govt. Print. Off., 1980. iii, 273 p. : ill. ; 23 cm. "Serial 96-79." Includes bibliographical references. LC Card 80-602814 DDC 344.73/022 19
1. Insurance, Health - United States. 2. Medical care, Cost of - Law and legislation - United States. I. Title.
KF27 .W344 1980

United States. Congress. House. Committee on Ways and Means. Subcommittee on Oversight.
Airport and airway trust fund : hearing before the Subcommittee on Oversight of the Committee on Ways and Means, House of Representatives, Ninety-sixth Congress, second session, February 28, 1980. Washington : U. S. Govt. Print. Off., 1980. iii, 30 p. ; 23 cm. "Serial 96-71." LC Card 80-602085 DDC 353.0072/6 19
1. Airports - United States - Safety measures. 2. Airports - United States - Finance. 3. Aeronautics, Commercial - Taxation - United States. I. Title.
KF27 .W345 1980a

Employer liability for taxes under the Railroad retirement tax act : hearing before the Subcommittee on Oversight of the Committee on Ways and Means, House of Representatives, Ninety-sixth Congress, first session ... November 27, 1979. Washington : U. S. Govt. Print. Off., 1980. iii, 128 p. ; 24 cm. "Serial no. 96-61." Includes bibliographical references. LC Card 80-602012 DDC 353.0087/5068 19
1. Railroads - United States - Pensions. I. Title.
KF27 .W345 1979j

Energy conservation tax incentives : field hearings before the Subcommittee on Oversight of the Committee on Ways and Means, House of Representatives, Ninety-sixth Congress, second session, on tax incentives to maximize the use of natural resources, June 7, 1980--Bend, Oregon, June 9, 1980--Portland, Oregon. Washington : U. S. G.P.O., 1980. iv, 177 p. : ill. ; 24 cm. "Serial 96-120." Includes bibliographical references. LC Card 81-600611 DDC 336.2/06 19
1. Energy tax credits - Oregon. 2. Energy conservation - Oregon. 3. Energy development - Oregon. I. Title.
KF27 .W345 1980j

Examination of special jobless benefit programs : hearing before the Subcommittee on Oversight of the Committee on Ways and Means, House of Representatives, Ninety-sixth Congress, second session, February 21, 1980. Washington : U. S. Govt. Print. Off., 1980. iii, 91 p. ; 24 cm. "Serial 96-86." LC Card 80-602951 DDC 368.4/4/00973 19
1. Insurance, Unemployment - United States. 2. Supplemental unemployment benefits - United States. I. Title.
KF27 .W345 1980c

Federal noncompliance with tax law reporting requirements : hearing before the Subcommittee on Oversight of the Committee on Ways and Means, House of Representatives, Ninety-sixth Congress, second session, September 18, 1980. Washington : U. S. G.P.O., 1981. iii, 37 p. ; 24 cm. "Serial 96-131." Item 1028 Includes bibliographical references. LC Card 81-601371 DDC 353.0072/4 19
1. Tax administration and procedure - United States. 2. Administrative agencies - United States. I. Title.
KF27 .W345 1980l

Guaranteed student loan tax-exempt financing : hearing before the Subcommittee on Oversight of the Committee on Ways and Means, House of Representatives, Ninety-sixth Congress, second session, June 26, 1980. Washington : U. S. G.P.O., 1980. iii, 96 p. : graphs ; 24 cm. LC Card 80-603435 DDC 379.1/3 19
1. Student loan funds - United States. 2. Loans - United States - Government guaranty. 3. Securities, Tax-exempt - United States. I. Title.
KF27 .W345 1980h

Income tax treaties : hearing before the Subcommittee on Oversight of the Committee on Ways and Means, House of Representatives, Ninety-sixth Congress, second session, April 29, 1980. Washington : U. S. Govt. Print. Off., 1980. iii, 161 p. ; 23 cm. "Serial 96-102." LC Card 80-603644 DDC 341.4/84 19
1. Taxation, Double - United States - Treaties. I. Title.
KF27 .W345 1980f

Review of progress on Teamsters' Central States pension fund reform : hearing before the Subcommittee on Oversight of the Committee on Ways and Means, House of Representatives, Ninety-sixty Congress, second session, March 24, 1980. Washington : U. S. Govt. Print. Off., 1980. iii, 236 p. ; 24 cm. "Serial 96-95." LC Card 80-602733 DDC 331.25/22 19
1. International Brotherhood of Teamsters, Chauffeurs, Warehousemen and Helpers of America. 2. Pension trusts - United States. I. Title.
KF27 .W345 1980b

Review of taxpayer privacy issues : hearing before the Subcommittee on Oversight of the Committee on Ways and Means, House of Representatives, Ninety-sixth Congress, second session, July 30, 1980. Washington : U. S. Govt. Print. Off., 1980. iii, 185 p. ; 24 cm. "Serial 96-112." LC Card 80-603900 DDC 323.44/83/0973 19
1. Confidential communications - Taxation - United States. 2. Privacy, Right of - United States. I. Title.
KF27 .W345 1980g

Shipp, P. Royal. Background material on work, retirement, and social security /. Washington , 1980. v, 24 p. ; LC Card 80-603060 DDC 368.4/3/00973 19
HD7125 .S527

Strategies to encourage older workers to voluntarily extend their worklives : hearing before the Subcommittee on Oversight of the Committee on Ways and Means, House of Representatives, Ninety-sixth Congress, second session, September 10, 1980. Washington : U. S. G.P.O., 1980. iii, 264 p. : ill. ; 24 cm. "Serial 96-116." Includes bibliographies. LC Card 80-604060 DDC 368.4/3/00973 19
1. Retirement age - United States. 2. Social security - United States. I. Title.
KF27 .W345 1980k

Taxpayer complaints : hearing before the Subcommittee on Oversight of the Committee on Ways and Means, House of Representatives, Ninety-sixth Congress, second session, May 20, 1980. Washington : U. S. G.P.O., 1980. iii, 178 p. ; 24 cm. "Serial 96-110." Includes bibliographical references. LC Card 80-604065 DDC 353.0072/4 19
1. United States. Internal Revenue Service. 2. Tax collection - United States. I. Title.
KF27 .W345 1980i

BIBLIOGRAPHIC GUIDE

United States. Congress. House. Committee on Ways and Means.

458

Underground economy : hearings before the Subcommittee on Oversight of the Committee on Ways and Means, House of Representatives, Ninety-sixth Congress, first session .... Washington : U. S. Govt. Print. Off., 1980. iv, 501 p. ; 24 cm. Hearings held July 16-Oct. 11, 1979. "Serial 96-70." LC Card 80-602166 DDC 353.0072/44 19
1. Tax collection - United States. 2. Tax evasion - United States. 3. Income tax - United States. 4. Self-employed - Taxation - United States. I. Title.
KF27 .W345 1979i

United States. Congress. House. Committee on Ways and Means. Subcommittee on Social Security. Social Security Administration office space problems . Washington , 1980. iii, 137 p. : LC Card 80-603328 DDC 353.0082/56/0682 19
KF27 .W347 1980a

Volunteer income tax assistance program : hearing before the Subcommittee on Oversight of the Committee on Ways and Means, House of Representatives, Ninety-sixth Congress, second session, April 21, 1980. Washington : U. S. Govt. Print. Off., 1980. iii, 79 p. ; 24 cm. "Serial 96-89." LC Card 80-602989 DDC 343.7305/2044 19
1. Volunteer workers in income tax return preparation - United States. I. Title.
KF27 .W345 1980d

United States. Congress. House. Committee on Ways and Means. Subcommittee on Public Assistance and Unemployment Compensation.
The administration's proposal for additional weeks of unemployment compensation : hearing before the Subcommittee on Public Assistance and Unemployment Compensation of the Committee on Ways and Means, House of Representatives, Ninety-Sixth Congress, second session, September 17, 1980. Washington : U. S. G.P.O., 1980. iii, 62 p. : ill. ; 24 cm. "Serial 96-126." LC Card 81-600849 DDC 344.73/024 347.30424 19
1. Insurance, Unemployment - United States. I. Title.
KF27 .W3464 1980b

Child abuse service programs : field hearings before the Subcommittee on Public Assistance and Unemployment Compensation of the Committee on Ways and Means, House of Representatives, Ninety-sixth Congress, second session, April 7, 8, 1980, Los Angeles, Calif. Washington : U. S. Govt. Print. Off., 1980. iv, 192 p. : ill. ; 23 cm. "Serial 96-108." LC Card 80-603414 DDC 362.7/044 19
1. Child abuse - Services - California. I. Title.
KF27 .W3464 1980

Fuel assistance legislation : field hearing before the Subcommittee on Public Assistance and Unemployment Compensation of the Committee on Ways and Means, House of Representatives, Ninety-sixth Congress, first session, November 26, 1979. Washington : U. S. Govt. Print. Off., 1980. iv, 102 p. ; 24 cm. "Serial 96-66." LC Card 80-601970 DDC 344.73/032583 19
1. Poor - Northeastern States - Energy assistance. 2. Aged - Northeastern States - Energy assistance. 3. Petroleum as fuel - Prices - Northeastern States. 4. Energy policy - United States. I. Title.
KF27 .W3464 1979g

Unemployment compensation benefits to servicemen released for the good of the service : hearing before the Subcommittee on Public Assistance and Unemployment Compensation of the Committee on Ways and Means, House of Representatives, Ninety-sixth Congress, first session, on H.R. 5533 ... November 1, 1979. Washington : U. S. Govt. Print. Off., 1979. iii, 28 p. ; 24 cm. "Serial 96-47." LC Card 80-600678 DDC 343.73/0116 19
1. Workmen's compensation - United States. 2. Veterans - Legal status, laws, etc. - United States. 3. Military discharge - United States. I. Title.
KF27 .W3464 1979c

Unemployment compensation bills : hearing before the Subcommittee on Public Assistance and Unemployment Compensation of the Committee on Ways and Means, House of Representatives, Ninety-sixth Congress, second session, on H.R. 6540, H.R. 6690, H.R. 7529, June 26, 1980. Washington : U. S. G.P.O., 1980. iv, 243 p. : forms ; 23 cm. Includes bibliographical references. "Serial 96-113." LC Card

80-603901 DDC 344.73/024 347.30424 19
1. Insurance, Unemployment - United States. I. Title.
KF27 .W3464 1980a

United States. Congress. House. Committee on Ways and Means. Subcommittee on Select Revenue Measures.
Expiring historic structure tax provisions : hearings before the Subcommittee on Select Revenue Measures of the Committee on Ways and Means House of Representatives, Ninety-sixth Congress, second session, on legislation to extend the expiring provisions of federal tax law which are designed to encourage the preservation of historic structures, San Francisco, California, October 17, 1980, Boston, Massachusetts, October 21, 1980, Chicago, Illinois, October 24, 1980. Washington : U. S. G.P.O., 1980. viii, 578 p. : ill. ; 24 cm. "Serial 96-130." Item 1028 Includes bibliographical references. LC Card 81-601397 DDC 343.7305/4 347.30354 19
1. Real property and taxation - United States. 2. Taxation, Exemption from - United States. 3. Historic buildings - Law and legislation - United States. I. Title.
KF27 .W3468 1980e

Foreign convention tax rules and minor tax bills : hearings before the Subcommittee on Select Revenue Measures of the Committee on Ways and Means, House of Representatives, Ninety-sixth Congress, second session, September 18, 1980. Washington : U. S. G.P.O., 1980 [i.e. 1981] vi, 283 p. ; 24 cm. "Serial 96-125." Item 1028 Includes bibliographical references. LC Card 81-600932 DDC 343.7305/2 347.30352 19
1. Taxation - Law and legislation - United States. 2. Income tax - United States - Deductions - Expenses. 3. Congresses and conventions - Attendance. I. Title.
KF27 .W3468 1980c

Minor tax bills : hearings before the Subcommittee on Select Revenue Measures of the Committee on Ways and Means, House of Representatives, Ninety-sixth Congress, second session, on June 19, 1980, H.R. 4175, H.R. 4511, H.R. 4544, H.R. 4640, H.R. 5512, H.R. 5847, H.R. 7220, H.R. 7553, and June 26, 1980, H.R. 4498, H.R. 5719, H.R. 6935, H.R. 7263, H.R. 7276, H.R. 7318, H.R. 7392, H.R. 7487, H.R. 7520, H.R. 7606. Washington : U. S. G.P.O., 1980. vii, 521 p. : ill. ; 24 cm. "Serial 96-115." Includes bibliographical references. LC Card 80-604098 DDC 343.7304/0262 347.30340262 19
1. Taxation - Law and legislation - United States. I. Title.
KF27 .W3468 1980b

Minor tax bills : hearing before the Subcommittee on Select Revenue Measures of the Committee on Ways and Means, House of Representatives, Ninety-sixth Congress, second session ... March 24, 1980. Washington : U. S. Govt. Print. Off., 1980. iii, 72 p. ; 24 cm. Hearing on H.R. 4070, H.R. 4155, H.R. 4725, H.R. 5124, H.R. 5716, and H.R. 5968. "Serial 96-84." LC Card 80-602528 DDC 343.7304/0262 19
1. Taxation - Law and legislation - United States. I. Title.
KF27 .W3468 1980

Payment of attorneys' fees in tax litigation : hearing before the Subcommittee on Select Revenue Measures of the Committee on Ways and Means, House of Representatives, Ninety-sixth Congress, second session, on H.R. 4584 ... Los Angeles, California, October 6, 1980. Washington : U. S. G.P.O., 1980 [i.e. 1981] iii, 111 p. ; 24 cm. "Serial 96-122." Item 1028 Includes bibliographical references. LC Card 81-600811 DDC 343.7304/0269 347.30340269 19
1. Tax protests and appeals - United States. 2. Lawyers - United States - Fees. 3. Government litigation - United States. I. Title.
KF27 .W3468 1980d

Written comments on certain aspects of H.R. 5043, Bankruptcy tax act of 1979 / Subcommittee on Select Revenue Measures of the Committee on Ways and Means, U. S. House of Representatives. Washington : U. S. Govt. Print. Off., 1980. v, 96 p. ; 24 cm. At head of title: 96th Congress, 2d session. Committee print, WMCP: 96-48. Includes bibliographical references. LC Card 80-602569 DDC 343.7305/23 19

1. Bankruptcy - Taxation - United States. I. Title.
KF6332 .A25 1980

United States. Congress. House. Committee on Ways and Means. Subcommittee on Social Security.
Koitz, David. Social Security and economic cycles /. Washington , 1980. vii, 21 p. ; LC Card 80-604122 DDC 338.4/336843/00973 19
HD7125 .K588

Receipt of Social Security benefits by persons incarcerated in penal institutions : hearing before the Subcommittee on Social Security of the Committee on Ways and Means, House of Representatives, Ninety-sixth Congress, second session, June 20, 1980. Washington : U. S. Govt. Print. Off., 1980. iv, 96 p. ; 23 cm. "Serial 96-103." LC Card 80-603715 DDC 368.4/00880692 19
1. Prisoners - Pensions - United States. 2. Social security - Law and legislation - United States. I. Title.
KF27 .W347 1980b

Social Security Administration office space problems : hearings before the Subcommittee on Social Security and Subcommittee on Oversight of the Committee on Ways and Means, House of Representatives, Ninety-sixth Congress, second session, May 20 and 21, 1980. Washington : U. S. Govt. Print. Off., 1980. iii, 137 p. : ill. ; 24 cm. "Serial 96-111." LC Card 80-603328 DDC 353.0082/56/0682 19
1. United States. Social Security Administration - Buildings. I. United States. Congress. House. Committee on Ways and Means. Subcommittee on Oversight. II. Title.
KF27 .W347 1980a

Social security dependents' benefits : field hearing before the Subcommittee on Social Security of the Committee on Ways and Means, House of Representatives, Ninety-sixth Congress, second session, July 28, 1980, Falls Church, Virginia. Washington : U. S. G.P.O., 1980. iii, 73 p. ; 24 cm. "Serial 96-111." Includes bibliographical references. LC Card 80-604069 DDC 368.4/3/00973 19
1. Social security - United States. I. Title.
KF27 .W347 1980c

Social security programs in the President's fiscal year 1981 budget : hearings before the Subcommittee on Social Security of the Committee on Ways and Means, House of Representatives, Ninety-sixth Congress, second session, February 21; March 17, 18, 1980. Washington : U. S. Govt. Print. Off., 1980. iii, 225 p. ; 23 cm. "Serial 96-77." LC Card 80-602523 DDC 353.0072 19
1. Social security - United States - Finance. I. Title.
KF27 .W347 1980

United States. Congress. House. Committee on Ways and Means. Subcommittee on Trade.
Auto situation, autumn 1980 : hearing before the Subcommittee on Trade of the Committee on Ways and Means, House of Representatives, Ninetysixth Congress, second session, November 18, 1980. Washington : U. S.G.P.O., 1980 [i.e. 1981] iv, 224 p. : ill. ; 23 cm. "Serial 96-132." Includes bibliographical references. Item 1028 LC Card 81-601391 DDC 338.4/76292/0973 19
1. Automobile industry and trade - United States. 2. Automobile industry and trade. 3. Automobile industry and trade - Law and legislation - United States.
KF27 .W348 1980i

Certain tariff and trade bills : hearing before the Subcommittee on Trade of the Committee on Ways and Means, House of Representatives, Ninety-sixth Congress, second session, March 17, April 17, and May 8, 1980. Washington : U. S. Govt. Print. Off., 1980. xi, 933 p. : ill. ; 24 cm. "Serial 96-105." Includes bibliographical references. LC Card 80-603420 DDC 343.73/087 19
1. Tariff - Law and legislation - United States. 2. Foreign trade regulations - United States. I. Title.
KF27 .W348 1980e

Gresser, Julian. High technology and Japanese industrial policy . Washington , 1980. xiii, 73 p. : LC Card 80-603865 DDC 338.4/5621381958/0952 19
HD9696.S43 J33

International sugar agreement : hearing before the Subcommittee on Trade of the Committee on Ways and Means, House of Representatives, Ninety-sixth Congress, first session ... December 11, 1979. Washington : U. S. Govt.

Print. Off., 1980. iii, 46 p. ; 24 cm. "Serial 96-65."
LC Card 80-601959   DDC 341.7/547/136 19
*1. Sugar laws and legislation. 2. Sugar laws and
legislation - United States. I. Title.*
KF27 .W348 1979n

Leather apparel and miscellaneous bills :
hearing before the subcommittee on Trade of
the Committee on Ways and Means, House of
Representatives, Ninety-sixth Congress, second
session, on H. Con. Res. 383, H.R. 6750, H.R.
7660, H.R. 7709, H.R. 7802, August 26, 1980.
Washington : U. S. G.P.O., 1981. iv, 148 p. :
24 cm. "Serial 96-124." Item 1028 Includes
bibliographical references.   LC Card 81-600942   DDC
343.7305/6 347.30356 19
*1. Tariff - Law and legislation - United States. 2.
Duty-free importation - United States. 3. Tariff on
leather garments - Law and legislation - United States.
I. Title.*
KF27 .W348 1980l

Market conditions and international trade in
semiconductors : field hearing before the
Subcommittee on Trade of the Committee on
Ways and Means, House of Representatives,
Ninety-sixth Congress, second session, April 28,
1980, Farmingdale, N.Y. Washington : U. S.
Govt. Print. Off., 1980. iii, 107 p. : graphs ; 23
cm. "Serial 96-90." Includes bibliographical references.
LC Card 80-602967   DDC
380.1/4562/38152/0973 19
*1. Semiconductor industry. 2. Semiconductor industry -
United States. I. Title.*
KF27 .W348 1980b

Oil import fees : the administration of the
program and its impact : hearings before the
Subcommittee on Trade of the Committee on
Ways and Means, House of Representatives,
Ninety-sixth Congress, second session, April 24,
May 9, 14, 1980. Washington : U. S. Govt.
Print. Off., 1980. iv, 443 p. : ill. ; 24 cm. "Serial
no. 96-106."   LC Card 80-603505   DDC 353.0082/75
19
1. Tariff on petroleum - United States. I. Title.
KF27 .W348 1980d

Operation of the generalized system of
preferences : hearing before the Subcommittee
on Trade of the Committee on Ways and
Means, House of Representatives, Ninety-sixth
Congress, second session ... May 8, 1980.
Washington : U. S. Govt. Print. Off., 1980. iii,
111 p. ; 24 cm. "Serial 96-96."   LC Card 80-603343
DDC 353.0082/7 19
*1. Tariff preferences - United States. 2. Duty-free
importation - United States. 3. Underdeveloped areas -
Commerce. I. Title.*
KF27 .W348 1980c

Quality of production and improvement in the
workplace : hearing before the Subcommittee
on Trade of the Committee on Ways and
Means, House of Representatives, Ninety-sixth
Congress, second session, San Diego, California,
October 14, 1980. Washington : U. S. G.P.O.,
1980 [i.e. 1981] iii, 186 p. : ill. ; 24 cm. "Serial
96-127." Item 1028 Includes bibliographical references.
LC Card 81-600833   DDC 338/.06 19
*1. Quality control - United States. 2. Quality of
products. 3. Industrial productivity - United States. 4.
Competition, International. I. Title.*
KF27 .W348 1980k

Trade functions authorizations for fiscal year
1981 : hearings before the Subcommittee on
Trade of the Committee on Ways and Means,
House of Representatives, Ninety-sixth
Congress, second session, February 7, 21, 1980.
Washington : U. S. Govt. Print. Off., 1980. iii,
177 p. ; 23 cm. "Serial 96-83."   LC Card 80-602818
DDC 353.0082/7 19
*1. United States - Commercial policy. 2. Foreign trade
regulation - United States. I. Title.*
KF27 .W348 1980

Trade with Japan : hearings before the
Subcommittee on Trade of the Committee on
Ways and Means, House of Representatives,
Ninety-sixth Congress, second session, August
26, September 18, 1980. Washington : U. S.
G.P.O. : For sale by the Supt. of Docs., U. S.
G.P.O., 1980. iv, 230 p. : ill. ; 24 cm. "Serial
96-121." Includes bibliographies.   LC Card 81-600633
DDC 382/.0973/052
*1. Foreign trade regulation - United States. 2. United
States - Commerce - Japan. 3. Japan - Commerce -
United States. I. Title.*
KF27 .W348 1980h

Trader waiver authority extension : hearing
before the Subcommittee on Trade of the
Committee on Ways and Means, House of
Representatives, Ninety-sixth Congress, second
session, on a presidential recommendation to
continue the waivers applicable to the Socialist
Republic of Romania, the Hungarian People's
Republic, and the People's Republic of China,
and to extend the waiver authority under the
Trade Act of 1974, June 10, 1980.
Washington : U. S. G.P.O., 1980 [i.e. 1981] v,
310 p. : ill. ; 24 cm. "Serial 96-123"   LC Card
81-600854   DDC 382/.0973/01717 19
*1. Foreign trade regulation - United States. 2.
Emigration and immigration. 3. United States -
Commerce - Communist countries. 4. Communist
countries - Commerce - United States. I. Title.*
KF27 .W348 1980j

U. S. trade policy : hearings before the
Subcommittee on Trade of the Committee on
Ways and Means, House of Representatives,
Ninety-sixth Congress, second session, June 26
and July 21, 1980. Washington : U. S. G.P.O.,
1980. v, 632 p. : ill. ; 24 cm. "Serial 96-119."
Includes bibliographies.   LC Card 81-600879   DDC
382/.3/0973 19
1. United States - Commercial policy. I. Title.
KF27 .W348 1980g

United States. Congress. House. Committee on
Ways and Means. Subcommittee on Trade.
United States-Japan Trade Task Force. United
States-Japan trade report /. Washington , 1980.
viii, 92 p. :   LC Card 80-603556   DDC
382/.0952/073 19
HF3127 .U52 1980

World auto trade : current trends and structural
problems : hearings before the Subcommittee on
Trade of the Committee on Ways and Means,
House of Representatives, Ninety-sixth
Congress, second session, March 7, 18, 1980.
Washington : U. S. Govt. Print. Off., 1980. iv,
363 p. : ill. ; 24 cm. "Serial 96-78." Includes
bibliographical references.   LC Card 80-602773   DDC
338.4/76292 19
*1. Automobile industry and trade - United States. 2.
Automobiles - United States - Design and construction.
3. Automobile industry and trade. 4. Automobiles -
Design and construction. I. Title.*
KF27 .W348 1980a

**United States. Congress. House. Committee on
Ways and Means. Subcommittee on Trade.
United States-Japan Trade Task Force.**
United States-Japan trade report / prepared for
the Subcommittee on Trade of the Committee
on Ways and Means by its chairman and the
members of its United States-Japan Trade Task
Force. Washington : U. S. Govt. Print. Off. :
for sale by the Supt. of Docs., U. S. Govt.
Print. Off., 1980. viii, 92 p. : ill. ; 24 cm. At
head of title: 96th Congress, 2d session. Committee
print. WMCP : 96-68. Subcommittee on Trade of the
Committee on Ways and Means, U. S. House of
Representatives. "September 5, 1980." Includes
bibliographical references.   LC Card 80-603556   DDC
382/.0952/073 19
*1. United States - Commerce - Japan. 2. Japan -
Commerce - United States. I. United States. Congress.
House. Committee on Ways and Means. Subcommittee
on Trade. II. Title.*
HF3127 .U52 1980

**United States. Congress. House. Committee on
Ways and Means. Subcommmittee on
Oversight.** Efficacy of medicare research
efforts : hearing before the Subcommittee on
Oversight of the Committee on Ways and
Means, House of Representatives, Ninety-sixth
Congress, second session, May 8, 1980.
Washington : U. S. Govt. Print. Off., 1980. iii,
333 p. : graphs ; 24 cm. "Serial 96-95."   LC Card
80-603309   DDC 353.0082/56 19
*1. Medicare - Cost effectiveness. 2. United States.
Health Care Financing Administration. I. Title.*
KF27 .W345 1980e

**UNITED STATES. CONGRESS. HOUSE -
COMMITTEES.**
United States. Congress. House. Select
Committee on Committees. Energy jurisdictions
of House committees . Washington , 1980. v.
509 p. ;   LC Card 80-603513   DDC 328.73/07652
19
KF27.5 .C57 1979a

**United States. Congress. House. Committes,
Select Committee on. see United States.**

Congress. House. Select Committee on
Committees.

**UNITED STATES. CONGRESS. HOUSE -
DATA PROCESSING.**
United States. Congress. House. Committee on
House Administration. Policy Group on
Information and Computers. Technical advisory
panel on the digital data communications
network . Washington , 1981. iv, 163 p. :   LC
Card 81-601775   DDC 328.73/072/0684 19
KF27 .H652 1981

**United States. Congress. House. Education,
Committee on. see United States. Congress.
House. Committee on Education.**

**UNITED STATES. CONGRESS. HOUSE -
ELECTIONS.**
United States. Laws, statutes, etc. Federal
election campaign laws relating to the U. S.
House of Representatives, as amended through
January 8, 1980 /. Washington , 1980. xiv, 232
p. ;   LC Card 80-602296   DDC 342.73/07 19
KF4914 .A3 1980

**United States. Congress. House. Emancipation
and Colonization, Select Committee on. see
United States. Congress. House. Select
Committee on Emancipation and
Colonization.**

**United States. Congress. House. Environment,
Energy and Natural Resources
Subcommittee. see United States. Congress.
House. Committee on Government
Operations. Environment, Energy, and
Natural Resources Subcommittee.**

**UNITED STATES. CONGRESS. HOUSE -
EXPULSION.**
United States. Congress. House. Committee on
Standards of Official Conduct. In the matter of
Representative Michael J. Myers . [Washington,
D.C. , 1980] 2 v. ;   LC Card 81-601430   DDC
328.73/0766 19
KF32 .S7 1980b

**United States. Congress. House. Government
Activities and Transportation Subcommittee.
see United States. Congress. House.
Committee on Government Operations.
Government Activities and Transportation
Subcommittee.**

**UNITED STATES. CONGRESS. HOUSE -
INFORMATION SERVICES.**
United States. Congress. House. Committee on
House Administration. Policy Group on
Information and Computers. Technical advisory
panel on the digital data communications
network . Washington , 1981. iv, 163 p. :   LC
Card 81-601775   DDC 328.73/072/0684 19
KF27 .H652 1981

**United States. Congress. House.
Intergovernmental Relations and Human
Resources Subcommittee. see United States.
Congress. House. Committee on Government
Operations. Intergovernmental Relations and
Human Resources Subcommittee.**

**United States. Congress. House Law Revision
Counsel, Office of the. see United States.
Congress. House. Office of the Law Revision
Counsel.**

**United States. Congress. House. Legislation and
National Security Subcommittee. see United
States. Congress. House. Committee on
Government Operations. Legislation and
National Security Subcommittee.**

**UNITED STATES. CONGRESS. HOUSE -
MANAGEMENT.**
United States. Congress. House. Commission on
Administrative Review. Final report of the
Commission on Administrative Review .
Washington , 1977. 2 v. (iii, 1389 p.) :   LC Card
81-600558   DDC 328.73/072/068 19
JK1433 .U54 1977

**United States. Congress. House. Manpower and
Housing Subcommittee. see United States.
Congress. House. Committee on Government
Operations. Manpower and Housing
Subcommittee.**

**United States. Congress. House. Narcotics Abuse
and Control, Select Committee on. see
United States. Congress. House. Select
Committee on Narcotics Abuse and Control.**

**United States. Congress. House of
Representatives. see United States. Congress.**

United States. Congress. House. Office of the Law Revision

BIBLIOGRAPHIC GUIDE

460

House.

United States. Congress. House. Office of the Law Revision Counsel. United States. Laws, statutes, etc. United States code. 1976 ed., supplement III . Washington , 1980- - v. ;
NYPL [*R-Econ. 78-895 Suppl. 3]

UNITED STATES. CONGRESS. HOUSE - OFFICIALS AND EMPLOYEES.
United States. Congress. House. Commission on Administrative Review. Final report of the Commission on Administrative Review . Washington , 1977. 2 v. (iii, 1389 p.) : LC Card 81-600558 DDC 328.73/072/068 19
JK1433 .U54 1977

United States. Congress. House. Permanent Select Committee on Intelligence. Subcommittee on Legislation. H.R. 6588, the National Intelligence Act of 1980 : hearings before the Subcommittee on Legislation of the Permanent Select Committee on Intelligence, House of Representatives, Ninety-sixth Congress, second session, March 18, 19, 27, and April 15, 22, 1980. Washington : U. S. G.P.O, 1980 [i.e. 1981] iv, 608 p. ; 24 cm. Item 1009 Includes bibliographical references. LC Card 81-600987 DDC 344.73/052 347.30452 19
1. Intelligence service - United States. 2. United States - National security. I. Title.
KF27.5 .I54 1980

United States. Congress. House. Permanent Select Committee on Intelligence. Subcommittee on Oversight.
CIA estimates of Soviet defense spending : hearing before the Subcommittee on Oversight of the Permanent Select Committee on Intelligence, House of Representatives, Ninety-sixth Congress, second session, September 3, 1980. Washington : U. S. G.P.O., 1980 [i.e. 1981] iii, 95 p. : ill. ; 24 cm. Item 1009 Includes bibliographical references. LC Card 81-600837 DDC 355/.033047 19
1. Soviet Union - Armed forces - Procurement. 2. Soviet Union - Military policy. 3. United States. Central Intelligence Agency. I. Title.
KF27.5 .I55 1980c

The Cuban emigres : was there a U. S. intelligence failure? : Staff report / Subcommittee on Oversight, Permanent Select Committee on Intelligence, U. S. House of Representatives. Washington : U. S. Govt. Print. Off., 1980. ii, 5 p. ; 24 cm. "June 1980." At head of title: Committee print. LC Card 80-602585 DDC 325/.27291/0973 19
1. Cubans in the United States. 2. Intelligence service - United States. I. Title.
E184.C97 U54 1980

Intelligence on the world energy outlook and its policy implications : hearings before the Subcommittee on Oversight of the Permanent Select Committee on Intelligence, House of Representatives, Ninety-sixth Congress, first session, October 17 and 18, 1979. Washington : U. S. Govt. Print. Off., 1980. iii, 235 p. : ill. ; 24 cm. LC Card 80-603479 DDC 333.79 19
1. Energy consumption - Forecasting. 2. Petroleum industry and trade. 3. United States. Central Intelligence Agency. 4. United States. Energy Information Administration. I. Title.
KF27.5 .I55 1979a

Pre-employment security procedures of the intelligence agencies : hearings before the Subcommittee on Oversight of the Permanent Select Committee on Intelligence, House of Representatives, Ninety-sixth Congress, first session .... Washington : U. S. Govt. Print. Off., 1980. iv, 213 p. ; 23 cm. Hearings held May 16-June 21, 1979. LC Card 80-602800 DDC 353.0074 19
1. Intelligence service - United States. 2. Loyalty-security program, 1947-. I. Title.
KF27.5 .I55 1979

Soviet biological warfare activities : a report of the Subcommittee on Oversight, Permanent Select Committee on Intelligence, U. S. House of Representatives. Washington : U. S. Govt. Print. Off., 1980. ii, 5 p. ; 24 cm. At head of title: Committee print. "June 1980." LC Card 80-603268 DDC 358/.38/0947 19
1. Biological warfare. 2. Military research - Russia. 3. Anthrax - Russian Republic - Sverdlousk. I. Title.
UG447.8 .U45 1980

Soviet covert action (the forgery offensive) :

hearings before the Subcommittee on Oversight of the Permanent Select Committee on Intelligence, House of Representatives, Ninety-sixth Congress, second session, February 6, 19, 1980. Washington : U. S. Govt. Print. Off., 1980. iii, 245 p. : ill. ; 24 cm. Includes bibliographical references. LC Card 80-603647 DDC 327.1/2/0947 19
1. Intelligence service - Russia. 2. Propaganda, Russian. 3. Forgery. I. Title.
KF27.5 .I55 1980b

Soviet strategic forces : hearings before the Subcommittee on Oversight of the Permanent Select Committee on Intelligence, House of Representatives, Ninety-sixth Congress, second session, February 7 and 20, 1980. Washington : U. S. Govt. Print. Off., 1980. iii, 76 p. ; 24 cm. LC Card 80-602765 DDC 358/.17/0947 19
1. Strategic forces - Russia. I. Title.
KF27.5 .I55 1980

The Sverdlovsk incident : Soviet compliance with the Biological weapons convention? : Hearing before the Subcommittee on Oversight of the Permanent Select Committee on Intelligence, House of Representatives, Ninety-sixth Congress, second session, May 29, 1980. Washington : U. S. Govt. Print. Off., 1980. iii, 18 p. ; 24 cm. LC Card 80-603451 DDC 358/.38/0947 19
1. Biological warfare. 2. Biological warfare - Research - Russian Republic - Sverdlovsk (Province). 3. Anthrax. I. Title.
KF27.5 .I55 1980a

United States. Congress. House. Permanent Select Committee on Intelligence. Subcommittee on Program and Budget Authorization. Soviet internal developments : hearings before the Subcommittee on Program and Budget Authorization of the Permanent Select Committee on Intelligence, House of Representatives, Ninety-sixth Congress, second session, January 24 and 25, 1980. Washington : U. S. Govt. Print. Off., 1980. iii, 134 p. ; 23 cm. Includes bibliographical references. LC Card 80-602084 DDC 947.085/3 19
1. Russia - Politics and government - 1953-. 2. Russia - Economic conditions - 1976-. I. Title.
KF27.5 .I56 1980

United States. Congress. House. Public Works and Transportation, Committee on. see **United States. Congress. House. Committee on Public Works and Transportation.**

UNITED STATES. CONGRESS. HOUSE - RULES AND PRACTICE.
United States. Congress. House. Committee on Rules. Subcommittee on the Rules and Organization of the House. Excerpts from hearings on congressional procedures . Washington , 1979. iii, 89 p. ; LC Card 79-601693 DDC 328.73/05 19
KF4992 .U55

United States. Congress. House. Science and Technology, Committee on. see **United States. Congress. House. Committee on Science and Technology.**

United States. Congress. House. Select Committee on Aging.
Age discrimination in the selection of Federal judges : hearing before the Select Committee on Aging, House of Representatives, Ninety-sixth Congress, second session, February 13, 1980. Washington : U. S. Govt. Print. Off., 1980. iii, 128 p. ; 24 cm. "Comm. pub. no. 96-228." LC Card 80-602715 DDC 347.73/2034 19 `
1. Judges - United States - Appointment, qualifications, tenure, etc. 2. Age discrimination - United States. I. Title.
KF27.5 .A3 1980

California. Legislature. Assembly. Committee on Aging. Crises in health care for older Americans . Washington , 1980. iii, 87 p. ; LC Card 80-602276 DDC 362.1/9897/00973 19
RA413.7.A4 C34 1979

DMSO, new hope for arthritis? : Hearing before the Select Committee on Aging, House of Representatives, Ninety-sixth Congress, second session, March 24, 1980. Washington : U. S. Govt. Print. Off. : for sale by the Supt. of Docs., U. S. Govt. Print. Off., 1980. iii, 180 p. ; 24 cm. "Comm. pub. no. 96-232." LC Card 80-603066 DDC 363.1/94 19
1. Methyl sulphoxide - Therapeutic use. 2. Arthritis. I.

Title.
KF27.5 .A3 1980a

Drug abuse in nursing homes : hearing before the Select Committee on Aging, House of Representatives, Ninety-sixth Congress, second session, June 25, 1980. Washington : U. S. Govt. Print. Off. : for sale by the Supt. of Docs., U. S. Govt. Print. Off., 1980. iv, 131 p. ; 24 cm. "Comm. pub. no. 96-244." LC Card 80-603430 DDC 362.1/6 19
1. Medication abuse - United States. 2. Nursing homes - United States - Pharmaceutical services. I. Title.
KF27.5 .A3 1980d

EEOC enforcement of the Age Discrimination in Employment Act : hearing before the Select Committee on Aging, House of Representatives, Ninety-sixth Congress, second session, June 18, 1980. Washington : U. S. G.P.O. : for sale by the Supt. of Docs., U. S. G.P.O., 1980. iii, 110 p. : ill. ; 24 cm. "Comm. pub. no. 96-265." Includes bibliographical references. LC Card 81-600653 DDC 331.3/98 19
1. Age discrimination in employment - United States. 2. Retirement, Mandatory - United States. 3. United States. Equal Employment Opportunity Commission. I. Title.
KF27.5 .A3 1980h

Families, aging and changing : hearing before the Select Committee on Aging, House of Representatives, Ninety-sixth Congress, second session, June 4, 1980. Washington : U. S. Govt. Print. Off. : for sale by the Supt. of Docs., U. S. Govt. Print. Off., 1980. iii, 118 p. : ill. ; 23 cm. "Comm. pub. no. 96-242." Bibliography: p. 112-113. LC Card 80-603635 DDC 362.8/2/0973 19
1. Family policy - United States. 2. Aged - Government policy - United States. I. Title.
KF27.5 .A3 1980e

Families, aging and changing (San Diego, Calif.) : hearing before the Select Committee on Aging, House of Representatives, Ninety-sixth Congress, second session, November 24, 1980, San Diego, Calif. Washington : U. S. G.P.O., 1981. iii, 85 p. : ill. ; 24 cm. "Comm. pub. no. 96-275A." Item 1009 Includes bibliographical references. LC Card 81-601767 DDC 306.8/7 19
1. Family policy - California. 2. Family policy - United States. 3. Aged - Government policy - California. 4. Aged - Government policy - United States. I. Title.
KF27.5 .A3 1980i

Frauds against the elderly : health quackery : hearing before the Select Committee on Aging, House of Representatives, Ninety-sixth Congress, second session, October 1, 1980. Washington : U. S. G.P.O., 1980 [i.e. 1981] iii, 144 p. : ill. ; 24 cm. "Comm. pub. no. 96-251." Item 1009 Bibliography: p. 143-144. LC Card 81-600945 DDC 364.1/63 19
1. Quacks and quackery - United States. 2. Fraud - United States. 3. Advertising, Fraudulent - United States. 4. Aged - United States - Care and hygiene. I. Title.
KF27.5 .A3 1980m

Frauds against the elderly : New York : hearing before the Subcommittee on Retirement Income and Employment of the Select Committee on Aging, House of Representatives, Ninety-sixth Congress, second session, October 23, 1980, New York, N.Y. Washington : U. S. G.P.O., 1981. iii, 51 p. ; 24 cm. "Comm. pub. no. 96-254." Item 1009 LC Card 81-601344 DDC 364.1/63 19
1. Aged - New York (N.Y.) - Crimes against. 2. Fraud - New York (N.Y.). I. Title.
KF27.5 .A3 1980k

Media portrayal of the elderly : hearing before the Select Committee on Aging, House of Representatives, Ninety-sixth Congress, second session, April 26, 1980, Los Angeles, Calif. Washington : U. S. Govt. Print. Off., 1980. iii, 99 p. : graphs ; 24 cm. "Comm. pub. no. 96-231." Bibliography: p. 94. LC Card 80-603012 DDC 305.2/6 19
1. Aged in television - United States. I. Title.
KF27.5 .A3 1980b

Medicare, a fifteen-year perspective : hearing before the Select Committee on Aging, House of Representatives, Ninety-sixth Congress, second session, July 30, 1980. Washington : U. S. G.P.O. : For sale by the Supt. of Docs., U. S. G.P.O., 1980. iii, 65 p. ; 24 cm. "Comm. pub. no. 96-258." S/N 052-070-05479-4 LC Card

GOVERNMENT PUBLICATIONS - U.S.: 1981

United States. Congress. House. Select Committee on Aging.

461

80-604061   DDC 368.4/26/00973 19
1. Medicare. I. Title.
KF27.5. .A3 1980g

Medicare after 15 years : has it become a broken promise to the elderly? : report (with supplemental views) / by the select Committee on Aging, U. S. House of Representatives, Ninety-sixth Congress, second session. Washington : U. S. Govt. Print. Off. : for sale by the Supt. of Docs., U. S. Govt. Print. Off., [1980] v, 112 p. ; 24 cm. At head of title: Committee print. "Comm. pub. no. 96-245." "November 17, 1980."   LC Card 80-603872   DDC 368.4/26/00973 19
1. Medicare. I. Title.
HD7102.U4 U53 1980a

Medicare oversight : hearing before the Select Committee on Aging, House of Representatives, Ninety-sixth Congress, second session, August 7, 1980, Miami, Fla. Washington : U. S. Govt. Print. Off., 1980- <v.> : ill. ; 23 cm. "Comm. pub. no. 96-"   LC Card 80-603487   DDC 362.1/0425/0973 19
1. Medicare - Florida. 2. Medicare. I. Title.
KF27.5 .A3 1980c

Michigan. Legislature. Joint Special Committee on Aging. Housing and in-house services . Washington , 1981. iv, 125 p. :   LC Card 81-601326   DDC 363.5/9 19
KF27.5 .A3 1930l

Oversight of Older Americans Act administration : hearing before the Select Committee on Aging, House of Representatives, Ninety-sixth Congress, second session, July 23, 1980. Washington : U. S. G.P.O., 1980. iii, 43 p. : ill. ; 24 cm. "Comm. pub. no. 96-257." Includes bibliographical references.   LC Card 80-604046   DDC 353.0084/6 19
1. Aged - Government policy - United States. 2. United States. Office of Human Development Services. I. Title.
KF27.5 .A3 1980f

Research Frontiers in Aging and Cancer : International Symposium for the 1980s : hearing before the Select Committee on Aging, House of Representatives, Ninety-sixth Congress, second session, September 26, 1980. Washington : U. S. G.P.O., 1981. iii, 48 p. ; 24 cm. "Comm. pub. no. 96-275." Item 1009   LC Card 81-601752   DDC 362.1/9699400973 19
1. Cancer - Age factors. 2. Research Frontiers in Aging and Cancer: International Symposium for the 1980s (1980 : Washington, D.C.). I. Title.
KF27.5 .A3 1980n

Retirement, the broken promise : hearing before the Select Committee on Aging, House of Representatives, Ninety-sixth Congress, second session, September 17, 1980. Washington : U. S. G.P.O., 1981. iii, 91 p. ; ill. ; 24 cm. "Comm. pub. no. 96-266." Item 1009   LC Card 81-601334   DDC 331.25/2/0973 19
1. Retirement income - United States. 2. Aged - United States - Economic conditions. 3. Old age pensions - United States. I. Title.
KF27.5 .A3 1980j

Teamwork in the delivery of Federal programs to the elderly : a report / by the Select Committee on Aging, U. S. House of Representatives, Ninety-sixth Congress, second session. Washington : U. S. Govt. Print. Off., 1980. v, 18 p. ; 24 cm. At head of title: Committee print. "Comm. pub. no. 96-227." "June 1980"   LC Card 80-602675   DDC 362.6/0973 19
1. Aged - Government policy - United States. I. Title.
HV1461 .U63 1980a

United States. Congress. Senate. Committee on the Judiciary. Subcommittee on Antitrust, Monopoly, and Business Rights. Cancer insurance and the elderly . Washington , 1980. vi, 524 p. :   LC Card 80-603736   DDC 368.3/82 19
KF26 .J835 1980b

United States. Congress. Senate. Special Committee on Aging. Elder abuse . Washington , 1980. iv, 166 p. :   LC Card 80-603798   DDC 362.6/042 19
KF26.5 .A3 1980d

University of California San Francisco. Innovative developments in aging . Washington , 1979. xi, 571 p. ;   LC Card 80-601011
HV1450 .U54 1979

*NYPL [*R-Econ. 80-4848]*

United States. Congress. House. Select Committee on Aging. Subcommittee No. 1. see United States. Congress. House. Select Committee on Aging. Subcommittee on Retirement Income and Employment.

United States. Congress. House. Select Committee on Aging. Subcommittee on Health and Long-Term Care.
Adult day care programs : hearing before the Subcommittee on Health and Long-Term Care of the Select Committee on Aging, House of Representatives, Ninety-sixth Congress, second session, April 23, 1980. Washington : U. S. G.P.O. : For sale by the Supt. of Docs., U. S. G.P.O., 1980. iv, 297 p. ; 24 cm. "Comm. pub. no. 96-260." Bibliography: p. 289-297.   LC Card 81-600606   DDC 362.6/3 19
1. Day care centers for the aged - United States. I. Title.
KF27.5 .A355 1980e

Catalyst altered water : a briefing / by the Subcommittee on Health and Long-Term Care of the Select Committee on Aging, U. S. House of Representatives, Ninety-sixth Congress, second session, July 7, 1980, Rapid City, S. Dak. Washington : U. S. G.P.O. : For sale by the Supt. of Docs., U. S. G.P.O., 1980. iii, 45 p. : ill. ; 24 cm. At head of title: Committee print. "Comm. pub. no. 96-240." S/N 052-070-05444-1 Item 1009   LC Card 81-601520   DDC 363.1/94 19
1. Drinking water - Therapeutic use. 2. Hydrotherapy - United States. I. Title.
RM813 .U54 1980

Long-term care for the 1980's : channeling demonstrations and other initiatives : hearing before the Subcommittee on Health and Long-Term Care of the Select Committee on Aging, House of Representatives, Ninety-sixth Congress, second session, February 27, 1980. Washington : U. S. Govt. Print. Off. : for sale by the Supt. of Docs., U. S. Govt. Print. Off., 1980. iii, 47 p. ; 24 cm. "Comm. pub. no. 96-234."   LC Card 80-603305   DDC 362.6/3 19
1. Aged - Home care - United States. 2. Home care services - United States. I. Title.
KF27.5 .A355 1980

Medicare and medicaid fraud : hearing before the Subcommittee on Health and Long-Term Care of the Select Committee on Aging, House of Representatives, Ninety-sixth Congress, second session, May 15, 1980. Washington : U. S. Govt. Print. Off. : for sale by the Supt. of Docs., U. S. Govt. Print. Off., 1980. iii, 39 p. ; 24 cm. "Comm. pub. no. 96-241."   LC Card 80-603434   DDC 364.1/63 19
1. Medicare fraud - United States. 2. Medicaid fraud - United States. I. Title.
KF27.5 .A355 1980a

Medicare reform : hearing before the Subcommittee on Health and Long-Term Care of the Select Committee on Aging, House of Representatives, Ninety-sixth Congress, second session, July 18, 1980, Longview, Wash. Washington : U. S. Govt. Print. Off., 1980. iii, 48 p. ; 24 cm. "Comm. pub. no. 96-237."   LC Card 80-603658   DDC 368.4/26/009797 19
1. Medicare - Washington (State). 2. Medicare. I. Title.
KF27.5 .A355 1980d

Nurse shortage and its impact on care for the elderly : hearing before the Subcommittee on Health and Long-Term Care of the Select Committee on Aging, House of Representatives, Ninety-sixth Congress, second session, August 20, 1980. Washington : U. S. G.P.O., 1981 [i.e. 1980] iii, 127 p. : ill. ; 24 cm. "Comm. Pub. no. 96-255." Item 1009   LC Card 81-601169   DDC 362.1/6 19
1. Nurses - United States - Supply and demand. 2. Geriatric nursing - United States. 3. Aged - United States - Care and hygiene. I. Title.
KF27.5 .A355 1980f

Problems of nursing home bed availability and placement : hearing before the Subcommittee on Health and Long-Term Care of the Select Committee on Aging, House of Representatives, Ninety-sixth Congress, second session, May 17, 1980, Shelton, Conn. Washington : U. S. Govt. Print. Off., 1980. iii, 63 p. ; 23 cm. "Comm. pub. no. 96-243."   LC Card 80-603433   DDC 362.1/6 19
1. Nursing homes - Connecticut. I. Title.
KF27.5 .A355 1980b

United States. Congress. House. Select Committee on Aging. Subcommittee on

Housing and Consumer Interests.
Alternative housing options for the elderly : hearing before the Subcommittee on Housing and Consumer Interests of the Select Committee on Aging, House of Representatives, Ninety-sixth Congress, second session, October 6, 1980, Denver, Colo. Washington : U. S. G.P.O., c1981. iii, 49 p. ; 24 cm. "Comm. pub. no. 96-270." Item 1009 Includes bibliographical references.   LC Card 81-601376   DDC 363.5/9 19
1. Aged - United States - Dwellings. 2. Housing policy - United States. I. Title.
KF27.5 .A358 1980d

Condominium conversions : hearing before the Subcommittee on Housing and consumer Interests of the Select Committee on Aging, House of Representatives, Ninety-sixth Congress, second session, May 15, 1980. Washington : U. S. G.P.O. : For sale by the Supt. of Docs., U. S. G.P.O., 1980. iii, 429 p. : ill. ; 24 cm. "Comm. pub. no. 96-246." Includes bibliographical references.   LC Card 80-604110   DDC 363.5/9 19
1. Condominium (Housing) - United States - Conversion. 2. Aged - United States - Dwellings. I. Title.
KF27.5 .A358 1980

Crime, transportation, and income maintenance : Denver, Colo. : hearing before the Subcommittee on Housing and Consumer Interests of the Select Committee on Aging, House of Representatives, Ninety-sixth Congress, second session, October 6, 1980, Denver, Colo. Washington : U. S. G.P.O., 1981. iii, 44 p. ; 24 cm. "Comm. pub. no. 96-256." Item 1009   LC Card 81-601354   DDC 362.6/09788 19
1. Aged - Colorado - Services for. I. Title.
KF27.5 .A358 1980e

Housing needs of the elderly : hearing before the Subcommittee on Housing and Consumer Interests of the Select Committee on Aging, House of Representatives, Ninety-sixth Congress, second session, September 13, 1980, North Hollywood, Calif. Washington : U. S. G.P.O., 1981 [i.e. 1980] iii, 52 p. : 24 cm. "Comm. rub. no. 96-268." Item 1009   LC Card 81-601318   DDC 363.5/9 19
1. Aged - California - Dwellings. I. Title.
KF27.5 .A358 1980b

The impact of thhe rising costs of energy, transportation, health, housing, and other necessities on senior citizens : hearings before the Subcommittee on Housing and Consumer Interests of the Select Committee on Aging, House of Representatives, Ninety-sixth Congress, second session, September 6 and 8, 1980, Columbia, Westminster and Reisterstown, Md. Washington : U. S. G.P.O., 1981. iv, 197 p. : ill. ; 24 cm. "Comm. pub. no. 96-274." Item 1009   LC Card 81-601751   DDC 330.9752/043/0880565 19
1. Aged - Maryland - Economic conditions. 2. Cost and standard of living - Maryland. 3. Inflation (Finance) - Maryland. I. Title.
KF27.5 .A358 1980f

Services for the elderly in Albuquerque, N. Mex. : hearing before the Subcommittee on Housing and Consumer Interests of the Select Committee on Aging, House of Representatives, Ninety-sixth Congress, second session, July 11, 1980, Albuquerque, N. Mex. Washington : U. S. G.P.O., 1980 [i.e. 1981] iv, 56 p. ; 24 cm. "Comm. pub. no. 96-252." Item 1009   LC Card 81-601154   DDC 362.6/3/0978961 19
1. Aged - Services for - New Mexico - Albuquerque. I. Title.
KF27.5 .A358 1980a

Social service needs of elder minorities : hearing before the Subcommittee on Housing and Consumer Interests of the Select Committee on Aging, House of Representatives, Ninety-sixth Congress, second session, September 13, 1980, Pacoima, Calif. Washington : U. S. G.P.O., 1981. iii, 39 p. ; 24 cm. "Comm. pub. no. 96-271." Item 1009   LC Card 81-601324   DDC 362.6/089 19
1. Minority aged - Services for - California. I. Title.
KF27.5 .A358 1980c

United States. Congress. House. Select Committee on Aging. Subcommittee on Human Services.
Domestic abuse of the elderly : a briefing / by the Subcommittee on Human Services of the

BIBLIOGRAPHIC GUIDE

United States. Congress. House. Select Committee on Aging.

462

Select Committee on Aging, U. S. House of Representatives, Ninety-sixth Congress, second session, April 28, 1980, Union, N.J. Washington : U. S. G.P.O., 1980. iii, 40 p. ; 23 cm. At head of title: Committee print. "Comm. pub. no. 96-259." Item 1009   LC Card 81-600670   DDC 362.6 19

1. Aged - Abuse of - United States. I. Title.

HV1461 .U63 1980b

Domestic violence against the elderly : hearing before the Subcommittee on Human Services of the Select Committee on Aging, House of Representatives, Ninety-sixth Congress, second session, April 21, 1980, New York, N.Y. Washington : U. S. Govt. Print. Off. : for sale by the Supt. of Docs., U. S. Govt. Print. Off., 1980. iii, 155 p. ; 24 cm. "Comm. pub. no. 96-233." LC Card 80-603108   DDC 362.6 19

1. Aged - New York (State) - Abuse of. 2. Aged - New York (State) - Crimes against. 3. Family violence - New York (State). I. Title.

KF27.5 .A36 1980b

Future directions for aging policy : a human service model : a report / by the Subcommittee on Human Services of the Select Committee on Aging, U. S. House of Representatives, Ninety-sixth Congress, second session. Washington : U. S. Govt. Print. Off. : for sale by the Supt. of Docs., U. S. Govt. Print. Off., 1980. vii, 141 p. : ill. ; 26 cm. "Comm. pub. no. 96-226." LC Card 80-602607   DDC 362.6/0973 19

1. Aged - Government policy - United States. 2. Aged, Services for - United States. I. Title.

HQ1064.U5 U53 1980

Reauthorization of the Older Americans Act, 1981 : hearing before the Subcommittee on Human Services of the Select Committee on Aging, House of Representatives, Ninety-sixth Congress, second session, August 8, 1980, Gloucester, N.J. Washington : U. S. G.P.O., 1980- v. <1> ; 23 cm. "United States. Congress. House. Comm. pub. no. 96-247." LC Card 80-603785   DDC 353.0084/6 19

1. Old age assistance - United States. 2. Old age assistance - New Jersey. I. Title.

KF27.5 .A36 1980c

United States. Congress. House. Select Committee on Aging. Subcommittee on Retirement Income and Employment. Income status of the rural elderly : hearing before the Subcommittee on Retirement Income and Employment of the Select Committee on Aging, House of Representatives, Ninety-sixth Congress, second session, August 29, 1980, Swannanoa, N.C. Washington : U. S. G.P.O., 1980. iii, 74 p. ; 24 cm. "Comm. pub. no. 96-253." Item 1009   LC Card 81-601192   DDC 362.6/042 19

1. Rural aged - North Carolina - Economic conditions. 2. Rural poor - North Carolina. 3. Retirement income - North Carolina. I. Title.

KF27.5 .A374 1980b

Inflation and New York's elderly : hearing before the Subcommittee on Retirement Income and Employment of the Select Committee on Aging, House of Representatives, Ninety-sixth Congress, second session, January 10, 1980, New York, N.Y. Washington : U. S. Govt. Print. Off., 1980. iv, 201 p. ; 24 cm. "Comm. pub. no. 96-229." LC Card 80-603004   DDC 330.9747/1043/0880565 19

1. Aged - New York (City) - Economic conditions. 2. Retirement income - New York (City) - Effect of inflation on. I. Title.

KF27.5 .A374 1980a

Oversight on recommendations of 1979 Social Security Advisory Council : hearings before the Subcommittee on Retirement Income and Employment of the Select Committee on Aging, House of Representatives, Ninety-sixth Congress, second session, March 11 and 13, 1980. Washington : U. S. Govt. Print. Off. : for sale by the Supt. of Docs., U. S. Govt. Print. Off., 1980. iv, 208 p. : graphs ; 24 cm. "Comm. pub. no. 96-230." Includes bibliographical references. LC Card 80-603006   DDC 368.4/00973 19

1. Social security - United States. 2. Old age pensions - Taxation - United States. 3. Retirement age - United States. I. United States. Advisory Council on Social Security (1978-1979). II. Title.

KF27.5 .A374 1980

Social security : a critique of recommendations to tax benefits and to raise the eligibility age for retirement benefits : a report with additional

views / by the Subcommittee on Retirement Income and Employment of the Select Committee on Aging, House of Representatives, Ninety-sixth Congress, second session. Washington : U. S. G.P.O. : for sale by the Supt. of Docs., U. S. G.P.O., 1980. v, 39 p. : graphs ; 24 cm. At head of title: Committee print. "September, 1980." "Comm. pub. no 96-235." LC Card 80-603864   DDC 353.0082/56 19

1. Social security - United States. 2. Old age pensions - Taxation - United States. 3. Retirement age - United States. I. Title.

HD7125 .U537 1980a

United States. Congress. House. Select Committee on Assassinations. Report of the Select Committee on Assassinations, U. S. House of Representatives, Ninety-fifth Congress, second session : findings and recommendations. Washington : U. S. Govt. Print. Off. : for sale by the Supt. of Docs., U. S. Govt. Print. Off., 1979. xiii, 686 p. ; 23 cm. (House report - 95th Congress, 2d session ; no. 95-1828, pt. 2) At head of title: Union calendar no. 962. "March 29, 1979." Includes bibliographical references. LC Card 79-603369   DDC 364.1/524/0973 19

1. Kennedy, John Fitzgerald, Pres. U. S., 1917-1963 - Assassination. 2. King, Martin Luther - Assassination. I. Series: United States. 95th Congress, 2d session, 1978. House. Report , no. 95-1828, pt. 2.

KF32.5 .A8 1979

United States. Congress. House. Select Committee on Committees. Energy jurisdictions of House committees : hearings before the Select Committee on Committees, House of Representatives, Ninety-sixth Congress, first session ... and markup meetings on H. Res. 549, December 18, 19, 20, and January 23. Washington : U. S. Govt. Print. Off., 1980. v. 509 p. ; 23 cm. Hearings held Oct. 30-Dec. 6, 1979.   LC Card 80-603513   DDC 328.73/07652 19

1. Energy policy - United States. 2. United States. Congress. House - Committees. I. Title.

KF27.5 .C57 1979a

United States. Congress. House. Select Committee on Emancipation and Colonization. Report of the Select Committee on Emancipation and Colonization : with an appendix. Washington : Govt. Print. Off., 1862. 83 p. ; 23 cm. Microfilm. 37th Cong., 2d sess. House. Report no. 148. "To accompany bill H. R. no. 576." "Address issued by a national emigration convention of colored people held at Cleveland, Ohio, August 24, 1854, written by M. R. Delany": p. 37-59.

1. Afro-Americans - Colonization. I. Delany, Martin Robison, 1812-1885. II. Title.

NYPL [Sc Micro R-3657]

United States. Congress. House. Select Committee on Narcotics Abuse and Control. Cocaine, a major drug issue of the seventies : hearings before the Select Committee on Narcotics Abuse and Control, House of Representatives, Ninety-sixth Congress, first session, July 24, 26, October 10, 1979. Washington : U. S. Govt. Print. Off., 1980. iii, 142 p. : maps ; 24 cm. "SCNAC-96-1-9." LC Card 80-601164   DDC 362.2/93 19

1. Cocaine. I. Title.

KF27.5 .N3 1979j

Diversion of licit drugs to illegal markets : hearing before the Select Committee on Narcotics Abuse and Control, House of Representatives, Ninety-sixth Congress, first session, October 31, 1979. Washington : U. S. Govt. Print. Off., 1980. iii, 90 p. : ill. ; 24 cm. "SCNAC-96-1-11." LC Card 80-601949   DDC 363.4/5 19

1. Psychotropic drugs - United States. 2. Drug abuse - United States. 3. Drugs - Prescribing - United States. I. Title.

KF27.5 .N3 1979i

Drug abuse in the Armed Forces of the United States : oversight update : hearing before the Select Committee on Narcotics Abuse and Control, House of Representatives, Ninety-sixth Congress, first session, November 7, 1979. Washington : U. S. Govt. Print. Off., 1980. iii, 144 p. ; 24 cm. "SCNAC-96-1-13." LC Card 80-601999   DDC 353.0084/29 19

1. Soldiers - United States - Drug use. 2. Narcotics, Control of - United States. 3. Drug abuse - Treatment -

United States. I. Title.

KF27.5 .N3 1979g

Drug abuse in the Armed Forces of the United States : oversight update : a report of the Select Committee on Narcotics Abuse and Control, Ninety-sixth Congress, second session. Washington : U. S. Govt. Print. Off., 1980. iii, 66 p. ; 24 cm. At head of title: 96th Congress, 2d session, House of Representatives. Committee print. "SCNAC-96-2-9." LC Card 80-603858   DDC 362.2/936 19

1. Soldiers - United States - Drug use. 2. United States - Armed Forces - Sanitary affairs. I. Title.

UH630 .U62 1980

Drug abuse in the Memphis, Tennessee schools : a report of the Select Committee on Narcotics Abuse and Control, Ninety-sixth Congress, second session. Washington : U. S. Govt. Print. Off., 1980. iii, 17 p. ; 24 cm. At head of title: Committee print. 96th Congress, 2d session, House of Representatives. "SCNAC 96-2-6." LC Card 80-603052   DDC 362.2/93/088375 19

1. Drug abuse - Study and teaching - Tennessee - Memphis. 2. High school students - Tennessee - Memphis - Drug use. I. Title.

HV5808 .U43 1980

Drug paraphernalia : a report of the Select Committee on Narcotics Abuse and Control, Ninety-sixth Congress, second session. Washington : U. S. G.P.O., 1980. iii, 46 p. : ill. ; 24 cm. At head of title: Committee print. 96th Congress, 2d session. House of Representatives. "SCNAC-96-1-6." Includes bibliographical references. LC Card 80-604119   DDC 381/.4568 19

1. Narcotics, Control of - United States. 2. Drug abuse - United States. 3. Youth - United States - Drug use. 4. Drug paraphernalia industry - United States. I. Title.

HV5825 .U563 1980

Drug use and abuse in the Memphis-Shelby County school system : hearings before the Select Committee on Narcotics Abuse and Control, House of Representatives, Ninety-sixth Congress, second session, January 17-18, 1980. Washington : U. S. Govt. Print. Off., 1980. iii, 184 p. ; 24 cm. "SCNAC-96-2-1." LC Card 80-602786   DDC 362.2/932/088375 19

1. Students - Tennessee - Memphis - Drug use. 2. Students - Tennessee - Shelby Co. - Drug use. I. Title.

KF27.5 .N3 1980a

Federal drug strategy : prospects for the 1980's : hearing before the Select Committee on Narcotics Abuse and Control, House of Representatives, Ninety-sixth Congress, second session, September 23, 1980. Washington : U. S. G.P.O., 1980. iii, 164 p. : ill. ; 24 cm. "SCNAC-96-2-14." Item 1009   LC Card 81-601321   DDC 363.4/5/0973 19

1. Drug abuse - United States. 2. Narcotics, Control of - United States. I. Title.

KF27.5 .N3 1980f

Health consequences of marihuana abuse : recent findings and the therapeutic uses of marihuana and the use of heroin to reduce pain : a report of the Select Committee on Narcotics Abuse and Control, Ninety-sixth Congress, second session. Washington : U. S. G.P.O., 1980 [i.e. 1981] v, 132 p. ; 24 cm. At head of title: Committee print. 96th Congress, 2d session. House of Representatives. "SCNAC-96-2-5." Item 1009   LC Card 81-602235   DDC 615/.7827 19

1. Marihuana - Physiological effect. 2. Marihuana - Therapeutic use. 3. Heroin - Therapeutic use. I. Title.

QP981.C14 U54 1981

Illicit methamphetamine laboratories in the Pennsylvania, New Jersey, Delaware area : hearing before the Select Committee on Narcotics Abuse and Control, House of Representatives, Ninety-sixth Congress, second session, July 7, 1980. Washington : U. S. G.P.O., 1980. iii, 167 p. ; 24 cm. "SCNAC-96-2-11." Includes bibliographical references. LC Card 80-603986   DDC 364.1/77 19

1. Metamphetamine - Pennsylvania. 2. Metamphetamine - New Jersey. 3. Metamphetamine - Delaware. I. Title.

KF27.5 .N3 1980e

Increased heroin supply and decreased Federal funds : impact on enforcement, prevention, and treatment : hearing before the Select Committee on Narcotics Abuse and Control, House of Representatives, Ninety-sixth Congress, second session, May 2, 1980. Washington : U. S. Govt.

463

GOVERNMENT PUBLICATIONS - U.S.: 1981

United States. Congress. House. Subcommittee on Courts, Civil

Print. Off., 1980. iii, 144 p. : ill. ; 23 cm. "SCNAC-96-2-7." LC Card 80-603349 DDC
362.2/93/0973 19
1. Heroin. 2. Heroin habit - Treatment - United States. 3. Narcotics, Control of - United States. I. Title.
KF27.5 .N3 1980c

Increased heroin supply and decreased federal funds : impact on enforcement, prevention, and treatment : a report of the Select Committee on Narcotics Abuse and Control, Ninety-sixth Congress, second session. Washington : U. S. G.P.O., 1980 [i.e. 1981] iii, 76 p. : ill. ; 24 cm. At head of title: Committee print. 96th Congress, 2d session. House of Representatives. "SCNAC-96-2-15."
Item 1009   LC Card 81-601275   DDC
362.2/9356/0973 19
1. Heroin. 2. Heroin habit - United States. 3. Heroin habit - Treatment - United States. 4. Narcotics, Control of - United States. I. Title.
HV5822.H4 U53 1980

Interdiction of drug trafficking in Georgia : a report of the Select Committee on Narcotics Abuse and Control, Ninety-sixth Congress, second session. Washington : U. S. G.P.O., 1980. iii, 17 p. ; 24 cm. At head of title: Committee print. 96th Congress, 2d session, House of Representatives. "SCNAC-96-2-4."   LC Card
80-603853   DDC 363.4/5/09758 19
1. Narcotics, Control of - Georgia. I. Title.
HV8079.N3 U53 1980

Interdiction of drug trafficking in Georgia : hearings before the Select Committee on Narcotics Abuse and Control, House of Representatives, Ninety-sixth Congress, second session, February 29, March 1 and 3, 1980. Washington : U. S. Govt. Print. Off., 1980. iv, 266 p. ; 24 cm. "SCNAC-96-2-3."   LC Card
80-603326   DDC 363.4/5/09758 19
1. Narcotics, Control of - Georgia. I. Title.
KF27.5 .N3 1980b

Oversight on federal drug strategy--1979 : a report of the select Committee on Narcotics Abuse and Control, Ninety-sixth Congress, second session. Washington : U. S. G.P.O., 1980 [i.e. 1981] iv, 63 p. : ill. ; 24 cm. At head of title: Committee print. 96th Congress, 2d session. House of Representatives. "SNAC-96-2-16." Item 1009
LC Card 81-601283   DDC 363.4/5/0973 19
1. Drug abuse - United States - Prevention. 2. Narcotics, Control of - United States. I. Title.
HV5825 .U563 1981

Therapeutic uses of marihuana and schedule I drugs : hearing before the Select Committee on Narcotics Abuse and Control, House of Representatives, Ninety-sixth Congress, second session, May 20, 1980. Washington : U. S. G.P.O., 1980. iii, 351 p. : ill. ; 24 cm. "SCNAC-96-8." Includes bibliographical references.
LC Card 80-603422   DDC 363.1/94 19
1. Marihuana - Therapeutic use. 2. Heroin - Therapeutic use. I. Title.
KF27.5 .N3 1980d

The use of drugs during pregnancy : hearing before the Select Committee on Narcotics Abuse and Control, House of Representatives, Ninety-sixth Congress, second session, February 6, 1980. Washington : U. S. Govt. Print. Off., 1980. iii, 99 p. ; 24 cm. "SCNAC-96-2-2." Bibliography: p. 83-84.   LC Card 80-602790   DDC
362.8/2 19
1. Pregnant women - United States - Drug use. 2. Drug abuse in pregnancy - United States. 3. Fetus - Effect of drugs on. I. Title.
KF27.5 .N3 1980

The use of paraquat to eradicate illicit marihuana crops and the health implications of paraquat-contaminated marihuana on the U. S. market : a report of the Select Committee on Narcotics Abuse and Control, Ninety-sixth Congress, second session. Washington : U. S. Govt. Print. Off., 1980. iii, 99 p. : graphs ; 24 cm. At head of title: Committee print. Includes bibliographical references.   LC Card 80-602592   DDC
363.4/5 19
1. Paraquat - Toxicology. 2. Marihuana - Contamination. 3. Narcotics, Control of - International cooperation. 4. Narcotics, Control of - United States. 5. Narcotics, Control of - Mexico. I. Title.
RA1242.P34 U54 1980

United States. Congress. House. Select Committee on the Outer Continental Shelf. Final report on the activities of the Select Committee on the Outer Continental Shelf :

including proposed legislative changes. Washington : United States Govt. Print. Off., 1980. vi, 133 p. ; 24 cm. (House report - 96th Congress, 2d session ; no. 96-1214) "July 31, 1980." Includes bibliographical references.   LC Card
80-603260   DDC 353.0082/325 19
1. Marine resources - Law and legislation - United States. 2. Continental shelf - United States. I. Series: United States. 96th Congress, 2d session, 1980. House. Report , no. 96-1214.
KF32.5 .O8 1980

United States. Congress. House. Small Business, Committee on. see United States. Congress. House. Committee on Small Business.

United States. Congress. House. Special Study Mission to Asia. Asian security environment, 1980 : report / submitted by a Special Study Mission to Asia, January 5-23, 1980, under the auspices of the Subcommittee on Asian and Pacific Affairs of the Committee on Foreign Affairs, U. S. House of Representatives. Washington : U. S. Govt. Print. Off., 1980. vii, 96 p. ; 24 cm. At head of title: 96th Congress, 2d session. Committee print.   LC Card 80-602264   DDC
355/.03305 19
1. Asia - Foreign relations - United States. 2. United States - Foreign relations - Asia. 3. Asia - Relations (military) with the United States. 4. United States - Relations (military) with Asia. 5. Asia - Politics and government. I. United States. Congress. House. Committee on Foreign Affairs. Subcommittee on Asian and Pacific Affairs. II. Title.
DS33.4.U6 U5 1980

United States. Congress. House. Special Study Mission to Mexico City. United States--Mexican relations and the energy crisis : report of a Special Study Mission to Mexico City, July 1-4, 1979 to the Committee on Foreign Affairs, U. S. House of Representatives. Washington : U. S. Govt. Print. Off., 1980. vii, 17 p. ; 24 cm. At head of title: 96th Congress, 2d session. Committee print. "Submitted to the Committee on Foreign Affairs by Representatives Michael D. Barnes and David R. Bowen."   LC Card 80-602869
DDC 327.73072 19
1. United States - Relations (general) with Mexico. 2. Mexico - Relations (general) with the United States. I. Barnes, Michael D. II. Bowen, David R. III. United States. Congress. House. Committee on Foreign Affairs. IV. Title.
E183.8.M6 U36 1980

United States. Congress. House. Special Study Mission to Venezuela, Barbados, Brazil, and Costa Rica. Assessment of trends and conditions in the Inter-American region : report of a Special Study Mission to Venezuela, Barbados, Brazil, and Costa Rica, January 13-20, 1980, to the Committee on Foreign Affairs, U. S. House of Representatives. Washington : U. S. Govt. Print. Off., 1980. vii, 33 p. ; 24 cm. At head of title: 96th Congress, 2d session. Committee print.   LC Card 80-602265   DDC
327.7308 19
1. Latin America - Relations (general) with the United States. 2. United States - Relations (general) with Latin America. 3. Latin America - Economic conditions - 1945-. I. United States. Congress. House. Committee on Foreign Affairs. II. Title.
F1418 .U44 1980

United States. Congress. House. Standards of Official Conduct, Committee on. see United States. Congress. House. Committee on Standards of Official Conduct.

United States. Congress. House. Study Mission to Morocco, the Western Sahara, Mauritania, Algeria, Liberia, Spain, and France. Arms for Morocco? : U. S. policy toward the conflict in the Western Sahara : report of a Study Mission to Morocco, the Western Sahara, Mauritania, Algeria, Liberia, Spain, and France, August 5-18, 1979, to the Committee on Foreign Affairs, U. S. House of Representatives, January 1980. Washington : U. S. Govt. Print. Off., 1979. viii, 26 p. : map ; 24 cm. At head of title: 96th Congress, 1st session. Committee print. Submitted by S.J. Solarz.   LC Card 80-601042   DDC
355/.032/64 19
1. United States - Relations (military) with Morocco. 2. Morocco - Relations (military) with the United States. 3. Sahara - Politics and government. 4. Military assistance, American - Morocco. 5. Frente Popular para la Liberación de Saguia el Hamath y Río de Oro. 6. Munitions - United States. 7. Munitions - Morocco. I.

Solarz, Stephen J. II. United States. Congress. House. Committee on Foreign Affairs. III. Title.
E183.8.M8 U54 1979

United States. Congress. House Subcommittee No. 1. see United States. Congress. House. Committee on Armed Services. Subcommittee No. 1.

United States. Congress. House. Subcommittee on Administrative Law and Governmental Relations. see United States. Congress. House. Committee on the Judiciary. Subcommittee on Administrative Law and Governmental Relations.

United States. Congress. House. Subcommittee on Advanced Energy Technologies and Energy Conservation Research, Development, and Demonstration. see United States. Congress. House. Committee on Science and Technology. Subcommittee on Advanced Energy Technologies and Energy Conservation Research, Development, and Demonstration.

United States. Congress. House. Subcommittee on Africa. see United States. Congress. House. Committee on Foreign Affairs. Subcommittee on Africa.

United States. Congress. House Subcommittee on Asian and Pacific Affairs. see United States. Congress. House. Committee on Foreign Affairs. Subcommittee on Asian and Pacific Affairs.

United States. Congress. House. Subcommittee on Aviation. see United States. Congress. House. Committee on Public Works and Transportation. Subcommittee on Aviation.

United States. Congress. House. Subcommittee on Census and Population. see United States. Congress. House. Committee on Post Office and Civil Service. Subcommittee on Census and Population.

United States. Congress. House. Subcommittee on Civil and Constitutional Rights. see United States. Congress. House. Committee on the Judiciary. Subcommittee on Civil and Constitutional Rights.

United States. Congress. House. Subcommittee on Coast Guard and Navigation. see United States. Congress. House. Committee on Merchant Marine and Fisheries. Subcommittee on Coast Guard and Navigation.

United States. Congress. House. Subcommittee on Communications. see United States. Congress. House. Committee on Interstate and Foreign Commerce. Subcommittee on Communications.

United States. Congress. House. Subcommittee on Compensation and Employee Benefits. see United States. Congress. House. Committee on Post Office and Civil Service. Subcommittee on Compensation and Employee Benefits.

United States. Congress. House. Subcommittee on Conservation and Credit. see United States. Congress. House. Committee on Agriculture. Subcommittee on Conservation and Credit.

United States. Congress. House. Subcommittee on Consumer Affairs. see United States. Congress. House. Committee on Banking, Finance and Urban Affairs. Subcommittee on Consumer Affairs.

United States. Congress. House. Subcommittee on Consumer Protection and Finance. see United States. Congress. House. Committee on Interstate and Foreign Commerce. Subcommittee on Consumer Protection and Finance.

United States. Congress. House. Subcommittee on Cotton. see United States. Congress. House. Committee on Agriculture. Subcommittee on Cotton.

United States. Congress. House. Subcommittee on Courts, Civil Liberties, and the Administration of Justice. see United States. Congress. House. Committee on the Judiciary. Subcommittee on Courts, Civil Liberties, and the Administration of Justice.

United States. Congress. House. Subcommittee on Crime. see United States. Congress. House. Committee on the Judiciary. Subcommittee on Crime.

United States. Congress. House. Subcommittee on Criminal Justice. see United States. Congress. House. Committee on the Judiciary. Subcommittee on Criminal Justice.

United States. Congress. House. Subcommittee on Dairy and Poultry. see United States. Congress. House. Committee on Agriculture. Subcommittee on Dairy and Poultry.

United States. Congress. House. Subcommittee on Department Investigations, Oversight, and Research. see United States. Congress. House. Committee on Agriculture. Subcommittee on Department Investigations, Oversight, and Research.

United States. Congress. House. Subcommittee on Departments of Labor, and Health, Education, and Welfare, and Related Agencies. see United States. Congress. House. Committee on Appropriations. Subcommittee on Departments of Labor, and Health, Education, and Welfare, and Related Agencies.

United States. Congress. House. Subcommittee on Dept. of the Interior and Related Agencies. see United States. Congress. House. Committee on Appropriations. Subcommittee on Dept. of the Interior and Related Agencies.

United States. Congress. House. Subcommittee on Dept. of Transportation and Related Agencies Appropriations. see United States. Congress. House. Committee on Appropriations. Subcommittee on Dept. of Transportation and Related Agencies Appropriations.

United States. Congress. House. Subcommittee on Domestic Marketing, Consumer Relations, and Nutrition. see United States. Congress. House. Committee on Agriculture. Subcommittee on Domestic Marketing, Consumer Relations, and Nutrition.

United States. Congress. House. Subcommittee on Domestic Monetary Policy. see United States. Congress. House. Committee on Banking, Finance, and Urban Affairs. Subcommittee on Domestic Monetary Policy.

United States. Congress. House. Subcommittee on Economic Stabilization. see United States. Congress. House. Committee on Banking, Finance and Urban Affairs. Subcommittee on Economic Stabilization.

United States. Congress. House. Subcommittee on Elementary, Secondary, and Vocational Education. see United States. Congress. House. Committee on Education and Labor. Subcommittee on Elementary, Secondary, and Vocational Education.

United States. Congress. House. Subcommittee on Employment Opportunities. see United States. Congress. House. Committee on Education and Labor. Subcommittee on Employment Opportunities.

United States. Congress. House. Subcommittee on Energy and Power. see United States. Congress. House. Committee on Interstate and Foreign Commerce. Subcommittee on Energy and Power.

United States. Congress. House. Subcommittee on Energy and the Environment. see United States. Congress. House. Committee on Interior and Insular Affairs. Subcommittee on Energy and the Environment.

United States. Congress. House. Subcommittee on Energy, Environment, Safety and Research. see United States. Congress. House. Committee on Small Business. Subcommittee on Energy, Environment, Safety and Research.

United States. Congress. House. Subcommittee on Family Farms, Rural Development, and Special Studies. see United States. Congress. House. Committee on Agriculture. Subcommittee on Family Farms, Rural Development, and Special Studies.

United States. Congress. House. Subcommittee on Financial Institutions Supervision, Regulation and Insurance. see United States. Congress. House. Committee on Banking, Finance and Urban Affairs. Subcommittee on Financial Institutions Supervision, Regulation and Insurance.

United States. Congress. House. Subcommittee on Fisheries and Wildlife Conservation and the Environment. see United States. Congress. House. Committee on Merchant Marine and Fisheries. Subcommittee on Fisheries and Wildlife Conservation and the Environment.

United States. Congress. House. Subcommittee on Flood Control and Internal Development. see United States. Congress. House. Committee on Public Works. Subcommittee on Flood Control and Internal Development.

United States. Congress. House. Subcommittee on Foreign Operations and Related Agencies Appropriations. see United States. Congress. House. Committee on Appropriations. Subcommittee on Foreign Operations and Related Agencies Appropriations.

United States. Congress. House. Subcommittee on Forests. see United States. Congress. House. Committee on Agriculture. Subcommittee on Forests.

United States. Congress. House. Subcommittee on General Oversight and Renegotiation. see United States. Congress. House. Committee on Banking, Finance and Urban Affairs. Subcommittee on General Oversight and Renegotiation.

United States. Congress. House. Subcommittee on Government Information and Individual Rights. see United States. Congress. House. Committee on Government Operations. Subcommittee on Government Information and Individual Rights.

United States. Congress. House. Subcommittee on Health. see United States. Congress. House. Committee on Ways and Means. Subcommittee on Health.

United States. Congress. House. Subcommittee on Health and Long-Term Care. see United States. Congress. House. Select Committee on Aging. Subcommittee on Health and Long-Term Care.

United States. Congress. House. Subcommittee on Health and the Environment. see United States. Congress. House. Committee on Interstate and Foreign Commerce. Subcommittee on Health and the Environment.

United States. Congress. House. Subcommittee on Housing. see United States. Congress. House. Committee on Veterans' Affairs. Subcommittee on Housing.

United States. Congress. House. Subcommittee on Housing and Community Development. see United States. Congress. House. Committee on Banking, Finance and Urban Affairs. Subcommittee on Housing and Community Development.

United States. Congress. House. Subcommittee on Housing and Consumer Interests. see United States. Congress. House. Select Committee on Aging. Subcommittee on Housing and Consumer Interests.

United States. Congress. House. Subcommittee on Indian Affairs and Public Lands. see United States. Congress. House. Committee on Interior and Insular Affairs. Subcommittee on Indian Affairs and Public Lands.

United States. Congress. House. Subcommittee on Inter-American Affairs. see United States. Congress. House. Committee on Foreign Affairs. Subcommittee on Inter-American Affairs.

United States. Congress. House. Subcommittee on International Development Institutions and Finance. see United States. Congress. House. Committee on Banking, Finance and Urban Affairs. Subcommittee on International Development Institutions and Finance.

United States. Congress. House. Subcommittee on International Organizations. see United States. Congress. House. Committee on Foreign Affairs. Subcommittee on International Organizations.

United States. Congress. House. Subcommittee on International Organizations and Movements. see United States. Congress. House. Committee on Foreign Affairs. Subcommittee on International Organizations and Movements.

United States. Congress. House. Subcommittee on International Trade, Investment and Monetary Policy. see United States. Congress. House. Committee on Banking, Finance and Urban Affairs. Subcommittee on International Trade, Investment and Monetary Policy.

United States. Congress. House. Subcommittee on Investigations. see United States. Congress. House. Committee on Armed Services. Subcommittee on Investigations; United States. Congress. House. Committee on Post Office and Civil Service. Subcommittee on Investigations.

United States. Congress. House. Subcommittee on Labor-Management Relations. see United States. Congress. House. Committee on Education and Labor. Subcommittee on Labor-Management Relations.

United States. Congress. House. Subcommittee on Labor Standards. see United States. Congress. House. Committee on Education and Labor. Subcommittee on Labor Standards.

United States. Congress. House. Subcommittee on Livestock and Grains. see United States. Congress. House. Committee on Agriculture. Subcommittee on Livestock and Grains.

United States. Congress. House. Subcommittee on Medical Facilities and Benefits. see United States. Congress. House. Committee on Veterans' Affairs. Subcommittee on Medical Facilities and Benefits.

United States. Congress. House. Subcommittee on Merchant Marine. see United States. Congress. House. Committee on Merchant Marine and Fisheries. Subcommittee on Merchant Marine.

United States. Congress. House. Subcommittee on Military Compensation. see United States. Congress. House. Committee on Armed Services. Subcommittee on Military Compensation.

United States. Congress. House. Subcommittee on Military Construction Appropriations. see United States. Congress. House. Committee on Appropriations. Subcommittee on Military Construction Appropriations.

United States. Congress. House. Subcommittee on Military Installations and Facilities. see United States. Congress. House. Committee on Armed Services. Subcommittee on Military Installations and Facilities.

United States. Congress. House. Subcommittee on Military Personnel. see United States. Congress. House. Committee on Armed Services. Subcommittee on Military Personnel.

United States. Congress. House. Subcommittee on Mines and Mining. see United States. Congress. House. Committee on Interior and Insular Affairs. Subcommittee on Mines and Mining.

United States. Congress. House. Subcommittee on Minority Enterprise and General Oversight. see United States. Congress. House. Committee on Small Business. Subcommittee on Minority Enterprise and General Oversight.

United States. Congress. House. Subcommittee on Monopolies and Commercial Law. see United States. Congress. House. Committee on the Judiciary. Subcommittee on Monopolies and Commercial Law.

United States. Congress. House. Subcommittee on Oceanography. see United States. Congress. House. Committee on Merchant Marine and Fisheries. Subcommittee on

Oceanography.

United States. Congress. House. Subcommittee on Oilseeds and Rice. see United States. Congress. House. Committee on Agriculture. Subcommittee on Oilseeds and Rice.

United States. Congress. House. Subcommittee on Oversight. see United States. Congress. House. Committee on Ways and Means. Subcommittee on Oversight.

United States. Congress. House. Subcommittee on Oversight and Investigations. see United States. Congress. House. Committee on Interstate and Foreign Commerce. Subcommittee on Oversight and Investigations.

United States. Congress. House. Subcommittee on Panama Canal. see United States. Congress. House. Committee on Merchant Marine and Fisheries. Subcommittee on Panama Canal.

United States. Congress. House. Subcommittee on Postal Operations and Services. see United States. Congress. House. Committee on Post Office and Civil Service. Subcommittee on Postal Operations and Services.

United States. Congress. House. Subcommittee on Public Assistance and Unemployment Compensation. see United States. Congress. House. Committee on Ways and Means. Subcommittee on Public Assistance and Unemployment Compensation.

United States. Congress. House. Subcommittee on Public Buildings and Grounds. see United States. Congress. House. Committee on Public Works and Transportation. Subcommittee on Public Buildings and Grounds.

United States. Congress. House. Subcommittee on Public Lands. see United States. Congress. House. Committee on Interior and Insular Affairs. Subcommittee on Public Lands.

United States. Congress. House. Subcommittee on Retirement Income and Employment. see United States. Congress. House. Select Committee on Aging. Subcommittee on Retirement Income and Employment.

United States. Congress. House. Subcommittee on SBA and SBIC Authority and General Small Business Problems. see United States. Congress. House. Committee on Small Business. Subcommittee on SBA and SBIC Authority and General Small Business Problems.

United States. Congress. House. Subcommittee on Science, Research, and Technology. see United States. Congress. House. Committee on Science and Technology. Subcommittee on Science, Research, and Technology.

United States. Congress. House. Subcommittee on Seapower and Strategic and Critical Materials. see United States. Congress. House. Committee on Armed Services. Subcommittee on Seapower and Strategic and Critical Materials.

United States. Congress. House. Subcommittee on Select Education. see United States. Congress. House. Committee on Education and Labor. Subcommittee on Select Education.

United States. Congress. House. Subcommittee on Social Security. see United States. Congress. House. Committee on Ways and Means. Subcommittee on Social Security.

United States. Congress. House. Subcommittee on Space Science and Applications. see United States. Congress. House. Committee on Science and Technology. Subcommittee on Space Science and Applications.

United States. Congress. House. Subcommittee on Surface Transporation. see United States. Congress. House. Committee on Public Works and Transportation. Subcommittee on Surface Transportation.

United States. Congress. House. Subcommittee on the City. see United States. Congress. House. Committee on Banking, Finance and Urban Affairs. Subcommittee on the City.

United States. Congress. House. Subcommittee on the Environment and the Atmosphere. see United States. Congress. House. Committee on Science and Technology. Subcommittee on the Environment and the Atmosphere.

United States. Congress. House. Subcommittee on Trade. see United States. Congress. House. Committee on Ways and Means. Subcommittee on Trade.

United States. Congress. House. Subcommittee on Transportation and Commerce. see United States. Congress. House. Committee on Interstate and Foreign Commerce. Subcommittee on Transportation and Commerce.

United States. Congress. House. Subcommittee on Water Resources. see United States. Congress. House. Committee on Public Works and Transportation. Subcommittee on Water Resources.

United States. Congress. House. Task Force on Budget Process. see United States. Congress. House. Committee on the Budget. Task Force on Budget Process.

United States. Congress. House. Task Force on Industrial Innovation. United States. Congress. House. Committee on Science and Technology. Technology trade . Washington , 1980. vii, 687 p. :   LC Card 80-604020   DDC 338.973 19
KF27 .S39 1980g

UNITED STATES. CONGRESS. HOUSE - TELEVISION BROADCASTING OF PROCEEDINGS.

Hall, Terry, 1954- Congress on the tube . Norman, Okla. , 1980. iii, 41, [4] leaves :   LC Card 80-623691   DDC 328.73 19
JK1444 .H44

United States. Congress. Joint Committee on Arrangements for the Commemoration of the Bicentennial. Women in Congress, 1917-1976. [Washington] 1976. iii, 112 p. :   LC Card 77-601008
JK1013 .W65

United States. Congress. Joint Committee on Internal Revenue Taxation. (Old Catalog form: United States. Internal Revenue Taxation, Joint Committee on) // Hearings printed in 1978 and later are available only in microform Please consult the librarians in the Economic and Public Affairs Division. Jeopardy and termination assessments, administrative summons, comprehensive administrative package, state conducted lotteries, and miscellaneous / prepared for the use of the Committee on Ways and Means by the staff of the Joint Committee on Internal Revenue Taxation. Washington : U. S. Govt. Print. Off., 1975. iii, 7 p. ; 23 cm.   LC Card 80-600755   DDC 353.0072/4 19
1. Tax administration and procedure - United States. I. United States. Congress. House. Committee on Ways and Means. II. Title.
KF6300 .A25 1975

United States. Congress. Joint Committee on Printing. (Old Catalog form: United States. Printing, Joint Committee on) Coopers & Lybrand. Analysis and evaluation of selected Government Printing Office operations /. Washington , 1979. xxii, 288, [40] p., [1] leaf of plates :   LC Card 79-601679   DDC 070.5/95 19
Z232.U6 C76 1979

Government depository libraries: the present law governing designated depository libraries / Joint Committee of Printing, Congress of the United States. Washington : U. S. Govt. Print. Off., 1973. 43 p. ; 24 cm. 93d Congress. 1st Session. Joint Committee Print.
1. Libraries, Storage - Law and legislation - United States. I. Title.   **NYPL   [JLE 81-116]**

United States. 96th Congress, 1st session, 1979. Memorial services held in the House of Representatives and Senate of the United States, together with remarks presented in eulogy of Leo J. Ryan, a late Representative from California /. Washington , 1979. vii, 88 p., [1] leaf of plates :   LC Card 79-603246
E840.8.R88 U5 1979   **NYPL   [JFE 81-694]**

United States. Federal Electronic Printing and Microform Committee. Electronic composition . Washington, D.C. , 1975. v, 191 p. :   LC Card 80-603603   DDC 686.2/2544 19
Z253.3 .U54 1975

United States. Congress. Joint Committee on Taxation.

Description of bills (S. 2402, S. 2403, S. 2404, and S. 2405) relating to disclosure of tax returns and return information listed for a hearing before the Subcommittee on Oversight of the Internal Revenue Service of the Committee on Finance, on June 20, 1980 / prepared for the use of the Committee on Finance by the staff of the Joint Committee on Taxation. Washington : U. S. Govt. Print. Off., 1980. iii, 18 p. ; 24 cm. At head of title: Joint Committee print.   LC Card 80-602679   DDC 343.7305/2 19
1. Confidential communications - Taxation - United States. 2. Tax returns - United States. I. United States. Congress. Senate. Committee on Finance. Subcommittee on Oversight of the Internal Revenue Service. II. Title.
KF6328 .A25 1980

Description of bills to provide tax incentives for savings : scheduled for a hearing before the Committee on Ways and Means of January 29-31, 1980 / prepared for the use of the Committee on Ways and Means by the Staff of the Joint Committee on Taxation. Washington : U. S. G.P.O., 1980. iii, 14 p. ; 24 cm. At head of title: Joint committee print. "January 28, 1980."   LC Card 81-600503   DDC 343.7305/23 347.303523 19
1. Interest and usury - Taxation - United States. 2. Taxation, Exemption from - United States. I. United States. Congress. House. Committee on Ways and Means. II. Title.
KF6417 .A25 1980

Description of legislation relating to Pension Benefit Guaranty Corporation plan termination insurance for multiemployer pension plans : scheduled for a hearing by the Subcommittee on Private Pension Plans and Employee Fringe Benefits of the Committee on Finance on March 18, 1980 / prepared for the use of the Committee on Finance by the staff of the Joint Committee on Taxation, March 14, 1980. Washington : U. S. Govt. Print. Off., 1980. iii, 56 p. ; 24 cm. At head of title: Joint committee print. Includes bibliographical references.   LC Card 80-602420   DDC 344.73/01252 19
1. Pension trusts - United States. 2. Pension Benefit Guaranty Corporation. I. United States. Congress. Senate. Committee on Finance. Subcommittee on Private Pension Plans and Employee Fringe Benefits. II. United States. Congress. Senate. Committee on Finance. III. Title.
KF3512 .A25 1980b

Description of proposals relating to the tax treatment of foreign investment in the United States, scheduled for a hearing before the Committee on Ways and Means on October 25, 1979 / prepared for the use of the Committee on Ways and Means by the staff of the Joint Committee on Taxation. Washington : U. S. Govt. Print. Off., 1979. iii, 8 p. ; 24 cm. "Joint committee print."   LC Card 80-602684   DDC 343.7305/248 19
1. Investments, Foreign - Taxation - United States. I. United States. Congress. House. Committee on Ways and Means. II. Title.
KF6419 .A25 1979

Description of S. 219, relating to the deduction for charitable contributions scheduled for hearings before the Subcommittee on Taxation and Debt Management Generally of the Committee on Finance, on January 30 and 31, 1980 / prepared for the use of the Committee on Finance by the staff of the Joint Committee on Taxation. Washington : U. S. Govt. Print. Off., 1980. iii, 14 p.; 24 cm. At head of title: Joint Committee print.   LC Card 80-602135   DDC 343-7305/232 19
1. Income tax - United States - Deductions - Charitable contributions. I. United States. Congress. Senate. Committee on Finance. II. United States. Congress. Senate. Committee on Finance. Subcommittee on Taxation and Debt Management Generally. III. Title.
KF6388 .A25 1980

Description of S. 983 and S. 1688 relating to state taxation of interstate business and foreign source corporate income : scheduled for a hearing before the Subcommittee on Taxation and Debt Management Generally of the Committee on Finance on June 24, 1980 /

BIBLIOGRAPHIC GUIDE

United States. Congress. Joint Committee on Taxation. (cont.)

466

prepared for the use of the Committee on Finance by the staff of the Joint Committee on Taxation. Washington : U. S. Govt. Print. Off., 1980. iii, 29 p. ; 24 cm. At head of title: Joint Committee print. "JCS-32-80." LC Card 80-602680 DDC 343.7305/267 19
1. Corporations - Taxation - United States - States. 2. Income tax - United States - States - Foreign income. 3. United States. Congress. Senate. Committee on Finance. I. Title.
KF6755 .A25 1980

Estimates of federal tax expenditures for fiscal years, 1980-1985 / prepared for the Committee on Ways and Means and the Committee on Finance by the Staff of the Joint Committee on Taxation. Washington : U. S. G.P.O., 1980. ii, 21 p. ; 24 cm. At head of title: Joint committee print. "March 6, 1980." LC Card 81-600720 DDC 336.2 19
1. Tax expenditures - United States. I. United States. Congress. House. Committee on Ways and Means. II. United States. Congress. Senate. Committee on Finance. III. Title.
HJ4652 .U627 1980

The income tax treatment of married couples and single persons : a report / prepared by the staff of the Joint Committee on Taxation for the use of the Committee on Ways and Means, U. S. House of Representatives and the Committee on Finance, United States Senate. Washington : U. S. Govt. Print Off. : for sale by the Supt. of Docs., U. S. Govt. Print. Off., 1980. iii, 68 p. ; 24 cm. LC Card 80-601745 DDC 343.7305/2/024065 19
1. Husband and wife - Taxation - United States. 2. Single people - Taxation - United States. I. United States. Congress. House. Committee on Ways and Means. II. United States. Congress. Senate. Committee on Finance. III. Title.
KF6355.5 .T38

Staff recommendations for simplication of tax rules relating to subchapter S corporations : a report / prepared by the staff of the Joint Committee on Taxation for the use of the Committe on Ways and Means, U. S. House of Representatives and the Committee on Finance, United States Senate. Washington : U. S. Govt. Print. Off., 1980. iii, 27 p. ; 24 cm. At head of title: Joint committee print. LC Card 80-602271 DDC 343.7306/8 19
1. Samll business - Taxation - United States. I. United States. Congress. House. Committee on Ways and Means. II. United States. Congress. Senate. Committee on Finance. III. Title.
KF6491 .A25 1980

Summary of H.R. 5741, and Mortgage subsidy bond tax act of 1979 : as reported with amendments by the Committee on Ways and Means on December 3, 1979 / prepared by the staffs of the Joint Committee on Taxation and the Committee on Ways and Means. Washington : U. S. Govt. Print. Off., 1979. iii, 8 p. ; 24 cm. At head of title: 96th Congress, 1st session. Committee print." WMCP 96-43." LC Card 80-602686 DDC 343.7305/23 19
1. Mortgage bonds, Tax-exempt - United States. I. United States. Congress. House. Committee on Ways and Means. II. Title.
KF6383 .A25 1979

United States. Congress. Joint Economic Committee. Hearings printed in 1978 and later are available only in microform. Please consult the librarians in the Economic and Public Affairs Division.
Capital formation and inflation : hearing before the Joint Economic Committee, Congress of the United States, Ninety-sixth Congress, second session, June 18, 1980. Washington : U. S. G.P.O., 1980. iii, 108 p. : ill. ; 24 cm. Includes bibliographical references. LC Card 80-604035 DDC 332/.0415/0973 19
1. Saving and investment - United States - Effect of inflation on. 2. Industrial productivity - United States - Effect of inflation on. I. Title.
KF25 .E2 1980g

Christainsen, Gregory. Environmental and health/safety regulations, productivity growth, and economic performance . Washington , 1980. v, 94 p. : LC Card 80-603059 DDC 339/.0973 19
HC110.E5 C5

Crisis in the bond market : hearing before the Joint Economic Committee, Congress of the

United States, Ninety-sixth Congress, second session, March 12, 1980. Washington : U. S. Govt. Print. Off. : for sale by the Supt. of Docs., U. S. Govt. Print. Off., 1980. iii, 44 p. : graphs ; 24 cm. LC Card 80-603031 DDC 332.63/23/0973 19
1. Bonds - United States. 2. Inflation (Finance) - United States. I. Title.
KF25 .E2 1980

Forecasting the supply side of the economy : hearing before the Joint Economic Committee, Congress of the United States, Ninety-sixth Congress, second session, May 21, 1980. Washington : U. S. G.P.O., 1980. iii, 87 p. ; 24 cm. G.P.O. sales statement incorrect in publication. Includes bibliographical references. LC Card 81-600591 DDC 338.5/443/0973 19
1. Economic forecasting - United States. 2. United States - Economic conditions - 1971-. I. Title.
KF25 .E2 1980i

Holt, Charles C. Inflation and the need for new economic policies . Austin, Tex. , 1980. 13 leaves ; LC Card 80-622266 DDC 332.4/15/0973 19
HG540 .H65

Housing and the economy : hearings before the Joint Economic Committee, Congress of the United States, Ninety-sixth Congress, second session, April 16 and September 17, 1980. Washington : U. S. G.P.O., 1981. iii, 116 p. : ill. ; 24 cm. G.P.O. sales information incorrect in publication. Item 1000 Includes bibliographical references. LC Card 81-601778 DDC 338.4/76908/0973 19
1. Housing - United States. 2. Housing policy - United States. I. Title.
KF25 .E2 1980j

How public welfare benefits are distributed in low-income areas, based on data collected by the General Accounting Office: a staff study/prepared for the use of the Subcommittee on Fiscal Policy of the Joint Economic Committee, Congress of the United States [by the staff of the Joint Economic Committee]. Washington : U. S. Govt. Print. Off., 1973. x, 144 p.; 23 cm. (Studies in public welfare. paper no. 6) At head of title: Joint committee print, 93 Congress, 1st session. Includes bibliographical references.
1. Public welfare - United States - Case studies. I. United States. Congress. Joint Economic Committee. Subcommittee on Fiscal Policy. II. Title.
NYPL [JLE 81-118]

Inflationary impact of Department of Agriculture paperwork : hearing before the Joint Economic Committee, Congress of the United States, Ninety-sixth Congress, second session, March 26, 1980. Washington : U. S. Govt. Print. Off., 1980. iii, 137 p. ; 24 cm. LC Card 80-603073 DDC 353.81 19
1. United States. Dept. of Agriculture. 2. Government paperwork - United States. 3. Inflation (Finance) - United States - Effect of government paperwork on. 4. Government paperwork - Law and legislation - United States. I. Title.
KF25 .E2 1980b

The minority business sector : a vehicle for regional growth : hearing before the Joint Economic Committee, Congress of the United States, Ninety-sixth Congress, first session, November 16, 1979. Washington : U. S. Govt. Print. Off., 1980. iii, 65 p. ; 24 cm. Includes bibliographical references. LC Card 80-602484 DDC 338.6/42/0973 19
1. Minority business enterprises - United States. I. Title.
KF25 .E2 1979n

A model income supplement bill: a staff study / prepared for the use of the Subcommittee on Fiscal Policy of the Joint Economic Committee, Congress of the United States [by the staff of the Joint Economic Committee]. Washington: U. S. Govt. Print. Off., 1974. v, 62 p.; 23 cm. (Studies in public welfare. paper no. 16) At head of title: Joint committee print, 93d Congress, 2d session.
1. Public welfare - Law and legislation - United States. 2. Income maintenance programs - Law and legislation - United States. I. United States. Congress. Joint Economic Committee. Subcommittee on Fiscal Policy. II. Title.
NYPL [JLE 81-116]

Monitoring inflation : hearings before the Joint Economic Committee, Congress of the United States, Ninety-sixth Congress, first session. Washington : U. S. G.P.O., 1979-<1980> v.<1-3> : ill. ; 24 cm. Pt. 1 for sale by Supt. of

Docs., U. S. G.P.O. ; pt. 4, G.P.O. sales statement incorrect in publication. Pt. 1: Apr. 26-July 26, 1979. Pt. 2: Sept. 25, 1979-Jan. 25, 1980. Pt. 3: "hearings ... Ninety-sixth Congress, second session, February 22, March 25, April 22, May 23, and June 24, 1980." S/N 052-070-05190-6 (pt. 1) GPO Item 1000 LC Card 81-601472 DDC 332.4/1/0973 19
1. Inflation (Finance) - United States. 2. Wage-price policy - United States. 3. United States - Economic policy - 1971-. I. Title.
KF25 .E2 1979p

Muller, Thomas, 1933- The impact of selected federal actions on municipal outlays . Washington , 1979. v, 53 p. ; LC Card 81-600798 DDC 336/.014/73 19
HJ9145 .M845

The President's new anti-inflation program : hearings before the Joint Economic Committee, Congress of the United States, Ninety-sixth Congress, second session, March 17, 20, and 27, 1980. Washington : U. S. Govt. Print. Off., 1980. iii, 172 p. ; 23 cm. LC Card 80-603703 DDC 332.4/15/0973 19
1. Inflation (Finance) - United States. 2. United States - Economic policy - 1971-. I. Title.
KF25 .E2 1980e

Productivity, the foundation of growth . Washington , 1980. v, 128 p. LC Card 81-601972 DDC 338/.06/0973 19
HC110.I52 P77

Public works as a countercyclical tool : hearing before the Joint Economic Committee, Congress of the United States, Ninety-sixth Congress, second session, June 17, 1980. Washington : U. S. Govt. Print. Off. : for sale by the Supt. of Docs., U. S. Govt. Print. Off., 1980. iii, 86 p. : graphs ; 24 cm. LC Card 80-603664 DDC 339.5/22 19
1. United States - Public works. 2. United States - Economic policy - 1971-. 3. Business cycles. 4. Economic stabilization. I. Title.
KF25 .E2 1980f

Savings and economic growth : hearing before the Joint Economic Committee, Congress of the United States, Ninety-sixth Congress, second session, July 30, 1980. Washington : U. S. G.P.O., 1981. iii, 54 p. ; 24 cm. Includes bibliographical references. Item 1000 LC Card 81-601400 DDC 332/.0415/0973 19
1. Saving and investment - United States. 2. Capital investments - United States. I. Title.
KF25 .E2 1980l

The state of the economy : hearings before the Joint Economic Committee, Congress of the United States, Ninety-sixth Congress, second session, May 28 and 29, 1980. Washington : U. S. Govt. Print. Off., 1980. iii, 77 p. ; 24 cm. Bibliography: p. 56. LC Card 80-603429 DDC 330.973/0926 19
1. United States - Economic conditions - 1971-. 2. United States - Economic policy - 1971-. I. Title.
KF25 .E2 1980c

U. S. export competitiveness : hearing before the Joint Economic Committee, Congress of the United States, Ninety-sixth Congress, second session, July 29, 1980. Washington : U. S. G.P.O., 1981. iii, 66 p. : ill. ; 24 cm. Item 1000 Includes bibliographical references. LC Card 81-601784 DDC 382/.6/0973 19
1. Foreign trade promotion - United States. 2. Competition, International. I. Title.
KF25 .E2 1980k

U. S. trade and investment policy : imports and the future of the American automobile industry : hearing before the Joint Economic Committee, Congress of the United States, Ninety-sixth Congress, second session, March 19, 1980. Washington : U. S. Govt. Print. Off. : for sale by the Supt. of Docs., U. S. Govt. Print. Off., 1980. iii, 148 p. : ill. ; 23 cm. Includes bibliographical references. LC Card 80-603497 DDC 338.4/76292/0973 19
1. Automobile industry and trade - United States. 2. Automobile industry and trade - Japan. 3. Foreign trade regulation - United States. 4. Tariff on automobile - United States. I. Title.
KF25 .E2 1980d

The underground economy : hearing before the Joint Economic Committee, Congress of the United States, Ninety-sixth Congress, first session, November 15, 1979. Washington : U. S. Govt. Print. Off. : for sale by Supt. of Docs.,

U. S. Govt. Print Off., 1980. iii, 76 p. : graphs ; 24 cm. LC Card 80-602483 DDC 353.0072/442 19
1. Tax collection - United States. 2. Tax evasion - United States. 3. Income tax - United States. 4. Self-employed - Taxation - United States.
KF25 .E2 1979m

United States. Library of Congress. Congressional Research Service. An inquiry into conflicting and duplicative regulatory requirements affecting selected industries and sectors . Washington , 1980. v, 40 p. ; LC Card 80-603057 DDC 343.73/08 347.3038 19
KF1600 .A25 1980

Welfare in the 70's: a national study of benefits available in 100 local areas: a staff study / prepared for the use of the Subcommittee on Fiscal Policy of the Joint Economic Committee, Congress of the United States [by the staff of the Joint Economic Committee]. Washington: U. S. Govt. Print. Off., 1974. ix, 300 p.; 23 cm. (Studies in public welfare. paper no. 15) At head of title: Joint committee print, 93 Congress, 2nd session.
1. Public welfare - United States - States. I. United States. Congress. Joint Economic Committee. Subcommittee on Fiscal Policy. II. Title.
NYPL [JLE 81-115]

The 1980 economic report of the President : hearings before the Joint Economic Committee, Congress of the United States, Ninety-sixth Congress, second session .... Washington : U. S. Govt. Print. Off., 1980. 2 v. : graphs ; 24 cm. Hearings held Jan. 30-Feb. 7, 1980. Pt. 2: Invited comments. LC Card 80-603018 DDC 330.973/0926 19
1. United States - Economic policy - 1971-. 2. United States - Economic conditions - 1971-. I. Title.
KF25 .E2 1980a

The 1980 midyear review of the economy : hearings before the Joint Economic Committee, Congress of the United States, Ninety-sixth Congress, second session, July 23 and August 1, 1980. Washington : U. S. G.P.O. : For sale by the Supt. of Docs., U. S. G.P.O., 1980. iii, 111 p. : ill. ; 24 cm. S/N 052-070-05388-7. LC Card 80-604050 DDC 330.973/0926 19
1. United States - Economic conditions - 1971-. 2. United States - Economic policy - 1971-. I. Title.
KF25 .E2 1980h

The 1980 midyear review of the economy : the recession and the recovery : report of the Joint Economic Committee, Congress of the United States, together with additional views. Washington : U. S. Govt. Print. Off. : for sale by the Supt. of Docs., U. S. Govt. Print. Off., 1980. iii, 24 p. ; 24 cm. "August 1980." At head of title: 96th Congress, 2d session. Joint committee print.
LC Card 80-603553 DDC 330.973/0926 19
1. United States - Economic policy - 1971-. I. Title.
HC106.7 .U543 1980

United States. Congress. Joint Economic Committee. Economic Change, Special Study on. see United States. Congress. Joint Economic Committee. Special Study on Economic Change.

United States. Congress. Joint Economic Committee. Special Study on Economic Change.
State and local government finances and the changing national economy : hearing before the Special Study on Economic Change of the Joint Economic Committee, Congress of the United States, Ninety-sixth Congress, second session, July 28, 1980. Washington : U. S. Govt. Print. Off., 1980. iii, 71 p. : graphs ; 24 cm. LC Card 80-603784 DDC 336.73 19
1. Finance, Public - United States - States. 2. Local finance - United States. 3. Intergovernmental fiscal relations - United States. 4. United States - Economic conditions - 1971-. I. Title.
KF25 .E23 1980

Willett, Thomas D. International liquidity issues /. Washington, D.C. , c1980. 114 p. : ISBN 0-8447-3388-1 LC Card 80-18074
HG3893 .W54

United States. Congress. Joint Economic Committee. Subcommittee on Economic Growth and Stabilization.
The impact of an accelerated coal-based synfuels program on western water resources : hearing before the Subcommittee on Economic Growth and Stabilization of the Joint Economic Committee, Congress of the United States,

Ninety-sixth Congress, first session, November 14, 1979. Washington, D.C. : U. S. Govt. Print. Off. : for sale by the Sup. of Docs., U. S. Govt. Print. Off., 1980. iii, 105 p. : ill. ; 24 cm. Includes bibliographical references. LC Card 80-602753 DDC 333.91/00978 19
1. Water-supply - The West. 2. Coal gasification - The West. 3. Synthetic fuels - The West. I. Title.
KF25 .E232 1979c

The impact of the Soviet grain embargo on rail and barge transportation : hearing before the Subcommittee on Economic Growth and Stabilization of the Joint Economic Committee, Congress of the United States, Ninety-sixth Congress, second session, February 4, 1980. Washington : U. S. Govt. Print. Off. : for sale by the Supt. of Docs., U. S. Govt. Print. Off., 1980. iii, 47 p. ; 24 cm. LC Card 80-602769 DDC 385/.1/0973 19
1. Railroads - Economic aspects - United States. 2. River boats - Economic aspects - United States. 3. Grain trade - United States. 4. Grain trade - Russia. I. Title.
KF25 .E232 1980

United States. Congress. Joint Economic Committee. Subcommittee on Energy.
Alcohol fuels policy : hearings before the Subcommittee on Energy of the Joint Economic Committee, Congress of the United States, Ninety-sixth Congress, second session. Washington : U. S. G.P.O. : [For sale by the Supt. of Docs., U. S. G.P.O.], 1980. 2 v. : ill. ; 24 cm. Hearings held Mar. 17 and June 25, 1980. Includes bibliographies. S/N 052-070-05435-2 (pt. 1) : 052-070-05464-6 (pt. 2) CONTENTS. - pt. 1. Energy self-sufficiency for rural America -- pt. 2. Potential for renewable resource alcohol fuels. LC Card 80-604078 DDC 338.4/7662669 19
1. Gasohol - Government policy - United States. 2. Gasohol. I. Title. II. Title: Energy self-sufficiency for rural America. III. Title: Potential for renewable resource alcohol fuels.
KF25 .E245 1980

Energy conservation . Washington , 1981. v, 39 p. : LC Card 81-601002 DDC 333.79/16/0973 19
TJ163.4.U6 E49

Farm and forest produced alcohol . Washington , 1980. v, 76 p. : LC Card 80-603552 DDC 333.95/3 19
TP358 .F37

Impact of energy prices and inflation on American families : hearing before the Subcommittee on Energy of the Joint Economic Committee, Congress of the United States, Ninety-sixth Congress, second session, July 8, 1980. Washington : U. S. G.P.O., 1981. iii, 74 p. : ill. ; 24 cm. Item 1000 LC Card 81-601606
1. Power resources - Prices - United States. 2. Cost and standard of living - United States. 3. Inflation (Finance) - United States. I. Title.
KF25 .E245 1980a

Safer, Arnold E. A strategy of oil proliferation . Washington , 1980. vii, 20 p. ; LC Card 80-603267 DDC 333.8/23215 19
TN870 .S22

United States. Congress. Joint Economic Committee. Subcommittee on Fiscal Policy.
United States. Congress. Joint Economic Committee. How public welfare benefits are distributed in low-income areas. Washington , 1973. x, 144 p.; NYPL [JLE 81-118]

United States. Congress. Joint Economic Committee. A model income supplement bill. Washington, 1974. v, 62 p.;
NYPL [JLE 81-116]

United States. Congress. Joint Economic Committee. Welfare in the 70's. Washington, 1974. ix, 300 p.;
NYPL [JLE 81-115]

United States. Congress. Joint Economic Committee. Subcommittee on International Economics.
Domestic and international implications of the Federal Reserve's new policy actions : hearing before the Subcommittee on International Economics of the Joint Economic Committee, Congress of the United States, Ninety-sixth Congress, first session, November 5, 1979. Washington : U. S. Govt. Print. Off. : for sale by the Supt. of Docs., U. S. Govt. Print. Off., 1980. iii, 88 p. ; 23 cm. LC Card 80-602731 DDC 332.4/973 19
1. United States. Board of Governors of the Federal

Reserve System. 2. Monetary policy - United States. 3. International finance. I. Title.
KF25 .E253 1979a

The global 2000 report : hearing before the Subcommittee on International Economics of the Joint Economic Committee, Congress of the United States, Ninety-sixth Congress, second session, September 4, 1980. Washington : U. S. Govt. Print. Off. : for sale by the Supt. of Docs., U. S. Govt. Print. Off., 1980. iii, 57 p. ; 24 cm. LC Card 80-603675 DDC 333.7/0973 19
1. United States. Council on Environmental Quality. The global 2000 report to the President of the U. S. 2. Environmental policy. 3. Natural resources. I. Title.
KF25 .E253 1980

United States. Congress. Library. see United States. Library of Congress.

United States. Congress. Office of Technology Assesment. Energy from biological processes. Washington, D.C. [1980] x, 195 p. : LC Card 81-152351 DDC 333.95/3 19
TP360 .E5 1980

United States. Congress. Office of Technology Assessment.
Alternative energy futures. Washington, D.C. : Congress of the United States, Office of Technology Assessment : for sale by the Supt. of Docs., U. S. Govt. Print. Off., [1980- 1 v. : ill. ; 26 cm. CONTENTS. - pt. 1. The future of liquified natural gas imports. LC Card 80-600046
1. Power resources - United States. 2. Energy policy - United States. I. Title.
TJ163.25.U6 U49 1980
NYPL [JLM 80-1009]

An assessment of oil shale technologies. Washington, D.C. : Congress of the United States, Office of Technology Assessment : for sale by the Supt. of Doc., U. S. Govt. Print. Off., 1980. vii, 517 p. : ill. ; 26 cm. "OTA-M-118." Includes bibliographical references. LC Card 80-600101
1. Oil-shales. I. Title.
TN858 .U54 1980 NYPL [JSF 80-1073]

Baham Corporation. Renewable ocean energy sources /. Washington, D.C. , 1978- v. : LC Card 80-502142 DDC 333.91/64 19
TK1056 .B33 1978

Conservation and solar energy programs of the Department of Energy : a critique. Washington, D.C. : Congress of the U. S., Office of Technology Assessment : for sale by the Supt. of Docs., U. S. Govt. Print. Off., [1980] viii, 80 p. : diagrs. ; 27 cm. "OTA-E-120." LC Card 80-600092
1. Energy conservation - United States. 2. Solar energy - United States. 3. United States. Dept. of Energy. I. Title.
TJ163.4.U6 U5445 1980
NYPL [JSF 80-1097]

Impact of advanced group rapid transit technology. Washington, D.C. : Congress of the United States, Office of Technology Assessment : for sale by the Supt. of Docs., U. S. Govt. Print. Off., [1980] viii, 58 p. : ill. ; 26 cm. Includes bibliographical references. LC Card 80-600001
1. Urban transportation. 2. Local transit. 3. Personal rapid transit. I. Title.
HE305 .U555 1980 NYPL [JLF 80-1368]

The implications of cost-effectiveness analysis of medical technology. Washington, D.C. : Congress of the United States, Office of Technology Assessment : for sale by the Supt. of Docs., U. S. Govt. Print. Off., [1980] vii, 219 p. : ill. ; 26 cm. Prepared for the Senate Committees on Labor and Human Resources and on Finance. "August 1980." "OTA-H-126." Bibliography: p. 197-219. LC Card 80-600130 DDC 362.1/068/1 19
1. Medical care - Cost effectiveness. 2. Medical innovations - Cost effectiveness. 3. Medical care - United States - Cost effectiveness. 4. Medical innovations - United States - Cost effectiveness. 5. Medical policy - United States. I. United States. Congress. Senate. Committee on Labor and Human Resources. II. United States. Congress. Senate. Committee on Finance. III. Title. IV. Title: Cost-effectiveness analysis of medical technology.
RA410.5 .U54 1980

OTA background paper .
(OTA-BP-T-4) OTA Seminar on the Discrete Address Beacon System (DABS), Washington, D.C., 1980. Proceedings of the

BIBLIOGRAPHIC GUIDE

United States. Congress. Office of Technology Assessment. (cont.)

468

OTA Seminar on the Discrete Address Beacon System (DABS). Washington, D.C. [1980] vii, 46 p. ;   LC Card 80-600093   DDC 387.7/4042/0973 19
TL696.R25 O18 1980

OTA-T.
(83) United States. Congress. Office of Technology Assessment. Technology assessment of changes in the future use and characteristics of the automobile transportation system. Washington [1979] 2 v. :   LC Card 79-600030
HE5623 .U53 1979   **NYPL** *[JLM 81-210]*

A preliminary analysis of the IRS tax administration system. - Washington : The Office ; Springfield, Va. : available from the National Technical Information Service, U. S. Dept. of Commerce, 1977. x, 206 p. ; 27 cm. Microfiche (neg.) NTIS. 3 sheets. 11 x 15 cm. (PB 273 143)
1. Tax administration and procedure. 2. Information storage and retrieval systems - Tax administration and procedure. I. Title.   **NYPL** *[*XME-9377]*

A preliminary assessment of the National Crime Information Center and the Computerized Criminal History System. Washington : Congress of the United States, Office of Technology Assessment : for sale by the Supt. of Docs., U. S. Govt. Print. Off., [1978] vii, 84 p. ; 26 cm. "OTA-1-80." Includes bibliographical references.   LC Card 78-600164   DDC 025/.06364973 19
1. National Crime Information Center (United States). I. Title.
HV6791 .U52 1978

Recent developments in ocean thermal energy. Washington, D.C. : Congress of the United States, Office of Technology Assessment : for sale by the Supt. of Docs., U. S. Govt. Print. Off., 1980. 32 p. : ill. ; 26 cm. (A Technical memorandum - Congress of the United States, Office of Technology Assessment) "April 1980." "OTA-TM-O-3." Updates Renewable ocean energy sources, published in 1978. Includes bibliographical references.   LC Card 80-600074   DDC 621.31/243 19
1. Ocean thermal power plants. I. Series: United States. Congress. Office of Technology Assessment. Technical memorandum - Congress of the United States, Office of Technology Assessment. II. Title.
TK1056 .U52 1980

Renewable ocean energy sources. Washington : Congress of the United States, Office of Technology Assessment : for sale by the Supt. of Docs., U. S. Govt. Print. Off., 1978- v. : ill. ; 27 cm. "OTA-0-62." Includes bibliographical references. CONTENTS. - v. 1. Ocean thermal energy conversion.   LC Card 78-600053   DDC 333.91/64 19
1. Ocean energy resources. I. Title.
TJ163.2 .U48 1978

A review of selected Federal vaccine and immunization policies : based on case studies of pneumococcal vaccine. Washington : Congress of the U. S., Office of Technology Assessment : for sale by the Supt. of Docs., U. S. Govt. Print. Off., 1979. xvi, 208 p. : ill. ; 26 cm. Bibliography: p. 199-208.   LC Card 79-600165   DDC 614.4/7/0973 19
1. Vaccination - United States. 2. Vaccines - Research - United States. 3. Vaccines industry - United States. 4. Pneumococcal vaccine - United States. 5. Pneumonia, Pneumococcal - United States - Preventive inoculation - Cost effectiveness. 6. Vaccination - Complications and sequelae - United States. 7. Medical policy - United States. 8. Pharmaceutical policy - United States. I. Title.
RA638 .U48 1979

Technical memorandum - Congress of the United States, Office of Technology Assessment.
United States. Congress. Office of Technology Assessment. Recent developments in ocean thermal energy. Washington, D.C. , 1980. 32 p. :   LC Card 80-600074   DDC 621.31/243 19
TK1056 .U52 1980

United States. Congress. Office of Technology Assessment. World petroleum availability, 1980-2000. Washington, D.C. [1980] vii, 77 p. :   LC Card 80-600164   DDC 338.2/7282 19
HD9560.5 .U62 1980

Technical options for conservation of metals : case studies of selected metals and products.

Washington, D.C. : Congress of the U. S., Office of Technology Assessment : for sale by the Supt. of Docs., U. S. Govt. Print. Off., [1979] x, 125 p. : ill. ; 26 cm. Bibliography: p. 125.   LC Card 79-600172
1. Metals - Conservation - United States. 2. Scrap metals - United States - Recycling. 3. Manufacturing processes - United States. I. Title.
TA459 .U615 1979   **NYPL** *[JSF 81-158]*

Technology and East-West trade. Washington, D.C. : Congress of the United States, Office of Technology Assessment : for sale by the Supt. of Docs., U. S. Govt. Print. Off., 1979. viii, 303 p. : ill. ; 26 cm. Prepared for the House Committee on Foreign Affairs and the Senate Committee on Commerce, Science, and Transportation. "OTA-ISC-101." Includes bibliographical references.   LC Card 79-600203
1. East-West trade (1945-). 2. United States - Commerce - Communist countries. 3. Communist countries - Commerce - United States. 4. Technology transfer. I. United States. Congress. House. Committee on Foreign Affairs. II. United States. Congress. Senate. Committee on Commerce, Science, and Transportation. III. Title.
HF1411 .U615 1979   **NYPL** *[JLF 81-165]*

Technology and steel industry competitiveness. Washington, D.C. : Congress of the United States, Office of Technology Assessment : for sale by the Supt. of Docs., U. S. Govt. Print. Off., 1980. vii, 374 p. : ill. ; 26 cm. "OTA-M-122." Includes bibliographical references.   LC Card 80-600111
1. Steel industry and trade - United States. I. Title.
TS303 .U54 1980   **NYPL** *[JLF 80-1648]*

Technology assessment in business and government : summary and analysis of the hearings held by the Technology Assessment Board, June 8, 9, 10 and 14, 1976. - [Washington] : The Office ; for sale by Supt. of Docs., U. S. Govt. Print. Off., 1977. xii, 32 [i. e. 33] p. : ill. ; 26 cm. Microfiche (neg.) NTIS. 1 sheet. 11 x 15 cm. (PB 273 164). Report No. OTA-X-42.
1. Technology assessment. 2. Business - Information services. 3. Political science research. I. Title.
NYPL *[*XME-9383]*

Technology assessment of changes in the future use and characteristics of the automobile transportation system. Washington : Congress of the United States, Office of Technology Assessment : for sale by the Supt. of Docs., U. S. Govt. Print. Off., [1979] 2 v. : ill. ; 27 cm. (United States. Congress. Office of Technology Assessment. OTA-T. 83) "OTA-T-83." "OTA-T-84." Bibliography: v. 2, p. 373-375. CONTENTS. - [1] Summary and findings.--v. 2. Technical report.   LC Card 79-600030
1. Transportation, Automotive - United States. 2. Automobile industry and trade - United States. 3. Automobiles - Social aspects - United States. 4. Technology assessment - United States. I. Title. II. Title: Changes in the future use and characteristics of the automobile transportation system. III. Series.
HE5623 .U53 1979   **NYPL** *[JLM 81-210]*

World petroleum availability, 1980-2000. Washington, D.C. : Congress of the United States, Office of Technology Assessment : for sale by the Supt. of Docs., U. S. Govt. Print. Off., [1980] vii, 77 p. : graphs ; 26 cm. (A Technical memorandum - Congress of the United States, Office of Technology Assessment) "October 1980." "OTA-TM-E-5." Includes bibliographical references.   LC Card 80-600164   DDC 338.2/7282 19
1. Petroleum industry and trade. I. Series: United States. Congress. Office of Technology Assessment. Technical memorandum - Congress of the United States, Office of Technology Assessment. II. Title.
HD9560.5 .U62 1980

UNITED STATES. CONGRESS - SALARIES, PENSIONS, ETC.
United States. Congress. House. Committee on Post Office and Civil Service. Subcommittee on Compensation and Employee Benefits. Executive level and congressional pay . Washington , 1980. iii, 55 p. ;   LC Card 80-604034   DDC 353.001/23 19
KF27 .P638 1980k

United States. Congress. Senate. (Old Catalog form: United States. Senate) // Hearings printed in 1978 and later are available only in microform. Please consult the librarians in Economic and Public Affairs Division.

Document .
(no. 96-46) United States. Congress. Senate. Standing rules of the Senate (pursuant to the adoption of S. Res. 274 and S. Res. 389, 96th Cong., Nov. 14, 1979, and Mar. 25, 1980, respectively). Washington , 1980. iv, 69 p. ;   LC Card 80-603245   DDC 328.73/05 19
KF4982 .S75

Standing rules for conducting business in the United States Senate / (pursuant to the adoption of S. Res. 274, 96th Cong., Nov. 14, 1979). Washington : U. S. Govt. Print. Off., 1979. iv, 77 p. ; 24 cm. At head of title: 96th Congress, 1st session. Committee print. "December 10, 1979." Includes index.   LC Card 80-602241   DDC 328.73/05 19
1. United States. Congress. Senate - Rules and practice. I. Title.
KF4982 .S74

Standing rules of the Senate (pursuant to the adoption of S. Res. 274 and S. Res. 389, 96th Cong., Nov. 14, 1979, and Mar. 25, 1980, respectively). Washington : U. S. Govt. Print. Off., 1980. iv, 69 p. ; 24 cm. (Document - 96th Congress, 2d session, Senate . no. 96-46) Includes index.   LC Card 80-603245   DDC 328.73/05 19
1. United States. Congress. Senate - Rules and practice. I. Series: United States. Congress. Senate. Document , no. 96-46. II. Title.
KF4982 .S75

United States. Congress. Senate. Agriculture, Nutrition, and Forestry, Committee on. see United States. Congress. Senate. Committee on Agriculture, Nutrition, and Forestry.

United States. Congress. Senate. Armed Services, Committee on. see United States. Congress. Senate. Committee on Armed Services.

United States. Congress. Senate. Atomic Energy, Special Committee on. see United States. Congress. Senate. Special Committee on Atomic Energy.

UNITED STATES. CONGRESS. SENATE - BIOGRAPHY.
Pressler, Larry, 1942- U. S. senators from the prairie /. Washington, D.C. [1980] p. cm.   ISBN 0-88249-033-8 :   LC Card 80-25220   DDC 328.73/092/2 B 920 19
E747 .P83

Trefousse, Hans Louis. Carl Schurz, a biography /. Knoxville , c1981. p. cm.   ISBN 0-87049-326-4 :   LC Card 81-3370   DDC 973.8/092/4 B 19
E664.S39 T7

UNITED STATES. CONGRESS. SENATE - BIOGRAPHY - ADDRESSES, ESSAYS, LECTURES.
United States. 92d Congress, 2d session, 1972. Memorial addresses and other tributes in the Congress of the United States on the life and contributions of James F. Byrnes, Ninety-second Congress, second session. Washington , 1972. vii, 161 p., [1] leaf of plates ;   LC Card 80-603558   DDC 973.9/092/4 B 19
E748.B975 U54 1972

United States. Congress. Senate. Budget, Committee on the. see United States. Congress. Senate. Committee on the Budget.

United States. Congress. Senate. Commerce, Science, and Transportation, Committee on. see United States. Congress. Senate. Committee on Commerce, Science, and Transportation.

United States. Congress. Senate. Committee on Agriculture and Forestry. (Old Catalog form: United States. Agriculture and Forestry, Committee on (Senate)) // Hearings printed in 1978 and later are available only in microform. Please consult the librarians in the Economic and Public Affairs Division.
United States. Dept. of Agriculture. Foreign meat inspection. Washington.   LC Card 79-640123   **NYPL** *[JLM 80-791]*

United States. Congress. Senate. Committee on Agriculture, Nutrition, and Forestry.
Agricultural Outlook Conference (1980 : Washington, D.C.) 1981 agricultural outlook . Washington , 1981. vi, 565 p. :   LC Card 81-601003   DDC 338.1/0973 19
HD1755 .A38 1980

Amendments to the Food and agriculture act of 1977 : hearing before the Committee on Agriculture, Nutrition, and Forestry, United States Senate, Ninety-sixth Congress, first session ... November 27, 1979. Washington : U. S. Govt. Print. Off., 1980. iii, 94 p. ; 24 cm. Hearing on S. 1696, 2016, 2028, 2029, 2036, and H.R. 3398. LC Card 80-601462 DDC 343.73/076 19
1. Agricultural laws and legislation - United States. 2. Food law and legislation - United States. I. Title.
KF26 .A35 1979l

Effects of the drought on Georgia farmers and the agricultural economy : hearing before the Committee on Agriculture, Nutrition, and Forestry, United States Senate, Ninety-sixth Congress, second session, September 16, 1980. Washington : U. S. G.P.O., 1980 [i.e. 1981] iv, 128 p. : ill. ; 24 cm. Item 1032-B LC Card 81-601181 DDC 338.1/09758 19
1. Droughts - Georgia. 2. Agriculture - Economic aspects - Georgia. I. Title.
KF26 .A35 1980e

Emergency agricultural act of 1980 : hearings before the Committee on Agriculture, Nutrition, and Forestry, United States Senate, Ninety-sixth Congress, second session .... Washington : U. S. Govt. Print. Off., 1980. iv, 197 p. : graphs ; 24 cm. Hearings on S. 2199, S. 2258, S.2264, S.2277, and S.2315, held Feb. 25-March 6, 1980. LC Card 80-602798 DDC 343.73/076 19
1. Agricultural laws and legislation - United States. 2. Agricultural credit - United States. I. Title.
KF26 .A35 1980b

Increase in minimum level price support on 1980 and 1981 quota peanuts : hearing before the Committee on Agriculture, Nutrition, and Forestry, United States Senate, Ninety-sixth Congress, second session, on S. 2249 ... March 12, 1980. Washington : U. S. Govt. Print. Off., 1980. iii, 80 p. ; 24 cm. LC Card 80-602531 DDC 343.73/0763368 19
1. Peanuts - United States. 2. Agricultural price supports - United States. I. Title.
KF26 .A35 1980a

Nominations of Ralph Raikes and William D. Wampler : hearing before the Committee on Agriculture, Nutrition, and Forestry, United States Senate, Ninety-sixth Congress, second session, on the nominations of Ralph Raikes, of Nebraska, and William D. Wampler, of Virginia, to be members of the Federal Farm Credit Board, Farm Credit Administration, August 20, 1980. Washington : U. S. G.P.O., 1980. iii, 31 p. : ill. ; 24 cm. LC Card 80-604017 DDC 353.0082/33045 19
1. Raikes, Ralph, 1907-. 2. Wampler, William D., 1928-. 3. United States. Federal Farm Credit Board - Officials and employees. I. Title.
KF26 .A35 1980c

United States. Commodity Futures Trading Commission. Report of the Commodity Futures Trading Commission on recent developments in the silver futures markets [prepared for the] Committee on Agriculture, Nutrition, and Forestry, United States Senate. Washington , 1980. viii, 123 p. : LC Card 80-602270 DDC 332.63/28 19
HG307.U5 U54 1980

United States. Dept. of Agriculture. U. S. agricultural export development efforts /. Washington , 1980. v, 36 p. : LC Card 80-603056 DDC 382/.41/0973 19
HD9006 .U557 1980

1981 farm legislation : hearings before the Committee on Agriculture, Nutrition, and Forestry, United States Senate, Ninety-sixth Congress, second session, August 28, 29, and 30, 1980, St. Paul, Minn. Washington : U. S. G.P.O., 1980. iv, 213 p. : ill. ; 24 cm. LC Card 81-600584 DDC 343.73/076 347.30376 19
1. Agriculture and state - Minnesota. 2. Agricultural laws and legislation - United States. I. Title.
KF26 .A35 1980d

United States. Congress. Senate. Committee on Agriculture, Nutrition, and Forestry. Subcommittee on Agricultural Credit and Rural Electrification.
United States. Congress. Senate. Committee on Agriculture, Nutrition, and Forestry. Subcommittee on Agricultural Research and General Legislation.
United States. Congress. Senate. Committee on Agriculture, Nutrition, and Forestry.

Subcommittee on Agricultural Production, Marketing, and Stabilization of Prices.
Agricultural waste products as alternative energy sources : hearing before the Subcommittee on Agricultural Research and General Legislation of the Committee on Agriculture, Nutrition, and Forestry, United States Senate, Ninety-sixth Congress, second session, March 21, 1980, Tallahassee Fla. Washington : U. S. Govt. Print. Off., 1980. iii, 74 p. ; 24 cm. LC Card 80-602751 DDC 333.79/38 19
1. Agricultural wastes - United States - Recycling. 2. Renewable energy sources - United States. 3. Agricultural wastes - Florida - Recycling. I. Title.
KF26 .A3534 1980

Amendments to the U. S. grain standards act : hearing before the Subcommittee on Agricultural Production, Marketing, and Stabilization of Prices and the Subcommittee on Foreign Agricultural Policy of the Committee on Agriculture, Nutrition, and Forestry, United States Senate, Ninety-sixth Congress, second session, on S. 2569 ... and S. 2886 ... July 29, 1980. Washington : U. S. Govt. Print. Off., 1980. iv, 95 p. ; 23 cm. LC Card 80-603493 DDC 343.73/085131 347.30385131 19
1. Grain trade - Law and legislation - United States. I. United States. Congress. Senate. Committee on Agriculture, Nutrition, and Forestry. Subcommittee on Foreign Agricultural Policy. II. Title. III. Title: Grain standards act.
KF26 .A35334 1980a

Energy research and extension : hearing before the Subcommittee on Agricultural Research and General Legislation of the Committee on Agriculture, Nutrition, and Forestry, United States Senate, Ninety-sixth Congress, second session ... March 11, 1980. Washington : U. S. Govt. Print. Off., 1980. iii, 56 p. ; 24 cm. LC Card 80-602749 DDC 333.95/3 19
1. Alcohol as fuel - Research - United States. 2. Biomass energy - Research - United States. 3. Energy crops - Research - United States. I. Title.
KF26 .A3534 1980b

FmHA biomass energy program : hearing before the Subcommittee on Agricultural Credit and Rural Electrification of the Committee on Agriculture, Nutrition, and Forestry, United States Senate, Ninety-sixth Congress, second session, October 17, 1980--Lincoln, Nebr. Washington : U. S. G.P.O., 1981. iii, 94 p. : ill. ; 24 cm. Item 1032-B Includes bibliographical references. LC Card 81-601763 DDC 338.4/7662669 19
1. Biomass energy - Government policy - United States. 2. Gasohol - Government policy - United States. 3. United States. Farmers Home Administration. I. Title.
KF26 .A3533 1980b

Interest rate levels of FmHA loan programs : hearing before the Subcommittee on Agricultural Credit and Rural Electrification and the Subcommittee on Rural Development of the Committee on Agriculture, Nutrition, and Forestry, United States Senate, Ninety-sixth Congress, second session, June 10, 1980. Washington : U. S. Govt. Print. Off., 1980. iii, 25 p. ; 24 cm. LC Card 80-603100 DDC 332.7/1/0973 19
1. United States. Farmers Home Administration. 2. Agricultural credit - United States. 3. Interest and usury - United States. I. United States. Congress. Senate. Committee on Agriculture, Nutrition, and Forestry. Subcommittee on Rural Development. II. Title.
KF26 .A3533 1980

Oversight on the Commodity Futures Trading Commission : hearing before the Subcommittee on Agricultural Research and General Legislation of the Committee on Agriculture, Nutrition, and Forestry, United States Senate, Ninety-sixth Congress, second session, February 21, 1980. Washington : U. S. Govt. Print. Off., 1980. iii, 135 p. ; 24 cm. Includes bibliographical references. LC Card 80-602999 DDC 332.63/28 19
1. United States. Commodity Futures Trading Commission. 2. Commodity exchanges - United States. 3. Commodity exchanges - Law and legislation - United States. I. Title.
KF26 .A3534 1980c

Plant Variety Protection Act : hearings before the Subcommittee on Agricultural Research and General Legislation of the Committee on

Agriculture, Nutrition, and Forestry, United States Senate, Ninety-sixth Congress, second session, on S. 23 ... S. 1580 ... and S. 2820 ... June 17 and 18, 1980. Washington : U. S. G.P.O., 1980. iv, 211 p. : ill. ; 24 cm. Includes bibliographical references. LC Card 80-604101 DDC 346.7304/86 347.306486 19
1. Plants - Patents. 2. Plants, Cultivated - Varieties - Law and legislation - United States. I. Title.
KF26 .A3534 1980d

Price volatility in the silver futures market : hearings before the Subcommittee on Agricultural Research and General Legislation of the Committee on Agriculture, Nutrition, and Forestry, United States Senate, Ninety-sixth Congress, second session, May 1 and 2, 1980. Washington : U. S. Govt. Print. Off., 1980. iv, 619 p. ; 24 cm. LC Card 80-602947 DDC 332.63/28 19
1. Silver - Prices. 2. Silver - Prices - United States. 3. Commodity exchanges - United States. I. Title.
KF26 .A3534 1980a

To prohibit futures trading of potatoes on commodity exchanges : hearing before the Subcommittee on Agricultural Research and General Legislation of the Committee on Agriculture, Nutrition, and Forestry, U. S. Senate, Ninety-sixth Congress, first session, on S. 770 ... November 15, 1979. Washington : U. S. Govt. Print. Off., 1980. v, 257 p. : graphs ; 24 cm. LC Card 80-601327 DDC 343.73/085134091/0262 19
1. Potato industry - Law and legislation - United States. 2. Commodity exchanges - Law and legislation - United States. I. Title.
KF26 .A3534 1979e

United States. Congress. Senate. Committee on Agriculture, Nutrition, and Forestry. Subcommittee on Environment, Soil Conservation, and Forestry.
Multiple-use management for North Carolina's national forests : hearing before the Subcommittee on Environment, Soil Conservation, and Forestry of the Committee on Agriculture, Nutrition, and Forestry, United States Senate, Ninety-sixth Congress, second session, on S. 2861 ... August 5, 1980. Washington : U. S. Govt. Print. Off., 1980. iii, 59 p. ; 23 cm. LC Card 80-603802 DDC 346.75604/675 347.56064675 19
1. Forest reserves - North Carolina. I. Title.
KF26 .A3543 1980b

Oversight on Resources planning act : hearing before the Subcommittee on Environment, Soil Conservation, and Forestry of the Committee on Agriculture, Nutrition, and Forestry, United States Senate, Ninety-sixth Congress, first session, October 2, 1979. Washington : U. S. Govt. Print. Off., 1980. iii, 144 p. : ill. ; 24 cm. Includes bibliographical references. LC Card 80-600839 DDC 353.0082/338 19
1. United States - Forest policy. I. Title.
KF26 .A3543 1979f

Resource Conservation and Development Act : hearing before the Subcommittee on Environment, Soil Conservation, and Forestry of the Committee on Agriculture, Nutrition, and Forestry, United States Senate, Ninety-sixth Congress, second session, on S. 1942 ... Tuesday, July 29, 1980. Washington : U. S. G.P.O., 1980. iv, 206 p. : ill. ; 24 cm. Includes bibliographical references. LC Card 80-603906 DDC 346.7304/4 347.30644 19
1. Conservation of natural resources - Law and legislation - United States. 2. Rural development - Law and legislation - United States. 3. United States. Dept. of Agriculture. I. Title.
KF26 .A3543 1980d

Resources planning act : management of the nation's forests : hearings before the Subcommittee on Environment, Soil Conservation, and Forestry of the Committee on Agriculture, Nutrition, and Forestry, United States Senate, Ninety-sixth Congress, second session, May .27, 1980, June 27, 1980. Washington : U. S. Govt. Print. Off., 1980. iii, 67 p. ; graphs ; 24 cm. LC Card 80-603686 DDC 346.7304/675/0262 347.30646750262 19
1. Forest reserves - United States. I. Title.
KF26 .A3543 1980a

Soil conservation : hearings before the Subcommittee on Environment, Soil Conservation, and Forestry of the Committee

on Agriculture, Nutrition, and Forestry, United States Senate, Ninety-sixth Congress, second session, August 13, 1980--Waterloo, Iowa, August 14, 1980--Ames, Iowa, August 15, 1980--Fairfield, Iowa. Washington : U. S. G.P.O., 1980. v. 332 p. : ill. ; 24 cm. Includes bibliographical references. LC Card 80-603997 DDC 333.76/16/09777 19
1. Soil conservation - Iowa. I. Title.
KF26 .A3543 1980c

United States. Congress. Senate. Committee on Agriculture, Nutrition, and Forestry. Subcommittee on Foreign Agricultural Policy.
Public law 480 aid for refugees : hearing before the Subcommittee on Foreign Agricultural Policy of the Committee on Agriculture, Nutrition, and Forestry, United States Senate, Ninety-sixth Congress, second session, March 4, 1980. Washington : U. S. Govt. Print. Off., 1980. iii, 29 p. ; 24 cm. LC Card 80-602524 DDC 344.73/03287 19
1. Food relief, American. 2. Refugees - Legal status, laws, etc. - United States. I. Title.
KF26 .A3549 1980

United States. Congress. Senate. Committee on Agriculture, Nutrition, and Forestry. Subcommittee on Agricultural Production, Marketing, and Stabilization of Prices. Amendments to the U. S. grain standards act . Washington , 1980. iv, 95 p. ; LC Card 80-603493 DDC 343.73/085131 347.30385131 19
KF26 .A35334 1980a

United States. Congress. Senate. Committee on Agriculture, Nutrition, and Forestry. Subcommittee on Nutrition.
Nutrition needs of the elderly : hearings before the Subcommittee on Nutrition of the Committee on Agriculture, Nutrition, and Forestry, United States Senate, Ninety-sixth Congress, second session, August 12, 1980, Wichita and Kansas City, Kans. Washington : U. S. G.P.O., 1981. iv, 122 p. ; 24 cm. Item 1032-B Includes bibliographical references. LC Card 81-601607 DDC 362.1/9897639 19
1. Aged - Kansas - Nutrition. I. Title.
KF26 .A3559 1980b

Review of child nutrition programs : hearings before the Subcommittee on Nutrition of the Committee on Agriculture, Nutrition, and Forestry, United States Senate, Ninety-sixth Congress, second session, April 15 and 17, 1980. Washington : U. S. Govt. Print. Off., 1980. iv, 130 p. ; 24 cm. LC Card 80-603080 DDC 363.8/0880544 19
1. Children - United States - Nutrition. 2. School children - Food - United States. I. Title.
KF26 .A3559 1980a

Trends in the American diet : hearing before the Subcommittee on Nutrition of the Committee on Agriculture, Nutrition, and Forestry, United States Senate, Ninety-sixth Congress, second session, February 22, 1980, Fort Lauderdale, Fla. Washington : U. S. Govt. Print. Off., 1980. iii, 66 p ; 24 cm. LC Card 80-602728 DDC 362.1/9639/073 19
1. Nutrition - United States. 2. Diet - United States. I. Title.
KF26 .A3559 1980

United States. Congress. Senate. Committee on Agriculture, Nutrition, and Forestry. Subcommittee on Rural Development.
Accuracy of census taking in small communities and rural areas : hearing before the Subcommittee on Rural Development of the Committee on Agriculture, Nutrition, and Forestry, United States Senate, Ninety-sixth Congress, second session, September 18, 1980. Washington : U. S. Govt. Print. Off., 1980. iii, 32 p. ; 24 cm. LC Card 80-603442 DDC 001.4/33 19
1. United States - Census, 20th, 1980. 2. United States - Population, rural. 3. Rural development - United States. I. Title.
KF26 .A3574 1980a

Administration's rural development policy : hearing before the Subcommittee on Rural Development of the Committee on Agriculture, Nutrition, and Forestry, United States Senate, Ninety-sixth Congress, second session, March 25, 1980. Washington : U. S. Govt. Print. Off., 1980. iii, 80 p. ; 24 cm. LC Card 80-603035

DDC 338.973 19
1. Rural development - United States. I. Title.
KF26 .A3574 1980

United States. Congress. Senate. Committee on Agriculture, Nutrition, and Forestry. Subcommittee on Agricultural Credit and Rural Electrification. Interest rate levels of FmHA loan programs . Washington , 1980. iii, 25 p. ; LC Card 80-603100 DDC 332.7/1/0973 19
KF26 .A3533 1980

United States. Congress. Senate. Committee on Agriculture, Nutrition, and Forestry. Subcommittee on Agricultural Credit and Rural Electrification. REA and energy conservation : hearing before the Subcommittee on Agricultural Credit and Rural Electrification of the Committee on Agriculture, Nutrition, and Forestry, United States Senate, Ninety-sixth Congress, second session, on energy conservation and its effect on rural electric cooperatives, May 6, 1980. Washington : U. S. G.P.O., 1980. iii, 113 p. : ill. ; 24 cm. LC Card 81-600598 DDC 334/.68136362 19
1. United States. Rural Electrification Administration. 2. Rural electrification - United States. 3. Electric power - United States - Conservation. I. Title.
KF26 .A3533 1980a

United States. Congress. Senate. Committee on Appropriations. (Old Catalog form: United States. Appropriations, Committee on (Senate)) // Hearings printed in 1978 and later are available only in microform. Please consult the librarians in the Economic and Public Affairs Division.
Disaster assistance Pacific Northwest--Mount Saint Helens eruption : hearing before the Committee on Appropriations, United States Senate, Ninety-sixth Congress, first session : special fiscal year 1980 supplemental hearing .... Washington : U. S. Govt. Print. Off. : for sale by the Supt. of Docs., U. S. Govt. Print. Off., 1980. iv, 241 p. : ill. ; 24 cm. LC Card 80-603023 DDC 363.3/495/0979788 19
1. Saint Helens, Mount, Wash. - Eruption, 1980. 2. Disaster relief - Northwest Pacific. I. Title.
KF26 .A6 1980

Economic overview : hearings before the Committee on Appropriations, United States Senate, Ninety-seventh Congress, first session : special hearings, budget of the U. S. Government. Washington : U. S. G.P.O. : For sale by the Supt. of Docs., U. S. G.P.O., 1981. iii, 577, vi p. : ill. ; 24 cm. Spine title: Economic overview, 1982. Includes index. S/N 052-070-05557-0 Item 1033, 1033-A (microfiche) LC Card 81-601646 DDC 330.973/0927 19
1. United States - Economic conditions - 1971-. 2. United States - Economic policy - 1971-. 3. Budget - United States. I. Title. II. Title: Economic overview, 1982.
KF26 .A6 1981

Fraud, abuse, waste, and error in government : hearing before the Committee on Appropriations, United States Senate, Ninety-sixth Congress, second session : special hearing, General Accounting Office [and] Office of Management and Budget. Washington : U. S. Govt. Print. Off. : for sale by the Supt. of Docs., U. S. Govt. Print. Off., 1980. ii, 124 p. : graphs ; 24 cm. Hearing held Feb. 27, 1980. LC Card 80-603298 DDC 353.009 19
1. Administrative agencies - United States. 2. Fraud - United States. 3. Misconduct in office - United States. 4. Whistle blowing - United States. I. Title.
KF26 .A6 1980a

Legislative branch appropriations for fiscal year 1968. Hearings before a subcommittee of the Committee on Appropriations, United States Senate, Ninetieth Congress, first session, on H. R. 10368, making appropriations for the legislative branch for the fiscal year ending June 30, 1968, and for other purposes. Washington., Govt. Print. Off., 1967. 281, x p. illus., tables. 24 cm.
1. United States. Congress - Appropriations and expenditures. I. Title. **NYPL [JLE 81-395]**

National Institute of Arthritis, Metabolism, and Digestive Diseases. Office of the Associate Director for Arthritis, Bone, and Skin Diseases. Progress against the rheumatic diseases (1967-1977) . [Bethesda, Md.] , 1978. vii, 39 p. ; LC Card 79-602034 DDC 616.7/23/0072073

19
RC927 .N38 1978

United States. Congress. Senate. Committee on Appropriations. Subcommittee on Agriculture, Rural Development, and Related Agencies. Agriculture, rural development, and related agencies appropriations for fiscal year 1981 : hearings before a subcommittee of the Committee on Appropriations, United States Senate, Ninety-sixth Congress, second session. Washington : U. S. Govt. Print. Off. : for sale by the Supt. of Docs., U. S. Govt. Print. Off., 1980. 3 v. : ill. ; 24 cm. Includes indexes. CONTENTS. - pt. 1 Commodity Futures Trading Commission. Department of Agriculture.--pt. 2. Department of Agriculture. Farm Credit Administration.--pt. 3. Congressional witnesses. Department of Agriculture. General Accounting Office. Nondepartmental witnesses. LC Card 80-603090 DDC 353.0072/23682/33 19
1. United States. Dept. of Agriculture - Appropriations and expenditures. 2. United States - Appropriations and expenditures, 1981. I. Title.
KF26 .A643 1980

United States. Congress. Senate. Committee on Appropriations. Subcommittee on Department of the Interior and Related Agencies. Rangeland management policy and wood energy development : hearings before a subcommittee of the Committee on Appropriations, United States Senate, Ninety-sixth Congress, second session : special hearing, Department of the Interior, Bureau of Land Management, nondepartmental witnesses, rangeland programs, Idaho, Nevada, New Mexico, Utah, wood energy programs, Vermont. Washington : U. S. G.P.O. : For sale by the Supt. of Docs., U. S. G.P.O., 1980. iii, 883, vii p. : ill. ; 24 cm. Includes bibliographical references. LC Card 80-603996 DDC 353.0082/326 19
1. Range policy - West (U. S.). 2. Fuelwood industry - Vermont. I. Title.
KF26 .A652 1979a

United States. Congress. Senate. Committee on Appropriations. Subcommittee on Departments of State, Justice, and Commerce, the Judiciary, and Related Agencies. Chrysler Corporation loan guarantees program : hearing before a subcommittee of the Committee on Appropriations, United States Senate, Ninety-sixth Congress, first session. Washington : U. S. Govt. Print. Off. : for sale by the Supt. of Docs., U. S. Govt. Print. Off., 1980. iii, 35 p. ; 24 cm. "Special hearing, Department of the Treasury, nondepartmental witnesses." LC Card 80-602994 DDC 353.0082/42 19
1. Chrysler Corporation - Finance. 2. Loans - United States - Government guaranty. I. Title.
KF26 .A659 1979a

Disaster loan fund budget amendment : hearing before a subcommittee of the Committee on Appropriations, United States Senate, Ninety-sixth Congress, second session : special hearing, Small Business Administration. Washington : U. S. Govt. Print. Off. : for sale by the Supt. of Docs., U. S. Govt. Print. Off., 1980. ii, 26 p. ; 24 cm. LC Card 80-603494 DDC 353.0082/33045 19
1. Agricultural credit - United States. 2. Disaster relief - United States. 3. United States. Small Business Administration - Appropriations and expenditures. I. Title.
KF26 .A659 1980a

Federal drug enforcement and supply control efforts : hearings before a subcommittee of the Committee on Appropriations, United States Senate, Ninety-sixth Congress, first session : special hearing. Washington : U. S. G.P.O. : For sale by the Supt. of Docs., U. S. G.P.O., 1980. iii, 325, vi p. : ill. ; 24 cm. Includes indexes. LC Card 80-603504 DDC 353.0076/5 19
1. Narcotics, Control of - United States. I. Title.
KF26 .A659 1979b

United States. General Accounting Office. States are funding juvenile justice projects that conform to legislative objectives . [Washington, D.C.] , 1980. iii, 129 p. ; LC Card 80-601282 DDC 353.9/38492 19
HV9104 .U52 1980

United States. Congress. Senate. Committee on Appropriations. Subcommittee on Dept. of

GOVERNMENT PUBLICATIONS - U.S.: 1981

471

United States. Congress. Senate. Committee on Armed Services.

the Interior and Related Agencies.
Department of the Interior and related agencies
appropriations for fiscal year 1980 : hearings
before a subcommittee of the Committee on
Appropriations, United States Senate,
Ninety-sixth Congress, first session, on H.R.
4930 .... Washington : U. S. Govt. Print. Off. :
for sale by the Supt. of Docs., U. S. Govt.
Print. Off., 1980- v. <1-4> ; 23 cm. On spine:
Interior appropriations, 1980 (H.R. 4930) Hearings held
<May 1, 1979-Sept. 24, 1979> Includes indexes. LC
Card 80-603500 DDC 353.0072/236 19
*1. United States. Dept. of the Interior - Appropriations
and expenditures. 2. United States - Appropriations and
expenditures, 1980. I. Title. II. Title: Interior
appropriations, 1980 (H.R. 4930).*
KF26 .A652 1980

**United States. Congress. Senate. Committee on
Appropriations. Subcommittee on Energy
and Water Development.**
Energy and water development appropriations
for fiscal year 1981 : hearings before a
Subcommittee of the Committee on
Appropriations, United States Senate,
Ninety-sixth Congress, second session.
Washington : U. S. Govt. Print. Off. : for sale
by the Supt. of Docs., U. S. Govt. Print. Off.,
1980- v. ; 24 cm. Includes index. LC Card
80-603292 DDC 353.0072/23682325 19
*1. Water resources development - United States -
Finance. 2. Energy development - United States -
France. 3. United States - Appropriations and
expenditures, 1981. I. Title.*
KF26 .A6469 1980a

Power program of the Tennessee Valley
Authority : hearing before a subcommittee of
the Committee on Appropriations, United
States Senate, Ninety-sixth Congress, second
session, special hearing, General Accounting
Office, Tennessee Valley Authority,
nondepartmental witnesses. Washington : U. S.
G.P.O. : For sale by the Supt. of Docs., U. S.
G.P.O., 1981. iii, 192 p. : ill. ; 24 cm. S/N
052-070-05589-9 Item 1033, 1033-A (microfiche) LC
Card 81-601951 DDC 353.0082/3/09768 19
*1. Tennessee Valley Authority. 2. Electric utilities -
Tennessee Valley - Rates. I. Title.*
KF26 .A6469 1980b

Tennessee-Tombigbee Waterway : hearing
before a subcommittee of the Committee on
Appropriations, United States Senate,
Ninety-sixth Congress, second session : special
hearing, Department of the Army, Corps of
Engineers. Washington : U. S. Govt. Print.
Off. : for sale by the Supt. of Docs., U. S.
Govt. Print. Off., 1980. ii, 56 p. : ill. ; 24 cm.
LC Card 80-603362 DDC 353.0087/6/09768 19
*1. Tennessee-Tombigbee waterway. I. United States.
Army. Corps of Engineers. II. Title.*
KF26 .A6469 1980

**United States. Congress. Senate. Committee on
Appropriations. Subcommittee on Foreign
Assistance and Related Programs. see United
States. Congress. Senate. Committee on
Appropriations. Subcommittee on Foreign
Operations.**

**United States. Congress. Senate. Committee on
Appropriations. Subcommittee on Foreign
Operations.**
Foreign assistance and related programs
appropriations for fiscal year 1981 : hearings
before a subcommittee of the Committee on
Appropriations, United States Senate,
Ninety-sixth Congress, second session.
Washington : U. S. G.P.O. : For sale by the
Supt. of Docs., U. S. G.P.O., c1980- v. : ill. ;
24 cm. Spine title: Foreign assistance appropriations,
1981. Includes bibliographical references and indexes.
CONTENTS. - pt. 1. Agency for International
Development, Congressional Research Service,
Department of State, Department of the Treasury,
Export-Import Bank, Inter-American Foundation,
International Development Cooperation Agency, Peace
Corps, public witnesses, Senate legal counsel. LC Card
89-2356
*1. Economic assistance, American. 2. Military
assistance, American. 3. United States - Appropriations
and expenditures, 1981. I. Title. II. Title: Foreign
assistance appropriations, 1981.*
HC60 .U5912 1981b

Foreign assistance and related programs,
appropriations for fiscal year 1981 : hearings
before a subcommittee of the Committee on

Appropriations, United States Senate,
Ninety-sixth Congress, second session.
Washington : U. S. Govt. Print. Off. ; for sale
by the Supt. of Docs., U. S. Govt. Print. Off.,
1980- v.<1>: ill. ; 24 cm. Includes index. LC
Card 80-603464 DDC 353.0072/23689 19
*1. Economic assistance, American. 2. Military
assistance, American. 3. United States - Appropriations
and expenditures, 1981. I. Title.*
KF26 .A647 1980

**United States. Congress. Senate. Committee on
Appropriations. Subcommittee on HUD-
Independent Agencies.**
Department of Housing and Urban
Development, and certain independent agencies
appropriations for fiscal year 1981 : hearings
before a subcommittee of the Committee on
Appropriations, United States Senate,
Ninety-sixth Congress, second session, on H.R.
7631 ... Washington : U. S. G.P.O. : For sale
by the Supt. of Docs., U. S. G.P.O., 1980. 2 v.
(iii, 2553, xiii p.) : ill. ; 24 cm. Spine title:
HUD-independent agencies appropriations, 1981.
Includes bibliographical references and indexes.
CONTENTS. - pt.1. Consumer Information Center ... --
pt. 2. American Battle Monuments Commission ... LC
Card 80-604053 DDC 353.0072/236865 19
*1. United States. Dept. of Housing and Urban
Development - Appropriations and expenditures. 2.
United States - Appropriations and expenditures, 1981.
I. Title. II. Title: HUD-independent agencies
appropriations, 1981.*
KF26 .A6486 1980a

Management of HUD's multi-family properties,
the Cliffton Terrace case : hearings before a
subcommittee of the Committee on
Appropriations, United States Senate,
Ninety-sixth Congress, first session : special
hearing, Department of Housing and Urban
Development, General Accounting Office,
nondepartmental witnesses. Washington : U. S.
Govt. Print. Off. : for sale by the Supt. of
Docs., U. S. Govt. Print. Off., 1980. iii, 375, vi
p. ; 24 cm. Includes bibliographical references and
index. LC Card 80-602962 DDC
353.0086/5043/09753 19
*1. Washington, D.C. Clifton Terrace - Management. 2.
Pride, inc. 3. Public housing - United States -
Management. 4. United States. Dept. of Housing and
Urban Development. I. United States. Dept. of Housing
and Urban Development. II. United States. General
Accounting Office. III. Title.*
KF26 .A6486 1979b

Military draft registration : hearings before a
subcommittee of the Committee on
Appropriations, United States Senate,
Ninety-sixth Congress, second session : special
hearing, congressional witnesses,
nondepartmental witnesses, selective service
system. Washington : U. S. Govt. Print. Off. :
for sale by the Supt. of Docs., U. S. Govt.
Print. Off., 1980. iii, 212 p. ; 23 cm. LC Card
80-603341 / DDC 355.2/2363/0973 19
1. Military service, Compulsory - United States. I. Title.
KF26 .A6486 1980

Nuclear and hazardous waste problems in New
Hampshire : hearing before a subcommittee of
the Committee on Appropriations, United
States Senate, Ninety-sixth Congress, second
session : special hearing, Department of Energy,
Envioronmental Protection Agency,
nondepartmental witnesses. Washington : U. S.
G.P.O., 1980 [i.e. 1981] iii, 122 p. ; 23 cm. Item
1033, 1033-A (microfiche) Includes bibliographical
references. LC Card 81-601754 DDC 363.7/28 19
*1. Hazardous wastes - New Hampshire. 2. Radioactive
waste disposal - New Hampshire. 3. United States.
Dept. of Energy. 4. United States. Environmental
Protection Agency. I. Title.*
KF26 .A6486 1980b

Space shuttle and Galileo mission : hearings
before a subcommittee of the Committee on
Appropriations, United States Senate,
Ninety-sixth Congress, first session : special
hearing, Department of Housing and Urban
Development. Washington : U. S. Govt. Print.
Off. : for sale by the Supt. of Docs., U. S.
Govt. Print. Off., 1980. iv, 132 p. ; 24 cm.
Hearings held Oct. 30 and Nov. 29, 1979. LC Card
80-601987 DDC 353.0072/2368778 19
*1. Reusable space vehicles. 2. Galileo Project. 3. United
States. National Aeronautics and Space
Administration - Appropriations and expenditures. 4.
United States - Appropriations and expenditures, 1980.*

I. Title.
KF26 .A6486 1979c

**United States. Congress. Senate. Committee on
Appropriations. Subcommittee on Military
Construction.**
Installation realinements : hearing before a
Subcommittee of the Committee on
Appropriations, United States Senate,
Ninety-sixth Congress, first session, special
hearing, Department of Defense. Washington :
U. S. Govt. Print. Off. : for sale by the Supt. of
Docs., U. S. Govt. Print. Off., 1980. iv, 145 p. :
maps ; 24 cm. LC Card 80-602722 DDC
355.7/0973 19
*1. Military bases - United States. 2. Military bases -
Economic aspects - United States. I. Title.*
KF26 .A655 1979

MX missile basing mode : hearings before a
subcommittee of the Committee on
Appropriations, United States Senate,
Ninety-sixth Congress, second session : special
hearing, Department of Defense. Washington :
U. S. G.P.O. : For sale by the Supt. of Docs.,
U. S. G.P.O., 1980. iii, 269 p. : ill. ; 24 cm.
Includes bibliographical references.
052-070-05478-6 LC Card 80-604099 DDC
358/.174/0973 19
*1. MX (Weapons system). 2. United States. Dept. of
Defense - Appropriations and expenditures. I. Title.*
KF26 .A655 1980

United States. Congress. Senate. Committee on
Armed Services. Subcommittee on Military
Construction and Stockpiles. Military
construction authorization, fiscal year 1981 .
Washington , 1980. iv, 694, xv p. : LC Card
80-603503 DDC 355.6/22/0973 19
KF26 .A756 1980

**United States. Congress. Senate. Committee on
Appropriations. Subcommittee on the Dept.
of the Treasury, U. S. Postal Service, and
General Government Appropriations.**
Treasury, Postal Service, and general
government appropriations for fiscal year 1981 :
hearings before a subcommittee of the
Committee on Appropriations, United States
Senate, Ninety-sixth Congress, second session,
on H.R. 7583 .... Washington : U. S. Govt.
Print. Off. : for sale by the Supt. of Docs., U.
S. Govt. Print. Off., 1980- v. <1> ; 24 cm.
Hearings held Apr. 15-<22>, 1980. Includes indexes.
LC Card 80-603729 DDC 353.0072/236 19
*1. United States. Treasury Dept. - Appropriations and
expenditures. 2. United States. Postal Service -
Appropriations and expenditures. 3. United States -
Appropriations and expenditures, 1981. I. Title.*
KF26 .A662 1980

**United States. Congress. Senate. Committee on
Appropriations. Subcommittee on
Transportation and Related Agencies.**
Department of Transportation and related
agencies appropriations for fiscal year 1981 :
hearings before a subcommittee of the
Committee on Appropriations, United States
Senate, Ninety-sixth Congress, second session.
Washington : U. S. Govt. Print. Off. : for sale
by the Supt. of Docs., U. S. Govt. Print. Off.,
1980- v. <1> : ill. ; 24 cm. Includes
bibliographical references and indexes. CONTENTS. -
pt. 1. Civil Aeronautics Board, Department of
Transportation, Interstate Commerce Commission,
National Railroad Passenger Corporation, National
Transportation Safety Board, Panama Canal
Commission. LC Card 80-603482 DDC
353.0072/236875 19
*1. United States. Dept. of Transportation -
Appropriations and expenditures. 2. United States -
Appropriations and expenditures, 1981. I. Title.*
KF26 .A66 1980

**United States. Congress. Senate. Committee on
Appropriations. Transportation and Related
Agencies, Subcommittee on. see United
States. Congress. Senate. Committee on
Appropriations. Subcommittee on
Transportation and Related Agencies.**

**United States. Congress. Senate. Committee on
Armed Services.** (Old Catalog form: United
States. Armed Services, Committee on
(Senate)) // Hearings printed in 1978 and
later are available only in microform. Please
consult the librarians in the Economic and
Public Affairs Division.
Department of Defense authorization for
appropriations for fiscal year 1981 : hearings

BIBLIOGRAPHIC GUIDE

United States. Congress. Senate. Committee on Armed Services.

472

before the Committee on Armed Services, United States Senate, Ninety-sixth Congress, second session, on S. 2294 .... Washington : U. S. Govt. Print. Off., 1980- v. : ill. ; 24 cm. Hearings held Jan. 31- Includes index. LC Card 80-602755 DDC 355.6/22/0973 19
1. *United States. Dept. of Defense - Appropriations and expenditures. I. Title.*
KF26 .A7 1980a

Department of Defense authorization for appropriations for fiscal year 1982 : hearings before the Committee on Armed Services, United States Senate, Ninety-seventh Congress, first session, on S. 815 .... Washington : U. S. G.P.O., 1981- v. <1-2> : ill. ; 24 cm. Pt. 1: "January 28, March 4, 1981." Pt. 2: "January 29, February 3, 5, 6, 1981." Includes indexes. Item 1034-A, 1034-B (microfiche) CONTENTS. - pt. 1. Posture statement, Secretary of Defense Caspar Weinberger, General David C. Jones, chairman, Joint Chiefs of Staff, budget amendments -- pt. 2. Defense management report, Army programs, Navy-Marine Corps programs, Air Force programs. LC Card 81-601875 DDC 353.0072/234 19
1. *United States. Dept. of Defense - Appropriations and expenditures. I. Title.*
KF26 .A7 1981e

Nomination of Caspar W. Weinberger to be Secretary of Defense : hearing before the Committee on Armed Services, United States Senate, Ninety-seventh Congress, first session, on nomination of Caspar W. Weinberger to be Secretary of Defense, January 6, 1981. Washington : U. S. G.P.O., 1981. ii, 61 p. ; 24 cm. Item 1034-A, 1034-B (microfiche) LC Card 81-600831 DDC 353.6 19
1. *Weinberger, Caspar W. 2. United States. Dept. of Defense - Officials and employees. I. Title.*
KF26 .A7 1981

Nomination of Charles W. Snodgrass : hearing before the Committee on Armed Services, United States Senate, Ninety-sixth Congress, second session, on nomination of Charles W. Snodgrass to be Assistant Secretary of the Air Force for Financial Management, June 12, 1980. Washington : U. S. Govt. Print. Off., 1980. ii, 7 p. ; 24 cm. LC Card 80-602952 DDC 353.63 19
1. *Snodgrass, Charles William, 1940-. 2. United States. Dept. of the Air Force - Officials and employees. I. Title.*
KF26 .A7 1980b

Nomination of David C. Jones : hearing before the Committee on Armed Services, United States Senate, Ninety-sixth Congress, second session, on nomination of Gen. David C. Jones to be Chairman of the Joint Chiefs of Staff for an additional two-year term ... June 16, 1980. Washington : U. S. Govt. Print. Off., 1980. ii, 64 p. ; 23 cm. LC Card 80-603324 DDC 355.3/3042/0973 19
1. *Jones, David C., 1921-. 2. United States. Joint Chiefs of Staff - Officials and employees. I. Title.*
KF26 .A7 1980e

Nomination of Frank C. Carlucci III to be Deputy Secretary of Defense : hearing before the Committee on Armed Services, United States Senate, Ninety-seventh Congress, first session, on nomination of Frank C. Carlucci III to be deputy secretary of defense, January 13, 1981. Washington : U. S. G.P.O., 1981. ii, 45 p. ; 24 cm. Item 1034-A, 1034-B (microfiche) LC Card 81-600832 DDC 353.6 19
1. *Carlucci, Frank Charles, 1930-. 2. United States. Dept. of Defense - Officials and employees. I. Title.*
KF26 .A7 1981a

Nomination of George Vernon Orr, Jr., to be secretary of the Air Force : hearing before the Committee on Armed Sevices, United States Senate, Ninety-seventh Congress, first session, on nomination of George Vernon Orr, Jr., to be Secretary of the Air Force, January 28, 1981. Washington : U. S. G.P.O., 1981. ii, 12 p. ; 24 cm. Item 1034-A, 1034-B (microfiche) LC Card 81-601412 DDC 353.63 19
1. *Orr, George Vernon, 1916-. 2. United States. Dept. of the Air Force - Officials and employees. I. Title.*
KF26 .A7 1981b

Nomination of Jack R. Borsting : hearing before the Committee on Armed Services, United States Senate, Ninety-sixth Congress, second session, on nomination of Jack R. Borsting to be Assistant Secretary of Defense

(Comptroller), July 28, 1980. Washington : U. S. Govt. Print. Off., 1980. 6 p. ; 23 cm. LC Card 80-603338 DDC 353.6 19
1. *Borsting, Jack Raymond, 1929-. 2. United States. Dept. of Defense - Officials and employees. I. Title.*
KF26 .A7 1980d

Nomination of John F. Lehman, Jr., to be Secretary of the Navy : hearing before the Committee on Armed Services, United States Senate, Ninety-seventh Congress, first session, on nomination of John F. Lehman, Jr., to be Secretary of the Navy, January 28, 1981. Washington : U. S. G.P.O., 1981. ii, 30 p. ; 24 cm. Item 1034-A, 1034-B (microfiche) LC Card 81-601340 DDC 353.7 19
1. *Lehman, John F. 2. United States. Navy Dept. - Officials and employees. I. Title.*
KF26 .A7 1981c

Nomination of John O. Marsh, Jr., to be secretary of the Army : hearing before the Committee on Armed Services, United States Senate, Ninety-seventh Congress, first session, on nomination of John O. Marsh, Jr., to be secretary of the army, January 26, 1981. Washington : U. S. G.P.O., 1981. iii, 22 p. ; 24 cm. LC Card 81-601158 DDC 353.62 19
1. *Marsh, John O., 1926-. 2. United States. Dept. of the Army - Officials and employees. I. Title.*
KF26 .A7 1981d

Nominations of Fred C. Ikle, to be under secretary of defense for policy, and William H. Taft, IV, to be general counsel of the Department of Defense : hearing before the Committee on Armed Services United States Senate, Ninety-seventh Congress, first session, on nominations of Fred C. Ikle, of Maryland, to be under secretary of defense for policy, and William H. Taft, IV, of Virginia, be general counsel of the Department of Defense, March 26, 1981. Washington : U. S. G.P.O., 1981. ii, 24 p. ; 24 cm. Item 1034-A, 1034-B (microfiche) LC Card 81-602261 DDC 353.6 19
1. *Iklé, Fred Charles. 2. Taft, William Howard, 1945-. 3. United States. Dept. of Defense - Officials and employees. I. Title.*
KF26 .A7 1981f

Nominations of Michael Blumenfeld, John A. Bushnell, John W. Clark, Clifford B. O'Hara, William Sidell, Robinson O. Everett, and William E. Peacock : hearing before the Committee on Armed Services, United States Senate, Ninety-sixth Congress, second session ..., March 7, 1980. Washington : U. S. Govt. Print. Off., 1980. ii, 49 p. ; 24 cm. "Nominations of Michael Blumenfeld, Assistant Secretary of the Army; John Alden Bushnell; John W. Clark; Clifford Bradley O'Hara; and William Sidell, to be Members of the Board of the Panama Canal Commission (new positions). Robinson O. Everett, to be a judge of the U. S. Court of Military Appeals. William Eldred Peacock, to be an Assistant Secretary of the Army." LC Card 80-602497 DDC 353.0087/6444 19
1. *United States. Panama Canal Commission - Officials and employees. 2. United States. Dept. of Defense - Officials and employees. 3. United States. Court of Military Appeals - Officials and employees. I. Title.*
KF26 .A7 1980c

Panama Canal Commission authorization fiscal year 1981 : hearing before the Committee on Armed Services, United States Senate, Ninety-sixth Congress, second session, June 12, 1980. Washington : U. S. G.P.O., 1980 [i.e. 1981] ii, 32 p. ; 24 cm. Item 1034 LC Card 81-600852 DDC 353.0072/234 19
1. *United States. Panama Canal Commission - Appropriations and expenditures. I. Title.*
KF26 .A7 1980f

United States. Congress. Senate. Committee on Armed Services. Subcommittee on Arms Control. Fiscal year 1981 Department of Energy authorization for national security programs : hearings before the Subcommittee on Arms Control of the Committee on Armed Services, United States Senate, Ninety-sixth Congress, second session, on S. 2341 ... April 28, June 24, 1980. Washington : U. S. Govt. Print. Off., 1980. iii, 205 p. : ill. ; 24 cm. LC Card 80-603337 DDC 353.0072/23682/3 19
1. *United States. Dept. of Energy - Appropriations and expenditures. 2. United States - National security - Finance. I. Title.*
KF26 .A7435 1980

United States. Congress. Senate. Committee on Armed Services. Subcommittee on General Procurement. Soviet defense expenditures and related programs : hearings before the Subcommittee on General Procurement of the Committee on Armed Services, United States Senate, Ninety-sixth Congress, first and second sessions, November 1, 8, 1979, February 4, 1980. Washington : U. S. G.P.O., 1980. iv, 215 p. : ill. ; 24 cm. Includes bibliographical references. LC Card 81-600583 DDC 355.6/212/0947 19
1. *Soviet Union - Armed forces - Procurement. I. Title.*
KF26 .A7543 1979a

United States. Congress. Senate. Committee on Armed Services. Subcommittee on Manpower and Personnel. Military compensation : hearing before the Subcommittee on Manpower and Personnel of the Committee on Armed Services, United States Senate, Ninety-sixth Congress, second session, June 2, 1980. Washington : U. S. G.P.O., 1980. ii, 73 p. ; 24 cm. LC Card 81-600589 DDC 355.6/4/0973 19
1. *United States - Armed Forces - Pay, allowances, etc. I. Title.*
KF26 .A7548 1980a

Military medical programs and proposed revisions of military medical pay : hearing before the Subcommittee on Manpower and Personnel of the Committee on Armed Services, United States Senate, Ninety-sixth Congress, first session, on S. 523 ... S. 1100 ... H.R. 5235 ... December 5, 1979. Washington : U. S. Govt. Print. Off., 1980. iii, 78 p. : graph ; 24 cm. LC Card 80-601938 DDC 343.73/013 19
1. *United States - Armed Forces - Pay, allowances, etc. - Law and legislation. 2. Medical personnel - Salaries, pensions, etc. - United States. I. Title.*
KF26 .A7548 1979e

Proposed changes to military compensation : hearing before the Subcommittee on Manpower and Personnel of the Committee on Armed Services, United States Senate, Ninety-sixth Congress, second session, January 22, 1980. Washington : U. S. Govt. Print. Off., 1980. iii, 101 p. ; 24 cm. LC Card 80-602795 DDC 355.6/4/0973 19
1. *United States - Armed Forces - Pay, allowances, etc. I. Title.*
KF26 .A7548 1980

Providing greater flexibility for the armed forces in ordering reserves to active duty : hearing before the Subcommittee on Manpower and Personnel of the Committee on Armed Services, United States Senate, Ninety-sixth Congress, second session, on H.R. 7682 ... September 18, 1890. Washington : U. S. G.P.O., 1980 [i.e. 1981] iii, 32 p. ; 24 cm. Item 1034 LC Card 81-600808 DDC 343.73/012 347.30312 19
1. *United States - Armed Forces - Reserves. 2. United States - Armed Forces - Mobilization. I. Title.*
KF26 .A7548 1980b

United States. Congress. Senate. Committee on Armed Services. Subcommittee on Military Construction and Stockpiles. Military construction authorization, fiscal year 1981 : joint hearings before the Subcommittee on Military Construction and Stockpiles of the Committee on Armed Services and the Subcommittee on Military Construction of the Committee on Appropriations, United States Senate, Ninety-sixth Congress, second session, on S. 2333 .... Washington : U. S. Govt. Print. Off. : For sale by the Supt. of Docs., U. S. Govt. Print. Off., 1980. iv, 694, xv p. : ill. ; 24 cm. Hearings held Mar. 3-Apr. 30, 1980. Includes index. LC Card 80-603503 DDC 355.6/22/0973 19
1. *United States. Dept. of Defense - Appropriations and expenditures. 2. United States - Armed Forces - Military construction operations. I. United States. Congress. Senate. Committee on Appropriations. Subcommittee on Military Construction. II. Title.*
KF26 .A756 1980

United States. Congress. Senate. Committee on Armed Services. Subcommittee on Procurement Policy and Reprograming. NATO support agreements : hearing before the Subcommittee on Procurement Policy and Reprograming of the Committee on Armed Services, United States Senate, Ninety-sixth Congress, second session, on H.R. 5580 ... January 30, 1980. Washington : U. S. Govt.

GOVERNMENT PUBLICATIONS - U.S.: 1981

473

United States. Congress. Senate. Committee on Banking, Housing

Print. Off., 1980. iii, 17 p. ; 24 cm. LC Card 80-603045 DDC 341.7/2 19
1. North Atlantic Treaty Organization. 2. United States - Armed Forces - Europe. I. Title.
KF26 .A768 1980

Vinson-Trammell act repeal or revision : hearings before the Subcommittee on Procurement Policy and Reprograming of the Committee on Armed Services, United States Senate, Ninety-sixth Congress, second session, on S. 1687 ... S. 2232 ... S. 2331 ... February 25, April 2, 1980. Washington : U. S. Govt. Print. Off., 1980. iii, 171 p. ; 24 cm. LC Card 80-603036 DDC 346.73/023 19
1. Defense contracts - United States. 2. United States - Armed Forces - Procurement. 3. Profit - United States. I. Title.
KF26 .A768 1980a

United States. Congress. Senate. Committee on Armed Services. Subcommittee on Research and Development. Davison, Richard H. The U. S. sea-based strategic force . [Washington, D.C.] [1980] xx, 62 p. : LC Card 80-601190 DDC 359.8/3 19
V993 .D38

United States. Congress. Senate. Committee on Banking, Housing, and Union Affairs. Federal Reserve's second monetary policy report for 1980 : hearings before the Committee on Banking, Housing, and Urban Affairs, United States Senate, Ninety-sixth Congress, second session ... July 21 and 22, 1980. Washington : U. S. Govt. Print. Off., 1980. vii, 329 p. : ill. ; 24 cm. LC Card 80-603797 DDC 332.4/973 19
1. Monetary policy - United States. 2. Federal Reserve banks. I. Title.
KF26 .B39 1980v

United States. Congress. Senate. Committee on Banking, Housing and Urban Affairs. (Old Catalog form: United States. Banking, Housing and Urban Affairs, Committee on (Senate)) // Hearings printed in 1978 and later are available only in microform. Please consult the librarians in the Economic and Public Affairs Division.
Ansett loan and export-import aircraft financing policies : hearings before the Committee on Banking, Housing, and Urban Affairs, United States Senate, Ninety-sixth Congress, second session ... May 12 and 13, 1980. Washington : U. S. Govt. Print. Off., 1980. v, 354 p. : ill. ; 23 cm. LC Card 80-603409 DDC 332.1/54 19
1. Export-Import Bank of Washington. 2. Export credit - United States. 3. Ansett Transport Industries. I. Title.
KF26 .B39 1980t

Banks and narcotics money flow in south Florida : hearings before the Committee on Banking, Housing, and Urban Affairs, United States Senate, Ninety-sixth Congress, second session, on S. 2236 ... June 5 and 6, 1980. Washington : U. S. Govt. Print. Off., 1980. v, 245 p. ; 23 cm. LC Card 80-603356 DDC 346.73/082 19
1. Money - Law and legislation - United States. 2. Banking law - United States. 3. Money - Law and legislation - Florida. 4. Banking law - Florida. 5. Narcotics, Control of - Florida. I. Title.
KF26 .B39 1980j

Chrysler Corporation loan guarantee act : hearing before the Committee on Banking, Housing, and Urban Affairs, United States Senate, Ninety-sixth Congress, second session ... May 20, 1980. Washington : U. S. Govt. Print. Off., 1980. iv, 114 p. ; 24 cm. LC Card 80-603673 DDC 353.0082/42 19
1. Chrysler Corporation - Finance. 2. Automobile industry and trade - United States. - Finance. 3. Loans - United States - Government guaranty. I. Title.
KF26 .B39 1980r

Competition in Banking Act of 1980 : hearing before the Committee on Banking, Housing, and Urban Affairs, United States Senate, Ninety-sixth Congress, second session, on S. 39 ... S. 380 ... H.R. 2255 ... July 1, 1980. Washington : U. S. G.P.O., 1980. v, 322 p. : ill. ; 23 cm. LC Card 80-603440 DDC 346.73/082 347.30682 19
1. Bank holding companies - United States. 2. Banking law - United States. 3. Insurance law - United States. I. Title.
KF26 .B39 1980w

Cross-industry takeovers between commercial banks and thrift institutions : hearing before the Committee on Banking, Housing, and Urban Affairs, United States Senate, Ninety-sixth Congress, second session, on amendment to H.R. 5625 as passed by Senate, November 21, 1980. Washington : U. S. G.P.O., 1980 [i.e. 1981] iv, 148 p. ; 24 cm. Item 1035 Includes bibliographical references. LC Card 81-601367 DDC 346.73/082 347.30682 19
1. Banking law - United States. 2. Saving-banks - Law and legislation - United States. 3. Bank mergers - United States. 4. Antitrust law - United States. I. Title.
KF26 .B39 1980aa

Depository Institutions Deregulation Committee : hearing before the Committee on Banking, Housing, and Urban Affairs, United States Senate, Ninety-sixth Congress, second session ... August 5, 1980. Washington : U. S. Govt. Print. Off., 1980. vi, 307 p. ; 24 cm. LC Card 80-603707 DDC 346.73/082 19
1. Banking law - United States. 2. Usury laws - United States. I. Title.
KF26 .B39 1980o

Export promotion, export disincentives, and U. S. competitiveness . Washington , 1980. iii, 612 p. : LC Card 80-603880 DDC 382/.63/0973 19
HF1455 .E93

Extension of the Council on Wage and Price Stability and review of the President's anti-inflation policies : hearings before the Committee on Banking, Housing, and Urban Affairs, United States Senate, Ninety-sixth Congress, second session, on S. 2352 .... Washington, D.C. : U. S. Govt. Print. Off., 1980. v, 452 p. : ill. ; 24 cm. Hearings held Mar. 10-Apr. 21, 1980. LC Card 80-602778 DDC 343.73/034 347.30334 19
1. United States. Council on Wage and Price Stability. 2. Inflation (Finance) - United States. I. Title.
KF26 .B39 1980h

Farm credit and the banking system : hearing before the Committee on Banking, Housing, and Urban Affairs, United States Senate, Ninety-sixth Congress, second session ... June 26, 1980. Washington : U. S. Govt. Print. Off., 1980. iv, 113 p. ; 24 cm. LC Card 80-603335 DDC 332.7/1/0973 19
1. Agricultural credit - United States. 2. Banks and banking - United States. 3. Farm Credit System (United States.). I. Title.
KF26 .B39 1980k

Federal Reserve's first monetary policy report for 1981 : hearings before the Committee on Banking, Housing, and Urban Affairs, United States Senate, Ninety-seventh Congress, first session, on oversight on monetary policy report to Congress pursuant to Public Law 95-523, February 25 and March 4, 1981. Washington : U. S. G.P.O., 1981. iv, 245 p. : ill. ; 24 cm. "97-8." Item 1035-C, 1035-D (microfiche) Bibliography: p. 133. LC Card 81-601769 DDC 332.4/973 19
1. Monetary policy - United States. 2. Board of Governors of the Federal Reserve System (U. S.). I. Title.
KF26 .B39 1981e

Financial institutions and export trading companies : hearing before the Committee on Banking, Housing, and Urban Affairs, United States Senate, Ninety-sixth Congress, second session on S. 2718 ... July 25, 1980. Washington : U. S. Govt. Print. Off., 1980. iv, 363 p. ; 24 cm. Includes bibliographical references. LC Card 80-603702 DDC 346.73/082 347.30682 19
1. Export associations - Law and legislation - United States. 2. Banking law - United States. I. Title.
KF26 .B39 1980q

Foreign takeovers of United States banks . [Washington, D.C.] , Washington , 1980. vi, 75 p. ; LC Card 81-601509 DDC 332.1/6 19
HG2491 .F64

Fourth meeting on the condition of the financial system : hearing before the Committee on Banking, Housing, and Urban Affairs, United States Senate, Ninety-sixth Congress, second session ... May 21, 1980. Washington : U. S. Govt. Print. Off., 1980. viii, 1096 p. : graphs ; 24 cm. LC Card 80-603722 DDC 332.1/0973 19
1. Banks and banking - United States. 2. Credit unions - United States. 3. Building and loan

associations - United States. I. Title.
KF26 .B39 1980u

Further matters relating to the nomination of G. William Miller : hearing before the Committee on Banking, Housing, and Urban Affairs, United States Senate, Ninety-sixth Congress, second session, on the nomination of G. William Miller to be chairman of the Board of Governors of the Federal Reserve System, February 8, 1980. Washington : U. S. G.P.O., c1980 [i.e. 1981]-1980. 2 v. ; 24 cm. Item 1035 CONTENTS. - pt. I. Testimony before the Committee -- pt. II. Appendix--consisting of staff report of Securities and Exchange Commission and complaint in re Textron, Inc. LC Card 81-601175 DDC 353/.0082/5 19
1. Miller, G. William (George William), 1925-. 2. Board of Governors of the Federal Reserve System (U. S.) - Officials and employees. I. Title.
KF26 .B39 1980z

Home mortgage disclosure amendments of 1980 : hearings before the Committee on Banking, Housing, and Urban Affairs, United States Senate, Ninety-sixth Congress, second session, on S. 2290 ... S. 2291 .... Washington : U. S. Govt. Print. Off., 1980- v. : ill. ; 24 cm. CONTENTS. - Pt. 1. Proceedings of Feb. 19-March 3, 1980. LC Card 80-603511 DDC 346.7304/364 19
1. Mortgage loans - United States. 2. Discrimination in mortgage loans - Law and legislation - United States. I. Title.
KF26 .B39 1980m

Implementation and enforcement of Fair mortgage lending laws and regulations : hearings before the Committee on Banking, Housing, and Urban Affairs, United States, Senate, Ninety-sixth Congress, first session ... December 20 and 21, 1979. Washington : U. S. Govt. Print. Off., 1980. iv, 314 p. ; 23 cm. LC Card 80-602520 DDC 353.0082/5 19
1. Discrimination in mortgage loans - United States. 2. Discrimination in mortgage loans - Law and legislation - United States. I. Title.
KF26 .B39 1979al

Implementation of the Credit control act : hearing before the Committee on Banking, Housing, and Urban Affairs, United States Senate, Ninety-sixth Congress, second session ... March 18, 1980. Washington : U. S. Govt. Print. Off., 1980. iii, 223 p. : ill. ; 23 cm. LC Card 80-602532 DDC 353.0082/5 19
1. Credit control - Law and legislation - United States. 2. Credit control - United States. I. Title.
KF26 .B39 1980f

Margin requirements for transactions in financial instruments : hearings before the Committee on Banking, Housing, and Urban Affairs, United States Senate, Ninety-sixth Congress, second session, on S. 2704 ... May 29 and 30, 1980. Washington : U. S. Govt. Print. Off., 1980. vii, 850 p. : ill. ; 24 cm. Includes bibliographical references. LC Card 80-603509 DDC 346.73/0922 19
1. Commodity exchanges - Law and legislation - United States. 2. Government securities - Law and legislation - United States. 3. Precious metals - Law and legislation - United States. 4. Speculation. I. Title. II. Title: Financial instruments.
KF26 .B39 1980r

Nominations of Robert E. Herzstein, Frank B. Sollars, Alexis M. Herman, and Alfred R. Marane : hearing before the Committee on Banking, Housing, and Urban Affairs, United States Senate, Ninety-sixth Congress, second session ... May 28, 1980. Washington : U. S. Govt. Print. Off., 1980. iii, 78 p. ; 24 cm. Hearing on the nominations of Robert E. Herzstein, to be Under Secretary of Commerce for International Trade; Frank B. Sollars, to be a Director of the National Consumer Cooperative Bank; Alexis M. Herman, to be a Director of the National Consumer Cooperative Bank; and Alfred R. Marane, to be General Manager, New Community Development Corporation. LC Card 80-603063 DDC 353.82 19
1. United States. Dept. of Commerce - Officials and employees. 2. National Consumer Cooperative Bank - Employees. 3. United States. Dept. of Housing and Urban Development - Officials and employees. I. Title.
KF26 .B39 1980i

Nomination of Barbara S. Thomas : hearing before the Committee on Banking, Housing, and Urban Affairs, United States Senate, Ninety-sixth Congress, second session, on the

BIBLIOGRAPHIC GUIDE

United States. Congress. Senate. Committee on Banking, Housing

474

nomination of Barbara S. Thomas to be a member of the Securities and Exchange Commission, August 19, 1980. Washington : U. S. Govt. Print. Off., 1980. ii, 61 p. ; 23 cm.
LC Card 80-603679   DDC 353.0082/58 19
1. Thomas, Barbara S., 1946-. 2. United States. Securities and Exchange Commission - Officials and employees. I. Title.
KF26 .B39 1980s

Nomination of Donald I. Hovde : hearing before the Committee on Banking, Housing, and Urban Affairs, United States Senate, Ninety-seventh Congress, first session, on the nomination of Donald I. Hovde to be under secretary of the Department of Housing and Urban Development, February 24, 1981. Washington : U. S. G.P.O., 1981. iii, 49 p. ; 24 cm. "97-7." Item 1035-C, 1035-D (microfiche)   LC Card 81-601780   DDC 353.85 19
1. Hovde, Donald I., 1931-. 2. United States. Dept. of Housing and Urban Development - Officials and employees. I. Title.
KF26 .B39 1981b

Nomination of John S. R. Shad : hearing before the Committee on Banking, Housing, and Urban Affairs, United States Senate, Ninety-seventh Congress, first session, on the nomination of John S.R. Shad, to be a member of the Securities and Exchange Commission for the remainder of the term expiring June 5, 1982, and to be a member of the Securities and Exchange Commission for the term of 5 years expiring June 5, 1986, April 6, 1981. Washington : U. S. Govt. Print. Off., 1981. ii, 34 p. ; 24 cm. "97-11." Item 1035-C, 1035-D (microfiche)   LC Card 81-601937   DDC 353.0082/58 19
1. Shad, John S. R., 1923-. 2. United States. Securities and Exchange Commission - Officials and employees. I. Title.
KF26 .B39 1981h

Nomination of Lyle E. Gramley : hearings before the Committee on Banking, Housing, and Urban Affairs, United States Senate, Ninety-sixth Congress, second session, on the nomination of Lyle E. Gramley to be a member of the Board of Governors of the Federal Reserve System, April 15 and 16, 1980. Washington, D.C. : U. S. Govt. Print. Off., 1980. iii, 124 p. : graphs ; 24 cm.   LC Card 80-602772   DDC 353.0082/5 19
1. Gramley, Lyle E. 2. United States. Board of Governors of the Federal Reserve System - Officials and employees. I. Title.
KF26 .B39 1980g

Nomination of Murray L. Weidenbaum : hearing before the Committee on Banking, Housing, and Urban Affairs, United States Senate, Ninety-seventh Congress, first session, on the nomination of Murray L. Weidenbaum to be chairman of the Council of Economic Advisers, February 5, 1981. Washington : U. S. G.P.O., 1981. iii, 114 p. ; 24 cm. "97-3." Item 1035-C, 1035-D (microfiche)   LC Card 81-601619   DDC 353.0082 19
1. Weidenbaum, Murray L. 2. Council of Economic Advisers (U. S.) - Officials and employees. I. Title.
KF26 .B39 1981a

Nomination of Richard T. Pratt : hearing before the Committee on Banking, Housing, and Urban Affairs, United States Senate, Ninety-seventh Congress, first session, on the nomination of Richard T. Pratt, to be a member of the Federal Home Loan Bank Board for the remainder of the term expiring June 30, 1981, and to be a member of the Federal Home Loan Bank Board for the term expiring June 30, 1985 (reappointment), April 6, 1981. Washington : U. S. G.P.O., 1981. iii, 49 p. ; 24 cm. "97-10." Item 1035-C, 1035-D (microfiche)   LC Card 81-601950   DDC 353.0082/5 19
1. Pratt, Richard Thomas, 1937-. 2. United States. Federal Home Loan Bank Board - Officials and employees. I. Title.
KF26 .B39 1981d

Nomination of Samuel R. Pierce, Jr. : hearing before the Committee on Banking, Housing, and Urban Affairs, United States Senate, Ninety-seven Congress, first session, on the nomination of Samuel R. Pierce, Jr., to be secretary of the Department of Housing and Urban Development, January 13, 1981. Washington : U. S. G.P.O., 1981. iii, 95 p. ; 24

cm. "97-2." Item 1035-C, 1035-D (microfiche)   LC Card 81-601350   DDC 353.85 19
1. Pierce, Samuel R., 1922-. 2. United States. Dept. of Housing and Urban Development - Officials and employees. I. Title.
KF26 .B39 1981c

Nomination of Stephen M. Goldfeld : hearing before the Committee on Banking, Housing, and Urban Affairs, United States Senate, Ninety-sixth Congress, second session, on the nomination of Stephen M. Goldfeld to be a member of the Council of Economic Advisers, July 23, 1980. Washington : U. S. Govt. Print. Off., 1980. ii 23 p. ; 24 cm.   LC Card 80-603302   DDC 353.09/3 19
1. Goldfeld, Stephen M. 2. United States. Council of Economic Advisers - Officials and employees. I. Title.
KF26 .B39 1980l

Nomination of Wayman D. Palmer : hearing before the Committee on Banking, Housing, and Urban Affairs, United States Senate, Ninety-sixth Congress, second session ... September 8, 1980. Washington : U. S. Govt. Print. Off., 1980. ii, 13 p. ; 24 cm.   LC Card 80-603651   DDC 353.0082/52045 19
1. Palmer, Wayman DuBois, 1927-. 2. National Consumer Cooperative Bank - Employees. I. Title.
KF26 .B39 1980p

Nominations of Herta Lande Seidman and Stephen J. Friedman : hearing before the Committee on Banking, Housing, and Urban Affairs, United States Senate, Ninety-sixth Congress, second session ... April 1, 1980. Washington : U. S. Govt. Print. Off., 1980. iii, 53 p. : forms ; 23 cm. Hearing on nominations of H. L. Seidman, to be Assistant Secretary for Trade Development, Dept. of Commerce, S. J. Friedman, to be Commissioner, Securities and Exchange Commission.
LC Card 80-602446   DDC 353.82 19
1. Seidman, Herta Lande, 1939-. 2. Friedman, Stephen J., 1938-. 3. United States. Dept. of Commerce - Officials and employees. 4. United States. Securities and Exchange Commission - Officials and employees. I. Title.
KF26 .B39 1980c

Nominations of Philip D. Winn, John J. Knapp, Emanuel S. Savas, and Arthur E. Teele, Jr., : hearing before the Committee on Banking, Housing, and Urban Affairs, United States Senate, Ninety-seventh Congress, first session, on the nominations of Philip D. Winn, to be assistant secretary for housing--FHA commissioner, John J. Knapp, to be general counsel, and Emanuel S. Savas, to be assistant secretary for policy development and research for the Department of Housing and Urban Development, and Arthur E. Teele, Jr., to be urban mass transportation administrator, March 24, 1981. Washington : U. S. G.P.O., 1981. iii, 136 p. ; 24 cm. "97-9." Item 1035-C, 1035-D (microfiche)   LC Card 81-601958   DDC 353.85 19
1. United States. Dept. of Housing and Urban Development - Officials and employees. 2. United States. Dept. of Transportation - Officials and employees. I. Title.
KF26 .B39 1981f

Suspension of United States exports of high technology and grain to the Soviet Union : hearings before the Committee on Banking, Housing, and Urban Affairs, United States Senate, Ninety-sixth Congress, second session, to assess the effectiveness of trade measures taken by the president under authority provided by the Export Administration Act of 1979, August 19 and 20, 1980. Washington : U. S.G.P.O., 1980. v, 156 p. : ill. ; 24 cm.   LC Card 80-604066   DDC 382/.4131/0973 19
1. Export controls - United States. 2. Grain trade - United States. 3. United States - Foreign economic relations - Soviet Union. 4. Soviet Union - Foreign economic relations - United States. I. Title.
KF26 .B39 1980x

Transfer of Cost Accounting Standards Board : hearing before the Committee on Banking, Housing, and Urban Affairs, United States Senate, Ninety-sixth Congress, second session, on proposals to transfer the residual functions of the Cost Accounting Standards Board to the Office of Management and Budget, September 23, 1980. Washington : U. S. G.P.O., 1980. iii, 67 p. ; 24 cm.   LC Card 80-604039   DDC 353.0071/2044 19
1. United States. Cost Accounting Standards Board. 2.

United States. Office of Management and Budget. 3. Cost accounting - Standards - United States. 4. Defense contracts - United States. I. Title.
KF26 .B39 1980y

United States. Securities and Exchange Commission. Report of the Securities and Exchange Commission on beneficial ownership reporting requirements pursuant to section 13(h) of the Securities exchange act of 1934. Washington , 1980. viii, 242 p. ;   LC Card 80-602870   DDC 346.73/0666 19
KF1448 .A88

United States. Securities and Exchange Commission. Division of Corporation Finance. Staff report on corporate accountability . Washington , 1980. 782 p. ;   LC Card 80-603877   DDC 346.73/0666 347.306666 19
KF1448 .A8837

1980 budgets of the Federal bank regulatory agencies : hearing before the Committee on Banking, Housing, and Urban Affairs, United States Senate, Ninety-sixth Congress, second session ... January 25, 1980. Washington : U. S. Govt. Print. Off., 1980. v, 1323 p. ; 24 cm.   LC Card 80-601901   DDC 353.0072/236825 19
1. United States. Board of Governors of the Federal Reserve System - Appropriations and expenditures. 2. United States. Comptroller of the Currency - Appropriations and expenditures. 3. Federal Deposit Insurance Corporation - Appropriations and expenditures. I. Title.
KF26 .B39 1980e

United States. Congress. Senate. Committee on Banking, Housing and Urban Affairs. Subcommittee on Consumer Affairs.
Cash Discount Act : hearing before the Subcommittee on Consumer Affairs of the Committee on Banking, Housing, and Urban Affairs, United States Senate, Ninety-seventh Congress, first session, on S. 414 ... February 18, 1981. Washington : U. S. G.P.O., c1981. iv, 136 p. ; 24 cm. "97-5." Item 1035-C, 1035-D (microfiche)   LC Card 81-601610   DDC 346.73/074 347.30673 19
1. Discount, Cash - Law and legislation - United States. I. Title.
KF26 .B3939 1981

Fair financial information practices act : hearings before the Subcommittee on Consumer Affairs of the Committee on Banking, Housing, and Urban Affairs, United States Senate, Ninety-sixth Congress, second session on S. 1928 ... January 31, and March 10 and 11, 1980. Washington : U. S. Govt. Print. Off., 1980- v. <1- > ; 24 cm. Includes bibliographical references. CONTENTS. - pt. 1. Insurance, title V.
LC Card 80-603510   DDC 343.73/071 347.30371 19
1. Consumer credit - Law and legislation - United States. 2. Consumer protection - Law and legislation - United States. 3. Data protection - United States. I. Title.
KF26 .B3939 1980

United States. Congress. Senate. Committee on Banking, Housing, and Urban Affairs. Subcommittee on Economic Stabilization.
Economic impact of payroll taxes : hearing before the Subcommittee on Economic Stabilization of the Committee on Banking, Housing, and Urban Affairs, United States Senate, Ninety-sixth Congress, second session ... March 13, 1980. Washington : U. S. Govt. Print. Off., 1980. iv, 65 p. : ill. ; 24 cm. Includes bibliographical references.   LC Card 80-602496   DDC 330.973/0926 19
1. Withholding tax - Economic aspects - United States. 2. Social security taxes - Economic aspects - United States. I. Title.
KF26 .B39425 1980a

The effect of expanding Japanese automobile imports on the domestic economy : hearing before the Subcommittee on Economic Stabilization of the Committee on Banking, Housing, and Urban Affairs, United States Senate, Ninety-sixth Congress, second session, April 3, 1980. Washington : U. S. Govt. Print. Off., 1980. iv, 114 p. : ill. ; 23 cm. Includes bibliographical references.   LC Card 80-602726   DDC 330.973/0926 19
1. Automobile industry and trade - United States. 2. Automobile industry and trade - Japan. 3. Automobile industry and trade. 4. Foreign trade regulation - United

States. I. Title.
KF26 .B39425 1980b

Interest rates and inflation : hearing before the Subcommittee on Economic Stabilization of the Committee on Banking, Housing, and Urban Affairs, United States Senate, Ninety-sixth Congress, second session ... February 1, 1980. Washington : U. S. Govt. Print. Off., 1980. iv, 85 p. : graphs ; 24 cm.   LC Card 80-601980
    DDC 332.4/15/0973 19
1. Interest and usury - United States - Effect of inflation on. I. Title.
KF26 .B39425 1980

United States. Congress. Senate. Committee on Banking, Housing and Urban Affairs. Subcommittee on Financial Institutions.
Money market mutual funds : hearings before the Subcommittee on Financial Institutions of the Committee on Banking, Housing, and Urban Affairs, United States Senate, Ninety-sixth Congress, second session ... January 24 and 30, 1980. Washington : U. S. Govt. Print. Off., 1980. vii, 644 p. : ill. ; 23 cm. Includes bibliographical references.   LC Card 80-602492   DDC 353.0082/58 19
1. Investment trusts - United States. 2. Certificates of deposit - United States. I. Title.
KF26 .B3943 1980

United States. Congress. Senate. Committee on Banking, Housing and Urban Affairs. Subcommittee on Housing and Urban Affairs.
Amending the Urban mass transportation act : hearings before the Subcommittee on Housing and Urban Affairs of the Committee on Banking, Housing, and Urban Affairs, United States Senate, Ninety-sixth Congress, second session ... March 6 and 19, 1980. Washington : U. S. Govt. Print. Off., 1980. v, 504 p. ; 24 cm. Bibliography: p. 131-132.   LC Card 80-602812 DDC 343.73/098 19
1. Local transit - Law and legislation - United States. I. Title.
KF26 .B3945 1980a

Federal role in conventional home financing : hearing before the Subcommittee on Housing and Urban Affairs of the Committee on Banking, Housing, and Urban Affairs, United States Senate, Ninety-seventh Congress, first session, oversight on the current status of home finance, particularly alternative mortgage instruments, and the role and status of the secondary mortgage market, April 7, 1981. Washington : U. S. G.P.O., 1981. iv, 215 p. : ill. ; 23 cm. "97-13." Item 1035-C, 1035-D (microfiche) Includes bibliographical references.   LC Card 81-602181   DDC 353.0086/5045 19
1. Mortgages - United States. 2. Housing - United States - Finance. 3. Housing policy - United States. I. Title.
KF26 .B39 1981i

Housing and community development act of 1980 : hearings before the Subcommittee on Housing and Urban Affairs of the Committee on Banking, Housing, and Urban Affairs, United States Senate, Ninety-sixth Congress, second session, on S. 2383 .... Washington, D.C. : U. S. Govt. Print. Off., 1980. xi, 1015 p. ; 24 cm. Hearings held Mar. 25-Apr. 29, 1980. Includes bibliographical references.   LC Card 80-603287   DDC 344.73/063635 19
1. Housing - Law and legislation - United States. 2. Community development - Law and legislation - United States. I. Title.
KF26 .B3945 1980c

Rental housing : hearing before the Subcommittee on Housing and Urban Affairs of the Committee on Banking, Housing, and Urban Affairs, United States Senate, Ninety-sixth Congress, second session. Washington : U. S. Govt. Print. Off., 1980. 3 v. : ill. ; 24 cm. Hearings held in Washington, D.C. and Bayonne, N.J., Feb. 27-Apr. 18, 1980. CONTENTS. - pt. 1. Administration's views on rental housing legislation.--pt. 2-3. Problems and solutions.
    LC Card 80-602974   DDC 338.4/73635/0973 19
1. Rental housing - United States. 2. Housing policy - United States. 3. Rental housing - New Jersey. 4. Rental housing - Law and legislation - United States. I. Title.
KF26 .B3945 1980b

United States. Congress. Senate. Committee on Banking, Housing and Urban Affairs.

Subcommittee on International Finance.
Competitive export financing : hearing before the Subcommittee on International Finance of the Committee on Banking, Housing, and Urban Affairs, United States Senate, Ninety-sixth Congress, second session, on S. 2339 ... S. 2340 ... May 22, 1980. Washington : U. S. Govt. Print. Off., 1980. iv, 208 p. : ill. ; 24 cm.   LC Card 80-603294   DDC 346.73/082154 347.30682154 19
1. Export credit - United States. 2. Foreign trade promotion - Law and legislation - United States. I. Title.
KF26 .B3946 1980e

Export trading company act of 1980 : hearings before the Subcommittee on International Finance of the Committee on Banking, Housing, and Urban Affairs, United States Senate, Ninety-sixth Congress, second session, on S. 2379 ... S. 864 ... and Amendment no. 1674 to S. 864, March 17 and 18, and April 3, 1980. Washington : U. S. Govt. Print. Off., 1980. vi, 372 p. ; 24 cm. Includes bibliographical references.   LC Card 80-602761 DDC 343.73/0878/0262 19
1. Export associations - Law and legislation. 2. Export sales - Law and legislation. 3. Business enterprises - United States. 4. Foreign trade regulation - United States. I. Title.
KF26 .B3946 1980b

International Monetary Fund and related legislation : hearings before the Subcommittee on International Finance of the Committee on Banking, Housing, and Urban Affairs, United States Senate, Ninety-sixth Congress, second session, on S. 2514 ... S. 2271 ... S. 1963 ... March 31 and April 15 and 16, 1980. Washington : U. S. Govt. Print. Off., 1980. iii, 237 p. ; 24 cm.   LC Card 80-602906 DDC 346.73/082152 19
1. United States. Treasury Dept. - Appropriations and expenditures. 2. International Monetary Fund. 3. Gold - Law and legislation - United States. I. Title.
KF26 .B3946 1980c

Small business export assistance : hearing before the Subcommittee on International Finance of the Committee on Banking, Housing, and Urban Affairs, United States Senate, Ninety-sixth Congress, second session, on S. 2040, S. 2097, and S. 2104 ... April 28, 1980. Washington : U. S. Govt. Print. Off., 1980. iv, 143 p. ; 24 cm.   LC Card 80-603092   DDC 343.73/0878 19
1. Small business - Law and legislation - United States. 2. Foreign trade promotion - Law and legislation - United States. I. Title.
KF26 .B3946 1980d

U. S. embargo of food and technology to the Soviet Union : hearings before the Subcommittee on International Finance of the Committee on Banking, Housing, and Urban Affairs, United States Senate, Ninety-sixth Congress, second session ... January 22, and March 24, 1980. Washington : U. S. Govt. Print. Off., 1980. v, 250 p. ; 23 cm.   LC Card 80-602113   DDC 382/.64/0973 19
1. Export controls - United States. 2. United States - Foreign relations - Russia. 3. Russia - Foreign relations - United States. 4. Russia - Foreign relations - Afghanistan. 5. Afghanistan - Foreign relations - Russia. I. Title.
KF26 .B3946 1980a

United States. Congress. Senate. Committee on Banking, Housing, and Urban Affairs. Subcommittee on Rural Housing and Development.
Energy conservation, rural housing, and the use of urea-formaldehyde foamed-in place insulation : hearing before the Subcommittee on Rural Housing and Development of the Committee on Banking, Housing, and Urban Affairs, United States Senate, Ninety-sixth Congress, first session ... December 19, 1979. Washington : U. S. Govt. Print. Off., 1980. iv, 127 p. ; 24 cm.   LC Card 80-601943 DDC 693.8/32/028 19
1. Dwellings - United States - Insulation. 2. Urethane foam - United States. 3. Urethane foam - Toxicology. I. Title.
KF26 .B3953 1979a

Rural housing oversight and reauthorizations : hearings before the Subcommittee on Rural Housing and Development of the Committee on Banking, Housing, and Urban Affairs, United

States Senate, Ninety-sixth Congress, second session, on S. 2647 ... S. 2650 ... April 1 and 30, 1980. Washington : U. S. Govt. Print. Off., 1980. iv, 234 p. : graphs ; 23 cm.   LC Card 80-602981   DDC 344.73/063635 19
1. Housing, Rural - Law and legislation - United States. 2. Housing, Rural - United States - Finance. I. Title.
KF26 .B3953 1980

United States. Congress. Senate. Committee on Banking, Housing and Urban Affairs. Subcommittee on Securities.
Authorization request for the Securities and Exchange Commission : hearing before the Subcommittee on Securities of the Committee on Banking, Housing, and Urban Affairs, United States Senate, Ninety-sixth Congress, second session, on S. 2465 ... March 24, 1980. Washington : U. S. Govt. Print. Off., 1980. iii, 163 p. : ill. ; 24 cm.   LC Card 80-602805   DDC 346.73/0666 19
1. United States. Securities and Exchange Commission - Appropriations and expenditures. I. Title.
KF26 .B3954 1980

Federal securities laws and small business legislation : hearings before the Subcommittee on Securities of the Committee on Banking, Housing, and Urban Affairs, United States Senate, Ninety-sixth Congress, second session, on S. 1533 ... S. 1940 ... S. 2699 ... April 29, May 16, and June 2, 1980. Washington : U. S. Govt. Print. Off., 1980. ix, 812 p. ; 23 cm.
    LC Card 80-603327   DDC 346.73/0666 19
1. Securities - United States. 2. Small business - Law and legislation - United States. 3. Small business investment companies. I. Title.
KF26 .B3954 1980a

Protection of Shareholders' Rights Act of 1980 : hearing before the Subcommittee on Securities of the Committee on Banking, Housing, and Urban Affairs, United States Senate, Ninety-sixth Congress, second session, on S. 2567 ... November 19, 1980. Washington : U. S. G.P.O., 1981. iv, 479 p. : ill. ; 24 cm. Item 1035 Includes bibliographic references.   LC Card 81-601417   DDC 346.73/0666 347.306666 19
1. Corporation law - United States. 2. Directors of corporations - Legal status, laws, etc. - United States. 3. Stockholders - Legal status, laws, etc. - United States. I. Title.
KF26 .B3954 1980b

United States. Congress. Senate. Committee on Commerce, Science, and Transportation.
Hearings printed in 1978 and later are available only in microform. Please consult the librarians in the Economic and Public Affairs Division.
Agreement governing the activities of states on the moon and other celestial bodies /. Washington , 1980. ix, 264 p. ;   LC Card 80-602580   DDC 341.4/6 19
JX5810 .A37

Beverage container reuse and recycling act of 1979 : hearing before the Committee on Commerce, Science, and Transportation, United States Senate, Ninety-sixth Congress, second session, on S. 50 ... March 3, 1980. Washington : U. S. Govt. Print. Off., 1980. iii, 69 p. ; 24 cm. "Serial no. 96-102." LC Card 80-602792 DDC 344.73/04622 19
1. Beverage containers - Law and legislation - United States. 2. Recycling (Waste, etc.) - Law and legislation - United States. 3. Refuse and refuse disposal - Law and legislation - United States. 4. Beverage containers - United States - Recycling. I. Title.
KF26 .C69 1980j

Christainsen, Gregory. Environmental and health/safety regulations, productivity growth, and economic performance . Washington , 1980. v, 94 p. :   LC Card 80-603059   DDC 339/.0973 19
HC110.E5 C5

Coast Guard authority : hearing before the Committee on Commerce, Science, and Transportation, United States Senate, Ninety-sixth Congress, second session on S. 2523 ... and H.R. 1198 ... May 21, 1980. Washington : U. S. G.P.O., 1980. iii, 104 p. ; 24 cm. "Serial no. 96-123." LC Card 81-600824 DDC 343.73/0965 347.303965 19
1. Ships - Inspection - United States. 2. Ships - Manning - Law and legislation - United States. 3. Coastwise navigation - Law and legislation - United

States. 4. *Territorial waters - United States. 5. United States. Coast Guard. I. Title.*
KF26 .C69 1980x

Coast Guard authorizations : hearing before the Committee on Commerce, Science, and Transportation, United States Senate, Ninety-sixth Congress, second session, on S. 2489 ... April 23, 1980. Washington : U. S. Govt. Print. Off., 1980. iii, 59 p. ; 24 cm. "Serial no. 96-100." LC Card 80-602815 DDC 353.0072/23674 19
1. United States. Coast Guard - Appropriations and expenditures. I. Title.
KF26 .C69 1980l

Coastal Zone Management Act amendments of 1980 : hearing before the Committee on Commerce, Science, and Transportation, United States Senate, Ninety-sixth Congress, second session, on S. 2622 ... April 30, 1980. Washington : U. S. G.P.O., 1980. iv, 142 p. ; 24 cm. "Serial no. 96-116." LC Card 80-604037 DDC 346.7304/6917 347.30646917 19
1. Coastal zone management - Law and legislation - United States. I. Title.
KF26 .C69 1980t

Energy from open ocean kelp farms /. Washington , 1980. ix, 82 p. : LC Card 80-603976 DDC 333.95/3 19
TP360 .E54

Georges Bank protection act : joint hearing before the Committee on Commerce, Science, and Transportation and the Subcommittee on Energy Resources and Materials Production of the Committee on Energy and Natural Resources, United States Senate, Ninety-sixth Congress, second session, on S. 2119 ... March 25, 1980. Washington : U. S. Govt. Print. Off., 1980. iii, 123 p. ; 24 cm. "Serial no. 96-89." "Energy committee publication no. 96-96." Bibliography: p. 47-52. LC Card 80-602169 DDC 346.7304/695616/0262 19
1. Fishery law and legislation - Georges Bank. 2. Fishery law and legislation - United States. I. United States. Congress. Senate. Committee on Energy and Natural Resources. Subcommittee on Energy Resources and Materials Production. II. Title.
KF26 .C69 1980f

The goals of the Committee on Commerce, Science, and Transportation for the first session of the 97th Congress / printed at the direction of Hon. Bob Packwood, chairman, for the use of the Committee on Commerce, Science, and Transportation, United States Senate. Washington : U. S. G.P.O., 1981. vii, 47 p. ; 24 cm. At head of title: 97th Congress, 1st session. Committee print. "February 26, 1981. Item 1041-A, 1041-B (microfiche) LC Card 81-601277 DDC 328.73/07652 19
1. United States. Congress. Senate. Committee on Commerce, Science, and Transportation. I. Packwood, Bob. II. Title.
JK1240.C57 U54 1981

The hazardous materials transportation amendments of 1980 : hearing before the Committee on Commerce, Science, and Transportation, United States Senate, Ninety-sixth Conress, second session, on staff working draft, "The hazardous materials transportation amendments of 1980," July 10, 1980. Washington : U. S. G.P.O., 1980. iii, 44 p. ; 23 cm. "Serial no. 96-121." LC Card 81-600580 DDC 343.73/093 347.30393 19
1. Hazardous substances - Transportation - Law and legislation - United States. I. Title.
KF26 .C69 1980u

Household goods transportation act of 1979 : hearings before the Committee on Commerce, Science, and Transportation, United States, Ninety-sixth Congress, first session, on S. 1798 ... June 19, September 26, and October 11, 1979. Washington : U. S. Govt. Print. Off., 1979 [i.e. 1980] iv, 413 p. ; 24 cm. "Serial no. 96-59." Includes bibliographical references. LC Card 80-601172 DDC 343.73/08856489 19
1. Storage and moving trade - Law and legislation - United States. 2. Storage and moving trade - Prices - United States. I. Title.
KF26 .C69 1979ac

Mount St. Helens impact : hearing before the Committee on Commerce, Science, and Transportation, United States Senate, Ninety-sixth Congress, second session ... June 13, 1980. Washington : U. S. Govt. Print. Off.,

1980. iv, 146 p. : ill. ; 24 cm. "Serial no. 96-108." LC Card 80-603517 DDC 363.3/495 19
1. Saint Helens, Mount, Wash. - Eruption, 1980. I. Title.
KF26 .C69 1980r

National Transportation Safety Board authorization : hearing before the Committee on Commerce, Science, and Transportation, United States Senate, Ninety-sixth Congress, second session, on S. 2459 ... March 27, 1980. Washington : U. S. Govt. Print. Off., 1980. iii, 26 p. ; 24 cm. "Serial no. 96-88." LC Card 80-602102 DDC 353.0072/236875 19
1. United States. National Transportation Safety Board - Appropriations and expenditures. 2. Transportation - Law and legislation - United States. I. Title.
KF26 .C69 1980h

Nomination--deputy secretary of commerce : hearing before the Committee on Commerce, Science, and Transportation, United States Senate, Ninety-seventh Congress, first session, on nomination of Joseph Robert Wright, Jr., to be deputy secretary of commerce, March 31, 1981. Washington : U. S. G.P.O., 1981. iii, 8 p. ; 24 cm. "Serial no. 97-11." Item 1041-A, 1041-B (microfiche) LC Card 81-601776 DDC 353.82 19
1. Wright, Joseph Robert, 1938-. 2. United States. Dept. of Commerce - Officials and employees. I. Title.
KF26 .C69 1981c

Nomination--deputy secretary of transportation : hearing before the Committee on Commerce, Science, and Transportation, United States Senate, Ninety-seventh Congress, first session, on nomination of Darrell Trent to be deputy secretary, Department of Transportation, January 19, 1981. Washington : U. S. G.P.O., 1981. iii, 25 p. ; 24 cm. Item 1041-A, 1041-B (microfiche) "Serial no. 97-3." LC Card 81-600981 DDC 353.86 19
1. Trent, Darrell Melvin, 1938-. 2. United States. Dept. of Transportation - Officials and employees. I. Title.
KF26 .C69 1981

Nomination--DOT : hearing before the Committee on Commerce, Science, and Transportation, United States Senate, Ninety-sixth Congress, second session, on nomination of Thomas G. Allison, to be General Counsel, Department of Transportation, May 6, 1980. Washington : U. S. Govt. Print. Off., 1980. iii, 13 p. ; 24 cm. "Serial no. 96-99." LC Card 80-602746 DDC 353.86 19
1. Allison, Thomas George, 1946-. 2. United States. Dept. of Transportation - Officials and employees. I. Title.
KF26 .C69 1980n

Nomination--National Transportation Board : hearing before the Committee on Commerce, Science, and Transportation, United States Senate, Ninety-sixth Congress, second session, on nomination of G. H. Patrick Bursley, to be a member, National Transportation Safety Board, May 22, 1980. Washington : U. S. Govt. Print. Off., 1980. iii, 8 p. ; 24 cm. "Serial no. 96-101." LC Card 80-602720 DDC 353.0087/5 19
1. Bursley, George Herbert Patrick, 1925-. 2. United States. National Transportation Safety Board - Officials and employees. I. Title.
KF26 .C69 1980k

Nomination--secretary of commerce : hearing before the Committee on Commerce, Science, and Transportation, United States Senate, Ninety-seventh Congress, first session, on nomination of Malcolm Baldrige to be secretary, Department of Commerce, January 6, 1981. Washington : U. S. G.P.O., 1981. iii, 46 p. ; 24 cm. "Serial no. 97-1." Item 1041-A, 1041-B (microfiche) LC Card 81-600818 DDC 353.82 19
1. Baldrige, Malcolm, 1922-. 2. United States. Dept. of Commerce - Officials and employees. I. Title.
KF26 .C69 1981a

Nomination--Secretary of Transportation : hearing before the Committee on Commerce, Science, and Transportation, United States Senate, Ninety-seventh Congress, first session, on nomination of Andrew L. Lewis, Jr., to be secretary, Department of Transportation, January 7, 1981. Washington : U. S. G.P.O., 1981. iii, 54 p. ; 24 cm. "Serial no. 97-2." Item 1041-A, 1041-B (microfiche) LC Card 81-600815 DDC 353.86 19
1. Lewis, Andrew Lindsay, 1931-. 2. United States. Dept. of Transportation - Officials and employees. I.

Title.
KF26 .C69 1981e

Nominations--Amtrak : hearing before the Committee on Commerce, Science, and Transportation, United States Senate, Ninety-sixth Congress, second session, on nomination of Athalie Range, James R. Mills, and Frank H. Neel, to be members, Board of Directors of Amtrak, April 15, 1980. Washington : U. S. Govt. Print. Off., 1980. iii, 24 p. ; 24 cm. "Serial no. 96-91." LC Card 80-602501 DDC 353.0087/5 19
1. Range, Athalie, 1916-. 2. Mills, James R., 1927-. 3. Neel, Frank H., 1916-. 4. Amtrak - Officials and employees. I. Title.
KF26 .C69 1980m

Nominations--assistant secretaries of commerce : hearing before the Committee on Commerce, Science, and Transportation, United States Senate, Ninety-seventh Congress, first session, on nominations of Arlene A. Triplett, to be assistant secretary of commerce for administration and Paul A. Vander Myde, to be assistant secretary of commerce for congressional affairs, April 29, 1981. Washington : U. S. G.P.O., 1981. iii, 4 p. ; 24 cm. "Serial no. 97-20." Item 1041-A, 1041-B (microfiche) LC Card 81-602035 DDC 353.82 19
1. Triplett, Arlene A. 2. Vander Myde, Paul A. 3. United States. Dept. of Commerce - Officials and employees. I. Title.
KF26 .C69 1981h

Nominations--August : hearings before the Committee on Commerce, Science, and Transportation, United States Senate, Ninety-sixth Congress, second session .... Washington : U. S. Govt. Print. Off., 1980. iii, 48 p. ; 23 cm. Hearings on nominations of Aug. 5 and 22, 1980. "Serial no. 96-114." LC Card 80-603804 DDC 353.0082 19
1. United States - Officials and employees. I. Title.
KF26 .C69 1980s

Nominations--Department of Commerce and Federal Maritime Commission : hearing before the Committee on Commerce, Science, and Transportation, United States Senate, Ninety-sixth Congress, first session, on nominations of Philip M. Klutznick, to be Secretary of Commerce; Luther H. Hodges, Jr., to be Deputy Secretary of Commerce; Homer E. Moyers, Jr., to be General Counsel, Department of Commerce; and James V. Day, to be a Commissioner, Federal Maritime Commission, December 19, 1979. Washington : U. S. Govt. Print. Off., 1980. iii, 81 p. ; 23 cm. "Serial no. 96-72." LC Card 80-601935 DDC 353.82 19
1. United States. Dept. of Commerce - Officials and employees. 2. United States. Federal Maritime Commission - Officials and employees. I. Title.
KF26 .C69 1979ak

Nominations--Departments of Commerce and Transportation : hearing before the Committee on Commerce, Science, and Transportation, United States Senate, Ninety-seventh Congress, first session, on nominations of Donald A. Derman, to be assistant secretary of transportation for budget and programs, Department of Transportation, and Sherman E. Unser, to be general counsel, Department of Commerce, April 24, 1981. Washington : U. S. G.P.O., 1981. iii, 5 p. ; 24 cm. "Serial no. 97-19." 1041-A, 1041-B (microfiche) LC Card 81-601952 DDC 353.82 19
1. Derman, Donald Allan, 1933-. 2. Unger, Sherman E., 1927-. 3. United States. Dept. of Transportation - Officials and employees. 4. United States. Dept. of Commerce - Officials and employees. I. Title.
KF26 .C69 1981g

Nominations--DOT : hearing before the Committee on Commerce, Science, and Transportation, United States Senate, Ninety-seventh Congress, first session, on nominations of Lee L.Verstandis, to be assistant secretary of transportation for governmental affairs, John M. Fowler, to be general counsel, Judith T. Connor, to be assistant secretary of transportation for policy and international affairs, and Robert W. Blanchette to be administrator, Federal Railroad Administration, March 4, 1981. Washington : U. S. G.P.O., 1981. iii, 35 p. ; 24 cm. "Serial no. 97-7." Item 1041-A, 1041-B (microfiche) LC Card 81-601783

DDC 353.86 19
1. United States. Dept. of Transportation - Officials and
employees. 2. United States. Federal Railroad
Administration - Officials and employees. I. Title.
KF26 .C69 1981b

Ocean thermal energy conversion act of 1980 :
hearings before the Committee on Commerce,
Science, and Transportation, United States
Senate, Ninety-sixth Congress, second session,
on S. 2492 ... April 10 and May 1, 1980.
Washington : U. S. Govt. Print. Off., 1980. iv,
164 p. : ill. ; 24 cm. "Serial no. 96-103." Includes
bibliographical references. LC Card 80-603076 DDC
346.7304/688 347.3064688 19
1. Ocean thermal power plants - Law and legislation -
United States. I. Title.
KF26 .C69 1980o

Recreational Boating Safety and Facilities
Improvement Act of 1979 : hearing before the
Committee on Commerce, Science, and
Transportation, United States Senate,
Ninety-sixth Congress, second session, on S.
1957 and H.R. 4310 ... June 19, 1980.
Washington : U. S. G.P.O., 1980. iii, 70 p. ; 24
cm. "Serial no. 96-120." LC Card 81-600592 DDC
344.73/0476 347.304476 19
1. Boats and boating - Law and legislation - United
States. I. Title.
KF26 .C69 1980v

Service Industries Development Act : hearings
before the Committee on Commerce, Science,
and Transportation, United States Senate,
Committee on Commerce, Science, and
Transportation, United States Senate,
Ninety-sixth Congress, second session, on S.
3003 ... September 24 and 25, 1980.
Washington : U. S.G.P.O., 1981. iii, 137 p. :
ill. ; 24 cm. "Serial no. 96-125." Bibliography: p.
113-114. Item 1041 LC Card 81-600931 DDC
343.73/078 347.30378 19
1. Service industries - Law and legislation - United
States. 2. United States - Commercial policy. 3. Service
industries. I. Title.
KF26 .C69 1980 w

U. S. commuter airline industry : hearings
before the Committee on Commerce, Science,
and Transportation, United States Senate,
Ninety-seventh Congress, first session, on status
of the U. S. commuter airline industry,
February 9 and 12, 1981. Washington : U. S.
G.P.O., 1981. iii, 91 p. : ill. ; 24 cm. "Serial no.
97-6." Item 1041-A, 1041-B (microfiche) LC Card
81-601625 DDC 387.7/42/0973 19
1. Aeronautics, Commercial - United States - Passenger
traffic. 2. Air lines, Local service - United States. I.
Title.
KF26 .C69 1981d

Unfairness . Washington , 1980. iii, 248 p. ;
   LC Card 80-602217 DDC 343.73/072 19
KF1603.5 .U55

United States. Congress. Office of Technology
Assessment. Technology and East-West trade.
Washington, D.C. , 1979. viii, 303 p. : LC Card
79-600203
HF1411 .U615 1979   NYPL [JLF 81-165]

United States. Congress. Senate. Committee on
Commerce, Science, and Transportation.
Subcommittee on Science, Technology, and
Space. Laser research and applications /.
Washington , 1980. xi, 32 p. ; LC Card
80-604121 DDC 621.36/6 19
TA1677 .U54 1980

United States. Congress. Senate. Committee on
Labor and Human Resources. Subcommittee on
Education, Arts, and Humanities.
Reauthorization of the national sea grant
college program . Washington , 1980. iii, 204
p. ; LC Card 80-603079 DDC 346.7304/695 19
KF26 .L2735 1980a

United States. Treaties, etc. Treaties and other
international agreements on fisheries,
oceanographic resources, and wildlife involving
the United States /. Washington , 1977. xv,
1201 p. ; LC Card 81-601815 DDC 341.7/62/026
19
JX236 1977 .U54

Washington State's salmon and steelhead
resources : hearings before the Committee on
Commerce, Science, and Transportation, United
States Senate, Ninety-sixth Congress, second
session, on S. 2163 ... February 11 and 12,
1980. Washington : U. S. Govt. Print. Off.,

1980. iv, 208 p. ; 24 cm. "Serial no. 96-80." LC
Card 80-603093 DDC 346.7304/6956 19
1. Salmon-fisheries - Law and legislation - Washington
(State). 2. Steelhead fishing - Law and legislation -
Washington (State). 3. Indians of North America -
Washington (State) - Legal status, laws, etc. 4. Indians
of North America - Washington (State) - Fishing. I.
Title.
KF26 .C69 1980p

**UNITED STATES. CONGRESS. SENATE.
COMMITTEE ON COMMERCE,
SCIENCE, AND TRANSPORTATION.**
United States. Congress. Senate. Committee on
Commerce, Science, and Transportation. The
goals of the Committee on Commerce, Science,
and Transportation for the first session of the
97th Congress /. Washington , 1981. vii, 47 p. ;
   LC Card 81-601277 DDC 328.73/07652 19
JK1240.C57 U54 1981

**United States. Congress. Senate. Committee on
Commerce, Science, and Transportation.
Aviation, Subcommittee on. see United States.
Congress. Senate. Committee on Commerce,
Science, and Transportation. Subcommittee
on Aviation.**

**United States. Congress. Senate. Committee on
Commerce, Science, and Transportation.
Merchant Marine and Tourism.
Subcommittee on . see United States.
Congress. Senate. Committee on Commerce,
Science, and Transportation. Subcommittee
on Merchant Marine and Tourism.**

**United States. Congress. Senate. Committee on
Commerce, Science, and Transportation.
Subcommittee for Consumers.**
Administrative law judge system : hearings
before the Subcommittee for Consumers of the
Committee on Commerce, Science, and
Transportation, United States Senate,
Ninety-sixth Congress, second session ...
September 4 and 5, 1980. Washington : U. S.
G.P.O., 1980. iii, 132 p. ; 23 cm. "Serial no.
96-117." LC Card 80-603889 DDC 342.73/0664
347.302664 19
1. Examiners (Administrative procedure) - United
States. I. Title.
KF26 .C693 1980c

Alcohol-impaired driver act : hearing before the
Subcommittee for Consumers of the Committee
on Commerce, Science, and Transportation,
United States Senate, Ninety-sixth Congress,
second session, on S. 2816 ... July 1, 1980.
Washington : U. S. Govt. Print. Off., 1980. iii,
95 p. : graphs ; 24 cm. "Serial no. 96-109." LC
Card 80-603636 DDC 345.73/0247 347.305247
19
1. Drunk driving - United States. I. Title.
KF26 .C693 1980b

Fire Prevention and Control Act
reauthorization : hearing before the
Subcommittee for Consumers of the Committee
on Commerce, Science, and Transportation,
United States Senate, Ninety-seventh Congress,
Science, first session, on reauthorization of the
Fire Prevention and Control Act of 1974,
March 11, 1981. Washington : U. S. G.P.O.,
1981. iii, 56 p. ; 24 cm. "Serial no. 97-9." Item
1041-A, 1041-B (microfiche) LC Card 81-601855
DDC 353.0078/2 19
1. Federal aid to fire prevention - United States. 2.
United States Fire Administration - Appropriations and
expenditures. I. Title.
KF26 .C693 1981

FTC mobile home sales and service rule :
hearing before the Subcommittee for Consumers
of the Committee on Commerce, Science, and
Transportation, United States Senate,
Ninety-sixth Congress, second session ... August
20, 1980. Washington : U. S. Govt. Print. Off.,
1980. iii, 187 p. : graphs ; 24 cm. "Serial no.
96-112." LC Card 80-603706 DDC 346.7304/3 19
1. Mobile homes - Law and legislation - United States.
2. Mobile homes - United States - Purchasing. 3.
Mobile homes - United States - Maintenance and
repair. I. Title.
KF26 .C693 1980a

Reauthorization of the Federal fire prevention
and control act : hearing before the
Subcommittee for Consumers of the Committee
on Commerce, Science, and Transportation,
United States Senate, Ninety-sixth Congress,
second session ... March 27, 1980.
Washington : U. S. Govt. Print. Off., 1980. iii,

77 p. ; 24 cm. "Serial no. 96-93." LC Card
80-602434 DDC 353.0078/2 19
1. Fire prevention - Law and legislation - United States.
2. Fire prevention - United States - Finance. I. Title.
KF26 .C693 1980

**United States. Congress. Senate. Committee on
Commerce, Science, and Transportation.
Subcommittee on Aviation.**
Airport and airway system development :
hearings before the Subcommittee on Aviation
of the Committee on Commerce, Science, and
Transportation, United States Senate,
Ninety-seventh Congress, first session, on S.
508 ... February 24 and 25, 1981. Washington :
U. S. G.P.O., 1981. iv, 276 p. : ill. ; 24 cm.
"Serial no. 97-8." Item 1041-A, 1041-B (microfiche)
   LC Card 81-601789 DDC 343.73/0977
347.303977 19
1. Airports - Law and legislation - United States. I.
Title.
KF26 .C692 1981

Aviation safety : hearings before the
Subcommittee on Aviation of the Committee on
Commerce, Science, and Transportation, United
States Senate, Ninety-sixth Congress, second
session ... August 25, 26, and 27, 1980.
Washington : U. S. G.P.O., 1980. iii, 165 p. ;
24 cm. "Serial no. 96-119." LC Card 80-604036
   DDC 363.1/24/0973 19
1. Aeronautics - United States - Safety measures. 2.
Aeronautics - United States - Accidents. 3. Air traffic
control - United States. I. Title.
KF26 .C6925 1980

Oversight on Civil Aeronautics Board : hearing
before the Subcommittee on Aviation of the
Committee on Commerce, Science, and
Transportation, United States Senate,
Ninety-sixth Congress, second session ... May
20, 1980. Washington : U. S. Govt. Print. Off.,
1980. iii, 57 p. : graphs ; 24 cm. "Serial no.
96-113." LC Card 80-603444 DDC 353.0087/7712
19
1. Air lines - United States - Rates. 2. United States.
Civil Aeronautics Board. I. Title.
KF26 .C692 1980

**United States. Congress. Senate. Committee on
Commerce, Science, and Transportation.
Subcommittee on Communications.** Cable
television : hearings before the Subcommittee
on Communications of the Committee on
Commerce, Science, and Transportation, United
States Senate, Ninety-fifth Congress, first
session ... June 6, 7, and 8, 1977. Washington :
U. S. Govt. Print. Off., 1977. iv, 338 p. : ill. ;
24 cm. "Serial no. 95-32." LC Card 77-604597
1. Community antenna television - United States. 2.
Community antenna television - Law and legislation -
United States. I. Title.
KF26 .C6925 1977a   NYPL [JLE 81-581]

**United States. Congress. Senate. Committee on
Commerce, Science, and Transportation.
Subcommittee on Merchant Marine and
Tourism.**
Amend the Shipping act, 1916 : hearing before
the Subcommittee on Merchant Marine and
Tourism of the Committee on Commerce,
Science, and Transportation, United States
Senate, Ninety-sixth Congress, second session,
on H.R. 6613 ... June 4, 1980. Washington : U.
S. Govt. Print. Off., 1980. iv, 111 p. ; 23 cm.
"Serial no. 96-107." LC Card 80-603361 DDC
344.73/01890413875 19
1. Collective labor agreements - Merchant marine -
United States. I. Title.
KF26 .C695 1980c

Ocean shipping act of 1979 : hearings before
the Subcommittee on Merchant Marine and
Tourism of the Committee on Commerce,
Science, and Transportation, United States
Senate, Ninety-sixth Congress, first session, on
S. 1460 ... S. 1462 ... S. 1463 .... Washington :
U. S. Govt. Print. Off., 1979. v, 707 p. : ill. ;
23 cm. "Serial no. 96-77." Hearings held Sept. 18-Nov.
28, 1979. Includes bibliographical references. LC Card
80-602185 DDC 343.73/0968 19
1. Maritime law - United States. 2. Merchant marine -
United States. I. Title.
KF26 .C695 1979d

War risk insurance : hearing before the
Subcommittee on Merchant Marine and
Tourism of the Committee on Commerce,
Science, and Transportation, United States
Senate, Ninety-sixth Congress, first session, on

BIBLIOGRAPHIC GUIDE

United States. Congress. Senate. Committee on Commerce,   478

S. 1452 ... December 11, 1979. Washington : U. S. Govt. Print. Off., 1980. iii, 52 p. ; 24 cm. "Serial no. 96-70." LC Card 80-601958   DDC 346.73/08614/0262 19
1. Insurance, War risk - United States. 2. Insurance, Marine - United States. I. Title.
KF26 .C695 1979e

United States. Congress. Senate. Committee on Commerce, Science, and Transportation. Subcommittee on Science, Technology, and Space.
Authorizations for NBS : hearing before the Subcommittee on Science, Technology, and Space of the Committee on Commerce, Science, and Transportation, United States Senate, Ninety-sixth Congress, second session, on S. 2320 ... March 12, 1980. Washington : U. S. Govt. Print. Off., 1980. iii, 67 p. : ill. ; 24 cm. "Serial no. 96-79." LC Card 80-602152   DDC 353.0072/236821 19
1. United States. National Bureau of Standards - Appropriations and expenditures. I. Title.
KF26 .C697 1980

Automotive technology and fuel economy standards : hearing before the Subcommittee on Science, Technology, and Space of the Committee on Commerce, Science, and Transportation, United States Senate, Ninety-sixth Congress, second session, on S. 2015 .... Washington : U. S. Govt. Print. Off., 1980. iv, 372 p. : ill. ; 24 cm. "Serial no. 96-110." Hearings held April 30-May 14, 1980. Includes bibliographical references.   LC Card 80-603668   DDC 343.73/078629222 347.30378629222 19
1. Automobile engineering research - Law and legislation - United States. 2. Automobiles - Fuel consumption - Law and legislation - United States. I. Title.
KF26 .C697 1980d

Civil remote sensing satellite system : hearings before the Subcommittee on Science, Technology, and Space of the Committee on Commerce, Science, and Transportation, United States Senate, Ninety-sixth Congress, second session ... June 26 and July 24, 1980. Washington : U. S. Govt. Print. Off., 1980. iv, 237 p. : ill. ; 23 cm. "Serial no. 96-111." Includes bibliographical references.   LC Card 80-603670   DDC 338.4/76213678 19
1. Landsat satellites. 2. Remote sensing - Government policy - United States. I. Title.
KF26 .C697 1980e

Congress/Science Forum, Washington, D.C., 1979. Risk/benefit analysis in the legislative process . Washington , 1980. vi, 228 p. :   LC Card 80-601466   DDC 328.73/077 19
KF27 .S399 1979n

Industrial applications of recombinant DNA techniques : hearing before the Subcommittee on Science, Technology, and Space of the Committee on Commerce, Science, and Transportation, United States Senate, Ninety-sixth Congress, second session ... May 20, 1980. Washington : U. S. Govt. Print. Off., 1980. iii, 90 p. : ill. ; 24 cm. "Serial no. 96-105." LC Card 80-603025   DDC 338.4/766062 19
1. Recombinant DNA - Industrial applications. I. Title.
KF26 .C697 1980c

Laser research and applications / prepared at the request of Hon. Howard W. Cannon, chairman, Committee on Commerce, Science, and Transportation, United States Senate. Washington : U. S. G.P.O., 1980. xi, 32 p. ; 24 cm. At head of title: 96th Congress, 2d session. Committee print. "November 1980." Item 1041 LC Card 80-604121   DDC 621.36/6 19
1. Lasers. 2. Lasers - Research - United States. I. Cannon, Howard W. II. United States. Congress. Senate. Committee on Commerce, Science, and Transportation. III. Title.
TA1677 .U54 1980

Laser technology development and applications : hearings before the Subcommittee on Science, Technology, and Space of the Committee on Commerce, Science, and Transportation, United States Senate, Ninety-sixth Congress, first and second sessions .... Washington : U. S. Govt. Print. Off., 1980. iv, 269 p. : ill. ; 24 cm. Hearings held Dec. 12, 1979-Jan. 12, 1980. "Serial no. 96-106." Includes bibliographical references.   LC Card 80-603091   DDC 338.4/7621366/0973 19

1. Lasers. I. Title.
KF26 .C697 1979j

The Moon treaty : hearings before the Subcommittee on Science, Technology, and Space of the Committee on Commerce, Science, and Transportation, United States Senate, Ninety-sixth Congress, second session ... July 29 and 31, 1980. Washington : U. S. G.P.O., 1980. iv, 267 p. : ill. ; 24 cm. "Serial no. 96-115." LC Card 80-603774   DDC 341.4/7 19
1. Space law. I. Title.
KF26 .C697 1980f

Office of Science and Technology Policy : hearing before the Subcommittee on Science, Technology, and Space of the Committee on Commerce, Science, and Transportation, United States Senate, Ninety-sixth-Congress, second session ... September 19, 1980. Washington : U. S. G.P.O., 1980. iii, 72 p. ; 24 cm. "Serial no. 96-118." LC Card 80-603897   DDC 353.0085/5 19
1. United States. Office of Science and Technology Policy. 2. Science and state - United States. 3. Technology and state - United States. I. Title.
KF26 .C697 1980g

Reauthorization of National climate program act : hearing before the Subcommittee on Science, Technology, and Space of the Committee on Commerce, Science, and Transportation, United States Senate, Ninety-sixth Congress, second session, on S. 1391 ... April 17, 1980. Washington : U. S. Govt. Print. Off., 1980. iii, 28 p. ; 24 cm. "Serial no. 96-98." LC Card 80-602777   DDC 353.0072/23682324 19
1. Weather control - Law and legislation - United States. 2. Weather control - United States - Finance. I. Title.
KF26 .C697 1980b

Reauthorization of National earthquake hazards reduction act : hearing before the Subcommittee on Science, Technology, and Space of the Committee on Commerce, Science, and Transportation, United States Senate, Ninety-sixth Congress, second session, on S. 1393 ... April 2, 1980. Washington : U. S. Govt. Print. Off., 1980. iii, 84 p. : maps ; 24 cm. "Serial no. 96-90." LC Card 80-602466   DDC 353.0085/4 19
1. Seismological research - Law and legislation - United States. 2. Seismological research - United States - Finance. I. Title.
KF26 .C697 1980a

United States. Congress. Senate. Committee on Energy and Natural Resources. Subcommittee on Energy Research and Development.
Methane Transportation Research, Development, and Demonstration Act of 1980 . Washington , 1980 [i.e. 1981] iii, 162 p. :   LC Card 81-601152   DDC 346.7304/6793 347.30646793 19
KF26 .E554 1980d

United States. Library of Congress. Congressional Research Service. Risk/benefit analysis in the legislative process . Washington , 1980. ix, 36 p. ;   LC Card 80-602214   DDC 363.1/056/0973 19
T174.5 .U57 1980

United States. Congress. Senate. Committee on Commerce, Science, and Transportation. Subcommittee on Surface Transportation.
Amendments to the Federal railway safety act of 1970 : hearing before the Subcommittee on Surface Transportation of the Committee on Commerce, Science, and Transportation, United States Senate, Ninety-sixth Congress, second session ... March 24, 1980. Washington : U. S. Govt. Print. Off., 1980. iii, 156 p. : graphs ; 24 cm. "Serial no. 96-97." LC Card 80-602782   DDC 343.73/095 19
1. Railroads - Safety regulations - United States. 2. United States. Federal Railroad Administration - Appropriations and expenditures. I. Title.
KF26 .C698 1980d

Amtrak reauthorization : hearings before the Subcommittee on Surface Transportation of the Committee on Commerce, Science, and Transportation, United States Senate, Ninety-seventh Congress, first session, on Amtrak reauthorization, March 13 and 17, 1981. Washington : U. S. G.P.O., 1981. iv, 177 p. : ill. ; 24 cm. "Serial no. 97-10." Item 1041-A, 1041-B (microfiche) Includes bibliographical references.   LC Card 81-601888   DDC 353.0072/234 19

1. Amtrak - Appropriations and expenditures. I. Title.
KF26 .C698 1981a

Conrail reauthorization : hearings before the Subcommittee on Surface Transportation of the Committee on Commerce, Science, and Transportation, United States Senate, Ninety-seventh Congress, first session, on Conrail reauthorization, March 24 and 25, 1981. Washington : U. S. G.P.O., 1981. iv, 166 p. ; 23 cm. "Serial no. 97-13." Item 1041-A, 1041-B (microfiche)   LC Card 81-601879   DDC 353.0072/234 19
1. ConRail - Appropriations and expenditures. 2. ConRail - Finance. I. Title.
KF26 .C698 1981

Northeast corridor completion act of 1979 : hearing before the Subcommittee on Surface Transportation of the Committee on Commerce, Science, and Transportation, United States Senate, Ninety-sixth Congress, second session, on S. 2156 ... February 29, 1980. Washington : U. S. Govt. Print. Off., 1980. iii, 89 p. ; 24 cm. "Serial no. 96-82." LC Card 80-602086   DDC 343.73/095 347.30395 19
1. Railroad law - Northeastern States. 2. Railroads - Northeastern States - Finance. 3. Railroad law - United States. I. Title.
KF26 .C698 1980

Rail restructuring assistance act of 1979 : hearing before the Subcommittee on Surface Transportation of the Committee on Commerce, Science, and Transportation, United States Senate, Ninety-sixth Congress, second session, on S. 1151 ... March 31, 1980. Washington : U. S. Govt. Print. Off., 1980. iii, 59 p. : maps ; 23 cm. "Serial no. 96-92." LC Card 80-602440   DDC 343.73/095/0262 19
1. Railroad law - United States. 2. Railroads - United States - Finance. I. Title.
KF26 .C698 1980a

Rock Island transition act : hearing before the Subcommittee on Surface Transportation of the Committee on Commerce, Science, and Transportation, United States Senate, Ninety-sixth Congress, on S. 2246 ... S. 2253 ... S.J. Res. 139 ... February 20, 1980. Washington : U. S. Govt. Print. Off., 1980. iv, 146 p. : maps ; 23 cm. "Serial no. 96-95." LC Card 80-602527   DDC 343.73/095 19
1. Chicago, Rock Island and Pacific Railway. 2. Railroad law - United States. I. Title.
KF26 .C698 1980b

USRA--nomination, authorization, Conrail plant rationalization, and employee protection program : hearing before the Subcommittee on Surface Transportation of the Committee on Commerce, Science, and Transportation, United States Senate, Ninety-sixth Congress, second session, on nomination of Stephen Berger, to be chairman of the Board, United States Railway Association and S. 2527 ... and S. 2530 ..., April 16, 1980. Washington : U. S. Govt. Print. Off., 1980. iv, 125 p. ; 23 cm. "Serial no. 96-96." LC Card 80-602781   DDC 343.73/095 19
1. Railroad law - United States. 2. Berger, Stephen, 1939- . 3. United States Railway Association. 4. Conrail. I. Title.
KF26 .C698 1980c

United States. Congress. Senate. Committee on Energy and Natural Resources.
Alaska Federal-civilian energy efficiency swap act of 1979 : hearing before the Committee on Energy and Natural Resources, United States Senate, Ninety-sixth Congress, second session, on S. 1784 ... March 27, 1980. Washington : U. S. Govt. Print. Off., 1980. ii, 43 p. ; 24 cm. "Publication no. 96-112." LC Card 80-603038   DDC 343.73/0929 19
1. Electric utilities - Law and legislation - Alaska. I. Title.
KF26 .E55 1980d

Brown, Russell Ray, 1941- Potential for hydroelectric power generation, Island of Ponape, Ponape District, Trust Territory of the Pacific. Washington , 1979. v, 83 p. :   LC Card 80-601032   DDC 333.91/4 19
TK1524.P66 B76

Clyde O. Martz nomination : hearing before the Committee on Energy and Natural Resources, United States Senate, Ninety-sixth Congress, second session, on the nomination of Clyde O. Martz to be Solicitor, Department of the Interior, May 12, 1980. Washington : U. S.

GOVERNMENT PUBLICATIONS - U.S.: 1981

479
United States. Congress. Senate. Committee on Energy and

Govt. Print. Off., 1980. iii, 72 p. ; 24 cm.
"Publication no. 96-104." Includes bibliographical
references. LC Card 80-602816 DDC 353.3 19
*1. Martz, Clyde O. 2. United States. Dept. of the
Interior - Officials and employees. I. Title.*
KF26 .E55 1980a

Coal exports : hearings before the Committee
on Energy and Natural Resources, United
States Senate, Ninety-sixth congress, second
session on coal exports, September 16, 18, and
19, 1980. Washington : U. S. G.P.O., 1981. iv,
544 p. : ill. ; 24 cm. "Publication no. 96-159." Item
1040 LC Card 81-601408 DDC 382/.4224/0973 19
*1. Coal trade - United States. 2. Coal trade. 3.
Harbors - United States. I. Title.*
KF26 .E55 1980o

Coal severance tax : hearing before the
Committee on Energy and Natural Resources,
United States Senate, Ninety-sixth Congress,
second session, on S. 2695 ... August 6, 1980.
Washington : U. S. G.P.O., 1980. v, 607 p. :
ill. ; 24 cm. "Publication no. 96-143. Bibliography: p.
523-524. LC Card 81-600620 DDC
343.7305/58566262 347.303558566262 19
1. Coal - Taxation - United States. I. Title.
KF26 .E55 1980n

Davis, David Howard. A critique of the Energy
management partnership act (EMPA) /.
Washington , 1979. vii, 44 p. ; LC Card
79-603227 DDC 346.7304/679 19
HD9502.U52 D29

Donald Paul Hodel nomination : hearing before
the Committee on Energy and Natural
Resources, United States Senate,
Ninety-seventh Congress, first session, on the
nomination of Donald Paul Hodel to be the
under secretary of the Department of the
Interior, February 5, 1981. Washington : U. S.
G.P.O., 1981. iii, 133 p. ; 24 cm. "Publication no.
97-5." Item 1040-A, 1040-B (microfiche) LC Card
81-601395 DDC 353.3 19
*1. Hodel, Donald Paul, 1935-. 2. United States. Dept.
of the Interior - Officials and employees. I. Title.*
KF26 .E55 1981b

Effects of acid rain : hearing before the
Committee on Energy and Natural Resources,
United States Senate, Ninety-sixth Congress,
second session ... May 28, 1980. Washington :
U. S. Govt. Print. Off., 1980- v. <1-> : ill. ;
23 cm. "Publication no. 96-126." Includes
bibliographies. LC Card 80-603417 DDC 363.7/394
19
*1. Acid rain - Environmental aspects - United States. 2.
Atmospheric circulation - United States. 3. Sulphur
compounds - Environmental aspects - United States. I.
Title.*
KF26 .E55 1980f

Effects of carbon dioxide buildup in the
atmosphere : hearing before the Committee on
Energy and Natural Resources, United States
Senate, Ninety-sixth Congress, second session ...
April 3, 1980. Washington, : U. S. Govt. Print.
Off., 1980. iii, 341 p. : ill. ; 24 cm. "Publication
no. 96-107." Includes bibliographical references. LC
Card 80-602991 DDC 333.9/21 19
*1. Atmospheric carbon dioxide. 2. Climatic changes. I.
Title.*
KF26 .E55 1980b

Energy in transition, 1985-2010 : hearing before
the Committee on Energy and Natural
Resources, United States Senate, Ninety-sixth
Congress, second session ... April 18, 1980.
Washington : U. S. Govt. Print. Off., 1980. iii,
61 p. ; 24 cm. "Publication no. 96-110." LC Card
80-602968 DDC 333.79 19
*1. National Research Council. Committee on Nuclear
and Alternative Energy Systems. Energy in transition,
1985-2010. 2. Power resources - United States. 3.
Energy policy - United States. I. Title.*
KF26 .E55 1980c

Extending the antitrust exemption in the
Energy Policy and Conservation Act : hearing
before the Committee on Energy and Natural
Resources, United States Senate,
Ninety-seventh Congress, first session, on S.
573 ... March 2, 1981. Washington : U. S.
G.P.O., 1981. iii, 42 p. : ill. ; 24 cm. "Publication
no. 97-7." Item 1040-A, 1040-B (microfiche) Includes
bibliographical references. LC Card 81-601762 DDC
343.73/072 347.30372 19
*1. Antitrust law - United States. 2. Petroleum law and
legislation - United States. I. Title.*
KF26 .E55 1981c

Geopolitics of oil : hearings before the
Committee on Energy and Natural Resources,
United States Senate, Ninety-sixth Congress,
second session ... Washington : U. S. G.P.O.,
1980. 2 v. : ill. ; 24 cm. "Publication no. 96-119."
Hearings held Feb. 5-July 31, 1980. LC Card
80-603788 DDC 333.8/232/0973 19
*1. Petroleum industry and trade. 2. Energy policy -
United States. I. Title.*
KF26 .E55 1980j

Gold, Fern R. Access to oil . [Washington ,
1977. xiii, 113 p. ; LC Card 78-600524
HD9566 .G64   *NYPL [JLE 81-460]*

James B. Edwards nomination : hearing before
the Committee on energy and Natural
Resources, United States Senate,
Ninety-seventh Congress, first session, on the
proposed nomination of Governor James B.
Edwards to be Secretary of Energy, January 12,
1981. Washington : U. S. G.P.O., 1981. ii, 216
p. : ill. ; 24 cm. "Publication no. 97-2." Item 1040-A,
1040-B (microfiche) LC Card 81-600846 DDC
353.87 19
*1. Edwards, James B., 1927-. 2. United States. Dept. of
Energy - Officials and employees. I. Title.*
KF26 .E55 1981a

James G. Watt nomination : hearings before the
Committee on Energy and Natural Resources,
United States Senate, Ninety-seventh Congress,
first session, on the proposed nomination of
James G. Watt to be secretary of the interior,
January 7 and 8, 1981. Washington : U. S.
G.P.O., 1981. 2 v. : ill. ; 24 cm. "Publication no.
97-1." Item 1040-A, 1040-B (microfiche) LC Card
81-600871 DDC 353.3 19
*1. Watt, James G., 1938-. 2. United States. Dept. of the
Interior - Officials and employees. I. Title.*
KF26 .E55 1981

Johnson, Odle, and Heffelfinger nominations :
hearing before the Committee on Energy and
Natural Resources, United States Senate,
Ninety-seventh Congress, first session, on the
nominations of R. Tenney Johnson, to be
general counsel, Department of Energy, Robert
C. Odle, Jr., to be assistant secretary for
congressional, intergovernmental, and public
affairs, Department of Energy, and William S.
Heffelfinger, to be assistant secretary for
management and administration, Department of
Energy, April 30, 1981. Washington : U. S.
G.P.O., 1981. iii, 140 p. : ill. ; 24 cm.
"Publication no. 97-9." LC Card 81-601965 DDC
353.87 19
*1. Heffelfinger, William S., 1925-. 2. Johnson, Richard
Tenney, 1930-. 3. Odle, Robert Charles, 1944-. 4.
United States. Dept. of Energy - Officials and
employees. I. Title.*
KF26 .E55 1981d

Lindsay D. Norman, Jr., and John D. Hughes
nominations : hearing before the Committee on
Energy and Natural Resources, United States
Senate, Ninety-sixth Congress, second session ...
August 4, 1980. Washington : U. S. Govt.
Print. Off., 1980. iii, 123 p. : ill. ; 24 cm.
"Publication no. 96-132." LC Card 80-603780 DDC
353.0082/327 19
*1. Norman, Lindsay D. 2. United States. Bureau of
Mines - Officials and employees. 3. Hughes, John
David, 1935-. 4. United States. Federal Energy
Regulatory Commission - Officials and employees. I.
Title.*
KF26 .E55 1980g

The national coal production, distribution, and
utilization act of 1980 : hearings before the
Committee on Energy and Natural Resources,
United States Senate, Ninety-sixth Congress,
second session, on S. 2665, a bill to amend the
Mineral leasing act of 1920, and for other
purposes, May 20, 30, and June 16, 1980.
Washington : U. S. Govt. Print. Off., 1980. iv,
435 p. : ill. ; 24 cm. "Publication no. 96-127."
Includes bibliographical references. LC Card
80-603714 DDC 343.73/07752 347.3037752 19
*1. Coal - Pipe lines - Law and legislation - United
States. I. Title.*
KF26 .E55 1980d

Omnibus Geothermal Energy
Commercialization Act of 1979 : hearing before
the Committee on Energy and Natural
Resources, United States Senate, Ninety-sixth
Congress, second session, on S. 1388 ... March
18, 1980. Washington : U. S. P.P.O., 1980. iii,
69 p. ; 24 cm. "Publication no. 96-129." LC Card

80-604105 DDC 346.7304/688 347.3064688 19
*1. Geothermal resources - Law and legislation - United
States. 2. Geothermal leases - United States. I. Title.*
KF26 .E55 1980m

Omnibus territorial legislation--1980 : hearing
before the Committee on Energy and Natural
Resources, United States Senate, Ninety-sixth
Congress, second session, on S. 2735 ... S.
2992 ... H.R. 7330 ... August 26, 1980.
Washington : U. S. G.P.O., 1980. iv, 679 p. :
ill. ; 24 cm. "Publication no. 96-146." Bibliography: p.
469-472. LC Card 81-600632 DDC 349.73 347.3 19
*1. Law - United States - Territories and possessions. 2.
United States - Insular possessions. I. Title.*
KF26 .E55 1980l

Pacific basin energy : hearings before the
Committee on Energy and Natural Resources,
United States Senate, Ninety-sixth Congress,
second session, on H.R. 7330 ... Honolulu,
Hawaii, July 10 and 11, 1980. Washington : U.
S. G.P.O., 1980. iv, 546 p. : ill. ; 24 cm.
"Publication no. 96-145." Includes bibliographical
references. LC Card 81-600636 DDC 346.7304/679
347.3064679 19
*1. United States - Insular possessions. 2. Renewable
energy sources - Law and legislation - United States. 3.
Energy development - Law and legislation - Pacific
area. I. Title.*
KF26 .E55 1980i

Potential for improved automobile fuel economy
between 1985 and 1995 : hearing before the
Committee on Energy and Natural Resources,
United States Senate, Ninety-sixth Congress,
second session ... April 30, 1980. [Washington :
U. S. Govt. Print. Off., 1980] iii, 516 p. : ill. ;
24 cm. "Publication no. 96-123." Includes
bibliographical references. LC Card 80-603426 DDC
333.8/232 19
*1. Automobiles - United States - Fuel consumption. I.
Title.*
KF26 .E55 1980e

Pugash, James Z. The geopolitics of oil .
Washington , 1980. v. 89 p. ; LC Card
80-604126 DDC 333.8/232 19
HD9560.5 .P76

Readings on the protection and management of
marine and submerged resources of the national
parks . Washington , 1980. ix, 157 p. : LC Card
80-603550 DDC 333.91/0973 19
QH91.75.U6 R4

Residential and commercial energy
conservation : hearing before the Committee on
Energy and Natural Resources, United States
Senate, Ninety-sixth Congress, first session, on
S. 932 (title IV) ... S. 1308 (amendment no,
388) ... S. 180 ... October 2, 1979.
Washington : U. S. Govt. Print. Off., 1980. iii,
296 p. : ill. ; 24 cm. "Publication no. 96-78." LC
Card 80-601488 DDC 346.7304/67916/0262 19
*1. Energy conservation - Law and legislation - United
States. 2. Energy conservation - United States -
Finance. I. Title.*
KF26 .E55 1979aa

Submittal of the Senate Committee on Energy
and Natural Resources to the Senate Budget
Committee pursuant to Section 301(c) of the
Congressional Budget Act / prepared by the
Committee on Energy and Natural Resources,
United States Senate. Washington : U. S.
G.P.O., 1977. vii, 45 p. ; 24 cm. At head of title:
95th Congress, 1st session. Committee print.
"Publication no. 95-7." LC Card 81-601121 DDC
328.73/07652 19
*1. United States. Congress. Senate. Committee on
Energy and Natural Resources. I. United States.
Congress. Senate. Committee on the Budget. II. Title.*
JK1240.E53 U54 1977

Synfuels from coal and the national synfuels
production program . Washington , 1981. x, 304
p. : LC Card 81-601287 DDC
338.4/76626622/0973 19
TP360 .S939

Synthetic Fuels Corporation nominations :
hearings before the Committee on Energy and
Natural Resources, United States Senate,
Ninety-sixth Congress, second session ...
September 18 and 24, 1980. Washington : U. S.
Govt. Print. Off., 1980. iii, 185 p. ; 24 cm.
Hearings on the nominations of John Crittendon
Sawhill to be Chairman of the Board, and John D.
deButts, and others, to be members of the Board of
Directors, U. S. Synthetic Fuels Corporation.

BIBLIOGRAPHIC GUIDE

United States. Congress. Senate. Committee on Energy and

480

"Publication no. 96-130." LC Card 80-603446 DDC 353.09/2 19
1. Sawhill, John C., 1936-. 2. Synthetic Fuels Corporation (U. S.) - Employees. I. Title.
KF26 .E55 1980h

Synthetic fuels legislation : hearings before the Committee on Energy and Natural Resources, United States Senate, Ninety-sixth Congress, first session on S. 932 ... S. 1308 ... S. 1377 ... July 23 and 24, 1979. Washington : U. S. Govt. Print. Off., 1980. iii, 407 p. ; 24 cm. "Publication no. 96-88." LC Card 80-601946 DDC 343.73/07866266/0262 19
1. Synthetic fuels - Law and legislation - United States. I. Title.
KF26 .E55 1979ad

Wallace O. Green nomination : hearing before the Committee on Energy and Natural Resources, United States Senate, Ninety-sixth Congress, second session, on the nomination of Wallace O. Green to be assistant secretary of the Interior for territorial and international affairs, Department of the Interior, September 23, 1980. Washington : U. S. G.P.O., 1980. iii, 68 p. ; 24 cm. "Publication no. 96-134." LC Card 80-604077 DDC 353.3 19
1. Green, Wallace Orphesus, 1948-. 2. United States. Dept. of the Interior - Officials and employees. I. Title.
KF26 .E55 1980k

World petroleum outlook--1981 : hearing before the Committee on Energy and Natural Resources, United States Senate, Ninety-seventh Congress, first session, on the outlook for world oil availability during 1981, January 22, 1981. Washington : U. S. G.P.O., 1981. iii, 152 p. : ill. ; 24 cm. "Publication no. 97-4." 1040-A, 1040-B (microfiche) LC Card 81-601403 DDC 333.8/232 19
1. Petroleum industry and trade. 2. Petroleum - Reserves. I. Title.
KF26 .E55 1981e

UNITED STATES. CONGRESS. SENATE. COMMITTEE ON ENERGY AND NATURAL RESOURCES.
United States. Congress. Senate. Committee on Energy and Natural Resources. Submittal of the Senate Committee on Energy and Natural Resources to the Senate Budget Committee pursuant to Section 301(c) of the Congressional Budget Act /. Washington , 1977. vii, 45 p. ;
LC Card 81-601121 DDC 328.73/07652 19
JK1240.E53 U54 1977

United States. Congress. Senate. Committee on Energy and Natural Resources. Subcommittee on Energy Conservation and Supply.
Community energy efficiency act of 1979 : hearing before the Subcommittee on Energy Conservation and Supply of the Committee on Energy and Natural Resources, United States Senate, Ninety-sixth Congress, first session, on S. 1829 ... December 12, 1979. Washington : U. S. Govt. Print. Off., 1980. iii, 68 p. ; 24 cm. "Publication no. 96-84." LC Card 80-601867 DDC 346.7304/67916/0262 19
1. Energy conservation - Law and legislation - United States. 2. Grants-in-aid - United States. I. Title.
KF26 .E553 1979h

Deferring repayment of certain reimbursable costs incurred by the Southwestern Power Administration : hearing before the Subcommittee on Energy Conservation and Supply of the Committee on Energy and Natural Resources, United States Senate, Ninety-sixth Congress, second session, on S. 1519 ... May 23, 1980. Washington : U. S. Govt. Print. Off., 1980. ii, 37 p. ; 24 cm. "Publication no. 96-109." LC Card 80-603007 DDC 343.79/0929 19
1. United States. Southwestern Power Administration - Management. 2. Electric utilities - Southwestern States - Costs. I. Title.
KF26 .E553 1980b

Department of Energy fiscal years 1981-82 authorization (civilian applications) : hearing before the Subcommittee on Energy Conservation and Supply of the Committee on Energy and Natural Resources, United States Senate, Ninety-sixth Congress, second session, on S. 2332 ... March 18, 1980. Washington : U. S. Govt. Print. Off., 1980. iii, 106 p. : graphs ; 23 cm. "Publication no. 96-106." LC Card 80-602997 DDC 353.0072/236823 19

1. United States. Dept. of Energy - Appropriations and expenditures. 2. Energy development - Law and legislation - United States. I. Title.
KF26 .E553 1980a

Energy management partnership act of 1979 : hearing before the Subcommittee on Energy Conservation and Supply of the Committee on Energy and Natural Resources, United States Senate, Ninety-sixth Congress, first session on S. 1280 ... July 27, 1979. Washington : U. S. Govt. Print. Off., 1980. iii, 74 p. ; 24 cm. "Publication no. 96-92." LC Card 80-602009 DDC 346.7304/679158/0262 19
1. Energy conservation - Law and legislation - United States. 2. Grants-in-aid - United States. 3. Intergovernmental fiscal relations - United States. I. Title.
KF26 .E553 1979i

International applications of renewable energy resources : hearings before the Subcommittee on Energy Conservation and Supply of the Committee on Energy and Natural Resources, United States Senate, Ninety-sixth Congress, second session, to examine the potential impacts of such applications on the growth of fossil fuel consumption, the domestic solar industry, and global environmental problems, August 19 and September 5, 1980. Washington : U. S. G.P.O., 1980. iii, 240 p. : ill. ; 24 cm. "Publication no. 96-147." Bibliography: p. 51-53. LC Card 81-600634 DDC 333.79 19
1. Renewable energy sources - United States. 2. Underdeveloped areas - Renewable energy sources. 3. Technical assistance, American. I. Title.
KF26 .E553 1980d

Municipal solid waste to energy act of 1979 : hearings before the Subcommittee on Energy Conservation and Supply of the Committee on Energy and Natural Resources, United States Senate, Ninety-sixth Congress, second session, on S. 1934 ... February 27 and 28, 1980. Washington : U. S. Govt. Print. Off., 1980. iii, 217 p. : ill. ; 24 cm. "Publication no. 96-99." LC Card 80-602495 DDC 344.73/04622 19
1. Refuse as fuel - Law and legislation - United States. 2. Refuse and refuse disposal - Law and legislation - United States. 3. Refuse as fuel - United States - Finance. I. Title.
KF26 .E553 1980

Proposed Community Energy Efficiency Act : hearings before the Subcommittee on Energy Conservation and Supply of the Committee on Energy and Natural Resources, United States Senate, Ninety-sixth Congress, second session, to examine the proposed Community Energy Act, Boston, Mass., March 7, 1980, Durham, N.H., April 12, 1980. Washington : U. S. G.P.O., c1981. iv, 186 p. ; 23 cm. "Publication no. 96-154." Item 1040 LC Card 81-600952 DDC 346.7304/67916 347.306467916 19
1. Energy conservation - Law and legislation - United States. 2. Grants-in-aid - United States. 3. Energy conservation - New England. 4. Grants-in-aid - New Zealand. I. Title.
KF26 .E553 1980e

United States. Congress. Senate. Committee on Energy and Natural Resources. Subcommittee on Energy Regulation.
Building Energy Performance Standards Implementation Act of 1980 : hearings before the Subcommittee on Energy Regulation of the Committee on Energy and Natural Resources, United States Senate, Ninety-sixth Congress, second session, on the status and issues associated with the building energy performance standards program and S. 2862 ... June 5 and 26, 1980. Washington : U. S. G.P.O., 1980. v, 1845 p. : ill. ; 24 cm. "Publication no. 96-138." Includes bibliographical references. LC Card 80-604054 DDC 346.7304/67916/0262 347.3064679160262 19
1. Buildings - Energy conservation - Law and legislation - United States. I. Title.
KF26 .E5535 1980b

Department of Energy fiscal years, 1981-82 authorization (civilian applications) : hearings before the Subcommittee on Energy Regulation of the Committee on Energy and Natural Resources, United States Senate, Ninety-sixth Congress, second session, on S. 2332 ... April 15 and 28, 1980. Washington : U. S. Govt. Print. Off., 1980. iii, 265 p. ; 24 cm. "Publication no. 96-116." LC Card 80-603317 DDC

353.0072/23682/3 19
1. United States. Dept. of Energy - Appropriations and expenditures. I. Title.
KF26 .E5535 1980a

Emergency Motor Fuel Demand Rationing Act of 1980 : hearing before the Subcommittee on Energy Regulation of the Committee on Energy and Natural Resources, United States Senate, Ninety-sixth Congress, second session, on S. 2754 ... June 2, 1980. Washington : U. S. G.P.O., 1980. iii, 96 p. ; 23 cm. "Publication no. 96-120." LC Card 80-603436 DDC 346.7304/6823217 347.30646823217 19
1. Gasoline - Law and legislation - United States. 2. Diesel fuels - Law and legislation - United States. 3. Gasoline supply - United States. I. Title.
KF26 .E5535 1980c

Federal gasoline allocation process : hearing before the Subcommittee on Energy Regulation of the Committee on Energy and Natural Resources, United States Senate, Ninety-sixth Congress, second session ... June 9, 1980. Washington : G.P.O., 1980. iii, 202 p. : ill. ; 23 cm. "Publication no. 96-122." LC Card 80-603652 DDC 353.0082/6566553827 19
1. Gasoline supply - United States. 2. Petroleum industry and trade - United States. I. Title.
KF26 .E5535 1980d

July report on the current fuel situation from the Energy Information Administration : hearing before the Subcommittee on Energy Regulation of the Committee on Energy and Natural Resources, United States Senate, Ninety-sixth Congress, first session ... July 23, 1979. Washington : U.S Print. Off., 1980. iii, 176 p. : graphs ; 24 cm. "Publication no. 96-94." Includes bibliographical references. LC Card 80-602079 DDC 338.4/7665538/0973 19
1. Petroleum products - United States. 2. Gasoline supply - United States. 3. Petroleum industry and trade. I. Title.
KF26 .E5535 1979n

Limiting oil imports : hearing before the Subcommittee on Energy Regulation of the Committee on Energy and Natural Resources, United States Senate, Ninety-sixth Congress, first session ... September 18, 1979. Washington : U. S. Govt. Print. Off., 1980. iii, 221 p. ; 23 cm. Hearings on S. 1134, 1205, 1417, and 1470. "Publication no. 96-63." LC Card 80-602100 DDC 343.73/0872282/0262 19
1. Petroleum law and legislation - United States. 2. Import quotas - United States. I. Title.
KF26 .E5535 1979l

October report on the current fuel situation from the Energy Information Administration : hearing before the Subcommittee on Energy Regulation of the Committee on Energy and Natural Resources, United States Senate, Ninety-sixth Congress, first session ... October 22, 1979. Washington : U. S. Govt. Print. Off., 1980. iii, 217 p. : ill. ; 24 cm. "Publication no. 96-101." Includes bibliographical references. LC Card 80-602534 DDC 338.4/766553827/0973 19
1. Petroleum as fuel. 2. Gasoline supply - United States. 3. United States. Energy Information Administration. I. Title.
KF26 .E5535 1979m

Powerplant fuels conservation act of 1980 : hearings before the Subcommittee on Energy Regulation of the Committee on Energy and Natural Resources, United States Senate, Ninety-sixth Congress, second session, on S. 2470 ... April 23 and 25, 1980. Washington : U. S. Govt. Print. Off., 1980. iv, 1228 p. : ill. ; 23 cm. "Publication no. 96-121." Includes bibliographical references. LC Card 80-603723 DDC 346.7304/6793216 347.30646793216 19
1. Electric power-plants - Fuel consumption - Law and legislation - United States. 2. Electric power-plants - Conversion to coal - Law and legislation - United States. I. Title.
KF26 .E5527 1980

United States. Congress. Senate. Committee on Energy and Natural Resources. Subcommittee on Energy Research and Development.
Crooked River Project Act of August 6, 1956 : hearing before the Subcommittee on Energy Research and Development of the Committee on Energy and Natural Resources, United States Senate, Ninety-sixth Congress, second session, on S. 2616 ... Prineville, Oreg., July 3,

GOVERNMENT PUBLICATIONS - U.S.: 1981

481

United States. Congress. Senate. Committee on Energy and

1980. Washington : U. S. G.P.O., 1980. iii, 82 p. ; 24 cm. "Publication no. 96-136." LC Card 80-603805 DDC 346.7304/6916 347.30646916 19
1. Prineville Reservoir (Ore.). I. Title.
KF26 .E554 1980b

Department of Energy fiscal years 1981-82 authorization (civilian applications) : hearings before the Subcommittee on Energy Research and Development of the Committee on Energy and Natural Resources, United States Senate, Ninety-sixth Congress, second session, on S. 2332 ... Washington : U. S. G.P.O., 1980. iv, 1037 p. : ill. ; 24 cm. Hearings held Mar. 17-Apr. 23, 1980. "Publication no. 96-135." Includes bibliographical references. LC Card 80-604097 DDC 353.0072/236823 19
1. United States. Dept. of Energy - Appropriations and expenditures. 2. Synthetic fuels - Law and legislation - United States. I. Title.
KF26 .E554 1980

Energy supply act (Title VIII) : hearings before the Subcommittee on Energy Research and Development of the Committee on Energy and Natural Resources, United States Senate, Ninety-sixth Congress, first session, on S. 750 ... S. 1308 ... Boise, Idaho, July 2, 1979, Washington, D.C., July 12 and 19, 1979. Washington : U. S. Govt. Print. Off., 1980 iv, 391 p. : ill. ; 24 cm. "Publication no. 96-97." Includes bibliographical references. LC Card 80-602175 DDC 346.7304/679/0262 19
1. Alcohol as fuel - Law and legislation - United States. 2. Petroleum law and legislation - United States. 3. Energy policy - United States. I. Title.
KF26 .E554 1979e

Library of Congress. Congressional Research Service. Petroleum industry involvement in alternative sources of energy /. Washington , 1977. 385 p., [1] folded leaf of plates : LC Card 81-601738 DDC 333.79/0973 19
HD9565 .L48 1977

Magnetic Fusion Engineering Act of 1980 : hearings before the Subcommittee on Energy Research and Development of the Committee on Energy and Natural Resources, United States Senate, Ninety-sixth Congress, second session, on S. 2926 ... July 28 and August 5, 1980. Washington : U. S. G.P.O., 1981. iii, 162 p. : ill. ; 24 cm. Item 1040 "Publication no. 96-156." Includes bibliographical references. LC Card 81-601352 DDC 346.7304/67924/072 347.306467924072 19
1. Fusion reactors - Research - Law and legislation - United States. I. Title.
KF26 .E554 1980c

Methane Transportation Research, Development, and Demonstration Act of 1980 : joint hearing hearing before the Subcommittee on Energy Research and Development of the Committee on Energy and Natural Resources and the Subcommittee on Science, Technology, and Space of the Committee on Commerce, Science, and Transportation, United States Senate, Ninety-sixth Congress, second session on H.R. 6889 ... September 23, 1980. Washington : U. S. G.P.O., 1980 [i.e. 1981] iii, 162 p. : ill. ; 24 cm. "Energy Committee serial no. 96-160." "Commerce Committee publication no. 96-126." Item 1040 Includes bibliographical references. LC Card 81-601152 DDC 346.7304/6793 347.30646793 19
1. Methane - Law and legislation - United States. 2. Motor fuels - Law and legislation - United States. I. United States. Congress. Senate. Committee on Commerce, Science, and Transportation. Subcommittee on Science, Technology, and Space. II. Title.
KF26 .E554 1980d

Reclamation authorizations : hearing before the Subcommittee on Energy Research and Development of the Committee on Energy and Natural Resources, United States Senate, Ninety-sixth Congress, second session ... May 2, 1980. Washington : U. S. G.P.O., 1980. iii, 200 p. : ill. ; 24 cm. Hearing on S.2431, S.2545, S.2546, S.2616, H.R.507, and H.R.2111. "Publication no. 96-137." LC Card 80-603810 DDC 353.0082/326 19
1. Reclamation of land - Law and legislation - United States. 2. Reclamation of land - United States - Finance. I. Title.
KF26 .E554 1980a

United States. Congress. Senate. Committee on Energy and Natural Resources. Subcommittee on Energy Resources and Material Production.
United States. Congress. Senate. Committee on Energy and Natural Resources. Subcommittee on Energy Resources and Materials Production.
Amending the Mineral leasing act of 1920 and for the relief of Keith C. Hayes and Dorothy Smith : hearing before the Subcommittee on Energy Resources and Materials Production of the Committee on Energy and Natural Resources, United States Senate, Ninety-sixth Congress, second session, on S. 1455 ... S. 1529 ... April 15, 1980. Washington : U. S. Govt. Print. Off., 1980. iii, 66 p. : ill. ; 24 cm. "Publication no. 96-103." LC Card 80-602537 DDC 346.7304/6822 19
1. Coal leases - United States. 2. Mining claims - United States. 3. Hayes, Keith C. 4. Smith, Dorothy I. I. Title.
KF26 .E5543 1980b

Coal leases on BLM lands in New Mexico : hearing before the Subcommittee on Energy Resources and Materials Production of the Committee on Energy and Natural Resources, United States Senate, Ninety-sixth Congress, first session ... Farmington, N. Mex., August 9, 1979. Washington : U. S. Govt. Print. Off., 1980. iii, 211 p. ; 23 cm. "Publication no. 96-66." LC Card 80-601117 DDC 333.33/9 19
1. Coal leases - New Mexico. 2. United States - Public lands. 3. United States. Bureau of Land Management. I. Title.
KF26 .E5543 1979d

Federal oil and gas leasing act of 1979 : hearing before the Subcommittee on Energy Resources and Materials Production of the Committee on Energy and Natural Resources, United States Senate, Ninety-sixth Congress, first session, on S. 1637 ... October 12, 1979. Washington : U. S. Govt. Print. Off., 1980. iii, 259 p. : ill. ; 24 cm. "Publication no. 96-89." LC Card 80-601767 DDC 346.7304/6823 19
1. Oil and gas leases - United States. 2. United States - Public lands. I. Title.
KF26 .E5543 1979a

Materials Policy, Research, and Development Act : hearings before the Subcommittee on Energy Resources and Materials Production of the Committee on Energy and Natural Resources, United States Senate, Ninety-sixth Congress, second session, on H.R. 2743 ... July 29 and 31, 1980. Washington : U. S. G.P.O., 1980. iii, 252 p. : ill. ; 24 cm. "Publication no. 96-142." Includes bibliographical references. LC Card 80-604015 DDC 343.73/07862011/072073 347.3037862011072073 19
1. Materials - Law and legislation - United States. 2. Materials research - Law and legislation - United States. I. Title.
KF26 .E5543 1980e

Oil shale leasing : hearing before the Subcommittee on Energy Resources and Materials Production of the Committee on Energy and Natural Resources, United States Senate, Ninety-sixth Congress, second session, on S. 2858 ... September 9, 1980. Washington : U. S. G.P.O., 1980. iii, 143 p. : ill. ; 24 cm. "Publication no. 96-144." LC Card 80-604059 DDC 343.73/077 347.30377 19
1. Oil-shale industry - Law and legislation - United States. 2. Mining leases - United States. I. Title.
KF26 .E5543 1980g

Oversight on the Federal coal leasing program : hearing before the Subcommittee on Energy Resources and Materials Production of the Committee on Energy and Natural Resources, United States Senate, Ninety-sixth Congress, second session, on the review of the Dept. of the Interior's Federal coal management program, June 12, 1980. Washington : U. S. Govt. Print. Off., 1980. iii, 315 p. : ill. ; 24 cm. "Publication no. 96-124." LC Card 80-603709 DDC 353.0071/32 19
1. Coal leases - United States. I. Title.
KF26 .E5543 1980c

Production of oil from tar sand and other hydrocarbon deposits : hearing before the Subcommittee on Energy Resources and Materials Production of the Committee on Energy and Natural Resources, United States

Senate, Ninety-sixth Congress, second session, on S. 2717 ... H.R. 7242 ... September 4, 1980. Washington : U. S. G.P.O., 1980. iii, 142 p. : ill. ; 24 cm. "Publication no. 96-148." Includes bibliographical references. LC Card 81-600562 DDC 343.73/0772 347.303772 19
1. Oil sands - Law and legislation - United States. 2. Oil and gas leases - United States. I. Title.
KF26 .E5543 1980h

Reinstatement of oil and gas lease, New Mexico 33955 : hearing before the Subcommittee on Energy Resources and Materials Production of the Committee on Energy and Natural Resources, United States Senate, Ninety-sixth Congress, second session, on S. 2279 ... August 5, 1980. Washington : U. S. G.P.O., 1980. iii, 32 p. ; 24 cm. "Publication no. 96-133." LC Card 80-603814 DDC 346.78904/6823 347.890646823 19
1. Oil and gas leases - New Mexico. I. Title.
KF26 .E5543 1980d

Strategic petroleum reserve and the naval petroleum reserve : hearing before the Subcommittee on Energy Resources and Materials Production of the Committee on Energy and Natural Resources, United States Senate, Ninety-sixth Congress, second session ... April 18, 1980. Washington : U. S. Govt. Print. Off., 1980. iii, 65 p. ; 24 cm. "Publication no. 96-102." LC Card 80-602779 DDC 333.8/23211/0973 19
1. Petroleum - United States - Reserves. 2. Petroleum - United States - Storage. 3. United States - Armed Forces - Fuel. 4. Energy policy - United States. I. Title.
KF26 .E5543 1980a

Transfer of certain land and facilities used by the Bureau of Mines to Carnegie-Mellon University : hearing before the Subcommittee on Energy Resources and Materials Production of the Committee on Energy and Natural Resources, United States Senate, Ninety-sixth Congress, second session, on S. 2734 ... August 1, 1980. Washington : U. S. Govt. Print. Off., 1980. iii, 35 p. : ill. ; 23 cm. "Publication no. 96-141." LC Card 80-603896 DDC 343.73/025 347.30325 19
1. United States - Public lands. 2. United States. Bureau of Mines. 3. Carnegie-Mellon University. I. Title.
KF26 .E5543 1980f

United States. Congress. Senate. Committee on Commerce, Science, and Transportation. Georges Bank protection act . Washington , 1980. iii, 123 p. ; LC Card 80-602169 DDC 346.7304/695616/0262 19
KF26 .C69 1980f

United States. Congress. Senate. Committee on Energy and Natural Resources. Subcommittee on Parks, Recreation, and Renewable Resources.
The Archaeological resources protection act of 1979, and the Frederick Law Olmsted National Historic Site : hearing before the Subcommittee on Parks, Recreation, and Renewable Resources of the Committee on Energy and Natural Resources, United States Senate, Ninety-sixth Congress, first session on S. 490 ... S. 495 ... May 1, 1979. Washington : U. S. Govt. Print. Off., 1979. iii, 148 p. ; 24 cm. "Publication no. 96-26." LC Card 79-603538 DDC 344.73/094 19
1. Archaeology - Law and legislation - United States. 2. Cultural property, Protection of - Law and legislation - United States. 3. Historic sites - Law and legislation - United States. 4. Frederick Law Olmsted National Historic Site, Mass. I. Title.
KF26 .E5565 1979d

Barrier island protection system : hearing before the Subcommittee on Parks, Recreation, and Renewable Resources of the Committee on Energy and Natural Resources, United States Senate, Ninety-sixth Congress, second session, on S. 2686 ... June 12, 1980. Washington : U. S. G.P.O., 1980. iii, 465 p. : ill., maps ; 24 cm. "Publication no. 96-139." Bibliography: p. 281-283. LC Card 80-604056 DDC 346.7304/6784 347.30646784 19
1. Barrier islands - Law and legislation - United States. 2. National parks and reserves - United States. 3. Coastal zone management - Law and legislation - United States. I. Title.
KF26 .E5565 1980e

The Big Sur Coast National Scenic Area Act : hearing before the Subcommittee on Parks, Recreation, and Renewable Resources of the

United States. Congress. Senate. Committee on Energy and

BIBLIOGRAPHIC GUIDE

482

Committee on Energy and Natural Resources, United States Senate, Ninety-sixth Congress, second session, on S. 2551 ... April 24, 1980. Washington : U. S. G.P.O., 1980. iii, 391 p. : ill., maps ; 24 cm. "Publication no. 96-125." Includes bibliographical references.   LC Card 80-604084   DDC 346.7304/6784 347.30646784 19
1. Big Sur Coast National Scenic Area (Calif.). I. Title.
KF26 .E5565 1980f

Biscayne National Park, Florida ; Valley Forge National Historical Park, Pennsylvania; Vietnam Veterans Memorial ; and Salinas National Monument in New Mexico : hearing before the Subcommittee on Parks, Recreation, and Renewable Resources of the Committee on Energy and Natural Resources, United States Senate, Ninety-sixth Congress, second session ... March 12, 1980. Washington : U. S. Govt. Print. Off., 1980. iii, 195 p. : ill. ; 24 cm. Hearings on S. 1431, S. 1924, S. 2025, S. 2299, H.R. 5926, and S.J. Res. 119. "Publication no. 96-111."   LC Card 80-602956   DDC 346.7304/6783/0262 19
1. National parks and reserves - United States. I. Title.
KF26 .E5565 1980

Bureau of Land Management wilderness review and rangeland management programs : hearings before the Subcommittee on Parks, Recreation, and Renewable Resources of the Committee on Energy and Natural Resources, United States Senate, Ninety-sixth Congress, second session ... February 22 and March 11, 1980. Washington : U. S. Govt. Print. Off., 1980. iii, 189 p. ; 24 cm. "Publication no. 96-105." LC Card 80-602719 DDC 346.7304/6782/0262 19
1. United States. Bureau of Land Management. 2. Wilderness areas - The West. 3. Range management - The West. 4. The West - Public lands. I. Title.
KF26 .E5565 1980a

Colorado national forest wilderness act : hearing before the Subcommittee on Parks, Recreation, and Renewable Resources of the Committee on Energy and Natural Resources, United States Senate, Ninety-sixth Congress, second session, on S. 2123 ... H.R. 5487 ... March 13, 1980. Washington : U. S. Govt. Print. Off., 1980- v. : ill. ; 23 cm. "Publication no. 96-117."   LC Card 80-603318   DDC 346.7304/6784 19
1. Forest reserves - Colorado. 2. Forest reserves - South Dakota. I. Title.
KF26 .E5565 1980c

Missouri, South Dakota, and New Mexico wilderness : hearing before the Subcommittee on Parks, Recreation, and Renewable Resource of the Committee on Energy and Natural Resources, United States Senate, Ninety-sixth Congress, second session, on S. 1685 ... S. 1769 ... S. 2583 ... May 29, 1980. Washington : U. S. G.P.O., 1980. iii, 407 p. : ill., maps ;·24 cm. "Publication no. 96-140." Includes bibliographies.   LC Card 80-604055   DDC 346.7304/6782/0262 347.306467820262 19
1. Wilderness areas - Law and legislation - Missouri. 2. Wilderness areas - Law and legislation - New Mexico. 3. Black Hills National Forest (S.D. and Wyo.). I. Title.
KF26 .E5565 1980g

National heritage policy act of 1979 : hearing before the Subcommittee on Parks, Recreation, and Renewable Resources of the Committee on Energy and Natural Resources, United States Senate, Ninety-sixth Congress, second session, on S. 1842 ... April 17, 1980. Washington : U. S. Govt. Print. Off., 1980. iv, 517 p. : ill. ; 23 cm. "Publication no. 96-118." LC Card 80-603718 DDC 344.73/094 19
1. Historic sites - Law and legislation - United States. 2. Natural areas - Law and legislation - United States. I. Title.
KF26 .E5565 1980d

Oregon wilderness act of 1979 : hearings before the Subcommittee on Parks, Recreation, and Renewable Resources of the Committee on Energy and Natural Resources, United States Senate, Ninety-sixth Congress, first session, on S. 812 ... S. 1369 ... Pendleton, Oreg., July 3, 1979, Salem, Oreg., July 6, 1979, Washington, D.C., September 27, 1979. Washington : U. S. Govt. Print. Off., 1980. vii, 696 p. : ill. ; 24 cm. "Publication no. 96-114."   LC Card 80-603319   DDC 346.7304/6782/0262 19
1. Wilderness areas - Law and legislation - Oregon. I. Title.
KF26 .E5565 1979j

Preservation and protection of the Potomac

River shoreline : hearing before the Subcommittee on Parks, Recreation, and Renewable Resources of the Committee on Energy and Natural Resources, United States Senate, Ninety-sixth Congress, second session, on S. 1495 ... March 3, 1980. Washington : U. S. Govt. Print. Off., 1980. iii, 79 p. ; 24 cm. "Publication no. 96-108."   LC Card 80-602980   DDC 346.7304/6784 19
1. Potomac River - Shorelines - Law and legislation. 2. Government purchasing of real property - District of Columbia. 3. Waterfronts - Law and legislation - District of Columbia. I. Title.
KF26 .E5565 1980b

Rattlesnake roadless area : hearing before the Subcommittee on Parks, Recreation, and Renewable Resources of the Committee on Energy and Natural Resources, United States Senate, first session ... December 3, 1979. Washington : U. S. Govt. Print. Off., 1980. iii, 119 p. : ill. ; 24 cm. "Publication no. 96-98." Includes bibliographical references.   LC Card 80-602500   DDC 346.7304/6782 347.30646782 19
1. Lolo National Forest, Montana. 2. Wilderness areas - Montana. 3. Recreation areas - Montana. I. Title.
KF26 .E5565 1979k

Various parks and Bureau of Land Management related legislation : hearing before the Subcommittee on Parks, Recreation, and Renewable Resources of the Committee on Energy and Natural Resources, United States Senate, Ninety-sixth Congress, second session, on S. 1506, H.R. 1762, S. 1715, S. 1803, H.R. 3928, S. 1910, S. 1923, S. 1972, S. 1985, S. 1997, H.R. 1967, S. 2209, S. 2261, S. 2307, H.R. 920, S. 2363, S. 2364, and S. 2398, March 25, 1980. Washington : U. S. G.P.O., 1980. iii, 194 p. : ill. ; 24 cm. "Publication no. 96-149." 1040   LC Card 81-600804   DDC 346.7304/6783/0262 347.306467830262 19
1. National parks and reserves - United States. I. United States. Bureau of Land Management. II. Title.
KF26 .E5565 1980h

Yaquina Head Outstanding Natural Area : hearing before the Subcommittee on Parks, Recreation, and Renewable Resources of the Committee on Energy and Natural Resources, United States Senate, Ninety-sixth Congress, first session, on S. 1567 ... November 15, 1979. Washington : U. S. Govt. Print. Off., 1980. iii, 23 p. : ill. ; 24 cm. "Publication no. 96-85."   LC Card 80-601869   DDC 346.7304/6917 347.30646917 19
1. Yaquina Head Outstanding Natural Area, Or. I. Title.
KF26 .E5565 1979l

United States. Congress. Senate. Committee on Energy on Natural Resources. Energy Research and Development. Subcommittee on. see United States. Congress. Senate. Committee on Energy and Natural Resources. Subcommittee on Energy Research and Development.

United States. Congress. Senate. Committee on Environment and Public Works. Hearings printed in 1978 and later are available only in microform. Please consult the librarians in the Economic and Public Affairs Division.
Animal damage control program : policy changes oversight : hearings before the Committee on Environment and Public Works, United States Senate, Ninety-sixth Congress, second session, April 24 and 25, 1980. Washington : U. S. Govt. Print. Off., 1980. iv, 595 p. : ill. ; 24 cm. "Serial no. 96-H52."   LC Card 80-603724   DDC 639.9/6 19
1. Predator control - Government policy - United States. 2. Coyotes - Control - Government policy - United States. I. Title.
KF26 .E6 1980i

Architectural barriers in Federal buildings : implementation of the Architectural barriers act of 1968. Washington : U. S. Govt. Print. Off., 1979. viii, 50 p. : ill. ; 24 cm. At head of title: 96th Congress, 1st session. Committee print. "Serial no. 96-8."   LC Card 80-600819   DDC 353.0086/2 19
1. United States - Public buildings. 2. Architecture and the physically handicapped - Law and legislation - United States. I. Title.
KF5765 .A25 1979

Architectural competitions : hearing before the Committee on Environment and Public Works,

United States Senate, Ninety-sixth Congress, first session, on S. 461, a bill to require that competitions be conducted to enhance the Nation's architecture and determine the design of certain new Federal office buildings, October 15, 1979. Washington : U. S. Govt. Print. Off., 1979. iii, 87 p. : ill. ; 23 cm. "Serial no. 96-H28."   LC Card 80-600699   DDC 344.73/067251/0262 19
1. Architecture - Competitions - Law and legislation - United States. 2. United States - Public buildings. I. Title.
KF26 .E6 1979k

Federal building financing and user charges : hearing before the Committee on Environment and Public Works, United States Senate, Ninety-sixth Congress, first session, September 18, 1979. Washington : U. S. Govt. Print. Off., 1979. iii, 39 p. ; 23 cm. "Serial no. 96-H26."   LC Card 80-600570   DDC 353.0086/2 19
1. United States - Public buildings. I. Title.
KF26 .E6 1979l

Fish restoration act of 1979 : hearing before the Committee on Environment and Public Works, United States Senate, Ninety-sixth Congress, second session, on S. 1631 ... May 20, 1980. Washington : U. S. Govt. Print. Off., 1980. iv, 229 p. : maps ; 24 cm. "Serial no. 96-H51."   LC Card 80-603307   DDC 343.73/07692 19
1. Fishery law and legislation - United States. I. Title.
KF26 .E6 1980h

Leasing of unoccupied space : hearing before the Committee on Environment and Public Works, United States Senate, Ninety-sixth Congress, second session, January 25, 1980. Washington : U. S. Govt. Print. Off., 1980. ii, 83 p. ; 23 cm. "Serial no. 96-H37."   LC Card 80-601863   DDC 353.0071/23 19
1. Office leases - United States. 2. United States - Public buildings. I. Title.
KF26 .E6 1980j

Nomination of Albert Carnesale : hearing before the Committee on Environment and Public Works, United States Senate, Ninety-sixth Congress, second session, on the nomination of Albert Carnesale to be a member of the Nuclear Regulatory Commission, August 5, 1980. Washington : U. S. Govt. Print. Off., 1980. iii, 138 p. ; 24 cm. "Serial no. 96-H54."   LC Card 80-603300   DDC 353.0087/22 19
1. Carnesale, Albert. 2. United States. Nuclear Regulatory Commission - Officials and employees. I. Title.
KF26 .E6 1980f

Nomination of John S. Hassell, Jr. : hearing before the Committee on Environment and Public Works, United States Senate, Ninety-sixth Congress, second session, on the nomination of John S. Hassell to be Federal Highway Administrator, June 3, 1980. Washington : U. S. Govt. Print. Off., 1980. iii, 39 p. ; 24 cm. "Serial no. 96-H49."   LC Card 80-603010   DDC 353.0086/42 19
1. Hassell, John S. 2. United States. Federal Highway Administration - Officials and employees. I. Title.
KF26 .E6 1980e

Nomination of Ray A. Barnhart : hearing before the Committee on Environment and Public Works, United States Senate, Ninety-seventh Congress, first session, on the nomination of Ray A. Barnhart to be administrator of the Federal Highway Administration, February 4, 1981. Washington : U. S. G.P.O., 1981. iii, 38 p. ; 24 cm. "Serial no. 97-H2." Item 1045-A, 1945-B (microfiche)   LC Card 81-601612   DDC 353.0086/42 19
1. Barnhart, Ray A., 1928-. 2. United States. Federal Highway Administration - Officials and employees. I. Title.
KF26 .E6 1981

Public buildings proposals : hearings before the Committee on Environment and Public Works, United States Senate, Ninety-sixth Congress, second session ... May 2 and June 16, 1980. Washington : U. S. Govt. Print. Off., 1980. iv, 318 p. : ill. ; 23 cm. "Serial no. 96-H47."   LC Card 80-603295   DDC 353.0086/2 19
1. United States - Public buildings. I. Title.
KF26 .E6 1980g

Recycling of used oil : hearing before the Committee on Environment and Public Works, United States Senate, Ninety-sixth Congress, second session, on S. 2412 ... May 5, 1980.

Washington : U. S. Govt. Print. Off., 1980. iii, 111 p. ; 24 cm. "Serial no. 96-H48." Includes bibliographical references. LC Card 80-603011 DDC 346.73/04622 19
1. Petroleum waste - Law and legislation - United States. 2. Petroleum waste - Recycling - United States. I. Title.
KF26 .E6 1980d

Report of the Steel Tripartite Committee : hearing before the Committee on Environment and Public Works, United States Senate, Ninety-sixth Congress, second session, December 4, 1980. Washington : U. S. G.P.O., 1981. iii, 124 p. ; 24 cm. "Serial no. 96-H60." Bibliography: p. 119. Item 1045 LC Card 81-601353 DDC 338.4/7669142/0973 19
1. United States. Steel Tripartite Committee. 2. Steel industry and trade - United States. I. Title.
KF26 .E6 1980k

S. 344, the Highway beautification assistance act of 1979 : prevailing and nonprevailing views of the Committee on Environment and Public Works. Washington : U. S. Govt. Print. Off., 1980. iii, 9 p. ; 23 cm. At head of title: 96th Congress, 2d session. Committee print. "Serial no. 96-11." "March 1980." LC Card 80-601737 DDC 346.7304/5 19
1. Roadside improvement - Law and legislation - United States. 2. Roadside improvement - United States - Finance. I. Title. II. Title: Highway beautification assistance act of 1979.
KF5532 .A25 1980

Testimony of Andrew L. Lewis, Jr. : hearing before the Committee on Environment and Public Works, United States Senate, Ninety-seventh Congress, first session, to receive testimony from Andrew L. Lewis, Jr., secretary-designate, Department of Transportation, January 13, 1981. Washington : U. S. G.P.O., 1981. iii, 34 p. ; 24 cm. "Serial no. 97-H 1." Item 1045-A, 1045-B (microfiche) LC Card 81-601349 DDC 353.0087/5 19
1. Transportation and state - United States. 2. Lewis, Andrew Lindsay, 1931-. I. Title.
KF26 .E6 1981a

United States. Congress. Senate. Committee on Environment and Public Works. Subcommittee on Nuclear Regulation. Nuclear accident and recovery at Three Mile Island . Washington , 1980. vii, 423 p. : LC Card 80-603139 DDC 363.1/79 19
TK1345.H37 U5 1980

United States. Congress. Senate. Select Committee on Small Business. Economic impact of acid rain . Washington , 1980. iii, 224 p. : LC Card 81-600642 DDC 330.973/0926 19
KF26.5 .S6 1980u

United States. Library of Congress. Congressional Research Service. State and national water use trends to the year 2000 . Washington , 1980. x, 297 p. : LC Card 80-602584 DDC 333.91/13/0973 19
TD223 .U53 1980a

Viessman, Warren. Assessing the nation's water resources . Washington , 1980. [76] p. : LC Card 81-600801 DDC 333.91/0028/7 19
TD223 .V53

United States. Congress. Senate. Committee on Environment and Public Works. Environmental Pollution, Subcommittee on. see United States. Congress. Senate. Committee on Environment and Public Works. Subcommittee on Environmental Pollution.

United States. Congress. Senate. Committee on Environment and Public Works. Subcommittee on Environmental Pollution. Environmental effects of the increased use of coal : hearings before the Subcommittee on Environmental Pollution of the Committee on Environment and Public Works, United States Senate, Ninety-sixth Congress, second session, March 19, April 21 and 24, 1980. Washington : U. S. Govt. Print. Off., 1980. iii, 453 p. : ill. ; 24 cm. "Serial no. 96-H45." Includes bibliographies. LC Card 80-603081 DDC 333.8/2215/0973 19
1. Coal - Combustion - Environmental aspects - United States. 2. Acid rain - United States. I. Title.
KF26 .E645 1980b

Implementation of certain sections of the Clean water act : hearings before the Subcommittee on Environmental Pollution of the Committee

on Environment and Public Works, United States Senate, Ninety-sixth Congress, second session, June 23, 24, and July 1, 1980. Washington : U. S. Govt. Print. Off., 1980. iv, 376 p. : ill. ; 24 cm. "Serial no. 96-H55." Includes bibliographical references. LC Card 80-603477 DDC 353.0082/326 19
1. Wetlands conservation - Government policy - United States. I. Title. II. Title: Clean water act.
KF26 .E645 1980c

Industrial cost recovery : hearing before the Subcommittee on Environmental Pollution of the Committee on Environment and Public Works, United States Senate, Ninety-sixth Congress, second session, March 18, 30, and 31, 1980. Washington : U. S. Govt. Print. Off., 1980. iii, 342 p. ; 24 cm. "Serial no. 96-H42." LC Card 80-602810 DDC 353.0082/325 19
1. Factory and trade waste - United States - Costs. 2. Sewage disposal - United States - Costs. 3. Sewage disposal - United States - Finance. 4. Water - Pollution - Economic aspects - United States. I. Title.
KF26 .E645 1980a

United States. Congress. Senate. Select Committee on Small Business. Impact of funding EPA sewer treatment construction program on small business contractors . Washington , 1980. iii, 180 p. : LC Card 80-603692 DDC 338.4/36283/0977595 19
KF26.5 .S6 1980p

United States. Congress. Senate. Committee on Environment and Public Works. Subcommittee on Nuclear Regulation. Nuclear accident and recovery at Three Mile Island . Washington , 1980. vii, 423 p. : LC Card 81-600709 DDC 363.1/79 19
TK1344.P4 N82

Nuclear accident and recovery at Three Mile Island : a report / prepared by the Subcommittee on Nuclear Regulation for the Committee on Environment and Public Works, U. S. Senate. Washington : U. S. Govt. Print. Off., 1980. vii, 423 p. : ill. ; 26 cm. At head of title: 96th Congress, 2d session. Committee print. "Serial no. 96-14." "June 1980." Includes bibliographical references. LC Card 80-603139 DDC 363.1/79 19
1. Three Mile Island Nuclear Power Plant, Pa. 2. Atomic power-plants - Pennsylvania - Accidents. I. United States. Congress. Senate. Committee on Environment and Public Works. II. Title.
TK1345.H37 U5 1980

United States. Congress. Senate. Committee on Environment and Public Works. Subcommittee on Regional and Community Development. Commercialization of guayule rubber : hearing before the Subcommittee on Regional and Community Development of the Committee on Environment and Public Works, United States Senate, Ninety-sixth Congress, second session ... March 20, 1980. Washington : U. S. Govt. Print. Off., 1980. iii, 172 p. : graphs ; 24 cm. "Serial no. 96-46." LC Card 80-602785 DDC 338.1/73895 19
1. Guayule - Research - United States. I. Title.
KF26 .E674 1980

United States. Congress. Senate. Committee on Environment and Public Works. Subcommittee on Resource Protection. Elephant Protection Act of 1979 and the International Wildlife Resources Conservation Act of 1980 : hearing before the Subcommittee on Resource Protection of the Committee on Environment and Public Works, United States Senate, Ninety-sixth Congress, second session, on H.R. 4685 ... June 30, 1980. Washington : U. S. G.P.O., 1980. iii, 220 p. : facsims. ; 23 cm. "Serial no. 96-H53." Includes bibliographical references. LC Card 80-603406 DDC 346.7304/6954 347.30646954 19
1. Elephants - Law and legislation - United States. 2. Wildlife conservation - Law and legislation - United States. I. Title.
KF26 .E675 1980a

Fish and wildlife conservation act of 1980 and authorizations for wildlife refuges : hearing before the Subcommittee on Resource Protection of the Committee on Environment and Public Works, United States Senate, Ninety-sixth Congress, second session on S. 2181 ... February 4, 1980. Washington : U. S. Govt. Print. Off., 1980. iv, 351 p. : ill. ; 24 cm. "Serial no. 96-H39." LC Card 80-602456 DDC 346.7304/69516/0262 19

1. Wildlife conservation - Law and legislation - United States. 2. Wildlife refuges - Law and legislation - United States. 3. Wildlife refuges - United States - Finance. I. Title.
KF26 .E675 1980

United States. Congress. Senate. Committee on Environment and Public Works. Subcommittee on Transportation. Automobile use management : hearing before the Subcommittee on Transportation of the Committee on Environment and Public Works, United States Senate, Ninety-sixth Congress, second session, July 22, 1980. Washington : U. S. G.P.O., 1980. iii, 133 p. : ill. ; 23 cm. "Serial no. 96-H57." LC Card 80-603909 DDC 388.4/1321 19
1. Car pools - United States. 2. Transportation and state - United States. 3. Automobiles - United States - Fuel consumption. 4. Energy conservation - United States. I. Title.
KF26 .E679 1980b

Funding for the Federal-aid highway program : hearings before the Subcommittee on Transportation of the Committee on Environment and Public Works, United States Senate, Ninety-sixth Congress, second session, on S. 2913 ... August 19 and September 9, 1980. Washington : U. S. Govt. Print. Off., 1980. iv, 552 p. : ill. ; 24 cm. "Serial no. 96-H59." LC Card 80-603903 DDC 343.73/0942 347.303942 19
1. Highway law - United States. 2. Roads - United States - Finance. I. Title.
KF26 .E679 1980a

To provide compliance with the national maximum speed limit : hearing before the Subcommittee on Transportation of the Committee on Environment and Public Works, United States Senate, Ninety-sixth Congress, second session, on S. 1337 ... June 3, 1980. Washington : U. S. Govt. Print. Off., 1980. iii, 141 p. : ill. ; 24 cm. "Serial no. 96-H50." LC Card 80-603026 DDC 343.73/0946 19
1. Speed limits - Law and legislation - United States. I. Title.
KF26 .E679 1980

United States. Congress. Senate. Committee on Environment and Public Works. Subcommittee on Water Resources. To establish a national water policy : hearings before the Subcommittee on Water Resources of the Committee on Environment and Public Works, United States Senate, Ninety-fifth Congress ... Washington : U. S. Govt. Off., 19<78> v. <2> : ill. ; 23 cm. Hearings held in various cities, Aug. 10-Dec. 6, 1978. "Serial no. 95-H16." LC Card 81-461639 DDC 333.91/00973 19
1. Water resources development - Government policy - United States. I. Title.
KF26 .E683 1978

Transportation needs of increased coal production and completion of the Tennessee-Tombigbee Waterway : hearings before the Subcommittee on Water Resources of the Committee on Environment and Public Works, United States, Senate, Ninety-sixth Congress, second session, July 25, 28, and 29, 1980. Washington : U. S. Govt. Print. Off., 1980. iv, 550 p. : ill. ; 23 cm. "Serial no. 96-H56." LC Card 80-603720 DDC 386/.3/09761 19
1. Coal - United States - Transportation. 2. Tennessee-Tombigbee waterway. I. Title.
KF26 .E683 1980

United States. Congress. Senate. Committee on Expenditures in the Executive Departments. see United States. Congress. Senate. Committee on Government Operations.

United States. Congress. Senate. Committee on Finance. (Old Catalog form: United States. Finance, Committee on (Senate) // Hearings printed in 1978 and later are available only in microform. Please consult the librarians in the Economic and Public Affairs Division. Employee stock ownership plans : an employer handbook / prepared by the staff of the Committee on Finance, United States Senate. Washington : U. S. Govt. Print. Off. : for sale by the Supt. of Docs., U. S. Govt. Print. Off., [1980] v, 63 p. : ill. ; 24 cm. At head of title: 96th Congress, 2d session. Committee print. CP 96-25. "April 1980." LC Card 80-602272 DDC 658.3/225 19

BIBLIOGRAPHIC GUIDE

United States. Congress. Senate. Committee on Finance. *(cont.)*

484

1. *Employee ownership - United States. I. Title.*
HD2984 .U53 1980

The Environmental Emergency Response Act : hearings before the Committee on Finance, United States Senate, Ninety-sixth Congress, second session, on S. 1480, September 11 and 12, 1980. Washington : U. S. G.P.O., 1980. v, 679 p. : ill. ; 24 cm. Includes bibliographical references. LC Card 80-603786   DDC 344.73/0462 347.304462 19
1. *Hazardous substances - Law and legislation - United States. 2. Hazardous wastes - Law and legislation - United States. 3. Liability for hazardous substances pollution damages - United States. I. Title.*
KF26 .F5 1980e

Nomination of Curtis A. Hessler : hearing before the Committee on Finance, United States Senate, Ninety-sixth Congress, second session, on the nomination of Curtis A. Hessler, to be an Assistant Secretary of the Treasury for Economic Policy, March 26, 1980. Washington : U. S. Govt. Print. Off., 1980. iii, 22 p. ; 24 cm.   LC Card 80-603001   DDC 353.2 19
1. *Hessler, Curtis A. 2. United States. Treasury Dept. - Officials and employees. I. Title.*
KF26 .F5 1980c

Nomination of Richard S. Schweiker : hearing before the Committee on Finance, United States Senate Ninety-seventh Congress, first session, on nomination of Richard S. Schweiker to be secretary of health and human services, January 6, 1981. Washington : U. S. G.P.O., c1981. iii, 39 p. ; 24 cm. Item 1038-A, 1038-B (microfiche)   LC Card 81-600829   DDC 353.842 19
1. *Schweiker, Richard Schultz, 1926-. 2. United States. Dept. of Health and Human Services - Officials and employees. I. Title.*
KF26 .F5 1981

Nomination of William E. Brock III : Hearing before the Committee on Finance, United States Senate, Ninety-seventh Congress, first session, on nomination of William E. Brock III to be U. S. trade representative. Washington : U. S. G.P.O., 1981. ii, 43 p. ; 24 cm. Item 1038-A, 1038-B (microfiche)   LC Card 81-601985   DDC 353.0082/7 19
1. *Brock, William Emerson, d 1930-. 2. United States. Office of the U. S. Trade Representative - Officials and employees. I. Title.*
KF26 .F5 1981c

Nominations of Abraham Katz, William J. Driver, and John L. Palmer : hearing before the Committee on Finance, United States Senate, Ninety-sixth Congress, second session ... March 19, 1980. Washington : U. S. Govt. Print. Off., 1980. iii, 19 p. ; 24 cm.   LC Card 80-602760   DDC 353.842 19
1. *Katz, Abraham, 1926-. 2. Driver William J. 3. Palmer, John Logan. 4. United States. Dept. of Commerce - Officials and employees. 5. United States. Social Security Administration - Officials and employees. 6. United States. Dept. of Health, Education, and Welfare - Officials and employees. I. Title.*
KF26 .F5 1980b

Nominations of John E. Chapoton, Roscoe L. Egger, Jr., and Paul C. Roberts : hearing before the Committee on Finance, United States Senate, Ninety-seventh Congress, first session, on nomination of John E. Chapoton, to be assistant secretary of the treasury for tax policy; Roscoe L. Egger, Jr., to be the commissioner of internal revenue; and Paul C. Roberts, to be assistant secretary of the treasury for economic policy, March 5, 1981. Washington : U. S. G.P.O., 1981. iii, 40 p. ; 24 cm. Item 1038-A, 1038-B (microfiche)   LC Card 81-601602   DDC 353.2 19
1. *Chapoton, John E. 2. Egger, Roscoe L. 3. Roberts, Paul Craig, 1939-. 4. United States. Dept. of the Treasury - Officials and employees. 5. United States. Internal Revenue Service - Officials and employees. I. Title.*
KF26 .F5 1981d

Nominations of Norman B. Ture and Beryl Wayne Sprinkel : hearing before the Committee on Finance, United States Senate, Ninety-seventh Congress, first session, on nominations of Norman B. Ture, to be under secretary of the treasury and Beryl Wayne Sprinkel, to be under secretary of the treasury for monetary affairs, March 20, 1981.

Washington : U. S. G.P.O., 1981. iii, 17 p. ; 24 cm. Item 1038-A, 1038-B (microfiche)   LC Card 81-601959   DDC 353.2 19
1. *Ture, Norman B. 2. Sprinkel, Beryl Wayne, 1923-. 3. United States. Dept. of the Treasury - Officials and employees. I. Title.*
KF26 .F5 1981e

Nominations of Robert E. Herzstein, C. Moxley Featherston, William M. Fay, Charles R. Simpson, Edna Parker, and Sheldon V. Ekman : hearings before the Committee on Finance, United States Senate, and the Subcommittee on International Trade, Ninety-sixth Congress, second session ... April 29, May 12 and 14, 1980. Washington : U. S. G.P.O., 1980. iii, 80 p. ; 24 cm. "HG 96-83." LC Card 80-603685   DDC 353.0072/4 19
1. *United States. Tax Court - Officials and employees. 2. United States. Dept. of Commerce - Officials and employees. I. United States. Congress. Senate. Committee on Finance. Subcommittee on International Trade. II. Title.*
KF26 .F5 1980f

Proposed residential energy efficiency plan : hearing before the Committee on Finance, United States Senate, Ninety-sixth Congress, first session, on S. 1800 ... September 26, 1979. Washington : U. S. Govt. Print. Off., 1979. iii, 74 p. ; 24 cm.   LC Card 80-600624   DDC 346.7304/67916/0262 19
1. *Energy conservation - Law and legislation - United States. 2. Dwellings - United States - Energy conservation. I. Title.*
KF26 .F5 1979l

Staff data and materials relating to social and child welfare services / Committee on Finance, United States Senate. Washington : U. S. Govt. Print. Off., 1979. iv, 65 p. ; 24 cm. At head of title: 96th Congress, 1st session. Committee print, CP 96-29. Prepared for the use of the Subcommittee on Public Assistance. LC Card 79-603783   DDC 362.7 19
1. *Child welfare - United States - Finance - Statistics. 2. Children - Legal status, laws, etc. - United States. I. Title.*
HV741 .U523 1979a

Staff data and materials relating to the International sugar stabilization act of 1979 / Committee on Finance, United States Senate. Washington : U. S. Govt. Print. Off., 1979. iii, 70 p. ; 24 cm. At head of title: 96th Congress, 1st session. Committee print, CP 96-8. "For use of the Subcommittee on Tourism and Sugar." LC Card 79-601697   DDC 343.73/08756641 347.3038756641 19
1. *Sugar laws and legislation - United States. 2. Sugar laws and legislation. I. United States. Congress. Senate. Committee on Finance. Subcommittee on Tourism and Sugar. II. Title.*
KF1996.S8 A25 1979

Tax cut proposals : hearings before the Committee on Finance, United States Senate, Ninety-sixth Congress, second session. Washington : U. S. Govt. Print. Off., 1980- v. : graphs ; 24 cm. Hearings held July 23-31, 1980. Pt. 1 has also special title: Administration witness and communications. Includes bibliographical references. LC Card 80-603089   DDC 343.7304/0262 19
1. *Income tax - Law and legislation - United States. 2. Taxation - Law and legislation - United States. I. Title.*
KF26 .F5 1980d

United States. [Social Security Act.] The Social Security Act and related laws /. Washington , 1980. viii, 856, xxx p. ;   LC Card 81-601049   DDC 344.73/02 347.3042 19
KF3644 1980

United States. Congress. Joint Committee on Taxation. Description of legislation relating to Pension Benefit Guaranty Corporation plan termination insurance for multiemployer pension plans . Washington , 1980. iii, 56 p. ;   LC Card 80-602420   DDC 344.73/01252 19
KF3512 .A25 1980b

United States. Congress. Joint Committee on Taxation. Description of S. 219, relating to the deduction for charitable contributions scheduled for hearings before the Subcommittee on Taxation and Debt Management Generally of the Committee on Finance, on January 30 and 31, 1980 /. Washington , 1980. iii, 14 p.;   LC Card 80-602135   DDC 343-7305/232 19
KF6388 .A25 1980

United States. Congress. Joint Committee on Taxation. Estimates of federal tax expenditures for fiscal years, 1980-1985 /. Washington , 1980. ii, 21 p. ;   LC Card 81-600720   DDC 336.2 19
HJ4652 .U627 1980

United States. Congress. Joint Committee on Taxation. The income tax treatment of married couples and single persons . Washington , 1980. iii, 68 p. ;   LC Card 80-601745   DDC 343.7305/2/024065 19
KF6355.5 .T38

United States. Congress. Joint Committee on Taxation. Staff recommendations for simplication of tax rules relating to subchapter S corporations . Washington , 1980. iii, 27 p. ;   LC Card 80-602271   DDC 343.7306/8 19
KF6491 .A25 1980

United States. Congress. Office of Technology Assessment. The implications of cost-effectiveness analysis of medical technology. Washington, D.C. [1980] vii, 219 p. :   LC Card 80-600130   DDC 362.1/068/1 19
RA410.5 .U54 1980

United States. General Accounting Office. Employee stock ownership plans . Washington, D.C. [1980] v, 52 p. ;   LC Card 80-603177   DDC 658.3/225 19
HD5660.U5 U54 1980

UNITED STATES. CONGRESS. SENATE. COMMITTEE ON FINANCE.
United States. Congress. Joint Committee on Taxation. Description of S. 983 and S. 1688 relating to state taxation of interstate business and foreign source corporate income . Washington , 1980. iii, 29 p. ;   LC Card 80-602680   DDC 343.7305/267 19
KF6755 .A25 1980

United States. Congress. Senate. Committee on Finance. Social Security, Subcommittee on.
see United States. Congress. Senate. Committee on Finance. Subcommittee on Social Security.

United States. Congress. Senate. Committee on Finance. Subcommittee on Health.
Comprehensive community based noninstitutional long-term care for the elderly and disabled : hearing before the Subcommittee on Health of the Committee on Finance, United States Senate, Ninety-sixth Congress, second session, on S. 2809 ... August 27, 1980. Washington : U. S. G.P.O., 1980 [i.e. 1981] iv, 401 p. : ill. ; 24 cm. Item 1038 Includes bibliographical references.   LC Card 81-600839   DDC 344.73/03263 347.3043263 19
1. *Community health services for the aged - Law and legislation - United States. 2. Community health services - Law and legislation - United States. 3. Aged - Home care - Law and legislation - United States. 4. Long-term care of the sick - Law and legislation - United States. I. Title.*
KF26 .F5538 1980b

Medicare and medicaid fraud : hearing before the Subcommittee on Health of the Committee on Finance, United States Senate, Ninety-sixth Congress, second session, July 22, 1980. Washington : U. S. G.P.O., c1980. iii, 49 p. ; 24 cm. Item 1038   LC Card 81-600588   DDC 364.1/63 19
1. *Medicare fraud. 2. Medicaid fraud. I. Title.*
KF26 .F5538 1980c

Proposals to stimulate health care competition : hearings before the Subcommittee on Health of the Committee on Finance, United States Senate, Ninety-sixth Congress, second session, on S. 1968 ... March 18 and 19, 1980. Washington : U. S. Govt. Print. Off., 1980. iv, 462 p. : ill. ; 24 cm.   LC Card 80-602729   DDC 344.73/022 19
1. *Insurance, Health - United States. 2. Medical care, Cost of - Law and legislation - United States. I. Title.*
KF26 .F5538 1980

United States. Congress. Senate. Committee on Finance. Subcommittee on International Trade.
Authorization of appropriations for the U. S. Customs Service, U. S. International Trade Commission, and Office of the U. S. Trade Representative, for fiscal year 1981 : hearing before the Subcommittee on International Trade of the Committee on Finance, United States Senate, Ninety-sixth Congress, second session,

March 13, 1980. Washington : U. S. Govt.
Print. Off., 1980. iii, 79 p. : graphs ; 24 cm.
LC Card 80-603102 DDC 353.0072/23682/7 19
*1. United States. Customs Service - Appropriations and
expenditures. 2. United States. International Trade
Commission - Appropriations and expenditures. 3.
United States. Office of the U. S. Trade
Representative - Appropriations and expenditures. I.
Title.*
KF26 .F554 1980b

Conference on U. S. Competitiveness (1980 :
Harvard University) Conference on U. S.
Competitiveness . Washington , 1980. viii, 109
p. ; LC Card 80-603876 DDC 382/.0973 19
HF1436 .C65 1980

Extension of the president's authority to waive
section 402 (freedom of emigration
requirements) of the Trade Act of 1974 :
hearing before the Subcommittee on
International Trade of the Committee on
Finance, United States Senate, Ninety-sixth
Congress, second session, July 21, 1980.
Washington : U. S. G.P.O., 1980. v, 515 p. :
ill. ; 24 cm. Includes bibliographical references. LC
Card 81-600640 DDC 342.73/082
347.3028202646 19
*1. Emigration and immigration law - United States. 2.
Refugees, Political - Legal status, laws, etc. - United
States. I. Title.*
KF26 .F554 1980d

Import relief to the domestic industry
producing certain leather coats and jackets :
hearing before the Subcommittee on
International Trade of the Committee on
Finance, United States Senate, Ninety-sixth
Congress, second session, on S. Con. Res.
108 ... August 19, 1980. Washington : U. S.
G.P.O., 1980. iii, 192 p. ; 24 cm. Item1038
Includes bibliographical references. LC Card
81-600635 DDC 382/.4568502/0973 19
*1. Tariff on leather garments - Law and legislation -
United States. I. Title.*
KF26 .F554 1980h

Issues relating to the domestic auto industry :
hearings before the Subcommittee on
International Trade of the Committee on
Finance, United States Senate, Ninety-seventh
Congress, first session .... Washington : U. S.
G.P.O., 1981- v. <1 > : ill. ; 24 cm. Item
1038-A, 1038-B (microfiche) CONTENTS: - Pt. 1.
"January 14 and 15, 1981" -- LC Card 81-601788
DDC 338.4/76292/0973 19
*1. Automobile industry and trade - United States. 2.
Automobiles - United States - Design and construction.
3. Competition, International. I. Title.*
KF26 .F554 1981a

Jackson, John Howard, 1932- MTN and the
legal institutions of international trade .
Washington , 1979. ii, 22 p. ; LC Card
79-603786 DDC 341.7/543 19
K4602.2 1979

Miscellaneous tariff bills : hearing before the
Subcommittee on International Trade of the
Committee on Finance, United States Senate,
Ninety-sixth Congress, second session ...
February 5, 1980. Washington : U. S. Govt.
Print. Off., 1980. v, 322 p. : ill. ; 24 cm. Hearing
on H.R. 2492 (S. 1258), H.R. 2535, H.R. 2537, H.R.
3046 (S. 1004), H.R. 3317, H.R. 3591, H.R. 3755, H.R.
4309 (S. 1275), H.R. 4738, H.R. 6089, S. 1851, S.
1852. LC Card 80-601975 DDC 343.7305/6/0262
19
1. Tariff - Law and legislation - United States. I. Title.
KF26 .F554 1980

Miscellaneous tariff bills : hearing before the
Subcommittee on International Trade of the
Committee on Finance, United States Senate,
Ninety-sixth Congress, second session, on H.R.
3122, H.R. 5047, and H.R. 7139, September 9,
1980. Washington : U. S. G.P.O., 1980 [i.e.
1981] iii, 158 p. : ill. ; 24 cm. Item 1038 Includes
bibliographical references. LC Card 81-601217 DDC
343.7305/6/0262 347.303560262 19
1. Tariff - Law and legislation - United States. I. Title.
KF26 .F554 1980f

North American economic interdependence :
hearing before the Subcommittee on
International Trade of the Committee on
Finance, United States Senate, Ninety-sixth
Congress, first session, June 6, 1979.
Washington : U. S. Govt. Print. Off., 1979. iii,
110 p. ; 24 cm. LC Card 80-601405 DDC
337.1/7 19

*1. United States - Relations (general) with Canada. 2.
Canada - Relations (general) with the United States. 3.
United States - Relations (general) with Mexico. 4.
Mexico - Relations (general) with the United States. I.
Title.*
KF26 .F554 1979j

Possible amendments to the "1916 Antidumping
act" : hearing before the Subcommittee on
International Trade of the Committee on
Finance, United States Senate, Ninety-sixth
Congress, second session, March 11, 1980.
Washington : U. S. Govt. Print. Off., 1980. iii,
148 p. ; 24 cm. Includes bibliographical references.
LC Card 80-603689 DDC 343.7/04626 19
1. Antidumping duties - United States. I. Title.
KF26 .F554 1980c

Protocol to the MTN customs valuation
agreement : hearing before the Subcommittee
on International Trade of the Committee on
Finance, United States Senate, Ninety-sixth
Congress, second session, April 2, 1980.
Washington : U. S. Govt. Print. Off., 1980. 23
p. ; 23 cm. LC Card 80-602438 DDC 353.0082/7
19
*1. Customs appraisal. 2. Customs appraisal - United
States. I. Title.*
KF26 .F554 1980a

Review of the U. S. generalized system of
preferences : hearing before the Subcommittee
on International Trade of the Committee on
Finance, United States Senate, Ninety-sixth
Congress, second session, November 25, 1980.
Washington : U. S. G.P.O., 1981. iv, 300 p. :
ill. ; 24 cm. Item 1038 Includes bibliographical
references. LC Card 81-601603 DDC
382.7/53/0973 19
*1. Tariff preferences - United States. 2. Underdeveloped
areas - Commerce. I. Title.*
KF26 .F554 1980g

U. S. international trade strategy : hearings
before the Subcommittee on International Trade
of the Committee on Finance, United States
Senate, Ninety-sixth Congress, second session,
July 28, August 1, September 10, 1980.
Washington : U. S. G.P.O., : for sale by the
Supt. of Docs., U. S. G.P.O., 1980. iii, 494 p. :
graphs ; 23 cm. LC Card 80-603898 DDC
382/.3/0973 19
*1. International economic relations. 2. Commercial
policy. 3. United States - Commercial policy. 4. United
States - Foreign economic relations. I. Title.*
KF26 .F554 1980e

United States. Congress. Senate. Committee on
Finance. Nominations of Robert E. Herzstein,
C. Moxley Featherston, William M. Fay,
Charles R. Simpson, Edna Parker, and Sheldon
V. Ekman . Washington , 1980. iii, 80 p. ; LC
Card 80-603685 DDC 353.0072/4 19
KF26 .F5 1980f

United States. International Trade Commission.
Agreements being negotiated at the mutilateral
trade negotiations in Geneva-- U. S.
International Trade Commission investigation
no. 332-101 . Washington , 1979- v. ; LC Card
79-603800 DDC 341.7/54/0265 19
K4603 1973 .U54

Unpaid claims of U. S. citizens against
Czechoslovakia : hearing before the
Subcommittee on International Trade of the
Committee on Finance, United States Senate,
Ninety-sixth Congress, second session, on S.
2721 ... September 9, 1980. Washington : U. S.
G.P.O., c1980 [i.e. 1981] iii, 217 p. : ill. ; 24
cm. Item 1038 Includes bibliographical references.
LC Card 81-600978 DDC 342.73/082 347.30282
19
*1. United States - Claims vs. Czechoslovakia. 2. United
States - Commerce - Czechoslovakia. 3.
Czechoslovakia - Commerce - United States. I. Title.*
KF26 .F554 1981

**United States. Congress. Senate. Committee on
Finance. Subcommittee on Oversight of the
Internal Revenue Service.**
IRS and nontax related criminal enforcement
investigation : hearing before the Subcommittee
on Oversight of the Internal Revenue Service of
the Committee on Finance, United States
Senate, Ninety-sixth Congress, second session
on S. 2402, S. 2403, S. 2404, S. 2405, June 20,
1980. Washington : U. S. G.P.O., 1980. iii, 371
p. ; 24 cm. LC Card 80-603799 DDC
345.73/0233 347.305233 19
1. Confidential communications - Taxation - United

*States. 2. United States. Internal Revenue Service. 3.
Law enforcement - United States. I. Title.*
KF26 .F56 1980

United States. Congress. Joint Committee on
Taxation. Description of bills (S. 2402, S. 2403,
S. 2404, and S. 2405) relating to disclosure of
tax returns and return information listed for a
hearing before the Subcommittee on Oversight
of the Internal Revenue Service of the
Committee on Finance, on June 20, 1980 /.
Washington , 1980. iii, 18 p. ; LC Card
80-602679 DDC 343.7305/2 19
KF6328 .A25 1980

**United States. Congress. Senate. Committee on
Finance. Subcommittee on Private Pension
Plans and Employee Fringe Benefits.**
Pension plan termination insurance for
multiemployer pension plans : hearing before
the Subcommittee on Private Pension Plans and
Employee Fringe Benefits of the Committee on
Finance, United States Senate, Ninety-sixth
Congress, second session, on S. 1076 ... March
18, 1980. Washington : U. S. Govt. Print. Off.,
1980. iii, 315 p. ; 24 cm. LC Card 80-602745
DDC 344.73/01252 19
*1. Pension trusts - United States. 2. Pension Benefit
Guaranty Corporation. I. Title.*
KF26 .F565 1980

United States. Congress. Joint Committee on
Taxation. Description of legislation relating to
Pension Benefit Guaranty Corporation plan
termination insurance for multiemployer
pension plans . Washington , 1980. iii, 56 p. ;
LC Card 80-602420 DDC 344.73/01252 19
KF3512 .A25 1980b

**United States. Congress. Senate. Committee on
Finance. Subcommittee on Revenue Sharing,
Intergovernmental Revenue Impact, and
Economic Problems.** Proposed general
revenue sharing extension : hearings before the
Subcommittee on Revenue Sharing,
Intergovernmental Revenue Impact, and
Economic Problems of the Committee on
Finance, United States Senate, Ninety-sixth
Congress, second session ... March 6 and May
21, 1980. Washington : U. S. Govt. Print. Off.,
1980. iv, 650 p. : graphs ; 24 cm. Hearings on S.
2414, 2574, 2678, and 2681. Includes bibliographical
references. LC Card 80-603507 DDC 343.73/034 19
*1. Revenue sharing - Law and legislation - United
States. I. Title.*
KF26 .F567 1980

**United States. Congress. Senate. Committee on
Finance. Subcommittee on Social Security.**
Social security financing : hearing before the
Subcommittee on Social Security of the
Committee on Finance, United States Senate,
Ninety-sixth Congress, second session, February
22 and 25, 1980. Washington : U. S. Govt.
Print. Off., 1980. iii, 169 p. ; 23 cm. LC Card
80-602164 DDC 353.0072 19
*1. Social security - United States - Management. 2.
Social security taxes - United States. I. Title.*
KF26 .F568 1980

Social security retirement test : hearing before
the Subcommittee on Social Security of the
Committee on Finance, United States Senate,
Ninety-sixth Congress, second session ... April
21, 1980. Washington : U. S. Govt. Print. Off.,
1980. iv, 305 p. ; 23 cm. LC Card 80-603289
DDC 344.73/023 19
*1. Social security - Law and legislation - United States.
2. Old age pensions - United States. 3. Income - United
States. I. Title.*
KF26 .F568 1980a

**United States. Congress. Senate. Committee on
Finance. Subcommittee on Taxation and
Debt Management.** Public debt limit-- 1981 :
hearings before the Subcommittee on Taxation
and Debt Management of the Committee on
Finance, United States Senate, Ninety-seventh
Congress, first session, February 4, 1981.
Washington : U. S. G.P.O., 1981. iii, 86 p. ; 24
cm. Item 1038-A, 1038-B (microfiche) Includes
bibliographical references. LC Card 81-600957 DDC
336.3/46/0973 19
*1. Debts, Public - United States. 2. Budget - United
States. I. Title.*
KF26 .F5694 1981

**United States. Congress. Senate. Committee on
Finance. Subcommittee on Taxation and
Debt Management Generally.**
Airport and airway trust fund : hearing before

United States. Congress. Senate. Committee on Finance. **BIBLIOGRAPHIC GUIDE**

486

the Subcommittee on Taxation and Debt Management Generally of the Committee on Finance, United States Senate, Ninety-sixth Congress, second session, on S. 1649 ... September 8, 1980. Washington : U. S.G.P.O., c1980. iv, 216 p. : ill. ; 24 cm. Includes bibliographical references. Item 1038 LC Card 81-600659 DDC 343.7305/5853877 347.30355853877 19
1. Airports - Law and legislation - United States. 2. Aeronautics, Commercial - Taxation - United States. 3. Airports - United States - Finance. I. Title.
KF26 .F5695 1980h

Charitable contribution deductions : hearings before the Subcommittee on Taxation and Debt Management Generally of the Committee on Finance, United States Senate, Ninety-sixth Congress, second session, on S. 219 ... January 30 and 31, 1980. Washington : U. S. Govt. Print. Off., 1980. vi, 572 p. : ill. ; 24 cm. Includes bibliographical references. LC Card 80-602151 DDC 343.7305/232/0262 19
1. Income tax - United States - Deductions - Charitable contributions. I. Title.
KF26 .F5695 1980

Extension of the temporary limit on public debt : hearings before the Subcommittee on Taxation and Debt Management Generally of the Committee on Finance, United States Senate, Ninety-sixth Congress, second session, April 2 and 16, 1980. Washington : U. S. Govt. Print. Off., 1980. iii, 168 p. : graph ; 24 cm. LC Card 80-603293 DDC 336.4/46/0973 19
1. Debts, Public - United States. I. Title.
KF26 .F5695 1980a

Family Enterprise Estate and Gift Tax Equity Act and miscellaneous tax bills : hearing before the Subcommittee on Taxation and Debt Management Generally of the Committee on Finance, United States Senate, Ninety-sixth Congress, second session, on S. 2775, S. 2805, S. 2818, S. 2904, S. 2967, and H.R. 7171, August 4, 1980. Washington : U. S. G.P.O., 1980. v, 514 p. : ill. ; 24 cm. Includes bibliographical references. LC Card 81-600624 DDC 343.7306/7 347.30367 19
1. Inheritance and transfer tax - United States. 2. Family corporations - Taxation - United States. 3. Taxation - Law and legislation - United States. I. Title.
KF26 .F5695 1980f

Marriage penalty tax : hearing before the Subcommittee on Taxation and Dept Management Generally of the Committee on Finance, United States Senate, Ninety-sixth Congress, second session, on S. 336 ... S. 1247 ... S. 1877 ... August 5, 1980. Washington : U. S. G.P.O., 1980. iii, 296 p. : ill. ; 24 cm. Includes bibliographical references. LC Card 81-600660 DDC 343.7305/23 347.303523 19
1. Husband and wife - Taxation - United States. 2. Income tax - United States - Deductions. I. Title.
KF26 .F5695 1980g

Public debt limit : hearing before the Subcommittee on Taxation and Debt Management Generally of the Committee on Finance, United States Senate, Ninety-sixth Congress, second session, December 2, 1980. Washington : U. S. G.P.O., 1980 [i.e. 1981] iii, 27 p. ; 24 cm. Item 1038 LC Card 81-601333 DDC 336.3/46/0973 19
1. Debts, Public - United States. 2. Budget - United States. I. Title.
KF26 .F5695 1980i

Small royalty owners exemption from the windfall profit tax : hearings before the Subcommittee on Taxation and Debt Management Generally of the Committee on Finance, United States Senate, Ninety-sixth Congress, second session, on S. 2521 ... Friday, May 23 and Thursday, July 17, 1980. Washington : U. S. G.P.O., 1980. vii, 442 p. ; 24 cm. LC Card 81-600593 DDC 343.7305/244 347.3035244 19
1. Excess profits tax - United States. 2. Petroleum - Taxation - United States. I. Title.
KF26 .F5695 1980d

Special oil taxes : hearings before the Subcommittee on Taxation and Debt Management Generally of the Committee on Finance, United States Senate, Ninety-sixth Congress, second session, November 11, December 11, and 12, 1980. Washington : U. S.

G.P.O., 1980 [i.e. 1981] iii, 222 p. : ill. ; 23 cm. Item 1038 Includes bibliographical references. LC Card 81-601139 DDC 336.2/783338232/0973 19
1. Tariff on petroleum - United States. 2. Petroleum - Taxation - United States. 3. Petroleum conservation - United States. I. Title.
KF26 .F5695 1980j

State taxation of interstate commerce and worldwide corporate income : hearing before the Subcommittee on Taxation and Debt Management Generally of the Committee on Finance, United States Senate, Ninety-sixth Congress, second session, on S. 983 ... S. 1688 ... June 24, 1980. Washington : U. S. G.P.O., 1980. 2 v. (v, 983 p.) ; 24 cm. Includes bibliographical references. CONTENTS. - pt. 1. Oral testimony -- pt. 2. Communications. LC Card 80-604089 DDC 343.7305/267 347.3035267 19
1. Interstate commerce - Taxation - United States - States. 2. Corporations - Taxation - United States - States. 3. Income tax - United States - States - Foreign income. I. Title.
KF26 .F5695 1980e

Taxation of foreign earned income : hearing before the Subcommittee on Taxation and Debt Management Generally of the Committee on Finance, United States Senate, Ninety-sixth Congress, second session, on S. 2283 ... S. 2321 ... S. 2418 ... June 26, 1980. Washington : U. S. G.P.O., 1980. iv, 777 p. : ill. ; 24 cm. Includes bibliographical references. LC Card 80-604096 DDC 343.7305/248 347.3035248 19
1. Income tax - United States - Foreign income. I. Title.
KF26 .F5695 1980c

United States. Congress. Joint Committee on Taxation. Description of S. 219, relating to the deduction for charitable contributions scheduled for hearings before the Subcommittee on Taxation and Debt Management Generally of the Committee on Finance, on January 30 and 31, 1980 /. Washington , 1980. iii, 14 p.; LC Card 80-602135 DDC 343-7305/232 19
KF6388 .A25 1980

United States. Congress. Senate. Committee on Finance. Subcommittee on Tourism and Sugar. United States. Congress. Senate. Committee on Finance. Staff data and materials relating to the International sugar stabilization act of 1979 /. Washington , 1979. iii, 70 p. ; LC Card 79-601697 DDC 343.73/08756641 347.3038756641 19
KF1996.S8 A25 1979

United States. Congress. Senate. Committee on Finance. Subcommittee on Unemployment and Related Problems. Repayment of loans made to state unemployment compensation programs : hearing before the Subcommittee on Unemployment and Related Problems of the Committee on Finance, United States Senate, Ninety-sixth Congress, second session, on H.R. 4007 ... April 28, 1980. Washington : U. S. Govt. Print. Off., 1980. iii, 188 p. : graphs ; 24 cm. LC Card 80-603704 DDC 344.73/024 347.30424 19
1. Insurance, Unemployment - United States. 2. Government lending - United States. 3. Intergovernmental fiscal relations - United States. I. Title.
KF26 .F58 1980

United States. Congress. Senate. Committee on Finance. Taxation and Debt. Management Generally, Subcommittee on. see United States. Congress. Senate. Committee on Finance. Subcommittee on Taxation and Debt Management Generally.

United States. Congress. Senate. Committee on Foreign Relations. (Old Catalog form: United States. Foreign Relations, Committee on (Senate)) // Hearings printed in 1978 and later are available only in microform. Please consult the librarians in the Economic and Public Affairs Division.
Baker, Pauline H. The birth of Zimbabwe . Washington , 1980. v, 21 p. ; LC Card 80-602587 DDC 968.91/04 19
DT962.8 .B34

China claims : hearing before the Committee on Foreign Relations, United States Senate, Ninety-sixth Congress, second session, on S. 2141 ... April 23, 1980. Washington : U. S. Govt. Print. Off., 1980. iii, 42 p. ; 24 cm. "April

23, 1980." LC Card 80-602966 DDC 341.5/5 19
1. United States - Claims vs. China. I. Title.
KF26 .F6 1980i

Department of State authorization act, fiscal years 1980 and 1981 : hearing before the Committee on Foreign Relations, United States Senate, Ninety-sixth Congress, second session, on S. 2444 ... and S. 2445 ... March 25, 1980. Washington : U. S. Govt. Print. Off., 1980. iii, 71 p. ; 24 cm. LC Card 80-602739 DDC 353.0072/23689 19
1. United States. Dept. of State - Appropriations and expenditures. I. Title.
KF26 .F6 1980h

Galbraith, Peter. Cambodian relief . Washington , 1980. vii, 14 p. : LC Card 80-603871 DDC 362.8/7/09596 19
HV640 .G34

Implementation of the Taiwan relations act : the first year : a staff report to the Committee on Foreign Relations, United States Senate. Washington : U. S. Govt. Print. Off., 1980. v, 61 p. ; 23 cm. At head of title: 96th Congress, 2d session. Committee print. "June 1980." LC Card 80-603554 DDC 327.73051/249 19
1. United States - Foreign relations - Taiwan. 2. Taiwan - Foreign relations - United States.
E183.8.T3 U54 1980

India-Pakistan nuclear issues : hearing before the Committee on Foreign Relations, United States Senate, Ninety-sixth Congress, second session ... March 18, 1980. Washington : U. S. Govt. Print. Off., 1980. iii, 19 p. ; 24 cm. LC Card 80-602998 DDC 327.73054 19
1. United States - Foreign relations - India. 2. India - Foreign relations - United States. 3. United States - Foreign relations - Pakistan. 4. Pakistan - Foreign relations - United States. 5. Nuclear nonproliferation. I. Title.
KF26 .F6 1980K

International natural rubber agreement of 1979 : hearing before the Committee on Foreign Relations, United States Senate, Ninety-sixth Congress, second session, April 23, 1980. Washington : U. S. Govt. Print. Off., 1980. iii, 52 p. : ill. ; 23 cm. LC Card 80-603353 DDC 341.7/547/1389520265 19
1. Rubber - Law and legislation. I. Title.
KF26 .F6 1980o

McGovern, George Stanley, 1922- Impressions of southern Africa . Washington , 1979. v, 38 p. ; LC Card 80-601034 DDC 327.68073 19
DT747.U6 M33

Maritime boundary settlement treaty and East coast fishery resources agreement : hearings before the Committee on Foreign Relations, United States Senate, Ninety-sixth Congress, second session, on Ex. U, 96-1 ... and Ex. V, 96-1 ... April 15 and 17, 1980. Washington : U. S. Govt. Print. Off., 1980. iv, 223 p. : ill., maps ; 24 cm. Includes bibliographical references. LC Card 80-603064 DDC 341.4/48/026673071 19
1. United States - Boundaries - Canada. 2. Canada - Boundaries - United States. 3. Fishery law and legislation - United States. 4. Territorial waters - United States. 5. Fishery law and legislation - Canada. 6. Territorial waters - Canada. I. Title. II. Title: East coast fishery resources agreement.
KF26 .F6 1980m

The maritime boundary treaty with Canada : hearing before the Committee on Foreign Relations, United States Senate, Ninety-seventh Congress, first session, on EX. V, 96-1, the maritime boundary settlement treaty with Canada, March 18, 1981. Washington : U. S. G.P.O., 1981. iii, 46 p. ; 24 cm. Item 1039-A, 1039-B (microfiche) LC Card 81-601779 DDC 341.4/48/026673071 19
1. United States - Boundaries - Canada. 2. Canada - Boundaries - United States. 3. Territorial waters - Canada. 4. Territorial waters - United States. I. Title.
KF26 .F6 1981b

The national security adviser : role and accountability : hearing before the Committee on Foreign Relations, United States Senate, Ninety-sixth Congress, second session, April 17, 1980. Washington : U. S. Govt. Print. Off., 1980. v, 243 p. : diagrs. ; 23 cm. Includes bibliographical references. LC Card 80-602957 DDC 353.03/1 19
1. United States. Special Assistant to the President for

487

GOVERNMENT PUBLICATIONS - U.S.: 1981

United States. Congress. Senate. Committee on Foreign Relations.

National Security Affairs. I. Title.
KF26 .F6 1980n

NATO--a status report . Washington , 1980.
viii, 24 p. ;   LC Card 80-603869   DDC
355/.031/091821 19
UA646.3 .N225

Nomination of Alexander M. Haig, Jr. :
hearings before the Committee on Foreign
Relations, United States Senate, Ninety-seventh
Congress, first session, on the nomination of
Alexander M. Haig, Jr., to be Secretary of
State, January 9, 10, 12, 13, 14, 15, 1981.
Washington : U. S. G.P.O., 1981. 2 v. ; 24 cm.
Includes bibliographical references.   LC Card
81-600880   DDC 353.1 19
1. Haig, Alexander Meiss, 1924-. 2. United States.
Dept. of State - Officials and employees. I. Title.
KF26 .F6 1981

Nomination of Edmund S. Muskie : hearing
before the Committee on Foreign Relations,
United States Senate, Ninety-sixth Congress,
second session, on the nomination of Edmund
S. Muskie, of Maine, to be Secretary of State,
May 7, 1980. Washington : U. S. Govt. Print.
Off., 1980. iii, 44 p. ; 24 cm.   LC Card 80-602965
DDC 353.1 19
1. Muskie, Edmund S., 1914-. 2. United States. Dept.
of State - Officials and employees. I. Title.
KF26 .F6 1980j

Nomination of James L. Malone : hearings
before the Committee on Foreign Relations,
United States Senate, Ninety-seventh Congress,
first session, on nomination of James L.
Malone, to be assistant secretary of state for
oceans and international environmental and
scientific affairs, March 16, and April 2, 1981.
Washington : U. S. G.P.O., 1981. iii, 80 p. ; 24
cm. Item 1039-A, 1039-B (microfiche)   LC Card
81-601860   DDC 353.1 19
1. Malone, James L. 2. United States. Dept. of State -
Officials and employees. I. Title.
KF26 .F6 1981d

Nomination of Jeane J. Kirkpatrick : hearing
before the Committee on Foreign Relations,
United States Senate, Ninety-seventh Congress,
first session, on the nomination of Jeane J.
Kirkpatrick to be representative to the United
nations, January 15, 1981. Washington : U. S.
G.P.O., 1981. iii, 110 p. ; 24 cm. Item 1039-A,
1039-B (microfiche)   LC Card 81-601348   DDC
353.1 19
1. Kirkpatrick, Jeane J. 2. United States. Dept. of
State - Officials and employees. 3. United Nations -
United States. I. Title.
KF26 .F6 1981a

Nomination of Justice William Patrick Clark :
hearings before the Committee on Foreign
Relations, United States Senate, Ninety-seventh
Congress, first session, on nomination of Justice
William Patrick Clark, of California, to be
deputy secretary of state, February 2 and 3,
1981. Washington : U. S. G.P.O., 1981. iii, 84
p. : ill. ; 24 cm. Item 1039-A, 1039-B (microfiche)
LC Card 81-601174   DDC 353.1 19
1. Clark, William Patrick, 1931-. 2. United States. Dept.
of State - Officials and employees. I. Title.
KF26 .F6 1981c

Nuclear war strategy : hearing before the
Committee on Foreign Relations, United States
senate, Ninety-sixth Congress, second session,
on Presidential Directive 59, September 16,
1980. Washington : U. S. G.P.O., 1981. iii, 40
p. ; 24 cm. "Top secret hearing held on September
16, 1980; sanitized and printed on February 18, 1981."
Item 1039 LC Card 81-601145   DDC
355/.0217/0973 19
1. Atomic warfare. 2. Deterrence (Strategy). 3. United
States - Military policy. 4. Strategic Arms Limitation
Talks. I. Title.
KF26 .F6 1980s

Overseas Private Investment Corporation :
hearings before the Committee on Foreign
Relations, United States Senate, Ninety-sixth
Congress, second session, on S. 2186 ... June
11, 12, 1980. Washington : U. S. G.P.O., 1980.
iv, 246 p. : ill. ; 24 cm. Includes bibliographical
references.   LC Card 80-604067   DDC 346.73/07
347.3067 19
1. Overseas Private Investment Corporation. 2.
Insurance, Investment guaranty - United States. 3.
Investments, American. I. Title.
KF26 .F6 1980q

Pell, Claiborne, 1918- Earthquake in Italy .
Washington , 1980. vii, 17 p. :   LC Card
80-604120   DDC 363.3/495 19
DG851 .P44

Pell, Claiborne, 1918- Earthquake in the
Azores . Washington , 1980. vii, 21 p. :   LC
Card 80-603275   DDC 363.3/495 19
HV555.A96 P44

Perspectives on NATO's southern flank .
Washington , 1980. v, 46 p. ;   LC Card
80-603559   DDC 355/.0330182/2 19
UA646.55 .P47

Rhodesia : hearings before the Committee on
Foreign Relations, United States Senate,
Ninety-sixth Congress, first session ....
Washington : U. S. Govt. Print. Off., 1980. iii,
59 p. ; 23 cm. Hearings held Nov. 27-Dec. 3, 1979.
LC Card 80-601055   DDC 968.91/04 19
1. Zimbabwe - Politics and government - 1980-. I. Title.
KF26 .F6 1979ab

Rousseau, Rudolph. An assessment of the
refugee situation in Somalia . Washington ,
1980. v, 19 p. :   LC Card 80-603863   DDC
362.8/7/096773 19
HV640.4.S58 R68

S. 1916 : hearing before the Committee on
Foreign Relations, United States Senate,
Ninety-sixth Congress, second session, on S.
1916, a bill to authorize operations by the
Overseas Private Investment Corporation
[OPIC] in the People's Republic of China,
March 3, 1980. Washington : U. S. Govt. Print.
Off., 1980. iii, 32 p. ; 24 cm.   LC Card 80-601997
DDC 346.51/07 19
1. Overseas Private Investment Corporation. 2.
Investments, American - China. I. Title.
KF26 .F6 1980a

The situation in Iran : hearing before the
Committee on Foreign Relations, United States
Senate, Ninety-sixth Congress, second session,
May 8, 1980. Washington : U. S. G.P.O., 1980
[i.e. 1981] v, 48 p. ; 24 cm. "(Top secret hearing
held on May 8, 1980; sanitized and printed on
February 18, 1981)." Item 1039 LC Card 81-601146
DDC 353.03/22 19
1. Iran Hostage Crisis, 1979-1981. 2. War and
emergency powers - United States. I. Title.
KF26 .F6 1980t

Taiwan, one year after United States-China
normalization . Washington , 1980. v, 170 p. :
LC Card 80-603279   DDC 327.73051/249 19
E183.8.T3 T34

The Tarapur nuclear fuel export issue : joint
hearings before the Committee on Foreign
Relations and the Committee on Governmental
Affairs, United States Senate, Ninety-sixth
Congress, second session ... June 18, 19, 1980.
Washington : U. S. Govt. Print. Off., 1980. iii,
134 p. : graphs ; 24 cm. Includes bibliographical
references.   LC Card 80-602987   DDC
382/.4562148335/0973 19
1. Technical assistance, American - India. 2. Nuclear
fuels - India. 3. Nuclear nonproliferation. 4. Export
controls - United States. I. United States. Congress.
Senate. Committee on Governmental Affairs. II. Title.
KF26 .F6 1980l

U. S. conventional arms transfer policy : a
report to the Senate from the Committee on
Foreign Relations, United States Senate.
Washington : U. S. G.P.O., 1980. v, 11 p. ; 24
cm. At head of title: 96th Congress, 2d session.
Committee print. "June 1980." LC Card 80-604139
DDC 355/.032/0973 19
1. Munitions - United States. 2. Military assistance,
American. 3. Munitions. 4. Military assistance. I. Title.
HD9743.U6 U57 1980

U. S. Middle East policy : hearing before the
Committee on Foreign Relations, United States
Senate, Ninety-sixth Congress, second session ...
March 20, 1980. Washington : U. S. Govt.
Print. Off., 1980. iii, 55 p. ; 24 cm.   LC Card
80-602819   DDC 327.73056 19
1. United States - Foreign relations - Near East. 2.
Near East - Foreign relations - United States. I. Title.
KF26 .F6 1980g

U. S. security interests and policies in
Southwest Asia : hearings before the Committee
on Foreign Relations, United States Senate and
its Subcommittee on Near Eastern and South
Asian Affairs, Ninety-sixth Congress, second
session .... Washington : U. S. Govt. Print. Off.,

1980. iii, 368 p. : ill. ; 23 cm. Hearings held Feb.
6-Mar. 18, 1980. Includes bibliographies.   LC Card
80-603283   DDC 355/.033056 19
1. Near East - Strategic aspects. 2. Persian Gulf
region - Strategic aspects. 3. United States - National
security. I. United States. Congress. Senate. Committee
on Foreign Relations. Subcommittee on Near Eastern
and South Asian Affairs. II. Title.
KF26 .F6 1980p

United States. Delegation to the Ad Hoc
Meeting of the Canada-United States
Interparliamentary Group, 1980, Ottawa, Ont.
Ad hoc meeting of the Canada-United States
Interparliamentary Group to discuss
international wheat marketing, July 26, 1980.
Washington , 1981. v, 12 p. ;   LC Card
81-600997   DDC 382/.41311/0971 19
HD9049.W5 C33 1980

United States. General Accounting Office.
Statistical data on Department of Defense
training of foreign military personnel .
[Washington, D.C.] , 1980. 2, 107 p. ;   LC Card
80-602018   DDC 355/.032/0973 19
U408.3 .U54 1980

World population trends : hearings before the
Committee on Foreign Relations, United States
Senate, Ninety-sixth Congress, second session ...
April 29 and June 5, 1980. Washington : U. S.
Gov. Print. Off., 1980. iv, 346 p. : ill., charts ;
24 cm.   LC Card 80-603894   DDC 304.6 19
1. Population. 2. Population policy. 3. Population
assistance, American. I. Title.
KF26 .F6 1980r

1980 summer Olympics boycott : hearing before
the Committee on Foreign Relations, United
States Senate, Ninety-sixth Congress, second
session ... January 28, 1980. Washington : U. S.
Govt. Print. Off., 1980. iii, 97 p. ; 24 cm.   LC
Card 80-602014   DDC 796.4/8/094731 19
1. Olympic Games, Moscow, 1980. 2. United States -
Foreign relations - Russia. 3. Russia - Foreign
relations - United States.
KF26 .F6 1980d

**United States. Congress. Senate. Committee on
Foreign Relations. Subcommittee on African
Affairs.** Library of Congress. Congressional
Research Service. Imports of minerals from
South Africa by the United States and the
OECD countries /. Washington , 1980. xviii, 46
p. ;   LC Card 80-603854   DDC 382/.42/0968 19
HD9506.S72 L52 1980

**United States. Congress. Senate. Committee on
Foreign Relations. Subcommittee on Arms
Control, Oceans, International Operations,
and Environment.**
Law of the sea negotiations : hearing before the
Subcommittee on Arms Control, Oceans,
International Operations and Environment of
the Committee on Foreign Relations, United
States Senate, Ninety-seventh Congress, first
session, March 5, 1981. Washington : U. S.
G.P.O., 1981. iii, 301 p. ; 24 cm. Item 1039-A,
1039-B (microfiche) Includes bibliographical references.
LC Card 81-601946   DDC 341.4/5 19
1. United Nations Conference on the Law of the Sea
(3rd : 1973- : New York, etc.). 2. Ocean mining - Law
and legislation - United States. I. Title.
KF26 .F6286 1981

The Non-proliferation Treaty : hearing before
the Subcommittee on Arms Control, Oceans,
International Operations and Environment of
the Committee on Foreign Relations, United
States Senate, Ninety-sixth Congress, second
session ... July 24, 1980. Washington : U. S.
G.P.O., 1980. iii, 99 p. : ill. ; 24 cm. Includes
bibliographical references.   LC Card 80-603656   DDC
327.1/74 19
1. Nuclear nonproliferation. I. Title.
KF26 .F6286 1980

**United States. Congress. Senate. Committee on
Foreign Relations. Subcommittee on East
Asian and Pacific Affairs.**
Oversight of the Taiwan relations act : hearing
before the Subcommittee on East Asian and
Pacific Affairs of the Committee on Foreign
Relations, United States Senate, Ninety-sixth
Congress, second session, May 14, 1980.
Washington : U. S. Govt. Print. Off., 1980. iii,
44 p. ; 24 cm.   LC Card 80-602822   DDC
327.73051/249 19
1. United States - Foreign relations - Taiwan. 2.
Taiwan - Foreign relations - United States. I. Title.
KF26 .F6354 1980a

BIBLIOGRAPHIC GUIDE

United States. Congress. Senate. Committee on Foreign Relations.

488

Southeast Asia : hearings before the Subcommittee on East Asian and Pacific Affairs of the Committee on Foreign Relations, United States Senate, Ninety-sixth Congress, second session ... March 24 and 25, 1980. Washington : U. S. Govt. Print. Off., 1980. iii, 92 p. ; 24 cm. LC Card 80-602433 DDC 959/.053 19
1. Cambodian-Vietnamese Conflict, 1977-. 2. Refugees - Asia, Southeastern. 3. Food relief - Asia, Southeastern. I. Title.
KF26 .F6354 1980

United States. Congress. Senate. Committee on Foreign Relations. Subcommittee on European Affairs. United States. Library of Congress. Foreign Affairs and National Defense Division. The role of the North Atlantic Assembly /. Washington , 1979. vii, 55 p. ; LC Card 80-601029 DDC 341.24/3 19
JX1393.N67 U519 1979

United States. Congress. Senate. Committee on Foreign Relations. Subcommittee on International Economic Policy. The U. S. stake in the global economy : hearings before the Subcommittee on International Economic Policy of the Committee on Foreign Relations, United States Senate, Ninety-seventh Congress, first session ... February 25 and 27, 1981. Washington : U. S. G.P.O., 1981. iv, 298 p. : ill. ; 24 cm. Item 1039-A, 1039-B (microfiche) Includes bibliographical references. LC Card 81-602271 DDC 337.73 19
1. United States - Foreign economic relations. 2. International economic relations. 3. Underdeveloped areas. I. Title.
KF26 .F648 1981

United States. Congress. Senate. Committee on Foreign Relations. Subcommittee on Near Eastern and South Asian Affairs. United States. Congress. Senate. Committee on Foreign Relations. U. S. security interests and policies in Southwest Asia . Washington , 1980. iii, 368 p. : LC Card 80-603283 DDC 355/.033056 19
KF26 .F6 1980p

United States. Congress. Senate. Committee on Government Affairs. Permanent Subcommittee on Investigations. Oversight of Labor Department's investigation of Teamsters central states pension fund : hearing before the Permanent Subcommittee on Investigations of the Committee on Governmental Affairs, United States Senate, Ninety-sixth Congress, second session, August 25 and 26 and September 29 and 30, 1980. Washington : U. S. G.P.O., 1981. v, 521 p. : ill. ; 24 cm. Item 1037-A Includes bibliographical references. LC Card 81-601398 DDC 332.6/7254 19
1. International Brotherhood of Teamsters, Chauffeurs, Warehousemen and Helpers of America. 2. Pension trusts - United States. I. United States. Dept. of Labor. II. Title.
KF26 .G674 1980f

United States. Congress. Senate. Committee on Government Affairs. Subcommittee on Intergovernmental Relations. Oversight of the administration of the Federal Freedom of Information Act : hearings before the Subcommittee on Intergovernmental Relations of the Committee on Governmental Affairs, United States Senate, Ninety-sixth Congress, second session, August 19 and November 18, 1980. Washington : U. S. G.P.O., 1980 [i.e. 1981] iv, 543, p. ; 24 cm. Item 1037-A Includes bibliographical references. LC Card 81-600809 DDC 353.0081/1 19
1. Government information - United States. 2. Freedom of information - United States. I. Title.
KF26 .G6738 1980c

United States. Congress. Senate. Committee on Government Operations. (Old Catalog form: United States. Government Operations, Committee on (Senate)) // Hearings printed in 1978 and later are available only in microform. Please consult the librarians in the Economic and Public Affairs Division. Staff study of computer security in Federal programs / Committee on Government Operations, United States Senate. Washington : U. S. Govt. Print. Off., 1977. v, 2,8 p. : ill. ; 24 cm. At head of title: 95th Congress, 1st session. Committee print. LC Card 79-602721
1. Administrative agencies - United States. 2. Electronic data processing departments - Security measures. 3.

Computer crimes - United States. 4. Privacy, Right of - United States. I. Title.
JK468.A8 U47 1977   **NYPL [JLE 81-477]**

United States. Congress. Senate. Committee on Government Operations. Permanent Subcommittee on Investigations. Prepaid health plans : / hearings before the Permanent Subcommittee on Investigations of the Committee on Government Operations, United States Senate, Ninety-fourth Congress, second session, December 14 and 15, 1976. Washington: U. S. Govt. Print. Off., 1977. 1 v.: ill., charts; 23 cm.
1. Insurance, Health - United States. I. Title.
                    NYPL [JLE 81-117]

United States. Congress. Senate. Committee on Governmental Affairs. Annual report of the Postmaster General : hearing before the Committee on Governmental Affairs, United States Senate, Ninety-sixth Congress, second session, May 1, 1980. Washington : U. S. Govt. Print. Off., 1980. iii, 19 p. ; 24 cm. LC Card 80-602955 DDC 353.0087/3/06 19
1. Postal service - Law and legislation - United States. 2. Postal service - United States. I. Title.
KF26 .G67 1980d

Civil Service reform act of 1978 and Reorganization Plan no. 2 of 1978 : hearings before the Committee on Governmental Affairs, United States Senate, Ninety-fifth Congress, second session, on S. 2640, S. 2707, and S. 2830. Washington, D.C. : U. S. Govt. Print. Off., 1978. viii, 1439 p. : graphs ; 24 cm. Hearings held Apr. 6-May 9, 1978. Includes bibliographical references. LC Card 80-602518 DDC 353.006 19
1. Civil service - United States. 2. Civil service reform. I. Title.
KF26 .G67 1978j

Commission on wartime relocation and internment of civilians act : hearing before the Committee on Governmental Affairs, United States Senate, Ninety-sixth Congress, second session, on S. 1647, March 18, 1980. Washington : U. S. Govt. Print. Off., 1980. iv, 365 p. : ill. ; 24 cm. LC Card 80-602970 DDC 342.73/0873 19
1. United States. Commission on Wartime Relocation and Internment of Civilians. 2. Japanese Americans - Legal status, laws, etc. 3. Japanese Americans - Evacuations and relocation, 1942-1945. I. Title.
KF26 .G67 1980e

Consultant Reform Act of 1980 : hearings before the Committee on Governmental Affairs, United States Senate, Ninety-sixth Congress, second session, on S. 2880 ... August 19 and 20, 1980. Washington : U. S. G.P.O., 1981. iv, 668 p. ; 24 cm. Item 1037-A LC Card 81-601616 DDC 342.73/068 347.30268 19
1. Government consultants - Legal status, laws, etc. - United States. 2. Public contracts - United States. I. Title.
KF26 .G67 1980o

Debt Collection Act of 1980 : hearings before the Committee on Governmental Affairs, United States Senate, Ninety-sixth Congress, second session, on S. 3160 ... November 19 and 20, 1980. Washington : U. S. G.P.O., 1981. iv, 211 p. ; 23 cm. Item 1037-A Includes bibliographical references. LC Card 81-601387 DDC 343.73/037 347.30337 19
1. Debts, Public - United States. 2. Collection laws - United States. I. Title.
KF26 .G67 1980p

Federal Employees Compensation Reform Act of 1979 : hearing before the Committee on Governmental Affairs, United States Senate, Ninety-sixth Congress, first session, on S. 1340 ... August 2, 1979. Washington : U. S. G.P.O., 1980. iii, 219 p. ; 24 cm. LC Card 81-600825 DDC 342.73/068 347.30268 19
1. United States - Officials and employees - Salaries, allowances, etc. I. Title.
KF26 .G67 1979ar

Federal Interagency Medical Resources Sharing and Coordination Act of 1980 : hearing before the Committee on Governmental Affairs, United States Senate, Ninety-sixth Congress, second session, on S. 2958 ... July 30, 1980. Washington : U. S. G.P.O., 1980. iv, 324 p. : maps ; 24 cm. Includes bibliographical references. LC Card 80-604081 DDC 343.73/0115

347.303115 19
1. United States. Veterans Administration. 2. United States. Dept. of Defense. 3. Veterans - Medical care - Law and legislation - United States. 4. United States - Armed Forces - Medical care - Law and legislation - United States. I. Title.
KF26 .G67 1980k

Federal regulation of radiation health and safety : organizational problems and possible remedies / prepared by the Committee on Governmental Affairs, United States Senate. Washington : U. S. Govt. Print. Off., 1978. v, 180 p. ; 24 cm. At head of title: 95th Congress, 2d session. Committee print. LC Card 80-602517 DDC 363.1/79 19
1. Radiation - Safety measures. 2. Radiation - Safety measures - Government policy - United States. 3. Radiation - Safety regulations - United States. I. Title.
RA569 .U4962 1978

Legislation to authorize the establishment of senior executive positions for NSA, DEA, and the Export-Import Bank : hearing before the Committee on Governmental Affairs, United States Senate, Ninety-sixth Congress, second session, on S. 2116, S. 2267, and S. 2327, September 4, 1980. Washington : U. S.G.P.O., 1980. iii, 44 p. ; 24 cm. LC Card 80-603902 DDC 342.73/068 347.30268 19
1. United States. National Security Agency/Central Security Service - Officials and employees. 2. United States. Drug Enforcement Administration - Officials and employees. 3. Export-Import Bank of the United States - Employees. 4. Government executives - Legal status, laws, etc. - United States. I. Title.
KF26 .G67 1980l

Massachusetts Institute of Technology. Center for Policy Alternatives. Benefits of environmental, health, and safety regulation /. Washington , 1980. vii, 100 p. ; LC Card 80-601784 DDC 363.7/00973 19
HC110.E5 M38 1980

Nomination of David A. Stockman : hearing before the Committee on Governmental Affairs, United States Senate, Ninety-seventh Congress, first session, on nomination of David A. Stockman to be director of the Office of Management and Budget, January 8, 1981. Washington : U. S. G.P.O., 1981. iii, 169 p. ; 24 cm. Item 1037-C (microfiche) LC Card 81-601411 DDC 353.0071 19
1. Stockman, David Alan, 1946-. 2. United States. Office of Management and Budget - Officials and employees. I. Title.
KF26 .G67 1981a

Nomination of Edwin L. Harper : hearing before the committee on Governmental Affairs, United States Senate, Ninety-seventh Congress, first session, on nomination of Edwin L. Harper, to be deputy director of the Office of Management and Budget, February 17, 1981. Washington : U. S. G.P.O., 1981. iii, 25 p. ; 24 cm. Item 1032-B, 1032-C (microfiche) LC Card 81-601771 DDC 353.0071 19
1. Harper, Edwin Leland 1941-. 2. United States. Office of Management and Budget - Officials and employees. I. Title.
KF26 .G67 1981b

Nomination of Henry Bowen Frazier III : hearing before the Committee on Governmental Affairs, United States Senate, Ninety-sixth Congress, second session, on nomination of Henry Bowen Frazier III, to be a member of the Federal Labor Relations Authority, June 3, 1980. Washington : U. S. Govt. Print. Off., 1980. iii, 24 p. ; 24 cm. LC Card 80-602712 DDC 353.0083/2 19
1. Frazier, Henry Bowen, 1934-. 2. United States. Federal Labor Relations Authority - Officials and employees. I. Title.
KF26 .G67 1980b

Nomination of James Bert Thomas, Jr. : hearing before the Committee on Governmental Affairs, United States Senate, Ninety-sixth Congress, second session, on nomination of James Bert Thomas, Jr., to be inspector general of the Department of Education, July 31, 1980. Washington : U. S. G.P.O., 1980 [i.e. 1981] iii, 33 p. ; 24 cm. LC Card 81-601163 DDC 353.844 19
1. Thomas, James Bert, 1935-. 2. United States. Dept. of Education - Officials and employees. I. Title.
KF26 .G67 1980n

Nomination of Karen Hastie Williams : hearing

before the Committee on Governmental Affairs,
United States Senate, Ninety-sixth Congress,
second session, on nomination of Karen Hastie
Williams to be administrator of Federal
procurement policy, March 14, 1980.
Washington : U. S. Govt. Print. Off., 1980. iii,
73 p. ; 23 cm. LC Card 80-602444 DDC
353.0071/2 19
1. Williams, Karen Hastie, 1944-. 2. United States.
Office of Federal Procurement Policy - Officials and
employees. I. Title.
KF26 .G67 1980a

Nomination of William C. Gardner : hearing
before the Committee on Governmental Affairs,
United States Senate, Ninety-sixth Congress,
second session ... July 2, 1980. Washington : U.
S. Govt. Print. Off., 1980. iii, 26 p. ; 24 cm.
LC Card 80-603340 DDC 353.008/8/09753 19
1. Gardner, William C., 1917-. 2. Judges - District of
Columbia. 3. District of Columbia. Superior Court -
Officials and employees. I. Title.
KF26 .G67 1980h

Nomination to be a member of the Postal Rate
Commission and nominations to be governors
of the U. S. Postal Service : hearing before the
Committee on Governmental Affairs, United
States Senate, Ninety-sixth Congress, second
session ... July 28, 1980. Washington : U. S.
G.P.O., 1980. iii, 78 p. ; 24 cm. Hearing on
nominations of Janet Dempsey Steiger to be a member
of the Postal Rate Commission; Timothy L. Jenkins,
Paula D. Hughes, and David E. Babcock to be
governors of the U. S. Postal Service. LC Card
80-603489 DDC 353.0087/3 19
1. United States. Postal Rate Commission - Officials
and employees. 2. United States Postal Service -
Employees. I. Title.
KF26 .G67 1980j

Nominations of Dorothy Sellers and Ricardo
M. Urbina : hearing before the Committee on
Governmental Affairs, United States Senate,
Ninety-sixth Congress, second session, on
nominations of Dorothy Sellers and Ricardo M.
Urbina to be associate judges of the Supreme
Court of the District of Columbia, September
26, 1980. Washington : U. S. G.P.O., 1980. iii,
34 p. ; 24 cm. Item 1037-A LC Card 81-600816
DDC 353.008/8/09753 19
1. Sellers, Dorothy Ann, 1943-. 2. Urbina, Ricardo
Manuel, 1945-. 3. District of Columbia. Superior
Court - Officials and employees. 4. Judges -
Washington (D.C.). I. Title.
KF26 .G67 1980m

Office of Government Ethics and Federal
post-employment restrictions . Washington ,
1980. vi, 304 p. ; LC Card 80-603840 DDC
342.73/068 347.30268 19
KF4568.A315 A15 1980

Omnibus antiterrorism act of 1979 : hearings
before the Committee on Governmental Affairs,
United States Senate, Ninety-sixth Congress,
first session, on S. 333 ... March 30 and May 7,
1979. Washington : U. S. Govt. Print. Off. : for
sale by the Supt. of Docs., U. S. Govt. Print.
Off., 1979. iv, 448 p. ; 24 cm. Bibliography: p.
208-209. LC Card 80-602011 DDC 345.73/023 19
1. Terrorism - United States. I. Title.
KF26 .G67 1979am

Oversight of GPO's direct deal printing
procurement system : hearing before the
Committee on Governmental Affairs, United
States Senate, Ninety-sixth Congress, second
session, April 30, 1980. Washington : U. S.
Govt. Print. Off., 1980. iii, 94 p. : ill. ; 23 cm.
LC Card 80-602743 DDC 353.0081/9 19
1. United States. Government Printing Office -
Procurement. 2. Printing, Public - United States. 3.
Contracts, Letting of - United States. 4. Public
contracts - United States. I. Title.
KF26 .G67 1980c

Oversight of the structure and management of
the Department of Energy . Washington , 1980
[i.e. 1981] iii, 434 p. : LC Card 81-601669 DDC
353.87 19
TJ163.25.U6 O93

Reorganization plan no. 1 of 1980 : hearings
before the Committee on Governmental Affairs,
United States Senate, Ninety-sixth Congress,
second session ... April 17, 18, and 29, 1980.
Washington : U. S. Govt. Print. Off., 1980. iv,
402 p. ; 24 cm. Includes bibliographical references.
LC Card 80-603288 DDC 353.0087/22 19
1. United States. Nuclear Regulatory Commission. I.

Title.
KF26 .G67 1980g

Shipper's export declarations : hearing before
the Committee on Governmental Affairs,
United States Senate, Ninety-sixth Congress,
second session, on S. 2419 ... May 7, 1980.
Washington : U. S. Govt. Print. Off., 1980. iii,
149 p. ; 23 cm. LC Card 80-603643 DDC
343.73/0878 347.303878 19
1. Bills of lading - United States. 2. United States -
Commerce - Statistical services - Law and legislation. 3.
Data protection - United States. I. Title.
KF26 .G67 1980i

Structure of corporate concentration :
institutional shareholders and interlocking
directorates among major U. S. corporations :
staff study / Committee on Governmental
Affairs, United States Senate. Washington : U.
S. G.P.O. : For sale by tahe Supt. of Docs., U.
S. G.P.O., 1980 [i.e. 1981] 2 v. : ill. ; 24 cm. At
head of title: 96th Congress, 2d session. Committee
print. "Prepared by E. Winslow Turner"--P. iii.
December 1980. S/N 052-070-05512-0 (v. 1) S/N
052-070-05513-8 (v. 2) Item 1037-A LC Card 81-601004 DDC
338.8/0973 19
1. Institutional investments - United States. 2. Directors
of corporations - United States. 3. Disclosure of
information (Securities law) - United States. 4.
Industrial concentration - United States. I. Turner, E.
Winslow. II. Title.
HG4910 .U54 1981

To establish a Commission on the International
Application of Antitrust Laws : hearings before
the Committee on Governmental Affairs,
United States Senate, Ninety-sixth Congress,
first [and second] session[s], on S. 1010 ...
October 31, 1979, and April 3, 1980.
Washington : U. S. Govt. Print. Off., 1980. iii,
187 p. ; 24 cm. LC Card 80-603105 DDC
343.73/072 19
1. United States. Commission on the International
Application of the United States Antitrust Laws. 2.
Antitrust law - United States. I. Title.
KF26 .G67 1979ap

To extend the reorganization authority of the
President : hearing before the Committee on
Governmental Affairs, United States Senate,
Ninety-sixth Congress, second session, on S.
2458, April 2, 1980. Washington : U. S. Govt.
Print. Off., 1980. iii, 44 p. ; 24 cm. LC Card
80-603039 DDC 353/.073 19
1. Administrative agencies - United States -
Reorganization. I. Title.
KF26 .G67 1980f

Transfer of authorities for implementation of
building energy performance standards : hearing
before the Committee on Governmental Affairs,
United States Senate, Ninety-sixth Congress,
first session, on S. 1604, November 20, 1979.
Washington : U. S. Govt. Print. Off., 1980. iii,
196 p. : ill. ; 23 cm. Includes bibliographical
references. LC Card 80-601881 DDC 353.0082/32
19
1. Buildings - Energy conservation - Law and
legislation - United States. 2. United States. Dept. of
Energy. 3. United States. Dept. of Housing and Urban
Development. I. Title.
KF26 .G67 1979aj

United States. Congress. Senate. Committee on
Foreign Relations. The Tarapur nuclear fuel
export issue . Washington , 1980. iii, 134 p. :
LC Card 80-602987 DDC
382/.4562148335/0973 19
KF26 .F6 1980l

United States. Congress. Senate. Committee on
Governmental Affairs. Subcommittee on
Energy, Nuclear Proliferation, and Federal
Services. Nuclear waste management
reorganization act of 1979 . Washington , 1980.
iv, 772 p. : LC Card 80-602895 DDC
344.73/04622 19
KF26 .G6728 1979m

United States. Library of Congress.
Congressional Research Service. Energy
information . Washington , 1980. ix, 114 p. ;
LC Card 80-602583 DDC 333.79/07 19
TJ163.17 .U54 1980

United States. Library of Congress.
Congressional Research Service. The Federal
executive establishment . Washington , 1980. v,

76 p. ; LC Card 80-602577 DDC 353.04 19
JK411 .U54 1980

**United States. Congress. Senate. Committee on
Governmental Affairs. Permanent
Subcommittee on Investigations.**
Alcohol fuels : hearing before the Permanent
Subcommittee on Investigations of the
Committee on Governmental Affairs, United
States Senate, Ninety-sixth Congress, second
session, August 12, 1980. Washington : U. S.
G.P.O., 1980 [i.e. 1981] iii, 86 p. : ill. ; 24 cm.
Item 1037-A LC Card 81-601179 DDC 662/.669 19
1. Alcohol as fuel. 2. Gasohol. I. Title.
KF26 .G674 1980e

Department of Energy gasoline allocation
program : hearings before the Permanent
Subcommittee on Investigations of the
Committee on Governmental Affairs, United
States Senate, Ninety-sixth Congress, second
session, July 25 and 26, 1980. Washington : U.
S. Govt. Print. Off., 1980. v, 411 p. : ill. ; 23
cm. Includes bibliographical references. LC Card
80-603734 DDC 333.8/232 19
1. Gasoline supply - United States. 2. Gasoline -
Prices - United States. 3. Gasoline - Law and
legislation - United States. 4. Gasoline - Law and legislation - United
States. I. Title.
KF26 .G674 1980c

Energy security : hearing before the Permanent
Subcommittee on Investigations of the
Committee on Governmental Affairs, United
States Senate, Ninety-sixth Congress, second
session, September 22, 1980. Washington : U.
S. Govt. Print. Off., 1980. iii, 154 p. : graphs ;
23 cm. LC Card 80-603907 DDC 333.79/0973 19
1. Energy policy - United States. 2. Power resources -
United States. 3. Petroleum - United States - Storage. I.
Title.
KF26 .G674 1980d

Illegal narcotics profits : index to hearings
before the Permanent Subcommittee on
Investigations of the Committee on
Governmental Affairs, United States Senate,
Ninety-sixth Congress, second session,
November 1, 1980. Washington : U. S. Govt.
Print. Off., 1980. xix p. ; 24 cm. LC Card
80-603428 DDC 338.4/3364177/0973 19
1. United States. Congress. Senate. Committee on
Governmental Affairs. Permanent Subcommittee on
Investigations. Illegal narcotics profits - Indexes. 2.
Narcotics, Control of - United States - Indexes. 3.
Narcotics - Economic aspects - United States - Indexes.
I. Title.
KF26 .G674 1980b

**ILLEGAL NARCOTICS PROFITS -
INDEXES.**
United States. Congress. Senate. Committee
on Governmental Affairs. Permanent
Subcommittee on Investigations. Illegal
narcotics profits . Washington , 1980. xix p. ;
LC Card 80-603428 DDC 338.4/3364177/0973
19
KF26 .G674 1980b

Labor union insurance activities of Joseph
Hauser and his associates : report of the
Committee on Governmental Affairs, United
States Senate, made by its Permanent
Subcommittee on Investigations together with
additional and separate views. Washington : U.
S. Govt. Print Off., 1979. viii, 202 p. ; 24 cm.
(Report - 96th Congress, 1st session, Senate ; no.
96-426) Includes bibliographical references. LC Card
80-600763 DDC 364.1/68 19
1. Welfare funds (Trade-union) - United States. 2.
Insurance companies - United States. 3. Hauser, Joseph.
I. Series: United States. 96th Congress, 1st session,
1979. Senate. Report , no. 96-426. II. Title.
KF31 .G684 1979

Organized crime and use of violence : hearings
before the Permanent Subcommittee on
Investigations of the Committee on
Governmental Affairs, United States Senate,
Ninety-sixth Congress, second session .....
Washington : U. S. Govt. Print. Off., 1980- v. :
ill. ; 24 cm. Hearings held Apr. 28, 1980- LC Card
80-603084 DDC 364.1/06/073 19
1. Organized crime - United States. 2. Violence -
United States. I. Title.
KF26 .G674 1980a

Professional motor vehicle theft and chop
shops : hearings before the Permanent
Subcommittee on Investigations of the
Committee on Governmental Affairs, United

States Senate, Ninety-sixth Congress, first session ... Washington : U. S. Govt. Print. Off., 1980. vi, 491 p. : ill. ; 24 cm. Hearings held Nov. 27-Dec. 4, 1979.   LC Card 80-601876   DDC 364.1/62 19

1. *Automobile theft - United States.* 2. *Automobile theft investigation - United States.* 3. *Automobiles - United States - Parts.* 4. *Automobile wrecking and used parts industry - United States - Corrupt practices.* I. *Title.* II. *Title: Chop shops.*
KF26 .G674 1979b

Staff study of the emergency building temperature regulations /. Washington , 1980 [i.e. 1981] v, 36 p. ;   LC Card 81-600667   DDC 333.79 19
TJ163.5.B84 S7

Transfer of technology to the Soviet bloc : hearing before the Permanent Subcommittee on Investigations of the Committee on Governmental Affairs, United States Senate, Ninety-sixth Congress, second session, February 20, 1980. Washington : U. S. Govt. Print. Off., 1980. iii, 156 p. ; 24 cm.   LC Card 80-602191   DDC 338.91/73/047 19

1. *United States - Commerce - Russia.* 2. *Russia - Commerce - United States.* 3. *United States - Commerce - Europe, Eastern.* 4. *Europe, Eastern - Commerce - United States.* 5. *Technology transfer.* 6. *Export controls - United States.* I. *Title.*
KF26 .G674 1980

United States. Congress. Senate. Committee on Governmental Affairs. Subcommittee on Civil Service and General Services.
Civil service retirement legislation : hearing before the Subcommittee on Civil Service and General Services of the Committee on Governmental Affairs, United States Senate, Ninety-sixth Congress, second session, on S. 358, H.R. 2583, S. 2449, and S. 2450, April 16, 1980. Washington : U. S. G.P.O. : 1980 [i.e. 1981] iii, 169 p. ; 24 cm. Item 1037-A   LC Card 81-601150   DDC 353.005 19

1. *Civil service pensions - United States.* I. *Title.*
KF26 .G6724 1980a

Federal consulting service contracts : joint hearings before the Subcommittee on Civil Service and General Services of the Committee on Governmental Affairs, United States Senate and the Subcommittee on Human Resources of the Committee on Post Office and Civil Service, House of Representatives, Ninety-sixth Congress, second session, March 27 and April 3, 1980. Washington : U. S. Govt. Print. Off., 1980- v. ; 23 cm. Serial no. 96-72.   LC Card 80-603411   DDC 353.09/3 19

1. *Government consultants - United States.* 2. *Public contracts - United States.* I. *United States. Congress. House. Committee on Post Office and Civil Service. Subcommittee on Human Resources.* II. *Title.*
KF26 .G6724 1980

Federal employee life insurance, tax withholding, and personal assistants : hearing before the Subcommittee on Civil Service and General Services of the Committee on Governmental Affairs, United States Senate, Ninety-sixth Congress, second session, on H.R. 6372, H.R. 7466, and H.R. 7666, September 17, 1980. Washington : U. S. G.P.O., 1980 [i.e. 1981] iii, 68 p. ; 24 cm. Item 1037-A   LC Card 81-601144   DDC 353.001/234 19

1. *Insurance, Government employees' life - Law and legislation - United States.* 2. *Withholding tax - United States - States.* 3. *Civil service pensions - Law and legislation - United States.* 4. *Handicapped - Employment - Law and legislation - United States.* 5. *Handicapped - Services for - Law and legislation - United States.* I. *Title.*
KF26 .G6724 1980b

United States. Congress. Senate. Committee on Governmental Affairs. Subcommittee on Governmental Efficiency and the District of Columbia. Status of implementation of the Part-Time Career Employment Act of 1978 . Washington , 1980 [i.e. 1981] iv, 77 p. :   LC Card 81-601317   DDC 353.001/4 19
KF26 .G6735 1980d

United States. Congress. Senate. Committee on Governmental Affairs. Subcommittee on Energy, Nuclear Proliferation, and Federal Services.
The Decennial census . Washington , 1980. ix, 465 p. ;   LC Card 81-601006   DDC 001.4/33 19
HA37.U55 D42

The Department of Energy's fiscal year 1981 budget request for energy research, development, and applications and energy conservation : a report / prepared for John Glenn by the staff of the Subcommittee on Energy, Nuclear Proliferation, and Federal Services of the Committee on Governmental Affairs, United States Senate. Washington : U. S. G.P.O., 1980. vii, 73 p. ; 24 cm. At head of title: 96th Congress, 2d session. Committee print. "July 16, 1980." Includes bibliographical references.   LC Card 80-604124   DDC 353.0072/236823 19

1. *United States. Dept. of Energy - Appropriations and expenditures.* I. *Glenn, John, 1921-.* II. *Title.*
HD9502.U52 U5 1980

DOE's safety and health program for enrichment plant workers : hearing before the Subcommittee on Energy, Nuclear Proliferation, and Federal Services of the Committee on Governmental Affairs, United States Senate, Ninety-sixth Congress, second session, July 21, 1980, Washington : U. S. G.P.O., 1980. iii, 377 p. : ill. ; 23 cm.   LC Card 80-603790   DDC 363.1/79 19

1. *Uranium industry - Hygienic aspects - United States.* 2. *Uranium industry - Safety measures - United States.* 3. *United States. Dept. of Energy.* I. *Title.*
KF26 .G6728 1980c

Energy impact assistance act : hearings before the Subcommittee on Energy, Nuclear Proliferation, and Federal Services of the Committee on Governmental Affairs, United States Senate, Ninety-sixth Congress, second session, on S. 1699, March 11 and 12, 1980. Washington : U. S. Govt. Print. Off., 1980. iv, 377 p. : maps ; 24 cm.   LC Card 80-602894   DDC 346.7304/679 19

1. *Economic assistance, Domestic - Law and legislation - United States.* 2. *Intergovernmental fiscal relations - United States - Finance.* 3. *Municipal services - United States - Finance.* 4. *Energy development - Economic aspects - United States.* I. *Title.*
KF26 .G6728 1980a

Federal advisory committees : index to the membership of Federal advisory committees listed in the sixth annual report of the President to the Congress covering calender year 1977 : index / Subcommittee on Energy, Nuclear Proliferation, and Federal Services of the Committee on Governmental Affairs, United States Senate. Washington : U. S. Govt. Print. Off., 1978. xvii, 1094 p. ; 20 x 26 cm. At head of title: 95th Congress, 2d session. Committee print. "December 1978." Index for 1974 issued by the Subcommittee on Reports, Accounting, and Management of the Senate Committee on Government Operations.   LC Card 79-601130   DDC 353.09/3/025 19

1. *Executive advisory bodies - United States - Directories.* I. *United States. President. Federal advisory committees.* II. *Title.*
JK468.C7 U53 1978

Impact abroad of the accident at the Three Mile Island Nuclear Power Plant . Washington , 1980. xii, 81 p. ;   LC Card 80-603262   DDC 333.79/24 19
TK9055 .I44

Nine-digit zip codes : hearing before the Subcommittee on Energy, Nuclear Proliferation, and Federal Services of the Committee on Governmental Affairs, United States Senate, Ninety-sixth Congress, second session, November 25, 1980. Washington : U. S. G.P.O., 1981. iii, 274 p. : ill. ; 24 cm. Item 1037-A   LC Card 81-610629   DDC 383/.145 19

1. *United States Postal Service.* 2. *Zip code - United States.* I. *Title.*
KF26 .G6728 1980d

Nuclear waste management reorganization act of 1979 : hearings before the Committee on Governmental Affairs and its Subcommittee on Energy, Nuclear Proliferation and Federal Services, United States Senate, Ninety-sixth Congress, first session on S. 742 ... July 5, 1979 (Chicago, Ill.), October 19, 1979, and February 13, 1980 (Washington, D.C.). Washington : U. S. Govt. Print. Off., 1980. iv, 772 p. : ill. ; 24 cm. Bibliography: p. 751-765. Includes index.   LC Card 80-602895   DDC 344.73/04622 19

1. *Radioactive waste disposal - Law and legislation - United States.* 2. *Spent reactor fuels - Storage - Law and legislation - United States.* I. *United States. Congress. Senate. Committee on Governmental Affairs.*

II. *Title.*
KF26 .G6728 1979m

Postal service act of 1980 : hearings before the Subcommittee on Energy, Nuclear Proliferation, and Federal Services of the Committee on Governmental Affairs, United States Senate, Ninety-sixth Congress, second session, on S. 2558, H.R. 79, and H.R. 826 .... Washington : U. S. Govt. Print. Off., 1980. v, 669 p. : ill. ; 24 cm. Hearings held Apr. 15-May 1, 1980.   LC Card 80-603728   DDC 343.73/0992/0262 347.3039920262 19

1. *Postal service - Law and legislation - United States.* 2. *Postal service - Employees - Legal status, laws, etc. - United States.* I. *Title.*
KF26 .G6728 1980b

Reader on nuclear nonproliferation /. Washington , 1980. x, 344 p. :   LC Card 81-600802   DDC 327.1/74 19
JX1974.73 .R4

United States. Library of Congress. Environment and Natural Resources Policy Division. Nuclear proliferation factbook /. Washington , 1980. xi, 531 p. :   LC Card 80-603879   DDC 327.1/74 19
JX1974.73 .U55 1980

1980 census, counting illegal aliens : hearing before the Subcommittee on Energy, Nuclear Proliferation, and Federal Services of the Committee on Governmental Affairs, United States Senate, Ninety-sixth Congress, second session, on S. 2366 ... March 26, 1980. Washington : U. S. Govt. Print. Off., 1980. iii, 254 p. ; 24 cm.   LC Card 80-602802   DDC 342.73/08 19

1. *United States - Census, 20th, 1980.* 2. *Aliens - United States.* I. *Title.*
KF26 .G6728 1980

United States. Congress. Senate. Committee on Governmental Affairs. Subcommittee on Federal Spending Practices and Open Government.
Continued oversight of the Small Business Association's [i.e. Administration's] 8 (a) program : hearing before the Subcommittee on Federal Spending Practices and Open Government of the Committee on Governmental Affairs and the Select Committee on Small Business, United States Senate, Ninety-sixth Congress, first session, October 5, 1979. Washington : U. S. Govt. Print. Off., 1980. iii, 105 p. ; 24 cm.   LC Card 80-603071   DDC 353.0082/048 19

1. *Federal aid to minority business enterprises - United States.* 2. *Minority business enterprises - United States - Corrupt practices.* 3. *Public contracts - United States.* 4. *United States. Small Business Administration.* I. *United States. Congress. Senate. Select Committee on Small Business.* II. *Title.*
KF26 .G6732 1979j

Continued investigation into fraud and mismanagement in General Services Administration : hearings before the Subcommittee on Federal Spending Practices and Open Government of the Committee on Governmental Affairs, United States Senate, Ninety-sixth Congress, first session .... Washington : U. S. Govt. Print. Off., 1980- v. : ill. ; 24 cm. Hearing held July 18, 1979-   LC Card 80-603087   DDC 364.1/63 19

1. *United States. General Services Administration.* 2. *Art Metal. - U. S.A., inc.* I. *Title.*
KF26 .G6732 1979i

Fraud and abuse in programs found in the Community Service Administration, Departments of Labor, Agriculture, and Health and Human Services : a report / prepared by the Subcommittee on Federal Spending Practices and Open Government of the Committee on Governmental Affairs, United States Senate. Washington : U. S. G.P.O., 1980 [i.e. 1981] v, 163 p. : ill. ; 24 cm. At head of title: 96th Congress, 2d session. Committee print. "December 1980." Item 1037-A   LC Card 81-600998   DDC 364.1/323 19

1. *Economic assistance, Domestic - United States - Corrupt practices.* I. *Title.*
HC110.P63 U478 1981

Paperwork and redtape reduction act of 1979 : hearing before the Subcommittee on Federal Spending Practices and Open Government of the Committee on Governmental Affairs, United States Senate, Ninety-sixth Congress,

GOVERNMENT PUBLICATIONS - U.S.: 1981

491

United States. Congress. Senate. Committee on Labor and Human

first session, on S. 1411 ... November 1, 1979. Washington : U. S. Govt. Print. Off., 1980. iii, 190 p. ; 23 cm. LC Card 80-602188 DDC 342.73/066 19

1. Government paperwork - Law and legislation - United States. 2. Government information - United States. I. Title.
KF26 .G6732 1979h

United States. Congress. Senate. Committee on Governmental Affairs. Subcommittee on Governmental Efficiency and the District of Columbia. Annual report of the Inspector General of the Department of Energy . Washington , 1980. iii, 50 p. ; LC Card 80-603994 DDC 353.87 19
KF26 .G6735 1980a

United States. Congress. Senate. Committee on Governmental Affairs. Subcommittee on Governmental Efficiency and the District of Columbia.
Annual report of the Inspector General of the Department of Energy : hearing before the Subcommittee on Governmental Efficiency and the District of Columbia and the Subcommittee on Federal Spending Practices and Open Government of the Committee on Governmental Affairs, United States Senate, Ninety-sixth Congress, second session, May 21, 1980. Washington : U. S. G.P.O., 1980. iii, 50 p. ; 24 cm. LC Card 80-603994 DDC 353.87 19
1. United States. Dept. of Energy. Office of Inspector General. I. United States. Congress. Senate. Committee on Governmental Affairs. Subcommittee on Federal Spending Practices and Open Government. II. Title.
KF26 .G6735 1980a

Chesapeake Bay Research Coordination Act : hearing before the Subcommittee on Governmental Efficiency and the District of Columbia of the Committee on Governmental Affairs, United States Senate, Ninety-sixth Congress, second session, on S. 1316 and H.R. 4417, July 31, 1980. Washington : U. S. G.P.O., 1980. iv, 199 p. ; 23 cm. LC Card 80-603783 DDC 346.7304/69164 347.306469164 19
1. Chesapeake Bay (Md. and Va.) - Research - Law and legislation. 2. Water resources development - Law and legislation - Chesapeake Bay region (Md. and Va.). I. Title.
KF26 .G6735 1980b

District of Columbia interest rate modification : hearing before the Subcommittee on Governmental Efficiency of the Committee on Governmental Affairs, United States Senate, Ninety-sixth Congress, first session, on S. 1992 and S. 2005, November 14, 1979. Washington : U. S. Govt. Print. Off., 1980. iii, 252 p. ; 23 cm. LC Card 80-602468 DDC 346.753/073 19
1. Usury laws - District of Columbia. 2. Home rule (District of Columbia). I. Title.
KF26 .G6735 1979j

Inspector General Act of 1980 : hearing before the Subcommittee on Governmental Efficiency and the District of Columbia of the Committee on Governmental Affairs, United States Senate, Ninety-sixth Congress, second session, on S. 3025 ... August 26, 1980. Washington : U. S. G.P.O., 1981. iii, 67 p. ; 24 cm. Item 1037-A LC Card 81-601380 DDC 342.73/0664 347.302664 19
1. Governmental investigations - United States. 2. Finance, Public - United States - Accounting. I. Title.
KF26 .G6735 1980c

Resolution to disapprove Location of chanceries amendment act of 1979 : hearing before the Subcommittee on Governmental Efficiency and the District of Columbia of the Committee on Governmental Affairs, United States Senate, Ninety-sixth Congress, first session, on S. Con. Res. 63 ... December 17, 1979. Washington : U. S. Govt. Print. Off., 1980. iv, 98 p. ; 23 cm. LC Card 80-602103 DDC 346.75304/5 19
1. Diplomatic and consular services in the United States. 2. Zoning law - District of Columbia. 3. Washington, D. C. - Public buildings. I. Title.
KF26 .G6735 1979i

Status of implementation of the Part-Time Career Employment Act of 1978 : hearings before the Subcommittee on Governmental Efficiency and the District of Columbia and the Subcommittee on Civil Services [sic] and General Services of the Committee on

Governmental Affairs, United States Senate, Ninety-sixth Congress, second session, June 10 and 17, 1980. Washington : U. S. G.P.O., 1980 [i.e. 1981] iv, 77 p. : ill. ; 24 cm. Item 1037-A Includes bibliographical references. LC Card 81-601317 DDC 353.001/4 19
1. Part-time employment - United States. 2. Civil service positions - United States. I. United States. Congress. Senate. Committee on Governmental Affairs. Subcommittee on Civil Service and General Services. II. Title.
KF26 .G6735 1980d

United States. Congress. Senate. Committee on Governmental Affairs. Subcommittee on Intergovernmental Relations.
Amendments to the uniform relocation assistance and property acquisitions policies act of 1970 : hearings before the Subcommittee on Intergovernmental relations of the Committee on Governmental Affairs, United States Senate, Ninety-sixth Congress, first session, on S. 1108, September 5, and November 6 and 7, 1979. Washington : U. S. Govt. Print. Off., 1980. vi, 813 p. ; 24 cm. Includes bibliographies. LC Card 80-601495 DDC 343.73/025 19
1. Relocation (Housing) - Law and legislation - United States. 2. Eminent domain - United States. 3. Government purchasing of real property - United States. 4. Compensation (Law) - United States. I. Title.
KF26 .G6738 1979g

Fiscal notes for state and local governments : hearing before the Subcommittee on Intergovernmental Relations of the Committee on Governmental Affairs, United States Senate, Ninety-sixth Congress, second session, on S. 3087 ... S. 2691, September 4, 1980. Washington : U. S. Govt. Print. Off., 1980- v. <1> ; 24 cm. LC Card 80-603488 DDC 343.73/03 347.3033 19
1. Legislation - United States - Compliance costs. 2. Finance, Public - Law and legislation - United States. 3. Local finance - Law and legislation - United States. I. Title.
KF26 .G6738 1980b

Nonprofit organization participation in the federal aid system : hearing before the Subcommittee on Intergovernmental Relations of the Committee on Governmental Affairs, United States Senate, Ninety-sixth Congress, second session .... Washington : U. S. G.P.O., 1980. 2 v. ; 24 cm. Pt. 1: "October 15, 1980, Minneapolis, Minnesota." Pt. 2: "October 20, 1980. Item 1037-A Includes bibliographical references. CONTENTS. - pt. 1. The Minnesota experience -- pt. 2. The national perspective. LC Card 81-600646 DDC 361.3/7/0973 19
1. Volunteer workers in social service - United States. 2. Volunteer workers in social service - Minnesota. 3. Economic assistance, Domestic - United States. I. Title. II. Title: Minnesota experience. III. Title: National perspective.
KF26 .G6738 1980d

Scope of the general revenue sharing program : hearings before the Subcommittee on Intergovernmental Relations of the Committee on Governmental Affairs, United States Senate, Ninety-sixth Congress, second session, March 20 and 25, 1980. Washington : U. S. Govt. Print. Off., 1980. iii, 227 p. ; 24 cm. Includes bibliographical references. LC Card 80-602990 DDC 336.1/85 19
1. Revenue sharing - United States. I. Title.
KF26 .G6738 1980a

United States. Congress. Senate. Committee on Governmental Affairs. Subcommittee on Oversight of Government Management.
HUD moratorium on single family sales programs / prepared by the Subcommittee on Oversight of Government Management for the Committee on Governmental Affairs, United States Senate. Washington : U. S. Govt. Print. Off., 1980. v, 24 p. : ill. ; 24 cm. At head of title: 96th Congress, 2d session. Committee print. "June 1980." Includes bibliographical references. LC Card 80-602589 DDC 363.5/8 19
1. Housing policy - United States. 2. United States. Dept. of Housing and Urban Development. I. Title.
HD7293 .U45 1980

HUD's moratorium on single family sales program : hearing before the Sucommittee on Oversight of Government Management of the Committee on Governmental Affairs, United States Senate, Ninety-sixth Congress, second

session, Detroit, Mich., April 11, 1980. Washington : U. S. Govt. Print. Off., 1980. 98 p. ; 23 cm. LC Card 80-603485 DDC 332.7/33/0973 19
1. Housing policy - United States. 2. United States. Dept. of Housing and Urban Development. 3. Housing - Michigan - Detroit. I. Title.
KF26 .G6735 1980

"Hurry-up" spending : a report / prepared by the Subcommittee on Oversight of Government Management of the Committee on Governmental Affairs, United States Senate. Washington : U. S. G.P.O. : For sale by the Supt. of Docs., U. S. G.P.O., 1980. v, 45 p. ; 24 cm. "July 23, 1980." "96th Congress, 2d session. Committee print." Includes bibliographical references. LC Card 81-601507 DDC 353.0072/232 19
1. Government spending policy - United States. 2. United States - Appropriations and expenditures. I. Title.
HJ7539 .U535 1980

Internal Revenue Service collection practices : impact on small businesses : a report / prepared by the Subcommittee on Oversight of Government Management of the Committee on Governmental Affairs, United States Senate, October 8, 1980. Washington : U. S. Govt. Print. Off., 1980. v, 29 p. ; 23 cm. At head of title: Committee print. 96th Congress, 2d session. LC Card 80-603867 DDC 353.0072/4 19
1. Small business - Taxation - United States. 2. United States. Internal Revenue Service. I. Title.
HD2346.U5 U515 1980a

IRS summary collection policy impact on small business : hearing before the Subcommittee on Oversight of Government Management of the Committee on Governmental Affairs, United States Senate, Ninety-sixth Congress, second session, July 31, 1980. Washington : U. S. Govt. Print. Off., 1980. iv, 415 p. ; 24 cm. LC Card 80-603735 DDC 338.6/42/0973 19
1. Tax collection - United States. 2. Tax penalties - United States. 3. Small business - Taxation - United States. 4. United States. Internal Revenue Service. I. Title.
KF26 .G676 1980a

United States. Congress. Senate. Committee on Governmental Affairs. Subcommittee on Reports, Accounting, and Management.
Consultants and contractors . Washington, D.C. [1977] viii, 610 p. : LC Card 81-601555 DDC 353/.0722 19
JK468.C7 C666

United States. Congress. Senate. Committee on Interior and Insular Affairs. Environment and Land Resources Subcommittee. To amend the Wild and scenic rivers act : hearing before the Subcommittee on the Environment and Land Resources of the Committee on Interior and Insular Affairs, United States Senate, Ninety-fourth Congress, first session. Washington : U. S. Govt. Print. Off., 1975- v. : ill., fold. maps ; 24 cm. Pt. 3 has also special title: Missouri River, Mont. Pt. 3 has title: To amend the Wild and scenic rivers act and to designate certain lands as wilderness. Hearings held in various cities, July 9, 1975- on S. 10, 1004, 1506, 2708, 3613, 3788 LC Card 76-600555
1. Housatonic River. 2. Allegheny River. 3. Missouri River. 4. Wild and scenic rivers - Law and legislation - United States. I. Title.
KF26 .I526 1975d

United States. Congress. Senate. Committee on Interior and Insular Affairs. Subcommittee on the Environment and Land Resources. see **United States. Congress. Senate. Committee on Interior and Insular Affairs. Environment and Land Resources Subcommittee.**

United States. Congress. Senate. Committee on Labor and Human Resources.
Asbestos Health Hazards Compensation Act of 1980 : hearings before the Committee on Labor and Human Resources, United States Senate, Ninety-sixth Congress, second session, on S. 2847 ... August 26 and 27, 1980. Washington : U. S. G.P.O., 1980 [i.e. 1981] iv, 367 p. : ill. ; 24 cm. Item 1043 Bibliography: p. 327-329. LC Card 81-600863 DDC 344.73/0217 347.304217 19
1. Workers' compensation - Law and legislation - United States. 2. Asbestos - Law and legislation - United States. I. Title.
KF26 .L27 1980p

Community Home Health Services Act of

BIBLIOGRAPHIC GUIDE

United States. Congress. Senate. Committee on Labor and Human

492

1981 : hearing before the Committee on Labor and Human Resources, United States Senate, Ninety-seventh Congress, first session, on S. 234 ... March 4, 1981. Washington : U. S. G.P.O., 1981. iv, 181 p. ; 24 cm. Item 1043-A, 1043-B (microfiche)   LC Card 81-601873   DDC 344.73/03214 347.3043214 19
1. Home care services - Law and legislation - United States. 2. Community health services - Law and legislation - United States. I. Title.
KF26 .L27 1981b

Employee protection and community stabilization act of 1980 : hearing before the Committee on Labor and Human Resources, United States Senate, Ninety-sixth Congress, second session, on S. 1609 ..., March 7, 1980, Cleveland, Ohio. Washington : U. S. Govt. Print. Off., 1980. v, 340 p. : ill. ; 24 cm.   LC Card 80-603818   DDC 343.73/0742 347.303742 19
1. Economic assistance, Domestic - Law and legislation - United States. 2. Community development - Law and legislation - United States. 3. Business relocation - United States. I. Title.
KF26 .L27 1980i

Health and other effects of unemployment : joint hearing before the Committee on Labor and Human Resources, United States Senate and the Subcommittee on Employment Opportunities of the Committee on Education and Labor, House of Representatives, Ninety-sixth Congress, second session, on examination on how unemployment affects the health, attitudes, and living conditions of individuals, July 24, 1980. Washington : U. S. G.P.O., 1980 [i.e. 1981] iii, 84 p. ; 24 cm. Item 1043   LC Card 81-601598   DDC 362.1/042/0973 19
1. Unemployment - Social aspects - United States. I. United States. Congress. House. Committee on Education and Labor. Subcommittee on Employment Opportunities. II. Title.
KF26 .L27 1980r

Home health care, future policy : joint hearing before the Committee on Labor and Human Resources and the Special Committee on Aging, United Ststes Senate, Ninety-sixth Congress, second session, on evaluation of federal policy, program administration, the delivery of services in community programs, and those who work to serve the real needs of elderly and disabled persons, November 23, 1980, Princeton, N.J. Washington : U. S. G.P.O.. 1981. iii, 332 p. ; 24 cm. Item 1043   LC Card 81-601630   DDC 362.1/4/09749 19
1. Aged - Home care - New Jersey. 2. Community health services for the aged - New Jersey. 3. Home care services - New Jersey. I. United States. Congress. Senate. Special Committee on Aging. II. Title.
KF26 .L27 1980u

Labor statistics respondent privacy protection act of 1980 : hearing before the Committee on Labor and Human Resources, United States Senate, Ninety-sixth Congress, second session, on S. 2887 ... July 23, 1980. Washington : U. S. G.P.O., 1980. iii, 43 p. ; 23 cm.   LC Card 80-603782   DDC 342.73/0853 347.302853 19
1. United States. Bureau of Labor Statistics. 2. Labor and laboring classes - Statistical services - Law and legislation - United States. I. Title.
KF26 .L27 1980k

Legislative history of the Pregnancy discrimination act of 1978, Public law 95-555 . Washington , 1979 [i.e. 1980] vi, 212 p. ;   LC Card 80-602871   DDC 344.73/014133 19
KF3467.A314 A15 1980

National workers' compensation standards act of 1979 : hearings before the Committee on Labor and Human Resources, United States Senate, Ninety-sixth Congress, first session, on S. 420 ... March 28, April 2 and 3, 1979. Washington : U. S. Govt. Print. Off., 1980. vi, 794 p. : ill. ; 24 cm. Includes bibliographical references.   LC Card 80-602897   DDC 344.73/021 19
1. Workmen's compensation - United States - States. I. Title.
KF26 .L27 1979y

Nomination : hearing before the Committee on Labor and Human Resources, United States Senate, Ninety-sixth Congress, second session, on John Brooks Slaughter, of Washington, to be director of the National Science Foundation, August 1, 1980. Washington : U. S. G.P.O., 1980 ii 28 p. ; 24 cm.   LC Card 80-604090 DDC

353.0085/5 19
1. Slaughter, John Brooks, 1934-. 2. National Science Foundation (U. S.) - Officials and employees. I. Title.
KF26 .L27 1980m

Nomination : hearing before the Committee on Labor and Human Resources, United States Senate, Ninety-sixth Congress, second session, on James E. Jones, Jr., of Wisconsin, to be chairman, Special Panel on Appeals. Washington : U. S. G.P.O., 1980. ii, 41 p. ; 23 cm. "August 1, 1980."   LC Card 80-603645   DDC 353.001/04 19
1. Jones, James E. 2. United States. Special Panel on Appeals - Officials and employees. I. Title.
KF26 .L27 1980n

Nomination : hearing before the Committee on Labor and Human Resources, United States Senate, Ninety-sixth Congress, second session, on Don Alan Zimmerman, of Maryland, to be a member of the National Labor Relations Board, June 10, 1980. Washington : U. S. Govt. Print. Off., 1980. ii, 14 p. ; 24 cm.   LC Card 80-602910   DDC 353.0085/2 19
1. Zimmerman, Don Alan, 1940-. 2. United States. National Labor Relations Board - Officials and employees.
KF26 .L27 1980c

Nomination : hearing before the Committee on Labor and Human Resources, United States Senate, Ninety-sixth Congress, second session, on William L. Smith, of Maryland, to be Commissioner of the Department of Education, January 23, 1980. Washington : U. S. Govt. Print. Off., 1980. ii, 29 p. : forms ; 24 cm.   LC Card 80-602538   DDC 353.842 19
1. Smith, William Lee, 1929-. 2. United States. Dept. of Education - Officials and employees.
KF26 .L27 1980b

Nomination : hearing before the Committee on Labor and Human Resources, United States Senate, Ninety-sixth Congress, second session, on Margaret J. Giannini, of New York, to be director of the National Institute of Handicapped Research, January 23, 1980. Washington : U. S. Govt. Print. Off., 1980. ii, 76 p. ; 24 cm.   LC Card 80-603359   DDC 353.0084/4 19
1. Giannini, Margaret Joan, 1921-. 2. National Institute of Handicapped Research - Employees.
KF26 .L27 1980f

Nomination : hearings before the Committee on Labor and Human Resources, United States Senate, Ninety-sixth Congress, second session, on John C. Truesdale, of Maryland, to be a member of the National Labor Relations Board (reappointment), August 22 and September 5, 1980. Washington : U. S. Govt. Print. Off., 1980. iv, 452 p. ; 23 cm.   LC Card 80-603891   DDC 353.0083/2 19
1. Truesdale, John C., 1921-. 2. United States. National Labor Relations Board - Officials and employees.
KF26 .L27 1980j

Nomination : hearing before the Committee on Labor and Human Resources, United States Senate, Ninety-sixth Congress, second session, on John Richard Rios, of California, to be Director and Michael T. Blouin, of Iowa, to be Assistant Director (of Community Action), Community Services Administration, June 11, 1980. Washington : U. S. Govt. Print. Off., 1980. ii, 46 p. ; 24 cm.   LC Card 80-602975   DDC 353.0084 19
1. Rios, Richard John, 1942-. 2. Blouin, Michael T., 1945-. 3. United States. Community Services Administration - Officials and employees. I. Title.
KF26 .L27 1980d

Nomination : hearings before the Committee on Labor and Human Resources, United States Senate, Ninety-seventh Congress, first session, on Dr. Terrel H. Bell, of Utah, to be secretary, Department of Education, January 15, 1981. Washington : U. S. G.P.O., 1981. 114 p. ; 24 cm. Item 1043-A, 1043-B (microfiche)   LC Card 81-601605   DDC 353.844 19
1. Bell, Terrel Howard, 1921-. 2. United States. Dept. of Education - Officials and employees. I. Title.
KF26 .L27 1981a

Nomination : hearings before the Committee on Labor and Human Resources, United States Senate, Ninety-seventh Congress, first session, on Raymond J. Donovan, of New Jersey, to be secretary of labor, January 12 and 27, 1981. Washington : U. S.G.P.O., c1981. ii, 378 p. ;

ill. ; 24 cm. Item 1043-A, 1043-B (microfiche)   LC Card 81-600954   DDC 353.83
1. Donovan, Raymond James, 1930-. 2. United States. Dept. of Labor - Officials and employees. I. Title.
KF26 .L27 1981

Nominations : hearing before the Committee on Labor and Human Resources, United States Senate, Ninety-sixth Congress, second session, on Martha E. Keys, of Kansas, to be Assistant Secretary of Education (For Legislation), and Daniel B. Taylor, of Massachusetts, to be Assistant Secretary (For Vocational and Adult Education), June 5, 1980. Washington : U. S. Govt. Print. Off., 1980. ii, 54 p. ; 23 cm.   LC Card 80-603437   DDC 353.844 19
1. Keys, Martha E., 1930-. 2. Taylor, Daniel B., 1933-. 3. United States. Dept. of Education - Officials and employees.
KF26 .L27 1980g

Nominations : hearing before the Committee on Labor and Human Resources, United States Senate, Ninety-sixth Congress, second session ... June 12, 1980. Washington : U. S. Govt. Print. Off., 1980. ii, 86 p. ; 23 cm. Hearing on nominations of Edwin W. Martin, Jr., to be Assistant Secretary (for Special Education and Rehabilitative Services) and Cynthia G. Brown to be Assistant Secretary (for Civil Rights) Dept. of Education.   LC Card 80-603445   DDC 353.842 19
1. Martin, Edwin W., 1931-. 2. Brown, Cynthia G., 1943-. 3. United States. Dept. of Education - Officials and employees.
KF26 .L27 1980h

Nominations : hearing before the Committee on Labor and Human Resources, United States Senate, Ninety-sixth Congress, second session, on Steven A. Minter, of Ohio, to be Under Secretary of Education; Albert H. Bowker, of California, to be Assistant Secretary (for postsecondary education) ; Thomas Kendall Minter, of Pennsylvania, to be Assistant Secretary (for elementary and secondary education); and F. James Rutherford, of the District of Columbia, to be Assistant Secretary (for educational research and improvement), April 30, 1980. Washington : U. S. Govt. Print. Off., 1980. ii, 122 p. ; 24 cm. Includes bibliographical references.   LC Card 80-602807 DDC 353.844 19
1. United States. Dept. of Education - Officials and employees.
KF26 .L27 1980e

Occupational Safety and Health Improvements Act of 1980 : hearings before the Committee on Labor and Human Resources, United States Senate, Ninety-Sixth Congress, second session, on S. 2153 ... April 15, 17, and 25, 1980. Washington : U. S. G.P.O., 1980. vii, 1170 p. : ill. ; 24 cm. Includes bibliographical references.   LC Card 81-600656   DDC 344.73/0465 347.304465 19
1. Industrial safety - Law and legislation - United States. 2. Industrial hygiene - Law and legislation - United States. I. Title.
KF26 .L27 1980l

Oversight on the Longshoremen's and Harbor Workers' Compensation Act, 1980 : hearing before the Committee on Labor and Human Resources, United States Senate, Ninety-sixth Congress, second session, on oversight on the administration of the Longshoremen's and Harbor Workers' Compensation Act, September 16, 1980. Washington : U. S. G.P.O., 1981. v, 472 p. : ill. ; 24 cm. Item 1043 Includes bibliographical references.   LC Card 81-601328   DDC 353.0082/56 19
1. Stevedores - Legal status, laws, etc. - United States. 2. Workers' compensation - Law and legislation - United States. 3. Stevedores - United States. 4. Workers' compensation - United States. I. Title.
KF26 .L27 1980t

Railroad retirement annuity increase--1980 : hearing before the Committee on Labor and Human Resources, United States Senate, Ninety-sixth Congress, second session, on S. 2979 ... September 25, 1980. Washington : U. S. G.P.O., 1980. iii, 78 p. ; 24 cm. Item 1043   LC Card 81-600578   DDC 344.73/012529 347.30412529 19
1. Railroads - United States - Pensions. I. Title.
KF26 .L27 1980o

State support for health professions education /. Washington , 1981. xiii, 109 p. ;   LC Card

GOVERNMENT PUBLICATIONS - U.S.: 1981

493

United States. Congress. Senate. Committee on Labor and Human

81-601289   DDC 610/.7/1173 19
R745 .S74

United States Commission on Proposals for the National Academy of Peace and Conflict Resolution. Interim report of the U. S. Commission on Proposals for the National Academy of Peace and Conflict Resolution . Washington , 1980. iii, 16, vii p. ;   LC Card 80-604123   DDC 327.1/72/071173 19
JX1963 .U14 1980

United States. Congress. Office of Technology Assessment. The implications of cost-effectiveness analysis of medical technology. Washington, D.C. [1980] vii, 219 p. ;   LC Card 80-600130   DDC 362.1/068/1 19
RA410.5 .U54 1980

United States. Health Resources Administration. Bureau of Health Manpower. A report on public and community health personnel . Washington, D.C. , 1980. viii, 220 p. ;   LC Card 80-602370   DDC 331.12/913621 19
RA440.9 .U47 1980

Workers and the evolving economy of the eighties : hearings before the Committee on Labor and Human Resources, United States Senate, Ninety-sixth Congress, second session, on examination of work force dislocation and exploring ways to enhance worker mobility and retraining to ensure full utilization of our work force's potential, September 17 and 18, 1980. Washington : U. S. G.P.O., 1981. iv, 387 p. : ill. ; 24 cm. Item 1043 Bibliography: p. 307.   LC Card 81-601377   DDC 331.12/042/0973 19
1. Employees, Relocation of - United States. 2. Plant shutdowns - United States. 3. Labor mobility - United States. 4. Occupational retraining - United States. I. Title.
KF26 .L27 1980s

Workplace and higher education : perspective for the coming decade, 1979 : hearings before the Committee on Labor and Human Resources, United States Senate, Ninety-sixth Congress, second session, on examination on the future of higher education and the provision of well-trained persons for the public and private employment sectors of the economy, June 6 and 7, 1979. Washington : U. S. G.P.O., 1980. v, 336 p. ; 24 cm. Includes bibliographical references.   LC Card 80-604012   DDC 378.73 19
1. Education, Higher - Economic aspects - United States. 2. Human capital - United States. I. Title.
KF26 .L27 1979z

United States. Congress. Senate. Committee on Labor and Human Resources. Subcommittee on Aging.
Home energy assistance act : hearings before the Subcommittee on Aging of the Committee on Labor and Human Resources, United States Senate, Ninety-sixth Congress, first session, on S. 1724 ... June 7, 1979, Washington, D.C., June 15, 1979, Kansas City, Mo. Washington : U. S. Govt. Print. Off., 1980- v. ; 23 cm. Includes bibliographical references.   LC Card 80-602480   DDC 344.73/03263 19
1. Aged - Energy assistance - Law and legislation - United States. 2. Poor - Energy assistance - Law and legislation - United States. I. Title.
KF26 .L2716 1979

Impact of Alzheimer's disease on the nation's elderly : joint hearing before the Subcommittee on Aging of the Committee on Labor and Human Resources, United States Senate, and the Subcommittee on Labor, Health, Education, and Welfare of the Committee on Appropriations, House of Representatives, Ninety-sixth Congress, second session, on to analyze the impact of Alzheimer's disease and other dimentias [i.e. dementias] of aging on our society, July 15, 1980. Washington : U. S. G.P.O., 1980 [i.e. 1981] vi, 199 p. ; 23 cm. Item 1043 Includes bibliographies.   LC Card 81-601182   DDC 362.1/989768983 19
1. Presenile dementia. 2. Brain - Aging. I. United States. Congress. House. Committee on Appropriations. Subcommittee on Departments of Labor, and Health, Education, and Welfare, and Related Agencies. II. Title.
KF26 .L2716 1980

United States. Congress. Senate. Special Committee on Aging. Regulations to implement the Comprehensive older Americans act amendments of 1978 . Washington , 1980- v. ;   LC Card 80-603040   DDC 353.0084/6 19
KF26.5 .A3 1979i

United States. Congress. Senate. Committee on Labor and Human Resources. Subcommittee on Child and Human Development.
Domestic Violence Prevention and Services Act, 1980 : hearing before the Subcommittee on Child and Human Development of the Committee on Labor and Human Resources, United States Senate, Ninety-sixth Congress, second session, on S. 1843 ... and related bill, February 6, 1980. Washington : U. S. G.P.O., 1980. iv, 584 p. : ill. ; 24 cm. Includes bibliographies.   LC Card 81-600639   DDC 344.73/03283 347.3043283 19
1. Abused wives - Legal status, laws, etc. - United States. 2. Abused wives - United States - Services for. 3. Conjugal violence - United States. I. Title.
KF26 .L273 1980b

Oversight on efforts to reduce infant mortality and to improve pregnancy outcome : hearing before the Subcommittee on Child and Human Development of the Committee on Labor and Human Resources, United States Senate, Ninety-sixth Congress, second session, to examine the overall efforts by the federal government and certain medical services to reduce infant mortality, birth defects, and improve pregnancy outcome, June 30, 1980. Washington : U. S. G.P.O., 1980 [i.e. 1981] v, 700 p. : ill. ; 24 cm. Item 1043 Includes bibliographies.   LC Card 81-601360   DDC 362.1/982/00973 19
1. Maternal health services - United States. 2. Infants - United States - Mortality. 3. Infants (Newborn) - United States - Mortality. 4. Abnormalities, Human - United States. I. Title.
KF26 .L273 1980c

Parental kidnaping, 1979 : hearing before the Subcommittee on Child and Human Development of the Committee on Labor and Human Resources, United States Senate, Ninety-sixth Congress, first session, on examination of the problem of "child snatching," April 17, 1979, Los Angeles, Calif. Washington : U. S. Govt. Print. Off., 1979. iv, 285 p. : ill. ; 23 cm. Includes bibliographical references.   LC Card 80-600739   DDC 364.1/54 19
1. Kidnapping, Parental - United States. 2. Custody of children - United States. I. Title.
KF26 .L273 1979d

Presidential Commission on National Service and National Commission on Volunteerism : hearing before the Subcommittee on Child and Human Development of the Committee on Labor and Human Resources, United States Senate, Ninety-sixth Congress, second session, on establishment of a Presidential Commission on National Service and a National Commission on Volunteerism, March 13, 1980. Washington : U. S. G.P.O., 1980. v, 606 p. : ill. ; 24 cm. Bibliography: p. 428.   LC Card 80-604000   DDC 361.3/7/0973 19
1. United States. Presidential Commission on National Service. 2. United States. National Commission on Volunteerism. 3. National service - United States. 4. National service - Law and legislation - United States. I. Title.
KF26 .L273 1980a

Save the Children Day, 1980 : hearing before the Subcommittee on Child and Human Development of the Committee on Labor and Human Resources, United States Senate, Ninety-sixth Congress, second session ... May 1, 1980. Washington : U. S. Govt. Print. Off., 1980. iii, 18 p. ; 24 cm.   LC Card 80-603311   DDC 362.7/95/0973 19
1. Child welfare - United States. I. Title.
KF26 .L273 1980

United States. Congress. Senate. Committee on the Judiciary. Subcommittee on Criminal Justice. Parental kidnaping prevention act of 1979, S. 105 . Washington , 1980. iv, 156 p. ;   LC Card 80-602799   DDC 345.73/0254 19
KF26 .J8377 1980c

United States. Congress. Senate. Committee on the Judiciary. Subcommittee on Criminal Justice. Parental kidnaping prevention act of 1979, S.105 . Washington , 1980. iii, 378 p. :   LC Card 80-602982   DDC 345.73/0254 19
KF26 .J8377 1980b

United States. Congress. Senate. Committee on Labor and Human Resources. Subcommittee on Education, Arts, and Humanities.
Asbestos school hazard detection and control

act of 1979 : hearing before the Subcommittee on Education, Arts and Humanities of the Committee on Labor and Human Resources, United States Senate, Ninety-sixth Congress, second session, on S. 1658 ... New York, N.Y., March 17, 1980. Washington, D.C. : U. S. Govt. Print. Off., 1980. iv, 277 p. : ill. ; 24 cm. Includes bibliographical references.   LC Card 80-602756   DDC 344.73/07 19
1. Asbestos - Law and legislation - United States. 2. School buildings - Law and legislation - United States. 3. Students - United States - Health and Hygiene. 4. Asbestos - Toxicology. I. Title.
KF26 .L2735 1980

Chartrand, Robert Lee. International information exchange . Washington , 1980. xii, 156 p. :   LC Card 80-603261   DDC 021.6/4 19
Z690 .C47

Family contribution schedule for the Basic educational opportunity grant program, 1980 : hearing before the Subcommittee on Education, Arts, and Humanities of the Committee on Labor and Human Resources, United States Senate, Ninety-sixth Congress, first session ... September 14, 1979. Washington : U. S. Govt. Print. Off., 1980. iii, 49 p. : forms ; 24 cm.   LC Card 80-602447   DDC 378/.3/0973 19
1. Student aid - United States. I. Title.
KF26 .L2735 1979c

Higher education amendments of 1979 : hearings before the Subcommittee on Education, Arts, and Humanities of the Committee on Labor and Human Resources, United States Senate, Ninety-sixth Congress, first session, on S. 1839 .... Washington : U. S. Govt. Print. Off., 1980- v. ; 24 cm. Hearings held October 2-5, 1979.   LC Card 80-602896   DDC 344.73/074 19
1. Universities and colleges - Law and legislation - United States. 2. Federal aid to higher education - United States. I. Title.
KF26 .L2735 1979d

Reauthorization of the national sea grant college program : joint hearing before the Subcommittee on Education, Arts, and Humanities of the Committee on Labor and Human Resources and the Committee on Commerce, Science, and Transportation, United States Senate, Ninety-sixth Congress, second session, on S. 2589 ... April 25, 1980. Washington : U. S. Govt. Print. Off., 1980. iii, 204 p. ; 24 cm. Bibliography: p. 113-115.   LC Card 80-603079   DDC 346.7304/695 19
1. National Sea Grant Program. 2. Oceanographic research - Law and legislation - United States. 3. Federal aid to higher education - United States. I. United States. Congress. Senate. Committee on Commerce, Science, and Transportation. II. Title.
KF26 .L2735 1980a

Youth Act of 1980 : hearings before the Subcommittee on Education, Arts, and Humanities of the Committee on Labor and Human Resources, United States Senate, Ninety-sixth Congress, second session, on S. 2385 ... March 7, June 17 and 18, 1980. Washington : U. S. G.P.O., 1980. vi, 681 p. : ill. ; 24 cm. Includes bibliographies.   LC Card 80-604088   DDC 344.73/01342592 347.3041342592 19
1. Occupational training - Law and legislation - United States. 2. Youth - Employment - United States. I. Title.
KF26 .L2735 1980b

United States. Congress. Senate. Committee on Labor and Human Resources. Subcommittee on Employment, Poverty, and Migratory Labor.
Oversight of the Legal Services Corporation, 1980 : hearing before the Subcommittee on Employment, Poverty, and Migratory Labor of the Committee on Labor and Human Resources, United States Senate, Ninety-sixth Congress, second session ... February 5, 1980. Washington : U. S. Govt. Print. Off., 1980. iv, 324 p. ; 24 cm. Includes bibliographical references.   LC Card 80-602105   DDC 353.0084/5 19
1. Legal Services Corporation. 2. Legal services - United States. I. Title.
KF26 .L2737 1980

Oversight on issues affecting Hispanics and migrant and seasonal farmworkers : hearing before the Subcommittee on Employment, Poverty, and Migratory Labor of the Committee on Labor and Human Resources,

BIBLIOGRAPHIC GUIDE

United States. Congress. Senate. Committee on Labor and Human

494

United States Senate, Ninety-sixth Congress, second session, on examination on whether and to what extent existing federal programs affectively and efficiently meet the needs of Hispanics and migrant and seasonal farmworkers, Milwaukee, Wis., September 6, 1980. Washington : U. S. G.P.O., 1981. iii, 127 p. ; 23 cm. Includes bibliographical references. Item 1043 LC Card 81-601138 DDC 353.0083/6 19
1. Hispanic Americans - Wisconsin - Economic conditions. 2. Migrant agricultural laborers - Wisconsin. I. Title.
KF26 .L2737 1980c

Staff evaluation of the Legal Services Corporation's responses to the recommendations made by the U. S. General Accounting Office in three reports issued in 1978 and 1979 / prepared by the Subcommittee on Employment, Poverty, and Migratory Labor of the Committee on Labor and Human Resources, United States Senate. Washington : U. S. Govt. Print. Off., 1980. ii, 15 p. ; 24 cm. At head of title: 96th Congress, 2d session. Committee print. "May 1980." LC Card 80-602593 DDC 353.0084/5 19
1. Legal Services Corporation. 2. Legal aid - United States. I. Title.
KF336 .A717

Youth employment act, 1980 : hearing before the Subcommittee on Employment, Poverty, and Migratory Labor of the Committee on Labor and Human Resources, United States Senate, Ninety-sixth Congress, second session on S. 2021 ... February 15, 1980, Cleveland, Ohio. Washington : U. S. Govt. Print. Off., 1980. iii, 111 p. ; 24 cm. LC Card 80-603336 DDC 344.73/0134 19
1. Children - Legal status, laws, etc. - United States. 2. Youth - Employment - United States. I. Title.
KF26 .L2737 1980a

Youth employment and welfare reform jobs, 1980 : hearings before the Subcommittee on Employment, Poverty, and Migratory Labor of the Committee on Labor and Human Resources, United States Senate, Ninety-sixth Congress, second session, on examination on legislative proposals relating to youth employment and the administration's welfare reform jobs bill, March 5, 6, 12, and 13, 1980. Washington : U. S. G.P.O., 1980. vi, 892 p. : ill. ; 24 cm. Includes bibliographical references. LC Card 81-600874 DDC 344.73/01342592 347.3041342592 19
1. Occupational training - Law and legislation - United States. 2. Public welfare - Law and legislation - United States. 3. Youth - Employment - United States. I. Title.
KF26 .L2737 1980b

United States. Congress. Senate. Committee on Labor and Human Resources. Subcommittee on Health and Scientific Research.
Blood assurance act of 1979 : hearing before the Subcommittee on Health and Scientific Research of the Committee on Labor and Human Resources, United States Senate, Ninety-sixth Congress, second session, on S. 1610 ... May 21, 1980. Washington : U. S. Govt. Print. Off., 1980. iv, 108 p. ; 24 cm. LC Card 80-603681 DDC 344.73/03217 347.3043217 19
1. Blood banks - Law and legislation - United States. I. Title.
KF26 .L274 1980c

Consumer-patient radiation safety and health act of 1979 : hearing before the Subcommittee on Health and Scientific Research of the Committee on Labor and Human Resources, United States Senate, Ninety-sixth Congress, second session, on S. 500 ... April 3, 1980. Washington : U. S. Govt. Print. Off., 1980. iv, 316 p. : ill. ; 24 cm. LC Card 80-603350 DDC 344.73/0472 19
1. Radiation - Safety regulations - United States. 2. X-rays - Safety regulations - United States. 3. Medical laws and legislation - United States. I. Title.
KF26 .L274 1980c

Health effects of hazardous waste disposal practices, 1980 : joint hearing before the Subcommittee on Health and Scientific Research of the Committee on Labor and Human Resources and the Committee on the Judiciary, United States Senate, Ninety-sixth Congress, second session ... June 6, 1980. Washington : U. S.G.P.O., 1980. iv, 110 p. ; 23 cm. LC Card 80-603890 DDC 363.1/79 19

1. Hazardous wastes - Toxicology - United States. I. United States. Congress. Senate. Committee on the Judiciary. II. Title.
KF26 .L274 1980j

Health Professions Education and Distribution Act of 1980 : hearings before the Subcommittee on Health and Scientific Research of the Committee on Labor and Human Resources, United States Senate, Ninety-sixth Congress, second session, on S. 2375 ... S. 2144 ... S. 2378 ... March 10 and 12, 1980. Washington : U. S. G.P.O., 1980. iii, 1034 p. : ill. ; 23 cm. Includes bibliographical references. LC Card 80-603787 DDC 344.73/0769 347.3.04769 19
1. Medical education - Law and legislation - United States. 2. Federal aid to medical education - United States. 3. Medical personnel - United States - Supply and demand. I. Title.
KF26 .L274 1980h

Implications of the President's health budget, 1979 : hearing before the Subcommittee on Health and Scientific Research of the Committee on Labor and Human Resources, United States Senate, Ninety-sixth Congress, first session ... January 26, 1979. Washington : U. S. Govt. Print. Off., 1979. iii, 422 p. : ill. ; 24 cm. LC Card 80-602525 DDC 353.0072/236841 19
1. Medical policy - United States. 2. Budget - United States. I. Title.
KF26 .L274 1979t

Infant Formula Act of 1980 : hearing before the Subcommittee on Health and Scientific Research of the Committee on Labor and Human Resources, United States Senate, Ninety-sixth Congress, second session, on S. 2490 ... June 12, 1980. Washington : U. S. G.P.O., 1980. iv, 164 p. ; 24 cm. LC Card 81-600630 DDC 344.73/04232 347.3044232 19
1. Infant formulas - Law and legislation - United States. I. Title.
KF26 .L274 1980i

International Health Act of 1980 : hearing before the Subcommittee on Health and Scientific Research of the Committee on Labor and Human Resources, United States Senate, Ninety-sixth Congress, second session, on S. 1424 ... July 2, 1980. Washington : U. S. G.P.O., 1980. iii, 147 p. ; 24 cm. LC Card 81-600608 DDC 344.73/04 347.3044 19
1. Public health laws, International. I. Title.
KF26 .L274 1980k

National Science Foundation authorization act for fiscal years 1981 and 1982 : hearing before the Subcommittee on Health and Scientific Research of the Committee on Labor and Human Resources, United States Senate, Ninety-sixth Congress, second session, on S. 2462 ... March 25, 1980. Washington : U. S. Govt. Print. Off., 1980. iv, 132 p. : ill. ; 24 cm. LC Card 80-602713 DDC 353.0072/236855 19
1. United States. National Science Foundation - Appropriations and expenditures. I. Title.
KF26 .L274 1980a

Nutrition labeling and information amendments of 1979 to the Federal food, drug, and cosmetic act : hearings before the Subcommittee on Health and Scientific Research of the Committee on Labor and Human Resources, United States Senate, Ninety-sixth Congress, second session, on S. 1652 ... February 20 and March 19, 1980. Washington : U. S. Govt. Print. Off., 1980. v, 738 p. : ill. ; 24 cm. Includes bibliographical references. LC Card 80-602890 DDC 344.73/04232 19
1. Food - Labeling - Law and legislation - United States. 2. Nutrition - Law and legislation - United States. I. Title.
KF26 .L274 1980b

Oversight of the National Health Service Corps : hearing before the Subcommittee on Health and Scientific Research of the Committee on Labor and Human Resources, United States Senate, Ninety-sixth Congress, second session, on examination on the implementation of the National Health Service Corps program of the Health Services Administration under the Department of Health and Human Services, September 24, 1980. Washington : U. S. G.P.O., 1980. iv, 167 p. : ill. ; 24 cm. Includes bibliographical references. LC Card 81-600609 DDC 362.1/0973 19

1. National Health Service Corps (U. S.). I. Title.
KF26 .L274 1980l

Oversight on financially distressed hospitals : hearing before the Subcommittee on Health and Scientific Research of the Committee on Labor and Human Resources, United States Senate, Ninety-sixth Congress, second session ... June 25, 1980. Washington : U. S. Govt. Print. Off., 1980. iv, 172 p. ; 23 cm. LC Card 80-603458 DDC 362.1/04252 19
1. Federal aid to hospitals - United States. 2. Hospitals - United States - Finance. 3. Poor - Hospital care - United States. I. Title.
KF26 .L274 1980f

Preclinical and clinical testing by the pharmaceutical industry, 1980--DMSO : hearing before the Subcommittee on Health and Scientific Research of the Committee on Labor and Human Resources, United States Senate, Ninety-sixth Congress, second session, on examination of the testing of DMSO and FDA's role in the process, July 31, 1980. Washington : U. S. G.P.O., 1980. iii, 103 p. ; 24 cm. LC Card 81-600617 DDC 363.1/9464 19
1. Dimethyl sulphoxide - Testing. 2. Dimethyl sulphoxide - Therapeutic use. 3. Dimethyl sulphoxide - Therapeutic use - Side effects - United States. I. Title.
KF26 .L274 1980n

Radiation exposure compensation act of 1979 : joint hearing before the Subcommittee on Health and Scientific Research of the Committee on Labor and Human Resources and the Committee on the Judiciary, United States Senate, Ninety-sixth Congress, second session, on S. 1865 ... June 10, 1980. Washington : U. S. Govt. Print. Off., 1980. iv, 132 p. : graphs ; 24 cm. Includes bibliographical references. LC Card 80-603432 DDC 346.7303/8 347.30638 19
1. Liability for nuclear damages - United States. 2. Government liability - United States. 3. Atomic weapons - Testing. 4. Uranium mines and mining - Employees - Diseases and hygiene - The West. I. United States. Congress. Senate. Committee on the Judiciary. II. Title.
KF26 .L274 1980d

Short- and long-term health effects on the surviving population of a nuclear war : hearing before the Subcommittee on Health and Scientific Research of the Committee on Labor and Human Resources, United States Senate, Ninety-sixth Congress, second session, on to [sic] examining some of the consequences that could affect the surviving population of a nuclear war, June 19, 1980. Washington : U. S. G.P.O., 1980 [i.e. 1981] iv, 133 p. ; 24 cm. Item 1043 LC Card 81-601151 DDC 363.1/79 19
1. Atomic bomb - Blast effect. 2. Atomic bomb - Physiological effect. 3. Atomic warfare and society. I. Title.
KF26 .L274 1980m

Toxic shock syndrome, 1980 : hearing before the Subcommittee on Health and Scientific Research of the Committee on Labor and Human Resources, United States Senate, Ninety-sixth Congress, second session ... June 6, 1980. Washington : U. S. Govt. Print. Off., 1980. iii, 12 p. ; 24 cm. LC Card 80-603321 DDC 616.9 19
1. Toxic shock syndrome - United States. I. Title.
KF26 .L274 1980g

United States. Congress. Senate. Committee on Labor and Human Resources. Subcommittee on the Handicapped.
Oversight on Education for all handicapped children act, 1979 : hearings before the Subcommittee on the Handicapped of the Committee on Labor and Human Resources, United States Senate, Ninety-sixth Congress, first session ... Washington : U. S. Govt. Print. Off., 1980. vi, 1215 p. : ill. ; 24 cm. Hearings held July 19-Oct. 10, 1979. Includes bibliographical references. LC Card 80-601923 DDC 353.0085/1 19
1. Handicapped children - Education - United States. I. Title.
KF26 .L2739 1979b

Oversight on Education for all handicapped children act, 1980 : hearing before the Subcommittee on the Handicapped of the Committee on Labor and Human Resources, United States Senate, Ninety-sixth Congress, second session ... March 3, 1980. Washington : U. S. Govt. Print. Off., 1980. iii, 156 p. :

GOVERNMENT PUBLICATIONS - U.S.: 1981

495

United States. Congress. Senate. Committee on the Judiciary.

graphs ; 24 cm. LC Card 80-602464 DDC 353.0085/1 19
1. Handicapped children - Education - United States. I. Title.
KF26 .L2739 1980

Oversight on programs for the deaf and hearing impaired, 1980 : hearing before the Subcommittee on the Handicapped of the Committee on Labor and Human Resources, United States Senate, Ninety-sixth Congress, second session ... February 6, 1980. Washington : U. S. Govt. Print. Off., 1980. iv, 238 p. ; 24 cm. LC Card 80-602742 DDC 362.4/28/0973 19
1. Deaf - Government policy - United States. 2. Deaf - United States - Services for. I. Title.
KF26 .L2739 1980a

United States. Congress. Senate. Committee on Labor and Public Welfare. (Old Catalog form: United States. Labor and Public Welfare, Committee on (Senate))
Nomination : hearing before the Committee on Labor and Public Welfare, United States Senate, Ninety-fourth Congress, first session, on Morton Corn, of Pennsylvania, to be an Assistant Secretary of Labor for Occupational Safety and Health, October 22, 1975. Washington : U. S. Govt. Print. Off., 1976. iii, 70 p. : ill. ; 24 cm. Includes bibliographical references. LC Card 76-601909
1. Corn, Morton, 1933-. I. Title.
KF26 .L3 1975o

United States. Congress. Senate. Committee on Labor and Public Welfare. Subcommittee on Labor. Scotia Mine disaster, 1976 : joint hearings before the Subcommittee on Labor of the Committee on Labor and Public Welfare, United States Senate, and the Committee on Education and Labor, U. S. House of Representatives, Ninety-fourth Congress, second session .... Washington : U. S. Govt. Print. Off., 1976. vi, 279 p. ; 24 cm. Hearings held in Whitesburg, Ky., and Washington, D.C., May 7-June 16, 1976. LC Card 76-602873
1. Scotia Mine Disaster, Oven Fork, Ky., 1976. 2. Coal mines and mining - Kentucky - Safety measures. I. United States. Congress. House. Committee on Education and Labor. II. Title.
KF26 .L363 1976f   **NYPL [JLE 81-466]**

United States. Congress. Senate. Committee on Labor and Public Welfare. Subcommittee on the Handicapped. Education for all handicapped children, 1973-74. Hearings, Ninety-third Congress, first session, on S. 6 ... Washington, U. S. Govt. Print. Off., 1973- v. (vi, 1763 p.) illus. 24 cm. Hearings held in various cities, Apr 9, 1973 Bibliography: v. 2, p. 713-714. LC Card 74-601834
1. Handicapped children - Education - United States. 2. Handicapped children - Law and legislation - United States. I. Title.
KF26 .L3515 1973d

United States. Congress. Senate. Committee on Public Works. (Old Catalog form: United States. Public Works, Committee on (Senate))

United States. Congress. Senate. Committee on Public Works. Panel on Environmental Science and Technology. Choosing our environment : can we anticipate the future? : Hearing before the Panel on Environmental Science and Technology of the Subcommittee on Environmental Pollution of the Committee on Public Works, United States Senate, Ninety-fourth Congress, first session, December 15, 1975. Washington : U. S. Govt. Print. Off., 1976- v. : ill. ; 23 cm. "Serial no. 94-H31." "Selected readings": v. 1, p. [173]-454. Includes bibliographical references. CONTENTS. - v. 1. Futures analysis and the environment. LC Card 76-601829
1. Environmental policy - United States. 2. Environmental policy research - United States. I. Title.
KF26 .P838 1975

United States. Congress. Senate. Committee on Rules and Administration. (Old Catalog form: United States. Rules and Administration, Committee on (Senate)) // Hearings printed in 1978 and later are available only in microform. Please consult the librarians in the Economic and Public Affairs Division.
To create a Select Committee on Narcotics Abuse and Control : hearing before the Committee on Rules and Administration, United States Senate, Ninety-sixth Congress,

second session, on S. Res. 207 ... April 23, 1980. Washington : U. S. Govt. Print. Off., 1980. iv, 224 p. : ill. ; 23 cm. LC Card 80-602455 DDC 353.0076/5 19
1. United States. Congress. Senate. Select Committee on Narcotics Abuse and Control. 2. Narcotics, Control of - United States. I. Title.
KF26 .R8 1980

To makethe Select Committee on Indian Affairs a permanent committee of the Senate : hearing before the Committee on Rules and Administration, United States Senate, Ninety-sixth Congress, second session, on S. Res. 448 ... June 25, 1980. Washington : U. S. Govt. Print. Off., 1980. v, 70 p. ; 24 cm. LC Card 80-603072 DDC 328.73/07652 19
1. United States. Congress. Senate. Select Committee on Indian Affairs. I. Title.
KF26 .R8 1980a

United States. Congress. Senate. Committee on Small Business. see United States. Congress. Senate. Select Committee on Small Business.

United States. Congress. Senate. Committee on the Budget. Hearings printed in 1978 and later are available only in microform. Please consult the librarians in the Economic and Public Affairs Division.
Inflation and recession : are high interest rates the cause or the cure? : Hearing before the Committee on the Budget, United States Senate, Ninety-sixth Congress, first session, Nashville, Tenn., November 3, 1979. Washington : U. S. Govt. Print. Off., 1980. iii, 50 p. ; 24 cm. Includes index. LC Card 80-603332 DDC 332.4/1/0973 19
1. Interest and usury - United States - Effect of inflation on. 2. Inflation (Finance) - United States. 3. United States - Economic policy - 1971-. I. Title.
KF26 .B8 1979e

The present state of the American economy : strategies to restore stability : hearings before the Committee on the Budget, United States Senate, Ninety-seventh Congress, first session .... Washington : U. S. G.P.O., 1981- v. <1 > : ill. ; 24 cm. Vol. 1: "January 21, 1981." Item 1035-A-1, 1035-A-2 (microfiche) CONTENTS. - v. 1. The Threat of inflation -- LC Card 81-600968 DDC 338.973 19
1. United States - Economic conditions - 1971-. 2. United States - Economic policy - 1971-. 3. Inflation (Finance) - United States. I. Title. II. Title: Threat of inflation.
KF26 .B8 1981

Reconciliation (S. 2885) and special rules for its consideration together with the reports to the Budget Committee of the instructed committees / Committee on the Budget, United States Senate. Washington : U. S. Govt. Print. Off., 1980. vii, 390 p. ; 24 cm. "September 15, 1980." At head of title: 96th Congress, 2d session. Committee print. LC Card 80-603544 DDC 343.73/034 19
1. Budget - United States. 2. United States. Congress. Senate - Rules and practice. I. Title.
KF6221.A55 C666

Second concurrent resolution on the budget--fiscal year, 1981 : hearings before the Committee on the Budget, United States Senate, Ninety-sixth Congress, second session, July 22 and 24, 1980, economic background ; July 23, 1980, CBO re-estimates, President's mid-year budget review. Washington : U. S. Govt. Print. Off., 1980. iv, 412 p. : graphs ; 24 cm. Includes index. LC Card 80-603471 DDC 353.0072/2 19
1. Budget - United States. I. Title.
KF26 .B8 1980b

United States. Congress. Senate. Committee on Energy and Natural Resources. Submittal of the Senate Committee on Energy and Natural Resources to the Senate Budget Committee pursuant to Section 301(c) of the Congressional Budget Act /. Washingon , 1977. vii, 45 p. ; LC Card 81-601121 DDC 328.73/07652 19
JK1240.E53 U54 1977

United States. Congressional Budget Office. Entering the 1980s . [Washington, D.C.] [1980] xxi, 101 p. : LC Card 80-602038 DDC 336.73 19
HJ257.2 .U57 1980

United States. Congress. Senate. Committee on the Budget. Special Subcommittee on

Control of Federal Credit. Control of Federal credit : hearings before the Special Subcommittee on Control of Federal Credit of the Committee on the Budget, United States Senate, Ninety-sixth Congress, second session, June 19, 23, and July 1, 1980. Washington : U. S. Govt. Print. Off., 1980. iv, 223 p. ; 24 cm. Bibliography: p. 87. Includes index. LC Card 80-603316 DDC 353.0082/5 19
1. Government lending - United States. 2. Insurance, Government - United States. 3. Loans - United States - Government guaranty. 4. Credit - United States.
KF26 .B83 1980

United States. Congress. Senate. Committee on the Judiciary. (Old Catalog form: United States. Judiciary, Committee on the (Senate)) // Hearings printed in 1978 and later are available only in // Hearings printed in 1978 and later are available only in microform. Please consult the librarians in the Economic and Public Affairs Division.
Caribbean refugee crisis, Cubans and Haitians : hearing before the Committee on the Judiciary, United States Senate, Ninety-sixth Congress, second session, May 12, 1980. Washington : U. S. Govt. Print. Off., 1980. iii, 288 p. ; 24 cm. "Serial no. 96-58." LC Card 80-602964 DDC 325/.21/09729 19
1. Refugees, Political - United States. 2. Refugees, Political - Cuba. 3. Refugees, Political - Haiti. I. Title.
KF26 .J8 1980c

Citizens' Right to Standing in Federal Courts Act, S. 680 : hearing before the Committee on the Judiciary, United States Senate, Ninety-sixth Congress, second session, on S. 680, October 12, 1979. Washington : U. S. G.P.O., 1981. iii, 232 p. ; 24 cm. "Serial no. 96-91." Item 1042 Includes bibliographical references. LC Card 81-601639 DDC 347.73/5 347.3075 19
1. Locus standi - United States. 2. Government litigation - United States. 3. Citizen suits (Civil procedure) - United States. I. Title.
KF26 .J8 1979v

Confirmation hearing on Edward C. Schmults, nominee, to be deputy attorney general : hearing before the Committee on the Judiciary, United States Senate, Ninety-seventh Congress, first session, on the nomination of Edward C. Schmults to be deputy attorney general, February 5, 1981. Washington : U. S. G.P.O., 1981. iii, 62 p. ; 24 cm. "Serial no. J-97-2." Item 1042-A, 1042-B (microfiche) LC Card 81-601773 DDC 353.5 19
1. Schmults, Edward C., 1931-. 2. United States. Dept. of Justice -Officials and employees. I. Title.
KF26 .J8 1981a

Confirmation hearing on William French Smith, nominee, to be attorney general : hearing before the Committee on the Judiciary, United States Senate, Ninety-seventh Congress, first session, on the nomination of William French Smith to be attorney general, January 15, 1981. Washington : U. S. G.P.O., 1981. iv, 179 p. ; 24 cm. "Serial no. J-97-1." LC Card 81-601872 DDC 353.5 19
1. Smith, William French, 1917-. 2. United States. Dept. of Justice -Officials and employees. I. Title.
KF26 .J8 1981

Confirmation hearings on Benjamin R. Civiletti, nominee, Attorney General : hearings before the Committee on the Judiciary, United States Senate, Ninety-sixth Congress, first session ... July 25, 26, and 27, 1979. Washington : U. S. Govt. Print. Off., 1980. iv, 213 p. ; 24 cm. "Serial no. 96-45." LC Card 80-601952 DDC 353.5 19
1. Civiletti, Benjamin R. 2. United States. Dept. of Justice -Officials and employees. I. Title.
KF26 .J8 1979q

Constitutional amendment to balance the federal budget : hearings before the Committee on the Judiciary, United States Senate, Ninety-sixth Congress, second session, on S.J. Res. 126, January 14 and February 22, 1980. Washington : U. S. G.P.O., 1980. iii, 130 p. ; 24 cm. "Serial no. 96-67." Includes bibliographical references. LC Card 80-603988 DDC 343.73/034 347.30334 19
1. Budget - United States. 2. United States - Constitutional law - Amendments. I. Title.
KF26 .J8 1980d

Department of Justice authorization and oversight, 1981 : hearings before the Committee

BIBLIOGRAPHIC GUIDE

United States. Congress. Senate. Committee on the Judiciary.

496

on the Judiciary, United States Senate, Ninety-sixth Congress, second session ... March 11, 12, 13, 17, 19, 20, 27, April 2, 3, 16, 23, 28, 30, and May 1, 1980. Washington : U. S. G.P.O., 1980. vi, 1293 p. : ill. ; 24 cm. "Serial no. 96-63." Includes bibliographical references.   LC Card 81-600649   DDC 353.5 19
1. United States. Dept. of Justice - Appropriations and expenditures. I. Title.
KF26 .J8 1980e

FBI charter act of 1979, S. 1612 : hearings before the Committee on the Judiciary, United States Senate, Ninety-sixth Congress, first session, on S. 1612 .... Washington : U. S. Govt. Print., 1980- v. : ill. ; 24 cm. Vol. 1: "Serial no. 96-53." Hearings held Aug. 2- 1979. Includes bibliographical references.   LC Card 80-603508   DDC 344.73/0525 19
1. United States. Federal Bureau of Investigation. I. Title.
KF26 .J8 1979t

Federal charter for Italian American War Veterans : hearing before the Committee on the Judiciary, United States Senate, Ninety-sixth Congress, second session, on S. 2542, November 20, 1980. Washington : U. S.G.P.O., 1981. iii, 83 p. ; 24 cm. "Serial no. 96-87." Item 1042   LC Card 81-600939   DDC 343.73/011 347.30311 19
1. Italian American War Veterans of the United States, Incorporated. I. Title.
KF26 .J8 1980g

Federal restraints on competition in the trucking industry : antitrust immunity and economic regulation : report of the Committee on the Judiciary, United States Senate, Ninety-sixth Congress, second session. Washington : U. S. Govt. Print. Off., 1980. xxxvii, 351 p. : ill. ; 24 cm. At head of title: 96th Congress, 2d session. Committee print. "April 1980." Includes bibliographical references.   LC Card 80-603054   DDC 343.73/09483 19
1. Transportation, Automotive - Law and legislation - United States. 2. Transportation, Automotive - United States - Rates. I. Title.
KF2265 .A25 1980.

Jurisdictional amendments act of 1979, S. 679 : hearings before the Committee on the Judiciary, United States Senate, Ninety-sixth Congress, first session ... March 21, June 4, and 5, 1979. Washington : U. S. Govt. Print. Off., 1980. iv, 313 p. : graph ; 23 cm. "Serial no. 96-51."   LC Card 80-602159   DDC 347.73/12 19
1. Jurisdiction - United States. I. Title.
KF26 .J8 1979r

Masanz, Sharon D. History of the Immigration and Naturalizaton Service . Washington , 1980 [i.e. 1981] vii, 91 p. :   LC Card 81-600999   DDC 353.0081/7 19
JV6483 .M3

Moore, Charlotte J. Review of U. S. refugee resettlement programs and policies . Washington , 1980. viii, 342 p. :   LC Card 80-603884   DDC 362.8/7/0973 19
HV640.4.U54 M66

Oversight of Department of Justice Public Integrity Section : hearing before the Committee on the Judiciary, United States Senate, Ninety-sixth Congress, second session, on oversight of DOJ's Public Integrity Section, June 11, 1980. Washington : U. S. G.P.O., 1980. iii, 12 p. ; 24 cm. "Serial no. 96-76." Item 1042   LC Card 81-600613   DDC 353.5 19
1. United States. Dept. of Justice. Public Integrity Section. I. Title.
KF26 .J8 1980h

Privacy protection act : hearing be[f]ore the Committee on the Judiciary, United States Senate, Ninety-sixth Congress, second session, on S. 115, S. 1790 , and S. 1816, March 28, 1980. Washington : U. S. Govt. Print. Off., 1980. iv, 233 p. ; 24 cm. "Serial no. 96-59." Includes bibliographical references.   LC Card 80-602900   DDC 342.73/0853 19
1. Searches and seizures - United States. 2. Confidential communications - Press - United States. 3. Confidential communications - Third parties - United States. 4. Privacy, Right of - United States. I. Title.
KF26 .J8 1980b

Reauthorization of the Juvenile Justice and Delinquency Prevention Act of 1974 : hearings before the Committee on the Judiciary, United

States Senate, Ninety-sixth Congress, second session, on S. 2434, S. 2441, and S. 2442, Ninety-sixth Congress, second session, on S. 2434, S. 2441, and S. 2442, March 27 and 28, 1980. Washington : U. S. G.P.O., 1981. viii, 555 p. : ill. ; 24 cm. "Serial no. 96-84. Item 1042 Includes bibliographical references.   LC Card 81-602037   DDC 344.73/03274 347.3043274 19
1. Juvenile justice, Administration of - United States. 2. Rehabilitation of juvenile delinquents - United States. I. Title.
KF26 .J8 1980i

Refugee consultation : hearing before the Committee on the Judiciary, United States Senate, Ninety-sixth Congress, first session ... October 16, 1979. Washington : U. S. G.P.O., 1980. iii, 22 p. ; 23 cm. "Serial no. 96-40." LC Card 80-603491   DDC 342.73/082 347.30282 19
1. Refugees - Legal status, laws, etc. - United States. 2. Emigration and immigration law - United States. I. Title.
KF26 .J8 1979u

U. S. refugee programs : hearing before the Committee on the Judiciary, United States Senate, Ninety-sixth Congress, second session, April 17, 1980. Washington : U. S. Govt. Print. Off., 1980. iii, 412 p. (p. 412 blank) : ill. ; 24 cm. "Serial no. 96-55."   LC Card 80-602735   DDC 362.8/7/0973 19
1. Refugees - United States. 2. United States - Emigration and immigration. 3. Economic assistance, American. I. Title.
KF26 .J8 1980a

United States. Congress. Senate. Committee on Labor and Human Resources. Subcommittee on Health and Scientific Research. Health effects of hazardous waste disposal practices, 1980 . Washington , 1980. iv, 110 p. ;   LC Card 80-603890   DDC 363.1/79 19
KF26 .L274 1980j

United States. Congress. Senate. Committee on Labor and Human Resources. Subcommittee on Health and Scientific Research. Radiation exposure compensation act of 1979 . Washington , 1980. iv, 132 p. :   LC Card 80-603432   DDC 346.7303/8 347.30638 19
KF26 .L274 1980d

United States. Select Commission on Immigration and Refugee Policy. Semiannual report to Congress /. Washington , 1980. v, 74 p. ;   LC Card 80-603270   DDC 353.0081/7 19
JV6481 1980 .S44

United States. Congress. Senate. Committee on the Judiciary. Constitution, Subcommittee on the. see United States. Congress. Senate. Committee on the Judiciary. Subcommittee on the Constitution.

United States. Congress. Senate. Committee on the Judiciary. Subcommittee on Antitrust, Monopoly, and Business Rights.
Cancer insurance and the elderly : joint hearing before the Subcommittee on Antitrust, Monopoly, and Business Rights of the Committee on the Judiciary, United States Senate and Select Committee on Aging, House of Representatives, Ninety-sixth Congress, second session ... March 20, 1980. Washington : U. S. Govt. Print. Off., 1980. vi, 524 p. : ill. ; 24 cm. "Serial no. 96-61."   LC Card 80-603736   DDC 368.3/82 19
1. Insurance, Cancer - United States. 2. Insurance, Health - United States. 3. Aged - Medical care - United States. I. United States. Congress. House. Select Committee on Aging. II. Title.
KF26 .J835 1980b

Concentration in the book-publishing and bookselling industry : hearing before the Subcommittee on Antitrust, Monopoly, and Business Rights of the Committee on the Judiciary, United States Senate, Ninety-sixth Congress, second session, on monopolization of the publishing industry, March 13, 1980. Washington : U. S. Govt. Print. Off., 1980. iii, 98 p. : ill. ; 24 cm. "Serial no. 96-56." Includes bibliographical references.   LC Card 80-603301   DDC 338.8/2610705/0973 19
1. Book industries and trade - United States. 2. Industrial concentration - United States. I. Title.
KF26 .J835 1980a

Credit life insurance : hearing before the Subcommittee on Antitrust, Monopoly, and Business Rights of the Committee on the

Judiciary, United States Senate, Ninety-sixth Congress, first session ... November 14, 1979. Washington : U. S. Govt. Print. Off., 1980. iii, 169 p. : ill. ; 24 cm. "Serial no. 96-44."   LC Card 80-602469   DDC 368.8/7/00973 19
1. Insurance, Credit - United States. I. Title.
KF26 .J835 1979m

DOE's role in the solar energy industry, and possible anticompetitive trends : hearing before the Subcommittee on Antitrust, Monopoly, and Business Rights of the Committee on the Judiciary, United States Senate, Ninety-sixth Congress, second session, on DOE and the solar energy industry, November 14, 1980. Washington : U. S. G.P.O., 1981. iii, 105 p. : ill. ; 1981. "Serial no. 96-95." Item 1042 Includes bibliographical references. LC Card 81-601624   DDC 338.4/76147/0973 19
1. Solar energy industries - Government policy - United States. 2. United States. Dept. of Energy. 3. Monopolies - United States. I. Title.
KF26 .J835 1980f

Gasohol competition act of 1979, S. 2251 : hearing before the Subcommittee on Antitrust, Monopoly, and Business Rights of the Committee on the Judiciary and the Select Committee on Small Business, United States Senate, Ninety-sixth Congress, second session, on S. 2251, March 5, 1980. Washington : U. S. Govt. Print. Off., 1980. iii, 201 p. : ill. ; 24 cm. "Serial no. 96-58." Bibliography: p. 183-188. LC Card 80-603339   DDC 343.73/078662669 19
1. Alcohol as fuel - Law and legislation - United States. 2. Petroleum law and legislation - United States. I. United States. Congress. Senate. Select Committee on Small Business. II. Title.
KF26 .J835 1980

Insurance Competition Improvement Act, S. 2474 : hearing before the Subcommittee on Antitrust, Monopoly, and Business Rights of the Committee on the Judiciary, United States Senate, Ninety-sixth Congress, second session, on S. 2474, May 29, 1980. Washington : U. S. G.P.O., c1981. iii, 344 p. : ill. ; 24 cm. "Serial no. 96-92." Item 1042 Bibliography: p. 280.   LC Card 81-601632   DDC 346.73/086 347.3086 19
1. Insurance law - United States. 2. Antitrust law - United States. I. Title.
KF26 .J835 1980g

International Energy Agreement, S. 1413 : hearings before the Subcommittee on Antitrust, Monopoly, and Business Rights of the Committee on the Judiciary, United States Senate, Ninety-sixth Congress, first session, on S. 1413, October 3 and 5, 1979. Washington : U. S. G.P.O., 1980 [i.e. 1981] iii, 175 p. ; 24 cm. "Serial no. 96-71." Item 1042 Includes bibliographical references.   LC Card 81-600938   DDC 341.7/5472282/0973 19
1. Petroleum law and legislation - United States. 2. Antitrust law - United States. 3. International Energy Agency. I. Title.
KF26 .J835 1979o

Nondiscrimination in Insurance Act, S. 2477 : hearing before the Subcommittee on Antitrust, Monopoly, and Business Rights, of the Committee on the Judiciary, United States Senate, Ninety-sixth Congress, second session, on S. 2477, April 30, 1980. Washington : U. S. G.P.O., 1980 [i.e. 1981] iii, 416 p. : ill. ; 24 cm. "Serial no. 96-80." Item 1042 Includes bibliographical references.   LC Card 81-601316   DDC 346.73/086 347.30686 19
1. Discrimination in insurance - Law and legislation - United States. I. Title.
KF26 .J835 1980e

Small Business Motor Fuel Marketer Preservation Act of 1980 : hearings before the Subcommittee on Antitrust, Monopoly and Business Rights of the Committee on the Judiciary, United States Senate, Ninety-sixth Congress, second session, on S. 2828 and S. 2798, September 9 and 25, 1980. Washington : U. S. G.P.O., 1981. v, 491 p. : ill. ; 24 cm. "Serial no. 96-93." Item 1042 Includes bibliographical references.   LC Card 81-601869   DDC 343.73/088566553827 347.30388566553827 19
1. Automobiles - Service stations - Law and legislation - United States. 2. Petroleum law and legislation - United States. 3. Loans - United States - Government guaranty. I. Title.
KF26 .J835 1980d

Unfair Foreign Competition Act of 1979, S.

GOVERNMENT PUBLICATIONS - U.S.: 1981

497

United States. Congress. Senate. Committee on the Judiciary.

938 : hearing before the Subcommittee on Antitrust, Monopoly, and Business Rights of the Committee on the Judiciary, United States Senate, Ninety-sixth Congress, first session, on S. 938, December 6, 1979. Washington : U. S. G.P.O., 1980. iii, 42 p. ; 24 cm. "Serial no. 96-74." LC Card 80-604014   DDC 343.73/072 347.30372 19
1. Foreign trade regulation - United States. 2. Antidumping duties - United States. 3. Competition, Unfair - United States. I. Title.
KF26 .J835 1979n

Why gasoline prices remain high : hearing before the Subcommittee on Antitrust, Monopoly, and Business Rights of the Committee on the Judiciary, United States Senate, Ninety-sixth Congress, second session, on gasoline prices, June 18, 1980. Washington : U. S. G.P.O., 1980 [i.e. 1981] iii, 52 p. ; 24 cm. "Serial no. 96-76" incorrect in publication. Item 1042 LC Card 81-600930   DDC 338.4/366553827/0973 19
1. Gasoline - Prices - United States. 2. Gasoline supply - United States. 3. Petroleum industry and trade - United States. I. Title.
KF26 .J835 1980c

United States. Congress. Senate. Committee on the Judiciary. Subcommittee on Criminal Justice.
Arson for profit : hearing before the Subcommittee on Criminal Justice of the Committee on the Judiciary, United States Senate, Ninety-sixth Congress, second session, September 10, 1980. Washington : U. S. G.P.O., 1981. iii, 141 p. ; 23 cm. "Serial no. 96-86" incorrect in publication. Item 1042 LC Card 81-601327   DDC 364.1/64 19
1. Arson - United States. 2. Insurance, Fire - United States - Adjustment of claims. 3. Insurance, Fire - Law and legislation - United States. I. Title.
KF26 .J8377 1980g

Automobile Theft Prevention Act of 1979, S. 1214 : hearing before the Subcommittee on Criminal Justice, Committee on the Judiciary, Ninety-sixth Congress, second session on S. 1214, April 14, 1980. Washington : U. S. G.P.O., 1980 [i.e. 1981] iii, 70 p. : ill. ; 24 cm. "Serial no. 96-76" incorrect in publication. Item 1042 LC Card 81-601177   DDC 345.73/0262 347.305262 19
1. Automobile theft - United States. 2. Crime prevention - United States. I. Title.
KF26 .J8377 1980e

Drug control program of the Federal Government : hearings before the Subcommittee on Criminal Justice of the Committee on the Judiciary, United States Senate, Ninety-sixth Congress, first session ... September 11, 13, and 19, 1979. Washington : U. S. Govt. Print. Off., 1980. iv, 157 p. : ill. ; 23 cm. "Serial no. 96-50." LC Card 80-602793   DDC 363.4/5/0973 19
1. Narcotics, Control of - United States. I. Title.
KF26 .J8377 1979

Drug paraphernalia and youth : hearing before the Subcommittee on Criminal Justice of the Committee on the Judiciary, United States Senate, Ninety-sixth Congress, second session ... November 16, 1979. Washington : U. S. G.P.O., 1980. iii, 349 p. : ill. ; 24 cm. "Serial no. 96-68." Includes bibliographical references.   LC Card 80-603781   DDC 362.2/93/088055 19
1. Drug paraphernalia - United States. 2. Drug abuse - United States. 3. Youth - United States - Drug use. I. Title.
KF26 .J8377 1979a

Forfeiture of narcotics proceeds : hearings before the Subcommittee on Criminal Justice of the Committee on the Judiciary, United States Senate, Ninety-sixth Congress, second session, on forfeiture of profits of narcotics traffickers, July 23 and 24, 1980. Washington : U. S. G.P.O., 1981. iii, 165 p. ; 24 cm. "Serial no. 96-81." Item 1042 LC Card 81-600972   DDC 363.4/5 19
1. Narcotics, Control of - United States. 2. Forfeiture - United States. I. Title.
KF26 .J8377 1980h

Graymail, S. 1482 : hearing before the Subcommittee on Criminal Justice of the Committee on the Judiciary, United States Senate, Ninety-sixth Congress, second session, on S. 1482, February 7, 1980. Washington : U.

S. Govt. Print. Off., 1980. iii, 189 p. ; 24 cm. "Serial no. 96-57." LC Card 80-603342   DDC 345.73/064 19
1. Evidence, Documentary - United States. 2. Security classification (Government documents) - United States. 3. Government litigation - United States. I. Title.
KF26 .J8377 1980d

Parental kidnaping prevention act of 1979, S. 105 : joint hearing before the Subcommittee on Criminal Justice of the Committee on the Judiciary and the Subcommittee on Child and Human Development of the Committee on Labor and Human Resources, United States Senate, Ninety-sixth Congress, second session, on S. 105, January 30, 1980. Washington : U. S. Govt. Print. Off., 1980. iv, 156 p. ; 24 cm. "Serial no. 96-54."   LC Card 80-602799   DDC 345.73/0254 19
1. Kidnapping, Parental - United States. I. United States. Congress. Senate. Committee on Labor and Human Resources. Subcommittee on Child and Human Development. II. Title.
KF26 .J8377 1980c

Parental kidnaping prevention act of 1979, S.105 : addendum to joint hearing before the Subcommittee on Criminal Justice of the Committee on the Judiciary and the Subcommittee on Child and Human Development of the Committee on Labor and Human Resources, United States Senate, Ninety-sixth Congress, second session, on S.105, January 30, 1980. Washington : U. S. Govt. Print. Off., 1980. iii, 378 p. : ill. ; 24 cm. "Serial no. 96-54."   LC Card 80-602982   DDC 345.73/0254 19
1. Kidnapping, Parental - United States. I. United States. Congress. Senate. Committee on Labor and Human Resources. Subcommittee on Child and Human Development. II. Title.
KF26 .J8377 1980b

Pretrial service agencies : hearing before the Subcommittee on Criminal Justice of the Committee on the Judiciary, United States Senate, Ninety-sixth Congress, second session, on S. 2705, May 13, 1980. Washington : U. S. G.P.O., c1981. iii, 112 p. : ill. ; 24 cm. "Serial no. 96-72." Item 1042 Includes bibliographical references.   LC Card 81-600953   DDC 347.73/72 347.30772 19
1. Pre-trial service agencies - United States. 2. Pre-trial release - United States. I. Title.
KF26 .J8377 1980i

United States. Congress. Senate. Committee on the Judiciary. Subcommittee on Criminal Laws and Procedures. The erosion of law enforcement intelligence and its impact on the public security : report of the Subcommittee on Criminal Laws and Procedures to the Committee on the Judiciary, United States Senate, Ninety-fifth Congress, second session. Washington : U. S. Govt. Print. Off. : for sale by the Supt. of Docs., U. S. Govt. Print. Off., 1978. iii, 179 p. ; 24 cm. At head of title: 95th Congress, 2d session. Committee print. "Information contained in this report is the product of investigative and oversight hearings ... conducted initially under the auspices of the Senate Internal Security Subcommittee and subsequent to July of 1977, by the Subcommittee on Criminal Laws and Procedures."   LC Card 79-600797   DDC 363.2/52 19
1. Law enforcement - United States. 2. Intelligence service - United States. 3. Privacy, Right of - United States. I. United States. Congress. Senate. Committee on the Judiciary. Subcommittee to Investigate the Administration of the Internal Security Act and Other Internal Security Laws. II. Title.
HV8141 .U52 1978

United States. Congress. Senate. Committee on the Judiciary. Subcommittee on Improvements in Judicial Machinery.
Bankruptcy fraud oversight : hearings before the Subcommittee on Improvements in Judicial Machinery of the Committee on the Judiciary, United States Senate, Ninety-sixth Congress, first and second sessions ... October 17, 18, 1979, and February 1, 1980. Washington : U. S. Govt. Print. Off., 1980. iv, 187 p. : ill. ; 24 cm. "Serial no. 96-52." LC Card 80-602801   DDC 353.0082 19
1. Fraudulent conveyances - United States. I. Title.
KF26 .J855 1980

Federal diversity of citizenship jurisdiction : hearings before the Subcommittee on

Improvements in Judicial Machinery of the Committee on the Judiciary, United States Senate, Ninety-fifth Congress, second session, on S. 2094, S. 2389, and H.R. 9622 ... March 17 and 20, and April 25, 1978. Washington : U. S. G.P.O., 1978. vi, 428 p. ; 23 cm. LC Card 81-601817   DDC 347.73/202 347.30712 19
1. Jurisdiction - United States. I. Title.
KF26 .J855 1978g

Federal venue statutes : hearing before the Subcommittee on Improvements in Judicial Machinery of the Committee on the Judiciary, United States Senate, Ninety-sixth Congress, second session, on S. 739 and S. 1472, February 20, 1980. Washington : U. S. G.P.O., 1981. iv, 176 p. ; 24 cm. "Serial no. 96-78" incorrect in publication. Item 1042 Includes bibliographical references.   LC Card 81-600928   DDC 347.73/12 347.30712 19
1. Venue - United States. I. Title.
KF26 .J855 1980d

Judicial Conference and Councils in the Sunshine act, S. 2045 : hearing before the Subcommittee on Improvements in Judicial Machinery of the Committee on the Judiciary, United States Senate, Ninety-sixth Congress, second session ... March 7, 1980. Washington : U. S. Govt. Print. Off., 1980. iv, 191 p. ; 24 cm. "Serial no. 96-60." Includes bibliographical references.   LC Card 80-603410   DDC 353.0081/9 19
1. Judicial Conference of the United States. 2. Judicial councils - United States - Public meetings. I. Title.
KF26 .J855 1980a

Preference section of the Bankruptcy Code, S. 3023 : hearing before the Subcommittee on Judicial Machinery of the Committee on the Judiciary, United States Senate, Ninety-sixth Congress, second session, on S. 3023, August 18, 1980. Washington : U. S. G.P.O., 1981. iii, 34 p. ; 24 cm. "Serial no. 96-89." Item 1042 LC Card 81-601155   DDC 346.73/078/0262 347.306780262 19
1. Bankruptcy - United States. 2. Negotiable instruments - United States. I. Title.
KF26 .J855 1980e

Spanish in the courtrooms of Puerto Rico, H.R. 5563 : hearing before the Subcommittee on Improvements in Judicial Machinery of the Committee on the Judiciary, United States Senate, Ninety-sixth Congress, second session, on H.R. 5563, May 19, 1980. Washington : U. S. G.P.O., 1980. iii, 86 p. ; 24 cm. "Serial no. 96-64." LC Card 80-603690   DDC 347.73/222 347.30722 19
1. United States. District Court (Puerto Rico). 2. Conduct of court proceedings - Puerto Rico. 3. Spanish language - Political aspects. I. Title.
KF26 .J855 1980b

To amend The Copyright Act, S. 2082 : hearings before the Subcommittee on Improvements in Judicial Machinery of the Committee on the Judiciary, United States Senate, Ninety-sixth Congress, second session, on S. 2082, August 20 and November 19, 1980. Washington : U. S. G.P.O., 1981. iv, 152 p. : ill. ; 23 cm. "Serial no. 96-90." Item 1042 Includes bibliographical references.   LC Card 81-601346   DDC 346.7304/82 347.306482 19
1. Copyright - Royalties - United States. 2. Copyright - Music - United States. 3. Corporations, Nonprofit - United States. I. Title.
KF26 .J855 1980c

United States. Congress. Senate. Committee on the Judiciary. Subcommittee on Jurisprudence and Governmental Relations.
Judicial impact statements : hearing before the Subcommittee on Jurisprudence and Governmental Relations of the Committee on the Judiciary, United States Senate, Ninety-sixth Congress, first session, on judicial impact statements, November 14, 1979. Washington : U. S. Govt. Print. Off., 1980. iii, 41 p. ; 24 cm. "Serial no. 96-48." LC Card 80-602157   DDC 347.73/2 19
1. Judicial impact statements - United States. I. Title.
KF26 .J8556 1979a

Judicial impact statements : hearings before the Subcommittee on Jurisprudence and Governmental Relations of the Committee on the Judiciary, United States Senate, Ninety-sixth Congress, second session, on judicial impact statements, September 24 and December 2, 1980. Washington : U. S. G.P.O.,

BIBLIOGRAPHIC GUIDE

United States. Congress. Senate. Committee on the Judiciary.

498

1980 [i.e. 1981] iii, 72 p. : ill. ; 24 cm. "Serial no. 96-73." Item 1042 LC Card 81-601322 DDC
   347.73/1 347.3071 19
1. Judicial impact statements - United States. I. Title.
KF26 .J8556 1980a

Role of the federal government in state and local law enforcement : hearings before the Subcommittee on Jurisprudence and Governmental Relations of the Committee on the Judiciary, United States Senate, Ninety-six Congress, second session, on role of the federal government in state and local law enforcement in criminal justice, December 3 and 22, 1980. Washington : U. S. G.P.O., 1981. iv, 388 p. : ill. ; 24 cm. "Serial no. 96-88." Item 1042 Bibliography: p. 243-245. LC Card 81-601785 DDC
   364/.973 19
1. Federal aid to law enforcemnt agencies - United States. 2. Law enforcement - United States. 3. Criminal justice, Administration of - United States. I. Title.
KF26 .J8556 1980b

State Justice Institute act of 1979 : hearings before the Subcommittee on Jurisprudence and Governmental Relations of the Committee on the Judiciary, United States Senate, Ninety-sixth Congress, first and second sessions on S. 2387, October 18, November 19, 1979, and March 19, 1980. Washington : U. S. Govt. Print. Off., 1980. iv, 229 p. ; 24 cm. "Serial no. 96-49." Includes bibliographical references. LC Card
   80-602173 DDC 347.73 19
1. State Justice Institute (U. S.). 2. Court administration - United States - States. 3. Justice, Administration - United States - States. I. Title.
KF26 .J8556 1979

State of judiciary address, S. 2483 : hearing before the Subcommittee on Jurisprudence and Governmental Relations of the Committee on the Judiciary, United States, Nineth-sixth Congress, second session, on a bill which would request the chief justice to address on a periodic basis a joint session of Congress on the state of the judiciary, June 23, 1980. Washington : U. S. G.P.O., 1980. iii, 35 p. ; 24 cm. "Serial no. 96-78." Includes bibliographical references. LC Card 81-600615 DDC 347.73/00262
   347.30700262 19
1. Courts - United States. I. Title.
KF26 .J8556 1980

United States. Congress. Senate. Committee on the Judiciary. Subcommittee on Limitations of Contracted and Delegated Authority.
Federal preemption of state energy policies : hearings before the Subcommittee on Limitations of Contracted and Delegated Authority of the Committee on the Judiciary, United States Senate, Ninety-sixth Congress, second session, on the federal preemption of state energy policies, October 14 and 20, 1980. Washington : U. S. G.P.O., 1980 [i.e. 1981] iii, 194 p. : ill. ; 24 cm. "Serial no. 96-82." Item 1042 Includes bibliographical references. LC Card
   81-601358 DDC 333.79/0973 19
1. Energy policy - United States - States. 2. Energy policy - United States. 3. Federal government - United States. I. Title.
KF26 .J857 1980a

Federal use of contractors and consultants : hearings before the Subcommittee on Limitations of Contracted and Delegated Authority of the Committee on the Judiciary, United States Senate, Ninety-sixth Congress, second session, on federal use of contractors and consultants, September 25 and October 7, 1980. Washington : U. S. G.P.O., 1981. iv, 342 p. ; 24 cm. "Serial no. 96-95" incorrect in publication. Item 1042 LC Card 81-601757 DDC 353/.0722 19
1. Abuse of administrative power - United States. 2. Government consultants - United States. 3. Public contracts - United States. I. Title.
KF26 .J857 1980

Oversight of the General Services Administration : hearings before the Subcommittee on Limitations of Contracted and Delegated Authority of the Committee on the Judiciary, United States Senate, Ninety-sixth Congress, first session ... September 26 and 27, 1979. Washington : U. S. G.P.O., 1980. iii, 89 p. : ill. ; 24 cm. "Serial no. 96-70." LC Card
   80-604043 DDC 353.0071 19
1. United States. General Services Administration. I. Title.
KF26 .J857 1979a

United States. Congress. Senate. Committee on the Judiciary. Subcommittee on Limitations on Contracted and Delegated Authority. Title III of the Higher education act of 1965 : hearings before the Subcommittee on Limitations of Contracted and Delegated Authority of the Committee on the Judiciary, United States Senate, Ninety-sixth Congress, first session, ... November 14 and December 12, 1979. Washington : U. S. Govt. Print. Off., 1980. iv, 345 p. : forms ; 23 cm. "Serial no. 96-38." LC Card 80-602424 DDC 353.0085/1 19
1. Universities and colleges - Law and legislation - United States. 2. Federal aid to higher education - United States. I. Title.
KF26 .J857 1979

United States. Congress. Senate. Committee on the Judiciary. Subcommittee on the Constitution.
Citizen's guide to individual rights under the Constitution of the United States of America / prepared by the Subcommittee on the Constitution of the Committee on the Judiciary, United States Senate, Ninety-sixth Congress, second session. 6th ed. Washington : U. S. Govt. Print. Off. : for sale by the Supt. of Docs., U. S. Govt. Print. Off., 1980. v, 47 p. ; 24 cm. At head of title: 96th Congress, 2d session. Committee print. "July 1980." LC Card 80-603263
   DDC 342.73/085 19
1. Civil rights - United States. I. Title.
KF4743.5 .J8 1980

Constitutional convention procedures : hearing before the Subcommittee on the Constitution of the Committee on the Judiciary, United States Senate, Ninety-sixth Congress, first session, on S. 3, S. 520 and S. 1710 ... November 29, 1979. Washington : U. S. G.P.O., 1980. vi, 1372 p. ; 24 cm. "Serial no. 96-77." Includes bibliographies. LC Card 80-604085 DDC 342.73/032/0262
   347.302320262 19
1. Constitutional conventions - United States. 2. United States - Constitutional law - Amendments. I. Title.
KF26 .J8359 1979f

Gun control and constitutional rights : hearing before the Subcommittee on the Constitution of the Committee on the Judiciary, United States Senate, Ninety-sixth Congress, second session, on constitutional oversight of a regulatory agency--the Bureau of Alcohol, Tobacco and Firearms, Department of the Treasury--on the enforcement of the Gun Control Act of 1969, September 15, 1980. Washington : U. S. G.P.O., 1981. v, 735 p. : ill. ; 24 cm. "Serial no. 96-83." Item 1042 Bibliography: p. 720-735. LC Card 81-601620 DDC 353.0075 19
1. Firearms - Law and legislation - United States. I. Title.
KF26 .J8359 1980b

Homeless youth : the saga of "pushouts" and "throwaways" in America : report of the Subcommittee on the Constitution of the Committee on the Judiciary, United States Senate, Ninety-sixth Congress, second session. Washington : U. S.G.P.O. : For sale by the Supt. of Docs., U. S.G.P.O., 1980. vii, 256 p. : ill. ; 24 cm. At head of title: 96th Congress, 2d session. Committee print. "December 1980." S/N 052-070-05481-6 Item 1042 Bibliography: p. 89-97.
   LC Card 81-600668 DDC 362.7/4 19
1. Runaway youth - United States. 2. Homelessness - United States. 3. Children - Services for - United States. 4. Juvenile delinquency - United States - Prevention. I. Title.
HV881 .U54 1980

An Investigation by children of the inappropriate incarceration of children . Washington , 1980. x, 190 p. : LC Card
   80-603875 DDC 365/.42/0973 19
HV9104 .I56

The National Guard tort claims act : hearing before the Subcommittee on the Constitution of the Committee on the Judiciary, United States Senate, Ninety-sixth Congress, second session, on S. 1858 ... April 3, 1980. Washington : U. S. Govt. Print. Off., 1980. v, 780 p. ; 24 cm. "Serial no. 96-66." Includes bibliographical references.
   LC Card 80-603086 DDC 343.73/013 19
1. Government liability - United States. 2. United States. National Guard. 3. Medical personnel - Malpractice - United States. I. Title.
KF26 .J8359 1980

U. S. Commission on Civil Rights fiscal year

1981 authorization : hearing before the Committee on the Judiciary, United States Senate, Ninety-sixth Congress, second session, on S. 2511 ... April 3, 1980. Washington : U. S. Govt. Print. Off., 1980. iii, 69 p. ; 24 cm. "Serial no. 96-62." LC Card 80-603460 DDC
   353.0072/236811 19
1. United States. Commission on Civil Rights - Appropriations and expenditures. I. Title.
KF26 .J835 1980a

United States. Congress. Senate. Committee on the Judiciary. Subcommittee to Investigate the Administration of the Internal Security Act and Other Internal Security Laws.
The Puerto Rican Revolutionary Workers Organization : a staff study / prepared by the Subcommittee to Investigate the Administration of the Internal Security Act and Other Internal Security Laws of the Committee on the Judiciary, United States Senate, Ninety-fourth Congress, second session. Washington : U. S. G.P.O., 1976. v, 47, viii p. ; 24 cm. "March 1976." Includes bibliographical references and index.
   LC Card 76-601803 DDC 322.4/2/0973 19
1. Terrorism - United States. 2. Subversive activities - United States. 3. Organización Obrera Revolucionaria Puertorriqueña. I. Title.
HV6432 .U54 1976

United States. Congress. Senate. Committee on the Judiciary. Subcommittee on Criminal Laws and Procedures. The erosion of law enforcement intelligence and its impact on the public security . Washington , 1978. iii, 179 p. ;
   LC Card 79-600797 DDC 363.2/52 19
HV8141 .U52 1978

United States. Congress. Senate. Committee on the Judiciary, United States Senate, Ninety-sixth Congress, second session, September 19, 1980. U. S. refugee programs, 1981 : hearing before the Committee on the Judiciary, United States Senate, Ninety-sixth Congress, second session, September 19, 1980. Washington : U. S. G.P.O., 1980. iii, 288 p. : ill. ; 24 cm. "Serial no. 96-79." Includes bibliographical references. LC Card 80-604094 DDC 362.8/7/0973 19
1. Refugees - United States. 2. United States - Emigration and immigration. 3. Economic assistance, American. 4. Refugees. I. Title.
KF26 .J8 1980f

United States. Congress. Senate. Committee on Veterans' Affairs. (Old Catalog form: United States. Veterans' Affairs, Committee on (Senate)) // Hearings printed in 1978 and later are available only in microform. Please consult the librarians in the Economic and Public Affairs Division.
Disabled Veterans Rehabilitation Act of 1980 : hearing before the Committee on Veterans' Affairs, United States Senate, Ninety-sixth Congress, second session, on S. 1188 and amdt. no. 1661, February 28, 1980. Washington : U. S. G.P.O., 1980. iv, 827 p. ; 24 cm. Includes bibliographical references. LC Card 81-600875 DDC 343.73/0116 347.303116 19
1. Veterans, Disabled - Rehabilitation - Law and legislation - United States. I. Title.
KF26 .V4 1980c

Educational incentives and the all-volunteer force : hearing before the Committee on Veterans' Affairs, United States Senate, Ninety-sixth Congress, second session, on S. 2020, S. 2596 and related bills. Washington : U. S.G.P.O., 1980. iv, 195 p. : ill. ; 24 cm. Includes bibliographical references. Item 1046-A LC Card 81-600866 DDC 343.73/011 347.30311 19
1. Military service, Voluntary - United States. 2. United States - Armed Forces - Recruiting, enlistment, etc. 3. Veterans - Education - United States. I. Title.
KF26 .V4 1980f

Fy 80 legislative recommendations of veterans' organizations : hearings before the Committee on Veterans' Affairs, United State Senate, Ninety-sixth Congress, first and second sessions .... Washington : U. S. Govt. Print. Off., 1980. iv, 387 p. : ill. ; 24 cm. Hearings held Sept. 25, 1979-March 27, 1980. Includes index. LC
   Card 80-603467 DDC 343.73/011 19
1. Veterans - Legal status, laws, etc. - United States. I. Title.
KF26 .V4 1980

Louis Harris and Associates. Myths and realities . Washington , 1980. xlviii, 481 p. :

GOVERNMENT PUBLICATIONS - U.S.: 1981

499

United States. Congress. Senate. Select Committee on Indian

LC Card 80-603127   DDC 355.1/15/0973 19
UB357 .L58 1980

Medal of Honor recipients, 1863-1978 : "In the name of the Congress of the United States" / prepared by the Committee on Veterans' Affairs, United States Senate. Washington : U. S. Govt. Print. Off., 1979. xix, 1113 p. : ill. ; 24 cm. At head of title: 96th Congress, 1st session. Senate committee print no. 3.   LC Card 80-603561   DDC 355.1/34 19
1. Medal of Honor. 2. United States - Armed Forces - Biography. I. Title.
UB433 .U55 1979

Minneapolis VA medical center construction proposal : hearing before the Committee on Veterans' Affairs, United States Senate, Ninety-sixth Congress, second session, April 8, 1980. Washington : U. S. G.P.O., 1980. iii, 459 p. : ill. ; 24 cm. Includes bibliographical references.   LC Card 81-600637   DDC 355.1/156/09776579 19
1. Veterans' Administration Medical Center at Minneapolis. I. Title.
KF26 .V4 1980e

Oversight of VA pacemaker policy : hearing before the Committee on Veterans' Affairs, United States Senate, Ninety-sixth Congress, second session, Wednesday, April 23, 1980. Washington : U. S. G.P.O., 1980. iii, 190 p. : ill. ; 24 cm. Includes bibliographical references. LC Card 80-604040   DDC 355.1/156/0973 19
1. Pacemaker, Artificial (Heart). 2. Veterans - Medical care - United States. 3. United States. Veterans Administration. I. Title.
KF26 .V4 1980b

Oversight on activities of the VA's Inspector General : hearing before the Committee on Veterans' Affairs, United States Senate, Ninety-sixth Congress, second session, June 11, 1980. Washington : U. S. G.P.O., 1980. iii, 212 p. ; 24 cm. Includes bibliographical references. LC Card 81-600655   DDC 353.0081/2 19
1. United States. Veterans Administration. Inspector General. I. Title.
KF26 .V4 1980d

United States. Congress. House. Committee on Veterans' Affairs. Oversight on admission policies to VA medical care facilities . Washington, D.C. , 1980. vi, 373 p. :   LC Card 80-601953   DDC 353.0081/2 19
KF27 .V4 1979f

United States. Veterans Administration. Overseas beneficiaries . Washington, 1980. xviii, 403 p. ;   LC Card 80-602866   DDC 355.1/151/0973 19
UB373 .U54 1980

VA debt collection : hearing before the Committee on Veterans' Affairs, United States Senate, Ninety-sixth Congress, first session, on S. 1518, Thursday, August 2, 1979. Washington : U. S. Govt. Print. Off., 1979. iv, 252 p. : ill. ; 24 cm.   LC Card 80-601119   DDC 346.73/077 19
1. Collection laws - United States. 2. Collection agencies - Law and legislation - United States. 3. Veterans - Legal status, laws, etc. - United States. 4. United States. Veterans Administration. I. Title.
KF26 .V4 1979i

VA Health-Care Personnel Act of 1980 : hearing before the Committee on Veterans' Affairs, United States Senate, Ninety-sixth Congress, second session, on S. 2534 and related bills, April 16, 1980. Washington : U. S. G.P.O., 1980. v, 895 p. : ill. ; 24 cm. Item 1046-A Includes bibliographical references.   LC Card 81-601756   DDC 343.73/0115/0262 347.3031150262 19
1. United States. Veterans Administration. Dept. of Medicine and Surgery - Officials and employees. 2. Medical personnel - Salaries, pensions, etc. - Law and legislation - United States. 3. Medical personnel - United States - Supply and demand. I. Title.
KF26 .V4 1980g

Veteran senior citizen health care act of 1979 : hearing before the Committee on Veterans' Affairs, United States Senate, Ninety-sixth Congress, first session, on S. 1523 and H.R 4015, Monday, October 29, 1979. Washington : U. S. Govt. Print. Off., 1980. iv, 348 p. : ill. ; 24 cm.   LC Card 80-602454   DDC 343.73/0115/0262 19
1. Veterans - Legal status, laws, etc. - United States. 2.

Aged - Legal status, laws, etc. - United States. 3. Veterans - Medical care - United States. 4. Aged - Medical care - United States. I. Title.
KF26 .V4 1979n

Veterans' Administration health-care programs : hearing before the Committee on Veterans' Affairs, United States Senate, Ninety-sixth Congress, first session, November 10, 1979, Orlando, Fla. Washington : U. S. Govt. Print. Off., 1980. iii, 220 p. : maps ; 24 cm.   LC Card 80-602487   DDC 355.1/154/09759 19
1. Veterans - Medical care - Florida. 2. United States. Veterans Administration. I. Title.
KF26 .V4 1979m

Veterans' disability compensation and survivors' benefits amendments of 1980 : hearings before the Committee on Veterans' Affairs, United States Senate, Ninety-sixth Congress, second session, on S. 2649, Amdt. no. 1888, S. 1212, S. 2330, S. 2755, S. 2758, and S. 2806, June 17, 1980. Washington : U. S. G.P.O., 1980, [i.e. 1981] iv, 601 p. : ill. ; 24 cm. Item 1046-A Includes bibliographical references.   LC Card 81-601405   DDC 343.73/0116 347.303116 19
1. Veterans, Disabled - Legal status, laws, etc. - United States. 2. Survivors' benefits - United States. I. Title.
KF26 .V4 1981h

Vietnam veterans' readjustment : hearings before the Committee on Veterans' Affairs, United States Senate, Ninety-sixth Congress, second session ... Washington : U. S. G.P.O., 1980. 2 v. (iv, 2082 p.) : ill., maps ; 24 cm. Hearings held in various cities, Jan. 25-May 21, 1980. Includes bibliographies.   LC Card 81-600647   DDC 355.1/15/0973 19
1. Veterans - United States. 2. Vietnamese Conflict, 1961-1975 - United States. I. Title.
KF26 .V4 1980a

United States. Congress. Senate. Energy and Natural Resources, Committee on. see United States. Congress. Senate. Committee on Energy and Natural Resources.

United States. Congress. Senate. Environment and Land Resources Subcommittee. see United States. Congress. Senate. Committee on Interior and Insular Affairs. Environment and Land Resources Subcommittee.

United States. Congress. Senate. Environment and Public Works, Committee on. see United States. Congress. Senate. Committee on Environment and Public Works.

United States. Congress. Senate. Governmental Affairs, Committee on. see United States. Congress. Senate. Committee on Governmental Affairs.

United States. Congress. Senate. Indian Affairs, Select Committee on. see United States. Congress. Senate. Select Committee on Indian Affairs.

United States. Congress. Senate. Intelligence, Select Committee on. see United States. Congress. Senate. Select Committee on Intelligence.

United States. Congress. Senate. National Ocean Policy Study. Energy from ocean kelp farms /. Washington , 1980. ix, 82 p. :   LC Card 80-603976   DDC 333.95/3 19
TP360 .E54

United States. Congress. Senate. Panel on Environmental Science and Technology. see United States. Congress. Senate. Committee on Public Works. Panel on Environmental Science and Technology.

United States. Congress. Senate. Permanent Subcommittee on Investigations. see United States. Congress. Senate. Committee on Government Operations. Permanent Subcommittee on Investigations; United States. Congress. Senate. Committee on Governmental Affairs. Permanent Subcommittee on Investigations.

UNITED STATES. CONGRESS. SENATE - RULES AND PRACTICE.
United States. Congress. Senate. Standing rules for conducting business in the United States Senate /. Washington , 1979. iv, 77 p. ;   LC Card 80-602241   DDC 328.73/05 19
KF4982 .S74

United States. Congress. Senate. Standing rules of the Senate (pursuant to the adoption of S.

Res. 274 and S. Res. 389, 96th Cong., Nov. 14, 1979, and Mar. 25, 1980, respectively). Washington , 1980. iv, 69 p. ;   LC Card 80-603245   DDC 328.73/05 19
KF4982 .S75

United States. Congress. Senate. Committee on the Budget. Reconciliation (S. 2885) and special rules for its consideration together with the reports to the Budget Committee of the instructed committees /. Washington , 1980. vii, 390 p. ;   LC Card 80-603544   DDC 343.73/034 19
KF6221.A55 C666

United States. Congress. Senate. Select Committee on Indian Affairs.
Conveyance of Federal land to the Ute Mountain Ute Tribe : hearing before the Select Committee on Indian Affairs, United States Senate, Ninety-sixth Congress, second session, on S. 2066 ... February 26, 1980. Washington, D.C. : U. S. Govt. Print. Off., 1980. iii, 51 p. : ill., maps ; 24 cm.   LC Card 80-602176   DDC 346.7304/3/08997 19
1. Ute Indians - Land transfers. 2. United States - Public lands. 3. Colorado - Public lands. 4. Indians of North America - Land transfers. I. Title.
KF26.5 .I4 1980b

Development of native American culture and art : hearing before the Select Committee on Indian Affairs, United States Senate, Ninety-sixth Congress, second session, on S. 2166 ... April 14, 1980, Santa Fe, N. Mex. Washington : U. S. Govt. Print. Off., 1980. iv, 108 p. ; 24 cm.   LC Card 80-602903   DDC 344.73/097/08997 19
1. Indians of North America - Arts - Law and legislation. 2. Indians of North America - Legal status, laws, etc. 3. Indians of North America - Education - Law and legislation. I. Title.
KF26.5 .I4 1980h

Disposition of the Gila River Pima-Maricopa Indian Community judgment funds : hearing before the Select Committee on Indian Affairs, United States Senate, Ninety-sixth Congress, second session, on S. 2508 ... April 30, 1980, Washington, D.C. Washington : U. S. Govt. Print. Off., 1980. iii, 14 p. ; 24 cm.   LC Card 80-603103   DDC 342.73/0872 347.302872 19
1. Gila River Indian Community - Claims. 2. Indians of North America - Arizona - Claims. I. Title.
KF26.5 .I4 1980j

Establishment of a Siletz Indian reservation : hearing before the Select Committee on Indian Affairs, United States Senate, Ninety-sixth Congress, first session, on S. 2055 ... January 30, 1980. Washington : U. S. Govt. Print. Off., 1980. iii, 183 p. : map ; 24 cm. Includes bibliographical references.   LC Card 80-601313   DDC 346.7304/32/08997 19
1. Siletz Indians - Legal status, laws, etc. 2. Indians of North America - Legal status, laws, etc. 3. Siletz Indians - Reservations. I. Title.
KF26.5 .I4 1980

Federal acknowledgment process : hearing before the Select Committee on Indian Affairs, United States Senate, Ninety-sixth Congress, second session, on oversight of the federal acknowledgment process and the federal acknowledgment project of the Bureau of Indian Affairs, June 2, 1980, Washington, D.C. Washington : U. S. G.P.O., 1980 [i.e. 1981] iii, 102 p. : ill. ; 24 cm. Item 1009 Includes bibliographical references.   LC Card 81-600843   DDC 353.0081/497 19
1. Indians of North America - Legal status, laws, etc. 2. Indians of North America - Government relations. I. Title.
KF26.5 .I4 1980t

Federal Indian housing programs : hearing before the Select Committee on Indian Affairs, United States Senate, Ninety-sixth Congress, second session, on federal Indian housing programs, August 19, 1980, Washington, D.C. Washington : U. S. G.P.O., 1980 [i.e. 1981] iii, 124 p. : ill. ; 24 cm. Item 1009   LC Card 81-600977   DDC 363.5/9 19
1. Indians of North America - Housing. I. Title.
KF26.5 .I4 1980s

Implementation of the Indian Judgment Funds Distribution Act : hearing before the Select Committee on Indian Affairs, United States Senate, Ninety-sixth Congress, second session, on oversight of the implementation of the Indian Judgment Funds Distribution Act, June

BIBLIOGRAPHIC GUIDE

United States. Congress. Senate. Select Committee on Indian

500

4, 1980, Washington, D.C. Washington : U. S. G.P.O., 1980. iii, 45. ; 28 cm. Item 1009 Includes bibliographical references. LC Card 81-600812 DDC 353.009/1 19

1. Indians of North America - Claims. I. Title.
KF26.5 .I4 1980u

Implementation of the Tribally controlled community colleges assistance act : hearing before the Select Committee on Indian Affairs, United States Senate, Ninety-sixth Congress, second session, on P.L. 95-471 ... June 10, 1980, Washington, D.C. Washington : U. S. Govt. Print. Off., 1980. iii, 70 p. ; ill. ; 23 cm.
LC Card 80-603520 DDC 379.1/214/0973 19

1. Indians of North America - Education. 2. Community colleges - United States. 3. Federal aid to higher education - United States. I. Title.
KF26.5 .I4 1980m

Indian education oversight : hearing before the Select Committee on Indian Affairs, United States Senate, Ninety-sixth Congress, second session, on oversight of Indian education (Public Laws 95-561--95-608), July 24, 1980, Washington, D.C. Washington : U. S. G.P.O., 1980 [i.e. 1981] iv, 373 p. ; ill. ; 24 cm. Item 1009 LC Card 81-601325 DDC 353.0085/1/08897 19

1. Indians of North America - Education. I. Title.
KF26.5 .I4 1980v

Inheritance of trust or restricted land on the Standing Rock Sioux Reservation : hearing before the Select Committee on Indian Affairs, United States Senate, Ninety-sixth Congress, second session, on H.R. 2102 ... April 17, 1980, Washington, D.C. Washington : U. S. Govt. Print. Off., 1980. iii, 14 p. ; 24 cm. Includes bibliographical references. LC Card 80-603114 DDC 346.7305/2/08997 19

1. Dakota Indians - Inheritance and succession. 2. Dakota Indians - Land transfers. 3. Standing Rock Indian Reservation, S.D. and N.D. 4. Indians of North America - Inheritance and succession. I. Title.
KF26.5 .I4 1980l

Investigation of Indian Health Service expenditures, Billings area : a report / prepared by the Select Committee on Indian Affairs of the United States Senate, during the Ninety-sixth Congress, second session, 1980. Washington : U. S. G.P.O., 1980. iv, 59 p. ; 24 cm. At head of title: 96th Congress, 2d session. Committee print. Item 1009 LC Card 81-600672 DDC 353.009/92 19

1. United States. Indian Health Service. Billings Area - Appropriations and expenditures. I. Title.
RA448.5.I5 U525 1980

Jurisdiction on Indian reservations : hearings before the Select Committee on Indian Affairs, United States Senate, Ninety-sixth Congress, second session, on S. 1181 ... S. 1722 ... and S. 2832 ... March 17, 18, and 19, 1980. Washington : U. S. Govt. Print. Off., 1980. iv, 467 p. ; 24 cm. Includes bibliographical references. LC Card 80-602898 DDC 349.73/08997 19

1: Indians of North America - Legal status, laws, etc. 2. Indians of North America - Government relations. 3. Indians of North America - Tribal government. 4. United States magistrates. I. Title.
KF26.5 .I4 1980f

Leases involving the Secretary of the Interior and the Northern Cheyenne Indian Reservation : hearing before the Select Committee on Indian Affairs, United States Senate, Ninety-sixth Congress, second session, on S. 2126 ... March 28, 1980, Billings, Mont. Washington : U. S. Govt. Print. Off., 1980. iii, 46 p. ; 24 cm. LC Card 80-602714 DDC 346.7304/6822 19

1. Coal leases - Montana. 2. United States. Dept. of the Interior. 3. Cheyenne Indians - Legal status, laws, etc. 4. Indians of North America - Legal status, laws, etc. I. Title.
KF26.5 .I4 1980i

Nomination of Thomas W. Fredericks to Assistant Secretary of the Interior : hearing before the Select Committee on Indian Affairs, United States Senate, Ninety-sixth Congress, second session ... July 1, 1980, Washington, D.C. Washington : U. S. Govt. Print. Off., 1980. iii, 126 p. ; 24 cm. LC Card 80-603457 DDC 353.3 19

1. Fredericks, Thomas W. 2. United States. Dept. of the Interior - Officials and employees. I. Title.
KF26.5 .I4 1980n

Oil and gas leases on Indian lands : hearing before the Select Committee on Indian Affairs, United States Senate, Ninety-seventh Congress, first session, on federal supervision of oil and gas leases on Indian lands ... Washington : U. S. G.P.O., 1981- v. <1 > : ill. ; 24 cm. Item 1009-B, 1009-C (microfiche) CONTENTS. - Pt. 1: "February 27, 1981, Billings, Montana." LC Card 81-601766 DDC 346.7304/6823 347.30646823 19

1. Indians of North America - Land tenure. 2. Oil and gas leases - United States. I. Title.
KF26.5 .I4 1981

Oversight of Indian health services in the Pacific Northwest and Alaska : hearing before the Select Committee on Indian Affairs, United States Senate, Ninety-sixth Congress, second session, on the Indian Health Care Improvement Act (Public Law 94-437), September 20, 1980, Portland, Oreg. Washington : U. S. G.P.O., c1980 [i.e. 1981] iv, 124 p. ; ill. ; 23 cm. Item 1009 Includes bibliographical references. LC Card 81-601184 DDC 353.0081/497/09795 19

1. Indians of North America - Northwest, Pacific - Medical care. 2. Indians of North America - Alaska - Medical care. I. Title.
KF26.5 .I4 1980r

Oversight of the Indian Child Welfare Act : hearing before the Select Committee on Indian Affairs, United States Senate, Ninety-sixth Congress, second session, on oversight of the Indian Child Welfare Act (Public Law 95-608), June 30, 1980, Washington, D.C. Washington : U. S. G.P.O., 1980. iii, 148 p. ; ill. ; 24 cm. LC Card 80-604076 DDC 353.0084/7/08997 19

1. Indians of North America - Child welfare. 2. Indians of North America - Children - Legal status, laws, etc. I. Title.
KF26.5 .I4 1980q

Per capita payments to Indians by tribal governments : hearing before the Select Committee on Indian Affairs, United States Senate, Ninety-sixth Congress, second session, on S. 2767 ... June 4, 1980, Washington, D.C. Washington : U. S. Govt. Print. Off., 1980. iii, 8 p. ; 24 cm. LC Card 80-603107 DDC 342.73/0872 347.302872 19

1. Indians of North America - Legal status, laws, etc. 2. Indians of North America - Tribal government. 3. Indians of North America - Financial affairs. I. Title.
KF26.5 .I4 1980k

Proposed settlement of Maine Indian land claims : hearings before the Select Committee on Indian Affairs, United States Senate, Ninety-sixth Congress, second session, on S. 2829 ... July 1 and 2, 1980, Washington, D.C. Washington : U. S. G.P.O., 1980 [i.e. 1981- v <1 > (iv, <421 > p.) : ill. ; 24 cm. Item 1009 Includes bibliographical references. LC Card 81-601172 DDC 346.74104/32/08897 347.410643208897 19

1. Indians of North America - Maine - Claims. 2. Indians of North America - Maine - Land tenure. I. Title.
KF26.5 .I4 1980w

Settlement of San Luis Rey River water claims : hearing before the Select Committee on Indian Affairs, United States Senate, Ninety-sixth Congress, second session, on S. 1507 ... March 6, 1980, Washington, D.C. Washington : U. S. Govt. Print. Off., 1980. iii, 56 p. ; 24 cm. LC Card 80-602905 DDC 346.7304/691 19

1. Indians of North American - California - Water rights. 2. Indians of North America - California - Claims. 3. San Luis Rey River, Calif. - Water-rights. I. Title.
KF26.5 .I4 1980g

Trade between Indians and Federal employees : hearing before the Select Committee on Indian Affairs, United States Senate, Ninety-sixth Congress, second session, on H.R. 3979 ... January 21, 1980, Washington, D.C. Washington : U. S. Govt. Print. Off., 1980. iii, 21 p. ; 24 cm. LC Card 80-601960 DDC 343.73/088/08997 19

1. Indians of North America - Legal status, laws, etc. 2. Indian agents - Legal status, laws, etc. - United States. 3. Indians of North America - Commerce. 4. Indians of North America - Government relations. I. Title.
KF26.5 .I4 1980e

Transfer of Indian lands to heirs or lineal

descendants : hearing before the Select Committee on Indian Affairs, United States Senate, Ninety-sixth Congress, second session, on S. 2223 ... February 28, 1980, Washington, D.C. Washington : U. S. Govt. Print. Off., 1980. iii, 17 p. ; 24 cm. LC Card 80-602489 DDC 346.7304/32/08997 19

1. Indians of North America - Land transfers. 2. Indians of North American - Wills. I. Title.
KF26.5 .I4 1980c

UNITED STATES. CONGRESS. SENATE. SELECT COMMITTEE ON INDIAN AFFAIRS.

United States. Congress. Senate. Committee on Rules and Administration. To makethe Select Committee on Indian Affairs a permanent committee of the Senate . Washington , 1980. v, 70 p. ; LC Card 80-603072 DDC 328.73/07652 19

KF26 .R8 1980a

United States. Congress. Senate. Select Committee on Intelligence.

Intelligence identities protection legislation : hearings before the Select Committee on Intelligence of the United States Senate, Ninety-sixth Congress, second session on S. 2216, et al. ... June 24, 25, 1980. Washington : U. S. G.P.O. : For sale by the Supt. of Docs., U. S. G.P.O., 1980. iii, 118 p. ; 24 cm. S/N 052-070-05487-5 Includes bibliographical references. LC Card 81-600614 DDC 344.73/0176132712 347.304176132712 19

1. Intelligence officers - Legal status, laws, etc. - United States. 2. Intelligence service - United States. 3. Official secrets - United States. I. Title.
KF26.5 .I5 1980a

National Intelligence Act of 1980 : hearings before the Select Committee on Intelligence of the United States Senate, Ninety-sixth Congress, second session, on S. 2284 ... February 21, 28, March 24, 25, 27, 31, April 1, 2, and 16, 1980. Washington : U. S. G.P.O., 1980. vi, 658 p. ; ill. ; 24 cm. Includes bibliographical references. LC Card 81-600623 DDC 344.73/052 347.30452 19

1. Intelligence service - United States. I. Title.
KF26.5 .I5 1980

Nomination of Admiral B.R. Inman : hearing before the Select Committee on Intelligence of the United States Senate, Ninety-seventh Congress, first session, on nomination of Admiral B.R. Inman to be deputy director of Central Intelligence, February 3, 1981. Washington : U. S. G.P.O., 1981. iii, 36 p. ; 24 cm. Item 1009-B, 1009-C (microfiche) LC Card 81-601774 DDC 327.1/2/06073 19

1. Inman, Bobby Ray, 1931-. 2. United States. Central Intelligence Agency - Officials and employees. I. Title.
KF26.5 .I5 1981

Nomination of William J. Casey : hearing before the Select Committee on Intelligence, of the United States Senate, Ninety-seventh Congress, first session, on nomination of William J. Casey, to be director of Central Intelligence, Tuesday, January 13, 1981. Washington : U. S. G.P.O., 1981. iv, 51 p. ; 24 cm. Item 1009-B, 1009-C (microfiche) LC Card 81-601604 DDC 327.1/2/06073 19

1. Casey, William J. 2. United States. Central Intelligence Agency - Officials and employees. I. Title.
KF26.5 .I5 1981a

UNITED STATES. CONGRESS. SENATE. SELECT COMMITTEE ON NARCOTICS ABUSE AND CONTROL.

United States. Congress. Senate. Committee on Rules and Administration. To create a Select Committee on Narcotics Abuse and Control . Washington , 1980. iv, 224 p. : LC Card 80-602455 DDC 353.0076/5 19

KF26 .R8 1980

United States. Congress. Senate. Select Committee on Small Business. (Old Catalog form: United States. Small Business, Committee on (Senate))

Agricultural research policy : report of the Select Committee on Small Business, United States Senate. Washington : U. S. Govt. Print. Off., 1980. iii, 32 p. ; 24 cm. At head of title: 96th Congress, 2d session. Committee print. "April 16, 1980." Includes bibliographical references. LC Card 80-603264 DDC 630/.72073 19

1. Agricultural research - Government policy - United States. 2. United States. Dept. of Agriculture. 3.

GOVERNMENT PUBLICATIONS - U.S.: 1981

501   *United States. Congress. Senate. Select Committee on Small*

Agricultural extension work - Government policy - United States. 4. Farms, Small - Government policy - United States. I. Title.
S541 .U652 1980

Blewer, Cecilia. Economic growth .
Washington , 1980. v, 56 p. ;   LC Card
    80-603061   DDC 338.973 19
HC106.7 .B59

Business economic outlook : hearings before the Select Committee on Small Business, United States Senate, Ninety-sixth Congress, first session ... October 23 and November 6, 1979. Washington : U. S. Govt. Print. Off., 1980. iii, 145 p. : graphs ; 24 cm. Includes bibliographical references.   LC Card 80-602443   DDC
    338.5/443/0973 19
1. Economic forecasting - United States. 2. United States - Economic conditions - 1971-. 3. United States - Economic policy - 1971-. 4. Small business - United States. I. Title.
KF26.5 .S6 1979w

Crime and its impact on small business : hearing before the Select Committee on Small Business, United States Senate, Ninety-sixth Congress, second session ... May 29, 1980. Washington : U. S. Govt. Print. Off., 1980. iii, 115 p. ; 24 cm. Includes bibliographical references.
    LC Card 80-603285   DDC 338.6/42/0973 19
1. Crime and criminals - United States. 2. Retail trade - United States - Security measures. 3. Small business - United States - Security measures. I. Title.
KF26.5 .S6 1980k

Customer pickup proposals and their impact on small business and the Robinson-Patman act : hearing before the Select Committee on Small Business, United States Senate, Ninety-sixth Congress, second session ... April 3, 1980. Washington : U. S. Govt. Print. Off., 1980. iii, 266 p. : ill. ; 24 cm. Includes bibliographical references.   LC Card 80-602985   DDC 338.5/2 19
1. Delivered pricing. 2. Price discrimination - United States. 3. Food prices - Law and legislation - United States. 4. Small business - Law and legislation - United States. I. Title.
KF26.5 .S6 1980d

Economic growth : hearings before the Select Committee on Small Business, United States Senate, Ninety-sixth Congress, second session .... Washington : U. S. Govt. Print. Off., 1980- v. : graphs ; 23 cm. Hearings held June 18
    LC Card 80-603331   DDC 338.973 19
1. Small business - United States. 2. Small business - United States - Taxation. 3. Industry and state - United States. 4. Industrial productivity - United States. I. Title.
KF26.5 .S6 1980j

Economic impact of acid rain : hearing before the Select Committee on Small Business and the Committee on Environment and Public Works, United States Senate, Ninety-sixth Congress, second session, on economic impact of acid rain, September 23, 1980. Washington : U. S. G.P.O., 1980. iii, 224 p. : ill. ; 24 cm. Includes bibliographical references.   LC Card 81-600642   DDC 330.973/0926 19
1. Acid rain - United States. 2. Acid rain - Economic aspects - United States. I. United States. Congress. Senate. Committee on Environment and Public Works. II. Title.
KF26.5 .S6 1980u

Effects of paperwork elimination and management : hearing before the Select Committee on Small Business, United States Senate, Ninety-sixth Congress, second session ... Green Bay, Wis., February 13, 1980. Washington : U. S. Govt. Print. Off., 1980. iii, 60 p. ; 24 cm.   LC Card 80-603443   DDC 353.0071/4 19
1. Government paperwork - United States. I. Title.
KF26.5 .S6 1980q

H.R. 5612, to amend the Small Business Act to extend the current SBA 8(a) pilot program : hearing before the Select Committee on Small Business, United States Senate, Ninety-sixth Congress, second session, on H.R. 5612, to amend the Small Business Act to extend the current SBA 8(a) pilot program, August 4, 1980. Washington : U. S. G.P.O., 1980. iii, 211 p. : ill. ; 24 cm. Includes bibliographical references.
    LC Card 80-604024   DDC 346.73/0652 347.306652 19
1. Small business - Law and legislation - United States. 2. Federal aid to minority business enterprises - United

States. 3. Public contracts - United States. I. Title. II. Title: To amend the Small Business Act to extend the current SBA 8(a) pilot program.
KF26.5 .S6 1980u

Impact of funding EPA sewer treatment construction program on small business contractors : hearing before the Select Committee on Small Business and the Subcommittee on Environmental Pollution of the Committee on Environment and Public Works, United States Senate, Ninety-sixth Congress, second session ... Milwaukee, Wis., July 9, 1980. Washington : U. S. Govt. Print. Off., 1980. iii, 180 p. : ill. ; 24 cm.   LC Card 80-603692   DDC 338.4/36283/0977595 19
1. Federal aid to water quality management - Wisconsin - Milwaukee metropolitan area. 2. Sewage disposal plants - Wisconsin - Milwaukee metropolitan area - Costs. 3. Sewage disposal plants - Wisconsin - Milwaukee metropolitan area - Finance. I. United States. Congress. Senate. Committee on Environment and Public Works. Subcommittee on Environmental Pollution. II. Title.
KF26.5 .S6 1980p

Impact of non-tariff barriers on the ability of small business to export to Japan : hearing before the Select Committee on Small Business, United States Senate, Ninety-sixth Congress, second session ... June 25, 1980. Washington : U. S. Govt. Print. Off., 1980. iii, 424 p. : ill. ; 24 cm.   LC Card 80-603719   DDC 382/.64 19
1. Nontariff trade barriers - Japan. 2. Small business - United States. 3. United States - Commerce - Japan. 4. Japan - Commerce - United States. I. Title.
KF26.5 .S6 1980r

The investment of pension funds in farmland : hearing before the Select Committee on Small Business, United States Senate, Ninety-sixth Congress, second session ... October 8, 1980. Washington : U. S. Govt. Print. Off., 1980. iii, 350 p. : ill. ; 23 cm. Includes bibliographical references.   LC Card 80-603904   DDC 332.63/242 19
1. Pension trusts - United States - Investments. 2. Family farms - United States. I. Title.
KF26.5 .S6 1980o

Nomination of Michael Cardenas to be administrator of the Small Business Administration : hearing before the Select Committee on Small Business, United States Senate, Ninety-seventh Congress, first session, on nomination of Michael Cardenas to be administrator of the Small Business Administration, March 23, 1981. Washington : U. S. G.P.O., 1981. iii, 64 p. ; 24 cm. Item 1049-J, 1049-K (microfiche)   LC Card 81-602263   DDC 353.0082/048 19
1. Cardenas, Michael. 2. United States. Small Business Administration - Officials and employees. I. Title.
KF26.5 .S6 1981c

Report by the White House Commission on Small Business : hearing before the Select Committee on Small Business, United States Senate, Ninety-sixth Congress, second session ... May 15, 1980. Washington : U. S. Govt. Print. Off., 1980. iii, 44 p. ; 24 cm.   LC Card 80-603047   DDC 338.6/42/0973 19
1. Small business - United States. I. White House Commission on Small Business (U. S.).
KF26.5 .S6 1980i

The role of small business in the nation's economic recovery : hearing before the Select Committee on Small Business, United States Senate, Ninety-seventh Congress, first session, on the role of small business in the nation's economic recovery, March 9, 1981. Washington : U. S. G.P.O., 1981. iii, 207 p. : ill. ; 24 cm. Item 1049-J, 1049-K (microfiche) Includes bibliographical references.   LC Card 81-601882   DDC 338.6/42/0973 19
1. Small business - United States. 2. Small business - Government policy - United States. I. Title.
KF26.5 .S6 1981a

S. 1860, Small Business Innovation Act of 1979 : hearings before the Select Committee on Small Business, United States Senate, Ninety-sixth Congress, second session, on S. 1860 ... March 18, April 2, 15, and 16, 1980. Washington : U. S. G.P.O., 1980 [i.e. 1981] iv, 611 p. : ill. ; 24 cm. Item 1049 Includes bibliographical references.   LC Card 81-601186   DDC 346.73/0652 347.306652 19
1. Small business - Law and legislation - United States. 2. Technological innovations - Law and legislation -

United States. I. Title. II. Title: Small Business Innovation Act of 1979.
KF26.5 .S6 1980x

S. 2040, the Small business export expansion act, S. 2104, the Small business export development act : hearings before the Select Committee on Small Business, United States Senate, Ninety-sixth Congress, second session ... March 12 and 13, 1980. Washington : U. S. Govt. Print. Off., 1980. iii, 178 p. ; 24 cm.   LC Card 80-602190   DDC 343.73/0878 19
1. Small business - Law and legislation - United States. 2. Foreign trade promotion - United States.
KF26.5 .S6 1980c

S. 2224, small business energy loan program : hearing before the Select Committee on Small Business, United States Senate, Ninety-sixth Congress, second session ... March 4, 1980. Washington : U. S. Govt. Print. Off., 1980. iii, 148 p. : ill. ; 24 cm.   LC Card 80-602162   DDC 346.7304/679158/0262 19
1. Energy development - Law and legislation - United States. 2. Small business - Law and legislation - United States. 3. Energy development - United States - Finance. I. Title. II. Title: Small business energy loan program.
KF26.5 .S6 1980a

S. 2635, the Small business energy conservation act : hearing before the Select Committee on Small Business, United States Senate, Ninety-sixth Congress, second session ... May 2, 1980. Washington : U. S. Govt. Print. Off., 1980. iii, 30 p. ; 24 cm.   LC Card 80-603682   DDC 346.7304/67916/02632 347.30646791602632 19
1. Small business - Law and legislation - United States. 2. Energy conservation - Law and legislation - United States. 3. Small business - United States - Finance. I. Title.
KF26.5 .S6 1980l

SBA' paperwork measurement and reduction program : hearing before the Select Committee on Small Business, United State Senate, Ninety-sixth Congress, second session ... January 4, 1980. Washington : U. S. Govt. Print. Off., 1980. iii, 153 p. : ill. ; 24 cm.   LC Card 80-603688   DDC 353.0082/048 19
1. United States. Small Business Administration - Records and correspondence. 2. Government paperwork - United States. I. Title.
KF26.5 .S6 1980n

SBA surety bond guarantee program : hearings before the Select Committee on Small Business, United States Senate, Ninety-sixth Congress, second session, on SBA surety bond guarantee program, June 30 and September 25, 1980. Washington : U. S. G.P.O., 1980 [i.e. 1981] iv, 320 p. : ill. ; 23 cm. Item 1049   LC Card 81-601160   DDC 353.0082/048045 19
1. Insurance, Surety and fidelity - United States. 2. Small business - United States. 3. United States. Small Business Administration. I. Title.
KF26.5 .S6 1980w

Small Business Administration 8(a) pilot program : hearing before the Select Committee on Small Business, United States Senate, Ninety-seventh Congress, first session, on Small Business Administration 8(a) pilot program, January 23, 1981. Washington : U. S. G.P.O., 1981. iii, 84 p. ; 24 cm. Item 1049-J, 1049-K (microfiche) Includes bibliographical references.   LC Card 81-601381   DDC 353.0071/2 19
1. United States. Small Business Administration. 2. Minority business enterprises - United States. 3. Government purchasing - United States. I. Title.
KF26.5 .S6 1981b

Small Business Administration's veterans' assistance programs : hearing before the Select Committee on Small Business, United States Senate, Ninety-sixth Congress, second session ... June 4, 1980. Washington : U. S. Govt. Print. Off., 1980. iii, 97 p. ; 24 cm.   LC Card 80-603678   DDC 355.1/15 19
1. Veterans - Loans - United States. 2. United States. Small Business Administration. I. Title.
KF26.5 .S6 1980m

Small business and Department of Energy research and development programs : hearing before the Select Committee on Small Business, United States Senate, Ninety-sixth Congress, second session ... April 30, 1980. Washington : U. S. Govt. Print. Off., 1980. iii, 77 p. : ill. ; 24 cm.   LC Card 80-602727   DDC 353.0082/048045 19

BIBLIOGRAPHIC GUIDE

United States. Congress. Senate. Select Committee on Small

502

1. Research and development contracts, Government - United States. 2. Small business - United States. 3. United States. Dept. of Energy - Procurement. I. Title.
KF26.5 .S6 1980e

Small business automobile dealers : their status and the impact of foreign auto imports on them : hearings before the Select Committee on Small Business, United States Senate, Ninety-sixth Congress, second session ... April 3 and 21, 1980. Washington : U. S. Govt. Print. Off., 1980. iii, 294 p. : ill. ; 23 cm. Includes bibliographical references.   LC Card 80-602971   DDC 381/.456292/0973 19
1. Automobile industry and trade - United States. 2. Small business - United States. 3. Automobiles, Foreign. I. Title.
KF26.5 .S6 1980f

To consider and report to the Senate Budget Committee recommendations for Small Business Administration programs : hearing before the Select Committee on Small Business, United States Senate, Ninety-seventh Congress, first session, on to consider and report to the Senate Budget Committee recomendations for Small Business Administration programs, March 13, 1981. Washington : U. S. G.P.O, 1981. iii, 53 p. ; 24 cm. Item 1049-J, 1049-K (microfiche)   LC Card 81-601795   DDC 353.0072/048 19
1. United States. Small Business Administration - Appropriations and expenditures. I. Title.
KF26.5 .S6 1981

United States. Congress. House. Committee on Science and Technology. Innovation .
Washington , 1980. v, 228 p. ;   LC Card 80-602110   DDC 338/.06 19
KF27 .S39 1979f

United States. Congress. Senate. Committee on Governmental Affairs. Subcommittee on Federal Spending Practices and Open Government. Continued oversight of the Small Business Association's [i.e. Administration's] 8 (a) program . Washington , 1980. iii, 105 p. ;   LC Card 80-603071   DDC 353.0082/048 19
KF26 .G6732 1979j

United States. Congress. Senate. Committee on the Judiciary. Subcommittee on Antitrust, Monopoly, and Business Rights. Gasohol competition act of 1979, S. 2251 . Washington , 1980. iii, 201 p. :   LC Card 80-603339   DDC 343.73/078662669 19
KF26 .J835 1980

Women-in-business programs in the Federal government : hearing before the Select Committee on Small Business, United States Senate, Ninety-sixth Congress, second session ... May 29, 1980. Washington : U. S. Govt. Print. Off., 1980. iii, 207 p. ; 24 cm.   LC Card 80-603041   DDC 353.0082/048 19
1. Women in business - United States. 2. Women-owned business enterprises - United States. 3. Small business - United States. I. Title.
KF26.5 .S6 1980h

United States. Congress. Senate. Select Committee on Small Business. Subcommittee on Government Procurement. S. 2873, to provide SBA loans to small businesses in the communications industry : hearing before the Subcommittee on Government Procurement of the Select Committee on Small Business, United States Senate, Ninety-sixth Congress, second session, on S. 2873 ... July 24, 1980. Washington : U. S. Govt. Print. Off., 1980. iii, 52 p. ; 24 cm.   LC Card 80-603716   DDC 346.73/0652 347.3016652 19
1. Small business - Law and legislation - United States. 2. Small business - United States - Finance. 3. Communication and traffic - Law and legislation - United States. 4. United States. Small Business Administration. I. Title.
KF26.5 .S625 1980

United States. Congress. Senate. Select Committee on Small Business. Subcommittee on Government Regulation and Paperwork. Oversight of SBA's management assistance programs : hearing before the Subcommittee on Government Regulation and Paperwork of the Select Committee on Small Business, United States Senate, Ninety-sixth Congress, first session ... September 25, 1979. Washington : U. S. Govt. Print. Off., 1980. iii, 201 p. : ill. ; 24 cm.   LC Card 80-602431   DDC 353.0082/048 19
1. Small business - United States - Management. 2.

United States. Small Business Administration. I. Title.
KF26.5 .S629 1979b

United States. Congress. Senate. Select Committee on Small Business. Subcommittee on Taxation, Financing, and Investment.
Procedural difficulties encountered by smaller business in dealing with the IRS : hearings before the Subcommittee on Taxation, Financing, and Investment of the Select Committee on Small Business, United States Senate, Ninety-sixth Congress, second session ... July 31 and August 19, 1980. Washington : U. S. Govt. Print. Off., 1980. iii, 122 p. ; 24 cm.
   LC Card 80-603483   DDC 353.0072/4 19
1. Small business - Taxation - United States. 2. Tax administration and procedure - United States. 3. United States. Internal Revenue Service. I. Title.
KF26.5 .S686 1980

United States. Congress. Senate. Special Committee on Aging. (Old Catalog form: United States. Aging, Special Committee on (senate))
Abuse of the medicare home health program : hearing before the Special Committee on Aging, United States Senate, Ninety-sixth Congress, first session, Miami, Fla., August, 28, 1979. Washington : U. S. Govt. Print. Off. : for sale by the Supt. of Docs., U. S. Govt. Print. Off., 1980. iii, 83 p. ; 24 cm.   LC Card 80-602488   DDC 364.1/63 19
1. Medicare fraud - Florida. 2. Home care services - Florida. 3. Medicare fraud. 4. Home care services - United States. I. Title.
KF26.5 .A3 1979e

Adapting social security to a changing work force : hearing before the Special Committee on Aging, United States Senate, Ninety-sixth Congress, first session, Washington, D.C. November 28, 1979. Washington : U. S. Govt. Print. Off. : for sale by the Supt. of Docs., U. S. Govt. Print. Off., 1980. iii, 102 p. : graphs ; 23 cm.   LC Card 80-602460   DDC 368.4/3/00973 19
1. Social security - United States. 2. Women - United States - Pensions. I. Title.
KF26.5 .A3 1979d

Aging and mental health : overcoming barriers to service : hearing before the Special Committee on Aging, United States Senate, Ninety-sixth Congress, second session, April 4, 1980. Washington : U. S. Govt. Print. Off., 1980- v. ; 24 cm. CONTENTS. - pt. 1. Little Rock, Ark.   LC Card 80-603082   DDC 362.2/0425/0880565 19
1. Aged - Mental health - Arkansas. 2. Aged - Mental health services - Arkansas. 3. Aged - Mental health - United States. 4. Aged - Mental health services - United States. I. Title.
KF26.5 .A3 1980a

Bechill, William D. Developments and trends in State programs and services for the elderly .
Washington , 1974. viii, 107 p. ;   LC Card 74-603212
HV1461 .B42   **NYPL   [JLE 81-99]**

Crime and the elderly : what your community can do : hearing before the Special Committee on Aging, United States Senate, Ninety-sixth Congress, second session, Albuquerque, N. Mex., June 23, 1980. Washington : U. S. G.P.O. : For sale by the Supt. of Docs., U. S. G.P.O., 1981. iv, 154 p. : ill. ; 24 cm. 052-070-05517-1   LC Card 81-600934   DDC 364.4/0458/0880565 19
1. Aged - New Mexico - Crimes against - Prevention. I. Title.
KF26.5 .A3 1980h

Elder abuse : joint hearing before the Special Committee on Aging, United States Senate and the Select Committee on Aging, U. S. House of Representatives, Ninety-sixth Congress, second session, Washington, D.C., June 11, 1980. Washington : U. S. G.P.O. : for sale by the Supt. of Docs., U. S. G.P.O., 1980. iv, 166 p. : ill. ; 23 cm. Includes bibliographical references.   LC Card 80-603798   DDC 362.6/042 19
1. Aged - United States - Abuse of. I. United States. Congress. House. Select Committee on Aging. II. Title.
KF26.5 .A3 1980d

Energy assistance for the elderly : hearing before the Special Committee on Aging, United States Senate, Ninety-sixth Congress, first session, August 30, 1979. Washington : U. S. Govt. Print. Off., 1980- v. ; 24 cm. Includes

bibliographical references. CONTENTS. - pt. 1. Akron, Ohio.   LC Card 80-601872   DDC 363.6/2/080565 19
1. Aged - United States - Energy assistance. 2. Energy policy - United States. 3. Energy consumption - United States. I. Title.
KF26.5 .A3 1979g

Energy equity and the elderly in the 80's : hearing before the Special Committee on Aging, United States Senate, Ninety-sixth Congress, second session .... Washington : U. S. G.P.O, 1981. 2 v. (iv, 147 p.) ; 24 cm. Pt. 1: "October 24, 1980." Pt. 2: "October 28, 1980." G.P.O. sales statement incorrect in pt. 2 of publication. Item 1009 CONTENTS. - pt. 1. Boston, Mass. -- pt. 2. St. Petersburg, Fla.   LC Card 81-601131   DDC 362.6/3 19
1. Aged - United States - Energy assistance. I. Title.
KF26.5 .A3 1980g

How old is "old"? : the effects of aging on learning and working : hearing before the Special Committee on Aging, United States Senate, Ninety-sixth Congress, second session, Washington, D.C., April 30, 1980. Washington : U. S. G.P.O. : For sale by the Supt. of Docs., U. S. G.P.O., 1980. iii, 57 p. ; 24 cm. S/N 052-070-05469-7.   LC Card 80-604031   DDC 305.2/6 19
1. Aging - Longitudinal studies. I. Title.
KF26.5 .A3 1980b

Impact of federal estate tax policies on rural women : hearing before the Special Committee on Aging, United States Senate, Ninety-seventh Congress, first session, Washington, D.C., February 4, 1981. Washington : U. S. G.P.O., 1981. iii, 57 p. ; 24 cm. Item 1009-B, 1009-C (microfiche) Includes bibliographical references.   LC Card 81-601884   DDC 330.973/0927/088042 19
1. Inheritance and transfer tax - United States. 2. Family farms - United States. 3. Rural women - United States. 4. Aged - United States - Economic conditions. I. Title.
KF26.5 .A3 1981

Innovative developments in aging .
Washington , 1980. xi, 372 p. ;   LC Card 80-603859   DDC 362.6/0973 19
HV1450 .I55

Koitz, David. Summary of recommendations and surveys on social security and pension policies . Washington , 1980. vii, 48 p. ;   LC Card 80-603856   DDC 368.4/3/00973 19
HD7125 .K59

Maine's rural elderly : independence without isolation : hearing before the Special Committee on Aging, United States Senate, Ninety-sixth Congress, second session, Bangor, Maine, June 9, 1980. Washington : U. S. G.P.O., 1980. iv, 125 p. ; 24 cm.   LC Card 80-604071   DDC 362.6/09741 19
1. Rural aged - Maine. 2. Rural aged - Government policy - Maine. I. Title.
KF26.5 .A3 1980c

Medicare reimbursement for elderly participation in health maintenance organizations and health benefit plans : hearing before the Special Committee on Aging, United States Senate, Ninety-sixth Congress, first session, Philadelphia, Pa., October 29, 1979. Washington : U. S. Govt. Print. Off. : for sale by the Supt. of Docs., U. S. Govt. Print. Off., 1980. iii, 61 p. ; 24 cm. Includes bibliographical references.   LC Card 80-603117   DDC 362.1/0425 19
1. Medicare. 2. Aged - Medical care - United States. 3. Federal aid to health maintenance organizations - United States. 4. Health maintenance organizations - Pennsylvania. I. Title.
KF26.5 .A3 1979j

Minority elderly : economics and housing in the 80's : hearing before the Special Committee on Aging, United States, Ninety-sixth Congress, second session, Philadelphia, Pa., May 7, 1980. Washington : U. S. G.P.O., 1981. iii, 61 p. ; 24 cm. Item 1009   LC Card 81-601366   DDC 363.5/9 19
1. Minority aged - Housing - Pennsylvania - Philadelphia. 2. Minority aged - Pennsylvania - Philadelphia - Economic conditions. 3. Minority aged - Housing - United States. 4. Minority aged - United States - Economic conditions. I. Title.
KF26.5 .A3 1980i

Occupational health hazards of older workers in New Mexico : hearing before the Special Committee on Aging, United States Senate,

Ninety-sixth Congress, first session, Grants, N. Mex., August 30, 1979. Washington : U. S. Govt. Print. Off., 1980. iv, 95 p. ; 24 cm. LC Card 80-602736   DDC 363.1/1962234932 19
1. Uranium mines and mining - Employees - Diseases and hygiene - New Mexico. 2. Aged - New Mexico - Care and hygiene. I. Title.
KF26.5 .A3 1979h

The proposed fiscal 1981 budget : what it means for older Americans : an information paper / prepared by the staff of the Special Committee on Aging, United States Senate. Washington : U. S. Govt. Print. Off., 1980. ii, 18 p. : graphs ; 24 cm. At head of title: 96th Congress, 2d session. Committee print.   LC Card 80-601777   DDC 362.6/3/0973 19
1. Old age assistance - United States. 2. Budget - United States. I. Title.
HV1461 .U63 1980

Regulations to implement the Comprehensive older Americans act amendments of 1978 : joint hearing before the Special Committee on Aging and the Subcommittee on Aging of the Committee on Labor and Human Resources, United States Senate, Ninety-sixth Congress, first-[second] session[s] .... Washington : U. S. Govt. Print. Off., 1980- v. ; 24 cm. Hearing held Oct. 18, 1979- CONTENTS. - pts. 1-2. Washington, D.C.   LC Card 80-603040   DDC 353.0084/6 19
1. Aged - Legal status, laws, etc. - United States. I. United States. Congress. Senate. Committee on Labor and Human Resources. Subcommittee on Aging. II. Title.
KF26.5 .A3 1979i

Retirement benefits, are they fair and are they enough? : hearing before the Special Committee on Aging, United States Senate, Ninety-sixth Congress, second session, Fort Leavenworth, Kans., November 8, 1980. Washington : U. S. G.P.O., 1981. iii, 74 p. ; 24 cm.   LC Card 81-602039   DDC 331.25/2/0973 19
1. Old age pensions - United States. 2. Old age pensions - Kansas. 3. Retirement income - United States. 4. Retirement income - Kansas. I. Title.
KF26.5 .A3 1980j

Rural elderly--the isolated population : a look at services in the 80's : hearing before the Special Committee on Aging, United States Senate, Ninety-sixth Congress, second session, Las Vegas, N. Mex., April 11, 1980. Washington : U. S. G.P.O., 1980. iv, 94 p. : ill. ; 24 cm. Item 1009 Includes bibliographical references.   LC Card 81-600599   DDC 362.6/09789 19
1. Rural aged - Government policy - New Mexico. I. Title.
KF26.5 .A3 1980f

Social security, what changes are necessary? : hearings before the Special Committee on Aging, United States Senate, Ninety-sixth Congress, second session .... Washington : U. S. G.P.O., 1981. 4 v. : ill. ; 24 cm. Pt. 1: "Washington, D.C., November 21, 1980." Pt. 2: "Washington, D.C., December 2, 1980." Pt. 3: "Washington, D.C., December 3, 1980." Pt. 4: "Washington, D.C., December 4, 1980." Item 1009 Includes bibliographical references.   LC Card 81-600970   DDC 368.4/3/00973 19
1. Social security - United States. I. Title.
KF26.5 .A3 1980e

State offices on aging . Washington , 1980. vii, 37 p. ;   LC Card 81-600673   DDC 362.6/0973 19
KF3737.Z95 S73

United States. Congress. Senate. Committee on Labor and Human Resources. Home health care, future policy . Washington , 1981. iii, 332 p. ;   LC Card 81-601630   DDC 362.1/4/09749 19
KF26 .L27 1980u

Urban Institute. Emerging options for work and retirement policy (an analysis of major income and employment issues with an agenda for research priorities) . Washington , 1980. vi, 186 p. 23 cm.   LC Card 80-603277   DDC 331.25/2/0973 19
HD7106.U5 U7 1980

Work after 65 : options for the 80's : hearing before the Special Committee on Aging, United States Senate, Ninety-sixth Congress, second session .... Washington : U. S. Govt. Print. Off. : for sale by the Supt. of Docs., U. S. Govt. Print. Off., 1980- v. ; 24 cm. Hearings held Apr. 24, 1980- Includes bibliographical references. CONTENTS. - pt. 1. Washington, D.C.   LC Card

80-603005   DDC 331.3/98/0973 19
1. Aged - Employment - United States. I. Title.
KF26.5 .A3 1980

United States. Congress. Senate. Special Committee on Atomic Energy. (Old Catalog form: United States. Atomic energy, Special Committee on.)
Atomic energy act of 1946 : hearings before the Special Committee on Atomic Energy, United States Senate, Seventy-ninth Congress, Second session, on S. 1717, a bill for the development and control of atomic energy. Washington : U. S. Govt. Print. Off., 1946. 5 pts. (539 p.) ; 23 cm. Microfilm. Hearings held Jan. 22-April 8, 1946.   LC Card 46-25891
1. Atomic energy. I. Title.   **NYPL [*ZT-1247]**

United States. Congress. Senate. Subcommittee for Consumers. see **United States. Congress. Senate. Committee on Commerce, Science, and Transportation. Subcommittee for Consumers.**

United States. Congress. Senate. Subcommittee on African Affairs. see **United States. Congress. Senate. Committee on Foreign Relations. Subcommittee on African Affairs.**

United States. Congress. Senate. Subcommittee on Agricultural Credit and Rural Electrification. see **United States. Congress. Senate. Committee on Agriculture, Nutrition, and Forestry. Subcommittee on Agricultural Credit and Rural Electrification.**

United States. Congress. Senate. Subcommittee on Agricultural Production, Marketing, and Stabilization of Prices. see **United States. Congress. Senate. Committee on Agriculture, Nutrition, and Forestry. Subcommittee on Agricultural Production, Marketing, and Stabilization of Prices.**

United States. Congress. Senate. Subcommittee on Agricultural Research and General Legislation. see **United States. Congress. Senate. Committee on Agriculture, Nutrition, and Forestry. Subcommittee on Agricultural Research and General Legislation.**

United States. Congress. Senate. Subcommittee on Arms Control. see **United States. Congress. Senate. Committee on Armed Services. Subcommittee on Arms Control.**

United States. Congress. Senate. Subcommittee on Aviation. see **United States. Congress. Senate. Committee on Commerce, Science, and Transportation. Subcommittee on Aviation.**

United States. Congress. Senate. Subcommittee on Civil Service and General Services. see **United States. Congress. Senate. Committee on Governmental Affairs. Subcommittee on Civil Service and General Services.**

United States. Congress. Senate. Subcommittee on Communications. see **United States. Congress. Senate. Committee on Commerce, Science, and Transportation. Subcommittee on Communications.**

United States. Congress. Senate. Subcommittee on Consumer Affairs. see **United States. Congress. Senate. Committee on Banking, Housing and Urban Affairs. Subcommittee on Consumer Affairs.**

United States. Congress. Senate. Subcommittee on Criminal Laws and Procedures. see **United States. Congress. Senate. Committee on the Judiciary. Subcommittee on Criminal Laws and Procedures.**

United States. Congress. Senate. Subcommittee on Departments of State, Justics, and Commerce, the Judiciary and Related Agencies. see **United States. Congress. Senate. Committee on Appropriations. Subcommittee on Departments of State, Justice, and Commerce, the Judiciary, and Related Agencies.**

United States. Congress. Senate. Subcommittee on Energy, Nuclear Proliferation, and Federal Services. see **United States. Congress. Senate. Committee on Governmental Affairs. Subcommittee on Energy, Nuclear Proliferation, and Federal Services.**

United States. Congress. Senate. Subcommittee on Energy Research and Development. see

United States. Congress. Senate. Committee on Energy and Natural Resources. Subcommittee on Energy Research and Development.

United States. Congress. Senate. Subcommittee on Environment, Soil Conservation, and Forestry. see **United States. Senate. Committee on Agriculture, Nutrition, and Forestry. Subcommittee on Environment, Soil Conservation, and Forestry.**

United States. Congress. Senate. Subcommittee on Environmental Pollution. see **United States. Congress. Senate. Committee on Environment and Public Works. Subcommittee on Environmental Pollution.**

United States. Congress. Senate. Subcommittee on Financial Institutions. see **United States. Congress. Senate. Committee on Banking, Housing and Urban Affairs. Subcommittee on Financial Institutions.**

United States. Congress. Senate. Subcommittee on Foreign Operations. see **United States. Congress. Senate. Committee on Appropriations. Subcommittee on Foreign Operations.**

United States. Congress. Senate. Subcommittee on Government Procurement. see **United States. Congress. Senate. Select Committee on Small Business. Subcommittee on Government Procurement.**

United States. Congress. Senate. Subcommittee on Health. see **United States. Congress. Senate. Committee on Finance. Subcommittee on Health.**

United States. Congress. Senate. Subcommittee on Housing and Urban Affairs. see **United States. Congress. Senate. Committee on Banking, Housing and Urban Affairs. Subcommittee on Housing and Urban Affairs.**

United States. Congress. Senate. Subcommittee on HUD-Independent Agencies. see **United States. Congress. Senate. Committee on Appropriations. Subcommittee on HUD-Independent Agencies.**

United States. Congress. Senate. Subcommittee on Improvements in Judicial Machinery. see **United States. Congress. Senate. Committee on the Judiciary. Subcommittee on Improvements in Judicial Machinery.**

United States. Congress. Senate. Subcommittee on Intergovernmental Relations. see **United States. Congress. Senate. Committee on Governmental Affairs. Subcommittee on Intergovernmental Relations.**

United States. Congress. Senate. Subcommittee on International Finance. see **United States. Congress. Senate. Committee on Banking, Housing and Urban Affairs. Subcommittee on International Finance.**

United States. Congress. Senate. Subcommittee on International Trade. see **United States. Congress. Senate. Committee on Finance. Subcommittee on International Trade.**

United States. Congress. Senate. Subcommittee on Labor. see **United States. Congress. Senate. Committee on Labor and Public Welfare. Subcommittee on Labor.**

United States. Congress. Senate. Subcommittee on Manpower and Personnel. see **United States. Congress. Senate. Committee on Armed Services. Subcommittee on Manpower and Personnel.**

United States. Congress. Senate. Subcommittee on Merchant Marine and Tourism. see **United States. Congress. Senate. Committee on Commerce, Science, and Transportation. Subcommittee on Merchant Marine and Tourism.**

United States. Congress. Senate. Subcommittee on Military Construction. see **United States. Congress. Senate. Committee on Appropriations. Subcommittee on Military Construction.**

United States. Congress. Senate. Subcommittee on Military Construction and Stockpiles. see **United States. Congress. Senate. Committee on Armed Services. Subcommittee on Military Construction and Stockpiles.**

BIBLIOGRAPHIC GUIDE

United States. Congress. Senate. Subcommittee on Near Eastern

504

United States. Congress. Senate. Subcommittee
on Near Eastern and South Asian Affairs.
see United States. Congress. Senate.
Committee on Foreign Relations.
Subcommittee on Near Eastern and South
Asian Affairs.

United States. Congress. Senate. Subcommittee
on Nuclear Regulation. see United States.
Congress. Senate. Committee on
Environment and Public Works.
Subcommittee on Nuclear Regulation.

United States. Congress. Senate. Subcommittee
on Nutrition. see United States. Congress.
Senate. Committee on Agriculture, Nutrition,
and Forestry. Subcommittee on Nutrition.

United STates. Congress. Senate. Subcommittee
on Private Pension Plans and Employee
Fringe Benefits. see United States. Congress.
Senate. Committee on Finance.
Subcommittee on Private Pension Plans and
Employee Fringe Benefits.

United States. Congress. Senate. Subcommittee
on Regional and Community Development.
see United States. Congress. Senate.
Committee on Environment and Public
Works. Subcommittee on Regional and
Community Development.

United States. Congress. Senate. Subcommittee
on Reports, Accounting, and Management.
see United States. Congress. Senate.
Committee on Governmental Affairs.
Subcommittee on Reports, Accounting, and
Management.

United States. Congress. Senate. Subcommittee
on Research and Development. see United
States. Congress. Senate. Committee on
Armed Services. Subcommittee on Research
and Development.

United States. Congress. Senate. Subcommittee
on Resource Protection. see United States.
Congress. Senate. Committee on
Environment and Public Works.
Subcommittee on Resource Protection.

United States. Congress. Senate. Subcommittee
on Rural Development. see United States.
Congress. Senate. Committee on Agriculture,
Nutrition, and Forestry. Subcommittee on
Rural Development.

United States. Congress. Senate. Subcommittee
on Science, Technology and Space. see
United States. Congress. Senate. Committee
on Commerce, Science, and Transportation.
Subcommittee on Science, Technology, and
Space.

United States. Congress. Senate. Subcommittee
on Securities. see United States. Congress.
Senate. Committee on Banking, Housing and
Urban Affairs. Subcommittee on Securities.

United States. Congress. Senate. Subcommittee
on Surface Transportation. see United States.
Congress. Senate. Committee on Commerce,
Science, and Transportation. Subcommittee
on Surface Transportation.

United States. Congress. Senate. Subcommittee
on the Dept. of the Treasury, U. S. Postal
Service, and General Government
Appropriations. see United States. Congress.
Senate. Committee on Appropriations.
Subcommittee on the Dept. of the Treasury,
U. S. Postal Service, and General
Government Appropriations.

United States. Congress. Senate. Subcommittee
on the Handicapped. see United States.
Congress. Senate. Committee on Labor and
Public Welfare. Subcommittee on the
Handicapped.

United States. Congress. Senate. Subcommittee
on Transportation. see United States.
Congress. Senate. Committee on
Environment and Public Works.
Subcommittee on Transportation.

United States. Congress. Senate. Subcommittee
on Water Resources. see United States.
Congress. Senate. Committee on
Environment and Public Works.
Subcommittee on Water Resources.

United States. Congress. Senate. Subcommittee
to Investigate the Administration of the
Internal Security Act and Other Internal

Security Laws. see United States. Congress.
Senate. Committee on the Judiciary.
Subcommittee to Investigate the
Administration of the Internal Security Act
and Other Internal Security Laws.

United States. Congress. Senate. Veterans'
Affairs, Committee on. see United States.
Congress. Senate. Committee on Veterans'
Affairs.

United States. Congress. Subcommittee on
Economic Growth and Stabilization. see
United States. Congress. Joint Economic
Committee. Subcommittee on Economic
Growth and Stabilization.

United States. Congress. Subcommittee on
Energy. see United States. Congress. Joint
Economic Committee. Subcommittee on
Energy.

United States. Congress. Subcommittee on Fiscal
Policy. see United States. Congress. Joint
Economic Committee. Subcommittee on
Fiscal Policy.

United States. Congress. Subcommittee on
International Economics. see United States.
Congress. Joint Economic Committee.
Subcommittee on International Economics.

United States. Congress. Subcommittee on
Postsecondary Education. see United States.
Congress. House. Committee on Education
and Labor. Subcommittee on Postsecondary
Education.

United States. Congress. Taxation, Joint
Committee on. see United States. Congress.
Joint Committee on Taxation.

United States. Congress. Technology Assessment
Board. Technology assessment activities in
the industrial, academic, and governmental
communities : hearings before the Technology
Assessment Board of the Office of Technology
Assessment, Congress of the United States,
Ninety-fourth Congress, second session ....
Washington : U. S. Govt. Print. Off., 1976. v,
391 p. : ill. ; 24 cm. Microfiche (neg.) NTIS. 5
sheets. 11 x 15 cm. (PB-273 435) Hearings held June
8-14, 1976. LC Card 77-600690
1. Technology assessment - United States.
T174.5 .U56 1976a   *NYPL [*XME-9524]*

United States. Congress. Technology Assessment,
Office of. see United States. Congress. Office
of Technology Assessment.

United States. 14th Congress, 2d session, 1816-
1817. Joint resolution for abolishing the
traffick in slaves, and the colinization of the
free people of colour of the United States :
February 11, 1817. [Washington? D. C. : s. n.],
1817. 2 p. ; 21 cm. Microfiche (neg.) 1 sheet. 11 x
15 cm. (NYPL FSN Sc 017,758) Caption title. "Read
and committed to a committee of the Whole House ..."
House document 77.
1. Afro-Americans - Colonization - Africa. 2.
Slave-trade.   *NYPL [Sc Micro F-8079]*

United States. 56th Congress, 1st session, 1899-
1900. House. Cannon, Joseph Gurney,
1836-1926. $1,050,000 into the pockets of the
American tobacco trust. [Washington? D. C. ,
1900] 16 p. ;   *NYPL [Arents S 1607]*

United States. 95th Congress, 2d session, 1978.
House.
Report .
    (no. 95-1828, pt. 2) United States. Congress.
    House. Select Committee on Assassinations.
    Report of the Select Committee on
    Assassinations, U. S. House of
    Representatives, Ninety-fifth Congress,
    second session . Washington , 1979. xiii, 686
    p. ; LC Card 79-603369 DDC 364.1/524/0973
    19
KF32.5 .A8 1979

United States. 96th Congress, 1st session. House.
Document .
    (no. 96-202, pt. 11) United States. Dept. of
    the Interior. Georgetown waterfront,
    Washington, D.C. . Washington , 1979. 53
    p. ; LC Card 80-602644 DDC 333.78/3 19
HT177.D6 U52 1979

United States. 96th Congress, 1st session, 1979.
Memorial addresses and other tributes in the
Congress of the United States on the life and
contributions of Nelson A. Rockefeller /
Ninety-sixth Congress, first session.

Washington : U. S. Govt. Print. Off., 1979. xi,
279 p., [1] leaf of plates : port. ; 24 cm. (Senate
document - 96th Congress, 1st session . no. 96-20)
Cover title: Nelson A. Rockefeller, late Vice President,
United States of America; memorial tributes in the
Congress of the United States and various articles and
editorials relating to his life and work. LC Card
80-603613   DDC 973.925/092/4 B 19
1. Rockefeller, Nelson Aldrich, 1908- - Addresses,
essays, lectures. 2. Vice-Presidents - United States -
Biography - Addresses, essays, lectures. I. Series: United
States. 96th Congress, 1st session, 1979. Senate.
Document , no. 96-20. II. Title.
E748.R673 U56 1979

Memorial services held in the House of
Representatives and Senate of the United
States, together with remarks presented in
eulogy of Leo J. Ryan, a late Representative
from California / Ninety-sixth Congress, first
session ; [compiled under the direction of the
Joint Committee on Printing]. Washington : U.
S. Govt. Print. Off., 1979. vii, 88 p., [1] leaf of
plates : port. ; 24 cm. LC Card 79-603246
1. Ryan, Leo J. - Addresses, essays, lectures. 2.
Legislators - United States - Biography - Addresses,
essays, lectures. 3. United States. Congress. House -
Biography - Addresses, essays, lectures. I. United
States. Congress. Joint Committee on Printing. II. Title.
E840.8.R88 U5 1979   *NYPL [JFE 81-694]*

United States. 96th Congress, 1st session, 1979.
House.
Document .
    (no. 96-167) Should the Federal government
    significantly strengthen the regulation of mass
    media communication in the United States? .
    Washington , 1979. ix, 425 p. : LC Card
    80-602647 DDC 343.73/099 19
KF2750.A75 S48

    (no. 96-202, pt. 16) United States. Dept. of
    the Interior. Alexandria waterfront, Virginia .
    Washington , 1979. 86 p. : LC Card 80-602643
    DDC 333.73/17/09755296 19
HT177.A44 U54 1979

Report .
    (no. 96-413) United States. Congress. House.
    Committee on Government Operations.
    Emergency planning around U. S. nuclear
    powerplants . Washington , 1979. v, 105 p. ;
    LC Card 79-604246 DDC 363.3/497 19
KF32 .G6 1979a

United States. 96th Congress, 1st session, 1979.
Senate.
Document .
    (no. 96-20) United States. 96th Congress, 1st
    session, 1979. Memorial addresses and other
    tributes in the Congress of the United States
    on the life and contributions of Nelson A.
    Rockefeller /. Washington , 1979. xi, 279 p.,
    [1] leaf of plates : LC Card 80-603613 DDC
    973.925/092/4 B 19
E748.R673 U56 1979

Report .
    (no. 96-426) United States. Congress. Senate.
    Committee on Governmental Affairs.
    Permanent Subcommittee on Investigations.
    Labor union insurance activities of Joseph
    Hauser and his associates . Washington ,
    1979. viii, 202 p. ; LC Card 80-600763 DDC
    364.1/68 19
KF31 .G684 1979

United States. 96th Congress, 2d session. House.
Document .
    (no. 96-265) United States. President, 1977-
    (Carter) Selective Service reform .
    Washington , 1980. ix, 62 p. ; LC Card
    80-601724 DDC 343.73/0122 19
KF7263 .A25 1980

United States. 96th Congress, 2d session, 1980.
House Document .
    (no. 96-303) United States. President, 1977-
    (Carter) Use of U. S. Armed Forces in
    attempted rescue of hostages in Iran .
    Washington, D.C. , 1980. 2 p. ; LC Card
    80-602258 DDC 327.73055 19
E183.8.I55 U54 1980

Memorial services held in the House of
Representatives and Senate of the United
States, together with remarks presented in
eulogy of John M. Slack, late a Representative
from West Virginia / Ninety-sixth Congress,
second session. Washington : U. S. Govt. Print.
Off., 1980. vii, 69 p., [1] leaf of plates : port. ;

24 cm. Cover title: John M. Slack; late a Representative from West Virginia, memorial addresses delivered in Congress. LC Card 80-603140 DDC 328.73/092/4 19

1. Slack, John Mark, 1915-1980 - Addresses, essays, lectures. 2. Legislators - United States - Biography - Addresses, essays, lectures. 3. United States. Congress. House - Biography - Addresses, essays, lectures. I. Title. II. Title: John M. Slack, late a Representative from West Virginia.
E840.8.S55 U54 1980

United States. 96th Congress, 2d session, 1980.
  House.
    Report .
    (no. 96-1068) United States. Congress. House. Committee on Small Business. Petroleum products . Washington , 1980. v, 99 p. : LC Card 80-602595 DDC 338.4/766553/0973 19
KF32 .S6 1980

    (no. 96-1214) United States. Congress. House. Select Committee on the Outer Continental Shelf. Final report on the activities of the Select Committee on the Outer Continental Shelf . Washington , 1980. vi, 133 p. ; LC Card 80-603260 DDC 353.0082/325 19
KF32.5 .O8 1980

United States. 96th Congress, 2d session, 1980.
  Senate.
    Document .
    (no. 96-43) How can the interests of United States consumers best be protected? . Washington , 1980. vii, 636 p. : LC Card 80-602855 DDC 381/.34/0973 19
HC110.C63 H68

United States. Congressional Budget Office.
An Analysis of President Carter's budgetary proposals for fiscal year 1982 /. [Washington, D.C.] , 1981. xix, 167 p. ; LC Card 81-601303 DDC 353.0072/225 19
HJ2051 .A778

Assisting the developing countries : foreign aid and trade policies of the United States / Congress of the United States, Congressional Budget Office. Washington, D.C. : The Office : for sale by the Supt. of Docs., U. S. Govt. Print. Off., [1980] xviii, 126 p. ; 26 cm. (Background paper - Congress of the United States, Congressional Budget Office) "September 1980." Includes bibliographical references. LC Card 80-603389 DDC 338.91/73/01724 19
1. Economic assistance, American. 2. United States - Commercial policy. I. Series: United States. Congressional Budget Office. Background paper - Congressional Budget Office. II. Title.
HC60.U6 C66 1980

Backgroud paper - Congressional Budget Office.
United States. Congressional Budget Office. Indexing the individual income tax for inflation /. [Washington, D.C.] [1980] xv, 81 p. ; LC Card 80-603390 DDC 336.24/2/0973 19
HJ4637 .U53 1980

Background paper - Congressional Budget Office.
Davison, Richard H. The U. S. sea-based strategic force . [Washington, D.C.] [1980] xx, 62 p. : LC Card 80-601190 DDC 359.8/3 19
V993 .D38

United States. Congressional Budget Office. Assisting the developing countries . Washington, D.C. [1980] xviii, 126 p. ; LC Card 80-603389 DDC 338.91/73/01724 19
HC60.U6 C66 1980

United States. Congressional Budget Office. Compensation reform for Federal white-collar employees . [Washington] [1980] xiv, 37 p. ; LC Card 80-602373 DDC 353.001/23 19
JK775 1980 .C66

United States. Congressional Budget Office. Forest Service timber sales . Washington, D.C. [1980] xviii, 64 p. ; LC Card 80-602605 DDC 338.4/36748/0973 19
HD9754 .U546 1980

United States. Congressional Budget Office. State profits on tax-exempt student loan bonds . [Washington] [1980] xvi, 57 p. ; LC Card 80-601571 DDC 379.1/214/0973 19
HG4946 .U52 1980

Chaikind, Stephen. Paying for social security . [Washington, D.C.], 1981. xix, 47 p. ; LC Card 81-601225 DDC 353.0082/56 19
HD7125 .C47

Compensation reform for Federal white-collar employees : the administration's proposal and budgetary options for 1981. [Washington] : Congress of the United States, Congressional Budget Office : for sale by the Supt. of Docs., U. S. Govt. Print. Off., [1980] xiv, 37 p. ; 26 cm. (Background paper - Congressional Budget Office) "Prepared by Earl A. Armbrust and David M. DelQuadro." "May 1980." Includes bibliographical references. LC Card 80-602373 DDC 353.001/23 19
1. United States - Officials and employees - Salaries, allowances, etc. I. Armbrust, Earl A. II. Delquadro, David M. III. Series: United States. Congressional Budget Office. Background paper - Congressional Budget Office. IV. Title.
JK775 1980 .C66

Conference on the Economics of Federal Credit Activity (1980 : Washington, D.C.) Conference on the Economics of Federal Credit Activity, April 10-11, 1980 /. [Washington, D.C.] , 1980- v. <1 > : LC Card 81-600545 DDC 336.3/44/0973 19
HG3729.U5 C62 1980

Costs of manning the active-duty military / The Congress of the United States, Congressional Budget Office. Washington, D.C. : The Office : for sale by the Supt. of Docs., U. S. Govt. Print. Off., [1980] xiv, 44 p. ; 26 cm. (Staff working paper - Congressional Budget Office) Includes bibliographical references. LC Card 80-603176 DDC 355.6/4/0973 19
1. United States - Armed Forces - Pay, allowances, etc. 2. Military service, Voluntary - United States. I. Series: United States. Congressional Budget Office. Staff working paper - Congressional Budget Office. II. Title.
UC74 .U54 1980

The economic outlook / the Congress of the United States, Congressional Budget Office. Washington, D.C. : The Office : for sale by the Supt. of Docs., U. S. Govt. Print. Off., [1978] xvi, 53 p. : ill. ; 27 cm. "February 1978." "A report to the Senate and House Committees on the Budget--Part II." Includes bibliographical references. LC Card 81-453019 DDC 338.5/443/0973 19
1. United States - Economic conditions - 1971-. 2. Fiscal policy - United States. I. Title.
HC106.7 .U544 1978b

Ehrlich, Everett M. Delays in nuclear reactor licensing and construction . [Washington, D.C.] [1979] xv, 64 p. : LC Card 81-600745 DDC 333.79/24 19
TK9023 .E37

Entering the 1980s : fiscal policy choices / The Congress of the United States, Congressional Budget Office. [Washington, D.C.] : The Office : for sale by the Supt. of Docs., U. S. Govt. Print. Off., [1980] xxi, 101 p. : ill. ; 26 cm. "A report to the Senate and House Committees on the Budget--part I." "January 1980." Includes bibliographical references. LC Card 80-602038 DDC 336.73 19
1. Fiscal policy - United States. 2. United States - Economic policy - 1971-. 3. United States - Economic conditions - 1971-. I. United States. Congress. Senate. Committee on the Budget. II. United States. Congress. House. Committee on the Budget. III. Title.
HJ257.2 .U57 1980

An evaluation of the strategic petroleum reserve : a report / prepared at the request of the Subcommittee on Energy and Power, Committee on Interstate and Foreign Commerce, United States, House of Representatives by the Congressional Budget Office. Washington : U. S. Govt. Print. Off., 1980. xv, 36 p. : ill. ; 24 cm. At head of title: 96th Congress, 2d session. Committee print 96-IFC 50. LC Card 80-602590 DDC 333.8/2311/0973 19
1. Energy policy - United States. 2. Petroleum - United States - Reserves. I. United States. Congress. House. Committee on Interstate and Foreign Commerce. Subcommittee on Energy and Power. II. Title.
HD9502.U52 U512 1980a

Federal credit activities . [Washington, D.C.] , 1981. xix, 106 p. ; LC Card 81-601827 DDC 353.0072/6 19
HJ8119 .F39

Federal energy research : an analysis of fiscal year 1977 program funding levels and

alternative budget paths through fiscal year 1986 / [prepared by Kendrick W. Wentzel]. Washington : Congress of the United States, Congressional Budget Office : for sale by the Supt. of Docs., U. S. Govt. Print. Off., 1976. xvi, 77 p. : graphs ; 27 cm. (Technical staff working paper - Congressional Budget Office) LC Card 77-602336 DDC 333.79/15/0973 19
1. Power resources - Research - United States - Finance. I. Wentzel, Kendrick W. II. Series: United States. Congressional Budget Office. Technical staff working paper - Congressional Budget Office. III. Title.
TJ163.25.U6 U513 1976a

Federal student assistance : issues and options / The Congress of the United States, Congressional Budget Office. Washington, D.C. : The Office : for sale by the Supt. of Docs., U. S. Govt. Print. Off., [1980] xvii, 73 p. ; 26 cm. (Budget issue paper for fiscal year 1981) Written by David Longanecker, with the assistance of D. Kalcevic and F. J. Lim, under the direction of D. S. Mundel. Includes bibliographical references. LC Card 80-602039 DDC 379.1/214/0973 19
1. Student aid - United States. 2. Federal aid to education - United States. I. Longanecker, David, 1946-. II. Title. III. Series.
LB2337.4 .U515 1980

Feeding children : Federal child nutrition policies in the 1980s / The Congress of the United States, Congressional Budget Office. [Washington] : The Office : for sale by the Supt. of Docs., U. S. Govt. Print. Off., [1980] xxiii, 149 p. : ill. ; 26 cm. (Budget issue paper for fiscal year 1981) "May 1980." Prepared by G.W. Hoagland. Includes bibliographical references. LC Card 80-603241 DDC 362.7/1 19
1. Food relief - United States. 2. Children - United States - Nutrition. 3. School children - Food - United States. I. Hoagland, G. William. II. Title. III. Series.
HV696.F6 U6146 1980

Fleisis, Heywood W. The effect of OPEC oil pricing on output, prices, and exchange rates in the United States and other industrial countries /. [Washington, D.C.] , 1981. xx, 107 p. : LC Card 81-601242 DDC 338.2/3 19
HD9560.4 .F58

Forest Service timber sales : their effect on wood product prices / The Congress of the United States, Congressional Budget Office. Washington, D.C. : The Office ; for sale by the Supt. of Docs., U. S. Govt. Print. Off., [1980] xviii, 64 p. ; 26 cm. (Background paper - Congressional Budget Office) Includes bibliographical references. LC Card 80-602605 DDC 338.4/36748/0973 19
1. Lumber trade - United States. 2. Word - Prices - United States. I. Series: United States. Congressional Budget Office. Background paper - Congressional Budget Office. II. Title.
HD9754 .U546 1980

Ginsburg, Paul B. The CBO hospital cost containment model . [Washington, D.C.] , 1981. xiv, 36 p. : LC Card 81-601120 DDC 362.1/1 19
RA981.A2 G49

Hillier, Pat. U. S. ground forces . [Washington, D.C.] , 1980. xxiii, 87 p. : LC Card 81-600683 DDC 355/.033073 19
UA23 .H513

Huck, Daniel F. Alternative approaches to adjusting compensation for federal bluecollar employees /. [Washington, D.C.] , c1980. xxii, 59 p. ; LC Card 80-604160 DDC 353.001/2 19
JK776 .H8

Iden, George. The productivity problem . [Washington, D.C.] , 1981. xvii, 137 p. ; LC Card 81-600899 DDC 331.11/8/0973 19
HC110.C3 I32

Index to the legislative history of the Congressional budget and impoundment control act of 1974 / [prepared at the request of the Committee on the Budget, U. S. House of Representatives]. [Washington] : Congress of the United States, Congressional Budget Office, [1980] xi, 481 p. ; 20 x 26 cm. "September 1980." Prepared by Barbara and Ken LePoer. LC Card 80-603388 DDC 343.73/034 347.30334 19
1. United States. Laws, statutes. etc. Congressional budget and impoundment control act of 1974 - Indexes. 2. Budget - United States - Indexes. 3. Executive impoundment of appropriated funds - United States - Indexes. I. LePoer, Barbara. II. LePoer, Kendall T. III. United States. Congress. House. Committee on the

Budget. IV. Title.
KF6222.115 .A15 1980

Indexing the individual income tax for inflation / the Congress of the United States, Congressional Budget Office. [Washington, D.C.] : The Office : for sale by the Supt. of Docs., U. S. Govt. Print. Off., [1980] xv, 81 p. ; 26 cm. (Background paper - Congress of the United States, Congressional Budget Office) "Written by Hyman Sanders and Joshua Greene." "Edited by Francis Pierce." Includes bibliographical references. LC Card 80-603390 DDC 336.24/2/0973 19
1. Income tax - United States - Effect of inflation on. I. Sanders, Hyman. II. Greene, Joshua E. III. Pierce, Francis. IV. Series: United States. Congressional Budget Office. Backgroud paper - Congressional Budget Office. V. Title.
HJ4637 .U53 1980

Koretz,Daniel M. The impact of PSROs on health care-costs . [Washington, D.C.] , 1971 [i.e. 1981] xvi, 56 p. ; LC Card 81-600900 DDC 362.1/1/0973 19
RA399.A3 K6

The Marine Corps in the 1980s : prestocking proposals, the rapid deployment force, and other issues. [Washington, D.C.] : Congress of the United States, Congressional Budget Office : for sale by the Supt. of Docs., U. S. Govt. Print. Off., [1980] xxii, 74 p. : ill. ; 26 cm. (Budget issue paper for fiscal year 1981) Prepared by Dov S. Zakheim. "May 1980." Includes bibliographical references. LC Card 80-602374 DDC 359.9/6/0973 19
1. United States. Marine Corps. 2. United States - Military policy. I. Zakheim, Dov S. II. Title. III. Series.
VE23 .A5 1980

Planning U. S. general purpose forces : forces related to Asia / the Congress of the United States, Congressional Budget Office ; [prepared by Charles A. Sorrels]. Washington : The Office : for sale by the Supt. of Docs., U. S. Govt. Print. Off., 1977. xxiii, 95 p. : 2 maps ; 26 cm. (Budget issue paper) Includes bibliographical references. LC Card 77-603153
1. United States - Armed Forces - Pacific area. 2. United States - Military policy. I. Sorrels, Charles A. II. Title.
UA26.E27 U54 1977

Reducing the Federal budget . Washington, D.C. [1981] xi, 187 p. ; LC Card 81-601803 DDC 353.0072/22 19
HJ2051 .R42

Saunders, Hyman. A review of the accuracy of treasury revenue forecasts, 1963-1978 /. [Washington, D.C.] , 1981. xi, 42 p. ; LC Card 81-601118 DDC 353.0072/2252 19
HJ2051 .S26

Shaping the general purpose Navy of the eighties : issues for fiscal years 1981-1985 / The Congress of the United States, Congressional Budget Office. Washington, D.C. : The Office : for sale by the Supt. of Docs., U. S. Govt. Print. Office, 1980. xxvii, 145 p. : ill. ; 26 cm. (Budget issue paper for fiscal year 1981) Prepared by D. S. Zakheim, A. Hamilton, M. Hoyler and P. Tarpgaard under the general supervision of D. S. C. Chu and R. F. Hale. Includes bibliographical references. LC Card 80-600968 DDC 359/.03/0973 19
1. United States. Navy. 2. Sea-power. 3. Russia (1923- U. S. S. R.). Voenno-Morskoĭ flot. I. Zakheim, Dov S. II. Title. III. Series.
VA53 .U52 1980

Slackman, Joel N. Costs of the National Service Act (H.R. 2206) . [Washington, D.C.] , c1980. xii, 42 p. ; LC Card 81-600733 DDC 355.2/236/0973 19
HD6273 .S57

Staff working paper - Congressional Budget Office.
United States. Congressional Budget Office. Costs of manning the active-duty military /. Washington, D.C. [1980] xiv, 44 p. ; LC Card 80-603176 DDC 355.6/4/0973 19
UC74 .U54 1980

State profits on tax-exempt student loan bonds : analysis and options. [Washington] : Congress of the United States, Congressional Budget Office, [1980] xvi, 57 p. ; 26 cm. (Background paper - Congressional Budget Office) Prepared by C. F. Gensheimer. "March 1980." Includes bibliographical references. LC Card 80-601571 DDC

379.1/214/0973 19
1. State bonds - United States - States. 2. Student loan funds - United States - States. 3. State bonds - Taxation - United States - States. 4. Taxation, Exemption from - United States - States. I. Gensheimer, Cynthia Francis. II. Series: United States. Congressional Budget Office. Background paper - Congressional Budget Office. III. Title.
HG4946 .U52 1980

Technical staff working paper - Congressional Budget Office.
United States. Congressional Budget Office. Federal energy research . Washington , 1976. xvi, 77 p. : LC Card 77-602336 DDC 333.79/15/0973 19
TJ163.25.U6 U513 1976a

U. S. tactical air forces : overview and alternative forces, fiscal years, 1976-81. Washington : Congress of the United States, Congressional Budget Office, 1976. 35 p. : graphs ; 26 cm. (Staff working paper - Congressional Budget Office) Cover title. "Prepared by ... Nancy J. Bearg." Errata sheet inserted. LC Card 76-602204
1. Aeronautics, Military - United States. 2. United States - Armed Forces. I. Bearg, Nancy J. II. Title.
UG633 .U52 1976

Vertrees, James G. Food and agriculture policy in the 1980s . [Washington, D.C.] , 1981. xvii, 52 p. : LC Card 81-601427 DDC 338.1/9/73 19
HD1761 .V45

Youth employment and education : possible Federal approaches / the Congress of the United States, Congressional Budget Office. [Washington] : The Office : for sale by the Supt. of Docs., U. S. Govt. Print. Off., [1980] xviii, 85 p. ; 26 cm. (Budget issue paper for fiscal year 1981) Prepared by J. Grassmuck and J. Greene. "July 1980." Includes bibliographical references. LC Card 80-602880 DDC 331.3/411/0973 19
1. Youth - Employment - United States. 2. Manpower policy - United States. I. Grassmuck, Janice. II. Greene, Joshua E. III. Title. IV. Series.
HD6273 .U5 1980

Youth unemployment : the outlook and some policy strategies / The Congress of the United States, Congressional Budget Office. Washington : The Office : for sale by the Supt. of Docs., U. S. Govt. Print. Off., 1978. xvii, 45 p. : graphs ; 27 cm. (Budget issue paper for fiscal year 1979) Prepared by G. Iden and T. Gibbons. Includes bibliographical references. LC Card 78-601457
1. Youth - Employment - United States. 2. Unemployed - United States. I. Iden, George. II. Gibbons, Toni. III. Title.
HD6273 .U5 1978

United States. Congressional Research Service. see United States. Library of Congress. Congressional Research Service.

UNITED STATES - CONSTITUTIONAL LAW - AMENDMENTS.
United States. Congress. Senate. Committee on the Judiciary. Constitutional amendment to balance the federal budget . Washington , 1980. iii, 130 p. ; LC Card 80-603988 DDC 343.73/034 347.30334 19
KF26 .J8 1980d

United States. Congress. Senate. Committee on the Judiciary. Subcommittee on the Constitution. Constitutional convention procedures . Washington , 1980. vi, 1372 p. ; LC Card 80-604085 DDC 342.73/032/0262 347.302320262 19
KF26 .J8359 1979f

UNITED STATES - CONSTITUTIONAL LAW - DIGESTS.
Fein, Bruce E. Significant decisions of the Supreme Court, 1976-1977 term /. - Washington , c1978. 168 p. ;
NYPL [JLE 80-1347]

United States. Consumer Product Safety Commission.
Bike-ed '77 . Washington, D. C. , 1977. i, 105 p. : LC Card 77-604118
GV1055 .B54   *NYPL [JFF 80-1530]*

United States. Consumer Product Safety Commission. Bureau of Epidemiology.
Nelson, Theresa. Hazard analysis of injuries relating to cribs . Washington , 1975. 66 p. ; LC Card 76-600895
TS886.5.C74 N44   *NYPL [JLF 80-1346]*

United States. Consumer Product Safety Commission. Communications, Directorate for. see United States. Consumer Product Safety Commission. Directorate for Communications.

United States. Consumer Product Safety Commission. Directorate for Communications. Consumer complaint contact system, annual report. 1st- ; 1977/78- [Washington] illus. 22 x 28 cm. Report year ends Sept. 30. LC Card 79-643680
1. Consumer protection - United States - Data processing - Periodicals. I. Title.
NYPL [JLM 80-887]

United States. Consumer Product Safety Commission. Directorate for Hazard Identification and Analysis. Division of Program Analysis.

United States. Consumer Product Safety Commission. Directorate for Hazard Identification and Analysis. Division of Human Factors. Hazard analysis injuries associated with skateboards (product code 1333) / Directorate of Hazard Identification and Analysis, Division of Program Analysis, Division of Human Factors. [Washington] : The Directorate : [for sale by the Supt. of Docs., U. S. Govt. Print. Off.], 1978. 130, [1] p. : ill. ; 27 cm. (HIA hazard analysis report) Bibliography: p. 130-[131] LC Card 78-602300
1. Skateboarding - Accidents and injuries. 2. Skateboarding - United States - Accidents and injuries - Statistics. I. United States. Consumer Product Safety Commission. Directorate for Hazard Identification and Analysis. Division of Human Factors. II. Title.
GV859.8 .U54 1978   *NYPL [JLF 81-381]*

United States. Consumer Product Safety Commission. Directorate for Hazard Identification and Analysis. Division of Program Analysis. Hazard analysis injuries associated with skateboards (product code 1333) /. [Washington] , 1978. 130, [1] p. : LC Card 78-602300
GV859.8 .U54 1978   *NYPL [JLF 81-381]*

United States. Consumer Product Safety Commission. Directorate for Hazard Identification and Analysis-Epidemiology. Division of Special Studies. Kessler, Eileen. Consumer product-related injuries treated in hospital emergency rooms, contiguous United States, January 1, 1976-December 31, 1976 /. Washington , 1978. i, 63 p. : LC Card 78-602486
TS175 .K47

United States. Consumer Product Safety Commission. Directorate for Hazard Identification and Analysis. Human Factors, Division of. see United States. Consumer Product Safety Commission. Directorate for Hazard Identification and Analysis. Division of Human Factors.

United States. Consumer Product Safety Commission. Directorate for Hazard Identification and Analysis. Program Analysis, Division of. see United States. Consumer Product Safety Commission. Directorate for Hazard Identification and Analysis. Division of Program Analysis.

United States. Consumer Product Safety Commission. Epidemiology, Bureau of. see United States. Consumer Product Safety Commission. Bureau of Epidemiology.

UNITED STATES. CONSUMER PRODUCT SAFETY COMMISSION - OFFICALS AND EMPLOYEES.
United States. Congress. House. Committee on Interstate and Foreign Commerce. Subcommittee on Consumer Protection and Finance. Consumer Product Safety Commission post-employment restrictions . Washington , 1980. iii, 8 p. ; LC Card 80-602437 DDC 343.73/071 19
KF27 .I554 1980

United States. Consumer Protection and Environmental Health Service. Environmental Control Administration. Water chlorine (residual). no. 1- Cincinnati, Ohio, 1969-   *NYPL [JSP 81-89]*

United States. Consumer Protection, Bureau of. see United States. Bureau of Consumer Protection.

United States. Contract Adjustment Board. see
United States. Dept. of Energy. Contract
Adjustment Board.

United States. Corps of Engineers. see United
States. Army. Corps of Engineers.

**UNITED STATES. COST ACCOUNTING
STANDARDS BOARD.**
United States. Congress. Senate. Committee on
Banking, Housing and Urban Affairs. Transfer
of Cost Accounting Standards Board .
Washington , 1980. iii, 67 p. ;   LC Card
   80-604039   DDC 353.0071/2044 19
KF26 .B39 1980y

United States. Cost of Living Council. Effective
managerial control of acute care hospitals under
the phase IV regulations. [Washington, 1974.] v,
53 p.   *NYPL   [JLF 80-451]*

United States. Council of Economic Advisers.
(Old Catalog form: United States. Economic
Advisers Council.)

**UNITED STATES. COUNCIL OF
ECONOMIC ADVISERS - OFFICIALS
AND EMPLOYEES.**
United States. Congress. Senate. Committee on
Banking, Housing and Urban Affairs.
Nomination of Stephen M. Goldfeld .
Washington , 1980. ii, 23 p. ;   LC Card
   80-603302   DDC 353.09/3 19
KF26 .B39 1980l

**United States. Council on Environmental
Quality.**
Charles River Associates. The economic effects
of pollution controls on the nonferrous metals
industry : copper /. Cambridge, Mass. , 1971.
ii, 159 leaves :   *NYPL   [JLF 81-131]*

Conservation Foundation. Coastal
environmental management. Washington, 1980.
161 p.:   *NYPL   [JSF 80-1124]*

The Economic impact of pollution control.
[Washington?] 1972. 332 p.   LC Card 72-601528
TD180 .E25   *NYPL   [JLF 81-274]*

**THE GLOBAL 2000 REPORT TO THE
PRESIDENT OF THE U. S.**
United States. Congress. Joint Economic
Committee. Subcommittee on International
Economics. The global 2000 report .
Washington , 1980. iii, 57 p. ;   LC Card
   80-603675   DDC 333.7/0973 19
KF25 .E253 1980

Global 2000 Study (U. S.) The global 2000
report to the President--entering the twenty-first
century . Washington, D.C. , 1980- v. <1-2> :
   LC Card 80-602859   DDC 333.7 19
HC79.E5 G59 1980b

The President's environmental program, 1979.
Washington, D.C. [1979] v, 57 p. ;   LC Card
   80-148627   DDC 363.7/00973 19
TD171 .P734

Solar energy, progress and promise / Council
on Environmental Quality. Washington : The
Council : for sale by the Supt. of Docs., U. S.
Govt. Print. Off., 1978. vii, 52 p. ; 26 cm.
Includes bibliographical references.   LC Card
78-601990
1. Solar energy - United States. I. Title.
TJ810 .U58 1978

Worldwatch Institute. The global environment
and basic human needs . [Washington] , 1978.
55 p. :   LC Card 78-602557   DDC 304.2 19
GF41 .W67 1978

**United States. Council on Equality of
Educational Opportunity, National Advisory.**
see United States. National Advisory Council
on Equality of Educational Opportunity.

**United States. Council on Wage and Price
Stability.** Pay and price standards : a
compendium / Executive Office of the
President, Council on Wage and Price Stability.
Washington : The Council : for sale by the
Supt. of Docs., U. S. Govt. Print Off., 1979. 95
p. in various pagings ; 28 cm.   LC Card
79-603044
1. Wage-price policy - United States. I. Title.
KF6067 .A88   *NYPL   [JLF 81-439]*

**UNITED STATES. COUNCIL ON WAGE
AND PRICE STABILITY.**
United States. Congress. House. Committee on
Banking, Finance and Urban Affairs.
Subcommittee on Economic Stabilization.

Amendments to the Council on Wage and Price
Stability act . Washington , 1977. iv, 415 p. :
   LC Card 77-602660
KF27 .B542 1977b   *NYPL   [JLE 81-450]*

United States. Congress. House. Committee on
Banking, Finance and Urban Affairs.
Subcommittee on Economic Stabilization. To
authorize the extension of the Council on Wage
and Price Stability . Washington , 1980. iv, 475
p. ;   LC Card 80-602791   DDC 343.73/034 19
KF27 .B542 1980

United States. Congress. House. Committee on
Government Operations. Commerce, Consumer,
and Monetary Affairs Subcommittee. Adequacy
of COWPS enforcement of price standards for
petroleum products . Washington , 1980. iii,
280 p. :   LC Card 80-602969   DDC
   353.0082/62282044 19
KF27 .G634 1980a

United States. Congress. Senate. Committee on
Banking, Housing and Urban Affairs. Extension
of the Council on Wage and Price Stability and
review of the President's anti-inflation policies .
Washington, D.C. , 1980. v, 452 p. :   LC Card
   80-602778   DDC 343.73/034 347.30334 19
KF26 .B39 1980h

**United States - Court-martial and courts of
inquiry.** see Courts-martial and courts of
inquiry - United States.

**UNITED STATES. COURT OF APPEALS
(5TH CIRCUIT)**
United States. Congress. House. Committee on
the Judiciary. Subcommittee on Courts, Civil
Liberties, and the Administration of Justice.
Federal court organization and fifth circuit
division . Washington , 1980 [i.e. 1981] v, 463
p. :   LC Card 81-601347   DDC 347.73/242
   347.307332 19
KF27 .J857 1980b

**UNITED STATES. COURT OF MILITARY
APPEALS.** (Old Catalog form: United States.
Courts. Court of Military Appeals.)
United States. Congress. House. Committee on
Armed Services. Subcommittee on Military
Personnel. Hearings on H.R. 6406 and H.R.
6298 . Washington , 1980. ii, 117 p. ;   LC Card
   80-604104   DDC 343.73/0143 347.303143 19
KF27 .A76398 1980c

**UNITED STATES. COURT OF MILITARY
APPEALS - OFFICIALS AND
EMPLOYEES.**
United States. Congress. Senate. Committee on
Armed Services. Nominations of Michael
Blumenfeld, John A. Bushnell, John W. Clark,
Clifford B. O'Hara, William Sidell, Robinson O.
Everett, and William E. Peacock . Washington ,
1980. ii, 49 p. ;   LC Card 80-602497   DDC
   353.0087/6444 19
KF26 .A7 1980c

United States. Courts. Court of Military Appeals.
see United States. Court of Military
Appeals.

**United States. Courts. District Court. New York.
Southern District. *09N.** see United States.
District Court. New York (Southern
District)

United States. Courts of Appeals. Federal rules
of appellate procedure, with forms, October 1,
1979. Washington : U. S. Govt. Print. Off. : for
sale by the Supt. of Docs., U. S. Govt. Print.
Off., 1979. x, 33 p. : forms ; 24 cm. At head of
title: 96th Congress, 1st session. Committee print. No.
4. "Promulgated and amended by the United States
Supreme Court." "Printed for the use of the Committee
on the Judiciary, House of Representatives."   LC Card
   80-600983   DDC 347.73/8 19
1. Appellate procedure - United States. I. United States.
Supreme Court. II. United States. Congress. House.
Committee on the Judiciary. III. Title.
KF9052 .A4 1979

United States. Courts. Supreme Court. see
United States. Supreme Court.

United States. Courts. Tax Court. see United
States. Tax Court.

United States. Crop Reporting Board.
Honey production : final estimates for 1970-75.
Washington, D.C. : Crop Reporting Board,
Economics, Statistics, and Cooperatives Service,
U. S. Dept. of Agriculture, 1978. 10 p. ; 26 cm.
(Statistical bulletin - U. S. Department of Agriculture ;

no. 614) "December 1978." Tables.   LC Card
80-601072   DDC 338.1/0973 s 338.1/7816/0973
19
1. Honey trade - United States - Statistics. I. Series:
United States. Dept. of Agriculture. Statistical bulletin ,
no. 614. II. Title.
HD1751 .A5 no. 614 HD9120.U52

Stocks of grains, oilseeds, and hay .
Washington, D.C. , 1981. 71 p. ;   LC Card
   81-601041   DDC 338.1/0973 s 338.1/731/0973
19
HD1751 .A5 no. 649 HD9034

United States. Customs Service.
Customs information series .
   (T:78-5) United States. Customs Service. U.
S. Customs guide for private flyers.
[Washington, D.C. , 1978] 55 p. :   LC Card
79-603485   DDC 343.7305/6/0243877 19
KF6694 .A32 1978

U. S. Customs guide for private flyers.
September 1978 ed. [Washington, D.C. : Dept.
of the Treasury, U. S. Customs Service] : for
sale by the Supt. of Docs., U. S. Govt. Print.
Off., [1978] 55 p. : ill. ; 23 cm. (Customs
information series ; T:78-5)   LC Card 79-603485
   DDC 343.7305/6/0243877 19
1. Customs administration - United States. 2. Airplanes,
Private. I. Title. II. Title: Guide for private flyers. III.
Series: United States. Customs Service. Customs
information series , T:78-5.
KF6694 .A32 1978

**UNITED STATES. CUSTOMS SERVICE -
APPROPRIATIONS AND
EXPENDITURES.**
United States. Congress. Senate. Committee on
Finance. Subcommittee on International Trade.
Authorization of appropriations for the U. S.
Customs Service, U. S. International Trade
Commission, and Office of the U. S. Trade
Representative, for fiscal year 1981 .
Washington , 1980. iii, 79 p. :   LC Card
   80-603102   DDC 353.0072/23682/7 19
KF26 .F554 1980b

UNITED STATES - DEFENSE.
United States. Congress. House. Committee on
Armed Services. Subcommittee on Seapower
and Strategic and Critical Materials. Submarine
alternatives study . Washington , 1980. ii, 182
p. ;   LC Card 80-603515   DDC 623.8/2574 19
KF27 .A769 1979d

**United States. Defense Advanced Research
Projects Agency.**
Rudins, George. U. S. and USSR MHD
electrode materials development. - Santa
Monica , 1974. vii, 71 p. :
                                    NYPL   [JSF 81-299]

Urick, Robert J. Sound propagation in the sea
/. [Arlington, Va.] , Washington, D.C. , 1979.
ca. 300 p. in various pagings :   LC Card
   80-601623   DDC 534/.23 19
QC233 .U76

United States. Defense Atomic Support Agency.
The effects of nuclear weapons. The effects of
nuclear weapons / compiled and edited by
Samuel Glasstone and Philip J. Dolan ;
prepared and published by the U. S. Dept. of
Defense and the U. S. Dept. of Energy. 3d
ed. [Washington] , 1977. 653 p. :   LC Card
78-600832
UF767 .E33 1977   *NYPL   [JSE 81-290]*

**United States. Defense Communications Agency.
National Military Command System Support
Center.** see United States. National Military
Command System Support Center.

United States. Defense Dept. see United States.
Dept. of Defense.

United States. Defense Documentation Center.
ASTIA subject headings. - 4th ed. Arlington,
Va.: Armed Services Technical Information
Agency, 1959. v, 758 p.; 27 cm. First ed.
published in 1948 by the Science and Technology
Project of the Library of Congress under title: List of
subject headings.   LC Card 59-61320
1. Subject headings - Science. 2. Subject headings -
Technology. I. United States. Library of Congress.
Science and Technology Project. List of subject
headings. II. Title.   *NYPL   [JSF 80-818]*

Performance measurement / Defense
Documentation Center. Alexandria, Va.: D. D.
C., 1976. 1 v. (various pagings) Microfiche (neg.)
NTIS. 6 sheets. 11 x 15 cm. (AD-A029 850) "A DDC

bibliography."
1. Performance - Bibliography. 2. Ability - Testing - Bibliography. 3. Work measurement - Bibliography. I. Title. *NYPL [*XME-9314]*

United States. Defense Documentation Center. Directorate of Technical Service. Delimited AD document index / Directorate of Technical Service. - Alexandria, Va. : Defense Documentation Center, Defense Logistics Agency, 1977. 116 p. ; 28 cm. Microfiche (neg.) NTIS. 2 sheets. 11 x 15 cm. (AD/A-037600) Cover title. "DDC/TR-77/1."
1. Science - Indexes. 2. Technology - Indexes. I. Title. *NYPL [*XMQ-2162]*

United States. Defense Logistics Agency. Quality assurance technical development program course catalog. Alexandria Va. 28 cm. Issued by the U. S. Defense Supply Agency, 1974-77. Issues for 1974-77 also called DSAH 8220.1; 1980- , also called DLAH 8220.1.
1. Quality control - Study and teaching - Handbooks, manuals, etc. I. United States. Defense Supply Agency. II. Title. *NYPL [JLM 80-723]*

Registers of planned emergency producers. Washington : U. S. Govt. Print. Off., 1980. 290 p. in various pagings : maps ; 26 cm. Cover title. "DOD H 005.3-H." "Planned manufacturers of war materiel for all military departments and agencies registered under the Dept. of Defence Industrial Preparedness Planning Program."
1. United States - Armed Forces - Supplies and stores - Directories. 2. Defense contracts - United States. - Directories. I. Title. *NYPL [JLF 80-1284]*

UNITED STATES. DEFENSE PRODUCTION ACT (1950) Compilation of the Energy Security Act of 1980, and 1980 amendments to the Defense Production Act of 1950 /. Washington , 1980. 3 v. (v. 2252 p.) ; LC Card 80-603878 DDC 346.7304/679 347.3064679 19
KF2120.A32 A15 1980

United States. Defense Supply Agency. United States. Defense Logistics Agency. Quality assurance technical development program course catalog. Alexandria Va.
NYPL [JLM 80-723]

UNITED STATES - DEFENSES. Hillier, Pat. U. S. ground forces . [Washington, D.C.] , 1980. xxiii, 87 p. : LC Card 81-600683 DDC 355/.033073 19
UA23 .H513

Mickey, V. V. Defense of the United States /. Maxwell Air Force Base, Ala. , Washington, D.C. , 1976. vi, 144 p. : LC Card 80-602629 DDC 355/.00973 19
UA23 .M524

United States. Congress. House. Committee on Armed Services. Capability of U. S. defense industrial base . Washington , 1980 [i.e. 1981] ii, 1796, ii p. : LC Card 81-600988 DDC 355.2/6/0973 19
KF27 .A7 1980K

United States. Congress. House. Committee on Armed Services. Procurement and Military Nuclear Systems Subcommittee. Readiness Panel. Review of readiness considerations in the development of the defense budget . Washington , 1980 [i.e. 1981] ii, 161 p. : LC Card 81-600960 DDC 355/.033073 19
KF27 .A7657 1980d

United States. Congress. House. Committee on Armed Services. Subcommitee on Investigations. National defense funding levels for fiscal year 1981 . Washington , 1980. ii, 27 p. ; LC Card 80-602709 DDC 355.6/22/0973 19
KF27 .A753 1980a

United States. Congress. House. Committee on the Budget. Military readiness and the Rapid Deployment Joint Task Force (RDJTF) . Washington , 1980. iii, 70 p. ; LC Card 80-604107 DDC 355.3/5 19
KF27 .B8 1980d

UNITED STATES - DEFENSES - PERIODICALS. United States. Joint Chiefs of Staff. United States military posture. [Washington] LC Card 79-642632 *NYPL [JLM 80-756]*

United States. Delegation to the Ad Hoc Meeting of the Canada-United States Interparliamentary Group, 1980, Ottawa,

Ont. Ad hoc meeting of the Canada-United States Interparliamentary Group to discuss international wheat marketing, July 26, 1980 : report / by the United States delegation, pursuant to Public Law 42, 96th Congress. Washington : U. S. G.P.O., 1981. v, 12 p. ; 24 cm. At head of title: 96th Congress, 2d session. Committee print. "Printed for the use of the Committee on Foreign Relations." "January 1981." Item 1039 LC Card 81-600997 DDC 382/.41311/0971 19
1. Wheat trade - Canada - Congresses. 2. Wheat trade - United States - Congresses. I. United States. Congress. Senate. Committee on Foreign Relations. II. Canada-United States Interparliamentary Group. III. Title.
HD9049.W5 C33 1980

United States. Dept. of Agricultural. Rural Development Service. see United States. Rural Development Service.

United States. Dept. of Agriculture. (Old Catalog form: United States. Agriculture Dept.

United States. Department of Agriculture. Agricultural Outlook Conference (1980 : Washington, D.C.) 1981 agricultural outlook . Washington , 1981. vi, 565 p. : LC Card 81-601003 DDC 338.1/0973 19
HD1755 .A38 1980

Agriculture Handbook.
(no. 516) Adhesives in building construction /. Washington, D.C. , 1978. iv, 160 p. : LC Card 77-600020 DDC 630 s 668/.3 19
S21 .A37 no. 516 TA455.A34

Agriculture information bulletin .
(no. 435) Lewis, James A., 1946- Landownership in the United States, 1978 /. [Washington, D.C.] [1980] ii, 98 p. : LC Card 80-602057 DDC 630 s 333.3/232/0973 19
S21 .A74 no. 435 HD205 1978

(no. 436) Henderson, Peter Louis, 1918- Farmer-to-consumer direct marketing in six states /. Washington, D.C. , 1980. iii, 44 p. ; LC Card 80-603170 DDC 630 s 381/.41/0973 19
S21 .A74 no. 436 HD9005

The Arkansas agricultural economist. v. 1-23, no. 1; Feb. 1959-Jan. 1980 (incomplete). [Little Rock] *NYPL [AM-10 159]*

Cutting energy costs. [Washington, D.C.] , 1980. x, 397 p. : LC Card 80-600168 DDC 630/.5 s 333.79 19
S21 .A35 1980 TJ163.4.U6

Food costs and wages the world over / United States Department of Agriculture. [Washington] : The Dept., [1979] 15 p. : ill. ; 22 cm. Cover title. LC Card 80-603156 DDC 338.4/36413 19
1. Food prices. 2. Wages. I. Title.
HD9000.4 .U476 1979

Foreign meat inspection. Washington. illus. 26 cm. Annual. "Report of the Secretary of Agriculture to the Committee on Agriculture, House of Representatives, and the Committee on Agriculture and Forestry, U. S. Senate." LC Card 79-640123
1. Meat inspection - United States - Periodicals. 2. Meat inspection - Periodicals. I. United States. Congress. House. Committee on Agriculture. II. United States. Congress. Senate. Committee on Agriculture and Forestry. III. Title. *NYPL [JLM 80-791]*

Henderson, Dennis R. Feeder calf production and marketing patterns, southeast Ohio/. [Columbus], 1974. iii, 41 leaves;
*NYPL [*ZT-1260]*

Miscellaneous publication.
(no. 1063) United States. Dept. of Agriculture. Office of Governmental and Public Affairs. Fact book of U. S. agriculture /. Washington, D.C. , 1979. viii, 119 p. ; LC Card 80-601547 DDC 630 s 338.1/0973 19
S21 .A46 no. 1063 1979 S441

(no. 1379) Holmes, Beatrice Hort. History of Federal water resources programs and policies, 1961-70 /. Washington, D.C. [1979] ix, 331 p. ; LC Card 80-601049 DDC 630 s 363.6 19
S21 .A46 no. 1379 HD1694.A5

(no. 867) United States. Agricultural Marketing Service. Tobacco in the United States. [Washington] [1979] 27 p. : LC Card 79-601924 DDC 633.7/1/0973 19
SB273 .U44 1979

Periodic reports of agricultural economics and statistics. Washington. *NYPL [JLM 80-812]*

Small-scale fuel alcohol production / prepared with the assistance of Development Planning and Research Associates. Washington, D.C. : U. S. Dept. of Agriculture, [1980] 221 p. in various pagings : graphs ; 28 cm. Includes bibliographical references. LC Card 80-601860 DDC 662/.669 19
1. Alcohol as fuel. I. Development Planning & Research Associates. II. Title.
TP358 .U7 1980

Statistical bulletin .
(no. 614) United States. Crop Reporting Board. Honey production . Washington, D.C. , 1978. 10 p. ; LC Card 80-601072 DDC 338.1/0973 s 338.1/7816/0973 19
HD1751 .A5 no. 614 HD9120.U52

(no. 631) United States. Economics, Statistics, and Cooperatives Service. U. S. fats and oils statistics, 1963-78. [Washington, D.C.] [1980] iv, 104 p. ; LC Card 80-601591 DDC 338.1/0973 s 338.1/7385/0973 19
HD1751 .A5 no. 631 HD9490.U6

(no. 632) Torgerson, David. Energy and U. S. agriculture, 1974 and 1978 /. [Washington, D.C.] [1980] ii, 115 p. ; LC Card 80-602126 DDC 338.1/0973 s 333.79 19
HD1751 .A5 no. 632 S494.5.E5

(no. 640) Holder, Shelby Herbert, 1931- U. S. rice distribution update /. Washington, D.C. [1980] ii, 50 p. ; LC Card 80-603201 DDC 338.1/0973 s 381/.41318/0973 19
HD1751 .A5 no. 640 HD9066.U45

Symposium on Rangeland Policies for the Future, Tucson, Ariz., 1979. Rangeland policies for the future . [Washington, D.C.] , 1979. v, 114 p. ; LC Card 80-600538 DDC 333.74/0973 19
HD241 .S95 1979

Tree Wardens, Arborists, and Utilities Conference, Chicopee, Mass., 1979. Proceedings of the Tree Wardens, Arborists, and Utilities Conference, March 13-15, 1979 /. [Amherst, Mass.] [1979] 94 p. : LC Card 80-622844 DDC 635.9/77 19
SB436 .T756 1979

U. S. agricultural export development efforts / prepared by the U. S. Department of Agriculture for the Committee on Agriculture, Nutrition, and Forestry, United States Senate. Washington : U. S. Govt. Print. Off., 1980. v, 36 p. : graphs ; 24 cm. At head of title: 96th Congress, 2d session. Committee print. "August 1980." LC Card 80-603056 DDC 382/.41/0973 19
1. Produce trade - United States. 2. Foreign trade promotion - United States. I. United States. Congress. Senate. Committee on Agriculture, Nutrition, and Forestry. II. Title.
HD9006 .U557 1980

Utilization research report .
(no. 5) Soybeans as human food . [Washington] , 1979. iv, 54 p. : LC Card 79-603033 DDC 641.3/5655 19
TX558.S7 S69 1979b

UNITED STATES. DEPT. OF AGRICULTURE. United States. Congress. Joint Economic Committee. Inflationary impact of Department of Agriculture paperwork . Washington , 1980. iii, 137 p. ; LC Card 80-603073 DDC 353.81 19
KF25 .E2 1980b

United States. Congress. Senate. Committee on Agriculture, Nutrition, and Forestry. Subcommittee on Environment, Soil Conservation, and Forestry. Resource Conservation and Development Act . Washington , 1980. iv, 206 p. : LC Card 80-603906 DDC 346.7304/4 347.30644 19
KF26 .A3543 1980d

United States. Congress. Senate. Select Committee on Small Business. Agricultural research policy . Washington , 1980. ii, 32 p. : LC Card 80-603264 DDC 630/.72073 19
S541 .U652 1980

United States. Dept. of Agriculture. Agricultural Marketing Service. see United States. Agricultural Marketing Service.

United States. Dept. of Agriculture. Agricultural Research Service. see United States. Agricultural Research Service.

United States. Dept. of Agriculture. Agricultural Stabilization and Conservation Service. see United States. Agricultural Stabilization and Conservation Service.

UNITED STATES. DEPT. OF AGRICULTURE - APPROPRIATIONS AND EXPENDITURES.
United States. Congress. Senate. Committee on Appropriations. Subcommittee on Agriculture, Rural Development, and Related Agencies. Agriculture, rural development, and related agencies appropriations for fiscal year 1981 . Washington , 1980. 3 v. : LC Card 80-603090 DDC 353.0072/23682/33 19
KF26 .A643 1980

UNITED STATES. DEPT. OF AGRICULTURE - BIBLIOGRAPHY.
Periodic reports of agricultural economics and statistics. Washington. *NYPL [JLM 80-812]*

United States. Dept. of Agriculture. Cooperative Marketing and Purchasing Division. Bunje, Ralph B. Cooperative farm bargaining and price negotiations /. Washington, D.C. , 1980. xviii, 194 p. ; LC Card 80-600078 DDC 334/.683/0688 19
HD9005 .B82

United States. Dept. of Agriculture. Economic Research Service. (Old Catalog form: United States. Agriculture Dept. Economic Research Service.)
Agricultural economic report. no. 1- Washington, 1961- LC Card 62-117

Farm real estate market developments. CD. 58-82; May 1961-Jan. 1978. Washington. 25 no. in 2 v. illus. 27 cm. Semiannual (slightly irregular) For earlier file, whose numbering it continues, see: United States. Agricultural Research Service. Current developments in the farm real estate market (in Old catalog) Title varies: 1961, Current developments in the farm real estate market, CD. Supplements included. For later file, which continues its numbering, see: United States. Dept. of Agriculture. Economics, Statistics and Cooperatives Service. Farm real estate market developments. CD.
1. Land use - United States - Periodicals. 2. Real estate business - United States - Periodicals. I. Title.
NYPL [M-10 7260]

Foreign agricultural trade of the United States. June, 1961-1977 (incomplete) Washington. 27 cm. Monthly. Formed by the union of: United States. Foreign Agricultural Relations Office. Foreign agricultural trade of the United States; digest, and: United States. Foreign Agricultural Relations Office. Foreign agricultural trade of the United States; statistical report (see those entries in Old Catalog). For later file, see: United States. Dept. of Agriculture. Economics, Statistics, and Cooperatives Service. FATUS; Foreign agricultural trade of the United States. Includes various supplements.
1. Produce Trade - United States - Periodicals. I. Title.

National food situation. NFS-96-161; May 1961-Sept. 1977. [Washington] 66 no. in 3 v. 28 cm. Quarterly. For earlier file, whose numbering it continues, see (in Old Catalog): United States. Agricultural Marketing Service. The National food situation. NFS. Superseded by National food review. LC Card 59-33311
1. Produce Trade - United States - Periodicals. I. Title.
NYPL [M-10 6174]

Poultry and egg situation. PES. 213-296; May 1961-1977. [Washington] illus. 27 cm. Bimonthly. For earlier file, whose numbering it continues, see: United States. Agricultural Marketing Service. Poultry and egg situation. PES. (in Old Catalog) Title varies slightly. For later file, which continues its numbering, see: United States. Dept. of Agriculture. Economics, Statistics and Cooperatives Service. Poultry and egg situation. PES.
1. Poultry industry - United States - Periodicals. 2. Egg trade - United States - Periodicals.
NYPL [M-10 6134]

United States. Dept. of Agriculture. Economic Research Service. Economic Development Divison. Voelker, Stanley W. Population changes within census county divisions of North Dakota, 1950-1970 /. Fargo, N.D. [Washington] , 1971. 23 leaves, [4] leaves of plates : LC Card 80-621261 DDC 312/.8/09784 19
HA566 .V63

United States. Dept. of Agriculture. Economics Division. see United States. Dept. of

Agriculture. Natural Resource Economics Division.

United States. Dept. of Agriculture. Economics, Statistics, and Cooperatives Service.
Agricultural economic report. no. 1- Washington, 1961- LC Card 62-117

An analysis of a ban on nitrite use in curing bacon. Washington : U. S. Dept. of Agriculture, Economics, Statistics, and Cooperatives Service ; Springfield, Va. : available from National Technical Information Service, 1979. iv, 23 p. ; 26 cm. (ESCS ; 48) Includes bibliographical references. LC Card 79-602021 DDC 338.1/0973 s 363.1/929 19
1. Bacon. 2. Nitrites. 3. Chemical preservatives. 4. Pork industry and trade - United States. I. Series: United States. Dept. of Agriculture. Economics, Statistics, and Cooperatives Service. ESCS , 48. II. Title.
HD1759 .U56a no. 48 HD9435.U52

Economics, statistics, cooperatives : program results and plans. [Washington, D.C.] : U. S. Dept. of Agriculture, Economics, Statistics, and Cooperative Services, [1979] iv, 59 p. : graphs ; 26 cm. Cover title. "December 1979." "ESCS-76." LC Card 80-601693 DDC 338.1/0973 19
1. Agriculture - Economic aspects - United States. I. Title.
HD1761 .U55 1979

ESCS .
(32) Daugherty, Arthur Berry, 1936- Open space preservation . Washington , Springfield, Va. , 1978. v, 32 p. ; LC Card 79-601799 DDC 338.1/0973 s 336.24/216 19
HD1759 .U56a no. 32 HJ4653.C73

(47) Grant, Warren R. Factors affecting supply, demand, and prices of U. S. rice /. Washington , 1979. iv, 57 p. : LC Card 79-602178 DDC 338.1/0973 s 338.1/7318/0973 19
HD1759 .U56a no. 47 HD9066.U45

(48) United States. Dept. of Agriculture. Economics, Statistics, and Cooperatives Service. An analysis of a ban on nitrite use in curing bacon. Washington , Springfield, Va. , 1979. iv, 23 p. ; LC Card 79-602021 DDC 338.1/0973 s 363.1/929 19
HD1759 .U56a no. 48 HD9435.U52

(60) ESCS Small-Farm Workshop, Alexandria, Va., 1978. Small-farm issues . Washington , Springfield, Va. , 1979. v, 73 p. : LC Card 79-602951 DDC 338.1/0973 s 338.1/6 19
HD1759 .U56a no. 60 HD1476.U5

(74) Roads of rural America /. Washington, D.C. , Springfield, Va. , 1979. iii, 57 p. : LC Card 80-602646 DDC 388.1/0973 19
HE355 .R57

Estimating agricultural costs of production--workshop proceedings. Washington, D.C. [1979] i, 82 p. ; LC Card 80-600979 DDC 338.1/3 19
S567 .E87

Global food assessment, 1980. Washington, D.C. : U. S. Dept. of Agriculture, Economics, Statistics, and Cooperatives Service, [1980] vii, 119 p. ; 26 cm. (Foreign agricultural economic report . no. 159) Cover title. "July 1980." LC Card 80-603393 DDC 338.1 s 338.1/9 19
1. Food supply. 2. Food industry and trade. I. Title. II. Series.
HD1411 .F59 no. 159 HD9000.5

Hager, Christine J. Textiles, U. S. trade agreements, imports, and consumption /. Washington, D.C. [1979] iii, 17 p. ; LC Card 80-601609 DDC 382/.45677/00973 19
HD9856 .H33

Henderson, Peter Louis, 1918- Farmer-to-consumer direct marketing in six states /. Washington, D.C. , 1980. iii, 44 p. ; LC Card 80-603170 DDC 630 s 381/.41/0973 19
S21 .A74 no. 436 HD9005

Holder, Shelby Herbert, 1931- U. S. rice distribution update /. Washington, D.C. [1980] ii, 50 p. ; LC Card 80-603201 DDC 338.1/0973 s 381/.41318/0973 19
HD1751 .A5 no. 640 HD9066.U45

Lewis, James A., 1946- Landownership in the United States, 1978 /. [Washington, D.C.] [1980] ii, 98 p. ; LC Card 80-602057 DDC 630 s

333.3/232/0973 19
S21 .A74 no. 435 HD205 1978

Roads of rural America /. Washington, D.C. , Springfield, Va. , 1979. iii, 57 p. : LC Card 80-602646 DDC 388.1/0973 19
HE355 .R57

Rowe, Gene A. The hired farm working force of 1977 /. Washington, D.C. , 1979. 53 p. : LC Card 79-604210 DDC 338.1 s 331.7/63/0973 19
HD1751 .A91854 no. 437 HD1525

Torgerson, David. Energy and U. S. agriculture, 1974 and 1978 /. [Washington, D.C.] [1980] ii, 115 p. ; LC Card 80-602126 DDC 338.1/0973 s 333.79 19
HD1751 .A5 no. 632 S494.5.E5

Update--impact of agricultural trade restrictions on the Soviet Union. [Washington, D.C.] [1980] 9 p. ; LC Card 80-603822 DDC 338.1 s 330.947/0853 19
HD1411 .F59 no. 160 HD9036

Voelker, Stanley W. A functional classification of agricultural trade centers in North Dakota /. Fargo [1978] 51 p. : LC Card 78-623601 DDC 338.1 s 381/.41/09784 19
SB205.S7 N64 no. 125 HT123.5.N9

United States. Dept. of Agriculture. Economics, Statistics, and Cooperatives Service. Cooperative Management Division. The changing financial structure of farmer cooperatives / Nelda Griffin ... [et al.]. Washington, D.C. : United States Dept. of Agriculture, Economics, Statistics, and Cooperatives Service, 1980. iv, 172 p. ; 26 cm. (Farmer cooperative research report . no. 17) Cover title. "March 1980." LC Card 80-602277 DDC 334/.683/0973 s 334/.683/0973 19
1. Agriculture, Cooperative - United States - Finance. I. Griffin, Nelda, 1925-. II. Title. III. Series.
HD1491.U5 F35 no. 17

United States. Dept. of Agriculture. Economics, Statistics, and Cooperatives Service. Economic Development Division. ESCS Small-Farm Workshop, Alexandria, Va., 1978. Small-farm issues . Washington , Springfield, Va. , 1979. v, 73 p. : LC Card 79-602951 DDC 338.1/0973 s 338.1/6 19
HD1759 .U56a no. 60 HD1476.U5

United States. Dept. of Agriculture. Economics, Statistics, and Cooperatives Service. National Economic Analysis Division. Economic effects of a prohibition on the use of selected animal drugs / [National Economic Analysis Division, Economics, Statistics, and Cooperatives Service, U. S. Department of Agriculture]. Washington, D.C. : The Service, 1978. iv, 68 p. : graphs ; 27 cm. (Agricultural economic report . no. 414) Includes bibliographical references. LC Card 79-603395 DDC 338.1 s 338.1/76/00973 19
1. Medicated feeds - Economic aspects - United States. I. Title. II. Series.
HD1751 .A91854 no. 414 SF98.M4

National food review. NFR-1- ; 1978- [Washington] LC Card 78-643276
NYPL [JLM 80-1081]

United States. Dept. of Agriculture. Economics, Statistics, and Cooperatives Service. National Economics Division. The Cotton industry in the United States . [Washington, D.C.] , Lubbock, Tex. , 1980. v, 76 p. : LC Card 80-622867 DDC 338.1/7351/0973 19
HD9875 .C74

United States. Dept. of Agriculture. Economics, Statistics & Cooperatives Services. Crop Reporting Board. see United States. Crop Reporting Board.

United States. Dept. of Agriculture. Extension Service (1970-) see United States. Extension Service (1970-)

United States. Dept. of Agriculture. Farmers Home Administration. see United States. Farmers Home Administration.

United States. Dept. of Agriculture. Federal Extension Service. see United States. Federal Extension Service.

United States. Dept. of Agriculture. Food and Nutrition Service. see United States. Food and Nutrition Service.

BIBLIOGRAPHIC GUIDE

United States. Dept. of Agriculture. Foreign Agricultural Service.

510

United States. Dept. of Agriculture. Foreign Agricultural Service. (1953-) see United States. Foreign Agricultural Service (1953-)

United States. Dept. of Agriculture. Forest Service. see United States. Forest Service.

United States. Dept. of Agriculture. Governmental and Public Affairs, Office of. see United States. Dept. of Agriculture. Office of Governmental and Public Affairs.

United States. Dept. of Agriculture. National Agricultural Library. see United States. National Agricultural Library.

United States. Dept. of Agriculture. Natural Resource Economics Division. Foreign ownership of U. S. agricultural land / [Natural Resource Economics Division, Economics, Statistics, and Cooperatives Service, U. S. Department of Agriculture]. Washington, D.C. : The Service, 1980. iv, 33 p. : form ; 26 cm. (Agricultural economic report . no. 447) Cover title. Prepared by Marilyn E. Eichler ... [et al.]. "February 1980." Page 33 is p. 3 of cover. Includes bibliographical references. LC Card 80-601679 DDC 338.1 s 333.33/5 19
1. Farms - United States - Foreign ownership. I. Eichler, Marilyn E. II. Title. III. Series.
HD1751 .A91854 no. 447 HD205 1980

United States. Dept. of Agriculture. Office of Communication.
Fact book of U. S. Agriculture. United States. Dept. of Agriculture. Office of Governmental and Public Affairs. Fact book of U. S. agriculture / compiled from Department sources by the Office of Governmental and Public Affairs. Rev. Washington, D.C. , 1979. vii, 119 p. ; LC Card 80-601547 DDC 630 s 338.1/0973 19
S21 .A46 no. 1063 1979 S441

United States. Dept. of Agriculture. Office of Foreign Agricultural Relations. see United States. Office of Foreign Agricultural Relations.

United States. Dept. of Agriculture. Office of Governmental and Public Affairs. Fact book of U. S. agriculture / compiled from Department sources by the Office of Governmental and Public Affairs. Rev. Washington, D.C. : U. S. Dept. of Agriculture : for sale by the Supt. of Docs., U. S. Govt. Print. Off., 1979. vii, 119 p. ; 24 cm. (Miscellaneous publication - United States Department of Agriculture ; no. 1063) Edition for 1976 by the Office of Communication, U. S. Dept. of Agriculture. LC Card 80-601547 DDC 630 s 338.1/0973 19
1. Agriculture - United States. 2. Agriculture - Economic aspects - United States. I. United States. Dept. of Agriculture. Office of Communication. Fact book of U. S. Agriculture. II. Series: United States. Dept. of Agriculture. Miscellaneous publication, no. 1063. III. Title.
S21 .A46 no. 1063 1979 S441

United States. Dept. of Agriculture. Office of the Special Coordinator for Grain Elevator Safety and Security. Prevention of dust explosions in grain elevators--an achievable goal : a task force report. [Washington] : United States Dept. of Agriculture, Office of the Special Coordinator for Grain Elevator Safety and Security, [1980] xii, 172 p. : ill. ; 28 cm. Cover title. Includes bibliographical references. LC Card 80-601550 DDC 363.1/89 19
1. Grain elevators - Fires and fire prevention. 2. Grain elevators - Dust control. I. Title.
TH9445.G7 U54 1980

United States. Dept. of Agriculture. Rural Electrification Administration. see United States. Rural Electrification Administration.

United States. Dept. of Agriculture. Science and Education Administration. see United States. Science and Education Administration.

United States. Dept. of Agriculture. Soil Conservation Service. see United States. Soil Conservation Service.

United States. Dept. of Agriculture. Statistical Reporting Service. Crop Reporting Board. see United States. Crop Reporting Board.

United States. Dept. of Commerce. (Old Catalog form: United States. Commerce Dept.)
Earl R. Combs Inc. A study to determine the export and domestic markets for currently underutilized fish and shellfish /. [Washington] 1978 [i. e. 1979] xxxv, 416 p. : LC Card 79-603273 *NYPL [JLF 81-419]*

The Economic impact of pollution control. [Washington?] 1972. 332 p. LC Card 72-601528
TD180 .E25 *NYPL [JLF 81-274]*

United States. Dept. of Commerce. Task Force on Corporate Social Perfomance. Business and society . [Washington, D.C.?] , 1980 [i.e. 1981] xviii, 193 p. : LC Card 81-601109 DDC 658.4/08/0973 19
HD60.5.U5 U55 1981

United States. Dept. of Commerce. Task Force on Product Liability and Accident Compensation. Report on product liability insurance ratemaking /. Washington, D.C. , 1980. xxiv, 164, [250] p. : LC Card 81-601189 DDC 368.5 19
HG9995.3 .U63 1980

United States. President's Export Council. The export imperative . Washington, D.C. , 1980. 2 v. : LC Card 81-600767 DDC 382/.63/0973 19
HF1455 .U475 1980

United States. Dept. of Commerce. Bureau of Standards. see United States. National Bureau of Standards.

United States. Dept. of Commerce. Area Redevelopment Administration. see United States. Area Redevelopment Administration.

United States. Dept. of Commerce. Bureau of Economic Analysis. see United States. Bureau of Economic Analysis.

United States. Dept. of Commerce. Bureau of International Commerce. see United States. Bureau of International Commerce.

United States. Dept. of Commerce. Bureau of Mines. see United States. Bureau of Mines.

United States. Dept. of Commerce. Bureau of the Census. see United States. Bureau of the Census.

United States. Dept. of Commerce. Economic Development Administration. see United States. Economic Development Administration.

United States. Dept. of Commerce. Environmental Affairs, Office of. see United States. Dept. of Commerce. Office of Environmental Affairs.

United States Department of Commerce final environmental impact statement . United States. Maritime Administration. [Washington] [1979] ca. 350 p. in various pagings : LC Card 79-602128 DDC 333.91/1/0973 19
TD427.P4 U58 1979

United States. Dept. of Commerce. Industry and Trade Administration. see United States. Industry and Trade Administration.

United States. Dept. of Commerce. Interagency Study Group. Economic study of Puerto Rico : report to the President / prepared by the Interagency Task Force coordinated by the United States Department of Commerce. [Washington] : The Dept. : for sale by the Supt. of Docs., U. S. Govt. Print. Off., 1979. 2 v. : ill. ; 27 cm. Includes bibliographical references. LC Card 80-601545 DDC 330.97295/053 19
1. Puerto Rico - Economic conditions - 1952-. I. Title.
HC154.5 .U54 1979

United States. Dept. of Commerce. Interagency Task Force on Product Liability. see United States. Interagency Task Force on Product Liability.

United States. Dept. of Commerce. Maritime Administration. see United States. Maritime Administration.

United States. Dept. of Commerce. Minority Business Development Agency. see United States. Minority Business Development Agency.

United States. Dept. of Commerce. National Bureau of Standards. see United States. National Bureau of Standards.

United States. Dept. of Commerce. National Oceanic and Atmospheric Administration. see United States. National Oceanic and Atmospheric Administration.

United States. Dept. of Commerce. National Technical Information Service. see United States. National Technical Information Service.

United States. Dept. of Commerce. Office of Environmental Affairs.
Marketing and financing aspects of resource recovery / U. S. Department of Commerce, Office of Environmental Affairs. [Washington, D.C.] : The Office, 1980. 63 p. ; 27 cm. : LC Card 80-601647 DDC 338.4/36046/0973 19
1. Waste products - United States - Abstracts. 2. Recycling (Waste, etc.) - United States - Abstracts. I. Title.
HD9975.U52 U54 1980

US/USSR Environmental Economics Symposium. Proceedings. 1st- [Washington] 1978- LC Card 79-602348
NYPL [JLM 80-1005]

United States. Dept. of Commerce. Office of Federal Statistical Policy and Standards. see United States. Office of Federal Statistical Policy and Standards.

United States. Dept. of Commerce. Office of Minority Business Enterprise. see United States. Office of Minority Business Enterprise.

United States. Dept. of Commerce. Office of Technical Services. Joint Publications Research Service. see United States. Joint Publications Research Service.

United States. Dept. of Commerce. Office of the Assistant Secretary for Policy. Consad Research Corporation. A study of public works investment in the United States /. [Washington] , 1980. 826 p. in various pagings : LC Card 80-603199 DDC 336.3/9/0973 19
HD3885 .C66 1980

UNITED STATES. DEPT. OF COMMERCE - OFFICIALS AND EMPLOYEES.
United States. Congress. Senate. Committee on Banking, Housing and Urban Affairs. Nominations of Robert E. Herzstein, Frank B. Sollars, Alexis M. Herman, and Alfred R. Marane . Washington , 1980. iii, 78 p. ; LC Card 80-603063 DDC 353.82 19
KF26 .B39 1980i

United States. Congress. Senate. Committee on Banking, Housing and Urban Affairs. Nominations of Herta Lande Seidman and Stephen J. Friedman . Washington , 1980. iii, 53 p. ; LC Card 80-602446 DDC 353.82 19
KF26 .B39 1980c

United States. Congress. Senate. Committee on Commerce, Science, and Transportation. Nomination--deputy secretary of commerce . Washington , 1981. iii, 8 p. ; LC Card 81-601776 DDC 353.82 19
KF26 .C69 1981c

United States. Congress. Senate. Committee on Commerce, Science, and Transportation. Nomination--secretary of commerce . Washington , 1981. iii, 46 p. ; LC Card 81-600818 DDC 353.82 19
KF26 .C69 1981a

United States. Congress. Senate. Committee on Commerce, Science, and Transportation. Nominations--assistant secretaries of commerce . Washington , 1981. iii, 4 p. ; LC Card 81-602035 DDC 353.82 19
KF26 .C69 1981h

United States. Congress. Senate. Committee on Commerce, Science, and Transportation. Nominations--Department of Commerce and Federal Maritime Commission . Washington , 1980. iii, 81 p. ; LC Card 80-601935 DDC 353.82 19
KF26 .C69 1979ak

United States. Congress. Senate. Committee on Commerce, Science, and Transportation. Nominations--Departments of Commerce and Transportation . Washington , 1981. iii, 5 p. ; LC Card 81-601952 DDC 353.82 19
KF26 .C69 1981g

United States. Congress. Senate. Committee on Finance. Nominations of Abraham Katz, William J. Driver, and John L. Palmer . Washington , 1980. iii, 19 p. ; LC Card 80-602760 DDC 353.842 19
KF26 .F5 1980b

GOVERNMENT PUBLICATIONS - U.S.: 1981

511   *United States. Dept. of Defense - Officials and employees.*

United States. Congress. Senate. Committee on Finance. Nominations of Robert E. Herzstein, C. Moxley Featherston, William M. Fay, Charles R. Simpson, Edna Parker, and Sheldon V. Ekman . Washington , 1980. iii, 80 p. ; LC Card 80-603685 DDC 353.0072/4 19
KF26 .F5 1980f

United States. Dept. of Commerce. Task Force on Corporate Social Perfomance. Business and society : strategies for the 1980's : report of the Task Force on Corporate Social Performance. [Washington, D.C.?] : U. S. Dept. of Commerce, 1980 [i.e. 1981] xviii, 193 p. : charts ; 24 cm. "December 1980." Includes index. Item 128 Bibliography: p. 177-183. LC Card 81-601109 DDC 658.4/08/0973 19
1. Industry - Social aspects - United States - Addresses, essays, lectures. I. United States. Dept. of Commerce. II. Title.
HD60.5.U5 U55 1981

United States. Dept. of Commerce. Task Force on Corporate Social Performance. Corporate social reporting in the United States and Western Europe : report of the Task Force on Corporate Social Performance. [Washington, D.C.] : U. S. Dept. of Commerce, 1979. xii, 177 p. ; 23 cm. Bibliography: p. 166-172. Includes index. LC Card 79-604245
1. Industry - Social aspects - United States. 2. Industry - Social aspects - Europe. I. Title.
HD60.5.U5 U55 1979   NYPL [JLE 81-481]

United States. Dept. of Commerce. Task Force on Product Liability and Accident Compensation.
Report on product liability insurance ratemaking / U. S. Department of Commerce, Task Force on Product Liability and Accident Compensation. Washington, D.C. : The Dept. : For sale by the Supt. of Docs., U. S. G.P.O., 1980. xxiv, 164, [250] p. : forms ; 28 cm. S/N 003-000-00565-5 Includes bibliographical references. LC Card 81-601189 DDC 368.5 19
1. Insurance, Products liability - United States - Rates and tables. I. United States. Dept. of Commerce.
HG9995.3 .U63 1980

Uniform product liability act : a model for the States. [Washington] : U. S. Dept. of Commerce, Task Force on Product Liability and Accident Compensation : for sale by the Supt. of Docs., U. S. Govt. Print. Off., 1979. 44 p. ; 31 cm. "Victor E. Schwartz, chairman." LC Card 80-601839 DDC 346.7303/82 19
1. Products liability - United States. I. Schwartz, Victor E. II. United States. Laws, statutes, etc. Uniform product liability act. 1979. III. Title.
KF1296 .A8168

United States. Dept. of Defense. (Old Catalog form: United States. Defense Dept.) Basic research program / Department of Defense. [Washington, D.C.?] : The Dept., [1980] 71 p. : ill. ; 28 cm. Cover title. "1 August 1980." LC Card 80-603588 DDC 355/.07/0973 19
1. Military research - United States. 2. Research - United States. I. Title.
.U393 .U524 1980

Berry, J. F. Managing knowledge as a corporate resource /. [Washington] 1976. 68 p.:
*NYPL [*XME-9312]*

The effects of nuclear weapons /. [Washington] , 1977. 653 p. : LC Card 78-600832
UF767 .E33 1977   NYPL [JSE 81-290]

Steadman, Richard C. The national military command structure . Washington , 1978. iii, 79 p. ; LC Card 79-602790
UA23.3 .S73

UNITED STATES. DEPT. OF DEFENSE. UNITED STATES. DEPARTMENT OF DEFENSE.
Steadman, Richard C. The national military command structure . Washington , 1978. iii, 79 p. ; LC Card 79-602790
UA23.3 .S73

United States. Congress. House. Committee on Armed Services. Procurement and Military Nuclear Systems Subcommittee. Coordination of Department of Energy/Department of Defense nuclear weapons materials requirements . Washington , 1980. ii, 23 p. ; LC Card 80-602992 DDC 355.8/25119/0973 19
KF27 .A7657 1980c

United States. Congress. House. Committee on Armed Services. Subcommittee on Investigations. Department of Defense petroleum requirements and supplies . Washington , 1980. iii, 17 p. ; LC Card 80-603555 DDC 355.2/4/0973 19
UC263 .U517 1980

United States. Congress. House. Committee on Banking, Finance and Urban Affairs. Subcommittee on Economic Stabilization. Defense Production Act Amendments of the Energy Security Act of 1980 . Washington , 1980. iii, 114 p. : LC Card 80-604041 DDC 343.73/07866266/0262 347.30378662660262 19
KF27 .B542 1980b

United States. Congress. Senate. Committee on Governmental Affairs. Federal Interagency Medical Resources Sharing and Coordination Act of 1980 . Washington , 1980. iv, 324 p. : LC Card 80-604081 DDC 343.73/0115 347.303115 19
KF26 .G67 1980k

United States. General Accounting Office. The Congress should mandate formation of a military-VA-civilian contingency hospital system . Washington, D.C. [1980] vi, 51 p. ; LC Card 80-602693 DDC 355.3/45/0973 19
RA981.A2 U53 1980

United States. Dept. of Defense. Advanced Research Projects Agency. see United States. Advanced Research Projects Agency.

United States. Dept. of Defense. Advisory Group on Electron Devices. see United States. Advisory Group on Electron Devices.

UNITED STATES. DEPT. OF DEFENSE - APPROPRIATIONS AND EXPENDITURES.
United States. Congress. House. Committee on Appropriations. Subcommittee on Military Construction Appropriations. Military construction appropriations for 1982 . Washingon , 1981. 2 v. : LC Card 81-601195 DDC 358/.22/0973 19
KF27 .A655 1981

United States. Congress. House. Committee on Armed Services. Hearings on H.R. 8390 . Washington , 1977. ii, 471 p. : LC Card 78-601218
KF27 .A7 1977q

United States. Congress. House. Committee on Armed Services. Hearings on military posture and H.R. 6495 (H.R. 6974) Department of Defense authorization for appropriations for fiscal year 1981 before the Committee on Armed Services, House of Representatives, Ninety-sixth Congress, second session. Washington , 1980- v. in : LC Card 80-602996 DDC 355.6/22/0973 19
KF27 .A7 1980

United States. Congress. House. Committee on Armed Services. Subcommitee on Investigations. National defense funding levels for fiscal year 1981 . Washington , 1980. ii, 27 p. ; LC Card 80-602709 DDC 355.6/22/0973 19
KF27 .A753 1980a

United States. Congress. House. Committee on Armed Services. Subcommittee on Military Installations and Facilities. Hearings on H.R. 6493 (H.R. 7301) ... and fiscal year 1980 supplemental request, and fiscal year 1981 Budget amendment for the Military construction program before the Military Istallations and Facilities Subcommittee of the Committee on Armed Services, House of Representatives, Ninety-sixth Congress, second session. Washington , 1980. liii, 662, x p. : LC Card 80-602757 DDC 355.6/22/0973 19
KF27 .A76397 1980a

United States. Congress. Senate. Committee on Appropriations. Subcommittee on Military Construction. MX missile basing mode . Washington , 1980. iii, 269 p. : LC Card 80-604099 DDC 358/.174/0973 19
KF26 .A655 1980

United States. Congress. Senate. Committee on Armed Services. Department of Defense authorization for appropriations for fiscal year 1981 . Washington , 1980- v. : LC Card 80-602755 DDC 355.6/22/0973 19
KF26 .A7 1980a

United States. Congress. Senate. Committee on Armed Services. Department of Defense authorization for appropriations for fiscal year 1982 . Washington , 1981- v. <1-2> : LC Card 81-601875 DDC 353.0072/234 19
KF26 .A7 1981e

United States. Congress. Senate. Committee on Armed Services. Subcommittee on Military Construction and Stockpiles. Military construction authorization, fiscal year 1981 . Washington , 1980. iv, 694, xv p. : LC Card 80-603503 DDC 355.6/22/0973 19
KF26 .A756 1980

United States. Dept. of Defense. Assistant Secretary of Defense (International Security Affairs) see United States. Assistant Secretary of Defense (International Security Affairs)

UNITED STATES. DEPT. OF DEFENSE - AUDITING AND INSPECTION.
United States. General Accounting Office. Correct balance of Defense's foreign military sales trust fund unknown . Washington, DC [1980] iii, 23 p. ; LC Card 80-602832 DDC 355/.032/0973 19
UA12 .U527 1980

United States. Dept. of Defense. Defense Advanced Research Projects Agency. see United States. Defense Advanced Research Projects Agency.

United States. Dept. of Defense. Defense Documentation Center. see United States. Defense Documentation Center.

United States. Dept. of Defense. Defense Logistics Agency. see United States. Defense Logistics Agency.

United States. Dept. of Defense. Defense Supply Agency. see United States. Defense Supply Agency.

United States. Dept. of Defense. Dept. of the Army. see United States. Dept. of the Army.

United States. Dept. of Defense. Dept. of the Navy. see United States. Navy Dept.

United States. Dept. of Defense. Historical Office. Kaplan, Lawrence S. A community of interests . Washington, D.C. , 1980. xii, 251 p. : LC Card 81-600535 DDC 355/.032/4 19
UA12 .K28

UNITED STATES. DEPT. OF DEFENSE - MANAGEMENT.
Daleski, Richard J. Defense management in the 1980s . Washington, D.C. , 1980. vi, 57 p. : LC Card 81-600682 DDC 355.6/0973 19
UA23.6 .D34

United States. Dept. of Defense. Office of the Assistant Secretary of Defense (Manpower, Reserve Affairs, and Logistics) see United States. Office of the Assistant Secretary of Defense (Manpower, Reserve Affairs, and Logistics)

UNITED STATES. DEPT. OF DEFENSE - OFFICIALS AND EMPLOYEES.
Daleski, Richard J. Defense management in the 1980s . Washington, D.C. , 1980. vi, 57 p. : LC Card 81-600682 DDC 355.6/0973 19
UA23.6 .D34

United States. Congress. Senate. Committee on Armed Services. Nomination of Caspar W. Weinberger to be Secretary of Defense . Washington , 1981. iii, 61 p. ; LC Card 81-600831 DDC 353.6 19
KF26 .A7 1981

United States. Congress. Senate. Committee on Armed Services. Nomination of Frank C. Carlucci III to be Deputy Secretary of Defense . Washington , 1981. ii, 45 p. ; LC Card 81-600832 DDC 353.6 19
KF26 .A7 1981a

United States. Congress. Senate. Committee on Armed Services. Nomination of Jack R. Borsting . Washington , 1980. 6 p. ; LC Card 80-603338 DDC 353.6 19
KF26 .A7 1980d

United States. Congress. Senate. Committee on Armed Services. Nominations of Fred C. Ikle, to be under secretary of defense for policy, and William H. Taft, IV, to be general counsel of the Department of Defense . Washington , 1981. ii, 24 p. ; LC Card 81-602261 DDC 353.6

19
KF26 .A7 1981f

United States. Congress. Senate. Committee on Armed Services. Nominations of Michael Blumenfeld, John A. Bushnell, John W. Clark, Clifford B. O'Hara, William Sidell, Robinson O. Everett, and William E. Peacock . Washington , 1980. ii, 49 p. ;   LC Card 80-602497 DDC 353.0087/6444 19
KF26 .A7 1980c

United States. Dept. of Education.
Facts; official publication of the U. S. Department of Education. May 1980- [Washington]   *NYPL [Econ. Div.]*

Gill, Clark C. The educational system of Costa Rica /. Washington, D.C. , 1980. iii, 30 p. :   LC Card 80-603837 DDC 370/.97286 19
LA446 .G46

Smith, B. Othanel (Bunnie Othanel) A design for a school of pedagogy /. Washington, D.C. , 1980. ix, 118 p. :   LC Card 80-603928 DDC 370/.7/30973 19
LB1715 .S47

Veltman, Calvin J. The role of language characteristics in the socioeconomic attainment process of Hispanic origin men and women /. [Washington, D.C.?] , 1980. iv, 103 p. ;   LC Card 81-601023 DDC 305.8/68073 19
E184.S75 V44

United States. Dept. of Education. Office for Civil Rights. Directory of elementary and secondary school districts, and schools in selected school districts . Washington, D.C. , 1980. 2 v. (xlvii, 1605 p.) ;   LC Card 81-601659 DDC 379.1/535 19
L901 .D5116

UNITED STATES. DEPT. OF EDUCATION - OFFICIALS AND EMPLOYEES.
United States. Congress. Senate. Committee on Governmental Affairs. Nomination of James Bert Thomas, Jr. . Washington , 1980 [i.e. 1981] iii, 33 p. ;   LC Card 81-601163 DDC 353.844 19
KF26 .G67 1980n

United States. Congress. Senate. Committee on Labor and Human Resources. Nomination . Washington , 1980. ii, 29 p. :   LC Card 80-602538 DDC 353.842 19
KF26 .L27 1980b

United States. Congress. Senate. Committee on Labor and Human Resources. Nomination . Washington , 1981. 114 p. ;   LC Card 81-601605 DDC 353.844 19
KF26 .L27 1981a

United States. Congress. Senate. Committee on Labor and Human Resources. Nominations . Washington , 1980. ii, 122 p. ;   LC Card 80-602807 DDC 353.844 19
KF26 .L27 1980e

United States. Congress. Senate. Committee on Labor and Human Resources. Nominations . Washington , 1980. ii, 86 p. ;   LC Card 80-603445 DDC 353.842 19
KF26 .L27 1980h

United States. Congress. Senate. Committee on Labor and Human Resources. Nominations . Washington , 1980. ii, 54 p. ;   LC Card 80-603437 DDC 353.844 19
KF26 .L27 1980g

United States. Dept. of Energy.
Earth covered buildings . [Washington, D.C.] [Springfield, Va. , foreword 1979] vi, 272 p. :   LC Card 79-600114 DDC 690 19
TH4819.E27 E38

Earth covered buildings and settlements /. [Washington, D.C.] [Springfield, Va. , 1979?] iv, 355 p. :   LC Card 79-600115 DDC 690 19
TH4819.E27 E37

The effects of nuclear weapons /. [Washington] , 1977. 653 p. :   LC Card 78-600832
UF767 .E33 1977   *NYPL [JSE 81-290]*

Energy insider. v. 1, no. 25- ; Sept. 18, 1978- Washington.   *NYPL [Econ. Div.]*

Erley, Duncan. Site planning for solar access . [Washington] [1979] 149 p. :   LC Card 80-600615
TH7414 .E74   *NYPL [JSF 81-159]*

Final report to the President on oil supply shortages during 1979. Washington, D.C. : U. S. Dept. of Energy : for sale by the Supt. of Docs., U. S. Govt. Print. Off., [1980] 58 p. : graphs ; 28 cm. "DOE/S-0011." "July 1980."   LC Card 80-602863 DDC 338.2/7282/0973 19
1. Petroleum industry and trade - United States. 2. Petroleum products - United States. I. Title.
HD9566 .U533 1980

Hawkins, Donna. Energy in Mexico . Golden, Colo. , Washington, D.C. [1980] 35 p. ;   LC Card 80-602377 DDC 333.79/23/0972 19
TJ810 .H363

International Conference on Nuclear Cross Sections for Technology (1979 : University of Tennessee) Nuclear cross sections for technology . [Washington, D.C.?] , 1980. xvi, 1039 p. :   LC Card 80-600128 DDC 602/.18 s 539.7/54 19
QC100 .U57 no. 594 QC794.6.C7

Lewis, R. E. Geothermal resources in the Banbury Hot Springs area, Twin Falls County, Idaho /. Reston, Va. , 1981. p. cm.   LC Card 81-607876 DDC 553.7/09796/37 19
GB1199.7.I2 L48

Motor gasoline deregulation and the gasoline tilt : final environmental impact statement. [Washington] : U. S. Dept. of Energy, 1979- v. ; 28 cm. Cover title. "DOE/EIS-0039." Includes bibliographical references.   LC Card 79-602143
1. Gasoline supply - United States. 2. Petroleum industry and trade - Environmental aspects - United States. 3. Environmental impact statements. I. Title.
HD9579.G4 U52 1979a

Oregon. State University, Corvallis. Federal Cooperative Extension Service. Oregon Energy Extension Service State plan /. [Corvallis] [1980] 38 p. :   LC Card 80-621871 DDC 630/.9795 s 333.79/16/09795 19
S105 .E43 no. 569 TJ163.4.U6

Solar energy objectives, calendar year 1980 / Department of Energy. Washington, D.C. : The Dept. : for sale by the Supt. of Docs., U. S. Govt. Print. Off., 1980. iii, 354, 73 p. ; 28 cm. "DOE/CS-0155." "April 1980." Includes bibliographical references.   LC Card 80-602116 DDC 333.79/23/0973 19
1. Solar energy policy - United States. I. Title.
HD9681.U62 U53 1980

Symposium on Biotechnology in Energy Production and Conservation, 1st, Gatlinburg, Tenn., 1978. Biotechnology in energy production and conservation . New York , c1979. vi, 513 p. :   ISBN 0-471-05745-2 (pbk.)   LC Card 80-128733
TJ163.7 .S97 1978   *NYPL [JSE 80-1362]*

Transcript from the National Hearings on the Federal nonnuclear energy R&D program . Washington, D.C. , 1980 i.e. 1981. xix, 207 p. :   LC Card 81-601492 DDC 333.79/23/0973 19
HD9502.U52 T7

United States/Canada electricity exchanges / prepared by United States Department of Energy, Canadian Department of Energy, Mines, and Resources. [Oak Ridge, Tenn.] : U. S. Dept. of Energy ; Washington : for sale by the Supt. of Docs., U. S. Govt. Print. Off., 1979. iii, 103, [120] p., [2] leaves of plates : ill., maps (2 fold.) ; 28 cm. "DOE/ERA-0053, Dist. category UC-66j." Includes bibliographical references.   LC Card 79-602608
1. Electric utilities - United States. 2. Electric utilities - Canada. I. Canada. Dept. of Energy, Mines and Resources. II. Title.
HD9685.U5 U495 1979 NYPL [JLF 81-451]

United States/Mexico electricity exchanges / prepared by United States Department of Energy [and] Comision Federal De Electricidad. Washington, D.C. : The Dept., [1980] 242 p. in various pagings : ill. ; 28 cm. "May 1980." "DOE/RG-0033." On spine: Electricity exchanges, United States/Mexico.   LC Card 80-603171 DDC 382/.45621319/0972 19
1. Electric utilities - United States. 2. Electric utilities - Mexico. I. México. Comisión Federal de Electricidad. II. Title. III. Title: Electricity exchanges, United States/Mexico.
HD9685.U5 U495 1980

UNITED STATES. DEPT. OF ENERGY.
Transcript from the national hearing on the Federal nonnuclear energy RD&D program .

Washington, D.C. , 1980. xv, 161 p. ;   LC Card 81-600788 DDC 333.79/15/0973 19
TD195.E49 T7

United States. Congress. House. Committee on Armed Services. Procurement and Military Nuclear Systems Subcommittee. Coordination of Department of Energy/Department of Defense nuclear weapons materials requirements . Washington , 1980. ii, 23 p. ;   LC Card 80-602992 DDC 355.8/25119/0973 19
KF27 .A7657 1980c

United States. Congress. House. Committee on Banking, Finance and Urban Affairs. Subcommittee on Economic Stabilization. Defense Production Act Amendments of the Energy Security Act of 1980 . Washington , 1980. iii, 114 p. :   LC Card 80-604041 DDC 343.73/07866266/0262 347.30378662660262 19
KF27 .B542 1980b

United States. Congress. House. Committee on Government Operations. Environment, Energy, and National Resources Subcommittee. Department of Energy's emergency energy conservation programs . Washington , 1980 [i.e. 1981] iii, 200 p. :   LC Card 81-600860 DDC 333.79/17/0973 19
KF27 .G655 1980f

United States. Congress. House. Committee on Government Operations. Environment, Energy, and Natural Resources Subcommittee. Department of Energy gasohol policy . Washington , 1980. iii, 175 p. :   LC Card 80-603776 DDC 333.8/232 19
KF27 .G655 1980d

United States. Congress. House. Committee on Government Operations. Environment, Energy, and Natural Resources Subcommittee. Home heating oil price and supply issues, the Department of Energy's record . Washington , 1980. iii, 216 p. ;   LC Card 80-603000 DDC 338.4/36655384 19
KF27 .G655 1980

United States. Congress. House. Committee on Government Operations. Environment, Energy, and Natural Resources Subcommittee. The petroleum import fee, Department of Energy Oversight . Washington , 1980. iii, 271 p. :   LC Card 80-602747 DDC 382/.42282/0973 19
KF27 .G655 1980a

United States. Congress. House. Committee on Interstate and Foreign Commerce. Subcommittee on Energy and Power. West Valley Demonstration Project Act . Washington , 1980. iv, 173 p. :   LC Card 80-603899 DDC 344.73/04622 347.3044622 19
KF27 .I5542 1980m

United States. Congress. House. Committee on Interstate and Foreign Commerce. Subcommittee on Oversight and Investigations. DOE gasoline allocation regulations and enforcement . Washington , 1980. iii, 216 p. :   LC Card 80-604027 DDC 353.0082/6566553827 19
KF27 .I5547 1980m

United States. Congress. House. Committee on Science and Technology. Subcommittee on Energy Development and Applications. Oversight, DOE solar and conservation programs . Washington , 1980. iii, 210 p. :   LC Card 81-600834 DDC 353.0082/3 19
KF27 .S3934 1980e

United States. Congress. House. Committee on Science and Technology. Subcommittee on Energy Research and Production. The Department of Energy's public information programs . Washington , 1980 [i.e. 1981] vii, 34 p. ;   LC Card 81-601001 DDC 353.87 19
HD9502.U52 U5 1980a

United States. Congress. House. Committee on Small Business. Subcommittee on Energy, Environment, Safety and Research. DOE petroleum allocation regulations--new stations vs. allocation problems for existing stations . Washington , 1980 [i.e. 1981] iv, 233 p. :   LC Card 81-600975 DDC 346.7304/68232 347.306468232 19
KF27 .S639 1980

United States. Congress. Office of Technology Assessment. Conservation and solar energy programs of the Department of Energy . Washington, D.C. [1980] viii, 80 p. :   LC Card

80-600092
TJ163.4.U6 U5445 1980
                    NYPL [JSF 80-1097]

United States. Congress. Senate. Committee on
Appropriations. Subcommittee on
HUD-Independent Agencies. Nuclear and
hazardous waste problems in New Hampshire .
Washington , 1980 [i.e. 1981] iii, 122 p. ; LC
    Card 81-601754   DDC 363.7/28 19
KF26 .A6486 1980b

United States. Congress. Senate. Committee on
Governmental Affairs. Transfer of authorities
for implementation of building energy
performance standards . Washington , 1980. iii,
196 p. : LC Card 80-601881   DDC 353.0082/32 19
KF26 .G67 1979aj

United States. Congress. Senate. Committee on
Governmental Affairs. Permanent Subcommittee
on Investigations. Department of Energy
gasoline allocation program . Washington ,
1980. v, 411 p. : LC Card 80-603734   DDC
    333.8/232 19
KF26 .G674 1980c

United States. Congress. Senate. Committee on
Governmental Affairs. Subcommittee on
Energy, Nuclear Proliferation, and Federal
Services. DOE's safety and health program for
enrichment plant workers . Washington , 1980.
iii, 377 p. : LC Card 80-603790   DDC 363.1/79 19
KF26 .G6728 1980c

United States. Congress. Senate. Committee on
the Judiciary. Subcommittee on Antitrust,
Monopoly, and Business Rights. DOE's role in
the solar energy industry, and possible
anticompetitive trends . Washington , 1981. iii,
105 p. : LC Card 81-601624   DDC
    338.4/76147/0973 19
KF26 .J835 1980f

United States. Dept. of Energy. Office of
Inspector General. Report on compensation
paid to consulting firms under selected
support-service contracts /. [Washington, D.C.]
[1979] 29, [29] p. ; LC Card 80-601687   DDC
    353.09/3 19
JK468.C7 U534 1979

United States. General Accounting Office.
Gasoline allocation . [Washington, D.C.]
[1980] vii, 96 p. : LC Card 80-602016   DDC
    353.0082/6566553827 19
HD9579.G4 U54 1980

United States. General Accounting Office.
Residential energy conservation outreach
activities . Washington, D.C. , 1981. iv, 31 p. ;
    LC Card 81-601119   DDC 333.79/16/0973 19
HD7287.5 .U49 1981

United States. General Accounting Office. U. S.
fast breeder reactor program needs direction .
Washington, D.C. , 1980. vii, 54 p. ; LC Card
    80-603953   DDC 353.0087/22 19
TK9203.B7 U5 1980

**UNITED STATES. DEPT. OF ENERGY -
    APPROPRIATIONS AND
    EXPENDITURES.**
United States. Congress. House. Committee on
Appropriations. Subcommittee on Energy and
Water Development. Energy and water
development supplemental appropriations for
1981 . Washington , 1980. ii, 60 p. : LC Card
    80-603978   DDC 353.0072/23687 19
KF27 .A64 1980a

United States. Congress. House. Committee on
Armed Services. Procurement and Military
Nuclear Systems Subcommittee. Hearings on
H.R. 6621 (H.R. 7265), Department of Energy
authorization legislation (national security
programs) for fiscal year 1981, before the
Procurement and Military Nuclear Systems
Subcommittee of the Committee on Armed
Services, House of Representatives, Ninety-sixth
Congress, second session .... Washington , 1980.
xiv, 1088, vi p. : LC Card 80-602721   DDC
    353.0072/236823 19
KF27 .A7657 1980a

United States. Congress. House. Committee on
Armed Services. Procurement and Military
Nuclear Systems Subcommittee. Naval nuclear
propulsion program--1980 . Washington , 1980.
vi, 246, iv p. : LC Card 80-602476   DDC
    343.73/0194 19
KF27 .A7657 1980

United States. Congress. House. Committee on
Foreign Affairs. Subcommittee on International
Security and Scientific Affairs. Department of
Energy fiscal year 1981 budget . Washington ,
1980. iii, 46 p. ; LC Card 80-603009   DDC
    353.0082/236823 19
KF27 .F64825 1980d

United States. Congress. House. Committee on
Interior and Insular Affairs. Subcommittee on
Energy and the Environment. Department of
Energy authorizations for fiscal year 1981 .
Washington , 1980. iii, 116 p. : LC Card
    80-603650   DDC 353.0072/236823 19
KF27 .I518 1980a

United States. Congress. House. Committee on
Interstate and Foreign Commerce.
Subcommittee on Energy and Power. Fiscal
year 1981 authorization for the Department of
Energy and the Federal Energy Regulatory
Commission . Washington , 1980. vi, 1012 p. :
    LC Card 80-603496   DDC 353.0072/236823 19
KF27 .I5542 1980e

United States. Congress. House. Committee on
Science and Technology. 1981 DOE
authorization . Washington , 1980- v. ; LC
    Card 80-602945   DDC 353.0072/236823 19
KF27 .S39 1980a

United States. Congress. House. Committee on
Science and Technology. Subcommittee on
Natural Resources and Environment. 1981
DOE authorization . Washington , 1980. iii,
600 p. : LC Card 80-602948   DDC
    353.0072/236823 19
KF27 .S398 1980a

United States. Congress. Senate. Committee on
Armed Services. Subcommittee on Arms
Control. Fiscal year 1981 Department of
Energy authorization for national security
programs . Washington , 1980. iii, 205 p. : LC
    Card 80-603337   DDC 353.0072/23682/3 19
KF26 .A7435 1980

United States. Congress. Senate. Committee on
Energy and Natural Resources. Subcommittee
on Energy Conservation and Supply.
Department of Energy fiscal years 1981-82
authorization (civilian applications) .
Washington , 1980. iii, 106 p. : LC Card
    80-602997   DDC 353.0072/236823 19
KF26 .E553 1980a

United States. Congress. Senate. Committee on
Energy and Natural Resources. Subcommittee
on Energy Regulation. Department of Energy
fiscal years, 1981-82 authorization (civilian
applications) . Washington , 1980. iii, 265 p. ;
    LC Card 80-603317   DDC 353.0072/23682/3 19
KF26 .E5535 1980a

United States. Congress. Senate. Committee on
Energy and Natural Resources. Subcommittee
on Energy Research and Development.
Department of Energy fiscal years 1981-82
authorization (civilian applications) .
Washington , 1980. iv, 1037 p. : LC Card
    80-604097   DDC 353.0072/236823 19
KF26 .E554 1980

United States. Congress. Senate. Committee on
Governmental Affairs. Subcommittee on
Energy, Nuclear Proliferation, and Federal
Services. The Department of Energy's fiscal
year 1981 budget request for energy research,
development, and applications and energy
conservation . Washington , 1980. vii, 73 p. ;
    LC Card 80-604124   DDC 353.0072/236823 19
HD9502.U52 U5 1980

**United States. Dept. of Energy. Basic Energy
    Sciences, Office of. see United States. Dept.
    of Energy. Office of Basic Energy Sciences.**

**United States. Dept. of Energy. Board of
    Contract Appeals.**
Guide. [Washington] 23 cm. (United States. Dept.
of Energy. DOE/S) Full title: Guide of the U. S. Dept.
of Energy, Board of Contract Appeals and Contract
Adjustment Board. Superseded by its Guide to Practice
and Procedure (not in the library)
*1. United States. Dept. of Energy. Board of Contract
Appeals - Periodicals. I. United States. Dept. of Energy.
Contract Adjustment Board. II. Title: Guide of the U.
S. Dept. of Energy, Board of Contract Appeals and
Contract Adjustment Board.* **NYPL [JLL 81-33]**

**UNITED STATES. DEPT. OF ENERGY.
    BOARD OF CONTRACT APPEALS -
    PERIODICALS.**

United States. Dept. of Energy. Board of
Contract Appeals. Guide. [Washington]
                    NYPL [JLL 81-33]

**United States. Dept. of Energy. Chemical
    Sciences, Division of. see United States.
    Dept. of Energy. Division of Chemical
    Sciences.**

**UNITED STATES. DEPT. OF ENERGY -
    CONGRESSES.**
Transcript from the National Hearings on the
Federal nonnuclear energy R&D program .
Washington, D.C. , 1980 i.e. 1981. xix, 207 p. :
    LC Card 81-601492   DDC 333.79/23/0973 19
HD9502.U52 T7

**United States. Dept. of Energy. Conservation and
    Solar Applications, Office of. see United
    States. Dept. of Energy. Office of
    Conservation and Solar Applications.**

**United States. Dept. of Energy. Contract
    Adjustment Board.** United States. Dept. of
Energy. Board of Contract Appeals. Guide.
[Washington]   **NYPL [JLL 81-33]**

**United States. Dept. of Energy. Contract
    Appeals, Board of. see United States. Dept.
    of Energy. Board of Contract Appeals.**

**United States. Dept. of Energy. Division of
    Chemical Sciences.** Summaries of research in
the chemical sciences. Washington, U. S. Dept.
of Energy, Office of Energy Research, Division
of Chemical Sciences. 27 cm. Annual. Report year
ends Sept. 30.   LC Card 79-644349
*1. Chemical research - Abstracts - Periodicals. 2.
Chemistry - Abstracts - Periodicals. I. Title.*
                    NYPL [JSP 80-279]

**United States. Dept. of Energy. Division of
    Geothermal Energy.** DiPippo, Ronald.
Geothermal energy as a source of electricity .
Washington, D.C. , 1980. xiii, 370 p. : LC Card
    80-602938   DDC 621.31/213 19
TK1055 .D56

**United States. Dept. of Energy. Division of
    Utility Regulatory Assistance.** Illinois. Office
of Consumer Services. A consumer's guide to
the economics of electric utility ratemaking /.
Washington, D.C. , Springfield, Va. , 1980. ix,
233 p. : LC Card 80-602857   DDC 338.4/336362
19
HD9685.U5 I44 1980

**United States. Dept. of Energy. Energy
    Extension Service.** JRB Associates. The
resource file . [Washington, D.C.] [Springfield,
Va. , 1980] 189 p. in various pagings ; LC Card
    80-602300   DDC 016.33379/16/0973 19
Z5853.P83 J16 1980 TJ163.3

**United States. Dept. of Energy. Energy
    Information Administration. see United
    States. Energy Information Administration.**

**United States. Dept. of Energy. Federal Energy
    Regulatory Commission. see United States.
    Federal Energy Regulatory Commission.**

**United States. Dept. of Energy. Fuels Conversion,
    Office of. see United States. Dept. of Energy.
    Office of Fuels Conversion.**

**UNITED STATES. DEPT. OF ENERGY.
    MANAGEMENT.**
Oversight of the structure and management of
the Department of Energy . Washington , 1980
[i.e. 1981] iii, 434 p. : LC Card 81-601669   DDC
    353.87 19
TJ163.25.U6 O93

**United States. Dept. of Energy. National Energy
    Information Center. see National Energy
    Information Center.**

**United States. Dept. of Energy. Office of
    Assistant Secretary for Conservation and
    Solar Applications.** Hurricane wind speeds in
the United States /. Washington, D.C. [1980]
viii, 30, 11 p. : LC Card 80-600039   DDC
    690/.02/18 s 551.5/52 19
TA435 .U58 no. 124 QC933

**United States. Dept. of Energy. Office of Basic
    Energy Sciences.** Lawrence Symposium on
Systems and Decision Sciences. Proceedings.
1- ; 1977- North Hollywood , Calif..
                    NYPL [JSP 80-446]

**United States. Dept. of Energy. Office of
    Buildings and Community Systems.** Knab,
Lawrence I. The effect of moisture on the
thermal conductance of roofing systems /.

[Washington] , 1980. x, 46 p. :   LC Card
80-600031   DDC 690/.0218 s 690/.15 19
TA435 .U58 no. 123 TH2401

**United States. Dept. of Energy. Office of
Competition.** Delaney, James B. The state of
competition in gasoline marketing . Washington,
D.C. [Springfield, Va.] 1980- v. :   LC Card
80-602541   DDC 338.6/048 19
HD9565 .D44

**United States. Dept. of Energy. Office of
Conservation and Solar Applications.**
Flat-plate Solar Collector Conference, Orlando,
Fla., 1977. Proceedings / . [Washington] , 1978.
x, 662 p. :   LC Card 78-601524
TJ810 .F56 1977   ***NYPL [JSF 81-189]***

United States. Dept. of Energy. Office of the
Assistant Secretary for Policy and Evaluation.
The role of the States in energy / . Washington
[Springfield, Va.] 1978. iii, 39 p. ;   LC Card
79-601823
HD9502.U52 U5125 1978

**United States. Dept. of Energy. Office of
Conservation and Solar Applications. Passive
Systems Development Program.** National
Passive Solar Conference. Proceedings. Newark,
Del.   ***NYPL [JSP 80-342]***

**United States. Dept. of Energy. Office of
Consumer Affairs.** Consumer energy atlas / .
Washington, D.C. [1980] xx, 251 p. ;   LC Card
80-603744   DDC 350.82/3/02573 19
HD9502.U52 U683

**United States. Dept. of Energy. Office of
Education, Business, and Labor Affairs.**
Northwest Regional Energy Conference, Seattle,
1978. Proceedings of the Northwest Regional
Energy Conference, May 31-June 1, 1978,
Seattle, Washington / . [Washington] , 1978. vii,
201 p. ;   LC Card 79-602539
HD9502.U53 A1964 1978
                         NYPL [JLE 81-480]

**United States. Dept. of Energy. Office of Energy
Research. Division of Chemical Sciences. see
United States. Dept. of Energy. Division of
Chemical Sciences.**

**United States. Dept. of Energy. Office of Energy
Technology.** Environmental development plan
ocean thermal energy conversion. Washington :
U. S. Dept. of Energy ; Springfield, Va. :
available from National Technical Information
Service, U. S. Dept. of Commerce, 1979. vii, 48
p. ; 28 cm. "DOE/EDP-0034." Includes
bibliographical references.   LC Card 79-603982   DDC
333.91/4 19
*1. Ocean thermal power plants - Environmental aspects.
I. Title.*
TD195.E4 U522 1979

**United States. Dept. of Energy. Office of Fuels
Conversion.** Fuel use act : final environmental
impact statement / [Department of Energy,
Economic Regulatory Administration, Fuels
Regulation, Office of Fuels Conversion].
Washington, D.C. : The Dept. ; Springfield,
Va. : available from National Technical
Information Service, U. S. Dept. of Commerce,
1979. ca. 600 p. in various pagings : ill., maps ;
28 cm. "April 1979." "DOE/EIS; UC-11, 13." Includes
bibliographies.   LC Card 80-601417
*1. Fossil fuels - Environmental aspects - United States.
2. Energy development - Environmental aspects -
United States. 3. Environmental impact statements -
United States. 4. Fossil fuels - Law and legislation -
United States. 5. Energy policy - United States. I. Title.*
TD196.F67 U54 1979   NYPL [JSF 81-226]

**United States. Dept. of Energy. Office of Fuels
Regulation. Office of Fuels Conversion. see
United States. Dept. of Energy. Office of
Fuels Conversion.**

**United States. Dept. of Energy. Office of Health
and Environmental Research.**
The Canine as a biomedical research model .
[Oak Ridge, TN] , Springfield, Va. , 1980. x,
425 p. :   ISBN 0-87079-122-2 (pbk.) :   LC Card
80-24174   DDC 619/.7 19
RB125 .C36

Hanford Life Sciences Symposium, 19th,
Richland, Wash., 1979. Pulmonary toxicology
of respirable particles . Oak Ridge, Tenn. ,
1980. xi, 676 p. :   ISBN 0-87079-121-4   LC Card
80-22907   DDC 616.2/44 19
RC756 .H3 1979

**United States. Dept. of Energy. Office of
Inspector General.**
**Report - U. S. Department of Energy, Office
of Inspector General** .
(no. IGA-79-13) United States. Dept. of
Energy. Office of Inspector General. Report
on compensation paid to consulting firms
under selected support-service contracts /.
[Washington, D.C.]   [1979] 29, [29] p. ;   LC
Card 80-601687   DDC 353.09/3 19
JK468.C7 U534 1979

Report on compensation paid to consulting
firms under selected support-service contracts /
U. S. Department of Energy, Office of
Inspector General. [Washington, D.C.] : The
Office, [1979] 29, [29] p. ; 28 cm. (Report - U. S.
Department of Energy, Office of Inspector General ;
no. IGA-79-13) "December 3, 1979."   LC Card
80-601687   DDC 353.09/3 19
*1. Government consultants - Salaries, pensions, etc. -
United States. 2. Business consultants - Salaries,
pensions, etc. - United States. 3. United States. Dept. of
Energy. I. Series: United States. Dept. of Energy. Office
of Inspector General. Report - U. S. Department of
Energy, Office of Inspector General ; no. IGA-79-13.
II. Title.*
JK468.C7 U534 1979

**UNITED STATES. DEPT. OF ENERGY.
OFFICE OF INSPECTOR GENERAL.**
United States. Congress. Senate. Committee on
Governmental Affairs. Subcommittee on
Governmental Efficiency and the District of
Columbia. Annual report of the Inspector
General of the Department of Energy .
Washington , 1980. iii, 50 p. ;   LC Card
80-603994   DDC 353.87 19
KF26 .G6735 1980a

**United States. Dept. of Energy. Office of
Regulations and Emergency Planning.**
Standby gasoline rationing plan. Washington,
D.C. : U. S. Dept. of Energy, Economic
Regulatory Administration, Office of
Regulations and Emergency Planning ;
[Springfield, Va. : Available from National
Technical Information Service, U. S. Dept. of
Commerce, 1980] 114 p. ; 28 cm.
"DOE/RG-0029. "Standby rationing plan no. 80-1.""
June 1980."   LC Card 80-603194   DDC 333.8/232 19
*1. Gasoline supply - United States. 2. Rationing,
Consumer - United States. I. Title.*
HD9579.G5 U58 1980

**United States. Dept. of Energy. Office of Solar
Applications and Commercialization.** PRC
Energy Analysis Company. Solar energy
commercialization for African countries / .
[Washington] , Springfield, Va. [1978] ix, 103
p. :   LC Card 79-602118   DDC 333.79/23/0967 19
TJ810 .P27 1978

**United States. Dept. of Energy. Office of the
Assistant Secretary for Intergovernmental
and Institutional Relations.** United States.
Dept. of Energy. Office of the Assistant
Secretary for Policy and Evaluation. The role of
the States in energy / . Washington
[Springfield, Va.] 1978. iii, 39 p. ;   LC Card
79-601823
HD9502.U52 U5125 1978

**United States. Dept. of Energy. Office of the
Assistant Secretary for Policy and
Evaluation.** The role of the States in energy /
prepared by the U. S. Department of Energy,
Office of the Assistant Secretary for Policy and
Evaluation, Office of the Assistant Secretary for
Intergovernmental and Institutional Relations,
Office of the Assistant Secretary for
Conservation and Solar Applications.
Washington : The Department ; [Springfield,
Va. : available from National Technical
Information Service, U. S. Dept. of Commerce],
1978. iii, 39 p. ; 28 cm. "DOE/PE-0009. UC-13."
Bibliography: p. 39.   LC Card 79-601823
*1. Energy policy - United States - States. I. United
States. Dept. of Energy. Office of the Assistant
Secretary for Intergovernmental and Institutional
Relations. II. United States. Dept. of Energy. Office of
Conservation and Solar Applications. III. Title.*
HD9502.U52 U5125 1978

**United States. Dept. of Energy. Office of
Transportation Programs.**
The charge of the future : an introduction to
electric and hybrid vehicles. Washington, D.C. :
U. S. Dept. of Energy, Assistant Secretary for
Conservation and Solar Energy, Office of

Transportation Programs : [for sale by the Supt.
of Docs., U. S. Govt. Print. Off., 1979] vii, 66
p. : ill. ; 15 x 23 cm. Includes bibliographical
references.   LC Card 80-601797   DDC 629.2/293 19
1. Automobiles, Electric. I. Title.
TL220 .U47 1979

**UNITED STATES. DEPT. OF ENERGY.
OFFICE OF TRANSPORTATION
PROGRAMS - APPROPRIATIONS AND
EXPENDITURES.**
United States. Congress. House. Committee on
Science and Technology. Subcommittee on
Transportation, Aviation, and Communications.
1982 DOE authorization (program review) .
Washington , 1980. iii, 54 p. ;   LC Card
80-604028   DDC 353.0072/234 19
KF27 .S3997 1980f

**United States. Dept. of Energy. Office of Utility
Systems.** The national power grid study.
Washington, D.C. : U. S. Dept. of Energy,
Economic Regulatory Administration, Office of
Utility Systems ; [Springfield, Va. : available
from National Technical Information Service,
U. S. Dept. of Commerce, 1980] 2 v. : ill. ; 28
cm. Vol. 1: "January 1980"; v. 2: "September 1979."
Vol. 1: "DOE/ERA-0056/1"; v. 2: "DOE/ERA-0056-2."
Includes bibliographical references. CONTENTS. - v. 1.
Final report.--v. 2. Technical study reports.   LC Card
80-601760   DDC 363.6/2 19
*1. Electric power systems - United States. 2. Electric
utilities - United States. I. Title.*
TK23 .U52 1980

**UNITED STATES. DEPT. OF ENERGY -
OFFICIALS AND EMPLOYEES.**
United States. Congress. House. Committee on
Post Office and Civil Service. Subcommittee on
Civil Service. Energy Department violation of
SES 120-day rule--the Tina Hobson case .
Washington , 1981. iii, 90 p. ;   LC Card
81-601878   DDC 353.87 19
KF27 .P635 1981

United States. Congress. Senate. Committee on
Energy and Natural Resources. James B.
Edwards nomination . Washington , 1981. ii,
216 p. :   LC Card 81-600846   DDC 353.87 19
KF26 .E55 1981a

United States. Congress. Senate. Committee on
Energy and Natural Resources. Johnson, Odle,
and Heffelfinger nominations . Washington ,
1981. iii, 140 p. :   LC Card 81-601965   DDC
353.87 19
KF26 .E55 1981d

**UNITED STATES. DEPT. OF ENERGY -
PROCUREMENT.**
United States. Congress. Senate. Select
Committee on Small Business. Small business
and Department of Energy research and
development programs . Washington , 1980. iii,
77 p. :   LC Card 80-602727   DDC 353.0082/048045
19
KF26.5 .S6 1980e

**United States. Dept. of Energy. Strategic
Petroleum Reserve Office. see United States.
Strategic Petroleum Reserve Office.**

**United States. Dept. of Energy. Technical
Information Center.** Energy . Oak Ridge,
Tenn. , Springfield, Va. , 1980. 660, 277, 8 p. ;
LC Card 81-600702   DDC 016.33379/0973 19
Z7164.E6 E53 HD9502.U52

**United States. Dept. of Health and Human
Services.**
DHHS publication.
(no. (ADM) 80-842) Taber, Merlin. The
social context of helping . Rockville, Md. ,
Washington , 1980. v, 259 p. ;   LC Card
80-602564   DDC 362.4/048 19
HV1568 .T33

(no. (ADM) 80-861) Lawton, Mortimer
Powell. Social and medical services in
housing for the aged / . Rockville, Md. ,
Washington, D.C. , 1980. vii, 112 p. ;   LC
Card 80-603249   DDC 363.5/9 19
HD7287.92.U54 L383

(no. (ADM) 80-946) Workshop for
Ethnographers and Single State Agency
Policymakers and Planners, Chicago, 1979.
Ethnography . Rockville, Md. , 1980. xvi,
128 p. ;   LC Card 80-602292   DDC 362.2/9 19
HV5809 .W67 1979

(no. (ADM) 80-962) Blehar, Mary.
Development of mental health in infancy /.

Rockville, Md. , Washington, D.C. [1980] v, 105, [106] p. ; LC Card 80-600037 DDC 618.92/8905 19
RJ502.5 .B55

(no. (HRA) 80-45) Hall, Thomas L. Schools of public health . [Washington] [1980] vi, 58 p. ; LC Card 80-602405 DDC 614/.07/1173 19
RA440.7.U6 H34

(no. (HRA) 80-46) Association of Schools of Public Health. Schools of public health . [Washington] , 1980. x, 149 p. ; LC Card 80-602404 DDC 614/.07/1173 19
RA440.7.U6 A87 1980

(no. (HSA) 80-5135) National Clearinghouse for Human Genetic Diseases. Clinical genetic service centers . [Rockville, Md.] [1980] iii, 117 p. ; LC Card 80-602604 DDC 362.1/96042/02573 19
RB155 .N37 1980

(no. (PHS) 81-1714) Bloom, Barbara, 1950- Utilization patterns and financial characteristics of nursing homes in the United States, 1977 /. Hyattsville, Md. , 1981. p. cm. ISBN 0-8406-0215-4 LC Card 80-606876 DDC 362.1/1/0973 s 362.1/6/0973 19
RA407.3 .A349 no. 53 RA997

United States. Dept. of Health and Human Services. Office of Human Development Services. see United States. Office of Human Development Services.

United States. Dept. of Health and Human Services. Office of the Deputy Assistant Secretary for Planning and Evaluation/Health. Developing the national health plan . [Washington, D.C.?] , 1980. 2 v. ; LC Card 81-601466 DDC 368.4/2/00973 19
HD7102.U4 D4

UNITED STATES. DEPT. OF HEALTH AND HUMAN SERVICES - OFFICIALS AND EMPLOYEES.
United States. Congress. Senate. Committee on Finance. Nomination of Richard S. Schweiker . Washington , c1981. iii, 39 p. ; LC Card 81-600829 DDC 353.842 19
KF26 .F5 1981

United States. Dept. of Health, Education, and Welfare. (Old Catalog form: United States. Health, Education and Welfare, Dept. of)
United States. Department of Health, Education, and Welfare.
Cost principles and procedures for establishing indirect cost and other rates for grants and contracts with the Department of Health, Education, and Welfare : a guide for non-profit institutions. Washington : The Department, 1974. vii, 64 p. ; 26 cm. "OASC-5, rev."
1. Grants-in-aid - United States - Handbooks, manuals, etc. 2. Public contracts - United States. I. Title.
NYPL [JLF 80-867]

DHEW publication.
((FDA) 76-8037) National Conference on Measurements of Laser Emissions for Regulatory Purposes, Rockville, Md., 1974. National Conference on Measurements of Laser Emissions for Regulatory Purposes . [Rockville, Md.] , Washington , 1976 i.e. 1977. vii, 255 p. : LC Card 77-602983 DDC 535.5/8 19
QC689.5.L37 N37 1974

((FDA) 80-8116) Torchia, Marion. Chest X-ray screening practices . Rockville, Md. , Washington, D.C. [1980] v, 57 p. ; LC Card 80-602827 DDC 363.1/79 19
RA645.R4 T67

((HSA) 79-12040) United States. Indian Health Service. Illness among Indians and Alaska Natives, 1970 to 1978. [Washington] [1979?]. viii, 58 p. ; LC Card 80-601653 DDC 312/.3/08997 19
RA408.I49 U54 1979a

((OS) 76-132) United States. Dept. of Health, Education, and Welfare. Secretary's Advisory Committee on the Rights and Responsibilities of Women. The rights & responsibilities of women . [Washington] [1976?] ii, 103 p. ; LC Card 77-603753 DDC 362.8/3/0973 19
HQ1426 .U52 1976

(no. (ADM) 74-35)) United States. National Institute of Mental Health. Division of Scientific and Technical Information. Guide

to mental health education materials . Rockville, Md. , Washington , 1974. vi, 50 p. ; LC Card 74-603098 DDC 016.3622 19
Z6664.N5 U557 1974 RA790

(no. (ADM) 76-361) National Institute on Alcohol Abuse and Alcoholism. The whole college catalog about drinking. Rockville, Md. , Washington [1976] xii, 129 p. : LC Card 76-603043 DDC 362.2/9286/088375 19
HV5292 .N33 1976

(no. (ADM) 77-515) National Institute on Drug Abuse. Referral strategies for polydrug abusers /. Rockville, Md. [1977] viii, 60 p. ; LC Card 78-602531 DDC 362.2/938 19
HV5825 .N35 1977

(no. (ADM) 78-660) Fisher, Anne. Women's worlds . Rockville, Md. , Washington [1978] xiii, 106 p. ; LC Card 78-603680 DDC 305.4/0973 19
HQ1420 .F57

(no. (ADM) 79-321) National Institute on Drug Abuse. National directory of drug abuse and alcoholism treatment programs. Rockville, Md. , Washington, D.C. , 1979. xi, 350 p. ; LC Card 80-601556 DDC 362.2/9 19
HV5825 .N35 1979

(no. (ADM) 79-675) Tierney, Kathleen J. Crisis intervention programs for disaster victims . Rockville, Md. , Washington [1979] xvi, 203 p. ; LC Card 79-603002 DDC 362.2 19
HV555.U6 T53

(no. (ADM) 79-782) Friedman, Lucy N. The wildcat experiment . Rockville, Md. , Washington [1978] ix, 147 p. ; LC Card 79-602059 DDC 362.2/9386 19
HV5833.N45 F74

(no. (ADM) 79-790) Grady, Kathleen E. The male sex role . Rockville, Md. , Washington, D.C. , 1979. x, 196 p. ; LC Card 79-604183 DDC 016.3053 19
Z7164.S42 G7 HQ1075

(no. (ADM) 79-831) Schwitzgebel, Ralph K., 1934- Legal aspects of the enforced treatment of offenders /. Rockville, Md. , Washington, D.C. [1979] vii, 133 p. ; LC Card 80-600988 DDC 344.73/044 347.30444 19
KF3828 .S38

(no. (ADM) 79-858) LoSciuto, Leonard A. Professional and paraprofessional drug abuse counselors . Rockville, Md. , 1979. v, 244 p. ; LC Card 79-604153 DDC 362.2/9386 19
HV5825 .L67

(no. (ADM) 79-877) Johnston, Lloyd. Drugs and the class of '78 . Rockville, Md. , Washington , 1979. xxi, 335 p. : LC Card 79-604015 DDC 362.2/9 19
HV5824.Y68 J622

(no. (ADM) 79-891) Alcohol and drug abuse in medical education /. Rockville, Md. , Washington, D.C. , 1980. ix, 131 p. ; LC Card 80-602242 DDC 616.86/007/11 19
RC565 .A37

(no. (ADM) 80-920) SRI International. Consequences of alcohol & marijuana use . Rockville, Md. , Washington, D.C. , 1980. xii, 227 p. : LC Card 80-601619 DDC 616.86/1 19
RC564 .S18 1980

(no. (ADM) 80-943) National Clearinghouse for Alcohol Information. Occupational alcoholism programs bibliography /. Rockville, Md. , 1980. iii, 42 p. ; LC Card 80-602280 DDC 016.6583/822 19
Z7164.C81 N257 1980 HF5549.5.A4

(no. (CDC) 80-8383) Center for Disease Control. Laboratory Training and Consultation Division. Common blood and tissue parasites of man . Atlanta, Ga. , 1979, 1980 printing. iii, 39 p. : LC Card 80-602354 DDC 616.9/6 19
RC119 .C33 1979

(no. (CDS) 79-8378) Center for Disease Control. Family Planning Evaluation Division. Surgical sterilization surveillance . Atlanta, Ga. [1979] 22 p. ; LC Card 79-600096 DDC 363.9/7/0973 19
RG138 .C46 1979

(no. (HCEA) 03008 9-79) Muller, Charlotte

Feldman, 1921- Study of physician reimbursement under medicare and medicaid /. [Washington] 1979- v. : LC Card 80-601289 DDC 338.4/33621/0973 19
R728.5 .M84

(no. (HDS) 79-21025) Santamour, Miles. Retardation, corrections, and retarded offenders . Washington [1979] i, 156 p. ; LC Card 79-604176 DDC 016.3646 19
Z5703.4.M46 S26 1979 HV6791

(no. (HRA) 79-14001) National Health Planning Information Center. Mental health planning . [Washington] [1978] v, 159 p. ; LC Card 80-601593 DDC 362.2/068 19
Z6664.N5 N34 1978 RA790

(no. (HRA) 79-18) United States. Health Resources Administration. Bureau of Health Manpower. Supply of optometrists in the United States . [Bethesda? Md.] , 1978. iii, 23 p. ; LC Card 79-603959 DDC 331.12/916177/00973 19
RE959 .U54 1978

(no. (HRA) 80-15) United States. Health Resources Administration. Bureau of Health Manpower. Program Management Information Systems Branch. Health professions schools . [Washington, D.C.] , OPD [1980] xii, 322 p. ; LC Card 80-601769 DDC 610/.7/1173 19
R745 .U485 1980

(no. (HRA) 80-43) United States. Health Resources Administration. Bureau of Health Manpower. A report on public and community health personnel . Washington, D.C. , 1980. viii, 220 p. ; LC Card 80-602370 DDC 331.12/913621 19
RA440.9 .U47 1980

(no. (HRA) 80-651) United States. Health Resources Administration. Report on health personnel in the United States. [Washington, D.C.] [1979] 38 p. ; LC Card 80-601525 DDC 331.12/3161/0973 19
RA410.7 .U555 1979

(no. (HSA) 79-5290) Moore, Coralie B. A reader's guide for parents of children with mental, physical, or emotional disabilities /. Rockville, Md. , Washington, D.C. , 1979. viii, 144 : LC Card 79-601825 DDC 016.3624/088054 19
Z5814.C52 M66 1979 HV888

(no. (HSA) 79-5623) Alan Guttmacher Institute. Family planning, contraception, voluntary sterilization, and abortion . Rockville, Md. , Washington, D.C. , 1978. xix, 380 p. ; LC Card 80-601267 DDC 344.73/048 19
KF3771.Z95 A37

(no. (HSA) 80-5264) National Conference on Mental Health Issues Related to Sudden Infant Death Syndrome, Baltimore, Md., 1977. Mental health issues in grief counseling . Rockville, Md. , Washington, D.C. , 1979 i.e. 1980. 133 p. ; LC Card 80-602299 DDC 362.8/286 19
RJ59 .N37 1977

(no. (NIH) 76-890) National Cancer Institute Symposium on Biohazards and Zoonotic Problems of Primate Procurement, Quarantine, and Research, Frederick Cancer Research Center, 1975. Biohazards and zoonotic problems of primate procurement, quarantine, and research . [Bethesda, Md.] 1975. 137 p. : LC Card 76-600529 DDC 614.4/3 19
RA641.P7 N37 1975

(no. (NIH) 78-714) National Sickle Cell Disease Program. Directory of national, Federal, and local sickle cell disease programs /. Bethesda, Md. [1978] 30 p. ; LC Card 79-601535 DDC 362.1/96152700973 19
RC641.7/S5 N36 1978

(no. (NIH) 79-1600) National Institute of Arthritis, Metabolism, and Digestive Diseases. Office of the Associate Director for Arthritis, Bone, and Skin Diseases. Progress against the rheumatic diseases (1967-1977) . [Bethesda, Md.] , 1978. vii, 39 p. ; LC Card 79-602034 DDC 616.7/23/0072073 19
RC927 .N38 1978

(no. (NIH) 79-1645) United States. National

BIBLIOGRAPHIC GUIDE

United States. Department of Health, Education, and Welfare.

516

Institutes of Health. Office of HEW Case Coordinator. HEW support for universities and colleges, medical and other health professional schools, research centers and hospitals, fiscal year 1969-1977 /. Bethesda, Md. [1979?] v, 79 p. : LC Card 79-602074 DDC 379.1/18/0973 19
LB2342 .U5864 1979

(no. (NIH) 80-1938) International Conference on Bone Measurement, 4th, University of Toronto, 1978. Fourth International Conference on Bone Measurement . [Washington] [1980] xii, 543 p. : LC Card 80-602926 DDC 599.04/71 19
QP88.2 .I58 1978

(no. (NIH)78-785) Gabovich, Rafail Davidovich. Fluorine in stomatology and hygiene =. Bethesda, Md. , Washington , 1977. vi, 1028 p. : LC Card 78-600559 DDC 612/.3924 19
RK331 .G313

(no. (OE) 78-19004) Pike, Lewis W. Other nations, other peoples . [Washington, D.C.] , 1979. xxiii, 139 p. : LC Card 80-600989 DDC 370.19/6 19
LC1099 .P54

(no. (OE) 79-19137) Bodenman, Paul S., 1912- The educational system of Switzerland /. Washington, D.C. , 1979 i.e. 1980. 35 p. : LC Card 80-602306 DDC 371.2/009485 19
LB2936 .B6

(no. (OE) 79-19140) Rosen, Seymour Michael, 1924- Education in the U. S.S.R., current status of higher education /. Washington , 1980. vi, 64 p. ; LC Card 80-603405 DDC 378.47 19
LA838 .R58

(no. (OHD) 75-72) Tips on the care and adjustment of Vietnamese and other Asian children in the United States. [Washington] [1975] 11, 11, [6] p. ; LC Card 75-602431 DDC 649/.145 19
RJ102 .T56

(no. (OHDS) 79-20170) United States. Laws, statutes, etc. Older Americans act of 1965, as amended . Washington, D.C. [1979] viii, 173 p. ; LC Card 80-602137 DDC 344.73/0326/02632 19
KF3737 .A3 1979

(no. (OHDS) 79-21017) Friedman, Paul R. Mental retardation and the law . [Washington, D.C.] 1978. 37 p. ; LC Card 79-603796 DDC 346.7301/38/02648 19
KF480.A59 F73

(no. (OHDS) 79-30225) Selected readings on mother-infant bonding. [Washington, D.C. , 1979] 115 p. : LC Card 79-604305 DDC 306.8/7 19
HQ759 .S44

(no. (OHDS) 79-30226) Child abuse and developmental disabilities essays . [Washington] [1980] iii, 45 p. : LC Card 80-602267 DDC 362.7/044 19
HV713 .C3817

(no. (OHDS) 80-20249) Kirschner Associates. Longitudinal evaluation of the National Nutrition Program for the Elderly . [Washington, D.C.] [1980] xiv, 333 p. : LC Card 80-601632 DDC 362.6/3 19
HV696.F6 K57 1980

(no. (OHDS) 80-20960) Mental health and the elderly . [Washington, D.C.] , 1979. iii, 126 p. ; LC Card 80-601603 DDC 362.2/0880565 19
RC451.4.A5 M44

(no. (PHS) 80-1240) Haupt, Barbara J. The Nation's use of health resources, 1979 /. [Washington] [1980] x, 169 p. ; LC Card 80-602252 DDC 362.1/0973 19
RA410.53 .H38

(no. (PHS) 80-50116-80-50117) Group Health Foundation Library (U. S.) Comprehensive bibliography on health maintenance organizations, 1974-1978 /. Washington, D.C. , 1980. 2 v. ; LC Card 80-602118 DDC 016.3621/0425 19
Z6675.H4 G76 1980 RA413

(no. (PHS) 80-50127) United States. Office of Health Maintenance Organization. National HMO census of prepaid plans. Rockville, Md.

[Washington, D.C.] [1979] 34 p., [3] leaves of plates : LC Card 80-602548 DDC 368.3/82/00973 19
HG9396 .U55 1979

(no. (SSA) 13-11728) Urban Systems Research & Engineering. Survey of blind and disabled children receiving supplemental security income benefits /. [Washington, D.C.] , 1980. xii, 94, [178] p. : LC Card 80-602123 DDC 362.4/0482/088054 19
HV1791 .U7 1980

(no. HRA 80-2) Longitudinal study of nurse practitioners . Hyattsville, Md. , Washington, D.C. , 1980. xv, 221 p. : LC Card 80-602207 DDC 610.73/0692 19
RT82.8 .L67

(no. HRA 80-31) Franklin Research Center. Continuing education in nursing . Hyattsville, Md. [1980] x, 196 p. ; LC Card 80-602706 DDC 610.73/07/15 19
Z5818.N8 F7 1980 RT76

(no. OS-76-130) Project SHARE. Issues in domestic violence /. [Rockville, Md.] [1980] v, 25 p. ; LC Card 80-602672 DDC 362.8/3 19
HV6626 .P76 1980

(no. 13-11921) United States. Social Security Administration. Office of Research and Statistics. Public assistance recipients and cash payments by State and county-February 1979. Washington, D.C. , 1980. v, 85 p. ; LC Card 80-600053 DDC 361/.973/0212 19
HV85 .U54 1980

DHEW publication .
(no. (OHDS) 80-22007) United States. Office for Handicapped Individuals. Directory of national information sources on handicapping conditions and related services /. [Washington, D.C.] , 1980. vii, 236 p. ; LC Card 80-602225 DDC 362.4/048/02573 19
HV1553 .U49 1980

A guide for colleges and universities : cost principles and procedures for establishing indirect cost and other rates for grants and contracts with the Dept. of Health, Education and Welfare. Washington, D. C., U. S. Govt. Print. Off., 1974. 97 p. ; 26 cm.
1. Research and development contracts - United States. 2. Universities and colleges - United States - Finance. I. Title. **NYPL [JLF 80-937]**

Publication.
(no. (FDA) 79-8035) United States. Bureau of Radiological Health. Regulations for the administration and enforcement of the Radiation control for health and safety act of 1968. Rockville, Md. , Washington, D.C. , 1978. vi, 68 p. : LC Card 79-603753 DDC 344.73/0472 19
KF3948.A355 A2 1978

Setzer, Florence. The Seattle-Denver income maintenance experiment . [[Washington] , 1978. xv, 54 p. ; LC Card 78-603699
HC110.I5 S4 **NYPL [JLF 81-429]**

United States. General Accounting Office. Returning the mentally disabled to the community . [Washington] 1977. x, 254 p. ; LC Card 77-601175
RA790.6 .U55 1977

Visual environmental adaptation problems of the partially sighted . [Santa Monica, Calif.] , 1979. xvii, 198 p. ; **NYPL [JLF 80-1465]**

United States. Dept. of Health, Education and Welfare. Administration on Aging. see United States. Administration on Aging.

United States. Dept. of Health, Education and Welfare. Asian American Affairs, Division of. see United States. Dept. of Health, Education, and Welfare. Division of Asian American Affairs.

UNITED STATES. DEPT. OF HEALTH, EDUCATION AND WELFARE - AUDITING AND INSPECTION.
United States. General Accounting Office. HEW must improve control over billions in cash advances . [Washington] , 1979. v, 40 p. ; LC Card 80-602661 DDC 353.84 19
HV85 .U53 1979

United States. Dept. of Health, Education, and Welfare. Division of Asian American Affairs.
JWK International Corporation. Summary and recommendations . Washington , 1978. iii

leaves, 46, 5, 227 p. ; LC Card 78-602799
E184.O6 J18 1978 **NYPL [JLF 81-294]**

United States. Dept. of Health, Education, and Welfare. Education Division. National Center for Education Statistics. see National Center for Education Statistics.

United States. Dept. of Health, Education, and Welfare. Finance, Office of the Deputy Assistant Secretary. see United States. Dept. of Health, Education, and Welfare. Office of the Deputy Assistant Secretary, Finance.

United States. Dept. of Health, Education and Welfare. Health Care Financing Administration. see United States. Health Care Financing Administration.

United States. Dept. of Health, Education, and Welfare. National Advisory Council on Equality of Educational Opportunity. see United States. National Advisory Council on Equality of Educational Opportunity.

United States. Dept. of Health Education and Welfare. National Institute on Drug Abuse. see National Institute on Drug Abuse.

United States. Dept. of Health, Education and Welfare. National Institutes of Health. see United States. National Institutes of Health.

United States. Dept. of Health, Education, and Welfare. New Drug Regulation, Review Panel on. see United States. Dept. of Health, Education, and Welfare. Review Panel on New Drug Regulation.

United States. Dept. of Health Education, and Welfare. Office of Education. see United States. Office of Education.

United States. Dept. of Health, Education and Welfare. Office of Special Concerns. Division of Asian American Affairs. see United States. Dept. of Health, Education, and Welfare. Division of Asian American Affairs.

United States. Dept. of Health, Education, and Welfare. Office of the Assistant Secretary for Health. see United States. Office of the Assistant Secretary for Health.

United States. Dept. of Health, Education, and Welfare. Office of the Assistant Secretary for Health and Surgeon General. see United States. Office of the Assistant Secretary for Health and Surgeon General.

United States. Dept. of Health, Education, and Welfare. Office of the Assistant Secretary for Human Development. Office for Handicapped Individuals. see United States. Office for Handicapped Individuals.

United States. Dept. of Health, Education, and Welfare. Office of the Assistant Secretary for Planning and Evaluation.

United States. Dept. of Health, Education, and Welfare. Office of the Assistant Secretary for Planning and Evaluation/Health. The appropriateness of the Federal interagency day care requirements : report of findings and recommendations. Washington : U. S. Dept. of Health, Education, and Welfare, Office of the Assistant Secretary for Planning and Evaluation : for sale by the Supt. of Docs., U. S. Govt. Print. Off., 1978. xxxvii, 304 p. ; 26 cm. Bibliography: p. 187-206. Appendices (p. 225-304): A. Text of the FIDCR: Federal interagency day care requirements.--B. Legislative history of the FIDCR.--C. Summary of comments from panel members.--D. Abt Associates. Preliminary findings of the National day care study. LC Card 79-601795
1. Day care centers - United States. 2. Day care centers - Standards - United States. 3. Day care aides - United States. 4. Federal aid to day care centers - United States. I. Title. II. Title: Federal interagency day care requirements.
HV854 .U517 1978

Marieskind, Helen I. An evaluation of caesarean section in the United States . [Washington, D.C.] , 1979. iv, 252 p. ; LC Card 80-602147 DDC 362.1/9886 19
RG761 .M37

Urban and Rural Systems Associates. Improving family planning services for teenagers . [Washington] , 1976. i, 85, 23 p. : LC Card 77-601716
HQ766.5.U5 U72 1976 **NYPL [JLF 81-163]**

United States. Dept. of Health, Education, and Welfare. Office of the Deputy Assistant Secretary, Finance.
Financial assistance by geographic area: Region 1, Boston, Mass. [Washington] illus. 27 cm. (DHEW publication (OS)) Annual. Report year ends Sept. 30. LC Card 79-6403026
1. Economic assistance, Domestic - New England - Statistics - Periodicals. 2. Grants-in-aid - New England - Statistics - Periodicals. I. Title.
NYPL [JLM 80-1057]

Financial assistance by geographic area: Region 10, Seattle, Washington. [Washington] illus. 27 cm. (DHEW publication (OS)) Annual. Report year ends Sept. 30. LC Card 79-643095
1. Economic assistance, Domestic - Northwest, Pacific - Statistics - Periodicals. 2. Grants-in-aid - Northwest, Pacific - Statistics - Periodicals. I. Title.
NYPL [JLM 80-1065]

Financial assistance by geographic area: Region 2, New York, N. Y. [Washington] illus. 27 cm. (DHEW publication (OS)) Annual. Report year ends Sept. 30. LC Card 79-643013
1. Economic assistance, Domestic - New York (State) - Statistics - Periodicals. 2. Economic assistance, Domestic - New Jersey - Statistics - Periodicals. 3. Economic assistance, Domestic - Puerto Rico - Statistics - Periodicals. 4. Economic assistance, Domestic - Virgin Islands of the United States - Statistics - Periodicals. I. Title.
NYPL [JLM 80-1058]

Financial assistance by geographic area: Region 3, Philadelphia, Penna. [Washington] illus. 27 cm. (DHEW publication (OS)) Annual. Report year ends Sept. 30. LC Card 79-643018
1. Economic assistance, Domestic - Middle Atlantic States - Statistics - Periodicals. 2. Grants-in-aid - Middle Atlantic States - Statistics - Periodicals. I. Title.
NYPL [JLM 80-1059]

Financial assistance by geographic area: Region 4, Atlanta, Georgia. [Washington] illus. 27 cm. (DHEW publication (OS)) Annual. Report year ends Sept. 30. LC Card 79-643014
1. Economic assistance, Domestic - Southern States - Statistics - Periodicals. 2. Grants-in-aid - Southern states - Statistics - Periodicals. I. Title.
NYPL [JLM 80-1060]

Financial assistance by geographic area: Region 5, Chicago, Illinois. [Washington] illus. 27 cm. (DHEW publication (OS)) Annual. Report year ends Sept. 30. LC Card 79-643015
1. Economic assistance, Domestic - Middle West - Statistics - Periodicals. 2. Grants-in-aid - Middle West - Statistics - Periodicals. I. Title.
NYPL [JLM 80-1061]

Financial assistance by geographic area: Region 6, Dallas, Taxas. [Washington] illus. 27 cm. (DHEW publication (OS)) Annual. Report year ends Sept. 30. LC Card 79-643039
1. Economic assistance, Domestic - Southwestern States - Statistics - Periodicals. 2. Grants-in-aid - Southern states - Statistics - Periodicals. I. Title.
NYPL [JLM 80-1062]

Financial assistance by geographic area: Region 8, Denver, Colorado. [Washington] illus. 27 cm. (DHEW publication (OS)) Annual. Report year ends Sept. 30. LC Card 79-643094
1. Economic assistance, Domestic - Rocky Mountain region - Statistics - Periodicals. 2. Grants-in-aid - Rocky Mountain region - Statistics - Periodicals. I. Title.
NYPL [JLM 80-1063]

Financial assistance by geographic area: Region 9, San Francisco, California. [Washington] illus. 27 cm. (DHEW publication (OS)) Annual. Report year ends Sept. 30. LC Card 79-643093
1. Economic assistance, Domestic - United States - Statistics - Periodicals. 2. Grants-in-aid - United States - Statistics - Periodicals. I. Title.
NYPL [JLM 80-1064]

United States. Dept. of Health, Education, and Welfare. Office of the Deputy Assistant Secretary for Planning and Evaluation/Health. Bureau of Social Science Research, Washington, D. C. Directory of rural health care programs, 1979 /. [Washington, D.C.] [1980] ix, 499 p. ; LC Card 80-602309 DDC 362.1/0425 19
RA771.5 .B87 1980

UNITED STATES. DEPT. OF HEALTH, EDUCATION, AND WELFARE - OFFICIALS AND EMPLOYEES.
United States. Congress. Senate. Committee on

Finance. Nominations of Abraham Katz, William J. Driver, and John L. Palmer . Washington , 1980. iii, 19 p. ; LC Card 80-602760 DDC 353.842 19
KF26 .F5 1980b

United States. Dept. of Health, Education, and Welfare. Planning and Evaluation, Office of the Assistant Secretary for. see United States. Dept. of Health, Education, and Welfare. Office of the Assistant Secretary for Planning and Evaluation.

United States. Dept. of Health, Education, and Welfare. Public Health Service. see United States. Public Health Service.

United States. Dept. of Health, Education, and Welfare. Review Panel on New Drug Regulation. Final report / Review Panel on New Drug Regulation. [Washington] : Dept. of Health, Education, and Welfare, 1977. 117, [85] p. ; 27 cm. Cover title. Includes bibliographical references. LC Card 77-602914
1. Pharmaceutical policy - United States. 2. United States. Food and Drug Administration. 3. Pharmaceutical research - United States.
RA401.A3 U52 1977 **NYPL [JLF 81-208]**

United States. Dept. of Health, Education, and Welfare. Rights and Responsabilities of Women, Secretary's Advisory Committee on the. see United States. Dept. of Health, Education, and Welfare. Secretary's Advisory Committee on the Rights and Responsibilities of Women.

United States. Dept. of Health, Education, and Welfare. Secretariat for IYC. United States. Federal Interagency Committee for the International Year of the Child. Report on Federal Government programs that relate to children, 1979 /. [Washington, D.C.] , 1979. vi, 125 p. ; LC Card 79-603379
HV741 .U5245 1979 **NYPL [JLF 81-458]**

United States. Dept. of Health, Education, and Welfare. Secretary's Advisory Committee on the Rights and Responsibilities of Women. The rights & responsibilities of women : recommendations of the Secretary's Advisory Committee on the Rights and Responsibilities of Women, 1973, 1974. [Washington] : Dept. of Health, Education, and Welfare : for sale by the Supt. of Docs., U. S. Govt. Print. Off., [1976?] ii, 103 p. ; 27 cm. ([DHEW publication] ; (OS) 76-132) Includes bibliographical references. LC Card 77-603753 DDC 362.8/3/0973 19
1. Women's rights - United States. 2. Women - Legal status, laws, etc. - United States. I. Series: United States. Dept. of Health, Education and Welfare. DHEW publication, (OS) 76-132. II. Title.
HQ1426 .U52 1976

United States. Dept. of Health, Education, and Welfare. Secretary's Committee on Mental Health and Illness of the Elderly. Report of the Secretary's Committee on Mental Health and Illness of the Elderly. 1979. Mental health and the elderly . [Washington, D.C.] , 1979. iii, 126 p. ; LC Card 80-601603 DDC 362.2/0880565 19
RC451.4.A5 M44

United States. Dept. of Health, Education, and Welfare. Social and Rehabilitation Service. see United States. Social and Rehabilitation Service.

United States. Dept. of Health, Education, and Welfare. Social Security Administration. see United States. Social Security Administration.

United States. Dept. of Housing and Urban Affairs. Office of Community Planning and Development. see United States. Office of Community Planning and Development.

United States. Dept. of Housing and Urban Development. (Old Catalog form: United States. Housing and Urban Development, Dept. of.)
Adams, Francis Gerard, 1929- An economic model of Mississippi . Jackson , 1973. v, 40 leaves ; **NYPL [*ZT-1264]**

California. Metropolitan Transportation Commission. BART in the San Francisco Bay Area . Washington, D.C. , Springfield, Va. , 1979 i.e. 1980. 227 p. : LC Card 80-603256 DDC 388.4/2/097946 19
HE4491.S45 C34 1980

Challenge! [Washington] v. 9, no. 10- ; Oct. 1978- Washington. **NYPL [JLM 81-3]**

Developmental needs of small cities : a study required by section 113 of the Housing and community development act of 1977 / U. S. Department of Housing and Urban Development. [Washington] : The Dept., 1979. vii, 294 p. : ill. ; 27 cm. Bibliography: p. 287-294. "HUD-PDR-374." LC Card 79-602073
1. Cities and towns - United States - Statistics. 2. Community development - United States. 3. Social surveys - United States. I. Title.
HT123 .U43 1979

Erley, Duncan. Site planning for solar access . [Washington] [1979] 149 p. : LC Card 80-600615
TH7414 .E74 **NYPL [JSF 81-159]**

Fifth biennial HUD awards for design excellence. Washington, for sale by the Supt. of Docs., U. S. Govt. Print. Office [1973] 58 p.: ill.; 24 x 29 cm. NYPL copy imperfectly bound. LC Card 76-16353
1. Architecture, Domestic - United States. 2. Housing - United States. 3. City planning - United States. I. Title.
NYPL [3-MRG 80-1639]

Graff, Donald Louis, 1935- Environmental impacts of BART . Washington [Springfield, Va.] 1980. ca. 150 p. in various pagings : LC Card 80-603252 DDC 388.4/2/097946 19
TD195.S9 G7

Regulation X. 1979. Real estate settlement procedures act. Washington, D.C. [1979] 7, 39, [12] p. : LC Card 80-601047 DDC 346.7304/373 19
KF681 .R4

Revitalizing North American neighborhoods : a comparison of Canadian and U. S. programs for neighborhood preservation and housing rehabilitation / U. S. Department of Housing and Urban Development, Central Mortgage and Housing Corporation, and Ministry of State Urban Affairs Canada. [Washington] : The Department, [1978] 28 p. ; 28 cm. Cover title. Prepared by David Carlson. Bibliography: p. 28. LC Card 79-602727 DDC 307.7/6/0973 19
1. Community development, Urban - United States. 2. Community development, Urban - Canada. 3. Housing rehabilitation - United States. 4. Housing rehabilitation - Canada. I. Carlson, David. II. Central Mortgate and Housing Corporation. III. Canada. Ministry of State for Urban Affairs. IV. Title.
HN90.C6 U6 1978

Schafer, Robert. Equal credit opportunity, accessibility to mortgage funds by women and minorities . Washington , 1980. 2 v. ;
NYPL [JLM 80-1138]

Settlement costs. 1979. Real estate settlement procedures act. Washington, D.C. [1979] 7, 39, [12] p. : LC Card 80-601047 DDC 346.7304/373 19
KF681 .R4

Struyk, Raymond J. Improving the elderly's housing . Cambridge, Mass. , c1980. xxii, 325 p. : ISBN 0-88410-495-8 LC Card 79-3008
HD7287.92.U55 S77 **NYPL [JLE 80-2769]**

United States. Civil Service Commission. Bureau of Training. Personnel Management Training Center. Instructors' guide for workshop in employee development /. [Washington?] , 1973. 305 p. in various pagings :
NYPL [JLF 80-1341]

United States. Congress. Senate. Committee on Appropriations. Subcommittee on HUD-Independent Agencies. Management of HUD's multi-family properties, the Cliffton Terrace case . Washington , 1980. iii, 375, vi p. ; LC Card 80-602962 DDC 353.0086/5043/09753 19
KF26 .A6486 1979b

UNITED STATES. DEPT. OF HOUSING AND URBAN DEVELOPMENT.
Targeting community development . Washington, D.C. [1980] xvii, 212, [154] p. ; LC Card 80-602935 DDC 307 19
HN90.C6 T37

United States. Congress. House. Committee on Government Operations. Manpower and Housing Subcommittee. Department of Housing and Urban Development's cooperative housing programs . Washington , 1980 [i.e. 1981] iii,

130 p. ;   LC Card 81-601644   DDC 363.5/8 19
KF27 .G6678 1980f

United States. Congress. House. Committee on
Government Operations. Manpower and
Housing Subcommittee. Fiscal and accounting
systems of the Department of Housing and
Urban Development :hearing before a
subcommittee of the Committee on
Government Operations, House of
Representatives, Ninety-sixth Congress, first
session, November 8, 1979. Washington , 1980.
iii, 90 p. ;   LC Card 80-602076   DDC 353.85 19
KF27 .G6678 1979e

United States. Congress. Senate. Committee on
Appropriations. Subcommittee on
HUD-Independent Agencies. Management of
HUD's multi-family properties, the Cliffton
Terrace case . Washington , 1980. iii, 375, vi
p. ;   LC Card 80-602962   DDC
353.0086/5043/09753 19
KF26 .A6486 1979b

United States. Congress. Senate. Committee on
Governmental Affairs. Transfer of authorities
for implementation of building energy
performance standards . Washington , 1980. iii,
196 p. :   LC Card 80-601881   DDC 353.0082/32 19
KF26 .G67 1979aj

United States. Congress. Senate. Committee on
Governmental Affairs. Subcommittee on
Oversight of Government Management. HUD
moratorium on single family sales programs /.
Washington , 1980. v, 24 p. :   LC Card
80-602589   DDC 363.5/8 19
HD7293 .U45 1980

United States. Congress. Senate. Committee on
Governmental Affairs. Subcommittee on
Oversight of Government Management. HUD's
moratorium on single family sales program .
Washington , 1980. 98 p. ;   LC Card 80-603485
DDC 332.7/33/0973 19
KF26 .G676 1980

United States. General Accounting Office.
Ways of providing a fairer share of Federal
housing support to rural areas . [Washington,
D.C. , 1980] v, 86 p. :   LC Card 80-601694
DDC 363.5/8 19
HD7289.U6 U55 1980

United States. General Accounting Office. Why
the formula for allocating community
development block grant funds should be
improved, Department of Housing and Urban
Development /. [Washington , 1976] v, 50 p. ;
LC Card 76-603691
HN90.C6 U62 1976   *NYPL [JLF 81-401]*

**UNITED STATES. DEPT. OF HOUSING
AND URBAN DEVELOPMENT -
APPROPRIATIONS AND
EXPENDITURES.**
United States. Congress. House. Committee on
Post Office and Civil Service. Subcommittee on
Human Resources. Department of Housing and
Urban Development year-end spending .
Washington , 1980. iii, 38 p. ;   LC Card
80-603115   DDC 353.0072/232 19
KF27 .P6456 1980

United States. Congress. Senate. Committee on
Appropriations. Subcommittee on
HUD-Independent Agencies. Department of
Housing and Urban Development, and certain
independent agencies appropriations for fiscal
year 1981 . Washington , 1980. 2 v. (iii, 2553,
xiii p.) :   LC Card 80-604053   DDC
353.0072/236865 19
KF26 .A6486 1980a

**United States. Dept. of Housing and Urban
Development. Federal Housing
Administration. see United States. Federal
Housing Administration.**

**United States. Dept. of Housing and Urban
Development. Federal Insurance
Administration. see United States. Federal
Insurance Administration.**

**United States. Dept. of Housing and Urban
Development. Fire Administration. see
United States. Fire Administration.**

**United States. Dept. of Housing and Urban
Development. Library and Information
Division.**

**Built environment for the elderly and the
handicapped.** United States. Dept. of
Housing and Urban Development. Library
Division. The built environment for the
elderly and the handicapped : a selective
bibliography. 2d ed., rev. [Washington] ,
1979. iii, 66 p. ;   LC Card 79-602339
Z7164.O4 U484 1979 HV1451
                             NYPL [JLF 81-414]

**United States. Dept. of Housing and Urban
Development. Library Division.**
The built environment for the elderly and the
handicapped : a selective bibliography. 2d ed.,
rev. [Washington] : U. S. Dept. of Housing and
Urban Development, Library Division, 1979. iii,
66 p. ; 27 cm. First ed. issued by the Division under
its earlier name: Library and Information Division.
Includes index.   LC Card 79-602339
*1. Aged - Bibliography. 2. Aged - Dwellings -
Bibliography. 3. Handicapped - Bibliography. 4.
Handicapped - Housing - Bibliography. I. United States.
Dept. of Housing and Urban Development. Library and
Information Division. Built environment for the elderly
and the handicapped. II. Title.*
Z7164.O4 U484 1979 HV1451
                             NYPL [JLF 81-414]

United States. Dept. of Housing and Urban
Development. Office of International Affairs.
Children in the built environment .
[Washington, D.C.] , 1980. 21 p. ;   LC Card
80-602399   DDC 016.3052/3 19
Z7164.C5 U567 1980 HT206

**United States. Dept. of Housing and Urban
Development. Office of International Affairs.**
Children in the built environment : a
bibliography, 1979 / prepared by the Office of
International Affairs and the Library,
Department of Housing and Urban
Development. [Washington, D.C.] : The Office,
1980. 21 p. ; 28 cm.   LC Card 80-602399   DDC
016.3052/3 19
*1. City children - Bibliography. I. United States. Dept.
of Housing and Urban Development. Library Division.
II. Title.*
Z7164.C5 U567 1980 HT206

Housing and urban development energy
research abroad : a bibliography / U. S.
Department of Housing and Urban
Development, Office of International Affairs.
[Washington, D.C.] : The Office, 1980. i, 27
p. ; 28 cm.   LC Card 80-601814   DDC 016.33379
19
*1. Power resources - Bibliography. 2. Dwellings -
Energy conservation - Bibliography. I. Title.*
Z5853.P83 U525 1980 TJ163.2

Housing and urban development planning in
Mexico : a bibliography / Department of
Housing and Urban Development (HUD),
Office of International Affairs (OIA).
Washington, D.C. : The Office, [1980] 54 p. ;
28 cm. Prepared by L. F. Pozo-Ledezma. "May 1980."
"HUD-IA-568.   LC Card 80-602924   DDC
307.7/6/0972 19
*1. Housing policy - Mexico - Bibliography. 2. City
planning - Mexico - Bibliography. I. Pozo-Ledezma,
Leo F. II. Title.*
Z7164.H8 U4495 1980 HD7306.A3

Housing finance institutions abroad : a
directory. [Washington, D.C.] : U. S. Dept. of
Housing and Urban Development, Office of
International Affairs, 1979. 49 p. ; 28 cm.   LC
Card 80-602630   DDC 332.7/2/025 19
*1. Housing - Finance - Directories. 2. Mortgage banks -
Directories. I. Title.*
HD7287.55 .U54 1979

Housing finance institutions abroad; a directory.
Washington.   *NYPL [JLM 80-1155]*

HUD international information series. 32-39,
41-47; Feb. 1975-July, 1976, Dec. 1976-Apr.
1978. Washington.   *NYPL [JLM 80-799]*

International bulletin. v. 1, no. 1- ; Apr. 1978-
Washington. Supersedes H. U. D. international
information sources series. Title varies: Apr.-May, 1978,
HUD international bulletin.
I. Title: H. U. D. international bulletin.
                             NYPL [Econ. Div.]

Ma, Laurence J. C., 1937- Cities and city
planning in the People's Republic of China .
Washington, D.C. , 1980. vii, 62 p. ;   LC Card
81-601007   DDC 016.3077/6/0951 19
Z5942 .M13 HT169.C6

Soviet housing and urban design /.
[Washington, D.C.] [1980] v, 68 p. :   LC Card
80-603575   DDC 363.7/0947 19
HD7345.A3 S64

Underhill, Jack A. French national urban policy
and the Paris region new towns . [Washington]
[1980] 131 p. :   LC Card 80-602925   DDC
307.7/6/0944 19
HT165.P37 U52

**United States. Dept. of Housing and Urban
Development. Office of Neighborhoods,
Voluntary Associations, and Consumer
Protection.** Real estate settlement procedures
act. Washington, D.C. [1979] 7, 39, [12] p. :
LC Card 80-601047   DDC 346.7304/373 19
KF681 .R4

**United States. Dept. of Housing and Urban
Development. Office of Policy Development
and Research.**
Burchell, Robert W. The fiscal impact
guidebook . [Washington] , 1979. xxii, 617 p. ;
LC Card 79-602895
HD4431 .B85 1979

Chi, Peter S. K. Population redistribution and
changes in housing tenure status in the United
States /. [Washington, D.C.] [1980] 27 p. ;
LC Card 80-601677   DDC 304.8/2/0973 19
HD7287.82.U6 C45

Conference on Local Financial Management,
1st, Detroit, 1979. Local financial management
in the '80s . Washington, D.C. [1980] ix, 306
p. :   LC Card 80-602329
HJ9141 .C66 1979   *NYPL [JLF 80-1653]*

The Deployment of emergency services / Dept.
of Housing and Urban Development, Office of
Policy Development and Research. Washington,
D. C. : The Department: For sale by the
Superintendent of Documents, U. S. Govt.
Print. Off., 1977. ix, 61 p. : ill. ; 27 cm.
Previously issued as a Rand Corporation report,
R-1867-HUD. Bibliography: p. 59-61.
*1. Emergency transportation. 2. Emergency
transportation - Mathematical models. I. Title.*
                             NYPL [JLF 81-350]

Design and construction of large-panel concrete
structures : supplemental report C, "seismic
tests of horizontal joints" / U. S. Department of
Housing and Urban Development, Office of
Policy Development and Research.
[Washington] : The Office, [1979] xii, 49 p. :
ill. ; 28 cm. Cover title. Includes bibliographical
references.   ISBN 0-08-931238-3   LC Card 79-603976
DDC 693.8/52 19
*1. Earthquake resistant design. 2. Concrete panels -
Design and construction. 3. Concrete construction -
Joints - Testing. 4. Precast concrete construction. I.
Title.*
TA658.44 .U52 1979

Franklin Research Center. The first passive
solar home awards, January 1979 /.
[Washington] , 1979. 226 p. :   LC Card
79-603049
TH7414 .F73 1979   *NYPL [JSF 81-210]*

HRB-Singer, inc., State College, Pa. Energy and
Natural Resources Program Dept. The nature
and distribution of subsidence problems
affecting HUD and urban areas (task A) /.
[Washington, D.C.] , 1979. x, 113 p. ;   LC Card
79-603258
TH1094 .H17 1979   *NYPL [JSF 81-154]*

How well are we housed? / U. S. Department
of Housing and Urban Development, Office of
Policy Development and Research.
Washington : The Office, 1978-1979. 4 v. : ill. ;
28 cm. (United States. Dept. of Housing and Urban
Development. HUD-PDR. 333, 344, 366, 413)
Summaries, by Ruth Limmer, of a report written by
Anthony Yezer under contract with HUD.
CONTENTS: - 1. Hispanics. - 2. Female-headed
households. - 3. Blacks. - 4. The elderly.
*1. Housing - United States. 2. Households - United
States. I. Limmer, Ruth. II. Yezer, Anthony. III. Title.*
                             NYPL [JLM 80-448]

Howenstine, Emanuel Jay. Housing costs in the
United States and other industrialized countries,
1970-1977 /. [Washington, D.C.] [1980] 23
p. ;   LC Card 80-601699   DDC 338.4/33635/0973
19
HD7293 .H8

HUD National Conference on Housing Costs,
Washington, D.C., 1979. Reducing the

GOVERNMENT PUBLICATIONS - U.S.: 1981

519   United States. Dept. of Justice. Immigration and Naturalization

development costs of housing . [Washington, D.C.] , 1979. xv, 275 p. : LC Card 80-601844
DDC 338.4/36908/0973 19
HD7293 .H82 1979

Joint Center for Urban Studies. The behavioral foundations of neighborhood change /. Washington [1979] 205 p. ; LC Card 79-601949
HT123 .J63 1979   **NYPL [JLF 81-252]**

Jones, Ronald, 1945- Problems affecting low-rent public housing projects . [Washington, D.C.] [1979] x, 317 p. : LC Card 80-600612
HD7293 .J66

Lower Income Housing Assistance Program (Section 8) : nationwide evaluation of the existing housing program / by Margaret Drury ... [et al.]. [Washington] : U. S. Dept. of Housing and Urban Development, Office of Policy Development and Research ; Washington : for sale by the Supt. of Docs., U. S. Govt. Print. Off., 1978 i.e. 1979. xx, 101 p. : ill. ; 26 cm. "HUD-PDR-359." Bibliography: p. 99-101. LC Card 79-602087
1. Rent subsidies - United States. 2. United States. Dept. of Housing and Urban Development. Section 8 Housing Assistance Payment Program for Lower Income Families. I. Drury, Margaret J. II. Title.
HD7293 .A5 1979b   **NYPL [JLF 81-553]**

Miller, Mary Lenn. Affirmative action planning. [Garland, Tex.], 1977. 121 p.;
                          NYPL [JLF 80-1394]

National Association of Housing and Redevelopment Officials. Designing rehab programs . [Washington, D.C.] , 1980. iv, 90, [75] p. : LC Card 80-602368 DDC 352.7/5/0973 19
HD7293 .N3325 1980

National Training and Information Center. Home mortgage disclosure act and reinvestment strategies . [Washington] , 1979. ii, 94 p. : LC Card 79-603975
HG2040.5.U5 N43 1979
                          NYPL [JLF 81-232]

Nelson, Kathryn P. Recent suburbanization of Blacks, how much, who, and where /. [Washington] , 1979. 34 p. : LC Card 79-602959
HD7288.72.U5 N44

Phipps, Antony A. Homebuyer's information package . [Washington, D.C.?] , 1979. 1 v. (loose-leaf) : LC Card 81-600743 DDC 643/.12 19
HD1379 .P468

Rahenkamp, Sachs, Wells, and Associates. Innovative zoning: a local officials guidebook /. [Washington] , 1977. 28 p.:
                          NYPL [*XME-8967]

Real Estate Research Corporation. Urban infill . [Washington, D.C.] [1980] 76 p. ; LC Card 80-602851 DDC 016.33377/13/0973 19
Z7164.L3 R4 1980 HD205

Residents' satisfaction in HUD-assisted housing . Washington [1979] ca. 200 p. in various pagings : LC Card 79-601946
HD7293 .R372   **NYPL [JLF 81-344]**

Rouse, W. Victor. Crime in public housing . Washington, D.C. , 1978 [i.e. 1979- v. ; LC Card 79-603818
HV6791 .R67

Schafer, Robert. Equal credit opportunity . [Washington, D.C.] , 1980. 2 v. : LC Card 80-602636 DDC 332.7/22 19
HG2040.2 .S3

Silver, Jennifer. Condominium conversion controls . Washington, D.C. , 1979 [i.e.] 1980. 61 p. ; LC Card 80-601762 DDC 346.7304/33 19
KF581 .S54

United States Conference of Mayors. The private development process . [Washington] [1979] iii, 49 p. ; LC Card 79-601943
HD259 .U53 1979

William Brill Associates. Comprehensive security planning . Washington , 1977. 196 p. in various pagings : LC Card 78-601532
HV8290 .W54 1977   **NYPL [JLF 81-371]**

United States. Dept. of Housing and Urban Development. Office of Policy Development and Research. Division of Energy, Building Technology and Standards. see United States. Division of Energy, Building Technology and Standards.

United States. Dept. of Housing and Urban Development. Office of Policy Development and Research. Division of Policy Studies.
United States. Dept. of Housing and Urban Development. Office of Policy Development and Research. Division of Evaluation.
Measuring racial discrimination in American housing markets : the housing market practices survey / by Ronald E. Wienk ... [et al.]. [Washington, D.C.] : Division of Evaluation, U. S. Dept. of Housing and Urban Development, Office of Policy Development and Research, 1979. vii, 30, 206, [93] p. : forms ; 27 cm. "HUD-PDR-444." Includes bibliographical references. LC Card 79-603351
1. Discrimination in housing - United States. 2. Afro-Americans - Housing. I. Wienk, Ronald E. II. Title.
HD7293 .A5 1979d

Peroff, Kathleen A. Gautreaux housing demonstration . Washington, D.C. [1979] x, 202 p. : LC Card 80-602934 DDC 363.5/1 19
HD7288.78.U52 C46

United States. Dept. of Housing and Urban Development. Office of Policy Development and Research. Lower Income Housing Assistance Program (Section 8) Yap, Lorene. Lower Income Housing Assistance Program (Section 8) . Washington , 1978 i.e. 1979. ix, 232 p. ; LC Card 79-602558
HD7293 .A5 1979b Suppl.
                          NYPL [JLF 81-460]

United States. Dept. of Housing and Urban Development. Office of Policy Research and Development. Ma, Laurence J. C., 1937- Cities and city planning in the People's Republic of China . Washington, D.C. , 1980. vii, 62 p. ; LC Card 81-601007 DDC 016.3077/6/0951 19
Z5942 .M13 HT169.C6

UNITED STATES. DEPT. OF HOUSING AND URBAN DEVELOPMENT - OFFICIALS AND EMPLOYEES.
United States. Congress. Senate. Committee on Banking, Housing and Urban Affairs. Nominations of Robert E. Herzstein, Frank B. Sollars, Alexis M. Herman, and Alfred R. Marane . Washington , 1980. iii, 78 p. ; LC Card 80-603063 DDC 353.82 19
KF26 .B39 1980i

United States. Congress. Senate. Committee on Banking, Housing and Urban Affairs. Nomination of Donald I. Hovde . Washington , 1981. iii, 49 p. ; LC Card 81-601780 DDC 353.85 19
KF26 .B39 1981b

United States. Congress. Senate. Committee on Banking, Housing and Urban Affairs. Nomination of Samuel R. Pierce, Jr. . Washington , 1981. iii, 95 p. ; LC Card 81-601350 DDC 353.85 19
KF26 .B39 1981c

United States. Congress. Senate. Committee on Banking, Housing and Urban Affairs. Nominations of Philip D. Winn, John J. Knapp, Emanuel S. Savas, and Arthur E. Teele, Jr., . Washington , 1981. iii, 136 p. ; LC Card 81-601958 DDC 353.85 19
KF26 .B39 1981f

United States. Dept. of Housing and Urban Development. Policy Development and Research, Office of. see United States. Dept. of Housing and Urban Development. Office of Policy Development and Research.

UNITED STATES. DEPT. OF HOUSING AND URBAN DEVELOPMENT. SECTION 8 HOUSING ASSISTANCE PAYMENT PROGRAM FOR LOWER INCOME FAMILIES - STATISTICS.
Yap, Lorene. Lower Income Housing Assistance Program (Section 8) . Washington , 1978 i.e. 1979. ix, 232 p. ; LC Card 79-602558
HD7293 .A5 1979b Suppl.
                          NYPL [JLF 81-460]

United States. Dept. of Housing and Urban Development. Task Force on Housing Costs. see United States. Task Force on Housing Costs.

United States. Dept. of Interior. Teton Dam Failure Review Group. see United States. Teton Dam Failure Review Group.

United States. Dept. of Justice. (Old Catalog form: United States. Justice Dept.) Employment fact book. July/Dec. 1977- [Washington]
I. Title.   **NYPL [Econ. Div.]**

Legal activities. [Washington] 26-28 cm. Cover title. LC Card 68-67189
1. United States. Dept. of Justice - Periodicals. 2. Justice, Administration of - United States - Periodicals.
I. Title. **NYPL [JLM 80-971 & *XME-1955]**

Tompkins, Joseph B. National priorities for the investigation and prosecution of white collar crime . Washington, D.C. , 1980. x, 50, 21-a p. ; LC Card 80-603918 DDC 364.1/68/0973 19
HV8079.W47 T65

UNITED STATES. DEPT. OF JUSTICE - ACCOUNTING.
United States. Congress. House. Committee on Government Operations. Subcommittee on Government Information and Individual Rights. Department of Justice internal audit operations . Washington , 1980 [i.e. 1981] iv, 263 p. ; LC Card 81-601331 DDC 353.5 19
KF27 .G6628 1980b

United States. Dept. of Justice. Antitrust Division. (Old Catalog form: United States. Justice Dept. Antitrust Laws, Division for Enforcement of)
Antitrust Division manual / U. S. Department of Justice, Antitrust Division. [Washington, D.C.] : The Division, 1980. 457 p. in various pagings : map ; 28 cm. Cover title. Includes bibliography. LC Card 80-601264 DDC 343.73/072/02636 19
1. United States. Dept. of Justice. Antitrust Division. 2. Antitrust law - United States. I. Title.
KF1653 .A8322

UNITED STATES. DEPT. OF JUSTICE. ANTITRUST DIVISION.
United States. Dept. of Justice. Antitrust Division. Antitrust Division manual /. [Washington, D.C.] , 1980. 457 p. in various pagings : LC Card 80-601264 DDC 343.73/072/02636 19
KF1653 .A8322

UNITED STATES. DEPT. OF JUSTICE - APPROPRIATIONS AND EXPENDITURES.
United States. Congress. House. Committee on the Judiciary. Department of Justice authorization--fiscal year 1981 . Washington , 1981. iii, 53 p. ; LC Card 81-601368 DDC 353.0072/234 19
KF27 .J8 1980

United States. Congress. Senate. Committee on the Judiciary. Department of Justice authorization and oversight, 1981 . Washington , 1980. vi, 1293 p. : LC Card 81-600649 DDC 353.5 19
KF26 .J8 1980e

United States. Department of Justice. Bureau of Investigation. see United States. Federal Bureau of Investigation.

United States. Dept. of Justice. Bureau of Justice statistics. see United States. Bureau of Justice Statistics.

United States. Dept. of Justice. Civil Rights Division. Task Force on Sex Discrimination. see United States. Dept. of Justice. Task Force on Sex Discrimination.

United States. Dept. of Justice. Criminal Division. Tompkins, Joseph B. National priorities for the investigation and prosecution of white collar crime . Washington, D.C. , 1980. x, 50, 21-a p. ; LC Card 80-603918 DDC 364.1/68/0973 19
HV8079.W47 T65

United States. Department of Justice. Division of Investigation. see United States. Federal Bureau of Investigation.

United States. Dept. of Justice. Drug Enforcement Administration. see United States. Drug Enforcement Administration.

United States. Department of Justice. Federal Bureau of Investigation. see United States. Federal Bureau of Investigation.

United States. Dept. of Justice. Immigration and Naturalization Service. see United States. Immigration and Naturalization Service.

United States. Department of Justice. Investigation Bureau. see United States. Federal Bureau of Investigation.

United States. Dept. of Justice. Law Enforcement Assistance Administration. see United States. Law Enforcement Assistance Administration.

United States. Dept. of Justice. Law Enforcement Assistance Administration. National Criminal Justice Information and Statistics Service. see United States. National Criminal Justice Information and Statistics Service.

United States. Dept. of Justice. National Institute of Justice (U. S.) see National Institute of Justice.

UNITED STATES. DEPT. OF JUSTICE - OFFICIALS AND EMPLOYEES.
United States. Congress. House. Committee on the Judiciary. Subcommittee on Civil and Constitutional Rights. Equal employment opportunities at the Department of Justice . Washington , 1981. iii, 147 p. : LC Card 81-601922 DDC 353.5 19
KF27 .J847 1979h

United States. Congress. Senate. Committee on the Judiciary. Confirmation hearing on Edward C. Schmults, nominee, to be deputy attorney general . Washington , 1981. iii, 62 p. ; LC Card 81-601773 DDC 353.5 19
KF26 .J8 1981a

United States. Congress. Senate. Committee on the Judiciary. Confirmation hearing on William French Smith, nominee, to be attorney general . Washington , 1981. iv, 179 p. ; LC Card 81-601872 DDC 353.5 19
KF26 .J8 1981

United States. Congress. Senate. Committee on the Judiciary. Confirmation hearings on Benjamin R. Civiletti, nominee, Attorney General . Washington , 1980. iv, 213 p. ; LC Card 80-601952 DDC 353.5 19
KF26 .J8 1979q

UNITED STATES. DEPT. OF JUSTICE - PERIODICALS.
United States. Dept. of Justice. Legal activities. [Washington] LC Card 68-67189
*NYPL [JLM 80-971 & *XME-1955]*

UNITED STATES. DEPT. OF JUSTICE. PUBLIC INTEGRITY SECTION.
United States. Congress. Senate. Committee on the Judiciary. Oversight of Department of Justice Public Integrity Section . Washington , 1980. iii, 12 p. ; LC Card 81-600613 DDC 353.5 19
KF26 .J8 1980h

United States. Dept. of Justice. Sex Discrimination, Task Force on. see United States. Dept. of Justice. Task Force on Sex Discrimination.

United States. Dept. of Justice. Task Force on Sex Discrimination. The pension game : the American pension system from the viewpoint of the average woman : report of the Task Force on Sex Discrimination, Civil Rights Division, U. S. Department of Justice. Washington : The Task Force : for sale by the Supt. of Docs., U. S. Govt. Print. Off., 1979. 78 p. ; 28 cm. Includes bibliographical references. LC Card 79-602270
1. Women - United States - Pensions. I. Title.
HD6080.2.U5 U52 1979   NYPL [Jlf 81-399]

United States. Dept. of Labor. (Old Catalog form: United States. Labor Dept.) Choice mechanisms in the migration decision. Columbus] 1974. vii, 129 p.
NYPL [JLF 80-1365]

Important events in American labor history, 1778-1978 / U. S. Department of Labor. [Washington, D.C.] : The Dept. : for sale by the Supt. of Docs., U. S. Govt. Print. Off., [1979?] [36] p. : ill. ; 14 x 22 cm. Cover title. LC Card 80-602346 DDC 331.88/0973 19
1. Labor and laboring classes - United States - Chronology. 2. Trade-unions - United States - Chronology. I. Title.
HD8066 .U54 1979

Protecting people at work . Washington, D.C. , 1980. 361, [3] p. : LC Card 80-602208 DDC 363.1/1/0973 19
HD7262.5.U6 P76

United States. Congress. Senate. Committee on Government Affairs. Permanent Subcommittee on Investigations. Oversight of Labor Department's investigation of Teamsters central states pension fund . Washington , 1981. v, 521 p. : LC Card 81-601398 DDC 332.6/7254 19
KF26 .G674 1980f

United States. National Archives and Records Service. Selected documents pertaining to black workers among the records of the Department of Labor and its component bureaus, 1902-1969 /. Washington , 1977. viii, 55 p. ; LC Card 77-12904
Z1361.N39 U63 1977 E185.8
NYPL [Sc F 81-48]

UNITED STATES. DEPARTMENT OF LABOR. - ARCHIVES - CATALOGS.
United States. National Archives and Records Service. Selected documents pertaining to black workers among the records of the Department of Labor and its component bureaus, 1902-1969 /. Washington , 1977. viii, 55 p. ; LC Card 77-12904
Z1361.N39 U63 1977 E185.8
NYPL [Sc F 81-48]

United States. Dept. of Labor. Assistant Secretary for Policy, Evaluation and Research, Office of the. see United States. Dept. of Labor. Office of the Assistant Secretary for Policy, Evaluation and Research.

United States. Dept. of Labor. Bureau of International Labor Affairs. see United States. Bureau of International Labor Affairs.

United States. Dept. of Labor. Bureau of Labor Statistics. see United States. Bureau of Labor Statistics.

United States. Dept. of Labor. Division of Public Employee Labor Relations. see United States. Division of Public Employee Labor Relations.

United States. Dept. of Labor. Employment and Training Administration. see United States. Employment and Training Administration.

United States. Dept. of Labor. Employment Service. see United States. Employment Service.

United States. Dept. of Labor. Employment Standards Administration. see United States. Employment Standards Administration.

United States. Dept. of Labor. Labor-Management Services Administration. see United States. Labor-Management Services Administration.

United States. Dept. of Labor. Library. (Old Catalog form: United States. Labor Dept. Library)
Apprenticeship in the United States, a bibliography. [Washington ; For sale by the Supt. of Docs., U. S. Govt. Print. Off., 1974] 55 p. ; 27 cm. "Includes primarily material published from 1965 through Spring 1974." LC Card 77-89406
1. Apprentices - United States - Bibliography. I. Title.
NYPL [JLF 80-869]

Black lung benefits program : selected references / U. S. Department of Labor, [Office of the] Assistant Secretary for Administration and Management, Library. Washington, D.C. : The Library : for sale by the Supt. of Docs., U. S. Govt. Print. Off., [1979] iii, 28 p. ; 28 cm. "November 1979." LC Card 80-601667 DDC 016.3684/1 19
1. Coal-miners - United States - Pensions - Bibliography. 2. Workmen's compensation - United States - Bibliography. 3. Lungs - Dust diseases - Bibliography. I. Title.
Z7164.L1 U686 1979 HD7116.M6152

The Davis-Bacon act : selected references / U. S. Department of Labor, Office of the Assistant Secretary for Administration and Management, Library. Washington, D.C. : The Library : for sale by the Supt. of Docs., U. S. Govt. Print. Off., [1979] 28 p. ; 28 cm. Cover title. LC Card 79-603951 DDC 016.34473/01289 19
1. Wages - Construction workers - United States - Bibliography. I. Title.
KF3505.C65 A123

Occupational safety and health : a bibliography / U. S. Department of Labor, Assistant Secretary for Administration and Management, Library. [Washington] : The Library, 1978 i.e. 1979. vii, 648 p. ; 28 cm. Prepared by E. K. Van Staaveren. Includes indexes. LC Card 79-603966
1. Industrial safety - Bibliography. 2. Industrial hygiene - Bibliography. I. Van Staaveren, Elizabeth K. II. Title.
Z7914.S17 U54 1979 T55

The Practice of management . [Washington, D.C.] , 1980. ii, 101 p. ; LC Card 80-604143 DDC 016.658 19
Z7164.O7 P68 HD30.5

United States. Dept. of Labor. Manpower Administraiton. United States. Bureau of the Census. Urban atlas, tract data for standard metropolitan areas . Washington, D.C. , 1974 [i.e. 1975] [15] p. : LC Card 80-600869 DDC 912/.1312/0976819
G1337.M4E25 U5 1975

United States. Dept. of Labor. Manpower Administration. (Old Catalog form: United States. Manpower Administration)
Bickner, Mei Liang. Women at work . [Los Angeles] , 1977. 1 v. ; LC Card 77-622630
Z7963.E7 B52 HD6095
NYPL [JLM 80-1110]

United States. Bureau of the Census. Urban atlas, tract data for standard metropolitan statistical areas . Washington, D.C. , 1974 [i.e. 1975] [16] p. : LC Card 80-600861 DDC 912/.1312/0979474
G1527.S33E25 U5 1975

United States. Bureau of the Census. Urban atlas, tract data for standard metropolitan statistical areas . Washington, D.C. , 1974 [i.e. 1975] [15] p. : LC Card 80-600872 DDC 912/.1312/0975662
G1302.G7E25 U5 1975

United States. Bureau of the Census. Urban atlas, tract data for standard metropolitan statistical areas . Washington, D.C. , 1974 [i.e. 1975] [43] p. : LC Card 80-600845 DDC 912/.1312/0977311
G1407.C54E25 U5 1975

United States. Bureau of the Census. Urban atlas, tract data for standard metropolitan statistical areas . Washington, D.C. , 1974 [i.e. 1975] [31] p. : LC Card 80-600856 DDC 912/.1312/097526
G1272.B3E25 U5 1975

United States. Bureau of the Census. Urban atlas, tract data for standard metropolitan statistical areas . Washington, D.C. , 1974 [i.e. 1975] [30] p. : LC Card 80-600863 DDC 912/.1312/0974932
G1257.N5E25 U5 1975

Walther, Regis H. The measurement of work-relevant attitudes . - Washington , 1975. 19, 2. [4] p. ;   *NYPL [*XM-13884]*

United States. Dept. of Labor. Manpower Administration. Office of Manpower Policy, Evaluation, and Research. see United States. Dept. of Labor. Office of Manpower Policy, Evaluation, and Research.

United States. Dept. of Labor. Manpower Administraton. United States. Bureau of the Census. Urban atlas, tract data for standard metropolitan statistical areas . Washington, D.C. , 1974 [i.e. 1975] [29] p. ; LC Card 80-600871 DDC 912/.1312/09778411
G1437.K2E25 U5 1975

United States. Dept. of Labor. Occupational Safety and Health Administration. see United States. Occupational Safety and Health Administration.

United States. Dept. of Labor. Office Federal Contract Compliance Programs. see United States. Office of Federal Contract Compliance Programs.

United States. Dept. of Labor. Office of Manpower Policy, Evaluation, and Research. (Old Catalog form: United States. Manpower Policy, Evaluation and Research, Office of) Ultrasystems, inc. Evaluation and analysis of the Cleff job matching system: final report /. - Irvine, Calif. , 1975. 2 v. in 1 :
*NYPL [*XME-9380]*

United States. Dept. of Labor. Office of the
Assistant Secretary for Administration and
Management. Library. see United States.
Dept. of Labor. Library.

United States. Dept. of Labor. Office of the
Assistant Secretary for Policy, Evaluation
and Research.
Conference on Evaluation of the Economic
Stimulus Package, Brookings Institution, 1977.
Conference report on evaluating the 1977
economic stimulus package /. [Washington] ,
1978. iii, 127 p. ; LC Card 79-602314
HC106.7 .C665 1977   NYPL [JLF 81-172]

An interim report to Congress on occupational
diseases : submitted to Congress June 1980 /
United States Department of Labor, Assistant
Secretary for Policy, Evaluation, and Research.
[Washington] : The Dept., [1980] 138 p. ; 28
cm. Includes bibliographical references. LC Card
80-602704 DDC 363.1/1/0973 19
1. Occupational diseases - United States. 2.
Occupational diseases - United States - Statistics. I.
Title.
RC964 .U54 1980

Lerman, Robert I. The nature of the youth
employment problem . [Washington, D.C.]
[Springfield, Va.] 1980. 105, 4 p. ; LC Card
80-602227 DDC 331.3/4137973 19
HD6273 .L46

Technical analysis paper - U. S. Department of
Labor, Office of the Assistant Secretary
for Policy, Evaluation, and Research .
(no. 69) Lerman, Robert I. The nature of the
youth employment problem . [Washington,
D.C.] [Springfield, Va.] 1980. 105, 4 p. ;
LC Card 80-602227 DDC 331.3/4137973 19
HD6273 .L46

UNITED STATES. DEPT. OF LABOR -
OFFICIALS AND EMPLOYEES.
United States. Congress. Senate. Committee on
Labor and Human Resources. Nomination .
Washington , c1981. ii, 378 p. : LC Card
81-600954 DDC 353.83
KF26 .L27 1981

United States. Dept. of Labor. Wage and Hour
and Public Contracts Divisons. see United
States. Wage and Hour and Public Contracts
Divisions.

United States. Dept. of Labor. Women's Bureau.
see United States. Women's Bureau.

United States. Dept. of State. (Old Catalog form:
United States. State Dept.)
Clark, G. Edward (Gilbert Edward), 1917-
Sub-Saharan Africa and the United States .
[Washington, D.C.] , 1980. 46 p., [1] leaf of
plates : LC Card 80-603396 DDC 967 19
DT353.5.U6 C55 1980

Communist interference in El Salvador .
[Washington, D.C.?] , 1981. 1 v. (various
pagings), [3] leaves of plates (1 folded) : LC
Card 81-601684 DDC 322.4/2/097284 19
HX148.5 C65

The global legal framework for narcotics and
prohibitive substances : prepared for Bureau of
International Narcotics Matters. Washington,
D.C. : U. S. Dept. of States : [for sale by the
Supt. of Docs., U. S. Govt. Print. Off.], 1979.
86, 14 p. ; 28 cm. Cover title. Includes index. LC
Card 79-603788
1. Narcotic laws. 2. Drugs - Law and legislation. I.
United States. Bureau of International Narcotics
Matters. II. Title.
K5282 .U54   NYPL [JLF 81-316]

Global 2000 Study (U. S.) The global 2000
report to the President--entering the twenty-first
century . Washington, D.C. , 1980- v. <1-2> :
LC Card 80-602859 DDC 333.7 19
HC79.E5 G59 1980b

Publication.
(7491) United States. National Commission
for the United Nations Educational, Scientific
and Cultural Organization. UNESCO and the
U. S. National Commission for UNESCO .
Washington, D.C. , 1977. viii, 48 p. ; LC
Card 78-602328 DDC 341.7/67 19
AS4.U825 U6 1977

The United States-Japan Cooperative Medical
Science Program . [Washington, D.C.?] 1980.
xiv, 214 p. : LC Card 81-600759 DDC 610/.72 19
R853.I57 U54

UNITED STATES. DEPT. OF STATE.
Communist interference in El Salvador .
[Washington, D.C.?] , 1981. 1 v. (various
pagings), [3] leaves of plates (1 folded) : LC
Card 81-601684 DDC 322.4/2/097284 19
HX148.5 C65

United States. Dept. of State. African Affairs,
Bureau of. see United States. Dept. of State.
Bureau of African Affairs.

United States. Dept. of State. Agency for
International Development. see United
States. Agency for International
Development.

UNITED STATES. DEPT. OF STATE -
APPROPRIATIONS AND
EXPENDITURES.
United States. Congress. House. Committee on
Foreign Affairs. Subcommittee on International
Operations. Authorizing appropriations for fiscal
years 1980-81 for the Department of State, the
International Communication Agency, and the
Board for International Broadcasting.
Washington , 1980. iii, 24 p. ; LC Card
80-603032 DDC 353.0072/23689 19
KF27 .F647 1979d

United States. Congress. Senate. Committee on
Foreign Relations. Department of State
authorization act, fiscal years 1980 and 1981 .
Washington , 1980. iii, 71 p. ; LC Card
80-602739 DDC 353.0072/23689 19
KF26 .F6 1980h

United States. Dept. of State. Bureau of African
Affairs. AF press clips. Washington, D. C..
NYPL [Sc Ser.-M .A145]

United States. Dept. of State. Bureau of
Educational and Cultural Affairs. see United
States. Bureau of Educational and Cultural
Affairs.

United States. Dept. of State. Bureau of
International Narcotics Matters. see United
States. Bureau of International Narcotics
Matters.

UNITED STATES. DEPT. OF STATE.
BUREAU OF OCEANS AND
INTERNATIONAL ENVIRONMENTAL
AND SCIENTIFIC AFFAIRS.
United States. Congress. House. Committee on
Science and Technology. Subcommittee on
Science, Research, and Technology. Natural
resources and environment in the Bureau of
Oceans and International Environmental and
Scientific Affairs . Washington , 1980. iii, 159
p. ; LC Card 80-603700 DDC 353.0085/5 19
KF27 .S399 1980e

United States. Dept. of State. Foreign Service
Institute. see United States. Foreign Service
Institute.

United States. Dept. of State. Information
Systems Office. United Nations. General
Assembly. 32d session, 1977. Votes at the
thirty-second regular session of the General
Assembly, 20 September-21 December, 1977.
[Washington, D.C.] [1978?] lix, 469 p. ; LC
Card 80-601606 DDC 341.23/22 19
JX1977.8.V6 U54 1977

United States. Dept. of State. International
Cooperation Administration. see United
States. International Cooperation
Administration.

United States. Dept. of State. Oceans and
International Environmental and Scientific
Affairs, Bureau of. see United States. Dept.
of State. Bureau of Oceans and International
Environmental and Scientific Affairs.

United States. Dept. of State. Office of
Multilateral Affairs. Reference and
Documents Section. United Nations. General
Assembly. 32d session, 1977. Votes at the
thirty-second regular session of the General
Assembly, 20 September-21 December, 1977.
[Washington, D.C.] [1978?] lix, 469 p. ; LC
Card 80-601606 DDC 341.23/22 19
JX1977.8.V6 U54 1977

United States. Dept. of State. Office of Public
Communication.
Selected documents - The Department of State,
Office of Public Communication .
(no. 5, rev) Human rights. [Washington]
[1978] 63 p. ; LC Card 79-602106 DDC

341.4/81 19
K3238.A1 H84

UNITED STATES. DEPT. OF STATE -
OFFICIALS AND EMPLOYEES.
United States. Congress. Senate. Committee on
Foreign Relations. Nomination of Alexander M.
Haig, Jr. . Washington , 1981. 2 v. ; LC Card
81-600880 DDC 353.1 19
KF26 .F6 1981

United States. Congress. Senate. Committee on
Foreign Relations. Nomination of Edmund S.
Muskie . Washington , 1980. iii, 44 p. ; LC
Card 80-602965 DDC 353.1 19
KF26 .F6 1980j

United States. Congress. Senate. Committee on
Foreign Relations. Nomination of James L.
Malone . Washington , 1981. iii, 80 p. ; LC
Card 81-601860 DDC 353.1 19
KF26 .F6 1981d

United States. Congress. Senate. Committee on
Foreign Relations. Nomination of Jeane J.
Kirkpatrick . Washington , 1981. iii, 110 p. ;
LC Card 81-601348 DDC 353.1 19
KF26 .F6 1981a

United States. Congress. Senate. Committee on
Foreign Relations. Nomination of Justice
William Patrick Clark . Washington , 1981. iii,
84 p. : LC Card 81-601174 DDC 353.1 19
KF26 .F6 1981c

United States. Dept. of the Air Force. (Old
Catalog form: United States. Air Force Dept.)
Educational opportunities on Air Force bases /
[writer-editor, J. Comeaux]. [Washington,
D.C.] : Dept. of the Air Force, [1980] ca. 150
p. in various pagings : ill. ; 28 cm. Cover title. At
head of title: Educational Services Program. "1 August
1980." "AF pamphlet ; 213-2." Includes indexes. LC
Card 80-603210 DDC 378.73 19
1. Soldiers - Education, Non-military - United States -
Directories. 2. University extension - United States -
Directories. I. Comeaux, J. II. Title.
U716 .A533 1980

UNITED STATES. DEPT. OF THE AIR
FORCE - OFFICIALS AND EMPLOYEES.
United States. Congress. Senate. Committee on
Armed Services. Nomination of Charles W.
Snodgrass . Washington , 1980. ii, 7 p. ; LC
Card 80-602952 DDC 353.63 19
KF26 .A7 1980b

United States. Congress. Senate. Committee on
Armed Services. Nomination of George Vernon
Orr, Jr., to be secretary of the Air Force .
Washington , 1981. ii, 12 p. ; LC Card
81-601412 DDC 353.63 19
KF26 .A7 1981b

United States. Dept. of the Army. (Old Catalog
form: United States. Army Dept.)
Assignment Canal Zone: facts you need to
know / [Department of the Army].
[Washington: The Dept., 1974] 24 p.; 22 cm.
Microfiche (neg.) 1 sheet. 11 x 15 cm. (NYPL FSN
35,273) "Department of the Army pamphlet, 608-8."
"Supersedes DA Pam 608-8, 10 October 1969."
1. Canal Zone - Description and travel. I. Title. II.
Title: Canal Zone: facts you need to know.
NYPL [*XMB-1398]

China, an analytical survey of literature. 1978
ed. Washington : Dept. of the Army : [for sale
by the supt. of Docs., U. S. Govt. Print. Off.]
1978. 231 p. : ill., maps (3 fold. in pocket ; 28
cm. Cover title. Earlier editions published under title:
Communist China. "DA pamphlet 550-9-1." LC Card
76-26660
1. China - History - 1949-1976 - Bibliography. I. Title.
Z3108 .A5U5 1978 DS777.55
NYPL [JFF 81-146]

Combat readiness : the army's goal. [Baltimore,
Md. : Department of the Army, U. S. Army
AG Publication Center], 1973. [4] p. ; 28
cm. (Its: Pamphlets. DA PAM 525-10) Microfilm.
1. United States. Army - Handbooks, manuals, etc. I.
Title.   NYPL [*Z-3211]

Firearm and archery safety / Department of the
Army. [Washington]: Headquarters, Dept. of
the Army, 1974. 22 p.: ill.; 23 cm. (Its:
Pamphlets. no. 385-7) Microfiche (neg.) 1 sheet. 11 x
15 cm. (NYPL FSN 34,051) Cover title.
1. Shooting - Safety measures. 2. Archery - Safety
measures. I. Title.   NYPL [*XM-13354]

Human self-development in confinement /

Department of the Army. Washington: Headquarters, Dept. of the Army, 1973. 24 p.; 28 cm. Microfiche (neg.) 1 sheet. 11 x 15 cm. (NYPL FSN 34,890 Cover title. "DA pamphlet no. 165-12."
1. Ethics - United States. 2. Prisons - Employees. 3. Prisons, Military - United States. I. Title.
NYPL [*XM-13534]

United States. Dept. of the Army. Adjutant-General's Office. see United States. Adjutant-General's Office.

United States. Dept. of the Army. Deputy Chief of Staff for Research Development and Acquisition. see United States. Dept. of the Army. Office of the Deputy Chief of Staff for Research, Development, and Acquisition.

United States. Dept. of the Army. General Staff. (Old Catalog form: United States. General Staff)
A framework for molding the Army of the 1980s into a disciplined, well-trained fighting force : white paper / Chief of Staff, US Army. [Washington, D.C.] : Dept. of the Army, United States of America, 1980. 17 p. : ill. ; 24 cm. Cover title. LC Card 80-602648 DDC 355.3/0973 19
1. United States. Army - Addresses, essays, lectures. I. Title.
UA24 .A7 1980

United States. Dept. of the Army. Office of the Chief of Engineers. see United States. Army. Corps of Engineers.

United States. Dept. of the Army. Office of the Chief of Legislative Liaison. Fact book for the 96th Congress. [Washington, D.C.] : Dept. of the Army, Legislative Liaison, [1979] ca. 150 p. in various pagings ; 27 cm. Cover title. Includes index. LC Card 79-602107 DDC 355.2/024/328 19
1. United States. Army - Handbooks, manuals, etc. I. Title.
UA24 .A7 1979

United States. Dept. of the Army. Office of the Comptroller of the Army. see United States. Office of the Comptroller of the Army.

United States. Dept. of the Army. Office of the Deputy Chief of Staff for Personnel. Army War College. see United States. Army War College.

United States. Dept. of the Army. Office of the Deputy Chief of Staff for Research, Development, and Acquisition. Army Science Conference. Proceedings. Washington.
NYPL [JSP 81-56]

UNITED STATES. DEPT. OF THE ARMY - OFFICIALS AND EMPLOYEES.
United States. Congress. Senate. Committee on Armed Services. Nomination of John O. Marsh, Jr., to be secretary of the Army . Washington , 1981. iii, 22 p. ; LC Card 81-601158 DDC 353.62 19
KF26 .A7 1981d

United States. Dept. of the Army. Research, Development, and Acquisition, Office of the Deputy Chief of Staff. see United States. Dept. of the Army. Office of the Deputy Chief of Staff for Research, Development, and Acquisition.

United States. Dept. of the Army. Research Institute for the Behavioral and Social Sciences. Hirshfeld, Stephen F. Algebraic systems ; applications in the behavioral and social sciences /. Alexandria, Va. , 1978. 119 p. ; **NYPL [JLF 80-1630]**

United States. Dept. of the Interior. (Old Catalog form: United States. Interior Dept.) Alexandria waterfront, Virginia : submitted as an accompanying part of the communication from the Secretary of the Interior transmitting reports on studies of new areas with potential for inclusion in the national park system. Washington : U. S. Govt. Print. Off., 1979. 86 p. : ill. ; 26 cm. (Houe document - 96th Congress, 1st session ; no 96-202, pt. 16) "October 9, 1979." "Referred to the Committee on Interior and Insular Affairs." Bibliography: p. 83-84. LC Card 80-602643 DDC 333.73/17/09755296 19
1. Urban renewal - Virginia - Alexandria. 2. Waterfronts - Virginia - Alexandria. 3. Land use, Urban - Virginia - Alexandria. I. Series: United States. 96th Congress, 1st session, 1979. House. Document , no. 96-202, pt. 16. II. Title.
HT177.A44 U54 1979

BIA profile . Washington, D.C. , 1981. 72 p. : LC Card 81-601834 DDC 323.1/197/073 19
E93 .B18

Brusse, David M. A history of the Chaco Navajos /. Albuquerque, N.M. , Washington, D.C. , 1980. viii, 542 p. : LC Card 81-601717 DDC 978.9/8200497 19
E99.N3 B76

Burger, Carl. Environmental surveillance of gravel removal on the Trans-Alaska Pipeline System, with recommendations for future gravel mining /. Anchorage, Alaska , 1977. 35 leaves : LC Card 79-625780 DDC 333.95/4 19
TD195.S3 B87

Doors to the future : careers for women / United States, Department of the Interior ; [editors, Kathy Wood Loveless, Margaret B. Hushelpeck ; photography editor, Clare Ralston ; contributing writer, Cassandra Larkins]. [Washington, D.C.] : The Dept., 1978. 58 p. : ill. (some col.) ; 26 cm. Cover title. LC Card 79-603728
1. United States. Dept. of the Interior - Officials and employees. I. Loveless, Kathy Wood. II. Hushelpeck, Margaret B. III. Title. IV. Title: Careers for women.
JK865 1978 .D46   **NYPL [JLF 81-226]**

Final environmental impact statement : proposed Alaska Peninsula National Wildlife Refuge, Alaska / prepared by the Department of the Interior. [Washington] : The Dept., [1980] xv, 339 p. : ill. ; 28 cm. Title on cover: Alaska Peninsula National Wildlife Refuge. Bibliography: p. 276-309. Includes index. LC Card 80-602694 DDC 333.95/1/09798 19
1. Wildlife refuges - Alaska - Alaska peninsula. 2. Environmental impact analysis - Alaska - Alaska peninsula. 3. Alaska Peninsula. I. Title. II. Title: Alaska Peninsula National Wildlife Refuge.
QH76.5.A4 U54 1980

Final environmental supplement : alternative administrative actions, Alaska national interest lands / prepared by the Department of the Interior. Washington : The Department, [1978?] ca. 600 p. in various pagings : map (fold. in pocket) ; 27 cm. Includes a bibliography. LC Card 79-601643
1. Research natural areas - Alaska - Management. 2. Alaska - Public lands - Management. 3. Nature conservation - Alaska - Management. I. Title.
QH76.5.A4 U54 1978   **NYPL [JLF 81-375]**

Final report on Phase I of water policy implementation . [Washington, D.C.?] , 1980. 99 p. in various pagings ; LC Card 81-600744 DDC 333.91/160973 19
TC423 .F57

Georgetown waterfront, Washington, D.C. : submitted as an accompanying part of the communication from the Secretary of the Interior, transmitting reports on studies of new areas with potential for inclusion in the national park system. Washington : U. S. Govt. Print. Off., 1979. 53 p. : ill. ; 26 cm. (House document - 96th Congress, 1st session ; no. 96-202, pt. 11) Covertitle. Bibliography: p. 51. LC Card 80-602644 DDC 333.78/3 19
1. Urban renewal - Washington, D.C. 2. Waterfronts - Washington, D.C. 3. Land use, Urban - Washington, D.C. 4. Georgetown, D. C. I. Series: United States. 96th Congress, 1st session. House. Document , no. 96-202, pt. 11. II. Title.
HT177.D6 U52 1979

The Secretary of the Interior's standards for historic preservation projects : with guidelines for applying the standards / developed by W. Brown Morton III, Gary L. Hume. Washington, D. C. : U. S. Dept. of the Interior, Heritage Conservation and Recreation Service, Technical Preservation Services Division, 1973. vi, 46 p. ; 28 cm. Microfilm.
1. Historic buildings - Preservation - Standards. I. Morton, W. Brown. II. Hume, Gary L. III. Title.
NYPL [*ZM-150]

UNITED STATES. DEPT. OF THE INTERIOR.
United States. Congress. House. Committee on Interior and Insular Affairs. Briefing by the secretary of the Interior . Washington , 1981. iii, 79 p. ; LC Card 81-601759 DDC 353.3 19
KF27 .I5 1981

United States. Congress. Senate. Select Committee on Indian Affairs. Leases involving the Secretary of the Interior and the Northern

Cheyenne Indian Reservation . Washington , 1980. iii, 46 p. ; LC Card 80-602714 DDC 346.7304/6822 19
KF26.5 .I4 1980i

UNITED STATES. DEPT. OF THE INTERIOR - APPROPRIATIONS AND EXPENDITURES.
United States. Congress. House. Committee on Appropriations. Subcommittee on Dept. of the Interior and Related Agencies. Department of the Interior and related agencies appropriations for 1982 . Washington , 1981. 4 v. : LC Card 81-601601 DDC 353.0072/2368232 19
KF27 .A6484 1981

United States. Congress. Senate. Committee on Appropriations. Subcommittee on Dept. of the Interior and Related Agencies. Department of the interior and related agencies appropriations for fiscal year 1980 . Washington , 1980- v. <1-4> ; LC Card 80-603500 DDC 353.0072/236 19
KF26 .A652 1980

United States. Dept. of the Interior. Bonneville Power Administration. see United States. Bonneville Power Administration.

United States. Dept. of the Interior. Bureau of Indian Affairs. see United States. Bureau of Indian Affairs.

United States. Dept. of the Interior. Bureau of Land Management. see United States. Bureau of Land Management.

United States. Dept. of the Interior. Bureau of Mines. see United States. Bureau of Mines.

United States. Dept. of the Interior. Bureau of Outdoor Recreation. see United States. Bureau of Outdoor Recreation.

United States. Dept. of the Interior. Bureau of Reclamation. see United States. Bureau of Reclamation.

United States. Dept. of the interior. Census office. see United States. Census Office.

United States. Dept. of the Interior. Federal Water Pollution Control Administration. see United States. Federal Water Pollution Control Administration.

United States. Dept. of the Interior. Fish and Wildlife Service. see United States. Fish and Wildlife Service.

United States. Dept. of the Interior. Geological Survey. see United States. Geological Survey.

United States. Dept. of the Interior. Heritage Conservation and Recreation Service. see United States. Heritage Conservation and Recreation Service.

United States. Dept. of the Interior. National Park Service. see United States. National Park Service.

United States. Dept. of the Interior. Office of Education. see United States. Office of Education.

United States. Dept. of the Interior. Office of Minerals Policy and Research Analysis. see United States. Office of Minerals Policy and Research Analysis.

United States. Dept. of the Interior. Office of Water Research and Technology.
Bella, David A. Environment, technology, and future generations /. Corvallis , 1978. ii, 36 p. ; LC Card 79-625127 DDC 333.91/009795 s 363.7/05 19
HD1694.O7 A13 no. 57 TD170

Bovee, Eugene C. Effects of heavy metals, especially selenium, vanadium, and zirconium on the movement, growth, and survival of certain animal aquatic life /. [Manhattan] , 1978. i, 24 leaves : LC Card 79-624987 DDC 591.5/263 19
QH545.H42 B68

Brockway, Charles E., 1936- Evaluation of urbanization and changes in land use on the water resources of mountain valleys . Moscow, Idaho [1978?] ix, 104 p. [1] fold. leaf of plates : LC Card 79-625237 DDC 333.91/2/09796 19
TD224.I2 B76

Geologic applications of Landsat images in

GOVERNMENT PUBLICATIONS - U.S.: 1981

United States. Dept. of Transportation. Office of Environment and

523

northeastern Arizona to the location of water supplies for municipal and industrial uses / by Elizabeth Babcock ... [et al.]. Washington, D.C. : Office of Water Research and Technology, U. S. Dept. of Interior, [1979] iv leaves, 92 p. : ill. ; 28 cm. "A final report of work performed under OWRT matching grant B-066-ARIZ, agreement number 14-34-0001-8060." Cooperating organizations, Office of Arid Lands Studies, University of Arizona and others. "April 1979." Bibliography: p. 62-69. LC Card 80-622485 DDC 628.1/14 19
1. Water, Underground - Arizona - Remote sensing. 2. Landsat satellites. I. Babcock, Elizabeth, 1954-. II. Arizona. University. Office of Arid Lands Studies. III. Title.
TD224.A7 U52 1979

Marzolf, G. Richard. Kansas River limnology . Manhattan , 1979. 56 p. : LC Card 79-625208 DDC 574.5/26323/09781 19
QH105.K3 M37

Rabe, Fred W. Aquatic natural areas in Idaho /. Moscow, Idaho [1977] 103 p., [7] leaves of plates : LC Card 80-621482 DDC 333.95/2/09796 19
QH76.5.I2 R33

Turner, James Harold, 1942- Improvement of the steady floating random walk Monte Carlo method near straight line and circular boundaries, with application to groundwater flow . [Manhattan, Kan.] , 1978, cover 1977. iv, 96 p. : LC Card 79-624986 DDC 551.49/0724 19
GB1197.7 .T87

UNITED STATES. DEPT. OF THE INTERIOR - OFFICIALS AND EMPLOYEES.

United States. Congress. Senate. Committee on Energy and Natural Resources. Clyde O. Martz nomination . Washington , 1980. iii, 72 p. ; LC Card 80-602816 DDC 353.3 19
KF26 .E55 1980a

United States. Congress. Senate. Committee on Energy and Natural Resources. Donald Paul Hodel nomination . Washington , 1981. iii, 133 p. ; LC Card 81-601395 DDC 353.3 19
KF26 .E55 1981b

United States. Congress. Senate. Committee on Energy and Natural Resources. James G. Watt nomination . Washington , 1981. 2 v. : LC Card 81-600871 DDC 353.3 19
KF26 .E55 1981

United States. Congress. Senate. Committee on Energy and Natural Resources. Wallace O. Green nomination . Washington , 1980. iii, 68 p. ; LC Card 80-604077 DDC 353.3 19
KF26 .E55 1980k

United States. Congress. Senate. Select Committee on Indian Affairs. Nomination of Thomas W. Fredericks to Assistant Secretary of the Interior . Washington , 1980. iii, 126 p. ; LC Card 80-603457 DDC 353.3 19
KF26.5 .I4 1980n

United States. Dept. of the Interior. Doors to the future . [Washington, D.C.] , 1978. 58 p. : LC Card 79-603728
JK865 1978 .D46   ***NYPL [JLF 81-226]***

United States. Dept. of the Interior. Water and Power Resources Service.
Brown, Patricia Eyring. Archaeological investigations at AZ U:6:61 (ASU), a prehistoric limited activity site in south-central Arizona /. [Tempe, Ariz.] 1980. vi, 84 p. : LC Card 80-620023 DDC 979.1/73 19
E78.A7 B73

United States. Dept. of the Interior. Water and Power Resources Service. Engineering Staff.
The world's major dams, man-made lakes, and hydroelectric plants / prepared by the Engineering Staff, Office of Science and Technology, Water and Power Resources Service, Department of the Interior. Washington, D.C. : The Service, [1980] 5 leaves ; 28 cm. "January 1980." LC Card 80-603189 DDC 627/.8/0212 19
1. Dams - Statistics. 2. Lakes - Statistics. 3. Hydroelectric power plants - Statistics. I. Title.
TC540 .U617 1980

United States. Dept. of the Interior. Water Research and Technology, Office of. see United States. Dept. of the Interior. Office of Water Research and Technology.

United States. Dept. of the Treasury.
United States savings bonds program . [Washington, D.C.] 1981. 2, iii,90 p. : LC Card 81-601928 DDC 332.63/23 19
HG4936 .U54

UNITED STATES. DEPT. OF THE TREASURY - OFFICIALS AND EMPLOYEES.

United States. Congress. Senate. Committee on Finance. Nominations of John E. Chapoton, Roscoe L. Egger, Jr., and Paul C. Roberts . Washington , 1981. iii, 40 p. ; LC Card 81-601602 DDC 353.2 19
KF26 .F5 1981d

United States. Congress. Senate. Committee on Finance. Nominations of Norman B. Ture and Beryl Wayne Sprinkel . Washington , 1981. iii, 17 p. ; LC Card 81-601959 DDC 353.2 19
KF26 .F5 1981e

United States. Dept. of Transportation. (Old Catalog form: United States. Transportation Dept.)
Alcohol and highway safety, 1978 : a review of the state of knowledge : summary volume. Washington, D.C. : U. S. Dept. of Transportation, National Highway Traffic Safety Administration : for sale by the Supt. of Docs., U. S. Govt. Print. Off., 1980. viii, 87 p. : ill. ; 28 cm. "DOT HS-805-172." "December 1979." Bibliography: p. 69-83. Includes index. LC Card 80-602371 DDC 363.1/251 19
1. Drinking and traffic accidents. 2. Drinking and traffic accidents - United States. I. Title.
HE5620.D7 U5 1980

Ayres, Robert U. Economic impact of mass production of alternative low emissions automotive power systems /. Springfield, Va. , 1973. 244 p. :   ***NYPL [JLF 80-387]***

Bike-ed '77 . Washington, D. C. , 1977. i, 105 p. : LC Card 77-604118
GV1055 .B54   ***NYPL [JFF 80-1530]***

California. Metropolitan Transportation Commission. BART in the San Francisco Bay Area . Washington, D.C. , Springfield, Va. , 1979 i.e. 1980. 227 p. : LC Card 80-603256 DDC 388.4/2/097946 19
HE4491.S45 C34 1980

Design, art & architecture in transportation 1st- ; 1978- [Washington]
NYPL [JLM 80-1118]

Graff, Donald Louis, 1935- Environmental impacts of BART . Washington [Springfield, Va.] 1980. ca. 150 p. in various pagings : LC Card 80-603252 DDC 388.4/2/097946 19
TD195.S9 G7

Guidelines for the railroad industry in a national emergency. Dept. of Transportation ; Interstate Commerce Commission ; Association of American Railroads. [Washington : U. S. Govt. Print. Off.], 1974. 54 p. : ill. ; 26 cm. Bibliography: p. 54.
1. Emergency transportation. 2. Railroads - United States. I. United States. Interstate Commerce Commission. II. Association of American Railroads. III. Title.   ***NYPL [JLF 80-736]***

The national highway safety needs report : report of the Secretary of Transportation to the United States Congress pursuant to section 225 of the Highway safety act of 1973. Washington : U. S. Dept. of Transportation, 1976. 148 p. in various pagings : ill. ; 27 cm. Cover title. Includes bibliographical references. LC Card 76-601953
1. Traffic safety - United States. I. Title.
HE5614.2 .U56 1976   ***NYPL [JLF 80-1698]***

Public Technology, inc. Elderly and handicapped transportation . Washington, 19. 28 p.;   ***NYPL [*XME-9106]***

R & D Planning Workshop, Transportation Systems Center, 1977. Tire rolling losses and fuel economy . Troy, MI , c1977. iii, 202 p. : LC Card 78-51861
TL151.6 .R18 1977

A revised estimate of the cost of completing the national system of interstate and defense highways : communication from the secretary of transportation transmitting a revised estimate of the cost of completing the national system of interstate and defense highways, pursuant to the provisions of Section 104(b)5, Title 23, United

States Code. Washington : U. S. G.P.O., 1981. iii, 27 p. : maps ; 24 cm. At head of title: 97th Congress, 1st session. Committee print. "Printed for the use of the Committee on Public Works and Transportation." "97-1." "January 1981." Item 1024-A, 1024-B (microfiche) LC Card 81-601266 DDC 338.1/12/0973 19
1. Express highways - United States - Estimates. 2. Express highways - United States - Finance. 3. Federal aid to transportation - United States. I. United States. Congress. House. Committee on Public Works and Transportation. II. Title.
HE355.3.E3 U54 1981

United States. Geological Survey. Summary of geologic and hydrologic information pertinent to tunneling in selected urban areas/. Washington, 1974. [370] p.:
NYPL [JSF 81-3]

United States. Interagency Task Force on Safety and Design Issue. Alaska natural gas transportation system: [safety and design] /. [Washington], 1977. 44 p.
NYPL [*XMQ-2151]

Voorhees (Alan M.) and Associates. Blue Streak bus rapid transit demonstration project . Seattle, 1973. 6, 11 p. LC Card 74-132895
NYPL [*ZT-1265]

UNITED STATES. DEPT. OF TRANSPORTATION.

United States. Congress. House. Committee on Public Works and Transportation. Subcommittee on Aviation. DOT/FAA proposed new policy for airports in the metropolitan Washington area . Washington , 1980. viii, 923 p. : LC Card 80-604030 DDC 387.7/4042/09753 19
KF27 .P89624 1980n

UNITED STATES. DEPT. OF TRANSPORTATION - APPROPRIATIONS AND EXPENDITURES.

United States. Congress. House. Committee on Appropriations. Subcommittee on Dept. of Transportation and Related Agencies Appropriations. Department of transportation and related agencies appropriations for 1982 . Washington , 1981- v. <1-3> ; LC Card 81-601415 DDC 353.0072/236875 19
KF27 .A667 1981

United States. Congress. Senate. Committee on Appropriations. Subcommittee on Transportation and Related Agencies. Department of Transportation and related agencies appropriations for fiscal year 1981 . Washington , 1980- v. <1> : LC Card 80-603482 DDC 353.0072/236875 19
KF26 .A66 1980

United States. Dept. of Transportation. Assistant Secretary for Policy, Plans, and International Affairs, Office of the. see United States. Dept. of Transportation. Office of the Assistant Secretary for Policy, Plans, and International Affairs.

United States. Dept. of Transportation. Climatic Impact Assessment Program Office. Garvin, David, 1923- Chemicl kinetics data survey VII. Washington, 1974. 101 p.
NYPL [JSF 80-995]

United States. Dept. of Transportation. Coast Guard. see United States. Coast Guard.

United States. Dept. of Transportation. Federal Aviation Administration. see United States. Federal Aviation Administration.

United States. Dept. of Transportation. Federal Highway Administration. see United States. Federal Highway Administration.

United States. Dept. of Transportation. Materials Transportation Bureau. see United States. Materials Transportation Bureau.

United States. Dept. of Transportation. National Highway Traffic Safety Administration. see United States. National Highway Traffic Safety Administration.

United States. Dept. of Transportation. National Transportation Safety Board. see United States. National Transportation Safety Board.

United States. Dept. of Transportation. Office of Environment and Safety. Webber, Margo B. Reuse of historically and architecturally significant railroad stations for transportation

BIBLIOGRAPHIC GUIDE

United States. Dept. of Transportation. Office of Hazardous

524

and other community needs . Washington, D.C. , 1978. ii, 126 p. : LC Card 79-603620 DDC 725/.31/0288 19
NA6311 .W4

United States. Dept. of Transportation. Office of Hazardous Materials. see United States. Office of Hazardous Materials.

United States. Dept. of Transportation. Office of Intergovernmental Affairs. Gladstone Associates. Innovative financing techniques . [Washington, D.C.] , Washington, D.C. [1978] ca. 350 p. in various pagings : LC Card 80-601836 DDC 388.4/042 19
HE4351 .G57 1978

Institute of Public Administration, Washington, D. C. Financing transit . [Washington] [1979] v, 331 p. : LC Card 80-601587 DDC 388.4/042 19
HE206.2 .I57 1979

United States. Dept. of Transportation. Office of International Programs. De Neufville, Richard, 1939- Investment strategies for developing areas : models of transport. Cambridge, 1973. 83 p.
NYPL [JLF 80-1121]

United States. Dept. of Transportation. Office of Policy and Plans Development. The barge mixing rule problem : a report to the Congress / U. S. Department of Transportation, [Office of Policy and Plans Development]. Washington : U. S. Dept. of Transportation, 1973. 1 v. Microfiche (neg.) NTIS. 3 sheets. 11 x 15 cm. (AD-762 349) CONTENTS. - v. 1. Report of the study.
1. Inland water transportation - United States. I. Title.
*NYPL [*XME-9626]*

United States. Dept. of Transportation. Office of the Assistant Secretary for Policy, Plans, and International Affairs. Moavenzadeh, Fred. Investment strategies for developing areas. [Washington] 1973. xvii, 224 p.
NYPL [JLF 80-1167]

Werner, Pamela A. A survey of national geocoding systems. [Cambridge, Mass.], 1974. xi, 344 p. LC Card 76-51887
NYPL [JFF 80-1538]

United States. Dept. of Transportation. Office of the Secretary. Bicycle transportation for energy conservation : including a comprehensive bicycle transportation program : a report of the Secretary of Transportation to the President and the Congress pursuant to the Section 682 of the National energy conservation policy act (P.L. 95-619) Washington, D.C. : U. S. Dept. of Transportation, Office of the Secretary, 1980. 42 p. ; 28 cm. Includes bibliographical references. LC Card 80-602140 DDC 388.4/11 19
1. Cycling - United States. 2. Bicycle commuting - United States. 3. Energy conservation - United States. I. Title.
GV1045 .U54 1980

Truck-top markings for visual identification. Washington; Dept. of Transportation, office of the Secretary, 1973. v, 70 p. illus. (some col.); 24 cm. "DOT P 5200.8." "August 1973." Bibliography: p. 13-14.
1. Motor-trucks. 2. Motor-trucks - Trailers. I. Title.
NYPL [JSE 81-6]

United States. Dept. of Transportation. Office of Transportation Economic Analysis. see United States. Office of Transportation Economic Analysis.

United States. Dept. of Transportation. Office of Transportation Security. Cargo security literature survey. Washington, D.C. : Dept. of Transportation, Office of Transportation Security, 1979. 135 p. ; 27 cm. LC Card 80-600986 DDC 016.3805/24 19
1. Freight and freightage - Security measures - Bibliography. I. Title.
Z7164.P76 U524 1979 HV8290

Executive Services, inc. A cooperative approach to cargo security in the trucking industry /] Washington , 1973. 89 p. in various pagings ;
NYPL [JLF 80-1486]

United States. Dept. of Transportation. Office of Transportation Systems Analysis and Information. see United States. Office of Transportation Systems Analysis and

Information.

United States. Dept. of Transportation. Office of University Research. Jennings, Kenneth M. Study of unions, management rights, and the public interest in mass transit . Washington , 1977. 276 p. : LC Card 77-604540
HD6976.T72 U55   *NYPL [*XME-9441]*

Kaitz, Gary M. An economic history of five midwestern railroads /. Washington , Springfield, Va. [1977] viii, 79 p. : LC Card 78-600991
HE2231 .K27   *NYPL [*XME-9388]*

UNITED STATES. DEPT. OF TRANSPORTATION - OFFICIALS AND EMPLOYEES. United States. Congress. Senate. Committee on Banking, Housing and Urban Affairs. Nominations of Philip D. Winn, John J. Knapp, Emanuel S. Savas, and Arthur E. Teele, Jr., . Washington , 1981. iii, 136 p. ; LC Card 81-601958 DDC 353.85 19
KF26 .B39 1981f

United States. Congress. Senate. Committee on Commerce, Science, and Transportation. Nomination--deputy secretary of transportation . Washington , 1981. iii, 25 p. ; LC Card 81-600981 DDC 353.86 19
KF26 .C69 1981

United States. Congress. Senate. Committee on Commerce, Science, and Transportation. Nomination--DOT . Washington , 1980. iii, 13 p. ; LC Card 80-602746 DDC 353.86 19
KF26 .C69 1980n

United States. Congress. Senate. Committee on Commerce, Science, and Transportation. Nomination--Secretary of Transportation . Washington , 1981. iii, 54 p. ; LC Card 81-600815 DDC 353.86 19
KF26 .C69 1981e

United States. Congress. Senate. Committee on Commerce, Science, and Transportation. Nominations--Departments of Commerce and Transportation . Washington , 1981. iii, 5 p. ; LC Card 81-601952 DDC 353.82 19
KF26 .C69 1981g

United States. Congress. Senate. Committee on Commerce, Science, and Transportation. Nominations--DOT . Washington , 1981. iii, 35 p. ; LC Card 81-601783 DDC 353.86 19
KF26 .C69 1981b

United States. Dept. of Transportation Policy and Plans Development, Office of. see United States. Dept. of Transportation. Office of Policy and Plans Development.

United States. Dept. of Transportation. Transportation Security, Office of. see United States. Dept. of Transportation. Office of Transportation Security.

United States. Dept. of Transportation. Transportation Systems Center. see United States. Dept. of Transportation. Transportation Systems Center.

United States. Dept. of Transportation. University Research, Office of. see United States. Dept. of Transportation. Office of University Research.

United States. Dept. of Transportation. Urban Mass Transportation Administration. see United States. Urban Mass Transportation Administration.

UNITED STATES. DEPT. OF VETERANS BENEFITS. (Old Catalog form: United States. Veterans Benefits, Dept. of) United States. Congress. House. Committee on Veterans' Affairs. Subcommittee on Compensation, Pension, Insurance, and Memorial Affairs. Workloads in the Department of Veterans Benefits and the Board of Veterans Appeals . Washington , 1980. iii, 45 p. ; LC Card 80-603663 DDC 353.0081/2 19
KF27 .V43 1980d

UNITED STATES. DEPT. OF HOUSING AND URBAN DEVELOPMENT. SECTION 8 HOUSING ASSISTANCE PAYMENT PROGRAM FOR LOWER INCOME FAMILIES. United States. Dept. of Housing and Urban Development. Office of Policy Development and Research. Lower Income Housing Assistance Program (Section 8) . [Washington] ,

Washington , 1978 i.e. 1979. xx, 101 p. : LC Card 79-602087
HD7293 .A5 1979b   *NYPL [JLF 81-553]*

United States - Departmental salaries. see United States - Officials and employees - Salaries, allowances, etc.

UNITED STATES. DEPOSITORY INSTITUTIONS DEREGULATION COMMITTEE. United State. Congress. House. Committee on Banking, Finance, and Urban Affairs. Subcommittee on Financial Institutions Supervision, Regulation and Insurance. Oversight hearings on Depository Institutions Deregulation Committee . Washington , 1980. vi, 582 p. : LC Card 81-600873 DDC 353.0082/52 19
KF27 .B544 1980c

DOE symposium series. (53) Hanford Life Sciences Symposium, 19th, Richland, Wash., 1979. Pulmonary toxicology of respirable particles . Oak Ridge, Tenn. , 1980. xi, 676 p. : ISBN 0-87079-121-4 LC Card 80-22907 DDC 616.2/44 19
RC756 .H3 1979

United States. Dept. of the Army. US Army Military History Institute. see US Army Military History Institute.

UNITED STATES - DESCRIPTION AND TRAVEL - 1865-1900. Kipling, Rudyard, 1865-1936. American notes /. Norman , c1981. p. cm. ISBN 0-8061-1682-X LC Card 81-40289 DDC 917.3/0486 19
E168 .K56 1981

United States. Developmental Disabilities Office. Haskins, James, 1941- He will lift up his head . [Washington] [1978?] 55 p. : LC Card 79-602502
E99.N3 H33   *NYPL [HBC 81-604]*

UNITED STATES - DIPLOMATIC AND CONSULAR SERVICE - AFRICA, WEST. United States. Congress. House. Committee on Government Operations. Legislation and National Security Subcommittee. U. S. mission and office operations--West Africa . Washington , 1980. iii, 75 p. ; LC Card 80-603676 DDC 353.008/92/0966 19
KF27 .G6676 1980j

UNITED STATES - DIPLOMATIC AND CONSULAR SERVICE - APPOINTMENTS, PROMOTIONS, SALARIES, ETC. United States. Congress. House. Committee on Foreign Affairs. Hostage Relief Act of 1980 . Washington , 1980. iii, 57 p. ; LC Card 81-600840 DDC 342.73/0412 347.302412 19
KF27 .F6 1980i

UNITED STATES - DIPLOMATIC AND CONSULAR SERVICE - EGYPT. United States. Congress. House. Committee on Government Operations. Legislation and National Security Subcommittee. U. S. mission and office operations--Egypt . Washington , 1980. iii, 161 p. ; LC Card 80-603495 DDC 353.008/92/0962 19
KF27 .G6676 1980h

United States. Disease Control, Center for. see Center for Disease Control.

United States. District Court. New York (Southern District) (Old Catalog form: United States. Courts. District Court. New York. Southern District.) 13 Communists speak to the Court /. New York , 1953. 95 p. ; LC Card 54-43867
NYPL [Sc Micro R-3647]

UNITED STATES. DISTRICT COURT (PUERTO RICO) United States. Congress. Senate. Committee on the Judiciary. Subcommittee on Improvements in Judicial Machinery. Spanish in the courtrooms of Puerto Rico, H.R. 5563 . Washington , 1980. iii, 86 p. ; LC Card 80-603690 DDC 347.73/222 347.30722 19
KF26 .J855 1980b

United States. District of Columbia, Committee on the (House) see United States. Congress. House. Committee on the District of Columbia.

United States. Division of Energy, Building Technology and Standards. Kovacs, William D. Soil and rock anchors for mobile homes . Washington, D.C. , 1979. xvi, 147 p. : LC Card 79-600143 DDC 690/.02/18 s 690/.79 19
TA435 .U58 no. 107 TH4819.M6

United States. Division of Intergovernmental Science & Public Technology. see **United States. National Science Foundation. Division of Intergovernmental Science & Public Technology.**

United States. Division of Labor Market Information. Career and labor market information . Columbus, Ohio , Washington, D.C. [1980] v, 71 p. ; LC Card 80-602937 DDC 331.12/0973 19
HD5724 .C33

United States. Division of Public Employee Labor Relations. Friedman, Marvin, 1923- The use of economic data in collective bargaining . [Washington] , 1978. vi, 128 p. ; LC Card 79-602392
HD6508 .F74   ***NYPL [JLF 81-432]***

UNITED STATES. DRUG ENFORCEMENT ADMINISTRATION.
United States. Drug Enforcement Administration. Management Analysis Division. Drug enforcement administration . [Washington, D.C.] [1980] 34 p. : LC Card 80-602842 DDC 353.0076/5 19
HV5825 .U565 1980

United States. Drug Enforcement Administration. Management Analysis Division. Drug enforcement administration : a profile / prepared by Office of Program Planning and Evaluation, Management Analysis Division. [Washington, D.C.] : The Office, [1980] 34 p. : ill. ; 28 cm. "January 1980." LC Card 80-602842 DDC 353.0076/5 19
1. United States. Drug Enforcement Administration. I. Title.
HV5825 .U565 1980

UNITED STATES. DRUG ENFORCEMENT ADMINISTRATION - OFFICIALS AND EMPLOYEES.
United States. Congress. Senate. Committee on Governmental Affairs. Legislation to authorize the establishment of senior executive positions for NSA, DEA, and the Export-Import Bank . Washington , 1980. iii, 44 p. ; LC Card 80-603902 DDC 342.73/068 347.30268 19
KF26 .G67 1980l

United States. Economic Adjustment Committee, President's. see **United States. President's Economic Adjustment Committee.**

United States. Economic Advisers Council. see **United States. Council of Economic Advisers.**

United States. Economic Analysis, Bureau of. see **United States. Bureau of Economic Analysis.**

United States - Economic conditions. Here are entered works on the economic history or conditions of the United States. Works on the discipline of economics in the United States are entered under: Economics - United States.

UNITED STATES - ECONOMIC CONDITIONS - 1945- - PERIODICALS.
United States. Bureau of the Census. Statistical profile. Ser. SP. no. 1-136; Feb. 1962-Aug. 1962. Washington. 136 no. in 3 v. LC Card A62-9234   *NYPL [TAA (United States. Census Bureau. Statistical profile. Ser. SP.)]*

UNITED STATES - ECONOMIC CONDITIONS - 1961- - PUBLIC OPINION.
Campbell, Angus, 1910- The sense of well-being in America . New York , c1981. xiii, 263 p. ; ISBN 0-07-009683-X LC Card 80-14379
HN59 .C29   ***NYPL [JLE 81-367]***

UNITED STATES - ECONOMIC CONDITIONS - 1961-1971 - BIBLIOGRAPHY.
United States. Economic Development Administration. Economic research studies of the Economic Development Administration . [Washington] , 1974. v, 121 p. ; LC Card 74-603105
Z7165.U5 U49 1974 HC106.6
NYPL [*XME-9405]

UNITED STATES - ECONOMIC CONDITIONS - 1971-
Allen, John William, 1936- The foundations of free enterprise /. College Station, Tex. , 1979. 24 p. ; LC Card 81-622050 DDC 330.12/2 19
HC106.7 .A367

Fleisis, Heywood W. The effect of OPEC oil pricing on output, prices, and exchange rates in the United States and other industrial countries /. [Washington, D.C.] , 1981. xx, 107 p. : LC Card 81-601242 DDC 338.2/3 19
HD9560.4 .F58

Port Authority of New York and New Jersey. Planning and Development Dept. Economic impact of the U. S. merchant marine and shipbuilding industries . New York, 1977. viii, 272 p.;
HE746 .C48   ***NYPL [*XME-9407]***

Productivity, the foundation of growth . Washington , 1980. v, 128 p. LC Card 81-601972 DDC 338/.06/0973 19
HC110.I52 P77

United States. Bureau of the Census. Center for Applied User Research. Guide to county census data for planning economic development. [Washington, D.C.] , 1979. iii, 123 p. ; LC Card 80-601079 DDC 330.973 19
HA37.U55 U54 1979

United States. Congress. House. Committee on the Budget. Economic issues for fiscal year 1981 . Washington , 1980. 2 v. (vi, 1355 p.) : LC Card 80-602893 DDC 330.973/0926 19
KF27 .B8 1980

United States. Congress. House. Committee on the Budget. Mid-year perspective on the economy . Washington , 1980. iii, 432 p. : LC Card 80-603475 DDC 338.5/443/0973 19
KF27 .B8 1980b

United States. Congress. Joint Economic Committee. Forecasting the supply side of the economy . Washington , 1980. iii, 87 p. ; LC Card 80-600591 DDC 338.5/443/0973 19
KF25 .E2 1980i

United States. Congress. Joint Economic Committee. The state of the economy . Washington , 1980. iii, 77 p. ; LC Card 80-603429 DDC 330.973/0926 19
KF25 .E2 1980c

United States. Congress. Joint Economic Committee. The 1980 economic report of the President . Washington , 1980. 2 v. : LC Card 80-603018 DDC 330.973/0926 19
KF25 .E2 1980a

United States. Congress. Joint Economic Committee. The 1980 midyear review of the economy . Washington , 1980. iii, 111 p. : LC Card 80-604050 DDC 330.973/0926 19
KF25 .E2 1980h

United States. Congress. Joint Economic Committee. Special Study on Economic Change. State and local government finances and the changing national economy . Washington , 1980. iii, 71 p. : LC Card 80-603784 DDC 336.73 19
KF25 .E23 1980

United States. Congress. Senate. Committee on Appropriations. Economic overview . Washington , 1981. iii, 577, vi p. : LC Card 81-601646 DDC 330.973/0927 19
KF26 .A6 1981

United States. Congress. Senate. Committee on the Budget. The present state of the American economy . Washington , 1981- v. <1 > : LC Card 81-600968 DDC 338.973 19
KF26 .B8 1981

United States. Congress. Senate. Select Committee on Small Business. Business economic outlook . Washington , 1980. iii, 145 p. : LC Card 80-602443 DDC 338.5/443/0973 19
KF26.5 .S6 1979w

United States. Congressional Budget Office. The economic outlook /. Washington, D.C. [1978] xvi, 53 p. : LC Card 81-453019 DDC 338.5/443/0973 19
HC106.7 .U544 1978b

United States. Congressional Budget Office. Entering the 1980s . [Washington, D.C.] [1980] xxi, 101 p. : LC Card 80-602038 DDC 336.73 19
HJ257.2 .U57 1980

United States. Maritime Administration. What U. S. ports mean to the economy /. [Washington] , 1978. 58 p., [1] leaf of plates : LC Card 79-602661
HE553 .U643 1978

Weintraub, Robert E., 1925- The impact of the Federal Reserve System's monetary policies on the nation's economy (second report) . Washington , c1980 [i.e. 1981] xii, 51 p. : LC Card 81-601005 DDC 330.973/0926 19
HG2565 .W44

UNITED STATES - ECONOMIC CONDITIONS - 1971- - CHARTS, DIAGRAMS, ETC.
Graphic summary of the 1977 economic censuses. Washington, D.C. , 1981. 128 p. : LC Card 81-1210 DDC 330.973/0926 19
HC106.7 .G7

UNITED STATES - ECONOMIC CONDITIONS - 1971- - MAPS.
Graphic summary of the 1977 economic censuses. Washington, D.C. , 1981. 128 p. : LC Card 81-1210 DDC 330.973/0926 19
HC106.7 .G7

UNITED STATES - ECONOMIC CONDITIONS - 1971- - PERIODICALS.
Federal Reserve chart book. 1979- Washington.
NYPL [JLK 80-199]

UNITED STATES - ECONOMIC CONDITIONS - ADDRESSES, ESSAYS, LECTURES.
Reflections of America . Washington, D.C. [1981] p. cm. LC Card 80-607843 DDC 317.3 19
HC103 .R43

United States. Economic Development Administration.
Consad Research Corporation. A study of public works investment in the United States /. [Washington] , 1980. 826 p. in various pagings : LC Card 80-603199 DDC 336.3/9/0973 19
HD3885 .C66 1980

Economic research studies of the Economic Development Administration : an annotated bibliography, reports received August 1965 through December 1973. [Washington] : U. S. Dept. of Commerce : for sale by the Supt. of Docs., U.S. Govt. Print. Off., 1974. v, 121 p. ; 26 cm. Microfilm (neg.) NTIS. 2 sheets 11 x 15 cm. (PB-265 193) Includes indexes. LC Card 74-603105
1. United States - Economic conditions - 1961-1971 - Bibliography. 2. Economic assistance, Domestic - United States - Bibliography. I. Title.
Z7165.U5 U49 1974 HC106.6
NYPL [*XME-9405]

EDA qualified areas, July 1978. [Washington] 1978. map 62 x 99 cm. Scale ca. 1:5,000,000. Insets: Puerto Rico, Virgin Is. -- Alaska. -- Hawaii. -- Gvam. -- A. Samoa.
1. Economic assistance, Domestic - United States - Maps. 2. United States - Maps.
G3701.G17 1976 .U5
NYPL [Map Div. 80-3385]

Edmonds, Robert H. A human investent tax credit program, second report . [Washington] , 1977. 24, 49 p. ; LC Card 77-604090
HC106.7 .E348

GMA Research Corporation. Alternate use and marketing study: southwest portion of the Umatilla Army Depot /. [Pendleton], 1974. 75 l.:   ***NYPL [JLF 80-198]***

Guide for communities: planning civilian reuse of defense installations. A handbook for community officials and others engaged in the conversion process. Washington, 1974. iv, 174 p. 28 cm. LC Card 76-10894
1. Military bases - United States. I. Title.
NYPL [JLF 80-1096]

National Urban League. National Urban League Entrepreneurial Development Program . [New York] , 1972. 54 p. in various pagings ;
NYPL [JLF 80-1689]

North Dakota. State University of Agriculture and Applied Science, Fargo. Center for Economic Development. A program of management and technical assistance in EDA designated areas in North Dakota . Fargo, N. D. , 1974. 70 p. :   ***NYPL [JLF 80-1351]***

SMS Associates. A directory of Federal

Government business assistance programs for women business owners . [Washington, D.C.] [1980] iv, 71 p. ; LC Card 80-602878 DDC 353.0082/048 19
HD2346.U5 S17 1980

United States. Economic Development Administration. Economic Research, Office of. see **United States. Economic Development Administration. Office of Economic Research.**

United States. Economic Development Administration. Office of Economic Research. (Old Catalog form: United States. Economic Development Administration. Economic Research, Office of.)
United States. Bureau of the Census. Guide to county census data. Washington , 1979. 123 p.;
NYPL [*R-Econ. 80-2970]

United States. Economic Development Administration. Office of Technical Assistance. Checchi and Company, Washington, D. C. Final report : feasibility of establishing a recording studio in the District of Columbia . Washington , 1973. 124 p. :
NYPL [*LE 80-1766]

United States. Economic Development Administration. Technical Assistance Project. see **United States. Economic Development Administration.**

UNITED STATES - ECONOMIC POLICY - 1933-1945.
Saloutos, Theodore. The American farmer and the New Deal /. Ames , 1982, c1981. p. cm.
ISBN 0-8138-1076-0 LC Card 81-12396 DDC 338.1/873 19
HD1761 .S2 1982

UNITED STATES - ECONOMIC POLICY - 1971-
Panel on the American Economy: Employment, Productivity, and Inflation (U. S.) The American economy--employment, productivity, and inflation in the eighties . Washington , 1980. 82 p. ; LC Card 81-357 DDC 330.973/0926 19
HC106.7 .P345 1981

United States. Congress. House. Committee on Banking, Finance and Urban Affairs. The administration's economic program . Washington , 1981. iii, 76 p. ; LC Card 81-601944 DDC 338.954 19
KF27 .B5 1981

United States. Congress. House. Committee on Banking, Finance and Urban Affairs. World War II and the problems of the eighties . Washington , 1980. iii, 70 p. ; LC Card 80-603655 DDC 338.973 19
KF27 .B5 1980a

United States. Congress. House. Committee on Banking, Finance and Urban Affairs. Subcommittee on Economic Stabilization. Amendments to the Council on Wage and Price Stability act . Washington , 1977. iv, 415 p. : LC Card 77-602660
KF27 .B542 1977b   *NYPL [JLE 81-450]*

United States. Congress. House. Committee on Banking, Finance and Urban Affairs. Subcommittee on Economic Stabilization. Productivity performance and the American economy . Washington , 1980. iv, 318 p. : LC Card 80-603669 DDC 338/.06/0973 19
KF27 .B542 1980a

United States. Congress. House. Committee on Education and Labor. Subcommittee on Employment Opportunities. Oversight hearing on employment impact of current and proposed economic policies . Washington , c1980 [i.e. 1981] iii, 51 p. ; LC Card 81-601627 DDC 339.5/0973 19
KF27 .E3366 1980c

United States. Congress. House. Committee on Education and Labor. Subcommittee on Employment Opportunities. Oversight on the Full employment and balanced growth act . Washington , 1979. v, 234 p. : LC Card 80-603323 DDC 353.0083 19
KF27 .E3366 1980

United States. Congress. House. Committee on Small Business. Subcommittee on General Oversight and Minority Enterprise. Impact of inflation on small business . Washington , 1980.

iv, 343 p. : LC Card 80-603791 DDC 338.6/42/0973 19
KF27 .S64 1980f

United States. Congress. House. Committee on the Budget. Economic issues for fiscal year 1981 . Washington , 1980. 2 v. (vi, 1355 p.) : LC Card 80-602893 DDC 330.973/0926 19
KF27 .B8 1980

United States. Congress. House. Committee on the Budget. President's economic revitalization program . Washington , 1980. iii, 205 p. : LC Card 80-604100 DDC 338.973 19
KF27 .B8 1980c

United States. Congress. Joint Economic Committee. Monitoring inflation . Washington , 1979-<198. v.<1-3> : LC Card 81-601472 DDC 332.4/1/0973 19
KF25 .E2 1979p

United States. Congress. Joint Economic Committee. The President's new anti-inflation program . Washington , 1980. iii, 172 p. ; LC Card 80-603703 DDC 332.4/15/0973 19
KF25 .E2 1980e

United States. Congress. Joint Economic Committee. Public works as a countercyclical tool . Washington , 1980. iii, 86 p. : LC Card 80-603664 DDC 339.5/22 19
KF25 .E2 1980f

United States. Congress. Joint Economic Committee. The state of the economy . Washington , 1980. iii, 77 p. ; LC Card 80-603429 DDC 330.973/0926 19
KF25 .E2 1980c

United States. Congress. Joint Economic Committee. The 1980 economic report of the President . Washington , 1980. 2 v. : LC Card 80-603018 DDC 330.973/0926 19
KF25 .E2 1980a

United States. Congress. Joint Economic Committee. The 1980 midyear review of the economy . Washington , 1980. iii, 111 p. : LC Card 80-604050 DDC 330.973/0926 19
KF25 .E2 1980h

United States. Congress. Joint Economic Committee. The 1980 midyear review of the economy . Washington , 1980. iii, 24 p. ; LC Card 80-603553 DDC 330.973/0926 19
HC106.7 .U543 1980

United States. Congress. Senate. Committee on Appropriations. Economic overview . Washington , 1981. iii, 577, vi p. : LC Card 81-601646 DDC 330.973/0927 19
KF26 .A6 1981

United States. Congress. Senate. Committee on the Budget. Inflation and recession . Washington , 1980. iii, 50 p. ; LC Card 80-603332 DDC 332.4/1/0973 19
KF26 .B8 1979e

United States. Congress. Senate. Committee on the Budget. The present state of the American economy . Washington , 1981- v. <1 > : LC Card 81-600968 DDC 338.973 19
KF26 .B8 1981

United States. Congress. Senate. Select Committee on Small Business. Business economic outlook . Washington , 1980. iii, 145 p. : LC Card 80-602443 DDC 338.5/443/0973 19
KF26.5 .S6 1979w

United States. Congressional Budget Office. Entering the 1980s . [Washington, D.C.] [1980] xxi, 101 p. : LC Card 80-602038 DDC 336.73 19
HJ257.2 .U57 1980

United States. General Accounting Office. An analytical framework for federal policies and programs influencing capital formation in the United States . Washington, D.C. , 1980. v, 80 p. : LC Card 80-603955 DDC 332/.0415/0973 19
HC110.S3 U63 1980

United States. President's Commission for a National Agenda for the Eighties. A national agenda for the eighties . Washington , 1980. 214 p. ; LC Card 81-356 DDC 973.926 19
HC106.7 .U577 1980

UNITED STATES - ECONOMIC POLICY - 1971- - CONGRESSES.
Blewer, Cecilia. Economic growth . Washington , 1980. v, 56 p. ; LC Card

80-603061 DDC 338.973 19
HC106.7 .B59

Conference on Evaluation of the Economic Stimulus Package, Brookings Institution, 1977. Conference report on evaluating the 1977 economic stimulus package /. [Washington] , 1978. iii, 127 p. ; LC Card 79-602314
HC106.7 .C665 1977   *NYPL [JLF 81-172]*

UNITED STATES - ECONOMIC POLICY - ADDRESSES, ESSAYS, LECTURES.
The Business cycle and public policy, 1929-80 . Washington , 1980. x, 379 p. : LC Card 81-600652 DDC 338.5/42/0973 19
HB3711 .B93

United States. Economics, Statistics, and Cooperatives Service. U. S. fats and oils statistics, 1963-78. [Washington, D.C.] : U. S. Dept. of Agriculture, Economics, Statistics, and Cooperatives Service, [1980] iv, 104 p. ; 27 cm. (Statistical bulletin ; no. 631) Cover title. "Supersedes Statistical bulletin no. 574 ... published in June 1977." LC Card 80-601591 DDC 338.1/0973 s 338.1/7385/0973 19
1. Oil industries - United States - Statistics. I. Series: United States. Dept. of Agriculture. Statistical bulletin , no. 631. II. Title.
HD1751 .A5 no. 631 HD9490.U6

United States. Education and Labor, Committee on (House) see **United States. Congress. House. Committee on Education and Labor.**

UNITED STATES. EDUCATION APPEAL BOARD.
United States. Congress. House. Committee on Education and Labor. Subcommittee on Elementary, Secondary, and Vocational Education. Hearings on dismissing certain cases pending before the Education Appeal Board . Washington , 1981. v, 568 p. : LC Card 81-601633 DDC 344.73/076 347.30476 19
KF27 .E3364 1980h

United States. Education Bureau. see **United States. Office of Education.**

United States. Education, Dept. of. see **United States. Dept. of Education.**

United States Education of Disadvantaged Children, National Advisory Council on the. see **United States. National Advisory Council on the Education of Disadvantaged Children.**

United States. Education, Office of. see **United States. Office of Education.**

United States. Educational and Cultural Affairs, Bureau of. see **United States. Bureau of Educational and Cultural Affairs.**

United States - Elections. see **Elections - United States.**

United States. Electron Devices, Advisory Group on. see **United States. Advisory Group on Electron Devices.**

UNITED STATES - EMIGRATION AND IMMIGRATION.
United States. Commission on Civil Rights. California Advisory Committee. A study of Federal immigration policies and practices in Southern California . Washington, D.C. [1980] ix, 61 p. : LC Card 80-602885 DDC 353.0081/7/097949 19
JV6920 .U54 1980

United States. Congress. House. Committee on the Judiciary. Subcommittee on Immigration, Refugees, and International Law. U. S. immigration policy regarding Iranian nationals . Washington , 1981. iii, 60 p. ; LC Card 81-601599 DDC 325/.255/0973 19
KF27 .J8645 1980d

United States. Congress. Senate. Committee on the Judiciary. U. S. refugee programs . Washington , 1980. iii, 412 p. (p. 412 blank) : LC Card 80-602735 DDC 362.8/7/0973 19
KF26 .J8 1980a

United States. Congress. Senate. Committee on the Judiciary, United States Senate, Ninety-sixth Congress, second session, September 19, 1980. U. S. refugee programs, 1981 . Washington , 1980. iii, 288 p. : LC Card 80-604094 DDC 362.8/7/0973 19
KF26 .J8 1980f

United States. General Accounting Office. Illegal aliens, estimating their impact on the United States . [Washington, D.C. , 1980] v,

128 p. : LC Card 80-601428 DDC 331.6/2/72073 19
JV6481 1980 .G46

Weintraub, Sidney, 1922- The illegal alien from Mexico . [Austin] , c1980. ix, 65 p. ; ISBN 0-292-73822-6 (pbk.) LC Card 80-80323 DDC 325/.272/0973 19
E184.M5 W46

UNITED STATES - EMIGRATION AND IMMIGRATION - ABSTRACTS.
North, Jeannette H. Immigration literature . Washington , 1979. viii, 89 p. ; LC Card 79-604155
JV6455 .N67 **NYPL [JLF 81-424]**

UNITED STATES - EMIGRATION AND IMMIGRATION - ADDRESSES, ESSAYS, LECTURES.
Greenwood, Michael J. Staff report companion papers. [Washington] [1979] ii leaves, 234 p. : LC Card 79-603817
JV6471 .G73 **NYPL [JLF 81-360]**

UNITED STATES - EMIGRATION AND IMMIGRATION - BIOGRAPHY.
Epstein, Helen, 1947- A study in American pluralism through oral histories of holocaust survivors /. [New York] [1977?] 157, xciv leaves ; LC Card 77-153163
E184.J5 E613 **NYPL [*PXY 80-4926]**

United States - Emigration and immigration law. see Emigration and immigration law - United States.

UNITED STATES - EMMIGRATION AND IMMIGRATION.
United States. Select Commission on Immigration and Refugee Policy. Semiannual report to Congress /. Washington , 1980. v, 74 p. ; LC Card 80-603270 DDC 353.0081/7 19
JV6481 1980 .S44

United States - Employees. see United States - Officials and employees.

United States. Employment and Training Administration.
Barton, Paul E. Between two worlds. Washington, 1978. 4 v.;
NYPL [JLF 80-1274]

Conference on the National Longitudinal Surveys of Mature Women, United States Department of Labor, 1978. Women's changing roles at home and on the job . Washington , 1978. iii, 331 p. : LC Card 79-601912
HQ1403 .C53 1978 **NYPL [JLF 81-250]**

DiPillo, Salvatore A. Connecticut occupational staffing patterns . [Hartford] [1980] 86 p. : LC Card 80-623517 DDC 331.12/5/09746 19
HD5725.C8 D553

Environmental protection careers guidebook. Washington, D.C. , 1980. xiv, 205 p. : LC Card 81-600895 DDC 628/.023 19
TD170.2 .E59

Glover, Robert W. Placing minority women in professional jobs /. Washington , 1978. vii, 75 p. ; LC Card 78-600751
HD5701 .U53 no. 55 HD6053.6.U5
NYPL [Sc F 81-49]

Indiana. Employment Security Division. Staffing patterns in the manufacturing industries in Indiana . [Indianapolis] , 1976. xv, 85 p. : LC Card 77-621779
HD5725.I6 I53 1976 **NYPL [*XME-9536]**

Indiana. Employment Security Division. Research and Statistics Section. Staffing patterns in wholesale and retail trade industries in Indiana . [Indianapolis, Ind.] , 1978. viii, 67 p. : LC Card 79-625864 DDC 331.12/51381/09772 19
HD5725.I6 I53 1978a

Layoff time training : a key to upgrading workforce utilization and EEOC affirmative action : a case study in the Northern California canning industry / prepared by Curtis C. Aller ... [et al.], for the Employment and Training Administration, U. S. Department of Labor. Berley, CA.: Center for Applied Manpower Research, 1977. v, 115, [1] p. ; 28 cm. Microfilm. (neg.) NTIS. 2 sheets. 11 x 15 cm. (PB 272 523) Includes bibliographical references.
1. Cannery workers - California - Contra Costa County. 2. Occupational retraining - California - Contra Costa County. 3. Affirmative action programs - California - Contra Costa County. 4. Layoff systems - California -

Contra Costa County. I. Aller, Curtis. II. Title.
HD5701 .U53 no. 61 HD5718.C272
NYPL [*XME-9433]

Lenihan, Kenneth J. Unlocking the second gate . [Washington] , 1977. iv, 71 p. : LC Card 77-600960
HD5701 .U53 no. 45 HV9306.B2
NYPL [*XME-9551]

Montana. Division of Employment Security. Research and Analysis Section. Selected wage information 1980 for Montana and 14 labor market areas /. Helena, MT [1980] ii, 209 p. : LC Card 80-623620 DDC 331.2/9786 19
HD4976.M84 M63 1980

Mott, Frank. The socioeconomic status of households headed by women . Washington, D.C. , 1979, 1980 printing. xiii, 68 p. : LC Card 80-601212 DDC 331.11/0973 s 305.4/8 19
HD5701 .U53 no. 72 HQ536

New Hampshire. Dept. of Employment Security. Economic Analysis and Reporting Section. New Hampshire staffing patterns in selected nonmanufacturing industries, 1978 . [Concord, N.H.] , 1979. i, 172 p. : LC Card 80-621986 DDC 331.12/5/09742 19
HD5725.N4 N45 1979

Pennsylvania. Bureau of Employment Security. Research and Statistics Division. Occupational staffing patterns of selected regulated industries in Pennsylvania. [Harrisburg] , 1979. ii, 73 p. ; LC Card 79-624037
HD5725.P4 P45 1979 **NYPL [JLF 80-1646]**

Pennsylvania. Office of Employment Security. Research and Statistics Division. Occupational staffing patterns of selected nonmanufacturing industries in Pennsylvania . Harrisburg, Pa. [1980] iii, 326 p. ; LC Card 80-622719 DDC 331.12/5/09748 19
HD5725.P4 P458 1980

Ratner, Ronnie Steinberg, 1947- A modest Magna Carta . [New York City, N. Y.] 19. 2 v. (xxxiv, 880 leaves) ; **NYPL [*XME-9376]**

Research and development, a 16-year compendium (1963-78) / U. S. Department of Labor, Employment and Training Administration. Washington, D.C. : For sale by the Supt. of Docs., U. S. Govt. Print. Off., 1979. xiv, 608 p. ; 29 cm. LC Card 80-601625 DDC 331.11/0973 19
1. Manpower policy - United States - Abstracts. 2. Labor and laboring classes - United States - Abstracts. I. Title.
HD5724 .U6285 1979

Seven years later, the experiences of the 1970 cohort of immigrants in the United States. [Washington, D.C.] : U. S. Dept. of Labor, Employment and Training Administration, 1979. v, 172 p. : graphs ; 28 cm. (R & D monograph. 71) Includes bibliographical references. LC Card 80-601560 DDC 331.11/0973 s 331.6/2/0973 19
1. Alien labor - United States. I. Title.
HD5701 .U53 no. 71 HD8081.A5

Symposium . Washington , 1977. ix, 141 p. ; LC Card 77-601861
HD5875 .S95 **NYPL [*XME-9409]**

Virginia. Employment Commission. Manpower Research Division. Labor market information for Affirmative Action programs . [Richmond] [1979] 67, xiv p. ; LC Card 80-621171 DDC 331.12/09755 19
HD5725.V8 V53 1979a

Virginia. Employment Commission. Manpower Research Division. Labor Market Analysis Unit. Special youth report, State of Virginia /. Richmond, Va. [1979] 24 p. : LC Card 79-625797 DDC 331.3/4/09755 19
HD6274.V8 V57 1979

Wisconsin. Dept. of Industry, Labor and Human Relations. Bureau of Administration, Planning, and Analysis. Occupational employment estimates for selected nonmanufacturing industries, 1978 /. [Madison, Wis.] [1980] iv, 212 p. : LC Card 80-623196 DDC 331.12/51/0009775 19
HD5725.W5 W55 1980

United States. Employment and Training Administration. Office of Policy, Evaluation, and Research. Office of Research and Development. see United States.

Employment and Training Administration. Office of Research and Development.

United States. Employment and Training Administration. Office of Research and Development. Kaufman, Bruce E. Wage-price expectations and cyclical strike activity /. Washington , 1979. vi, 257 leaves :
NYPL [JLF 80-1484]

United States. Employment and Training Administration. Office of Youth Programs.
Report on SPEDY conferences : Summer Program for Economically Disadvantaged Youth / U. S. Department of Labor, Employment and Training Administration, Office of Youth Programs. [Washington] : The Administration, [1979] viii, 297 p. ; 28 cm. Cover title. "Lab-441." The SPEDY conferences conducted in the fall of 1978: King of Prussia, Pa., Oct. 15-17, 1978; Chicago, Ill., Oct. 18-20. 1978; Los Angeles, Calif., Oct 29-31, 1978; Houston, Tex., Nov. 1-3, 1978. LC Card 79-603023
1. Youth - Employment - United States - Congresses. I. Title. II. Title: SPEDY conferences. III. Title: Summer Program for Economically Disadvantaged Youth.
HD6273 .U514 1979a

United States. Employment and Training Administration. Youth Programs, Office of. see United States. Employment and Training Administration. Office of Youth Programs.

United States. Employment of the Handicapped, President's Committee on. see United States. President's Committee on Employment of the Handicapped.

UNITED STATES. EMPLOYMENT SERVICE.
United States. Congress. House. Committee on Government Operations. Manpower and Housing Subcommittee. Operation of the U. S. Employment Service . Washington , 1976. iv, 359 p. : LC Card 76-603085
KF27 .G6678 1976b

UNITED STATES. EMPLOYMENT SERVICE - CONGRESSES.
Symposium . Washington , 1977. ix, 141 p. ; LC Card 77-601861
HD5875 .S95 **NYPL [*XME-9409]**

United States. Employment Standards Administration.
Motion picture theaters / U. S. Department of Labor, Employment Standards Administration. [Washington] : The Administration, 1979. 93 p. in various pagings ; 28 cm. Prepared by D. Ridzon. Includes bibliographical references. LC Card 79-602947
1. Wages - Moving-picture theaters - United States. I. Ridzon, David. II. Title.
HD4966.M79 U58 1979
NYPL [JLF 81-423]

United States. Employment Standards Administration. Wage and Hour Division.
Working children. Washington.
NYPL [JLL 80-212]

United States. Energy, Building Technology and Standards, Division of. see United States. Division of Energy, Building Technology and Standards.

United States. Energy, Dept. of. see United States. Dept. of Energy.

United States. Energy Information Administration.
Major extra high voltage transmission lines, December 31, 1977. Washington ; For sale by Supt. of Docs., U. S. Govt. Print. Off., 1979. col. map 55 x 71 cm. Scale 1:7,200,000. Includes numbered "Ownership list" keyed to map.
1. Electric power distribution - United States - Maps. 2. Electric power-plants - United States - Maps. 3. United States - Maps. **NYPL [Map Div. 80-3272]**

Major extra high voltage transmission lines, December 31, 1978: [United States] / Department of Energy, Energy Information Administration. Washington : The Administration : for sale by the Supt. of Docs., U. S. Govt. Print. Off., [1979] 1 map : col. ; 44 x 70 cm. Scale ca. 1:7,000,000. "DOE/EIA-0165(78)." Includes index to owners.
1. Electric power distribution - United States - High tension - Maps. 2. United States - Maps. I. Title.
G3701.N4 1977 .U5
NYPL [Map Div 81-3045]

Monthly petroleum product price report. Washington. **NYPL** *[JLM 80-1101]*

UNITED STATES. ENERGY INFORMATION ADMINISTRATION.
United States. Congress. House. Permanent Select Committee on Intelligence. Subcommittee on Oversight. Intelligence on the world energy outlook and its policy implications . Washington , 1980. iii, 235 p. :
LC Card 80-603479 DDC 333.79 19
KF27.5 .I55 1979a

United States. Congress. Senate. Committee on Energy and Natural Resources. Subcommittee on Energy Regulation. October report on the current fuel situation from the Energy Information Administration . Washington , 1980. iii, 217 p. : LC Card 80-602534 DDC 338.4/766553827/0973 19
KF26 .E5535 1979m

United States. Energy Information Administration. Division of Electric Power Statistics. Electric power monthly. June 1980- Washington. **NYPL** *[Econ. Div.]*

United States. Energy Information Administration. Electric Power Statistics, Division of. . see United States. Energy Information Administration. Division of Electric Power Statistics.

United States. Energy Information Administration. National Energy Information Center. see National Energy Information Center.

United States. Energy Information Administration. Office of Applied Analysis. Brazzel, John M. A distributional analysis of trends in energy expenditures by Black households . Washington, D.C. [1980] xvii, 106 p. : LC Card 80-602125 DDC 339.4/86626/08996073 19
HD9502.U52 B686

United States. Energy Information Administration. Office of Coal and Electric Power Statistics. Division of Electric Power Statistics. see United States. Energy Information Administration. Division of Electric Power Statistics.

United States. Energy Information Administration. Office of Economic Analysis. Ryan, Paul, 1930- An analysis of petroleum company investments in non-petroleum energy sources /. Washington, D.C. [Springfield, VA , 1979] 2 v. : LC Card 80-601258 DDC 332.6/7254 19
HD9565 .R9

United States. Energy Information Administration. Office of Energy Data Operations. Slatick, Eugene R. Coal data, a reference /. Washington, D.C. , 1980. vii, 53 p. : LC Card 80-603221 DDC 553.2/4/0973 19
HD9545 .S5 1980

United States. Energy Research and Development Administration. International Conference on Nuclear Systems Reliability Engineering and Risk Assessment, Gatlinburg, Tenn., 1977. Nuclear systems reliability engineering and risk assessment . Philadelphia , 1977. xi, 849 p. : LC Card 77-91478
TK9152 .I48 1977 **NYPL** *[JSF 81-47]*

International Meeting on Advanced LMFBR Fuels, Tucson, Ariz., 1977. Advanced LMFBR fuels . Hindsdale, Ill. , c1977. xi, 694 p. : LC Card 77-88497
TK9360 .I63 1977 **NYPL** *[JSD 80-865]*

R & D Planning Workshop, Transportation Systems Center, 1977. Tire rolling losses and fuel economy . Troy, MI , c1977. iii, 202 p. : LC Card 78-51861
TL151.6 .R18 1977

United States. Energy Research and Development Administration. Basic Energy Sciences, Division of. see United States. Energy Research and Development Administration. Division of Basic Energy Sciences.

United States. Energy Research and Development Administration. Division of

Basic Energy Sciences. Lawrence Symposium on Systems and Decision Sciences. Proceedings. 1- ; 1977- North Hollywood , Calif..
NYPL *[JSP 80-446]*

United States. Energy Research and Development Administration. Nonhighway Transport Systems and Special Projects. Data Analysis Branch. United States. National Laboratory, Oak Ridge, Tenn. Transportation energy conservation data book /. Oak Ridge, Tenn. , 1977. xxv, 536 p. :
HE18 1977 .N37 1977 **NYPL** *[JLF 81-192]*

UNITED STATES. ENERGY SECURITY ACT. Compilation of the Energy Security Act of 1980, and 1980 amendments to the Defense Production Act of 1950 /. Washington , 1980. 3 v. (v. 2252 p.) ; LC Card 80-603878 DDC 346.7304/679 347.3064679 19
KF2120.A32 A15 1980

United States. Engineer Bureau (Army) see United States. Army. Corps of Engineers.

United States. Engineers, Corps of. see United States. Army. Corps of Engineers.

United States. Engineers for Rivers and Harbors, Board of. see United States. Board of Engineers for Rivers and Harbors.

United States. Environmental Data Service. National Climatic Center. see National Climatic Center.

United States. Environmental Data Service. National Geophysical and Solar-Terrestrial Data Center. see National Geophysical and Solar-Terrestrial Data Center.

United States. Environmental Health Service. Bureau of Radiological Health. see United States. Bureau of Radiological Health.

United States. Environmental Protection Agency. Abt Associates. Factors affecting pollution referenda. Washington, 1971. v, 331 p. LC Card 73-614491
HG4952 .A6

Available information materials on solid waste management : total listing, 1966 to 1979. [Washington] : U. S. Environmental Protection Agency, 1979. v, 240 p. ; 28 cm. "An environmental protection publication (SW-203) in the solid waste management series." Includes indexes. LC Card 80-601846 DDC 016.3637/28 19
1. Refuse and refuse disposal - Indexes. 2. United States. Office of Solid Waste - Bibliography. I. Title.
Z5853.S22 U4285 1979a TD791

EPA's position on the health implications of airborne lead / prepared by U. S. Environmental Protection Agency. Washington : The Agency, 1973. 1 v. of various pagings; 28 cm. Cover title. Includes bibliographies.
1. Lead - Physiological effect. 2. Lead-poisoning. 3. Air - Pollution - Physiological effect. I. Title.
NYPL *[JSF 80-279]*

The Economic impact of pollution control. [Washington?] 1972. 332 p. LC Card 72-601528
TD180 .E25 **NYPL** *[JLF 81-274]*

The economics of clean water. Washington, U. S. Govt. Print. off. 26 cm. "Annual report of the administrator of the Environmental Protection Agency to the Congress of the United States in compliance with section 26(a), Federal Water Pollution Control Act." For earlier file, see: United States. Federal Water Pollution Control Administration. The economics of clean water. At head of title: Committee print.
1. Water - Pollution - Economic aspects - United States - Periodicals. I. Title.
NYPL *[JLM 80-772]*

Environmental protection careers guidebook. Washington, D.C. , 1980. xiv, 205 p. : LC Card 81-600895 DDC 628/.023 19
TD170.2 .E59

Guidance for facilities planning. Washington, 1974. 81 p.; 28 cm.
1. Water-supply. 2. Water - Pollution. I. Title.
NYPL *[JSF 80-618]*

Hazardous waste management facilities in the United States. Cincinnati.
NYPL *[JSP 81-81]*

Legislation, programs, and organization / United States Environmental Protection Agency. Rev. [Washington, D.C.] : The Agency, [1979] 56 p. ; 28 cm. Cover title. LC Card 80-602042 DDC 353.0082/321 19

1. Environmental law - United States. 2. Environmental policy - United States. I. Title.
KF3775 .A843 1979

UNITED STATES. ENVIRONMENTAL PROTECTION AGENCY.
United States. Congress. House. Committee on Government Operations. Environment, Energy, and Natural Resources Subcommittee. Automobile fuel economy, EPA oversight . Washington , 1980. iv, 572 p. : LC Card 80-601926 DDC 339.4/866553827/0973 19
KF27 .G655 1980c

United States. Congress. House. Committee on Interstate and Foreign Commerce. Subcommittee on Oversight and Investigations. Clean air act amendments of 1977-oversight . Washington , 1980. ii, 52 p. ; LC Card 80-602530 DDC 353.0082/324 19
KF27 .I5547 1979q

United States. Congress. House. Committee on Interstate and Foreign Commerce. Subcommittee on Oversight and Investigations. EPA's action concerning nitrilotriacetic acid (NTA) . Washington , 1980. iv, 393 p. ; LC Card 80-603817 DDC 363.1/79 19
KF27 .I5547 1980r

United States. Congress. House. Committee on Interstate and Foreign Commerce. Subcommittee on Oversight and Investigations. Hazardous waste matters . Washington , 1980. iii, 117 p. ; LC Card 80-603987 DDC 353.0077/2 19
KF27 .I5547 1980k

United States. Congress. House. Committee on Science and Technology. Posture hearings (EPA and NOAA) . Washington , 1980. iii, 70 p. ;
LC Card 80-604052 DDC 353.0082/321 19
KF27 .S39 1980e

United States. Congress. Senate. Committee on Appropriations. Subcommittee on HUD-Independent Agencies. Nuclear and hazardous waste problems in New Hampshire . Washington , 1980 [i.e. 1981] iii, 122 p. ; LC Card 81-601754 DDC 363.7/28 19
KF26 .A6486 1980b

United States. General Accounting Office. The Environmental Protection Agency needs congressional guidance and support to guard the public in a period of radiation proliferation . [Washington] 1978. vii, 81 p. ; LC Card 78-602990
TD171 .U57 1978 **NYPL** *[JLF 81-156]*

United States. General Accounting Office. Improving the scientific and technical information available to the Environmental Protection Agency in its decisionmaking process . [Washington, D.C. , 1979] v, 60 p. ; LC Card 79-603730 DDC 353.0082/32 19
TD171 .U57 1979

United States. Environmental Protection Agency. Air Pollution Training Institute. see Air Pollution Training Institute.

United States. Environmental Protection Agency. Air Quality Planning and Standards, Office of. see United States. Environmental Protection Agency. Office of Air Quality Planning and Standards.

UNITED STATES. ENVIRONMENTAL PROTECTION AGENCY. CHESAPEAKE BAY PROGRAM.
Virginia. State Water Control Board. Data organization, technical support, and coordination for the Environmental Protection Agency's Chesapeake Bay Program . [Richmond] [1979] 17 leaves ; LC Card 80-621161 DDC 353.0082/325 19
TD223.1 .V57 1979

United States. Environmental Protection Agency. Division of Oil and Special Materials Control. see United States. Environmental Protection Agency. Oil and Special Materials Control Division.

United States. Environmental Protection Agency. Energy, Minerals, and Industry, Office of. see United States. Environmental Protection Agency. Office of Energy, Minerals, and Industry.

United States. Environmental Protection Agency. Environmental Studies Division. Booz, Allen Public Administration Services, inc. The quality

of life concept . [Washington] , 1973. 1 v.
(various pagings). **NYPL [*XME-9624]**

**United States. Environmental Protection Agency.
General Radiation Standards Branch.** Cook,
John R. (John Richard), 1950- Occupational
exposure to ionizing radiation in the United
States . Washington, D.C. , 1980 [i.e. 1981] x,
74, [68] p. :   LC Card 81-601500   DDC 363.1/79
19
RC965.R25 C66

**United States. Environmental Protection Agency.
Noise Abatement and Control, Office of.** see
**United States. Environmental Protection
Agency. Office of Noise Abatement and
Control.**

**United States. Environmental Protection Agency.
Office of Air and Waste Management. Office
of Air Quality Planning and Standards.** see
**United States. Environmental Protection
Agency. Office of Air Quality Planning and
Standards.**

**United States. Environmental Protection Agency.
Office of Air and Water Programs Office of
Air Quality Planning and Standards.** see
**United States. Environmental Protection
Agency. Office of Air Quality Planning and
Standards.**

**United States. Environmental Protection Agency.
Office of Air Quality Planning and
Standards.**
American Society of Planning Officials. Legal
issues of emission density zoning /. Research
Triangle Park, N.C. , 1978. vi, 278 p. :   LC
Card 79-601742   DDC 344.73/046342 19
KF3812.5.E55 A94

Osag, T. R. Control of odors from
inedibles-rendering plants /. Research Triangle
Park, N. C. , 1974. vi, 51 p. in various pagings.
NYPL [JSF 80-793]

**United States. Environmental Protection Agency.
Office of Education and Manpower Planning.
Public Service Careers Section.** see **United
States. Environmental Protection Agency.
Public Service Careers Section.**

**United States. Environmental Protection Agency.
Office of Energy, Minerals, and Industry.**
National Conference on the Interagency R&D
Program, 4th, Washington, D.C., 1979.
Energy/environment IV . [Cincinnati, Ohio] ,
1980. v, 330 :   LC Card 80-602220   DDC
333.79/0973 19
TJ163.15 .N37 1979

National Conference on the Interagency Energy
/ Environment R&D Program.
Energy/environment: proceedings. Washington.
NYPL [JLM 80-1115]

National Conference on the Interagency R&D
Program, 2d Washington, D.C., 1977.
Energy/environment II /. [Cincinnati] , 1977.
v, 563 p., [1] leaf of plates :   LC Card 78-603659
TJ163.15 .N37 1977   **NYPL [JLF 81-191]**

**United States. Environmental Protection Agency.
Office of Environmental Engineering and
Technology.** Transcript from the national
hearing on the Federal nonnuclear energy
RD&D program . Washington, D.C. , 1980. xv,
161 p. ;   LC Card 81-600788   DDC 333.79/15/0973
19
TD195.E49 T7

**United States. Environmental Protection Agency.
Office of Environmental Protection Agency.
Office of Environmental Engineering and
Technology.** Transcript from the National
Hearings on the Federal nonnuclear energy
R&D program . Washington, D.C. , 1980 i.e.
1981. xix, 207 p. :   LC Card 81-601492   DDC
333.79/23/0973 19
HD9502.U52 T7

**United States. Environmental Protection Agency.
Office of Noise Abatement and Control.**
Official docket for proposed revision to rail
carrier noise emission regulation / United States
Environmental Protection Agency, Office of
Noise Abatement and Control. Washington: The
Office, 1980. 1 v.; 28 cm. Cover title. "EPA
550/9-80-215."
*1. Noise control - Law and legislation - United States.
2. Railroads - United States - Noise control. I. Title.*
NYPL [JLM 81-95]

**United States. Environmental Protection Agency.
Office of Pesticide Programs.** Savage, Eldon
P. National household pesticide usage study,
1976-1977 . Washington, D.C. [1979] cover
1980. ix, 126 p. :   LC Card 80-603384   DDC
363.7/384 19
TX325 .S28

**United States. Environmental Protection Agency.
Office of Planning and Evaluation.** Howarth,
John T. Economic analysis of proposed effluent
guidelines, the rubber processing industry
(phase II) /. Washington , 1974. 60, 5 p. :
NYPL [JLF 80-559]

**United States. Environmental Protection Agency.
Office of Radiation Programs.**
Cook, John R. (John Richard), 1950-
Occupational exposure to ionizing radiation in
the United States . Washington, D.C. , 1980
[i.e. 1981] x, 74, [68] p. :   LC Card 81-601500
DDC 363.1/79 19
RC965.R25 C66

Radioactivity in consumer products /.
Washington , Springfield, Va. , 1978. xi, 509
p. :   LC Card 79-602786
RA569 .R29

**United States. Environmental Protection Agency.
Office of Research and Development.**
Terrestrial microcosms and environmental
chemistry . [Washington] [1978?] xv, 147 p. :
LC Card 79-601829   DDC 574.5/264 19
QH541.2 .T45

**UNITED STATES. ENVIRONMENTAL
PROTECTION AGENCY. OFFICE OF
RESEARCH AND DEVELOPMENT -
APPROPRIATIONS AND
EXPENDITURES.**
United States. Congress. House. Committee on
Science and Technology. Subcommittee on
Natural Resources and Environment. 1981
authorization for the Office of Research and
Development, Environmental Protection
Agency . Washington , 1980. iii, 267 p. :   LC
Card 80-604013   DDC 353.0072/23682321 19
KF27 .S398 1980d

**United States. Environmental Protection Agency.
Office of Water and Hazardous Materials.
Effluent Guidelines Division.** Development
document for effluent limitations guidelines and
new source performance standards : soap and
detergent manufacturing point source category.
- Washington : The Division : for sale by the
Supt. of Docs., U. S. Govt. Print. Off., 1974.
xiii, 202 p. : diagrs. ; 27 cm. Spine title: Soap and
detergent. "EPA-440/1-74-018a." Bibliography: p.
189-194.
*1. Soap - Waste disposal. 2. Detergents, Synthetic -
Waste disposal. I. Title.*   **NYPL [JSF 80-270]**

**United States. Environmental Protection Agency.
Office of Water Program Operations.**
Association of Boards of Certification for
Operating Personnel in Water and Wastewater
Utilities. A classification system for water and
wastewater facilities and personnel. Milbrae,
Calif., 1974. 33 p.   LC Card 77-95256
NYPL [*ZT-1264]

Estimating laboratory needs for municipal
wastewater treatment facilities. Washington,
1973. i, 23, [104] p. : ill. ; 27 cm.
EPA-430/9-74-022
*1. Water - Pollution. 2. Sewerage. 3. Sewage disposal. I.
Title.*   **NYPL [JSF 80-271]**

**United States. Environmental Protection Agency.
Office of Water Program Operations.
Municipal Permits and Operations Division.**
Operation of wastewater treatment plants .
Sacramento , <1980-. v. <3 > :   LC Card
81-114782   DDC 628.3 19
TD746 .O64 1980

**United States. Environmental Protection Agency.
Office of Water Program Operations. Oil
and Special Materials Control Division.** see
**United States. Environmental Protection
Agency. Oil and Special Materials Control
Division.**

**UNITED STATES. ENVIRONMENTAL
PROTECTION AGENCY - OFFICIALS
AND EMPLOYEES - HEALTH AND
HYGIENE.**
United States. General Accounting Office.
Health monitoring needed for laboratory
employees, Environmental Protection Agency .

Washington , 1976. iv, 26 p. ;   LC Card
76-603278   DDC 363.1/79 19
RA566.26 .U47 1976

**United States. Environmental Protection Agency.
Oil and Special Materials Control Division.**
Proposed revisions to ocean dumping criteria :
final environmental impact statement /
prepared by Oil and Special Materials Control
Division, Office of Water Program Operations,
U. S. Environmental Protection Agency.
Washington : U. S. Environmental Protection
Agency, 1977. 2 v. ; 28 cm.
1. Waste disposal in the ocean - United States. I. Title.
NYPL [JSF 80-969]

**United States. Environmental Protection Agency.
Planning and Evaluation, Office of.** see
**United States. Environmental Protection
Agency. Office of Planning and Evaluation.**

**United States. Environmental Protection Agency.
Procurement and Contracts Management
Division.** Professional minority consulting
firms. Washington. 28 cm.
*1. Business consultants - United States - Directories. 2.
Minority business enterprises - United States -
Directories. I. Title.*   **NYPL [*R-Econ.
80-2054 & JLM 80-1149]**

**United States. Environmental Protection Agency.
Public Service Careers Section.** Guidelines to
career development for wastewater
treatment-plant personnel, for the Public
Service Careers Section, Office of Education
and Manpower Planning, Environmental
Protection Agency. Washington, The Agency,
1973. viii, 100 p. ill. 28 cm. Career development
planning grid (folded) inserted. LC Card 76-87266
*1. Water treatment plants. 2. Water - Purification -
Study and teaching. I. Title.*   **NYPL [JSF 80-487]**

**United States. Environmental Protection Agency.
Radiation Programs, Office of.** see **United
States. Environmental Protection Agency.
Office of Radiation Programs.**

**United States. Environmental Protection Agency.
Region III. Montana. Water Quality Bureau.**
Water quality in Montana-1980 /. [Helena] ,
1980. 247, [7] p. :   LC Card 80-623056   DDC
363.7/3942/09786 19
TD224.M9 M68 1980

**United States. Environmental Protection Agency.
Region VII. Public Involvement Branch.**
Directory of environmental groups, Region 7.
1980 ed. Kansas City, Mo. : U. S.
Environmental Protection Agency, Public
Involvement Branch, 1980. 36 p. : ill. ; 28 cm.
Cover title: EPA directory, Region 7, environmental
groups, Iowa, Kansas, Nebraska, Missouri. LC Card
80-603239   DDC 363.7/0025/73 19
*1. Environmental protection - Middle West -
Directories. I. Title.*
TD169.6 .U48 1980

**United States. Environmental Protection Agency.
Water Planning Division.** Association of
New Jersey Environmental Commissions. Tools
and rules . [Washington] , 1978 printing. 69, xii
p. ;   LC Card 79-602335
KF3775 .A97 1978   **NYPL [JLF 81-387]**

**United States. Environmental Protection Agency.
Water Program Operations, Office of.** see
**United States. Environmental Protection
Agency. Office of Water Program
Operations.**

**United States. Environmental Protection Agency.
Water Quality Section. Massachusetts.**
Divison of Water Pollution Control. Rumford
and Three Mile Rivers . Boston [1971] 63 p. :
LC Card 80-118665   DDC 363.7/3942/0974485
19
TD224.M4 M36 1971b

**United States. Environmental Protection Agency.
Water Supply Research Division.** Ozone,
chlorine dioxide, and chloramines as
alternatives to chlorine for disinfection of
drinking water : state-of-the-art : presented at
Second Conference on Water Chlorination:
Environmental Impact and Health Effects,
Gatlinburg, Tennessee, October 31-November 4,
1977. Rev. Cincinnati, Ohio : Water Supply
Research, Office of Research and Development,
U. S. Environmental Protection Agency, [1977]
1979 printing. 84 p. : ill. ; 28 cm. Includes
bibliographical references. LC Card 80-601552   DDC
628.1/66 19

1. Water - Purification. 2. Drinking water. I. Conference on Water Chlorination: Environmental Impact and Health Effects, 2d, Gatlinburg, Tenn., 1977. II. Title.
TD459 .U54 1977

United States. Environmental Quality, Council on. see United States. Council on Environmental Quality.

United States. Environmental Research Laboratories. see Environmental Research Laboratories.

United States. Equal Employment Opportunity Commission.
Hearings before the United States Equal Employment Opportunity Commission on religious accommodation : hearings held in New York, N.Y., Los Angeles, CA. & Milwaukee, WI., April-May 1978. [Washington] : U. S. Govt. Print. Off., 1979. x, 649 p. ; 24 cm. LC Card 80-601627 DDC 331.13/3 19
1. Discrimination in employment - United States. 2. Religious tolerance - United States. I. Title.
HD4903.5.U58 U536 1979

Minorities and women in private industry : 1978 report. [Washington] : U. S. Equal Employment Opportunity Commission : [for sale by the Supt. of Docs., U. S. Govt. Print. Off., 1980] 2 v. : forms ; 28 cm. Cover title. Edition for 1977 entered under K. A. McMillan. "February 1980." Chiefly tables. LC Card 80-602340 DDC 331.13/3/0973 19
1. Minorities - Employment - United States - Statistics. 2. Women - Employment - United States - Statistics. 3. Discrimination in employment - United States - Statistics. I. McMillan, Kathleen A. Minorities and women in private industry, 1975. II. Title.
HD8081.A5 U54 1980

UNITED STATES. EQUAL EMPLOYMENT OPPORTUNITY COMMISSION.
United States. Congress. House. Select Committee on Aging. EEOC enforcement of the Age Discrimination in Employment Act . Washington , 1980. iii, 110 p. ; LC Card 81-600653 DDC 331.3/98 19
KF27.5 .A3 1980h

United States. Equality of Educational Opportunity, National Advisory Council on. see United States. National Advisory Council on Equality of Educational Opportunity.

UNITED STATES - ETHNIC RELATIONS - ADDRESSES, ESSAYS, LECTURES.
Civil rights issues of Euro-ethnic Americans in the United States . Washington, D.C. , 1980. vii, 592 p. : LC Card 81-600724 DDC 305.8/4 19
E184.E95 C58

United States-European communities relations : focusing on the differences, Washington, January 1979 : report on the fourteenth meeting of members of Congress and the European Parliament, January 30-31, 1979, pursuant to H. Res. 981 ... Washington [D.C.] : U. S. G.P.O., 1979. x, 44 p. ; 24 cm. "96th Congress, 1st Session. Committee Print." "Printed for the use of the Committee on Foreign Affairs." LC Card 80-603969 DDC 337/.09/047 19
1. International economic relations. 2. Nuclear nonproliferation. 3. Near East - Strategic aspects. I. European Parliament. II. United States. Congress. House. Committee on Foreign Affairs.
HF1411 .U64

UNITED STATES - EXECUTIVE DEPARTMENTS.
United States. Laws, statutes, etc. Compiled statutes--Committee on Government Operations . Washington , 1980. xiv, 1065 p. ; LC Card 80-603543 DDC 342.73/06/02632 347.302602632 19
KF5102 1980

United States. Library of Congress. Congressional Research Service. The Federal executive establishment . Washington , 1980. v, 76 p. ; LC Card 80-602577 DDC 353.04 19
JK411 .U54 1980

UNITED STATES - EXECUTIVE DEPARTMENTS - BIBLIOGRAPHY.
Federal information sources & systems. 1976- Washington.
*NYPL [*R-Econ. 81-135 & JLM 81-123]*

Requirements for recurring reports to the Congress. 1976- Washington.
*NYPL [*R-Econ. 77-323 & JLM 77-313]*

UNITED STATES - EXECUTIVE DEPARTMENTS - DIRECTORIES.
United States. Office of the Federal Register. Directory of Federal regional structure /. [Washington] [1978] iii, 94 p. : LC Card 79-603213
JK464 1978 .U54   *NYPL [JLF 81-410]*

UNITED STATES - EXECUTIVE DEPARTMENTS - EVALUATION.
Federal program evaluations. 1976- Washington.
*NYPL [*R-Econ. 81-136 & JLM 81-130]*

UNITED STATES - EXECUTIVE DEPARTMENTS - MANAGEMENT - DATA PROCESSING.
United States. General Accounting Office. Wider use of better computer software technology can improve management control and reduce costs . Washington, DC [1980] iii, 57 p. ; LC Card 80-602401 DDC 353/.075 19
JK468.A8 U5 1980

UNITED STATES - EXECUTIVE DEPARTMENTS - OFFICIALS AND EMPLOYEES.
United States. Congress. House. Committee on Government Operations. Legislation and National Security Subcommittee. Inspector General Act Amendments of 1980 . Washington , 1980. iv, 261 p. ; LC Card 80-604018 DDC 342.73/066 347.30266 19
KF27 .G6676 1980k

United States. Executive Office of the President. Council of Economic Advisers. see United States. Council of Economic Advisers.

United States. Executive Office of the President. Council on Environmental Quality. see United States. Council on Environmental Quality.

United States. Executive Office of the President. Council on Wage and Price stability. see United States. Council on Wage and Price Stability.

United States. Executive Office of The President. Office of Management and Budget. see United States. Office of Management and Budget.

United States. Export-Import Bank. see Export-Import Bank of the United States.

United States. Extension Service (1970-)
Extension service review. v. 1-49, no. 1; May, 1930-Jan./Feb. 1978. Washington. 49 v.
NYPL [VPG (U. S.) (Extension service review)]

United States. Fair Employment Practice, Committee on. see United States. Committee on Fair Employment Practice (1941-1943); United States. Committee on Fair Employment Practice (1943-1946)

United States. Farmers Home Administration.
A brief history of FmHA / United States Department of Agriculture, Farmers Home Administration. [Washington, D.C.] : The Administration, [1980] 17, [32] p. : graphs ; 28 cm. LC Card 80-602652 DDC 353.0082/33045 19
1. United States. Farmers Home Administration - History. I. Title.
HG2051.U5 U54 1980

National Strategy Conference on Improving Service Delivery to the Rural Elderly (1979 : Des Moines, Iowa) Improving services for the rural elderly . Washington, D.C. [1980] ix, 62 p. ; LC Card 80-69618 DDC 362.6/0973 19
HV1465 .N36 1979

UNITED STATES. FARMERS HOME ADMINISTRATION.
United States. Congress. Senate. Committee on Agriculture, Nutrition, and Forestry. Subcommittee on Agricultural Credit and Rural Electrification. FmHA biomass energy program . Washington , 1981. iii, 34 p. : LC Card 81-601763 DDC 338.4/7662669 19
KF26 .A3533 1980b

United States. Congress. Senate. Committee on Agriculture, Nutrition, and Forestry. Subcommittee on Agricultural Credit and Rural Electrification. Interest rate levels of FmHA loan programs . Washington , 1980. iii, 25 p. ; LC Card 80-603100 DDC 332.7/1/0973 19
KF26 .A3533 1980

United States. General Accounting Office. Ways of providing a fairer share of Federal

housing support to rural areas . [Washington, D.C. , 1980] v, 86 p. : LC Card 80-601694 DDC 363.5/8 19
HD7289.U6 U55 1980

UNITED STATES. FARMERS HOME ADMINISTRATION - HISTORY.
United States. Farmers Home Administration. A brief history of FmHA /. [Washington, D.C.] [1980] 17, [32] p. : LC Card 80-602652 DDC 353.0082/33045 19
HG2051.U5 U54 1980

United States. Federal Agencies Task Force.
American Indian religious freedom act report : P. L. 95-341 / Federal Agencies Task Force, chairman, Cecil D. Andrus. [Washington] : The Task Force, 1979. 215 p. in various pagings ; 28 cm. Cover title. LC Card 79-604018 DDC 353.0081/497 19
1. Indians of North America - Religious liberty. 2. Indians of North America - Legal status, laws, etc. 3. Indians of North America - Religion and mythology. I. Title.
KF8210.R37 A833

United States. Federal Aviation Administration.
International flight information manual. v. 15- ; 1967- Washington. 26 cm.
1. Air-pilot guides - Periodicals. I. Title.
NYPL [JSP 80-448]

List of certificated pilot flight and ground schools. Washington. 27 cm. (United States. Federal Aviation Administration. AC) Annual. Cover title. Vol. for 1967 issued by the Administration under its earlier name, Federal Aviation Agency. Superseded by its List of certificated pilot schools.
1. Flight training - United States - Directories. I. United States. Federal Aviation Agency. II. Title.
NYPL [JLM 81-99]

List of certificated pilot schools. Washington. 28 cm. (United States. Federal Aviation Administration. AC) Supersedes its List of certificated pilot flight and ground schools.
1. Flight training - United States - Directories. I. Title.
NYPL [JLM 81-98]

Monitoring of Concorde operations at Dulles International Airport, May 24 through November 30, 1976 / Department of Transportation, Federal Aviation Administration. Washington, D.C. : The Administration, [1977] 56 p. : ill. ; 26 cm. Cover title: Concorde monitoring. "January 1977." LC Card 79-604296 DDC 363.7/41 19
1. Concorde (Jet transports) - Noise. 2. Dulles International Airport, Washington, D. C. I. Title. II. Title: Concorde monitoring.
TL671.65 .U54 1977b

Report.
(FAA-EE-79-20) United States. Federal Aviation Administration. Office of Environment and Energy. Energy conservation potential of general aviation activity. [Washington] , 1979. iii, 43 p. : LC Card 80-601430 DDC 333.79 19
TJ163.5.T7 U52 1979

United States. Civil Aeronautics Board. Airport activity statistics of certificated route air carriers. Washington. LC Card 63-4959
NYPL [VDS (United States. Civil Aeronautics Board. Airport activity Statistics of certificated route air carriers)]

UNITED STATES. FEDERAL AVIATION ADMINISTRATION.
United States. Congress. House. Committee on Government Operations. Government Activities and Tansportation Subcommittee. FAA-OSHA jurisdiction over workplace safety in the aviation industry . Washington , 1980. iii, 192 p. : LC Card 81-600596 DDC 353.0087/77/0289 19
KF27 .G6626 1980c

United States. Congress. House. Committee on Public Works and Transportation. Subcommittee on Aviation. DOT/FAA proposed new policy for airports in the metropolitan Washington area . Washington , 1980. viii, 923 p. : LC Card 80-604030 DDC 387.7/4042/09753 19
KF27 .P89624 1980n

United States. Congress. House. Committee on Public Works and Transportation. Subcommittee on Aviation. To enhance the safety mission of the FAA . Washington , 1980. iv, 560 p. : LC

Card 80-604032   DDC 343.73/097 347.30397 19
KF27 .P89624 1980m

United States. Congress. House. Committee on
Science and Technology. Posture hearings
(NASA and FAA) . Washington , 1980. iii, 107
p. ;   LC Card 80-602953   DDC 353.0085/6 19
KF27 .S39 1980

**United States. Federal Aviation Administration.
Aviation Forecast Branch. see United States.
Aviation Forecast Branch.**

**United States. Federal Aviation Administration.
Civil Aviation Security Service. see United
States. Civil Aviation Security Service.**

**United States. Federal Aviation Administration.
Flight Standards Service. see United States.
Flight Standards Service.**

**United States. Federal Aviation Administration.
Office of Environment and Energy.** Energy
conservation potential of general aviation
activity. [Washington] : U. S. Dept. of
Transportation, Federal Aviation
Administration, Office of Environment and
Energy, 1979. iii, 43 p. : ill. ; 28 cm. (Report -
Federal Aviation Administration ; FAA-EE-79-20)
Cover title. "September 1979." Includes bibliographical
references.   LC Card 80-601430   DDC 333.79 19
*1. Aeronautics, Commercial - United States - Energy
conservation. I. Series: United States. Federal Aviation
Administration. Report, FAA-EE-79-20.*
TJ163.5.T7 U52 1979

United States. Federal Aviation Agency.
Air carrier operations inspector's handbook.
Washington [1964] 1 v. (loose-leaf) ill. 26 cm.
(FS P 8430.13) "An FAA handbook."
1. Transport planes. 2. Airplanes - Inspection.
                                    NYPL [JSF 78-777]

Flight training handbook. United States. Flight
Standards Service. Flight training handbook.
Rev. [Oklahoma City, Okla.] , Washington,
D.C. , 1980. xvi, 325 p. :   LC Card 80-601809
DDC 629.132/52 19
TL710 .U64 1980

International flight information manual.
Washington. 26 cm. Published by the U. S. Civil
Aeronautics Administration, Office of Aviation
Information. For later file, which continues its
numbering, see: United States. Federal Aviation
Administration. International flight information manual.
*1. Air-pilot guides - Periodicals. I. United States. Office
of Aviation Information. II. Title.*   ***NYPL [VDS***
(U. S. Federal Aviation Agency.
International flight information manual)]

United States. Civil Aeronautics Board. Airport
activity statistics of certificated route air
carriers. Washington.   LC Card 63-4959
            NYPL [VDS (United States. Civil
            Aeronautics Board. Airport activity
            Statistics of certificated route air
                                    carriers)]

United States. Federal Aviation Administration.
List of certificated pilot flight and ground
schools. Washington.   ***NYPL [JLM 81-99]***

United States. Federal Bureau of Investigation.
(Old Catalog form: United States. Justice
Dept. Investigation Bureau.)
Japanese pre-war colonization. [Washington :
Federal Bureau of Investigation, [1935?] [18]
p. : all maps (some col.) ; 30 x 42 cm. Cover
title. English and Japanese, with ms. Spanish
translations of Japanese captions. CONTENTS. -
Japanese nationals, enterprises, consulates.--Resources
and Japanese ship routes.--Japanese nationals living
abroad.--Agricultural production--Mineral
production.--Provinces of Manchuria and their
capitals.--Location of railroads and Japanese immigrant
colonies.   LC Card 80-675188   DDC 912/.1325352
*1. Japanese in foreign countries - Maps. 2. Japan -
Colonies - Maps. I. Title.*
G1046.E27 U5 1935

The science of fingerprints : classification and
uses. Rev. [Washington] : United States Dept.
of Justice, Federal Bureau of Investigation ;
Washington, D.C. : for sale by the Supt. of
Docs., U. S. Govt. Print. Off., [1979] v, 209
p. : ill. ; 24 cm.   LC Card 80-602568   DDC
363.2/58 19
1. Fingerprints. I. Title.
HV6074 .U6 1979

**UNITED STATES. FEDERAL BUREAU OF
INVESTIGATION.**
United States. Commission on Civil Rights.
Federal Bureau of Investigation--Indian
reservations police abuse . Washington, D.C.
[1979] iii, 69 p. ;   LC Card 80-601782   DDC
323.1/197/073 19
E93 .U53 1979

United States. Congress. House. Committe on
the Judiciary. Subcommittee on Civil and
Constitutional Rights. FBI oversight .
Washington , 1980. iii, 256 p. :   LC Card
80-604016   DDC 353.0074 19
KF27 .J847 1979f

United States. Congress. House. Committee on
the Judiciary. Subcommittee on Civil and
Constitutional Rights. Legislative charter for the
FBI . Washington , 1980 [i.e. 1981] iv, 560 p. ;
LC Card 81-600983   DDC 344.73/0525
347.304525 19
KF27 .J843 1979a

United States. Congress. Senate. Committee on
the Judiciary. FBI charter act of 1979, S. 1612 .
Washington , 1980- v. :   LC Card 80-603508
DDC 344.73/0525 19
KF26 .J8 1979t

United States. General Accounting Office.
From quantity to quality . [Washington] [1980]
iv, 41 p. ;   LC Card 80-602224   DDC 363.2/5 19
HV6658 .U55 1980

**United States. Federal Committee on Statistical
Methodology. Subcommittee on Matching
Techniques.** Report on exact and statistical
matching techniques / prepared by
Subcommittee on Matching Techniques, Federal
Committee on Statistical Methodology.
[Washington] : U. S. Dept. of Commerce,
Office of Federal Statistical Policy and
Standards : [for sale by the Supt. of Docs., U.
S. Govt. Print. Off., 1980] vii, 57 p. ; 26 cm.
(Statistical policy working paper . 5) Authors, Daniel
Radner, and others. "Issued June 1980." Bibliography: p.
55-[58]   LC Card 80-603147   DDC 001.4/224 19
*1. Dual record systems. I. Radner, Daniel. II. Title. III.
Title: Statistical matching techniques. IV. Series.*
HB849.49 .U53 1980

**United States. Federal Committee on Statistical
Methodology. Subcommittee on Statistical
Uses of Administrative Records.** Report on
statistical uses of administrative records /
prepared by Subcommitte on Statistical Uses of
Administrative Records, Federal Committee on
Statistical Methodology. [Washington, D.C.?] :
U. S. Dept. of Commerce, Office of Federal
Statistical Policy and Standards, 1980 [i.e.
1981] xii, 106 p. : 1 chart, forms ; 26 cm.
(Statistical policy working paper . v. 6) "Issued
December 1980." S/N 003-005-00185-9 Item 126-D-7
Bibliography: p. 104-106.   LC Card 81-601438   DDC
353.0081/9 19
*1. United States - Statistical services. 2. Administrative
agencies - United States - Records and Correspondence.
I. United States. Office of Federal Statistical Policy and
Standards. II. Title. III. Series.*
HA37.U55 U55 1981

**United States. Federal Committee on Statistical
Methodology. Subcommittee on Statistics for
Allocation of Funds.** Correlation between the
United States and international standard
industrial classifications / prepared by
Subcommittee on Statistics for Allocation of
Funds, Federal Committee on Statistical
Methodology. [Washington] : U. S. Dept. of
Commerce, Office of Federal Statistical Policy
and Standards : for sale by the Supt. of Docs.,
U. S. Govt. Print. Off., 1979. 101 ; 28 cm.
(Technical paper ; U. S. Department of Commerce,
Office of Federal Statistical Policy and Standards ; 1)
LC Card 80-601531   DDC 338/.02/0973 19
*1. Industry - Classification. I. Series: United States.
Office of Federal Statistical Policy and Standards.
Technical paper - U. S. Department of Commerce,
Office of Federal Statistical Policy and Standards , 1.
II. Title.*
HD2328 .U54 1979

**United States. Federal Communications
Commission.**
A study of maritime public coast station
operations, services, and industry : report to the
Congress of the United States / Federal
Communications Commission. [Washington,
D.C.] : The Commission, [1979] 48, 31, [15]
p. ; 28 cm. "December 1979." LC Card 80-602044

DDC 353.0087/45453 19
1. Marine radio stations - United States. I. Title.
VK397 .U47 1979

**United States. Federal Communications
Commission. EEO-Minority Enterprise
Division.** Minority ownership of broadcast
facilities : a report. [Washington, D.C.] :
Federal Communications Commission, Office of
Public Affairs, EEO-Minority Enterprise
Division, 1980. 64 p. : ill. ; 18 x 23 cm.
"December 1979." Outgrowth of a Conference on
Minority Ownership, held in Washington, D.C. in 1977,
this report summarizes findings of CCG, Inc.
Bibliography: p. 63-64.   LC Card 80-601583   DDC
384.54 19
*1. Minorities in broadcasting - United States. I.
Conference on Minority Ownership, Washington, D.C.,
1977. II. CCG, inc. III. Title.*
HE8689.8 .U547 1980

**United States. Federal Contract Compliance
Programs, Office of. see United States.
Office of Federal Contract Compliance
Programs.**

**United States. Federal Coordinating Council for
Science, Engineering, and Technology.**
Reports of the Subcommittees on National
Needs and Problems; Data Collection, Storage,
and Distribution; Monitoring; Research and
Development. Springfield, Va. , 1979. v, 177
p. :   ***NYPL [JSF 80-409]***

United States. Federal Council on the Aging.
The impact of the tax structure on the elderly.
Washington : Federal Council on the Aging :
for sale by the Supt. of Docs., U. S. Govt.
Print. Off., 1975. iv, 119 p. ; 24 cm. (DHEW
publication. no. (OHD) 76-20954) Includes
bibliographical references.   LC Card 76-601234
*1. Aged - Taxation - United States. 2. Income tax -
United States. 3. Social security taxes - United States.
4. Sales tax - United States. 5. Property tax - United
States. I. Title.*
HJ4653.A82 U55 1975   ***NYPL [JLF 80-1411]***

Public policy and the frail elderly : a staff
report, December 1978. Washington, D.C. : U.
S. Dept. of Health, Education, and Welfare,
Office of Human Development Services,
Federal Council on [the] Aging, 1979. viii, 170
p. ; 28 cm. (United States. Dept. of Health,
Education, and Welfare. DHEW publication (OHDS)
79-20959) Bibliography: p. 150-159.   LC Card
80-600607
*1. Aged, Services for - United States. 2. Aged -
Medical care - United States. I. Title.*
HV1457 .U52 1979   ***NYPL [JLF 81-261]***

**United States. Federal Council on the Arts and
the Humanities. see Federal Council on the
Arts and the Humanities.**

United States. Federal Election Commission.
Regulations / Federal Election Commission.
Washington, D.C. : The Commission, [1980]
178 p. ; 23 cm. Regulations for compliance with the
Federal election campaign act of 1971, as amended.
"April 1980." Includes indexes.   LC Card 80-602940
DDC 342.73/07 19
*1. Election law - United States. 2. Elections - United
States - Campaign funds. I. United States. Laws,
statutes, etc. Federal election campaign act of 1971.*
KF4885 .A33 1980

Smolka, Richard G. Handbook of state election
agencies and election officials /. [Springfield,
Va.] , 1976. 176, 23, 56 p. ;   LC Card 76-603434
JK2021 .S58   ***NYPL [*XME-9548]***

United States. Federal election campaign laws
/. Washington, D.C. (1325 K Street, N.W.,
Washington, D.C., 20463) , 1980. xi, 140 p. ;
LC Card 80-603772   DDC 342.73/078 347.30278
19
KF4885 .A3 1980a

United States. Laws, statutes, etc. Federal
election campaign laws (including the Federal
election campaign act amendments of 1979,
Pub. L. no. 96-187) /. Washington, D.C.
[1980] ix, 90 p. ;   LC Card 80-602594   DDC
342.73/07 19
KF4885 .A3 1980

United States. Library of Congress.
Congressional Research Service. American Law
Division. Election law updates. 1978-
[Washington].   ***NYPL [JLM 81-184]***

United States. Federal Electronic Printing and Microform Committee. Electronic composition : a study of costs / prepared at the direction of the Federal Electronic Printing and Microform Committee under the supervision of the Joint Committee on Printing, 1975. Washington, D.C. : U. S. Govt. Print. Off. : for sale by the Supt. of Docs., U. S. Govt. Print. Off., 1975. v, 191 p. : ill. ; 28 cm. At head of title: 94th Congress, 1st session. Joint Committee print. Update of the 1970 ed. issued by the Committee under its earlier name: Federal Electronic Printing Committee, under title: A review of the costs of electronic composition. LC Card 80-603603 DDC 686.2/2544 19
1. Computerized typesetting - Costs. I. United States. Congress. Joint Committee on Printing. II. United States. Federal Electronic Printing Committee. Review of the costs of electronic composition. III. Title.
Z253.3 .U54 1975

United States. Federal Electronic Printing Committee.
Review of the costs of electronic composition.
United States. Federal Electronic Printing and Microform Committee. Electronic composition : a study of costs / prepared at the direction of the Federal Electronic Printing and Microform Committee under the supervision of the Joint Committee on Printing, 1975. Washington, D.C. , 1975. v, 191 p. : LC Card 80-603603 DDC 686.2/2544 19
Z253.3 .U54 1975

United States. Federal Emergency Management Agency.
Munson, Michael J. Indirect costs of residential fires /. [Washington] , 1979 [i.e. 1980] vi, 30 p. : LC Card 80-602415 DDC 363.3/79 19
TH9445.D9 M86

Stockpile report to the Congress. Apr./Sept. 1979- Washington. Supersedes: United States. General Services Administration. Office of Preparedness. Stockpile report to the Congress.
I. Title.　　　**NYPL [Econ. Div.]**

Telephone directory. AUG. 1980- [Washington]
NYPL [Econ. Div.]

UNITED STATES. FEDERAL EMERGENCY MANAGEMENT AGENCY.
United States. Congress. House. Committee on Science and Technology. Posture hearings (NSF, NBS, and FEMA) . Washington , 1980. iii, 200 p. : LC Card 80-604103 DDC 353.008 19
KF27 .S39 1980f

United States. Congress. House. Committee on Science and Technology. Subcommittee on Science, Research, and Technology. Earthquake and Fire Act authorization . Washington , 1980. iv, 720 p. : LC Card 80-604029 DDC 353.0072/23675 19
KF27 .S399 1980f

United States. Federal Energy Administration.
Nossman, Waters, Krueger, Marsh & Riordan. Summary: an evaluation of the options of the U. S. Government in its relationship to U. S. firms in international petroleum affairs. Los Angeles, 1975. 122 p.;　　**NYPL [JLF 80-599]**

United States. Federal Energy Administration. National Energy Information Center. see National Energy Information Center.

United States. Federal Energy Administration. Strategic Petroleum Reserve Office. see United States. Strategic Petroleum Reserve Office.

UNITED STATES. FEDERAL ENERGY REGULATORY COMMISSION - APPROPRIATIONS AND EXPENDITURES.
United States. Congress. House. Committee on Interstate and Foreign Commerce. Subcommittee on Energy and Power. Fiscal year 1981 authorization for the Department of Energy and the Federal Energy Regulatory Commission . Washington , 1980. vi, 1012 p. : LC Card 80-603496 DDC 353.0072/236823 19
KF27 .I5542 1980e

United States. Federal Energy Regulatory Commission. Office of Pipeline and Producer Regulation. Prudhoe Bay project final environmental impact statement : construction and operation of a sales gas conditioning facility at Prudhoe Bay, Alaska : Northwest Alaskan

Natural Gas Transportation Company, docket no. CP78-123 et al. / Federal Energy Regulatory Commission, Office of Pipeline and Producer Regulation. Washington, D.C. : The Office, 1980. xv, 416 p. : ill. ; 28 cm. R. Arvedlund, project manager. "July 1980." "FERC/EIS 0009." Bibliography: p. 209-217. LC Card 80-603226 DDC 333.8/2331/09798 19
1. Gas industry - Environmental aspects - Alaska - Prudhoe Bay region. 2. Environmental impact statements - Alaska - Prudhoe Bay region. I. Arvedlund, Robert A. II. Title.
TD195.G3 U55 1980

UNITED STATES. FEDERAL ENERGY REGULATORY COMMISSION - OFFICIALS AND EMPLOYEES.
United States. Congress. Senate. Committee on Energy and Natural Resources. Lindsay D. Norman, Jr., and John D. Hughes nominations . Washington , 1980. iii, 123 p. : LC Card 80-603780 DDC 353.0082/327 19
KF26 .E55 1980g

United States. Federal Executive Institute. see Federal Executive Institute.

United States. Federal Extension Service. (Old Catalog form: United States. Agriculture Dept. Extension Service)
Extension service review. v. 1-49, no. 1; May, 1930-Jan./Feb. 1978. Washington. 49 v.
NYPL [VPG (U. S.) (Extension service review)]

UNITED STATES. FEDERAL FARM CREDIT BOARD - OFFICIALS AND EMPLOYEES.
United States. Congress. Senate. Committee on Agriculture, Nutrition, and Forestry. Nominations of Ralph Raikes and William D. Wampler . Washington , 1980. iii, 31 p. : LC Card 80-604017 DDC 353.0082/33045 19
KF26 .A35 1980c

United States. Federal Highway Administration.
Alaska. Dept. of Transportation and Public Facilities. Transportation Planning Division. State of Alaska coal haul road system report /. [Juneau] [1978?] 27, [13] leaves : LC Card 79-622823 DDC 333.8/22152/09798 19
HE199.5.C6 A44 1978

Arizona. Transportation Planning Division. Traffic on the county federal-aid highway system. [Phoenix, Ariz.] , 1976. 53 p., [21] leaves of plates : LC Card 80-620909 DDC 388.3/142/09791 19
HE371.A6 A55 1976

Bishop, A. Bruce. Socio-economic and community factors in planning urban freeways. [Washington] 1970. xiii, 216 p. : LC Card 73-610102
HE356.C2 B5　　　**NYPL [JLF 81-276]**

Comsis Corporation. Traffic assignment . Washington, 1973. 205 p.
NYPL [JLF 81-601]
FHWA-OEP/HEV. 80/1- Washington.
NYPL [Econ. Div.]
Gallagher, V. P. Contrast requirements of urban drivers . Philadelphia , Springfield, Va. , 1974. viii, 72 p. :　　　**NYPL [JSF 80-828]**

A handbook of highway safety design and operating practices. Revised 1973. Washington; For sale by the Supt. of Docs., U. S. Govt. Print. Off. [1973] 1 v. (loose-leaf). illus. 20x26 cm. "To keep the Handbook current, revisions and new material will be issued through looseleaf supplements."
1. Roads - Safety measures. 2. Roads - Accessories. I. Title. II. Title: Highway safety design and operating practices.　　**NYPL [JLF 80-1456]**

Highway functional classification : concepts, criteria and procedures. [Washington] 1974. [34] p. in various pagings : ill., graphs ; 26 cm. Microfilm. Cover title. At head of title: Transmittal 155, volume 20, appendix 12.
1. Roads - United States. I. Title.
NYPL [*ZT-1259]
Highway joint development and multiple use. [Washington : U. S. Dept. of Transportation, Federal Highway Administration ; Washington : for sale by the Supt. of Docs., U. S. Govt. Print. Off., 1979] 132 p. : ill. ; 20 x 27 cm. Cover title. Includes bibliographical references. LC Card 79-602134
1. Roads - Right of way - Multiple use. 2. Express

highways - United States. I. Title.
HE355.8 .U54 1979

Marshall Kaplan, Gans, and Kahn. Social characteristics of neighborhoods as indicators of the effects of highway improvements. Washington, 1972. vii, 81, A88 p. LC Card 73-601292 DDC 388.1/22/0973 19
HE355.3.E3 M37 1972

National Research Council. Transportation Research Board. Motor vehicle size and weight regulations, enforcement, and permit operations. Washington, D.C. [1980] 45 p. ISBN 0-390-03019-6 (pbk.) : LC Card 80-66742 DDC 629.2/24 19
TL230 .N27 1980

National Research Council (U. S.) Transportation Research Board. Direction finding from arterials to destinations . Washington, D.C. , 1980. 50 p. : ISBN 0-309-03031-5 (pbk.) : LC Card 80-54090 DDC 388.3/122 19
TE228 .N32 1980

Nevada. Dept. of Transportation. Safety Section. 1978 Nevada fatal traffic accident report /. [Carson City?] [1979?] 34, 44 leaves, [6] leaves of plates (1 fold.) : LC Card 80-623180 DDC 312/.274/09793 19
HE5614.3.N42 N47 1979

Palmquist, Raymond B. Impact of highway improvements on property values in Washington /. Olympia, WA [1980] 247 p. : LC Card 80-622759 DDC 333.33/2/09797 19
HD266.W2 P34

Robertson, Richard Neal, 1940- Impact of removal of tolls on travel in Tidewater Virginia /. Charlottesville, Va. [1977?] 3 v. : LC Card 79-625466 DDC 388.1/14 19
HE376.A2 V87

Roy Jorgenson Associates. Construction engineering manpower management : system design manual /. [Gaithersburg, Md.], 1978. 1 v. (loose-leaf);　　**NYPL [JSF 80-656]**

South Dakota. Dept. of Transportation. Office of System Analysis. Highway traffic report, 1979 /. [Pierre] [1980] 146 p. : LC Card 80-622944 DDC 388.3/142/09783 19
HE371.S8 S68 1980

South Dakota. Division of Highway Safety. State & Community Programs. South Dakota highway safety plan, fiscal year 1980 /. [Pierre, S.D.] [1980?] 237 p. : LC Card 80-621619 DDC 363.1/256/09783 19
HE5614.3.S8 S68 1980

Urban origin-destination surveys: dwelling unit survey; truck and taxi surveys; external surveys / U. S. Dept. of Transportation, Federal Highway Administration. Washington: U. S. Govt. Print. Off., 1973. viii, 309 p.: ill. 26 cm. Includes bibliographical references.
1. Traffic surveys - United States. 2. Highway research. 3. Traffic engineering - United States. I. Title.
NYPL [JLF 81-455]

Vermont. Agency of Transportation. Planning Division. Vermont travel information study . [Montpelier] , 1978. v, 77 p. : LC Card 78-623822 DDC 388.3/124 19
G155.U6 V37 1978

Virginia. University. Civil Engineering Dept. Bridges on secondary highways and local roads . Washington, D.C. , 1980. 132 p. : ISBN 0-309-03025-0 (pbk.) : LC Card 80-51497 DDC 625.7 s 624.2 19
TE7 .N25 no. 222 TG153

Washington (State). Division of Public Transportation and Planning. Annual traffic report. [Olympia]　　**NYPL [JLM 80-967]**

Washington (State). State Highway Commission. Annual traffic report. [Olympia]
NYPL [N-10 2121]

United States. Federal Highway Administration. Bureau of Public Roads. see United States. Bureau of Public Roads.

United States. Federal Highway Administration. Office of Environmental Policy. The consideration of archeology and paleontology in the Federal-aid highway program. [Washington] : U. S. Dept. of Transportation, Federal Highway Administration, Office of Environmental Policy, 1979. 79 p. : ill., maps ;

GOVERNMENT PUBLICATIONS - U.S.: 1981

533   *United States. Federal Railroad Administration. Policy and*

22 x 26 cm. Cover title. "January 1979." Bibliography: p. 58-69. LC Card 79-602652
1. United States - Antiquities. 2. Archaeological surveying - United States. 3. Paleontology - United States. 4. Indians of North America - Antiquities. 5. Roads - United States - Surveying. I. Title.
E159.5 .U54 1978   **NYPL [HBC 81-515]**

United States. Federal Highway Administration. Office of Program and Policy Planning.
Cooper, Thomas W. The State highway finance outlook /. [Washington] , 1978. viii, 101 p. : LC Card 79-601548
HE355 .C66

United States. Federal Highway Administration. Offices of Research and development. Traffic Systems Division. see United States. Federal Highway Administration. Traffic Systems Division.

UNITED STATES. FEDERAL HIGHWAY ADMINISTRATION - OFFICIALS AND EMPLOYEES.
United States. Congress. Senate. Committee on Environment and Public Works. Nomination of John S. Hassell, Jr. . Washington , 1980. iii, 39 p. ; LC Card 80-603010 DDC 353.0086/42 19
KF26 .E6 1980e

United States. Congress. Senate. Committee on Environment and Public Works. Nomination of Ray A. Barnhart . Washington , 1981. iii, 38 p. ; LC Card 81-601612 DDC 353.0086/42 19
KF26 .E6 1981

United States. Federal Highway Administration. Traffic Systems Division. Abrams, Charles M. Measures of effectiveness for multimodal urban traffic management - Washington , Springfield, Va. , 1979. 1 v. :
NYPL [JLM 80-740]

United States. Federal Home Loan Bank Board.
Summary of savings accounts by geographic area : based on survey of savings accounts by office, FSLIC-insured savings and loan associations. Washington, D.C. : Federal Home Loan Bank Board, [1979] 2, 141 p. ; 28 cm. Cover title. LC Card 80-602040 DDC 332.3/2/0973 19
1. Building and loan associations - United States - Statistics. 2. Savings accounts - United States - Statistics. I. Title.
HG2151 .U52 1979

UNITED STATES. FEDERAL HOME LOAN BANK BOARD.
United States. Congress. House. Committee on Government Operations. Commerce, Consumer, and Monetary Affairs Subcommittee. "Renegotiable rate" mortgage proposals of Federal Home Loan Bank Board . Washington , 1980. v, 776 p. ; LC Card 80-602892 DDC 332.7/22 19
KF27 .G634 1980b

UNITED STATES. FEDERAL HOME LOAN BANK BOARD - OFFICIALS AND EMPLOYEES.
United States. Congress. Senate. Committee on Banking, Housing and Urban Affairs. Nomination of Richard T. Pratt . Washington , 1981. iii, 49 p. ; LC Card 81-601950 DDC 353.0082/5 19
KF26 .B39 1981d

United States. Federal Housing Administration.
Dealers and individuals: subject to the provisions of section 201.8(b) and 201.8(d) of the title I regulations, revised Dec. 31, 1972 / U. S. Dept. of Housing and Urban Development. Washington: U. S. Dept. of Housing and Urban Development, Federal Housing Administration, 1972. 58 p.; 26 cm.
1. Betterments - United States - Directories. I. Title.
NYPL [JLF 80-1690]

FHA regulations : home, mortgage insurance. Washington : U. S. Govt. Print. Off., 1973. 224 p. ; 24 cm. Cover title. "FHA 3000." "Reprinted to include all amendments through Dec. 1972, including transmittal 3000-90."
1. Housing - United States - Finance. 2. Insurance, Mortgage guaranty - United States. I. Title.
NYPL [JLE 80-2356]

United States. Federal Insurance Administration.
Areas eligible for flood insurance: master index. [Washington] U. S. Dept. of Housing and Urban Development, Federal Insurance Administration [1973?] 1 v. (various pagings)

26 cm. Caption title.
1. Insurance, Flood - United States. 2. Disaster relief - United States. I. Title.   **NYPL [JLF 80-866]**

United States. Federal Interagency Committee for the International Year of the Child.
Report on Federal Government programs that relate to children, 1979 / prepared by the representatives of the Federal Interagency Committee for the International Year of the Child and compiled by the the HEW Secretariat for IYC. [Washington, D.C.] : U. S. Dept. of Health, Education, and Welfare, 1979. vi, 125 p. ; 27 cm. (DHEW publication. no. (OHDS) 79-30180) "HEW-393." LC Card 79-603379
1. Child welfare - United States. 2. Federal aid to child welfare - United States. I. United States. Dept. of Health, Education, and Welfare. Secretariat for IYC. II. Title.
HV741 .U5245 1979   **NYPL [JLF 81-458]**

United States. Federal Interagency Committee on Education. Education and Work, Sub-Committee on. see United States. Federal Interagency Committee on Education. Sub-Committee on Education and Work.

United States. Federal Interagency Committee on Education. Sub-Committee on Education and Work. Olympus Research Corporation. Education service and work . [Washington] , for sale by the Supt. of Docs., U. S. Govt. Print. Off., 1977. 99 p. ; LC Card 78-600742
LB1029.C6 O48 1977   **NYPL [JFE 81-723]**

UNITED STATES. FEDERAL LABOR RELATIONS AUTHORITY - OFFICIALS AND EMPLOYEES.
United States. Congress. Senate. Committee on Governmental Affairs. Nomination of Henry Bowen Frazier III . Washington , 1980. iii, 24 p. ; LC Card 80-602712 DDC 353.0083/2 19
KF26 .G67 1980b

United States. Federal Labor Relations Council.
Report of the Federal Labor Relations Council, January 1, 1970-December 31, 1976. Washington : The Council : for sale by the Supt. of Docs., U. S. Govt. Print. Off., 1977. 90 p. ; 24 cm. "FLRC-77-2." Includes bibliographical references. LC Card 78-600833 DDC 344.73/0189041353 19
1. Employee-management relations in government - United States. 2. Collective labor agreements - Government employees - United States. I. Title.
KF5365 .A837

United States. Federal Maritime Commission. Office of Economic Analysis. Virgin Islands trade study : an economic analysis / prepared by the Federal Maritime Commission, Bureau of Industry Economics, Office of Economic Analysis. Washington, D.C. : The Commission : for sale by the Supt. of Docs., U. S. Govt. Print. Off., [1979] ca. 500 p. in various pagings : ill. ; 27 cm. "October 1979." Includes bibliography. LC Card 80-601213 DDC 387/.0097297/22 19
1. Shipping - Virgin Islands of the United States. 2. Virgin Islands of the United States - Commerce. I. Title.
HE796.3 .U54 1979

UNITED STATES. FEDERAL MARITIME COMMISSION - OFFICIALS AND EMPLOYEES.
United States. Congress. Senate. Committee on Commerce, Science, and Transportation. Nominations--Department of Commerce and Federal Maritime Commission . Washington , 1980. iii, 81 p. ; LC Card 80-601935 DDC 353.82 19
KF26 .C69 1979ak

United States. Federal Mediation and Conciliation Service. Office of Research.
Impact of the 1974 health care amendments to the NLRA on collective bargaining in the health care industry / U. S. Department of Labor, Labor-Management Services Administration ; Federal Mediation and Conciliation Service, [Office of Research] . [Washington] : The Administration, 1979. x, 473 p. : ill. ; 28 cm. "This report is based on a study financed by the Labor-Management Services Administration, U. S. Department of Labor, and prepared in the Federal Mediation and Conciliation Service by Lucretia Dewey Tanner, Harriet Goldberg Weinstein, and Alice Lynn Ahmuty, of the Office of Research." Bibliography: p. 443-473. LC Card 79-603053

1. Collective bargaining - Health facilities - United States. 2. Collective labor agreements - Health facilities - United States. I. Tanner, Lucretia Dewey. II. Weinstein, Harriet Goldberg. III. Ahmuty, Alice Lynn. IV. United States. Labor-Management Services Administration. V. Title.
RA971.35 .U54 1979

United States. Federal Mine Safety and Health Review Commission. Decisions. v. 1 (no. [1]-); Apr. 1979- [Washington] 27 cm. Monthly. Includes an introductory number, issued Mar. 1979. LC Card 79-643482
1. Mine safety - Law and legislation - United States - Cases - Periodicals. 2. Mine sanitation - Law and legislation - United States - Cases - Periodicals. 3. Coal mines and mining - Safety regulations - United States - Cases - Periodicals.   **NYPL [JLM 80-957]**

United States. Federal National Mortgage Association. see Federal National Mortgage Association.

United States. Federal Paperwork, Commission on. see United States. Commission on Federal Paperwork.

United States. Federal Power Commission. Transmission, Distribution, and Storage Technical Advisory Task Force on Rate Design.
United States. Federal Power Commission. Transmission, Distribution, and Storage Technical Advisory Task Force, Rate Design. see United States. Federal Power Commission. Transmission, Distribution, and Storage Technical Advisory Task Force on Rate Design.

National gas survey : report of the Transmission, Distribution, and Storage Technical Advisory Task Force Rate Design to the Federal Power Commission. Washington : United States Federal Power Commission, 1977. ca. 250 p. : graphs ; 28 cm. Includes bibliographical references. LC Card 78-601032
1. Gas, Natural - United States - Rates. 2. Gas industry - United States. I. Title.
HD9581.U5 U53 1977

UNITED STATES. FEDERAL PROTECTIVE SERVICE.
United States. Congress. House. Committee on Public Works and Transportation. Subcommittee on Public Buildings and Grounds. Federal Protective Service . Washington , 1980. iv, 174 p. : LC Card 80-603638 DDC 344.73/052 347.30452 19
KF27 .P8964 1979d

UNITED STATES. FEDERAL RAILROAD ADMINISTRATION - APPROPRIATIONS AND EXPENDITURES.
United States. Congress. Senate. Committee on Commerce, Science, and Transportation. Subcommittee on Surface Transportation. Amendments to the Federal railway safety act of 1970 . Washington , 1980. iii, 156 p. : LC Card 80-602782 DDC 343.73/095 19
KF26 .C698 1980d

United States. Federal Railroad Administration. Office of Policy and Program Development.
The Railroad situation . Washington , 1979. 487 p. : LC Card 79-602934
HE2751 .R13   **NYPL [JLF 81-372]**

United States. Geological Survey. Transportation map of ... [Washington] 1975-76. 41 col. maps on sheets 43 x 56 cm. and 56 x 43 cm. Scales vary. Each sheet separately titled. "Transportation zone edition." Shows lines that may be subject to abandonment, those operating under rail service continuation provisions, and other operating lines. Includes "Index to railroads." Accompanied by text. [2] p.   **NYPL [Map Div. 80-3426]**

UNITED STATES. FEDERAL RAILROAD ADMINISTRATION - OFFICIALS AND EMPLOYEES.
United States. Congress. Senate. Committee on Commerce, Science, and Transportation. Nominations--DOT . Washington , 1981. iii, 35 p. ; LC Card 81-601783 DDC 353.86 19
KF26 .C69 1981b

United States. Federal Railroad Administration. Policy and Program Development, Office of. see United States. Federal Railroad Administration. Office of Policy and Program Development.

United States. Federal Register, Office of. see **United States. Office of the Federal Register.**

United States. Federal Reserve Board. see **United States. Board of Governors of the Federal Reserve System.**

United States. Federal Reserve System. see **United States. Board of Governors of the Federal Reserve System.**

United States. Federal Security Agency. Office of Education. see **United States. Office of Education.**

United States. Federal Statistical Policy and Standards, Office of. see **United States. Office of Federal Statistical Policy and Standards.**

United States. Federal Theatre Project. see **Federal Theatre Project.**

United States. Federal Trade Commission.
FTC staff report on television advertising to children. [Washington : Federal Trade Commission] : for sale by the Supt. of Docs., U. S. Govt. Print. Off., 1978 394 p. in various pagings ; 28 cm. Cover title. Includes bibliographical references.   LC Card 79-601465
1. Television advertising and children - United States. 2. Advertising - Psychological aspects. 3. Youth as consumers - United States. 4. Children - Nutrition. I. Title.
HF6146.T42 U55 1978   NYPL [JLF 81-278]

Media policy session : technology and legal change (edited) / Federal Trade Commission. Washington, D.C. : The Commission : for sale by the Supt. of Docs., U. S. Govt. Print. Off., 1980. vi, 167, [37] p. ; 28 cm. Cover title. Includes bibliography.   LC Card 80-602844   DDC 343.73/0994 19
1. Mass media - Law and legislation - United States. 2. Telecommunications - Law and legislation - United States. 3. Advertising laws - United States. I. Title.
KF2765 .A355

Report of the presiding officer on proposed trade regulation rule : credit practices, 16 CFR part 444, public record 215-42 / Federal Trade Commission ; Henry B. Cabell, presiding officer. [Washington, D.C.] : The Commission : [for sale by the Supt. of Docs., U. S. Govt. Print. Off., 1978] vii, 373 p. ; 28 cm. Cover title. Spine title: Credit practices, presiding officer's report. "August 1978."   LC Card 79-602495   DDC 346.73/073 19
1. Consumer credit - Law and legislation - United States. 2. Debtor and creditor - United States. I. Cabell, Henry B. II. Title. III. Title: Credit practices, presiding officer's report.
KF1040 .A68

Report of the presiding officer on proposed trade regulation rule : health spas, 16 CFR Part 443; Public record 215-50 / Federal Trade Commission, Roger J. Fitzpatrick, presiding officer. [Washington] : The Commission : for sale by the Supt. of Docs., U. S. Govt. Print. Off., 1979. ii, 213 p. ; 28 cm. Cover title. Includes bibliographical references.   LC Card 79-602972   DDC 344.73/099 19
1. Physical fitness centers - Law and legislation - United States. I. Fitzpatrick, Roger J. II. Title.
KF2042.P49 A877

State restrictions on vision care providers . [Washington, D.C.?] , 1980. xix, 289 p. ;   LC Card 81-600519   DDC 343.73/078681411 347.30378681411 19
KF2036.E93 Z957

United States. Bureau of Consumer Protection. Disclosure of energy cost and consumption information in labeling and advertising of consumer appliances . [Washington] , 1979. 227 p. in various pagings ;   LC Card 79-602022   DDC 343.73/085568383 19
KF1620.A6 A825

United States. Bureau of Consumer Protection. Funeral industry practices . [Washington] , 1978. 526, [12] p. ;   LC Card 78-603684
KF2042.U5 A8137   NYPL [JLF 81-308]

United States. Bureau of Consumer Protection. Life insurance cost disclosure . [Washington, D.C.] [1979] ca. 500 p. in various pagings ;   LC Card 79-603257
HG8951 .U54 1979   NYPL [JLF 81-342]

Whitten, Ira Taylor. Brand performance in the

cigarette industry and the advantage to early entry, 1913-74 /. [Washington] , 1979. 54 p. :   LC Card 79-603962
HD9149.C42 U695   NYPL [JLD 81-574]

UNITED STATES. FEDERAL TRADE COMMISSION.
Future developments in the food industry and their implications for the Federal Trade Commission /. [Washington, D.C.?] 1980. i, 163 p. :   LC Card 80-604179   DDC 338.1/973 19
HD9006 .F88

Unfairness . Washington , 1980. iii, 248 p. ;   LC Card 80-602217   DDC 343.73/072 19
KF1603.5 .U55

United States. Congress. House. Committee on Post Office and Civil Service. Subcommittee on Investigations. Administrative law judge program of the Federal Trade Commission . Washington , 1980. iii, 66 p. ;   LC Card 80-603347   DDC 342.73/0664 19
KF27 .P646 1980a

United States. Congress. House. Committee on the Judiciary. Subcommittee on Courts, Civil Liberties, and the Administration of Justice. Trademarks and the Federal Trade Commission . Washington , 1980. iii, 199 p. ;   LC Card 80-602813   DDC 346.7304/88 19
KF27 .J857 1979j

United States. Federal Trade Commission. Bureau of Competition. see **United States. Bureau of Competition.**

United States. Federal Trade Commission. Bureau of Consumer Protection. see **United States. Bureau of Consumer Protection.**

United States. Federal Trade Commission. Bureau of Economics. (Old Catalog form: United States. Federal Trade Commission. Economics, Bureau of)
Economic report [on] effects of restrictions on advertising and commercial practice in the professions : the case of optometry / by Ronald S. Bond ... [et al.]. Washington, D.C. : Federal Trade Commission, Bureau of Economics : for sale by the Supt. of Docs., U. S. Govt. Print. Off., [1980] viii, 120 p. : graphs. ; 28 cm. Cover title: Staff report on effects of restrictions on advertising and commercial practice in the professions. "April 1980."   LC Card 80-602861   DDC 338.4/761775/0973 19
1. Optometry - United States - Practice. 2. Optometry - Economic aspects - United States. 3. Advertising - Optometry - United States. I. Bond, Ronald S. II. Title. III. Title: Effects of restrictions on advertising and commercial practice in the professions. IV. Title: Staff report on effects of restrictions on advertising and commercial practice in the professions.
RE959.3 .U53 1980

The Economics of firm size, market structure, and social performance . [Washington, D.C.?] , 1980. viii, 388 p. ;   LC Card 81-600757   DDC 338.6/4/0973 19
HD60.5.U5 E26

Ippolito, Richard A. Staff report on consumer responses to cigarette health information /. [Washington] , 1979. 64 p. ;   LC Card 79-604242
HV5760 .I66   NYPL [JLF 81-240]

Kass, David I. Physician control of Blue Shield plans . [Washington, D.C.] [1979] v, 139 p. ;   LC Card 80-601542   DDC 368.3/8 19
RA413.3.B49 K37

Morkre, Morris E. The effects of restrictions on United States imports . [Washington, D.C.] [1980] xv, 212 p. ;   LC Card 80-603259   DDC 382/.5/0973 19
HF1731 .M67

United States. Bureau of Consumer Protection. Life insurance cost disclosure . [Washington, D.C.] [1979] ca. 500 p. in various pagings ;   LC Card 79-603257
HG8951 .U54 1979   NYPL [JLF 81-342]

United States. Federal Trade Commission. Economics, Bureau of. see **United States. Federal Trade Commission. Bureau of Economics.**

United States. Federal Trade Commission. Office of Policy Planning and Evaluation. Housing policy session. Edited version. [Washington, D.C. : Federal Trade Commission, Office of Policy Planning and Evaluation, 1978] 50, [20] p. ; 28 cm. Cover title. Includes bibliographical

references.   LC Card 80-601655   DDC 363.5/0973 19
1. Housing policy - United States. I. Title.
HD7293 .U46 1978

United States. Federal Water Pollution Control Administration.
The cost of clean water. United States. Federal Water Pollution Control Administration. The economics of clean water. 1968- Washington.
NYPL [JLM 80-773]

The cost of clean water and its economic impact. United States. Federal Water Pollution Control Administration. The economics of clean water. 1968- Washington.
NYPL [JLM 80-773]

The economics of clean water. 1968- Washington. 26 cm. Annual. Title varies: 1968, The cost of clean water; 1969, The cost of clean water and its economic impact. Vols. for 1968-70 issued in parts. For later file, see: United States. Environmental Protection Agency. The economics of clean water.
1. Water - Pollution - Economic aspects - United States - Periodicals. I. United States. Federal Water Pollution Control Administration. The cost of clean water. II. United States. Federal Water Pollution Control Administration. The cost of clean water and its economic impact. III. Title.   NYPL [JLM 80-773]

United States. Finance, Committee on (Senate) see **United States. Congress. Senate. Committee on Finance.**

United States. Fire Administration.
Report to Congress on firefighter safety and health / submitted by Federal Emergency Management Agency, U. S. Fire Administration. [Washington, D.C.] : The Agency, [1980] ii, 56 p. : ill. ; 28 cm. (FEMA . 5) Cover title. "September 1980." Includes bibliographical references.   LC Card 80-603745   DDC 363.1/19628925/0973 19
1. Fire extinction - Safety measures. 2. Fire fighters - United States. I. Title. II. Series.
TH9182 .U54 1980

United States Fire Administration catalog / Federal Emergency Management Agency, National Fire Data Center, United States Fire Administration. [Washington, D.C.] : The Center, [1980] 80 p. ; 31 cm. "March 1980." "MP-90." Includes index.   LC Card 80-602124   DDC 016.3633/7 19
1. Fire prevention - Bibliography - Catalogs.
Z5853.F6 U53 1980 TH9503

UNITED STATES FIRE ADMINISTRATION - APPROPRIATIONS AND EXPENDITURES.
United States. Congress. Senate. Committee on Commerce, Science, and Transportation. Subcommittee for Consumers. Fire Prevention and Control Act reauthorization . Washington , 1981. iii, 56 p. ;   LC Card 81-601855   DDC 353.0078/2 19
KF26 .C693 1981

United States. Fire Administration. National Fire Academy. see **National Fire Academy.**

United States. Fire Administration. National Fire Data Center. see **National Fire Data Center (U. S.)**

United States. Fire Safety and Research Office, National. see **United States. National Fire Safety and Research Office.**

United States. Fish and Wildlife Service.
Bailey, Robert G., 1939- Description of the ecoregions of the United States /. Ogden, Utah , 1978. iv, 77 p. :   LC Card 79-601521
QH104 .B34

Biological evaluation of environmental impacts . Washington, D.C. , 1980. iv, 237 p. :   LC Card 80-604147   DDC 333.951/028 19
QH545.A .B564

Directory, Pacific States Region National Wildlife Refuges and Fish Hatcheries. [Washington? : Dept. of the Interior, U. S. Fish & Wildlife Service, 1980] 32 p. : ill. ; 28 cm. Cover title. "March 1980."   LC Card 80-602853   DDC 333.95/025/78 19
1. Wildlife refuges - The West - Directories. 2. Fish hatcheries - The West - Directories. I. Title.
QL84.22.W47 U54 1980

Predator damage in the West : a study of coyote management alternatives / prepared by U. S. Fish and Wildlife Service, Department of the Interior. [Washington] : The Service, 1978.

vii, 168 p. : ill. ; 27 cm. Cover title. Includes bibliographies. LC Card 79-602347 DDC 636.08/3 19
1. Coyotes - Control - The West. 2. Wildlife depredation - The West. 3. Predator control - Environmental aspects - The West. I. Title.
SF810.7.C88 U54 1978

Research report - U. S. Fish and Wildlife Service .
(80) Benson, Norman Gustaf, 1928- Effects of post-impoundment shore modifications on fish populations in Missouri River reservoirs /. Washington, D.C. , 1980. p. cm. LC Card 80-21800 DDC 639.9/0973 s 639.9/77 19
SH11 .A3 no. 80 SH173.5

Resource publication - United States, Fish and Wildlife Service .
(138) Birkenstein, Lillian R. Native names of Mexican birds . Washington , 1981. p. cm. LC Card 80-606886 DDC 333.95/4 s 598.2972/014 19
S914 .A3 no. 138 QL686

Scott, Kevin M., 1935- Erosion and sedimentation in the Kenai River, Alaska /. Washington , 1981. p. cm. LC Card 81-6755 DDC 553.7/8/097983 19
QE571 .S412

Technical papers of the U. S. Fish and Wildlife Service .
(104) Sanders, Herman O. Abate - effects of the organophosphate insecticide on bluegills and invertebrates in ponds /. Washington, D.C. , 1981. 6 p. : LC Card 80-606806 DDC 639 s 628.9/657 19
SH11 .A313 no. 104 SH177.P44

United States. Fish and Wildlife Service. Bureau of Sport Fisheries and Wildlife. see United States. Bureau of Sport Fisheries and Wildlife.

United States. Fish and Wildlife Service. Coal Project.
A Biologist's manual for the evaluation of impacts of coal-fired power plants on fish, wildlife, and their habitats /. [Washington] , 1978. xix p., 146 leaves, p. 147-206 : LC Card 79-100195
QH76 .U54a 78/75 QH545.C57

Impacts of coal-fired power plants on fish, wildlife, and their habitats /. [Washington] , 1978. xii, 261 p. : LC Card 78-602648 DDC 574.5/222 19
QH545.C57 I47

United States. Fish and Wildlife Service. Division of Ecological Services. Office of Environmental Contaminants Evaluation. see United States. Fish and Wildlife Service. Office of Environmental Contaminants Evaluation.

United States. Fish and Wildlife Service. Environmental Contaminants Evaluation, Office of. see United States. Fish and Wildlife Service. Office of Environmental Contaminants Evaluation.

United States. Fish and Wildlife Service. Federal Wildlife Permit Office. Convention of International Trade in Endangered Species of Wild Fauna and Flora. Annual report by the United States of America. 1977- Washington.
NYPL [JLM 80-800]

United States. Fish and Wildlife Service. Geothermal Project. Suter, Glenn W. Effects of geothermal energy development on fish and wildlife /. [Washington, D.C.] , 1978. 20 p. : LC Card 79-603793 DDC 333.8/81 19
QH545.G46 S87

United States. Fish and Wildlife Service. National Coastal Ecosystems Team. see National Coastal Ecosystems Team.

United States Fish and Wildlife Service. Office of Biological Services.
Camp, Dresser & McKee. Environmental Sciences Division. Effect of peat mining on fish and other aquatic organisms in the Upper Midwest /. Washington, DC [1981] p. cm. LC Card 81-607838 DDC 622/.331 19
SH177.P4 C35 1981

Leedy, Daniel L. Planning for wildlife in cities and suburbs /. [Washington] , 1978. vii, 64 p. : LC Card 79-603493 DDC 639.9/09173/2 19
QH541.5.C6 L43 1978

Texas barrier islands region ecological characterization . Washington, D.C.?] , 1980. 2 v. : LC Card 81-600915 DDC 333.91/09764/1 19
QH105.T4 T52

United States. Fish and Wildlife Service. Office of Biological Services. Coal Project. see United States. Fish and Wildlife Service. Coal Project.

United States. Fish and Wildlife Service. Office of Biological Services. Power Plant Project. see United States. Fish and Wildlife Service. Power Plant Project.

United States. Fish and Wildlife Service. Office of Coastal Management. Wetlands Conference, Anchorage, Alaska, 1979. Proceedings of the Wetlands Conference, February 5, 1979 /. [Juneau] , 1979. 35 p. ; LC Card 79-625932 DDC 333.91/8/09798 19
QH76.5.A4 W47 1979

United States. Fish and Wildlife Service. Office of Endangered Species. Liaison conservation directory for endangered and threatened species /. Washington, D.C. , 1980. v, 129 p. : LC Card 81-601550 DDC 333.95/16/0973 19
QH35 .L49 1980

United States. Fish and Wildlife Service. Office of Environmental Contaminants Evaluation.
A Biologist's manual for the evaluation of impacts of coal-fired power plants on fish, wildlife, and their habitats /. [Washington] , 1978. xix p., 146 leaves, p. 147-206 : LC Card 79-100195
QH76 .U54a 78/75 QH545.C57

Impacts of coal-fired power plants on fish, wildlife, and their habitats /. [Washington] , 1978. xii, 261 p. : LC Card 78-602648 DDC 574.5/222 19
QH545.C57 I47

United States. Fish and Wildlife Service. Power Plant Project.
A Biologist's manual for the evaluation of impacts of coal-fired power plants on fish, wildlife, and their habitats /. [Washington] , 1978. xix p., 146 leaves, p. 147-206 : LC Card 79-100195
QH76 .U54a 78/75 QH545.C57

Impacts of coal-fired power plants on fish, wildlife, and their habitats /. [Washington] , 1978. xii, 261 p. : LC Card 78-602648 DDC 574.5/222 19
QH545.C57 I47

Suter, Glenn W. Effects of geothermal energy development on fish and wildlife /. [Washington, D.C.] , 1978. 20 p. : LC Card 79-603793 DDC 333.8/81 19
QH545.G46 S87

United States. Fish and Wildlife Service. Region 2. Office of Environment. Gulf of Mexico Coastal Ecosystems Workshop, Port Aransas, Tex., 1979. Proceedings of the Gulf of Mexico Coastal Ecosystems Workshop /. [Washington] [1980] vi, 214 p. : LC Card 80-603154 DDC 333.91/7/0916364 19
QH105.T4 G84 1979

United States. Fish and Wildlife Service. Wildlife Permit Office. see United States. Fish and Wildlife Service. Federal Wildlife Permit Office.

United States. Fisheries Development, Office of. see United States. Office of Fisheries Development.

United States fisheries systems and social science . Orbach, Michael K. Washington, D.C. , 1979. v, 162 p. : LC Card 80-601229 DDC 016.3383/714/0973 19
Z5974.U5 O72 HD8039.F66

United States. Flight Standards Service. Flight training handbook. Rev. [Oklahoma City, Okla.] : U. S. Dept. of Transportation, Federal Aviation Administration, Flight Standards Service ; Washington, D.C. : for sale by the Supt. of Docs., U. S. Govt. Print. Off., 1980. xvi, 325 p. : ill. ; 26 cm. Cover title. "AC 61-21A." Issued in 1965 by U. S. Federal Aviation Agency. LC Card 80-601809 DDC 629.132/52 19
1. Airplanes - Piloting. I. United States. Federal Aviation Agency. Flight training handbook. II. Title.
TL710 .U64 1980

United States. Food and Drug Administration. Over-the-counter drugs. United States. Food and Drug Administration. Preamble compilation: over-the-counter drugs. Mar. 1936/Mar. 1978- Washington.
*NYPL [*R-Econ. 80-2052 & JLL 80-360]*

Preamble compilation: over-the-counter drugs. Mar. 1936/Mar. 1978- Washington. 24 cm. Kept up to date by annual cumulative pocket supplements. Cover title, Mar. 1936/Mar. 1978- : Over-the-counter drugs.
1. Drugs - Law and legislation - United States. I. United States. Food and Drug Administration. Over-the-counter drugs. II. Title: Over-the-counter drugs.
*NYPL [*R-Econ. 80-2052 & JLL 80-360]*

Radiological health, March 1936-March 1978 . [Rockville, Md.] [1979] xii, 232 p. ; LC Card 80-602315 DDC 344.73/0472 19
KF3948 .A33 1979

Requirements of laws and regulations enforced by the U. S. Food and Drug Administration. Rockville, Md. : U. S. Dept. of Health, Education, and Welfare, Public Health Service, Food and Drug Administration ; Washington, D.C. : for sale by the Supt. of Docs., U. S. Govt. Print. Off., 1979] vi, 72 p. ; 24 cm. (United States. Dept. of Health, Education, and Welfare. DHEW publication (FDA) 79-1042) Previous ed. published under title: Requirements of the United States Food, drug, and cosmetic act. LC Card 79-601809
1. Food law and legislation - United States. 2. Drugs - Law and legislation - United States. 3. Cosmetics - Law and legislation - United States. I. Title.
KF3869 .A32 1979   *NYPL [JLE 81-479]*

UNITED STATES. FOOD AND DRUG ADMINISTRATION.
United States. Congress. House. Committee on Interstate and Foreign Commerce. Subcommittee on Health and the Environment. Drug regulation reform--oversight . Washington , 1980- v. <1- > ; LC Card 80-603639 DDC 353.0077/84 19
KF27 .I5543 1980j

United States. Dept. of Health, Education, and Welfare. Review Panel on New Drug Regulation. Final report /. [Washington] , 1977. 117, [85] p. ; LC Card 77-602914
RA401.A3 U52 1977   *NYPL [JLF 81-208]*

United States. General Accounting Office. FDA drug approval--a lengthy process that delays the availability of important new drugs .
Washington, DC [1980] vi, 83 p. ; LC Card 80-602514 DDC 363.1/946/0973 19
RS189 .U54 1980

United States. General Accounting Office. Lack of authority hampers attempts to increase cosmetic safety . [Washington , 1978] viii, 136 p. ; LC Card 78-603000 DDC 363.1/966/0973 19
RA1270.C65 U54 1978

United States. Food and Drug Administration. Bureau of Radiological Health. see United States. Bureau of Radiological Health.

United States. Food and Drug Administration. Division of Federal-State Relations. State Services Branch. State programs and services in food and drug control / Richard A. Moats [acting director], State Services Branch, Division of Federal-State Relations, Executive Director of Regional Operations, Food and Drug Administration. Rockville, Md. : The Administration, 1978. xiv, 68 p. : ill. ; 27 cm. LC Card 79-600638 DDC 353.0077/82 19
1. Food adulteration and inspection - United States - States. 2. Pharmaceutical policy - United States - States. 3. Drug adulteration - United States - States. I. Moats, Richard A. II. Title.
TX531 .U536 1978

United States. Food and Nutrition Service. Characteristics of food stamp households, February 1978. [Washington, D.C.] : U. S. Dept. of Agriculture, Food and Nutrition Service, 1980. 37, [75] p. : graphs ; 27 cm. Cover title. Chiefly tables. "FNS-204." LC Card 80-601585 DDC 363.8/82/0973 19
1. Food stamp program - United States - Statistics. I. Title.
HV696.F6 U617 1980

National survey of food stamp and food distribution program recipients: summary of

findings on income sources and amounts and incidence of multiple benefits. A study prepared for the use of the Subcommittee on Fiscal Policy of the Joint Economic Committee, Congress of the United States, [by the Food and Nutrition Service, U. S. Department of Agriculture] Washington, U. S. Govt. Print. Off., 1974. v, 47 p. 23 cm. (Studies in public welfare. paper no. 17.) At head of title: Joint committee print, 93d Congress, 2d session.
1. Food stamp program - United States. I. Title.
NYPL [JLE 81-549]

United States. Food and Nutrition Service. Office of Policy, Planning, and Evaluation.
Factors influencing school and student participation in the school breakfast program, 1977-78. [Washington] : Office of Policy, Planning and Evaluation, Food and Nutrition Service, U. S. Dept. of Agriculture, 1980. x, 54 p. ; 27 cm. Bibliography: p. 53-54. LC Card 80-602327 DDC 371.7/16/0973 19
1. School breakfast programs - United States. I. Title.
LB3479 .U55 1980

United States. Foreign Affairs, Committee on (House) see United States. Congress. House. Committee on Foreign Affairs.

United States. Foreign Agricultural Relations, Office of. see United States. Office of Foreign Agricultural Relations.

United States. Foreign Agricultural Service.
Update--impact of agricultural trade restrictions on the Soviet Union. [Washington, D.C.] [1980] 9 p. ; LC Card 80-603822 DDC 338.1 s 330.947/0853 19
HD1411 .F59 no. 160 HD9036

United States. Foreign Agricultural Service (1953-) (Old Catalog form: United States. Foreign Agricultural Relations Office)
Emerson, L. P. Bill. Preview of Mexico's vegetable production for export /. [Washington, D.C.] [1980] 74 p. : LC Card 80-603534 DDC 338.1/75/0972 19
HD9220.M42 E43

FAS .
(M-294) Emerson, L. P. Bill. Mexico's expanding olive industry /. [Washington, D.C.] [foreword 1980] 14 p. : LC Card 80-602696 DDC 338.1 s 338.1/7463/0972 19
S21 .Z2383 no. 294 HD9019.O4M6

FAS-M .
(292) Emerson, L. P. Bill. Mexico's grape industry . [Washington, D.C.] , 1979. ii, 22 p. : LC Card 80-601857 DDC 338.1 s 338.1/748/0972 19
S21 .Z2383 no. 292 HD9259.G7M6

(295) Wilson, John Harvard, 1953- Brazil's orange juice industry /. [Washington, D.C.] , 1980. ii, 17 p. : LC Card 80-602547 DDC 338.1 s 338.4/766363 19
S21 .Z2383 no. 295 HD9348.5.O723B6

(296) Petges, Richard. Pakistan's cotton industry /. [Washington, D.C.] [1980] 20 p. : LC Card 80-602637 DDC 338.1 s 338.1/7351/095491 19
S21 .Z2383 no. 296 HD9086.P3

Foreign agriculture report. no. 1-133. Washington, 1942-71. 133 no. illus., maps. 24-27 cm. Irregular. Issued by the Office of Foreign Agricultural Relations, 1942-Jan. 1953. No more published?
1. Agriculture - Collected works. I. United States. Office of Foreign Agricultural Relations. II. Title.
NYPL [VPZ (U. S. Foreign Agricultural Relations Office. Foreign agriculture report)]

United States. Foreign Demographic Analysis Division. see United States. Bureau of the Census. Foreign Demographic Analysis Division.

UNITED STATES - FOREIGN ECONOMIC RELATIONS.
Nossman, Waters, Krueger, Marsh & Riordan. Summary: an evaluation of the options of the U. S. Government in its relationship to U. S. firms in international petroleum affairs. Los Angeles, 1975. 122 p.; **NYPL [JLF 80-599]**

United States. Congress. House. Committee on Banking, Finance and Urban Affairs. Subcommittee on International Trade, Investment and Monetary Policy. To amend the

Bretton Woods agreements act to authorize consent to an increase in the United States quota in the International Monetary Fund . Washington , 1980. iv, 621 p. : LC Card 80-602758 DDC 343.73/032 19
KF27 .B577 1980

United States. Congress. House. Committee on Foreign Affairs. Resolution of inquiry concerning human rights policies . Washington , 19. iii, 29 p. ; LC Card 81-600587 DDC 323.4/0973 19
KF27 .F6 1980m

United States. Congress. House. Committee on Foreign Affairs. Subcommittee on International Economic Policy and Trade. North-South dialog . Washington , 1980. iii, 267 p. ; LC Card 80-603478 DDC 337/.09/048 19
KF27 .F6465 1980a

United States. Congress. Senate. Committee on Finance. Subcommittee on International Trade. U. S. international trade strategy . Washington , 1980. iii, 494 p. : LC Card 80-603898 DDC 382/.3/0973 19
KF26 .F554 1980e

United States. Congress. Senate. Committee on Foreign Relations. Subcommittee on International Economic Policy. The U. S. stake in the global economy . Washington , 1981. iv, 298 p. : LC Card 81-602271 DDC 337.73 19
KF26 .F648 1981

UNITED STATES - FOREIGN ECONOMIC RELATIONS - CANADA.
United States. General Accounting Office. Prospects for cooperation and trade of energy resources between the United States and Canada . [Washington, D.C. , 1979] iii, 33 p. ; LC Card 80-600527 DDC 333.79/0971 19
HD9502.C32 U56 1979

UNITED STATES - FOREIGN ECONOMIC RELATIONS - CHINA - CONGRESSES.
The People's Republic of China and the U. S. . Atlanta, Ga. [1979] v, 118 p. ; LC Card 80-622176 DDC 382/.0951/073 19
HF3128 .P46

UNITED STATES - FOREIGN ECONOMIC RELATIONS - EUROPE, EASTERN.
United States. Congress. House. Committee on Foreign Affairs. Subcommittee on International Economic Policy and Trade. Review of implementation of Basket II of the Helsinki Final Act . Washington , 1980. iii, 82 p. ; LC Card 80-604051 DDC 337.73047 19
KF27 .F6465 1980d

UNITED STATES - FOREIGN ECONOMIC RELATIONS - JAPAN.
United States. Congress. House. Committee on Foreign Affairs. United States-Japan economic relations . Washington , 1981. vi, 337 p. : LC Card 81-601171 DDC 337.52073 19
KF27 .F6 1980K

UNITED STATES - FOREIGN ECONOMIC RELATIONS - JAPAN - ADDRESSES, ESSAYS, LECTURES.
U. S.-Japan economic relations . [Berkeley] , 1980. x, 57 p. ; ISBN 0-912966-25-4 (pbk.) : LC Card 80-620017 DDC 337.52073 19
HF1456.5.J3 U554

UNITED STATES - FOREIGN ECONOMIC RELATIONS - RUSSIA.
United States. Central Intelligence Agency. National Foreign Assessment Center. Soviet strategy and tactics in economic and commercial negotiations with the United States /. Washington , 1979. v, 11 p. ; LC Card 79-602793
*HF1456.5.R9 U54 1979 NYPL [*XME-9336]*

UNITED STATES - FOREIGN ECONOMIC RELATIONS - SOVIET UNION.
United States. Congress. Senate. Committee on Banking, Housing and Urban Affairs. Suspension of United States exports of high technology and grain to the Soviet Union . Washington , 1980. v, 156 p. : LC Card 80-604066 DDC 382/.4131/0973 19
KF26 .B39 1980x

Update--impact of agricultural trade restrictions on the Soviet Union. [Washington, D.C.] [1980] 9 p. ; LC Card 80-603822 DDC 338.1 s 330.947/0853 19
HD1411 .F59 no. 160 HD9036

UNITED STATES - FOREIGN ECONOMIC RELATIONS - TURKEY.
United States. Congress. House. Committee on Foreign Affairs. Subcommittee on Europe and the Middle East. United States-Turkey defense and economic cooperation agreement, 1980 . Washington , 1980. iii, 69 p. ; LC Card 80-603044 DDC 327.730561 19
KF27 .F64214 1980a

UNITED STATES - FOREIGN RELATIONS.
United States. General Accounting Office. Formulation of U. S. international energy policies . Washington, D.C. , 1980. iii, 115 p. : LC Card 80-603937 DDC 353.0082/3 19
HD9502.U52 U55 1980a

United States. General Accounting Office. Meeting U. S. political objectives through economic aid in the Middle East and southern Africa . [Washington] , 1979. iv, 42 p., [1] leaf of plates : LC Card 79-602541 DDC 338.91/56/073 19
HC415.15 .U54 1979

UNITED STATES - FOREIGN RELATIONS - 1933-1945 - CONGRESSES.
Three faces of Midwestern isolationism /. Iowa City, Iowa , 1981. p. cm. ISBN 0-87414-019-6 (pbk.) : LC Card 81-2741 DDC 327.73 19
E806 .T58

UNITED STATES - FOREIGN RELATIONS - 1945-
United States. President's Commission for a National Agenda for the Eighties. A national agenda for the eighties . Washington , 1980. 214 p. ; LC Card 81-356 DDC 973.926 19
HC106.7 .U577 1980

United States. President's Commission for a National Agenda for the Eighties. Panel on the United States and the World Community. The United States and the world community in the eighties . Washington, D.C. , 1980. 109 p. ; LC Card 80-28709 DDC 327.73 19
E840 .U67 1980

UNITED STATES - FOREIGN RELATIONS - 1945-1953.
Buhite, Russell D. Soviet-American relations in Asia, 1945-1954 /. Norman , 1981. p. cm. ISBN 0-8061-1729-X LC Card 81-40285 DDC 327.47073 19
E183.8.S65 B83

Rostow, W. W. (Walt Whitman), 1916- The division of Europe after World War II, 1946 /. Austin , 1981. p. cm. ISBN 0-292-70358-9 LC Card 81-11640 DDC 940.55/4 19
D816 .R67

UNITED STATES - FOREIGN RELATIONS - 1963-1969.
United States. Congress. House. Committee on Foreign Affairs. Subcommittee on International Organizations and Movements. Behavioral sciences and the national security . Washington , 1965. vi, 1OR, iii, 203 p. : LC Card 80-503601 DDC 327.73 s 327.1/1 19
E840.2 .A3 no. 4 E846

UNITED STATES - FOREIGN RELATIONS - 1977-
United States. Congress. House. Committee on Foreign Affairs. Subcommittee on Europe and the Middle East. U. S. interests in, and policies toward, the Persian Gulf, 1980 . Washington , 1980. iv, 471 p. ; LC Card 80-603806 DDC 355/.0330536 19
KF27 .F64214 1980c

UNITED STATES - FOREIGN RELATIONS - 1977- - ADDRESSES, ESSAYS, LECTURES.
Should the United States significantly increase its foreign military commitments? . Washington , 1980. v, 484 p. : LC Card 80-603968 DDC 355/.031/0973 19
UA23 .S485

UNITED STATES - FOREIGN RELATIONS - 1977-1981.
United States. Congress. House. Committee on Foreign Affairs. Resolution of inquiry concerning human rights policies . Washington , 19. iii, 29 p. ; LC Card 81-600587 DDC 323.4/0973 19
KF27 .F6 1980m

UNITED STATES - FOREIGN RELATIONS ADMINISTRATION.
United States. Congress. House. Committee on

Government Operations. Legislation and National Security Subcommittee. U. S. mission and office operations, East Africa . Washington , 1980. iii, 72 p. ; LC Card 80-603484   DDC 353.008/92/09676 19
KF27 .G6676 1980f

United States. Congress. House. Committee on Government Operations. Legislation and National Security Subcommittee. U. S. mission and office operations--Egypt . Washington , 1980. iii, 161 p. ; LC Card 80-603495 DDC 353.008/92/0962 19
KF27 .G6676 1980h

UNITED STATES - FOREIGN RELATIONS - AFRICA, EASTERN.
United States. Congress. House. Committee on Government Operations. Legislation and National Security Subcommittee. U. S. mission and office operations, East Africa .
Washington , 1980. iii, 72 p. ; LC Card 80-603484   DDC 353.008/92/09676 19
KF27 .G6676 1980f

UNITED STATES - FOREIGN RELATIONS - AFRICA, NORTH.
United States. Congress. House. Committee on Foreign Affairs. Subcommittee on Africa. Current situationin the western Sahara, 1980 . Washington , 1981. iii, 24 p. ; LC Card 81-600927 DDC 327.73061 19
KF27 .F625 1980f

UNITED STATES - FOREIGN RELATIONS - AFRICA, SOUTHERN.
McGovern, George Stanley, 1922- Impressions of southern Africa . Washington , 1979. v, 38 p. ; LC Card 80-601034   DDC 327.68073 19
DT747.U6 M33

UNITED STATES - FOREIGN RELATIONS - AFRICA, WEST.
United States. Congress. House. Committee on Government Operations. Legislation and National Security Subcommittee. U. S. mission and office operations--West Africa .
Washington , 1980. iii, 75 p. ; LC Card 80-603676   DDC 353.008/92/0966 19
KF27 .G6676 1980j

UNITED STATES - FOREIGN RELATIONS - ANGOLA.
United States. Congress. House. Committee on Foreign Affairs. Subcommittee on Africa. United States policy toward Angola--update . Washington , 1980. iii, 76 p. : LC Card 81-600629 DDC 327.73067/3 19
KF27 .F625 1980e

UNITED STATES - FOREIGN RELATIONS - ASIA.
Buhite, Russell D. Soviet-American relations in Asia, 1945-1954 /. Norman , 1981. p. cm.
ISBN 0-8061-1729-X LC Card 81-40285 DDC 327.47073 19
E183.8.S65 B83

United States. Congress. House. Special Study Mission to Asia. Asian security environment, 1980 . Washington , 1980. vii, 96 p. ; LC Card 80-602264 DDC 355/.03305 19
DS33.4.U6 U5 1980

UNITED STATES - FOREIGN RELATIONS - ASIA, SOUTHEASTERN.
United States. Congress. House. Committee on Foreign Affairs. Subcommittee on Asian and Pacific Affairs. POW/MIA's . Washington , 1980. v, 49 p. ; LC Card 80-603653 DDC 959.704/37 19
KF27 .F638 1980a

UNITED STATES - FOREIGN RELATIONS - CANADA.
United States. Congress. House. Committee on Foreign Affairs. Subcommittee on Inter-American Affairs. Update, United States-Canadian/Mexican relations .
Washington , 1980. iii, 71 p. ; LC Card 80-603028 DDC 327.73071 19
KF27 .F646 1980b

UNITED STATES - FOREIGN RELATIONS - CENTRAL AMERICA.
United States. Congress. House. Committee on Foreign Affairs. Subcommittee on Inter-American Affairs. Assessment of conditions in Central America . Washington , 1980. iii, 137 p. ; LC Card 80-602995 DDC 972.8/052 19
KF27 .F646 1980

UNITED STATES - FOREIGN RELATIONS - CHINA.
Henson, Curtis T., 1931- Commissioners and commodores . University, Ala. , c1982. p. cm.
ISBN 0-8173-0087-2 LC Card 81-10359 DDC 327.73051 19
E183.8.C5 H46

Sutter, Robert G. Executive-legislative consultations on China policy, 1978-79 /. Washington , 1980. vii, 42 p. ; LC Card 80-602678 DDC 327.73051 19
JX1428.C6 S97

United States. Congress. House. Committee on Foreign Affairs. Subcommittee on Asian and Pacific Affairs. The United States and the People's Republic of China . Washington , 1980 [i.e. 1981] v, 163 p. ; LC Card 81-600985 DDC 327.73051 19
KF27 .F638 1980d

United States. Library of Congress. Foreign Affairs and National Defense Division. Sino-American relations . Washington , 1980. iii, 12 p. ; LC Card 80-603273 DDC 327.73051 19
E183.8.C5 U58 1980

UNITED STATES - FOREIGN RELATIONS - CHINA - CONGRESSES.
Chinese communism and the United States . [Tempe] , 1975. 69 p. ; LC Card 77-621162
E183.8.C5 C538   **NYPL [*XMB-1422]**

United States. Foreign Relations, Committee on (Senate) see United States. Congress. Senate. Committee on Foreign Relations.

UNITED STATES - FOREIGN RELATIONS - EGYPT.
United States. Congress. House. Committee on Government Operations. Legislation and National Security Subcommittee. U. S. mission and office operations--Egypt . Washington , 1980. iii, 161 p. ; LC Card 80-603495 DDC 353.008/92/0962 19
KF27 .G6676 1980h

UNITED STATES - FOREIGN RELATIONS - EUROPE.
United States. Congress. House. Committee on Foreign Affairs. Subcommittee on Europe and the Middle East. United States-Western European relations in 1980 . Washington , 1980. xi, 320 p. : LC Card 80-603423 DDC 327.7304 19
KF27 .F64214 1980b

UNITED STATES - FOREIGN RELATIONS - INDIA.
United States. Congress. Senate. Committee on Foreign Relations. India-Pakistan nuclear issues . Washington , 1980. iii, 19 p. ; LC Card 80-602998 DDC 327.73054 19
KF26 .F6 1980K

UNITED STATES - FOREIGN RELATIONS - IRAN.
Gold, Fern R. Access to oil . [Washington , 1977. xiii, 113 p. ; LC Card 78-600524
HD9566 .G64   **NYPL [JLE 81-460]**

United States. President, 1977- (Carter) Use of U. S. Armed Forces in attempted rescue of hostages in Iran . Washington, D.C. , 1980. 2 p. ; LC Card 80-602258 DDC 327.73055 19
E183.8.I55 U54 1980

UNITED STATES - FOREIGN RELATIONS - JORDAN.
United States. Congress. House. Committee on Foreign Affairs. Subcommittee on Europe and the Middle East. United States-Jordanian relations and arms supply issues . Washington , 1980. iii, 71 p. ; LC Card 80-604082 DDC 327.7305695 19
KF27 .F64214 1980d

UNITED STATES - FOREIGN RELATIONS - KOREA - CONGRESSES.
The United States and Korea . Kalamazoo , 1979. 262 p. ; LC Card 78-65924 DDC 327.730519 19
E183.8.K6 U54

UNITED STATES - FOREIGN RELATIONS - KOREA (SOUTH)
United States. Congress. House. Committee on Foreign Affairs. Subcommittee on Asian and Pacific Affairs. United States-South Korean relations . Washington , 1980. v, 60 p. ; LC Card 80-604073 DDC 327.730519/5 19
KF27 .F638 1980b

UNITED STATES - FOREIGN RELATIONS - LATIN AMERICA.
United States. Congress. House. Committee on Foreign Affairs. Subcommittee on Inter-American Affairs. U. S. national interest in Latin America . Washington , 1981. iii, 67 p. : LC Card 81-601864 DDC 327.7308 19
KF27 .F646 1981

UNITED STATES - FOREIGN RELATIONS - MEXICO.
United States. Congress. House. Committee on Foreign Affairs. Subcommittee on Inter-American Affairs. Update, United States-Canadian/Mexican relations .
Washington , 1980. iii, 71 p. ; LC Card 80-603028 DDC 327.73071 19
KF27 .F646 1980b

UNITED STATES - FOREIGN RELATIONS - NEAR EAST.
United States. Congress. Senate. Committee on Foreign Relations. U. S. Middle East policy . Washington , 1980. iii, 55 p. ; LC Card 80-602819 DDC 327.73056 19
KF26 .F6 1980g

UNITED STATES - FOREIGN RELATIONS - PAKISTAN.
United States. Congress. Senate. Committee on Foreign Relations. India-Pakistan nuclear issues . Washington , 1980. iii, 19 p. ; LC Card 80-602998 DDC 327.73054 19
KF26 .F6 1980K

UNITED STATES - FOREIGN RELATIONS - RUSSIA.
United States. Congress. Committee on Foreign Affairs. Subcommittee on Europe and the Middle East. East-West relations in the aftermath of Soviet invasion of Afghanistan . Washington , 1980. iii, 125 p. ; LC Card 80-602490 DDC 327.73047 19
KF27 .F64214 1980

United States. Congress. House. Committee on Agriculture. Recent developments pertaining to grain embargo . Washington , 1980. iii, 44 p. ;
LC Card 80-603662 DDC 382/.4131/0973 19
KF27 .A3 1980b

United States. Congress. House. Committee on Foreign Affairs. U. S. participation in the 1980 summer Olympic games . Washington , 1980. iii, 88 p. ; LC Card 80-602748 DDC 796.4/8/0947431 19
KF27 .F6 1980d

United States. Congress. House. Committee on Interstate and Foreign Commerce. Subcommittee on Transportation and Commerce. Alternatives to the Moscow Olympics . Washington , 1980. iii, 83 p. ; LC Card 80-602442 DDC 353.0085/8 19
KF27 .I5589 1980a

United States. Congress. Senate. Committee on Banking, Housing and Urban Affairs. Subcommittee on International Finance. U. S. embargo of food and technology to the Soviet Union . Washington , 1980. v, 250 p. ; LC Card 80-602113 DDC 382/.64/0973 19
KF26 .B3946 1980a

United States. Congress. Senate. Committee on Foreign Relations. 1980 summer Olympics boycott . Washington , 1980. iii, 97 p. ; LC Card 80-602014 DDC 796.4/8/094731 19
KF26 .F6 1980d

UNITED STATES - FOREIGN RELATIONS - SAUDI ARABIA.
Gold, Fern R. Access to oil . [Washington , 1977. xiii, 113 p. ; LC Card 78-600524
HD9566 .G64   **NYPL [JLE 81-460]**

UNITED STATES - FOREIGN RELATIONS - SOUTH AFRICA.
Study Commission on U. S. Policy toward Southern Africa (U. S.) South Africa . Berkeley , c1981. xxvii, 517 p., [26] p. of plates : ISBN 0-520-04504-1 LC Card 81-2742
DDC 327.73068 19
E183.8.S6 S78 1981

United States. Congress. House. Committee on Foreign Affairs. Subcommittee on International Economic Policy and Trade. U. S. policy toward South Africa . Washington , 1980. iv, 912 p. : LC Card 80-603998 DDC 327.73068 19
KF27 .F6465 1980b

UNITED STATES - FOREIGN RELATIONS - SOVIET UNION.

Buhite, Russell D. Soviet-American relations in Asia, 1945-1954 /. Norman , 1981. p. cm.
ISBN 0-8061-1729-X LC Card 81-40285 DDC 327.47073 19
E183.8.S65 B83

Update--impact of agricultural trade restrictions on the Soviet Union. [Washington, D.C.] [1980] 9 p. ; LC Card 80-603822 DDC 338.1 s 330.947/0853 19
HD1411 .F59 no. 160 HD9036

UNITED STATES - FOREIGN RELATIONS - TAIWAN.

Sutter, Robert G. Executive-legislative consultations on China policy, 1978-79 /. Washington , 1980. vii, 42 p. ; LC Card 80-602678 DDC 327.73051 19
JX1428.C6 S97

United States. Congress. House. Committee on Foreign Affairs. Subcommittee on Asian and Pacific Affairs. Implementation of the Taiwan Relations Act . Washington , 1981. v, 107 p. ;
LC Card 81-600827 DDC 327.73051/249 19
KF27 .F638 1980e

United States. Congress. Senate. Committee on Foreign Relations. Implementation of the Taiwan relations act . Washington , 1980. v, 61 p. ; LC Card 80-603554 DDC 327.73051/249 19
E183.8.T3 U54 1980

United States. Congress. Senate. Committee on Foreign Relations. Subcommittee on East Asian and Pacific Affairs. Oversight of the Taiwan relations act . Washington , 1980. iii, 44 p. ;
LC Card 80-602822 DDC 327.73051/249 19
KF26 .F6354 1980a

UNITED STATES - FOREIGN RELATIONS - TAIWAN - CONGRESSES.

Taiwan, one year after United States-China normalization . Washington , 1980. v, 170 p. :
LC Card 80-603279 DDC 327.73051/249 19
E183.8.T3 T34

UNITED STATES - FOREIGN RELATIONS - TREATIES.

United States. Treaties, etc. Treaties and other international agreements on fisheries, oceanographic resources, and wildlife involving the United States /. Washington , 1977. xv, 1201 p. ; LC Card 81-601815 DDC 341.7/62/026 19
JX236 1977 .U54

UNITED STATES - FOREIGN RELATIONS - TURKEY.

United States. Congress. House. Committee on Foreign Affairs. Subcommittee on Europe and the Middle East. United States-Turkey defense and economic cooperation agreement, 1980 . Washington , 1980. iii, 69 p. ; LC Card 80-603044 DDC 327.730561 19
KF27 .F64214 1980a

UNITED STATES - FOREIGN RELATIONS - ZIMBABWE.

United States. Congress. House. Committee on Foreign Affairs. Rhodesian sanctions, should the United States lift them? . Washington , 1980. iii, 80 p. ; LC Card 80-601130 DDC 327.7306891 19
KF27 .F6 1979j

United States. Foreign Service Institute.
De La Cruz, Nina. Russian. Washington, 1973. xxix, 138 p. LC Card 73-602523
PG2121 .D4 1973   NYPL [*QCI 81-322]

MacDougall, Bonnie G. Sinhala . [Washington, D.C.] , 1979. 3 v. : LC Card 80-601818 DDC 491/.4883421 19
PK2812 .M25

Testing kit, French and Spanish / with articles by Claudia P. Wilds ... [et al.] ; pref. by James R. Frith ; [edited by Marianne Lehr Adams and James R. Frith]. [Washington, D.C.] : Dept. of State, Foreign Service Institute : for saleby the Supt. of Docs., U. S. Govt. Print. Off., [1979] x, 140 p. (p. 140 blank) : ill. ; 27 cm. English, French and Spanish. LC Card 80-602389 DDC 440[.76 19
1. Languages, Modern - Examinations - Addresses, essays, lectures. 2. Languages, Modern - Examinations, questions, etc. 3. French language - Examinations, questions, etc. 4. Spanish language - Examinations, questions, etc. I. Wilds, Claudia P. II. Frith, James

Robert, 1917-. III. Adams, Marianne Lehr. IV. Title.
PB36 .U54 1979

United States. Foreign Service Institute. Overseas Briefing Center. Harner, Annie Lai. Living and working in the People's Republic of China . [Arlington, Va.] , 1980. 38 p. ; LC Card 80-133373 DDC 951.05/7 19
DS779.23 .H37

United States. Forest Experiment station, Southern, New Orleans. see United States. Southern Forest Experiment Station, New Orleans.

United States. Forest Insect and Disease Management. A guide to common insects and diseases of forest trees in the Northeastern United States / Forest Insect and Disease Management, Forest Service, U. S. Department of Agriculture, Northeastern Area, State and Private Forestry. Broomall, PA. : Forest Insect and Disease Management ; Washington, D.C. : for sale by the Supt. of Docs., U. S. Govt. Print. Off., 1979. vi, 127 p. : ill. ; 23 cm. "NA-FR-4." Includes index. LC Card 80-601798 DDC 634.9/67/0974 19
1. Forest insects - Northeastern States - Identification. 2. Trees - Diseases and pests - Northeastern States - Identification. I. Title.
SB763.N67 U54 1979

UNITED STATES - FOREST POLICY.

United States. Congress. Senate. Committee on Agriculture, Nutrition, and Forestry. Subcommittee on Environment, Soil Conservation, and Forestry. Oversight on Resources planning act . Washington , 1980. iii, 144 p. : LC Card 80-600839 DDC 353.0082/338 19
KF26 .A3543 1979f

United States. Forest Service. Pacific Northwest Region. Final environmental statement: land use plan. Olympic, Wash., 1975? 300 p. :
NYPL [JLF 80-871]

United States. Forest Service. Annual report. United States. Forest Service. Report of the Chief of the Forest Service. 1882/83- [Washington] NYPL [VQO (U. S. Forest Service. Report of the Chief of the Forest Service)]

Camp, Wallace Jefferson, 1906- Soil survey of Greenwood and McCormick Counties, South Carolina /. [Washington, D.C. , 1980] iv, 68 p., [42] fold. leaves of plates : LC Card 80-602310 DDC 631.4/7/75733 19
S599.S58 C36

Forest service standard specifications for construction of roads and bridges. Washington : Forest Service, U. S. Dept. of Agriculture : for sale by the Supt. of Docs., U. S. Govt. Print. Off., 1979. xiv, 461 p. : graphs ; 28 cm. "EM-7720-100." LC Card 79-603953 DDC 625.7/0212 19
1. Road construction - Contracts and specifications - United States. 2. Forest roads - Design and construction - Contracts and specifications - United States. 3. Bridge construction - Contracts and specifications - United States. I. Title.
TE180 .U66 1979

Garner, Billy A. Soil survey of Crawford County, Arkansas /. [Washington] , 1979. viii, 91, [22] fold. leaves of plates : LC Card 80-601639 DDC 631.4/7/76735 19
S599.A75 G37

King, John M. Soil survey of Henderson County, North Carolina /. [Washington, D.C. , 1980] viii, 89 p., [15] fold. leaves of plates :
LC Card 80-602311 DDC 631.4/7/75692 19
S599.N8 K55

Long, Bobby M. Soil survey of Berkeley County, South Carolina /. [Washington, D.C.] 1980. viii, 94 p., [51] fold. leaves of plates :
LC Card 80-601634 DDC 631.4/7/75793 19
S599.S58 L66

Meland, Arvid C. Soil survey of Lawrence County, South Dakota /. [Washington, D.C. , 1979] viii, 173 p., [25] fold. leaves of plates :
LC Card 80-601071 DDC 631.4/7/78391 19
S599.S6 M44

Planning considerations for winter sports resort development / U. S. Department of Agriculture, Forest Service, in cooperation with National Ski Areas Association. [Washington] : The Service,

1973. iii, 53 p. : ill. ; 21x26 cm. Cover title.
1. Winter sport facilities - Planning. 2. Skis and skiing - Economic aspects - United States. I. National Ski Areas Association. II. Title.   NYPL [JLF 79-1344]

Report of the Chief of the Forest Service. 1882/83- [Washington] 23-26 cm. Annual. Not published 1952/53. Vols. for 1882/83-1884/85 included in the Report of the Secretary of Agriculture (in Old Catalog). Title varies: 1885/86-1886/87, Annual report; 1888/89-1933/34, Report of the Forester. For later years, see its Report of the Forest Service, highlights.
1. Forests and forestry - United States - Periodicals. I. United States. Forest Service. Annual report. II. United States. Forest Service. Report of the Forester. III. Title.
NYPL [VQO (U. S. Forest Service. **Report of the Chief of the Forest Service)]**

Report of the Forest Service, highlights. 1976/77- [Washington] illus. 28 cm. Annual. Report year ends Sept. 30. For earlier years, see its: Report of the Chief of the Forest Service. LC Card 80-648919
1. Forests and forestry - United States - Periodicals. I. Title.   NYPL [JLM 81-47]

Report of the Forester. United States. Forest Service. Report of the Chief of the Forest Service. 1882/83- [Washington]
NYPL [VQO (U. S. Forest Service. **Report of the Chief of the Forest Service)]**

Townsend, William R. Soil survey of Conway County, Arkansas /. [Washington] [1980] vii, 91 p., [27] fold. leaves of plates : LC Card 80-603205 DDC 631.4/7/76731 19
S599.A75 T67

Tweed, William C. Recreation site planning and improvement in national forests, 1891-1942 /. Washington, D.C. , 1980 [i.e. 1981] vi, 29 p. :
LC Card 80-601100 DDC 333.78/3/0973 19
GV191.4 .T83

United States. Geological Survey. Water power of the world . Washington , 1918. [7] leaves of plates : LC Card 80-675255 DDC 912/.133391 19
G1046.N33 U53 1918

United States. Soil Conservation Service. Burns, roads, and facilities, Entiat River Basin, Chelan County, Washington /. Portland, Or. , 1979. 1 map : LC Card 81-691538
G4282.E5K5 1978 .U5

United States. Soil Conservation Service. Precipitation and runoff, Entiat River Basin, Chelan County, Washington /. Portland, Or. , 1979. 1 map : LC Card 81-691528
G4282.E5C88 1978 .U5

United States. Soil Conservation Service. Soil survey of Ashley County, Arkansas /. [Washington, D.C. , 1979] vii, 92 p., [40] fold. leaves of plates : LC Card 80-601804 DDC 631.4/7/76783 19
S599.A75 U54 1979

United States. Soil Conservation Service. Soil survey of Rapides Parish, Louisiana /. [Washington] , 1980. iii, 86 p., [59] fold. leaves of plates : LC Card 80-602333 DDC 631.4/7/76369 19
S599.L6 U54 1980

USDA Forest Service general technical report WO.
(17) Symposium on Rangeland Policies for the Future, Tucson, Ariz., 1979. Rangeland policies for the future . [Washington, D.C.] , 1979. v, 114 p. ; LC Card 80-600538 DDC 333.74/0973 19
HD241 .S95 1979

The 1980 report to Congress on the nation's renewable resources / United States Department of Agriculture, Forest Service. [Washington, D.C.] : The Service, [1980] xvii, 155 p. : ill. ; 28 cm. Includes bibliographical references and index. LC Card 80-602939 DDC 333.7/0973 19
1. Renewable natural resources - United States. I. Title.
HC103.7 .U52 1980

United States. Forest Service. California Region. Klamath National Forest (Goosenest Ranger District) California and Oregon. Compiled and drawn at Regional Office, San Francisco, Calif., 1968. [San Francisco] 1978. col. map 77 x 81 cm. Scale 1:126,720; 1/2˝ = 1 mile. "Polyconic projection; 1927 North American datum. Willamette and Mt. Diablo meridians." Includes "Vicinity map" and "Key map."

1. Klamath National Forest - Maps. I. Title: Goosenest Ranger District.
G4362.K5 1968 .U52
NYPL [Map Div. 80-3412]

United States. Forest Service. Pacific Northwest Region.
Final environmental statement: land use plan, Soleduck Planning Unit [of the Olympic National Forest] Prepared in accordance with section 102 (2) (c) of P. L. 91-190. Olympic, Wash., U. S. Dept. of Agriculture, Forest Service, Pacific Northwest Region, Olympic National Forest, 1975? 300 p. : maps ; 28 cm.
Cover title: Soleduck Planning Unit; final environmental statement. Bibliography: p. 297-300.
1. Forest management - Washington (State). 2. United States - Forest policy. **NYPL [JLF 80-871]**

Oregon. Dept. of Fish and Wildlife. A statewide comprehensive plan for fish and wildlife on the national forests in the State of Oregon .
[Portland] [1979?] 84 p. : LC Card 80-621380
SK439 .O75 1979 **NYPL [JLF 81047]**

Wallowa-Whitman National Forest [north half] Oregon. Compiled in the U. S. F. S. Regional Office, Portland, Oregon, 1975. Supplemental recreation data has been added 1977. Portland : The Office, 1979. 1 map : col. ; on sheet 66 x 102 cm. Scale ca. 1:126,720. Relief shown by hachures and spot heights. Map printed on both sides of sheet. Map includes Hells Canyon National Recreation Area, Oregon-Idaho.
1. Wallowa-Whitman National Forest - Maps. 2. Hells Canyon National Recreation Area - Maps. 3. Outdoor recreation - Hells Canyon National Recreation Area - Maps.
G4292.W31 1975 .U53
NYPL [Map Div. 80-3406]

Wallowa - Whitman National Forest [south half] Oregon. Compiled in the U. S. F. S. Regional Office, Portland, Oregon, 1975. Supplemental recreation data has been added 1977. Portland : The Office, 1979. 1 map : col. ; on sheet 66 x 91 cm. Scale ca. 1: 126,720. Relief shown by hachures and spot heights. Shows forest lands in color. Includes location map, list of "Recreation sites," text, and col. illus. Map printed on both sides of sheet.
1. Wallowa-Whitman National Forest - Maps.
G4292.W31 1975 .U54
NYPL [Map Div. 80-3393]

United States. Forest Service. Rocky Mountain Region.
Arapaho National Forest, Colorado, 1974. Compiled in the Regional Office, Denver, Colorado in 1972 ... Partial revision 1977. [Denver] 1977. col. map on sheet 66 x 107 cm. Scale 1:126,720; 11/2" = 1 mile. Printed on both sides of sheet. Relief shown by hachures and spot heights. "Polyconic projection." "Sixth principal meridian." "Forest visitors map."
1. Arapaho National Forest. Colo, - Maps. 2. Outdoor recreation - Colorado - Arapaho National Forest - Maps. **NYPL [Map Div. 80-3424]**

Bighorn National Forest, Wyoming. Compiled in the Regional Office, Denver, Colorado in 1973 ... [Denver], 1974. col. map. on sheet 65 x 103 cm. Scale 1:126,720; 1/2" = 1 mile. Printed on both sides of sheet. Relief Shawn by hachures and spot heights. "Polyconic projection." "Sixth principal meridian." Includes location map, 2 map Keys, 2 indexes to recreation areas, text, and col. illus.
1. Bighorn National Forest - Maps. 2. Outdoor recreation - Wyoming - Bighorn National Forest - Maps. **NYPL [Map Div. 80-3361]**

Black Hills Nacional Forest, South Dakota, Wyoming, 1972. Compiled in the Regional Office, Denver, Colorado in 1960-1961 ... Partial revision 1976. [Denver] 1976. col. map on sheet 114 x 66 cm. Scale 1:126,720; 1/2" = 1 mile. Printed on both sides of sheet. Relief shown by hachures and spot heights. "Polyconic projection. Black Hills meridian, sixth principal meridian." "Forest visitors map." Includes map keys, "Vicinity maps," text, col. illus., "Recreation site directory," and "Pactola Reservoir vicinity map," "Sheridan Lake vicinity map," and "Deerfield Lake vicinity map." Includes map keys, "Vicinity maps," text, col. illus., "Recreation site directory," and "Pactola Reservoir vicinity map," "Sheridan Lake vicinity map," and "Deerfield Lake vicinity map."
1. Black Hills National Forest - Maps. 2. Outdoor

recreation - Black Hills National Forest - Maps.
G4182.B51 1972 .U5
NYPL [Map Div. 80-3419]

Buffalo Gap National Grassland, South Dakota. Compiled in the regional office, Denver, Colorado in 1964. Partial revision 1974. [Denver] 1974. col. map on sheet 65 x 120 cm. Scale 1:126,720; 1/2" = 1 mile. Printed on both sides of sheet. "Polyconic projection. Black Hills meridian and sixth principal meridian." Relief shown by hachures and spot heights. "Forest Service map class A." "Grassland visitors map." Includes text, col. illus., "Recreation directory," "Map key," and "Vicinity map."
LC Card 77-691258
1. Buffalo Gap National Grassland, S. D. - Maps. 2. Outdoor recreation - South Dakota - Buffalo Gap National Grassland - Maps.
G4182.B82 1974 .U5
NYPL [Map Div. 80-3351]

Cimarron National Grassland, Kansas. Compiled in the regional office, Denver, Colo. in 1969. Denver, 1971. col. map 54 x 78 cm. Scale 1:126,720; 1/2" = 1 mile. Relief shown by spot heights. "Polyconic projection; 1927 North American datum. Sixth principal meridian." "Forest service map class A." Includes "Key map." LC Card GM72-1077
1. Cimarron National Grassland, Kan. - Maps.
G4202.C55 1971 .U5
NYPL [Map Div. 80-3354]

Comanche National Grassland (north half) Colorado. Compiled in the Regional Office, Denver, Colorado in 1967 ... Partial revision 1977. [Denver] 1977. col. map on sheet 61 x 111 cm. Scale ca. 1:126,720; 1/2" = 1 mile. "Polyconic projection; 1927 North American datum. Sixth principal meridian." "Forest Service map." Inset: Key map. On verso: Comanche National Grassland (South half). Colorado, compiled in 1969, partial revision 1977.
1. Comanche National Grassland - Maps. I. Title.
G4312.C64 1969 .U5
NYPL [Map Div. 80-3363]

Grand Mesa National Forest, Colorado, 1976. Compiled in the Regional Office, Denver, Colo., in 1975. [Denver] 1976. col. map 65 x 90 cm. Scale 1:126,720; 1/2" = 1 mile. Relief shown by hachures and spot heights. "Polyconic projection." "Sixth principal and Ute meridians." "Forest visitors map." Includes map of "Fruita Division," location map, "Index to Geological Survey topographic maps," recreation index, text, and col. illus. On verso: map of "Grand Mesa lakes country," scale ca. 1:42,500; key map; text; col. illus. LC Card 77-694720
1. Grand Mesa National Forest, Colo - Maps. 2. Outdoor recreation - Colorado - Grand Mesa National Forest - Maps.
G4312.G6 1976 .U5
NYPL [Map Div. 80-3420]

Gunnison National Forest, Colorado. Compiled in the Regional Office, Denver, Colorado in 1975... [Denver], 1976. col. map on sheet 143 x 66 cm. Scale 1:126,720; 1/2" = 1 mile. Printed on both sides of sheet. Relief shown by hachures and spot heights. "Polyconic projection." "New Mexico and sixth principal meridians." Includes inset of "Black Canyon of the Gunnison National Monument," 2 vicinity maps, "Index to Geological Survey topographical maps," recreation indexes, text, and col. illus. LC Card 77-694719
1. Gunnison National Forest, Colo. - Maps. 2. Outdoor recreation - Colorado - Gunnison National Forest - Maps.
G4312.G8 1976 .U5
NYPL [Map Div. 80-3349]

Medicine Bow National Forest, Wyoming. Compiled in the Regional Office, Denver, Colorado 1969-70 ... [Denver] 1973. col. map on sheet 65 x 114 cm. Scale 1:126,720; 1/2" = 1 mile. Folded title: The Medicine Bow National Forest in Wyoming. Printed on both sides of sheet. Relief shown by hachures and spot heights. "Polyconic projection ... Sixth principal meridian." "Forest visitors map." "Forest Service map, class A." Includes col. illus., text, index to "Points of interest," "Recreation directory," 2 key maps, and location map. LC Card 74-696309
1. Medicine Bow National Forest, Wyo. - Maps. 2. Outdoor recreation - Wyoming - Medicine Bow National Forest - Maps.
G4262.M4 1973 .U5
NYPL [Map Div. 80-3343]

Pawnee National Grassland, Colorado. Compiled in the regional office, Denver, Colo.

in 1966-67. [Denver] 1969. col. map 55 x 101 cm. Scale 1:126,720; 1/2" = 1 mile. "Polyconic projection; 1927 North American Datum. Sixth principal meridian." "Forest Service map." Includes source diagram and key map. Text and illus. on verso. "Reprinted 1977." LC Card GM69-1310
1. Pawnee National Grassland - Maps.
G4312.P3 1969 .U5
NYPL [Map Div. 80-3367]

Pike National Forest, Colorado; west-[east] half. Compiled in the Regional Office, Denver, Colorado in 1970 ... [Denver] 1970. 2 col. maps on sheet 106 x 65 cm. Scale 1:126,720; 1/2" = 1 mile. Printed on both sides of sheet. "Reprinted 1977." "Polyconic projection, 1927 North American datum." Relief shown by hachures and spot heights. Forest Service map. Includes text, col. illus., index to recreation sites, and location map. LC Card GM72-1927
1. Pike National Forest, Colo. - Maps. 2. Recreation areas - Colorado - Pike National Forest - Maps.
G4312.P48 1970 .U5
NYPL [Map Div. 80-3344]

Rio Grande National Forest, Colorado, 1975. Compiled in the Regional Office, Denver, Colorado in 1974. [Denver] 1975] col. map on sheet 142 x 67 cm. Scale 1:126,720; 1/2" = 1 mile. Folded title: Rio Grande National Forest, Colorado. Printed on both sides of sheet. "Polyconic projection. New Mexico and sixth principal meridians." Relief shown by hachures and spot heights. "Forest visitors map." Includes key maps, "Vicinity map," recreation indexes, text, and col. illus. LC Card 76-690740
1. Rio Grande National Forest - Maps. 2. Outdoor recreation - Colorado - Rio Grande National Forest - Maps.
G4312.R5 1975 .U5
NYPL [Map Div. 80-3418]

Roosevelt National Forest, Colorado. Compiled in the Regional Office, Denver, Colorado in 1973 and 1974. [Denver] 1974. col. map on sheet 66 x 92 cm. Scale 1:126,720; 1/2" = 1 mile. Printed on both sides of sheet. "Polyconic projection. Sixth principal meridian." Relief shown by hachures and spot heights. "Forest Service map class A." "Forest visitors map." Includes text, 2 recreation directories, "Vicinity map," 2 key maps, and col. illus. LC Card 76-690738
1. Roosevelt National Forest, Colo. - Maps. 2. Outdoor recreation - Colorado - Roosevelt National Forest - Maps.
G4312.R66 1974 .U5
NYPL [Map Div 80-3346]

San Isabel National Forest, Colorado. Compiled in the Regional Office, Denver, Colorado in 1964 ... Partial revision 1972. [Denver] 1972. col. map on sheet 115 x 66 cm. Scale 1:126,720; 1/2" = 1 mile. Printed on both sides of sheet. Relief shown by hachures and spot heights. "Polyconic projection ... New Mexico and sixth principal meridians." "Forest Service map." "Forest visitors map." Includes col. illus., text, map keys, listings of "Forest Service recreation sites," index to "Points of interest," and "Vicinity map." "Reprinted 1978." LC Card 74-696335
1. San Isabel National Forest, Colo. - Maps. 2. Outdoor recreation - Colorado - San Isabel National Forest - Maps.
G4312.S2 1972 .U5
NYPL [Map Div. 80-3362]

San Juan National Forest, Colorado. Compiled in the Regional Office, Denver, Colorado in 1972 and 1973 ... [Denver], 1974. col. map. on sheet 66 x 105 cm. Scale 1:126,720; 1/2" = 1 mile. Printed on both sides of sheet. Relief shown by hachures and spot heights. "Polyconic projection." "New Mexico principal meridian." "Reprinted 1976." "Forest visitors map." "Forest Service map class A." Includes inset of Mesa Verde National Park, 2 map keys, "Vicinity map," "Recreation directory," text, and col. illus.
1. San Juan National Forest, Colo. - Maps. 2. Outdoor recreation - Colorado - San Juan National Forest - Maps. **NYPL [Map Div. 80-3365]**

Shoshone National Forest, Wyoming. Compiled in the Regional Office, Denver, Colorado in 1967 ... [Denver] 1969. col. map on sheet 66 x 92 cm. Scale 1:126,720; 1/2" = 1 mile. Folded title: North half Shoshone National Forest, Wyoming. Printed on both sides of sheet. Relief shown by hachures and spot heights. "Polyconic projection ... Sixth principal meridian, Wind River meridian." "Forest visitors map." "Forest Service map, class A." Includes

BIBLIOGRAPHIC GUIDE

United States. Forest Service. Rocky Mountain Region. (cont.)

540

col. illus., text, index to "Forest Service recreation sites," 2 key maps, and "Vicinity map." LC Card 74-696308

1. Shoshone National Forest, Wyo. - Maps. 2. Outdoor recreation - Wyoming - Shoshone National Forest - Maps. I. Title: North half Shoshone National Forest, Wyoming.

G4262.S5 1969 .U5

NYPL [Map Div. 80-3348]

Shoshone National Forest, Wyoming. Compiled in the Regional Office, Denver, Colorado in 1967 ... [Denver] 1971. col. map on sheet 67 x 92 cm. Scale 1:126,720; 1/2″ = 1 mile. Folded title: Shoshone National Forest, Wyoming, south half. Printed on both sides of sheet. Relief shown by hachures and spot heights. "Polyconic projection ... Sixth principal meridian, Wind River meridian." "Forest visitors map." "Forest Service map, class A." Includes col. illus., text, indexes to "Forest Service recreation sites," and "State recreation sites," 2 key maps, and "Vicinity map." LC Card 74-696307

1. Shoshone National Forest, Wyo. - Maps. 2. Outdoor recreation - Wyoming - Shoshone National Forest - Maps. I. Title: Shoshone National Forest, Wyoming, south half.

G4262.S5 1971 .U5

NYPL [Map Div. 80-3347]

Thunder Basin National Grassland, Wyoming. 1973. Compiled in the Regional Office, Denver, Colorado in 1969. [Denver] 1973. col. map 117 x 105 cm. Scale 1:126,720; 1/2″ = 1 mile. Relief shown by hachures and spot heights. "Polyconic projection." "Sixth principal meridian." "Forest Service map class A." Includes inset, "Source diagram," and "Key map." LC Card 76-690850

1. Thunder Basin National Grassland, Wyo. - Maps.

G4262.T55 1973 .U5

NYPL [Map Div. 80-3355]

Uncompahgre National Forest, Colorado. Compiled in the regional office, Denver, Colorado in 1966. [Denver] 1972. col. map on sheet 65 x 97 cm. Scale 1:126,720; 1/2″ = 1 mile. Printed on both sides of sheet. Relief shown by hachures and spot heights. "New Mexico, Sixth, Ute principal meridians." Includes text, col. illus., "Vicinity map," "Map key[s]," and "Recreation site directory." "Reprinted 1976." "Polyconic projection." LC Card 75-690673

1. Uncompahgre National Forest, Colo. - Maps. 2. Outdoor recreation - Colorado - Uncompahgre National Forest - Maps.

G4312.U6 1972 .U5

NYPL [Map Div. 80-3364]

White River National Forest, Colorado. Compiled in the regional office, Denver, Colorado in 1969. Partial revision 1973. [Denver] 1973. col. map on sheet 66 x 143 cm. Scale 1:126,720; 1/2″ = 1 mile. Relief shown by hachures and spot heights. Printed on both sides of sheet. "Polyconic projection. Sixth principal meridian." "Forest visitors map." Includes col. illus., text, "Key map," "Vicinity map," "Recreation directory," and indexes to "Ski areas" and "Points of interest." "Forest Service map class A." LC Card 75-690675

1. White River National Forest, Colo. - Maps. 2. Outdoor recreation - Colorado - White River National Forest - Maps.

G4312.W5 1973 .U5

NYPL [Map Div. 80-3350]

United States. Forest Service. Southern Forest Experiment Station, New Orleans. see **United States. Southern Forest Experiment Station, New Orleans.**

United States. Forest Service. Southwestern Region. Berman, Mary Jane. Cultural resources overview of Socorro, New Mexico /. Albuquerque, N.M. : Santa Fe, N.M. : v, 128 p. : LC Card 80-602245 DDC 978.9/62 19

E78.N65 B36

United States. Forest Sevice. Dolezel, Raymond. Soil survey of Nacogdoches County, Texas /. [Washington] , 1980. vii, 146 p., [30] fold. leaves of plates : LC Card 80-602411 DDC 631.4/7/764182 19

S599.T4 D63

UNITED STATES - FULL EMPLOYMENT POLICIES.
Edmonds, Robert H. A human investent tax credit program, second report . [Washington] , 1977. 24, 49 p. ; LC Card 77-604090

HC106.7 .E348

United States. Congress. House. Committee on

Education and Labor. Subcommittee on Employment Opportunities. Oversight hearing on employment impact of current and proposed economic policies . Washington , c1980 [i.e. 1981] iii, 51 p. ; LC Card 81-601627 DDC 339.5/0973 19

KF27 .E3366 1980c

United States. Congress. House. Committee on Education and Labor. Subcommittee on Employment Opportunities. Oversight on the Full employment and balanced growth act . Washington , 1979. v, 234 p. : LC Card 80-603323 DDC 353.0083 19

KF27 .E3366 1980

UNITED STATES - FULL EMPLOYMENT POLICIES - CONGRESSES.
Labor's views on employment policy . Washington , 1978. 132 p. ; LC Card 78-603516

HD5724 .L23 **NYPL [JLF 81-279]**

Unemployment, problems and policies . Los Angeles [1976] 73 p. : LC Card 77-621485

HD5724 .U614 **NYPL [*XME-9401]**

United States. Gelogical Survey.
Bulletin 1482-B.
Johnson, Ronald Carl, 1950- A study of the Cretaceous-Tertiary unconformity in the Piceance Creek Basin, Colorado . Washington , 1980. iii, 27 p. : LC Card 80-607774 DDC 551.7/7 19

QE688 .J63

UNITED STATES - GENEALOGY.
United States. Bureau of the Census. Census descriptions of geographic subdivisions and enumeration districts, 1830-1950. Washington , 1978. 6 microfilm reels ; **NYPL [*ZI-283]**

United States. General Accounting Office.
Action needed to improve management and effectiveness of drug abuse treatment : report to the Congress / by the Comptroller General of the United States. [Washington, D.C.] : U. S. General Accounting Office, [1980] v, 92 p. ; 28 cm. Cover title. "HRD-80-32." "April 14, 1980." LC Card 80-601701 DDC 362.2/938 19

1. Drug abuse - Treatment - Evaluation. 2. Drug abuse - Treatment - United States - Evaluation. I. Title.

RC564 .U54 1980

Actions needed to increase federal onshore oil and gas exploration and development : report to the Congress / by the Comptroller General of the United States. Washington, D.C. : U. S. General Accounting Office, 1981. xi, 203 p. ; 27 cm. Cover title. Feb. 11, 1981. "EMD-81-40." "B-201799"--Prelim. p. Item 546-D (microfiche) Includes bibliographical references. LC Card 81-601214 DDC 353.0082/388 19

1. Petroleum industry and trade - Government policy - United States. 2. Gas industry - Government policy - United States. 3. Energy development - Government policy - United States. 4. Oil and gas leases - United States. 5. United States - Public lands. I. Title.

HD9566 .U543 1981

Agency for International Development needs to strengthen its management of study, research, and evaluation activities : report / by the Comptroller General of the United States. [Washington : U. S. General Accounting Office], 1979. iii, 30 p. ; 27 cm. Cover title. "ID-79-13." "B-133220." LC Card 79-601658 DDC 353.0089 19

1. United States. Agency for International Development. 2. Research and development contracts - United States. I. Title.

HC60.U6 G4 1979

AID must consider social factors in establishing cooperatives in developing countries : report to the Congress of the United States / by the Comptroller General. [Washington, D.C.] : U. S. General Accounting Office : for sale by Supt. of Docs., U. S. Govt. Print. Off., [1980] iv, 42 p. ; 27 cm. Cover title. "ID-80-39." "B-199397." LC Card 80-602922 DDC 334/.09172/4 19

1. Underdeveloped areas - Cooperative societies. 2. United States. Agency for International Development. I. Title.

HD3575 .U54 1980

The Air Force can reduce its stated requirements for strategic airlift crews : report / by the Comptroller General of the United States. [Washington : U. S. General Accounting Office], 1979. v, 23 p. ; 27 cm. Cover title. "LCD-79-411." "B-146896." LC Card 79-603765 DDC 358.4/161/0973 19

1. United States. Air Force - Personnel management. 2. Flight crews - United States. 3. Jet transports. 4. Strategic forces - United States. I. Title.

UG773 .U54 1979

Alternatives for eliminating Amtrak's debt to the Government : report to the Congress / by the Comptroller General of the United States. [Washington, D.C. : U. S. General Accounting Office, 1980] iv, 45 p. ; 27 cm. Cover title. "PAD-80-45." "B-197385." "March 28, 1980." LC Card 80-601698 DDC 385/.1 19

1. Amtrak - Finance. I. Title.

HE2705 1980 .E5

American seaports--changes affecting operations and development : report to the Congress / by the Comptroller General of the United States. [Washington, D.C.] : U. S. General Accounting Office, [1979] v, 49 p. : graphs ; 27 cm. Cover title. "November 16, 1979." "CED-80-8." "B-195850." LC Card 79-604293 DDC 387.1/0973 19

1. Harbors - United States. I. Title.

HE553 .U642 1979

An analytical framework for federal policies and programs influencing capital formation in the United States : report to the Congress / by the Comptroller General of the United States. Washington, D.C. : U. S. General Accounting Office, 1980. v, 80 p. : ill. ; 27 cm. Cover title. Sept. 23, 1980. "PAD-80-24." "B-199822"--Prelim. p. G.P.O. sales statement incorrect in publication. Item 546-D (microfiche) Includes bibliographical references. LC Card 80-603955 DDC 332/.0415/0973 19

1. Saving and investment - United States. 2. Capital - United States. 3. United States - Economic policy - 1971-. I. Title.

HC110.S3 U63 1980

Antirecession assistance--an evaluation : report to the Congress / by the Comptroller General of the United States. [Washington : U. S. General Accounting Office], 1977. v, 128 p. : ill. ; 28 cm. Cover title. "PAD-78-20." "B-146285." Includes bibliographical references. LC Card 77-604896

1. Public service employment - United States. 2. Economic assistance, Domestic - United States. 3. Revenue sharing - United States. I. Title.

HD5724 .U629 1977 **NYPL [JLF 81-298]**

Background information bearing upon Panama Canal treaty implementing legislation : study / by the staff of the U. S. General Accounting Office. [Washington] : The Office, [1979] 62 p. ; 27 cm. Cover title. "June 4, 1979." "B-114839." Errata slip inserted. LC Card 79-602532 DDC 353.0087/6444 19

1. Panama Canal Treaties, 1977. 2. United States. Panama Canal Commission. I. Title.

JX1398.73 .U54 1979

Better evaluations needed to weed out useless Federal advisory committees : report to the Congress / by the Comptroller General of the United States. Washington : General Accounting Office, [1977] iv, 74 p. ; 27 cm. Microfiche (neg.) NTIS. 1 sheet. 11 x 15 cm. (PB-268 686) Cover title. Publication date stamped on t.p. "GGD-76-104." LC Card 77-601732

1. Executive advisory bodies - United States. I. Title.

JK468.C7 U54 1977 **NYPL [*XME-9541]**

Better Navy management of shipbuilding contracts could save millions of dollars : report to the Congress / by the Comptroller General of the United States. [Washington] : U. S. General Accounting Office, [1980] v, 40 p. ; 27 cm. Cover title. "January 10, 1980." "PSAD-80-18." "B-196771." LC Card 80-602619 DDC 359.6/211/0973 19

1. Ship-building - United States. 2. Defense contracts - United States. 3. United States. Navy - Management. I. Title.

VM299.6 .U55 1980

A central manager is needed to coordinate the military diagnostic and calibration program, Department of Defense / United States General Accounting Office. [Washington] : The Office, 1977. 12, 4 leaves : diagr. ; 27 cm. Cover title. "LCD-77-427." LC Card 77-603003 DDC 355.6/213 19

1. Calibration. 2. United States - Armed Forces - Facilities - Management. I. Title: A central manager is needed ...

UG455 .U54 1977

Changes needed to improve government's knowledge of OPEC financial influence in the

United States : report to the Congress / by the Comptroller General of the United States. [Washington : U. S. General Accounting Office], 1979. vi, 71 p. ; 27 cm. Cover title. "December 19, 1979." "EMD-80-23." "B-172255." Includes bibliographical references. LC Card 80-600965 DDC 332.6/73/0973 19

1. Investments, Foreign - United States. 2. Organization of Petroleum Exporting Countries. I. Title.

HG4910 .U5434 1979a

Child Care Food Program : better management will yield better nutrition and fiscal integrity : report to the Congress / by the Comptroller General of the United States. Washington, D.C. : U. S. General Accounting Office, [1980] vii, 64 p. ; 27 cm. Cover title. "June 6, 1980." "CED-80-91." LC Card 80-602698 DDC 362.7/1 19

1. Food relief - United States - Evaluation. 2. Children - United States - Nutrition. I. Title.

HV696.F6 U623 1980

Commercializing solar heating : a national strategy needed : report to the Congress / by the Comptroller General of the United States. [Washington : U. S. General Accounting Office], 1979. xii, 66 p. ; 27 cm. Cover title. "EMD-79-19." "B-178205." LC Card 79-603062 DDC 338.4/769778/0973 19

1. Solar energy policy - United States. 2. Solar heating - Economic aspects - United States. I. Title.

HD9681.U62 U54 1979

A compilation of Federal laws and Executive orders for nondiscrimination and equal opportunity programs / study by the staff of the U. S. General Accounting Office. [Washington] : The Office, 1978. i, 72 p. ; 27 cm. Cover title. "HRD-78-138." LC Card 78-603607 DDC 353.0081/1 19

1. Discrimination - United States. I. Title.

KF4755 .A87

Conditions of older people, national information system needed : report to the Congress / by the Comptroller General of the United States. [Washington, D.C.] : United States General Accounting Office, 1979. vi, 52 p. : ill. ; 27 cm. Cover title. "HRD-79-95." "B-165430." LC Card 79-603736 DDC 362.6/09771/32 19

1. Aged - Ohio - Cleveland - Social conditions. 2. Aged, Services for - United States. 3. Aged - United States - Government policy. 4. Aged - Information services - United States. I. Title.

HQ1064.U6 O375 1979

The Congress should mandate formation of a military-VA-civilian contingency hospital system : report to the Congress / by the Comptroller General of the United States. Washington, D.C. : U. S. General Accounting Office, [1980] vi, 51 p. ; 27 cm. Cover title. "HRD-80-76." "B-196409." "June 26, 1980." LC Card 80-602693 DDC 355.3/45/0973 19

1. Hospitals - United States - Military aspects. 2. Hospitals, Military - United States - Planning. 3. Health facilities - United States - Affiliations. 4. War wounds - United States. 5. United States. Department of Defense. I. Title.

RA981.A2 U53 1980

Congressional sourcebook series. see Congressional sourcebook series.

Contracting for computer software development serious problems require management attention to avoid wasting additional millions : report to the Congress / by the Comptroller General of the United States. [Washington, D.C.] : U. S. General Accounting Office, 1979. v, 84 p. ; 27 cm. Cover title. "FGMSD-80.4." LC Card 79-604267 DDC 353.0071/1 19

1. Administrative agencies - United States - Management - Data processing. 2. Computer programs - Contracts and specifications. 3. Government consultants - United States. 4. Public contracts - United States. I. Title.

JK468.A8 U5 1979a

Controls over DOD's management support service contracts need strengthening : report to Congresswoman Geraldine Ferraro and Senator David Pryor / by the Comptroller General of the United States. Washington, D.C. : U. S. General Accounting Office, 1981. v, 76 p. ; 27 cm. Cover title. Mar. 31, 1981. "MASAD-81-14." "B201534"--Prelim. p. Item 546-D (microfiche) Includes bibliographical references. LC Card 81-601728 DDC 355.6/211/0973 19

1. Defense contracts - United States. 2. Government consultants - United States. I. Ferraro, Geraldine. II.

Pryor, David. III. Title.

UC263 .U54 1981

Correct balance of Defense's foreign military sales trust fund unknown : report to the chairman, Committee on Appropriations, House of Representatives / by the Comptroller General of the United States. Washington, DC : U. S. General Accounting Office, [1980] iii, 23 p. ; 27 cm. Cover title. "B-198131." "FGMSD-80-47." "June 3, 1980." LC Card 80-602832 DDC 355/.032/0973 19

1. Security Assistance Program - Auditing and inspection. 2. United States. Dept. of Defense - Auditing and inspection. 3. Munitions - United States. I. United States. Congress. House. Committee on Appropriations. II. Title.

UA12 .U527 1980

Costs of Federal personnel security investigations could and should be cut : report / by the Comptroller General of the United States. [Washington, D.C.] : United States General Accounting Office, 1979. 2, v, 42 p. ; 27 cm. Cover title. "FPCD-79-79." LC Card 79-603767 DDC 353.0013/242 19

1. Loyalty-security program, 1947-. I. Title.

JK734 .U54 1979

The Department of Justice can do more to help improve conditions at State and local correctional facilities : report to the Congress / by the Comptroller General of the United States. Washington, D.C. : U. S. General Accounting Office, 1980. v, 52 p. ; 27 cm. Sept. 15, 1980. "GGD-80-77." "B-198054"--Prelim. p. G.P.O. sales statement incorrect in publication. Item 546-D (microfiche) LC Card 80-603948 DDC 365/.7/0973 19

1. Prisoners - Legal status, laws, etc. - United States - Collected works. 2. Prisoners - Health and hygiene - United States - Collected works. 3. Prison administration - United States - Collected works. I. Title.

HV9471 .U53 1980a

Developing markets for fish not traditionally harvested by the United States : the problems and the Federal role : report / by the Comptroller General of the United States. [Washington, D.C. : U. S. General Accounting Office, 1980] v, 60 p. ; 27 cm. Cover title. "CED-80-73." "B-197669." "May 7, 1980." LC Card 80-602253 DDC 380.1/4370973 19

1. Fish trade - United States. 2. Fisheries - Economic aspects - United States. I. Title.

HD9455 .U53 1980

Effects in Washington, D.C., area of 1979 gasoline shortage : supplies less than national average, price increases comparable : report to Senator John W. Warner / by the Comptroller General of the United States. Washington, D.C. : U. S. General Accounting Office, [1980] viii, 47 p. ; 27 cm. Cover title. "EMD-80-70." "B-197378." LC Card 80-602653 DDC 338.4/766553827/09753 19

1. Gasoline supply - Washington metropolitan area. 2. Gasoline - Prices - Washington metropolitan area. 3. Rationing, Consumer - Washington metropolitan area. I. Warner, John W., 1927-. II. Title.

HD9579.G5 U595 1980

Efforts to charge for using government-owned assets for foreign military sales: marked improvement but additional action needed : report / by the Comptroller General of the United States. [Washington] : U. S. General Accounting Office, 1979. iv, 21 p. ; 27 cm. Cover title. "FGMSD-79-36." LC Card 79-602498 DDC 353.0071/13 19

1. Munitions - United States - Finance. I. Title.

HD9743.U6 U59 1979c

Employee stock ownership plans : who benefits most in closely held companies? : Report to the Committee on Finance, United States Senate / by the Comptroller General of the United States. Washington, D.C. : United States General Accounting Office, [1980] v, 52 p. ; 27 cm. Cover title. "June 20, 1980." "HRD-80-88." "B-199055." LC Card 80-603177 DDC 658.3/225 19

1. Employee ownership - United States. 2. Close corporations - United States. I. United States. Congress. Senate. Committee on Finance. II. Title.

HD5660.U5 U54 1980

Endangered species--a controversial issue needing resolution : report to the Congress / by the Comptroller General of the United States. [Washington] : U. S. General Accounting

Office, 1979. vii, 123 p. : ill. ; 27 cm. Cover title. "CED-79-65." "B-118370." LC Card 79-603243 DDC 333.95/0973 19

1. Endangered species - United States. 2. Endangered species - Law and legislation - United States. I. Title.

QL84.2 .U56 1979

The Environmental Protection Agency needs congressional guidance and support to guard the public in a period of radiation proliferation : report to the Congress / by the Comptroller General of the United States. [Washington : U. S. General Accounting Office], 1978. vii, 81 p. ; 27 cm. Cover title. LC Card 78-602990

1. United States. Environmental Protection Agency. 2. Radioactive pollution - United States. I. Title.

TD171 .U57 1978   NYPL [JLF 81-156]

Evaluating a performance measurement system : a guide for the Congress and Federal agencies : report to the chairwoman, Subcommittee on Civil Service, House Committee on Post Office and Civil Service / by the Comptroller general of the United States. [Washington, D.C. : U. S. General Accounting Office, [1980] 24 p. ; 27 cm. Cover title. "May 12, 1980." "FGMSD-80-57." "B-198677." LC Card 80-602699 DDC 353.07/6 19

1. Government productivity - United States. 2. Organizational effectiveness. I. Title.

JK468.P75 U56 1980

An evaluation of the Intergovernmental personnel act of 1970 : report to the Congress / by the Comptroller General of the United States. [Washington, D.C. : U. S. General Accounting Office, 1979] v, 96 p. : graphs ; 27 cm. Cover title. "December 19, 1979." "FPCD-80-11." "B-157936." LC Card 80-602660 DDC 350.1/0973 19

1. Personnel management - United States. 2. Intergovernmental personnel programs - United States. I. Title.

JK765 .U57 1979

Factors influencing the size of the U. S. strategic petroleum reserve : report to the Congress / by the Comptroller General of the United States. [Washington, D.C. : U. S. General Accounting Office, 1979] iii, 42 p. ; 27 cm. Cover title. "ID-79-8." "June 15, 1979." Includes bibliographical references. LC Card 79-602708 DDC 333.8/23211/0973 19

1. Petroleum - United States - Storage. I. Title.

TP692.5 .U624 1979

FDA drug approval--a lengthy process that delays the availability of important new drugs : report to the Subcommittee on Science, Research, and Technology, House Committee on Science and Technology / by the Comptroller General of the United States. Washington, DC : U. S. General Accounting Office, [1980] vi, 83 p. ; 27 cm. Cover title. "May 28, 1980." "HRB-80-64." "B-198724." LC Card 80-602514 DDC 363.1/946/0973 19

1. Drugs - United States - Testing. 2. Drug trade - United States - Quality control. 3. United States. Food and Drug Administration. I. United States. Congress. House. Committee on Science and Technology. II. Title.

RS189 .U54 1980

Federal assistance system should be changed to permit greater involvement by state legislatures : report to the Congress / by the Comtroller General of the United States. Washington, D.C. : U. S. General Accounting Office, 1980. v, 88 p. ; 27 cm. Cover title. Dec. 15, 1980. "GGD-81-3." "B-128043"--Prelim. p. G.P.O. sales statement incorrect in publication. Item 546-D (microfiche) Includes bibliographical references. LC Card 81-601073 DDC 353.0072/52 19

1. Grants-in-aid - United States. 2. Intergovernmental fiscal relations - United States. I. Title.

HJ275 .U54 1980b

Federal capital budgeting : a collection of haphazard practices : report to the Congress / by the Comptroller General of the United States. Washington, D.C. : U. S. General Accounting Office, 1981. iv, 139 p. ill. ; 27 cm. Cover title. Feb. 26, 1981. "PAD-81-19." Item 546-D (microfiche) Includes bibliographical references. LC Card 81-601452 DDC 353.0072/22534 19

1. Capital budget - United States. 2. Capital investments - United States. I. Title.

HJ2052 .U56 1981

Federal demonstrations of solar heating and cooling on commercial buildings have not been

very effective : report to the Congress / by the Comptroller General of the United States. [Washington, D.C. : U. S. General Accounting Office, 1980] v, 36 p. : ill. ; 27 cm. Cover title. "April 15, 1980." "EMD-80-41." "B-197809." LC Card 80-601697 DDC 697/.78 19
1. Solar heating - United States. 2. Solar air conditioning - United States. 3. Solar energy policy - United States. I. Title.
TH7413 .U53 1980

The Federal drive to acquire private lands should be reassessed : report / by the Comptroller General of the United States. [Washington, D.C. : U. S. General Accounting Office, 1979] viii, 172 p. : maps ; 27 cm. Cover title. "CED-80-14." "B-196787." "December 14, 1979." LC Card 80-600998 DDC 353.0082/326 19
1. Government purchasing of real property - United States. 2. Conservation of natural resources - United States. I. Title.
HD205 1979 .U54

The Federal Government needs a comprehensive program to curb its energy use : report to the Congress / by the Comptroller General of the United States. [Washington, D.C.] : United States General Accounting Office, [1979] v, 56 p. ; 27 cm. Cover title. "December 12, 1979." "EMD-80-11." LC Card 80-601719 DDC 333.79 19
1. Energy conservation - United States. 2. Energy policy - United States. I. Title.
TJ163.4.U6 U55 1979

Federal information sources & systems. 1976- Washington.
NYPL [*R-Econ. 81-135 & JLM 81-123]

The federal payment to the District of Columbia : experience since home rule ; analysis of proposals for change : report to the Congress / by the Comptroller General of the United States. Washington, D.C. : U. S. General Accounting Office, 1981. viii, 81 p. : ill. ; 27 cm. Cover title. Apr. 23, 1981. "GGD-81-67." Includes bibliographical references. "B-201788"--Prelim. LC Card 81-601896 DDC 353.0072/5/09753 19
1. Finance, Public - Washington (D.C.). I. Title.
HJ9215 .U54 1981

Federal program evaluations. 1976- Washington.
NYPL [*R-Econ. 81-136 & JLM 81-130]

A Federal strategy is needed to help improve medical and dental care in prisons and jails : report to the Congress / by the Comptroller General of the United States. [Washington, D.C.] : U. S. General Accounting Office, 1978. v, 74 p. : ill. ; 27 cm. Cover title "GGD-78-96." "B-133223." LC Card 79-603770 DDC 365/.66 19
1. Prisoners - Medical care - United States. 2. Prisoners - Dental care - United States. I. Title.
HV8843 .U54 1978

Federally-financed research and communication on Soviet affairs : capabilities and needs : report to the Congress / by the Comptroller General of the United States. [Washington, D.C. : U. S. General Accounting Office, 1980] ii, 37 p. ; 27 cm. Cover title. "B-199095." "ID-80-48." "July 2, 1980." Includes bibliographical references. LC Card 80-602671 DDC 947/.007/073 19
1. Russia - Study and teaching - United States. 2. Europe, Eastern - Study and teaching - United States. 3. Social scientists in government - United States. 4. Federal aid to research - United States. I. Title.
DK38.8 .U54 1980

Financial and other constraints prevent Eximbank from consistently offering competitive financing for U. S. exports : report to the Congress / by the Comptroller General of the United States. Washington, DC : U. S. General Accounting Office, [1980] vi, 47 p. ; 27 cm. Cover title "April 30, 1980." "B-80-16." "B-196942." LC Card 80-602393 DDC 332.1/54 19
1. Export-Import Bank of the United States. 2. Export credit - United States. I. Title.
HG3754.U5 U54 1980

Flexibility--key to administering Fulbright-Hays exchange program : report to the Congress / by the Comptroller General of the United States. [Washington, D.C.] : U. S. General Accounting Office, 1979. v, 73 p. ; 27 cm. Cover title. "December 10, 1979." "ID-80-3." LC Card 80-601041 DDC 370.19/62/0973 19
1. Educational exchanges - United States. I. Title.
LB2376 .U54 1979

Food price inflation in the United States and

other countries : report / by the Comptroller General of the United States. [Washington, D.C.] : U. S. General Accounting Office, 1979. ii, 28 p. : graphs ; 27 cm. Cover title. "CED-80-24." "B-114824." LC Card 80-601077 DDC 338.4/36413/00973 19
1. Food prices - United States. 2. Food prices. I. Title.
HD9004 .U57 1979

Foreign direct investment in the United States--the Federal role : report to the Congress / by the Comptroller General of the United States. Washington, DC : U. S. General Accounting Office, [1980] v, 83 p. ; 27 cm. Cover title. "ID-80-24." "B-197843." "June 3, 1980." LC Card 80-602513 DDC 332.6/73/0973 19
1. Investments, Foreign - United States. I. Title.
HG4910 .U5434 1980

Formulation of U. S. international energy policies : report to the Congress / by the Comptroller General of the United States. Washington, D.C. : U. S. General Accounting Office, 1980. iii, 115 p. : charts ; 27 cm. Cover title. Sept. 30, 1980. "ID-80-21." "B-197454"--Prelim. p. G.P.O. sales statement incorrect in publication. Item 546-D (microfiche) LC Card 80-603937 DDC 353.0082/3 19
1. Energy policy - United States. 2. United States - Foreign relations. I. Title.
HD9502.U52 U55 1980a

From auditing to editing / [by U. S. General Accounting Office.] Washington: U. S. Government Printing Office, [1974] vii, 80 p.: ill.; 28 cm. Bibliography: p. 79-80.
1. Authorship - Handbooks, manuals, etc. 2. Editing. I. Title.
NYPL [JLF 80-681]

From quantity to quality : changing FBI emphasis on interstate property crimes : report to the Congress / by the Comptroller General of the United States. [Washington] : U. S. General Accounting Office, [1980] iv, 41 p. ; 27 cm. Cover title. "GGD-80-43." "B-198539." "May 8, 1980." LC Card 80-602224 DDC 363.2/5 19
1. Offenses against property - United States. 2. United States. Federal Bureau of Investigation. I. Title.
HV6658 .U55 1980

GAO documents. Washington. 28 cm. Monthly. "Catalog of reports, decisions and opinions, testimonies and speeches." LC Card 79-643268
1. United States. General Accounting Office - Bibliography - Periodicals. I. Title.
NYPL [JLM 80-801]

GAO findings on Federal internal audit, a summary : report to the Congress / by the Comptroller General of the United States. Washington, D.C. : U. S. General Accounting Office, [1980] iv, 47 p. ; 27 cm. Cover title. "FGMSD-80-39." LC Card 80-602395 DDC 353.0072/32 19
1. Finance, Public - United States - Accounting. 2. Auditing, Internal - United States. I. Title.
HJ9801 .A3 1980

Gasoline allocation : a chaotic program in need of overhaul : report to the Congress / by the Comptroller General of the United States. [Washington, D.C.] : U. S. General Accounting Office, [1980] vii, 96 p. : ill. ; 27 cm. Cover title. "EMD-80-34." "B-196941." LC Card 80-602016 DDC 353.0082/6566553827 19
1. Gasoline supply - United States. 2. United States. Dept. of Energy. I. Title.
HD9579.G4 U54 1980

Geothermal energy : obstacles and uncertainties impede its widespread use : report to the Congress / by the Comptroller General of the United States. [Washington, D.C.] : U. S. General Accounting Office, [1980] v, 41 p. ; 27 cm. Cover title. "EMD-80-36." "B-197250." LC Card 80-601046 DDC 333.8/8/0973 19
1. Geothermal engineering - United States. 2. Geothermal resources - United States. I. Title.
TJ280.7 .U54 1980

Government agencies need effective planning to curb unnecessary year-end spending : report to the Chairman, Subcommittee on Human Resources, Committee on Post Office and Civil Service, House of Representatives / by the Comptroller General of the United States. [Washington, D.C. : U. S. General Accounting Office] : for sale by the Supt. of Docs., U. S. Govt. Print. Off., [1980] viii, 101 p. ; 27 cm. Cover title. "July 28, 1980." "PSAD-80.67." LC Card 80-603214 DDC 353.0072 19

1. Government spending policy - United States. I. United States. Congress. House. Committee on Post Office and Civil Service. Subcommittee on Human Resources. II. Title.
HJ2051 .U55 1980

Government earns low marks on proper use of consultants : report to the Congress / by the Comptroller General of the United States. Washington, D.C. : U. S. General Accounting Office, [1980] viii, 66 p. ; 27 cm. Cover title. "June 5, 1980." "FPCD-80-48." "B-197806." LC Card 80-602701 DDC 353.07/22 19
1. Government consultants - United States. I. Title.
JK468.C7 U54 1980a

Ground water overdrafting must be controlled : report to the Congress / by the Comptroller general of the United States. Washington, D.C. : U. S. General Accounting Office, 1980. iv, 52 p. ; 27 cm. Cover title. Sept. 12, 1980. "CED-80-96." Item 546-D (microfiche) Includes bibliographical references. LC Card 81-600550 DDC 333.91/0416/0973 19
1. Water, Underground - United States. 2. Water-supply - United States. 3. Water conservation - United States. I. Title.
TD223 .U525 1980

Health maintenance organizations can help control health care costs : report to the Congress / by the Comptroller General of the United States. [Washington, D.C.] : U. S. General Accounting Office, [1980] v, 75 p. : forms ; 27 cm. Cover title. Bibliography: p. 68-71. LC Card 80-602228 DDC 362.1/0425 19
1. Health maintenance organizations - United States - Costs. I. Title.
RA413.5.U5 U58 1980

Health monitoring needed for laboratory employees, Environmental Protection Agency : report to the Congress / by the Comptroller General of the United States. Washington : U. S. General Accounting Office, 1976. iv, 26 p. ; 27 cm. Cover title. Date of publication stamped on t.p. "CED-76-160." "B-163375." LC Card 76-603278 DDC 363.1/79 19
1. Environmental laboratories - Hygienic aspects - United States. 2. Toxicology laboratories - Hygienic aspects - United States. 3. United States. Environmental Protection Agency - Officials and employees - Health and hygiene. I. Title.
RA566.26 .U47 1976

HEW must improve control over billions in cash advances : report to the Congress / by the Comptroller General of the United States. [Washington] : U. S. General Accounting Office, 1979. v, 40 p. ; 27 cm. Cover title. "FGMSD-80-6." "B-164031." "December 28, 1979." LC Card 80-602661 DDC 353.84 19
1. United States. Dept. of Health, Education and Welfare - Auditing and Inspection. I. Title.
HV85 .U53 1979

How Federal programs affect migrant and seasonal farmworkers in the Connecticut River Valley : Department of Health, Education, and Welfare, Department of Labor, Office of Economic Opportunity : report of the Comptroller General of the United States. [Washington : U. S. General Accounting Office, 1976] iv, 48 leaves ; 27 cm. "B-177486." Publication date stamped on cover: "Feb. 27, 1976." LC Card 80-601674 DDC 353.0082/33 19
1. Migrant agricultural laborers - Services for - Connecticut Valley. I. Title.
HD1527.A11 U54 1976

How revenue sharing formulas distribute aid : urbanrural implications : report / by the Comptroller General of the United States. [Washington, D.C.] : U. S. General Accounting Office, [1980] iii, 61 p. : ill. ; 27 cm. Cover title. "PAD-80-23." "B-198287." LC Card 80-602651 DDC 353.0072/5 19
1. Revenue sharing - United States. 2. Revenue sharing - New York (State). I. Title.
HJ275 .U54 1980

How the petroleum refining industry approaches energy conservation--a case study : report to the Congress / by the Comptroller General of the United States. [Washington, D.C.] : U. S. General Accounting Office, [1980] v, 60 p. ; 27 cm. Cover title. "June 13, 1980." "EMD-80-55." "B-197477." LC Card 80-602620 DDC 333.79 19
1. Petroleum industry and trade - United States - Energy conservation. I. Title.
TP690.2.U6 U54 1980

How to burn coal efficiently and economically, and meet air pollution requirements--the fluidized-bed combustion process : report to the Congress / by the Comptroller General of the United States. [Washington, D.C.] : U. S. General Accounting Office, [1979] v, 45 p. ; 27 cm. Cover title. "EMD-80-12." "B-192938." "November 9, 1979." LC Card 80-600524 DDC 621.402/3 19
1. Fluidized-bed furnaces. 2. Coal - Combustion. I. Title.
TH7140 .U54 1979

Illegal aliens, estimating their impact on the United States : report to the Congress / by the Comptroller General of the United States. [Washington, D.C. : U. S. General Accounting Office, 1980] v, 128 p. : ill. ; 27 cm. Cover title. "March 14, 1980." "PAD-80-22." "B-125051." LC Card 80-601428 DDC 331.6/2/72073 19
1. Aliens - United States. 2. Emigration and immigration - Economic aspects - United States. 3. United States - Emigration and immigration. I. Title.
JV6481 1980 .G46

Impact of eliminating the States from the general revenue sharing program--a nine-state assessment : report to the Congress / by the Comptroller General of the United States. Washington, D.C. : U. S. General Accounting Office, [1980] iv, 39 p. : graphs ; 27 cm. Cover title. "GGD-80-68." "June 27, 1980." B-198603." LC Card 80-603192 DDC 353.0072/5 19
1. Revenue sharing - United States - States. 2. Intergovernmental fiscal relations - United States. I. Title.
HJ275 .U54 1980a

Implementing the Panama Canal treaty of 1977--good planning but many issues remain : report to the Congress / by the Comptroller General of the United States. Washington, D.C. : U. S. General Accounting Office, 1980. vii, 101 p. : ill. ; 27 cm. Cover title. "May 15, 1980." "ID-80-30." "B-197827." LC Card 80-602506 DDC 353.0087/6444 19
1. Panama Canal Treaties, 1977. 2. Canal Zone. I. Title.
JX1398.73 .U54 1980

Implications of highly sophisticated weapon systems on military capabilities ; report to the Congress / by the Comptroller General of the United States. [Washington, D.C.] : U. S. General Accounting Office, [1980] iv, 24 p. ; 27 cm. Cover title. "PSAD-80-61." "B-199275." "June 30, 1980." LC Card 80-603238 DDC 355.8/2/0973 19
1. United States - Armed Forces - Weapons systems. 2. United States - Armed Forces - Cost control. I. Title.
UF503 .U56 1980

Improving the scientific and technical information available to the Environmental Protection Agency in its decisionmaking process : report to the Congress / by the Comptroller General of the United States. [Washington, D.C.] : U. S. General Accounting Office, 1979] v, 60 p. ; 27 cm. Cover title. "CED-79-115." "September 21, 1979." "B-166506." LC Card 79-603730 DDC 353.0082/32 19
1. United States. Environmental Protection Agency. I. Title.
TD171 .U57 1979

Increasing commuting by transit and ridesharing : many factors should be considered : report to the Congress / by the Comptroller General of the United States. Washington, D.C. : U. S. General Accounting Office : for sale by Supt. of Docs., U. S. Govt. Print. Off., [1980] v, 82 p. ; 27 cm. Cover title. "CED-81-13." "B-199857." "November 14, 1980." LC Card 80-603842 DDC 388.4/068 19
1. Local transit - United States - Planning. 2. Car pools - United States - Planning. 3. Van pools - United States - Planning. I. Title.
HE4451 .U54 1980

Increasing costs, competition may hinder U. S. position of leadership in high energy physics : report to the Congress / by the Comptroller General of the United States. Washington, D.C. : U. S. General Accounting Office, 1980. v, 222 p. : ill., maps ; 27 cm. Cover title. Sept. 16, 1980. "EMD-80-58." "B-197675"--Prelim. p. Item 546-D (microfiche) Includes bibliographical references. LC Card 80-603949 DDC 539.7/6/072073 19
1. Particles (Nuclear physics) - Research - United States. 2. Nuclear research - United States. 3. Science and state - United States. I. Title.
QC793.4 .U54 1980

Industrial wastes : an unexplored source of valuable minerals : report to the Congress / by the Comptroller General of the United States. [Washington, D.C. : U. S. General Accounting Office, 1980] 68 p. ; 27 cm. "May 15, 1980." Cover title. "EMD-80-45." "B-197285." LC Card 80-602287 DDC 363.7/28 19
1. Factory and trade waste - United States. 2. Metals - Recycling. I. Title.
TD897.7 .U54 1980

The interaction of federal and state aid in New York State : trends and patterns, 1969-75 : report to the Congress / by the Comptroller General of the United States. Washington, D.C. : U. S. General Accounting Office, 1980. iv, 36 p. : ill. ; 27 cm. Cover title. Dec. 16, 1980. "PAD-81.10 "B-197848"--Prelim. p. Item 546-D (microfiche) Includes bibliographical references. LC Card 81-601066 DDC 353.97470072/52 19
1. Intergovernmental fiscal relations - New York (State). 2. Intergovernmental fiscal relations - United States. I. Title.
HJ605 .U64 1980

The interstate organized crime index : report / by the Comptroller General of the United States. [Washington, D.C.] : U. S. General Accounting Office, 1979. ii, 53 p. ; 27 cm. Cover title. "GGD-79-37." "B-171019." LC Card 79-602616 DDC 353.0075 19
1. Information storage and retrieval systems - Organized crime - United States. 2. Organized crime - Information services - United States. I. Title.
HV8079.O73 U54 1979

Issues and needed improvements in State regulation of the insurance business : report to the Congress / by the Comptroller General of the United States. [Washington, D.C. : U. S. General Accounting Office], 1980. viii, 275 p. ; 27 cm. Cover title. "October 9, 1979." "PAD-79-72." "B-192813." Includes bibliographical references. LC Card 80-601847 DDC 353.0082/55 19
1. Insurance law - United States - States. 2. Insurance - United States - State supervision. I. Title.
KF1165 .U54

Issues surrounding the Surface mining control and reclamation act : report / by the Comptroller General of the United States. [Washington, D.C.] : U. S. General Accounting Office, 1979. v, 45 p. : ill. ; 27 cm. Cover title. "CED-79-83." "B-190642." LC Card 79-603742 DDC 353.0082/382 19
1. Strip mining - Law and legislation - United States - States. 2. Coal mines and mining - United States - States. I. Title.
KF1823.Z95 U53

Lack of authority hampers attempts to increase cosmetic safety : report to the Congress / by the Comptroller General of the United States. [Washington : U. S. General Accounting Office, 1978] viii, 136 p. ; 27 cm. Cover title. "HRD-78-139." Publication date stamped on cover. Includes bibliographical references. LC Card 78-603000 DDC 363.1/966/0973 19
1. Cosmetics - Toxicology. 2. Cosmetics industry - United States. 3. Cosmetics - Law and legislation - United States. 4. United States. Food and Drug Administration. I. Title.
RA1270.C65 U54 1978

Major deficiencies in Army's Washington, D.C. finance and accounting operation : report to the Congress / by the Comptroller General of the United States. Washington, D.C. : U. S. General Accounting Office, [1980] iii, 47 p. ; 27 cm. Cover title. "June 5, 1980." "B-198588." "FGMSD-80-53." LC Card 80-602702 DDC 355.6/22 19
1. United States. Army. Military District of Washington. Finance and Accounting Office - Auditing and inspection. I. Title.
UB194.D6 U54 1980

Major factors inhibit expansion of the school breakfast program : report to the Congress / by the Comptroller General of the United States. [Washington, D.C. : United States General Accounting Office, 1980] vi, 65 p. ; 27 cm. Cover title. "June 16, 1980." "CED-80-35." "B-198282." Includes bibliographical references. LC Card 80-602650 DDC 371.7/16/0973 19
1. School breakfast programs - United States. I. Title.
LB3479 .U55 1980a

Making public buildings accessible to the handicapped : more can be done : report to the Congress / by the Comptroller General of the

United States. Washington, D.C. : U. S. General Accounting Office, [1980] vi, 48 p. ; 27 cm. Cover title. "FPCD-80-51." "B-182030." "June 6, 1980." LC Card 80-602707 DDC 353.0086/2 19
1. United States - Public buildings - Access for the physically handicapped. I. Title.
NA2545.P5 U53 1980

Meeting U. S. political objectives through economic aid in the Middle East and southern Africa : report to the Congress / by the Comptroller General of the United States. [Washington] : U. S. General Accounting Office, 1979. iv, 42 p., [1] leaf of plates : maps ; 28 cm. Cover title. "ID-79-23." "B-125029." LC Card 79-602541 DDC 338.91/56/073 19
1. Economic assistance, American - Near East. 2. Economic assistance, American - Africa, Southern. 3. United States - Foreign relations. I. Title.
HC415.15 .U54 1979

Military child advocacy programs, victims of neglect : report to the Congress / by the Comptroller General of the United States. [Washington] : U. S. General Accounting Office, 1979. iv, 36 p. ; 27 cm. Cover title. "HRD-79-75." LC Card 79-602651 DDC 355.1/29 19
1. Children of military personnel - United States. 2. Child abuse - Services - United States.
UB403 .U55 1979

Military commissaries : justification as fringe benefit needed, consolidation can reduce dependence on appropriations : report to the Congress / by the Comptroller General of the United States. [Washington, D.C.] : U. S. General Accounting Office, 1980. 46 p. ; 27 cm. Cover title. "FPCD-80-1." Includes bibliographical references. LC Card 80-600969 DDC 355.3/41 19
1. United States - Armed Forces - Commissariat. 2. United States - Armed Forces - Personnel management. I. Title.
UC703 .U54 1980

Millions of dollars for rehabilitating housing can be used more effectively : report to the Congress / by the Comptroller General of the United States. [Washington, D.C.] : U. S. General Accounting Office, [1979?] v, 50 p. ; 27 cm. Cover title. "December 7, 1979." "CED-80-19." "B-171630." LC Card 80-600530 DDC 353.0086/5045 19
1. Housing rehabilitation - United States. I. Title.
HD7293 .U47 1979a

Models, data, and war : a critique of the foundation for defense analyses : report to the Congress / by the Comptroller General of the United States. [Washington, D.C.] : GAO, 1980. v, 153 p. : ill. ; 27 cm. Cover title. "PAD-80-21." Bibliography: p. 131-142. LC Card 80-601429 DDC 355/.0335/73072 19
1. United States - Military policy - Decision making. 2. Operations research.
UA23 .U475 1980

More benefits to jobless can be attained in public service employment, Department of Labor : report to the Congress / by the Comptroller General of the United States. Washington : U. S. General Accounting Office, 1977. x, 99 p. ; 27 cm. Microfiche (neg.) NTIS 2 sheets. 11 x 15 cm. (PB 268 691) Covetitle.on t.p. "B-163922." "HRD-77-53." LC Card 77-601735 DDC 353.0082/56 19
1. Public service employment - United States. I. Title.
HD5724 .U629 1977a   **NYPL [*XME-9418]**

More can be done to achieve greater efficiency in contracting for medicare claims processing : report to the Congress / by the Comptroller General of the United States. [Washington] : U. S. General Accounting Office, 1979. ix, 220 p. : maps ; 27 cm. Cover title. "HRD-79-76." LC Card 79-602881 DDC 353.0082/56 19
1. Medicare - Claims administration. I. Title.
HD7102.U4 U55 1979a

More can be done to speed the entry of international travelers : report / by the Comptroller General of the United States. [Washington, D.C. : U. S. General Accounting Office, 1979) vi, 59 p. : ill. ; 27 cm. Cover title. "GGD-79-84." "B-114898." "August 30, 1979." LC Card 80-601083 DDC 353.0082/6591 19
1. Tourist trade - United States. 2. Visitors, Foreign - United States. I. Title.
G155.U6 U54 1979

More competence in foreign languages needed by Federal personnel working overseas : report

United States. General Accounting Office. (cont.)

/ by the Comptroller General of the United States. [Washington, D.C. : U. S. General Accounting Office], 1980. iv, 77 p. : forms ; 27 cm. Cover title. "ID-80-31." "B-198078." LC Card 80-602021 DDC 353.0013/23 19
1. *United States - Officials and employees in foreign countries - Appointment, qualifications, tenure, etc. 2. United States - Officials and employees in foreign countries - Foreign language competency. I. Title.*
JK736 .U54 1980

The multinational F-16 aircraft program : its progress and concerns : report to the Congress / by the Comptroller General of the United States. [Washington : U. S. General Accounting Office], 1979. v, 32 p. ; 27 cm. Cover title. "PSAD-79-63." "B-163058." LC Card 79-603054 DDC 358.4/183/0973 19
1. *Munitions - United States. 2. Munitions - International cooperation. 3. Foreign licensing agreements. 4. North Atlantic Treaty Organization. 5. F-16 (Fighter planes). I. Title.*
UF533 .U52 1979a

Multiple problems with the 1974 amendments to the Federal employees' compensation act : report to the Congress / by the Comptroller General of the United States. [Washington] : U. S. General Accounting Office, 1979. vi, 85 p. ; 27 cm. Cover title. "HRD-79-80." "B-157593." LC Card 79-602706 DDC 344.73/0217 19
1. *Workmen's compensation - United States. 2. United States - Officials and employees - Salaries, allowances, etc. I. Title.*
KF3626 .A85

The MX weapon system : issues and challenges : report to the Congress / by the Comptroller General of the United States. Washington, D.C. : General Accounting Office, 1981. iii, 43 p. : ill. ; 24 cm. Cover title. Feb. 17, 1981. "MASAD-81-1." "B-196893"--Prelim. p. Item 546-D (microfiche) Includes bibliographical references. LC Card 81-601213 DDC 358.1/74/0973 19
1. *MX (Weapons system). I. Title.*
UG1312.I2 U55 1981

Natural gas plan needed to provide greater protection for highpriority and critical uses : report to the Congress / by the Comptroller General of the United States. Washington, D.C. : U. S. General Accounting Office, 1981. v, 46 p. ; 27 cm. Cover title. Mar. 23, 1981. "EMD-81-27." "B-201827"--Prelim. p. Includes bibliographical references. LC Card 81-601431 DDC 333.8/233/0973 19
1. *Gas industry - Government policy - United States. 2. Gas, Natural - Law and legislation - United States. 3. Energy policy - United States. 4. Energy conservation - United States. I. Title.*
HD9581.U5 U54 1981

Need for more effective regulation of direct additives to food : report to the Congress / by the Comptroller General of the United States. Washington, D.C. : [U. S. General Accounting Office] : for sale by Supt. of Docs., U. S. Govt. Print. Off., [1980] vi, 42 p. ; 28 cm. Cover title. "August 14, 1980." "HRD-80-90." LC Card 80-603222 DDC 353.0077/82 19
1. *Food additives - Law and legislation - United States. I. Title.*
KF3879.P7 A836

New alien identification system : little help in stopping illegal aliens : report / by the Comptroller General of the United States. [Washington : U. S. General Accounting Office], 1979. iii, 40 p. ; 27 cm. Cover title. "GGD-79-44." "B-125051." LC Card 79-602501 DDC 353.0081/7 19
1. *Aliens, Illegal - United States. 2. Identification cards - Forgeries - United States. I. Title.*
JV6505 1979 .G45

A new approach is needed for weapon systems coproduction programs between the United States and its allies : report to the Congress / by the Comptroller General of the United States. [Washington, D.C. : U. S. General Accounting Office], 1979. v, 29 p. ; 27 cm. Cover title. "PSAD-79-24." "B-163058." LC Card 79-603384 DDC 355.8/2/0973 19
1. *Munitions - United States. 2. Munitions - International cooperation. 3. Foreign licensing agreements. I. Title.*
UF533 .U52 1979

New York City's efforts to improve its accounting systems, Department of the Treasury : report to the Congress / by the

Comptroller General of the United States. [Washington] : U. S. General Accounting Office, 1977. 29 p. ; 27 cm. Microfiche (neg.) 1 sheet. 11 x 15 cm. (PB 268 768) Cover title. Date of publication stamped on t.p. "FGMSD-77-15." "B-185522." LC Card 77-601736
1. *Finance, Public - New York (City) - Accounting. I. Title.*
HJ9777.N42 N48 1977   **NYPL [*XME-9396]**

No easy choice : NATO collaboration and the U. S. arms export control issue : report to the Congress / by the Comptroller General of the United States. Washington, D.C. : U. S. General Accounting Office, 1981. vii, 84 p. : charts ; 27 cm. Cover title. Jan. 19, 1981. "ID 81-18. "B-197529"--Prelim. p. Item 546-D (microfiche) LC Card 81-600892 DDC 382/.456234/0973 19
1. *Munitions - United States. 2. Export control - United States. 3. Arms control. I. Title. II. Title: NATO collaboration and the U. S. arms export control issue.*
HD9743.U6 U59 1981

Nuclear energy's dilemma : disposing of hazardous radioactive waste safely : report to the Congress / by the Comptroller General of the United States. [Washington] : U. S. General Accounting Office, 1977. xvii, 73 p. : ill. ; 27 cm. Cover title. "EMD-77-41." "B-164052." Publication date stamped on cover. LC Card 77-603908
1. *Radioactive waste disposal - United States. I. Title.*
TD898 .U54 1977

The Nuclear Regulatory Commission, more aggressive leadership needed : report to the Congress / by the Comptroller General of the United States. [Washington, D.C. : U. S. General Accounting Office, 1980] viii, 93 p. ; 27 cm. Cover title. "January 15, 1980." "EMD-80-17." "B-197263." LC Card 80-601236 DDC 353.0087/22 19
1. *United States. Nuclear Regulatory Commission. 2. Atomic power - Law and legislation - United States. I. Title.*
HD9698.U52 U55 1980a

Operational and support costs of the Navy's F/A-18 can be substantially reduced : report to the Congress / by the Comptroller General of the United States. Washington, D.C. : U. S. General Accounting Office, [1980] iii, 58 p., [1] leaf of plates : ill. ; 27 cm. Cover title. "LCD-80-65." Includes bibliographical references. LC Card 80-602400 DDC 358.4/183 19
1. *United States. Navy - Aviation. 2. United States. Navy - Aviation supplies and stores. 3. Hornet (Jet fighter plane). I. Title.*
VG93 .U54 1980

Policy conflict--energy, environmental, and materials : automotive fuel-economy standards' implications for materials : report to the Congress / by the Comptroller General of the United States. [Washington, D.C.] : U. S. General Accounting Office, [1980] iv, 38 p. : ill. ; 27 cm. Cover title. "February 5, 1980." "EMD-80-22." "B-118678." LC Card 80-602621 DDC 333.8/232 19
1. *Energy policy - United States. 2. Environmental policy - United States. 3. Materials. 4. Automobiles - Fuel consumption. I. Title.*
HD9502.U52 U55 1980

Policy needed to guide natural gas regulation on Federal lands : report to the Congress / by the Comptroller General of the United States. [Washington] : U. S. General Accounting Office, 1979. vii, 71 p. : ill. ; 27 cm. Cover title. "EMD-78-86." "B-178205." LC Card 79-602690 DDC 353.0087/23 19
1. *Gas, Natural - United States. 2. United States - Public lands. 3. Oil and gas leases - United States. I. Title.*
HD9581.U5 U54 1979

The problem of disposing of nuclear low-level waste : where do we go from here? : Report to the Congress / by the Comptroller General of the United States. [Washington, D.C.] : U. S. General Accounting Office, 1980. vii, 30 p. ; 27 cm. Cover title. "EMD-80-68." "B-194786." LC Card 80-601696 DDC 363.7/28 19
1. *Radioactive waste disposal - United States. 2. Waste disposal sites - United States. I. Title.*
TD898 .U54 1980

Problems in assessing the cancer risks of low-level ionizing radiation exposure : report to the Congress / by the Comptroller General of the United States. Washington, D.C. : U. S. General Accounting Office, 1981. 2 v. : ill. (1

col.) ; 27 cm. Cover title. Jan. 2, 1981. Item 546-D (microfiche) "EMD-81-1." "B-196841"--Vol. 1, Prelim. Includes bibliographical references. LC Card 81-600890 DDC 616.99/4071 19
1. *Tumors, Radiation-induced. 2. Ionizing radiation - Toxicology. 3. Ionizing radiation - Dose-response relationship. 4. Cancer research - United States. I. Title.*
RC268.55 .U54 1981

Procedures to adjust 1980 census counts have limitations : report / by the Comptroller General of the United States. Washington, D.C. : U. S. General Accounting Office, 1980. v, 37 p. ; 27 cm. Cover title. Dec. 24, 1980. "GGD-81-28." "N-201114"--Prelim. p. Includes bibliographical references. LC Card 81-600763 DDC 353.0081/9 19
1. *United States - Census, 20th, 1980. 2. United States. Bureau of the Census. 3. Census undercounts - United States. I. Title.*
HA201 1980

Prospects for cooperation and trade of energy resources between the United States and Canada : report to the Congress / by the Comptroller General of the United States. [Washington, D.C. : U. S. General Accounting Office, 1979] iii, 33 p. ; 23 cm. Cover title. "November 8, 1979." "ID-80-2." "B-178205." LC Card 80-600527 DDC 333.79/0971 19
1. *Power resources - Canada. 2. Economic policy - Canada. 3. United States - Foreign economic relations - Canada. 4. Canada - Foreign economic relations - United States. I. Title.*
HD9502.C32 U56 1979

Public Management Research Conference, Brookings Institution, 1979. Setting public management research agendas . [Washington, D.C.] [1980] iv, 95 p. : LC Card 80-602841 DDC 350/.00072/073 19
JF1338.A2 P85 1979

Public representation on boards and Blue Shield allowances : important relationship not found : report / by the Comptroller General of the United States. Washington, D.C. : U. S. General Accounting Office, 1980. v, 96 p. ; 27 cm. Cover title. "Dec. 31, 1980." "HRD-81-31." "B-201262"--Prelim. p. G.P.O. sales statement incorrect in publication. Includes bibliographical references. LC Card 80-600715 DDC 362.1/0681 19
1. *Blue Shield Association - Management. 2. Insurance, Health - United States - Management - Citizen participation. 3. Insurance, Health - United States - Cost control. 4. Medical fees - United States. I. Title.*
RA413.3.B5 U55 1980

Quality civil legal services for the poor and near poor are possible through improved productivity : report / by the Comptroller General of the United States. [Washington, D.C. : U. S. General Accounting Office, 1979] iii, 23 p. ; 27 cm. Cover title. "October 19, 1979." "FGMSD-79-46." "B-163762." LC Card 80-600508 DDC 362.5/8 19
1. *Legal aid - United States - Costs. 2. Prepaid legal services - United States - Costs. 3. Legal Services Corporation. I. Title.*
KF336 .A718

Radiation control programs provide limited protection : report / by the Comptroller General of the United States. [Washington, D.C. : U. S. General Accounting Office, 1979] iv, 62 p. ; 26 cm. Cover title. "HRD-80-25." "December 4, 1979." LC Card 80-601720 DDC 363.1/79 19
1. *Radiation - Safety measures. 2. Radiation - Safety measures - Government policy - United States. 3. Radiation - Safety regulations - United States. I. Title.*
RA569 .U4966 1979

Requirements for recurring reports to the Congress. 1976- Washington.
NYPL [*R-Econ. 77-323 & JLM 77-313]

Residential energy conservation outreach activities : a new federal approach needed : report to the Congress / by the Comptroller General of the United States. Washington, D.C. : U. S. General Accounting Office, 1981. iv, 31 p. ; 27 cm. Cover title. Feb. 11, 1981. "EMD-81-8." "B-200892"--Prelim. p. Item 546-D (microfiche) Includes bibliographical references. LC Card 81-601119 DDC 333.79/16/0973 19
1. *Dwellings - United States - Energy conservation. 2. Energy conservation - United States. 3. United States. Dept. of Energy. I. Title.*
HD7287.5 .U49 1981

Returning the mentally disabled to the community : government needs to do more, Department of Health, Education, and Welfare and other Federal agencies : report to the Congress / by the Comptroller General of the United States. [Washington : U. S. General Accounting Office], 1977. x, 254 p. ; 27 cm. Cover title. "HRD-76-152." "B-164031 (5)." Publication date stamped on cover. LC Card 77-601175
1. Community mental health services - United States. 2. Mental retardation services - United States. I. United States. Dept. of Health, Education, and Welfare. II. Title.
RA790.6 .U55 1977

Rising hospital costs can be restrained by regulating payments and improving management : report to the Congress / by the Comptroller General of the United States. Washington, D.C. : U. S. General Accounting Office, 1980. vi, 210 p. ; 28 cm. Cover title. Sept. 19, 1980. "HRD-80-72." "B-198503"--Prelim. G.P.O. sales statement incorrect in publication. 546-D (microfiche) LC Card 81-600511 DDC 362.1/1/0681 19
1. Hospitals - United States - Rates. 2. Hospitals - United States - Cost control. 3. Hospitals - United States - Cost of operation. 4. Medicare. I. Title.
RA981.A2 U53 1980a

A single agency needed to manage port-of-entry inspections--particularly at U. S. airports, Department of Justice, Department of the Treasury, Department of Agriculture, Department of Health, Education, and Welfare; report to the Congress by the Comptroller General of the Untied States. [Washington] 1973. 33 p. illus. 27 cm. Cover title. "B-114898." LC Card 73-602073 DDC 353.007 19
1. International airports - United States. 2. Ports of entry - United States. 3. Customs administration - United States. I. Title.
HE9797.5.U5 U52 1973

States are funding juvenile justice projects that conform to legislative objectives : report to the Subcommittee on State, Justice, Commerce, the Judiciary, and Related Agencies, Committee on Appropriations, United States Senate / by the Comptroller General. [Washington, D.C.] : U. S. General Accounting Office, 1980. iii, 129 p. ; 27 cm. Cover title. "GGD-80-40." "B-197161." LC Card 80-601282 DDC 353.9/38492 19
1. Juvenile corrections - United States - Finance - Case studies. 2. Grants-in-aid - United States - Case studies. I. United States. Congress. Senate. Committee on Appropriations. Subcommittee on Departments of State, Justice, and Commerce, the Judiciary, and Related Agencies. II. Title.
HV9104 .U52 1980

Statistical data on Department of Defense training of foreign military personnel : report to the chairman, Committee on Foreign Relations, United States Senate / by the Comptroller General of the United States. [Washington, D.C.] : U. S. General Accounting Office, 1980. 2, 107 p. ; 27 cm. Cover title. Chiefly tables. "FGMSD-80-48." LC Card 80-602018 DDC 355/.032/0973 19
1. Military education - United States - Statistics. 2. Military assistance, America - Statistics. I. United States. Congress. Senate. Committee on Foreign Relations. II. Title.
U408.3 .U54 1980

Suggested State auditing acts and constitutional amendments / by the Comptroller General of the United States. [Washington, D. C.] : General Accounting Office, 1974. 73 p. ; 23 cm. Cover title. LC Card 77-33784
1. Finance, Public - United States - States - Accounting. 2. Auditing. I. Title. **NYPL [JLE 80-3204]**

Two contracts for nuclear attack submarines modified by Public law 85-804--status as of December 23, 1978 : report to the Congress / by the Comptroller General of the United States. Washington, D.C. : U. S. General Accounting Office, 1979. ii, 16 p. ; 27 cm. Cover title. "PSAD-79-107." LC Card 79-603739 DDC 359.6/212/0973 19
1. United States. Navy - Procurement. 2. Defense contracts - United States - Auditing and inspection. 3. Atomic submarines. 4. Electric Boat Company. I. Title.
VC263 .U54 1979

U. S. coal development--promises, uncertainties : report to the Congress / by the Comptroller General of the United States.

[Washington] : U. S. General Accounting Office, 1977. ca. 350 p. in various pagings : ill. ; 27 cm. Cover title. "B-151071." Includes bibliography. LC Card 77-604230
1. Coal - United States. I. Title.
TN805 .A353 1977 **NYPL [JSF 81-165]**

U. S. fast breeder reactor program needs direction : report to the Congress / by the Comptroller General of the United States. Washington, D.C. : U. S. General Accounting Office, 1980. vii, 54 p. ; 27 cm. Cover title. Sept. 22, 1980. "EMD-80-81." "B-199272"--Prelim. p. G.P.O. sales statement incorrect in publication. Item 546-D (microfiche) Includes bibliographical references. LC Card 80-603953 DDC 353.0087/22 19
1. Breeder reactors. 2. United States. Dept. of Energy. I. Title.
TK9203.B7 U5 1980

U. S. ground troops in South Vietnam were in areas sprayed with herbicide orange : report / by the Comptroller General of the United States. [Washington, D.C.] : U. S. General Accounting Office, 1979. 9, 12 p. : ill. ; 27 cm. Cover title. "FPCD-80-23." "B-159451." LC Card 79-604309 DDC 363.1/79 19
1. Vietnamese Conflict, 1961-1975 - Chemistry. 2. Herbicides - War use. 3. Dichlorophenoxyacetic acid. 4. Trichlorophenoxyacetic acid. 5. Tetrachlorodibenzodioxin. I. Title.
DS559.8.C5 U54 1979

U. S. import restrictions : alternatives to present dairy programs, Department of Agriculture and other agencies : report to the Congress / by the Comptroller General of the United States. [Washington : U. S. General Accounting Office, 1976] v, 72 p. : ill. ; 27 cm. Cover title. "ID-76-44." "B-114824." Publication date stamped on cover. LC Card 77-600705
1. Dairy products - United States. 2. Import quotas - United States. I. Title.
HD9275.U6 U56 1976 **NYPL [JLF 81-320]**

U. S. nuclear non-proliferation policy: impact on exports and nuclear industry could not be determined : report to the Congress / by the Comptroller General of the United States. Washington, D.C. : U. S. General Accounting Office, 1980. vi, 78 p. ; 27 cm. Cover title. Sept. 23, 1980. "ID-80-42." "B-199974"--Prelim. p. G.P.O. sales statement incorrect in publication. Item 546-D (microfiche) LC Card 80-603954 DDC 382/.4562345119/0973 19
1. Atomic energy industries - United States. 2. Nuclear nonproliferation. I. Title.
HD9698.U52 U55 1980b

U. S. strategic petroleum reserve at a turning point : management of cost, oil supply problems, and future site development : report to the chairman, Subcommittee on Energy and Power, House Committee on Interstate and Foreign Commerce / by the Comptroller General of the United States. Washington, D.C. : U. S. General Accounting Office, 1980. iv p., 28 leaves : ill. ; 27 cm. Cover title. LC Card 80-601078 DDC 333.8/23211/0973 19
1. Petroleum - United States - Storage. 2. Strategic materials - United States - Storage. I. United States. Congress. House. Committee on Interstate and Foreign Commerce. Subcommittee on Energy and Power. II. Title.
TP692.5 .U624 1980

Unanswered questions on educating handicapped children in local public schools : report to the Congress / by the Comptroller General of the United States. Washington, D.C. : U. S. General Accounting Office, 1981. v, 122 p. : ill. ; 27 cm. Cover title. Feb. 5, 1981. "HRD-81-43." "B-199396"--Prelim. p. Item 546-D (microfiche) Includes bibliographical references. LC Card 81-601129 DDC 371.9/0973 19
1. Handicapped children - Education - United States. 2. Federal aid to education - United States. I. Title.
LC4031 .U5 1981

United States. Congress. Senate. Committee on Appropriations. Subcommittee on HUD-Independent Agencies. Management of HUD's multi-family properties, the Cliffton Terrace case . Washington , 1980. iii, 375, vi p. ; LC Card 80-602962 DDC 353.0086/5043/09753 19
KF26 .A6486 1979b

United States. Office of Federal Elections. Survey of election boards . Washington , 1974. 229 p. ; **NYPL [JLF 80-1622]**

Unresolved issues impede Federal debt collection efforts : a status report : report to the Congress / by the Comptroller General of the United States. [Washington, D.C. : U. S. General Accounting Office, 1980] iv, 17 p. ; 27 cm. Cover title. "January 15, 1980." "CD-80-1." LC Card 80-603132 DDC 353.0072/6 19
1. Government lending - United States. 2. Collecting of accounts - United States. 3. Accounts receivable - United States. 4. Debts, Public - United States. I. Title.
HG3729.U5 U55 1980

The value-added tax : what else should we know about it? : report to the Congress / by the Comptroller General of the United States. Washington, D.C. : U. S. General Accounting Office, 1981. vii, 44 p. ; 28 cm. Cover title. Mar. 3, 1981. "PAD-81-60." "B-202032"--Prelim. p. Item 546-D (microfiche) LC Card 81-601434 DDC 336.2/714/0973 19
1. Value-added tax - United States. I. Title.
HJ5715.U6 U63 1981

Water supply for urban areas : problems in meeting future demand : report to the Congress / by the Comptroller General of the United States. [Washington : U. S. General Accounting Office], 1979. iv, 50 p. ; 27 cm. Cover title. "CED-79-56." "B-114885." LC Card 79-602696 DDC 363.6/1/0973 19
1. Water-supply - United States. 2. Urbanization - United States. I. Title.
TD223 .U525 1979

Ways of providing a fairer share of Federal housing support to rural areas : report to the Congress / by the Comptroller General of the United States. [Washington, D.C. : U. S. General Accounting Office, 1980] v, 86 p. : ill. ; 27 cm. Cover title. "CED-80-1." "B-197850." "March 28, 1980." LC Card 80-601694 DDC 363.5/8 19
1. Housing, Rural - United States - Finance. 2. United States. Farmers Home Administration. 3. United States. Dept. of Housing and Urban Development. 4. United States. Veterans Administration. I. Title.
HD7289.U6 U55 1980

What foods should Americans eat? : Better information needed on nutritional quality of foods : report to the Congress / by the Comptroller General of the United States. [Washington, D.C. : U. S. General Accounting Office, 1980] iv, 92 p. ; 27 cm. Cover title. "CED-80-68." "B198160." "April 30, 1980." LC Card 80-602052 DDC 641.1/07/1073 19
1. Food. 2. Nutrition. 3. Nutrition policy - United States. I. Title.
TX353 .U495 1980

Why the formula for allocating community development block grant funds should be improved, Department of Housing and Urban Development / by the Comptroller General of the United States. [Washington : U. S. General Accounting Office, 1976] v, 50 p. ; 27 cm. Cover title. Publication date stamped on cover. "CED-77-2." "B-171630." LC Card 76-603691
1. Community development - United States - Finance. 2. Block grants - United States. 3. United States. Dept. of Housing and Urban Development. I. Title: Why the formula for allocating community development block grant funds ...
HN90.C6 U62 1976 **NYPL [JLF 81-401]**

Wider use of better computer software technology can improve management control and reduce costs : report to the Congress / by the Comptroller General of the United States. Washington, DC : U. S. General Accounting Office, [1980] iii, 57 p. ; 27 cm. Cover title. "April 29, 1980." "FGMSD-80-38." "B-115369." LC Card 80-602401 DDC 353/.075 19
1. Administrative agencies - United States - Management - Data processing. 2. United States - Executive departments - Management - Data processing. I. Title.
JK468.A8 U5 1980

Women in prison : inequitable treatment requires action : report to the Congress / by the Comptroller General of the United States. Washington, D.C. : U. S. General Accounting Office, 1980. v, 50 p. ; 57 cm. Cover title. Dec. 10, 1980. "GGD-81-6 "B-200741"--Prelim. p. Item 546-D (microfiche) Includes bibliographical references. LC Card 81-600746 DDC 365/.43/0973 19
1. Women prisoners - United States. 2. Sex discrimination against women - United States. I. Title.
HV9471 .U53 1980

UNITED STATES. GENERAL ACCOUNTING OFFICE.

A Glossary of terms used in the Federal budget process and related accounting, economic, and tax terms. Washington, D.C. [1981] p. cm.
    LC Card 81-607987   DDC 353.0072/2/0321 19
HJ2052 .G6 1981

UNITED STATES. GENERAL ACCOUNTING OFFICE - BIBLIOGRAPHY - PERIODICALS.

United States. General Accounting Office. GAO documents. Washington.   LC Card 79-643268   ***NYPL [JLM 80-801]***

United States. General Accounting Office. Office of Federal Elections. see United States. Office of Federal Elections.

United States. General Accounting Office. Office of Program Analysis.
Federal information sources & systems. 1976- Washington.
    NYPL [*R-Econ. 81-135 & JLM 81-123]

Federal program evaluations. 1976- Washington.
    NYPL [*R-Econ. 81-136 & JLM 81-130]

Requirements for recurring reports to the Congress. 1976- Washington.
    NYPL [*R-Econ. 77-323 & JLM 77-313]

United States. General Accounting Office. Program Analysis, Office of. see United States. General Accounting Office. Office of Program Analysis.

United States. General Services Administration.
The National Archives celebrates the bicentennial / General Services Administration. Washington, D. C. : The Administration, 1975. 15 p. ; 24 cm. Microfiche (neg.) 1 sheet. 11 x 15 cm. (NYPL FSN 35,118) Cover title.
    1. United States. National Archives and Records Service. I. Title.   ***NYPL [*XME-9265]***

UNITED STATES. GENERAL SERVICES ADMINISTRATION.

Report on the sale of Carson City silver dollars by General Services Administration .
Washington , 1981. v, 20 p. ;   LC Card 81-601279   DDC 737.4973 19
CJ1835 .R46

United States. Congress. House. Committee on Banking, Finance and Urban Affairs. Subcommittee on Consumer Affairs. Sale of Carson City silver dollars by the General Services Administration . Washington , 1980. iii, 65 p. ;   LC Card 80-603492   DDC 353.0082/2 19
KF27 .B535 1980d

United States. Congress. Senate. Committee on Governmental Affairs. Subcommittee on Federal Spending Practices and Open Government. Continued investigation into fraud and mismanagement in General Services Administration . Washington , 1980- v. :   LC Card 80-603087   DDC 364.1/63 19
KF26 .G6732 1979i

United States. Congress. Senate. Committee on the Judiciary. Subcommittee on Limitations of Contracted and Delegated Authority. Oversight of the General Services Administration . Washington , 1980. iii, 89 p. :   LC Card 80-604043   DDC 353.0071 19
KF26 .J857 1979a

United States. General Services Administration. Automated Data and Telecommunications Service. see United States. Automated Data and Telecommunications Service.

United States. General Services Administration. National Archives. see United States. National Archives.

United States. General Services Administration. National Archives and Records Service. see United States. National Archives and Records Service.

United States. General Services Administration. Office of Finance. Worldwide geographical location codes / [prepared by] General Services Administration, Office of Finance. [Washington, D.C.] : The Office : [for sale by the Supt. of Docs., U. S. Govt. Print. Off.], 1972. i, 356 p. ; 21 x 27 cm. Cover title.   LC Card 79-123353   DDC 910/.0148 19
1. Geographical location codes. I. Title.
G108.7 .U56 1972

United States. General Staff. see United States. Dept. of the Army. General Staff.

United States. Geodynamics Committee. Working Group 10b on Data Centers and Repositories. Directory of U. S. data repositories supporting the International Geodynamics Project / compiled by Working Group 10b on Data Centers and Repositories, U. S. Geodynamics Committee. Boulder, Colo. : World Data Center A for Solid Earth Geophysics, U. S. Dept. of Commerce, National Oceanic and Atmospheric Administration, Environmental Data and Information Service, 1978. v, 40 p. ; 28 cm. (Report - World Data Center A for Solid Earth Geophysics . SE-14) "August 1978." Includes bibliographical references and index.
    LC Card 79-109815   DDC 551 s 551/.072 19
1. Geodynamics - Information services. I. World Data Center A for Solid Earth Geophysics. II. Series: World Data Center A for Solid Earth Geophysics. Report , SE-14. III. Title.
QE500 .W67a no. 14 QE501

United States. Geological Survey.
Ackerman, D. J. Ground-water resources of Morton County, North Dakota /. Bismarck, N.D. , 1980. v, 51 p. :   LC Card 80-622722   DDC 553.7/9/09784 s 553.7/9/0978485 19
GB705.N9 A25 no. 27, pt. 3 GB1025.N9

Anna, Lawrence O. Ground-water data for Billings, Golden Valley, and Slope Counties, North Dakota /. Bismarck, N. D. , 1980. v, 241 p. :   LC Card 80-623714   DDC 553.7/9/09784 s 553.7/9/0978494 19
GB705.N9 A25 no. 29, pt. 2 GB1025.N9

Bedell, Douglas J. Irrigation in Michigan, 1977 /. [Lansing, Mich.] [1979] iii, 37 p. :   LC Card 80-623184   DDC 333.91/3/09774 19
S616.U6 B42

Bolke, E. L. Hydrologic reconnaissance of the Fish Springs Flat area, Tooele, Juab, and Millard counties, Utah /. [Salt Lake City] , 1978. iv, 30 p. :   LC Card 79-621928   DDC 553/.09792 s 553.7/9/097924 19
TA7 .U77 no. 64 GB705.U8

Bulletin .

(1470) Marchand, Denis E. Late Cenozoic stratigraphic units, northeastern San Joaquin Valley, California /. Washington , 1981. iv, 70 p. :   LC Card 80-607167   DDC 557.3 s 551.7/8 19
QE75 .B9 no. 1470 QE690

(1471) Reed, John Calvin, 1930- The river and the rocks . Washington , 1980. vii, 75 p. :   LC Card 80-600023   DDC 557.3 s 557.52 19
QE75 .B9 no. 1471 QE122.G7

(1478) Gard, Leonard Meade, 1923- The Pleistocene geology of Amchitka Island Aleutian Islands, Alaska /. Washington , 1980. iv, 38 p. :   LC Card 80-607888   DDC 557.3 s 551.7/92/097984 19
QE75 .B9 no. 1478 QE84.A38

(1495) Mineral resources of the Snow Mountain Wilderness study area, California /. Washington , 1981. p. cm.   LC Card 80-606866   DDC 557.3 s 553/.09794/3 19
QE75 .B9 no. 1495 TN24.C2

(1510) Lesure, Frank Gardner, 1927- Mineral resources of the Mill Creek, Mountain Lake, and Peters Mountain wilderness study areas, Craig and Giles Counties, Virginia, and Monroe County, West Virginia /. Washington , 1981. p. cm.   LC Card 80-607815   DDC 557.3 s 553/.09755/795 19
QE75 .B9 no. 1510 TN24.V8

(1512) Mineral-resource evaluation of the Round Lake Wilderness study area, Price and Vilas Counties, Wisconsin . Washington , 1980. p. cm.   LC Card 80-607793   DDC 557.3 s 553/.09715/23 19
QE75 .B9 no. 1512 TN24.W6

(1515) Lesure, Frank Gardner, 1927- Mineral resources of the Craggy Mountain wilderness study area and extension, Buncombe County, North Carolina /. Washington [1981] p. cm.   LC Card 80-607863   DDC 557.3 s 553/.09756/88 19
QE75 .B9 no. 1515 TN24.N8

(1517) Watt, Arthur Dwight, 1921- Index of generic names of fossil plants, 1974-1978 . Washington , 1981. p. cm.   LC Card 80-606811

    DDC 557.3 s 561/.014 19
QE75 .B9 no. 1517 QE903

Burkart, M. R. Ground-water data for Sheridan County, North Dakota /. Bismark, N.D. , 1980. iv, 302 p. :   LC Card 80-622724   DDC 557.84 s 553.7/9/0978476 19
GB705.N9 A25 no. 32, pt. 2 GB1025.N9

Catalog of selected offices of the Office of Surface Mining, Bureau of Land Management, and Geological Survey relating to coal, 1981. Reston, Va. : U. S. Geological Survey, 1980. p. cm. (Geological Survey circular ; 840) Bibliography: p.   LC Card 80-607870   DDC 557.3 s 353.0082/382 19
1. United States. Office of Surface Mining, Reclamation, and Enforcement - Directories. 2. United States. Bureau of Land Management - Directories. 3. United States. Geological Survey - Directories. I. Series: United States. Geological Survey. Circular , 840. II. Title.
QE75 .C5 no. 840 TN12

Channel conditions in the lower Toutle and Cowlitz rivers resulting from the mudflows of May 18, 1980 /. [Reston, Va.?] , Alexandria, Va. (604 S. Pickett Street, Alexandria, Va. 22304) , 1981. v, 16 p. :   LC Card 81-600040   DDC 557.3 s 551.48/9/0979788 19
QE75 .C5 no. 850-c QE599.U5

Circular .

(812) Structural framework, stratigraphy, and petroleum geology of the area of oil and gas lease Sale no. 49 on the U. S. Atlantic Continental Shelf and slope /. Arlington, Va. , 1980. v, 101 p. :   LC Card 80-600090   DDC 557.3 s 553.2/82/0974 19
QE75 .C5 no. 812 QE78.3

(814) Landa, Edward. Isolation of uranium mill tailings and their component radionuclides from the biosphere--some earth science perspectives /. Arlington, VA , 1980. iii, 32 p. :   LC Card 79-600148   DDC 622 s 621.48/38 19
QE75 .C5 no. 814 TD899.U73

(816) Hays, Walter W. Program and plans of the U. S. Geological Survey for producing information needed in national seismic hazards and risk assessment, fiscal years 1980-84 /. [Arlington, Va.] , 1979. iv, 40 p. :   LC Card 80-602831   DDC 557.3 s 363.3/495 19
QE75 .C5 no. 816 QE535.2.U6

(834) United States. Geological Survey. Worldwide directory of national earth-science agencies and related international organizations /. Reston, Va. , 1981. iv, 87 p. :   LC Card 80-607795   DDC 557.3 s 351.85/5 19
QE75 .C5 no. 834 QE61

(840) United States. Geological Survey. Catalog of selected offices of the Office of Surface Mining, Bureau of Land Management, and Geological Survey relating to coal, 1981. Reston, Va. , 1980. p. cm.   LC Card 80-607870   DDC 557.3 s 353.0082/382 19
QE75 .C5 no. 840 TN12

Coastal mapping handbook / Melvin Y. Ellis, editor ; cooperating organizations, U. S. Department of the Interior, Geological Survey [and] U. S. Department of Commerce, National Ocean Survey, Office of Coastal Zone Management. Washington : U. S. Govt. Print. Off. : for sale by the Supt. of Docs., U. S. Govt. Print. Off., 1978. vi, 199 p. : ill. ; 29 cm. Bibliography: p. 100-101.   LC Card 78-600000
1. Coasts - Maps - Handbooks, manuals, etc. 2. Geomorphological mapping - Handbooks, manuals, etc. I. Ellis, Melvin Y. II. National Ocean Survey. Office of Coastal Zone Management. III. Title.
GB452.2 .U54 1978
    NYPL [Map Div. 81-155]

Colorado, base map with highways / compiled, edited, and published by the Geological Survey. Rev. 1980. Reston, Va. : The Survey, 1980. 1 map : col. ; 93 x 127 cm. Relief shown by spot heights. Title in upper margin: State of Colorado. Title in upper right margin: Colorado. "Compiled in 1968."
    LC Card 81-691605
1. Colorado - Maps. I. Title: State of Colorado.
G4310 1980 .U5

Contributions to economic geology.

Cornwall, Henry Rowland, 1913- Chromite deposits in the Seiad Valley and Scott Bar

quadrangles, Siskiyou County, California /. Washington , 1981. iii, 17 p. : LC Card 80-606881 DDC 557.3 s 553.4/643 19
QE75 .B9 no. 1382-D TN490.C4

Crittenden, Max D. The Facer Formation, a new early Proterozoic unit in northern Utah /. [Reston, Va.?] , Washington, D.C. , 1980. iv, F28 p. : LC Card 80-600144 DDC 557.3 s 551.7/15/09792 19
QE75 .B9 no. 1482-F QE653

Dalsin, G. J. Water for industrial and agricultural development in Bolivar, Carroll, Leflore, Sunflower, and Tallahatchie Counties, Mississippi . Jackson, Miss. , 1978. 67 p. : LC Card 80-621547 DDC 553.7/09762/4 19
TD224.M65 D33

Dickerman, David C. Geohydrologic data for the Beaver-Pasquiset ground-water reservoir, Rhode Island . [Providence, R.I.] , 1977. 128 p. : LC Card 80-622751 DDC 553.7/9/09745 19
GB1025.R4 D53

Eissler, Benjamin B. Low-flow data and frequency analysis of streams in New York, excluding New York City and Long Island /. Albany, N.Y. , 1979. v, 176 p. : LC Card 80-622145 DDC 551.48/3/09747 19
GB1225.N7 E37

Eissler, Benjamin B. Summary and evaluation of crest-stage-gage data in New York. Albany, N. Y., 1974. 24 p. **NYPL [JSF 81-23]**

Evapotranspiration before and after clearing phreatophytes, Gila River Flood Plain, Graham County, Arizona /. Washington , 1981. p. cm. LC Card 81-607801 DDC 551.57/2 19
QC915.7.U5 E9

Fader, Stuart Wesley, 1919- Geohydrology of the Great Bend Prairie, southcentral Kansas /. Lawrence , 1978. 19 p. : LC Card 78-624087 DDC 553.7/9/097818 19
GB1025.K2 F3

Floods of May 1978 in southeastern Montana and northeastern Wyoming /. Washington [1981] p. cm. LC Card 81-607843 DDC 551.48/9/097863 19
GB1399.4.M9 F46

Forbes, Max J., 1930- Low-flow characteristics of Louisiana streams /. Baton Rouge, La. , 1980. iv, 95 p., [1] fold. leaf of plates : LC Card 80-623625 DDC 551.48/3/09763 19
GB1225.L6 F67

Geologic map of Colorado / by the United States Geological Survey in cooperation with Colorado State Geological Survey Board and Colorado Metal Mining Fund; compiled by W. S. Burbank ... [et al.] ; edited by George W. Stose. Denver : Colorado Geological Survey, [1975] 1 map : col. ; 93 x 127 cm. Scale 1:500,000. "Modified polyconic projection." Reprinted in 1975 from the 1935 ed. Includes "Index map of Colorado, showing principal sources of geologic data." Bibliography. LC Card 78-695857
1. Geology - Colorado - Maps. 2. Colorado - Maps. I. Burbank, Wilbur Swett, 1898-. II. Stose, George Willis, 1869-1960. III. Colorado. Geological Survey.
G4311.C5 1935 .U51
NYPL [Map Div. 81-3090]

Glancy, Patrick A. A reconnaissance of streamflow and fluvial sediment transport, Incline Village area, Lake Tahoe, Nevada . Carson City , 1976. v, 42 p. ; LC Card 80-623612 DDC 551.48/09793/57 19
GB1225.N3 G56

Hansen, Wallace R., 1920- Environmental geology of the Front Range Urban Corridor and vicinity, Colorado /. Washington , 1981. p. cm. LC Card 81-4280 DDC 624.1/51/097883 19
QE92.F7 H36

Harr, C. Albert. Ground-water resources and geology of Columbia County, Wisconsin /. Madison, Wis. , 1978. vii, 30 p. : LC Card 80-623464 DDC 557.75 s 553.7/9/0977581 19
QE179 .A33 no. 37 GB1025.W6

Harrill, J. R. Pumping and depletion of ground-water storage in Las Vegas Valley, Nevada, 1955-74 /. [Carson City] , 1976. vii, 70 p. : LC Card 80-623616 DDC 333.91/2/0979313 19
GB705.N3 A35 no. 44 TD224.N2

Harrill, J. R. Water-level changes associated with ground-water development in Las Vegas

Valley, Nevada, March 1975 to March 1976 /. Carson City , 1976 i.e. 1977. iv, 31 p. : LC Card 80-624035 DDC 553.7/9/0979313 19
GB1025.N4 H38

Hutchinson, Rickard D. Ground-water resources of Ramsey County, North Dakota /. Bismarck, N.D. , 1980. 36 p. : LC Card 80-622721 DDC 553.7/9/09784 s 553.7/9/0978436 19
GB705.N9 A25 no. 26, pt. 3 GB1025.N9

Johnstown-western Pennsylvania storm and floods of July 19-20, 1977 / by L. Ray Hoxit ... [et al.] ; report prepared jointly by the U. S. Geological Survey and the National Oceanic and Atmospheric Administration. Washington : U. S. Govt. Print. Off., 1981. p. cm. (Geological Survey professional paper ; 1211) Bibliography: p. LC Card 80-607777 DDC 551.48/9/0974877 19
1. Johnstown metropolitan area, Pa. - Storm, 1977. 2. Johnstown metropolitan area, Pa. - Flood, 1977. I. Hoxit, Lee R. II. United States. National Oceanic and Atmospheric Administration. III. Series: United States. Geological Survey. Professional paper, 1211. IV. Title.
QC943.5.U6 U53

Macpherson, George S. Outer Continental Shelf oil and gas activities in the mid-Atlantic and their onshore impacts . Reston, VA [1980] viii, 63 p. : LC Card 80-129968 DDC 338.2/728/0974 19
TN872.A5 M32

Montana. State Bureau of Mines and Geology. Ground water of the Fort Union coal region, eastern Montana /. Butte, Mont. , 1978. 47 p. : LC Card 79-621779 DDC 553.7/9/09786 19
GB1025.M9 M54 1978

THE NATIONAL ATLAS OF THE UNITED STATES OF AMERICA - INDEXES. United States. Geological Survey. [National atlas of the United States of America. Location index.] Location index. McLean, Va. , 1975. 309 p. ; LC Card 80-107197 DDC 912/.73
G1200 .U57 1975 Index

[National atlas of the United States of America. Location index] Location index. McLean, Va. : Documents Index, 1975. 309 p. ; 28 cm. At head of title: Guide to U. S. government maps. Reprinted from the National atlas of the United States of America published in 1970 by the U. S. Geological Survey. LC Card 80-107197 DDC 912/.73
1. United States - Maps. 2. United States. Geological Survey. The national atlas of the United States of America - Indexes. I. Title. II. Title: Guide to U. S. government maps.
G1200 .U57 1975 Index

Oregon, base map with highways and contours / compiled, edited, and published by the Geological Survey. Rev. 1979, highways corr. to 1979. Reston, Va. : The Survey, 1979. 1 map : col. ; 100 x 132 cm. "Advance copy, subject to corrections." Relief shown by contours and spot heights. Title in upper margin: State of Oregon. Title in upper right margin: Oregon. "Compiled in 1964-1965." LC Card 81-691602
1. Oregon - Maps. I. Title: State of Oregon.
G4290 1979 .U5

Organic substances in water /. Reston, Va. [1981] p. cm. LC Card 81-607886 DDC 557.3 s 628.1/61 19
QE75 .C5 no. 848-C GB855

Poppe, Barbara B. Directory of world seismograph stations. Boulder, Colo. , 1980- v. <1, pt. 1 > : LC Card 80-603927 DDC 551 s 551.2/2/2025 19
QE500 .W67a no. 25 QE540.U6

Professional paper.
(1048) Geology of the Apollo 16 area, Central Lunar Highlands . Washington , 1980. p. cm. LC Card 80-607170 DDC 559.9/1 19
QB592 .G47

(1049-C) Olson, Jerry Chipman, 1917- Alkalic rocks and resources of thorium and associated elements in the Powderhorn District, Gunnison County, Colorado /. Washington , 1980. p. cm. LC Card 80-607811 DDC 552/.1 19
QE462.A4 O44

(1062) Imlay, Ralph Willard, 1908- Jurassic paleobiogeography of the conterminous United States in its continental setting /.

Washington , 1980. v, 134 p. : LC Card 80-600017 DDC 560/.176 19
QE681 .I48

(1126-A-J) Shorter contributions to stratigraphy and structural geology, 1979. Washington , 1980. ca. 150 p. in various pagings : LC Card 80-600016 DDC 557.3 19
QE77 .S47

(1130) Matthai, Howard Frederick, 1913- Hydrologic and human aspects of the 1976-77 drought /. Washington , 1979. v, 84 p. : LC Card 79-600188 DDC 363.3/492 19
GB701 .M37

(1140) Schefter, John E. An economic analysis of selected strategies for dissolved-oxygen management, Chattahoochee River, Georgia /. Washington , 1980. iv, 26 p. : LC Card 80-600113 DDC 363.7/394 19
TD225.C35 S33

(1141) Research in the Geysers-Clear Lake geothermal area, northern California /. Washington , U. S. Govt. Print. Off. , 1981. viii, 259 p. : LC Card 80-607169 DDC 557.94 19
QE90.G45 R45

(1143) Spicer, Robert A., 1950- The sorting and deposition of allochthonous plant material in a modern environment at Silwood Lake, Silwood Park, Berkshire, England /. Washington , 1981. v, 77 p. : LC Card 80-607854 DDC 560/.1/78 19
QE931.3 .S64

(1151-D) Trace, Robert Denny, 1917- Stratigraphy and structure of the western Kentucky fluorspar district /. Washington , 1981. p. cm. LC Card 80-607000 DDC 551.7/009769 19
QE672 .T7

(1157) King, Philip Burke, 1903- Geology of the eastern part of the Marathon Basin, Texas /. Washington , 1980. iii, 40 p. : LC Card 80-607171 DDC 551.7/009764 19
QE168.M36 K49

(1159) Monroe, Watson Hiner, 1907- Some tropical landforms of Puerto Rico . Washington , 1980. iv, 39 p. : LC Card 80-600071 DDC 551.4/097295 19
GB428.5.P9 M66

(1163-A-D) Studies of the Permian Phosphoria formation and related rocks, Great Basin-Rocky Mountain region /. Washington , 1979. iii, 22 p. : LC Card 79-607907 DDC 551.7/5 19
QE674 .S78

(1170-A) Hietanen, Anna Martha, 1909- Geology west of the Melones Fault between the feather and Yuba Rivers /. Washington , 1980. p. cm. LC Card 80-607168 DDC 557.94/29 19
QE90.P57 H53

(1176) Irradiation of samples for $^{40}Ar/^{39}Ar$ dating using the Geological Survey TRIGA reactor /. Washington , 1980. p. cm. LC Card 80-607859 DDC 551.7/01 19
QE508 .I77

(1177-A) Dolan, Robert. Geographical analysis of Fenwick Island, Maryland, a Middle Atlantic coast barrier island /. Washington, D.C. , 1980. 24 p. : LC Card 79-600212 DDC 333.7 19
GB126.M3 D64

(1210) Colman, Steven M. Weathering rinds on andesitic and basaltic stones as a Quaternary age indicator, Western United States /. Washington , 1981. iv, 56 p. : LC Card 80-607840 DDC 551.7/9/0978 19
QE696 .C656

(1211) United States. Geological Survey. Johnstown-western Pennsylvania storm and floods of July 19-20, 1977 /. Washington , 1981. p. cm. LC Card 80-607777 DDC 551.48/9/0974877 19
QC943.5.U6 U53

(1218) Aeroradioactivity maps in heavy-mineral exploration--Charleston, South Carolina area /. Washington [1981] p. cm. LC Card 80-607879 DDC 622/.18 19
TN269 .A28

(1219) Pettinger, Lawrence R. Digital

classification of landsat data for vegetation and land cover mapping in the Blackfoot River watershed, southeastern Idaho . Washington , 1980. p. cm. LC Card 80-606816 DDC 581.9/028 19
QK63 .P47

(1220) Cater, Frederick William, 1912- Intrusive rocks of the Holden and Lucerne quadrangles, Washington . Washington , 1981. p. cm. LC Card 80-607844 DDC 551.8/8/0979759 19
QE611.5.U6 C37

(1222) Valentine, Page C. Upper Cretaceous subsurface stratigraphy and structure of coastal Georgia and South Carolina /. Washington, D.C. [1981] p. cm. LC Card 80-607868 DDC 551.7/7/09757 19
QE688 .V35

(1224) Ruppel, Edward Thompson, 1925- Cenozoic block uplifts in east-central Idaho and southeast Montana /. Washington , 1981. p. cm. LC Card 80-607875 DDC 551.7/8/09796 19
QE691 .R85

(831-D) Warner, Lawrence Allen, 1914- Geology of the eastern part of the Harold D. Roberts Tunnel, Colorado (Stations 690+00 to 1238+58) /. Washington , 1980. p. cm. LC Card 80-607839 DDC 624.1/92 19
QE92.H37 W37

(954-E) Feder, Gerald L. Geochemical survey of waters of Missouri . Washington , 1979. iv, 78 p. : LC Card 79-600129 DDC 551.48/09778 19
GB705.M8 F4

(954-G) Ebens, Richard J. Geochemistry of loess and carbonate residuum /. Washington , 1980. iii, 32 p. : LC Card 80-607796 DDC 553.6 19
QE499 .E23

Randich, Philip G., 1909- Ground-water resources of Grant and Sioux Counties, North Dakota /. Bismarck, N.D. , 1979. vi, 49 p. : LC Card 80-621090 DDC 553.7/9/09784 s 553.7/9/0978487 19
GB705.N9 A25 no. 24, pt. 3 TD224.N9

The river and the rocks. Reed, John Calvin, 1930- The river and the rocks : the geologic story of Great Falls and Potomac River Gorge / by John C. Reed, Jr., Robert S. Sigafoos, and George W. Fisher.[2d ed.]. Washington , 1980. vii, 75 p. : LC Card 80-600023 DDC 557.3 s 557.52 19
QE75 .B9 no. 1471 QE122.G7

Rush, F. Eugene. Geohydrology of Smith Valley, Nevada, with special reference to the water-use period, 1953-72 /. [Carson City] , 1976. 95 p. : LC Card 80-623615 DDC 553.7/09793/58 19
GB705.N3 R87

Schroer, C. V. Nevada streamflow characteristics /. Carson City [1978] 478 p. : LC Card 80-623614 DDC 551.48/3/09793 19
GB1225.N3 S37

Shorter contributions to general geology. Hietanen, Anna Martta, 1909- The Feather River area as a part of the Sierra Nevada suture system in California . Washington , 1981. p. cm. LC Card 80-606891 DDC 551.8/709794 19
QE90.F4 H5

Nokleberg, Warren J. Stratigraphy and structure of the Strawberry mine roof pendant, central Sierra Nevada, California /. Washington , 1980. p. cm. LC Card 80-607173 DDC 551.7/6/097944 19
QE675 .N64

Pomeroy, John S., 1929- Mass movement in two selected areas of western Washington County, Pennsylvania /. Washington , 1981. p. cm. LC Card 80-607835 DDC 551.3 19
QE599.U5 P65

Poore, Richard Z. Biostratigraphy and paleoecology of the upper Miocene (Messinian) and lower Pliocene (?) Cerro de Almendral section, Alermía Basin, southern Spain /. Washington , 1981. iii, 11 p., [2] leaves of plates : LC Card 80-607164 DDC 551.7/86/094681 19
QE694 .P67

State of New Jersey / compiled, edited, and published by the Geological Survey. Reston, Va. : The Survey, 1978. 1 map : col. ; 61 x 53 cm. Scale 1:500,000; 1 in. equals approx. 8 miles. Title in right lower margin: New Jersey, base map with highways and contours, shaded, relief. "Lambert conformal conic projection, standard parallels 33° and 45°." Relief shown by contours, spot heights, and shading. Date under population legend: 1974.
1. New Jersey - Maps. 2. New Jersey - Maps, Topographic.
G3810 1974 .U51

                              NYPL [Map Div. 80-3383]
State of Pennsylvania. Reston, Va., 1977. col. map 62 x 104 cm. Scale 1:500,000; 1 in. equals approx. 8 miles. Alternate title: Pennsylvania, base map with highways and contours, shaded relief. "Lambert conformal conic projection." Relief shown by contours, spot heights, and shading. In bottom margin: 1975.
1. Pennsylvania - Maps. 2. Pennsylvania - Maps, topographic.
G3820 1975 .U5   NYPL [Map Div. 80-3384]

State of Washington, base map with highway and contours / compiled, edited, and published by the Geological Survey. Rev. in 1976. Reston, Va. : The Survey, 1979. 1 map : col. ; 85 x 123 cm. "Advance copy subject to corrections." Relief shown by contours and spot heights. Title in upper right margin: Washington. "Compiled in 1961."
       LC Card 81-691603
1. Washington (State) - Maps.
G4280 1976 .U5

Summary of geologic and hydrologic information pertinent to tunneling in selected urban areas/ by E. M. Cushing and Rachel M. Barker; prepared by the U. S. Department of The Interior, Geological Survey. Washington: U. S. Dept. of Transportation, Office of the Secretary, Office of Systems Engineering, 1974. [370] p.: ill.; 28 cm. "DOT-TST; 75-49. "Administrative report prepared for and at the request of U. S. Dept. of Transportation ... Office of Systems Engineering." Includes bibliographical references.
1. Tunneling. I. Cushing, Elliot Morse, 1914-. II. Barker, Rachel M. III. United States. Dept. of Transportation. IV. Title. V. Title: Geologic and hydrologic information pertinent to tunneling in selected urban areas.   *NYPL [JSF 81-3]*

Summary of hydrologic testing in Tertiary limestone aquifer, Tenneco offshore exploratory well-Atlantic OCS, lease-block 427 (Jacksonville NH 17-5) / by Richard H. Johnston ... [et al.]. Washington : U. S. Govt. Print. Off. : for sale by the Supt. of Docs., U. S. Govt. Off., 1981. p. cm. (Geological Survey water-supply paper ; 2180) Bibliography: p. LC Card 80-606901 DDC 553/.79/09759 19
1. Aquifers - Atlantic coast (United States). 2. Saltwater encroachment - Atlantic coast (United States). 3. Tenneco Inc. I. Johnston, Richard H. II. Series: United States. Geological Survey. Water supply paper , 2180. III. Title.
GB1199.2 .U54 1981

Synthetic fuels development : earth-science considerations / U. S. Department of the Interior/Geological Survey ; edited by D. A. Rickert, W. J. Ulman, and E. R. Hampton. Washington, D.C. : U. S. Govt. Print. Off. : for sale by the Supt. of Docs., U. S. Govt. Print. Off., 1979. 45 p. : col. ill. ; 24 x 29 cm. Bibliography: p. 44-45. LC Card 79-600206 DDC 662/.66/0973 19
1. Synthetic fuels - United States. 2. Fossil fuels - United States. 3. Water-supply - United States. I. Rickert, David A., 1940-. II. Ulman, W. J. III. Hampton, E. R. IV. Title.
TP360 .U584 1979

Transportation map of ... Prepared by U. S. Geological Survey for the Office of Policy and Program Development, Federal Railroad Administration, United States Department of Transportation. [Washington, Office of Policy and Program Development ; available from Supt. of Docs., U. S. Govt. Print. Off.] 1975-76. 41 col. maps on sheets 43 x 56 cm. and 56 x 43 cm. Scales vary. Each sheet separately titled. "Transportation zone edition." Shows lines that may be subject to abandonment, those operating under rail service continuation provisions, and other operating lines. Includes "Index to railroads." Accompanied by text. [2] p.
1. United States - Maps. 2. Transportation - United States - Maps. 3. Railroads - United States - Maps. I.

United States. Federal Railroad Administration. Office of Policy and Program Development.
                              NYPL [Map Div. 80-3426]
Trimble, Stanley Wayne. Soil conservation, erosion, and sedimentation, Coon Creek Basin, Wisconsin /. Reston, Va. [1981] p. cm. LC Card 81-607057 DDC 631.4/5/0977554 19
S624.W5 T74

Trust Territory of the Pacific Islands. Ed. 1-DMATC. [Washington] 1975. col. map 64 x 128 cm. Scale 1:4,000,000. Depths shown by gradient tints. "Lambert conformal conic projection based on standard parallels 6° and 30°." "Compiled and edited for the Trust Territory of the Pacific Islands by the U. S. Geological Survey from charts compiled by the U. S. Air Force, U. S. Army, and various other sources to 1973." Includes location map. Insets: Yap Islands.--Rota.--Saipan and Tinian.--Truk Islands.--Palau Islands.--Kwajalein Atoll.--Ponape Islands.--Majuro and Arno Atolls. LC Card 78-691550
1. Pacific Islands (Ter.) - Maps. I. Title.
G9405 1973 .U5

United States. Soil Conservation Service. Adams County, Illinois /. Lincoln, Nebr. , 1980. 1 map : LC Card 81-691410
G4103.A2 1980 .U5

United States. Soil Conservation Service. Adams County, Iowa /. Lincoln, Nebr. , 1979. 1 map : LC Card 81-691195
G4153.A3 1979 .U5

United States. Soil Conservation Service. Adams County, Nebraska /. Lincoln, Neb. , 1980. 1 map : LC Card 81-691081
G4193.A2 1980 .U5

United States. Soil Conservation Service. Allegany County, Maryland /. Hyattsville, MD , 1979. 1 map : LC Card 81-690001
G3843.A4 1979 .U5

United States. Soil Conservation Service. Anne Arundel County, Maryland /. Lanham, MD , 1980. 1 map : LC Card 81-690011
G3843.A5 1977 .U5

United States. Soil Conservation Service. Baltimore County, Maryland /. Lanham, MD , 1980. 1 map : LC Card 81-690004
G3843.B3 1977 .U5

United States. Soil Conservation Service. Barbour County, West Virginia /. Lanham, MD , 1980. 1 map : LC Card 81-690038
G3893.B3 1975 .U5

United States. Soil Conservation Service. Berkeley County, West Virginia /. Lanham, MD , 1980. 1 map : LC Card 81-690039
G3893.B4 1976 .U5

United States. Soil Conservation Service. Black Hawk County, Iowa /. [Lincoln, Neb.] [1979?] 1 map : LC Card 81-691194
G4153.B4 1979 .U5

United States. Soil Conservation Service. Boone County, Illinois /. Lincoln, Nebr. , 1980. 1 map : LC Card 81-691411
G4103.B6 1980 .U5

United States. Soil Conservation Service. Boone County, Iowa /. Lincoln, Nebr. , 1979. 1 map : LC Card 81-691193
G4153.B5 1979 .U5

United States. Soil Conservation Service. Bremer County, Iowa /. Lincoln, Nebr. , 1979. 1 map : LC Card 81-691192
G4153.B6 1979 .U5

United States. Soil Conservation Service. Brevard County, Florida . Fort Worth, Tex. , 1980. 1 map : LC Card 81-690350
G3933.B7H5 1980 .U5

United States. Soil Conservation Service. Carroll County, Illinois /. Lincoln, Nebr. , 1980. 1 map : LC Card 81-691412
G4103.C25 1980 .U5

United States. Soil Conservation Service. Carroll County, Maryland /. Hyattsville, MD , 1979. 1 map : LC Card 81-690006
G3843.C4 1979 .U5

United States. Soil Conservation Service. Charles County, Maryland /. Hyattsville, MD , 1979. 1 map : LC Card 81-690003
G3843.C6 1979 .U5

United States. Soil Conservation Service. Chittenden County, Vermont /. Lanham, MD ,

1979. 1 map : LC Card 81-690027
G3753.C5 1972 .U5

United States. Soil Conservation Service. Clark County, Illinois /. Lincoln, Nebr. , 1980. 1 map : LC Card 81-691413
G4103.C5 1980 .U5

United States. Soil Conservation Service. Clay County, Iowa /. Lincoln, Nebr. , 1979. 1 map : LC Card 81-691191
G4153.C65 1979 .U5

United States. Soil Conservation Service. Clinton County, Iowa /. Lincoln, Nebr. , 1979. 1 map : LC Card 81-691190
G4153.C8 1979 .U5

United States. Soil Conservation Service. Cook County, Illinois /. Lincoln, Nebr. , 1980. 1 map : LC Card 81-691414
G4103.C7 1980 .U5

United States. Soil Conservation Service. Crawford County, Iowa /. [Lincoln, Neb.] [1979?] 1 map : LC Card 81-691189
G4153.C9 1979 .U5

United States. Soil Conservation Service. Dakota County, Nebraska /. Lincoln, Neb. , 1980. 1 map : LC Card 81-691080
G4193.D2 1980 .U5

United States. Soil Conservation Service. Dawson County, Nebraska /. Lincoln, Neb. , 1980. 1 map : LC Card 81-691079
G4193.D4 1980 .U5

United States. Soil Conservation Service. De Kalb County, Illinois /. Lincoln, Nebr. , 1980. 1 map : LC Card 81-691415
G4103.D4 1980 .U5

United States. Soil Conservation Service. Dorchester County, Maryland /. Hyattsville, MD , 1979. 1 map : LC Card 81-690010
G3843.D6 1979 .U5

United States. Soil Conservation Service. Douglas County, Illinois /. Lincoln, Nebr. , 1980. 1 map : LC Card 81-691416
G4103.D6 1980 .U5

United States. Soil Conservation Service. Du Page County, Illinois /. Lincoln, Nebr. , 1980. 1 map : LC Card 81-691417
G4103.D8 1980 .U5

United States. Soil Conservation Service. Edwards County, Illinois /. Lincoln, Nebr. , 1980. 1 map : LC Card 81-691418
G4103.E3 1980 .U5

United States. Soil Conservation Service. Fayette County, West Virginia /. Lanham, MD , 1980. 1 map : LC Card 81-690032
G3893.F3 1978 .U5

United States. Soil Conservation Service. Franklin County, Vermont /. Lanham, MD , 1980. 1 map : LC Card 81-690026
G3753.F7 1979 .U5

United States. Soil Conservation Service. Frederick County, Maryland /. Hyattsville, MD , 1979. 1 map : LC Card 81-690005
G3843.F7 1979 .U5

United States. Soil Conservation Service. Garrett County, Maryland /. Hyattsville, MD , 1979. 1 map : LC Card 81-690008
G3843.G3 1979 .U5

United States. Soil Conservation Service. Grand Isle County, Vermont /. Lanham, MD [1979?] 1 map : LC Card 81-690028
G3753.G7 1972 .U5

United States. Soil Conservation Service. Greenbrier County, West Virginia /. [Lanham, Md.] [1980] 1 map : LC Card 81-690015
G3893.G8 1973 .U5

United States. Soil Conservation Service. Greene County, Illinois /. Lincoln, Nebr. , 1980. 1 map : LC Card 81-691419
G4103.G7 1980 .U5

United States. Soil Conservation Service. Harford County, Maryland /. Lanham, MD , 1980. 1 map : LC Card 81-690012
G3843.H3 1978 .U5

United States. Soil Conservation Service. Harrison County, West Virginia /. Lanham, MD , 1980. 1 map : LC Card 81-690040
G3893.H5 1979 .U5

United States. Soil Conservation Service.

Howard County, Maryland /. Hyattsville, MD , 1979. 1 map : LC Card 81-690007
G3843.H6 1979 .U5

United States. Soil Conservation Service. Iowa County, Iowa /. [Lincoln, Neb.] [1979?] 1 map : LC Card 81-691188
G4153.I6 1979 .U5

United States. Soil Conservation Service. Jackson County, Illinois /. Lincoln, Nebr. , 1980. 1 map : LC Card 81-691420
G4103.J2 1980 .U5

United States. Soil Conservation Service. Jackson County, West Virginia /. Lanham, MD , 1980. 1 map : LC Card 81-690035
G3893.J2 1978 .U5

United States. Soil Conservation Service. Jefferson County, Iowa /. Lincoln, Nebr. , 1979. 1 map : LC Card 81-691187
G4153.J4 1979 .U5

United States. Soil Conservation Service. Jefferson County, West Virginia /. Lanham, MD , 1980. 1 map : LC Card 81-690037
G3893.J4 1977 .U5

United States. Soil Conservation Service. Kanawha County, West Virginia /. [Lanham, Md.] [1980] 1 map : LC Card 81-690016
G3893.K3 1979 .U5

United States. Soil Conservation Service. Kane County, Illinois /. Lincoln, Nebr. , 1980. 1 map : LC Card 81-691421
G4103.K2 1980 .U5

United States. Soil Conservation Service. Kendall County, Illinois /. Lincoln, Nebr. , 1980. 1 map : LC Card 81-691422
G4103.K4 1980 .U5

United States. Soil Conservation Service. Kennebec County, Maine /. Lanham, MD , 1980. 1 map : LC Card 81-690041
G3733.K4 1978 .U5

United States. Soil Conservation Service. La Salle County, Illinois /. Lincoln, Nebr. , 1980. 1 map : LC Card 81-691424
G4103.L3 1980 .U5

United States. Soil Conservation Service. Lake County, Illinois /. Lincoln, Nebr. , 1980. 1 map : LC Card 81-691423
G4103.L2 1980 .U5

United States. Soil Conservation Service. Lenawee County, Michigan /. Lincoln, Nebr. , 1980. 1 map : LC Card 81-691403
G4113.L4 1980 .U5

United States. Soil Conservation Service. Linn County, Iowa /. Lincoln, Nebr. , 1979. 1 map : LC Card 81-691186
G4153.L5 1979 .U5

United States. Soil Conservation Service. Litchfield County, Connecticut /. Lanham, MD , 1979. 1 map : LC Card 81-690029
G3783.L5 1976 .U5

United States. Soil Conservation Service. Logan County, Illinois /. Lincoln, Nebr. , 1980. 1 map : LC Card 81-691425
G4103.L7 1980 .U5

United States. Soil Conservation Service. Madison County, Iowa /. Lincoln, Nebr. , 1979. 1 map : LC Card 81-691185
G4153.M2 1979 .U5

United States. Soil Conservation Service. Manatee County, Florida, phosphate holdings /. Fort Worth, Tex. , 1980. 1 map : LC Card 81-690257
G3933.M3H5 1980 .U5

United States. Soil Conservation Service. Mason County, West Virginia /. Lanham, MD , 1980. 1 map : LC Card 81-690034
G3893.M36 1973 .U5

United States. Soil Conservation Service. Monroe County, West Virginia /. Lanham, MD , 1980. 1 map : LC Card 81-690033
G3893.M8 1978 .U5

United States. Soil Conservation Service. Montgomery County, Maryland /. Hyattsville, MD , 1979. 1 map : LC Card 81-690009
G3843.M6 1979 .U5

United States. Soil Conservation Service. New Castle County, Delaware /. Hyattsville, MD ,

1979. 1 map : LC Card 81-690013
G3833.N4 1979 .U5

United States. Soil Conservation Service. New Haven County, Connecticut /. Lanham, MD , 1979. 1 map : LC Card 81-690030
G3783.N3 1978 .U5

United States. Soil Conservation Service. Orange County, Vermont /. Lanham, MD , 1979. 1 map : LC Card 81-690025
G3753.O6 1977 .U5

United States. Soil Conservation Service. Preston County, West Virginia /. Lanham, MD , 1980. 1 map : LC Card 81-690036
G3893.P7 1978 .U5

United States. Soil Conservation Service. Richland County, Illinois /. Lincoln, Nebr. , 1980. 1 map : LC Card 81-691426
G4103.R5 1980 .U5

United States. Soil Conservation Service. Saline County, Kansas /. [Lincoln? Neb.] [1979?] 1 map : LC Card 81-691133
G4203.S2 1979 .U5

United States. Soil Conservation Service. Scotts Bluff County, Nebraska /. Lincoln, Neb. , 1980. 1 map : LC Card 81-691078
G4193.S4 1980 .U5

United States. Soil Conservation Service. Shelby County, Iowa /. [Lincoln, Neb.] [1979?] 1 map : LC Card 81-691184
G4153.S5 1979 .U5

United States. Soil Conservation Service. Stephenson County, Illinois /. Lincoln, Nebr. , 1980. 1 map : LC Card 81-691429
G4103.S9 1980 .U5

United States. Soil Conservation Service. Sussex County, Delaware /. Lanham, MD , 1980. 1 map : LC Card 81-690014
G3833.S8 1980 .U5

United States. Soil Conservation Service. Wabash County, Illinois /. Lincoln, Nebr. , 1980. 1 map : LC Card 81-691430
G4103.W2 1980 .U5

United States. Soil Conservation Service. Wayne County, Iowa /. Lincoln, Nebr. , 1979. 1 map : LC Card 81-691183
G4153.W35 1979 .U5

United States. Soil Conservation Service. Webster County, Iowa /. [Lincoln, Neb.] [1979?] 1 map : LC Card 81-691182
G4153.W4 1979 .U5

United States. Soil Conservation Service. Winneshiek County, Iowa /. Lincoln, Nebr. , 1979. 1 map : LC Card 81-691181
G4153.W6 1979 .U5

United States. Soil Conservation Service. Woodbury County, Iowa /. [Lincoln, Neb.] [1979?] 1 map : LC Card 81-691180
G4153.W7 1979 .U5

Utah. Division of Water Resources. Developing a state water plan; ground water conditions in Utah. [Salt Lake City]. **NYPL [JSP 81-11]**

Water power of the world : distribution of water power resources and developed water power by countries : atlas / prepared by the Department of the Interior, United States Geological Survey in cooperation with the Department of Agriculture, United States Forest Service. Washington : The Survey, 1918. [7] leaves of plates : [6] maps ; 76 cm. LC Card 80-675255 DDC 912/.133391
1. Water-power - Maps. 2. Water-supply - Maps. 3. Water resources development. I. United States. Forest Service. II. Title.
G1046.N33 U53 1918

Water resources of Boulder County, Colorado / by Dennis C. Hall ... [et al.] ; prepared by the U. S. Geological Survey in cooperation with the Colorado Geological Survey and the Boulder County Health Department. Denver, Colo. : Colorado Geological Survey, Dept. of Natural Resources, State of Colorado, 1980. vii, 97 p. : ill. (1 fold. in pocket) ; 28 cm. (Bulletin - Colorado Geological Survey . 42) Bibliography: p. 92-94. LC Card 80-623575 DDC 553.7/09788/63
19
1. Hydrology - Colorado - Boulder Co. 2. Water quality - Colorado - Boulder Co. I. Hall, Dennis C. II. Colorado. Geological Survey. III. Boulder Co., Colo. Health Dept. IV. Series: Colorado. Geological Survey.

Bulletin , 42. V. Title.
GB705.C6 U54 1980

Water supply paper .
(2061) Knott, J. M. Reconnaissance assessment of erosion and sedimentation in the Cañada de los Alamos basin, Los Angeles and Ventura Counties, California /. Washington, D.C. , 1980. iv, 26 p. : LC Card 80-600012   DDC 551.3/009794/93 19
QE571 .K54

(2080) Puckett, Larry J. Dendroclimatic estimates of a drought index for northern Virginia /. Washington, D.C. [1981] p. cm. LC Card 80-607816   DDC 551.6/4 19
QC929.D8 P84

(2081) McDonald, M. G. Hydraulic characteristics of an underdrained irrigation circle, Muskegon County wastewater disposal system, Michigan /. Reston, VA , 1981. p. cm. LC Card 80-607871   DDC 628.3/623 19
TD760 .M32

(2083) Bingham, Roy H., 1930- Low-flow characteristics of Alabama streams /. Washington , 1981. p. cm. LC Card 80-607849   DDC 551.48/3/09761 19
GB1225.A2 B56 1981

(2180) United States. Geological Survey. Summary of hydrologic testing in Tertiary limestone aquifer, Tenneco offshore exploratory well-Atlantic OCS, lease-block 427 (Jacksonville NH 17-5) /. Washington , 1981. p. cm. LC Card 80-606901   DDC 553/.79/09759 19
GB1199.2 .U54 1981

(2182) Trujillo, L. F. Trap-efficiency study, highland creek flood retarding reservoir near Kelseyville, California, water years 1966-77 /. Washington , 1980. p. cm. LC Card 80-606911   DDC 627/.44 19
TC424.C2 T78

Wells, Deborah K. Chemical analyses of water from the Minnelusa Formation and equivalents in the Powder River Basin and adjacent areas, northeastern Wyoming . Cheyenne [1979] iii, 27 p., [1] leaf of plates : LC Card 79-622599   DDC 553.7/9/097871 19
TD224.W8 W44

Wells, Frank C. Hydrology and water quality of the lower Mississippi River /. Baton Rouge, La. , 1980. vii, 83 p., [5] leaves of plates (4 fold.) : LC Card 80-622932   DDC 553.7/8/09763 19
TD223.4 .W44

West Virginia. Geological Survey. Land use statistics for West Virginia. [Morgantown, WV] [Reston, VA] , 1979- 1 v. ; LC Card 80-621498
QE177 .E58 no. 18, etc. HD211.W4
NYPL [JSK 75-100 no. 18-1]

Williams, James Frank, 1944- Simulated changes in water level in the Piney Point aquifer in Maryland /. [Baltimore, Md.] , 1979. v, 50 p. : LC Card 80-621643   DDC 557.52 s 551.49/09752/4 19
QE121 .A23 no. 31 GB1199.3.M3

Worldwide directory of national earth-science agencies and related international organizations / compiled by Wenonah E. Bergquist ... [et al.]. Reston, Va. : U. S. Geological Survey, 1981. iv, 87 p. : maps ; 26 cm. (Geological Survey circular ; 834) LC Card 80-607795   DDC 557.3 s 351.85/5 19
1. Earth sciences - Directories. 2. Geological surveys - Directories. I. Bergquist, Wenonah E. II. Series: United States. Geological Survey. Circular , 834. III. Title.
QE75 .C5 no. 834 QE61

Wyoming, base map / compiled, edited, and published by the Geological Survey. Rev. 1980. Reston, Va. : The Survey, 1980. 1 map ; 47 x 61 cm. Relief shown by spot heights. Title in upper margin: State of Wyoming. Title in upper right margin: Wyoming. "Compiled in 1964." LC Card 81-691604
1. Wyoming - Maps. I. Title: State of Wyoming.
G4260 1980 .U5

Wyoming, base map with highways / compiled, edited, and published by the Geological Survey. Rev. 1980, highways corr. to 1980. Reston, Va. : The Survey, 1980. 1 map : col. ; 94 x 121 cm. Relief shown by spot heights. Title in upper margin: State of Wyoming. Title in upper right margin: Wyoming. "Compiled in 1964." LC Card 81-691607

1. Wyoming - Maps. I. Title: State of Wyoming.
G4260 1980 .U51

Young, H. L. Ground-water resources and geology of Washington and Ozaukee Counties, Wisconsin /. [Washington] , Madison, Wis. [1980] iv, 37 p. : LC Card 80-622195 DDC 557.75 s 553.7/9/0977591 19
QE179 .A33 no. 38 GB1025.W6

UNITED STATES. GEOLOGICAL SURVEY.
U. S. Geological Survey research in radioactive waste disposal--fiscal year 1979 /. Reston, Va. , 1981. p. cm. LC Card 81-607990   DDC 557.3 s 621.48/38 19
QE75 .C5 no. 847 TD898

UNITED STATES. GEOLOGICAL SURVEY - DIRECTORIES.
United States. Geological Survey. Catalog of selected offices of the Office of Surface Mining, Bureau of Land Management, and Geological Survey relating to coal, 1981. Reston, Va. , 1980. p. cm. LC Card 80-607870   DDC 557.3 s 353.0082/382 19
QE75 .C5 no. 840 TN12

United States. Geological Survey. Library.
Catalog of the united States Geological Survey Library. Supplement. 1- ; 1972- Boston, G. K. Hall. Each supplement published in 4 or more vols. LC Card 76-646208
1. Geology - Bibliography - Catalogs - Collected works.
2. United States. Geological Survey. Library. I. Title.
NYPL [PT+ (U. S. Geological Survey. Library. Catalog. Supplement.)]

UNITED STATES. GEOLOGICAL SURVEY. LIBRARY.
United States. Geological Survey. Library. Catalog of the united States Geological Survey Library. Supplement. 1- ; 1972- Boston. LC Card 76-646208   ***NYPL [PT+ (U. S. Geological Survey. Library. Catalog. Supplement.)]***

United States. Geological Survey. National Cartographic Information Center. see National Cartographic Information Center.

United States. Geologicl Survey. United States. Soil Conservation Service. Rock Island County, Illinois /. Lincoln, Nebr. , 1980. 1 map : LC Card 81-691427
G4103.R6 1980 .U5

United States. Geology Survey. United States. Soil Conservation Service. Middlesex County, Connecticut /. Lanham, MD , 1979. 1 map : LC Card 81-690031
G3783.M5 1978 .U5

United States - Government. see United States - Politics and government.

United States - Government buildings. see United States - Public buildings.

United States - Government employees. see United States - Officials and employees.

United States. Government Operations, Committee on (House) see United States. Congress. House. Committee on Government Operations.

United States. Government Operations, Committee on (Senate) see United States. Congress. Senate. Committee on Government Operations.

United States government policy and supporting positions / Committee on Post Office and Civil Service, House of Representatives, 96th Congress, 2d session. Washington : U. S. G.P.O. : For sale by the Supt. of Docs. U. S. G.P.O., 1980. vii, 161 p. ; 31 cm. Spine title: U. S. government policy and supporting positions. At head of title: Committee print. Includes index. Tables. "November 18, 1980. S/N 052-070-05436-1 Item 1022 LC Card 80-604162   DDC 353.001/03 19
1. United States - Officials and employees. 2. Government executives - United States - Registers. I. United States. Congress. House. Committee on Post Office and Civil Service. II. Title: U. S. government policy and supporting positions.
JK661 .U54

UNITED STATES. GOVERNMENT PRINTING OFFICE.
Coopers & Lybrand. Analysis and evaluation of selected Government Printing Office operations /. Washington , 1979. xxii, 288, [40] p., [1] leaf of plates : LC Card 79-601679   DDC 070.5/95 19
Z232.U6 C76 1979

United States. Congress. House. Committee on Government Operations. Legislation and National Security Subcommittee. National publications act of 1980 . Washington , 1980. iii, 277 p. ; LC Card 80-603037   DDC 343.73/0998 19
KF27 .G6676 1980e

United States. Congress. House. Committee on Rules. Subcommittee on Rules of the House. The National Publications Act of 1980 . Washington , 1980. iii, 126 p. ; LC Card 81-600621   DDC 343.73/0998 347.303998 19
KF27 .R8737 1980

UNITED STATES. GOVERNMENT PRINTING OFFICE - PROCUREMENT.
United States. Congress. Senate. Committee on Governmental Affairs. Oversight of GPO's direct deal printing procurement system . Washington , 1980. iii, 94 p. : LC Card 80-602743   DDC 353.0081/9 19
KF26 .G67 1980c

UNITED STATES - GOVERNMENT PROPERTY.
United States. Congress. House. Committee on Public Works and Transportation. Subcommittee on Public Buildings and Grounds. Federal Protective Service . Washington , 1980. iv, 174 p. : LC Card 80-603638   DDC 344.73/052 347.30452 19
KF27 .P8964 1979d

UNITED STATES - GOVERNMENT PUBLICATIONS.
Schroyer, Helen Q. A guide to a course in government documents /. [Champaign, Ill.] , 1978. 51 p. ; LC Card 79-625738   DDC 026/.01573 19
Z688.G6 S36

United States. Congress. House. Committe on House Administration. National publications act of 1980 . Washington , 1980. iv, 179 p. ; LC Card 80-601753   DDC 343.73/0998 19
KF32 .H6 1980

United States. Congress. House. Committee on Rules. Subcommittee on Rules of the House. The National Publications Act of 1980 . Washington , 1980. iii, 126 p. ; LC Card 81-600621   DDC 343.73/0998 347.303998 19
KF27 .R8737 1980

UNITED STATES - GOVERNMENT PUBLICATIONS - BIBLIOGRAPHY.
Federal information sources & systems. 1976- Washington.
NYPL [*R-Econ. 81-135 & JLM 81-123]

Requirements for recurring reports to the Congress. 1976- Washington.
NYPL [*R-Econ. 77-323 & JLM 77-313]

UNITED STATES - GOVERNMENT PUBLICATIONS - BIBLIOGRAPHY - CATALOGS.
United States. National Technical Information Service. A directory of computer software & related technical reports, 1980. [Springfield, VA] , 1980. vii, 202, [108] p. ; LC Card 80-602222   DDC 001.64/25/029473 19
Z5644 .U54 1980 QA76.6

UNITED STATES - GOVERNMENT PUBLICATIONS - BIBLIOGRAPHY - UNION LISTS.
Olsgaard, John N. Union list of items received by South Dakota Federal document depositories /. Vermillion, S.D. , c1980. 107 leaves ; LC Card 80-623201   DDC 015.73 19
Z1223.Z7 O55 J83

UNITED STATES - GOVERNMENT PUBLICATIONS (STATE GOVERNMENTS) - DIRECTORIES.
Lane, Margaret T. State publications . Austin, TX , 1980. iii, 178, 4 p. ; LC Card 80-622732   DDC 027.5 19
Z1223.5.A1 L36

United States. Gross National Product Data Improvement, Advisory Committee on. see United States. Advisory Committee on Gross National Product Data Improvement.

United States. HEW Secretariat for IYC. see United States. Dept. of Health, Education, and Welfare. Secretariat for IYC.

United States Habitat and Human Settlements Foundation. Policies on human settlements in Bolivia : summary of the report / prepared by

GOVERNMENT PUBLICATIONS - U.S.: 1981

551   *United States. Health Resources Administration. Division of*

the Mission of the United Nations Habitat and Human Settlements Foundation, September 1976-March 1977. [New York : United Nations], 1977. 55 p. ; 30 cm. "Project no. GF/RBOL/76/06." LC Card 80-117387 DDC 363.5/8/0984 19
1. Housing policy - Bolivia. 2. Housing - Bolivia. 3. City planning - Bolivia. I. Title.
HD7322.A3 U54 1977

United States. Handicapped Individuals, Office for. see United States. Office for Handicapped Individuals.

United States. Handicapped, President's Committee on Employment of the. see United States. President's Committee on Employment of the Handicapped.

United States. Hazardous Materials, Office of. see United States. Office of Hazardous Materials.

United States. Health and Human Services, Dept. of. see United States. Dept. of Health and Human Services.

United States. Health Care Financing Administration.
The International classification of diseases, 9th revision, clinical modification . [Washington, D.C.?] , 1980. 3 v. ; LC Card 81-601048 DDC 616/.0012 19
RB115 .I49 1980

Muller, Charlotte Feldman, 1921- Study of physician reimbursement under medicare and medicaid /. [Washington] 1979- v. : LC Card 80-601289 DDC 338.4/33621/0973 19
R728.5 .M84

National monthly medicaid statistics. Sept. 1978- Baltimore.   *NYPL [Econ. Div.]*

UNITED STATES. HEALTH CARE FINANCING ADMINISTRATION.
United States. Congress. House. Committee on Ways and Means. Subcommmittee on Oversight. Efficacy of medicare research efforts . Washington , 1980. iii, 333 p. : LC Card 80-603309 DDC 353.0082/56 19
KF27 .W345 1980e

United States. Health Care Financing Administration. Office of Policy, Planning, and Research. Selected characteristics of the living arrangements and institutionalization of the elderly in the States, HEW regions, and the United States : 1970 census data / Office of Policy, Planning, and Research, Health Care Financing Administration. Washington : U. S. Govt. Print. Off., 1978. vii, 501 p. : maps ; 28 cm. LC Card 79-603338
1. Aged - United States - Dwellings - Statistics. 2. Aged - United States - States - Dwellings - Statistics. 3. Old age homes - United States - Statistics. 4. Old age homes - United States - States - Statistics. I. Title.
HD7287.8 .U5 1978   *NYPL [JLF 81-290]*

United States. Health Care Financing Administration. Office of Research, Demonstrations, and Statistics.
Health care financing research report. see Health care financing research report.

Professional standards review organization; program evaluation. [Washington] 28 cm. (Health care financing research report) Annual. "HHS publication no. (HCFA)"
1. Professional standards review organizations (Medicine) - United States - Evaluation - Periodicals. 2. Medical care - Evaluation - Periodicals. I. Title. II. Series.   *NYPL [JLM 81-32]*

United States Health Care Financing Administration. Research, Demonstrations, and Statistics, Office of. see United States. Health Care Financing Administration. Office of Research, Demonstrations, and Statistics.

United States. Health, Education, and Welfare, Dept. of. see United States. Dept. of Health, Education, and Welfare.

United States. Health Manpower, Bureau of. see United States. Health Resources Administration. Bureau of Health Manpower.

United States. Health, Office of the Assistant Secretary for. see United States. Office of the Assistant Secretary for Health.

United States. Health Planning, Bureau of. see United States. Bureau of Health Planning.

United States. Health Resources Administration.
Epidemiology as a fundamental science, its uses in health services planning, administration, and evaluation /. New York , 1976. xv, 235 p. : ISBN 0-19-502081-2 LC Card 75-46369
RA651 .E66   *NYPL [JLD 80-3374]*

Health planning information series. see Health planning information series.

Report on health personnel in the United States. [Washington, D.C.] : U. S. Dept. of Health, Education, and Welfare, Public Health Service, Health Resources Administration : [for sale by the Supt. of Docs., U. S. Govt. Print. Off., 1979] 38 p. ; 24 cm. (Health resources studies) DHEW publication ; no. (HRA) 80-651 "October 1979." LC Card 80-601525 DDC 331.12/3161/0973 19
1. Medical personnel - United States - Supply and demand. 2. Medical education policy - United States. I. Series. II. Series: United States. Dept. of Health, Education and Welfare. DHEW publication, no. (HRA) 80-651. III. Title.
RA410.7 .U555 1979

United States. Health Resources Administration. Associated Health Professions, Division of. see United States. Health Resources Administration. Division of Associated Health Professions.

United States. Health Resources Administration. Bureau of Health Manpower.
Budde, Norbert W. Characteristics of physicians . [Hyattsville, Md.] [1979- -v. ; LC Card 80-602072
RA410.7 .B82   *NYPL [JLM 81-120]*

Minorities & women in the health fields : applicants, students, and workers. [Hyattsville, Md.] : U. S. Dept. of Health, Education, and Welfare, Public Health Service, Health Resources Administration, Bureau of Health Manpower ; Washington : for sale by Supt. of Docs., U. S. Govt. Print. Off., 1978. xiii, 122 p. : graphs ; 27 cm. (DHEW publication no. (HRA) 79-22) "Prepared by Wilbertine P. Philpot." Updates and expands the ed. of 1975 by M. E. Altenderfer. "Health manpower references." Chiefly tables. LC Card 79-602970
1. Minorities in medicine - United States - Statistics. 2. Women in medicine - United States - Statistics. I. Philpot, Wilbertine P. II. Altenderfer, Marion E. Minorities & women in the health fields. III. Title.
R693 .U55 1978   *NYPL [JLF 81-355]*

A report on public and community health personnel : prepared for the Committee on Interstate and Foreign Commerce, House of Representatives and the Committee on Labor and Human Resources, United States Senate, as required by section 793 of the Public health service act. Washington, D.C. : U. S. Dept. of Health, Education, and Welfare, Public Health Service, Health Resources Administration, Bureau of Health Manpower : for sale by the Supt. of Docs., U. S. Govt. Print. Off., 1980. viii, 220 p. ; 28 cm. (DHEW publication ; no. (HRA) 80-43) "December 7, 1979." Includes bibliographical references. LC Card 80-602370 DDC 331.12/913621 19
1. Public health personnel - United States. 2. Public health personnel - Training of - United States. 3. Public health personnel - Supply and demand. I. United States. Congress. House. Committee on Interstate and Foreign Commerce. II. United States. Congress. Senate. Committee on Labor and Human Resources. III. Series: United States. Dept. of Health, Education and Welfare. DHEW publication, no. (HRA) 80-43. IV. Title.
RA440.9 .U47 1980

Sherman, Charles Roger, 1944- A second exploratory analysis of the relations among institutional variables . Washington , 1977. vi, 34 p. ; LC Card 77-153938
R745 .S493   *NYPL [*XME-9427]*

Supply of optometrists in the United States : current and future. [Bethesda? Md.] : U. S. Dept. of Health, Education, and Welfare, Public Health Service, Health Resources Administration, Bureau of Health Manpower, 1978. iii, 23 p. ; 26 cm. (DHEW publication ; no. (HRA) 79-18) "Health manpower references." "Prepared by Stuart Bernstein." "October 1978." LC Card 79-603959 DDC 331.12/916177/00973 19
1. Optometrists - United States - Supply and demand. 2. Optometrists - United States - Supply and demand - Statistics. I. Bernstein, Stuart. II. Series: United States. Dept. of Health, Education and Welfare. DHEW publication, no. (HRA) 79-18. III. Title.
RE959 .U54 1978

United States. Health Resources Administration. Bureau of Health Manpower. Division of Dentistry. see United States. Health Resources Administration. Division of Dentistry.

United States. Health Resources Administration. Bureau of Health Manpower. Division of Nursing. see United States. Health Resources Administration. Division of Nursing.

United States. Health Resources Administration. Bureau of Health Manpower. Program Management Information Systems Section.
United States. Health Resources Administration. Bureau of Health Manpower. Program Management Information Systems Branch.
Construction grants for education facilities, fiscal years 1965-77. [Washington] : U. S. Dept. of Health, Education, and Welfare, Public Health Service, Health Resources Administration, Bureau of Health Manpower, Program Management Information Systems Section, 1978. ix, 138 p. ; 21 x 28 cm. (DHEW publication (HRA) 78-28) "Health manpower references." LC Card 78-602588
1. Health occupations schools - United States - Design and construction - Finance - Statistics. 2. Federal aid to medical education - United States - Statistics. I. Title.
R745 .U485 1978b   *NYPL [JLF 81301]*

Health professions schools : selected enrollment data, 1970-71/1981-82. [Rockville, Md.] : U. S. Dept. of Health, Education, and Welfare, Public Health Service, Health Resources Administration, Bureau of Health Manpower, Program Management Information Systems Section, PELB, OBD, 1978. vi, 268, 72 p. : graphs ; 20 x 26 cm. (DHEW publication (HRA) 78-46) Tables. "Health manpower references." "Prepared in the Bureau of Health Manpower's Planning, Evaluation, and Legislation Branch by Mr. Samuel Rosenthal." LC Card 78-601985
1. Health professions schools - United States - Statistics. I. Rosenthal, Samuel. II. Title.
R745 .U485 1978   *NYPL [JLF 81-386]*

Health professions schools : selected BHM support data FY 1965-77. [Washington, D.C.] : U. S. Dept. of Health, Education, and Welfare, Public Health Service, Health Resources Administration, Bureau of Health Manpower, Program Management Information Systems Branch, OPD [1980] xii, 322 p. ; 23 x 15 cm. (DHEW publication ; no. (HRA) 80-15) "Health manpower references." LC Card 80-601769 DDC 610/.7/1173 19
1. Federal aid to medical education - United States - Statistics. 2. Federal aid to paramedical education - United States - Statistics. 3. Health occupations schools - United States - Finance - Statistics. I. Series: United States. Dept. of Health, Education, and Welfare. DHEW publication, no. (HRA) 80-15. II. Title.
R745 .U485 1980

United States. Health Resources Administration. Bureau of Health Planning. see United States. Bureau of Health Planning.

United States. Health Resources Administration. Bureau of Health Resources Development. see United States. Bureau of Health Resources Development.

United States. Health Resources Administration. Dentistry, Division of. see United States. Health Resources Administration. Division of Dentistry.

United States. Health Resources Administration. Division of Associated Health Professions.
Association of Schools of Public Health. Schools of public health . [Washington] , 1980. x, 149 p. ; LC Card 80-602404 DDC 614/.07/1173 19
RA440.7.U6 A87 1980

Hall, Thomas L. Schools of public health . [Washington] [1980] vi, 58 p. ; LC Card 80-602405 DDC 614/.07/1173 19
RA440.7.U6 H34

United States. Health Resources Administration. Division of Dentistry. Dental quality assurance : bibliography and abstracts. [Washington] : U. S. Dept. of Health, Education, and Welfare, Public Health Service, Health Resources Administration, Bureau of Health Manpower, Division of Dentistry, 1977. vii, 122 p. ; 27 cm. (DHEW publication (HRA) 78-47) At head of title: Health manpower references. Includes indexes. LC Card 78-603581
1. Dental care - Quality control - Abstracts. 2. Dental care - Evaluation - Abstracts. 3. Dental care - United States - Quality control - Abstracts. 4. Dental care - United States - Evaluation - Abstracts. I. Title. II. Title: Health manpower references.
RK52.8 .U54 1977   *NYPL [JLF 81-180]*

United States. Health Resources Administration. Division of Nursing. Nurse planning information series. 1- Hyattsville, Md., 1977-
   NYPL [JLM 81-4]

United States. Health Resources Administration. Health Manpower, Bureau of. see **United States. Health Resources Administration. Bureau of Health Manpower.**

United States. Health Resources Administration. National Center for Health Services Research. see **National Center for Health Services Research.**

United States. Health Resources Development, Bureau of. see **United States. Bureau of Health Resources Development.**

United States. Health Services Administration. National Symposium on Patients' Rights in Health Care, Washington, D.C., 1976. Proceedings /. [Rockville, Md.] [1976] ii, 91 p. ; LC Card 76-603462
KF3825.A75 N3 1976

United States. Health Services Administration. Bureau of Community Health Services. Directory of community health centers. [Washington?] 21 x 28 cm.
1. Community health services - United States - Directories. I. Title.   *NYPL [JLM 81-171]*

National Family and Reproductive Health Association. A directory of national health, education, and social service organizations concerned with youth /. Rockville, Md. [1979] 56 p. ; LC Card 80-601714
HV741 .N316 1979   *NYPL [JLF 80-1557]*

UNITED STATES. HEALTH SERVICES ADMINISTRATION. BUREAU OF COMMUNITY HEALTH SERVICES - BIBLIOGRAPHY - CATALOGS. United States. Health Services Administration. Bureau of Community Health Services. Publications of the Bureau of Community Health Services. [Rockville, Md.] , 1979. iii, 35 p. ; LC Card 79-603998
Z6673 .U435 1979 RA425

United States. Health Services Administration. Bureau of Community Health Services. Office for Maternal and Child Health. see **United States. Office for Maternal and Child Health.**

United States. Health Services Administration. Community Health Services, Bureau of. see **United States. Health Services Administration. Bureau of Community Health Services.**

United States. Health Services Administration. Office for Family Planning. Alan Guttmacher Institute. Family planning, contraception, voluntary sterilization, and abortion . Rockville, Md. , Washington, D.C. , 1978. xix, 380 p. ; LC Card 80-601267 DDC 344.73/048 19
KF3771.Z95 A37

United States. Health Services and Mental Health Administration. Center for Disease Control. see **Center for Disease Control.**

United States. Health Services and Mental Health Administration. Indian Health Service. see **United States. Indian Health Service.**

United States. Health Services and Mental Health Administration. National Center for Health Services Research and Development. see **National Center for Health Services Research and Development.**

United States. Health Services and Mental Health Administration. National Institute

for Occupational Safety and Health. see **National Institute for Occupational Safety and Health.**

United States. Health Services and Mental Health Administration. National Institute of Mental Health. see **United States. National Institute of Mental Health.**

United States. Heritage Conservation and Recreation Service. Economics of revitalization . [Washington, D.C.?] , 1981 i.e. 1980. 94 p. : LC Card 81-601655 DDC 352.94/18/0973 19
HT175 .E27

Eighmy, Jeffrey L. Archeomagnetism . [Washington, D.C.?] , 1980. 104 p. : LC Card 81-600714 DDC 930.1/028/5 19
CC79.M33 E37

HCRS publication.
(no. 19) White, Richard, 1924- Olmsted Park System, Jamaica Pond boathouse, Jamaica Plain, Massachusetts . Washington, D.C. , 1979. 51 p. : LC Card 80-601622 DDC 690/.587/0288 19
TH2401 .W47

(no. 20) Planning for exterior work on the First Parish Church, Portland, Maine, using photographs as project documentation. Washington, D.C. , 1979. 55 p. : LC Card 80-601858 DDC 726/.5/0288 19
NA5235.P7 P57

(no. 22) Historic American Engineering Record. Rehabilitation, Claremont 1978 . Washington, D.C. [1979] 89 p. : LC Card 80-601586 DDC 711/.5524 19
NA2793 .H57 1979a

(no. 46) Parrott, Charles A., 1944- Historic buildings access for the disabled . Washington, D.C. , 1980. p. cm. LC Card 80-23427 DDC 720/.42 19
NA2545.P5 P37

(no. 52) Smith, Baird M. Dampness in historic buildings . Washington, DC , 1980. p. cm. LC Card 80-607172 DDC 690/.24 19
TH9031 .S64

(no. 7) Morton, W. Brown. The Secretary of the Interior's standards for historic preservation projects . Washington, D.C. , 1979. vi, 46 p. ; LC Card 80-603172 DDC 720/.28/8 19
NA106 .M67

Historic American Engineering Record. Rehabilitation, Claremont 1978 . Washington, D.C. [1979] 89 p. : LC Card 80-601586 DDC 711/.5524 19
NA2793 .H57 1979a

National urban recreation study : executive report. [Washington : U. S. Dept. of the Interior, Heritage Conservation and Recreation Service : for sale by the Supt. of Docs., U. S. Govt. Print. Off., 1978] 184 p. : ill. ; 27 cm. Prepared by the Heritage Conservation and Recreation Service and the National Park Service. Bibliography: p. 180-184. LC Card 78-602420
1. Recreation - United States. 2. Open spaces - United States. 3. Recreational surveys - United States. I. United States. National Park Service. II. Title.
GV53 .U54 1978

A proposal for protection of eleven Alaskan rivers / U. S. Department of the Interior, Heritage Conservation and Recreation Service. [Washington, D.C.] : The Service, [1980] ca. 200 p. in various pagings : ill. ; 28 cm. Cover title. Includes a bibliography. LC Card 80-602406 DDC 333.78/45/09798 19
1. Nature conservation - Alaska. 2. Wild and scenic rivers - Alaska. I. Title.
QH76.5.A4 U56 1980

Urban waterfront revitalization . Washington [1980]. 2 v.   *NYPL [JLM 80-739]*

United States. Heritage Conservation and Recreation Service. Division of State Plans and Grants. New directions in rural preservation. Washington, D.C. [1980?] xi, 115 p. : LC Card 81-601043 DDC 307.7/2/0973 19
HN59 .N398

United States Heritage Conservation and Recreation Service. Northeast Regional Office. Final environmental impact statement: proposed comprehensive management plan for the Pinelands National Reserve /. Washington ,

1981. 1 v. of various pagings :
   NYPL [JSF 81-289]

United States. Heritage Conservation and Recreation Service. Technical Preservation Services Division. Guthrie, Susan. Main Street historic district, Van Buren, Arkansas . Washington, D.C. , 1980. 31 p. : LC Card 80-603967 DDC 363.6/9/0976735 19
F419.V36 G87

United States. High Altitude Pollution Program. Cutchis, Pythagoras. On the linkage of solar ultraviolet radiation to skin cancer . Washington, D.C. , 1978. xiv, 146, [13] p. : LC Card 79-602135 DDC 616.99/477071 19
RC280.S5 C83

United States. Higher and Continuing Education, Bureau of. see **United States. Bureau of Higher and Continuing Education.**

United States. Highway Administration. see **United States. Federal Highway Administration.**

United States. Historic Preservation, Advisory Council on. see **United States. Advisory Council on Historic Preservation.**

UNITED STATES - HISTORIOGRAPHY - ADDRESSES, ESSAYS, LECTURES. Bell, Whitfield Jenks. 'Towards a national spirit' . Boston , 1979. ix, 37 p. : LC Card 78-10486   *NYPL [*KSD 80-202 no. 6]*

UNITED STATES - HISTORY - COLONIAL PERIOD, CA. 1600-1775 - MANUSCRIPTS - UNION LISTS. Gehring, Charles. A guide to Dutch manuscripts relating to New Netherland in United States repositories /. Albany , 1978. ix, 138 p. ; LC Card 79-624962
Z1361.D8 G45 E184.D9 NYPL [IF 80-2567]

UNITED STATES - HISTORY - COLONIAL PERIOD, CA. 1600-1775 - SOURCES - ABSTRACTS. Wells, Carolyn M. Index and abstracts of colonial documents in the Eugene P. Watson Memorial Library /. Natchitoches, La. , c1980. xi, 75 p. ; LC Card 81-128135 DDC 016.9763/65 19
Z674.5.U52 L848

UNITED STATES - HISTORY - COLONIAL PERIOD, CA. 1600-1775 - SOURCES - BIBLIOGRAPHY - UNION LISTS. Gehring, Charles. A guide to Dutch manuscripts relating to New Netherland in United States repositories /. Albany , 1978. ix, 138 p. ; LC Card 79-624962
Z1361.D8 G45 E184.D9 NYPL [IF 80-2567]

UNITED STATES - HISTORY - REVOLUTION, 1775-1783 - BIBLIOGRAPHY - CATALOGS. Gephart, Ronald M. Revolutionary America, 1763-1789 . Washington , 1982. p. cm. ISBN 0-8444-0359-8 LC Card 80-606802 DDC 016.9733 19
Z1238 .G43 E208

UNITED STATES - HISTORY - REVOLUTION, 1775-1783 - CONGRESSES. Library of Congress Symposia on the American Revolution, 1st, 1972. The development of a revolutionary mentality. Washington, 1972. 157 p. ISBN 0-8444-0045-9 LC Card 72-11849
E204 .L53 1972   *NYPL [IG 80-3121]*

Library of Congress Symposia on the American Revolution, 3d, 1974. Leadership in the American Revolution . Washington , 1974. x, 135 p. ; ISBN 0-8444-0149-8 LC Card 74-30110
E204 .L53 1974   *NYPL [IG 80-3122]*

UNITED STATES - HISTORY - REVOLUTION, 1775-1783 - SOURCES - BIBLIOGRAPHY - CATALOGS. Gephart, Ronald M. Revolutionary America, 1763-1789 . Washington , 1982. p. cm. ISBN 0-8444-0359-8 LC Card 80-606802 DDC 016.9733 19
Z1238 .G43 E208

UNITED STATES - HISTORY - CONFEDERATION, 1783-1789 - BIBLIOGRAPHY - CATALOGS. Gephart, Ronald M. Revolutionary America, 1763-1789 . Washington , 1982. p. cm. ISBN 0-8444-0359-8 LC Card 80-606802 DDC

016.9733 19
Z1238 .G43 E208

UNITED STATES - HISTORY - CONFEDERATION, 1783-1789 - SOURCES - BIBLIOGRAPHY - CATALOGS.
Gephart, Ronald M. Revolutionary America, 1763-1789 . Washington , 1982. p. cm. ISBN 0-8444-0359-8 LC Card 80-606802 DDC 016.9733 19
Z1238 .G43 E208

UNITED STATES - HISTORY - WAR WITH MEXICO, 1845-1848 - PERSONAL NARRATIVES.
Gibson, George Rutledge, 1810 (ca.)-1885. Over the Chihuahua and Santa Fe trails, 1847-1848 . Albuquerque , c1981. p. cm. ISBN 0-8263-0590-3 : LC Card 81-52054 DDC 973.6/2 19
E411 .G44

United States - History - Civil War, 1861-1865 - Campaigns and battles - 1865 - Appomattox. see Appomattox Campaign, 1865.

UNITED STATES - HISTORY - CIVIL WAR, 1861-1865 - JOURNALISTS.
Marszalek, John F., 1939- Sherman's other war . Memphis, TN , c1981. p. cm. ISBN 0-87870-203-2 : LC Card 81-9483 DDC 973.7 19
E609 .M37

UNITED STATES - HISTORY - CIVIL WAR, 1861-1865 - NAVAL OPERATIONS - BIBLIOGRAPHY.
Watts, Gordon P. The Monitor . [Kure Beach, N.C.] [1978?] [87] leaves ; LC Card 80-622593 DDC 016.9737/52 19
Z1242 .W37 E595.M7

UNITED STATES - HISTORY - CIVIL WAR, 1861-1865 - PRISONERS AND PRISONS.
Paludan, Phillip S., 1938- Victims . Knoxville , c1981. p. cm. ISBN 0-87049-316-7 LC Card 81-2578 DDC 973.7/33 19
F262.M25 P34

UNITED STATES - HISTORY - WAR OF 1898.
Johnston, William Andrew, 1871- History up to date . New York , 1899. 257 p. :
NYPL [*ZH-665]

UNITED STATES - HISTORY - WAR OF 1898 - SOURCES.
Rudd, Robert R. [Papers] [1875-1906] 2 boxes.
NYPL [Sc Rare Mss-51]

United States. History and Historic Architecture, Office of. see United States. Office of History and Historic Architecture.

UNITED STATES - HISTORY - BIBLIOGRAPHY.
National Endowment for the Humanities. Bicentennial reading, viewing, listening . Chicago [1976] [12] p. ;   *NYPL [*ZH-661]*

United States - History, Economic. see United States - Economic conditions.

UNITED STATES - HISTORY, LOCAL.
Trementozzi, Miriam, 1947- Preservation, an ethic for planning /. Concord, N.H. , 1980. p. cm. LC Card 80-26731 DDC 363.6/9 19
E159 .T795

UNITED STATES - HISTORY, MILITARY.
Mickey, V. V. Defense of the United States /. Maxwell Air Force Base, Ala. , Washington, D.C. , 1976. vi, 144 p. : LC Card 80-602629 DDC 355/.00973 19
UA23 .M524

UNITED STATES - HISTORY, MILITARY - 20TH CENTURY - MANUSCRIPTS - MICROFORM CATALOGS.
Zeidlik, Hannah M. Catalog and index to historical manuscripts, 1940-1966 /. Washington, DC , 1979. 2 v. ; LC Card 79-604297 DDC 016.355/00973 19
Z1249.M5 Z44 E745

UNITED STATES - HISTORY, MILITARY - 20TH CENTURY - SOURCES - BIBLIOGRAPHY - MICROFORM CATALOGS.
Zeidlik, Hannah M. Catalog and index to historical manuscripts, 1940-1966 /. Washington, DC , 1979. 2 v. ; LC Card 79-604297 DDC 016.355/00973 19
Z1249.M5 Z44 E745

UNITED STATES - HISTORY, NAVAL.
Henson, Curtis T., 1931- Commissioners and commodores . University, Ala. , c1982. p. cm. ISBN 0-8173-0087-2 LC Card 81-10359 DDC 327.73051 19
E183.8.C5 H46

UNITED STATES - HISTORY, NAVAL - 20TH CENTURY.
Vlahos, Michael, 1951- The blue sword . Newport, R.I. , Washington, D.C. , 1980 [i.e. 1981] p. cm. LC Card 81-9654 DDC 359/.07/1173 19
V420 .V55

UNITED STATES - HISTORY, NAVAL - ARCHIVAL RESOURCES - UNITED STATES.
Allard, Dean C., 1933- U. S. naval history sources in the United States /. Washington, D.C. , 1979. vii, 235 p. : LC Card 79-600070 DDC 026/.359/00973 19
Z1249.N3 A48 E182

UNITED STATES - HISTORY, NAVAL - LIBRARY RESOURCES - UNITED STATES.
Allard, Dean C., 1933- U. S. naval history sources in the United States /. Washington, D.C. , 1979. vii, 235 p. : LC Card 79-600070 DDC 026/.359/00973 19
Z1249.N3 A48 E182

United States - History, Political. see United States - Politics and government.

UNITED STATES - HISTORY - SOCIETIES, ETC. - ADDRESSES, ESSAYS, LECTURES.
Bell, Whitfield Jenks. 'Towards a national spirit' . Boston , 1979. ix, 37 p. : LC Card 78-10486   *NYPL [*KSD 80-202 no. 6]*

UNITED STATES - HISTORY - SOURCES.
Noggle, Burl. Working with history . Baton Rouge , c1981. p. cm. ISBN 0-8071-0881-2 : LC Card 81-5789 DDC 976.3 19
F369 .N63

United States. National Historical Publications and Records Commission. Report to the President /. Washington , 1978 i.e. 1979. 59 p. ; LC Card 80-601723 DDC 027.5 19
E175.4 .U55 1978

United States. Home Loan Bank Board. see United States. Federal Home Loan Bank Board.

United States. House. see United States. Congress. House.

United States. House Administration, Committee on (House) see United States. Congress. House. Committee on House Administration.

United States. House of Representatives. see United States. Congress. House.

United States. Housing Administration. see United States. Federal Housing Administration.

United States. Housing and Development Dept. see United States. Dept. of Housing and Urban Development.

United States. Housing and Urban Development, Dept. of. see United States. Dept. of Housing and Urban Development.

United States. Human Development Services, Office of. see United States. Office of Human Development Services.

United States. Hydrographic Office.
United States. Hydrographic Office. Division of Chart Construction. Tracks for full powered steam vessels with the shortest navigable distances in nautical miles /. Washington , 1900. 1 map : LC Card 81-690532
G3201.P54 1900 .U5

United States. Hydrographic Office. Division of Chart Construction. Tracks for full powered steam vessels with the shortest navigable distances in nautical miles / Division of Chart Construction, G.W. Littlehales, hydrographic engineer in charge ; drawn by H.G. Brewer, A.C. Roberts, and G. Noetzel ; engraved by C.E. Birch, J.A. Waddey, and V.L. Ourdan. Washington : Hydrographic Office, 1900. 1 map : col. ; 60 x 112 cm. From the Sophonisba P. Breckinridge papers. Includes tables of "Speed per hour with daily and weekly distances in nautical miles" and "Reduction of knots or nautical miles to statue miles"

and distance charts. "No. 1262." LC Card 81-690532
1. Shipping - Maps. 2. World maps. I. Littlehales, G. W. (George Washington), 1860-1943. II. Breckinridge, Sophonisba Preston, 1866-1948. III. United States. Hydrographic Office. IV. Title.
G3201.P54 1900 .U5

United States - Immigration. see United States - Emigration and immigration.

United States. Immigration and Naturalization Service.
Basic guide to naturalization / United States Department of Justice, Immigration and Naturalization Service. [Washington, D.C.] : The Service : [for sale by the Supt. of Docs., U. S. Govt. Print. Off., 1980] 115 p. : ill. ; 28 cm. Cover title. "Form M 230." LC Card 80-603228 DDC 323.6/23/0973 19
1. Naturalization - United States. I. Title.
KF4819 .K316

Citizenship day and Constitution week guide. Washington. 24 cm. Title varies: 1965-71, Citizenship day and Constitution week bulletin. LC Card 75-645688
1. Citizenship - United States. - Handbooks, manuals, etc. I. Title.   *NYPL [L-10 9674]*

UNITED STATES. IMMIGRATION AND NATURALIZATION SERVICE.
United States. Congress. House. Committee on the Judiciary. Subcommittee on Immigration, Refugees, and International Law. Efficiency of the Immigration and Naturalization Service . Washington , 1980. iii, 88 p. ; LC Card 80-602462 DDC 353.0081/7 19
KF27 .J8645 1979d

United States. Congress. House. Committee on the Judiciary. Subcommittee on Immigration, Refugees, and International Law. Immigration and Naturalization Service oversight . Washington , 1980. iii, 230 p. ; LC Card 80-604019 DDC 353.0081/7 19
KF27 .J8645 1980b

UNITED STATES. IMMIGRATION AND NATURALIZATION SERVICE - HISTORY.
Masanz, Sharon D. History of the Immigration and Naturalizaton Service . Washington , 1980 [i.e. 1981] vii, 91 p. : LC Card 81-600999 DDC 353.0081/7 19
JV6483 .M3

United States. Immigration and Naturalization Service. Office of Planning, Evaluation, and Budgeting. North, Jeanette H. Immigration literature . Washington , 1979. viii, 89 p. ; LC Card 79-604155
JV6455 .N67   *NYPL [JLF 81-424]*

UNITED STATES. IMMIGRATION STATION, ELLIS ISLAND, N.Y. MAIN BUILDING.
Building Conservation Technology/The Ehrenkrantz Group. Mechanical and electrical rehabilitation, Main Building, Ellis Island, Statue of Liberty National Monument, New York . Denver, Colo. , 1980. 97 leaves, ca. 500 leaves of plates : LC Card 80-601419 DDC 725/.1 19
NA4510.I6 B84 1980a

UNITED STATES - IMPRINTS.
Colorado. State University, Fort Collins. Libraries. A bibliography of Colorado State University imprints in the Colorado State University Libraries /. Fort Collins, Colo. , 1980. iii, 201 p. ; LC Card 80-622676 DDC 027.7788 s 015.788 19
Z881.F72 P8 no. 20, 1980 Z5055.U5 AS36.C58

UNITED STATES IN ART - EXHIBITIONS.
Florida. University, Gainsville. University Gallery. The Gallery Guild, in cooperation with the University Gallery, are pleased to present the American scene . [Gainesville] [1979?] [63] p. : LC Card 79-623238 DDC 759.13/074/015979 19
ND212 .F563 1979

United States - Income tax. see Income tax - United States.

United States. Indian Affairs, Bureau of. see United States. Bureau of Indian Affairs.

United States. Indian Affairs Office. see United States. Bureau of Indian Affairs.

United States. Indian Bureau. see United States. Bureau of Indian Affairs.

United States. Indian Health Service.
Illness among Indians and Alaska Natives, 1970
to 1978. [Washington] : U. S. Dept. of Health,
Education, and Welfare, Public Health Service,
Health Services Administration, Indian Health
Service, Division of Resource Coordination,
Office of Program Statistics, [1979?]. viii, 58
p. ; 28 cm. (DHEW publication ; no. (HSA)
79-12040) Chiefly tables.   LC Card 80-601653   DDC
   312/.3/08997 19
1. Indians of North America - Diseases - Statistics. 2.
Eskimos - Alaska - Diseases - Statistics. 3.
Communicable diseases - United States - Statistics. 4.
United States - Statistics, Medical. I. Series: United
States. Dept. of Health, Education and Welfare. DHEW
publication, (HSA) 79-12040. II. Title.
RA408.I49 U54 1979a

**UNITED STATES. INDIAN HEALTH
SERVICE - APPROPRIATIONS AND
EXPENDITURES.**
United States. Congress. House. Committee on
Interior and Insular Affairs. Bureau of Indian
Affairs and Indian Health Service budget
request for fiscal year 1981 . Washington ,
1980. iii, 102 p. ;   LC Card 81-600586   DDC
   353.0072/23671497 19
KF27 .I5 1980b

**UNITED STATES. INDIAN HEALTH
SERVICE. BILLINGS AREA -
APPROPRIATIONS AND
EXPENDITURES.**
United States. Congress. Senate. Select
Committee on Indian Affairs. Investigation of
Indian Health Service expenditures, Billings
area . Washington , 1980. iv, 59 p. ;   LC Card
   81-600672   DDC 353.009/92 19
RA448.5.I5 U525 1980

United States Indian population and land, 1960.
United States. Bureau of Indian Affairs.
Washington , 1960. v, 32 p. ;   LC Card
   80-505734   DDC 929/.3/08997 19
E98.C3 U453 1960

United States. Indian Service. see **United States.
Bureau of Indian Affairs.**

UNITED STATES - INDUSTRIES.
United States. Bureau of Economic Analysis.
The detailed input-output structure of the U. S.
economy, 1972. [Washington, D.C.] , 1979- v. ;
   LC Card 80-601759   DDC 339.2/3/0973 19
HC106.7 .U537 1979

United States. Congress. House. Committee on
Armed Services. Capability of U. S. defense
industrial base . Washington , 1980 [i.e. 1981]
ii, 1796, ii p. :   LC Card 81-600988   DDC
   355.2/6/0973 19
KF27 .A7 1980K

**UNITED STATES - INDUSTRIES - CHARTS,
DIAGRAMS, ETC.**
Graphic summary of the 1977 economic
censuses. Washington, D.C. , 1981. 128 p. :
   LC Card 81-1210   DDC 330.973/0926 19
HC106.7 .G7

**UNITED STATES - INDUSTRIES -
CLASSIFICATION - INDEXES.**
United States. Bureau of the Census. 1980
census of population . Washington, D.C. , 1980.
xviii, 111, 157 p. ;   LC Card 80-24960   DDC
   331.7/0016 19
HC106.7 .U542 1980a

**UNITED STATES - INDUSTRIES - ENERGY
CONSERVATION.**
United States. Congress. House. Committee on
Science and Technology. Subcommittee on
Energy Development and Applications.
Industrial energy conservation . Washington ,
1979 [i.e. 1980] iii, 323 p. :   LC Card 80-602230
   DDC 333.79/16/0973 19
KF27 .S3934 1979l

**UNITED STATES - INDUSTRIES -
HISTORY - CONGRESSES.**
Yankee enterprise, the rise of the American
system of manufactures . Washington. D.C. ,
1981. p. cm.   ISBN 0-87474-631-0 LC Card
   81-607315   DDC 338.0973 19
HC103 .Y36

**UNITED STATES - INDUSTRIES -
INDEXES - PERIODICALS.**
United States. Bureau of the Census. 1980
census of population: alphabetical index of
industries and occupations. 1st- ed. Washington,

1980-
   *NYPL [*R-Econ. 81-164 & JLM 81-159]*
United States. Bureau of the Census. 1980
census of population: classified index of
industries and occupations. 1st- ed. Washington,
1980-
   *NYPL [*R-Econ. 81-163 & JLM 81-158]*

**UNITED STATES - INDUSTRIES -
STATISTICAL SERVICES.**
United States. Bureau of the Census. History of
the 1977 economic censuses. Washington,
D.C. , 1980. vii, 549 p. :   LC Card 80-607818
   DDC 330.973/0926 19
HF3001 .U54 1980

**UNITED STATES - INDUSTRIES -
STATISTICS.**
General report on industrial organization.
Washington , 1981. 468 p. in various pagings ;
   LC Card 81-607798   DDC 338.0973 s
   338.6/0973 19
HC106.7 .A14 ES77-1

Spencer, Vivian Eberle, 1907- Raw materials in
the United States economy, 1900-1977 /.
Washington, D.C. , 1980. 90 p. :   LC Card
   80-603173   DDC 333.7/0973 19
HF1052 .S63

**UNITED STATES - INDUSTRIES -
STATISTICS - COLLECTED WORKS.**
1977 enterprise statistics. Washington [1981] p.
cm.   LC Card 81-607012   DDC 338.0973 19
HC106.7 .A14

**United States. Industry and Trade
Administration.**
Country market survey. CMS 79-111; Feb.
1979- [Washington].   *NYPL [Econ. Div.]*

The motor vehicle leasing & rental industry :
trends and prospects. Washington : U. S. Dept.
of Commerce, Industry and Trade
Administration : for sale by the Supt. of Docs.,
U. S. Govt. Print. Off., 1979. iv, 48 p. ill. ; 24
cm. Prepared by Renee L. Gallop. Bibliography: p.
47-48.   LC Card 79-603251
1. Automobiles, Rental - United States. 2. Lease and
rental services - United States. I. Gallop, Renee L. II.
Title.
HD9710.U52 U488 1979
   NYPL [JLE 81-483]

Nelson, Theodore A. Measuring markets .
[Washington] , 1979. iv, 101 p. ;   LC Card
   79-603999
HF5415.3 .N44 1979

Overseas business reports. OBR 77-62- ; Nov.
1977- Washington. 26 cm. (International marketing
information series) Irregular. For earlier file, whose
numbering it continues, see: United States. Domestic
and International Business Administration. Overseas
business reports.
1. Commerce - Collected works. I. Title.
   NYPL [JLM 80-840]

**United States. Industry and Trade
Administration. Office of East-West Country
Affairs.** U. S.-Hungarian trade relations .
[Washington] , 1979. 64 p. ;   LC Card 80-600608
   DDC 341.7/54/0266439073 19
HF3097.5 .U54

**United States. Industry and Trade
Administration. Office of Producer Goods.** A
report on the U. S. semiconductor industry.
Washington, D.C. : U. S. Dept. of Commerce,
Industry and Trade Administration, Office of
Producer Goods : for sale by the Supt. of
Docs., U. S. Govt. Print. Off., 1979. ix, 132 p. ;
27 cm. "September 1979." Includes bibliographical
references.   LC Card 79-604001
1. Semiconductor industry - United States. I. Title. II.
Title: U. S. semiconductor industry.
HD9696.S43 U54 1979   NYPL [JLF 81-168]

**United States. Industry and Trade
Administration. Office of Textiles. Market
Analysis Division.**
**United States textiles production, imports &
import/production ratios for cotton, wool &
man-made fiber textiles & apparel.** United
States. International Trade Administration. U.
S. production, imports & import/production
ratios for cotton, wool & man-made fiber
textiles & apparel. [Washington] [1980] 143
p. ;   LC Card 80-602836   DDC 338.4/7677/00973
   19
HD9854 .U55 1980

**United States. Information Agency. Office of
Research and Assessment. Research Service.**
see **United States. Information Agency.
Research Service.**

**United States. Information Agency. Research
Service.** External information and cultural
relations programs : United Kingdom. -
[Washington] : 1973. 192 p. 27 cm.   LC Card
   77-88645
1. Great Britain - Diplomatic and consular service. 2.
Great Britain - Foreign relations - 1945-. I. Title.
   NYPL [JLF 80-402]

**United States. Institute for Applied Technology.
Technical Analysis Division.** City I player's
manual. Edited by John E. Moriarty.
Washington, D.C., 1973. viii, 142 p. illus.; 28
cm. (United States. National Bureau of Standards.
NBSIR. 73-110) "Final report." "March, 1973."
"Sponsored by National Technical Information Service."
1. Municipal government - United States - Simulation
methods. 2. Urban policy - United States - Simulation
methods. 3. City planning - Data processing. I.
Moriarty, John E., ed. II. United States. National
Technical Information Service. III. Title.
   NYPL [JLF 80-1361]

**United States. Institute for Basic Standards.
Cryogenics Division.**
Publications and services of the Cryogenics
Division, National Bureau of Standards,
1953-1977 / D.J. Frizén, J.R. Mendenhall.
[Washington] : The Bureau : for sale by the
Supt. of Docs., U. S. Govt. Print. Off., 1978.
vii, 101 p. : ill. ; 27 cm. (NBS technical note. 1005)
Includes indexes.   LC Card 79-602766   DDC 602/.18
   s 016.536/56 19
1. Low temperatures - Bibliography. 2. United States.
Institute for Basic Standards. Cryogenics Division -
Bibliography. I. Frizén, D. J. II. Mendenhall, J. R. III.
Series: United States. National Bureau of Standards.
Technical note , 1005.
QC100 .U5753 no. 1005 Z7144.L6 QC278

**UNITED STATES. INSTITUTE FOR BASIC
STANDARDS. CRYOGENICS DIVISION -
BIBLIOGRAPHY.**
United States. Institute for Basic Standards.
Cryogenics Division. Publications and services
of the Cryogenics Division, National Bureau of
Standards, 1953-1977 /. [Washington] , 1978.
vii, 101 p. :   LC Card 79-602766   DDC 602/.18 s
   016.536/56 19
QC100 .U5753 no. 1005 Z7144.L6 QC278

United States. Institute of Heraldry. see **United
States. Army. Institute of Heraldry.**

**UNITED STATES - INSULAR
POSSESSIONS.**
United States. Congress. House. Committee on
Interior and Insular Affairs. Subcommittee on
Pacific Affairs. Activities of the Subcommittee
on Pacific Affairs, including a report of the
oversight inspection trip of January 3 to 17,
1980 . Washington , 1981. v, 12 p. ;   LC Card
   81-601831   DDC 328.73/07652 19
F970 .U577 1981

United States. Congress. Senate. Committee on
Energy and Natural Resources. Omnibus
territorial legislation--1980 . Washington , 1980.
iv, 679 p. :   LC Card 81-600632   DDC 349.73
   347.3 19
KF26 .E55 1980l

United States. Congress. Senate. Committee on
Energy and Natural Resources. Pacific basin
energy . Washington , 1980. iv, 546 p. :   LC
   Card 81-600636   DDC 346.7304/679
   347.3064679 19
KF26 .E55 1980i

**United States. Interagency Archeological
Services Division.**
Scholars as contractors . Washington , 1979.
265 p. in various pagings :   LC Card 79-603005
CC136 .S36   *NYPL [JLF 81-76]*

Workshop on Management Techniques Applied
to Archeology, Texas Tech University, 1977.
Scholars as managers, or how can the managers
do it better . Washington , 1978. vii, 21 p., [2]
leaves of plates :   LC Card 79-602641
CC51 .W67 1977

**United States. Interagency Committee for the
International Year of the Child, Federal.** see
**United States. Federal Interagency
Committee for the International Year of the
Child.**

United States. Interagency Committee on Ocean Pollution Research, Development, and Monitoring.
Reports of the Subcommittees on National Needs and Problems; Data Collection, Storage, and Distribution; Monitoring; Research and Development. Springfield, Va. , 1979. v, 177 p. :   *NYPL [JSF 80-409]*

Reports of the Subcommittees on National Needs and Problems, Data Collection, Storage, and Distribution, Monitoring, Research and Development : working papers 2-5 for the Federal plan for ocean pollution research development, and monitoring, fiscal years, 1979-83. [Washington, D.C.] : Interagency Committee on Ocean Pollution Research, Development, and Monitoring, Federal Coordinating Council for Science, Engineering, and Technology ; Springfield, VA : sold by National Technical Information Service, 1979. v, 177 p. : ill. ; 27 cm. "August 1979." LC Card 80-601835   DDC 363.7/394 19
1. Marine pollution - Research - United States. 2. Oceanography and state - United States. I. Title.
GC511 .U625 1979

United States. Interagency Regulatory Liaison Group. Hazardous substances summary and full development plan / Interagency Regulatory Liaison Group. Washington : The Group, 1978. iv, 236 p. ; 28 cm. Bibliography: p. 217-220.   LC Card 79-602378   DDC 353.0077/2 19
1. Hazardous substances - Law and legislation - United States. 2. Chemicals - Law and legislation - United States. I. Title.
KF3958 .A854

United States. Interagency Task Force on Compensation and Liability for Releases of Hazardous Substances. The superfund concept : report of the Interagency Task Force on Compensation and Liability for Releases of Hazardous Substances. [Washington] : Land and Natural Resources Division, Dept. of Justice, 1979. 315 p. in various pagings: ill. ; 28 cm. Includes bibliographical references.   LC Card 79-603356   DDC 344.73/04632 19
1. Liability for environmental damages - United States. 2. Personal injuries - United States. 3. Hazardous substances - Law and legislation - United States. 4. Compensation (Law) - United States. 5. Insurance, Liability - United States. I. Title.
KF1298 .A83

United States. Interagency Task Force on Immigration Policy.
Staff report. Greenwood, Michael J. Staff report companion papers. [Washington] [1979] ii leaves, 234 p. :   LC Card 79-603817
JV6471 .G73   NYPL [JLF 81-360]

United States. Interagency Task Force on International Air Transportation Policy of the United States. International air transportation policy of the United States / [Interagency Task Force on International Air Transportation Policy of the United States ; co-chaired by Department of State, Department of Transportation]. [Washington] : The Task Force, [1976] ii, 31 p. ; 24 cm. "September 1976." LC Card 77-602263   DDC 387.7/068 19
1. Aeronautics and state - United States. 2. Aeronautics, Commercial. I. Title.
HE9803.A4 U55 1976

United States. Interagency Task Force on Product Liability. Interagency Task Force on Product Liability : final report. [Washington] : U. S. Dept. of Commerce 1977. 1 v. (various pagings); 28 cm. Microfiche (neg.) NTIS. 8 sheets. 11 x 15 cm. (PB 273 220)
1. Products liability - United States. 2. Insurance, Products liability - United States. I. Title.
*NYPL [*XME-9329]*

United States. Inter-Agency Task Force on Regulation Q, President's. see United States. President's Inter-Agency Task Force on Regulation Q.

United States. Interagency Task Force on Safety and Design Issue. Alaska natural gas transportation system: [safety and design] / Interagency Task Force on Safety and Design Issue; lead agency: Department of Transportation. [Washington]: The Task Force, 1977. 44 p. Microfiche (neg.) U. S. Govt. Print. Off. 1 sheet. 11 x 15 cm. (SUPT DOCS TD 1.2:AL 1 S)
1. Gas, Natural - Alaska - Pipe lines - Design and construction. 2. Gas, Natural - United States -

Transportation. I. United States. Dept. of Transportation. II. Title.   *NYPL [*XMQ-2151]*

United States. Interagency Task force on Thrift Institutions. The report of the Interagency Task Force on Thrift Institutions : Department of the Treasury, June 30, 1980, Committee on Banking, Finance, and Urban Affairs, House of Representatives, 96th Congress, second session. Washington : U. S. Govt. Print. Off. : for sale by the Supt. of Docs., U. S. Govt. Print. Off, 1980. viii, 267 p. ; 23 cm. "[Committee print 96-14]." LC Card 80-603280   DDC 332.2/0973 19
1. Building and loan associations - United States. 2. Savings-banks - United States. 3. Credit unions - United States. I. United States. Congress. House. Committee on Banking, Finance and Urban Affairs. II. Title. III. Title: Thrift institutions.
HG2151 .U53 1980

United States. Interagency Task Force on Workplace Safety and Health. First recommendations report / Interagency Task Force on Workplace Safety and Health. Rosslyn, Va. : The Task Force, 1978. 134 leaves in various foliations : diagrs. ; 27 cm. Includes bibliographical references.   LC Card 79-601550
1. Industrial safety - United States. 2. Industrial hygiene - United States. I. Title.
HD7654 .U546 1978   NYPL [JLF 81-183]

United States. Interdepartmental Workers' Compensation Task Force. Research report of the Interdepartmental Workers' Compensation Task Force. Washington, 1979. 1 v.;
NYPL [JLM 80-745]

United States. Intergovernmental Personnel Programs. EEO statistical report on employment in State and local government : employment security, health, and welfare programs : comparison of 1970, 1974, 1976. Washington : United States of America, Office of Personnel Management, Intergovernmental Personnel Programs, 1979. [52] p. ; 27 cm. Cover title. Prepared by D. R. Hunt. "IPP 152-101." LC Card 79-602132
1. Civil service - United States - States - Minority employment - Statistics. 2. Women in the civil service - United States - States - Statistics. 3. Local officials and employees - United States - Statistics. I. Hunt, Donald R. II. Title.
JK2480.M5 U56 1979   NYPL [JLF 81-448]

United States. Intergovernmental Relations, Advisory Commission on. see United States. Advisory Commission on Intergovernmental Relations.

United States. Interior and Insular Affairs, Committee on (House) see United States. Congress. House. Committee on Interior and Insular Affairs.

United States. Interior Dept. see United States. Dept. of the Interior.

United States. Internal Revenue Office. see United States. Internal Revenue Service.

United States. Internal Revenue Service. (Old Catalog form: United States. Internal Revenue Office)
Tax rates and tables for prior years. Rev. 5-80. [Washington, D.C.?] : Dept. of the Treasury, Internal Revenue Service, 1980. ii leaves, 89 p. : forms ; 28 cm. (Document. 6583) Cover title. LC Card 80-603934   DDC 343.7305/2 347.30352 19
1. Taxation - United States - Rates and tables. I. Series: Document (United States. Internal Revenue Service) , 6583. II. Title.
HJ2381 .U55 1980

UNITED STATES. INTERNAL REVENUE SERVICE.
United States. Congress. House. Commitee on Government Operations. Commerce, Consumer, and Monetary Affairs Subcommittee. IRS' administration of the tax laws (income information document matching) . Washington , 1980. iii, 178 p. :   LC Card 81-600661   DDC 353.00072/4 19
KF27 .G634 1980f

United States. Congress. House. Committee on Ways and Means. Subcommittee on Oversight. Taxpayer complaints . Washington , 1980. iii, 178 p. ;   LC Card 80-604065   DDC 353.0072/4 19
KF27 .W345 1980i

United States. Congress. Senate. Committee on

Finance. Subcommittee on Oversight of the Internal Revenue Service. IRS and nontax related criminal enforcement investigation . Washington , 1980. iii, 371 p. ;   LC Card 80-603799   DDC 345.73/0233 347.305233 19
KF26 .F56 1980

United States. Congress. Senate. Committee on Governmental Affairs. Subcommittee on Oversight of Government Management. Internal Revenue Service collection practices . Washington , 1980. v, 29 p. ;   LC Card 80-603867   DDC 353.0072/4 19
HD2346.U5 U515 1980a

United States. Congress. Senate. Committee on Governmental Affairs. Subcommittee on Oversight of Government Management. IRS summary collection policy impact on small business . Washington , 1980. iv, 415 p. ;   LC Card 80-603735   DDC 338.6/42/0973 19
KF26 .G676 1980a

United States. Congress. Senate. Select Committee on Small Business. Subcommittee on Taxation, Financing, and Investment. Procedural difficulties encountered by smaller business in dealing with the IRS . Washington , 1980. iii, 172 p. ;   LC Card 80-603483   DDC 353.0072/4 19
KF26.5 .S686 1980

UNITED STATES. INTERNAL REVENUE SERVICE - OFFICIALS AND EMPLOYEES.
United States. Congress. Senate. Committee on Finance. Nominations of John E. Chapoton, Roscoe L. Egger, Jr., and Paul C. Roberts . Washington , 1981. iii, 40 p. ;   LC Card 81-601602   DDC 353.2 19
KF26 .F5 1981d

United States. Internal Revenue Taxation, Joint Committee on. see United States. Congress. Joint Committee on Internal Revenue Taxation.

United States. International Commerce, Bureau of. see United States. Bureau of International Commerce.

United States. International Communication Agency.
Directory of resources for cultural and educational exchanges and international communication. [Washington]
NYPL [JLM 81-45]

UNITED STATES. INTERNATIONAL COMMUNICATION AGENCY - APPROPRIATIONS AND EXPENDITURES.
United States. Congress. House. Committee on Foreign Affairs. Subcommittee on International Operations. Authorizing appropriations for fiscal years 1980-81 for the Department of State, the International Communication Agency, and the Board for International Broadcasting . Washington , 1980. iii, 24 p. ;   LC Card 80-603032   DDC 353.0072/23689 19
KF27 .F647 1979d

United States. International Cooperation Administration. Regional Irrigation Practices Leadership Seminar : NESA Region, 1st, Izmir, 1956. First Regional Irrigation Practices Leadership Seminar, Izmir, Turkey. [Washington] [195-] 91 p. :   LC Card 80-500427   DDC 631.7/0956 19
S616.N34 R33 1956

United States. International Development Agency. see United States. Agency for International Development.

United States International Environmental Referral Center.
U. S. directory of environmental sources / United States International Environmental Referral Center, national focal point of the United Nations Environment Program/International Referral System. 2d ed. Washington : Office of Administration, Assistant Administrator for Planning & Management, U. S. Environmental Protection Agency, 1977. 193, 496, [49] p. ; 27 cm. Microfiche (neg.) NTIS. 8 sheets. 11 x 15 cm. (PB-274 110)"EPA-840-77-009." First ed. published in 1976 under title: United States directory of sources.   LC Card 77-604804
1. Environmental protection - United States - Directories. 2. United States International

Environmental Referral Center - Directories. I. Title.
*TD171 .U58 1977   NYPL [*XME-9521]*

**UNITED STATES INTERNATIONAL
ENVIRONMENTAL REFERRAL
CENTER - DIRECTORIES.**
United States International Environmental
Referral Center. U. S. directory of
environmental sources /. Washington , 1977.
193, 496, [49] p. ;   LC Card 77-604804
*TD171 .U58 1977   NYPL [*XME-9521]*

**United States. International Labor Affairs,
Bureau of.** see United States. Bureau of
International Labor Affairs.

**United States. International Labor Affairs, Office
of.** see United States. Bureau of
International Labor Affairs.

**United States. International Narcotics Matters,
Bureau of.** see United States. Bureau of
International Narcotics Matters.

**United States. International Trade
Administration.**
Attracting foreign investment to the United
States . Washington, D.C. , 1981. 254 p. in
various pagings :   LC Card 81-601726   DDC
332.6/732273 19
HG4910 .A82

European market : apparel. [Washington,
D.C.] : U. S. Dept. of Commerce, International
Trade Administration, [1980] 39 p. ; 28 cm.
(Global market survey) "March 1980." Cover title.   LC
Card 80-602369   DDC 382/.45687/0973 19
*1. Clothing trade - Europe. 2. Market surveys - Europe.
I. Title.*
HD9940.E82 U53 1980

U. S. production, imports & import/production
ratios for cotton, wool & man-made fiber
textiles & apparel. [Washington] : U. S. Dept.
of Commerce, International Trade
Administration, [1980] 143 p ; 28 cm. Cover
title. "Prepared by James Bennett and Laurie McKenna,
under the supervision of Leonard A. Mobley." Edition
of 1978 prepared by the Market Analysis Division,
Office of Textiles, U. S. Industry and Trade
Administration. "June 1980."   LC Card 80-602836
DDC 338.4/7677/00973 19
*1. Textile industry - United States - Statistics. 2.
Clothing trade - United States - Statistics. 3. Foreign
trade regulation - United States. I. Bennett, James,
1949-. II. McKenna, Laurie. III. United States. Industry
and Trade Administration. Office of Textiles. Market
Analysis Division. United States production, imports &
import/production ratios for cotton, wool & man-made
fiber textiles & apparel. IV. Title. V. Title: Cotton,
wool & man-made fiber textiles & apparel.*
HD9854 .U55 1980

**United States. International Trade
Administration. Office of Country
Marketing.** A business guide to the
Association of Southeast Asian Nations.
[Washington] : U. S. Dept. of Commerce,
International Trade Administration, Office of
Country Marketing : for sale by the Supt. of
Docs., U. S. Govt. Print. Off., 1980. 58 p. ; 24
cm. "March 1980." LC Card 80-601616   DDC
332.6/732259 19
*1. Market surveys - Asia, Southeastern. 2. Asia,
Southeastern - Industries. 3. Asia, Southeastern -
Commerce. 4. Asia, Southeastern - Description and
travel. I. Association of Southeast Asian Nations. II.
Title.*
HC441 .U54 1980

**United States. International Trade
Administration. Office of Export Planning
and Evaluation.** Maurer, Alan O. U. S. trade
opportunities resulting from the MTN
agreement on tariff cuts /. Washington, D.C. ,
1980. vi, 40 p. ;   LC Card 81-600731   DDC
382/.0973/04 19
HF3092.8 .M38

**United States. International Trade
Administration. Office of Trade Policy.** The
Tokyo round trade agreements: subsidies and
countervailing measures. v. 1- Washington,
1980-   *NYPL [Econ. Div.]*

United States. International Trade Commission.
Agreements being negotiated at the mutilateral
trade negotiations at Geneva--U. S.
International Trade Commission investigation
no. 332-101 : analysis of nontariff agreements :
a report / prepared at the request of the
Committee on Finance, United States Senate,

Subcommittee on International Trade, August
1979. Washington : U. S. Govt. Print. Off.,
1979. Washington : U. S. Govt. Print. Off., : for
sale by the Supt. of Docs., U. S. Govt. Print.
Off., 1979- v. ; 26 cm. (MTN studies . 6) At head
of title: 96th Congress, 1st session. Committee print CP
96-27. Title on spine: U. S. International Trade
Commission investigation. Principal author: J. M. Lang.
Includes bibliographical references. CONTENTS. - pt.
1. Introduction and overview of legal issues.
Subsidies/countervailing duty measures agreement.--pt.
2. Customs valuation agreement. Agreement on import
licensing procedures.--pt. 3. Agreement on technical
barriers to trade. Agreement on government
procurement.--pt. 4. International diary arrangement.
Agreement on trade in civil aircraft. Group
"Framework." Proof-gallon method of tax and duty
assessment.--pt. 5. Industry/agriculture sector analysis.
LC Card 79-603800   DDC 341.7/54/0265 19
*1. Tariff - Law and legislation. 2. Foreign trade
regulation. 3. Tariff - Law and legislation - United
States. 4. Foreign trade regulation - United States. I.
Lang, Jeffrey M. II. United States. Congress. Senate.
Committee on Finance. Subcommittee on International
Trade. III. Title. IV. Title: United States. International
Trade Commission investigation. V. Series.*
K4603 1973 .U54

Bicycle tires and tubes : report to the President
on investigation TA-201-33 under section 201
of the Trade act of 1974 / [Marion M. Jacks,
investigator ; John M. MacHatton, supervisory
investigator]. Washington, D.C. : United States
International Trade Commission, 1978. iv, 21,
131 p. ; 29 cm. (USITC publication. 910) Cover title.
Includes bibliographical references.   LC Card
79-601748   DDC 382/.4567832 19
*1. Tariff on bicycle tires - United States. 2. Tariff on
bicycle inner tubes - United States. I. Jacks, Marion M.
II. Series: United States. International Trade
Commission USITC publication, 910. III. Title.*
HF2651.B49 U58 1978

Certain carbon steel products from Belgium, the
Federal Republic of Germany, France, Italy,
Luxembourg, the Netherlands, and the United
Kingdom : determinations of the Commission in
investigations nos. 731-TA-18--24 (preliminary)
under the Tariff act of 1930, together with the
information obtained in the investigations.
Washington, D.C. : United States International
Trade Commission, [1980] vii, 71, 180 p. ; 28
cm. (USITC publication ; 1064) Cover title. "Prepared
principally by Quay Williams [and others]." Includes
bibliographical references.   LC Card 80-602282   DDC
382/.45672 19
*1. Tariff on steel - United States. I. Williams, Quay. II.
Series: United States. International Trade Commission
USITC publication, 1064. III. Title.*
HF2651.S76 U54 1980

Certain marine radar systems from the United
Kingdom : determination of no injury in
investigation no. AA1921-210 under the
Antidumping act, 1921, as amended, together
with the information obtained in the
investigation. Washington, D.C. : U. S.
International Trade Commission, [1979] ii, 8,
50 p. ; 29 cm. (USITC publication ; 1016) Cover
title. "November 1979."   LC Card 80-602625   DDC
382/.45623863 19
*1. Tariff on marine radar systems - United States. I.
Series: United States. International Trade Commission
USITC publication, 1016. II. Title.*
HF2651.M385 U58 1979

Color television receivers and subassemblies
thereof : report to the President on
investigation no. TA-203-6 under section 203 of
the Trade act of 1974. Washington, D.C. :
United States International Trade Commission,
[1980] 144 p. in various pagings : graphs ; 28
cm. (USITC publication ; 1068) Cover title. "May
1980." Includes bibliographical references. LC Card
80-602557   DDC 382/.4562138804/0973 19
*1. Television industry - United States. 2. Color
television - Receivers and reception. 3. Import quotas -
United States. 4. Television industry - Asia. I. Series:
United States. International Trade Commission USITC
publication, 1068. II. Title.*
HD9696.T463 U68 1980

Cook, C. Lee. Textiles and textile products of
cotton from Pakistan . Washington, D.C.
[1980] vi, 56, 105 p. ;   LC Card 80-602856   DDC
382/.4567721/0973 19
HD9856 .C66

Greer, T. Vernon. Sugar from Belgium, France,
and West Germany . Washington , 1979. 21, 62

p. ;   LC Card 79-602639   DDC 382/.4136/0973 19
HF2651.S8 U54

Leather wearing apparel from Uruguay :
determination of the Commission in
investigation no. 701-TA-68 (preliminary) under
the Tariff Act of 1930, together with the
information obtained in the investigation.
Washington, D.C. : United States International
Trade Commission, 1980. ii, 9, 47 p. ; 28 cm.
(USITC publication. 1114) Cover title. Prepared
principally by Patrick J. Magrath, Jackie Worrell;
assisted by Jeffrey Neeley, Andrew V. Valiunas.
"December 1980." Includes bibliographical references.
LC Card 81-600775   DDC 382/.4568522/0973
19
*1. Tariff on leather garments - United States. 2. Leather
industry and trade - United States. 3. Leather industry
and trade - Uruguay. I. Magrath, Patrick J. II. Worrell,
Jackie. III. Neeley, Jeffrey. IV. Valiunas, Andrew. V.
Title.*
HF2651.L45 U64 1980

Magrath, Patrick J. Leather wearing apparel .
Washington, D.C. [1980] iii, 15, 51 p. :   LC
Card 80-602342   DDC 382/.456852/0973 19
HF2651.L45 U496

Mushrooms, report to the President on
investigation no. TA-201-29, under section 201
of the Trade act of 1974. Washington, D.C. :
U. S. International Trade Commission, [1980]
iv, 27, 78 p. : graphs ; 28 cm. (USITC publication.
1089) Cover title. "August 1980." Includes
bibliographical references.   LC Card 80-603136   DDC
382/.4158/0973 19
*1. Tariff on mushrooms - United States. I. Series:
United States. International Trade Commission USITC
publication, 1089. II. Title.*
HF2651.M83 U53 1980

Pipes and tubes of iron or steel from Japan :
determination of the Commission in
Investigation no. 731-TA-15 (preliminary) under
the Tariff act of 1930, together with the
information obtained in the investigation.
Washington, D.C. : United States International
Trade Commission, [1980] ii, 29, 37 p. ; 29 cm.
(USITC publication ; 1058) Cover title. Prepared by W.
Schechter and J. J. Lukes. "April 1980."   LC Card
80-602337   DDC 382/.4567283/0973 19
*1. Tariff on steel pipe - United States. 2. Tariff on steel
tubes - United States. 3. Tariff on iron pipe - United
States. 4. United States - Commerce - Japan. 5. Japan -
Commerce - United States. I. Schechter, William I. II.
Lukes, James J. III. Series: United States. International
Trade Commission USITC publication, 1058. IV. Title.*
HF2651.S76 U54 1980a

Portable electric typewriters from Japan :
determination of material injury in investigation
no. 731-TA-12 (final) under Section 735(b) of
the Tariff act of 1930. Washington, D.C. : U. S.
International Trade Commission, [1980] ii, 15,
A-41 p. ; 29 cm. (USITC publication ; 1062) Cover
title. "May 1980."   LC Card 80-602317   DDC
382/.4568161 19
*1. Typewriter industry - Japan. I. Series: United States.
International Trade Commission USITC publication,
1062. II. Title.*
HD9802.J32 U5 1980

Stahmer, C. B. Butter cookies from Denmark .
Washington, D.C. [1980] ii, 15, 50 p. ;   LC
Card 80-602669   DDC 382/.456647525 19
HD9057.D42 S7

USITC publication.
(1016) United States. International Trade
Commission. Certain marine radar systems
from the United Kingdom . Washington, D.C.
[1979] ii, 8, 50 p. ;   LC Card 80-602625   DDC
382/.45623863 19
HF2651.M385 U58 1979

(1030) Magrath, Patrick J. Leather wearing
apparel . Washington, D.C. [1980] iii, 15, 51
p. :   LC Card 80-602342   DDC 382/.456852/0973
19
HF2651.L45 U496

(1047) Greer, T. Vernon. Sugars and sirups
from Canada . Washington, D.C. [1980] ii,
17, 66 p. ;   LC Card 80-602338   DDC
382/.4136/0973 19
HF2651.S8 U55

(1058) United States. International Trade
Commission. Pipes and tubes of iron or steel
from Japan . Washington, D.C. [1980] ii, 29,
37 p. ;   LC Card 80-602337   DDC

382/.4567283/0973 19
HF2651.S76 U54 1980a

(1059) Burket, Stephen D. Fresh cut roses . Washington, D.C. , 1980. iii, 9, 44 p. : LC Card 80-602339 DDC 382/.415933372/0973 19
HF2651.R85 U63

(1062) United States. International Trade Commission. Portable electric typewriters from Japan . Washington, D.C. [1980] ii, 15, A-41 p. ; LC Card 80-602317 DDC 382/.4568161 19
HD9802.J32 U5 1980

(1064) United States. International Trade Commission. Certain carbon steel products from Belgium, the Federal Republic of Germany, France, Italy, Luxembourg, the Netherlands, and the United Kingdom . Washington, D.C. [1980] vii, 71, 180 p. ; LC Card 80-602282 DDC 382/.45672 19
HF2651.S76 U54 1980

(1068) United States. International Trade Commission. Color television receivers and subassemblies thereof . Washington, D.C. [1980] 144 p. in various pagings : LC Card 80-602557 DDC 382/.4562138804/0973 19
HD9696.T463 U68 1980

(1077) Stahmer, C. B. Butter cookies from Denmark . Washington, D.C. [1980] ii, 15, 50 p. ; LC Card 80-602669 DDC 382/.456647525 19
HD9057.D42 S7

(1086) Cook, C. Lee. Textiles and textile products of cotton from Pakistan . Washington, D.C. [1980] vi, 56, 105 p. ; LC Card 80-602856 DDC 382/.4567721/0973 19
HD9856 .C66

(1089) United States. International Trade Commission. Mushrooms, report to the President on investigation no. TA-201-43, under section 201 of the Trade act of 1974. Washington, D.C. [1980] iv, 27, 78 p. : LC Card 80-603136 DDC 382/.4158/0973 19
HF2651.M83 U53 1980

(910) United States. International Trade Commission. Bicycle tires and tubes . Washington, D.C. , 1978. iv, 21, 131 p. ; LC Card 79-601748 DDC 382/.4567832 19
HF2651.B49 U58 1978

(972) Greer, T. Vernon. Sugar from Belgium, France, and West Germany . Washington , 1979. 21, 62 p. ; LC Card 79-602639 DDC 382/.4136/0973 19
HF2651.S8 U54

UNITED STATES. INTERNATIONAL TRADE COMMISSION - APPROPRIATIONS AND EXPENDITURES.
United States. Congress. Senate. Committee on Finance. Subcommittee on International Trade. Authorization of appropriations for the U. S. Customs Service, U. S. International Trade Commission, and of the U. S. Trade Representative, for fiscal year 1981 . Washington , 1980. iii, 79 p. : LC Card 80-603102 DDC 353.0072/23682/7 19
KF26 .F554 1980b

United States. International Trade Commission investigation. United States. International Trade Commission. Agreements being negotiated at the multilateral trade negotiations in Geneva--U. S. International Trade Commission investigation no. 332-101 . Washington , 1979- v. ; LC Card 79-603800 DDC 341.7/54/0265 19
K4603 1973 .U54

United States. International Year of the Child, Federal Interagency Committee for the. see United States. Federal Interagency Committee for the International Year of the Child.

United States. InternationalTrade Commission. ITC publication .
(1066) Lopp, Thomas G. Fish, fresh, chilled, or frozen, whether or not whole, but not otherwise prepared or preserved, from Canada . Washington, D.C. [1980] vi, 32, 121 p. : LC Card 80-602376 DDC 382/.4566494 19
HF2651.F5 U44

United States. Interstate and Foreign Commerce, Committee on (House) see United States.

Congress. House. Committee on Interstate and Foreign Commerce.

United States. Interstate Commerce Commission. Classification of operating expenses as prescribed by the Interstate Commerce Commission. United States. Interstate Commerce Commission. Supplement to the third revised issue of the Classification of operating expenses as prescribed by the Interstate Commerce Commission for steam roads in accordance with section 20 of the Act to regulate commerce. Washington , 1908-1913. 2 v. ; LC Card 81-459319 DDC 657/.8 19
HE2241 .U5 1908d Suppl

Federal State Workshop on Motor Carrier Regulation, 1st, Washington, D.C., 1979. Proceedings of the Federal State Workshop on Motor Carrier Regulation, October 22-24, 1979 /. [Washington, D.C. , 1980] 194 p. ; LC Card 80-602343 DDC 388.3/24/0973 19
HE5623 .F43 1979

Supplement to the third revised issue of the Classification of operating expenses as prescribed by the Interstate Commerce Commission for steam roads in accordance with section 20 of the Act to regulate commerce. Washington : Govt. Print. Off., 1908-1913. 2 v. ; 22 cm. "Effective on July 1, 1908 [and July 1, 1913]" LC Card 81-459319 DDC 657/.8 19
1. Railroads - United States - Accounts, bookkeeping, etc. 2. Railroads - United States - Equipment and supplies. I. United States. Interstate Commerce Commission. Classification of operating expenses as prescribed by the Interstate Commerce Commission.
HE2241 .U5 1908d Suppl

Uniform system of accounts for railroad companies / prescribed by the Interstate Commerce, issue of January 1, 1968. Washington, D. C.: U. S. Govt. Print. Off., 1974. 117 p.; 23 cm. "Revised as of October 1, 1973."
1. Railroads - United States - Accounts, bookkeeping, etc. I. Title. **NYPL [JLE 81-288]**

United States. Dept. of Transportation. Guidelines for the railroad industry in a national emergency. [Washington] 1974. 54 p. :
NYPL [JLF 80-736]

United States. Interstate Commerce Commission. Motor Carrier Task Force. Initial report of the Motor Carrier Task Force . Washington , 1979. 146 p. ; LC Card 79-603515
HE5623 .A4 1979b

UNITED STATES. INTERSTATE COMMERCE COMMISSION.
United States. Congress. House. Committee on Interstate and Foreign Commerce. Subcommittee on Oversight and Investigations. ICC ratemaking in noncompetitive markets--oversight . Washington , 1980. iii, 87 p. ; LC Card 80-603486 DDC 353.0087/512 19
KF27 .I5547 1980i

United States. Interstate Commerce Commission. Motor Carrier Task Force. Initial report of the Motor Carrier Task Force : recommended policy statement and proposed regulatory reform measures to the Honorable A. Daniel O'Neal, Chairman, Interstate Commerce Commission. Washington : ICC, 1979. 146 p. ; 27 cm. LC Card 79-603515
1. Transportation, Automotive - United States - Freight. 2. Carriers - United States. I. United States. Interstate Commerce Commission.
HE5623 .A4 1979b

The United States-Japan Cooperative Medical Science Program : third five-year report, 1975-1980. [Washington, D.C.? : U. S. Dept. of State] : For sale by the Supt. of Docs., U. S. G.P.O., 1980. xiv, 214 p. : ill. ; 28 cm. (Department of State publication. 9127. 217) "Released September 1980"--T.p. verso. S/N 044-000-017989 Item 870 Includes bibliographies. LC Card 81-600759 DDC 610/.72 19
1. United States-Japan Cooperative Medical Science Program. 2. Medical research - International cooperation. 3. Medical research - United States. 4. Medical research - Japan. I. United States. Dept. of State. II. Series: Department of State publication, 9127.
R853.I57 U54

UNITED STATES-JAPAN COOPERATIVE MEDICAL SCIENCE PROGRAM.
The United States-Japan Cooperative Medical

Science Program . [Washington, D.C.?] 1980. xiv, 214 p. : LC Card 81-600759 DDC 610/.72 19
R853.I57 U54

United States-Japan Cooperative Program in Natural Resources. Panel on Wind and Seismic Effects. Wind and seismic effects : proceedings of the tenth joint panel conference of the U. S.-Japan Cooperative Program in Natural Resources, May 23-26, 1978, National Bureau of Standards, Gaithersburg, Maryland / H.S. Lew, editor. Washington, D.C. : U. S. Dept. of Commerce, National Bureau of Standards : For sale by the Supt. of Docs., U. S. G.P.O., c1980. 604 p. in various pagings : ill. ; 26 cm. (NBS special publication . 560) "Center for Building Technology, National Engineering Laboratory, National Bureau of Standards." "Issued October 1980." S/N 003-003-02252-7 Item 247 Includes bibliographies. LC Card 79-600134 DDC 602/.18 s 624.1/76 19
1. Wind-pressure - Congresses. 2. Earthquake engineering - Congresses. 3. Earthquakes and building - Congresses. I. Lew, Hai Sans. II. United States. National Engineering Laboratory. Center for Building Technology. III. United States. National Bureau of Standards. IV. Title. V. Series.
QC100 .U57 no. 560 TA654.5

United States-Japan economic relations . United States. Congress. House. Committee on Foreign Affairs. Washington , 1981. vi, 337 p. : LC Card 81-601171 DDC 337.52073 19
KF27 .F6 1980K

United States-Japan trade report /. United States. Congress. House. Committee on Ways and Means. Subcommittee on Trade. United States-Japan Trade Task Force. Washington , 1980. viii, 92 p. : LC Card 80-603556 DDC 382/.0952/073 19
HF3127 .U52 1980

United States. Japan-United States Friendship Commission. see Japan-United States Friendship Commission.

United States. Joint Chiefs of Staff.
United States military posture. [Washington] illus. 27 cm. Report covers fiscal year. LC Card 79-642632
1. United States - Defenses - Periodicals. 2. United States - Military policy - Periodicals. 3. United States - Armed forces - Periodicals. I. Title.
NYPL [JLM 80-756]

UNITED STATES. JOINT CHIEFS OF STAFF - OFFICIALS AND EMPLOYEES.
United States. Congress. Senate. Committee on Armed Services. Nomination of David C. Jones . Washington , 1980. ii, 64 p. ; LC Card 80-603324 DDC 355.3/3042/0973 19
KF26 .A7 1980e

United States. Joint Council on Food and Agricultural Sciences.
United States. Joint Council on Food and Agricultural Sciences. Ad Hoc Committee on Human Nutrition. Human nutrition programs . Washington, D.C. [1980] v, 120, [21] p. : LC Card 80-601855 DDC 613.2/07/073 19
TX367 .U56 1980

United States. Joint Council on Food and Agricultural Sciences. Ad Hoc Committee on Human Nutrition. Human nutrition programs : research, extension, and higher education programs, supported by the United States Department of Agriculture : prepared for the Joint Council on Food and Agricultural Sciences. Washington, D.C. : U. S. Dept. of Agriculture, [1980] v, 120, [21] p. : forms ; 27 cm. Cover title. LC Card 80-601855 DDC 613.2/07/073 19
1. Nutrition - Research - United States. 2. Nutrition - Study and teaching - United States. I. United States. Joint Council on Food and Agricultural Sciences. II. Title.
TX367 .U56 1980

United States. Joint Economic Committee.
Freund, William Curt, 1926- Productivity and inflation . Washington , 1980. v, 14 p. ; LC Card 80-602572 DDC 332.4/1 19
HG229 .F655

United States. Joint Federal-State Land Use Planning Commission for Alaska. see Joint Federal-State Land Use Planning Commission for Alaska.

United States. Joint Financial Management Improvement Program. Financial Management Conference, 9th, Washington, D.C., 1980. "A new decade--the outlook for financial management" . [Washington, D.C.] , 1980. i, 64 p. : LC Card 80-602663 DDC 351.72 19
HJ257.2 .F55 1980

United States. Joint Publications Research Service. Malinovskiĭ, Aleksandr Aleksandrovich, 1909- Science of organization and organization of science /. [Washington] 1972. 18 p. *NYPL [*XMQ-2148]*

United States-Jordanian relations and arms supply issues . United States. Congress. House. Committee on Foreign Affairs. Subcommittee on Europe and the Middle East. Washington , 1980. iii, 71 p. ; LC Card 80-604082 DDC 327.7305695 19
KF27 .F64214 1980d

United States. Judge Advocate General's School, Ann Arbor, Mich. see United States. Judge Advocate General's School, Charlottesville, Va.

United States. Judge Advocate General's School, Charlottesville, Va. Procurement law case book . [Charlottesville] , 1957 [i.e. 1958] iii, 390 p. ; LC Card 79-107788 DDC 346.73/023 347.30623 19
KF845 .P76 1958

United States. Judiciary, Committee on the (House) see United States. Congress. House. Committee on the Judiciary.

United States. Judiciary, Committee on the (Senate) see United States. Congress. Senate. Committee on the Judiciary.

United States. Justice Dept. see United States. Dept. of Justice.

United States. Justice Dept. Antitrust Laws, Division for Enforcement of. see United States. Dept. of Justice. Antitrust Division.

United States. Justice, Dept. of. see United States. Dept. of Justice.

United States. Justice Statistics, Bureau of. see United States. Bureau of Justice Statistics.

United States. Kommission für Bürgerrechte. see United States. Commission on Civil Rights.

United States. Labor and Public Welfare, Committee on (Senate) see United States. Congress. Senate. Committee on Labor and Public Welfare.

United States. Labor, Dept. of. see United States. Dept. of Labor.

United States. Labor-Management and Welfare-Pension Reports, Office of. see United States. Office of Labor-Management and Welfare-Pension Reports.

United States. Labor-Management Services Administration. United States. Federal Mediation and Conciliation Service. Office of Research. Impact of the 1974 health care amendments to the NLRA on collective bargaining in the health care industry /. [Washington] , 1979. x, 473 p. : LC Card 79-603053
RA971.35 .U54 1979

Zack, Arnold. Understanding fact finding and arbitration in the public sector. [Washington, D.C.] , 1980. 105, 23 p. ; LC Card 80-601261 DDC 331.89/041353 19
HD8005.6.U5 Z33 1980

Zack, Arnold. Understanding grievance arbitration in the public sector. [Washington, D.C.] , 1980. 111, 23 p. ; LC Card 80-602268 DDC 353.001/76 19
JK768.8 .Z32 1980

United States. Labor-Management Services Administration. Division of Public Employee Labor Relations. see United States. Division of Public Employee Labor Relations.

United States. Labor Relations Board. see United States. National Labor Relations Board.

United States. Labor Statistics Bureau. see United States. Bureau of Labor Statistics.

United States. Land Management Bureau. see United States. Bureau of Land Management.

United States, Langley Research Center, Hampton, Va. Nuclear-pumped lasers. [Washington], 1979. vi, 136 p.: *NYPL [JSF 80-528]*

Workshop on Earth Radiation Budget Science, Williamsburg, Va., 1978. Earth radiation budget science, 1978 . [Washington, D.C.] , Springfield, Va. , 1979. vi, 72 p. : LC Card 80-601801 DDC 551.5/272 19
QC809.E6 W67 1978

UNITED STATES, LANGLEY RESEARCH CENTER, HAMPTON, VA. Anderton, David A. Sixty years of aeronautical research, 1917-1977 /. Washington , 1978. 89 p. : LC Card 79-601508
TL521.312 .A65 *NYPL [JSF 81-171]*

United States. Langley Research Center, Hampton, Va. Environmental Quality Projects Office. Remote sensing and problems of the hydrosphere . Washington, D.C. , 1980. iv, 30 p. ; LC Card 80-603169 DDC 553.7/028/7 19
TD419.5 .R45

United States - Law. see Law - United States.

United States. Law Enforcement Assistance Administration. (Old Catalog form: United States. Law Enforcement Assistance, Office of)
National Academy of Public Administration. LEAA Criminal Justice Planning Panel. Criminal justice planning in the governing process . [Washington] , 1979. ca. 200 p. in various pagings ; LC Card 79-602883
HV8138 .N269 1979

National Association of State Drug Abuse Program Coordinators. TASC, an approach for dealing with the substance abusing offender . Washington , 1978 [i.e. 1979] iv, 77, [83] p. : LC Card 79-602048
HV5825 .N32 1979

Viano, Emilio. Victim/witness services . [Washington, D.C.] , 1979. 69 p. ;
HV6250.3.U5 V49 *NYPL [JLF 81-398]*

United States. Law Enforcement Assistance Administration. Criminal Conspiracies Division. Walsh, Marilyn E. Computerized tracking of stolen office equipment . Washington , 1979. vi, 107 p. : LC Card 79-602794 DDC 363.2/5 19
HV6658 .W295

What happened : an examination of recently terminated anti-fencing operations : a special report to the Administrator. Washington, D.C. : Criminal Conspiracies Division, Office of Criminal Justice Programs, Law Enforcement Assistance Administration, U. S. Dept. of Justice, 1979. 62 p. in various pagings ; 28 cm. Includes a bibliography. LC Card 79-602151 DDC 364.1/62 19
1. Offenses against property - United States. I. Title. II. Title: Anti-fencing: a special report to the administrator.
HV6635 .U54 1979

United States. Law Enforcement Assistance Administration. Criminal Justice Education and Training, Office of. see United States. Law Enforcement Assistance Administration. Office of Criminal Justice Education and Training.

United States. Law Enforcement Assistance Administration. Juvenile Justice and Deliquency Prevention, Office of. see United States. Law Enforcement Assistance Administration. Office of Juvenile Justice and Delinquency Prevention.

United States. Law Enforcement Assistance Administration. National Criminal Justice Reference Service. see United States. National Criminal Justice Reference Service.

United States. Law Enforcement Assistance Administration. National Institute of Law Enforcement and Criminal Justice. see National Institute of Law Enforcement and Criminal Justice.

United States. Law Enforcement Assistance Administration. Office of Criminal Justice Education and Training. National Symposium on Job-Task Analysis in Criminal Justice, Dallas, 1978. National Symposium on Job-Task Analysis in Criminal Justice . Washington, D.C. , 1979. ix, 465 p. ; LC Card 79-603983

DDC 363.2/2 19
HV8143 .N39 1978

United States. Law Enforcement Assistance Administration. Office of Juvenile Justice and Delinquency Prevention. Johnson, Grant. Delinquency prevention, theories and strategies /. [Washington] [1979] vii leaves, 203 p. : LC Card 80-602136 DDC 362.7/4 19
HV9104 .J64

King, Jane L. A comparative analysis of juvenile codes /. Washington, D.C. , 1980. 90 p. ; LC Card 81-601206 DDC 345.73/08 347.3058 19
KF9795.Z95 K56

National Youth Workers Alliance, Washington, D.C. Runaway youth program directory /. [Washington, D.C.] [1979] 109 p. : LC Card 79-604199
HV1431 .N37 1979 *NYPL [JLD 81-606]*

Shepherd, Jack R. Police-juvenile diversion . Washington, D.C. , 1980. x, 77, [91] p. : LC Card 81-601094 DDC 364.6/8 19
HV9105.M5 S5 1980

United States. Laws, statutes, etc. (Old Catalog form: United States. Statutes)
Code of federal regulations. Title 3: The President. 1936/38- [Washington] 24 cm. "Containing the full text of Presidential documents published in the Federal Register." Published by the Office of the Federal Register. INDEXES: 1936/65. 1 v.
1. Administrative law - Periodicals. I. United States. Office of the Federal Register. II. Title.
*NYPL [*R-Econ. 81-3]*

Compilation of energy-related legislation / prepared by the staff, Committee on Interstate and Foreign Commerce, U. S. House of Representatives. Washington : U. S. Govt. Print. Off., 1979. 3 v. ; 24 cm. At head of title: 96th Congress, 1st session. Committee print 96-IFC 26. CONTENTS. - v. 1. Oil, gas, and coal.--v. 2. Electric and nuclear energy.--v. 3. Energy conservation, organization, and related matters. LC Card 79-603457
1. Power resources - Law and legislation - United States. I. United States. Congress. House. Committee on Interstate and Foreign Commerce. II. Title.
KF2120 .A3 1979

Compilation of selected acts within the jurisdiction of the Committee on Interstate and Foreign Commerce : prepared for the use of the House Committee on Interstate and Foreign Commerce. Washington : U. S. Govt. Print. Off., 1980- v. ; 24 cm. At head of title: 96th Congress, 2d session. Committee print 96-IFC 44. CONTENTS. - v. 1. Health law. LC Card 80-601741 DDC 344.73/04/02632 19
1. Public health laws - United States. 2. Environmental law - United States. 3. Consumer protection - Law and legislation - United States. I. United States. Congress. House. Committee on Interstate and Foreign Commerce. II. Title.
KF3775 .A3 1980

Compiled statutes--Committee on Government Operations : being a compilation of acts of Congress reported from or connected with the Committee on Government Operations. 4th ed. Washington : U. S. Govt. Print. Off., 1980. xiv, 1065 p. ; 24 cm. On cover: 96th Congress, 2d session. House of Representatives. Committee print. "July 1980." Includes index. LC Card 80-603543 DDC 342.73/06/02632 347.302602632 19
1. United States - Executive departments. I. United States. Congress. House. Committee on Government Operations. II. Title.
KF5102 1980

CONGRESSIONAL BUDGET AND IMPOUNDMENT CONTROL ACT OF 1974 - INDEXES. United States. Congressional Budget Office. Index to the legislative history of the Congressional budget and impoundment control act of 1974 /. [Washington] [1980] xi, 481 p. ; LC Card 80-603388 DDC 343.73/034 347.30334 19
KF6222.115 .A15 1980

ELEMENTARY AND SECONDARY EDUCATION ACT OF 1965. United States. Office of Education. Title I ESEA. Washington, D. C., 1973. vi, 67 p.:
NYPL [JLF 81-40]

Fair labor standards act of 1938. United States. Wage and Hour and Public Contracts Division. [Interpretative bulletin of the Fair labor standards act of 1938. Part 776. Subpart A. Coverage of wage-hour law.] Coverage of wage-hour law : text of official explanation on general coverage of the wage-hour law, together with BNA editorial analysis. Washington, D.C. , 1950. x, 29 p. ;   LC Card 80-116713   DDC 344.73/0121   347.304121 19
KF3489 .A36

Federal election campaign act of 1971. United States. Federal Election Commission. Regulations / Federal Election Commission. Washington, D.C. [1980] 178 p. ;   LC Card 80-602940   DDC 342.73/07 19
KF4885 .A33 1980

Federal election campaign laws (including the Federal election campaign act amendments of 1979, Pub. L. no. 96-187) / compiled by the Federal Election Commission. Washington, D.C. : For sale by the Supt. of Docs., U. S. Govt. Print. Off., [1980] ix, 90 p. ; 24 cm. "January 1980." LC Card 80-602594 DDC 342.73/07 19
1. Election law - United States. I. United States. Federal Election Commission. II. Title.
KF4885 .A3 1980

Federal election campaign laws relating to the U. S. House of Representatives, as amended through January 8, 1980 / Committee on House Administration. Washington : U. S. Govt. Print. Off. : for sale by the Supt. of Docs., U. S. Govt. Print. Off., 1980. xiv, 232 p. ; 24 cm. (Document - 96th Congress, 2nd session, House of Representatives ; no. 96-301) "April 1980." LC Card 80-602296 DDC 342.73/07 19
1. United States. Congress. House - Elections. 2. Election law - United States. I. United States. Congress. House. Committee on House Administration. II. Title. III. Series.
KF4914 .A3 1980

[National environmental policy act of 1969] Erickson, Paul A. Environmental impact assessment : principles and applications / Paul A. Erickson. New York , 1979. xviii, 395 p. :   ISBN 0-12-241550-7   LC Card 78-22522
TD194.6 .E74   *NYPL [JLE 80-2797]*

Older Americans act of 1965, as amended : history and related acts. Washington, D.C. : Administration on Aging, Office of Human Development Services, U. S. Dept. of Health, Education, and Welfare, [1979] viii, 173 p. ; 24 cm. (DHEW publication ; no. (OHDS) 79-20170) Includes index. LC Card 80-602137 DDC 344.73/0326/02632 19
1. Aged - Legal status, laws, etc. - United States. I. United States. Administration on Aging. II. Series: United States. Dept. of Health, Education and Welfare. DHEW publication, no. (OHDS) 79-20170. III. Title.
KF3737 .A3 1979

OMNIBUS INSULAR AREAS ACT OF 1979-1980.
Legislative history of the Omnibus insular areas act of 1979-1980, (H.R. 3756), (Public law 96-205) /. Washington , 1980. iv, 185 p. ;   LC Card 80-602286   DDC 342.73/0413 19
KF4635.A315 A15 1980

Omnibus insular areas act of 1979-1980. 1980. Legislative history of the Omnibus insular areas act of 1979-1980, (H.R. 3756), (Public law 96-205) / compiled by Subcommittee on National Parks and Insular Affairs of the Committee on Interior and Insular Affairs of the U. S. House of Representatives, Ninety-sixth Congress, second session. Washington , 1980. iv, 185 p. ;   LC Card 80-602286   DDC 342.73/0413 19
KF4635.A315 A15 1980

PREGNANCY DISCRIMINATION ACT OF 1978.
Legislative history of the Pregnancy discrimination act of 1978, Public law 95-555 . Washington , 1979 [i.e. 1980] vi, 212 p. ;   LC Card 80-602871   DDC 344.73/014133 19
KF3467.A314 A15 1980

Real estate settlement procedures act of 1974.
1979. Real estate settlement procedures act. Washington, D.C. [1979] 7, 39, [12] p. :

LC Card 80-601047   DDC 346.7304/373 19
KF681 .R4

SOCIAL SECURITY ACT. TITLE 20.
United States. Office of Human Development Services. Guide to federal financial participation under Title XX of the Social Security act /. [Washington] , 1980. 1 v. (various pagings) ;   *NYPL [JLM 81-18]*

Uniform product liability act. 1979. United States. Dept. of Commerce. Task Force on Product Liability and Accident Compensation. Uniform product liability act : a model for the States. [Washington] , 1979. 44 p. ;   LC Card 80-601839   DDC 346.7303/82 19
KF1296 .A8168

United States code. 1976 ed., supplement III : containing the general and permanent laws of the United States, enacted during the 95th Congress and 96th Congress, first session. Prepared and published ... by the Office of the Law Revision Counsel of the House of Representatives. Washington : U. S. Govt. Print. Off., 1980- - v. ; 27 cm. Contents. - v. 2. Title 19 - Customs duties to Title 41 - Public contracts (Jan. 4, 1977, to Jan. 8, 1980).
1. Law - United States. I. United States. Laws, etc. II. United States. Congress. House. Office of the Law Revision Counsel. II. Title.
        *NYPL [*R-Econ. 78-895 Suppl. 3]*

United States. Lewis Research Center, Cleveland. Aeropropulsion 1979 . Washington, D.C. , Springfield, Va. , 1979. vi, 463 p. :   LC Card 79-604273
TL701 .A37

The Rotary combustion engine . [Washington, D.C.] , Springfield, Va. , 1978. v, 190 p. :   LC Card 79-603405
TL701.1 .R58

Wind energy developments in the 20th century. Rev. 1979. Cleveland, Ohio : Lewis Research Center, National Aeronautics and Space Administration, 1980. 32 p. : ill. ; 28 cm. Bibliography: p. 22-32.   LC Card 80-602418   DDC 621.31/2136 19
1. Wind power. 2. Air-turbines. I. Title.
TK1541 .U56 1980

United States. Libraries and Information Science, National Commission on. see United States. National Commission on Libraries and Information Science.

United States. Libraries and Learning Resources, Office of. see United States. Office of Libraries and Learning Resources.

United States. Library of Congress.
Audiovisual materials. United States. Library of Congress. Library of Congress catalogs: Audiovisual materials. Jan./Mar. 1979- Washington.   *NYPL [*R-Theatre 80-409]*

Belgium België Belgique "shall constitute an independent state" : an exhibition in honor of the 150th anniversary of the independence of Belgium, April 22-June 2, 1980. Washington : Library of Congress, 1980. iv, 36 p. : ill. ; 28 cm.   LC Card 80-602019   DDC 949.3/03/0740153 19
1. Belgium - History - Revolution, 1830-1839 - Exhibitions. 2. Belgium - Civilization - Exhibitions. I. Title.
Z2419 .U54 1980 DH651

Bibliographic guide to maps and atlases. Boston.   *NYPL [Map. Div. 81-27]*

[Dime novels collection] /. Washington [197-] 83 reels ;   *NYPL [*ZAN-5163 - *ZAN-5191]*

Films and other materials for projection. United States. Library of Congress. Library of Congress catalogs: Films and other materials for projection. 1973/77-1978. Washington. 6 v. in 8.   *NYPL [*R-Theatre 80-408]*

Gephart, Ronald M. Revolutionary America, 1763-1789 . Washington , 1982. p. cm.   ISBN 0-8444-0359-8   LC Card 80-606802   DDC 016.9733 19
Z1238 .G43 E208

Hilker, Helen-Anne. Ten First Street, Southeast . Washington , 1980. iii, 102 p. :   ISBN 0-8444-0351-2   LC Card 80-607808   DDC 027.5753 19
Z679.2.U54 H54

Library of Congress catalogs: Audiovisual

materials. Jan./Mar. 1979- Washington. 28 cm. Quarterly, with annual and quinquennial cumulations. For earlier file, see its: Library of Congress catalogs: Films and other materials for projection.
1. Audio-visual materials - Catalogs. I. United States. Library of Congress. Audiovisual materials. II. Title.
        *NYPL [*R-Theatre 80-409]*

Library of Congress catalogs: Films and other materials for projection. 1973/77-1978. Washington. 6 v. in 8. 27 cm. Quarterly, with annual and quinquennial cumulations. For earlier years, see its: Library of Congress catalogs: Motion pictures and filmstrips. For later years, see its: Library of Congress catalogs: Audiovisual materials.
1. Moving-pictures - Catalogs. 2. Filmstrips - Catalogs. I. United States. Library of Congress. Films and other materials for projection. II. Title.
        *NYPL [*R-Theatre 80-408]*

Library of Congress Symposia on the American Revolution, 1st, 1972. The development of a revolutionary mentality. Washington, 1972. 157 p.   ISBN 0-8444-0045-9   LC Card 72-11849
E204 .L53 1972   *NYPL [IG 80-3121]*

Library of Congress Symposia on the American Revolution, 3d, 1974. Leadership in the American Revolution . Washington , 1974. ix, 135 p. ;   ISBN 0-8444-0149-8   LC Card 74-30110
E204 .L53 1974   *NYPL [IG 80-3122]*

The Portuguese manuscripts collection of the Library of Congress : a guide / compiled by Christopher C. Lund and Mary Ellis Kahler ; edited by Mary Ellis Kahler. Washington : The Library, 1980. xi, 187 p. ; 24 cm. Bibliography: p. 157-158. Includes index.   ISBN 0-8444-0329-6   LC Card 80-607039
1. Manuscripts, Portuguese - Washington, D. C. - Catalogs. 2. United States. Library of Congress. Manuscript Division - Catalogs. I. Lund, Christopher C. II. Kahler, Mary Ellis. III. Title.
Z6621.U582 P68   *NYPL [JFE 81216]*

Select list of recent purchases in certain departments of literature, 1901-1903 / Library of Congress. Washington : Government Printing Office, 1904. vi, 326 p. ; 24 cm. "Reprinted from the Report of the Librarian of Congress for the fiscal year ending June 30, 1903."   LC Card 80-495444   DDC 018/.1/09753 19
1. United States. Library of Congress - Catalogs. I. Title.
Z881 .U5 1904

The Textbook in American society . Washington , 1981. x, 55 p. ;   ISBN 0-8444-0355-5 (pbk.) :   LC Card 80-27657   DDC 371.3/2/0973 19
LB3047 .T48

UNITED STATES. LIBRARY OF CONGRESS.
Library of Congress Network Advisory Group. Toward a national library and information service network . Washington [1977] vii, 54 p. ;   LC Card 80-601614   DDC 021.6/5 19
Z674.8 .L52 1977

United States. Library of Congress. African Section. (Old Catalog form: United States. Library of Congress. Division of Bibliography)
Aradoum, Fassil. University of Malawi publications . Washington , 1979. viii, 41 p. ;   ISBN 0-8444-0324-5   LC Card 79-607918
Z3577 .A72 DT858
        NYPL [Sc Micro F-9346]

Conover, Helen Field. African libraries, book production and archives . Washington, D. C. , 1962. vi, 64 p. ;   LC Card 62-64603
        NYPL [Sc F 81-66]

United States. Library of Congress. American Folklife Center. see American Folklife Center.

United States. Library of Congress. Bibliography, Division of. see United States. Library of Congress. Division of Bibliography.

United States. Library of Congress. Blind and Physically Handicapped, Division for the. see United States. Library of Congress. Division for the Blind and Physically Handicapped.

United States. Library of Congress. Broadcasting, Recorded Sound, and motion Picture Division. see United States. Library of Congress. Motion Picture, Broadcasting, and Recorded Sound Division.

UNITED STATES. LIBRARY OF CONGRESS - CATALOGS.
United States. Library of Congress. Select list of recent purchases in certain departments of literature, 1901-1903 /. Washington , 1904. vi, 326 p. ; LC Card 80-495444 DDC 018/.1/09753 19
Z881 .U5 1904

United States. Library of Congress. Center for the book. see **Center for the Book.**

United States. Library of Congress. Children's Literature Center. The audience for children's books . Washington , 1980. 42 p. : ISBN 0-8444-0330-X LC Card 80-12397
Z1037.A1 A9 ***NYPL [JFD 81-1348]***

United States. Library of Congress. Congressional Research Service.
Alternative breeding cycles for nuclear power : an analysis : report / prepared for the Committee on Science and Technology, U. S. House of Representatives, Ninety-sixth Congress, second session, by the Congressional Research Service, Library of Congress.Rev. Aug. 1980. Washington : U. S. Govt. Print. Off., 1980. xx, 124 p. : ill. ; 24 cm. At head of title: Committee print. Prepared by Marcia S. Smith, Carl E. Behrens, and Warren H. Donnelly. "August 1980." "Serial AAA." Includes bibliographical references. LC Card 80-603560 DDC 333.79/24/0973 19
1. Breeder reactors. 2. Atomic power industry - United States. 3. Nuclear nonpooliferation. 4. Energy policy - United States. I. Smith, Marcia S. II. Behrens, Carl E. III. Donnelly, Warren H. IV. United States. Congress. House. Committee on Science and Technology. V. Title.
TK9203.B7 U53 1980

Congress and foreign policy series. no. 1- ; June, 1980- Washington.
I. Title. ***NYPL [Econ. Div.]***

Corporate crime / Subcommittee on Crime of the Committee on the Judiciary, House of Representatives, Ninety-sixth Congress, second session, May, 1980. Washington : U. S. Govt. Print. Off., 1980. iii, 106 p. ; 24 cm. At head of title: 96th Congress, 2d session. Committee print. No. 10. Prepared by the Congressional Research Service and the Law Library of the Library of Congress for the Subcommittee on Crime. Includes bibliographical references. LC Card 80-602274 DDC 364.1/68 19
1. Commercial crimes - United States. 2. Corporations - United States - Corrupt practices. I. United States. Library of Congress. Law Library. II. United States. Congress. House. Committee on the Judiciary. Subcommittee on Crime. III. Title.
HV6769 .U55 1980

Effects of chronic exposure to low-level pollutants in the environment : prepared for the Subcommittee on the Environment and the Atmosphere of the Committee on Science and Technology, U. S. House of Representatives, Ninety-fourth Congress, first session / by the Congressional Research Service, Library of Congress. Washington : U. S. Govt. Print. Off., 1975. ii, 402 p. ; 24 cm. At head of title: Committee print. "Serial O." Includes bibliographical references. LC Card 75-603631
1. Pollution - Environmental aspects. 2. Pollution - Toxicology. I. United States. Congress. House. Committee on Science and Technology. Subcommittee on the Environment and the Atmosphere. II. Title. III. Title: Low-level pollutants in the environment.
QH545.A1 U54 1975 ***NYPL [JSE 81-285]***

Energy information : a workshop on current progress and problems / prepared for the Committee on Governmental Affairs, United States Senate by the Congressional Research Service, Library of Congress. Washington : U. S. Govt. Print. Off. : for sale by the Supt. of Docs., U. S. Govt. Print. Off., 1980. ix, 114 p. ; 23 cm. At head of title: 96th Congress, 2d session. Committee print. Summary of the Energy Information Workshop held Feb. 6, 1980 at the Library of Congress. LC Card 80-602583 DDC 333.79/07 19
1. Power resources - Information services - United States - Congresses. 2. Energy policy - Information services - United States - Congresses. I. United States. Congress. Senate. Committee on Governmental Affairs. II. Energy Information Workshop, Library of Congress, 1980. III. Title.
TJ163.17 .U54 1980

The Federal executive establishment : evolution and trends / prepared for the Committee on Governmental Affairs, United States Senate by the Congressional Research Service, Library of Congress. Washington : U. S. Govt. Print. Off., 1980. v, 76 p. ; 23 cm. Bibliography: p. 70-76. LC Card 80-602577 DDC 353.04 19
1. United States - Executive departments. 2. Administrative agencies - United States. I. United States. Congress. Senate. Committee on Governmental Affairs. II. Title.
JK411 .U54 1980

Federal responsibility to the elderly : executive programs and legislative jurisdiction : charts / compiled by the Congressional Research Service of the Library of Congress for the Select Committee on Aging, House of Representatives, Ninety-fifth Congress, second session.Rev. ed. Washington : U. S. Govt. Print. Off., 1979. iii, 16 p. : ill. ; 26 cm. At head of title: Committee print. "Comm. pub. no. 95-167." LC Card 79-600867 DDC 362.6/3/0973 19
1. Old age assistance - United States. I. United States. Congesss. House. Select Committee on Aging. II. Title.
HV1461 .U645 1979

How can the interests of United States consumers best be protected? . Washington , 1980. vii, 636 p. : LC Card 80-602855 DDC 381/.34/0973 19
HC110.C63 H68

An inquiry into conflicting and duplicative regulatory requirements affecting selected industries and sectors : a background study, prepared for the use of the Joint Economic Committee, Congress of the United States. Washington : U. S. Govt. Print. Off. : for sale by the Supt. of Docs., U. S. Govt. Print. Off., 1980. v, 40 p. ; 24 cm. At head of title: 96th Congress, 2d session. Joint committee print. "July 31, 1980." Includes bibliographical references. LC Card 80-603057 DDC 343.73/08 347.3038 19
1. Trade regulation - United States. 2. Administration procedure - United States. I. United States. Congress. Joint Economic Committee. II. Title.
KF1600 .A25 1980

Morrison, Robert Eugene, 1930- Possible effects on the atmosphere of large-scale helium extraction from the atmosphere /. Washington , 1979. vii, 14 p. ; LC Card 79-603780 DDC 333.9/2 19
TD888.G37 M67

Nuclear safeguards : an update analysis of the concept of safeguards as a national and international institution : report / prepared for the Subcommittee on Energy Research and Production of the Committee on Science and Technology, U. S. House of Representatives, Ninety-sixth Congress, second session, by the Congressional Research Service, Library of Congress. Washington : U. S. Govt. Print. Off. : for sale by the Supt. of Docs., 1980. xi, 50 p. ; 24 cm. At head of title: Committee print. Prepared by Frederick Forscher. "Serial VV." Includes bibliographical references. LC Card 80-602868 DDC 363.1/79 19
1. Atomic energy industries - United States - Security measures. 2. Atomic power - Law and legislation - United States. I. Forscher, Frederick. II. United States. Congress. House. Committee on Science and Technology. Subcommittee on Energy Research and Production. III. Title.
HD9698.U52 U57 1980a

Risk/benefit analysis in the legislative process : summary of a Congress/science joint forum / prepared by the Congressional Research Service, Library of Congress, for the Subcommittee on Science, Research and Technology of the Committee on Science and Technology, U. S. House of Representatives, and the Subcommittee on Science, Technology, and Space of the Committee on Commerce, Science, and Transportation, United States Senate, Ninety-sixth Congress, second session. Washington : U. S. Govt. Print. Off. : for sale by the Supt. of Docs., U. S. Govt. Print. Off., 1980. ix, 36 p. ; 24 cm. At head of title: Joint committee print. "Serial KK." Forum held July 24-25, 1979, co-sponsored by two congressional subcommittees and the American Association for the Advancement of Science. LC Card 80-602214 DDC 363.1/056/0973 19
1. Technology assessment - Congresses. 2. Risk - Congresses. I. United States. Congress. House. Committee on Science and Technology. Subcommittee on Science, Research, and Technology. II. United States. Congress. Senate. Committee on Commerce, Science, and Transportation. Subcommittee on Science, Technology, and Space. III. Title.
T174.5 .U57 1980

Shipp, P. Royal. Background material on work, retirement, and social security /. Washington , 1980. v, 24 p. : LC Card 80-603060 DDC 368.4/3/00973 19
HD7125 .S527

Should the Federal government significantly strengthen the regulation of mass media communication in the United States? . Washington , 1979. ix, 425 p. : LC Card 80-602647 DDC 343.73/099 19
KF2750.A75 S48

State and national water use trends to the year 2000 : a report / prepared by the Congressional Research Service of the Library of Congress for the Committee on Environment and Public Works, U. S. Senate, May 1980. Washington : U. S. Govt. Print. Off., 1980. x, 297 p. : ill. ; 23 cm. At head of title: Committee print. 96th Congress, 2d session. Authors: Warren Viessman, Jr., and Christine DeMoncada. "Serial no. 96-12." Includes bibliographical references. LC Card 80-602584 DDC 333.91/13/0973 19
1. Water use - United States. 2. Water consumption - United States. 3. Water quality - United States. I. Viessman, Warren. II. DeMoncada, Christine. III. United States. Congress. Senate. Committee on Environment and Public Works. IV. Title.
TD223 .U53 1980a

Sutter, Robert G. Executive-legislative consultations on China policy, 1978-79 /. Washington , 1980. vii, 42 p. ; LC Card 80-602678 DDC 327.73051 19
JX1428.C6 S97

Taiwan, one year after United States-China normalization . Washington , 1980. v, 170 p. : LC Card 80-603279 DDC 327.73051/249 19
E183.8.T3 T34

U. S. refineries : a background study : a study / prepared at the request of the Subcommittee on Energy and Power, Committee on Interstate and Foreign Commerce, United States House of Representatives by the Congressional Research Service, Library of Congress. Washington : U. S. Govt. Print. Off. : for sale by the Supt. of Docs., U. S. Govt. Print. Off., 1980. v, 169 p. : ill. ; 24 cm. "Coordinated and edited by David M. Lindahl." "July 1980." At head of title: 96th Congress, 2d session. Committee print. Committee print 96-IFC54. Includes bibliographical references. LC Card 80-603551 DDC 665.5/3/0973 19
1. Petroleum refineries - United States. I. Lindahl, David M. II. United States. Congress. House. Committee on Interstate and Foreign Commerce. Subcommittee on Energy and Power. III. Title.
TP690.3 .U538 1980

United States and Soviet progress in space : summary data through 1979 and a forward look : report / prepared for the Subcommittee on Space Science and Applications of the Committee on Science and Technology, U. S. House of Representatives, Ninety-sixth Congress, second session, by the Congressional Research Service, Library of Congress. Washington : U. S. Govt. Print. Off. : for sale by the Supt. of Docs., U. S. Govt. Print. Off., 1980. xiii, 91 p. ; 24 cm. At head of title: Committee print. Prepared by Charles S. Sheldon II. "Serial LL." Edition for 1978 by Science Policy Research Division, Congressional Research Service, Library of Congress. LC Card 80-602269 DDC 387.8 19
1. Astronautics - United States. 2. Astronautics - Russia. I. Sheldon, Charles S. II. United States. Congress. House. Committee on Science and Technology. Subcommittee on Space Science and Applications. III. United States. Library of Congress. Science Policy Research Division. United States and Soviet progress in space. IV. Title.
TL789.8.U5 U54 1980

What should be the energy policy of the United States? . Washington , 1978. ix, 518 p. : LC Card 80-603542 DDC 333.79/0973 19
HD9502.U52 W48

Workshop on Energy Conservation in Cities, Library of Congress, 1978. Energy conservation in cities /. Washington , 1979. vii, 117 p. : LC Card 80-602834 DDC 333.79/16/0973 19
TJ163.4.U6 W67 1978

United States. Library of Congress. Congressional Research Service. American

GOVERNMENT PUBLICATIONS - U.S.: 1981

561 *United States. Library of Congress. Photoduplication Service.*

Law Division.
Election law updates. 1978- [Washington]. 28 cm. Quarterly, with annual cumulations (Library retains annual cumulations only). Supersedes in part its Federal-State election law survey. Prepared for the Federal Election Commission. Title also as: Federal-state election law updates.
1. Election law - United States - States - Periodicals. 2. Election law - United States - Periodicals. I. United States. Federal Election Commission. II. United States. Library of Congress. Congressional Research Service. American Law Division. Federal-state election law updates. III. Title. IV. Title: Federal-state election law updates. ***NYPL [JLM 81-184]***

Federal-state election law updates. United States. Library of Congress. Congressional Research Service. American Law Division. Election law updates. 1978- [Washington]. ***NYPL [JLM 81-184]***

United States. Library of Congress. Congressional Research Service. Environment and Natural Resources Policy Division. see United States. Library of Congress. Environment and Natural Resources Policy Division.

United States. Library of Congress. Congressional Research Service. Science Policy Research Division. see United States. Library of Congress. Science Policy Research Division.

United States. Library of Congress. Congressional Research Services. Impact abroad of the accident at the Three Mile Island Nuclear Power Plant . Washington , 1980. xii, 81 p. ;   LC Card 80-603262 DDC 333.79/24 19
TK9055 .I44

United States. Library of Congress. Division for the Blind and Physically Handicapped. Government Studies & Systems, inc. Braille reader survey analysis /. Philadelphia , 1974. viii, 17 p., [45] p. of tables ; ***NYPL [*Z-3211]***

The Musical mainstream. v. 4, no. 3- ; May/June 1980- Washington. LC Card 76-640164 ***NYPL [Music Div.]***

The New braille musician. Washington. LC Card 70-608593 ***NYPL [JMM 80-45]***

United States. Library of Congress. Division of Bibliography. United States. Library of Congress. General Reference and Bibliography Division. [Select list of references. no. 1-1611]. Washington, 1910-50. 71 v. ***NYPL [*ZAN-T5190]***

United States. Library of Congress. Division of Fine Arts. see United States. Library of Congress. Prints and Photographs Division.

United States. Library of Congress. Division of Manuscripts. see United States. Library of Congress. Manuscript Division.

United States. Library of Congress. Division of Prints. see United States. Library of Congress. Prints and Photographs Division.

United States. Library of Congress. Environment and Natural Resources Policy Division. Nuclear proliferation factbook / prepared for the Subcommittee on Energy, Nuclear Proliferation, and Federal Services of the Committee on Governmental Affairs, U. S. Senate and the Subcommittee on International Economic Policy and Trade of the Committee on Foreign Affairs, U. S. House of Representatives, by the Environment and Natural Resources Policy Division, Congressional Research Service, Library of Congress. Washington : U. S. Govt. Print. Off. : for sale by the Supt. of Docs., U. S. Govt. Print. Off., 1980. xi, 531 p. : ill. ; 24 cm. At head of title: 96th Congress, 2d session. Joint committee print. "September 1980." Bibliography: p. 520-525. LC Card 80-603879 DDC 327.1/74 19
1. Nuclear nonproliferation. I. United States. Congress. Senate. Committee on Governmental Affairs. Subcommittee on Energy, Nuclear Proliferation, and Federal Services. II. United States. Congress. House. Committee on Foreign Affairs. Subcommittee on International Economic Policy and Trade. III. Title.
JX1974.73 .U55 1980

United States. Library of Congress. European Division.
Hoskins, Janina W. Casimir Pulaski,

1747-1779 . [Washington , 1979] 24 p. : LC Card 79-124952
Z8716.5 .H67 E207.P8 ***NYPL [JFE 80-4304]***

Hoskins, Janina W. Tadeusz Kościuszko, 1746-1817 . Washington , 1980. iv, 24 p. : LC Card 80-149054 DDC 016.9438/02/0924 19
Z8467.5 .H67 E207.K8

United States. Library of Congress. Foreign Affairs and National Defense Division.
The role of the North Atlantic Assembly / prepared for the Subcommittee on European Affairs of the Committee on Foreign Relations, United States Senate by the Foreign Affairs and National Defense Division, Congressional Research Service, Library of Congress. Washington : U. S. Govt. Print. Off., 1979. vii, 55 p. ; 24 cm. At head of title: 96th Congress, 1st session. Committee print. "July 1979." Includes bibliographical references. LC Card 80-601029 DDC 341.24/3 19
1. North Atlantic Assembly. I. United States. Congress. Senate. Committee on Foreign Relations. Subcommittee on European Affairs. II. Title.
JX1393.N67 U519 1979

Sino-American relations : from the Shanghai communique to the present : report / prepared for the Subcommittee on Asian and Pacific Affairs of the Committee on Foreign Affairs, U. S. House of Representatives, by the Foreign Affairs and National Defense Division, Congressional Research Service, Library of Congress. Washington : U. S. Govt. Print. Off., 1980. iii, 12 p. ; 24 cm. At head of title: Committee print. 96th Congress, 2d session. LC Card 80-603273 DDC 327.73051 19
1. United States - Foreign relations - China. 2. China - Foreign relations - United States. I. United States. Congress. House. Committee on Foreign Affairs. Subcommittee on Asian and Pacific Affairs. II. Title.
E183.8.C5 U58 1980

United States. Library of Congress. General Reference and Bibliography Division. (Old Catalog form: United States. Library of Congress. Division of bibliography)
Official publications of French West Africa, 1946-1958: a guide / compiled by Helen F. Conover. Washington, D. C.: Library of Congress, General Reference and Bibliography Division, 1961. x, 88 p.; 27 cm. Reprint of the 1960 ed.
1. Africa, French-speaking West - Government publications - Bibliography. I. Conover, Helen Field, comp. II. Title. ***NYPL [Sc F 80-133]***

[Select list of references. no. 1-1611]. Washington, 1910-50. 71 v. 27 cm. Microfilm. Lists issued at irregular intervals. Numbers assigned as cataloged, and do not appear on issues. Vols. for 1910-1943 issued by Division of Bibliography of Library of Congress. Later years cataloged separately as monographs, see separate entries.
I. United States. Library of Congress. Division of Bibliography. ***NYPL [*ZAN-T5190]***

United States. Library of Congress. General Reference and Bibliography Division. African Section. see United States. Library of Congress. African Section.

United States. Library of Congress. Geography and Map Division. The bibliography of cartography. Supplement. 1 st- ; 1980- Boston, G. K. Hall & Co. 37 cm. LC Card 73-12977
1. Cartography - Bibliography - Catalogs. 2. United States. Library of Congress. Geography and Map Division. I. Hall (G. K.) & Company. II. Title. ***NYPL [Map. Div. 73-602 Suppl.]***

UNITED STATES. LIBRARY OF CONGRESS. GEOGRAPHY AND MAP DIVISION.
United States. Library of Congress. Geography and Map Division. The bibliography of cartography. Supplement. 1 st- ; 1980- Boston. LC Card 73-12977 ***NYPL [Map. Div. 73-602 Suppl.]***

United States. Library of Congress. Law Division. see United States. Library of Congress. Law Library.

United States. Library of Congress. Law Library. Baik, ChungSook. Korean law . Washington, D.C. , 1980. viii, 14 p. ; LC Card 80-600114 DDC 016.349519 016.34519 19
LAW

Government financing of national elections, political parties, and campaign spending in

various foreign countries / by members of the staff. Washington, D.C. : Law Library, Library of Congress, 1980. 48 p. ; 28 cm. Includes bibliographical references. LC Card 80-600064 DDC 324.7/8 19
1. Elections - Campaign funds. I. Title.
JF1085 .U55 1980

Law Library publications.
Shroff, Kersi B. Individualized sentencing and the use of social inquiry (presentence) reports in England /. Washington , 1978. 20 p. ; LC Card 78-600143 DDC 345.42/0772 19
KD8406 .S55

United States. Library of Congress. Congressional Research Service. Corporate crime /. Washington , 1980. iii, 106 p. ; LC Card 80-602274 DDC 364.1/68 19
HV6769 .U55 1980

United States. Library of Congress. Manuscript Division. (Old Catalog form: United States. Library of Congress. Manuscripts Division)
Members of Congress : a checklist of their papers in the Manuscript Division, Library of Congress / compiled by John J. McDonough, with the assistance of Marlyn K. Parr, Washington : Manuscript Division, Research Services, Library of Congress, 1980. xiii, 217 p. : ill. ; 24 cm. ISBN 0-8444-0272-9
1. Legislators - United States - Manuscripts - Catalogs. 2. United States - Politics and government - Manuscripts - Catalogs. 3. Manuscripts - United States - Catalogs. 4. United States. Library of Congress. Manuscript Division - Catalogs. I. McDonough, John J., 1926-. II. Parr, Marilyn K., 1947-. III. Title.
Z1236 .U613 1979 E176 ***NYPL [JLE 81-85]***

UNITED STATES. LIBRARY OF CONGRESS. MANUSCRIPT DIVISION - CATALOGS.
United States. Library of Congress. The Portuguese manuscripts collection of the Library of Congress . Washington , 1980. xi, 187 p. ; ISBN 0-8444-0329-6 LC Card 80-607039
Z6621.U582 P68 ***NYPL [JFE 81216]***

United States. Library of Congress. Manuscript Division. Members of Congress . Washington , 1980. xiii, 217 p. : ISBN 0-8444-0272-9
Z1236 .U613 1979 E176 ***NYPL [JLE 81-85]***

United States. Library of Congress. Manuscripts Division. see United States. Library of Congress. Manuscript Division.

United States. Library of Congress. Motion Picture, Broadcasting, and Recorded Sound Division. The George Kleine collection of early motion pictures in the Library of Congress : a catalog / prepared by Rita Horwitz and Harriet Harrison, with the assistance of Wendy White. Washington : Motion Picture, Broadcasting, and Recorded Sound Division, Library of Congress : for sale by the Supt. of Documents, U. S. Govt. Print. Off., 1980. xxxvi, 270 p. : ill. ; 21 x 27 cm. Includes bibliographical references and indexes. ISBN 0-8444-0331-8 LC Card 79-607073
1. George Kleine Film Collection - Catalogs. 2. Silent films - Catalogs. I. Horwitz, Rita. II. Harrison, Harriet. III. White, Wendy. IV. Title.
PN1998.A1 U57 1980
NYPL [MFLE 81-199]

United States. Library of Congress. National Serials Data Program. see National Serials Data Program.

United States. Library of Congress. Office for Descriptive Cataloging Policy. Bibliographic description of rare books : rules formulated under AACR 2 and ISBD(A) for the descriptive cataloging of rare books and other special printed materials / Office for Descriptive Cataloging Policy, Processing Services. Washington : Library of Congress : available from the Cataloging Distribution Service, 1981. vii, 62 p. ; 28 cm. ISBN 0-8444-0358-X LC Card 80-29100 DDC 025.3/24 19
1. Cataloging of rare books - Rules. I. Title.
Z695.74 U54 1981

United States. Library of Congress. Photoduplication Service. Johnston, William Andrew, 1871- History up to date . New York , 1899. 257 p. : ***NYPL [*ZH-665]***

BIBLIOGRAPHIC GUIDE

United States. Library of Congress. Prints and Photographs

562

United States. Library of Congress. Prints and Photographs Division. Counts, I. Wilmer. A photographic legacy /. Bloomington, Ind. , c1979. 72 p. : *NYPL [IT 80-2223]*

United States. Library of Congress. Processing Dept. Subject Cataloging Division. see **United States. Library of Congress. Subject Cataloging Division.**

United States. Library of Congress. Rare Book Division. [Dime novels collection] /. Washington [197-] 83 reels ; *NYPL [*ZAN-5163 - *ZAN-5191]*

United States. Library of Congress. Recorded Sound, Broadcasting, and Motion Picture Division. see **United States. Library of Congress. Motion Picture, Broadcasting, and Recorded Sound Division.**

United States. Library of Congress. Reference Dept. General Reference and Bibliography Division. see **United States. Library of Congress. General Reference and Bibliography Division.**

United States. Library of Congress. Research Services. Manpower for science and engineering in China / prepared for the Subcommittee on Science, Research, and Technology of the Committee on Science and Technology, U. S. House of Representatives, Ninety-sixth Congress, second session, by the Research Services Division, Library of Congress. Washington : U. S. Govt. Print. Off. : for sale by the Supt. of Docs., U. S. Govt. Print. Off., 1980. v, 36 p. ; 24 cm. (Science and technology in the People's Republic of China, background study ; no. 4) At head of title: Committee print. "Serial YY." "June 1980." Includes bibliographical references. LC Card 80-603062 DDC 331.12/9150951 19
1. Scientists - China. 2. Engineers - China. 3. Science - Study and teaching - China - History. 4. Engineering - Study and teaching - China - History. 5. Manpower planning - China. I. United States. Congress. House. Committee on Science and Technology. Subcommittee on Science, Research, and Technology. II. Title.
Q149.C5 U56 1980

United States. Library of Congress. Research Services. European Division. see **United States. Library of Congress. European Division.**

United States. Library of Congress. Science and Technology Project.
List of subject headings. United States. Defense Documentation Center. ASTIA subject headings. - 4th ed. Arlington, Va., 1959. v, 758 p.; LC Card 59-61320
NYPL [JSF 80-818]

United States. Library of Congress. Science Policy Research Division.
Energy from biomass and solid wastes : prospects and constraints / prepared for the Subcommittee on Natural Resources and Environment and the Subcommittee on Science, Research, and Technology and the Subcommittee on Energy Development and Applications of the Committee on Science and Technology, U. S. House of Representatives, Ninety-sixth Congress, second session, by the Science Policy Research Division, Congressional Research Service, Library of Congress. Washington : U. S. Govt. Print. Off. : for sale by the Supt. of Docs., U. S. Govt. Print. Off., 1980. xix, 169 p. : ill. ; 24 cm. At head of title: Committee print. "Serial RR." LC Card 80-603278 DDC 333.79/38 19
1. Biomass energy. 2. Waste products as fuel. I. United States. Congress. House. Committee on Science and Technology. Subcommittee on Natural Resources and Environment. II. United States. Congress. House. Committee on Science and Tecnology. Subcommittee on Science, Research, and Technology. III. United States. Congress. House. Committee on Science and Tecnology. Subcommittee on Energy Development and Applications. IV. Title.
TP360 .U59 1980

Societal aspects of hydrogen energy systems /. Washington , 1979. vii, 161 p. : LC Card 80-602232 DDC 338.4/766581/0973 19
TP359.H8 S58

United States and Soviet progress in space. United States. Library of Congress. Congressional Research Service. United States and Soviet progress in space : summary data

through 1979 and a forward look : report / prepared for the Subcommittee on Space Science and Applications of the Committee on Science and Technology, U. S. House of Representatives, Ninety-sixth Congress, second session, by the Congressional Research Service, Library of Congress. Washington , 1980. xiii, 91 p. ; LC Card 80-602269 DDC 387.8 19
TL789.8.U5 U54 1980

Workshop on Research Needed to Improve the Quality of Socioeconomic Data Used in Regulatory Decisionmaking, Library of Congress, 1979. Workshop on Research Needed to Improve the Quality of Socioeconomic Data Used in Regulatory Decisionmaking . Washington , 1980. xiii, 296 p. ; LC Card 80-602262 DDC 361.6/1/072073 19
H22 .W67 1979

United States. Library of Congress. Subject Cataloging Division.
Classification, Class H, Subclasses H-HJ, social sciences, economics / Subject Cataloging Division, Processing Services, Library of Congress. 4th ed. Washington : The Library : for sale by the Cataloging Distribution Service, 1981. xiii, 400 p. ; 26 cm. Title on spine: Library of Congress classification, social sciences, economics. Includes index. ISBN 0-8444-0353-9 (pbk.) LC Card 80-607827 DDC 025.4/63 19
1. Classification - Books - Social sciences. 2. Classification, Library of Congress. I. Title. II. Title: Social sciences, economics. III. Title: Library of Congress classification, social sciences, economics.
Z696.U5 H-HJ 1981

Classification, Class Z, bibliography and library science / Subject Cataloging Division, Processing Services, Library of Congress. 5th ed. Washington : Library of Congress, 1980. p. cm. Edited by Lawrence Buzard and Susan Williams. ISBN 0-8444-0340-7 LC Card 80-607921
1. Classification - Books - Bibliography. 2. Classification - Books - Library science. 3. Classification, Library of Congress. I. Buzard, Lawrence. II. Williams, Susan, 1947-. III. Title.
Z696.U5 Z 1980

Library of Congress subject headings / Subject Cataloging Division, Processing Services. 9th ed. Washington : Library of Congress, 1980. 2 v. (xxiii, 2591 p.) ; 31 cm. Incorporates material through 1978. Kept up to date by cumulative supplements issued quarterly, with annual cumulations, 1979- ISBN 0-8444-0299-0 LC Card 79-22742
1. Subject headings. I. Title.
Z695 .U4749 1980
NYPL [Perf. Arts Ref. 81-651]

UNITED STATES. LIBRARY OF CONGRESS. THOMAS JEFFERSON BUILDING - HISTORY - EXHIBITIONS.
Hilker, Helen-Anne. Ten First Street, Southeast . Washington , 1980. iii, 102 p. : ISBN 0-8444-0351-2 LC Card 80-607808 DDC 027.5753 19
Z679.2.U54 H54

UNITED STATES. LIBRARY OF CONGRESSES - CATALOGS.
Gephart, Ronald M. Revolutionary America, 1763-1789 . Washington , 1982. p. cm. ISBN 0-8444-0359-8 LC Card 80-606802 DDC 016.9733 19
Z1238 .G43 E208

UNITED STATES MAGISTRATES.
United States. Congress. Senate. Select Committee on Indian Affairs. Jurisdiction on Indian reservations . Washington , 1980. iv, 467 p. ; LC Card 80-602898 DDC 349.73/08997 19
KF26.5 .I4 1980f

United States. Manpower Administration. see **United States. Dept. of Labor. Manpower Administration.**

United States. Manpower Policy, Evaluation, and Research, Office of. see **United States. Dept. of Labor. Office of Manpower Policy, Evaluation, and Research.**

United States. Manpower Policy, National Commission for. see **United States. National Commission for Manpower Policy.**

UNITED STATES - MANUFACTURES.
Aho, C. Michael, 1949- An empirical analysis of the structure of U. S. manufacturing trade, 1964-1976 /. [Washington, D.C.] [Springfield,

Va. , 1980] 45 p. : LC Card 80-602633 DDC 382/.0973 19
HD9725 .A63

UNITED STATES - MANUFACTURES - EMPLOYEES - STATISTICS.
United States. Bureau of Labor Statistics. Occupational employment in manufacturing industries, 1977 /. Washington, D.C. [1980] vi, 91 p., [1] leaf of plates : LC Card 80-602314 DDC 331.12/57/0973 19
HD5724 .U625 1980a

UNITED STATES - MAPS.
(1970) United States. Geological Survey. [National atlas of the United States of America. Location index.] Location index. McLean, Va. , 1975. 309 p. ; LC Card 80-107197 DDC 912/.73
G1200 .U57 1975 Index

(1975) United States. Geological Survey. Transportation map of ... [Washington] 1975-76. 41 col. maps on sheets 43 x 56 cm. and 56 x 43 cm. Scales vary. Each sheet separately titled. "Transportation zone edition." Shows lines that may be subject to abandonment, those operating under rail service continuation provisions, and other operating lines. Includes "Index to railroads." Accompanied by text. [2] p. *NYPL [Map Div. 80-3426]*

(1978) United States. Economic Development Administration. EDA qualified areas, July 1978. [Washington] 1978. map 62 x 99 cm. Scale ca. 1:5,000,000. Insets: Puerto Rico, Virgin Is. -- Alaska. -- Hawaii. - Gvam. -- A. Samoa.
G3701.G17 1976 .U5
NYPL [Map Div. 80-3385]

(1979) United States. Energy Information Administration. Major extra high voltage transmission lines. Washington , 1979. col. map 55 x 71 cm. Scale ca. 1:7,200,000. Includes numbered "Ownership list" keyed to map.
NYPL [Map Div. 80-3272]

(1979) United States. Energy Information Administration. Major extra high voltage transmission lines, December 31, 1978. Washington [1979] 1 map : 44 x 70 cm. Scale ca. 1:7,000,000. "DOE/EIA-0165(78)." Includes index to owners.
G3701.N4 1977 .U5
NYPL [Map Div 81-3045]

United States. Marine Corps.
Marine Corps manual. Washington, D.C. : Dept. of the Navy, Headquarters U. S. Marine Corps : [for sale by the Supt. of Docs., U. S. Govt. Print. Off.], 1980- 1 v. ; 28 cm. Cover title. "Supersedes for the Marine Corps manual, 1961." Loose-leaf for updating. LC Card 80-602364 DDC 359.9/6/0973 19
1. United States. Marine Corps - Regulations. I. Title.
VE153 .U54 1980

UNITED STATES. MARINE CORPS.
United States. Congressional Budget Office. The Marine Corps in the 1980s . [Washington, D.C.] [1980] xxii, 74 p. : LC Card 80-602374 DDC 359.9/6/0973 19
VE23 .A5 1980

UNITED STATES. MARINE CORPS. ATTACK SQUADRON 223 - HISTORY.
Jones, Brett A. A history of Marine Attack Squadron 223 /. Washington , 1978. vii, 39 p. : LC Card 79-601756
D790 .J66
NYPL [JFF 80-1164]

United States. Marine Corps. History and Museums Division.
Bartlett, Merrill L. George Barnett, 1859-1930 . Washington, D.C. , 1980. vii, 18 p. ; LC Card 81-600912 DDC 016.355/0092/4 19
Z6616.B3215 B37 E746.B37

Jones, Brett A. A history of Marine Attack Squadron 223 /. Washington , 1978. vii, 39 p. : LC Card 79-601756
D790 .J66
NYPL [JFF 80-1164]

Parker, Gary W. A history of Marine Medium Helicopter Squadron 161 /. Washington , 1978. vii, 47 P. : LC Card 79-601669
VG94.6.M38 P37
NYPL [JFF 81-182]

Santelli, James S. A brief history of the 7th Marines /. Washington, D.C. , 1980. vii, 83 p. : LC Card 81-600697 DDC 359.9/6/0973 19
VE23.25 7th .S25

UNITED STATES. MARINE CORPS. HISTORY AND MUSEUMS DIVISION - CATALOGS.

Bartlett, Merrill L. George Barnett, 1859-1930 . Washington, D.C. , 1980. vii, 18 p. ; LC Card 81-600912 DDC 016.355/0092/4 19
Z6616.B3215 B37 E746.B37

UNITED STATES. MARINE CORPS. - HISTORY - SOURCES - BIBLIOGRAPHY - CATALOGS.
Bartlett, Merrill L. George Barnett, 1859-1930 . Washington, D.C. , 1980. vii, 18 p. ; LC Card 81-600912 DDC 016.355/0092/4 19
Z6616.B3215 B37 E746.B37

UNITED STATES. MARINE CORPS. MARINES, 7TH HISTORY.
Santelli, James S. A brief history of the 7th Marines /. Washington, D.C. , 1980. vii, 83 p. : LC Card 81-600697 DDC 359.9/6/0973 19
VE23.25 7th .S25

UNITED STATES. MARINE CORPS - REGULATIONS.
United States. Marine Corps. Marine Corps manual. Washington, D.C. , 1980- 1 v. ; LC Card 80-602364 DDC 359.9/6/0973 19
VE153 .U54 1980

UNITED STATES. MARINE MEDIUM HELICOPTER SQUADRON 161 - HISTORY.
Parker, Gary W. A history of Marine Medium Helicopter Squadron 161 /. Washington , 1978. vii, 47 P. : LC Card 79-601669
VG94.6.M38 P37   *NYPL [JFF 81-182]*

United States. Maritime Administration.
Analysis of the North American cruise industry /. [Washington, D.C.?] [1980] v, 145 p. : LC Card 80-604175 DDC 387.5/42 19
G550 .A56

Computer Sciences Corporation. Shipping operations information system /. Falls Church, Va., 1973. 2 v.   *NYPL [*XMQ-2149]*

Port Authority of New York and New Jersey. Planning and Development Dept. Economic impact of the U. S. merchant marine and shipbuilding industries . New York, 1977. viii, 272 p.;
HE746 .C48   *NYPL [*XME-9407]*

Relative cost of shipbuilding. Washington. 26 cm. (United States. Dept. of Commerce. Publication) Annual.
1. *Ship-building - Costs - Yearbooks. I. Title.*
          NYPL [JLM 80-1114]

Report. Washington. illus., tables, 24-28 cm. Annual. Supersedes in part: United States. Federal Maritime Board. Annual report of the Federal Maritime Board and Maritime Administration (in Old Catalog).
1. *Shipping - United States - Periodicals.*
          NYPL [JLM 80-989]

Seafaring guide & directory of labor management affiliations. Washington, D.C. : U. S. Dept. of Commerce, Maritime Administration : for sale by the Supt. of Docs., U. S. Govt. Print. Off., [1980] iv, 49 p. ; 24 cm. Ed. published in 1969 authored by U. S. Office of Maritime Manpower, Division of Labor Studies. "January 1980." LC Card 80-602281 DDC 331.88/113875/0973 19
1. *Trade-unions - Merchant seamen - United States - Directories. 2. Merchant marine - United States - Directories. I. United States. Office of Maritime Manpower. Division of Labor Studies. Seafaring guide and directory of labor management affiliations. II. Title.*
HD6515.S42 U46 1980

Stanford Research Institute. SRI International. Cost effectiveness of marine fire protection programs . [Washington] , 1978. xvii, 212 p. : LC Card 79-602278
VK1258 .S18 1979   *NYPL [JLF 81-262]*

United States Department of Commerce final environmental impact statement : Maritime Administration Title XI tank vessels engaged in domestic trade. [Washington] : The Administration, [1979] ca. 350 p. in various pagings : ill. ; 27 cm. "MA-EIS-7302-79016-F." Cover title. LC Card 79-602128 DDC 333.91/1/0973 19
1. *Oil spills - Environmental aspects - United States. 2. Tankers - Environmental aspects - United States. 3. Water - Pollution - United States. 4. Environmental impact statements - United States. I. Title.*
TD427.P4 U58 1979

What U. S. ports mean to the economy / [written by Jerome Gilbert, project leader,

Nai-Ching Sun, Amos Ilan; consulting editor, Walter Hamshar]. [Washington] : U. S. Dept. of Commerce, Maritime Administration : for sale by the Supt. of Docs., U. S. Govt. Print. Off., 1978. 58 p., [1] leaf of plates : ill. ; 28 cm. LC Card 79-602661
1. *Harbors - United States. 2. United States - Economic conditions - 1971-. I. Gilbert, Jerome. II. Title.*
HE553 .U643 1978

United States. Maritime Administration. Division of Trade Studies and Statistics. Foreign flag mechant ships owned by U. S. parent companies as of June 30, 1974 / U. S. Department of Commerce, Maritime Administration, Office of Subsidy Administration, Division of Trade Studies and Statistics. Washington : U. S. Govt. Print. Off., [1975?] 54 p. ; 26 cm.
1. *Ships - Nationality - Directories. I. Title.*
          NYPL [JLF 79-1500]

United States. Maritime Administration. Office of Policy and Plans. The maritime aids of the six major maritime nations, / prepared by Temple, Barker & Sloane, Inc. and Chase Econometric Associates [for the] Office of Policy and Plans, Maritime Administrations, U. S. Dept. of Commerce. [Washington] : U. S. Dept. of Commerce, Maritime Administration, Office of Policy and Plans, 1977. ca. 500 p. in various pagings : ill. ; 29 cm. Microfiche (neg.) NTIS. 6 sheets. 11 x 15 cm. (PB 273 013) Bibliography: p. E[1]-E13. LC Card 78-600514
1. *Shipping bounties and subsidies. 2. Merchant marine - Finance. 3. Ship-building - Finance. I. Temple, Barker & Sloane. II. Chase Econometric Associates. III. Title.*
HE741 .U55 1977   *NYPL [*XME-9415]*

United States. Maritime Administration. Office of Port and Intermodal Development. see United States. Office of Port and Intermodal Development.

United States. Maritime Administration. Office of Subsidy Administration. Division of Trade Studies and Statistics. see United States. Maritime Administration. Division of Trade Studies and Statistics.

United States. Maritime Administration. Policy and Plans, Office of. see United States. Maritime Administration. Office of Policy and Plans.

United States. Maritime Fire Prevention and Control Administration. Stanford Research Institute. SRI International. Cost effectiveness of marine fire protection programs . [Washington] , 1978. xvii, 212 p. : LC Card 79-602278
VK1258 .S18 1979   *NYPL [JLF 81-262]*

United States. Materials Transportation Bureau. Annual report of pipeline safety. Washington. illus. 26 cm. Title varies: 1977, Annual report on the administration of the Natural Gas Pipeline Safety Act.
1. *Gas, Natural - Pipe lines - Safety regulations - United States - Periodicals. 2. Gas, Natural - Pipe line failures - United States - Periodicals. I. United States. Materials Transportation Bureau. Annual report on the administration of the Natural Gas Pipeline Safety Act. II. Title.*   *NYPL [JLM 81-321]*

Annual report on the administration of the Natural Gas Pipeline Safety Act. United States. Materials Transportation Bureau. Annual report of pipeline safety. Washington.
          NYPL [JLM 81-321]

United States. Maternal and Child Health, Office for. see United States. Office for Maternal and Child Health.

United States. Mental Retardation, President's Committee on. see United States. President's Committee on Mental Retardation.

United States. Merchant Marine and Fisheries, Committee on (House) see United States. Congress. House. Committee on Merchant Marine and Fisheries.

UNITED STATES METRIC BOARD.
United States. Congress. House. Committee on Science and Technology. Subcommittee on Science, Research, and Technology. Oversight hearing, United States Metric Board . Washington , 1980. iii, 34 ; LC Card 80-602077 DDC 353.0082/1 19
KF27 .S399 1979m

United States--Mexican relations and the energy crisis . United States. Congress. House. Special Study Mission to Mexico City. Washington , 1980. vii, 17 p. ; LC Card 80-602869 DDC 327.73072 19
E183.8.M6 U36 1980

United States/Mexico electricity exchanges /. United States. Dept. of Energy. Washington, D.C. [1980] 242 p. in various pagings : LC Card 80-603171 DDC 382/.45621319/0972 19
HD9685.U5 U495 1980

United States-Mexico scientific and technological cooperation . United States. Congress. House. Committee on Science and Technology. Subcommittee on Science, Research, and Technology. Washington , 1979. iii, 289 p. : LC Card 80-602192 DDC 338.9 19
KF27 .S399 1979k

United States - Military air defenses. see United States - Air defenses, Military.

United States. Military Appeals, Court of. see United States. Court of Military Appeals.

UNITED STATES. MILITARY ASSISTANCE COMMAND, VIETNAM. CIVIL OPERATIONS AND RURAL DEVELOPMENT SUPPORT.
Scoville, Thomas W. Reorganizing for pacification support /. Washington, D.C. [1981] p. cm. LC Card 81-10204 DDC 959.704/3373 19
DS558.2 .S27

United States. Military History Institute. see US Army Military History Institute.

UNITED STATES - MILITARY POLICY.
Gervasi, Sean. The United States and the arms embargo against South Africa . [Binghamton] , c1978. 49 p. ; LC Card 78-112749 DDC 382/.456234/0968 19
HD9743.S62 G47

Giddings, Edward N. Unilateral U. S. force reduction in Western Europe. Carlisle Barracks, Pa., 1972. iii, 45 leaves.   *NYPL [*XM-13703]*

New Jersey. State Legislature. General Assembly. Revenue, Finance, and Appropriations Committee. Public hearing before Assembly Revenue, Finance, and Appropriations Committee on Assembly Resolution Number 50 (memorializes Congress to transfer funding from unnecessary military spending to domestic spending for human services) . [Trenton] [1980] 49, 23x p. ; LC Card 81-621305 DDC 353.97490084 19
KFN1811.4 .R45 1980b

United States. Congress. House. Committee on Armed Services. Hearings on military posture and H.R. 6495 (H.R. 6974) Department of Defense authorization for appropriations for fiscal year 1981 before the Committee on Armed Services, House of Representatives, Ninety-sixth Congress, second session. Washington , 1980- v. in : LC Card 80-602996 DDC 355.6/22/0973 19
KF27 .A7 1980

United States. Congress. House. Committee on Armed Services. Subcommittee on Seapower and Strategic and Critical Materials. National policy objectives and the adequacy of our current navy forces . Washington , 1980 [i.e. 1981] ii, 137 p. : LC Card 81-601761 DDC 359/.03/0973 19
KF27 .A769 1979e

United States. Congress. Senate. Committee on Foreign Relations. Nuclear war strategy . Washington , 1981. iii, 40 p. ; LC Card 81-601145 DDC 355/.0217/0973 19
KF26 .F6 1980s

United States. Congressional Budget Office. The Marine Corps in the 1980s . [Washington, D.C.] [1980] xxii, 74 p. : LC Card 80-602374 DDC 359.9/6/0973 19
VE23 .A5 1980

United States. Congressional Budget Office. Planning U. S. general purpose forces . Washington , 1977. xxiii, 95 p. : LC Card 77-603153
UA26.E27 U54 1977

UNITED STATES - MILITARY POLICY - ADDRESSES, ESSAYS, LECTURES.
Should the United States significantly increase its foreign military commitments? .

Washington , 1980. v, 484 p. : LC Card
80-603968   DDC 355/.031/0973 19
UA23 .S485

UNITED STATES - MILITARY POLICY - CONGRESSES.
National Security Affairs Conference, 6th,
National Defense University, 1979. Continuity
and change in the eighties and beyond .
[Washington, D.C.] , 1979. xiii, 222 p. ; LC
Card 80-601820   DDC 355/.033073 19
UA23 .N248 1979

UNITED STATES - MILITARY POLICY - DECISION MAKING.
United States. General Accounting Office.
Models, data, and war . [Washington, D.C.] ,
1980. v, 153 p. : LC Card 80-601429   DDC
355/.0335/73072 19
UA23 .U475 1980

UNITED STATES - MILITARY POLICY - PERIODICALS.
United States. Joint Chiefs of Staff. United
States military posture. [Washington]   LC Card
79-642632   *NYPL [JLM 80-756]*

United States military posture. United States.
Joint Chiefs of Staff. [Washington]   LC Card
79-642632   *NYPL [JLM 80-756]*

UNITED STATES. MILITARY SEALIFT COMMAND.
United States. Congress. House. Committee on
Merchant Marine and Fisheries. Defense sealift
capability . Washington , 1980. iv, 301 p. : LC
Card 80-604083   DDC 359.9/82/0973 19
KF27 .M4 1979c

**United States. Minerals Policy and Research
Analysis, Office of.** see **United States. Office
of Minerals Policy and Research Analysis.**

United States. Mines Bureau. see **United States.
Bureau of Mines.**

**United States. Minority Business Development
Agency.**
Guide to federal assistance programs for
minority business development enterprises.
[Washington?]   *NYPL [JLM 80-821]*

Guide to federal assistance programs for
minority business development enterprises /
prepared by the Minority Business
Development Agency. [Washington] : The
Agency, [1979] xi, 90 p. : maps ; 27 cm. Title
on spine: Federal assistance program. "October 1979."
LC Card 80-601260   DDC 353.0082/048 19
1. Federal aid to minority business enterprises - United
States. 2. Minority business enterprises - United States -
Finance. 3. Minority business enterprises - United
States - Information services - United States. I. Title. II.
Title: Minority business development enterprises. III.
Title: Federal assistance program.
HD2346.U5 U54 1979

Guide to Federal assistance programs for
minority business development enterprises / U.
S. Department of Commerce, Minority Business
Development Agency. [Washington] : The
Agency, [1980] viii, 95 p. ; 28 cm. "February
1980." LC Card 80-602054   DDC 353.0082/048 19
1. Federal aid to minority business enterprises - United
States. 2. Minority business enterprises - United States -
Information services - United States. 3. Minority
business enterprises - United States - Finance.
HD2346.U5 U54 1980

UNITED STATES. MINORITY BUSINESS DEVELOPMENT AGENCY.
United States. Congress. House. Committee on
Small Business. Subcommittee on General
Oversight and Minority Enterprise.
Establishment of a Minority Business
Development Administration in the Department
of Commerce . Washington , 1980. iv, 203 p. :
LC Card 81-600618   DDC 353.0082/048 19
KF27 .S64 1980h

**United States. Minority Business Enterprise,
Office of.** see **United States. Office of
Minority Business Enterprise.**

UNITED STATES - MORAL CONDITIONS.
Fellman, Anita Clair. Making sense of self .
Philadelphia , 1981. p. cm. ISBN 0-8122-7810-0
LC Card 81-51141   DDC 613/.07/073 19
RA440.3.U5 F43

Tipton, Steven M. Getting saved from the
sixties . Berkeley , c1981. p. cm. ISBN
0-520-03868-1 LC Card 81-3033   DDC 973.92

19
HN59 .T58

**United States. National Advisory Committee for
Aeronautics. Ames Aeronautical Laboratory,
Moffett Field, Calif.** see **United States. Ames
Research Center, Moffett Field, Calif.**

**United States. National Advisory Committee on
Black Higher Education and Black Colleges
and Universities.** Access of Black Americans
to higher education : how open is the door?.
Washington : National Advisory Committee on
Black Higher Education and Black Colleges and
Universities : for sale by the Supt. of Docs., U.
S. Govt. Print. Off., 1979. xv, 59 p. ; 26 cm.
"January 1979." Bibliography: p. 55-57. LC Card
79-602775   DDC 378.73 19
1. Afro-Americans - Education (Higher). I. Title.
LC2781 .U54 1979

**United States. National Advisory Committee on
Oceans and Atmosphere. National Sea Grant
Program.** see **National Sea Grant Program.**

**United States. National Advisory Council on
Equality of Educational Opportunity.** Final
report, September 30, 1979 / National Advisory
Council on Equality of Educational
Opportunity. [Washington] : The Council,
[1979] 145 p. ; 28 cm. Cover title. LC Card
79-604002
1. Educational equalization - United States.
LC213.2 .U54 1979   *NYPL [JFF 81-164]*

**United States. National Advisory Council on the
Education of Disadvantaged Children.** (Old
Catalog form: United States. Education of
Disadvantaged Children, National Advisory
Council on the.)
Special report on rural education. Washington,
D.C. : National Advisory Council on the
Education of Disadvantaged Children, [1979]
82 p. ; 27 cm. Cover title. LC Card 80-602041
DDC 370.19/346/0973 19
1. Education, Rural - United States. I. Title.
LC5146 .U54 1979

**United States. National Advisory Council on
Women's Educational Programs. Information
Resources Committee.** Young, Tasia. Report
of the Southwest Consultation on the
Educational Needs of Rural Girls and Women,
convened by the Information Resources
Committee, Advisory Council on Women's
Educational Programs in Santa Fe, New
Mexico, September 10 and 11, 1976 /.
Albuquerque [1976?] 25 leaves ; LC Card
79-623319   DDC 376/.9789 19
LC1758.N6 Y68

**United States. National Aeronautics and Space
Administration.** (Old Catalog form: United
States, Aeronautics, National advisory
committee for)
Anderton, David A. Sixty years of aeronautical
research, 1917-1977 /. Washington , 1978. 89
p. : LC Card 79-601508
TL521.312 .A65   *NYPL [JSF 81-171]*

Geology of the Apollo 16 area, Central Lunar
Highlands . Washington , 1980. p. cm. LC Card
80-607170   DDC 559.9/1 19
QB592 .G47

NASA conference proceedings .
(CP2111) Scientific research with the space
telescope . [Huntsville, Ala.] , Washington,
D.C. [1979] xii, 327 p. : LC Card 80-601618
DDC 520 19
QB61 .S33

NASA conference publication .
(2089) Symposium on Space Missions to
Comets, Goddard Space Flight Center, 1977.
Space missions to comets . [Washington] ,
1979. v, 226 p. : LC Card 79-604295   DDC
523.6 19
QB721 .S97 1977

(2100) Workshop on Earth Radiation Budget
Science, Williamsburg, Va., 1978. Earth
radiation budget science, 1978 . [Washington,
D.C.] , Springfield, Va. , 1979. vi, 72 p. : LC
Card 80-601801   DDC 551.5/272 19
QC809.E6 W67 1978

(2116) Workshop on Operational
Applications of Satellite Snowcover
Observations, Sparks, Nev., 1979. Operational
applications of satellite snowcover
observations . Washington, D.C. , 1980. vi,
301 p. : LC Card 80-602361   DDC 551.57/846

19
GB2601.72.A83 W67 1979

(2126) General aviation propulsion .
Washington, D.C. , Springfield, Va. , 1980.
vi, 432 p. : LC Card 80-602545   DDC
629.134/35 19
TL701 .G45

(2132) Remote sensing and problems of the
hydrosphere . Washington, D.C. , 1980. iv,
30 p. ; LC Card 80-603169   DDC 553.7/028/7
19
TD419.5 .R45

NASA conference publications. NASA-CP.
(2101) Flight technology improvement.
[Washington], 1979. 709 p.;
NYPL [JSF 80-531]

(2107) Nuclear-pumped lasers. [Washington],
1979. vi, 136 p.:   *NYPL [JSF 80-528]*

NASA reference publication .
(1050) Classical aerodynamic theory /.
[Washington, D.C.] , Springfield, Va. , 1979.
vi, 311 p. : LC Card 80-601716   DDC
629.132/3 19
TL570 .C54

(1054) Wilson, Gregory Sims.
Thunderstorm-environment interactions
determined with three-dimensional
trajectories /. [Washington] , 1980. viii, 153
p. : LC Card 80-603200   DDC 551.5/54 19
QC968 .W54

NASA SP.
(428) Ames Summer Study on Space
Settlements and Industrialization Using
Nonterrestrial Materials, Ames Research
Center, 1977. Space resources and space
settlements . Washington, D.C. , 1979. x, 288
p. : LC Card 79-603821   DDC 629.44/2 19
TL795.7 .A45 1977

(438) Batson, Raymond M. Atlas of Mars .
Washington, D.C. , 1979. xi, 146 p. : LC
Card 79-600164   DDC 912/.99/23 19
QB641 .B27

(444) Carr, Michael H. Images of Mars .
Washington, D.C. , 1980. iii, 32 p. : LC Card
80-602703   DDC 559.9/23 19
QB641 .C36

North Atlantic Treaty Organization. Advisory
Group for Aerospace Research and
Development. How to obtain information in
different fields of science and technology.
Langley Field, Va., 1974. 1 v. of various
pagings;   *NYPL [JSG 80-127]*

The Rotary combustion engine . [Washington,
D.C.] , Springfield, Va. , 1978. v, 190 p. : LC
Card 79-603405
TL701.1 .R58

Space photography index. Washington. 10 x 15
cm.
1. Space photography - Indexes - Periodicals. I. Title.
NYPL [JSP 81-22]

Voyager 1, encounter with Jupiter.
[Washington] : National Aeronautics and Space
Administration, 1979. 43 p. : ill. ; 28 cm. LC
Card 79-602497
1. Jupiter (Planet) - Photographs from space. 2. Project
Voyager. I. Title.
QB661 .U54 1979a   *NYPL [JSF 81-36]*

Workshop on Operational Applications of
Satellite Snowcover Observations, Sparks, Nev.,
1979. Operational applications of satellite
snowcover observations . Washington, D.C. ,
1980. vi, 301 p. : LC Card 80-602361   DDC
551.57/846 19
GB2601.72.A83 W67 1979

UNITED STATES. NATIONAL AERONAUTICS AND SPACE ADMINISTRATION.
Ahn, Chung-Hae. NASA's biomedical research
program /. Washington, D.C. , 1981. p. cm.
LC Card 81-607969   DDC 616.9/80214 19
RC1150 .A35

Bell, Trudy. Technologies for the handicapped
and the aged . [Washington] , 1979. iii, 43 p. :
LC Card 80-601228   DDC 617 19
R856 .B4

United States civilian space programs,
1958-1978 . Washington , 1981- v. <1 > :
LC Card 81-602024   DDC 629.4 19
TL789.8.U5 U58

United States. Congress. House. Committee on Science and Technology. Posture hearings (NASA and FAA) . Washington , 1980. iii, 107 p. ; LC Card 80-602953 DDC 353.0085/6 19
KF27 .S39 1980

United States. Congress. House. Committee on Science and Technology. Subcommittee on Transportation, Aviation, and Communications. 1982 NASA authorization (program review) . Washington , 1980- v. <1> : LC Card 80-604026 DDC 353.0087/78 19
KF27 .S3997 1980e

United States. National Aeronautics and Space Administration. Ames Research Center, Moffett Field, Calif. see United States. Ames Research Center, Moffett Field, Calif.

UNITED STATES. NATIONAL AERONAUTICS AND SPACE ADMINISTRATION - APPROPRIATIONS AND EXPENDITURES.
United States. Congress. Senate. Committee on Appropriations. Subcommittee on HUD-Independent Agencies. Space shuttle and Galileo mission . Washington , 1980. iv, 132 p. ; LC Card 80-601987 DDC 353.0072/2368778 19
KF26 .A6486 1979c

UNITED STATES. NATIONAL AERONAUTICS AND SPACE ADMINISTRATION - BIBLIOGRAPHY.
Looney, John J. Bibliography of space books and articles from non-aerospace journals, 1957-1977 /. Washington, DC , 1979 [i.e. 1980] xv, 243 p. ; LC Card 80-601815 DDC 016.6294 19
Z5065.U5 L66 TL521.312

United States National Aeronautics and Space Administration. Langley Research Center, Hampton, Va. see United States, Langley Research Center, Hampton, Va.

United States. National Aeronautics and Space Administration. Lydon B. Johnson Space Center. see Lyndon B. Johnson Space Center.

United States. National Aeronautics and Space Administration. Office of Aeronautics and Space Technology. see United States. Office of Aeronautics and Space Technology.

United States. National Aeronautics and Space Administration. Office of Space Science. see United States. Office of Space Science.

United States. National Aeronautics and Space Administration. Scientific and Technical Information Branch.
Knight, Keith Shelburne. Atmospheric structure determined from satellite data /. Washington, D.C. [Springfield, Va.] 1981. x, 95 p. : LC Card 81-601075 DDC 551.5/14 19
QC879.59.A .K58

Remote sensing and problems of the hydrosphere . Washington, D.C. [Springfield, Va.] 1979. v, 56 p. : LC Card 81-601298 DDC 551.4/028/7 19
TD370 .R45

Research in nonlinear structural and solid mechanics . Washington, D.C. [Springfield, Va.] 1980. viii, 289 p. : LC Card 81-601087 DDC 624.1/71/0724 19
TA646 .R38

Viking orbiter views of Mars /. Washington, D.C. , 1980. vii, 182 p. : LC Card 80-600167 DDC 356/.00634 19
QB641 .V55

Walisora, J. M. The physiological basis for spacecraft environmental limits /. Washington, D.C. , Washington , D.C.] c1979. xvii, 217 p. : LC Card 81-600766 DDC 612/.0145 19
RC1150 .W34

United States. National Aeronautics and Space Administration. Scientific and Technical Information Office.
Hohl, Frank. Collisionless galaxy simulations /. Washington, D.C. [Springfield, Va.] 1979. iii, 145 p. : LC Card 81-600552 DDC 523.1/12/0724 19
QB857 .H64

The Stratosphere . Washington, D.C. [Springfield, Va.] 1979. xiv, 432 p. : LC Card

81-600765 DDC 551.5/142 19
QC881.2.S8 S85

United States. National Aeronautics and Space Agency. see United States. National Aeronautics and Space Administration.

United States. National Agricultural Library. Food and Nutrition Information and Educational Materials Center. Index to the proceedings of 10 USDA-Land-Grant university seminars for food service supervisory personnel 1969-1970-1971. [Washington] U. S. Dept. of Agriculture, National Agricultural Library [1974] xiii, 27 p. 28 cm. Microfilm.
1. School children - Food - Bibliography. 2. Children - Nutrition - Bibliography. 3. Nutrition - Bibliography. I. Title. ***NYPL [*Z-3211]***

United States. National Alcohol Fuels Commission. Federal agency compendium : Federal agency and department alcohol fuels programs / U. S. National Alcohol Fuels Commission. Washington, D.C. : The Commission, 1980. iii, 47 p. ; 28 cm. Cover title. "Prepared by Lloyd Costley ... [et al.]" LC Card 80-602837 DDC 353.0072/2368242 19
1. Alcohol as fuel. I. Costley, Lloyd. II. Title.
TP358 .U73 1980

UNITED STATES. NATIONAL ARCHIVES.
United States. Committee on Fair Employment Practice (1941-1943) Guide to the microfilm record of selected documents of records of the Committee on Fair Employment Practice in the custody of the National Archives /. Glen Rock, N. J. , 1970. iii, 131 p. ;
NYPL [Sc Micro R-3644]

United States. National Archives and Records Service.
Agricultural maps in the National Archives of the United States, ca. 1860-1930 / compiled by William J. Heynen. Washington : National Archives and Records Service, General Services Administration, 1976. vii, 25 p. : maps ; 23 cm. (Reference information paper . no. 75) LC Card 79-124956 DDC 015.73 s 912/.163/0973 19
1. Agricultural mapping - United States - History. 2. Agriculture - United States - Maps - History. 3. United States. National Archives and Records Service - Catalogs. I. Heynen, William J. II. Title. III. Series.
CD3023 .A35 no. 75 S494.5.C3

The National Archives and Records Service in 1978 / by James B. Rhoads, archivist of the United States. [Washington, D.C.] : The Service, [1979?] 20 p. : ill. ; 26 cm. Caption title. LC Card 80-601808 DDC 027.5753 19
1. United States. National Archives and Records Service. I. Rhoads, James Berton. II. Title.
CD3023 .U54 1979a

Preliminary inventory .
(195) United States. National Archives and Records Service. Preliminary inventory of the cartographic records of the Soil Conservation Service /. Washington , 1981. p. cm. LC Card 81-3988 DDC 016.3530082/326 19
CD3026 .A32 no. 195 CD3038

Preliminary inventory - National Archives and Records Service .
(11 (Rev.)) United States. National Archives and Records Service. Preliminary inventory of the records of the Civilian Conservation Corps . Washington , 1980. vii, 23 p. ; LC Card 80-28921 DDC 016.973 s 016.3337/2/0973 19
CD3026 .A32 no. 11, 1980 CD3035

(192) United States. National Archives and Records Service. Preliminary inventory of the Pueblo records created by field offices of the Bureau of Indian Affairs . Washington , 1980. vii, 34 p. ; LC Card 80-607174 DDC 016.973 s 016.3231/197/073 19
CD3026 .A32 no. 192 Z1210.P8 E99.P9

Preliminary inventory of the cartographic records of the Soil Conservation Service / compiled by William Heynen. Washington : National Archives & Records Service, General Services Administration, 1981. p. cm. (Preliminary inventory / National Archives & Records Service . 195) Includes indexes. LC Card 81-3988 DDC 016.3530082/326 19
1. United States. Soil Conservation Service - Archives - Catalogs. 2. Soil-surveys - United States - Bibliography - Catalogs. 3. United States. National Archives and Records Service - Catalogs. I. Heynen, William J. II. Series: United States. National Archives

and Records Service. Preliminary inventory , 195. III. Title.
CD3026 .A32 no. 195 CD3038

Preliminary inventory of the Pueblo records created by field offices of the Bureau of Indian Affairs : record group 75 / compiled by Robert Svenningsen. Washington : National Archives & Records Service, General Services Administration, 1980. vii, 34 p. ; 27 cm. (Preliminary inventory - National Archives and Records Service . 192) LC Card 80-607174 DDC 016.973 s 016.3231/197/073 19
1. Pueblo Indians - Government relations - Bibliography - Catalogs. 2. Indians of North America - Southwest, New - Government relations - Bibliography - Catalogs. 3. United States. Bureau of Indian Affairs - Bibliography - Catalogs. 4. United States. National Archives and Records Service - Catalogs. I. Svenningsen, Robert, 1941-. II. United States. Bureau of Indian Affairs. III. Series: United States. National Archives and Records Service. Preliminary inventory - National Archives and Records Service , 192. IV. Title.
CD3026 .A32 no. 192 Z1210.P8 E99.P9

Preliminary inventory of the records of the Civilian Conservation Corps : record group 35 / compiled by Douglas Helms. Washington : National Archives & Records Service, General Services Administration, 1980. vii, 23 p. ; 27 cm. (P[reliminary] i[nventory] - National Archives and Records Service . PI11 (Rev.)) "A revision of the Preliminary inventory of the records of the Civilian Conservation Corps, PI 11, compiled by Harold T. Pinkett (Washington, D.C.: NARS, 1948)." LC Card 80-28921 DDC 016.973 s 016.3337/2/0973 19
1. United States. Civilian Conservation Corps - Archives - Catalogs. 2. Reclamation of land - United States - History - Sources - Bibliography - Catalogs. 3. United States. National Archives. - Catalogs. I. Helms, Douglas, 1945-. II. United States. National Archives. Preliminary inventory of the records of the Civilian Conservation Corps. III. Series: United States. National Archives and Records Service. Preliminary inventory - National Archives and Records Service , 11 (Rev.). IV. Title.
CD3026 .A32 no. 11, 1980 CD3035

Selected documents pertaining to black workers among the records of the Department of Labor and its component bureaus, 1902-1969 / compiled by Debra L. Newman. Washington : National Archives and Records Service, General Services Administration, 1977. viii, 55 p. ; 27 cm. Special list - National Archives and Records Service, no. 40. LC Card 77-12904
1. Afro-Americans - Economic conditions - Sources - Bibliography - Catalogs. 2. Afro-Americans - Employment - Sources - Bibliography - Catalogs. 3. United States. Department of Labor. - Archives - Catalogs. 4. United States. National Archives and Records Service - Catalogs. I. Newman, Debra L. II. United States. Dept. of Labor. III. Title: Selected documents pertaining to black workers among the records of the Department of Labor ...
Z1361.N39 U63 1977 E185.8
NYPL [Sc F 81-48]

United States. Bureau of the Census. Census descriptions of geographic subdivisions and enumeration districts, 1830-1950. Washington , 1978. 6 microfilm reels ; ***NYPL [*ZI-283]***

United States. Census Office. 12th census, 1900. Descriptions of the enumeration districts of the ... Twelfth census, June 1, 1900. [Washington, D. C., 1977?] 2 reels.
NYPL [*ZI-275]

United States. Committee on Fair Employment Practice (1941-1943) Guide to the microfilm record of selected documents of records of the Committee on Fair Employment Practice in the custody of the National Archives /. Glen Rock, N. J. , 1970. iii, 131 p. ;
NYPL [Sc Micro R-3644]

UNITED STATES. NATIONAL ARCHIVES AND RECORDS SERVICE.
United States. General Services Administration. The National Archives celebrates the bicentennial /. Washington, D. C. , 1975. 15 p. ; ***NYPL [*XME-9265]***

United States. National Archives and Records Service. The National Archives and Records Service in 1978 /. [Washington, D.C.] [1979?] 20 p. : LC Card 80-601808 DDC 027.5753 19
CD3023 .U54 1979a

BIBLIOGRAPHIC GUIDE

United States. National Archives and Records Service - Catalogs.

566

UNITED STATES. NATIONAL ARCHIVES AND RECORDS SERVICE - CATALOGS.

United States. National Archives and Records Service. Agricultural maps in the National Archives of the United States, ca. 1860-1930 /. Washington , 1976. vii, 25 p. : LC Card 79-124956 DDC 015.73 s 912/.163/0973 19
CD3023 .A35 no. 75 S494.5.C3

United States. National Archives and Records Service. Preliminary inventory of the cartographic records of the Soil Conservation Service /. Washington , 1981. p. cm. LC Card 81-3988 DDC 016.3530082/326 19
CD3026 .A32 no. 195 CD3038

United States. National Archives and Records Service. Preliminary inventory of the Pueblo records created by field offices of the Bureau of Indian Affairs . Washington , 1980. vii, 34 p. ; LC Card 80-607174 DDC 016.973 s 016.3231/197/073 19
CD3026 .A32 no. 192 Z1210.P8 E99.P9

United States. National Archives and Records Service. Selected documents pertaining to black workers among the records of the Department of Labor and its component bureaus, 1902-1969 /. Washington , 1977. viii, 55 p. ; LC Card 77-12904
Z1361.N39 U63 1977 E185.8

NYPL [Sc F 81-48]

UNITED STATES. NATIONAL ARCHIVES AND RECORDS SERVICE - MANAGEMENT.

United States. Congress. House. Committee on Government Operations. Subcommittee on Government Information and Individual Rights. National Archives and Records Service documents preservation program and trust fund operation . Washington , 1980. v, 913 p. ; LC Card 80-602891 DDC 353.0071/46 19
KF27 .G6628 1979a

UNITED STATES. NATIONAL ARCHIVES. - CATALOGS.

United States. National Archives and Records Service. Preliminary inventory of the records of the Civilian Conservation Corps . Washington , 1980. vii, 23 p. ; LC Card 80-28921 DDC 016.973 s 016.3337/2/0973 19
CD3026 .A32 no. 11, 1980 CD3035

UNITED STATES. NATIONAL ARCHIVES - MICROFORM CATALOGS.

Zeidlik, Hannah M. Catalog and index to historical manuscripts, 1940-1966 /. Washington, DC , 1979. 2 v. ; LC Card 79-604297 DDC 016.355/00973 19
Z1249.M5 Z44 E745

United States. National Archives. Preliminary inventory of the records of the Civilian Conservation Corps. United States. National Archives and Records Service. Preliminary inventory of the records of the Civilian Conservation Corps . Washington , 1980. vii, 23 p. ; LC Card 80-28921 DDC 016.973 s 016.3337/2/0973 19
CD3026 .A32 no. 11, 1980 CD3035

United States. National Arthritis Advisory Board.
Arthritis research & education in nursing & allied health . [Bethesda, Md.] , 1980. xvii, 114 p. ; LC Card 80-603577 DDC 616.7/22/0072 19
RC933.A2 A77

Public policy & chronic disease . [Washington] , 1979. x, 122 p. : LC Card 79-602729
RA644.6 .P82   **NYPL [JLF 81-366]**

United States. National Bureau of Standards.
(Old Catalog form: United States. Standards Bureau)
Adler, Sanford C. A history of walkway slip-resistance research at the National Bureau of Standards /. [Washington] , 1979. iv, 31 p. : LC Card 79-600179 DDC 602/.18 s 698/.9 19
QC100 .U57 No. 565 TA418.72

American National Standards Institute. Subcommittee N43-3.2. American National Standard N538, classification of industrial ionizing radiation gauging devices /. Washington, D.C. , 1979. ix, 19 p. : LC Card 79-600113
QC795.5 .A48 1979

Audit and evaluation of computer security II . [Washington, D.C.] [1980] ca. 250 p. in various pagings : LC Card 80-600034 DDC

602/.18 s 658.4/78 19
QC100 .U57 no. 500-57 HF5548.2

Building science series .
(107) Kovacs, William D. Soil and rock anchors for mobile homes . Washington, D.C. , 1979. xvi, 147 p. : LC Card 79-600143 DDC 690/.02/18 s 690/.79 19
TA435 .U58 no. 107 TH4819.M6

(121) Yokel, Felix Y. Soil classification for construction practice in shallow trenching /. Washington, D.C. [1980] xiv, 76 p. : LC Card 80-600014 DDC 690/.02/18 s 624.1/51/012 19
TA435 .U58 no. 121 TA710

(122) A Study of lumber used for bracing trenches in the United States . Washington, D.C. [1980] 218 p. in various pagings : LC Card 80-600015 DDC 690/.02/18 s 624.1/52 19
TA435 .U58 no. 122 TA770

(123) Knab, Lawrence I. The effect of moisture on the thermal conductance of roofing systems /. [Washington] , 1980. x, 46 p. : LC Card 80-600031 DDC 690/.0218 s 690/.15 19
TA435 .U58 no. 123 TH2401

(124) Hurricane wind speeds in the United States /. Washington, D.C. [1980] viii, 30, 11 p. : LC Card 80-600039 DDC 690/.02/18 s 551.5/52 19
TA435 .U58 no. 124 QC933

(127) Yokel, Felix Y. Recommended technical provisions for construction practice in shoring and sloping of trenches and excavations /. Washington, DC [1980] xvi, 68 p. : LC Card 80-600068 DDC 690/.02/18 s 624.1/52 19
TA435 .U58 no. 127 TA770

Chapman, Robert E. Cost estimation and cost variability in residential rehabilitation . Washington, D.C. , 1980. x, 109 p. : LC Card 80-600174 DDC 690/.0218 s 690/.8/0286 19
TA435 .U58 vol. 129 HD7293

Data base directions, the conversion problem . [Washington, D.C.?] , 1980. x, 167 p. : LC Card 80-600129 DDC 602/.18 s 658.4/0388 19
QC100 .U57 no. 500-64 QA76.9.D3

Fire investigation handbook /. [Washington, D.C.?] , 1980. ix, 187 p. : LC Card 80-600095 DDC 363.3/765 19
TH9180 .F48

Guidance on requirements analysis for office automation systems. Washington, D.C. , c1980. 125 p. in various pagings : LC Card 80-600179 DDC 602/.18 s 651.8/4 19
QC100 .U57 no. 500-72 HF5548.2

Handbook. For other vols. in this series, see entry in Old Catalog: United States. Standards Bureau. Handbook.
(130) National Conference on Weights and Measures. Model state laws and regulations /. Washington, D.C. [1980] 119 p. in various pagings : LC Card 79-600214 DDC 343.73/075/02632 19
KF1665.Z95 N37 1979

(131) Using ANS FORTRAN /. Washington, D.C. [1980] vi, 100 p. ; LC Card 80-600009 DDC 001.64/24 19
QA76.73.F25 U84

(132) Marshall, Harold E. Energy conservation in buildings . Washington, D.C. [1980] xii, 144 p. : LC Card 80-600056 DDC 333.79 19
TJ163.5.B84 M36

Implant retrieval . Washington, D.C. , 1981. xi, 776 : LC Card 80-600194 DDC 602/.18 s 617/.307 19
QC100 .U57 no. 601 RD755.5

International Conference on Nuclear Cross Sections for Technology (1979 : University of Tennessee) Nuclear cross sections for technology . [Washington, D.C.?] , 1980. xvi, 1039 p. : LC Card 80-600128 DDC 602/.18 s 539.7/54 19
QC100 .U57 no. 594 QC794.6.C7

Minicomputer trends and applications, 1973; symposium record. New York [1973] iii, 58 p. LC Card 73-174854
TK7888.3 .M56   **NYPL [JSF 81-17]**

Monograph .
(165) Steiner, Bruce W. An institutional plan for developing national standards . [Washington, D.C.] , 1979. vi, 17 p., [7] leaves of plates (2 fold.) : LC Card 79-600116 DDC 602/.18 s 620/.00218 19
QC100 .U556 no. 165 TA368

National Conference on Measurements of Laser Emissions for Regulatory Purposes, Rockville, Md., 1974. National Conference on Measurements of Laser Emissions for Regulatory Purposes . [Rockville, Md.] , Washington , 1976 i.e. 1977. vii, 255 p. : LC Card 77-602983 DDC 535.5/8 19
QC689.5.L37 N37 1974

National standard reference data series .
(NSRDS-NBS 69) Hug, Gordon L. Optical spectra of nonmetallic inorganic transient species in aqueous solution /. Washington [1981] vi, 159 p. : LC Card 80-606826 DDC 602/.18 s 543/.0858 19
QC100 .U573 no. 69 QC454.A2

NBS/NCSBCS Joint Conference on Research and Innovation in the Building Regulatory Process, 3d, Annapolis, 1978. Research and innovation in the building regulatory process . Washington , 1979. x, 360 p. : LC Card 79-600090 DDC 602/.18 s 343.73/07869 19
QC100 .U57 no. 552 KF5701

Roundtable Discussion of Radon in Buildings, National Bureau of Standards, 1979. Radon in buildings . Washington, D.C. [1980] x, 77 p. : LC Card 80-600069 DDC 602/.18 s 628.5/35 19
QC100 .U57 no. 581 TD885.5.R33

Snowdon, John C. Vibration isolation . Washington , 1979. ix, 119 p. : LC Card 79-600062
TA355 .S55

Societal aspects of hydrogen energy systems /. Washington , 1979. vii, 161 p. : LC Card 80-602232 DDC 338.4/766581/0973 19
TP359.H8 S58

Special publication.
(250) United States. National Bureau of Standards. Office of Measurement Services. Calibration and related measurement services of the National Bureau of Standards . Washington , 1978. vii, 100 p. ; LC Card 79-603214 DDC 602/.8/7 19
T50 .U57 1978

(400-16) Kenney, James M. Modulation measurements for microwave mixers /. [Washington, D.C.] , 1980. v, 80 p. : LC Card 79-600161 DDC 602/.18 s 621.381/33 19
QC100 .U57 no. 400-16 TK7872.M5

(400-61) Bullis, W. Murray, 1930- Metrology for submicrometer devices and circuits /. Washington, D.C. , 1980. vi, 34 p. : LC Card 80-600054 DDC 602/.18 s 621.381/73/0287 19
QC100 .U57 no. 400-61 TK7874

(426, suppl. 1) Gallagher, J. W. Bibliography of low energy electron and photon cross section data, (January 1975 through December 1977) /. Washington , 1979. vi, 106 p. ; LC Card 78-600156 DDC 602/.18 s 539.7/54 19
QC100 .U57 no. 426, suppl. 1 Z7144.N8 QC794.6.C7

(500-40) Guideline on major job accounting systems . [Gaithersburg, Md.] , Washington , 1978. ix, 162 p. : LC Card 78-600113 DDC 602/.18 s 001.64/25 19
QC100 .U57 no. 500-40 QA76.9.E94

(500-50) Westin, Alan F. Computer science & technology . Washington , 1979. xxiv, 439 p. : LC Card 79-600081 DDC 602.18 s 658.3/00973 19
QC100 .U57 no. 500-50 HF5549.2.U5

(500-51) Fips Task Group on Database Management System Standards. Recommendations for database management system standards /. Washington , 1979. x, 88 p. ; LC Card 79-600087 DDC 001.64/0218 19
QC100 .U57 no. 500-51 QA76.9.D3

(500-53) Wilson, Carol B. Technology assessment . Washington, D.C. [1979] iv, 32 p. ; LC Card 79-600154 DDC 602/.18 s 001.64 19
QC100 .U57 no. 500-53 QA76.9E95

(500-56) Branstad, Martha A. Validation, verification, and testing for the individual programmer /. Washington, D.C. , 1980. iii, 22 p. ; LC Card 80-600005 DDC 602/.18 s 001.64/25 19
QC100 .U57 no. 500-56 QA76.6

(500-57) Audit and evaluation of computer security II . [Washington, D.C.] [1980] ca. 250 p. in various pagings : LC Card 80-600034 DDC 602/.18 s 658.4/78 19
QC100 .U57 no. 500-57 HF5548.2

(500-58) Amer, Paul D. Application of measurement criteria in the selection of interactive computer services /. Washington, D.C. , 1980. v, 84 p. : LC Card 80-600035 DDC 602/.18 s 001.64 19
QC100 .U57 no. 500-58 QA76.9.I58

(500-60) Mamrak, Sandra A., 1944- Sizing distributed systems . Washington, D.C. [1980] iv, 16 p. : LC Card 80-600061 DDC 001.64 s 001.64 19
QC100 .U57 no. 500-60 QA76.9.D5

(500-63) Treu, Siegfried. A testbed for providing uniformity to user-computer interaction languages /. [Washington, D.C.] , 1980. 72 p. in various pagings : LC Card 80-603146 DDC 602/.18 s 001.64/24 19
QC100 .U57 no. 500-63 QA76.7

(525) Ultrasonic tissue characterization II . Washington , 1979. xi, 362 p. : LC Card 79-600026 DDC 602/.18 s 616.07/543 19
QC100 .U57 no. 525 RC78.7.U4

(533) Microbeam Analysis Society. Characterization of particles . Washington, D.C. [1980] vi, 223 p. : LC Card 80-600033 DDC 602/.18 s 620/.43 19
QC100 .U57 no. 533 TA418.8

(540) UJNR Panel on Fire Research and Safety. Fire research and safety . Washington, D.C. , 1979. x, 718 p. : LC Card 79-600054 DDC 602/.18 s 628.9/22 19
QC100 .U57 no. 540 TH9112

(546) Leedy, K. O. Catalog of Federal metrology and calibration capabilities /. [Gaithersburg, Md.] , Washington , 1979. iii, 48 p. : LC Card 79-600075 DDC 602/.18 s 530.8/025/73 19
QC100 .U57 no. 546 QC51.U6

(547) Mechanical Failures Prevention Group. Detection, diagnosis, and prognosis . [Washington] , 1979. vi, 370 p. : LC Card 79-600078 DDC 602/.18 s 620.1/126 19
QC100 .U57 no. 547 TA409

(549) National Conference on Regulatory Aspects of Building Rehabilitation, National Bureau of Standards, 1978. Proceedings of the National Conference on Regulatory Aspects of Building Rehabilitation, held at the National Bureau of Standards, October 30, 1978 /. [Washington, D.C.] , 1979. ix, 201, 30 p. : LC Card 79-600095 DDC 602.18 s 343.73/078690/24 19
QC100 .U57 no. 549 KF5701

(552) NBS/NCSBCS Joint Conference on Research and Innovation in the Building Regulatory Process, 3d, Annapolis, 1978. Research and innovation in the building regulatory process . Washington , 1979. x, 360 p. : LC Card 79-600090 DDC 602/.18 s 343.73/07869 19
QC100 .U57 no. 552 KF5701

(554) Conference on Neutrons from Electron Medical Accelerators, National Bureau of Standards, 1979. Proceedings of a Conference on Neutrons from Electron Medical Accelerators . Washington , 1979. vii, 175 p. ; LC Card 79-600133 DDC 602/.18 s 615.8/422 19
QC100 .U57 no. 554 RM849

(558) Marshall, Harold E. Efficient allocation of research funds . Washington, D.C. [1979] viii, 47 p. : LC Card 79-600210 DDC 602/.18 s 338.4/569/0072073 19
QC100 .U57 no. 558 TH23

(559) National Measurement Laboratory (U. S.). Time and Frequency Division. Time and frequency users' manual /. Washington, D.C. , 1979. xvi, 248 p. : LC Card 79-600169 DDC 602/.18 s 529/.7 19
QC100 .U57 no. 559 QB209

(562) Symposium on the Science of Ceramic Machining and Surface Finishing, 2d, National Bureau of Standards, 1978. The science of ceramic machining and surface finishing II . Gaithersburg, Md. , Washington, D.C. , 1979. xii, 532 p. : LC Card 79-600149 DDC 602/.18 s 666 19
QC100 .U57 no. 562 TP814

(565) Adler, Sanford C. A history of walkway slip-resistance research at the National Bureau of Standards /. [Washington] , 1979. iv, 31 p. : LC Card 79-600179 DDC 602/.18 s 698/.9 19
QC100 .U57 No. 565 TA418.72

(567) Symposium on Accuracy in Powder Diffraction, National Bureau of Standards, 1979. Accuracy in powder diffraction . [Washington, D.C.] [1980] x, 572 p. : LC Card 80-600010 DDC 602/.18 s 548/.83 19
QC100 .U57 no. 567 QC482.D5

(571) Paffenbarger, George Corbly, 1902- Organizations engaged in preparing standards for dental materials and therapeutic agents with a list of standards /. [Washington, D.C.] [1980] iii, 51 p. ; LC Card 80-600041 DDC 602/.18 s 362.1/7 19
QC100 .U57 no. 571 RK681

(574) Topical Conference on Basic Optical Properties of Materials, Gaithersburg, Md., 1980. Basic optical properties of materials . Washington, D.C. [1980] x, 241 p. : LC Card 80-600038 DDC 602/.18 s 620.1/1295 19
QC100 .U57 no. 574 QC374

(577) Development of a probability based load criterion for American national standard A58 . [Washington, D.C.] , 1980. v, 222 p. : LC Card 80-600067 DDC 602/.18 s 690/.21 19
QC100 .U57 no. 577 TH845

(579) Symposium on International Standards Information and Isonet, National Bureau of Standards, 1979. Symposium on International Standards Information and ISONET . Washington, D.C. [1980] vii, 59 p. : LC Card 80-600073 DDC 602/.18 s 389/.6/0601 19
QC100 .U57 no. 579 T59.A1

(581) Roundtable Discussion of Radon in Buildings, National Bureau of Standards, 1979. Radon in buildings . Washington, D.C. [1980] x, 77 p. : LC Card 80-600069 DDC 602/.18 s 628.5/35 19
QC100 .U57 no. 581 TD885.5.R33

(585) Conference on Fire Safety for the Handicapped, National Bureau of Standards, 1979. Fire and life safety for the handicapped . Washington, D.C. , 1980. ix, 144 p. ; LC Card 80-600082 DDC 602/.18 s 362.4/38 19
QC100 .U57 no. 585 TH9112

Spencer, L. V. (Lewis Van Clief), 1924- Structure shielding against fallout gamma rays from nuclear detonations /. [Washington, D.C.?] , 1980. xvi, 967 p : LC Card 80-600120 DDC 602/.18 s 363.1/89 19
QC100 .U57 no. 570 UF787

Standard reference materials.
Mavrodineanu, Radu, 1910- Metal-on-quartz filters as a standard reference material for spectrophotometry--SRM 2031 /. [Washington, D.C.] [1980] xiii, 110 p. : LC Card 79-600192 DDC 602/.18 s 681/.414 19
QC100 .U57 no. 260-68 QC465

National Measurement Laboratory (U. S.) Standard reference materials . Washington, D.C. , 1980. xiv, 99 p. : LC Card 80-600091 DDC 602/.18 s 616.07/56 19
QC100 .U57 no. 260-69 RB46

Velapoldi, R. A. A Fluorescence standard reference material, quinine sulfate dihydrate /. Washington, D.C. , 1980. xvi, 122 p. : LC Card 79-600119 DDC 602/.18 s 535/.35 19
QC100 .U57 no. 260-64 QC477

Stanford Research Institute. SRI International. Cost effectiveness of marine fire protection programs . [Washington] , 1978. xvii, 212 p. : LC Card 79-602278
VK1258 .S18 1979   NYPL [JLF 81-262]

Survey of properties of the hydrgen isotopes below their critical temperatures /. Washington, 1973. vii, 113 p. :
NYPL [JSF 81-57]

Symposium on International Standards Information and Isonet, National Bureau of Standards, 1979. Symposium on International Standards Information and ISONET . Washington, D.C. [1980] vii, 59 p. : LC Card 80-600073 DDC 602/.18 s 389/.6/0601 19
QC100 .U57 no. 579 T59.A1

Symposium on the Science of Ceramic Machining and Surface Finishing, 2d, National Bureau of Standards, 1978. The science of ceramic machining and surface finishing II . Gaithersburg, Md. , Washington, D.C. , 1979. xii, 532 p. : LC Card 79-600149 DDC 602/.18 s 666 19
QC100 .U57 no. 562 TP814

Technical note .
(1005) United States. Institute for Basic Standards. Cryogenics Division. Publications and services of the Cryogenics Division, National Bureau of Standards, 1953-1977 /. [Washington] , 1978. vii, 101 p. : LC Card 79-602766 DDC 602/.18 s 016.536/56 19
QC100 .U5753 no. 1005 Z7144.L6 QC278

(1108) Peacock, Richard D. SPEED2, a computer program for the reduction of data from automatic data acquisition systems /. [Washington, D.C.] [1979] 58, 68, 22, [7] p. ; LC Card 79-603987 DDC 602/.18 s 001.6 19
QC100 .U5753 no. 1108 QA276

Topical Conference on Basic Optical Properties of Materials, Gaithersburg, Md., 1980. Basic optical properties of materials . Washington, D.C. [1980] x, 241 p. : LC Card 80-600038 DDC 602/.18 s 620.1/1295 19
QC100 .U57 no. 574 QC374

Tucker, Jane C. New serial holdings, 1977 /. [Washington] [Springfield, Va.] 1977. vi, 232 p. ; LC Card 77-602720
Z7403 .T79 Q158.5   NYPL [JSF 81-153]

United States-Japan Cooperative Program in Natural Resources. Panel on Wind and Seismic Effects. Wind and seismic effects . Washington, D.C. , c1980. 604 p. in various pagings : LC Card 79-600134 DDC 602/.18 s 624.1/76 19
QC100 .U57 no. 560 TA654.5

Workshop on Eddy Current Nondestructive Testing, (1977 : National Bureau of Standards) Eddy current nondestructive testing . Washington, D.C. , 1981. viii, 158 p. : LC Card 80-600172 DDC 602/.18 s 620.1/67 19
QC100 .U57 no. 589 TA417.35

UNITED STATES. NATIONAL BUREAU OF STANDARDS.
United States. Congress. House. Committee on Science and Technology. Posture hearings (NSF, NBS, and FEMA) . Washington , 1980. iii, 200 p. ; LC Card 80-604103 DDC 353.008 19
KF27 .S39 1980f

United States. National Bureau of Standards. Office of Measurement Services. Calibration and related measurement services of the National Bureau of Standards /. Washington , 1978. vii, 100 p. ; LC Card 79-603214 DDC 602/.8/7 19
T50 .U57 1978

UNITED STATES. NATIONAL BUREAU OF STANDARDS - APPROPRIATIONS AND EXPENDITURES.
United States. Congress. House. Committee on Science and Technology. Subcommittee on Science, Research, and Technology. 1981 National Bureau of Standards authorization . Washington , 1980. iii, 424 p. : LC Card 80-602738 DDC 353.0072/23682/1 19
KF27 .S399 1980a

United States. Congress. Senate. Committee on Commerce, Science, and Transportation. Subcommittee on Science, Technology, and Space. Authorizations for NBS . Washington , 1980. iii, 67 p. : LC Card 80-602152 DDC 353.0072/236821 19
KF26 .C697 1980

United States. National Bureau of Standards. Library.
Abstract and index collection, National Bureau of Standards Library / compiled by Diane Cunningham. Springfield, Va. : Order From National Technical Information Service, 1980. 59 p. ; 22 x 28 cm. "NBSIR 80-2009."
1. Technology - Abstracts - Bibliography. 2.

BIBLIOGRAPHIC GUIDE

United States. National Bureau of Standards. Library - Catalogs.

568

Technology - Indexes - Bibliography. I. Cunningham, Diane. II. Title. **NYPL [JSF 80-657]**

UNITED STATES. NATIONAL BUREAU OF STANDARDS. LIBRARY - CATALOGS.
Tucker, Jane C. New serial holdings, 1977 /. [Washington] [Springfield, Va.] 1977. vi, 232 p. ; LC Card 77-602720
Z7403 .T79 Q158.5 **NYPL [JSF 81-153]**

UNITED STATES. NATIONAL BUREAU OF STANDARDS. MUSEUM.
United States. National Bureau of Standards. Museum. Catalog of artifacts on display in the NBS Museum /. Washington, D.C. , 1977. ca. 200 p. : LC Card 79-603912
Q185.7 .U54 1977

United States. National Bureau of Standards. Office of Measurement Services. Calibration and related measurement services of the National Bureau of Standards / B.C. Belanger, editor. 1978 ed. Washington : Office of Measurement Services, National Bureau of Standards : for sale by the Supt. of Docs., U. S. Govt. Print. Off., 1978. vii, 100 p. ; 26 cm. (NBS special publication . 250) "Supersedes NBS special publication 250-1970 edition." Includes bibliographical references and index. LC Card 79-603214 DDC 602/.8/7 19
1. United States. National Bureau of Standards. 2. Calibration. 3. Testing. I. Belanger, Brian C. II. Series. III. Series: United States. National Bureau of Standards Special publication, 250. IV. Title.
T50 .U57 1978

United States. National Bureau of Standards. Planning Office. Barth, James R. Evaluating the impact of securities regulation on venture capital markets /. Washington, D.C. , 1980. iv, 38 p. : LC Card 80-600036 DDC 602.18 s 332/.0414 19
QC100 .U556 no. 166 HG4963

United States. National Bureau of Standards. Technical Analysis Division. see United States. Institute for Applied Technology. Technical Analysis Division.

United States. National Cancer Institute. Monograph.
(52) Aspects of cancer research, 1971-1978 . Bethesda, Md. , Washington, D.C. [1979] 531 p. : LC Card 80-601790 DDC 616.99/4 s 616.99/4 19
RC261 .A448 no. 52 RC267

National Cancer Institute Symposium on Biohazards and Zoonotic Problems of Primate Procurement, Quarantine, and Research, Frederick Cancer Research Center, 1975. Biohazards and zoonotic problems of primate procurement, quarantine, and research . [Bethesda, Md.] 1975. 137 p. : LC Card 76-600529 DDC 614.4/3 19
RA641.P7 N37 1975

National cancer program; Director's report and annual plan. 1979- [Bethesda, Md.] 28 cm. (NIH publication) Annual. Vols. for 1979- cover report period 1978- . Formed by the union of its: National cancer program; report of the Director and its: National cancer program; annual plan.
1. Cancer research - United States - Periodicals. I. Title. **NYPL [JLM 80-1047]**

Transfer RNA and transfer RNA modification in differentiation and neoplasia . [Washington] 1971 [i.e. 1974] p. 591-724 : LC Card 78-601843 DDC 616.99/4 s 616.99/2071 19
RC261 .A274 vol. 31 QP623

UNITED STATES. NATIONAL CANCER INSTITUTE.
United States. Congress. House. Committee on Interstate and Foreign Commerce. Subcommittee on Oversight and Investigations. Community-based cancer control programs . Washington, 1980. iii, 89 p. ; LC Card 80-603286 DDC 362.1/96994009747 19
KF27 .I5547 1980d

United States. National Cancer Institute. Journal. Aspects of cancer research, 1971-1978 . Bethesda, Md. , Washington, D.C. [1979] 531 p. : LC Card 80-601790 DDC 616.99/4 s 616.99/4 19
RC261 .A448 no. 52 RC267

United States. National Cancer Institute. Preventive Medicine Branch. Known effects of low-level radiation exposure . [Bethesda, Md.] [1980] 147 p. : LC Card 80-601671 DDC

616.9/897 19
RA1231.R2 K59

United States. National Capital Planning Commission. Downtown design and development : a staff proposal establishing design guidelines for revitalization of downtown, Washington, 1974 / National Capital Planning Commission, Washington, D. C. Washington, The Commission, 1974. 28 p. ill. (some col.), maps (some col.) 23 x 30 cm.
1. Urban renewal - Washington, D.C. 2. Washington, D. C. - City planning. I. Title. **NYPL [JLG 80-72]**

United States. National Cartographic Information Center. see National Cartographic Information Center.

United States - National cemeteries. see National cemeteries - United States.

United States. National Center for Education Statistics. see National Center for Education Statistics.

United States. National Center for Educational Statistics.
Basic student charges. Washington. 26 cm. At head of title: 1966/67- Higher education.
1. Education, Higher - United States - Costs - Statistics - Periodicals. I. United States. National Center for Educational Statistics. Higher education, basic student charges. II. Title. **NYPL [JLM 80-771]**

Higher education, basic student charges.
United States. National Center for Educational Statistics. Basic student charges. Washington. **NYPL [JLM 80-771]**

United States. National Center for Health Sciences Research. see National Center for Health Services Research.

United States. National Center for Health Statistics.
Bloom, Barbara, 1950- Utilization patterns and financial characteristics of nursing homes in the United States, 1977 /. Hyattsville, Md. , 1981. p. cm. ISBN 0-8406-0215-4 LC Card 80-606876 DDC 362.1/1/0973 19
RA407.3 .A349 no. 53 RA997

Directory : family planning service sites, United States. [Hyattsville, Md.] : U. S. Dept. of Health, Education, and Welfare, Public Health Service, National Center for Health Statistics ; Washington : for sale by the Supt. of Docs., U. S. Govt. Print. Off., 1977 [i.e. 1978] iv, 177 p. ; 26 cm. (United States. Dept. of Health, Education, and Welfare. DHEW publication no. (PHS) 78-1239) Title on spine: Directory of family planning service sites. LC Card 78-601080
1. Birth control clinics - United States - Directories. I. Title: Directory of family planning service sites.
HQ766.5.U5 U57 1978 **NYPL [JLF 81-251]**

NCHS publications on ... no. 1- ; Jan. 1979- Washington.
I. Title. **NYPL [Econ Div.]**

Publications and data tapes of the National Center for Health Statistics available from the National Technical Information Service. Hyattsville, Md. : The Center, 1978. 260 p. ; 27 cm. (DHEW publication no. (PHS) 78-1308) Includes indexes. LC Card 79-602913
1. Health surveys - United States - Bibliography - Catalogs. 2. United States - Statistics, Medical - Bibliography - Catalogs. 3. United States - Statistics, Vital - Bibliography - Catalogs. 4. Health surveys - United States - Data tape catalogs. 5. United States - Statistics, Medical - Data tape catalogs. 6. United States - Statistics, Vital - Data tape catalogs. 7. United States. National Center for Health Statistics - Bibliography - Catalogs. 8. United States. National Technical Information Service - Catalogs. I. United States. National Technical Information Service. II. Title.
Z7553.M43 U54 1978 RA407.3 **NYPL [JLF 81-340]**

Social and economic implications of cancer in the United States : based on a presentation to the Expert Committee on Cancer Statistics of the World Health Organization and International Agency for Research on Cancer at Madrid, Spain, June 20 to 26, 1978. Hyattsville, Md. : Dept. of Health and Human Services, Public Health Service, Office of the Assistant Secretary for Health, National Center for Health Statistics ; Washington : for sale by the Supt. of Docs., U. S. Govt. Print. Off., [1981]. iv, 43 p. : ill. ; 26 cm. (Vital and health statistics : Series 3, analytical studies . no. 20) DHHS

publication ; (PHS) 80-1404 Prepared by D.P. Rice and T.A. Hodgson. ISBN 0-8406-0203-0 LC Card 80-607176 DDC 362.1/96994 19
1. Cancer - Economic aspects - United States - Congresses. 2. Cancer - United States - Statistics - Congresses. I. Rice, Dorothy P. II. Hodgson, Thomas A. III. World Health Organization. Expert Committee on Cancer Statistics. IV. International Agency for Research on Cancer. V. Series: United States. National Center for Health Statistics. Vital and health statistics ; Series 3, analytical studies , no. 20. VI. Title.
RC276 .U56 1981

Vital and health statistics : Series 2, Data evaluation and methods research .
(no. 88) Kozak, Lola Jean. The status of hospital discharge data in Denmark, Scotland, West Germany, and the United States /. Hyattsville, Md. , 1981. p. cm. ISBN 0-8406-0211-1 LC Card 80-607865 DDC 312/.07/23 s 362.1/1/0684 19
RA409 .U45 no. 88 RA971.6

Vital and health statistics ; Series 3, analytical studies .
(no. 20) United States. National Center for Health Statistics. Social and economic implications of cancer in the United States . Hyattsville, Md. , Washington [1981]. iv, 43 p. : ISBN 0-8406-0203-0 LC Card 80-607176 DDC 362.1/96994 19
RC276 .U56 1981

Vital and health statistics : Series 11, Data from National Health Survey, data from the health examination survey .
(no. 222) O'Brien, Richard J. Basic data on spirometry in adults 25-74 years of age, United States, 1971-75 /. Hyattsville, Md. , 1980. p. cm. LC Card 80-607829 DDC 312/.0973 s 312/.6 19
RA407.3 .A347 no. 222 RC734.S65

Vital and health statistics : Series 11, Data from the National Health Survey, Data from the health examination survey .
(no. 218) Hadden, Wilbur Crane, 1946- Basic data on health care needs of adults 25-74 years of age, United States, 1971-75. Hyattsville, MD , 1980. vi, 45 p. ; ISBN 0-8406-0197-2 LC Card 80-607810 DDC 312/.0973 s 362.1 19
RA407.3 .A347 no. 218 RA410.53

(no. 221) Roberts, Jean, 1918- Hypertension in adults 25-74 years of age, United States, 1971-1975 /. Hyattsville, Md. , 1980. p. cm. ISBN 0-8406-0207-3 LC Card 80-607834 DDC 312/.0973 s 614.5/9132/0973 19
RA407.3 .A347 no. 221 RC685.H8

(no. 223) Harvey, Clair R. Decayed, missing, and filled teeth among persons 1-74 years, United States, 1971-74 . Hyattsville, Md. , 1980. p. cm. ISBN 0-8406-0209-X LC Card 80-607837 DDC 312/.0973 s 312/.30476 19
RA407.3 .A347 no. 223 RK52.2

Vital and health statistics : Series 13, Data from the National Health Survey, Data from the hospital discharge survey .
(no. 52) Cardocki, Gloria J. Utilization of short-stay hospitals by persons with heart disease and malignant neoplasms . Hyattsville, Md. [1981] p. cm. ISBN 0-8406-0214-6 LC Card 80-28017 DDC 362.1/1/0973 s 362.1/9612/00973 19
RA407.3 .A349 no. 52 RA981.A2

Vital and health statistics : Series 14, Data from the National Health Survey, Data on health resources, manpower, and facilities .
(no. 24) Strahan, Genevieve W. Inpatient health facilities statistics, United States, 1978 /. Hyattsville, Md. , 1980. p. cm. ISBN 0-8406-0204-9 LC Card 80-607845 DDC 362.1/1/0973 19
RA981.A2 S78

Vital and health statistics : Series 20, Data from the National Vital Statistics System, Data on mortality .
(no. 17) Klebba, A. Joan. Mortality from diseases associated with smoking. Hyattsville, Md. , 1980. p. cm. ISBN 0-8406-0208-1 LC Card 80-607855 DDC 312/.2/0973 s 615.9/52379 19
HB1335 .A18 no. 17 RA1242.T6

Vital and health statistics : Series 23, Data from the National Survey of Family Growth .

(no. 7) Mosher, William D. Contraceptive utilization, United States /. Hyattsville, Md. , Washington , 1981. iv, 58 p. ; ISBN 0-8406-0210-3 LC Card 80-39981 DDC 613.9/4/0973 19
HQ776.5.U5 M67

Workshop on Synthetic Estimates, Princeton, N. J., 1978. Synthetic estimates for small areas . Rockville, Md. , Washington , 1979. viii, 282 p. : LC Card 79-600067
RC563.2 .W67 1978

UNITED STATES. NATIONAL CENTER FOR HEALTH STATISTICS - BIBLIOGRAPHY - CATALOGS.
United States. National Center for Health Statistics. Publications and data tapes of the National Center for Health Statistics available from the National Technical Information Service. Hyattsville, Md. , 1978. 260 p. ; LC Card 79-602913
Z7553.M43 U54 1978 RA407.3
      NYPL [JLF 81-340]

United States. National Center for Productivity and Quality of Working Life. see National Center for Productivity and Quality of Working Life.

United States. National Center on Child Abuse and Neglect. see National Center on Child Abuse and Neglect.

United States. National Climatic Center. see National Climatic Center.

United States. National Commission for Employment Policy.
Best, Fred. Exchanging earnings for leisure . Washington, D.C. , 1980. vi, 184 p. : LC Card 80-602865 DDC 331.11/0973 s 331.25/76 19
HD5701 .U53 no. 79 HD5124

Special report - National Commission for Employment Policy .
(no. 36) National Commission for Manpower Policy, the first five years, 1974-1979 . Washington, D.C. , 1979 [i.e. 1980] ii, 166 p. ; LC Card 80-602132 DDC 353.0083/06 19
HD5724 .N22

United States. National Commission for Manpower Policy.
Conference on Creating Job Opportunities in the Private Sector, Washington, D.C., 1978. Increasing job opportunities in the private sector . Washington, D.C. , 1979. 242 p. ; LC Card 79-604184
HD5724 .C673 1978   *NYPL [JLF 81-323]*

Conference on Labor Market Intermediaries, Washington, D.C., 1977. Labor market intermediaries . Washington , 1978. 372 p. ; LC Card 78-602599
HD5875 .C66 1977   *NYPL [JLF 81-181]*

Conference on the National Longitudinal Surveys of Mature Women, United States Department of Labor, 1978. Women's changing roles at home and on the job . Washington , 1978. iii, 331 p. ; LC Card 79-601912
HQ1403 .C53 1978   *NYPL [JLF 81-250]*

Conference on the Role of Private Sector Employers in National Employment Policies, Washington, D.C., 1978. The business sector role in employment policy . Washington , 1978. 111 p. ; LC Card 79-602115 DDC 331.11/0973 19
HD5724 .C688 1978

Labor's views on employment policy . Washington , 1978. 132 p. ; LC Card 78-603516
HD5724 .L23   *NYPL [JLF 81-279]*

National Commission for Manpower Policy, the first five years, 1974-1979 . Washington, D.C. , 1979 [i.e. 1980] ii, 166 p. ; LC Card 80-602132 DDC 353.0083/06 19
HD5724 .N22

Special report.
(no. 22) Conference on Labor Market Intermediaries, Washington, D.C., 1977. Labor market intermediaries . Washington , 1978. 372 p. ; LC Card 78-602599
HD5875 .C66 1977   *NYPL [JLF 81-181]*

(no.25) Labor's views on employment policy . Washington , 1978. 132 p. ; LC Card 78-603516
HD5724 .L23   *NYPL [JLF 81-279]*

(no. 26) Conference on the National Longitudinal Surveys of Mature Women,

United States Department of Labor, 1978. Women's changing roles at home and on the job . Washington , 1978. iii, 331 p. : LC Card 79-601912
HQ1403 .C53 1978   *NYPL [JLF 81-250]*

(no. 29) Conference on Creating Job Opportunities in the Private Sector, Washington, D.C., 1978. Increasing job opportunities in the private sector . Washington, D.C. , 1979. 242 p. ; LC Card 79-604184
HD5724 .C673 1978   *NYPL [JLF 81-323]*

Special report - National Commission for Manpower Policy .
(no. 30) Trade and employment . Washington, D.C. , 1979. 336 p. : LC Card 80-601562 DDC 331.12/0973 19
HD5710.75.U6 T7

(no. 31) Conference on the Role of Private Sector Employers in National Employment Policies, Washington, D.C., 1978. The business sector role in employment policy . Washington , 1978. 111 p. ; LC Card 79-602115 DDC 331.11/0973 19
HD5724 .C688 1978

Trade and employment . Washington, D.C. , 1979. 336 p. : LC Card 80-601562 DDC 331.12/0973 19
HD5710.75.U6 T7

UNITED STATES. NATIONAL COMMISSION FOR MANPOWER POLICY.
National Commission for Manpower Policy, the first five years, 1974-1979 . Washington, D.C. , 1979 [i.e. 1980] ii, 166 p. ; LC Card 80-602132 DDC 353.0083/06 19
HD5724 .N22

United States. National Commission for the Protection of Human Subjects of Biomedical and Behavioral Research. Research on the fetus : report and recommendations / National Commission for the Protection of Human Subjects of Biomedical and Behavioral Research. [Bethesda, Md.] : The Commission, 1975. 88 p. ; 27 cm. (DHEW publication (OS) no. 76-127) LC Card 76-603269
1. Fetus - Research. 2. Human experimentation in medicine. 3. Fetus - Research - United States. 4. Human experimentation in medicine - United States. I. Title.
RG600 .U53 1975   *NYPL [JFF 80-1527]*

United States. National Commission for the United Nations Educational, Scientific and Cultural Organization. UNESCO and the U. S. National Commission for UNESCO : basic documents. 8th ed. Washington, D.C. : The Commission, 1977. viii, 48 p. ; 24 cm. (Department of State publication. 7491) International organization and conference series ; 37 "September 1977." Edition of 1948 published under title: UNESCO and the National Commission. LC Card 78-602328 DDC 341.7/67 19
1. United Nations Educational, Scientific and Cultural Organization. 2. United States. National Commission for the United Nations Educational, Scientific and Cultural Organization. I. Series: United States. Dept. of State. Publication, 7491. II. Title.
AS4.U825 U6 1977

UNITED STATES. NATIONAL COMMISSION FOR THE UNITED NATIONS EDUCATIONAL, SCIENTIFIC AND CULTURAL ORGANIZATION.
United States. National Commission for the United Nations Educational, Scientific and Cultural Organization. UNESCO and the U. S. National Commission for UNESCO . Washington, D.C. , 1977. viii, 48 p. ; LC Card 78-602328 DDC 341.7/67 19
AS4.U825 U6 1977

United States. National Commission on Employment and Unemployment Statistics.
Background paper - National Commission on Employment and Unemployment Statistics .
(no. 8) Goldfarb, Robert S. Measuring types of unemployment . Washington , 1978. ix, 52 p. ; LC Card 79-602636 DDC 331.13/704/0973 19
HD5724 .G63

United States. National Commission on Libraries and Information Science.
Chartrand, Robert Lee. White House

Conference on Library and Information Services pre-conference meetings on special themes, July 31, 1979 . Washington, D.C. [1979] 18 p. ; LC Card 80-143975 DDC 021.6/4 19
Z690 .C48

Ladd, Boyd, 1915- Inventory of library needs, 1975, New York . [Albany, N.Y.] [1978] 62 p. : LC Card 80-623351 DDC 021 19
Z732.N7 L32

White House Conference on Library and Information Services. (1979 : Washington, D.C. Information for the 1980's . Washington, D.C. , 1980. viii, 808 p. : LC Card 80-603771 DDC 027.073 19
Z731 .W69 1979a

United States. National Commission on Neighborhoods. People, building neighborhoods : final report to the President and the Congress of the United States / the National Commission on Neighborhoods. [Washington?] : The Commission ; Washington : for sale by the Supt. of Docs., U. S. Govt. Print. Off., [1979] xi, 358 p. : ill. ; 28 cm. Includes bibliographies. LC Card 79-602955
1. Community development - United States. 2. Neighborhood. I. Title.
HN90.C6 U66 1979

United States. National Commission on Productivity and Work Quality. see National Commission on Productivity and Work Quality.

United States. National Commission on the International Year of the Child.
Report to the President / United States National Commission on the International Year of the Child. Washington, D.C. : The Commission : for sale by the Supt. of Docs., U. S. Govt. Print. Off., [1980] xi, 227 p. : ill. ; 23 cm. "March 1980." Includes bibliographical references. LC Card 80-602206 DDC 353.0084/7 19
1. International Year of the Child, 1979 - United States. I. Title.
HQ767.9 .I57 1979z

United States. National Commission on the International Year of the Child. Children's Advisory Panel. No time for mud pies : new roles for children & youth in child advocacy : Children's Advisory Panel action report to America's children and youth. [Washington, D.C.] : The Panel ; Auburn, AL : available from N. Spears, [1980] 31 p. : ill. ; 19 x 22 cm. Cover title. Includes phonodisc, Across the oceans (2 s. : 7 in. ; 33 1/3 rpm.) "Presented to the President of the United States of America, April 1980, along with the full report of the U. S. Commission." Presents the action plan for bettering children's lives written by the 25 young people aged 10 to 18 who compose the Children's Advisory Panel to the U. S. National Commission on the International Year of the Child. LC Card 80-600049 DDC 323.3 19
1. Children's rights - United States - Juvenile literature. I. Title.
HQ789 .U55 1980

United States. National Commission on the Observance of International Women's Year. Homemakers Committee. Bersch, Blanche E. The legal status of homemakers in California /. [Washington, D.C.] [1977] ix, 36 p. ; LC Card 77-603975
KFC120 .B47

United States. National Commission on Unemployment Compensation. First interim report of the National Commission on Unemployment Compensation, November 1978. Rosslyn, Va. : The Commission, [1978] 151 p. : ill. ; 27 cm. LC Card 79-602138
1. Insurance, Unemployment - United States. I. Title.
HD7096.U5 U6494 1978
      NYPL [JLF 81-379]

UNITED STATES. NATIONAL COMMISSION ON VOLUNTEERISM.
United States. Congress. Senate. Committee on Labor and Human Resources. Subcommittee on Child and Human Development. Presidential Commission on National Service and National Commission on Volunteerism. Washington , 1980. v, 606 p. : LC Card 80-604000 DDC 361.3/7/0973 19
KF26 .L273 1980a

United States. National Commission on Water Quality. see National Commission on Water Quality.

United States. National Credit Union Administration.
Board of directors manual for Federal credit unions/ National Credit Union Administration. Washington: The Administration, 1974. v, 60 p.; 26 cm.
1. Banks and banking, Cooperative - United States. I. Title. **NYPL [JLF 80-199]**

NCUA quarterly. v. 1-5, no. 3; 1973-Oct. 1977. [Washington] 5 v. in 2. illus. 26 cm. Supersedes its NCUA bulletin. LC Card 73-641622
1. Banks and banking, Cooperative - United States - Periodicals. I. Title. **NYPL [JLM 80-978]**

The NCUA review. SEPT. 1980- Washington. **NYPL [Econ. Div.]**

Telephone directory. May/Aug. 1980- Washington, D. C. **NYPL [Econ. Div.]**

United States. National Criminal Justice Information and Statistics Service.
National prisoner statistics special report; SD-NPS-SR. Washington.
1. Prisoners - United States - Statistics - Collected works. I. Title. **NYPL [JLM 81-137]**

Privacy and security of criminal history information. Privacy and security of criminal history information : analyses of State privacy legislation : 1979 supplement / [prepared by SEARCH Group, inc.]. Washington, D.C. , c1979. xi, 545 p. ; LC Card 80-601565 DDC 342.73/0858 19
KF9751.Z95 N37 Suppl

United States. National Criminal Justice Reference Service.
Brantley, James R. The etiology of criminality . Washington, D.C. , 1979. vii, 45 p. ; LC Card 80-601563 DDC 016.3643 19
Z5703 .B72 HV6115

Brousseau, Bill. Affirmative action, equal employment opportunity in the criminal justice system . [Washington, D.C.] [1980] vii, 49 p. ; LC Card 80-602931 DDC 016.33113/3 19
HV8143 .B76

Cain, Anthony A. Paralegals, a selected bibliography /. Washington, D.C. , 1978 [i.e. 1979] vii, 40 p. ; LC Card 79-603300 DDC 016.34/0023 19
KF320.L4 C34

Caplan, Marc H. Police manpower management . Washington, D.C. , 1980. vii, 50 p. ; LC Card 81-601200 DDC 350.74/068/ 19
HV8141 .C34

Duncan, J. T. Skip. Citizen crime prevention tactics . Washington, D.C. [1980] v, 116 p. ; LC Card 80-602862 DDC 016.3628/8 19
HV6791 .D86

Eskin, Marian. Child abuse and neglect . [Washington, D.C.] [1980] v, 118 p. ; LC Card 80-602301 DDC 362.7/044 19
HV741 .E83

Ferry, John. Police training . Washington, D.C. [1980] vii, 38 p. ; LC Card 80-602850 DDC 363.2/2/0715 19
HV8143 .F47

Freimund, Justus. Police productivity /. [Washington] , 1978. vii, 47 p. ; LC Card 79-602774 DDC 331.11/8 19
HV7936.P7 F73

Klein, Carol. Bibliographies in criminal justice /. Washington, D.C. [1980] vii, 47 p. ; LC Card 80-602056 DDC 016.016364 19
Z5703.A1 K58 HV7921

Levine, Mark. Jail-based inmate programs . [Washington, D.C.] , 1979. vii, 24 p. ; LC Card 80-601763 DDC 016.365/66 19
HV9304 .L43

Levine, Mark. Standards of care in adult and juvenile correctional institutions . Washington, D.C. , 1980. vii, 40 p. ; LC Card 80-602119 DDC 016.365/973/0218 19
HV9304 .L44

Lockard, James L. Directory of community crime prevention programs, national and State levels /. Washington , 1978. xiii, 129 p. ; LC Card 79-603996
HV6789 .L62

National Institute of Law Enforcement and Criminal Justice. Publications of the National Institute of Law Enforcement and Criminal

Justice . [Washington] , 1978. vii, 230 p. ; LC Card 79-601977 DDC 016.364/973 19
Z7164.P76 N37 HV8138

Selected bibliography - National Criminal Justice Reference Service.
Cain, Anthony A. Paralegals, a selected bibliography /. Washington, D.C. , 1978 [i.e. 1979] vii, 40 p. ; LC Card 79-603300 DDC 016.34/0023 19
KF320.L4 C34

Ferry, John. Police training . Washington, D.C. [1980] vii, 38 p. ; LC Card 80-602850 DDC 363.2/2/0715 19
HV8143 .F47

Freimund, Justus. Police productivity /. [Washington] , 1978. vii, 47 p. ; LC Card 79-602774 DDC 331.11/8 19
HV7936.P7 F73

Johnson, Carolyn, 1948- Prison industries . [Washington] , 1978. vii, 32 p. ; LC Card 79-602384 DDC 016.365/65/0973 19
HV8925 .J63

Klein, Carol. Bibliographies in criminal justice /. Washington, D.C. [1980] vii, 47 p. ; LC Card 80-602056 DDC 016.016364 19
Z5703.A1 K58 HV7921

Levine, Mark. Standards of care in adult and juvenile correctional institutions . Washington, D.C. , 1980. vii, 40 p. ; LC Card 80-602119 DDC 016.365/973/0218 19
HV9304 .L44

United States. National Defense University. see **National Defense University.**

United States. National Diabetes Advisory Board.
Annual report. National Conference on Diabetes : Current Status and Future Directions, Reston, Va., 1979. Report of the National Conference on Diabetes : Current Status and Future Directions, October 9-12, 1979, Sheraton International Conference Center, Reston, Virginia : appendix to the third Annual report of the National Diabetes Advisory Board / sponsored by the National Diabetes Advisory Board. [Bethesda, Md.] [1980] xxx, 170 p. ; LC Card 80-602553 DDC 616.4/62 19
RC660 .N37 1979

National Conference on Diabetes : Current Status and Future Directions, Reston, Va., 1979. Report of the National Conference on Diabetes . [Bethesda, Md.] [1980] xxx, 170 p. ; LC Card 80-602553 DDC 616.4/62 19
RC660 .N37 1979

United States. National Endowment for the Arts. see **National Endowment for the Arts.**

United States. National Endowment for the Humanities. see **National Endowment for the Humanities.**

United States. National Engineering Laboratory. Center for Building Technology.
Chapman, Robert E. Cost estimation and cost variability in residential rehabilitation /. Washington, D.C. , 1980. x, 109 p. : LC Card 80-600174 DDC 690/.0218 s 690/.8/0286 19
TA435 .U58 vol. 129 HD7293

United States-Japan Cooperative Program in Natural Resources. Panel on Wind and Seismic Effects. Wind and seismic effects . Washington, D.C. , c1980. 604 p. in various pagings : LC Card 79-600134 DDC 602/.18 s 624.1/76 19
QC100 .U57 no. 560 TA654.5

United States. National Engineering Laboratory. Center for Fire Research. Fire investigation handbook /. [Washington, D.C.?] , 1980. ix, 187 p. : LC Card 80-600095 DDC 363.3/765 19
TH9180 .F48

United States. National Environmental Satellite Service. Environmental satellite imagery, March 1974 / prepared by National Environmental Satellite Service. Washington, D. C.: Environmental Data Service, 1974. [86] p. : chiefly ill. ; 31 cm. (United States. Weather Bureau. Key to meteorological records documentation. No. 5.4)
Bibliography: p. [3]
1. Clouds - Photographs from space. 2. Meteorological satellites. I. Title. **NYPL [JSF 80-263]**

United States. National Fertilizer Development Center, Muscle Shoals, Ala. (Old Catalog

form: United States. Tennessee Valley Authority. National Fertilizer Development Center)
Bulletin Y.
(145) TVA Fertilizer Conference, St. Louis, 1979. Situation 79 . [Muscle Shoals, Ala. , 1979] 76 p. ; LC Card 80-602627 DDC 631.8/1 s 338.4/766862/0973 19
S631 .U48 no. 145 HD9483.U52

TVA Fertilizer Bulk Blending Conference, Louisville, Ky., 1973. TVA Fertilizer Bulk Blending Conference. [Muscle Shoals, Ala., 1973] 126 p. **NYPL [JLF 80-1485]**

United States. National Fire Academy. see **National Fire Academy.**

United States. National Fire Data Center. see **National Fire Data Center (U. S.)**

United States. National Fire Prevention and Control Administration. National Fire Safety and Research Office. see **United States. National Fire Safety and Research Office.**

United States. National Fire Safety and Research Office. Johns Hopkins University. Applied Physics Laboratory. Assessment of the potential impact of fire protection systems on actual fire incidents /. [Laurel, Md.] , Washington , 1978. v, 62 p. : LC Card 79-601981
TH9503 .J63 1978 **NYPL [JSF 81-194]**

United States. National Foreign Assessment Center. see **United States. Central Intelligence Agency. National Foreign Assessment Center.**

United States. National Foundation on the Arts and the Humanities. see **National Foundation on the Arts and the Humanities.**

United States. National Gallery of Art. (Old Catalog form: Washington, D. C. National Gallery of Art.)
American paintings: an illustrated catalogue. Washington : National Gallery of Art, 1980. 311 p. : ill. ; 25 cm. Includes index. LC Card 80-11221
1. Painting, American - Catalogs. 2. Painting - Washington, D. C. - Catalogs. 3. United States. National Gallery of Art - Catalogs. I. Title.
ND205 .U54 1980 **NYPL [3-MAVY (Washington, D. C.) 80-2649]**

Catalogue of the Italian paintings / by Fern Rusk Shapley. Washington : National Gallery of Art, c1979. 2 v. : ill. ; 24 cm. Includes bibliographical references and index. CONTENTS. - v. 1. Text.--v. 2. Plates. LC Card 79-4410
1. Painting, Italian - Washington, D. C. - Catalogs. 2. United States. National Gallery of Art - Catalogs. I. Shapley, Fern Rusk. II. Title. III. Title: Italian paintings.
ND611 .U54 1979
NYPL [MAVY (Washinton, D. C.) 81-62]

UNITED STATES. NATIONAL GALLERY OF ART - CATALOGS.
United States. National Gallery of Art. American paintings. Washington , 1980. 311 p. : LC Card 80-11221
ND205 .U54 1980 **NYPL [3-MAVY (Washington, D. C.) 80-2649]**

United States. National Gallery of Art. Catalogue of the Italian paintings /. Washington , c1979. 2 v. : LC Card 79-4410
ND611 .U54 1979
NYPL [MAVY (Washinton, D. C.) 81-62]

United States. National Geophysical and Solar-Terrestrial Data Center. see **National Geophysical and Solar-Terrestrial Data Center.**

UNITED STATES. NATIONAL GUARD.
United States. Congress. Senate. Committee on the Judiciary. Subcommittee on the Constitution. The National Guard tort claims act . Washington , 1980. v, 780 p. ; LC Card 80-603086 DDC 343.73/013 19
KF26 .J8359 1980

UNITED STATES - NATIONAL GUARD - PERSONNEL MANAGEMENT.
United States. Congress. House. Committee on Post Office and Civil Service. Subcommittee on Investigations. Civilian technician program . Washington , 1980. iii, 131 p. ; LC Card 80-603291 DDC 355.3/7/0973 19
KF27 .P646 1980b

571 GOVERNMENT PUBLICATIONS - U.S.: 1981

United States. National Institute of Mental Health. Disaster

United States. National Health Planning
Information Center. see National Health
Planning Information Center.

United States. National Health Service Corps.
National Health Service Corps scholarship
program; report to Congress. United
States. National Health Service Corps.
Scholarship program; report to Congress.
[Hyattsville, Md.]   NYPL [JLM 81-63]

Scholarship program; report to Congress.
[Hyattsville, Md.] U. S. Dept. of Health and
Human Services, Public Health Service, Health
Resources Administration, Bureau of Health
Manpower. 22 x 28 cm. (DHHS publication no.
(HRA)) Annual. Vol. for 1978/79 issued as DHEW
publication (HRA). "Report of the Secretary of Health
and Human Services." Title varies: 1978/79, National
Health Service Corps scholarship program; report to
Congress.
1. United States. National Health Service Corps -
Statistics - Periodicals. 2. Medicine - Scholarships,
fellowships, etc. - United States - Statistics - Periodicals.
I. United States. National Health Service Corps.
National Health Service Corps scholarship program;
report to Congress. II. Title.   NYPL [JLM 81-63]

UNITED STATES. NATIONAL HEALTH
SERVICE CORPS - STATISTICS -
PERIODICALS.
United States. National Health Service Corps.
Scholarship program; report to Congress.
[Hyattsville, Md.]   NYPL [JLM 81-63]

United States. National Heart, Lung, and Blood
Institute. see National Heart, Lung, and
Blood Institute.

United States. National Highway Safety
Advisory Committee. Alcohol and
Adjudication, Subcommittee. see United
States. National Highway Safety Advisory
Committee. Subcommittee on Alcohol and
Adjudication.

United States. National Highway Safety
Advisory Committee. Subcommittee on
Alcohol and Adjudication. Rural courts and
highway safety / [Subcommittee on Alcohol
and Adjudication]. Washington : Dept. of
Transportation, National Highway Traffic Safety
Administration, 1977. viii, 52 p. : ill. ; 28 cm.
"DOT HS 802 479." Bibliography: p. 48-50. LC Card
77-604399
1. Drunk driving - United States. 2. Justices of the
peace - United States. 3. Traffic regulations - United
States. I. Title.
KF2231 .A86

United States. National Highway Traffic Safety
Administration.
Alcohol safety action projects evaluation
methodology and overall program impact.
Washington, D.C. : U. S. Dept. of
Transportation, National Highway Traffic Safety
Administration, 1979. 92 p. : graphs ; 28 cm.
"Volume 3." Third volume of a group of related studies.
"DOT HS 803 896." Bibliography: p. 91-92. LC Card
80-601087
1. Drinking and traffic accidents - United States -
Statistics. I. Title.
HE5620.D7 U56 1979

Automobile Inspection, Maintenance & Repair
Conference, National Academy of Sciences,
1979. Automobile Inspection, Maintenance &
Repair Conference. [Washington] [1979] iv,
126 p. : LC Card 80-601649 DDC 629.28/25 19
TL154 .A82 1979

Flynn, Lois. Passive restraints . [Washington,
D.C.] , Springfield, Va. [1979] 184 leaves, 190
p. ; LC Card 80-602367 DDC 016.6292/76 19
Z5173.S2 F58 TL242

Marijuana, other drugs and their relation to
highway safety : a report to Congress.
Washington, D.C. : U. S. Dept. of
Transportation, National Highway Traffic Safety
Administration : for sale by the Supt. of Docs.,
U. S. Govt. Print. Off., [1980] iv, 36 p. ; 28
cm. Bibliography: p. 33-35. LC Card 80-602375
DDC 363.1/251 19
1. Automobile drivers - Drug use. I. Title.
HE5620.D65 U54 1980

Results of national alcohol safety action projects
/ U. S. Department of Transportation, National
Highway Traffic Safety Administration.
Washington, D.C. : The Administration, 1979.
118 p. : ill. ; 28 cm. Cover title. On spine: Results

of the national ASAP program. "DOT HS-804-033."
Includes bibliographical references. LC Card
80-601080
1. Drinking and traffic accidents - United States. I.
Title. II. Title: Results of the national ASAP program.
HE5620.D7 U56 1979a   NYPL [JLF 81-157]

Special bibliography .
(SB-06) Flynn, Lois. Alcohol and highway
safety . Washington, D.C. , 1976. 512 p. ;
LC Card 80-601803 DDC 016.3631/251 19
Z7164.T81 F55 HE5620.D7

Waller, Patricia F., 1932- Truck drivers .
Chapel Hill, N.C. , Springfield, Va. [1979]
xxvi, 222 p. : LC Card 80-622449 DDC
353.0087/8324 19
HE5614.2 .W34

United States. National Highway Traffic Safety
Administration. Region VIII. South Dakota.
Division of Highway Safety. State &
Community Programs. South Dakota highway
safety plan, fiscal year 1980 /. [Pierre, S.D.]
[1980?] 237 p. : LC Card 80-621619 DDC
363.1/256/09783 19
HE5614.3.S8 S68 1980

United States. National Highway Traffic Safety
Administration. Technical Services Division.
Flynn, Lois. Alcohol and highway safety .
Washington, D.C. , 1976. 512 p. ; LC Card
80-601803 DDC 016.3631/251 19
Z7164.T81 F55 HE5620.D7

United States. National Historical Publications
and Records Commission.
Report to the President / National Historical
Publications and Records Commission.
Washington : The Commission, 1978 i.e. 1979.
59 p. ; 24 cm. Includes bibliographical references.
LC Card 80-601723 DDC 027.5 19
1. United States. National Historical Publications and
Records Commission. 2. United States - History -
Sources. I. Title.
E175.4 .U55 1978

UNITED STATES. NATIONAL HISTORICAL
PUBLICATIONS AND RECORDS
COMMISSION.
United States. National Historical Publications
and Records Commission. Report to the
President /. Washington , 1978 i.e. 1979. 59
p. ; LC Card 80-601723 DDC 027.5 19
E175.4 .U55 1978

UNITED STATES. NATIONAL HISTORICAL
PUBLICATIONS AND RECORDS
COMMISSION - APPROPRIATIONS
AND EXPENDITURES.
United States. Congress. House. Committee on
Government Operations. Subcommittee on
Government Information and Individual Rights.
Reauthorization of appropriation for the
National Historical Publications and Records
Commission . Washington , 1980. iii, 66 p. :
LC Card 80-603008 DDC 344.73/092 19
KF27 .G6628 1979b

United States. National Institute for Juvenile
Justice and Delinquency Prevention. see
National Institute for Juvenile Justice and
Delinquency Prevention.

United States. National Institute for
Occupational Safety and Health. see
National Institute for Occupational Safety
and Health.

United States. National Institute of Alcohol
Abuse and Alcoholism. see National Institute
on Alcohol Abuse and Alcoholism.

United States. National Institute of Child Health
and Human Development. Center for
Population Research. CPR population
research. [Bethesda, Md.]
NYPL [JLM 81-10]

United States. National Institute of Dental
Research.
Gabovich, Rafail Davidovich. Fluorine in
stomatology and hygiene =. Bethesda, Md. ,
Washington , 1977. vi, 1028 p. : LC Card
78-600559 DDC 612/.3924 19
RK331 .G313

Oral motor behavior . [Bethesda, Md.] , 1979.
vi, 261 p. : LC Card 79-604290 DDC 617/.522 19
RK480 .O7

United States. National Institute of Education.
Lasker, Harry. Adult development and
approaches to learning /. Washington, D.C. ,

1980. viii, 74 p. : LC Card 81-601188 DDC
374/.973 19
LC5251 .L35

United States. National Institute of Health. see
United States. National Institutes of Health.

United States. National Institute of Justice. see
National Institute of Justice (U. S.)

United States. National Institute of Law
Enforcement and Criminal Justice. see
National Institute of Law Enforcement and
Criminal Justice.

United States. National Institute of Mental
Health.
Directory of halfway houses and community
residences for the mentally ill. Rockville, Md.
26 cm. (United States. Dept. of Health, Education,
and Welfare. DHEW publication (ADM)) Irregular.
Vol. for 1977 is the result of "a cooperative effort
between the Division of Biometry and Epidemiology of
the National Institut of Mental Health and various
governmental and nongovernmental sources." Title
varies: 1972, Directory of halfway houses for the
mentally ill and alcoholics.
1. Halfway houses - United States - Directories. 2.
Mentally ill - United States. I. United States. National
Institute of Mental Health. Directory of halfway houses
for the mentally ill and alcoholics. II. Title. III. Title:
Directory of halfway houses for the mentally ill and
alcoholics.   NYPL [JLM 81-196]

Directory of halfway houses for the mentally
ill and alcoholics. United States. National
Institute of Mental Health. Directory of
halfway houses and community residences for
the mentally ill. Rockville, Md.
NYPL [JLM 81-196]

Lawton, Mortimer Powell. Social and medical
services in housing for the aged /. Rockville,
Md. , Washington, D.C. , 1980. vii, 112 p. ;
LC Card 80-603249 DDC 363.5/9 19
HD7287.92.U54 L383

Mental health statistics; Series A: mental health
facilities report. Rockville, Md..
NYPL [JLM 80-1073]

Mental health statistics ; series B : analytical
and special study reports. 1- Rockville, Md.,
1968-   NYPL [JLM 80-1006]

Mental health statistics; series C: methodology
reports. Rockville, Md. [etc.]
NYPL [JLM 80-1069]

The Older woman . [Bethesda, Md.] ,
Washington, D.C. , 1979. 51 p. ; LC Card
79-604218
HQ1064.U5 O42   NYPL [JLF 81-395]

Silber, Stanley C. Handbook : foundation
support for mental health and related services /
edited by Stanley Silber. Rockville, Md. , 1974.
v, 89 p. ; LC Card NUC75-137492
NYPL [JLE 80-2424]

United States. National Institute of Mental
Health. Center for Studies of Crime and
Delinquency.
Dangerous behavior, a problem in law and
mental health /. Rockville, Md. , Washington
[1978] vii, 191 p. ; LC Card 79-600623
KF480.A75 D36

Graduated release / National Institute of
Mental Health. Center for Studies of Crime and
Delinquency. Rockville, Md. : The Center,
1971. 30 p. ; 24 cm. (Crime and delinquency topics)
Microfiche (neg.) 1 sheet. 11 x 15 cm. (NYPL FSN.
34,769 "United States. Public Health Service.
Publication no. 2128" Bibliography: p. 25-30.
1. Rehabilitation of criminals - United States. I. Title.
NYPL [*XME-9048]

United States. National Institute of Mental
Health. Center for Studies of Metropolitan
Problems. Conference on Mental Health and
the Economy, Hunt Valley, Md., 1978. Mental
health and the economy . Kalamazoo, Mich.
[1979] viii, 423 p. : ISBN 0-911558-69-1 LC
Card 79-25809
RC455 .C625 1978   NYPL [JLE 80-2456]

United States. National Institute of Mental
Health. Disaster Assistance and Emergency
Mental Health Section. Tierney, Kathleen J.
Crisis intervention programs for disaster
victims . Rockville, Md. , Washington [1979]
xvi, 203 p. ; LC Card 79-603002 DDC 362.2 19
HV555.U6 T53

BIBLIOGRAPHIC GUIDE

United States. National Institute of Mental Health. Division of

572

United States. National Institute of Mental Health. Division of Biometry. Survey and Reports Branch. Reference data on halfway houses for the mentally ill and alcoholics, United States, 1973 / prepared by Survey and Reports Branch, Division of Biometry, National Institute of Mental Health, Alcohol, Drug Abuse and Mental Health Administration. Rockville, Md. : U. S. Alcohol, Drug Abuse, and Mental Health Administration, 1974. 28 p. : 27 cm. Microfilm. Cover title. Chiefly tables. "July 1974."
1. Halfway houses - United States - Statistics. 2. Mentally ill - United States - Rehabilitation. - Statistics. 3. Alcoholics - Rehabilitation - United States - Statistics. I. Title. **NYPL [*ZT-1264]**

United States. National Institute of Mental Health. Division of Scientific and Technical Information. Guide to mental health education materials : a directory for mental health educators / prepared by Division of Scientific and Technical Information, Alcohol, Drug Abuse, and Mental Health Administration. Rockville, Md. : National Institute of Mental Health ; Washington : for sale by the Supt. of Docs., U. S. Govt. Print. Off., 1974. vi, 50 p. ; 24 cm. (DHEW publication ; no. (ADM) 74-35) LC Card 74-603098 DDC 016.3622 19
1. Mental health - Bibliography. 2. Mental health - United States - Directories. I. Series: United States. Dept. of Health, Education and Welfare. DHEW publication, no. (ADM) 74-35). II. Title.
Z6664.N5 U557 1974 RA790

United States. National Institute of Mental Health. Patient Rights and Advocacy Program. Symposium on Safeguarding the Rights of Recipients of Mental Health Services, East Lansing, Mich., 1977. Proceedings /. [Rockville, Md.] [1978] x, 59 p. ; LC Card 79-602277 DDC 344.73/044 19
KF3828.A75 S95 1977

United States. National Institute of Mental Health. Psychopharmacology Research Branch. see United States. Psychopharmacology Research Branch.

United States. National Institute of Neurological and Communicative Disorders and Stroke. see National Institute of Neurological and Communicative Disorders and Stroke.

United States. National Institute on Drug Abuse. see National Institute on Drug Abuse.

United States. National Institute of Health. (Old Catalog form: United States. National Institute of Health.) **Publication.**
(no. 79-1272) Joint US-USSR Symposium on Hypertension, 1st, Sochi, Russia, 1978. Proceedings /. [Bethesda, Md.] , Washington, D.C. [1979] xiv, 436 p. : LC Card 80-601230 DDC 616.1/32 19
RC685.H8 J64 1978

(no. 79-1845) Oral motor behavior . [Bethesda, Md.] , 1979. vi, 261 p. : LC Card 79-604290 DDC 617/.522 19
RK480 .O7

(no. 79-1906) International Nutrition Conference on the Behavioral Effects of Energy and Protein Deficits, Washington, D.C., 1977. Behavioral effects of energy and protein deficits . [Bethesda, Md.] , Washington , 1979. vii, 370 p. : LC Card 79-604003 DDC 155.9/16 19
RJ399.M26 I57 1977

(no. 79-1913) Panel on Convulsive and Neuromuscular Disorders (U. S.) Report of the Panel on Convulsive and Neuromuscular Disorders to the National Advisory Neurological and Communicative Disorders and Stroke Council, National Institute of Neurological and Communicative Disorders and Stroke. [Bethesda, Md.] [1979] xiii, 124 p. : LC Card 80-601220 DDC 616.7/4/0072073 19
RC925.5 .P26 1979

(no. 79-1914) Panel on Communicative Disorders (U. S.) Report of the Panel on Communicative Disorders to the National Advisory Neurological and Communicative Disorders and Stroke. [Bethesda, Md.]

[1979] xvii, 351 p. ; LC Card 80-601219 DDC 616.85/5/0072073 19
RC423 .P24 1979

(no. 79-1916) Panel on Inflammatory, Demyelinating and Degenerative Diseases (U. S.) Report of the Panel on Inflammatory, Demyelinating, and Degenerative Diseases to the National Advisory Neurological and Communicative Disorders and Stroke Council [prepared for the] National Institute of Neurological and Communicative Disorders and Stroke. [Bethesda, Md.] [1979] ix, 129 p. ; LC Card 80-601215 DDC 616.8/072073 19
RC346 .P275 1979

(no. 79-1952) Gibbs, Clarence J., 1924- Bibliography of Creutzfeldt-Jakob disease /. [Washington] , 1979. vii, 169 p. ; LC Card 79-602886 DDC 016.6168/32 19
Z6664.J34 G5 RC394.J34

(no. 80-1529) Prenatal approaches to the diagnosis of fetal hemoglobinopathies . [Bethesda, Md.] , 1980. xiii, 259 p. : LC Card 80-602909 DDC 618.3/2 19
RG629.H45 P73

(no. 80-1872) National Diabetes Information Clearinghouse (U. S.) Diet and nutrition for people with diabetes . [Bethesda, Md.] , 1979. iii, 58 p. ; LC Card 80-601526 DDC 016.6164/620654 19
Z6664.D5 N37 1979 RC662

(no. 80-1970) The Biomedical and behavioral basis of clinical nutrition . [Bethesda, Md.] , Washington, D.C. , 1979. xii, 217 p. ; LC Card 80-601711 DDC 616.3/9 19
RC620.5 .B52

(no. 80-2018) Coronary-prone behavior and coronary heart disease . [Bethesda, Md.] [1980] v, 50 p. ; LC Card 80-602612 DDC 016.6161/23/0019 19
Z6664.H3 C67 RC685.C6

(no. 80-2051) Biomedical research in Latin America . [Bethesda, Md.] , Washington, D.C. [1980] xiv, 239 p. ; LC Card 80-602567 DDC 610/.7208 19
R854.L35 B56

(no. 80-2071) Freiherr, Gregory. The seeds of artificial intelligence . Bethesda, Md. , Washington, D.C. [1980] 74 p. ; LC Card 80-602247 DDC 001.64 19
R858 .F73

(no. 80-2073) National Conference on Diabetes : Current Status and Future Directions, Reston, Va., 1979. Report of the National Conference on Diabetes . [Bethesda, Md.] [1980] xxx, 170 p. ; LC Card 80-602553 DDC 616.4/62 19
RC660 .N37 1979

(no. 80-2079) Eating hints . [Bethesda, Md.] [1980] iii, 86 p. : LC Card 80-602402 DDC 641.5/631 19
RC271.D52 M67 1980

(no. 80-2087) Known effects of low-level radiation exposure . [Bethesda, Md.] [1980] 147 p. : LC Card 80-601671 DDC 616.9/897 19
RA1231.R2 K59

(no. 80-233) John E. Fogarty International Center for Advanced Study in the Health Sciences. International Cooperation and Geographic Studies Branch. U. S.-U. S.S.R. health cooperation, 1972-77 /. [Bethesda, Md.] , 1979. vi, 108 p. ; LC Card 80-601277 DDC 610/.72 19
R853.I57 J63 1979

(no. 80-388) Young, Patrick. Asthma and allergies . [Bethesda, Md.] , Washington, D.C. , 1980. 179 p. : LC Card 80-603185 DDC 616.97 19
RC584 .Y68

(no. 80-940) United States. Task Force on Immunology and Disease. Immunology, its role in disease and health . Bethesda, Md. , Washington, D.C. [1980] xi, 157 p. : LC Card 80-602884 DDC 616.07/9 19
QR181 .U53 1980

(nos. 79-1623-79-1631) National Heart, Lung, and Blood Institute. Hypertension Task Force. Report of the Hypertension Task Force. [Bethesda, Md.] [Washington, D.C.] 1979. 9 v. ; LC Card 80-601819 DDC

616.1/32/072073 19
RC685.H8 N38 1979

(79-1920) National Advisory Neurological and Communicative Disorders and Stroke Council (United States). Task Force on Basic Science. Report of the Task Force on Basic Science to the National Advisory Neurological and Communicative Disorders and Stroke Council. [Washington, D.C.] , 1979. ix, 129 p. ; LC Card 80-601253 DDC 612.8/072073 19
QP356 .N28 1979

Research and development contracts. [Bethesda, Md.] 25 cm. Report for 1974/75 forms part of DHEW publication no. (NIH); 1978/79- forms part of NIH publication. LC Card 76-646048
1. Medical research - United States - Periodicals. 2. Research and development contracts - United States - Periodicals. 3. Research support - Directories. 4. United States. National Institutes of Health.
NYPL [JLL 80-227]

UNITED STATES. NATIONAL INSTITUTES OF HEALTH.
United States. Congress. House. Committee on Interstate and Foreign Commerce. Subcommittee on Health and the Environment. Health research act of 1980 . Washington , 1980. viii, 596 p. : LC Card 80-602806 DDC 344.73/04 19
KF27 .I5543 1980d

United States. National Institutes of Health. Research and development contracts. [Bethesda, Md.] LC Card 76-646048 **NYPL [JLL 80-227]**

United States. National Institutes of Health. Clinical Center. Diagnostic Radiology Dept. Ultrasonic tissue characterization II . Washington , 1979. xi, 362 p. : LC Card 79-600026 DDC 602/.18 s 616.07/543 19
QC100 .U57 no. 525 RC78.7.U4

United States. National Institutes of Health. Division of Research Resources. Workshop on Biological X-ray Microanalysis by Electron Beam Excitation, Boston, 1977. Microbeam analysis in biology /. New York , 1979. xx, 672 p. : ISBN 0-12-440340-9 LC Card 79-24948
QH324.9.X2 W67 1977
NYPL [JSE 80-1320]

United States. National Institutes of Health. National Cancer Institute. see United States. National Cancer Institute.

United States. National Institutes of Health. National Heart, Lung, and Blood Institute. see National Heart, Lung, and Blood Institute.

United States. National Institutes of Health. National Institute of Dental Research. see United States. National Institute of Dental Research.

United States. National Institutes of Health. National Institute of Neurological and Communicative Disorders and Stroke. see National Institute of Neurological and Communicative Disorders and Stroke.

United States. National Institutes of Health. Nutrition Coordinating Committee. The Biomedical and behavioral basis of clinical nutrition . [Bethesda, Md.] , Washington, D.C. , 1979. xii, 217 p. ; LC Card 80-601711 DDC 616.3/9 19
RC620.5 .B52

United States. National Institutes of Health. Office of HEW Case Coordinator. HEW support for universities and colleges, medical and other health professional schools, research centers and hospitals, fiscal year 1969-1977 / U. S. Department of Health, Education, and Welfare. Bethesda, Md. : Office of HEW Case Coordinator, Division of Resources Analysis, National Institutes of Health, [1979?] v, 79 p. : graphs ; 29 cm. (DHEW publication ; no. (NIH) 79-1645) LC Card 79-602074 DDC 379.1/18/0973 19
1. Federal aid to higher education - United States - Statistics. 2. Federal aid to medical education - United States - Statistics. 3. Federal aid to hospitals - United States - Statistics. 4. Federal aid to research - United States - Statistics. 5. Federal aid to medical research - United States - Statistics. I. Series: United States. Dept. of Health, Education and Welfare. DHEW publication, no. (NIH) 79-1645. II. Title.
LB2342 .U5864 1979

**United States. National Institutes of Health.
Office of Resources Analysis.** Brown, Carol
M. Trends in graduate enrollment and Ph.D.
output in scientific fields, 1960-61 through
1967-68. [Washington] , 1969 [i.e. 1970] vii,
204 p. ; LC Card 73-606834 DDC 610/.7 s
610/.7/073 19
RA440.6 .R4 no. 18 R854.U5

**United States. National Institutes of Health.
Research Resources, Division of. see United
States. National Institutes of Health.
Division of Research Resources.**

**United States. National Institutes of Health.
Toxicology Study Section.** Workshop on
Behavioral Toxicology, National Institutes of
Health, 1975. Proceedings /. [Bethesda, Md.]
[1976?] v, 109 p. : LC Card 77-601979
RA1191 .W67 1975 **NYPL [JSF 81-141]**

**UNITED STATES. NATIONAL LABOR
RELATIONS BOARD.**
Truesdale, John C., 1921- The NLRB and
arbitration . Amherst , 1979. 18 p. ; LC Card
80-624267 DDC 344.73/0189143 347.304189143
19
KF3372.Z9 T78

**UNITED STATES. NATIONAL LABOR
RELATIONS BOARD - OFFICIALS AND
EMPLOYEES.**
United States. Congress. Senate. Committee on
Labor and Human Resources. Nomination .
Washington , 1980. iv, 452 p. ; LC Card
80-603891 DDC 353.0083/2 19
KF26 .L27 1980j

United States. Congress. Senate. Committee on
Labor and Human Resources. Nomination .
Washington , 1980. ii, 14 p. ; LC Card
80-602910 DDC 353.0085/2 19
KF26 .L27 1980c

**United States. National Laboratory, Oak Ridge,
Tenn.**
Monte Carlo Seminar-Workshop, Oak Ridge
National Laboratory, 1970. A review of the
Monte Carlo method for radiation transport
calculations. Oak Ridge, Tenn. [1971] vii, 144
p.: **NYPL [JSF 80-645]**

Oak Ridge National Laboratory Life Sciences
Symposium, 1st, Oak Ridge, Tenn., 1978.
Synthetic fossil fuel teachnology. Ann Arbor,
Mich. , c1980. xiii, 288 p. : LC Card 80-68338
NYPL [JSF 81-116]

Symposium on Biotechnology in Energy
Production and Conservation, 1st, Gatlinburg,
Tenn., 1978. Biotechnology in energy
production and conservation . New York ,
c1979. vi, 513 p. : ISBN 0-471-05745-2 (pbk.)
LC Card 80-128733
TJ163.7 .S97 1978 **NYPL [JSE 80-1362]**

Transportation energy conservation data book /
D. B. Shonka, A. S. Loebl, P. D. Patterson ;
prepared for Data Analysis Branch,
Nonhighway Transport Systems and Special
Projects, Transportation Energy Conservation
Division, Office of Conservation, Energy
Research and Development Administration.
Edition 2. Oak Ridge, Tenn. : The Laboratory;
available for National Technical Inofrmation
service, U. S. Dept of Commerce, Springfield,
Va., 1977. xxv, 536 p. : ill. ; 28 cm.
"ORNL-5320." Contract no. W-7405-eng.-26. Includes
bibliographies and index.
*1. Transportation - United States - Energy
consumption - Statistics. 2. Energy conservation -
United States - Statistics. I. Shonka, D. B. II. United
States. Energy Research and Development
Administration. Nonhighway Transport Systems and
Special Projects. Data Analysis Branch. III. Title.*
HE18 1977 .N37 1977 **NYPL [JLF 81-192]**

**United States. National Laboratory, Oak Ridge,
Tenn. Analytical Chemistry Division.**
Conference on Analytical Chemistry in Energy
Technology, 23d, Gatlinburg, Tenn., 1979.
Radioelement analysis . Ann Arbor, Mich. ,
1980. xii, 424 p. : ISBN 0-250-40343-9 LC Card
79-55145
QD605 .C66 1979 **NYPL [JSE 80-1475]**

**United States. National Laboratory, Oak Ridge,
Tenn. Environmental Sciences Division.**
Sourcebook of hydrologic and ecological
features : water resource regions of the
conterminous United States / Robert M.
Cushman ... [et al.]. Ann Arbor, Mich. : Ann

Arbor Science Publishers, c1980. x, 126 p. :
ill. ; 24 cm. Bibliography: p. 111-118. Includes index.
ISBN 0-250-40355-2 LC Card 79-56108
*1. Hydrology - United States. 2. Water-supply - United
States. 3. Aquatic ecology - United States. I. Cushman,
Robert M. II. Title.*
GB701 .U54 1980 **NYPL [JSE 80-1263]**

United States. National Library of Medicine.
Health sciences serials. APR. 1979- Rockville,
Md.. **NYPL [Econ. Div.]**

**United States. National Marine Fisheries
Service.**
Breithaupt, Rob L. A study of the southern
oyster drill (Thais haemastoma) distribution and
density on the oyster seed grounds /. New
Orleans, La. [1979] vii, 20 p. : LC Card
80-621421 DDC 639/.411/09763 19
QL430.5.M9 B73

Fish meal and oil market review. Jan. 1979-
Washingtgton. LC Card 79-643011
I. Title. **NYPL [Econ. Div.]**

Hoyt, Robert D. Population dynamics and
catch susceptibility of smallmouth buffalo in
Rough River Reservoir /. [Frankfort, Ky.] ,
1976. vii, 67 p. : LC Card 79-624983 DDC
639/.2 s 597/.52 19
SH222.K4 A3 no. 62 QL638.C27

Ritchie, Theodore P. A comprehensive review
of the commercial clam industries in the United
States /. Washington , 1977. ix, 106 p. : LC
Card 77-602000
HD9472.C53 U57 **NYPL [*XME-9426]**

**United States. National Marine Fisheries Service.
Office of Fisheries Development. see United
States. Office of Fisheries Development.**

**United States. National Military Command
System Support Center.** United States
population data methodology /. Alexandria,
Va. , 1973. v, 258 p. ; **NYPL [JLF 81-353]**

**United States. National Museum. National
Gallery of Art. see Smithsonian Institution.
National Collection of Fine Arts; United
States. National Gallery of Art.**

**United States. National Ocean Survey. see
National Ocean Survey.**

**United States. National Oceanic and
Atmospheric Administration.**
Climate Diagnostics Workshop. Proceeding of
the annual Climate Diagnostics Workshop.
[Washington, etc.]. LC Card 79-640997
NYPL [JSP 80-293]

Floods of May 1978 in southeastern Montana
and northeastern Wyoming /. Washington
[1981] p. cm. LC Card 81-607843 DDC
551.48/9/097863 19
GB1399.4.M9 F46

International Symposium on Problems Related
to the Redefinition of North American
Geodetic Networks, 2d, Arlington, Va., 1978.
Proceedings /. [Rockville, Md.] , Washington ,
1979. xiii, 645 p. : LC Card 78-15124
QB301 .I66 1978 **NYPL [JSE 81-179]**

NOAA professional paper.
(10) Hatcher, Patrick G. The organic
geochemistry of Mangrove Lake, Bermuda /.
Rockville, Md. , 1978. vi, 92 p. : LC Card
78-601738 DDC 551.46 s 551.9/097299 19
GC1 .U42c no. 10 GB1657.B47

Red River Valley tornadoes of April 10, 1979 :
a report to the administrator. Rockville, Md. :
U. S. Dept. of Commerce, National Oceanic
and Atmospheric Administration, [1980] v, 60
p., [2] leaves of plates : ill. ; 27 cm. (Natural
disaster survey report . 80-1) "January 1980." LC
Card 80-601568 DDC 363.3/492 19
*1. Tornado warning systems - Texas. 2. Tornado
warning systems - Oklahoma. 3. Wichita Falls, Tex. -
Tornado, 1979. 4. Vernon, Tex. - Tornado, 1979. 5.
Lawton, Okla. - Tornado, 1979. I. Title. II. Series.*
QC955.5.T4 U54 1980

Report to the Congress on ocean pollution and
offshore development. Oct. 1977/Sept. 1978-
[Washington] illus. 28 cm. For earlier years, see its
Report to the Congress on ocean pollution, overfishing
and offshore development. Report year ends Sept. 30th.
*1. Marine pollution - Periodicals. 2. Marine resources
and state - United States - Periodicals. 3. Marine
resources conservation - Periodicals. I. Title.*
NYPL [JSP 81-88]

The story of the Pribilof fur seals.
[Washington] : U. S. Dept. of Commerce,
National Oceanic and Atmospheric
Administration, [1976] 34 p. : ill. ; 27 cm. LC
Card 77-601364 DDC 333.95/9 19
*1. Sealing - Alaska - Pribilof Islands. 2. Northern fur
seal. 3. Pribilof Islands. I. Title.*
SH361 .U75 1976

United States. Geological Survey.
Johnstown-western Pennsylvania storm and
floods of July 19-20, 1977 /. Washington ,
1981. p. cm. LC Card 80-607777 DDC
551.48/9/0974877 19
QC943.5.U6 U53

**UNITED STATES. NATIONAL OCEANIC
AND ATMOSPHERIC
ADMINISTRATION.**
United States. Congress. House. Committee on
Science and Technology. Posture hearings (EPA
and NOAA) . Washington , 1980. iii, 70 p. ;
LC Card 80-604052 DDC 353.0082/321 19
KF27 .S39 1980e

United States. Congress. House. Committee on
Science and Technology. Subcommittee on
Natural Resources and Environment. Research
and development programs of the National
Oceanic and Atmospheric Adminstration .
Washington , 1979, [i.e. 1980] iii, 229 p. ; LC
Card 80-602771 DDC 353.0082/32 19
KF27 .S398 1979i

**UNITED STATES. NATIONAL OCEANIC
AND ATMOSPHERIC
ADMINISTRATION -
APPROPRIATIONS AND
EXPENDITURES.**
United States. Congress. House. Committee on
Science and Technology. Subcommittee on
Natural Resources and Environment. 1981
NOAA authorization . Washington , 1980. iii,
279 p. ; LC Card 80-602732 DDC
353.0072/2368232 19
KF27 .S398 1980b

**United States. National Oceanic and
Atmospheric Administration. Environmental
Data and Information Service.** Poppe,
Barbara B. Directory of world seismograph
stations. Boulder, Colo. , 1980- v. <1, pt. 1
> : LC Card 80-603927 DDC 551 s 551.2/2/2025
19
QE500 .W67a no. 25 QE540.U6

**United States. National Oceanic and
Atmospheric Administration. Environmental
Research Laboratories. see Environmental
Research Laboratories.**

**United States. National Oceanic and
Atmospheric Administration. Marine
Minerals Division.** Andrews, Benjamin V.
Relative costs of U. S. and foreign nodule
transport ships /. Rockville, Md. , 1978. vi, 70
p. : LC Card 78-602299
HE746 .A75

**United States. National Oceanic and
Atmospheric Administration. National
Marine Fisheries Service. see United States.
National Marine Fisheries Service.**

**United States. National Oceanic and
Atmospheric Administration. National Ocean
Survey. see National Ocean Survey.**

**United States. National Oceanic and
Atmospheric Administration. National
Weather Service. see United States. National
Weather Service.**

**United States. National Oceanic and
Atmospheric Administration. Office of
Coastal Zone Management. see United
States. Office of Coastal Zone Management.**

**United States. National Oceanic and
Atmospheric Administration. Office of Policy
and Planning. Marine Minerals Divisions.
see United States. National Oceanic and
Atmospheric Administration. Marine
Minerals Division.**

**United States. National Oceanic and
Atmospheric Administration. Office of Sea
Grant.** Hale, Stuart O., 1917- Narragansett
Bay . Narragansett, RI [1980] ix, 122 p. :
ISBN 0-938412-19-1 (pbk.) : LC Card 80-52813
DDC 974.5 19
F87.N2 H34

United States. National Oceanic and Atmospheric Administration. Sea Grant, Office of. see **United States. National Oceanic and Atmospheric Administration. Office of Sea Grant.**

United States. National Park Service.
Anderson, Susan H. The most splendid carpet /. Philadelphia , Washington , 1978. x, 93 [3] p. : LC Card 79-602679
NK3012.S46 A52 **NYPL [3-MOP 81-683]**

Anthropological papers. see **Anthropological papers.**

Brusse, David M. A history of the Chaco Navajos /. Albuquerque, N.M. , Washington, D.C. , 1980. viii, 542 p. : LC Card 81-601717 DDC 978.9/8200497 19
E99.N3 B76

Clara Barton, Clara Barton National and Historic Site, Maryland / produced by the Division of Publications, National Park Service, U. S. Dept. of the Interior. Washington, D.C. : The Division, 1981. p. cm. (National park handbook ; 110) Includes index. CONTENTS. - Clara Barton and her times.--Pryor, E. B. The professional angel.--Guide and adviser. LC Card 80-607838 DDC 361.7/63 B 19
1. Barton, Clara Harlowe, 1821-1912. 2. Clara Barton House National Historic Site, Md. I. Series: United States. National Park Service. Handbook - National Park Service , 110. II. Title.
HV569.B3 U65 1981

Hageman, Fred C. An archeological and restoration study of Mission La Purísima Concepción . Santa Barbara, Calif. , Glendale, Calif. , 1980. xxxi, 307 p. : LC Card 79-64806
F869.P89 H33 **NYPL [IXH (Purísima Concepción Mission) 81-684]**

Handbook - National Park Service .
(110) United States. National Park Service. Clara Barton, Clara Barton National and Historic Site, Maryland /. Washington, D.C. , 1981. p. cm. LC Card 80-607838 DDC 361.7/63 B 19
HV569.B3 U65 1981

An inventory of international park possibilities: Point Roberts, Boundary Bay, San Juan and Gulf Islands Archipelago; a joint report prepared [by] U. S. National Park Service [and] Parks Canada for the International Point Roberts Board. [Washington?] 1973. 87 l. illus. 22 x 37 cm. LC Card 81-461454 DDC 333.78/3/0979773 19
1. Parks - Washington (State) - Point Roberts. 2. Parks - Washington (State). 3. Parks - British Columbia. 4. Parks - United States. 5. Parks - Canada. I. Canada. Dept. of Indian Affairs and Northern Development. National and Historic Parks Branch. II. International Point Roberts Board. III. Title. IV. Title: International park possibilities.
SB482.W2 U54 1973

McClellan, Carole. The archeology of Lake Mead National Recreation Area . Tucson, Ariz. [Washington, D.C.?] , 1980. x,188 p. : LC Card 81-600707 DDC 979.3/12 19
F788 .M163

Mount Rainier National Park / National Park Service, U. S. Department of the Interior. [Washington] : The Service, [1981] 1 map : col. ; 47 x 61 cm., folded to 24 x 11 cm. Relief shown by shading and spot heights. Panel title: Mount Rainier. "Reprint 1981." Text and ill. (some col.) on verso. LC Card 81-691569
1. Mount Rainier National Park (Wash.) - Maps.
G4282.M6 1981 .U5

Paine, Judith. Theodate Pope Riddle, her life and work. [Washington?] , 1979. [26] p. : LC Card 79-52952
NA737.R53 A4 1979
NYPL [3-MQZ (Riddle) 81-627]

Richard T. Greener . [Washington, D. C.] , 1980. 16 p. : **NYPL [Sc F 80-218]**

Snake River : Idaho, Washington, Oregon : final wild and scenic river study report and environmental statement. [Washington] : National Park Service, [1980] viii, 302 p. : ill. ; 27 cm. "February 1980." LC Card 80-602290 DDC 333.78/45/097961 19
1. Nature conservation - Snake River. 2. Environmental impact analysis - Snake River. 3. Snake River. I. Title.
QH76.5.S62 U54 1980

United States. Heritage Conservation and Recreation Service. National urban recreation study . [Washington , 1978] 184 p. : LC Card 78-602420
GV53 .U54 1978

Washington, D.C. / National Park Service, U. S. Department of the Interior. Washington : The Service : For sale by the Supt. of Docs., U. S. Govt. Print. Off., [1978] 1 map : col. ; 23 x 49 cm. Scale not given. Folded title: Welcome to Washington. "Reprint 1978." "Stock Number 024-005-00669-9." Covers the National Mall, major government buildings, and tourist sites in downtown Washington. Includes text, tourist information, and col. ill. Text, tourist information, map of Washington region, and col. ill. on verso. LC Card 78-696267
1. Washington, D. C. - Maps, Tourist. 2. Central business districts - Washington D. C. - Maps. 3. Washington, D. C. - Maps. I. Title: Welcome to Washington.
G3851.E635 1978 .U5
NYPL [Map Div. 81-3038]

United States. National Park Service. Cultural Resources Management Division. Cultural resources remote sensing /. Washington, D.C. , 1980. ix, 390 p. : LC Card 81-601114 DDC 973/.028 19
E77.9 .C84

United States. National Park Service. Denver Service Center.
Building Conservation Technology/The Ehrenkrantz Group. Mechanical and electrical rehabilitation, Main Building, Ellis Island, Statue of Liberty National Monument, New York . Denver, Colo. , 1980. 97 leaves, ca. 500 leaves of plates : LC Card 80-601419 DDC 725/.1 19
NA4510.I6 B84 1980a

Final environmental statement, FES-78-7 : proposed wilderness recommendation, Everglades National Park, Florida / prepared by Denver Service Center, National Park Service, United States Department of the Interior. [Denver] : The Center, [1978] vii, 211 p. : ill. ; 27 cm. Bibliography: p. 207-211. LC Card 79-601941 DDC 333.91/8/0975939 19
1. Wilderness areas - Florida - Everglades National Park. 2. Nature conservation - Florida - Everglades National Park. 3. Everglades National Park.
QH76.5.F6 U54 1978

United States. National Park Service. Denver Service Center. Mid-Atlantic/North Atlantic Team. Branch of Historic Preservation.
Rogers, Rebecca M. The dependencies of the Nelson, Smith, and Ballard houses, Colonial National Historical Park, Yorktown, Virginia . [Washington] , 1979. vii, 25 p., [27] leaves of plates : LC Card 79-603752 DDC 975.5/423 19
F234.Y6 R63

United States. National Park Service. Division of Publications.
Devils Tower . Washington, D.C. , 1981. p. cm. LC Card 81-607961 DDC 978.7/13 19
F767.D47 D48

Fort Vancouver . Washington, D.C. , 1981. p. cm. LC Card 81-607951 DDC 979.7/86 19
F899.V2 F67

Great Smoky Mountains National Park, North Carolina and Tennessee / produced by the Division of Publications, National Park Service. Washington, D.C. : U. S. Dept. of the Interior, 1981. p. cm. (Handbook / National Park Service . 112) Includes index. LC Card 81-11320 DDC 976.8/89 19
1. Great Smoky Mountains National Park (N.C. and Tenn.). I. Series: Handbook (United States. National Park Service. Division of Publications) , 112. II. Title.
F443.G7 U63 1981

Independence, Independence National Historical Park / produced by the Division of Publications, National Park Service. Washington, D.C. : National Park Service, U. S. Dept. of the Interior, 1981. p. cm. (National Park handbook . 116) LC Card 81-607080 DDC 917.48/11 19
1. Independence National Historical Park (Pa.). 2. Philadelphia (Pa.) - Parks. I. Series: Handbook (United States. National Park Service. Division of Publications) , 116. II. Title.
F158.65.I3 U54 1981

United States. National Park Service. Historic American Buildings Survey. see **Historic**

American Buildings Survey.

United States. National Park Service. Historic American Engineering Record. see **Historic American Engineering Record.**

United States. National Park Service. Office of History and Historic Architecture. see **United States. Office of History and Historic Architecture.**

UNITED STATES. NATIONAL RAILROAD ADJUSTMENT BOARD.
Lazar, Joseph, 1916- Due process in disciplinary hearings . Los Angeles , c1980. 459 p. ; LC Card 80-135569 DDC 344.73/012598 19
KF3580.R2 L38 1980

United States. National Science Foundation.
An analysis of Federal R & D funding by function, fiscal years 1969-1975. - Washington : National Science Foundation : for sale by the Supt. of Docs. U. S. Govt. Print. Off., [1974] x, 69 p. : graphs ; 24 x 30 cm. (United States. National Science Foundation. Surveys of science resources series) "NSF 74-313". Includes bibliographical references. LC Card 74-601163
1. Research - United States - Finance. I. Title.
NYPL [JLF 80-1457]

Databook / National Science Foundation. [Washington] : NSF, 1973. vii, 68 p. ; 11 x 16 cm. "NSF 73-3." Chiefly tables.
1. Federal aid to research - United States. 2. Grants-in-aid - United States. 3. United States. National Science Foundation. **NYPL [JLB 80-5]**

Deep sea drilling project; ocean sediment coring program. [Washington, D. C., U. S. Govt. Print. Off.] 1974. 19 p. illus. 22 x 28 cm. LC Card 75-44202
1. Oil well drilling, Submarine. I. Title.
NYPL [JSF 80-400]

The five-year outlook : problems, opportunities, and constraints in science and technology. [Washington, D.C.] : National Science Foundation : for sale by the Supt. of Docs., U. S. Govt. Print. Off., [1980?- v. ; 28 cm. Includes index. LC Card 80-603198 DDC 509/.73 19
1. Science - United States. 2. Technology - United States. 3. Science and state - United States. 4. Technology and state - United States. I. Title.
Q127.U6 U489 1980

The Five-year outlook: problems, opportunities, and constraints in science and technology. 1980- [Washington]. illus. 27 cm.
1. Science and state - United States - Periodicals. 2. Technology and state - United States - Periodicals. I. Title. **NYPL [JSP 81-1]**

Hurricane wind speeds in the United States /. Washington, D.C. [1980] viii, 30, 11 p. : LC Card 80-600039 DDC 690/.02/18 s 551.5/52 19
TA435 .U58 no. 124 QC933

International Conference on the Biogeochemistry of Amino Acids, Airlie House, 1978. Biogeochemistry of amino acids . New York , c1980. xviii, 558 p. : ISBN 0-471-05493-3 : LC Card 79-25824
QH344 .I56 1978 **NYPL [JSE 80-1214]**

MODE-1 Scientific Council. Mid-Ocean Dynamics Experiment - One. Washington, 1973. 38 p.; **NYPL [JSF 80-781]**

Scientists and engineers from abroad. Washington, D. C. 29 cm. (Its: NSF) Its: Surveys of science resource series. Title varies: 1966/67-1969/70, Scientists, engineers, and physicians from abroad.
1. Scientist - United States - Statistics - Periodicals. 2. Engineers - United States - Statistics - Periodicals. I. United States. National Science Foundation. Scientists, engineers, and physicians from abroad. II. Title.
NYPL [M-11 4663]

Scientists, engineers, and physicians from abroad. United States. National Science Foundation. Scientists and engineers from abroad. Washington, D. C.
NYPL [M-11 4663]

Site characterization & exploration . New York , c1979. vi, 395 p. : LC Card 79-115992
TA705 .S537 **NYPL [JSd 81-100]**

Using ANS FORTRAN /. Washington, D.C. [1980] vi, 100 p. ; LC Card 80-600009 DDC 001.64/24 19
QA76.73.F25 U84

UNITED STATES. NATIONAL SCIENCE FOUNDATION.

United States. National Science Foundation. Databook /. [Washington] , 1973. vii, 68 p. ;
NYPL [JLB 80-5]

United States. National Science Foundation. Access Improvement Program. Gellman Research Associates. The role of scientific and technical information in critical period management. /. Jenkintown, Pa. , 1977. 2 v. (various pagings) LC Card 77-604051
*HD30.3 .G45 1977 NYPL [*XME-9434]*

United States. National Science Foundation. Advanced Productivity Research and Technology, Division of. see United States. National Science Foundation. Division of Advanced Productivity Research and Technology.

UNITED STATES. NATIONAL SCIENCE FOUNDATION - APPROPRIATIONS AND EXPENDITURES.

United States. Congress. House. Committee on Science and Technology. Subcommittee on Science, Research, and Technology. 1981 National Science Foundation authorization . Washington , 1980. iv, 853 p. : LC Card 80-603468 DDC 353.0072/236855 19
KF27 .S399 1980c

United States. Congress. Senate. Committee on Labor and Human Resources. Subcommittee on Health and Scientific Research. National Science Foundation authorization act for fiscal years 1981 and 1982 . Washington , 1980. iv, 132 p. : LC Card 80-602713 DDC 353.0072/236855 19
KF26 .L274 1980a

United States. National Science Foundation. Directorate for Science Education. Office of Program Integration. Science education databook/ [prepared by staff of Office of Program Integration]. [Washington, D.C.] : Directorate for Science Education, National Science Foundation, [1980] ix, 154 p. : graphs ; 21 x 26 cm. "SE 80-3." Bibliography: p. 145-154. LC Card 80-602336 DDC 507/.1073 19
1. Science - Study and teaching - United States - Statistics. I. Title.
Q183.3.A1 U55 1980

United States. National Science Foundation. Division of Advanced Productivity Research and Technology.
Extending the human life span . [Chicago] , Washington [1977] v, 70 p. : LC Card 77-604795
*HQ1064.U5 E9 NYPL [*XME-9403]*

Research on the effects of television advertising on children . [Washington] [1977] viii, 229 p. : LC Card 77-604793
*HQ784.T4 R47 NYPL [*XME-9373]*

United States. National Science Foundation. Division of Intergovernmental Science & Public Technology. Wisconsin. Legislative Council. Science and technology intern program . Madison, Wis. , 1979. iv, 152 p. ; LC Card 79-624457 DDC 328.775/0761 19
Q127.U6 W57 1979

United States. National Science Foundation. Division of Polar Programs. Survival in Antarctica. 1979 ed. Washington, D.C. : National Science Foundation, Division of Polar Programs : for sale by the Supt. of Docs., U. S. Govt. Print. Off., 1979. v, 90 p. : ill. ; 24 cm. Bibliography: p. 98-99. LC Card 80-601811 DDC 613.6/9/09989 19
1. Wilderness survival - Antarctic regions. I. Title.
GV200.5 .U54 1979

United States. National Science Foundation. Division of Problem-Focused Research Applications.
Terrestrial microcosms and environmental chemistry . [Washington] [1978?] xv, 147 p. : LC Card 79-601829 DDC 574.5/264 19
QH541.2 .T45

Workshop on Terrestrial Microcosms, Newport, Or., 1977. Terrestrial microcosms . [Washington] [1978?] xii, 35 p. : LC Card 79-602306 DDC 574.5/264 19
QH541.28 .W67 1977

United States. National Science Foundation. National Science Board. Subcommittee on

Environmental Programs. Strengthening environmental programs / National Science Board, Subcommittee on Environmental Programs, Programs Committee. [Washington] : The Board : for sale by the Supt. of Docs., U. S. Govt. Print. Off., 1976. 27 p. ; 26 cm. "NSB 77-450." Includes bibliographical references. LC Card 78-601436 DDC 551.48/072073 19
1. Hydrology - United States - Research. 2. Meteorological research - United States. 3. Environmental protection - United States - Research. I. Title.
GB658.7 .U57 1976

United States. National Science Foundation. Office of Experimental Projects and Programs. College science improvement programs; COSIP A & B report [Ruth Ann Verell and Robert F. Watson, editors] Washington, D. C. [For sale by the Supt of Docs., U. S. Govt. Print. Off., 1974] v, 191 p. 26 cm. At head of title: An index to undergraduate science.
1. Science - Study and teaching (Higher) - United States. I. Verell, Ruth Ann, ed. II. Watson, Robert F. III. Title. NYPL [JSF 80-775]

United States. National Science Foundation. Office of Intergovernmental Science Programs. Reid, George Willard, 1917- Final report on the Governor's Conference on Research and Development Priorities for the State of Oklahoma /. [Norman, Okla. , 1973] 293 p. in various pagings : LC Card 80-621267 DDC 338.9766 19
T176 .R4

United States. National Science Foundation. Office of Science Information Service.
Shapero, Albert. Exit, a high communicator of long standing leaves . Austin , 1978. 31 p. : LC Card 79-621448 DDC 302.3/5 19
HM131 .S446

United States. National Science Foundation. Research Applied to National Needs Program.
Environmental Design Conference on City Centers in Transition, University of North Carolina at Chapel Hill, 1976. City centers in transition . Chapel Hill , 1976. xii, 90 leaves ; LC Card 76-29226 *NYPL [JLF 80-1605]*

General Electric Company. Automation and Control Laboratory. Product system productivity research. Washington, 1976. 3 v.
*NYPL [*XME-9310]*

Ostrom, Elinor. Policing metropolitan America /. [Washington] [1977] viii, 49 p. : LC Card 77-603798
*HV8138 .O76 NYPL [*XME-9420]*

Ultrasonic tissue characterization II . Washington , 1979. xi, 362 p. : LC Card 79-600026 DDC 602/.18 s 616.07/543 19
QC100 .U57 no. 525 RC78.7.U4

UNITED STATES - NATIONAL SECURITY.

United States. Congress. House. Committee on Armed Services. Procurement and Military Nuclear Systems Subcommittee. Hearings on H.R. 6621 (H.R. 7265), Department of Energy authorization legislation (national security programs) for fiscal year 1981, before the Procurement and Military Nuclear Systems Subcommittee of the Committee on Armed Services, House of Representatives, Ninety-sixth Congress, second session .... Washington , 1980. xiv, 1088, vi p. : LC Card 80-602721 DDC 353.0072/236823 19
KF27 .A7657 1980a

United States. Congress. House. Committee on Armed Services. Procurement and Military Nuclear Systems Subcommittee. Readiness Panel. Review of readiness considerations in the development of the defense budget . Washington , 1980 [i.e. 1981] ii, 161 p. : LC Card 81-600960 DDC 355/.033073 19
KF27 .A7657 1980d

United States. Congress. House. Committee on Armed Services. Subcommittee on Investigations. Leaks of classified national defense information--stealth aircraft . Washington , 1980 [i.e. 1981] iii, 9 p. ; LC Card 81-601284 DDC 353.0071/45 19
UB247 .U53 1981

United States. Congress. House. Committee on Armed Services. Subcommittee on

Investigations. Leaks of classified national defense information--stealth aircraft . Washington , 1980 [i.e. 1981] ii, 228 p. ; LC Card 81-601135 DDC 353.0071/45 19
KF27 .A753 1980c

United States. Congress. House. Committee on Armed Services. Subcommittee on Seapower and Strategic and Critical Materials. National policy objectives and the adequacy of our current navy forces . Washington , 1980 [i.e. 1981] ii, 137 p. : LC Card 81-601761 DDC 359/.03/0973 19
KF27 .A769 1979e

United States. Congress. House. Committee on Foreign Affairs. Subcommittee on International Organizations and Movements. Behavioral sciences and the national security . Washington , 1965. vi, 1OR, iii, 203 p. : LC Card 80-503601 DDC 327.73 s 327.1/1 19
E840.2 .A3 no. 4 E846

United States. Congress. House. Permanent Select Committee on Intelligence. Subcommittee on Legislation. H.R. 6588, the National Intelligence Act of 1980 . Washington , 1980 [i.e. 1981] iv, 608 p. ; LC Card 81-600987 DDC 344.73/052 347.30452 19
KF27.5 .I54 1980

United States. Congress. Senate. Committee on Foreign Relations. U. S. security interests and policies in Southwest Asia . Washington , 1980. iii, 368 p. : LC Card 80-603283 DDC 355/.033056 19
KF26 .F6 1980p

UNITED STATES - NATIONAL SECURITY - ADDRESSES, ESSAYS, LECTURES.

Evolving strategic realities . Washington, DC , 1980. xi, 222 p. ; LC Card 80-602927 DDC 355/.033073 19
UA23 .E97

UNITED STATES. NATIONAL SECURITY AGENCY/CENTRAL SECURITY SERVICE - OFFICIALS AND EMPLOYEES.

United States. Congress. Senate. Committee on Governmental Affairs. Legislation to authorize the establishment of senior executive positions for NSA, DEA, and the Export-Import Bank . Washington , 1980. iii, 44 p. ; LC Card 80-603902 DDC 342.73/068 347.30268 19
KF26 .G67 1980l

UNITED STATES - NATIONAL SECURITY - CONGRESSES.

National Security Affairs Conference, 6th, National Defense University, 1979. Continuity and change in the eighties and beyond . [Washington, D.C.] , 1979. xiii, 222 p. ; LC Card 80-601820 DDC 355/.033073 19
UA23 .N248 1979

UNITED STATES - NATIONAL SECURITY - FINANCE.

United States. Congress. Senate. Committee on Armed Services. Subcommittee on Arms Control. Fiscal year 1981 Department of Energy authorization for national security programs . Washington , 1980. iii, 205 p. : LC Card 80-603337 DDC 353.0072/23682/3 19
KF26 .A7435 1980

United States. National Technical Information Service.
Appropriate technology information for developing countries : selected abstracts from the NTIS data file / prepared by the U. S. Department of Commerce, National Technical Information Service, in collaboration with the Volunteers in Technical Assistance, Inc.2d ed.-Nov. 1979. [Washington, D.C.] : NTIS, [c1980] xxiv, 384 p. (p. 383-384 ordering instructions) ; 28 cm. Editor: Paul L. Bundick. Earlier ed. (1979) published under title: Selected appropriate technologies for developing countries. On cover: International technical information network, a project of the U. S. Agency for International Development. "PB80-117666." LC Card 80-601640 DDC 600 19
1. Underdeveloped areas - Technology - Abstracts. I. Bundick, Paul L. II. Volunteers in Technical Assistance. III. United States. Agency for International Development. IV. Title.
T49.5 .U56 1980

A directory of computer software & related technical reports, 1980. [Springfield, VA] : U. S. Dept. of Commerce, National Technical

Information Service, c1980. vii, 202, [108] p. ; 28 cm. Cover title. Running title: Software and related technical reports. "PB80-110232." Includes indexes.
LC Card 80-602222   DDC 001.64/25/029473 19
1. Computer programs - Bibliography - Catalogs. 2. United States - Government publications - Bibliography - Catalogs. I. Title. II. Title: Software and related technical reports.
Z5644 .U54 1980 QA76.6

A directory of computer software applications : minicomputers & microcomputers, August 1977-1980. [Springfield, Va.] : U. S. Dept. of Commerce, National Technical Information Service, 1980. iii, 180 p. ; 28 cm. Cover title. "PB80-105513." Includes indexes.   LC Card 80-603142   DDC 016.00164/25/0973 19
1. Computer service industry - United States - Directories. I. Title.
HD9696.C63 U593 1980

A directory of computer software applications, atmospheric sciences, 1970-October, 1978. Springfield, Va. : U. S. Dept. of Commerce, National Technical Information Service, c1978. vii, 114 p. ; 28 cm. "PB-286 256." Includes indexes.
LC Card 80-602673   DDC 016.5515/028/5425 19
1. Meteorology - Data processing - Bibliography. I. Title. II. Title: Atmospheric sciences.
Z6683.D37 U54 1978 QC874.3

A directory of computer software applications, electrical & electronics engineering : 1970-September 1978. Springfield, Va. : U. S. Dept. of Commerce, National Technical Information Service, c1978. vii, 115 p. ; 28 cm. "PB-284 924." Includes indexes.   LC Card 80-602676   DDC 621.3/028/54 19
1. Electric engineering - Data processing - Bibliography - Catalogs. 2. Electronics - Data processing - Bibliography - Catalogs. 3. Computer programs - Catalogs. I. Title. II. Title: Electrical & electronics engineering.
Z5834.D37 U55 1978

A Directory of computer software applications: environmental pollution & control. [Springfield, Va.]   *NYPL [JSP 81-8]*

A directory of computer software applications, library & information sciences, 1970-March 1978. Springfield, Va. : U. S. Dept. of Commerce, National Technical Information Service, c1978. vii, 71 p. ; 28 cm. "PB278 452." Includes indexes.   LC Card 80-601076   DDC 016.02/028/54 19
1. Library science - Data processing - Bibliography. 2. Libraries - Automation - Bibliography. 3. Information storage and retrieval systems - Bibliography. 4. Information science - Bibliography. I. Title.
Z678.9.A2 U54 1978

A directory of computer software applications, physics, 1970-May 1978. Springfield, Va. : U. S. Dept. of Commerce, National Technical Information Service, c1978. vii, 208, 114 p. ; 28 cm. Includes indexes. "June 1978." "PB-281 642."   LC Card 80-602674
1. Physics - Computer programs - Bibliography. I. Title. II. Title: Computer software applications, physics, 1970-May 1978.
Z7144.C74 U54 1978 QC52
NYPL [JSF 81-190]

United States. Institute for Applied Technology. Technical Analysis Division. City I player's manual. Washington, D.C., 1973. viii, 142 p.
NYPL [JLF 80-1361]

United States. National Center for Health Statistics. Publications and data tapes of the National Center for Health Statistics available from the National Technical Information Service. Hyattsville, Md. , 1978. 260 p. ;   LC Card 79-602913
Z7553.M43 U54 1978 RA407.3
NYPL [JLF 81-340]

UNITED STATES. NATIONAL TECHNICAL INFORMATION SERVICE - CATALOGS.
United States. National Center for Health Statistics. Publications and data tapes of the National Center for Health Statistics available from the National Technical Information Service. Hyattsville, Md. , 1978. 260 p. ;   LC Card 79-602913
Z7553.M43 U54 1978 RA407.3
NYPL [JLF 81-340]

United States. National Transportation Safety Board.

Marine accident report, NTSB-MAR. no. 78-2- ; Nov. 1975- - Washington.
I. Title.   *NYPL [Sci. & Tech. Div.]*

Preliminary analysis of aircraft accident data: United States civil aviation. Washington. 28 cm. Annual.
1. Aeronautics - United States - Accidents - Periodicals. I. Title.   *NYPL [JLM 80-909]*

Report no. NTSB-HSS. 79/1- Washington.
NYPL [Econ. Div.]

UNITED STATES. NATIONAL TRANSPORTATION SAFETY BOARD - APPROPRIATIONS AND EXPENDITURES.
United States. Congress. House. Committee on Public Works and Transportation. Subcommittee on Aviation. To amend the Hazardous materials transportation act and to amend the Independent safety board act . Washington , 1980. v, 97 p. ;   LC Card 80-603697   DDC 343.73/093 347.30393 19
KF27 .P89624 1980j

United States. Congress. Senate. Committee on Commerce, Science, and Transportation. National Transportation Safety Board authorization . Washington , 1980. iii, 26 p. ;
LC Card 80-602102   DDC 353.0072/236875 19
KF26 .C69 1980h

UNITED STATES. NATIONAL TRANSPORTATION SAFETY BOARD - OFFICIALS AND EMPLOYEES.
United States. Congress. Senate. Committee on Commerce, Science, and Transportation. Nomination--National Transportation Board . Washington , 1980. iii, 8 p. ;   LC Card 80-602720   DDC 353.0087/5 19
KF26 .C69 1980k

United States. National Weather Service.
Average monthly weather outlook. v. 24, no. 20- ; Oct. 16, 1970- Washington. illus. 30 cm. Semimonthly. For earlier file, whose numbering it continues, see (in Old Catalog): United States. Weather Bureau. Average monthly weather resume and outlook.
1. Long-range weather forecasting - United States - Periodicals. I. Title.   *NYPL [JSP 80-443]*

University of Alaska, Fairbanks. Geophysical Institute. Alaska's weather and climate . Fairbanks, Alaska [1979] v, 153 leaves :   LC Card 80-621244   DDC 551.69798 19
QC984.A4 U54 1979

United States. Natural Resource Economics Division (Dept. of Agriculture) see United States. Dept. of Agriculture. Natural Resource Economics Division.

United States - Naturalization. see Naturalization - United States.

United States. Nautical Almanac Office.
American ephemeris and nautical almanac. 1855-1980. Washington, U. S. Govt. Print. Off. 126 v. illus. 27 cm. Annual. Vols. for 1960-80, issued simultaneously in London by the Great Britain, Nautical Office with title: the Astronomical ephemeris. Beginning with 1981, only one edition issued for both countries; see: The Astronomical almanac. Includes supplements.   LC Card 70-35435
1. Nautical almanacs. I. Title.   *NYPL [ONR (United States. Nautical Almanac Office. American ephemeris and nautical almanac)]*

The Astronomical almanac. 1981- Washington.
LC Card 80-647548   *NYPL [JSP 81-85]*

United States. Naval Academy, Annapolis.
International Meeting of Directors and Chiefs of Naval Material, 1st, Annapolis, 1972. [Proceedings] Annapolis [1973] [62] p.
NYPL [JLF 80-886]

United States Naval Academy History Symposium, 3rd, 1977. Changing interpretations and new sources in naval history . New York , 1980. xi, 471 p. :   ISBN 0-8240-9517-0 :   LC Card 80-5
D27 .U63 1977   *NYPL [JFE 81-505]*

United States Naval Academy History Symposium, 3rd, 1977. Changing interpretations and new sources in naval history : papers from the Third United States Naval Academy History Symposium / edited by Robert William Love, Jr., co-editors, P. Robert Artigiani ... [et al]. New York : Garland Pub., 1980. xi, 471 p. : ill. ; 24 cm.   ISBN

0-8240-9517-0 :   LC Card 80-5
1. Naval history - Congresses. I. Love, Robert William, 1944-. II. United States. Naval Academy, Annapolis. III. Title.
D27 .U63 1977   *NYPL [JFE 81-505]*

United States. Naval Air Systems Command.
Project Squid Workshop on Gas Turbine Combustor Design Problems, Purdue University, 1978. Gas turbine combustor design problems /. Washington , c1980. xvi, 431 p. :   ISBN 0-89116-177-5   LC Card 79-222350
TJ778 .P74 1978   *NYPL [JSE 81-58]*

United States. Naval Education and Training, Chief of. see United States. Chief of Naval Education and Training.

United States. Naval Education and Training Command.
Gunner's Mate M 1 & C / Naval Education and Training Command. [Rev.]. [Pensacola, Fla. : Naval Education and Training Program Development Center ; Washington, D.C. : U. S. Govt. Print. Off., 1979] iii, 329, 75 p., [1] fold. leaf of plates : ill. ; 26 cm. (Rate training manual and nonresident career course) Cover title. "NAVEDTRA 10200-C." Includes index.   LC Card 80-601852   DDC 623.4/519 19
1. United States. Navy - Gunner's mates (Missiles). 2. Guided missiles. I. Naval Education and Training Program Development Center. II. Title.
VF347 .U56 1979

Pastoral care in alcoholism/alcohol abuse / Naval Education and Training Command. [Pensacola, Fla. : Naval Education and Training Program Development Center], 1980. iii, 164 p. : ill. ; 26 cm. Cover title. "NAVEDTRA 10805-A." Bibliography: p. 149-162. Includes index.   LC Card 80-603166   DDC 362.2/9286 19
1. Church work with alcoholics - United States. 2. Alcoholism - Study and teaching. 3. Chaplains, Military - United States. I. Title.
BV4460.5 .U54 1980

United States. Naval Education and Training Program Development Center. see Naval Education and Training Program Development Center.

United States. Naval Education and Training Support Command. Naval Education and Training Program Development Center. Human behavior and leadership /. [Washington?] [1977] i.e. 1978. iii, 163, [51] p. :   LC Card 78-601716   DDC 158/.4/024359 19
VB203 .N38 1978

United States. Naval Facilities Engineering Command. Chesapeake Division. Washington Navy Yard master plan. [Washington, D.C.] : Chesapeake Division, Naval Facilities Engineering Command, [1979] v, 102 p. : ill. (some col.) ; 20 x 27 cm. "Updates the 1967 Washington Navy Yard master plan."   LC Card 80-602046   DDC 359.7/5/09753 19
1. Washington Navy Yard. 2. Buildings - Washington, D.C. - Remodeling for other use. I. Title.
VA70.W3 U54 1979

United States. Naval History Division. (Old Catalog form: United States. Naval History Office.)
Allard, Dean C., 1933- U. S. naval history sources in the United States /. Washington, D.C. , 1979. vii, 235 p. :   LC Card 79-600070   DDC 026/.359/00973 19
Z1249.N3 A48 E182

United States. Naval Material Command. United States. Navy Dept. Office of Information. Ships, aircraft, and weapons of the United States Navy. [Washington, D.C. , 1980] 51 p. :   LC Card 80-603251   DDC 359.3/2/0973 19
VF347 .U57 1980

United States. Naval Observatory. Circular.
(no. 153) United States. Naval Observatory. Coordinates Committee. Coordinates of U. S. Naval Observatory installations /. Washington, D.C. , 1975. 35 p. :   LC Card 80-602058   DDC 520 s 522/.2/0973 19
QB4 .W34 no. 153 QB86

(no. 153) United States. Naval Observatory. Coordinates Committee. Coordinates of U. S. Naval Observatory installations /. Washington, D.C. , 1975. 35 p. :   LC Card 80-602058   DDC 520 s 522/.2/0973 19
QB4 .W34 no. 153 QB86

(no. 158) Fiala, Alan D. Total solar eclipse of 16 February 1980 /. Washington, D.C. [1978] 42 p. : LC Card 80-601567 DDC 520 s 523.7/8 19
QB4 .W34 no. 158 QB544.80

UNITED STATES. NAVAL OBSERVATORY.
United States. Naval Observatory. Coordinates Committee. Coordinates of U. S. Naval Observatory installations /. Washington, D.C. , 1975. 35 p. : LC Card 80-602058 DDC 520 s 522/.2/0973 19
QB4 .W34 no. 153 QB86

United States. Naval Observatory. Coordinates Committee. Coordinates of U. S. Naval Observatory installations / by James A. Hughes (chairman) ... [et al.] ; Coordinates Committee, Naval Observatory. Washington, D.C. : U. S. Naval Observatory, 1975. 35 p. : ill. ; 27 cm. (United States. Naval Observatory. Circular. no. 153) Includes bibliographical references. LC Card 80-602058 DDC 520 s 522/.2/0973 19
1. Astronomical instruments. 2. Latitude. 3. Longitude. 4. United States. Naval Observatory. I. Hughes, James A. II. Series. III. Series: United States. Naval Observatory. Circular, no. 153. IV. Title.
QB4 .W34 no. 153 QB86

United States. Naval Oceanographic Office.
World port index. 1st-4th ed.; 1953-71. Washington. illus., maps. 27 cm. (Its: Publication. no. 150.) For later file, see World port index.
1. Harbors - Directories. I. Title. **NYPL [VDN (United States. Naval Oceanographic Office. World port index)]**

United States. Naval Oceanography Command.
United States. Naval Oceanography Command Detachment, Asheville, N.C. Climatic study of the Persian Gulf and Gulf of Oman . [Washington] [1980] viii, 125 p. : LC Card 80-602634 DDC 551.69165/35 19
QC994.5 .U53 1980

United States. Naval Oceanography Command Detachment, Asheville, N.C. Guide to standard weather summaries and climatic services /. [Asheville, N.C.] 1980. ix, 92, 102, [6] p. ; LC Card 80-601710 DDC 551.6 19
QC982.5.U6 U53 1980

United States. Naval Oceanography Command Detachment, Asheville, N.C.
Climatic study of the Persian Gulf and Gulf of Oman : near coastal zone / prepared by Naval Oceanography Command Detachment, Asheville, N.C. for the Commander, Naval Oceanography Command. [Washington] : Naval Oceanography Command [1980] viii, 125 p. : chiefly maps ; 28 cm. Bibliography: p. vii-viii. Title on spine: Near coastal zone, Persian Gulf and Gulf of Oman. LC Card 80-602634 DDC 551.69165/35 19
1. Persian Gulf - Climate - Charts, diagrams, etc. 2. Oman, Gulf of - Climate - Charts, diagrams, etc. 3. Meteorology, Maritime - Persian Gulf - Charts, diagrams, etc. 4. Meteorology, Maritime - Oman, Gulf of - Charts, diagrams, etc. I. United States. Naval Oceanography Command. II. Title. III. Title: Near coastal zone, Persian Gulf and Gulf of Oman.
QC994.5 .U53 1980

Guide to standard weather summaries and climatic services / edited by J. W. Ownbey for the Commander, Naval Oceanography Command ; [prepared by NOCD Asheville]. [Asheville, N.C. : Naval Oceanography Command Detachment], 1980. ix, 92, 102, [6] p. ; 28 cm. "NAVAIR 50-1C-534 as of January 1980." "Supersedes NAVAIR 50-1C-534 dated January 1978." Chiefly tables. Edition of 1978 prepared by the detachment under its earlier name: Naval Weather Service Detachment. LC Card 80-601710 DDC 551.6 19
1. United States - Climate - Tables. 2. United States - Climate - Indexes. 3. Climatology - Indexes. 4. Climatology - Tables. I. Ownbey, J. W. II. United States. Naval Oceanography Command. III. United States. Naval Weather Service Detachment. Guide to standard weather summaries and climatic services. IV. Title.
QC982.5.U6 U53 1980

United States. Naval Personnel, Bureau of. see **United States. Bureau of Naval Personnel.**

United States. Naval Research Laboratory, Washington, D. C.
NRL report .
(8300) Gebhard, Louis A. Evolution of naval radio-electronics and contributions of the

Naval Research Laboratory /. Washington, D.C. , 1979. xvi, 448 p. : LC Card 79-600083 DDC 500 s 623.7/34/0973 19
QC453 .U54 no. 8300 VM480.3

UNITED STATES. NAVAL RESEARCH LABORATORY, WASHINGTON, D.C. - HISTORY.
Gebhard, Louis A. Evolution of naval radio-electronics and contributions of the Naval Research Laboratory /. Washington, D.C. , 1979. xvi, 448 p. : LC Card 79-600083 DDC 500 s 623.7/34/0973 19
QC453 .U54 no. 8300 VM480.3

United States. Naval Research, Office of. see **United States. Office of Naval Research.**

United States. Naval Safety Center. see **Naval Safety Center.**

United States. Naval School of Aviation Medicine, Pensacola, Fla.
Monograph series .
(report no. 2) Wilbanks, William A. The measurement of color blindness . Pensacola, Fla. , 1956. iv, 44 p. : LC Card 81-462888 DDC 617.7/59 19
RE921 .W7

United States. Naval Sea Systems Command.
Building patrol frigates for the United States Navy. Washington , 1974. 8 p. :
NYPL [*XMQ-2114]

United States. Naval Ship Systems Command.
Supervisor of Diving. U. S. Navy diving operations: handbook. Supervisor of Diving, Naval Ship Systems Command. Washington, Navy Dept.; for sale by the Supt. of Docs., U. S. Govt. Print. Off., 1974. 198 p. illus. 30 cm. "Issued as an addendum to the U. S. Navy diving manual (NAVSHIPS 0994-001-9010)" "NAVSHIPS 0994-009-6010." LC Card 76-86691
1. Diving, Submarine. I. United States. Navy Dept. Diving manual. II. Title. **NYPL [JSG 80-103]**

United States. Naval Training Command.
Human behavior and leadership. Naval Education and Training Program Development Center. Human behavior and leadership / Naval Education and Training Support Command ; [prepared by the Naval Education and Training Program Development Center, Pensacola, Florida, for the Chief of Naval Education and Training]. [Washington?] [1977] i.e. 1978. iii, 163, [51] p. : LC Card 78-601716 DDC 158/.4/024359 19
VB203 .N38 1978

Machinist's mate 3 & 2. Naval Education and Training Program Development Center. Machinist's mate 3 & 2. Rev. [Washington, D.C. , 1978]. iv, 399, iii, 106 p., [3] fold. leaves of plates : LC Card 80-601617 DDC 623.8/72 19
VG803 .N38 1978

United States. Naval Weather Service Detachment.
Guide to standard weather summaries and climatic services. United States. Naval Oceanography Command Detachment, Asheville, N.C. Guide to standard weather summaries and climatic services / edited by J. W. Ownbey for the Commander, Naval Oceanography Command ; [prepared by NOCD Asheville]. [Asheville, N.C.] 1980. ix, 92, 102, [6] p. ; LC Card 80-601710 DDC 551.6 19
QC982.5.U6 U53 1980

UNITED STATES. NAVY.
Building patrol frigates for the United States Navy. Washington , 1974. 16 p. :
NYPL [*XMQ-2114]

United States. Congress. House. Committee on Armed Services. Procurement and Military Nuclear Systems Subcommittee. Naval nuclear propulsion program--1980 . Washington , 1980. vi, 246, iv p. : LC Card 80-602476 DDC 343.73/0194 19
KF27 .A7657 1980

United States. Congress. House. Committee on Armed Services. Subcommittee on Seapower and Strategic and Critical Materials. National policy objectives and the adequacy of our current navy forces . Washington , 1980 [i.e. 1981] ii, 137 p. : LC Card 81-601761 DDC 359/.03/0973 19
KF27 .A769 1979e

United States. Congressional Budget Office. Shaping the general purpose Navy of the eighties . Washington, D.C. , 1980. xxvii, 145 p. : LC Card 80-600968 DDC 359/.03/0973 19
VA53 .U52 1980

United States. Navy. Air Systems Command. see **United States. Naval Air Systems Command.**

UNITED STATES. NAVY - AVIATION.
United States. General Accounting Office. Operational and support costs of the Navy's F/A-18 can be substantially reduced . Washington, D.C. [1980] iii, 58 p., [1] leaf of plates : LC Card 80-602400 DDC 358.4/183 19
VG93 .U54 1980

UNITED STATES. NAVY - AVIATION SUPPLIES AND STORES.
United States. General Accounting Office. Operational and support costs of the Navy's F/A-18 can be substantially reduced . Washington, D.C. [1980] iii, 58 p., [1] leaf of plates : LC Card 80-602400 DDC 358.4/183 19
VG93 .U54 1980

United States. Navy. Coast Guard. see **United States. Coast Guard.**

UNITED STATES. NAVY - COMMUNICATION SYSTEMS - HISTORY.
Gebhard, Louis A. Evolution of naval radio-electronics and contributions of the Naval Research Laboratory /. Washington, D.C. , 1979. xvi, 448 p. : LC Card 79-600083 DDC 500 s 623.7/34/0973 19
QC453 .U54 no. 8300 VM480.3

United States. Navy. Court-martial (Allen: 1944)
Allen, Julius J. (defendant) Record and proceedings of a general court martial. [San Francisco?, 1945?] 8 v. (1655 leaves);
NYPL [Sc Micro R-3912]

United States. Navy Dept.
Diving manual. United States. Naval Ship Systems Command. Supervisor of Diving. U. S. Navy diving operations: handbook. Supervisor of Diving, Naval Ship Systems Command. Washington, 1974. 198 p. : LC Card 76-86691 **NYPL [JSG 80-103]**

United States. Navy Dept. Bureau of Naval Personnel. see **United States. Bureau of Naval Personnel.**

United States. Navy Dept. Bureau of Ordnance. see **United States. Bureau of Ordnance (Navy Dept.)**

United States. Navy Dept. Coast Guard. see **United States. Coast Guard.**

United States. Navy Dept. Hydrographic Office. see **United States. Hydrographic Office.**

United States. Navy Dept. Marine Corps. see **United States. Marine Corps.**

United States. Navy Dept. Naval History Division. see **United States. Naval History Division.**

United States. Navy Dept. Naval Material Command. see **United States. Naval Material Command.**

United States. Navy Dept. Naval Oceanography Command. see **United States. Naval Oceanography Command.**

United States. Navy Dept. Naval Sea Systems Command. see **United States. Naval Sea Systems Command.**

United States. Navy Dept. Office of Information.
Ships, aircraft, and weapons of the United States Navy. [Washington, D.C. : Office of Information, Navy Dept. : for sale by the Supt. of Docs., U. S. Govt. Print. Off., 1980] 51 p. : ill. ; 28 cm. Cover title. "Compiled by the staffs of the Office of Information and the Naval Material Command." "NAVSO P-3564." LC Card 80-603251 DDC 359.3/2/0973 19
1. United States. Navy - Weapons systems. 2. Warships - United States. 3. Airplanes, Military. I. United States. Naval Material Command. II. Title.
VF347 .U57 1980

United States. Navy Dept. Office of Naval Research. see **United States. Office of Naval Research.**

UNITED STATES. NAVY DEPT. - OFFICIALS AND EMPLOYEES.
United States. Congress. Senate. Committee on

Armed Services. Nomination of John F. Lehman, Jr., to be Secretary of the Navy . Washington , 1981. ii, 30 p. ; LC Card 81-601340 DDC 353.7 19
KF26 .A7 1981c

UNITED STATES. NAVY. EAST INDIA SQUADRON - HISTORY.
Henson, Curtis T., 1931- Commissioners and commodores . University, Ala. , c1982. p. cm. ISBN 0-8173-0087-2 LC Card 81-10359 DDC 327.73051 19
E183.8.C5 H46

UNITED STATES. NAVY - ELECTRONIC INSTALLATIONS - HISTORY.
Gebhard, Louis A. Evolution of naval radio-electronics and contributions of the Naval Research Laboratory /. Washington, D.C. , 1979. xvi, 448 p. : LC Card 79-600083 DDC 500 s 623.7/34/0973 19
QC453 .U54 no. 8300 VM480.3

UNITED STATES. NAVY - FUEL.
United States. Congress. House. Committee on Interstate and Foreign Commerce. Subcommittee on Energy and Power. Filling the strategic petroleum reserve, oversight, and H.R. 7252, use of the naval petroleum reserves . Washington , 1980. iv, 410 p. : LC Card 81-600602 DDC 346.7304/6823216 347.30646823216 19
KF27 .I5542 1980l

UNITED STATES. NAVY - GUNNER'S MATES.
Naval Education and Training Program Development Center. Gunner's mate G 1 & C. [Pensacola, Fla. , Washington, D.C. , 1980] ca. 500 p. in various pagings : LC Card 80-603250 DDC 623/.553 19
VF160 .N38 1980

UNITED STATES. NAVY - GUNNER'S MATES (MISSILES)
United States. Naval Education and Training Command. Gunner's Mate M 1 & C /. [Pensacola, Fla. , Washington, D.C. , 1979] iii, 329, 75 p., [1] fold. leaf of plates : LC Card 80-601852 DDC 623.4/519 19
VF347 .U56 1979

UNITED STATES. NAVY - HISTORY - 20TH CENTURY.
Vlahos, Michael, 1951- The blue sword . Newport, R.I. , Washington, D.C. , 1980 [i.e. 1981] p. cm. LC Card 81-9654 DDC 359/.07/1173 19
V420 .V55

UNITED STATES. NAVY - MACHINIST'S MATES.
Naval Education and Training Program Development Center. Machinist's mate 3 & 2. [Washington, D.C. , 1978]. iv, 399, iii, 106 p., [3] fold. leaves of plates : LC Card 80-601617 DDC 623.8/72 19
VG803 .N38 1978

UNITED STATES. NAVY - MANAGEMENT.
United States. General Accounting Office. Better Navy management of shipbuilding contracts could save millions of dollars . [Washington] [1980] v, 40 p. ; LC Card 80-602619 DDC 359.6/211/0973 19
VM299.6 .U55 1980

UNITED STATES. NAVY - MOBILIZATION.
United States. Congress. House. Committee on Merchant Marine and Fisheries. Report on the strategic implications of the Omnibus maritime bill, H.R. 6899 . Washington , 1980. ii, 35 p. : LC Card 80-602266 DDC 359.2/7/0973 19
VA77 .U56 1980

United States. Navy. Naval Air Systems Command. see United States. Naval Air Systems Command.

UNITED STATES. NAVY - ORDNANCE AND ORDNANCE STORES.
Naval Education and Training Program Development Center. Gunner's mate G 1 & C. [Pensacola, Fla. , Washington, D.C. , 1980] ca. 500 p. in various pagings : LC Card 80-603250 DDC 623/.553 19
VF160 .N38 1980

UNITED STATES. NAVY - PETTY OFFICERS.
Naval Education and Training Program Development Center. Human behavior and leadership /. [Washington?] [1977] i.e. 1978.

iii, 163, [51] p. : LC Card 78-601716 DDC 158/.4/024359 19
VB203 .N38 1978

UNITED STATES. NAVY - PROCUREMENT.
Cole, Brady M. Procurement of Naval ships . Washington, D.C. , 1979. vi, 52 p. (p. 52 advertisements) : LC Card 79-604212 DDC 338.7/6238/200973 19
VM299.6 .C64

Davison, Richard H. The U. S. sea-based strategic force . [Washington, D.C.] [1980] xx, 62 p. : LC Card 80-601190 DDC 359.8/3 19
V993 .D38

United States. Congress. House. Committee on Armed Services. Subcommittee on Seapower and Strategic and Critical Materials. Submarine alternatives study . Washington , 1980. ii, 182 p. ; LC Card 80-603515 DDC 623.8/2574 19
KF27 .A769 1979d

United States. General Accounting Office. Two contracts for nuclear attack submarines modified by Public law 85-804--status as of December 23, 1978 . Washington, D.C. , 1979. ii, 16 p. ; LC Card 79-603739 DDC 359.6/212/0973 19
VC263 .U54 1979

UNITED STATES. NAVY - RADIO INSTALLATIONS - HISTORY.
Gebhard, Louis A. Evolution of naval radio-electronics and contributions of the Naval Research Laboratory /. Washington, D.C. , 1979. xvi, 448 p. : LC Card 79-600083 DDC 500 s 623.7/34/0973 19
QC453 .U54 no. 8300 VM480.3

United States Navy uniform regulations. United States. Bureau of Naval Personnel. [Washington, 1978] 1 v.
NYPL [JFF 78-1006]

UNITED STATES. NAVY - UNIFORMS.
United States. Bureau of Naval Personnel. United States Navy uniform regulations. [Washington, 1978] 1 v.
NYPL [JFF 78-1006]

UNITED STATES. NAVY - WEAPONS SYSTEMS.
United States. Navy Dept. Office of Information. Ships, aircraft, and weapons of the United States Navy. [Washington, D.C. , 1980] 51 p. : LC Card 80-603251 DDC 359.3/2/0973 19
VF347 .U57 1980

United States. Neighborhoods, National Commissioon on. see United States. National Commission on Neighborhoods.

UNITED STATES - NEUTRALITY - CONGRESSES.
Three faces of Midwestern isolationism /. Iowa City, Iowa , 1981. p. cm. ISBN 0-87414-019-6 (pbk.) : LC Card 81-2741 DDC 327.73 19
E806 .T58

United States. New England River Basins Commission.
Kennebec River Basin overview / New England River Basins Commission. [Boston, Mass.] : The Commission, [1979] ix, 158, [22] p. : maps ; 28 cm. "Decmeber, 1979." Includes bibliography. LC Card 80-622003 DDC 333.91/02/0974122 19
1. Water resources development - Maine - Kennebec River watershed. I. Title.
TC424.M2 U54 1979

Lake Champlain Basin Study (United States.) Shaping the future of Lake Champlain . [Boston, Mass.] [1979] x, 124, 45 p. ; LC Card 80-622025 DDC 333.91/6316/097454 19
TD225.L252 L34 1979

United States. Noise Abatement and Control, Office of. see United States. Office of Noise Abatement and Control.

United States - Noncontiguous possessions. see United States - Insular possessions.

United States. North Central Forest Experiment Station, St. Paul.
United States D.A. Forest Service resource bulletin NC .
(39) Blyth, James E. Primary forest products industry & timber use, Minnesota, 1973 /. St. Paul , 1979. 34 p. : LC Card 79-602962 DDC 333.75/0977 s 338.1/7498/09776 19
SD11 .A45533 no. 39 HD9757.M6

USDA Forest Service research paper NC .
(27) Tubbs, Carl H. The influence of light, moisture, and seedbed on yellow birch regeneration /. St. Paul , 1969. 12 p. : LC Card 71-603400 DDC 634.9/0977 s 634.9/726 19
SD11 .A45476 no. 27 SD397.Y44

United States. Northeastern Forest Experiment Station, Upper Darby, Pa.
United States D.A. Forest Service research paper .
(NE-161) Shigo, Alex L., 1930- Some effects of paraformaldehyde on wood surrounding tapholes in sugar maple trees /. Upper Darby, Pa. , 1970. 11 p. : LC Card 81-460882 DDC 634.9/0974 s 633.6/49 19
SD11 .A455493 no. 161 SB608.S913

United States D.A. Forest Service research paper NE .
(141) Gibbs, Carter B. The effect of xylem age on volume yield & sugar content of sugar maple sap /. Upper Darby, Pa. , 1969. 11 p. :ill. LC Card 75-605745 DDC 333.76/0974 s 633.3/4 19
SD11 .A455493 no. 141 SB239.M3

United States. Nuclear Regulatory Commission. Program summary report. [Washington]. 28 cm. (Its: NUREG) Monthly. Prepared by the Office of Management and Program Analysis, Sept. 1978- LC Card 79-643217
1. Atomic power plants - United States - Statistics - Periodicals. 2. Atomic power industry - United States - Statistics - Periodicals. 3. Atomic energy industries - United States - Statistics - Periodicals. I. United States. Nuclear Regulatory Commission. Office of Management and Program Analysis.   *NYPL [JLM 80-951]*

United States. Ad Hoc Interagency Population Dos Assessement Group. Population dose and health impact of the accident at the Three Mile Island Nuclear Station . Washington , 1979. 77, [16] p. : LC Card 79-602730
RA569 .U46 1979

United States. Congress. House. Committee on Interior and Insular Affairs. Subcommittee on Energy and the Environment. Three Mile Island cleanup and rehabilitation . Washington , 1980. iv, 236 p. : LC Card 80-604111 DDC 363.7/28 19
KF27 .I518 1980b

UNITED STATES. NUCLEAR REGULATORY COMMISSION.
United States. Congress. House. Committee on Government Operations. Emergency planning around U. S. nuclear powerplants . Washington , 1979. v, 105 p. ; LC Card 79-604246 DDC 363.3/497 19
KF32 .G6 1979a

United States. Congress. House. Committee on Government Operations. Environment, Energy, and Natural Resources Subcommittee. Construction problems at Marble Hill nuclear facility . Washington , 1980. iv, 349 p. : LC Card 80-601154 DDC 363.1/79 19
KF27 .G655 1979k

United States. Congress. House. Committee on Government Operations. Environment, Energy, and Natural Resources Subcommittee. Nuclear Regulatory Commission--the Rogovin report . Washington , 1980. iii, 90 p. ; LC Card 80-602901 DDC 363.1/79 19
KF27 .G655 1980b

United States. Congress. House. Committee on Government Operations. Legislation and National Security Subcommittee. Reorganization plan no. 1 of 1980 (Nuclear Regulatory Commission) . Washington , 1980. iii, 100 p. ; LC Card 80-602817 DDC 353.0087/22 19
KF27 .G6676 1980b

United States. Congress. House. Committee on Interior and Insular Affairs. Subcommittee on Energy and the Environment. Nuclear plant shutdowns . Washington , 1980. v, 346 p. : LC Card 80-603454 DDC 363.1/79 19
KF27 .I518 1979j

United States. Congress. House. Committee on Interior and Insular Affairs. Subcommittee on Energy and the Environment. Nuclear siting and licensing process (Limerick Atomic Power Station, Pa.) . Washington , 1980. iv, 305 p. : LC Card 81-600605 DDC 343.73/0925

579

GOVERNMENT PUBLICATIONS - U.S.: 1981

United States. Office of Aeronautics and Space Technology.

347.303925 19
KF27 .I518 1980c

United States. Congress. House. Committee on
Interstate and Foreign Commerce.
Subcommittee on Oversight and Investigations.
Regulation and construction of nuclear
powerplants--South Texas nuclear project .
Washington , c1981. iii, 198 p. ;   LC Card
   81-601168   DDC 343.73/0925 347.303925 19
KF27 .I5547 1980u

United States. Congress. Senate. Committee on
Governmental Affairs. Reorganization plan no.
1 of 1980 . Washington , 1980. iv, 402 p. ;   LC
   Card 80-603288   DDC 353.0087/22 19
KF26 .G67 1980g

United States. General Accounting Office. The
Nuclear Regulatory Commission, more
aggressive leadership needed . [Washington,
D.C. , 1980] vii, 93 p. ;   LC Card 80-601236
   DDC 353.0087/22 19
HD9698.U52 U55 1980a

United States. Office of Nuclear Reactor
Regulation. NRC views and analysis of the
recommendations of the President's Commission
on the Accident at Three Mile Island / .
Washington, D.C. , 1979. 51 p. in various
pagings ;   LC Card 80-601286   DDC 363.1/79 19
TK1343 .U57 1979

**UNITED STATES. NUCLEAR REGULATORY
COMMISSION - APPROPRIATIONS
AND EXPENDITURES.**
United States. Congress. House. Committee on
Interior and Insular Affairs. Subcommittee on
Energy and the Environment. Nuclear
Regulatory Commission authorizations for fiscal
year 1981 . Washington , 1980. iv, 503 p. :   LC
   Card 80-603512   DDC 353.0072/2368722 19
KF27 .I518 1980

**United States Nuclear Regulatory Commission.
Division of Siting, Health, and Safeguards
Standards.** The Feasibility of epidemiologic
investigations of the health effects of low-level
ionizing radiation . Washington, D.C. . xxiii,
421 p. ;   LC Card 81-600796   DDC 363.1/79 19
RA569 .F4

**United States. Nuclear Regulatory Commission.
Office of Management and Program
Analysis.** United States. Nuclear Regulatory
Commission. Program summary report.
[Washington].   LC Card 79-643217
               NYPL [JLM 80-951]

**United States. Nuclear Regulatory Commission.
Office of Nuclear Reactor Regulation. see
United States. Office of Nuclear Reactor
Regulation.**

**United States. Nuclear Regulatory Commission.
Office of Standards Development.**
Federal-State Reports, inc. Compilation of state
laws and regulations on transportation of
radioactive materials / . Washington, D.C. ,
1980. ca. 300 p. ;   LC Card 80-601610   DDC
   343.73//093 19
KF3948.Z95 F4

Radioactivity in consumer products / .
Washington , Springfield, Va. , 1978. xi, 509
p. :   LC Card 79-602786
RA569 .R29

**United States. Nuclear Regulatory Commission.
Office of State Programs.** Federal-State
Reports, inc. Compilation of state laws and
regulations on transportation of radioactive
materials / . Washington, D.C. , 1980. ca. 300
p. ;   LC Card 80-601610   DDC 343.73//093 19
KF3948.Z95 F4

**UNITED STATES. NUCLEAR REGULATORY
COMMISSION - OFFICIALS AND
EMPLOYEES.**
United States. Congress. Senate. Committee on
Environment and Public Works. Nomination of
Albert Carnesale . Washington , 1980. iii, 138
p. ;   LC Card 80-603300   DDC 353.0087/22 19
KF26 .E6 1980f

**United States. Nuclear Regulatory Commission.
Standards Development, Office of. see
United States. Nuclear Regulatory
Commission. Office of Standards
Development.**

**United States. Nuclear Regulatory Commission.
T. M. I. Program Office. see United States.
Nuclear Regulatory Commission. Three Mile**

Island Program Office.

**United States. Nuclear Regulatory Commission.
Three Mile Island Program Office.** Final
environmental assessment for decontamination
of the Three Mile Island Unit 2 reactor building
atmosphere: final NRC staff report / Prepared
for TMI support staff, office of Nuclear Reactor
Regulation, U. S. Nuclear Regulatory
Commission. Washington : Available from GPO
Sales Program, Division of Technical
Information and Document Control, U. S.
Nuclear Regulatory Commission, 1980. 1 v. :
ill. ; 28 cm. "NUREG - 0662."
*1. Three Mile Island Nuclear Power Plant, Pa. 2.
Radioactive decontamination.*
               NYPL [JSK 80-129]

United States. Nutrition and Agribusiness Group.
Low-cost extrusion cookers . [Fort Collins,
Colo. , 1979] vii, 288 p. :   LC Card 80-601551
   DDC 664/.02 19
TP373 .L68

**United States. Oak Ridge National Laboratory.
see United States. National Laboratory, Oak
Ridge, Tenn.**

**United States. Occupational Safety and Health
Administration.**
Lost in the workplace . [Washington, D.C.]
[1980?] 468 p. ;   LC Card 80-601645   DDC
   363.1/1/0973 19
HD7265.5.U5 L67

A Study of lumber used for bracing trenches in
the United States . Washington, D.C. [1980]
218 p. in various pagings :   LC Card 80-600015
   DDC 690/.02/18 s 624.1/52 19
TA435 .U58 no. 122 TA770

Yokel, Felix Y. Recommended technical
provisions for construction practice in shoring
and sloping of trenches and excavations / .
Washington, DC [1980] xvi, 68 p. :   LC Card
   80-600068   DDC 690/.02/18 s 624.1/52 19
TA435 .U58 no. 127 TA770

Yokel, Felix Y. Soil classification for
construction practice in shallow trenching / .
Washington, D.C. [1980] xiv, 76 p. :   LC Card
   80-600014   DDC 690/.02/18 s 624.1/51/012 19
TA435 .U58 no. 121 TA710

**UNITED STATES. OCCUPATIONAL SAFETY
AND HEALTH ADMINISTRATION.**
United States. Congress. House. Committee on
Government Operations. Government Activities
and Transportation Subcommittee. FAA-OSHA
jurisdiction over workplace safety in the
aviation industry . Washington , 1980. iii, 192
p. :   LC Card 81-600596   DDC 353.0087/77/0289
   19
KF27 .G6626 1980c

United States. Congress. House. Committee on
Government Operations. Manpower and
Housing Subcommittee. Performance of the
Occupational Safety and Health
Administration . Washington , 1977. iv, 163 p. ;
   LC Card 80-603631   DDC 353.008/3/0289 19
KF27 .G6678 1977f

United States. Occupational Safety and Health
Administration. Policy Analysis and Integration
Staff. Occupational Safety and Health
Administration's impact on small business .
[Washington] , 1976. v, 55, [71] p. :   LC Card
   77-602353
HD7654 .U55 1976   ***NYPL [*XME-9522]***

**United States. Occupational Safety and Health
Administration. Policy Analysis and
Integration Staff.** Occupational Safety and
Health Administration's impact on small
business : a policy paper / prepared for the
Assistant Secretary by OSHA's Policy Analysis
and Integration Staff. [Washington] : U. S.
Dept. of Labor, Occupational Safety & Health
Administration, 1976. v, 55, [71] p. : graphs ;
28 cm. Microfiche (neg.) 2 sheets. 11 x 16 cm.
(PB-263 855) Includes bibliographical references.   LC
   Card 77-602353
*1. United States. Occupational Safety and Health
Administration. 2. Small business. 3. Industrial safety -
United States. 4. Industrial hygiene - United States. I.
Title.*
HD7654 .U55 1976   ***NYPL [*XME-9522]***

**United States. Occupational Safety and Health
Review Commission.** Citator of the decisions
of the Occupational Safety and Health Review
Commission. Oct. 1979- Washington. Continues:

Citator of the decisions of the Occupational Safety and
Health Review Commission. (Ceased with July 1979
issue; not in the library)   LC Card 80-644589
I. Title.   ***NYPL [Econ. Div.]***

UNITED STATES - OCCUPATIONS.
Johnson, Gordon C. Metropolitan professional
sexual differentiation . [Madison] [1979] 27
p. ;   LC Card 80-622903   DDC 331.11/4 19
HD8038.U5 J6

**UNITED STATES - OCCUPATIONS -
CLASSIFICATION - INDEXES.**
United States. Bureau of the Census. 1980
census of population . Washington, D.C. , 1980.
xviii, 111, 157 p. ;   LC Card 80-24960   DDC
   331.7/0016 19
HC106.7 .U542 1980a

**UNITED STATES - OCCUPATIONS -
INDEXES - PERIODICALS.**
United States. Bureau of the Census. 1980
census of population: alphabetical index of
industries and occupations. 1st- ed. Washington,
1980-
     NYPL [*R-Econ. 81-164 & JLM 81-159]

United States. Bureau of the Census. 1980
census of population: classified index of
industries and occupations. 1st- ed. Washington,
1980-
     NYPL [*R-Econ. 81-163 & JLM 81-158]

**UNITED STATES - OCCUPATIONS -
STATISTICS.**
Keitt, Barbara L. Occupational employment in
selected nonmanufacturing industries.
Washington, D.C. , 1981. vi, 78 p. ;   LC Card
   81-601842   DDC 331.12/5/0973 19
HD5724 .K42

United States. Bureau of Labor Statistics.
Occupational employment in manufacturing
industries, 1977 / . Washington, D.C. [1980] vi,
91 p., [1] leaf of plates :   LC Card 80-602314
   DDC 331.12/57/0973 19
HD5724 .U625 1980a

**United States. Ocean Pollution Research,
Development, and Monitoring, Interagency
Committee on. see United States.
Interagency Committee on Ocean Pollution
Research, Development, and Monitoring.**

**United States. Oceanographic Office. see United
States. Naval Oceanographic Office.**

**United States. Office for Emergency
Management. Committee on Fair
Employment Practice. see United States.
Committee on Fair Employment Practice
(1943-1946)**

**United States. Office for Handicapped
Individuals.**
Directory of national information sources on
handicapping conditions and related services.
Washington.   ***NYPL [JLM 81-38]***

Directory of national information sources on
handicapping conditions and related services /
U. S. Department of Health, Education, and
Welfare, Office of Human Development
Services, Office for Handicapped Individuals.
[2d ed.]. [Washington, D.C.] : HDS : for sale
by the Supt. of Docs., U. S. Govt. Print. Off.,
1980. vii, 236 p. ; 28 cm. (DHEW publication. no.
(OHDS) 80-22007) "May 1980." Bibliography: p.
182-185. Includes index.   LC Card 80-602225   DDC
   362.4/048/02573 19
*1. Handicapped services - United States - Directories. I.
Series: United States. Department of Health, Education,
and Welfare. DHEW publication , no. (OHDS)
80-22007. II. Title.*
HV1553 .U49 1980

**United States. Office for Maternal and Child
Health.** Tri-Regional Workshop for Social
Workers in Maternal and Child Health Services
(1980 : Raleigh, N.C.) Social work in a
state-based system of child health care . Chapel
Hill [1981?] v, 156 p. :   LC Card 81-50559
   DDC 362.1/9892/000973 19
RJ102 .T74 1980

**United States. Office of Aeronautics and Space
Technology.**
Ames Summer Study on Space Settlements and
Industrialization Using Nonterrestrial Materials,
Ames Research Center, 1977. Space resources
and space settlements . Washington, D.C. ,
1979. x, 288 p. :   LC Card 79-603821   DDC

BIBLIOGRAPHIC GUIDE

United States. Office of Aeronautics and Space Technology.

580

629.44/2 19
TL795.7 .A45 1977

Flight technology improvement. [Washington], 1979. 709 p.; *NYPL [JSF 80-531]*

United States. Office of Archeology and Historic Preservation. Interagency Archeological Services Division. see United States. Interagency Archeological Services Division.

United States. Office of Archeology and Historic Preservation. Technical Preservation Services Division. Morton, W. Brown. The Secretary of the Interior's standards for historic preservation projects . Washington, D.C. , 1979. vi, 46 p. ; LC Card 80-603172 DDC 720/.28/8 19
NA106 .M67

United States. Office of Aviation Information. (Old Catalog form: United States. Civil Aeronautics Administration. Aviation Information, Office of)
United States. Federal Aviation Agency. International flight information manual. Washington. *NYPL [VDS (U. S. Federal Aviation Agency. International flight information manual)]*

United States. Office of Civil Rights Compliance. Civil rights enforcement under the Crime Control Act of 1976 and the Justice System Improvement Act of 1979 : progress report, 1976-1980. Washington, D.C. : Office of Civil Rights Compliance, Office of Justice Assistance, Research and Statistics, U. S. Dept. of Justice, 1980. 47 p. ; 28 cm. "U. S. Department of Justice, Office of Justice Assistance, Research, and Statistics"--Cover. Item 717 Includes bibliographical references. LC Card 81-600902 DDC 353.008/8 19
1. Criminal justice personnel - Legal status, laws, etc. - United States. 2. Discrimination in employment - Law and legislation - United States. 3. Federal aid to law enforcement agencies - United States. I. United States. Office of Justice Assistance, Research, and Statistics. II. Title.
KF5398.P6 A833

United States. Office of Civilian Health and Medical Program of the Uniformed Services. CHAMPUS chartbook / Department of Defense, Office of Civilian Health and Medical Program of the Uniformed Services. 2d ed. [Aurora, Colo.] : Department of Defense, Office of Civilian Health and Medical Program of the Uniformed Services, Program Evaluation Division, Statistics Branch, [1979] ix, 121 leaves : ill. ; 21 x 28 cm. Includes index. LC Card 80-602030 DDC 355.6/4 19
1. CHAMPUS. 2. Military dependents - Medical care - United States - Statistics. I. Title.
UB403 .U56 1979

United States. Office of Coastal Zone Management. Center for Natural Areas. An annotated bibliography of coastal zone management work products . Washington, D.C. [1980] iii, 391 p. ; LC Card 80-602351 DDC 016.33391/7/0973 19
Z7164.R33 C45 1980 HT392

United States. Office of Community Planning and Development. United States Conference of Mayors. The private development process . [Washington] [1979] iii, 49 p. ; LC Card 79-601943
HD259 .U53 1979

United States. Office of Conservation and Solar Applications. see United States. Dept. of Energy. Office of Conservation and Solar Applications.

United States. Office of Construction of Standard Weights and measures. see United States. National Bureau of Standards.

United States. Office of Consumer Affairs. Consumer Information Division. Consumer's resource handbook / edited by Midge Shubow ; prepared by Anthony J. Anastasi ... [et al.]. [Washington] : White House Office of the Special Assistant for Consumer Affairs ; Pueblo, Colo. : additional single copies ... Consumer Information Center, [1979] iv, 76 p. : ill. ; 28 cm. "December 1979." LC Card 80-603215 DDC 381/.33/0973 19
1. Consumer protection - Information services - United States. I. Shubow, Midge. II. Anastasi, Anthony J. III. Title.
HC110.C63 U5 1979

People power : what communities are doing to

counter inflation / U. S. Office of Consumer Affairs, Consumer Information Division ; [Margo R. Friedman, project director ; Mary S. Gordon, editor]. [Washington] : The Office, [1980] ix, 411 p. : ill. ; 28 cm. Includes bibliographies.
1. Community development - United States. 2. Consumer cooperatives - United States. I. Title.
NYPL [JLF 80-1637]

United States. Office of Criminal Justice Education and Training. see United States. Law Enforcement Assistance Administration. Office of Criminal Justice Education and Training.

United States. Office of Economic Research. see United States. Economic Development Administration. Office of Economic Research.

United States. Office of Education. (Old Catalog form: United States. Education Bureau) Bodenman, Paul S., 1912- The educational system of Switzerland /. Washington, D.C. , 1979 i.e. 1980. 35 p. : LC Card 80-602306 DDC 371.2/009485 19
LB2936 .B6

Career education and organized labor /. [Washington, D.C.] , 1979] iii, 98 p. ; LC Card 79-602090 DDC 370.11/3/0973 19
LC1037.5 .C385

Commissioner's National Conference on Career Education, Houston, Tex., 1976. Career education . [Washington] , 1977. iii, 64 p. : LC Card 78-601755
LC1032 .C65 1976

Examining the role of the workplace in citizen education / U. S. Department of Health, Education, and Welfare, Office of Education. Washington : The Office, [1978] viii, 102 p. ; 24 cm. (HEW publication; no. (OE) 78-07004) Includes bibliographical references. LC Card 79-602660
1. Labor and laboring classes - Education - United States. 2. Career education - United States. 3. Industry - Social aspects - United States. 4. Trade-unions - Social aspects - United States. I. Title.
LC5051 .U54 1978 NYPL [JFE 81736]

McIntyre, Pat Kern. Study and teaching opportunities abroad . Washington, D.C. , 1980. v, 68 p. ; LC Card 80-602357 DDC 370.19/6 19
LB2376 .M25 1980

Miscellaneous .
(no. 52) Munse, Albert Ralph, 1923- State programs for public school support /. Washington , 1965. vii, 113 p. ; LC Card 80-502015 DDC 370/.973 s 379.1/22/0973 19
L111 .A614 no. 52 LB2828

National Conference of Senior Officials to Consider Unesco Recommendations on Physical Education and Sport, Washington, D.C., 1977. Report of the National Conference of Senior Officials to Consider Unesco Recommendations on Physical Education and Sport, held in Washington, D.C., November 16-18, 1977. [Washington] , 1979. vii, 143 p. ; LC Card 80-601246 DDC 613.7 19
GV205 .N234 1977

Selected list of postsecondary education opportunities for minorities and women. [Washington] : U. S. Dept. of Health, Education, and Welfare, Office of Education : for sale by Supt. of Docs., U. S. Govt. Print. Off., 1978. 87 p. ; 27 cm. Cover title. LC Card 78-603500
1. Minorities - Education (Higher) - United States. 2. Higher education of women - United States. I. Title.
LC3731 .U58 1978 NYPL [JFF 81-168]

Title I ESEA: how it works: a guide for parents and parent advisory councils / U. S. Dept. of Health, Education and Welfare, Office of Education. Washington, D. C.: U. S. Govt. Print. Off., 1973. vi, 67 p.: ill.; 27 cm. (DHEW publication; (OE) no. 73-07104)
1. United States. Laws, statutes, etc. Elementary and secondary education act of 1965. I. Title.
NYPL [JLF 81-40]

UNITED STATES. OFFICE OF EDUCATION. Barkin, Tom. Legal implications of the Office [of] Education criteria for the self-supporting student /. [Madison] , 1974. 38 p. ; LC Card 77-621624
*KF4235 .B47 NYPL [*XME-9435]*

United States. Office of Education. Bureau of Student Financial Assistance. Basic educational opportunity grant program, end-of-year report. United States. Office of Education. Bureau of Student Financial Assistance. End of year report, basic grants. [Washington] LC Card 79-644063
NYPL [JLM 80-975]

Basic grants. United States. Office of Education. Bureau of Student Financial Assistance. End of year report, basic grants. [Washington] LC Card 79-644063
NYPL [JLM 80-975]

End of year report, basic grants. [Washington] 28 cm. Annual. Other title, 1977/78- : Basic educational opportunity grant program, end-of-year report. LC Card 79-644063
1. Student aid - United States - Statistics - Periodicals. I. United States. Office of Education. Bureau of Student Financial Assistance. Basic educational opportunity grant program, end-of-year report. II. United States. Office of Education. Bureau of Student Financial Assistance. Basic grants. III. Title.
NYPL [JLM 80-975]

Student financial aid : 1979-80 handbook. [Washington] : U. S. Dept. of Health, Education, and Welfare, Office of Education, Bureau of Student Financial Assistance, [1979] ca. 300 p. in various pagings : forms ; 28 cm. LC Card 80-601252 DDC 378/.3/0973 19
1. Student aid - United States. I. Title.
LB2337.4 .U55 1979

United States. Office of Education. Citizen Education Staff. Farquhar, Elizabeth C. Citizen education today . Washington, D.C. , 1979. xiv, 186 p. ; LC Card 79-604201
H62.5.U5 F37 NYPL [JLE 81-518]

United States. Office of Education. Division of Vocational and Technical Education. (Old Catalog form: United States. Education Bureau. Vocational Division)
Resurge '79 : manual for identifying, classifying and serving the disadvantaged and handicapped under the Vocational Education Amendments of 1976 (P. L. 94-482). Washington, D. C. : For sale by the Supt. of Docs., U. S. Govt. Print Off., 1980. 81 p. ; 26 cm. Replaces the document: Revised edition of Suggested Utilization or Resources and Guide for Expenditures (Resurge) issued in 1972. Bibliography: p. [79]-81.
1. Vocational education - United States. 2. Socially handicapped - Education - United States. I. Title.
NYPL [JLF 81-624]

United States. Office of Education. Migrant Program Branch. Massachusetts. Division of Curriculum and Instruction. Commonwealth of Massachusetts Migrant Education Program . [Boston] [1979] ix, 100, [57], 25 p. : LC Card 80-621683 DDC 371.96/75/09744 19
LC5152.M37 M32 1979

United States. Office of Education. National Center for Educational Statistics. see United States. National Center for Educational Statistics.

United States. Office of Education. Office of Career Education. Hall, Linda, 1953- Bibliography on career education /. Washington, D.C. [1979] v, 20, 23, [11] p. ; LC Card 80-601669 DDC 016.37011/3 19
Z5815.U5 H34 LC1037.5

United States. Office of Education. Office of Libraries and Learning Resources. see United States. Office of Libraries and Learning Resources.

United States. Office of Education. Office of Planning, Budgeting, and Evaluation. Achievement testing of disadvantaged and minority students for educational program evaluation /. [Monterey, CA] [1979] viii, 464 p. : LC Card 78-4519
LB3051 .A528 NYPL [Sc D 80-645]

Patrick, Ruth J. A study of library cooperatives, networks, and demonstration projects . New York , 1980. p. cm. ISBN 0-89664-313-1 : LC Card 79-20231
Z731 .P34

United States. Office of Education. Planning, Budgeting, and Evaluation, Office of. see United States. Office of Education. Office of Planning, Budgeting, and Evaluation.

GOVERNMENT PUBLICATIONS - U.S.: 1981

581   United States. Office of Labor-Management and Welfare-Pension

United States. Office of Education. Vocational and Technical Education, Division of. see **United States. Office of Education. Division of Vocational and Technical Education.**

United States. Office of Educational Research and Improvement. National Institute of Education. Conference on the Educational and Occupational Needs of American Indian Women, Albuquerque, N.M., 1976. Conference on the Educational and Occupational Needs of American Indian Women, October 12 and 13, 1976. [Washington, D.C.] [1980] vi, 312 p. ;
LC Card 80-603566   DDC 305.4/8 19
E98.W8 C64 1976

United States. Office of Experimental Projects and Programs. see **United States. National Science Foundation. Office of Experimental Projects and Programs.**

UNITED STATES. OFFICE OF FEDERAL CONTRACT COMPLIANCE PROGRAMS.
United states. Office of Federal Contract Compliance Programs. Task Force. A preliminary report on the revitalization of the Federal Contract Compliance Program. Washington , 1977. xxix, 301 p. ;   LC Card 78-602378
KF3464 .A86   **NYPL [JLF 81-198]**

United states. Office of Federal Contract Compliance Programs. Task Force. A preliminary report on the revitalization of the Federal Contract Compliance Program. Washington : U. S. Dept. of Labor, Office of Federal Contract Compliance Programs Task Force, 1977. xxix, 301 p. ; 28 cm. Includes bibliographical references.   LC Card 78-602378
1. Discrimination in employment - Law and legislation - United States. 2. Public contracts - United States. 3. United States. Office of Federal Contract Compliance Programs. I. Title.
KF3464 .A86   **NYPL [JLF 81-198]**

United States. Office of Federal Elections. Analytic Systems, inc. Survey of election boards. Washington, D. C., 1974. 1 v.
                                        NYPL [JLM 81-5]

Analytic Systems, inc. Survey of election boards . Washington, D.C. [1974] ii, 111 p. ;
LC Card 74-602978   DDC 353.008 19
JK1980 .A55 1974

Survey of election boards : data base / Office of Federal Elections, United States General Accounting Office. Washington : The Office, for sale by the Supt. of Docs., U. S. Govt. Print. Off., 1974. 229 p. ; 21 x 27 cm. Cover title. - "... For a more complete description of the data base and project refer to the final report ... entitled Survey of election boards: final report." Chiefly tables.
1. Elections - United States - States - Statistics. I. United States. General Accounting Office. II. Title.
                                        NYPL [JLF 80-1622]

United States. Office of Federal Elections. Clearinghouse on Election Administration. see **United States. Clearinghouse on Election Administration.**

UNITED STATES. OFFICE OF FEDERAL PROCUREMENT POLICY - OFFICIALS AND EMPLOYEES.
United States. Congress. Senate. Committee on Governmental Affairs. Nomination of Karen Hastie Williams . Washington , 1980. iii, 73 p. ;
LC Card 80-602444   DDC 353.0071/2 19
KF26 .G67 1980a

United States. Office of Federal Statistical Policy and Standards.
A framework for planning U. S. Federal statistics for the 1980's / U. S. Department of Commerce, Office of Federal Statistical Policy and Standards. Washington : The Office : for sale by the Supt. of Docs., U. S. Govt. Print. Off., 1978. vii, 440 p. ; 26 cm. On spine: Framework for statistics for the 1980's. Bibliography: p. 437-440.   LC Card 79-601484
1. United States - Statistical services. I. Title. II. Title: Framework for statistics for the 1980's.
HA37 .U549 1978   **NYPL [JLF 81-221]**

Technical paper - U. S. Department of Commerce, Office of Federal Statistical Policy and Standards .
(1) United States. Federal Committee on Statistical Methodology. Subcommittee on Statistics for Allocation of Funds. Correlation between the United States and international

standard industrial classifications /.
[Washington] , 1979. 101 ;   LC Card 80-601531
DDC 338/.02/0973 19
HD2328 .U54 1979

United States. Advisory Committee on Gross National Product Data Improvement. Gross national product data improvement project report . Washington , 1979. xii, 204 p. ;   LC Card 79-602253
HC110.15 U48 1979   **NYPL [JLF 81-487]**

United States. Federal Committee on Statistical Methodology. Subcommittee on Statistical Uses of Administrative Records. Report on statistical uses of administrative records /. [Washington, D.C.?] , 1980 [i.e. 1981] xii, 106 p. :   LC Card 81-601438   DDC 353.0081/9 19
HA37.U55 U55 1981

United States. Office of Fisheries Development. A comprehensive review of the commercial oyster industries in the United States / prepared by Office of Fisheries Development, National Marine Fisheries Service. Washington : The Service : for sale by the Supt. of Docs., U. S. Govt. Print. Off., 1977. vi, 63 p. ; 27 cm. Microfiche (neg.) NTIS. 1 sheet. 11 x 15 cm. (PB 273 678 Bibliography: p. 62-63.   LC Card 77-602004
1. Oysters. 2. Shellfish trade - United States. I. Title.
HD9472.O83 U56   **NYPL [*XME-9429]**

United States. Office of Foreign Agricultural Relations. (Old Catalog form: United States. Foreign agricultural relations office)
United States. Foreign Agricultural Service (1953-) Foreign agriculture report. no. 1-133. Washington, 1942-71. 133 no.   **NYPL [VPZ**
(U. S. Foreign Agricultural Relations Office. Foreign agriculture report)]

United States. Office of Foreign Investment in the United States. Hawaii. International Services Agency. Foreign direct investment in the United States . [Honolulu] [Washington] [1980] ix, 132 p. ;   LC Card 80-602318   DDC 332.6/73/09969 19
HG5128.H3 H38 1980

United States. Office of Geography. Kenya. Defense Mapping Agency. Topographic Center. Kenya, official standard names approved by the United States Board on Geographic Names /. Washington , 1978. vii, 470 p., [1] leaf of plates :   LC Card 79-601438
DT433.52 .D43 1978

United States. Office of Hazardous Materials. (Old Catalog form: United States. Hazardous materials, office of)
California Institute of Technology, Pasadena. Jet Propulsion Laboratory. An index to the Hazardous Materials Regulations ; Title 49, Code of Federal Regulations (October 1, 1972 Revision) parts 170-180. Washington, D. C. [1973] 81 p. ;   LC Card 77-4094
                                        NYPL [JSE 80-480]

United States. Office of Health Maintenance Organization. National HMO census of prepaid plans. Rockville, Md. : U. S. Dept. of Health, Education, and Welfare, Public Health Service, Division of Program Promotion : [Washington, D.C.] : for sale by the Supt. of Docs., U. S. Govt. Print. Off., [1979] 34 p., [3] leaves of plates : ill. ; 28 cm. (DHEW publication. no. (PHS) 80-50127) "June 30, 1979."   LC Card 80-602548   DDC 368.3/82/00973 19
1. Insurance, Health - United States - Statistics. 2. Health maintenance organizations - United States - Statistics. I. Series: United States. Dept. of Health, Education and Welfare. DHEW publication, no. (PHS) 80-50127. II. Title.
HG9396 .U55 1979

United States. Office of Health Maintenance Organizations.
Group Health Foundation Library (U. S.) Comprehensive bibliography on health maintenance organizations, 1974-1978 /. Washington, D.C. , 1980. 2 v. ;   LC Card 80-602118   DDC 016.3621/0425 19
Z6675.H4 G76 1980 RA413

HMO development in Chicago . [Rockville, Md.?] , Washington, D.C. , 1980. 84 p. :   LC Card 81-600748   DDC 362.1/0425 19
RA413.5.U6 I464

United States. Office of History and Historic Architecture. (Old Catalog form: United

States. National Park Service)
Hatch, Charles E. "Par Force" (Reef Bay) Estate Great House and Reef Bay Sugar Factory in Virgin Islands National Park. [Washington] 1969. iii, 18 l.   LC Card 80-503016
DDC 972.97/22 19
F2136.9.R43 H37 1969

United States. Office of Human Development. Administration for Children, Youth and Families. see **United States. Administration for Children, Youth and Families.**

United States. Office of Human Development. Developmental Disabilities Office. see **United States. Developmental Disabilities Office.**

United States. Office of Human Development. Rehabilitation Services Administration. see **United States. Rehabilitation Services Administration.**

United States. Office of Human Development Services.
Guide to federal financial participation under Title XX of the Social Security act / U. S. Department of Health and Human Services, Office of Human Development Services. [Washington] : The Office, 1980. 1 v. (various pagings) ; 28 cm. (DHHS publication. no. (OHDS) 80-02034) Cover title. Updated by unbound supplements shelved with main work.
1. Federal aid to public welfare - United States - Handbooks, manuals, etc. 2. United States. Laws, statutes, etc. Social security act. Title 20. I. Title.
                                        NYPL [JLM 81-18]

UNITED STATES. OFFICE OF HUMAN DEVELOPMENT SERVICES.
United States. Congress. House. Select Committee on Aging. Oversight of Older Americans Act administration . Washington , 1980. iii, 43 p. :   LC Card 80-604046   DDC 353.0084/6 19
KF27.5 .A3 1980f

United States. Office of Human Development Services. Administration for Public Services. Caulfield, Barbara A. The legal aspects of protective services for abused and neglected children . [Washington] , 1978. xii, 121 p. :
LC Card 79-602174   DDC 344.73/03271 19
KF9323 .C38

United States. Office of Indian Affairs. see **United States. Bureau of Indian Affairs.**

United States. Office of Intergovernmental Personnel Programs. see **United States. Office of Personnel Management. Office of Intergovernmental Personnel Programs.**

United States. Office of Internal Revenue. see **United States. Internal Revenue Service.**

United States. Office of International Labor Affairs. see **United States. Bureau of International Labor Affairs.**

United States. Office of Justice Assistance, Research, and Statistics. United States. Office of Civil Rights Compliance. Civil rights enforcement under the Crime Control Act of 1976 and the Justice System Improvement Act of 1979 . Washington, D.C. , 1980. 47 p. ;   LC Card 81-600902   DDC 353.008/8 19
KF5398.P6 A833

United States. Office of Juvenile Justice and Delinquency Prevention. National Institute for Juvenile Justice and Delinquency Prevention. see **National Institute for Juvenile Justice and Delinquency Prevention.**

United States. Office of Juvenile Justice and Deliquency Prevention. see **United States. Law Enforcement Assistance Administration. Office of Juvenile Justice and Delinquency Prevention.**

United States. Office of Labor-Management and Welfare-Pension Reports. (Old Catalog form: United States. Labor-management reports, Bureau of)
Characteristics of plans on file under the Welfare and pension plans disclosure act. [Washington] tables. 27 cm. Title varies: 1965, Welfare and pension plan statistics: characteristics of plans.
1. Pensions - United States - Periodicals. 2. Non-wage payments - United States - Periodicals. 3. Welfare funds (Trade-union) - United States - Periodicals. I. United States. Office of Labor-Management and

BIBLIOGRAPHIC GUIDE

United States. Office of Labor-Management and Welfare-Pension

582

Welfare-Pension Reports. Welfare and pension plan statistics: characteristics of plans. II. Title. III. Title: Welfare and pension plan statistics: characteristics of plans. **NYPL [JLM 80-866]**

Welfare and pension plan statistics: characteristics of plans. United States. Office of Labor-Management and Welfare-Pension Reports. Characteristics of plans on file under the Welfare and pension plans disclosure act. [Washington] **NYPL [JLM 80-866]**

United States. Office of Libraries and Learning Resources.
Conference on Networks for Networkers, Indianapolis, 1979. Networks for networkers . New York, N.Y., London , 1980. xvi, 444 p. : ISBN 0-7201-1599-X : LC Card 80-40016
Z674.8 .C66 1979 **NYPL [*R-*HB 80-3875]**

Directory of library research & demonstration projects, 1966-1975 / [Office of Libraries & Learning Resources]. Preliminary ed. Washington : U. S. Dept. of Health, Education, and Welfare, Office of Education, 1978. v, 117 p. ; 28 cm. At head of title: Higher education act, Title II-B. Includes indexes. LC Card 79-601743
1. Library science - Research - United States - Directories. I. Title.
Z669.7 .U56 1978 **NYPL [JFF 81-141]**

United States. Office of Management and Budget.
Administration of the Employee retirement income security act, ERISA : a report to Congress in fulfillment of provisions of Section 107 of Reorganization plan no. 4 of 1978. [Washington, D.C.] : Executive Office of the President, Office of Management and Budget, [1980] xvi, 81 p. ; 28 cm. LC Card 80-601600 DDC 353.0083/5 19
1. Pension trusts - United States. I. Title.
KF3512 .A863

Managing Federal assistance in the 1980's : a report to the Congress of the United States pursuant to the Federal grant and cooperative agreement act of 1977 (Pub. L. 95-224) : public comments on the draft working papers issued August 1979. [Washington, D.C.] : Executive Office of the President, Office of Management and Budget, 1980. ca. 600 p. in various pagings ; 28 cm. "June 1980." LC Card 80-603124 DDC 353.0072/53 19
1. Grants-in-aid - United States. I. Title.
HJ275 .U57 1980b

Managing Federal assistance in the 1980's : a report to the Congress of the United States pursuant to the Federal grant and cooperative agreement act of 1977 (Pub. L. 95-224) : working papers. Washington, D.C. : Executive Office of the President, Office of Management and Budget : for sale by the Supt. of Docs., U. S. Govt. Print. Off., 1980- v. ; 28 cm. "June 1980." Includes bibliographical references. LC Card 80-603125 DDC 353.0072/53 19
1. Grants-in-aid - United States. I. Title.
HJ275 .U57 1980a

Paperwork and red tape : new perspectives, new directions : a report to the President and the Congress / from the Office of Management and Budget. Washington : For sale by the Supt. of Doc., U. S. Govt. Print. Off., 1979. 133 p. in various pagings ; 24 cm. "... Third semi-annual report ..."
1. Government paperwork - United States. I. Title.
NYPL [JLE 81-478]

UNITED STATES. OFFICE OF MANAGEMENT AND BUDGET.
United States. Congress. Senate. Committee on Banking, Housing and Urban Affairs. Transfer of Cost Accounting Standards Board . Washington , 1980. iii, 67 p. ; LC Card 80-604039 DDC 353.0071/2044 19
KF26 .B39 1980y

UNITED STATES. OFFICE OF MANAGEMENT AND BUDGET - OFFICIALS AND EMPLOYEES.
United States. Congress. Senate. Committee on Governmental Affairs. Nomination of David A. Stockman . Washington , 1981. iii, 169 p. ; LC Card 81-601411 DDC 353.0071 19
KF26 .G67 1981a

United States. Congress. Senate. Committee on Governmental Affairs. Nomination of Edwin L. Harper . Washington , 1981. iii, 25 p. ; LC

Card 81-601771 DDC 353.0071 19
KF26 .G67 1981b

United States. Office of Marine Pollution Assessment. Environmental assessment of the Alaskan continental shelf . [Rockville, Md.?] , 1980. xv, 313 p. : LC Card 81-600735 DDC 574.5/2636/09798 19
QH105.A4 E586

United States. Office of Maritime Manpower. Division of Labor Studies.
Seafaring guide and directory of labor management affiliations. United States. Maritime Administration. Seafaring guide & directory of labor management affiliations. Washington, D.C. [1980] v, 49 p. ; LC Card 80-602281 DDC 331.88/113875/0973 19
HD6515.S42 U46 1980

United States. Office of Minerals Policy and Research Analysis.
Energy and Environmental Analysis, inc. Benefit/cost analyses of laws and regulations affecting coal . Washington , 1977. ca. 750 p. : LC Card 77-603790
TD195.C58 E53 1977

Final report of the 105(b) economic and policy analysis / [prepared by the U. S. Department of the Interior, Office of Minerals Policy and Research Analysis] ; study team, Roger Anderson ... [et al.]. [Washington] : The Office : for sale by the Supt. of Docs., U. S. Govt. Print. Off., 1980. vii, 145 p. : ill. ; 28 cm. On spine: 105(b) economic and policy analysis. "December 15, 1979." Includes bibliographical references. LC Card 80-601683 DDC 333.8/2315/097987 19
1. Petroleum industry and trade - Alaska. I. Anderson, Roger. II. Title. III. Title: 105(b) economic and policy analysis.
HD9567.A4 U565 1980

United States. Office of Minority Business Enterprise. Guide to federal assistance programs for minority business development enterprises. [Washington?]
NYPL [JLM 80-821]

United States. Office of National Parks, Buildings and Reservations. see United States. National Park Service.

United States. Office of Naval Operations. Chief of Naval Education and Training. see United States. Chief of Naval Education and Training.

United States. Office of Naval Operations. Coast Guard. see United States. Coast Guard.

United States. Office of Naval Operations. Naval Education and Training Command. see United States. Naval Education and Training Command.

United States. Office of Naval Operations. Naval History Division. see United States. Naval History Division.

United States. Office of Naval Research. (Old Catalog form: United States. Naval research Office)
Environmental Research Institute of Michigan. Infrared Information and Analysis (IRIA) Center. The infrared handbook / . Washington , 1978. ca. 1600 p. in various pagings : LC Card 77-90786
TA1570 .E56 1978 **NYPL [JSE 80-1602]**

MODE-1 Scientific Council. Mid-Ocean Dynamics Experiment - One. Washington, 1973. 38 p.: **NYPL [JSF 80-781]**

National Conference on Numerical Methods in Heat Transfer. Proceedings. 1st- ; 1979- [College Park, Md.] **NYPL [JSP 81-105]**

Naval research logistics quarterly. v. 1- ; Mar. 1954- [Washington] **NYPL [*ZAN-5064]**

Project Squid Workshop on Gas Turbine Combustor Design Problems, Purdue University, 1978. Gas turbine combustor design problems /. Washington , c1980. xvi, 431 p. : ISBN 0-89116-177-5 LC Card 79-22350
TJ778 .P74 1978 **NYPL [JSE 81-58]**

United States. Office of Naval Research. Ocean Science and Technology Division.
Oceanic sound scattering prediction /. New York , c1977. xii, 859 p. : ISBN 0-306-35505-1 LC Card 77-3445
QC242 .O25 **NYPL [JSF 81-96]**

Report availability notice : Summer 1974 : physical oceanography, marine geophysics, ocean biology, chemical oceanography, ocean technology, sea floor acoustics, environmental acoustics. Arlington, VA. : Office of Naval Research, 1974. ii, 308 p. ; 26 cm. Cover title. Its: ONR report ACR-199.
1. Oceanography - Bibliography - Catalogs. I. Title.
NYPL [JSF 80-767]

United States. Office of Naval Research. Project Squid. see Project Squid.

United States. Office of Noise Abatement and Control. Information on levels of environmental noise requisite to protect public health and welfare with an adequate margin of safety. Washington, 1974. ca 159 p. in various pagings: ill.; 28 cm. (Its: Report. no. 550/9-74-004) Includes bibliographical references. LC Card 76-11078
1. Noise. 2. Health. I. Society of Naval Architects and Marine Engineers, New York. Panel M-16 Modernization of Propulsion Shaft System). II. Title.
NYPL [JSF 80-574]

United States. Office of Nuclear Reactor Regulation. NRC views and analysis of the recommendations of the President's Commission on the Accident at Three Mile Island / Office of Nuclear Reactor Regulation, U. S. Nuclear Regulatory Commission. Washington, D.C. : The Office : [available from GPO Sales Program, Division of Technical Information and Document Control, U. S. Nuclear Regulatory Commission], 1979. 51 p. in various pagings ; 28 cm. "NUREG-0632." LC Card 80-601286 DDC 363.1/79 19
1. Atomic power-plants - United States. 2. Atomic power industry - United States. 3. United States. Nuclear Regulatory Commission. I. Title.
TK1343 .U57 1979

United States. Office of Personnel Management.
Annual report. 1st- ; 1979- [Washington] 28 cm. Supersedes: United States. Civil Service Commission. Annual report.
1. United States. Office of Personnel Management - Periodicals. 2. United States - Officials and employees - Periodicals. **NYPL [JLM 80-854]**

Federal forecast for engineers. winter/spring. 1979- [Washington].
NYPL [Sci. & Tech. Div.]

General schedule salary table. no. 64- ; 1979- [Washington]. 30 cm. For earlier file, whose numbering it continues, see: United States. Civil Service Commission, Salary table. Title varies: no. 64, Salary table.
1. United States - Officials and employees - Salaries, allowances, etc. - Statistics - Periodicals. 2. Withholding tax - United States - Rates and tables - Periodicals. I. United States. Office of Personnel Management. Salary table. II. Title. **NYPL [JLM 81-193]**

Manager's handbook. [Washington, D.C.] : U. S., Office of Personnel Management, [1979] viii, 252 p. ; 22 cm. "November 1979." "OPA-6." Cover title. LC Card 80-601755 DDC 353.1 19
1. Personnel management - Handbooks, manuals, etc. I. Title.
HF5549 .U445 1979

OPM-EV. Washington. **NYPL [Econ. Div.]**

OPM document .
(127-53-1) Public Management Research Conference, Brookings Institution, 1979. Setting public management research agendas . [Washington, D.C.] [1980] iv, 95 p. : LC Card 80-602841 DDC 350/.00072/073 19
JF1338.A2 P85 1979

(128-06-6) United States. Office of Personnel Management. Selective Placement Programs Office. Statistical profile of handicapped Federal civilian employees. [Washington, D.C.] [1980] 41 p. : LC Card 80-602254 DDC 353.001/04 19
JK723.H3 U56 1980

Salary table. United States. Office of Personnel Management. General schedule salary table. no. 64- ; 1979- [Washington].
NYPL [JLM 81-193]

United States. Office of Personnel Management. Intergovernmental Personnel Programs.
United States. Office of Personnel Management. Library. Public personnel management . Washington , 1979. 77 p. ; LC Card 79-601906
Z7164.C6 U66 1979 JK765
NYPL [JLF 81-315]

United States. Office of Personnel Management. Intergovernmental Personnel Programs, Office of. see United States. Office of Personnel Management. Office of Intergovernmental Personnel Programs.

United States. Office of Personnel Management. Labor-Management Relations, Office of. see United States. Office of Personnel Management. Office of Labor-Management Relations.

United States. Office of Personnel Management. Library.
Personnel bibliography series. no. 103- ; 1979- Washington. 27 cm. Supersedes: United States. Civil Service Commission. Library. Personnel bibliography series.
1. Personnel management - United States - Bibliography - Periodicals. 2. Civil service - United States - Bibliography - Periodicals. I. Title.
Z7164.C6 U66 1979 JK765
           NYPL [JLM 80-974]

Public personnel management : reform and improvement : bibliography. Washington : Office of Personnel Management, Intergovernmental Personnel Programs : [for sale by the Supt. of Docs., U. S. Govt. Print. Off.], 1979. 77 p. ; 27 cm. Cover title. "Prepared by the Library of the Office of Personnel Management (OPM) at the request of the Office of Intergovernmental Personnel Programs." LC Card 79-601906
1. Civil service - United States - Personnel management - Bibliography. I. United States. Office of Personnel Management. Intergovernmental Personnel Programs. II. Title.
Z7164.C6 U66 1979 JK765
           NYPL [JLF 81-315]

United States. Office of Personnel Management. Office of Intergovernmental Personnel Programs. Personnel management reform; progress in state and local governments. v. 1, no. 2- ; Aug. 1980- [Washington]
           NYPL [Econ. Div.]

United States. Office of Personnel Management. Office of Labor-Management Relations.
Union recognition in the federal government. Washington.   *NYPL [M-11 4907]*

UNITED STATES. OFFICE OF PERSONNEL MANAGEMENT - PERIODICALS.
United States. Office of Personnel Management. Annual report. 1st- ; 1979- [Washington]
           NYPL [JLM 80-854]

United States. Office of Personnel Management. Selective Placement Programs Office.
Statistical profile of handicapped Federal civilian employees. [Washington, D.C.] : U. S. Office of Personnel Management, Selective Placement Programs Office, Office of Affirmative Employment Programs, [1980] 41 p. : ill. ; 27 cm. (OPM document ; 128-06-6) Cover title. "February 1980." LC Card 80-602254 DDC 353.001/04 19
1. Handicapped - Employment - United States - Statistics. 2. United States - Officials and employees - Statistics. I. Series: United States. Office of Personnel Management. OPM document ; 128-06-6. II. Title.
JK723.H3 U56 1980

United States. Office of Pesticide Programs. see United States. Environmental Protection Agency. Office of Pesticide Programs.

United States. Office of Pipeline and Producer Regulation. see United States. Federal Energy Regulatory Commission. Office of Pipeline and Producer Regulation.

United States. Office of Port and Intermodal Development.
National port assessment, 1980-1990 : an analysis of future U. S. port requirements. [Washington] : U. S. Dept. of Commerce, Maritime Administration, Office of Commercial Development, Office of Port and Intermodal Development, [1980] ix, 127 p. : maps (2 fold. in pocket) ; 28 cm. "June 1980." Bibliography: p. 118-122. LC Card 80-603149 DDC 387.1/0973 19
1. Harbors - United States - Planning. I. Title.
HE553 .U644 1980a

United States port development expenditure survey / U. S. Department of Commerce, Maritime Administration, Office of Port and Intermodal Development. [Washington] : The Office : for sale by the Supt. of Docs., U. S. Govt. Print. Off., [1980] vi, 45 p. ; 28 cm.

"January 1980." Tables. LC Card 80-601703 DDC 387.1 19
1. Harbors - United States - Finance. 2. Marine terminals - United States - Finance. I. Title.
HE553 .U644 1980

United States. Office of Production Management. Committee on Fair Employment Practice. see United States. Committee on Fair Employment Practice (1941-1943)

United States. Office of Quality Control Management. see United States. Social and Rehabilitation Service. Office of Quality Control Management.

UNITED STATES. OFFICE OF SCIENCE AND TECHNOLOGY POLICY.
United States. Congress. Senate. Committee on Commerce, Science, and Transportation. Subcommittee on Science, Technology, and Space. Office of Science and Technology Policy . Washington , 1980. iii, 72 p. ; LC Card 80-603897 DDC 353.0085/5 19
KF26 .C697 1980g

United States. Office of Science Information Service. see United States. National Science Foundation. Office of Science Information Service.

United States. Office of Scientific Research (Air Force) see United States. Air Force. Office of Scientific Research.

UNITED STATES. OFFICE OF SOLID WASTE - BIBLIOGRAPHY.
United States. Environmental Protection Agency. Available information materials on solid waste management . [Washington] , 1979. v, 240 p. ; LC Card 80-601846 DDC 016.3637/28 19
Z5853.S22 U4285 1979a TD791

United States. Office of Solid Waste Management Programs. Hazardous Waste Management Division. An environmental assessment of potential gas and leachate problems at land disposal sites / prepared by the Hazardous Waste Management Division, Office of Solid Waste Management Programs. - [Washington] : U. S. Environmental Protection Agency, 1973 [i. e. 1975] v, 33 p. ; 26 cm. (Open-file report - Office of Solid Waste Management Programs. SW-110. of) Microfilm. Includes bibliographies.
1. Sanitary landfills - United States. 2. Waste disposal in the ground - United States. 3. Soils - Leaching. I. Title.   *NYPL [*ZV-185 Reel 1]*

United States. Office of Space and Terrestrial Applications.
Remote sensing and problems of the hydrosphere . Washington, D.C. [Springfield, Va.] 1979. v, 56 p. : LC Card 81-601298 DDC 551.4/028/7 19
TD370 .R45

Remote sensing and problems of the hydrosphere . Washington, D.C. , 1980. iv, 30 p. ; LC Card 80-603169 DDC 553.7/028/7 19
TD419.5 .R45

United States. Office of Space Science.
Ames Summer Study on Space Settlements and Industrialization Using Nonterrestrial Materials, Ames Research Center, 1977. Space resources and space settlements . Washington, D.C. , 1979. x, 288 p. : LC Card 79-603821 DDC 629.44/2 19
TL795.7 .A45 1977

Symposium on Space Missions to Comets, Goddard Space Flight Center, 1977. Space missions to comets . [Washington] , 1979. v, 226 p. : LC Card 79-604295 DDC 523.6 19
QB721 .S97 1977

United States. Office of Space Transportation Systems. Ames Summer Study on Space Settlements and Industrialization Using Nonterrestrial Materials, Ames Research Center, 1977. Space resources and space settlements . Washington, D.C. , 1979. x, 288 p. : LC Card 79-603821 DDC 629.44/2 19
TL795.7 .A45 1977

United States. Office of Standard Weights and Measures. see United States. National Bureau of Standards.

UNITED STATES. OFFICE OF SURFACE MINING, RECLAMATION, AND ENFORCEMENT - DIRECTORIES.

United States. Geological Survey. Catalog of selected offices of the Office of Surface Mining, Bureau of Land Management, and Geological Survey relating to coal, 1981. Reston, Va. , 1980. p. cm. LC Card 80-607870 DDC 557.3 s 353.0082/382 19
QE75 .C5 no. 840 TN12

United States. Office of Tax Analysis.
Carlson, George N. Value-added tax . [Washington, D.C.?] , 1980. 85 p. : LC Card 80-604142 DDC 351.72/47 19
HJ5715.E95 C37

Compendium of tax research. Washington.
           NYPL [JLL 81-3]

United States. Office of Technical Assistance (EDA) see United States. Economic Development Administration. Office of Technical Assistance.

United States. Office of Technology Assessment. see United States. Congress. Office of Technology Assessment.

United States. Office of Telecommunications. OT report.
(77-121) Alleman, James H. The pricing structure of local telephone service . [Boulder, Colo.] , 1977. 21 p. ; LC Card 77-602916 DDC 384.6/3 19
HE8825 .A6

United States. Office of the Army Research Center. see United States. Army Research Office.

United States. Office of the Assistant Secretary for Health. National Conference on Health Promotion Programs in Occupational Settings, Washington, D.C., 1979. Proceedings of the National Conference on Health Promotion Programs in Occupational Settings, January 17, 18, and 19, 1979 /. Washington, D.C. [1979] xii, 69 p. ; LC Card 80-600621 DDC 362.1/0883317 19
HD7654 .N28 1979

United States. Office of the Assistant Secretary for Health and Surgeon General.
Healthy people. Institute of Medicine. Healthy people : the Surgeon General's report on health promotion and disease prevention : background papers : report to the Surgeon General on health promotion and disease prevention / by the Institute of Medicine, National Academy of Sciences. Washington , 1979. viii, 484 p. : LC Card 79-603264
RA445 .I57 1979   *NYPL [JLD 80-3780]*

Institute of Medicine. Healthy people . Washington , 1979. viii, 484 p. : LC Card 79-603264
RA445 .I57 1979   *NYPL [JLD 80-3780]*

Promoting health/preventing disease . [Washington, D.C.?] , 1980. xiv, 197 p. ; LC Card 80-604164 DDC 362.1/0973 19
RA445 .P7

United States. Office of the Assistant Secretary of Defense (Manpower, Reserve Affairs, and Logistics) Pathways to military service for men and women. [Washington] : Dept. of Defense, Office of the Assistant Secretary of Defense (Manpower, Reserve Affairs, and Logistics) : for sale by the Supt. of Docs., U. S. Govt. Print. Off., 1978. 68 p. ; 20 x 26 cm. LC Card 78-603689
1. United States - Armed Forces - Vocational guidance. I. Title.
UB147 .U49 1978

United States. Office of the Comptroller of the Army. (Old Catalog form: United States. Comptroller of the Army, Office of the.) Resource management journal. 1st.- ct. [1980?]- [Washington]   *NYPL [Econ. Div.]*

United States, Office of the Director of Defense Research and Engineering. Advisory Group on Electron Devices. see United States. Advisory Group on Electron Devices.

United States. Office of the Director of Defense Research and Engineering. Defense Advanced Research Projects Agency. see United States. Defense Advanced Research Projects Agency.

United States. Office of the Federal Register. (Old Catalog form: United States. Federal register, Office of the) Directory of Federal regional structure / Office of the Federal Register, National Archives and Records Service, General Services Administration. [Washington] : The Office : for sale by the Supt. of Docts., U. S. Govt. Print. Off., [1978] iii, 94 p. : maps ; 28 cm.   LC Card 79-603213

1. *United States - Executive departments - Directories.* 2. *Administrative agencies - United States - Directories.* I. *Title.*

JK464 1978 .U54   **NYPL** *[JLF 81-410]*

The Federal register : what it is and how to use it : a guide for the user of the Federal register, Code of Federal regulations system. [Washington] : Office of the Federal Register, National Archives and Records Service, General Services Administration, [1980] iv, 132 p. : ill. ; 28 cm. "Editor of this revision ... Judie Craine." Includes index.   LC Card 80-602839 DDC 348.73/25 19

1. *Legal research - United States.* 2. *United States. Federal register.* 3. *Code of federal regulations.* I. *Craine, Judie.* II. *Title.*

KF240 .F5 1980

United States. Laws, statutes, etc. Code of federal regulations. Title 3: The President. 1936/38- [Washington]

    NYPL *[*R-Econ. 81-3]*

UNITED STATES. OFFICE OF THE U. S. TRADE REPRESENTATIVE - APPROPRIATIONS AND EXPENDITURES.
United States. Congress. Senate. Committee on Finance. Subcommittee on International Trade. Authorization of appropriations for the U. S. Customs Service, U. S. International Trade Commission, and Office of the U. S. Trade Representative, for fiscal year 1981 . Washington , 1980. iii, 79 p. :   LC Card 80-603102   DDC 353.0072/23682/7 19
KF26 .F554 1980b

UNITED STATES. OFFICE OF THE U. S. TRADE REPRESENTATIVE - OFFICIALS AND EMPLOYEES.
United States. Congress. Senate. Committee on Finance. Nomination of William E. Brock III . Washington , 1981. ii, 43 p. ;   LC Card 81-601985   DDC 353.0082/7 19
KF26 .F5 1981c

United States. Office of Transportation Economic Analysis. Control Data Corporation. Trends in bus transit financial and operating characteristics, 1960-1975 /. [Washington] [Springfield, Va.] 1978, cover 1977. ca. 300 p. in various pagings :   LC Card 79-602177
HE5623 .A4 1977d   **NYPL** *[JLF 81-376]*

United States. Office of Transportation Security. see **United States. Dept. of Transportation. Office of Transportation Security.**

United States. Office of Transportation Systems Analysis and Information. Ernst and Ernst. Rail system investment analysis. Washington, 1977. 66 p. in various pagings
    NYPL *[*XME-9311]*

United States. Office of Water Research and Technology. Collins, D. Cheryl. A state of knowledge on Indian water rights in Kansas . Manhattan, Kan. , 1980. 44 p. :   LC Card 80-623437   DDC 346.78104/32 347.8106432 19
KFK505.6.W38 C64

United States. Office of Weights and Measures. see **United States. National Bureau of Standards.**

UNITED STATES - OFFICIALS AND EMPLOYEES.
United States. Congress. House. Committee on Post Office and Civil Service. Subcommittee on Civil Service. Personal assistants for handicapped federal employees . Washington , 1980. iii, 84 p. :   LC Card 80-604075 DDC 342.73/068 347.30268
KF27 .P635 1980c

United States. Congress. Senate. Committee on Commerce, Science, and Transportation. Nominations--August . Washington , 1980. iii, 48 p. ;   LC Card 80-603804   DDC 353.0082 19
KF26 .C69 1980s

United States government policy and supporting positions /. Washington , 1980. vii, 161 p. ;   LC Card 80-604162   DDC 353.001/03 19
JK661 .U54

UNITED STATES - OFFICIALS AND EMPLOYEES - ACCIDENTS.
United States. Congress. House. Committee on Education and Labor. Subcommittee on Health and Safety. Oversight hearings on OSHA--occupational safety and health for Federal employees . Washington , 1980- v. :   LC Card 80-602740   DDC 353.001/6 19
KF27 .E3394 1979a

UNITED STATES - OFFICIALS AND EMPLOYEES - HEALTH AND HYGIENE.
United States. Congress. House. Committee on Education and Labor. Subcommittee on Health and Safety. Oversight hearings on OSHA--occupational safety and health for Federal employees . Washington , 1980- v. :   LC Card 80-602740   DDC 353.001/6 19
KF27 .E3394 1979a

United States - Officials and employees - Health insurance. see **Insurance, Government employees' health - United States.**

UNITED STATES - OFFICIALS AND EMPLOYEES IN FOREIGN COUNTRIES.
United States. Congress. House. Committee on the Judiciary. Subcommittee on Administrative Law and Governmental Relations. Compensation of military personnel and government employees for loss of personal property incident to their foreign service . Washington , 1980. iii, 110 p. :   LC Card 80-602775   DDC 346.7304/7 19
KF27 .J832 1980

UNITED STATES - OFFICIALS AND EMPLOYEES IN FOREIGN COUNTRIES - APPOINTMENT, QUALIFICATIONS, TENURE, ETC.
United States. General Accounting Office. More competence in foreign languages needed by Federal personnel working overseas . [Washington, D.C.] 1980. iv, 77 p. :   LC Card 80-602021   DDC 353.0013/23 19
JK736 .U54 1980

UNITED STATES - OFFICIALS AND EMPLOYEES IN FOREIGN COUNTRIES - FOREIGN LANGUAGE COMPETENCY.
United States. General Accounting Office. More competence in foreign languages needed by Federal personnel working overseas . [Washington, D.C.] 1980. iv, 77 p. :   LC Card 80-602021   DDC 353.0013/23 19
JK736 .U54 1980

UNITED STATES - OFFICIALS AND EMPLOYEES - PERIODICALS.
United States. Office of Personnel Management. Annual report. 1st- ; 1979- [Washington]
    NYPL *[JLM 80-854]*

UNITED STATES - OFFICIALS AND EMPLOYEES - RATING OF.
United States. Congress. House. Committee on Post Office and Civil Service. Subcommittee on Civil Service. Civil service reform oversight, 1980--performance appraisal . Washington , 1980. iv, 335 p. :   LC Card 80-603315   DDC 353.006 19
KF27 .P635 1980b

UNITED STATES - OFFICIALS AND EMPLOYEES, RETIRED - EMPLOYMENT.
United States. Congress. House. Committee on Interstate and Foreign Commerce. Subcommittee on Consumer Protection and Finance. Consumer Product Safety Commission post-employment restrictions . Washington , 1980. iii, 8 p. ;   LC Card 80-602437   DDC 343.73/071 19
KF27 .I554 1980

UNITED STATES - OFFICIALS AND EMPLOYEES - SALARIES, ALLOWANCES, ETC.
Huck, Daniel F. Alternative approaches to adjusting compensation for federal bluecollar employees /. [Washington, D.C.] , c1980. xxii, 59 p. ;   LC Card 80-604160   DDC 353.001/2 19
JK776 .H8

United States. Congress. House. Committee on Education and Labor. Subcommittee on Labor Standards. Oversight hearings on the Federal employees' compensation act . Washington , D.C. , 1980- v. :   LC Card 80-603447 DDC

353.0082/56 19
KF27 .E348 1980a

United States. Congress. House. Committee on Foreign Affairs. Special Central America economic assistance ; Compensation for hostages in Iran ; International conference on Cambodia . Washington , 1980. iii, 130 p. ;   LC Card 80-601146   DDC 338.91/730596 19
KF27 .F6 1979k

United States. Congress. House. Committee on Government Operations. Government Activities and Transportation Subcommittee. Government travel per diem reimbursement rate . Washington , 1980. iii, 141 p. ;   LC Card 80-602902   DDC 353.001/6 19
KF27 .G6626 1980

United States. Congress. House. Committee on Post Office and Civil Service. Subcommittee on Compensation and Employee Benefits. Conversion of nonappropriated fund employees to competitive service . Washington , 1980. iii, 52 p. ;   LC Card 81-600627   DDC 353.001/23 19
KF27 .P638 1980l

United States. Congress. House. Committee on Post Office and Civil Service. Subcommittee on Compensation and Employee Benefits. Federal pay continuity act . Washington , 1980. iii, 128 p. ;   LC Card 80-602950   DDC 353.001/23 19
KF27 .P638 1980c

United States. Congress. Senate. Committee on Governmental Affairs. Federal Employees Compensation Reform Act of 1979 . Washington , 1980. iii, 219 p. ;   LC Card 81-600825   DDC 342.73/068 347.30268 19
KF26 .G67 1979ar

United States. Congressional Budget Office. Compensation reform for Federal white-collar employees . [Washington] [1980] xiv, 37 p. ;   LC Card 80-602373   DDC 353.001/23 19
JK775 1980 .C66

United States. General Accounting Office. Multiple problems with the 1974 amendments to the Federal employees' compensation act . [Washington] , 1979. vi, 85 p. ;   LC Card 79-602706   DDC 344.73/0217 19
KF3626 .A85

UNITED STATES - OFFICIALS AND EMPLOYEES - SALARIES, ALLOWANCES, ETC. - COST OF LIVING ADJUSTMENTS - PUERTO RICO.
United States. Congress. House. Committee on Post Office and Civil Service. Subcommittee on Compensation and Employee Benefits. Cost of living allowances (Virgin Islands and Puerto Rico) . Washington , 1978. iii, 87 p. ;   LC Card 81-601487   DDC 353.001/232 19
KF27 .P638 1978i

UNITED STATES - OFFICIALS AND EMPLOYEES - SALARIES, ALLOWANCES, ETC. - COST OF LIVING ADJUSTMENTS - VIRGIN ISLANDS OF THE UNITED STATES.
United States. Congress. House. Committee on Post Office and Civil Service. Subcommittee on Compensation and Employee Benefits. Cost of living allowances (Virgin Islands and Puerto Rico) . Washington , 1978. iii, 87 p. ;   LC Card 81-601487   DDC 353.001/232 19
KF27 .P638 1978i

UNITED STATES - OFFICIALS AND EMPLOYEES - SALARIES, ALLOWANCES, ETC. - STATISTICS - PERIODICALS.
United States. Office of Personnel Management. General schedule salary table. no. 64- ; 1979- [Washington].   **NYPL** *[JLM 81-193]*

UNITED STATES - OFFICIALS AND EMPLOYEES - STATISTICS.
United States. Office of Personnel Management. Selective Placement Programs Office. Statistical profile of handicapped Federal civilian employees. [Washington, D.C.] [1980] 41 p. :   LC Card 80-602254   DDC 353.001/04 19
JK723.H3 U56 1980

UNITED STATES - OFFICIALS AND EMPLOYEES - TRAVEL REGULATIONS.
United States. Congress. House. Committee on Government Operations. Government Activities and Transportation Subcommittee. Government travel per diem reimbursement rate . Washington , 1980. iii, 141 p. ;   LC Card

80-602902 DDC 353.001/6 19
KF27 .G6626 1980

United States. Organization of the Joint Chiefs of Staff. Logistics Directorate. WorldWide Strategic Mobility Conference, National Defense University, 1977. The WorldWide Strategic Mobility Conference 1977, 2-4 May 1977 /. [Washington, D.C., 1977] ca. 100 p. in various pagings ; LC Card 80-601611 DDC 355.2/7 19
UC273 .W67 1977

United States. Outdoor Recreation, Bureau of. see **United States. Bureau of Outdoor Recreation.**

United States - Outlying possessions. see **United States - Insular possessions.**

United States. Ozarks Regional Commission. Campbell, Rex R. Population change in the Ozarks region, 1970-1975 . [Washington] , 1978. v, 29 p. : LC Card 80-622359 DDC 304.6/2/097671 19
HB3517 .C35

Missouri, socioeconomic strata health analysis : report of the Ozarks Regional Commission. [Washington] : The Commission, 1975. xi, 432 p. : ill. ; 28 cm. Document no. 1021-0037. Chiefly tables. LC Card 78-622054 DDC 362.1/09778 19
1. Missouri - Statistics, Medical. 2. Ozark Mountain region - Statistics, Medical. 3. Sick - Missouri - Socioeconomic status - Statistics. 4. Sick - Ozark Mountain region - Socioeconomic status - Statistics. 5. Missouri - Population - Statistics. 6. Ozark Mountain region - Population - Statistics. 7. Missouri - Statistics, Vital. 8. Ozark Mountain region - Statistics, Vital. I. Title.
RA407.4.M8 U54 1975

United States. Pacific Northwest Forest and Range Experiment Station, Portland, Or. USDA Forest Service research paper PNW . (93) Berndt, H. W. Forest land use and streamflow in central Oregon /. Portland, Or. , 1970. 15 p. : LC Card 71-608738 DDC 634.9/09795 s 553.7/09795/83 19
SD11 .A45614 no. 93 SD387.M8

(94) Radwan, M. A., 1926- Impregnating and coating with endrin to protect Douglas-fir seed from rodents /. Portland, Or., 1970. 17 p. : LC Card 77-608734 DDC 634.9/0979 s 634.9/75466 19
SD11 .A45614 no. 94 SB608.D6

(96) Ruth, Robert H. Effect of shade on germination and growth of salmonberry /. Portland, Or. , 1970. 10 p. : LC Card 70-608740 DDC 634.9/09795 s 634/.711 19
SD11 .A45614 no. 96 QK495.R78

(99) Fahnestock, George R. Two keys for appraising forest fire fuels /. Portland, Or. , 1970. 26 p. : LC Card 70-609148 DDC 634.9/0979 s 634.9/618 19
SD11 .A45614 no. 99 SD421

United States. Pacific Northwest Regional Commission. see **Pacific Northwest Regional Commission.**

United States. Pacific Northwest River Basins Commission. (Old Catalog form: Pacific northwest river basins commission) Evergreen State College. Applied Environmental Studies Program. Yakima River Basin carrying capacity study project /. [Olympia, Wash.] , 1975. 63 p. : LC Card 76-620920 DDC 330.9797/55043 19
HC107.W2 E9 1975

Water--today and tomorrow. [Vancouver, Wash. : Pacific Northwest River Basins Commission, 1979] 3 v. : ill. ; 28 cm. Cover title. Vols. 2-3 have special subtitle: A Pacific Northwest regional program for water and related resources. Includes bibliography. CONTENTS. - v. 1. Program summary.--v. 2. The region.--v. 3. The States. LC Card 80-622316 DDC 333.91/009795 19
1. Water resources development - Northwestern States. I. Title.
TC423.7 .U54 1979

United States. Pacific Northwest River Basins Commission. Washington State Study Team. The Big Bend Basin level B study of the water & related land resources / prepared by the Washington State Study Team for the Pacific Northwest River Basins Commission. [Vancouver, Wash.] : The Commission, 1976. x,

106, [64] p., [1] fold. leaf of plates : ill. ; 28 cm. Cover title. Bibliography: p. 104-105. LC Card 77-624406
1. Water resources development - Washington (State) - Big Bend Basin. 2. Land use - Washington (State) - Big Bend Basin. I. Title.
TC425.B44 U54 1976

UNITED STATES. PANAMA CANAL COMMISSION.
United States. Congress. House. Committee on Merchant Marine and Fisheries. Subcommittee on Panama Canal. Panama Canal oversight . Washington , 1980. iii, 158 p. : LC Card 80-603322 DDC 353.0087/6444 19
KF27 .M475 1980a

United States. General Accounting Office. Background information bearing upon Panama Canal treaty implementing legislation . [Washington] [1979] 62 p. ; LC Card 79-602532 DDC 353.0087/6444 19
JX1398.73 .U54 1979

UNITED STATES. PANAMA CANAL COMMISSION - APPROPRIATIONS AND EXPENDITURES.
United States. Congress. Senate. Committee on Armed Services. Panama Canal Commission authorization fiscal year 1981 . Washington , 1980 [i.e. 1981] ii, 32 p. ; LC Card 81-600852 DDC 353.0072/234 19
KF26 .A7 1980f

UNITED STATES. PANAMA CANAL COMMISSION - OFFICIALS AND EMPLOYEES.
United States. Congress. Senate. Committee on Armed Services. Nominations of Michael Blumenfeld, John A. Bushnell, John W. Clark, Clifford B. O'Hara, William Sidell, Robinson O. Everett, and William E. Peacock . Washington , 1980. ii, 49 p. ; LC Card 80-602497 DDC 353.0087/6444 19
KF26 .A7 1980c

United States. Panel on Government and the Regulation of Corporate and Individual Decisions. Government and the regulation of corporate and individual decisions in the eighties : report of the Panel on Government and the Regulation of Corporate and Individual Decisions. Washington : President's Commission for a National Agenda for the Eighties : for sale by the Supt. of Docs., U. S. Govt. Print. Off., 1980. 113 p. ; 23 cm. LC Card 80-29251 DDC 343.73/08 19
1. Industrial laws and legislation - United States. 2. Trade regulation - United States. 3. Social legislation - United States. I. Title. II. Title: Government regulation.
KF1600 .A843

United States. Panel on Policies and Priorities for Metropolitan and Nonmetropolitan Areas. Urban America in the eighties : perspectives and prospects / report of the Panel on Policies and Priorities for Metropolitan and Nonmetropolitan Areas. Washington : President's Commission for a National Agenda for the Eighties, 1980. p. cm. LC Card 80-27894 DDC 307.7/6/0973 19
1. Urban policy - United States - Congresses. I. Title.
HT123 .U465 1980

United States. Panel on the Quality of American Life. The quality of American life in the eighties : report of the Panel on the Quality of American Life. Washington : President's Commission for a National Agenda for the Eighties : For sale by the Supt. of Docs., U. S.G.P.O., 1980. 140 p. : ill. ; 23 cm. Includes bibliographical references. LC Card 81-281 DDC 361.6/1/0973 19
1. Quality of life - United States. 2. United States - Social policy. I. Title.
HN60 .U545 1980

United States. Patent and Trademark Office. Concordance, United States patent classification to international patent classification. 4th ed. [Washington, D.C.] : U. S. Dept. of Commerce, Patent and Trademark Office, Patent Documentation Organizations ; Washington : for sale by the Supt. of Docs., U. S. Govt. Print. Off., 1980. 148 p. ; 28 cm. Second ed. issued by United States Patent Office, Office of Search Systems and Documentation. "January 1980." LC Card 79-603986 DDC 608.773/012 19
1. Patents - United States - Classification. I. United States. Patent Office. Office of Search Systems and

Documentation. Concordance. II. Title.
T223.F4 U54 1980

Directory of patent attorneys and agents. McLean, Va.. **NYPL [*VBL 81-125]**

Patent and trademark forms booklet / United States Department of Commerce, Patent and Trademark Office. Washington : The Office ; [For sale by the Superintendent of Documents, U. S. Govt. Print. Off.], 1979 [i. e. 1980] 1 v. : 28 cm. Cover title. "October 1979".
1. Patent laws and legislation - United States - Forms. 2. Trade-marks - United States - Forms. I. Title.
NYPL [*VBE 81-231]

U. S. design patents. Nov. 9, 1842- Woodbridge, Conn., Research Publications inc. Microfilm in cartridges. Running title: United States patents design.
1. Patents - United States. 2. Design protection - United States. I. United States Patent and Trademark Office. United States patents design. II. Title. III. Title: United States patents design. **NYPL [*XFR-10]**

United States patents design. United States. Patent and Trademark Office. U. S. design patents. Nov. 9, 1842- Woodbridge, Conn..
NYPL [*XFR-10]

United States. Patent and Trademark Office. Office of Technology Assessment and Forecast. Solar energy. [Washington, D.C.] : U. S. Dept. of Commerce, Patent and Trademark Office, Office of Technology Assessment and Forecast, [1980] iii, 190 p. : ill. ; 29 cm. (Patent profiles) "January 1980." LC Card 80-601594 DDC 621.47/0272 19
1. Solar energy - Patents. I. Title. II. Series.
TJ810 .U63 1980

Synthetic fuels. Washington, D.C. : U. S. Dept. of Commerce, Patent and Trademark Office, Office of Technology Assessment and Forecast : for sale by the Supt. of Docs., U. S. Govt. Print. Off., [1979] iii, 230 p. : graphs ; 29 cm. (Patent profiles) "December 1979." LC Card 80-601527 DDC 662/.66/0272 19
1. Synthetic fuels - Patents. I. Title. II. Series.
TP360 .U63 1979

United States. Patent Office. Office of Search Systems and Documentation. Concordance. United States. Patent and Trademark Office. Concordance, United States patent classification to international patent classification. 4th ed. [Washington, D.C.] , Washington , 1980. 148 p. ; LC Card 79-603986 DDC 608.773/012 19
T223.F4 U54 1980

United States patents design. United States. Patent and Trademark Office. U. S. design patents. Nov. 9, 1842- Woodbridge, Conn..
NYPL [*XFR-10]

United States - Pensions, Civil Service. see Civil service pensions - United States.

United States - Pensions, Military. see Pensions, Military - United States.

United States. Personnel Management, Office of. see **United States. Office of Personnel Management.**

United States - Police. see Police - United States.

United States policy toward Angola--update . United States. Congress. House. Committee on Foreign Affairs. Subcommittee on Africa. Washington , 1980. iii, 76 p. : LC Card 81-600629 DDC 327.73067/3 19
KF27 .F625 1980e

UNITED STATES - POLITICS AND GOVERNMENT.
United States. President's Commission for a National Agenda for the Eighties. Panel on the Electoral and Democratic Process. The electoral and democratic process in the eighties . Washington , 1980. 101 p. : LC Card 81-86 DDC 320.973 19
JK271 .U56 1981

UNITED STATES - POLITICS AND GOVERNMENT - 1815-1861.
Watson, Harry L. Jacksonian politics and community conflict /. Baton Rouge , c1981. p. cm. ISBN 0-8071-0857-X : LC Card 81-2414 DDC 324/.09756/373 19
F262.C9 W37

UNITED STATES - POLITICS AND GOVERNMENT - 1865-1933 - SOURCES - BIBLIOGRAPHY - CATALOGS.
Library of Congress. Manuscript Division. The La Follette family collection. Washington , 1981. p. cm. ISBN 0-8444-0360-1 LC Card 81-1165 DDC 016.97391/092/2 19
CD3029.5.L2 L52 1981

UNITED STATES - POLITICS AND GOVERNMENT - 1865-1869.
Gambill, Edward L. (Edward Lee), 1936- Conservative ordeal, northern Democrats and Reconstruction, 1865-1868 /. Ames , 1981. viii, 188 p. ; ISBN 0-8138-1385-9 LC Card 81-1560 DDC 973.8/1 19
E668 .G18

UNITED STATES - POLITICS AND GOVERNMENT - 20TH CENTURY - SOURCES.
Pressler, Larry, 1942- U. S. senators from the prairie /. Washington, D.C. [1980] p. cm. ISBN 0-88249-033-8 : LC Card 80-25220 DDC 328.73/092/2 B 920 19
E747 .P83

UNITED STATES - POLITICS AND GOVERNMENT - 1901-1953 - CARICATURES AND CARTOONS.
Caswell, Lucy Shelton. Billy Ireland /. Columbus, Ohio , 1980. ix, 235 p. : ISBN 0-88215-051-0 (pbk.) LC Card 81-119198 DDC 741.5/092/4 B 19
E743 .C28

UNITED STATES - POLITICS AND GOVERNMENT - 1945-
United States. President's Commission for a National Agenda for the Eighties. A national agenda for the eighties . Washington , 1980. 214 p. ; LC Card 81-356 DDC 973.926 19
HC106.7 .U577 1980

UNITED STATES - POLITICS AND GOVERNMENT - 1963-1969 - CONGRESSES.
Exploring the Johnson years /. Austin, Tex. , c1981. p. cm. ISBN 0-292-72031-9 LC Card 81-2269 DDC 973.923/092/4 19
E846 .E94

UNITED STATES - POLITICS AND GOVERNMENT - 1977- - ADDRESSES, ESSAYS, LECTURES.
Fallows, James M. An old capital and a new president /. Bloomington, Ind. , c1979. 16 p. ; LC Card 80-140042 DDC 973.926/092/4 19
E873 .F34

United States. President, 1977- (Carter) State of the Union address and State of the Union message. [Washington? D.C.] 1980. 96 p. ; LC Card 80-602059 DDC 353.03/52 19
J82 .E44 1980

UNITED STATES - POLITICS AND GOVERNMENT - ADDRESSES, ESSAYS, LECTURES.
Latin American populism in comparative perspective /. Albuquerque , c1981. p. cm. ISBN 0-8263-0580-6 : LC Card 80-54572 DDC 320.98 19
JL966 .L36

UNITED STATES - POLITICS AND GOVERNMENT - DATA PROCESSING - PERIODICALS.
United States. Automated Data and Telecommunications Service. Automatic data processing equipment inventory in the United States government. Washington.
NYPL [JLM 80-1067]

UNITED STATES - POLITICS AND GOVERNMENT - HANDBOOKS, MANUALS, ETC.
United States. Immigration and Naturalization Service. Our Constitution and government. [1st]- ed. Washington, 1940- *NYPL [Pub. Cat. 80-967 & IB (United States. Immigration and Naturalization Service. Our Constitution and government.)]*

UNITED STATES - POLITICS AND GOVERNMENT - MANUSCRIPTS - CATALOGS.
United States. Library of Congress. Manuscript Division. Members of Congress . Washington , 1980. xiii, 217 p. ; ISBN 0-8444-0272-9
Z1236 .U613 1979 E176 NYPL [JLE 81-85]

UNITED STATES - POPULAR CULTURE - ADDRESSES, ESSAYS, LECTURES.
Rituals and ceremonies in popular culture /. Bowling Green, Ohio , c1980. 349 p. : ISBN 0-87972-160-X LC Card 80-83188 DDC 306/.4 19
E169.12 .R55

UNITED STATES - POPULAR CULTURE - PERIODICALS.
Journal of American culture. v. 1- Spring 1978- [Bowling Green, Ohio] LC Card 79-642570
NYPL [JFL 80-314]

UNITED STATES - POPULATION.
Baldassare, Mark. The growth dilemma . Berkeley , c1981. p. cm. ISBN 0-520-04302-2 LC Card 81-1449 DDC 304.6/2/0973 19
HB3505 .B298

United States. Bureau of the Census. Selected characteristics of persons in physical science, 1978. Washington, D.C. , U. S. Dept. of Commerce, Bureau of the Census. iv, 30 p. : LC Card 80-607850 DDC 312/.0973 s 509/.02/2 19
HA203 .A218 no. 108 Q149.U5

United States. Congress. House. Committee on Science and Tecnology. Subcommittee on Energy Research and Production. Population and energy . Washington , 1981. iii, 154 p. : LC Card 81-601357 DDC 333.79/13/0973 19
KF27 .S3936 1980f

UNITED STATES - POPULATION - ADDRESSES, ESSAYS, LECTURES.
Nonmetropolitan America in transition /. Chapel Hill , c1981. p. cm. ISBN 0-8078-1490-3 LC Card 81-3511 DDC 307.7/2/0973 19
HT123 .N65

United States population data methodology / [David J. Hyams, Paul T. Strickler] Alexandria, Va. : [Obtainable] from the Defense Documentation Center, 1973. v, 258 p. ; 28 cm. Cover title. At head of title: National Military Command System Support Center. Technical memorandum TM 6-73.
1. United States - Population density. 2. Atomic bomb - Safety measures. I. Hyams, David J. II. Strickler, Paul T. III. United States. National Military Command System Support Center. **NYPL [JLF 81-353]**

UNITED STATES - POPULATION DENSITY.
Baldassare, Mark. The growth dilemma . Berkeley , c1981. p. cm. ISBN 0-520-04302-2 LC Card 81-1449 DDC 304.6/2/0973 19
HB3505 .B298

United States population data methodology /. Alexandria, Va. , 1973. v, 258 p. ;
NYPL [JLF 81-353]

UNITED STATES - POPULATION - MAPS.
Borchert, David J. Recent population change in the United States. Minneapolis [1978]. [32] p. : LC Card 80-223350
NYPL [Map Div. 81-43]

UNITED STATES - POPULATION - PUBLIC OPINION.
Baldassare, Mark. The growth dilemma . Berkeley , c1981. p. cm. ISBN 0-520-04302-2 LC Card 81-1449 DDC 304.6/2/0973 19
HB3505 .B298

UNITED STATES - POPULATION, RURAL.
United States. Congress. Senate. Committee on Agriculture, Nutrition, and Forestry. Subcommittee on Rural Development. Accuracy of census taking in small communities and rural areas . Washington , 1980. iii, 32 p. ; LC Card 80-603442 DDC 001.4/33 19
KF26 .A3574 1980a

UNITED STATES - POPULATION - STATISTICS.
1980 census of population. Washington [1982]- p. cm. LC Card 81-607939 DDC 312/.0973 19
HA201 1980 .A132

1980 census of population and housing. Washington [1981]- p. cm. LC Card 81-607944
HA201 1980 .A143

1980 census of population and housing. Washington [1981]- p. cm. LC Card 81-607960 DDC 312/.0973 19
HA201 1980 .A142

1980 census of population and housing. Washington [1981]- p. cm. LC Card 81-607959 DDC 312/.0973 19
HA201 1980 .A147

United States. Port and Intermodal Development, Office of. see United States. Office of Port and Intermodal Development.

United States port development expenditure survey /. United States. Office of Port and Intermodal Development. [Washington] [1980] vi, 45 p. ; LC Card 80-601703 DDC 387.1 19
HE553 .U644 1980

United States. Post Office and Civil Service, Committee on (House) see United States. Congress. House. Committee on Post Office and Civil Service.

United States. Postal Rate Commission .
United States Postal Service. Board of Governors. Action of the Governors under 39 U. S. C.. [Washington] [1977?] 802 p. in various pagings. *NYPL [*XME-9307]*

UNITED STATES. POSTAL RATE COMMISSION - OFFICIALS AND EMPLOYEES.
United States. Congress. Senate. Committee on Governmental Affairs. Nomination to be a member of the Postal Rate Commission and nominations to be governors of the U. S. Postal Service . Washington , 1980. iii, 78 p. ; LC Card 80-603489 DDC 353.0087/3 19
KF26 .G67 1980j

United States Postal Service.
All about letters / produced by the United States Postal Service in cooperation with the National Council of Teachers of English. [Washington, D.C.] : The Service, [c1979] 64 p. : ill. ; 27 cm. Cover title. Bibliography: p. 56-57. LC Card 79-600199 DDC 808.6 19
1. Letter-writing. I. National Council of Teachers of English. II. Title.
BJ2101 .U54 1979

Personnel series, handbook P. 40- ; Oct. 1980- [Washington]
I. Title. *NYPL [Econ. Div.]*

Proceedings, West Virginia University-United States Postal Service workshop . Morgantown [1973?] 50 p. ; LC Card 77-623862 DDC 383/.14/0973 19
HE6497.D35 P76

UNITED STATES POSTAL SERVICE.
United States. Congress. House. Committee on Government Operations. Subcommittee on Government Information and Individual Rights. U. S. Postal Service Plan for nine-digit zip code . Washington , 1980. v, 462 p. : LC Card 81-601386 DDC 383/.145 19
KF27 .G6628 1980a

United States. Congress. House. Committee on Post Office and Civil Service. Subcommittee on Postal Operations and Services. USPS role in registering male citizens . Washington , 1980. iii, 40 p. ; LC Card 80-603591 DDC 355.2/2363/0973 19
KF27 .P6674 1980a

United States. Congress. House Committee on Post Office and Civil Service. Subcommittee on Postal Personnel and Modernization. Electronic message service systems . Washington , 1980. iv, 317 p. : LC Card 80-602988 DDC 384.1/4 19
KF27 .P6677 1980

United States. Congress. House Committee on Post Office and Civil Service. Subcommittee on Postal Personnel and Modernization. Safety and health within U. S. Postal Service . Washington , 1980. vi, 392 p. : LC Card 80-603078 DDC 363.1/193834973 19
KF27 .P6677 1980a

United States. Congress. Senate. Committee on Governmental Affairs. Subcommittee on Energy, Nuclear Proliferation, and Federal Services. Nine-digit zip codes . Washington , 1981. iii, 274 p. : LC Card 81-610629 DDC 383/.145 19
KF26 .G6728 1980d

UNITED STATES. POSTAL SERVICE - APPROPRIATIONS AND EXPENDITURES.
United States. Congress. House. Committee on Post Office and Civil Service. Implications of proposed reductions in Postal Service appropriations . Washington , 1980. iii, 90 p. ; LC Card 80-602977 DDC 383/.4973 19
KF27 .P6 1980

United States. Congress. Senate. Committee on

Appropriations. Subcommittee on the Dept. of the Treasury, U. S. Postal Service, and General Government Appropriations. Treasury, Postal Service, and general government appropriations for fiscal year 1981 . Washington , 1980- v. <1> ;   LC Card 80-603729   DDC 353.0072/236 19
KF26 .A662 1980

United States Postal Service. Board of Governors.
Action of the Governors under 39 U. S. C., Section 3625, and supporting record in the matter of the mail classification schedule, 1976, before the Postal Rate Commission concerning stipulated proposal for zone-rated military mail. [Washington]: The Service, [1977?] 802 p. in various pagings. (Its: Docket. no. MC 76-1-4) Microfiche (neg.) U. S. Govt. Print. Off. 9 sheets. 11 x 15 cm. (SUPTDOCS Y3.P84/4:9/MC76-1-4) Cover title.
1. Postal service - United States - Rates. I. United States. Postal Rate Commission. II. Title: Zone-rated military mail.   **NYPL [*XME-9307]**

Action of the Governors under 39 U. S. C., section 3625, and supporting record in the matter of the mail classification schedule, 1976, before the Postal Rate Commission, concerning elimination of airmail from the domestic mail classification schedule. [Washington]: The Service, [1977] 619 p. in various pagings. (Its: Docket. no. MC76-1) Microfiche (neg.) U. S. Govt. Print. Off. 7 sheets. 11 x 15 cm. (SUPTDOCS Y.3P84/4:9/MC76-1)
1. Air mail service - United States. I. Title: Elimination of airmail from the domestic mail classification schedule.   **NYPL [*XME-9313]**

UNITED STATES POSTAL SERVICE - EMPLOYEES.
United States. Congress. House Committee on Post Office and Civil Service. Subcommittee on Postal Personnel and Modernization. Equal employment opportunity and sexual harassment in the Postal Service . Washington , 1981. iii, 85 p. :   LC Card 81-602045   DDC 353.001/04 19
KF27 .P6677 1980d

United States. Congress. Senate. Committee on Governmental Affairs. Nomination to be a member of the Postal Rate Commission and nominations to be governors of the U. S. Postal Service . Washington , 1980. iii, 78 p. ;   LC Card 80-603489   DDC 353.0087/3 19
KF26 .G67 1980j

United States Postal Service. Research and Engineering Dept. United States Postal Service damage reduction program . Morgantown , 1975. 99 leaves ;   LC Card 77-623861   DDC 383/.14/0973 19
HE6497.D35 U52

United States. President.
Federal advisory committees. United States. Congress. Senate. Committee on Governmental Affairs. Subcommittee on Energy, Nuclear Proliferation, and Federal Services. Federal advisory committees : index to the membership of Federal advisory committees listed in the sixth annual report of the President to the Congress covering calender year 1977 : index / Subcommittee on Energy, Nuclear Proliferation, and Federal Services of the Committee on Governmental Affairs, United States Senate. Washington , 1978. xvii, 1094 p. ;   LC Card 79-601130   DDC 353.09/3/025 19
JK468.C7 U53 1978

United States. President - Powers. see **Executive power - United States.**

United States. President, 1977- (Carter)
The President's environmental program, 1979. Washington, D.C. : [1979] v, 57 p. ;   LC Card 80-148627   DDC 363.7/00973 19
TD171 .P734

Selective Service reform : message from the President of the United States .... Washington : U. S. Govt. Print. Off., 1980. ix, 62 p. ; 24 cm. (House document - 96th Congress, 2d session ; no. 96-265) Added t.p.: Presidential recommendations for Selective Service reform. Bibliography: p. 61.   LC Card 80-601724   DDC 343.73/0122 19
1. United States. Selective Service System. 2. Military service, Compulsory - United States. I. Title. II. Title: Presidential recommendations for Selective Service reform. III. Series: United States. 96th Congress, 2d

session. House. Document , no. 96-265.
KF7263 .A25 1980

State of the Union address and State of the Union message. [Washington? D.C. : s.n.], 1980. 96 p. ; 28 cm. Cover title.   LC Card 80-602059   DDC 353.03/52 19
1. United States - Politics and government - 1977- - Addresses, essays, lectures. I. Title.
J82 .E44 1980

Use of U. S. Armed Forces in attempted rescue of hostages in Iran : communication from the President of the United States transmitting a report on the use of United States Armed Forces in an attempt to rescue the American hostages held in Iran, pursuant to section 4(a) of the War Powers Resolution of 1973 (Public Law 93-148). Washington, D.C. : U. S. Govt. Print. Off., 1980. 2 p. ; 24 cm. (Document - 96th Congress, 2d session, House ; no. 96-303) "April 28, 1980."   LC Card 80-602258   DDC 327.73055 19
1. United States - Foreign relations - Iran. 2. Iran - Foreign relations - United States. 3. Hostages - Iran. 4. Hostages - United States. I. Series: United States. 96th Congress, 2d session, 1980. House Document , no. 96-303. II. Title.
E183.8.I55 U54 1980

United States. President (1977-1981 : Carter)
Export promotion, export disincentives, and U. S. competitiveness . Washington , 1980. iii, 612 p. :   LC Card 80-603880   DDC 382/.63/0973 19
HF1455 .E93

Planning for trilateral scientific and technological cooperation by Egypt, Israel, and the United States . Washington , 1980. vii, 49 p. ;   LC Card 80-603873   DDC 327.1/7 19
Q127.U6 P53

UNITED STATES. PRESIDENT (1981- : REAGAN)
Federal credit activities . [Washington, D.C.] , 1981. xix, 106 p. ;   LC Card 81-601827   DDC 353.0072/6 19
HJ8119 .F39

UNITED STATES. PRESIDENTIAL COMMISSION ON NATIONAL SERVICE.
United States. Congress. House. Committee on Education and Labor. Subcommittee on Select Education. Proposed Presidential Commission on National Service Act of 1980 . Washington , 1980. iii, 69 p. ;   LC Card 80-604048   DDC 344.73/03137 347.3043137 19
KF27 .E373 1980c

United States. Congress. Senate. Committee on Labor and Human Resources. Subcommittee on Child and Human Development. Presidential Commission on National Service and National Commission on Volunteerism . Washington , 1980. v, 606 p. :   LC Card 80-604000   DDC 361.3/7/0973 19
KF26 .L273 1980a

United States. Presidential Commission on World Hunger.
Overcoming world hunger : the challenge ahead : report of the Presidential Commission on World Hunger. Washington, DC : The Commission : for sale by Supt. of Docs., U. S. Govt. Print. Off., [1980] xiii, 251 p. ; 29 cm.   LC Card 80-600057   DDC 338.1/9 19
1. Food supply. 2. Food supply - United States. 3. Hunger. I. Title.
HD9000.5 .U55 1980a

Overcoming world hunger. 1980. United States. Congress. House. Committee on Agriculture. Subcommittee on Family Farms, Rural Development, and Special Studies. Small and medium-sized family farms and Presidential Commission on World Hunger report : hearing before the Subcommittee on Family Farms, Rural Development, and Special Studies of the Committee on Agriculture, House of Representatives, Ninety-sixth Congress, second session, June 25, 1980. Washington , 1980. iii, 167 p. ;   LC Card 80-603660   DDC 338.1/9 19
KF27 .A344 1980b

Technical papers, June 1980. [Washington, D.C.] : Presidential Commission on World Hunger, [1980] ii, 201 p. ; 28 cm. Includes bibliographical references. Cover title.   LC Card 80-603138   DDC 338.1/9 19
1. Food supply - Addresses, essays, lectures. 2.

Hunger - Addresses, essays, lectures. I. Title.
HD9000.5 .U55 1980b

United States. President's Commission for a National Agenda for the Eighties.
A national agenda for the eighties : report of the President's Commission for a National Agenda for the Eighties. Washington : The Commission : For sale by The Supt. of Docs., U. S. G.P.O., 1980. 214 p. ; 23 cm.   LC Card 81-356   DDC 973.926 19
1. United States - Economic policy - 1971-. 2. United States - Social policy. 3. United States - Politics and government - 1945-. 4. United States - Foreign relations - 1945-. I. Title.
HC106.7 .U577 1980

Reports of the President's Commission for a National Agenda for the Eighties.
United States. President's Commission for a National Agenda for the Eighties. Panel on Science and Technology. Science and technology . Washington , 1981. p. cm.   LC Card 80-28290   DDC 306/.4 19
T21 .U56 1981

United States. President's Commission for a National Agenda for the Eighties. Panel on Government and the Advancement of Social Justice: Health, Welfare, Education, and Civil Rights. Government and the advancement of social justice : health, welfare, education, and civil rights in the eighties : report of the Panel on Government and the Advancement of Social Justice: Health, Welfare, Education, and Civil Rights. Washington : President's Commission for a National Agenda for the Eighties : for sale by the Supt. of Docs., U. S. Gov't Print. Off., 1980. 130 p. : ill. ; 23 cm. Includes bibliographical references.   LC Card 81-256   DDC 361.6/1/0973 19
1. United States - Social policy. I. Title.
HN59 .U544 1980

United States. President's Commission for a National Agenda for the Eighties. Panel on Science and Technology. Science and technology : promises and dangers in the eighties : report of the Panel on Science and Technology. Washington : President's Commission for a National Agenda for the Eighties, 1981. p. cm. (Reports of the President's Commission for a National Agenda for the Eighties)   LC Card 80-28290   DDC 306/.4 19
1. Technology and state - United States. 2. Science and state - United States. I. Series: United States. President's Commission for a National Agenda for the Eighties. Reports of the President's Commission for a National Agenda for the Eighties. II. Title.
T21 .U56 1981

United States. President's Commission for a National Agenda for the Eighties. Panel on the Electoral and Democratic Process. The electoral and democratic process in the eighties : report of the Panel on the Electoral and Democratic Process. Washington : President's Commission for a National Agenda for the Eighties : [for sale by the Supt. of Docs., U. S. Gov't. Print. Off.], 1980. 101 p. : ill. ; 23 cm. Includes bibliographies.   LC Card 81-86   DDC 320.973 19
1. United States - Politics and government. I. Title.
JK271 .U56 1981

United States. President's Commission for a National Agenda for the Eighties. Panel on the United States and the World Community. The United States and the world community in the eighties : report of the Panel on the United States and the World Community. Washington, D.C. : President's Commission for a National Agenda for the Eighties : for sale by the Supt. of Docs., U. S. Govt. Print. Off., 1980. 109 p. ; 23 cm.   LC Card 80-28709   DDC 327.73 19
1. United States - Foreign relations - 1945-. I. Title.
E840 .U67 1980

United States. President's Commission on Coal.
Coal, a data book / the President's Commission on Coal. [Washington] : The Commission, 1979. 233 p. : ill. ; 28 cm. Cover title.   LC Card 79-602066
1. Coal - United States. I. Title.
TN800 .U56 1979   **NYPL [JSF 81-169]**

Coal data book / The President's Commission on Coal. Washington, D.C. : The Commission : for sale by the Supt. of Docs., U. S. Govt. Print. Off., [1980] 235 p. : ill. ; 28 cm. "February

BIBLIOGRAPHIC GUIDE

United States. President's Commission on Mental Health. Task

588

1980." ISBN 0-9603806-2-0 LC Card 80-600026
DDC 333.8/22/0973 19
1. Coal - Handbooks, manuals, etc. I. Title.
TN800 .U56 1980

United States. President's Commission on Mental Health. Task Panel on the Elderly. Report of the Task Panel on Mental Health of the Elderly. 1979. Mental health and the elderly . [Washington, D.C.] , 1979. iii, 126 p. ;
LC Card 80-601603 DDC 362.2/0880565 19
RC451.4.A5 M44

United States. President's Commission on Pension Policy.
An interim report / The President's Commission on Pension Policy. Chicago, Ill. : Commerce Clearing House, 1980. 51, [13] p. : ill. ; 23 cm. At head of title: Pension plan guide.
LC Card 80-132555 DDC 331.25/2/0973 19
1. Pensions - United States. 2. Retirement income - United States. I. Title.
HD7106.U5 U644 1980a

An interim report / the President's Commission on Pension Policy. Washington, D.C. (736 Jackson Place, N.W., Washington, D.C. 20006) : The Commission, 1980. 66 p. in various pagings : ill. ; 28 cm. "Second Interim Report"--P. 2. "November 1980." Item 851-J Includes bibliographical references. LC Card 81-600721 DDC 331.25/2/0973 19
1. Old age pensions - United States. 2. Retirement income - United States. I. Title.
HD7106.U5 U644 1981

Torrey, Barbara Boyle. An international comparison of pension systems /. [Washington, D.C.] , 1980. v, 52, [46] p. ; LC Card 80-602549 DDC 331.25/2 19
HD7105.3 .T67

Working papers - President's Commission on Pension Policy.
Meier, Elizabeth L. Retirement income goals /. Washington, D.C. [1980] v, 60 p. ; LC Card 80-602550 DDC 331.25/2/0973 19
HD7106.U5 M37

Torrey, Barbara Boyle. An international comparison of pension systems /. [Washington, D.C.] , 1980. v, 52, [46] p. ; LC Card 80-602549 DDC 331.25/2 19
HD7105.3 .T67

United States. President's Commission on the Accident at Three Mile Island. Public Health and Safety Task Force. Reports of the Public Health and Safety Task Force on public health and safety summary, health physics and dosimetry, radiation health effects, behavioral effects, public health and epidemiology. Washington, D.C. : for sale by the Supt. of Docs., U. S. Govt. Print. Off., [1980] 423 p. : ill. ; 26 cm. "October 1979." Includes bibliographical references. LC Card 80-601717 DDC 363.1/79 19
1. Atomic power-plants - Accidents - Hygienic aspects - Pennsylvania - Three Mile Island. 2. Atomic power-plants - Pennsylvania - Three Mile Island - Accidents. 3. Three Mile Island Nuclear Power Plant, Pa. 4. Radioactive pollution - Pennsylvania - Harrisburg region. 5. Radiation - Dosage. 6. Radiation - Toxicology. I. Title.
RA569 .U4977 1980

United States. President's Commission on the Accident at Three Mile Island. Public's Right to Information Task Force. Report of the Public's Right to Information Task Force / by David M. Rubin ... [et al.]. Washington, D.C. : For sale by the Supt. of Docs., U. S. Govt. Print. Off., [1980] 262 p. ; 27 cm. "October 1979." Includes bibliographical references. LC Card 80-601569 DDC 363.1/79 19
1. Metropolitan Edison Company - Public relations. 2. Three Mile Island Nuclear Power Plant, Pa. 3. Atomic power-plants - Pennsylvania - Accidents. I. Rubin, David M.
HD9698.U54 M478 1980

United States. President's Committee on Employment of the Handicapped.
Resources for the vocational preparation of disabled youth. Washington, D.C. : President's Committee on Employment of the Handicapped : [for sale by the Supt. of Docs., U. S. Govt. Print. Off., 1980] iii, 44 p. ; 28 cm. Cover title. Written by M. L. Hippolitus. LC Card 80-602690 DDC 016.3624/088055 19
1. Handicapped - Employment - United States -

Bibliography. 2. Vocational rehabilitation - United States - Bibliography. I. Hippolitus, Mona L. II. Title.
Z7164.L1 U873 1980 HD7256.U5

A survey of state laws to remove barriers. - Washington : The Committee, 1973. 31 p. ; 26 cm. Microfiche (neg.) 1 sheet. 11 x 15 cm. (NYPL FSN 35,884) Cover title.
1. Handicapped - Law and legislation - United States. 2. Discrimination in employment - Law and legislation - United States. I. Title. **NYPL [*XME-9572]**

United States. President's Committee on Employment of the Handicapped. Women's Committee. Schwab, Lois. Rehabilitation for independent living . Washington, D.C. , 1980. 47 p. ; LC Card 80-601692 DDC 016.3624/048 19
Z7254 .S37 HV3000

United States. President's Committee on Mental Retardation. Friedman, Paul R. Mental retardation and the law . [Washington, D.C.] 1978. 37 p. ; LC Card 79-603796 DDC 346.7301/38/02648 19
KF480.A59 F73

United States. President's Economic Adjustment Committee. Communities in transition : community response to reduced defense activity / the President's Economic Adjustment Committee. Washington : Defense Office of Economic Adjustment, 1977. 56 p. : ill. ; 28 cm. Cover title. LC Card 79-603393
1. Community development - United States - Case studies. I. Title.
HN90.C6 U68 1977 **NYPL [JLF 81-268]**

United States. President's Export Council. The export imperative : report to the President / submitted by the President's Export Council. Washington, D.C. : U. S. Dept. of Commerce, 1980. 2 v. : ill., charts ; 28 cm. "December 1980." Item 851-J LC Card 81-600767 DDC 382/.63/0973 19
1. Foreign trade promotion - United States. 2. United States - Commercial policy. 3. United States - Commerce. I. United States. Dept. of Commerce. II. Title.
HF1455 .U475 1980

United States. President's Inter-Agency Task Force on Deposit Interest Rate Ceilings and Housing credit. see United States. President's Inter-Agency Task Force on Regulation Q.

United States. President's Inter-Agency Task Force on Regulation Q. Deposit interest rate ceilings and housing credit : the report of the President's Inter-Agency Task Force on Regulation Q. [Washington, D.C.] : Dept. of the Treasury : [for sale by the Supt. of Docs., U. S. Govt. Print. Off.], 1979. xii, 266 p. : graphs ; 27 cm. Cover title. Includes bibliographical references. LC Card 79-604165
1. Interest and usury - United States. 2. Mortgage loans - United States. I. Title.
HG1623.U5 U54 1979 **NYPL [JLF 81-361]**

United States. Printing, Joint Committee on. see United States. Congress. Joint Committee on Printing.

United States. Product Liability, Interagency Task Force on. see United States. Interagency Task Force on Product Liability.

United States. Psychopharmacology Research Branch. (Old Catalog form: United States. National institute of mental health. Psychopharmacology research branch) The documentation of clinical psychotropic drug trials; [a workbook and user's guide to understanding and interpreting the data processing and output of the Biometric Laboratory George Washington University, and the Early Clinical Drug Evaluation Unit (ECDEU), NIMH. Edited by Thomas McGlashan] Rockville, Md., National Institute of Mental Health [1973] 2 v. illus. 27 cm. [v. 2:20 x 26 cm.] (DHEW publication. no. (HSM) 72-9308, 73-9309) On cover of v. 2: Early clinical drug evaluation units analyses. Contents. - v. 1. Workbook. - v. 2. Sample output package.
1. Psychopharmacological research. I. McGlashan, Thomas, ed. II. George Washington University, Washington, D. C. Biometric Laboratory. III. Title.
NYPL [JSK 80-137]

UNITED STATES - PUBLIC BUILDINGS.
United States. Congress. House. Committee on Public Works and Transportation. Subcommittee

on Public Buildings and Grounds. Public building needs . Washington , 1980. vi, 430 p. :
LC Card 81-600628 DDC 353.0086/2 19
KF27 .P8964 1980

United States. Congress. Senate. Committee on Environment and Public Works. Architectural barriers in Federal buildings . Washington , 1979. viii, 50 p. : LC Card 80-600819 DDC 353.0086/2 19
KF5765 .A25 1979

United States. Congress. Senate. Committee on Environment and Public Works. Architectural competitions . Washington , 1979. iii, 87 p. :
LC Card 80-600699 DDC 344.73/067251/0262 19
KF26 .E6 1979k

United States. Congress. Senate. Committee on Environment and Public Works. Federal building financing and user charges . Washington , 1979. iii, 39 p. ; LC Card 80-600570 DDC 353.0086/2 19
KF26 .E6 1979l

United States. Congress. Senate. Committee on Environment and Public Works. Leasing of unoccupied space . Washington , 1980. ii, 83 p. ; LC Card 80-601863 DDC 353.0071/23 19
KF26 .E6 1980j

United States. Congress. Senate. Committee on Environment and Public Works. Public buildings proposals . Washington , 1980. iv, 318 p. : LC Card 80-603295 DDC 353.0086/2 19
KF26 .E6 1980g

UNITED STATES - PUBLIC BUILDINGS - ACCESS FOR THE PHYSICALLY HANDICAPPED.
United States. General Accounting Office. Making public buildings accessible to the handicapped . Washington, D.C. [1980] vi, 48 p. ; LC Card 80-602707 DDC 353.0086/2 19
NA2545.P5 U53 1980

UNITED STATES - PUBLIC BUILDINGS - ENERGY CONSERVATION.
United States. Congress. House. Committee on Public Works and Transportation. Subcommittee on Public Buildings and Grounds. Review of Title V of the National energy conservation policy act . Washington , 1980. iv, 240 p. : LC Card 80-601868 DDC 346.7304/67916/0262 19
KF27 .P8964 1979b

UNITED STATES - PUBLIC BUILDINGS - EXHIBITIONS.
Smithsonian Institution. National Collection of Fine Arts. Across the nation . Washington, D.C. , c1980. 35 p. : LC Card 80-51702 DDC 709/.73/0740153 19
N6512 .S6 1980

UNITED STATES - PUBLIC BUILDINGS - HEATING AND VENTILATION.
United States. Congress. House. Committee on Public Works and Transportation. Subcommittee on Public Buildings and Grounds. Review of Title V of the National energy conservation policy act . Washington , 1980. iv, 240 p. : LC Card 80-601868 DDC 346.7304/67916/0262 19
KF27 .P8964 1979b

United States - Public documents. see United States - Government publications.

United States. Public Employee Labor Relations, Division of. see United States. Division of Public Employee Labor Relations.

United States. Public Health Service.
Developing the national health plan . [Washington, D.C.?] , 1980. 2 v. : LC Card 81-601466 DDC 368.4/2/00973 19
HD7102.U4 D4

Pollution of interstate waters: Missouri River; transcript of hearing. [Washington] U. S. Dept. of Health, Education, and Welfare, Public Health Service, 1959. 2 v. illus., maps. 29 cm. Cover title. Contents. - v. 1. [Hearing at] Sioux City, Iowa, March 23-24, 1959. - v. 2. [Hearing at] St. Joseph, Missouri, July 27-30, 1959. LC Card 75-80621
1. Water - Pollution - Missouri River watershed. 2. Sewage disposal - Missouri River watershed. I. Sioux City, Iowa. II. St. Joseph, Mo. III. Title.
NYPL [JSF 81-65]

Publication.
(no. 1860) United States. National Institute of Mental Health. Biometry Branch. Survey

and Reports Section. Patients in public institutions for the mentally retarded, 1967. Chevy Chase, Md. , Washington , 1969. ii, 79 p. ;   LC Card 81-452003   DDC 362.3/850973 19
RC570.5.U6 U65 1969

Wilson, Elaine Blume. At the edge of life . [Bethesda, Md.?] , Washington, D.C. , 1980. 75 p. :   LC Card 80-604128   DDC 616.9/25 19
RC114.5 .W54

United States. Public Health Service. Bureau of Radiological Health. see United States. Bureau of Radiological Health.

United States. Public Health Service. Dept. of Health and Human Services. see United States. Dept. of Health and Human Services.

UNITED STATES. PUBLIC HEALTH SERVICE. DIVISION OF HOSPITALS AND CLINICS.
United States. Congress. House. Committee on Merchant Marine and Fisheries. United States Public Health Service hospitals and clinics . Washington , 1980. iv, 182 p. ;   LC Card 80-603303   DDC 362.1/1/0973 19
KF27 .M4 1979b

United States. Public Health Service. Division of Nursing. (Old Catalog form: United States. Public health service. Nursing. Division of)
Doyle, Timothy C. The impact of health system changes on the nation's requirements for registered nurses in 1985 /. Hyattsville, Md. , Washington , 1978. vi, 71 p. :   LC Card 79-602562
RT86.73 .D68   ***NYPL [JLF 81-185]***

Taylor, Deane B. Systematic nursing assessment. Bethesda, U. S [1974] viii, 164 p.
NYPL [JSF 80-1012]

United States. Public Health Service. Health Resources Administration. see United States. Health Resources Administration.

United States Public Health Service hospitals and clinics . United States. Congress. House. Committee on Merchant Marine and Fisheries. Washington , 1980. iv, 182 p. ;   LC Card 80-603303   DDC 362.1/1/0973 19
KF27 .M4 1979b

United States. Public Health Service. National Cancer Institute. see United States. National Cancer Institute.

United States. Public Health Service. National Center for Health Statistics. see United States. National Center for Health Statistics.

United States. Public Health Service. National Institute for Occupational Safety and Health. see National Institute for Occupational Safety and Health.

United States. Public Health Service. National Institute of Mental Health. see United States. National Institute of Mental Health.

United States. Public Health Service. National Institute on Alcohol Abuse and Akoholism. see National Institute on Alcohol Abuse and Alcoholism.

United States. Public Health Service. National Institutes of Health. see United States. National Institutes of Health.

United States. Public Health Service. Nursing, Division of. see United States. Public Health Service. Division of Nursing.

United States. Public Health Service. Office of the Surgeon General. National Health Service Corps. see United States. National Health Service Corps.

United States. Public Health Services. Health Services Administration. see United States. Health Services Administration.

United States. Public Health Services. National Library of Medicine. see United States. National Library of Medicine.

UNITED STATES - PUBLIC LANDS.
Alaska. Division of Forest, Land, and Water Management. Water Management Section. Federal lands in Alaska and their reserved water rights . Anchorage, Alaska [1979] 222 leaves in various foliations :   LC Card 80-622413   DDC 346.79804/691 347.98064691 19
KFA1646 .A844

United States. Advisory Commission on Intergovernmental Relations. The adequacy of federal compensation to local governments for tax exempt federal lands . Washington , 1978. x, 203 p. :   LC Card 79-601477
HJ4182.A3 U54 1978   ***NYPL [JLF 81-314]***

United States. Congress. Senate. Committee on Energy and Natural Resources. Subcommittee on Energy Resources and Materials Production. Coal leases on BLM lands in New Mexico . Washington , 1980. iii, 211 p. ;   LC Card 80-601117   DDC 333.33/9 19
KF26 .E5543 1979d

United States. Congress. Senate. Committee on Energy and Natural Resources. Subcommittee on Energy Resources and Materials Production. Federal oil and gas leasing act of 1979 . Washington , 1980. iii, 259 p. ;   LC Card 80-601767   DDC 346.7304/6823 19
KF26 .E5543 1979a

United States. Congress. Senate. Committee on Energy and Natural Resources. Subcommittee on Energy Resources and Materials Production. Transfer of certain land and facilities used by the Bureau of Mines to Carnegie-Mellon University . Washington , 1980. iii, 35 p. :   LC Card 80-603896   DDC 343.73/025 347.30325 19
KF26 .E5543 1980f

United States. Congress. Senate. Select Committee on Indian Affairs. Conveyance of Federal land to the Ute Mountain Ute Tribe . Washington, D.C. , 1980. iii, 51 p. :   LC Card 80-602176   DDC 346.7304/3/08997 19
KF26.5 .I4 1980b

United States. General Accounting Office. Actions needed to increase federal onshore oil and gas exploration and development . Washington, D.C. , 1981. xi, 203 p. ;   LC Card 81-601214   DDC 353.0082/388 19
HD9566 .U543 1981

United States. General Accounting Office. Policy needed to guide natural gas regulation on Federal lands . [Washington] , 1979. vii, 71 p. :   LC Card 79-602690   DDC 353.0087/23 19
HD9581.U5 U54 1979

Wyant, William K. Westward in Eden /. Berkeley, Calif. , c1982. p. cm.   ISBN 0-520-04377-4   LC Card 81-7519   DDC 333.1/0973 19
HD205 1982 .W9

UNITED STATES - PUBLIC LANDS - CONGRESSES.
Symposium on Rangeland Policies for the Future, Tucson, Ariz., 1979. Rangeland policies for the future . [Washington, D.C.] , 1979. v, 114 p. ;   LC Card 80-600538   DDC 333.74/0973 19
HD241 .S95 1979

UNITED STATES - PUBLIC LANDS - MANAGEMENT.
United States. Bureau of Land Management. Managing the Nation's public lands . [Washington] [1980] 166 p. ;   LC Card 80-603164   DDC 333.1/0973 19
HD216 .U54 1980

United States - Public property. see United States - Government property.

United States. Public Roads Bureau. see United States. Bureau of Public Roads.

UNITED STATES - PUBLIC WORKS.
Consad Research Corporation. A study of public works investment in the United States /. [Washington] , 1980. 826 p. in various pagings :   LC Card 80-603199   DDC 336.3/9/0973 19
HD3885 .C66 1980

United States. Congress. Joint Economic Committee. Public works as a countercyclical tool . Washington , 1980. iii, 86 p. :   LC Card 80-603664   DDC 339.5/22 19
KF25 .E2 1980f

United States. Public Works Administration. Projects Division. Research Section. Allotments for educational building construction . [Washington] , 1936. 158 leaves ;   LC Card 81-456134
LB3218.A1 U55 1963

United States. Public Works Administration. Projects Division. Research Section.
Allotments for educational building construction : list of projects, by state and county, showing the number of buildings and classrooms with student capacity, the total estimated cost, and amount of allotment with loan and grant portions : authorized under the National industrial recovery act of 1933, Emergency appropriation act, fiscal year 1935, Emergency relief appropriation act of 1935, and the first Deficiency appropriation act, fiscal year, 1936. [Washington] : Federal Emergency Administration of Public Works, Projects Division, Research Section, 1936. 158 leaves ; 23 x 28 cm. Cover title. Tables. "Supplement to 'P.W.A. non-Federal allotments for educational building construction" showing additional allotments and rescissions as of January 15, 1938" (58 leaves) inserted at end.   LC Card 81-456134
1. School buildings - United States - Statistics. 2. School facilities - United States - Statistics. 3. United States - Public works. I. Title.
LB3218.A1 U55 1963

United States. Public Works, Committee on (Senate) see United States. Congress. Senate. Committee on Public Works.

UNITED STATES - PUBLIC WORKS - CONGRESSES.
Conference on Evaluation of the Economic Stimulus Package, Brookings Institution, 1977. Conference report on evaluating the 1977 economic stimulus package /. [Washington] , 1978. iii, 127 p. ;   LC Card 77-603314
HC106.7 .C665 1977   ***NYPL [JLF 81-172]***

UNITED STATES - RACE RELATIONS.
Dovidio, John F. The subtlety of white racism . Newark , 1977. 85 leaves :   LC Card 78-621433   DDC 305.8/96073 19
E185.615 .D67

United States Radiation Policy Council. Progress report and preliminary 1981-83 agenda. Washington, D.C. (Room 3026, New Executive Office Building, 726 Jackson Place, N.W., Washington, D.C., 20503) : U. S. Radiation Policy Council, 1980. 177 p. in various pagings ; 28 cm. "September 30, 1980." Includes bibliographical references. "RPC-80-001."   LC Card 81-600523   DDC 353.0075 19
1. Radiation - Safety measures - Government policy - United States. 2. United States Radiation Policy Council. I. Title.
RA569 .U17 1980

UNITED STATES RADIATION POLICY COUNCIL.
United States Radiation Policy Council. Progress report and preliminary 1981-83 agenda. Washington, D.C. (Room 3026, New Executive Office Building, 726 Jackson Place, N.W., Washington, D.C., 20503) , 1980. 177 p. in various pagings ;   LC Card 81-600523   DDC 353.0075 19
RA569 .U17 1980

United States. Radiological Health, Bureau of. see United States. Bureau of Radiological Health.

United States. Railroad Adjustment Board. see United States. National Railroad Adjustment Board.

United States. Railroad Retirement Board.
Handbook on railroad retirement and unemployment insurance systems. [Chicago?] 1974. 1 v. (various pagings) 26 cm. Loose-leaf. Added title page: Informational conference handbook, 1974.   LC Card 78-3501
1. Railroads - United States - Pensions. I. Title. II. Title: Informational conference handbook, 1974.
NYPL [JLF 80-1047]

Monthly benefit statistics. Mar. 1968- Chicago [etc.] 28-31 cm. "Railroad retirement and unemployment insurance programs." Prepared by the board's Bureau of Research.   LC Card 76-646293
1. Railroads - United States - Pensions - Statistics - Periodicals. I. Title.   ***NYPL [JLN 80-91]***

UNITED STATES RAILWAY ASSOCIATION.
United States. Congress. Senate. Committee on Commerce, Science, and Transportation. Subcommittee on Surface Transportation. USRA--nomination, authorization, Conrail plant rationalization, and employee protection program . Washington , 1980. iv, 125 p. ;   LC Card 80-602781   DDC 343.73/095 19
KF26 .C698 1980c

UNITED STATES RAILWAY ASSOCIATION - APPROPRIATIONS AND EXPENDITURES.

United States. Congress. House. Committee on Interstate and Foreign Commerce. Subcommittee on Transportation and Commerce. Reauthorization for the U. S. Railway Association for fiscal year 1981 . Washington , 1980. iii, 73 p. ; LC Card 80-603452 DDC 353.0072/236875 19
KF27 .I5589 1980d

UNITED STATES. RAPID DEPLOYMENT FORCE.
United States. Congress. House. Committee on the Budget. Military readiness and the Rapid Deployment Joint Task Force (RDJTF) . Washington , 1980. iii, 70 p. ; LC Card 80-604107 DDC 355.3/5 19
KF27 .B8 1980d

United States. Reclamation Service. see United States. Bureau of Reclamation.

United States. Regulation Q, President's Inter-Agency Task Force on. see United States. President's Inter-Agency Task Force on Regulation Q.

United States. Regulation Q Task Force. see United States. President's Inter-Agency Task Force on Regulation Q.

United States. Regulatory Council.
The Automobile calendar . [Washington, D.C.] , 1981. ii, 392 p. ; LC Card 81-601095 DDC 343.73/078629222/02636 347.037862922202636 19
KF2204.6 1981

Regulatory reform highlights : an inventory of initiatives, 1978-1980 / United States Regulatory Council. [Washington, D.C.] : The Council, [1980] xi, 172 p. ; 28 cm. LC Card 80-602350 DDC 353.09/3 19
1. Trade regulation - United States. 2. Administrative agencies - United States. I. Title.
KF1600 .A877

United States. Rehabilitation and Social Service. see United States. Social and Rehabilitation Service.

United States. Rehabilitation Services Administration.
American rehabilitation. v. 1- ; Sept./Oct. 1975- [Washington] LC Card 75-648421
NYPL [JLM 80-958]

Program and financial plan for state vocational rehabilitation agencies. Washington. 26 cm. Annual Cover title, 1979- : State vocational rehabilitation agency: program and financial plan. LC Card 78-645637
1. Vocational rehabilitation - United States - States - Periodicals. 2. Vocational rehabilitation - United States - States - Finance - Periodicals. I. United States. Rehabilitation Services Administration. State vocational rehabilitation agency: program and financial plan. II. Title.
NYPL [JLM 80-870]

Rehabilitation service series. 63/32-69/13 (incomplete) Washington, U. S. Dept. of Health, Education, and Welfare, Social and Rehabilitation Service, Rehabilitation Services Administration, [1968-69] 27 cm. Issues 69-4, 69-11, 69-13, 1968, comprise reports of the fifth and sixth Institute on Rehabilitation Services, May 22, 1967-Mar 22, 1968. Superseded by its Information memorandum (not in the library)
1. Vocational rehabilitation - United States - Collected works. I. Institute on Rehabilitation Services. [Report]. II. Title.
NYPL [JLM 81-302]

State vocational rehabilitation agency: program and financial plan. United States. Rehabilitation Services Administration. Program and financial plan for state vocational rehabilitation agencies. Washington. LC Card 78-645637
NYPL [JLM 80-870]

UNITED STATES - RELATIONS (GENERAL) WITH CANADA.
United States. Congress. Senate. Committee on Finance. Subcommittee on International Trade. North American economic interdependence . Washington , 1979. iii, 110 p. ; LC Card 80-601405 DDC 337.1/7 19
KF26 .F554 1979j

UNITED STATES - RELATIONS (GENERAL) WITH LATIN AMERICA.
United States. Congress. House. Special Study Mission to Venezuela, Barbados, Brazil, and Costa Rica. Assessment of trends and

conditions in the Inter-American region . Washington , 1980. vii, 33 p. ; LC Card 80-602265 DDC 327.7308 19
F1418 .U44 1980

UNITED STATES - RELATIONS (GENERAL) WITH MEXICO.
United States. Congress. House. Committee on Science and Technology. Subcommittee on Science, Research, and Technology. United States-Mexico scientific and technological cooperation . Washington , 1979. iii, 289 p. : LC Card 80-602192 DDC 338.9 19
KF27 .S399 1979k

United States. Congress. House. Special Study Mission to Mexico City. United States--Mexican relations and the energy crisis . Washington , 1980. vii, 17 p. ; LC Card 80-602869 DDC 327.73072 19
E183.8.M6 U36 1980

United States. Congress. Senate. Committee on Finance. Subcommittee on International Trade. North American economic interdependence . Washington , 1979. iii, 110 p. ; LC Card 80-601405 DDC 337.1/7 19
KF26 .F554 1979j

UNITED STATES - RELATIONS (GENERAL) WITH RUSSIA.
United States. Congress. House. Committee on Foreign Affairs. Subcommittee on International Security and Scientific Affairs. United States scientific and technical exchanges with the Soviet Union . Washington , 1980. iii, 57 p. ; LC Card 80-602821 DDC 327.73047 19
KF27 .F64825 1980c

UNITED STATES - RELATIONS (GENERAL) WITH SUB-SAHARAN AFRICA.
Clark, G. Edward (Gilbert Edward), 1917- Sub-Saharan Africa and the United States . [Washington, D.C.] , 1980. 46 p., [1] leaf of plates : LC Card 80-603396 DDC 967 19
DT353.5.U6 C55 1980

UNITED STATES - RELATIONS (MILITARY) WITH AFRICA.
United States. Congress. House. Committee on Armed Services. Delegation to Africa. Report of the delegation to Africa . Washington , 1980. iii, 29 p. ; LC Card 80-601793 DDC 355/.03306 19
DT30 .U58 1980

UNITED STATES - RELATIONS (MILITARY) WITH ASIA.
United States. Congress. House. Special Study Mission to Asia. Asian security environment, 1980 . Washington , 1980. vii, 96 p. ; LC Card 80-602264 DDC 355/.03305 19
DS33.4.U6 U5 1980

UNITED STATES - RELATIONS (MILITARY) WITH MOROCCO.
United States. Congress. House. Study Mission to Morocco, the Western Sahara, Mauritania, Algeria, Liberia, Spain, and France. Arms for Morocco? . Washington , 1979. viii, 26 p. : LC Card 80-601042 DDC 355/.032/64 19
E183.8.M8 U54 1979

UNITED STATES - RELIGION.
Kirschner Associates. Religious requirements and practices of certain selected groups . [Washington] , 1980. vi, 200 p. in various pagings ; LC Card 80-602248 DDC 291/.0973 19
BL2530.U6 K57 1980

United States. Reserve Officers' Training Corps. see United States. Army. Reserve Officers' Training Corps.

United States. Resource Conservation Committee. Choices for conservation : Resource Conservation Committee final report to the President and Congress, July, 1979. [Washington, D.C.] : The Committee ; [Cincinnati, OH : available from Solid Waste Information, U. S. Environmental Protection Agency, 1980] xxii, 130 p. ; 23 cm. "Resource Conservation Committee reports and records": p. 122-129. LC Card 80-601284 DDC 333.7/16/0973 19
1. Environmental policy - United States. I. Title.
HC110.E5 U6 1980

United States - Revenue. see Tariff - United States; Taxation - United States.

United States. Review of the National Policy toward gambling, Commission on the. see

United States. Commission on the Review of the National Policy toward Gambling.

United States. Rivers and Harbors, Board of Engineers for. see United States. Board of Engineers for Rivers and Harbors.

United States. Rocky Mountain Forest and Range Experiment Station, Fort Collins, Colo.
USDA Forest Service general technical report RM.
(65) Mitigation Symposium, Colorado State University, 1979. The Mitigation Symposium . Fort Collins, Colo , 1979. xi, 684 p. : LC Card 80-602560 DDC 639.9/2/0973 19
SK361 .M57 1979

United States. Rules and Administration, Committee on (Senate) see United States. Congress. Senate. Committee on Rules and Administration.

UNITED STATES - RURAL CONDITIONS.
New directions in rural preservation. Washington, D.C. [1980?] xi, 115 p. : LC Card 81-601043 DDC 307.7/2/0973 19
HN59 .N398

Sargent, Merle J. Rural health and rural health care, U. S. and Idaho /. Moscow , 1980. 43, [11] p. : LC Card 80-622141 DDC 362.1/0425 19
RA771.5 .S27

United States. Rural Development Service. How USDA can help you involve youth in community development. Washington: U. S. Govt. Print. Off., 1973. 15 p.: ill.; 24 cm. Microfiche (neg.) 1 sheet. 11 x 15 cm. (NYPL FSN 35,309) "Program aid no. 1042."
1. Rural youth. 2. Youth. I. Title.
*NYPL [*XME-9362]*

UNITED STATES. RURAL ELECTRIFICATION ADMINISTRATION.
United States. Congress. Senate. Committee on Agriculture, Nutrition, and Forestry. Subcommittee on Agricultural Credit and Rural Electrification. REA and energy conservation . Washington , 1980. iii, 113 p. ; LC Card 81-600598 DDC 334/.68136362 19
KF26 .A3533 1980a

UNITED STATES. RURAL TRANSPORTATION ADVISORY TASK FORCE.
United States. Congress. House. Committee on Agriculture. Subcommittee on Family Farms, Rural Development, and Special Studies. Agricultural subterminal facilities act of 1979 and Rural Transportation Advisory Task Force report . Washington , 1980. iii, 89 p. : LC Card 80-603304 DDC 343.73/0851 19
KF27 .A344 1980

United States S. New Jersey Battleship Commission (N.J.) Report of the U. S.S. New Jersey Battleship Commission (created by JR-6 of 1975). [Trenton, N.J.? : The Commission, 1977?] 28, 4 p. ; 28 cm. LC Card 80-620534 DDC 359.3/252 19
1. New Jersey (Battleship, BB-62). I. Title.
VA65.N5 U22 1977

United States. Safety and Design Issue, Interagency Task Force on. see United States. Interagency Task Force on Safety and Design Issue.

United States. St. Elizabeths Hospital.
United States. National Archives and Records Service. Preliminary inventory of the records of St. Elizabeths Hospital . Washington , 1981. p. cm. LC Card 81-607004 DDC 016.973 s 016.3622/1/09753 19
CD3026 .A32 no. 193 Z6675.H75 RC445.W19W37

UNITED STATES. ST. ELIZABETHS HOSPITAL - ARCHIVES - CATALOGS.
United States. National Archives and Records Service. Preliminary inventory of the records of St. Elizabeths Hospital . Washington , 1981. p. cm. LC Card 81-607004 DDC 016.973 s 016.3622/1/09753 19
CD3026 .A32 no. 193 Z6675.H75 RC445.W19W37

United States. Saint Elizabeths Hospital, Washington, D. C. see Saint Elizabeths Hospital, Washington, D. C.

United States savings bonds program : a study

prepared for the Committee on Ways and Means, U. S. House of Representatives / by the Department of the Treasury. [Washington, D.C. : U. S. Dept. of the Treasury], 1981. 2, iii,90 p. : ill.,charts ; 28 cm. Cover title. "January 1981." Item 925 LC Card 81-601928 DDC 332.63/23 19
1. Bonds - United States. I. United States. Dept. of the Treasury. II. United States. Congress. House. Committee on Ways and Means.
HG4936 .U54

United States. Science and Education Administration.
Extension review. v. 49, no. 2- ; Mar./Apr. 1978- [Washington] LC Card 78-645572
NYPL [Econ. Div.]

Salley, E. Jean. Checklist of types in the U. S. national parasite collection /. [Washington] , 1978. iv, 233 p. ; LC Card 78-602796 DDC 591.52/49/0740153 19
QL757 .S23

Soybeans as human food . [Washington] , 1979. iv, 54 p. : LC Card 79-603033 DDC 641.3/5655 19
TX558.S7 S69 1979b

Synectics Corporation. The Expanded Food and Nutrition Education Program . [Washington] [1979] xi, 131 p. : LC Card 79-601895 DDC 641.1/07/073 19
TX364 .S96 1979

United States. Science and Education Administration. Extension. Evaluation of economic and social consequences of cooperative extension programs / United States, Department of Agriculture, Science and Education Administration-Extension. Washington, D.C. : The Administration : for sale by the Supt. of Docs., U. S. Govt. Print. Off., 1980. xiii, 188 p. : graphs ; 28 cm. "January 1980." Includes bibliographical references. LC Card 80-601705 DDC 378/.104/0973 19
1. Non-formal education - Economic aspects - United States - Evaluation. 2. Non-formal education - Social aspects - United States - Evaluation. 3. Agricultural extension work - United States - Evaluation. I. Title.
LC45.4 .U54 1980

United States. Science and Education Administration. Federal Research. Rogers, Charlie Ellic, 1938- Selected bibliography of insect pests of sunflower /. College Station, Tex. [Beltsville, Md.] [1979] 41 p. ; LC Card 80-621131 DDC 016.6338/5 19
Z5354.P3 S867 SB608.S92

United States. Science and Education Administration. Southern Regional Research Center. Publications and patents with abstracts. July/Dec. 1970- [New Orleans, La.]
NYPL [*VA 80-314]

United States. Science, Engineering, and Technology, Federal Coordinating Council for. see United States. Federal Coordinating Council for Science, Engineering, and Technology.

United States. Science Information Service, Office of. see United States. National Science Foundation. Office of Science Information Service.

United States scientific and technical exchanges with the Soviet Union . United States. Congress. House. Committee on Foreign Affairs. Subcommittee on International Security and Scientific Affairs. Washington , 1980. iii, 57 p. ; LC Card 80-602821 DDC 327.73047 19
KF27 .F64825 1980c

United States. Scientific Laboratory, Los Alamos, N. M. Hamilton, Michael S. Environmental, legal, and political constraints on power plant siting in the Southwestern United States . Fort Collins, Colo. , 1980. viii, 175 p. : LC Card 80-67305 DDC 338.6/042 19
TK1193.U5 H35

United States. Scientific Laboratory, Los Alamos, N. M. Office of Public Relations. see United States. Scientific Laboratory, Los Alamos, N. M.

United States. Scientific Laboratory, Los Alamos, N. M. Personnel Dept. see United States. Scientific Laboratory, Los Alamos, N. M.

United States. Scientific Laboratory, Los Alamos, N. M. Wage and Salary Dept. see United

States. Scientific Laboratory, Los Alamos, N. M.

United States. Secretary of Transportation. see United States. Dept. of Transportation.

United States. Securities and Exchange Commission.
Report of the Securities and Exchange Commission on beneficial ownership reporting requirements pursuant to section 13(h) of the Securities exchange act of 1934. Washington : U. S. Govt. Print. Off., 1980. viii, 242 p. ; 24 cm. At head of title: 96th Congress, 2d session. Committee print. "Printed for the use of the Committee on Banking, Housing, and Urban Affairs, United States Senate." Includes bibliographical references. LC Card 80-602870 DDC 346.73/0456 19
1. Stock ownership - United States. 2. Disclosure of information (Securities law) - United States. 3. Shareholders - Legal status, laws, etc. - United States. I. United States. Congress. Senate. Committee on Banking, Housing and Urban Affairs. II. Title.
KF1448 .A88

SEC monthly statistical review. v. 39, no. 8- ; Aug. 1980- [Washington] For earlier file, whose numbering it continues, see its: Statistical bulletin.
I. Title. ***NYPL [Econ. Div.]***

UNITED STATES. SECURITIES AND EXCHANGE COMMISSION.
United States. Congress. House. Committee on Government Operations. Commerce, Consumer, and Monetary Affairs Subcommittee. Silver prices and the adequacy of Federal actions in the marketplace, 1979-80 . Washington , 1980. v, 1203 p. : LC Card 80-603499 DDC 332.63/28 19
KF27 .G634 1980c

UNITED STATES. SECURITIES AND EXCHANGE COMMISSION - APPROPRIATIONS AND EXPENDITURES.
United States. Congress. House. Committee on Interstate and Foreign Commerce. Subcommittee on Consumer Protection and Finance. Securities and Exchange Commission authorizations for fiscal years 1981, 1982, and 1983 . Washington , 1980. iii, 158 p. : LC Card 80-603892 DDC 353.0072/2368258 19
KF27 .I554 1980b

United States. Congress. Senate. Committee on Banking, Housing and Urban Affairs. Subcommittee on Securities. Authorization request for the Securities and Exchange Commission . Washington , 1980. iii, 163 p. : LC Card 80-602805 DDC 346.73/0666 19
KF26 .B3954 1980

United States. Securities and Exchange Commission. Directorate of Economic and Policy Research.
Bank participation in municipal revenue board underwriting : impact on securities industry revenues / Securities and Exchange Commission, Directorate of Economic and Policy Research. [Washington, D.C.] : The Directorate, [1979] 18, 8, [7] leaves ; 28 cm. Cover title. "October 9, 1979." Includes bibliographical references. LC Card 80-602682 DDC 332.63/233/0973 19
I. Title.
HG4952 .U55 1979

Staff report on the securities industry in 1977 / Directorate of Economic and Policy Research. [Washington] : The Directorate, [1978] 21, [30] leaves : graphs ; 28 cm. Cover title. "May 22, 1978." Tables. LC Card 80-602626 DDC 332.6/2/0973 19
1. Brokers - United States. 2. Stock-exchange - United States. 3. Securities - United States. I. Title.
HG4910 .U55 1978

United States. Securities and Exchange Commission. Division of Corporation Finance. Staff report on corporate accountability : a re-examination of rules relating to shareholder communications, shareholder participation in the corporate electoral process, and corporate governance generally / Division of Corporation Finance, Securities and Exchange Commission. Washington : U. S.G.P.O., 1980. 782 p. ; 24 cm. "September 4, 1980." "Prepared for the use of the Committee on Banking, Housing, and Urban Affairs, United States Senate." At head of title: 96th Congress, 2d session. Committee print. LC Card 80-603877

DDC 346.73/0666 347.306666 19
1. Stockholders - Legal status, laws, etc. - United States. 2. Stockholders' voting - United States. I. United States. Congress. Senate. Committee on Banking, Housing and Urban Affairs. II. Title.
KF1448 .A8837

United States. Securities and Exchange Commission. Office of Reports and Information Services. Classification, assets, and location of registered investment companies under the Investment company act of 1940. 27 cm. Annual. Report year ends September 30. Continues: United States. Securities and Exchange Commission. Division of corporate Regulation. Classification, assets, and location of registered investment companies under the Investment company act of 1940. (Not in the library). Cover title. LC Card 79-643058
1. Investment trusts - United States - Directories. I. Title. ***NYPL [JLM 80-722]***

UNITED STATES. SECURITIES AND EXCHANGE COMMISSION - OFFICIALS AND EMPLOYEES.
United States. Congress. Senate. Committee on Banking, Housing and Urban Affairs. Nomination of Barbara S. Thomas . Washington , 1980. ii, 61 p. ; LC Card 80-603679 DDC 353.0082/58 19
KF26 .B39 1980s

United States. Congress. Senate. Committee on Banking, Housing and Urban Affairs. Nomination of John S. R. Shad . Washington , 1981. ii, 34 p. ; LC Card 81-601937 DDC 353.0082/58 19
KF26 .B39 1981h

United States. Congress. Senate. Committee on Banking, Housing and Urban Affairs. Nominations of Herta Lande Seidman and Stephen J. Friedman . Washington , 1980. iii, 53 p. : LC Card 80-602446 DDC 353.82 19
KF26 .B39 1980c

United States. Securities and Exchange Commission. Reports and Information Services, Office of. see United States. Securities and Exchange Commission. Office of Reports and Information Services.

United States. Select Commission on Immigration and Refugee Policy.
Masanz, Sharon D. History of the Immigration and Naturalizaton Service . Washington , 1980 [i.e. 1981] vii, 91 p. : LC Card 81-600999 DDC 353.0081/7 19
JV6483 .M3

Semiannual report to Congress. 1st- ; Mar. 1980- Washington. ***NYPL [Econ. Div.]***

Semiannual report to Congress / Select Commission on Immigration and Refugee Policy. Washington : U. S. Govt. Print. Off., 1980. v, 74 p. ; 24 cm. At head of title: 96th Congress, 2d session. Joint committee print. "Printed for the use of Committees on the Judiciary, United States Senate and House of Representatives, Ninety-sixth Congress, second session." "March 1980." LC Card 80-603270 DDC 353.0081/7 19
1. United States - Emmigration and immigration. 2. Refugees - United States. I. United States. Congress. Senate. Committee on the Judiciary. II. United States. Congress. House. Committee on the Judiciary.
JV6481 1980 .S44

UNITED STATES. SELECTIVE SERVICE SYSTEM.
United States. President, 1977- (Carter) Selective Service reform . Washington , 1980. ix, 62 p. ; LC Card 80-601724 DDC 343.73/0122 19
KF7263 .A25 1980

United States. Senate. Committee on Veterans' Affairs. United States. Veterans Administration. Study of former prisoners of war . Washington , 1980. v, 181 p. ; LC Card 80-602576 DDC 35.1/156/0973 19
UB369 .U57 1980

United States - Shipping. see Shipping - United States.

United States. Small Business Administration. SMS Associates. A directory of Federal Government business assistance programs for women business owners . [Washington, D.C.] [1980] iv, 71 p. ; LC Card 80-602878 DDC 353.0082/048 19
HD2346.U5 S17 1980

Sullivan, A. Charlene. Credit and collections for small stores /. Washington, D.C., 1980. v, 67 p. : LC Card 81-600882 DDC 658.8/8 19
HD30 .U5 no. 43 HG3751

UNITED STATES. SMALL BUSINESS ADMINISTRATION.
United States. Congress. House. Committee on Small Business. Subcommittee on General Oversight and Minority Enterprise. SBA proposed size standards. Washington, 1980-
v. ; LC Card 80-603083 DDC 338.6/42/0973 19
KF27 .S64 1980b

United States. Congress. House. Committee on Small Business. Subcommittee on Minority Enterprise and General Oversight. H.R. 2377, H.R. 2379, and Small Business Administration activities. Washington, 1977. iv, 188 p. ; LC Card 77-604012
KF27 .S65 1977c

United States. Congress. House. Committee on Veterans' Affairs. Subcommittee on Special Investigations. Small Business Administration loans to veterans. Washington, 1981. iii, 223 p. ; LC Card 81-600813 DDC 353.0082/048045 19
KF27 .V458 1980c

United States. Congress. Senate. Committee on Governmental Affairs. Subcommittee on Federal Spending Practices and Open Government. Continued oversight of the Small Business Association's [i.e. Administration's] 8 (a) program. Washington, 1980. iii, 105 p. ;
LC Card 80-603071 DDC 353.0082/048 19
KF26 .G6732 1979j

United States. Congress. Senate. Select Committee on Small Business. SBA surety bond guarantee program. Washington, 1980 [i.e. 1981] iv, 320 p. : LC Card 81-601160 DDC 353.0082/048045 19
KF26.5 .S6 1980w

United States. Congress. Senate. Select Committee on Small Business. Small Business Administration 8(a) pilot program. Washington, 1981. iii, 84 p. ; LC Card 81-601381 DDC 353.0071/2 19
KF26.5 .S6 1981b

United States. Congress. Senate. Select Committee on Small Business. Small Business Administration's veterans' assistance programs. Washington, 1980. iii, 97 p. ; LC Card 80-603678 DDC 355.1/15 19
KF26.5 .S6 1980m

United States. Congress. Senate. Select Committee on Small Business. Subcommittee on Government Procurement. S. 2873, to provide SBA loans to small businesses in the communications industry. Washington, 1980. iii, 52 p. ; LC Card 80-603716 DDC 346.73/0652 347.3016652 19
KF26.5 .S625 1980

United States. Congress. Senate. Select Committee on Small Business. Subcommittee on Government Regulation and Paperwork. Oversight of SBA's management assistance programs. Washington, 1980. iii, 201 p. : LC Card 80-602431 DDC 353.0082/048 19
KF26.5 .S629 1979b

UNITED STATES. SMALL BUSINESS ADMINISTRATION - APPROPRIATIONS AND EXPENDITURES.
United States. Congress. Senate. Committee on Appropriations. Subcommittee on Departments of State, Justice, and Commerce, the Judiciary, and Related Agencies. Disaster loan fund budget amendment. Washington, 1980. ii, 26 p. ; LC Card 80-603494 DDC 353.0082/33045 19
KF26 .A659 1980a

United States. Congress. Senate. Select Committee on Small Business. To consider and report to the Senate Budget Committee recommendations for Small Business Administration programs. Washington, 1981. iii, 53 p. ; LC Card 81-601795 DDC 353.0082/048 19
KF26.5 .S6 1981

United States. Small Business Administration. Chief Counsel for Advocacy, Office of the. see United States. Small Business Administration. Office of the Chief Counsel for Advocacy.

United States. Small Business Administration. Office of the Chief Counsel for Advocacy.
Directory of state small business programs. Washington.
NYPL [*R-Econ. 81-178 & JLM 81-180]

Small business & innovation : a report of an SBA Office of Advocacy Task Force / Office of the Chief Counsel for Advocacy, U. S. Small Business Administration. [Washington] : The Office, 1979. 130 p. in various pagings : graphs ; 28 cm. Bibliography: p. 53-54. LC Card 79-603309
1. Small business - United States. 2. Technological innovations - United States. I. Title.
HD2346.U5 U57 1979   NYPL [JLF 81-384]

UNITED STATES. SMALL BUSINESS ADMINISTRATION - OFFICIALS AND EMPLOYEES.
United States. Congress. Senate. Select Committee on Small Business. Nomination of Michael Cardenas to be administrator of the Small Business Administration. Washington, 1981. iii, 64 p. ; LC Card 81-602263 DDC 353.0082/048 19
KF26.5 .S6 1981c

United States. Small Business Administration. Paperwork Measurement and Reduction Program. Government paperwork and small business : problems and solutions / U. S. Small Business Administration, Office of Chief Counsel for Advocacy, Paperwork Measurement and Reduction Program. [Washington] : The Program, [1980?] iv, 86 p. : ill. ; 28 cm. Cover title. "December 1979." LC Card 80-601425 DDC 353.0082/048 19
1. Small business - United States. 2. Government paperwork - United States. 3. Industry and state - United States. I. Title.
HD2346.U5 U57 1980

UNITED STATES. SMALL BUSINESS ADMINISTRATION - RECORDS AND CORRESPONDENCE.
United States. Congress. Senate. Select Committee on Small Business. SBA' paperwork measurement and reduction program. Washington, 1980. iii, 153 p. : LC Card 80-603688 DDC 353.0082/048 19
KF26.5 .S6 1980n

United States. Small Business, Committee on (Senate) see United States. Congress. Senate. Select Committee on Small Business.

United States. Social and Rehabilitation Service. Administration on Aging. see United States. Administration on Aging.

United States. Social and Rehabilitation Service. Assistance Payments Administration. Child support payments control, Massachusetts and Washington. [Washington] : U. S. Dept. of Health, Education, and Welfare, Social and Rehabilitation Service, Assistance Payments Administration, [1974] 100 p. : forms ; 27 cm. (Its: How-they-do-it series) On cover: "Illustrations of practice in the administration of AFDC."
1. Child welfare. - Massachusetts. 2. Child welfare - Washington (State). 3. Public welfare - Massachusetts. I. Title.   *NYPL [JLF 80-1363]*

United States. Social and Rehabilitation Service. Office of Quality Control Management. Training for federal quality control review / U. S. Department of Health, Education and Welfare, Social and Rehabilitation Service, Office of Quality Control Management. Washington D. C. : [s. n.], 1974. 167 p. ; 28 cm. "SRS 74-04007"
1. Public welfare administration - Quality control. I. Title.   *NYPL [JLF 81-28]*

United States. Social and Rehabilitation Service. Quality Control Management, Office of. see United States. Social and Rehabilitation Service. Office of Quality Control Management.

United States. Social and Rehabilitation Service. Rehabilitation Services Administration. see United States. Rehabilitation Services Administration.

United States - Social conditions. Here are entered works on the Social history or conditions of the United States. Works on the discipline of sociology in the United States are entered under Sociology - United States.

UNITED STATES - SOCIAL CONDITIONS - 1865-1918.
Fellman, Anita Clair. Making sense of self. Philadelphia, 1981. p. cm. ISBN 0-8122-7810-0 LC Card 81-51141 DDC 613/.07/073 19
RA440.3.U5 F43

UNITED STATES - SOCIAL CONDITIONS - 1960- - ADDRESSES, ESSAYS, LECTURES.
Nonmetropolitan America in transition /. Chapel Hill, c1981. p. cm. ISBN 0-8078-1490-3 LC Card 81-3511 DDC 307.7/2/0973 19
HT123 .N65

UNITED STATES - SOCIAL CONDITIONS - 1960- - PUBLIC OPINION.
Campbell, Angus, 1910- The sense of well-being in America. New York, c1981. xiii, 263 p. ; ISBN 0-07-009683-X LC Card 80-14379
HN59 .C29   NYPL [JLE 81-367]

UNITED STATES - SOCIAL CONDITIONS - ADDRESSES, ESSAYS, LECTURES.
Reflections of America. Washington, D.C. [1981] p. cm. LC Card 80-607843 DDC 317.3 19
HC103 .R43

UNITED STATES - SOCIAL LIFE AND CUSTOMS - 1865-1918.
First person America /. New York, 1980. xxv, 287 p. : ISBN 0-394-41397-0 : LC Card 80-7660
E169 .56   NYPL [ILH 81-601]

Kipling, Rudyard, 1865-1936. American notes /. Norman, c1981. p. cm. ISBN 0-8061-1682-X LC Card 81-40289 DDC 917.3/0486 19
E168 .K56 1981

UNITED STATES - SOCIAL LIFE AND CUSTOMS - 1865-1918 - ADDRESSES, ESSAYS, LECTURES.
Plain folk. Urbana, c1981. p. cm. ISBN 0-252-00884-7 LC Card 81-3026 DDC 973.91/1/0922 B 19
E168 .P7

UNITED STATES - SOCIAL LIFE AND CUSTOMS - 20TH CENTURY - ADDRESSES, ESSAYS, LECTURES.
Rituals and ceremonies in popular culture /. Bowling Green, Ohio, c1980. 349 p. : ISBN 0-87972-160-X LC Card 80-83188 DDC 306/.4 19
E169.12 .R55

UNITED STATES - SOCIAL LIFE AND CUSTOMS - 1918-1945.
First person America /. New York, 1980. xxv, 287 p. : ISBN 0-394-41397-0 : LC Card 80-7660
E169 .56   NYPL [ILH 81-601]

UNITED STATES - SOCIAL POLICY.
United States. Congress. House. Committee on the Budget. Task Force on Human Resources and Block Grants. Human resources programs and block grants. Washington, 1981. 2 v. : LC Card 81-602053 DDC 361.6/1/0973 19
KF27 .B85 1981

United States. Panel on the Quality of American Life. The quality of American life in the eighties. Washington, 1980. 140 p. : LC Card 81-281 DDC 361.6/1/0973 19
HN60 .U545 1980

United States. President's Commission for a National Agenda for the Eighties. A national agenda for the eighties. Washington, 1980. 214 p. ; LC Card 81-356 DDC 973.926 19
HC106.7 .U577 1980

United States. President's Commission for a National Agenda for the Eighties. Panel on Government and the Advancement of Social Justice: Health, Welfare, Education, and Civil Rights. Government and the advancement of social justice. Washington, 1980. 130 p. : LC Card 81-256 DDC 361.6/1/0973 19
HN59 .U544 1980

UNITED STATES - SOCIAL POLICY - CONGRESSES.
Extending the human life span. [Chicago], Washington [1977] v, 70 p. : LC Card 77-604795
HQ1064.U5 E9   NYPL [*XME-9403]

United States. Social Security Administration. (Old Catalog form: United States. Social Security board)
How to see. Washington, D. C., U. S. Govt. Print. Off.] 1973. 71 p. illus. 21 cm. (United States. Dept. of Health, Education and Welfare. DHEW

publication (SSA) no. 73-10063)

I. Title. **NYPL** *[JLD 80-3345]*

SSA publication .
(no. 13-11727) United States. Social Security Administration. Office of Research and Statistics. Income & resources of the aged /. [Washington, D.C.] [1980] 35 p. : LC Card 80-600019

HD7106.U5 U65 1980

United States. Social Security Administration. Actuary, Division of the. see United States. Social Security Administration. Division of the Actuary.

United States. Social Security Administration. Actuary, Office of the. see United States. Social Security Administration. Office of the Actuary.

UNITED STATES. SOCIAL SECURITY ADMINISTRATION - APPROPRIATIONS AND EXPENDITURES.
United States. Congress. House. Committee on Appropriations. Subcommittee on Departments of Labor, and Health, Education, and Welfare, and Related Agencies. Departments of Labor and Health, Education, and Welfare, and Related Agencies appropriations for 1981 . Washington , 1979. ii, 55, i p. ; LC Card 80-602536 DDC 353.0072/23682/56 19

KF27 .A652 1980a

UNITED STATES. SOCIAL SECURITY ADMINISTRATION - BUILDINGS.
United States. Congress. House. Committee on Ways and Means. Subcommittee on Social Security. Social Security Administration office space problems . Washington , 1980. iii, 137 p. : LC Card 80-603328 DDC 353.0082/56/0682 19

KF27 .W347 1980a

United States. Social Security Administration. Division of Program Research. see United States. Social Security Administration. Office of Research and Statistics.

United States. Social Security Administration. Division of Research and Statistics. see United States. Social Security Administration. Office of Research and Statistics.

United States. Social Security Administration. Division of the Actuary. United States. Social Security Administration. Office of the Actuary. Actuarial study. [Washington?]

NYPL *[JLM 81-126]*

United States. Social Security Administration. Office of Policy. Urban Systems Research & Engineering. Survey of blind and disabled children receiving supplemental security income benefits /. [Washington, D.C.] , 1980. xii, 94, [178] p. : LC Card 80-602123 DDC 362.4/0482/088054 19

HV1791 .U7 1980

United States. Social Security Administration. Office of Research and Statistics. (Old Catalog form: United States. Social Security board. Research and statistics bureau) Horlick, Max. Private pension plans in West Germany and France /. Washington, D.C. , c1980. v, 70 p. ; LC Card 80-600176 DDC 368.4/3/00973 331.25/2/0943 19

HD7123 .A39 no. 55 HD7106.F8

Income & resources of the aged / U. S. Department of Health, Education, and Welfare, Social Security Administration, Office of Policy, Office of Research and Statistics. [Washington, D.C.] : ORS : [for sale by the Supt. of Docs., U. S. Govt. Print. Off., 1980] 35 p. : ill. ; 23 cm. (SSA publication ; no. 13-11727) "Produced by the ORS Publications Staff. Robert Robinson, Marilyn Thomas, and G. Ricardo Campbell contributed to the writing and editing." "January 1980." Based on Income of the population 55 and over, 1976, by S. Grad and K. Foster. LC Card 80-600019
1. Retirement income - United States. 2. Aged - United States - Economic conditions. I. Robinson, Robert, 1920-. II. Thomas, Marilyn R. III. Campbell, Gary Ricardo. IV. Grad, Susan. Income of the population 55 and over, 1976. V. Series: United States. Social Security Administration. SSA publication , no. 13-11727. VI. Title.

HD7106.U5 U65 1980

Leimer, Dean R. The role of the replacement

rate in the design of the social security benefit structure /. Washington, D.C. , 1979. iv, 15 p. : LC Card 79-600182 DDC 368.4/3/00973 s 368.4/3/00973 19

HD7123 .A395 no. 36 HD7125

Muller, L. Scott. Replacement of earnings of the disabled under social security . Washington, D.C. , 1980] vi, 45 p. : LC Card 80-600107 DDC 368.4/3/00973 s 368.4/3/00973 19

HD7123 .A39 no. 53 HD7106.U5

1974 followup of disabled & nondisabled adults / U. S. Department of Health, Education, and Welfare, Social Security Administration, Office of Policy, Office of Research and Statistics. Washington : The Office, 1979. 2 v. in 1 ; 27 cm. "SSA publication no. 13-11725." CONTENTS: - no. 1. General characteristics, by R. E. Ferguson. - no. 2. Work experience of the disabled, 1972 and 1974, by Evan S. Schechter.
1. Social security - United States. 2. Insurance, Disability - United States. I. Ferguson, Robert E. II. Schechter, Evan S. III. Title.

NYPL *[JLF 80-1201]*

Public assistance recipients & cash payments by state & county. [Washington] LC Card 78-640797 **NYPL** *[JLM 81-20]*

Public assistance recipients and cash payments by State and county-February 1979. Washington, D.C. : U. S. Dept. of Health, Education, and Welfare, Social Security Administration, Office of Policy, Office of Research and Statistics : for sale by the Supt. of Docs., U. S. Govt. Print. Off., 1980. v, 85 p. ; 28 cm. (SSA publication. no. 13-11921) Tables. LC Card 80-600053 DDC 361/.973/0212 19
1. Public welfare - United States - States - Statistics. I. Series: United States. Dept. of Health, Education and Welfare. DHEW publication, no. 13-11921. II. Title.

HV85 .U54 1980

Public assistance statistics. Mar. 1977- [Washington] 27 cm. (Its: ORS report) Monthly. Supersedes: National Center for Social Statistics. Public assistance statistics. Issues for Apr. 1977- also called "HEW publication no. (SSA)" LC Card 77-643177
1. Public welfare - United States - Statistics - Periodicals. I. Title. **NYPL** *[JLM 80-970]*

Staff paper.
(no. 36) Leimer, Dean R. The role of the replacement rate in the design of the social security benefit structure /. Washington, D.C. , 1979. iv, 15 p. : LC Card 79-600182 DDC 368.4/3/00973 s 368.4/3/00973 19

HD7123 .A395 no. 36 HD7125

Studies from interagency data links. Report. no. 9- ; Nov. 1979- Washington.
I. Title. **NYPL** *[Econ. Div.]*

Urban Systems Research & Engineering. Survey of blind and disabled children receiving supplemental security income benefits /. [Washington, D.C.] , 1980. xii, 94, [178] p. : LC Card 80-602123 DDC 362.4/0482/088054 19

HV1791 .U7 1980

1974 followup of disabled & nondisabled adults. [Washington, D.C.] [1979- v. ; LC Card 80-602409 DDC 362.4/042/0973 19

HV1553 .N56

United States. Social Security Administration. Office of the Actuary. Actuarial study. [Washington?] 26-28 cm. Issued as DHEW pub. no. (SSA), 1974-77; as HEW pub. no. (SSA), 1978; as SSA pub., 1980- For earlier file, whose numbering it continues, see: United States. Social Security Board. Office of the Actuary. Actuarial study. Issued by the administration's Division of the Actuary, 1949-65.
1. Old age pensions - United States - Periodicals. I. United States. Social Security Administration. Division of the Actuary. II. Title. **NYPL** *[JLM 81-126]*

UNITED STATES. SOCIAL SECURITY ADMINISTRATION - OFFICIALS AND EMPLOYEES.
United States. Congress. Senate. Committee on Finance. Nominations of Abraham Katz, William J. Driver, and John L. Palmer . Washington , 1980. iii, 19 p. ; LC Card 80-602760 DDC 353.842 19

KF26 .F5 1980b

UNITED STATES. SOCIAL SECURITY ADMINISTRATION - RECORDS AND CORRESPONDENCE.
United States. Congress. House. Committee on

Interstate and Foreign Commerce. Subcommittee on Oversight and Investigations. Data transfer restrictions impede epidemiological research . Washington , c1980 [i.e. 1981] v, 32 p. ; LC Card 81-600797 DDC 363.1/1/0723 19

RA652.4 .U54 1981

United States. Social Security Administration. Technical Documents Branch. Legislative history, titles I-XX of the Social security act . Washington, 1980. ca. 1060 p. ;

NYPL *[JLE 81-598]*

United States. Social Security Board. Actuary, Office of the. see United States. Social Security Board. Office of the Actuary.

United States. Social Security Board. Office of the Actuary. Actuarial study. no. [1]-19 (incomplete). [Washington?] 1937-44. 26 cm. For later file, which continues its numbering, see: United States. Social Security Administration. Office of the Actuary. Actuarial study.
1. Old age pensions - United States - Periodicals. I. Title. **NYPL** *[SIW (U. S. Social Security Board. Actuary Office. Actuarial study)]*

United States. Soil Conservation Service.
Adams County, Illinois / U. S. Department of Agriculture, Soil Conservation Service [and] United States Department of the Interior, Geological Survey. Lincoln, Nebr. : USDA-SCS, 1980. 1 map : col. ; 37 x 37 cm. "Base source: USGS 1/100,000 compiled in 1978." Includes location map. "5,P-38,077." LC Card 81-691410
1. Adams County, Ill. - Maps. I. United States. Geological Survey.

G4103.A2 1980 .U5

Adams County, Iowa / U. S. Department of Agriculture, Soil Conservation Service [and] United States Department of the Interior, Geological Survey. Lincoln, Nebr. : USDA-SCS, 1979. 1 map : col. ; 27 x 35 cm. "Base source: USGS 1:100,000 county base compiled in 1978." Includes location map. "5,P-37,701." LC Card 81-691195
1. Adams County (Iowa) - Maps. I. United States. Geological Survey.

G4153.A3 1979 .U5

Adams County, Nebraska / U. S. Department of Agriculture, Soil Conservation Service [and] United States Department of the Interior, Geological Survey. Lincoln, Neb. : USDA-SCS, 1980. 1 map : col. ; 43 x 43 cm. "Base source: USGS 1/100,000 compiled in 1979." Includes location map. "5,P-38,089." LC Card 81-691081
1. Adams County (Neb.) - Maps. I. United States. Geological Survey.

G4193.A2 1980 .U5

Allegan County, Michigan / U. S. Department of Agriculture, Soil Conservation Service. Lincoln, Nebr. : USDA-SCS, 1971. 1 map ; 26 x 45 cm. "8-25-71." "Source: General highway map, Allegan County 1968." "5,O-29459." Includes location map. LC Card 81-691407
1. Allegan County (Mich.) - Maps.

G4113.A5 1971 .U5

Allegany County, Maryland / United States Department of Agriculture, Soil Conservation Service ; edited by the Geological Survey. Hyattsville, MD : USDA-SCS, 1979. 1 map : col. ; 28 x 54 cm. "Compiled by USGS from USGS 1:24,000-scale topographic maps dated 1959-1972." "Planimetry revised from aerial photographs taken 1974 and other source data." LC Card 81-690001
1. Allegany County (Md.) - Maps. I. United States. Geological Survey.

G3843.A4 1979 .U5

Anne Arundel County, Maryland / United States Department of Agriculture, Soil Conservation Service ; edited by the Geological Survey. Lanham, MD : USDA-SCS, 1980. 1 map : col. ; 47 x 36 cm. Title in lower margin: Anne Arundel County : N3842.5-W7620/32 x 31.5, 1977. "Compiled in 1977 from USGS 1:24,000-scale topographic maps dated 1970-1974." "Planimetry revised from aerial photographs taken 1976 and other source data." "1-16174." LC Card 81-690011
1. Anne Arundel County, Md. - Maps. I. United States. Geological Survey.

G3843.A5 1977 .U5

Appendix B, project map A, Wheeling Creek watershed, Pennsylvania and West Virginia / U. S. Department of Agriculture, Soil Conservation

United States. Soil Conservation Service. (cont.)   BIBLIOGRAPHIC GUIDE

594

Service. Lanham, MD : USDA-SCS, 1980. 1 map : col. ; 35 x 25 cm. Shows flood control dams, reservoirs, and benefited areas. "September 1980." Includes location map. "1-12,194."   LC Card 81-690293
1. Flood control - Wheeling Creek watershed (Pa. and W.Va.) - Maps. I. Title.
G3892.W44N22 1980 .U5

Augusta County, Virginia / United States Department of Agriculture, Soil Conservation Service. Lanham, MD : USDA-SCS, 1980. 1 map : col. ; 54 x 56 cm. Title in lower margin: Augusta Co., Va. : N3752.5-W7844.5/36.5x48, 1979. "Compiled from 1:24,000-scale topographic maps dated 1964-1973." "Planimetry revised from aerial photographs taken 1977-1978 and other source data."   LC Card 81-690000
1. Augusta County (Va.) - Maps.
G3883.A9 1979 .U5

Average annual precipitation in inches, 1931-60, southwest Ohio River basin study area, Ohio / U. S. Department of Agriculture. Lincoln, Nebr. : USDA-SCS, 1978. 1 map : col. ; 46 x 26 cm. Shows southwestern Ohio. At head of title: Map 5-1. "7-7-78." "Source: Family of maps SCS draw. no. 5,R-34,214 (6-74) and information from field technicians." Includes location map. "5,S-36,951."   LC Card 81-691036
1. Precipitation (Meteorology) - Ohio - Maps. I. Title: Southwest Ohio River basin study area, Ohio. II. Title: Ohio River basin study area, Ohio.
G4081.C88 1960 .U5

Average annual precipitation, Kentucky River Basin : drainage area 6966 square miles / U. S. Department of Agriculture, Soil Conservation Service. Fort Worth, Tex. : USDA-SCS, 1980. 1 map : col. ; 27 x 20 cm. "March 1980 4-R-37393. March 1980 base 4-R-34039-1." "Compiled from 1:250,000 USGS map sheets." "Plate A-2." Includes location map.   LC Card 81-692250
1. Precipitation (Meteorology) - Kentucky - Kentucky River watershed - Maps. I. Title.
G3952.K44C3 1980 .U5

Average annual precipitation, Walla Walla County Soil Conservation District, Walla Walla County, Washington / U. S. Department of Agriculture, Soil Conservation Service. Portland, Or. : USDA-SCS, 1979. 1 map : col. ; on sheet 28 x 43 cm. "March 1979." "Thematic detail compiled by staff from U. S. Weather Bureau and a number of independent observers." "Base map prepared by SCS, WTSC Carto Unit from 1:126,720 General highway maps." Includes location map. "M7-EN-24020-6."   LC Card 81-691505
1. Precipitation (Meteorology) - Washington (State) - Walla Walla County - Maps. I. Title. II. Title: Walla Walla County Soil Conservation District, Walla Walla County, Washington.
G4283.W3C88 1979 .U5

Average annual rainfall, Whitman County, Washington / U. S. Department of Agriculture, Soil Conservation Service. Portland, Or. : USDA-SCS, 1977. 1 map : col. ; on sheet 27 x 41 cm. "January 1977." "Thematic detail compiled by Washington state staff." "Base map prepared by SCS from 1:126,720 General highway map." Relief shown by hachures. Includes location map. "M7-N-23725-3."   LC Card 81-691519
1. Rain and rainfall - Washington (State) - Whitman County - Maps. I. Title.
G4283.W6C883 1977 .U5

Awalt, F. L. Soil survey of Clark County, Illinois /. [Washington, D.C. , 1980] iii, 104 p., [38] fold. leaves of plates :   LC Card 80-602050   DDC 631.4/7/77371 19
S599.I5 A92

Baldwin County, Georgia : soil interpretive map of limitations for septic tank absorption fields / U. S. Department of Agriculture, Soil Conservation Service. Fort Worth, Tex. : USDA-SCS, 1979. 1 map : col. ; 35 x 46 cm. "Base map compiled from USGS quadrangle sheets and Georgia county highway map ..." "10,000 meter universal transverse Mercator grid, zone 17." Includes text and location map. "April 1978 base 4-R-36583."   LC Card 81-690364
1. Sewage disposal in the ground - Georgia - Baldwin County - Maps. 2. Septic tanks - Georgia - Baldwin County - Maps.
G3923.B26N46 1978 .U5

Baltimore County, Maryland / United States Department of Agriculture, Soil Conservation Service ; edited by the Geological Survey.

Lanham, MD : USDA-SCS, 1980. 1 map : col. ; 51 x 45 cm. Title in lower margin: Baltimore Co., Md. : N3909--W7615/35X39.5, 1977. "Compiled in 1977 from USGS 1:24,000-scale topographic maps dated 1953-1974." "Planimetry revised from photographs taken 1976 and other source data." "1-16171."   LC Card 81-690004
1. Baltimore County, Md. - Maps. I. United States. Geological Survey.
G3843.B3 1977 .U5

Barbour County, West Virginia / United States Department of Agriculture, Soil Conservation Service ; cartographic mapping by the Geological Survey. Lanham, MD : USDA-SCS, 1980. 1 map : col. ; 41 x 37 cm. Title in lower margin: Barbour Co., W.Va. : N3856.5-W7948.5/22 x 25.5, 1975. "Compiled in 1975 from USGS 1:24,000-scale topographic maps dated 1958-1969." "Planimetry revised from aerial photographs taken 1975." "1,P-13167."   LC Card 81-690038
1. Barbour County (W.Va.) - Maps. I. United States. Geological Survey.
G3893.B3 1975 .U5

Barnhill, William L. Soil survey of Greene County, North Carolina /. [Washington] [1980] vii, 83 p., [2] fold. leaves of plates :   LC Card 80-602829   DDC 631.4/7/756393 19
S599.N6 B37

Base map, Little Whitestick and Cranberry Creeks watershed, Raleigh County, West Virginia : March 1980 / U. S. Department of Agriculture, Soil Conservation Service. Lanham, MD : USDA-SCS, 1980. 1 map : col. ; 27 x 19 cm. "Aerial photography flown April 1977. Photobase rectified to 7 1/2′ Topographic Quadrangle." Includes location map. "Lib. No. 1-15864."   LC Card 81-690294
1. Little Whitestick Creek watershed (W.Va.) - Photo maps. 2. Cranberry Creek watershed (W.Va.) - Photo maps. I. Title.
G3892.L58A4 1980 .U5

Beard, Leo R. Flood control effects of headwater reservoirs, Trinity River, Texas /. Austin , 1979. iii, 50, [78] p. :   LC Card 79-625849   DDC 627/.44/097645 19
TC557.T39 B4

Belknap County, New Hampshire / United States Department of Agriculture, Soil Conservation Service. Lanham, MD : USDA-SCS, 1980. 1 map : col. ; 43 x 37 cm. Title in lower margin: Belknap Co., N.H. : N4317-W7109.5/29 x 34.5, 1974. "Compiled in 1975 from USGS 1:62,500-scale topographic maps dated 1956-1958." "Planimetry revised from aerial photographs taken 1974."   LC Card 81-690022
1. Belknap County (N.H.) - Maps.
G3743.B4 1974 .U5

Berkeley County, West Virginia / United States Department of Agriculture, Soil Conservation Service ; cartographic mapping by the Geological Survey. Lanham, MD : USDA-SCS, 1980. 1 map : col. ; 41 x 37 cm. Title in lower margin: Berkeley Co., W.Va. : N3915.5--W7749/22X25.5, 1976. "Compiled in 1976 from USGS 1:24,000-scale topographic maps dated 1953-1972." "Planimetry revised from aerial photographs taken 1976 and other source data." "1,P-13168."   LC Card 81-690039
1. Berkeley County, W. Va. - Maps. I. United States. Geological Survey.
G3893.B4 1976 .U5

Black Hawk County, Iowa / U. S. Department of Agriculture, Soil Conservation Service [and] United States Department of the Interior, Geological Survey. [Lincoln, Neb.] : The Service, [1979?] 1 map : col. ; 34 x 36 cm. "Base source: USGS 1:100,000 county base compiled from 1963-1972 topographic maps." Includes location map. "5,P-37,500."   LC Card 81-691194
1. Black Hawk County, Iowa - Maps. I. United States. Geological Survey.
G4153.B4 1979 .U5

Boone County, Illinois / U. S. Department of Agriculture, Soil Conservation Service [and] United States Department of the Interior, Geological Survey. Lincoln, Nebr. : USDA-SCS, 1980. 1 map : col. ; 43 x 24 cm., on sheet 64 x 49 cm. "Base source: USGS 1/100,000 compiled in 1978." Includes location map. "5,P-38,080."   LC Card 81-691411
1. Boone County (Ill.) - Maps. I. United States. Geological Survey.
G4103.B6 1980 .U5

Boone County, Iowa / U. S. Department of Agriculture, Soil Conservation Service [and] United States Department of the Interior, Geological Survey. Lincoln, Nebr. : USDA-SCS, 1979. 1 map : col. ; 34 x 33 cm. "Base source: USGS 1:100,000 county base compiled in 1979." Includes location map. "5,P-37,707."   LC Card 81-691193
1. Boone County (Iowa) - Maps. I. United States. Geological Survey.
G4153.B5 1979 .U5

Bowman, Roy H. Soil survey of Santa Cruz County, California /. [[Washington] [1980] vii, 148 p., [2] fold. leaves of plates :   LC Card 80-603187   DDC 631.4/7/79471 19
S599.C2 B68

Bremer County, Iowa / U. S. Department of Agriculture, Soil Conservation Service [and] United States Department of the Interior, Geological Survey. Lincoln, Nebr. : USDA-SCS, 1979. 1 map : col. ; 27 x 34 cm. "Base source: USGS 1:100,000 county base compiled in 1972." Includes location map. "5,P-37,703."   LC Card 81-691192
1. Bremer County (Iowa) - Maps. I. United States. Geological Survey.
G4153.B6 1979 .U5

Brent, Floyd V. Soil survey of Lowndes County, Mississippi /. [Washington] [1979] viii, 137 p., [24] fold. leaves of plates :   LC Card 80-602618   DDC 631.4/7/762973 19
S599.M5 B7

Brevard County, Florida : soil interpretive map for source of sand / U. S. Department of Agriculture, Soil Conservation Service. Fort Worth, Tex. : USDA-SCS, 1980. 1 map : col. ; 87 x 44 cm. Title in lower margin: Brevard Co., Fla. "Base map prepared by the Geological Survey in cooperation with the Soil Conservation Service." "Compiled from USGS 1:24,000-scale topographic maps dated 1949-1976. UTM grid. Includes text and location map.   LC Card 81-690350
1. Sand - Florida - Brevard County - Maps. 2. Sandy soils - Florida - Brevard County - Maps. I. United States. Geological Survey.
G3933.B7H5 1980 .U5

Bristol County, Massachusetts / United States Department of Agriculture, Soil Conservation Service. Lanham, MD : USDA-SCS, 1980. 1 map : col. ; 56 x 43 cm. Title in lower margin: Bristol Co., Mass. : N4128.5-W7045/38x38.5, 1978. "Compiled from USGS 1:24,000-scale topographic maps dated 1949-1977." "Planimetry revised from aerial photographs taken 1977 and other source data."   LC Card 81-690017
1. Bristol County (Mass.) - Maps.
G3763.B7 1978 .U5

Brown, James Henry, 1946- Soil survey of Randolph County, Arkansas /. [Washington] [1980] viii, 103 p., [30] fold. leaves of plates :   LC Card 80-602554   DDC 631.4/7/76724 19
S599.A75 B76

Buffalo County, Nebraska / U. S. Department of Agriculture, Soil Conservation Service. Lincoln, Nebr. : USDA-SCS, 1980. 1 map : col. ; 41 x 57 cm. "6-28-80." "Source: 1976 general county highway map." Includes location map. "5,P-37,741.1."   LC Card 81-691015
1. Buffalo County (Neb.) - Maps.
G4193.B8 1980 .U5

Burgess, Dent Louis, 1913- Soil survey of Marshall County, Oklahoma /. [Washington, D. C. , 1980] vii, 92 p., [20] fold. leaves of plates :   LC Card 80-602509   DDC 631.4/7/76661 19
S599.O4 B88

Burns, roads, and facilities, Entiat River Basin, Chelan County, Washington / U. S. Department of Agriculture, Soil Conservation Service. Portland, Or. : USDA-SCS, 1979. 1 map : col. ; on sheet 44 x 28 cm. "April 1979." Relief shown by hachures. "Thematic detail compiled by U. S. Forest Service." "Base map prepared by SCS, WTSC Carto Staff from U. S. Forest Service compilation." "U. S.D.A. eastern Washington cooperative river basin study." Includes location map. "M7-SN-23919-5."   LC Card 81-691538
1. Forest fires - Washington (State) - Entiat River watershed - Maps. 2. Entiat River watershed (Wash.) - Road maps. I. United States. Forest Service. II. Title.
G4282.E5K5 1978 .U5

Bushue, Lester J., 1930- Soil survey of Adams County, Illinois /. [Washington] , 1979. i, 143,

[66] fold. leaves of plates : LC Card 80-601805
DDC 631.4/9773 s 631.4/7/77344 19
S599.I5 A3 no. 101

Caldwell County, Missouri / U. S. Department
of Agriculture, Soil Conservation Service.
[Lincoln, Neb.] : The Service, [1979?] 1 map :
col. ; 26 x 33 cm. "Base source: USGS 1:100,000
county base compiled in 1975." Includes location map.
"5,O-37,513." LC Card 81-691212
1. Caldwell County (Mo.) - Maps.
G4163.C2 1979 .U5

Camp, Wallace Jefferson, 1906- Soil survey of
Greenwood and McCormick Counties, South
Carolina /. [Washington, D.C. , 1980] iv, 68 p.,
[42] fold. leaves of plates : LC Card 80-602310
DDC 631.4/7/75733 19
S599.S58 C36

Candland, David M. Soil survey of Big Smoky
Valley Area, Nevada, part of Nye County /.
[Washington] 1980. iii, 140 p. [2] fold. leaves
of plates : LC Card 80-601637 DDC
631.4/7/79334 19
S599.N425 C36

Carlson, Carroll Richard, 1928- Soil survey of
Freeborn County, Minnesota /. [Washington,
D.C.] [1979] ix, 228 p., [56] fold. leaves of
plates : LC Card 80-601843 DDC 631.4/7/77618
19
S599.M45 C37

Carroll County, Illinois / U. S. Department of
Agriculture, Soil Conservation Service [and]
United States Department of the Interior,
Geological Survey. Lincoln, Nebr. :
USDA-SCS, 1980. 1 map : col. ; 33 x 56 cm.
"Base source: USGS 1/100,000 compiled in 1976."
Includes location map. "5,P-38,081." LC Card
81-691412
1. Carroll County, Ill. - Maps. I. United States.
Geological Survey.
G4103.C25 1980 .U5

Carroll County, Maryland / United States
Department of Agriculture, Soil Conservation
Service ; edited by the Geological Survey.
Hyattsville, MD : USDA-SCS, 1979. 1 map :
col. ; 34 x 37 cm. "Compiled by USGS in 1976 from
USGS 1:24,000-scale topographic maps dated
1966-1974." "Planimetry revised from aerial photographs
taken 1973." LC Card 81-690006
1. Carroll County (Md.) - Maps. I. United States.
Geological Survey.
G3843.C4 1979 .U5

Carroll County, New Hampshire / United
States Department of Agriculture, Soil
Conservation Service. Lanham, MD :
USDA-SCS, 1980. 1 map : col. ; 72 x 42 cm.
"Compiled from 1:24,000- and 1:62,500-scale
topographic maps dated 1928-1964." "Planimetry revised
from aerial photographs taken 1974 and other source
data." LC Card 81-690020
1. Carroll County (N.H.) - Maps.
G3743.C3 1980 .U5

Charles County, Maryland / United States
Department of Agriculture, Soil Conservation
Service ; edited by the Geological Survey.
Hyattsville, MD : USDA-SCS, 1979. 1 map :
col. ; 48 x 47 cm. "Compiled by USGS in 1975 from
USGS 1:24,000-scale topographic maps dated
1943-1971." "Planimetry revised from aerial photographs
taken 1973." LC Card 81-690003
1. Charles County, Md. - Maps. I. United States.
Geological Survey.
G3843.C6 1979 .U5

Chittenden County, Vermont / U. S.
Department of Agriculture, Soil Conservation
Service ; edited by the Geological Survey.
Lanham, MD : USDA-SCS, 1979. 1 map :
col. ; 63 x 46 cm. Title in lower margin: Chittenden
Co., Vt. : 1972. "Compiled in 1975 from USGS
1:24,000 and 1:62,500-scale topographic maps dated
1948-1971." "Planimetry revised from aerial photographs
taken 1972." LC Card 81-690027
1. Chittenden County, Vt. - Maps. I. United States.
Geological Survey.
G3753.C5 1972 .U5

Christian County, Illinois / U. S. Department
of Agriculture, Soil Conservation Service.
Lincoln, Nebr. : USDA-SCS, 1976. 1 map :
col. ; 41 x 57 cm. "4-20-76." "Source: 1972 general
county highway map." Includes location map.
"5,S-35,631.1." LC Card 81-691439
1. Christian County, Ill. - Maps.
G4103.C45 1976 .U5

Clark County, Illinois / U. S. Department of
Agriculture, Soil Conservation Service [and]
United States Department of the Interior,
Geological Survey. Lincoln, Nebr. :
USDA-SCS, 1980. 1 map : col. ; 39 x 45 cm.
"Base source: USGS 1/100,000 compiled in 1980."
Includes location map. "5,P-38,110." LC Card
81-691413
1. Clark County (Ill.) - Maps. I. United States.
Geological Survey.
G4103.C5 1980 .U5

Clatsop County, Oregon / U. S. Department of
Agriculture, Soil Conservation Service.
Portland, Or. : USDA-SCS, 1979. 1 map : col. ;
on sheet 28 x 22 cm. "October 1979." "Base map
prepared by SCS, WTSC Carto Unit from 1:126,720
General highway maps." Includes location map.
"M7-OL-24072." LC Card 81-691563
1. Clatsop County (Or.) - Maps.
G4293.C5 1979 .U5

Clay County, Iowa / U. S. Department of
Agriculture, Soil Conservation Service [and]
United States Department of the Interior,
Geological Survey. Lincoln, Nebr. :
USDA-SCS, 1979. 1 map : col. ; 33 x 33 cm.
"Base source: USGS 1:100,000 county base compiled in
1978." Includes location map. "5,P-37,704." LC Card
81-691191
1. Clay County (Iowa) - Maps. I. United States.
Geological Survey.
G4153.C65 1979 .U5

Clinton County, Iowa / U. S. Department of
Agriculture, Soil Conservation Service [and]
United States Department of the Interior,
Geological Survey. Lincoln, Nebr. :
USDA-SCS, 1979. 1 map : col. ; 30 x 53 cm.
"Base source: USGS 1:100,000 county base compiled in
1979." Includes location map. "5,P-37,708." LC Card
81-691190
1. Clinton County (Iowa) - Maps. I. United States.
Geological Survey.
G4153.C8 1979 .U5

Cloud County, Kansas / U. S. Department of
Agriculture, Soil Conservation Service. Lincoln,
Nebr. : USDA-SCS, 1979. 1 map ; 20 x 27 cm.
"6-1-73." "Source: 1967 general county highway map."
Includes location map. "5-P-32,0392.2." LC Card
81-691136
1. Cloud County (Kan.) - Maps.
G4203.C65 1973 .U5

Clower, Dennis F. Soil survey of Brown and
Mills Counties, Texas. [Washington, D.C.?] ,
1980. vii, 170 p., 92 fold. p. of plates : LC
Card 81-601467 DDC 631.4/7/764512 19
S599.T4 C57

Coal resources map, Kansas / U. S. Department
of Agriculture, Soil Conservation Service.
Lincoln, Nebr. : USDA-SCS, 1979. 1 map :
col. ; 18 x 23 cm. "6-8-79." "Source: Family of maps
S.C.S. drwg. no. 5,S-32,550 (rev. 1-76) and information
from S.C.S. field technicians." "5,S-37,434." LC Card
81-691127
1. Coal - Kansas - Maps.
G4201.H9 1979 .U5

Cochran, Rex. Soil survey of Grayson County,
Texas /. [Washington? , 1980] vii, 141 p., [41]
leaves of plates : LC Card 80-602304 DDC
631.4/7/764557 19
S599.T4 C593

Coffee, Daniel R., 1919- Soil survey of Dallas
County, Texas /. [Washington] [1980] vii, 153
p., [38] fold. leaves of plates : LC Card
80-601832 DDC 631.4/7/7642811 19
S599.T4 C63

Collett, Russell A. Soil survey of Ada County
area, Idaho /. [Washington] , 1980. ix, 327 p.,
[39] fold. leaves of plates : LC Card 80-603366
DDC 631.4/7/79628 19
S599.I2 C64

Cook County, Illinois / U. S. Department of
Agriculture, Soil Conservation Service [and]
United States Department of the Interior,
Geological Survey. Lincoln, Nebr. :
USDA-SCS, 1980. 1 map : col. ; 51 x 42 cm.
"Base source: USGS 1/100,000 compiled in 1976."
Includes location map. "5,P-38,073." LC Card
81-691414
1. Cook County (Ill.) - Maps. I. United States.
Geological Survey.
G4103.C7 1980 .U5

Coos County, New Hampshire / U. S.

Department of Agriculture, Soil Conservation
Service. Lanham, MD : USDA-SCS, 1979. 1
map ; 67 x 54 cm. "Base Source: New Hampshire
family of maps 1:500,000." Includes location map. "1-15
507." LC Card 81-690120
1. Coos County (N.H.) - Maps.
G3743.C6 1979 .U5

Counties grouped to form yield subareas,
western South Dakota river basins / U. S.
Department of Agriculture, Soil Conservation
Service. Rev. 7-18-79. Lincoln, Nebr. :
USDA-SCS, 1979. 1 map : col. ; 18 x 26 cm.
"Source: Family of maps S.C.S. drwg. no. 5,R-30,116
(5-8-72) and information from field technicians." At
head of title: Figure C-2. Includes location map. Text
on verso. "5,N-36,987." LC Card 81-691115
1. Crop yields - South Dakota - Maps.
G4181.J6 1979 .U5

Cox, Frank R., 1918- Soil survey of McLean
and Muhlenberg Counties, Kentucky /.
[Washington] [1980] viii, 124 p., 61 fold p. of
plates : LC Card 80-604148 DDC 631.4/7/769826
19
S599.K4 C68

Crawford County, Iowa / U. S. Department of
Agriculture, Soil Conservation Service [and]
United States Department of the Interior,
Geological Survey. [Lincoln, Neb.] : The
Service, [1979?] 1 map : col. ; 34 x 42 cm. "Base
source: USGS 1:100,000 county base compiled from
1969-1978 topographic maps. Includes location map.
"5,P-37,510." LC Card 81-691189
1. Crawford County (Iowa) - Maps. I. United States.
Geological Survey.
G4153.C9 1979 .U5

Critical erosion, Walla Walla County Soil
Conservation District, Walla Walla County,
Washington / U. S. Department of Agriculture,
Soil Conservation Service. Portland, Or. :
USDA-SCS, 1979. 1 map : col. ; on sheet 28 x
43 cm. "March 1979." "Thematic detail compiled by
state staff." "Base map prepared by SCS, WTSC Carto
Unit from 1:126,720 General highway maps." Includes
location map. "M7-EN-24020-4." LC Card 81-691507
*1. Erosion - Washington (State) - Walla Walla County -
Maps. I. Title. II. Title: Walla Walla County Soil
Conservation District, Walla Walla County,
Washington.*
G4283.W3J4 1979 .U5

Crockett County, Tennessee : gross erosion /
prepared by Soil Conservation Service for
Crockett County Soil Conservation District.Rev.
Sept. 1977. Fort Worth, Tex. : USDA-SCS,
1980. 1 map : col. ; 45 x 58 cm. "Base
4-R-30876." "Base map compiled from Tennessee
general highway map ..." Includes location map. LC
Card 81-692293
*1. Soil erosion - Tennessee - Crockett County - Maps.
2. Flood control - Tennessee - Crockett County - Maps.
I. Title.*
G3963.C7N22 1977 .U5

Crockett County, Tennessee : upland land use /
prepared by Soil Conservation Service for
Crockett County Soil Conservation District.
Rev. Sept. 1977. Fort Worth, Tex. :
USDA-SCS, 1980. 1 map : col. ; 45 x 58 cm.
"Base 4-R-30876." "Base compiled from Tennessee
general highway map ..." Includes location map. LC
Card 81-692292
*1. Land use - Tennessee - Crockett County - Maps. I.
Title.*
G3963.C7G4 1977 .U5

Da Moude, Dean W. Soil survey Burt County,
Nebraska. [Washington, D.C.?] , 1980. vii, 165
p., 44 folded p. of plates : LC Card 81-601021
DDC 631.4/7/782243 19
S599.N2 D34

Dakota County, Nebraska / U. S. Department
of Agriculture, Soil Conservation Service [and]
United States Department of the Interior,
Geological Survey. Lincoln, Neb. : USDA-SCS,
1980. 1 map : col. ; 32 x 37 cm. "Base source:
USGS 1/100,000 compiled in 1976." Includes location
map. "5,P-38,092." LC Card 81-691080
1. Dakota County (Neb.) - Maps. I. United States.
Geological Survey.
G4193.D2 1980 .U5

Dawson County, Nebraska / U. S. Department
of Agriculture, Soil Conservation Service [and]
United States Department of the Interior,
Geological Survey. Lincoln, Neb. : USDA-SCS,
1980. 1 map : col. ; 38 x 57 cm. "Base source:

United States. Soil Conservation Service. (cont.)

USGS 1/100,000 compiled in 1978." Includes location map. "5,P-38,091." LC Card 81-691079
1. Dawson County (Neb.) - Maps. I. United States. Geological Survey.
G4193.D4 1980 .U5

De Kalb County, Illinois / U. S. Department of Agriculture, Soil Conservation Service [and] United States Department of the Interior, Geological Survey. Lincoln, Nebr. : USDA-SCS, 1980. 1 map : col. ; 49 x 25 cm. "Base source: USGS 1/100,000 compiled in 1978." Includes location map. "5,P-38,082." LC Card 81-691415
1. DeKalb County (Ill.) - Maps. I. United States. Geological Survey.
G4103.D4 1980 .U5

De Witt County, Illinois / U. S. Department of Agriculture, Soil Conservation Service. Lincoln, Nebr. : USDA-SCS, 1976. 1 map : col. ; 41 x 52 cm. "4-9-76." "Source: 1972 county highway map." Includes location map. "5,P-35,633.1." LC Card 81-691440
1. De Witt County (Ill.) - Maps.
G4103.D5 1976 .U5

Deer population, upper Little Nemaha watershed, Lancaster, Cass, and Otoe Counties, Nebraska / U. S. Department of Agriculture, Soil Conservation Service. Lincoln, Nebr. : USDA-SCS, 1979. 1 map ; 17 x 26 cm. "12-29-78." "Source: SCS drawing 5,R-23,485 (7-66) and information from field technicians." Includes location map. "5,0-37,204." LC Card 81-691092
1. Deer - Nebraska - Little Nemaha River watershed - Maps.
G4192.L5D4 1978 .U5

Dodge County, Nebraska / U. S. Department of Agriculture, Soil Conservation Service. Lincoln, Nebr. : USDA-SCS, 1977. 1 map : col. ; 46 x 59 cm. "6-3-77." "Source: 1969 general county highway map." Includes location map. "5,P-36,307.1." LC Card 81-691014
1. Dodge County (Neb.) - Maps.
G4193.D7 1977 .U5

Dolezel, Raymond. Soil survey of Nacogdoches County, Texas /. [Washington] , 1980. vii, 146 p., [30] fold. leaves of plates :   LC Card 80-602411   DDC 631.4/7/764182 19
S599.T4 D63

Dorchester County, Maryland / United States Department of Agriculture, Soil Conservation Service ; edited by the Geological Survey. Hyattsville, MD : USDA-SCS, 1979. 1 map : col. ; 54 x 46 cm. "Compiled by USGS from USGS 1:24,000-scale topographic maps dated 1942-1973." "Planimetry revised from aerial photographs taken 1973-1975 and other source data." LC Card 81-690010
1. Dorchester County (Md.) - Maps. I. United States. Geological Survey.
G3843.D6 1979 .U5

Douglas County, Illinois / U. S. Department of Agriculture, Soil Conservation Service [and] United States Department of the Interior, Geological Survey. Lincoln, Nebr. : USDA-SCS, 1980. 1 map : col. ; 30 x 50 cm. "Base source: USGS 1/100,000 compiled in 1980." Includes location map. "5,S-38,112." LC Card 81-691416
1. Douglas County (Ill.) - Maps. I. United States. Geological Survey.
G4103.D6 1980 .U5

Douglas County, Nebraska / U. S. Department of Agriculture, Soil Conservation Service. Lincoln, Nebr. : USDA-SCS, 1978. 1 map : col. ; 46 x 59 cm. "7-18-78." "Source: 1971 general county highway map." Includes location map. "5,P-36,982.1." LC Card 81-691013
1. Douglas County (Neb.) - Maps.
G4193.D8 1978 .U5

Drainage area map, Mellette County, South Dakota : IV-3 / U. S. Department of Agriculture, Soil Conservation Service. Lincoln, Nebr. : USDA-SCS, 1978. 1 map : col. ; 26 x 34 cm. "Source: 1976 general county highway map and information from field technicians." Includes location map. "5,S-36,998." LC Card 81-691104
1. Drainage - South Dakota - Mellette County - Maps.
G4183.M6C315 1978 .U5

Drainage map, Gray County, Kansas / U. S. Department of Agriculture, Soil Conservation Service. Lincoln, Nebr. : USDA-SCS, 1979. 1 map ; 26 x 36 cm. "5-5-79." "Source: Family of maps

SCS drwg. no. 5,S-34,957 (rev. 4-79) and information from field technicians." Includes location map. "5,S-37,273." LC Card 81-691141
1. Drainage - Kansas - Gray County - Maps.
G4203.G6C315 1979 .U5

Drainage map, Ness County, Kansas / U. S. Department of Agriculture, Soil Conservation Service. Lincoln, Nebr. : USDA-SCS, 1979. 1 map : col. ; 41 x 57 cm. "1-24-79." "Source: Family of maps S.C.S. drwg. no. 5,S-36,165 (3-77) and information from field technicians." Includes location map. "5,S-37,183." LC Card 81-691146
1. Drainage - Kansas - Ness County - Maps.
G4203.N5C315 1979 .U5

Du Page County, Illinois / U. S. Department of Agriculture, Soil Conservation Service [and] United States Department of the Interior, Geological Survey. Lincoln, Nebr. : USDA-SCS, 1980. 1 map : col. ; 38 x 34 cm. "Base source: USGS 1/100,000 compiled in 1976." Includes location map. "5,P-38,076." LC Card 81-691417
1. DuPage County (Ill.) - Maps. I. United States. Geological Survey.
G4103.D8 1980 .U5

Dutchess County, New York / United States, Department of Agriculture, Soil Conservation Service. Lanham, MD : USDA-SCS, 1981. 1 map : col. ; 58 x 37 cm. Title in right lower margin: Dutchess Co., N.Y., N4126-W7328.5/39.5x33, 1979. "Compiled from 1:24,000-scale topographic maps dated 1953-1963." "Planimetry revised from aerial photographs taken 1978 and other source data." UTM grid. LC Card 81-692936
1. Dutchess County, N. Y. - Maps.
G3803.D8 1979 .U5

Dyer County, Tennessee / prepared by Soil Conservation Service for Dyer County Soil Conservation District. Fort Worth, Tex. : USDA-SCS, 1980. 1 map : col. ; 46 x 59 cm. Shows upland cropland by capability classes. "Base compiled from Tennessee general highway map ..." Includes location map. "Revised August 1977 base 4-R-22415." LC Card 81-692283
1. Land capability for agriculture - Tennessee - Dyer County - Maps. I. Title.
G3963.D9J3 1980 .U5

Edwards County, Illinois / U. S. Department of Agriculture, Soil Conservation Service [and] United States Department of the Interior, Geological Survey. Lincoln, Nebr. : USDA-SCS, 1980. 1 map : col. ; 39 x 21 cm., on sheet 64 x 49 cm. "Base source: USGS 1/100,000 compiled in 1979." Includes location map. "5,P-38,113." LC Card 81-691418
1. Edwards County, Ill. - Maps. I. United States. Geological Survey.
G4103.E3 1980 .U5

El Paso County, Colorado / U. S. Department of Agriculture, Soil Conservation Service. Portland, Or. : USDA-SCS, 1979. 1 map ; on sheet 48 x 64 cm. "November 1969." "Base map prepared by SCS, WTSC Carto Unit from 1:126,720 General highway maps." Relief shown by hachures. Includes location map. "M7-0-21205-21." LC Card 81-691552
1. El Paso County (Colo.) - Maps.
G4313.E5 1969 .U5

Entiat River Basin, Chelan County, Washington / U. S. Department of Agriculture, Soil Conservation Service. Portland, Or. : USDA-SCS, 1979. 1 map : col. ; on sheet 44 x 28 cm. "April 1978." Relief shown by hachures. "Base map prepared by SCS, WTSC, Carto Staff from U. S. Forest Service compilation." "U. S.D.A. eastern Washington cooperative river basin study." Includes location map. "M7-SN-23916." LC Card 81-691530
1. Entiat River watershed (Wash.) - Maps.
G4282.E5 1978 .U5

Ernst, James Edgar. Soil survey of Seneca County, Ohio. [Washington, D.C.?] , 1980. vii, 143 p., 81 folded p. of plates :   LC Card 80-604150   DDC 631.4/7/77124 19
S599.O3 E77

Erosion areas map, Kansas / U. S. Department of Agriculture, Soil Conservation Service. Lincoln, Nebr. : USDA-SCS, 1979. 1 map : col. ; 18 x 23 cm. "5-31-79." "Source: Family of maps S.C.S. drwg. no. 5,S-32,550 (rev. 1-76) and information from S.C.S. field technicians." "5,S-37,422." LC Card 81-691126

1. Soil erosion - Kansas - Maps.
G4201.J4 1979 .U5

Erosion potential of Wisconsin soils / U. S. Department of Agriculture, Soil Conservation Service. Lincoln, Nebr. : USDA-SCS, 1979. 1 map : col. ; 24 x 18 cm. "4-19-79." "Source: Drwg. no. 5,S-32,817 (2-74) and information from field technicians. "5,R-37,303." LC Card 81-691253
1. Soil erosion - Wisconsin - Maps.
G4121.J4 1979 .U5

Evaluaion reach map, Los Olmos Creek watershed, Jim Hogg and Starr Counties, Texas. Rev. Nov. 1979 base 4R-33919. [Temple? Tex. : U. S. Dept. of Agriculture, Soil Conservation Service, [1979] 1 map : col. ; 26 x 29 cm. "November 1979 4R-37322." Shows evaluation reach and floodwater damage area. "Base compiled from 1973 Texas general highway maps ..." "Source: Data compiled by Watershed Planning Staff." Includes inset of Rio Grande City area and location map.   LC Card 81-692270
1. Flood damage - Texas - Los Olmos Creek watershed - Maps. I. Title.
G4032.L67C32 1979 .U5

Fairfax County, Virginia / U. S. Department of Agriculture, Soil Conservation Service. Lanham, MD : USDA-SCS, 1980. 1 map : col. ; 29 x 26 cm. "Compiled in 1977 from USGS 1:24,000-scale topographic maps dated 1965-1973." "Planimetry revised from aerial photographs taken 1973 and other source data." LC Card 81-690095
1. Fairfax County, Va. - Maps.
G3883.F2 1977 .U5

Fayette County, West Virginia / United States Department of Agriculture, Soil Conservation Service ; cartographic mapping by the Geological Survey. Lanham, MD : USDA-SCS, 1980. 1 map : col. ; 52 x 58 cm. Title in lower margin: Fayette Co., W.Va. : N 3748.5-W8044.5/28x39, 1978. "Compiled from 1:24,000-scale topographic maps dated 1965-1969." "Planimetry revised from aerial photographs taken 1976-1977 and other source data." "1,S-13402." LC Card 81-690032
1. Fayette County (W.Va.) - Maps. I. United States. Geological Survey.
G3893.F3 1978 .U5

Flat Rock Creek watershed, Lunenburg County, Virginia : December 1979 / U. S. Department of Agriculture, Soil Conservation Service. Lanham, MD : USDA-SCS 1980. 1 map : col. ; 26 x 39 cm. "Source: USGS Topo Quad Sheets 1:24,000." "Contour interval 50 feet." Oriented with north to the left. Includes location map. "1-15447." LC Card 81-690290
1. Flat Rock Creek watershed (Va.) - Maps, Topographic.
G3882.F5 1979 .U5

Flood insurance studies status map, Virginia : November 1979 / U. S. Department of Agriculture, Soil Conservation Service. Lanham, MD : USDA-SCS, 1980. 1 map : col. ; 25 x 53 cm. Indexed. "1-15596." LC Card 81-690103
1. Insurance, Flood - Virginia - Maps. I. Title.
G3881.C32 1979 .U5

Fox, Richard W. Soil survey of Bowie County, Texas. [Washington, D.C.?] , 1980. vii, 128 p., 76 fold. p. of plates :   LC Card 81-601439   DDC 631.4/7/764197 19
S599.T4 F678

Fox, Robert E. Soil survey of Dodge County, Wisconsin /. [Washington] [1980] ix, 201 p., [71] fold. leaves of plates :   LC Card 80-602249   DDC 631.4/7/776153 19
S599.W5 F69

Franklin County, Massachusetts / United States Department of Agriculture, Soil Conservation Service. Lanham, MD : USDA-SCS, 1980. 1 map : col. ; 39 x 53 cm. Title in lower margin: Franklin Co., Mass. : N4218-W7213.5/26.5x48, 1972. "Compiled in 1975 from USGS 1:24,000-scale topographic maps dated 1960-1971." "Planimetry revised from aerial photographs taken 1972." LC Card 81-690024
1. Franklin County (Mass.) - Maps.
G3763.F7 1972 .U5

Franklin County, Vermont / U. S. Department of Agriculture, Soil Conservation Service ; edited by the Geological Survey. Lanham, MD : USDA-SCS, 1980. 1 map : col. ; 45 x 60 cm. Title in lower margin: Franklin Co., Vt. : 1979. "Compiled from USGS 1:24,000- and 1:62,500-scale topogrphic maps dated 1963-1966." "Planimetry revised

from aerial photographs taken 1976 and other source data." "15444." LC Card 81-690026
1. Franklin County (Vt.) - Maps. I. United States. Geological Survey.
G3753.F7 1979 .U5

Frederick County, Maryland / United States Department of Agriculture, Soil Conservation Service ; edited by the Geological Survey. Hyattsville, MD : USDA-SCS, 1979. 1 map : col. ; 45 x 40 cm. "Compiled by USGS in 1976 USGS 1:24,000-scale topographic maps dated 1969-1971." "Planimetry revised from aerial photographs taken 1973." LC Card 81-690005
1. Frederick County, Md. - Maps. I. United States. Geological Survey.
G3843.F7 1979 .U5

Froedge, Ronald D. Soil survey of Grant and Pendleton Counties, Kentucky /. [Washington] , 1980. vii, 85 p., [40] fold. leaves of plates : LC Card 80-602321 DDC 631.4/7/76933 19
S599.K4 F76

Gage County, Nebraska / U. S. Department of Agriculture, Soil Conservation Service. Lincoln, Nebr. : USDA-SCS, 1979. 1 map : col. ; 57 x 41 cm. "10-24-78." "Source: 1975 general county highway map." Includes location map. "5,S-37,076.1." LC Card 81-691012
1. Gage County (Neb.) - Maps.
G4193.G2 1978 .U5

Garner, Billy A. Soil survey of Crawford County, Arkansas /. [Washington] , 1979. viii, 91, [22] fold. leaves of plates : LC Card 80-601639 DDC 631.4/7/76735 19
S599.A75 G37

Garrett County, Maryland / United States Department of Agriculture, Soil Conservation Service ; edited by the Geological Survey. Hyattsville, MD : USDA-SCS, 1979. 1 map : col. ; 48 x 41 cm. "Compiled by USGS from 1:24,000-scale topographic maps dated 1946-1967." "Planimetry revised from aerial photographs taken 1974 and 1977 and other source data." LC Card 81-690008
1. Garrett County (Md.) - Maps. I. United States. Geological Survey.
G3843.G3 1979 .U5

General availability of groundwater map, Seward County, Kansas / U. S. Department of Agriculture, Soil Conservation Service. Lincoln, Nebr. : USDA-SCS, 1979. 1 map : col. ; 23 x 30 cm. "4-19-79." "Source: SCS family of maps drawing no. 5,P-36,087, rev. 3-79 ..." Includes location map. "5,P-37,294." LC Card 81-691145
1. Water, Underground - Kansas - Seward County - Maps.
G4203.S45C34 1979 .U5

General geology map, western South Dakota river basins / U. S. Department of Agriculture, Soil Conservation Service. Rev. 7-18-79. Lincoln, Nebr. : USDA-SCS, 1979. 1 map : col. ; 26 x 45 cm. "Source: SCS drawing no. 5,R-30,116 (5-72) ..." At head of title: Fig. A-4. Includes "Idealized cross sections of western South Dakota" and location maps. "5,S-36,672." LC Card 81-691117
1. Geology - South Dakota - Maps.
G4181.C5 1979 .U5

General precipitation, Grant County, Washington / U. S. Department of Agriculture, Soil Conservation Service. Portland, Or. : USDA-SCS, 1978. 1 map : col. ; on sheet 51 x 28 cm. "January 1978." "Thematic detail compiled by state staff. "Base map prepared by SCS, WTSC Carto Unit from 1:126,720 General highway maps." Relief shown by hachures. Includes location map. "M7-RN-23716-5." LC Card 81-691511
1. Precipitation (Meteorology) - Washington (State) - Grant County - Maps.
G4283.G7C88 1978 .U5

General road map, Mellette County, South Dakota : III-2 / U. S. Department of Agriculture, Soil Conservation Service. Lincoln, Nebr. : USDA-SCS, 1978. 1 map : col. ; 26 x 34 cm. "Source: 1976 general county highway map and information from field technicians." Includes location map. "5,S-36,995." LC Card 81-691103
1. Mellette County (S.D.) - Road maps.
G4183.M6P2 1978 .U5

General soil map, Adams County, Wisconsin / U. S. Department of Agriculture, Soil Conservation Service [and] Research Division of the College of Agricultural and Life Sciences, University of Wisconsin. Lincoln, Nebr. :

USDA-SCS, 1980. 1 map : col. ; 41 x 27 cm. "Compiled 1979." LC Card 81-691244
1. Soils - Wisconsin - Adams County - Maps. I. University of Wisconsin-Madison. College of Agricultural and Life Sciences. Research Division.
G4123.A2J3 1979 .U5

General soil map, Armstrong County, Pennsylvania / U. S. Department of Agriculture, Soil Conservation Service, [and] Pennsylvania State University, College of Agriculture, [and] Pennsylvania Department of Environmental Resources, State Conservation Commission. [Lanham, Md.] : The Service, [1980?] 1 map : col. ; 39 x 26 cm. "Compiled 1974." Includes note. LC Card 81-690078
1. Soils - Pennsylvania - Armstrong County - Maps. I. Pennsylvania. State University. College of Agriculture. II. Pennsylvania. State Conservation Commission. III. Title.
G3823.A6J3 1974 .U5

General soil map, Burt County, Nebraska / U. S. Department of Agriculture, Soil Conservation Service. Rev. 6-79. Lincoln, Nebr. : USDA-SCS, 1979. 1 map : col. ; 26 x 36 cm. "Source: 1970 county highway map and information from field technicians." Includes location map. "5,P-36,924." LC Card 81-691073
1. Soils - Nebraska - Burt County - Maps.
G4193.B85J3 1979 .U5

General soil map, Butler County, Iowa / U. S. Department of Agriculture, Soil Conservation Service. Lincoln, Nebr. : USDA-SCS, 1978. 1 map ; 26 x 36 cm. "4-21-78." "Source: 1976 general county highway map and information from field technicians." Includes location map. "5,O-36,848." LC Card 81-691196
1. Soils - Iowa - Butler County - Maps.
G4153.B9J3 1978 .U5

General soil map, Chisago County, Minnesota / U. S. Department of Agriculture, Soil Conservation Service. Lincoln, Nebr. : USDA-SCS, 1979. 1 map : col. ; 27 x 20 cm. "6-26-79." "Source: Family of maps SCS drawing 5,S-35,088 (3-31-75) and information from SCS field personnel." Includes location map. "5,P-37,438." LC Card 81-691228
1. Soils - Minnesota - Chisago County - Maps.
G4143.C45J3 1979 .U5

General soil map, Custer County, South Dakota / USDA, Soil Conservation Service and South Dakota Agricultural Experiment Station cooperating. Lincoln, Nebr. : USDA-SCS, 1979. 1 map : col. ; 26 x 41 cm. "2-15-79." "Source: Family of maps, SCS drwg. no 5,R-31,381 (2-79) and information from field technicians." Includes location map. "5,R-37,163." LC Card 81-691164
1. Soils - South Dakota - Custer County - Maps. I. South Dakota Agricultural Experiment Station.
G4183.C8J3 1979 .U5

General soil map, Dallas County, Iowa / U. S. Department of Agriculture, Soil Conservation Service. Lincoln, Nebr. : USDA-SCS, 1980. 1 map ; 26 x 36 cm. "4-30-80." "Source: 1980 general county highway map." Includes location map. "5,P-37,824." LC Card 81-691197
1. Soils - Iowa - Dallas County - Maps.
G4153.D2J3 1980 .U5

General soil map, Dickinson County, Iowa / U. S. Department of Agriculture, Soil Conservation Service. Lincoln, Nebr. : USDA-SCS, 1979. 1 map ; 26 x 49 cm. "12-3-79." "Source: 1978 county highway map and information from SCS field personnel." Includes location map. "5,O-37,646." LC Card 81-691199
1. Soils - Iowa - Dickinson County - Maps.
G4153.D7J3 1979 .U5

General soil map, Fayette and Union Counties, Indiana. [Lincoln, Neb. : USDA-SCS, 1980?] 1 map : col. ; 21 x 30 cm. LC Card 81-691259
1. Soils - Indiana - Fayette County - Maps. 2. Soils - Indiana - Union County - Maps.
G4093.F3J3 1980 .U5

General soil map, Galveston County, Texas / Soil Conservation Service, in cooperation with Texas Agricultural Experiment Station. [Fort Worth, Tex.] : The Service, [1980] 1 map : col. ; 46 x 59 cm. "August 1980 4-R-37515." "Base compiled from Texas general highway map, polyconic projection." Depth shown by form lines. Includes descriptive index, location map, and table of "Proportion of association in the county." Text, list of "Associated features," and table of "Soil interpretations

for selected uses" on verso. LC Card 81-692258
1. Soils - Texas - Galveston County - Maps. I. Texas Agricultural Experiment Station. II. Title.
G4033.G25J3 1980 .U5

General soil map, Gosper County, Nebraska / U. S. Department of Agriculture, Soil Conservation Service. Rev. 3-1-79. Lincoln, Nebr. : USDA-SCS, 1979. 1 map ; 20 x 27 cm. "Source: General county highway map (1974) and information from field technicians." Includes location map. "5,P-36,772." LC Card 81-691075
1. Soils - Nebraska - Gosper County - Maps.
G4193.G6J3 1979 .U51

General soil map, Johnson County, Iowa / U. S. Department of Agriculture, Soil Conservation Service. Lincoln, Nebr. : USDA-SCS, 1979. 1 map ; 36 x 26 cm. "10-5-79." "Source: 1978 general county highway map and information from SCS field personnel." Includes location map. "5,O-37,566." LC Card 81-691404
1. Soils - Iowa - Johnson County - Maps.
G4153.J5J3 1979 .U5

General soil map, Kanabec County, Minnesota / U. S. Department of Agriculture, Soil Conservation Service. Lincoln, Nebr. : USDA-SCS, 1979. 1 map : col. ; 27 x 20 cm. "6-15-79." "Source: Family of maps SCS drawing 5,S-35,088 (3-31-75) and information from SCS field personnel." Includes location map. "5,P-37,437." LC Card 81-691229
1. Soils - Minnesota - Kanabec County - Maps.
G4143.K3J3 1979 .U5

General soil map, Kewaunee County, Wisconsin / U. S. Department of Agriculture, Soil Conservation Service [and] Research Division of the College of Agricultural and Life Sciences, University of Wisconsin. Lincoln, Nebr. : USDA-SCS, 1979. 1 map : col. ; 26 x 36 cm. "Compiled 1979." "9-10-79." "Source: SCS drawing 5,P-37,383 (1979)." Includes location map. "5,N-37,553." LC Card 81-691242
1. Soils - Wisconsin - Kewaunee County - Maps. I. University of Wisconsin-Madison. College of Agricultural and Life Sciences. Research Division.
G4123.K5J3 1979 .U5

General soil map, Kossuth County, Iowa / U. S. Department of Agriculture, Soil Conservation Service. Lincoln, Nebr. : USDA-SCS, 1980. 1 map ; 36 x 26 cm. "7-11-80." "Source: 1977 general county highway map and information from SCS field personnel." Includes location map. "5,O-38,050." LC Card 81-691200
1. Soils - Iowa - Kossuth County - Maps.
G4153.K6J3 1980 .U5

General soil map, Mellette County, South Dakota / U. S. Department of Agriculture, Soil Conservation Service, U. S. Department of the Interior, Bureau of Indian Affairs [and] South Dakota Agricultural Experiment Station. [Lincoln, Neb.] : The Service, [1978?] 1 map : col. ; 26 x 39 cm. "Compiled 1973." LC Card 81-691165
1. Soils - South Dakota - Mellette County - Maps. I. United States. Bureau of Indian Affairs. II. South Dakota Agricultural Experiment Station.
G4183.M6J3 1973 .U5

General soil map, Mille Lacs County, Minnesota / U. S. Department of Agriculture, Soil Conservation Service. Lincoln, Nebr. : USDA-SCS, 1979. 1 map : col. ; 27 x 19 cm. "6-29-79." "Source: Family of maps SCS drawing 5,S-35,088 (3-31-75) and information from SCS field personnel." Includes location map. "5,P-37,439." LC Card 81-691230
1. Soils - Minnesota - Mille Lacs County - Maps.
G4143.M5J3 1979 .U5

General soil map of Scott County, Minnesota / prepared by U. S. Department of Agriculture, Soil Conservation Service. Lincoln, Nebr. : USDA-SCS, 1980. 1 map : col. ; 16 x 27 cm., on sheet 49 x 64 cm. "March 1980." Includes text, location map, and "A block diagram depicting the soil associations in a west to east direction across Scott County." Text and table of "Estimated soil limitations or suitability for selected uses, Scott County, Minnesota" on verso. "5,P-37,862." LC Card 81-691232
1. Soils - Minnesota - Scott County - Maps.
G4143.S3J3 1980 .U5

General soil map, Oneida County, Wisconsin / U. S. Department of Agriculture, Soil Conservation Service. Lincoln, Nebr. : USDA-SCS, 1980. 1 map : col. ; 26 x 41 cm.

"11-31-79." "Source: Family of maps S.C.S. drawing no. 5,S-36,363 (1977) ..." Includes location map. "5,S-37,567." LC Card 81-691233
1. Soils - Wisconsin - Oneida County - Maps.
G4123.O5J3 1979 .U5

General soil map, Outagamie County, Wisconsin / U. S. Department of Agriculture, Soil Conservation Service [and] Research Division of the College of Agricultural and Life Sciences, University of Wisconsin. Lincoln, Nebr. : USDA-SCS, 1980. 1 map : col. ; 26 x 38 cm. "Compiled 1977." "4-4-80." Includes location map. "5,O-37,667." LC Card 81-691241
1. Soils - Wisconsin - Outagamie County - Maps. I. University of Wisconsin-Madison. College of Agricultural and Life Sciences. Research Division.
G4123.O8J3 1977 .U5

General soil map, Pine County, Minnesota / U. S. Department of Agriculture Soil Conservation Service. Lincoln, Nebr. : USDA-SCS, 1979. 1 map : col. ; 27 x 19 cm. "7-6-79." "Source: Family of maps SCS drawing 5,S-35,088 (3-31-75) and information from SCS field personnel." Includes location map. "5,P-37,440." LC Card 81-691231
1. Soils - Minnesota - Pine County - Maps.
G4143.P4J3 1979 .U5

General soil map, Roscommon County, Michigan / U. S. Department of Agriculture, Soil Conservation Service. Lincoln, Nebr. : USDA-SCS, 1979. 1 map ; 23 x 29 cm. "5,S-37,421." "Source: Family of maps SCS drwg. no. 5,P-32,531 (rev. 10-2-74) ..." Includes location map. "5,S-37,421." LC Card 81-691401
1. Soils - Michigan - Roscommon County - Maps.
G4113.R6J3 1979 .U5

General soil map, Seward County, Kansas / U. S. Department of Agriculture, Soil Conservation Service. Lincoln, Nebr. : USDA-SCS, 1979. 1 map : col. ; 23 x 30 cm. "4-6-79." "Source: SCS family of maps drawing no. 5,P-36,087, rev. 3-79 ..." Includes location map. "5,P-37,276." LC Card 81-691144
1. Soils - Kansas - Seward County - Maps.
G4203.S45J3 1979 .U5

General soil map, Stafford County, Kansas / U. S. Department of Agriculture, Soil Conservation Service [and] Kansas Agricultural Experiment Station. [Lincoln, Neb.] : The Service, [1977?] 1 map : col. ; 27 x 41 cm. "Compiled 1977." LC Card 81-691171
1. Soils - Kansas - Stafford County - Maps. I. Kansas Agricultural Experiment Station.
G4203.S7J3 1977 .U5

General soil map, Virginia / U. S. Department of Agriculture, Soil Conservation Service ; prepared in cooperation with Virginia Polytechnic Institute and State University, July 1979. Lanham, MD : USDA-SCS, 1979. 1 map : col. ; 22 x 48 cm. Title on verso: General soil map of Virginia : compiled to scale of 1:750,000. Text, list of soil association names, and tables of soil characteristics on verso. "1-13480." LC Card 81-690105
1. Soils - Virginia - Maps. I. Virginia Polytechnic Institute and State University. II. Title.
G3881.J3 1979 .U5

General soil map, Walla Walla County Soil Conservation District, Walla Walla County, Washington / U. S. Department of Agriculture, Soil Conservation Service. Portland, Or. : USDA-SCS, 1979. 1 map : col. ; on sheet 28 x 43 cm. "March 1979." "Thematic detail compiled by state staff." "Base map prepared by SCS, WTSC Carto Unit from 1:126,720 General highway maps." Includes location map. "M7-EN-24020-5." LC Card 81-691504
1. Soils - Washington (State) - Walla Walla County - Maps. I. Title: Walla Walla County Soil Conservation District, Walla Walla County, Washington.
G4283.W3J3 1979 .U5

General soil map, West Virginia / U. S. Department of Agriculture, Soil Conservation Service. Lanham, MD : USDA-SCS, 1980. 1 map : col. ; 52 x 59 cm. "Base Source: U. S.G.S. 1:500,000 base map." "December 1979." Includes text. Soil characteristics table on verso. "15334." LC Card 81-690096
1. Soils - West Virginia - Maps. I. Title.
G3891.J3 1979 .U5

General soil map, White County, Illinois / U. S. Department of Agriculture, Soil Conservation Service. Lincoln, Nebr. : USDA-SCS, 1978. 1 map : col. ; 23 x 30 cm., on sheet 31 x 51 cm.

"11-27-78." "Source: Family of maps, SCS drwg. no. 5,P-36,229 and information from field tehnicians. Includes location map. "5,O-37,148." LC Card 81-691445
1. Soils - Illinois - White County - Maps.
G4103.W5J3 1978 .U51

General soil map, Whitman County, Washington / U. S. Department of Agriculture, Soil Conservation Service. Portland, Or. : USDA-SCS, 1977. 1 map : col. ; on sheet 27 x 41 cm. "January 1977." "Thematic detail compiled by Washington state staff." "Base map prepared by SCS from 1:126,720 General highway map." Relief shown by hachures. Includes location map. "M7-N-23725-2." LC Card 81-691518
1. Soils - Washington (State) - Whitman County - Maps.
G4283.W6J3 1977 .U5

General soil map, Wood County, Wisconsin / U. S. Department of Agriculture, Soil Conservation Service. Lincoln, Nebr. : USDA-SCS, 1978. 1 map : col. ; 26 x 18 cm. "9-27-78." "Source: SCS base map 5,P-37,037 (9-78), NCSS general soil map (1976), and information from field technicians." Includes location map. "5,P-37,038." LC Card 81-691237
1. Soils - Wisconsin - Wood County - Maps.
G4123.W9J3 1978 .U5

Generalized geologic map, Kentucky River Basin, Kentucky / U. S. Department of Agriculture, Soil Conservation Service. Fort Worth, Tex. : USDA-SCS, 1980. 1 map : col. ; 24 x 19 cm. "August 1980 4-R-37506. August 1980 base 4-R-34039-2." "Base compiled from 1:250,000 U. S.G.S. quadrangle sheets ..." "Source: Kentucky Geological Survey, 1979." "Plate A-4." Includes location map. LC Card 81-692308
1. Geology - Kentucky - Kentucky River watershed - Maps. I. Title.
G3952.K44C5 1980 .U5

Geologic map, Gray County, Kansas / U. S. Department of Agriculture, Soil Conservation Service. Lincoln, Nebr. : USDA-SCS, 1979. 1 map : col. ; 26 x 36 cm. "5-5-79." "Source: Family of maps SCS drwg. no. 5,S-34,957 (rev. 4-79) and information from field technicians." Includes location map. "5,S-37,272." LC Card 81-691140
1. Geology - Kansas - Gray County - Maps.
G4203.G6C5 1979 .U5

Geology map, Allamakee County, Iowa / U. S. Department of Agriculture, Soil Conservation Service. Rev. 1-11-80. Lincoln, Nebr. : USDA-SCS, 1980. 1 map : col. ; 41 x 49 cm. "Source: S.C.S. drawing no. 5,R-31,511 (3-73) and information from S.C.S. field personnel." Includes location map. "5,P-37,414." LC Card 81-691201
1. Geology - Iowa - Allamakee County - Maps.
G4153.A5C5 1980 .U5

Geology map, Clayton County, Iowa / U. S. Department of Agriculture, Soil Conservation Service. Rev. 1-16-80. Lincoln, Nebr. : USDA-SCS, 1980. 1 map : col. ; 41 x 58 cm. "Source: S.C.S. drawing no. 5,R-31,511 (3-73) and information from S.C.S. field personnel." Includes location map. "5,P-37,415." LC Card 81-691202
1. Geology - Iowa - Clayton County - Maps.
G4153.C7C5 1980 .U5

Geology map, Cloud County, Kansas / U. S. Department of Agriculture, Soil Conservation Service. Lincoln, Nebr. : USDA-SCS, 1979. 1 map ; 20 x 27 cm. "8-14-74." "Source: Kansas State Geological Survey." Includes location map. "5-P-34,486.3." LC Card 81-691137
1. Geology - Kansas - Cloud County - Maps.
G4203.C65C5 1974 .U5

Geology map, Delaware County, Iowa / U. S. Department of Agriculture, Soil Conservation Service. Rev. 1-18-80. Lincoln, Nebr. : USDA-SCS, 1980. 1 map : col. ; 41 x 49 cm. "Source: S.C.S. drawing no. 5,R-31,511 (3-73) and information from S.C.S. field personnel." Includes location map. "5,P-37,416." LC Card 81-691203
1. Geology - Iowa - Delware County - Maps.
G4153.D5C5 1980 .U5

Geology map, Dubuque County, Iowa / U. S. Department of Agriculture, Soil Conservation Service. Rev. 1-23-80. Lincoln, Nebr. : USDA-SCS, 1980. 1 map : col. ; 41 x 49 cm. "Source: S.C.S. drawing no. 5,R-31,511 (3-73) and information from S.C.S. field personnel." Includes location map. "5,P-37,417." LC Card 81-691204

1. Geology - Iowa - Dubuque County - Maps.
G4153.D8C5 1980 .U5

Geology map, Fayette County, Iowa / U. S. Department of Agriculture, Soil Conservation Service. Rev. 1-25-80. Lincoln, Nebr. : USDA-SCS, 1980. 1 map : col. ; 41 x 49 cm. "Source: S.C.S. drawing no. 5,R-31,511 (3-73) and information from S.C.S. field personnel." Includes location map. "5,P-37,4/8." LC Card 81-691205
1. Geology - Iowa - Fayette County - Maps.
G4153.F2C5 1980 .U5

Geology map, Howard County, Iowa / U. S. Department of Agriculture, Soil Conservation Service. Rev. 1-30-80. Lincoln, Nebr. : USDA-SCS, 1980. 1 map : col. ; 41 x 49 cm. "Source: S.C.S. drawing no. 5,R-31,511 (3-73) and information from S.C.S. field personnel." Includes location map. "5,P-37,419." LC Card 81-691206
1. Geology - Iowa - Howard County - Maps.
G4153.H7C5 1980 .U5

Geology map, Republic County, Kansas / U. S. Department of Agriculture, Soil Conservation Service. Lincoln, Nebr. : USDA-SCS, 1974. 1 map ; 23 x 30 cm. "8-7-74." "Source: Kansas State Geological Survey." Includes location map. "5,P-34,484.3." LC Card 81-691154
1. Geology - Kansas - Republic County - Maps.
G4203.R4C5 1974 .U5

Geology map, Winneshiek County, Iowa / U. S. Department of Agriculture, Soil Conservation Service. Rev. 2-1-80. Lincoln, Nebr. : USDA-SCS, 1980. 1 map : col. ; 41 x 49 cm. "Source: S.C.S. drawing no. 5,R-31,511 (3-73) and information from S.C.S. field personnel." Includes location map. "5,P-37,420." LC Card 81-691207
1. Geology - Iowa - Winneshiek County - Maps.
G4153.W6C5 1980 .U5

Geology map, Wood County, Wisconsin / U. S. Department of Agriculture, Soil Conservation Service. Lincoln, Nebr. : USDA-SCS, 1978. 1 map : col. ; 26 x 18 cm. "9-27-78." "Source: SCS base map 5,P-37,037 (9-78) and information from field technicians." Includes location map. "5,P-37,039." LC Card 81-691235
1. Geology - Wisconsin - Wood County - Maps.
G4123.W9C5 1978 .U5

Gierbolini, Roberto E. Soil survey of Ponce area of southern Puerto Rico /. [Washington] [1979] iii, 80 p., [22] fold. leaves of plates :
LC Card 80-602349   DDC 631.4/7/72957 19
S599.25.P832 P663

Glacial deposits, Wood County, Wisconsin / U. S. Department of Agriculture, Soil Conservation Service. Lincoln, Nebr. : USDA-SCS, 1978. 1 map : col. ; 26 x 18 cm. "9-27-78." "Source: SCS base map 5,P-37,037 (9-78) and information from field technicians." Includes location map. "5,P-37,040." LC Card 81-691239
1. Glacial landforms - Wisconsin - Wood County - Maps.
G4123.W9C38 1978 .U5

Gonick, Walter N. General soil map of Connecticut /. Hyattsville, Md. , 1978. 1 map :
LC Card 81-690080
G3781.J3 1978 .G6

Gordon County, Georgia : soil interpretive map of characteristics for depth to seasonal high water table / U. S. Department of Agriculture, Soil Conservation Service. Fort Worth, Tex. : USDA-SCS, 1979. 1 map : col. ; 34 x 46 cm. "Base compiled from U. S.G.S. quadrangle sheets and Georgia county highway map ..." UTM grid. Includes note and location map. "April 1978 base 4-R-36590." LC Card 81-690450
1. Water table - Georgia - Gordon County - Maps.
G3923.G6C34 1978 .U5

Gosper County, Nebraska / U. S. Department of Agriculture, Soil Conservation Service. Lincoln, Nebr. : USDA-SCS, 1981. 1 map : col. ; 46 x 59 cm. "4-10-80." "Source: Late date 7 1/2' USGS quadrangle maps and 1974 county highway map." Includes location map. "5,P-37,656." LC Card 81-691011
1. Gosper County (Neb.) - Maps.
G4193.G6 1980 .U5

Grand Isle County, Vermont / U. S. Department of Agriculture, Soil Conservation Service ; edited by the Geological Survey. Lanham, MD : USDA-SCS, [1979?] 1 map : col. ; 51 x 16 cm., on sheet 61 x 51 cm. Title in lower right corner: Grand Isle Co., Vt. : 1972.

"Compiled in 1975 from USGS 1:24,000-scale topographic maps dated 1948-1972." "Planimetry revised from photographs taken 1972." "1-13147." LC Card 81-690028
1. Grand Isle County (Vt.) - Maps. I. United States. Geological Survey.
G3753.G7 1972 .U5

Grand Traverse, Michigan / U. S. Department of Agriculture, Soil Conservation Service. [Lincoln, Neb.] : The Service, [1979?] 1 map : col. ; 44 x 33 cm. "Base source: USGS 1:100,000 county base compiled in 1975." Includes location map. "5,P-37,515." LC Card 81-691405
1. Grand Traverse County, Mich. - Maps.
G4113.G7 1979 .U5

Grantham, Dana R., 1936- Soil survey of Winnebago and Boone Counties, Illinois /. [Washington] , 1980. ix, 279 p., [53] leaves of plates : LC Card 80-602556   DDC 631.4/9773 s 631.4/7/77329 19
S599.I5 A3 no. 107

Gravel pit location map, Mellette County, South Dakota : IV-6 / U. S. Department of Agriculture, Soil Conservation Service. Lincoln, Nebr. : USDA-SCS, 1978. 1 map : col. ; 26 x 34 cm. "Source: 1976 general county highway map and information from field technicians." Includes location map. "5,S-36,682." LC Card 81-691102
1. Gravel - South Dakota - Mellette County - Maps.
G4183.M6H5 1978 .U5

Greenbrier County, West Virginia / United States Department of Agriculture, Soil Conservation Service ; cartographic mapping by the Geological Survey. [Lanham, Md.] : The Service, [1980] 1 map : col. ; 66 x 83 cm. "February 1980." "Compiled in 1976 from USGS 1:24,000-scale topographic maps dated 1961-1972." "Planimetry revised from aerial photographs taken 1973." Title in lower margin: Greenbrier Co., W.Va. : N3741-W7957.5/35.5 x 56.5, 1973. Stamped on LC copy: Produced under contract printing. "1,S-13169." LC Card 81-690015
1. Greenbrier County (W.Va.) - Maps. I. United States. Geological Survey.
G3893.G8 1973 .U5

Greene County, Illinois / U. S. Department of Agriculture, Soil Conservation Service [and] United States Department of the Interior, Geological Survey. Lincoln, Nebr. : USDA-SCS, 1980. 1 map : col. ; 49 x 45 cm. "Base source: USGS 1/100,000 compiled in 1979." Includes location map. "5,S-38,075." LC Card 81-691419
1. Greene County (Ill.) - Maps. I. United States. Geological Survey.
G4103.G7 1980 .U5

Ground water availability map, Cloud County, Kansas / U. S. Department of Agriculture, Soil Conservation Service. Lincoln, Nebr. : USDA-SCS, 1979. 1 map ; 20 x 27 cm. "8-14-74." "Source: Kansas State Geological Survey." Includes location map. "5,P-34,486.4." LC Card 81-691134
1. Water, Underground - Kansas - Cloud County - Maps.
G4203.C65C34 1974 .U5

Ground water availability map, Republic County, Kansas / U. S. Department of Agriculture, Soil Conservation Service. Lincoln, Nebr. : USDA-SCS, 1974. 1 map ; 23 x 30 cm. "8-9-74." "Source: Kansas State Geological Survey." Includes location map. "5,P-34,484.4." LC Card 81-691152
1. Water, Underground - Kansas - Republic County - Maps.
G4203.R4C34 1974 .U5

Gully erosion problem areas, Missouri / U. S. Department of Agriculture, Soil Conservation Service. Lincoln, Nebr. : USDA-SCS, 1978. 1 map : col. ; 26 x 18 cm. "4-7-78." "Source: Family of maps SCS drawing no. 5,S-32,925.1 (3-5-74) and information from field technicians." "5,N-36,549.7." LC Card 81-691213
1. Soil erosion - Missouri - Maps. I. Title.
G4161.J4 1978 .U51

Gundlach, Howard F. Soil survey of Sauk County, Wisconsin /. [Washington] [1980] ix, 248 p., [67] fold. leaves of plates : LC Card 80-602384   DDC 631.4/7/77576 19
S599.W5 G86

Hall County, Nebraska / U. S. Department of Agriculture, Soil Conservation Service. Lincoln,

Nebr. : USDA-SCS, 1979. 1 map : col. ; 46 x 59 cm. "12-11-78." "Source: 1977 general county highway map." Includes location map. "5,P-37,087.1." LC Card 81-691010
1. Hall County (Neb.) - Maps.
G4193.H2 1978 .U5

Hamilton, Vernon Leroy, 1932- Soil survey of Mitchell County, Kansas /. [Washington], 1980. vii, 94 p., [30] fold. leaves of plates : LC Card 80-602876   DDC 631.4/7/78123 19
S599.K2 H315

Hampden County, Massachusetts / United States Department of Agriculture, Soil Conservation Service. Lanham, MD : USDA-SCS, 1980. 1 map : col. ; 32 x 63 cm. Title in lower margin: Hampden Co., Mass. : N4159.5-W7207.5/21.5 x 57.5, 1976. "Compiled in 1976 from USGS 1:24,000-scale topographic maps dated 1958-1973." "Planimetry revised from aerial photographs taken 1975." LC Card 81-690042
1. Hampden County (Mass.) - Maps.
G3763.H3 1976 .U5

Hampshire County, Massachusetts / United States Department of Agriculture, Soil Conservation Service. Lanham, MD : USDA-SCS, 1980. 1 map : col. ; 35 x 58 cm. "Map edited 1979." Title in lower margin: Hampshire Co., Mass. : N4210.5-W7211.5/23.5x53, 1964. "Compiled from USGS 1:24,000-scale topographic maps dated 1964-1973. Planimetry revised from aerial photographs taken 1975 and other source data." LC Card 81-690019
1. Hampshire County (Mass.) - Maps.
G3763.H4 1979 .U5

Harford County, Maryland / United States Department of Agriculture, Soil Conservation Service ; edited by the Geological Survey. Lanham, MD : USDA-SCS, 1980. 1 map : col. ; 41 x 38 cm. Title in lower margin: Harford Co., Md. : N3916-W7601.5/28x33.5, 1978. "Compiled from USGS 1:24,000-scale topographic maps dated 1948-1957." "Planimetry revised from aerial photographs taken 1974 and other source data." "1-16170." LC Card 81-690012
1. Harford County (Md.) - Maps. I. United States. Geological Survey.
G3843.H3 1978 .U5

Harrison County, West Virginia / United States Department of Agriculture, Soil Conservation Service ; cartographic mapping by the Geological Survey. Lanham, MD : USDA-SCS, 1980. 1 map : col. ; 43 x 39 cm. Title in lower margin: Harrison Co., W.Va. : N 3905.5-W8009.5/23x27, 1979. "Compiled from USGS 1:24,000-scale topographic maps dated 1958-1964." "Planimetry revised from aerial photographs taken 1976 and other source data." "1,S-15448." LC Card 81-690040
1. Harrison County (W.Va.) - Maps. I. United States. Geological Survey.
G3893.H5 1979 .U5

Hartman, George William, 1935- General soil map with soil interpretations for land use planning: [Maricopa County, Arizona] /. Portland, Or., 1973. 49 p.:
NYPL [Map Div. 80-258]

Heil, Dennis M. Soil survey of Beadle County, South Dakota /. [Washington] , 1979. viii, 169 p., [98] fold. leaves of plates : LC Card 80-602070   DDC 631.4/7/783274 19
S599.S6 H43

Heil, Dennis M. Soil survey of McCook County, South Dakota /. [Washington] , 1980. vii, 123 p., [25] fold. leaves of plates : LC Card 80-601638   DDC 631.4/7/783372 19
S599.S6 H44

Herren, Edward C. Soil survey of Abbeville County, South Carolina /. [Washington] [1980] viii, 82 p., [25] fold. leaves of plates : LC Card 80-602551   DDC 631.4/7/75735 19
S599.S58 H46

Herren, Edward C. Soil survey of Anderson County, South Carolina /. [Washington , 1979] viii, 79 p., [34] leaves of plates : LC Card 79-604161   DDC 631.4/7/75725 19
S599.S58 H47

Hettinger County, North Dakota / U. S. Department of Agriculture, Soil Conservation Service. Lincoln, Nebr. : USDA-SCS, 1980. 1 map ; 46 x 61 cm. "Source: General county highway map 1975." Relief shown by hachures and spot heights.

Includes location map. LC Card 81-691260
1. Hettinger County (N.D.) - Maps.
G4173 H4 1980 .U5

Hickman, Glenn L. Soil survey of Mobile County, Alabama /. [Washington] , 19. vii, 134 p., [60] fold. leaves of plates : LC Card 80-603367   DDC 631.4/7/76122 19
S599.A4 H53

Hillis, John H. Soil survey of Lagrange County, Indiana /. [Washington] [1980] vii, 135 p., [19] fold. leaves of plates : LC Card 80-602561   DDC 631.4/7/77279 19
S599.I63 H54

Hillsborough County, New Hampshire / U. S. Department of Agriculture, Soil Conservation Service. Lanham, Md. : USDA-SCS, 1980. 1 map ; 59 x 59 cm. "Base Source: New Hampshire family of maps 1:500,000." Includes location map. "1-15828." LC Card 81-690126
1. Hillsborough County (N.H.) - Maps.
G3743.H4 1980 .U5

Historical and recreational sites, Whitman County, Washington / U. S. Department of Agriculture, Soil Conservation Service. Portland, Or. : USDA-SCS, 1977. 1 map : col. ; on sheet 27 x 41 cm. "January 1977." Relief shown by hachures. "Thematic detail compiled by Washington state staff." "Base map prepared by SCS from 1:126,720 general highway map." Includes location map. "M7-N-23725-6." LC Card 81-691525
1. Historic sites - Washington (State) - Whitman County - Maps. 2. Outdoor recreation - Washington (State) - Whitman County - Maps.
G4283.W6E635 1977 .U5

Historical districts, Okanogan County Conservation District, Okanogan County, Washington / U. S. Department of Agriculture, Soil Conservation Service. Portland, Or. : USDA-SCS, 1980. 1 map : col. ; on sheet 28 x 44 cm. "July 1980." Relief shown by hachures. "Thematic detail compiled by state staff." "Base map prepared by SCS, WTSC Carto Unit from 1:126,720 General highway maps." Includes location map. "M7-EN-24119." LC Card 81-691539
1. Historic sites - Washington (State) - Okanogan County - Maps. I. Title. II. Title: Okanogan County Conservation District, Okanogan County, Washington.
G4283.O3E635 1980 .U5

Historical trails and sites, upper Little Nemaha watershed, Lancaster, Cass, and Otoe Counties, Nebraska / U. S. Department of Agriculture, Soil Conservation Service. Lincoln, Nebr. : USDA-SCS, 1979. 1 map : col. ; 26 x 39 cm. "12-28-78." "Source: SCS drawing no. 5,R-23,485 (7-66) and information from field technicians." Includes indexes and location map. "5,R-37,209." LC Card 81-691090
1. Trails - Nebraska - Little Nemaha River watershed - Maps. 2. Historic sites - Nebraska - Little Nemaha River watershed - Maps.
G4192.L5P25 1978 .U5

Historical, utilities, and quarries map, lower Little Nemaha watershed, Johnson, Nemaha, Otoe, and Richardson Counties, Nebraska / U. S. Department of Agriculture, Soil Conservation Service. Lincoln, Nebr. : USDA-SCS, 1979. 1 map : col. ; 26 x 50 cm. "1-18-79." "Source: SCS drwg. no. 5,R-24,031 (rev. 12-78) and information from field technicians." Includes index to historical points of interest and location map. "5,S-37,202." LC Card 81-691089
1. Historic sites - Nebraska - Little Nemaha River watershed - Maps. 2. Public utilities - Nebraska - Little Nemaha River watershed - Maps. 3. Quarries and quarrying - Nebraska - Little Nemaha River watershed - Maps.
G4192.L5E635 1979 .U5

Hole, Thornton J. F. Soil survey of Ocean County, New Jersey /. [Washington] [1980] vii, 102 p., [35] fold. leaves of plates : LC Card 80-602312   DDC 631.4/7/74948 19
S599.N5 H64

Holmes County, Florida : soil interpretive map of limitations for soil drainage and water table depths / U. S. Department of Agriculture, Soil Conservation Service. Fort Worth, Tex. : USDA-SCS, 1980. 1 map : col. ; 44 x 57 cm. "Base compiled from U. S.G.S. quadrangle sheets and Florida county general highway map, polyconic projection." "10,000 meter universal transverse Mercator grid, zone 16." Includes notes and location map. "August 1979 4-R-37204." LC Card 81-690356

United States. Soil Conservation Service. (cont.)

1. Soil percolation - Florida - Holmes County - Maps.
2. Water table - Florida - Holmes County - Maps.
G3933.H8C34 1979 .U5

Holt County, Nebraska / U. S. Department of
Agriculture, Soil Conservation Service. [Lincoln,
Nebr.] : The Service, [1980] 1 map : col. ; 46 x
50 cm. "5-12-80." "Source: 1974 general county
highway map." Includes location map. "5,R-37,858.1."
LC Card 81-691009
1. Holt County (Neb.) - Maps.
G4193.H7 1980 .U5

Horsch, Marcellus L. Soil survey of Cowley
County, Kansas /. [Washington] [1980] viii,
123 p., [47] fold. leaves of plates :   LC Card
80-601849   DDC 631.4/7/78189 19
S599.K2 H578

Howard County, Maryland / United States
Department of Agriculture, Soil Conservation
Service ; edited by the Geological Survey.
Hyattsville, MD : USDA-SCS, 1979. 1 map :
col. ; 25 x 36 cm. "Compiled by USGS from USGS
1:24,000-scale topographic maps dated 1944-1965."
"Planimetry revised from aerial photographs taken 1975
and 1976 and other source data."   LC Card 81-690007
1. Howard County, Md. - Maps. I. United States.
Geological Survey.
G3843.H6 1979 .U5

Howard County, Nebraska / U. S. Department
of Agriculture, Soil Conservation Service.
Lincoln, Nebr. : USDA-SCS, 1978. 1 map :
col. ; 46 x 59 cm. "12-5-78." "Source: 1964 general
county highway map." Includes location map.
"5,P-37,133.1."   LC Card 81-691008
1. Howard County (Neb.) - Maps.
G4193.H9 1978 .U5

Hydrologic soil groups, Chickies Creek
watershed, Lancaster and Lebanon Counties,
Pennsylvania / U. S. Department of
Agriculture, Soil Conservation Service.
Hyattsville, Md. : USDA-SCS, 1977. 1 map :
col. ; 25 x 34 cm. "Source: 1969 U. S. Geological
Survey quadrangles." Includes location map.   LC Card
81-690273
1. Soils - Pennsylvania - Chickies Creek watershed -
Maps. 2. Hydrology - Pennsylvania - Chickies Creek
watershed - Maps. I. Title.
G3822.C45J3 1977 .U5

Hydrologic unit map, Wisconsin, 1974 / U. S.
Department of Agriculture, Soil Conservation
Service. Lincoln, Nebr. : USDA-SCS, 1978. 1
map : col. ; 24 x 18 cm., on sheet 51 x 31 cm.
"11-2-78." "Source: USDA map and the USGS
hydrologic unit map of Wisconsin (1974)." "5,S-37,113."
LC Card 81-691250
1. Hydrology - Wisconsin - Maps.
G4121.C3 1974 .U51

Important farmland of New York / U. S.
Department of Agriculture, Soil Conservation
Service. [Lanham? Md.] : The Service, 1979. 1
map : col. ; 70 x 90 cm. Also shows soil classes.
"Interpretations derived from general soil map compiled
by Cornell University Agricultural Experiment Station,
constructed 1977 by Cartographic Division, Soil
Conservation Service, U. S. Department of Agriculture."
"August 1979." "Source Data: U. S. Geological Survey
1:500,000 Base Map." Base map "Revised 7-78."
"1,P-12,771." Stamped on LC copy: Produced under
contract printing.   LC Card 81-693111
1. Agricultural resources - New York (State) - Maps. 2.
Land use, Rural - New York (State) - Maps. 3. Land
capability for agriculture - New York (State) - Maps. 4.
Soils - New York (State) - Maps. I. Title.
G3801.J15 1977 .U5

Indian reservations, Wisconsin / U. S.
Department of Agriculture, Soil Conservation
Service. Lincoln, Nebr. : USDA-SCS, 1980. 1
map : col. ; 26 x 20 cm., on sheet 51 x 31 cm.
"2-20-74." "Source: 1970 national atlas of the United
States of America." "5,S-32,817.1."   LC Card
81-691251
1. Indians of North America - Wisconsin -
Reservations - Maps.
G4121.G6 1974 .U5

Iowa County, Iowa / U. S. Department of
Agriculture, Soil Conservation Service [and]
United States Department of the Interior,
Geological Survey. [Lincoln, Neb.] : The
Service, [1979?] 1 map : col. ; 34 x 33 cm. "Base
source: USGS 1:100,000 county base compiled from
1965-1973 topographic maps." Includes location map.
"5,O-37,512."   LC Card 81-691188
1. Iowa County (Iowa) - Maps. I. United States.

Geological Survey.
G4153.I6 1979 .U5

Irrigated acres map, Kansas / U. S. Department
of Agriculture, Soil Conservation Service.
Lincoln, Nebr. : USDA-SCS, 1979. 1 map :
col. ; 18 x 23 cm. "Source: Family of maps S.C.S.
drwg. no. 5,S-32,550 (rev. 1-76) and information from
S.C.S. field technicians." "5,S-37,429."   LC Card
81-691124
1. Irrigation - Kansas - Maps. I. Title.
G4201.J4 1979 .U51

Irrigated land map, Seward County, Kansas /
U. S. Department of Agriculture, Soil
Conservation Service. Lincoln, Nebr. :
USDA-SCS, 1979. 1 map : col. ; 23 x 30 cm.
"Source: SCS family of maps drawing no. 5,P-36,087,
rev. 3-79 ..." Includes location map. "5,P-37,278."   LC
Card 81-691143
1. Irrigation - Kansas - Seward County - Maps. I. Title.
G4203 S45J4 1979 .U5

Irrigation map, Gray County, Kansas / U. S.
Department of Agriculture, Soil Conservation
Service. Lincoln, Nebr. : USDA-SCS, 1979. 1
map : col. ; 26 x 36 cm. "Source: Family of maps
SCS drwg. no. 5,S-34,957 (rev. 4-79) and information
from field technicians." Includes location map.
"5,S-37,269."   LC Card 81-691139
1. Irrigation - Kansas - Gray County - Maps.
G4203.G6J4 1979 .U5

Irrigation map, Ness County, Kansas / U. S.
Department of Agriculture, Soil Conservation
Service. Lincoln, Nebr. : USDA-SCS, 1979. 1
map : col. ; 41 x 57 cm. "Source: Family of maps
S.C.S. drwg. no. 5,S-36,165 (3-77) and information from
field technicians." Includes location map. "5,S-37,182."
LC Card 81-691151
1. Irrigation - Kansas - Ness County - Maps.
G4203.N5J4 1979 .U5

Jackson County, Illinois / U. S. Department of
Agriculture, Soil Conservation Service [and]
United States Department of the Interior,
Geological Survey. Lincoln, Nebr. :
USDA-SCS, 1980. 1 map : col. ; 37 x 40 cm.
"Base source: USGS 1/100,000 compiled in 1979."
Includes location map. "5,P-38,079."   LC Card
81-691420
1. Jackson County, Ill. - Maps. I. United States.
Geological Survey.
G4103.J2 1980 .U5

Jackson County, West Virginia / United States
Department of Agriculture, Soil Conservation
Service ; cartographic mapping by the
Geological Survey. Lanham, MD : USDA-SCS,
1980. 1 map : col. ; 62 x 37 cm. Title in lower
margin: Jackson Co., W.Va. : N3832.5-W8130/33.5X25,
1978. "Compiled from 1:24,000-scale topographic maps
dated 1957-1968." "Planimetry revised from aerial
photographs taken 1976-1977 and other source data."
"1,S-13170."   LC Card 81-690035
1. Jackson County (W.Va.) - Maps. I. United States.
Geological Survey.
G3893.J2 1978 .U5

Jakel, Dale E. Soil survey of Adams County,
Wisconsin. [Washington, D.C.?] , 1980. vii, 142
p., 57 folded p. of plates :   LC Card 81-600526
DDC 631.4/7/77556 19
S599.W5 J34

Jefferson County, Iowa / U. S. Department of
Agriculture, Soil Conservation Service [and]
United States Department of the Interior,
Geological Survey. Lincoln, Nebr. :
USDA-SCS, 1979. 1 map : col. ; 27 x 34 cm.
"Base source: USGS 1:100,000 county base compiled in
1978." Includes location map. "5,P-37,702."   LC Card
81-691187
1. Jefferson County (Iowa) - Maps. I. United States.
Geological Survey.
G4153.J4 1979 .U5

Jefferson County, West Virginia / United States
Department of Agriculture, Soil Conservation
Service ; cartographic mapping by the
Geological Survey. Lanham, MD : USDA-SCS,
1980. 1 map : col. ; 43 x 29 cm. Title in lower
margin: Jefferson Co., W.Va. :
N3707.5--W7743/23X19.5, 1977. "Compiled in 1977
from USGS 1:24,000-scale topographic maps dated
1966-1971." "Planimetry revised from aerial photographs
taken 1975-1976 and other source data." "1,P-13263."
LC Card 81-690037
1. Jefferson County, W. Va. - Maps. I. United States.
Geological Survey.
G3893.J4 1977 .U5

Johnson County, Indiana / U. S. Department of
Agriculture, Soil Conservation Service. [Lincoln,
Neb.] : The Service, [1979?] 1 map : col. ; 28 x
22 cm. "Base source: USGS 1:100,000 county base
compiled from 1961-1973 topographic maps." Includes
location map. "5,O-37,505."   LC Card 81-691258
1. Johnson County, Ind. - Maps.
G4093.J7 1979 .U5

Kanawha County, West Virginia / United States
Department of Agriculture, Soil Conservation
Service ; cartographic mapping by the
Geological Survey. [Lanham, Md.] : The
Service, [1980] 1 map : col. ; 75 x 65 cm. Title
in lower margin: Kanawha Co., W.Va. :
N3757.5-W8111/40.5x44.5, 1979. "Compiled from
USGS 1:24,000-scale topographic maps dated
1957-1967." "Planimetry revised from aerial photographs
taken 1977 and other source data." Stamped on LC
copy: Produced under contract printing. "1,S-11036."
"February 1980."   LC Card 81-690016
1. Kanawha County (W.Va.) - Maps. I. United States.
Geological Survey.
G3893.K3 1979 .U5

Kane County, Illinois / U. S. Department of
Agriculture, Soil Conservation Service [and]
United States Department of the Interior,
Geological Survey. Lincoln, Nebr. :
USDA-SCS, 1980. 1 map : col. ; 53 x 35 cm.
"Base source: USGS 1:100,000 compiled in 1976."
Includes location map. "5,P-37,893."   LC Card
81-691421
1. Kane County (Ill.) - Maps. I. United States.
Geological Survey.
G4103.K2 1980 .U5

Kendall County, Illinois / U. S. Department of
Agriculture, Soil Conservation Service [and]
United States Department of the Interior,
Geological Survey. Lincoln, Nebr. :
USDA-SCS, 1980. 1 map : col. ; 32 x 33 cm.
"Base source: USGS 1:100,000 compiled in 1978."
Includes location map. "5,P-37,892."   LC Card
81-691422
1. Kendall County (Ill.) - Maps. I. United States.
Geological Survey.
G4103.K4 1980 .U5

Kennebec County, Maine / United States
Department of Agriculture, Soil Conservation
Service ; cartographic mapping by the
Geological Survey. Lanham, MD : USDA-SCS,
1980. 1 map : col. ; 56 x 50 cm. Title in lower
margin: Kennebec Co., Me. : N4406--W6921.5/38x47,
1978. "Compiled in 1978 from USGS 1:24,000 and
1:62,500-scale topographic maps dated 1956-1970."
"Planimetry revised from aerial photographs taken
1976-1977 and other source data." "1-13507."   LC
Card 81-690041
1. Kennebec County (Me.) - Maps. I. United States.
Geological Survey.
G3733.K4 1978 .U5

Kerr, James W. Soil survey of Pickaway
County, Ohio /. [Washington, D.C.] [1980] vii,
172 p., [36] fold. leaves of plates :   LC Card
80-602251   DDC 631.4/7/771815 19
S599.O3 K47

King, John M. Soil survey of Henderson
County, North Carolina /. [Washington, D.C. ,
1980] viii, 89 p., [15] fold. leaves of plates :
LC Card 80-602311   DDC 631.4/7/75692 19
S599.N8 K55

La Salle County, Illinois / U. S. Department of
Agriculture, Soil Conservation Service [and]
United States Department of the Interior,
Geological Survey. Lincoln, Nebr. :
USDA-SCS, 1980. 1 map : col. ; 51 x 33 cm.
"Base source: USGS 1:100,000 compiled in 1975."
Includes location map. "5,P-37,894."   LC Card
81-691424
1. La Salle County, Ill. - Maps. I. United States.
Geological Survey.
G4103.L3 1980 .U5

Lake County, Illinois / U. S. Department of
Agriculture, Soil Conservation Service [and]
United States Department of the Interior,
Geological Survey. Lincoln, Nebr. :
USDA-SCS, 1980. 1 map : col. ; 34 x 32 cm.
"Base source: USGS 1:100,000 county base compiled in
1976." Includes location map. "5,P-37,507."   LC Card
81-691423
1. Lake County, Ill. - Maps. I. United States.
Geological Survey.
G4103.L2 1980 .U5

Lancaster County, Nebraska / U. S.

Department of Agriculture, Soil Conservation
Service. Lincoln, Nebr. : USDA-SCS, 1979. 1
map : col. ; 61 x 39 cm. "10-31-78." "Source: 1968
general county highway map." Includes location map.
"5,S-37,108.1."   LC Card 81-691007
1. Lancaster County (Neb.) - Maps.
G4193.L3 1978 .U5

Lancaster County, Nebraska / U. S.
Department of Agriculture, Soil Conservation
Service. Rev. 2-80. Lincoln, Neb. : USDA-SCS,
1980. 1 map : col. ; 59 x 46 cm. "Source:
Lancaster County general highway map (1978) and
information from SCS field personnel." Includes location
map. "5,P-31,264."   LC Card 81-691076
1. Lancaster County (Neb.) - Maps.
G4193.L3 1980 .U5

Land capability classes, Chickies Creek
watershed, Lancaster and Lebanon Counties,
Pennsylvania / U. S. Department of
Agriculture, Soil Conservation Service.
Hyattsville, Md. : USDA-SCS, [1978] 1 map :
col. ; 25 x 34 cm. "Source: 1969 U. S. Geological
Survey quadrangles." "3-23-78." Includes location map.
"126888."   LC Card 81-690269
1. Land capability, Agricultural - Pennsylvania -
Chickies Creek watershed - Maps. I. Title.
G3822.C45G4 1978 .U5

Land ownership, Grant County, Washington /
U. S. Department of Agriculture, Soil
Conservation Service. Portland, Or. :
USDA-SCS, 1977. 1 map : col. ; on sheet 49 x
28 cm. Shows major public land holdings. "June 1977."
"Thematic detail compiled by state staff." "Base map
prepared by SCS, WTSC Carto Unit from 1:126,720
General highway maps." Relief shown by hachures.
Includes location map. "M7-RN-23716-1."   LC Card
   81-691515
1. Grant County (Wash.) - Public lands - Maps.
G4283.G7G5 1977 .U5

Land ownership, Stevens County Conservation
District, Stevens County, Washington / U. S.
Department of Agriculture, Soil Conservation
Service. Portland, Or. : USDA-SCS, 1980. 1
map : col. ; on sheet 57 x 28 cm. Shows major
public land holdings. "June 1979." "Thematic detail
compiled by state staff." "Base map prepared by SCS,
WTSC Carto Unit from 1:126,720 General highway
maps." Relief shown by hachures. Includes location
map. "M7-RN-24051-1."   LC Card 81-691516
1. Stevens County (Wash.) - Public lands - Maps. I.
Title. II. Title: Stevens County Conservation District,
Stevens County, Washington.
G4283.S8G5 1979 .U5

Land ownership, Walla Walla County Soil
Conservation District, Walla Walla County,
Washington / U. S. Department of Agriculture,
Soil Conservation Service. Portland, Or. :
USDA-SCS, 1979. 1 map : col. ; on sheet 28 x
43 cm. Shows major public lands. "March 1979."
"Thematic detail compiled by state staff." "Base map
prepared by SCS, WTSC Carto Unit from 1:126,720
General highway maps." Includes location map.
"M7-EN-24020-2."   LC Card 81-691503
1. Walla Walla County (Wash.) - Public lands - Maps.
I. Title. II. Title: Walla Walla County Soil Conservation
District, Walla Walla County, Washington.
G4283.W3G4 1979 .U51

Land use and natural plant communities,
Chaffee County, Colorado / U. S. Department
of Agriculture, Soil Conservation Service.
Portland, Or. : USDA-SCS, 1979. 1 map : col. ;
on sheet 63 x 48 cm. "February 1979." Shows land
use, range sites, and woodlands. "Thematic detail
prepared by state staff." "Base map prepared by SCS,
WTSC Carto Unit from 1:126,720 General highway
maps." Relief shown by hachures. Includes location map
and inset. "M7-E-23444-8."   LC Card 81-691557
1. Land use - Colorado - Chaffee County - Maps. 2.
Phytogeography - Colorado - Chaffee County - Maps.
G4313.C2G4 1979 .U5

Land use and natural plant communities, Custer
County, Colorado / U. S. Department
of Agriculture, Soil Conservation Service.
Portland, Or. : USDA-SCS, 1979. 1 map : col. ;
on sheet 48 x 63 cm. "February 1979." Shows land
use, range sites, and woodlands. "Thematic detail
compiled by state staff." "Base map prepared by SCS,
WTSC Carto Unit from 1:126,720 General highway
maps." Relief shown by hachures. Includes location
map. "M7-E-23444-14."   LC Card 81-691555
1. Land use - Colorado - Custer County - Maps. 2.
Phytogeography - Colorado - Custer County - Maps.
G4313.C8G4 1979 .U5

Land use and natural plant communities, Eagle
County, Colorado / U. S. Department of
Agriculture, Soil Conservation Service.
Portland, Or. : USDA-SCS, 1979. 1 map on 2
sheets : col. ; 52 x 64 cm., sheets 63 x 49 cm.
"June 1978." Shows land use, range sites, and
woodlands. "Thematic detail compiled by state staff."
"Base map prepared by SCS, WTSC Carto Unit from
1:126,720 General highway maps." Relief shown by
hachures. Includes location map. "M7-O-23444-19."
   LC Card 81-691548
1. Land use - Colorado - Eagle County - Maps. 2.
Phytogeography - Colorado - Eagle County - Maps.
G4313.E2G4 1978 .U5

Land use and natural plant communities,
Jefferson County, Colorado / U. S. Department
and Agriculture, Soil Conservation Service.
Portland, Or. : USDA-SCS, 1980. 1 map : col. ;
on sheet 64 x 49 cm. "June 1979." Shows land use,
range sites, and woodlands. "Thematic detail compiled
by state staff." "Base map prepared by SCS, WTSC
Carto Unit from 1:126,720 General highway maps."
Relief shown by hachures. Includes location map and
inset of Pike National Forest area. "M7-O-23444-30."
   LC Card 81-691558
1. Land use - Colorado - Jefferson County - Maps. 2.
Phytogeography - Colorado - Jefferson County - Maps.
G4313.J4G4 1979 .U5

Land use and natural plant communities, Lake
County, Colorado / U. S. Department of
Agriculture, Soil Conservation Service.
Portland, Or. : USDA-SCS, 1979. 1 map : col. ;
on sheet 48 x 63 cm. "June 1978." Shows land use,
range sites, and woodlands. "Thematic detail compiled
by state staff." "Base map prepared by SCS, WTSC
Carto Unit from 1:126,720 General highway maps."
Includes location map. "M7-E-23444-33."   LC Card
   81-691554
1. Land use - Colorado - Lake County - Maps. 2.
Phytogeography - Colorado - Lake County - Maps.
G4313.L2G4 1978 .U5

Land use and natural plant communities, San
Miguel County, Colorado / U. S. Department
of Agriculture, Soil Conservation Service.
Portland, Or. : USDA-SCS, 1979. 1 map on 2
sheets : col. ; 93 x 45 cm., sheets 48 x 63 cm.
"June 1978." Shows land use, range sites, and
woodlands. "Thematic detail compiled by state staff."
"Base map prepared by SCS, WTSC Carto Unit from
1:126,720 General highway maps." Relief shown by
hachures. Includes sheet index and location map.
"M7-E-23444-57."   LC Card 81-691549
1. Land use - Colorado - San Miguel County - Maps. 2.
Phytogeography - Colorado - San Miguel County -
Maps.
G4313.S4G4 1978 .U5

Land use and natural plant communities,
Summit County, Colorado / U. S. Department
of Agriculture, Soil Conservation Service.
Portland, Or. : USDA-SCS, 1979. 1 map : col. ;
on sheet 63 x 48 cm. "June 1978." Shows land use,
range sites, and woodlands. "Thematic detail compiled
by state staff." "Base map prepared by SCS, WTSC
Carto Unit from 1:126,720 General highway maps."
Relief shown by hachures. Includes location map.
"M7-0-23444-59."   LC Card 81-691545
1. Land use - Colorado - Summit County - Maps. 2.
Phytogeography - Colorado - Summit County - Maps.
G4313.S8G4 1978 .U5

Land use and natural plant communities, Teller
County, Colorado / U. S. Department of
Agriculture, Soil Conservation Service.
Portland, Or. : USDA-SCS, 1979. 1 map : col. ;
on sheet 63 x 48 cm. "June 1978." Shows land use,
range sites, and woodlands. "Thematic detail compiled
by Colorado State Staff." "Base map prepared by SCS,
Portland Carto. Unit from General highway map."
Relief shown by hachures. Includes location map.
"M7-0-23444-60."   LC Card 81-691544
1. Land use - Colorado - Teller County - Maps. 2.
Phytogeography - Colorado - Teller County - Maps.
G4313.T4G4 1978 .U5

Land use, Grant County, Washington / U. S.
Department of Agriculture, Soil Conservation
Service. Portland, Or. : USDA-SCS, 1977. 1
map : col. ; on sheet 49 x 28 cm. "November
1976." "Thematic detail compiled by Washington State
Staff." "Base map prepared by SCS, Portland Carto.
Unit from General highway map." Includes location
map. Includes location map. "M7-RN-23716."   LC
Card 81-691514
1. Land use - Washington (State) - Grant County -

Maps.
G4283.G7G4 1976 .U5

Land use map, Arapahoe County, Colorado /
U. S. Department of Agriculture, Soil
Conservation Service. Portland, Or. :
USDA-SCS, 1980. 1 map : col. ; on sheet 48 x
64 cm. "October 1979." "Thematic detail compiled by
state staff." "Base map prepared by SCS, WTSC Carto
Unit fom 1:126,720 General highway maps." Includes
location map. "M7-E-22527-3."   LC Card 81-691560
1. Land use - Colorado - Arapahoe County - Maps.
G4313.A6G4 1979 .U5

Land use map, Cloud County, Kansas / U. S.
Department of Agriculture, Soil Conservation
Service. Lincoln, Nebr. : USDA-SCS, 1979. 1
map ; 20 x 27 cm. "8-15-74. Source: University of
Kansas Space Technology Center. Includes location
map. "5,P-34,486.5."   LC Card 81-691135
1. Land use, Rural - Kansas - Cloud County - Maps.
G4203.C65G4 1974 .U5

Land use map, Franklin County, Tennessee /
U. S. Department of Agriculture, Soil
Conservation Service. Fort Worth, Tex. :
USDA-SCS, 1979. 1 map : col. ; 25 x 40 cm.
"February 1979 4-R-36973." "Base compiled from
original field material." Includes location map.   LC
   Card 81-692254
1. Land use - Tennessee - Franklin County - Maps. I.
Title.
G3963.F7G4 1979 .U5

Land use map, Gray County, Kansas / U. S.
Department of Agriculture, Soil Conservation
Service. Lincoln, Nebr. : USDA-SCS, 1979. 1
map : col. ; 26 x 36 cm. "5-5-79." "Source: Family
of maps SCS drwg. no. 5,S-34,957 (rev. 4-79) and
information from field technicians." Includes location
map. "5,S-37,268."   LC Card 81-691138
1. Land use, Rural - Kansas - Gray County - Maps.
G4203.G6G4 1979 .U5

Land use map, Kansas / U. S. Department of
Agriculture, Soil Conservation Service. Lincoln,
Nebr. : USDA-SCS, 1979. 1 map : col. ; 18 x
23 cm. "5-31-79." "Source: Family of maps S.C.S.
drwg. no. 5,S-32,550 (rev. 1-76) and information from
S.C.S. field technicians." "5,S-37,423."   LC Card
   81-691123
1. Land use, Rural - Kansas - Maps.
G4201.G4 1979 .U5

Land use map, Kishacoquillas Creek watershed,
parts of Mifflin, Centre, Snyder, and
Huntingdon Counties, Pennsylvania / United
States Department of Agriculture, Soil
Conservation Service. [Lanham? Md.] : The
Service, [1980?] 1 map : col. ; 26 x 30 cm. "Base
Source: 1:24,000 topographic maps." "25,000 foot grid
ticks based on Pennsylvania coordinate system" Includes
location map. "1-16237."   LC Card 81-690276
1. Land use - Pennsylvania - Kishacoquillas Creek
watershed - Maps. I. Title.
G3822.K58G4 1980 .U5

Land use map, Mifflin County, Pennsylvania /
United States Department of Agriculture, Soil
Conservation Service. Lanham, MD :
USDA-SCS, 1980. 1 map : col. ; 27 x 37 cm.
"Base Source: 1:24,000 topographic maps." Includes
location map. "1-16189."   LC Card 81-690077
1. Land use - Pennsylvania - Mifflin County - Maps. I.
Title.
G3823.M5G4 1980 .U51

Land use map, Ness County, Kansas / U. S.
Department of Agriculture, Soil Conservation
Service. Lincoln, Nebr. : USDA-SCS, 1979. 1
map : col. ; 41 x 57 cm. "1-30-79." "Source: Family
of maps SCS drawing no. 5,S-36,165 (3-77) ..." Includes
location map. "5,S-37,178."   LC Card 81-691150
1. Land use, Rural - Kansas - Ness County - Maps.
G4203.N5G4 1979 .U5

Land use map, Republic County, Kansas / U. S.
Department of Agriculture, Soil Conservation
Service. Lincoln, Nebr. : USDA-SCS, 1974. 1
map ; 23 x 30 cm. "8-9-74." Source: University of
Kansas Space Technology Center. Includes location
map. "5,P-34,484.5."   LC Card 81-691153
1. Land use, Rural - Kansas - Republic County - Maps.
G4203.R4G4 1974 .U5

Land use map, Seward County, Kansas / U. S.
Department of Agriculture, Soil Conservation
Service. Lincoln, Nebr. : USDA-SCS, 1979. 1
map : col. ; 23 x 30 cm. "4-13-79." "Source: SCS
family of maps drawing no. 5,P-36,087, rev. 3-79 ..."
Includes location map. "5,P-37,291."   LC Card
   81-691142

1. Land use, Rural - Kansas - Seward County - Maps.
G4203.S45G4 1979 .U5

Land use map, upper Tioga River watershed,
Tioga and Bradford Counties, Pennsylvania / U.
S. Department of Agriculture, Soil Conservation
Service. Hyattsville, Md. : USDA-SCS, 1979. 1
map : col. ; 26 x 41 cm. "April 1979." "Base source:
USGS 1:24,000 Topo Quads (1969, 1970)" Includes
location map. "1-14-064." LC Card 81-690278
1. Land use - Tioga River watershed (Pa. and N.Y.) -
Maps. I. Title.
G3822.T55G4 1979 .U5

Land use plan for town of Cato. Hyattsville,
Md. : USDA-SCS ; Auburn, N.Y. : Cayuga
County Soil & Water Conservation District
[distributor], 1978. 1 map : col. ; on sheet 45 x
54 cm. Photomap. Includes text. "A plan for Cato"
[text] on verso. "Exhibit 507.19." "13,419." LC Card
81-690187
1. Land use - New York (State) - Cato - Planning -
Maps. 2. Cato (N.Y.) - Photo maps. I. Title.
G3804.C296G4 1978 .U5

Land use, upper Little Nemaha watershed,
Lancaster, Cass, and Otoe Counties, Nebraska /
U. S. Department of Agriculture, Soil
Conservation Service. Lincoln, Nebr. :
USDA-SCS, 1979. 1 map : col. ; 26 x 39 cm.
"1-30-79." "Source: USGS unedited advance print
quadrangles, Douglas, Firth, Lincoln ... Drainage stereo
interpreted from aerial photographs ..." Includes location
map. "5,P-37,232." LC Card 81-691087
1. Land use, Rural - Nebraska - Little Nemaha River
watershed - Maps.
G4192.L5G4 1979 .U51

Land use, Walla Walla County Soil
Conservation District, Walla Walla County,
Washington / U. S. Department of Agriculture,
Soil Conservation Service. Portland, Or. :
USDA-SCS, 1979. 1 map : col. ; on sheet 28 x
43 cm. "March 1979." "Thematic detail compiled by
state staff." "Base map prepared by SCS, WTSC Carto
Unit from 1:126,720 General highway maps." Includes
location map. "M7-EN-24020-1." LC Card 81-691506
1. Land use - Washington (State) - Walla Walla
County - Maps. I. Title: Walla Walla County Soil
Conservation District, Walla Walla County,
Washington.
G4283.W3G4 1979 .U5

Land use, Whitman County, Washington / U.
S. Department of Agriculture, Soil Conservation
Service. Portland, Or. : USDA-SCS, 1977. 1
map ; on sheet 27 x 41 cm. "January 1977."
"Thematic detail compiled by Washington state staff."
"Base map prepared by SCS from 1:126,720 General
highway map." Relief shown by hachures. Includes
location map. "M7-N-23725-7." LC Card 81-691521
1. Land use, Rural - Washington (State) - Whitman
County - Maps.
G4283.W6G4 1977 .U5

Larsen, Lynn Seymour, 1913- Soil survey of
Elbert County, Colorado, western part /.
[Washington, D.C.] [1980] viii, 135 p., [2] fold.
leaves of plates : LC Card 80-603150 DDC
631.4/7/78887 19
S599.C6 L382

Larson, Jerry D. Soil survey of Berrien County,
Michigan. [Washington, D.C.?] , 1980. vii, 192
p. 90 folded p. of plates : LC Card 81-600705
DDC 631.4/7/77411 19
S599.M4 L363

Lazaretto Creek watershed, Nottoway County,
Virginia : December 1979 / U. S. Department
of Agriculture. Lanham, MD : USDA-SCS,
1980. 1 map : col. ; 26 x 56 cm. "Source: USGS
Topo Quad Sheets 1:24,000." "Contour interval 50 feet."
Oriented with north toward the upper left. Includes
location map. "1-15448." LC Card 81-690289
1. Lazaretto Creek watershed (Va.) - Maps,
Topographic.
G3882.L38 1979 .U5

Leifer, Lewis. Soil survey of Los Angeles
County, California, west San Fernando Valley
area /. [Washington , 1980] viii, 107 p., [2]
fold. leaves of plates : LC Card 80-602305 DDC
631.4/7/79493 19
S599.C2 L44

Lenawee County, Michigan / U. S. Department
of Agriculture, Soil Conservation Service [and]
United States Department of the Interior,
Geological Survey. Lincoln, Nebr. :
USDA-SCS, 1980. 1 map : col. ; 35 x 41 cm.
"Base source: USGS 1/100,000 compiled in 1978."

Includes location map. "5,P-38,083." LC Card
81-691403
1. Lenawee County, Mich. - Maps. I. United States.
Geological Survey.
G4113.L4 1980 .U5

Lerch, Norbert K. Soil survey of Butler County,
Ohio /. [Washington] [1980] vii, 175 p., [38]
fold. leaves of plates : LC Card 80-602516 DDC
631.4/7/77175 19
S599.O3 L36

Lincoln County, Nebraska / U. S. Department
of Agriculture, Soil Conservation Service.
Lincoln, Nebr. : USDA-SCS, 1979. 1 map :
col. ; "11-7-78." "Source: 1976 general
county highway map." Includes location map.
"5,R-37,130.1." LC Card 81-691006
1. Lincoln County, Neb. - Maps.
G4193.L4 1978 .U5

Linn County, Iowa / U. S. Department of
Agriculture, Soil Conservation Service [and]
United States Department of the Interior,
Geological Survey. Lincoln, Nebr. :
USDA-SCS, 1979. 1 map : col. ; 43 x 36 cm.
"Base source: USGS 1:100,000 county base compiled in
1976." Includes location map. "5,P-37,392." LC Card
81-691186
1. Linn County (Iowa) - Maps. I. United States.
Geological Survey.
G4153.L5 1979 .U5

Linsemier, Lyle H. Soil survey of Huron
County, Michigan. [Washington] , 1979. vii,
145 p., [39] fold. leaves of plates : LC Card
80-602145 DDC 631.4/7/77444 19
S599.M4 L56

Litchfield County, Connecticut / United States
Department of Agriculture, Soil Conservation
Service. Lanham, MD : USDA-SCS, 1979. 1
map : col. ; 66 x 54 cm. Title in lower margin:
Litchfield Co., Conn. : N4128-W7253/35.5 x 38.5,
1976. "Compiled by USGS in 1976 from USGS
1:24,000-scale topographic maps dated 1955-1972."
"Planimetry revised from aerial photographs taken
1974." LC Card 81-690029
1. Litchfield County (Conn.) - Maps. I. United States.
Geological Survey.
G3783.L5 1976 .U5

Livingston County, Illinois / U. S. Department
of Agriculture, Soil Conservation Service.
Lincoln, Nebr. : USDA-SCS, 1979. 1 map :
col. ; 41 x 58 cm. "10-27-78." "Source: 1975 general
county highway map." Includes location map.
"5,S-37,109.1." LC Card 81-691441
1. Livingston County, Ill. - Maps.
G4103.L6 1978 .U5

Logan County, Illinois / U. S. Department of
Agriculture, Soil Conservation Service [and]
United States Department of the Interior,
Geological Survey. Lincoln, Nebr. :
USDA-SCS, 1980. 1 map : col. ; 38 x 34 cm.
"Base source: USGS 1/100,000 compiled in 1975."
Includes location map. "5,P-37,878." LC Card
81-691425
1. Logan County (Ill.) - Maps. I. United States.
Geological Survey.
G4103.L7 1980 .U5

Long, Bobby M. Soil survey of Berkeley
County, South Carolina /. [Washington, D.C.]
1980. viii, 94 p., [51] fold. leaves of plates :
LC Card 80-601634 DDC 631.4/7/75793 19
S599.S58 L66

Lovell, Burrell B. Soil survey of Malheur
County, Oregon, northeastern part /.
[Washington, D.C.] 1980. viii, 94 p., [22]
folded leaves of plates : LC Card 80-603621
DDC 631.4/7/79597 19
S599.O7 L68

Lower use map, lower Little Nemaha
watershed, Johnson, Nemaha, Otoe and
Richardson Counties, Nebraska / U. S.
Department of Agriculture, Soil Conservation
Service. Lincoln, Nebr. : USDA-SCS, 1979. 1
map : col. ; 26 x 45 cm. "3-28-79." "Source: SCS
drawing no. 5,R-24,031 (1-67) and information from
field technicians." Includes location map. "5,S-37,246."
LC Card 81-691084
1. Land use, Rural - Nebraska - Little Nemaha River
watershed - Maps.
G4192.L5G4 1979 .U5

McLoda, N. A. Soil survey of Franklin County,
Ohio /. [Washington] [1980] viii, 188 p., [37]
fold. leaves of plates : LC Card 80-602372 DDC

631.4/7/77156 19
S599.O3 M32

Macon County, Illinois / U. S. Department of
Agriculture, Soil Conservation Service. Lincoln,
Nebr. : USDA-SCS, 1977. 1 map : col. ; 37 x
47 cm. "4-5-77." "Source: 1972 general county highway
map." Includes location map. "5,P-36,208.1." LC Card
81-691442
1. Macon County (Ill.) - Maps.
G4103.M3 1977 .U5

Madison County, Iowa / U. S. Department of
Agriculture, Soil Conservation Service [and]
United States Department of the Interior,
Geological Survey. Lincoln, Nebr. :
USDA-SCS, 1979. 1 map : col. ; 33 x 31 cm.
"Base source: USGS 1:100,000 county base compiled in
1978." Includes location map. "5,P-37,700." LC Card
81-691185
1. Madison County (Iowa) - Maps. I. United States.
Geological Survey.
G4153.M2 1979 .U5

Madison County, Nebraska / U. S. Department
of Agriculture, Soil Conservation Service.
Lincoln, Nebr. : USDA-SCS, 1978. 1 map :
col. ; 46 x 59 cm. "11-14-78." "Source: 1971 general
county highway map." Includes location map.
"5,P-37,127.1." LC Card 81-691005
1. Madison County (Neb.) - Maps.
G4193.M3 1978 .U5

Maine, status of flood insurance studies / U. S.
Department of Agriculture, Soil Conservation
Service. Lanham, MD : USDA-SCS, 1979. 1
map : col. ; 24 x 19 cm. Legend title: Status of
flood insurance studies program conducted by SCS in
Maine as of October 1, 1979. "1-10051." LC Card
81-690091
1. Insurance, Flood - Maine - Maps. I. Title.
G3731.C32 1979 .U5

Major drainage basins, South Dakota / U. S.
Department of Agriculture, Soil Conservation
Service. Lincoln, Nebr. : USDA-SCS, 1977. 1
map : col. ; 18 x 23 cm. "Source: Family of maps
SCS drawing no. 5,S-32,929 (4-77) and information
from field technicians." Indexed. "5,O-36,219." LC
Card 81-691100
1. Watersheds - South Dakota - Maps. I. Title:
Drainage basins, South Dakota.
G4181.C315 1977 .U5

Major land use areas, Columbia County,
Washington / U. S. Department of Agriculture,
Soil Conservation Service. Portland, Or. :
USDA-SCS, 1979. 1 map : col. ; on sheet 28 x
22 cm. "June 1979." "Thematic detail compiled by
state staff." "Base map prepared by SCS, WTSC Carto
Unit from 1:126,720 General highway maps." Relief
shown by hachures. Includes location map.
"M7-EL-24052." LC Card 81-691501
1. Land use, Rural - Washington - Columbia County -
Maps.
G4283.C6G4 1979 .U5

[Major rivers of Wisconsin] / U. S. Department
of Agriculture, Soil Conservation Service.
Lincoln, Nebr. : USDA-SCS, 1981. 1 map :
col. ; 24 x 17 cm., on sheet 51 x 31 cm. LC
Card 81-691249
1. Rivers - Wisconsin - Maps.
G4121.C3 1981 .U5

Major streams and drainages, Whitman County,
Washington / U. S. Department of Agriculture,
Soil Conservation Service. Portland, Or. :
USDA-SCS, 1977. 1 map : col. ; on sheet 27 x
41 cm. "January 1977." Relief shown by hachures.
"Thematic detail compiled by Washington state staff."
"Base map prepared by SCS from 1:126,720 General
highway map." Includes location map. "M7-N-23725-5."
LC Card 81-691522
1. Rivers - Washington (State) - Whitman County -
Maps. 2. Drainage - Washington (State) - Whitman
County - Maps. I. Title.
G4283.W6C3 1977 .U5

Manatee County, Florida, phosphate holdings /
U. S. Department of Agriculture, Soil
Conservation Service. Fort Worth, Tex. :
USDA-SCS, 1980. 1 map : col. ; 41 x 56 cm.
"Base map prepared by the Geological Survey in
cooperation with the Soil Conservation Service."
"Compiled from USGS 1:24,000-scale topographic maps
dated 1956-1973." Includes notes, statistical data, and
location map. LC Card 81-690257
1. Phosphate leases - Florida - Manatee County - Maps.
I. United States. Geological Survey.
G3933.M3H5 1980 .U5

Mason County, West Virginia / United States Department of Agriculture, Soil Conservation Service ; cartographic mapping by the Geological Survey. Lanham, MD : USDA-SCS, 1980. 1 map : col. ; 63 x 40 cm. Title in lower margin: Mason Co., W.Va. : N3828-W8146/34 x 27.5, 1973. "Compiled in 1976 from USGS 1:24,000-scale topographic maps dated 1957-1968." "Planimetry revised from aerial photographs taken 1973." "1,S-13264." LC Card 81-690034
1. Mason County (W.Va.) - Maps. I. United States. Geological Survey.
G3893.M36 1973 .U5

Massachusetts : 1979 / U. S. Department of Agriculture, Soil Conservation Service. Lanham, MD ; USDA-SCS, 1980. 1 map : col. ; 24 x 38 cm. "Base map constructed by the Cartographic Division, Soil Conservation Service, USDA, from USGS maps, 1:250,000 Series." "Town lines and names from Massachusetts Department of Community Affairs map, October 1970." In lower margin: Figure 7. Without legend. Some town areas tinted yellow or green. "1,P-12,701." LC Card 81-690116
1. Massachusetts - Maps.
G3760 1979 .U5

Meherrin River watershed, Brunswick and Greensville Counties, Virginia : December 1979 / U. S. Department of Agriculture, Soil Conservation Service. Lanham, MD : USDA-SCS, 1980. 1 map : col. ; 25 x 37 cm. "Source: USGS Topo Quad Sheets 1:24,000." "Contour interval 50 feet." Oriented with north to the right. Includes location map. "1-15502." LC Card 81-690291
1. Meherrin River watershed (Va. and N.C.) - Maps, Topographic.
G3882.M43 1979 .U5

Meland, Arvid C. Soil survey of Lawrence County, South Dakota /. [Washington, D.C. , 1979] viii, 173 p., [25] fold. leaves of plates : LC Card 80-601071 DDC 631.4/7/78391 19
S599.S6 M44

Merrimack County, New Hampshire / U. S. Department of Agriculture, Soil Conservation Service. Lanham, MD : USDA-SCS, 1980. 1 map ; 59 x 59 cm. "Base Source: New Hampshire family of maps 1:500,000." Includes location map. "1-15826." LC Card 81-690121
1. Merrimack County (N.H.) - Maps.
G3743.M4 1980 .U5

Michigan / U. S. Department of Agriculture, Soil Conservation Service. Lincoln, Nebr. : USDA-SCS, 1979. 1 map ; 52 x 41 cm. "11-21-79." "Source: Michigan state family of maps drawing no. 5,S-32,577." "5,O-37,599." LC Card 81-691408
1. Michigan - Maps.
G4110 1979 .U5

Middlesex County, Connecticut / United States Department of Agriculture, Soil Conservation Service. Lanham, MD : USDA-SCS, 1979. 1 map : col. ; 46 x 39 cm. Title in lower margin: Middlesex Co., Conn. : 1978. "Compiled by USGS from USGS 1:24,000-scale topographic maps dated 1953-1967." "Planimetry revised from aerial photographs taken 1972 and other source data." LC Card 81-690031
1. Middlesex County (Conn.) - Maps. I. United States. Geology Survey.
G3783.M5 1978 .U5

Miles, Ray L. Soil survey of Summit County area, Colorado /. [Washington] [1980] vii, 74 p., [2] fold. leaves of plates : LC Card 80-602603 DDC 631.4/7/78845 19
S599.C6 M54

Mines, utilities, and pipeline map, upper Little Nemaha watershed, Lancaster, Cass, and Otoe Counties, Nebraska / U. S. Department of Agriculture, Soil Conservation Service. Lincoln, Nebr. : USDA-SCS, 1979. 1 map : col. ; 26 x 39 cm. "12-27-78." "Source: SCS drwg. no. 5,R-23,485 and information from field technicians." Includes location map. "5,S-37,206." LC Card 81-691086
1. Mines and mineral resources - Nebraska - Little Nemaha River watershed - Maps. 2. Public utilities - Nebraska - Little Nemaha River watershed - Maps. 3. Pipe lines - Nebraska - Little Nemaha River watershed - Maps.
G4192.L5H1 1978 .U5

Minnehaha County, South Dakota / U. S. Department of Agriculture, Soil Conservation Service. [Lincoln, Neb.] : The Service, [1979?] 1 map : col. ; 34 x 46 cm. "Base source: USGS 1:100,000 county base compiled in 1975." "5,P-37,502." LC Card 81-691101
1. Minnehaha County (S.D.) - Maps.
G4183.M8 1979 .U5

Missouri, status of PL-566 watershed projects / U. S. Department of Agriculture, Soil Conservation Service. Rev. 4-16-79. Lincoln, Nebr. : USDA-SCS, 1979. 1 map : col. ; 26 x 33 cm. "Source: Family of maps SCS drawing no. 5,S-32,925 (3-5-74) and information from field technicians." "5,S-34,618." LC Card 81-691209
1. Watersheds - Missouri - Maps. I. Title: PL-566 watershed projects.
G4161.C315 1979 .U5

Missouri, status of PL-566 watershed projects / U. S. Department of Agriculture, Soil Conservation Service. Rev. 3-5-80. Lincoln, Nebr. : USDA-SCS, 1980. 1 map : col. ; 26 x 33 cm. "Source: Family of maps SCS drawing no. 5,S-32,925 (3-5-74) and information from field technicians." "5,S-34,618." LC Card 81-691208
1. Watersheds - Missouri - Maps. I. Title: PL-566 watershed projects.
G4161.C315 1980 .U5

Mitchell, Michael J. Soil survey of Winnebago County, Wisconsin /. [Washington] [1980] vii, 182 p., [23] fold. leaves of plates : LC Card 80-602659 DDC 631.4/7/77564 19
S599.W5 M58

Mitigation and construction requirements, Lost-Duck Creeks watershed, Kay County, Oklahoma. Fort Worth, Tex. : USDA-SCS, 1980. 2 maps : col. ; on sheet 51 x 28 cm. "May 1980 4-R-37448." Shows recommended mitigation area, woodland, wetland, rangeland, farmstead, cropland, excavated side, selected clearing and snagging, and stream bank stabilization. "Compiled from field information." CONTENTS. - Lost Creek -- Duck Creek. LC Card 81-692269
1. Lost Creek watershed (Kay County, Okla.) - Channelization - Maps. 2. Duck Creek watershed (Kay County, Okla.) - Channelization - Maps. 3. Lost Creek watershed (Kay County, Okla.) - Regulation - Maps. 4. Duck Creek watershed (Kay County, Okla.) - Regulation - Maps. I. Title.
G4022.L6N2 1980 .U5

Monroe County, West Virginia / United States Department of Agriculture, Soil Conservation Service ; cartographic mapping by the Geological Survey. Lanham, MD : USDA-SCS, 1980. 1 map : col. ; 42 x 59 cm. Title in lower margin: Monroe Co., W.Va. : N 3722-W8012.5/22.5x40, 1978. "Compiled from USGS 1:24,000-scale topographic maps dated 1965-1971." "Planimetry revised from aerial photographs taken 1976-1977 and other source data." "1,P-13342." LC Card 81-690033
1. Monroe County (W.Va.) - Maps. I. United States. Geological Survey.
G3893.M8 1978 .U5

Montgomery County, Maryland / United States Department of Agriculture, Soil Conservation Service ; edited by the Geological Survey. Hyattsville, MD : USDA-SCS, 1979. 1 map : col. ; 38 x 45 cm. "Compiled by USGS in 1976 from USGS 1:24,000-scale topographic maps dated 1968-1972." "Planimetry revised from aerial photographs taken 1976 and other source data." LC Card 81-690009
1. Montgomery County, Md. - Maps. I. United States. Geological Survey.
G3843.M6 1979 .U5

Montgomery County, Ohio / U. S. Department of Agriculture, Soil Conservation Service. [Lincoln, Neb.] : The Service, [1979?] 1 map : col. ; 32 x 31 cm. "Base source: USGS 1:100,000 county base compiled in 1976." "5,O-37,506." LC Card 81-691082
1. Montgomery County (Ohio) - Maps.
G4083.M65 1979 .U5

Morton County, North Dakota / U. S. Department of Agriculture, Soil Conservation Service. Lincoln, Nebr. : USDA-SCS, 1977. 1 map ; 41 x 59 cm. "5-19-77." "Source: 1972 general county highway map." Includes location map. "5,R-36,231.1." LC Card 81-691446
1. Morton County (N.D.) - Maps.
G4173.M7 1977 .U5

Murphree, Leland C., 1912- Soil survey of Itawamba County, Mississippi /. [Washington] [1979] viii, 86 p., [25] fold. leaves of plates : LC Card 80-602033 DDC 631.4/7/762982 19
S599.M5 M89

Murphy, James O. Soil survey of Clayton, Fayette, and Henry Counties, Georgia/. [Washington] [1979] viii, 74 p., [32] fold. leaves of plates : LC Card 80-602614 DDC 631.4/7/75843 19
S599.G4 M87

Nantucket County, Massachusetts / United States Department of Agriculture, Soil Conservation Service. Lanham, MD : USDA-SCS, 1980. 1 map : col. ; 15 x 26 cm. Title in lower margin: Nantucket Co., Mass. : N 4114-W6957/10x23, 1979. "Compiled from USGS 1:24,000-scale topographic maps dated 1972-1977." "Planimetry revised from aerial photographs taken 1969-1977 and other source data." LC Card 81-690021
1. Nantucket (Mass.) - Maps.
G3762.N3 1979 .U5

Natural soil groups, St. Marys County, Maryland / United States Department of Agriculture, Soil Conservation Service. [Lanham? Md.] : The Service, [1981] 1 map : col. ; 87 x 79 cm. "March 1981." "This natural soil group map is a generalization of the detailed soil map of St. Marys County Soil Survey ..." Includes notes and location map. "1-16590." Stamped on LC copy: Produced under contract printing. LC Card 81-693031
1. Soils - Maryland - St. Marys County - Maps. I. Title.
G3843.S3J3 1981 .U5

Natural soil groups, Worcester County, Maryland / United States Department of Agriculture, Soil Conservation Service. [Lanham? Md.] : The Service, [1980?] 1 map : col. ; 82 x 100 cm. "This natural soil group map is a generalization of the detailed soil map of Worcester County Soil Survey ..." Includes notes and location map. "1-11892." Stamped on LC copy: Produced under contract printing. LC Card 81-693029
1. Soils - Maryland - Worcester County - Maps. I. Title.
G3843.W6J3 1980 .U5

Nebraska / U. S. Department of Agriculture, Soil Conservation Service. Lincoln, Nebr. : USDA-SCS, 1966. 1 map ; 18 x 26 cm. "57M-244." LC Card 81-691016
1. Nebraska - Maps.
G4190 1966 .U5

Neher, R. E. Soil survey of Luna County, New Mexico /. [Washington, D.C.] 1980. iii, 80 p., [81] folded leaves of plates : DDC 631.4/7/78968 19
S599.N6 N4

NETSC location, Broomall, Pennsylvania / U. S. Department of Agriculture, Soil Conservation Service. Lanham, MD : USDA-SCS, 1980. 1 map : col. ; 18 x 26 cm. Shows approach routes to the Northeast Technical Service Center of the Soil Conservation Service. LC Card 81-690189
1. Broomall region (Pa.) - Maps. I. Title.
G3824.B84A1 1980 .U5

New Castle County, Delaware / United States Department of Agriculture, Soil Conservation Service ; edited by the Geological Survey. Hyattsville, MD : USDA-SCS, 1979. 1 map : col. ; 49 x 27 cm. "Compiled by USGS in 1975 from USGS 1:24,000-scale topographic maps dated 1948-1973." "Planimetry revised from aerial photographs taken 1973." LC Card 81-690013
1. New Castle County (Del.) - Maps. I. United States. Geological Survey.
G3833.N4 1979 .U5

New Haven County, Connecticut / United States Department of Agriculture, Soil Conservation Service. Lanham, MD : USDA-SCS, 1979. 1 map : col. ; 54 x 67 cm. Title in lower margin: New Haven Co., Conn. : 1978. "Compiled by USGS in 1978 from USGS 1:24,000 topographic maps dated 1955-1968." "Planimetry revised from aerial photographs taken 1974 and other source data." LC Card 81-690030
1. New Haven County, Conn. - Maps. I. United States. Geological Survey.
G3783.N3 1978 .U5

Newaygo County, Michigan / U. S. Department of Agriculture, Soil Conservation Service. Lincoln, Nebr. : USDA-SCS, 1976. 1 map ; 39 x 26 cm. "3-8-76." "Source: General highway map, Newaygo County, 1969, and information from field technicians." Includes location map. "5,O-29,470." LC Card 81-691402

1. Newaygo County (Mich.) - Maps.
G4113.N4 1976 .U5

Nicholson, John C. Soil survey of Goochland
County, Virginia /. [Washington] , 1980. ix,
137 p., [22] fold. leaves of plates :   LC Card
80-601854   DDC 631.4/7/755455 19
S599.V8 N52

Nielson, Woodrow. Soil survey of Navajo
Indian Reservation, San Juan County, Utah /.
[Washington] [1980] viii, 119 p., [12] fold.
leaves of plates :   LC Card 80-602348   DDC
631.4/7/79259 19
S599.U8 N53

Northwest River-Indian Creek watershed,
Chesapeake City, Virginia : December 1979 /
U. S. Department of Agriculture, Soil
Conservation Service. Lanham, MD :
USDA-SCS, 1980. 1 map : col. ; 27 x 38 cm.
"Source: USGS Topo Quad Sheets 1:24,000." "Contour
interval 10 feet." Includes location map. "1-15600." LC
Card 81-690292
*1. Northwest River watershed (Va. and N.C.) - Maps,
Topographic. 2. Indian Creek watershed (Chesapeake,
Va.) - Maps, Topographic. I. Title.*
G3882.N67 1979 .U5

Obion County, Tennessee / prepared by Soil
Conservation Service for Obion County
Conservation District. Fort Worth, Tex. :
USDA-SCS, 1980. 1 map : col. ; 58 x 27 cm.
"3-80 4-R-36 533." Shows distribution of amount of
erosion per acre per year. "Planimetry revised from
aerial photographs taken 1975." "Base map prepared by
the Geological Survey in cooperation with the Soil
Conservation Service." Includes location map.   LC
Card 81-692275
*1. Soil erosion - Tennessee - Obion County - Maps. I.
Title.*
G3963.O2J4 1980 .U5

Ohio status of soil surveys, October 1980 / U.
S. Department of Agriculture, Soil Conservation
Service. Rev. 6-10-80. Lincoln, Nebr. :
USDA-SCS, 1980. 1 map : col. ; 26 x 19 cm.
"Source: Family of maps SCS drawing no. 5, S-32,927
(4-74) and SCS field personnel." "5,S-35,213." LC Card
81-691033
1. Soil-surveys - Ohio - Maps.
G4081.J3 1980 .U5

Ohio status of soil survyes, October 1979 / U.
S. Department of Agriculture, Soil Conservation
Service. Rev. 6-29-79. Lincoln, Nebr. :
USDA-SCS, 1979. 1 map : col. ; 24 x 18 cm.
"Source: Family of maps SCS drawing no. 5,S-32,927
(4-74) and SCS field personnel." "5,S-35,213." LC
Card 81-691035
1. Soil-surveys - Ohio - Maps.
G4081.J3 1979 .U5

Orange County, Vermont / U. S. Department
of Agriculture, Soil Conservation Service ;
edited by the Geological Survey. Lanham,
MD : USDA-SCS, 1979. 1 map : col. ; 53 x 63
cm. Title in lower margin: Orange Co., Vt. : 1977.
"Compiled in 1977 from USGS 1:24,000 scale
topographic maps dated 1970-1973." "1-13148." LC
Card 81-690025
*1. Orange County (Vt.) - Maps. I. United States.
Geological Survey.*
G3753.O6 1977 .U5

Otter, Augustine J. Soil survey of Calumet and
Maitowoc Counties, Wisconsin /. [Washington,
D.C.] 1980. vii, 176 p., [64] fold. leaves of
plates :   LC Card 80-602383   DDC 631.4/7/77566
19
S599.W5 O86

P.L. 566 watershed status, southwest Ohio
River basin study area, Ohio / U. S.
Department of Agriculture. Lincoln, Nebr. :
USDA-SCS, 1978. 1 map : col. ; 46 x 26 cm.
Shows southwestern Ohio. "6-8-78." At head of title:
Map 5-7. "Source: Family of maps SCS draw. no.
5,R-34,214 (6-74) and information from field
technicians." Includes location map. "5,S-36,948." LC
Card 81-691040
*1. Watersheds - Ohio - Maps. I. Title: Southwest Ohio
River basin study area, Ohio. II. Title: Ohio River basin
study area, Ohio.*
G4081.C315 1978 .U5

Pannell, James P., 1926- Soil survey of Rio
Grande County area, Colorado /.
[Washington] , 1980. iv, 89 p., [2] fold. leaves
of plates :   LC Card 80-602320   DDC
631.4/7/78837 19
S599.C6 P36

Parke County, Indiana / U. S. Department of
Agriculture, Soil Conservation Service. Lincoln,
Nebr. : USDA-SCS, 1980. 1 map : col. ; 46 x
59 cm. "9-22-80." "Source: 1976 general county
highway map and information from SCS field
personnel." Includes location map. "5,P-36,273.1." LC
Card 81-691257
1. Parke County (Ind.) - Maps.
G4093.P2 1980 .U5

Parker, John Leon, 1912- Soil survey of
Stillwater County area, Montana /.
[Washington, D.C.]. [1980] vii, 131, 98, [4] p.,
[1] fold. leaf of plates :   LC Card 80-603196
DDC 631.4/7/786651 19
S599.M9 P37

Pasture production and soil loss areas, western
South Dakota river basins / U. S. Department
of Agriculture, Soil Conservation Service.
Lincoln, Nebr. : USDA-SCS, 1979. 1 map :
col. ; 18 x 26 cm. "7-18-79." "Source: Family of
maps S.C.S drwg. no. 5,30,116 (5-8-72) and information
from field technicians." At head of title: Figure C-3.
Includes location map. Table on verso. "5,N-37,477."
LC Card 81-691116
*1. Pastures - South Dakota - Maps. 2. Soil erosion -
South Dakota - Maps.*
G4181.J67 1979 .U5

Paulk, Herschel Leverne, 1934- Soil survey of
Candler, Evans, and Tattnall Counties, Georgia
/. [Washington] [1980] viii, 96 p., [42] fold.
leaves of plates :   LC Card 80-601838   DDC
631.4/7/75877 19
S599.G4 P315

Penner, Harold L. Soil survey of Sedgwick
County, Kansas /. [Washington , 1979] vii, 126
p., [41] fold. leaves of plates :   LC Card
79-603621   DDC 631.4/7/78186 19
S599.K2 P44

Pesoado, Pedro. Soil survey of Richland
County, Montana. [Washington, D.C.?] , C1980.
iv, 71 p., 142 folded p. of plates :   LC Card
80-604152   DDC 631.4/7/78623 19
S599.M57 P47

Pitts, J. J. Soil survey of Marion County, South
Carolina /. [Washington] , 1980. vii, 99 p., [27]
fold. leaves of plates :   LC Card 80-603206   DDC
631.4/7/75786 19
S599.S58 P58

Plymouth County, Massachusetts / United
States Department of Agriculture, Soil
Conservation Service. Lanham, MD :
USDA-SCS, 1980. 1 map : col. ; 70 x 37 cm.
"Compiled in 1976 from USGS 1:24,000-scale
topographic maps dated 1961-1972." "Planimetry revised
from aerial photographs taken 1972." LC Card
81-690018
1. Plymouth County (Mass.) - Maps.
G3763.P5 1980 .U5

Poch, George A. Soil survey of Olmsted
County, Minnesota /. [Washington, D.C.]
[1980] ix, 202 p., [53] fold. leaves of plates :
LC Card 80-602323   DDC 631.4/7/776155 19
S599.M45 P62

Population density, 1975, persons per square
mile, South Dakota / U. S. Department of
Agriculture, Soil Conservation Service. Lincoln,
Nebr. : USDA-SCS, 1977. 1 map : col. ; 18 x
27 cm. "5-2-77." "Source: Family of maps SCS drawing
no. 5,S-32,929 (Rev. 4-77) and information from field
technicians." "5,O-36,221." LC Card 81-691168
1. South Dakota - Population - Maps.
G4181.E2 1975 .U5

Potential irrigation water erosion hazard, Grant
County, Washington / U. S. Department of
Agriculture, Soil Conservation Service.
Portland, Or. : USDA-SCS, 1977. 1 map : col. ;
on sheet 49 x 28 cm. "December 1977." "Thematic
detail compiled by state staff." "Base map prepared by
SCS, WTSC Carto Unit from 1:126,720 General
highway maps." Relief shown by hachures. Includes
location map. "M7-RN-23716-4." LC Card 81-691513
*1. Erosion - Washington (State) - Grant County -
Maps. 2. Irrigation - Washington (State) - Grant
County - Maps. I. Title.*
G4283.G7J4 1977 .U5

Precipitation and runoff, Entiat River Basin,
Chelan County, Washington / U. S.
Department of Agriculture, Soil Conservation
Service. Portland, Or. : USDA-SCS, 1979. 1
map : col. ; on sheet 44 x 28 cm. "April 1978."
Relief shown by hachures. "Thematic detail compiled by

U. S. Forest Service." "Base map prepared by SCS,
WTSC Carto Staff from U. S. Forest Service
compilation." "USDA eastern Washington cooperative
river basin study." Includes location map.
"M7-SN-23916-4." LC Card 81-691528
*1. Precipitation (Meteorology) - Washington (State) -
Entiat River watershed - Maps. 2. Runoff - Washington
(State) - Entiat River watershed - Maps. I. United
States. Forest Service.*
G4282.E5C88 1978 .U5

Precipitation map, Franklin County
Conservation District, Franklin County,
Washington / U. S. Department of Agriculture
Soil Conservation Service. Portland, Or. :
USDA-SCS, 1980. 1 map : col. ; on sheet 22 x
28 cm. "August 1980." "Thematic detail compiled by
state staff." "Base map prepared by SCS, WTSC Carto
Unit from 1:126,720 General highway maps." Includes
location map. "M7-L-24129-2." LC Card 81-691510
*1. Precipitation (Meteorology) - Washington (State) -
Franklin County - Maps. I. Title: Franklin County
Conservation District, Franklin County, Washington.*
G4283.F7C88 1980 .U5

Preston County, West Virginia / United States
Department of Agriculture, Soil Conservation
Service ; cartographic mapping by the
Geological Survey. Lanham, MD : USDA-SCS,
1980. 1 map : col. ; 60 x 39 cm. Title in lower
margin: Preston Co., W.Va. : N3911-W7928/32.5x26.5,
1978. "Compiled from USGS 1:24,000-scale topographic
maps dated 1947-1967." "Planimetry revised from aerial
photographs taken 1976 and other source data."
"1,P-13273." LC Card 81-690036
*1. Preston County (W.Va.) - Maps. I. United States.
Geological Survey.*
G3893.P7 1978 .U5

Prince Georges County, Maryland / United
States Department of Agriculture, Soil
Conservation Service ; edited by the Geological
Survey. Hyattsville, MD : USDA-SCS, 1979. 1
map : col. ; 54 x 33 cm. Title in lower margin:
Prince Georges Co., Md. : N3831.5-W7637.5/36.5 x
28, 1977. "Compiled by USGS from 1977 from USGS and
Army Map Service 1:24,000-scale topographic maps
dated 1953-1971." "Planimetry revised from aerial
photographs taken 1976 and other source data." LC
Card 81-690002
1. Prince Georges County, Md. - Maps.
G3843.P7 1977 .U5

Problem location map, Limestone-Muddy Creek
watershed, portions of Duplin, Jones, and
Onslow Counties, North Carolina. Fort Worth,
Tex. : USDA-SCS, 1979. 1 map : col. ; 46 x 25
cm. "September 1979 4-R-37268. January 1979 base
4-R-36967." Shows swamp and wet sub class soil. "Base
compiled from NCSS atlas sheets and uncontrolled
mosaic." Includes location map.   LC Card 81-692265
*1. Wetlands - North Carolina - Limestone Creek
watershed - Maps. 2. Wetlands - North Carolina -
Muddy Creek watershed (Duplin County) - Maps. I.
Title.*
G3902.L48G4 1979 .U5

Progress of soil surveys, January 1, 1979, state
of South Dakota / U. S. Department of
Agriculture, Soil Conservation Service. Lincoln,
Nebr. : USDA-SCS, 1979. 1 map : col. ; 18 x
26 cm. "1-2-79." "Source: 1963 U. S.G.S. 1/1,000,000
base map and information from field technicians."
"5,S-36,019." LC Card 81-691098
1. Soil-surveys - South Dakota - Maps.
G4181.J3 1979 .U5

Project map, Baker River watershed, Grafton
County, New Hampshire / U. S. Department of
Agriculture, Soil Conservation Service.
[Lanham? Md.] : The Service, [1979?] 1 map :
col. ; 25 x 19 cm. Shows flood control dams,
reservoirs, and benefited areas. Includes location map.
LC Card 81-690286
*1. Flood control - New Hmpshire - Baker River
watershed - Maps. I. Title.*
G3742.B33N22 1979 .U5

Project map, Carney Creek watershed, Choctaw
County, Oklahoma. Fort Worth, Tex. :
USDA-SCS, 1980. 1 map : col. ; 35 x 25 cm.
Shows area benefited, drainage area controlled by
structure, and floodwater retarding structure. "May
1980 4-R-37447." "Base compiled from USGS
quadrangle sheets and Oklahoma County general
highway map." Includes text and location map. LC
Card 81-692268
*1. Flood control - Oklahoma - Carney Creek
watershed - Maps. I. Title.*
G4022.C38N22 1980 .U5

Project map, Elm Creek (1250) watershed, portions of Coleman, Runnels, and Taylor Counties, Texas. Fort Worth, Tex. : USDA-SCS, 1979. 1 map ; 36 x 24 cm. "September 1978 4-R-36836. September 1978 base 4-R-36834." Shows drainages, area benefited, drainage area controlled by structure, and floodwater retarding structure. "Base compiled from USGS quadrangle sheets and Texas general highway maps, polyconic projection." "Appendix F." Includes location map and list of sites and their areas in acres. LC Card 81-692267
1. Elm Creek watershed (Taylor County and Runnels County, Tex.) - Maps. I. Title.
G4032.E62 1978 .U5

Project map, Limestone-Muddy Creek watershed, portions of Duplin, Jones, and Onslow Counties, North Carolina. Fort Worth, Tex. : USDA-SCS, 1979. 1 map : col. ; 44 x 24 cm. "January 1979 4-R-36968. January 1979 base 4-R-36967." Shows channel restoration and excavation, fishing access areas, recreational impoundment and development, benefited area, wet woodland, and swamp. "Base compiled from NCSS atlas sheets and uncontrolled mosaic." Includes location map. LC Card 81-692266
1. Limestone Creek watershed (N.C.) - Maps. 2. Muddy Creek watershed (Duplin County, N.C.) - Maps. I. Title.
G3902.L48 1979 .U5

Project map, Los Olmos Creek watershed, Jim Hogg and Starr Counties, Texas. Rev. Nov. 1979 base 4R-33919. Temple, Tex. : U. S. Dept. of Agriculture, Soil Conservation Service, [1979] 1 map : col. ; 49 x 26 cm. "November 1979 4R-37322." Shows dike, floodwater retarding structure, drainage area controlled by structure, and benefited area. "Base compiled from 1973 Texas general highway maps ..." "Source: Data compiled by Watershed Planning Staff." Includes location map. LC Card 81-692271
1. Flood control - Texas - Los Olmos Creek watershed - Maps. I. Title.
G4032.L67N22 1979 .U5

Project map, Meadow Creek watershed, Fayette County, West Virginia, Drainage Area 6530 AC / U. S. Department of Agriculture, Soil Conservation Service. Lanham, MD : USDA-SCS, 1980. 1 map : col. ; 26 x 39 cm. Shows flood control dam, reservoir, and benefited area. "Base source: U. S.G.S. Topo Quad Sheets 1:24,000." "July 1978." Includes location map. LC Card 81-690287
1. Flood control - West Virginia - Meadow Creek watershed (Fayette County) - Maps. I. Title.
G3892.M4N22 1978 .U5

Project map, South Fork, Licking River watershed, Fairfield, Licking, and Perry Counties, Ohio / U. S. Department of Agriculture, Soil Conservation Service. Lincoln, Nebr. : USDA-SCS, 1980. 1 map : col. ; 33 x 26 cm. "2-15-80." "Source: Late date 7 1/2 min. USGS quadrangles and information from SCS field personnel." Includes location map. "5,S-37,744." LC Card 81-691028
1. Licking River, South Fork, watershed (Ohio) - Maps.
G4082.L5 1980 .U5

Project map, Spring Creek watershed, Colbert and Franklin Counties, Alabama / U. S. Department of Agriculture, Soil Conservation Service. Fort Worth, Tex. : USDA-SCS, 1979. 1 map : col. ; 35 x 25 cm. "April 1979 4-R-36445. September 1976 base 4-R-35682." Shows floodwater retarding structure, benefited area, channel work, drainage area controlled by structure, and grade control structure. "Source: Data compiled by Watershed Planning Staff." "Base compiled from USGS quadrangle sheets ..." Includes location map. LC Card 81-692287
1. Flood control - Alabama - Spring Creek watershed (Colbert and Franklin Counties) - Maps. I. Title.
G3972.S6N22 1979 .U5

Public and private parks and recreation areas, Wood County, Wisconsin / U. S. Department of Agriculture, Soil Conservation Service. Lincoln, Nebr. : USDA-SCS, 1978. 1 map : col. ; 26 x 18 cm. "9-27-78." "Source: SCS base map 5,P-37,037 (9-78) and information from field technicians." Includes location map. "5,P-37,041." LC Card 81-691238
1. Parks - Wisconsin - Wood County - Maps. 2. Recreation areas - Wisconsin - Wood County - Maps.
G4123.W9G52 1978 .U5

Quail population, upper Little Nemaha watershed, Lancaster, Cass, and Otoe Counties,

Nebraska / U. S. Department of Agriculture, Soil Conservation Service. Lincoln, Nebr. : USDA-SCS, 1979. 1 map ; 17 x 26 cm. "12-29-78." "Source: SCS drawing 5,R-23,485 (7-66) and information from field technicians." Includes location map. "5,O-37,203." LC Card 81-691091
1. Quails - Nebraska - Little Nemaha River watershed - Maps.
G4192.L5D4 1978 .U51

Rainfall distribution, Whitman County, Washington / U. S. Department of Agriculture, Soil Conservation Service. Portland, Or. : USDA-SCS, 1979. 1 map : col. ; on sheet 48 x 63 cm. "October 1978." "Thematic detail prepared by state staff." "Base map prepared by SCS, WTSC Carto Unit from 1:126,720 General highway maps." Relief shown by hachures. Includes location map. "7-E-16830." LC Card 81-691526
1. Rain and rainfall - Washington (State) - Whitman County - Maps. I. Title.
G4283.W6C883 1978 .U5

Readle, Elmer L. Soil survey of Osceola County area, Florida /. [Washington] , 1979. x, 151 p., [59] fold. leaves of plates : LC Card 79-602772 DDC 631.4/7/75925 19
S599.F6 R42

Red Willow County, Nebraska / U. S. Department of Agriculture, Soil Conservation Service. Lincoln, Nebr. : USDA-SCS, 1978. 1 map : col. ; 46 x 59 cm. "11-12-78." "Source: 1973 general county highway map." Includes location map. "5,P-37,131.1." LC Card 81-691004
1. Red Willow County (Neb.) - Maps.
G4193.R4 1978 .U5

Redmond, Charles Edward, 1932- Soil survey of Ashland County, Ohio /. [Washington] [1980] vii, 179 p., [31] fold. leaves of plates : LC Card 80-602507 DDC 631.4/7/77129 19
S599.O3 R39

Reineback, L. M. Soil survey of Grundy County, Illinois /. [Washington] [1980] vii, 131 p., [35] fold. leaves of plates : LC Card 80-602552 DDC 631.4/9773 s 631.4/7/773265 19
S599.I5 A3 no. 142

Reynolds, Charles Arthur, 1937- Soil survey of Middlesex County, Connecticut /. [Washington] [1979] ix, 155 p., [28] fold. leaves of plates : LC Card 80-601842 DDC 631.4/7/7444 19
S599.C76 R5

Richland County, Illinois / U. S. Department of Agriculture, Soil Conservation Service [and] United States Department of the Interior, Geological Survey. Lincoln, Nebr. : USDA-SCS, 1980. 1 map : col. ; 36 x 37 cm. "Base source: USGS 1/100,000 compiled in 1980." Includes location map. "5,P-38,111." LC Card 81-691426
1. Richland County (Ill.) - Maps. I. United States. Geological Survey.
G4103.R5 1980 .U5

Richmond, Davie L. General soil map, Greenlee County, Arizona. Portland, Or., 1973. 49 p. **NYPL [JSF 80-721]**

River basin and watershed progress, Colorado / U. S. Department of Agriculture, Soil Conservation Service. Portland, Or. : USDA-SCS, 1979. 1 map : col. ; on sheet 27 x 41 cm. "September 1979." "Thematic detail compiled by state staff." "Base map prepared by SCS, WTSC Cartographic Unit from USGS 1:1,000,000 National atlas." Indexed. "M7-EN-23547-2." LC Card 81-691540
1. Watersheds - Colorado - Maps. I. Title.
G4311.C315 1979 .U5

River basin studies, Oregon / U. S. Department of Agriculture, Soil Conservation Service. Portland, Or. : USDA-SCS, 1979. 1 map : col. ; on sheet 22 x 28 cm. "November 1979." "Thematic detail compiled by state staff." "Base map prepared by SCS, WTSC Carto Unit from USGS 1:1,000,000 Nat. atlas." Indexed. "M7-OL-24073." LC Card 81-691562
1. Watersheds - Oregon - Maps.
G4291.C315 1979 .U51

Rives, Jerry L. Soil survey of Pecos County, Texas /. [Washington] [1980] vii, 97 p., [77] fold. leaves of plates : LC Card 80-602640 DDC 631.4/7/764923 19
S599.T4 R59

Rock Island County, Illinois / U. S. Department of Agriculture, Soil Conservation

Service [and] United States Department of the Interior, Geological Survey. Lincoln, Nebr. : USDA-SCS, 1980. 1 map : col. ; 35 x 51 cm. "Base source: USGS 1:100,000 compiled in 1976." Includes location map. "5,P-37,882." LC Card 81-691427
1. Rock Island County, Ill. - Maps. I. United States. Geological Survey.
G4103.R6 1980 .U5

Rockingham County, New Hampshire / U. S. Department of Agriculture, Soil Conservation Service. Lanham, Md. : USDA-SCS, 1980. 1 map ; 59 x 59 cm. "Base Source: New Hampshire family of maps 1:500,000." Includes location map. "1-15827." LC Card 81-690125
1. Rockingham County, N. H. - Maps.
G3743.R6 1980 .U5

Rolling, R. E. Soil survey of Cottonwood County, Minnesota /. [Washington] [1979] viii, 142 p., [28] fold. leaves of plates : LC Card 80-602397 DDC 631.4/7/77622 19
S599.M45 R64

Russell, Robert Cone, 1917- Soil survey of Marion County, Iowa /. [Washington, D.C.] [1980] ix, 183 p., [72] fold. leaves of plates : LC Card 80-602332 DDC 631.4/7/77783 19
S599.I8 R88

St. Clair County, Illinois / U. S. Department of Agriculture, Soil Conservation Service. Rev. 5-28-80. Lincoln, Nebr. : USDA-SCS, 1980. 1 map ; 36 x 26 cm. "Source: 1976 county highway map." Includes location map. "5,N-31,980." LC Card 81-691443
1. St. Clair County, Ill. - Maps.
G4103.S2 1980 .U49

Saline County, Kansas / U. S. Department of Agriculture, Soil Conservation Service [and] United States, Department of the Interior, Geological Survey. [Lincoln? Neb.] : The Service, [1979?] 1 map : col. ; 33 x 42 cm. "Base source: USGS 1:100,000 county base compiled from 1955--1978 topographic maps." "25,000-foot grid ticks based on Kansas coordinate system." Includes location map. "5,P-37,516." LC Card 81-691133
1. Saline County, Kan. - Maps. I. United States. Geological Survey.
G4203.S2 1979 .U5

Sarpy County, Nebraska / U. S. Department of Agriculture, Soil Conservation Service. Lincoln, Nebr. : USDA-SCS, 1978. 1 map : col. ; 37 x 51 cm. "7-23-78." "Source: 1970 general county highway map." Includes location map. "5,P-36,983.1." LC Card 81-691003
1. Sarpy County (Neb.) - Maps.
G4193.S3 1978 .U5

Saunders County, Nebraska / U. S. Department of Agriculture, Soil Conservation Service. Lincoln, Nebr. : USDA-SCS, 1978. 1 map : col. ; 39 x 62 cm. "9-30-78." "Source: 1974 general county highway map." Includes location map. "5,S-36,984.1." LC Card 81-691002
1. Saunders County (Neb.) - Maps.
G4193.S35 1978 .U5

Schumacher, Thomas M. Soil survey of Campbell County, South Dakota /. [Washington] [1979] vii, 175 p., [32] fold. leaves of plates : LC Card 80-602616 DDC 631.4/7/78317 19
S599.S6 S4

Scotts Bluff County, Nebraska / U. S. Department of Agriculture, Soil Conservation Service [and] United States Department of the Interior, Geological Survey. Lincoln, Neb. : USDA-SCS, 1980. 1 map : col. ; 33 x 50 cm. "Base source: USGS 1/100,000 compiled in 1978." Includes location map. "5,P-38,090." LC Card 81-691078
1. Scotts Bluff County (Neb.) - Maps. I. United States. Geological Survey.
G4193.S4 1980 .U5

Sediment sources map, Kansas / U. S. Department of Agriculture, Soil Conservation Service. Lincoln, Nebr. : USDA-SCS, 1979. 1 map : col. ; 46 x 58 cm. Shows sediment load to streams in 1980. "Source: Family of maps S.C.S. drwg. no. 5,S-32,550 (rev. 1-76) and information from S.C.S. field technicians." "5,S-37,432." LC Card 81-691121
1. Sediment, suspended - Kansas - Maps.
G4201.J4 1980 .U5

Seward County, Nebraska / U. S. Department of Agriculture, Soil Conservation Service.

Lincoln, Nebr. : USDA-SCS, 1979. 1 map :
col. ; 46 x 59 cm. "Source: 1974 general county
highway map." Includes location map. "5,S-37,145.1."
    LC Card 81-691001
1. Seward County (Neb.) - Maps.
G4193.S5 1979 .U5

Sheet erosion for all lands, Missouri / U. S.
Department of Agriculture, Soil Conservation
Service. Lincoln, Nebr. : USDA-SCS, 1978. 1
map : col. ; 26 x 18 cm. "12-13-77." "Source:
Family of maps SCS drawing no. 5,S-32,925.1 (3-5-74)
and information from field technicians." "5,N-36,549.1."
    LC Card 81-691219
1. Soil erosion - Missouri - Maps. I. Title.
G4161.J4 1977 .U5

Sheet erosion for cropland, hay, and pasture,
Missouri / U. S. Department of Agriclture, Soil
Conservation Service. Lincoln, Nebr. :
USDA-SCS, 1978. 1 map : col. ; 26 x 18 cm.
"12-13-77." "Source: Family of maps SCS drawing no.
5,S-32,925.1 (3-5-74) and information from field
technicians." "5,N-36,549.6."   LC Card 81-691218
1. Soil erosion - Missouri - Maps. I. Title.
G4161.J4 1977 .U51

Sheet erosion for grazed forest land, Missouri /
U. S. Department of Agriculture, Soil
Conservation Service. Lincoln, Nebr. :
USDA-SCS, 1978. 1 map : col. ; 26 x 18 cm.
"12-13-77." "Source: Family of maps SCS drawing no.
5,S-32,925.1 (3-5-74) and information from field
technicians." "5,N-36,549.4."   LC Card 81-691217
1. Soil erosion - Missouri - Maps. I. Title.
G4161.J4 1977 .U52

Sheet erosion for non-grazed forest, Missouri /
U. S. Department of Agriculture, Soil
Conservation Service. Lincoln, Nebr. :
USDA-SCS, 1978. 1 map : col. ; 26 x 18 cm.
"12-13-77." "Source: Family of maps SCS drawing no.
5,S-32,925.1 (3-5-74) and information from field
technicians." "5,N-36,549.2."   LC Card 81-691216
1. Soil erosion - Missouri - Maps. I. Title.
G4161.J4 1977 .U53

Sheet erosion for permanent pasture, Missouri /
U. S. Department of Agriculture, Soil
Conservation Service. Lincoln, Nebr. :
USDA-SCS, 1978. 1 map : col. ; 26 x 18 cm.
"12-13-77." "Source: Family of maps SCS drawing no.
5,S-32,925.1 (3-5-74) and information from field
technicians." "5,N-36,549.5."   LC Card 81-691215
1. Soil erosion - Missouri - Maps. I. Title.
G4161.J4 1977 .U54

Sheet erosion for tilled land, Missouri / U. S.
Department of Agriculture, Soil Conservation
Service. Lincoln, Nebr. : USDA-SCS, 1978. 1
map : col. ; 26 x 18 cm. "12-13-77." "Source:
Family of maps SCS drawing no. 5,S-32,925.1 (3-5-74)
and information from field technicians." "5,N-36,549.3."
    LC Card 81-691214
1. Soil erosion - Missouri - Maps. I. Title.
G4161.J4 1977 .U55

Shelby County, Iowa / U. S. Department of
Agriculture, Soil Conservation Service [and]
United States Department of the Interior,
Geological Survey. [Lincoln, Neb.] : The
Service, [1979?] 1 map : col. ; 35 x 37 cm. "Base
source: USGS 1:100,000 county base compiled from
1971 and 1978 topographic maps." Includes location
map. "5,P-37,511."   LC Card 81-691184
*1. Shelby County (Iowa) - Maps. I. United States.
Geological Survey.*
G4153.S5 1979 .U5

Slope class map, Chickies Creek watershed,
Lancaster and Lebanon Counties, Pennsylvania
/ U. S. Department of Agriculture, Soil
Conservation Service. Hyattsville, Md. :
USDA-SCS, [1978] 1 map : col. ; 25 x 34 cm.
"Source: 1969 U. S. Geological Survey quadrangles."
"3-23-78." Includes location map. "12688."   LC Card
81-690268
*1. Slopes (Physical geography) - Pennsylvania -
Chickies Creek watershed - Maps. I. Title.*
G3822.C45C28 1978 .U5

Smallwood, Benjamin F. Soil survey of Marshall
County, Indiana. [Washington, D.C.?] , 1980.
vii, 136 p., 63 folded p. of plates :   LC Card
81-601062   DDC 631.4/7/77288 19
S599.I63 S6

Soil areas of Nebraska / U. S. Department of
Agriculture, Soil Conservation Service. Lincoln,
Nebr. : USDA-SCS, 1979. 1 map : col. ; 18 x
23 cm. "2-15-79." "Source: State family of maps, SCS
drwg. no. 5,S-32,930 (4-77) and information from SCS

field personnel." "5,O-37,195."   LC Card 81-691022
1. Soils - Nebraska - Maps.
G4191.J3 1979 .U5

Soil areas of Wisconsin / U. S. Department of
Agriculture, Soil Conservation Service. Lincoln,
Nebr. : USDA-SCS, 1980. 1 map : col. ; 24 x
18 cm., on sheet 51 x 31 cm. "5-25-80." "Source:
Family of maps SCS drwg. no. 5,S-32,817 (2-74) and
information from SCS field personnel. "5,O-37,841."
    LC Card 81-691248
1. Soils - Wisconsin - Maps.
G4121.J3 1980 .U5

Soil association map, Franklin County
Conservation District, Franklin County,
Washington / U. S. Department of Agriculture,
Soil Conservation Service. Portland, Or. :
USDA-SCS, 1980. 1 map : col. ; on sheet 22 x
28 cm. "August 1980." "Thematic detail compiled by
state staff." "Base map prepared by SCS, WTSC Carto
Unit from 1:126,720 General highway maps." Includes
location map. "M7-L-24129-1."   LC Card 81-691509
*1. Soils - Washington (State) - Franklin County - Maps.
I. Title. II. Title: Franklin County Conservation District,
Franklin County, Washington.*
G4283.F7J3 1980 .U51

Soil erosion hazard map, Nebraska / U. S.
Department of Agriculture, Soil Conservation
Service. Lincoln, Nebr. : USDA-SCS, 1980. 1
map : col. ; 26 x 49 cm. "9-80." "Source: SCS map
5,S-32,930 and information from SCS field personnel."
Includes text. "5,O-38,087."   LC Card 81-691020
1. Soil erosion - Nebraska - Maps.
G4191.J4 1980 .U5

Soil survey area status map, as of December 31,
1980, New Hampshire / U. S. Department of
Agriculture, Soil Conservation Service. Lanham,
MD : USDA-SCS, 1981. 1 map : col. ; 61 x 41
cm. Shows minor civil divisions. "Source: U. S.G.S.
Topo Map 1:500,000." In lower right corner: January
1981. "1-10923."   LC Card 81-692784
1. Soil-surveys - New Hampshire - Maps. I. Title.
G3741.J3 1980 .U5

Soil survey of Ashley County, Arkansas / [by
Hiram V. Gill ... et al.] ; United States
Department of Agriculture, Soil Conservation
Service and Forest Service, in cooperation with
Arkansas Agricultural Experiment Station.
[Washington, D.C. : National Cooperative Soil
Survey, 1979] vii, 92 p., [40] fold. leaves of
plates : ill. ; 28 cm. Cover title. Bibliography: p. 54.
    LC Card 80-601804   DDC 631.4/7/76783 19
*1. Soils - Arkansas - Ashley Co. - Maps. I. Gill, Hiram
V. II. United States. Soil Conservation Service. III.
United States. Forest Service. IV. Arkansas.
Agricultural Experiment Station, Fayetteville. V. Title.*
S599.A75 U54 1979

Soil survey of Blount County, Alabama / [by
Charles D. Bowen ... et al.] ; United States
Department of Agriculture, Soil Conservation
Service, in cooperation with Alabama
Department of Agriculture and Industries, and
Alabama Agricultural Experiment Station.
[Washington] : The Service, [1979] iii, 73 p., [2]
fold. leaves of plates : ill. ; 29 cm. Cover title.
"Issued December 1979." Bibliography: p. 71.   LC Card
80-601827   DDC 631.4/7/76172 19
*1. Soils - Alabama - Blount Co. - Maps. I. Bowen,
Charles D. II. Alabama. Dept. of Agriculture and
Industries. III. Alabama. Agricultural Experiment
Station, Auburn. IV. Title.*
S599.A4 U54 1979

Soil survey of Caddo Parish, Louisiana / [by
Jimmy P. Edwards ... et al.] ; United States
Department of Agriculture, Soil Conservation
Service, in cooperation with the Louisiana
Agricultural Experiment Station. [Washington] :
The Service, [1980] vii, 137 p., [43] fold. leaves
of plates : ill. ; 28 cm. Cover title. "Issued June
1980." Bibliography: p. 76-77.   LC Card 80-603369
    DDC 631.4/7/76399 19
*1. Soils - Louisiana - Caddo Parish - Maps. I. Edwards,
Jimmy P. II. Louisiana. Agricultural Experiment
Station, Baton Rouge. III. Title.*
S599.L6 U54 1980a

Soil survey of Calhoun and Dallas Counties,
Arkansas / [by Hiram V. Gill ... et al.] ; United
States Department of Agriculture, Soil
Conservation Service, in cooperation with
Arkansas Agricultural Experiment Station.
[Washington] : The Service, [1980] vii, 80 p.,
[59] fold. leaves of plates : ill. ; 29 cm. Cover
title. Bibliography: p. 46.   LC Card 80-601636   DDC
631.4/7/76764 19

*1. Soils - Arkansas - Calhoun Co. - Maps. 2. Soils -
Arkansas - Dallas Co. - Maps. I. Gill, Hiram V. II.
United States. Soil Conservation Service. III. Arkansas.
Agricultural Experiment Station, Fayetteville. IV. Title.*
S599.A75 U54 1980

Soil survey of Chaves County, New Mexico,
southern part / [by Max V. Hodson ... et al.] ;
United States Department of Agriculture, Soil
Conservation Service and United States
Department of the Interior, Bureau of Land
Management, in cooperation with New Mexico
Agricultural Experiment Station. [Washington] :
The Service, [1980] iv, 143 p., [90] fold. leaves
of plates : ill. ; 28 cm. Cover title. "Issued April
1980." Bibliography: p. 141.   LC Card 80-602510
    DDC 631.4/7/78943 19
*1. Soils - New Mexico - Chaves Co. - Maps. I. Hodson,
Max V. II. United States. Bureau of Land Management.
III. New Mexico. Agricultural Experiment Station,
University Park. IV. Title.*
S599.N6 U54 1980

Soil survey of Conejos County area, Colorado.
[Washington, D.C.?], 1980. vii, 144 p. :   LC
Card 81-600706   DDC 631.4/7/78833 19
S599.C6 S66

Soil survey of Glacier County area and part of
Pondera County, Montana / [by June G.
Haigh ... et al.] ; United States Department of
Agriculture, Soil Conservation Service, and
United States Department of the Interior,
Bureau of Indian Affairs, in cooperation with
Montana Agricultural Experiment Station.
[Washington, D.C.] : The Service, [1980] v, 161
p., [92] leaves of plates : ill. ; 29 cm. Cover title.
Bibliography: p. 158.   LC Card 80-602512   DDC
    631.4/7/78652 19
*1. Soils - Montana - Glacier County - Maps. 2. Soils -
Montana - Pondera County - Maps. I. Haigh, June G.
II. United States. Bureau of Indian Affairs. III.
Montana. Agricultural Experiment Station, Bozeman.
IV. Title.*
S599.M57 U54 1980

Soil survey of Gloucester County, Virginia.
[Washington, D.C.?] , 1980. vii, 88 p., 35
folded p. of plates :   LC Card 80-604149   DDC
    631.4/7/75532 19
S599.V8 S64

Soil survey of Keya Paha County, Nebraska.
[Washington, D.C.?] , 1980. ix, 224 p., 62
folded p. of plates :   LC Card 81-600561   DDC
    631.4/7/782725 19
S599.N2 S63

Soil survey of Logan County, Arkansas.
[Washington, D.C.?] , 1980. vii, 100 p., 42
folded p. of plates :   LC Card 81-600695   DDC
    631.4/7/76737 19
S599.A75 S66

Soil survey of Ogle County, Illinois / [by
Lawrence L. Acker ... et al.] ; United States
Department of Agriculture, Soil Conservation
Service, in cooperation with the Illinois
Agricultural Experiment Station. [Washington] :
The Service, [1980] ix, 242 p., [58] fold. leaves
of plates : ill. ; 28 cm. Cover title.   LC Card
80-602563   DDC 631.4/7/77332 19
*1. Soils - Illinois - Ogle Co. - Maps. I. Acker, Lawrence
L. II. Illinois. Agricultural Experiment Station, Urbana.
III. Title.*
S599.I5 U54 1980

Soil survey of Rapides Parish, Louisiana / [by
Alexander Kerr, Jr. ... et al.] ; United States
Department of Agriculture, Soil Conservation
Service and Forest Service, in cooperation with
Louisiana Agricultural Experiment Station.
[Washington] : Soil Conservation Service, 1980.
iii, 86 p., [59] fold. leaves of plates : ill., maps ;
28 cm. Cover title. "Issued March 1980." Bibliography:
p. 84-85.   LC Card 80-602333 DDC 631.4/7/76369
    19
*1. Soils - Louisiana - Rapides Parish - Maps. I. Kerr,
Alexander. II. United States. Forest Service. III.
Louisiana. Agricultural Experiment Station, Baton
Rouge. IV. Title.*
S599.L6 U54 1980

Soil survey of Rush County, Kansas / [by
Darold A. Dodge ... et al.] ; United States
Department of Agriculture, Soil Conservation
Service, in cooperation with Kansas Agricultural
Experiment Station. [Washington, D.C.] : The
Service, [1980] vi, 62 p., [31] fold. leaves of
plates : ill. ; 28 cm. Cover title. Bibliography: p. 37.
    LC Card 80-603364   DDC 631.4/7/78148 19

1. Soils - Kansas - Rush Co. - Maps. I. Dodge, Darold Ardale, 1917-. II. Kansas Agricultural Experiment Station, Manhattan. III. Title.
S599.K2 U54 1980

Soil survey of Santa Rosa County, Florida / [by Herbert H. Weeks ... et al.] ; United States Department of Agriculture, Soil Conservation Service, in cooperation with University of Florida Institute of Food and Agricultural Sciences [and] Agricultural Experiment Stations and Soil Science Department, and Florida Department of Agriculture and Consumer Services. [Washington] : U. S. Dept. of Agriculture, Soil Conservation Service, [1980] vii, 150 p., [47] fold. leaves of plates : ill. ; 29 cm. Cover title. "Issued May 1980". Bibliography: p. 85.   LC Card 80-602511   DDC 631.4/7/759985 19
1. Soils - Florida - Santa Rosa Co. - Maps. I. Weeks, Herbert H., 1929-. II. Florida. University, Gainesville. Institute of Food and Agricultural Sciences. III. Title.
S599.F6 U54 1980a

Soil survey of Shelby County, Kentucky / [by Carl W. Hail ... et al.], United States Department of Agriculture, Soil Conservation Service, in cooperation with the Kentucky Agricultural Experiment Station and the Kentucky Department for Natural Resources and Environmental Protection. [Washington, D.C. : National Cooperative Soil Survey, 1980] vii, 84 p., [20] leaves of plates : ill., maps ; 29 cm. Cover title. Bibliography: p. 50. Includes index.
    LC Card 80-602322   DDC 631.4/7/769435 19
1. Soils - Kentucky - Shelby Co. - Maps. I. Hail, Carl W. II. Kentucky. Agricultural Experiment Station, Lexington. III. Kentucky. Dept. for Natural Resources and Environmental Protection. IV. Title.
S599.K4 U54 1980

Soil survey of Thomas County, Kansas / [by Wesley L. Barker ... et al.] ; United States Department of Agriculture, Soil Conservation Service, in cooperation with Kansas Agricultural Experiment Station. [Washington] : The Service, [1980] vii, 57 p., [43] fold. leaves of plates : ill. ; 28 cm. Cover title. "Issued June 1980."
Bibliography: p. 34.   LC Card 80-603122   DDC 631.4/7/781132 19
1. Soils - Kansas - Thomas Co. - Maps. I. Barker, Wesley L. II. Kansas. Agricultural Experiment Station, Manhattan. III. Title.
S599.K2 U54 1980a

Soil survey of Volusia County, Florida / [by Robert Baldwin ... et al.] ; United States Department of Agriculture, Soil Conservation Service, in cooperation with the University of Florida, Institute of Food and Agricultural Sciences, Agricultural Experiment Stations, Soil Science Department. [Washington, D.C.] : The Service, [1980] ix, 207 p., [55] fold. leaves of plates : ill. ; 28 cm. Cover title. "Issued February 1980." Bibliography: p. 105-106.   LC Card 80-602334   DDC 631.4/7/75921 19
1. Soils - Florida - Volusia Co. - Maps. I. Baldwin, Robert, 1944-. II. Florida. Agricultural Experiment Station, Gainesville. Soil Science Dept. III. Title.
S599.F6 U54 1980

Soil survey of Whitman County, Washington /. [Washington?] [1980] v, 185 p., [75] folded leaves of plates :   LC Card 80-602555   DDC 631.4/7797/39 19
S599.W32 S63

Soil survey status, Oregon / U. S. Department of Agriculture, Soil Conservation Service. Portland, Or. : USDA-SCS, 1980. 1 map : col. ; on sheet 28 x 44 cm. "May 1979." "Thematic detail compiled by state staff." "Base map prepared by SCS, WTSC Carto Unit from USGS 1:1,000,000 Nat. atlas." Indexed. "M7-EN-22493."   LC Card 81-691564
1. Soils - Oregon - Maps.
G4291.J3 1979 .U5

Soil survey status, Washington / U. S. Department of Agriculture, Soil Conservation Service. Portland, Or. : USDA-SCS, 1979. 1 map : col. ; 14 x 21 cm., on sheet 22 x 28 cm. "May 1979." "Thematic detail compiled by state staff." "Base map prepared by SCS, WTSC Carto Unit from USGS 1:1,000,000 Nat. atlas." Indexed. List of published and unpublished soil surveys on verso. "M7-PL-24009."   LC Card 81-691502
1. Soil-surveys - Washington(State) - Maps. I. Title.
G4281.J3 1979 .U5

Soil texture, Franklin County Conservation District, Franklin County, Washington / U. S. Department of Agriculture, Soil Conservation

Service. Portland, Or. : USDA-SCS, 1980. 1 map : col. ; on sheet 22 x 28 cm. "August 1980." "Thematic detail compiled by state staff. "Base map prepared by SCS, WTSC Carto Unit from 1:126,720 General highway maps." Includes location map. "M7-L-24129-3."   LC Card 81-691508
1. Soil texture - Washington (State) - Franklin County - Maps. I. Title: Franklin County Conservation District, Franklin County, Washington.
G4283.F7J3 1980 .U5

Soils, Chickies Creek watershed, Lancaster and Lebanon Counties, Pennsylvania / U. S. Department of Agriculture, Soil Conservation Service. Hyattsville, Md. : USDA-SCS, [1978] 1 map ; 25 x 34 cm. "Source: 1969 U. S. Geological Survey quadrangles." "3-23-78." Includes location map. "12688."   LC Card 81-690272
1. Soils - Pennsylvania - Chickies Creek watershed - Maps. I. Title.
G3822.C45J3 1978 .U5

Soils map, Kansas / U. S. Department of Agriculture, Soil Conservation Service. Lincoln, Nebr. : USDA-SCS, 1979. 1 map : col. ; 18 x 23 cm. "6-1-79." "Source: Family of maps S.C.S. drwg. no. 5,S-32,550 (rev. 1-76) and information from S.C.S. field technicians." "5-S-37,425."   LC Card 81-691120
1. Soils - Kansas - Maps.
G4201.J3 1979 .U5

Soils map, Kansas / U. S. Department of Agriculture, Soil Conservation Service. Rev. 7-7-80. Lincoln, Nebr. : USDA-SCS, 1980. 1 map : col. ; on sheet 31 x 51 cm. "Source: Family of maps S.C.S. drwg. no. 5,S-32,550 (rev. 1-76) and information from S.C.S. field technicians." "5,S-37,425."
    LC Card 81-691119
1. Soils - Kansas - Maps.
G4201.J3 1980 .U5

Soils of South Dakota / U. S. Department of Agriculture, Soil Conservation Service. Lincoln, Nebr. : USDA-SCS, 1976. 1 map : col. ; on sheet 44 x 57 cm. "8-5-76." "Source: 'Soils of the Great Plains' by Andrew R. Aandahl, 1972 ..." "5,S-35818."   LC Card 81-691113
1. Soils - South Dakota - Maps.
G4181.J3 1976 .U5

South Central New York Resource Conservation and Development Project / U. S. Department of Agriculture, Soil Conservation Service. [Lanham? Md.] : The Service, [1967?] 1 map ; 25 x 32 cm. Does not show resource conservation and development data. Covers Binghamton region (Tompkins, Tioga, Cortland, Broome, Madison, Chenango, Otsego, and Delaware Counties) In lower right corner: March 1967.   LC Card 81-692937
1. Binghamton region (N.Y.) - Maps. I. Title.
G3804.B6A1 1967 .U5

South Dakota, average annual precipitation (inches) 1941-70 / U. S. Department of Agriculture, Soil Conservation Service. Lincoln, Nebr. : USDA-SCS, 1976. 1 map : col. ; 16 x 23 cm. "6-14-76." "Source: Family of maps SCS drwg. no. 5,S-32,929 (4-74) and information from the U. S. Department of Commerce Environmental Data Service." "5,O-35,735."   LC Card 81-691114
1. Precipitation (Meteorology) - South Dakota - Maps.
G4181.C88 1970 .U5

South Dakota land use map / U. S. Department of Agriculture, Soil Conservation Service. Lincoln, Nebr. : USDA-SCS, 1976. 1 map : col. ; 26 x 33 cm. "Land use percentages are total land area (1975)." "6-15-76." "Source: Family of maps SCS drwg. no. 5,S-32,929 (4-74) and information from county CNI committees." "5,P-35,736."   LC Card 81-691109
1. Land use, Rural - South Dakota - Maps.
G4181.G4 1975 .U5

South Dakota, natural vegetation / U. S. Department of Agriculture, Soil Conservation Service. Lincoln, Nebr. : USDA-SCS, 1974. 1 map : col. ; 18 x 26 cm. "5-17-24." "Source: SCS drawing no. 5,S-32,929 (4-77) and information from field technicians." "5,L-34,081.1."   LC Card 81-691111
1. Phytogeography - South Dakota - Maps.
G4181.D2 1974 .U5

South Dakota natural vegetation / U. S. Department of Agriculture, Soil Conservation Service. Lincoln, Nebr. : USDA-SCS, 1976. 1 map : col. ; 26 x 33 cm. "6-15-76." "Source: Family of maps SCS drwg. no. 5,S-32,929 (4-74) and information from SRM/OWRC Advisory Board." "5,P-35,738."   LC Card 81-691110

1. Phytogeography - South Dakota - Maps.
G4181.D2 1976 .U5

South Dakota range condition classes / U. S. Department of Agriculture, Soil Conservation Service. Lincoln, Nebr. : USDA-SCS, 1976. 1 map : col. ; 26 x 33 cm. "Range condition based on SCS field estimates as of 1975." "6-15-76." "Source: Family of maps SCS drwg. no. 5,S-32,929 (4-74) and information from field technicians." "5-P-35,737."   LC Card 81-691108
1. Range management - South Dakota - Maps.
G4181.J1 1975 .U5

South Dakota river basins study areas / U. S. Department of Agriculture, Soil Conservation Service. Rev. 3-6-80. Lincoln, Nebr. : USDA-SCS, 1980. 1 map : col. ; 18 x 27 cm. "Source: Family of maps SCS drawing no. 5,S-32,929 (4-77) and information from field technicians." "5,S-36,666."   LC Card 81-691105
1. Watersheds - South Dakota - Maps. I. Title: River basins study areas.
G4181.C315 1980 .U5

Status of detailed soil surveys, Vermont. Lanham, MD : USDA-SCS, 1980. 1 map : col. ; 25 x 19 cm. "April 1980." "1-14,847."   LC Card 81-690085
1. Soil-surveys - Vermont - Maps. I. Title.
G3751.J3 1980 .U5

Status of New York soil surveys : October 1, 1980 / U. S. Department of Agriculture, Soil Conservation Service. Lanham, MD : USDA-SCS, 1980. 1 map : col. ; 18 x 25 cm. "I,P-11,280."   LC Card 81-690084
1. Soil-surveys - New York (State) - Maps. I. Title.
G3801.J3 1980 .U5

Status of P.L.566 watersheds in Washington / U. S. Department of Agriculture, Soil Conservation Service. Portland, Or. : USDA-SCS, 1979. 1 map : col. ; 26 x 36 cm. Relief shown by shading. Title in upper right margin: Washington. "Thematic detail compiled by state staff." "Base map prepared by SCS, WTSC Carto Unit from USGS 1:500,000 series."   LC Card 81-691500
1. Watersheds - Washington (State) - Maps.
G4281.C315 1979 .U5

Status of recent soil surveys in Nebraska, Oct. 1, 1978 / U. S. Department of Agriculture, Soil Conservation Service. Rev. 7-26-78. Lincoln, Nebr. : USDA-SCS, 1978. 1 map : col. ; 18 x 23 cm. "Source: Family of maps, SCS drwg. no. 5,S-32,930 (6-76) and information from field technicians." "5,L-25,690."   LC Card 81-691095
1. Soil-surveys - Nebraska - Maps.
G4191.J3 1978 .U5

Status of recent soil surveys in Nebraska, Oct. 1, 1979 / U. S. Department of Agriculture, Soil Conservation Service. Rev. 8-79. Lincoln, Nebr. : USDA-SCS, 1979. 1 map : col. ; 18 x 23 cm. "Source: Family of maps, SCS drwg. no. 5,S-32,930 (6-76) and information from field technicians." "5,L-25,690."   LC Card 81-691096
1. Soil-surveys - Nebraska - Maps.
G4191.J3 1979 .U52

Status of recent soil surveys in Nebraska, Oct. 1, 1980 / U. S. Department of Agriculture, Soil Conservation Service. Rev. 8-80. Lincoln, Nebr. : USDA-SCS, 1980. 1 map : col. ; 18 x 23 cm. "Source: Family of maps, SCS drawing 5,S-32,930 (6-76) and information from SCS field personnel." "5,P-37,754."   LC Card 81-691097
1. Soil-surveys - Nebraska - Maps.
G4191.J3 1980 .U51

Status of soil surveys in Kansas, October 1, 1978 / U. S. Department of Agriculture, Soil Conservation Service. Rev. 9-5-78. Lincoln, Nebr. : USDA-SCS, 1978. 1 map : col. ; 18 x 23 cm. "Source: SCS drawings no. 5,S-34,550, 5,R-31,052, and information from field technicians." "5,S-32,917."   LC Card 81-691130
1. Soil-surveys - Kansas - Maps.
G4201.J3 1978 .U5

Status of soil surveys in Kansas, October 1, 1979 / U. S. Department of Agriculture, Soil Conservation Service. Rev. 7-27-79. Lincoln, Nebr. : USDA-SCS, 1979. 1 map : col. ; 18 x 23 cm. "Source: SCS drawings no. 5,S-34,550, 5,R-31,052, and information from SCS field technicians." "5,S-32,917."   LC Card 81-691129
1. Soil-surveys - Kansas - Maps.
G4201.J3 1979 .U51

Status of soil surveys in Kansas, October 1,

1980 / U. S. Department of Agriculture, Soil Conservation Service. Rev. 6-23-80. Lincoln, Nebr. : USDA-SCS, 1980. 1 map : col. ; 18 x 23 cm. "Source: SCS drawing no. 5,S-32,550 and information from SCS field personnel." "5,S-32,917." LC Card 81-691128
1. Soil-surveys - Kansas - Maps.
G4201.J3 1980 .U51

Status of soil surveys in North Dakota, FY-1979 / U. S. Department of Agriculture, Soil Conservation Service. Rev. 12-11-78. Lincoln, Nebr. : USDA-SCS, 1978. 1 map : col. ; 18 x 24 cm. "Source: Family of maps SCS drawing no. 5,S-32,814, January 1974, and information from SCS field technicians." "5,S-34,845." LC Card 81-691263
1. Soil-surveys - North Dakota - Maps.
G4171.J3 1979 .U5

Status of soil surveys in North Dakota, FY 1980 / U. S. Department of Agriculture, Soil Conservation Service. Rev. 10-1-79. Lincoln, Nebr. : USDA-SCS, 1979. 1 map : col. ; 18 x 24 cm. "Source: Family of maps SCS drawing no. 5,S-32,814, January 1974, and information from SCS field technicians." "5,S-34,845." LC Card 81-691262
1. Soil-surveys - North Dakota - Maps.
G4171.J3 1980 .U5

Status of soil surveys in North Dakota, FY 1981 / U. S. Department of Agriculture, Soil Conservation Service. Rev. 10-1-80. Lincoln, Nebr. : USDA-SCS, 1980. 1 map : col. ; 18 x 34 cm. "Source: Family of maps SCS drawing no. 5,S-32,814 (1-74) and information from SCS field personnel." "5,S-34,845." LC Card 81-691261
1. Soil-surveys - North Dakota - Maps.
G4171.J3 1981 .U5

Status of soil surveys, Michigan, August 1979 / U. S. Department of Agriculture, Soil Conservation Service. Rev. 8-2-79. Lincoln, Nebr. : USDA-SCS, 1979. 1 map : col. ; 23 x 18 cm. "Source: Family of maps drwg. no. 5,S-32,577 (7-74) and information from SCS field personnel." "5,P-36,339." LC Card 81-691406
1. Soil-surveys - Michigan - Maps.
G4111.J3 1979 .U5

Status of soil surveys, Michigan, August 1980 / U. S. Department of Agriculture, Soil Conservation Service. Rev. 8-80. Lincoln, Nebr. : USDA-SCS, 1980. 1 map : col. ; 23 x 18 cm., on sheet 51 x 31 cm. "Source: Family of maps drwg. no. 5,S-32,577 (7-74) and information from SCS field personnel." "5,O-36,339." LC Card 81-691409
1. Soil-surveys - Michigan - Maps.
G4111.J3 1980 .U5

Status of soil surveys South Dakota, January 1, 1980 / U. S. Department of Agriculture, Soil Conservation Service. Lincoln, Nebr. : USDA-SCS, 1980. 1 map : col. ; 36 x 46 cm. "1-2-80." "Source: Family of maps, SCS drawing no. 5,S-32,929 (4-74) and information from SCS field personnel." "5,N-37,674." LC Card 81-691112
1. Soil-surveys - South Dakota - Maps.
G4181.J3 1980 .U5

Status of soil surveys, State of Indiana, October 1979 / U. S. Department of Agriculture, Soil Conservation Service. Rev. 7-10-79. Lincoln, Nebr. : USDA-SCS, 1979. 1 map : col. ; 23 x 18 cm. "Source: Family of maps SCS drwg. no. 5,S-32,450 (3-15-74) and information from field personnel." "5,P-34,218." LC Card 81-691255
1. Soil-surveys - Indiana - Maps.
G4091.J3 1979 .U5

Status of soil surveys, State of Indiana, October 1980 / U. S. Department of Agriculture, Soil Conservation Service. Rev. 7-80. Lincoln, Nebr. : USDA-SCS, 1980. 1 map : col. ; 26 x 18 cm. "Source: Family of maps SCS drwg. no. 5,S-32,450 (3-74) and information from field personnel." "5,O-34,218." LC Card 81-691256
1. Soil-surveys - Indiana - Maps.
G4091.J3 1980 .U5

Status of soil surveys, Virginia. Lanham, Md. : USDA-SCS, 1979. 1 map : col. ; 26 x 40 cm. "Base Source: USDA, SCS, in cooperation with VPI&SU and Virginia SWCC." "October 1979." Indexed. "1,O-12,727." LC Card 81-690106
1. Soil-surveys - Virginia - Maps. I. Title.
G3881.J3 1979 .U51

Status of soil surveys, Virginia. Lanham, Md. : USDA-SCS, 1981. 1 map : col. ; 26 x 40 cm. In lower right corner: January 1981. "Base Source: USDA,

SCS in cooperation with VPI&SU and Virginia SWCC." Indexed for independent cities. "1,O-12,727." LC Card 81-692880
1. Soil-surveys - Virginia - Maps. I. Title.
G3881.J3 1981 .U5

Status of soil surveys, Wisconsin, October 1, 1980 / U. S. Department of Agriculture, Soil Conservation Service. Rev. 9-16-80. Lincoln, Nebr. : USDA-SCS, 1980. 1 map : col. ; 26 x 20 cm., on sheet 51 x 31 cm. "Source: Family of maps SCS drwg. no. 5,S-32,817 (2-74) and information from SCS field technicians. "5,P-34,995." LC Card 81-691247
1. Soil-surveys - Wisconsin - Maps.
G4121.J3 1980 .U51

Status of soil surveys, Wisconsin, September 30, 1979 / U. S. Department of Agriculture, Soil Conservation Service. Rev. 5-29-79. Lincoln, Nebr. : USDA-SCS, 1979. 1 map : col. ; 24 x 18 cm., on sheet 51 x 31 cm. Coloring differs from other ed. "Source: Family of maps SCS drwg. no. 5,S-32,817 (2-74) and information from field technicians. "5,P-34,995." LC Card 81-691245
1. Soil-surveys - Wisconsin - Maps.
G1421.J3 1979 .U51

Status of the national cooperative soil survey in Missouri / U. S. Department of Agriculture, Soil Conservation Service. Rev. 1-25-79. Lincoln, Nebr. : USDA-SCS, 1979. 1 map : col. ; 18 x 23 cm. "Source: Family of maps SCS drwg. no. 5,S-32,925 (3-5-74) and information from field technicians." "5,S-35,293." LC Card 81-691211
1. Soil-surveys - Missouri - Maps.
G4161.J3 1979 .U5

Status of the national cooperative soil survey in Missouri, July 1, 1980 / U. S. Department of Agriculture, Soil Conservation Service. Rev. 6-19-80. Lincoln, Nebr. : USDA-SCS, 1980. 1 map : col. ; 18 x 23 cm. "Source: Family of maps SCS drwg. no. 5,S-32,925 (3-5-74) and information from field technicians." "5,S-35,293." LC Card 81-691210
1. Soil-surveys - Missouri - Maps.
G4161.J3 1980 .U5

Status of watershed assistance under P.L.566, Oregon / U. S. Department of Agriculture, Soil Conservation Service. Portland, Or. : USDA-SCS, 1979. 1 map : col. ; on sheet 22 x 28 cm. "November 1979." "Thematic detail compiled by state staff." "Base map prepared by SCS, WTSC Carto Unit from USGS 1:1,000,000 Nat. atlas." Indexed. "M7-OL-16506." LC Card 81-691561
1. Watersheds - Oregon - Maps. I. Title.
G4291.C315 1979 .U5

Steinkamp, James F. Soil survey of Sangamon County, Illinois /. [Washington, D.C.] [1980] vii, 139 p., [71] fold. leaves of plates : LC Card 80-602641 DDC 631.4/7/77356 19
S599.I5 S73

Stephenson County, Illinois / U. S. Department of Agriculture, Soil Conservation Service [and] United States Department of the Interior, Geological Survey. Lincoln, Nebr. : USDA-SCS, 1980. 1 map : col. ; 38 x 48 cm. Base source: USGS 1:100,000 compiled in 1976." Includes location map. "5,S-37,883." LC Card 81-691429
1. Stephenson County, Ill. - Maps. I. United States. Geological Survey.
G4103.S9 1980 .U5

Strafford County, New Hampshire / United States Department of Agriculture, Soil Conservation Service. Lanham, MD : USDA-SCS, 1980. 1 map : col. ; 44 x 29 cm. Title in lower margin: Strafford Co., N.H. : N4304.5-W7048.5/30 x 26.5, 1975. "Compiled in 1975 from USGS 1:24,000 and 1:62,500-scale topographic maps dated 1957-1973." "Planimetry revised from aerial photographs taken 1975." LC Card 81-690023
1. Strafford County (N.H.) - Maps.
G3743.S7 1975 .U5

Stringer, Billy R. Soil survey of Bosque County, Texas /. [Washington, D.C.] [1980] vii, 102 p., [31] fold. leaves of plates : LC Card 80-602639 DDC 631.4/7/764518 19
S599.T4 S75

Sussex County, Delaware / United States Department of Agriculture, Soil Conservation Service ; edited by the Geological Survey. Lanham, MD : USDA-SCS, 1980. 1 map : col. ; 46 x 49 cm. "Compiled by USGS in 1977 from USGS 1:24,000 scale topographic maps dated

1942-1967." "Planimetry revised from photographs taken 1973 and other source data." "1-13115." LC Card 81-690014
1. Sussex County (Del.) - Maps. I. United States. Geological Survey.
G3833.S8 1980 .U5

Talbot County, Maryland / United States Department of Agriculture, Soil Conservation Service. [Lanham, MD] : The Service, [1980] 1 map : col. ; 69 x 80 cm. "This natural soil group map is a generalization of the detailed soil map of Talbot County and is suitable only for broad land use planning." Relief shown by contours and spot heights. Stamped on LC copy: Produced under contract printing. "July 1980." Includes notes and location map. "1-16206." LC Card 81-690094
1. Soils - Maryland - Talbot County - Maps.
G3843.T3J3 1980 .U5

Thurston County, Nebraska / U. S. Department of Agriculture, Soil Conservation Service. Lincoln, Nebr. : USDA-SCS, 1980. 1 map : col. ; 46 x 59 cm. "12-12-79." "Source: 1970 general county highway map." Includes location map. "5,P-37,583.1." LC Card 81-691000
1. Thurston County (Neb.) - Maps.
G4193.T6 1979 .U5

Toombs County, Georgia : soil interpretive map of limitations for septic tank absorption fields / U. S. Department of Agriculture, Soil Conservation Service. Fort Worth, Tex. : USDA-SCS, 1979. 1 map : col. ; 50 x 38 cm. "Base compiled from USGS quadrangle sheets and Georgia county highway map ..." UTM grid. Includes text and location map. "April 1978 base 4-R-36581." LC Card 81-690349
1. Sewage disposal in the ground - Georgia - Toombs County - Maps. 2. Septic tanks - Georgia - Toombs County - Maps.
G3923.T6N46 1978 .U5

Townsend, William R. Soil survey of Conway County, Arkansas /. [Washington] [1980] vii, 91 p., [27] fold. leaves of plates : LC Card 80-603205 DDC 631.4/7/76731 19
S599.A75 T67

Township, school, and hospital district map, Ness County, Kansas / U. S. Department of Agriculture, Soil Conservation Service. Lincoln, Nebr. : USDA-SCS, 1979. 1 map : col. ; 41 x 57 cm. "1-24-79." "Source: Family of maps SCS drawing no. 5,S-36,165 (3-77) ..." Includes location map. "5,S-37,181." LC Card 81-691149
1. Ness County (Kan.) - Administrative and political divisions - Maps. 2. School districts - Kansas - Ness County - Maps. 3. Hospitals - Kansas - Ness County - Maps. I. Title.
G4203.N5F7 1979 .U5

Transportation network, Greater Southwest Regional Planning Commission, Kansas / U. S. Department of Agriculture, Soil Conservation Service. Lincoln, Nebr. : USDA-SCS, 1979. 1 map : col. ; 46 x 58 cm. Covers 19 counties. "3-1-75." "Source: Family of maps SCS drawing no. 5,R-32,488 (1-1975) ..." Includes location map. "5,O-34,967." LC Card 81-691161
1. Transportation - Kansas - Maps. 2. Greater Southwest Regional Planning Commission - Maps.
G4201.P1 1975 .U52

Tributary flooding map, Kansas / U. S. Department of Agriculture, Soil Conservation Service. Lincoln, Nebr. : USDA-SCS, 1979. 1 map : col. ; 46 x 58 cm. "6-8-79." "Source: Family of maps S.C.S. drwg. no. 5,S-32,550 (rev. 1-76) and information from S.C.S. field technicians." "5-S-37,433." LC Card 81-691131
1. Floods - Kansas - Maps. I. Title.
G4201.C32 1979 .U5

Trujillo, L. F. Trap-efficiency study, highland creek flood retarding reservoir near Kelseyville, California, water years 1966-77 /. Washington , 1980. p. cm. LC Card 80-606911 DDC 627/.44 19
TC424.C2 T78

United States. Soil Conservation Service. Soil survey of Ashley County, Arkansas /. [Washington, D.C. , 1979] vii, 92 p., [40] fold. leaves of plates : LC Card 80-601804 DDC 631.4/7/76783 19
S599.A75 U54 1979

United States. Soil Conservation Service. Soil survey of Calhoun and Dallas Counties, Arkansas /. [Washington] [1980] vii, 80 p., [59] fold. leaves of plates : LC Card 80-601636

DDC 631.4/7/76764 19
S599.A75 U54 1980

Upper Schoharie Creek watershed, Delaware, Greene, and Schoharie Counties, New York. Lanham, MD : USDA-SCS, 1980. 1 map : col. ; 27 x 19 cm. "Source: New York State base map 1:250,000, central part." "September 1980." Includes location map. "1-12057." LC Card 81-690285
1. Schoharie Creek watershed (N.Y.) - Maps. I. Title.
G3802.S42 1980 .U5

Van Buren County, Michigan / U. S. Department of Agriculture, Soil Conservation Service. Lincoln, Nebr. : USDA-SCS, 1971. 1 map ; 26 x 41 cm. "9-7-71." "Source: General highway map, Van Buren County 1968." Includes location map. "5,O-29474." LC Card 81-691400
1. Van Buren County (Mich.) - Maps.
G4113.V3 1971 .U5

Vermont. State Planning Office. Chittenden County, Vermont, land capability plan, 1972 /. Lanham, MD , 1980. 1 map ; LC Card 81-690127
G3753.C5 1972 .V4

Vinar, Kenneth R. Soil survey of Washington and Ramsey Counties, Minnesota /. [Washington] [1980] ix, 246 p., [56] fold. leaves of plates : LC Card 80-602943 DDC 631.4/7/77658 19
S599.M52 V56

Virginia Polytechnic Institute and State University. Soil survey of Hanover County, Virginia /. [Washington, D.C. , 1980] ix, 218 p., [35] fold. leaves of plates : LC Card 80-602048 DDC 631.4/7/755462 19
S599.V8 V57 1980

Voy, Kermit D. Soil survey of Franklin County, Iowa /. [Washington, D.C.] [1980] ix, 183 p., [37] fold. leaves of plates : LC Card 80-602539 DDC 631.4/7/77728 19
S599.I8 V68

Wabash County, Illinois / U. S. Department of Agriculture, Soil Conservation Service [and] United States Department of the Interior, Geological Survey. Lincoln, Nebr. : USDA-SCS, 1980. 1 map : col. ; 39 x 33 cm. "Base source: USGS 1:100,000 compiled in 1978." Includes location map. "5,P-37,881." LC Card 81-691430
1. Wabash County, Ill. - Maps. I. United States. Geological Survey.
G4103.W2 1980 .U5

Waqua Creek watershed, Lunenburg and Brunswick Counties, Virginia / U. S. Department of Agriculture, Soil Conservation Service. Lanham, MD : USDA-SCS, 1979. 1 map : col. ; 27 x 58 cm. "Source: USGS Topo Quad Sheets 1:24,000." "December 1979." "Contour interval 50 feet." Includes location map. "1-15518." LC Card 81-690288
1. Waqua Creek watershed (Va.) - Maps, Topographic.
G3882.W27 1979 .U5

Washichek, Jack N. Summary of snow survey measurements for Colorado and New Mexico, 1971-1977 . Denver, Colo. [1978] xxiii, 128 p. : LC Card 79-601670 DDC 551.57/9/788 19
GB2625.C6 W37

Washington County, Nebraska / U. S. Department of Agriculture, Soil Conservation Service. [Lincoln, Neb.] : The Service, [1979?] 1 map : col. ; 29 x 38 cm. "Base source: USGS 1:100,000 county base compiled in 1975." Includes location map. "5,O-37,514." LC Card 81-691077
1. Washington County, Neb. - Maps.
G4193.W2 1979 .U5

Water, fisheries, and pollution resources map lower Little Nemaha watershed, Johnson, Nemaha, Otoe and Richardson Counties, Nebraska / U. S. Department of Agriculture, Soil Conservation Service. Lincoln, Nebr. : USDA-SCS, 1978. 1 map : col. ; 26 x 45 cm. "12-20-78." "Source: SCS drawing 5,R-24,031 (rev. 12-78) and information from field technicians." Includes location map. "5,S-37,162." LC Card 81-691088
1. Water resources development - Nebraska - Little Nemaha River watershed - Maps. 2. Fisheries - Nebraska - Little Nemaha River watershed - Maps. 3. Water - Pollution - Nebraska - Little Nemaha River watershed - Maps.
G4192.L5C3 1978 .U5

Water quality characteristics of major streams, western South Dakota river basins / U. S.

Department of Agriculture, Soil Conservation Service. Lincoln, Nebr. : USDA-SCS, 1978. 3 maps on sheet : col. ; 7 x 9 cm. on sheet 26 x 18 cm. "7-10-78." "Source: Mineral and water resources of South Dakota (U. S.G.S. 1975) ..." "5,N-36,973." CONTENTS. - Total dissolved solids in water from major streams -- Predominant chemical constituents in water from major streams -- Suspended-sediment concentration in major streams. LC Card 81-691107
1. Water quality - South Dakota - Maps.
G4181.C35 1978 .U5

Water resource map, Ness County, Kansas / U. S. Department of Agriculture, Soil Conservation Service. Lincoln, Nebr. : USDA-SCS, 1979. 1 map : col. ; 41 x 57 cm. Shows generalized well yields. "1-19-79." "Source: Family of maps S.C.S. drwg. no. 5,S-36,165 (3-77) ..." Includes location map. "5,S-37,180." LC Card 81-691148
1. Water, Underground - Kansas - Ness County - Maps.
G4203.N5C34 1979 .U5

Water resources map, upper Little Nemaha watershed, Lancaster, Cass, and Otoe Counties, Nebraska / U. S. Department of Agriculture, Soil Conservation Service. Lincoln, Nebr. : USDA-SCS, 1979. 1 map : col. ; 26 x 39 cm. "1-15-79." "Source: SCS drwg. no. 5,R-23,485 (7-66) and information from field technicians." Includes location map. "5,S-37,212." LC Card 81-691085
1. Water resources development - Nebraska - Little Nemaha River watershed - Maps.
G4192.L5C3 1979 .U5

Watershed map, Ness County, Kansas / U. S. Department of Agriculture, Soil Conservation Service. Lincoln, Nebr. : USDA-SCS, 1979. 1 map : col. ; 41 x 57 cm. "1-25-79." "Source: Family of maps S.C.S. drwg. no. 5,S-36,165 (3-77) ..." Includes location map. "5,S-37,179." LC Card 81-691147
1. Watersheds - Kansas - Ness County - Maps.
G4203.N5C315 1979 .U51

Watershed (P.L. 566) projects South Dakota, January 1979 / U. S. Department of Agriculture, Soil Conservation Service. Rev. 1-9-79. Lincoln, Nebr. : USDA-SCS, 1979. 1 map : col. ; 41 x 58 cm. "Source: USGS base map and official highway map of South Dakota watershed informaion from field technicians." Indexed. "5,P-20,630." LC Card 81-691106
1. Watersheds - South Dakota - Maps. I. Title.
G4181.C315 1979 .U5

Watershed (P.L. 566) projects, South Dakota, January 1980 / U. S. Department of Agriculture, Soil Conservation Service. Rev. 3-12-80. Lincoln, Nebr. : USDA-SCS, 1980. 1 map : col. ; 18 x 26 cm. "Source: USGS base map ... Watershed information from SCS field personnel." Indexed. "5P-37,759." LC Card 81-691099
1. Watersheds - South Dakota - Maps. I. Title.
G4181.C315 1980 .U52

Watersheds, Whitman County, Washington / U. S. Department of Agriculture, Soil Conservation Service. Portland, Or. : USDA-SCS, 1977. 1 map : col. ; on sheet 27 x 41 cm. "January 1977." "Thematic detail compiled by Washington state staff." "Base map prepared by SCS from 1:126,720 general highway map." Relief shown by hachures. Includes location map. "M7-N-23725-4." LC Card 81-691520
1. Watersheds - Washington (State) - Whitman County - Maps.
G4283.W6C315 1977 .U5

Watts, Frank C. Soil survey of St. Lucie County area, Florida /. [Washington] [1980] vii, 183 p., [26] fold. leaves of plates : LC Card 80-602562 DDC 631.4/7/75929 19
S599.F6 W37

Wayne County, Iowa / U. S. Department of Agriculture, Soil Conservation Service [and] United States Department of the Interior, Geological Survey. Lincoln, Nebr. : USDA-SCS, 1979. 1 map : col. ; 31 x 33 cm. "Base source: USGS 1:100,000 county base compiled in 1973." Includes location map. "5,P-37,706." LC Card 81-691183
1. Wayne County, Iowa - Maps. I. United States. Geological Survey.
G4153.W35 1979 .U5

Webster County, Iowa / U. S. Department of Agriculture, Soil Conservation Service [and] United States Department of the Interior, Geological Survey. [Lincoln, Neb.] : The Service, [1979?] 1 map : col. ; 40 x 35 cm. "Base source: USGS 1:100,000 county base compiled in 1976."

Includes location map. "5,P-37,509." LC Card 81-691182
1. Webster County (Iowa) - Maps. I. United States. Geological Survey.
G4153.W4 1979 .U5

Weesies, Glenn A. Soil survey of Bay County, Michigan /. [Washington, D.C.] , 1980. vii, 105 p., [23] fold. leaves of plates : LC Card 80-602508 DDC 631.4/7/77447 19
S599.M4 W43

Weisel, Charles J. Soil survey of Benewah County area, Idaho /. [Washington] [1980] x, 188 p., [25] fold. leaves of plates : LC Card 80-602396 DDC 631.4/7/79693 19
S599.I2 W44

Wet soils, Chickies Creek watershed, Lancaster and Lebanon Counties, Pennsylvania / U. S. Department of Agriculture, Soil Conservation Service. Hyattsville, Md. : USDA-SCS, 1977. 1 map : col. ; 25 x 34 cm. "Source: 1969 U. S. Geological Survey quadrangles." Includes location map. LC Card 81-690274
1. Soil moisture - Pennsylvania - Chickies Creek watershed - Maps. I. Title.
G3822.C45J3 1977 .U51

White County, Illinois / U. S. Department of Agriculture, Soil Conservation Service. Lincoln, Nebr. : USDA-SCS, 1980. 1 map : col. ; 37 x 47 cm. "8-1-78." "Source: 1974 general county highway map." Includes location map. "5,P-36,229.1." LC Card 81-691444
1. White County, Ill. - Maps.
G4103.W5 1978 .U5

Wildlife habitat evaluation map, upper Little Nemaha watershed, Lancaster, Cass, and Otoe Counties, Nebraska / U. S. Department of Agriculture, Soil Conservation Service. Lincoln, Nebr. : USDA-SCS, 1978. 1 map : col. ; 26 x 39 cm. "Source: SCS drawing no 5,R-23,485, (7-66) and information from field technicians." Includes location map. "5,S-37,211." LC Card 81-691083
1. Wildlife habitat improvement - Nebraska - Little Nemaha River watershed - Maps.
G4192.L5D5 1978 .U5

Wingard, Robert C. Soil survey of Dubois County, Indiana /. [Washington, D.C. , 1980] vii, 117 p., [36] fold. leaves of plates : LC Card 80-602049 DDC 631.4/7/77237 19
S599.I63 W57

Winneshiek County, Iowa / U. S. Department of Agriculture, Soil Conservation Service [and] United States Department of the Interior, Geological Survey. Lincoln, Nebr. : USDA-SCS, 1979. 1 map : col. ; 40 x 34 cm. "Base source: USGS 1:100,000 county base compiled in 1978." Includes location map. "5,P-37,705." LC Card 81-691181
1. Winneshiek County, Iowa - Maps. I. United States. Geological Survey.
G4153.W6 1979 .U5

Wisconsin / U. S. Department of Agriculture, Soil Conservation Service. Lincoln, Nebr. : USDA-SCS, 1979. 1 map : col. ; 24 x 18 cm. "Source: 1970 national atlas of the United States of America." "5,S-32,817." LC Card 81-691254
1. Wisconsin - Maps.
G4120 1979 .U5

Woodbury County, Iowa / U. S. Department of Agriculture, Soil Conservation Service [and] United States Department of the Interior, Geological Survey. [Lincoln, Neb.] : The Service, [1979?] 1 map : col. ; 35 x 57 cm. "Base source: USGS 1:100,000 county base compiled from 1962-1971 topographic maps." Includes location map. "5,P-37,501." LC Card 81-691180
1. Woodbury County (Iowa) - Maps. I. United States. Geological Survey.
G4153.W7 1979 .U5

Woodruff, George A. Soil survey of San Bernardino County, southwestern part, California /. [Washington] [1980] ii, 64 p., [2] fold. leaves of plates : LC Card 80-601256 DDC 631.4/7/79495 19
S599.C2 W66

1977 land use map, Chickies Creek watershed, Lancaster and Lebanon Counties, Pennsylvania / U. S. Department of Agriculture, Soil Conservation Service. Hyattsville, Md. : USDA-SCS, [1978] 1 map : col. ; 25 x 34 cm. "Source: 1969 U. S. Geological Survey quadrangles." "3-23-78." Includes location map. "12688." LC Card

81-690270
*1. Land use - Pennsylvania - Chickies Creek
watershed - Maps. I. Title.*
G3822.C45G4 1977 .U5

**UNITED STATES. SOIL CONSERVATION
SERVICE.**
Schlepp, Richard L. Soil survey of Aurora
County, South Dakota. [Washington, D.C.?] ,
c1980. vii, 148 p., 58 folded p. of plates : LC
Card 81-600698   DDC 631.4/7/783375 19
S599.S6 S34

**UNITED STATES. SOIL CONSERVATION
SERVICE - ARCHIVES - CATALOGS.**
United States. National Archives and Records
Service. Preliminary inventory of the
cartographic records of the Soil Conservation
Service /. Washington , 1981. p. cm.   LC Card
81-3988   DDC 016.3530082/326 19
CD3026 .A32 no. 195 CD3038

**United States. Solicitor for the Dept. of the
Interior. Portland Region.** Althaus, Helen F.
Public trust rights /. [Washington] , 1978.
xxxix, 421 p. ;   LC Card 80-602390   DDC
346.7304/691 19
KF5571 .A94

United States. Solid Waste, Office of. see United
States. Office of Solid Waste.

United States-South Korean relations . United
States. Congress. House. Committee on Foreign
Affairs. Subcommittee on Asian and Pacific
Affairs. Washington , 1980. v, 60 p. ;   LC Card
80-604073   DDC 327.730519/5 19
KF27 .F638 1980b

**United States. Southern Forest Experiment
Station, New Orleans.** (Old Catalog form:
United States. Forest experiment Station,
New Orleans)
Bertelson, Daniel F. Arkansas forest industries,
1971 /. New Orleans , 1973. 29 p. :   LC Card
80-505836   DDC 333.75/0976 s
338.4/7674/009767 19
SD11 .A45793 no. 38 HD9757.A9

Resource bulletin SO .
(38) Bertelson, Daniel F. Arkansas forest
industries, 1971 /. New Orleans , 1973. 29
p. :   LC Card 80-505836   DDC 333.75/0976 s
338.4/7674/009767 19
SD11 .A45793 no. 38 HD9757.A9

**UNITED STATES. SOUTHWESTERN
POWER ADMINISTRATION -
MANAGEMENT.**
United States. Congress. Senate. Committee on
Energy and Natural Resources. Subcommittee
on Energy Conservation and Supply. Deferring
repayment of certain reimbursable costs
incurred by the Southwestern Power
Administration . Washington , 1980. ii, 37 p. ;
LC Card 80-603007   DDC 343.79/0929 19
KF26 .E553 1980b

United States. Space Science, Office of. see
United States. Office of Space Science.

**UNITED STATES. SPECIAL ASSISTANT TO
THE PRESIDENT FOR NATIONAL
SECURITY AFFAIRS.**
United States. Congress. Senate. Committee on
Foreign Relations. The national security
adviser . Washington , 1980. v, 243 p. :   LC
Card 80-602957   DDC 353.03/1 19
KF26 .F6 1980n

**United States. Special Committee on Atomic
Energy.** see United States. Congress. Senate.
Special Committee on Atomic Energy.

**UNITED STATES. SPECIAL PANEL ON
APPEALS - OFFICIALS AND
EMPLOYEES.**
United States. Congress. Senate. Committee on
Labor and Human Resources. Nomination .
Washington , 1980. ii, 41 p. ;   LC Card
80-603645   DDC 353.001/04 19
KF26 .L27 1980n

**United States. Sport Fisheries and Wildlife,
Bureau of.** see United States. Bureau of
Sport Fisheries and Wildlife.

United States Standards Bureau. see United
States. National Bureau of Standards.

United States. Standards, National Bureau of.
see United States. National Bureau of
Standards.

**United States. Standards of Official Conduct,
Committee on (House)** see United States.
Congress. House. Committee on Standards of
Official Conduct.

United States. State Dept. see United States.
Dept. of State.

**UNITED STATES - STATES - RACE
RELATIONS.**
Civil rights issues of Asian and Pacific
Americans . [Washington, D.C.] , 1980. xiii,
834, 20 p. ;   LC Card 80-602622   DDC
323.1/195/073 19
E184.O6 C58

UNITED STATES - STATISTICAL SERVICES.
Nelson, Theodore A. Measuring markets .
[Washington] , 1979. iv, 101 p. ;   LC Card
79-603999
HF5415.3 .N44 1979

United States. Bureau of the Census. Center for
Applied User Research. Guide to county census
data for planning economic development.
[Washington, D.C.] , 1979. iii, 123 p. ;   LC
Card 80-601079   DDC 330.973 19
HA37.U55 U54 1979

United States. Federal Committee on Statistical
Methodology. Subcommittee on Statistical Uses
of Administrative Records. Report on statistical
uses of administrative records /. [Washington,
D.C.?] , 1980 [i.e. 1981] xii, 106 p. :   LC Card
81-601438   DDC 353.0081/9 19
HA37.U55 U55 1981

United States. Office of Federal Statistical
Policy and Standards. A framework for
planning U. S. Federal statistics for the 1980's
/. Washington , 1978. vii, 440 p. ;   LC Card
79-601484
HA37 .U549 1978   NYPL [JLF 81-221]

**UNITED STATES - STATISTICAL
SERVICES - CONGRESSES.**
A Numerator and denominator for measuring
change . Washington , 1975. 195 p. :   LC Card
75-619192   DDC 001.4/33 19
HA37 .U52 1975

UNITED STATES - STATISTICS, MEDICAL.
Cardocki, Gloria J. Utilization of short-stay
hospitals by persons with heart disease and
malignant neoplasms . Hyattsville, Md. [1981]
p. cm.   ISBN 0-8406-0214-6   LC Card 80-28017
DDC 362.1/1/0973 s 362.1/9612/00973 19
RA407.3 .A349 no. 52 RA981.A2

Cypress, Beulah K. Patients' reasons for visiting
physicians . Hyattsville, Md. [1981] p. cm.
ISBN 0-8406-0225-1   LC Card 81-607915   DDC
362.1/1/0973 362.1 19
RA407.3 .A349 no. 56 RA410.7

Feller, Barbara A. Health characteristics of
persons with chronic activity limitation .
Hyattsville, Md. , 1981. p. cm.   ISBN
0-8406-0229-4   LC Card 81-11249   DDC
312/.0973 s 312/.3 19
RA407.3 .A346 no. 137 RA644.6

Hadden, Wilbur Crane, 1946- Basic data on
health care needs of adults 25-74 years of age,
United States, 1971-75. Hyattsville, MD , 1980.
vi, 45 p. ;   ISBN 0-8406-0197-2   LC Card
80-607810   DDC 312/.0973 s 362.1 19
RA407.3 .A347 no. 218 RA410.53

Haupt, Barbara J. The Nation's use of health
resources, 1979 /. [Washington] [1980] x, 169
p. ;   LC Card 80-602252   DDC 362.1/0973 19
RA410.53 .H38

Hing, Esther. Use of health services by women
65 years and over. Hyattsville, Md. [1981] p.
cm.   LC Card 81-607865   DDC 362.1/1/0973 s
362.1/9/0880565 19
RA407.3 .A349 no. 59 RA408.W65

Jack, Susan S. Current estimates from the
health interview survey, United States, 1979 .
Hyattsvile, Md. , 1981. p. cm.   ISBN
0-8406-0219-7   LC Card 81-607002   DDC
312/.3/0973 19
RA407.3 .J32

Klebba, A. Joan. Mortality from diseases
associated with smoking . Hyattsville, Md. ,
1980. p. cm.   ISBN 0-8406-0208-1   LC Card
80-607855   DDC 312/.2/0973 s 615.9/52379 19
HB1335 .A18 no. 17 RA1242.T6

McCarthy, Eileen. Inpatient utilization of
short-stay hospitals by diagnosis, United States,

1978 /. Hyattsville, Md. [1981] p. cm.   ISBN
0-8406-0220-0   LC Card 81-5000   DDC
M362.1/1/0973 s 362.1/1/0973
RA407.3 .A349 no. 55 RA981.A2

Rosenstein, Marilyn. The characteristics of
persons served by the federally funded
community mental health centers program,
1974 /. Rockville, Md. , Washington, D.C.
[1979] iv, 19, [33] p. ;   LC Card 80-602392
DDC 312/.389/00973 19
RA790.6 .R67

Seiling, Virginia. Health characteristics of
veterans and nonveterans . Washington, D.C.
[1980] v, 75 p. :   LC Card 80-602055   DDC
362.1/9 19
RA408.M4 S44

United States. Indian Health Service. Illness
among Indians and Alaska Natives, 1970 to
1978. [Washington] [1979?]. viii, 58 p. ;   LC
Card 80-601653   DDC 312/.3/08997 19
RA408.I49 U54 1979a

**UNITED STATES - STATISTICS, MEDICAL -
BIBLIOGRAPHY - CATALOGS.**
United States. National Center for Health
Statistics. Publications and data tapes of the
National Center for Health Statistics available
from the National Technical Information
Service. Hyattsville, Md. , 1978. 260 p. ;   LC
Card 79-602913
Z7553.M43 U54 1978 RA407.3
NYPL [JLF 81-340]

**UNITED STATES - STATISTICS, MEDICAL -
DATA TAPE CATALOGS.**
United States. National Center for Health
Statistics. Publications and data tapes of the
National Center for Health Statistics available
from the National Technical Information
Service. Hyattsville, Md. , 1978. 260 p. ;   LC
Card 79-602913
Z7553.M43 U54 1978 RA407.3
NYPL [JLF 81-340]

**UNITED STATES - STATISTICS, MEDICAL -
PERIODICALS.**
Tuberculosis statistics; states & cities. Atlanta
NYPL [JLM 80-839]

UNITED STATES - STATISTICS, VITAL.
Klebba, A. Joan. Mortality from diseases
associated with smoking . Hyattsville, Md. ,
1980. p. cm.   ISBN 0-8406-0208-1   LC Card
80-607855   DDC 312/.2/0973 s 615.9/52379 19
HB1335 .A18 no. 17 RA1242.T6

**UNITED STATES - STATISTICS, VITAL -
BIBLIOGRAPHY - CATALOGS.**
United States. National Center for Health
Statistics. Publications and data tapes of the
National Center for Health Statistics available
from the National Technical Information
Service. Hyattsville, Md. , 1978. 260 p. ;   LC
Card 79-602913
Z7553.M43 U54 1978 RA407.3
NYPL [JLF 81-340]

**UNITED STATES - STATISTICS, VITAL -
DATA TAPE CATALOGS.**
United States. National Center for Health
Statistics. Publications and data tapes of the
National Center for Health Statistics available
from the National Technical Information
Service. Hyattsville, Md. , 1978. 260 p. ;   LC
Card 79-602913
Z7553.M43 U54 1978 RA407.3
NYPL [JLF 81-340]

United States. Statutes. see United States. Laws,
statutes, etc.

**UNITED STATES. STEEL TRIPARTITE
COMMITTEE.**
United States. Congress. Senate. Committee on
Environment and Public Works. Report of the
Steel Tripartite Committee . Washington , 1981.
iii, 124 p. ;   LC Card 81-601353   DDC
338.4/7669142/0973 19
KF26 .E6 1980k

**United States. Strategic Petroleum Reserve
Office.**
Annual strategic petroleum reserve report.
[Washington], United States Dept. of Energy.
illus. 28 cm. Cover title: Strategic petroleum reserve
annual report.   LC Card 78-645585
*1. Petroleum - United States - Storage - Periodicals. 2.
Strategic materials - United States - Storage -
Periodicals. I. United States. Strategic Petroleum
Reserve Office. Strategic petroleum reserve annual*

report. II. Title. III. Title: *Strategic petroleum reserve annual report.*   **NYPL [JSP 80-382]**

Strategic petroleum reserve : final environmental impact statement. [Washington] : Federal Energy Administration, Strategic Petroleum Reserve Office, 1976- v. : ill. ; 27 cm. "FES 76-2." "FEA/S-76/487." Includes bibliography.   LC Card 77-602345
1. Petroleum - Storage. I. Title.
TP692.5 .U627 1976a

Strategic petroleum reserve annual report.
United States. Strategic Petroleum Reserve Office. Annual strategic petroleum reserve report. [Washington].   LC Card 78-645585
NYPL [JSP 80-382]

United States. Student Financial Assistance, Bureau of. see United States. Office of Education. Bureau of Student Financial Assistance.

United States. Supreme Court. (Old Catalog form: United States. Courts. Supreme Court)
Bakke, Allan Paul, petitioner. Allan Bakke versus Regents of the University of California /. Dobbs Ferry, N.Y. , 1978- v. ; ISBN 0-379-20297-2 :   LC Card 78-3573
KF228.B34 A3   **NYPL [Sc E 80-286]**

Fein, Bruce E. Significant decisions of the Supreme Court, 1976-1977 term /. - Washington , c1978. 168 p. ;
NYPL [JLE 80-1347]

Rules of the Supreme Court of the United States, adopted April 14, 1980, effective June 30, 1980. [Washington] : U. S. Govt. Print. Off., 1980. ii, 78 p. ; 23 cm. Cover title. Includes index.   LC Card 80-602260   DDC 347.73/265 19
1. Court rules - United States. I. Title.
KF9056.A315 A2 1980

United States. Courts of Appeals. Federal rules of appellate procedure, with forms, October 1, 1979. Washington , 1979. x, 33 p. :   LC Card 80-600983   DDC 347.73/8 19
KF9052 .A4 1979

UNITED STATES. SUPREME COURT.
The Criminal law revolution and its aftermath, 1960-1977. Supplement, Supreme Court, 1977-1978, 1978-1979, and 1979-1980 terms /. Washington, D.C. , 1981. p. cm. ISBN 0-87179-350-4 LC Card 81-607008   DDC 345.73 347.305 19
KF9614 .C7 1978 Suppl

United States. Congress. House. Committee on the Judiciary. Subcommittee on Courts, Civil Liberties, and the Administration of Justice. Prayer in public schools and buildings--federal court jurisdiction . Washington , 1981. iv, 976 p. ;   LC Card 81-601626   DDC 344.73/0796 347.304796 19
KF27 .J857 1980a

United States - Tariff. see Tariff - United States.

United States. Tariff Commission. Peanuts ; supplemental investigation under section 22, Agricultural adjustment act, as amended. Washington, 1955. 42 l. tables. 27 cm. Cover title.   LC Card 55-60610
1. Peanuts - United States. 2. Tariff on peanuts - United States.   **NYPL [JLF 75-1381]**

United States. Task Force on Asthma and the Other Allergic Diseases.
Asthma and the other allergic diseases. Young, Patrick. Asthma and allergies : an optimistic future / by Patrick Young. [Bethesda, Md.] , Washington, D.C. , 1980. 179 p. :   LC Card 80-603185   DDC 616.97 19
RC584 .Y68

United States. Task Force on Design, Art and Architecture in Transportation. Design, art & architecture in transportation 1st- ; 1978- [Washington]   **NYPL [JLM 80-1118]**

United States. Task Force on Housing Costs.
Final report of the Task Force on Housing Costs. Washington : U. S. Dept. of Housing and Urban Development, 1978. viii, 106 p. ; 27 cm. Cover title.   LC Card 78-601758
1. Housing - United States - Costs.
HD7293 .A5 1978d   **NYPL [JLF 81-380]**

United States. Task Force on Immunology and Disease. Immunology, its role in disease and health : summary report of the Task Force on Immunology and Disease. Rev. Bethesda, Md. : U. S. Dept. of Health and Human Services,

Public Health Service, National Institutes of Health, National Institute of Allergy and Infectious Diseases ; Washington, D.C. : for sale by the Supt. of Docs., U. S. Govt. Print. Off., [1980] xi, 157 p. : ill. ; 23 cm. (NIH publication ; no. 80-940)   LC Card 80-602884   DDC 616.07/9 19
1. Immunology. 2. Immunologic diseases. I. Series: United States. National Institutes of Health. Publication, no. 80-940. II. Title.
QR181 .U53 1980

United States. Task Force on Regulation Q, President's Inter-Agency. see United States. President's Inter-Agency Task Force on Regulation Q.

United States. Task Force on Safety and Design Issue. see United States. Interagency Task Force on Safety and Design Issue.

United States. Task Force on Sex Discrimination. see United States. Dept. of Justice. Task Force on Sex Discrimination.

United States. Task Force on Workplace Safety and Health, Interagency. see United States. Interagency Task Force on Workplace Safety and Health.

United States. Tax Analysis, Office of. see United States. Office of Tax Analysis.

UNITED STATES. TAX COURT. (Old Catalog form: United States. Courts. Tax Court)
United States. Congress. House. Committee on Ways and Means. Organization and administration of the United States Tax Court . Washington , 1980. iii, 38 p. ;   LC Card 80-602486   DDC 343.7304/0269 19
KF27 .W3 1980d

UNITED STATES. TAX COURT - OFFICIALS AND EMPLOYEES.
United States. Congress. Senate. Committee on Finance. Nominations of Robert E. Herzstein, C. Moxley Featherston, William M. Fay, Charles R. Simpson, Edna Parker, and Sheldon V. Ekman . Washington , 1980. iii, 80 p. ;   LC Card 80-603685   DDC 353.0072/4 19
KF26 .F5 1980f

United States - Taxation. see Taxation - United States.

United States. Technology Assessment Board. see United States. Congress. Technology Assessment Board.

United States. Tennessee Valley Authority. see Tennessee Valley Authority.

United States. Teton Dam Failure Review Group.
Failure of Teton Dam : final report / by U. S. Department of the Interior, Teton Dam Failure Review Group ; F. William Eikenberry, chairman. Washington, D.C. : For sale by the Supt. of Docs., U. S. Govt. Print. Off., 1980. ca. 800 p. in various pagings, [1] leaf of plates : ill. ; 27 cm. Includes bibliographical references.   LC Card 80-601802   DDC 627/.83/0979656 19
1. Teton Dam, Idaho. I. Eikenberry, F. William. II. Title.
TC557.I22 T488 1980

United States. Trade Commission. see United States. Federal Trade Commission.

United States. Transportation, Dept. of. see United States. Dept. of Transportation.

United States. Transportation Economic Analysis, Office of. see United States. Office of Transportation Economic Analysis.

United States. Transportation Systems Analysis and Information, Office of. see United States. Office of Transportation Systems Analysis and Information.

United States. Transportation Systems Center. see Transportation Systems Center.

United States Travel Data Center. Travel in Virginia, 1978 : an economic analysis / prepared by the U. S. Travel Data Center for the Virginia State Travel Service. [Richmond, Va. : The Service, 1978] 12 p. : ill. ; 22 x 28 cm. Cover title.   LC Card 80-622616   DDC 381/.45917550443 19
1. Tourist trade - Virginia - Statistics. I. Virginia. State Travel Service. II. Title.
G155.U6 U58 1978

United States. Travel Service. Research and Analysis Division. Starch INRA Hooper. Italy . [Washington] , 1978. vi, 65 p. :   LC Card 78-601739
G155.U6 S65 1978a

United States. Treasury Dept.
President's cash management initiatives / submitted by Secretary of the Treasury G. William Miller [to] Committee on Ways and Means, U. S. House of Representatives on December 21, 1979. Washington : U. S. Govt. Print. Off., 1980. vi, 94 p. ; 24 cm. At head of title: 96th Congress, 2d session. Committee print, WMCP: 96-51.   LC Card 80-601795   DDC 353.0072/4 19
1. Tax administration and procedure - United States. 2. Tax collection - United States. 3. Cash management - United States. I. United States. Congress. House. Committee on Ways and Means. II. Title.
HJ3252 .U58 1980

Taxation of foreign investment in U. S. real estate. [Washington] : Dept. of the Treasury : for sale by the Supt. of Docs., U. S. Govt. Print. Off., 1979. 68 p. ; 26 cm. Includes bibliographical references.   LC Card 79-602968
1. Investments, Foreign - Law and legislation - United States. 2. Real property - United States - Foreign ownership. I. Title.
KF6441 .A85   **NYPL [JLF 81-449]**

UNITED STATES. TREASURY DEPT.
Saunders, Hyman. A review of the accuracy of treasury revenue forecasts, 1963-1978 /. [Washington, D.C.] , 1981. xi, 42 p. ;   LC Card 81-601118   DDC 353.0072/2252 19
HJ2051 .S26

UNITED STATES. TREASURY DEPT. - APPROPRIATIONS AND EXPENDITURES.
United States. Congress. Senate. Committee on Appropriations. Subcommittee on the Dept. of the Treasury, U. S. Postal Service, and General Government Appropriations. Treasury, Postal Service, and general government appropriations for fiscal year 1981 . Washington , 1980- v. <1> ;   LC Card 80-603729   DDC 353.0072/236 19
KF26 .A662 1980

United States. Congress. Senate. Committee on Banking, Housing and Urban Affairs. Subcommittee on International Finance. International Monetary Fund and related legislation . Washington , 1980. iii, 237 p. ;   LC Card 80-602906   DDC 346.73/082152 19
KF26 .B3946 1980c

United States. Treasury Dept. Coast Guard. see United States. Coast Guard.

United States. Treasury Dept. Customs Service. see United States. Customs Service.

United States. Treasury Dept. General Accounting Office. see United States. General Accounting Office.

United States. Treasury Dept. Internal Revenue Service. see United States. Internal Revenue Service.

United States. Treasury Dept. Office of Tax Analysis. see United States. Office of Tax Analysis.

United States. Treasury Dept. Office of Weights and Measures. see United States. National Bureau of Standards.

UNITED STATES. TREASURY DEPT. - OFFICIALS AND EMPLOYEES.
United States. Congress. Senate. Committee on Finance. Nomination of Curtis A. Hessler . Washington , 1980. iii, 22 p. ;   LC Card 80-603001   DDC 353.2 19
KF26 .F5 1980c

United States - Treaties. see United States - Foreign relations - Treaties.

United States. Treaties, etc. Treaties and other international agreements on fisheries, oceanographic resources, and wildlife involving the United States / prepared at the request of Warren G. Magnuson for the use of the Committee on Commerce, Science, and Transportation, United States Senate, by the Congressional Research Service, the Library of Congress. Washington : U. S. G.P.O., 1977. xv, 1201 p. ; 24 cm. At head of title: 95th Congress, 1st session. Committee print. "October 31, 1977."   LC

Card 81-601815   DDC 341.7/62/026 19
1. United States - Foreign relations - Treaties. 2. Fishery law and legislation - United States. 3. Marine resources conservation - Law and legislation - United States. 4. Wildlife conservation - Law and legislation - United States. I. United States. Congress. Senate. Committee on Commerce, Science, and Transportation. II. Library of Congress. Congressional Research Service. III. Title.
JX236 1977 .U54

United States. Treaties, etc. Panama, Sept. 7, 1977. Tratados sobre el Canal de Panamá suscritos entre la República de Panamá y los Estados Unidos de América = Treaties on the Panama Canal signed between the United States of America and the Republic of Panama. Washington, D.C. : Secretaría General, Organización de los Estados Americanos, 1979. 2 v. : ill. ; 24 cm. (Serie sobre tratados . 57-57A) OEA Documentos oficiales ; OEA/Ser.A/34-OEA/Ser.A/34, Add. 1 (español-inglés) "79-11-054-SE" CONTENTS. - [v. 1] pt. 1. Tratado concerniente a la neutralidad permanente del Canal y al funcionamiento del Canal de Panamá y Protocol anexo. pt. 2. Tratado del Canal de Panamá.--[v. 2] Documentos de ratificación.   LC Card 80-121836   DDC 341.4/46/02667307287 19
1. Panama Canal Treaties, 1977. I. Title. II. Title: Treaties on the Panama Canal signed between the United States of America and the Republic of Panama. III. Series. IV. Series: Organization of American States. Documentos oficiales , OEA/Ser. A/34-OEA/Ser.A/34, Add. 1.
JX1398.72 1979 .U54 1977

United States-Turkey defense and economic cooperation agreement, 1980 . United States. Congress. House. Committee on Foreign Affairs. Subcommittee on Europe and the Middle East. Washington , 1980. iii, 69 p. ;
    LC Card 80-603044   DDC 327.730561 19
KF27 .F64214 1980a

United States /U. S.S.R. Urban Transportation Team. Transportation and the urban environment : the rational relationship between automobile and public transit development : a joint report of the U. S./U. S.S.R. Urban Transportation Team under the "Agreement on Cooperation in the Field of Environmental Protection". Washington : for sale by the Supt. of Docs., U. S. Govt. Print. Off., 1978. xii, 173 p. : ill. ; 27 cm. Includes bibliographies.   LC Card 79-600645
1. Urban transportation - Environmental aspects - United States. 2. Urban transportation - Environmental aspects - Russia. 3. Automobiles - Environmental aspects. I. Title.
HE308 .U568 1978

UNITED STATES. UMATILLA ARMY DEPOT.
GMA Research Corporation. Alternate use and marketing study: southwest portion of the Umatilla Army Depot /. [Pendleton], 1974. 75 l.:   *NYPL [JLF 80-198]*

United States. Unemployment Compensation, National Commission on. see United States. National Commission on Unemployment Compensation.

United States. Urban High School Reform Initiative. Federal educational law and urban secondary school reform : a legislative analysis / prepared by the Urban High School Reform Initiative ; Thomas J. Burns ... [et al.]. [Washington, D.C.] : U. S. Dept. of Health, Education, and Welfare, Office of Education, 1979. 2 v. ; 28 cm. Cover title: Federal education law and urban secondary school reform. Title on spine: Urban high school. "September 1979." CONTENTS. - v. 1. Reform recommendations.--v. 2. Federal support.
    LC Card 80-600029   DDC 344.73/074 19
1. Educational law and legislation - United States. 2. Federal aid to education - United States. 3. Education, Secondary - United States. 4. Education, Urban - United States. I. Burns, Thomas Joseph, 1937-. II. Title. III. Title: Urban high school.
KF4199 .A873

United States. Urban Mass Transportation Administration.
Draft environmental impact statement : Washington Metrorail system, Branch/Rosecroft (F) route / [prepared by the Urban Mass Transportation Administration (UMTA) in cooperation with the Washington Metropolitan Area Transportation Authority (WMATA)].

[Washington] : U. S. Dept. of Transportation, Urban Mass Transportation Administration, 1979. 204 p. in various pagings, [17] fold. leaves of plates : ill. ; 28 cm. Cover title.   LC Card 79-602769   DDC 388.4/2/09753 19
1. Subways - Environmental aspects - Washington metropolitan area. 2. Environmental impact statements - Washington metropolitan area. I. Washington Metropolitan Area Transportation Authority. II. Title.
TD195.S9 U54 1979

Golembiewski, Robert T. The MARTA code of ethics . [Atlanta? , 197-] 36 p. ;
                    *NYPL [*ZT-1259]*

Innovation in public transportation : a directory of research, development, and demonstration projects / United States Department of Transportation, Urban Mass Transportation Administration. Washington : The Administration ; for sale by the Supt. of Docs., U. S. Govt. Print. Off., 1974. ix, 147 p. : ill. ; 27 cm. Includes bibliographical references and indexes.
1. Transportation - Research - United States. 2. Urban transportation - United States. I. Title. II. Title: Directory of research, development, and demonstration projects in public transportation.
                    NYPL [JLF 80-1675]

The legal framework for collective bargaining in the urban transit industry /. Madison, Wisc. , 1976. iv, 188 p. ;   *NYPL [*XME-9332]*

A section 147 rural public transportation demonstration manual. Washington , 1979. 5 v. in 1 ;   *NYPL [JLF 80-1345]*

Womack, Katie N. Costs of public transportation in Texas, 1973-1977 /. College Station, Tex. , 1979. viii, 81 p. :   LC Card 80-621655   DDC 388.4/042 19
HE4487.T4 W65

UNITED STATES. URBAN MASS TRANSPORTATION ADMINISTRATION.
United States. Congress. House. Committee on Science and Technology. Subcommittee on Transportation, Aviation, and Communications. Urban mass transit R. & D. . Washington , 1980. iii, 200 p. ;   LC Card 80-603002   DDC 388.4/072073 19
KF27 .S3997 1980b

United States. Urban Mass Transportation Administration. Office of Intergovernmental Affairs. Institute of Public Administration, Washington, D. C. Financing transit . [Washington, D.C.] , 1979. ii, xii, 79 p. :   LC Card 80-602705   DDC 388.4/042 19
HE308 .I56 1979

United States. Urban Mass Transportation Administration. Office of Planning Assistance. Booz, Allen and Hamilton, inc. Transportation Consulting Division. Planning for the phase-in of fixed-route accessible buses : interim report /. Washington , 1980. 1 v. :
                    NYPL [JLM 80-1153]

United States. Urban Mass Transportation Administration. Office of Policy and Program Development.
Institute of Public Administration, Washington, D. C. Financing transit . [Washington, D.C.] , 1979. ii, xii, 79 p. :   LC Card 80-602705   DDC 388.4/042 19
HE308 .I56 1979

Institute of Public Administration, Washington, D. C. Financing transit . [Washington] [1979] v, 331 p. :   LC Card 80-601587   DDC 388.4/042 19
HE206.2 .I57 1979

United States. Urban Mass Transportation Administration. Office of Policy Research.
Gladstone Associates. Innovative financing techniques . [Washington, D.C.] , Washington, D.C. [1978] ca. 350 p. in various pagings /   LC Card 80-601836   DDC 388.4/042 19
HE4351 .G57 1978

United States. Urban Mass. Transportation Administration. Planning Assistance, Office of. see United States. Urban Mass Transportation Administration. Office of Planning Assistance.

United States. Veterans Administration.
Louis Harris and Associates. Myths and realities . Washington , 1980. xlviii, 481 p. :   LC Card 80-603127   DDC 355.1/15/0973 19
UB357 .L58 1980

Overseas beneficiaries : a study / prepared by the Veteran's Administration, pursuant to Section 308 of Public law 95-588, submitted to the Committee on Veteran's Affairs, United States Senate. Washington : U. S. Govt. Print. Off., 1980. xviii, 403 p. ; 24 cm. At head of title: 96th Congress, 2d session. Senate committee print no. 27. "June 24, 1980."   LC Card 80-602866   DDC 355.1/151/0973 19
1. Pensions, Military - United States. I. United States. Congress. Senate. Committee on Veterans' Affairs. II. Title.
UB373 .U54 1980

Study of former prisoners of war : a study / prepared by the Veterans' Administration (pursuant to Section 305 of Public Law 95-479) ; submitted to the Committee on Veterans' Affairs, United States Senate. Washington : U. S. Govt. Print. Off., 1980. v, 181 p. ; 24 cm. At head of title: 96th Congress, 2d session. Senate Committee print, no. 25. "June 3, 1980." Bibliography: p. 173-181.   LC Card 80-602576   DDC 35.1/156/0973 19
1. Veterans, Disabled - Medical care - United States. 2. Pensions, Military - United States. 3. Prisoners of war - United States. I. United States. Senate. Committee on Veterans' Affairs. II. Title.
UB369 .U57 1980

Survey of factors relating to job satisfaction among VA nurses : (1960 and 1970). [Washington] : U. S. Gov. Printing Office, 1973. 20, [45] p. : graphs; 26 cm. Cover title. "June 1, 1973" "1B 11-40" Bibliography: p. [45].
1. Job satisfaction - United States - Statistics. 2. Nursing - United States - Statistics. I. Title.
                    NYPL [JLF 80-1691]

UNITED STATES. VETERANS ADMINISTRATION.
United States. Congress. House. Committee on Veterans' Affairs. Subcommittee on Education, Training, and Employment. Hearing on the rehabilitation, education, and training programs administered by the Veterans' Administration--Nashville, Tenn. . Washington , 1981. iii, 181 p. ;   LC Card 81-601153   DDC 355.1/15/09768 19
KF27 .V436 1980a

United States. Congress. House. Committee on Veterans' Affairs. Subcommittee on Housing. Hearings regarding the VA home loan program . Washington , 1980. iii, 54 p. ;   LC Card 80-603111   DDC 353.0081/2 19
KF27 .V446 1980a

United States. Congress. House. Committee on Veterans' Affairs. Subcommittee on Medical Facilities and Benefits. Oversight of veterans' health care program in Florida . Washington , 1980. iii, 67 p. ;   LC Card 80-603075   DDC 355.1/156/09759 19
KF27 .V459 1979b

United States. Congress. House. Committee on Veterans' Affairs. Subcommittee on Medical Facilities and Benefits. Veterans' Administration 5-year medical construction plan for fiscal years 1981-85 . Washington , 1981. iii, 29 p. ;   LC Card 81-601369   DDC 353.0086/2 19
KF27 .V459 1980d

United States. Congress. House. Committee on Veterans' Affairs. Subcommittee on Special Investigations. Hearing on the collection of debts owed the Veterans' Administration . Washington , 1980. iii, 180 p. ;   LC Card 80-602904   DDC 353.0081/2 19
KF27 .V458 1980a

United States. Congress. Senate. Committee on Governmental Affairs. Federal Interagency Medical Resources Sharing and Coordination Act of 1980 . Washington , 1980. iv, 324 p. :   LC Card 80-604081   DDC 343.73/0115 347.303115 19
KF26 .G67 1980k

United States. Congress. Senate. Committee on Veterans' Affairs. Oversight of VA pacemaker policy . Washington , 1980. iii, 190 p. :   LC Card 80-604040   DDC 355.1/156/0973 19
KF26 .V4 1980b

United States. Congress. Senate. Committee on Veterans' Affairs. VA debt collection . Washington , 1979. iv, 252 p. :   LC Card 80-601119   DDC 346.73/077 19
KF26 .V4 1979i

United States. Congress. Senate. Committee on Veterans' Affairs. Veterans' Administration health-care programs . Washington , 1980. iii, 220 p. :   LC Card 80-602487   DDC 355.1/154/09759 19
KF26 .V4 1979m

United States. General Accounting Office. Ways of providing a fairer share of Federal housing support to rural areas . [Washington, D.C. , 1980] v, 86 p. :   LC Card 80-601694   DDC 363.5/8 19
HD7289.U6 U55 1980

UNITED STATES. VETERANS ADMINISTRATION - APPROPRIATIONS AND EXPENDITURES.
United States. Congress. House. Committee on Veterans' Affairs. Proposed Veterans' Administration budget for fiscal year 1982 . Washington , 1981. iii 87 p. :   LC Card 81-601758   DDC 353.0072/236812 19
KF27 .V4 1981a

United States. Veterans Administration. Biometrics Division. Gee, Susan. Psychiatric drug study /. Washington, D.C. , 1979- v. <1> :   LC Card 79-604263   DDC 616.89/18 19
RM315 .G43

United States. Veterans Administration. Controller, Office of the. see United States. Veterans Administration. Office of the Controller.

UNITED STATES. VETERANS ADMINISTRATION. DEPT. OF MEDICINE AND SURGERY - OFFICIALS AND EMPLOYEES.
United States. Congress. House. Committee on Veterans' Affairs. Subcommittee on Medical Facilities and Benefits. Oversight in the recruitment and retention of Veterans' Administration physicians and dentists, and H.R. 6153 . Washington , 1981. iv, 168 p. :   LC Card 81-601384   DDC 353.001/31 19
KF27 .V459 1980c

United States. Congress. Senate. Committee on Veterans' Affairs. VA Health-Care Personnel Act of 1980 . Washington , 1980. v, 895 p. :   LC Card 81-601756   DDC 343.73/0115/0262 347.3031150262 19
KF26 .V4 1980g

United States. Veterans Administration. Dept. of Veterans Benefits. see United States. Dept. of Veterans Benefits.

UNITED STATES. VETERANS ADMINISTRATION. INSPECTOR GENERAL.
United States. Congress. Senate. Committee on Veterans' Affairs. Oversight on activities of the VA's Inspector General . Washington , 1980. iii, 212 p. ;   LC Card 81-600655   DDC 353.0081/2 19
KF26 .V4 1980d

UNITED STATES. VETERANS ADMINISTRATION - MANAGEMENT - DATA PROCESSING.
United States. Congress. House. Committee on Government Operations. Subcommittee on Government Information and Individual Rights. Veterans Administration planning for medical automated data processing needs . Washington , 1980 [i.e. 1981] iv, 334 p. ;   LC Card 81-600933   DDC 353.0081/2 19
KF27 .G6628 1980c

United States. Congress. House. Committee on Veterans' Affairs. Subcommittee on Special Investigations. VA target system . Washington , 1980 [i.e. 1981] iii, 36 p. ;   LC Card 81-600822   DDC 362.1/1/0687 19
KF27 .V458 1980e

United States. Veterans Administration. Office of Construction. Heimbuch, Raymond J. Evaluation of alternative interment methods for national cemeteries. Washington, D.C. , 1980. 214 p. in various pagings :   LC Card 81-600537   DDC 353.0086 19
UB393 .H44

United States. Veterans Administration. Office of Planning and Program Evaluation. Study of former prisoners of war / Studies and Analysis Service, Office of Planning and Program Evaluation. Washington, D.C. : The Office : for sale by the Supt. of Docs., U. S. Govt. Print.

Off., 1980. iii, 181 p. ; 28 cm. Bibliography: p. 173-181. Cover title: POW.   LC Card 80-602667   DDC 355.1/15 19
1. Veterans, Disabled - Medical care - United States. 2. Pensions, Military - United States. 3. Prisoners of war - United States. I. Title. II. Title: POW.
UB369 .U57 1980a

United States. Veterans Administration. Office of the Controller.
Controller monograph .
   (no. 11) Seiling, Virginia. Health characteristics of veterans and nonveterans . Washington, D.C. [1980] v, 75 p. :   LC Card 80-602055   DDC 362.1/9 19
RA408.M4 S44

   (no. 4) United States. Veterans Administration. Office of the Controller. The most frequently occurring diagnoses in VA hospitals, 1971-1976 . Washington , 1977. viii, 75 p. :   LC Card 77-601849   DDC 362.1/0973 19
UB369 .U57 1977a

   (no. 9) Gee, Susan. Psychiatric drug study /. Washington, D.C. , 1979- v. <1> :   LC Card 79-604263   DDC 616.89/18 19
RM315 .G43

The most frequently occurring diagnoses in VA hospitals, 1971-1976 : a statistical review : data developed from VA patient treatment file / Louis Mesard, Virginia Seiling. Washington : Reports & Statistics Service, Office of Controller, Veterans Administration : for sale by the Supt. of Docs., U. S. Govt. Print. Off., 1977. viii, 75 p. : graphs ; 27 cm. (Controller monograph . no. 4) Includes bibliographical references.   LC Card 77-601849   DDC 362.1/0973 19
1. Veterans - Diseases - United States - Statistics. 2. Hospitals, Veterans - United States - Statistics. I. Mesard, Louis. II. Seiling, Virginia. III. Series: United States. Veterans Administration. Office of the Controller. Controller monograph , no. 4. IV. Title.
UB369 .U57 1977a

UNITED STATES. VETERANS ADMINISTRATION - PROCUREMENT.
United States. Congress. House. Committee on Veterans' Affairs. Subcommittee on Special Investigations. Computer systems for the Veterans' Administration and procurement practices . Washington , 1981. iv, 230 p. ;   LC Card 81-601147   DDC 362.1/1/0687 19
KF27 .V458 1980d

UNITED STATES. VETERANS ADMINISTRATION - RECORDS AND CORRESPONDENCE - DATA PROCESSING.
United States. Congress. House. Committee on Veterans' Affairs. Subcommittee on Special Investigations. VA target system . Washington , 1980 [i.e. 1981] iii, 36 p. ;   LC Card 81-600822   DDC 362.1/1/0687 19
KF27 .V458 1980e

United States. Veterans Administration. Reports and Statistics Service. Seiling, Virginia. Health characteristics of veterans and nonveterans . Washington, D.C. [1980] v, 75 p. :   LC Card 80-602055   DDC 362.1/9 19
RA408.M4 S44

United States. Veterans' Affairs, Committee on (House) see United States. Congress. House. Committee on Veterans' Affairs.

United States. Veterans Benefits, Dept. of. see United States. Dept. of Veterans Benefits.

United States - Vital statistics. see United States - Statistics, Vital.

United States. Wage and Hour and Public Contracts Division.
[Interpretative bulletin of the Fair labor standards act of 1938. Part 776. Subpart A. Coverage of wage-hour law]
Coverage of wage-hour law : text of official explanation on general coverage of the wage-hour law, together with BNA editorial analysis. Washington, D.C. : Bureau of National Affairs, 1950. x, 29 p. ; 23 cm. (BNA special report) Cover title.   LC Card 80-116713   DDC 344.73/0121 347.304121 19
1. Wages - Minimum wage - United States. 2. Overtime - United States. I. Bureau of National Affairs, Washington, D. C. II. United States. Laws, statutes, etc. Fair labor standards act of 1938. III. Title.
KF3489 .A36

United States. Wage and Hour and Public Contracts Divisions. (Old Catalog form: United States. Labor Dept. Wage and Hour Division)
Working children. Washington.
               NYPL [JLL 80-212]

United States. Wage and Price Stability, Council on. see United States. Council on Wage and Price Stability.

United States. War Dept. Adjutant-General's Office. see United States. Adjutant-General's Office.

United States. War Dept. Office of Indian Affairs. see United States. Bureau of Indian Affairs.

United States. War Food Administration. Federal Extension Service. see United States. Federal Extension Service.

United States. War Production Board. Labor Division. Committee on Fair Employment Practice. see United States. Committee on Fair Employment Practice (1941-1943)

UNITED STATES. WAR RELOCATION CENTER, MANZANAR, CALIF.
Camp and community . Fullerton , c1977. xvi, 233 p. :   ISBN 0-930046-00-5   LC Card 77-75817
D769.8.A6 C23
        NYPL [IXH (Manzanar) 80-2530]

United States. Water and Power Resources Service. Water and land resource accomplishments, Federal reclamation projects. 1978- [Washington] illus. 28 cm. Annual. For earlier years, see: United States. Bureau of Reclamation. Water and land resource accomplishments, Federal reclamation projects. Vols. for 1978- includes statistical appendix.
1. Field crops - United States - Statistics - Periodicals. 2. Irrigation farming - United States - Periodicals. I. Title.   *NYPL [JLM 80-707]*

United States. Water Conservation Task Force 6a. Water conservation Federal agency program changes : final summary report. [Washington] : Water Conservation Task Force 6a, 1979. 43 p. ; 28 cm. Cover title. "June 6, 1979."   LC Card 79-604000   DDC 333.91/16/0973 19
1. Water conservation - United States. I. Title.
TD223 .U547 1979

United States. Water Resources Council.
The Nation's water resources, 1975-2000. Kansas. State Water Resources Board. Compilation of socio-economic, land use, and water use information and projections for the 1975 national water assessment. [Topeka] , 1979. 54 p. :   LC Card 80-622138   DDC 333.91/13/09781 19
HD211.K2 K36 1979

Utah. Division of Water Resources. Specific problem analysis summary report . [Salt Lake City] , 1977. 87 p., [1] leaf of plates :   LC Card 80-620890   DDC 333.9/1/09792 19
TC423.6 .U82 1977

United States. Ways and Means, Committee on (House) see United States. Congress. House. Committee on Ways and Means.

United States-Western European relations in 1980 . United States. Congress. House. Committee on Foreign Affairs. Subcommittee on Europe and the Middle East. Washington , 1980. xi, 320 p. :   LC Card 80-603423   DDC 327.7304 19
KF27 .F64214 1980b

United States. Western Interstate Nuclear Board. see Western Interstate Nuclear Board.

United States. Woman in Industry Service. see United States. Women's Bureau.

United States. Women's Bureau.
The earnings gap between women and men / U. S. Department of Labor, Women's Bureau. [Washington, D.C.] : The Bureau : for sale by the Supt. of Docs., U. S. Govt. Print. Off., 1979. 22 p. ; 28 cm. Chiefly tables. Includes bibliographical references.   LC Card 80-602542   DDC 331.2/1 19
1. Equal pay for equal work - United States. 2. Women - Employment - United States. 3. Discrimination in employment - United States. 4. Sex discrimination against women - United States. I. Title.
HD6061.2.U6 U53 1979

Employment goals of the world : plan of
action : developments and issues in the United
States : report for the World Conference on the
United Nations Decade for Women, 1976-1985
/ U. S. Department of Labor, Women's Bureau.
Washington, D.C. : The Bureau : for sale by the
Supt. of Docs., U. S. Govt. Print. Off., [1980]
vi, 54, [22] p. : ill. ; 28 cm. "July 1980."
Bibliography: p. [19]-[22] (3d group)   LC Card
80-602858   DDC 331.4/133/0973 19
*1. Women - Employment - United States. 2. Sex
discrimination in employment - United States. I. World
Conference on the United Nations Decade for Women,
Copenhagen, 1980. II. Title.*
HD6095 .U54 1980

Native American women and equal
opportunity : how to get ahead in the Federal
Government / U. S. Department of Labor,
Women's Bureau. [Washington, D.C.] : The
Bureau : for sale by the Supt. of Docs., U. S.
Govt. Print. Off., 1979. vii, 81 p. : ill. ; 28 cm.
Includes bibliographical references.   LC Card
80-600536
*1. Indians of North America - Women. 2. Indians of
North America - Employment. 3. Women in the civil
service - United States. 4. Discrimination in
employment - United States. I. Title.*
E98.W8 U54 1979   *NYPL   [HBC 81-449]*

**United States. Work Projects Administration.
Federal Theatre Project. see Federal Theatre
Project.**

**United States. Work Projects Administration.
Federal Writers' Project. see Federal
Writers' Project.**

**United States. Workers' Compensation Task
Force, Interdepartmental. see United States.
Interdepartmental Workers' Compensation
Task Force.**

**United States. Workplace Safety and Health,
Interagency Task Force on. see United
States. Interagency Task Force on
Workplace Safety and Health.**

**UnitedStates. Congress. Senate. Special
Committee on Aging.** Energy and the aged :
a challenge to the quality of life in a time of
declining energy availability : hearing before the
Special Committee on Aging, United States
Senate, Ninety-sixth Congress, first session,
Washington, D.C., November 26, 1979.
Washington : U. S.Govt. Print. Off., 1980. iii,
40 p. : graphs ; 24 cm. Includes bibliographical
references.   LC Card 80-601941   DDC 363.6/2 19
*1. Power resources - United States. 2. Energy policy -
United States. 3. Aged - United States. I. Title.*
KF26.5 .A3 1979f

**UnitedStates. Health Resources Administration.
Bureau of Health Profession. Office of
Program Development. Planning, Evaluation,
and Legislation Branch.** Becker, Dorothy D.
Health professions legislation . [Hyattsville,
Md?] , 1980. 1 v. in various pagings ;   LC Card
81-601013   DDC 344.73/041 347.30441 19
KF2905 .A372

UNITEDSTATES - INDUSTRIES - MAPS.
Graphic summary of the 1977 economic
censuses. Washington, D.C. , 1981. 128 p. :
LC Card 81-1210   DDC 330.973/0926 19
HC106.7 .G7

**Universidad de San Marcos, Lima. see Lima.
Universidad de San Marcos.**

**Universidad Nacional Mayor de San Marcos,
Lima. see Lima. Universidad de San Marcos.**

Université du Québec à Montréal.
Rassemblement en études urbaines. Veltman,
Calvin J. The role of language characteristics in
the socioeconomic attainment process of
Hispanic origin men and women /.
[Washington, D.C.?] , 1980. iv, 103 p. ;   LC
Card 81-601023   DDC 305.8/68073 19
E184.S75 V44

**UNIVERSITIES AND COLLEGES -
ADMISSION - LAW AND
LEGISLATION - UNITED STATES.**
United States. Congress. House. Committee on
Education and Labor. Subcommittee on
Elementary, Secondary, and Vocational
Education. Truth in testing act of 1979, the
Educational testing act of 1979 . Washington ,
1980. viii, 1194 p. :   LC Card 80-601862   DDC
344.73/07 19
KF27 .E3364 1979r

**UNIVERSITIES AND COLLEGES - CHINA -
ENTRANCE EXAMINATIONS.**
The 1978 national college entrance examination
in the People's Republic of China /.
[Washington, D.C.] , 1979. vii, 110 p. :   LC
Card 80-601841   DDC 378/.1057/0951 19
LB2353.8.C6 N56

**UNIVERSITIES AND COLLEGES -
ENTRANCE EXAMINATIONS - LAW
AND LEGISLATION - UNITED STATES.**
United States. Congress. House. Committee on
Education and Labor. Subcommittee on
Elementary, Secondary, and Vocational
Education. The Educational testing act of
1979 . Washington , 1980. iv, 407 p. :   LC Card
80-603455   DDC 344.73/079 19
KF27 .E3364 1980d

**UNIVERSITIES AND COLLEGES - LAW
AND LEGISLATION - ALASKA.**
Alaska Commission on Postsecondary
Education. Bylaws and personnel regulations.
Juneau, Alaska [1979?] 6, 21 leaves ;   LC Card
80-620964   DDC 344.798/074 19
KFA1596 .A862

**UNIVERSITIES AND COLLEGES - LAW
AND LEGISLATION - UNITED STATES.**
United States. Congress. Senate. Committee on
Labor and Human Resources. Subcommittee on
Education, Arts, and Humanities. Higher
education amendments of 1979 . Washington ,
1980- v. ;   LC Card 80-602896   DDC 344.73/074
19
KF26 .L2735 1979d

United States. Congress. Senate. Committee on
the Judiciary. Subcommittee on Limitations on
Contracted and Delegated Authority. Title III
of the Higher education act of 1965 .
Washington , 1980. iv, 345 p. :   LC Card
80-602424   DDC 353.0085/1 19
KF26 .J857 1979

**UNIVERSITIES AND COLLEGES -
MARYLAND - DIRECTORIES.**
State directory of higher education institutions
and agencies in Maryland. Annapolis.   LC Card
75-643681   *NYPL   [JLL 80-277]*

**UNIVERSITIES AND COLLEGES - NEW
JERSEY - ADMISSION - STATISTICS.**
O'Connor, Linda. Applications/admissions
information, by sector for fall 1977, by
institution for fall 1978 . [Trenton]   [1979]   [42]
p. ;   LC Card 80-621681   DDC 378/.1056/09749 19
LB2351.3.N5 O26

**UNIVERSITIES AND COLLEGES - NEW
JERSEY - EXAMINATIONS -
STATISTICS.**
New Jersey Basic Skills Council. Report to the
Board of Higher Education on the results of the
New Jersey college basic skills placement
testing, May 1, 1978-September 28, 1978,
aggregated according to sending high schools /.
[Trenton? N.J.]   [1978]   [76] p. in various
pagings :   LC Card 80-622753   DDC 370/.9749 19
LC1035.7.N5 N48 1978

**UNIVERSITIES AND COLLEGES - NEW
MEXICO - ENTRANCE
EXAMINATIONS - STATISTICS.**
Nochumson, Bayla S. New Mexico ACT and
SAT results, 1978-79 /. Santa Fe, N.M.   [1980]
v, 35 p. :   LC Card 80-623171   DDC 378/.1664 19
LB2353.42 .N6

**UNIVERSITIES AND COLLEGES - NEW
YORK (STATE)**
New York (State). University. The master plan.
Albany [1961] 72 p.   *NYPL   [JFF 78-1282]*

**UNIVERSITIES AND COLLEGES -
PENNSYLVANIA - STATISTICS.**
Pennsylvania. Dept. of Education. Programs
approved for teacher education in Pennsylvania
colleges and universities. Harrisburg, PA , 1979.
ii, 102 leaves ;   LC Card 80-621835   DDC
370/.7/309748 19
LB2167.P4 P46 1979

**UNIVERSITIES AND COLLEGES - UNITED
STATES.**
Linking science and technology to public
policy . [Albany]   [1979]   viii, 156 p. (p.
155-156 blank) :   ISBN 0-915194-03-1   LC Card
78-22608   DDC 353.9/172 19
Q127.U6 L56

United States. Congress. House. Committee on
Science and Technology. Subcommittee on

Science, Research, and Technology. The
Government-university accountability
relationship in the field of scientific research .
Washington , 1980. iii, 251 p. ;   LC Card
80-602710   DDC 001.4/4 19
KF27 .S399 1980b

**UNIVERSITIES AND COLLEGES - UNITED
STATES - CURRICULA.**
National Institute on Alcohol Abuse and
Alcoholism. The whole college catalog about
drinking. Rockville, Md. , Washington [1976]
xii, 129 p. :   LC Card 76-603043   DDC
362.2/9286/088375 19
HV5292 .N33 1976

**UNIVERSITIES AND COLLEGES - UNITED
STATES - FINANCE.**
United States. Dept. of Health, Education, and
Welfare. A guide for colleges and universities .
Washington, D. C., 1974. 97 p. ;
NYPL   [JLF 80-937]

**UNIVERSITIES AND COLLEGES - UNITED
STATES - STATISTICS.**
Virginia. State Council of Higher Education.
Out-of-state institutions operating in Virginia,
1978-79. [Richmond]   [1979] 42 p. ;   LC Card
80-622044   DDC 378.73 19
LA227.3 .V57 1979

**UNIVERSITIES AND COLLEGES -
VIRGINIA - DIRECTORIES.**
Virginia. State Council of Higher Education.
Fact book . [Richmond, Va.]   [1980] 59 p. ;
LC Card 80-621790   DDC 378.755 19
L903.V8 V52 1980

**UNIVERSITIES AND COLLEGES -
VIRGINIA - STATISTICS.**
Virginia. State Council of Higher Education.
Out-of-state institutions operating in Virginia,
1978-79. [Richmond]   [1979] 42 p. ;   LC Card
80-622044   DDC 378.73 19
LA227.3 .V57 1979

**UNIVERSITIES AND COLLEGES -
WASHINGTON (STATE)**
Jons, Tom. The formula manual . [Olympia]
[1980] iii, 260 p. :   LC Card 80-623853   DDC
378.797 s 378.797 19
LC148 .W336a no. 81-1 LA382.5

**UNIVERSITIES AND COLLEGES -
WASHINGTON (STATE) - COSTS.**
Fischer, Norman M. 1976-77 unit expenditures
study /. [Olympia]   [1980] viii, 91 p. :   LC Card
80-621763   DDC 379.1/214/09797 19
LB2342 .F57

**UNIVERSITIES AND COLLEGES -
UNITED STATES - FACULTY.**
Nelson, Elizabeth Ness. Women's studies as a
catalyst for faculty development /. Washington,
D.C. , 1980. xii, 43 p. ;   LC Card 80-602285
DDC 378/.12/0973 19
LB2331.72 .N44

**University, Ala. Alabama Law Institute. see
Alabama. Law Institute.**

**UNIVERSITY EXTENSION - UNITED
STATES.**
Calvert, Robert, 1922- Free universities and
learning referral centers, 1978 /. [Washington]
[1979] vi, 36 p. ;   LC Card 79-602964   DDC
378/.1554/0973 19
LC6251 .C3

**UNIVERSITY EXTENSION - UNITED
STATES - CONGRESSES.**
Gross, Ronald. Future directions for open
learning . Washington, D.C. : [Lincoln, Neb.] :
x, 82 p. :   LC Card 80-601828   DDC
378/.1554/0973 19
LC6251 .G75

**UNIVERSITY EXTENSION - UNITED
STATES - DIRECTORIES.**
United States. Dept. of the Air Force.
Educational opportunities on Air Force bases /.
[Washington, D.C.]   [1980] ca. 150 p. in
various pagings :   LC Card 80-603210   DDC
378.73 19
U716 .A533 1980

University of Alabama. see Alabama. University.

University of Alaska, Anchorage. Library.
Rollins, Alden M., 1946- The Anchorage
documents file, 1970- /. Anchorage, Alaska ,
1978. 47, 1, 9 leaves ;   LC Card 80-622423   DDC
016.9798 19
Z1256.A52 R64 F914.A5

**University of Alaska, Fairbanks. Center for
Northern Educational Research.** New school
districts in rural Alaska : a report on the
REAAs after one year / Kathryn A. Hecht,
principal investigator, Ronald K. Inouye,
co-investigator. Fairbanks : Center for Northern
Educational Research, University of Alaska,
1978. v, 247 p., [1] fold. leaf of plates : ill. ; 28
cm. "March 1978." Includes bibliographical references.
LC Card 78-622541   DDC 370.19/346 19
*1. Education, Rural - Alaska. 2. School districts -
Alaska. I. Hecht, Kathryn A. II. Inouye, Ronald K. III.
Title.*
LC5147.A4 U54 1978

**University of Alaska, Fairbanks. Geophysical
Institute.**
Alaska's weather and climate : a collection of
articles written for the educated layman / by
staff members of the Geophysical Institute and
the National Weather Service in Alaska ; edited
by Gunter Weller. Fairbanks, Alaska : The
Institute, [1979] v, 153 leaves : ill. ; 28 cm.
"July 1979." Includes bibliographies.   LC Card
80-621244   DDC 551.69798 19
*1. Alaska - Climate - Addresses, essays, lectures. I.
Weller, Gunter. II. United States. National Weather
Service. III. Title.*
QC984.A4 U54 1979

Davis, T. Neil. Probability of earthquake
occurrence in the vicinity of the Chena Flood
Control Dam near Fairbanks, Alaska .
Fairbanks , 1978. i, 18 leaves, [10] leaves of
plates :   LC Card 79-622804   DDC 551.2/2/097986
19
QE535.2.U6 D38

**University of Alaska, Fairbanks. Institute of
Marine Science.**
Institute of Marine Science report .
(R78-1) Feder, Howard M. Survey of the
epifaunal invertebrates of Norton Sound,
southeastern Chukchi Sea, and Kotzebue
Sound /. Fairbanks , 1978. vii, 124 p. :   LC
Card 79-622468   DDC 551.46 s 592.09798 19
GC1.A497 R78-1 QL161

(R78-3) University of Alaska, Fairbanks.
Institute of Marine Science. Some aspects of
the carrying capacity of Prince William
Sound, Alaska, for hatchery released pink and
chum salmon fry /. Fairbanks , 1978. ix, 98
p. :   LC Card 78-624148   DDC 551.46 s
639.3/755 19
GC1 .A497 no. 78-3 SH167.S17

(R78-7) Feder, Howard M. A preliminary
survey of the benthos of Resurrection Bay
and Aialik Bay, Alaska /. Fairbanks, Alaska ,
1979. iii, 53 p. :   LC Card 80-623129   DDC
551.46 s 591.9798/3 19
GC1 .A497 R78-7 QL161

(79-2) Niebauer, H. J. Recent fluctuations in
meteorological and oceanographic parameters
in Alaska waters /. Fairbanks, Alaska [1980]
iv, 34 p. :   LC Card 80-623130   DDC 551.46
551.46/634 19
GC1 .A497 no. 79-2 QC994.6

Some aspects of the carrying capacity of Prince
William Sound, Alaska, for hatchery released
pink and chum salmon fry / R. Ted Cooney ...
[et al.]. Fairbanks : Institute of Marine Science,
University of Alaska, 1978. ix, 98 p. : ill. ; 28
cm. (Sea grant report ; 78-4) (IMS report ; R78-3
Includes bibliographies.   LC Card 78-624148   DDC
551.46 s 639.3/755 19
*1. Pink salmon. 2. Pacific salmon. 3. Fishes - Migration.
4. Fishes - Stocking. 5. Fish-culture - Alaska - Prince
William Sound. I. Cooney, R. Ted. II. Series: Alaska
sea grant report, 78-4. III. Title.*
GC1 .A497 no. 78-3 SH167.S17

**University of Alaska, Fairbanks. Institute of
Social and Economic Research.**
Goldsmith, Scott. Historic and projected oil and
gas consumption /. [Juneau?] , 1980. 55 leaves ;
LC Card 80-622464   DDC 338.2/728/09798 19
HD9567.A4 G63

Scott, Michael James, 1948- Standards for
determining child support obligations in Alaska
/. Anchorage [1978] 156 p. in various
pagings :   LC Card 79-622825   DDC 362.7/95 19
HV742.A4 S37

**University of Alaska, Fairbanks. School of
Agriculture and Land Resources
Management.**

**Special publication - School of Agriculture and
Land Resources Management, University
of Alaska, Fairbanks .**
(1) The Subsistence lifestyle in Alaska .
Fairbanks [1979] iii, 180 p. :   LC Card
79-623800   DDC 330.9798/05/08997 19
E78.A3 S9

The Subsistence lifestyle in Alaska . Fairbanks
[1979] iii, 180 p. :   LC Card 79-623800   DDC
330.9798/05/08997 19
E78.A3 S9

University of Alaska (System).
Biological papers of the University of Alaska .
(no. 19) Vladykov, Vadim Dmitrij, 1898- A
new nonparasitic species of the holarctic
lamprey genus Lethenteron Creaser and
Hubbs, 1922, (Petromyzonidae) from
northwestern North America, with notes on
other species of the same genus /.
[Fairbanks] 1978. 74 p. :   LC Card 78-622997
DDC 574 s 597/.2 19
QH1 .A258 no. 19 QL638.25.P48

**University of Alaska (System). Cooperative
Extension Service.**
Epps, Alan C. Landscape plant materials for
Alaska /. [Fairbanks] [Washington] , c1979. iii,
66 p. :   LC Card 80-623301   DDC 635.9/77/09798
19
SB435.52.A4 E66

What's a second class city? : An information
manual for operation of second class cities
under Alaska statutes title 29. Rev.
[Anchorage] : Cooperative Extension Service,
University of Alaska : Dept. of Community and
Regional Affairs, State of Alaska, 1980- 1 v. :
forms ; 28 cm. Loose-leaf for updating.   LC Card
80-622652   DDC 352/.00724/09798 19
*1. Municipal corporations - Alaska. 2. Municipal
corporations - Alaska - Forms. I. Alaska. Dept. of
Community and Regional Affairs. II. Title.*
KFA1631 .U54 1980

**University of Alaska (System). Office of the
President.** Alaska. Instructional Television. A
report on the feasibility of telecommunications
for instruction in the State of Alaska /.
[Juneau] [1980] 225 p. in various pagings ;
LC Card 80-622196   DDC 371.3/358/09798 19
LB1044.8 .A43 1980

University of Arizona. see Arizona. University.

**University of Arkansas. Agricultural Experiment
Station.** Soil survey of Logan County,
Arkansas. [Washington, D.C.?] , 1980. vii, 100
p., 42 folded p. of plates :   LC Card 81-600695
DDC 631.4/7/76737 19
S599.A75 S66

University of Arkansas anthropological papers .
(no. 1) Archaeological whale bone--a northern
resource . Fayetteville, ARK , 1979. xx, 558
p. :   LC Card 80-624409   DDC 971.9/5 19
E99.E7 A73

**University of Birmingham. Centre for Russian
and East European Studies.** Davis,
Christopher, 1948- Rising infant mortality in
the U. S.S.R. in the 1970's /. Washington,
D.C. , 1980. 33 p. ;   LC Card 81-600791   DDC
304.6 s 304.6/4 19
HC331 .U52 no. 74 HB1323.I4

**University of California. see California.
University.**

**University of California, Berkeley. Institute of
East Asian Studies.** Chŏn, Pong-dŏk, 1910-
Traditional Korean legal attitudes /. Berkeley,
Calif. , c1980. vii, 101 p. ;   ISBN 0-912966-30-0
(pbk.) :   LC Card 80-620036   DDC 349.519/09
345.1909 19
LAW

**University of California, Davis. University
Extension.** Managing revenue reductions .
Davis, Calif. , 1981. 94 leaves ;   LC Card
81-156255   DDC 350.72/6/0973 19
HJ2051 .M36

**University of California, Los Angeles. Chicano
Studies Research Center.**
Quien sabe? : a preliminary list of Chicano
reference materials / compiled and edited by
Francisco García-Ayvens, Darien Fisher, Hilda
Villarreal ; with a foreword by Roberto G.
Trujillo. Los Angeles, Calif. : Bibliographic
Research & Collection Development Unit,
Chicano Studies Research Center, UCLA, 1981.

p. cm. (Bibliographic and reference series. no. 11)
Annotated list of materials in the reference collection of
the Chicano Studies Research Library, UCLA. Includes
indexes. ISBN 0-89551-000-6   LC Card 81-10156
DDC 016.973/046872 19
*1. Reference books - Mexican Americans - Catalogs. 2.
Mexican Americans - Bibliography - Catalogs. 3.
University of California, Los Angeles. Chicano Studies
Research Center - Catalogs. I. García-Ayvens,
Francisco, 1948-. II. Fisher, Darien, 1955-. III.
Villarreal, Hilda, 1951-. IV. Title.*
Z1361.M4 U55 1981 E184.M5

**UNIVERSITY OF CALIFORNIA, LOS
ANGELES. CHICANO STUDIES
RESEARCH CENTER - CATALOGS.**
University of California, Los Angeles. Chicano
Studies Research Center. Quien sabe? . Los
Angeles, Calif. , 1981. p. cm.   ISBN
0-89551-000-6   LC Card 81-10156   DDC
016.973/046872 19
Z1361.M4 U55 1981 E184.M5

**University of California, Los Angeles. Museum of
Cultural History.** The people and art of the
Philippines / Gabriel Casal ... [et al.]. Los
Angeles : Museum of Cultural History,
University of California, Los Angeles, c1981. p.
cm. Catalogue of an exhibition presented at Honolulu
Academy of Arts, Spring/Summer 1981, and other
museums. Bibliography: p.   LC Card 81-2328   DDC
709/.599/074013 19
*1. Art, Philippine - Exhibitions. 2. Ethnic art -
Philippines - Exhibitions. 3. Philippines - Antiquities -
Exhibitions. 4. Philippines - Civilization - Exhibitions. I.
Casal, Gabriel, 1938-. II. Honolulu Academy of Arts.
III. Title.*
N7327 .U54 1981

**University of California, Los Angeles. School of
Law.** Estate planning, 1980. Los Angeles
[S.l.] , c1980. xii, 249 p. ;   LC Card 80-69720
DDC 343.7305/3 347.30353 19
KF750.A2 E83

**University of California publications: Folklore
and mythology studies.** Folklore and mythology
studies. Berkeley.   *NYPL   [JFM 81-58]*

**University of California publications in
entomology .**
(v. 93) Gordh, Gordon. Taxonomic studies of
the Encyrtidae with the descriptions of new
species and a new genus (Hymenoptera,
Chalcicoidea) /. Berkeley , 1981. p. cm.   ISBN
0-520-09629-0   LC Card 81-1327   DDC 595.79
19
QL568.E6 G67

(v. 95) Kimsey, Lynn Siri. Systematics of bees
of the genus Eufriesia (Hymenoptera, Apidae)
/. Berkeley, CA , 1981. p. cm.   ISBN
0-520-09643-6   LC Card 81-7400   DDC
595.79/9 19
QL568.A6 K465

**University of California publications. Near
Eastern studies .**
(v. 22) The Creation of sacred literature .
Berkeley, CA [1981] p. cm.   ISBN
0-520-09637-1   LC Card 81-2547   DDC 221.6
19
BS1192 .C73

University of California San Francisco.
Innovative developments in aging : area
agencies on aging : a directory / compiled by
the University of California for the use of the
Select Committee on Aging, U. S. House of
Representatives, Ninety-sixth Congress, first
session, December, 1979. Washington : U. S.
Govt. Print. Off. : for sale by the Supt. of
Docs., U. S. Govt. Print. Off., 1979. xi, 571 p. ;
24 cm. "Comm. pub. no. 96-197." Includes index.   LC
Card 80-601011
*1. Aged, Services for - United States - Directories. I.
United States. Congress. House. Select Committee on
Aging. II. Title.*
HV1450 .U54 1979

*NYPL   [*R-Econ. 80-4848]*

Innovative developments in aging .
Washington , 1980. xi, 372 p. ;   LC Card
80-603859   DDC 362.6/0973 19
HV1450 .I55

**University of Cincinnati. see Cincinnati.
University.**

**University of Colorado, Boulder. see Colorado.
University.**

BIBLIOGRAPHIC GUIDE

University of Colorado. Cooperative Institute for Research in

616

University of Colorado. Cooperative Institute for Research in Environmental Sciences. Berry, George W. Thermal springs list for the United States /. Boulder, Colo. , Boulder, Colo. (Code D64, 325 Broadway, Boulder, Colo. 80303) , 1980. 59 p. ; LC Card 81-600521 DDC 553.7 19
GB1198.2 .B47

University of Colorado Health Sciences Center. Center for Health Services Research. An Evaluation of swing bed experiments to provide long-term care in rural hospitals. Denver, Colo. (4200 East Ninth Ave., Denver 80262) [1980] 2 v. ; LC Card 80-65248 DDC 362.1/1/091734 19
RA975.R87 E9

University of Florida. Center for Gerontological Studies and Programs. Programs for older Americans . Gainesville , 1981. p. cm. ISBN 0-8130-0705-4 LC Card 81-11645 DDC 305.2/6/0973 19
HQ1064.U5 P73

University of Georgia. Institute of Government. Jackson, Edwin L. Handbook for Georgia legislators /. Athens , c1980. xii, 214 p., [1] leaf of plates : LC Card 81-154019 DDC 328.758/00202 19
JK4331 1980 .J32

University of Georgia. International Trade and Development Center. A small business export development program / developed by the International Trade and Development Center, Small Business Development Center, College of Business Administration, University of Georgia ; A.G. Stell Kefalas, director ; and Karen P. Palmour, coordinator. Athens, Ga. : ITDC, c1980. 24 p. : ill. ; 22 cm. LC Card 80-624106 DDC 658.8/48 19
1. Export marketing. 2. Foreign trade promotion. 3. Small business. I. Palmour, Karen P. II. Title.
HF1009.5 .U55 1980

University of Hawaii at Manoa. Center for Governmental Development. An Analytical study of alternative gasoline rationing plans for Hawaii /. Honolulu , 1975. 32 p. ; LC Card 76-622980 DDC 333.8/232 19
HD9579.G45 H32

University of Hawaii at Manoa. Dept. of Electrical Engineering. Pacific Telecommunications Conference, Honolulu, 1979. Pacific Telecommunications Conference . Honolulu , 1979. ca. 500 p. in various pagings : LC Card 79-110059
TK5102.3.P32 P32 1979

NYPL [JLF 80-1628]

University of Hawaii at Manoa. Plant Science Instructional Arboretum.
A catalog of plants in the Plant Science Instructional Arboretum, College of Tropical Agriculture and Human Resources, University of Hawaii / Robert M. Warner. [3rd ed.] [Honolulu] : Hawaii Institute of Tropical Agriculture and Human Resources, University of Hawaii, 1981. p. cm. (Miscellaneous publication . 98) LC Card 81-2897 DDC 582.16/061/074099691 19
1. University of Hawaii at Manoa. Plant Science Instructional Arboretum - Catalogs. 2. Tree crops - Hawaii - Waimanalo region - Catalogs and collections. 3. Woody plants - Hawaii - Waimanalo region - Catalogs and collections. I. Warner, Robert Malcolm, 1908-. II. Series: Miscellaneous publication (Hawaii Institute of Tropical Agriculture and Human Resources) , 98. III. Title.
SB171.U6 U54 1981

UNIVERSITY OF HAWAII AT MANOA. PLANT SCIENCE INSTRUCTIONAL ARBORETUM - CATALOGS.
University of Hawaii at Manoa. Plant Science Instructional Arboretum. A catalog of plants in the Plant Science Instructional Arboretum, College of Tropical Agriculture and Human Resources, University of Hawaii /. [Honolulu] , 1981. p. cm. LC Card 81-2897 DDC 582.16/061/074099691 19
SB171.U6 U54 1981

University of Hawaii at Manoa. Sea Grant College Program. Environmental survey techniques for coastal water assessment . [Honolulu, Hawaii] [1980] iv, 229 p. : LC Card 80-621111 DDC 628.1/686162/0287 19
TD763 .E58

University of Hawaii at Manoa. Social Development & Research Center.

Report - Social Development & Research Center, University of Hawaii .
(no. 121) University of Hawaii at Manoa. Social Welfare Development & Research Center. Evaluation & report of progress, 1972-73. [Manoa] [1973] viii, 78, [33] leaves ; LC Card 80-494222 DDC 365/.42/099693 19
HV9106.K182 H348 1973

university of Hawaii at Manoa. Social Science Research Institute. Pacific Telecommunications Conference, Honolulu, 1979. Pacific Telecommunications Conference . Honolulu , 1979. ca. 500 p. in various pagings : LC Card 79-110059
TK5102.3.P32 P32 1979

NYPL [JLF 80-1628]

University of Hawaii at Manoa. Social Welfare Development & Research Center.
Evaluation & report of progress, 1972-73. [Manoa] : Social Welfare Development & Research Center, School of Social Work, College of Health Sciences & Social Welfare, University of Hawaii, [1973] viii, 78, [33] leaves ; 29 cm. (Report - Social Welfare Development & Research Center, University of Hawaii ; no. 121) "Hawaii Youth Correctional Facility, Division of Corrections, Department of Social Services & Housing [and] Olomana School (fourth annual report) Windward Oahu District, Department of Education." "September 1973." LC Card 80-494222 DDC 365/.42/099693 19
1. Hawaii Youth Correctional Facility - Evaluation. 2. Olomana School - Evaluation. I. Series: University of Hawaii at Manoa. Social Development & Research Center. Report - Social Development & Research Center, University of Hawaii , no. 121.
HV9106.K182 H348 1973

University of Hawaii at Manoa. Water Resources Research Center.
Environmental survey techniques for coastal water assessment . [Honolulu, Hawaii] [1980] iv, 229 p. : LC Card 80-621111 DDC 628.1/686162/0287 19
TD763 .E58

Lau, Leung-Ku Stephen. Recycling of sewage effluent by sugarcane irrigation . Honolulu, Hawaii [1978?] x, 59 p. : LC Card 79-625336 DDC 628.3/62 19
TC1 .H36 no. 121 TD760

Technical report - Water Resources Research Center, University of Hawaii .
(no. 121) Lau, Leung-Ku Stephen. Recycling of sewage effluent by sugarcane irrigation . Honolulu, Hawaii [1978?] x, 59 p. : LC Card 79-625336 DDC 628.3/62 19
TC1 .H36 no. 121 TD760

University of Hawaii. College of Tropical Agriculture. Crop improvement in Hawaii--past, present, future . [Honolulu] [1981] p. cm. LC Card 81-4885 DDC 631.5/3/09969 19
SB123 .C82

University of Idaho newspaper holdings as of December 31, 1979 /. Idaho. University. Library. [Moscow, Idaho] , 1979. 28 p. ; LC Card 80-622444 DDC 016.07 19
Z6952.I2 I2 1979 PN4897.I23

University of Illinois at Urbana-Champaign. Spencer, L. V. (Lewis Van Clief), 1922- Structure shielding against fallout gamma rays from nuclear detonations /. [Washington, D.C.?] , 1980. xvi, 967 p. : LC Card 80-600120 DDC 602/.18 s 363.1/89 19
QC100 .U57 no. 570 UF787

University of Illinois at Urbana-Champaign. Community Research Forum. King, Jane L. A comparative analysis of juvenile codes /. Washington, D.C. , 1980. 90 p. ; LC Card 81-601206 DDC 345.73/08 347.3058 19
KF9795.Z95 K56

University of Illinois at Urbana-Champaign. Dept. of Agriculture Economics. London, Alan C. Coarse grain consumption and import relationships in the European Community /. [Urbana, Ill.] [1979] 36 p. : LC Card 80-623669 DDC 338.1 s 382/.4131/094 19
HD1401 .I42 no. 177 HD9045.E82

University of Indiana. see Indiana. University.

University of Iowa. Institute of Public Affairs.
1980 Iowa constitutional issues. Iowa City

[1980] 23 p. ; LC Card 80-624270 DDC 342.777/087 347.770287 19
KFI4611.7.Z9 A15

University of Iowa. Museum of Art. Centering on contemporary clay . Iowa City, Iowa , c1981. 68 p. : LC Card 81-50916 DDC 730/.0973/0740177655 19
NK4008 .C46

University of Lagos. (Old Catalog form: Lagos. Univversity)
New York University. School of Commerce, Accounts and Finance. Final report, New York University-University of Lagos Project. [New York , 1970] 45 leaves ; LC Card 80-503704 DDC 650/.07/106691 19
HF1176.N62 L334 1970

UNIVERSITY OF LAGOS.
New York University. School of Commerce, Accounts and Finance. Final report, New York University-University of Lagos Project. [New York , 1970] 45 leaves ; LC Card 80-503704 DDC 650/.07/106691 19
HF1176.N62 L334 1970

University of Louisville. see Louisville, Ky. University.

University of Louisville studies in paleontology and stratigraphy .
(no. 12) Conkin, James Elvin. Devonian black shale in the Eastern United States /. Louisville, Ky. , c1980- v. <1 > : LC Card 80-54589 DDC 552/.5 19
QE471.15.S5 C66

University of Maine at Orono. Bureau of Public Administration. Division of Research and Public Services. Maine municipal series. Orono, Me. *NYPL [JLM 80-769]*

University of Maine at Orono. Bureau of Public Administration. Research and Public Services, Division of. see University of Maine at Orono. Bureau of Public Administration. Division of Research and Public Services.

University of Maine at Orono. Division of Research and Public Services. see University of Maine at Orono. Bureau of Public Administration. Division of Research and Public Services.

University of Maine at Orono. Social Science and Research Institute. Maine. State Science, Engineering, and Technology Study Group. Science in the Statehouse . Orono , 1979. iii leaves, 57, cxxvi p. ; LC Card 79-624434 DDC 353.97410085/5 19
Q127.U6 M27 1979

UNIVERSITY OF MALAWI - CATALOGS.
Aradoum, Fassil. University of Malawi publications . Washington , 1979. viii, 41 p. ; ISBN 0-8444-0324-5 LC Card 79-607918
Z3577 .A72 DT858

NYPL [Sc Micro F-9346]

University of Malawi publications . Aradoum, Fassil. Washington , 1979. viii, 41 p. ; ISBN 0-8444-0324-5 LC Card 79-607918
Z3577 .A72 DT858

NYPL [Sc Micro F-9346]

University of Maryland, Baltimore County. Library Gallery. Lapinski, Tadeusz, 1928- Color lithography . Catonsville, Md. , c1980. [20] p. : LC Card 80-51345 DDC 769.92/4 19
NE2371.P6 L36

University of Maryland. Fire & Rescue Institute. Fire investigation handbook /. [Washington, D.C.?] , 1980. ix, 187 p. : LC Card 80-600095 DDC 363.3/765 19
TH9180 .F48

University of Massachusetts at Amherst. Citizen Involvement Training Project.
Dale, Duane, 1946- How to make citizen involvement work . Amherst , c1978. iii, 92 p. : LC Card 79-624734
JK1764 .D34 *NYPL [JLF 80-1677]*

Dale, Duane, 1946- Planning, for a change . Amherst , c1978. 88 p. : LC Card 79-624733
JK1764 .D35 *NYPL [JLF 81-311]*

Gordon, Robbie. We interrupt this program . Amherst , 1980, c1978. 117 p. : LC Card 79-624735
HM263 .G63 *NYPL [JLF 81-53]*

University of Massachusetts at Amherst.
Cooperative Extension Service. Tree
Wardens, Arborists, and Utilities Conference,
Chicopee, Mass., 1979. Proceedings of the Tree
Wardens, Arborists, and Utilities Conference,
March 13-15, 1979 /. [Amherst, Mass.] [1979]
94 p. : LC Card 80-622844 DDC 635.9/77 19
SB436 .T756 1979

University of Massachusetts at Amherst. Dept. of
Anthropology.
Research reports - Department of
Anthropology, University of Massachusetts,
Amherst .
(no. 18) Ecological anthropology of the
Middle Connecticut River Valley /.
Amherst , 1979. iv, 161 p. : LC Card
80-621530 DDC 974 19
F12.C7 E26

(no. 19) Conference on Northeastern
Archaeology, University of Massachusetts,
1979. Proceedings of the Conference on
Northeastern Archaeology /. Amherst , 1980.
vi, 219 p. : LC Card 80-623704 DDC 974 19
F106 .C75 1979

University of Massachusetts at Amherst.
Technical Guidance Center for
Environmental Quality. Energy, environment,
and economics in Massachusetts : a register of
scientists, engineers, and centers for community
use. [Amherst] : Technical Guidance Center for
Environmental Quality, Division of Continuing
Education, University of Massachusetts at
Amherst, 1978. v, 68 p. ; 28 cm. LC Card
79-621744 DDC 304.2/025/744 19
1. Environmental protection - Massachusetts -
Directories. 2. Energy development - Massachusetts -
Directories. 3. Economics - Information services -
Massachusetts - Directories. I. Title.
TD169.6 .U52 1978

University of Massachusetts at Amherst.
University Gallery. Davies, Hugh Marlais.
1948- Al Souza /. [Amherst] , c1979. [24] p. :
LC Card 79-4894
TR647 .S69 1979
NYPL [MFX (Souza) 80-2495]

University of Massachusetts at Amherst. Water
Resources Research Center.
Completion report - Water Resources Research
Center, University of Massachusetts at
Amherst.
(FY-76-8) Kaul, Jawahar Lal. A floodplain
management framework with structural and
nonstructural measures /. [Amherst] , 1975.
vi, 114 p. : LC Card 78-622289 DDC
333.91/009744 s 363.3/49356 19
TD224.M4 M37 no. 61 TC424.C8

(72-4) Robinton, Elizabeth Dorothy. The Mill
River and its floodplain in Northampton and
Williamsburg, Massachusetts . Amherst
[1972?] vii leaves, 72 p. : LC Card 80-497906
DDC 581.5/26323 19
QK166 .R67

Rich, Peter, 1955- Measuring certain
intangible benefits of water pollution
abatement by use of changes of impacted real
estate values /. Amherst, Mass. [1979] 52
leaves : LC Card 80-621812 DDC 333.33/22 19
HD268.L44 R5

Lake-shoreland management programs .
Amherst , 1976. 224 p. ; LC Card 78-622978
DDC 333.91/009744 s 333.91/7 19
TD224.M4 M37 no. 69 HT391

Publication - Water Resources Research
Center, University of Massachusetts at
Amherst .
(no. 104) University of Massachusetts at
Amherst. Water Resources Research Center.
Urbanization and water quality planning .
Amherst, Mass. [1979] viii, 121 [14] p. ;
LC Card 80-623703 DDC 333.91/009744 s
363.7/39456/068 19
TD224.M4 M37 no. 104

(no. 69) Lake-shoreland management
programs . Amherst , 1976. 224 p. ; LC Card
78-622978 DDC 333.91/009744 s 333.91/7 19
TD224.M4 M37 no. 69 HT391

(no. 73) Kreplick, Ruth. Effectiveness of
information transfer through water resources
researcher/user group interaction /.
Amherst , 1976. xvii, 144 p. ; LC Card
78-622292 DDC 333.91/009744 s 333.91/0072

19
TD224.M4 M37 no. 73

(no. 90) Ludlam, Stuart D. The recent history
of productivity in selected Berkshire lakes /.
Amherst , 1977. ii, 66 p. : LC Card 79-624503
DDC 333.91/009744 s 581.5/26322/097441 19
TD224.M4 M37 no. 90 QH105.M4

Urbanization and water quality planning : the
208 experience in Massachusetts / by Harry E.
Schwarz, principal investigator ; Branden B.
Johnson, Robert J. Caiazzo, Debra E. Pincus,
graduate research assistants ; Environmental
Affairs Program, Clark University. Amherst,
Mass. : Water Resources Research Center,
University of Massachusetts at Amherst, [1979]
viii, 121 [14] p. ; 28 cm. (Publication - Water
Resources Research Center, University of Massachusetts
at Amherst . no. 104) Completion report - Water
Resources Research Center, University of Massachusetts
at Amherst "January 1979." "Project no. A-104-MASS."
Bibliography: p. [14] (3d group) LC Card 80-623703
DDC 333.91/009744 s 363.7/39456/068 19
1. Water quality management - Massachusetts -
Planning. 2. Land use - Massachusetts - Planning. 3.
Urbanization - Massachusetts. I. Schwarz, Harry E. II.
Clark University, Worcester, Mass. Environmental
Affairs Program. III. Series: University of Massachusetts
at Amherst. Water Resources Research Center.
Publication - Water Resources Research Center,
University of Massachusetts at Amherst , no. 104. IV.
Title.
TD224.M4 M37 no. 104

University of Massachusetts (System). Institute
for Governmental Services.
Motor vehicle excise tax program. [Boston] :
Committee on Post Audit and Oversight, Post
Audit and Oversight Bureau, [1980] xvi, 25, 6
leaves ; 29 cm. "PAB-1-1-80." "A report to the Joint
Legislative Committee on Post Audit and Oversight."
LC Card 80-622436 DDC 353.97440072/471 19
1. Motor vehicles - Taxation - Massachusetts. I.
Massachusetts. General Court. Joint Committee on Post
Audit and Oversight. II. Massachusetts. Post Audit and
Oversight Bureau. III. Title.
HJ5780.V4 U54 1980

Sheehan, David M. The children's puzzle .
Boston , 1977. 41, [18] leaves ; LC Card
79-621668 DDC 362.7/95/09744 19
HV742.M4 S53

University of Michigan. Center for Continuing
Education of Women. Women's lives . [Ann
Arbor, Mich.] , 1980. xiv, 451 p. : LC Card
81-134376 DDC 305.4/2/0973 19
HQ1420 .W65

University of Michigan. Graduate School of
Business Administration. Division of
Research. Applications of economic principles
in public utility industries /. [Ann Arbor] ,
c1981. ix, 155 p. ; ISBN 0-87712-211-3 LC Card
81-936 DDC 338.4/33636/0973 19
HD2763 .A66

University of Michigan. Medical School. Office
of Educational Resources and Research.
Audiovisual resources for diabetes education.
Ann Arbor, Mich. , c1980. vii, 344 p. ; LC
Card 81-621409 DDC 016.6164/62 19
RC660 .A9 1980

University of Michigan. Survey Research Center.
Conte, Michael. Employee ownership /. Ann
Arbor, Mich. , 1981. vi, 65 p. ; ISBN
0-87944-255-7 (pbk.) LC Card 81-150054
DDC 331.2/164 19
HD5660.U5 C66

Marans, Robert W. Evaluating built
environments . [Ann Arbor] , 1981. p. cm.
ISBN 0-87944-272-7 : LC Card 81-6709 DDC
725/.1 19
TH6025 .M37

University of Mid-America. Gross, Ronald.
Future directions for open learning .
Washington, D.C. : [Lincoln, Neb.] : x, 82 p. :
LC Card 80-601828 DDC 378/.1554/0973 19
LC6251 .G75

University of Minnesota. Division of Pediatric
Nephrology. Someone special . Minneapolis,
Minn. , 1981. p. cm. ISBN 0-940210-00-2 LC
Card 81-51347 DDC 618.92/61 19
RJ476.K5 S65

University of Minnesota (Minneapolis-St. Paul
campus). University Gallery. Minnesota
pottery, a potter's view . Minneapolis [1981]

32 p. : LC Card 81-50237 DDC
738/.09776/0740176579 19
NK4025.M6 M56

University of Missouri, Columbia. Public Affairs
Information Service. Enrollment projections
for elementary and secondary public schools in
Missouri, 1979-1984 /. [Jefferson City] [1979]
5, 1, 10 p. : LC Card 80-623486 DDC
371.2/19/778 19
LC144.M8 E57

University of Missouri--Columbia. Dept. of
Economics. Evaluations of the fee structures
of the Missouri Department of Mental Health /
provided by Department of Economics, College
of Arts and Sciences, University of
Missouri--Columbia, for the Division of Budget
and Planning, Office of Administration, State of
Missouri. [Jefferson City, Mo.] : The Division,
[1979] vi, 68 p. ; 28 cm. Cover title. "September,
1979." Bibliography: p. 68. LC Card 79-625947
DDC 338.4/33622/09778 19
1. Mental health services - Missouri - Fees. 2. Mentally
ill - Missouri - Socio-economic status. 3. Missouri.
Dept. of Mental Health. I. Missouri. Division of Budget
and Planning. II. Title.
RA790.65.M8 U54 1979

University of Missouri--Columbia. Dept. of
Geology. Davis, Peter N. Missouri instream
flow requirements . Jefferson City, Mo. [1980]
xviii, 415 p., [1] fold. leaf of plates : LC Card
80-623733 DDC 346.77804/691 347.78064691
19
KFM8246 .D36

University of Missouri--Columbia. Dept. of
Mechanical and Aerospace Engineering.
Product and professional liability. [Columbia,
1967?] 138 l. LC Card 74-632752 DDC 620 s
346.7303/82 19
TA7 .M538 no. 10 KF1296

University of Missouri--Columbia. School of Law.
Davis, Peter N. Missouri instream flow
requirements . Jefferson City, Mo. [1980] xviii,
415 p., [1] fold. leaf of plates : LC Card
80-623733 DDC 346.77804/691 347.78064691
19
KFM8246 .D36

University of Nebraska at Omaha. Center for
Applied Urban Research. Frost, Murray.
Survey of Nebraska women's employment
participation, attitudes, and needs /. Omaha,
Neb. , 1979. vi, 97 p. ; LC Card 80-621228
DDC 331.4/09782 19
HD6096.N3 F76

University of Nebraska (Central Administration).
Medical Center. Library.
KWOC index to the serials holdings list /
editors, Georgene E. Fawcett, Deborah L.
McMaster. Omaha : University of Nebraska
Medical Center, 1978. 67 p. ; 28 cm. (Library of
Medicine publication series ; no. 5) LC Card
79-625355 DDC 016.61/05 19
1. University of Nebraska (Central administration).
Medical Center. Library. Serials holdings list - Indexes.
2. Medicine - Periodicals - Indexes. I. Fawcett,
Georgene E. II. McMaster, Deborah L. III. Series:
University of Nebraska (Central Administration).
Medical Center. Library. Library of Medicine
publication , no. 5. IV. Title.
Z6660 .U692 1978 R129

Library of Medicine publication .
(no. 5) University of Nebraska (Central
Administration). Medical Center. Library.
KWOC index to the serials holdings list /.
Omaha , 1978. 67 p. : LC Card 79-625355
DDC 016.61/05 19
Z6660 .U692 1978 R129

SERIALS HOLDINGS LIST - INDEXES.
University of Nebraska (Central
Administration). Medical Center. Library.
KWOC index to the serials holdings list /.
Omaha , 1978. 67 p. ; LC Card 79-625355
DDC 016.61/05 19
Z6660 .U692 1978 R129

University of Nebraska-Lincoln. Remote Sensing
Center. General land use in
Nebraska--summer 1973. This map was
prepared in cooperation with the State Office of
Planning and Programming and the Nebraska
Natural Resources Commission. Cartography by
Carmen Eucker, Arleen Faulkner, and John
Roy. [Lincoln] 1974. col. map 43 x 76 cm. Scale
ca. 1:1,000,000. Relief shown by spot heights. Includes

text. LC Card 78-691032
1. Land use - Nebraska - Maps. I. Eucker, Carmen C.
II. Faulkner, Arleen. III. Roy, John. IV. Nebraska. State
Office of Planning and Programming. V. Nebraska.
Natural Resources Commission. VI. Title.
G4191.G4 1973 .U5
                    NYPL [Map Div. 81-3033]

University of Nebraska studies.
(new series no. 59) Karch, Dieter. Neuberg am
Rhein . Lincoln, Neb. , c1978. x, 215 p. :
         NYPL [*EA N363 new series no. 59]

University of Nebraska--Lincoln. Area Studies
    Committee in Linguistics. Mid-America
Linguistics Conference, 14th, University of
Nebraska--Lincoln, 1979. Papers from the 1979
Mid-America Linguistics Conference, November
2-3, University of Nebraska--Lincoln /.
[Lincoln] , 1980. v leaves, 421 p. : LC Card
    80-52825 DDC 410 19
P21 .M5 1979

University of Nebraska--Lincoln. Civil
    Engineering Dept.
Research report - Civil Engineering
    Department, University of Nebraska--
    Lincoln .
    (TRP-04-001-78) McCoy, Patrick T. Legal
    obstacles to car/vanpooling in Nebraska /.
    Lincoln, Neb. [1978] 14, 16 p. : LC Card
        80-623554 DDC 343.782/0982 347.8203982 19
KFN298 .M32

University of Nebraska--Lincoln. Conservation
    and Survey Division.
Da Moude, Dean W. Soil survey Burt County,
Nebraska. [Washington, D.C.?] , 1980. vii, 165
p., 44 folded p. of plates : LC Card 81-601021
    DDC 631.4/7/782243 19
S599.N2 D34

Soil survey of Keya Paha County, Nebraska.
[Washington, D.C.?] , 1980. ix, 224 p., 62
folded p. of plates : LC Card 81-600561 DDC
    631.4/7/782725 19
S599.N2 S63

Souders, Vernon L. Geology and groundwater
supplies of Box Butte County, Nebraska /.
[Lincoln] [1980] vii, 205 p. : LC Card
    80-623050 DDC 553/.7/09782 s
    551.7/9/0978294 19
GB1025.N2 N42 no. 47 QE136.B67

University of Nebraska--Lincoln. Dept. of
    Agricultural Economics.
Report - Department of Agricultural
    Economics .
    (no. 100) Johnson, Bruce B. Agricultural crop
    pesticide usage in Nebraska, 1978 /.
    [Lincoln] [1979] iv, 30, [11] p. : LC Card
        80-621253 DDC 632/.95/09782 19
SB950.2.N4 J63

University of Nebraska--Lincoln. Water
    Resources Research Institute.
A cost-benefit presentation of several artificial
recharge schemes in the Upper Big Blue River
Basin : final report : in fulfillment of a contract
with the State Office of Planning and
Programming / submitted by Nebraska Water
Resources Research Institute, University of
Nebraska-Lincoln ; prepared by Deane M.
Manbeck ... [et al.]. Lincoln, Neb. : NWRRI,
[1975] 40 leaves : ill. ; 28 cm. "September 1975."
    LC Card 79-623375 DDC 333.91/04153/097822
    19
1. Water, Underground - Big Blue River watershed,
Kan. & Neb. - Artificial recharge - Cost effectiveness. I.
Manbeck, Deane M. II. Nebraska. State Office of
Planning and Programming. III. Title.
TD404 .U54 1975

Water resources publications related to the
    State of Nebraska. Nebraska Water
Resources Center. Water resources
publications related to the State of Nebraska.
4th ed. [Lincoln] [1979] 129 p. : LC Card
    80-621398 DDC 016.33391/009782 19
Z7935 .N4 1979 TC424.N2

University of Nevada, Las Vegas. Dept. of
    Anthropology. Lyneis, Margaret M. Impacts,
damage to cultural resources in the California
desert /. Riverside, Calif. , 1980. viii, 171 p. :
    LC Card 81-600782 DDC 979.4/9 19
F863 .L95

University of Nevada, Reno. Workshop on
Operational Applications of Satellite Snowcover
Observations, Sparks, Nev., 1979. Operational

applications of satellite snowcover observations .
Washington, D.C. , 1980. vi, 301 p. : LC Card
    80-602361 DDC 551.57/846 19
GB2601.72.A83 W67 1979

University of Nevada System. Water Resources
    Center. Mifflin, Martin D. Pluvial lakes and
estimated pluvial climates of Nevada /. Reno ,
1979. 57 p. : LC Card 80-621829 DDC
    551.48/2/09793 19
QC884 .M53

University of New Mexico. General Library.
A million stars . Albuquerque , 1981. p. cm.
    ISBN 0-913630-05-5 LC Card 81-7396 DDC
    025.2/187789/81 19
Z675.U5 M54

UNIVERSITY OF NEW MEXICO. GENERAL
LIBRARY - ADDRESSES, ESSAYS,
LECTURES.
A million stars . Albuquerque , 1981. p. cm.
    ISBN 0-913630-05-5 LC Card 81-7396 DDC
    025.2/187789/81 19
Z675.U5 M54

University of New Mexico. Medical Center
    Library. Hendryson, Elizabeth. Health and
safety aspects of mining . Albuquerque, N.M.
[1980] iv, 76 p. : LC Card 81-621701 DDC
    016.622/8 19
Z6664.L9 H46 RC965.M48

University of New Orleans. Division of Business
    and Economic Research.
Research study - Division of Business and
    Economic Research, University of New
    Orleans .
    (no. 30) Wildgen, John K. A political atlas of
    Louisiana gubernatorial elections /. [New
    Orleans] , 1979. 14 leaves : LC Card
    79-625553 DDC 330.9763 s 912/.13249763 19
HC107.L8 L58 no.30 G1361.F9

University of North Carolina at Chapel Hill.
    Bush Institute for Child and Family Policy.
    see Bush Institute for Child and Family
    Policy.

University of North Carolina at Chapel Hill.
    Center for Urban and Regional Studies.
Burby, Raymond J., 1942- Managing flood
hazard areas . Chapel Hill, N.C. [1980] viii,
212 p. ; LC Card 80-66830 DDC 363.3/493 19
HD1691 .B85

Environmental Design Conference on City
Centers in Transition, University of North
Carolina at Chapel Hill, 1976. City centers in
transition . Chapel Hill , 1976. xii, 90 leaves ;
    LC Card 76-29226   ***NYPL [JLF 80-1605]***

University of North Carolina at Chapel Hill.
    Dept. of Maternal and Child Health.
Tri-Regional Workshop for Social Workers in
Maternal and Child Health Services (1980 :
Raleigh, N.C.) Social work in a state-based
system of child health care . Chapel Hill
[1981?] v, 156 p. : LC Card 81-50559 DDC
    362.1/9892/000973 19
RJ102 .T74 1980

University of North Carolina at Chapel Hill.
    Highway Safety Research Center.
Clark, Verneta J. Single variable tabulations for
1973-1976 North Carolina accidents /. Chapel
Hill, N.C. [1977] xiii, 20, ca. 200 p. : LC Card
    80-622768 DDC 312/.44/09756 19
HE5614.3.N6 C52

Hunter, William W. Mopeds, an analysis of
1976-1978 North Carolina accidents /. Chapel
Hill, N.C. [1979] 194 p. in various pagings :
    LC Card 80-622241 DDC 363.1/259 19
HE5614.3.N6 H86

University of North Carolina at Chapel Hill.
    Institute of Government.
Administration of justice memoranda .
    (no. 79/06) Rankin, Sue B. Applying the
    Uniform child custody jurisdiction act /.
    Chapel Hill , 1979, c1978. 7 p. ; LC Card
        80-620669 DDC 347.756 s 346.75601/7 19
KFN7908.A15 U6 No. 79/06 KFN7504

    (no. 80/01) Farb, Robert L. The public's
    right to attend criminal proceedings in North
    Carolina /. Chapel Hill, N.C. [1980], c1978.
    10 p. ; LC Card 80-622371 DDC 347.756 s
        345.756/05 19
KFN7908.A15 U6 no. 80/01 KFN7910.5.C6

    (no. 80/03) Crowell, Michael. Entering a
    home to arrest without a warrant /. Chapel

Hill [1980] c1978. 4 p. ; LC Card 80-622792
    DDC 347.756 s 345.756/0527 19
KFN7908.A15 U6 no. 80/03 KFN7976

    (no. 80/04) Farb, Robert L. The impact of
    Baldasar v. Illinois on uncounseled
    misdemeanor convictions in North Carolina
    /. Chapel Hill, N.C. , 1980, c1978. 4 p. ; LC
        Card 80-622793 DDC 347.756 s 345.756/056 19
KFN7908.A15 U6 no. 80/04 KFN7978

Davis, Bonnie E. Disclosure of adoption records
/. [Chapel Hill] , 1980. 10 p. ; LC Card
    81-621375 DDC 346.75601/78 347.5606178 19
KFN7504.5.Z9 D38

Drennan, James C. Punishment chart for crimes
of general interest in the Superior Courts of
North Carolina /. [Chapel Hill] , 1978. ix, 40
p. ; LC Card 78-624325 DDC 345.756/077 19
KFN7983.2.Z9 D73

Phay, Robert E. The public library . [Chapel
Hill] , 1980. 69 p. : LC Card 81-620731 DDC
    021.8/2/09756 19
Z681.5 .P45 1980

Sawyer, Ann L. Procedures to be followed for
the placement of children with special needs in
educational programs . Chapel Hill [1979] 58
p. ; LC Card 81-621674 DDC 344.756/0791
    347.5604791 19
KFN7795.9.H3 S28

University of North Carolina at Chapel Hill.
    Library. Southern Historical Collection.
Guide to the microfilm edition of the Penn
School papers, 1862-1976 : a project of the
Southern Historical Collection of the University
of North Carolina Library, Chapel Hill. [Chapel
Hill : The Collection, 1977] 42 p. ; 28 cm.
1. Penn School, St. Helena Island, S. C. - Sources. 2.
Afro-Americans - South Carolina - St. Helena Island -
Sources. I. Title.   ***NYPL [Sc F 80-196]***

University of North Carolina (System). Water
    Resources Research Institute.
Knopf, Bruce J. M. The impacts of rural water
systems in North Carolina . [Raleigh, N.C.] ,
1979. xii, 120 p. : LC Card 80-621889 DDC
    333.91/009756 s 363.6/1/09756 19
HD1694.N8 N6 no. 151 TD224.N8

Nunnally, Nelson R. Use of fluvial processes to
minimize adverse effects of stream
channelization /. [Raleigh, N.C.] , 1979. viii,
115 p. : LC Card 80-620990 DDC 333.91/009756
    s 627/.12 19
HD1694.N8 N6 no. 144 TC424.N8

Report .
    (no. 129) North Carolina. State University,
    Raleigh. Dept. of Botany. Response of
    phytoplankton to water quality in the
    Chowan River system /. [Raleigh, N.C.]
    [1979] xv, 204 p. : LC Card 79-626203 DDC
        589.4 19
HD1694.N8 N6 no. 129 QK571.5.N8

    (no. 137) Campbell, William A., 1940- Legal
    aspects of flood plain management /.
    [Raleigh] , 1979. xiii, 49 p. ; LC Card
        79-624322 DDC 333.91/009756 s
        344.756/0633391 19
HD1694.N8 N6 no. 137 KFN7847.8

    (no. 139) Kuenzler, Edward J. Nutrient
    kinetics of phytoplankton in the Pamlico
    River, North Carolina /. [Raleigh] [1979]
    xxii, 163 p. : LC Card 79-626205 DDC
        333.91/009756 s 589.4 19
HD1694.N8 N6 no. 139 QK571.5.N8

    (no. 141) Pal, Dhiraj. Assessment of land
    treatment technology for petroleum refinery
    solid wastes /. [Raleigh, N.C.] 1980, vi, 30
    leaves, [1] leaf of plates : LC Card 80-623569
        DDC 333.91/009756 s 628.5/46 19
HD1694.N8 N6 no. 141 TD899.P4

    (no. 144) Nunnally, Nelson R. Use of fluvial
    processes to minimize adverse effects of
    stream channelization /. [Raleigh, N.C.] ,
    1979. viii, 115 p. : LC Card 80-620990 DDC
        333.91/009756 s 627/.12 19
HD1694.N8 N6 no. 144 TC424.N8

    (no. 151) Knopf, Bruce J. M. The impacts of
    rural water systems in North Carolina .
    [Raleigh, N.C.] , 1979. xii, 120 p. : LC Card
        80-621889 DDC 333.91/009756 s
        363.6/1/09756 19
HD1694.N8 N6 no. 151 TD224.N8

    (no. 154) Kuenzler, Edward J. Phosphorus

GOVERNMENT PUBLICATIONS - U.S.: 1981

619

University of Wisconsin-Madison. College of Agricultural and Life

dynamics in a North Carolina Piedmont reservoir /. Raleigh, N.C. [1980] xii, 56 p. : LC Card 80-622281 DDC 333.91/009756 s 628.1/32 19
HD1694.N8 N6 no. 154 TD427.P56

(no. 156) Malcom, H. Rooney. A study of detention in urban stormwater management /. [Raleigh, N.C.] [1980] xvi, 78 p. : LC Card 80-623571 DDC 333.91/009756 s 628/.212 19
HD1694.N8 N6 no. 156 TD657

(no. 158) Sherwani, Jabbar K. Public policy for the management of groundwater in the coastal plain of North Carolina /. [Raleigh, N.C.] [1980] xv, 63 p. : LC Card 80-623572 DDC 333.91/009756 s 333.91/04/09756 19
HD1694.N8 N6 no. 158 TD224.N8

WRRI report .
(no. 142) Overcash, Michael R. Characterization and land application of seafood industry wastewaters /. Raleigh [1980] ix, 34 leaves : LC Card 80-623929 DDC 664/.94996 19
TD774 .O92

(no. 149) Hargett, David. Guidelines for socioeconomic impact analyses of environmental regulations /. [Raleigh, N.C.] 1979. vi, 68 p. : LC Card 80-622155 DDC 333.91/009756 s 363.7/056 19
HD1694.N8 N6 no. 149 TD170.2

University of North Dakota. Bureau of Governmental Affairs. The Structure of North Dakota state government . Bismarck, ND [1979] 76 leaves in various foliations ; LC Card 80-622720 DDC 353.978404 19
JK6431 1979 .S77

University of Northern Colorado. Museum of Anthropology.
Abrams, H. Leon. A partial working bibliography on the Amerindians of New Jersey /. Greeley, Colo. , 1980. 10 leaves ;
NYPL [HBA 80-381 no. 41]

Miscellaneous series.
(no. 41) Abrams, H. Leon. A partial working bibliography on the Amerindians of New Jersey /. Greeley, Colo. , 1980. 10 leaves ;
NYPL [HBA 80-381 no. 41]

(no. 22) Abrams, H. Leon. A partial working bibliography on the Amerindians of New York /. Greeley, Colo. , 1979. 22 leaves ; LC Card 80-622303 DDC 909/.09812 s 016.9747/00497 19
GN4 .U53 no. 22 Z1209.2.U52N65

University of Northern Iowa. Library. Women's studies bibliography / [University of Northern Iowa Library]. [Cedar Falls, Iowa : UNI Library, 1973] 54 p. in various pagings ; 28 cm.
-- --- Supplement 1. Prepared by Janet Dellinger. Cedar Falls, 1975. 47 p.; 28 cm.
1. Women's studies - Bibliography. 2. Women's studies - United States - Bibliography. 3. Women - Social conditions - Bibliography. 4. Women - United States - Social conditions - Bibliography. I. Title.
NYPL [*R-Econ. 80-1012]

UNIVERSITY OF OKLAHOMA - FACULTY.
Cross, George Lynn. Professors, presidents, and politicians . Norman , c1981. p. cm. ISBN 0-8061-1781-8 LC Card 81-40288 DDC 378.766/37 19
LD4323 .C75

UNIVERSITY OF OKLAHOMA - PRESIDENTS.
Cross, George Lynn. Professors, presidents, and politicians . Norman , c1981. p. cm. ISBN 0-8061-1781-8 LC Card 81-40288 DDC 378.766/37 19
LD4323 .C75

UNIVERSITY OF OREGON.
Sheldon, Henry Davidson, 1874-1948. Henry Davidson Sheldon and the University of Oregon, 1874-1948 . Bellingham, Wash. , 1979. xvi, 192 p. : LC Card 81-110768 DDC 378/.111 19
LD4362.8.S53 A34

University of Oregon. Bureau of Governmental Research and Service. Mattis, James. Boundary determination procedures for Oregon local governments. [Eugene] , 1979-1980. 2 v. : LC Card 80-623933 DDC 349.795 s 342.795/09 349.795 s 347.95029 19
KFO2831.A7 L34 no. 16 KFO2830

University of Pennsylvania. Middle East Research Institute. The Middle East challenge, 1980-1985 /. Carbondale , c1981. p. cm. ISBN 0-8093-1042-2 LC Card 81-5651 DDC 320.956 19
DS63.1 .M486

University of Pennsylvania publications in conduct and communication.
Hymes, Dell H. "In vain I tried to tell you" . Philadelphia , 1981. p. cm. ISBN 0-8122-7806-2 LC Card 81-51138 DDC 897 19
PM483.5 .H9

University of Rhode Island. see Rhode Island. University.

University of South Dakota. Business Research Bureau. Historic sites of South Dakota . [Vermillion, S.D.] , 1980. x, 126 p. : LC Card 80-623927 DDC 917.83/0433 19
F652 .H57

University of South Dakota. Human Factors Laboratory. Osga, Glenn A. An investigation of the riding experiences of MSF rider course participants in South Dakota /. Pierre, S.D. [1980] xi, 231 leaves : LC Card 80-624202 DDC 629.28/475/0715 19
TL440.5 .O83

University of Southern Maine. New Enterprise Institute. Maine. State Development Office. Maine metalworking directory, 1979-1980 /. Augusta, Me. [1980] vi, 104 p. ; LC Card 80-622393 DDC 338.4/7671/025741 19
TS203 .M253 1980

University of Southern Mississippi, Hattiesburg. see Mississippi. University of Southern Mississippi, Hattiesburg.

University of Tennessee, Knoxville. Center for Business and Economic Research. An economic report to the Governor of the State of Tennessee on the State's economic outlook / prepared by Center for Business and Economic Research, College of Business Administration, University of Tennessee, Knoxville, in cooperation with the Tennessee State Planning Office ; William C. Goolsby, project director. Nashville, Tenn. : The Office, [1979] xiv, 246 p. ; 29 cm. "February 1979." LC Card 79-623072 DDC 338.5/443/09768 19
1. Tennessee - Economic conditions. I. Goolsby, William. II. Tennessee. State Planning Office. III. Title.
HC107.T3 U53 1979

University of Tennessee, Knoxville. Dept. of Nuclear Engineering. International Conference on Nuclear Systems Reliability Engineering and Risk Assessment, Gatlinburg, Tenn., 1977. Nuclear systems reliability engineering and risk assessment . Philadelphia , 1977. xi, 849 p. : LC Card 77-91478
TK9152 .I48 1977 **NYPL [JSF 81-47]**

University of Tennessee, Knoxville. Nuclear Engineering, Dept. of. see University of Tennessee, Knoxville. Dept. of Nuclear Engineering.

University of Tennessee, Knoxville. Public Law Institute.
Tennessee domestic relations law for attorneys and legal assistants /. Knoxville, Tenn. (1505 W. Cumberland Ave., Knoxville 37916) , c1980. 1 v. (various pagings) : LC Card 81-132962 DDC 346.76801/5 347.680615 19
KFT94 .T45

Tennessee law of criminal procedure /. Knoxville , c1980. 1 v. (various pagings) : LC Card 81-135057 DDC 345.768/05 347.68055 19
KFT575 .T46

University of Tennessee, Knoxville. Water Resources Research Center.
Research report - Water Resources Research Center, University of Tennessee, Knoxville .
(no. 68) Bonner, William P. Effects of wastewater process operation on organics in potable water supplies /. Knoxville , 1978. ix, 109 leaves : LC Card 79-624195 DDC 628.1/62 19
TD758.5.O75 B66

University of Texas at Austin. Center for Mexican American Studies. Cuantos somos . Austin , 1977. xvi, 238 p. ; ISBN 0-292-71045-3 (pbk.) LC Card 77-93093 DDC 304.6/089687

19
E184.M5 C8

University of Texas at Austin. Institute of Latin American Studies. McGinn, Noel F., 1934- Higher education policies in Mexico /. Austin , 1980. 11 p. ; LC Card 81-621755 DDC 370/.972 19
LC177.M6 M23

University of Texas at Austin. Petroleum Extension Service.
Fundamental principles of gas turbines. [Austin] , 1980. v, 81 p. : LC Card 80-154782 DDC 621.43/3 19
TJ778 .F86

A Primer of oil-well service and workover. Austin, Tex. , Dallas, Tex. , 1979. v, 106 p. : LC Card 80-154730 DDC 622/.3382 19
TN871 .P7164 1979

University of Texas at San Antonio. Center for Archaeological Research.
McGraw, A. Joachim. A preliminary archaeological survey for the Conquista project in Gonzales, Atascosa, and Live Oak Counties, Texas /. [San Antonio] , 1979. iii, 31 leaves : LC Card 80-620819 DDC 976.4/445 19
E78.T4 M317

Special report - Center for Archaeological Research, The University of Texas at San Antonio .
(no. 5) Gunn, Joel. Hop Hill . San Antonio , 1977. x, 295 p. : LC Card 78-621351 DDC 976.4/65 19
E78.T4 G86

University of Texas Health Science Center at Houston. School of Public Health. Project for the Early Prevention of Individual Violence. Harris, Robert L. Health and crime abstracts, 1960-1971 /. Houston, Tex. , 1972. xi, 149 p. ; LC Card 73-621328 DDC 016.3642/4 19
HV6131 .H37

University of Texas Press poetry series .
(no. 7) Moore, Prentiss, 1947- The garden in winter and other poems /. Austin , 1981. p. cm. ISBN 0-292-72721-6 : LC Card 81-13117 DDC 811/.54 19
PS3563.O627 G3

University of Texas System. Institute of Higher Education Management. Proceedings of the Texas postsecondary education outlook, 1980-1985 . [Austin] , c1979. xv, 166 p. : LC Card 80-623590 DDC 378.764 19
LB2329.5 .P76

University of Toronto. Institute for Environmental Studies. International Symposium on the Analysis of Hydorcarbons and Halogenated Hydrocarbons in the Aquatic Environment, McMaster University, 1978. Hydrocarbons and halogenated hydrocarbons in the aquatic environment /. New York , c1980. xiii, 588 p. : ISBN 0-306-40329-3 LC Card 79-26462
QH545.H92 I54 1978 **NYPL [JSF 80-1049]**

University of Vermont. Historic Preservation Program. The Burlington book . Wheeler, VT (Wheeler House, University of Vermont, Burlington 05405) , c1980. 111 p. : LC Card 81-622322 DDC 720/.9743/17 19
NA735.B85 B87

University of Virginia. Institute of Government. Abramowitz, Alan. Party activists in Virginia . Charlottesville , 1981. x, 106 p. ; LC Card 81-142700 DDC 324.5/6/09755 19
JK2295.V83 A24

University of Washington. Center for Contemporary Chinese and Soviet Studies. The Sino-Soviet conflict . Seattle , c1981. p. cm. ISBN 0-295-95854-5 : LC Card 81-51279 DDC 327.51047 19
DS740.5.S65 S56

University of Washington, Seattle. see Washington (State). University.

University of West Virginia. see West Virginia. University.

University of Wisconsin-Madison. College of Agricultural and Life Sciences. Research Division.
United States. Soil Conservation Service. General soil map, Adams County, Wisconsin /. Lincoln, Nebr. , 1980. 1 map : LC Card

BIBLIOGRAPHIC GUIDE

University of Wisconsin-Madison. College of Agricultural and Life

620

81-691244
G4123.A2J3 1979 .U5

United States. Soil Conservation Service.
General soil map, Kewaunee County, Wisconsin
/. Lincoln, Nebr. , 1979. 1 map : LC Card
81-691242
G4123.K5J3 1979 .U5

United States. Soil Conservation Service.
General soil map, Outagamie County,
Wisconsin /. Lincoln, Nebr. , 1980. 1 map :
LC Card 81-691241
G4123.O8J3 1977 .U5

**University of Wisconsin--Extension. Women's
Education Resources.** Violence against
women, causes and prevention . Rockville, Md.
(P.O. Box 2309, Rockville 20852) , 1980. vii,
37 p. ; LC Card 80-603151 DDC 016.3628/8 19
HV6250.4.W65 V56 1980

**University of Wisconsin--Milwaukee. Center for
Architecture and Urban Planning Research.**
Community Design Center (Milwaukee, Wis.)
Recommendations for child care centers /.
Milwaukee , 1979. 453 leaves in various
foliations : LC Card 80-153764 DDC 362.7/12 19
HV851 .C65 1979

**UNIVERSITY READERS. see COLLEGE
READERS.**

**A university's approach to delinquency
prevention .** Ku, Richard. [Washington] , 1977.
ii, 128 p. : LC Card 77-602177
HV9106.U7 K8 **NYPL [JLF 81-166]**

Unkeless, Elaine, 1945- Women in Joyce /.
Urbana , c1982. p. cm. ISBN 0-252-00891-X LC
Card 81-4663 DDC 823/.912
PR6019.O9 Z654

Unlocking the second gate . Lenihan, Kenneth J.
[Washington] , 1977. iv, 71 p. : LC Card
77-600960
HD5701 .U53 no. 45 HV9306.B2
NYPL [*XME-9551]

**Unnecessary exposure to radiation from medical
and dental x-rays .** United States. Congress.
House. Committee on Interstate and Foreign
Commerce. Subcommittee on Oversight and
Investigations. Washington , 1980. v, 15 p. ;
LC Card 80-603049 DDC 363.1/89 19
RC78 .U534 1980

**Unpaid claims of U. S. citizens against
Czechoslovakia .** United States. Congress.
Senate. Committee on Finance. Subcommittee
on International Trade. Washington , c1980 [i.e.
1981] iii, 217 p. : LC Card 81-600978 DDC
342.73/082 347.30282 19
KF26 .F554 1981

**Unresolved issues impede Federal debt collection
efforts .** United States. General Accounting
Office. [Washington, D.C. , 1980] iv, 17 p. ;
LC Card 80-603132 DDC 353.0072/6 19
HG3729.U5 U55 1980

"The unsearchable wisdom of God . Fortuna,
James Louis, 1943- Gainesville , c1980. viii, 130
p. ; ISBN 0-8130-0676-7 : LC Card 80-14919
PR3664.P4 F6 **NYPL [L-10 3842 no. 49]**

Unsicker, Joan I. Archeological explorations at
Jubilee College historic site, 1979 : report /
submitted to the Illinois Department of
Conservation by Joan I. Unsicker. [Normal,
Ill.] : Illinois State University, 1979, c1980. xii,
81 p., [3] fold. leaves of plates : ill. (1 fold. in
pocket) ; 26 cm. (Illinois State University
archeological surveys research report . no. 1)
Bibliography: p. 78-81. LC Card 80-623248
*1. Jubilee College State Park, Ill. - Antiquities. 2.
Illinois - Antiquities. 3. Excavations (Archaeology) -
Illinois - Jubilee College State Park. I. Illinois. Dept. of
Conservation. II. Series: Illinois. State University,
Normal. Illinois State University archeological surveys
research report , no. 1. III. Title.*
F547.P4 U57

**Update--impact of agricultural trade restrictions
on the Soviet Union .** [Washington, D.C.] : U.
S. Dept. of Agriculture, [1980] 9 p. ; 27 cm.
(Foreign agricultural economic report . no. 160)
Prepared by the Foreign Agricultural Service and the
Economics, Statistics, and Cooperatives Service. "July
1980." LC Card 80-603822 DDC 338.1 s
330.947/0853 19
*1. Grain trade - Political aspects - United States. 2.
Grain trade - Political aspects - Soviet Union. 3. United
States - Foreign economic relations - Soviet Union. 4.*

*Soviet Union - Foreign economic relations - United
States. 5. United States - Foreign relations - Soviet
Union. 6. Soviet Union - Foreign relation - United
States. 7. Soviet Union - Economic conditions - 1976-.
I. United States. Foreign Agricultural Service. II. United
States. Dept. of Agriculture. Economics, Statistics, and
Cooperatives Service. III. Series.*
HD1411 .F59 no. 160 HD9036

Update on juvenile crime and justice in Arizona .
Arizona. State Justice Planning Agency.
Statistical Analysis Center. Phoenix, Ariz.
[1979] 32 p. : LC Card 80-620799 DDC
364.3/6/09791 19
HV9105.A68 A74 1979

**Update, United States-Canadian/Mexican
relations .** United States. Congress. House.
Committee on Foreign Affairs. Subcommittee
on Inter-American Affairs. Washington , 1980.
iii, 71 p. ; LC Card 80-603028 DDC 327.73071 19
KF27 .F646 1980b

Updike, Randall G. Surficial geology and
processes : Prudhoe Bay Oil Field, Alaska, with
hydrologic implications / by Randall G. Updike
and Mark D. Howland. Anchorage, Alaska :
Division of Geological and Geophysical
Surveys, 1979. iii, 6 p., 17 leaves (14 fold.) of
plates : ill., maps ; 51 cm. (Special report -
Division of Geologic and Geophysical Surveys . 16)
Scale of principal maps 1:12,000. Bibliography: p. 6.
LC Card 79-626004 DDC 912/.1551/097987 19
*1. Geology - Alaska - Prudhoe Bay region - Maps. 2.
Hydrology - Alaska - Prudhoe Bay region - Maps. I.
Howland, Mark D., joint author. II. Series: Alaska.
Division of Geological and Geophysical Surveys.
Special report - Division of Geological & Geophysical
Surveys , 16. III. Title.*
G1532.P7C5 U6 1979

Uphaus, Robert W. Beyond tragedy : structure &
experience in Shakespeare's romances / Robert
W. Uphaus. Lexington : University Press of
Kentucky, 1981. p. cm. Includes bibliographical
references and index. ISBN 0-8131-1441-1 : LC
Card 80-5184 DDC 822.3/3 19
*1. Shakespeare, William, 1564-1616 - Tragicomedies. I.
Title.*
PR2981.5 .U6

**Upper Cretaceous subsurface stratigraphy and
structure of coastal Georgia and South
Carolina /.** Valentine, Page C. Washington,
D.C. [1981] p. cm. LC Card 80-607868 DDC
551.7/7/09757 19
QE688 .V35

Upper Great Plains Transportation Institute.
Griffin, Gene C. North Dakota grain and
oilseed transportation statistics, 1978-79 /.
Fargo, N.D. , 1979. iii, 70 p. : LC Card
80-621931 DDC 388.044 19
HE2321.G7 G74

UGPTI report .
(no. 35) Griffin, Gene C. North Dakota grain
and oilseed transportation statistics, 1978-79
/. Fargo, N.D. , 1979. iii, 70 p. : LC Card
80-621931 DDC 388.044 19
HE2321.G7 G74

Upper Mystic Lake . Chesebrough, Eben W.
Westborough, Mass. [1975] 75 p. : LC Card
79-620591 DDC 363.7/3942/097444 19
TD224.M4 C488

**Upper Niobrara-White Natural Resources
District.** Souders, Vernon L. Geology and
groundwater supplies of Box Butte County,
Nebraska /. [Lincoln] [1980] vii, 205 p. : LC
Card 80-623050 DDC 553/.7/09782 s
551.7/9/0978294 19
GB1025.N2 N42 no. 47 QE136.B67

**The upper Quaboag River basin, Dunn
Brook-Seven Mile River .** Massachusetts.
Water Quality and Research Section.
Westborough [1978] 48 p. : LC Card 79-620590
DDC 363.7/3942/0974426 19
TD224.M4 M368 1978

**Upper Schoharie Creek watershed, Delaware,
Greene, and Schoharie Counties, New York.**
United States. Soil Conservation Service.
Lanham, MD , 1980. 1 map : LC Card
81-690285
G3802.S42 1980 .U5

Uptake and release of phenol by algal cells /.
Bofill, Jordi. Austin, Tex. [1979] vii leaves, 49
p. : LC Card 80-622520 DDC 589.3/133 19
QK565 .B57

Upton, Helen M. The Everett report in historical
perspective : the Indians of New York / Helen
M. Upton. Albany, N.Y. : New York State
American Revolution Bicentennial Commission,
c1980. xiii, 248 p. : ill. ; 23 cm. Bibliography: p.
233-240. Includes index. LC Card 80-623134 DDC
974.7/00497 19
*1. Iroquois Indian Government relations. 2. New York
(State). Indian Commission. 3. Indians of North
America - New York (State). 4. Indians of North
America - Government relations. 5. Iroquois Indians -
Legal status, laws, etc. 6. Indians of North America -
Legal status, laws, etc. I. Title.*
E99.I7 U75

**URANIUM INDUSTRY - ENVIRONMENTAL
ASPECTS - UNITED STATES.**
Landa, Edward. Isolation of uranium mill
tailings and their component radionuclides from
the biosphere--some earth science perspectives
/. Arlington, VA , 1980. iii, 32 p. : LC Card
79-600148 DDC 622 s 621.48/38 19
QE75 .C5 no. 814 TD899.U73

**URANIUM INDUSTRY - HYGIENIC
ASPECTS - UNITED STATES.**
United States. Congress. Senate. Committee on
Governmental Affairs. Subcommittee on
Energy, Nuclear Proliferation, and Federal
Services. DOE's safety and health program for
enrichment plant workers . Washington , 1980.
iii, 377 p. : LC Card 80-603790 DDC 363.1/79 19
KF26 .G6728 1980c

**URANIUM INDUSTRY - SAFETY
MEASURES - UNITED STATES.**
United States. Congress. Senate. Committee on
Governmental Affairs. Subcommittee on
Energy, Nuclear Proliferation, and Federal
Services. DOE's safety and health program for
enrichment plant workers . Washington , 1980.
iii, 377 p. : LC Card 80-603790 DDC 363.1/79 19
KF26 .G6728 1980c

**URANIUM INDUSTRY - UNITED STATES -
WASTE DISPOSAL.**
Landa, Edward. Isolation of uranium mill
tailings and their component radionuclides from
the biosphere--some earth science perspectives
/. Arlington, VA , 1980. iii, 32 p. : LC Card
79-600148 DDC 622 s 621.48/38 19
QE75 .C5 no. 814 TD899.U73

URANIUM INDUSTRY - WASTE DISPOSAL.
United States. Congress. House. Committee on
Interior and Insular Affairs. Subcommittee on
Energy and the Environment. Mill tailings dam
break at Church Rock, New Mexico .
Washington , 1980. iv, 232 p. : LC Card
80-601962 DDC 622/.8 19
KF27 .I518 1979i

**URANIUM INDUSTRY - WYOMING -
EMPLOYEES.**
Wyoming. Dept. of Labor and Statistics.
Wyoming uranium, mining and milling .
[Cheyenne, Wyo. , 1980] iii, 41 p. : LC Card
80-622020 DDC 331.12/52234932/09787 19
HD4966.U72 U68 1979

URANIUM - METALLURGY.
(1981) Feed grade versus extraction correlations
on uranium ores from New Mexico /.
Avondale, Md. , 1981. p. cm. LC Card
80-607857 DDC 622 s 622/.34932 19
TN23 .U43 TN490.U7

(1981) Schultze, L. E. (Lawrence E.) Extracting
uranium from carbonaceous ores /.
[Washington, D.C.] [1981] p. cm. LC Card
81-10150 DDC 622 s 669/.2931 19
TN23 .U43 TN799.U7

**URANIUM MILL TAILINGS - UNITED
STATES.**
Landa, Edward. Isolation of uranium mill
tailings and their component radionuclides from
the biosphere--some earth science perspectives
/. Arlington, VA , 1980. iii, 32 p. : LC Card
79-600148 DDC 622 s 621.48/38 19
QE75 .C5 no. 814 TD899.U73

Uranium mine ventilation costs /. Bates, Robert
C. [Washington, D.C.] [1981] p. cm. LC Card
81-607862 DDC 622 s 338.2/3 19
TN295 .U4

URANIUM MINES AND MINING.
Nigbor, M. T. (Michael T.) Case history of a
pilot scale acidic in situ uranium leaching
experiment /. Avondale, MD , 1981. p. cm.

LC Card 81-607873 DDC 622 s 622/.34932 19
TN23 .U43 TN799.U7

Savanick, George A. Water jet perforation .
Washington, D.C. , 1981. p. cm. LC Card
80-607781 DDC 622 s 622/.184932 19
TN23 .U43 TN278.3

Tweeton, Daryl R. Selection of lixiviants for in
situ uranium leaching /. Avondale, MD [1981]
p. cm. LC Card 81-6103 DDC 622 s 622/.34932
19
TN295 .U4 TN490.U7

**URANIUM MINES AND MINING -
EMPLOYEES - DISEASES AND
HYGIENE - NEW MEXICO.**
United States. Congress. Senate. Special
Committee on Aging. Occupational health
hazards of older workers in New Mexico .
Washington , 1980. iv, 95 p. ; LC Card
80-602736 DDC 363.1/1962234932 19
KF26.5 .A3 1979h

**URANIUM MINES AND MINING -
EMPLOYEES - DISEASES AND
HYGIENE - THE WEST.**
United States. Congress. Senate. Committee on
Labor and Human Resources. Subcommittee on
Health and Scientific Research. Radiation
exposure compensation act of 1979 .
Washington , 1980. iv, 132 p. ; LC Card
80-603432 DDC 346.7303/8 347.30638 19
KF26 .L274 1980d

**URANIUM MINES AND MINING -
HYGIENIC ASPECTS - BIBLIOGRAPHY.**
Hendryson, Elizabeth. Health and safety aspects
of mining . Albuquerque, N.M. [1980] iv, 76
p. ; LC Card 81-621701 DDC 016.622/8 19
Z6664.L9 H46 RC965.M48

**URANIUM MINES AND MINING - SAFETY
MEASURES.**
Bates, Robert C. Uranium mine ventilation
costs /. [Washington, D.C.] [1981] p. cm. LC
Card 81-607862 DDC 622 s 338.2/3 19
TN295 .U4

URANIUM - NEW MEXICO - SOCORRO CO.
Chapin, Charles Edward, 1932- Coal, uranium,
oil, and gas potential of the Riley-Puertecito
area, Socorro County, New Mexico /. Socorro
[1979] v, 33 p., [3] fold. leaves of plates : LC
Card 79-626216 DDC 553.2/09789/62 19
TN805.N6 C47

URANIUM ORES - NEW MEXICO.
Feed grade versus extraction correlations on
uranium ores from New Mexico /. Avondale,
Md. , 1981. p. cm. LC Card 80-607857 DDC
622 s 622/.34932 19
TN23 .U43 TN490.U7

URANIUM ORES - TEXAS.
Galloway, William E. Catahoula formation of
the Texas Coastal Plain . Austin, Tex. , 1980.
vi, 81 p. : LC Card 80-623081 DDC 553/.09764 s
553.4/932/09764 19
QE167 .T42 no. 100 QE693

URANIUM ORES - UNITED STATES.
Schultze, L. E. (Lawrence E.) Extracting
uranium from carbonaceous ores /.
[Washington, D.C.] [1981] p. cm. LC Card
81-10150 DDC 622 s 669/.2931 19
TN23 .U43 TN799.U7

**Uranium-series dating of mollusks and corals and
age of Pleistocene deposits, Chesapeake Bay
area, Virginia and Maryland /.** Mixon, Robert
B. Washington , 1981. p. cm. LC Card
81-607014 DDC 551.7/92/097521 19
QE697 .M7

**Urban abandonment and property tax
delinquency /.** Neuhaus, William B. Frankfort,
Ky. , 1978. iii, 22 p. ; LC Card 79-621078 DDC
343.76905/4 347.690354 19
KFK1679 .N48

Urban America in the eighties . United States.
Panel on Policies and Priorities for
Metropolitan and Nonmetropolitan Areas.
Washington , 1980. p. cm. LC Card 80-27894
DDC 307.7/6/0973 19
HT123 .U465 1980

Urban and Rural Systems Associates. Improving
family planning services for teenagers : final
report submitted to Office of the Assistant
Secretary for Planning and Evaluation/Health,
Department of Health, Education, and Welfare,
contract HEW-OS-74-304 / submitted by

Urban and Rural Systems Associates.
[Washington] : The Office, 1976. i, 85, 23 p. :
forms ; 28 cm. Bibliography: p. [1]-23 (3d group)
LC Card 77-601716
*1. Birth control clinics - United States. 2. Youth -
United States - Sexual behavior. I. United States. Dept.
of Health, Education, and Welfare. Office of the
Assistant Secretary for Planning and Evaluation. II.
Title.*
HQ766.5.U5 U72 1976   **NYPL [JLF 81-163]**

**Urban atlas, tract data for standard metropolitan
areas .** United States. Bureau of the Census.
Washington, D.C. , 1974 [i.e. 1975] [15] p. :
LC Card 80-600869 DDC 912/.1312/0976819
G1337.M4E25 U5 1975

**Urban atlas, tract data for standard metropolitan
statistical areas .** United States. Bureau of the
Census. Washington, D.C. , 1974 [i.e. 1975]
[15] p. : LC Card 80-600872 DDC
912/.1312/0975662
G1302.G7E25 U5 1975

**Urban atlas, tract data for standard metropolitan
statistical areas .** United States. Bureau of the
Census. Washington, D.C. , 1974 [i.e. 1975]
[29] p. : LC Card 80-600871 DDC
912/.1312/09778411
G1437.K2E25 U5 1975

**Urban atlas, tract data for standard metropolitan
statistical areas .** United States. Bureau of the
Census. Washington, D.C. , 1974 [i.e. 1975]
[43] p. : LC Card 80-600845 DDC
912/.1312/0977311
G1407.C54E25 U5 1975

**Urban atlas, tract data for standard metropolitan
statistical areas .** United States. Bureau of the
Census. Washington, D.C. , 1974 [i.e. 1975]
[16] p. : LC Card 80-600861 DDC
912/.1312/0979474
G1527.S33E25 U5 1975

**Urban atlas, tract data for standard metropolitan
statistical areas .** United States. Bureau of the
Census. Washington, D.C. , 1974 [i.e. 1975]
[30] p. : LC Card 80-600863 DDC
912/.1312/0974932
G1257.N5E25 U5 1975

**Urban atlas, tract data for standard metropolitan
statistical areas .** United States. Bureau of the
Census. Washington, D.C. , 1974 [i.e. 1975]
[31] p. : LC Card 80-600856 DDC
912/.1312/097526
G1272.B3E25 U5 1975

Urban, Charles W. (joint author) Page, Steven J.
Effectiveness of wet cutter bars in reducing salt
mine dust /. Washington [1980] p. cm. LC
Card 80-607782 DDC 622 s 622/.3632 19
TN23 .U43 TN312

**URBAN COMMUNITY DEVELOPMENT. see
COMMUNITY DEVELOPMENT, URBAN.**

Urban Consortium for Technology Initiatives.
Elderly and handicapped transportation : local
government approaches / prepared by Public
Technology, inc., secretariat to the Urban
Consortium for Technology Initiatives ....
Washington, D.C. : U. S. Dept. of
Transportation, Urban Mass Transportation
Administration, Office of the Secretary : for
sale by the Supt. of Docs., U. S. Govt. Print.
Off., 1979. 60 p. (p. 59-60 blank) : ill. ; 22 x 28
cm. LC Card 79-602755
*1. Aged - United States - Transportation. 2.
Handicapped - United States - Transportation. I. Title.*
HV1465 .U72 1979   **NYPL [JLF 81-378]**

Information bulletin - Urban Consortium.
Gonder, John. The housing needs of
"non-traditional" households . Washington,
D.C. , 1979 [i.e. 1980] 56 p. ; LC Card
80-602223 DDC 363.5/0973 19
HD7293 .G59

Silver, Jennifer. Condominium conversion
controls . Washington, D.C. , 1979 [i.e.]
1980. 61 p. ; LC Card 80-601762 DDC
346.7304/33 19
KF581 .S54

Public Technology, inc. Elderly and
handicapped transportation . Washington, 19.
28 p.;   **NYPL [*XME-9106]**

**Urban Consortium for Technology Initiatives.
Community and Economic Development Task
Force.**
Gonder, John. The housing needs of

"non-traditional" households . Washington,
D.C. , 1979 [i.e. 1980] 56 p. ; LC Card
80-602223 DDC 363.5/0973 19
HD7293 .G59

Silver, Jennifer. Condominium conversion
controls . Washington, D.C. , 1979 [i.e.] 1980.
61 p. ; LC Card 80-601762 DDC 346.7304/33 19
KF581 .S54

URBAN DESIGN. see CITY PLANNING.

Urban design primer, Hawaii. Hawaii. Dept. of
Planning and Economic Development.
[Honolulu] , 1975. vi, 101 p. : LC Card
76-624060
HT167.5.H3 H34 1975   **NYPL [JLF 80-1338]**

**URBAN DEVELOPMENT. see CITY
PLANNING.**

Urban Development Corporation.
Roosevelt Island Development Plan. New York,
1978. map 32 x 76 cm. Scale ca. 1:4,700. Blue line
print. North oriented toward upper right corner.
*1. Roosevelt Island, N. Y. - Maps. 2. City planning -
New York (State).*   **NYPL [Map Div. 80-3265]**

A step-by-step guide to resources for economic
development / New York State Urban
Development Corporation [and] State of New
York Department of State. New York, N.Y. :
The Corporation, c1980. 208 p. ; 28 cm.
Bibliography: p. 199-201. Includes index. LC Card
80-620009 DDC 353.0082/09747 19
*1. Economic assistance, Domestic - New York (State) -
Handbooks, manuals, etc. 2. Community development -
New York (State) - Finance - Handbooks, manuals, etc.
I. New York (State). Dept. of State. II. Title.*
HC107.N73 P6385 1980

**Urban Development Corporation. New York
Convention Center Development
Corporation. see New York Convention
Center Development Corporation.**

**URBAN ECONOMIC DEVELOPMENT. see
COMMUNITY DEVELOPMENT, URBAN.**

URBAN ECONOMICS.
Voelker, Stanley W. A functional classification
of agricultural trade centers in North Dakota /.
Fargo [1978] 51 p. : LC Card 78-623601 DDC
338.1 s 381/.41/09784 19
SB205.S7 N64 no. 125 HT123.5.N9

**URBAN EDUCATION. see EDUCATION,
URBAN.**

URBAN FAUNA.
Leedy, Daniel L. Planning for wildlife in cities
and suburbs /. [Washington] , 1978. vii, 64 p. :
LC Card 79-603493 DDC 639.9/09173/2 19
QH541.5.C6 L43 1978

Urban forestry . Albrecht, Jean. St. Paul, Minn.
[1980] 100 p. ; LC Card 80-622738 DDC
016.6349/09173/2 19
Z5996.T74 A4 SB436

URBAN FORESTRY - BIBLIOGRAPHY.
Albrecht, Jean. Urban forestry . St. Paul, Minn.
[1980] 100 p. ; LC Card 80-622738 DDC
016.6349/09173/2 19
Z5996.T74 A4 SB436

Urban gaming/simulation '77 : an ongoing
conference for educators and trainers / edited
by Larry C. Coppard, Frederick L. Goodman.
Ann Arbor : School of Education, University of
Michigan, c1977. x, 57, 376 p. ; 23 cm.
Bibliography: p. 50-57. LC Card 77-151140 DDC
307.7/6/0724 19
*1. City planning - Study and teaching - United States.
2. Community life - Study and teaching - United States.
3. Land use, Urban - Study and teaching - United
States. 4. Regional planning - Study and teaching -
United States. 5. Community development - Study and
teaching - United States. 6. Simulation games in
education. I. Coppard, Larry C. II. Goodman, Frederick
L.*
HT165.52 .U7

Urban high school. United States. Urban High
School Reform Initiative. Federal educational
law and urban secondary school reform .
[Washington, D.C.] , 1979. 2 v. ; LC Card
80-600029 DDC 344.73/074 19
KF4199 .A873

URBAN HOUSING. see HOUSING.

Urban infill . Real Estate Research Corporation.
[Washington, D.C.] [1980] 76 p. ; LC Card
80-602851 DDC 016.33377/13/0973 19
Z7164.L3 R4 1980 HD205

Urban Institute.
Emerging options for work and retirement
policy (an analysis of major income and
employment issues with an agenda for research
priorities) : an information paper / prepared for
use by the Special Committee on Aging, United
States Senate. Washington : U. S. Govt. Print.
Off. : for sale by the Supt. of Docs., U. S.
Govt. Print. Off., 1980. vi, 186 p. 23 cm. At
head of title: 96th Congress, 2d session. Committee
print. Principal author: James R. Storey. Includes
bibliographies. LC Card 80-603277 DDC
331.25/2/0973 19
*1. Retirement income - United States. 2. Aged -
Employment - United States. 3. Aged - United States -
Economic conditions. I. Storey, James R. II. United
States. Congress. Senate. Special Committee on Aging.
III. Title.*
HD7106.U5 U7 1980

How effective are your community recreation
services? [Washington] , 1973. 189 p. in various
pagings :   *NYPL [JFF 80-1149]*

Urban Land Institute. United States Conference
of Mayors. The private development process .
[Washington] [1979] iii, 49 p. ; LC Card
79-601943
HD259 .U53 1979

URBAN LAND USE. see LAND USE, URBAN.

**Urban League, National. see National Urban
League.**

Urban mass transit R. & D. . United States.
Congress. House. Committee on Science and
Technology. Subcommittee on Transportation,
Aviation, and Communications. Washington ,
1980. iii, 200 p. : LC Card 80-603002 DDC
388.4/072073 19
KF27 .S3997 1980b

**Urban Observatory, Garland, Tex. see Garland
Urban Observatory.**

**Urban observatory research report. see National
League of Cities. NLC urban observatory
research report.**

Urban origin-destination surveys. United States.
Federal Highway Administration. Washington,
1973. viii, 309 p.:   *NYPL [JLF 81-455]*

URBAN PLANNING. see CITY PLANNING.

URBAN POLICY - FRANCE.
Underhill, Jack A. French national urban policy
and the Paris region new towns . [Washington]
[1980] 131 p. : LC Card 80-602925 DDC
307.7/6/0944 19
HT165.P37 U52

URBAN POLICY - IRELAND.
Huff, David Lynch, 1931- Ireland's urban
system /. Austin , 1978. 49 p. : LC Card
79-621433 DDC 307.7/6/09417 19
HT145.I7 H83

URBAN POLICY - NEW JERSEY.
New Jersey. Cabinet Committee on Urban
Policy. An assessment of New Jersey's urban
programs /. Trenton , 1978. 192 p. in various
pagings ; LC Card 79-623364
HT123.5.N5 N46 1978

URBAN POLICY - UNITED STATES.
United States. Congress. House. Committee on
Banking, Finance and Urban Affairs.
Subcommittee on the City. Compact cities .
Washington , 1980. viii, 86 p. ; LC Card
80-602867 DDC 333.79/0973 19
HD108.2 .U54 1980

United States. Congress. House. Committee on
Banking, Finance and Urban Affairs.
Subcommittee on the City. Urban revitalization
and industrial policy . Washington , 1980. iv,
388 p. : LC Card 81-600638 DDC 338.973 19
KF27 .B52 1980

**URBAN POLICY - UNITED STATES -
ADDRESSES, ESSAYS, LECTURES.**
Nonmetropolitan America in transition /.
Chapel Hill , c1981. p. cm. ISBN 0-8078-1490-3
LC Card 81-3511 DDC 307.7/2/0973 19
HT123 .N65

Urban professionals and the future of the
metropolis /. Port Washington, N.Y. , 1980. ix,
122 p. : ISBN 0-8046-9261-0 : LC Card 79-29748
HT123 .U76   *NYPL [JLD 81-113]*

**URBAN POLICY - UNITED STATES - CASE
STUDIES.**
Henig, Jeffrey R., 1951- Neighborhood

mobilization . New Brunswick, N.J. , c1981. p.
cm. ISBN 0-8135-0933-5 : LC Card 81-5234
DDC 307.7/6/0977311 19
HT177.C5 H45

**URBAN POLICY - UNITED STATES -
CONGRESSES.**
United States. Panel on Policies and Priorities
for Metropolitan and Nonmetropolitan Areas.
Urban America in the eighties . Washington ,
1980. p. cm. LC Card 80-27894 DDC
307.7/6/0973 19
HT123 .U465 1980

**URBAN POLICY - UNITED STATES -
SIMULATION METHODS.**
United States. Institute for Applied Technology.
Technical Analysis Division. City I player's
manual. Washington, D.C., 1973. viii, 142 p.
                    NYPL [JLF 80-1361]

**URBAN POPULATION MOVEMENTS. see
RESIDENTIAL MOBILITY.**

**Urban professionals and the future of the
metropolis /** edited by Paula Dubeck and Zane
L. Miller. Port Washington, N.Y. : Kennikat
Press Corp., 1980. ix, 122 p. : ill. ; 23 cm.
(Interdisciplinary urban series) Papers from four
symposia sponsored by the University of Cincinnati.
Includes bibliographical references.Bibliography: p.
ISBN 0-8046-9261-0 : LC Card 79-29748
*1. Urban policy - United States - Addresses, essays,
lectures. 2. Housing policy - United States - Addresses,
essays, lectures. 3. Medical policy - United States -
Addresses, essays, lectures. I. Miller, Zane L. II.
Dubeck, Paula J., 1944-. III. Cincinnati. University.*
HT123 .U76   *NYPL [JLD 81-113]*

Urban rail in America . Pushkarev, Boris.
Bloomington , c1981. p. cm. ISBN
0-253-37555-X LC Card 81-47293 DDC
388.4/2/0973 19
HE4451 .P87

**URBAN REDEVELOPMENT. see URBAN
RENEWAL.**

URBAN RENEWAL - CONGRESSES.
Environmental Design Conference on City
Centers in Transition, University of North
Carolina at Chapel Hill, 1976. City centers in
transition . Chapel Hill , 1976. xii, 90 leaves /
LC Card 76-29226   *NYPL [JLF 80-1605]*

**URBAN RENEWAL - ILLINOIS - CHICAGO -
CITIZEN PARTICIPATION - CASE
STUDIES.**
Henig, Jeffrey R., 1951- Neighborhood
mobilization . New Brunswick, N.J. , c1981. p.
cm. ISBN 0-8135-0933-5 : LC Card 81-5234
DDC 307.7/6/0977311 19
HT177.C5 H45

**URBAN RENEWAL - MINNESOTA -
MINNEAPOLIS - CITIZEN
PARTICIPATION - CASE STUDIES.**
Henig, Jeffrey R., 1951- Neighborhood
mobilization . New Brunswick, N.J. , c1981. p.
cm. ISBN 0-8135-0933-5 : LC Card 81-5234
DDC 307.7/6/0977311 19
HT177.C5 H45

URBAN RENEWAL - NEW YORK (N.Y.)
Danielson, Michael N. New York, the politics
of urban regional development . Berkeley ,
c1981. p. cm. ISBN 0-520-04371-5 LC Card
81-7480 DDC 307.7/6 19
HT393.N7 D3

URBAN RENEWAL - OHIO - CLEVELAND.
Cleveland. City Planning Commission. Impact
of new construction on the market for existing
dowtown office space. Cleveland, Ohio, 1974.
31 leaves .   *NYPL [*ZT-1250]*

**URBAN RENEWAL - PENNSYLVANIA -
PHILADELPHIA.**
Philadelphia. City Planning Commission. Penn
Center. [Philadelphia] 1952. 22 p. LC Card
81-471288
HT177.P47 P44 1952

Urban renewal review. v. 4-16, no. 2; Mar.
1965-1977 (incomplete) Chicago, Dept. of
Urban Renewal. 28 cm. Bimonthly, Mar. 1965-Nov.
1965; quarterly (slightly irregular), 1966-77. Superseded
by Planning & development review.
*1. City planning - Illinois - Chicago - Periodicals. I.
Chicago. Dept. of Urban Renewal.*
                    NYPL [JLM 80-1122]

URBAN RENEWAL - TEXAS.
Texas. Dept. of Community Affairs. Recycling

neighborhoods . [Austin] [1978] 2 v. : LC
Card 79-622456 DDC 363.5/8 19
HD7293 .T46 1978

URBAN RENEWAL - UNITED STATES.
Cohen, Rick. Partnerships for neighborhood
preservation . [Harrisburg] , 1978. vii, 200 p. ;
LC Card 79-622460 DDC 307.7/6/0973 19
HN90.C6 C626

Urban waterfront revitalization . Washington
[1980]. 2 v.   *NYPL [JLM 80-739]*

**URBAN RENEWAL - UNITED STATES -
CASE STUDIES.**
United States. Advisory Council on Historic
Preservation. The contribution of historic
preservation to urban revitalization /.
Washington , 1979. 176 p. in various pagings :
LC Card 79-602153
HT175 .U58 1979   *NYPL [JLF 81-453]*

**URBAN RENEWAL - UNITED STATES -
HANDBOOKS, MANUALS, ETC.**
Economics of revitalization . [Washington,
D.C.?] , 1981 i.e. 1980. 94 p. : LC Card
81-601655 DDC 352.94/18/0973 19
HT175 .E27

**URBAN RENEWAL - UNITED STATES -
PERIODICALS.**
Challenge! [Washington] v. 9, no. 10- ; Oct.
1978- Washington.   *NYPL [JLM 81-3]*

**URBAN RENEWAL - VIRGINIA -
ALEXANDRIA.**
United States. Dept. of the Interior. Alexandria
waterfront, Virginia . Washington , 1979. 86 p. :
LC Card 80-602643 DDC 333.73/17/09755296
19
HT177.A44 U54 1979

URBAN RENEWAL - WASHINGTON, D.C.
United States. Dept. of the Interior.
Georgetown waterfront, Washington, D.C. .
Washington , 1979. 53 p. : LC Card 80-602644
DDC 333.78/3 19
HT177.D6 U52 1979

United States. National Capital Planning
Commission. Downtown design and
development . Washington, 1974. 28 p.
                    NYPL [JLG 80-72]

Urban revitalization and industrial policy .
United States. Congress. House. Committee on
Banking, Finance and Urban Affairs.
Subcommittee on the City. Washington , 1980.
iv, 388 p. : LC Card 81-600638 DDC 338.973 19
KF27 .B52 1980

URBAN RUNOFF - CONGRESSES.
International Symposium on Urban Storm
Runoff, University of Kentucky, 1980.
International Symposium on Urban Storm
Runoff, July 28-31, 1980 . Lexington , c1980.
319 p. : ISBN 0-89779-040-5 (pbk.) LC Card
80-52482 DDC 551.48/8/091732 19
GB980 .I58 1980

**URBAN RUNOFF - NORTH CAROLINA -
CHARLOTTE - MATHEMATICAL
MODELS.**
Malcom, H. Rooney. A study of detention in
urban stormwater management /. [Raleigh,
N.C.] [1980] xvi, 78 p. : LC Card 80-623571
DDC 333.91/009756 s 628/.212 19
HD1694.N8 N6 no. 156 TD657

**URBAN RUNOFF - SOUTHERN STATES -
CONGRESSES.**
Southeast Conference on Urban Stormwater
Management, North Carolina State University,
1979. Urban stormwater management .
[Raleigh, N.C.] [1980] vi, 252 p. : LC Card
80-623271 DDC 363.6/1 19
TD657 .S68 1979

Urban stormwater management . Southeast
Conference on Urban Stormwater Management,
North Carolina State University, 1979. [Raleigh,
N.C.] [1980] vi, 252 p. : LC Card 80-623271
DDC 363.6/1 19
TD657 .S68 1979

**Urban Studies Center, University of Louisville.
see Louisville, Ky. University. Urban Studies
Center.**

**Urban Studies of the Massachusetts Institute of
Technology and Harvard University, Joint
Center for. see Joint Center for Urban
Studies.**

Urban Systems Research & Engineering. Survey of blind and disabled children receiving supplemental security income benefits / prepared for U. S. Department of Health, Education, and Welfare, Social Security Administration, Office of Policy, Office of Research and Statistics by Urban Systems Research & Engineering, inc. [Washington, D.C.] : Office of Research and Statistics, 1980. xii, 94, [178] p. : ill. ; 28 cm. (DHEW publication. no. (SSA) 13-11728) LC Card 80-602123 DDC 362.4/0482/088054 19
1. Children, Blind - United States. 2. Supplemental security income - United States - Statistics. 3. Federal aid to child welfare - United States - Statistics. I. United States. Social Security Administration. Office of Policy. II. United States. Social Security Administration. Office of Research and Statistics. III. Series: United States. Dept. of Health, Education and Welfare. DHEW publication. no. (SSA) 13-11728. IV. Title.
HV1791 .U7 1980

URBAN TRAFFIC. see TRAFFIC ENGINEERING.

URBAN TRANSIT. see LOCAL TRANSIT.

URBAN TRANSPORTATION.
United States. Congress. Office of Technology Assessment. Impact of advanced group rapid transit technology. Washington, D.C. [1980] viii, 58 p. : LC Card 80-600001
HE305 .U555 1980   **NYPL [JLF 80-1368]**

URBAN TRANSPORTATION AND STATE. see URBAN TRANSPORTATION POLICY.

URBAN TRANSPORTATION - ENVIRONMENTAL ASPECTS - RUSSIA.
United States /U. S.S.R. Urban Transportation Team. Transportation and the urban environment . Washington , 1978. xii, 173 p. : LC Card 79-600645
HE308 .U568 1978

URBAN TRANSPORTATION - ENVIRONMENTAL ASPECTS - UNITED STATES.
United States /U. S.S.R. Urban Transportation Team. Transportation and the urban environment . Washington , 1978. xii, 173 p. : LC Card 79-600645
HE308 .U568 1978

URBAN TRANSPORTATION - FINANCE.
Gladstone Associates. Innovative financing techniques . [Washington, D.C.] , Washington, D.C. [1978] ca. 350 p. in various pagings : LC Card 80-601836 DDC 388.4/042 19
HE4351 .G57 1978

URBAN TRANSPORTATION - NEW YORK (CITY)
Regional Plan Association, New York. Transportation and economic opportunity. [New York, 1973] 206 p.   **NYPL [JLF 81-23]**

URBAN TRANSPORTATION - PLANNING - ADDRESSES, ESSAYS, LECTURES.
Advances in urban transportation planning /. Washington, D.C. , 1980. iv, 22 p. : ISBN 0-309-03115-X (pbk.) LC Card 81-4761 DDC 380.5 s 388.4/068 19
TE7 .H5 no. 771 HE305

URBAN TRANSPORTATION POLICY - ILLINOIS - CHICAGO METROPOLITAN AREA - PERIODICALS.
Transportation system management plan for northeastern Illinois. Chicago.
       NYPL [JLM 80-1096]

URBAN TRANSPORTATION POLICY - UNITED STATES.
Abrams, Charles M. Measures of effectiveness for multimodal urban traffic management . - Washington , Springfield, Va. , 1979. 1 v. :
       NYPL [JLM 80-740]

United States. Congress. House. Committee on Public Works and Transportation. Subcommittee on Oversight and Review. Mobility for Americans in an era of increasing energy, environmental, and financial constraints . Washington , 1980. v, 578 p. : LC Card 80-603419 DDC 380.5/0973 19
KF27 .P89636 1980a

Urban Transportation Team, U. S. - U. S. S. R. see United States /U. S.S.R. Urban Transportation Team.

URBAN TRANSPORTATION - UNITED STATES.
Alternative work schedules . Washington, D.C. , 1980. 54 p. : ISBN 0-309-03153-2 (pbk.) : LC Card 80-54556 DDC 388.4/13143/0973 19
HE308 .A62

Rothenberg, Morris Jerome, 1934- Public transportation . [Washington, D.C.] [1980] viii, 200, [160] p. : LC Card 80-602279 DDC 388.4/0973 19
HE308 .R67

United States. Bureau of the Census. Selected characteristics of travel to work in 20 metropolitan areas, 1977. Washington , 1981. p. cm. LC Card 80-606807 DDC 312/.0973 s 388.4/0973 19
HA203 .A218 no. 105 HE308

United States. Congress. House. Committee on Public Works and Transportation. Subcommittee on Oversight and Review. Mobility for Americans in an era of increasing energy, environmental, and financial constraints . Washington , 1980. v, 578 p. : LC Card 80-603419 DDC 380.5/0973 19
KF27 .P89636 1980a

United States. Urban Mass Transportation Administration. Innovation in public transportation . Washington , 1974. ix, 147 p. :
       NYPL [JLF 80-1675]

Urban waterfront revitalization : the role of recreation and heritage / Heritage Conservation and Recreation Service. Washington : The Service, [1980]. 2 v. ill., maps. ; 26 cm. CONTENTS: v. 1. [pt. 1] Key factors, needs and goals: summary. [pt. 2] Key factors, needs and goals. - v. 2. Eighteen case studies.
1. Urban renewal - United States. 2. Waterfronts - United States. 3. Recreation areas - United States. I. United States. Heritage Conservation and Recreation Service.   **NYPL [JLM 80-739]**

URBAN WILDLIFE. see URBAN FAUNA.

URBANISM. see CITIES AND TOWNS.

URBANIZATION.
United Nations. Dept. of International Economic and Social Affairs. Patterns of urban and rural population growth. New York , 1980. ix, 175 p. : LC Card 80-138417 DDC 081 s 304.6/2 19
JX1977 .A2 ST/ESA/SER.A/68 HB1951

URBANIZATION - AFRICA - BIBLIOGRAPHY.
Schatzberg, Michael G. Bibliography of small urban centers in rural development in Africa /. [Madison] , 1979. ix, 246 p. ; LC Card 80-623484 DDC 016.3077/6/096 19
Z7164.U7 S25 HT148.A2

URBANIZATION - AFRICA - RESEARCH - PERIODICALS.
African urban notes. Ser. B. v. [1]-2; winter, 1974/75-fall/winter, 1976/77. East Lansing, Mich. [etc.] 2 v. in 1.   **NYPL [JLM 80-802]**

Urbanization and water quality planning .
University of Massachusetts at Amherst. Water Resources Research Center. Amherst, Mass. [1979] viii, 121 [14] p. ; LC Card 80-623703 DDC 333.91/009744 s 363.7/39456/068 19
TD224.M4 M37 no. 104

URBANIZATION - CONGRESSES.
United Nations Conference on Human Settlements, Vancouver, B.C., 1976. Global review of human settlements . [New York?] 1976. 237 p. : LC Card 80-515666 DDC 330 s 307.7/6 19
JX1977 .A2 A/CONF.70/A/1

URBANIZATION - ENVIRONMENTAL ASPECTS - FLORIDA - TAMPA BAY REGION - MAPS.
Tampa Bay Regional Planning Council. Tampa Bay region preliminary environmental assessment of development atlas /. [Tampa Bay? Fla.] , 1972. 1 portfolio (21 fold. leaves of plates : LC Card 80-675325 DDC 912/.133373/0975965 19
G1317.T3 T34 1972

URBANIZATION - EUROPE - HISTORY.
Hall, Peter Geoffrey. Growth centres in the European urban system /. Berkeley , 1980. xxii, 278 p. : ISBN 0-520-04198-4 LC Card 81-135069 DDC 307.7/6/094 19
HT334.E85 H34

URBANIZATION - INDIANA.
Yamin, Hadi. Relationship of highway development and city development for non-metropolitan places in Indiana . West Lafayette, Ind. , 1979. xii, 175 leaves : LC Card 80-620933 DDC 388.1/1 19
TE24.I6 Y35

URBANIZATION - MASSACHUSETTS.
University of Massachusetts at Amherst. Water Resources Research Center. Urbanization and water quality planning . Amherst, Mass. [1979] viii, 121 [14] p. ; LC Card 80-623703 DDC 333.91/009744 s 363.7/39456/068 19
TD224.M4 M37 no. 104

URBANIZATION - UNITED STATES.
United States. General Accounting Office. Water supply for urban areas . [Washington] 1979. iv, 50 p. ; LC Card 79-602696 DDC 363.6/1/0973 19
TD223 .U525 1979

URBANIZATION - WEST (U. S.) - HISTORY - 19TH CENTURY.
Reps, John William. The forgotten frontier . Columbia , 1982, c1981. p. cm. ISBN 0-8262-0351-5 LC Card 81-10322 DDC 307.7/6/0978 19
HT123 .R44 1982

URBINA, RICARDO MANUEL, 1945-
United States. Congress. Senate. Committee on Governmental Affairs. Nominations of Dorothy Sellers and Ricardo M. Urbina . Washington , 1980. iii, 34 p. ; LC Card 81-600816 DDC 353.008/8/09753 19
KF26 .G67 1980m

URETHANE FOAM.
(1980) United States. Congress. Senate. Committee on Banking, Housing, and Urban Affairs. Subcommittee on Rural Housing and Development. Energy conservation, rural housing, and the use of urea-formaldehyde foamed-in place insulation . Washington , 1980. iv, 127 p. ; LC Card 80-601943 DDC 693.8/32/028 19
KF26 .B3953 1979a

URETHANE FOAM - TOXICOLOGY.
United States. Congress. Senate. Committee on Banking, Housing, and Urban Affairs. Subcommittee on Rural Housing and Development. Energy conservation, rural housing, and the use of urea-formaldehyde foamed-in place insulation . Washington , 1980. iv, 127 p. ; LC Card 80-601943 DDC 693.8/32/028 19
KF26 .B3953 1979a

The urge to mobilize . Yaney, George L. Urbana , c1982. p. cm. ISBN 0-252-00910-X LC Card 81-11527 DDC 333.3/1/47 19
HD1333.S65 Y36

Urick, Robert J. Sound propagation in the sea / written for Defense Advanced Research Projects Agency [by] R. J. Urick. [Arlington, Va.] : DARPA ; Washington, D.C. : for sale by the Supt. of Docs., U. S. Govt. Print. Off., 1979. ca. 300 p. in various pagings : ill. ; 28 cm. Includes bibliographical references and index. LC Card 80-601623 DDC 534/.23 19
1. Underwater acoustics. 2. Sound - Transmission - Measurement. I. United States. Defense Advanced Research Projects Agency. II. Title.
QC233 .U76

URINE - ANALYSIS.
Mutagen screening in an isolated high lung cancer mortality area of Montana /. Helena, Mont. [1979] 30 leaves : LC Card 79-626214 DDC 616.9/8 19
RA576 .M85

Urofsky, Melvin I. A voice that spoke for justice : the life and times of Stephen S. Wise / Melvin I. Urofsky. Albany : State University of New York Press, 1981. p. cm. (SUNY series in modern Jewish history) Bibliography: p. Includes index. ISBN 0-87395-538-2 LC Card 81-5676 DDC 296.8/346/0924 B 19
1. Wise, Stephen Samuel, 1874-1949. 2. Rabbis - United States - Biography. 3. Zionists - United States - Biography. I. Title. II. Series.
BM755.W53 U76

URS Company, Seattle, Wash. Dynamics of polychlorinated biphenyls in the upper Mississippi River : final report : phase 1 / by R. N. Dexter ... [et al.] ; project officer, Robert

Little ; performed for Columbia National Fishery Research Laboratory, Fish and Wildlife Service, U. S. Department of the Interior. Columbia, Mo. : The Service ; Washington : for sale by the Supt. of Docs., U. S. Govt. Print. Off., 1978- v. : ill. ; 27 cm. Vol. 1: April 1978; vol. 2: July 1978. "Contract number 14-16-009-78-026." Includes bibliographies. CONTENTS. - task 1. Compilation of information.--task 2. Evaluation of compiled information. LC Card 79-602554 DDC 363.7/394 19
1. Polychlorinated biphenyls - Environmental aspects - Mississippi River watershed. 2. Water - Pollution - Mississippi River Watershed. I. Dexter, R. N. II. Columbia National Fisheries Research Laboratory. III. Title.
TD427.P65 U18 1978

URS Company/Las Vegas. Land application of wastewater in Nevada : prepared for State of Nevada, Division of Water Planning / prepared by URS Company/Las Vegas. Carson City, Nev. : The Division, [1979] xv, 267 p. : ill. ; 28 cm. (Water planning report . 2) Information series - State of Nevada, Division of Water Planning "September 1979." Bibliography: p. 223-229. LC Card 80-623617 DDC 628.3/62 19
1. Sewage irrigation - Nevada. I. Title. II. Series.
TD760 .U17 1979

Urton, Gary, 1946- At the crossroads of the earth and the sky : an Andean cosmology / by Gary Urton. Austin : University of Texas Press, c1981. p. cm. (Latin American monographs. no. 55) Originally presented as the author's thesis (Ph.D.--University of Illinois at Urbana-Champaign) 1979. Bibliography: p. Includes index. ISBN 0-292-70349-X LC Card 81-4331 DDC 520/.985/37 19
1. Quechua Indians - Astronomy. 2. Quechua Indians - Philosophy. 3. Indians of South America - Peru - Cuzco (Dept.) - Astronomy. 4. Indians of South America - Peru - Cuzco (Dept.) - Philosophy. 5. Cuzco, Peru (Dept.) - Social life and customs. I. Series. II. Series: Latin American monographs (University of Texas at Austin. Institute of Latin American Studies) , no. 55. III. Title.
F2230.2.K4 U77 1981

Urwin, David William. Cambridge, Eng. Dept. of Architecture and Planning. Offices in Cambridge . [Cambridge] , 1976. 29 leaves in various pagings : ISBN 0-902696-04-1 LC Card 81-458609 DDC 338.6/042/0942659 19
HT169.G72 C2932 1976

US financing of East-West trade ; the political economy of government credits and the national interest / edited by Paul Marer. Bloomington : International Development Research Center, Indiana University, 1975. xiv, 442 p. ; 24 cm. (Studies in East European and Soviet planning, development, and trade . no. 22) Includes updated versions of the original papers presented at a panel discussion held in San Francisco, Dec. 28, 1974 and jointly sponsored by the American Economic Association and the Association for the Study of Grants Economy. Bibliography: p. 433-442. LC Card 79-129495 DDC 382/.63 19
1. Export credit - United States - Congresses. 2. Export-Import Bank of the United States - Congresses. 3. East-West trade (1945-) - Congresses. 4. United States - Commerce - Europe, Eastern - Congresses. 5. Europe, Eastern - Commerce - United States - Congresses. I. Marer, Paul. II. American Economic Association. III. Association for the Study of Grants Economy (U. S.). IV. Series.
HG3754.U5 U17

The US position in world markets. United States. Central Intelligence Agency. National Foreign Assessment Center. Washington , 1979. iii, 13 p. : LC Card 79-602644
HF3031 .U54 1979   *NYPL [*XME-9339]*

USDA/FDA announcement on nitrites and related issues . United States. Congress. House. Committee on Agriculture. Washington , 1980. iv, 221 p. : LC Card 81-600861 DDC 363.1/92 19
KF27 .A3 1980c

Use of amphetamine and its substitutes /. Spotts, James V. Rockville, Md. , Washington, D.C. , 1980. xvi, 560 p. ; LC Card 80-601718 DDC 362.2/9 19
RC568.A45 S68

Use of a cataloging center's bibliographic records as a means to check and balance acquisitions activities at an academic health sciences library /. Bristor, Patricia R. Detroit , 1980. 6,

[5] leaves ; LC Card 80-622445 DDC 025.2/18661 19
Z688.M4 B74

Use of arthropods to evaluate water quality of streams /. Hilsenhoff, William LeRoy, 1929- Madison, WI , 1977. 15 p. : LC Card 78-623368 DDC 639.9/09775 s 628.1/68/028/7 19
SK463 .A27 no. 100 QH105.W6

Use of casino gambling revenues to assist senior citizens and disabled. New Jersey. Legislature. General Assembly. Revenue, Finance, and Appropriations Committee. Public hearing before Assembly Revenue, Finance and Appropriations Committee on Assembly concurrent resolution no. 139 O[i.e. A]CR (use of casino gambling revenues to assist senior citizens and disabled) held June 30, 1980, Assembly Majority Conference Room, State House, Trenton, New Jersey. [Trenton] [1980] 3, 32 p. ; LC Card 80-623450
KFN1811.4 .R45 1980

Use of classified information in federal criminal cases . United States. Congress. House. Committee on the Judiciary. Subcommittee on Civil and Constitutional Rights. Washington , 1980 [i.e. 1981] iii, 103 p. ; LC Card 81-600944 DDC 347.73/64 347.30764 19
KF27 .J847 1980f

Use of cost-benefit analysis by regulatory agencies . United States. Congress. House. Committee on Interstate and Foreign Commerce. Subcommittee on Oversight and Investigations. Washington , 1980. v, 482 p. : LC Card 80-603329 DDC 353.09/1 19
KF27 .I5547 1979v

The use of drugs during pregnancy . United States. Congress. House. Select Committee on Narcotics Abuse and Control. Washington , 1980. iii, 99 p. ; LC Card 80-602790 DDC 362.8/2 19
KF27.5 .N3 1980

The use of economic data in collective bargaining . Friedman, Marvin, 1923- [Washington] , 1978. vi, 128 p. ; LC Card 79-602392
HD6508 .F74   *NYPL [JLF 81-432]*

The use of fiscal indicators to predict financial emergencies in Florida local governments /. Florida. Advisory Council on Intergovernmental Relations. Tallahassee, Fla. , 1980. x, 163 p. ; LC Card 80-621993 DDC 336/.014/759 19
HJ9218 .F39 1980a

Use of fluvial processes to minimize adverse effects of stream channelization /. Nunnally, Nelson R. [Raleigh, N.C.] , 1979. viii, 115 p. : LC Card 80-620990 DDC 333.91/009756 s 627/.12 19
HD1694.N8 N6 no. 144 TC424.N8

Use of health services by women 65 years and over. Hing, Esther. Hyattsville, Md. [1981] p. cm. LC Card 81-607865 DDC 362.1/1/0973 s 362.1/9/0880565 19
RA407.3 .A349 no. 59 RA408.W65

The use of independent hearing officers for administrative adjudications. California. Legislature. Senate. Interim Committee on Administrative Regulations and Adjudications. First report of the Senate Interim Committee on Administrative Regulations and Adjudications to the 1957 session of the California Legislature concerning the use of independent hearing officers for administrative adjudications. [Sacramento] , 1957. 131 p. ; LC Card 79-129502 DDC 342.794/066 347.940266 19
KFC782.5 .A25 1975

USE OF LAND. see LAND USE.

The use of paraquat to eradicate illicit marihuana crops and the health implications of paraquat-contaminated marihuana on the U. S. market . United States. Congress. House. Select Committee on Narcotics Abuse and Control. Washington , 1980. iii, 99 p. : LC Card 80-602592 DDC 363.4/5 19
RA1242.P34 U54 1980

Use of U. S. Armed Forces in attempted rescue of hostages in Iran . United States. President, 1977- (Carter) Washington, D.C. , 1980. 2 p. ; LC Card 80-602258 DDC 327.73055 19
E183.8.I55 U54 1980

Use of wetland habitats by birds in the National Petroleum Reserve--Alaska /. Derksen, Dirk V. Washington, D.C. , 1981. p. cm. LC Card 81-607937 DDC 639.9/784109798 19
S914 .A3 no.141 QL684A4

USE TAX - MAINE.
Maine. Legislature. Committee on Taxation. Report of the Joint Standing Committee on Taxation of the statutory review of the sales and use tax exemptions contained in Title 36 Section 1760, Sub-sections 15-23 and 25-29. Augusta, Me. [1980] 43, [17] leaves ; LC Card 80-622574 DDC 343.74105/5 347.410355 19
KFM11.62 .T3 1980

USE TAX - NEW MEXICO.
New Mexico. Taxation and Revenue Dept. Gross receipts & compensating tax regulations /. [Santa Fe, N.M.] [1980] x, 174, 58 p. ; LC Card 80-623312 DDC 343.78906/8 19
KFN4080.A434 A2 1980

USED CAR TRADE - LAW AND LEGISLATION - CALIFORNIA.
California. Legislature. Assembly. Labor, Employment & Consumer Affairs Committee. Hearing on consumer protection in the sale of new and used cars, San Diego, California, December 14-15, 1979 /. [Sacramento, CA] [1980?] iv, 435 p. : LC Card 80-621713 DDC 343.794/08556292222/0262 19
KFC10.4 .L27 1979

USEFUL ARTS. see INDUSTRIAL ARTS; TECHNOLOGY.

User manual series.
Borgman, Robert D. Crisis intervention . [Washington, D.C.] , 1979. ix, 33, [2] p. ; LC Card 79-603994 DDC 362.7/1 19
HV873 .B65

Users guide to the information system on transnational corporations . United Nations. Centre on Transnational Corporations. New York , 1980. iii, 30 p. ; LC Card 80-131497 DDC 300 s 025/.0633888 19
JX1977 .A2 ST/CTC/13 HD2755.5

The uses of paraprofessionals in the delivery of manpower and social services through public service employment. Stanfield, Robert E. [Montpelier, Vt.] 1973. xiii, 64 p.
*NYPL [*XME-9293]*

Using ANS FORTRAN / Gordon Lyon, editor ; contributors, Frances E. Holberton, J. Larmouth, M. D. McIlroy ; sponsored by National Science Foundation. Washington, D.C. : U. S. Dept. of Commerce, National Bureau of Standards : for sale by the Supt. of Docs., U. S. Govt. Print. Off., [1980] vi, 100 p. ; 27 cm. (NBS handbook ; 131) Includes bibliographical references. LC Card 80-600009 DDC 001.64/24 19
1. FORTRAN (Computer program language). I. Lyon, Gordon. II. Holberton, Frances E. III. Larmouth, John. IV. McIlroy, M. D. V. United States. National Science Foundation. VI. Series: United States. National Bureau of Standards. Handbook, 131.
QA76.73.F25 U84

USPS role in registering male citizens . United States. Congress. House. Committee on Post Office and Civil Service. Subcommittee on Postal Operations and Services. Washington , 1980. iii, 40 p. ; LC Card 80-603591 DDC 355.2/2363/0973 19
KF27 .P6674 1980a

USRA. see United States Railway Association.

USRA--nomination, authorization, Conrail plant rationalization, and employee protection program . United States. Congress. Senate. Committee on Commerce, Science, and Transportation. Subcommittee on Surface Transportation. Washington , 1980. iv, 125 p. ; LC Card 80-602781 DDC 343.73/095 19
KF26 .C698 1980c

USS Dewey DDG-45 Unitas XX. Unitas XX June 16, 1979-December 13, 1979. [Washington, D.C.? , 1980?] 128 p. : LC Card 80-603957 DDC 359.3/252/0973 19
VA65.D45 U54

USSR administrative divisions, 1979. United States. Central Intelligence Agency. [Washington , 1980] 1 map : LC Card 81-692775
G7001.F7 1979 .U5

USSR, coal industry problems and prospects.

United States. Central Intelligence Agency. National Foreign Assessment Center. Washington, D.C. [1980] iv, 20 p. : LC Card 80-602025 DDC 338.2/724/0947 19
HD9555.R82 U54 1980

Ustach, Joseph F. Effects of sub-lethal oil levels on the reproduction of a copepod, Nitocra affinis / Joseph F. Ustach. [Raleigh : UNC Sea Grant, North Carolina State University], 1977. 16 leaves : graphs ; 28 cm. (Sea grant publication. UNC-SG 76-10) Bibliography: leaves 14-16. LC Card 79-623524 DDC 595.3/4 19
1. Copepoda - Effect of water pollution on. 2. Copepoda - Reproduction. 3. Oil pollution of the sea - Environmental aspects. I. Title. II. Title: Nitocra affinis. III. Series: Sea grant publication (Raleigh) , UNC-SG-76-10.
QL444.C74 U87

USURY. see INTEREST AND USURY.

USURY LAWS - CALIFORNIA.
California. Legislature. Assembly. Committee on Finance, Insurance, and Commerce. Public hearing on economic statistical indicators, indexing, proposed Federal Trade Commission, consumer credit rules and credit union, interest rates and costs of funds . Sacramento, CA (Box 90, Sacramento 95814) [1980] 220 p. : LC Card 81-621157 DDC 332.7/09794 19
KFC10.4 .F56 1980

USURY LAWS - DISTRICT OF COLUMBIA.
United States. Congress. Senate. Committee on Governmental Affairs. Subcommittee on Governmental Efficiency and the District of Columbia. District of Columbia interest rate modification . Washington , 1980. iii, 252 p. ; LC Card 80-602468 DDC 346.753/073 19
KF26 .G6735 1979j

USURY LAWS - UNITED STATES.
United States. Congress. Senate. Committee on Banking, Housing and Urban Affairs. Depository Institutions Deregulation Committee . Washington , 1980. vi, 307 p. ; LC Card 80-603707 DDC 346.73/082 19
KF26 .B39 1980o

USURY LAWS - UNITED STATES - STATES.
United States. Congress. House. Committee on Small Business. Subcommittee on General Oversight and Minority Enterprise. State usury ceilings and their impact on small businesses . Washington , 1980. iii, 294 p : LC Card 81-600855 DDC 338.6/42/0973 19
KF27 .S64 1980g

Utah. Agricultural Experiment Station, Logan.
Nielson, Woodrow. Soil survey of Navajo Indian Reservation, San Juan County, Utah /. [Washington] [1980] viii, 119 p., [12] fold. leaves of plates : LC Card 80-602348 DDC 631.4/7/79259 19
S599.U8 N53

UTAH - ANTIQUITIES.
Castleton, Kenneth Bitner, 1903- Petroglyphs and pictographs of Utah /. Salt Lake City , 1978-1979. 2 v. : LC Card 78-53941 DDC 709/.01/1309792 19
E78.U55 C37

Hauck, Forrest Richard, 1938- Cultural resource evaluation in central Utah, 1977 /. [Salt Lake City, Utah] [1979] xiv, 389 p. : LC Card 80-600539 DDC 979.2/01 19
F828 .H37

Hauck, Forrest Richard, 1938- Cultural resource evaluation in south central Utah, 1977-1978 /. [Salt Lake City] [1979] xi, 346 p. : LC Card 80-601615 DDC 979.2/51 19
F828 .H38

Utah - Archaeology. see Utah - Antiquities.

Utah. Bureau of Health Statistics.
Annual report of Utah vital statistics. Salt Lake City. 28 cm. Issued by the State Dept. of Health, Bureau of Records and Statistics, 1957; by the Bureau of Vital Statistics, 1958-60; by the Division of Vital Statistics, 1961-65; by the State Division of Health, Bureau of Statistical Services, 1971. Title varies: 1957-62, Utah vital statistics; annual report (varies slightly); 1963-65, Division of Vital Statistics annual report. Cover title, 1963-76: Utah vital statistics; annual report (varies slightly) For later file, see its: Utah vital statistics; annual report.
1. Utah - Statistics, Vital - Periodicals. 2. Utah - Statistics, Medical - Periodicals. I. Utah. Bureau of Records and Statistics. II. Utah. Bureau of Vital

Statistics. III. Utah. Division of Vital Statistics. IV. Utah. State Division of Health. Bureau of Statistical Services. V. Title. ***NYPL [SDG (Utah. Health Board. Utah vital statistics; report)]***
Utah vital statistics; annual report. Salt Lake City. 28 cm. For earlier file, see its: Annual report of Utah vital statistics.
1. Utah - Statistics, Vital - Periodicals. 2. Utah - Statistics, Medical - Periodicals. I. Title.
NYPL [JLM 80-984]

Utah. Bureau of Records and Statistics. Utah. Bureau of Health Statistics. Annual report of Utah vital statistics. Salt Lake City.
NYPL [SDG (Utah. Health Board. Utah vital statistics; report)]

Utah. Bureau of Vital Statistics. Utah. Bureau of Health Statistics. Annual report of Utah vital statistics. Salt Lake City. ***NYPL [SDG (Utah. Health Board. Utah vital statistics; report)]***

Utah. Constitution. Constitution of the State of Utah : original as amended. [Salt Lake City] : Dept. of Finance, State Archives and Records Service, 1979. [91] p. ; 28 cm. Includes index. LC Card 80-624132 DDC 342.792/023 19
1. Utah - Constitutional law. I. Title.
KFU401 1895 .A337

UTAH - CONSTITUTIONAL LAW.
Utah. Constitution. Constitution of the State of Utah . [Salt Lake City] , 1979. [91] p. ; LC Card 80-624132 DDC 342.792/023 19
KFU401 1895 .A337

Utah. Council on Criminal Justice Administration. Safe streets, 1968-1980 : What has been done with all that LEAA money in Utah? / Utah Council on Criminal Justice Administration. Salt Lake City, Utah : The Council, [1980] 13 leaves ; 28 cm. Cover title. "May 1980." LC Card 80-623598 DDC 364/.9792 19
1. Crime prevention - Utah - Finance. 2. Federal aid to law enforcement agencies - Utah. 3. Utah. Law Enforcement Planning Agency - Appropriations and expenditures. I. Title.
HV7294 .A6 1980

Utah. Dept. of Employment Security. (Old Catalog form: Utah. Employment Security Dept.)
Coverston, G. Scott. Report on youth in the Utah labor force /. [Salt Lake City] , 1979. vii, 50 p. ; LC Card 80-620745 DDC 331.3/4125/09792 19
HD6274.U8 C66

Utah. Dept. of Employment Security. Reports and Analysis Section. Utah employment, wages, and reporting units by firm size, 1979. Salt Lake City, Utah : Job Service, Utah Dept. of Employment Security, [1979] iii, 51 p. ; 22 x 28 cm. "December 1979." Chiefly tables. LC Card 80-621434 DDC 331.12/5/09792 19
1. Labor supply - Utah - Statistics. 2. Wages - Utah - Statistics. 3. Industries, Size of - Utah - Statistics. I. Title.
HD5725.U8 U82 1979a

Utah. Dept. of Natural Resources. Technical publication.
(no. 64) Bolke, E. L. Hydrologic reconnaissance of the Fish Springs Flat area, Tooele, Juab, and Millard counties, Utah /. [Salt Lake City] , 1978. iv, 30 p. : LC Card 79-621928 DDC 553/.09792 s 553.7/9/097924 19
TA7 .U77 no. 64 GB705.U8

Utah. Dept. of Natural Resources. Division of Water Resources. see Utah. Division of Water Resources.

Utah. Dept. of Natural Resources. Division of Water Rights. see Utah. Division of Water Rights.

UTAH. DEPT. OF SOCIAL SERVICES - APPROPRIATIONS AND EXPENDITURES.
Utah. Dept. of Social Services. Office of Planning & Research. Appropriation, direction & priorities for FY 1979 /. [Salt Lake City] , 1978. 38 p. : LC Card 79-623076 DDC 353.97920072/23684 19
HV86 .U89 1978

Utah. Dept. of Social Services. Office of Planning & Research. Appropriation, direction & priorities for FY 1979 / prepared by the Office of Planning & Research. [Salt Lake City] : State of Utah, Dept. of Social Services, 1978. 38 p. : ill. ; 22 x 28 cm. LC Card 79-623076 DDC 353.97920072/23684 19
1. Utah. Dept. of Social Services - Appropriations and expenditures. I. Title.
HV86 .U89 1978

Utah. Div. of Education Support Services. State & Federal Data Support Services. Salary schedule information on Utah school districts. Salt Lake City, Utah : Utah State Office of Education, Div. of Education Support Services, State & Federal Data Support Services, [1979] 201 p. 28 cm. "November 1979." LC Card 80-622337 DDC 331.2/813711/009792 19
1. Teachers - Utah - Salaries pensions, etc. 2. School administrators - Utah - Salaries, pensions, etc. 3. School employees - Utah - Salaries, pensions, etc. I. Title.
LB2842.2 .U85 1979

UTAH. DIVISION OF FINE ARTS.
Utah. Office of the Legislative Auditor General. A performance audit of the Division of Fine Arts /. [Salt Lake City] , 1980. 39, 8 p. ; LC Card 80-621609 DDC 353.97920085/4 19
NX24.U8 U7938 1980

UTAH. DIVISION OF PURCHASING - AUDITING AND INSPECTION.
Utah. Office of the Legislative Auditor General. A performance audit of the Division of Purchasing in the Department of Finance /. [Salt Lake City] (412 State Capitol, Salt Lake City, 84114) [1980] ii, 62, 4 p. ; LC Card 80-623434 DDC 353.97920071/2 19
JK8488.A1 U86 1980

Utah. Division of Rehabilitation Services. A program report, fiscal year 1979 / Utah State Office of Education, Division of Rehabilitation Services. Salt Lake City, Utah : The Division, [1979] v, 13, 4 leaves ; 28 cm. "November 1979." LC Card 80-622338 DDC 362/.0425 19
1. Vocational rehabilitation - Utah.
HD7256.U6 U88 1979

Utah. Division of State History. Antiquities Section.
Antiquities Section selected papers .
(no. 16) Fremont perspectives /. [Salt Lake City] , c1980. 83 p. : LC Card 80-149987 DDC 979.2 19
E78.U55 F73

Utah. Division of Vital Statistics. Utah. Bureau of Health Statistics. Annual report of Utah vital statistics. Salt Lake City. ***NYPL [SDG (Utah. Health Board. Utah vital statistics; report)]***

Utah. Division of Water Resources.
Cooperative investigations report.
Utah. Division of Water Resources. Developing a state water plan; ground water conditions in Utah. [Salt Lake City].
NYPL [JSP 81-11]

Developing a state water plan; ground water conditions in Utah. [Salt Lake City]. illus. 28 cm. (Its: Cooperative investigations report) Annual. Prepared in cooperation with U. S. Geological Survey.
1. Water resources development - Utah - Periodicals. 2. Water, Underground - Utah - Periodicals. I. United States. Geological Survey. II. Title. III. Title: Ground water conditions in Utah. IV. Series.
NYPL [JSP 81-11]

The Escalante River Basin multiobjective resource planning /. [Salt Lake City] [1978] xi, 127 p. : LC Card 79-624078 DDC 333.91/02/0979251 19
TC424.U8 E72

Specific problem analysis summary report : 1975 national assessment of water and related land resources, Great Basin Region / prepared by Utah Division of Water Resources, Nevada Division of Water Resources for U. S. Water Resources Council. [Salt Lake City] : Utah Division of Water Resources, 1977. 87 p., [1] leaf of plates : ill. ; 29 cm. (Technical memorandum - Utah Division of Water Resources ; no. 4) Cover title: 1975 water assessment, Great Basin Region. LC Card 80-620890 DDC 333.9/1/09792 19
1. Water resources development - Great Basin. 2. Land use - Great Basin. 3. Irrigation - Great Basin. I. Nevada. Division of Water Resources. II. United States.

Water Resources Council. III. Title. IV. Title: 1975
water assessment, Great Basin Region. V. Series: Utah.
Division of Water Resources. Technical memorandum -
Utah Division of Water Resources , no. 4.
TC423.6 .U82 1977

Technical memorandum - Utah Division of Water Resources .
(no. 4) Utah. Division of Water Resources. Specific problem analysis summary report . [Salt Lake City] , 1977. 87 p., [1] leaf of plates : LC Card 80-620890   DDC 333.9/1/09792 19
TC423.6 .U82 1977

Utah. Division of Water Rights. Bolke, E. L. Hydrologic reconnaissance of the Fish Springs Flat area, Tooele, Juab, and Millard counties, Utah /. [Salt Lake City] , 1978. iv, 30 p. : LC Card 79-621928 DDC 553/.09792 s 553.7/9/097924 19
TA7 .U77 no. 64 GB705.U8

Utah. Division of Wildlife Resources. Publication .
(no. 79-11) Zwank, Phillip J., 1944- Reduced recruitment in Utah mule deer relative to winter condition /. [Salt Lake City] [1979] ix, 80 p. : LC Card 80-621214 DDC 333.95/5 s 599.73/57 19
SK453 .A25 no. 79-11 QL737.U55

UTAH - ECONOMIC POLICY.
Utah. Office of the Utah State Planning Coordinator. Utah:2000 . Salt Lake City, Utah , 1980. iii, 65 leaves : LC Card 80-622474 DDC 338.5/443/09792 19
HC107.U8 U55 1980

Utah. Employment Security, Dept. of. see Utah. Dept. of Employment Security.

Utah employment, wages, and reporting units by firm size, 1979. Utah. Dept. of Employment Security. Reports and Analysis Section. Salt Lake City, Utah [1979] iii, 51 p. ; LC Card 80-621434 DDC 331.12/5/09792 19
HD5725.U8 U82 1979a

UTAH - GENEALOGY.
Utah. State Archives. Veterans with Federal service buried in the State of Utah, Territorial period to 1965. [Salt Lake City] , 1965- v. ; LC Card 80-53986 DDC 929/.3792 19
F825 .U85 1965

UTAH - GENEALOGY - BIBLIOGRAPHY - CATALOGS.
Utah. State Archives and Records Service. Guide to official records of genealogical value in the State of Utah. [Salt Lake City] , 1980. 23 p., [1] leaf of plates : LC Card 80-622068 DDC 025.17/1/09792 19
Z1341 .U68 1980 F825

Utah. Geological and Mineral Survey. Dustin, Jacob D. Hydrogeology of Utah Lake with emphasis on Goshen Bay /. [Salt Lake City, Utah] [1980] ii, 50 p. : LC Card 80-623593 DDC 553.7/09792 s 553.7/9/0979224 19
TD224.U8 A3 no. 23 GB1025.U8

Utah. Health Statistics, Bureau of. see Utah. Bureau of Health Statistics.

UTAH - HISTORY.
Stegner, Wallace Earle, 1909- Mormon country /. Lincoln , 1981, c1970. p. cm. ISBN 0-8032-4129-1 LC Card 81-3410 DDC 979.2 19
F826 .S75 1981

UTAH. INSURANCE DEPT. - AUDITING AND INSPECTION.
Utah. Office of the Legislative Auditor General. A performance audit of the State Department of Insurance /. [Salt Lake City] [1980] iii, 42 p. : LC Card 80-622523 DDC 353.97920082/55 19
HG8538.U8 U85 1980

UTAH. LAW ENFORCEMENT PLANNING AGENCY - APPROPRIATIONS AND EXPENDITURES.
Utah. Council on Criminal Justice Administration. Safe streets, 1968-1980 . Salt Lake City, Utah [1980] 13 leaves ; LC Card 80-623598 DDC 364/.9792 19
HV7294 .A6 1980

UTAH. MOTOR VEHICLE BUSINESS ADMINISTRATION - AUDITING AND INSPECTION.
Utah. Office of the Legislative Auditor General. A performance audit of the Motor Vehicle

Business Administration /. [Salt Lake City] [1980] 48, 13 p. ; LC Card 80-621605 DDC 353.97920087/834 19
HD9710.U53 U88 1980

Utah. Office of Legislative Research.
Digest of legislation as enacted by the budget session of the 43rd Legislature, convened January 14, 1980, adjourned February 2, 1980 / prepared by the Office of Legislative Research. [Salt Lake City] : The Office, 1980. v, 29 leaves ; 22 x 28 cm. (Research report - Office of Legislative Research, State of Utah . no. 33) Includes indexes. LC Card 80-622627 DDC 348.792/026 347.920826 19
1. Legislation - Utah. I. Series: Utah. Office of Legislative Research. Research report - Office of Legislative Research, State of Utah , no. 33. II. Title.
KFU15.2 1980

Research report - Office of Legislative Research, State of Utah .
(no. 33) Utah. Office of Legislative Research. Digest of legislation as enacted by the budget session of the 43rd Legislature, convened January 14, 1980, adjourned February 2, 1980 /. [Salt Lake City] , 1980. v, 29 leaves ; LC Card 80-622627 DDC 348.792/026 347.920826 19
KFU15.2 1980

Utah. Office of the Legislative Auditor General.
A performance audit of electronic repair dealer registration in Utah : audit / performed by audit manager Roy Dunn, auditor in charge, Sumner Newman. [Salt Lake City] : Office of Legislative Auditor General, State of Utah, [1979] ii, 14, 3 leaves ; 28 cm. (Report to Utah State Legislature . no. 79-14) "October 1979." LC Card 79-626149 DDC 353.97920082/42 19
1. Consumer protection - Utah - Auditing and inspection. 2. Electronic apparatus and appliances - Maintenance and repair. 3. Trade regulation - Utah - Auditing and inspection. I. Dunn, Roy. II. Newman, Sumner. III. Title. IV. Series.
HC107.U83 C637 1979

A performance audit of mental health programs funded by the State of Utah. [Salt Lake City] : Legislative Auditor General, State of Utah, 1976. 177 p. : ill. ; 28 cm. (Report to Utah State Legislature . no. 76-7A) Includes bibliographical references. LC Card 77-621216 DDC 353.97920084/2045 19
1. Mental health services - Utah - Auditing and inspection. 2. Mental health services - Utah - Finance. I. Title. II. Series.
RA790.65.U8 U86 1976

A performance audit of the Division of Fine Arts / audit performed by audit manager, Wayne Welsh ... [et al.]. [Salt Lake City] : Office of Legislative Auditor General, State of Utah, 1980. 39, 8 p. ; 28 cm. (Report to Utah State Legislature . no. 80-5) LC Card 80-621609 DDC 353.97920085/4 19
1. Utah. Division of Fine Arts. I. Welsh, Wayne. II. Title. III. Series.
NX24.U8 U7938 1980

A performance audit of the Division of Purchasing in the Department of Finance / audit performed by Wayne Welsh ... [et al.]. [Salt Lake City] (412 State Capitol, Salt Lake City, 84114) : Office of Legislative Auditor General, State of Utah, [1980] ii, 62, 4 p. ; 28 cm. (Report to Utah State Legislature . no. 80-10) "June 1980." LC Card 80-623434 DDC 353.97920071/2 19
1. Utah. Division of Purchasing - Auditing and inspection. I. Welsh, Wayne. II. Title. III. Series.
JK8488.A1 U86 1980

A performance audit of the Motor Vehicle Business Administration / audit performed by audit manager, Wayne Welsh, audit senior, Susan Elmer, audit staff, Kirk Anderson. [Salt Lake City] : Office of Legislative Auditor General, State of Utah, [1980] 48, 13 p. ; 28 cm. (Report to Utah State Legislature . report no. 80-1) "January 1980." LC Card 80-621605 DDC 353.97920087/834 19
1. Utah. Motor Vehicle Business Administration - Auditing and inspection. I. Welsh, Wayne. II. Elmer, Susan. III. Anderson, Kirk. IV. Title. V. Series.
HD9710.U53 U88 1980

A performance audit of the State Department of Insurance / audit performed by audit manager, Roy Dunn, audit supervisor, Bruce R. Peterson, audit staff, Byron Jorgenson, Kent

Mohlman, Scott Tingey. [Salt Lake City] : Office of Legislative Auditor General, State of Utah, [1980] iii, 42 p. : ill. ; 28 cm. (Report to Utah State Legislature . report no. 80-6) "April 1980." LC Card 80-622523 DDC 353.97920082/55 19
1. Utah. Insurance Dept. - Auditing and inspection. I. Dunn, Roy. II. Title. III. Series.
HG8538.U8 U85 1980

A performance audit of the Utah Schools for the Deaf and Blind / audit performed by audit manager Wayne Welsh, auditor in charge Byron Jorgenson, audit staff Summer Newman, Craig Monson. [Salt Lake City, Utah] : Office of Legislative Auditor General, State of Utah, 1979. iii, 41, 10 leaves ; 28 cm. (Report to Utah State Legislature ; report no. 79-11) LC Card 79-626146 DDC 371.91/1/09792 19
1. Utah Schools for the Deaf and the Blind - Evaluation. I. Welsh, Wayne. II. Series: Report to Utah State Legislature , no. 79-11. III. Title.
HV2561.U82 U857 1979

A program audit of equal employment opportunity in Utah State Government / audit performed by audit manager, Wayne L. Welsh, audit senior, Byron Jorgenson, audit staff, Sandra Dredge, Roger Bagley. [Salt Lake City] : Office of Legislative Auditor General, State of Utah, 1979. ii, 58 p. : graphs ; 29 cm. (Report to Utah State Legislature . no. 79-4) LC Card 79-624189 DDC 353.9792001/04 19
1. Afirmative action programs - Utah. 2. Civil service - Utah - Minority employment. 3. Discrimination in employment - Utah. I. Welsh, Wayne. II. Title. III. Series.
JK8460.A33 U82 1979

Welsh, Wayne. A performance audit of the WICHE student exchange program . [Salt Lake City] , 1978. iii, 45 leaves ; LC Card 78-622932 DDC 370.19/62 19
R847.6.U8 W44

Utah. Office of the Utah State Planning Coordinator. Utah:2000 : a high development scenario. Salt Lake City, Utah : State Planning Coordinator, Office of Governor Scott M. Matheson, 1980. iii, 65 leaves : ill. ; 28 cm. (Toward a Utah growth management strategy . 1) "Documents related to the development of policy and planning coordination": leaf 65. LC Card 80-622474 DDC 338.5/443/09792 19
1. Utah - Economic policy. 2. Economic forecasting - Utah. I. Title. II. Series.
HC107.U8 U55 1980

UTAH - PUBLIC LANDS.
United States. Congress. House. Committee on Interior and Insular Affairs. Subcommittee on Public Lands. The MX missile system . Washington , 1980. vii, 906 p. : LC Card 80-603306 DDC 358/.174/0973 19
KF27 .I544 1979a

Utah. Records and Statistics, Bureau of. see Utah. Bureau of Records and Statistics.

Utah school finance reference manual. Utah. State Board of Education. [Salt Lake City, Utah] , 1979. v leaves, 93 p., [1] leaf of plates : LC Card 80-621052 DDC 379.1/13/09792 19
LB2826.U8 U84 1979

UTAH SCHOOLS FOR THE DEAF AND THE BLIND - EVALUATION.
Utah. Office of the Legislative Auditor General. A performance audit of the Utah Schools for the Deaf and Blind /. [Salt Lake City, Utah] , 1979. iii, 41, 10 leaves ; LC Card 79-626146 DDC 371.91/1/09792 19
HV2561.U82 U857 1979

Utah. State Archives. Veterans with Federal service buried in the State of Utah, Territorial period to 1965. [Salt Lake City] : the Archives, 1965- v. ; 28 cm. LC Card 80-53986 DDC 929/.3792 19
1. Utah - Genealogy. 2. Registers of births, etc. - Utah. 3. United States - Armed Forces - Registers of dead. I. Title.
F825 .U85 1965

Utah. State Archives and Records Service. Guide to official records of genealogical value in the State of Utah. [Salt Lake City] : Dept. of Finance, Utah State Archives and Records Service, 1980. 23 p., [1] leaf of plates : diagr. ; 28 cm. Cover title. LC Card 80-622068 DDC 025.17/1/09792 19
1. Utah - Genealogy - Bibliography - Catalogs. 2. Utah.

State Archives and Records Service - Catalogs. I. Title.
Z1341 .U68 1980 F825

UTAH. STATE ARCHIVES AND RECORDS SERVICE - CATALOGS.
Utah. State Archives and Records Service. Guide to official records of genealogical value in the State of Utah. [Salt Lake City] , 1980. 23 p., [1] leaf of plates :   LC Card 80-622068   DDC 025.17/1/09792 19
Z1341 .U68 1980 F825

Utah. State Board of Education. Utah school finance reference manual. [Salt Lake City, Utah] : Utah State Board of Education, 1979. v leaves, 93 p., [1] leaf of plates : graphs ; 29 cm. LC Card 80-621052   DDC 379.1/13/09792 19
1. Education - Utah - Finance - Handbooks, manuals, etc. I. Title.
LB2826.U8 U84 1979

Utah. State Climatologists Office. Hubbard, Kenneth G. Tabulation and application of pan evaporation data for Utah through 1976 . Logan, Utah , 1979. vi, 76 p. :   LC Card 80-622271   DDC 551.57/2/09792 19
QC915.7.U5 H82

Utah. State Dept. of Agriculture. Hubbard, Kenneth G. Tabulation and application of pan evaporation data for Utah through 1976 . Logan, Utah , 1979. vi, 76 p. :   LC Card 80-622271   DDC 551.57/2/09792 19
QC915.7.U5 H82

Utah. State Dept. of Health. Bureau of Records and Statistics. see **Utah. Bureau of Records and Statistics.**

Utah. State Dept. of Health. Bureau of Vital Statistics. see **Utah. Bureau of Vital Statistics.**

Utah. State Dept. of Health. Division of Vital Statistics. see **Utah. Division of Vital Statistics.**

Utah. State Division of Health. Bureau of Health Statistics. see **Utah. Bureau of Health Statistics.**

Utah. State Division of Health. Bureau of Statistical Services. Utah. Bureau of Health Statistics. Annual report of Utah vital statistics. Salt Lake City.   *NYPL [SDG (Utah. Health Board. Utah vital statistics; report)]*

Utah. State Division of Health. Statistical Services, Bureau of. see **Utah. State Division of Health. Bureau of Statistical Services.**

Utah. State Planning Coordinator. see **Utah. Office of the Utah State Planning Coordinator.**

Utah. State University of Agriculture and Applied Science, Logan. Institute for Social Science Research on Natural Resources. Research monograph - Institute for Social Science Research on Natural Resources, Utah State University.
(no. 5) Andrews, Wade H. Social effects of changes in uses of Bear Lake, an interstate body of water /. Logan , 1975. x, 119 p. :   LC Card 77-623439   DDC 333.91/63/0979213 19
HD1695.B38 A52

Utah. State University of Agriculture and Applied Science, Logan. Utah Water Research Laboratory. see **Utah Water Research Laboratory.**

UTAH - STATISTICS, MEDICAL - PERIODICALS.
Utah. Bureau of Health Statistics. Annual report of Utah vital statistics. Salt Lake City.
NYPL [SDG (Utah. Health Board. Utah vital statistics; report)]

Utah. Bureau of Health Statistics. Utah vital statistics; annual report. Salt Lake City.
NYPL [JLM 80-984]

UTAH - STATISTICS, VITAL - PERIODICALS.
Utah. Bureau of Health Statistics. Annual report of Utah vital statistics. Salt Lake City.
NYPL [SDG (Utah. Health Board. Utah vital statistics; report)]

Utah. Bureau of Health Statistics. Utah vital statistics; annual report. Salt Lake City.
NYPL [JLM 80-984]

Utah. University. American West Center.
A Canadian-United States conference on American Indian curriculum development, May 1-3, 1978, Santa Fe, New Mexico. Salt Lake City , 1978. 417 p. ;   LC Card 79-624051   DDC 375/.970004/97 19
E76.6 .C36

Occasional papers--American West Center, University of Utah .
(no. 11) A Canadian-United States conference on American Indian curriculum development, May 1-3, 1978, Santa Fe, New Mexico. Salt Lake City , 1978. 417 p. ;   LC Card 79-624051   DDC 375/.970004/97 19
E76.6 .C36

Utah. University. Bureau of Economic and Business Research. (Old Catalog form: Utah. University. Business School. Economic and Business Research Bureau)
Travel Research Association. The 80's, its impact on travel and tourism marketing . Salt Lake City, Utah , c1977. xv, 221 p. :   LC Card 80-141505   DDC 380.1/459104 19
G154.9 .T72 1977

Utah. University. Economic and Business Research, Bureau of. see **Utah. University. Bureau of Economic and Business Research.**

Utah. University. School of Business. Bureau of Economic and Business Research. see **Utah. University. Bureau of Economic and Business Research.**

Utah vital statistics; annual report. Utah. Bureau of Health Statistics. Salt Lake City.
NYPL [JLM 80-984]

Utah. Vital Statistics, Bureau of. see **Utah. Bureau of Vital Statistics; Utah. Division of Vital Statistics.**

Utah Water Research Laboratory.
Bagley, Jay M. Feasibility study of establishing a water rights banking/brokering service in Utah /. Logan, Utah [1980] vii, 33 p. ;   LC Card 80-623594   DDC 363.6/1 19
HD1694.U8 B34

Estimation of water surface elevation probabilities and associated damages for the Great Salt Lake / by L. Douglas James ... [et al.]. Logan, Utah : Utah Water Research Laboratory, College of Engineering, Utah State University, 1979. xi, 182 p. : ill. ; 28 cm. (Water resources planning series ; UWRL/P-79/03) "Project no. B-153-UTAH. Contract no. 14-34-0001-8122." Bibliography: p. 109-113.   LC Card 80-621436   DDC 551.48/2/0979242 19
1. Great Salt Lake - Water level. I. James, Leonard Douglas, 1936- . II. Series: Water resources planning series , P-79/03. III. Title.
TC425.G72 U85 1979

Hubbard, Kenneth G. The Great Basin climate study for range fire management /. Logan , 1978. vi, 25 p. :   LC Card 80-620825   DDC 634.9/618/015516 19
SD421.37 .H8

Hubbard, Kenneth G. Tabulation and application of pan evaporation data for Utah through 1976 . Logan, Utah , 1979. vi, 76 p. :   LC Card 80-622271   DDC 551.57/2/09792 19
QC915.7.U5 H82

Integrating water resources and land use planning /. Logan , 1979. xii, 114 p. :   LC Card 79-624686   DDC 333.91/00973 19
HD1694.A5 I56

Larson, Dean T. Levels of analysis in comprehensive river basin planning /. Logan, Utah , 1979. ix, 110 p. :   LC Card 80-621123   DDC 333.91/02 19
TC425.C6 L37

Studies on viruses in water / Rex S. Spendlove ... [et al.]. Logan, Utah : Utah Water Research Laboratory, Utah State University, 1979. viii, 35 p. : ill. ; 28 cm. (Water quality series . UWRL/Q-79/02) Includes bibliographies.   LC Card 80-621126   DDC 628.3 19
1. Sanitary microbiology. 2. Viruses - Identification. 3. Fluorescent antibody technique. 4. Water - Purification. I. Spendlove, Rex S. II. Title. III. Series.
QR48 .U8 1979

Utah's 1977 drought /. Logan , 1978. viii, 49 p. :   LC Card 79-624684   DDC 363.3/492 19
QC929.D8 U72

Utah. Water Resources, Division of. see **Utah. Division of Water Resources.**

Utah:2000 . Utah. Office of the Utah State Planning Coordinator. Salt Lake City, Utah , 1980. iii, 65 leaves :   LC Card 80-622474   DDC 338.5/443/09792 19
HC107.U8 U55 1980

Utah's 1977 drought / by Trevor C. Hughes ... [et al.] ; data gathering and/or analysis by U. S. Bureau of Reclamation ... [et al.]. Logan : Utah Water Research Laboratory, College of Engineering, Utah State University, 1978. viii, 49 p. : ill. ; 28 cm. (Water resources planning series . UWRL/P-78/07) "In cooperation with Utah Division of Water Resources and Utah State University Extension Service." Bibliography: p. 49.   LC Card 79-624684   DDC 363.3/492 19
1. Droughts - Utah. I. Hughes, Trevor C. II. United States. Bureau of Reclamation. III. Utah Water Research Laboratory. IV. Series.
QC929.D8 U72

UTE INDIANS - LAND TRANSFERS.
United States. Congress. Senate. Select Committee on Indian Affairs. Conveyance of Federal land to the Ute Mountain Ute Tribe . Washington, D.C. , 1980. iii, 51 p. :   LC Card 80-602176   DDC 346.7304/3/08997 19
KF26.5 .I4 1980b

UTILITARIANISM.
The Limits of utilitarianism /. Minneapolis , 1981. p. cm.   ISBN 0-8166-1044-4 :   LC Card 81-14698   DDC 144/.6 19
B843 .L55

UTILITIES. see **PUBLIC UTILITIES.**

Utilities and energy conservation : prospects and problems : a report from a workshop / sponsored by the Subcommittee on Energy Development and Applications of the Committee on Science and Technology and the Subcommittee on Energy and Power of the Committee on Interstate and Foreign Commerce, U. S. House of Representatives, Ninety-sixth Congress, second session. Washington : U. S. G.P.O., 1980 [i.e. 1981] vii, 78 p. ; 24 cm. At head of title: Joint committee print. "Serial MMM." "December 1980." Item 1025-A   LC Card 81-601265   DDC 333.79 19
1. Electric utilities - United States - Rates. 2. Energy conservation - United States. I. United States. Congress. House. Committee on Science and Technology. Subcommittee on Energy Development and Applications. II. United States. Congress. House. Committee on Interstate and Foreign Commerce. Subcommittee on Energy and Power.
HD9685.U5 U87

Utility preparedness . United States. Congress. House. Committee on the District of Columbia. Ad Hoc Task Force on Utility Preparedness. Washington , 1980. v, 250 p. :   LC Card 80-603354   DDC 363.6/2 19
KF27 .D59 1979

Utility rules of the Georgia Public Service Commission, effective January 1, 1976 . Georgia. Public Service Commission. Atlanta, Ga. [1976?] 126 p. ;   LC Card 77-620988   DDC 343.758/09/02636 19
KFG285.A433 A2 1976

UTILIZATION OF DRUGS. see **DRUG UTILIZATION.**

UTILIZATION OF LAND. see **LAND USE.**

Utilization of short-stay hospitals by persons with heart disease and malignant neoplasms . Cardocki, Gloria J. Hyattsville, Md. [1981] p. cm.   ISBN 0-8406-0214-6   LC Card 80-28017   DDC 362.1/1/0973 s 362.1/9612/00973 19
RA407.3 .A349 no. 52 RA981.A2

UTILIZATION OF WASTE. see **WASTE PRODUCTS.**

UTILIZATION OF WASTE PRODUCTS. see **SALVAGE (WASTE, ETC.)**

Utilization patterns and financial characteristics of nursing homes in the United States, 1977 /. Bloom, Barbara, 1950- Hyattsville, Md. , 1981. p. cm.   ISBN 0-8406-0215-4   LC Card 80-606876   DDC 362.1/1/0973 s 362.1/6/0973 19
RA407.3 .A349 no. 53 RA997

Utter, Jack. Wild river management : the use allocation issue / by Jack Utter, Stephen F. McCool, William Gleason, School of Forestry, University of Montana. Bozeman, MT :

Montana Water Resources Research Center, Montana State University, [1980] xiii, 117 leaves : ill. ; 28 cm. (MWRRC report ; no. 103) "March 1980." "Final report. Project no. A-103-MONT." Bibliography: leaves 101-106. LC Card 80-623137 DDC 333.78/45 19
1. Water use - Montana. 2. Wild and scenic rivers - Montana. 3. Nature conservation - Montana. 4. Water-rights - Montana. I. McCool, Stephen F., joint author. II. Gleason, William, 1949- joint author. III. Montana. University, Missoula. School of Forestry. IV. Series: Montana University Joint Water Resources Research Center. Report , no. 103. V. Title.
TD224.M9 U88

UVALDE CO., TEX. - ANTIQUITIES.
Two sites in Uvalde County. [Austin, Tex.] [1979] vi, 15, vi, 19 p., : LC Card 80-622621 DDC 976.4/432 19
E78.T4 T89

Uyeno, Teruya. (joint author) Miller, Robert Rush, 1916- Allodontichthys hubbsi, a new species of Goodeid fish from southwestern Mexico /. Ann Arbor, Mich. , 1980. 13 p. : LC Card 80-622059 DDC 597/.53 19
QL638.G82 M54

VA debt collection . United States. Congress. Senate. Committee on Veterans' Affairs. Washington , 1979. iv, 252 p. : LC Card 80-601119 DDC 346.73/077 19
KF26 .V4 1979i

VA direct loans for residential solar energy systems . United States. Congress. House. Committee on Veterans' Affairs. Subcommittee on Housing. Washington , 1980. iii, 20 p. ; LC Card 80-603113 DDC 343.73/011 19
KF27 .V446 1980

VA Health-Care Personnel Act of 1980 . United States. Congress. Senate. Committee on Veterans' Affairs. Washington , 1980. v, 895 p. : LC Card 81-601756 DDC 343.73/0115/0262 347.3031150262 19
KF26 .V4 1980g

VA target system . United States. Congress. House. Committee on Veterans' Affairs. Subcommittee on Special Investigations. Washington , 1980 [i.e. 1981] iii, 36 p. ; LC Card 81-600822 DDC 362.1/1/0687 19
KF27 .V458 1980e

VACCINATION - COMPLICATIONS AND SEQUELAE - UNITED STATES.
United States. Congress. Office of Technology Assessment. A review of selected Federal vaccine and immunization policies . Washington , 1979. xvi, 208 p. : LC Card 79-600165 DDC 614.4/7/0973 19
RA638 .U48 1979

VACCINATION OF CHILDREN - LAW AND LEGISLATION - WASHINGTON (STATE)
Washington (State). Office of Community Health Services. Child Health Section. Washington State school immunization manual. Olympia, Wash. [1980] 146 p. : LC Card 80-622798 DDC 344.797/043 19
KFW357.9.I44 A836 1980

VACCINATION - UNITED STATES.
United States. Congress. Office of Technology Assessment. A review of selected Federal vaccine and immunization policies . Washington , 1979. xvi, 208 p. : LC Card 79-600165 DDC 614.4/7/0973 19
RA638 .U48 1979

VACCINES INDUSTRY - UNITED STATES.
United States. Congress. Office of Technology Assessment. A review of selected Federal vaccine and immunization policies . Washington , 1979. xvi, 208 p. : LC Card 79-600165 DDC 614.4/7/0973 19
RA638 .U48 1979

VACCINES - RESEARCH - UNITED STATES.
United States. Congress. Office of Technology Assessment. A review of selected Federal vaccine and immunization policies . Washington , 1979. xvi, 208 p. : LC Card 79-600165 DDC 614.4/7/0973 19
RA638 .U48 1979

Vadus, Joseph R. International status and utilization of undersea vehicles, 1976 / by Joseph R. Vadus. Rockville, Md. : U. S. Dept. of Commerce, National Oceanic and Atmospheric Administration ; Washington : for sale by the Supt. of Docs., U. S. Govt. Print.

Off., [1976] 29 p. : ill. ; 28 cm. "Prepared for Inter Ocean '76 Conference; June 15-19, 1976, Düsseldorf, Germany." Includes bibliographical references. LC Card 80-497559 DDC 387.2/7 19
1. Oceanographic submersibles. I. Interocean, 3rd, Düsseldorf, Ger., 1976. II. Title.
GC67 .V32

Vale, M. G. A. (Malcolm Graham Allan) War and chivalry : warfare and aristocratic culture in England, France, and Burgundy at the end of the Middle Ages / Malcolm Vale. Athens, Ga. : University of Georgia Press, 1981. p. cm. Bibliography: p. Includes index. ISBN 0-8203-0571-5 LC Card 81-3046 DDC 355/.00942 19
1. Military art and science - England - History. 2. Military art and science - France - History. 3. Military art and science - France - Burgundy - History. 4. Chivalry. 5. Great Britain - History, Military - Medieval period, 1066-1485. 6. France - History, Military - 1328-1589. 7. Burgundy (France) - History Military. I. Title.
U43.G7 V34 1981

Valentine, Page C. Upper Cretaceous subsurface stratigraphy and structure of coastal Georgia and South Carolina / by Page C. Valentine. Washington, D.C. : U. S. Govt. Print. Off., [1981] p. cm. (Geological Survey professional paper ; 1222) "A study based on 24 wells along transects from the southeast Georgia embayment northeastward to the Cape Fear Arch and offshore to the Outer Continental shelf." Bibliography: p. LC Card 80-607868 DDC 551.7/7/09757 19
1. Geology, Stratigraphic - Cretaceous. 2. Geology - Georgia. 3. Geology - South Carolina. 4. Coasts - Georgia. 5. Coasts - South Carolina. I. Series: United States. Geological Survey. Professional paper, 1222. II. Title.
QE688 .V35

VALÉRY, PAUL, 1871-1945 - ADDRESSES, ESSAYS, LECTURES.
Wellek, René. Four critics . Seattle , c1981. p. cm. ISBN 0-295-95800-6 LC Card 80-54429 DDC 801.95/0904 19
PN94 .W44

Validation of selection procedures for welfare specialists /. Nelson, David D. [St. Paul] , 1976. 46 p. ; LC Card 77-622755 DDC 361/.0076 19
HV98.M65 N44

Validation, verification, and testing for the individual programmer /. Branstad, Martha A. Washington, D.C. , 1980. iii, 22 p. ; LC Card 80-600005 DDC 602/.18 s 001.64/25 19
QC100 .U57 no. 500-56 QA76.6

Valiunas, Andrew. United States. International Trade Commission. Leather wearing apparel from Uruguay . Washington, D.C. , 1980. ii, 9, 47 p. ; LC Card 81-600775 DDC 382/.4568522/0973 19
HF2651.L45 U64 1980

Valk, Barbara G. HAPI thesaurus and name authority, 1975-1977 / Barbara G. Valk, compiler, assisted by Mary E. Greco, Maj-Britt V. Nilsson, Steven K. Phillips. Los Angeles : UCLA Latin American Center Publications, University of California, c1979. 113 p. ; 26 cm. "An adjunct to the UCLA Latin American Center Publications reference series." ISBN 0-87903-403-3 LC Card 79-620062 DDC 980/.005 19
1. Hispanic American periodicals index. 2. Subject headings - Latin America. 3. Names, Personal (Cataloging). I. HAPI, Hispanic American periodicals index. II. California. University. University at Los Angeles. Latin American Center. Reference series. III. Title.
Z1605.H162 V34 F1408

VALUATION OF LAND. see FARMS - VALUATION; REAL PROPERTY - VALUATION.

Value-added tax . Carlson, George N. [Washington, D.C.?] , 1980. 85 p. : LC Card 80-604142 DDC 351.72/47 19
HJ5715.E95 C37

The value-added tax . United States. General Accounting Office. Washington, D.C. , 1981. vii, 44 p. ; LC Card 81-601434 DDC 336.2/714/0973 19
HJ5715.U6 U63 1981

VALUE-ADDED TAX - EUROPEAN ECONOMIC COMMUNITY COUNTRIES.
Carlson, George N. Value-added tax .

[Washington, D.C.?] , 1980. 85 p. : LC Card 80-604142 DDC 351.72/47 19
HJ5715.E95 C37

VALUE-ADDED TAX - MEXICO - PERIODICALS.
Mexico. Laws, statutes, etc. Mexican income and commercial receipts tax laws. Chicago.
NYPL [JLL 80-229]

VALUE-ADDED TAX - UNITED STATES.
Carlson, George N. Value-added tax . [Washington, D.C.?] , 1980. 85 p. : LC Card 80-604142 DDC 351.72/47 19
HJ5715.E95 C37

United States. Congress. House. Committee on Ways and Means. Hearing announcement on the "Tax restructuring act of 1979", H.R. 5665 . Washington , 1979. iii, 44 p. ; LC Card 80-602685 DDC 343.7304 19
KF6275.5 .W245

United States. General Accounting Office. The value-added tax . Washington, D.C. , 1981. vii, 44 p. ; LC Card 81-601434 DDC 336.2/714/0973 19
HJ5715.U6 U63 1981

Vaman Rao. see Rao, Vaman.

Van Arsdall, Roy Neuman, 1924- (joint author) Gee, C. Kerry. U. S. fed-beef production costs, 1976-77, and industry structure /. Washington , 1979. i, 29 p. ; LC Card 79-602695 DDC 338.1 s 338.1/36213/0973 19
HD1751 .A91854 no. 424 SF203

Van Blokland, P. J. An investigation on the role of commercial banks in financing Florida agriculture / P. J. van Blokland. Gainesville : Food and Resource Economics Dept., College of Agriculture, Institute of Food and Agricultural Sciences, University of Florida, [1979] 19 leaves ; 28 cm. (Economic report ; 95) Bibliography: leaf 19. LC Card 80-622177 DDC 332.7/1/09759 19
1. Agricultural credit - Florida. 2. Banks and banking - Florida. I. Series: Economics report , 95. II. Title.
HG2051.U6 F68

VAN BUREN (ARK.) - BUILDINGS - CONSERVATION AND RESTORATION.
Guthrie, Susan. Main Street historic district, Van Buren, Arkansas . Washington, D.C. , 1980. 31 p. : LC Card 80-603967 DDC 363.6/9/0976735 19
F419.V36 G87

Van Buren (Ark.) Community Development Program. Guthrie, Susan. Main Street historic district, Van Buren, Arkansas . Washington, D.C. , 1980. 31 p. : LC Card 80-603967 DDC 363.6/9/0976735 19
F419.V36 G87

VAN BUREN COUNTY (MICH.) - MAPS.
United States. Soil Conservation Service. Van Buren County, Michigan /. Lincoln, Nebr. , 1971. 1 map ; LC Card 81-691400
G4113.V3 1971 .U5

Van de Vate, Dwight, 1929- Romantic love, a philosophical inquiry / Dwight Van de Vate, Jr. University Park [Pa.] : Pennsylvania State University Press, c1981. 150 p. ; 24 cm. Includes bibliographical references and index. ISBN 0-271-00288-3 : LC Card 81-47171 DDC 306.7 19
1. Love. I. Title.
BD436 .V36

Van Dusen, Michael H. (joint author) Gulick, Lewis. Economic support fund programs in the Middle East . Washington , 1979. vii, 79 p. ; LC Card 79-602515 DDC 338.91/73/0174927 19
HC498 .G84

Van Dyke, John B. West Virginia private proprietary schools : the role and scope / by John B. Van Dyke, Jr. Charleston, W. Va. : West Virginia Postsecondary Education Commission, [1978] 50 p. ; 28 cm. LC Card 79-124128 DDC 607/.11754 19
1. Trade schools - West Virginia. I. West Virginia. Postsecondary Education Commission. II. Title.
T74.W4 V36

Van Esterik, Penny. Cognition and design production in Ban Chiang painted pottery / by Penny Van Esterik. [Athens, Ohio] : Ohio University Center for International Studies, 1981. p. cm. (Papers in international studies.

Southeast Asia series . no. 58) Bibliography: p. ISBN 0-89680-078-4 LC Card 81-11172 DDC 738.3/7 19
1. Pottery - Thailand - Ban Chiang. 2. Decoration and ornament - Thailand - Ban Chiang. 3. Cognition and culture - Thailand - Ban Chiang. 4. Ban Chiang, Thailand - Antiquities. 5. Thailand - Antiquities. I. Title. II. Series.
NK4156.6.B36 V37

Van Gogh, Vincent. see Gogh, Vincent van, 1853-1890.

Van Herik, Judith. Freud on femininity and faith / Judith Van Herik. Berkeley : University of California Press, c1981. p. cm. Bibliography: p. Includes index. ISBN 0-520-04368-5 LC Card 81-3413 DDC 155.3/33/0924 19
1. Freud, Sigmund, 1856-1939. 2. Religion and psychoanalysis. 3. Femininity (Psychology). 4. Masculinity (Psychology). 5. Self-realization. 6. Renunciation (Philosophy). I. Title.
BF173.F85 V26

Van Houten, John. Occupational employment statistics, non-manufacturing industries, Alaska, 1978 / prepared by John O. Van Houten, Nancy Thornburgh, Kelly Wheeler. [Juneau] : State of Alaska, Dept. of Labor, Research and Analysis, 1979. 68 p. : ill. ; 22 x 28 cm. LC Card 80-620795 DDC 331.12/51/0009798 19
1. Labor supply - Alaska - Statistics. 2. Alaska - Occupations - Statistics. 3. Employment forecasting - Alaska - Statistics. I. Thornburgh, Nancy, joint author. II. Wheeler, Kelly, joint author. III. Alaska. Dept. of Labor. Research and Analysis Section. IV. Title.
HD5725.A4 V32

VAN POOLS - LAW AND LEGISLATION - NEBRASKA.
McCoy, Patrick T. Legal obstacles to car/vanpooling in Nebraska /. Lincoln, Neb. [1978] 14, 16 p. ; LC Card 80-623554 DDC 343.782/0982 347.8203982 19
KFN298 .M32

VAN POOLS - UNITED STATES - PLANNING.
United States. General Accounting Office. Increasing commuting by transit and ridesharing . Washington, D.C. [1980] v, 82 p. ; LC Card 80-603842 DDC 388.4/068 19
HE4451 .U54 1980

Van Rensburg, W. C. J. The future utilization of Texas lignites : a review / by W. C. J. van Rensburg. Austin, Tex. : Mining and Mineral Resources Research Institute, Bureau of Economic Geology, University of Texas at Austin, 1979. iv, 57 p. : ill. ; 28 cm. (Mineral resource circular . no. 63) Bibliography: p. 56-57. LC Card 80-621659 DDC 553.2/2/09764 19
1. Lignite - Texas. I. Texas. University at Austin. Mining and Mineral Resources Research Institute. II. Title. III. Series.
TP329 .V36

Van Rixport, Theresa C. Seminar on Industrial Pretreatment, Federal, State, and Local Government Perspectives and Industry's Interests, New Jersey Institute of Technology, 1979. Proceedings . [Trenton] [1980] vii, 73 p. ; LC Card 80-620966 DDC 628.1/683 19
TD896 .S45 1979

Van Staaveren, Elizabeth K. United States. Dept. of Labor. Library. Occupational safety and health . [Washington] , 1978 i.e. 1979. vii, 648 p. ; LC Card 79-603966
Z7914.S17 U54 1979 T55

Van Til, Ronald L. (joint author) Bedell, Douglas J. Irrigation in Michigan, 1977 /. [Lansing, Mich.] [1979] iii, 37 p. : LC Card 80-623184 DDC 333.91/3/09774 19
S616.U6 B42

Van Velson, Rodney C. The McConaughy rainbow : life history and a management plan for the North Platte River Valley / by Rodney C. Van Velson ; editor, Elizabeth Huff ; layout and design, Steve O'Hare. Lincoln, Nebraska : Nebraska Game and Parks Commission, 1978. 83 p. : ill. (some col.) ; 28 cm. (Nebraska technical series . no. 2) "A contribution of Federal Aid in Sport Fish Restoration Project F-4-R Nebraska." Bibliography: p. 48-49. LC Card 79-626007 DDC 639.3/755 19
1. Rainbow trout. 2. Fishery management - Nebraska. 3. Fishes - Nebraska - North Platte River. 4. Fishes - Nebraska - McConaughy, Lake. I. Huff, Elizabeth. II. Nebraska. Game and Parks Commission. III. Title. IV.

Series.
QL638.S2 V36

VANCOUVER, WASH. - BRIDGES.
United States. Congress. House. Committee on Public Works and Transportation. Subcommittee on Surface Transportation. Proposed third bridge crossing on the Columbia River between Vancouver, Washington, and Portland, Oregon . Washington , 1980. iii, 89 p. : LC Card 80-603449 DDC 388.1/32/0979549 19
KF27 .P8966 1980

VANDALISM - NEW JERSEY.
Report of the Assembly Judiciary, Law, Public Safety, and Defense Committee, Juvenile Justice Subcommittee, on juvenile violence, vandalism, and the juvenile justice system /. Trenton, N.J. [1980] ii, 30 p. ; LC Card 80-624394 DDC 364.3/6/09749 19
HV9105.N5 R46

VANDER MYDE, PAUL A.
United States. Congress. Senate. Committee on Commerce, Science, and Transportation. Nominations--assistant secretaries of commerce . Washington , 1981. iii, 4 p. ; LC Card 81-602035 DDC 353.82 19
KF26 .C69 1981h

Vanderleest, Henry W., 1941- International marketing bibliography / Henry W. Vanderleest ; edited by Sandra W. Marsh. Muncie, Ind. : College of Business, Bureau of Business Research, Ball State University, 1981. p. cm. LC Card 81-9963 DDC 016.6588/48 19
1. Export marketing - Bibliography. I. Marsh, Sandra W. II. Title.
Z7164.C8 V35 HF1009.5

Vanderlip, R. L. (joint author) Bark, Laurence Dean, 1926- Cloud seeding . Manhattan [1979] 24 p. : LC Card 80-621773 DDC 630/.2/516876 19
S600.7.R35 B37

Vandrovec, Eugene. (joint author) O'Leary, William. Family planning statistics, 1965 to 1973 . Washington , 1975. 74 p., [1] fold. leaf of plates ; LC Card 75-600039 DDC 363.9/6/091724 19
HQ766.7 .O43

Vanguard of expansion . Schubert, Frank N. Washington, D.C. [1980] xii, 160 p. : LC Card 80-144567 DDC 358/.22/0973 19
UG23 .S38

VanHulle, Frank D. Inventory and cataloging . [Juneau] , 1977. 118 p. : LC Card 78-102830 DDC 333.95/611/09798 19
QL628.A4 I58

Vanishing roadside America /. Anderson, Warren H. Tucson , c1981. p. cm. ISBN 0-8165-0746-5 : LC Card 81-11529 DDC 741.973 19
NC998.5.A1 A5

VanVooren, Allan R. Survey of fish species in Ohio waters of Lake Erie, July 1, 1973 to June 30, 1974 : performance report / prepared by Allan R. VanVooren, David H. Davies. [Columbus] : Ohio Dept. of Natural Resources, Division of Wildlife, 1974. 68 leaves : ill. ; 28 cm. On cover: Lake Erie fisheries investigations. "Dingell-Johnson project, F-35-R-12, Study II." Bibliography: leaf 68. LC Card 75-622209 DDC 597.092/9771/2 19
1. Fishes - Erie, Lake. 2. Fishes - Ohio. I. Davies, David H., joint author. II. Title.
QL625.5 .V36

VAPOR-PHASE CHROMATOGRAPHY. see GAS CHROMATOGRAPHY.

VARIATION (BIOLOGY)
(1981) King, James C., 1904- The biology of race /. Berkeley , c1981. p. cm. ISBN 0-520-04223-9 LC Card 81-1345 DDC 572 19
QH401 .K55 1981

Variety and distribution of occupations in Massachusetts . Meisner, Charlotte. Boston, MA. [1980] ii, 61 p. : LC Card 80-623644 DDC 331.12/5/09744 19
HB2615.M4 M44

Various medicaid proposals . United States. Congress. House. Committee on Interstate and Foreign Commerce. Subcommittee on Health and the Environment. Washington , 1980. iv, 205 p. : LC Card 80-603816 DDC 344.73/032104252 347.30432104252 19
KF27 .I5543 1980k

Various parks and Bureau of Land Management related legislation . United States. Congress. Senate. Committee on Energy and Natural Resources. Subcommittee on Parks, Recreation, and Renewable Resources. Washington , 1980. iii, 194 p. : LC Card 81-600804 DDC 346.7304/6783/0262 347.306467830262 19
KF26 .E5565 1980h

Världsbanken. see International Bank for Reconstruction and Development.

VARMA, MAHA DEVI, 1907- - CRITICISM AND INTERPRETATION.
Schomer, Karine. Mahadevi Varma and the chhayavad age of modern Hindi poetry /. Berkeley , 1981, c1982. p. cm. ISBN 0-520-04255-7 LC Card 81-13002 DDC 891/.4316 19
PK2098.V3 Z878 1982

Varney, Katy. Tennessee. General Assembly. Special Joint Committee Created Pursuant to House Joint Resolution No. 308. Sudy of the laws concerning annexation, 1980 . Nashville, Tenn. (Suite G-10, War Memorial Bldg., Nashville, Tenn. 37219) [1980] 105 p. : LC Card 80-624151 DDC 352/.006/09768 19
KFT431.9.A5 A25 1980

VASCULAR PLANTS. see BOTANY.

Vasquez, John A., 1945- The power of power politics : a critique / John A. Vasquez. New Brunswick, N.J. : Rutgers University Press, c1981. p. cm. Bibliography: p. Includes index. ISBN 0-8135-0919-X : LC Card 81-5849 DDC 327/.072 19
1. International relations - Research. 2. Balance of power - Research. I. Title.
JX1291 .V38

VAUGHN, HENRY, 1622-1695 - CRITICISM AND INTERPRETATION.
Seelig, Sharon Cadman. The shadow of eternity . Lexington, Ky , 1981. p. cm. ISBN 0-8131-1444-6 : LC Card 80-51018 DDC 821/.3/09 19
PR545.M4 S4

Vause, W. Gary. Labor arbitration in state and local government / [W. Gary Vause]. Tallahassee, Fla. : Center for Employment Relations and Law, College of Law, Florida State University, 1981. viii, 214 p. : forms ; 26 cm. (CERL monograph . no. 3) Includes bibliographical references. LC Card 81-622006 DDC 344.73/0189143 347.304189143 19
1. Arbitration, Industrial - United States. 2. State governments - Officials and employees. 3. Local officials and employees - United States. I. Florida State University. Center for Employment Relations and Law. II. Title. III. Series.
KF3450.P8 V38

Vaz, Edmund W. The professionalization of young hockey players / Edmund W. Vaz, with technical assistance from Wesley Clarke. Lincoln : University of Nebraska Press, c1982. p. cm. Bibliography: p. Includes index. ISBN 0-8032-4652-8 LC Card 81-12938 DDC 796.96/2 19
1. Hockey - Social aspects - Canada. 2. Violence in sports - Canada. 3. Hockey players - Canada - Attitudes. 4. Hockey - Rules. I. Clarke, Wesley. II. Title.
GV847 .V39

VD facts in the District of Columbia /. District of Columbia. Dept. of Human Resources. Research and Statistics Division. [Washington] , 1976. ii, 17 p. ; LC Card 78-620889 DDC 312/.3951/09753 19
RA644.V4 D57 1976

VD facts in the District of Columbia. District of Columbia. Dept. of Human Resources. Research and Statistics Division. [Washington] , 1977. iii leaves, [19] p. ; LC Card 79-624170 DDC 312/.3951/09753 19
RA644.V4 D57 1977

VEGETABLE KINGDOM. see BOTANY.

VEGETABLE TRADE - MEXICO.
Emerson, L. P. Bill. Preview of Mexico's vegetable production for export /. [Washington, D.C.] [1980] 74 p. : LC Card 80-603534 DDC 338.1/75/0972 19
HD9220.M42 E43

VEGETABLES - WOUNDS AND INJURIES.
Nishimoto, R. K. (Roy Katsuto), 1944- Effects

of Polado on several horticultural crops /.
Honolulu , 1981. p. cm.   LC Card 81-2796   DDC
633.6/14 19
SB608.V4 N57

**VEGETATION CLASSIFICATION - IDAHO -
BLACKFOOT RIVER WATERSHED.**
Pettinger, Lawrence R. Digital classification of
landsat data for vegetation and land cover
mapping in the Blackfoot River watershed,
southeastern Idaho . Washington , 1980. p. cm.
LC Card 80-606816   DDC 581.9/028 19
QK63 .P47

**VEGETATION MAPPING - REMOTE
SENSING - DATA PROCESSING.**
Pettinger, Lawrence R. Digital classification of
landsat data for vegetation and land cover
mapping in the Blackfoot River watershed,
southeastern Idaho . Washington , 1980. p. cm.
LC Card 80-606816   DDC 581.9/028 19
QK63 .P47

**Vegetation of the Yellow Water Triangle,
Montana** /. Jorgensen, Henry E. [Helena] ,
1979. vii, 57 p. :   LC Card 79-626265   DDC
581.5/2643/09786 19
QK171 .J67

**Vehicle emission inspection and maintenance
legislation and programs in California and
other states** /. Grow, William S. [Sacramento,
CA] [1980] ii, 54 leaves ;   LC Card 81-621486
DDC 343.794/0944 347.9403944 19
KFC614 .A25 1980a

Velapoldi, R. A.
A Fluorescence standard reference material,
quinine sulfate dihydrate / R. A. Velapoldi and
K. D. Mielenz. Washington, D.C. : U. S. Dept.
of Commerce, National Bureau of Standards :
for sale by the Supt. of Docs., U. S. Govt.
Print. Off., 1980. xvi, 122 p. : ill. ; 26 cm.
(Standard reference materials) NBS special publication ;
260-64 Includes bibliographical references.   LC Card
79-600119   DDC 602/.18 s 535/.35 19
*1. Fluorescence - Standards. 2. Quinine sulfate - Optical
properties - Standards. 3. Materials - Standards - United
States. I. Mielenz, K. D., joint author. II. Title. III.
Title: Standard reference material. IV. Series: United
States. National Bureau of Standards. Standard
reference materials.*
QC100 .U57 no. 260-64 QC477

National Measurement Laboratory (U. S.)
Standard reference materials . Washington,
D.C. , 1980. xiv, 99 p. :   LC Card 80-600091
DDC 602/.18 s 616.07/56 19
QC100 .U57 no. 260-69 RB46

**Veliger larvae of the European oyster, Ostrea
edulis Linné.** Waller, Thomas R. Functional
morphology and development of veliger larvae
of the European oyster, Ostrea edulis Linné /.
Washington , 1981. iii, 70 p. :   LC Card 80-23129
DDC 591 s 594/.11 19
QL1 .S54 no. 328 QL430.7.O9

Vella, Jane Kathryn, 1931- Learning to listen : a
guide to methods of adult nonformal education
/ Jane Kathryn Vella ; [cover graphics, Pepper
Peterson] Amherst, MA : Center for
International Education, University of
Massachusetts, c1979. vii, 58 p. : ill. ; 28 cm.
Bibliography: p. 58.   ISBN 0-932288-57-X (pbk.)   LC
Card 80-131689   DDC 374 19
*1. Adult education. 2. Nonformal education. 3.
Listening. I. Title.*
LC5219 .V44

**VELOCITY OF CHEMICAL REACTION. see
CHEMICAL REACTION, RATE OF.**

Veltman, Calvin J. The role of language
characteristics in the socioeconomic attainment
process of Hispanic origin men and women /
Calvin J. Veltman ; Department of Sociology,
The State University of New York at
Plattsburgh, and Rassemblement en études
urbaines, Université du Québec à Montréal.
[Washington, D.C.?] : The Center : For sale by
the Supt. of Docs., U. S. G.P.O., 1980. iv, 103
p. ; 28 cm. "Prepared for the National Center for
Education Statistics under contract OE-300-78-0503
with the U. S. Department of Education." Contract
report"--Cover. "June, 1980." NCES 81-103." S/N
065-000-00067-9 Bibliography: p. 102-103.   LC Card
81-601023   DDC 305.8/68073 19
*1. Hispanic Americaan - Economic conditions. 2.
Hispanic Americaans - Social conditions. I. United
States. Dept. of Education. II. State University of New
York College at Plattsburgh. Dept. of Sociology. III.*

Université du Québec à Montréal. Rassemblement en
études urbaines. IV. National Center for Educational
Statistics. V. Title.
E184.S75 V44

**VENEREAL DISEASES - IDAHO -
STATISTICS.**
Idaho. Bureau of Preventive Medicine. Selected
venereal disease statistics, Idaho, 1974. [Boise]
[1975] 19 leaves :   LC Card 75-622999   DDC
312.39/51/009796 19
RA644.V4 I3 1975

**VENEREAL DISEASES - WASHINGTON, D.C.
- STATISTICS.**
District of Columbia. Dept. of Human
Resources. Research and Statistics Division. VD
facts in the District of Columbia.
[Washington] , 1977. iii leaves, [19] p. ;   LC
Card 79-624170   DDC 312/.3951/09753 19
RA644.V4 D57 1977

**VENEREAL DISESASE - WASHINGTON, D.C.
- STATISTICS.**
District of Columbia. Dept. of Human
Resources. Research and Statistics Division. VD
facts in the District of Columbia /.
[Washington] , 1976. ii, 17 p. ;   LC Card
78-620889   DDC 312/.3951/09753 19
RA644.V4 D57 1976

Venezuela . United States. Bureau of International
Commerce. [Washington] , 1976. 154 p. ;   LC
Card 77-600918
HC237 .U52 1976   NYPL [JLF 81-312]

VENEZUELA - ECONOMIC CONDITIONS.
Childers, Victor Ernest, 1931- Human resources
development: Venezuela. Bloomington, 1974.
184 p.   LC Card 76-48532
NYPL [JLE 80-1683]

**VENEZUELA - ECONOMIC CONDITIONS -
1918-**
United States. Bureau of International
Commerce. Venezuela . [Washington] , 1976.
154 p. ;   LC Card 77-600918
HC237 .U52 1976   NYPL [JLF 81-312]

VENEZUELA - INDUSTRIES.
United States. Bureau of International
Commerce. Venezuela . [Washington] , 1976.
154 p. ;   LC Card 77-600918
HC237 .U52 1976   NYPL [JLF 81-312]

**VENEZUELA - INTELLECTUAL LIFE - CASE
STUDIES.**
El Intelectual y el estado, Venezuela-Chile /.
College Park, Md. , 1980. 69 p. ;   LC Card
80-54441   DDC 305.5/5 19
HM213 .I54

VENEZUELA - SOCIAL CONDITIONS.
Childers, Victor Ernest, 1931- Human resources
development: Venezuela. Bloomington, 1974.
184 p.   LC Card 76-48532
NYPL [JLE 80-1683]

Venini glass / organized by Venini International,
S.R.L., and the Smithsonian Institution
Traveling Exhibition Service. [Washington,
D.C.] : The Service, 1981. p. cm.   ISBN
0-86528-012-6   LC Card 81-14395   DDC
748.295/31 19
*1. Venini International - Exhibitions. 2. Glassware -
Italy - Venice - History - 20th century - Exhibitions. I.
Venini International. II. Smithsonian Institution.
Traveling Exhibition Service.*
NK5198.V38 A4 1981

Venini International.
Venini glass /. [Washington, D.C.] , 1981. p.
cm.   ISBN 0-86528-012-6   LC Card 81-14395
DDC 748.295/31 19
NK5198.V38 A4 1981

VENINI INTERNATIONAL - EXHIBITIONS.
Venini glass /. [Washington, D.C.] , 1981. p.
cm.   ISBN 0-86528-012-6   LC Card 81-14395
DDC 748.295/31 19
NK5198.V38 A4 1981

Venture capital and the New Orleans economy /.
Klaasen, Thomas A. [New Orleans] , 1980. 30
leaves ;   LC Card 80-622446   DDC 330 s
332/.04154 19
HC107.L8 L58 no. 34 HG3729.U5

Venture Capital Improvements Acts of 1980 .
United States. Congress. House. Committee on
Interstate and Foreign Commerce.
Subcommittee on Consumer Protection and
Finance. Washington , 1980. iii, 244 p. :   LC
Card 81-600877   DDC 346.73/0922 347.306922

19
KF27 .I554 1980e

**VENTURE CAPITAL - LAW AND
LEGISLATION - UNITED STATES.**
United States. Congress. House. Committee on
Interstate and Foreign Commerce.
Subcommittee on Consumer Protection and
Finance. Venture Capital Improvements Acts of
1980 . Washington , 1980. iii, 244 p. :   LC Card
81-600877   DDC 346.73/0922 347.306922 19
KF27 .I554 1980e

**VENTURE CAPITAL - LOUISIANA - NEW
ORLEANS METROPOLITAN AREA.**
Klaasen, Thomas A. Venture capital and the
New Orleans economy /. [New Orleans] ,
1980. 30 leaves ;   LC Card 80-622446   DDC 330 s
332/.04154 19
HC107.L8 L58 no. 34 HG3729.U5

VENTURE CAPITAL - UNITED STATES.
Barth, James R. Evaluating the impact of
securities regulation on venture capital markets
/. Washington, D.C. , 1980. iv, 38 p. :   LC Card
80-600036   DDC 602.18 s 332/.0414 19
QC100 .U556 no. 166 HG4963

Klaasen, Thomas A. Venture capital and the
New Orleans economy /. [New Orleans] ,
1980. 30 leaves ;   LC Card 80-622446   DDC 330 s
332/.04154 19
HC107.L8 L58 no. 34 HG3729.U5

VENTURES, JOINT. see JOINT VENTURES.

VENUE - UNITED STATES.
United States. Congress. Senate. Committee on
the Judiciary. Subcommittee on Improvements
in Judicial Machinery. Federal venue statutes .
Washington , 1981. iv, 176 p. ;   LC Card
81-602008   DDC 347.73/12 347.30712 19
KF26 .J855 1980d

Verburg, Kenneth. Michigan local property tax
primer / by Kenneth VerBurg. 4th ed. East
Lansing : Institute for Community
Development, Lifelong Education Programs,
Michigan State University, [1980] vi, 55 p. ; 27
cm. (Technical bulletin - The Institute for Community
Development, Michigan State University . B25) "July
1980."   LC Card 80-620026   DDC 361.6/09774 s
343.77405/4 361.6/09774 s 347.740354 19
*1. Property tax - Michigan. I. Series: Michigan. State
University, East Lansing. Institute for Community
Development and Services. Technical bulletin , B25. II.
Title.*
JK5801 .M48 no. B25 KFM4691.P7

Verell, Ruth Ann. (ed) United States. National
Science Foundation. Office of Experimental
Projects and Programs. College science
improvement programs. Washington, D. C
[1974] v, 191 p.   *NYPL [JSF 80-775]*

Verenigde Staten. see United States.

**VERGENNES, CHARLES GRAVIER, COMTE
DE, 1719-1787.**
Murphy, Orville Theodore. Charles Gravier,
comte de Vergennes . Albany [1981] p. cm.
ISBN 0-87395-482-3   LC Card 81-2281   DDC
327.2/092/ B 19
DC131.9.V3 M84

Verich, Thomas. (joint author) Brodsky, Louis
Daniel. William Faulkner's gifts of friendship .
[University] c1980. [60] p. :   LC Card 80-136569
DDC 813/.52 19
PS3511.A86 Z636

Vermeule, Cornelius Clarkson, 1925- Greek and
Roman sculpture in America / Cornelius C.
Vermeule. Berkeley, Calif. : University of
California Press, c1981. p. cm. Includes indexes.
ISBN 0-520-04324-3   LC Card 81-3057   DDC
733/.074/013 19
1. Sculpture, Classical - United States. I. Title.
NB86 .V47

Vermont.
Adult education report : Vermont plan,
1980-1982. Montpelier, Vt. : [State of Vermont,
1979] 82, 4 p. : ill. ; 28 cm. Cover title. "May
1979."   LC Card 80-621210   DDC 374/.9743 19
1. Adult education - Vermont - Planning. I. Title.
LC5252.V4 V47 1979

State of Vermont program and financial plan
for vocational rehabilitation agencies.
[Montpelier : State of Vermont, 1979] 56
leaves ; 28 cm.   LC Card 80-621209   DDC
353.97430083 19

1. Vocational rehabilitation - Vermont. I. Title.
HD7256.U6 V42 1979

Vermont. Agency of Environmental Conservation. Division of Planning. Vermont State comprehensive outdoor recreation plan : Vermont's future in recreation, eligibility period September 6, 1978-June 30, 1983 / prepared by Vermont Agency of Environmental Conservation, Division of Planning, for the Interagency Committee on Natural Resources. [Montpelier] : The Division, 1978. ca. 500 p. in various pagings, [17] fold. leaves of plates (8 fold. in pocket) : ill. ; 30 cm. Cover title: SCORP 1978.   LC Card 80-622420   DDC 790/.09743 19
1. Outdoor recreation - Vermont - Planning. I. Vermont. Interagency Committee on Natural Resources. II. Title. III. Title: SCORP 1978.
GV191.42.V5 V48 1978

Vermont. Agency of Transportation. Planning Division. Vermont travel information study : an evaluation of the statewide travel information program / prepared by Vermont Agency of Transportation, Planning Division, in cooperation with the Federal Highway Administration, U. S. Department of Transportation. [Montpelier] : The Division, 1978. v, 77 p. : ill., forms (5 in pocket, 1 fold.) ; 28 cm.   LC Card 78-623822   DDC 388.3/124 19
1. Tourist trade - Information services - Vermont. I. United States. Federal Highway Administration. II. Title.
G155.U6 V37 1978

Vermont Criminal Justice Training Council. Rules and regulations / Vermont Criminal Justice Training Council. [Montpelier?] : The Council, [1979?] 24 p. ; 23 x 11 cm. Cover title.   LC Card 80-623937   DDC 345.743/052 347.430552 19
1. Police training - Law and legislation - Vermont. 2. Criminal justice personnel, Training of - Law and legislation - Vermont. I. Title.
KFV435.8.S7 A32 1979

Vermont. Dept. of Education. 1978-1979 Vermont school enrollment : statistics and information / Department of Education. [Montpelier, Vt.] : The Dept., [1979?] [6], 27 p. ; 22 x 28 cm. Cover title.   LC Card 80-621761   DDC 371.2/19/743 19
1. School attendance - Vermont - Statistics. I. Title.
LC144.V4 V47 1979

Vermont. Dept. of Employment Security. (Old Catalog form: Vermont. Employment Security, Dept. of)
Burleson, Erica. The role of the coach in public service employment. [Montpelier, Vt.] 1973. ix, 43 p.   *NYPL [*XME-9294]*

Mattson, Robert E. Considerations in the selection of public service employers. [Montpelier, Vt.] 1973. xiii, 51 p.
                    *NYPL [*XME-9291]*

Mattson, Robert E. An evaluation of individualized and pool slot development for public service employment. [Montpelier, Vt.] 1973. xv, 32 p.   *NYPL [*XME-9289]*

Mattson, Robert E. Final upgrading report. [Montpelier, Vt.] 1973. xiv, 126 p.
                    *NYPL [*XME-9292]*

Stanfield, Robert E. The uses of paraprofessionals in the delivery of manpower and social services through public service employment. [Montpelier, Vt.] 1973. xiii, 64 p.
                    *NYPL [*XME-9293]*

Vermont. Dept. of Health. Division of Public Health Statistics. Physicians in Vermont, 1979. Burlington, Vt. : State of Vermont, Department of Health, Division of Public Health Statistics, [1980] iv, 45 p. : ill. ; 28 cm. Cover title: Vermont health manpower report. "Prepared by Steven Kappel under the direction of Mary Anne Freedman." "April 1980."   LC Card 80-623433   DDC 331.12/9161/09743 19
1. Physicians - Vermont - Statistics. 2. Osteopaths - Vermont - Statistics. I. Kappel, Steven. II. Freedman, Mary Anne. III. Vermont health manpower report. IV. Title.
RA410.8.V5 V47 1980

Vermont. Dept. of Health. Public Health Statistics, Division of. see Vermont. Dept. of Health. Division of Public Health Statistics.

Vermont. Dept. of Labor and Industry. Boiler and pressure vessel rules : adopted pursuant to 21 V.S.A. [paragraph symbol] 242. [Montpelier, Vt. : State of Vermont, Dept. of Labor and Industry, 1980] 28 leaves : ill. ; 28 cm. "January 1980."   LC Card 80-623908   DDC 363.1/89 19
1. Boilers - Standards - Vermont. 2. Pressure vessels - Standards - Vermont. I. Title.
TJ263.5 .V47 1980

Vermont. Dept. of Public Service. Burleson, Richard A. SWP versus PEP. [Montpelier, Vt.] 1973. xi, 77 p.   *NYPL [*XME-9290]*

Vermont. Electricians' Licensing Board. State of Vermont Electricians' Licensing Board rules. [Montpelier] : The Board, [1978?] 8 leaves ; 28 cm.   LC Card 80-623527   DDC 344.743/01762131924 19
1. Electricians - Licenses - Vermont. 2. Vermont. Electricians' Licensing Board - Rules and practice. I. Title.
KFV282.E4 A32 1980

VERMONT. ELECTRICIANS' LICENSING BOARD - RULES AND PRACTICE. Vermont. Electricians' Licensing Board. State of Vermont Electricians' Licensing Board rules. [Montpelier] [1978?] 8 leaves ;   LC Card 80-623527   DDC 344.743/01762131924 19
KFV282.E4 A32 1980

Vermont. Employment Security, Dept. of. see **Vermont. Dept. of Employment Security.**

Vermont. Governor's Commission on the Status of Women. Morse, Phoebe. Women and the law . [Montpelier, VT , 1979] 31 p. ;   LC Card 80-620943   DDC 342.743/0878 19
KFV91.W6 M67 1979

Vermont Governor's Conference for Better Libraries, 2d, Montpelier, Vt., 1979. Final report of the Second Vermont Governor's Conference for Better Libraries. Montpelier, Vt. : Vermont Dept. of Libraries, [1979?] 29 p., 30-77 leaves : ill. ; 28 cm.   LC Card 80-622314   DDC 027.0743 19
1. Libraries - Vermont. 2. Library science - Congresses.
Z732.V5 V633 1979

Vermont health manpower report. Vermont. Dept. of Health. Division of Public Health Statistics. Physicians in Vermont, 1979. Burlington, Vt. [1980] iv, 45 p. :   LC Card 80-623433   DDC 331.12/9161/09743 19
RA410.8.V5 V47 1980

Vermont. Interagency Committee on Natural Resources. Vermont. Agency of Environmental Conservation. Division of Planning. Vermont State comprehensive outdoor recreation plan . [Montpelier] , 1978. ca. 500 p. in various pagings, [17] fold. leaves of plates (8 fold. in pocket) :   LC Card 80-622420   DDC 790/.09743 19
GV191.42.V5 V48 1978

VERMONT - POPULATION - STATISTICS. Vermont. State Planning Office. The people book. Montpelier, Vt. , 1978. v, 70 p. :   LC Card 79-623073   DDC 312/.8/09743 19
HA673 .S72 1978

Vermont State comprehensive outdoor recreation plan . Vermont. Agency of Environmental Conservation. Division of Planning. [Montpelier] , 1978. ca. 500 p. in various pagings, [17] fold. leaves of plates (8 fold. in pocket) :   LC Card 80-622420   DDC 790/.09743 19
GV191.42.V5 V48 1978

Vermont. State Planning Office. Chittenden County, Vermont, land capability plan, 1972 / State Planning Office. Lanham, MD : USDA-SCS, 1980. 1 map ; on sheet 59 x 46 cm. Does not show land capability. Relief shown by hachures and spot heights.   LC Card 81-690127
1. Chittenden County, Vt. - Maps. I. United States. Soil Conservation Service. II. Title.
G3753.C5 1972 .V4

The people book. Montpelier, Vt. : Vermont State Planning Office, 1978. v, 70 p. : ill. ; 28 cm. Prepared by M. Slajchert. Chiefly tables. Bibliography: p. 68-70.   LC Card 79-623073   DDC 312/.8/09743 19
1. Vermont - Population - Statistics. 2. Population forecasting - Vermont. I. Slajchert, Margaret. II. Title.
HA673 .S72 1978

Vermont travel information study . Vermont. Agency of Transportation. Planning Division.

[Montpelier] , 1978. v, 77 p. :   LC Card 78-623822   DDC 388.3/124 19
G155.U6 V37 1978

Vermont. University. Robert Hull Fleming Museum. Hewitt, Karen. Educational toys in America, 1800 to the present /. Burlington, Vt. , c1979. 141 p. :   LC Card 80-131686   DDC 688.7/25 19
LB1029.T6 H48

Recent gifts and acquisitions, 1976-1980. Burlington : Robert Hull Fleming Museum, University of Vermont, [1980] 60 p. : ill. ; 21 x 22 cm. Includes bibliographical references.   LC Card 80-622800   DDC 708.143/17 19
1. Art - Vermont - Burlington - Catalogs. 2. Vermont. University. Robert Hull Fleming Museum - Catalogs. I. Title.
N525.7 .A66

VERMONT. UNIVERSITY. ROBERT HULL FLEMING MUSEUM - CATALOGS. Vermont. University. Robert Hull Fleming Museum. Recent gifts and acquisitions, 1976-1980. Burlington [1980] 60 p. :   LC Card 80-622800   DDC 708.143/17 19
N525.7 .A66

Vermont. University. Vermont Resources Research Center. Stinebring, Warren R. Endotoxin in waters of the State of Vermont /. [Montpelier] [1978?] iv leaves, 25 p. ;   LC Card 79-624701   DDC 363.7/394 19
QR48 .S74

VERNON, TEX. - TORNADO, 1979. United States. National Oceanic and Atmospheric Administration. Red River Valley tornadoes of April 10, 1979 . Rockville, Md. [1980] v, 60 p., [2] leaves of plates :   LC Card 80-601568   DDC 363.3/492 19
QC955.5.T4 U54 1980

VERS LIBRE. see FREE VERSE.

The vertebrate faunas of the Pliocene Ringold Formation, south-central Washington /. Gustafson, Eric Paul. Eugene, Or. , 1978. 62 p. :   LC Card 79-625683   DDC 574.979 s 566/.09797/51 19
QH1 .O7 no. 23 QE841

VERTEBRATES, FOSSIL. Gustafson, Eric Paul. The vertebrate faunas of the Pliocene Ringold Formation, south-central Washington /. Eugene, Or. , 1978. 62 p. :   LC Card 79-625683   DDC 574.979 s 566/.09797/51 19
QH1 .O7 no. 23 QE841

VERTEBRATES, FOSSIL - ADDRESSES, ESSAYS, LECTURES. Fossil vertebrates from the Bahamas . Washington , 1982. p. cm.   LC Card 81-13543   DDC 560 s 566/.097296 19
QE701 .S56 no. 48 QE841

VERTEBRATES - NORTH DAKOTA. Steinhaus, Virginia S. A list of vertebrates of northcentral North Dakota /. Grand Forks, N.D. [1979] 29 p. ;   LC Card 80-622454   DDC 596.09784 19
QL197 .S85

Steinhaus, Virginia S. A list of vertebrates of northwestern North Dakota /. Grand Forks, N.D. [1979] 28 p. ;   LC Card 80-622453   DDC 596.09784/7 19
QL197 .S86

Steinhaus, Virginia S. A list of vertebrates of southcentral North Dakota /. Grand Forks, N.D. [1979] 30 p. ;   LC Card 80-622452   DDC 596.09784 19
QL197 .S87

Steinhaus, Virginia S. A list of vertebrates of southeastern North Dakota /. Grand Forks, N.D. [1979] 29 p. :   LC Card 80-622451   DDC 596.09784 19
QL197 .S88

Vertical deformation, stress accumulation, and secondary faulting in the vicinity of the transverse ranges of southern California /. Rodgers, Donald A. Sacramento, Calif. , 1979. v, 74 p. :   LC Card 79-625539   DDC 557.94 s 551.8 19
TN24.C2 A3 no. 203 QE604

VERTICAL RISING AIRCRAFT. see VERTICALLY RISING AIRCRAFT.

VERTICAL TAKE-OFF AND LANDING AIRCRAFT. see **VERTICALLY RISING AIRCRAFT.**

VERTICALLY RISING AIRCRAFT.
Kohlman, David L., 1937- Introduction to V/STOL airplanes /. Ames , 1981. xii, 231 p. :
    ISBN 0-8138-0660-7   LC Card 81-3776   DDC 629.133/35 19
TL685 .K64

Vertrees, James G. Food and agriculture policy in the 1980s : major crops and milk / the Congress of the United States, Congressional Budget Office. [Washington, D.C.] : The Office : For sale by the Supt. of Docs., U. S. G.P.O., 1981. xvii, 52 p. : ill. ; 27 cm. (A CBO study) "March 1981"--Cover. S/N 052-070-05548-1 Item 1005-C Includes bibliographical references.   LC Card 81-601427   DDC 338.1/9/73 19
1. Agriculture and state - United States. 2. Agricultural price supports - United States. 3. Dairying - Economic aspects - United States. I. United States. Congressional Budget Office. II. Title. III. Series.
HD1761 .V45

Verzariu, Pompiliu. Countertrade practices in East Europe, the Soviet Union, and China : an introductory guide to business / by Pompiliu Verzariu. [Washington] : U. S. Dept. of Commerce, International Trade Administration, [1980] vi, 102 p. : ill. ; 24 cm. An expansion of the work by P. Verzariu, S. Bozek, and J. Matheson published in 1978 under title: East-West countertrade practices. Includes bibliographical references.   LC Card 80-602143   DDC 382/.3/0947 19
1. East-West trade (1945-). 2. Commercial policy. I. Title.
HF1411 .V444 1980

VESICULAR STOMATITIS - PREVENTION.
Rio de Janeiro. Pan American Foot and Mouth Disease Center. Manual de procedimientos para la prevención y erradicación de las enfermedades vesiculares de los animales /. Washington , 1975. 77 p. ;   LC Card 79-123539
SF793 .R55 1975

VESSELS (SHIPS) see **SHIPS.**

VESTIBULE SCHOOLS. see **EMPLOYEES, TRAINING OF.**

Vesy, Carl J. Energy self-sufficiency for the big island of Hawaii / Carl J. Vesy and Justus Muller. [Honolulu] : Hawaii Natural Energy Institute, 1977. 34 p. : ill. ; 28 cm. Includes bibliographical references.   LC Card 79-624185   DDC 333.79/09969 19
1. Energy policy - Hawaii. I. Muller, Justus, joint author. II. Hawaii Natural Energy Institute. III. Title.
HD9502.U53 H388

The veteran in New Jersey, 1978 . Seidel, Laurence H. Trenton, N.J. , 1979. 16, [7] leaves :   LC Card 80-620973   DDC 355.1/154/09749 19
UB358.N5 S4

Veteran senior citizen health care act of 1979 .
United States. Congress. Senate. Committee on Veterans' Affairs. Washington , 1980. iv, 348 p. :   LC Card 80-602454   DDC 343.73/0115/0262 19
KF26 .V4 1979n

Veterans' Administration health-care programs .
United States. Congress. Senate. Committee on Veterans' Affairs. Washington , 1980. iii, 220 p. :   LC Card 80-602487   DDC 355.1/154/09759 19
KF26 .V4 1979m

VETERANS' ADMINISTRATION MEDICAL CENTER AT MINNEAPOLIS.
United States. Congress. Senate. Committee on Veterans' Affairs. Minneapolis VA medical center construction proposal . Washington , 1980. iii, 459 p. :   LC Card 81-600637   DDC 355.1/156/09776579 19
KF26 .V4 1980e

Veterans Administration planning for medical automated data processing needs . United States. Congress. House. Committee on Government Operations. Subcommittee on Government Information and Individual Rights. Washington , 1980 [i.e. 1981] iv, 334 p. ;   LC Card 81-600933   DDC 353.0081/2 19
KF27 .G6628 1980c

Veterans' Administration 5-year medical construction plan for fiscal years 1980-84 .
United States. Congress. House. Committee on

Veterans' Affairs. Subcommittee on Medical Facilities and Benefits. Washington , 1980. iii, 54 p. :   LC Card 80-602752   DDC 362.11/0973 19
KF27 .V459 1980a

Veterans' Administration 5-year medical construction plan for fiscal years 1981-85 .
United States. Congress. House. Committee on Veterans' Affairs. Subcommittee on Medical Facilities and Benefits. Washington , 1981. iii, 29 p. ;   LC Card 81-601369   DDC 353.0086/2 19
KF27 .V459 1980d

VETERANS - CALIFORNIA - SAN FRANCISCO BAY REGION.
United States. Congress. House. Committee on Veterans' Affairs. Status of Vietnam veterans in the bay area . Washington , 1980. iii, 64 p. ;   LC Card 80-604108   DDC 355.1/15/097946 19
KF27 .V4 1980a

Veterans characteristics as related to employment activities . South Dakota. Dept. of Labor. Research and Statistics. Aberdeen , 1979. ii, 37 p. :   LC Card 79-623547
UB358.S8 S68 1979   *NYPL [*XME-9453]*

Veterans' disability compensation and survivors' benefits amendments of 1980 . United States. Congress. Senate. Committee on Veterans' Affairs. Washington , 1980, [i.e. 1981] iv, 601 p. :   LC Card 81-601405   DDC 343.73/0116 347.303116 19
KF26 .V4 1981h

VETERANS, DISABLED - LEGAL STATUS, LAWS, ETC. - UNITED STATES.
United States. Congress. House. Committee on Veterans' Affairs. 1981 legislative program of the Disabled American Veterans . Washington , 1981. iii, 27 p. ;   LC Card 81-601622   DDC 343.73/0115/0262 347.3031150262 19
KF27 .V4 1981b

United States. Congress. Senate. Committee on Veterans' Affairs. Veterans' disability compensation and survivors' benefits amendments of 1980 . Washington , 1980, [i.e. 1981] iv, 601 p. :   LC Card 81-601405   DDC 343.73/0116 347.303116 19
KF26 .V4 1981h

VETERANS, DISABLED - MEDICAL CARE - UNITED STATES.
United States. Congress. House. Committee on Veterans' Affairs. Subcommittee on Compensation, Pension, Insurance, and Memorial Affairs. Benefits and services for former prisoners of war . Washington , 1980. iii, 71 p. :   LC Card 80-603807   DDC 343.73/0115 347.303115 19
KF27 .V43 1980e

United States. Veterans Administration. Study of former prisoners of war . Washington , 1980. v, 181 p. ;   LC Card 80-602576   DDC 35.1/156/0973 19
UB369 .U57 1980

United States. Veterans Administration. Office of Planning and Program Evaluation. Study of former prisoners of war /. Washington, D.C. , 1980. iii, 181 p. ;   LC Card 80-602667   DDC 355.1/15 19
UB369 .U57 1980a

VETERANS, DISABLED - REHABILITATION - LAW AND LEGISLATION - UNITED STATES.
United States. Congress. Senate. Committee on Veterans' Affairs. Disabled Veterans Rehabilitation Act of 1980 . Washington , 1980. iv, 827 p. ;   LC Card 81-600875   DDC 343.73/0116 347.303116 19
KF26 .V4 1980c

VETERANS, DISABLED - UNITED STATES.
United States. Congress. House. Committee on Veterans' Affairs. Subcommittee on Compensation, Pension, Insurance, and Memorial Affairs. Review of compensation and DIC programs . Washington , 1980. iii, 93 p. ;   LC Card 80-603330   DDC 343.73/0112 19
KF27 .V43 1980a

VETERANS, DISABLED - VOCATIONAL REHABILITATION - TENNESSEE.
United States. Congress. House. Committee on Veterans' Affairs. Subcommittee on Education, Training, and Employment. Hearing on the rehabilitation, education, and training programs administered by the Veterans' Administration--Nashville, Tenn. . Washington ,

1981. iii, 181 p. ;   LC Card 81-601153   DDC 355.1/15/09768 19
KF27 .V436 1980a

VETERANS - DISEASES - UNITED STATES.
United States. Congress. House. Committee on Interstate and Foreign Commerce. Subcommittee on Oversight and Investigations. Involuntary exposure to agent orange and other toxic spraying . Washington , 1980. iv, 256 p. :   LC Card 80-602744   DDC 363.1/79 19
KF27 .I5547 1979r

United States. Congress. House. Committee on Veterans' Affairs. Subcommittee on Medical Facilities and Benefits. Oversight hearing to receive testimony on Agent Orange . Washington , 1980. iii, 121 p. ;   LC Card 80-602984   DDC 363.7/384 19
KF27 .V459 1980

VETERANS - DISEASES - UNITED STATES - STATISTICS.
Seiling, Virginia. Health characteristics of veterans and nonveterans . Washington, D.C. [1980] v, 75 p. :   LC Card 80-602055   DDC 362.1/9 19
RA408.M4 S44

United States. Veterans Administration. Office of the Controller. The most frequently occurring diagnoses in VA hospitals, 1971-1976 . Washington , 1977. viii, 75 p. :   LC Card 77-601849   DDC 362.1/0973 19
UB369 .U57 1977a

VETERANS - EDUCATION - TENNESSEE.
United States. Congress. House. Committee on Veterans' Affairs. Subcommittee on Education, Training, and Employment. Hearing on the rehabilitation, education, and training programs administered by the Veterans' Administration--Nashville, Tenn. . Washington , 1981. iii, 181 p. ;   LC Card 81-601153   DDC 355.1/15/09768 19
KF27 .V436 1980a

VETERANS - EDUCATION - UNITED STATES.
United States. Congress. House. Committee on Veterans' Affairs. Subcommittee on Education, Training, and Employment. Review of education, training, and employment programs administered by the Veterans' Administration . Washington , 1980. iv, 275 p. :   LC Card 80-602986   DDC 355.1/152/0973 19
KF27 .V436 1980

United States. Congress. Senate. Committee on Veterans' Affairs. Educational incentives and the all-volunteer force . Washington , 1980. iv, 195 p. :   LC Card 81-600866   DDC 343.73/011 347.30311 19
KF26 .V4 1980f

VETERANS - EMPLOYMENT - CALIFORNIA.
California. Legislature. Assembly. Select Committee on Veterans Affairs. Transcript of proceedings, hearing on veterans employment problems, California State Capitol, room 2117, Sacramento, California, October 21, 1980 /. Sacramento, CA (Box 90, State Capitol, Sacramento, 95814) [1980] ii, 139 p. ;   LC Card 81-621312   DDC 331.5/2/09794 19
KFC10.4 .V47 1980

VETERANS - EMPLOYMENT - ILLINOIS - STATISTICS - PERIODICALS.
Veterans in Illinois. 1977- [Chicago]   LC Card 79-643725   *NYPL [JLM 80-714]*

VETERANS - EMPLOYMENT - NEW JERSEY.
Seidel, Laurence H. The veteran in New Jersey, 1978 . Trenton, N.J. , 1979. 16, [7] leaves :   LC Card 80-620973   DDC 355.1/154/09749 19
UB358.N5 S4

Veterans employment problems. California. Legislature. Assembly. Select Committee on Veterans Affairs. Transcript of proceedings, hearing on veterans employment problems, California State Capitol, room 2117, Sacramento, California, October 21, 1980 /. Sacramento, CA (Box 90, State Capitol, Sacramento, 95814) [1980] ii, 139 p. ;   LC Card 81-621312   DDC 331.5/2/09794 19
KFC10.4 .V47 1980

VETERANS - EMPLOYMENT - SOUTH DAKOTA - STATISTICS.
South Dakota. Dept. of Labor. Research and

Statistics. Veterans characteristics as related to employment activities . Aberdeen , 1979. ii, 37 p. : LC Card 79-623547
UB358.S8 S68 1979 **NYPL [*XME-9453]**

VETERANS - EMPLOYMENT - UNITED STATES.
Northrup, James P. Old age, handicapped, and Vietnam-era antidiscrimination legislation /. Philadelphia , c1978. vii, 92 p. ; ISBN 0-89546-008-4 LC Card 78-70927 DDC 344.73/01133 347.3041133 19
KF3464 .N6 Suppl

United States. Congress. House. Committee on Veterans' Affairs. Subcommittee on Education, Training, and Employment. Oversight hearings on employment programs for veterans and veterans' preference in federal employment . Washington , 1981. iii, 221 p. : LC Card 81-601161 DDC 354.1/154/0973 19
KF27 .V436 1980b

United States. Congress. House. Committee on Veterans' Affairs. Subcommittee on Education, Training, and Employment. Review of education, training, and employment programs administered by the Veterans' Administration . Washington , 1980. iv, 275 p. ; LC Card 80-602986 DDC 355.1/152/0973 19
KF27 .V436 1980

Veterans in Illinois. 1977- [Chicago] Dept. of Labor, Bureau of Employment Security, Research & Analysis. illus. 28 cm. Annual. LC Card 79-643725
1. Veterans - Employment - Illinois - Statistics - Periodicals. I. Illinois. Bureau of Employment Security. Research and Analysis Division.
NYPL [JLM 80-714]

Veterans in New Mexico /. New Mexico. Employment Security Dept. Research and Statistics Section. Alburquerque, N.M. , 1978. 34 leaves : LC Card 79-626217 DDC 355.1/15/09789 19
UB358.N6 N42 1978

VETERANS - IOWA - STATISTICS.
Iowa. Dept. of Job Service. Research and Analysis Dept. Veterans report, fiscal year 1979, State of Iowa /. Des Moines, Iowa [1980] v, 100 p. : LC Card 80-621461 DDC 355.1/15/09777 19
UB358.I8 I59 1980

VETERANS - LEGAL STATUS, LAWS, ETC. - MAINE.
Maine. Legislature. Joint Standing Committee on Aging, Retirement, and Veterans. Report of the Joint Standing Committee on Aging, Retirement, and Veterans of the statutory review of the rules of the Bureau of Veterans' Services. [Augusta, Me.] [1980?] 27 leaves ; LC Card 80-623270 DDC 343.741/011 347.410311 19
KFM11.62 .A34 1980

VETERANS - LEGAL STATUS, LAWS, ETC. - UNITED STATES.
United States. Congress. House. Committee on Veterans' Affairs. The American Legion legislative goals . Washington , 1980. iii, 38 p. ; LC Card 81-601142 DDC 343.73/011 347.30311 19
KF27 .V4 1980b

United States. Congress. House. Committee on Veterans' Affairs. Legislative priorities of our national service organizations . Washington , 1981. iii, 97 ; LC Card 81-601764 DDC 343.73/011 347.30311 19
KF27 .V4 1981

United States. Congress. House. Committee on Veterans' Affairs. Legislative recommendations of the American Legion for fiscal year 1978 . Washington , 1977. iii, 26 p. ; LC Card 81-601481 DDC 343.73/011 347.30311 19
KF27 .V4 1977c

United States. Congress. House. Committee on Veterans' Affairs. Veterans organizations legislative recommendations . Washington , 1980. iii, 108 p. ; LC Card 80-602461 DDC 343.73/011 19
KF27 .V4 1980

United States. Congress. House. Committee on Veterans' Affairs. Subcommittee on Compensation, Pension, Insurance, and Memorial Affairs. Hearings on H.R. 4367 and H.R. 6688 . Washington , 1980. iv, 353 p. :

LC Card 80-603310 DDC 343.73/011 19
KF27 .V43 1980b

United States. Congress. House. Committee on Veterans' Affairs. Subcommittee on Compensation, Pension, Insurance, and Memorial Affairs. Life insurance programs for veterans and service persons . Washington , 1981. v, 314 p. : LC Card 81-601337 DDC 353.001/234 19
KF27 .V43 1980f

United States. Congress. House. Committee on Veterans' Affairs. Subcommittee on Special Investigations. Judicial review of veteran's claims . Washington , 1981. v, 371 p. ; LC Card 81-601404 DDC 343.73/011 347.30311 19
KF27 .V458 1980g

United States. Congress. House. Committee on Ways and Means. Subcommittee on Public Assistance and Unemployment Compensation. Unemployment compensation benefits to servicemen released for the good of the service . Washington , 1979. iii, 28 p. ; LC Card 80-600678 DDC 343.73/0116 19
KF27 .W3464 1979c

United States. Congress. Senate. Committee on Veterans' Affairs. Fy 80 legislative recommendations of veterans' organizations . Washington , 1980. iv, 387 p. : LC Card 80-603467 DDC 343.73/011 19
KF26 .V4 1980

United States. Congress. Senate. Committee on Veterans' Affairs. VA debt collection . Washington , 1979. iv, 252 p. : LC Card 80-601119 DDC 346.73/077 19
KF26 .V4 1979i

United States. Congress. Senate. Committee on Veterans' Affairs. Veteran senior citizen health care act of 1979 . Washington , 1980. iv, 348 p. : LC Card 80-602454 DDC 343.73/0115/0262 19
KF26 .V4 1979n

VETERANS - LOANS - ALASKA.
Alaska. Division of Legislative Audit. A review of Division of Veterans' Affairs, Department of Commerce and Economic Development, July 1, 1976-June 30, 1977. Juneau, Alaska [1978] 29 leaves ; LC Card 78-624010 DDC 353.97980081/2 19
UB358.A4 A29 1978

VETERANS - LOANS - CALIFORNIA.
California. Legislature. Senate. Committee on Governmental Organization. Transcript of proceedings . Sacramento, Calif. [1980] iiii, 154 p. ; LC Card 80-622919 DDC 355.1/15/09794 19
KFC10.3 .G6 1980

VETERANS - LOANS - UNITED STATES.
United States. Congress. House. Committee on Veterans' Affairs. Subcommittee on Housing. Hearings regarding the VA home loan program . Washington , 1980. iii, 54 p. ; LC Card 80-603111 DDC 353.0081/2 19
KF27 .V446 1980a

United States. Congress. House. Committee on Veterans' Affairs. Subcommittee on Housing. VA direct loans for residential solar energy systems . Washington , 1980. iii, 20 p. ; LC Card 80-603113 DDC 343.73/011 19
KF27 .V446 1980

United States. Congress. House. Committee on Veterans' Affairs. Subcommittee on Special Investigations. Small Business Administration loans to veterans . Washington , 1981. iii, 223 p. ; LC Card 81-600813 DDC 353.0082/048045 19
KF27 .V458 1980c

United States. Congress. Senate. Select Committee on Small Business. Small Business Administration's veterans' assistance programs . Washington , 1980. iii, 97 p. ; LC Card 80-603678 DDC 355.1/15 19
KF26.5 .S6 1980m

VETERANS - MEDICAL CARE - FLORIDA.
United States. Congress. House. Committee on Veterans' Affairs. Subcommittee on Medical Facilities and Benefits. Oversight of veterans' health care program in Florida . Washington , 1980. iii, 67 p. ; LC Card 80-603075 DDC 355.1/156/09759 19
KF27 .V459 1979b

United States. Congress. Senate. Committee on

Veterans' Affairs. Veterans' Administration health-care programs . Washington , 1980. iii, 220 p. : LC Card 80-602487 DDC 355.1/154/09759 19
KF26 .V4 1979m

VETERANS - MEDICAL CARE - LAW AND LEGISLATION - UNITED STATES.
United States. Congress. Senate. Committee on Governmental Affairs. Federal Interagency Medical Resources Sharing and Coordination Act of 1980 . Washington , 1980. iv, 324 p. : LC Card 80-604081 DDC 343.73/0115 347.303115 19
KF26 .G67 1980k

VETERANS - MEDICAL CARE - TENNESSEE.
United States. Congress. House. Committee on Veterans' Affairs. Subcommittee on Medical Facilities and Benefits. State delegation on Tennessee Veterans' Administration medical services . Washington , 1980. iii, 57 p. ; LC Card 80-603034 DDC 355.1/156/09768 19
KF27 .V459 1980b

VETERANS - MEDICAL CARE - UNITED STATES.
United States. Congress. House. Committee on Veterans' Affairs. Oversight on admission policies to VA medical care facilities . Washington, D.C. , 1980. vi, 373 p. : LC Card 80-601953 DDC 353.0081/2 19
KF27 .V4 1979f

United States. Congress. House. Committee on Veterans' Affairs. Subcommittee on Compensation, Pension, Insurance, and Memorial Affairs. Benefits and services for former prisoners of war . Washington , 1980. iii, 71 p. : LC Card 80-603807 DDC 343.73/0115 347.303115 19
KF27 .V43 1980e

United States. Congress. Senate. Committee on Veterans' Affairs. Oversight of VA pacemaker policy . Washington , 1980. iii, 190 p. : LC Card 80-604040 DDC 355.1/156/0973 19
KF26 .V4 1980b

United States. Congress. Senate. Committee on Veterans' Affairs. Veteran senior citizen health care act of 1979 . Washington , 1980. iv, 348 p. : LC Card 80-602454 DDC 343.73/0115/0262 19
KF26 .V4 1979n

VETERANS - MEDICAL CARE - UNITED STATES - DATA PROCESSING.
United States. Congress. House. Committee on Government Operations. Subcommittee on Government Information and Individual Rights. Veterans Administration planning for medical automated data processing needs . Washington , 1980 [i.e. 1981] iv, 334 p. ; LC Card 81-600933 DDC 353.0081/2 19
KF27 .G6628 1980c

United States. Congress. House. Committee on Veterans' Affairs. Subcommittee on Special Investigations. Computer systems for the Veterans' Administration and procurement practices . Washington , 1981. iv, 230 p. ; LC Card 81-601147 DDC 362.1/1/0687 19
KF27 .V458 1980d

VETERANS - MEDICAL CARE - UNITED STATES - STATISTICS.
Seiling, Virginia. Health characteristics of veterans and nonveterans . Washington, D.C. [1980] v, 75 p. : LC Card 80-602055 DDC 362.1/9 19
RA408.M4 S44

VETERANS - MEDICAL CARE - UNITED STATES - TRAVEL EXPENSE REIMBURSEMENT.
United States. Congress. House. Committee on Veterans' Affairs. Subcommittee on Special Investigations. VA beneficiary travel . Washington , 1980. iii, 37 p. ; LC Card 80-603717 DDC 355.1/156/0973 19
KF27 .V458 1980b

VETERANS - NEW MEXICO.
New Mexico. Employment Security Dept. Research and Statistics Section. Veterans in New Mexico /. Alburquerque, N.M. , 1978. 34 leaves ; LC Card 79-626217 DDC 355.1/15/09789 19
UB358.N6 N42 1978

Veterans organizations legislative recommendations . United States. Congress. House. Committee on Veterans' Affairs. Washington , 1980. iii, 108 p. ; LC Card 80-602461   DDC 343.73/011 19
KF27 .V4 1980

Veterans report, fiscal year 1979, State of Iowa /. Iowa. Dept. of Job Service. Research and Analysis Dept. Des Moines, Iowa [1980] v, 100 p. : LC Card 80-621461   DDC 355.1/15/09777 19
UB358.I8 I59 1980

VETERANS - UNITED STATES.
Louis Harris and Associates. Myths and realities . Washington , 1980. xlviii, 481 p. : LC Card 80-603127   DDC 355.1/15/0973 19
UB357 .L58 1980

United States. Congress. Senate. Committee on Veterans' Affairs. Vietnam veterans' readjustment . Washington , 1980. 2 v. (iv, 2082 p.) : LC Card 81-600647   DDC 355.1/15/0973 19
KF26 .V4 1980a

VETERANS - UNITED STATES - DATA PROCESSING.
United States. Congress. House. Committee on Veterans' Affairs. Subcommittee on Special Investigations. Target system . Washington , 1980. iii, 40 p. : LC Card 80-602467   DDC 353.0081/2 19
KF27 .V458 1980

VETERANS - UNITED STATES - STATISTICS.
West Virginia. Dept. of Employment Security. Labor and Economic Research. Special report on veterans. Charleston, 1978. 29 p. ;
NYPL [*ZT-1245]

VETERANS - WEST VIRGINIA - STATISTICS.
West Virginia. Dept. of Employment Security. Labor and Economic Research. Special report on veterans. Charleston, 1978. 29 p. ;
NYPL [*ZT-1245]

Veterans with Federal service buried in the State of Utah, Territorial period to 1965. Utah. State Archives. [Salt Lake City] , 1965- v. ; LC Card 80-53986   DDC 929/.3792 19
F825 .U85 1965

VETERINARIANS - CONNECTICUT - DIRECTORIES.
Connecticut. State Board of Veterinary Registration and Examination. Roster of registered veterinarians as of April 1, 1980. Hartford, Conn. [1980] [17] leaves ; LC Card 80-621971   DDC 636.089/025/746 19
SF611 .C66 1980

VETERINARIANS - LEGAL STATUS, LAWS, ETC. - ILLINOIS.
Illinois. Laws, statutes, etc. Veterinary medicine and surgery practice act /. Springfield, Ill. , 1961. 19 p. ; LC Card 81-461542   DDC 347.773/049/02632 347.73044902632 19
KFI1529.V48 A32 1961

VETERINARIANS - SALARIES, PENSIONS, ETC. - UNITED STATES.
United States. Congress. House. Committee on Armed Services. Subcommittee on Military Compensation. Special pay for military veterinary officers . Washington , 1980 [i.e. 1981] ii, 59 p. : LC Card 81-600607   DDC 331.2/81636089/0973 19
KF27 .A76392 1980

VETERINARIANS - SUPPLY & DISTRIBUTION - ARKANSAS - STATISTICS - PERIODICALS.
Arkansas health manpower statistis: veterinarians. 1978- Little Rock.
NYPL [JLM 80-1089]

VETERINARIANS - TEXAS - SUPPLY AND DEMAND - STATISTICS.
Texas. Bureau of State Health Planning & Resource Development. Division of Data Collection and Analysis. Texas health manpower report, veterinarians, 1978 /. Austin, Tex. [1979?] 124 p. ; LC Card 80-622856   DDC 331.12/91636089/09764 19
SF611 .T49 1979

VETERINARY DRUGS - PHYSIOLOGICAL EFFECT.
Boyd, Joseph H. New York State Racing and

Wagering Board drug medication study . [Albany] , 1976. 69 leaves ; LC Card 78-621360   DDC 636.1/089558 19
SF951 .B79

VETERINARY HYGIENE - LAW AND LEGISLATION - ILLINOIS.
Illinois. Laws, statutes, etc. [Bovine brucellosis control law.] Illinois Bovine brucellosis control law. [Springfield] 1951. 14 p. ; LC Card 81-452404   DDC 344.773/049/02632 19
KFI1569.B7 A32 1951

Veterinary medicine and surgery practice act /. Illinois. Laws, statutes. etc. Springfield, Ill. , 1961. 19 p. ; LC Card 81-461542   DDC 347.773/049/02632 347.73044902632 19
KFI1529.V48 A32 1961

VETERINARY MEDICINE - STUDY AND TEACHING - THE WEST.
Welsh, Wayne. A performance audit of the WICHE student exchange program . [Salt Lake City] , 1978. iii, 45 leaves ; LC Card 78-622932   DDC 370.19/62 19
R847.6.U8 W44

VETERINARY ONCOLOGY.
United States. Congress. House. Committee on Agriculture. Subcommittee on Department Investigations, Oversight, and Research. Animal Cancer Research Act . Washington , 1980. iv, 101 p. ; LC Card 80-604025   DDC 344.73/0436994 347.304436994 19
KF27 .A33265 1980c

VETERINARY PUBLIC HEALTH.
Rio de Janeiro. Pan American Foot and Mouth Disease Center. Manual de procedimientos para la prevención y erradicación de las enfermedades vesiculares de los animales /. Washington , 1975. 77 p. ; LC Card 79-123539
SF793 .R55 1975

VETERINARY PUBLIC HEATLH - HANDBOOKS, MANUALS, ETC.
Rio de Janeiro. Pan American Foot and Mouth Disease Center. Manual de procedimientos para la atención de un predio donde ocurre fiebre aftosa /. Washington , 1974. 45 p. ; LC Card 79-123524
SF793 .R55 1974

VETERINARY SURGERY.
Dougherty, R. W. (Robert Watson), 1904- Experimental surgery in farm animals /. Ames , 1981. p. cm. ISBN 0-8138-1540-1 LC Card 81-3693   DDC 636.089/79/0724 19
RD29 .D68

VETO - ILLINOIS.
Illinois. Governor, 1973- (Walker) Governor's special messages and veto messages to the 80th Illinois General Assembly, 1977 session /. [Springfield] 1978. 214 p. ; LC Card 79-622756   DDC 348.773/01 19
KFI1215.2 1977b

Veto messages and other messages to 80th Illinois General Assembly, 1977. Illinois. Governor, 1973- (Walker) Governor's special messages and veto messages to the 80th Illinois General Assembly, 1977 session /. [Springfield] 1978. 214 p. ; LC Card 79-622756   DDC 348.773/01 19
KFI1215.2 1977b

VETO - NEW JERSEY.
New Jersey. Governor, 1911-13 (Wilson) Vetoes of Woodrow Wilson, /. [Trenton ; 1912.] 35 l.   *NYPL [*ZT-1251]*

Vetoes of Woodrow Wilson, /. New Jersey. Governor, 1911-13 (Wilson) [Trenton ; 1912.] 35 l.   *NYPL [*ZT-1251]*

Viano, Emilio. Victim/witness services : a review of the model / prepared by Emilio C. Viano ; prepared for the U. S. Department of Justice, Law Enforcement Assistance Administration by the National Institute for Advanced Studies sub-contracted to Public Management and Research, inc. [Washington, D.C.] : The Administration, 1979. 69 p. ; 28 cm. "Contract no. J-LEAA-019-78." Bibliography: p. 39.
1. Victims of crimes - United States. 2. Victims of crimes - United States - Bibliography. I. United States. Law Enforcement Assistance Administration. II. National Institute for Advanced Studies (U. S.). III. Public Management and Research, inc. IV. Title.
HV6250.3.U5 V49   NYPL [JLF 81-398]

VIBRATION.
(1979) Snowdon, John C. Vibration isolation . Washington , 1979. ix, 119 p. : LC Card 79-600062
TA355 .S55

Vibration isolation . Snowdon, John C. Washington , 1979. ix, 119 p. : LC Card 79-600062
TA355 .S55

VICE-PRESIDENTS - UNITED STATES - BIOGRAPHY - ADDRESSES, ESSAYS, LECTURES.
United States. 96th Congress, 1st session, 1979. Memorial addresses and other tributes in the Congress of the United States on the life and contributions of Nelson A. Rockefeller /. Washington , 1979. xi, 279 p., [1] leaf of plates : LC Card 80-603613   DDC 973.925/092/4 B 19
E748.R673 U56 1979

Victim/witness services . Viano, Emilio. [Washington, D.C.] , 1979. 69 p. ;
HV6250.3.U5 V49   NYPL [JLF 81-398]

Victims . Paludan, Phillip S., 1938- Knoxville , c1981. p. cm. ISBN 0-87049-316-7 LC Card 81-2578   DDC 973.7/33 19
F262.M25 P34

Victims, authority, and terror . Kelly, George Armstrong, 1932- Chapel Hill , c1982. p. cm. ISBN 0-8078-1495-4 LC Card 81-10298   DDC 944.04 19
DC138 .K35

VICTIMS OF CRIME SURVEYS - UNITED STATES.
United States. Bureau of Justice Statistics. Intimate victims . Washington, D.C. [1980] v, 52, 4 p. : LC Card 80-601656   DDC 362.8/8 19
HV6250 .U52 1980

VICTIMS OF CRIMES - UNITED STATES.
Carrow, Deborah. Crime victim compensation /. [Washington, D.C.] [1980] i, 235 p. : LC Card 80-602243   DDC 362.8/8 19
HV6250.3.U5 C37

Viano, Emilio. Victim/witness services . [Washington, D.C.] , 1979. 69 p. ;
HV6250.3.U5 V49   NYPL [JLF 81-398]

VICTIMS OF CRIMES - UNITED STATES - BIBLIOGRAPHY.
Viano, Emilio. Victim/witness services . [Washington, D.C.] , 1979. 69 p. ;
HV6250.3.U5 V49   NYPL [JLF 81-398]

VICTIMS OF CRIMES - UNITED STATES - CONGRESSES.
Restitution and victims of crime . Arlington, Tex. [1977?] iv, 86 p. : LC Card 80-621838   DDC 364.6/8 19
HV6250.2 .R47

Victor, Frances Fuller, 1826-1902. Bancroft, Hubert Howe, 1832-1918. History of Nevada, 1540-1888 /. Reno, Nev. , 1981. p. cm. ISBN 0-87417-068-0 LC Card 81-13145   DDC 979.3/01 19
F841 .B2 1981

The Victorian experience, the poets / edited by Richard A. Levine. Athens : Ohio University Press, 1981. p. cm. Includes bibliographical references. CONTENTS. - Introduction / Richard A. Levine -- The persistence of Tennyson / Jerome H. Buckley -- Browning's irony / Clyde de L. Ryals -- Arthur Hugh Clough / Michael Timko -- Matthew Arnold / Miriam Allot -- The feminization of D.G. Rossetti / Barbara Charlesworth Gelpi -- Sifting and sorting Meredith's poetry / Wendell Harris -- Swinburne / Robert Peters -- Reading oneself into Hopkins / Wendell Stacy Johnson -- Thomas Hardy, poet / Paul Zietlow. ISBN 0-8214-0447-4 LC Card 81-4020   DDC 821/.8/09 19
1. English poetry - 19th century - History and criticism - Addresses, essays, lectures. I. Levine, Richard A.
PR593 .V48

Victoria's world . Texas. University at Austin. Humanities Research Center. [Austin] , c1980. [36] p. : ISBN 0-87959-008-4 (pbk.) LC Card 80-131516   DDC 779/.9941081 19
DA551 .T483 1980

VIDEO ART - EXHIBITIONS.
Long Beach, Calif. Museum of Art. California video, Long Beach Museum of Art, June 29-August 24, 1980. [Long Beach, Calif.] ,

c1980. [40] p. : LC Card 80-82817   DDC 700 19
PN1992.8.V5 L6 1980

Vien, Cao Van. The final collapse / Cao Van
Vien. Washington, D.C. : Center of Military
History, U. S. Army, 1981. p. cm. Includes
bibliographical references and index.   LC Card
81-607989   DDC 959.704/3 19
1. Vietnamese Conflict, 1961-1975. I. Title.
DS557.7 .V48

Viessman, Warren.
Assessing the nation's water resources : issues
and options : a report / prepared by the
Congressional Research Service of the Library
of Congress for the Committee on Environment
and Public Works, U. S. Senate. Washington :
U. S. G.P.O., 1980. [76] p. : ill. ; 24 cm. At
head of title: 96th Congress, 2d session. Committee
print. "Serial no. 96-19." "December 1980." Item 1045
Includes bibliographical references.   LC Card
81-600801   DDC 333.91/0028/7 19
1. Water-supply - United States. I. United States.
Congress. Senate. Committee on Environment and
Public Works. II. Library of Congress. Congressional
Research Service. III. Title.
TD223 .V53

United States. Library of Congress.
Congressional Research Service. State and
national water use trends to the year 2000 .
Washington , 1980. x, 297 p. : LC Card
80-602584   DDC 333.91/13/0973 19
TD223 .U53 1980a

VIETNAM - ADMINISTRATIVE AND
   POLITICAL DIVISIONS - MAPS.
United States. Central Intelligence Agency.
Office of Basic and Geographical Intelligence.
South Vietnam, provincial maps. [Washington] ,
1967. [52] leaves : LC Card 80-675252   DDC
912/.597
G2371.F7 U54 1967

VIETNAM - ARMED FORCES.
Hinh, Nguyen Duy. Vietnamization and the
cease-fire /. Washington, D.C. [1980] viii, 194
p. : LC Card 79-607982   DDC 959.704/3325 19
DS557.7 .H56

VIETNAM - BIBLIOGRAPHY - CATALOGS.
Library of Congress. Vietnamese holdings in the
Library of Congress . Washington , 1981. p.
cm.   ISBN 0-8444-0362-8   LC Card 81-2847   DDC
016.9597 19
Z3228.V5 L52 1981 DS556.3

VIETNAM CONFLICT, 1961-1975. see
   VIETNAMESE CONFLICT, 1961-1975.

VIETNAM - FOREIGN RELATIONS.
Pike, Douglas Eugene, 1924- Vietnam's foreign
relations, 1975-78 . Washington , 1979. vii, 21
p. ; LC Card 80-603974   DDC 327.597 19
DS559.912 P54

VIETNAM - FOREIGN RELATIONS -
   CAMBODIA.
United States. Congress. House. Committee on
Foreign Affairs. Subcommittee on Asian and
Pacific Affairs. 1979--tragedy in Indochina .
Washington , 1980. viii, 233 p.   LC Card
80-601996   DDC 959/.053 19
KF27 .F638 1979h

VIETNAM - HISTORY - TO 939.
Taylor, Keith Weller. The birth of Vietnam /.
Berkeley , c1982. p. cm.   ISBN 0-520-04428-2
   LC Card 81-11590   DDC 959.7/03 19
DS556.6 .T39 1982

VIETNAM - OFFICIALS AND EMPLOYEES -
   DIRECTORIES.
Directory of officials of the Socialist Republic
of Vietnam . Washington,. D.C. , 1980. xii, 204
p. ; LC Card 81-600559   DDC 354.597002 19
JQ821 .D48

VIETNAM - REGISTERS.
Directory of officials of the Socialist Republic
of Vietnam . Washington, D.C. , 1980. xii, 204
p. ; LC Card 81-600559   DDC 354.597002 19
JQ821 .D48

Vietnam veterans' readjustment . United States.
Congress. Senate. Committee on Veterans'
Affairs. Washington , 1980. 2 v. (iv, 2082 p.) :
   LC Card 81-600647   DDC 355.1/15/0973 19
KF26 .V4 1980a

VIETNAM WAR, 1961-1975. see
   VIETNAMESE CONFLICT, 1961-1975.

VIETNAMESE-CAMBODIAN CONFLICT,
   1977- see CAMBODIAN-VIETNAMESE

CONFLICT, 1977-

VIETNAMESE CONFLICT, 1961-1975.
Hinh, Nguyen Duy. Vietnamization and the
cease-fire /. Washington, D.C. [1980] viii, 194
p. : LC Card 79-607982   DDC 959.704/3325 19
DS557.7 .H56

Vien, Cao Van. The final collapse /.
Washington, D.C. , 1981. p. cm.   LC Card
81-607989   DDC 959.704/3 19
DS557.7 .V48

VIETNAMESE CONFLICT, 1961-1975 -
   AERIAL OPERATION, AMERICAN.
Buckingham, William A. Operation Ranch
Hand . Washington, D.C. , 1981. p. cm.   LC
Card 81-11244   DDC 959.704/348 19
DS559.8.C5 B82

VIETNAMESE CONFLICT, 1961-1975 -
   AERIAL OPERATIONS, AMERICAN.
Ballard, Jack S. The development and
employment of fixed-wing gunships, 1962-1972
/. Washington, D.C. , 1981. p. cm.   LC Card
80-25422   DDC 959.704/348 19
DS558.8 .B35

Futrell, Robert Frank. The advisory years in
Southeast Asia, to 1965 /. Washington, D.C. ,
1980. p. cm.   LC Card 80-24547   DDC
959.704/348 19
DS558.8 .F87

Gropman, Alan L., 1938- Airpower and the
airlift evacuation of Kham Duc /.
[Washington] , 1979. viii, 87 p. : LC Card
80-601630   DDC 959.704/348 19
DS558.8 .G76   **NYPL   [JFL 77-126 v. 5, monograph 7]**

McCarthy, James R. Linebacker II .
[Montgomery] Ala. , Washington , 1979. xvi,
208 p. : LC Card 79-603001
DS558.8 .M32

VIETNAMESE CONFLICT, 1961-1975 -
   CAMPAIGNS - LAOS.
Vongsavanh, Soutchay. RLG military operations
and activities in the Laotian panhandle /.
Washington, D.C. , 1981. p. cm.   LC Card
81-10934   DDC 959.704/34 19
DS557.8.L3 V66

VIETNAMESE CONFLICT, 1961-1975 -
   CHEMISTRY.
Buckingham, William A. Operation Ranch
Hand . Washington, D.C. , 1981. p. cm.   LC
Card 81-11244   DDC 959.704/348 19
DS559.8.C5 B82

United States. General Accounting Office. U. S.
ground troops in South Vietnam were in areas
sprayed with herbicide orange . [Washington,
D.C.] , 1979. 9, 12 p. : LC Card 79-604309
   DDC 363.1/79 19
DS559.8.C5 U54 1979

VIETNAMESE CONFLICT, 1961-1975 -
   FOREIGN PUBLIC OPINION,
   AMERICAN.
Louis Harris and Associates. Myths and
realities . Washington , 1980. xlviii, 481 p. :
   LC Card 80-603127   DDC 355.1/15/0973 19
UB357 .L58 1980

VIETNAMESE CONFLICT, 1961-1975 -
   MISSING IN ACTION.
United States. Congress. House. Committee on
Foreign Affairs. Subcommittee on Asian and
Pacific Affairs. POW/MIA's . Washington ,
1980. v, 49 p. ; LC Card 80-603653   DDC
959.704/37 19
KF27 .F638 1980a

VIETNAMESE CONFLICT, 1961-1975 -
   PRISONERS AND PRISONS.
United States. Congress. House. Committee on
Foreign Affairs. Subcommittee on Asian and
Pacific Affairs. POW/MIA's . Washington ,
1980. v, 49 p. ; LC Card 80-603653   DDC
959.704/37 19
KF27 .F638 1980a

VIETNAMESE CONFLICT, 1961-1975 -
   UNDERGROUND MOVEMENTS.
Scoville, Thomas W. Reorganizing for
pacification support /. Washington, D.C.
[1981] p. cm.   LC Card 81-10204   DDC
959.704/3373 19
DS558.2 .S27

VIETNAMESE CONFLICT, 1961-1975 -
   UNITED STATES.
Scoville, Thomas W. Reorganizing for

pacification support /. Washington, D.C.
[1981] p. cm.   LC Card 81-10204   DDC
959.704/3373 19
DS558.2 .S27

United States. Congress. House. Committee on
Veterans' Affairs. Status of Vietnam veterans in
the bay area . Washington , 1980. iii, 64 p. ;
   LC Card 80-604108   DDC 355.1/15/097946 19
KF27 .V4 1980a

United States. Congress. Senate. Committee on
Veterans' Affairs. Vietnam veterans'
readjustment . Washington , 1980. 2 v. (iv,
2082 p.) : LC Card 81-600647   DDC
355.1/15/0973 19
KF26 .V4 1980a

Vietnamese holdings in the Library of Congress .
Library of Congress. Washington , 1981. p. cm.
   ISBN 0-8444-0362-8   LC Card 81-2847   DDC
016.9597 19
Z3228.V5 L52 1981 DS556.3

VIETNAMESE WAR, 1961-1975. see
   VIETNAMESE CONFLICT, 1961-1975.

Vietnamization and the cease-fire /. Hinh,
Nguyen Duy. Washington, D.C. [1980] viii,
194 p. : LC Card 79-607982   DDC 959.704/3325
19
DS557.7 .H56

Vietnam's foreign relations, 1975-78 . Pike,
Douglas Eugene, 1924- Washington , 1979. vii,
21 p. ; LC Card 80-603974   DDC 327.597 19
DS559.912 P54

Viets, Victor F. Minnesota coal transport
evaluations / prepared by Victor F. Viets and
Herbert R. Schaal (Earth Sciences Associates).
St. Paul, Minn. : Minnesota Environmental
Quality Board, [1979] 126 p. in various
pagings : ill. ; 28 cm. "January 1979." Includes
bibliographical references.   LC Card 79-625704   DDC
380.5/24 19
1. Coal - Minnesota - Transportation. I. Schaal, Herbert
R., joint author. II. Earth Sciences Associates. III.
Minnesota. Environmental Quality Board. IV. Title.
HE2321.C6 V53

Viewpoints in teaching and learning .
(v. 56, no. 2 0160-8398) New concerns in
educational administration. Bloomington, Ind. ,
1980. iii, 117 p. : LC Card 80-128415   DDC
371.2/00973 19
LB2805 .N487

Viewpoints in teaching and learning, 0160-8398 .
(v. 56, no. 4) On teaching philosophy /.
Bloomington, Ind. , 1980. v. 93 p. ; LC Card
81-620733   DDC 371.1/02 19
LB41 .O576

(v. 57, no. 1) Comprehensive programming for
multiply handicapped children and youth /.
Bloomington, Ind. , 1981. v, 101 p. : LC Card
81-622010   DDC 371.9 19
LC4019 .C56

Vigdorchik, Michael E. Arctic Pleistocene history
and the development of submarine permafrost /
Michael E. Vigdorchik. Boulder, Colo. :
Westview Press, 1980. xviii, 286 p. : ill. ; 26
cm. (Westview special studies in earth sciences) Errata
slip inserted. "Published in cooperation with Institute of
Arctic and Alpine Research, University of Colorado,
Boulder, Colorado." Bibliography: p. 271-286.   ISBN
0-89158-658-X   LC Card 79-13561
1. Glacial epoch - Arctic regions. 2. Frozen ground -
Arctic regions. 3. Submarine topography - Arctic
regions. I. Colorado. University. Institute of Arctic and
Alpine Research. II. Title.
QE697 .V48   **NYPL   [JSF 80-1146]**

VIKING MARS PROGRAM.
Viking orbiter views of Mars /. Washington,
D.C. , 1980. vii, 182 p. : LC Card 80-600167
   DDC 356/.00634 19
QB641 .V55

Viking Orbiter Imaging Team. Viking orbiter
views of Mars /. Washington, D.C. , 1980. vii,
182 p. : LC Card 80-600167   DDC 356/.00634 19
QB641 .V55

Viking orbiter views of Mars / by the Viking
Orbiter Imaging Team, Cary R. Spitzer, editor.
Washington, D.C. : Scientific and Technical
Information Branch, National Aeronautics and
Space Administration : For sale by the Supt. of
Docs., U. S. G.P.O., 1980. vii, 182 p. : ill.
(some col.), maps ; 30 cm. (NASA SP. v 441) "For
stereo images, a collapsible viewer is included on the

inside back cover of this book"--P. vii. S/N
033-000-00795-7 Item 830-I Includes bibliographical
references. LC Card 80-600167 DDC 356/.00634 19
*1. Viking Mars Program. 2. Mars (Planet) -
Exploration. 3. Mars (Planet) - Photographs from space.
I. Spitzer, Cary R. II. United States. National
Aeronautics and Space Administration. Scientific and
Technical Information Branch. III. Viking Orbiter
Imaging Team.*
QB641 .V55

**VILLAGE INDUSTRIES. see COTTAGE
INDUSTRIES.**

Villarreal, Hilda, 1951- University of California,
Los Angeles. Chicano Studies Research Center.
Quien sabe? . Los Angeles, Calif. , 1981. p. cm.
    ISBN 0-89551-000-6 LC Card 81-10156 DDC
    016.973/046872 19
Z1361.M4 U55 1981 E184.M5

VILLAS. see ARCHITECTURE, DOMESTIC.

Vinar, Kenneth R. Soil survey of Washington and
Ramsey Counties, Minnesota / [by Kenneth R.
Vinar] ; United States Department of
Agriculture, Soil Conservation Service, in
cooperation with the Minnesota Agricultural
Experiment Station. [Washington] : The
Service, [1980] ix, 246 p., [56] fold. leaves of
plates : ill. ; 28 cm. Cover title. Bibliography: p. 148.
    LC Card 80-602943 DDC 631.4/7/77658 19
*1. Soils - Minnesota - Washington Co. - Maps. 2.
Soils - Minnesota - Ramsey Co. - Maps. I. United
States. Soil Conservation Service. II. Minnesota.
Agricultural Experiment Station, St. Anthony Park. III.
Title.*
S599.M52 V56

**The Vincent Thrust, Eastern San Gabriel
Mountains, California /.** Evans, James George,
1938- Washington , 1981. p. cm.   LC Card
    81-607914 DDC 557.3 s 551.8/7/0979493 19
QE75 .B9 no. 1507 QE606.5.U6

**Vincent van Gogh, the influences of nineteenth
century illustrations .** Werness, Hope B.
[Tallahassee, Fla. , 1980] 44 p. :   LC Card
    80-66125 DDC 760/.092/4 19
N6953.G63 A4 1980

Vines, Robert A., 1907- Trees of north Texas /
by Robert A. Vines. Austin : University of
Texas Press, c1981. p. cm. Includes index.   ISBN
0-292-78018-4 :   LC Card 81-1644 DDC
582.1609764 19
*1. Trees - Texas - Identification. I. Title. II. Title:
North Texas.*
QK484.T4 V53

Vinson-Trammell act repeal or revision . United
States. Congress. Senate. Committee on Armed
Services. Subcommittee on Procurement Policy
and Reprograming. Washington , 1980. iii, 171
p. ;   LC Card 80-603036 DDC 346.73/023 19
KF26 .A768 1980a

Vintage Nevada series.
Bancroft, Hubert Howe, 1832-1918. History of
Nevada, 1540-1888 /. Reno, Nev. , 1981. p.
cm. ISBN 0-87417-068-0 LC Card 81-13145
    DDC 979.3/01 19
F841 .B2 1981

VIOLENCE - ABSTRACTS.
Violence against women, causes and
prevention . Rockville, Md. (P.O. Box 2309,
Rockville 20852) , 1980. vii, 37 p. ;   LC Card
    80-603151 DDC 016.3628/8 19
HV6250.4.W65 V56 1980

Violence against women, causes and prevention :
a literature search and annotated bibliography /
prepared by Women's Education Resources,
University of Wisconsin--Extension ; Carolyn F.
Wilson, Kathryn F. Clarenbach, project
director.2nd ed. Rockville, Md. (P.O. Box 2309,
Rockville 20852) : National Clearinghouse on
Domestic Violence, 1980. vii, 37 p. ; 27 cm.
(Domestic violence monograph series . no. 3) Includes
bibliographical references. LC Card 80-603151 DDC
016.3628/8 19
*1. Women - Crimes against - Abstracts. 2. Violence -
Abstracts. I. Wilson, Carolyn F. II. Clarenbach, Kathryn
F. III. University of Wisconsin--Extension. Women's
Education Resources. IV. Series.*
HV6250.4.W65 V56 1980

VIOLENCE IN SPORTS - CANADA.
Vaz, Edmund W. The professionalization of
young hockey players /. Lincoln , c1982. p. cm.
    ISBN 0-8032-4652-8 LC Card 81-12938 DDC

*796.96/2 19
GV847 .V39*

**VIOLENCE IN THE HOME. see CONJUGAL
VIOLENCE.**

VIOLENCE - NEW JERSEY.
Report of the Assembly Judiciary, Law, Public
Safety, and Defense Committee, Juvenile
Justice Subcommittee, on juvenile violence,
vandalism, and the juvenile justice system /.
Trenton, N.J. [1980] ii, 30 p. ;   LC Card
    80-624394 DDC 364.3/6/09749 19
HV9105.N5 R46

VIOLENCE - PREDICTION.
Monahan, John, 1946- The clinical prediction
of violent behavior /. Rockville, Md. (5600
Fishers Lane, Rockville, Md. 20857) ,
Washington, D.C. , 1980 i.e.1981. xi, 134 p. :
    LC Card 81-601072 DDC 616.85/82 19
RC569.5.V55 M64

VIOLENCE RESEARCH - TEXAS.
Texas. Dept. of Mental Health and Mental
Retardation. The forensic psychiatric patient in
Texas . Austin, Tex. [1980] 367 p. in various
pagings ;   LC Card 80-622802 DDC 364.3/8/09764
19
HV6133 .T43 1980

VIOLENCE - UNITED STATES.
United States. Congress. Senate. Committee on
Governmental Affairs. Permanent Subcommittee
on Investigations. Organized crime and use of
violence . Washington , 1980- v. :   LC Card
    80-603084 DDC 364.1/06/073 19
KF26 .G674 1980a

**VIOLENT DEATHS - NEVADA -
STATISTICS.**
Nevada. Dept. of Transportation. Safety
Section. 1978 Nevada fatal traffic accident
report /. [Carson City?] [1979?] 34, 44 leaves,
[6] leaves of plates (1 fold.) :   LC Card
    80-623180 DDC 312/.274/09793 19
HE5614.3.N42 N47 1979

Viral pesticides : present knowledge and potential
effects on public and environmental health :
symposium proceedings / edited by Max D.
Summers and Clinton Y. Kawanishi. Research
Triangle Park, N.C. : Health Effects Research
Laboratory, Office of Health and Ecological
Effects, U. S. Environmental Protection
Agency, 1978. xix, 312 p. : ill. ; 28 cm.
"EPA-600/9-78-026." Symposium held at Myrtle Beach,
S.C. in 1977; sponsored by Health Effects Research
Laboratory. Includes bibliographical references. LC
Card 79-601644 DDC 632/.96 19
*1. Insect viruses - Congresses. 2. Insect viruses - Safety
measures - Congresses. 3. Insect control - Biological
control - Environmental aspects - Congresses. I.
Summers, Max. II. Kawanishi, Clinton Y. III. Health
Effects Research Laboratory.*
SB942 .V57

Virgilio, Keven. (joint author) Phillips, Glenn S.
Race relations in Oklahoma /. Oklahoma City,
Okla. , 1979. 81 p. ;   LC Card 80-621086 DDC
305.8/009766 19
F705.A1 P48

**VIRGIN ISLANDS OF THE UNITED
STATES - COMMERCE.**
United States. Federal Maritime Commission.
Office of Economic Analysis. Virgin Islands
trade study . Washington, D.C. [1979] ca. 500
p. in various pagings :   LC Card 80-601213 DDC
387/.0097297/22 19
HE796.3 .U54 1979

Virgin Islands trade study . United States.
Federal Maritime Commission. Office of
Economic Analysis. Washington, D.C. [1979]
ca. 500 p. in various pagings :   LC Card
    80-601213 DDC 387/.0097297/22 19
HE796.3 .U54 1979

Virginia. Agricultural Opportunities Commission.
Report of the Agricultural Opportunities
Commission to the Governor and the General
Assembly of Virginia. Richmond, Va. :
Commonwealth of Virginia, 1980. 151 p. : ill. ;
28 cm. (Senate document - Commonwealth of
Virginia . no. 15) LC Card 80-621793 DDC
300/.9755 s 338.1/09755 19
*1. Agriculture - Economic aspects - Virginia. I. Series:
Virginia. General Assembly, 1980. Senate. Document ,
no. 15.*
J87 .V9 1980b, no. 15 HD1775.V5

Virginia. Alcoholic Beverage Control Commission.
Regulations of the Virginia Alcoholic Beverage
Control Commission, in force and effect as of
January 15, 1980, including rules of practice
before hearing officers and the Commission.
[Richmond] : Commonwealth of Virginia, Dept.
of Alcoholic Beverage Control, [1980] 36 p. ;
23 cm. LC Card 80-622997 DDC 344.755/0541 19
*1. Liquor laws - Virginia. 2. Virginia. Alcoholic
Beverage Control Commission - Rules and practice. I.
Title.*
KFV2775.A439 A2 1980

**VIRGINIA. ALCOHOLIC BEVERAGE
CONTROL COMMISSION - RULES AND
PRACTICE.**
Virginia. Alcoholic Beverage Control
Commission. Regulations of the Virginia
Alcoholic Beverage Control Commission, in
force and effect as of January 15, 1980,
including rules of practice before hearing
officers and the Commission. [Richmond]
[1980] 36 p. ;   LC Card 80-622997 DDC
    344.755/0541 19
KFV2775.A439 A2 1980

**Virginia. Attorney General. see Virginia.
Attorney General's Office.**

Virginia. Attorney General's Office. (Old Catalog
form: Virginia. Law Dept.)
**Annual report of the Attorney General to the
Governor.** Virginia. Attorney General's
Office. Opinions of the Attorney General and
report to the Governor of Virginia.
Richmond.   *NYPL [XMZ (Virginia. Law
Dept. Annual report)]*

Index to the opinions of the Attorney General
of Virginia, included in the annual reports.
1967/77- [Richmond] 23 cm. Decennial. Earlier
years included in its Opinions of the Attorney General
of Virginia and report to the Governor of Virginia (see
that entry).
*1. Attorneys general's opinions - Virginia - Indexes. I.
Virginia. Attorney General's Office. Opinions of the
Attorney General and report to the Governor of
Virginia. (Indexes). II. Title.   NYPL [JLL 80-312]*

Opinions of the Attorney General and report to
the Governor of Virginia. Richmond. 23 cm.
Annual (slightly irregular). Report year varies. Title
varies: 1903-21, Annual report of the Attorney General
to the Governor ; 1921/22-1930/31, Report of the
Attorney General to the Governor. INDEXES: July 1,
1930-June 30, 1947. 1. v. - July 1, 1947-June 30, 1957,
with 1956/57. - July 1, 1957-June 30, 1967. 1 v. -
Later indexes cataloged separately as its Index to
opinions of the Attorney General of Virginia, included
in the annual reports (see that entry).
*1. Justice, Administration of - Virginia - Periodicals. 2.
Attorney general's opinions - Virginia. I. Virginia.
Attorney General's office. Annual report of
the Attorney General to the Governor. II. Virginia.
Attorney General's Office. Report of the Attorney
General to the Governor. III. Title.   NYPL [XMZ
(Virginia. Law Dept. Annual report)]*

**Opinions of the Attorney General and report
to the Governor of Virginia. (Indexes)**
Virginia. Attorney General's Office. Index to
the opinions of the Attorney General of
Virginia, included in the annual reports.
1967/77- [Richmond]   *NYPL [JLL 80-312]*

**Report of the Attorney General to the
Governor.** Virginia. Attorney General's
Office. Opinions of the Attorney General and
report to the Governor of Virginia.
Richmond.   *NYPL [XMZ (Virginia. Law
Dept. Annual report)]*

**Virginia. Banking Bureau. see Virginia. Bureau of
Banking.**

**Virginia. Banking Division. see Virginia. State
Corporation Commission. Banking Division.**

VIRGINIA - BIBLIOGRAPHY - CATALOGS.
McCombs, Dorothy F. The Appalachian region
of Virginia . Blacksburg, Va. , 1981. p. cm. LC
Card 81-11487 DDC 016.9755 19
Z1345 .M36 F226

Virginia. Board of Behavioral Science.
Regulations of the Boards . Richmond, Va. (2
South Ninth St., P.O. Box 1-X, Richmond, Va.
23202) [1977?] 36 p. ;   LC Card 80-623907
DDC 344.755/0176115 347.5504176115 19
KFV2726.5.P73 A3 1977

637

GOVERNMENT PUBLICATIONS - U.S.: 1981

Virginia. Dept. of Corrections. Bureau of Research, Reporting and

Virginia. Board of Funeral Directors and Embalmers. Rules, regulations, and by-laws and Chapter 10.2, Code of Virginia. [Richmond] : Virginia Board of Funeral Directors and Embalmers, [1979?] 24 p. ; 23 cm. LC Card 80-621938 DDC 344.755/045 347.550445 19

1. Undertakers and undertaking - Law and legislation - Virginia. I. Virginia. Laws, statutes, etc. Code of Virginia, 1950. Chapter 10.2. 1979.
KFV2682.U5 A32 1979a

Virginia. Bureau of Banking. (Old Catalog form: Virginia. Banking Bureau) Annual report. Richmond. 23 cm. "Showing the condition of banks, savings and loan associations, industrial loan associations, credit unions operating in Virginia." Issued by the Corporation Commission, 1904-08; by the Banking Division of the Corporation Commisssion, 1910-27; by the Bureau of Insurance and Banking, 1928-37. Title varies: 1904-20, Statements showing the condition of incorporated state banks operating in Virginia (other slight variations) Issues for 1904, 1908 include the statutes of Virginia regulating or affecting state banks. Superseded by: Virginia. Bureau of Financial Institutions. Annual report.
1. Banks and banking - Virginia - Periodicals. 2. Financial institutions - Virginia - Periodicals. I. Virginia. State Corporation Commission. II. Virginia. State Corporation Commission. Banking Division. III. Virginia. Bureau of Insurance and Banking. IV. Virginia. Bureau of Banking. Statements showing the condition of incorporated state banks operating in Virginia. V. Title.
NYPL [THB (Virginia. Bureau of Banking. Annual report)]

Statements showing the condition of incorporated state banks operating in Virginia. Virginia. Bureau of Banking. Annual report. Richmond. *NYPL [THB (Virginia. Bureau of Banking. Annual report)]*

Virginia. Bureau of Financial Institutions. Annual report. 1978- Richmond. 23 cm. "Showing the condition of banks, savings and loan associations, industrial loan associations, credit unions operating in Virginia." Supersedes; Virginia. Bureau of Banking. Annual report. Includes supplements.
1. Banks and banking - Virginia - Periodicals. 2. Financial institutions - Virginia - Periodicals. I. Title.
NYPL [JLL 80-301]

Virginia. Bureau of Health Planning. Virginia. Statewide Health Coordinating Council. State health plan, Commonwealth of Virginia /. [Richmond, Va.] [1979] 2 v. : LC Card 80-620762 DDC 362.1/09755 19
RA395.A4 V88 1979

Virginia. Bureau of Insurance and Banking. (Old Catalog form: Virginia. Insurance Bureau) Virginia. Bureau of Banking. Annual report. Richmond. *NYPL [THB (Virginia. Bureau of Banking. Annual report)]*

Virginia. Bureau of Water Control Management. Basic data bulletin - Bureau of Water Control Management .
(33A) Virginia. Bureau of Water Control Management. Flow characteristics of Virginia streams, North Atlantic slope basin. Richmond, Va. [1979] xv, 254 p. : LC Card 80-622495 DDC 551.48/3/09755 19
GB1225.V8 V57 1979

(35A) Virginia. Bureau of Water Control Management. Flow characteristics of Virginia streams, Ohio River basin. Richmond, Va. [1979] xxv, 197 p. : LC Card 80-622497 DDC 551.48/3/09755 19
GB1225.V8 V57 1979a

Flow characteristics of Virginia streams, North Atlantic slope basin. Richmond, Va. : Virginia State Water Control Board, Bureau of Water Control Management, [1979] xv, 254 p. : ill. ; 28 cm. (Basic data bulletin - Bureau of Water Control Management . 33A) "March 1979." Chiefly tables. Bibliography: p. xv. Includes index. LC Card 80-622495 DDC 551.48/3/09755 19
1. Stream measurements - Virginia - Tables. I. Series: Virginia. Bureau of Water Control Management. Basic data bulletin - Bureau of Water Control Management , 33A. II. Title.
GB1225.V8 V57 1979

Flow characteristics of Virginia streams, Ohio River basin. Richmond, Va. : Virginia State Water Control Board, Bureau of Water Control Management, [1979] xxv, 197 p. : ill. ; 28 cm.

(Basic data bulletin - Bureau of Water Control Management . 35A) "March 1979." Chiefly tables. Bibliography: p. xxv. Includes index. LC Card 80-622497 DDC 551.48/3/09755 19
1. Stream measurements - Virginia - Tables. 2. Stream measurements - Ohio River watershed - Tables. I. Series: Virginia. Bureau of Water Control Management. Basic data bulletin - Bureau of Water Control Management , 35A. II. Title.
GB1225.V8 V57 1979a

Flow characteristics of Virginia streams, South Atlantic slope basin. Richmond, Va. [1979] xvi, 421 p. : LC Card 80-622496 DDC 551.48/3/09755 19
GB1225.V8 F58

Virginia. Children and Youth in Trouble in Virginia Advisory Group. Virginia. State Crime Commission. Children and youth in trouble in Virginia . Richmond, Va. [1977] xvi, 188 p. ; LC Card 80-622757 DDC 364.3/6/09755 19
HV9105.V7 V53 1977

Virginia. Coastal Erosion Abatement Commission. Interim report of the Coastal Erosion Abatement Commission to the Governor and the General Assembly of Virginia. Richmond : Commonwealth of Virginia, Division of Purchases and Supply, 1979. 17 p. ; 28 cm. (Senate document - Commonwealth of Virginia ; no. 23) LC Card 79-623624 DDC 300/.9755 s 627/.58/09755 19
1. Shore protection - Virginia. 2. Beach erosion - Virginia. 3. Coast changes - Virginia. I. Virginia. Governor. II. Virginia. General Assembly. III. Series: Virginia. General Assembly, 1979. Senate. Document , no. 23.
J87 .V9 1979b, no. 23 TC224.V8

Report of the Coastal Erosion Abatement Commission to the Governor and the General Assembly of Virginia. Richmond : Commonwealth of Virginia, Division of Purchases and Supply, 1979. 52 p. : ill. ; 28 cm. (Senate document - Commonwealth of Virginia ; no. 4) Cover title. Includes bibliographical references. LC Card 80-621165 DDC 300/.9755 s 333.91/716/09755 19
1. Shore protection - Virginia. 2. Beach erosion - Virginia. I. Series: Virginia. General Assembly, 1979. Senate. Document , no. 4.
J87 .V9 1979b, no. 4a TC224.V8

Virginia (Colony). Laws, statutes, etc. Anno regni Georgii II, Regis Angliae, Scotiae, Franciae & Hiberniae, vicessimo quinto: At a General Assembly, begun and held at the college, in Williamsburg, on Thursday the twenty seventh day of February, in the twenty fifth year of the reign of our Sovereign Lord George II by the Grace of God, of Great-Britain, France, and Ireland, King, Defender of the Faith, &c. and in the year of our Lord, 1752. [Williamsburg, Printed by W. Hunter, 1752] 47 p. 35 cm. Bound with Virginia (Colony). Laws, statutes, etc. The acts of Assembly, now in force, in the Colony of Virginia. Williamsburg, 1752. Caption title. Evans 6942. LC Card 80-492689
1. Legislation - Virginia.
KFV2430 1752 .A23 KFV25.2

Virginia. Commission for the Visually Handicapped. Annual report. [Richmond] 23-28 cm. For earlier years, see Virginia Commission for the Blind. Report (in Old Catalog) Report year ends June 30.
1. Blind - Virginia. *NYPL [JLM 81-73]*

Virginia. Commission to Study the Containment of Health Care Costs. Report of the Commission to Study the Containment of Health Care Costs to the Governor and the General Assembly of Virginia. Richmond : Commonwealth of Virginia, 1980. 25 p. ; 28 cm. (Senate document - Commonwealth of Virginia ; no. 31) LC Card 80-621791 DDC 300/.9755 s 362.1 19
1. Medical care - Virginia - Cost control. 2. Health maintenance organizations - Law and legislation - Virginia. 3. Insurance, Health - Virginia. I. Series: Virginia. General Assembly, 1980. Senate. Document , no. 31.
J87 .V9 1980b, no. 31 RA410.54.V8

Virginia. Corporation Commission. see Virginia. State Corporation Commission.

Virginia. Corrections, Dept. of. see Virginia. Dept. of Corrections.

Virginia. Council of Higher Education. see Virginia. State Council of Higher Education.

Virginia. Crime Commission. see Virginia. State Crime Commission.

Virginia. Dept. of Commerce. Interim report of the Department of Commerce to the Governor and the General Assembly of Virginia : response to House Resolution no. 45 requesting the Department of Commerce to study the feasibility and desirability of licensure of audio stress examiners. Richmond, Va. : Commonwealth of Virginia, 1980. 58 p. in various pagings : ill. ; 28 cm. (House document -- Commonwealth of Virginia . no. 34) Includes bibliographical references. LC Card 80-622978 DDC 300/.9755 s 363.2/54 19
1. Lie detectors and detection - Virginia. I. Series: Virginia. General Assembly, 1980. House of Delegates. Document , no. 34.
J87 .V9 1980c, no. 34 HV8078

Virginia. Dept. of Corrections. Published reports : an annotated index, 1975-1977 / Virginia Department of Corrections. [Richmond] : Bureau of Research, Reporting, and Evaluation, Division of Administration, Dept. of Corrections, 1978. [15] leaves ; 28 cm. LC Card 79-622562 DDC 364.6/09755 19
1. Correctional institutions - Virginia - Abstracts. 2. Virginia. Dept. of Corrections - Abstracts.
HV8366 .V8 1978

VIRGINIA. DEPT. OF CORRECTIONS - ABSTRACTS.
Virginia. Dept. of Corrections. Published reports . [Richmond] , 1978. [15] leaves ; LC Card 79-622562 DDC 364.6/09755 19
HV8366 .V8 1978

Virginia. Dept. of Corrections. Bureau of Research, Reporting and Evaluation. Evaluation concepts and planning guide. [Richmond] : Virginia Dept. of Corrections, Division of Administration, Bureau of Research, Reporting, and Evaluation, 1977. iv, 68 leaves ; 28 cm. Cover title. "Report no. 7727." Bibliography: leaf 64. LC Card 79-621989 DDC 364.6 19
1. Corrections - Evaluation. 2. Evaluation research (Social action programs). I. Title.
HV9275 .V57 1977

Evaluation of Classification and Records training sessions, March 1, 1978, and March 15, 1978. [Richmond] : Virginia Dept. of Corrections, Division of Administration, Bureau of Research, Reporting & Evaluation, 1978. iv, 37 p. ; 28 cm. Cover title. "Written by J. Allen Hinshaw." "Report no. 7825." Bibliography: p. 32. LC Card 79-621994 DDC 365/.6 19
1. Virginia. Dept. of Corrections. Classification and Records Services - Officials and employees - Training of - Evaluation. I. Hinshaw, J. Allen. II. Title.
HV8754 .V53 1978

Index of selected out-of-State studies. [Richmond] : Virginia Dept. of Corrections, Division of Administration, Bureau of Research, Reporting, and Evaluation, [1978?] [35] p. ; 28 cm. Cover title. LC Card 79-621942 DDC 016.3646/0973 19
1. Corrections - United States - States. I. Title.
HV7296 .A6 1978a

The Mecklenburg evaluation. [Richmond] : Virginia Dept. of Corrections, Division of Administration, Bureau of Research, Reporting, and Evaluation, 1977-1978. 5 v. : ill. ; 28 cm. Vol. 4 prepared by the Bureau under its later name, Virginia Dept. of Corrections, Division of Program Development and Evaluation, Research and Reporting Unit. "Reports no. 7625, 7726, 7729, 7730, 7806." Bibliography: v. 2, p. 29. CONTENTS. - v. 1. The task force interviews.--v. 2. The research project. The Mecklenburg inmate.--v. 3. Follow-up evaluation plan for Mecklenburg inmates. Development of an inmate tracking system.--v. 4. Impact on the correctional system.--v. 5. First assignments. LC Card 79-621981 DDC 365/.9755645 19
1. Mecklenburg Correctional Center - Evaluation - Collected works. I. Virginia. Dept. of Corrections. Research and Reporting Unit. II. Title.
HV9481.M432 M438 1978

NYPUM program evaluation. [Richmond] : Virginia Dept. of Corrections, Division of Administration, Bureau of Research, Reporting & Evaluation, 1977. 171 p. ; 28 cm. Cover title. Includes bibliographical references. LC

BIBLIOGRAPHIC GUIDE

Virginia. Dept. of Corrections. Bureau of Research, Reporting and

638

Card 79-621982   DDC 365/.9755462 19
1. Rehabilitation of juvenile delinquents - Virginia -
Evaluation. 2. Juvenile detention homes - Virginia -
Evaluation. I. Title.
HV9105.V7 V5 1977

A study of recidivism. [Richmond] : Virginia
Dept. of Corrections, Division of
Administration, Bureau of Research, Reporting,
and Evaluation, 1977. i, 16 leaves ; 28 cm.
Cover title. "Compiled by J. Allen Hinshaw and Brian
Stamas." "Report no. 7707."   LC Card 78-621733
    DDC 364.3 19
1. Recidivists - Virginia. I. Hinshaw, J. Allen. II.
Stamas, Brian. III. Title.
HV7296 .A6 1977b

**Virginia. Dept. of Corrections. Bureau of
Research, Reporting, and Evaluation.
Reporting Section.** The Virginia State penal
system, felons committed, fiscal years
1972-1976 ; the Virginia State penal system,
felons confined, fiscal years 1972-1976 /
prepared by Department of Corrections, Bureau
of Research, Reporting & Evaluation, Reporting
Section. [Richmond] : The Section, [1977?] 17
p. ; 28 cm. Tables. "Report no. RS-377."   LC Card
80-623252   DDC 364.3/09755 19
1. Prisoners - Virginia - Statistics. I. Title. II. Title:
Virginia State penal system, felons confined, fiscal years
1972-1976.
HV8366 .V82 1977

**VIRGINIA. DEPT. OF CORRECTIONS.
CLASSIFICATION AND RECORDS
SERVICES - OFFICIALS AND
EMPLOYEES - TRAINING OF -
EVALUATION.**
Virginia. Dept. of Corrections. Bureau of
Research, Reporting and Evaluation. Evaluation
of Classification and Records training sessions,
March 1, 1978, and March 15, 1978.
[Richmond] , 1978. iv, 37 p. ;   LC Card
79-621994   DDC 365/.6 19
HV8754 .V53 1978

**Virginia. Dept. of Corrections. Evaluation and
Monitoring Unit.** Impacts of the first year of
the 1977 Juvenile code revision / prepared by
Virginia Department of Corrections, Division of
Program Development & Evaluation, Evaluation
and Monitoring Unit. [Richmond] : The Unit,
1978. 13, x p. : map ; 28 cm. (Impacts ; 12) Cover
title: The first year, Virginia's Juvenile code revision,
1977.   LC Card 79-622561   DDC 345.755/08 19
1. Juvenile justice, Administration of - Virginia. 2.
Juvenile courts - Virginia. 3. Status offenders - Legal
status, laws, etc. - Virginia. I. Title. II. Title: First year,
Virginia's Juvenile code revision, 1977. III. Series:
Impacts (Richmond, Va.) , 12.
KFV2995 .A83

**Virginia. Dept. of Corrections. Research and
Reporting Unit.**
Criminal justice prediction scales : a survey of
the 50 States. [Richmond] : Dept. of
Corrections, Research and Reporting Unit,
1978. ii, 29 p. ; 48 cm. Cover title. Compiled by
J.A. Hinshaw. "Report no. 7837."   LC Card 79-624252
    DDC 364.3/0973 19
1. Crime forecasting - United States - Methodology. 2.
Criminal justice, Administration of - United States. I.
Hinshaw, J. Allen. II. Title.
HV6791 .V57 1978

Self-mutilation at the penitentiary and
Powhatan : supplement / Research and
Reporting Unit, Division of Program
Development and Evaluation, Virginia
Department of Corrections. [Richmond] : The
Unit, [1978] 10 leaves : graph ; 28 cm.
"Supplement to Report #7821, September 1978."   LC
    Card 79-622551   DDC 365/.641 19
1. Virginia. Penitentiary, Richmond - Case studies -
Statistics. 2. Self-mutilation - Statistics. I. Title.
HV9475.V82 R57 1978

Virginia. Dept. of Corrections. Bureau of
Research, Reporting and Evaluation. The
Mecklenburg evaluation. [Richmond] ,
1977-1978. 5 v. :   LC Card 79-621981   DDC
365/.9755645 19
HV9481.M432 M438 1978

**Virginia. Dept. of Corrections. Research,
Reporting and Evaluation, Bureau of.** see
**Virginia. Dept. of Corrections. Bureau of
Research, Reporting and Evaluation.**

Virginia. Dept. of Education. Virginia. Office of
the Secretary of Human Resources. The revised

State plan for the identification and diagnosis of
children who are handicapped . Richmond ,
1979. [73] p. ;   LC Card 79-624128   DDC
    300/.9755 s 362.4/048 19
J87 .V9 1979c no. 37 RJ102.5.V8

Virginia. Dept. of Highways and Transportation.
Virginia. University. Civil Engineering Dept.
Bridges on secondary highways and local
roads . Washington, D.C. , 1980. 132 p. :
    ISBN 0-309-03025-0 (pbk.) :   LC Card 80-51497
    DDC 625.7 s 624.2 19
TE7 .N25 no. 222 TG153

**VIRGINIA. DEPT. OF HIGHWAYS AND
TRANSPORTATION.**
Virginia. General Assembly. Joint Legislative
Audit and Review Commission. Interim report
of the Joint Legislative Audit and Review
Commission and the SJR 50 Subcommittee on
the organization and administration of the
Department of Highways and Transportation to
the Governor and the General Assembly of
Virginia. Richmond, Va. (910 Capitol St.,
Richmond 23219) , 1981. 85 p. :   LC Card
81-622025   DDC 300/.9755 s
353.97550087/8/06 19
J87 .V9 1981b, no. 14 HE28.V8

**Virginia. Dept. of Highways and Transportation.
Division of Traffic and Safety.** see **Virginia.
Division of Traffic and Safety.**

**Virginia. Dept. of Highways and Transportation.
Virginia Highway & Transportation Research
Council.** see **Virginia Highway &
Transportation Research Council.**

**Virginia. Dept. of Housing and Community
Development.** Status of local planning in
Virginia, 1979 / prepared by the Virginia
Department of Housing and Community
Development, in cooperation with Virginia's
local governments and planning district
commissions. Richmond, Va. : The Dept.,
[1979] 55 p. : maps ; 28 cm. Cover title.   LC
    Card 80-622615   DDC 352.9/6/025755 19
1. City planning - Virginia - Statistics. 2. City
planning - Virginia - Directories. 3. Zoning - Virginia. I.
Title.
HT167.5.V8 V53 1979

Virginia. Dept. of Industry and Labor. see
Virginia. Dept. of Labor and Industry.

**Virginia. Dept. of Intergovernmental Affairs.
Office of Human Resources.** An overview of
nutrition programs in Virginia / prepared by
Office of Human Resources, Department of
Intergovernmental Affairs under the auspices of
the U. S. Community Services Administration.
[Richmond] : The Office, 1978. 93, [2] p. ; 29
cm. Cover title. "Volume II." Corrections sheet
inserted. Bibliography: p. [95]   LC Card 79-621946
    DDC 363.8/8/09755 19
1. Food relief - Virginia. 2. Food stamp program -
Virginia. I. United States. Community Services
Administration. II. Title.
HV696.F6 V57 1978

Virginia. Dept. of Labor and Industry. (Old
Catalog form: Virginia. Labor and Industry
Dept.)
Virginia rules and regulations declaring
hazardous occupations, as promulgated by
Commissioner, Virginia Department of Labor
and Industry, effective date November 1, 1979
/ issued by the Virginia Department of Labor
and Industry. Richmond, Va. : The Dept.,
[1979] 16, [5] p. ; 23 cm.   LC Card 80-622803
    DDC 344.755/0134 19
1. Children - Employment - Virginia. 2. Children -
Legal status, laws, etc. - Virginia. 3. Occupations,
Dangerous. I. Title.
KFV2735.5.A435 A2 1979

**Virginia. Dept. of Planning and Budget.
Economic Research Section.** Jones, Daniel G.
Commonwealth of Virginia--demographic and
economic trends /. Richmond, Va. , 1978. 56
p. :   LC Card 79-625625   DDC 312/.8/09755 19
HB3525.V8 J66

Virginia. Dept. of Rehabilitative Services. Interim
state plan for independent living rehabilitation
services under section 705 of the Rehabilitation
act of 1973, as amended through 1978.
Richmond, VA : Virginia Dept. of
Rehabilitation Serv., [1979] iii, 26, [9] leaves ;
28 cm. Caption title. "VA(G)-SP-79.2."   LC Card
79-626035

1. Virginia. Dept. of Rehabilitative Services. I. Title.
HV2561.V8 V58 1979

**VIRGINIA. DEPT. OF REHABILITATIVE
SERVICES.**
Virginia. Dept. of Rehabilitative Services.
Interim state plan for independent living
rehabilitation services under section 705 of the
Rehabilitation act of 1973, as amended through
1978. Richmond, VA [1979] iii, 26, [9] leaves ;
    LC Card 79-626035
HV2561.V8 V58 1979

Virginia. Dept. of Taxation. Virginia tax facts.
[Richmond, Va.] : Virginia Dept. of Taxation,
[1979] 57 p. ; 22 cm. "March 1979."   LC Card
79-625802   DDC 343.75504 19
1. Taxation - Law and legislation - Virginia - Outlines,
syllabi, etc. I. Title.
KFV2870 .A87

Virginia. Dept. of Transportation Safety.
Simpson, Clinton H. The development of a
methodology for transportation safety planning
in Virginia /. Charlottesville, Va. [1980] 37,
[24] p. ;   LC Card 80-622408   DDC
363.1/206/09755 19
HE5614.3.V8 S57

Virginia. Dept. of Welfare. Directory of homes
for adults and adult day care centers.
Richmond : Commonwealth of Virginia, Dept.
of Welfare, [1979] 34 p. ; 28 cm. "April 23, 1979."
    LC Card 79-626034   DDC 362.6/1/025755 19
1. Day care centers for the aged - Virginia -
Directories. I. Title.
HV1450 .V57 1979

**VIRGINIA - DESCRIPTION AND TRAVEL -
1951- - GUIDE-BOOKS.**
Robertson, James I. Civil War sites in Virginia .
Charlottesville , 1981. p. cm.   ISBN
0-8139-0907-4   LC Card 81-7426   DDC
917.55/0443 19
F227 .R59

**Virginia. Division of Consolidated Laboratory
Services.** Regulations. [Richmond] : Division
of Consolidated Laboratory Services, [1980] 9
leaves ; 28 cm. Caption title.   LC Card 80-623523
    DDC 345.755/0247 347.5505247 19
1. Drunk driving - Virginia. 2. Chemistry, Forensic -
Virginia. 3. Blood alcohol. 4. Alcohol in the body.
KFV2697.8.A45 A2 1980

Virginia. Division of Industrial Development.
(Old Catalog form: Virginia. Industrial
Development, Division of)
A guide for establishing a manufacturing
business in Virginia. Richmond, 1974. 33 p.
illus. 28 cm. Microfilm
1. Virginia - Manufactures. I. Title.
*NYPL [*ZT-1259]*

An outline of state and local taxes in Virginia.
Richmond, Va. : Commonwealth of Virginia
Governor's Office, Division of Industrial
Development, [1977] iii leaves, 18 p. ; 28 cm.
"July 1977."   LC Card 80-621940   DDC
336.2/009755 19
1. Taxation - Virginia. 2. Business enterprises -
Taxation - Virginia. I. Title.
HF2438 .A7 1977

**Virginia. Division of Justice and Crime
Prevention.**
The Criminal justice system in Virginia .
Richmond, Va. (8501 Mayland Dr., Richmond
23229) [1980] x, 98 p. :   LC Card 81-621748
    DDC 364/.9755 19
HV7296 .A6 1980

**Virginia. Division of Justice and Crime
Prevention. Statistical Analysis Center.**
Wohlford, Laura. The State agency resource
compendium . Richmond, Va. [1979] 242 p. in
various pagings ;   LC Card 80-622046   DDC
364/.07 19
HV8145.V8 W63

Virginia. Division of Legislative Services.
Summary of the regular 1980 legislative session
of the Virginia General Assembly / prepared by
the Division of Legislative Services. [Richmond,
Va.] : The Division, [1980] 53 p. ; 28 cm.   LC
    Card 80-622921   DDC 348.755/01 19
1. Bills, Legislative - Virginia. I. Title.
KFV2415.2 1980

**Virginia. Division of Local and Regional
Planning.** Local government information :
1977 survey report. [Richmond] :
Commonwealth of Virginia, Dept. of Housing

GOVERNMENT PUBLICATIONS - U.S.: 1981

639   Virginia. General Assembly. Joint Subcommittee Studying the

and Community Development, Division of Local and Regional Planning, [1978?] 18 p. ; 28 cm. "December 1, 1978." LC Card 79-624115 DDC 352.0755 19
1. Local government - Virginia. I. Title.
JS451 .V6 1978

Virginia. Division of Mineral Resources. Virginia Division of Mineral Resources publication .
(16) Bartlett, Charles S. Geology of the Abingdon, Wyndale, Holston Valley, and Shady Valley quadrangles / . Charlottesville, Va. , 1980. 39 p. : LC Card 80-623838 DDC 557.55/725 19
QE174.W34 B37

(20) Geology of the Oak Grove core. Charlottesville, Va. , 1980. 88 p. : LC Card 80-623839 DDC 551.7/8/09755366 19
QE691 .G47

(5) Kreisa, Ronald D. Geology of the Omega, south Boston, Cluster Springs, and Virgilina quadrangles / . Charlottesville, Va. , 1980. 22 p. : LC Card 80-622511 DDC 557.55/661 19
QE174.H34 K73

Virginia. Division of State Planning and Community Affairs. Virginia, planning, housing & districting legislation. [Richmond]
NYPL [JLM 80-935]

Virginia. Division of Traffic and Safety. City and town map atlas / [prepared by Virginia Department of Highways and Transportation, Traffic and Safety Division]. [Richmond : Commonwealth Traffic and Safety Division, c1980] 229 [i.e. 308] leaves (1 fold.) : col. ill., maps (1 fold. col.) ; 49 x 71 cm. Cover title. Edition for 1976 published under title: City & town maps. "Streets correct through December 31, 1979." Includes index. LC Card 80-675310 DDC 912/.755
1. Cities and towns - Virginia - Maps. I. Title.
G1294.A1 V32 1980

VIRGINIA - ECONOMIC CONDITIONS.
Jones, Daniel G. Commonwealth of Virginia--demographic and economic trends / . Richmond, Va. , 1978. 56 p. : LC Card 79-625625 DDC 312/.8/09755 19
HB3525.V8 J66

Virginia. Employment Commission. Manpower Research Division.
Labor market information for Affirmative Action programs : [1979 supplement, based on 1978 data] / prepared by Manpower Research Division, Virginia Employment Commission, affiliated with Employment and Training Administration, U. S. Department of Labor. [Richmond] : The Division, [1979] 67, xiv p. ; 28 cm. LC Card 80-621171 DDC 331.12/09755 19
1. Labor supply - Virginia - Statistics. 2. Minorities - Employment - Virginia - Statistics. 3. Women - Employment - Virginia - Statistics. 4. Affirmative action programs - Virginia - Statistics. I. United States. Employment and Training Administration. II. Title.
HD5725.V8 V53 1979a

Occupational employment statistics : selected nonmanufacturing industries, Virginia, 1978 / prepared by Manpower Research Division, Virginia Employment Commission. [Richmond] : The Division, [1980] ix, 198 p. : graphs ; 28 cm. "April 1980." LC Card 80-622341 DDC 331.12/5/09755 19
1. Labor supply - Virginia - Statistics. 2. Virginia - Occupations - Statistics. I. Title.
HD5725.V8 V53 1980

Virginia. Employment Commission. Manpower Research Division. Labor Market Analysis Unit. Special youth report, State of Virginia / prepared by Labor Market Analysis Unit, Manpower Research, Virginia Employment Commission, affiliated with Employment and Training Administration, U. S. Dept. of Labor. Richmond, Va. : The Commission, [1979] 24 p. : graphs ; 28 cm. "September 1979." LC Card 79-625797 DDC 331.3/4/09755 19
1. Youth - Employment - Virginia. I. United States. Employment and Training Administration. II. Title.
HD6274.V8 V57 1979

Virginia. Financial Institutions, Bureau of. see **Virginia. Bureau of Financial Institutions.**

Virginia Fisheries Laboratory, Gloucester Point. see **Virginia Institute of Marine Science, Gloucester Point.**

VIRGINIA - GENEALOGY.
Nugent, Nell Marion. Cavaliers and pioneers . Richmond , 1980. iii, 18 p. ; ISBN 0-88490-088-6 (pbk.) LC Card 80-141230 DDC 929/.3755 19
F225 .N842 1934 Suppl.

VIRGINIA. GENERAL ASEMBLY. HOUSE OF BURGESSES - BIOGRAPHY.
Kukla, Jon, 1948- Speakers and clerks of the Virginia House of Burgesses, 1643-1776 / . Richmond , 1981. x, 163 p. : ISBN 0-88490-075-4 LC Card 81-5051 DDC 328.755/0762/0922 B 19
JK83.V8 K84

Virginia. General Assembly.
Virginia. Coastal Erosion Abatement Commission. Interim report of the Coastal Erosion Abatement Commission to the Governor and the General Assembly of Virginia. Richmond , 1979. 17 p. ; LC Card 79-623624 DDC 300/.9755 s 627/.58/09755 19
J87 .V9 1979b, no. 23 TC224.V8

Virginia. General Assembly. Joint Subcommittee to Study Real Property Tax Exemptions. Report of the Joint Subcommittee to Study Real Property Tax Exemptions to the Governor and the General Assembly of Virginia. Richmond , 1980. 73 p. ; LC Card 80-622737 DDC 300/.9755 s 343.75505/43 19
J87 .V9 1980c no. 35 KFV2411.62

Virginia. General Assmebly. House of Delegates. Committee for Courts of Justice. Report of the subcommittee of the Committee for Courts of Justice studying the jurisdictional limits of general district courts and juvenile and domestic relations district courts to the General Assembly of Virginia. Richmond, Va. , 1980. 27 p. ; LC Card 80-623901 DDC 300/.9755 s 347.755/012 300/.9755 s 347.550712 19
J87 .V9 1980c, no. 27 KFV2411.82.C

Virginia. General Assembly. House of Delegates. Document .
(no. 4) Virginia. Secretary of Education. Report of the Secretary of Education and the Secretary of Public Safety on Senate joint resolution 159 to the General Assembly of Virginia. Richmond, Va. , 1980. iii, 10 p. ; LC Card 80-621140 DDC 300/.9755 s 362.7/4/09755 19
J87 .V9 1980c, no. 4 HV9105.V7

Virginia. General Assembly. House of Delegates. Committee on Labor and Commerce. Workmen's Compensation Subcommittee.
Report of the Workmen's Compensation Subcommittee of the House Committee on Labor and Commerce to the Governor and General Assembly of Virginia. Richmond : Commonwealth of Virginia, 1980. 202 p. ; 28 cm. (House document - Commonwealth of Virginia ; no. 39) LC Card 80-623143 DDC 300/.9755 s 368.4/09755 19
1. Workmen's compensation - Virginia. I. Series: Virginia. General Assembly, 1980. House of Delegates. Document , no. 39.
J87 .V9 1980c no. 39 KFV2411.82.L

Virginia. General Assembly. Joint Committee for the Courts of Justice. Report of the Joint Committee for the Courts of Justice of the House and Senate studying sentencing in criminal cases to the General Assembly of Virginia. Richmond, Va. : Commonwealth of Virginia, 1980. 19 p. ; 28 cm. (House document -- Commonwealth of Virginia . no. 26) LC Card 80-623756 DDC 300/.9755 s 345.755/0772 300/.9755 s 347.5505772 19
1. Sentences (Criminal procedure) - Virginia. I. Series: Virginia. General Assembly, 1979. House of Delegates. Document , no. 26. II. Title.
J87 .V9 1979c no. 26 KFV2411.62

Virginia. General Assembly. Joint Legislative Audit & Review Commission.
Virginia. General Assembly. Joint Legislative Audit and Review Commission.
Deinstitutionalization and community services : special report / Joint Legislative Audit and Review Commission. [Richmond] : The Commission, [1979] 84 p. : ill. ; 28 cm. "September 1979." LC Card 80-622409 DDC 362.2/1/09755 19
1. Mentally handicapped - Care and treatment - Virginia. 2. Community mental health services - Virginia. I. Title.
HV3006.V7 V59 1979

Homes for adults in Virginia / Joint Legislative Audit and Review Commission, Virginia General Assembly. [Richmond, Va.] : JLARC, [1979] iv, 73 p. : ill. ; 29 cm. Cover title. On spine: JLARC, program evaluation, homes for adults in Virginia, December 1979. LC Card 80-622566 DDC 362.6/1/09755 19
1. Old age homes - Virginia. I. Title. II. Title: JLARC, program evaluation, homes for adults in Virginia.
HV1468.V8 V5 1979

Interim report of the Joint Legislative Audit and Review Commission and the SJR 50 Subcommittee on the organization and administration of the Department of Highways and Transportation to the Governor and the General Assembly of Virginia. Richmond, Va. (910 Capitol St., Richmond 23219) : Commonwealth of Virginia, 1981. 85 p. : ill. ; 28 cm. (Senate document . no. 14) LC Card 81-622025 DDC 300/.9755 s 353.97550087/8/06 19
1. Virginia. Dept. of Highways and Transportation. 2. Transportation and state - Virginia. I. Virginia. General Assembly. SJR 50 Subcommittee. II. Series: Senate document (Virginia. General Assembly. Senate) , 1981, no. 14. III. Title.
J87 .V9 1981b, no. 14 HE28.V8

Management and use of consultants by state agencies / Join Legislative Audit and Review Commission, the Virginia General Assembly ; [JLARC staff for this report, Mark S. Fleming, project director, Ronald L. Tillett, Glen S. Tittermary]. [Richmond, Va.] : The Commission, 1980. iv, 73 p. : ill. ; 28 cm. Cover title. On spine: Operational review--management and use of consultants by the state agencies. LC Card 80-623858 DDC 353.975507/22 19
1. Government consultants - Virginia. I. Fleming, Mark S. II. Title. III. Title: Operational review--management and use of consultants by the state agencies.
JK3949.C7 V54 1980

Report of the Joint Legislative audit and Review Commission on federal funds in Virginia to the Governor and the General Assembly of Virginia. Richmond, Va. : Commonwealth of Virginia, 1981. vii, 122 p. : ill. ; 28 cm. (House document -- Commonwealth of Virginia . no. 6) Cover title. LC Card 81-621744 DDC 300/.9755 s 353.97550072/52 19
1. Intergovernmental fiscal relations - Virginia. 2. Grants-in-aid - Virginia. 3. Intergovernmental fiscal relations - United States. 4. Grants-in-aid - United States. I. Series: House document (Virginia. General Assembly. House of Delegates) , no. 6. II. Title.
J87 .V9 1981c no. 6 HJ745

Virginia. State Council of Higher Education. Graduate marine science education in Virginia . Richmond, Va. [1978] 3, v, 155 p. ; LC Card 79-624103 DDC 551.46/007/11755 19
GC31.6 .V575 1978

Virginia. General Assembly. Joint Subcommittee of the Courts of Justice Committees of the Senate and House of Delegates Studying Virginia's Mechanic's Lien Laws Under House Joint Resolution No. 229. Report of the Joint Subcommittee of the Courts of Justice Committees of the Senate and House of Delegates Studying Virginia's Mechanic's Lien Laws Under House Joint Resolution No. 229 to the Governor and the General Assembly of Virginia. Richmond : Commonwealth of Virginia, 1980. 10 p. ; 28 cm. (House document -- Commonwealth of Virginia . no. 32) LC Card 80-623941 DDC 346.755/024 19
1. Mechanic's liens - Virginia. I. Series: Virginia. General Assembly, 1980. House of Delegates. Document , no. 32. II. Title.
J87 .V9 1980c, no. 32 KFV2411.62.M

Virginia. General Assembly. Joint Subcommittee Studying the Commonwealth's Insurance Coverage. Final report of the Joint Subcommittee Studying the Commonwealth's Insurance Coverage to the Governor and the General Assembly of Virginia. Richmond : Commonwealth of Virginia, 1980. 67 p. : ill. ; 28 cm. (House document -- Commonwealth of Virginia . no. 41) LC Card 80-624123 DDC 300/.9755 s 368.5 19
1. Insurance, Government - Virginia. I. Series: Virginia. General Assembly, 1980. House of Delegates. Document , no. 41. II. Title.
J87 .V9 1980c, no. 41 HG8215.V8

Virginia. General Assembly. Joint Subcommittee Studying the Virginia Resource Information System. Report of the Joint Subcommittee Studying the Virginia Resource Information System (VARIS) to the Governor and the General Assembly of Virginia. Richmond : Commonwealth of Virginia, 1980. 134 p. ; 28 cm. (House document - Commonwealth of Virginia ; no. 20) Bibliography: p. 134. LC Card 80-622729 DDC 300/.9755 s 025/.063337/09755 19
1. Natural resources - Virginia - Information services - Virginia. I. Series: Virginia. General Assembly, 1980. House of Delegates. Document , no. 20. II. Title.
J87 .V9 1980c no. 20 HC107.V8

Virginia. General Assembly. Joint Subcommittee to Study Real Property Tax Exemptions. Report of the Joint Subcommittee to Study Real Property Tax Exemptions to the Governor and the General Assembly of Virginia. Richmond : Commonwealth of Virginia, 1980. 73 p. ; 28 cm. (House document -- Commonwealth of Virginia . no. 35) Includes bibliographical references. LC Card 80-622737 DDC 300/.9755 s 343.75505/43 19
1. Real property tax - Virginia. 2. Taxation, Exemption from - Virginia. I. Virginia. Governor. II. Virginia. General Assembly. III. Series: Virginia. General Assembly, 1979. House of Delegates. Document , no. 35.
J87 .V9 1980c no. 35 KFV2411.62

Virginia. General Assembly. Joint Subcommittee to Study the Care of the Impaired Elderly. Report of the Joint Subcommittee to Study the Care of the Impaired Elderly to the Governor and the General Assembly of Virginia. Richmond : Commonwealth of Virginina, 1980. 43, 7, [8] p. ; 29 cm. (House document -- Commonwealth of Virginia . no. 20) LC Card 81-621718 DDC 300/.9755 s 362.6/09755 19
1. Aged - Services for - Virginia. 2. Aged - Virginia - Care and hygiene. 3. Long-term care of the sick - Virginia. I. Series: House document (Virginia. General Assembly. House of Delegates) , no. 20. II. Title.
J87 .V9 1980c, no. 20a HV1468.V8

Virginia. General Assembly. Joint Subcommittee to Study the Virginia Industrial Income Tax Structure. Report of the Joint Subcommittee to Study the Virginia Individual Income Tax Structure to the Governor and the General Assembly of Virginia. Richmond, Va. : Commonwerlth of Virginia, 1980. 133 p. ; 28 cm. (Senate document - Commonwealth of Virginia ; no. 16) LC Card 80-623141 DDC 300/.9755 s 343.75505/2 19
1. Income tax - Law and legislation - Virginia. I. Series: Virginia. General Assembly, 1980. Senate. Document , no. 16. II. Title.
J87 .V9 1980b no. 16 KFV2411.62.S75

Virginia. General Assembly. SJR 50 Subcommittee. Virginia. General Assembly. Joint Legislative Audit and Review Commission. Interim report of the Joint Legislative Audit and Review Commission and the SJR 50 Subcommittee on the organization and administration of the Department of Highways and Transportation to the Governor and the General Assembly of Virginia. Richmond, Va. (910 Capitol St., Richmond 23219) , 1981. 85 p. : LC Card 81-622025 DDC 300/.9755 s 353.97550087/8/06 19
J87 .V9 1981b, no. 14 HE28.V8

Virginia. General Assembly, 1979. House of Delegates. Document .
(no. 26) Virginia. General Assembly. Joint Committee for the Courts of Justice. Report of the Joint Committee for the Courts of Justice of the House and Senate studying sentencing in criminal cases to the General Assembly of Virginia. Richmond, Va. , 1980. 19 p. ; LC Card 80-623756 DDC 300/.9755 s 345.755/0772 300/.9755 s 347.5505772 19
J87 .V9 1979c no. 26 KFV2411.62

(no. 31) Virginia. Retirement Study Commission. Report of the Virginia Retirement Study Commission to the Governor and the General Assembly of Virginia. Richmond , 1980. 129 p. ; LC Card 80-623142 DDC 300/.9755 s 353.9755005 19
J87 .V9 1980c no. 31 JK3960.P4

(no. 35) Virginia. General Assembly. Joint Subcommittee to Study Real Property Tax Exemptions. Report of the Joint

Subcommittee to Study Real Property Tax Exemptions to the Governor and the General Assembly of Virginia. Richmond , 1980. 73 p. ; LC Card 80-622737 DDC 300/.9755 s 343.75505/43 19
J87 .V9 1980c no. 35 KFV2411.62

(no. 37) Virginia. Office of the Secretary of Human Resources. The revised State plan for the identification and diagnosis of children who are handicapped . Richmond , 1979. [73] p. ; LC Card 79-624128 DDC 300/.9755 s 362.4/048 19
J87 .V9 1979c no. 37 RJ102.5.V8

Virginia. General Assembly, 1979. Senate. Document .
(no. 23) Virginia. Coastal Erosion Abatement Commission. Interim report of the Coastal Erosion Abatement Commission to the Governor and the General Assembly of Virginia. Richmond , 1979. 17 p. ; LC Card 79-623624 DDC 300/.9755 s 627/.58/09755 19
J87 .V9 1979b, no. 23 TC224.V8

(no. 4) Virginia. Coastal Erosion Abatement Commission. Report of the Coastal Erosion Abatement Commission to the Governor and the General Assembly of Virginia. Richmond , 1979. 52 p. : LC Card 80-621165 DDC 300/.9755 s 333.91/716/09755 19
J87 .V9 1979b, no. 4a TC224.V8

Virginia. General Assembly, 1980. House of Delegates. Document .
(no. 20) Virginia. General Assembly. Joint Subcommittee Studying the Virginia Resource Information System. Report of the Joint Subcommittee Studying the Virginia Resource Information System (VARIS) to the Governor and the General Assembly of Virginia. Richmond , 1980. 134 p. ; LC Card 80-622729 DDC 300/.9755 s 025/.063337/09755 19
J87 .V9 1980c no. 20 HC107.V8

(no. 27) Virginia. General Assmebly. House of Delegates. Committee for Courts of Justice. Report of the subcommittee of the Committee for Courts of Justice studying the jurisdictional limits of general district courts and juvenile and domestic relations district courts to the General Assembly of Virginia. Richmond, Va. , 1980. 27 p. ; LC Card 80-623901 DDC 300/.9755 s 347.755/012 300/.9755 s 347.550712 19
J87 .V9 1980c, no. 27 KFV2411.82.C

(no. 29) Virginia. Statewide Grand Jury Commission. Report of the Statewide Grand Jury Commission to the Governor and the General Assembly of Virginia. Richmond, Va. , 1980. 12 p. ; LC Card 80-622980 DDC 300/.9755 s 345.755/075 19
J87 .V9 1980c no. 29 KFV2977

(no. 32) Virginia. General Assembly. Joint Subcommittee of the Courts of Justice Committees of the Senate and House of Delegates Studying Virginia's Mechanic's Lien Laws Under House Joint Resolution No. 229. Report of the Joint Subcommittee of the Courts of Justice Committees of the Senate and House of Delegates Studying Virginia's Mechanic's Lien Laws Under House Joint Resolution No. 229 to the Governor and the General Assembly of Virginia. Richmond , 1980. 10 p. ; LC Card 80-623941 DDC 346.755/024 19
J87 .V9 1980c, no. 32 KFV2411.62.M

(no. 34) Virginia. Dept. of Commerce. Interim report of the Department of Commerce to the Governor and the General Assembly of Virginia . Richmond, Va. , 1980. 58 p. in various pagings : LC Card 80-622978 DDC 300/.9755 s 363.2/54 19
J87 .V9 1980c, no. 34 HV8078

(no. 39) Virginia. General Assembly. House of Delegates. Committee on Labor and Commerce. Workmen's Compensation Subcommittee. Report of the Workmen's Compensation Subcommittee of the House Committee on Labor and Commerce to the Governor and the General Assembly of Virginia. Richmond , 1980. 202 p. ; LC Card 80-623143 DDC 300/.9755 s 368.4/1/009755 19
J87 .V9 1980c no. 39 KFV2411.82.L

(no. 41) Virginia. General Assembly. Joint

Subcommittee Studying the Commonwealth's Insurance Coverage. Final report of the Joint Subcommittee Studying the Commonwealth's Insurance Coverage to the Governor and the General Assembly of Virginia. Richmond , 1980. 67 p. : LC Card 80-624123 DDC 300/.9755 s 368.5 19
J87 .V9 1980c, no. 41 HG8215.V8

Virginia. General Assembly, 1980. Senate. Document .
(no. 15) Virginia. Agricultural Opportunities Commission. Report of the Agricultural Opportunities Commission to the Governor and the General Assembly of Virginia. Richmond, Va. , 1980. 151 p. : LC Card 80-621793 DDC 300/.9755 s 338.1/09755 19
J87 .V9 1980b, no. 15 HD1775.V5

(no. 16) Virginia. General Assembly. Joint Subcommittee to Study the Virginia Industrial Income Tax Structure. Report of the Joint Subcommittee to Study the Virginia Individual Income Tax Structure to the Governor and the General Assembly of Virginia. Richmond, Va. , 1980. 133 p. ; LC Card 80-623141 DDC 300/.9755 s 343.75505/2 19
J87 .V9 1980b no. 16 KFV2411.62.S75

(no. 22) Virginia. Telecommunications Study Commission. Telecommunications, a new Virginia initiative . Richmond, Va. , 1980. 79 p. ; LC Card 80-621795 DDC 300/.9755 s 353.975504 19
J87 .V9 1980b, no. 22 JK3949.C65

(no. 25) Virginia. Solid Waste Commission. Report of the Solid Waste Commission to the Governor and the General Assembly of Virginia. Richmond, Va. , 1980. 16 p. ; LC Card 80-621794 DDC 300/.9755 s 363.7/2 19
J87 .V9 1980b, no. 25 TD788.4.V8

(no. 29) Allen, Gary R. An analysis of state imposed taxes and fees on motor carriers of passengers /. Charlottesville, Va. , 1980. 26, 1, vi p. ; LC Card 80-623479 DDC 300/.9755 s 353.97550072/6 19
J87 .V9 1980b no. 29 HE5633.V8

(no. 31) Virginia. Commission to Study the Containment of Health Care Costs. Report of the Commission to Study the Containment of Health Care Costs to the Governor and the General Assembly of Virginia. Richmond , 1980. 25 p. ; LC Card 80-621791 DDC 300/.9755 s 362.1 19
J87 .V9 1980b, no. 31 RA410.54.V8

(no. 32) Chesapeake Bay Legislative Advisory Commission (U. S.) Report of the Chesapeake Bay Legislative Advisory Commission to the Governors of Maryland and Virginia, the General Assembly of the Commonwealth of Virginia, and the General Assembly of the State of Maryland. Richmond, Va. , 1980. iii, 67 p. ; LC Card 80-622736 DDC 300/.9755 s 333.91/7/0975518 19
J87 .V9 1980b no. 32 HT392.5.C45

Virginia. General Assmebly. House of Delegates. Committee for Courts of Justice. Report of the subcommittee of the Committee for Courts of Justice studying the jurisdictional limits of general district courts and juvenile and domestic relations district courts to the General Assembly of Virginia. Richmond, Va. : Commonwealth of Virginia, 1980. 27 p. ; 28 cm. (House document -- Commonwealth of Virginia . no. 27) LC Card 80-623901 DDC 300/.9755 s 347.755/012 300/.9755 s 347.550712 19
1. Jurisdiction - Virginia. I. Virginia. General Assembly. II. Series: Virginia. General Assembly, 1980. House of Delegates. Document , no. 27. III. Title.
J87 .V9 1980c, no. 27 KFV2411.82.C

Virginia. Governor.
Virginia. Coastal Erosion Abatement Commission. Interim report of the Coastal Erosion Abatement Commission to the Governor and the General Assembly of Virginia. Richmond , 1979. 17 p. ; LC Card 79-623624 DDC 300/.9755 s 627/.58/09755 19
J87 .V9 1979b, no. 23 TC224.V8

Virginia. General Assembly. Joint Subcommittee to Study Real Property Tax Exemptions. Report of the Joint Subcommittee to Study Real Property Tax Exemptions to the Governor and the General Assembly of Virginia. Richmond ,

1980. 73 p. ; LC Card 80-622737 DDC 300/.9755
s 343.75505/43 19
J87 .V9 1980c no. 35 KFV2411.62

Virginia Governor's Conference on Library and Information Services, Richmond, 1979. Final report / Virginia Governor's Conference on Library and Information Services. [Richmond] : The Conference, [1979] 39 p. ; 28 cm. Caption title. LC Card 80-622797 DDC 027.0755 19
1. Libraries - Virginia. 2. Library science - Congresses.
Z732.V8 V837 1979

Virginia. Higher Education, State Council of. see Virginia. State Council of Higher Education.

Virginia Highway & Transportation Research Council.
Allen, Gary R. An analysis of state imposed taxes and fees on motor carriers of passengers /. Charlottesville, Va. , 1980. 26, 1, vi p. ; LC Card 80-623479 DDC 300/.9755 s 353.97550072/6 19
J87 .V9 1980b no. 29 HE5633.V8

Robertson, Richard Neal, 1940- Impact of removal of tolls on travel in Tidewater Virginia /. Charlottesville, Va. [1977?] 3 v. : LC Card 79-625466 DDC 388.1/14 19
HE376.A2 V87

Simpson, Clinton H. The development of a methodology for transportation safety planning in Virginia /. Charlottesville, Va. [1980] 37, [24] p. ; LC Card 80-622408 DDC 363.1/206/09755 19
HE5614.3.V8 S57

Virginia. University. Civil Engineering Dept. Bridges on secondary highways and local roads . Washington, D.C. , 1980. 132 p. : ISBN 0-309-03025-0 (pbk.) : LC Card 80-51497 DDC 625.7 s 624.2 19
TE7 .N25 no. 222 TG153

Virginia. Highways and Transportation, Dept. of. see Virginia. Dept. of Highways and Transportation.

VIRGINIA - HISTORY - COLONIAL PERIOD, CA. 1600-1775 - COLLECTED WORKS.
Smith, John, 1580-1631. [Works. 1983.] The complete works of Captain John Smith (1580-1631) /. Chapel Hill, c1983. p. cm. ISBN 0-8078-1525-X LC Card 81-10364 DDC 975.5/02 19
F229 .S59 1983

VIRGINIA - HISTORY - CIVIL WAR, 1861-1865.
Robertson, James I. Civil War sites in Virginia . Charlottesville , 1981. p. cm. ISBN 0-8139-0907-4 LC Card 81-7426 DDC 917.55/0443 19
F227 .R59

Virginia. Industrial Development, Division of. see Virginia. Division of Industrial Development.

Virginia Institute of Marine Science, Gloucester Point. The Chesapeake Bay . Gloucester Point, Va. [1975] 2 v. : LC Card 80-621270 DDC 363.7/3942/0916347 19
TD223.1 .C44

Virginia. Insurance and Banking, Bureau of. see Virginia. Bureau of Insurance and Banking.

Virginia. Insurance Bureau. see Virginia. Bureau of Insurance and Banking.

Virginia. Laws, statutes, etc. (Old Catalog form: Virginia. Statutes)
Code of Virginia, 1950. Chapter 10.2. 1979.
Virginia. Board of Funeral Directors and Embalmers. Rules, regulations, and by-laws and Chapter 10.2, Code of Virginia. [Richmond] [1979?] 24 p. ; LC Card 80-621938 DDC 344.755/045 347.550445 19
KFV2682.U5 A32 1979a

VIRGINIA. LAWS, STATUTES, ETC.
Virginia, planning, housing & districting legislation. [Richmond] *NYPL [JLM 80-935]*

Virginia. Legislature. see Virginia. General Assembly.

VIRGINIA - MANUFACTURES.
Virginia. Division of Industrial Development. A guide for establishing a manufacturing business in Virginia. Richmond, 1974. 33 p.
*NYPL [*ZT-1259]*

Virginia Museum of Fine Arts, Richmond.
Virginia Museum state services, 1976-1978. [Richmond] : The Museum, [197-] 79 p. : ill. ; 22 cm. Cover title. Supplement for 1976 (5 leaves) inserted. LC Card 80-623145 DDC 069.5/6 19
1. Art rental and lending services - Virginia - Catalogs.
2. Virginia Museum of Fine Arts, Richmond - Catalogs. I. Title.
N716.M8 A73

VIRGINIA MUSEUM OF FINE ARTS, RICHMOND - CATALOGS.
Virginia Museum of Fine Arts, Richmond. Virginia Museum state services, 1976-1978. [Richmond] [197-] 79 p. : LC Card 80-623145 DDC 069.5/6 19
N716.M8 A73

Virginia Museum state services, 1976-1978.
Virginia Museum of Fine Arts, Richmond. [Richmond] [197-] 79 p. : LC Card 80-623145 DDC 069.5/6 19
N716.M8 A73

VIRGINIA - OCCUPATIONS - STATISTICS.
Virginia. Employment Commission. Manpower Research Division. Occupational employment statistics . [Richmond] [1980] ix, 198 p. : LC Card 80-622341 DDC 331.12/5/09755 19
HD5725.V8 V53 1980

Virginia. Office of Emergency and Energy Services. Line, Lloyd E. Energy in the 80's . Richmond, Va. (310 Turner Rd., Richmond, 23225) [1980] xviii, 203 p. : LC Card 81-622013 DDC 333.79/09755 19
TJ163.25.U6 L56

Virginia. Office of the Attorney General. see Virginia. Attorney General's Office.

Virginia. Office of the Secretary of Human Resources.
The effects of services integration in Virginia at the local and state level / prepared by Office of the Secretary of Human Resources. Richmond : The Office, [1978] 58 p. ; 28 cm. Cover title. "Author-editor: Patti Chrzan-Seelig." Bibliography: p. 47-48. LC Card 79-624121 DDC 361.6/09755 19
1. Public welfare - Virginia - Planning. 2. Social service - Virginia - Planning. I. Chrzan-Seelig, Patti. II. Title.
HV86 .V86 1978

The revised State plan for the identification and diagnosis of children who are handicapped : joint report of the Secretary of Human Resources and the Secretary of Education to the Governor and the General Assembly of Virginia. Richmond : Commonwealth of Virginia, Division of Purchases and Supply, 1979. [73] p. ; 28 cm. (House document - the General Assembly of Virginia . no. 37) LC Card 79-624128 DDC 300/.9755 s 362.4/048 19
1. Children - Medical examinations - Virginia - Planning. 2. Handicapped children - Virginia - Identification - Planning. 3. Medical screening - Virginia. I. Virginia. Dept. of Education. II. Series: Virginia. General Assembly, 1979. House of Delegates. Document , no. 37. III. Title.
J87 .V9 1979c no. 37 RJ102.5.V8

VIRGINIA. PENITENTIARY, RICHMOND - CASE STUDIES - STATISTICS.
Virginia. Dept. of Corrections. Research and Reporting Unit. Self-mutilation at the penitentiary and Powhatan . [Richmond] [1978] 10 leaves : LC Card 79-622551 DDC 365/.641 19
HV9475.V82 R57 1978

Virginia, planning, housing & districting legislation. [Richmond] 20-28 cm. Issued by the Virginia Division of State Planning and community Affairs. Title varies: 1970, Virginia planning legislation.
1. Virginia. Laws, statutes, etc. I. Virginia. Division of State Planning and Community Affairs. II. Title: Virginia planning legislation.
NYPL [JLM 80-935]

Virginia planning legislation. Virginia, planning, housing & districting legislation. [Richmond]
NYPL [JLM 80-935]

VIRGINIA - POLITICS AND GOVERNMENT - 1951-
Virginia. Telecommunications Study Commission. Telecommunications, a new Virginia initiative . Richmond, Va. , 1980. 79 p. ; LC Card 80-621795 DDC 300/.9755 s 353.975504 19
J87 .V9 1980b, no. 22 JK3949.C65

Virginia Polytechnic Institute and State University.
Nicholson, John C. Soil survey of Goochland County, Virginia /. [Washington] , 1980. ix, 137 p., [22] fold. leaves of plates : LC Card 80-601854 DDC 631.4/7/755455 19
S599.V8 N52

Soil survey of Gloucester County, Virginia. [Washington, D.C.?] , 1980. vii, 88 p., 35 folded p. of plates : LC Card 80-604149 DDC 631.4/7/755532 19
S599.V8 S64

Soil survey of Hanover County, Virginia / [by Robert L. Hodges ... et al.] / United States Department of Agriculture, Soil Conservation Service, in cooperation with Virginia Polytechnic Institute and State University. [Washington, D.C. : National Cooperative Soil Survey, 1980] ix, 218 p., [35] fold. leaves of plates : ill., maps ; 29 cm. Cover title. Bibliography: p. 126. Includes index. LC Card 80-602048 DDC 631.4/7/755462 19
1. Soils - Virginia - Hanover Co. - Maps. I. Hodges, Robert L. II. United States. Soil Conservation Service. III. Title.
S599.V8 V57 1980

United States. Soil Conservation Service. General soil map, Virginia /. Lanham, MD , 1979. 1 map : LC Card 81-690105
G3881.J3 1979 .U5

Virginia Polytechnic Institute and State University. Dept. of Management, Housing, and Family Development. Sharp, Bobby H. Books consumerists (and others) should know about . Blacksburg, Va. [1980] iii, 30 p. ; LC Card 80-622383 DDC 016.64073 19
Z5776.C65 S5 TX335

Virginia Polytechnic Institute and State University. Extension Division. Sharp, Bobby H. Books consumerists (and others) should know about . Blacksburg, Va. [1980] iii, 30 p. ; LC Card 80-622383 DDC 016.64073 19
Z5776.C65 S5 TX335

VIRGINIA POLYTECHNIC INSTITUTE AND STATE UNIVERSITY. LEARNING RESOURCES CENTER - CATALOGS.
McCombs, Dorothy F. The Appalachian region of Virginia . Blacksburg, Va. , 1981. p. cm. LC Card 81-11487 DDC 016.9755 19
Z1345 .M36 F226

Virginia Polytechnic Institute and State University. Research Division.
Bulletin .
(135) Orden, David. Small farm programs . Blacksburg , 1978. xvi, 200 p. : LC Card 79-623060 DDC 081 s 338.1/8755 19
AS36 .V512 no. 135 HD1476.U5

(146) Hamon, Avas B. Morphology and systematics of the first instars of the genus Cerococcus (Homoptera:Coccoidea:Cerococcidae) /. Blacksburg, Va. [1979] v, 122 p. : LC Card 80-622297 DDC 595.7/52 19
AS36 .V512 no. 146 QL527.C43

(149) Buccola, Steven T. Potential efficiencies through coordination of milk assembly and milk manufacturing plant location in the northeastern United States /. Blacksburg, Va. , 1979. viii, 64 p. : LC Card 79-625090 DDC 081 s 381/.4171/0974 19
AS36 .V512 no. 149 HD9282.U5A115

(153) Orden, David. Cooperative extension small-farm programs in the South . Blacksburg [1980] xii, 86 p. : LC Card 80-622494 DDC 081 s 334/.683/0975 19
AS36 .V512 no. 153 HD1476.U5

Virginia Polytechnic Institute and State University. Water Resources Research Center.
Buikema, Arthur L. Rotifer sensitivity to combinations of inorganic water pollutants /. Blacksburg , 1977. vi, 216 p. : LC Card 78-621510 DDC 333.91/09755 s 595.1/81 19
TD201 .V57 no. 92 QL391.R8

Bulletin.
(109) Lake, Carol A. Phosphate and tripolyphosphate adsorption by clay minerals and estuarine sediments /. Blacksburg , 1977. v, 58 p. : LC Card 77-624071 DDC 333.91/009755 s 551.46/09 19
TD201 .V57 no. 109 GC97.8.V8

(110) Collins, Edmond R. Swine lagoon effluent on a soil-plant environment . Blacksburg , 1978. v, 38 p. ; LC Card 78-624385 DDC 333.91/009755 s 636.4/0831 19
TD201 .V57 no. 110 TD930

(118) Wendt, Stephen L. Occurrence and distribution of human bacterial pathogens in Virginia surface waters /. Blacksburg, Va. , 1979. vii, 68 p. : LC Card 79-625812 DDC 333.91/009755 s 363.7/394 19
TD201 .V57 no. 118 TD224.V8

(119) Contractor, D. N. Streamflow and water quality modeling of the Chowan River /. Blacksburg, Va. [1980] vii, 71 p. : LC Card 80-623862 DDC 333.91/009755 s 363.7/3942/0724 19
TD201 .V57 no. 119 TD225.C53

(121) Navigation user charges impact the transportation of agricultural products /. Blacksburg, Va. [1979] viii, 97 p. : LC Card 79-626057 DDC 551.4/8 s 386/.242 19
TD201 .V57 no. 121 HE629

(125) Smolen, M. D. Agricultural land use . Blacksburg, Va. , 1980. vii, 82 p. : LC Card 80-622278 DDC 333.91/009755 s 363.7/3941 19
TD201 .V57 no. 125 TD428.A37

(126) Erkenbrecher, Carl W. Sediment bacteria as a water quality indicator in the Lynnhaven estuary /. Blacksburg, Va. [1980] x, 118 p. : LC Card 80-622517 DDC 333.91/009755 s 628.168/028/7 19
TD201 .V57 no. 126 QR48

(39) Flood damage abatement . Blacksburg , 1970. 138 p. : LC Card 75-634086 DDC 333.91/009755 s 363.3/49356/09755 19
TD201 .V57 no. 39

(85) A Model for evaluating the effect of land uses on flood flows /. Blacksburg , 1978. x, 137 p. : LC Card 79-621996 DDC [551.48/9/0724] 19
TD201 .V57 no. 85 GB1399

(92) Buikema, Arthur L. Rotifer sensitivity to combinations of inorganic water pollutants /. Blacksburg , 1977. vi, 42 p. : LC Card 78-621510 DDC 333.91/09755 s 595.1/81 19
TD201 .V57 no. 92 QL391.R8

Collins, Edmond R. Swine lagoon effluent on a soil-plant environment . Blacksburg , 1978. v, 38 p. : LC Card 78-624385 DDC 333.91/009755 s 636.4/0831 19
TD201 .V57 no. 110 TD930

Flood damage abatement . Blacksburg , 1970. 138 p. : LC Card 75-634086 DDC 333.91/009755 s 363.3/49356/09755 19
TD201 .V57 no. 39

Special report - Virginia Water Resources Research Center, Virginia Polytechnic Institute and State University .
(no. 7) Cox, William Edward, 1944- Virginia water law . Blacksburg, Va. , 1979. 15 p. ; LC Card 80-622367 DDC 346.75504/691 19
KFV2846.Z9 C68

VIRGINIA - POPULATION.

Jones, Daniel G. Commonwealth of Virginia--demographic and economic trends /. Richmond, Va. , 1978. 56 p. : LC Card 79-625625 DDC 312/.8/09755 19
HB3525.V8 J66

Virginia Port Authority. Virginia ports : Port of Hampton Roads : first in world trade, 1607-1974 : no. 1 export port, no. 1 railnetwork, no. 2 east coast container port. Norfolk : Virginia Port Authority, [1974?] [15] p. : col. ill., maps ; 28 cm. Cover title.
1. Harbors - Virginia - Hampton Roads region.
NYPL [JLF 81-623]

Virginia. Public Safety, Secretary of. see **Virginia. Secretary of Public Safety.**

The Virginia quarterly review. v. 1- ; Apr. 1925- Charlottesville [etc.] University of Virginia. 25 cm. Microfilm. INDEXES: Vols. 1-20, 1925-44, with v. 1.
1. American periodicals (General). I. Virginia. University.
NYPL [*ZAN-4648]

Virginia. Rehabilitative Services, Dept. of. see **Virginia. Dept. of Rehabilitative Services.**

Virginia. Retirement Study Commission. Report of the Virginia Retirement Study Commission to the Governor and the General Assembly of Virginia. Richmond : Commonwealth of Virginia, 1980. 129 p. ; 28 cm. (House document - Commonwealth of Virginia ; no. 31) LC Card 80-623142 DDC 300/.9755 s 353.9755005 19
1. Civil service pensions - Virginia. 2. Judges - Salaries, pensions, etc. - Virginia. 3. Police - Salaries, pensions, etc. - Virginia. I. Series: Virginia. General Assembly, 1979. House of Delegates. Document , no. 31.
J87 .V9 1980c no. 31 JK3960.P4

Virginia. Revenue Resources and Economic Commission. Inflation and the Virginia income tax ; Personal property taxation in Virginia localities ; Transportation taxation in Virginia. Richmond, Va. , 1979. x, 210 p. ; LC Card 80-623840 DDC 336.2/009755 19
HJ4655.V88 I64

Virginia rules and regulations declaring hazardous occupations, as promulgated by Commissioner, Virginia Department of Labor and Industry, effective date November 1, 1979 /. Virginia. Dept. of Labor and Industry. Richmond, Va. [1979] 16, [5] p. ; LC Card 80-622803 DDC 344.755/0134 19
KFV2735.5.A435 A2 1979

Virginia. Secretary of Education. Report of the Secretary of Education and the Secretary of Public Safety on Senate joint resolution 159 to the General Assembly of Virginia. Richmond, Va. : Commonwealth of Virginia, 1980. iii, 10 p. ; 29 cm. (House document -- Commonwealth of Virginia . no. 4) LC Card 80-621140 DDC 300/.9755 s 362.7/4/09755 19
1. Juvenile delinquency - Virginia - Prevention. 2. Juvenile courts - Virginia - Public relations. 3. Schools - Virginia - Public relations. I. Virginia. Secretary of Public Safety. II. Series: Virginia. General Assembly. House of Delegates. Document , no. 4.
J87 .V9 1980c, no. 4 HV9105.V7

Virginia. Secretary of Public Safety. Virginia. Secretary of Education. Report of the Secretary of Education and the Secretary of Public Safety on Senate joint resolution 159 to the General Assembly of Virginia. Richmond, Va. , 1980. iii, 10 p. ; LC Card 80-621140 DDC 300/.9755 s 362.7/4/09755 19
J87 .V9 1980c, no. 4 HV9105.V7

Virginia. Soil and Water Conservation Commission. Directory of the Virginia soil & water conservation districts, 1979 / prepared by Virginia Soil & Water Conservation Commission. Richmond : The Commission, 1979. 40 p. : maps ; 28 cm. LC Card 79-624120 DDC 631.4/025/755 19
1. Soil conservation districts - Virginia - Directories. 2. Water districts - Virginia - Directories. I. Title.
S624.V8 V57 1979

Virginia. Solid Waste Commission. Report of the Solid Waste Commission to the Governor and the General Assembly of Virginia. Richmond, Va. : Commonwealth of Virginia, 1980. 16 p. ; 28 cm. (Senate document - Commonwealth of Virginia ; no. 25) LC Card 80-621794 DDC 300/.9755 s 363.7/2 19
1. Refuse and refuse disposal - Virginia. 2. Hazardous wastes - Virginia. I. Series: Virginia. General Assembly, 1980. Senate. Document , no. 25.
J87 .V9 1980b, no. 25 TD788.4.V8

Virginia. State Board of Architects, Professional Engineers, and Land Surveyors. Rules and regulations, adopted May 30, 1975, amended December 17, 1976, March 10, 1977, March 2, 1979, published June 1, 1979, effective July 1, 1979 ; Statutes, March 2, 1979, chapter 1.1, title 54, Chapter 3, title 54, chapter 24, title 54, chapter 7, title 13.1 / Commonwealth of Virginia, The State Board of Architects, Professional Engineers and Land Surveyors. Richmond, Va. : Dept. of Commerce, [1979] 39 p. ; 29 cm. Cover title. LC Card 80-621955 DDC 344.755/01762 19
1. Architects - Legal status, laws, etc. - Virginia. 2. Engineers - Legal status, laws, etc. - Virginia. 3. Surveyors - Legal status, laws, etc. - Virginia. I. Title.
KFV2729.A7 A32 1979

Virginia. State Board of Professional Counselors. Regulations of the Boards . Richmond, Va. (2 South Ninth St., P.O. Box 1-X, Richmond, Va. 23202) [1977?] 36 p. ; LC Card 80-623907 DDC 344.755/0176115 347.5504176115 19
KFV2726.5.P73 A3 1977

Virginia. State Corporation Commission. (Old Catalog form: Virginia. Corporation Commission)
Virginia. Bureau of Banking. Annual report. Richmond. **NYPL [THB (Virginia. Bureau of Banking. Annual report)]**

Virginia. State Corporation Commission. Banking Division. (Old Catalog form: Virginia. Corporation Commission. Banking Division)
Virginia. Bureau of Banking. Annual report. Richmond. **NYPL [THB (Virginia. Bureau of Banking. Annual report)]**

Virginia. State Corporation Commission. Bureau of Banking. see **Virginia. Bureau of Banking.**

Virginia. State Corporation Commission. Bureau of Financial Institutions. see **Virginia. Bureau of Financial Institutions.**

Virginia. State Council of Higher Education. (Old Catalog form: Virginia. Higher Education, Council of)
Enrollment projections, Virginia's state-supported institutions, 1980-82 biennium. [Richmond, Va.] : State Council of Higher Education for Virginia, [1980] 70 p. ; 28 cm. (Staff technical report . STR 79-12) "Council staff responsible for preparation of this report: James M. Alessio ... Mona N. Mallory." "January, 1980." Chiefly tables. LC Card 80-622506 DDC 378/.1059755 19
1. College attendance - Virginia - Planning - Statistics. I. Alessio, James M. II. Mallory, Mona N. III. Title. IV. Series.
LC148 .V52 1980

Fact book : higher education in Virginia, 1979-80. [Richmond, Va.] : State Council of Higher Education for Virginia, [1980] 59 p. ; 22 x 11 cm. Cover title. LC Card 80-621790 DDC 378.755 19
1. Education, Higher - Virginia - Directories. 2. Universities and colleges - Virginia - Directories. I. Title. II. Title: Higher education in Virginia, 1979-80.
L903.V8 V52 1980

Graduate marine science education in Virginia : a report to the Governor and the Joint Legislative Audit and Review Commission / by the State Council of Higher Education for Virginia. Richmond, Va. : The Council, [1978] 3, v, 155 p. ; 28 cm. "December 1978." Includes bibliographical references. LC Card 79-624103 DDC 551.46/007/11755 19
1. Oceanography - Study and teaching (Higher) - Virginia. 2. Marina biology - Study and teaching (Higher) - Virginia. I. Virginia. General Assembly. Joint Legislative Audit & Review Commission. II. Title.
GC31.6 .V575 1978

Out-of-state institutions operating in Virginia, 1978-79. [Richmond] : State Council of Higher Education for Virginia, [1979] 42 p. ; 28 cm. (Staff technical report . 79-13) LC Card 80-622044 DDC 378.73 19
1. Universities and colleges - United States - Statistics. 2. Universities and colleges - Virginia - Statistics. I. Title. II. Series.
LA227.3 .V57 1979

Virginia. State Crime Commission.
Children and youth in trouble in Virginia : a report / by the Virginia State Crime Commission and Advisory Group. Richmond, Va. : The Commission, [1977] xvi, 188 p. ; 28 cm. "December, 1977." LC Card 80-622757 DDC 364.3/6/09755 19
1. Juvenile delinquents - Virginia. 2. Social work with delinquents and criminals - Virginia. 3. Rehabilitation of juvenile delinquents - Virginia. I. Virginia. Children and Youth in Trouble in Virginia Advisory Group. II. Title.
HV9105.V7 V53 1977

Children and youth in trouble in Virginia : phase II, a report / by the Virginia State Crime Commission. Richmond, Va. : The Commission, [1979] xxii, 179 p. : ill. ; 28 cm. "May 1979." Cover title. Includes bibliographical references. LC Card 80-622758 DDC 364.3/6/09755 19
1. Juvenile justice, Administration of - Virginia. I. Title.
HV9105.V7 V53 1979

Virginia State health plan, 1979-83. Virginia. Statewide Health Coordinating Council. State health plan, Commonwealth of Virginia /. [Richmond, Va.] [1979] 2 v. : LC Card 80-620762 DDC 362.1/09755 19
RA395.A4 V88 1979

Virginia. State Library, Richmond.
Publications. For other vols. in this series, see
Old Catalog.
(no. 47) Nugent, Nell Marion. Cavaliers and
pioneers . Richmond , 1980. iii, 18 p. ; ISBN
0-88490-088-6 (pbk.) LC Card 80-141230
DDC 929/.3755 19
F225 .N842 1934 Suppl.

The Virginia State penal system, felons
committed, fiscal years 1972-1976 ; the
Virginia State penal system, felons confined,
fiscal years 1972-1976 /. Virginia. Dept. of
Corrections. Bureau of Research, Reporting,
and Evaluation. Reporting Section. [Richmond]
[1977?] 17 p. ; LC Card 80-623252 DDC
364.3/09755 19
HV8366 .V82 1977

Virginia State penal system, felons confined,
fiscal years 1972-1976. Virginia. Dept. of
Corrections. Bureau of Research, Reporting,
and Evaluation. Reporting Section. The Virginia
State penal system, felons committed, fiscal
years 1972-1976 ; the Virginia State penal
system, felons confined, fiscal years 1972-1976
/. [Richmond] [1977?] 17 p. ; LC Card
80-623252 DDC 364.3/09755 19
HV8366 .V82 1977

Virginia. State Planning and Community Affairs,
Division of. see **Virginia. Division of State**
Planning and Community Affairs.

Virginia. State Travel Service. United States
Travel Data Center. Travel in Virginia, 1978 .
[Richmond, Va. , 1978] 12 p. : LC Card
80-622616 DDC 381/.45917550443 19
G155.U6 U58 1978

Virginia. State Water Control Board.
Data organization, technical support, and
coordination for the Environmental Protection
Agency's Chesapeake Bay Program :
semi-annual report for the period 5 June to 31
December, 1978. [Richmond] : Commonwealth
of Virginia, State Water Control Board, [1979]
17 leaves ; 28 cm. Cover title. "EPA grant number
R805859." "February 1979." LC Card 80-621161
DDC 353.0082/325 19
1. United States. Environmental Protection Agency.
Chesapeake Bay Program. I. Title.
TD223.1 .V57 1979

Planning bulletin - Virginia State Water
Control Board .
(312) Dawson, James W. Groundwater
resources of Henry County, Virginia /.
Richmond, Va. , 1979. xviii, 69, [35] p. : LC
Card 79-625459 DDC 553.7/9/09755692 19
GB1025.V8 D38

Virginia. Statewide Grand Jury Commission.
Report of the Statewide Grand Jury
Commission to the Governor and the General
Assembly of Virginia. Richmond, Va. :
Commonwealth of Virginia, 1980. 12 p. ; 28
cm. (House document - Commonwealth of Virginia ;
no. 29) LC Card 80-622980 DDC 300/.9755 s
345.755/075 19
1. Grand jury - Virginia. I. Series: Virginia. General
Assembly, 1980. House of Delegates. Document , no.
29.
J87 .V9 1980c no. 29 KFV2977

Virginia. Statewide Health Coordinating Council.
State health plan, Commonwealth of Virginia /
prepared by the Statewide Health Coordinating
Council and the Bureau of Health Planning,
State Health Department. [Richmond, Va.] :
The Council, [1979] 2 v. : ill. ; 28 cm. Cover
title: Virginia State health plan, 1979-83. "April, 1979."
Includes bibliographies. LC Card 80-620762 DDC
362.1/09755 19
1. Health planning - Virginia. 2. Medical policy -
Virginia. 3. Public health - Virginia. 4. Medical care -
Virginia. I. Virginia. Bureau of Health Planning. II.
Title. III. Title: Virginia State health plan, 1979-83.
RA395.A4 V88 1979

Virginia. Statutes. see **Virginia. Laws, statutes,**
etc.

Virginia. Supreme Court. Rules of the Supreme
Court of Virginia governing practice and
procedure in courts, with the admission of
foreign attorneys, with amendments adopted
through February 1, 1980. [Richmond] : The
Court, c1979. 178 p. : forms ; 23 cm. Previous
ed. issued by this body under its earlier name: Virginia,
Supreme Court of Appeals under title: Rules of the
Supreme Court of Appeals of Virginia, February 1,

1950. LC Card 80-624098 DDC 347.755/0355
347.5507355 19
1. Court rules - Virginia. I. Virginia. Supreme Court of
Appeals. Rules of Supreme Court of Appeals of
Virginia, February 1, 1950. II. Title.
KFV2958.A445 A2 1980

Virginia. Supreme Court of Appeals.
Rules of Supreme Court of Appeals of Virginia,
February 1, 1950. Virginia. Supreme Court.
Rules of the Supreme Court of Virginia
governing practice and procedure in courts
and the admission of foreign attorneys, with
amendments adopted through February 1,
1980. [Richmond] , c1979. 178 p. : LC Card
80-624098 DDC 347.755/0355 347.5507355 19
KFV2958.A445 A2 1980

Virginia tax facts. Virginia. Dept. of Taxation.
[Richmond, Va.] [1979] 57 p. ; LC Card
79-625802 DDC 343.75504 19
KFV2870 .A87

Virginia. Telecommunications Study Commission.
Telecommunications, a new Virginia initiative :
the report of the Telecommunications Study
Commission to the Governor and the General
Assembly of Virginia. Richmond, Va. :
Commonwealth of Virginia, 1980. 79 p. ; 28
cm. (Senate document - Commonwealth of Virginia ;
no. 22) LC Card 80-621795 DDC 300/.9755 s
353.975504 19
1. Administrative agencies - Virginia. 2. Virginia -
Politics and government - 1951-. 3.
Telecommunication - Virginia. I. Series: Virginia.
General Assembly, 1980. Senate. Document , no. 22. II.
Title.
J87 .V9 1980b, no. 22 JK3949.C65

Virginia. Traffic and Safety, Division of. see
Virginia. Division of Traffic and Safety.

Virginia. University.
The Virginia quarterly review. v. 1- ; Apr.
1925- Charlottesville [etc.]
*NYPL [*ZAN-4648]*

Virginia. University. Alderman Library. see
Virginia. University. Library.

Virginia. University. Bibliographical Society.
Life, Page West. Sir Thomas Malory and the
Morte Darthur . Charlottesville , 1980. xiii, 297
p. ; ISBN 0-8139-0868-X LC Card 80-16180
Z8545.5 .L53 PR2045 NYPL [JFE 80-3924]

MacMahon, Candace W. Elizabeth Bishop .
Charlottesville , 1980. xviii, 227 p. : ISBN
0-8139-0783-7 LC Card 79-13063
Z8098.9 .M34 PS3503.I785
*NYPL [*RS-NBC (Bishop) 81-802]*

Virginia. University. Civil Engineering Dept.
Bridges on secondary highways and local
roads : rehabilitation and replacement /
University of Virginia Civil Engineering
Department, Virginia Highway and
Transportation Research Council, and Virginia
Department of Highways and Transportation.
Washington, D.C. : Transportation Research
Board, National Research Council, 1980. 132
p. : ill. ; 28 cm. (National Cooperative Highway
Research Program report ; 222 0077-5614) "Research
sponsored by the American Association of State
Highway and Transportation Officials, in cooperation
with the Federal Highway Administration." "Project
12-20 FY '78." Includes bibliographies. ISBN
0-309-03025-0 (pbk.) : LC Card 80-51497
DDC 625.7 s 624.2 19
1. Bridges. I. Virginia Highway & Transportation
Research Council. II. Virginia. Dept. of Highways and
Transportation. III. American Association of State
Highway and Transportation Officials. IV. United
States. Federal Highway Administration. V. Series:
National Cooperative Highway Research Program.
Report , 222. VI. Title.
TE7 .N25 no. 222 TG153

Virginia. University. Dept. of Engineering:
Virginia Highway & Transportation Research
Council. see **Virginia Highway &**
Transportation Research Council.

Virginia. University. Library. Computer catalog
of nineteenth-century American-imprint sheet
music. Charlottesville, 1977. 12 p.
NYPL [JNF 78-151]

Virginia. Visually Handicapped, Commission for
the. see **Virginia. Commission for the**
Visually Handicapped.

Virginia water law . Cox, William Edward, 1944-

Blacksburg, Va. , 1979. 15 p. ; LC Card
80-622367 DDC 346.75504/691 19
KFV2846.Z9 C68

Virginia. Welfare, Dept. of. see **Virginia. Dept. of**
Welfare.

VIRUS DISEASES.
Wilson, Elaine Blume. At the edge of life .
[Bethesda, Md.?] , Washington, D.C. , 1980. 75
p. : LC Card 80-604128 DDC 616.9/25 19
RC114.5 .W54

VIRUSES - IDENTIFICATION.
Utah Water Research Laboratory. Studies on
viruses in water /. Logan, Utah , 1979. viii, 35
p. : LC Card 80-621126 DDC 628.3 19
QR48 .U8 1979

VISCERAL LEARNING. see **BIOFEEDBACK**
TRAINING.

VISIBILITY.
Gallagher, V. P. Contrast requirements of urban
drivers . Philadelphia , Springfield, Va. , 1974.
viii, 72 p. : *NYPL [JSF 80-828]*

VISIBILITY - ADDRESSES, ESSAYS,
LECTURES.
Grade crossings, devices, visibility, and freeway
operations /. Washington, D.C. , 1980. iv, 49
p. : ISBN 0-309-03117-6 LC Card 81-4730 DDC
380.5 s 625.7/94 19
TE7 .H5 no. 773 TE228

VISIBILITY - FLATHEAD RIVER
WATERSHED, B.C. AND MONT.
Montana. Air Quality Bureau. Flathead River
Basin environmental impact study /. Helena,
Mont. [1979] vi, 86, [170] p. : LC Card
80-620860 DDC 363.7/3942/097868 19
TD883.5.F56 M66 1979

VISITORS, FOREIGN - UNITED STATES.
United States. General Accounting Office.
More can be done to speed the entry of
international travelers . [Washington, D.C. ,
1979] vi, 59 p. : LC Card 80-601083 DDC
353.0082/6591 19
G155.U6 U54 1979

Visual environmental adaptation problems of the
partially sighted : final report / S. M.
Genensky ... [et al.] [Santa Monica, Calif.] :
Center for the Partially Sighted, Santa Monica
Hospital Medical Center, 1979. xvii, 198 p. ; 28
cm. "Prepared for the Department of Health,
Education, and Welfare." "CPS-100-HEW."
Bibliography: p. 187-198.
1. Visually handicapped. I. Genensky, Samuel M. II.
United States. Dept. of Health, Education, and Welfare.
III. Center for the Partially Sighted.
NYPL [JLF 80-1465]

VISUALLY HANDICAPPED.
Visual environmental adaptation problems of
the partially sighted . [Santa Monica, Calif.] ,
1979. xvii, 198 p. ; *NYPL [JLF 80-1465]*

Vital and health statistics. Series 10, Data from
the national health survey .
(no. 137) Feller, Barbara A. Health
characteristics of persons with chronic activity
limitation . Hyattsville, Md. , 1981. p. cm.
ISBN 0-8406-0229-4 LC Card 81-11249 DDC
312/.0973 s 312/.3 19
RA407.3 .A346 no. 137 RA644.6

VITAL STATISTICS - YEARBOOKS.
World tables: from the data files of the World
Bank. Baltimore. *NYPL [*R-Econ 77-2973]*

VITICULTURE - FOUR CORNERS REGION.
Grape and wine production in the Four Corners
Region /. [Tucson, Ariz. , 1980] 116 p. : LC
Card 80-623372 DDC 634/.8/0978 19
SB389 .G76

VITICULTURE - SOUTH CAROLINA -
STATISTICS.
South Carolina Crop and Livestock Reporting
Service. South Carolina fruit tree survey, 1978 .
[Clemson, S.C.] [Washington] [1979] 26 p. :
LC Card 80-621005 DDC 338.1 s
338.1/7411/09757 19
HD1775.S6 S6 no. 404 SB320.7.S6

Viven-Bessières rifle grenade. France. Ministère
de la guerre. Notes on the use of the
Viven-Bessières rifle grenade /. Washington,
1918. 12 p.: *NYPL [*ZV-179]*

Vivian, James F. Fritz, Chester. The journal of
Chester Fritz . Grand Forks , 1981. 120 p., [1]
folded leaf of plates : LC Card 81-148265 DDC

Vizenor, Gerald Robert, 1934- Earthdivers : tribal narratives on mixed descent / Gerald Vizenor ; with illustrations by Jaune Quick-to-See Smith. Minneapolis : University of Minnesota Press, c1981. xxii, 191 p., [1] leaf of plates : ill. ; 24 cm. ISBN 0-8166-1048-7 : LC Card 81-150279 DDC 813/.54 19
1. Indians of North America - Mixed bloods - Fiction. I. Title.
PS3572.I9 E2

Vladykov, Vadim Dmitrij, 1898- A new nonparasitic species of the holarctic lamprey genus Lethenteron Creaser and Hubbs, 1922, (Petromyzonidae) from northwestern North America, with notes on other species of the same genus / by Vadim D. Valdykov and Edward Kott. [Fairbanks : University of Alaska], 1978. 74 p. : ill. ; 23 cm. (Biological papers of the University of Alaska . no. 19) Bibliography: p. 68-74. LC Card 78-622997 DDC 574 s 597/.2 19
1. Lethenteron alaskense - Classification. 2. Lethenteron - Classification. 3. Fishes - Classification. 4. Fishes - Alaska - Classification. 5. Fishes - Northwest Territories, Can. - Classification. I. Kott, Edward, joint author. II. Series: University of Alaska (System). Biological papers of the University of Alaska , no. 19. III. Title.
QH1 .A258 no. 19 QL638.25.P48

Vlahos, Michael, 1951- The blue sword : the Naval War College and the American mission, 1919-1941 / by Michael Vlahos.1st ed. Newport, R.I. : Naval War College Press ; Washington, D.C. : For sale by the Supt. of Docs., U. S. G.P.O., 1980 [i.e. 1981] p. cm. (Historical monograph series / U. S. Naval War College . no. 4) Bibliography: p. Includes index. LC Card 81-9654 DDC 359/.07/1173 19
1. Naval War College (U. S.) - History - 20th century. 2. United States. Navy - History - 20th century. 3. Naval art and science - History - 20th century. 4. United States - History, Naval - 20th century. I. Series: Historical monograph series (Naval War College (U. S.)). II. Title.
V420 .V55

VOCATIONAL ASPIRATIONS. see **VOCATIONAL INTERESTS.**

VOCATIONAL EDUCATION - ALABAMA - PLANNING - CONGRESSES.
Conference on Postsecondary Statewide Planning for 1980-1985, Montgomery, Ala., 1978. Statewide postsecondary planning for 1980-1985 . Montgomery, Ala. [1979?] 109 p. ; LC Card 79-623281 DDC 378/.107/09761 19
LA231.5 .C66 1978

VOCATIONAL EDUCATION - CONNECTICUT - STATISTICS.
Connecticut. Bureau of Vocational Program Planning & Development. Summary of selected statistics . [Hartford] [1979] 29 p. : LC Card 79-624847 DDC 379.1/552/09746 19
LC1046.C8 C663 1979

VOCATIONAL EDUCATION - IDAHO - PLANNING.
Idaho. State Board for Vocational Education. Idaho State plan for the administration of vocational education under Public law 94-482 . [Boise] [1977] ii leaves, 208 p. : LC Card 80-621264 DDC 375/.008 s 379.1/552/09796 19
LC1046.I2 A3 no. 105a

VOCATIONAL EDUCATION - INDIANA.
Indiana. State Board of Vocational and Technical Education. Secondary area vocational system, spring 1980. Bloomington, IN , c1980. v, 114 p. : LC Card 80-623920 DDC 373/.01/1309772 19
LC1046.I4 I55 1980

Smalley, Shirley F. A local school implementation plan for performance based vocational education . Bloomington , 1980. ix, 70 p. : LC Card 81-622007 DDC 373.2/46/09772 19
LC1046.I4 S55

VOCATIONAL EDUCATION - IOWA - ADMINISTRATION - COLLECTED WORKS.
Iowa. Dept. of Public Instruction. Career Education Division. Iowa state plan for the administration of vocational education within career education under the Vocational

education act of 1976, P.L. 94-482, fiscal years 1978-1982 . Des Moines, Iowa [1979?]- v. <1> : LC Card 80-623153 DDC 379.1/552/09777 19
LC1046.I8 I67 1979

VOCATIONAL EDUCATION - IOWA - PLANNING - STATISTICS.
Iowa. Dept. of Job Service. Labor Market Information Unit. Planning information for vocational education, State of Iowa, fiscal year 1981. Des Moines, Iowa [1980] 112 p. : LC Card 80-622458 DDC 373.2/46/09777 19
LC1046.I8 I65 1980

VOCATIONAL EDUCATION - MISSOURI - ACCREDITATION.
Missouri. Dept. of Elementary and Secondary Education. Accreditation standards and procedures for Missouri public school districts providing adult preparatory vocational education. [Jefferson City, Mo.] , 1980. iv, 35 p. ; LC Card 80-622460 DDC 379.1/58/09778 19
LC1046.M8 M54 1980

VOCATIONAL EDUCATION - NEVADA - PERIODICALS.
Nevada. State Dept. of Education. Vocational-Technical and Adult Education Branch. A survey of adult and continuing educaton programs in Nevada. Carson City.
NYPL [JLM 80-726]

VOCATIONAL EDUCATION - NEW MEXICO.
New Mexico. Board of Educational Finance--Commission of Postsecondary Education. Factbook on New Mexico public two-year community colleges and vocational schools, 1978-79. Santa Fe, N.M. [1979] vi, 90 p. : LC Card 80-622001 DDC 379.1/552/09789 19
LC1046.N45 N47 1979

VOCATIONAL EDUCATION - NEW YORK (STATE)
New York (State). Legislative Commission on Expenditure Review. Occupational education in secondary schools . Albany, N.Y. [1980] 5, ii, 70 p. : LC Card 80-623681 19
LC1046.N5 N48 1980

New York (State). State Consumer Protection Board. The profits of failure . Albany, N.Y. [1978] 114 p. ; LC Card 80-621030 19
LC1046.N5 N48 1978 NYPL [JLF 80-1578]

VOCATIONAL EDUCATION - NORTH CAROLINA.
North Carolina. State University, Raleigh. Center for Occupational Education. A prospectus for a vocational education policy resource center. Raleigh , 1975. 47 leaves ; LC Card 79-622866 DDC 370.11/3/09756 19
LC1046.N8 N68 1975

VOCATIONAL EDUCATION - OKLAHOMA - FINANCE - STATISTICS.
Oklahoma. State Dept. of Vocational and Technical Education. FY 1978-79 cost per program report . Stillwater, Okla. [1979] 78 leaves ; LC Card 80-622152 DDC 379.1/552/09766 19
LC1046.O5 O6 1979

VOCATIONAL EDUCATION - SOUTH CAROLINA - EDUCATION.
South Carolina. Dept. of Education. Assessment of vocational and technical education needs in South Carolina. [Columbia, S.C.] [1978] 497 p. in various pagings : LC Card 80-621836 DDC 379/.155 19
LC1046.S7 S68 1978

VOCATIONAL EDUCATION - UNITED STATES.
United States. Congress. House. Committee on Education and Labor. Subcommittee on Elementary, Secondary, and Vocational Education. Current issues in vocational education . Washington , 1980 [i.e. 1981] iv, 1178 p. : LC Card 81-601613 DDC 370.11/3 19
KF27 .E3364 1980i

United States. Office of Education. Division of Vocational and Technical Education. Resurge '79 . Washington, D. C. , 1980. 81 p. :
NYPL [JLF 81-624]

VOCATIONAL GUIDANCE FOR GIRLS. see **VOCATIONAL GUIDANCE FOR WOMEN.**

VOCATIONAL GUIDANCE FOR WOMEN - UNITED STATES - CONGRESSES.
Women as third-party neutrals . Ithaca , 1978. vi, 55 p. ; ISBN 0-87546-066-6 : LC Card 78-620003 DDC 331.89/14/02373 19
HD6058 .W6894

VOCATIONAL GUIDANCE - HAWAII.
Job hunter's guide to Hawaii . [Honolulu] , c1980. xvi, 263 p. : LC Card 81-144474 DDC 650.1/4/09969 19
HF5382.5.U6 H33

VOCATIONAL GUIDANCE - INFORMATION SERVICES - UNITED STATES - CONGRESSES.
Career and labor market information . Columbus, Ohio , Washington, D.C. [1980] v, 71 p. ; LC Card 80-602937 DDC 331.12/0973 19
HD5724 .C33

VOCATIONAL INTERESTS - UNITED STATES - STATISTICS.
Johns Hopkins University. Office of Health Manpower Studies. Career patterns of unaccepted applicants to medical school . [Bethesda? Md.] , 1974. vi, 207 p. : LC Card 76-600905
*R838.4 .J63 1974 NYPL [*XME-9527]*

VOCATIONAL OPPORTUNITIES. see **VOCATIONAL GUIDANCE.**

VOCATIONAL REHABILITATION - ILLINOIS.
Illinois. Dept. of Rehabilitation Services. Three year interim state plan for vocational rehabilitation, fiscal years 1980, 1981 & 1982. Springfield, Ill. [1979] iv, 51, [33] p. : LC Card 80-622136 DDC 353.97730083/3 19
HD7256.U6 I266 1979

Illinois. Division of Vocational Rehabilitation. Program and financial plan fiscal years 1980, 1981, and 1985. [Springfield, Ill.] [1979] 35 p. ; LC Card 80-621705 DDC 362/.0425 19
HV1555.I3 I4 1979

VOCATIONAL REHABILITATION - LAW AND LEGISLATION - FLORIDA.
United States. Congress. House. Committee on Education and Labor. Subcommittee on Select Education. To amend the Rehabilitation act of 1973, relating to State agency organization requirements . Washington , 1980. v, 560 p. : LC Card 80-602471 DDC 344.73/0769 19
KF27 .E373 1979e

VOCATIONAL REHABILITATION - LAW AND LEGISLATION - UNITED STATES.
United States. [Rehabilitation Act of 1973.] Rehabilitation, comprehensive services, and developmental disabilities legislation ... . Washington [1979] viii, 94 p. ; LC Card 80-603984 DDC 344.73/0159 347.304159 19
KF3738 .A3 1979

United States. Congress. House. Committee on Education and Labor. Subcommittee on Select Education. To amend the Rehabilitation act of 1973, relating to State agency organization requirements . Washington , 1980. v, 560 p. : LC Card 80-602471 DDC 344.73/0769 19
KF27 .E373 1979e

VOCATIONAL REHABILITATION - NEBRASKA.
Nebraska. Division of Rehabilitation Services. Three-year interim state plan for Nebraska Rehabilitation Services, fiscal years 1980-81-82. [Lincoln , 1979?] iv, 64 p. ; LC Card 80-622103 DDC 362/.0425 19
HD7256.U6 N34 1979

VOCATIONAL REHABILITATION - TEXAS.
Texas. Rehabilitation Commission. Texas Rehabilitation Commission State plan . [Austin] [1979] v, 45, [20] leaves : LC Card 80-622857 DDC 362/.0425 19
HD7256.U6 T437 1979

VOCATIONAL REHABILITATION - TEXAS - PLANNING.
Texas. Rehabilitation Commission. Interim state plan for independent living rehabilitation services, under title VII of the Rehabilitation act of 1973, as amended through 1978 /. [Austin] [1979] 40 leaves ; LC Card 80-622344 DDC 362/.0425 19
HV1555.T4 T49 1979

VOCATIONAL REHABILITATION - UNITED STATES - BIBLIOGRAPHY.

United States. President's Committee on Employment of the Handicapped. Resources for the vocational preparation of disabled youth. Washington, D.C. , 1980] iii, 44 p. ; LC Card 80-602690 DDC 016.3624/088055 19
Z7164.L1 U873 1980 HD7256.U5

VOCATIONAL REHABILITATION - UNITED STATES - COLLECTED WORKS.
United States. Rehabilitation Services Administration. Rehabilitation service series. 63/32-69/13 (incomplete) Washington [1968-69] 27 cm.   *NYPL [JLM 81-302]*

VOCATIONAL REHABILITATION - UNITED STATES - DIRECTORIES.
Olympus Research Corporation. Education service and work . [Washington] , for sale by the Supt. of Docs., U. S. Govt. Print. Off., 1977. 99 p. ;   LC Card 78-600742
LB1029.C6 O48 1977   NYPL [JFE 81-723]

VOCATIONAL REHABILITATION - UNITED STATES - STATES - FINANCE - PERIODICALS.
United States. Rehabilitation Services Administration. Program and financial plan for state vocational rehabilitation agencies. Washington. LC Card 78-645637
NYPL [JLM 80-870]

VOCATIONAL REHABILITATION - UNITED STATES - STATES - PERIODICALS.
United States. Rehabilitation Services Administration. Program and financial plan for state vocational rehabilitation agencies. Washington. LC Card 78-645637
NYPL [JLM 80-870]

VOCATIONAL REHABILITATION - UTAH.
Utah. Division of Rehabilitation Services. A program report, fiscal year 1979 /. Salt Lake City, Utah [1979] v, 13, 4 leaves ; LC Card 80-622338 DDC 362/.0425 19
HD7256.U6 U88 1979

VOCATIONAL REHABILITATION - VERMONT.
Vermont. State of Vermont program and financial plan for vocational rehabilitation agencies. [Montpelier , 1979] 56 leaves ; LC Card 80-621209 DDC 353.97430083 19
HD7256.U6 V42 1979

VOCATIONAL TRAINING. see OCCUPATIONAL TRAINING.

Voda, Ann M. (Ann Mae), 1930- Changing perspectives on menopause /. Austin , c1981. p. cm.   ISBN 0-292-71069-0 : LC Card 81-11714 DDC 612/.665 19
RG186 .C45

Voelker, Stanley W.
A functional classification of agricultural trade centers in North Dakota / Stanley W. Voelker, Delmer L. Helgeson, Harvey G. Vreugdenhil. Fargo : Agricultural Economics Dept., North Dakota Agricultural Experiment Station, North Dakota State University : Economics, Statistics, and Cooperatives Service, U. S. Dept. of Agriculture, [1978] 51 p. : ill. ; 28 cm. (Agricultural economics report . no. 125) Cover title. "March 1978." Includes bibliographical references. LC Card 78-623601 DDC 338.1 s 381/.41/09784 19
1. Cities and towns - North Dakota. 2. Urban economics. 3. Central places - North Dakota. I. Helgeson, Delmer L., joint author. II. Vreugdenhil, Harvey G., joint author. III. North Dakota. State University of Agriculture and Applied Science, Fargo. Dept. of Agricultural Economics. IV. United States. Dept. of Agriculture. Economics, Statistics, and Cooperatives Service. V. Series: North Dakota. Agricultural Experiment Station, Fargo. Agricultural economics report , no. 125. VI. Title.
SB205.S7 N64 no. 125 HT123.5.N9

Population changes within census county divisions of North Dakota, 1950-1970 / Stanley W. Voelker and Thomas K. Ostenson. Fargo, N.D. : Dept. of Agricultural Economics, Agricultural Experiment Station, North Dakota State University of Agriculture and Applied Sciences ; [Washington] : Economic Development Division, Economic Research Service, U. S. Dept. of Agriculture, 1971. 23 leaves, [4] leaves of plates : maps ; 28 cm. Includes bibliographical references. LC Card 80-621261 DDC 312/.8/09784 19
1. North Dakota - Population - Statistics. I. Ostenson, Thomas K., joint author. II. North Dakota. State University of Agriculture and Applied Sciences, Fargo.

Dept. of Agricultural Economics. III. United States. Dept. of Agriculture. Economic Research Service. Economic Development Divison. IV. Title.
HA566 .V63

Vogele, Louis E. Reproduction of smallmouth bass, Micropterus dolomieui, in Bull Shoals Lake, Arkansas / by Louis E. Vogele. Washington, D.C. : U. S. Dept. of the Interior, Fish and Wildlife Service, 1981. p. cm. (Technical papers of the U. S. Fish and Wildlife Service . 106) LC Card 81-607977 DDC 639 s 597/.58 19
1. Smallmouth bass - Reproduction. 2. Fishes - Reproduction. 3. Fishes - Bull Shoals Lake (Ark. and Mo.) - Reproduction. I. Title.
SH11 .A313 no. 106 QL638.C3

Vogler, Lawrence. Reports on data recovery operations at two sites in the Papago Indian Reservation, Arizona : Sonora C:3:2 and Arizona Z:14:47 / by Lawrence E. Vogler ; submitted by Cultural Resource Management Section, Arizona State Museum, University of Arizona. [Tucson, Ariz.] : The Museum, [1978] v, 45, v, 44, leaves : ill. ; 28 cm. (Archaeological series ; no. 119) Includes bibliographies. LC Card 80-622637 DDC 979.1/77 19
1. Hohokam culture. 2. Papago Indian Reservation, Ariz. - Antiquities. 3. Arizona - Antiquities. I. Arizona. State Museum, Tucson. Cultural Resource Management Section. II. Series: Archaeological series (Tucson) , no. 119. III. Title.
E99.H68 V63

A voice that spoke for justice . Urofsky, Melvin I. Albany , 1981. p. cm.   ISBN 0-87395-538-2 LC Card 81-5676 DDC 296.8/346/0924 B 19
BM755.W53 U76

Voices and choices . California Governor's Conference on Libraries and Information Services, Sacramento, 1979. Sacramento , 1979. 32 p. : LC Card 80-623065 DDC 027.0794 19
Z732.C2 C47 1979

Voices of Oklahoma families . Oklahoma. Dept. of Economic and Community Affairs. Children's Services Coordination Project. [Oklahoma City] , 1978. ix, 300 p. : LC Card 79-621197 DDC 362.7/1/09766 19
HV742.O5 O35 1978

The Voices of time : a cooperative survey of man's views of time as expressed by the sciences and by the humanities / edited with a new introduction by J.T. Fraser.2nd ed. Amherst : University of Massachusetts Press, 1981. lx, 710 p. : ill. ; 23 cm. Includes bibliographical references and index. ISBN 0-87023-337-8 LC Card 81-3025 DDC 115 19
1. Time - Addresses, essays, lectures. I. Fraser, J. T. (Julius Thomas), 1923-.
BD638 .V59 1981

The voir dire examination, juror challenges, and adversary advocacy /. Bermant, Gordon. [Washington] , 1978. v, 50 p. : LC Card 79-602041 DDC 347.73/752 19
KF8979 .B48

The Volga Germans . Scheuerman, Richard D. Moscow, Idaho , c1980. 245 p. : ISBN 0-89301-073-1 LC Card 80-52314 DDC 979.5 19
F855.2.R85 S33

Volk, Garth W. Ohio. Dept. of Agriculture. Agricultural land use in Ohio. [Columbus [1979] 97 p. : LC Card 80-621589 DDC 333.76/13/09771 19
HD211.O3 O37 1979

Volkwein, Jon C.
Canopy air curtain dust reductions on a gathering-arm loader / by Jon C. Volkwein, Steven J. Page, and Edward D. Thimons. [Avondale, Md.] : U. S. Dept. of the Interior, Bureau of Mines, [1981] p. cm. (Report of investigations / Bureau of Mines) Bibliography: p. LC Card 81-10148 DDC 622 s 622/.2 19
1. Mine dusts. 2. Mineral industries - Dust control. 3. Loaders (machines) - Safety measures. 4. Air curtains. I. Page, Steven J. II. Thimons, Edward D. III. Series: Report of investigations (United States. Bureau of Mines). IV. Title.
TN23 .U43 TN312

(joint author) Page, Steven J. Effectiveness of wet cutter bars in reducing salt mine dust /. Washington [1980] p. cm. LC Card 80-607782

DDC 622 s 622/.3632 19
TN23 .U43 TN312

Vinson, Robert P. SF$_6$ tracer gas tests of bagging-machine hood enclosures /. [Avondale, Md.] , 1981. p. cm. LC Card 80-606907 DDC 661/.06832 19
TN23 .U43 TH7697.C54

VOLTA LAKE, GHANA.
Freeman, Peter H. The environmental impact of a large tropical reservoir . Washington , 1974. 86 p., [1] fold. leaf of plates : LC Card 81-450719 DDC 333.78/46 19
QH195.G53 F73

VOLUNTARISM - AFRICA - DIRECTORIES.
United Nations. Economic Commission for Africa. Directory of activities of international voluntary agencies in rural development in Africa /. New York , 1977. iii, 173 p. ; LC Card 79-109825 DDC 300 s 361.7/7/0256 19
JX1977 .A2 E/CN.14/SWCD/68

VOLUNTARISM - ALABAMA.
Alabama Year of the Child Commission. Alabama children, a matter of commitment and priority . Montgomery, Ala. [1980-] c1981- p. cm. LC Card 80-620054 DDC 305.2/3/09761 19
HQ796 .A452 1980

Voluntary retirements under the civil service retirement system . United States. Congress. House. Committee on Post Office and Civil Service. Subcommittee on Compensation and Employee Benefits. Washington , 1980. iii, 72 p. ; LC Card 80-603099 DDC 353.005 19
KF27 .P638 1980g

The voluntary water quality monitoring project report, 1979 /. Welch, Barbara. [Augusta] [1980] 16 p. : LC Card 80-623367 DDC 363.7/3942/09741 19
TD224.M2 W44

Voluntary withholding of State income tax for civil service annuitants . United States. Congress. House. Committee on Post Office and Civil Service. Subcommittee on Compensation and Employee Benefits. Washington , 1980. iii, 24 p. ; LC Card 80-603116 DDC 343.7305/242 19
KF27 .P638 1980e

Volunteer income tax assistance program . United States. Congress. House. Committee on Ways and Means. Subcommittee on Oversight. Washington , 1980. iii, 79 p. ; LC Card 80-602989 DDC 343.7305/2044 19
KF27 .W345 1980d

VOLUNTEER WORKERS IN EDUCATION - UNITED STATES.
Los Angeles. University of Southern California. Center for International Education. An evaluation of the Volunteers to America program, 1967-1968 . Los Angeles , 1968. 133, [32] leaves ; LC Card 79-111308 DDC 370.19/0973 19
LB2376 .L67 1968

VOLUNTEER WORKERS IN IMMUNIZATION.
National League for Nursing. Guidelines for volunteer participation in childhood immunization programs. New York , c1980. xv, 333 p. : LC Card 80-132263
RJ240 .N37 1980   NYPL [JLF 81-445]

VOLUNTEER WORKERS IN INCOME TAX RETURN PREPARATION - UNITED STATES.
United States. Congress. House. Committee on Ways and Means. Subcommittee on Oversight. Volunteer income tax assistance program . Washington , 1980. iii, 79 p. ; LC Card 80-602989 DDC 343.7305/2044 19
KF27 .W345 1980d

VOLUNTEER WORKERS IN SOCIAL SERVICE - MINNESOTA.
United States. Congress. Senate. Committee on Governmental Affairs. Subcommittee on Intergovernmental Relations. Nonprofit organization participation in the federal aid system . Washington , 1980. 2 v. ; LC Card 81-600646 DDC 361.3/7/0973 19
KF26 .G6738 1980d

VOLUNTEER WORKERS IN SOCIAL SERVICE - UNITED STATES.
Los Angeles. University of Southern California. Center for International Education. An

BIBLIOGRAPHIC GUIDE

Volunteer workers in social service - United States. (cont.)

646

evaluation of the Volunteers to America program, 1967-1968 . Los Angeles , 1968. 133, [32] leaves :   LC Card 79-111308   DDC 370.19/0973 19
LB2376 .L67 1968

United States. Congress. Senate. Committee on Governmental Affairs. Subcommittee on Intergovernmental Relations. Nonprofit organization participation in the federal aid system . Washington , 1980. 2 v. ;   LC Card 81-600646   DDC 361.3/7/0973 19
KF26 .G6738 1980d

VOLUNTEER WORKERS IN SOCIAL SERVICE - WASHINGTON (STATE) - CONGRESSES.
Pasco Volunteers Conference, Columbia Basin College, 1976. Pasco Volunteers Conference . Olympia, 1976. 19 p.;   *NYPL [*XME-9108]*

Volunteers Conference, Pasco. see Pasco Volunteers Conference, Columbia Basin College, 1976.

Volunteers in Technical Assistance.
Mathur, Brij. International directory of appropriate technology resources /. [Washington] , 1980. ca. 500 p. ;   LC Card 80-602130   DDC 333.91/0025 19
T49.5 .M37

United States. National Technical Information Service. Appropriate technology information for developing countries . [Washington, D.C.] [c1980] xxiv, 384 p. (p. 383-384 ordering instructions) ;   LC Card 80-601640   DDC 600 19
T49.5 .U56 1980

Von Groschwitz, Gustave, 1906- Lapinski, Tadeusz, 1928- Color lithography . Catonsville, Md. , c1980. [20] p. :   LC Card 80-51345   DDC 769.92/4 19
NE2371.P6 L36

Vongsavanh, Soutchay. RLG military operations and activities in the Laotian panhandle / by Soutchay Vongsavanh. Washington, D.C. : U. S. Army Center of Military History, 1981. p. cm. (Indochina monographs)   LC Card 81-10934   DDC 959.704/34 19
1. Vietnamese Conflict, 1961-1975 - Campaigns - Laos. 2. Laos - History. I. Title. II. Title: R.L.G. military operations and activities in the Laotian Panhandle. III. Series.
DS557.8.L3 V66

Voorhees (Alan M.) and Associates. Blue Streak bus rapid transit demonstration project : final report [summary]. Prepared for Washington State ... Department of Highways and the City of Seattle Department of Transportation. Seattle, 1973. 6, 11 p. 28 cm. Microfilm. U. S. Dept. of Transportation Demonstration project no. WASH-MTD-2. LC Card 74-132895
1. Local transit - Washington (State) - Seattle. 2. Seattle - Transit systems. I. Washington (State). Dept. of Highways. II. Seattle. Dept of Transportation. III. United States. Dept. of Transportation. IV. Title.
*NYPL [*ZT-1265]*

Voss, Frederick. We never sleep : the first fifty years of the Pinkerton men / by Frederick Voss and James Barber. Washington, D.C. : Published for the National Portrait Gallery by the Smithsonian Institution Press : For sale by U. S.G.P.O., 1981. p. cm. Catalog of an exhibition held at the National Portrait Gallery, July 31, 1981, to January 3, 1982. LC Card 81-607851 DDC 363.2/89/0973 19
1. Pinkerton's National Detective Agency - History - Exhibitions. 2. Pinkerton, Allan, 1819-1884 - Exhibitions. 3. Detectives - United States - Biography - Exhibitions. 4. Smithsonian Institution. National Portrait Gallery. I. Barber, James, 1952-. II. Title.
HV8087.P75 V67

Voss, Robert. Male accessory glands and the evolution of copulatory plugs in rodents / Robert Voss. Ann Arbor, Mich. : Museum of Zoology, University of Michigan, 1979. 27 p. ; 23 cm. (Occasional papers of the Museum of Zoology, University of Michigan . no. 689) Caption title. Bibliography: p. 22-27. LC Card 79-624538 DDC 599.32/32 19
1. Generative organs, Male - Evolution. 2. Rodentia - Reproduction. I. Title. II. Title: Copulatory plugs in rodents. III. Series: Michigan. University. Museum of Zoology. Occasional papers , no. 689.
QP257 .V67

VOTERS, REGISTRATION OF - UNITED STATES.
United States. Congress. House. Committee on the Judiciary. Subcommittee on Civil and Constitutional Rights. Minority language provisions of the Voting Rights Act . Washington , 1980. iii, 29 p. ;   LC Card 81-601330   DDC 324.6/4/0973 19
KF27 .J847 1980e

Votes at the thirty-second regular session of the General Assembly, 20 September-21 December, 1977. United Nations. General Assembly. 32d session, 1977. [Washington, D.C.] [1978?] lix, 469 p. ;   LC Card 80-601606   DDC 341.23/22 19
JX1977.8.V6 U54 1977

Voth, Donald E. (joint author) Fryar, Michelle Davis. The impact of nutrition programs on the health status of elderly Arkansans /. Fayetteville , 1979. 24 p. :   LC Card 80-620832   DDC 362.1/9897/009767 19
RA564.8 .F78

VOTING, ABSENT - UNITED STATES.
United States. Congress. House. Committee on Post Office and Civil Service. Subcommittee on Postal Operations and Services. Absentee ballot legislation . Washington , 1980. iii, 94 p. ;   LC Card 80-603110   DDC 324.6/5 19
KF27 .P6674 1980

The Voting Rights Act and Rome (Georgia) city elections /. Mathis, Douglas J., 1960- Athens , 1981. p. cm. ISBN 0-89854-074-7 :   LC Card 81-6707   DDC 342.758/35072 347.58350272 19
KFX2263.R582 G625

Voy, Kermit D. Soil survey of Franklin County, Iowa / [by Kermit D. Voy] ; United States Department of Agriculture, Soil Conservation Service in cooperation with the Iowa Agriculture and Home Economics Experiment Station, and the Cooperative Extension Service, Iowa State University, and the Department of Soil Conservation, State of Iowa. [Washington, D.C.] : The Service, [1980] ix, 183 p., [37] fold. leaves of plates : ill. ; 28 cm. Cover title. "Issued March 1980." Bibliography: p. 101. LC Card 80-602539 DDC 631.4/7/77728 19
1. Soils - Iowa - Franklin Co. - Maps. I. United States. Soil Conservation Service. II. Title.
S599.I8 V68

Voyager 1, encounter with Jupiter. United States. National Aeronautics and Space Administration. [Washington] , 1979. 43 p. :   LC Card 79-602497
QB661 .U54 1979a   *NYPL [JSF 81-36]*

VOYAGER PROJECT. see PROJECT VOYAGER.

The Voynich manuscript . D'Imperio, M. E. Fort George E. Mead, Md. , 1978. ix, 140 p. :   LC Card 79-602687   DDC 091 19
Z105.5.V65 D55

VOYNICH MANUSCRIPT.
D'Imperio, M. E. The Voynich manuscript . Fort George E. Mead, Md. , 1978. ix, 140 p. :   LC Card 79-602687   DDC 091 19
Z105.5.V65 D55

Vredenburg, Harvey L. Trading stamps in the service station. Iowa City, Iowa, Bureau of Business and Economic Research, College of Business Administration, State University of Iowa, 1959. v, 34 p. : illus. ; 24 cm. Microfiche (neg.) 1 sheet. 11 x 15 cm. (NYPL FSN 36,315) Includes bibliographical references.
1. Premiums (Retail trade). 2. Automobiles - Service stations. I. Iowa. University. Bureau of Business and Economic Research.   *NYPL [*XME-9742]*

Vreugdenhil, Harvey G. (joint author) Voelker, Stanley W. A functional classification of agricultural trade centers in North Dakota /. Fargo [1978] 51 p. :   LC Card 78-623601   DDC 338.1 s 381/.41/09784 19
SB205.S7 N64 no. 125 HT123.5.N9

Vsemirnaia konferentsiia oon voprosam narodonaseleniia. see World Population Conference.

Vsemirnaia konferentsiia po narodonaseleniiu. see World Population Conference.

Vsemirnaia konferentsiia po voprosam narodonaseleniia. see World Population Conference.

Vsesoiuznaia Kommunisticheskaia Partiia (Bol'shevikov) see Kommunisticheskaia partiia Sovetskogo Soiuza.

VULCANITE. see RUBBER.

W. E. U. For corporate body referred to by these initials, see: **Western European Union.**

W. H. O. see World Health Organization.

W. I. C. H. E. see Western Interstate Commission for Higher Education.

W. R. C. see United States. Water Resources Council.

W.W.U. subtidal study, Huxley College. Smith, Gary Frederick. A quantitative sampling program of benthic communities in nearshore subtidal areas within the Rosario Strait region of Northern Puget Sound, Washington State (1976) /. [Olympia] [1979] vi, 105 p. :   LC Card 80-622612   DDC 591.9797/7 19
QH105.W2 S65

WABASH COUNTY, ILL. - MAPS.
(1980) United States. Soil Conservation Service. Wabash County, Illinois /. Lincoln, Nebr. , 1980. 1 map :   LC Card 81-691430
G4103.W2 1980 .U5

WABASH VALLEY - ANTIQUITIES.
Winters, Howard D. The Riverton culture . Springfield , 1969. xiii, 164 p., 48 [i.e. 24] leaves of plates :   LC Card 79-629858   DDC 977.3 s 977.2/401 19
AM101 .I374 no. 13 E78.I3

Wachter, Michael L. (joint author) Greenwood, Michael J. Staff report companion papers. [Washington] [1979] ii leaves, 234 p. :   LC Card 79-603817
JV6471 .G73   *NYPL [JLF 81-360]*

WADENA CO., MINN. - PUBLIC LANDS - MAPS.
Minnesota. Dept. of Iron Range Resources and Rehabilitation. Land ownership, Wadena County /. [Hibbing? Minn.] [1976] 1 leaf :   LC Card 80-675212   DDC 912/.77687
G1428.W3G46 M5 1976

WADING BIRDS. see CICONIIFORMES.

WAGE-FUND. see WAGES.

WAGE-PRICE CONTROLS. see WAGE-PRICE POLICY.

Wage-price expectations and cyclical strike activity /. Kaufman, Bruce E. Washington , 1979. vi, 257 leaves :   *NYPL [JLF 80-1484]*

WAGE-PRICE GUIDELINES. see WAGE-PRICE POLICY.

WAGE-PRICE POLICY - UNITED STATES.
Holt, Charles C. Inflation and the need for new economic policies . Austin, Tex. , 1980. 13 leaves ;   LC Card 80-622266   DDC 332.4/15/0973 19
HG540 .H65

United States. Congress. Joint Economic Committee. Monitoring inflation . Washington , 1979-<198. v.<1-3> :   LC Card 81-601472   DDC 332.4/1/0973 19
KF25 .E2 1979p

United States. Council on Wage and Price Stability. Pay and price standards . Washington , 1979. 95 p. in various pagings ;   LC Card 79-603044
KF6067 .A88   *NYPL [JLF 81-439]*

WAGE SURVEYS - BIBLIOGRAPHY.
United States. Bureau of Labor Statistics. Directory of occupational wage surveys, Jan. 1970-Dec. 1977. [Washington] , 1979. i, 94 p. ;   LC Card 79-602338   DDC 331.1/0973 s 016.3312/973 19
HD8051 .A7876 no. 53 Z7164.W1 HD4975

WAGES.
United States. Dept. of Agriculture. Food costs and wages the world over /. [Washington] [1979] 15 p. :   LC Card 80-603156   DDC 338.4/36413 19
HD9000.4 .U476 1979

WAGES - BENTONITE INDUSTRY - WYOMING.
Wyoming. Dept. of Labor and Statistics. Wyoming bentonite & trona industries . [Cheyenne, Wyo.] 1980. iii, 59 p. :   LC Card 80-623151   DDC 338.2/761 19
HD4966.B452 U69 1980

WAGES - CALIFORNIA - STATISTICS - PERIODICALS.

California employment and payrolls. [Sacramento]   NYPL [JLM 81-164]

WAGES - COAL-MINERS - WYOMING - STATISTICS.
Wyoming. Dept. of Labor and Statistics. Wyoming coal strip mining . Cheyenne, Wyo. , 1979] iii, 40 p. ;   LC Card 79-625469   DDC 331.12/522334/09787 19
HD4966.M63 U59 1979

WAGES - CONSTRUCTION WORKERS - UNITED STATES - BIBLIOGRAPHY.
United States. Dept. of Labor. Library. The Davis-Bacon act . Washington, D.C. [1979] 28 p. ;   LC Card 79-603951   DDC 016.34473/01289 19
KF3505.C65 A123

WAGES - HANDICAPPED - UNITED STATES.
United States. Congress. House. Committee on Education and Labor. Subcommittee on Labor Standards. Oversight hearings on section 14(C) of the Fair Labor Standards Act . Washington , 1980. v, 540 p. ;   LC Card 80-603995   DDC 353.0083/6 19
KF27 .E348 1980d

WAGES - LOUISIANA - STATISTICS - PERIODICALS.
Employment - wages. Baton Rouge.
        NYPL [JLM 72-96]

WAGES - MASSACHUSETTS - PERIODICALS.
Massachusetts. Dept. of Labor and Industries. Division of Statistics. Employment and earnings of nonmanufacturing workers in the areas in Massachusetts. 1952-Mar. 1973 (incomplete) Boston.   NYPL [TDV+ (Mass. Labor and Industries Dept. Statistics Div. Employment and earnings of workers ...]

WAGES - MASSACHUSETTS - STATISTICS.
Massachusetts. Division of Employment Security. Job Market Research Service. Employment and wages State summary, 1978. [Boston] [1979?] 21 leaves ;   LC Card 80-621279   DDC 331.12/5/09744 19
HD5725.M4 M37 1979

WAGES - MASSACHUSETTS - STATISTICS - PERIODICALS.
Massachusetts. Dept. of Labor and Industries. Division of Statistics. Employment and earnings in wholesale and retail trade establishments in Massachusetts. Dec. 1929-July, 1973 (Incomplete). Boston.   NYPL [*ZAN-T1514]

WAGES - MINIMUM WAGE - UNITED STATES.
United States. Wage and Hour and Public Contracts Division. [Interpretative bulletin of the Fair labor standards act of 1938. Part 776. Subpart A. Coverage of wage-hour law.] Coverage of wage-hour law . Washington, D.C. , 1950. x, 29 p. ;   LC Card 80-116713   DDC 344.73/0121 347.304121 19
KF3489 .A36

WAGES - MINIMUM WAGE - UNITED STATES - HISTORY.
Ratner, Ronnie Steinberg, 1947- A modest Magna Carta . [New York City, N. Y.] 19. 2 v. (xxxiv, 880 leaves) ;   NYPL [*XME-9376]

WAGES - MONTANA - STATISTICS.
Montana. Division of Employment Security. Research and Analysis Section. Selected wage information 1980 for Montana and 14 labor market areas /. Helena, MT [1980] ii, 209 p. :   LC Card 80-623620   DDC 331.2/9786 19
HD4976.M84 M63 1980

WAGES - MOVING-PICTURE THEATERS - UNITED STATES.
United States. Employment Standards Administration. Motion picture theaters /. [Washington] , 1979. 93 p. in various pagings ;   LC Card 79-602947
HD4966.M79 U58 1979
        NYPL [JLF 81-423]

WAGES - NORTH CAROLINA.
Fearn, Robert M. Employment and wage changes in North Carolina /. Raleigh, N.C. [1980] 38 p. ;   LC Card 80-624073   DDC 331.12/5/09756 19
S97 .Z4 no. 60 HD5725.N8

WAGES - NORTH CAROLINA - PERIODICALS.
North Carolina. Bureau of Employment

Security Research. North Carolina wage rates and weekly earnings in selected occupations. 1973- Raleigh.   NYPL [JLM 81-14]

WAGES - OHIO - STATISTICS.
Number of active employer accounts, covered workers, taxable wages and contributions under Ohio Unemployment Compensaton Law. Columbus [1978] 15 leaves ;
        NYPL [*ZT-1259]

Ohio. Bureau of Employment Services. Division of Research and Statistics. Average weekly earnings of workers under Ohio Unemployment Compensation Law, by industrial division since 1939 /. Columbus, 1979. 2 leaves ;
        NYPL [*ZT-1265]

Ohio. Bureau of Employment Services. Division of Research and Statistics. Employers, workers, total and taxable payroll, and contributions under Ohio Unemployment Compensation Law since 1938 /. Columbus , 1979. 2 leaves ;
        NYPL [*ZT-1264]

Ohio. Bureau of Employment Services. Division of Research and Statistics. Employment, payroll, and earnings under the Ohio unemployment compensation law by county, 1972 through 1978. Columbus [1979?] 90 leaves ;   LC Card 80-623537   DDC 331.12/5/09771 19
HD5725.O3 O37 1979a

Ohio. Bureau of Employment Services. Division of Research and Statistics. Employment, payroll, and earnings under the Ohio unemployment compensation law by county, 1972 through 1979. Columbus [1980] 90 leaves ;   LC Card 80-623675   DDC 331.12/5/09771 19
HD5725.O3 O37 1980

Ohio. Bureau of Employment Services. Division of Research and Statistics. Number of active employer accounts, covered workers, total wages, taxable wages and contributions under Ohio Employment Compensation Law. Columbus, 1977. 14 leaves;
        NYPL [*ZT-1264]

WAGES - OHIO - STATISTICS - PERIODICALS.
Ohio. Bureau of Employment Services. Division of Research and Statistics. Average employment, total payroll, and average weekly earnings of educational local government employees covered under Ohio unemployment compensation law, by county. RS 203.8. Columbus.   NYPL [JLM 81-22]

Ohio. Bureau of Employment Services. Division of Research and Statistics. Average hourly earnings of production workers in Ohio [and various metropolitan areas] Table RS-790-4. Columbus.   NYPL [JLM 80-999]

Ohio. Bureau of Employment Services. Division of Research and Statistics. Average weekly earnings of production workers in Ohio [and various metropolitan areas] Table RS-790-2. Columbus.   NYPL [JLM 80-997]

Ohio. Bureau of Employment Services. Division of Research and Statistics. Average weekly earnings of workers under Ohio unemployment compensation law, by industrial division and county. RS 203.3-B. Columbus.
        NYPL [JLM 81-26]

Ohio. Bureau of Employment Services. Division of Research and Statistics. Payrolls and contributions under Ohio unemployment compensation law, by industry. RS 203.2-1. Columbus.   NYPL [JLM 81-28]

WAGES - OREGON.
Oregon. Bureau of Labor and Industries. Technical Assistance Unit. A handbook of Oregon wage and hour laws. [Salem, Or.] , 1980. iv, 41 p. ;   LC Card 80-623410   DDC 344.795/0121 347.9504121 19
KFO2734 .A853

WAGES - RAILROADS - UNITED STATES.
United States. Congress. House. Committee on Interstate and Foreign Commerce. Subcommittee on Transportation and Commerce. Title V authorization under the Regional rail reorganization act of 1973 . Washington , 1980. iii, 38 p. ;   LC Card 80-603098   DDC 331.25/5 19
KF27 .I5589 1980b

WAGES - TRONA INDUSTRY - WYOMING.
Wyoming. Dept. of Labor and Statistics. Wyoming bentonite & trona industries . [Cheyenne, Wyo.] 1980. iii, 59 p. :   LC Card 80-623151   DDC 338.2/761 19
HD4966.B452 U69 1980

WAGES - UNITED STATES.
Huck, Daniel F. Alternative approaches to adjusting compensation for federal bluecollar employees /. [Washington, D.C.] , c1980. xxii, 59 p. ;   LC Card 80-604160   DDC 353.001/2 19
JK776 .H8

WAGES - UNITED STATES - BIBLIOGRAPHY.
United States. Bureau of Labor Statistics. Directory of occupational wage surveys, Jan. 1970-Dec. 1977. [Washington] , 1979. i, 94 p. ;   LC Card 79-602338   DDC 331.1/0973 s 016.3312/973 19
HD8051 .A7876 no. 53 Z7164.W1 HD4975

WAGES - UNITED STATES - MATHEMATICAL MODELS.
Dickinson, Jonathan, 1943- Revealed preferences, functional form, and labor supply /. [Madison] , 1979. 50 p. :   LC Card 80-622900   DDC 331.2/973 19
HD5724 .D52 1979

WAGES - URANIUM INDUSTRY - WYOMING.
Wyoming. Dept. of Labor and Statistics. Wyoming uranium, mining and milling . [Cheyenne, Wyo. , 1980] iii, 41 p. :   LC Card 80-622020   DDC 331.12/52234932/09787 19
HD4966.U72 U68 1979

WAGES - UTAH - STATISTICS.
Utah. Dept. of Employment Security. Reports and Analysis Section. Utah employment, wages, and reporting units by firm size, 1979. Salt Lake City, Utah [1979] iii, 51 p. ;   LC Card 80-621434   DDC 331.12/5/09792 19
HD5725.U8 U82 1979a

WAGES - WEST VIRGINIA - STATISTICS.
Clay, Rex J. Occupational demand, supply, and wages in West Virginia /. [Charleston, W. Va.] [1980] iv leaves, 424 p. ;   LC Card 80-621755   DDC 331.12/09754 19
HD5725.W4 C52

Employment and wages, calendar year 1978 /. Charleston, W. Va. (112 California Ave., Charleston 25305) [1980] iv, 101 leaves ;   LC Card 80-624425   DDC 331.12/5/09754 19
HD4976.W4 E47

West Virginia. Dept. of Employment Security. Labor and Economic Research Section. Insured workers in West Virginia /. Charleston, WV , 1979. ii, 40 leaves ;   LC Card 80-623169   DDC 331.12/5/09754 19
HD7096.U6 W448 1979

WAGES - WOMEN - UNITED STATES.
Garfinkel, Irwin. The effect of income and wage rates on the labor supply of prime age women /. [Madison] , 1974. ia, leaves ;   LC Card 77-621617
HD6095 .G37   NYPL [*XME-9544]

WAGES - WYOMING - STATISTICS.
Wyoming. Employment Security Commission Research and Analysis Section. Wyoming covered employment and wage data by industry and county, 1976-1978 /. Casper, Wyo. [1979?] 26 leaves ;   LC Card 80-623146   DDC 331.12/5/09787 19
HD5725.W9 W96 1979

Wagner, D. Patricia. (joint author) Stosberg, Don. Kentucky's Black teacher gap . Frankfort , 1975. 20 p. ;   LC Card 77-621256
LC214.32.K4 S76   NYPL [*XME]

Wagner, David H., 1945- (joint author) Siddall, Jean L. Rare, threatened, and endangered vascular plants in Oregon . Salem, Or. [1979] iv, 109 p. :   LC Card 80-621881   DDC 582.09795 19
QK86.U6 S52

Wagner, Robert T. Characteristics and needs of the aged in South Dakota, 1980-1990 / by Robert T. Wagner, Edward P. Hogan, and Charles H. Blazey. Brookings, S.D. : South Dakota State University, Dept. of Rural Sociology, 1978. ix, 238 leaves : ill. ; 28 cm. Cover title: Research in sociology in South Dakota. Bibliography: leaves [165]-170. LC Card 80-622161

DDC 305.2/6/09783 19
1. *Aged - South Dakota - Statistics. 2. Aged - South Dakota - Social conditions. 3. Social indicators - South Dakota. I. Hogan, Edward Patrick, 1939- joint author. II. Blazey, Charles H., joint author. III. South Dakota. Agricultural Experiment Station, Brookings. Rural Sociology Dept. IV. Title. V. Title: Research in sociology in South Dakota.*
HQ1064.U6 S7

WAILAKI INDIANS - WARS - 1815-1875.
Carranco, Lynwood. Genocide and vendetta . Norman , c1981. p. cm.   ISBN 0-8061-1549-1   LC Card 81-7469   DDC 979.4/1504 19
F868.M5 C3

Waisman, Carlos H. (Carlos Horacio), 1943- Modernization and the working class : the politics of legitimacy / by Carlos H. Waisman.1st ed. Austin : University of Texas Press, c1982. p. cm. (The Dan Danciger publication series) Includes index.   ISBN 0-292-75065-X   LC Card 81-10397   DDC 306/.2 19
1. *Labor and laboring classes - Political activity. 2. Legitimacy of governments. 3. Political sociology. I. Title.*
HD8031 .W34

Wait, Walter K. The Star lake archaeological project . Carbondale , c1982. p. cm.   ISBN 0-8093-0949-1   LC Card 81-13596   DDC 978.9/83 19
E78.N65 S75

Waite, Alan T. (joint author) Hoyt, Robert D. Population dynamics and catch susceptibility of smallmouth buffalo in Rough River Reservoir /. [Frankfort, Ky.] , 1976. vii, 67 p. :   LC Card 79-624983   DDC 639/.2 s 597/.52 19
SH222.K4 A3 no. 62 QL638.C27

Waite, Thomas D. (joint author) Gemmell, Robert S. Economic impact of revisions of the public water supply regulations, R77-13 /. [Chicago] , 1978. [82] p. in various pagings ;   LC Card 78-623933   DDC 363.6/1 19
TD224.I3 G45

Waiver of nonimmigrant visa requirements . United States. Congress. House. Committee on the Judiciary. Subcommittee on Immigration, Refugees, and International Law. Washington , 1980. iv, 146 p. ;   LC Card 80-603043   DDC 342.73/082 19
KF27 .J8645 1980a

Waking their neighbors up . Young, Thomas Daniel, 1919- Athens , c1982. p. cm.   ISBN 0-8203-0600-2   LC Card 81-14736   DDC 810/.9/975 19
PS261 .Y63

Wald, Michael L. Municipal government wage surveys, Washington, D.C., October 1978. Philadelphia, Pa. (P.O. Box 13309, Philadelphia 19101) : U. S. Dept. of Labor, Bureau of Labor Statistics, Mideast Region, [1979] v, 70 p. ; 29 cm. (Regional report / U. S. Department of Labor, Bureau of Labor Statistics . 39) "October 1979."   LC Card 80-603374   DDC 352/.005123/09753 19
1. *Washington (D.C.) - Officials and employees - Salaries, allowances, etc. I. United States. Bureau of Labor Statistics. Mideast Regional Office. II. Series: Regional report (United States. Bureau of Labor Statistics. Mideast Regional Office) , 39. III. Title.*
JK2757 .W34

Waldhorn, Steven A. Picket fence planning in California: a study of local government planning / Sacramento : Special Subcommittee on Community Development, California Assembly, 1976-77. XII, 62 p. ill. ; 29 cm. Microfiche (neg.) NTIS. 1 sheet. 11 x 15 cm. (PB 000 1534) Bibliography: p. 51-52.
1. *Local government - California. 2. Local finance - California. 3. Regional planning - California. I. California. Legislature. Assembly. Special Subcommittee on Community Development. II. Title.*
JS451.C25 W34   **NYPL [*XME-9440]**

Waldman, Elizabeth. (joint author) Norwood, Janet Lippe. Women in the labor force . [Washington, D.C.] , 1979. 9 p. :   LC Card 80-601713   DDC 331.1/0973 s 331.4/12/0973 19
HD8051 .A7876 no. 575 HD6094

Waldrop, John S. MacFadden, Bruce J. Nannippus phlegon (Mammalia, Equidae) from the Pliocene (Blancan) of Florida /. Gainesville (Museum Rd., University of Florida, Gainesville, FL 32611) , 1980. 37 p. :   LC Card

81-621398   DDC 569/.72 19
QE882.U6 M28

Walecka, Scott. (joint author) Sagiv, Yehoshua. Subset dependencies as an alternative to embedded multivalued dependencies /. Urbana, Ill. , 1979. 25 p. :   LC Card 80-621695   DDC 001.64 s 519.7 19
QA76 .I4 no. 980 QA76.9.D3

Walisora, J. M. The physiological basis for spacecraft environmental limits / J.M. Walisora, coordinator. Washington, D.C. : National Aeronautics and Space Administration, Scientific and Technical Information Branch ; [Springfield, Va. : For sale by the National Technical Information Service], c1979. xvii, 217 p. : ill. ; 27 cm. (NASA reference publication. 1045) "Lyndon B. Johnson Space Center." Nov. 1979. Includes bibliographical references and index.   LC Card 81-600766   DDC 612/.0145 19
1. *Space flight - Physiological effect. I. United States. National Aeronautics and Space Administration. Scientific and Technical Information Branch. II. Lyndon B. Johnson Space Center. III. Title.*
RC1150 .W34

Walker, A. S. (Alta Sharon), 1942- Annotated bibliography of remote sensing methods for monitoring desertification / by A.S. Walker and Charles J. Robinove. Washington : U. S. G.P.O., 1981. p. cm. (Geological survey circular . 851)   LC Card 81-607078   DDC 557.3 s 016.508315/4 19
1. *Desertification - Remote sensing - Bibliography. I. Robinove, Charles Joseph, 1931-. II. Title.*
QE75 .C5 no. 851 Z6004.D4 GB612

Walker, Clarence Earl. A rock in a weary land : the African Methodist Episcopal Church during the Civil War and Reconstruction / Clarence E. Walker. Baton Rouge : Louisiana State University Press, c1981. p. cm. Revision of thesis (Ph. D.)--University of California, Berkeley. Bibliography: p. Includes index.   ISBN 0-8071-0883-9 :   LC Card 81-11731   DDC 287/.83 19
1. *African Methodist Episcopal Church - History. I. Title.*
BX8443 .W27 1981

Walker, Ernest Winfield. Evaluation of investment alternatives : a conceptual model integrating the investment and financing decisions / Ernest W. Walker, Peter A. DeVito. Austin, Tex. : Graduate School of Business, University of Texas at Austin : distributed by Bureau of Business Research, University of Texas at Austin, [1980] 23 leaves : graphs ; 28 cm. (Working paper - Graduate School of Business, University of Texas at Austin ; 80-5) "February 1980." Bibliography: leaf 23.   LC Card 80-622513   DDC 658.1/52 19
1. *Capital investments - Evaluation - Mathematical models. I. DeVito, Peter A., joint author. II. Series: Texas. University at Austin. Graduate School of Business. Working paper - Graduate School of Business, University of Texas at Austin , 80-5. III. Title.*
HG4028.C4 W34

Walker, James L., 1940- (joint author) Fox, Warren H. Nevada occupational information use and needs assessment . Reno, Nev. [1979] 141, 96 p. :   LC Card 80-620637   DDC 025/.06331702 19
HB2615.N3 F69

Walker, Jeanne Murray. Nailing up the home sweet home / Jeanne Murray Walker. [Cleveland] : Cleveland State University Poetry Center ; Oberlin, Ohio : Distributed by NACSCORP., c1980. 60 p. ; 22 cm. (CSU poetry series . 9)   ISBN 0-914946-24-2 (pbk.) :   LC Card 80-68027   DDC 811/.54 19
I. *Title. II. Series.*
PS3573.A425336 N3

Walker, Richard, 1947- (joint author) Storper, Michael. Systems and marxist theories of industrial location . Berkeley , 1979. viii, 92, [6] p. ;   LC Card 80-623098   DDC 338.6/042/01 19
HD58 .S679

Walker, Sheila S. The religious revolution in the Ivory Coast : the prophet Harris and the Harrist church / by Sheila S. Walker. Chapel Hill : University of North Carolina Press, c1982. p. cm. (Studies in religion) Bibliography: p. Includes index.   ISBN 0-8078-1503-9   LC Card 81-13010   DDC 289/.9 19
1. *Harris, William Wadé. 2. Ivory Coast - Church history. I. Series: Studies in religion (Chapel Hill, N.C.)*

II. *Title.*
BV3785.H348 W34

Walker, William A. Mead, James G. Biological observations on Mesoplodon carlhubbsi (Cetacea:Ziphiidae) /. Washington, D.C. , 1981. p. cm.   LC Card 81-9311   DDC 591 s 599.5/3 19
QL1 .S54 no. 344 QL237.C438

Walker, William R.
(joint author) Cox, William Edward, 1944- Virginia water law . Blacksburg, Va. , 1979. 15 p. ;   LC Card 80-622367   DDC 346.75504/691 19
KFV2846.Z9 C68

Flood damage abatement . Blacksburg , 1970. 138 p. :   LC Card 75-634086   DDC 333.91/009755 s 363.3/49356/09755 19
TD201 .V57 no. 39

Walkiewicz, J. W. (John W.) Magnetic properties of alloys containing mischmetal cobalt, copper, iron, and magnesium / by J.W. Walkiewicz, J.S. Winston and M.M. Wong. Avondale, MD : U. S. Dept. of the Interior, Bureau of Mines, 1981. p. cm. (Report of investigations) Bibliography: p.   LC Card 81-607845   DDC 622 s 620.1/697 19
1. *Alloys - Magnetic properties. 2. Magnets, Permanent. I. Winston, J. S. (John S.). II. Wong, M. M. (Morton M.). III. Series: Report of investigations (United States. Bureau of Mines). IV. Title.*
TN23 .U43 TN690

Walla Walla County Soil Conservation District, Walla Walla County, Washington. United States. Soil Conservation Service. Average annual precipitation, Walla Walla County Soil Conservation District, Walla Walla County, Washington /. Portland, Or. , 1979. 1 map :   LC Card 81-691505
G4283.W3C88 1979 .U5

Walla Walla County Soil Conservation District, Walla Walla County, Washington. United States. Soil Conservation Service. Critical erosion, Walla Walla County Soil Conservation District, Walla Walla County, Washington /. Portland, Or. , 1979. 1 map :   LC Card 81-691507
G4283.W3J4 1979 .U5

Walla Walla County Soil Conservation District, Walla Walla County, Washington. United States. Soil Conservation Service. General soil map, Walla Walla County Soil Conservation District, Walla Walla County, Washington /. Portland, Or. , 1979. 1 map :   LC Card 81-691504
G4283.W3J3 1979 .U5

Walla Walla County Soil Conservation District, Walla Walla County, Washington. United States. Soil Conservation Service. Land ownership, Walla Walla County Soil Conservation District, Walla Walla County, Washington /. Portland, Or. , 1979. 1 map :   LC Card 81-691503
G4283.W3G4 1979 .U51

Walla Walla County Soil Conservation District, Walla Walla County, Washington. United States. Soil Conservation Service. Land use, Walla Walla County Soil Conservation District, Walla Walla County, Washington /. Portland, Or. , 1979. 1 map :   LC Card 81-691506
G4283.W3G4 1979 .U5

WALLA WALLA COUNTY (WASH.) - PUBLIC LANDS - MAPS.
United States. Soil Conservation Service. Land ownership, Walla Walla County Soil Conservation District, Walla Walla County, Washington /. Portland, Or. , 1979. 1 map :   LC Card 81-691503
G4283.W3G4 1979 .U51

Wallace O. Green nomination . United States. Congress. Senate. Committee on Energy and Natural Resources. Washington , 1980. iii, 68 p. ;   LC Card 80-604077   DDC 353.3 19
KF26 .E55 1980k

Wallace, Robert W. (joint author) Cook, C. Lee. Textiles and textile products of cotton from Pakistan . Washington, D.C. [1980] vi, 56, 105 p. ;   LC Card 80-602856   DDC 382/.4567721/0973 19
HD9856 .C66

Wallace School of Community Service and Public Affairs. Bureau of Governmental Research and Service. The development standards document, with section-by-section explanation.

[Eugene] : Bureau of Governmental Research and Service, School of Community Service and Public Affairs, University of Oregon, [1979] 172 p. ; 28 cm. Cover title. "Volume 2 of a project conducted under a contract with the Oregon Department of Land Conservation and Development." Companion to: A model land development ordinance format. 1979. "December 1979." Includes bibliographical references. LC Card 80-624205 DDC 346.7304/5 347.30645 19
1. Land use - Standards - United States. 2. Land use - Law and legislation - United States. 3. Real estate development - Standards - United States. 4. Real estate development - Law and legislation - United States. 5. Real property - United States. 6. Zoning law - United States. 7. Environmental protection - United States. I. Title.
HD205 1979 .W34

Wallace Stevens . Litz, A. Walton. Washington , 1981. p. cm. ISBN 0-8444-0370-9 LC Card 81-607906 DDC 811/.52 19
PS3537.T4753 Z676

WALLENBERG, RAOUL.
United States. Congress. House. Committee on Foreign Affairs. Human rights in Eastern Europe and the Soviet Union . Washington , 1980 [i.e. 1981] iv, 248 p. ; LC Card 81-600864 DDC 232.4/0947 19
KF27 .F6 1980n

Waller, Patricia F., 1932- Truck drivers : licensing and monitoring : an analysis with recommendations : final report / Patricia F. Waller, Livia K. Li ; prepared for U. S. Department of Transportation, National Highway Traffic Safety Administration. Chapel Hill, N.C. : University of North Carolina, Highway Safety Research Center; Springfield, Va. : available to the public through the National Technical Information Service, [1979] xxvi, 222 p. : ill. ; 28 cm. "December 1979." Bibliography: p. 183-189. LC Card 80-622449 DDC 353.0087/8324 19
1. Truck drivers - Licenses - United States. I. Li, Livia K., joint author. II. United States. National Highway Traffic Safety Administration. III. Title.
HE5614.2 .W34

Waller, Thomas R. Functional morphology and development of veliger larvae of the European oyster, Ostrea edulis Linné / Thomas R. Waller. Washington : Smithsonian Institution Press, 1981. iii, 70 p. : ill. ; 27 cm. (Smithsonian contributions to zoology ; no. 328) Bibliography: p. 66-70. LC Card 80-23129 DDC 591 s 594/.11 19
1. European oyster - Development. 2. Mollusks - Larvae. 3. Mollusks - Development. I. Title. II. Title: Veliger larvae of the European oyster, Ostrea edulis Linné. III. Series: Smithsonian Institution. Smithsonian contributions to zoology ; no. 328.
QL1 .S54 no. 328 QL430.7.O9

WALLOWA-WHITMAN NATIONAL FOREST - MAPS.
(1979) United States. Forest Service. Pacific Northwest Region. Wallowa-Whitman National Forest [north half] Oregon. Portland , 1979. 1 map : on sheet 66 x 102 cm. Scale ca. 1:126,720. Relief shown by hachures and spot heights. Map printed on both sides of sheet. Map includes Hells Canyon National Recreation Area, Oregon-Idaho.
G4292.W31 1975 .U53
NYPL [Map Div. 80-3406]

(1979) United States. Forest Service. Pacific Northwest Region. Wallowa - Whitman National Forest [south half] Oregon. Portland , 1979. 1 map : on sheet 66 x 91 cm. Scale ca. 1: 126,720. Relief shown by hachures and spot heights. Shows forest lands in color. Includes location map, list of "Recreation sites," text, and col. illus. Map printed on both sides of sheet.
G4292.W31 1975 .U54
NYPL [Map Div. 80-3393]

WALLS, RETAINING. see RETAINING WALLS.

WALNUT - MARKETING - LAW AND LEGISLATION - UNITED STATES.
United States. Congress. House. Committee on Agriculture. Subcommittee on Domestic Marketing, Consumer Relations, and Nutrition. Marketing orders for walnuts and olives and Freestone Peach Research and Education Act . Washington , 1980. iii, 74 p. ; LC Card 80-604106 DDC 343.73/08514/0262 347.30385140262 19
KF27 .A3336 1980b

Walpole, Mass. Correctional Institution. see **Massachusetts. Correctional Institution, Walpole.**

Walsh, David F. (joint author) Sanders, Herman O. Abate - effects of the organophosphate insecticide on bluegills and invertebrates in ponds /. Washington, D.C. , 1981. 6 p. : LC Card 80-606806 DDC 639 s 628.9/657 19
SH11 .A313 no. 104 SH177.P44

Walsh, Marilyn E. Computerized tracking of stolen office equipment : a new enforcement offensive in the making : a special report to the administrator / prepared by Marilyn E. Walsh. Washington : Criminal Conspiracies Division, Office of Criminal Justice Programs, Law Enforcement Assistance Administration, U. S. Dept. of Justice, 1979. vi, 107 p. : maps ; 28 cm. LC Card 79-602794 DDC 363.2/5 19
1. Larceny - United States. 2. Offenses against property - United States - Data processing. 3. Office equipment and supplies - Data processing. I. United States. Law Enforcement Assistance Administration. Criminal Conspiracies Division. II. Title.
HV6658 .W295

Walsh, Richard G., 1930- An economic evaluation of the general management plan for Yosemite National Park / by Richard G. Walsh. Fort Collins, Colo. : Water Resources Research Institute, Colorado State University, [1980] xii, 102 p. : ill. ; 28 cm. (Technical report - Colorado Water Resources Research Institute . no. 19) "March 1980." Bibliography: p. 99-102. LC Card 80-623117 DDC 333.78/3/0979447 19
1. Yosemite National Park. I. Series: Colorado Water Resources Research Institute. Technical report - Colorado Water Resources Research Institute , no. 19. II. Title.
F868.Y6 W34

Wålstedt, Bertil. State manufacturing enterprise in a mixed economy : the Turkish case / Bertil Wålstedt. Baltimore : Published for the World Bank [by] the Johns Hopkins University Press, c1980. xxii, 354 p. : ill. ; 23 cm. Includes bibliographical references and index. ISBN 0-8018-2226-2 : LC Card 78-21398
1. Government business enterprises - Turkey. 2. Turkey - Manufactures. I. International Bank for Reconstruction and Development. II. Title.
HD4276.7 .W34 **NYPL [JLE 81-426]**

Walt Whitman review. 1980, Leaves of grass at 125 . Detroit , 1980. 78 p., [1] leaf of plates : LC Card 81-136978 DDC 811/.3 19
PS3231 .A515

Walter, Edward, 1932- The immorality of limiting growth / by Edward Walter. Albany : State University of New York Press, 1981. p. cm. Bibliography: p. Includes index. ISBN 0-87395-478-5 LC Card 81-166 DDC 338.9 19
1. Economic development. 2. Liberalism. I. Title. II. Title: Limiting growth.
HD88 .W34

Walter Havighurst, novelist of the heartland /. Throne, Marilyn. Columbus , 1979. 20 p. ; LC Card 80-137524 DDC 813/.54 19
PS3515.A8694 Z89

Walter, Paul C. Reznik, Gerd. Clinical anatomy of the European hamster . Washington [1978] xi, 247 p. : LC Card 79-602139 DDC 619/.93 19
QL813.H35 R49

Walter, William H. (joint author) Cardwell, George T., 1922- Pumpage of water in Louisiana, 1975 /. Baton Rouge, La. , 1979. iv, 15 p. : LC Card 80-620624 DDC 333.91/13/09763 19
TD224.L8 C37

Walters, A. A. (joint author) Feibel, Charles. Ownership and efficiency in urban buses /. Washington, D.C. , 1980. 19 p. ; LC Card 80-114661 DDC 388.4/042 19
HE5613 .F44

Walther, Regis H. The measurement of work-relevant attitudes : final report / by Regis H. Walther. - Washington : Manpower Research Projects, The George Washington University. 1975. 19, 2. [4] p. ; 29 cm. Microfiche (neg.) N T I S. 1 sheet. 11 x 15 cm. (PB 246 260) Final report of the development of a work-relevant attitudes inventory for use in diagnosing the needs of individuals and evaluating the effectiveness of manpower programs. The inventory was used in two studies: four Neighborhood Youth Corps programs and a demonstration education project. Prepared for the

Manpower Administration, U. S. Department of Labor, under research and development grant no. 41-0-003-09.
1. Attitude (Psychology). 2. Socially handicapped - United States. 3. Socially handicapped - Education - United States. I. George Washington University, Washington, D. C. Manpower Research Projects. II. United States. Dept. of Labor. Manpower Administration. III. Title. **NYPL [*XM-13884]**

Walton, James M. (joint author) Ilg, Janet. An annotated bibliography of the lingcod, Ophiodon elongatus /. [Olympia, Wash.] , 1979. 25 p. ; LC Card 80-621496 DDC 016.597/58 19
QL638.H49 I43

Walton, Todd L. Littoral drift estimates along the coastline of Florida / T.L. Walton, Jr. Gainesville : Marine Advisory Program, University of Florida, 1976. ii, 41, [89] p. : ill. ; 28 cm. (Sea Grant report - State University System of Florida, Sea Grant Program . no. 13) Includes bibliographical references. LC Card 77-622038 DDC 551.46/34 19
1. Ocean currents - Atlantic coast (United States). 2. Ocean currents - Florida - Gulf region. 3. Coasts - Florida. I. Series: Florida Sea Grant Program. Report - Florida Sea Grant Program , no. 13. II. Title.
GC272 .W34

Walvin, James. The Abolition of the Atlantic slave trade . Madison , 1981. p. cm. ISBN 0-299-08490-6 : LC Card 80-52290 DDC 382/.44 19
HT855 .A26

Walzer, Norman.
Financing local services in Illinois / Norman Walzer. [Urbana] : Cooperative Extension Service, Agricultural Experiment Station, College of Agriculture, University of Illinois at Urbana-Champaign, 1979. 222 p. ; 28 cm. Includes bibliographical references. LC Card 80-622079 DDC 352.1/09773 19
1. Local government - Illinois - Finance. I. Title.
HJ9227 .W3

Financing township services / prepared by Norman Walzer and Peter J. Stratton. [Macomb] : Public Policy Research Institute, Western Illinois University ; [Urbana-Champaign] : Cooperative Extension Service, Agricultural Experiment Station, College of Agriculture, University of Illinois at Urbana-Champaign, [1979?] 84 p. : ill. ; 23 cm. Includes bibliographical references. LC Card 80-621226 DDC 352.1/09773 19
1. Local finance - Illinois. I. Stratton, Peter J., joint author. II. Title.
HJ9227 .W32

Fiscal note and reimbursement programs for state mandates / Norman Walzer, with the assistance of John Carroll. Macomb, Ill. : Public Policy Research Institute, Western Illinois University. 1978. 5, 65 p. ; 28 cm. On cover: Illinois Cities and Villages Municipal Problems Commission. Includes bibliographical references. LC Card 79-624292
1. Local finance - United States. 2. Intergovernmental fiscal relations - United States - States. I. Carroll, John, 1945- joint author. II. Illinois. Cities and Villages Municipal Problems Commission. III. Title.
HJ9157 .W34 **NYPL [JLF 80-1340]**

Revenue sharing in Illinois municipalities / by Norman Walzer and Randy Nyberg. Springfield, IL : Cities and Villages Municipal Problems Commission, [1979] 6, 47, [67] p. : ill. ; 28 cm. "December 1979." Includes bibliographical references. LC Card 80-623316 DDC 336.1/85 19
1. Municipal finance - Illinois. 2. Revenue sharing - Illinois. I. Nyberg, Randy, joint author. II. Title.
HJ9227 .W345

WAMPLER, WILLIAM D., 1928-
United States. Congress. Senate. Committee on Agriculture, Nutrition, and Forestry. Nominations of Ralph Raikes and William D. Wampler . Washington , 1980. iii, 31 p. : LC Card 80-604017 DDC 353.0082/33045 19
KF26 .A35 1980c

Wandering in the garden, waking from a dream /. Pai, Hsien-yung, 1937- [Yu yüan ching meng. English.] Bloomington , c19., p. cm. ISBN 0-253-19981-6 LC Card 81-47165 DDC 895.1/35 19
PL2892.A345 A24

Wang, Hwa Lih, 1921- Soybeans as human food . [Washington] , 1979. iv, 54 p. : LC Card

79-603033   DDC 641.3/5655 19
TX558.S7 S69 1979b

Wang, Kung-Lee. (joint author) Opyrchal, Anthony
M. Economic significance of the Florida
phosphate industry . [Washington, D.C.] [1981]
p. cm.   LC Card 80-606892   DDC 622 s 338.2/764
19
TN295 .U4 HD9484.P5U5

Wang, Tong-eng, 1933- Economic policies and
price stability in China / Tong-eng Wang.
Berkeley : Center for Chinese Studies, Institute
of East Asian Studies, University of California,
c1980 xvi, 146 p. : ill. ; 23 cm. (China research
monographs. no. 16) Bibliography: p. 133-146.   ISBN
0-912966-24-6 (pbk.) :   LC Card 80-620008
DDC 338.5/26/0951 19
*1. Price regulation - China - History. 2. China -
Economic policy. I. Title. II. Series.*
HB236.C55 W36   **NYPL [*OVA no. 16]**

Wang, Zhen. Early and Middle Devonian
charophytes of eastern Guangxi, China /.
Louisville, Ky. , c1980. iv, 16 p., leaves 17-18 :
LC Card 80-623043   DDC 561/.93 19
QE955 .E25

WANKEL ENGINE - CONGRESSES.
The Rotary combustion engine . [Washington,
D.C.] , Springfield, Va. , 1978. v, 190 p. :   LC
Card 79-603405
TL701.1 .R58

**WAQUA CREEK WATERSHED (VA.) - MAPS,
TOPOGRAPHIC.**
United States. Soil Conservation Service.
Waqua Creek watershed, Lunenburg and
Brunswick Counties, Virginia /. Lanham, MD ,
1979. 1 map :   LC Card 81-690288
G3882.W27 1979 .U5

War and chivalry . Vale, M. G. A. (Malcolm
Graham Allan) Athens, Ga. , 1981. p. cm.
ISBN 0-8203-0571-5   LC Card 81-3046   DDC
355/.00942 19
U43.G7 V34 1981

**WAR AND EMERGENCY POWERS -
UNITED STATES.**
United States. Congress. Senate. Committee on
Foreign Relations. The situation in Iran .
Washington , 1980 [i.e. 1981] v, 48 p. ;   LC
Card 81-601146   DDC 353.03/22 19
KF26 .F6 1980t

WAR AND PEACE. see PEACE.

**WAR DAMAGE CONTROL IN INDUSTRY.
see WAR DAMAGE, INDUSTRIAL.**

WAR DAMAGE, INDUSTRIAL.
Ramberg, Bennett. Destruction of nuclear
energy facilities in war . Lexington, Mass. ,
c1980. xvi, 203 p. :   LC Card 80-7691
UA929.95.A87 R35   **NYPL [JLE 81-179]**

**WAR - ECONOMIC ASPECTS - UNITED
STATES.**
Ennis, Harry F. Peacetime industrial
preparedness for wartime ammunition
production /. Washington, D.C. [1980] vi, 122
p. :   LC Card 80-603600   DDC 355.2/6/0973 19
HC110.D4 E56

**WAR OF NERVES. see PSYCHOLOGICAL
WARFARE.**

War risk insurance . United States. Congress.
Senate. Committee on Commerce, Science, and
Transportation. Subcommittee on Merchant
Marine and Tourism. Washington , 1980. iii, 52
p. ;   LC Card 80-601958   DDC 346.73/08614/0262
19
KF26 .C695 1979e

WAR-SHIPS. see WARSHIPS.

**WAR USE OF HERBICIDES. see
HERBICIDES - WAR USE.**

WAR WOUNDS - UNITED STATES.
United States. General Accounting Office. The
Congress should mandate formation of a
military-VA-civilian contingency hospital
system . Washington, D.C. [1980] vi, 51 p. ;
LC Card 80-602693   DDC 355.3/45/0973 19
RA981.A2 U53 1980

Ward, Delbert B. Flat-plate Solar Collector
Conference, Orlando, Fla., 1977. Proceedings /.
[Washington] , 1978. x, 662 p. :   LC Card
78-601524
TJ810 .F56 1977   **NYPL [JSF 81-189]**

Ward, Keith J. Property tax administration :
reappraisal in Alabama / by Keith J. Ward,
Betty D. Sparkman. Auburn, Ala. : Office of
Public Service & Research, School of Arts &
Sciences, Auburn University, [1980] xiv, 167
p. : ill. ; 23 cm. (Monograph series - Office of Public
Service & Research, School of Arts & Sciences, Auburn
University ; no. 4) Bibliography: p. 161-165.   LC Card
80-622123   DDC 353.97610072/42 19
*1. Property tax - Alabama. 2. Tax administration and
procedure - Alabama. I. Sparkman, Betty D., joint
author. II. Auburn University. Office of Public Service
and Research. III. Series: Auburn University. Office of
Public Service and Research. OPSR monograph series ,
no. 4. IV. Title.*
HJ4121.A22 W37

Ward, Sheila J. Powers, Jane VanDeMark.
Adolescent health care services in Michigan .
Lansing , 1978. vi, 159 p. :   LC Card 79-620710
DDC 362.1/9 19
RJ102.5.M5 P68

Wardlaw, Bruce R. Studies of the Permian
Phosphoria formation and related rocks, Great
Basin-Rocky Mountain region /. Washington ,
1979. iii, 22 p. :   LC Card 79-607907   DDC
551.7/5 19
QE674 .S78

WAREHOUSE RECEIPTS - ILLINOIS.
Illinois. Laws, statutes, etc. The Public grain
warehouse and warehouse receipts act ; Rules
and regulations. Springfield, Ill. [1973?] 13 p. ;
LC Card 80-622697   DDC 343.773/07631 19
KFI1484.A335 A2 1973

**WAREHOUSES - LAW AND LEGISLATION -
ILLINOIS.**
Illinois. Laws, statutes, etc. The Public grain
warehouse and warehouse receipts act ; Rules
and regulations. Springfield, Ill. [1973?] 13 p. ;
LC Card 80-622697   DDC 343.773/07631 19
KFI1484.A335 A2 1973

Wargo, M. J. Achievement testing of
disadvantaged and minority students for
educational program evaluation /. [Monterey,
CA] [1979] viii, 464 p. :   LC Card 78-4519
LB3051 .A528   **NYPL [Sc D 80-645]**

Warlick, Jennifer L. (joint author) Burkhauser,
Richard V. Disentangling the annuity from the
redistributive aspects of social security /.
[Madison] , 1979. 30 p. :   LC Card 80-622901
DDC 368.4/4 19
HD7125 .B84

WARM SPRINGS LAKE, CALIF.
Baumhoff, Martin A. An archaeological assay
on Dry Creek, Sonoma County, California /.
Berkeley , 1979. xi, 244 p. :   LC Card 80-620631
DDC 979.4/18 19
E51 .C2 no. 40 E78.C15

Warmack, William B. Readle, Elmer L. Soil
survey of Osceola County area, Florida /.
[Washington] , 1979. x, 151 p., [59] fold. leaves
of plates :   LC Card 79-602772   DDC
631.4/7/75925 19
S599.F6 R42

Warner, Deborah Jean. Perfect in her place :
women at work in industrial America /
Deborah J. Warner. Washington, D.C. :
Published for the National Museum of
American History by the Smithsonian
Institution Press : for sale by Supt. of Docs., U.
S. G.P.O., 1981. p. cm. "Prepared in conjunction
with an exhibit at the National Museum of American
History, Smithsonian Institution." Includes
bibliographical references.   LC Card 81-607826   DDC
331.4/0973 19
*1. Women - Employment - United States - History. I.
National Museum of American History (U. S.). II.
Title.*
HD6095 .W198

Warner, John W., 1927- United States. General
Accounting Office. Effects in Washington, D.C.,
area of 1979 gasoline shortage . Washington,
D.C. [1980] viii, 47 p. ;   LC Card 80-602653
DDC 338.4/766553827/09753 19
HD9579.G5 U595 1980

Warner, John Ward, 1944- Scientific research
with the space telescope . [Huntsville, Ala.] ,
Washington, D.C. [1979] xii, 327 p. :   LC Card
80-601618   DDC 520 19
QB61 .S33

Warner, Judith S. (joint author) Budde, Norbert W.
Characteristics of physicians . [Hyattsville, Md.]

[1979- -v. ;   LC Card 80-602072
RA410.7 .B82   **NYPL [JLM 81-120]**

Warner, Lawrence Allen, 1914- Geology of the
eastern part of the Harold D. Roberts Tunnel,
Colorado (Stations 690+00 to 1238+58) / by
Lawrence A. Warner and Charles S. Robinson.
Washington : U. S. Govt. Print. Off., 1980. p.
cm. (Engineering geology of the Harold D. Roberts
Tunnel, Colorado) Geological Survey professional
paper ; 831-D Bibliography: p.   LC Card 80-607839
DDC 624.1/92 19
*1. Geology - Colorado - Harold D. Roberts Tunnel. 2.
Engineering geology - Colorado - Harold D. Roberts
Tunnel. I. Robinson, Charles Sherwood, 1920- joint
author. II. Series. III. Series: United States. Geological
Survey. Professional paper, 831-D. IV. Title.*
QE92.H37 W37

Warner, Robert Malcolm, 1908- University of
Hawaii at Manoa. Plant Science Instructional
Arboretum. A catalog of plants in the Plant
Science Instructional Arboretum, College of
Tropical Agriculture and Human Resources,
University of Hawaii /. [Honolulu] , 1981. p.
cm.   LC Card 81-2897   DDC 582.16/061/074099691
19
SB171.U6 U54 1981

Warner, Robert Mark, 1927- The anatomy of a
speech : Lyndon Johnson's Great Society
address / Robert M. Warner. Ann Arbor,
Mich. : Michigan Historical Collections, Bentley
Historical Library, University of Michigan,
[1978] 15 p. : ill. ; 23 cm. (Bulletin - Michigan
Historical Collections . no. 28) Includes bibliographical
references.   LC Card 80-623114   DDC
973.923/092/4 19
*1. Johnson, Lyndon Baines, Pres. U. S., 1908-1973 -
Literary art. I. Series: Michigan. University. Michigan
Historical Collections. Bulletin, no. 28. II. Title.*
E847 .W37

Warner, Ronald R. Workshop on Biological X-ray
Microanalysis by Electron Beam Excitation,
Boston, 1977. Microbeam analysis in biology /.
New York , 1979. xx, 672 p. :   ISBN
0-12-440340-9   LC Card 79-24948
QH324.9.X2 W67 1977
     NYPL [JSE 80-1320]

Warnick, Wendy. (joint author) Skaggs, Samuel. A
design for agriculture in the Tanana Loop .
[Juneau] , 1978. ii, 61 p. :   LC Card 79-620899
DDC 338.1/09798/6 19
S451.A3 S58

**WARRANTS, AGRICULTURAL. see
AGRICULTURAL CREDIT.**

WARRANTS (LAW) - UNITED STATES.
National Institute of Law Enforcement and
Criminal Justice. Model Program Development
Division. Managing criminal warrants /.
Washington , 1978. vii, 92 p. :   LC Card
79-602012
KF9625 .N37   **NYPL [JLF 81-324]**

WARRANTY - CALIFORNIA.
California. Legislature. Assembly. Labor,
Employment & Consumer Affairs Committee.
Hearing on consumer protection in the sale of
new and used cars, San Diego, California,
December 14-15, 1979 /. [Sacramento, CA]
[1980?] iv, 435 p. :   LC Card 80-621713   DDC
343.794/08556292222/0262 19
KFC10.4 .L27 1979

WARRANTY - MAINE.
Maine. Legislature. Committee on Business
Legislation. [Final report of the Joint Standing
Committee on Business Legislation on its study
of H.P. 1459]. [Augusta, Me. , 1980]. 12, [9]
leaves ;   LC Card 80-622698   DDC
343.741/078629222 19
KFM11.62 .B8 1980

WARRANTY - UNITED STATES.
United States. Congress. House. Committee on
Interstate and Foreign Commerce.
Subcommittee on Consumer Protection and
Finance. Automobile warranty and repair act .
Washington , 1980. vi, 720 p. :   LC Card
80-603473   DDC 343.73/0944 19
KF27 .I554 1979h

Warren, Elizabeth, 1934- Lyneis, Margaret M.
Impacts, damage to cultural resources in the
California desert /. Riverside, Calif. , 1980. viii,
171 p. :   LC Card 81-600782   DDC 979.4/9 19
F863 .L95

Warren, Guylyn. Mutagen screening in an isolated high lung cancer mortality area of Montana /. Helena, Mont. [1979] 30 leaves : LC Card 79-626214 DDC 616.9/8 19
RA576 .M85

Warren, Kay B., 1947- Bourque, Susan Carolyn, 1943- Women of the Andes . Ann Arbor , c1981. p. cm. ISBN 0-472-09330-4 : LC Card 81-811 DDC 305.4/2/0985 19
HQ1572 .B68 1981

WARREN, ROBERT PENN, 1905- - BIBLIOGRAPHY.
Grimshaw, James A. Robert Penn Warren . Charlottesville , 1981. p. cm. ISBN 0-8139-0891-4 LC Card 81-3003 DDC 016.813/52 19
Z8949.73 .G75 PS3545.A748

WARREN, ROBERT PENN, 1905- - CRITICISM AND INTERPRETATION.
Justus, James H. The achievement of Robert Penn Warren /. Baton Rouge , c1981. p. cm. ISBN 0-8071-0875-8 : LC Card 81-3714 DDC 813/.52 19
PS3545.A748 Z73

WARS. see NAVAL HISTORY; WAR.

Warsaw Treaty Organization. see Organizatsiia stran Varshavskogo dogovora.

WARSHIPS - UNITED STATES.
United States. Navy Dept. Office of Information. Ships, aircraft, and weapons of the United States Navy. [Washington, D.C. , 1980] 51 p. : LC Card 80-603251 DDC 359.3/2/0973 19
VF347 .U57 1980

Washburn, H. Gordon. (joint author) Kunkle, John H. Plea negotiation in Pennsylvania . [Harrisburg] [1979] ii, 105, [76] p. : LC Card 80-622816 DDC 345.748/072 19
KFP578.5 .K86

Washichek, Jack N. Summary of snow survey measurements for Colorado and New Mexico, 1971-1977 : report / prepared by Jack N. Washichek, Bernard A. Shafer, Judy Raye Teilborg. Denver, Colo. : Soil Conservation Service, [1978] xxiii, 128 p. : maps ; 27 cm. "Federal-State-private cooperative snow surveys, U. S. Department of Agriculture, Soil Conservation Service." "Issued summer 1978." Chiefly tables. Includes index. LC Card 79-601670 DDC 551.57/9/788 19
1. Snow surveys - Colorado. 2. Snow surveys - New Mexico. 3. Water-supply - Colorado. 4. Water-supply - New Mexico. I. Shafer, Bernard A., joint author. II. Teilborg, Judy Raye, joint author. III. United States. Soil Conservation Service.
GB2625.C6 W37

The washing away of wrongs . Sung, Tz'u, 1186-1249. [Hsi yüan chi lu. English.] Ann Arbor , 1981. p. cm. ISBN 0-89264-801-5 : LC Card 81-6195 DDC 614/.1 19
RA1063 .S9613

Washington coastal geology between the Hoh and Quillayute Rivers /. Rau, Weldon W. Olympia, Wash. , 1980. xii, 57 p. : LC Card 80-623473 DDC 557.9794 19
QE176.O43 R38

WASHINGTON COUNTY, NEB. - MAPS.
(1979) United States. Soil Conservation Service. Washington County, Nebraska /. [Lincoln, Neb.] [1979?] 1 map : LC Card 81-691077
G4193.W2 1979 .U5

Washington, D. C. American Folklife Center. see American Folklife Center.

Washington, D. C. Army War College. see United States. Army War College.

WASHINGTON, D. C. ARTHUR CAPPER DWELLINGS - SECURITY MEASURES.
William Brill Associates. Comprehensive security planning . Washington , 1977. 196 p. in various pagings : LC Card 78-601532
HV8290 .W54 1977   NYPL [JLF 81-371]

Washington, D. C. Biblioteca Conmemorativa de Colón. see Columbus Memorial Library.

WASHINGTON, D. C. - BIOGRAPHY.
Hutchinson, Louise Daniel. Anna J. Cooper, a voice from the South /. Washington (A&I Building-2280, Washington, D.C. 20560) , 1981. p. cm. LC Card 81-5323 DDC 370/.92/4 B 19
F205.N4 C664

Washington, D. C. Brookings Institution. see Brookings Institution, Washington, D. C.

Washington, D. C. Bureau of National Affairs. see Bureau of National Affairs, Washington, D. C.

Washington, D. C. Bureau of Social Science Research. see Bureau of Social Science Research, Washington, D. C.

Washington, D. C. Carnegie Institution. see Carnegie Institution of Washington.

WASHINGTON, D. C. - CITY PLANNING.
United States. National Capital Planning Commission. Downtown design and development . Washington, 1974. 28 p.
NYPL [JLG 80-72]

Washington, D. C. Columbus Memorial Library. see Columbus Memorial Library.

Washington, D. C. Dulles International Airport. see Dulles International Airport, Washington, D. C.

WASHINGTON, D. C. - ECONOMIC CONDITIONS.
United States. Congress. House. Committee on the District of Columbia. Problems in urban centers . Washington , 1980 [i.e. 1981] ix, 936, x p. : LC Card 81-601760 DDC 361.6/09753 19
KF27 .D5 1980

WASHINGTON, D. C. ECONOMIC DEVELOPMENT INSTITUTE.
International Bank for Reconstruction and Development. The Economic Development Institute 1966-67. [Washington, D. C., 1966] 30 p.
*NYPL [*XME-9636]*

Washington, D. C. Export-Import Bank. see Export-Import Bank of Washington.

Washington, D. C. George Washington University. see George Washington University, Washington, D. C.

Washington, D. C. Hirshhorn (Joseph H.) Museum and Sculpture Garden. see Hirshhorn Museum and Sculpture Garden.

Washington, D. C. Hirshhorn Museum and Sculpture Garden. see Hirshhorn Museum and Sculpture Garden.

Washington, D. C. Inter-American Statistical Institute. see Inter-American Statistical Institute.

Washington, D. C. Joseph H. Hirshhorn Museum and Sculpture Garden. see Hirshhorn Museum and Sculpture Garden.

WASHINGTON, D. C. - MAPS.
(1978) United States. National Park Service. Washington, D.C. /. Washington [1978] 1 map : 23 x 49 cm. Scale not given. Folded title: Welcome to Washington. "Reprint 1978." "Stock Number 024-005-00669-9." Covers the National Mall, major government buildings, and tourist sites in downtown Washington. Includes text, tourist information, and col. ill. Text, tourist information, map of Washington region, and col. ill. on verso. LC Card 78-696267
G3851.E635 1978 .U5
NYPL [Map Div. 81-3038]

WASHINGTON, D. C. - MAPS, TOURIST.
United States. National Park Service. Washington, D.C. /. Washington [1978] 1 map : 23 x 49 cm. Scale not given. Folded title: Welcome to Washington. "Reprint 1978." "Stock Number 024-005-00669-9." Covers the National Mall, major government buildings, and tourist sites in downtown Washington. Includes text, tourist information, and col. ill. Text, tourist information, map of Washington region, and col. ill. on verso. LC Card 78-696267
G3851.E635 1978 .U5
NYPL [Map Div. 81-3038]

Washington, D. C. Mellon Gallery of Art. see United States. National Gallery of Art.

Washington, D. C. National Air and Space Museum. see National Air and Space Museum.

Washington, D. C. National Collection of Fine Arts. see Smithsonian Institution. National Collection of Fine Arts.

Washington, D. C. National Defense University. see National Defense University.

Washington, D. C. National Gallery of Art (Mellon Gallery) see United States. National Gallery of Art.

Washington, D. C. National Gallery of Art of the Smithsonian Institution. see Smithsonian Institution. National Collection of Fine Arts.

Washington, D. C. National Institute of Senior Centers. see National Institute of Senior Centers.

Washington, D. C. National Military Command System Support Center. see United States. National Military Command System Support Center.

Washington, D. C. National Museum of History and Technology. see National Museum of History and Technology.

Washington, D. C. National Portrait Gallery. see National Portrait Gallery, Washington, D. C.

Washington, D. C. Office of the Commonwealth of Puerto Rico. see Puerto Rico. Office of the Commonwealth of Puerto Rico, Washington, D. C.

Washington, D. C. Optical Society of America. see Optical Society of America.

WASHINGTON, D. C. - PUBLIC BUILDINGS.
United States. Congress. Senate. Committee on Governmental Affairs. Subcommittee on Governmental Efficiency and the District of Columbia. Resolution to disapprove Location of chanceries amendment act of 1979 . Washington , 1980. iv, 98 p. ; LC Card 80-602103 DDC 346.75304/5 19
KF26 .G6735 1979i

Washington, D. C. Renwick Gallery. see Renwick Gallery.

Washington, D. C. Saint Elizabeths Hospital. see Saint Elizabeths Hospital, Washington, D. C.

Washington, D. C. Smithsonian Institution. see Smithsonian Institution.

WASHINGTON, D. C. - SOCIAL CONDITIONS.
United States. Congress. House. Committee on the District of Columbia. Problems in urban centers . Washington , 1980 [i.e. 1981] ix, 936, x p. : LC Card 81-601760 DDC 361.6/09753 19
KF27 .D5 1980

Washington, D. C. Woodrow Wilson International Center for Scholars. see Woodrow Wilson International Center for Scholars.

Washington, D. C. Worldwatch Institute. see Worldwatch Institute.

WASHINGTON, D.C. - CITY PLANNING - CITIZEN PARTICIPATION.
District of Columbia. Municipal Planning Office. Citizen participation in comprehensive planning . [Washington] , 1977. 81 p. in various pagings ; LC Card 78-621432 DDC 307.7/6/09753 19
HT168.W3 D57 1977

WASHINGTON, D.C. CLIFTON TERRACE - MANAGEMENT.
United States. Congress. Senate. Committee on Appropriations. Subcommittee on HUD-Independent Agencies. Management of HUD's multi-family properties, the Cliffton Terrace case . Washington , 1980. iii, 375, vi p. ; LC Card 80-602962 DDC 353.0086/5043/09753 19
KF26 .A6486 1979b

WASHINGTON, D.C. - EXHIBITIONS.
Pachter, Marc. Champions, heroes of American sport /. [Washington] , New York [1981] p. cm. ISBN 0-8109-1602-9 (Abrams) : LC Card 80-28934 DDC 796/.092/2 B 19
GV697.A1 P28

WASHINGTON (D.C.) - OFFICIALS AND EMPLOYEES - SALARIES, ALLOWANCES, ETC.
Wald, Michael L. Municipal government wage surveys, Washington, D.C., October 1978. Philadelphia, Pa. (P.O. Box 13309, Philadelphia 19101) [1979] v, 70 p. ; LC Card 80-603374 DDC 352/.005123/09753 19
JK2757 .W34

Washington forest productivity study, phase II. Harding, Roger A. Forest inventory with Landsat . Olympia , 1978. ix, 221 p. : LC Card

79-621899   DDC 634.9/285 19
SD387.R4 H37

Washington historical quarterly. Pacific
Northwest quarterly. v. 1- ; Oct. 1906- Seattle.
LC Card 80-30966   *NYPL [IAA(Pacific
Northwest quarterly)]*

Washington, Institute of Public Administration.
see **Institute of Public Administration,
Washington, D. C.**

**WASHINGTON METROPOLITAN AREA -
ANTIQUITIES.**
Mid-Atlantic Archaeological Research, inc.
Cultural resources reconnaissance investigations
for the metropolitan Washington area water
supply study early action report . Newark, Del.
[1979] [92] leaves, [24] leaves of plates : LC
Card 80-601709   DDC 975.3 19
F195.5 .M53 1979

**WASHINGTON METROPOLITAN AREA -
CITY PLANNING.**
Metropolitan Washington Council of
Governments. Metropolitan growth policy
statement . [Washington , 1977] 21 p. ;
      NYPL [*XME-8652]

**Washington Metropolitan Area Transit
Authority** . United States. Congress. House.
Committee on the District of Columbia.
Subcommittee on Metropolitan Affairs.
Washington , 1980. iv, 92 p. : LC Card
80-603077   DDC 363.3/79 19
KF27 .D563 1980

**Washington Metropolitan Area Transit
Authority.**
Inauguration Day : [central Washington (D.C.)].
[Washington : The Authority, 1981] 1 map ; on
sheet 22 x 28 cm. Shows subway stations and routes
serving the Ronald Reagan inauguration site and parade
route 20 Jan. 1981. Includes notes. LC Card
81-690316
1. Subways - Washington, D. C. - Maps. I. Title.
G3851.P33 1981 .W3

Metro service : [Washington D.C., metropolitan
area]. Washington : Metropolitan Area Transit
Authority, [1980] 1 map : col. ; 34 x 43 cm.,
folded to 18 x 9 cm. Panel title on verso: All about
Metro, November 1980. Includes list of "Metro station
locations" and inset of central Washington. Text, fare
table, transit information, ill. (some col.), and
advertisement on verso. "10/80-12." LC Card
81-690217
*1. Subways - Washington, D. C. - Maps. 2. Subways -
Washington metropolitan area - Maps. I. Title. II. Title:
All about Metro, November 1980.*
G3851.P33 1980 .W31

**WASHINGTON METROPOLITAN AREA
TRANSIT AUTHORITY.**
United States. Congress. House. Committee on
the District of Columbia. Subcommittee on
Metropolitan Affairs. Washington Metropolitan
Area Transit Authority . Washington , 1980. iv,
92 p. : LC Card 80-603077   DDC 363.3/79 19
KF27 .D563 1980

**Washington Metropolitan Area Transportation
Authority.** United States. Urban Mass
Transportation Administration. Draft
environmental impact statement .
[Washington] , 1979. 204 p. in various pagings,
[17] fold. leaves of plates : LC Card 79-602769
  DDC 388.4/2/09753 19
TD195.S9 U54 1979

Washington Metropolitan Regional Conference.
see **Metropolitan Washington Council of
Governments.**

WASHINGTON NAVY YARD.
United States. Naval Facilities Engineering
Command. Chesapeake Division. Washington
Navy Yard master plan. [Washington, D.C.]
[1979] v, 102 p. : LC Card 80-602046   DDC
359.7/5/09753 19
VA70.W3 U54 1979

Washington Navy Yard master plan. United
States. Naval Facilities Engineering Command.
Chesapeake Division. [Washington, D.C.]
[1979] v, 102 p. : LC Card 80-602046   DDC
359.7/5/09753 19
VA70.W3 U54 1979

Washington Sea Grant Program.
Spencer, Wallace H. Environmental
management of Puget Sound . Seattle [1971]
50 p. ;   LC Card 80-505800   DDC 333.91/009797/7

19
HD1695.P83 S67

Thorne, Richard E. A portable hydroacoustic
data acquisition system for fish stock
assessment /. Seattle [1972] ii, 14 leaves : LC
Card 81-462262   DDC 639/.2 19
SH344.23.E3 T48

Washington sea grant publication (unnumb.)
Shorelines management '77 . Seattle [1978?] ix,
163 p. :   LC Card 79-624199   DDC 333.91/7/0973
19
HT392 .S54

Washington (State). Accountancy, Board of. see
Washington (State). Board of Accountancy.

Washington (State). Adult Corrections Division.
Master plan : adult corrections / Washington
State, Department of Social and Health
Services, Adult Corrections Division.
[Olympia] : The Division, [1979] iii, 108, [83]
p. : ill. ; 28 cm. "December 1979." LC Card
80-622610   DDC 365/.9797 19
1. Corrections - Washington (State). I. Title.
HV9305.W2 W36 1979

**WASHINGTON (STATE) - ANTIQUITIES -
ADDRESSES, ESSAYS, LECTURES.**
Lyman, R. Lee. Prehistoric butchering
techniques in the lower granite reservoir,
southeastern Washington /. [Pocatello] , 1978.
25 p. : LC Card 79-620641   DDC 979.7/4 19
E78.I18 T43 no. 13 E78.W3

**Washington (State). Asian American Affairs,
Commission on.** see **Washington (State).
Commission on Asian American Affairs.**

Washington (State). Board of Accountancy. (Old
Catalog form: Washington (State).
Accountancy, Board of.)
Rules of professional conduct of certified public
accountants, licensed public accountants, and
public accountants / Washington State Board of
Accountancy. [Olympia, WA] : The Board,
[1978?] [5] p. ; 28 cm. "Effective January 29, 1978."
"Amending the Code of professional conduct for
accountants licensed pursuant to provisions of chapter
18.04, RCW, by adopting WAC 4-16-300 through
WAC 4-16-410; repealing WAC 4-16-200 through
WAC 4-16-280." LC Card 80-620938   DDC
346.797/06648 19
*1. Accountants - Legal status, laws, etc. - Washington
(State). 2. Accountants, Professional ethics for. I. Title.*
KFW329.A252 A32 1978

Washington (State). Budget Committee. see
**Washington (State). Legislature. Budget
Committee.**

**Washington (State). Bureau of Community and
Residential Care.** Community-based care
systems for the functionally disabled . Olympia,
Wash. , 1979. xiv, 339 p. : LC Card 79-620045
  DDC 362.1/4/09797 19
RA645.36.W2 C65

**Washington (State). Bureau of Income
Maintenance.** Washington (State). Dept. of
Social and Health Services. Division of Analysis
and Information Services. Public assistance
programs in the State of Washington . Olympia,
Wash. [1979] iv, 151 p. ;   LC Card 79-625823
  DDC 361.6/09797 19
HV86 .W365 1979

**Washington (State). Center for Health Statistics.
Report - Washington State, Center for Health
Statistics.**
Starzyk, Patricia M. Chiropractors in
Washington State, 1978 /. Olympia, Wash.
[1979?] 36 p. : LC Card 80-621770   DDC
331.11/916155/3409797 19
RZ225.U6 S82

Starzyk, Patricia M. Pharmacists in
Washington State, 1977 /. Olympia, Wash.
[1979] 39 p. : LC Card 80-621514   DDC
331.11/916151/09797 19
RS67.U7 W37

Washington (State). Center for Health
Statistics. Boarding homes in Washington
State, 1978 /. Olympia, Wash. [1979] iv, 23
p. : LC Card 80-621771   DDC 362.6/1/09797 19
HV1468.W2 W35 1979

**Washington (State). Central Washington
University.** see **Central Washington
University.**

WASHINGTON (STATE) - COMMERCE.
Washington (State). Dept. of Commerce and

Economic Development. Economic and
Planning Analysis Division. International trade
and the Washington State economy. [Olympia],
1973. 31 p. ;   *NYPL [*ZT-1259]*

**Washington (State). Commission on Asian
American Affairs.** Ong, Paul M. Asians in
Washington . Olympia , 1976. vii. 69 p. : LC
Card 77-621579
F900.O6 O53   *NYPL [*XME-9406]*

**Washington (State) Community Affairs and
Planning Agency.** see **Washington (State).
Planning and Community Affairs Agency.**

**Washington (State). Community Development,
Office of.** see **Washington (State). Office of
Community Development.**

**Washington (State). Council for Postsecondary
Education.**
Fischer, Norman M. Research in Washington
higher education /. [Olympia] , 1978. 112 p. :
LC Card 79-623622
LB1028 .F484   *NYPL [JFF 80-1521]*

Fischer, Norman M. 1976-77 unit expenditures
study /. [Olympia] [1980] viii, 91 p. : LC Card
80-621763   DDC 379.1/214/09797 19
LB2342 .F57

Professional leave, fiscal 1979, follow-up report
/ State of Washington, Council for
Postsecondary Education ; contact person,
Jackie M. Johnson. [Olympia] : The Council,
[1980] 36 p. ; 28 cm. (Report - Council for
Postsecondary Education, State of Washington ; no.
80-8) "February 1980." Includes the author's
Professional leave, fiscal 1979, Washington public
colleges and universities, dated Oct. 1979, and issued as
Report no. 80-3 (p. 29-36) LC Card 80-621764
  DDC 331.25/763 19
*1. College teachers - Washington (State) - Leaves of
absence. I. Johnson, Jacquelin. II. Washington (State).
Council for Postsecondary Education. Professional
leave, fiscal 1979, Washington public colleges and
universities. 1980. III. Series: Washington (State).
Council for Postsecondary Education. Report - Council
for Postsecondary Education, State of Washington , no.
80-3 [etc.].*
LB2331.7 .W37 1980

**Professional leave, fiscal 1979, Washington
public colleges and universities. 1980.**
Washington (State). Council for
Postsecondary Education. Professional leave,
fiscal 1979, follow-up report / State of
Washington, Council for Postsecondary
Education ; contact person, Jackie M.
Johnson. [Olympia] [1980] 36 p. ; LC Card
80-621764   DDC 331.25/763 19
LB2331.7 .W37 1980

**Report - Council for Postsecondary Education,
State of Washington .**
(no. 80-3 [etc.]) Washington (State). Council
for Postsecondary Education. Professional
leave, fiscal 1979, follow-up report /.
[Olympia] [1980] 36 p. : LC Card 80-621764
  DDC 331.25/763 19
LB2331.7 .W37 1980

(no. 80-5) Washington (State). Council for
Postsecondary Education. Resident and
nonresident, undergraduate and graduate
tuition and/or required fees . [Olympia,
Wash.] [1980] 21 p. : LC Card 80-621762
  DDC 379.1/3/09797 19
LB2342 .W316 1980

(no. 80-7) Fischer, Norman M. 1976-77 unit
expenditures study /. [Olympia] [1980] viii,
91 p. : LC Card 80-621763   DDC
379.1/214/09797 19
LB2342 .F57

(no. 81-1) Jons, Tom. The formula manual .
[Olympia] [1980] iii, 260 p. : LC Card
80-623853   DDC 378.797 s 378.797 19
LC148 .W336a no. 81-1 LA382.5

Resident and nonresident, undergraduate and
graduate tuition and/or required fees : public
universities, colleges and state universities, and
community colleges / project officer, Jackie M.
Johnson. [Olympia, Wash.] : Council for
Postsecondary Education, State of Washington,
[1980] 21 p. : graphs ; 28 cm. (Report - Council
for Postsecondary Education, State of Washington ; no.
80-5) "January 1980." LC Card 80-621762   DDC
379.1/3/09797 19
*1. College costs - Washington (State) - Statistics. I.
Johnson, Jacquelin. II. Series: Washington (State).*

Council for Postsecondary Education. Report - Council for Postsecondary Education, State of Washington , no. 80-5. III. Title.
LB2342 .W316 1980

Washington (State). Dept. of Commerce and Economic Development. Economic and Planning Analysis Division. International trade and the Washington State economy; 1960-1972 [Olympia], 1973. 31 p. ; 28 cm. Microfilm.
1. Washington (State) - Commerce. 2. Washington (State) - Economic conditions. I. Title.
                        NYPL [*ZT-1259]

Washington (State). Dept. of Ecology. CH2M Hill, inc. Water quality in Capitol Lake, Olympia, Washington /. [Corvallis, Or.] , 1978. 116 p. in various pagings :   LC Card 79-621289
TD224.W2 C18 1978   **NYPL [JSF 81-45]**

Columbia River instream resource protection program : final program document. Olympia, Wash. : State of Washington, Dept. of Ecology, [1980] iii, 185, [79] p. : ill. ; 28 cm. "June 1980." Includes bibliographies. LC Card 80-623147 DDC 333.91/009797 19
1. Water resources development - Environmental aspects - Columbia River Valley. 2. Water resources development - Environmental aspects - Washington (State). I. Title.
HD1695.C73 W37 1980

Final environmental impact statement : proposed upper Lewis River cloud seeding program / prepared by State of Washington, Department of Ecology. [Olympia] : The Dept., [1974] ca. 100 p. in various pagings ; 28 cm. Includes bibliography. "January 23, 1974." LC Card 76-624014 DDC 333.9/2 19
1. Rain-making - Environmental aspects - Washington (State) - Lewis River watershed. 2. Silver iodide - Environmental aspects - Washington (State) - Lewis River watershed. 3. Environmental impact statement - Washington (State) - Lewis River watershed. I. Title.
TD195.R34 W37 1974

Final environmental impact statement (including program overview) : Western Washington instream resources protection program. [Olympia] : Washington State Dept. of Ecology, 1979. [78] p. : ill. ; 28 cm. Cover title. Includes bibliography. LC Card 79-625437 DDC 333.7/1/09797 19
1. Water resources development - Environmental aspects - Washington (State). I. Title.
HD1694.W2 W37 1979

Kramer, Chin & Mayo. Jefferson County solid waste management plan. Seattle, 1973. 1 v. (various pagings):   **NYPL [JSF 80-734]**

Kruger, Dan M. Effects of point-source discharges and other inputs on water quality in Budd Inlet, Washington /. Olympia, WA [1979] xiv, 40, 37 p. : LC Card 80-623150 DDC 333.91/64 19
TD224.W2 K78

Lakes constituting shorelines of the State Shoreline Management Act of 1971. Adopted June, 1972 ; amended effective August, 1973. [n. p., 1973] 27 p. 28 cm. Microfilm. At head of title: Chapter 173-20 WAC. Cover title.
1. Shore-lines - Law and legislation - Washington (State). 2. Lakes - Washington (State). I. Title.
                        NYPL [*ZT-1250]

Project report - Washington State Dept. of Ecology .
(no. DOE-PR-6) Yake, William E. Water quality trend analysis . Olympia, WA [1979] 39, 5 p. : LC Card 79-625821 DDC 363.7/3942/097973 19
TD225.S56 Y34

Report - State of Washington, Department of Ecology .
(no. 80-8) Washington (State). Dept. of Ecology. Shorelands Division. Overview, coastal aquatic management policies of Washington State and federal agencies /. Olympia, Wash. [1980] 29 p. ; LC Card 80-624143 DDC 333.91/7/09797 19
HT393.W3 W3 1980

Smith, Gary Frederick. A quantitative sampling program of benthic communities in nearshore subtidal areas within the Rosario Strait region of Northern Puget Sound, Washington State (1976) /. [Olympia] [1979] vi, 105 p. : LC

Card 80-622612 DDC 591.9797/7 19
QH105.W2 S65

Soltero, Raymond A. Further investigation as to the cause and effect of eutrophication in Long Lake, Washington. Cheney, Wash., 1974. x, 85 p.: LC Card 76-9604   **NYPL [JSF 80-397]**

Washington (State). Laws, statutes, etc. Compendium of State laws and regulations concerning solid waste management in Washington State. [Olympia] , 1974. 1 v. ; LC Card 74-622943
KFW359.R3 A2 1974   **NYPL [JLF 81-89]**

Washington (State). Dept. of Ecology. Shorelands Division. Overview, coastal aquatic management policies of Washington State and federal agencies / agency contributors, Nancy Nelson ... [et al.] ; edited by Steve Tilley. Olympia, Wash. : Shorelands Division, Dept. of Ecology, [1980] 29 p. ; 28 cm. (Report - Washington State Department of Ecology . no. 80-8) "August 1980." LC Card 80-624143 DDC 333.91/7/09797 19
1. Coastal zone management - Washington (State). I. Nelson, Nancy. II. Tilley, Steve. III. Series: Washington (State). Dept. of Ecology. Report - State of Washington, Department of Ecology , no. 80-8. IV. Title.
HT393.W3 W3 1980

Shorelines management '77 . Seattle [1978?] ix, 163 p. : LC Card 79-624199 DDC 333.91/7/0973 19
HT392 .S54

Washington (State). Dept. of Ecology. Water Quality Planning. Dryland agriculture water quality management plan : section 208, P.L. 95-217. Olympia, Wash. : Dept. of Ecology, Office of Water Programs, Water Quality Planning : Washington State Conservation Commission, [1979] 2 v. : maps ; 29 cm. "Final draft, September 1979." "D.O.E. 79-5d-(1)[-(2)]." Includes bibliographical references. LC Card 80-621082 DDC 363.7/39456/09797 19
1. Agricultural pollution - Washington (State). 2. Dry farming - Environmental aspects - Washington (State). 3. Water - Pollution - Washington (State). 4. Water quality management - Washington (State). I. Washington (State). State Conservation Commission. II. Title.
TD428.A37 W37 1979a

Forest practice water quality management plan : Section 208, P.L. 95-217. Olympia, Wash. : Water Quality Planning, Office of Water Programs, Dept. of Ecology, [1979] iii, 56 p. : ill. ; 29 cm. "DOE 79-5a." "October 1979." Includes bibliographical references. LC Card 80-621083 DDC 363.7/394 19
1. Forests and forestry - Environmental aspects - United States. 2. Water quality management - United States. 3. Forest management - United States. I. Title.
TD428.F67 W37 1979

WASHINGTON (STATE). DEPT. OF EDUCATION. (Old Catalog form: Washington (State). Education Dept.) Washington (State). Legislature. Budget Committee. Superintendent of Public Instruction, special education for the handicapped program. Olympia , 1979. iv, 35 p. ; LC Card 80-621134 DDC 371.9/042 19
HJ11 .W2453 no. 79-6 LC4032.W2

WASHINGTON (STATE). DEPT. OF EMERGENCY SERVICES - AUDITING AND INSPECTION. Washington (State). Legislature. Budget Committee. Department of Emergency Services. Olympia , 1980. vi, 120 p. : LC Card 80-621767 DDC 353.97970072/32 s 353.97970075/4 19
HJ11 .W2453 no. 80-2 UA928.W2

Washington (State). Dept. of Fisheries. Technical report .
(no. 18) Fraidenburg, Mike. 1974 recreational fisheries at four jetty and breakwater sites in the Grays Harbor and Columbia River mouth areas /. [Olympia] , 1976. ii, 12 p. : LC Card 76-623971 DDC 333.95/611/09797 19
SH559 .F72

(no. 40) Stern, Loren. 1977 summary of Department of Fisheries and treaty Indian commercial salmon fishing regulations in the Boldt case area /. [Olympia] , 1978. i, 44 p. ; LC Card 79-624606 DDC 343.979/07692755 19
KFW505.6.H85 S73

(no. 46) Campo, Joe. 1978 summary of commercial salmon fishing regulations in the Boldt case area /. [Olympia] , 1979. 174 p. : LC Card 79-625420 DDC 343.979/07692755 19
KFW505.6.H85 C35

(no. 49) Miller, Marc C. Trends in catch timing and distribution of the Washington commercial troll salmon fishery, 1960-1975 /. [Olympia, Wash.] , 1979. iii, 56 p. : LC Card 80-620830 DDC 338.3/72755 19
SH222.W2 M54

(no. 51) Ilg, Janet. An annotated bibliography of the lingcod, Ophiodon elongatus /. [Olympia, Wash.] , 1979. 25 p. ; LC Card 80-621496 DDC 016.597/58 19
QL638.H49 I43

Washington (State). Dept. of General Administration. (Old Catalog form: Washington (State). General Administration, Dept. of)of) CH2M Hill, inc. Water quality in Capitol Lake, Olympia, Washington /. [Corvallis, Or.] , 1978. 116 p in various pagings : LC Card 79-621289
TD224.W2 C18 1978   **NYPL [JSF 81-45]**

WASHINGTON (STATE). DEPT. OF GENERAL ADMINISTRATION - AUDITING AND INSPECTION. Washington (State). Legislature. Budget Committee. Central stores revolving fund and the motor transport account, Department of General Administration. Olympia , 1980. xi, 140 p. : LC Card 80-621766 DDC 353.97970072/32 s 353.97970071/2 19
HJ11 .W2453 No. 80-1 JK9288

Washington (State). Dept. of Highways. (Old Catalog form: Washington (State). Highway Dept.) Voorhees (Alan M.) and Associates. Blue Streak bus rapid transit demonstration project . Seattle, 1973. 6, 11 p. LC Card 74-132895
                      NYPL [*ZT-1265]

Washington (State). Dept. of Labor and Industries. Division of Safety. Management Information Section. 1976 occupational injury and illness survey / prepared by the Management Information Section. [Olympia] : State of Washington, Dept. of Labor and Industries, Division of Industrial Safety and Health, [1978] 43 p. : ill. ; 28 cm. Cover title: Washington State occupational injury and illness survey, 1976. "July 1978." LC Card 79-624249 DDC 312/.39803/09797 19
1. Occupational diseases - Washington (State) - Statistics. 2. Industrial accidents - Washington (State) - Statistics. I. Title. II. Title: Washington State occupational injury and illness survey, 1976.
RC964 .W36 1978

1977 occupational injury and illness survey / prepared by Management Information Section. Olympia : State of Washington, Dept. of Labor and Industries, Division of Industrial Safety and Health, 1979. 46 p. : ill. ; 28 cm. LC Card 80-620759 DDC 362.1/1/09797 19
1. Occupational diseases - Washington (State) - Statistics. 2. Industrial accidents - Washington (State) - Statistics. I. Title.
RC964 .W36 1979

Washington (State). Dept. of Natural Resources. (Old Catalog form: Washington (State). Natural Resources, Dept. of) Christy, Irene. Harbor area planning project, State of Washington /. Olympia, Wash. [1979] ii, 38, [140] : LC Card 80-622052 DDC 387.1/09797/9 19
HE554.W2 C47

Washington (State). Dept. of Natural Resources. Division of Geology and Earth Resources. see **Washington (State). Division of Geology and Earth Resources.**

Washington (State). Dept. of Natural Resources. Division of Technical Services. Harding, Roger A. Forest inventory with Landsat . Olympia , 1978. ix, 221 p. : LC Card 79-621899 DDC 634.9/285 19
SD387.R4 H37

Washington (State). Dept. of Personnel. (Old Catalog form: Washington (State). Personnel Dept.) Salary schedule and alpha listing of classes, October 1, 1979. [Olympia] : State of Washington, Dept. of Personnel, [1979] [57]

BIBLIOGRAPHIC GUIDE

Washington (State). Dept. of Revenue. Inheritance Tax Division.

654

p. ; 29 cm. LC Card 80-621509 DDC
331.2/813539797 19
1. Washington (State) - Officials and employees -
Salaries, allowances, etc. - Statistics. I. Title.
JK9257 .W36 1979

Washington (State). Dept. of Revenue.
Inheritance Tax Division. Washington
(State). Laws, statutes, etc. Laws and
regulations . [Olympia, Wash.] , 1979. iv, 71
p. ; LC Card 80-622380 DDC 343.79705/3/0263
19
KFW482 .A3 1979

Washington (State). Dept. of Revenue. Research
and Information Division. Conklin, John B.
A review of forest taxation in Washington /.
[Olympia, Wash.] [1980] vi, 116 p. : LC Card
80-623470 DDC 336.22/5 19
HJ4280.A3 C65

Washington (State). Dept. of Social and Health
Services.
Community-based care systems for the
functionally disabled . Olympia, Wash. , 1979.
xiv, 339 p. : LC Card 79-620045 DDC
362.1/4/09797 19
RA645.36.W2 C65

Report - Washington State Dept. of Social &
Health Services .
(01-24) Sykes, Thomas M. An analysis of
program needs of prison inmates in
Washington State /. Olympia, Wash. [1980]
xxi, 139 p. ; LC Card 80-620028 DDC
365/.66/09797 19
HV9475.W2 S93

The two-state collaborative mental health
outcome study, State of Washington /.
Olympia, 1980. 2 v.;   *NYPL [JLF 81-132]*

Washington (State). Dept. of Social and Health
Services. Analysis and Information Services
Division. Office of Research. An assessment
of the community adjustment and service needs
of former State hospital patients : a study of
deinstitutionalization / Gary W. Johnson ... [et
al.]. Olympia, Wash. : State of Washington,
Dept. of Social and Health Services, Analysis
and Information Services Division, Office of
Research, 1980. xxviii, 300 p. ; 28 cm. Includes
bibliographical references. LC Card 80-620020 DDC
362.2/0425 19
1. Mentally ill - Rehabilitation - Washington (State). 2.
Community mental health services - Washington
(State) - Evaluation. 3. Halway houses - Washington
(State) - Evaluation. I. Johnson, Gary W. II. Title.
RC439.5 .W37 1980

WASHINGTON (STATE). DEPT. OF SOCIAL
AND HEALTH SERVICES - AUDITING
AND INSPECTION.
Washington (State). Legislature. Budget
Committee. Adoption program and State child
care system, Department of Social and Health
Services . Olympia , 1978. 165 p. in various
pagings ; LC Card 79-620911 DDC
353.97970072/32 s 353.97970084/7 19
HJ11 .W2453 no. 77-8 HV875

Washington (State). Dept. of Social and Health
Services. Division of Analysis and
Information Services.
Public assistance programs in the State of
Washington : a program review / Analysis and
Information Services Division and Bureau of
Income Maintenance. Olympia, Wash. : Dept.
of Social and Health Services, [1979] iv, 151
p. ; 28 cm. "January 1979." LC Card 79-625823
DDC 361.6/09797 19
1. Public welfare - Washington (State). I. Washington
(State). Bureau of Income Maintenance. II. Title.
HV86 .W365 1979

Report - Washington State Dept. of Social &
Health Services, Analysis and Information
Services Division .
(01-22) Lichtenstein, Karen. Assessment of
variables used in presentence
recommendations and court decisions /.
Olympia, Wash. [1980] vii, 29 p. : LC Card
80-623909 DDC 345.797/77077/0723
347.977705770723 19
KFX2379.89 .L52

Washington (State). Dept. of Transportation.
Division of Public Transportation and
Planning. see Washington (State). Division
of Public Transportation and Planning.

Washington (State). Division of Geology and
Earth Resources.
Bulletin - Division of Geology and Earth
Resources .
(no. 72) Rau, Weldon W. Washington coastal
geology between the Hoh and Quillayute
Rivers /. Olympia, Wash. , 1980. xii, 57 p. :
LC Card 80-623473 DDC 557.9794 19
QE176.O43 R38

Information circular - State of Washington,
Division of Geology and Earth Resources .
(70) Manson, Connie. Theses on Washington
geology . [Olympia, Wash.] , 1980. iii, 212
p. : LC Card 80-623709 DDC 557.97 s
016.55797 19
TN24.W2 A33 no. 70 Z6034.U5 QE175

Moen, Wayne S. Placer gold mining in
Washington /. Olympia , 1979. 21 p. :
                                *NYPL [*ZQ-577]*

Washington (State). Division of Private Forestry.
Guide to regulations affecting harvesting and
marketing forest products in Washington. 8th
revision. Olympia, Wash. : Division of Private
Forestry, State of Washington, Dept. of Natural
Resources, [1980] vi, 49 p. ; 28 cm. "January
1980." LC Card 80-622924 DDC 343.797/076498
19
1. Forest products - Law and legislation - Washington
(State). I. Title.
KFW249 .A863

Washington (State). Division of Public
Transportation and Planning. Annual traffic
report. [Olympia] maps (part. fold.) 22 x 29 cm.
Supersedes: Washington (State). State Highway
Commission. Annual traffic report. Issued in
cooperation with the U. S. Federal Highway
Administration.
1. Traffic surveys - Washington (State) - Statistics -
Periodicals. I. United States. Federal Highway
Administration. II. Title.   *NYPL [JLM 80-967]*

Washington (State). Eastern Washington State
College, Cheney. Biology, Dept. of. see
Washington (State). Eastern Washington
State College, Cheney. Dept. of Biology.

Washington (State). Eastern Washington State
College, Cheney. Dept. of Biology. Soltero,
Raymond A. Further investigation as to the
cause and effect of eutrophication in Long
Lake, Washington. Cheney, Wash., 1974. x, 85
p.: LC Card 76-9604   *NYPL [JSF 80-397]*

Washington (State). Ecology, Dept. of. see
Washington (State). Dept. of Ecology.

WASHINGTON (STATE) - ECONOMIC
CONDITIONS.
Washington (State). Dept. of Commerce and
Economic Development. Economic and
Planning Analysis Division. International trade
and the Washington State economy. [Olympia],
1973. 31 p. ;   *NYPL [*ZT-1259]*

Washington (State). Economic Opportunity,
Office of. see Washington (State). Office of
Economic Opportunity.

WASHINGTON (STATE) - ECONOMIC
POLICY - DIRECTORIES.
Washington (State). Planning and Community
Affairs Agency. Directory of city, county,
regional, state & federal planning agencies.
Olympia , 1978. 47 p. ; LC Card 79-621293
DDC 350.007/2/025797 19
HT393.W3 W34 1978

Washington (State). Education Dept. see
Washington (State). Dept. of Education.

Washington (State). Energy Facility Site
Evaluation Council. Rules relating to siting
energy facilities : Title 463, Washington
administrative code. Olympia, Wash. : Energy
Facility Site Evaluation Council, 1978. 133 p. ;
22 cm. Cover title. LC Card 79-624605
1. Energy facilities - Location - Law and legislation -
Washington (State). I. Title.
KFW286 .A4 1978

Washington (State). Fiscal Management and
Program Planning, Office of. see Washington
(State). Office of Program Planning and
Fiscal Management.

WASHINGTON (STATE). FISHERIES
MANAGEMENT DIVISION - AUDITING
AND INSPECTION.
Washington (State). Legislature. Budget
Committee. Performance audit, Department of

Game--Fish program . Olympia , 1979. vi, 90
p. : LC Card 79-626054 DDC 353.97970072/32 s
353.97970082/362 19
HJ11 .W2453 no. 79-3 SH222.W2

WASHINGTON (STATE). FORMS
MANAGEMENT CENTER.
Washington (State). Legislature. Budget
Committee. State forms management program
/. Olympia 1979] v, 57 p. ; LC Card 79-626055
DDC 353.97970072/32 s 353.97970071/4 19
HJ11 .W2453 no. 79-4 JK9249.P36

Washington (State). General Administration,
Dept. of. see Washington (State). Dept. of
General Administration.

Washington (State). Geology and Earth
Resources, Division of. see Washington
(State). Division of Geology and Earth
Resources.

Washington (State). Governor. Commission on
Asian American Affairs. see Washington
(State). Commission on Asian American
Affairs.

Washington (State). Governor, 1977- (Ray)
Report on my third year in office / Dixy Lee
Ray. [Olympia, Wash. : State Print. Plant,
1980] iv, 31 p. ; 28 cm. Cover title. LC Card
80-622791 DDC 353.979703/5 19
1. Washington (State) - Politics and government -
1951- - Addresses, essays, lectures. I. Title.
J87 .W222 1980

Washington (State). Health, State Board of. see
Washington (State). State Board of Health.

Washington (State). Highway Commission. see
Washington (State). State Highway
Commission.

Washington (State). Highways Dept. see
Washington (State). Dept. of Highways.

Washington State Historical Society. Pacific
Northwest quarterly. v. 1- ; Oct. 1906- Seattle.
LC Card 80-30966   *NYPL [IAA(Pacific*
                                Northwest quarterly)]

WASHINGTON (STATE) - HISTORY -
PERIODICALS.
Washington (State). State Capitol Historical
Association. Annual report. Olympia, Wash.
                NYPL [IAA (Washington) 81-185]

WASHINGTON (STATE) - HISTORY -
SOURCES - BIBLIOGRAPHY -
CATALOGS.
Washington (State) State University, Pullman.
Library. William Compton Brown . Pullman,
Wash. , 1966. 25 p. ; LC Card 67-65327 DDC
016.9797/04/0924 19
Z6616.B855 W37 1966 F891

Washington (State). Indian Affairs Task Force.
"Are you listening, neighbor?" : Report of the
Indian Affairs Task Force and The people
speak : will you listen? 1st revision. [Olympia] :
State of Washington, 1978. 124 p. ; 28 cm.
Cover title. Includes bibliographical references. LC
Card 79-621905 DDC 979.7/00497 19
1. Indians of North America - Washington (State). 2.
Indians of North America - Government relations -
1934-. 3. Indians of North America - Washington
(State) - Legal status, laws, etc. I. Washington (State).
Indian Affairs Task Force. People speak. 1978. II. Title.
E78.W3 W27 1978

People speak. 1978. Washington (State). Indian
Affairs Task Force. "Are you listening,
neighbor?" : Report of the Indian Affairs Task
Force and The people speak : will you listen?
1st revision. [Olympia] , 1978. 124 p. ; LC
Card 79-621905 DDC 979.7/00497 19
E78.W3 W27 1978

Washington (State). Interagency Committee for
Outdoor Recreation. (Old Catalog form:
Washington (State). Outdoor recreation, Inter-
agency Committee on.)
Nash, A. E. Keir. Understanding and planning
for ORV recreation . Tumwater, Wash. , 19. v,
159 p. ; LC Card 79-625837 DDC 338.3/4 19
GV191.42.W2 N37

Washington (State). Laws, statutes, etc. (Old
Catalog form: Washington (State). Statutes)
Compendium of State laws and regulations
concerning solid waste management in
Washington State. [Olympia] : State of
Washington, Dept. of Ecology., 1974. 1 v. ; 28
cm. Loose-leaf for updating. LC Card 74-622943
1. Refuse and refuse disposal - Law and legislation -

GOVERNMENT PUBLICATIONS - U.S.: 1981

655

Washington (State). Office of the Governor. Office of Program

Washington (State). I. Washington (State). Dept. of Ecology. II. Title.
KFW359.R3 A2 1974 **NYPL [JLF 81-89]**

Laws and regulations : inheritance taxes, gift taxes, escheats / Inheritance Tax Division. [Olympia, Wash.] : State of Washington, Dept. of Revenue, 1979. iv, 71 p. ; 28 cm. Includes index. LC Card 80-622380 DDC 343.79705/3/0263 19
1. Inheritance and transfer tax - Washington (State). 2. Gifts - Taxation - Washington (State). 3. Escheat - Washington (State). I. Washington (State). Dept. of Revenue. Inheritance Tax Division.
KFW482 .A3 1979

Washington (State). Legislative Budget Committee. see Washington (State). Legislature. Budget Committee.

Washington (State). Legislature.
Final legislative report, 1980 : 46th regular session. Olympia, WA : [Washington State Legislature] : available from House Office of Program Research, [1980] xxiii, 158 p. ; 28 cm. LC Card 80-622922 DDC 348.7970/01 19
1. Legislation - Washington (State). I. Title.
KFW15 .2 1980

Washington (State). Legislature. Budget Committee. (Old Catalog form: Washington (State). Budget committee)
Adoption program and State child care system, Department of Social and Health Services : [a report to the Washington State Legislature]. Olympia : State of Washington, Legislative Budget Committee, 1978. 165 p. in various pagings ; 28 cm. (Performance audit . report no. 77-8) Includes bibliographies. LC Card 79-620911 DDC 353.97970072/32 s 353.97970084/7 19
1. Adoption - Washington (State). 2. Foster home care - Washington (State). 3. Child welfare - Washington (State). 4. Washington (State). Dept. of Social and Health Services - Auditing and inspection. I. Title.
HJ11 .W2453 no. 77-8 HV875

Central stores revolving fund and the motor transport account, Department of General Administration. Olympia : State of Washington, Legislative Budget Committee, 1980. xi, 140 p. : ill. ; 28 cm. (Performance audit . report no. 80-1) "A report to the Washington State Legislature." LC Card 80-621766 DDC 353.97970072/32 s 353.97970071/2 19
1. Government purchasing - Washington (State) - Accounting. 2. Automobiles, Government - Washington (State) - Accounting. 3. Washington (State). Dept. of General Administration - Auditing and inspection. I. Title.
HJ11 .W2453 No. 80-1 JK9288

Department of Emergency Services. Olympia : State of Washington, Legislative Budget Committee, 1980. vi, 120 p. : diagrams ; 28 cm. (Performance audit . report no. 80-2) "A report to the Washington State Legislature." "January 19, 1980." LC Card 80-621767 DDC 353.97970072/32 s 353.97970075/4 19
1. Washington (State). Dept. of Emergency Services - Auditing and inspection.
HJ11 .W2453 no. 80-2 UA928.W2

Performance audit, Department of Game--Fish program : a report to the Washington State Legislature. Olympia : State of Washington, Legislative Budget Committee, 1979. vi, 90 p. : ill. ; 28 cm. (Report - State of Washington, Legislative Budget Committee ; no. 79-3) Cover title. LC Card 79-626054 DDC 353.97970072/32 s 353.97970082/362 19
1. Fishery management - Washington (State) - Evaluation. 2. Washington (State). Fisheries Management Division - Auditing and inspection. 3. Legislative auditing - Washington (State). I. Series: Washington (State). Legislature. Budget Committee. Report, no. 79-3. II. Title.
HJ11 .W2453 no. 79-3 SH222.W2

Report.
(no. 79-3) Washington (State). Legislature. Budget Committee. Performance audit, Department of Game--Fish program . Olympia , 1979. vi, 90 p. : LC Card 79-626054 DDC 353.97970072/32 s 353.97970082/362 19
HJ11 .W2453 no. 79-3 SH222.W2

State forms management program / [State of Washington, Legislative Budget Committee]. Olympia : The Committee, [1979] v, 57 p. ; 28 cm. (Performance audit . report no. 79-4) "A report to

the Washington State Legislature." "September 14, 1979." LC Card 79-626055 DDC 353.97970072/32 s 353.97970071/4 19
1. Washington (State). Forms Management Center. 2. Government paperwork - Washington (State). 3. Public administration - Forms, blanks, etc. I. Title.
HJ11 .W2453 no. 79-4 JK9249.P36

Superintendent of Public Instruction, special education for the handicapped program. Olympia : State of Washington, Legislative Budget Committee, 1979. iv, 35 p. ; 28 cm. (Performance audit . report no. 79-6) "Audit was conducted by Bradley Duerr." LC Card 80-621134 DDC 371.9/042 19
1. Handicapped children - Education - Washington (State) - Finance. 2. Washington (State). Dept. of Education. 3. Handicapped children - Education - Law and legislation - Washington (State). I. Duerr, Bradley. II. Title.
HJ11 .W2453 no. 79-6 LC4032.W2

Washington (State). Legislature. House of Representatives. Revenue Committee.
Washington state taxes . [Olympia] [1980] 46 p. : LC Card 81-621438 DDC 343.79704 347.97034 19
HJ2439 .W27

Washington (State). Legislature. Legislative Budget Committee. Program and fiscal review of state comic book law (chapter 19.18 RCW). Olympia : State of Washington: Legislative Budget Committee, 1980. iii, 7 p. ; 28 cm. (Performance audit . report no. 80-5.) "A report to the Washington State Legislature" - Cover. LC Card 80-624258 DDC 353.97970072/32 s 343.797/08557415 353.97970072/32 s 347.97038557415 19
1. Comic books, strips, etc. - Law and legislation - Washington (State). I. Series: Performance audit , report no. 80-5. II. Title.
HJ11 .W2453 no. 80-5 KFW271.B64

Washington (State). Legislature. Senate. Energy and Utilities Committee.
Major energy legislation of the 1979 legislative session / Washington State Senate Energy and Utilities Committee. Olympia, WA : The Committee, [1979] 26 p. : graphs ; 28 cm. Cover title: The energy crunch. LC Card 80-621222 DDC 346.79704/679/02638 19
1. Power resources - Law and legislation - Washington (State). 2. Energy conservation - Law and legislation - Washington (State). I. Title. II. Title: The energy crunch.
KFW11.72 .E53 1979

Price, Eleonore B. From waste to energy--the recycling connection . [Olympia, Wash.] [1980] v leaves, 112 p. ; LC Card 81-621765 DDC 363.7/28 19
TD794.5 .P73

Watson, Richard H. Energy, transition to the '80s . Olympia, WA [1980] 52 p., [2] leaves : LC Card 80-623469 DDC 346.7304/679 19
KFW286 .W38

WASHINGTON (STATE) - MAPS.
(1979) United States. Geological Survey. State of Washington, base map with highway and contours /. Reston, Va. , 1979. 1 map : LC Card 81-691603
G4280 1976 .U5

Washington (State). Natural Resources, Dept. of. see Washington (State). Dept. of Natural Resources.

Washington State occupational injury and illness survey, 1976. Washington (State). Dept. of Labor and Industries. Division of Safety. Management Information Section. 1976 occupational injury and illness survey /. [Olympia] [1978] 43 p. : LC Card 79-624249 DDC 312/.39803/09797 19
RC964 .W36 1978

Washington (State). Office of Community Development.
A brief survey of CSA-related anti-poverty organizations in Washington State. [Olympia] : Office of Community Development [and] Office of Economic Opportunity, 1978. 64 p. ; 28 cm. Cover title. Prepared by C. Weinreich. LC Card 79-621288
1. Poor - Services for - Washington (State) - Directories. 2. Washington (State). Office of Community Development. 3. Social service - Washington (State) - Directories. I. Weinreich, Chris. II. Washington (State). Office of Economic

Opportunity. III. Title.
HV86 .W365 1978a **NYPL [JLF 81-121]**

WASHINGTON (STATE). OFFICE OF COMMUNITY DEVELOPMENT.
Washington (State). Office of Community Development. A brief survey of CSA-related anti-poverty organizations in Washington State. [Olympia] , 1978. 64 p. ; LC Card 79-621288
HV86 .W365 1978a **NYPL [JLF 81-121]**

Washington (State). Office of Community Development. Office of Voluntary Action.
Pasco Volunteers Conference, Columbia Basin College, 1976. Pasco Volunteers Conference . Olympia, 1976. 19 p.; **NYPL [*XME-9108]**

Washington (State). Office of Community Health Services. Child Health Section. Washington State school immunization manual. Rev. Olympia, Wash. : Dept. of Social and Health Services, Health Services Division, Office of Community Health Services, Child Health Section, [1980] 146 p. : forms ; 28 cm. Cover title: Manual, school immunization. "February 1980." Includes bibliographical references. LC Card 80-622798 DDC 344.797/043 19
1. Vaccination of children - Law and legislation - Washington (State). 2. School hygiene - Law and legislation - Washington (State). I. Title. II. Title: Manual, school immunization.
KFW357.9.I44 A836 1980

Washington (State). Office of Economic Opportunity. Washington (State). Office of Community Development. A brief survey of CSA-related anti-poverty organizations in Washington State. [Olympia] , 1978. 64 p. ; LC Card 79-621288
HV86 .W365 1978a **NYPL [JLF 81-121]**

Washington (State). Office of Financial Management. Forecasting and Support Services Division.
Special report - State of Washington, Office of Financial Management, Forecasting and Support Services Division . (no. 30) Washington (State). Office of Financial Management. Forecasting and Support Services Division. State and county population forecasts by age and sex, 1980-2000. [Olympia] [1980] [31] p. ; LC Card 80-622047 DDC 312/.8/09797 19
HA693 .W36 1980

State and county population forecasts by age and sex, 1980-2000. [Olympia] : State of Washington, Office of Financial Management, Forecasting and Support Services Division, [1980] [31] p. ; 28 cm. (Special report - State of Washington, Office of Financial Management, Forecasting and Support Services Division ; no. 30) "January 1980." Chiefly tables. Includes bibliographical references. LC Card 80-622047 DDC 312/.8/09797 19
1. Washington (State) - Population - Statistics. 2. Population forecasting - Washington (State). I. Series: Washington (State). Office of Financial Management. Forecasting and Support Services Division. Special report - State of Washington, Office of Financial Management, Forecasting and Support Services Division , no. 30. II. Title.
HA693 .W36 1980

Washington (State). Office of Nursing Home Affairs. Survey Section. Directory of licensed nursing homes. Olympia. 28 cm. For earlier years, see: Washington (State). Division of Health Services. Directory of licensed nursing homes.
1. Nursing homes - Washington (State) - Directories. I. Title. **NYPL [JLM 80-846]**

Washington (State). Office of Program Planning and Fiscal Management. State lands inventory; ownership, control and use summary. 1970- [Olympia]. 28 cm. Annual. Report period ends June 30. Cover title. LC Card 73-649668
1. Washington (State) - Public lands - Statistics - Periodicals. I. Title. **NYPL [JLM 80-900]**

Washington (State). Office of the Governor. Commission on Asian American Affairs. see Washington (State). Commission on Asian American Affairs.

Washington (State). Office of the Governor. Office of Community Development. see Washington (State). Office of Community Development.

Washington (State). Office of the Governor. Office of Program Planning and Fiscal

Management. see **Washington (State). Office of Program Planning and Fiscal Management.**

Washington (State). Office of Voluntary Action. see **Washington (State). Office of Community Development. Office of Voluntary Action.**

Washington (State). Office on Aging. An In-depth analysis of the needs assessment of the elderly, 1976, Washington State . [Salem] , 1978. 117 xvii p. ;   LC Card 79-621901   DDC 362.6/09797 19
HQ1064.U6 W295

Washington (State). Offices of Small and Minority Business. Minority business enterprises in Washington State / prepared by the Offices of Small and Minority Business, Washington State Department of Commerce & Economic Development. Olympia, WA : The Dept., [1980] iii, 72 p. ; 28 cm. "January 1980." Includes index.   LC Card 80-622766   DDC 338.6/422/025797 19
1. Minority business enterprises - Washington (State) - Directories. I. Title.
HD2346.U52 W3785 1980

WASHINGTON (STATE) - OFFICIALS AND EMPLOYEES - SALARIES, ALLOWANCES, ETC. - STATISTICS.
Washington (State). Dept. of Personnel. Salary schedule and alpha listing of classes, October 1, 1979. [Olympia] [1979] [57] p. ;   LC Card 80-621509   DDC 331.2/813539797 19
JK9257 .W36 1979

Washington (State). Outdoor Recreation, Interagency Committee for. see **Washington (State). Interagency Committee for Outdoor Recreation.**

Washington (State). Personnel Dept. see **Washington (State). Dept. of Personnel.**

Washington (State). Planning and Community Affairs Agency.
Directory of city, county, regional, state & federal planning agencies. Rev. Olympia : Planning & Community Affairs Agency, 1978. 47 p. ; 29 cm. Cover title.   LC Card 79-621293   DDC 350.007/2/025797 19
1. Regional planning - Washington (State) - Directories. 2. City planning - Washington (State) - Directories. 3. Washington (State) - Economic policy - Directories. I. Title.
HT393.W3 W34 1978

Washington (State). Planning and Community Affairs Agency. Local Government Services Division. Housing, the problems in Washington State. Olympia, Wash. : Washington State Planning and Community Affairs Agency, Local Government Services Division, [1980?] v, 29, [10] p. : map ; 28 cm. Prepared by R. Suko. Bibliography: p. [10] (2d group)   LC Card 80-622049   DDC 363.5/09797 19
1. Housing - Washington (State). I. Suko, Randy. II. Title.
HD7303.W2 W38 1980

Washington (State). Planning and Public Transportation Division.
Public transportation in Washington State. Olympia, Wash. : Washington State Dept. of Transportation, Division of Public Transportation and Planning, Public Transportation Office, [1980] iii, 126, [67] p., [1] leaf of plates : ill. ; 22 x 30 cm. "April 1980."   LC Card 80-623197   DDC 380.5/068 19
1. Transportation planning - Washington (State). 2. Local transit - Washington (State). I. Title.
HE213.W2 W36 1980

Washington (State). Planning and Public Transportation Division. Social and Economic Planning Section. Palmquist, Raymond B. Impact of highway improvements on property values in Washington /. Olympia, WA [1980] 247 p. :   LC Card 80-622759   DDC 333.33/2/09797 19
HD266.W2 P34

WASHINGTON (STATE) - POLITICS AND GOVERNMENT - 1951- - ADDRESSES, ESSAYS, LECTURES.
Washington (State). Governor, 1977- (Ray) Report on my third year in office /. [Olympia, Wash. , 1980] iv, 31 p. ;   LC Card 80-622791   DDC 353.979703/5 19
J87 .W222 1980

WASHINGTON (STATE) - POPULATION - STATISTICS.
Ong, Paul M. Asians in Washington . Olympia , 1976. vii. 69 p. :   LC Card 77-621579
F900.O6 O53   **NYPL [*XME-9406]**

Washington (State). Office of Financial Management. Forecasting and Support Services Division. State and county population forecasts by age and sex, 1980-2000. [Olympia] [1980] [31] p. ;   LC Card 80-622047   DDC 312/.8/09797 19
HA693 .W36 1980

Washington (State). Postsecondary Education, Council for. see **Washington (State). Council for Postsecondary Education.**

Washington (State). Program Planning and Fiscal Management, Office of. see **Washington (State). Office of Program Planning and Fiscal Management.**

Washington (State). Public Disclosure Commission. 1980 campaign instructions : Candidates, committees, organizations using full reporting / Public Disclosure Commission.Rev. Olympia, Wash. (403 Evergreen Plaza, FJ-42, Olympia 98504) : PDC, 1980. vi, 49 p. : ill. ; 28 cm. Cover title.   LC Card 80-623468   DDC 324.7/8/09797 19
1. Elections - Washington (State) - Campaign funds. I. Title. II. Title: Nineteen eighty campaign instructions.
JK1991.5.W37 W38 1980

WASHINGTON (STATE) - PUBLIC LANDS - STATISTICS - PERIODICALS.
Washington (State). Office of Program Planning and Fiscal Management. State lands inventory; ownership, control and use summary. 1970- [Olympia].   LC Card 73-649668
NYPL [JLM 80-900]

Washington (State). Public Transportation and Planning, Division of. see **Washington (State). Division of Public Transportation and Planning.**

Washington State school immunization manual.
Washington (State). Office of Community Health Services. Child Health Section. Olympia, Wash. [1980] 146 p. :   LC Card 80-622798   DDC 344.797/043 19
KFW357.9.I44 A836 1980

Washington (State). Social and Health Services, Dept. of. see **Washington (State). Dept. of Social and Health Services.**

Washington (State). State Board of Accountancy. see **Washington (State). Board of Accountancy.**

Washington (State). State Board of Education.
Requirements and guidelines for high school graduation. [Olympia : State of Washington, State Board of Education, 1980] iv, 20 p. ; 23 cm.   LC Card 80-623898   DDC 373.12/912/09797 19
1. High schools - Washington (State) - Graduation requirements. I. Title. II. Title: High school graduation.
LB1627.7 .W37 1980

Washington (State). State Board of Health.
Rules & regulations of the State Board of Health for environmental sanitation, primary & secondary schools. [Rev. March 1980]. Olympia, Wash. : Washington State Dept. of Social & Health Services, Office of Environmental Health Programs, Health Services Division, [1980] 10 p. ; 23 cm. Cover title. "DSHS 22-44."   LC Card 80-623897   DDC 344.797/07 347.94047 19
1. School hygiene - Law and legislation - Washington (State). 2. School buildings - Law and legislation - Washington (State). I. Title.
KFW459.S3 A32 1980

Washington (State). State Capitol Historical Association.
Annual report. Olympia, Wash. 28 cm.
1. Washington (State) - History - Periodicals. 2. Washington (State). State Capitol Historical Association - Periodicals.
NYPL [IAA (Washington) 81-185]

WASHINGTON (STATE). STATE CAPITOL HISTORICAL ASSOCIATION - PERIODICALS.
Washington (State). State Capitol Historical Association. Annual report. Olympia, Wash.
NYPL [IAA (Washington) 81-185]

Washington (State). State Commission on Asian American Affairs. see **Washington (State). Commission on Asian American Affairs.**

Washington (State). State Conservation Commission. Washington (State). Dept. of Ecology. Water Quality Planning. Dryland agriculture water quality management plan . Olympia, Wash. [1979] 2 v. :   LC Card 80-621082   DDC 363.7/39456/09797 19
TD428.A37 W37 1979a

Washington (State). State Highway Commission.
Annual traffic report. [Olympia] maps (Part. fold.) 22 x 32 cm. Vols. for 1958-69 issued in cooperation with the U. S. Bureau of Public Roads; vols. for 1970- issued in cooperation with the U. S. Federal Highway Administration. Superseded by: Washington (State). Division of Public Transportation and Planning. Annual traffic report.
1. Traffic surveys - Washington (State) - Statistics - Periodicals. I. United States. Bureau of Public Roads. II. United States. Federal Highway Administration. III. Title.   **NYPL [N-10 2121]**

Washington (State). State Highway Commission. Dept. of Highways. see **Washington (State). Dept. of Highways.**

Washington (State). State Library, Olympia.
Newspapers on microfilm in the Washington State Library / compiled by Kathryn S. Hamilton. [Olympia] : Washington State Library, [1980] iii, 86 p. ; 28 cm.   LC Card 80-622614   DDC 011/.35 19
1. American newspapers - Washington (State) - Bibliography - Microform catalogs. 2. Washington (State). State Library, Olympia - Microform catalogs. I. Hamilton, Kathryn S. II. Title.
Z6952.W31 W23 1980 PN4897.W3

WASHINGTON (STATE). STATE LIBRARY, OLYMPIA - MICROFORM CATALOGS.
Washington (State). State Library, Olympia. Newspapers on microfilm in the Washington State Library /. [Olympia] [1980] iii, 86 p. ;   LC Card 80-622614   DDC 011/.35 19
Z6952.W31 W23 1980 PN4897.W3

Washington (State). State Office of Economic Opportunity. see **Washington (State). Office of Economic Opportunity.**

Washington (State). State Office of Public Instruction. see **Washington (State). Dept. of Education.**

Washington (State). State University, Pullman. Civil and Environmental Engineering, Dept. of. see **Washington (State). State University, Pullman. Dept. of Civil and Environmental Engineering.**

Washington (State). State University, Pullman. College of Agriculture.
Circular - College of Agriculture Research Center, Washington State University . (0622) Kirkland, Jack J. Market potential of the Middle East /. [Pullman] , 1980. 82 p. :   LC Card 80-622499   DDC 330.956/04 19
HF3756.Z5 K57

Washington (State). State University, Pullman. Dept. of Civil and Environmental Engineering. Study of Silver Lake eutrophication : current problems and possible solutions / Surinder K. Bhagat ... [et al.]. Pullman, Wash. : State of Washington Water Research Center, [1975] xviii, 298 p. : ill. ; 28 cm. (Report - State of Washington Water Research Center . no. 9) "Date of report: July 3, 1975." Project completion report, DOE Project no. WF-PS-74-002, project period: Apr. 1, 1974- June 30, 1975. Bibliography: p. 175-179.   LC Card 79-625419   DDC 553.7/09797 s 363.7/3942/0979788 19
1. Eutrophication - Washington (State) - Silver Lake. 2. Silver Lake, Wash. I. Bhagat, Surinder K. II. Series: State of Washington Water Research Center. Report , no. 9. III. Title.
TD224.W2 S8 no. 9a QH105.W2

Washington (State). State University, Pullman. Extension Service. Recreation '76 Conference, University of Washington, 1976. Recreation '76 Conference proceedings, February 23 and 24, 1976, University of Washington . Seattle , Pullman [1976] iv, 114 p. :   LC Card 77-623136   DDC 333.78/4 19
GV191.42.W2 R42 1976

Washington (State) State University, Pullman. Library.
William Compton Brown : a calendar of his

GOVERNMENT PUBLICATIONS - U.S.: 1981

657   Waste disposal in the ocean - Law and legislation - United States.

papers in the Washington State University Library. Pullman, Wash. : Manuscripts-Archives Division, Washington State University Library, 1966. 25 p. ; 28 cm. LC Card 67-65327 DDC 016.9797/04/0924 19
1. Brown, William Compton, 1869-1963 - Archives - Catalogs. 2. Washington (State) - History - Sources - Bibliography - Catalogs. 3. Indians of North America - Washington (State) - History - Sources - Bibliography - Catalogs. 4. Washington (State). State University, Pullman. Library - Catalogs.
Z6616.B855 W37 1966 F891

WASHINGTON (STATE). STATE UNIVERSITY, PULLMAN. LIBRARY - CATALOGS.
Washington (State) State University, Pullman. Library. William Compton Brown . Pullman, Wash. , 1966. 25 p. ; LC Card 67-65327 DDC 016.9797/04/0924 19
Z6616.B855 W37 1966 F891

Washington (State). State University, Pullman. State of Washington Water Research Center. see State of Washington Water Research Center.

Washington (State). State University, Pullman. Water Research Center. see State of Washington Water Research Center.

WASHINGTON (STATE) - STATISTICS, MEDICAL - BIBLIOGRAPHY.
Health Policy Analysis Program (Wash.) The yellow pages . Seattle, Wash. [1978] v, 80 leaves ; LC Card 79-621291 DDC 362.1/09797 19
RA407.4.W3 H4 1978

Washington (State). Statutes. see Washington (State). Laws, statutes, etc.

Washington (State). Superintendent of Public Instruction. see Washington (State). Dept. of Education.

Washington state taxes : a resource manual, 1980. [Olympia] : House Revenue Committee, [1980] 46 p. : ill. ; 28 cm. Cover title. "December 1980." Errata slip inserted. LC Card 81-621438 DDC 343.79704 347.97034 19
1. Taxation - Washington (State) - Handbooks, manuals, etc. I. Washington (State). Legislature. House of Representatives. Revenue Committee.
HJ2439 .W27

Washington (State). Transportation Commission.
Palmquist, Raymond B. Impact of highway improvements on property values in Washington /. Olympia, WA [1980] 247 p. : LC Card 80-622759 DDC 333.33/2/09797 19
HD266.W2 P34

Washington (State). University.
Pacific Northwest quarterly. v. 1- ; Oct. 1906- Seattle. LC Card 80-30966
NYPL [IAA(Pacific Northwest quarterly)]

Washington State University. Agricultural Research Center. Soil survey of Whitman County, Washington /. [Washington?] [1980] v, 185 p., [75] folded leaves of plates : LC Card 80-602555 DDC 631.4/7797/39 19
S599.W32 S63

Washington (State). University. College of Forest Resources. Wooldridge, David D. Suspended sediment from truck traffic on forest roads, Meadow and Coal Creeks /. Seattle [1978] 33 p.: *NYPL [*ZV-185 Reel 1]*

Washington (State). University. Division of Environmental Health. Pacific Northwest Seminar on Clinical Laboratory Planning and Design, Seattle, 1956. Pacific Northwest Seminar on Clinical Laboratory Planning and Design. [Olympia, Wash., 1967?] 1 v. (various pagings) LC Card 81-462890 DDC 610/.28 19
RB36 .P32 1967

Washington (State). University. Fisheries Research Institute.
Circular.
(no. 79-2) Harris, Colin K. Forecast of the sockeye salmon run to Bristol Bay in 1979 /. Seattle , 1979. 50 p. : LC Card 79-624864 DDC 639/.2 s 597/.55 19
SH1 .W3352 no. 79-2 QL638.S2

Washington (State). University. Forest Resources, College of. see Washington (State). University. College of Forest Resources.

Washington (State). University. Institute for Marine Studies. Coastal Resources Program.

Recreation '76 Conference, University of Washington, 1976. Recreation '76 Conference proceedings, February 23 and 24, 1976, University of Washington /. Seattle , Pullman [1976] iv, 114 p. : LC Card 77-623136 DDC 333.78/4 19
GV191.42.W2 R42 1976

Shorelines management '77 . Seattle [1978?] ix, 163 p. : LC Card 79-624199 DDC 333.91/7/0973 19
HT392 .S54

WASHINGTON (STATE). UNIVERSITY. LIBRARY - CATALOGS.
Washington (State). University. Library. Manuscripts Section. An inventory-guide to the Wilbert McLeod Chapman Papers, 1939-1970, in the University of Washington Libraries. Seattle , 1977. xi, 61 p., [1] leaf of plates : LC Card 79-620831 DDC 016.33395/6/0979 19
Z6611.F55 W37 1977 SH221

Washington (State). University. Library. Manuscripts Section. An inventory-guide to the Wilbert McLeod Chapman Papers, 1939-1970, in the University of Washington Libraries. Seattle : Manuscripts Section, University of Washington Libraries, 1977. xi, 61 p., [1] leaf of plates : port. ; 28 cm. Cover title: Guide to the Wilbert McLeod Chapman collection. Includes index. LC Card 79-620831 DDC 016.33395/6/0979 19
1. Fisheries - United States - Manuscripts - Catalogs. 2. Chapman, Wilbert McLeod, 1910-1970 - Manuscripts - Catalogs. 3. Fishery scientists - United States - Biography. 4. Washington (State). University. Library - Catalogs. I. Title. II. Title: Guide to the Wilbert McLeod Chapman collection.
Z6611.F55 W37 1977 SH221

Washington (State). University. National Center for the Assessment of Delinquent Behavior and Its Prevention. Weis, Joseph G. Jurisdiction and the elusive status offender . Washington, D.C. [1980] c1979. ix, 135 p. : LC Card 80-602845 DDC 364.3/6/0973 19
HV9104 .W447

Washington (State). University. Washington University State Historical Society. Pacific Northwest quarterly. v. 1- ; Oct. 1906- Seattle. LC Card 80-30966 *NYPL [IAA(Pacific Northwest quarterly)]*

Washington (State) Utilities and Transportation Commission. Summary and analysis, heavy truck-hazardous material accidents. Olympia, Wash. : Washington Utilities and Transportation Commission, [letter, 1979] [13], 34 p. ; 28 cm. Cover title. LC Card 80-621084 DDC 363.1/259 19
1. Traffic accidents - Washington (State). 2. Trucks - Washington (State) - Accidents. 3. Hazardous substances - Washington (State) - Transportation - Accidents. I. Title.
HE5614.3.W2 W394 1979

Washington (State). Water Research Center. see State of Washington Water Research Center.

Washington (State). Water Resource Management Division. Policy Development Section. Deschutes River Basin instream resources protection program including proposed administrative rules : water resources inventory area 13 / prepared by Water Resource Policy Development Section, Washington State Department of Ecology ; project planner, Robert Kavanaugh. Olympia, Wash. : Washington State Dept. of Printing, [1980] 29, [52] p. : ill. ; 28 cm. (W.W.I.R.P.P. series . no. 8) Includes bibliographical references. LC Card 80-623859 DDC 333.91/0216/0979779 19
1. Water quality management - Washington (State) - Deschutes River watershed. 2. Watershed management - Washington (State) - Deschutes River watershed. I. Title. II. Series.
TD224.W2 W38 1980

Washington (State). Water Resources Management Division. Policy Development Section. Cedar-Sammamish Basin instream resources protection program, including proposed administrative rules, and supplemental environmental impact statement : water resource inventory area 8 / prepared by Water Resources, Policy Development Section, Washington State Department of Ecology. Olympia, Wash. : Washington State Dept. of Print., 1979. 148 p. in various pagings : ill. ; 28 cm. (W.W.I.R.P.P. series . no. 1) Errata slip inserted.

"Final, August 28, 1979, 173-508 WAC, adopted September 5, 1979." Includes bibliographies. LC Card 79-625825 DDC 333.91/0216/0979777 19
1. Water quality management - Washington (State). 2. Nature conservation - Washington (State). I. Title. II. Series.
TD224.W2 W38 1979

Washington (State). Western Washington University, Bellingham. see Western Washington University.

Washington State's salmon and steelhead resources . United States. Congress. Senate. Committee on Commerce, Science, and Transportation. Washington , 1980. iv, 208 p. ; LC Card 80-603093 DDC 346.7304/6956 19
KF26 .C69 1980p

Washington. United States International Environmental Referral Center. see United States International Environmental Referral Center.

Washington, Walter E., 1915- District of Columbia. Capital Improvements Program Technical Advisory Committee. District of Columbia 1975-1980 Capital Improvements Program. [Washington] 1974. 265 p.
NYPL [JLF 80-401]

The Washo Indians . Price, John A., 1933- [Carson City, Nev.] , c1980. vi, 82 p., [2] leaves of plates : LC Card 80-623850 DDC 970.004/97 19
E99.W38 P74

WASHO INDIANS.
Price, John A., 1933- The Washo Indians . [Carson City, Nev.] , c1980. vi, 82 p., [2] leaves of plates : LC Card 80-623850 DDC 970.004/97 19
E99.W38 P74

WASHOAN INDIANS. see WASHO INDIANS.

Wasserman, Paul.
(joint author) Bundy, Mary Lee, 1927- The academic library administrator and his situation : final report. [Washington?] 1970. vi, 89, 27 p. *NYPL [*XM-7266]*

(joint author) Bundy, Mary Lee, 1927- The administrator of a special library or information center and his situation: Final report. [Washington?] 1970. vii, 94, 25 p. *NYPL [*XM-7265]*

(joint author) Bundy, Mary Lee, 1927- The school library supervisor and her situation : final report. [Washington?] 1970. viii, 95, 25 p. *NYPL [*XM-7267]*

WASTE AS FUEL. see REFUSE AS FUEL.

WASTE DISPOSAL IN THE GROUND - FLORIDA - PINELLAS COUNTY.
Hickey, John J. Hydrogeology and results of injection tests at waste-injection test sites in Pinellas County, Florida /. Washington , 1981. p. cm. LC Card 81-607052 DDC 627/.57 19
TD761 .H52

WASTE DISPOSAL IN THE GROUND - UNITED STATES.
United States. Congress. House. Committee on Interstate and Foreign Commerce. Subcommittee on Health and the Environment. Hazardous waste and drinking water . Washington , 1981. v, 195 p. : LC Card 81-601136 DDC 363.7/394 19
KF27 .I5543 1980q

United States. Office of Solid Waste Management Programs. Hazardous Waste Management Division. An environmental assessment of potential gas and leachate problems at land disposal sites / . - [Washington] , 1973 [i. e. 1975] v, 33 p. ;
NYPL [*ZV-185 Reel 1]

WASTE DISPOSAL IN THE OCEAN - ENVIRONMENTAL ASPECTS - UNITED STATES.
United States. Congress. House. Committee on Merchant Marine and Fisheries. Dredge spoil disposal and PCB contamination . Washington , 1980. v, 698 p. : LC Card 81-600658 DDC 363.7/28 19
KF27 .M4 1980

WASTE DISPOSAL IN THE OCEAN - LAW AND LEGISLATION - UNITED STATES.
United States. Congress. House. Committee on

Merchant Marine and Fisheries. Subcommittee on Fisheries and Wildlife Conservation and the Environment. Ocean dumping . Washington , 1975- v. : LC Card 75-603626
KF27 .M447 1975e

United States. Congress. House. Committee on Merchant Marine and Fisheries. Subcommittee on Oceanography. Ocean dumping . Washington , 1980. viii, 404 p. : LC Card 80-603809   DDC 344.73/04626 347.3044626 19
KF27 .M473 1980b

WASTE DISPOSAL IN THE OCEAN - NEW YORK BIGHT.
Disposal of dredged material within the New York District /. McLean, Va., 1979. 1 v.:
NYPL [JSK 80-128]

WASTE DISPOSAL IN THE OCEAN - UNITED STATES.
United States. Environmental Protection Agency. Oil and Special Materials Control Division. Proposed revisions to ocean dumping criteria . Washington , 1977. 2 v. ;
NYPL [JSF 80-969]

WASTE, DISPOSAL OF. see FACTORY AND TRADE WASTE; REFUSE AND REFUSE DISPOSAL; SEWAGE DISPOSAL; WASTE PRODUCTS.

WASTE DISPOSAL SITES - CALIFORNIA - LOS ANGELES CO.
California. Dept. of Water Resources. Southern District. Potential waste disposal areas, northern Los Angeles County /. [Sacramento] [1979] vii, 58 p. : LC Card 80-621404   DDC 363.7/28 19
TD811.5 .C34 1979

WASTE DISPOSAL SITES - ENVIRONMENTAL ASPECTS - CONNECTICUT.
Iannicelli, Donald. Surface impoundment assessment . Hartford, Conn. [1979] x, 53 leaves : LC Card 80-623424   DDC 363.7/394 19
TD224.C8 I26

WASTE DISPOSAL SITES - NEW JERSEY.
United States. Congress. House. Committee on Interstate and Foreign Commerce. Subcommittee on Transportation and Commerce. Hazardous waste disposal . Washington , 1980 [i.e. 1981] iii, 97 p. ; LC Card 81-600820   DDC 363.7/28 19
KF27 .I5589 1980o

WASTE DISPOSAL SITES - UNITED STATES.
United States. General Accounting Office. The problem of disposing of nuclear low-level waste . [Washington, D.C.] , 1980. vii, 30 p. ; LC Card 80-601696   DDC 363.7/28 19
TD898 .U54 1980

WASTE HEAD RECOVERY. see HEAT RECOVERY.

WASTE MANAGEMENT. see SALVAGE (WASTE, ETC.)

Waste management and fuel cycles. Symposium on Waste Management. Waste management; proceedings. Tucson, Ariz.
NYPL [JSP 80-332]

Waste management; proceedings. Symposium on Waste Management. Tucson, Ariz.
NYPL [JSP 80-332]

Waste Management, Symposium on. see Symposium on Waste Management.

Waste oil, North Carolina's recovered resource /. Howard, Dick, 1937- [Lexington, Ky.] , c1980. 8 p. : LC Card 80-139998   DDC 353.9 s 363.7/28 19
JS308 .C6 no. 687 TP687

WASTE PAPER - RECYCLING.
Keller, Richard, 1955- Maryland's program for buying recycled paper /. [Lexington, Ky.] [1980] 6 p. ; LC Card 80-140050   DDC 353.9 s 353.97520071/25 19
JS308 .C6 no. 681 JK3888.P36

WASTE PRODUCTS AS FUEL.
United States. Congress. House. Committee on Science and Technology. Subcommittee on Energy Development and Applications. Energy from municipal solid wastes . Washington , 1980. v, 26 p. ; LC Card 80-603278   DDC 662/.8 19
TP360 .U55 1980

United States. Library of Congress. Science

Policy Research Division. Energy from biomass and solid wastes . Washington , 1980. xix, 169 p. : LC Card 80-603278   DDC 333.79/38 19
TP360 .U59 1980

WASTE PRODUCTS - UNITED STATES - ABSTRACTS.
United States. Dept. of Commerce. Office of Environmental Affairs. Marketing and financing aspects of resource recovery /. [Washington, D.C.] , 1980. 63 p. ; LC Card 80-601647   DDC 338.4/36046/0973 19
HD9975.U52 U54 1980

WASTE RECLAMATION. see SALVAGE (WASTE, ETC.)

WASTE RECYCLING. see RECYCLING (WASTE, ETC.)

WASTE REUSE. see RECYCLING (WASTE, ETC.)

WASTE STABILIZATION LAGOONS. see SEWAGE LAGOONS.

WASTE WATER RECLAMATION. see WATER REUSE.

WASTE WATERS. see SEWAGE.

Wasted health dollars . United States. Congress. House. Committee on Interstate and Foreign Commerce. Subcommittee on Oversight and Investigations. Washington , 1980. iv, 155 p. : LC Card 80-603470   DDC 353.0077 19
KF27 .I5547 1980f

Wasted health dollars . United States. Congress. House. Committee on Interstate and Foreign Commerce. Subcommittee on Oversight and Investigations. Washington , 1980. iii, 144 p. ; LC Card 80-602716   DDC 338.4/336210973 19
KF27 .I5547 1980a

Wasted surgical dollars . United States. Congress. House. Committee on Interstate and Foreign Commerce. Subcommittee on Oversight and Investigations. Washington , 1981. ii, 38 p. ; LC Card 81-601159   DDC 362.1/97/0973 19
KF27 .I5547 1980q

WASTES, HAZARDOUS. see HAZARDOUS WASTES.

Wastewater aerosols and disease . Symposium on Wastewater Aerosols and Disease (1979 : Cincinnati, Ohio) Cincinnati, Ohio , Springfield, Va. , 1980 [i.e. 1981] xv, 367 p. : LC Card 81-601460   DDC 363.7/28 19
RA567 .S94 1979

Wat ertown Free Public Library. see Watertown, Mass. Free Public Library.

WATCHES. see CLOCKS AND WATCHES.

WATER - ANALYSIS.
(1978) Galloway, G. E. Assessing man's impact on wetlands /. [Raleigh, N.C. , 1978] iv, 115 p. : LC Card 79-625636   DDC 333.91/81 19
QH76 .G34

(1978) Stinebring, Warren R. Endotoxin in waters of the State of Vermont /. [Montpelier] [1978?] iv leaves, 25 p. : LC Card 79-624701   DDC 363.7/394 19
QR48 .S74

(1981) Holland, Philip W. A method for determining helium in water /. Washington, D.C. [1981] p. cm. LC Card 81-607975   DDC 622 s 628.1/61 19
TN23 .U43 QD142

WATER - ANALYSIS - COLLECTED WORKS.
Water chlorine (residual). no. 1- Cincinnati, Ohio, 1969-
NYPL [JSP 81-89]

Water and land resource accomplishments, Federal reclamation projects. United States. Water and Power Resources Service. 1978- [Washington]
NYPL [JLM 80-707]

Water and power . Kahrl, William L. Berkeley , c1981. p. cm. ISBN 0-520-04431-2 LC Card 81-7428   DDC 333.91/009794/9 19
HD4464.L7 K33

Water as a parameter for development of energy resources in the Upper Great Plains . North Dakota. Agricultural Experiment Station, Fargo. Fargo, N.D. [1978] ii, 144 p. : LC Card 79-625649   DDC 630 s 333.8/22/0978 19
S99 .A5a no. 71 HD9502.U53N683

WATER - BACTERIOLOGY.
Taylor, Robert Gay, 1940- Effects of bacteria on nitrate and nitrite concentrations in

groundwater of the Ogallala aquifer /. Las Cruces, N.M. [1979] vii, 20 leaves : LC Card 80-622275   DDC 333.91/09789 s 628.1/68 19
GB856.N6 N64 no. 114 TD224.N6

Wendt, Stephen L. Occurrence and distribution of human bacterial pathogens in Virginia surface waters /. Blacksburg, Va. , 1979. vii, 68 p. : LC Card 79-625812   DDC 333.91/009755 s 363.7/394 19
TD201 .V57 no. 118 TD224.V8

WATER BALANCE (HYDROLOGY) - ARIZONA - GILA RIVER WATERSHED.
Evapotranspiration before and after clearing phreatophytes, Gila River Flood Plain, Graham County, Arizona /. Washington , 1981. p. cm. LC Card 81-607801   DDC 551.57/2 19
QC915.7.U5 E9

WATER BALANCE (HYDROLOGY) - TEXAS - GULF REGION.
Hillaker, Harry J. Atlas of water balance computations for 48 Texas coastal zone stations, 1941-1970 /. Austin , 1978. iv, 92 p. : LC Card 79-624055   DDC 551.5 s 551.48/097641 19
QC851 .T45 no. 50 GB705.T4

WATER BANKING - UTAH.
Bagley, Jay M. Feasibility study of establishing a water rights banking/brokering service in Utah /. Logan, Utah [1980] vii, 33 p. ; LC Card 80-623594   DDC 363.6/1 19
HD1694.U8 B34

WATER-BEARING FORMATIONS. see AQUIFERS.

WATER BIOLOGY. see AQUATIC BIOLOGY.

WATER-BIRDS - ALASKA - HABITAT.
Derksen, Dirk V. Use of wetland habitats by birds in the National Petroleum Reserve--Alaska /. Washington, D.C. , 1981. p. cm. LC Card 81-607937   DDC 639.9/784109798 19
S914 .A3 no.141 QL684A4

WATER-BIRDS - HABITAT.
Derksen, Dirk V. Use of wetland habitats by birds in the National Petroleum Reserve--Alaska /. Washington, D.C. , 1981. p. cm. LC Card 81-607937   DDC 639.9/784109798 19
S914 .A3 no.141 QL684A4

WATER-BIRDS - YELLOWSTONE RIVER WATERSHED - EFFECT OF WATER LEVELS ON.
Hinz, Tom. The effect of altered streamflow on migratory birds of the Yellowstone River Basin, Montana /. Helena , 1977. x, 107 p. : LC Card 78-623506   DDC 598.2/525 19
QL683.Y44 H56

WATER-BIRDS - YELLOWSTONE RIVER WATERSHED - EFFECT OF WATER QUALITY ON.
Hinz, Tom. The effect of altered streamflow on migratory birds of the Yellowstone River Basin, Montana /. Helena , 1977. x, 107 p. : LC Card 78-623506   DDC 598.2/525 19
QL683.Y44 H56

WATER BLOOM - NORTH CAROLINA - CHOWAN RIVER.
North Carolina. State University, Raleigh. Dept. of Botany. Response of phytoplankton to water quality in the Chowan River system /. [Raleigh, N.C.] [1979] xv, 204 p. : LC Card 79-626203   DDC 589.4 19
HD1694.N8 N6 no. 129 QK571.5.N8

WATER BLOOM - NORTH CAROLINA - PAMLICO RIVER.
Kuenzler, Edward J. Nutrient kinetics of phytoplankton in the Pamlico River, North Carolina /. [Raleigh] [1979] xxii, 163 p. : LC Card 79-626205   DDC 333.91/009756 s 589.4 19
HD1694.N8 N6 no. 139 QK571.5.N8

WATER CHEMISTRY.
(1977) Foggin, G. Thomas. Completion report, using topographic characteristics to predict total solute concentrations in streams draining small forested watersheds in Western Montana /. Bozeman, Mont. , 1977. 42 leaves : LC Card 79-624615   DDC 551.48/3/09786 19
GB855 .F63

(1979) Feder, Gerald L. Geochemical survey of waters of Missouri . Washington , 1979. iv, 78 p. : LC Card 79-600129   DDC 551.48/09778 19
GB705.M8 F4

WATER CHEMISTRY - ADDRESSES, ESSAYS, LECTURES.
Organic substances in water /. Reston, Va. [1981] p. cm.   LC Card 81-607886   DDC 557.3 s 628.1/61 19
QE75 .C5 no. 848-C GB855

WATER CHEMISTRY - MATHEMATICAL MODELS.
Brown, David Wayne, 1949- Development of a model to predict the adsorption of lead from solution on a natural streambed sediment /. Washington [1981] p. cm.   LC Card 81-607984   DDC 628.1/6836 19
QD547 .B76

WATER CHLORINATION. see WATER - PURIFICATION - CHLORINATION.

Water conservation & development projects . Idaho. Water Resource Board. [Boise, Idaho] [1979] 134 p. in various pagings : LC Card 80-621480   DDC 333.91/02/0979637 19
TC424.I2 I3 1979

WATER CONSERVATION - CALIFORNIA.
California. Advisory Panel on Agricultural Water Conservation. Report of findings /. Sacramento, Calif. [1979] v, 18 p. : LC Card 80-620554   DDC 631.7/09794 19
S494.5.W3 C34 1979

Water conservation Federal agency program changes . United States. Water Conservation Task Force 6a. [Washington] , 1979. 43 p. ; LC Card 79-604000   DDC 333.91/16/0973 19
TD223 .U547 1979

WATER CONSERVATION - IDAHO.
Idaho. Water Resource Board. Water conservation & development projects . [Boise, Idaho] [1979] 134 p. in various pagings : LC Card 80-621480   DDC 333.91/02/0979637 19
TC424.I2 I3 1979

Water conservation in Nevada . Gilbert (J. B.) & Associates. Carson City [1979] xvii, 273 p. : LC Card 80-622041   DDC 333.91/16/09793 19
TD224.N2 G54 1979

WATER CONSERVATION - MISSISSIPPI.
Cartee, Charles P. A study of factors related to the implementation and use of water conservation technology in Mississippi /. Mississippi State, Miss. , 1979. vi, 49 leaves : LC Card 80-622039   DDC 333.91/22 19
TD224.M65 C38

WATER CONSERVATION - NEVADA.
Gilbert (J. B.) & Associates. Water conservation in Nevada . Carson City [1979] xvii, 273 p. : LC Card 80-622041   DDC 333.91/16/09793 19
TD224.N2 G54 1979

WATER CONSERVATION - OREGON.
Oregon. Water Policy Review Board. Final report to the Pacific Northwest Regional Commission on Oregon's drought and conservation activities /. [Salem, Or.] [1979] 74 p. : LC Card 80-621882   DDC 333.91/16/09795 19
TD224.O7 O72 1979

WATER CONSERVATION - UNITED STATES.
United States. General Accounting Office. Ground water overdrafting must be controlled . Washington, D.C. , 1980. iv, 52 p. : LC Card 81-600550   DDC 333.91/0416/0973 19
TD223 .U525 1980

United States. Water Conservation Task Force 6a. Water conservation Federal agency program changes . [Washington] , 1979. 43 p. ; LC Card 79-604000   DDC 333.91/16/0973 19
TD223 .U547 1979

WATER CONSUMPTION - IDAHO - BLAINE CO.
Brockway, Charles E., 1936- Evaluation of urbanization and changes in land use on the water resources of mountain valleys . Moscow, Idaho [1978?] ix, 104 p. [1] fold. leaf of plates : LC Card 79-625237   DDC 333.91/2/09796 19
TD224.I2 B76

WATER CONSUMPTION - LOUISIANA.
Cardwell, George T., 1922- Pumpage of water in Louisiana, 1975 /. Baton Rouge, La. , 1979. iv, 15 p. : LC Card 80-620624   DDC 333.91/13/09763 19
TD224.L8 C37

WATER CONSUMPTION - UNITED STATES.
United States. Library of Congress. Congressional Research Service. State and national water use trends to the year 2000 . Washington , 1980. x, 297 p. : LC Card 80-602584   DDC 333.91/13/0973 19
TD223 .U53 1980a

WATER CONSUMPTION - UTAH.
Hughes, Trevor C. Domestic water demand in Utah /. Logan, Utah [1979] viii, 61 p. : LC Card 80-621122   DDC 333.91/22 19
TD224.U8 H83

WATER DEVELOPMENT - UNITED STATES - PLANNING.
Crist, Charles E. Public participation practices of the U. S. Army Corps of Engineers /. Fort Collins, Colo. , 1979. vi, 123 p. ; LC Card 79-626247   DDC 333.91/15/0973 19
TC423 .C76

WATER - DISSOLVED OXYGEN.
Schefter, John E. An economic analysis of selected strategies for dissolved-oxygen management, Chattahoochee River, Georgia /. Washington , 1980. iv, 26 p. : LC Card 80-600113   DDC 363.7/394 19
TD225.C35 S33

WATER - DISSOLVED OXYGEN - STATISTICAL METHODS.
Finney, Brad A. Random differential equations in water quality modeling /. Logan, Utah [1979] viii, 41 p. : LC Card 80-622173   DDC 553.7/028 19
TD367 .F56

WATER DISTRICTS - TEXAS.
Texas. Legislature. Senate. Texas water administration . [Austin] [197-] v, 87 p. ; LC Card 80-622555   DDC 353.97640082/325 19
HD1694.T4 T3 1970

WATER DISTRICTS - VIRGINIA - DIRECTORIES.
Virginia. Soil and Water Conservation Commission. Directory of the Virginia soil & water conservation districts, 1979 /. Richmond , 1979. 40 p. : LC Card 79-624120   DDC 631.4/025/755 19
S624.V8 V57 1979

WATER FARMING. see HYDROPONICS.

WATER - FILTRATION. see WATER - PURIFICATION - FILTRATION.

WATER - FLOURIDATION.
Gabovich, Rafail Davidovich. Fluorine in stomatology and hygiene =. Bethesda, Md. , Washington , 1977. vi, 1028 p. : LC Card 78-600559   DDC 612/.3924 19
RK331 .G313

WATER - FLOW. see HYDRAULICS.

Water for industrial and agricultural development in Bolivar, Carroll, Leflore, Sunflower, and Tallahatchie Counties, Mississippi . Dalsin, G. J. Jackson, Miss. , 1978. 67 p. : LC Card 80-621547   DDC 553.7/09762/4 19
TD224.M65 D33

WATER, GROUND. see WATER, UNDERGROUND.

WATER IN LANDSCAPE ARCHITECTURE - WYOMING.
Hampe, Gary D. Water-related aesthetic preferences of Wyoming residents /. Laramie [1974] 111 p. : LC Card 74-623922   DDC 553.7/09787 s 719 19
TD201 .W9 no. 46 BH301.L3

Water information series report .
(3) Dickerman, David C. Geohydrologic data for the Beaver-Pasquiset ground-water reservoir, Rhode Island . [Providence, R.I.] , 1977. 128 p. : LC Card 80-622751   DDC 553.7/9/09745 19
GB1025.R4 D53

Water jet perforation . Savanick, George A. Washington, D.C. , 1981. p. cm. LC Card 80-607781   DDC 622 s 622/.184932 19
TN23 .U43 TN278.3

WATER - LAW AND LEGISLATION - MISSOURI.
Davis, Peter N. Missouri instream flow requirements . Jefferson City, Mo. [1980] xviii, 415 p., [1] fold. leaf of plates : LC Card 80-623733   DDC 346.77804/691 347.78064691 19
KFM8246 .D36

WATER - LAW AND LEGISLATION - OKLAHOMA.
Oklahoma. Water Resources Board. Rules, regulations, and modes of procedure /. [Oklahoma City] [1979] iii, 73 p. ; LC Card 80-621865   DDC 333.91/009766 s 333.91/00766 s 346.76604/691/002636 347.66064691002636 19
TD224.O5 A3 no. 90 KFO1646

WATER - LAW AND LEGISLATION - VIRGINIA.
Cox, William Edward, 1944- Virginia water law . Blacksburg, Va. , 1979. 15 p. ; LC Card 80-622367   DDC 346.75504/691 19
KFV2846.Z9 C68

WATER - LAW AND LEGISLATION - WEST (U. S.) - ADDRESSES, ESSAYS, LECTURES.
Trelease, Frank J., 1913- Back to basics--taking the politics out of water law . [Sacramento? Calif.] [1979?] 29 leaves ; LC Card 81-621163   DDC 346.7304/691 347.3064691 19
KF5571 .T74

Water-level changes associated with ground-water development in Las Vegas Valley, Nevada, March 1975 to March 1976 /. Harrill, J. R. Carson City , 1976 i.e. 1977. iv, 31 p. : LC Card 80-624035   DDC 553.7/9/0979313 19
GB1025.N4 H38

The water link . Chasan, Daniel Jack. Seattle , 1981. p. cm ISBN 0-295-95782-4 (University of Washington Press) : LC Card 81-11457   DDC 333.91/64 19
HC107.W22 P838

WATER - MISSOURI - COMPOSITION.
Feder, Gerald L. Geochemical survey of waters of Missouri . Washington , 1979. iv, 78 p. : LC Card 80-600129   DDC 551.48/09778 19
GB705.M8 F4

WATER - PHOSPHORUS CONTENT.
Schroeder, David C. Phosphorus export from rural Maine watersheds /. [Orono, Me.] [1979] iv, 42 leaves : LC Card 80-623370   DDC 363.7/394 19
TD427.P56 S37

Smith, Richard A. A study of trends in total phosphorus measurements at NASQAN stations /. Reston, Va. [1981] p. cm. LC Card 81-607899   DDC 363.7/394 19
TD427.P56 S64

Water planning report .
(1) Gilbert (J. B.) & Associates. Water conservation in Nevada . Carson City [1979] xvii, 273 p. : LC Card 80-622041   DDC 333.91/16/09793 19
TD224.N2 G54 1979

(2) URS Company/Las Vegas. Land application of wastewater in Nevada . Carson City, Nev. [1979] xv, 267 p. : LC Card 80-623617   DDC 628.3/62 19
TD760 .U17 1979

Water planning studies .
Idaho economic base study for water requirements. [Boise, 1969] 2 v. LC Card 79-632346
HC107.I2 I19

Water policy implementation . Final report on Phase I of water policy implementation . [Washington, D.C.?] , 1980. 99 p. in various pagings ; LC Card 81-600744   DDC 333.91/160973 19
TC423 .F57

WATER - POLLUTION.
(1973) United States. Environmental Protection Agency. Office of Water Program Operations. Estimating laboratory needs for municipal wastewater treatment facilities. Washington, 1973. i, 23, [104] p. : **NYPL [JSF 80-271]**

(1974) United States. Environmental Protection Agency. Guidance for facilities planning. Washington, 1974. 81 p.;
NYPL [JSF 80-618]

(1978) Wooldridge, David D. Suspended sediment from truck traffic on forest roads, Meadow and Coal Creeks . Seattle [1978] 33 p.: **NYPL [*ZV-185 Reel 1]**

WATER - POLLUTION - BLACKSTONE RIVER WATERSHED.
Massachusetts. Division of Water Pollution Control. Water Quality Section. Blackstone River basin . Westborough [1974] 36 p. : LC

Card 80-120648   DDC 363.7/3942/097443 19
TD225.B65 M37 1974

Massachusetts. Water Quality and Research
Section. Blackstone River basin . Westborough ,
1976. 33 p. :   LC Card 79-620584   DDC
363.7/3942/097443 19
TD225.B65 M38 1976

Massachusetts. Water Quality and Research
Section. Blackstone River basin . Westborough
[1978] 34 p. :   LC Card 79-620585   DDC
363.7/3942/097443 19
TD225.B65 M38 1978

WATER - POLLUTION - CALIFORNIA.
California. Legislature. Assembly. Ad Hoc
Committee on Water Contamination. Transcript
/. [Sacramento, Calif.] [1979] 350 p. :   LC
Card 80-621897   DDC 344.794/046343
347.940446343 19
KFC10.4 .W35 1979

California. Legislature. Assembly. Ad Hoc
Committee on Water Contamination. Transcript
(investigation into DBCP) . Sacramento, CA ,
1980. 140 p. :   LC Card 80-623739   DDC
363.7/394 19
KFC10.4 .W35 1980

California. State Water Resources Control
Board. Significance of pesticides from irrigated
agriculture in California /. [Sacramento, CA] ,
1977, 1979 printing. vi, 152, [98] leaves of
plates :   LC Card 80-621350   DDC 628.1/68/09794
s 632/.95/09794 19
TD224.C3 A47 no. 62 SB950.2.C2

WATER - POLLUTION - CHICOPEE RIVER
WATERSHED.
Massachusetts. Water Quality Research Section.
Chicopee River basin . Westborough , 1976. 40
p. :   LC Card 77-622227   DDC 363.7/3942/0974426
19
TD224.M4 M39 1976

WATER - POLLUTION - CONNECTICUT
RIVER WATERSHED.
Massachusetts. Division of Water Pollution
Control. Water Quality Section. Connecticut
River . Westborough, Mass. [1976] 52 p. :   LC
Card 77-622207   DDC 363.7/3942/097442 19
TD225.C74 M37 1976

Massachusetts. Water Quality and Research
Section. Connecticut River . Westborough,
Mass. , 1977. 35 p. :   LC Card 79-620576   DDC
363.7/3942/097442 19
TD225.C74 M38 1977

Massachusetts. Water Quality and Research
Section. Connecticut River . Westborough,
Mass. , 1978. 58 p. :   LC Card 79-623996   DDC
363.7/3942/097442 19
TD225.C74 M38 1978

WATER - POLLUTION - DEERFIELD RIVER
WATERSHED.
Massachusetts. Division of Water Pollution
Control. Water Quality Section. Deerfield River
basin . Westborough , 1976. 22 p. :   LC Card
79-620577   DDC 363.7/3942/0974422 19
TD225.D24 M36 1976a

Massachusetts. Division of Water Pollution
Control. Water Quality Section. Deerfield River
basin . Westborough , 1976. 18 p. :   LC Card
77-622638   DDC 363.7/3942/0974422 19
TD225.D24 M36 1976

Massachusetts. Division of Water Pollution
Control. Water Quality Section. Deerfield River
basin /. Westborough , 1977- v. :   LC Card
79-620578   DDC 363.7/3942/0974422 19
TD225.D24 M36 1977

Massachusetts. Water Quality and Research
Section. Deerfield River basin . Westborough,
Mass. , 1978. 16 p. :   LC Card 79-623991   DDC
363.7/3942/0974422 19
TD225.D24 M38 1978

WATER - POLLUTION - ECONOMIC
ASPECTS - UNITED STATES.
United States. Congress. Senate. Committee on
Environment and Public Works. Subcommittee
on Environmental Pollution. Industrial cost
recovery . Washington , 1980. iii, 342 p. ;   LC
Card 80-602810   DDC 353.0082/325 19
KF26 .E645 1980a

WATER - POLLUTION - ECONOMIC
ASPECTS - UNITED STATES -
PERIODICALS.
United States. Environmental Protection

Agency. The economics of clean water.
Washington.   **NYPL [JLM 80-772]**

United States. Federal Water Pollution Control
Administration. The economics of clean water.
1968- Washington.   **NYPL [JLM 80-773]**

WATER - POLLUTION - ENVIRONMENTAL
ASPECTS - CONGRESSES.
International Symposium on the Analysis of
Hydorcarbons and Halogenated Hydrocarbons
in the Aquatic Environment, McMaster
University, 1978. Hydrocarbons and
halogenated hydorcarbons in the aquatic
environment /. New York , c1980. xiii, 588 p. :
ISBN 0-306-40329-3   LC Card 79-26462
QH545.H92 I54 1978   **NYPL [JSF 80-1049]**

WATER - POLLUTION - ENVIRONMENTAL
ASPECTS - GREAT LAKES.
Wisconsin. University, Madison. Sea Grant
College Program. The invisible menace .
Madison, WI [1980] 58 p. :   LC Card 80-622418
DDC 628.1/68677 19
QH104.5.G7 W57 1980

WATER - POLLUTION - GREAT LAKES.
United States. Congress. House. Committee on
Science and Technology. Subcommittee on
Natural Resources and Environment.
Coordination of Federal research and
monitoring programs for toxic and hazardous
substances in the Great Lakes region .
Washington , 1980. iii, 451 p. :   LC Card
80-602529   DDC 363.7/38 19
KF27 .S398 1979h

WATER - POLLUTION - GREAT LAKES
REGION.
United States. Congress. House. Committee on
Science and Technology. Subcommittee on
Natural Resources and Environment.
Coordination of Federal research and
monitoring programs for toxic and hazardous
substances in the Great Lakes region .
Washington , 1980. iii, 451 p. :   LC Card
80-602529   DDC 363.7/38 19
KF27 .S398 1979h

WATER - POLLUTION - ILLINOIS.
Ewing, Ben B. Economic impact of a proposed
change in lead effluent standards /. Chicago, IL
[1980] vi, 83 p. ;   LC Card 80-623378   DDC
363.7/394 19
TD427.H45 E92

Harza Engineering Company, Chicago.
Economic impact of proposed amendments to
water pollution regulations, R77-12, Docket A
/. Chicago , 1978. 95 p. in various pagings :
LC Card 78-623938   DDC 363.7/3946 19
TD224.I3 H37 1978

Huff, Linda L. The economic impact analysis of
effluent standards for total dissolved solids /.
Chicago , 1978. xiv, 77 p. ;   LC Card 79-621565
DDC 363.7/39462 19
TD224.I3 H832

Muchmore, C. B. Economic impact of the
proposed averaging rule, R76-21 /. Chicago,
IL , 1978. xi, 43 p. :   LC Card 80-622962   DDC
363.7/39462 19
TD224.I3 M84

WATER - POLLUTION - ILLINOIS -
KISHWAUKEE RIVER WATERSHED.
Illinois. Natural History Survey. Economic
impact of a suspension of rule 404(f) as it
applies to an unnamed tributary of the
Kishwaukee River (R77-8) /. Chicago, Il.
[1978] vi leaves, 70 p. :   LC Card 79-622686
DDC 363.7/394 19
TD224.I3 I583 1978

Matsunaga, Wallace O. A biological
investigation of the Kishwaukee River and its
tributaries (segment A-02 of the Rock River
Basin), April-July, 1976 /. [Springfield] [1978?]
iii, 38 p. :   LC Card 79-622704   DDC
363.7/3942/097732 19
QL173 .M37

WATER - POLLUTION - KANSAS.
Hargadine, Gerald D. Mineral intrusion in
Kansas surface waters . Topeka, Kan. , 1979.
xxii, 211 p., [2] fold. leaves of plates :   LC Card
79-625233   DDC 553.7/8/09781 19
TD224.K3 H37

WATER - POLLUTION - LAW AND
LEGISLATION - ECONOMIC ASPECTS -
ILLINOIS.

Brigham, Allison R. Economic impact of
changing the copper effluent standard, R76-21
/. Chicago, Ill. [1979] vii, 123 p. :   LC Card
80-621149   DDC 363.7/394 19
TD427.C66 B74

Brigham, Warren U. Economic impact of a
suspension of rule 203 as it applies to an
unnamed tributary of the Vermilion River,
Vermilion County, Illinois /. Chicago, IL
[1980] ix, 90 p. :   LC Card 80-622963   DDC
363.7/394 19
TD224.I3 B74

Harza Engineering Company, Chicago.
Economic impact of proposed amendments to
water pollution regulations, R77-12, Docket A
/. Chicago , 1978. 95 p. in various pagings :
LC Card 78-623938   DDC 363.7/3946 19
TD224.I3 H37 1978

Huff, Linda L. The economic impact analysis of
effluent standards for total dissolved solids /.
Chicago , 1978. xiv, 77 p. ;   LC Card 79-621565
DDC 363.7/39462 19
TD224.I3 H832

WATER - POLLUTION - LAW AND
LEGISLATION - ECONOMIC ASPECTS -
ILLINOIS - KISHWAUKEE RIVER
WATERSHED.
Illinois. Natural History Survey. Economic
impact of a suspension of rule 404(f) as it
applies to an unnamed tributary of the
Kishwaukee River (R77-8) /. Chicago, Il.
[1978] vi leaves, 70 p. :   LC Card 79-622686
DDC 363.7/394 19
TD224.I3 I583 1978

WATER - POLLUTION - LAW AND
LEGISLATION - ILLINOIS.
Illinois. Pollution Control Board. Public water
supplies /. [Springfield , 1979] 22 p. ;   LC Card
80-621932   DDC 353.97730082322 s
344.773/046343 19
KFI1554 .A4 1972 chap. 6 KFI1556

WATER - POLLUTION - LAW AND
LEGISLATION - UNITED STATES.
Deyak, Timothy A. The effect of water
pollution control regulations on the cost of
production of electric power /. Auburn, Ala. ,
1979. v, 24 p. :   LC Card 79-622808   DDC
333.91/009761 s 338.4/36213121/0973 19
TC1 .A85 no. 36 HD9685.U5

Fisher, Ann Broman. Coal mine water pollution
legal and regulatory issues . Chicago , 1978. iii,
43 p. ;   LC Card 79-621567   DDC 363.7/394 19
TD428.C6 F57

United States. Congress. House. Committee on
Public Works and Transportation. Subcommittee
on Water Resources. Industrial cost recovery .
Washington , 1980. iv, 447 p. :   LC Card
80-603642   DDC 344.73/046343 19
KF27 .P8968 1980

WATER - POLLUTION - MAINE.
Maine. Land Use Regulation Commission. A
survey of erosion and sedimentation problems
associated with logging in Maine /. [Augusta,
Me.] [1979] 56 p. :   LC Card 80-620932   DDC
333.75/16/09741 19
TD428.F67 M34 1979

WATER - POLLUTION - MASSACHUSETTS -
ASSABET RIVER WATERSHED.
Massachusetts. Division of Water Pollution
Control. Water Quality Section. SUASCO River
basin . Westborough, Mass. [1976] 36 p. :   LC
Card 77-622200   DDC 363.7/3942/097444 19
TD224.M4 M36 1976l

Massachusetts. Water Quality and Research
Section. SUASCO River basin . Westborough,
Mass. , 1977. 33 p. :   LC Card 79-622377   DDC
363.7/3942/097444 19
TD224.M4 M368 1977

WATER - POLLUTION - MASSACHUSETTS -
BOSTON.
Massachusetts. Division of Water Pollution
Control. Water Quality Section. Boston
Harbor . Westborough, Mass. [1976] 18 p. :
LC Card 77-622213   DDC 363.7/3942/097446
19
TD225.B7 M37 1976

Massachusetts. Division of Water Pollution
Control. Water Quality Section. Boston
Harbor . Westborough, Mass. , 1977. 20 p. :
LC Card 79-620586   DDC 363.7/3942/097446

19
TD225.B7 M37 1977

WATER - POLLUTION - MASSACHUSETTS - BOSTON BAY WATERSHED.
Massachusetts. Water Quality and Research Section. Boston Harbor . Westborough, Mass. , 1977. iv, 48 p. :   LC Card 79-620587   DDC 363.7/3942/097446 19
TD225.B7 M39 1977

WATER - POLLUTION - MASSACHUSETTS - BUZZARDS BAY WATERSHED - STATISTICS.
Massachusetts. Water Quality and Research Section. Buzzards Bay . Westborough, Mass. [1978] 62 p. :   LC Card 79-620588   DDC 363.7/3942/097448 19
TD224.M4 M39 1978g

WATER - POLLUTION - MASSACHUSETTS - CHARLES RIVER WATERSHED.
Massachusetts. Division of Water Pollution Control. Water Quality Section. Charles River . Westborough [1974] 33 p. :   LC Card 77-622229   DDC 363.7/3942/097447 19
TD224.M4 M36 1974d

Massachusetts. Division of Water Pollution Control. Water Quality Section. Charles River . Westborough, Mass. [1976] 55 p. :   LC Card 80-120642 DDC 363.7/3942/097447 19
TD224.M4 M36 1976f

WATER - POLLUTION - MASSACHUSETTS - CONCORD RIVER WATERSHED.
Massachusetts. Division of Water Pollution Control. Water Quality Section. SUASCO River basin . Westborough, Mass. [1976] 36 p. :   LC Card 77-622200   DDC 363.7/3942/097444 19
TD224.M4 M36 1976l

Massachusetts. Water Quality and Research Section. SUASCO River basin . Westborough, Mass. , 1977. 33 p. :   LC Card 79-622377 DDC 363.7/3942/097444 19
TD224.M4 M368 1977

WATER - POLLUTION - MASSACHUSETTS - FRENCH RIVER WATERSHED.
Massachusetts. Water Quality and Research Section. French and Quinebaug Rivers . Westborough [1978] 43 p. :   LC Card 79-620581 DDC 363.7/3942/097443 19
TD224.M4 M39 1978d

WATER - POLLUTION - MASSACHUSETTS - IPSWICH RIVER WATERSHED.
Massachusetts. Water Quality and Research Section. Parker and Ipswich Rivers . Westborough, Mass. [1977] 13 p. :   LC Card 79-620594   DDC 363.7/3942/097445 19
TD224.M4 M368 1977a

WATER - POLLUTION - MASSACHUSETTS - LEE - MATHEMATICAL MODELS.
Rich, Peter, 1955- *Measuring certain intangible benefits of water pollution abatement by use of changes of impacted real estate values* /. Amherst, Mass. [1979] 52 leaves :   LC Card 80-621812   DDC 333.33//22 19
HD268.L44 R5

WATER - POLLUTION - MASSACHUSETTS - MILLERS RIVER WATERSHED.
Massachusetts. Water Quality and Research Section. Millers River . Westborough, Mass. [1979] 39 p. :   LC Card 79-623981 DDC 363.7/3942/0974422 19
TD224.M4 M39 1979

WATER - POLLUTION - MASSACHUSETTS - MYSTIC RIVER WATERSHED.
Massachusetts. Division of Water Pollution Control. Water Quality Section. Mystic River . Westborough, Mass. [1976] 37 p. :   LC Card 77-622204   DDC 363.7/3942/097444 19
TD224.M4 M36 1976a

WATER - POLLUTION - MASSACHUSETTS - NEPONSET RIVER WATERSHED.
Massachusetts. Division of Water Pollution Control. Water Quality Section. Neponset River . Westborough [1976] 38, A-U p. :   LC Card 77-622675 DDC 363.7/3942/097447 19
TD224.M4 M36 1976h

WATER - POLLUTION - MASSACHUSETTS - NORTH RIVER WATERSHED.
Massachusetts. Division of Water Pollution Control. Water Quality Section. North River basin . Westborough , 1975. 16 p. :   LC Card

78-621331   DDC 363.7/3942/0974482 19
TD224.M4 M36 1975i

Massachusetts. Division of Water Pollution Control. Water Quality Section. North River basin . Westborough [1976] 22 p. :   LC Card 79-620607   DDC 363.7/3942/0974482 19
TD224.M4 M36 1976i

Massachusetts. Water Quality and Research Section. North River . Westborough , 1977. 53 p. :   LC Card 79-622379   DDC 363.7/3942/0974482 19
TD224.M4 M39 1977i

WATER - POLLUTION - MASSACHUSETTS - PARKER RIVER WATERSHED.
Massachusetts. Water Quality and Research Section. Parker and Ipswich Rivers . Westborough, Mass. [1977] 13 p. :   LC Card 79-620594   DDC 363.7/3942/097445 19
TD224.M4 M368 1977a

WATER - POLLUTION - MASSACHUSETTS - RUMFORD RIVER WATERSHED.
Massachusetts. Divison of Water Pollution Control. Rumford and Three Mile Rivers . Boston [1971] 63 p. :   LC Card 80-118665   DDC 363.7/3942/0974485 19
TD224.M4 M36 1971b

WATER - POLLUTION - MASSACHUSETTS - SOUTH WATUPPA POND WATERSHED.
Chesebrough, Eben W. *South Watuppa Pond* . Westborough, Mass. [1977] 69 p. :   LC Card 79-621235   DDC 363.7/3942/0974485 19
TD224.M4 C485

WATER - POLLUTION - MASSACHUSETTS - STATISTICS.
Massachusetts. Water Quality and Research Section. North Coastal water quality survey, 1976 /. Westborough, Mass. [1978] v, 53 p. :   LC Card 79-620601   DDC 363.7/3942/097445 19
TD224.M4 M39 1978c

Massachusetts. Water Quality and Research Section. South Coastal . Westborough [1977] 72 p. :   LC Card 79-620597   DDC 363.7/3942/0974482 19
TD224.M4 M39 1977h

WATER - POLLUTION - MASSACHUSETTS - SUDBURY RIVER WATERSHED.
Massachusetts. Division of Water Pollution Control. Water Quality Section. SUASCO River basin . Westborough, Mass. [1976] 36 p. :   LC Card 77-622200   DDC 363.7/3942/097444 19
TD224.M4 M36 1976l

Massachusetts. Water Quality and Research Section. SUASCO River basin . Westborough, Mass. , 1977. 33 p. :   LC Card 79-622377   DDC 363.7/3942/097444 19
TD224.M4 M368 1977

WATER - POLLUTION - MASSACHUSETTS - TAUNTON RIVER WATERSHED.
Massachusetts. Water Quality and Research Section. Taunton River Basin wastewater discharge survey, 1975, 1976, 1978, 1979 /. Westborough [Mass.] [1979] 133 p. :   LC Card 80-621549   DDC 363.7/3942/097448 19
TD224.M4 M368 1979

Salo, John E. *Taunton River study* . Boston [1971] 31 leaves :   LC Card 80-118663 DDC 363.7/3942/097448 19
TD224.M4 S25

WATER - POLLUTION - MASSACHUSETTS - TEN MILE RIVER WATERSHED.
Lord, Sabin M. *Ten Mile River study, 1968* /. [Boston] [1970]- v. :   LC Card 80-120118   DDC 363.7/3942/0974485 19
TD224.M4 L67

Massachusetts. Division of Water Pollution Control. Water Quality Section. Ten Mile River basin . Westborough, Mass. , 1976. 46 p. ;   LC Card 77-622202   DDC 363.7/39456/0974485 19
TD224.M4 M36 1976b

Massachusetts. Water Quality and Research Section. Ten Mile River basin . Westborough [1978] 42 p. :   LC Card 79-620593   DDC 363.7/3942/0974485 19
TD224.M4 M39 1978b

WATER - POLLUTION - MASSACHUSETTS - THREE MILE RIVER WATERSHED.
Massachusetts. Divison of Water Pollution Control. Rumford and Three Mile Rivers . Boston [1971] 63 p. :   LC Card 80-118665   DDC

363.7/3942/0974485 19
TD224.M4 M36 1971b

WATER - POLLUTION - MASSACHUSETTS - WESTFIELD RIVER WATERSHED.
Massachusetts. Water Quality and Research Section. Westfield River basin /. Westborough , 1975. 2 v. :   LC Card 77-622217   DDC 363.7/394/0974426 19
TD224.M4 M39 1975

WATER - POLLUTION - MASSACHUSETTS - WESTFIELD RIVER WATERSHED - STATISTICS.
Massachusetts. Water Quality and Research Section. Westfield River basin . Westborough, Mass. , 1978. 113 p. :   LC Card 79-623982   DDC 363.7/3942/0974426 19
TD224.M4 M39 1978f

WATER - POLLUTION - MASSACHUSETTS - WEYMOUTH BACK RIVER WATERSHED.
Massachusetts. Water Quality and Research Section. Weymouth Fore and Back River survey, 1975 /. Westborough [1976] 58 p. :   LC Card 79-620589   DDC 363.7/3942/097447 19
TD224.M4 M39 1976a

WATER - POLLUTION - MASSACHUSETTS - WEYMOUTH FORE RIVER WATERSHED.
Massachusetts. Water Quality and Research Section. Weymouth Fore and Back River survey, 1975 /. Westborough [1976] 58 p. :   LC Card 79-620589   DDC 363.7/3942/097447 19
TD224.M4 M39 1976a

WATER - POLLUTION - MERRIMACK RIVER WATERSHED, N.H. AND MASS.
Massachusetts. Water Quality and Research Section. Merrimack River basin . Westborough , 1977. 15 p. :   LC Card 79-620606   DDC 363.7/3942/097445 19
TD225.M514 M37 1977

Massachusetts. Water Quality and Research Section. Merrimack River basin . Westborough [1978] 30 p. :   LC Card 79-624447   DDC 363.7/3942/097445 19
TD225.M514 M37 1978

WATER - POLLUTION - MISSISSIPPI RIVER WATERSHED.
URS Company, Seattle, Wash. *Dynamics of polychlorinated biphenyls in the upper Mississippi River* . Columbia, Mo. , Washington , 1978- v. :   LC Card 79-602554   DDC 363.7/394 19
TD427.P65 U18 1978

WATER - POLLUTION - MISSOURI.
Missouri. Dept. of Conservation. *An inventory of point and non-point water pollution sources in Missouri* . [Jefferson City] , 1978. 160 p. ;   LC Card 78-622216   DDC 628.1/686778 19
QL628.M8 M49 1978

WATER - POLLUTION - MISSOURI RIVER WATERSHED.
United States. Public Health Service. *Pollution of interstate waters.* [Washington] 1959. 2 v.   LC Card 75-80621   *NYPL [JSF 81-65]*

WATER - POLLUTION - MONTANA.
Bahls, Loren L. *Biological water quality monitoring, southwest Montana, 1977-1978* /. Helena , 1979. v, 60 p. ;   LC Card 79-623384   DDC 553.7/8/097866 19
QH105.M9 B34

WATER - POLLUTION - MONTANA - FLINT CREEK RANGE.
Ingman, Gary L. *An assessment of mining impacts on quality of surface waters in the Flint Creek Range, Montana* . Helena [1979] 82 p. :   LC Card 80-621730   DDC 363.7/3942/097868 19
TD428.M56 I53

WATER - POLLUTION - NASHUA RIVER WATERSHED, MASS. AND N.H. - STATISTICS.
Massachusetts. Division of Water Pollution Control. Water Quality Section. Nashua River basin . Westborough [1975] 38 p. :   LC Card 79-620604   DDC 363.7/3942/097443 19
TD225.N2 M37 1975

Massachusetts. Water Quality and Research Section. Nashua River basin . Westborough,

Mass. [1978] 31 p. : LC Card 79-620603 DDC
363.7/3942/097444 19
TD225.N2 M38 1978

WATER - POLLUTION - NEBRASKA - LITTLE NEMAHA RIVER WATERSHED - MAPS.
United States. Soil Conservation Service. Water,
fisheries, and pollution resources map lower
Little Nemaha watershed, Johnson, Nemaha,
Otoe and Richardson Counties, Nebraska /.
Lincoln, Nebr. , 1978. 1 map : LC Card
81-691088
G4192.L5C3 1978 .U5

WATER - POLLUTION - NEW JERSEY.
United States. Congress. House. Committee on
Interstate and Foreign Commerce.
Subcommittee on Transportation and
Commerce. Hazardous waste disposal .
Washington , 1980 [i.e. 1981] iii, 97 p. ; LC
Card 81-600820 DDC 363.7/28 19
KF27 .I5589 1980o

WATER - POLLUTION - NORTH DAKOTA - STATISTICS.
North Dakota. State Dept. of Health. Nutrient
levels in North Dakota streams, 1972-1978 /.
[Bismarck, N.D.] [1980] 86 p. : LC Card
80-622821 DDC 363.7/3942/09784 19
TD224.N9 N65 1980

WATER - POLLUTION - QUINEBAUG RIVER WATERSHED, CONN. AND MASS.
Massachusetts. Water Quality and Research
Section. French and Quinebaug Rivers .
Westborough [1978] 43 p. : LC Card 79-620581
DDC 363.7/3942/097443 19
TD224.M4 M39 1978d

WATER - POLLUTION - REMOTE SENSING - CONGRESSES.
Remote sensing and problems of the
hydrosphere . Washington, D.C. , 1980. iv, 30
p. ; LC Card 80-603169 DDC 553.7/028/7 19
TD419.5 .R45

WATER - POLLUTION - SONORAN DESERT.
Jamail, Milton H. International water use
relations along the Sonoran Desert borderlands
/. Tuscon, Ariz. , 1979. iv leaves, 139 p., [1]
leaf of plates : LC Card 80-622139 DDC
333.91/13/0979 19
TD223.9 .J35

WATER - POLLUTION - TEXAS - HOUSTON SHIP CHANNEL.
Texas. Dept. of Water Resources. Enforcement
and Field Operations Division. District 7
Office. Houston Ship Channel monitoring
program data, 1973-1978. Deer Park, Tex.
[1980] iii leaves, 65 p. : LC Card 80-622407
DDC 363.7/39463/09764141 19
TD224.T4 T36 1980b

WATER - POLLUTION - UNITED STATES.
United States. Congress. House. Committee on
Interstate and Foreign Commerce.
Subcommittee on Health and the Environment.
Hazardous waste and drinking water .
Washington , 1981. v, 195 p. : LC Card
81-601136 DDC 363.7/394 19
KF27 .I5543 1980q

United States. Maritime Administration. United
States Department of Commerce final
environmental impact statement . [Washington]
[1979] ca. 350 p. in various pagings : LC Card
79-602128 DDC 333.91/1/0973 19
TD427.P4 U58 1979

WATER - POLLUTION - VERMILION RIVER WATERSHED, ILL. & IND.
Brigham, Warren U. Economic impact of a
suspension of rule 203 as it applies to an
unnamed tributary of the Vermilion River,
Vermilion County, Illinois /. Chicago, IL
[1980] ix, 90 p. : LC Card 80-622963 DDC
363.7/394 19
TD224.I3 B74

WATER - POLLUTION - VERMONT.
Stinebring, Warren R. Endotoxin in waters of
the State of Vermont /. [Montpelier] [1978?]
iv leaves, 25 p. ; LC Card 79-624701 DDC
363.7/394 19
QR48 .S74

WATER - POLLUTION - VIRGINIA.
Smolen, M. D. Agricultural land use .
Blacksburg, Va. , 1980. vii, 82 p. : LC Card

80-622278 DDC 333.91/009755 s 363.7/3941
19
TD201 .V57 no. 125 TD428.A37

Wendt, Stephen L. Occurrence and distribution
of human bacterial pathogens in Virginia surface
waters /. Blacksburg, Va. , 1979. vii, 68 p. :
LC Card 79-625812 DDC 333.91/009755 s
363.7/394 19
TD201 .V57 no. 118 TD224.V8

WATER - POLLUTION - WASHINGTON (STATE)
Washington (State). Dept. of Ecology. Water
Quality Planning. Dryland agriculture water
quality management plan . Olympia, Wash.
[1979] 2 v. : LC Card 80-621082 DDC
363.7/39456/09797 19
TD428.A37 W37 1979a

WATER - POLLUTION - WASHINGTON (STATE) - PUGET SOUND - HISTORY.
Chasan, Daniel Jack. The water link . Seattle ,
1981. p. cm ISBN 0-295-95782-4 (University of
Washington Press) : LC Card 81-11457 DDC
333.91/64 19
HC107.W22 P838

WATER - POLLUTION - WEST VIRGINIA.
Double, Mark L. Recovery of sanitary-indicator
bacteria from streams containing acid mine
water /. Morgantown , 1978. v, 30 p. : LC
Card 78-622769 DDC 333.91/009754 s
628.1/6832/0287 19
QC986.W4 W46 no. 11 QR48

WATER - POLLUTION - WISCONSIN - MEASUREMENT.
Hilsenhoff, William LeRoy, 1929- Use of
arthropods to evaluate water quality of streams
/. Madison, WI , 1977. 15 p. : LC Card
78-623368 DDC 639.9/09775 s 628.1/68/028/7
19
SK463 .A27 no. 100 QH105.W6

WATER-POWER - ARKANSAS.
Arkansas. State Geologist. Water powers of
Arkansas. [Fayettevillel, Ark.] 1911. x, 94, [4]
p. LC Card GS12-3   *NYPL [*ZV-180]*

WATER POWER - CALIFORNIA.
California. Dept. of Water Resources. A survey
of small hydroelectric potential at existing sites
in California. [Sacramento] , 1979. viii, 28 p. :
LC Card 80-620653 DDC 621.31/2134/09794
19
TK1424.C2 C34 1979

WATER-POWER ELECTRIC PLANTS - LAW AND LEGISLATION - MAINE.
Freeman, Martha. The Mill act, the Abandoned
dams act, and the Neglected dams act .
[Augusta, Me.] , 1979. ii, 54 p. ; LC Card
80-623039 DDC 346.74104/6914 19
KFM447.8 .F73

WATER-POWER - MAPS.
United States. Geological Survey. Water power
of the world . Washington , 1918. [7] leaves of
plates : LC Card 80-675255 DDC 912/.133391
G1046.N33 U53 1918

Water power of the world . United States.
Geological Survey. Washington , 1918. [7]
leaves of plates : LC Card 80-675255 DDC
912/.133391
G1046.N33 U53 1918

WATER-POWER - WASHINGTON (STATE)
State of Washington Water Research Center.
An assessment of potential hydroelectric power
and energy for the State of Washington /.
[Olympia] [1979] 5 v. : LC Card 80-622476
DDC 553.7/09797 s 333.91/4 19
TD224.W2 S8 no. 34 TK1424.W2

Water powers of Arkansas. Arkansas. State
Geologist. [Fayettevillel, Ark.] 1911. x, 94, [4]
p. LC Card GS12-3   *NYPL [*ZV-180]*

Water problems in an urbanizing state. Whipple,
William, 1909- Principles of water resources
planning (phase II) /. [New Brunswick] [1978]
26 leaves ; LC Card 79-623366 DDC 333.91 19
TC409 .W48

WATER - PURIFICATION.
(1977) United States. Environmental Protection
Agency. Water Supply Research Division.
Ozone, chlorine dioxide, and chloramines as
alternatives to chlorine for disinfection of
drinking water . Cincinnati, Ohio [1977] 1979
printing. 84 p. : LC Card 80-601552 DDC

628.1/66 19
TD459 .U54 1977

(1979) Utah Water Research Laboratory.
Studies on viruses in water /. Logan, Utah ,
1979. viii, 35 p. : LC Card 80-621126 DDC
628.3 19
QR48 .U8 1979

WATER - PURIFICATION - CHLORINATION.
Bonner, William P. Effects of wastewater
process operation on organics in potable water
supplies /. Knoxville , 1978. ix, 109 leaves :
LC Card 79-624195 DDC 628.1/62 19
TD758.5.O75 B66

WATER - PURIFICATION - FILTRATION.
Evaluation of in-line direct filtration for virus
removal /. Logan, Utah [1979]. xi, 93 p. : LC
Card 80-622171 DDC 628.1/64 19
TD753 .E88

Stanley, Donald A. Treatment of Florida
surface waters for use in phosphate
beneficiation /. [Washington, D.C.] [1981] p.
cm. LC Card 80-606882 DDC 622 s 661/.43 19
TN23 .U43

WATER - PURIFICATION - FLOCCULATION.
Stanley, Donald A. Treatment of Florida
surface waters for use in phosphate
beneficiation /. [Washington, D.C.] [1981] p.
cm. LC Card 80-606882 DDC 622 s 661/.43 19
TN23 .U43

WATER - PURIFICATION - NITROGEN REMOVAL.
Taylor, Robert Gay, 1940- Effects of bacteria
on nitrate and nitrite concentrations in
groundwater of the Ogallala aquifer /. Las
Cruces, N.M. [1979] vii, 20 leaves : LC Card
80-622275 DDC 333.91/09789 s 628.1/68 19
GB705.N6 N64 no. 114 TD224.N6

WATER PURIFICATION PLANTS. see
WATER TREATMENT PLANTS.

WATER - PURIFICATION - STUDY AND TEACHING.
United States. Environmental Protection
Agency. Public Service Careers Section.
Guidelines for career development for
wastewater treatment-plant personnel.
Washington, 1973. viii, 100 p. LC Card 76-87266
NYPL [JSF 80-487]

WATER - PURIFICATION - VIRUS REMOVAL.
Evaluation of in-line direct filtration for virus
removal /. Logan, Utah [1979]. xi, 93 p. : LC
Card 80-622171 DDC 628.1/64 19
TD753 .E88

WATER QUALITY BIOASSAY.
Biota and biological parameters as
environmental indicators /. Reston, Va. , 1981.
p. cm. LC Card 81-607891 DDC 557.3 s 628.1/61
19
QE75 .C5 no. 848-B QH96.8.B5

Biota and biological principles of the aquatic
environment /. Reston, Va. , 1980. p. cm. LC
Card 81-607921 DDC 557.3 s 574.5/263 19
QE75 .C5 no. 848-A QH90

Birge, Wesley J. Sensitivity of vertebrate
embryos to heavy metals as a criterion of water
quality, phase II . Lexington , 1975. iii, 36 p. :
LC Card 76-624547 DDC 628.1/6836 19
QH90.57.B5 B6

Buikema, Arthur L. Rotifer sensitivity to
combinations of inorganic water pollutants /.
Blacksburg , 1977. vi, 42 p. : LC Card 78-621510
DDC 333.91/09755 s 595.1/81 19
TD201 .V57 no. 92 QL391.R8

WATER QUALITY BIOASSAY - GILA RIVER.
Brandvold, D. K. Chemical and biological
survey of the Upper Gila River system in New
Mexico . Las Cruces, N.M. [1979] iii, 48 p. ;
LC Card 80-622273 DDC 333.91/009789 s
628.1/686789/692 19
GB705.N6 N64 no. 110 QH105.N6

WATER QUALITY BIOASSAY - MERRIMACK RIVER WATERSHED, N.H. AND MASS.
Bilger, Michael D. Merrimack River .
Westborough, Mass. [1976] i, 29 p. : LC Card
77-622236 DDC 363.7/3942/097445 19
TD225.M574 B54

WATER QUALITY BIOASSAY - MONTANA.
Bahls, Loren L. Biological water quality monitoring, southwest Montana, 1977-1978 /. Helena , 1979. v, 60 p. ;   LC Card 79-623384   DDC 553.7/8/097866 19
QH105.M9 B34

Montana. Water Quality Bureau. Biological water quality monitoring, northwest Montana, 1978-1979 /. Helena, Mont. [1979] v, 59 p. ;   LC Card 80-621281   DDC 628.1/686786 19
QH96.8.B5 M66 1979

WATER QUALITY BIOASSAY - NASHUA RIVER WATERSHED, MASS. AND N.H.
Bilger, Michael D. Nashua River . Westborough, Mass. [1978] iv leaves, 45 p. :   LC Card 79-624432   DDC 363.7/3942/097443 19
TD225.N2 B54

WATER QUALITY BIOASSAY - NEW MEXICO.
Brandvold, D. K. Chemical and biological survey of the Upper Gila River system in New Mexico . Las Cruces, N.M. [1979] iii, 48 p. ;   LC Card 80-622273   DDC 333.91/009789 s 628.1/686789/692 19
GB705.N6 N64 no. 110 QH105.N6

WATER QUALITY BIOASSAY - WISCONSIN.
Hilsenhoff, William LeRoy, 1929- Use of arthropods to evaluate water quality of streams /. Madison, WI , 1977. 15 p. :   LC Card 78-623368   DDC 639.9/09775 s 628.1/68/028/7 19
SK463 .A27 no. 100 QH105.W6

WATER QUALITY - BLACKSTONE RIVER WATERSHED.
Chesebrough, Eben W. Baseline water quality studies of selected lakes and ponds in the Blackstone River Basin, 1977 /. Westborough, Mass. , 19. 172 p. :   LC Card 80-620852   DDC 363.7/3942/097443 19
TD225.B65 C43

WATER QUALITY - BLACKSTONE RIVER WATERSHED - STATISTICS.
Massachusetts. Water Quality and Research Section. Blackstone River tributaries . Westborough [1978] 155 p. :   LC Card 79-624445   DDC 363.7/3942/097443 19
TD225.B65 M38 1978a

WATER QUALITY - CALIFORNIA - LOS ANGELES CO.
California. Dept. of Water Resources. Southern District. Areawide water quality monitoring program for the Raymond Basin . [Los Angeles?] [1979] vi, 56 p., 2 fold. leaves of plates :   LC Card 80-620668   DDC 553.7/9/0979493 19
TD224.C3 C24 1979d

California. Dept. of Water Resources. Southern District. Results of areawide water quality monitoring program for the Raymond Basin, July 1, 1978 - June 30, 1979 . [Los Angeles] [1980] v, 29 p., 1 fold. leaf of plates :   LC Card 80-621916   DDC 363.6/1 19
TD224.C3 C24 1980

WATER QUALITY - CALIFORNIA - SUSAN RIVER WATERSHED.
California. Dept. of Water Resources. Northern District. Susan River water quality study /. [Sacramento] , 1979. vii, 63 p. :   LC Card 80-621635   DDC 363.7/3942/0979426 19
TD224.C3 C24 1979e

WATER QUALITY - CHESAPEAKE BAY.
The Chesapeake Bay . Gloucester Point, Va. [1975] 2 v. :   LC Card 80-621270   DDC 363.7/3942/0916347 19
TD223.1 .C44

WATER QUALITY - CHOWAN RIVER WATERSHED - MATHEMATICAL MODELS.
Contractor, D. N. Streamflow and water quality modeling of the Chowan River /. Blacksburg, Va. [1980] vii, 71 p. :   LC Card 80-623862   DDC 333.91/009755 s 363.7/3942/0724 19
TD201 .V57 no. 119 TD225.C53

WATER QUALITY - COLORADO - BOULDER CO.
United States. Geological Survey. Water resources of Boulder County, Colorado /. Denver, Colo. , 1980. vii, 97 p. :   LC Card

80-623575   DDC 553.7/09788/63 19
GB705.C6 U54 1980

WATER QUALITY - CONNECTICUT RIVER WATERSHED.
Simpson, Kimball T. Connecticut River . Westborough, Mass. , 1975. 67 p. :   LC Card 77-622233   DDC 363.7/3942/097442 19
TD225.C74 S55

WATER QUALITY - CONNECTICUT RIVER WATERSHED - STATISTICS.
Kimball, Robert A. Connecticut River survey, 1966 /. Boston , 1970. 67 leaves :   LC Card 77-622170   DDC 363.7/3942/097442 19
TD225.C74 K55

Massachusetts. Division of Water Pollution Control. Water Quality Section. Connecticut River basin . Westborough , 1978. 147 p. :   LC Card 79-623997   DDC 363.7/3942/097442 19
TD225.C74 M37 1978

WATER QUALITY - DEERFIELD RIVER WATERSHED.
Massachusetts. Division of Water Pollution Control. Water Quality Section. Deerfield River /. Westborough , 1973- v. :   LC Card 77-622223   DDC 362.7/3942/0974422 19
TD225.D24 M36 1973

WATER QUALITY - FARMINGTON RIVER, WEST BRANCH, MASS. AND CONN.
Anderson, Paul R. Farmington River . Westborough , 1975. 70, [23] p. :   LC Card 79-620582   DDC 363.7/394/097441 19
TD225.F37 A52

WATER QUALITY - HOUSATONIC RIVER WATERSHED.
Cooperman, Alan N. Housatonic River study, 1969 /. Boston , 1969- v. :   LC Card 80-117974   DDC 363.7/3942/09441 19
TD225.H75 C66

WATER QUALITY - IDAHO - IDAHO NATIONAL ENGINEERING LABORATORY REGION.
Barraclough, Jack T. Hydrologic conditions at the Idaho National Engineering Laboratory, Idaho emphasis, 1974-1978 /. Denver, Colo. , 1981. p. cm.   LC Card 81-6821   DDC 553.7/9/0979659 19
TD224.I2 B37

WATER QUALITY - ILLINOIS - ILLINOIS RIVER WATERSHED.
Tucker, William Jacob, 1926- An intensive survey of Illinois River and its tributaries . [Springfield] [1979?] v, 158 p., [6] leaves of plates :   LC Card 80-622577   DDC 363.7/3942/097735 19
TD224.I3 T83

Water quality in Capitol Lake, Olympia, Washington /. CH2M Hill, inc. [Corvallis, Or.] , 1978. 116 p. in various pagings :   LC Card 79-621289
TD224.W2 C18 1978   *NYPL [JSF 81-45]*

Water quality in Montana-1980 /. Montana. Water Quality Bureau. [Helena] , 1980. 247, [7] p. :   LC Card 80-623056   DDC 363.7/3942/09786 19
TD224.M9 M68 1980

WATER QUALITY - IOWA.
Iowa. Chemicals and Water Quality Division. Planning Section. Water quality report /. [Des Moines] , 1977. 437 p. in various pagings :   LC Card 80-622135   DDC 363.7/3942/09777 19
TD224.I8 I56 1977

WATER QUALITY - LAKE CHAMPLAIN WATERSHED.
Lake Champlain Basin Study (United States.) Shaping the future of Lake Champlain . [Boston, Mass.] [1979] x, 124, 45 p. ;   LC Card 80-622025   DDC 333.91/6316/097454 19
TD225.L252 L34 1979

WATER QUALITY - MAINE.
Schroeder, David C. Phosphorus export from rural Maine watersheds /. [Orono, Me.] [1979] iv, 42 leaves :   LC Card 80-623370   DDC 363.7/394 19
TD427.P56 S37

WATER QUALITY - MAINE - MEASUREMENT.
Welch, Barbara. The voluntary water quality monitoring project report, 1979 /. [Augusta] [1980] 136 p. :   LC Card 80-623367   DDC

363.7/3942/09741 19
TD224.M2 W44

WATER QUALITY MANAGEMENT - ALASKA.
Alaska. Division of Water Programs. Alaska water quality management plan for non-point sources /. [Juneau] [1979] 50 p. :   LC Card 80-621564   DDC 363.7/39456/09798 19
TD224.A25 A54 1979

WATER QUALITY MANAGEMENT - BLACKSTONE RIVER WATERSHED.
Massachusetts. Division of Water Pollution Control. Water Quality Section. Blackstone River basin . Westborough , 1975. 125, [44] p. :   LC Card 77-622210   DDC 363.7/39456/097443 19
TD225.B65 M37 1975

WATER QUALITY MANAGEMENT - CHATTAHOOCHEE RIVER WATERSHED - COSTS.
Schefter, John E. An economic analysis of selected strategies for dissolved-oxygen management, Chattahoochee River, Georgia /. Washington , 1980. iv, 26 p. :   LC Card 80-600113   DDC 363.7/394 19
TD225.C35 S33

WATER QUALITY MANAGEMENT - CONNECTICUT.
Iannicelli, Donald. Surface impoundment assessment . Hartford, Conn. [1979] x, 53 leaves :   LC Card 80-623424   DDC 363.7/394 19
TD224.C8 I26

WATER QUALITY MANAGEMENT - CONNECTICUT - CONGRESSES.
Lake Management Conference, University of Connecticut, 1977. Proceedings, Lake Management Conference, held June 9, 1977, at the University of Connecticut, Storrs. Storrs [1979] iv, 127 p. :   LC Card 79-625225   DDC 333.91 s 333.91/63/09746 19
HD1694.C8 C7 no. 30 TC424.C8

WATER QUALITY MANAGEMENT - CONNECTICUT RIVER WATERSHED.
Massachusetts. Division of Water Pollution Control. Water Quality Section. Connecticut River basin . Westborough, Mass. , 1975. 96, [51] p. :   LC Card 80-119554   DDC 363.7/39456/097442 19
TD225.C74 M37 1975

WATER QUALITY MANAGEMENT - DEERFIELD RIVER WATERSHED.
Massachusetts. Division of Water Pollution Control. Water Quality Section. Deerfield River basin . Westborough, Mass. , 1975. 67, A-E, A-N p. :   LC Card 77-622231   DDC 363.7/39456/0974422 19
TD225.D24 M36 1975

WATER QUALITY MANAGEMENT - GEORGIA - COSTS.
Schefter, John E. An economic analysis of selected strategies for dissolved-oxygen management, Chattahoochee River, Georgia /. Washington , 1980. iv, 26 p. :   LC Card 80-600113   DDC 363.7/394 19
TD225.C35 S33

WATER QUALITY MANAGEMENT - GREAT LAKES - CONGRESSES.
Phosphorus managemnt strategies or lakes . Ann Arbor, Mich. , 1980. vi, 490 p. :   ISBN 0-250-40332-3   LC Card 79-55150
TD223.3 .P48

WATER QUALITY MANAGEMENT - ILLINOIS.
Huff, Linda L. Technical and economic review of control methods for total dissolved solids, sulfates, chlorides, iron, and manganese /. Chicago, Ill. [1980] ix, 214 p. :   LC Card 80-622964   DDC 628.1/6832 19
TD899.M47 H83

Water quality management in Ouachita Highland headwaters of Oklahoma . Miller, Robert L. [Oklahoma City] , 1980. xxvi, 109 p. :   LC Card 80-623044   DDC 363.7/39456/097666 19
TD224.O5 M54

WATER QUALITY MANAGEMENT - IOWA.
Iowa. Chemicals and Water Quality Division. Iowa statewide water quality management plan /. Des Moines, Iowa [1979] 172, 36, 8 p. :   LC Card 80-622459   DDC 363.7/39456/09777 19
TD224.I8 I56 1979

WATER QUALITY MANAGEMENT - MAINE.
Welch, Barbara. The voluntary water quality
monitoring project report, 1979 /. [Augusta]
[1980] 136 p. : LC Card 80-623367 DDC
363.7/3942/09741 19
TD224.M2 W44

**WATER QUALITY MANAGEMENT - MAINE -
PLANNING.**
Maine. Division of Water Quality Evaluation
and Planning. Detailed work plan for the fiscal
year 1978, Maine Statewide 208 Waste
Treatment Management Planning Program /.
[Augusta] [1980] 77 p. in various pagings :
LC Card 80-621395 DDC 363.7/28 19
TD788.4.M2 M32 1980

**WATER QUALITY MANAGEMENT -
MASSACHUSETTS - ASSABET RIVER
WATERSHED.**
Massachusetts. Division of Water Pollution
Control. Water Quality Section. SUASCO River
basin . Westborough [1976] 106, [37] p. : LC
Card 79-620596 DDC 363.7/39456/097444 19
TD224.M4 M36 1976k

**WATER QUALITY MANAGEMENT -
MASSACHUSETTS - BUZZARDS BAY
WATERSHED.**
Beauregard, Dennis G. Buzzards Bay basin .
Westborough, Mass. [1977] 109, [33] p. : LC
Card 79-620574 DDC 363.7/39456/097448 19
TD224.M4 B42

**WATER QUALITY MANAGEMENT -
MASSACHUSETTS - CAPE COD.**
Massachusetts. Division of Water Pollution
Control. Water Quality Section. Cape Cod .
Westborough , 1976. 61, [37] p. : LC Card
77-622178 DDC 363.7/39456/0974492 19
TD224.M4 M36 1976e

**WATER QUALITY MANAGEMENT -
MASSACHUSETTS - CHARLES RIVER
WATERSHED.**
Massachusetts. Division of Water Pollution
Control. Water Quality Section. Charles River
basin . Westborough, Mass. , 1976. 143, [56]
p. : LC Card 77-622228 DDC 363.7/39456/097447
19
TD224.M4 M36 1976g

**WATER QUALITY MANAGEMENT -
MASSACHUSETTS - CHICOPEE RIVER
WATERSHED.**
Massachusetts. Division of Water Pollution
Control. Water Quality Section. Chicopee River
basin . Westborough, Mass. [1976] 86, [42] p. :
LC Card 77-622226 DDC 363.7/39456/0974426
19
TD224.M4 M36 1976j

**WATER QUALITY MANAGEMENT -
MASSACHUSETTS - CONCORD RIVER
WATERSHED.**
Massachusetts. Division of Water Pollution
Control. Water Quality Section. SUASCO River
basin . Westborough [1976] 106, [37] p. : LC
Card 79-620596 DDC 363.7/39456/097444 19
TD224.M4 M36 1976k

**WATER QUALITY MANAGEMENT -
MASSACHUSETTS - FRENCH RIVER
WATERSHED.**
Massachusetts. Division of Water Pollution
Control. Water Quality Section. French and
Quinebaug River basin . Westborough , 1975.
84, [32] p. : LC Card 79-622327 DDC
363.7/39456/097443 19
TD224.M4 M36 1975g

**WATER QUALITY MANAGEMENT -
MASSACHUSETTS - IPSWICH RIVER
WATERSHED.**
Dalton, John D. Ipswich and Parker Rivers .
Westborough, Mass. [1977] 196, [74] p. : LC
Card 79-622328 DDC 363.7/39456/097445 19
TD224.M4 D34

**WATER QUALITY MANAGEMENT -
MASSACHUSETTS - PARKER RIVER
WATERSHED.**
Dalton, John D. Ipswich and Parker Rivers .
Westborough, Mass. [1977] 196, [74] p. : LC
Card 79-622328 DDC 363.7/39456/097445 19
TD224.M4 D34

**WATER QUALITY MANAGEMENT -
MASSACHUSETTS - PLANNING.**
University of Massachusetts at Amherst. Water
Resources Research Center. Urbanization and
water quality planning . Amherst, Mass. [1979]

viii, 121 [14] p. ; LC Card 80-623703 DDC
333.91/009744 s 363.7/39456/068 19
TD224.M4 M37 no. 104

**WATER QUALITY MANAGEMENT -
MASSACHUSETTS - SUDBURY RIVER
WATERSHED.**
Massachusetts. Division of Water Pollution
Control. Water Quality Section. SUASCO River
basin . Westborough [1976] 106, [37] p. : LC
Card 79-620596 DDC 363.7/39456/097444 19
TD224.M4 M36 1976k

**WATER QUALITY MANAGEMENT -
MASSACHUSETTS - TEN MILE RIVER
WATERSHED.**
Massachusetts. Division of Water Pollution
Control. Water Quality Section. Ten Mile River
basin . Westborough , 1975. 77, [45] p. : LC
Card 77-622203 DDC 363.7/39456/0974485 19
TD224.M4 M36 1975c

**WATER QUALITY MANAGEMENT -
MASSACHUSETTS - WESTFIELD RIVER
WATERSHED.**
Massachusetts. Water Quality and Research
Section. Westfield River basin /. Westborough ,
1975. 2 v. : LC Card 77-622217 DDC
363.7/394/0974426 19
TD224.M4 M39 1975

**WATER QUALITY MANAGEMENT -
MERRIMACK RIVER WATERSHED, N.H.
AND MASS.**
Massachusetts. Division of Water Pollution
Control. Water Quality Section. Merrimack
River basin . Westborough , 1975. 101, [42] p. :
LC Card 77-622212 DDC 363.7/39456/097445
19
TD225.M514 M36 1975

**WATER QUALITY MANAGEMENT -
NEBRASKA - BIBLIOGRAPHY.**
Nebraska Water Resources Center. Water
resources publications related to the State of
Nebraska. [Lincoln] [1979] 129 p. ; LC Card
80-621398 DDC 016.33391/009782 19
Z7935 .N4 1979 TC424.N2

**WATER QUALITY MANAGEMENT -
OKLAHOMA.**
Miller, Robert L. Water quality management in
Ouachita Highland headwaters of Oklahoma .
[Oklahoma City] , 1980. xxvi, 109 p. : LC Card
80-623044 DDC 363.7/39456/097666 19
TD224.O5 M54

**WATER QUALITY MANAGEMENT -
OUACHITA MOUNTAINS.**
Miller, Robert L. Water quality management in
Ouachita Highland headwaters of Oklahoma .
[Oklahoma City] , 1980. xxvi, 109 p. : LC Card
80-623044 DDC 363.7/39456/097666 19
TD224.O5 M54

**WATER QUALITY MANAGEMENT -
QUINEBAUG RIVER WATERSHED,
CONN. AND MASS.**
Massachusetts. Division of Water Pollution
Control. Water Quality Section. French and
Quinebaug River basin . Westborough , 1975.
84, [32] p. : LC Card 79-622327 DDC
363.7/39456/097443 19
TD224.M4 M36 1975g

**WATER QUALITY MANAGEMENT -
UNITED STATES.**
Washington (State). Dept. of Ecology. Water
Quality Planning. Forest practice water quality
management plan . Olympia, Wash. [1979] iii,
56 p. : LC Card 80-621083 DDC 363.7/394 19
TD428.F67 W37 1979

**WATER QUALITY MANAGEMENT -
WASHINGTON (STATE)**
Washington (State). Dept. of Ecology. Water
Quality Planning. Dryland agriculture water
quality management plan . Olympia, Wash.
[1979] 2 v. : LC Card 80-621082 DDC
363.7/39456/09797 19
TD428.A37 W37 1979a

Washington (State). Water Resources
Management Division. Policy Development
Section. Cedar-Sammamish Basin instream
resources protection program, including
proposed administrative rules, and supplemental
environmental impact statement . Olympia,
Wash. , 1979. 148 p. in various pagings : LC
Card 79-625825 DDC 333.91/0216/0979777 19
TD224.W2 W38 1979

**WATER QUALITY MANAGEMENT -
WASHINGTON (STATE) - DESCHUTES
RIVER WATERSHED.**
Washington (State). Water Resource
Management Division. Policy Development
Section. Deschutes River Basin instream
resources protection program including
proposed administrative rules . Olympia, Wash.
[1980] 29, [52] p. : LC Card 80-623859 DDC
333.91/0216/0979779 19
TD224.W2 W38 1980

**WATER QUALITY - MASSACHUSETTS -
ASSABET RIVER WATERSHED.**
Massachusetts. Division of Water Pollution
Control. Water Quality Section. Assabet River
/. Westborough , 1974-[1975] 2 v. : LC Card
77-622221 DDC 363.7/3942/097444 19
TD224.M4 M36 1974c

**WATER QUALITY - MASSACHUSETTS -
BUZZARDS BAY WATERSHED -
STATISTICS.**
Massachusetts. Division of Water Pollution
Control. Water Quality Section. Buzzards Bay
/. Westborough, Mass. , 1975-[1976] 2 v. : LC
Card 77-622214 DDC 363.7/3942/097448 19
TD224.M4 M36 1975j

**WATER QUALITY - MASSACHUSETTS -
CHARLES RIVER WATERSHED.**
Chesebrough, Eben W. Baseline water quality
studies of selected lakes and ponds in the
Charles River Basin, 1978 /. Westborough,
Mass. [1979] 145 p. : LC Card 80-621551
DDC 363.7/3942/097447 19
TD224.M4 C45

Erdmann, John B. Charles River and Charles
Basin . Westborough, Mass. [1977] 174 p. :
LC Card 80-620705 DDC 363.7/3942/097447
19
TD224.M4 E72

Massachusetts. Water Quality and Research
Section. Charles River /. Westborough, Mass. ,
1978- v. : LC Card 79-623994 DDC
363.7/3942/097447 19
TD224.M4 M39 1978e

Massachusetts. Water Quality and Research
Section. Charles River tributaries .
Westborough, Mass. [1979] 57 p. : LC Card
79-623993 DDC 363.7/3942/097447 19
TD224.M4 M39 1979a

**WATER QUALITY - MASSACHUSETTS -
CHARLES RIVER WATERSHED -
STATISTICS.**
Ferullo, Alfred F. Charles River study, 1967 /.
Boston [1969]- v. : LC Card 80-120632 DDC
363.7/3942/097444 19
TD224.M4 F47

Massachusetts. Division of Water Pollution
Control. Water Quality Section. Charles Basin .
Westborough [1975] 1976 printing. 111 p. :
LC Card 79-620575 DDC 363.7/3942/097447
19
TD224.M4 M36 1975h

Massachusetts. Division of Water Pollution
Control. Water Quality Section. Charles River .
Westborough [1974] 112 p. : LC Card
77-622211 DDC 363.7/3942/097447 19
TD224.M4 M36 1974e

**WATER QUALITY - MASSACHUSETTS -
CHICOPEE RIVER WATERSHED.**
Massachusetts. Division of Water Pollution
Control. Water Quality Section. The Chicopee
River basin /. Westborough [1974] 2 v. : LC
Card 77-622225 DDC 363.7/3942/0974426 19
TD224.M4 M36 1974g

**WATER QUALITY - MASSACHUSETTS -
COCHITUATE, LAKE - STATISTICS.**
Massachusetts. Water Quality and Research
Section. Lake Cochituate water quality data,
June, 1977-June, 1979 /. Westborough, Mass.
[1979] 38 p. : LC Card 80-622438 DDC
363.7/3942/097444 19
TD224.M4 M368 1979a

**WATER QUALITY - MASSACHUSETTS -
COCHITUATE, LAKE, WATERSHED -
STATISTICS.**
Massachusetts. Water Quality and Research
Section. Lake Cochituate . Westborough, Mass.
[1977] 36 p. : LC Card 79-621045 DDC
363.7/3942/09444 19
TD224.M4 M39 1977j

WATER QUALITY - MASSACHUSETTS - DUNN BROOK WATERSHED - STATISTICS.
Massachusetts. Water Quality and Research Section. The upper Quaboag River basin, Dunn Brook-Seven Mile River . Westborough [1978] 48 p. :   LC Card 79-620590   DDC 363.7/3942/0974426 19
TD224.M4 M368 1978

WATER QUALITY - MASSACHUSETTS - FRENCH RIVER WATERSHED.
Anderson, Paul R. French and Quinebaug Rivers . Westborough, Mass. [1975] 123 p. :   LC Card 79-622382   DDC 363.7/3942/097443 19
TD224.M4 A7

Smith, Jeffrey B. French and Quinebaug Rivers . Westborough, Mass. [1978] 94 p. :   LC Card 79-622381   DDC 363.7/3942/097443 19
TD224.M4 S64

WATER QUALITY - MASSACHUSETTS - INDIAN LAKE WATERSHED.
Chesebrough, Eben W. Indian Lake . Westborough, Mass. [1978] 44, A-M p. :   LC Card 79-623988   DDC 363.7/3942/097443 19
TD224.M4 C477

WATER QUALITY - MASSACHUSETTS - IPSWICH RIVER WATERSHED.
Massachusetts. Water Quality and Research Section. Ipswich and Parker River basins . Westborough, Mass. [1979] 93 p. :   LC Card 79-623985   DDC 363.7/3942/097445 19
TD224.M4 M368 1979b

Tennant, Peter A. Ipswich River study, 1968 /. Boston [1969] [16] p. :   LC Card 80-118035   DDC 363.7/3942/097445 19
TD224.M4 T462 1969

WATER QUALITY - MASSACHUSETTS - MATTAWA, LAKE.
Chesebrough, Eben W. Lake Mattawa . Westborough, Mass. [1978] 49, A-O p. :   LC Card 79-620592   DDC 363.7/3942/0974422 19
TD224.M4 C479

WATER QUALITY - MASSACHUSETTS - MEASUREMENT.
Massachusetts. Water Quality and Research Section. Water quality monitoring program /. Westborough, Mass. , 1978. 262, 1a-1d, 2a-2d p. :   LC Card 79-622387   DDC 363.7/39463/09744 19
TD224.M4 M39 1978h

WATER QUALITY - MASSACHUSETTS - MILLERS RIVER WATERSHED - STATISTICS.
Cooperman, Alan N. Millers River survey, 1965 /. [Boston] [1970] 30 leaves :   LC Card 80-119079   DDC 363.7/3942/0974422 19
TD224.M4 C66

WATER QUALITY - MASSACHUSETTS - MYSTIC LAKE WATERSHED.
Chesebrough, Eben W. Upper Mystic Lake . Westborough, Mass. [1975] 75 p. :   LC Card 79-620591   DDC 363.7/3942/097444 19
TD224.M4 C488

WATER QUALITY - MASSACHUSETTS - MYSTIC RIVER WATERSHED.
Massachusetts. Division of Water Pollution Control. Water Quality Section. Mystic River /. Westboro [1974]-<1975. v. <1-3 > :   LC Card 77-622205   DDC 363.7/3942/097444 19
TD224.M4 M36 1974b

WATER QUALITY - MASSACHUSETTS - MYSTIC RIVER WATERSHED - STATISTICS.
Tennant, Peter A. Mystic River study, 1967 /. Boston [1970] 11 leaves :   LC Card 80-118857   DDC 363.7/3942/097444 19
TD224.M4 T464

WATER QUALITY - MASSACHUSETTS - NANTUCKET.
Massachusetts. Water Quality and Research Section. Nantucket . Westborough , 1978. 50 p. :   LC Card 79-623987   DDC 363.7/3942/0974497 19
TD224.M4 M39 1978a

WATER QUALITY - MASSACHUSETTS - PARKER RIVER WATERSHED.
Massachusetts. Water Quality and Research Section. Ipswich and Parker River basins .

Westborough, Mass. [1979] 93 p. :   LC Card 79-623985   DDC 363.7/3942/097445 19
TD224.M4 M368 1979b

WATER QUALITY - MASSACHUSETTS - PARKER RIVER WATERSHED - STATISTICS.
McAnespie, Robert C. Parker River study, 1968 /. Boston [1969] [11] p. :   LC Card 80-118014   DDC 363.7/3942/097445 19
TD224.M4 M27

WATER QUALITY - MASSACHUSETTS - QUABOAG RIVER WATERSHED - STATISTICS.
Massachusetts. Water Quality and Research Section. The upper Quaboag River basin, Dunn Brook-Seven Mile River . Westborough [1978] 48 p. :   LC Card 79-620590   DDC 363.7/3942/0974426 19
TD224.M4 M368 1978

WATER QUALITY - MASSACHUSETTS - SEVENMILE RIVER WATERSHED - STATISTICS.
Massachusetts. Water Quality and Research Section. The upper Quaboag River basin, Dunn Brook-Seven Mile River . Westborough [1978] 48 p. :   LC Card 79-620590   DDC 363.7/3942/0974426 19
TD224.M4 M368 1978

WATER QUALITY - MASSACHUSETTS - SHAWSHEEN RIVER WATERSHED.
Massachusetts. Division of Water Pollution Control. Water Quality Section. Shawsheen River . Westborough [1975] 59 p. :   LC Card 79-620598   DDC 363.7/3942/09444 19
TD224.M4 M36 1975f

WATER QUALITY - MASSACHUSETTS - SHAWSHEEN RIVER WATERSHED - STATISTICS.
Cooperman, Alan N. Shawsheen River study, 1968 /. Boston , 1970. 16 leaves :   LC Card 80-118847   DDC 363.7/3942/097444 19
TD224.M4 C67

WATER QUALITY - MASSACHUSETTS - STONY BROOK - STATISTICS.
Massachusetts. Division of Water Pollution Control. Water Quality Section. Stony Brook . Westborough [1975] 51 p. :   LC Card 79-620595   DDC 363.7/3942/097444 19
TD224.M4 M36 1975a

WATER QUALITY - MASSACHUSETTS - TAUNTON RIVER WATERSHED.
Salo, John E. Taunton River study . Boston [1971] 31 leaves :   LC Card 80-118663   DDC 363.7/3942/097448 19
TD224.M4 S25

WATER QUALITY - MASSACHUSETTS - WESTFIELD RIVER WATERSHED.
Kimball, Warren A. Westfield River basin . Westborough, Mass. [1975] 76, a-d p. :   LC Card 77-622234   DDC 363.7/3942/0974426 19
TD224.M4 K55

WATER QUALITY - MASSACHUSETTS - WESTFIELD RIVER WATERSHED - STATISTICS.
Massachusetts. Division of Water Pollution Control. Water Quality Section. Westfield River . Westborough [1974] 50 p. :   LC Card 80-118658   DDC 363.7/3942/0974426 19
TD224.M4 M36 1974f

WATER QUALITY - MEASUREMENT - STATISTICAL METHODS.
Stochastic analysis of water quality /. Logan [1979] viii, 75 p. :   LC Card 80-621125   DDC 628.1/61 19
TD367 .S8

WATER QUALITY - MERRIMACK RIVER WATERSHED, N.H. AND MASS.
Bilger, Michael D. Merrimack River . Westborough, Mass. [1976] i, 29 p. :   LC Card 77-622236   DDC 363.7/3942/097445 19
TD225.M574 B54

WATER QUALITY - MERRIMACK RIVER WATERSHED, N.H. AND MASS. - STATISTICS.
Massachusetts. Division of Water Pollution Control. Water Quality Section. Merrimack River . Westborough , 1974. 86 p. :   LC Card 77-622235   DDC 363.7/3942/097445 19
TD225.M514 M36 1974

WATER QUALITY - MICHIGAN, LAKE.
Chicago. Water Quality Surveillance Section. Lake Michigan water quality report, January through December 1977 /. [Chicago] [1978] 86 p. :   LC Card 79-622168   DDC 363.7/3942/097731 19
TD223.3 .C48 1978

WATER QUALITY - MICHIGAN - SHIAWASSEE RIVER.
Roycraft, Philip R. Shiawassee River study . [Lansing] , 1979. 55 p. :   LC Card 80-620626   DDC 363.7/3942/09774 19
TD224.M5 R694

WATER QUALITY - MINNESOTA.
Singer, Rexford D. Ground water quality in southeastern Minnesota /. Minneapolis, Minn. [1980] vi, 79, 64 leaves :   LC Card 80-622728   DDC 553.7/9/097761 19
TD224.M6 S56

WATER QUALITY - MISSISSIPPI RIVER.
Wells, Frank C. Hydrology and water quality of the lower Mississippi River /. Baton Rouge, La. , 1980. vii, 83 p., [5] leaves of plates (4 fold.) :   LC Card 80-622932   DDC 553.7/8/09763 19
TD223.4 .W44

WATER QUALITY - MISSOURI.
Missouri. Division of Geological Survey and Water Resources. Water quality of Big, Bourbeuse and Meramec river basins. Jefferson City, 1964. 65 p.   LC Card 66-64012
TD224.M8 M55 1964   NYPL [JSF 80-915]

Water quality monitoring program /.
Massachusetts. Water Quality and Research Section. Westborough, Mass. , 1978. 262, 1a-1d, 2a-2d p. :   LC Card 79-622387   DDC 363.7/39463/09744 19
TD224.M4 M39 1978h

WATER QUALITY - MONTANA.
Bahls, Loren L. Biological water quality monitoring, southwest Montana, 1977-1978 /. Helena , 1979. v, 60 p. :   LC Card 79-623384   DDC 553.7/8/097866 19
QH105.M9 B34

Montana. State Bureau of Mines and Geology. Regional assessment of the saline-seep problem and a water-quality inventory of the Montana Plains . Bozeman, Mont. [1980] 24 p. :   LC Card 80-623140   DDC 363.7/3942/09786 19
TD224.M9 M64 1980

Montana. Water Quality Bureau. Biological water quality monitoring, northwest Montana, 1978-1979 /. Helena, Mont. [1979] v, 59 p. ;   LC Card 80-621281   DDC 628.1/686786 19
QH96.8.B5 M66 1979

Montana. Water Quality Bureau. Water quality in Montana-1980 /. [Helena] , 1980. 247, [7] p. :   LC Card 80-623056   DDC 363.7/3942/09786 19
TD224.M9 M68 1980

WATER QUALITY - NASHUA RIVER WATERSHED, MASS. AND N.H.
Bilger, Michael D. Nashua River . Westborough, Mass. [1978] iv leaves, 45 p. :   LC Card 79-624432   DDC 363.7/3942/097443 19
TD225.N2 B54

Chesebrough, Eben W. Baseline water quality surveys of selected lakes and ponds in the Nashua River basin, 1977 /. Westborough, Mass. [1978] 141 p. :   LC Card 79-620602   DDC 363.7/3942/097443 19
TD225.N2 C47

WATER QUALITY - NEBRASKA - STATISTICS.
Engberg, R. A. A statistical analysis of the quality of surface water in Nebraska /. Washington , 1981. p. cm.   LC Card 81-2161   DDC 553.7/9/09782 19
TD224.N18 E5

WATER QUALITY - NEW MEXICO - STATISTICS.
New Mexico. Environmental Improvement Division. Water Supply Section. Chemical quality of New Mexico community water supplies, 1980 . [Santa Fe] [1980] 256 p. ;   LC Card 80-624082   DDC 363.6/1 19
TD224.N6 N47 1980

WATER QUALITY - NORTH CAROLINA - CHOWAN RIVER.

WATER QUALITY - NORTH CAROLINA - CHOWAN RIVER. (cont.)

North Carolina. State University, Raleigh. Dept. of Botany. Response of phytoplankton to water quality in the Chowan River system /. [Raleigh, N.C.] [1979] xv, 204 p. : LC Card 79-626203 DDC 589.4 19
HD1694.N8 N6 no. 129 QK571.5.N8

WATER QUALITY - NORTH CAROLINA - UNIVERSITY LAKE.
Kuenzler, Edward J. Phosphorus dynamics in a North Carolina Piedmont reservoir /. Raleigh, N.C. [1980] xii, 56 p. : LC Card 80-622281 DDC 333.91/009756 s 628.1/32 19
HD1694.N8 N6 no. 154 TD427.P56

WATER QUALITY - NORTH DAKOTA - METIGOSHE LAKE.
North Dakota. Agricultural Experiment Station, Fargo. Bacteriological analyses of Lake Metigoshe water and sediments /. Fargo , 1978. ii, 14 p. : LC Card 79-625005 DDC 363.7/3942/0978461 19
QR48 .N67 1978

WATER QUALITY - NORTH DAKOTA - STATISTICS.
Ragan, James E. Water quality of selected North Dakota lakes /. [Bismarck, N.D.] , 1978. [112] p. : LC Card 79-626040 DDC 553.7/8/09784 19
TD224.N9 R33

Water quality of Big, Bourbeuse and Meramec river basins. Missouri. Division of Geological Survey and Water Resources. Jefferson City, 1964. 65 p. LC Card 66-64012
TD224.M8 M55 1964   NYPL [JSF 80-915]

Water quality of Livingston Reservoir on the Trinity River, Southeastern Texas /. Rawson, Jack. Austin, Tex. , 1979. v, 46 p. : LC Card 79-625432 DDC 553.7/8/0976416 19
TD224.T4 A333 no. 230

Water quality of selected North Dakota lakes /. Ragan, James E. [Bismarck, N.D.] , 1978. [112] p. : LC Card 79-626040 DDC 553.7/8/09784 19
TD224.N9 R33

WATER QUALITY - OHIO - OTTAWA RIVER WATERSHED.
Ohio. Division of Surveillance and Water Quality Standards. Water quality study of the Ottawa River, Allen and Putnam Counties, Ohio /. [Columbus] , 1979. 35, [35] p., [4] leaves of plates : LC Card 80-621710 DDC 363.7/3942/09771 19
TD224.O3 O254 1979

WATER QUALITY - POTOMAC RIVER WATERSHED.
Rasin, V. James. Potomac River Basin water quality, 1978-1979 /. Rockville, Md. (1055 1st St., Rockville 20850) [1980] vii, 77, 22 p. : LC Card 80-624161 DDC 363.7/3942/0972 19
TD225.P74 R373

WATER QUALITY - QUINEBAUG RIVER WATERSHED, CONN. AND MASS.
Anderson, Paul R. French and Quinebaug Rivers . Westborough, Mass. [1975] 123 p. : LC Card 79-622382 DDC 363.7/3942/097443 19
TD224.M4 A7

Smith, Jeffrey B. French and Quinebaug Rivers . Westborough, Mass. [1978] 94 p. : LC Card 79-622381 DDC 363.7/3942/097443 19
TD224.M4 S64

WATER QUALITY - REMOTE SENSING - CONGRESSES.
Remote sensing and problems of the hydrosphere . Washington, D.C. [Springfield, Va.] 1979. v, 56 p. : LC Card 81-601298 DDC 551.4/028/7 19
TD370 .R45

Water quality report /. Iowa. Chemicals and Water Quality Division. Planning Section. [Des Moines] , 1977. 437 p. in various pagings : LC Card 80-622135 DDC 363.7/3942/09777 19
TD224.I8 I56 1977

Water quality series :
(UWRL/Q-79/01) Stochastic analysis of water quality /. Logan [1979] viii, 75 p. : LC Card 80-621125 DDC 628.1/61 19
TD367 .S8

(UWRL/Q-79/02) Utah Water Research Laboratory. Studies on viruses in water /. Logan, Utah , 1979. viii, 35 p. : LC Card 80-621126   DDC 628.3 19
QR48 .U8 1979

(UWRL/Q-79/03) Cowan, Peter A. Modeling the performance of the intermittent sand filter /. Logan, Utah [1979] xii, 115 p. : LC Card 80-622170 DDC 628.3/52/0724 19
TD753 .C68

(UWRL/Q-79/04) Evaluation of in-line direct filtration for virus removal /. Logan, Utah [1979]. xi, 93 p. : LC Card 80-622171 DDC 628.1/64 19
TD753 .E88

(UWRL/Q-79/06) Finney, Brad A. Random differential equations in water quality modeling /. Logan, Utah [1979] viii, 41 p. : LC Card 80-622173 DDC 553.7/028 19
TD367 .F56

WATER QUALITY - SOUTH DAKOTA - MAPS.
United States. Soil Conservation Service. Water quality characteristics of major streams, western South Dakota river basins /. Lincoln, Nebr. , 1978. 3 maps on sheet : LC Card 81-691107
G4181.C35 1978 .U5

WATER QUALITY - SPOKANE RIVER WATERSHED, IDAHO AND WASH.
Yake, William E. Water quality trend analysis . Olympia, WA [1979] 39, 5 p. : LC Card 79-625821 DDC 363.7/3942/097973 19
TD225.S56 Y34

WATER QUALITY - STANDARDS - ECONOMIC ASPECTS - ILLINOIS.
Huff, Linda L. Economic impact analysis of proposed change in Illinois deoxygenating regulations, R77-12, docket C /. Chicago , 1979. xvii, 78 p. : LC Card 80-620894 DDC 363.7/394 19
TD224.I3 H833

WATER QUALITY - STANDARDS - OKLAHOMA.
Oklahoma. Water Resources Board. Oklahoma's water quality standards, 1976. Oklahoma City, Okla. [197-?] 91 p. : LC Card 80-622277 DDC 333.91/009766 s 363.7/39462/09766 19
TD224.O5 A3 no. 79

WATER QUALITY - STATISTICAL METHODS.
Finney, Brad A. Random differential equations in water quality modeling /. Logan, Utah [1979] viii, 41 p. : LC Card 80-622173 DDC 553.7/028 19
TD367 .F56

Water quality study of the Ottawa River, Allen and Putnam Counties, Ohio /. Ohio. Division of Surveillance and Water Quality Standards. [Columbus] , 1979. 35, [35] p., [4] leaves of plates : LC Card 80-621710 DDC 363.7/3942/09771 19
TD224.O3 O254 1979

Water quality survey. Ohio. Division of Surveillance and Water Quality Standards. Water quality study of the Ottawa River, Allen and Putnam Counties, Ohio /. [Columbus] , 1979. 35, [35] p., [4] leaves of plates : LC Card 80-621710 DDC 363.7/3942/09771 19
TD224.O3 O254 1979

WATER QUALITY - TAHOE, LAKE.
Brown, Randall L. Lake Tahoe water quality . [Sacramento] [1979] 78 p. : LC Card 80-621413 DDC 363.7/3942/0979438 19
TD225.T25 B76

WATER QUALITY - TEXAS.
Texas. Dept. of Water Resources. Construction Grants and Water Quality Planning Division. The State of Texas water quality inventory /. [Austin] , 1980. 540 p., 1 fold. leaf of plates : LC Card 80-622419 DDC 363.7/3942/09764 19
TD224.T4 T36 1980a

WATER QUALITY - TEXAS - LIVINGSTON, LAKE.
Rawson, Jack. Water quality of Livingston Reservoir on the Trinity River, Southeastern Texas /. Austin, Tex. , 1979. v, 46 p. : LC Card 79-625432 DDC 553.7/8/0976416 19
TD224.T4 A333 no. 230

WATER QUALITY - TEXAS - LYNDON B. JOHNSON, LAKE.
Texas. University at Austin. Center for Research in Water Resources. Before and after studies on the effects of a power plant installation on Lake Lyndon B. Johnson . Austin [1971?] xiv, 145 p. : LC Card 79-624702 DDC 333.91/62/0976462 19
TD224.T4 T42 1971

WATER QUALITY - TEXAS - TRINITY RIVER WATERSHED.
Trinity River Authority of Texas. Planning and Environmental Management Division. Low flow nutrient loss in the mid-Trinity River ; Runoff-related pollutant loadings in the mid-Trinity River /. [Austin] , 1978. iii, 72, iv, 73 p. : LC Card 80-622543 DDC 363.7/3942/097642 19
TD224.T4 T74 1978

Water quality trend analysis . Yake, William E. Olympia, WA [1979] 39, 5 p. : LC Card 79-625821 DDC 363.7/3942/097973 19
TD225.S56 Y34

WATER QUALITY - UNITED STATES.
Smith, Richard A. A study of trends in total phosphorus measurements at NASQAN stations /. Reston, Va. [1981] p. cm. LC Card 81-607899 DDC 363.7/394 19
TD427.P56 S64

United States. Congress. House. Committee on Interstate and Foreign Commerce. Subcommittee on Health and the Environment. Quality of drinking water--1980 . Washington, 1980. vii, 714 p. : LC Card 80-604005 DDC 363.6/1 19
KF27 .I5543 1980n

United States. Library of Congress. Congressional Research Service. State and national water use trends to the year 2000 . Washington , 1980. x, 297 p. : LC Card 80-602584 DDC 333.91/13/0973 19
TD223 .U53 1980a

WATER QUALITY - VIRGINIA.
Erkenbrecher, Carl W. Sediment bacteria as a water quality indicator in the Lynnhaven estuary /. Blacksburg, Va. [1980] x, 118 p. : LC Card 80-622517 DDC 333.91/009755 s 628.168/028/7 19
TD201 .V57 no. 126 QR48

WATER QUALITY - WASHINGTON (STATE)
Investigation to determine extent and nature of nonpoint source enrichment and hydrology of several recreational lakes of eastern Washington . Pullman , 1976. xvi, 309 p. : LC Card 79-623617 DDC 553.7/09797 s 333.91/631/09797 19
TD224.W2 S8 no. 26 GB1625.W2

WATER QUALITY - WASHINGTON (STATE) - BUDD INLET WATERSHED.
Kruger, Dan M. Effects of point-source discharges and other inputs on water quality in Budd Inlet, Washington /. Olympia, WA [1979] xiv, 40, 37 p. : LC Card 80-623150 DDC 333.91/64 19
TD224.W2 K78

WATER QUALITY - WASHINGTON (STATE) - CAPITOL LAKE.
CH2M Hill, inc. Water quality in Capitol Lake, Olympia, Washington /. [Corvallis, Or.] , 1978. 116 p. in various pagings : LC Card 79-621289
TD224.W2 C18 1978   NYPL [JSF 81-45]

WATER QUALITY - WYOMING.
Wells, Deborah K. Chemical analyses of water from the Minnelusa Formation and equivalents in the Powder River Basin and adjacent areas, northeastern Wyoming . Cheyenne [1979] iii, 27 p., [1] leaf of plates : LC Card 79-622599 DDC 553.7/9/097871 19
TD224.W8 W44

WATER RECLAMATION. see WATER REUSE.

Water-related aesthetic preferences of Wyoming residents /. Hampe, Gary D. Laramie [1974] 111 p. : LC Card 74-623922 DDC 553.7/09787 s 719 19
TD201 .W9 no. 46 BH301.L3

WATER RENOVATION. see WATER REUSE.

Water research progress at OSU : seminar, fall quarter 1978 / conducted by Water Resources Research Institute, Oregon State University. [Corvallis, Or.] : The Institute, 1979. 101 p. : ill. ; 27 cm. "SEMIN WR 025-79." Includes bibliographies. LC Card 79-626121 DDC 551.48 19
1. Hydrology - Research - Oregon - Congresses. I. Oregon. State University, Corvallis. Water Resources

Research Institute.
GB658.7 .W37

WATER RESOURCE DEVELOPMENT - EUROPE.
United Nations. Economic Commission for Europe. Manual for the compilation of balances of water resources and needs /. New York , 1974. viii, 80 p. :   LC Card 80-513013   DDC 300 s 333.91/0094 19
JX1977 .A2 ECE/WATER/5

Water resources and industrial development in Mississippi : opportunities and constraints / by Kenneth W. Hollman ... [et al.]. Mississippi State, Miss. : Water Resources Research Institute, Mississippi State University, [1979] v, 58 leaves : forms ; 28 cm. "Project no. A-128-MISS." Bibliography: leaves 42-46.   LC Card 80-622324   DDC 333.91/23/09762 19
1. Water-supply, Industrial - Mississippi. I. Hollman, Kenneth W.
TD224.M65 W35

WATER RESOURCES DEVELOPMENT.
United States. Geological Survey. Water power of the world . Washington , 1918. [7] leaves of plates :   LC Card 80-675255   DDC 912/.133391
G1046.N33 U53 1918

WATER RESOURCES DEVELOPMENT - BEAR LAKE REGION, IDAHO AND UTAH.
Andrews, Wade H. Social effects of changes in uses of Bear Lake, an interstate body of water /. Logan , 1975. x, 119 p. :   LC Card 77-623439   DDC 333.91/63/0979213 19
HD1695.B38 A52

WATER RESOURCES DEVELOPMENT - BIBLIOGRAPHY.
United Nations. Dag Hammarskjold Library. Water resources, planning, and management . New York , 1977. vi, 117 p. ;   LC Card 81-478046   DDC 300 s 016.33391 19
JX1977 .A2 ST/LIB/SER.B/23 TC405

WATER RESOURCES DEVELOPMENT - BIBLIOGRAPHY - PERIODICALS.
California. University. Water Resources Center. Archives. Dictionary catalog of the Water Resources Center Archives, University of California, Berkeley. Supplement. 1st- ; 1971- Boston.   **NYPL [JSK 73-123 Suppl.]**

WATER RESOURCES DEVELOPMENT - BLUESTONE RIVER WATERSHED, VA. AND W. VA.
West Virginia. Division of Water Resources. Comprehensive survey of the Bluestone River Basin. Charleston , [1978- v. <1> :   LC Card 79-624203   DDC 333.91/009754/74 19
TC425.B54 W47 1978

WATER RESOURCES DEVELOPMENT - CALIFORNIA.
California. Dept. of Water Resources. California water /. [Sacramento, CA [1979] 84 p. :   LC Card 80-621391   DDC 333.91/15/09794 19
TC424.C2 C28 1979

WATER RESOURCES DEVELOPMENT - CALIFORNIA - COST EFFECTIVENESS.
California. Dept. of Finance. Program Evaluation Unit. Review of Davis-Dolwig allocation methodology . [Sacramento] [1979] xviii, 85 p. :   LC Card 80-620662   DDC 333.78/09794 19
GV191.42.C2 C33 1979

WATER RESOURCES DEVELOPMENT - ENVIRONMENTAL ASPECTS - COLUMBIA RIVER VALLEY.
Washington (State). Dept. of Ecology. Columbia River instream resource protection program . Olympia, Wash. [1980] iii, 185, [79] p. :   LC Card 80-623147   DDC 333.91/009797 19
HD1695.C73 W37 1980

WATER RESOURCES DEVELOPMENT - ENVIRONMENTAL ASPECTS - THE WEST - BIBLIOGRAPHY.
Western Energy and Land Use Team. Western Energy and Land Use Team publications . Fort Collins, Colo. [1979] x, 35 p. ;   LC Card 80-601848   DDC 016.3337/0978 19
Z7164.L3 W48 1979 HD209

WATER RESOURCES DEVELOPMENT - ENVIRONMENTAL ASPECTS - WASHINGTON (STATE)
Washington (State). Dept. of Ecology. Columbia River instream resource protection program .

Olympia, Wash. [1980] iii, 185, [79] p. :   LC Card 80-623147   DDC 333.91/009797 19
HD1695.C73 W37 1980

Washington (State). Dept. of Ecology. Final environmental impact statement (including program overview) . [Olympia] , 1979. [78] p. :   LC Card 79-625437   DDC 333.7/1/09797 19
HD1694.W2 W37 1979

WATER RESOURCES DEVELOPMENT - GOVERNMENT POLICY - UNITED STATES.
United States. Congress. Senate. Committee on Environment and Public Works. Subcommittee on Water Resources. To establish a national water policy . Washington , 19<7. v. <2> :   LC Card 81-461639   DDC 333.91/00973 19
KF26 .E683 1978

WATER RESOURCES DEVELOPMENT - GREAT BASIN.
Utah. Division of Water Resources. Specific problem analysis summary report . [Salt Lake City] , 1977. 87 p., [1] leaf of plates :   LC Card 80-620890   DDC 333.9/1/09792 19
TC423.6 .U82 1977

WATER RESOURCES DEVELOPMENT - IDAHO.
Idaho. Water Resource Board. Water conservation & development projects . [Boise, Idaho] [1979] 134 p. in various pagings :   LC Card 80-621480   DDC 333.91/02/0979637 19
TC424.I2 I3 1979

WATER RESOURCES DEVELOPMENT - ILLINOIS - CANTEEN CREEK WATERSHED.
Booker Associates. Strategic planning study, Canteen Creek watershed, Madison & St. Clair Counties /. St. Louis, Mo. [1978] iiii, 46, [17] leaves, 19 fold. leaves of plates :   LC Card 79-623263   DDC 627/.12/0977386 19
TC424.I3 B66 1978

WATER RESOURCES DEVELOPMENT - KANSAS.
Kansas. State Water Resources Board. Compilation of socio-economic, land use, and water use information and projections for the 1975 national water assessment. [Topeka] , 1979. 54 p. :   LC Card 80-622138   DDC 333.91/13/09781 19
HD211.K2 K36 1979

WATER RESOURCES DEVELOPMENT - LAKE CHAMPLAIN WATERSHED.
Lake Champlain Basin Study (United States.) Shaping the future of Lake Champlain . [Boston, Mass.] [1979] x, 124, 45 p. ;   LC Card 80-622025   DDC 333.91/6316/097454 19
TD225.L252 L34 1979

WATER RESOURCES DEVELOPMENT - LAW AND LEGISLATION - CHESAPEAKE BAY REGION (MD. AND VA.)
United States. Congress. Senate. Committee on Governmental Affairs. Subcommittee on Governmental Efficiency and the District of Columbia. Chesapeake Bay Research Coordination Act . Washington , 1980. iv, 199 p. ;   LC Card 80-603783   DDC 346.7304/69164 347.306469164 19
KF26 .G6735 1980b

WATER RESOURCES DEVELOPMENT - LAW AND LEGISLATION - UNITED STATES.
United States. Congress. House. Committee on Public Works. Subcommittee on Flood Control and Internal Development. River basin monetary authorizations. Washington , 1972. iii, 50 p.   LC Card 72-600616
NYPL [JLE 81-118]

WATER RESOURCES DEVELOPMENT - LAW AND LEGISLATION - VIRGINIA.
Cox, William Edward, 1944- Virginia water law . Blacksburg, Va. , 1979. 15 p. ;   LC Card 80-622367   DDC 346.75504/691 19
KFV2846.Z9 C68

WATER RESOURCES DEVELOPMENT - MAINE - KENNEBEC RIVER WATERSHED.
United States. New England River Basins Commission. Kennebec River Basin overview /. [Boston, Mass.] [1979] ix, 158, [22] p. :   LC Card 80-622003   DDC 333.91/02/0974122 19
TC424.M2 U54 1979

WATER RESOURCES DEVELOPMENT - MINNESOTA - BUFFALO RIVER WATERSHED.
Minnesota. Water Resources Board. Overall plan, Buffalo-Red River Watershed District . [St. Paul] , 1979. iii, iv, 85 p. :   LC Card 79-624540   DDC 333.91/009776/9 19
HD1694.M6 M58 1979

WATER RESOURCES DEVELOPMENT - MINNESOTA - RED RIVER WATERSHED (RED RIVER OF THE NORTH)
Minnesota. Water Resources Board. Overall plan, Buffalo-Red River Watershed District . [St. Paul] , 1979. iii, iv, 85 p. :   LC Card 79-624540   DDC 333.91/009776/9 19
HD1694.M6 M58 1979

WATER RESOURCES DEVELOPMENT - MONTANA.
Future development projections and hydrologic modeling in the Yellowstone River Basin, Montana /. Helena, MT , 1977. xi, 141 p. :   LC Card 80-623619   DDC 333.91/009786/3 19
TC424.M9 F87

WATER RESOURCES DEVELOPMENT - NEBRASKA - BIBLIOGRAPHY.
Nebraska Water Resources Center. Water resources publications related to the State of Nebraska. [Lincoln] [1979] 129 p. ;   LC Card 80-621398   DDC 016.33391/009782 19
Z7935 .N4 1979 TC424.N2

WATER RESOURCES DEVELOPMENT - NEBRASKA - LITTLE NEMAHA RIVER WATERSHED - MAPS.
United States. Soil Conservation Service. Water, fisheries, and pollution resources map lower Little Nemaha watershed, Johnson, Nemaha, Otoe and Richardson Counties, Nebraska /. Lincoln, Nebr. , 1978. 1 map :   LC Card 81-691088
G4192.L5C3 1978 .U5

United States. Soil Conservation Service. Water resources map, upper Little Nemaha watershed, Lancaster, Cass, and Otoe Counties, Nebraska /. Lincoln, Nebr. , 1979. 1 map :   LC Card 81-691085
G4192.L5C3 1979 .U5

WATER RESOURCES DEVELOPMENT - NORTH CAROLINA.
North Carolina. Legislative Study Commission on Alternatives for Water Management. Alternatives for water management . [Raleigh, N.C.] [1980] ca. 100 p. in various pagings ;   LC Card 80-622778   DDC 333.91/15/09756 19
TC424.N8 N59 1980

WATER RESOURCES DEVELOPMENT - NORTHWEST, PACIFIC - FINANCE - CONGRESSES.
Non-Federal financing of water resources development . Corvallis, 1978. 80 p. ;   LC Card 79-621887
HD1695.N74 N66   **NYPL [JLF 80-1601]**

WATER RESOURCES DEVELOPMENT - NORTHWESTERN STATES.
United States. Pacific Northwest River Basins Commission. Water--today and tomorrow. [Vancouver, Wash. , 1979] 3 v. :   LC Card 80-622316   DDC 333.91/009795 19
TC423.7 .U54 1979

WATER RESOURCES DEVELOPMENT - OKLAHOMA.
Oklahoma. Water Resources Board. Oklahoma comprehensive water plan. [Oklahoma City] , 1980. ii, 248 p. :   LC Card 80-623045   DDC 333.91/009766 s 333.91/15/09766 19
TD224.O5 A3 no. 94 TC424.O5

WATER RESOURCES DEVELOPMENT - OKLAHOMA - PLANNING.
Westphal, Joseph W. Commitments, priorities, and organizational options for water resource planning in Oklahoma /. [Stillwater] [1979] xix, 346 p. :   LC Card 80-622933   DDC 333.91/15/09766 19
TC424.O5 W47

WATER RESOURCES DEVELOPMENT - PLANNING.
Whipple, William, 1909- Principles of water resources planning (phase II) /. [New Brunswick] [1978] 26 leaves ;   LC Card 79-623366   DDC 333.91 19
TC409 .W48

WATER RESOURCES DEVELOPMENT - PUGET SOUND AREA.
Spencer, Wallace H. Environmental management of Puget Sound . Seattle [1971] 50 p. ;   LC Card 80-505800   DDC 333.91/009797/7 19
HD1695.P83 S67

WATER RESOURCES DEVELOPMENT - RESEARCH - CALIFORNIA.
California. University. Water Resources Center. Chronicle of research /. Davis, CA [1980] vii, 148 p. ;   LC Card 80-623772   DDC 553.7/09794 s 333.91/00720794 19
TD224.C3 C3 no. 48

WATER RESOURCES DEVELOPMENT - RESEARCH - MASSACHUSETTS - EVALUATION.
Kreplick, Ruth. Effectiveness of information transfer through water resources researcher/user group interaction /. Amherst , 1976. xvii, 144 p. ;   LC Card 78-622292   DDC 333.91/009744 s 333.91/0072 19
TD224.M4 M37 no. 73

WATER RESOURCES DEVELOPMENT - RESEARCH - UNITED STATES.
United States. Bureau of Reclamation. Reclamation research . [Washington] , 1979. vi, 121 p. :   LC Card 80-602385   DDC 333.91/0072073 19
TC423 .U48 1979

WATER RESOURCES DEVELOPMENT - TEXAS.
Texas. Legislature. Senate. Texas water administration . [Austin] [197-] v, 87 p. ;   LC Card 80-622555   DDC 353.97640082/325 19
HD1694.T4 T3 1970

WATER RESOURCES DEVELOPMENT - UNITED STATES.
Final report on Phase I of water policy implementation . [Washington, D.C.?] , 1980. 99 p. in various pagings ;   LC Card 81-600744   DDC 333.91/160973 19
TC423 .F57

Integrating water resources and land use planning /. Logan , 1979. xii, 114 p. :   LC Card 79-624686   DDC 333.91/00973 19
HD1694.A5 I56

Platt, Rutherford H. Intergovernmental management of floodplains /. [Boulder] , 1980. xv, 317 p. :   LC Card 80-82675   DDC 350.82/329/0973 19
HD1694 .A5126 1980

WATER RESOURCES DEVELOPMENT - UNITED STATES - FINANCE.
United States. Congress. House. Committee on Appropriations. Subcommittee on Energy and Water Development. Energy and water development appropriations for 1982 . Washington , 1981. 2 v. (2710, xviii p.) ;   LC Card 81-601647   DDC 353.0072/236823 19
KF27 .A64 1981

United States. Congress. Senate. Committee on Appropriations. Subcommittee on Energy and Water Development. Energy and water development appropriations for fiscal year 1981 . Washington , 1980- v. ;   LC Card 80-603292   DDC 353.0072/23682325 19
KF26 .A6469 1980a

WATER RESOURCES DEVELOPMENT - UNITED STATES - HISTORY.
Holmes, Beatrice Hort. History of Federal water resources programs and policies, 1961-70 /. Washington, D.C. [1979] ix, 331 p. ;   LC Card 80-601049   DDC 630 s 363.6 19
S21 .A46 no. 1379 HD1694.A5

WATER RESOURCES DEVELOPMENT - UTAH - ESCALANTE RIVER WATERSHED.
The Escalante River Basin multiobjective resource planning /. [Salt Lake City] [1978] xi, 127 p. :   LC Card 79-624078   DDC 333.91/02/0979251 19
TC424.U8 E72

WATER RESOURCES DEVELOPMENT - UTAH - PERIODICALS.
Utah. Division of Water Resources. Developing a state water plan; ground water conditions in Utah. [Salt Lake City].   *NYPL [JSP 81-11]*

WATER RESOURCES DEVELOPMENT - WASHINGTON (STATE)
Spencer, Wallace H. Environmental management of Puget Sound . Seattle [1971] 50 p. ;   LC Card 80-505800   DDC 333.91/009797/7 19
HD1695.P83 S67

WATER RESOURCES DEVELOPMENT - WASHINGTON (STATE) - BIG BEND BASIN.
United States. Pacific Northwest River Basins Commission. Washington State Study Team. The Big Bend Basin level B study of the water & related land resources /. [Vancouver, Wash.] , 1976. x, 106, [64] p., [1] fold. leaf of plates ;   LC Card 77-624406
TC425.B44 U54 1976

WATER RESOURCES DEVELOPMENT - YELLOWSTONE RIVER WATERSHED.
Future development projections and hydrologic modeling in the Yellowstone River Basin, Montana /. Helena, MT , 1977. xi, 141 p. :   LC Card 80-623619   DDC 333.91/009786/3 19
TC424.M9 F87

Water resources-information series .
(report 23) Glancy, Patrick A. A reconnaissance of streamflow and fluvial sediment transport, Incline Village area, Lake Tahoe, Nevada . Carson City , 1976. v, 42 p. ;   LC Card 80-623612   DDC 551.48/09793/57 19
GB1225.N3 G56

(report 26) Harrill, J. R. Water-level changes associated with ground-water development in Las Vegas Valley, Nevada, March 1975 to March 1976 /. Carson City , 1976 i.e. 1977. iv, 31 p. :   LC Card 80-624035   DDC 553.7/9/0979313 19
GB1025.N4 H38

(report 28) Schroer, C. V. Nevada streamflow characteristics /. Carson City [1978] 478 p. :   LC Card 80-623614   DDC 551.48/3/09793 19
GB1225.N3 S37

Water Resources Information System. WRIS technical bulletin .
(no. 23) Olson, Theodore M. Ground water resources of Five Mile Prairie, Spokane County, Washington /. Olympia, Wash. [1979] iv, 30 p. :   LC Card 80-621127   DDC 553.7/9/0979737 19
GB1025.W2 O47

Water resources of Boulder County, Colorado /.
United States. Geological Survey. Denver, Colo. , 1980. vii, 97 p. :   LC Card 80-623575   DDC 553.7/09788/63 19
GB705.C6 U54 1980

Water resources, planning, and management .
United Nations. Dag Hammarskjold Library. New York , 1977. vi, 117 p. ;   LC Card 81-478046   DDC 300 s 016.33391 19
JX1977 .A2 ST/LIB/SER.B/23 TC405

Water resources planning series .
(P-79/03) Utah Water Research Laboratory. Estimation of water surface elevation probabilities and associated damages for the Great Salt Lake /. Logan, Utah , 1979. xi, 182 p. :   LC Card 80-621436   DDC 551.48/2/0979242 19
TC425.G72 U85 1979

(UWRL/P-78/07) Utah's 1977 drought /. Logan , 1978. viii, 49 p. :   LC Card 79-624684   DDC 363.3/492 19
QC929.D8 U72

(UWRL/P-79/01) Integrating water resources and land use planning /. Logan , 1979. xii, 114 p. :   LC Card 79-624686   DDC 333.91/00973 19
HD1694.A5 I56

(UWRL/P-79/04) Hughes, Trevor C. Domestic water demand in Utah /. Logan, Utah [1979] viii, 61 p. :   LC Card 80-621122   DDC 333.91/22 19
TD224.U8 H83

(UWRL/P-79/05) Larson, Dean T. Levels of analysis in comprehensive river basin planning /. Logan, Utah , 1979. ix, 110 p. :   LC Card 80-621123   DDC 333.91/02 19
TC425.C6 L37

(UWRL/P-79/07) Narayanan, Rangesan. An economic evaluation of the salinity impacts from energy development . Logan, Utah , 1979. x, 71 p. :   LC Card 80-622072   DDC 363.7/394 19
TD195.E5 N37

(UWRL/P-80/02) Bagley, Jay M. Feasibility

study of establishing a water rights banking/brokering service in Utah /. Logan, Utah [1980] vii, 33 p. ;   LC Card 80-623594   DDC 363.6/1 19
HD1694.U8 B34

Water resources publications related to the State of Nebraska.
Nebraska Water Resources Center. [Lincoln] [1979] 129 p. ;   LC Card 80-621398   DDC 016.33391/009782 19
Z7935 .N4 1979 TC424.N2

Water Resources Research Institute, New Mexico State University. see New Mexico State University. Water Resources Research Institute.

Water resources special report .
(no. 2) Cardwell, George T., 1922- Pumpage of water in Louisiana, 1975 /. Baton Rouge, La. , 1979. iv, 15 p. :   LC Card 80-620624   DDC 333.91/13/09763 19
TD224.L8 C37

Water Resources Support Center (U. S.)
The port of Buffalo, New York / prepared by Water Resources Support Center. Washington : U. S. Govt. Print. Off. ; Fort Belvoir, VA : for sale by the Center, 1980. vi, 55 p. : ill., map (fold. in pocket) ; 27 cm. (Port series . no. 41, rev. 1980) At head of title: Corps of Engineers, U. S. Army. Previous ed. prepared by Board of Engineers for Rivers and Harbors.   LC Card 80-601613   DDC 386./8/0974797 19
1. Buffalo - Harbor. I. United States. Board of Engineers for Rivers and Harbors. The port of Buffalo, New York. II. Title.
HE554.B8 W37 1980

The ports of Baton Rouge and Lake Charles, Louisiana / prepared by Water Resources Support Center. Rev. Washington : U. S. Govt. Print. Off. ; Fort Belvoir, VA : for sale by Water Resources Support Center, 1979. vi, 114 p., [1] leaf of plates : ill. ; 26 cm. (Port series . no. 21, rev. 1979) At head of title: Corps of Engineers, U. S. Army. Part of illustrative matter in pocket. Includes index.   LC Card 80-601764   DDC 387.1/09763/18 19
1. Baton Rouge, La. - Harbor. 2. Lake Charles, La. - Harbor. I. Title.
TC225.B37 W37 1979

Ports of Hawaii . Washington , Fort Belvoir, Va. , 1980. vi, 78 p. :   LC Card 80-603619   DDC 387.1/09969 19
HE554.A6 P63 1980

Water resources technical publication.
Jansen, Robert B., 1922- Dams and public safety /. Denver, Colo. , Washington, D.C. , 1980. xii, 332 p. :   LC Card 80-602658   DDC 627/.8/0289 19
TC556 .J36

Water resources technical report .
(no. 20) Whiteman, C. D. Measuring local subsidence with extensometers in the Baton Rouge area, Louisiana, 1975-1979 /. Baton Rouge, La. , 1980. iv, 18 p. :   LC Card 80-621814   DDC 551.4/4 19
QE600.3.U6 W48

(no. 21) Wells, Frank C. Hydrology and water quality of the lower Mississippi River /. Baton Rouge, La. , 1980. vii, 83 p., [5] leaves of plates (4 fold.) :   LC Card 80-622932   DDC 553.7/8/09763 19
TD223.4 .W44

(no. 22) Forbes, Max J., 1930- Low-flow characteristics of Louisiana streams /. Baton Rouge, La. , 1980. iv, 95 p., [1] fold. leaf of plates :   LC Card 80-623625   DDC 551.48/3/09763 19
GB1225.L6 F67

WATER REUSE - CALIFORNIA.
Bruvold, William H. Public attitudes toward community wastewater reclamation and reuse options /. Davis, Calif. , 1979. v, 51 p. ;   LC Card 80-621184   DDC 333.91/009794 s 363.6/1 19
GB705.C2 C27 no. 179 TD429

WATER-RIGHTS - ALASKA.
Alaska. Division of Forest, Land, and Water Management. Water Management Section. Federal lands in Alaska and their reserved water rights . Anchorage, Alaska [1979] 222 leaves in various foliations :   LC Card 80-622413   DDC 346.79804/691 347.98064691 19
KFA1646 .A844

WATER-RIGHTS - CALIFORNIA.
Archibald, Marybelle. Appropriative water
rights in California . [Sacramento] , 1977. 63
p. ;　LC Card 79-624937　DDC 346.79404/691 19
KFC790 .A97

WATER-RIGHTS - MISSOURI.
Davis, Peter N. Missouri instream flow
requirements . Jefferson City, Mo. [1980] xviii,
415 p., [1] fold. leaf of plates :　LC Card
　80-623733　DDC 346.77804/691 347.78064691
　19
KFM8246 .D36

WATER-RIGHTS - MONTANA.
Utter, Jack. Wild river management . Bozeman,
MT [1980] xiii, 117 leaves :　LC Card 80-623137
　DDC 333.78/45 19
TD224.M9 U88

WATER-RIGHTS - OHIO.
Callahan, Charles C. Principles of water rights
law in Ohio /. [Columbus, Ohio] [1979] xiii,
48 p. :　LC Card 80-622377　DDC 346.77104/691
　19
KFO446 .C34 1979

WATER-RIGHTS - UNITED STATES.
Alaska. Division of Forest, Land, and Water
Management. Water Management Section.
Federal lands in Alaska and their reserved
water rights . Anchorage, Alaska [1979] 222
leaves in various foliations :　LC Card 80-622413
　DDC 346.79804/691 347.98064691 19
KFA1646 .A844

Althaus, Helen F. Public trust rights /.
[Washington] , 1978. xxxix, 421 p. ;　LC Card
　80-602390　DDC 346.7304/691 19
KF5571 .A94

**WATER-RIGHTS - WEST (U. S.) -
　ADDRESSES, ESSAYS, LECTURES.**
Trelease, Frank J., 1913- Back to basics--taking
the politics out of water law . [Sacramento?
Calif.] [1979?] 29 leaves ;　LC Card 81-621163
　DDC 346.7304/691 347.3064691 19
KF5571 .T74

WATER SALVAGE. see WATER REUSE.

**WATER-STORAGE - CALIFORNIA -
　ORANGE CO.**
California. Dept. of Water Resources. Southern
District. Analysis of aquifer-system compaction
in the Orange County ground water basin .
[Los Angeles, Calif.] [1980] vi, 58 p. :　LC
　Card 80-623751　DDC 627/.56 19
TD224.C3 C24 1980a

**WATER-STORAGE - CALIFORNIA - SAN
　FERNANDO VALLEY.**
California. Dept. of Water Resources. A ground
water storage program for the State Water
Project . [Sacramento] , 1979. viii, 88 p. :　LC
　Card 80-620652　DDC 333.91/02153/0979493
　19
TD224.C3 C24 1979c

**WATER, SUBTERRANEAN. see WATER,
　UNDERGROUND.**

WATER-SUPPLY. Here are entered works on
　surveys of the water resources of a region,
　both superficial and underground, primarily
　with reference to the supply of water for
　domestic and manufacturing purposes, or for
　agriculture.
(1974) United States. Environmental Protection
Agency. Guidance for facilities planning.
Washington, 1974. 81 p.;
　　　　　　　　　　NYPL [JSF 80-618]

**WATER-SUPPLY, AGRICULTURAL -
　CALIFORNIA.**
California. Advisory Panel on Agricultural
Water Conservation. Report of findings /.
Sacramento, Calif. [1979] v, 18 p. :　LC Card
　80-620554　DDC 631.7/09794 19
S494.5.W3 C34 1979

**WATER-SUPPLY, AGRICULTURAL -
　MISSISSIPPI.**
Dalsin, G. J. Water for industrial and
agricultural development in Bolivar, Carroll,
Leflore, Sunflower, and Tallahatchie Counties,
Mississippi . Jackson, Miss. , 1978. 67 p. :　LC
　Card 80-621547　DDC 553.7/09762/4 19
TD224.M65 D33

Water supply and sewerage of Korea. United
States. Army. Corps of Engineers. [Washington]
1945. iii, 36, A-6 p.　LC Card 59-27970
　　　　　　　　　　NYPL [JSF 80-676]

**Water supply and sewerage of Manchuria (in one
　volume)** United States. Army. Corps of
Engineers. Washington, 1945. iii, 55, A 1-A 6
p.　LC Card 72-614996
TA7 .U53 no. 160 TD310.M3

**WATER SUPPLY - BIBLIOGRAPHY -
　PERIODICALS.**
California. University. Water Resources Center.
Archives. Dictionary catalog of the Water
Resources Center Archives, University of
California, Berkeley. Supplement. 1st- ; 1971-
Boston.　　　　　*NYPL [JSK 73-123 Suppl.]*

**WATER-SUPPLY - CALIFORNIA - LOS
　ANGELES CO.**
California. Interagency Task Force on Mono
Lake. Report of Interagency Task Force on
Mono Lake. [Los Angeles , 1980?] ix, 140 p. :
　LC Card 80-621319　DDC 333.91/63/0979448
　19
TC424.C2 C286 1980

**WATER-SUPPLY - CALIFORNIA - OWENS
　VALLEY.**
Kahrl, William L. Water and power . Berkeley ,
c1981. p. cm.　ISBN 0-520-04431-2　LC Card
　81-7428　DDC 333.91/009794/9 19
HD4464.L7 K33

WATER-SUPPLY - COLORADO.
Washichek, Jack N. Summary of snow survey
measurements for Colorado and New Mexico,
1971-1977 . Denver, Colo. [1978] xxiii, 128
p. :　LC Card 79-601670　DDC 551.57/9/788 19
GB2625.C6 W37

**WATER-SUPPLY ENGINEERING -
　PERSONNEL MANAGEMENT -
　CERTIFICATION.**
Association of Boards of Certification for
Operating Personnel in Water and Wastewater
Utilities. A classification system for water and
wastewater facilities and personnel. Milbrae,
Calif., 1974. 33 p.　LC Card 77-95256
　　　　　　　　　　*NYPL [*ZT-1264]*

**WATER-SUPPLY ENGINEERS - LICENSES -
　NEW JERSEY.**
New Jersey. Dept. of Environmental Protection.
Rules and regulations on licensing of
superintendents or operators of public water
supply systems, public water treatment plants,
and public sewage treatment plants. [Trenton] ,
1973. 19 p. :　LC Card 79-624793　[DDC
　344.749/0176281 19
KFN2129.E61 A32 1973

Water supply for urban areas . United States.
General Accounting Office. [Washington]
1979. iv, 50 p. ;　LC Card 79-602696　DDC
　363.6/1/0973 19
TD223 .U525 1979

WATER-SUPPLY - IDAHO.
Idaho economic base study for water
requirements. [Boise, 1969] 2 v.　LC Card
　79-632346
HC107.I2 I19

Kennedy, S. Koehler. An economic water
market as an alternative to reduce return flow
from irrigation /. [Boise, Idaho] , 1979. v, 165,
[20] p. :　LC Card 79-625878　DDC 333.91/009796
　19
HD1694.I2 K46

**WATER-SUPPLY, INDUSTRIAL -
　MISSISSIPPI.**
Dalsin, G. J. Water for industrial and
agricultural development in Bolivar, Carroll,
Leflore, Sunflower, and Tallahatchie Counties,
Mississippi . Jackson, Miss. , 1978. 67 p. :　LC
　Card 80-621547　DDC 553.7/09762/4 19
TD224.M65 D33

Water resources and industrial development in
Mississippi . Mississippi State, Miss. [1979] v,
58 leaves :　LC Card 80-622324　DDC
　333.91/23/09762 19
TD224.M65 W35

WATER-SUPPLY - KOREA.
United States. Army. Corps of Engineers.
Water supply and sewerage of Korea.
[Washington] 1945. iii, 36, A-6 p.　LC Card
59-27970　　　　　　　*NYPL [JSF 80-676]*

**WATER-SUPPLY - LAW AND
　LEGISLATION - NEW JERSEY.**
New Jersey. Legislature. General Assembly.
Energy and Natural Resources Committee.
Public hearing before Assembly Energy and

Natural Resources Committee on Assembly, no.
728 (Blue Acres Bond issue) held March 20,
1978, Wayne Township Municipal Building,
Wayne, New Jersey. [Trenton] [1978?] 38 p. ;
　LC Card 79-624644　DDC 343.749/0924
　347.4903924 19
KFN1811.4 .E53 1978b

WATER-SUPPLY - MANCHURIA.
United States. Army. Corps of Engineers.
Water supply and sewerage of Manchuria (in
one volume) Washington, 1945. iii, 55, A 1-A 6
p.　LC Card 72-614996
TA7 .U53 no. 160 TD310.M3

WATER-SUPPLY - MAPS.
United States. Geological Survey. Water power
of the world . Washington , 1918. [7] leaves of
plates :　LC Card 80-675255　DDC 912/.133391
G1046.N33 U53 1918

WATER-SUPPLY - MISSISSIPPI.
Frnka, Robert L. Forecasting the need for
surface water use conjunctive with ground water
/. Mississippi State, Miss. , 1979. vii, 91
leaves :　LC Card 80-622323　DDC
　333.91/12/09762 19
TD224.M65 F76

WATER-SUPPLY - MISSOURI.
Davis, Peter N. Missouri instream flow
requirements . Jefferson City, Mo. [1980] xviii,
415 p., [1] fold. leaf of plates :　LC Card
　80-623733　DDC 346.77804/691 347.78064691
　19
KFM8246 .D36

**WATER-SUPPLY - NEVADA - LAS VEGAS
　VALLEY.**
Harrill, J. R. Pumping and depletion of
ground-water storage in Las Vegas Valley,
Nevada, 1955-74 /. [Carson City] , 1976. vii,
70 p. :　LC Card 80-623616　DDC
　333.91/2/0979313 19
GB705.N3 A35 no. 44 TD224.N2

Harrill, J. R. Water-level changes associated
with ground-water development in Las Vegas
Valley, Nevada, March 1975 to March 1976 /.
Carson City , 1976 i.e. 1977. iv, 31 p. :　LC
　Card 80-624035　DDC 553.7/9/0979313 19
GB1025.N4 H38

**WATER-SUPPLY - NEVADA - SMITH
　VALLEY.**
Rush, F. Eugene. Geohydrology of Smith
Valley, Nevada, with special reference to the
water-use period, 1953-72 /. [Carson City] ,
1976. 95 p. :　LC Card 80-623615　DDC
　553.7/09793/58 19
GB705.N3 R87

**WATER-SUPPLY - NEW JERSEY -
　FINANCE.**
New Jersey. Legislature. General Assembly.
Energy and Natural Resources Committee.
Public hearing before Assembly Energy and
Natural Resources Committee on Assembly, no.
728 (Blue Acres Bond issue) held March 20,
1978, Wayne Township Municipal Building,
Wayne, New Jersey. [Trenton] [1978?] 38 p. ;
　LC Card 79-624644　DDC 343.749/0924
　347.4903924 19
KFN1811.4 .E53 1978b

WATER-SUPPLY - NEW MEXICO.
Washichek, Jack N. Summary of snow survey
measurements for Colorado and New Mexico,
1971-1977 . Denver, Colo. [1978] xxiii, 128
p. :　LC Card 79-601670　DDC 551.57/9/788 19
GB2625.C6 W37

WATER SUPPLY - NEW YORK (CITY)
Quirk, Lawler & Matusky Engineers. Hydraulic
analysis of the New York City water supply
system /. Tappan, N. Y. , 1974. xviii, 82,
A1-A9 p. :　　　　　　*NYPL [JSF 80-751]*

**WATER-SUPPLY - NORTH CAROLINA -
　MANAGEMENT.**
North Carolina. Legislative Study Commission
on Alternatives for Water Management.
Alternatives for water management . [Raleigh,
N.C.] [1980] ca. 100 p. in various pagings ;
　LC Card 80-622778　DDC 333.91/15/09756 19
TC424.N8 N59 1980

**WATER-SUPPLY, RURAL - NORTH
　CAROLINA.**
Knopf, Bruce J. M. The impacts of rural water
systems in North Carolina . [Raleigh, N.C.] ,
1979. xii, 120 p. :　LC Card 80-621889　DDC

333.91/009756 s 363.6/1/09756 19
HD1694.N8 N6 no. 151 TD224.N8

WATER-SUPPLY - TEXAS.
Muller, Daniel A. Ground-water availability in
Texas . Austin, Tex. [1979] vii, 77 p. : LC
Card 80-620811   DDC 333.91/009764 s
553.7/9/09764 19
TD224.T4 A333 no. 238 GB1025.T4

**WATER-SUPPLY - TEXAS - LUBBOCK CO. -
DATA PROCESSING.**
Texas. Dept. of Water Resources. Playa Lake
monitoring for the Llano Estacado total water
management study . [Austin] , 1980. 18 leaves,
[2] leaves of plates : LC Card 80-621333   DDC
553.7/8/0723 19
TD224.T4 T36 1980

**WATER-SUPPLY - TEXAS - LUBBOCK CO. -
MATHEMATICAL MODELS.**
Texas. Dept. of Water Resources. Playa Lake
monitoring for the Llano Estacado total water
management study . [Austin] , 1980. 18 leaves,
[2] leaves of plates : LC Card 80-621333   DDC
553.7/8/0723 19
TD224.T4 T36 1980

**WATER-SUPPLY - TEXAS - WILBARGER
CO.**
Price, Robert Donald, 1926- Occurrence,
quality, and quantity of ground water in
Wilbarger County, Texas /. Austin, Tex. , 1979.
viii, 229 p., [4] leaf of plates (3 fold.) : LC
Card 80-621331   DDC 333.91/009764 s
553.7/9/09764746 19
TD224.T4 A333 no. 240 GB1025.T4

WATER-SUPPLY - THE WEST.
United States. Congress. Joint Economic
Committee. Subcommittee on Economic
Growth and Stabilization. The impact of an
accelerated coal-based synfuels program on
western water resources . Washington, D.C. ,
1980. iii, 105 p. : LC Card 80-602753   DDC
333.91/00978 19
KF25 .E232 1979c

WATER-SUPPLY - UNITED STATES.
Matthai, Howard Frederick, 1913- Hydrologic
and human aspects of the 1976-77 drought /.
Washington , 1979. v, 84 p. : LC Card
79-600188   DDC 363.3/492 19
GB701 .M37

United States. General Accounting Office.
Ground water overdrafting must be controlled .
Washington, D.C. , 1980. iv, 52 p. ; LC Card
81-600550   DDC 333.91/0416/0973 19
TD223 .U525 1980

United States. General Accounting Office.
Water supply for urban areas . [Washington]
1979. iv, 50 p. ; LC Card 79-602696   DDC
363.6/1/0973 19
TD223 .U525 1979

United States. Geological Survey. Synthetic
fuels development . Washington, D.C. , 1979.
45 p. : LC Card 79-600206   DDC 662/.66/0973 19
TP360 .U584 1979

United States. National Laboratory, Oak Ridge,
Tenn. Environmental Sciences Division.
Sourcebook of hydrologic and ecological
features . Ann Arbor, Mich. , c1980. x, 126 p. :
ISBN 0-250-40355-2 LC Card 79-56108
GB701 .U54 1980   **NYPL [JSE 80-1263]**

Viessman, Warren. Assessing the nation's water
resources . Washington , 1980. [76] p. : LC
Card 81-600801   DDC 333.91/0028/7 19
TD223 .V53

WATER SUPPLY - UTAH.
Hughes, Trevor C. Domestic water demand in
Utah /. Logan, Utah [1979] viii, 61 p. : LC
Card 80-621122   DDC 333.91/22 19
TD224.U8 H83

**WATER-SUPPLY - WASHINGTON
METROPOLITAN AREA.**
Mid-Atlantic Archaeological Research, inc.
Cultural resources reconnaissance investigations
for the metropolitan Washington area water
supply study early action report . Newark, Del.
[1979] [92] leaves, [24] leaves of plates : LC
Card 80-601709   DDC 975.3 19
F195.5 .M53 1979

WATER-SUPPLY - WASHINGTON (STATE)
A summary of quantity, quality, and economic
methodology for establishing minimum flows .
Pullman , 1973- v. <1> : LC Card 75-620707

DDC 553.7/09797 s 333.9/0217/09797 19
TD224.W2 S8 no. 13 GB1225.W3

**WATER-SUPPLY - WISCONSIN -
STATISTICS - PERIODICALS.**
Wisconsin. Public Service Commission.
Accounts and Finance Division. Comparison of
net quarterly bills of Wisconsin water utilities.
1980- [Madison]   **NYPL [JLM 80-1150]**

**WATER - SUSPENDED SEDIMENT. see
SEDIMENT, SUSPENDED.**

**WATER TABLE - FLORIDA - HOLMES
COUNTY - MAPS.**
United States. Soil Conservation Service.
Holmes County, Florida . Fort Worth, Tex. ,
1980. 1 map : LC Card 81-690356
G3933.H8C34 1979 .U5

**WATER TABLE - GEORGIA - GORDON
COUNTY - MAPS.**
United States. Soil Conservation Service.
Gordon County, Georgia . Fort Worth, Tex. ,
1979. 1 map : LC Card 81-690450
G3923.G6C34 1978 .U5

**WATER TABLE - NEVADA - LAS VEGAS
VALLEY.**
Harrill, J. R. Water-level changes associated
with ground-water development in Las Vegas
Valley, Nevada, March 1975 to March 1976 /.
Carson City , 1976 i.e. 1977. iv, 31 p. : LC
Card 80-624035   DDC 553.7/9/0979313 19
GB1025.N4 H38

Water--today and tomorrow. United States.
Pacific Northwest River Basins Commission.
[Vancouver, Wash. , 1979] 3 v. : LC Card
80-622316   DDC 333.91/009795 19
TC423.7 .U54 1979

WATER TRANSPORTATION. see SHIPPING.

WATER TREATMENT PLANTS.
Meade, Thomas L. The technology of closed
system culture of salmonids /. [Narragansett ,
1974] i, 30 p. : LC Card 76-623379   DDC
639.3/755 19
SH154 .M4

United States. Environmental Protection
Agency. Public Service Careers Section.
Guidelines to career development for
wastewater treatment-plant personnel.
Washington, 1973. viii, 100 p. LC Card 76-87266
                                   NYPL [JSF 80-487]

**WATER TREATMENT PLANTS - LAW AND
LEGISLATION - UNITED STATES.**
United States. Congress. House. Committee on
Public Works and Transportation. Subcommittee
on Water Resources. Industrial cost recovery .
Washington , 1980. iv, 447 p. : LC Card
80-603642   DDC 344.73/046343 19
KF27 .P8968 1980

**WATER TREATMENT PLANTS - UNITED
STATES - FINANCE.**
United States. Congress. House. Committee on
Public Works and Transportation. Subcommittee
on Water Resources. Industrial cost recovery .
Washington , 1980. iv, 447 p. : LC Card
80-603642   DDC 344.73/046343 19
KF27 .P8968 1980

**WATER, UNDERGROUND - ARIZONA -
REMOTE SENSING.**
United States. Dept. of the Interior. Office of
Water Research and Technology. Geologic
applications of Landsat images in northeastern
Arizona to the location of water supplies for
municipal and industrial uses /. Washington,
D.C. [1979] iv leaves, 92 p. : LC Card
80-622485   DDC 628.1/14 19
TD224.A7 U52 1979

**WATER, UNDERGROUND - BIG BLUE
RIVER WATERSHED, KAN. & NEB. -
ARTIFICIAL RECHARGE - COST
EFFECTIVENESS.**
University of Nebraska--Lincoln. Water
Resources Research Institute. A cost-benefit
presentation of several artificial recharge
schemes in the Upper Big Blue River Basin .
Lincoln, Neb. [1975] 40 leaves : LC Card
79-623375   DDC 333.91/04153/097822 19
TD404 .U54 1975

**WATER, UNDERGROUND - CALIFORNIA -
ARROYO GRANDE REGION.**
California. Dept. of Water Resources. Southern
District. Ground water in the Arroyo Grande
area . [Los Angeles] , 1979. vii, 108 p. : LC

Card 79-625584   DDC 553.7/9/0979478 19
GB1025.C2 C14 1979b

**WATER, UNDERGROUND - CALIFORNIA -
MORRO BAY REGION.**
California. Dept. of Water Resources. Southern
District. Morro Bay sandspit investigation .
[Sacramento, Calif.] [1979] viii, 64 p., [1] leaf
of plates : LC Card 79-626228   DDC
553.7/9/0979478 19
GB1025.C2 C14 1979c

**WATER, UNDERGROUND - CALIFORNIA -
ORANGE CO.**
California. Dept. of Water Resources. Southern
District. Analysis of aquifer-system compaction
in the Orange County ground water basin .
[Los Angeles, Calif.] [1980] vi, 58 p. : LC
Card 80-623751   DDC 627/.56 19
TD224.C3 C24 1980a

**WATER, UNDERGROUND - CALIFORNIA -
SAN FERNANDO VALLEY.**
California. Dept. of Water Resources. A ground
water storage program for the State Water
Project . [Sacramento] , 1979. viii, 88 p. : LC
Card 80-620652   DDC 333.91/02153/0979493
19
TD224.C3 C24 1979c

**WATER, UNDERGROUND - FLORIDA -
PINELLAS COUNTY.**
Hickey, John J. Hydrogeology and results of
injection tests at waste-injection test sites in
Pinellas County, Florida /. Washington , 1981.
p. cm. LC Card 81-607052   DDC 627/.57 19
TD761 .H52

**WATER, UNDERGROUND - IDAHO -
BLAINE CO.**
Brockway, Charles E., 1936- Evaluation of
urbanization and changes in land use on the
water resources of mountain valleys . Moscow,
Idaho [1978?] ix, 104 p. [1] fold. leaf of
plates : LC Card 79-625237   DDC 333.91/2/09796
19
TD224.I2 B76

**WATER, UNDERGROUND - KANSAS -
CLOUD COUNTY - MAPS.**
United States. Soil Conservation Service.
Ground water availability map, Cloud County,
Kansas /. Lincoln, Nebr. , 1979. 1 map ; LC
Card 81-691134
G4203.C65C34 1974 .U5

**WATER, UNDERGROUND - KANSAS -
GREAT BEND PRAIRIE.**
Fader, Stuart Wesley, 1919- Geohydrology of
the Great Bend Prairie, southcentral Kansas /.
Lawrence , 1978. 19 p. : LC Card 78-624087
DDC 553.7/9/097818 19
GB1025.K2 F3

**WATER, UNDERGROUND - KANSAS - NESS
COUNTY - MAPS.**
United States. Soil Conservation Service. Water
resource map, Ness County, Kansas /. Lincoln,
Nebr. , 1979. 1 map : LC Card 81-691148
G4203.N5C34 1979 .U5

**WATER, UNDERGROUND - KANSAS -
REPUBLIC COUNTY - MAPS.**
United States. Soil Conservation Service.
Ground water availability map, Republic
County, Kansas /. Lincoln, Nebr. , 1974. 1
map ; LC Card 81-691152
G4203.R4C34 1974 .U5

**WATER, UNDERGROUND - KANSAS -
SEWARD COUNTY - MAPS.**
United States. Soil Conservation Service.
General availability of groundwater map,
Seward County, Kansas /. Lincoln, Nebr. ,
1979. 1 map : LC Card 81-691145
G4203.S45C34 1979 .U5

**WATER, UNDERGROUND - LAW AND
LEGISLATION - HAWAII.**
Hawaii. Hydrologic Advisory Committee.
Recommendations for ground water use
regulation . Honolulu, Hawaii [1980] x, 33 p. :
LC Card 80-622659   DDC 333.7/09969 s
346.96904/69104 333.7/09969 s 349.6906469104
19
GB832.H4 A43 no. C80 KFH446

**WATER, UNDERGROUND -
MASSACHUSETTS - NANTUCKET.**
Massachusetts. Water Quality and Research
Section. Nantucket . Westborough , 1978. 50
p. : LC Card 79-623987   DDC 363.7/3942/0974497

19
TD224.M4 M39 1978a

**WATER, UNDERGROUND - METIGOSHE,
LAKE, WATERSHED, N.D. AND MAN.**
Moran, Stephen R. Hydrogeology of the Lake
Metigoshe basin, North Dakota and Manitoba
/. Fargo , 1977. v, 59 leaves : LC Card
79-621837 DDC 553.7/9/0978461 19
GB1025.N9 M67

WATER, UNDERGROUND - MINNESOTA.
Singer, Rexford D. Ground water quality in
southeastern Minnesota /. Minneapolis, Minn.
[1980] vi, 79, 64 leaves : LC Card 80-622728
DDC 553.7/9/097761 19
TD224.M6 S56

WATER, UNDERGROUND - MISSISSIPPI.
Frnka, Robert L. Forecasting the need for
surface water use conjunctive with ground water
/. Mississippi State, Miss. , 1979. vii, 91
leaves : LC Card 80-622323 DDC
333.91/12/09762 19
TD224.M65 F76

**WATER, UNDERGROUND - MISSISSIPPI -
CATALOGS.**
Easom, William Davison. Electrical logs of
water wells and test holes on file at the Bureau
of Geology and Energy Resources /. Jackson,
Miss. , 1979. 306 p. : LC Card 80-620873 DDC
551.49/09762 19
GB1025.M7 E27

WATER, UNDERGROUND - MONTANA.
Montana. State Bureau of Mines and Geology.
Ground water of the Fort Union coal region,
eastern Montana /. Butte, Mont. , 1978. 47 p. :
LC Card 79-621779 DDC 553.7/9/09786 19
GB1025.M9 M54 1978

**WATER, UNDERGROUND - NEBRASKA -
BOX BUTTE COUNTY.**
Souders, Vernon L. Geology and groundwater
supplies of Box Butte County, Nebraska /.
[Lincoln] [1980] vii, 205 p. : LC Card
80-623050 DDC 553/.7/09782 s
551.7/9/0978294 19
GB1025.N2 N42 no. 47 QE136.B67

**WATER, UNDERGROUND - NEVADA - LAS
VEGAS VALLEY.**
Harrill, J. R. Pumping and depletion of
ground-water storage in Las Vegas Valley,
Nevada, 1955-74 /. [Carson City] , 1976. vii,
70 p. : LC Card 80-623616 DDC
333.91/2/0979313 19
GB705.N3 A35 no. 44 TD224.N2

**WATER, UNDERGROUND - NEW
ENGLAND.**
Sinnott, Allen, 1917- Summary appraisals of the
nation's ground-water resources--New England
region /. Washington , 1981. p. cm. LC Card
81-607880 DDC 553.7/9/0974 19
GB1016.3 .S57

**WATER, UNDERGROUND - NORTH
CAROLINA - MANAGEMENT.**
Sherwani, Jabbar K. Public policy for the
management of groundwater in the coastal plain
of North Carolina /. [Raleigh, N.C.] [1980] xv,
63 p. : LC Card 80-623572 DDC 333.91/009756 s
333.91/04/09756 19
HD1694.N8 N6 no. 158 TD224.N8

**WATER, UNDERGROUND - NORTH
DAKOTA - BILLINGS COUNTY.**
Anna, Lawrence O. Ground-water data for
Billings, Golden Valley, and Slope Counties,
North Dakota /. Bismarck, N.D. , 1980. v, 241
p. : LC Card 80-623714 DDC 553.7/9/09784 s
553.7/9/0978494 19
GB705.N9 A25 no. 29, pt. 2 GB1025.N9

**WATER, UNDERGROUND - NORTH
DAKOTA - BISMARCK REGION.**
Groenewold, Gerald H. Geologic and
hydrogeologic conditions affecting land use in
the Bismarck-Mandan area /. [Grand Forks] ,
1980. iv, 42 p. : LC Card 80-623715 DDC
557.84 s 624.1/51/0978477 19
TN24.N9 A3 no. 70 QE150.B57

**WATER, UNDERGROUND - NORTH
DAKOTA - GOLDEN VALLEY CO.**
Anna, Lawrence O. Ground-water data for
Billings, Golden Valley, and Slope Counties,
North Dakota /. Bismarck, N.D. , 1980. v, 241
p. : LC Card 80-623714 DDC
553.7/9/0978494 19
GB705.N9 A25 no. 29, pt. 2 GB1025.N9

**WATER, UNDERGROUND - NORTH
DAKOTA - GRANT CO.**
Randich, Philip G., 1909- Ground-water
resources of Grant and Sioux Counties, North
Dakota /. Bismarck, N.D. , 1979. vi, 49 p. :
LC Card 80-621090 DDC 553.7/9/09784 s
553.7/9/0978487 19
GB705.N9 A25 no. 24, pt. 3 TD224.N9

**WATER, UNDERGROUND - NORTH
DAKOTA - MORTON CO.**
Ackerman, D. J. Ground-water resources of
Morton County, North Dakota /. Bismarck,
N.D. , 1980. v, 51 p. : LC Card 80-622722
DDC 553.7/9/09784 s 553.7/9/0978485 19
GB705.N9 A25 no. 27, pt. 3 GB1025.N9

**WATER, UNDERGROUND - NORTH
DAKOTA - RAMSEY CO.**
Hutchinson, Rickard D. Ground-water resources
of Ramsey County, North Dakota /. Bismarck,
N.D. , 1980. 36 p. : LC Card 80-622721 DDC
553.7/9/09784 s 553.7/9/0978436 19
GB705.N9 A25 no. 26, pt. 3 GB1025.N9

**WATER, UNDERGROUND - NORTH
DAKOTA - SHERIDAN CO.**
Burkart, M. R. Ground-water data for Sheridan
County, North Dakota /. Bismark, N.D. , 1980.
iv, 302 p. : LC Card 80-622724 DDC 557.84 s
553.7/9/0978476 19
GB705.N9 A25 no. 32, pt. 2 GB1025.N9

**WATER, UNDERGROUND - NORTH
DAKOTA - SIOUX CO.**
Randich, Philip G., 1909- Ground-water
resources of Grant and Sioux Counties, North
Dakota /. Bismarck, N.D. , 1979. vi, 49 p. :
LC Card 80-621090 DDC 553.7/9/09784 s
553.7/9/0978487 19
GB705.N9 A25 no. 24, pt. 3 TD224.N9

**WATER, UNDERGROUND - NORTH
DAKOTA - SLOPE CO.**
Anna, Lawrence O. Ground-water data for
Billings, Golden Valley, and Slope Counties,
North Dakota /. Bismarck, N.D. , 1980. v, 241
p. : LC Card 80-623714 DDC 553.7/9/09784 s
553.7/9/0978494 19
GB705.N9 A25 no. 29, pt. 2 GB1025.N9

**WATER, UNDERGROUND - OHIO - KNOX
COUNTY - MAPS.**
Schmidt, James J. Ground-water resources of
Knox County /. Columbus , 1980. 1 map : LC
Card 81-691460
G4083.K6C34 1980 .S3

**WATER, UNDERGROUND - OHIO -
PICKAWAY COUNTY - MAPS.**
Schmidt, James J. Ground-water resources of
Pickaway County /. Columbus , 1980. 1 map :
LC Card 81-691459
G4083.P5C34 1980 .S3

**WATER, UNDERGROUND - OHIO - ROSS
COUNTY - MAPS.**
Schmidt, James J. Ground-water resources of
Ross County /. Columbus , 1980. 1 map : LC
Card 81-691461
G4083.R6C34 1980 .S3

**WATER, UNDERGROUND - OREGON -
WARNER VALLEY.**
Sammel, Edward A. The geothermal hydrology
of Warner Valley, Oregon . Washington , 1981.
p. cm. LC Card 81-607830 DDC 553.7 19
GB1199.7.O7 S24

**WATER, UNDERGROUND - POLLUTION -
ALABAMA - CALHOUN CO.**
Moore, James D. Effect of quarry blasting on
ground-water quality in a limestone terrane in
Calhoun County, Alabama /. Auburn, Ala.
[1979] vi, 72 p. : LC Card 79-625904 DDC
333.91/009761 s 628.1/683 19
TC1 .A85 no. 38 TD224.A2

**WATER, UNDERGROUND - POLLUTION -
CALIFORNIA - LOS ANGELES CO.**
California. Dept. of Water Resources. Southern
District. Potential waste disposal areas, northern
Los Angeles County /. [Sacramento] [1979]
vii, 58 p. : LC Card 80-621404 DDC 363.7/28 19
TD811.5 .C34 1979

**WATER, UNDERGROUND - POLLUTION -
IDAHO - IDAHO NATIONAL
ENGINEERING LABORATORY REGION.**
Barraclough, Jack T. Hydrologic conditions at
the Idaho National Engineering Laboratory,
Idaho emphasis, 1974-1978 /. Denver, Colo. ,
1981. p. cm. LC Card 81-6821 DDC

553.7/9/0979659 19
TD224.I2 B37

**WATER, UNDERGROUND - POLLUTION -
MONTANA.**
Peavy, Howard S. The effects of non-sewered
subdivisions on ground water quality /.
Bozeman, MT [1980?] iv, 65, 22 p. : LC Card
80-623175 DDC 363.7/394 19
TD224.M9 P33

**WATER, UNDERGROUND - POLLUTION -
NEW MEXICO.**
Taylor, Robert Gay, 1940- Effects of bacteria
on nitrate and nitrite concentrations in
groundwater of the Ogallala aquifer /. Las
Cruces, N.M. [1979] vii, 20 leaves : LC Card
80-622275 DDC 333.91/09789 s 628.1/68 19
GB705.N6 N64 no. 114 TD224.N6

**WATER, UNDERGROUND - RHODE
ISLAND.**
Dickerman, David C. Geohydrologic data for
the Beaver-Pasquiset ground-water reservoir,
Rhode Island . [Providence, R.I.] , 1977. 128
p. : LC Card 80-622751 DDC 553.7/9/09745 19
GB1025.R4 D53

**WATER, UNDERGROUND - SIERRA
NEVADA MOUNTAINS (CALIF. AND
NEV.)**
Geochemical evidence on the nature of the
basement rocks of the Sierra Nevada, California
/. Washington , 1981. p. cm. LC Card 81-607895
DDC 551.9/09794/4 19
QE515 .G354

WATER, UNDERGROUND - TEXAS.
Muller, Daniel A. Ground-water availability in
Texas . Austin, Tex. [1979] vii, 77 p. : LC
Card 80-620811 DDC 333.91/009764 s
553.7/9/09764 19
TD224.T4 A333 no. 238 GB1025.T4

**WATER, UNDERGROUND - TEXAS - SAN
ANTONIO REGION - DATA
PROCESSING.**
Texas. Dept. of Water Resources. Ground-water
resources and model applications for the
Edwards (Balcones Fault Zone) aquifer in the
San Antonio region, Texas /. Austin, Tex.
[1979] vi, 88 p., 30 leaves of plates : LC Card
80-622334 DDC 553.7/9/0976435 19
TD224.T4 A333 no. 239 GB1199.3.T4

**WATER, UNDERGROUND - TEXAS - SAN
ANTONIO REGION - MATHEMATICAL
MODELS.**
Texas. Dept. of Water Resources. Ground-water
resources and model applications for the
Edwards (Balcones Fault Zone) aquifer in the
San Antonio region, Texas /. Austin, Tex.
[1979] vi, 88 p., 30 leaves of plates : LC Card
80-622334 DDC 553.7/9/0976435 19
TD224.T4 A333 no. 239 GB1199.3.T4

**WATER, UNDERGROUND - TEXAS -
WILBARGER CO.**
Price, Robert Donald, 1926- Occurrence,
quality, and quantity of ground water in
Wilbarger County, Texas /. Austin, Tex. , 1979.
viii, 229 p., [4] leaf of plates (3 fold.) : LC
Card 80-621331 DDC 333.91/009764 s
553.7/9/09764746 19
TD224.T4 A333 no. 240 GB1025.T4

**WATER, UNDERGROUND - UNITED
STATES.**
United States. General Accounting Office.
Ground water overdrafting must be controlled .
Washington, D.C. , 1980. iv, 52 p. ; LC Card
81-600550 DDC 333.91/0416/0973 19
TD223 .U525 1980

**WATER, UNDERGROUND - UTAH -
PERIODICALS.**
Utah. Division of Water Resources. Developing
a state water plan; ground water conditions in
Utah. [Salt Lake City].   *NYPL [JSP 81-11]*

**WATER, UNDERGROUND - UTAH - UTAH
LAKE BASIN.**
Dustin, Jacob D. Hydrogeology of Utah Lake
with emphasis on Goshen Bay /. [Salt Lake
City, Utah] [1980] ii, 50 p. : LC Card
80-623593 DDC 553.7/09792 s
553.7/9/0979224 19
TD224.U8 A3 no. 23 GB1025.U8

**WATER, UNDERGROUND - VIRGINIA -
HENRY CO.**
Dawson, James W. Groundwater resources of
Henry County, Virginia /. Richmond, Va. ,

1979. xviii, 69, [35] p. : LC Card 79-625459
DDC 553.7/9/09755692 19
GB1025.V8 D38

**WATER, UNDERGROUND - WASHINGTON
(STATE) - SPOKANE CO.**
Olson, Theodore M. Ground water resources of
Five Mile Prairie, Spokane County, Washington
/. Olympia, Wash. [1979] iv, 30 p. : LC Card
80-621127   DDC 553.7/9/0979737 19
GB1025.W2 O47

**WATER, UNDERGROUND - WISCONSIN -
COLUMBIA CO.**
Harr, C. Albert. Ground-water resources and
geology of Columbia County, Wisconsin /.
Madison, Wis. , 1978. vii, 30 p. : LC Card
80-623464   DDC 557.75 s 553.7/9/0977581 19
QE179 .A33 no. 37 GB1025.W6

**WATER, UNDERGROUND - WISCONSIN -
OZAUKEE CO.**
Young, H. L. Ground-water resources and
geology of Washington and Ozaukee Counties,
Wisconsin /. [Washington] , Madison, Wis.
[1980] iv, 37 p. : LC Card 80-622195 DDC
557.75 s 553.7/9/0977591 19
QE179 .A33 no. 38 GB1025.W6

**WATER, UNDERGROUND - WISCONSIN -
WASHINGTON CO.**
Young, H. L. Ground-water resources and
geology of Washington and Ozaukee Counties,
Wisconsin /. [Washington] , Madison, Wis.
[1980] iv, 37 p. : LC Card 80-622195 DDC
557.75 s 553.7/9/0977591 19
QE179 .A33 no. 38 GB1025.W6

WATER USE - IDAHO.
Kennedy, S. Koehler. An economic water
market as an alternative to reduce return flow
from irrigation /. [Boise, Idaho] , 1979. v, 165,
[20] p. : LC Card 79-625878 DDC 333.91/009796
19
HD1694.I2 K46

**WATER USE - IDAHO - COST
EFFECTIVENESS.**
Allen, Rick G. Relationship of costs and water
use efficiency for irrigation projects in Idaho /.
Moscow, Idaho [1979] xvi, 288 p. : LC Card
80-622427   DDC 333.91/3/09796 19
HD1739.I2 A6

WATER USE - KANSAS.
Kansas. State Water Resources Board.
Compilation of socio-economic, land use, and
water use information and projections for the
1975 national water assessment. [Topeka] ,
1979. 54 p. : LC Card 80-622138 DDC
333.91/13/09781 19
HD211.K2 K36 1979

WATER USE - LOUISIANA.
Cardwell, George T., 1922- Pumpage of water
in Louisiana, 1975 /. Baton Rouge, La. , 1979.
iv, 15 p. : LC Card 80-620624 DDC
333.91/13/09763 19
TD224.L8 C37

WATER USE - MONTANA.
Utter, Jack. Wild river management . Bozeman,
MT [1980] xiii, 117 leaves : LC Card 80-623137
DDC 333.78/45 19
TD224.M9 U88

**WATER USE - RESEARCH -
MASSACHUSETTS - EVALUATION.**
Kreplick, Ruth. Effectiveness of information
transfer through water resources researcher/user
group interaction /. Amherst , 1976. xvii, 144
p. ; LC Card 78-622292 DDC 333.91/009744 s
333.91//0072 19
TD224.M4 M37 no. 73

WATER USE - SONORAN DESERT.
Jamail, Milton H. International water use
relations along the Sonoran Desert borderlands
/. Tuscon, Ariz. , 1979. iv leaves, 139 p., [1]
leaf of plates : LC Card 80-622139 DDC
333.91/13/0979 19
TD223.9 .J35

WATER USE - UNITED STATES.
United States. Library of Congress.
Congressional Research Service. State and
national water use trends to the year 2000 .
Washington , 1980. x, 297 p. : LC Card
80-602584   DDC 333.91/13/0973 19
TD223 .U53 1980a

**WATER - WATER QUALITY - HOUSATONIC
RIVER WATERSHED.**

Chesebrough, Eben W. Baseline water quality
surveys of selected lakes and ponds in the
Housatonic River basin, Berkshire County, 1976
/. Westborough, Mass. , 1976. 91 p. : LC Card
79-620583   DDC 363.7/3942/097441 19
TD225.H75 C45

WATERBORNE INFECTION.
Greeson, Phillip E. Infectious waterborne
diseases /. Reston, VA [1981] p. cm. LC Card
81-607881   DDC 557.3 s 614.4 19
QE75 .C5 no. 848-D RA642.W3

**WATERBORNE INFECTION -
CONGRESSES.**
National Symposium on Waterborne
Transmission of Giardiasis, Cincinnati, 1978.
Waterborne transmission of giardiasis .
Cincinnati , Springfield, Va. , 1979. xiv, 306 p. :
LC Card 79-603744   DDC 614.5/3 19
RC145 .N37 1978

Waterborne transmission of giardiasis . National
Symposium on Waterborne Transmission of
Giardiasis, Cincinnati, 1978. Cincinnati ,
Springfield, Va. , 1979. xiv, 306 p. : LC Card
79-603744   DDC 614.5/3 19
RC145 .N37 1978

Watercolor, wax & wool . LaCoste, Janet Shook.
[San Antonio] , c1980. [88] p. : ISBN
0-933164-81-5 (pbk.) LC Card 80-82780 DDC
746.44/2/0924 19
NK9198.L3 A4 1980

**Waterfowl and their wintering grounds in
Mexico, 1937-64 /.** Saunders, George Bradford,
1907- Washington, D.C. , 1981. p. cm. LC
Card 81-607010   DDC 333.95/4 s 598.4/1 19
S914 .A3 no. 138a QL696.A5

WATERFOWL - DISEASES.
McDonald, Malcolm Edwin, 1915- Key to
trematodes reported in waterfowl /.
Washington, D.C. , 1981. p. cm. LC Card
81-607044   DDC 333.95/4/0973 s 639.9/741 19
S914 .A3 no. 142 QL391.P7

WATERFOWL - MEXICO.
Saunders, George Bradford, 1907- Waterfowl
and their wintering grounds in Mexico, 1937-64
/. Washington, D.C. , 1981. p. cm. LC Card
81-607010   DDC 333.95/4 s 598.4/1 19
S914 .A3 no. 138a QL696.A5

WATERFOWL - MEXICO - WINTERING.
Saunders, George Bradford, 1907- Waterfowl
and their wintering grounds in Mexico, 1937-64
/. Washington, D.C. , 1981. p. cm. LC Card
81-607010   DDC 333.95/4 s 598.4/1 19
S914 .A3 no. 138a QL696.A5

**WATERFRONT WORKERS. see
STEVEDORES.**

**WATERFRONTS - LAW AND LEGISLATION -
DISTRICT OF COLUMBIA.**
United States. Congress. Senate. Committee on
Energy and Natural Resources. Subcommittee
on Parks, Recreation, and Renewable
Resources. Preservation and protection of the
Potomac River shoreline . Washington , 1980.
iii, 79 p. ; LC Card 80-602980 DDC
346.7304/6784 19
KF26 .E5565 1980b

WATERFRONTS - UNITED STATES.
Urban waterfront revitalization . Washington
[1980]. 2 v.   NYPL [JLM 80-739]

**WATERFRONTS - VIRGINIA -
ALEXANDRIA.**
United States. Dept. of the Interior. Alexandria
waterfront, Virginia . Washington , 1979. 86 p. :
LC Card 80-602643   DDC 333.73/17/09755296
19
HT177.A44 U54 1979

WATERFRONTS - WASHINGTON, D.C.
United States. Dept. of the Interior.
Georgetown waterfront, Washington, D.C. .
Washington , 1979. 53 p. : LC Card 80-602644
DDC 333.78/3 19
HT177.D6 U52 1979

**WATERSHED DEVELOPMENT. see
WATERSHED MANAGEMENT.**

**WATERSHED MANAGEMENT -
CALIFORNIA, SOUTHERN.**
Lee, Robert G. Brushland watershed fire
management policy in southern California .
Davis, Calif. [1978] iv, 74 p. : LC Card
80-620664   DDC 333.91/009794 s 363.3/79 19
GB705.C2 C27 no. 172 SD421.32.C2

**WATERSHED MANAGEMENT - COLORADO
RIVER WATERSHED - PLANNING.**
Larson, Dean T. Levels of analysis in
comprehensive river basin planning /. Logan,
Utah , 1979. ix, 110 p. : LC Card 80-621123
DDC 333.91/02 19
TC425.C6 L37

**WATERSHED MANAGEMENT -
CONNECTICUT - CONGRESSES.**
Lake Management Conference, University of
Connecticut, 1977. Proceedings, Lake
Management Conference, held June 9, 1977, at
the University of Connecticut, Storrs. Storrs
[1979] iv, 127 p. : LC Card 79-625225 DDC
333.91 s 333.91/63/09746 19
HD1694.C8 C7 no. 30 TC424.C8

**WATERSHED MANAGEMENT - NEW
JERSEY.**
New Jersey. Legislature. General Assembly.
Energy and Natural Resources Committee.
Public hearing before Assembly Energy and
Natural Resources Committee on Assembly, no.
728 (Blue Acres Bond issue) held March 20,
1978, Wayne Township Municipal Building,
Wayne, New Jersey. [Trenton] [1978?] 38 p. ;
LC Card 79-624644   DDC 343.749/0924
347.4903924 19
KFN1811.4 .E53 1978b

**WATERSHED MANAGEMENT - OREGON -
OCHOCO CREEK WATERSHED.**
Berndt, H. W. Forest land use and streamflow
in central Oregon /. Portland, Or. , 1970. 15
p. : LC Card 71-608738 DDC 634.9/09795 s
553.7/09795/83 19
SD11 .A45614 no. 93 SD387.M8

WATERSHED MANAGEMENT - PLANNING.
Larson, Dean T. Levels of analysis in
comprehensive river basin planning /. Logan,
Utah , 1979. ix, 110 p. : LC Card 80-621123
DDC 333.91/02 19
TC425.C6 L37

**WATERSHED MANAGEMENT - RESEARCH -
UNITED STATES.**
United States. Bureau of Reclamation.
Reclamation research . [Washington] , 1979. vi,
121 p. : LC Card 80-602385 DDC
333.91/0072073 19
TC423 .U48 1979

**WATERSHED MANAGEMENT - SOUTHERN
STATES - CONGRESSES.**
Southeast Conference on Urban Stormwater
Management, North Carolina State University,
1979. Urban stormwater management .
[Raleigh, N.C.] [1980] vi, 252 p. : LC Card
80-623271   DDC 363.6/1 19
TD657 .S68 1979

**WATERSHED MANAGEMENT -
WASHINGTON (STATE) - DESCHUTES
RIVER WATERSHED.**
Washington (State). Water Resource
Management Division. Policy Development
Section. Deschutes River Basin instream
resources protection program including
proposed administrative rules . Olympia, Wash.
[1980] 29, [52] p. : LC Card 80-623859 DDC
333.91/0216/0979779 19
TD224.W2 W38 1980

**Watershed (P.L. 566) projects South Dakota,
January 1979 /.** United States. Soil
Conservation Service. Lincoln, Nebr. , 1979. 1
map : LC Card 81-691106
G4181.C315 1979 .U5

**Watershed (P.L. 566) projects, South Dakota,
January 1980 /.** United States. Soil
Conservation Service. Lincoln, Nebr. , 1980. 1
map : LC Card 81-691099
G4181.C315 1980 .U52

WATERSHEDS - COLORADO - MAPS.
United States. Soil Conservation Service. River
basin and watershed progress, Colorado /.
Portland, Or. , 1979. 1 map : LC Card
81-691540
G4311.C315 1979 .U5

**WATERSHEDS - KANSAS - NESS COUNTY -
MAPS.**
United States. Soil Conservation Service.
Watershed map, Ness County, Kansas /.
Lincoln, Nebr. , 1979. 1 map : LC Card
81-691147
G4203.N5C315 1979 .U51

WATERSHEDS - KANSAS - TUTTLE CREEK RESERVOIR REGIONS.
Chelikowsky, Joseph Rudolph, 1907-
Pleistocene drainage reversal in the Upper Tuttle Creek reservoir area of Kansas /. Lawrence , 1976. 10 p. :   LC Card 76-623731   DDC 557.81 s 551.48/09781 19
QE113 .A2 no. 211, pt. 1 GB565.K2

WATERSHEDS - MANAGEMENT. see
WATERSHED MANAGEMENT.

WATERSHEDS - MASSACHUSETTS.
Massachusetts. Water Quality and Research Section. Compilation of lakes, ponds, and reservoirs relative to the Massachusetts Lake Classification Program /. Westborough, Mass. , 1976. 124 p. ;   LC Card 79-623986   DDC 551.48/2/09744 19
GB1625.M3 M37 1976

WATERSHEDS - MISSOURI - MAPS.
United States. Soil Conservation Service. Missouri, status of PL-566 watershed projects /. Lincoln, Nebr. , 1979. 1 map :   LC Card 81-691209
G4161.C315 1979 .U5

United States. Soil Conservation Service. Missouri, status of PL-566 watershed projects /. Lincoln, Nebr. , 1980. 1 map :   LC Card 81-691208
G4161.C315 1980 .U5

WATERSHEDS - MONTANA - BRIDGER NATIONAL FOREST - RESEARCH - HISTORY.
Weaver, Donald Kessler. Bridger Hydrometeorological Research Area development and operation, 1965-1968 /. [Bozeman] , 1975. 49, 4, 8 leaves ;   LC Card 76-624302   DDC 551.57/028/54 19
GB991.M9 W4

WATERSHEDS - OHIO - MAPS.
United States. Soil Conservation Service. P.L. 566 watershed status, southwest Ohio River basin study area, Ohio /. Lincoln, Nebr. , 1978. 1 map :   LC Card 81-691040
G4081.C315 1978 .U5

WATERSHEDS - OREGON - MAPS.
United States. Soil Conservation Service. River basin studies, Oregon /. Portland, Or. , 1979. 1 map :   LC Card 81-691562
G4291.C315 1979 .U51

United States. Soil Conservation Service. Status of watershed assistance under P.L.566, Oregon /. Portland, Or. , 1979. 1 map :   LC Card 81-691561
G4291.C315 1979 .U5

WATERSHEDS - SOUTH DAKOTA - MAPS.
United States. Soil Conservation Service. Major drainage basins, South Dakota /. Lincoln, Nebr. , 1977. 1 map :   LC Card 81-691100
G4181.C315 1977 .U5

United States. Soil Conservation Service. South Dakota river basins study areas /. Lincoln, Nebr. , 1980. 1 map :   LC Card 81-691105
G4181.C315 1980 .U5

United States. Soil Conservation Service. Watershed (P.L. 566) projects South Dakota, January 1979 /. Lincoln, Nebr. , 1979. 1 map :   LC Card 81-691106
G4181.C315 1979 .U5

United States. Soil Conservation Service. Watershed (P.L. 566) projects, South Dakota, January 1980 /. Lincoln, Nebr. , 1980. 1 map :   LC Card 81-691099
G4181.C315 1980 .U52

WATERSHEDS - STATISTICAL METHODS.
Finney, Brad A. Random differential equations in water quality modeling /. Logan, Utah [1979] viii, 41 p. :   LC Card 80-622173   DDC 553.7/028 19
TD367 .F56

WATERSHEDS - WASHINGTON (STATE) - MAPS.
United States. Soil Conservation Service. Status of P.L.566 watersheds in Washington /. Portland, Or. , 1979. 1 map :   LC Card 81-691500
G4281.C315 1979 .U5

WATERSHEDS - WASHINGTON (STATE) - WHITMAN COUNTY - MAPS.
United States. Soil Conservation Service. Watersheds, Whitman County, Washington /.

Portland, Or. , 1977. 1 map :   LC Card 81-691520
G4283.W6C315 1977 .U5

WATERSIDE WORKERS. see **STEVEDORES.**

Watertown, Mass. Free Public Library. Hodges, Maud deLeigh, 1888-1972. Crossroads on the Charles . Canaan, N.H. , c1980. vii, 243 p. :   ISBN 0-914016-68-7 :   LC Card 80-13753
F74.W33 H76 1980
NYPL [IQH+ (Watertown) 81-74]

WATERTOWN, MASS. - HISTORY.
Hodges, Maud deLeigh, 1888-1972. Crossroads on the Charles . Canaan, N.H. , c1980. vii, 243 p. :   ISBN 0-914016-68-7 :   LC Card 80-13753
F74.W33 H76 1980
NYPL [IQH+ (Watertown) 81-74]

Watkins, Elizabeth L. Tri-Regional Workshop for Social Workers in Maternal and Child Health Services (1980 : Raleigh, N.C.) Social work in a state-based system of child health care . Chapel Hill [1981?] v, 156 p. :   LC Card 81-50559   DDC 362.1/9892/000973 19
RJ102 .T74 1980

Watkins, L. V.
Human investment tax credit. Edmonds, Robert H. A human investent tax credit program, second report : a component of an anti-inflation and full employment alternative economic program : a discussion paper / prepared for the Economic Development Administration, U. S. Department of Commerce by Robert H. Edmonds with Mark Goldes. [Washington] , 1977. 24, 49 p. ;   LC Card 77-604090
HC106.7 .E348

Watson, Donald P. Hawaiian plumerias /. Honolulu , 1981. p. cm.   LC Card 81-6746   DDC 635.9/77375 19
SB413.P56 H38

Watson, Harry L. Jacksonian politics and community conflict / Harry L. Watson. Baton Rouge : Louisiana State University Press, c1981. p. cm. Bibliography: p. Includes index.   ISBN 0-8071-0857-X :   LC Card 81-2414   DDC 324/.09756/373 19
1. Cumberland County (N.C.) - Politics and government. 2. United States - Politics and government - 1815-1861. 3. Jackson, Andrew, 1767-1845. I. Title.
F262.C9 W37

Watson, Hugh Seton- see **Seton-Watson, Hugh.**

Watson, Richard H. Energy, transition to the '80s : a report on energy legislation in the 1980 regular session of the Washington State Legislature / prepared for the Senate Committee on Energy and Utilities by Richard H. Watson. Olympia, WA : The Committee, [1980] 52 p., [2] leaves : graphs ; 28 cm. Bibliography: leaves [53-54]   LC Card 80-623469   DDC 346.7304/679 19
1. Power resources - Law and legislation - Washington (State). 2. Power resources - Washington (State). I. Washington (State). Legislature. Senate. Energy and Utilities Committee. II. Title.
KFW286 .W38

Watson, Robert F. United States. National Science Foundation. Office of Experimental Projects and Programs. College science improvement programs. Washington, D. C [1974] v, 191 p.   **NYPL [JSF 80-775]**

Watson, Robert William Seton- see **Seton-Watson, Robert William, 1879-1951.**

Watt, Arthur Dwight, 1921- Index of generic names of fossil plants, 1974-1978 : based on the Compendium index of paleobotany of the U. S. Geological Survey / by Arthur D. Watt. Washington : U. S. Govt. Print. Off., 1981. p. cm. (Geological Survey bulletin ; 1517) Supplements Index of generic names of fossil plants, 1820-1965, by H. N. Andrews and Index of generic names of fossil plants, 1966-1973, by A. M. Blazer.   LC Card 80-606811   DDC 557.3 s 561/.014 19
1. Paleobotany - Nomenclators. 2. Paleobotany - Bibliography. I. Blazer, Anna M. Index of generic names of fossil plants, 1966-1973. II. Series: United States. Geological Survey. Bulletin ; 1517. III. Title.
QE75 .B9 no. 1517 QE903

WATT, JAMES G., 1938-
United States. Congress. House. Committee on Interior and Insular Affairs. Briefing by the

secretary of the Interior . Washington , 1981. iii, 79 p. ;   LC Card 81-601759   DDC 353.3 19
KF27 .I5 1981

United States. Congress. Senate. Committee on Energy and Natural Resources. James G. Watt nomination . Washington , 1981. 2 v. :   LC Card 81-600871   DDC 353.3 19
KF26 .E55 1981

Watt, William J. Indiana's citizen soldiers . Indianapolis , 1980. vi, 232 p. :   LC Card 80-620014   DDC 355.3/7/09772 19
UA180 .I53

Watts, Ann Chalmers. Literature and the urban experience . New Brunswick, N.J. , c1981. p. cm.   ISBN 0-8135-0929-7 :   LC Card 81-5857   DDC 810/.9/321732 19
PS169.C57 L5

Watts, Frank C. Soil survey of St. Lucie County area, Florida / [by Frank C. Watts and Daniel L. Stankey] ; United States Department of Agriculture, Soil Conservation Service, in cooperation with University of Florida, Institute of Food and Agricultural Sciences and Agricultural Experiment Stations, Soil Science Department, and Florida Department of Agriculture and Consumer Services. [Washington] : U. S. Dept. of Agriculture, Soil Conservation Service, [1980] vii, 183 p., [26] fold. leaves of plates : ill. ; 29 cm. Cover title. "Issued March 1980." Bibliography: p. 105-106.   LC Card 80-602562   DDC 631.4/7/75929 19
1. Soils - Florida - St. Lucie Co. - Maps. I. Stankey, Daniel L., joint author. II. United States. Soil Conservation Service. III. Title.
S599.F6 W37

Watts, Gordon P. The Monitor : a bibliography / compiled by Gordon P. Watts, Jr., James A. Pleasants, Jr. [Kure Beach, N.C.] : Underwater Archaeological Research Branch, Division of Archives and History, North Carolina Dept. of Cultural Resources, [1978?] [87] leaves ; 28 cm. Cover title.   LC Card 80-622593   DDC 016.9737/52 19
1. Monitor (Ironclad) - Bibliography. 2. United States - History - Civil War, 1861-1865 - Naval operations - Bibliography. I. Pleasants, James A., joint author. II. Title.
Z1242 .W37 E595.M7

Watts, W. F. (Winthrop F.) An introduction to the mine inspection data analysis system (MIDAS) /. Avondale, Md. , 1981. p. cm.   LC Card 81-607306   DDC 622 s 622/.8/0285425 19
TN23 .U43 TN295

Waugh, Charles. Woolrich, Cornell, 1903-1968. The fantastic stories of Cornell Woolrich /. Carbondale , c1981. p. cm.   ISBN 0-8093-1008-2   LC Card 81-4785   DDC 813/.54 19
PS3515.O6455 A6 1981

Wayman, Cooper H. Permits handbook for coal development / Cooper H. Wayman, Gail A. Genasci. Golden, CO : Colorado School of Mines Press, c1981. xxiii, 616 p. : ill. ; 29 cm. Includes bibliographical references and index.   ISBN 0-918062-40-3 :   LC Card 80-22500   DDC 353.0082/327 19
1. Coal mines and mining - Licenses - United States. 2. Coal leases - United States. I. Genasci, Gail A. II. Title.
KF1830 .W39

WAYNE COUNTY, IOWA - MAPS.
(1979) United States. Soil Conservation Service. Wayne County, Iowa /. Lincoln, Nebr. , 1979. 1 map :   LC Card 81-691183
G4153.W35 1979 .U5

WAYNE COUNTY, N. Y. - ADMINISTRATIVE AND POLITICAL DIVISIONS - MAPS.
Rice, Philip A. Wayne County, New York, highway system. Lyons, N. Y, 1976. col. map
NYPL [Map Div. 80-3337]

Wayne County, N. Y. Highways, Superintendent of. see **Wayne County, N. Y. Superintendent of Highways.**

WAYNE COUNTY, N. Y. - MAPS.
(1976) Rice, Philip A. Wayne County, New York, highway system. Lyons, N. Y., 1976. col. map   **NYPL [Map Div. 80-3337]**

WAYNE COUNTY, N. Y. - ROAD MAPS.
Rice, Philip A. Wayne County, New York, highway system. Lyons, N. Y, 1976. col. map
NYPL [Map Div. 80-3337]

Wayne County, N. Y. Superintendent of Highways. Rice, Philip A. Wayne County, New York, highway system. Lyons, N. Y, 1976. col. map   *NYPL [Map Div. 80-3337]*

Wayne State University. Center for Black Studies. National Invitational Symposium on the King Decision (1980 : Wayne State University) Black English and the education of Black children and youth . Detroit, Mich. , c1981. 441 p. :   LC Card 80-85071   DDC 371.97/96073 19
LC2771 .N37 1981

Wayne State University, Detroit. Archives of Labor and Urban Affairs. An American Federation of Teachers bibliography / compiled by Archives of Labor and Urban Affairs, Wayne State University. Detroit : Wayne State University Press, 1980. 222 p. ; 24 cm. Includes index.   ISBN 0-8143-1659-X   LC Card 80-13142
1. Teachers' unions - United States - Bibliography. 2. Academic freedom - United States - Bibliography. 3. American Federation of Teachers - Bibliography. I. Title.
Z5815.U5 W38 1980 LB2844.53.U6
                                    NYPL [JLE 81-27]

Wayne State University, Detroit. College of Liberal Arts. Dept. of English. see Wayne State University, Detroit. Dept. of English.

Wayne State University, Detroit. Dept. of English. Criticism; a quarterly for literature and the arts. v. 1- ; winter 1959- Detroit.
                                    *NYPL [*ZAN-4455]*

Wayne State University, Detroit. English Dept. see Wayne State University, Detroit. Dept. of English.

Wayne State University, Detroit. Folklore Archive.
    Annotated holdings list - Wayne State University Folklore Archive .
    (no. 3) Wayne State University, Detroit. Folklore Archive. German and German-American folklore collections /. Detroit , 1980. 20 p. ;   LC Card 80-621843   DDC 016.39/000943 19
Z5984.U6 W39 1980 GR111.G47

German and German-American folklore collections / compiled by Angela Dubicki and Christina S. Rostkowycz ; edited by Philip LaRonge. Detroit : Wayne State University, Folklore Archive, 1980. 20 p. ; 22 cm. (Annotated holdings list - Wayne State University, Folklore Archive ; no. 3) Cover title.   LC Card 80-621843   DDC 016.39/000943 19
1. German American folklore - Bibliography. 2. Folk-lore - Germany - Bibliography. 3. Wayne State University, Detroit. Folklore Archives - Catalogs. I. Dubicki, Angela. II. Rostkowycz, Christina S. III. LaRonge, Philip. IV. Series: Wayne State University, Detroit. Folklore Archive. Annotated holdings list - Wayne State University Folklore Archive , no. 3. V. Title.
Z5984.U6 W39 1980 GR111.G47

WAYNE STATE UNIVERSITY, DETROIT. FOLKLORE ARCHIVES - CATALOGS.
Wayne State University, Detroit. Folklore Archive. German and German-American folklore collections /. Detroit , 1980. 20 p. ;   LC Card 80-621843   DDC 016.39/000943 19
Z5984.U6 W39 1980 GR111.G47

Wayne State University, Detroit. Institute of Labor and Industrial Relations. see Institute of Labor and Industrial Relations (University of Michigan-Wayne State University)

Wayne State University, Detroit. Labor and Urban Affairs, Archives of. see Wayne State University, Detroit. Archives of Labor and Urban Affairs.

Wayne State University, Detroit. Medical Library.
    Report .
    (no. 63) Bristor, Patricia R. Use of a cataloging center's bibliographic records as a means to check and balance acquisitions activities at an academic health sciences library /. Detroit , 1980. 6, [5] leaves ;   LC Card 80-622445   DDC 025.2/18661 19
Z688.M4 B74

WAYNE STATE UNIVERSITY, DETROIT. MEDICAL LIBRARY.
Bristor, Patricia R. Use of a cataloging center's

bibliographic records as a means to check and balance acquisitions activities at an academic health sciences library /. Detroit , 1980. 6, [5] leaves ;   LC Card 80-622445   DDC 025.2/18661 19
Z688.M4 B74

Wayne State University, Detroit. Walter P. Reuther Library of Labor and Urban Affairs. Archives of Labor and Urban Affairs. see Wayne State University, Detroit. Archives of Labor and Urban Affairs.

Wayne State University. School of Medicine. PBB general population study . [Lansing , 1979] 269 p. in various pagings :   LC Card 80-621045   DDC 363.1/79 19
RA1242.P69 P16

Ways of providing a fairer share of Federal housing support to rural areas . United States. General Accounting Office. [Washington, D.C. , 1980] v, 86 p. :   LC Card 80-601694   DDC 363.5/8 19
HD7289.U6 U55 1980

Ways to Shiva . Dye, Joseph M., 1944- Philadelphia, PA , 1980. p. cm.   ISBN 0-87633-038-3 :   LC Card 80-25113   DDC 294.5 19
BL2001.2 .D93

Waytulonis, Robert W. State regulations pertaining to the use of internal-combustion engines underground / by Robert W. Waytulonis. [Avondale, Md.] : U. S. Dept. of the Interior, Bureau of Mines, [1981] p. cm. (Information circular)   LC Card 81-607000   DDC 622 s 363.1/89 19
1. Mine safety - United States. 2. Internal combustion engines - Safety measures. I. Series: Information circular (United States. Bureau of Mines) . II. Title.
TN295 .U4

... We come to dedicate a school /. New York (City). Intermediate School 201 Complex. [New York , 196-?]. 33 leaves ;
                                NYPL [Sc Micro R-3667]

We have all gone away /. Harnack, Curtis, 1927- Ames , 1981. 188 p. ;   ISBN 0-8138-1901-6   LC Card 81-3777   DDC 813/.54 B 19
PS3558.A62474 Z476 1981

We interrupt this program . Gordon, Robbie. Amherst , 1980, c1978. 117 p. :   LC Card 79-624735
HM263 .G63   *NYPL [JLF 81-53]*

We never sleep . Voss, Frederick. Washington, D.C. , 1981. p. cm.   LC Card 81-607851   DDC 363.2/89/0973 19
HV8087.P75 V67

WEALDEN FLORA. see PALEOBOTANY - CRETACEOUS.

WEALDEN FOSSILS. see PALEONTOLOGY - CRETACEOUS.

WEAPONS. see FIREARMS.

WEAPONS, ATOMIC. see ATOMIC WEAPONS.

WEATHER CONTROL - LAW AND LEGISLATION - UNITED STATES.
United States. Congress. Senate. Committee on Commerce, Science, and Transportation. Subcommittee on Science, Technology, and Space. Reauthorization of National climate program act . Washington , 1980. iii, 28 p. ;   LC Card 80-602777   DDC 353.0072/23682324 19
KF26 .C697 1980b

WEATHER CONTROL - UNITED STATES - FINANCE.
United States. Congress. Senate. Committee on Commerce, Science, and Transportation. Subcommittee on Science, Technology, and Space. Reauthorization of National climate program act . Washington , 1980. iii, 28 p. ;   LC Card 80-602777   DDC 353.0072/23682324 19
KF26 .C697 1980b

WEATHER SATELLITES. see METEOROLOGICAL SATELLITES.

WEATHERING.
Colman, Steven M. Chemical weathering of basalts and andesites . Washington , 1982. p. cm.   LC Card 81-6903   DDC 552/.26 19
QE462.B3 C64

Weathering rinds on andesitic and basaltic stones as a Quaternary age indicator, Western United States /. Colman, Steven M. Washington , 1981. iv, 56 p. :   LC Card 80-607840   DDC 551.7/9/0978 19
QE696 .C656

WEATHERING - THE WEST.
Colman, Steven M. Weathering rinds on andesitic and basaltic stones as a Quaternary age indicator, Western United States /. Washington , 1981. iv, 56 p. :   LC Card 80-607840   DDC 551.7/9/0978 19
QE696 .C656

Weatherization assistance for low income persons . Connecticut. General Assembly. Legislative Program Review and Investigations Committee. [Hartford, CT) (Legislative Office Building, 18 Trinity St., Hartford 06115) [1980] vii, 124 p. ;   LC Card 81-621601   DDC 353.97460084/5045 19
HC107.C83 P6325 1980

Weaver, Donald Kessler. Bridger Hydrometeorological Research Area development and operation, 1965-1968 / by Donald K. Weaver. [Bozeman] : Montana University Joint Water Resources Research Center, 1975. 49, 4, 8 leaves ; 29 cm. (Report - Montana University Joint Water Resources Research Center . no. 70) "Final report for WRRC projects B-006 Mont., instrumentation of remote areas; B-014, digital instrumentation and telemetry; A-021, operation of the Bridger data acquisition system." Series stamped on cover. "ERL report #2175."   LC Card 76-624302   DDC 551.57/028/54 19
1. Watersheds - Montana - Bridger National Forest - Research - History. I. Montana University Joint Water Resources Research Center. II. Series: Montana University Joint Water Resources Research Center. Report , no. 70. III. Title.
GB991.M9 W4

Weaver, Margaret G. Mushroom flora of Minnesota--a contribution / by Margaret G. Weaver and David J. McLaughlin. Minneapolis, Minn. : Bell Museum of Natural History, University of Minnesota, [1980] 89 p. : ill. ; 26 cm. (Occasional papers - Bell Museum of Natural History, University of Minnesota . no. 16) Bibliography: p. 68. Includes index. CONTENTS. - 1. Key to families of gilled mushrooms.--2. Tricholomataceae, keys to genera and species.   LC Card 80-623787   DDC 589.2/2209776 19
1. Tricholomataceae. 2. Mushrooms - Minnesota - Identification. 3. Fungi - Minnesota - Identification. I. McLaughlin, David Jordan, joint author. II. Series: Bell Museum of Natural History. Occasional papers , no. 16. III. Title.
QK629.T73 W4

Webb, Walter Prescott, 1888-1963. The Great Plains / Walter Prescott Webb. 1st Bison book print. Lincoln : University of Nebraska Press, 1981, c1959. p. cm. Reprint. Originally published: Boston : Ginn, 1931. Includes index.   ISBN 0-8032-9702-5 (pbk.)   LC Card 81-1821   DDC 978 19
1. Great Plains - History. 2. Mississippi Valley - History. I. Title.
F591 .W35 1981

Webber, Margo B. Reuse of historically and architecturally significant railroad stations for transportation and other community needs : documentation, analysis, evaluation : prepared for U. S. Department of Transportation, Office of the Secretary, Office of Environment and Safety ... Robert F. Crecco, technical representative / prepared by Anderson Notter Finegold Inc., with assistance from Russell Wright, Roger W. Foster, Dalton Dalton Little Newport . Washington, D.C. : U. S. Dept. of Transportation : for sale by the Supt. of Docs., U. S. Govt. Print. Off., 1978. ii, 126 p. : ill. ; 28 cm. Report prepared by M. B. Webber and P. J. McGinley. Cover title: Recycling historic railroad stations. "DOT-OST-77-002."   LC Card 79-603620   DDC 725/.31/0288 19
1. Railroads - United States - Stations - Remodeling for other use. I. McGinley, Paul J., joint author. II. Anderson Notter Finegold Inc. III. United States. Dept. of Transportation. Office of Environment and Safety. IV. Title. V. Title: Recycling historic railroad stations.
NA6311 .W4

Webbert, Charles A. Idaho. University. Library. University of Idaho newspaper holdings as of December 31, 1979 /. [Moscow, Idaho] , 1979.

28 p. ;   LC Card 80-622444   DDC 016.07 19
Z6952.I2 I2 1979 PN4897.I23

Weber, Margaret J. Boyer, Lester L. Energy and habitability aspects of earth sheltered housing in Oklahoma . Stillwater, Okla. [1980] viii, 88 p. :   LC Card 81-620560   DDC 690/.837 19
TH4819.E27 B68

Weber, Max, 1881-1961.
Rubenstein, Daryl R. Max Weber, prints and color variations . [Washington, D.C.] , c1980. 15 p. :   LC Card 80-51701   DDC 769.92/4 19
NE539.W38 A4 1980a

WEBER, MAX, 1881-1961 - EXHIBITIONS.
Rubenstein, Daryl R. Max Weber, prints and color variations . [Washington, D.C.] , c1980. 15 p. :   LC Card 80-51701   DDC 769.92/4 19
NE539.W38 A4 1980a

Weber, Michael T. (joint author) Riley, Peter, 1950- Food and agricultural marketing in developing countries . East Lansing, Mich. , 1979. 49 p. ;   LC Card 80-622267   DDC 016.381/41/091724 19
Z7164.F7 R54 HD9000.5

Weber, Polly. (joint author) Boyd, Joseph H. New York State Racing and Wagering Board drug medication study . [Albany] , 1976. 69 leaves ;   LC Card 78-621360   DDC 636.1/089558 19
SF951 .B79

Webfoots & Bunchgrassers. Folk art of the Oregon country /. [Salem?] , c1980. 128 p. :   LC Card 80-622779   DDC 745/.09795/074013 19
NK805.O7 F64

WEBSTER COUNTY (IOWA) - MAPS.
United States. Soil Conservation Service. Webster County, Iowa /. [Lincoln, Neb.] [1979?] 1 map :   LC Card 81-691182
G4153.W4 1979 .U5

Webster, Stephen H. A survey of arson and arson response capabilities in selected jurisdictions / by Stephen H. Webster, Kenneth E. Mathews, Jr. ; prepared for the National Institute of Law Enforcement and Criminal Justice, Law Enforcement Assistance Administration, U. S. Department of Justice, by Abt Associates Inc. [Washington] : National Institute of Law Enforcement and Criminal Justice, Office of Development, Testing, and Dissemination, 1979. 41 p. : ill. ; 28 cm.
Includes bibliographical references. LC Card 79-601901   DDC 364.1/64 19
1. Arson investigation - United States - Statistics. 2. Arson - United States - Statistics. I. Mathews, Kenneth E., joint author. II. Abt Associates. III. Title.
HV8079.A7 W4

Wedemeyer, Charles A. Learning at the back door : reflections on non-traditional learning in the lifespan / Charles A. Wedemeyer. Madison : University of Wisconsin Press, 1981. p. cm. Bibliography: p. Includes index. ISBN 0-299-08560-0 :   LC Card 80-52301   DDC 374 19
1. Nonformal education. 2. Continuing education. I. Title.
LC45.3 .W43

Wedemeyer, Dan J. Pacific Telecommunications Conference, Honolulu, 1979. Pacific Telecommunications Conference . Honolulu , 1979. ca. 500 p. in various pagings :   LC Card 79-110059
TK5102.3.P32 P32 1979
                                    NYPL [JLF 80-1628]

WEED CONTROL - BIBLIOGRAPHY.
Chykaliuk, P. B. Bibliography of glyphosate /. College Station, Tex. [1980] 87 p. ;   LC Card 80-622516   DDC 016.632/954 19
Z5074.P4 C48 SB952.G58

WEED KILLERS. see HERBICIDES.

WEEDICIDES. see HERBICIDES.

WEEDS - NORTHWEST, PACIFIC - IDENTIFICATION.
Gilkey, Helen Margaret, 1886- [Weeds of the Pacific Northwest.] Gilkey's Weeds of the Pacific Northwest /. [Corvallis] , c1980. 382 p. :   ISBN 0-88246-039-0 :   LC Card 80-82742 DDC 582/.0652/09795 19
SB612.N6 G5 1980

Weeds of the Pacific Northwest. Gilkey, Helen Margaret, 1886- [Weeds of the Pacific Northwest.] Gilkey's Weeds of the Pacific

Northwest /. [Corvallis] , c1980. 382 p. :   ISBN 0-88246-039-0 :   LC Card 80-82742 DDC 582/.0652/09795 19
SB612.N6 G5 1980

Weekly mortality from the principal causes of death. New York (City) Dept. of Health Bureau of Records and Statistics. 1876-77. New York.
                         NYPL [*ZAN-T5293]

Weeks, Edwin Lord, 1849-1903. The art of Edwin Lord Weeks, 1849-1903 [exhibition]/ University Art Galleries, University of New Hampshire, Durham, New Hampshire, 1976. Durham, N. H.: The Galleries, 1976. 34 p.: ill.; 31 cm.
Includes bibliographical references.
1. Weeks, Edwin Lord, 1849-1903. I. New Hampshire. University. University Art Galleries. II. Title.
                NYPL [3-MCX+ W39 80-1385]

WEEKS, EDWIN LORD, 1849-1903.
Weeks, Edwin Lord, 1849-1903. The art of Edwin Lord Weeks, 1849-1903 [exhibition]/. Durham, N. H., 1976. 34 p.:
                NYPL [3-MCX+ W39 80-1385]

Weeks, Herbert H., 1929- United States. Soil Conservation Service. Soil survey of Santa Rosa County, Florida /. [Washington] [1980] vii, 150 p., [47] fold. leaves of plates :   LC Card 80-602511   DDC 631.4/7/759985 19
S599.F6 U54 1980a

Weeks (I. D.) Library. Energy, a bibliography and index of related materials at the University of South Dakota / compiled by John E. Evans & John N. Olsgaard. Vermillion : I. D. Weeks Library, University of South Dakota, c1978. 546 p. ; 29 cm.   LC Card 79-621285
1. Power resources - Bibliography. 2. Power (Mechanics) - Bibliography. 3. Power resources - Indexes. 4. Power (Mechanics) - Indexes. 5. Weeks (I. D.) Library. I. Evans, John Edward 1951-. II. Olsgaard, John N. III. Title.
Z5853.P83 W4 1978 TJ163.2
                                    NYPL [JLF 80-1563]

WEEKS (I. D.) LIBRARY.
Weeks (I. D.) Library. Energy, a bibliography and index of related materials at the University of South Dakota /. Vermillion , c1978. 546 p. ;   LC Card 79-621285
Z5853.P83 W4 1978 TJ163.2
                                    NYPL [JLF 80-1563]

Weeks, J. Devereux. (joint author) Hardy, Paul T., 1953- Personal liability of public officials, under Federal law /. Athens, Ga. , c1980. p. cm.   ISBN 0-89854-068-2 :   LC Card 80-28931 DDC 342.73/068 19
KF1306.A2 H37 1980b

Weeks Library. see Weeks (I. D.) Library.

Weesies, Glenn A. Soil survey of Bay County, Michigan / [by Glenn A. Weesies] ; United States Department of Agriculture, Soil Conservation Service, in cooperation with Michigan Agricultural Experiment Station. [Washington, D.C.] : The Service, 1980. vii, 105 p., [23] fold. leaves of plates : ill. ; 28 cm.
Cover title. Bibliography: p. 57.   LC Card 80-602508 DDC 631.4/7/77447 19
1. Soils - Michigan - Bay Co. - Maps. I. United States. Soil Conservation Service. II. Michigan. Agricultural Experiment Station, East Lansing. III. Title.
S599.M4 W43

Wehmuller, William A. (joint author) Penner, Harold L. Soil survey of Sedgwick County, Kansas /. [Washington , 1979] vii, 126 p., [41] fold. leaves of plates :   LC Card 79-603621   DDC 631.4/7/78186 19
S599.K2 P44

Weicherding, Patrick J. (joint author) Albrecht, Jean. Urban forestry . St. Paul, Minn. [1980] 100 p. ;   LC Card 80-622738   DDC 016.6349/09173/2 19
Z5996.T74 A4 SB436

Weide, David L. Lyneis, Margaret M. Impacts, damage to cultural resources in the California desert /. Riverside, Calif. , 1980. viii, 171 p. :   LC Card 81-600782   DDC 979.4/9 19
F863 .L95

WEIDENBAUM, MURRAY L.
United States. Congress. Senate. Committee on Banking, Housing and Urban Affairs. Nomination of Murray L. Weidenbaum . Washington , 1981. iii, 114 p. :   LC Card

81-601619   DDC 353.0082 19
KF26 .B39 1981a

Weidman, Michael. Santa Ana's architectural heritage : a guide to Santa Ana's historic neighborhoods / produced by the Santa Ana Historic Survey ; photography by Michael Weidman ; text by Kathleen Les ; [historic research Suzanne Claire]. Santa Ana : City of Santa Ana : Santa Ana First Federal Savings, c1980. 65 p. : ill. ; 22 x 28 cm.   LC Card 80-137507   DDC 917.94/96 19
1. Santa Ana, Calif. - Buildings - Guide-books. 2. Santa Ana, Calif. - Dwellings - Guide-books. 3. Historic buildings - California - Santa Ana - Guide-books. I. Les, Kathleen. II. Santa Ana Historic Survey. III. Title.
NA735.S4 W44

WEIGHTS AND MEASURES - LAW AND LEGISLATION - UNITED STATES - STATES.
National Conference on Weights and Measures. Model state laws and regulations /. Washington, D.C. [1980] 119 p. in various pagings :   LC Card 79-600214   DDC 343.73/075/02632 19
KF1665.Z95 N37 1979

Weights and Measures, National Conference on. see National Conference on Weights and Measures.

WEIGHTS AND MEASURES - UNITED STATES - EXHIBITIONS.
United States. National Bureau of Standards. Museum. Catalog of artifacts on display in the NBS Museum /. Washington, D.C. , 1977. ca. 200 p. :   LC Card 79-603912
Q185.7 .U54 1977

Weigle, James Montgomery, 1919- (joint author) Achmad, Grufron. A quasi three-dimensional finite-difference ground-water flow model with a field application . Baltimore, Md. , 1979. iv, 22, [35] p. :   LC Card 80-621644   DDC 557.52 s 551.49/0724 19
QE121 .A23 no. 33 TC176

WEIL, SIMONE, 1909-1943 - ADDRESSES, ESSAYS, LECTURES.
Simone Weil, interpretations of a life /. Amherst, 1981. p. cm.   ISBN 0-87023-343-2 :   LC Card 81-7460   DDC 194 19
B2430.W474 S617

Wein, Frances Stevenson. Hussey, Jeannette M. The code duello in America /. Washington , 1980. p. cm.   LC Card 80-607828   DDC 394/.8 19
CR4595.U5 H87

Weinberg, Martin S. Bell, Alan P., 1932- Sexual preference, its development in men and women /. Bloomington , c1981. p. cm.   ISBN 0-253-16673-X   LC Card 81-47006   DDC 306.7/6 19
HQ76 .B438

WEINBERGER, CASPAR W.
United States. Congress. Senate. Committee on Armed Services. Nomination of Caspar W. Weinberger to be Secretary of Defense . Washington , 1981. iii, 61 p. ;   LC Card 81-600831   DDC 353.6 19
KF26 .A7 1981

Weinreich, Chris. Washington (State). Office of Community Development. A brief survey of CSA-related anti-poverty organizations in Washington State. [Olympia] , 1978. 64 p. ;   LC Card 79-621288
HV86 .W365 1978a   **NYPL [JLF 81-121]**

Weinstein, Allan. Implant retrieval . Washington, D.C. , 1981. xi, 776 :   LC Card 80-600194   DDC 602/.18 s 617/.307 19
QC100 .U57 no. 601 RD755.5

Weinstein, Harriet Goldberg. United States. Federal Mediation and Conciliation Service. Office of Research. Impact of the 1974 health care amendments to the NLRA on collective bargaining in the health care industry /. [Washington] , 1979. x, 473 p. :   LC Card 79-603053
RA971.35 .U54 1979

Weinstein, Richard A. Beau Mire, a late Tchula period site of the Tchefuncte culture, Ascension Parish, Louisiana / Richard A. Weinstein, Philip G. Rivet. Baton Rouge, La. : Dept. of Culture, Recreation, and Tourism : Louisiana Archaeological Survey and Antiquites Commission, 1978. vii, 125, [9] p. : ill. ; 23 cm.

(Anthropological report . no. 1) Bibliography: p. [127]-[134]   LC Card 80-137100   DDC 976.3/19 19
1. Beau Mire site, La. I. Rivet, Philip G., joint author. II. Louisiana. Dept. of Culture, Recreation & Tourism. III. Louisiana Archaeological Survey and Antiquities Commission. IV. Title. V. Series.
E78.L8 W44

Weinstein, Stanley E. National Conference on Mental Health Issues Related to Sudden Infant Death Syndrome, Baltimore, Md., 1977. Mental health issues in grief counseling . Rockville, Md. , Washington, D.C. , 1979 i.e. 1980. 133 p. ;   LC Card 80-602299   DDC 362.8/286 19
RJ59 .N37 1977

Weintraub, Robert E., 1925- The impact of the Federal Reserve System's monetary policies on the nation's economy (second report) : staff report of the Subcommittee on Domestic Monetary Policy of the Committee on Banking, Finance and Urban Affairs, House of Representatives, 96th Congress, second session. Washington : U. S. G.P.O., c1980 [i.e. 1981] xii, 51 p. : ill. ; 26 cm. At head of title: Committee print 96-21. "Updates a 1976 staff study"--P. iii. "December 1980." Item 1013   LC Card 81-601005   DDC 330.973/0926 19
1. Monetary policy - United States. 2. Board of Governors of the Federal Reserve System (U. S.). 3. United States - Economic conditions - 1971-. I. United States. Congress. House. Committee on Banking, Finance, and Urban Affairs. Subcommittee on Domestic Monetary Policy. II. Title.
HG2565 .W44

Weintraub, Sidney, 1922- The illegal alien from Mexico : policy choices for an intractable issue / by Sidney Weintraub and Stanley R. Ross. [Austin] : Mexico-United States Border Research Program, University of Texas at Austin : Distributed by University of Texas Press, c1980. ix, 65 p. ; 21 cm. Bibliography: p. 57-65. ISBN 0-292-73822-6 (pbk.)   LC Card 80-80323   DDC 325/.272/0973 19
1. Mexicans - United States. 2. Aliens - United States. 3. United States - Emigration and immigration. I. Ross, Stanley Robert, 1921-. II. Title.
E184.M5 W46

Weir, Adrianne W. Smith, Charles P., 1931- A national assessment of case disposition and classification in the juvenile justice system. Washington, D.C. , 1979-80. 3 v. :   LC Card 80-600043   DDC 364.3/6/0973 19
HV9104 .S6

Weir, Judith H. Treude, Mai. Windows to the past . Minneapolis, Minn. (311 Walter Library, 117 Pleasant St. S.E., University of Minnesota, Minneapolis, Minn. 55455) , 1980. ix, 187 p. :   LC Card 80-154529   DDC 016.912/776 19
Z6027.M65 T73 GA432

Weis, Joseph G. Jurisdiction and the elusive status offender : a comparison of involvement in delinquent behavior and status offenses / by Joseph G. Weis [with] Karleen Sakumoto, John Sederstrom, Carol Zeiss, research assistants. Washington, D.C. : U. S. Dept. of Justice, Law Enforcement Assistance Administration, Office of Juvenile Justice and Delinquency Prevention : for sale by the Supt. of Docs., U. S. Govt. Print. Off., [1980] c1979. ix, 135 p. : graph ; 28 cm. (Reports of the national juvenile justice assessment centers) At head of title: National Institute for Juvenile Justice and Delinquency Prevention. On spine: Jurisdiction and the status offender. "Prepared by the National Center for the Assessment of Delinquent Behavior and Its Prevention of the Center for Law and Justice, University of Washington." "June 1980." Bibliography: p. 131-135.   LC Card 80-602845   DDC 364.3/6/0973 19
1. Status offenders - United States. 2. Juvenile delinquency - United States. I. National Institute for Juvenile Justice and Delinquency Prevention. II. Washington (State). University. National Center for the Assessment of Delinquent Behavior and Its Prevention. III. Title. IV. Title: Jurisdiction and the status offender. V. Series.
HV9104 .W447

Weisberg, H. L. (Howard L.) Chamber of Commerce of the United States of America. International Dept. A national export policy . Washington, D.C. , c1981. iii, 49 p. ; ISBN 0-89834-037-3 (pbk.) :   LC Card 81-67315   DDC 382/.63/0973 19
HF1455 .C47 1981

Weisbrod, Burton Allen, 1931- (joint author) Geweke, John. Some economic consequences of technological advance in medical care . [Madison, Wis.] [1980] 52 p. : ;   LC Card 80-622910   DDC 338.4/33621963433061 19
RA645.P46 G48 1980

Weisel, Charles J. Soil survey of Benewah County area, Idaho / [by Charles J. Weisel] ; United States Department of Agriculture, Soil Conservation Service [and] United States Department of the Interior, Bureau of Indian Affairs, in cooperation with University of Idaho, Idaho Agricultural Experiment Station. [Washington] : The Service, [1980] x, 188 p., [25] fold. leaves of plates : ill. ; 29 cm. Cover title. Bibliography: p. 97.   LC Card 80-602396   DDC 631.4/7/79693 19
1. Soils - Idaho - Benewah Co. - Maps. I. United States. Soil Conservation Service. II. United States. Bureau of Indian Affairs. III. Idaho. Agricultural Experiment Station, Moscow. IV. Title.
S599.I2 W44

Weisel, George Ferdinand, 1915- (joint author) Neher, Michael A. Heavy metal accumulation and its effect on the biota of an industrial settling pond . Bozeman , 1977. viii, 96, 2 p., [1] leaf of plates ;   LC Card 79-624616   DDC 574.5/26322 19
QH545.H42 N44

Weisenberger, Billy C., 1916- (joint author) Froedge, Ronald D. Soil survey of Grant and Pendleton Counties, Kentucky /. [Washington] , 1980. vii, 85 p., [40] fold. leaves of plates :   LC Card 80-602321   DDC 631.4/7/76933 19
S599.K4 F76

Weishuhn, Larry L. An annotated bibliography of Texas white-tailed deer research and selected articles from other states / compiled by Larry L. Wieshuhn, Robert L. Cook, W. Fielding Harwell. [Austin. Tex. : Texas Parks and Wildlife Dept., 1979] 82 p. : ill. ; 29 cm. (FA series ; no. 17) "A contribution of Federal aid project W-109-R Texas Parks and Wildlife Department." "PWD booklet 7000-52." Includes index.   LC Card 80-621109   DDC 599.73/57 19
1. White-tailed deer - Abstracts. 2. White-tailed deer - Bibliography. 3. Mammals - Texas - Abstracts. 4. Mammals - Texas - Bibliography. I. Cook, Robert L., joint author. II. Harwell, W. Fielding, joint author. III. Series: FA report series , no. 17. IV. Title.
QL737.U55 W42

Weiss, Michael J. An annotated bibliography of the genus Stelidota Erichson (Coleoptera: Nitidulidae, Nitidulinae) / Michael J. Weiss and Roger N. Williams. Wooster, Ohio : Ohio Agricultural Research and Development Center, [1980] 37 p. ; 28 cm. (Research circular - Ohio Agricultural Research and Development Center . 255) Cover title. "February 1980." Includes index.   LC Card 80-623557   DDC 016.59576/43 19
1. Stelidota - Bibliography. I. Williams, Roger N., joint author. II. Series: Ohio. Agricultural Research and Development Center. Research circular, 255. III. Title.
Z5858.S74 W44 QL596.N58

Weiss, Shirley F. Environmental Design Conference on City Centers in Transition, University of North Carolina at Chapel Hill, 1976. City centers in transition . Chapel Hill , 1976. xii, 90 leaves ;   LC Card 76-29226
NYPL [JLF 80-1605]

Weissman, Judith. Carruth, Hayden, 1921- [Selections.] Working papers . Athens , c1981. p. cm.   ISBN 0-8203-0583-9   LC Card 81-4404   DDC 809/.04 19
PN771 .C336

Welch, Barbara. The voluntary water quality monitoring project report, 1979 / Barbara Welch, Judy Potvin. [Augusta] : State of Maine, Dept. of Environmental Protection, [1980] 136 p. : ill. ; 28 cm. Cover title. "April 1980."   LC Card 80-623367   DDC 363.7/3942/09741 19
1. Water quality - Maine - Measurement. 2. Water quality management - Maine. 3. Environmental monitoring - Maine. 4. Lakes - Maine. I. Potvin, Judy, joint author. II. Title.
TD224.M2 W44

Welcome to Washington. United States. National Park Service. Washington, D.C. /. Washington [1978] 1 map : 23 x 49 cm. Scale not given. Folded title: Welcome to Washington. "Reprint 1978." "Stock Number 024-005-00669-9." Covers the National Mall, major government buildings, and tourist sites in downtown Washington. Includes text, tourist information, and col. ill. Text, tourist information, map of Washington region, and col. ill. on verso.   LC Card 78-696267
G3851.E635 1978 .U5
NYPL [Map Div. 81-3038]

Weld County Genealogical Society. 1870 Colorado Territory census index. Greeley, Colo. : Weld County Genealogical Society, 1977. 13, 377 p. : map ; 28 cm.   LC Card 80-128759
1. Colorado - Census, 1870 - Indexes. 2. Colorado - Genealogy. I. United States. Census Office. 9th census, 1870. II. Title.
F775 .W52 1977
NYPL [APR (Colorado) 81-165]

WELDING - SAFETY MEASURES.
Derby, George K. Reduction of airborne contaminants from welding exhaust at surface mines /. Avondale, MD , 1981. p. cm.   LC Card 81-607864   DDC 622 s 671.5/2 19
TN295 .U4

Welfare and pension plan statistics: characteristics of plans. United States. Office of Labor-Management and Welfare-Pension Reports. Characteristics of plans on file under the Welfare and pension plans disclosure act. [Washington]   *NYPL [JLM 80-866]*

WELFARE FUNDS (TRADE-UNION) - UNITED STATES.
United States. Congress. Senate. Committee on Governmental Affairs. Permanent Subcommittee on Investigations. Labor union insurance activities of Joseph Hauser and his associates . Washington , 1979. viii, 202 p. ;   LC Card 80-600763   DDC 364.1/68 19
KF31 .G684 1979

WELFARE FUNDS (TRADE-UNION) - UNITED STATES - PERIODICALS.
United States. Office of Labor-Management and Welfare-Pension Reports. Characteristics of plans on file under the Welfare and pension plans disclosure act. [Washington]
NYPL [JLM 80-866]

Welfare in the 70's. United States. Congress. Joint Economic Committee. Washington, 1974. ix, 300 p.;   *NYPL [JLE 81-115]*

WELFARE RECIPIENTS - EMPLOYMENT - UNITED STATES - CASE STUDIES.
Setzer, Florence. The Seattle-Denver income maintenance experiment . [[Washington] , 1978. xv, 54 p. ;   LC Card 78-603699
HC110.I5 S4   *NYPL [JLF 81-429]*

WELFARE RECIPIENTS - MICHIGAN - STATISTICS.
Swanson, Robert William. Income and benefit receipt among Michigan AFDC families /. [Lansing] [1979] xix, 150 p. :   LC Card 80-621648   DDC 361/.9774 s 362.7/13/09774 19
HV86 .M536 no. 31 (11-79)
NYPL [JLM 75-1607 no. 13]

WELFARE RECIPIENTS - MISSOURI - STATISTICS.
Rao, Vaman. Evaluation of real income of welfare recipients in Missouri /. [Columbia] , 1978. 73 p. ;   LC Card 79-623417   DDC 362.5/2/09778 19
HV98.M8 R36

Well-being in old age . Texas. Joint Committee on Long-Term Care Alternatives. Austin, Tex. , 1978. xiii, 91 p. :   LC Card 80-620754   DDC 362.6/042/09764 19
HV1468.T4 T49 1978

Well drillers and contractors . Oregon. Legislative Assembly. Legislative Research. Salem, Or. (S-420 State Capitol, Salem 97310) [1980] iv, 40 p. ;   LC Card 81-620549   DDC 344.795/017627114 347.950417627114 19
KFO2849 .A25 1980

WELL DRILLERS - LICENSES - OREGON.
Oregon. Legislative Assembly. Legislative Research. Well drillers and contractors . Salem, Or. (S-420 State Capitol, Salem 97310) [1980] iv, 40 p. ;   LC Card 81-620549   DDC 344.795/017627114 347.950417627114 19
KFO2849 .A25 1980

WELL DRILLING, GAS. see GAS WELL DRILLING.

Wellek, René. Four critics : Croce, Valéry, Lukács, and Ingarden / by René Wellek.

Seattle : University of Washington Press, c1981.
p. cm. Based on four lectures at the University of
Washington, Oct. 11, 18, 24, and Nov. 1, 1979.
Includes bibliographical references and index. ISBN
0-295-95800-6   LC Card 80-54429   DDC
801.95/0904 19
1. Criticism - History - 20th century - Addresses,
essays, lectures. 2. Croce, Benedetto, 1866-1952 -
Addresses, essays, lectures. 3. Valéry, Paul, 1871-1945 -
Addresses, essays, lectures. 4. Lukács, György,
1885-1971 - Addresses, essays, lectures. 5. Ingarden,
Roman, 1893- - Addresses, essays, lectures. I. Title.
PN94 .W44

Weller, Gunter. University of Alaska, Fairbanks.
Geophysical Institute. Alaska's weather and
climate . Fairbanks, Alaska [1979] v, 153
leaves .   LC Card 80-621244   DDC 551.69798 19
QC984.A4 U54 1979

Wells, Carolyn M. Index and abstracts of colonial
documents in the Eugene P. Watson Memorial
Library / Carolyn M. Wells, compiler.
Natchitoches, La. : Archives Division, Eugene
P. Watson Memorial Library, Northwestern
State University of Louisiana, c1980. xi, 75 p. ;
23 cm.   LC Card 81-128135   DDC 016.9763/65 19
1. Eugene P. Watson Memorial Library - Bibliography -
Catalogs. 2. United States - History - Colonial period,
ca. 1600-1775 - Sources - Abstracts. I. Eugene P.
Watson Memorial Library. II. Title.
Z674.5.U52 L848

Wells, Deborah K. Chemical analyses of water
from the Minnelusa Formation and equivalents
in the Powder River Basin and adjacent areas,
northeastern Wyoming : a basic-data report /
by Deborah K. Wells, John F. Busby, and Kent
C. Glover ; prepared by the U. S. Geological
Survey. Cheyenne : Wyoming Water Planning
Program, State Engineer's Office, [1979] iii, 27
p., [1] leaf of plates : ill. ; 28 cm. (Report -
Wyoming Water Planning Program ; no. 18) Stamped
on t.p.: Jan 1979. Bibliography: p. 9.   LC Card
79-622599   DDC 553.7/9/097871 19
1. Water quality - Wyoming. I. Busby, John F., joint
author. II. Glover, Kent C., joint author. III. United
States. Geological Survey. IV. Series: Wyoming. State
Water Planning Program. Report, no. 18. V. Title.
TD224.W8 W44

Wells, Frank C. Hydrology and water quality of
the lower Mississippi River / by Frank C.
Wells ; [prepared by United States Department
of the Interior, Geological Survey, in
cooperation with Louisiana Department of
Transportation and Development, Office of
Public Works]. Baton Rouge, La. : The Office,
1980. vii, 83 p., [5] leaves of plates (4 fold.) :
ill. ; 28 cm. (Water resources technical report . no.
21) Bibliography: p. 79-83.   LC Card 80-622932
DDC 553.7/8/09763 19
1. Water quality - Mississippi River. 2. Hydrology -
Mississippi River watershed. I. United States.
Geological Survey. II. Louisiana. Office of Public
Works. III. Title. IV. Series.
TD223.4 .W44

Wells, Gary R. Idaho economic base study for
water requirements. [Boise, 1969] 2 v.   LC Card
79-632346
HC107.I2 I19

**WELLS, H. G. (HERBERT GEORGE), 1866-
1946 - PHILOSOPHY.**
Reed, John Robert, 1938- The natural history
of H.G. Wells /. Athens, c1981. p. cm.   ISBN
0-8214-0628-0   LC Card 81-11261   DDC
823/.912 19
PR5778.P5 R4 1981

Wells, Helen Fairman. The Archeology of Oak
Park, Ventura County, California /. Los
Angeles , 1978. 2 v.   LC Card 80-621558   DDC
979.4/92 19
E99.C815 A7

**WELLS, H.G. (HERBERT GEORGE), 1866-
1946 - CRITICISM AND
INTERPRETATION.**
Reed, John Robert, 1938- The natural history
of H.G. Wells /. Athens, c1981. p. cm.   ISBN
0-8214-0628-0   LC Card 81-11261   DDC
823/.912 19
PR5778.P5 R4 1981

Wells, John West, 1907- Fossil corals from
Midway atoll / by John W. Wells.
Washington : U. S. G.P.O., 1981. p. cm.
(Geology of the Midway Area, Hawaiian Islands)
Geological Survey professional paper ; 680-G

Bibliography: p.   LC Card 81-607875   DDC
563/.6/099699 19
1. Corals, Fossil. 2. Paleontology - Midway Islands. I.
Title. II. Series.
QE778 .W43

**WELLS - LAW AND LEGISLATION -
OREGON.**
Oregon. Legislative Assembly. Legislative
Research. Well drillers and contractors . Salem,
Or. (S-420 State Capitol, Salem 97310) [1980]
iv, 40 p. ;   LC Card 81-620549   DDC
344.795/017627114 347.950417627114 19
KFO2849 .A25 1980

Oregon. Water Resources Dept. Rules and
regulations prescribing general standards for the
construction and maintenance of water wells in
Oregon. [Salem, Or.] [1979] 27 p., [17] leaves
of plates :   LC Card 80-623342   DDC
353.97950087/1 19
KFO2849.A435 A2 1979

Wells Research Company. Control Data
Corporation. Trends in bus transit financial and
operating characteristics, 1960-1975 /.
[Washington] [Springfield, Va.] 1978, cover
1977. ca. 300 p. in various pagings :   LC Card
79-602177
HE5623 .A4 1977d   **NYPL [JLF 81-376]**

Welsh, Wayne.
A performance audit of the WICHE student
exchange program : audit / performed by
Wayne Welsh, Susan Elmer, Dan Dahlgren.
[Salt Lake City] : Office of Legislative Auditor
General, State of Utah, 1978. iii, 45 leaves ; 28
cm. (Report to Utah State Legislature . no. 78-7)   LC
Card 78-622932   DDC 370.19/62 19
1. State aid to paramedical education - Utah. 2.
Students, Interchange of - Utah. 3. Students,
Interchange of - The West. 4. Veterinary medicine -
Study and teaching - The West. 5. Dentistry - Study
and teaching - The West. 6. Podiatry - Study and
teaching - The West. 7. Optometry - Study and
teaching - The West. 8. Western Interstate Commission
for Higher Education. I. Elmer, Susan, joint author. II.
Dahlgren, Dan, joint author. III. Utah. Office of the
Legislative Auditor General. IV. Title. V. Series.
R847.6.U8 W44

Utah. Office of the Legislative Auditor General.
A performance audit of the Division of Fine
Arts /. [Salt Lake City] , 1980. 39, 8 p. ;   LC
Card 80-621609   DDC 353.97920085/4 19
NX24.U8 U7938 1980

Utah. Office of the Legislative Auditor General.
A performance audit of the Division of
Purchasing in the Department of Finance /.
[Salt Lake City] (412 State Capitol, Salt Lake
City, 84114) [1980] ii, 62, 4 p. ;   LC Card
80-623434   DDC 353.97920071/2 19
JK8488.A1 U86 1980

Utah. Office of the Legislative Auditor General.
A performance audit of the Motor Vehicle
Business Administration /. [Salt Lake City]
[1980] 48, 13 p. ;   LC Card 80-621605   DDC
353.97920087/834 19
HD9710.U53 U88 1980

Utah. Office of the Legislative Auditor General.
A performance audit of the Utah Schools for
the Deaf and Blind /. [Salt Lake City, Utah] ,
1979. iii, 41, 10 leaves ;   LC Card 79-626146
DDC 371.91/1/09792 19
HV2561.U82 U857 1979

Utah. Office of the Legislative Auditor General.
A program audit of equal employment
opportunity in Utah State Government /. [Salt
Lake City] , 1979. ii, 58 p. :   LC Card 79-624189
DDC 353.9792001/04 19
JK8460.A33 U82 1979

**Welthandels- und Entwicklungskonferenz der
Vereinten Nationen. see United Nations.
Conference on Trade and Development.**

Wendorf, Richard. William Collins and
eighteenth-century English poetry / Richard
Wendorf. Minneapolis : University of
Minnesota Press, 1981. p. cm. Bibliography: p.
Includes index.   ISBN 0-8166-1058-4 :   LC Card
81-14674   DDC 823/.8 19
1. Collins, William, 1721-1759 - Criticism and
interpretation. I. Title.
PR3354 .W46

Wendt, Stephen L. Occurrence and distribution of
human bacterial pathogens in Virginia surface
waters / Stephen L. Wendt, Bruce C. Parker,

Joseph O. Falkinham, Ill. Blacksburg, Va. :
Virginia Water Resources Research Center,
Virginia Polytechnic Institute and State
University, 1979. vii, 68 p. : ill. ; 24 cm.
(Bulletin - Virginia Water Resources Research Center ;
118) "Project B-098-VA, VPI-VWRRC-BULL 118."
Bibliography: p. 27-31.   LC Card 79-625812   DDC
333.91/009755 s 363.7/394 19
1. Water - Pollution - Virginia. 2. Water - Bacteriology.
3. Bacteria, Pathogenic. I. Parker, Bruce C., joint
author. II. Falkinham, Joseph O., joint author. III.
Series: Virginia Polytechnic Institute and State
University. Water Resources Research Center. Bulletin,
118. IV. Title.
TD201 .V57 no. 118 TD224.V8

Wengert, Norman I. (joint author) Hamilton,
Michael S. Environmental, legal, and political
constraints on power plant siting in the
Southwestern United States . Fort Collins,
Colo. , 1980. viii, 175 p. :   LC Card 80-67305
DDC 338.6//042 19
TK1193.U5 H35

Wentz, Walter J., 1928- Holmgren, John H.
Material management and purchasing for the
health care facility /. Ann Arbor , 1981. p. cm.
ISBN 0-914904-72-8 (pbk.)   LC Card 81-12753
DDC 362.1/1/0687 19
RA971.33 .H636

Wentzel, Kendrick W. United States.
Congressional Budget Office. Federal energy
research . Washington , 1976. xvi, 77 p. :   LC
Card 77-602336   DDC 333.79/15/0973 19
TJ163.25.U6 U513 1976a

**Wereldbevolkingsconferentie. see World
Population Conference.**

Werner, Pamela A. A survey of national
geocoding systems [by] Pamela A. Werner.
[Cambridge, Mass.]: Urban Systems Laboratory,
Massachusetts Institute of Technology, 1974. xi,
344 p. illus., tables, maps. 27 cm. "Report no.
DOT-TSC-OST-74-26." "November 1974." "Prepared for
U. S. Dept. of Tranportation Office of the Secretary,
Office of the Assistant Secretary for Policy, Plans and
International Affairs, Wash., D. C." Bibliography: p.
337-343.   LC Card 76-51887
1. Punched card systems - Names, Geographical. 2.
Information storage and retrieval systems - Code words.
3. Names, Geographical - United States. I. United
States. Dept. of Transportation. Office of the Assistant
Secretary for Policy, Plans, and International Affairs. II.
Title.   **NYPL [JFF 80-1538]**

Werner, Sanford L. California. Dept. of Water
Resources. Southern District. Potential waste
disposal areas, northern Los Angeles County /.
[Sacramento] [1979] vii, 58 p. :   LC Card
80-621404   DDC 363.7/28 19
TD811.5 .C34 1979

Werness, Hope B. Vincent van Gogh, the
influences of nineteenth century illustrations :
the University Fine Arts Gallery, Florida State
University, Tallahassee, April 18-May
10, 1980 / introduction by Albert Stewart ; text
by Hope B. Werness ; catalogue compiled by
Graduate Students, the Department of Art.
[Tallahassee, Fla. : Florida State University,
Fine Arts Gallery, 1980] 44 p. : ill. (some
col.) ; 27 cm. Bibliography: p. 42. Includes index.
LC Card 80-66125   DDC 760/.092/4 19
1. Gogh, Vincent van, 1853-1890 - Exhibitions. 2.
Magazine illustration - 19th century - Influence -
Exhibitions. 3. Humans in art - Exhibitions. I. Gogh,
Vincent van, 1853-1890. II. Florida State University.
Art Gallery. III. Florida State University. Dept. of Art.
IV. Title.
N6953.G63 A4 1980

Wershow, James S. (joint author) Simpson, James
R. Legal and ethical implications of the U. S.
agricultural structure controversy /. Gainesville,
Fla. [1980] 16 p. ;   LC Card 80-622541   DDC
343.73/076 19
KF1686.Z9 S55

Wertheimer, Barbara M. Women as third-party
neutrals. Ithaca , 1978. vi, 55 p. ;   ISBN
0-87546-066-6 :   LC Card 78-620003   DDC
331.89/14/02373 19
HD6058 .W6894

Wessel, Louis. Wyoming. Dept. of Labor and
Statistics. Wyoming coal strip mining .
Cheyenne, Wyo. , 1979] iii, 40 p. ;   LC Card
79-625469   DDC 331.12/522334/09787 19
HD4966.M63 U59 1979

West, Bernadette. (joint author) Santamour, Miles. Retardation, corrections, and retarded offenders . Washington [1979] i, 156 p. ; LC Card 79-604176 DDC 016.3646 19
Z5703.4.M46 S26 1979 HV6791

WEST CHESTER STATE COLLEGE - MAPS.
West Chester State College. Office of College Information & Publications. West Chester State College, campus map & guide /. West Chester, Pa. [1980?] 2 maps : LC Card 81-690412
G3824.W3:2W4 1980 .W4

West Chester State College. Office of College Information & Publications. West Chester State College, campus map & guide / Office of College Information & Publications. West Chester, Pa. : The Office, [1980?] 2 maps : on sheet 46 x 31 cm., folded to 23 x 16 cm. Title from verso. Includes text. Index, location map, and ill. on verso. CONTENTS. - North campus -- South campus. LC Card 81-690412
1. West Chester State College - Maps.
G3824.W3:2W4 1980 .W4

West German Federal Republic. see Germany (Federal Republic, 1949-)

THE WEST - HISTORY - TO 1848.
Schubert, Frank N. Vanguard of expansion . Washington, D.C. [1980] xii, 160 p. : LC Card 80-144567 DDC 358/.22/0973 19
UG23 .S38

THE WEST - HISTORY - 1848-1950.
Schubert, Frank N. Vanguard of expansion . Washington, D.C. [1980] xii, 160 p. : LC Card 80-144567 DDC 358/.22/0973 19
UG23 .S38

THE WEST - HISTORY - PERIODICALS.
Arizona and the West. v. 1- ; 1959- Tucson.
NYPL [IAA (Arizona and the West)]

THE WEST IN ART - EXHIBITIONS.
Thomas Hill, the grand view /. Oakland, Calif. , 1980. 64 p. : LC Card 80-82938 DDC 759.13 19
ND237.H615 A4 1980

West Los Angeles County Resource Conservation District. Leifer, Lewis. Soil survey of Los Angeles County, California, west San Fernando Valley area /. [Washington , 1980] viii, 107 p., [2] fold. leaves of plates : LC Card 80-602305 DDC 631.4/7/79493 19
S599.C2 L44

THE WEST - PERIODICALS.
Montana; the magazine of western history. v. 5, no. [2]- ; spring, 1955- Helena. *NYPL [IAA (Montana; the magazine of western history.)]*

West River Diversion Study (N.D.) Conference on Mining and Power Production, Dickinson State College, 1973. Conference on Mining and Power Production /. Fargo, N.D. , 1973. v, 130 p., [8] leaves of plates : LC Card 80-621258 DDC 333.8/2215/097848 19
TN805.N9 C66 1973

WEST (U. S.) - ECONOMIC CONDITIONS - 19TH CENTURY.
Haeger, John D. The investment frontier . Albany , 1981. p. cm. ISBN 0-87395-530-7 LC Card 81-741 DDC 330.978/02 19
HC107.A17 H33

WEST (U. S.) - HISTORIOGRAPHY - ADDRESSES, ESSAYS, LECTURES.
Sonnichsen, C. L. (Charles Leland), 1901- The ambidextrous historian . Norman , c1981. p. cm. ISBN 0-8061-1690-0 LC Card 81-2786 DDC 978/.0072 19
F591 .S67

WEST (U. S.) IN ART - CATALOGS.
Caylor, H. W. (Harvey Wallace), b. 1867. H.W. Caylor, frontier artist /. College Station , c1981. 125 p. : ISBN 0-89096-108-5 : LC Card 80-6112 DDC 759.13 19
ND237.C384 A4 1981

WEST (U. S.) - SOCIAL LIFE AND CUSTOMS.
Brown, Dee Alexander. The gentle tamers . Lincoln, NE , 1981, c1958. p. cm. ISBN 0-8032-5025-8 (pbk.) LC Card 81-3428 DDC 978/.0088042 19
F591 .B87 1981

West Valley Demonstration Project Act . United States. Congress. House. Committee on Interstate and Foreign Commerce.

Subcommittee on Energy and Power. Washington , 1980. iv, 173 p. p. : LC Card 80-603899 DDC 344.73/04622 347.3044622 19
KF27 .I5542 1980m

West Virginia. Agricultural and Forestry Experiment Station. see West Virginia. University. Agricultural and Forestry Experiment Station.

West Virginia. Agricultural Experiment Station, Morgantown.
Bulletin.
(594T) Layton, Ronald A. Estimated annual costs, production, and income for selected livestock and crop enterprises, eastern West Virginia. [Morgantown] 1970. 92 p. LC Card 80-515026 DDC 338.1/09754 19
S561.6.W4 L39

West Virginia. Archives and History, Dept. of. see West Virginia. Dept. of Archives and History.

West Virginia. Civil Service System. Regulations concerning compensation of civil service employees. [Charleston] : State of West Virginia, Civil Service System, [1976] 43 p. ; 28 cm. Cover title: Compensation manual. "Proposed June 1, 1976." Tables. LC Card 80-623167 DDC 353.9755001/23 19
1. West Virginia - Officials and employees - Salaries, allowances, etc. I. Title. II. Title: Compensation manual.
JK4057 .W47 1976

West Virginia. Community Development Division. Directory of regional planning and development councils / Governor's Office of Economic and Community Development, Community Development Division. [Charleston], W. Va. : The Division, 1979. 89 p. ; 24 cm. LC Card 80-621499 DDC 353.97540081/8/025 19
1. Regional planning - West Virginia - Directories. I. Title. II. Title: Regional planning and development councils.
HT393.W4 W47 1979

West Virginia. Dept. of Archives and History. (Old Catalog form: West Virginia. Archives and History Dept.)
West Virginia history; a quarterly magazine. v. 1- ; Oct. 1939- Charleston, W. Va. LC Card 42-50005
NYPL [IAA (West Virginia history)]

West Virginia. Dept. of Education. see West Virginia. State Dept. of Education.

West Virginia. Dept. of Employment Security. Labor and Economic Research.
Directory of publications dealing with labor market information. Charleston, W. Va. 28 cm. (Its: WVLER-LMI)
1. Labor supply - West Virginia - Bibliography. 2. West Virginia. Dept. of Employment Security. Labor and Economic Research. - Bibliography. I. Title.
NYPL [JLM 80-878]

WEST VIRGINIA. DEPT. OF EMPLOYMENT SECURITY. LABOR AND ECONOMIC RESEARCH. - BIBLIOGRAPHY.
West Virginia. Dept. of Employment Security. Labor and Economic Research. Directory of publications dealing with labor market information. Charleston, W. Va.
NYPL [JLM 80-878]

West Virginia. Dept. of Employment Security. Labor and Economic Research Section. Employment and wages, calendar year 1978 /. Charleston, W. Va. (112 California Ave., Charleston 25305) [1980] iv, 101 leaves ; LC Card 80-624425 DDC 331.12/5/09754 19
HD4976.W4 E47

Insured workers in West Virginia / prepared by West Virginia Department of Employment Security, Data Systems Division, Labor and Economic Research Section. Charleston, WV : The Department, 1979. ii, 40 leaves ; 28 cm. (LER ; 308) Chiefly tables. LC Card 80-623169 DDC 331.12/5/09754 19
1. Insurance, Unemployment - West Virginia - Statistics. 2. Wages - West Virginia - Statistics. I. Series: West Virginia. Dept. of Employment Security. Labor and Economic Research Section. LER series , 308. II. Title.
HD7096.U6 W448 1979

LER series .
(126) West Virginia. Dept. of Employment Security. Labor and Economic Research Section. West Virginia youth and the labor

market /. Charleston, W. Va. [1979] ii, 46 p. ; LC Card 80-621110 DDC 331.3/412/09754 19
HD6274.W4 W47 1979

(302) West Virginia. Dept. of Employment Security. Labor and Economic Research Section. Projections to 1982 by occupation and industry, West Virginia /. Charleston, W. Va. , 1979. i leaf, 99 p. ; LC Card 80-620829 DDC 331.12/3/09754 19
HD5725.W4 W38 1979a

(308) West Virginia. Dept. of Employment Security. Labor and Economic Research Section. Insured workers in West Virginia /. Charleston, WV , 1979. ii, 40 leaves ; LC Card 80-623169 DDC 331.12/5/09754 19
HD7096.U6 W448 1979

Projections to 1982 by occupation and industry, West Virginia / [prepared by Labor & Economic Research Section]. Charleston, W. Va. : West Virginia Dept. of Employment Security, Labor and Economic Research Section, 1979. i leaf, 99 p. ; 28 cm. (LER ; 302) Chiefly tables. LC Card 80-620829 DDC 331.12/3/09754 19
1. Employment forecasting - West Virginia - Statistics. 2. Labor supply - West Virginia - Statistics. 3. Job vacancies - West Virginia - Statistics. 4. West Virginia - Occupations - Statistics. I. Series: West Virginia. Dept. of Employment Security. Labor and Economic Research Section. LER series , 302. II. Title.
HD5725.W4 W38 1979a

West Virginia youth and the labor market / [prepared by Data Systems Division, Labor & Economic Research Section]. Charleston, W. Va. : The Section, [1979] ii, 46 p. ; 28 cm. (LER ; 126) "October 1979." LC Card 80-621110 DDC 331.3/412/09754 19
1. Youth - Employment - West Virginia. I. Series: West Virginia. Dept. of Employment Security. Labor and Economic Research Section. LER series , 126. II. Title.
HD6274.W4 W47 1979

West Virginia. Dept. of Employment Security. Research and Statistics Section. Occupational employment statistics : selected manufacturing industries. [Charleston] : West Virginia Dept. of Employment Security, Research and Statistics Section, [1975?] 78 p. ; 28 cm. (RS series. 100-C) LC Card 76-622476
1. Labor supply - West Virginia - Statistics. 2. West Virginia - Manufactures - Employees - Statistics. I. Title.
HD5725.W4 W38b no. 100-C
NYPL [JLF 80-1513]

West Virginia. Dept. of Natural Resources. Division of Water Resources. see West Virginia. Division of Water Resources.

West Virginia. Division of Instructional Learning Systems. Perry, Gerald K. Official State multiple list for elementary schools, K-8 . Charleston, W. Va. [1980] iv, 42, 10 p. ; LC Card 80-621060 DDC 016.3791/56/09754 19
Z5817 .P47 LB3047.5.W4

West Virginia. Division of Special Education and Student Support Systems. Standards for the education of exceptional children / Division of Special Education and Student Support Systems, Bureau of Learning Systems, West Virginia Department of Education. [Charleston] : The Division, 1979. iii, 109 p., [8] leaves of plates : ill. ; 28 cm. Cover title. LC Card 80-621051 DDC 371.9/09754 19
1. Exceptional children - Education - West Virginia. I. Title.
LC3982.W4 W47 1979

West Virginia. Division of Water Resources. (Old Catalog form: West Virginia. Water Resources, Division of.)
Comprehensive survey of the Bluestone River Basin. Charleston : West Virginia Dept. of Natural Resources, Division of Water Resources, 1978- v. <1> : ill. ; 28 cm. Bibliography: v. 1, p. 99-101. CONTENTS. - v. 1. Inventory. LC Card 79-624203 DDC 333.91/009754/74 19
1. Water resources development - Bluestone River watershed, Va. and W. Va. 2. Land use - Bluestone River watershed, Va. and W. Va. I. Title.
TC425.B54 W47 1978

The West Virginia dropout study, 1978-1979 /. Murray, Charles Robert, 1932- Charleston, W. Va. [1979] ii leaves, 30 p. : LC Card 80-622735

DDC 371.2/913/09754 19
LC144.W4 M87

**WEST VIRGINIA - ECONOMIC
CONDITIONS.**
West Virginia. Governor's Office of Economic
and Community Development. Economic
Development Division. West Virginia economic
profile. [Charleston, W. Va. , 1977] 75 p. : LC
Card 80-623864   DDC 330.9754/043 19
HC107.W5 W3 1977

West Virginia economic profile. West Virginia.
Governor's Office of Economic and Community
Development. Economic Development Division.
[Charleston, W. Va. , 1977] 75 p. : LC Card
80-623864   DDC 330.9754/043 19
HC107.W5 W3 1977

West Virginia. Education, State Dept. of. see
West Virginia. State Dept. of Education.

West Virginia Forage and Grassland Council.
International Hill Lands Symposium, West
Virginia University, 1976. Hill lands .
[Morgantown, WV] [1976?] xiv, 770 p. : LC
Card 80-100503   DDC 333.76/09143 19
S604.3 .I57 1976

West Virginia. Geological and Economic Survey.
see **West Virginia. Geological Survey.**

West Virginia. Geological Survey. Land use
statistics for West Virginia. [Morgantown,
WV] : West Virginia Geological and Economic
Survey ; [Reston, VA] : U. S. Geological
Survey, 1979- 1 v. ; 28 cm. (Environmental
geology bulletin. no. 18-1) Cover title. LC Card
80-621498
*1. Land use - West Virginia - Statistics. I. United
States. Geological Survey. II. Title. III. Series.*
QE177 .E58 no. 18, etc. HD211.W4
        NYPL [JSK 75-100 no. 18-1]

**West Virginia. Government and Finance, Joint
Committee on.** see **West Virginia. Legislature.
Joint Committee on Government and
Finance.**

**West Virginia. Governor's Office of Economic
and Community Development. Economic
Development Division.** West Virginia
economic profile. [Charleston, W. Va. :
Economic Development Division, 1977] 75 p. :
ill. ; 22 x 28 cm. Cover title. LC Card 80-623864
DDC 330.9754/043 19
1. West Virginia - Economic conditions. I. Title.
HC107.W5 W3 1977

West Virginia history; a quarterly magazine. v.
1- ; Oct. 1939- Charleston, W. Va. illus. 24 cm.
Issued by the Dept. of Archives and History of West
Virginia. LC Card 42-50005
*1. West Virginia - History - Periodicals. I. West
Virginia. Dept. of Archives and History.*
        NYPL [IAA (West Virginia history)]

**WEST VIRGINIA - HISTORY -
PERIODICALS.**
West Virginia history; a quarterly magazine. v.
1- ; Oct. 1939- Charleston, W. Va. LC Card
42-50005
        NYPL [IAA (West Virginia history)]

West Virginia. Human Rights Commission.
Women & minorities in the construction
industry : hearing report. [Charleston, W. Va.] :
West Virginia Human Rights Commission,
[1979?] ii, 41 leaves ; 29 cm. Cover title. LC
Card 80-622765   DDC 331/4/824/09754 19
*1. Construction workers - West Virginia. 2. Women -
Employment - West Virginia. 3. Minorities -
Employment - West Virginia. I. Title.*
HD8039.B92 U78 1979

**West Virginia. Legislature. Government and
Finance, Joint Committee on.** see **West
Virginia. Legislature. Joint Committee on
Government and Finance.**

**West Virginia. Legislature. Joint Committee on
Government and Finance.** (Old Catalog form:
West Virginia. Government and Finance,
Joint Committee on)
Schmidt, Richard A. A study of surface coal
mining in West Virginia. Menlo Park, Calif.,
1972. xiii, 180 p. LC Card 72-611225
TN805.W4 S28   ***NYPL [JLF 81-203]***

**WEST VIRGINIA - MANUFACTURES -
EMPLOYEES - STATISTICS.**
West Virginia. Dept. of Employment Security.
Research and Statistics Section. Occupational
employment statistics . [Charleston] [1975?] 78

p. ; LC Card 76-622476
HD5725.W4 W38b no. 100-C
        NYPL [JLF 80-1513]

**WEST VIRGINIA - OCCUPATIONS -
STATISTICS.**
West Virginia. Dept. of Employment Security.
Labor and Economic Research Section.
Projections to 1982 by occupation and industry,
West Virginia /. Charleston, W. Va. , 1979. i
leaf, 99 p. ; LC Card 80-620829   DDC
331.12/3/09754 19
HD5725.W4 W38 1979a

**WEST VIRGINIA - OFFICIALS AND
EMPLOYEES - SALARIES,
ALLOWANCES, ETC.**
West Virginia. Civil Service System.
Regulations concerning compensation of civil
service employees. [Charleston] [1976] 43 p. ;
LC Card 80-623167   DDC 353.9755001/23 19
JK4057 .W47 1976

**West Virginia. Postsecondary Education
Commission.** Van Dyke, John B. West
Virginia private proprietary schools .
Charleston, W. Va. [1978] 50 p. ; LC Card
79-124128   DDC 607/.11754 19
T74.W4 V36

West Virginia private proprietary schools . Van
Dyke, John B. Charleston, W. Va. [1978] 50
p. ; LC Card 79-124128   DDC 607/.11754 19
T74.W4 V36

West Virginia. Public Service Commission.
Appalachian Gas Measurement Short Course,
West Virginia University. Proceedings 32- ;
1972- [Morgantown]. LC Card 44-30134
        NYPL [JSP 81-112]

West Virginia. State Dept. of Education. (Old
Catalog form: West Virginia. Education
Dept.)
Murray, Charles Robert, 1932- The West
Virginia dropout study, 1978-1979 /.
Charleston, W. Va. [1979] ii leaves, 30 p. :
LC Card 80-622735   DDC 371.2/913/09754 19
LC144.W4 M87

**West Virginia. State Occupational Information
Coordinating Committee.** Clay, Rex J.
Occupational demand, supply, and wages in
West Virginia /. [Charleston, W. Va.] [1980] iv
leaves, 424 p. ; LC Card 80-621755   DDC
331.12/09754 19
HD5725.W4 C52

West Virginia University . Ernst, Harry W.
[Morgantown, W. Va. , c1980] vi, 106 p. : LC
Card 80-50600   DDC 378.754/53 19
LD5923 .E76

West Virginia. University.
International Hill Lands Symposium, West
Virginia University, 1976. Hill lands .
[Morgantown, WV] [1976?] xiv, 770 p. : LC
Card 80-100503   DDC 333.76/09143 19
S604.3 .I57 1976

Proceedings, West Virginia University-United
States Postal Service workshop . Morgantown
[1973?] 50 p. ; LC Card 77-623862   DDC
383/.14/0973 19
HE6497.D35 P76

West Virginia University Gerontology
Conference, 1st, 1979. Transitions of aging .
New York , 1980. xv, 221 p.; ISBN
0-12-203580-1
HQ1064.U5 W47 1979
        NYPL [JLE 80-2946]

**West Virginia. University. Agricultural and
Forestry Experiment Station.** Global
radiation in West Virginia. Morgantown : West
Virginia University, Agricultural and Forestry
Experiment Station, 1979. 51 p. : graphs ; 23
cm. (Bulletin - West Virginia University, Agricultural
and Forestry Experiment Station . 665T) Cover title.
"February 1979." Authors: R. Lee, and others. LC
Card 80-621504   DDC 551.5/271 19
*1. Global radiation - West Virginia. I. Lee, Richard,
1926-. II. Series: West Virginia. University. Agricultural
and Forestry Experiment Station - Bulletin - West
Virginia University Agricultural and Forestry
Experiment Station , 665T. III. Title.*
QC912.55 .W47 1979

**West Virginia. University. Agricultural and
Foretry Experiment Station.**
**Bulletin - West Virginia University
Agricultural and Forestry Experiment**

Station .
(665T) West Virginia. University. Agricultural
and Forestry Experiment Station. Global
radiation in West Virginia. Morgantown ,
1979. 51 p. : LC Card 80-621504   DDC
551.5/271 19
QC912.55 .W47 1979

**West Virginia. University. College of Agriculture
and Forestry. Agricultural and Forestry
Experiment Station.** see **West Virginia.
University. Agricultural and Forestry
Experiment Station.**

**West Virginia. University. College of Mineral
and Energy Resources.** Appalachian Gas
Measurement Short Course, West Virginia
University. Proceedings 32- ; 1972-
[Morgantown]. LC Card 44-30134
        NYPL [JSP 81-112]

**West Virginia. University. Engineering
Experiment Station.**
Appalachian Underground Corrosion Short
Course. Proceedings. 18- ; 1973- [Morgantown]
        NYPL [JSP 81-110]

Report.
(6) Zaltzman, Raul. Biological decomposition
of cellulose. Morgantown, 1969. iii, 107 p.
LC Card 72-628129   DDC 620 s 581.19/2482 19
TA1 .W393 no. 6 QR160

**West Virginia University Gerontology Conference,
1st, 1979.** Transitions of aging : [proceedings]
/ edited by Nancy Datan and Nancy Lohmann.
New York : Academic Press, 1980. xv, 221 p.;
24 cm. Includes bibliographies and index. ISBN
0-12-203580-1
*1. Gerontology - United States - Congresses. 2. Aged
women - United States - Congresses. 3. Aged policy -
United States - Congresses. I. Datan, Nancy. II.
Lohmann, Nancy. III. West Virginia. University. IV.
Title.*
HQ1064.U5 W47 1979
        NYPL [JLE 80-2946]

WEST VIRGINIA. UNIVERSITY - HISTORY.
Ernst, Harry W. West Virginia University .
[Morgantown, W. Va. , c1980] vi, 106 p. : LC
Card 80-50600   DDC 378.754/53 19
LD5923 .E76

**West Virginia. University. Mineral and Energy
Resources, College of.** see **West Virginia.
University. College of Mineral and Energy
Resources.**

**West Virginia. University. Water Research
Institute.**
Information report .
(11) Double, Mark L. Recovery of
sanitary-indicator bacteria from streams
containing acid mine water /. Morgantown ,
1978. v, 30 p. : LC Card 78-622769   DDC
333.91/009754 s 628.1/6832/0287 19
QC986.W4 W46 no. 11 QR48

Thompson, Frederick C. Tolerance and
synthetic ability of sewage microorganisms in
acid mine water /. Morgantown , 1975. ix, 60
p. : LC Card 76-622086   DDC 628.1/6832 19
QR88 .T48

West Virginia. Water Resources, Division of. see
West Virginia. Division of Water Resources.

West Virginia youth and the labor market /.
West Virginia. Dept. of Employment Security.
Labor and Economic Research Section.
Charleston, W. Va. [1979] ii, 46 p. ; LC Card
80-621110   DDC 331.3/412/09754 19
HD6274.W4 W47 1979

**Westchester and metropolitan area
transportation .** Westchester County, N. Y.
Dept. of Planning. White Plains, N.Y. [1976] 1
map : LC Card 81-692860
G3803.W5P1 1976 . W4

Westchester County, N. Y. Dept. of Planning.
(Old Catalog form: Westchester County, N.
Y. Planning Dept.)
Selected enrollment and financial data for
school districts in Westchester. White Plains, N.
Y., 1964. 29 p. fold. map. 28 cm. Microfilm.
*1. School attendance - New York (State) - Westchester
County. 2. Education - New York (State) - Westchester
County - Finance. 3. Westchester County, N. Y. -
History. I. Title.*   ***NYPL [*Z-3176]***

Westchester and metropolitan area
transportation : May 1976 / Westchester
County Department of Planning. White Plains,

N.Y. : The Department, [1976] 1 map : photocopy ; 54 x 40 cm. Indexed for bridges and tunnels. LC Card 81-692860
1. Transportation - New York (State) - Westchester County - Maps. 2. Transportation - New York (State) - New York metropolitan area - Maps. I. Title.
G3803.W5P1 1976 .W4

Westchester County (N.Y.). Office of Economic Development. Westchester County, New York, vacant land zoned commercial or industrial . White Plains, N.Y. [1978] 1 map : LC Card 81-692859
G3803.W5Q46 1978 .W4

WESTCHESTER COUNTY, N. Y. - HISTORY.
Westchester County, N. Y. Dept. of Planning. Selected enrollment and financial data for school districts in Westchester. White Plains, N. Y., 1964. 29 p.   *NYPL [*Z-3176]*

Westchester County, N. Y. Planning, Dept. of. see **Westchester County, N. Y. Dept. of Planning.**

Westchester County, New York, vacant land zoned commercial or industrial . Westchester County (N.Y.). Office of Economic Development. White Plains, N.Y. [1978] 1 map : LC Card 81-692859
G3803.W5Q46 1978 .W4

Westchester County (N.Y.). Office of Economic Development. Westchester County, New York, vacant land zoned commercial or industrial : spring 1978 / prepared by the Office of Economic Development. White Plains, N.Y. : Westchester Co. Dept. of Planning, [1978] 1 map : photocopy ; 46 x 35 cm. Includes notes. LC Card 81-692859
1. Store location - New York (State) - Westchester County - Maps. 2. Industrial sites - New York (State) - Westchester County - Maps. I. Westchester County, N. Y. Dept. of Planning. II. Title.
G3803.W5Q46 1978 .W4

Westerly Public Library. see **Westerly, R. I. Public Library.**

Westerly, R. I. Public Library. Berman, Susan Folsom. Municipal publications in the public library. Westerly, R. I. [197-] 28 p.;
*NYPL [*XM-13140]*

Western Archeological Center.
McClellan, Carole. The archeology of Lake Mead National Recreation Area . Tucson, Ariz. [Washington, D.C.?] , 1980. x,188 p. : LC Card 81-600707   DDC 979.3/12 19
F788 .M163

Ruppert, David E. Lake Mead national recreation area . Tucson, Ariz. , 1976. ix, 90 p. : LC Card 80-601435   DDC 979.3/12 19
E78.A7 R86

Western Energy and Land Use Team.
Holden, Paul B. Habitat requirements of juvenile Colorado River squawfish /. [Fort Collins, Colo.] , Washington , 1978. 71 p. : LC Card 79-602765   DDC 639.7/77092/9792 19
QL638.C94 H64

Western Energy and Land Use Team publications : an annotated bibliography. Fort Collins, Colo. : WELUT, [1979] x, 35 p. ; 27 cm. Cover title: Biological services program. "WELUT-79/10." "October 1979." Includes indexes.
LC Card 80-601848   DDC 016.3337/0978 19
1. Western Energy and Land Use Team - Bibliography. 2. Land use - Environmental aspects - The West - Bibliography. 3. Water resources development - Environmental aspects - The West - Bibliography. I. Title. II. Title: Biological services program.
Z7164.L3 W48 1979 HD209

WESTERN ENERGY AND LAND USE TEAM - BIBLIOGRAPHY.
Western Energy and Land Use Team. Western Energy and Land Use Team publications . Fort Collins, Colo. [1979] x, 35 p. ; LC Card 80-601848   DDC 016.3337/0978 19
Z7164.L3 W48 1979 HD209

Western Energy and Land Use Team publications . Western Energy and Land Use Team. Fort Collins, Colo. [1979] x, 35 p. ; LC Card 80-601848   DDC 016.3337/0978 19
Z7164.L3 W48 1979 HD209

Western European Union . Great Britain. Central Office of Information. Reference Division. New York [1966] 20 p. ; LC Card 81-468994   DDC

341.24/2 19
JN94.A2 G74 1966

WESTERN EUROPEAN UNION.
Great Britain. Central Office of Information. Reference Division. Western European Union . New York [1966] 20 p. ; LC Card 81-468994   DDC 341.24/2 19
JN94.A2 G74 1966

Western European Union. Assembly. see **Western European Union.**

Western frontier library .
(54) Kipling, Rudyard, 1865-1936. American notes /. Norman , c1981. p. cm. ISBN 0-8061-1682-X   LC Card 81-40289   DDC 917.3/0486 19
E168 .K56 1981

Western Interstate Commission for Higher Education.
Regional Legislative Workshop on Higher Education, 3d, San Francisco, 1961. The role of the universities in the economic development of the West /. Boulder, Colo. , 1962. x, 28 p. : LC Card 79-124780   DDC 378.78 19
LC67.65.W47 R43 1961

Report .
(80-2) Kaufman, Norman. Estimates of doctorates to be conferred by Western universities in English, philosophy, and history, 1980-1982 /. Boulder, Colo. [1980] 9, [5] leaves ; LC Card 80-622760   DDC 378.78 s 378/.24/0978 19
L107 .W47 vol. 80-2 LB2386

WESTERN INTERSTATE COMMISSION FOR HIGHER EDUCATION.
Welsh, Wayne. A performance audit of the WICHE student exchange program . [Salt Lake City] , 1978. iii, 45 leaves ; LC Card 78-622932   DDC 370.19/62 19
R847.6.U8 W44

Western Interstate Commission for Higher Education. Project on Expanding Regional Cooperation in Graduate & Professional Education. Kaufman, Norman. Estimates of doctorates to be conferred by Western universities in English, philosophy, and history, 1980-1982 /. Boulder, Colo. [1980] 9, [5] leaves ; LC Card 80-622760   DDC 378.78 s 378/.24/0978 19
L107 .W47 vol. 80-2 LB2386

Western Interstate Nuclear Board. Symposium on Waste Management. Waste management; proceedings. Tucson, Ariz.
NYPL [JSP 80-332]

Western Interstate Nuclear Compact. see **Western Interstate Nuclear Board.**

Western Michigan University. Center for Korean Studies. The United States and Korea . Kalamazoo , 1979. 262 p. ; LC Card 78-65924   DDC 327.730519 19
E183.8.K6 U54

Western Michigan University, Kalamazoo. see **Michigan. Western Michigan University, Kalamazoo.**

Western Regional Civil Rights and Women's Rights Conference, 4th, San Francisco, 1977. Recent developments, new opportunities in civil rights and women's rights : a report of the proceedings of the Western Regional Civil Rights and Women's Rights Conference IV, sponsored by the U. S. Commission on Civil Rights in San Francisco, California, June 29-July 1, 1977. - Washington : The Commission : for sale by the Supt. of Docs., U. S. Govt. Print. Off., [1977]. vi, 178 p. ; 23 cm.
1. Civil rights - United States - Congresses. 2. Women's rights - United States - Congresses. I. United States. Commission on Civil Rights. II. Title.
NYPL [JLE 80-2420]

Western State College, Gunnison, Colo. see **Colorado. Western State College, Gunnison.**

Western views and Eastern visions /. Ostroff, Eugene. Washington , 1981. 118 p. : ISBN 0-86528-005-3 (pbk.)   LC Card 81-70   DDC 779/.9978 19
TR23.6 .O87

Western Washington University. Smith, Gary Frederick. A quantitative sampling program of benthic communities in nearshore subtidal areas within the Rosario Strait region of Northern Puget Sound, Washington State (1976) /.

[Olympia] [1979] vi, 105 p. : LC Card 80-622612   DDC 591.9797/7 19
QH105.W2 S65

Westfield River. Kimball, Warren A. Westfield River basin . Westborough, Mass. [1975] 76, a-d p. : LC Card 77-622234   DDC 363.7/3942/0974426 19
TD224.M4 K55

Westfield River . Massachusetts. Division of Water Pollution Control. Water Quality Section. Westborough [1974] 50 p. : LC Card 80-118658   DDC 363.7/3942/0974426 19
TD224.M4 M36 1974f

Westfield River. Massachusetts. Water Quality and Research Section. Westfield River basin /. Westborough , 1975. 2 v. : LC Card 77-622217   DDC 363.7/394/0974426 19
TD224.M4 M39 1975

Westfield River. Massachusetts. Water Quality and Research Section. Westfield River basin . Westborough, Mass. , 1978. 113 p. : LC Card 79-623982   DDC 363.7/3942/0974426 19
TD224.M4 M39 1978f

Westfield River basin . Kimball, Warren A. Westborough, Mass. [1975] 76, a-d p. : LC Card 77-622234   DDC 363.7/3942/0974426 19
TD224.M4 K55

Westfield River basin /. Massachusetts. Water Quality and Research Section. Westborough , 1975. 2 v. : LC Card 77-622217   DDC 363.7/394/0974426 19
TD224.M4 M39 1975

Westfield River basin . Massachusetts. Water Quality and Research Section. Westborough, Mass. , 1978. 113 p. : LC Card 79-623982   DDC 363.7/3942/0974426 19
TD224.M4 M39 1978f

Westin, Alan F. Computer science & technology : computers, personnel administration, and citizen rights / Alan F. Westin. Washington : U. S. Dept. of Commerce, National Bureau of Standards : for sale by the Supt. of Docs., U. S. Govt. Print. Off., 1979. xxiv, 439 p. : ill. ; 26 cm. (NBS special publication ; 500-50) Bibliography: p. 325-377. LC Card 79-600081   DDC 602.18 s 658.3/00973 19
1. Personnel management - United States. 2. Personnel records - United States - Data processing. 3. Privacy, Right of - United States. I. Series: United States. National Bureau of Standards Special publication, 500-50. II. Title.
QC100 .U57 no. 500-50 HF5549.2.U5

Westin, Robert A. Polychlorinated biphenyls . [Washington, D.C.] , 1981. p. cm. LC Card 80-607190   DDC 622 s 363.1/79 19
TN295 .U4 T55.3.H3

WESTLANDS WATER DISTRICT.
Ely, George. Small-scale farming in the Westlands . Davis, Calif. [197-] viii, 64 leaves ; LC Card 79-626029   DDC 338.1/6 19
HD1476.U5 E49

Westphal, Joseph W. Commitments, priorities, and organizational options for water resource planning in Oklahoma / by Joseph W. Westphal and James J. Lawler. [Stillwater] : Oklahoma Water Resources Research Institute, [1979] xix, 346 p. : ill. ; 28 cm. "August, 1979." "Final technical completion report, A-076-OKLA. Contract no. 14-34-0001-9038." Includes bibliographical references. LC Card 80-622933   DDC 333.91/15/09766 19
1. Water resources development - Oklahoma - Planning. I. Lawler, James J., joint author. II. Oklahoma Water Resources Research Institute. III. Title.
TC424.O5 W47

Westward in Eden /. Wyant, William K. Berkeley, Calif. , c1982. p. cm. ISBN 0-520-04377-4   LC Card 81-7519   DDC 333.1/0973 19
HD205 1982 .W9

Wet soils, Chickies Creek watershed, Lancaster and Lebanon Counties, Pennsylvania /. United States. Soil Conservation Service. Hyattsville, Md. , 1977. 1 map : LC Card 81-690274
G3822.C45J3 1977 .U51

Wetland classification system for the Tennessee Valley region /. Carter, Virginia. [Norris] 1978. v, 36 p. : LC Card 79-103835   DDC 333.7/5/09768 s 574.5/26325/012 19
SD11 .T416 no. B24 QH541.5.M3

WETLAND CONSERVATION - ALASKA - CONGRESSES.
Wetlands Conference, Anchorage, Alaska, 1979. Proceedings of the Wetlands Conference, February 5, 1979 /. [Juneau] , 1979. 35 p. ; LC Card 79-625932 DDC 333.91/8/09798 19
QH76.5.A4 W47 1979

WETLAND CONSERVATION - UNITED STATES.
Galloway, G. E. Assessing man's impact on wetlands /. [Raleigh, N.C. , 1978] iv, 115 p. : LC Card 79-625636 DDC 333.91/81 19
QH76 .G34

WETLAND ECOLOGY.
Lefor, M. W. Inland wetland definitions /. [Storrs] , 1977. vii, 63 p. : LC Card 78-624194 DDC 333.91 s 574.5/26325 19
HD1694.C8 C7 no. 28 QH541.5.M3

WETLAND ECOLOGY - CLASSIFICATION.
Carter, Virginia. Wetland classification system for the Tennessee Valley region /. [Norris] 1978. v, 36 p. : LC Card 79-103835 DDC 333.7/5/09768 s 574.5/26325/012 19
SD11 .T416 no. B24 QH541.5.M3

WETLAND ECOLOGY - CONNECTICUT - BIBLIOGRAPHY.
Murphy, James Edward, 1943- Annotated bibliography of source materials for wetland habitats in Connecticut /. [Hartford] , 1979. i, 37 p. ; LC Card 79-624848 DDC 016.33391/8/09746 19
Z5322.W47 M87 QH105.C8

WETLAND ECOLOGY - DATA PROCESSING.
Kratz, Timothy K. A spatial simulation model of lake-edge wetland formation /. Madison , 1979. 59 p. : LC Card 80-621224 DDC 574.5/26325/0724 19
QH541.5.M3 K7

WETLAND ECOLOGY - FLORIDA.
Forested wetlands of Florida . Tallahassee , 1977. v, 348 p. : LC Card 78-621426 DDC 333.91/8/09759 19
QH105.F6 F67 1977

WETLAND ECOLOGY - ILLINOIS - MOMENCE.
Mitsch, William J. The Momence Wetlands of the Kankakee River in Illinois . Chicago , 1979. vi, 55 p. : LC Card 79-624911 DDC 333.91/8/0977363 19
QH105.I3 M57

WETLAND ECOLOGY - KANKAKEE RIVER.
Mitsch, William J. The Momence Wetlands of the Kankakee River in Illinois . Chicago , 1979. vi, 55 p. : LC Card 79-624911 DDC 333.91/8/0977363 19
QH105.I3 M57

WETLAND FLORA - ILLINOIS - IDENTIFICATION.
Winterringer, Glen Spelman, 1906- Aquatic plants of Illinois . Springfield , 1977. 142 p. (p. 142 blank) : LC Card 80-621674 DDC 581.92/9/773 19
QK157 .W54 1977

WETLAND FLORA - WISCONSIN.
Beule, John D. Control and management of cattails in southeastern Wisconsin wetlands /. Madison, Wis. , 1979. 39 p. : LC Card 80-621497 DDC 639.9/09775 s 632/.58 19
SK463 .A27 no. 112 SB615.T96

WETLANDS - ALASKA.
Derksen, Dirk V. Use of wetland habitats by birds in the National Petroleum Reserve--Alaska /. Washington, D.C. , 1981. p. cm. LC Card 81-607937 DDC 639.9/784109798 19
S914 .A3 no.141 QL684A4

WETLANDS - ALASKA - CONGRESSES.
Wetlands Conference, Anchorage, Alaska, 1979. Proceedings of the Wetlands Conference, February 5, 1979 /. [Juneau] , 1979. 35 p. : LC Card 79-625932 DDC 333.91/8/09798 19
QH76.5.A4 W47 1979

WETLANDS - CLASSIFICATION.
Carter, Virginia. Wetland classification system for the Tennessee Valley region /. [Norris] 1978. v, 36 p. : LC Card 79-103835 DDC 333.7/5/09768 s 574.5/26325/012 19
SD11 .T416 no. B24 QH541.5.M3

Wetlands Conference, Anchorage, Alaska, 1979.
Proceedings of the Wetlands Conference, February 5, 1979 / sponsored by Alaska

Department of Environmental Conservation [and] United States Fish and Wildlife Service, Office of Coastal Management. [Juneau] : The Dept., 1979. 35 p. ; 28 cm. LC Card 79-625932 DDC 333.91/8/09798 19
1. Wetland conservation - Alaska - Congresses. 2. Wetlands - Alaska - Congresses. I. Alaska. Dept. of Environmental Conservation. II. United States. Fish and Wildlife Service. Office of Coastal Management.
QH76.5.A4 W47 1979

WETLANDS - CONNECTICUT - BIBLIOGRAPHY.
Murphy, James Edward, 1943- Annotated bibliography of source materials for wetland habitats in Connecticut /. [Hartford] , 1979. i, 37 p. ; LC Card 79-624848 DDC 016.33391/8/09746 19
Z5322.W47 M87 QH105.C8

WETLANDS CONSERVATION - GOVERNMENT POLICY - UNITED STATES.
United States. Congress. Senate. Committee on Environment and Public Works. Subcommittee on Environmental Pollution. Implementation of certain sections of the Clean water act . Washington , 1980. iv, 376 p. : LC Card 80-603477 DDC 353.0082/326 19
KF26 .E645 1980c

WETLANDS - ECONOMIC ASPECTS - ILLINOIS - MOMENCE.
Mitsch, William J. The Momence Wetlands of the Kankakee River in Illinois . Chicago , 1979. vi, 55 p. : LC Card 79-624911 DDC 333.91/8/0977363 19
QH105.I3 M57

WETLANDS - ECONOMIC ASPECTS - KANKAKEE RIVER.
Mitsch, William J. The Momence Wetlands of the Kankakee River in Illinois . Chicago , 1979. vi, 55 p. : LC Card 79-624911 DDC 333.91/8/0977363 19
QH105.I3 M57

WETLANDS - LAW AND LEGISLATION - MASSACHUSETTS.
Massachusetts. Dept. of Environmental Quality Engineering. Division of Wetlands. A guide to the coastal wetlands regulations of the Massachusetts wetlands protection act (G.L. 131,s.40). Boston [1979] 158 p. : LC Card 79-623454
KFM2851.8 .A83

WETLANDS - NORTH CAROLINA - LIMESTONE CREEK WATERSHED - MAPS.
United States. Soil Conservation Service. Problem location map, Limestone-Muddy Creek watershed, portions of Duplin, Jones, and Onslow Counties, North Carolina. Fort Worth, Tex. , 1979. 1 map : LC Card 81-692265
G3902.L48G4 1979 .U5

WETLANDS - NORTH CAROLINA - MUDDY CREEK WATERSHED (DUPLIN COUNTY) - MAPS.
United States. Soil Conservation Service. Problem location map, Limestone-Muddy Creek watershed, portions of Duplin, Jones, and Onslow Counties, North Carolina. Fort Worth, Tex. , 1979. 1 map : LC Card 81-692265
G3902.L48G4 1979 .U5

WETLANDS - NORTHEASTERN STATES.
Lefor, M. W. Inland wetland definitions /. [Storrs] , 1977. vii, 63 p. : LC Card 78-624194 DDC 333.91 s 574.5/26325 19
HD1694.C8 C7 no. 28 QH541.5.M3

WETLANDS - TENNESSEE VALLEY REGION - CLASSIFICATION.
Carter, Virginia. Wetland classification system for the Tennessee Valley region /. [Norris] 1978. v, 36 p. : LC Card 79-103835 DDC 333.7/5/09768 s 574.5/26325/012 19
SD11 .T416 no. B24 QH541.5.M3

WETLANDS - TERMINOLOGY.
Lefor, M. W. Inland wetland definitions /. [Storrs] , 1977. vii, 63 p. : LC Card 78-624194 DDC 333.91 s 574.5/26325 19
HD1694.C8 C7 no. 28 QH541.5.M3

WETLANDS - UNITED STATES.
Galloway, G. E. Assessing man's impact on wetlands /. [Raleigh, N.C. , 1978] iv, 115 p. : LC Card 79-625636 DDC 333.91/81 19
QH76 .G34

Wetzel, Mark J.
(joint author) Brigham, Allison R. Economic impact of changing the copper effluent standard, R76-21 /. Chicago, Ill. [1979] vii, 123 p. : LC Card 80-621149 DDC 363.7/394 19
TD427.C66 B74

(joint author) Brigham, Warren U. Economic impact of a suspension of rule 203 as it applies to an unnamed tributary of the Vermilion River, Vermilion County, Illinois /. Chicago, IL [1980] ix, 90 p. : LC Card 80-622963 DDC 363.7/394 19
TD224.I3 B74

Weymouth Fore and Back River survey, 1975 /.
Massachusetts. Water Quality and Research Section. Westborough [1976] 58 p. : LC Card 79-620589 DDC 363.7/3942/097447 19
TD224.M4 M39 1976a

Weymouth River basin. Massachusetts. Water Quality and Research Section. Weymouth Fore and Back River survey, 1975 /. Westborough [1976] 58 p. : LC Card 79-620589 DDC 363.7/3942/097447 19
TD224.M4 M39 1976a

Whaite, Ralph H. (joint author) Colaizzi, Gary J. Pumped-slurry backfilling of abandoned coal mine workings for subsidence control at Rock Springs, Wyoming /. Washington , 1981. p. cm. LC Card 80-39876 DDC 622 s 622/.334 19
TN295 .U4 TN319

WHALE FISHERIES. see WHALING.

Whalen, Michael E. Settlement patterns of the Western Hueco Bolson / by Michael E. Whalen, with contributions by T.C. O'Laughlin ... [et al.] ; Rex E. Gerald, principal investigator ; prepared for the Corps of Engineers, Fort Worth District, Fort Worth, Texas. [El Paso] : El Paso Centennial Museum, University of Texas at El Paso, 1978. xv, 260 p., [1] leaf of plates : ill. ; 28 cm. (Historic and natural resources report . no. 1) Publications in anthropology ; no. 6 Bibliography : p. 257-260. LC Card 79-624053 DDC 976.4/96 19
1. Hueco Mountains region, Tex. and N.M. - Antiquities. 2. Land settlement - Hueco Mountains region, Tex. and N.M. 3. Excavations (Archaeology) - Hueco Mountains region, Tex. and N.M. 4. Indians of North America - Hueco Mountains region, Tex. and N.M. - Antiquities. 5. Texas - Antiquities. I. United States. Army. Corps of Engineers. Fort Worth District. II. Series. III. Series: Publications in anthropology (El Paso, Tex.) , no. 6. IV. Title.
F392.H82 W45

WHALES, FOSSIL - ADDRESSES, ESSAYS, LECTURES.
Archaeological whale bone--a northern resource . Fayetteville, ARK , 1979. xx, 558 p. : LC Card 80-624409 DDC 971.9/5 19
E99.E7 A73

WHALING - LAW AND LEGISLATION.
United States. Congress. House. Committee on Foreign Affairs. Subcommittee on International Organizations. Preparations for the 32d International Whaling Commission meeting . Washington , 1980. iii, 155 p. ; LC Card 80-602734 DDC 333.95/6 19
KF27 .F648 1980

United States. Congress. House. Committee on Foreign Affairs. Subcommittee on International Organizations. Review of the 32d International Whaling Commission meeting . Washington , 1980. iii, 97 p. ; LC Card 80-603893 DDC 341.7/622 19
KF27 .F648 1980c

WHALING - LAW AND LEGISLATION - UNITED STATES.
United States. Congress. House. Committee on Foreign Affairs. Subcommittee on International Organizations. Preparations for the 32d International Whaling Commission meeting . Washington , 1980. iii, 155 p. ; LC Card 80-602734 DDC 333.95/6 19
KF27 .F648 1980

Wharton, Charles H. Forested wetlands of Florida . Tallahassee , 1977. v, 348 p. : LC Card 78-621426 DDC 333.91/8/09759 19
QH105.F6 F67 1977

What can you do with a major in Black studies /. Daniel, Jack L. [Pittsburgh] , 1973. vii [i. e. iii], 21 leaves : *NYPL [Sc Micro R-3643]*

What foods should Americans eat? . United States. General Accounting Office. [Washington, D.C. , 1980] iv, 92 p. ; LC Card 80-602052 DDC 641.1/07/1073 19 *TX353 .U495 1980*

What happened . United States. Law Enforcement Assistance Administration. Criminal Conspiracies Division. Washington, D.C. , 1979. 62 p. in various pagings ; LC Card 79-602151 DDC 364.1/62 19 *HV6635 .U54 1979*

What Hawaii thinks about population/. Hawaii. Commission on Population and the Hawaiian Future. Honolulu [197-?] [12] p.: *NYPL [*XME-9364]*

What should be the energy policy of the United States? : National debate topic for high schools, 1978-1979, pursuant to Public law 88-246 / compiled by the Congressional Research Service, Library of Congress. Washington : U. S. Govt. Print. Off. : for sale by the Supt. of Docs., U. S. Govt. Print. Off., 1978. ix, 518 p. : ill. ; 24 cm. (Document - 95th Congress, 2d session, Senate . no. 95-116) Bibliography: p. 492-510. LC Card 80-603542 DDC 333.79/0973 19
1. Energy policy - United States - Addresses, essays, lectures. I. United States. Library of Congress. Congressional Research Service.
HD9502.U52 W48

What U. S. ports mean to the economy /. United States. Maritime Administration. [Washington] , 1978. 58 p., [1] leaf of plates : LC Card 79-602661 *HE553 .U643 1978*

What you never thought to ask about mining . Alaska. Division of Economic Enterprise. [Juneau] , 1979. 28 p. : LC Card 79-625931 DDC 338.2/09798 19 *HD9506.U63 A43 1979*

Whatever happened to agrarian reform? . Grindle, Merilee Serrill. Austin , 1980. 36 p. : LC Card 80-623135 DDC 338.1/88 19 *HD1333.L29 G74*

What's a second class city? . University of Alaska (System). Cooperative Extension Service. [Anchorage] , 1980- 1 v. : LC Card 80-622652 DDC 352/.00724/09798 19 *KFA1631 .U54 1980*

What's published about Colorado / compiled by C. R. Goeldner ... [et al.]. Boulder: Business Research Division, Graduate School of Business Administration, University of Colorado, c1978. iii, 138 leaves; 28 cm.
1. Colorado - Bibliography. I. Goeldner, Charles R. II. Colorado. University. Business Research Division.
NYPL [IWP 80-2840]

Wheat acreage response to changes in prices and government programs in Oregon and Washington /. Moe, Debra K. Corvallis , 1980. 55 p. : LC Card 80-622276 DDC 338.1/7311/09795 19 *HD9049.W5 U4456*

WHEAT - GREAT PLAINS - HARVESTING - HISTORY.
Isern, Thomas D. (Thomas Dean), 1952- Custom combining on the Great Plains . Norman, Okla. , 1981. p. cm. ISBN 0-8061-1681-1 LC Card 81-2781 DDC 338.1/73115/0978 19 *S699 .I78*

Wheat, Margaret M. (joint author) Mifflin, Martin D. Pluvial lakes and estimated pluvial climates of Nevada /. Reno , 1979. 57 p. : LC Card 80-621829 DDC 551.48/2/09793 19 *QC884 .M53*

WHEAT - PRICES - OREGON.
Moe, Debra K. Wheat acreage response to changes in prices and government programs in Oregon and Washington /. Corvallis , 1980. 55 p. : LC Card 80-622276 DDC 338.1/7311/09795 19 *HD9049.W5 U4456*

WHEAT - PRICES - WASHINGTON (STATE)
Moe, Debra K. Wheat acreage response to changes in prices and government programs in Oregon and Washington /. Corvallis , 1980. 55 p. : LC Card 80-622276 DDC 338.1/7311/09795 19 *HD9049.W5 U4456*

WHEAT - TRADE AND STATISTICS. see WHEAT TRADE.

WHEAT TRADE - CANADA - CONGRESSES.
United States. Delegation to the Ad Hoc Meeting of the Canada-United States Interparliamentary Group, 1980, Ottawa, Ont. Ad hoc meeting of the Canada-United States Interparliamentary Group to discuss international wheat marketing, July 26, 1980 . Washington , 1981. v, 12 p. ; LC Card 81-600997 DDC 382/.41311/0971 19 *HD9049.W5 C33 1980*

WHEAT TRADE - LATIN AMERICA.
Hall, Lana. The effects of P.L. 480 wheat imports on Latin American countries /. Ithaca, N.Y. [1980] 84 p. : LC Card 80-623682 DDC 382/.41311/098 19 *HD9049.W5 L294*

WHEAT TRADE - OREGON.
Moe, Debra K. Wheat acreage response to changes in prices and government programs in Oregon and Washington /. Corvallis , 1980. 55 p. : LC Card 80-622276 DDC 338.1/7311/09795 19 *HD9049.W5 U4456*

WHEAT TRADE - UNITED STATES - CONGRESSES.
United States. Delegation to the Ad Hoc Meeting of the Canada-United States Interparliamentary Group, 1980, Ottawa, Ont. Ad hoc meeting of the Canada-United States Interparliamentary Group to discuss international wheat marketing, July 26, 1980 . Washington , 1981. v, 12 p. ; LC Card 81-600997 DDC 382/.41311/0971 19 *HD9049.W5 C33 1980*

WHEAT TRADE - WASHINGTON (STATE)
Moe, Debra K. Wheat acreage response to changes in prices and government programs in Oregon and Washington /. Corvallis , 1980. 55 p. : LC Card 80-622276 DDC 338.1/7311/09795 19 *HD9049.W5 U4456*

WHEAT - UNITED STATES - VARIETIES.
Dalrymple, Dana G. Development and spread of semi-dwarf varieties of wheat and rice in the United States . Washington, D.C. [1980] xiv, 150 p. : LC Card 80-602635 DDC 338.1 s 633.1/17/0973 19 *HD1751 .A91854 no. 455 SB191.W5*

Wheatheart of the plains : an early history of Ochiltree County. 1st ed. [Perrytown?, Tex.] : Ochiltree County Historical Survey Committee, 1969. 653 p. : ill., ports. ; 28 cm. Includes index. LC Card 81-100404 DDC 976.4/81506/0922 B 19
1. Ochiltree County (Tex.) - History. 2. Ochiltree County (Tex.) - Biography. I. Ochiltree County Historical Survey Committee.
F392.O2 W45

Wheatley, J. McNeal. Maryland. Alcoholism Control Administration. Occupational program survey report /. Baltimore , 1977. 13, [4] leaves ; LC Card 79-621085 DDC 658.3/822 19 *HV5297.M3 M37 1977*

WHEELCHAIR BASKETBALL.
Owen, Edward S., 1946- Playing and coaching wheelchair basketball /. Urbana , c1982. p. cm. ISBN 0-252-00867-7 LC Card 81-10456 DDC 796.32/38 19 *GV886.5 .O93*

WHEELCHAIR BASKETBALL - COACHING.
Owen, Edward S., 1946- Playing and coaching wheelchair basketball /. Urbana , c1982. p. cm. ISBN 0-252-00867-7 LC Card 81-10456 DDC 796.32/38 19 *GV886.5 .O93*

Wheeler, H. William. (joint author) Savage, Eldon P. National household pesticide usage study, 1976-1977 . Washington, D.C. [1979] cover 1980. ix, 126 p. : LC Card 80-603384 DDC 363.7/384 19 *TX325 .S28*

Wheeler, Kelly. (joint author) Van Houten, John. Occupational employment statistics, non-manufacturing industries, Alaska, 1978 /. [Juneau] , 1979. 68 p. : LC Card 80-620795 DDC 331.12/51/0009798 19 *HD5725.A4 V32*

When government speaks . Yudof, Mark G.

Berkeley , c1982. p. cm. ISBN 0-520-04254-9 LC Card 81-1965 DDC 342.73/0853 347.302853 19 *KF5753 .Y83*

When is a stream a stream? . Rankin, Janna S. Bozeman, MT [1980] iv, 43 leaves : LC Card 80-623138 DDC 346.78604/69162/014 19 *GB1201.5 .R36*

Where are the children? /. Nebraska. Dept. of Public Welfare. Division of Research and Statistics. [Lincoln] [1976.] 88 p. : LC Card 78-621978 *HV875 .N27 1976* *NYPL [*XME-9432]*

Whipkey, Harry E.
Pennsylvania. Division of Archives and Manuscripts. Descriptive list of the map collection in the Pennsylvania State Archives . Harrisburg , 1976. 178 p. ; LC Card 77-623410 *Z6027.U5 P46 1976 GA447*
NYPL [Map Div. 81-152]
Pennsylvania. Historical and Museum Commission. Guide to the microfilm of the records of Pennsylvania's revolutionary governments, 1775-1790 (record group 27) in the Pennsylvania State Archives, 54 rolls . Harrisburg , 1978 [c1979] vii, 351 p. ; LC Card 79-624725 *E263.P4 P37 1979* *NYPL [ISC 80-2758]*

Whipper, Leigh Rollin, 1876-1975.
[Papers] [1861-1963, n. d.]. 1 box. Black actor. In Schomburg Center for Research in Black Culture. Papers include family papers (1861-1943); Correspondence (1926-1961); Contracts (1940-1942); Writings and Typescripts (1927, n. d.); Playscripts (n. d.); Programs (1924-1963) and a scrapbook. SCM: 76-13, 77-32, 77-37, 77-38, 77-61.
1. Whipper, Leigh Rollin, 1876-1975 - Correspondence. 2. Afro-American actors - Biography - Sources. I. Schomburg Center for Research in Black Culture.
NYPL [Sc Rare Mss-47 & Sc Micro R-3807]

WHIPPER, LEIGH ROLLIN, 1876-1975 - CORRESPONDENCE.
Whipper, Leigh Rollin, 1876-1975. [Papers] [1861-1963, n. d.]. 1 box. *NYPL [Sc Rare Mss-47 & Sc Micro R-3807]*

Whipple, William, 1909- Principles of water resources planning (phase II) / William Whipple, Jr. [New Brunswick] : Rutgers, the State University of New Jersey, Water Resources Research Institute, [1978] 26 leaves ; 28 cm. On cover: Water problems in an urbanizing state. "A partial technical completion report of research supported by funds from the Office of Water Research and Technology, Department of the Interior. Project no. A-048-N.J., agreement no. 14-34-0001-8032." "November 1978." Includes bibliographical references. LC Card 79-623366 DDC 333.91 19
1. Water resources development - Planning. I. Rutgers University, New Brunswick, N. J. Water Resources Research Institute. II. Title. III. Title: Water problems in an urbanizing state.
TC409 .W48

Whiskey Mountain. Wyoming. Game and Fish Dept. The status, mortality, and response to management of the bighorn sheep of Whiskey Mountain /. Cheyenne [1979] 213 p. ; LC Card 80-622756 DDC 639.9/797358 19 *QL737.U53 W96 1979*

WHISTLE BLOWING - UNITED STATES.
United States. Congress. House. Committee on Post Office and Civil Service. Subcommittee on Civil Service. Civil service reform oversight, 1980--whistleblower . Washington , 1980. iii, 330 p. ; LC Card 80-602092 DDC 353.001 19 *KF27 .P635 1980*
United States. Congress. Senate. Committee on Appropriations. Fraud, abuse, waste, and error in government . Washington , 1980. ii, 124 p. : LC Card 80-603298 DDC 353.009 19 *KF26 .A6 1980a*

Whitaker, Donald P.
Area handbook for the People's Republic of China. China, a country study / Foreign Area Studies, the American University ; edited by Frederica M. Bunge and Rinn-Sup Shinn. 3rd ed. Washington, D.C. , 1981. p. cm. LC Card 81-12878 DDC 951 19 *DS706 .C489 1981*

Whitaker, Gordon P. (joint author) Ostrom, Elinor. Policing metropolitan America /. [Washington]

[1977] viii, 49 p. : LC Card 77-603798
HV8138 .O76   **NYPL [*XME-9420]**

Whitaker, John O. Mumford, Russell E. Mammals of Indiana /. Bloomington , c1981. p. cm. ISBN 0-253-30387-7 LC Card 79-2175 DDC 599.09772 19
QL719.I6 M86

Whitcomb, Debra. Focus on robbery : the hidden cameras project, Seattle, Washington : an exemplary project / by Debra Whitcomb ; prepared for the National Institute of Law Enforcement and Criminal Justice, Law Enforcement Assistance Administration, U. S. Department of Justice by Abt Associates Inc. [Washington] : U. S. Dept. of Justice, Law Enforcement Assistance Administration, National Institute of Law Enforcement and Criminal Justice, Office of Development, Testing, and Dissemination : for sale by the Supt. of Docs., U. S. Govt. Print. Off., 1979. iii, 76 p. : ill. ; 26 cm. Includes bibliographical references. LC Card 79-602932 DDC 363.2/52 19
1. Law enforcement - Washington (State) - Seattle - Optical equipment. 2. Robbery - Washington (State) - Seattle. 3. Electric eye cameras. I. National Institute of Law Enforcement and Criminal Justice. II. Abt Associates. III. Title.
HV8145.W2 W45

White Burkett Miller Center. Commission on Presidential Press Conference (U. S.) Report of the Commission on Presidential Press Conferences. [Charlottesville] [Washington, D.C. , c1981] 9 p. ; ISBN 0-8191-1461-8 (pbk.) : LC Card 81-140872 DDC 353.03/5 19
JK518 .C62 1981

WHITE COLLAR CRIME INVESTIGATION - UNITED STATES.
Tompkins, Joseph B. National priorities for the investigation and prosecution of white collar crime . Washington, D.C. , 1980. x, 50, 21-a p. ; LC Card 80-603918 DDC 364.1/68/0973 19
HV8079.W47 T65

WHITE COLLAR CRIME - UNITED STATES.
Tompkins, Joseph B. National priorities for the investigation and prosecution of white collar crime . Washington, D.C. , 1980. x, 50, 21-a p. ; LC Card 80-603918 DDC 364.1/68/0973 19
HV8079.W47 T65

WHITE COLLAR CRIMES - CALIFORNIA.
California. Legislature. Assembly. Select Committee on Crime Prevention. Interim hearing on white collar crime, San Francisco, California, October 4, 1978. [Sacramento, Calif. , 1979] 118 p. ; LC Card 80-622949 DDC 345.794/0268 19
KFC10.4 .C67 1978

WHITE COUNTY, ILL. - MAPS.
(1980) United States. Soil Conservation Service. White County, Illinois /. Lincoln, Nebr. , 1980. 1 map : LC Card 81-691444
G4103.W5 1978 .U5

White, Craig. Geology and geochemistry of Mt. Hood volcano / Craig White. Portland, Or. (1069 State Office Bldg., Portland, Or. 97201) : State of Oregon, Dept. of Geology and Mineral Industries, 1980. iii, 26 p. : ill. ; 28 cm. (Special paper / State of Oregon, Department of Geology and Mineral Industries . 8) Bibliography: p. 26. "Contract EG-77-C-06-1040." LC Card 80-624065 DDC 552/.22/0979561 19
1. Lava - Oregon - Hood, Mount. 2. Dacite - Oregon - Hood, Mount. 3. Geology - Oregon - Hood, Mount. I. Oregon. Dept. of Geology and Mineral Industries. II. Series: Special paper (Oregon. Dept. of Geology and Mineral Industries) , 8. III. Title.
QE461 .W48

White, Doris, 1948- (joint author) Murray, Charles Robert, 1932- The West Virginia dropout study, 1978-1979 /. Charleston, W. Va. [1979] ii leaves, 30 p. : LC Card 80-622735 DDC 371.2/913/09754 19
LC144.W4 M87

White, Eston T.
Human resources for national strength.
Stephens, Richard H. Human resources / Richard H. Stephens. Washington , 1978. v, 150 p. : LC Card 78-602425 DDC 331.11/0973 19
HD5724 .S68

White, George Abbott. Simone Weil, interpretations of a life /. Amherst , 1981. p.

cm. ISBN 0-87023-343-2 : LC Card 81-7460 DDC 194 19
B2430.W474 S617

White, George Willard, 1903- Glacial geology of Ashtabula County, Ohio / by George W. White and Stanley M. Totten ; [cartographer, James A. Brown]. Columbus : State of Ohio, Dept. of Natural Resources, Division of Geological Survey, 1979. iv, 48 p. : ill., maps (1 fold. col.) ; 28 cm. (Report of investigations - State of Ohio, Division of Geological Survey ; no. 112) Bibliography: p. 47-48. LC Card 80-622748 DDC 557.71 s 551.7/92/0977134 19
1. Glacial epoch - Ohio - Ashtabula Co. I. Totten, Stanley M., joint author. II. Series: Ohio. Division of Geological Survey. Report of investigations , no. 112. III. Title.
QE151 .A186 no. 112 QE697

White, Gregory K. Institutional structures affecting on-site waste disposal in Maine / by Gregory K. White and Joel D. Davis. [Orono, Me.] : Life Sciences and Agriculture Experiment Station, University of Maine at Orono, 1979. 46 p. : graph ; 23 cm. (Bulletin - Life Sciences and Agriculture Experiment Station ; 761) Cover title. "Technical completion report project A-046-ME." Bibliography: p. 42-46. LC Card 80-622060 DDC 363.7/28 19
1. Septic tanks - Maine. 2. Sewage disposal, Rural - Law and legislation - Maine. I. Davis, Joel D., joint author. II. Series: Life Sciences and Agriculture Experiment Station. Bulletin - Life Sciences and Agriculture Experiment Station , 761. III. Title.
TD778 .W49

White House Commission on Small Business (U. S.) United States. Congress. Senate. Select Committee on Small Business. Report by the White House Commission on Small Business . Washington , 1980. iii, 44 p. ; LC Card 80-603047 DDC 338.6/42/0973 19
KF26.5 .S6 1980i

WHITE HOUSE CONFERENCE ON BALANCED NATIONAL GROWTH AND ECONOMIC DEVELOPMENT, WASHINGTON, D. C., 1978.
Oklahoma. Delegation to the White House Conference on Balanced National Growth and Economic Development, Washington, D.C., 1978. Report and recommendations to the Governor from the Oklahoma Delegation to the White House Conference on Balanced National Growth and Economic Development. [Oklahoma City] , 1978. 12, 2 [i.e. 3] leaves ; LC Card 79-620770 DDC 338.9766 19
HC107.O5 O44 1978

White House Conference on Children and Youth, Golden Anniversary. see Golden Anniversary White House Conference on Children and Youth, Washington, D. C., 1960.

White House Conference on Families, Washington, D.C., 1979. National Institute for Advance Studies (U. S.) Summary of national hearings of the White House Conference on Families /. Washington, D.C. [1980] ca. 150 p. in various pagings ; LC Card 80-602558 DDC 362.8/2/0973 19
HQ536 .N39 1980

White House Conference on Library and Information Services, Washington, D.C., 1979.
Chartrand, Robert Lee. International information exchange . Washington , 1980. xii, 156 p. : LC Card 80-603261 DDC 021.6/4 19
Z690 .C47

Chartrand, Robert Lee. White House Conference on Library and Information Services pre-conference meetings on special themes, July 31, 1979 . Washington, D.C. [1979] 18 p. ; LC Card 80-143975 DDC 021.6/4 19
Z690 .C48

The White House Conference on Library and Information Services, 1979 : summary. Washington, D.C. : The Conference : for sale by the Supt. of Docs., U. S. Govt. Print. Off., [1980] 101 p. ; 28 cm. "March 1980." LC Card 80-602664 DDC 027.073 19
1. Libraries - United States. 2. Information services - United States. 3. Library science - Congresses.
Z731 .W69 1979

White House Conference on Library and Information Services. (1979 : Washington, D.

C. Information for the 1980's : final report of the White House Conference on Library and Information Services, 1979. Washington, D.C. : National Commission on Libraries and Information Science : For sale by the Supt. of Docs., U. S. G.P.O., 1980. viii, 808 p. : ill. ; 28 cm. Item 1088 S/N 052-003-00764-9 Includes bibliographical references. LC Card 80-603771 DDC 027.073 19
1. Libraries - United States - Congresses. 2. Information services - United States - Congresses. I. United States. National Commission on Libraries and Information Science. II. Title.
Z731 .W69 1979a

White House Conference on Small Business.
White House Conference on Small Business, Washington, D.C., 1980. Delegate recommendations /. Washington , 1980. v, 77 p. ; LC Card 80-602062 DDC 338.6/42/0973 19
HD2346.U5 W54 1980

White House Conference on Small Business, Washington, D.C., 1980. Delegate recommendations / White House Conference on Small Business, ; Committee on Small Business, House of Representatives, Ninety-sixth Congress, second session, January 1980. Washington : U. S. Govt. Print. Off., 1980. v, 77 p. ; 24 cm. At head of title: 96th Congress, 2d session. Committee print. LC Card 80-602062 DDC 338.6/42/0973 19
1. Small business - United States - Congresses. I. United States. Congress. House. Committee on Small Business. II. Title. III. Title: White House Conference on Small Business.
HD2346.U5 W54 1980

White, J. C. (Jack C.) Removal of organic contaminants from aluminum chloride solutions / by Jack C. White, Jack L. Henry, and Charles J. Krogh. Avondale, Md. : U. S. Dept. of the Interior, Bureau of Mines, 1981. p. cm. (Report of investigations) Bibliography: p. LC Card 81-607812 DDC 622 s 622/.34926 19
1. Aluminum chloride. 2. Aluminum oxide. 3. Organic compounds. I. Henry, Jack L. II. Krogh, Charles J. III. Series: Report of investigations (United States. Bureau of Mines). IV. Title.
TN23 .U43 TP245.A4

White, John H. The John Bull, 150 years a locomotive / John H. White, Jr. Washington, D.C. : Smithsonian Institution Press, 1981. p. cm. Bibliography: p. ISBN 0-87474-961-1 LC Card 81-607054 DDC 625.2/61/09034 19
1. Locomotives - History. I. Title.
TJ603 .W527

White, Kerr L. Epidemiology as a fundamental science, its uses in health services planning, administration, and evaluation /. New York , 1976. xv, 235 p. : ISBN 0-19-502081-2 LC Card 75-46369
RA651 .E66   **NYPL [JLD 80-3374]**

White, Patrick, 1912-
VOSS.
Harris, Wilson. Fossil and psyche /. Austin [1974] 12 p. : LC Card 74-622729
PR9619.3.W5 V634   **NYPL [Sc 823-H]**

White, Phillip D. Macro-marketing Seminar, 2d, University of Colorado, 1977. Macro-marketing . Boulder , c1978. vii, 477 p. ; HF5415.125 .M32 1976
    NYPL [JLF 80-1496]

White, Richard, 1924- Olmsted Park System, Jamaica Pond boathouse, Jamaica Plain, Massachusetts : planning for preservation of the boathouse roof / by Richard White. Washington, D.C. : Heritage Conservation and Recreation Service, Technical Preservation Services, U. S. Dept. of the Interior : for sale by the Supt. of Docs., U. S. Govt. Print. Off., 1979. 51 p. : ill. ; 29 cm. (Preservation case studies) HCRS publication ; no. 19 LC Card 80-601622 DDC 690/.587/0288 19
1. Roofs - Maintenance and repair. 2. Boat-houses - Massachusetts - Jamaica Plain - Conservation and restoration. I. Series. II. Series: United States. Heritage Conservation and Recreation Service. HCRS publication, no. 19. III. Title.
TH2401 .W47

WHITE RIVER NATIONAL FOREST, COLO. - MAPS
(1973) United States. Forest Service. Rocky Mountain Region. White River National Forest, Colorado. [Denver] 1973. col. map on sheet 66

x 143 cm. Scale 1:126,720; 1/2˝ = 1 mile. Relief shown by hachures and spot heights. Printed on both sides of sheet. "Polyconic projection. Sixth principal meridian." "Forest visitors map." Includes col. illus., text, "Key map," "Vicinity map," "Recreation directory," and indexes to "Ski areas" and "Points of interest." "Forest Service map class A." LC Card 75-690675
G4312.W5 1973 .U5
NYPL [Map Div. 80-3350]

White, Sheldon Harold, 1928- Testing, teaching, and learning . Washington, D.C. , 1979. vii, 391, [43] p. : LC Card 80-601554 DDC 371.2/6/0973 19
LB3051 .T443

White, Stephen, 1945- Communist legislatures in comparative perspective /. Albany , 1982. p. cm. ISBN 0-87395-566-8 LC Card 81-9189 DDC 328/.3/091717 19
JC474 .C64 1982

WHITE-TAILED DEER - ABSTRACTS.
Weishuhn, Larry L. An annotated bibliography of Texas white-tailed deer research and selected articles from other states /. [Austin. Tex. , 1979] 82 p. : LC Card 80-621109 DDC 599.73/57 19
QL737.U55 W42

WHITE-TAILED DEER - BIBLIOGRAPHY.
Weishuhn, Larry L. An annotated bibliography of Texas white-tailed deer research and selected articles from other states /. [Austin. Tex. , 1979] 82 p. : LC Card 80-621109 DDC 599.73/57 19
QL737.U55 W42

WHITE TAILED DEER - PHYSIOLOGY.
Casey, Timothy J. Chemical and biological investigations of mice and deer in the vicinity of two coal-fired power plants near Stanton, North Dakota /. Grand Forks , 1976. viii, 58 p. : LC Card 77-621848 DDC 599.02/4 19
QH545.C57 C37

White, Teresa J. Rubinstein, Michael L. Alaska bans plea bargaining /. Washington, D.C. , 1980. viii, 312 p. : LC Card 81-601045 DDC 345.798/072 347.980572 19
KFA1778.5 .R8

White, Wendy. United States. Library of Congress. Motion Picture, Broadcasting, and Recorded Sound Division. The George Kleine collection of early motion pictures in the Library of Congress . Washington , 1980. xxxvi, 270 p. : ISBN 0-8444-0331-8 LC Card 79-607073
PN1998.A1 U57 1980
NYPL [MFLE 81-199]

White, William, 1910- 1980, Leaves of grass at 125 . Detroit , 1980. 78 p., [1] leaf of plates : LC Card 81-136978 DDC 811/.3 19
PS3231 .A515

White, William Allen, 1939- Land and water resources, historical changes, and dune criticality . Austin, Tex. , 1978. v, 46 p. : LC Card 79-623595 DDC 553/.09764 s 551.4/57/0976447 19
QE167 .T42 no. 92 GB459.4

Whitehead, Richard S. Hageman, Fred C. An archeological and restoration study of Mission La Purísima Concepción . Santa Barbara, Calif. , Glendale, Calif. , 1980. xxxi, 307 p. : LC Card 79-64806
F869.P89 H33   **NYPL [IXH (Purísima Concepción Mission) 81-684]**

Whiteman, C. D. Measuring local subsidence with extensometers in the Baton Rouge area, Louisiana, 1975-1979 / by C. D. Whiteman, Jr. Baton Rouge, La. : Louisiana Dept. of Transportation and Development, Office of Public Works, 1980. iv, 18 p. : ill. ; 28 cm. (Water resources technical report . no. 20) Bibliography: p. 13. LC Card 80-621814 DDC 551.4/4 19
1. Subsidences (Earth movements) - Louisiana - Baton Rouge region. I. Louisiana. Office of Public Works. II. Title. III. Series.
QE600.3.U6 W48

Whitemarsh Township (Pa.). Board of Township Supervisors. Zoning map, Whitemarsh Township, Montgomery Co., Pennsylvania : May 1958 / Board of Township Supervisors.Map revisions, 5-14-59 rev. zoning on Penna. Ave. added sub-divisions. [Lafayette Hill, Pa.] : The Board, [1959] 1 map : photocopy ; 63 x 137 cm. LC Card 81-690184

1. Whitemarsh Township (Pa.) - Zoning maps. I. Title.
G3824.W584G44 1959 .W4

WHITEMARSH TOWNSHIP (PA.) - ZONING MAPS.
Whitemarsh Township (Pa.). Board of Township Supervisors. Zoning map, Whitemarsh Township, Montgomery Co., Pennsylvania . [Lafayette Hill, Pa.] [1959] 1 map : LC Card 81-690184
G3824.W584G44 1959 .W4

Whiting, Carol. (joint author) Johnson, Edward R. An assessment of the impact of the management review and analysis program (MRAP) /. University Park, Pa. [1977] 202 leaves : LC Card 80-622450 DDC 026 19
Z675.R45 J63

Whitlock, Reid E. China (People's Republic of China, 1949-). Treaties, etc. Treaties of the People's Republic of China, 1949-1978 . Boulder, Colo. , 1980. ix, 207 p. : ISBN 0-89158-761-6 : LC Card 79-27904
JX926 1980 .C47   **NYPL [JFE 80-3747]**

WHITMAN, WALT, 1829-1892 - ADDRESSES, ESSAYS, LECTURES.
1980, Leaves of grass at 125 . Detroit , 1980. 78 p., [1] leaf of plates : LC Card 81-136978 DDC 811/.3 19
PS3231 .A515

Whitman, Warren C. Analysis of grassland vegetation on selected key areas in southwestern North Dakota : a report on a project of the North Dakota Regional Environmental Assessment Program / by Warren C. Whitman. [Bismarck : REAP, [1979?] x, 199 p. : ill. ; 28 cm. (REAP reports ; no. 79-14) Bibliography: p. 101-104. LC Card 80-622820 DDC 581.5/2643/09784 19
1. Grasslands - North Dakota. 2. Botany - North Dakota - Ecology. 3. Phytogeography - North Dakota - Maps. I. Series: North Dakota. Regional Environmental Assessment Program. REAP reports , no. 79-14. II. Title.
QK179 .W83

Whitney Canyon and Carter Creek natural gas processing projects. United States. Bureau of Land Management. District Office, Rock Springs, Wyo. Final environmental assessment: Whitney Canyon & Carter Creek natural gas processing projects /. Washington , 1980. vii, 82, A1-A105 p. :   **NYPL [JSF 81-67]**

Whittaker, Gerald W. (joint author) Oliveira, Ronald A. An examination of dynamic relationships--and the lack thereof--among U. S. lumber prices, U. S. housing starts, U. S. log exports to Japan, and Japanese housing starts /. Corvallis [1979] 34 p. ; LC Card 80-621302 DDC 338.4/7674/00973 19
HD9755 .O44

Whittaker, James Kramer, 1949- (joint author) Moe, Debra K. Wheat acreage response to changes in prices and government programs in Oregon and Washington /. Corvallis , 1980. 55 p. : LC Card 80-622276 DDC 338.1/7311/09795 19
HD9049.W5 U4456

Whitten, Ira Taylor. Brand performance in the cigarette industry and the advantage to early entry, 1913-74 / by Ira Taylor Whitten. [Washington] : Federal Trade Commission, Bureau of Economics : for sale by the Supt. of Docs., U. S. Govt. Print. Off., 1979. 54 p. : graphs ; 20 cm. "Staff report to the Federal Trade Commission." Bibliography: p. 53-54. LC Card 79-603962
1. Cigarette manufacture and trade - United States. 2. Brand choice - United States. I. United States. Federal Trade Commission. II. Title.
HD9149.C42 U695   **NYPL [JLD 81-574]**

Whitten, Norman E., 1937- Cultural transformations and ethnicity in modern Ecuador /. Urbana , c1981. p. cm. ISBN 0-252-00832-4 LC Card 81-44402 DDC 986.6 19
HN317 .C8

Whittow, G. Causey, 1930- (joint author) Balazs, George H. Revised bibliography of the Hawaiian monk seal . [Manoa] , 1979. iv, 27 p. ; LC Card 79-625332 DDC 016.59974/8 19
Z7996.P5 B27 QL737.P64

Whitwell, W. L. (William Livingston), 1936- The architectural heritage of the Roanoke Valley /

W.L. Whitwell, Lee W. Winborne ; special pictures by Judith Farb. Charlottesville : University Press of Virginia, 1982. p. cm. Bibliography: p. Includes index. ISBN 0-8139-0905-8 LC Card 81-12987 DDC 720/.9756/1 19
1. Architecture - Roanoke Valley (Va. and N.C.). I. Winborne, Lee W. II. Title.
NA730.V82 R68

Who perished . Hansen, Gladys C., 1925- San Francisco, CA , 1980. 4, [51] p. ; LC Card 80-126237 DDC 929/.379461 19
F869.S353 A23

The whole college catalog about drinking.
National Institute on Alcohol Abuse and Alcoholism. Rockville, Md. , Washington [1976] xii, 129 p. : LC Card 76-603043 DDC 362.2/9286/088375 19
HV5292 .N33 1976

WHOLESALE TRADE - DELAWARE - EMPLOYEES - STATISTICS.
Delaware. Dept. of Labor. Office of Planning, Research & Evaluation. Delaware occupational employment statistics, wholesale trade, 1973. Wilmington, DE , 1975. 10 p. ; LC Card 77-622507
HD5725.D3 D33 1975b   **NYPL [*ZT-1265]**

WHOLESALE TRADE - DELAWARE - WILMINGTON METROPOLITAN AREA - EMPLOYEES - STATISTICS.
Delaware. Dept. of Labor. Office of Planning, Research & Evaluation. Wilmington SMSA occupational employment statistics . Newark, DE , 1978. i, 80 leaves ; LC Card 78-624189
HD5725.D3 D33 1978a   **NYPL [JLF 81-109]**

WHOLESALE TRADE - INDIANA - EMPLOYEES - STATISTICS.
Indiana. Employment Security Division. Research and Statistics Section. Staffing patterns in wholesale and retail trade industries in Indiana . [Indianapolis, Ind.] , 1978. viii, 67 p. : LC Card 79-625864 DDC 331.12/51381/09772 19
HD5725.I6 I53 1978a

WHOOPING CRANE.
Whooping Crane Recovery Team. Whooping crane recovery plan, January 1980 /. [Albuquerque, N.M. , 1980] vi, 206 p. : LC Card 80-602324 DDC 639.9/7831 19
QL696.G84 W48 1980

Whooping crane recovery plan, January 1980 /.
Whooping Crane Recovery Team. [Albuquerque, N.M. , 1980] vi, 206 p. : LC Card 80-602324 DDC 639.9/7831 19
QL696.G84 W48 1980

Whooping Crane Recovery Team. Whooping crane recovery plan, January 1980 / prepared by the Whooping Crane Recovery Team ; David L. Olsen, team leader ... [et al.] ; editor, Scott R. Derrickson. [Albuquerque, N.M. : U. S. Fish and Wildlife Service, 1980] vi, 206 p. : ill. ; 28 cm. "Approved January 23, 1980." Bibliography: p. 127-129. LC Card 80-602324 DDC 639.9/7831 19
1. Whooping crane. 2. Birds, Protection of - United States. 3. Birds - United States. I. Olsen, David L., 1933-. II. Derrickson, Scott R. III. Title.
QL696.G84 W48 1980

Why gasoline prices remain high . United States. Congress. Senate. Committee on the Judiciary. Subcommittee on Antitrust, Monopoly, and Business Rights. Washington , 1980 [i.e. 1981] iii, 52 p. ; LC Card 81-600930 DDC 338.4/366553827/0973 19
KF26 .J835 1980c

Why the formula for allocating community development block grant funds ... United States. General Accounting Office. Why the formula for allocating community development block grant funds should be improved, Department of Housing and Urban Development /. [Washington , 1976] v, 50 p. ; LC Card 76-603691
HN90.C6 U62 1976   **NYPL [JLF 81-401]**

The WIC program in Illinois . Illinois. General Assembly. Legislative Investigating Commission. Chicago, Ill. [1979] vii, 169 p. : LC Card 80-622568 DDC 362.8/283 19
HV696.F6 I35 1979

WICHE. see Western Interstate Commission for Higher Education.

WICHITA FALLS, TEX. - TORNADO, 1979.
United States. National Oceanic and
Atmospheric Administration. Red River Valley
tornadoes of April 10, 1979 . Rockville, Md.
[1980] v, 60 p., [2] leaves of plates : LC Card
80-601568   DDC 363.3/492 19
QC955.5.T4 U54 1980

WICHITA, KANSAS - POLICE -
COMPLAINTS AGAINST.
United States. Commission on Civil Rights.
Kansas Advisory Committee. Police-community
relations in the city of Wichita and Sedgwick
County . Washington, D.C. [1980] xi, 95 p. :
    LC Card 80-603162   DDC 363.2/2/0978186 19
HV7936.P8 U53 1980

Wichita State University. University Gerontology
Center. Allegrucci, Robert L. An empirical
analysis of age-based lobbying strategies in
Kansas . Wichita, Kan. , 1981. 39 leaves ; LC
    Card 81-127338   DDC 328/.38/0880565 19
HQ1064.U6 K15

Wider use of better computer software
technology can improve management control
and reduce costs . United States. General
Accounting Office. Washington, DC [1980] iii,
57 p. ; LC Card 80-602401   DDC 353/.075 19
JK468.A8 U5 1980

Wiederanders, Mark R. Job survival skills of
youthful offenders : report of a needs
assessment and curriculum development
project : final report / Mark R. Wiederanders,
Albert Victor Luckey, Candace J. Cross-Drew ;
California Youth Authority, Division of
Research. [Washington] : U. S. Dept. of Health,
Education, and Welfare, Office of Education,
Bureau of Occupational and Adult Education,
1978. 105 p. ; 29 cm. Bibliography: p. 61-62. LC
    Card 79-621769   DDC 331.3/4 19
1. Ex-offenders - Employment - California. 2.
Occupational training - California. 3. Juvenile
delinquents - Employment - Study and teaching -
California. I. Luckey, Albert Victor, joint author. II.
Cross-Drew, Candace J., joint author. III. California.
Dept. of the Youth Authority. Division of Research and
Development. IV. Title.
HV9288 .W53

Wiegmann, Fred. (joint author) Reiling, Stephen D.
Louisiana agriculture, 1940-1977 . [Baton
Rouge] , 1979. 74 p. (p. 74 blank) : LC Card
79-624475   DDC 338.1/09763 19
HD1775.L8 R44

Wieland, James S. (joint author) Leholm, Arlen.
Profile of electric power plant construction
work force /. Fargo , 1976. ii, 53 p. : LC Card
77-621855   DDC 338.1/0212 s 331.11/99054 19
HD1407 .A33 no. 22 HD8039.B92U5

Wiener, William E. Oral History Library. see
William E. Wiener Oral History Library.

Wienk, Ronald E. United States. Dept. of
Housing and Urban Development. Office of
Policy Development and Research. Division of
Evaluation. Measuring racial discrimination in
American housing markets . [Washington,
D.C.] , 1979. vii, 30, 206, [93] p. : LC Card
79-603351
HD7293 .A5 1979d

Wierenga, Petrus Johannes. Soil salinity and
cotton yields as affected by surface and trickle
irrigation : partial technical completion report /
by P.J. Wierenga. Las Cruces, N.M. : New
Mexico Water Resources Research Institute, in
cooperation with Dept. of Agronomy, New
Mexico State University, [1979] vi, 212 p. :
graphs ; 28 cm. (WRRI report . no. 106) "EPA grant
no. 5803565." "August 1979." Bibliography: p. 76. LC
    Card 80-622502   DDC 333.91/009789 s
    631.4/16 19
1. Irrigation - New Mexico - Mesilla Valley. 2. Soils,
Salts in - New Mexico - Mesilla Valley. 3. Cotton
growing - New Mexico - Mesilla Valley. 4. Cotton -
New Mexico - Mesilla Valley - Irrigation. 5. Trickle
irrigation - New Mexico - Mesilla Valley. 6. Soils,
Irrigated - New Mexico - Mesilla Valley. I. New
Mexico State University. Water Resources Research
Institute. II. New Mexico State University. Dept. of
Agronomy. III. Series: New Mexico State University.
Water Resources Research Institute. WRRI report , no.
106. IV. Title.
GB705.N6 N64 no. 106 S616.U6

Wierer, Rudolf. Lovejoy Library. Slavic-American
imprints . [Edwardsville, Ill.] , 1979- v. ; LC

Card 80-622920   DDC 016.947 19
Z2483 .L68 1972 Suppl.

WIESENTHAL, SIMON - MEDALS.
United States. Congress. House. Committee on
Banking, Finance and Urban Affairs.
Subcommittee on Consumer Affairs. Legislation
authorizing issuance of gold medals to Canadian
Ambassador Kenneth Taylor, Simon
Wiesenthal, Gerald F. Spiess, and
commemorative medals for the United States
Capitol Historical Society . Washington , 1980.
iii, 73 p. ; LC Card 80-601297   DDC 344.73/091
    347.30491 19
KF27 .B535 1980c

WIFE ABUSE - BIBLIOGRAPHY.
Woodhull, S. Domestic violence bibliography .
[Lansing] [1980] 7 leaves ; LC Card 80-623994
    DDC 016.3068/7 19
Z5703.4.F35 W66 HQ809

WIFE ABUSE - KENTUCKY.
Schulman, Mark A. A survey of spousal
violence against women in Kentucky /.
Washington, D.C. , 1980 printing. 67, 13 p., p.
a-b : LC Card 80-602365   DDC 362.8/2 19
HV6626 .S38

WIFE ABUSE - MONTANA.
Adrian, Martha. A study of spouse battering in
Montana /. Helena, MT [1978] 117 p. ; LC
    Card 80-622328   DDC 362.8/3 19
HV6626 .A37

WIFE ABUSE - OREGON.
Miller, Marilyn G. Domestic violence in
Oregon /. [Salem] [1979] 43, [20] p. ; LC
    Card 80-621297   DDC 362.8/2 19
HV6626 .M54

WIFE ABUSE - UNITED STATES -
ABSTRACTS.
Project SHARE. Issues in domestic violence /.
[Rockville, Md.] [1980] v, 25 p. ; LC Card
    80-602672   DDC 362.8/3 19
HV6626 .P76 1980

WIFE ABUSE - UNITED STATES -
BIBLIOGRAPHY.
Woodhull, S. Domestic violence bibliography .
[Lansing] [1980] 7 leaves ; LC Card 80-623994
    DDC 016.3068/7 19
Z5703.4.F35 W66 HQ809

WIFE ABUSE - UNITED STATES -
CONGRESSES.
Prosecutor's responsibility in spouse abuse
cases. Washington, D.C. , 1980. 13, 24 [13] p. ;
    LC Card 80-602608   DDC 345.73/04555 19
KF9322.A75 P76

Wilbanks, William A. The measurement of color
blindness : report / by William A. Wilbanks ;
approved by Ashton Graybiel ; released by
Julius C. Early. Pensacola, Fla. : U. S. Naval
School of Aviation Medicine, 1956. iv, 44 p. :
graphs ; 26 cm. (Monograph series - U. S. Naval
School of Aviation Medicine . report no. 2) Includes
bibliographical references. LC Card 81-462888   DDC
    617.7/59 19
1. Color blindness - Diagnosis. 2. Colorimetry. I. Series:
United States. Naval School of Aviation Medicine,
Pensacola, Fla. Monograph series , report no. 2. II.
Title.
RE921 .W7

Wilbur Cross Library, Storrs, Conn. see
Connecticut. University. Library.

Wilbur, Henry M. (joint author) Collins, James P.
Breeding habits and habitats of the amphibians
of the Edwin S. George Reserve, Michigan ,
with notes on the local distribution of fishes /.
Ann Arbor , 1979. 34 p. : LC Card 79-623929
    DDC 597.6/09774/36 19
QL653.M5 C64

Wilbur Smith and Associates. see **Smith (Wilbur)**
and Associates.

Wilcox, Ralph. (joint author) Davis, Paul, 1950-
Spring characteristics of the western Roswell
artesian basin . Las Cruces, N.M. [1980] viii,
93 p. : LC Card 80-623165   DDC 333.91/009789 s
    551.49/8 19
GB705.N6 N64 no. 116 GB1198.3.N6

WILD AND SCENIC RIVERS - ALASKA.
United States. Heritage Conservation and
Recreation Service. A proposal for protection of
eleven Alaskan rivers /. [Washington, D.C.]
[1980] ca. 200 p. in various pagings : LC Card

80-602406   DDC 333.78/45/09798 19
QH76.5.A4 U56 1980

WILD AND SCENIC RIVERS - LAW AND
LEGISLATION - UNITED STATES.
United States. Congress. Senate. Committee on
Interior and Insular Affairs. Environment and
Land Resources Subcommittee. To amend the
Wild and scenic rivers act . Washington , 1975-
v. : LC Card 76-600555
KF26 .I526 1975d

WILD AND SCENIC RIVERS -
MINNESOTA - CANNON RIVER.
Minnesota. Dept. of Natural Resources. Cannon
River resource analysis. [St. Paul] [1979] 48
p. : LC Card 79-623707   DDC 333.91/62/09776 19
QH76.5.M6 M54 1979

WILD AND SCENIC RIVERS -
MINNESOTA - MINNESOTA RIVER.
Minnesota. Wild and Scenic Rivers Program.
Minnesota River resource analysis. [St. Paul] ,
1979. 55 p. : LC Card 79-625703   DDC
    333.91/621/097763 19
QH105.M55 M56 1979

WILD AND SCENIC RIVERS - MONTANA.
Utter, Jack. Wild river management . Bozeman,
MT [1980] xiii, 117 leaves : LC Card 80-623137
    DDC 333.78/45 19
TD224.M9 U88

WILD ANIMAL TRADE.
United States. Congress. House. Committee on
Merchant Marine and Fisheries. Subcommittee
on Fisheries and Wildlife Conservation and the
Environment. Oversight report on the
administration of the Endangered species act
and the Convention on International Trade in
Endangered Species of Wild Fauna and Flora /.
Washington , 1980. ii, 28 p. ; LC Card
    80-602275   DDC 353.0082/328 19
QL84.2 .U55 1980

WILD ANIMAL TRADE - PERIODICALS.
Convention of International Trade in
Endangered Species of Wild Fauna and Flora.
Annual report by the United States of America.
1977- Washington.   *NYPL [JLM 80-800]*

WILD FLOWERS - MISSOURI -
IDENTIFICATION.
Denison, Edgar. Missouri wildflowers .
Jefferson City, Mo. (P.O. Box 180, Jefferson
City, Mo. 65101) , 1978. x, 286 p. : LC Card
    80-624456   DDC 582.13/09778 19
QK170 .D46 1978

WILD FLOWERS, PROTECTION OF. see
PLANTS, PROTECTION OF.

Wild, free-roaming burros . Zarn, Mark.
[Washington] , Denver, Colo. , 1979. 29 p. ;
    LC Card 80-601254   DDC 639.9 s 016.59972/5
    19
QL84.2 .U54a vol. 297 Z7997.D76 QL737.U62

WILD LIFE - CONSERVATION OF - NEW
YORK (STATE) - PERIODICALS.
The Conservationist. v. 14, no. 5- ; Apr./May
1960- Albany.
    *NYPL [*ZAN-T5219 & M-10 5488]*

Wild reach of the Rogue River, Oregon. Purdom,
William B. Guide to the geology and lore of the
wild reach of the Rogue River, Oregon /.
Eugene , 1977. 67 p. : LC Card 77-622970
    DDC 917.95/2 19
QH1 .O7 no. 22 QH105.O7

Wild river management . Utter, Jack. Bozeman,
MT [1980] xiii, 117 leaves : LC Card 80-623137
    DDC 333.78/45 19
TD224.M9 U88

The wildcat experiment . Friedman, Lucy N.
Rockville, Md. , Washington [1978] ix, 147
p. ; LC Card 79-602059   DDC 362.2/9386 19
HV5833.N45 F74

WILDCAT SERVICE CORPORATION - CASE
STUDIES.
Friedman, Lucy N. The wildcat experiment .
Rockville, Md. , Washington [1978] ix, 147
p. ; LC Card 79-602059   DDC 362.2/9386 19
HV5833.N45 F74

WILDERNESS AREAS - FLORIDA -
EVERGLADES NATIONAL PARK.
United States. National Park Service. Denver
Service Center. Final environmental statement,
FES-78-7 . [Denver] [1978] vii, 211 p. : LC
Card 79-601941   DDC 333.91/8/0975939 19
QH76.5.F6 U54 1978

WILDERNESS AREAS - LAW AND LEGISLATION - MISSOURI.
United States. Congress. Senate. Committee on Energy and Natural Resources. Subcommittee on Parks, Recreation, and Renewable Resources. Missouri, South Dakota, and New Mexico wilderness . Washington , 1980. iii, 407 p. : LC Card 80-604055 DDC 346.7304/6782/0262 347.306467820262 19
KF26 .E5565 1980g

WILDERNESS AREAS - LAW AND LEGISLATION - NEW MEXICO.
United States. Congress. Senate. Committee on Energy and Natural Resources. Subcommittee on Parks, Recreation, and Renewable Resources. Missouri, South Dakota, and New Mexico wilderness . Washington , 1980. iii, 407 p. : LC Card 80-604055 DDC 346.7304/6782/0262 347.306467820262 19
KF26 .E5565 1980g

WILDERNESS AREAS - LAW AND LEGISLATION - OREGON.
United States. Congress. Senate. Committee on Energy and Natural Resources. Subcommittee on Parks, Recreation, and Renewable Resources. Oregon wilderness act of 1979 . Washington , 1980. vii, 696 p. : LC Card 80-603319 DDC 346.7304/6782/0262 19
KF26 .E5565 1979j

WILDERNESS AREAS - MONTANA.
United States. Congress. Senate. Committee on Energy and Natural Resources. Subcommittee on Parks, Recreation, and Renewable Resources. Rattlesnake roadless area . Washington , 1980. iii, 119 p. : LC Card 80-602500 DDC 346.7304/6782 347.30646782 19
KF26 .E5565 1979k

WILDERNESS AREAS - THE WEST.
United States. Congress. Senate. Committee on Energy and Natural Resources. Subcommittee on Parks, Recreation, and Renewable Resources. Bureau of Land Management wilderness review and rangeland management programs . Washington , 1980. iii, 189 p. ; LC Card 80-602719 DDC 346.7304/6782/0262 19
KF26 .E5565 1980a

WILDERNESS SURVIVAL - ANTARCTIC REGIONS.
United States. National Science Foundation. Division of Polar Programs. Survival in Antarctica. Washington, D.C. , 1979. v, 99 p. : LC Card 80-601811 DDC 613.6/9/09989 19
GV200.5 .U54 1979

WILDFIRES - CALIFORNIA, SOUTHERN - PREVENTION AND CONTROL.
Lee, Robert G. Brushland watershed fire management policy in southern California . Davis, Calif. [1978] iv, 74 p. : LC Card 80-620664 DDC 333.91/009794 s 363.3/79 19
GB705.C2 C27 no. 172 SD421.32.C2

Wildgen, John K. A political atlas of Louisiana gubernatorial elections / John K. Wildgen. [New Orleans] : Division of Business and Economic Research, College of Business Administration, University of New Orleans, 1979. 14 leaves : maps ; 28 cm. (Research study - Division of Business and Economic Research, University of New Orelans . no. 30) Illustrative matter in pocket. LC Card 79-625553 DDC 330.9763 s 912/.13249763 19
1. Louisiana - Elections - Maps. 2. Louisiana - Politics and government. I. Series: University of New Orleans. Division of Business and Economic Research. Research study - Division of Business and Economic Research, University of New Orleans , no. 30. II. Title.
HC107.L8 L58 no.30 G1361.F9

Wildlife atlas . Alaska Interagency Fish and Wildlife Team. [s.l.] , 1976. 30 leaves : LC Card 79-625526 DDC 912/.159909798
G1531.D4 A45 1976

WILDLIFE CONSERVATION - LAW AND LEGISLATION - UNITED STATES.
United States. Congress. Senate. Committee on Environment and Public Works. Subcommittee on Resource Protection. Elephant Protection Act of 1979 and the International Wildlife Resources Conservation Act of 1980 . Washington , 1980. iii, 220 p. : LC Card 80-603406 DDC 346.7304/6954 347.30646954 19
KF26 .E675 1980a

United States. Congress. Senate. Committee on Environment and Public Works. Subcommittee on Resource Protection. Fish and wildlife conservation act of 1980 and authorizations for wildlife refuges . Washington , 1980. iv, 351 p. : LC Card 80-602456 DDC 346.7304/69516/0262 19
KF26 .E675 1980

United States. Treaties, etc. Treaties and other international agreements on fisheries, oceanographic resources, and wildlife involving the United States /. Washington , 1977. xv, 1201 p. ; LC Card 81-601815 DDC 341.7/62/026 19
JX236 1977 .U54

WILDLIFE CONSERVATION - MISSOURI.
Sampson, Frank W. Missouri fur harvests /. Jefferson City, Mo. , 1980. 59 p. : LC Card 81-621615 DDC 381/.456753/09778 19
HD9944.U46 M87

WILDLIFE DEPREDATION - BOTSWANA.
Simpson, C. David. Effects of elephant and other wildlife on vegetation along the Chobe River, Botswana /. [Lubbock] , 1978. 15 p. : LC Card 78-621508 DDC 639.9/5 19
SK575.B6 S54

WILDLIFE DEPREDATION - OREGON.
Animal damage to coniferous plantations in Oregon and Washington /. Corvallis, Or. , 1979. 2 v. : LC Card 80-623387 DDC 634.9 s 634.9/7547 19
SD12 .O87 no. 25-26 SB608.D6

WILDLIFE DEPREDATION - THE WEST.
United States. Fish and Wildlife Service. Predator damage in the West . [Washington] , 1978. vii, 168 p. : LC Card 79-602347 DDC 636.08/3 19
SF810.7.C88 U54 1978

WILDLIFE DEPREDATION - WASHINGTON (STATE)
Animal damage to coniferous plantations in Oregon and Washington /. Corvallis, Or. , 1979. 2 v. : LC Card 80-623387 DDC 634.9 s 634.9/7547 19
SD12 .O87 no. 25-26 SB608.D6

Wildlife drawings /. Schwartz, Charles Walsh. Jefferson City, Mo. , c1980. 122 p. : LC Card 81-621407 DDC 599 19
QL46 .S395

WILDLIFE HABITAT IMPROVEMENT - NEBRASKA - LITTLE NEMAHA RIVER WATERSHED - MAPS.
United States. Soil Conservation Service. Wildlife habitat evaluation map, upper Little Nemaha watershed, Lancaster, Cass, and Otoe Counties, Nebraska /. Lincoln, Nebr. , 1978. 1 map : LC Card 81-691083
G4192.L5D5 1978 .U5

WILDLIFE HABITAT IMPROVEMENT - UNITED STATES.
Establishment of seeded grasslands for wildlife habitat in the prairie pothole region /. Washington, D.C. , 1981. p. cm. LC Card 81-607001 DDC 639.9/79/0973 s 639.9/79 19
SK361 .A256 no. 234

WILDLIFE HABITAT IMPROVEMENT - UNITED STATES - CONGRESSES.
Mitigation Symposium, Colorado State University, 1979. The Mitigation Symposium . Fort Collins, Colo , 1979. xi, 684 p. : LC Card 80-602500 DDC 639.9/2/0973 19
SK361 .M57 1979

WILDLIFE MANAGEMENT.
Leedy, Daniel L. Planning for wildlife in cities and suburbs /. [Washington] , 1978. vii, 64 p. : LC Card 79-603493 DDC 639.9/09173/2 19
QH541.5.C6 L43 1978

WILDLIFE MANAGEMENT - BOTSWANA.
Simpson, C. David. Effects of elephant and other wildlife on vegetation along the Chobe River, Botswana /. [Lubbock] , 1978. 15 p. : LC Card 78-621508 DDC 639.9/5 19
SK575.B6 S54

WILDLIFE MANAGEMENT - MISSOURI.
LaVal, Richard K. Ecological studies and management of Missouri bats, with emphasis on cave-dwelling species /. Jefferson City, Mo. , 1980. 53 p. : LC Card 80-623996 DDC 599.4/09778 19
QL737.C5 L32

WILDLIFE MANAGEMENT - OREGON.
Oregon. Dept. of Fish and Wildlife. A statewide comprehensive plan for fish and wildlife on the national forests in the State of Oregon . [Portland] [1979?] 84 p. : LC Card 80-621380
SK439 .O75 1979   **NYPL [JLF 81047]**

WILDLIFE MANAGEMENT - WYOMING - FREMONT CO.
Wyoming. Game and Fish Dept. The status, mortality, and response to management of the bighorn sheep of Whiskey Mountain /. Cheyenne [1979] 213 p. : LC Card 80-622756 DDC 639.9/797358 19
QL737.U53 W96 1979

WILDLIFE REFUGES - ALASKA - ALASKA PENINSULA.
United States. Dept. of the Interior. Final environmental impact statement . [Washington] [1980] xv, 339 p. : LC Card 80-602694 DDC 333.95/1/00798 19
QH76.5.A4 U54 1980

WILDLIFE REFUGES - LAW AND LEGISLATION - UNITED STATES.
United States. Congress. House. Committee on Merchant Marine and Fisheries. Subcommittee on Fisheries and Wildlife Conservation and the Environment. National wildlife refuges . Washington , 1980. vii, 584 p. : LC Card 80-602809 DDC 346.7304/695 19
KF27 .M447 1979f

United States. Congress. Senate. Committee on Environment and Public Works. Subcommittee on Resource Protection. Fish and wildlife conservation act of 1980 and authorizations for wildlife refuges . Washington , 1980. iv, 351 p. : LC Card 80-602456 DDC 346.7304/69516/0262 19
KF26 .E675 1980

WILDLIFE REFUGES - THE WEST - DIRECTORIES.
United States. Fish and Wildlife Service. Directory, Pacific States Region National Wildlife Refuges and Fish Hatcheries. [Washington? , 1980] 32 p. : LC Card 80-602853 DDC 333.95/025/78 19
QL84.22.W47 U54 1980

WILDLIFE REFUGES - UNITED STATES - FINANCE.
United States. Congress. Senate. Committee on Environment and Public Works. Subcommittee on Resource Protection. Fish and wildlife conservation act of 1980 and authorizations for wildlife refuges . Washington , 1980. iv, 351 p. : LC Card 80-602456 DDC 346.7304/69516/0262 19
KF26 .E675 1980

Wildlife research report .
(12) North American tortoises . Washington, D.C. , 1981. p. cm. LC Card 81-607867 DDC 597.92 19
QL666.C584 N67

Wildlife technical report .
(no. 1) Compton, Thomas. Sierra Madre elk-deer ecology study /. [Cheyenne] , 1975. ix, 125 p. : LC Card 76-622419 DDC 599.73/57 19
QL737.U55 C63

(no. 7) Wyoming. Game and Fish Dept. The status, mortality, and response to management of the bighorn sheep of Whiskey Mountain /. Cheyenne [1979] 213 p. : LC Card 80-622756 DDC 639.9/797358 19
QL737.U53 W96 1979

Wilds, Claudia P. United States. Foreign Service Institute. Testing kit, French and Spanish /. [Washington, D.C.] [1979] x, 140 p. (p. 140 blank) : LC Card 80-602389 DDC 440[.76 19
PB36 .U54 1979

Wiley, William N. The Judicial Retirement System, expansion? / Prepared by William Wiley. Frankfort, Ky. : Legislative Research Commission, [1979] vi, 27, 18 p. ; 27 cm. (Research report - Legislative Research Commission ; no. 154) "August 1979." Bibliography: p. 22. LC Card 79-625554 DDC 347.769/014 19
1. Judges - Kentucky - Retirement. I. Series: Kentucky. Legislative Research Commission. Research report , no. 154. II. Title.
KFK1725.5.A6 A25 1979

Wilhelm, Steven. (joint author) Blyth, James E. Primary forest products industry & timber use, Minnesota, 1973 /. St. Paul , 1979. 34 p. : LC

Card 79-602962   DDC 333.75/0977 s
338.1/7498/09776 19
SD11 .A45533 no. 39 HD9757.M6

Wilhite, Donald A. Drought in the Great Plains :
a bibliography / [compiled and edited by
Donald A. Wilhite, Richard O. Hoffman].
[Lincoln] : Agricultural Experiment Station,
University of Nebraska-Lincoln, Institute of
Agriculture and Natural Resources, [1980] 75
p. ; 28 cm. ([Miscellaneous publication] - Agricultural
Experiment Station, University of Nebraska-Lincoln .
MP 39) "Prepared for the Workshop on Research in
Great Plains Drought Management Strategies,
University of Nebraska-Lincoln, March 26-28, 1979."
"Issued June 1980." Includes indexes.   LC Card
80-624036   DDC 016.363/492 19
*1. Droughts - Great Plains - Bibliography. I. Hoffman,
Richard O., joint author. II. Series: Nebraska.
Agricultural Experiment Station, Lincoln. Miscellaneous
publication , MP 39. III. Title.*
Z6683.D7 W54 QC929.D8

Wilkie, Jane. Evaluation of discontinuities in
regional population projections/ by Jane Wilkie
and Everett Lee. Amherst : Water Resources
Research Center, University of Massachusetts,
1973. 21, iii p. ; 28 cm. Microfilm. On cover:
Completion report FY-73-9. Bibliographical footnotes.
*1. Population forecasting. I. Lee, Everett Spurgeon,
joint author. II. Massachusetts. University. Water
Resources Research Center. III. Title.*
                              NYPL [*ZT-1259]

Will the lights go on in 1990? . Kaufman, Alvin.
Washington , 1980. vii, 15 p. :   LC Card
80-603985   DDC 333.79/32/0973 19
TK1193.U5 K32

Willard, William A. Mechanical Failures
Prevention Group. Detection, diagnosis, and
prognosis . [Washington] , 1979. vi, 370 p. :
      LC Card 79-600078   DDC 602/.18 s 620.1/126
      19
QC100 .U57 no. 547 TA409

Willdan Associates. Mississippi Deltaic Plain
Region ecological characterization : a
socioeconomic study / prepared for National
Coastal Ecosystems Team, Office of Biological
Services, Fish and Wildlife Service, U. S.
Department of the Interior. [Washington] : The
Service, [1980- v. <1> : ill. ; 28 cm. On cover:
Biological Services Program. "FWS/OBS-79/05."
"March 1980." "This study co-sponsored by the Bureau
of Land Management." Bibliography: v. 1, p. 318-368.
CONTENTS. - v. 1. Larson, D.K., et al. Synthesis
papers.   LC Card 80-603195   DDC 330.9763/3063 19
*1. New Orleans region - Economic conditions -
Collected works. 2. Gulf region, Miss. - Economic
conditions - Collected works. 3. Mississippi River -
Delta - Collected works. 4. Natural resources -
Louisiana - New Orleans region - Collected works. 5.
Natural resources - Mississippi - Gulf region - Collected
works. 6. Natural resources - Mississippi River - Delta -
Collected works. I. Larson, Douglas K. II. National
Coastal Ecosystems Team. III. United States. Bureau of
Land Management. IV. Title.*
HC108.N42 W54 1980

Willeke, Gene E., 1934- (joint author) Bishop, A.
Bruce. Socio-economic and community factors
in planning urban freeways. [Washington] 1970.
xiii, 216 p. ;   LC Card 73-610102
HE356.C2 B5   *NYPL [JLF 81-276]*

Willers, W. B., 1938- Trout biology, an angler's
guide / W.B. Willers. Madison : University of
Wisconsin Press, 1981. p. cm. Includes index.
Includes index.   ISBN 0-299-08720-4 :   LC Card
81-50829   DDC 597/.55 19
1. Trout. 2. Trout fishing. I. Title.
QL638.S2 W55

Willett, K. World Bank. Agriculture and Rural
Development Dept. Resource Planning Unit.
Nepal /. Washington, D.C. , 1980. 1 remote
sensing image on 2 sheets :   LC Card 81-692612
G7761.A4 1980 .W6

William Benton Museum of Art.
Connecticut and American impressionism .
Storrs, c1980. 184 p. :
                              NYPL [MCW 80-2001]

A Handbook of twentieth century art. - Storrs,
Conn. , 1973. 71, iv p. :
                   NYPL [3-MAVZ (New York) 80-2266]

William Brill Associates. Comprehensive security
planning : a program for Arthur Capper
dwellings, Washington, D.C. : final draft /

prepared for U. S. Department of Housing and
Urban Development, Office of Policy
Development and Research by William Brill
Associates, Inc. Washington : The Office : for
sale by the Supt. of Docs., U. S. Govt. Print.
Off., 1977. 196 p. in various pagings : ill. ; 27
cm. Includes bibliographical references.   LC Card
78-601532
*1. Washington, D. C. Arthur Capper Dwellings -
Security measures. I. United States. Dept. of Housing
and Urban Development. Office of Policy Development
and Research. II. Title.*
HV8290 .W54 1977   *NYPL [JLF 81-371]*

**William Collins and eighteenth-century English
poetry /.** Wendorf, Richard. Minneapolis ,
1981. p. cm.   ISBN 0-8166-1058-4 :   LC Card
81-14674   DDC 823/.8 19
PR3354 .W46

William E. Wiener Oral History Library.
Epstein, Helen, 1947- A study in American
pluralism through oral histories of holocaust
survivors /. [New York] [1977?] 157, xciv
leaves ;   LC Card 77-153163
E184.J5 E613   *NYPL [*PXY 80-4926]*

William Faulkner's gifts of friendship . Brodsky,
Louis Daniel. [University] c1980. [60] p. :   LC
Card 80-136569   DDC 813/.52 19
PS3511.A86 Z636

**William Smith O'Brien and his Irish
revolutionary companions in penal exile /.**
Touhill, Blanche M. (Blanche Marie), 1931-
Columbia , 1981. p. cm.   ISBN 0-8262-0339-6
   LC Card 81-1899   DDC 941.5081/092/4 19
DA952.O22 T68

Williams and Heintz Map Corporation. World
Bank. Agriculture and Rural Development
Dept. Resource Planning Unit. Nepal /.
Washington, D.C. , 1980. 1 remote sensing
image on 2 sheets :   LC Card 81-692612
G7761.A4 1980 .W6

Williams, Bradford B. (joint author) Lesure, Frank
Gardner, 1927- Mineral resources of the Mill
Creek, Mountain Lake, and Peters Mountain
wilderness study areas, Craig and Giles
Counties, Virginia, and Monroe County, West
Virginia /. Washington , 1981. p. cm.   LC Card
80-607815   DDC 557.3 s 553/.09755/795 19
QE75 .B9 no. 1510 TN24.V8

Williams, Craig L. Motorcycle operator training
evaluation plan / C. L. Williams. [Springfield] :
Illinois Dept. of Transportation, Division of
Traffic Safety, [1978?] 19 leaves : maps ; 28
cm. Cover title: Motorcycle rider training evaluation
plan. On cover: Illinois traffic safety programs report of
evaluation or assessment. "September 1978."   LC Card
79-622180   DDC 629.28/475/0710773 19
*1. Motorcycling - Study and teaching - Illinois. I.
Illinois. Division of Traffic Safety. II. Title. III. Title:
Motorcycle rider training evaluation plan. IV. Title:
Illinois traffic safety programs report of evaluation or
assessment.*
TL440.5 .W54

Williams, D. C., 1929- (joint author) Cartee,
Charles P. A study of factors related to the
implementation and use of water conservation
technology in Mississippi /. Mississippi State,
Miss. , 1979. vi, 49 leaves :   LC Card 80-622039
      DDC 333.91/22 19
TD224.M65 C38

Williams, Frank Broyles, 1913- Tennessee's
presidents / by Frank B. Williams. 1st ed.
Knoxville : University of Tennessee Press,
c1981. p. cm. (Tennessee three star books) "Published
in cooperation with the Tennessee Historical
Commission." Bibliography: p. Includes index.   ISBN
0-87049-321-3 :   LC Card 81-3391   DDC
973/.09/92 B 19
*1. Presidents - United States - Biography. 2. Jackson,
Andrew, 1767-1845. 3. Polk, James K. (James Knox),
1795-1849. 4. Johnson, Andrew, 1808-1875. 5.
Tennessee - Biography. I. Tennessee Historical
Commission. II. Title.*
E176.1 .W7225

Williams, Fred T. Alaska. Division of Sport Fish.
Annual performance report for study no. G-I .
Juneau [1977?] 93 p. :   LC Card 79-625181
      DDC 333.95/611/09798 19
QL628.A4 A4 1977

Williams, James Frank, 1944- Simulated changes
in water level in the Piney Point aquifer in
Maryland / by James F. Williams III ; prepared

in cooperation with the United States
Department of the Interior, Geological Survey,
and the Boards of County Commissioners of
Calvert, Caroline, and St. Mary's Counties.
[Baltimore, Md.] : Dept. of Natural Resources,
Maryland Geological Survey, 1979. v, 50 p. :
ill., maps (7 fold. in pocket) ; 28 cm. (Report of
investigations - Maryland Geological Survey ; no. 31)
Bibliography: p. 47-49.   LC Card 80-621643   DDC
      557.52 s 551.49/09752/4 19
*1. Aquifers - Maryland - Mathematical models. 2.
Aquifers - Maryland - Data processing. I. United States.
Geological Survey. II. Series: Maryland. Geological
Survey. Report of investigations , no. 31. III. Title.*
QE121 .A23 no. 31 GB1199.3.M3

Williams, Jay R. Effects of labeling the
"drug-abuser" : an inquiry / by Jay R. Williams.
Rockville, Md. : National Institute on Drug
Abuse ; Springfield, Va. : for sale by National
Technical Information Service, 1976. v, 39 p. ;
27 cm. (NIDA research monograph series ; 6) DHEW
publication ; no. (ADM) 76-320 Bibliography: p. 25-39.
      LC Card 76-3101   DDC 364.1/77/019 19
*1. Drugs and youth - United States. 2. Deviant
behavior - Labeling theory. I. Series: National Institute
on Drug Abuse. NIDA research monograph series, 6.
II. Title.*
HV5824.Y68 W55

Williams, Jeffrey W. Students and schools /
compiled by Jeffrey W. Williams.
[Washington] : National Center for Education
Statistics, 1979. viii, 85 p. : ill., maps, graphs ;
27 cm. Includes bibliographical references.   LC Card
79-602036
*1. School children - United States - Statistics. 2.
Demography. I. National Center for Education
Statistics. II. Title.*
LC69 .W54   *NYPL [JLF 81-365]*

Williams, Jimmy R. HYMO: Problem-oriented
computer language for hydrologic modeling:
users manual / [by Jimmy R. Williams and Roy
W. Hann] Washington: U. S. Department of
Agriculture, Agricultural Research Service,
1973. 76 p.: ill.; 26 cm. Cover title. "ARS-S-9"
Southern Region. Published in cooperation with Texas
Agricultural Experiment Station, Texas A & M
University.
*1. Hydrology - Computer programs. 2. HYMO
(Computer program language). I. Hann, Roy W. II.
United States. Agricultural Research Service. III. Texas.
Agricultural Experiment Station, College Station. IV.
Title.*   *NYPL [JSF 80-689]*

WILLIAMS, KAREN HASTIE, 1944-
United States. Congress. Senate. Committee on
Governmental Affairs. Nomination of Karen
Hastie Williams . Washington , 1980. iii, 73 p. ;
      LC Card 80-602444   DDC 353.0071/2 19
KF26 .G67 1980a

Williams, Lawrence T.
Inmates released directly from a maximum
security institution during 1977 and 1978 /
prepared by Lawrence T. Williams. [Boston] :
Massachusetts Dept. of Correction, [1979] ii, 38
leaves ; 28 cm. "November, 1979."   LC Card
80-620616   DDC 365/.33 19
*1. Ex-convicts - Massachusetts. 2. Massachusetts.
Correctional Institution, Walpole. I. Title.*
HV9306.W342 M378

A profile of characteristics distinguishing
between program completers and program
non-completers, Charlotte House, 1977 and
1978 releases / prepared by Lawrence T.
Williams. [Boston] : Massachusetts Dept. of
Correction, 1980. 20 leaves ; 28 cm.
(Massachusetts. Dept. of Correction. Publication. 202)
Microfilm. "Publication #12032." Cover title.
Bibliography: leaf 20.
*1. Rehabilitation of criminals - Massachusetts -
Statistics. 2. Female offenders - Massachusetts -
Statistics. I. Massachusetts. Dept. of Correction. II.
Title.*   *NYPL [*ZT-1263]*

Williams, Martin T. A Smithsonian book of
comic-book comics /. [Washington, D.C.]
[New York] , 1981. p. cm.   ISBN 0-87474-228-5 :
      LC Card 81-607842   DDC 741.5/973 19
PN6726 .S58

Williams, Quay. United States. International
Trade Commission. Certain carbon steel
products from Belgium, the Federal Republic of
Germany, France, Italy, Luxembourg, the
Netherlands, and the United Kingdom .
Washington, D.C. [1980] vii, 71, 180 p. ;   LC

Card 80-602282   DDC 382/.45672 19
HF2651.S76 U54 1980

Williams, Roger N. (joint author) Weiss, Michael J. An annotated bibliography of the genus Stelidota Erichson (Coleoptera: Nitidulidae, Nitidulinae) /. Wooster, Ohio [1980] 37 p. ;   LC Card 80-623557   DDC 016.59576/43 19
Z5858.S74 W44 QL596.N58

Williams, Rosalind H. Dream worlds of the consumer in late nineteenth-century France / Rosalind H. Williams. Berkeley : University of California Press, c1981. p. cm. Bibliography: p. Includes iindex.   ISBN 0-520-04355-3   LC Card 81-4689   DDC 381./3/0944 19
1. Consumers - France - History. I. Title.
HC280.C6 W54

Williams, Sheldon W. The dairy industry / Sheldon W. Williams. Urbana, IL : Dept. of Agricultural Economics, Agricultural Experiment Station, University of Illinois at Urbana-Champaign, [1979] vii, 27 p. : ill. ; 28 cm. (Agriculture in Illinois, alternative futures for the 1980s) Aerr ; 172 "September 1979." Includes bibliographical references.   LC Card 80-623667   DDC 338.1 s 338.1/77/09773 19
1. Dairying - Illinois. I. Series. II. Series: Illinois. University at Urbana-Champaign. Dept. of Agricultural Economics. Aerr , 172. III. Title.
HD1401 .I42 no. 172 HD9275.U7

Williams, Susan, 1947- United States. Library of Congress. Subject Cataloging Division. Classification, Class Z, bibliography and library science / . Washington , 1980. p. cm.   ISBN 0-8444-0340-7   LC Card 80-607921
Z696.U5 Z 1980

Williams, William H. (William Hatton), 1934- The Limits of utilitarianism /. Minneapolis , 1981. p. cm.   ISBN 0-8166-1044-4 :   LC Card 81-14698   DDC 144/.6 19
B843 .L55

Williams, Wirt. The tragic art of Ernest Hemingway / Wirt Williams. Baton Rouge : Louisiana State University Press, c1981. p. cm. Includes index.   ISBN 0-8071-0884-7 :   LC Card 81-4740   DDC 813/.52 19
1. Hemingway, Ernest, 1899-1961 - Criticism and interpretation. 2. Tragic, The. I. Title.
PS3515.E37 Z952

Williamsburg, Va. Institute of Early American History and Culture. see Institute of Early American History and Culture, Williamsburg, Va.

WILLIAMSON COUNTY, ILL. - GENEALOGY.
Public Library, Winnetka, Ill. Genealogy Projects Committee. An index to the names of persons appearing in The History of Gallatin, Saline, Hamilton, Franklin and Williamson Counties, Illinois. (Chicago, The Goodspeed Pub. Co., 1887). Thomson, Ill. [c1973] 122 p. ;
NYPL [APR (Gallatin Co., Ill.) 80-1987]

Public Library, Winnetka, Ill. Genealogy Projects Committee. An index to the names of persons appearing in The History of Gallatin, Saline, Hamilton, Franklin and Williamson Counties, Illinois. (Chicago, The Goodspeed Pub. Co., 1887). Thomson, Ill. [c1973] 122 p. ;
NYPL [APR (Gallatin Co., Ill.) 80-1987]

Williamstown, Mass. Sterling and Francine Clark Art Institute. see Sterling and Francine Clark Art Institute, Williamstown, Mass.

Willis, Cleve E. (joint author) Kaul, Jawahar Lal. A floodplain management framework with structural and nonstructural measures /. [Amherst] , 1975. vi, 114 p. :   LC Card 78-622289   DDC 333.91/009744 s 363.3/49356 19
TD224.M4 M37 no. 61 TC424.C8

Williss, George F., 1939- Historical data, historic structure report, Fredericksburg and Spotsylvania County Battlefields Memorial National Military Park, Fredericksburg, Virginia / prepared by G. Frank Williss. Denver, Colo. : Denver Service Center, Historic Preservation Branch, Mid-Atlantic/North Atlantic Team, National Park Service, U. S. Dept. of the Interior, [1980] 99 p. : ill. ; 27 cm. Cover title: Fredericksburg and Spotsylvania County Battlefields Memorial. Stamped on t.p.: Ellwood-Lacy House. "April 1980." Bibliography: p. 93-99.   LC Card 80-602417   DDC 975.5/365 19

1. Ellwood House, Va. I. Title. II. Title: Fredericksburg and Spotsylvania County Battlefields Memorial.
F234.E45 W54

WILLKIE, WENDELL LEWIS, 1892-1944 - ICONOGRAPHY - EXHIBITIONS.
Lilly Library, Indiana University, Bloomington. Wendell Lewis Willkie, 1892-1944 . Bloomington , 1980. 24 p. :   LC Card 80-140105   DDC 016.973917/092/4 19
Z881.I42 P8 no. 32 E748.W7

Willman, H. B. (Harold Bowen), 1901- The glacial boundary in southern Illinois / H.B. Willman and John C. Frye. [Chicago] : Illinois Institute of Natural Resources ; Urbana, Ill. : Illinois State Geological Survey Division, 1980. 23 p. : maps ; 28 cm. (Circular / Illinois State Geological Survey Division . 511) Bibliography: p. 23.   LC Card 80-623959   DDC 557.73 s 551.7/92/09773 19
1. Glacial epoch - Illinois. I. Frye, John Chapman, 1912-. II. Series: Circular (Illinois State Geological Survey) , 511. III. Title.
QE105 .A45 no. 511 QE697

Willoughby, Charles Clark, 1857-1943. Indian antiquities of the Kennebec Valley / Charles Clark Willoughby ; with a foreword and notes by Arthur E. Spiess. Augusta, Me. : Maine Historic Preservation Commission : Maine State Museum, c1980. 128 p., [22] leaves of plates : ill. ; 32 cm. (Occasional publications in Maine archaeology . no. 1) Includes bibliography.   ISBN 0-913764-13-2   LC Card 81-119254   DDC 974.1/22 19
1. Indians of North America - Maine - Kennebec Valley - Antiquities. 2. Kennebec Valley (Me.) - Antiquities. 3. Maine - Antiquities. I. Spiess, Arthur E. II. Title. III. Series.
E78.M2 W54 1980

Willow Creek Reservoir. Nolting, Donald H. Electric fish screen efficiency, Willow Creek Reservoir /. Denver , 1962. iv, 24 p. :   LC Card 81-464857   DDC 639.9/7755 19
SH157.85.F54 N64

Wills, Wirth H. (joint author) Lyons, Thomas R. Aerial anthropological perspectives . Washington, D.C. , 1980. p. cm.   LC Card 80-25967   DDC 930.1/028 s 016.9301/028 19
CC76.4 .L96 Suppl., no. 3 Z5133.A34

WILMINGTON METROPOLITAN AREA, DEL. - OCCUPATIONS - STATISTICS.
Delaware. Dept. of Labor. Office of Planning, Research & Evaluation. Wilmington SMSA occupational employment statistics . Newark, DE , 1978. i, 80 leaves ;   LC Card 78-624189
HD5725.D3 D33 1978a   NYPL   [JLF 81-109]

Wilmington SMSA occupational employment statistics . Delaware. Dept. of Labor. Office of Planning, Research & Evaluation. Newark, DE , 1978. i, 80 leaves ;   LC Card 78-624189
HD5725.D3 D33 1978a   NYPL   [JLF 81-109]

Wilson, Carol B. Technology assessment : ADP installation performance measurement and reporting / Carol B. Wilson. Washington, D.C. : U. S. Dept. of Commerce, National Bureau of Standards : for sale by the Supt. of Docs., U. S. Govt. Print. Off., [1979] iv, 32 p. ; 27 cm. (Computer science & technology) NBS special publication ; 500-53 "Issued September 1979." Bibliography: p. 22-26.   LC Card 79-600154   DDC 602/.18 s 001.64 19
1. Electronic data processing - Evaluation. I. Series. II. Series: United States. National Bureau of Standards Special publication, 500-53. III. Title.
QC100 .U57 no. 500-53 QA76.9E95

Wilson, Carol M. Pennsylvania. Dept. of Commerce. Bureau of Statistics, Research and Planning. Pennsylvania manufacturing exports /. [Harrisburg] [1978?] [71] leaves :   LC Card 80-622589   DDC 382/.45/0009748 19
HF3161.P4 P45 1978

Wilson, Carolyn F. Violence against women, causes and prevention . Rockville, Md. (P.O. Box 2309, Rockville 20852) , 1980. vii, 37 p. ;   LC Card 80-603151   DDC 016.3628/8 19
HV6250.4.W65 V56 1980

Wilson, Curtis R. (joint author) Townsend, William R. Soil survey of Conway County, Arkansas /. [Washington] [1980] vii, 91 p., [27] fold. leaves of plates :   LC Card 80-603205   DDC 631.4/7/76731 19
S599.A75 T67

Wilson, D. A. (Donald A.) A pyrometallurgical method for processing Ni-Cd scrap batteries / by D.A. Wilson and H.V. Makar. [Washington, D.C.] : U. S. Dept. of the Interior, Bureau of Mines, [1981] p. cm. (Report of investigations) Bibliography: p.   LC Card 81-10151   DDC 622 s 669/.56 19
1. Nickel - Metallurgy. 2. Cadmium - Metallurgy. 3. Pyrometallurgy. 4. Nickel-cadmium batteries - Recycling. I. Makar, H. V. (Harry V.). II. Series: Report of investigations (United States. Bureau of Mines). III. Title.
TN23 .U43 TN799.N6

Wilson, David, 1936- Design and constructaion of tailings dams . Golden, Colo. , 1981. p. cm.   ISBN 0-918062-45-4 :   LC Card 81-10273   DDC 622/.7 19
TN292 .D46

Wilson, David Edwin, 1938- Low-cost extrusion cookers . [Fort Collins, Colo. , 1979] vii, 288 p. :   LC Card 80-601551   DDC 664/.02 19
TP373 .L68

Wilson, Elaine Blume. At the edge of life : an introduction to viruses : a report from the National Institute of Allergy and Infectious Diseases / by Elaine Blume Wilson. [Bethesda, Md.?] : U. S. Dept. of Health and Human Services, National Institutes of Health, Public Health Service ; Washington, D.C. : For sale by the Supt. of Docs., U. S. G.P.O., 1980. 75 p. : ill. ; 26 cm. (NIH publication. no. 80-433) Aug. 1980. S/N 017-044-00037-1 Item 505-A-1   LC Card 80-604128   DDC 616.9/25 19
1. Virus diseases. I. United States. Public Health Service. II. National Institute of Allergy and Infectious Diseases (U. S.). III. Series: DHHS publication, no. (NIH) 80-433. IV. Title.
RC114.5 .W54

Wilson, Floyd D. The Canine as a biomedical research model . [Oak Ridge, TN] , Springfield, Va. , 1980. x, 425 p. :   ISBN 0-87079-122-2 (pbk.) :   LC Card 80-24174   DDC 619/.7 19
RB125 .C36

Wilson, George Wilton, 1928- Inflation--causes, consequences, and cures / George W. Wilson. Bloomington : Indiana University Press, c1982. p. cm. Includes bibliographical references and index.   ISBN 0-253-33008-4   LC Card 81-47830   DDC 332.4/1 19
1. Inflation (Finance). I. Title.
HG229 .W55

Wilson, Gregory Sims. Thunderstorm-environment interactions determined with three-dimensional trajectories / Gregory Sims Wilson. [Washington] : National Aeronautics and Space Administration, Scientific and Technical Information Office, 1980. viii, 153 p. : ill. ; 27 cm. (NASA reference publication. 1054) Bibliography: p. 150-153.   LC Card 80-603200   DDC 551.5/54 19
1. Thunderstorms. 2. Atmospheric circulation. I. Series: United States. National Aeronautics and Space Administration. NASA reference publication , 1054. II. Title.
QC968 .W54

Wilson, Harold Albert, 1905- (joint author) Thompson, Frederick C. Tolerance and synthetic ability of sewage microorganisms in acid mine water /. Morgantown , 1975. ix, 60 p. :   LC Card 76-622086   DDC 628.1/6832 19
QR88 .T48

Wilson historic buildings inventory, Wilson, North Carolina /. Bainbridge, Robert C. [Raleigh?] , 1980. iv, 244 p. :   LC Card 81-621389   DDC 975.6/43 19
F264.W74 B34

Wilson, James Rollo, 1949- Occupational supply and demand / prepared by James R. Wilson. [Juneau] : State of Alaska, Dept. of Labor, [1979] 30 p. ; 28 cm. "In cooperation with the Employment and Training Administration, U. S. Department of Labor." "December 1979."   LC Card 80-622142   DDC 331.12/09798 19
1. Labor supply - Alaska. 2. Alaska - Occupations. I. Alaska. Dept. of Labor. II. Title.
HD5725.A4 W55

Wilson, John Harvard, 1953- Brazil's orange juice industry / [by John H. Wilson]. [Washington, D.C.] : U. S. Dept. of Agriculture, Foreign Agricultural Service, 1980. ii, 17 p. : ill. ; 27 cm. (FAS-M ; 295) Cover title. "April 1980." Map on p. [2] of cover.   LC Card 80-602547   DDC 338.1 s

338.4/766363 19
1. Orange juice industry - Brazil. I. Series: United States. Foreign Agricultural Service (1953-) FAS-M , 295. II. Title.
S21 .Z2383 no. 295 HD9348.5.O723B6

Wilson, Lawrence A. Ginsburg, Paul B. The CBO hospital cost containment model . [Washington, D.C.] , 1981. xiv, 36 p. : LC Card 81-601120 DDC 362.1/1 19
RA981.A2 G49

Wilson, Michael, 1948- Applied geology and archaeology . Laramie, Wyo. [1974] vi, 127 p. : LC Card 76-624236 DDC 557.87 s 551.7/93/09787 19
QE181 .A26 no. 10 QE699

WILSON (N.C.) - BUILDINGS.
Bainbridge, Robert C. Wilson historic buildings inventory, Wilson, North Carolina /. [Raleigh?] , 1980. iv, 244 p. : LC Card 81-621389 DDC 975.6/43 19
F264.W74 B34

WILSON (N.C.) - HISTORY.
Bainbridge, Robert C. Wilson historic buildings inventory, Wilson, North Carolina /. [Raleigh?] , 1980. iv, 244 p. : LC Card 81-621389 DDC 975.6/43 19
F264.W74 B34

Wilson, Rex L. Bottles on the western frontier / Rex L. Wilson ; edited by Edward Staski. Tucson, Ariz. : University of Arizona Press, c1981. p. cm. Bibliography: p. ISBN 0-8165-0414-8 : LC Card 81-11703 DDC 748.8/2/0973 19
1. Bottles - West (U. S.). I. Staski, Edward. II. Title.
NK5440.B6 W57

Wilson, Ted Y. Double jeopardy . Ann Arbor , c1979. 332 p. ; LC Card 80-621753 DDC 362.3/0880565 19
HV3006.M54 D68

Wilson, Tom, 1954- (joint author) Isaak, David. Solar system economics /. Salem, Or. , 1980. 119, [24] p. : LC Card 80-623275 DDC 338.4/362147/09795 19
HD9681.U63 O75

Wilson, William Edward, 1934- Estimated effects of projected ground-water withdrawals on movement of the saltwater front in the Floridan aquifer, 1976-2000, west-central Florida / by William E. Wilson ; prepared in cooperation with the Southwest Florida Water Management District. Washington : U. S. G.P.O. ; Arlington, VA : For sale by the Branch of Distribution, U. S. Geological Survey, 1981. p. cm. (U. S. Geological Survey water supply paper . 2189) Bibliography: p. LC Card 81-607085 DDC 628.1/1 19
1. Saltwater encroachment - Florida. 2. Aquifers - Florida. I. Southwest Florida Water Management District. II. Series: Geological Survey water-supply paper , 2189. III. Title.
GB1197.83.F6 W54

Wilson, William Henry, 1939- Dutch seventeenth century portraiture, the golden age / William H. Wilson ; presented under the auspices of the Royal Netherlands Embassy ; the John and Mable Ringling Museum of Art, Sarasota, Florida, the State Art Museum of Florida, December 4, 1980-February 8, 1981. Sarasota, Fla. : The Museum, c1980. [185] p. : ill. ; 28 cm. Includes bibliographical references and indexes. ISBN 0-916758-03-6 (pbk.) LC Card 80-53473 DDC 704.9/42/0942074015961 19
1. Portraits, Dutch - Exhibitions. 2. Portraits, Group - Netherlands - Exhibitions. 3. Netherlands - Biography - Portraits - Exhibitions. 4. Art, Modern - 17th-18th centuries - Netherlands - Exhibitions. I. John and Mable Ringling Museum of Art. II. Title. III. Title: The golden age.
N7607 .W54

Wilson (Woodrow) International Center for Scholars. see Woodrow Wilson International Center for Scholars.

WILSON, WOODROW, PRES. U. S., 1856-1924.
New Jersey. Governor, 1911-13 (Wilson) Vetoes of Woodrow Wilson, /. [Trenton ; 1912.] 35 l.   ***NYPL [*ZT-1251]***

Winborne, Lee W. Whitwell, W. L. (William Livingston), 1936- The architectural heritage of the Roanoke Valley /. Charlottesville , 1982. p. cm. ISBN 0-8139-0905-8 LC Card 81-12987

DDC 720/.9756/1 19
NA730.V82 R68

Wind and seismic effects . United States-Japan Cooperative Program in Natural Resources. Panel on Wind and Seismic Effects. Washington, D.C. , c1980. 604 p. in various pagings : LC Card 79-600134 DDC 602/.18 s 624.1/76 19
QC100 .U57 no. 560 TA654.5

WIND CIRCULATION. see ATMOSPHERIC CIRCULATION.

Wind energy developments in the 20th century. United States. Lewis Research Center, Cleveland. Cleveland, Ohio , 1980. 32 p. : LC Card 80-602418 DDC 621.31/2136 19
TK1541 .U56 1980

Wind energy systems act of 1980 . United States. Congress. House. Committee on Science and Technology. Subcommittee on Energy Development and Applications. Washington , 1980. iv, 429 p. : LC Card 80-603413 DDC 346.7304/6792 19
KF27 .S3934 1979m

WIND LOADS. see WIND-PRESSURE.

WIND POWER.
United States. Lewis Research Center, Cleveland. Wind energy developments in the 20th century. Cleveland, Ohio , 1980. 32 p. : LC Card 80-602418 DDC 621.31/2136 19
TK1541 .U56 1980

WIND POWER - LAW AND LEGISLATION - UNITED STATES.
United States. Congress. House. Committee on Science and Technology. Subcommittee on Energy Development and Applications. Wind energy systems act of 1980 . Washington , 1980. iv, 429 p. : LC Card 80-603413 DDC 346.7304/6792 19
KF27 .S3934 1979m

WIND-PRESSURE - CONGRESSES.
United States-Japan Cooperative Program in Natural Resources. Panel on Wind and Seismic Effects. Wind and seismic effects . Washington, D.C. , c1980. 604 p. in various pagings : LC Card 79-600134 DDC 602/.18 s 624.1/76 19
QC100 .U57 no. 560 TA654.5

WIND TUNNELS.
Baals, Donald D. Wind tunnels of NASA /. Washington, D.C. , 1981. p. cm. LC Card 81-607811 DDC 629.134/52 19
TL567.W5 B2

Wind tunnels of NASA /. Baals, Donald D. Washington, D.C. , 1981. p. cm. LC Card 81-607811 DDC 629.134/52 19
TL567.W5 B2

WINDHAM COUNTY, VT. REGIONAL PLANNING AND DEVELOPMENT COMMISSION.
Henke, Joseph T. A case study of Windham Regional Planning and Development Commission, Vermont /. Eugene, Or., 1970. 69 l. LC Card 73-101271   ***NYPL [JLF 80-1288]***

Windham, Michael P. (joint author) Finney, Brad A. Random differential equations in water quality modeling /. Logan, Utah [1979] viii, 41 p. : LC Card 80-622173 DDC 553.7/028 19
TD367 .F56

Windham Regional Planning and Development Commission. see Windham County, Vt. Regional Planning and Development Commission.

Windows into China . Parker, John, 1923- Boston , 1978. xi, 36 p. : LC Card 77-13191   ***NYPL [*KSD 80-202 no. 5]***

Windows to the past . Treude, Mai. Minneapolis, Minn. (311 Walter Library, 117 Pleasant St. S.E., University of Minnesota, Minneapolis, Minn. 55455) , 1980. ix, 187 p. : LC Card 80-154529 DDC 016.912/776 19
Z6027.M65 T73 GA432

WINDS - NORTHERN HEMISPHERE - MAPS.
United States. Aeronautical Chart Service. Isobars & prevailing winds chart, January . [Washington] [1946] 1 map : LC Card 81-690547
G3211.C842 1946 .U5

WINDS - SPEED - MEASUREMENT - MATHEMATICAL MODELS.

Hurricane wind speeds in the United States /. Washington, D.C. [1980] viii, 30, 11 p. : LC Card 80-600039 DDC 690/.02/18 s 551.5/52 19
TA435 .U58 no. 124 QC933

WINDS - UTAH - TABLES.
Hubbard, Kenneth G. Tabulation and application of pan evaporation data for Utah through 1976 . Logan, Utah , 1979. vi, 76 p. : LC Card 80-622271 DDC 551.57/2/09792 19
QC915.7.U5 H82

WINDSTORMS - CALIFORNIA.
California. Dept. of Water Resources. Division of Planning. Windstorms in California /. [Sacramento] , 1979. v, 34 p. : LC Card 80-620557 DDC 551.5/5 19
QC943.5.U6 C34 1979

Windstorms in California /. California. Dept. of Water Resources. Division of Planning. [Sacramento] , 1979. v, 34 p. : LC Card 80-620557 DDC 551.5/5 19
QC943.5.U6 C34 1979

Windy Ridge, a prehistoric site in the inter-riverine Piedmont in South Carolina /. House, John H. [Columbia] , 1978. xv, 158 p. : LC Card 78-624313
E78.S6 H69   ***NYPL [HBC 81-156]***

WINDY RIDGE SITE, S. C.
House, John H. Windy Ridge, a prehistoric site in the inter-riverine Piedmont in South Carolina /. [Columbia] , 1978. xv, 158 p. : LC Card 78-624313
E78.S6 H69   ***NYPL [HBC 81-156]***

WINE AND WINE MAKING - FOUR CORNERS REGION.
Grape and wine production in the Four Corners Region /. [Tucson, Ariz. , 1980] 116 p. : LC Card 80-623372 DDC 634/.8/0978 19
SB389 .G76

WINE MAKING. see WINE AND WINE MAKING.

WINEMAKING. see WINE AND WINE MAKING.

Winer, Elliot A. Employment requirements for Massachusetts by occupation, by industry, 1976-1985 / prepared by Elliot A. Winer, Susan P. Rico. Boston, MA : Massachusetts Division of Employment Security, Job Market Research, [1979] 58 leaves : ill. ; 28 cm. (Occupation/industry research publication) Cover title: Employment requirements by occupation, by industry, 1976-1985. "December 1979." LC Card 80-623635 DDC 331.12/3/09744 19
1. Labor supply - Massachusetts - Statistics. 2. Job vacancies - Massachusetts - Statistics. 3. Employment forecasting - Massachusetts - Statistics. I. Rico, Susan. II. Title. III. Title: Employment requirements by occupation, by industry, 1976-1985. IV. Series.
HD5725.M4 W56

Wines, Margaret. Oklahoma. Dept. of Economic and Community Affairs. Children's Services Coordination Project. Voices of Oklahoma families . [Oklahoma City] , 1978. ix, 300 p. : LC Card 79-621197 DDC 362.7/1/09766 19
HV742.O5 O35 1978

Wingard, Lemuel B. Conference on the Future of Enzyme Engineering Development, Tiflis, 1978. Enzyme engineering . New York , c1980. xiv, 521 p. : ISBN 0-306-40442-7 LC Card 80-12061
TP248.E5 C68 1978   ***NYPL [JSE 80-1231]***

Wingard, Robert C. Soil survey of Dubois County, Indiana / [by Robert C. Wingard] ; United States Department of Agriculture, Soil Conservation Service, in cooperation with Purdue University Agricultural Experiment Station and Indiana Department of Natural Resources, Soil and Water Conservation Committee. [Washington, D.C. : National Cooperative Soil Survey, 1980] vii, 117 p., [36] fold. leaves of plates : ill. ; 28 cm. Cover title. Bibliography: p. 73. Includes index. LC Card 80-602049 DDC 631.4/7/77237 19
1. Soils - Indiana - Dubois Co. - Maps. I. United States. Soil Conservation Service. II. Indiana. Agricultural Experiment Station, Lafayette. III. Indiana. Soil and Water Conservation Committee. IV. Title.
S599.I63 W57

Winkler, G. R. Nokleberg, Warren J. Stratiform zinc-lead deposits in the Drenchwater Creek area, Howard Pass quadrangle, northwestern Brooks Range, Alaska /. Menlo Park, CA ,

1981. p. cm.   LC Card 81-607994   DDC
553.4/4/097987 19
TN483.A64 N64

Winkler, Karen S. Nevada allied health education
and manpower . Carson City, Nev. , 1976. 98
p. :   LC Card 80-621254   DDC 331.12/3161 19
R847.6.N3 N48

Winner, Anthony. Characters in the twilight :
Hardy, Zola, and Chekhov / Anthony Winner.
Charlottesville : University Press of Virginia,
1981. p. cm. Includes bibliographical references.
CONTENTS. - Balzac's Le père Goriot: the character
of society -- Hardy's moderns: the ache of uncertain
character -- Zola: characters in the fields of force --
Chekhov's characters: true tears, real things.   ISBN
0-8139-0894-9   LC Card 81-10355   DDC
809.3/927 19
*1. Characters and characteristics in literature. 2.
Fiction - 19th century - History and criticism. I. Title.*
PN3411 .W56

WINNESHIEK COUNTY, IOWA - MAPS.
(1979) United States. Soil Conservation Service.
Winneshiek County, Iowa / . Lincoln, Nebr. ,
1979. 1 map :   LC Card 81-691181
G4153.W6 1979 .U5

**Winnetka Public Library. Genealogy Projects
Committee.**
An index to the names of persons appearing in
A history of Lake County, Illinois (by John J.
Halsey. Roy S. Bates, Publisher, 1912) /
prepared by Genealogy Projects Committee, the
Winnetka Public Library, Winnetka, Illinois.
Thomson, Ill. : Heritage House, c1973. 77 p. ;
29 cm. Preface signed: Jeanne Rabbitt Talamine,
indexer.
*1. Lake County, Ill. - Genealogy. 2. Lake County, Ill. -
History. I. Talamine, Jeanne Rabbitt. II. Halsey, John
Julius, b. 1848. A history of Lake county, Illinois. III.
Title.*   *NYPL*   *[IVF (Lake Co.) (Halsey, J.*
                Hist. of Lake Co. Index)]

An index to the names of persons appearing in
History of Du Page County, Illinois (by Rufus
Blanchard. Chicago, O. L. Baskin & Co., 1882).
Thomson, Ill., Heritage House [c1973] 105 p.
29 cm.
*1. Du Page County, Ill. - Genealogy. I. Blanchard,
Rufus, 1821-1904. History of Du Page County, Illinois.
II. Title.*
       NYPL   *[APR (Du Page Co., Ill.) 80-1729]*

Winnick, Joseph P. Train-a-champ . Albany,
N.Y. , c1979. vii, 95 p. :   LC Card 81-119267
DDC 371.9/044 19
GV445 .T73

Winship, Christopher. (joint author) Mare, Robert
D. Changes in the relative labor force status of
Black and white youths . [Madison] [1980] 43
p. ;   LC Card 80-623148   DDC 331.3/412/0973 19
HD6273 .M38

Winslow, Gerald R. Triage and justice / Gerald
R. Winslow. Berkeley : University of California
Press, c1982. p. cm. Bibliography: p. Includes index.
ISBN 0-520-04328-6   LC Card 81-10434   DDC
174/.2 19
*1. Triage (Medicine) - Moral and religious aspects. 2.
Social justice. I. Title.*
R725.5 .W56

Winslow, Hall. Public acquisition costs of
recreation land to the year 2000 / . New York ,
1968. 23 p. ;   *NYPL*   *[*ZT-1244]*

Winston, J. S. (John S.) Walkiewicz, J. W. (John
W.) Magnetic properties of alloys containing
mischmetal cobalt, copper, iron, and magnesium
/ . Avondale, MD , 1981. p. cm.   LC Card
81-607845   DDC 622 s 620.1/697 19
TN23 .U43 TN690

Winston, Mark L. (joint author) Michener, Charles
Duncan, 1918- Pollen manipulation and related
activities and structures in bees of the family
Apidae / . [Lawrence] 1978. p. 576-601 :   LC
Card 79-621073   DDC 500 s 595.79/9 19
Q1 .K17 vol. 51, no. 19 QL568.A6

WINSTON-SALEM, N.C. - CENSUS - MAPS.
United States. Bureau of the Census. Urban
atlas, tract data for standard metropolitan
statistical areas . Washington, D.C. , 1974 [i.e.
1975] [15] p. :   LC Card 80-600872   DDC
912/.1312/0975662
G1302.G7E25 U5 1975

Winter, H. Leabah. Consumer guide to health
care costs / H. Leabah Winter. Sacramento, CA

(555 Capitol Mall, Room 525, Sacramento
95814) : California Health Facilities
Commission, c1980. 115 p. : ill. (some col.) ; 28
cm. Includes bibliographical references. LC Card
80-620045   DDC 338.4/361/09794 19
*1. Medical care, Cost of - California. 2. Medical care,
Cost of - United States. 3. Medical care - California -
Cost control. I. California Health Facilities Commission.
II. Title.*
RA410.54.C3 W56

WINTER SPORT FACILITIES - PLANNING.
United States. Forest Service. Planning
considerations for winter sports resort
development / . [Washington] , 1973. iii, 53 p. :
       NYPL   *[JLF 79-1344]*

Winterringer, Glen Spelman, 1906- Aquatic
plants of Illinois : an illustrated manual
including species submersed, floating, and some
of shallow water and muddy shores / Glen S.
Winterringer, Alvin C. Lopinot.Reprinted 1977
with corrections. Springfield : Dept. of
Registration & Education, Illinois State
Museum Division : Dept. of Conservation,
Division of Fisheries, 1977. 142 p. (p. 142
blank) : ill. ; 23 cm. (Illinois State Museum popular
science series ; v. 6 0360-0297) Bibliography: p.
129-132. Includes index.   LC Card 80-621674   DDC
581.92/9/773 19
*1. Freshwater flora - Illinois - Identification. 2. Wetland
flora - Illinois - Identification. I. Lopinot, Alvin C., joint
author. II. Illinois. State Museum, Springfield. III.
Illinois. Division of Fisheries. IV. Series: Illinois. State
Museum, Springfield. Popular science series , v. 6. V.
Title.*
QK157 .W54 1977

Winters, Howard D. The Riverton culture : a
second millenium occupation in the central
Wabash Valley / by Howard Dalton Winters.
Springfield : Illinois State Museum, 1969. xiii,
164 p., 48 [i.e. 24] leaves of plates : ill. ; 28
cm. (Reports of investigations ; no. 13) Monograph -
Illinois Archaeological Survey ; no. 1 Bibliography: p.
155-164.   LC Card 79-629858   DDC 977.3 s
977.2/401 19
*1. Indians of North America - Wabash Valley -
Antiquities. 2. Wabash Valley - Antiquities. 3. Indians
of North America - Wabash Valley - Implements. 4.
Excavations (Archaeology) - Wabash Valley. 5. Illinois -
Antiquities. I. Series: Illinois. State Museum,
Springfield. Reports of investigations , no. 13. II. Title.*
AM101 .I374 no. 13 E78.I3

WIRE-TAPPING - TEXAS.
Texas. Legislature. House of Representatives.
Study Group. Wiretapping / . Austin, Tex.
[1980] 34 p. :   LC Card 80-622368   DDC
347.764/064 19
KFT1780.5.W5 A25 1980

WIRE-TAPPING - UNITED STATES.
Texas. Legislature. House of Representatives.
Study Group. Wiretapping / . Austin, Tex.
[1980] 34 p. :   LC Card 80-622368   DDC
347.764/064 19
KFT1780.5.W5 A25 1980

Wiretapping / . Texas. Legislature. House of
Representatives. Study Group. Austin, Tex.
[1980] 34 p. :   LC Card 80-622368   DDC
347.764/064 19
KFT1780.5.W5 A25 1980

Wirtenberg, Jeana. Characters in textbooks : a
review of the literature / [prepared by Jeana
Wirtenberg, Robin Murez, and Rose Ann
Alspektor]. [Washington, D.C.] : U. S.
Commission on Civil Rights : [for sale by the
Supt. of Docs.], U. S. Govt. Print. Off., 1980.
iii, 19 p. ; 26 cm. (Clearinghouse publication ; 62)
Includes bibliographical references.   LC Card
80-602697   DDC 323.4/0973 s 379.1/56 19
*1. Textbook bias - United States. 2. Minorities in
literature. I. Murez, Robin, joint author. II. Alspektor,
Rose Ann, joint author. III. Series: United States.
Commission on Civil Rights. Clearinghouse publication ,
62. IV. Title.*
KF4755 .A83 no. 62 LB3045.6

Wisconsin. Bureau of Planning and Budget.
Work force 1980. [1]- [Madison, Wis.] 1971-
       NYPL   *[JLM 80-1016]*

**Wisconsin. Bureau of Planning and Budget.
Information Systems Unit.** Wisconsin
statistical abstract / . Madison (202 S. Thornton
Ave., Madison, Wis.) [1974] ix, 215 p. :   LC
Card 78-621667   DDC 317.75 19
HA716 .W58 1974

Wisconsin. Business Development, Dept. of. see
Wisconsin. Dept. of Business Development.

**Wisconsin. Citizens Study Committee on Judicial
Organization. Citizens Study Committee on
Judicial Organization.** Wisconsin. Dept. of
Administration. Office of Program and
Management Analysis. 1977 status report on
judicial reform in Wisconsin . Madison , 1977.
45, 31 p. :   LC Card 78-621327   DDC 347.775/01
19
KFW2908 .A812

Wisconsin court rules and procedure, 1980 .
Wisconsin. Courts. St. Paul, Minn. , c1980. xiii,
774 p. :   LC Card 80-137814   DDC 347.775/051 19
KFW2929 .A2 1980

Wisconsin. Courts. Wisconsin court rules and
procedure, 1980 : state and Federal : with
amendments received to July 14, 1980. St. Paul,
Minn. : West Pub. Co., c1980. xiii, 774 p. :
forms ; 25 cm. Includes indexes.   LC Card
80-137814   DDC 347.775/051 19
1. Court rules - Wisconsin. I. Title.
KFW2929 .A2 1980

Wisconsin. Demographic Services Center. Kale,
Balkrishna Damodar, 1925- Wisconsin
population and households, March 1979 / .
Madison, Wis. , 1980. 20 p. ;   LC Card
80-623861   DDC 312/.09775 19
HA716 .K345

**Wisconsin. Dept. of Administration. Bureau of
Planning and Budget.** see **Wisconsin. Bureau
of Planning and Budget.**

**Wisconsin. Dept. of Administration. Demographic
Services Center.** see **Wisconsin. Demographic
Services Center.**

**Wisconsin. Dept. of Administration. Office of
Program and Management Analysis.**
Land records : the cost to the citizen to
maintain the present land information base : a
case study of Wisconsin : project / conducted
by the State of Wisconsin, Department of
Administration, Office of Program and
Management Analysis, in conjunction with the
University of Wisconsin-Madison, Institute for
Environmental Studies, Environmental
Monitoring and Data Acquisition Group ;
sponsored by the Council of State
Governments. [Madison] : The Dept., 1978. vi,
64 p. : ill. ; 28 cm. Bibliography: p. 39-42. LC
Card 79-622611   DDC 025/.063337313 19
*1. Information storage and retrieval systems - Land
use - Costs. 2. Land use - Wisconsin. I. Wisconsin.
University--Madison. Institute for Environmental
Studies. Environmental Monitoring and Data
Acquisition Group. II. Council of State Governments.
III. Title.*
HD211.W6 W63 1978

1977 status report on judicial reform in
Wisconsin : a follow-up on the final report of
the Citizens Study Committee on Judicial
Organization. Madison : Office of Program and
Management Analysis, Dept. of Administration,
1977. 45, 31 p. : ill. ; 28 cm.   LC Card 78-621327
DDC 347.775/01 19
*1. Courts - Wisconsin. 2. Judges - Wisconsin. 3.
Procedure (Law) - Wisconsin. I. Wisconsin. Citizens
Study Committee on Judicial Organization. Citizens
Study Committee on Judicial Organization. II. Title.*
KFW2908 .A812

Wisconsin. Dept. of Business Development.
Wisconsin manufacturing. Madison : Dept. of
Business Development, 1977. iv, 48 p. : ill. ; 28
cm. "Update to the fourth edition of the 'Geography of
Wisconsin manufacturing.'"   LC Card 77-623350
*1. Wisconsin - Manufactures. I. Wisconsin. Dept. of
Resource Development. Geography of Wisconsin
manufacturing. II. Title.*
HD9727.W6 W57 1977
       NYPL   *[JLF 80-1489]*

**Wisconsin. Dept. of Business Development.
Division of Tourism.** see **Wisconsin. Division
of Tourism.**

**Wisconsin. Dept. of Industry, Labor and Human
Relations. Bureau of Administration,
Planning, and Analysis.** Occupational
employment estimates for selected
nonmanufacturing industries, 1978 / prepared
by the Bureau of Administration, Planning and
Analysis of the Wisconsin Department of
Industry, Labor and Human Relations, in
cooperation with the Bureau of Labor Statistics

and Employment and Training Administration of the U. S. Department of Labor. [Madison, Wis.] : DILHR, [1980] iv, 212 p. : ill. ; 28 cm.
LC Card 80-623196   DDC 331.12/51/0009775 19
1. Labor supply - Wisconsin - Statistics. 2. Wisconsin - Occupations - Statistics. I. United States. Bureau of Labor Statistics. II. United States. Employment and Training Administration. III. Title.
HD5725.W5 W55 1980

Wisconsin. Dept. of Industry, Labor and Human Relations. State Employment Service Division. see Wisconsin. State Employment Service Division.

Wisconsin. Dept. of Local Affairs and Development. Division of Economic Development. see Wisconsin. Division of Economic Development.

Wisconsin. Dept. of Natural Resources.
Kubisiak, John F. Brood characteristics and summer habitats of ruffed grouse in central Wisconsin /. Madison, Wis. , 1978. 10, [1] p. :
LC Card 79-624430   DDC 639.9/09775 s 598/.616 19
SK463 .A27 no. 108 QL696.G285

Technical bulletin.
(no. 100) Hilsenhoff, William LeRoy, 1929- Use of arthropods to evaluate water quality of streams /. Madison, WI , 1977. 15 p. :
LC Card 78-623368   DDC 639.9/09775 s 628.1/68/028/7 19
SK463 .A27 no. 100 QH105.W6

(no. 108) Kubisiak, John F. Brood characteristics and summer habitats of ruffed grouse in central Wisconsin /. Madison, Wis. , 1978. 10, [1] p. : LC Card 79-624430 DDC 639.9/09775 s 598/.616 19
SK463 .A27 no. 108 QL696.G285

(no. 110) Avery, Eddie L. The influence of chemical reclamation on a small brown trout stream in southwestern Wisconsin /. Madison, Wis. , 1978. 35 p. : LC Card 79-624431 DDC 639.9/09775 s 597/.55 19
SK463 .A27 no. 110 QL638.S2

(no. 112) Beule, John D. Control and management of cattails in southeastern Wisconsin wetlands /. Madison, Wis. , 1979. 39 p. : LC Card 80-621497 DDC 639.9/09775 s 632/.58 19
SK463 .A27 no. 112 SB615.T96

Wisconsin. Dept. of Public Instruction. Bulletin.
(no. 3540) Wisconsin. Division for Instructional Services. Title I Unit. Educational programs for disadvantaged children, funded through Title I of the Elementary and secondary education act in Wisconsin school districts during 1972-73 /. [Madison] , 1973. iii, 411 p. ; LC Card 75-624181 DDC 370/.9775 s 371.96/7/09775 19
L216 .B36 no. 3540 LC4092.W6

Wisconsin. Dept. of Resource Development. Geography of Wisconsin manufacturing.
Wisconsin. Dept. of Business Development. Wisconsin manufacturing. Madison , 1977. iv, 48 p. : LC Card 77-623350
HD9727.W6 W57 1977

                    NYPL [JLF 80-1489]

Wisconsin. Dept. of Resource Development. Division of Economic Development. see Wisconsin. Division of Economic Development.

Wisconsin. Division for Instructional Services. Title I Unit. Educational programs for disadvantaged children, funded through Title I of the Elementary and secondary education act in Wisconsin school districts during 1972-73 / prepared by Title I Unit, Division of Instructional Services. [Madison] : Wisconsin Dept. of Public Instruction, 1973. iii, 411 p. ; 14 x 22 cm. (Bulletin - Wisconsin Department of Public Instruction . no. 3540) Chiefly tables. LC Card 75-624181 DDC 370/.9775 s 371.96/7/09775 19
1. Socially handicapped children - Education - Wisconsin - Statistics. 2. Federal aid to education - Wisconsin - Statistics. I. Series: Wisconsin. Dept. of Public Instruction. Bulletin. no. 3540. II. Title.
L216 .B36 no. 3540 LC4092.W6

Wisconsin. Division of Corrections. Office of Policy, Planning, and Budget.
Adult admissions and releases : ten-year trend

1970 through 1979, Wisconsin correctional institutions. Madison, Wis. : Dept. of Health and Social Services, Division of Corrections, Office of Policy, Planning, and Budget, [1980] 30 p. : graphs ; 28 cm. (Special report - Division of Corrections, Office of Policy, Planning, and Budget) Cover title. Prepared by Stephen M. Puckett. "June 1980." LC Card 80-623463 DDC 364.3/7/09775 19
1. Prisoners - Wisconsin - Statistics. I. Puckett, Stephen M. II. Series: Wisconsin. Division of Corrections. Office of Policy, Planning, and Budget. Special report - Division of Corrections, Office of Policy, Planning, and Budget. III. Title.
HV8369 .W62 1979a

Special report - Division of Corrections, Office of Policy, Planning, and Budget.
Wisconsin. Division of Corrections. Office of Policy, Planning, and Budget. Adult admissions and releases . Madison, Wis. [1980] 30 p. : LC Card 80-623463 DDC 364.3/7/09775 19
HV8369 .W62 1979a

Wisconsin. Division of Corrections. Office of Systems and Evaluation. Offenders admitted to the Mutual Agreement Program, calendar year 1978. Madison, Wis. : Dept. of Health and Social Services, Division of Corrections, Office of Systems and Evaluation, 1979. 25 p. ; 28 cm. Cover title. "September 1979." LC Card 80-620784 DDC 365/.66/09775 19
1. Prisoners - Wisconsin. 2. Prisoners - Wisconsin - Statistics. I. Title.
HV8369 .W62 1979

Wisconsin. Division of Corrections. Systems and Evaluation, Office of. see Wisconsin. Division of Corrections. Office of Systems and Evaluation.

Wisconsin. Division of Economic Development.
(Old Catalog form: Wisconsin. Economic Development, Division of.)
Work force 1980. [1]- [Madison, Wis.] 1971-
                    NYPL [JLM 80-1016]

Wisconsin. Division of Motor Vehicles.
Wisconsin. Laws, statutes, etc. Wisconsin motor vehicle laws, 1973-1974. [Madison] [1974?] 239 p. in various pagings ; LC Card 81-479063 DDC 343.775/0944/02632 347.750394402632 19
KFW2697 .A3 1974

Wisconsin. Division of State Energy. Wisconsin. University--Madison. Energy Systems & Policy Research Program. Industrial energy use in Wisconsin . [Madison] [1980] 196 p. : LC Card 80-622493 DDC 333.79 19
HC107.W6 W656 1980

Wisconsin. Division of Tourism. Bicentennial bike map of Wisconsin. Madison [1976?] 12 maps on sheet 87 x 56 cm. Scale varies. Includes 12 maps of County Bibycle Trails; Location map; text. On verso: 4 maps of State Bike Trails; 9 maps of City Bike Routes; text; table of camping areas, bike shops, local attractions, and sources of information, by county. Folded title: Wisconsin bicentennial bike map.
1. Wisconsin - Maps. 2. Cycling paths - Wisconsin - Maps. I. Title.   *NYPL [Map. Div. 80-3168]*

Wisconsin. Economic Development, Division of. see Wisconsin. Division of Economic Development.

Wisconsin. Employment Service Division. see Wisconsin. State Employment Service Division.

Wisconsin. Geological and Natural History Survey.
Harr, C. Albert. Ground-water resources and geology of Columbia County, Wisconsin /. Madison, Wis. , 1978. vii, 30 p. : LC Card 80-623464 DDC 557.75 s 553.7/9/0977581 19
QE179 .A33 no. 37 GB1025.W6

Information circular.
(no. 37) Harr, C. Albert. Ground-water resources and geology of Columbia County, Wisconsin /. Madison, Wis. , 1978. vii, 30 p. : LC Card 80-623464 DDC 557.75 s 553.7/9/0977581 19
QE179 .A33 no. 37 GB1025.W6

(no. 38) Young, H. L. Ground-water resources and geology of Washington and Ozaukee Counties, Wisconsin /. [Washington] , Madison, Wis. [1980] iv, 37 p. : LC Card 80-622195 DDC 557.75 s 553.7/9/0977591 19
QE179 .A33 no. 38 GB1025.W6

Wisconsin. Shore Erosion Study. Annotated bibliography of shore erosion and related physical materials concerning Wisconsin's Great Lakes coastal areas /. [Madison, Wis.] , 1976. 116 p. : LC Card 79-623658 DDC 016.5513/52 19
Z6004.C6 W57 1976 GB459.5.M5

Young, H. L. Ground-water resources and geology of Washington and Ozaukee Counties, Wisconsin /. [Washington] , Madison, Wis. [1980] iv, 37 p. : LC Card 80-622195 DDC 557.75 s 553.7/9/0977591 19
QE179 .A33 no. 38 GB1025.W6

Wisconsin Governor's Conference on Library and Information Services, Madison, 1978.
Wisconsin Governor's Conference on Library and Information Services, September 15-17, 1978, Sheraton Inn-Madison-Gateway, Madison, Wisconsin : conference report. [Madison] : Wisconsin Dept. of Public Instruction, [1978?] 18, 13 p. ; 28 cm. "Minutes ... alternates and delegates meeting, January 26, 1979." LC Card 80-622776 DDC 027.0775 19
1. Libraries - Wisconsin. 2. Wisconsin Governor's Conference on Library and Information Services, Madison, 1978. I. Wisconsin Governor's Conference on Library and Information Services, Madison, 1979.
Z732.W8 W57 1978

WISCONSIN GOVERNOR'S CONFERENCE ON LIBRARY AND INFORMATION SERVICES, MADISON, 1978.
Wisconsin Governor's Conference on Library and Information Services, Madison, 1978. Wisconsin Governor's Conference on Library and Information Services, September 15-17, 1978, Sheraton Inn-Madison-Gateway, Madison, Wisconsin . [Madison] [1978?] 18, 13 p. ; LC Card 80-622776 DDC 027.0775 19
Z732.W8 W57 1978

Wisconsin Governor's Conference on Library and Information Services, Madison, 1979.
Wisconsin Governor's Conference on Library and Information Services, Madison, 1978. Wisconsin Governor's Conference on Library and Information Services, September 15-17, 1978, Sheraton Inn-Madison-Gateway, Madison, Wisconsin . [Madison] [1978?] 18, 13 p. ; LC Card 80-622776 DDC 027.0775 19
Z732.W8 W57 1978

WISCONSIN - INDUSTRIES - ENERGY CONSERVATION.
Wisconsin. University--Madison. Energy Systems & Policy Research Program. Industrial energy use in Wisconsin . [Madison] [1980] 196 p. : LC Card 80-622493 DDC 333.79 19
HC107.W6 W656 1980

WISCONSIN - INDUSTRIES - ENERGY CONSUMPTION.
Wisconsin. University--Madison. Energy Systems & Policy Research Program. Industrial energy use in Wisconsin . [Madison] [1980] 196 p. : LC Card 80-622493 DDC 333.79 19
HC107.W6 W656 1980

Wisconsin. Joint Legislative Council. see Wisconsin. Legislative Council.

Wisconsin. Laws, statutes, etc. Wisconsin motor vehicle laws, 1973-1974. [Madison] : Dept. of Transportation, Division of Motor Vehicles, [1974?] 239 p. in various pagings ; 25 cm. Cover title. Includes index. LC Card 81-479063 DDC 343.775/0944/02632 347.750394402632 19
1. Motor vehicles - Law and legislation - Wisconsin. 2. Automobiles - Law and legislation - Wisconsin. 3. Traffic regulations - Wisconsin. I. Wisconsin. Division of Motor Vehicles. II. Title.
KFW2697 .A3 1974

Wisconsin. Legislative Council.
Discussion paper - Wisconsin Legislative Council staff .
(80-15) Wisconsin. Legislative Council. Issues relating to pretrial release pursuant to the issuance of a citation or summons /. Madison, Wis. [1980] 54 p. ; LC Card 80-624139 DDC 347.775/072 347.750772 19
KFW2976.6 .A25 1980

Hearing examiners and administrative review proceedings in Wisconsin State government / [prepared by Dan Fernbach and Keith Johnson]. Madison, Wis. : Wisconsin Legislative Council Staff, [1980] ii, 42 p. ; 28 cm. (Staff brief - Wisconsin Legislative Council Staff . 80-15) Cover title. LC Card 80-623541 DDC 300/.9775 s 342.775/066/0269 300/.9775 s 347.7502660269

19

1. Examiners (Administrative procedure) - Wisconsin. I. Fernbach, Dan. II. Johnson, Keith, 1952-. III. Series: Wisconsin. Legislative Council. Staff brief ; 80-15. IV. Title.
KFW2420 .L37 vol. 80-15 KFW2841.H4

Information on domestic violence in Wisconsin : extent and services available / Wisconsin Legislative Council staff. Madison : The Council, 1978. v, 75 p. : forms ; 28 cm. (Research bulletin - Wisconsin Legislative Council staff . 78-2) Cover title.　LC Card 78-622429　DDC 362.8/2 19
1. Conjugal violence - Wisconsin. 2. Family social work - Wisconsin. I. Series: Wisconsin. Legislative Council. Research bulletin - Wisconsin Legislative Council , 78-2. II. Title.
HV6626 .W57 1978

Issues relating to pretrial release pursuant to the issuance of a citation or summons / Wisconsin Legislative Council staff. Madison, Wis. : The Council, [1980] 54 p. ; 28 cm. (Discussion paper - Wisconsin Legislative Council staff ; 80-15) Cover title. "Prepared by Shaun P. Haas." "September 17, 1980." Includes bibliographical references.　LC Card 80-624139　DDC 347.775/066/0272 347.750772 19
1. Pre-trial release - Wisconsin. 2. Summons - Wisconsin. I. Haas, Shaun P. II. Series: Wisconsin. Legislative Council. Discussion paper - Wisconsin Legislative Council staff , 80-15. III. Title.
KFW2976.6 .A25 1980

Legislation and case law relating to the definition of death / Wisconsin Legislative Council staff. Madison : The Council, 1978. i, 54 p. ; 28 cm. (Research bulletin - Wisconsin Legislative Council ; 78-6) Cover title. "Prepared by Richard Sweet." LC Card 79-621977　DDC 346.77501/2 19
1. Death - Proof and certification - Wisconsin. I. Sweet, Richard N. II. Series: Wisconsin. Legislative Council. Research bulletin - Wisconsin Legislative Council , 78-6. III. Title.
KFW2767.D4 A25 1978

Research bulletin - Wisconsin Legislative Council .
(78-2) Wisconsin. Legislative Council. Information on domestic violence in Wisconsin . Madison , 1978. v, 75 p. :　LC Card 78-622429　DDC 362.8/2 19
HV6626 .W57 1978

(78-6) Wisconsin. Legislative Council. Legislation and case law relating to the definition of death /. Madison , 1978. i, 54 p. ;　LC Card 79-621977　DDC 346.77501/2 19
KFW2767.D4 A25 1978

Science and technology intern program : final project report / Wisconsin Legislative Council staff ; submitted to Division of Intergovernmental Science and Public Technology, National Science Foundation. Madison, Wis. : The Council, 1979. iv, 152 p. ; 28 cm.　LC Card 79-624457　DDC 328.775/0761 19
1. Science and Technology Intern Program. 2. Scientists in government - Wisconsin. 3. Engineers in government - Wisconsin. I. United States. National Science Foundation. Division of Intergovernmental Science & Public Technology. II. Title.
Q127.U6 W57 1979

Staff brief .
(80-15) Wisconsin. Legislative Council. Hearing examiners and administrative review proceedings in Wisconsin State government /. Madison, Wis. [1980] ii, 42 p. ;　LC Card 80-623541　DDC 300/.9775 s 342.775/066/0269 300/.9775 s 347.7502660269 19
KFW2420 .L37 vol. 80-15 KFW2841.H4

Staff memorandum. M-61, [no.] 2-M-69, [no.] 3 (incomplete). Madison, 1960-68. 28 cm. Irregular. The numbering of the memoranda corresponds to the year of the legislature for which it was prepared, e. g., in M-71, [no.] 2, 61 refers to the legislature of 1961. Each issue has also distinctive title: e. g., M65, no. 4, Administrative organization of higher education; M-69, no. 1, Court reorganization in Wisconsin; etc., etc. Ceased publication with M-69, no. 3, 1968?
1. Legislation - Wisconsin - Periodicals. 2. Legislative bodies - Wisconsin - Committees - Periodicals.
NYPL [M-10 5982]

Wisconsin. Legislative reference bureau. Information bulletin .
(80-IB-4) Wisconsin. Legislative reference

bureau. Wisconsin's outlook on energy /. Madison, Wis. [1980] 17 p. ;　LC Card 80-624141　DDC 300/.9775 s 346.77504/679 300/.9775 s 347.75064679 19
KFW2415 .L4 80-4 KFW2686

Research bulletin .
(80-RB-2) Wisconsin. Legislative reference bureau. The taxation and financing of transportation in Wisconsin . Madison, Wis. [1980] 101 p. ;　LC Card 80-621759　DDC 300/.9775 s 336.2/78 19
KFW2420 .L4 no. 80-2 HE213

Solomon, Jodee. The recent history and current status of abortion law. Madison, Wis. [1980] 12 p. ;　LC Card 80-624142　DDC 344.775/0419 347.7504419 19
KFW2415 .L4 80-5 KFW2753

The taxation and financing of transportation in Wisconsin : an overview of intermodal tax` relationships The State of Wisconsin, Legislative Reference Bureau. Madison, Wis. : The Bureau, [1980] 101 p. ; 28 cm. (Research bulletin - The State of Wisconsin, Legislative Reference Bureau ; 80-RB-2) Cover title. "January 1980." Bibliography: p. 99-101.　LC Card 80-621759　DDC 300/.9775 s 336.2/78 19
1. Transportation - Taxation - Wisconsin. 2. Transportation - Wisconsin - Finance. I. Series: Wisconsin. Legislative Reference Bureau. Research bulletin , 80-RB-2. II. Title.
KFW2420 .L4 no. 80-2 HE213

Wisconsin's outlook on energy / [prepared by Clark G. Radatz]. Madison, Wis. : State of Wisconsin, Legislative Reference Bureau, [1980] 17 p. ; 28 cm. (Informational bulletin / The State of Wisconsin, Legislative Reference Bureau . 80-IB-4) Cover title.　LC Card 80-624141　DDC 300/.9775 s 346.77504/679 300/.9775 s 347.75064679 19
1. Energy conservation - Law and legislation - Wisconsin. 2. Power resources - Law and legislation - Wisconsin. I. Radatz, Clark G. II. Series: Legislative Reference Bureau. Information bulletin , 80-IB-4. III. Title.
KFW2415 .L4 80-4 KFW2686

Wisconsin. Legislature. Joint Legislative Council. see Wisconsin. Legislative Council.

Wisconsin. Legislature. Law Revision Committee.
Wisconsin. Legislature. Legislative Council. Case and opinion review. Madison, Wis. [1980] 4 v. ;　LC Card 81-621133　DDC 347.775/012 347.750712 19
KFW2807 .A25 1980

Wisconsin. Legislature. Legislative Council. Case and opinion review. Madison, Wis. : [Wisconsin Legislative Council, 1980] 4 v. ; 28 cm. (Discussion paper - Wisconsin Legislative Council staff . 80-27, pt. 1-4) Cover title. "December 1, 1980." "Prepared for the Law Revision Committee ... by Don Dyke, Don Salm, and Mark Patronsky"--p. [1] CONTENTS. - pt. 1. Financial institution and commerce -- pt. 2. Criminal law and traffic -- pt. 3. Procedural law -- pt 4. General government.　LC Card 81-621133　DDC 347.775/012 347.750712 19
1. Judicial review - Wisconsin - Cases. 2. Law - Wisconsin - Interpretation and construction - Cases. I. Dyke, Don. II. Salm, Don. III. Patronsky, Mark C. IV. Wisconsin. Legislature. Law Revision Committee. V. Series: Discussion paper (Wisconsin. Legislature. Legislative Council) , 80-27, pt. 1-4. VI. Title.
KFW2807 .A25 1980

Wisconsin. Manpower Council, State. see Wisconsin. State Manpower Council.

WISCONSIN - MANUFACTURES.
Wisconsin. Dept. of Business Development. Wisconsin manufacturing. Madison , 1977. iv, 48 p. :　LC Card 77-623350
HD9727.W6 W57 1977
NYPL [JLF 80-1489]

Wisconsin manufacturing. Wisconsin. Dept. of Business Development. Madison , 1977. iv, 48 p. :　LC Card 77-623350
HD9727.W6 W57 1977
NYPL [JLF 80-1489]

WISCONSIN - MAPS.
(1976) Wisconsin. Division of Tourism. Bicentennial bike map of Wisconsin. Madison [1976?] 12 maps on sheet 87 x 56 cm. Scale varies. Includes 12 maps of County Bicycle Trails; Location map; text. On verso: 4 maps of State Bike Trails; 9 maps of City Bike Routes; text; table of camping areas, bike shops, local attractions, and sources

of information, by county. Folded title: Wisconsin bicentennial bike map.
NYPL [Map. Div. 80-3168]
(1979) United States. Soil Conservation Service. Wisconsin /. Lincoln, Nebr. , 1979. 1 map :　LC Card 81-691254
G4120 1979 .U5

Wisconsin medicine : historical perspectives / edited by Ronald L. Numbers and Judith Walzer Leavitt. Madison, Wis. : University of Wisconsin Press, 1981. ix, 212 p. : ill., map ; 24 cm. Map on lining papers. Bibliography: p. 185-200. Includes index. CONTENTS. - Frontier medicine in the Territory of Wisconsin / Peter T. Harstad -- From horse and buggy to automobile and telephone: medical practice in Wisconsin, 1848-1930 / Guenter B. Risse -- Sectarians and scientists: alternatives to orthodox medicine / Elizabeth Barnaby Keeney, Susan Eyrich Lederer, and Edmond P. Minihan -- Public protection and self-interest: medical societies in Wisconsin / Ronald L. Numbers -- From infirmaries to intensive care: hospitals in Wisconsin / Philip Shoemaker and Mary Van Hulle Jones -- One hundred years of health and healing in rural Wisconsin / Dale E. Treleven -- Health in urban Wisconsin: from bad to better / Judith Walzer Leavitt -- A note on medical education in Wisconsin / Ronald L. Numbers -- Selected sources on the history of medicine in Wisconsin / Deanna Reed Spring.　ISBN 0-299-08430-2 :　LC Card 80-52297　DDC 362.1/09775 19
1. Medicine - Wisconsin - History - Addresses, essays, lectures. I. Numbers, Ronald L. II. Leavitt, Judith Walzer.
R357 .W57

Wisconsin motor vehicle laws, 1973-1974. Wisconsin. Laws, statutes, etc. [Madison] [1974?] 239 p. in various pagings ;　LC Card 81-479063　DDC 343.775/0944/02632 347.750394402632 19
KFW2697 .A3 1974

Wisconsin. Natural History and Geological Survey. see Wisconsin. Geological and Natural History Survey.

Wisconsin. Natural Resources, Dept. of. see Wisconsin. Dept. of Natural Resources.

WISCONSIN - OCCUPATIONS - STATISTICS.
Wisconsin. Dept. of Industry, Labor and Human Relations. Bureau of Administration, Planning, and Analysis. Occupational employment estimates for selected nonmanufacturing industries, 1978 /. [Madison, Wis.] [1980] iv, 212 p. :　LC Card 80-623196　DDC 331.12/51/0009775 19
HD5725.W5 W55 1980

Wisconsin. Planning and Budget, Bureau of. see Wisconsin. Bureau of Planning and Budget.

Wisconsin population and households, March 1979 /. Kale, Balkrishna Damodar, 1925- Madison, Wis. , 1980. 20 p. ;　LC Card 80-623861　DDC 312/.09775 19
HA716 .K345

Wisconsin population by age and sex, 1958-1990 /. Kale, Balkrishna Damodar, 1925- Madison, Wis. [1979] 10 p. :　LC Card 79-625835　DDC 312/.8/09775 19
HA716 .K35

WISCONSIN - POPULATION - STATISTICS.
Kale, Balkrishna Damodar, 1925- Wisconsin population and households, March 1979 /. Madison, Wis. , 1980. 20 p. ;　LC Card 80-623861　DDC 312/.09775 19
HA716 .K345

Kale, Balkrishna Damodar, 1925- Wisconsin population by age and sex, 1958-1990 /. Madison, Wis. [1979] 10 p. :　LC Card 79-625835　DDC 312/.8/09775 19
HA716 .K35

WISCONSIN - PUBLIC BUILDINGS - ENERGY CONSUMPTION.
Energy use in state-owned facilities for fiscal year 1978-79 . [Madison, Wis.] [1980] 15 p. :　LC Card 80-623506　DDC 333.79 19
HD9502.U53 W584

Wisconsin public library building survey for handicapped accessibility /. Ross, Judith, 1947- Madison, WI [1979] 16, 2 p. :　LC Card 80-621510　DDC 727/.8/04209775 19
Z711.92.P5 R67

GOVERNMENT PUBLICATIONS - U.S.: 1981

693   Wisconsin. University, Madison. Institute for Research on

Wisconsin. Public Service Commission. Accounts and Finance Division.
Bulletin.
(no. 59) Wisconsin. Public Service Commission. Accounts and Finance Division. Periods of peak demand for utility service . [Madison, Wis.] [1979] iii, 30 p. : LC Card 79-626145 DDC 363.6/.09775 s 338.4/736362 19
HD2767.W6 A37 no. 59a HD9685.U6W6

Comparison of net quarterly bills of Wisconsin water utilities. 1980- [Madison] 22 x 28 cm. (Its: Bulletin. no. 25) Annual. For earlier file, see its Comparison of quarterly water bills for all incorporated Wisconsin communities.
1. Water-supply - Wisconsin - Statistics - Periodicals. I. Title.   **NYPL [JLM 80-1150]**

Periods of peak demand for utility service : Wisconsin electric utilities, 1978-1974. [Madison, Wis.] : Public Service Commission of Wisconsin, Accounts and Finance Division, [1979] iii, 30 p. : graphs ; 28 cm. (Bulletin - Public Service Commission of Wisconsin, Accounts and Finance Division ; no. 59) "October 1979." LC Card 79-626145 DDC 363.6/.09775 s 338.4/736362 19
1. Electric utilities - Wisconsin - Statistics. 2. Peak load - Economic aspects - Wisconsin. I. Series: Wisconsin. Public Service Commission. Accounts and Finance Division. Bulletin, no. 59. II. Title.
HD2767.W6 A37 no. 59a HD9685.U6W6

Wisconsin. Public Service Commission. Utility Accounts and Finance Division. see **Wisconsin. Public Service Commission. Accounts and Finance Division.**

Wisconsin Seminar on Natural Resource Policies in Relation to Economic Development and International Cooperation, University of Wisconsin--Madison, 1977-1978. Resources and development : natural resource policies and economic development in an interdependent world / edited by Peter Dorner, Mahmoud A. El-Shafie. Madison : University of Wisconsin Press ; London : Croom Helm, c1980. xv, 500 p. ; 24 cm. Co-sponsored by the University of Wisconsin--Madison and others. Includes bibliographies and index. ISBN 0-299-08250-4 : LC Card 80-10577
1. Natural resources - Congresses. 2. Economic development - Congresses. 3. International economic relations - Congresses. I. Dorner, Peter, 1925-. II. Shafie, Mahmoud A. III. Wisconsin. University, Madison. IV. Title.
HC55 .W57 1977a   **NYPL [JLE 80-3198]**

Wisconsin. Shore Erosion Study. Annotated bibliography of shore erosion and related physical materials concerning Wisconsin's Great Lakes coastal areas / Shore Erosion Study, Coastal Management Development Program. [Madison, Wis.] : Geological and Natural History Survey, Dept. of Natural Resources, 1976. 116 p. : 28 cm. Cover title: Shore erosion, a bibliography, 1976. LC Card 79-623658 DDC 016.5513/52 19
1. Shore-lines - Michigan, Lake - Bibliography. 2. Shore-lines - Superior, Lake - Bibliography. 3. Coast changes - Michigan, Lake - Bibliography. 4. Coast changes - Superior, Lake - Bibliography. I. Wisconsin. Geological and Natural History Survey. II. Title. III. Title: Shore erosion a bibliography, 1976.
Z6004.C6 W57 1976 GB459.5.M5

Wisconsin. State Bureau of Planning and Budget. see **Wisconsin. Bureau of Planning and Budget.**

Wisconsin. State Cartographer's Office. Fond du Lac County, Wisconsin, cartographic catalog / . Madison, WI (University of Wisconsin, 1555 Science Hall, Madison 53706) [1979] 1 v. (various pagings) : LC Card 80-624194 DDC 016.912/775/68 19
Z6027.U5 F65 GA458

Wisconsin. State Employment Service Division. Work force 1980. [1]- [Madison, Wis.] 1971-
NYPL [JLM 80-1016]

Wisconsin. State Manpower Council. Work force 1980. [1]- [Madison, Wis.] 1971-
NYPL [JLM 80-1016]

Wisconsin. State Planning Office. Huddleston, Jack R. Economic change and the urban poor . Madison, Wis. , 1976. 53 p. : LC Card 77-621328 DDC 330.9775/95043/0880624 19
HD5726.M5 H82

Wisconsin statistical abstract / prepared by Department of Administration, State Bureau of Planning and Budget, Information Systems Unit. 3rd ed. Madison (202 S. Thornton Ave., Madison, Wis.) : For sale by Wisconsin Dept. of Administration, Document Sales and Distribution, [1974] ix, 215 p. : chiefly tables ; 28 cm. "Document no. BSP-IS-74-6." "June 1974."   LC Card 78-621667 DDC 317.75 19
1. Wisconsin - Statistics. I. Wisconsin. Bureau of Planning and Budget. Information Systems Unit.
HA716 .W58 1974

WISCONSIN - STATISTICS.
Wisconsin statistical abstract / . Madison (202 S. Thornton Ave., Madison, Wis.) [1974] ix, 215 p. : LC Card 78-621667 DDC 317.75 19
HA716 .W58 1974

Wisconsin studies in contemporary literature. v. 1-8; winter 1960- autumn 1967. Madison, University of Wisconsin. 8 v. 23 cm. Microfilm. Three issues a year (slightly irregular) For later file, which continues its numbering, see Contemporary literature. LC Card 64-6922
1. Literature, Modern - 20th century - History and criticism - Periodicals. I. Wisconsin. University, Madison.   **NYPL [*ZAN-4597]**

Wisconsin. Tourism, Division of. see **Wisconsin. Division of Tourism.**

Wisconsin. University.
Land economics; a journal of planning, housing & public utilities. v. 1- ; 1925- Chicago [etc.] LC Card 26-19201
NYPL [*ZAN-T4596]

Wisconsin. University. Banking, Graduate School of. see **Wisconsin. University. Graduate School of Banking.**

Wisconsin. University. College of Agricultural and Life Sciences. Research Division. Jakel, Dale E. Soil survey of Adams County, Wisconsin. [Washington, D.C.?] , 1980. vii, 142 p., 57 folded p. of plates : LC Card 81-600526 DDC 631.4/7/77556 19
S599.W5 J34

Wisconsin. University. Graduate School of Banking. Madden, Carl Halford. Lecture on "current issues in a mixed economy" / . Washington , 1974. 24 p. :
NYPL [*XME-9134]

Wisconsin. University Library. see **Wisconsin. University, Madison. Library.**

Wisconsin. University, Madison.
Contemporary literature. v. 9- ; winter 1968- Madison.   **NYPL [*ZAN-4597]**

Wisconsin Seminar on Natural Resource Policies in Relation to Economic Development and International Cooperation, University of Wisconsin--Madison, 1977-1978. Resources and development . Madison , London , c1980. xv, 500 p. ; ISBN 0-299-08250-4 : LC Card 80-10577
HC55 .W57 1977a   **NYPL [JLE 80-3198]**

Wisconsin studies in contemporary literature. v. 1-8; winter 1960- autumn 1967. Madison. 8 v.   LC Card 64-6922   **NYPL [*ZAN-4597]**

Wisconsin. University, Madison. Bureau of Business Research and Services. Monograph. no. 1- Madison, 1968- illus. 23-29 cm. Cover title, 1968-71: Monograph series.
1. Business - Periodicals.   **NYPL [JLM 81-68]**

Wisconsin. University, Madison. Business Research and Services, Bureau of. see **Wisconsin. University, Madison. Bureau of Business Research and Services.**

Wisconsin. University, Madison. College of Agricultural and Life Sciences. Research Division.
Fox, Robert E. Soil survey of Dodge County, Wisconsin / . [Washington] [1980] ix, 201 p., [71] fold. leaves of plates : LC Card 80-602249 DDC 631.4/7/776153 19
S599.W5 F69

Gundlach, Howard F. Soil survey of Sauk County, Wisconsin / . [Washington] [1980] ix, 248 p., [67] fold. leaves of plates : LC Card 80-602384 DDC 631.4/7/77576 19
S599.W5 G86

Mitchell, Michael J. Soil survey of Winnebago County, Wisconsin / . [Washington] [1980] vii, 182 p., [23] fold. leaves of plates : LC Card

80-602659 DDC 631.4/7/77564 19
S599.W5 M58

Otter, Augustine J. Soil survey of Calumet and Maitowoc Counties, Wisconsin / . [Washington, D.C.] 1980. vii, 176 p., [64] fold. leaves of plates : LC Card 80-602383 DDC 631.4/7/77566 19
S599.W5 O86

Plant juice protein and moisture expression from organic materials . Madison [1978] 17 p. ; LC Card 79-625898 DDC 016.664/6 19
Z5524.P83 P53 TP453.P7

Wisconsin. University, Madison. Graduate School of Business. Bureau of Business Research and Services. see **Wisconsin. University, Madison. Bureau of Business Research and Services.**

Wisconsin. University-Madison. Industrial Relations Research Institute. The legal framework for collective bargaining in the urban transit industry / . Madison, Wisc. , 1976. iv, 188 p. ;   **NYPL [*XME-9332]**

Wisconsin. University, Madison. Institute for Research on Poverty.
Barkin, Tom. Legal implications of the Office [of] Education criteria for the self-supporting student / . [Madison] , 1974. 38 p. ; LC Card 77-621624
KF4235 .B47   **NYPL [*XME-9435]**

Discussion papers.
(# 562-79) Burkhauser, Richard V. Disentangling the annuity from the redistributive aspects of social security / . [Madison] , 1979. 30 p. ; LC Card 80-622901 DDC 368.4/4 19
HD7125 .B84

(# 588-79) Balcer, Yves. Family size, personal income tax credits, and horizontal equity / . [Madison] [1979] 30 p. : LC Card 80-622907 DDC 336.24/216 19
HJ4621 .B28

(# 592-79) Hauser, Robert Mason. On "Stratification in a dual economy" / . [Madison, Wis.] [1980] 29, [3] p. ; LC Card 80-622908 DDC 339.2/0973 19
HC110.I5 H36

(# 602-80) Geweke, John. Some economic consequences of technological advance in medical care . [Madison, Wis.] [1980] 52 p. : LC Card 80-622910 DDC 338.4/33621963433061 19
RA645.P46 G48 1980

(329-76) MacDonald, Maurice, 1947- Relative economic status and fertility . [Madison] [1976?] 25 p. ; LC Card 78-624376 DDC 304.6/3 19
HQ760 .M32

(331-76) Singer, Burton. Some methodological issues in the analysis of longitudinal surveys / . [Madison] , 1976. 56 p. ; LC Card 78-624379 DDC 330/.723 19
H62 .S4775

(359-76) Marwell, Gerald, 1937- Residence location, geographic mobility, and the attainments of women in academia / . Madison , 1976. 31 p. ; LC Card 78-623190 DDC 378/.12/0973 19
LB2331.72 .M37

(532-78) Bailey, William C., 1944- Deterrence and the celerity of the death penalty . [Madison] . 46 p. ; LC Card 79-625417 DDC 364.6/6/0973 19
HV8699.U5 B34

(546-79) Dickinson, Jonathan, 1943- Revealed preferences, functional form, and labor supply / . [Madison] , 1979. 50 p. : LC Card 80-622900 DDC 331.2/973 19
HD5724 .D52 1979

(583-79) Saupe, William E. Changes in farm poverty in Wisconsin / . [Madison] [1979] 24 p. ; LC Card 80-622902 DDC 338.1/3/09775 19
HC107.W63 P6246

(584-79) Johnson, Gordon C. Metropolitan professional sexual differentiation . [Madison] [1979] 27 p. ; LC Card 80-622903 DDC 331.11/4 19
HD8038.U5 J6

(585-79) Schwalbe, Rosanne M. Health insurance coverage of disabled persons under

Medicaid and private insurance /. [Madison] [1980] 55 p. ;   LC Card 80-622904   DDC 368.3/8/00880816 19
HG9396 .S28

(594-80) Sørensen, Aage Bøttger. Experimental matching of people to jobs /. [Madison] , 1980. 17 p. ;   LC Card 80-622909 DDC 658.3/128 19
HF5549.5.J63 S57

Garfinkel, Irwin. The effect of income and wage rates on the labor supply of prime age women /. [Madison] , 1974. ia, leaves ;   LC Card 77-621617
HD6095 .G37   **NYPL [*XME-9544]**

Special report .
(26) Mare, Robert D. Changes in the relative labor force status of Black and white youths . [Madison] [1980] 43 p. ;   LC Card 80-623148 DDC 331.3/412/0973 19
HD6273 .M38

Wisconsin. University, Madison. Land Tenure Center.
Horton, Douglas E. Land reform and reform enterprises in Peru . [Madison , 1974] xxxii, 182 p., [3] leaves of plates :   LC Card 80-623235 DDC 333.3/1/85 19
HD1333.P4 H67

Wisconsin. University, Madison. Library. (Old Catalog form: Wisconsin. University Library) Catalog of little magazines : a collection in the Rare Book Room, Memorial Library, University of Wisconsin--Madison / compiled and edited by Robert F. Roeming in cooperation with MINITEX, University of Minnesota, Wilson Library, Minneapolis, Minnesota. Madison : University of Wisconsin Press ; Ann Arbor : distributed on demand by University Microfilms International, 1979. xv, 137 p. ; 28 cm.   LC Card 79-5414
1. Little magazines - Bibliography - Catalogs. 2. Wisconsin. University, Madison Library - Catalogs. I. Roeming, Robert F. II. Title.
Z6944.L5 W57 1979 PN4836
     NYPL [*R-*D 80-3900]

WISCONSIN. UNIVERSITY, MADISON LIBRARY - CATALOGS.
Wisconsin. University, Madison. Library. Catalog of little magazines . Madison , Ann Arbor , 1979. xv, 137 p. ;   LC Card 79-5414
Z6944.L5 W57 1979 PN4836
     NYPL [*R-*D 80-3900]

Wisconsin. University, Madison. Sea Grant College Program. The invisible menace : contaminants in the Great Lakes : a report on the activities of the University of Wisconsin Sea Grant College Program. Madison, WI : The Program, [1980] 58 p. : ill. ; 28 cm. Prepared by C. Kohler ... et al. "WIS-SG-80-133; March 1980." Includes bibliographies.   LC Card 80-622418 DDC 628.1/68677 19
1. Water - Pollution - Environmental aspects - Great Lakes. 2. Great Lakes. I. Kohler, Christine. II. Title.
QH104.5.G7 W57 1980

Wisconsin. University. Memorial Library. see Wisconsin. University, Madison. Library.

Wisconsin. University--Madison. Center for Biotic Systems. Aquatic plants, lake management, and ecosystem consequences of lake harvesting . Madison, WI [1979] 435 p. :   LC Card 80-621513 DDC 632/.58/091692 19
SB614 .A687

Plant juice protein and moisture expression from organic materials. Plant juice protein and moisture expression from organic materials : a bibliography, addenda to R2386 published May, 1976 / by H. W. Ream ... [et al.]. Madison [1978] 17 p. ;   LC Card 79-625898 DDC 016.664/6 19
Z5524.P83 P53 TP453.P7

Wisconsin. University--Madison. Energy Research Center. ERC report .
(80-102) Wisconsin. University--Madison. Energy Systems & Policy Research Program. Industrial energy use in Wisconsin . [Madison] [1980] 196 p. :   LC Card 80-622493 DDC 333.79 19
HC107.W6 W656 1980

Wisconsin. University--Madison. Energy Systems & Policy Research Program.
Industrial energy use in Wisconsin :

consumption patterns and conservation measures / W. K. Foell ... [et al.] ; with contributions by M. E. Hanson ... [et al.]. [Madison] : Energy Systems & Policy Research Program, Energy Research Center, College of Engineering, University of Wisconsin--Madison, [1980] 196 p. : ill. ; 28 cm. (ERC report . 80-102) IES report ; 110 DSE special monograph Prepared in collaboration with Wisconsin Division of State Energy. "March 1980." Includes bibliographies.   LC Card 80-622493 DDC 333.79 19
1. Wisconsin - Industries - Energy consumption. 2. Wisconsin - Industries - Energy conservation. I. Foell, Wesley K. II. Wisconsin. Division of State Energy. III. Series: Wisconsin. University--Madison. Energy Research Center. ERC report , 80-102. IV. Title.
HC107.W6 W656 1980

Wisconsin. University--Madison. Institute for Environmental Studies. IES report .
(107) Kratz, Timothy K. A spatial simulation model of lake-edge wetland formation /. Madison , 1979. 59 p. :   LC Card 80-621224 DDC 574.5/26325/0724 19
QH541.5.M3 K7

Wisconsin. University--Madison. Institute for Environmental Studies. Environmental Monitoring and Data Acquisition Group.
Wisconsin. Dept. of Administration. Office of Program and Management Analysis. Land records . [Madison] , 1978. vi, 64 p. :   LC Card 79-622611 DDC 025/.063337313 19
HD211.W6 W63 1978

Research paper .
(no. 27-S) Johnson, Roger G. [Study of farm size and economic performance in old Santa Rosa, Rio Grande do Sul. Spanish.] Estudio sobre la extensión y el funcionamiento económico de las cranjas [i.e. granjas] en antigua Santa Rosa, Rio Grande do Sul /. Madison , 1972. 66 p. ;   LC Card 80-623239
HD107 .W52 no. 27-S HD1875.R5

(no. 73) Njeru, Enos Hudson Nthia. Land adjudication and its implications for the social organization of the Mbere /. Madison, Wis. [1978] i, 38 p. ;   LC Card 80-623243   DDC 333 s 306/.3 19
HD107 .W52 no. 73 DT433.545.M34

Wisconsin. University--Stevens Point. Museum of Natural History. Bowers, Frank D. Atlas of Wisconsin bryophytes /. Stevens Point, Wis. [1979] 2 v. (135 [i.e. 230] p.) :   LC Card 80-623149 DDC 574.9775 s 912/.1588/09775 19
QH105.W6 R43 no. 16 G1416.D2

Wisconsin's outlook on energy /. Wisconsin. Legislative reference bureau. Madison, Wis. [1980] 17 p. ;   LC Card 80-624141 DDC 300/.9775 s 346.77504/679 300/.9775 s 347.75064679 19
KFW2415 .L4 80-4 KFW2686

Wise, Edward M. Italy. Laws, statutes, etc. [Codice penale (1930). English.] The Italian penal code /. Littleton, Colo. , 1978. xlvi, 249 p. ;   ISBN 0-8377-0043-4   LC Card 78-54592
LAW   **NYPL [JLD 81-513]**

WISE, STEPHEN SAMUEL, 1874-1949.
Urofsky, Melvin I. A voice that spoke for justice . Albany , 1981. p. cm.   ISBN 0-87395-538-2   LC Card 81-5676   DDC 296.8/346/0924 B 19
BM755.W53 U76

Wisenbaker, Joseph M. (joint author) Eckland, Bruce Kent. A capsule description of young adults four and one-half years after high school /. [Washington, D.C.] , 1979. ix, 34 p. :   LC Card 80-601549 DDC 305.2/3/0973 19
HQ799.7 .E3

Wissig, George C. Bedrock geology of the Ossining quadrangle, New York / by George C. Wissig, Jr. ; New York State Museum. Albany : University of the State of New York, State Education Dept., 1979. 1 portfolio ; 31 cm. (Map and chart series . no. 30) Includes 1 pamphlet (viii, 53 p. : ill. ; 27 cm.) and 2 fold. maps. Bibliography: p. 51-53.   LC Card 80-621857 DDC 557.47/277 19
1. Geology - New York (State) - Westchester Co. I. New York (State) State Museum, Albany. II. Title. III. Series.
QE146.W35 W53

Wissler, Anne L. (joint author) Pecorella, Patricia A. Survey-guided development. [Washington?] , 1974. 1 v. (various pagings) ;
     NYPL [JLF 81-585]

Witherspoon, A. M. North Carolina. State University, Raleigh. Dept. of Botany. Response of phytoplankton to water quality in the Chowan River system /. [Raleigh, N.C.] [1979] xv, 204 p. :   LC Card 79-626203   DDC 589.4 19
HD1694.N8 N6 no. 129 QK571.5.N8

Withholding state income tax for annuitants and amending student survivor annuity provisions . United States. Congress. House. Committee on Post Office and Civil Service. Subcommittee on Compensation and Employee Benefits. Washington , 1981. iii, 31 p. ;   LC Card 81-601887   DDC 343.7305/242 347.3035242 19
KF27 .P638 1981

WITHHOLDING TAX - ECONOMIC ASPECTS - UNITED STATES.
United States. Congress. Senate. Committee on Banking, Housing, and Urban Affairs. Subcommittee on Economic Stabilization. Economic impact of payroll taxes . Washington , 1980. iv, 65 p. :   LC Card 80-602496 DDC 330.973/0926 19
KF26 .B39425 1980a

WITHHOLDING TAX - UNITED STATES.
United States. Congress. House. Committee on Ways and Means. President's proposal for withholding on interest and dividends . Washington , 1980. v, 310 p. :   LC Card 80-603348 DDC 353.0072/44 19
KF27 .W3 1980k

WITHHOLDING TAX - UNITED STATES - RATES AND TABLES - PERIODICALS.
United States. Office of Personnel Management. General schedule salary table. no. 64- ; 1979- [Washington].   **NYPL [JLM 81-193]**

WITHHOLDING TAX - UNITED STATES - STATES.
United States. Congress. House. Committee on Post Office and Civil Service. Subcommittee on Compensation and Employee Benefits. Voluntary withholding of State income tax for civil service annuitants . Washington , 1980. iii, 24 p. ;   LC Card 80-603116 DDC 343.7305/242 19
KF27 .P638 1980e

United States. Congress. House. Committee on Post Office and Civil Service. Subcommittee on Compensation and Employee Benefits. Withholding state income tax for annuitants and amending student survivor annuity provisions . Washington , 1981. iii, 31 p. ;   LC Card 81-601887 DDC 343.7305/242 347.3035242 19
KF27 .P638 1981

United States. Congress. Senate. Committee on Governmental Affairs. Subcommittee on Civil Service and General Services. Federal employee life insurance, tax withholding, and personal assistants . Washington , 1980 [i.e. 1981] iii, 68 p. ;   LC Card 81-601144 DDC 353.001/234 19
KF26 .G6724 1980b

Witinok, Patricia M. (joint author) Hallberg, George R. Changes in the channel area of the Missouri River in Iowa, 1879-1976 /. Iowa City, Iowa , 1979. iv, 32 p. :   LC Card 80-622112 DDC 551.48/3/097777 19
GB565.I8 H34

Witt, James M.
Terrestrial microcosms and environmental chemistry . [Washington] [1978?] xv, 147 p. :   LC Card 79-601829 DDC 574.5/264 19
QH541.2 .T45

Workshop on Terrestrial Microcosms, Newport, Or., 1977. Terrestrial microcosms . [Washington] [1978?] xii, 35 p. :   LC Card 79-602306 DDC 574.5/264 19
QH541.28 .W67 1977

Witteborg, Lothar P., 1927- Good show, a practical guide for temporary exhibitions / by Lother P. Witteborg for the Smithsonian Institution Traveling Exhibition Service, Washington, D.C. 1981 ; ill. by Steven D. Schindler ; editor, Andrea P. Stevens. Washington, D.C. : Smithsonian Institution Traveling Exhibition Service, 1981. 172 p. : ill. ; 26 cm. Bibliography: p. 164-168. Includes index. ISBN 0-86528-007-X   LC Card 80-39543   DDC 069.5 19

1. Art - Exhibitions, Traveling - Technique. I. Stevens, Andrea. II. Smithsonian Institution. Traveling Exhibition Service. III. Title.
N4396 .W57

Witter-Merithew, Anne. A Resource guide for interpreter training for the deaf programs /. [Washington, D.C. , 1980] 62 p. ; LC Card 80-602341 DDC 419 19
HV2395 .R45 1980

WIVES - EMPLOYMENT - UNITED STATES - STATISTICS.
Labor force participation and family formation among currently married women 15-44 years of age, United States /. Hyattsville, Md. [1981] p. cm. ISBN 0-8406-0233-2 LC Card 81-14015 DDC 305.4/3 19
HB915 .L25

Wogaman, Ronald W. (joint author) House, John H. Windy Ridge, a prehistoric site in the inter-riverine Piedmont in South Carolina /. [Columbia] , 1978. xv, 158 p. : LC Card 78-624313
E78.S6 H69 **NYPL [HBC 81-156]**

Wohlford, Laura. The State agency resource compendium : a criminal justice and crime prevention oriented index of services and data available through certain State agencies in Virginia / [author, Laura Wohlford]. Richmond, Va. : Commonwealth of Virginia, Division of Justice and Crime Prevention, Statistical Analysis Center, [1979] 242 p. in various pagings ; 28 cm. Cover title. "December 1979." LC Card 80-622046 DDC 364/.07 19
1. Criminal justice, Administration of - Information services - Virginia. 2. Crime prevention - Information services - Virginia. I. Virginia. Division of Justice and Crime Prevention. Statistical Analysis Center. II. Title.
HV8145.V8 W63

Wojowasito, Suwojo. Old Cat. (W- , S.)
A Kawi lexicon / by Soewojo Wojowasito ; edited by Roger F. Mills. Ann Arbor : University of Michigan, Center for South and Southeast Asian Studies, 1980. xv, 629 p. ; 23 cm. (Michigan papers on South and Southeast Asia. no. 17) ISBN 0-89148-017-X (pbk.) LC Card 78-57221 DDC 499/.2227 19
1. Kawi language - Dictionaries - English. I. Mills, Roger F. II. Title. III. Series.
PL5156 .W64

Wojtyła, Karol, Cardinal. see **John Paul II, Pope, 1920-**

Wolf, A. J. Wyoming. Dept. of Labor and Statistics. Wyoming coal strip mining . Cheyenne, Wyo. , 1979] iii, 40 p. ; LC Card 79-625469 DDC 331.12/522334/09787 19
HD4966.M63 U59 1979

Wolf, Andrew I. United States. Bureau of Consumer Protection. Disclosure of energy cost and consumption information in labeling and advertising of consumer appliances . [Washington] , 1979. 227 p. in various pagings ; LC Card 79-602022 DDC 343.73/085568383 19
KF1620.A6 A825

Wolfe, William L. Environmental Research Institute of Michigan. Infrared Information and Analysis (IRIA) Center. The infrared handbook /. Washington , 1978. ca. 1600 p. in various pagings ; LC Card 77-90786
TA1570 .E56 1978 **NYPL [JSE 80-1602]**

Wolken, Lawrence C.
Allen, John William, 1936- The foundations of free enterprise /. College Station, Tex. , 1979. 24 p. ; LC Card 81-622050 DDC 330.12/2 19
HC106.7 .A367

The exploration and colonization of space : lessons from history / Lawrence C. Wolken. College Station, Tex. : Center for Education and Research in Free Enterprise, Texas A&M University, c1980. 28 p. ; 23 cm. (Economic education series . no. 2) LC Card 81-621410 DDC 919.9/04 19
1. Outer space - Exploration - Economic aspects - United States. 2. Outer space - Exploration - Political aspects - United States. 3. Space colonies - Economic aspects - United States. 4. Space colonies - Political aspects - United States. I. Title. II. Series.
HC110.O93 W64

Woll, Allen. A functional past : the uses of history in nineteenth-century Chile / Allen Woll. Baton Rouge : Louisiana State University Press, c1982. p. cm. Bibliography: p. Includes index.

ISBN 0-8071-0977-0 : LC Card 81-12411 DDC 983/.06 19
1. Chile - Historiography. 2. Chile - History - 1824-1920. I. Title.
F3074 .W64

Wolski, Thomas R., 1947- Houpt, Katherine A. Domestic animal behavior for veterinarians and animal scientists /. Ames , 1981. p. cm. ISBN 0-8138-1060-4 LC Card 81-2811 DDC 636/.001/9 19
SF756.7 .H68

Womack, Katie N. Costs of public transportation in Texas, 1973-1977 / by Katie N. Womack, Dock Burke ; sponsored by the Texas State Department of Highways and Public Transportation and Urban Mass Transportation Administration, U. S. Department of Transportation. College Station, Tex. : Texas Transportation Institute, Texas A&M University, 1979. viii, 81 p. : graphs ; 28 cm. (Technical report - Texas Transportation Institute ; 1060-1) Bibliography: p. 67. LC Card 80-621655 DDC 388.4/042 19
1. Local transit - Texas - Costs. I. Burke, Dock, joint author. II. Texas. State Dept. of Highways and Public Transportation. III. United States. Urban Mass Transportation Administration. IV. Series: Texas Transportation Institute, College Station. Technical report - Texas Transportation Institute , 1060-1.
HE4487.T4 W65

WOMAN. see WOMEN.

A woman to deliver her people . Hopkins, James K., 1941- Austin , c1981. p. cm. ISBN 0-292-79017-1 : LC Card 81-10462 DDC 303.4/84 19
BF1815.S7 H66

The Women and culture series.
Bourque, Susan Carolyn, 1943- Women of the Andes . Ann Arbor , c1981. p. cm. ISBN 0-472-09330-4 : LC Card 81-811 DDC 305.4/2/0985 19
HQ1572 .B68 1981

Women & minorities in the construction industry . West Virginia. Human Rights Commission. [Charleston, W. Va.] [1979?] ii, 41 leaves ; LC Card 80-622765 DDC 331/4/824/09754 19
HD8039.B92 U78 1979

WOMEN AND RELIGION - ADDRESSES, ESSAYS, LECTURES.
Mother worship . Chapel Hill , c1981. p. cm. ISBN 0-8078-1471-7 LC Card 81-3336 DDC 306/.6 19
BL325.M6 M67

Women and the law . Morse, Phoebe. [Montpelier, VT , 1979] 31 p. ; LC Card 80-620943 DDC 342.743/0878 19
KFV91.W6 M67 1979

Women as third-party neutrals : gaining acceptability : proceedings from a conference / sponsored by the Institute for Education and Research on Women and Work, NYSSILR, Cornell University and the American Arbitration Association, February 12, 1977, New York, New York ; Barbara M. Wertheimer and Anne H. Nelson, editors. Ithaca : New York State School of Industrial and Labor Relations, Cornell University, 1978. vi, 55 p. ; 23 cm. ISBN 0-87546-066-6 : LC Card 78-620003 DDC 331.89/14/02373 19
1. Vocational guidance for women - United States - Congresses. 2. Arbitration, Industrial - United States - Vocational guidance - Congresses. 3. Mediation and conciliation, Industrial - United States - Vocational guidance - Congresses. I. Wertheimer, Barbara M. II. Nelson, Anne H. III. Cornell University. New York State School of Industrial and Labor Relations. Institute for Education and Research on Women and Work. IV. American Arbitration Association.
HD6058 .W6894

Women at work . Bickner, Mei Liang. [Los Angeles] , 1977. 1 v. ; LC Card 77-622630
Z7963.E7 B52 HD6095
NYPL [JLM 80-1110]

WOMEN COLLEGE TEACHERS - UNITED STATES - CONGRESSES.
Advancing women in higher education administration . Madison [1975?] 107 p. : LC Card 79-621418 DDC 378/.12/0973 19
LB2331.72 .A38

WOMEN - CRIMES AGAINST - ABSTRACTS.
Violence against women, causes and prevention . Rockville, Md. (P.O. Box 2309, Rockville 20852) , 1980. vii, 37 p. ; LC Card 80-603151 DDC 016.3628/8 19
HV6250.4.W65 V56 1980

WOMEN DENTAL STUDENTS - UNITED STATES - STATISTICS.
Ott, Mary Diederich. Women's participation in first-professional degree programs in medicine, dentistry, veterinary medicine, and law, 1969-70 through 1974-75 /. [Washington] , 1976. viii, 21 p. : LC Card 77-601995 DDC 610/.7/1173 19
R745 .O87

WOMEN DIPLOMATS - CONGRESSES.
The United Nations and decision-making . New York [c1978] 2 v. : LC Card 79-126238 DDC 354.1/03 19
JX1977 .U4257

WOMEN, DISCRIMINATION AGAINST. see **SEX DISCRIMINATION AGAINST WOMEN.**

WOMEN - DRUG USE.
Addicted women . Rockville, Md. [1979] vi, 130 p. : LC Card 80-601626 DDC 616.86/3/0088042 19
RC566 .A32

Characteristics of the drug-abusing woman. Rockville, Md. , Washington [1979] vii, 82 p. ; LC Card 79-602768
RC564 .C47 **NYPL [JLF 81-407]**

WOMEN - EMANCIPATION. see **WOMEN'S RIGHTS.**

WOMEN - EMPLOYMENT - ALABAMA - STATISTICS.
Alabama. Dept. of Industrial Relations. Research and Statistics Division. Women in Alabama. Montgomery, Ala. , 1979. 33 p. : LC Card 80-621563 DDC 331.4/125/09761 19
HD6096.A2 A4 1979

WOMEN - EMPLOYMENT - ALASKA.
United States. Commission on Civil Rights. Alaska Advisory Committee. Changing commitment into action . [Washington] , 1980. ix, 105 p. : LC Card 80-603134 DDC 353.9798001/04 19
HD6096.A4 U54 1980

WOMEN - EMPLOYMENT - LOUISIANA - STATISTICS.
Louisiana. Dept. of Labor. Office of Management and Finance. Louisiana women in the labor force, January 1980 /. Baton Rouge, La. [1980] 33 leaves ; LC Card 80-622130 DDC 331.4/12/09763 19
HD6096.L85 L68 1980

WOMEN - EMPLOYMENT - MONTANA.
Uda, Joan A. Montana working woman . [Helena, Mont.] [1979?] xi, 55 p. : LC Card 80-623400 DDC 344.786/014 19
KFM9334.5.D5 U3

WOMEN - EMPLOYMENT - NEBRASKA.
Frost, Murray. Survey of Nebraska women's employment participation, attitudes, and needs /. Omaha, Neb. , 1979. vi, 97 p. ; LC Card 80-621228 DDC 331.4/09782 19
HD6096.N3 F76

WOMEN - EMPLOYMENT - OREGON - STATISTICS.
Oregon. Employment Division. Oregon women at work. [Salem] 1977. 71 p. ; LC Card 78-621381
HD6096.O7 O73 1977 **NYPL [*XME-9535]**

WOMEN - EMPLOYMENT - UNITED STATES.
Garfinkel, Irwin. The effect of income and wage rates on the labor supply of prime age women /. [Madison] , 1974. ia, leaves ; LC Card 77-621617
HD6095 .G37 **NYPL [*XME-9544]**

United States. Women's Bureau. The earnings gap between women and men /. [Washington, D.C.] , 1979. 22 p. ; LC Card 80-602542 DDC 331.2/1 19
HD6061.2.U6 U53 1979

United States. Women's Bureau. Employment goals of the world . Washington, D.C. [1980] vi, 54, [22] p. : LC Card 80-602858 DDC 331.4/133/0973 19
HD6095 .U54 1980

WOMEN - EMPLOYMENT - UNITED STATES - BIBLIOGRAPHY.
Bickner, Mei Liang. Women at work . [Los Angeles] , 1977. 1 v. ;   LC Card 77-622630
Z7963.E7 B52 HD6095

WOMEN - EMPLOYMENT - UNITED STATES - HISTORY.
Warner, Deborah Jean. Perfect in her place . Washington, D.C. , 1981. p. cm.   LC Card 81-607826   DDC 331.4/0973 19
HD6095 .W198

WOMEN - EMPLOYMENT - UNITED STATES - INDEXES.
Bickner, Mei Liang. Women at work . [Los Angeles] , 1977. 1 v. ;   LC Card 77-622630
Z7963.E7 B52 HD6095

WOMEN - EMPLOYMENT - UNITED STATES - LONGITUDINAL STUDIES - CONGRESSES.
Conference on the National Longitudinal Surveys of Mature Women, United States Department of Labor, 1978. Women's changing roles at home and on the job . Washington , 1978. iii, 331 p. :   LC Card 79-601912
HQ1403 .C53 1978   **NYPL [JLF 81-250]**

WOMEN - EMPLOYMENT - UNITED STATES - STATISTICS.
Norwood, Janet Lippe. Women in the labor force . [Washington, D.C.] , 1979. 9 p. :   LC Card 80-601713   DDC 331.1/0973 s 331.4/12/0973 19
HD8051 .A7876 no. 575 HD6094

United States. Equal Employment Opportunity Commission. Minorities and women in private industry . [Washington] [1980] 2 v. :   LC Card 80-602340   DDC 331.13/3/0973 19
HD8081.A5 U54 1980

WOMEN - EMPLOYMENT - VIRGINIA - STATISTICS.
Virginia. Employment Commission. Manpower Research Division. Labor market information for Affirmative Action programs . [Richmond] [1979] 67, xiv p. ;   LC Card 80-621171   DDC 331.12/09755 19
HD5725.V8 V53 1979a

WOMEN - EMPLOYMENT - WEST VIRGINIA.
West Virginia. Human Rights Commission. Women & minorities in the construction industry . [Charleston, W. Va.] [1979?] ii, 41 leaves ;   LC Card 80-622765   DDC 331/4/824/09754 19
HD8039.B92 U78 1979

WOMEN HEADS OF HOUSEHOLDS - UNITED STATES.
Mott, Frank. The socioeconomic status of households headed by women . Washington, D.C. , 1979, 1980 printing. xiii, 68 p. :   LC Card 80-601212   DDC 331.11/0973 s 305.4/8 19
HD5701 .U53 no. 72 HQ536

WOMEN HEADS OF HOUSEHOLDS - UNITED STATES - STATISTICS.
Rawlings, Stephen, 1945- Families maintained by female householders, 1970 to 1979 /. [Washington] , 1980. p. cm.   LC Card 80-25731   DDC 312/.0973 s 306.8 19
HA203 .A218 no. 107 HQ536

WOMEN - HOURS OF LABOR. see HOURS OF LABOR.

Women in Alabama. Alabama. Dept. of Industrial Relations. Research and Statistics Division. Montgomery, Ala. , 1979. 33 p. :   LC Card 80-621563   DDC 331.4/125/09761 19
HD6096.A2 A4 1979

Women in business . United States. Congress. House. Committee on Small Business. Subcommittee on General Oversight and Minority Enterprise. Washington , 1980 [i.e. 1981] iv, 178 p. :   LC Card 81-600836   DDC 331.4/8165/00973 19
KF27 .S64 1980k

Women-in-business programs in the Federal government . United States. Congress. Senate. Select Committee on Small Business. Washington , 1980. iii, 207 p. ;   LC Card 80-603041   DDC 353.0082/048 19
KF26.5 .S6 1980h

WOMEN IN BUSINESS - UNITED STATES.
United States. Congress. House. Committee on Small Business. Subcommittee on General Oversight and Minority Enterprise. Women in business . Washington , 1980 [i.e. 1981] iv, 178 p. :   LC Card 81-600836   DDC 331.4/8165/00973 19
KF27 .S64 1980k

United States. Congress. Senate. Select Committee on Small Business. Women-in-business programs in the Federal government . Washington , 1980. iii, 207 p. ;   LC Card 80-603041   DDC 353.0082/048 19
KF26.5 .S6 1980h

Women in Congress, 1917-1976. [Washington : u.S. Govt. Print. Off.], 1976. iii, 112 p. : ports ; 26 cm. Cover title. "Printed for the use of the Joint Committee on Arrangements for the Commemoration of the Bicentennial." LC Card 77-601008
1. Legislators - United States - Biography. 2. Women legislators - United States - Biography. 3. Women legislators - United States - Directories. I. United States. Congress. Joint Committee on Arrangements for the Commemoration of the Bicentennial.
JK1013 .W65

Women in Joyce / edited by Suzette Henke and Elaine Unkeless. Urbana : University of Illinois Press, c1982. p. cm. Includes bibliographical references.   ISBN 0-252-00891-X   LC Card 81-4663   DDC 823/.912
1. Joyce, James, 1882-1941 - Characters - Women. 2. Women in literature. I. Henke, Suzette. II. Unkeless, Elaine, 1945-.
PR6019.O9 Z654

WOMEN IN LITERATURE.
Newton, Judith Lowder. Women, power, and subversion . Athens , c1981. p. cm.   ISBN 0-8203-0564-2   LC Card 81-1068   DDC 823/.009/9287 19
PR830.W62 N4

Women in Joyce /. Urbana , c1982. p. cm.   ISBN 0-252-00891-X   LC Card 81-4663   DDC 823/.912
PR6019.O9 Z654

WOMEN IN LITERATURE - ADDRESSES, ESSAYS, LECTURES.
Icons and fallen idols . Berkeley , c1982. p. cm.   ISBN 0-520-04291-3   LC Card 81-14663   DDC 860/.9 19
PQ6048.W6 I26

Vox feminae . Kalamazoo, Mich. , 1981. viii, 223 p. ;   ISBN 0-918720-12-5 (pbk.) :   LC Card 81-3981   DDC 809.1/9352042 19
CB351 .S83 vol. 15 PN691

WOMEN IN MEDICINE - PENNSYLVANIA - CONGRESSES.
Conference on Women and Health, Philadelphia, 1974. Proceedings of the Conference on Women and Health, June 27, 28, 29, 1974, Philadelphia, Pa. [Philadelphia] [1976?] 28 p. :   LC Card 76-623061   DDC 362.1/088042 19
RA564.85 .C66 1974

WOMEN IN MEDICINE - UNITED STATES - STATISTICS.
United States. Health Resources Administration. Bureau of Health Manpower. Minorities & women in the health fields . [Hyattsville, Md.] , Washington , 1978. xiii, 122 p. :   LC Card 79-602970
R693 .U55 1978   **NYPL [JLF 81-355]**

WOMEN IN POLITICS - UNITED STATES.
Levenson, Rosaline. Public acceptance of women in politics . Chico, Calif. [1980] 31 p. ;   LC Card 80-622812   DDC 320/.088042 19
HQ1391.U5 L48

Women in prison . United States. General Accounting Office. Washington, D.C. , 1980. v, 50 p. ;   LC Card 81-600746   DDC 365/.43/0973 19
HV9471 .U53 1980

WOMEN IN THE ARMED FORCES. see UNITED STATES - ARMED FORCES - WOMEN.

WOMEN IN THE CIVIL SERVICE - KENTUCKY.
Kentucky. Commission on Human Rights. Status of women in Kentucky State agencies . Frankfort, Ky. [1979] ii. 21 p. :   LC Card 80-622262   DDC 353.9769001/04 19
JK5360.5.W6 K46 1979

WOMEN IN THE CIVIL SERVICE - OHIO.
Ohio. Governor's Task Force on Women in State Government. Governor's Task Force on Women in State Government. [Columbus , 1978?] vi, 100 p. :   LC Card 80-117284   DDC 353.9771001/04 19
JK5560.5.W6 O34 1978

WOMEN IN THE CIVIL SERVICE - UNITED STATES.
United States. Congress. House. Committee on Post Office and Civil Service. Subcommittee on Civil Service. Civil service reform oversight--1980 . Washington , 1981. iv, 433 p. ;   LC Card 81-600955   DDC 353.001/04 19
KF27 .P635 1980d

United States. Congress. House. Committee on Post Office and Civil Service. Subcommittee on Investigations. Sexual harassment in the Federal Government /. Washington , 1980. iii, 32 p. ;   LC Card 80-602591   DDC 353-001/04 19
JK721 .U554 1980

United States. Women's Bureau. Native American women and equal opportunity . [Washington, D.C.] , 1979. vii, 81 p. :   LC Card 80-600536
E98.W8 U54 1979   **NYPL [HBC 81-449]**

WOMEN IN THE CIVIL SERVICE - UNITED STATES - STATISTICS.
United States. Intergovernmental Personnel Programs. EEO statistical report on employment in State and local government . Washington , 1979. [52] p. ;   LC Card 79-602132
JK2480.M5 U56 1979   **NYPL [JLF 81-448]**

WOMEN IN THE CIVIL SERVICE - UNITED STATES - STATISTICS.
United States. Congress. House. Committee on Education and Labor. Subcommittee on Employment Opportunities. Comparison of employment trends for women and minorities in forty-five selected Federal agencies, 1980 /. Washington , 1980. v, 192 p. :   LC Card 80-603058   DDC 331.12/51353 19
HD8008 .U56 1980

Women in the labor force . Norwood, Janet Lippe. [Washington, D.C.] , 1979. 9 p. :   LC Card 80-601713   DDC 331.1/0973 s 331.4/12/0973 19
HD8051 .A7876 no. 575 HD6094

Women in the military . United States. Congress. House. Committee on Armed Services. Subcommittee on Military Personnel. Washington , 1981. ii, 369 p. :   LC Card 81-601874   DDC 355/.0088/042 19
KF27 .A76398 1979d

WOMEN - LATIN AMERICA - SOCIAL CONDITIONS - ADDRESSES, ESSAYS, LECTURES.
Mujer y sociedad en América Latina /. Irvine [Santiago, Chile] [1980] 261 p. ;   LC Card 80-138107   DDC 305.4/2/098 19
HQ1460.5 .M85

WOMEN LAW STUDENTS - UNITED STATES - STATISTICS.
Ott, Mary Diederich. Women's participation in first-professional degree programs in medicine, dentistry, veterinary medicine, and law, 1969-70 through 1974-75 /. [Washington] , 1976. viii, 21 p. :   LC Card 77-601995   DDC 610/.7/1173 19
R745 .O87

WOMEN - LEGAL STATUS, LAWS, ETC. - KENTUCKY - POPULAR WORKS.
Roberts, W. Lewis (William Lewis), 1877-1960. Legal tidbits for women /. Lexington [Ky.] [1936] 97 p. ;   LC Card 80-144806   DDC 349.769 347.69 19
KFK1281 .R6

WOMEN - LEGAL STATUS, LAWS, ETC. - UNITED STATES.
United States. Dept. of Health, Education, and Welfare. Secretary's Advisory Committee on the Rights and Responsibilities of Women. The rights & responsibilities of women . [Washington] [1976?] ii, 103 p. ;   LC Card 77-603753   DDC 362.8/3/0973 19
HQ1426 .U52 1976

WOMEN - LEGAL STATUS, LAWS, ETC. - VERMONT.
Morse, Phoebe. Women and the law . [Montpelier, VT , 1979] 31 p. ;   LC Card 80-620943   DDC 342.743/0878 19
KFV91.W6 M67 1979

WOMEN LEGISLATORS - UNITED STATES - BIOGRAPHY.
Women in Congress, 1917-1976. [Washington] 1976. iii, 112 p. :　LC Card 77-601008
JK1013 .W65

WOMEN LEGISLATORS - UNITED STATES - DIRECTORIES.
Women in Congress, 1917-1976. [Washington] 1976. iii, 112 p. :　LC Card 77-601008
JK1013 .W65

WOMEN - LIBRARY RESOURCES - NEW YORK (CITY) - DIRECTORIES.
Nelson, Martha. A guide to collections on women in the New York area /. [New York, 1980?] 17 p.;　***NYPL [JLF 81-437]***

WOMEN MEDICAL STUDENTS - UNITED STATES - STATISTICS.
Ott, Mary Diederich. Women's participation in first-professional degree programs in medicine, dentistry, veterinary medicine, and law, 1969-70 through 1974-75 /. [Washington] , 1976. viii, 21 p. :　LC Card 77-601995　DDC 610/.7/1173 19
R745 .O87

WOMEN - OCCUPATIONS. see WOMEN - EMPLOYMENT.
Women of the Andes . Bourque, Susan Carolyn, 1943- Ann Arbor, c1981. p. cm.　ISBN 0-472-09330-4 :　LC Card 81-811　DDC 305.4/2/0985 19
HQ1572 .B68 1981

Women of the old Wild West. Brown, Dee Alexander. The gentle tamers . Lincoln, NE , 1981, c1958. p. cm.　ISBN 0-8032-5025-8 (pbk.)
LC Card 81-3428　DDC 978/.0088042 19
F591 .B87 1981

WOMEN - OREGON - BIO-BIBLIOGRAPHY.
Leasher, Evelyn M. Oregon women . Corvallis , 1980, c1981. viii, 54 p. ;　ISBN 0-87071-138-5 (pbk.)　LC Card 81-122472　DDC 016.3054/09795 19
HQ1438.O7 L4

WOMEN - OREGON - BIOGRAPHY.
Leasher, Evelyn M. Oregon women . Corvallis , 1980, c1981. viii, 54 p. ;　ISBN 0-87071-138-5 (pbk.)　LC Card 81-122472　DDC 016.3054/09795 19
HQ1438.O7 L4

WOMEN-OWNED BUSINESS ENTERPRISES - UNITED STATES.
SMS Associates. A directory of Federal Government business assistance programs for women business owners . [Washington, D.C.] [1980] iv, 71 p. ;　LC Card 80-602878　DDC 353.0082/048 19
HD2346.U5 S17 1980

United States. Congress. Senate. Select Committee on Small Business. Women-in-business programs in the Federal government . Washington , 1980. iii, 207 p. ;　LC Card 80-603041　DDC 353.0082/048 19
KF26.5 .S6 1980h

WOMEN - PERU - CASE STUDIES.
Bourque, Susan Carolyn, 1943- Women of the Andes . Ann Arbor , c1981. p. cm.　ISBN 0-472-09330-4 :　LC Card 81-811　DDC 305.4/2/0985 19
HQ1572 .B68 1981

WOMEN - PERU - CHUCCHÍN.
Bourque, Susan Carolyn, 1943- Women of the Andes . Ann Arbor , c1981. p. cm.　ISBN 0-472-09330-4 :　LC Card 81-811　DDC 305.4/2/0985 19
HQ1572 .B68 1981

WOMEN - PERU - MAYOBAMBA.
Bourque, Susan Carolyn, 1943- Women of the Andes . Ann Arbor , c1981. p. cm.　ISBN 0-472-09330-4 :　LC Card 81-811　DDC 305.4/2/0985 19
HQ1572 .B68 1981

WOMEN - POLITICAL ACTIVITY. see WOMEN IN POLITICS.
Women, power, and subversion . Newton, Judith Lowder. Athens , c1981. p. cm.　ISBN 0-8203-0564-2　LC Card 81-1068　DDC 823/.009/9287 19
PR830.W62 N4

WOMEN PRISONERS - UNITED STATES.
United States. General Accounting Office. Women in prison . Washington, D.C. , 1980. v,

50 p. ;　LC Card 81-600746　DDC 365/.43/0973 19
HV9471 .U53 1980

WOMEN - PSYCHOLOGY.
Characteristics of the drug-abusing woman. Rockville, Md. , Washington [1979] vii, 82 p. ;　LC Card 79-602768
RC564 .C47　　　　　　***NYPL [JLF 81-407]***

WOMEN - RIGHTS OF WOMEN. see WOMEN'S RIGHTS.

WOMEN - ROCKY MOUNTAIN REGION - CONGRESSES.
Energy resource development . Washington, D.C. [1979] xiii, 221 p. :　LC Card 79-604168
HD9502.U53 A1713　***NYPL [JLF 81-331]***

WOMEN - SOCIAL CONDITIONS - BIBLIOGRAPHY.
University of Northern Iowa. Library. Women's studies bibliography /. [Cedar Falls, Iowa , 1973] 54 p. in various pagings ;
NYPL [*R-Econ. 80-1012]

WOMEN - UNITED STATES - ALCOHOL USE - CONGRESSES.
Alcoholism and alcohol abuse among women, research issues . Rockville, Md. , Washington, D.C. [1980] xvii, 256 p. ;　LC Card 79-600166　DDC 362.2/92/088042 19
HV5137 .A42

WOMEN - UNITED STATES - CONGRESSES.
Women's lives . [Ann Arbor, Mich.] , 1980. xiv, 451 p. :　LC Card 81-134376　DDC 305.4/2/0973 19
HQ1420 .W65

WOMEN - UNITED STATES - PENSIONS.
United States. Congress. Senate. Special Committee on Aging. Adapting social security to a changing work force . Washington , 1980. iii, 102 p. :　LC Card 80-602460　DDC 368.4/3/00973 19
KF26.5 .A3 1979d

United States. Dept. of Justice. Task Force on Sex Discrimination. The pension game . Washington , 1979. 78 p. ;　LC Card 79-602270
HD6080.2.U5 U52 1979　***NYPL [Jlf 81-399]***

WOMEN - UNITED STATES - SOCIAL CONDITIONS - ADDRESSES, ESSAYS, LECTURES.
Fisher, Anne. Women's worlds . Rockville, Md. , Washington [1978] xiii, 106 p. ;　LC Card 78-603680　DDC 305.4/0973 19
HQ1420 .F57

WOMEN - UNITED STATES - SOCIAL CONDITIONS - BIBLIOGRAPHY.
University of Northern Iowa. Library. Women's studies bibliography /. [Cedar Falls, Iowa , 1973] 54 p. in various pagings ;
NYPL [*R-Econ. 80-1012]

WOMEN - UNITED STATES - SOCIAL CONDITIONS - LONGITUDINAL STUDIES - CONGRESSES.
Conference on the National Longitudinal Surveys of Mature Women, United States Department of Labor, 1978. Women's changing roles at home and on the job . Washington , 1978. iii, 331 p. :　LC Card 79-601912
HQ1403 .C53 1978　　***NYPL [JLF 81-250]***

Women versus men : a conflict of Navajo emergence / the Curly Tó Aheedlíinii version ; [recorded by] Berard Haile ; Navajo orthography by Irvy M. Goossen ; Karl W. Luckert, editor. Lincoln : University of Nebraska Press, 1982. p. cm. (American tribal religions . v. 6) English and Navaho.　ISBN 0-8032-2319-6　LC Card 81-7433　DDC 299/.72 19
1. Navaho Indians - Religion ad mythology. 2. Indians of North America - Southwest, New - Religion and mythology. 3. Navaho Indians - Legends. 4. Indians of North America - Southwest, New - Legends. I. Curly, Tó Aheedlíinii. II. Haile, Berard, 1874-1961. III. Goossen, Irvy W. IV. Luckert, Karl W., 1934-. V. Series.
E99.N3 W74

WOMEN VETERINARY STUDENTS - UNITED STATES - STATISTICS.
Ott, Mary Diederich. Women's participation in first-professional degree programs in medicine, dentistry, veterinary medicine, and law, 1969-70 through 1974-75 /. [Washington] , 1976. viii,

21 p. :　LC Card 77-601995　DDC 610/.7/1173 19
R745 .O87

WOMEN - WEST (U. S.) - HISTORY.
Brown, Dee Alexander. The gentle tamers . Lincoln, NE , 1981, c1958. p. cm.　ISBN 0-8032-5025-8 (pbk.)　LC Card 81-3428　DDC 978/.0088042 19
F591 .B87 1981

WOMEN WORKERS. see WOMEN - EMPLOYMENT.
Women's changing roles at home and on the job . Conference on the National Longitudinal Surveys of Mature Women, United States Department of Labor, 1978. Washington , 1978. iii, 331 p. :　LC Card 79-601912
HQ1403 .C53 1978　　***NYPL [JLF 81-250]***

WOMEN'S HEALTH SERVICES - PENNSYLVANIA - CONGRESSES.
Conference on Women and Health, Philadelphia, 1974. Proceedings of the Conference on Women and Health, June 27, 28, 29, 1974, Philadelphia, Pa. [Philadelphia] [1976?] 28 p. :　LC Card 76-623061　DDC 362.1/088042 19
RA564.85 .C66 1974

WOMEN'S LIB. see FEMINISM.

WOMEN'S LIBERATION. see WOMEN'S RIGHTS.

WOMEN'S LIBERATION MOVEMENT. see FEMINISM.
Women's lives : new theory, research & policy / edited by Dorothy G. McGuigan. [Ann Arbor, Mich.] : University of Michigan, Center for Continuing Education of Women, 1980. xiv, 451 p. : ill. ; 23 cm. Collection of papers from the 5th University of Michigan Center for Continuing Education of Women conference, held Nov. 7-8, 1979. Includes bibliographies and index.　LC Card 81-134376　DDC 305.4/2/0973 19
1. Women - United States - Congresses. 2. Life cycle, Human - Congresses. I. McGuigan, Dorothy Gies. II. University of Michigan. Center for Continuing Education of Women.
HQ1420 .W65

Women's participation in first-professional degree programs ... Ott, Mary Diederich. Women's participation in first-professional degree programs in medicine, dentistry, veterinary medicine, and law, 1969-70 through 1974-75 /. [Washington] , 1976. viii, 21 p. :　LC Card 77-601995　DDC 610/.7/1173 19
R745 .O87

Women's place . Morahan, Shirley, 1945- Albany , 1981. p. cm.　ISBN 0-87395-488-2 (pbk.)　LC Card 81-4802　DDC 808/.042 19
PE1417 .M618

WOMEN'S RIGHTS - UNITED STATES.
United States. Dept. of Health, Education, and Welfare. Secretary's Advisory Committee on the Rights and Responsibilities of Women. The rights & responsibilities of women . [Washington] [1976?] ii, 103 p. ;　LC Card 77-603753　DDC 362.8/3/0973 19
HQ1426 .U52 1976

WOMEN'S RIGHTS - UNITED STATES - CONGRESSES.
Western Regional Civil Rights and Women's Rights Conference, 4th, San Francisco, 1977. Recent developments, new opportunities in civil rights and women's rights . - Washington [1977]. vi, 178 p. ;　***NYPL [JLE 80-2420]***

Women's studies as a catalyst for faculty development /. Nelson, Elizabeth Ness. Washington, D.C. , 1980. xii, 43 p. ;　LC Card 80-602285　DDC 378/.12/0973 19
LB2331.72 .N44

Women's studies bibliography /. University of Northern Iowa. Library. [Cedar Falls, Iowa , 1973] 54 p. in various pagings ;
NYPL [*R-Econ. 80-1012]

WOMEN'S STUDIES - BIBLIOGRAPHY.
University of Northern Iowa. Library. Women's studies bibliography /. [Cedar Falls, Iowa , 1973] 54 p. in various pagings ;
NYPL [*R-Econ. 80-1012]

Women's studies monograph series.
Bose, Christine E. The relationship between women's studies, career development, and vocational choice /. Washington, D.C. , 1980.

xi, 59 p. ; LC Card 80-602291 DDC
305.4/2/072073 19
HQ1181.U5 B67

Howe, Florence. The impact of women's studies
on the campus and the disciplines /.
[Washington, D.C.] [1980] xiv, 132 p. ; LC
Card 80-602566 DDC 305.4/072073 19
HQ1181.U5 H69

Nelson, Elizabeth Ness. Women's studies as a
catalyst for faculty development /. Washington,
D.C. , 1980. xii, 43 p. ; LC Card 80-602285
DDC 378/.12/0973 19
LB2331.72 .N44

Porter, Nancy M. The effectiveness of women's
studies teaching /. Washington, D.C. [1980] ix,
76 p. ; LC Card 80-602283 DDC 305.4/07/073 19
HQ1181.U5 P67

WOMEN'S STUDIES - UNITED STATES.
Nelson, Elizabeth Ness. Women's studies as a
catalyst for faculty development /. Washington,
D.C. , 1980. xii, 43 p. ; LC Card 80-602285
DDC 378/.12/0973 19
LB2331.72 .N44

**WOMEN'S STUDIES - UNITED STATES -
BIBLIOGRAPHY.**
University of Northern Iowa. Library. Women's
studies bibliography /. [Cedar Falls, Iowa ,
1973] 54 p. in various pagings ;
NYPL [*R-Econ. 80-1012]

**WOMEN'S STUDIES - UNITED STATES -
EVALUATION.**
Bose, Christine E. The relationship between
women's studies, career development, and
vocational choice /. Washington, D.C. , 1980.
xi, 59 p. ; LC Card 80-602291 DDC
305.4/2/072073 19
HQ1181.U5 B67

Howe, Florence. The impact of women's studies
on the campus and the disciplines /.
[Washington, D.C.] [1980] xiv, 132 p. ; LC
Card 80-602566 DDC 305.4/072073 19
HQ1181.U5 H69

Porter, Nancy M. The effectiveness of women's
studies teaching /. Washington, D.C. [1980] ix,
76 p. ; LC Card 80-602283 DDC 305.4/07/073 19
HQ1181.U5 P67

Women's worlds . Fisher, Anne. Rockville, Md. ,
Washington [1978] xiii, 106 p. ; LC Card
78-603680 DDC 305.4/0973 19
HQ1420 .F57

Wones, David R. "The Caledonides in the USA" .
[Blacksburg, Va.] , 1980. iv, 329, 19 p. : LC
Card 81-134431 DDC 551.7/32/0973 19
QE661 .C34

Wong, M. M. (Morton M.)
Bennetts, J. (John) Preparation of platinum
flotation concentrate from stillwater complex
ore /. Avondale, Md. [1981] p. cm. LC Card
80-606913 DDC 622 s 622/.3424 19
TN23 .U43 TN523

Walkiewicz, J. W. (John W.) Magnetic
properties of alloys containing mischmetal
cobalt, copper, iron, and magnesium /.
Avondale, MD , 1981. p. cm. LC Card
81-607845 DDC 622 s 620.1/697 19
TN23 .U43 TN690

Wong, M. M. (Morton Min), 1924- Martinez, G.
M. (George M.) Recovery of byproduct heavy
minerals from Oregon and Washington sand
and gravel operations /. Washington , 1981. p.
cm. LC Card 81-6080 DDC 622 s 622/.751 19
TN23 .U43 TN939

WOOD AS FUEL - MARKETING.
Dammann, J. C. Economies in fuel wood
supply firms in New Hampshire /. Durham,
N.H. [1979] ii, 23 p. : LC Card 80-620870
DDC 338.4/366265/09742 19
HD9757.N4 D35

WOOD - BONDING.
Adhesives in building construction /.
Washington, D.C. , 1978. iv, 160 p. : LC Card
77-600020 DDC 630 s 668/.3 19
S21 .A37 no. 516 TA455.A34

WOOD CHIPS - CONGRESSES.
Conference on Wood Chips for Fuel and
Energy, Clarkson College, 1978. Conference on
Wood Chips for Fuel and Energy, Clarkson
College, Potsdam, New York, January 11, 1978
/. [Albany, N.Y.] [1978] 181 p. : LC Card

80-621929 DDC 662/.65 19
TP324 .C66 1978

Wood, Lindsay W. An evaluation of the
eutrophication process in Lake George, based
on historical and 1978 limnological data / by
Lindsay W. Wood and G. Wolfgang Fuhs.
[Albany, N.Y.] : New York State Dept. of
Health, [1979] 73 p. : ill. ; 29 cm. (Environmental
health report . no. 5) "May 1979." Bibliography: p.
53-59. LC Card 80-622774 DDC 551.48/2/097475
19
*1. Eutrophication - New York - George, Lake. 2.
George, Lake. I. Fuhs, Georg Wolfgang, joint author. II.
Title. III. Series.*
QH96.8.E9 W66

WOOD-LOTS - OREGON.
Oregon. Dept. of Forestry. Nursery stock for
nonindustrial private forest lands in Oregon.
Salem, Or. [1979] x, 35, [22] p. : LC Card
79-623541 DDC 634.9/564/09795 19
SD398.42.O7 O73 1979

**WOOD-PULP INDUSTRY - ADDRESSES,
ESSAYS, LECTURES.**
Appropriate industrial technology for paper
products and small pulp mills. New York ,
1979. xiii, 149 p. : LC Card 80-108650 DDC
300 s 338.4/7676 19
JX1977 .A2 ID/232/3, no. 3

Wood residue utilization act . United States.
Congress. House. Committee on Agriculture.
Subcommittee on Forests. Washington , 1980.
iv, 226 p. ; LC Card 80-602766 DDC
346.7304/67513 19
KF27 .A348 1979b

WOOD - TROPICS.
Chudnoff, Martin. Tropical timbers of the world
/. Madison, Wis. [1980] iv, 826 p. ; LC Card
80-602127 DDC 674/.13/0913 19
SD434 .C48

WOOD-USING INDUSTRIES - ARKANSAS.
Bertelson, Daniel F. Arkansas forest industries,
1971 /. New Orleans , 1973. 29 p. : LC Card
80-505836 DDC 333.75/0976 s
338.4/7674/009767 19
SD11 .A45793 no. 38 HD9757.A9

**WOOD-USING INDUSTRIES - ARKANSAS -
STATISTICS.**
Bertelson, Daniel F. Arkansas forest industries,
1977 /. New Orleans, La. , 1980. 18 p. : LC
Card 81-600548 DDC 333.75/0976 s
338.1/7498/09767 19
SD11 .A45793 no. 75 HD9757.A9

WOOD-USING INDUSTRIES - MINNESOTA.
Blyth, James E. Primary forest products
industry & timber use, Minnesota, 1973 /. St.
Paul , 1979. 34 p. : LC Card 79-602962 DDC
333.75/0977 s 338.1/7498/09776 19
SD11 .A45533 no. 39 HD9757.M6

**WOOD-USING INDUSTRIES - SOUTHERN
STATES - DIRECTORIES.**
Directory of forest products industries in 125
Tennessee Valley counties. [Norris, Tenn.].
NYPL [JLM 80-908]

WOOD WASTE.
Johnson, Leonard R. Quantities and costs of
wood biomass in Idaho /. Moscow, Idaho ,
1979. 10 p. : LC Card 79-624515 DDC 333.79/38
19
TP360 .J58

**WOOD WASTE - LAW AND LEGISLATION -
UNITED STATES.**
United States. Congress. House. Committee on
Agriculture. Subcommittee on Forests. Wood
residue utilization act . Washington , 1980. iv,
226 p. ; LC Card 80-602766 DDC
346.7304/67513 19
KF27 .A348 1979b

Woodard, Fredrick, 1939- Love songs and new
spirituals . [Iowa City] , c1980. [23] p. ; LC
Card 80-125470 DDC 811/.008/0896073 19
PS591.N4 L63

WOODBURY COUNTY (IOWA) - MAPS.
United States. Soil Conservation Service.
Woodbury County, Iowa /. [Lincoln, Neb.]
[1979?] 1 map : LC Card 81-691180
G4153.W7 1979 .U5

Woodhull, S. Domestic violence bibliography :
available resources / compiled by S. Woodhull.
[Lansing] : Domestic Violence Prevention and
Treatment Board, Michigan Dept. of Social

Services, [1980] 7 leaves ; 28 cm. "July 1980."
LC Card 80-623994 DDC 016.3068/7 19
*1. Family violence - Bibliography. 2. Wife abuse -
Bibliography. 3. Family violence - United States -
Bibliography. 4. Wife abuse - United States -
Bibliography. I. Title.*
Z5703.4.F35 W66 HQ809

Woodman, Mary. Salads for all the year round /
by Mary Woodman. New York : Gordon, 1981.
p. cm. Reprint. Originally published: London :
Foulsham, 1930. (Foulsham's home library) ISBN
0-8490-3210-5 LC Card 81-4204 DDC 641.8/3
19
1. Salads. I. Title.
TX740 .W6 1981

Woodman, Richard W. (joint author) Stone, Eugene
F. Relationships between growth need strength
and other individual differences measures
employed in job design research /. West
Lafayette, Ind. , 1977. 17 leaves ; LC Card
78-101255 DDC 658/.001/9 s 658.3/1422 19
HD6483 .P8 no. 644 HF5549.5.J63

**Woodrow Wilson International Center for
Scholars.** Dorr, Steven R. Scholars' guide to
Washington, D.C., for Middle Eastern studies /.
Washington, D.C. , 1981. p. cm. ISBN
0-87474-372-9 LC Card 81-607073 DDC
956/.00720753 19
Z3013.6 .D67 DS61.9.U6

**Woodrow Wilson International Center for
Scholars. Kennan Institute for Advanced
Russian Studies.** see Kennan Institute for
Advanced Russian Studies.

Woodruff, C. M. Land resource overview of the
Capital Area Planning Council region, Texas : a
nontechnical guide / by C. M. Woodruff, Jr.
Austin, Tex. : Bureau of Economic Geology,
University of Texas at Austin, 1979. v, 29 p. :
ill., maps (1 fold. in pocket) ; 28 cm.
Bibliography: p. 28-29. LC Card 80-621668 DDC
333.73/09764 19
*1. Land use - Texas. 2. Land use - Texas - Planning. I.
Title.*
HD211.T4 W66

Woodruff, George A. Soil survey of San
Bernardino County, southwestern part,
California / [by George A. Woodruff] ; United
States Department of Agriculture, Soil
Conservation Service, in cooperation with
University of California, Agricultural
Experiment Station. [Washington] : The
Service, [1980] ii, 64 p., [2] fold. leaves of
plates : ill. ; 29 cm. Cover title. "Issued January
1980." LC Card 80-601256 DDC 631.4/7/79495 19
*1. Soils - California - San Bernardino Co. - Maps. I.
United States. Soil Conservation Service. II. California.
Agricultural Experiment Station, Berkeley. III. Title.*
S599.C2 W66

Woods, Henry J. Texas A & M Research
Foundation. Ballot access /. - [Washington]
1978. 4 v. in 1 ; **NYPL [*XME-9374]**

Woodward, William, 1951- Studds, Gerry E.
Central America, 1981 . Washington , 1981. vii,
33 p. ; LC Card 81-601664 DDC 320.9728 19
F1439 .S88

**WOODWORKERS - DISEASES AND
HYGIENE - CALIFORNIA - STATISTICS.**
California. Dept. of Industrial Relations.
Division of Labor Statistics and Research.
California sawmills and planing mills industry .
San Francisco , 1978. v, 26 p. ; LC Card
79-623207 DDC 312/.43/09794 19
RC965.W6 C28 1978

Woodworth, Patrick. The write occasion / by
Patrick Woodworth and Catharine Keech.
Berkeley, Calif. : University of California,
Berkeley, Bay Area Writing Project, c1980. v,
72 p. ; 22 cm. (Collaborative research study . no. 1)
Bibliography: p. 44-45. LC Card 81-100412 DDC
808/.042 19
*1. English language - Rhetoric. 2. Creative writing. I.
Keech, Catharine. II. Bay Area Writing Project. III.
Title. IV. Series.*
PE1408 .W676

**WOODY PLANTS - HAWAII - WAIMANALO
REGION - CATALOGS AND
COLLECTIONS.**
University of Hawaii at Manoa. Plant Science
Instructional Arboretum. A catalog of plants in
the Plant Science Instructional Arboretum,
College of Tropical Agriculture and Human

Resources, University of Hawaii /. [Honolulu] , 1981. p. cm.   LC Card 81-2897   DDC 582.16/061/074099691 19
SB171.U6 U54 1981

WOOL TRADE AND INDUSTRY - UNITED STATES - STATISTICS - PERIODICALS.
United States. Bureau of the Census. General imports of cotton, wool, and man-made fiber manufacturers. Washington.
NYPL *[JLM 80-725]*

Wooldridge, David D. Suspended sediment from truck traffic on forest roads, Meadow and Coal Creeks / by David D. Wooldridge. Seattle : College of Forest Resources, University of Washington, [1978] 33 p.: ill.; 28 cm. Microfilm.
1. Water - Pollution. 2. Forest roads. 3. Motor-trucks - Environmental aspects. 4. Sediment, Suspended. I. Washington (State). University. College of Forest Resources. II. Title.   **NYPL** *[*ZV-185 Reel 1]*

Woolls, Blanche. Conference on Networks for Networkers, Indianapolis, 1979. Networks for networkers . New York, N.Y. , London , 1980. xvi, 444 p. :   ISBN 0-7201-1599-X :   LC Card 80-40016
Z674.8 .C66 1979   **NYPL** *[*R-*HB 80-3875]*

Woolrich, Cornell, 1903-1968. The fantastic stories of Cornell Woolrich / edited by Charles G. Waugh and Martin H. Greenberg ; with an introduction by Francis M. Nevins, Jr. ; afterword by Barry N. Malzberg. Carbondale : Southern Illinois University Press, c1981. p. cm. (Alternatives) CONTENTS. - The moon of Montezuma -- The lamp of memory -- My lips destroy -- Music from the dark -- Jane Brown's body -- Speak to me of death -- Steps ... coming near -- I'm dangerous tonight -- Kiss of the cobra -- Somebody's clothes--somebody's life -- Vision of murder -- The blue ribbon.   ISBN 0-8093-1008-2   LC Card 81-4785   DDC 813/.54 19
1. Fantastic fiction, American. I. Waugh, Charles. II. Greenberg, Martin Harry. III. Title.
PS3515.O6455 A6 1981

Wootton, Edward M. Galloway Township (N.J.). Township Engineer. Tax map, Galloway Township, Atlantic County, N.J. /. [Mays Landing] [1933] 2 maps on 2 sheets :   LC Card 81-690328
G3814.G17 s24 .G3

Worcester, Ellen.
Doerr, David R. Proposition 13 assessment issues . [Sacramento CA] , 1980] 1 v. (various pagings) :   LC Card 81-620793   DDC 333.33/2/09794 19
HJ4121.C22 D63

No-property-tax cities after Proposition 13 : a briefing book / prepared by the staffs of the Assembly Revenue and Taxation Committee and the Assembly Local Government Committee for joint committee interim hearing, November 6, 1980, Rolling Hills Estates. Sacramento, CA : California State Assembly ; Sacramento, CA (Box 90, State Capitol, Sacramento, CA 95814) : May be purchased from Assembly Publications Office, [1980] iii, 52 p. ; 28 cm. Cover title. Prepared by Ellen Worcester, Bob Leland, and Julie Castelli Nauman.
LC Card 81-620796   DDC 352.1/352/09794 19
1. Property tax - California. 2. Municipal finance - California. 3. Intergovernmental fiscal relations - California. I. Leland, Bob. II. Castelli, Julie Nauman. III. California. Legislature. Assembly. Committee on Revenue and Taxation. IV. California. Legislature. Assembly. Committee on Local Government. V. Title.
HJ4121.C22 W67

WORD - PRICES - UNITED STATES.
United States. Congressional Budget Office. Forest Service timber sales . Washington, D.C. [1980] xviii, 64 p. ;   LC Card 80-602605   DDC 338.4/36748/0973 19
HD9754 .U546 1980

Work accidents in nonprofit membership organizations /. New York (State). Workmen's Compensation Board. [Albany?] [1976] v, 63 p. ;   LC Card 80-622882   DDC 368.4/1/009747 s 363.1/1/09747 19
HD7816.U7 N687 no. 32 HD7262.5.U6

Work after 65 . United States. Congress. Senate. Special Committee on Aging. Washington , 1980- v. ;   LC Card 80-603005   DDC 331.3/98/0973 19
KF26.5 .A3 1980

WORK ENVIRONMENT - HYGIENIC ASPECTS. see INDUSTRIAL HYGIENE.

WORK EXPERIENCE. see APPRENTICES; VOCATIONAL EDUCATION.

Work experience programs & supportive services administered by Department of Personnel. New York (City). Dept. of Personnel. New York.   **NYPL** *[JLN 80-76]*

Work force 1980. [1]- [Madison, Wis.] 1971- 28 cm. Irregular. "A cooperative analysis by Wisconsin Department of Administration, Bureau of Planning and Budget, Wisconsin Department of Local Affairs and Development, Division of Economic Development, Wisconsin Department of Industry, Labor and Human Relations, State Employment Service Division, Wisconsin State Manpower Council Staff." Each issue has also a distinctive title: e. g.: Industry projections; Occupational projections, etc., etc.
1. Employment forecasting - Wisconsin - Periodicals. 2. Labor supply - Wisconsin - Periodicals. I. Wisconsin. Bureau of Planning and Budget. II. Wisconsin. Division of Economic Development. III. Wisconsin. State Employment Service Division. IV. Wisconsin. State Manpower Council.   **NYPL** *[JLM 80-1016]*

WORK MEASUREMENT - BIBLIOGRAPHY.
United States. Defense Documentation Center. Performance measurement /. Alexandria, Va., 1976. 1 v. (various pagings)
NYPL *[*XME-9314]*

Work plan, Western Michigan University-Technical College, Ibadan Project in cooperation with the United States Agency for International Development. [Kalamazoo] : The University, 1966. vii, 53 leaves : ill. ; 28 cm. Contract AID/afr-300."   LC Card 81-450648   DDC 607/.116692 19
1. Technical College, Ibadan, Nigeria. I. Michigan. Western Michigan University, Kalamazoo. II. United States. Agency for International Development.
T173.I27 W67

WORK RELIEF. see PUBLIC SERVICE EMPLOYMENT.

A Workbook of informational data : Orientation Conference for Louisiana Legislators, March 3-March 5, 1980, Baton Rouge, Lousiana / prepared by the staff of the Louisiana Legislative Council. Baton Rouge, LA (P.O. Box 44012, Baton Rouge 70804) ; The Council, [1980?] xi leaves, 212 p. : ill. ; 28 cm. Bibliography: p. 209-212.   LC Card 81-620884   DDC 353.9763 19
1. Finance, Public - Louisiana. 2. Louisiana - Economic policy. 3. Louisiana - Social policy. I. Orientation Conference for Louisiana Legislators (1980 :Baton Rouge, La.).
HJ465 .W67

Worker adjustment to liberalized trade . Glenday, Graham. Washington, D.C. (1818 H St., N.W., Washington) , 1980. 86 p. :   LC Card 80-154970   DDC 362.8/5 19
HD5710.75.C2 G57

WORKERS. see LABOR AND LABORING CLASSES.

Workers and the evolving economy of the eighties . United States. Congress. Senate. Committee on Labor and Human Resources. Washington , 1981. iv, 387 p. :   LC Card 81-601377   DDC 331.12/042/0973 19
KF26 .L27 1980s

Workers' attitudes toward productivity . Clarke, Ronald H. Washington, D.C. , c1980. 35 p. :   ISBN 0-89834-026-8 (pbk.) :   LC Card 80-67758   DDC 331.11/8/0973 19
HD57 .C565

Workers (Communist) Party of America. see Communist Party of the United States of America.

Worker's compensation /. Oregon State Bar. Continuing Legal Education. [Portland] [1980] xiii, 196, 36 p. :   LC Card 81-620533   DDC 344.795/021 347.950421 19
KFO2742 .O74

Workers' compensation . Tannenbaum, Kenneth A. [Springfield, Ill.] [1980] 51 p. ;   LC Card 80-623567   DDC 338.4/336841/009773 19
HD7103.65.U6 T35

WORKERS' COMPENSATION - LAW AND LEGISLATION - OREGON.
Oregon State Bar. Continuing Legal Education. Worker's compensation /. [Portland] [1980]

xiii, 196, 36 p. :   LC Card 81-620533   DDC 344.795/021 347.950421 19
KFO2742 .O74

WORKERS' COMPENSATION - LAW AND LEGISLATION - UNITED STATES.
United States. Congress. House. Committee on Education and Labor. Subcommittee on Labor Standards. Oversight hearings on the Longshoremen's and Harbor Workers' Compensation Act. Supplement . Washington , 1980. v, 57 p. ;   LC Card 80-604153   DDC 344.73/0217 347.304217 19
KF27 .E348 1979d Suppl

United States. Congress. Senate. Committee on Labor and Human Resources. Asbestos Health Hazards Compensation Act of 1980 . Washington , 1980 [i.e. 1981] iv, 367 p. :   LC Card 81-600863   DDC 344.73/0217 347.304217 19
KF26 .L27 1980p

United States. Congress. Senate. Committee on Labor and Human Resources. Oversight on the Longshoremen's and Harbor Workers' Compensation Act, 1980 . Washington , 1981. v, 472 p. :   LC Card 81-601328   DDC 353.0082/56 19
KF26 .L27 1980t

WORKERS' COMPENSATION - UNITED STATES.
United States. Congress. Senate. Committee on Labor and Human Resources. Oversight on the Longshoremen's and Harbor Workers' Compensation Act, 1980 . Washington , 1981. v, 472 p. :   LC Card 81-601328   DDC 353.0082/56 19
KF26 .L27 1980t

Workers covered under Ohio unemployment compensation law, by industrial group. RS 203.1. Ohio. Bureau of Employment Services. Division of Research and Statistics. Columbus.
NYPL *[JLM 81-25]*

Workers Party of America. see Communist Party of the United States of America.

Workers 45 and over in Hawaii. Hawaii. Dept. of Labor and Industrial Relations. Honolulu, Hawaii [1980] 16 p. :   LC Card 80-622184   DDC 331.3/9 19
HD6281.H3 H38 1980

Working children. Washington. tables. 23 cm. Report year for 1966/68 ends June 30; for 1968/69- ends June 20. Issued by the Wage and Hour and Public Contracts Divisions, U. S. Dept. of Labor, 1966/68; by the Wage and Hour Division, Wage and Labor Standards Administration, U. S. Dept. of Labor, 1968/69-
1. Children - Employment - United States - Periodicals. I. United States. Wage and Hour and Public Contracts Divisions. II. United States. Employment Standards Administration. Wage and Hour Division.
NYPL *[JLL 80-212]*

Working-class life . Shergold, Peter R., 1946- Pittsburgh, Pa. , c1981. p. cm.   ISBN 0-8229-3802-2   LC Card 81-50921   DDC 339.4/7/0973 19
HD6983 .S45

WORKING-CLASSES. see LABOR AND LABORING CLASSES.

WORKING-DAY. see HOURS OF LABOR.

WORKING LIFE. see LIFE SPAN, PRODUCTIVE.

WORKING-MEN'S ASSOCIATIONS. see TRADE-UNIONS.

WORKING-MEN'S LUNCH ROOMS. see RESTAURANTS, LUNCH ROOMS, ETC.

Working papers . Carruth, Hayden, 1921- [Selections.] Athens , c1981. p. cm.   ISBN 0-8203-0583-9   LC Card 81-4404   DDC 809/.04 19
PN771 .C336

Working with history . Noggle, Burl. Baton Rouge , c1981. p. cm.   ISBN 0-8071-0881-2 :   LC Card 81-5789   DDC 976.3 19
F369 .N63

WORKING WIVES. see WIVES - EMPLOYMENT.

WORKINGMEN. see LABOR AND LABORING CLASSES.

Workloads in the Department of Veterans Benefits and the Board of Veterans Appeals . United States. Congress. House. Committee on Veterans' Affairs. Subcommittee on Compensation, Pension, Insurance, and Memorial Affairs. Washington , 1980. iii, 45 p. ; LC Card 80-603663 DDC 353.0081/2 19
KF27 .V43 1980d

Workman, Clark M. (joint author) Lopp, Thomas G. Fish, fresh, chilled, or frozen, whether or not whole, but not otherwise prepared or preserved, from Canada . Washington, D.C. [1980] vi, 32, 121 p. ; LC Card 80-602376 DDC 382/.4566494 19
HF2651.F5 U44

Workman's compensation insurance . Illinois. General Assembly. Insurance Study Commission. Workmen's Compensation Insurance Subcommittee. [Springfield] , 1977. 74 p. ; LC Card 77-624212
KFI1542 .A25 1977 **NYPL [*XME-9540]**

WORKMEN'S COMPENSATION - ILLINOIS.
Illinois. General Assembly. Insurance Study Commission. Workmen's Compensation Insurance Subcommittee. Workman's compensation insurance . [Springfield] , 1977. 74 p. ; LC Card 77-624212
KFI1542 .A25 1977 **NYPL [*XME-9540]**

WORKMEN'S COMPENSATION - ILLINOIS - COST CONTROL.
Tannenbaum, Kenneth A. Workers' compensation . [Springfield, Ill.] [1980] 51 p. ; LC Card 80-623567 DDC 338.4/336841/009773 19
HD7103.65.U6 T35

WORKMEN'S COMPENSATION - MAINE.
Maine. Laws, statutes, etc. [Workers' compensation act.] Maine Workers' compensation act and Occupational disease law /. Augusta, Me. , 1979. 66 p. ; LC Card 80-622036 DDC 344.741/021/02632 19
KFM342.A3329 A2 1979

WORKMEN'S COMPENSATION - NEBRASKA.
Nebraska. Court Rules. Workmen's Compensation Court. Rules of procedure of the Nebraska Workmen's Compensation Court. Lincoln, Neb. [1978] 23 p. ; LC Card 78-111321 DDC 344.782/021/0269 19
KFN342.A435 A2 1978

WORKMEN'S COMPENSATION - NEW JERSEY.
New Jersey. Commission of Investigation. Interim report and recommendations of the State of New Jersey Commission of Investigation on incorrect injury leave practices in the counties. [Trenton, N.J. , 1979?] 64 p. ; LC Card 79-623334 DDC 352/.005164/09749 19
HD5115.6.U52 N56 1979

New Jersey. Legislature. Senate. Labor, Industry and Professions Committee. Public hearing before the Senate Labor, Industry & Proffessions [sic] Committee and the Assembly Labor Committee on workers' compensation, administrative aspects . [Trenton] [1979] 30 p. ; LC Card 79-625599
KFN1811.3 .L3 1979 **NYPL [*XMF-13771]**

WORKMEN'S COMPENSATION - NEW YORK (STATE)
New York (State). Joint Labor/Management Committee. 1978 report to the Governor and the legislature, January 1, 1978-October 15, 1978 /. [Albany] [1979] 11, [33] p. ; LC Card 79-624386 DDC 344.747/021 19
KFN5010.62 .L3 1979

New York (State). Legislature. Assembly. Standing Committee on Labor. Compilation of public hearing testimony on Assembly bill no. 7 . [Albany, N.Y.] [1979?] 151 p. ; LC Card 80-621872 DDC 344.747/021 19
KFN5010.4 .L3 1979

WORKMEN'S COMPENSATION - NEW YORK (STATE) - STATISTICS.
New York (State). Workmen's Compensation Board. Work accidents in nonprofit membership organizations /. [Albany?] [1976] v, 63 p. ; LC Card 80-622882 DDC 368.4/1/009747 s 363.1/1/09747 19
HD7816.U7 N687 no. 32 HD7262.5.U6

WORKMEN'S COMPENSATION - NORTH DAKOTA.
North Dakota. Laws, statutes, etc. [Workmen's compensation act.] North Dakota Workmen's compensation act and Crime victims reparations act and rules of procedure, effective July 1, 1979 /. [Bismarck] [1979] 105 p. ; LC Card 80-621922 DDC 344.784/021/02632 19
KFN8942.A335 A2 1979

WORKMEN'S COMPENSATION - UNITED STATES.
Research report of the Interdepartmental Workers' Compensation Task Force. Washington, 1979. 1 v.;
NYPL [JLM 80-745]

United States. Congress. House. Committee on Education and Labor. Subcommittee on Labor Standards. Oversight hearings on the Federal employees' compensation act . Washington, D.C. , 1980- v. : LC Card 80-603447 DDC 353.0082/56 19
KF27 .E348 1980a

United States. Congress. House. Committee on Education and Labor. Subcommittee on Labor Standards. Oversight hearings on the Longshoremen's and harbor workers' compensation act . Washington , 1980. viii, 1231 p. : LC Card 80-603416 DDC 353.0082/56 19
KF27 .E348 1979d

United States. Congress. House. Committee on Ways and Means. Subcommittee on Public Assistance and Unemployment Compensation. Unemployment compensation benefits to servicemen released for the good of the service . Washington , 1979. iii, 28 p. ; LC Card 80-600678 DDC 343.73/0116 19
KF27 .W3464 1979c

United States. General Accounting Office. Multiple problems with the 1974 amendments to the Federal employees' compensation act . [Washington] , 1979. vi, 85 p. ; LC Card 79-602706 DDC 344.73/0217 19
KF3626 .A85

WORKMEN'S COMPENSATION - UNITED STATES - BIBLIOGRAPHY.
United States. Dept. of Labor. Library. Black lung benefits program . Washington, D.C. [1979] iii, 28 p. ; LC Card 80-601667 DDC 016.3684/1 19
Z7164.L1 U686 1979 HD7116.M6152

WORKMEN'S COMPENSATION - UNITED STATES - STATES.
United States. Congress. House. Committee on Education and Labor. Subcommittee on Labor Standards. National workers' compensation standards act of 1979 . Washington , 1980. vi, 815 p. : LC Card 80-603427 DDC 344.73/021 19
KF27 .E348 1980c

United States. Congress. Senate. Committee on Labor and Human Resources. National workers' compensation standards act of 1979 . Washington , 1980. vi, 794 p. : LC Card 80-602897 DDC 344.73/021 19
KF26 .L27 1979y

WORKMEN'S COMPENSATION - VIRGINIA.
Virginia. General Assembly. House of Delegates. Committee on Labor and Commerce. Workmen's Compensation Subcommittee. Report of the Workmen's Compensation Subcommittee of the House Committee on Labor and Commerce to the Governor and the General Assembly of Virginia. Richmond , 1980. 202 p. ; LC Card 80-623143 DDC 300/.9755 s 368.4/1/009755 19
J87 .V9 1980c no. 39 KFV2411.82.L

Workplace and higher education . United States. Congress. Senate. Committee on Labor and Human Resources. Washington , 1980. v, 336 p. ; LC Card 80-604012 DDC 378.73 19
KF26 .L27 1979z

Works of art selected from collections of alumni of the University of Michigan: [exhibition].
Michigan. University. Museum of Art. [Ann Arbor, Mich.], 1967. xiv, 41 p., [62] p. of plates:
NYPL [3-MAW (Ann Arbor) 80-1921]

Workshop for Ethnographers and Single State Agency Policymakers and Planners, Chicago, 1979. Ethnography : a research tool for policymakers in the drug & alcohol fields / editors, Carl Akins, George Beschner. Rockville, Md. : U. S. Dept. of Health and Human Services, Public Health Service, Alcohol, Drug Abuse, and Mental Health Administration, National Institute on Drug Abuse, 1980. xvi, 128 p. ; 23 cm. (DHHS publication. no. (ADM) 80-946) On cover: National Institute on Drug Abuse, Services Research Branch. "NIDA contract no. 271-78-4609." Includes bibliographies. LC Card 80-602292 DDC 362.2/9 19
1. Drug abuse - Research - Congresses. 2. Ethnology - Methodology - Congresses. 3. Alcoholism - Research - Congresses. I. Akins, Carl. II. Beschner, George M. III. National Institute on Drug Abuse. Services Research Branch. IV. Series: United States. Dept. of Health and Human Services. DHHS publication, no. (ADM) 80-946. V. Title.
HV5809 .W67 1979

Workshop for Serving the Deaf-Blind and Multihandicapped Child, Honolulu, 1977.
Workshop for Serving the Deaf-Blind and Multihandicapped Child : identification, assessment, and training : proceedings. Sacramento : California State Dept. of Education, 1979. vi, 69 p. : ill. ; 28 cm. Includes bibliographical references. LC Card 79-625563 DDC 362.4 19
1. Blind-deaf - Congresses.
HV1597 .W58 1977

Workshop on Auto Theft Prevention, National. see **National Workshop on Auto Theft Prevention, New York, 1978.**

Workshop on Behavioral Toxicology, National Institutes of Health, 1975. Proceedings / Workshop on Behavioral Toxicology. [Bethesda, Md.] : U. S. Dept. of Health, Education, and Welfare, Public Health Service, National Institutes of Health, Toxicology Study Section, Division of Research Grants, [1976?] v, 109 p. : ill. ; 27 cm. (DHEW publication. no. (NIH) 76-1189) Includes bibliographies. LC Card 77-601979
1. Toxicology - Congresses. 2. Psychopharmacology - Congresses. 3. Toxicology, Experimental - Congresses. I. United States. National Institutes of Health. Toxicology Study Section.
RA1191 .W67 1975 **NYPL [JSF 81-141]**

Workshop on Biological X-ray Microanalysis by Electron Beam Excitation, Boston, 1977.
Microbeam analysis in biology / edited by Claude P. Lechene, Ronald R. Warner. New York : Academic Press, 1979. xx, 672 p. : ill. ; 24 cm. Sponsored by the Division of Research Resources, National Institutes of Health. Includes bibliographies and index. ISBN 0-12-440340-9 LC Card 79-24948
1. X-ray microanalysis - Congresses. I. Lechene, Claude P. II. Warner, Ronald R. III. United States. National Institutes of Health. Division of Research Resources. IV. Title.
QH324.9.X2 W67 1977
NYPL [JSE 80-1320]

Workshop on Earth Radiation Budget Science, Williamsburg, Va., 1978. Earth radiation budget science, 1978 : proceedings of a workshop / sponsored by NASA Langley Research Center, in cooperation with Colorado State University, and held at Williamsburg, Virginia, March 28-30, 1978. [Washington, D.C.] : NASA, Scientific and Technical Branch ; Springfield, Va. : for sale by National Technical Information Service, 1979. vi, 72 p. : ill. ; 28 cm. (NASA conference publication. 2100) Includes bibliographies. LC Card 80-601801 DDC 551.5/272 19
1. Energy budget (Geophysics) - Remote sensing - Congresses. 2. Climatology - Congresses. 3. Solar radiation - Congresses. 4. Astronautics in geophysics - Congresses. I. United States, Langley Research Center, Hampton, Va. II. Colorado. State University, Fort Collins. III. Series: United States. National Aeronautics and Space Administration. NASA conference publication , 2100. IV. Title.
QC809.E6 W67 1978

Workshop on Eddy Current Nondestructive Testing, (1977 : National Bureau of Standards) Eddy current nondestructive testing : proceedings of the Workshop on Eddy Current Nondestructive Testing, held at the National Bureau of Standards, Gaithersburg, Maryland, on November 3-4, 1977 / edited by George M. Free. Washington, D.C. : U. S.

Dept. of Commerce, National Bureau of
Standards : For sale by the Supt. of Docs., U.
S. G.P.O., 1981. viii, 158 p. : ill. ; 26 cm. (NBS
special publication . 589) "Center for Absolute Physical
Quantities, National Measurement Laboratory, National
Bureau of Standards." "Issued January 1981." S/N
003-003-02287-0 Item 247 Includes bibliographical
references. LC Card 80-600172 DDC 602/.18 s
620.1/67 19
*1. Electric testing - Congresses. 2. Eddy currents
(Electric) - Congresses. I. Free, George M. II. United
States. National Bureau of Standards. III. Center for
Absolute Physical Quantities (U. S.). IV. Title. V.
Series.*
QC100 .U57 no. 589 TA417.35

**Workshop on Energy Conservation in Cities,
Library of Congress, 1978.** Energy
conservation in cities / prepared for the
Subcommittee on Advanced Energy
Technologies and Energy Conservation
Research, Development, and Demonstration of
the Committee on Science and Technology, U.
S. House of Representatives, Ninety-fifth
Congress, second session, by the Congressional
Research Service, Library of Congress.
Washington : U. S. Govt. Print. Off. : for sale
by the Supt. of Docs., U. S. Govt. Print. Off.,
1979. vii, 117 p. : ill. ; 24 cm. (Foresight . v. 2)
At head of title: Committee print. Proceedings of a
workshop held Oct. 19, 1978, sponsored by the
Congressional Research Service, Library of Congress.
"Serial ZZZ." "December 1978." Includes bibliographical
references. LC Card 80-602834 DDC
333.79/16/0973 19
*1. Cities and towns - United States - Energy
conservation. I. United States. Library of Congress.
Congressional Research Service. II. United States.
Congress. House. Committee on Science and
Technology. Subcommittee on Advanced Energy
Technologies and Energy Conservation Research,
Development, and Demonstration. III. Title. IV. Series.*
TJ163.4.U6 W67 1978

**Workshop on Gas Turbine Combustor Design
Problems, Project Squid. see Project Squid
Workshop on Gas Turbine Combustor Design
Problems, Purdue University, 1978.**

**Workshop on Management Techniques Applied
to Archeology, Texas Tech University, 1977.**
Scholars as managers, or how can the managers
do it better : report of a workshop on
management techniques in archeology / edited
by Alice W. Portnoy ; formal contributions
from Jerry Alexander ... [et al.] ; informal
contributions from Phil Bandy ... [et al.].
Washington : U. S. Dept. of the Interior,
Cultural Resource Management Studies, Office
of Archeology and Historic Preservation
Division, Heritage Conservation and Recreation
Service, Interagency Archeological Services,
1978. vii, 21 p., [2] leaves of plates : ill. ; 28
cm. "Prepared under contract to Interagency
Archeological Services, Office of Archeology and
Historic Preservation, Heritage Conservation and
Recreation Service, Washington, D.C.; Cultural
Resources Institute, Department of Anthropology,
Texas Tech University, Lubbock, Texas." Includes
bibliographies. LC Card 79-602641
*1. Archaeology - Congresses. 2. Public contracts -
United States - Congresses. 3. United States -
Antiquities - Congresses. 4. Indians of North America -
Antiquities - Congresses. I. Portnoy, Alice W. II.
United States. Interagency Archeological Services
Division. III. Texas Tech University. Cultural Resources
Institute. IV. Title.*
CC51 .W67 1977

**Workshop on Operational Applications of
Satellite Snowcover Observations, Sparks,
Nev., 1979.** Operational applications of
satellite snowcover observations : proceedings of
a final workshop sponsored by the National
Aeronautics and Space Administration and the
University of Nevada, Reno, and held at
Sparks, Nevada, April 16-17, 1979 / editors,
Albert Rango, Ralph Peterson. Washington,
D.C. : NASA, Scientific and Technical
Information Office, 1980. vi, 301 p. : ill. ; 23
cm. (NASA conference publication . 2116) Includes
bibliographies. LC Card 80-602361 DDC
551.57/846 19
*1. Snow - Congresses. 2. Hydrological forecasting -
Congresses. 3. Runoff - Congresses. 4. Astronautics in
hydrology - Congresses. I. Rango, Albert. II. Peterson,
Ralph. III. United States. National Aeronautics and
Space Administration. IV. University of Nevada, Reno.*

*V. Series: United States. National Aeronautics and
Space Administration. NASA conference publication ,
2116. VI. Title.*
GB2601.72.A83 W67 1979

**Workshop on "Remote sensing and Problems of
the Hydrosphere" 1979 : Warner Springs,
Calif.)** Remote sensing and problems of the
hydrosphere . Washington, D.C. [Springfield,
Va.] 1979. v, 56 p. : LC Card 81-601298 DDC
551.4/028/7 19
TD370 .R45

**Workshop on Research Needed to Improve the
Quality of Socioeconomic Data Used in
Regulatory Decisionmaking, Library of
Congress, 1979.** Workshop on Research
Needed to Improve the Quality of
Socioeconomic Data Used in Regulatory
Decisionmaking : summary and proceedings /
prepared for the Subcommittee on Science,
Research and Technology of the Committee on
Science, and Technology, U. S. House of
Representatives, Ninety-sixth Congress, second
session, by the Science Policy Research
Division, Congressional Research Service,
Library of Congress. Washington : U. S. Govt.
Print. Off., 1980. xiii, 296 p. ; 24 cm. "May
1980." Includes bibliographical references. LC Card
80-602262 DDC 361.6/1/072073 19
*1. Policy sciences - Cost effectiveness - Congresses. 2.
Public administration - Cost effectiveness - Congresses.
3. Administrative agencies - United States - Congresses.
I. United States. Congress. House. Committee on
Science and Technology. Subcommittee on Science,
Research, and Technology. II. United States. Library of
Congress. Science Policy Research Division.*
H22 .W67 1979

**Workshop on Soybeans for Tropical and
Subtropical Conditions, University of Puerto
Rico Mayagüez Campus, 1974.** Proceedings
of the Workshop on Soybeans for Tropical and
Subtropical Conditions, February 4-6, 1974,
University of Puerto Rico Mayagüez campus.
[Urbana] : College of Agriculture, University of
Illinois at Urbana-Champaign, 1974, 1978
printing. 184 p. : ill. ; 28 cm. (INTSOY series .
no. 2) International agricultural publications "Sponsored
by the International Soybean Program." Includes
bibliographies. LC Card 80-620583 DDC
635/.655/0913 19
*1. Soybean - Tropics - Congresses. I. International
Soybean Program. II. Series.*
SB205.S7 W65 1974

**Workshop on Switching Requirements and R &
D for Fusion Reactors, Palo Alto, Calif.,
1976.** Proceedings of the Workshop on
Switching Requirements and R&D for Fusion
Reactors, Palo Alto, California, March 24-26,
1976/prepared by Department of Electrical
Engineering, Texas Tech University ...;
coordinator, M. Kristiansen. Palo Alto : Electric
Power Research Institute, 1977. 1 v. of various
pagings : ill.; 28 cm. "EPRI ER-376-SR. Special
report." Includes bibliographies.
*1. Fusion reactors - Congresses. I. Kristiansen, M. II.
Texas Tech University, Dept. of Electrical Engineering.
III. Electric Power Research Institute. IV. Title.*
NYPL [JSF 80-697]

**Workshop on Terrestrial Microcosms, Newport,
Or., 1977.** Terrestrial microcosms : the
proceedings of the Workshop on Terrestrial
Microcosms, Symposium on Terrestrial
Microcosms and Environmental Chemistry /
edited by James W. Gillett and James M. Witt ;
technical editor, C. J. Wyatt ; prepared for the
National Science Foundation, Directorate for
Applied Science and Research Applications,
Division of Problem-Focused Research
Applications. [Washington] : The Foundation,
[1978?] xii, 35 p. : ill. ; 28 cm. "NSF/RA 790034."
Bibliography : 29-30. LC Card 79-602306 DDC
574.5/264 19
*1. Energy - Technique - Congresses. 2. Ecology -
Research - Congresses. 3. Biological models -
Congresses. I. Gillett, James W. II. Witt, James M. III.
Symposium on Terrestrial Microcosms and
Environmental Chemistry, Oregon State University,
1977. IV. United States. National Science Foundation.
Division of Problem-Focused Research Applications. V.
Title.*
QH541.28 .W67 1977

**Workshop on the Estuarine Survival of Salmon,
Juneau, Alaska, 1979.** Proceedings of the
Workshop on the Estuarine Survival of Salmon,

Juneau, Alaska, February 8, 1979 / compiled
by Raymond S. Hadley. Fairbanks, Alaska :
Alaska Sea Grant Program, University of
Alaska, 1979. 38 p. ; 28 cm. (Alaska sea grant
report. 79-10) LC Card 80-621846 DDC 597/.55 19
*1. Pacific salmon - Congresses. 2. Fish habitat
improvement - Alaska - Congresses. 3. Estuarine
ecology - Alaska - Congresses. 4. Fish-culture -
Alaska - Congresses. 5. Fishes - Alaska - Ecology -
Congresses. I. Hadley, Raymond S. II. Alaska Sea
Grant Program. III. Title.*
QL638.S2 W67 1979

**WORKSHOPS FOR HANDICAPPED. see
SHELTERED WORKSHOPS.**

**Workshops in employee development for state
and local training officers.** United States. Civil
Service Commission. Bureau of Training.
Personnel Management Training Center.
Instructors' guide for workshop in employee
development /. [Washington?] , 1973. 305 p. in
various pagings : *NYPL [JLF 80-1341]*

**Workshops on Life Safety for the Handicapped,
Washington, D.C. and Sacramento, Calif.,
1979.** Conference on Fire Safety for the
Handicapped, National Bureau of Standards,
1979. Fire and life safety for the handicapped .
Washington, D.C. , 1980. ix, 144 p. ; LC Card
80-600082 DDC 602/.18 s 362.4/38 19
QC100 .U57 no. 585 TH9112

**The World Administrative Radio Conference and
international communications policy .** United
States. Congress. House. Committee on Foreign
Affairs. Subcommittee on International
Operations. Washington , 1980. iii, 135 p. : LC
Card 80-603991 DDC 384.54 19
KF27 .F647 1979e

World auto trade . United States. Congress.
House. Committee on Ways and Means.
Subcommittee on Trade. Washington , 1980. iv,
363 p. : LC Card 80-602773 DDC 338.4/76292 19
KF27 .W348 1980a

WORLD BANK.
United States. Congress. House. Committee on
Banking, Finance and Urban Affairs.
Subcommittee on International Development
Institutions and Finance. U. S. participation in
the multilateral development institutions .
Washington , 1981. iii, 258 p. ; LC Card
81-601948 DDC 332.1/53 19
KF27 .B547 1981

**World Bank. Agriculture and Rural Development
Dept. Resource Planning Unit.** Nepal /
prepared by the Resource Planning Unit,
Agriculture and Rural Development
Department, World Bank ; cartographic drafting
by Williams and Heintz Map Corp.,
Washington, D.C. ; compilation, design, and
supervision by W. Drewes and K. Willett,
World Bank. Washington, D.C. : World Bank,
1980. 1 remote sensing image on 2 sheets :
col. ; 72 x 169 cm., sheets 78 x 85 cm. and 78
x 95 cm. Relief shown by spot heights. "The Universal
transverse Mercator (UTM) grid overlay is based on the
Everest geodetic system." Distinctive recent map.
Includes location map, index to Landsat coverage,
"Stereoscopic pair of the Kathmandu Valley images,"
and insets of "Kathmandu Valley" and "Kathmandu
streets in city center." CONTENTS. - Western sheet --
Eastern sheet. LC Card 81-692612
*1. Nepal - Photo maps. I. Drewes, Wolfram U. II.
Willett, K. III. Williams and Heintz Map Corporation.*
G7761.A4 1980 .W6

**World Bank. East Asia and Pacific Regional
Office.** Indonesia--employment and income
distribution in Indonesia. Washington, D.C. ,
c1980. 2, xiii, 187 p. ; LC Card 80-138441 DDC
331.1/09598 19
HD5824.A6 I53

**World Bank. Employment and Rural
Development Division.**
Indonesia--employment and income distribution
in Indonesia. Washington, D.C. , c1980. 2, xiii,
187 p. ; LC Card 80-138441 DDC 331.1/09598 19
HD5824.A6 I53

**World Bank. Population and Human Resources
Division.** Indonesia--employment and income
distribution in Indonesia. Washington, D.C. ,
c1980. 2, xiii, 187 p. ; LC Card 80-138441 DDC
331.1/09598 19
HD5824.A6 I53

World Coal Study.
 COAL--BRIDGE TO THE FUTURE.
 United States. Congress. House. Committee
 on Interstate and Foreign Commerce.
 Subcommittee on Energy and Power. Final
 report of the World Coal Study .
 Washington , 1980. iii, 88 p. : LC Card
 80-603074 DDC 333.8/22 19
 KF27 .I5542 1980c

**World Conference on the United Nations Decade
 for Women, Copenhagen, 1980.** United
 States. Women's Bureau. Employment goals of
 the world . Washington, D.C. [1980] vi, 54,
 [22] p. : LC Card 80-602858 DDC
 331.4/133/0973 19
 HD6095 .U54 1980

**World Conference to Combat Racism and Racial
 Discrimination, Geneva, 1978.** United
 Nations. General Assembly. Committee on the
 Elimination of Racial Discrimination.
 Committee on the Elimination of Racial
 Discrimination and the progress made towards
 the achievement of the objectives of the
 International Convention on the Elimination of
 All Forms of Racial Discrimination . New
 York , 1979. vi, 35 p. ; LC Card 80-115627
 DDC 300 s 341.4/81 19
 JX1977 .A2 CERD/1 HT1521

**World Data Center A for Solid Earth
 Geophysics.**
 Poppe, Barbara B. Directory of world
 seismograph stations. Boulder, Colo. , 1980- v.
 <1, pt. 1 > : LC Card 80-603927 DDC 551 s
 551.2/2/2025 19
 QE500 .W67a no. 25 QE540.U6

Report
 (SE-14) United States. Geodynamics
 Committee. Working Group 10b on Data
 Centers and Repositories. Directory of U. S.
 data repositories supporting the International
 Geodynamics Project /. Boulder, Colo. ,
 1978. v, 40 p. ; LC Card 79-109815 DDC 551
 s 551/.072 19
 QE500 .W67a no. 14 QE501

Report SE .
 (13) International Association of Seismology
 and the Physics of the Earth's Interior.
 European Seismological Commission.
 Working Group on Statistical Methods.
 Bibliography of statistical aspects of
 seismicity /. Boulder, Colo. , 1978. iv, 74 p. ;
 LC Card 79-603198 DDC 551 551.2/2/072 19
 QE500 .W67a no. 13 Z6033.E1 QE539

United States. Geodynamics Committee.
 Working Group 10b on Data Centers and
 Repositories. Directory of U. S. data
 repositories supporting the International
 Geodynamics Project /. Boulder, Colo. , 1978.
 v, 40 p. ; LC Card 79-109815 DDC 551 s
 551/.072 19
 QE500 .W67a no. 14 QE501

World economic outlook. [Washington, D. C.]
 Washington, International Monetary Fund. 28
 cm.
 *1. Economic forecasting - Periodicals. I. International
 Monetary Fund.*
 NYPL [*R-Econ. 81-251 & JLM 81-268]

World economic trends : implications for Europe
 and the southeastern U. S. / [sponsored by]
 Georgia World Congress Institute, cosponsored
 by Credit suisse. Atlanta, Ga. : The Institute,
 [1979 or 1980] iii leaves, 33 p. ; 28 cm.
 (Conference series - Georgia World Congress Institute ;
 no. 6) Summary, papers, and discussion from a round
 table meeting held at the Georgia World Congress
 Center, Atlanta, May 23, 1979. Edited by R. P.
 Sheehan. LC Card 80-132705 DDC 337/.09/04 19
 *1. International economic relations - Congresses. 2.
 Investments, Foreign - Southern States - Congresses. 3.
 International finance - Congresses. I. Sheehan, Regis P.
 II. Georgia World Congress Institute. III. Crédit suisse.
 IV. Series: Georgia World Congress Institute.
 Conference series - Georgia World Congress Institute ,
 no. 6.*
 HF1410.5 .W67

**WORLD ECONOMICS. see COMMERCIAL
 POLICY; COMPETITION,
 INTERNATIONAL; ECONOMIC POLICY;
 GEOGRAPHY, ECONOMIC.**

The world encompassed . Boorstin, Daniel J.
 (Daniel Joseph), 1914- Washington , 1981. 11
 p. ; ISBN 0-8444-0369-5 LC Card 81-607916

DDC 027.573 19
 Z733.U58 B65

The world encompassed . Scammell, Geoffrey
 Vaughn. Berkeley , 1981. p. cm. ISBN
 0-520-04422-3 LC Card 81-4302 DDC 940.1
 19
 D104 .S35

**World Health Organization. Expert Committee
 on Cancer Statistics.** United States. National
 Center for Health Statistics. Social and
 economic implications of cancer in the United
 States . Hyattsville, Md. , Washington [1981].
 iv, 43 p. : ISBN 0-8406-0203-0 LC Card
 80-607176 DDC 362.1/96994 19
 RC276 .U56 1981

World industry since 1960 . United Nations.
 Industrial Development Organization. New
 York , 1979. xviii, 422 p. : LC Card 80-105073
 DDC 300 s 338.09/046 19
 JX1977 .A2 ID/CONF.4/2(ID/229)

WORLD LITERATURE. see LITERATURE.

WORLD MAPS.
 (1900) United States. Hydrographic Office.
 Division of Chart Construction. Tracks for full
 powered steam vessels with the shortest
 navigable distances in nautical miles /.
 Washington , 1900. 1 map : LC Card 81-690532
 G3201.P54 1900 .U5

(1976) United States. Central Intelligence
 Agency. World plotting series /. Washington
 [1976] 7 maps : 77 x 59 cm. or smaller. Scale
 1:18,000,000. "Lambert conformal conic, standard
 parallels 37°N and 65°N." "This map is designed to be
 used in conjunction with automated cartographic
 systems." 540931-540937. Includes "Index to sheets."
 "Series 1147." LC Card 79-691244
 G3201.A1 s18000 .U6
 NYPL [Map. Div. 80-3396]

(1978) United States. Central Intelligence
 Agency. Application of Soviet pressure,
 1946-53. [Washington , 1978] 1 map : LC Card
 81-690523
 G5701.F33 1953 .U5

(1978) United States. Central Intelligence
 Agency. Changing face of Europe and colonial
 tension, late 1945. [Washington , 1978] 1 map :
 LC Card 81-690522
 G5701.F33 1945 .U5

(1978) United States. Central Intelligence
 Agency. Collapse of colonial system, 1953-68.
 [Washington , 1978] 1 map : LC Card 81-690524
 G5701.F33 1968 .U5

(1978) United States. Central Intelligence
 Agency. Major European colonial empires on
 the eve of World War II, 1938. [Washington ,
 1978] 1 map : LC Card 81-690521
 G5701.F33 1938 .U5

(1978) United States. Central Intelligence
 Agency. Recent Soviet gains and possible
 targets, 1978. [Washington , 1978] 1 map : LC
 Card 81-690525
 G7001.F35 1978 .U5

(1980) United States. Central Intelligence
 Agency. Political map of the world .
 [Washington , 1980] 1 map : LC Card 81-690682
 G3200 1980 .U5

(1980) United States. Central Intelligence
 Agency. Selected world shipping lanes and
 straits. [Washington , 1980] 1 map : LC Card
 81-690686
 G3201.P54 1980 .U5

(1980) United States. Central Intelligence
 Agency. Standard time zones of the world.
 [Washington , 1980] 1 map : LC Card 81-690683
 G3201.B2 1980 .U5

(1980) United States. Central Intelligence
 Agency. 200-nautical-mile claims, January 1980.
 [Washington , 1980] 1 map : LC Card 81-690684
 G3201.F3 1980 .U5

**World Meteorological Organization. Global
 Atmospheric Research Programme. see
 Global Atmospheric Research Program.**

The world of the citizen in republican Rome /.
 Nicolet, Claude, 1930- [Métier de citoyen dans
 la Rome républicaine. English.] Berkeley , 1980.
 435 p. ; ISBN 0-520-03545-3 LC Card 77-80474
 DDC 323.6/0937 19
 DG83.1 .N513 1980b

The world oil market in the years ahead . United
 States. Central Intelligence Agency. Office of
 Economic Research. Washington , 1979. ix, 80
 p. : LC Card 79-603266
 HD9565.6 .U53 1979

World petroleum availability, 1980-2000. United
 States. Congress. Office of Technology
 Assessment. Washington, D.C. [1980] vii, 77
 p. : LC Card 80-600164 DDC 338.2/7282 19
 HD9560.5 .U62 1980

World petroleum outlook--1981 . United States.
 Congress. Senate. Committee on Energy and
 Natural Resources. Washington , 1981. iii, 152
 p. : LC Card 81-601403 DDC 333.8/232 19
 KF26 .E55 1981e

World plotting series /. United States. Central
 Intelligence Agency. Washington [1976] 7
 maps : 77 x 59 cm. or smaller. Scale 1:18,000,000.
 "Lambert conformal conic, standard parallels 37°N and
 65°N." "This map is designed to be used in conjunction
 with automated cartographic systems." 540931-540937.
 Includes "Index to sheets." "Series 1147." LC Card
 79-691244
 G3201.A1 s18000 .U6
 NYPL [Map. Div. 80-3396]

**WORLD POLITICS - 1900-1945 -
 CARICATURES AND CARTOONS.**
 Caswell, Lucy Shelton. Billy Ireland /.
 Columbus, Ohio , 1980. ix, 235 p. : ISBN
 0-88215-051-0 (pbk.) LC Card 81-119198
 DDC 741.5/092/4 B 19
 E743 .C28

WORLD POLITICS - 1945-
 Thompson, Kenneth W., 1921- Cold war
 theories /. Baton Rouge , c1981- p. cm. ISBN
 0-8071-0876-6 (v. 1) : LC Card 81-6001 DDC
 327.1/12 19
 D843 .T423

**WORLD POLITICS - 1945- - ADDRESSES,
 ESSAYS, LECTURES.**
 Evolving strategic realities . Washington, DC ,
 1980. xi, 222 p. ; LC Card 80-602927 DDC
 355/.033073 19
 UA23 .E97

WORLD POLITICS - 1955-1965.
 United States. Congress. House. Committee on
 Foreign Affairs. Subcommittee on International
 Organizations and Movements. Behavioral
 sciences and the national security .
 Washington , 1965. vi, 1OR, iii, 203 p. : LC
 Card 80-503601 DDC 327.73 s 327.1/1 19
 E840.2 .A3 no. 4 E846

WORLD POLITICS - 1975-1985.
 Pugash, James Z. The geopolitics of oil .
 Washington , 1980. v. 89 p. ; LC Card
 80-604126 DDC 333.8/232 19
 HD9560.5 .P76

United States. Congress. House. Committee on
 Foreign Affairs. Subcommittee on International
 Economic Policy and Trade. Review of
 implementation of Basket II of the Helsinki
 Final Act . Washington , 1980. iii, 82 p. ; LC
 Card 80-604051 DDC 337.73047 19
 KF27 .F6465 1980d

**WORLD POLITICS - 1975-1985 -
 CONGRESSES.**
 The Sino-Soviet conflict . Seattle , c1981. p.
 cm. ISBN 0-295-95854-5 : LC Card 81-51279
 DDC 327.51047 19
 DS740.5.S65 S56

World Population Conference. Latin American
 Preparatory Meeting for the World Population
 Conference, San José, Costa Rica, 1974.
 Informe de la reunión /. [New York] , 1974. v,
 248 p. ; LC Card 80-119992
 HB3530.5 .L37 1974

World population trends . United States.
 Congress. Senate. Committee on Foreign
 Relations. Washington , 1980. iv, 346 p. : LC
 Card 80-603894 DDC 304.6 19
 KF26 .F6 1980r

World port index. United States. Naval
 Oceanographic Office. 1st-4th ed.; 1953-71.
 Washington.   **NYPL [VDN (United States.
 Naval Oceanographic Office. World port
 index)]**

World shipping lanes and straits. United States.
 Central Intelligence Agency. Selected world
 shipping lanes and straits. [Washington , 1980]

1 map : LC Card 81-690686
G3201.P54 1980 .U5

World tables: from the data files of the World Bank. Baltimore, Johns Hopkins University Press. 29 cm. "Published for the World Bank."
1. Economic history - 1945- - Yearbooks. 2. Vital statistics - Yearbooks. I. International Bank for Reconstruction and Development.
NYPL [*R-Econ 77-2973]

World War II and the problems of the eighties . United States. Congress. House. Committee on Banking, Finance and Urban Affairs. Washington , 1980. iii, 70 p. ; LC Card 80-603655 DDC 338.973 19
KF27 .B5 1980a

WORLD WAR, 1914-1918 - AERIAL OPERATIONS, GERMAN.
Morrow, John Howard, 1944- German air power in World War I /. Lincoln , c1982. p. cm. ISBN 0-8032-3076-1 LC Card 81-11588 DDC 940.54/4943 19
D604 .M64

WORLD WAR, 1939-1945 - AERIAL OPERATIONS, AMERICAN.
Jones, Brett A. A history of Marine Attack Squadron 223 /. Washington , 1978. vii, 39 p. : LC Card 79-601756
D790 .J66   ***NYPL [JFF 80-1164]***

WORLD WAR, 1939-1945 - DEPORTATIONS FROM PERU.
Gardiner, C. Harvey (Clinton Harvey) Pawns in a triangle of hate . Seattle , c1981. p. cm. ISBN 0-295-95855-3 LC Card 81-51278 DDC 940.53/1 19
D769.8.A6 G37

WORLD WAR, 1939-1945 - ECONOMIC ASPECTS - UNITED STATES.
United States. Congress. House. Committee on Banking, Finance and Urban Affairs. World War II and the problems of the eighties . Washington , 1980. iii, 70 p. ; LC Card 80-603655 DDC 338.973 19
KF27 .B5 1980a

WORLD WAR, 1939-1945 - PEACE.
Rostow, W. W. (Walt Whitman), 1916- The division of Europe after World War II, 1946 /. Austin , 1981. p. cm. ISBN 0-292-70358-9 LC Card 81-11640 DDC 940.55/4 19
D816 .R67

WORLD WAR, 1939-1945 - PERU.
Gardiner, C. Harvey (Clinton Harvey) Pawns in a triangle of hate . Seattle , c1981. p. cm. ISBN 0-295-95855-3 LC Card 81-51278 DDC 940.53/1 19
D769.8.A6 G37

WORLD WAR, 1939-1945 - PRISONERS AND PRISONS, AMERICAN.
Gardiner, C. Harvey (Clinton Harvey) Pawns in a triangle of hate . Seattle , c1981. p. cm. ISBN 0-295-95855-3 LC Card 81-51278 DDC 940.53/1 19
D769.8.A6 G37

World Wildlife Fund. North American tortoises . Washington, D.C. , 1981. p. cm. LC Card 81-607867 DDC 597.92 19
QL666.C584 N67

The world's major dams, man-made lakes, and hydroelectric plants /. United States. Dept. of the Interior. Water and Power Resources Service. Engineering Staff. Washington, D.C. [1980] 5 leaves ; LC Card 80-603189 DDC 627/.8/0212 19
TC540 .U617 1980

Worldwatch Institute. The global environment and basic human needs : a report to the Council on Environmental Quality / by the Worldwatch Institute. [Washington] : The Council, 1978. 55 p. : graphs ; 26 cm. Includes bibliographical references. LC Card 78-602557 DDC 304.2 19
1. Human ecology. 2. Man - Influence on nature. 3. Environmental policy. I. United States. Council on Environmental Quality. II. Title.
GF41 .W67 1978

Worldwide directory of national earth-science agencies and related international organizations /. United States. Geological Survey. Reston, Va. , 1981. iv, 87 p. : LC Card 80-607795 DDC 557.3 s 351.85/5 19
QE75 .C5 no. 834 QE61

Worldwide geographical location codes /. United States. General Services Administration. Office of Finance. [Washington, D.C.] , 1972. i, 356 p. ; LC Card 79-123353 DDC 910/.0148 19
G108.7 .U56 1972

WorldWide Strategic Mobility Conference, National Defense University, 1977. The WorldWide Strategic Mobility Conference 1977, 2-4 May 1977 / sponsored by the Organization of the Joint Chiefs of Staff, Logistics Directorate ; hosted by the National Defense University. [Washington, D.C. : Organization of the Joint Chiefs of Staff, 1977] ca. 100 p. in various pagings ; 27 cm. LC Card 80-601611 DDC 355.2/7 19
1. United States - Armed Forces - Transportation - Congresses. 2. Logistics - Congresses. 3. Transportation, Military - Congresses. I. United States. Organization of the Joint Chiefs of Staff. Logistics Directorate.
UC273 .W67 1977

Worrell, Jackie. United States. International Trade Commission. Leather wearing apparel from Uruguay . Washington, D.C. , 1980. ii, 9, 47 p. ; LC Card 81-600775 DDC 382/.4568522/0973 19
HF2651.L45 U64 1980

Worsham, Mark P.
Alabama. Development Office. Annotated publications list: 1969-1978 /. Montgomery, Ala., 1979. 98 p. in various pagings:
NYPL [JLF 80-1610]

Alabama. Development Office. A selected bibliography of Alabama county and regional planning and development documents /. Montgomery , 1974. xiii, 254 p. : LC Card 74-623967
Z7165.U6 A416 1974 HC107.A4

Worthington, Hannah M. Directory of sources of technical assistance to municipalities in Maryland / prepared by Hannah M. Worthington. College Park, Md. : Maryland Technical Advisory Service, Division of Behavioral and Social Sciences, University of Maryland, 1979. vii, 142 p. ; 28 cm. Includes index. LC Card 79-625220 DDC 352/.00047/2209752 19
1. Municipal government - Maryland - Directories. 2. Government consultants - Maryland - Directories. I. Maryland Technical Advisory Service. II. Title.
JS451.M35 W67

Worthington, Virginia. (joint author) Regan, Dennis C. Wreck diving in North Carolina . Raleigh, N.C. [1978] 16 p. : LC Card 79-623528 DDC 910/.0916348 19
G525 .R375

Wouden, M. L. (Marinus L.) Salisbury, H. B. Beneficiation of low-grade California chromite ores /. [Avondale, Md.] , 1981. p. cm. LC Card 81-607307 DDC 622 s 622/.34643 19
TN23 .U43 TN538.C57

WOUNDS AND INJURIES - UNITED STATES - STATISTICS.
Jack, Susan S. Current estimates from the health interview survey, United States, 1979 . Hyattsville, Md. , 1981. p. cm. ISBN 0-8406-0219-7 LC Card 81-607002 DDC 312/.3/0973 19
RA407.3 .J32

McCarthy, Eileen. Inpatient utilization of short-stay hospitals by diagnosis, United States, 1978 /. Hyattsville, Md. [1981] p. cm. ISBN 0-8406-0220-0 LC Card 81-5000 DDC M362.1/1/0973 s 362.1/1/0973
RA407.3 .A349 no. 55 RA981.A2

Wrap-up report of Legislative Budget and Finance Committee study of State fees /. Pennsylvania. General Assembly. Legislative Budget and Finance Committee. Harrisburg, Pa. [1980] viii, 83 p. ; LC Card 80-622330 DDC 353.97480072/6 19
KFP11.62 .B8 1980

Wreck diving in North Carolina . Regan, Dennis C. Raleigh, N.C. [1978] 16 p. : LC Card 79-623528 DDC 910/.0916348 19
G525 .R375

Wright, Boyd L. The Structure of North Dakota state government . Bismarck, ND [1979] 76 leaves in various foliations ; LC Card 80-622720 DDC 353.978404 19
JK6431 1979 .S77

Wright, Delpha. Maryland. Alcoholism Control Administration. Occupational program survey report /. Baltimore , 1977. 13, [4] leaves ; LC Card 77-621085 DDC 658.3/822 19
HV5297.M3 M37 1977

Wright, Jacqueline S. Handbook for appellate advocacy in the Arkansas Supreme Court and Court of Appeals / Jacqueline S. Wright. [Little Rock] : Arkansas Judicial Dept., c1980. 1 v. (loose-leaf) : forms ; 28 cm. Cover title: Appellate advocacy handbook, 1980. Includes bibliography. LC Card 80-623894 DDC 347.767/08 347.67078 19
1. Appellate procedure - Arkansas. I. Title. II. Title: Appellate advocacy handbook, 1980.
KFA4155 .W73

WRIGHT, JOSEPH ROBERT, 1938-
United States. Congress. Senate. Committee on Commerce, Science, and Transportation. Nomination--deputy secretary of commerce . Washington , 1981. iii, 8 p. ; LC Card 81-601776 DDC 353.82 19
KF26 .C69 1981c

Wright, Laurie K. California. Governor's Office. Office of Planning and Research. California permit handbook. Sacramento, Calif. [1980] xxi, 270 p. : LC Card 80-623775 DDC 353.97940082/3 19
TD171.3.C2 C34 1980

Wright, Robert R. Zoning law in Arkansas : a comparative analysis / Robert R. Wright. Little Rock, Ark. : University of Arkansas at Little Rock, c1980. 60 p. ; 23 cm. (Monograph series / University of Arkansas at Little Rock) Includes bibliographical references. LC Card 80-84888 DDC 346.76704/5 347.670645 19
1. Zoning law - Arkansas. I. Series: Monograph series / University of Arkansas at Little Rock. II. Title.
KFA4058 .W73

Wright State University.
Records of Black and Mulatto persons [in Ohio]. [1804-57] 1 reel. ***NYPL [*ZI-276]***

Wright State University. Fine Arts Gallery.
Abish, Cecile. Firsthand /. Dayton, Ohio, 1978. [39] p.:   ***NYPL [3-MCX A149 80-1159]***

Acconci, Vito 1940- Think/leap/re-think/fall /. Dayton , c1976. [54] p. :
NYPL [3-MCF A172 80-2907]

Tacha, Athena. Athena Tacha. [Dayton] , 1978. 20 p. :   ***NYPL [3-MGO (Tacha) 81-880]***

Wright State University. University Art Galleries. see Wright State University. Fine Arts Gallery.

Wrigley, J. C. (joint author) Kennedy, S. Koehler. An economic water market as an alternative to reduce return flow from irrigation /. [Boise, Idaho] , 1979. v, 165, [20] p. : LC Card 79-625878 DDC 333.91/009796 19
HD1694.I2 K46

The write occasion /. Woodworth, Patrick. Berkeley, Calif. , c1980. v, 72 p. ; LC Card 81-100412 DDC 808/.042 19
PE1408 .W676

WRITERS' MARKETS. see AUTHORSHIP.

WRITING (AUTHORSHIP) see AUTHORSHIP; CREATIVE WRITING; JOURNALISM.

Writing class . Friss, Dick. [Berkeley] , c1979. iii, 37 p. : LC Card 81-100190 DDC 808/.042 19
PE1408 .F74

Writing for the inexperienced writer . Griffith, Marlene. Berkeley, Calif. , c1979. iii, 30 p. ; LC Card 80-155384 DDC 808/.042 19
PE1408 .G8654

Writings from the Beaver Trail / by residents of the Albany-Rensselaer area ; editors, Florence Boochever and Raymond H. Jackson. Albany, N.Y. : Albany Public Library, 1980, c1979. 291 p. : ill. ; 24 cm. ISBN 0-9605090-0-3 (pbk.) LC Card 80-154008 DDC 810/.8/0974741 19
1. American literature - New York (State). 2. American literature - 20th century. 3. Aged, Writings of the American. I. Boochever, Florence. II. Jackson, Raymond H. III. Albany. Public Library.
PS548.N7 W7 1980

WRITINGS OF THE AMERICAN AGED. see AGED, WRITINGS OF THE AMERICAN.

Written comments on certain aspects of H.R. 5043, Bankruptcy tax act of 1979 /. United

States. Congress. House. Committee on Ways and Means. Subcommittee on Select Revenue Measures. Washington , 1980. v, 96 p. ; LC Card 80-602569 DDC 343.7305/23 19
KF6332 .A25 1980

Wu, Ch'i-yüan, 1912- United Nations. Dept. of Technical Co-operation for Development. Organizational systems for national planning /. New York , 1979. vi, 177 p. : LC Card 79-123608 DDC 300 s 338.9/009172/4 19
JX1977 .A2 ST/ESA/SER.E/18

Wurmser, Leon. The mask of shame / Leon Wurmser. Baltimore : Johns Hopkins University Press, c1981. p. cm. Includes index. ISBN 0-8018-2527-X LC Card 81-964 DDC 152.4 19
1. Shame. 2. Psychoanalysis. 3. Psychotherapy. I. Title.
BF575.S45 W87

W.W.I.R.P.P. series .
(no. 1) Washington (State). Water Resources Management Division. Policy Development Section. Cedar-Sammamish Basin instream resources protection program, including proposed administrative rules, and supplemental environmental impact statement . Olympia, Wash. , 1979. 148 p. in various pagings : LC Card 79-625825 DDC 333.91/0216/0979777 19
TD224.W2 W38 1979

(no. 8) Washington (State). Water Resource Management Division. Policy Development Section. Deschutes River Basin instream resources protection program including proposed administrative rules . Olympia, Wash. [1980] 29, [52] p. : LC Card 80-623859 DDC 333.91/0216/0979779 19
TD224.W2 W38 1980

Wyandotté, or, The hutted knoll . Cooper, James Fenimore, 1789-1851. Albany , c1981. p. cm. ISBN 0-87395-414-9 LC Card 81-1132 DDC 813/.2 19
PS1419 .W7 1981

Wyant, William K. Westward in Eden / William K. Wyant. Berkeley, Calif. : University of California Press, c1982. p. cm. Bibliography: p. Includes index. ISBN 0-520-04377-4 LC Card 81-7519 DDC 333.1/0973 19
1. United States - Public lands. 2. Land use - Environmental aspects - United States. 3. Land use - Law and legislation - United States. I. Title.
HD205 1982 .W9

Wyatt, Jane. Terrestrial microcosms and environmental chemistry . [Washington] [1978?] xv, 147 p. : LC Card 79-601829 DDC 574.5/264 19
QH541.2 .T45

Wydler, John W.
Oversight of energy development in northern Europe : report to the Committee on Science and Technology, U. S. House of Representatives, Ninety-sixth Congress, second session. Washington : U. S. Govt. Print. Off. : for sale by the Supt. of Docs., U. S. Govt. Print. Off., 1980. v, 45 p. : ill. ; 24 cm. At head of title: Committee print. "Serial ZZ." "July 1980." LC Card 80-603051 DDC 333.79/24 19
1. Energy development - Europe, Northern. 2. Nuclear reactors - Sweden. 3. Nuclear reactors - Finland. I. United States. Congress. House. Committee on Science and Technology. II. Title.
TJ163.25.E853 W93

Oversight of energy development in South America : to the Committee on Science and Technology, U. S. House of Representatives, Ninety-sixth Congress, second session. Washington : U. S. Govt. Print. Off. : for sale by the Supt. of Docs., U. S. Govt. Print. Off., 1980. v, 167 p. : graphs ; 24 cm. At head of title: Committee print. "Serial XX." "July 1980." Includes bibliographical references. LC Card 80-603265 DDC 333.79/098 19
1. Energy development - South America. 2. Atomic power-plants - South America. I. United States. Congress. House. Committee on Science and Technology. II. Title.
TJ163.25.S65 W92

Wynar, Lubomyr Roman, 1932- Guide to ethnic museums, libraries, and archives in the United States / by Lubomyr R. Wynar and Lois Buttlar. Kent, Ohio : Program for the Study of Ethnic Publications, School of Library Science, Kent State University, 1978. xvi, 378 p. ; 23 cm. Includes indexes. LC Card 78-624077

1. Minorities - United States - Societies, etc. - Directories. 2. Archives - United States - Directories. 3. Historical museums - United States - Directories. 4. Ethnological museums and collections - United States - Directories. I. Buttlar, Lois, 1934- joint author. 0700. II. Ohio. State University, Kent. School of Library Science. III. Title.
E184.A1 W95

Wyoming bentonite & trona industries . Wyoming. Dept. of Labor and Statistics. [Cheyenne, Wyo.] 1980. iii, 59 p. : LC Card 80-623151 DDC 338.2/761 19
HD4966.B452 U69 1980

Wyoming coal strip mining . Wyoming. Dept. of Labor and Statistics. Cheyenne, Wyo. , 1979] iii, 40 p. ; LC Card 79-625469 DDC 331.12/522334/09787 19
HD4966.M63 U59 1979

Wyoming covered employment and wage data by industry and county, 1976-1978 /. Wyoming. Employment Security Commission Research and Analysis Section. Casper, Wyo. [1979?] 26 leaves : LC Card 80-623146 DDC 331.12/5/09787 19
HD5725.W9 W96 1979

Wyoming. Dept. of Administration and Fiscal Control. Statistics and Research Division.
Wyoming information source catalog. [3d ed.]. [Cheyenne : Dept. of Administration and Fiscal Control, Research and Statistics Division], 1978. 2 v. ; 28 cm. Cover title. CONTENTS. - v. 1. Agency index.--v. 2. Subject index. Alphabetical index. LC Card 78-623159 DDC 015.787 19
1. Wyoming - Government publications - Bibliography. I. Title.
Z1223.5.W82 W86 1978 J87.W8

Wyoming. Dept. of Economic Planning and Development. see **Wyoming. State Dept. of Economic Planning and Development.**

Wyoming. Dept. of Labor and Statistics. (Old Catalog form: Wyoming. Labor and Statistics Dept.)
Wyoming bentonite & trona industries : the nation's leading producers : a wage and employment survey. [Cheyenne, Wyo. : Wyoming Dept. of Labor & Statistics], 1980. iii, 59 p. : graphs ; 28 cm. LC Card 80-623151 DDC 338.2/761 19
1. Wages - Bentonite industry - Wyoming. 2. Wages - Trona industry - Wyoming. 3. Bentonite industry - Wyoming - Employees - Supply and demand. 4. Trona industry - Wyoming - Employees - Supply and demand. I. Title.
HD4966.B452 U69 1980

Wyoming coal strip mining : a wage and employment survey, 1979. Cheyenne, Wyo. : Wyoming Dept. of Labor & Statistics, 1979] iii, 40 p. ; 27 cm. Authors: A. J. Wolf, L. Wessel. LC Card 79-625469 DDC 331.12/522334/09787 19
1. Wages - Coal-miners - Wyoming - Statistics. 2. Coal-miners - Wyoming - Supply and demand - Statistics. 3. Strip mining - Wyoming - Statistics. I. Wolf, A. J. II. Wessel, Louis. III. Title.
HD4966.M63 U59 1979

Wyoming uranium, mining and milling : a wage and employment survey, 1979. [Cheyenne, Wyo. : Wyoming Dept. of Labor & Statistics, 1980] iii, 41 p. : ill. ; 28 cm. Includes bibliographical references. LC Card 80-622020 DDC 331.12/52234932/09787 19
1. Wages - Uranium industry - Wyoming. 2. Uranium industry - Wyoming - Employees. I. Title.
HD4966.U72 U68 1979

Wyoming. Division of Health and Medical Services. Wyoming medical facilities directory : licensure year, July 1, 1980 to June 30, 1981. [Cheyenne] : Division of Health and Medical Services, Wyoming Dept. of Health and Social Services, [1980] [14] leaves ; 28 cm. Cover title. LC Card 80-622352 DDC 362.1/1/025787 19
1. Health facilities - Wyoming - Directories. I. Title.
RA977 .W96 1980

Wyoming. Economic Planning and Development, State Dept. of. see **Wyoming. State Dept. of Economic Planning and Development.**

Wyoming. Employment Security Commission Research and Analysis Section.
Occupational employment of selected manufacturing industries, Wyoming, 1977 / prepared by Research and Analysis Section,

Wyoming Employment Security Commission. Casper, Wyo. : The Section, [197-?] 19 leaves : graphs ; 28 cm. Cover title: Wyoming occupational employment statistics, selected manufacturing, 1977. LC Card 80-622021 DDC 331.12/57/09787 19
1. Labor supply - Wyoming - Statistics. 2. Wyoming - Occupations - Statistics. I. Title. II. Title: Wyoming occupational employment statistics, selected manufacturing, 1977.
HD5725.W9 W96 1970

Wyoming covered employment and wage data by industry and county, 1976-1978 / prepared by Research & Analysis Section, Employment Security Commission of Wyoming. Casper, Wyo. : The Commission, [1979?] 26 leaves : graphs ; 28 cm. Cover title. LC Card 80-623146 DDC 331.12/5/09787 19
1. Labor supply - Wyoming - Statistics. 2. Wages - Wyoming - Statistics. I. Title.
HD5725.W9 W96 1979

Wyoming. Energy Conservation Office. Planning, conservation, and regulation . [Cheyenne] [1980] v, 108 p. : LC Card 80-622619 DDC 333.79/09787 19
HD9502.U53 W85

Wyoming. Fish Division. Yekel, Steve. Limnological investigation of the Shoshone River below Buffalo Bill Dam, Wyoming /. [Cheyenne] , 1978. v, 91 p. : LC Card 78-623439 DDC 574.5/26323/0978733 19
QL628.W8 Y44

Wyoming. Game and Fish Commission. Compton, Thomas. Sierra Madre elk-deer ecology study /. [Cheyenne] , 1975. ix, 125 p. : LC Card 76-622419 DDC 599.73/57 19
QL737.U55 C63

Wyoming. Game and Fish Dept. The status, mortality, and response to management of the bighorn sheep of Whiskey Mountain / by Tom Thorne ... [et al.]. Cheyenne : Wyoming Game & Fish Dept., [1979] 213 p. : ill. ; 28 cm. (Wildlife technical report . no. 7) "August 1979." "Completion report for Federal Aid in Wildlife Restoration Wyoming Project FW-3-R-24, Work plan 3, job no. 15W." Bibliography: p. 113-125. LC Card 80-622756 DDC 639.9/797358 19
1. Bighorn sheep. 2. Wildlife management - Wyoming - Fremont Co. 3. Mammals - Wyoming - Fremont Co. I. Thorne, Tom. II. Title. III. Title: Whiskey Mountain. IV. Series.
QL737.U53 W96 1979

Wyoming. Geological Survey. County resource series .
(no. 1) Lane, Donald W. Geologic map atlas and summary of economic mineral resources of Converse County, Wyoming /. Laramie , 1972. 22 p. : LC Card 74-623237 DDC 912/.1553/0978716
G1478.C6C5 L3 1972

Report of investigations .
(no. 10) Applied geology and archaeology . Laramie, Wyo. [1974] vi, 127 p. : LC Card 76-624236 DDC 557.87 s 551.7/93/09787 19
QE181 .A26 no. 10 QE699

(no. 22) Glass, Gary B. Coals and coal-bearing rocks of the Hanna Coal Field, Wyoming /. Laramie, Wyo. , 1980. iv, 43 p. (3 fold.) : LC Card 80-622620 DDC 557.87 s 553.2/4/0978786 19
QE181 .A26 no. 22 TN805.W8

WYOMING - GOVERNMENT PUBLICATIONS - BIBLIOGRAPHY.
Wyoming. Dept. of Administration and Fiscal Control. Statistics and Research Division. Wyoming information source catalog. [Cheyenne] 1978. 2 v. ; LC Card 78-623159 DDC 015.787 19
Z1223.5.W82 W86 1978 J87.W8

Wyoming. Health and Medical Services, Division of. see **Wyoming. Division of Health and Medical Services.**

Wyoming housing monitoring system /. Kelsey, Sharron. [Cheyenne] , 1979- 1 v. ; LC Card 80-621092 DDC 363.5/09787 19
HD7303.W9 K44

Wyoming information source catalog. Wyoming. Dept. of Administration and Fiscal Control. Statistics and Research Division. [Cheyenne] 1978. 2 v. ; LC Card 78-623159 DDC 015.787 19
Z1223.5.W82 W86 1978 J87.W8

Wyoming. Labor and Statistics, Dept. of. see **Wyoming. Dept. of Labor and Statistics.**

Wyoming. Laws, statutes, etc.
Real estate license act of 1971. 1979.
Wyoming. Real Estate Commission. Real estate manual / compiled under the auspices of the Wyoming Real Estate Commission. Cheyenne, Wyo. [1979] v, 320 p. : LC Card 79-625847 DDC 346.78704/37 19
KFW4482.R4 A87 1979

WYOMING - MAPS.
(1980) United States. Geological Survey. Wyoming, base map /. Reston, Va. , 1980. 1 map ; LC Card 81-691604
G4260 1980 .U5

(1980) United States. Geological Survey. Wyoming, base map with highways /. Reston, Va. , 1980. 1 map : LC Card 81-691607
G4260 1980 .U51

Wyoming medical facilities directory . Wyoming. Division of Health and Medical Services. [Cheyenne] [1980] [14] leaves ; LC Card 80-622352 DDC 362.1/1/025787 19
RA977 .W96 1980

Wyoming occupational employment statistics, selected manufacturing, 1977. Wyoming. Employment Security Commission Research and Analysis Section. Occupational employment of selected manufacturing industries, Wyoming, 1977 /. Casper, Wyo. [197-?] 19 leaves : LC Card 80-622021 DDC 331.12/57/09787 19
HD5725.W9 W96 1970

WYOMING - OCCUPATIONS - STATISTICS.
Wyoming. Employment Security Commission Research and Analysis Section. Occupational employment of selected manufacturing industries, Wyoming, 1977 /. Casper, Wyo. [197-?] 19 leaves : LC Card 80-622021 DDC 331.12/57/09787 19
HD5725.W9 W96 1970

Wyoming Platte County heritage /. Platte County Extension Homemaker's Council (Wyo.) Wheatland, Wyo. , c1981. p. cm. LC Card 81-2567 DDC 978.7/17 19
F767.P5 P58 1981

Wyoming. Public Service Commission. Planning, conservation, and regulation . [Cheyenne] [1980] v, 108 p. : LC Card 80-622619 DDC 333.79/09787 19
HD9502.U53 W85

Wyoming. Real Estate Commission. Real estate manual / compiled under the auspices of the Wyoming Real Estate Commission. Cheyenne, Wyo. : The Commission, [1979] v, 320 p. : ill. ; 23 cm. "Wyoming Real estate license act of 1971": p. [1]-12. "June 1979." Bibliography: p. 273-275. LC Card 79-625847 DDC 346.78704/37 19
1. Real estate business - Law and legislation - Wyoming. I. Wyoming. Laws, statutes, etc. Real estate license act of 1971. 1979. II. Title.
KFW4482.R4 A87 1979

Wyoming. State Dept. of Economic Planning and Development.
DEPAD statistical yearbook. 1972- [Cheyenne?] illus. (part. col.). 23 cm.
1. Wyoming - Statistics - Periodicals. I. Wyoming. State Dept. of Economic Planning and Development. Statistical yearbook. II. Title. III. Title: DEPAD statistical yearbook.   **NYPL [JLL 80-288]**

Planning, conservation, and regulation . [Cheyenne] [1980] v, 108 p. : LC Card 80-622619 DDC 333.79/09787 19
HD9502.U53 W85

Statistical yearbook. Wyoming. State Dept. of Economic Planning and Development. DEPAD statistical yearbook. 1972- [Cheyenne?]   **NYPL [JLL 80-288]**

Wyoming. State Dept. of Economic Planning and Development. Office of the Chief of State Planning. Kelsey, Sharron. Wyoming housing monitoring system /. [Cheyenne] , 1979- 1 v. ; LC Card 80-621092 DDC 363.5/09787 19
HD7303.W9 K44

Wyoming. State Land Use Commission. Wyoming State land use plan : a program for land use planning in the State of Wyoming. [Cheyenne?] : Wyoming State Land Use Commission, [1979] 180 p., [15] fold. leaves : ill. (3 fold. in pockets) ; 31 cm. "June 1979." Bibliography: p. 176-180. LC Card 79-625833 DDC

333.73/09787 19
1. Land use - Wyoming - Planning. I. Title.
HD211.W8 W97 1979

Wyoming State land use plan . Wyoming. State Land Use Commission. [Cheyenne?] [1979] 180 p., [15] fold. leaves : LC Card 79-625833 DDC 333.73/09787 19
HD211.W8 W97 1979

Wyoming. State Water Planning Program. Report.
(no. 18) Wells, Deborah K. Chemical analyses of water from the Minnelusa Formation and equivalents in the Powder River Basin and adjacent areas, northeastern Wyoming . Cheyenne [1979] iii, 27 p., [1] leaf of plates : LC Card 79-622599 DDC 553.7/9/097871 19
TD224.W8 W44

Report on reconnaissance studies of irrigation projects : Yellowstone Basin and adjacent coal area, level B study : Wind-Bighorn-Clarks Fork study area / State Engineer's Office, Wyoming Water Planning Program and Bureau of Reclamation, U. S. Dept. of the Interior. [Cheyenne, Wyo. : The Office], 1977. 41 leaves in various foliations, [7] leaves of plates : maps ; 28 cm. LC Card 79-622603 DDC 333.91/315/0978733 19
1. Irrigation - Wyoming. 2. Irrigation - Yellowstone River watershed. I. United States. Bureau of Reclamation. II. Title.
TC824.W8 W96 1977

WYOMING - STATISTICS - PERIODICALS.
Wyoming. State Dept. of Economic Planning and Development. DEPAD statistical yearbook. 1972- [Cheyenne?]   **NYPL [JLL 80-288]**

Wyoming. University. Dept. of Political Science. Government Research Bureau. see **Wyoming. University. Government Research Bureau.**

Wyoming. University. Government Research Bureau. Boyer, Edward C. Collective bargaining for municipal employees. [Laramie], 1973. iii, 34 p.;   **NYPL [JLM 75-1268 no. 1]**

Wyoming. University. Water Resources Research Institute.
Water resources series .
(no. 46) Hampe, Gary D. Water-related aesthetic preferences of Wyoming residents /. Laramie [1974] 111 p. : LC Card 74-623922 DDC 553.7/09787 s 719 19
TD201 .W9 no. 46 BH301.L3

Wyoming uranium, mining and milling . Wyoming. Dept. of Labor and Statistics. [Cheyenne, Wyo. , 1980] iii, 41 p. : LC Card 80-622020 DDC 331.12/52234932/09787 19
HD4966.U72 U68 1979

X-RAY DIAGNOSIS. see **DIAGNOSIS, RADIOSCOPIC.**

X-RAY MICROANALYSIS - CONGRESSES.
Workshop on Biological X-ray Microanalysis by Electron Beam Excitation, Boston, 1977. Microbeam analysis in biology /. New York , 1979. xx, 672 p. : ISBN 0-12-440340-9 LC Card 79-24948
QH324.9.X2 W67 1977
                    NYPL [JSE 80-1320]

X-RAYS - DIFFRACTION.
Ferrante, M. J. (Michael John), 1930- High-temperature enthalpy and x-ray powder diffraction data for aluminum sulfide (Al$_2$S$_3$) /. Washington , 1981. p. cm. LC Card 80-606912 DDC 622 s 546/.6732 19
TN23 .U43 QD181.A4

X-RAYS - DIFFRACTION - MEASUREMENT - CONGRESSES.
Symposium on Accuracy in Powder Diffraction, National Bureau of Standards, 1979. Accuracy in powder diffraction . [Washington, D.C.] [1980] x, 572 p. : LC Card 80-600010 DDC 602/.18 s 548/.83 19
QC100 .U57 no. 567 QC482.D5

X-RAYS - DOSAGE. see **RADIATION - DOSAGE.**

X-RAYS - PHYSIOLOGICAL EFFECT.
United States. Congress. House. Committee on Interstate and Foreign Commerce. Subcommittee on Oversight and Investigations. Unnecessary exposure to radiation from medical and dental x-rays . Washington , 1980. v, 15

p. ; LC Card 80-603049 DDC 363.1/89 19
RC78 .U534 1980

X-RAYS - SAFETY REGULATIONS - UNITED STATES.
United States. Congress. Senate. Committee on Labor and Human Resources. Subcommittee on Health and Scientific Research. Consumer-patient radiation safety and health act of 1979 . Washington , 1980. iv, 316 p. : LC Card 80-603350 DDC 344.73/0472 19
KF26 .L274 1980c

XEROPHYTES - CALIFORNIA.
California. Dept. of Water Resources. Plants for California landscapes . [Sacramento, Calif.] [1979] vi, 127 p. : LC Card 80-621393 DDC 635.9/52 19
SB472.32.U6 C34 1979

XYLEM.
Gibbs, Carter B. The effect of xylem age on volume yield & sugar content of sugar maple sap /. Upper Darby, Pa. , 1969. 11 p. :ill. LC Card 75-605745 DDC 333.76/0974 s 633.3/4 19
SD11 .A455493 no. 141 SB239.M3

Yake, William E. Water quality trend analysis : the Spokane River basin / by William E. Yake. Olympia, WA : Washington State Dept. of Ecology, Water and Wastewater Monitoring Section, [1979] 39, 5 p. : ill. ; 28 cm. (Project report - Washington State Dept. of Ecology ; no. DOE-PR-6) Cover title. "July 1979." Bibliography: p. 37-39. LC Card 79-625821 DDC 363.7/3942/097973 19
1. Water quality - Spokane River watershed, Idaho and Wash. I. Series: Washington State Dept. of Ecology. Project report - Washington State Dept. of Ecology , no. DOE-PR-6. II. Title.
TD225.S56 Y34

Yakima River Basin carrying capacity study project /. Evergreen State College. Applied Environmental Studies Program. [Olympia, Wash.] , 1975. 63 p. : LC Card 76-620920 DDC 330.9797/55043 19
HC107.W2 E9 1975

YAKIMA RIVER VALLEY - ECONOMIC CONDITIONS.
Evergreen State College. Applied Environmental Studies Program. Yakima River Basin carrying capacity study project /. [Olympia, Wash.] , 1975. 63 p. : LC Card 76-620920 DDC 330.9797/55043 19
HC107.W2 E9 1975

Yale-New Haven Medical Center. Eating hints . [Bethesda, Md.] [1980] iii, 86 p. : LC Card 80-622402 DDC 641.5/631 19
RC271.D52 M67 1980

Yamaichi International (America) Seminar on Investing in America, New York, 1973. Investing in America . [New York] 1973. 1 v. (various pagings) ;   **NYPL [JLE 80-1704]**

Yamin, Hadi. Relationship of highway development and city development for non-metropolitan places in Indiana : final report / by Hadi Yamin ; prepared as part of an investigation conducted by Joint Highway Research Project, Engineering Experiment Station, Purdue University, in cooperation with the Indiana State Highway Commission. West Lafayette, Ind. : Purdue University, 1979. xii, 175 leaves : ill. ; 28 cm. Bibliography: leaf 170-175. LC Card 80-620933 DDC 388.1/1 19
1. Roads - Indiana. 2. Urbanization - Indiana. 3. Land use - Indiana. I. Purdue University, Lafayette, Ind. Engineering Experiment Station. Joint Highway Research Project. II. Indiana. State Highway Commission. III. Title.
TE24.I6 Y35

Yanagida, John F. (joint author) Dovring, Folke. Monoculture and productivity . [Urbana] , 1979. 27 p. : LC Card 79-625880 DDC 338.1/09773 19
HD9037.I3 D68

Yanarella, Ann Marie. Coal and the social sciences . [Lexington, Ky.] [1979] 41 leaves ; LC Card 80-624324 DDC 016.622/334 19
Z6738.C6 C62 TN800

Yaney, George L. The urge to mobilize : agrarian reform in Russia, 1861-1930 / George Yaney. Urbana : University of Illinois Press, c1982. p. cm. Bibliography: p. Includes index. ISBN 0-252-00910-X LC Card 81-11527 DDC 333.3/1/47 19

1. Land reform - Soviet Union - History. 2. Stolypin, Petr Arkad'evich, 1862-1911. I. Title.
HD1333.S65 Y36

Yankee enterprise, the rise of the American system of manufactures : a symposium / sponsored by the United States Chamber of Commerce, held at the Dibner Rare Book Library, National Museum of American History, Smithsonian Institution ; Otto Mayr and Robert C. Post, editors. Washington. D.C. : Smithsonian Institution Press, 1981. p. cm.
Bibliography: p. Includes index. ISBN 0-87474-631-0 LC Card 81-607315 DDC 338.0973 19
1. United States - Industries - History - Congresses. 2. Industrial arts - United States - History - Congresses. 3. Industrial management - United States - History - Congresses. 4. Interchangeable mechanisms - Congresses. I. Mayr, Otto. II. Post, Robert C. III. Chamber of Commerce of the United States. IV. Dibner Library.
HC103 .Y36

Yans-McLaughlin, Virginia, 1943- Family and community : Italian immigrants in Buffalo, 1880-1930 / Virginia Yans-McLaughlin.Illini Books ed. Urbana : University of Illinois Press, 1981, c1977. p. cm. Reprint. Originally published: Ithaca : Cornell University Press, 1977. Bibliography: p. Includes index. ISBN 0-252-00916-9 (pbk.) LC Card 81-11475 DDC 305.8/51/074797 19
1. Italian Americans - New York (State) - Buffalo - Economic conditions. 2. Family - United States. 3. Buffalo (N.Y.) - Economic conditions. I. Title. II. Title: Italian immigrants in Buffalo, 1880-1930.
F129.B819 I89 1981

Yap, Lorene. Lower Income Housing Assistance Program (Section 8) : nationwide evaluation of the existing housing program : technical supplement / by Lorene Yap, Peter Greenston, and Robert Sadacca. Washington : U. S. Dept. of Housing and Urban Development, Office of Policy Development and Research ; for sale by the Supt. of Docs., U. S. Govt. Print. Off., 1978 i.e. 1979. ix, 232 p. ; 26 cm. "HUD-PDR-360." Chiefly tables. Includes bibliographical references. LC Card 79-602558
1. Rent subsidies - United States - Statistics. 2. United States. Dept. of Housing and Urban Development. Section 8 Housing Assistance Payment Program for Lower Income Families - Statistics. I. Greenston, Peter, joint author. II. Sadacca, Robert, joint author. III. United States. Dept. of Housing and Urban Development. Office of Policy Development and Research. Lower Income Housing Assistance Program (Section 8). IV. Title.
HD7293 .A5 1979b Suppl.
NYPL [JLF 81-460]

YAQUI INDIANS - WARS, 1740.
Hu-DeHart, Evelyn. Missionaries, miners, and Indians . Tucson, Ariz. , 1981. p. cm. ISBN 0-8165-0740-6 : LC Card 81-14658 DDC 972/.00497 19
F1221.Y3 H82

YAQUI INDIANS - GOVERNMENT RELATIONS.
Hu-DeHart, Evelyn. Missionaries, miners, and Indians . Tucson, Ariz. , 1981. p. cm. ISBN 0-8165-0740-6 : LC Card 81-14658 DDC 972/.00497 19
F1221.Y3 H82

YAQUI INDIANS - MISSIONS.
Hu-DeHart, Evelyn. Missionaries, miners, and Indians . Tucson, Ariz. , 1981. p. cm. ISBN 0-8165-0740-6 : LC Card 81-14658 DDC 972/.00497 19
F1221.Y3 H82

Yaquina Head Outstanding Natural Area . United States. Congress. Senate. Committee on Energy and Natural Resources. Subcommittee on Parks, Recreation, and Renewable Resources. Washington , 1980. iii, 23 p. : LC Card 80-601869 DDC 346.7304/6917 347.30646917 19
KF26 .E5565 19791

YAQUINA HEAD OUTSTANDING NATURAL AREA, OR.
United States. Congress. Senate. Committee on Energy and Natural Resources. Subcommittee on Parks, Recreation, and Renewable Resources. Yaquina Head Outstanding Natural Area . Washington , 1980. iii, 23 p. : LC Card 80-601869 DDC 346.7304/6917 347.30646917 19
KF26 .E5565 19791

Yates County, N. Y. Highways, Superintendent of. see Yates County, N. Y. Superintendent of Highways.

YATES COUNTY, N. Y. - MAPS.
(1976) Manning (H.A.) Company. Highway map of Yates County, New York, 1976. Greenfield, Mass., 1976. col. map 60 x 71 cm. Scale ca. 1:63,360 Includes index of roads and list of historical sites. Copyright, County of Yates, New York. At head of title: Thomas H. Sayles, Supt. of Highways. On verso illus, text and maps of Penn Yan, Dundee, Dresden, Rushville, and Keuka Park.
NYPL [Map Div. 80-3335]

YATES COUNTY, N. Y. - ROAD MAPS.
Manning (H.A.) Company. Highway map of Yates County, New York, 1976. Greenfield, Mass., 1976. col. map 60 x 71 cm. Scale ca. 1:63,360 Includes index of roads and list of historical sites. Copyright, County of Yates, New York. At head of title: Thomas H. Sayles, Supt. of Highways. On verso illus, text and maps of Penn Yan, Dundee, Dresden, Rushville, and Keuka Park.
NYPL [Map Div. 80-3335]

Yates County, N. Y. Superintendent of Highways. Manning (H.A.) Company. Highway map of Yates County, New York, 1976. Greenfield, Mass., 1976. col. map 60 x 71 cm. Scale ca. 1:63,360 Includes index of roads and list of historical sites. Copyright, County of Yates, New York. At head of title: Thomas H. Sayles, Supt. of Highways. On verso illus, text and maps of Penn Yan, Dundee, Dresden, Rushville, and Keuka Park.
NYPL [Map Div. 80-3335]

Yates, John J. Economic impact of incorporating RACT 1 guidelines for VOC emissions into the Illinois air pollution control regulations (R78-3 and R78-4) /. Chicago IL , 1979. xxii, 137, [125] p. : LC Card 79-624233 DDC 363.7/39262/09773 19
TD885.5.O74 E28

Yavno, Max. The photography of Max Yavno / pictures by Max Yavno ; text by Ben Maddow ; designed by Carl Seltzer. Berkeley, Calif. : University of California Press, c1981. ca. 150 p. : ill. ; 31 cm. ISBN 0-520-04238-7 (pbk.) LC Card 80-6060 DDC 779/.092/4 19
1. Photography, Artistic. 2. Yavno, Max. I. Maddow, Ben, 1909-. II. Title. III. Title: Max Yavno.
TR654 .Y35

YAVNO, MAX.
Yavno, Max. The photography of Max Yavno /. Berkeley, Calif. , c1981. ca. 150 p. : ISBN 0-520-04238-7 (pbk.) LC Card 80-6060 DDC 779/.092/4 19
TR654 .Y35

Yaworski, N. Tim. (joint author) Greer, T. Vernon. Sugars and sirups from Canada . Washington, D.C. [1980] ii, 17, 66 p. : LC Card 80-602338 DDC 382/.4136/0973 19
HF2651.S8 U55

Yearbook of agriculture .
(1980) Cutting energy costs. [Washington, D.C.] , 1980. x, 397 p. : LC Card 80-600168 DDC 630/.5 s 333.79 19
S21 .A35 1980 TJ163.4.U6

Yearwood, Lennox S. Black organizations . Washington, D.C. , c1980. xxi, 267 p. ; ISBN 0-8191-0897-9 : LC Card 79-5500
E185.5 .B538
NYPL [Sc D 80-631]

Yee, Warren, 1921-
The Lychee in Hawaii / Warren Yee. Honolulu : Cooperative Extension Service, College of Tropical Agriculture, and Human Resources, University of Hawaii at Manoa, 1981. p. cm. (Circular / Cooperative Extension Service, College of Tropical Agriculture and Human Resources, University of Hawaii at Manoa . 366) Bibliography: p. LC Card 81-6939 DDC 634/.65 19
1. Litchi chinensis. 2. Fruit-culture - Hawaii. I. Series: Circular (Hawaii Cooperative Extension Service) , 366. II. Title.
SB379.L8 Y44

Plum culture in Hawaii / authors, Warren Yee and Daniel Shigeta. Honolulu : Cooperative Extension Service, College of Tropical Agriculture and Human Resources, University of Hawaii at Manoa, 1981. p. cm. (Circular . 404) Bibliography: p. LC Card 81-6824 DDC 634/.22/09969 19
1. Plum - Hawaii. I. Shigeta, Daniel, 1928-. II. Hawaii Cooperative Extension Service. III. Series: Circular

(Hawaii Cooperative Extension Service) , 404. IV. Title.
SB377 .Y43

Yekel, Steve. Limnological investigation of the Shoshone River below Buffalo Bill Dam, Wyoming / by Steve Yekel. [Cheyenne] : Wyoming Game and Fish Dept., Fish Division, 1978. v, 91 p. : ill. ; 28 cm. "Completion report to contract no. 7-07-60-V0001, Bureau of Reclamation." Bibliography: p. 38. LC Card 78-623439 DDC 574.5/26323/0978733 19
1. Fishes - Wyoming - Shoshone River - Statistics. 2. Fishery management - Wyoming - Shoshone River - Statistics. I. Wyoming. Fish Division. II. Title.
QL628.W8 Y44

YELLOW BIRCH.
Tubbs, Carl H. The influence of light, moisture, and seedbed on yellow birch regeneration /. St. Paul , 1969. 12 p. : LC Card 71-603400 DDC 634.9/0977 s 634.9/726 19
SD11 .A45476 no. 27 SD397.Y44

The Yellow Dog peridotite and a possible buried igneous complex of lower Keweenawan age in the northern peninsula of Michigan / by John S. Klasner ... [et al.]. Lansing, Mich. : State of Michigan, Dept. of Natural Resources, Geological Survey Division, 1979. v, 31 p. : ill. ; 28 cm. (Report of investigation - State of Michigan, Geological Survey Division . 24) Bibliography: p. 30-31. LC Card 80-622270 DDC 557.74 s 552/.3 19
1. Peridotite - Michigan, Upper Peninsula. 2. Intrusions (Geology) - Michigan, Upper Peninsula. 3. Geology, Stratigraphic - Pre-Cambrian. 4. Geology - Michigan, Upper Peninsula. I. Klasner, J. S. II. Series: Michigan. Geological Survey Division. Report of investigation, 24.
QE125 .A417 no. 24 QE462.P45

The yellow pages . Health Policy Analysis Program (Wash.) Seattle, Wash. [1978] v, 80 leaves ; LC Card 79-621291 DDC 362.1/09797 19
RA407.4.W3 H4 1978

Yellowstone impact study .
(technical report no. 7) Hinz, Tom. The effect of altered streamflow on migratory birds of the Yellowstone River Basin, Montana /. Helena , 1977. x, 107 p. : LC Card 78-623506 DDC 598.2/525 19
QL683.Y44 H56

Yellowstone impact study ; technical report .
(no. 1) Future development projections and hydrologic modeling in the Yellowstone River Basin, Montana /. Helena, MT , 1977. xi, 141 p. : LC Card 80-623619 DDC 333.91/009786/3 19
TC424.M9 F87

YELLOWSTONE RIVER - REGULATION.
Hinz, Tom. The effect of altered streamflow on migratory birds of the Yellowstone River Basin, Montana /. Helena , 1977. x, 107 p. : LC Card 78-623506 DDC 598.2/525 19
QL683.Y44 H56

Yenter, James M.
(joint author) Pannell, James P., 1926- Soil survey of Rio Grande County area, Colorado /. [Washington] , 1980. iv, 89 p., [2] fold. leaves of plates : LC Card 80-602320 DDC 631.4/7/78837 19
S599.C6 P36

Soil survey of Conejos County area, Colorado. [Washington, D.C.?], 1980. vii, 144 p. : LC Card 81-600706 DDC 631.4/7/78833 19
S599.C6 S66

Yezer, Anthony. United States. Dept. of Housing and Urban Development. Office of Policy Development and Research. How well are we housed? /. Washington , 1978-1979. 4 v. :
NYPL [JLM 80-448]

Yhdysvallat. see United States.

Ylvisaker, Miriam. An experiment in encouraging fluency / by Miriam Ylvisaker. [Berkeley, Calif. (Tolman Hall, University of California, Berkeley, Calif. 94720)] : Bay Area Writing Project, University of California, Berkeley, c1979. iii, 26 p. ; 23 cm. (Curriculum publication . no. 8) Bibliography: p. 13. LC Card 81-100023 DDC 808/.042/071273 19
1. English language - Composition and exercises - Study and teaching - Addresses, essays, lectures. I. Title. II. Series.
PE1404 .Y57

Yoke, Carl B. Roger Zelazny and Andre Norton, proponents of individualism / Carl Yoke.

Columbus : State Library of Ohio, 1979. 26 p. ; 23 cm. (Ohio authors)   LC Card 80-137489   DDC 813/.54 19
1. Science fiction, American - History and criticism - Addresses, essays, lectures. 2. Zelazny, Roger - Criticism and interpretation - Addresses, essays, lectures. 3. Norton, Andre - Criticism and interpretation - Addresses, essays, lectures. I. Title. II. Series.
PS374.S35 Y6

Yokel, Felix Y.
(joint author) Kovacs, William D. Soil and rock anchors for mobile homes . Washington, D.C. , 1979. xvi, 147 p. :   LC Card 79-600143   DDC 690/.02/18 s 690/.79 19
TA435 .U58 no. 107 TH4819.M6

Recommended technical provisions for construction practice in shoring and sloping of trenches and excavations / Felix Y. Yokel ; prepared for the Occupational Safety and Health Administration, Department of Labor, and National Institute for Occupational Safety and Health, Department of Health, Education and Welfare. Washington : U. S. Dept. of Commerce, National Bureau of Standards : for sale by the Supt. of Docs., U. S. Govt. Print. Off., [1980] xvi, 68 p. : ill. ; 27 cm. (NBS building science series ; 127) "Issued June 1980." Bibliography: p. 53-54.   LC Card 80-600068   DDC 690/.02/18 s 624.1/52 19
1. Retaining walls. 2. Excavation. 3. Slopes (Soil mechanics). I. United States. Occupational Safety and Health Administration. II. National Institute for Occupational Safety and Health. III. Series: United States. National Bureau of Standards. Building science series ; 127. IV. Title.
TA435 .U58 no. 127 TA770

Soil classification for construction practice in shallow trenching / Felix Y. Yokel and Richard L. Tucker, Lymon C. Reese ; prepared for Occupational Safety and Health Administration, Department of Labor and National Institute for Occupational Safety and Health, Department of Health, Education and Welfare. Washington, D.C. : U. S. Dept. of Commerce, National Bureau of Standards : for sale by the Supt. of Docs., U. S. Govt. Print. Off., [1980] xiv, 76 p. : ill. ; 27 cm. (NBS building science series ; 121) "March 1980." Bibliography: p. 59-60.   LC Card 80-600014   DDC 690/.02/18 s 624.1/51/012 19
1. Soil mechanics. 2. Soils - Classification. 3. Excavation. I. Tucker, Richard L., joint author. II. Reese, Lymon C., joint author. III. United States. Occupational Safety and Health Administration. IV. National Institute for Occupational Safety and Health. V. Series: United States. National Bureau of Standards. Building science series ; 121. VI. Title.
TA435 .U58 no. 121 TA710

York, Marjorie. (joint author) Burke, Mary. Inter-American investigation of mortality in childhood . Washington, D.C. , 1979. v, 145 p. :   ISBN 92-75-11386-6 (pbk.) :   LC Card 80-132481   DDC 362.1/09181/2 s 304.6/4 19
RA10 .P252 no. 386 HB1323.C5

YORKTOWN, VA. BALLARD HOUSE.
Rogers, Rebecca M. The dependencies of the Nelson, Smith, and Ballard houses, Colonial National Historical Park, Yorktown, Virginia . [Washington] , 1979. vii, 25 p., [27] leaves of plates :   LC Card 79-603752   DDC 975.5/423 19
F234.Y6 R63

YORKTOWN, VA. NELSON HOUSE.
Rogers, Rebecca M. The dependencies of the Nelson, Smith, and Ballard houses, Colonial National Historical Park, Yorktown, Virginia . [Washington] , 1979. vii, 25 p., [27] leaves of plates :   LC Card 79-603752   DDC 975.5/423 19
F234.Y6 R63

YORKTOWN, VA. SMITH HOUSE.
Rogers, Rebecca M. The dependencies of the Nelson, Smith, and Ballard houses, Colonial National Historical Park, Yorktown, Virginia . [Washington] , 1979. vii, 25 p., [27] leaves of plates :   LC Card 79-603752   DDC 975.5/423 19
F234.Y6 R63

YOSEMITE NATIONAL PARK.
Walsh, Richard G., 1930- An economic evaluation of the general management plan for Yosemite National Park . Fort Collins, Colo. [1980] xii, 102 p. :   LC Card 80-623117   DDC 333.78/3/0979447 19
F868.Y6 W34

Yoshihara, Harvey T. Annual progress report for monitoring and evaluation of arctic waters, with emphasis on the North Slope drainages / by Harvey T. Yoshihara. [Juneau] : Alaska Dept. of Fish and Game, Division of Sport Fish, [1972] 49 p. : ill. ; 28 cm. On cover: Federal aid in fish restoration. "Volume 13. Report no. G-III-A." Bibliography: p. 49.   LC Card 81-463275   DDC 639.9/755 19
1. Fishes - Alaska - North Slope. 2. Arctic char. I. Alaska. Division of Sport Fisheries. II. Title: Annual progress report for monitoring and evaluation of arctic waters ... III. Title: Monitoring and evaluation of arctic waters ... IV. Title: Federal aid in fish restoration.
QL628.A4 Y67

Yoshinaka, Marvin S. Hood Canal, priorities for tomorrow : an initial report on fish and wildlife, developmental aspects and planning considerations for Hood Canal, Washington / Marvin S. Yoshinaka, Nancy J. Ellifrit ; ill. by Nancy J. Ellifrit. Portland, Or. : U. S. Dept. of the Interior, Fish and Wildlife Service, 1974. v, 97 p. [17] fold. leaves of plates : ill. ; 28 cm. Bibliography: p. 78-80.   LC Card 75-602160   DDC 333.95/09797/9 19
1. Marine biology - Washington (State) - Puget Sound. 2. Marine resources conservation - Washington (State) - Puget Sound. 3. Coastal zone management - Washington (State) - Puget Sound. I. Ellifrit, Nancy J., joint author. II. Title.
QH105.W2 Y67

Yost, Kathleen M. Selected readings on mother-infant bonding. [Washington, D.C. , 1979] 115 p. :   LC Card 79-604305   DDC 306.8/7 19
HQ759 .S44

Youmans, E. Grant. (joint author) Larson, Donald Keith, 1932- Problems of rural elderly households in Powell County, Kentucky /. [Washington] [Springfield, Va. , 1978] iii, 25 p. ;   LC Card 81-451882   DDC 362.6/09769/585 19
HV1468.K4 L37

YOUNG ADULTS - UNITED STATES.
Eckland, Bruce Kent. A capsule description of young adults four and one-half years after high school / . [Washington, D.C.] , 1979. ix, 34 p. :   LC Card 80-601549   DDC 305.2/3/0973 19
HQ799.7 .E3

Young (Arthur) and Company. Earl R. Combs Inc. A study to determine the export and domestic markets for currently underutilized fish and shellfish /. [Washington] 1978 [i. e. 1979] xxxv, 416 p. :   LC Card 79-603273
NYPL   [JLF 81-419]

Young, Brigham, 1801-1877. Diary of Brigham Young, 1857 / edited and introduction by Everett L. Cooley. Salt Lake City, Utah : Tanner Trust Fund, University of Utah Library, c1980. xxvi, 105 p. : ill., facsim., ports. ; 24 cm. (Utah, the Mormons, and the West. no. 10) Bibliography: p. 91-98. Includes index.   LC Card 80-52639   DDC 289.3/3 B 19
1. Young, Brigham, 1801-1877. 2. Mormons - United States - Biography. I. Cooley, Everett L. II. Title.
BX8695.Y7 A34

YOUNG, BRIGHAM, 1801-1877.
Young, Brigham, 1801-1877. Diary of Brigham Young, 1857 /. Salt Lake City, Utah , c1980. xxvi, 105 p. :   LC Card 80-52639   DDC 289.3/3 B 19
BX8695.Y7 A34

Young, Douglas, 1953- A brief history of the Staunton and James River Turnpike / by Douglas Young. 2d rev ed. Charlottesville, Va. : Virginia Highway & Transportation Research Council, [1980] vii, 22 p. : ill. ; 28 cm. (Historic roads of Virginia) "March 1980." "VHTRC 75-R59." Bibliography: p. 21-22.   LC Card 80-620005   DDC 388.1/22/0975548 19
1. Roads - Virginia. I. Title.
HE356.V8 Y68 1980

Young, George Anthony, 1919- Effects of the explosion of 45 tons of TNT under water at a depth scaled to test Baker / by G.A. Young, contributors, M.A. Cook ... [et al.]. White Oak, Md. : U. S. Naval Ordnance Laboratory, 1954. ix, 154 p. : ill. ; 27 cm. "NOL project 152." "Interim report no. 10."   LC Card 80-514235   DDC 662/.2 19
1. Underwater explosions. 2. Explosives, Military - Testing. 3. Ordnance, Naval - Testing. 4. Atomic weapons - Testing. I. Cook, Melvin Alonzo, joint

author. II. Title.
VF540 .Y68

Young, H. L. Ground-water resources and geology of Washington and Ozaukee Counties, Wisconsin / H.L. Young and W.G. Batten. [Washington] : United States Dept. of the Interior, Geological Survey ; Madison, Wis. : University of Wisconsin-Extension, Geological and Natural History Survey, [1980] iv, 37 p. : maps (2 fold. col. in pocket) ; 28 cm. (Information circular - University of Wisconsin-Extension, Geological and Natural History Survey . no. 38) Bibliography: p. 36-37.   LC Card 80-622195   DDC 557.75 s 553.7/9/0977591 19
1. Water, Underground - Wisconsin - Washington Co. 2. Water, Underground - Wisconsin - Ozaukee Co. I. Batten, W. G., joint author. II. United States. Geological Survey. III. Wisconsin. Geological and Natural History Survey. IV. Series: Wisconsin. Geological and Natural History Survey. Information circular, no. 38. V. Title.
QE179 .A33 no. 38 GB1025.W6

Young, H. W. (Harold William), 1942- Hydrology and geochemistry of thermal ground water in southwestern Idaho and north-central Nevada / by H.W. Young and R.E. Lewis. Reston, Va. : U. S. Geological Survey, 1981. p. cm. (Geohydrology of geothermal systems) Geological Survey professional paper ; 1044-J Bibliography: p.   LC Card 81-6817   DDC 553.7/09796/2 19
1. Geothermal resources - Idaho. 2. Geochemistry - Idaho. I. Lewis, R. E. (Robert Edward), 1935-. II. Title. III. Series.
GB1199.7.I2 Y68

Lewis, R. E. Geothermal resources in the Banbury Hot Springs area, Twin Falls County, Idaho /. Reston, Va. , 1981. p. cm.   LC Card 81-607876   DDC 553.7/09796/37 19
GB1199.7.I2 L48

Young, John Richard. The schooling of the horse / by John Richard Young ; with drawings by Randy Steffen and Claude (Skip) Johnson and diagrams by Larry Kumferman. Norman : University of Oklahoma Press, 1982. p. cm. "A completely revised edition of the book previously known as The schooling of the Western horse." Includes bibliographical references and index.   ISBN 0-8061-1787-7   LC Card 81-11539   DDC 636.1/0888 19
1. Horse-training. I. Title.
SF287 .Y6 1982

Young Joseph. see Joseph, Nez Percé Chief, 1840-1904.

Young, Martha W. Peterson, Charles Henry. The ecology of intertidal flats of North Carolina . Slidell, LA , 1979 [i.e. 1980] vi, 73 p. :   LC Card 80-601522   DDC 574.5/2636 19
QH105.N8 P45

Young, Patrick. Asthma and allergies : an optimistic future / by Patrick Young. [Bethesda, Md.] : United States Dept. of Health and Human Services, Public Health Service, National Institutes of Health ; Washington, D.C. : for sale by the Supt. of Docs., United States Govt. Print. Off., 1980. 179 p. : ill. ; 23 cm. (NIH publication ; no. 80-388) Based on the report of the Task Force on Asthma and the Other Allergic Diseases, National Institute of Allergy and Infectious Diseases. "March 1980."   LC Card 80-603185   DDC 616.97 19
1. Allergy. 2. Asthma. I. United States. Task Force on Asthma and the Other Allergic Diseases. Asthma and the other allergic diseases. II. Series: United States. National Institutes of Health. Publication, no. 80-388. III. Title.
RC584 .Y68

Young, Tasia. Report of the Southwest Consultation on the Educational Needs of Rural Girls and Women, convened by the Information Resources Committee, Advisory Council on Women's Educational Programs in Santa Fe, New Mexico, September 10 and 11, 1976 / prepared by Tasia Young. Albuquerque : New Mexico Commission on the Status of Women, [1976?] 25 leaves ; 28 cm.   LC Card 79-623319   DDC 376/.9789 19
1. Education of women - New Mexico. 2. Education, Rural - New Mexico. 3. Mexican Americans - Education - New Mexico. 4. Indians of North America - New Mexico - Education. I. Southwest Consultation on the Educational Needs of Rural Girls and Women, Santa Fe, N.M., 1976. II. United States. National Advisory Council on Women's Educational

Programs. Information Resources Committee. III. New Mexico. Commission on the Status of Women. IV. Title.
LC1758.N6 Y68

Young, Thomas Daniel, 1919-
Literary movements in Tennessee / by Thomas Daniel Young. 1st ed. Knoxville : Published in cooperation with Tennessee Historical Commission : University of Tennessee Press, c1981. p. cm. (Tennessee three star books)
Bibliography: p. Includes index. ISBN 0-87049-319-1 : LC Card 81-2206 DDC 810/.9/9768 19
1. American literature - Tennessee - History and criticism. 2. Criticism - Tennessee - History. 3. Tennessee - Intellectual life. I. Title.
PS266.T2 Y6

Waking their neighbors up : the Nashville Agrarians rediscovered / Thomas Daniel Young. Athens : University of Georgia Press, c1982. p. cm. (Lamar memorial lectures . no. 24)
Bibliography: p. Includes index. ISBN 0-8203-0600-2 LC Card 81-14736 DDC 810/.9/975 19
1. American literature - Southern States - History and criticism. 2. Authors, American - Southern States - Political and social views. 3. Literature and society - Southern States. 4. Southern States - Civilization. 5. Nashville (Tenn.) - Intellectual life. 6. American literature - 20th century - History and criticism. I. Title. II. Series.
PS261 .Y63

Young, Wayne C.
Elm Creek site. 1979. Two sites in Uvalde County. [Austin, Tex.] [1979] vi, 15, vi, 19 p., : LC Card 80-622621 DDC 976.4/432 19
E78.T4 T89

Young, William Russell, 1949- New Mexico dropout study, 1977-78 and 1978-79 / prepared by William R. Young, III. Santa Fe, N.M. : Evaluation, Assessment, and Testing Unit, New Mexico State Dept. of Education, [1980] [24] p. ; 28 cm. "Summer, 1980." LC Card 80-623587 DDC 373.12913/09789 19
1. Dropouts - New Mexico. I. New Mexico. Dept. of Education. Evaluation, Assessment, and Testing Unit. II. Title.
LC144.N6 Y68

YOUNG'S MODULUS. see ELASTICITY.

YOUTH.
United States. Rural Development Service. How USDA can help you involve youth in community development. Washington, 1973. 15 p.:   *NYPL [*XME-9362]*

Youth Act of 1980 . United States. Congress. Senate. Committee on Labor and Human Resources. Subcommittee on Education, Arts, and Humanities. Washington , 1980. vi, 681 p. : LC Card 80-604088 DDC 344.73/01342592 347.3041342592 19
KF26 .L2735 1980b

YOUTH, AFRO-AMERICAN. see AFRO-AMERICAN YOUTH.

YOUTH AND DRUGS. see DRUGS AND YOUTH.

YOUTH AS CONSUMERS - UNITED STATES.
United States. Federal Trade Commission. FTC staff report on television advertising to children. [Washington] 19. 394 p. in various pagings ; LC Card 79-601465
HF6146.T42 U55 1978   *NYPL [JLF 81-278]*

YOUTH CONSERVATION CORPS (OHIO)
Ohio. Division of Civilian Conservation. The new conservationists . [Columbus, Ohio] [1979?] ix, 41 p. : LC Card 80-623069 DDC 331.3/8133372/09771 19
HD6274.O3 O33 1979

YOUTH - EMPLOYMENT.
Sorrentino, Constance. Youth unemployment, an international perspective. Washington, D.C. [1981] p. cm. LC Card 81-607979 DDC 331.3/4137 19
HD6270 .S66

Youth employment act, 1980 . United States. Congress. Senate. Committee on Labor and Human Resources. Subcommittee on Employment, Poverty, and Migratory Labor. Washington , 1980. iii, 111 p. ; LC Card 80-603336 DDC 344.73/0134 19
KF26 .L2737 1980a

Youth employment and education . United States.

Congressional Budget Office. [Washington] [1980] xviii, 85 p. ; LC Card 80-602880 DDC 331.3/411/0973 19
HD6273 .U5 1980

Youth employment and welfare reform jobs, 1980 . United States. Congress. Senate. Committee on Labor and Human Resources. Subcommittee on Employment, Poverty, and Migratory Labor. Washington , 1980. vi, 892 p. : LC Card 81-600874 DDC 344.73/01342592 347.3041342592 19
KF26 .L2737 1980b

YOUTH - EMPLOYMENT - CONNECTICUT - STATISTICS.
Carle, Cynthia A. Youth in Connecticut's labor force /. [Wethersfield] [1979] iii leaves, 34 p. ; LC Card 80-621003 DDC 331.3/412/09746 19
HD6274.C8 C37

YOUTH - EMPLOYMENT - HAWAII.
Hawaii. Dept. of Labor and Industrial Relations. Youths in Hawaii's work force. Honolulu, Hawaii [1979] 16 p. : LC Card 80-621561 DDC 331.3/4125/09969 19
HD6274.H3 H38 1979

YOUTH - EMPLOYMENT - ILLINOIS.
Youth in the labor force, 1979, State of Illinois. [Chicago, Ill.] [1979] 31 p. ; LC Card 80-623384 DDC 331.3/4125/09773 19
HD6274.I3 Y68

YOUTH - EMPLOYMENT - MICHIGAN.
Michigan. Employment Security Commission. Youth in Michigan's work force . [Lansing?] [1979] x, 80 p. : LC Card 80-620866 DDC 331.3/412/09774 19
HD6274.M5 M47 1979

YOUTH - EMPLOYMENT - MICHIGAN - STATISTICS.
Michigan. Employment Security Commission. Youth in Michigan's work force . [Lansing?] [1979] x, 80 p. : LC Card 80-620866 DDC 331.3/412/09774 19
HD6274.M5 M47 1979

YOUTH - EMPLOYMENT - MONTANA.
Montana. Division of Employment Security. Youth in Montana labor force /. Helena, Mont. [1980] v leaves, 87, [74] p. ; LC Card 80-622327 DDC 331.3/412/09786 19
HD6274.M7 M66 1980

YOUTH - EMPLOYMENT - NORTH CAROLINA.
North Carolina. Bureau of Employment Security Research. North Carolina youth . Raleigh, N.C. [1979] ii, 83 p. ; LC Card 80-623680 DDC 331.3/412/09756 19
HD6274.N8 N83 1979

YOUTH - EMPLOYMENT - OKLAHOMA - STATISTICS.
Oklahoma. Employment Security Commission. Research and Planning Division. Youth in the labor force. [Oklahoma City, Okla.] [1979?] 15 p. : LC Card 80-620522 DDC 331.3/4125/09766 19
HD6274.O5 O34 1979

Youth employment programs in the Southwest . Briggs, Vernon M. Austin, Tex. , c1980. vii, 47 p. ; ISBN 0-87755-245-2 (pbk.) LC Card 81-620741 DDC 331.3/411/0979 19
HD6274.A165 B74

YOUTH - EMPLOYMENT - SOUTHWEST, NEW - CASE STUDIES.
Briggs, Vernon M. Youth employment programs in the Southwest . Austin, Tex. , c1980. vii, 47 p. ; ISBN 0-87755-245-2 (pbk.) LC Card 81-620741 DDC 331.3/411/0979 19
HD6274.A165 B74

YOUTH - EMPLOYMENT - STATISTICS.
Mushkin, Selma J., 1913- Indicators of youth unemployment and education in industrialized nations /. [Washington] , 1978. v, 181 p. : LC Card 79-602354
HD6270 .M87   *NYPL [JLG 81-24]*

YOUTH - EMPLOYMENT - UNITED STATES.
Barton, Paul E. Between two worlds. Washington, 1978. 4 v.;
   NYPL [JLF 80-1274]

Lerman, Robert I. The nature of the youth employment problem . [Washington, D.C.] [Springfield, Va.] 1980. 105, 4 p. ; LC Card

80-602227 DDC 331.3/4137973 19
HD6273 .L46

Mare, Robert D. Changes in the relative labor force status of Black and white youths . [Madison] [1980] 43 p. ; LC Card 80-623148 DDC 331.3/412/0973 19
HD6273 .M38

Slackman, Joel N. Costs of the National Service Act (H.R. 2206) . [Washington, D.C.] , c1980. xii, 42 p. ; LC Card 81-600733 DDC 355.2/236/0973 19
HD6273 .S57

United States. Congress. House. Committee on Education and Labor. Subcommittee on Elementary, Secondary, and Vocational Education. Hearings on the President's youth education and employment initiative . Washington , 1980. vi, 938 p. ; LC Card 80-603474 DDC 344.73/013411 19
KF27 .E3364 1980e

United States. Congress. Senate. Committee on Labor and Human Resources. Subcommittee on Education, Arts, and Humanities. Youth Act of 1980 . Washington , 1980. vi, 681 p. : LC Card 80-604088 DDC 344.73/01342592 347.3041342592 19
KF26 .L2735 1980b

United States. Congress. Senate. Committee on Labor and Human Resources. Subcommittee on Employment, Poverty, and Migratory Labor. Youth employment act, 1980 . Washington , 1980. iii, 111 p. ; LC Card 80-603336 DDC 344.73/0134 19
KF26 .L2737 1980a

United States. Congress. Senate. Committee on Labor and Human Resources. Subcommittee on Employment, Poverty, and Migratory Labor. Youth employment and welfare reform jobs, 1980 . Washington , 1980. vi, 892 p. : LC Card 81-600874 DDC 344.73/01342592 347.3041342592 19
KF26 .L2737 1980b

United States. Congressional Budget Office. Youth employment and education . [Washington] [1980] xviii, 85 p. ; LC Card 80-602880 DDC 331.3/411/0973 19
HD6273 .U5 1980

United States. Congressional Budget Office. Youth unemployment . Washington , 1978. xvii, 45 p. : LC Card 78-601457
HD6273 .U5 1978

YOUTH - EMPLOYMENT - UNITED STATES - CONGRESSES.
United States. Employment and Training Administration. Office of Youth Programs. Report on SPEDY conferences . [Washington] [1979] viii, 297 p. ; LC Card 79-603023
HD6273 .U514 1979a

YOUTH - EMPLOYMENT - UTAH.
Coverston, G. Scott. Report on youth in the Utah labor force /. [Salt Lake City] , 1979. vii, 50 p. ; LC Card 80-620745 DDC 331.3/4125/09792 19
HD6274.U8 C66

YOUTH - EMPLOYMENT - VIRGINIA.
Virginia. Employment Commission. Manpower Research Division. Labor Market Analysis Unit. Special youth report, State of Virginia /. Richmond, Va. [1979] 24 p. : LC Card 79-625797 DDC 331.3/4/09755 19
HD6274.V8 V57 1979

YOUTH - EMPLOYMENT - WEST VIRGINIA.
West Virginia. Dept. of Employment Security. Labor and Economic Research Section. West Virginia youth and the labor market /. Charleston, W. Va. [1979] ii, 46 p. ; LC Card 80-621110 DDC 331.3/412/09754 19
HD6274.W4 W47 1979

YOUTH - GOVERNMENT POLICY - ALABAMA.
Alabama Year of the Child Commission. Alabama children, a matter of commitment and priority . Montgomery, Ala. [1980-] c1981- p. cm. LC Card 80-620054 DDC 305.2/3/09761 19
HQ796 .A452 1980

Youth in Connecticut's labor force /. Carle, Cynthia A. [Wethersfield] [1979] iii leaves, 34 p. ; LC Card 80-621003 DDC 331.3/412/09746 19
HD6274.C8 C37

Youth in Michigan's work force . Michigan. Employment Security Commission. [Lansing?] [1979] x, 80 p. : LC Card 80-620866 DDC 331.3/412/09774 19
HD6274.M5 M47 1979

Youth in Montana labor force /. Montana. Division of Employment Security. Helena, Mont. [1980] v leaves, 87, [74] p. ; LC Card 80-622327 DDC 331.3/412/09786 19
HD6274.M7 M66 1980

Youth in the labor force. Oklahoma. Employment Security Commission. Research and Planning Division. [Oklahoma City, Okla.] [1979?] 15 p. : LC Card 80-620522 DDC 331.3/4125/09766 19
HD6274.O5 O34 1979

Youth in the labor force, 1979, State of Illinois. [Chicago, Ill.] : Publications and Project Development Section, [1979] 31 p. ; 28 cm. "September 1979." Includes bibliographical references. LC Card 80-623384 DDC 331.3/4125/09773 19 *1. Youth - Employment - Illinois. I. Illinois. Bureau of Employment Security. Research and Analysis Division.*
HD6274.I3 Y68

YOUTH - MEDICAL CARE - MICHIGAN. Powers, Jane VanDeMark. Adolescent health care services in Michigan . Lansing , 1978. vi, 159 p. : LC Card 79-620710 DDC 362.1/9 19
RJ102.5.M5 P68

YOUTH - MEDICAL CARE - MICHIGAN - KENT CO. Powers, Jane VanDeMark. Adolescent health care services in Michigan . Lansing , 1978. vi, 159 p. : LC Card 79-620710 DDC 362.1/9 19
RJ102.5.M5 P68

YOUTH MOVEMENT. International youth organizations and the United Nations /. New York , 1973. v, 95 p. ;
NYPL [JLM 74-1459 no. 17]

YOUTH - NEVADA - ALCOHOL USE - PREVENTION. Nevada. Legislative Commission. Juvenile crime and abuse of alcohol /. [Carson City] [1980] viii, 37 p. ; LC Card 81-621352 DDC 364.3/6/09793 19
HV5053 .N48 1980

YOUTH - NEW YORK (CITY) New York (City). Youth Board. The summer of 1962 . New York , 1962. iv, 64 p. ;
NYPL [JLF 80-1632]

YOUTH - NEW YORK (STATE) - DRUG USE. New York (State). Office of Drug Abuse Services. Bureau of Social Science Research and Program Evaluation. Drug abuse prevention . [Albany] , 1976. 33 p. ; LC Card 77-622761
*HV5824.Y68 N76 1976 NYPL [*XME-9523]*

YOUTH - NUTRITION. Tuckermanty, Elizabeth. Normal diet, adolescence /. Columbus, Ohio (456 Clinic Dr., Columbus 43210) , c1980. 31 p. : LC Card 81-620941 DDC 613.2/088055 19
RJ235 .T83

YOUTH - OREGON. Oregon. Governor's Commission on Youth. Report on the opinions and experiences of Oregon youth. Salem , 1976. 51, 10 p. ; LC Card 77-621410
*HQ796 .O647 1976   NYPL [*XME-9430]*

YOUTH - OREGON - ATTITUDES. Oregon. Governor's Commission on Youth. Report on the opinions and experiences of Oregon youth. Salem , 1976. 51, 10 p. ; LC Card 77-621410
*HQ796 .O647 1976   NYPL [*XME-9430]*

YOUTH, RURAL. see RURAL YOUTH.

Youth service bureaus in California; progress report. California. Dept. of the Youth Authority. [Sacramento]
NYPL [JLM 80-686]

YOUTH SERVICES - ALASKA. Alaska. Legislature. House of Representatives. Committee on Health, Education, and Social Services. Interim report /. [Juneau, Alaska] [1980] 349, 3 p. : LC Card 80-622417 DDC 362.7/09798 19
KFA1211.82 .H4 1980

YOUTH SERVICES - CALIFORNIA - DIRECTORIES. California. Council on Criminal Justice. An

assessment and directory of federally funded delinquency prevention projects in California . [Sacramento?] , 1973. viii, 118 p. ;
NYPL [JLF 80-1251]

YOUTH - SERVICES FOR - NEW YORK (STATE) New York (State). Legislative Commission on Expenditure Review. Delinquency prevention and youth development programs . [Albany, N.Y.] [1980] 4, ii, 68 p. ; LC Card 80-622881 DDC 364.3/6/09747 19
HV9105.N7 N44 1980

YOUTH - SERVICES FOR - UNITED STATES - DIRECTORIES. National Family and Reproductive Health Association. A directory of national health, education, and social service organizations concerned with youth /. Rockville, Md. [1979] 56 p. ; LC Card 80-601714
HV741 .N316 1979   NYPL [JLF 80-1557]

Youth unemployment . United States. Congressional Budget Office. Washington , 1978. xvii, 45 p. : LC Card 78-601457
HD6273 .U5 1978

Youth unemployment, an international perspective. Sorrentino, Constance. Washington, D.C. [1981] p. cm. LC Card 81-607979 DDC 331.3/4137 19
HD6270 .S66

YOUTH - UNITED STATES. National Council of State Committees for Children and Youth. The States report on children and youth. [Washington? 1960] 232 p. LC Card 60-61000   *NYPL [JLD 80-3271]*

YOUTH - UNITED STATES - ALCOHOL USE - PREVENTION. National Institute on Alcohol Abuse and Alcoholism. The whole college catalog about drinking. Rockville, Md. , Washington [1976] xii, 129 p. : LC Card 76-603043 DDC 362.2/9286/088375 19
HV5292 .N33 1976

YOUTH - UNITED STATES - CONDUCT OF LIFE. Tipton, Steven M. Getting saved from the sixties . Berkeley , c1981. p. cm. ISBN 0-520-03868-1 LC Card 81-3033 DDC 973.92 19
HN59 .T58

YOUTH - UNITED STATES - DRUG USE. United States. Congress. House. Select Committee on Narcotics Abuse and Control. Drug paraphernalia . Washington , 1980. iii, 46 p. : LC Card 80-604119 DDC 381/.4568 19
HV5825 .U563 1980

United States. Congress. Senate. Committee on the Judiciary. Subcommittee on Criminal Justice. Drug paraphernalia and youth . Washington , 1980. iii, 349 p. : LC Card 80-603781 DDC 362.2/93/088055 19
KF26 .J8377 1979a

YOUTH - UNITED STATES - SEXUAL BEHAVIOR. Urban and Rural Systems Associates. Improving family planning services for teenagers . [Washington] , 1976. i, 85, 23 p. : LC Card 77-601716
HQ766.5.U5 U72 1976   NYPL [JLF 81-163]

Youths in Hawaii's work force. Hawaii. Dept. of Labor and Industrial Relations. Honolulu, Hawaii [1979] 16 p. : LC Card 80-621561 DDC 331.3/4125/09969 19
HD6274.H3 H38 1979

Yuarn msuic dramas . Johnson, Dale R. Ann Arbor , 1980. p. cm. ISBN 0-89264-040-5 : LC Card 80-25372 DDC 895.1/24/09 19
PL2384 .J6

Yudof, Mark G. When government speaks : politics, law, and government expression in America / Mark G. Yudof. Berkeley : University of California Press, c1982. p. cm. Includes index. ISBN 0-520-04254-9 LC Card 81-1965 DDC 342.73/0853 347.302853 19 *1. Government information - United States. 2. Freedom of information - United States. 3. Government publicity - United States. 4. Liberty of speech - United States. I. Title.*
KF5753 .Y83

YUGOSLAVIA - HISTORY - CONGRESSES. The Creation of Yugoslavia, 1914-1918 /. Santa

Barbara, Calif. , c1980. viii, 228 p., [2] leaves of plates : LC Card 79-22331
DR363 .C7   NYPL [JFE 81-166]

YUGOSLAVIA - MAPS. (1980) United States. Central Intelligence Agency. Yugoslavia. [Washington , 1980] 1 map : LC Card 81-693055
G6840 1980 .U5

Yuill, Charles. Maine. State Planning Office. Investigation into the feasibility of establishing a statewide, natural resources, geographic information system for Maine . [Augusta] , 1979. 196, [64] p. : LC Card 80-620927 DDC 025/.063337/09741 19
HD211.M2 M34 1979

YUKIAN INDIANS - WARS - 1815-1875. Carranco, Lynwood. Genocide and vendetta . Norman , c1981. p. cm. ISBN 0-8061-1549-1 LC Card 81-7469 DDC 979.4/1504 19
F868.M5 C3

YUMA INDIANS - GOVERNMENT RELATIONS. Bee, Robert L. Crosscurrents along the Colorado . Tucson , c1981. p. cm. ISBN 0-8165-0558-6 : LC Card 81-7446 DDC 970.004/97 19
E99.Y94 B43

YUMA INDIANS - HISTORY. Bee, Robert L. Crosscurrents along the Colorado . Tucson , c1981. p. cm. ISBN 0-8165-0558-6 : LC Card 81-7446 DDC 970.004/97 19
E99.Y94 B43

Yuwipi, vision and experience in Oglala ritual /. Powers, William K. Lincoln , c1982. p. cm. ISBN 0-8032-3663-8 LC Card 81-10501 DDC 299/.74 19
E99.O3 P683

Zabriskie, Jan G., 1947- Plants of Deep Canyon and the central Coachella Valley, California / by Jan G. Zabriskie ; drawings by Carol Lewis. Riverside : Philip L. Boyd Deep Canyon Desert Research Center, University of California, c1979. 175 p. : ill. ; 23 cm. (The Deep Canyon series) Bibliography: p. [161] Includes index. LC Card 79-63644 DDC 581.9794/97 19 *1. Desert flora - California - Deep Canyon. 2. Desert flora - California - Coachella Valley. 3. Deep Canyon, Calif. 4. Coachella Valley, Calif. I. Series: Deep Canyon series. II. Title.*
QK149 .Z32

Zack, Arnold. Understanding fact finding and arbitration in the public sector. 3d ed. [Washington, D.C.] : U. S. Dept. of Labor, Labor Management Services Administration : for sale by the Supt. of Docs., U. S. Govt. Print. Off., 1980. 105, 23 p. ; 21 cm. LC Card 80-601261 DDC 331.89/041353 19 *1. Collective bargaining - Government employees - United States. 2. Arbitration, Industrial - United States. I. United States. Labor-Management Services Administration. II. Title. III. Title: Fact finding and arbitration in the public sector.*
HD8005.6.U5 Z33 1980

Understanding grievance arbitration in the public sector. [3d ed.]. [Washington, D.C.] : U. S. Dept. of Labor, Labor-Management Services Administration : for sale by the Supt. of Docs., U. S. Govt. Print. Off., 1980. 111, 23 p. ; 21 cm. LC Card 80-602268 DDC 353.001/76 19 *1. Grievance arbitration - United States. 2. Employee-management relations in government - United States. I. United States. Labor-Management Services Administration. II. Title.*
JK768.8 .Z32 1980

Zahuranec, Bernard J. Oceanic sound scattering prediction /. New York , c1977. xii, 859 p. : ISBN 0-306-35505-1 LC Card 77-3445
QC242 .O25   NYPL [JSF 81-96]

Zakheim, Dov S. United States. Congressional Budget Office. The Marine Corps in the 1980s . [Washington, D.C.] [1980] xxii, 74 p. : LC Card 80-602374 DDC 359.9/6/0973 19
VE23 .A5 1980

United States. Congressional Budget Office. Shaping the general purpose Navy of the eighties . Washington, D.C. , 1980. xxvii, 145 p. : LC Card 80-600968 DDC 359/.03/0973 19
VA53 .U52 1980

Zaltzman, Raul. Biological decomposition of cellulose; a literature review and annotated bibliography, by Raul Zaltzman and Anthony Tarquinio. Morgantown, Engineering Experiment Station, West Virginia University, 1969. iii, 107 p. 28 cm. (West Virginia. University. Engineering Experiment Station. Report. 6) LC Card 72-628129 DDC 620 s 581.19/2482 19
1. Cellulose - Biodegradation - Abstracts. I. Tarquinio, Anthony, joint author. II. Title. III. Series.
TA1 .W393 no. 6 QR160

Zammuto, Raymond F. Assessing organizational effectiveness : systems change, adaptation, and strategy / Raymond F. Zammuto. Albany : SUNY Press, 1982. p. cm. (SUNY Press series on administrative systems) Includes bibliographical references.   ISBN 0-87395-552-8   LC Card 81-9130   DDC 658.4/01 19
1. Organizational effectiveness. I. Title. II. Series.
HD58.9 .Z35

Zang, Thomas A. Hohl, Frank. Collisionless galaxy simulations /. Washington, D.C. [Springfield, Va.] 1979. iii, 145 p. :   LC Card 81-600552   DDC 523.1/12/0724 19
QB857 .H64

Zappolo, Aurora. Discharges from nursing homes : 1977 national nursing home survey / Aurora Zappolo. Hyattsville, Md. : U. S. Dept. of Health and Human Services, Public Health Service, National Center for Health Statistics, 1981. p. cm. (Vital and health statistics. Series 13) Data from the national health survey (Series 13) ; no. 54 DHHS publication ; no. (PHS) 81-1715   ISBN 0-8406-0216-2   LC Card 81-607016   DDC 362.1/6/0973 19
1. Nursing homes - United States - Utilization - Statistics. I. Series: Data from the national health survey (Series 13) , no. 54. II. Title.
RA997 .Z36

Zarn, Mark. Wild, free-roaming burros : an annotated bibliography / by Mark Zarn, Thomas Heller, and Kay Collins. [Washington] : U. S. Dept. of the Interior, Bureau of Land Management : U. S. Dept. of Agriculture, U. S. Forest Service ; Denver, Colo. : available from DSC, 1979. 29 p. ; 27 cm. (Technical note - U. S. Bureau of Land Management ; T/N 297) Cover title. "Date issued, March 1977."   LC Card 80-601254   DDC 639.9 s 016.59972/5 19
1. Donkeys - The West - Bibliography. 2. Equus - Bibliography. 3. Mammals - The West - Bibliography. I. Heller, Thomas, joint author. II. Collins, Kay, joint author. III. Series: United States. Bureau of Land Management. Technical note - Bureau of Land Management , 297. IV. Title.
QL84.2 .U54a vol. 297 Z7997.D76 QL737.U62

Zatko, Jalna R. Polymeric concentration determined by drag reduction / by Jalna R. Zatko. [Avondale, MD] : U. S. Dept. of Interior, Bureau of Mines, [1981] p. cm. (Report of investigations)   LC Card 81-607021   DDC 622 s 622/.7 19
1. Polymers and polymerization - Analysis. 2. Frictional resistance (Hydodynamics). I. Series: Report of investigations (United States. Bureau of Mines). II. Title.
TN23 .U43 QD381.8

Zdanowicz, Daniel P. (joint author) Cooperman, Alan N. Millers River survey, 1965 /. [Boston] [1970] 30 leaves :   LC Card 80-119079   DDC 363.7/3942/0974422 19
TD224.M4 C66

Zeidlik, Hannah M. Catalog and index to historical manuscripts, 1940-1966 / compiled by Hannah M. Zeidlik. Washington, D.C. : Center of Military History, Dept. of the Army, 1979. 2 v. ; 27 cm. CONTENTS. - v. 1. Headquarters, War Department, and Department of the Army.--v. 2. The Army Service Forces.   LC Card 79-604297   DDC 016.355/00973 19
1. United States - History, Military - 20th century - Manuscripts - Microform catalogs. 2. United States. Army - 20th century - History - Manuscripts - Microform catalogs. 3. United States - History, Military - 20th century - Sources - Bibliography - Microform catalogs. 4. United States. Army - 20th century - History - Sources - Microform catalogs. 5. United States. National Archives - Microform catalogs. 6. United States. Army Command and General Staff College, Fort Leavenworth, Kan. Library Services - Microform catalogs. I. Center of Military History. II. Title.
Z1249.M5 Z44 E745

Zeimetz, Kathryn A. Growing energy : land for biomass farms / by Kathryn A. Zeimetz. Washington, D.C. : U. S. Dept. of Agriculture, Economics, Statistics, and Cooperatives Service, [1980] ii, 35 p. : ill. ; 27 cm. (Agricultural economic report ; no. 425) Cover title. "June 1979." Bibliography: p. 33-35.   LC Card 80-601245   DDC 338.1 s 338.1/7389 19
1. Energy crops - United States. 2. Biomass energy - United States. I. Title. II. Series.
HD1751 .A91854 no. 425 SB288.3.U6

Zeisel, Rose N. United States. Bureau of Labor Statistics. Technology, productivity, and labor in the bituminous coal industry, 1950-79. Washington , 1980. p. cm.   LC Card 80-607858   DDC 331.7/622334/0973 19
HD9545 .U54 1980

ZELAZNY, ROGER - CRITICISM AND INTERPRETATION - ADDRESSES, ESSAYS, LECTURES.
Yoke, Carl B. Roger Zelazny and Andre Norton, proponents of individualism /. Columbus , 1979. 26 p. ;   LC Card 80-137489   DDC 813/.54 19
PS374.S35 Y6

Zembruski, Thomas J. (joint author) Eissler, Benjamin B. Summary and evaluation of crest-stage-gage data in New York. Albany, N. Y., 1974. 24 p.   *NYPL [JSF 81-23]*

Zemel, Jay N. Nato Advanced Study Institute on Nondestructive Evaluation of Semiconductor Materials and Devices, Villa Tuscolano, Italy, 1978. Nondestructive evaluation of semiconductor materials and devices . New York , c1979. xi, 782 p. :   ISBN 0-306-40293-9   LC Card 79-16499
TK7871.85 .N376 1978   NYPL [JSF 80-961]

Zevelechi Wells, Maria Xenia. The Ranuzzi manuscripts / selected and described by Maria Xenia Zevelechi Wells. [Austin] : Humanities Research Center, University of Texas, c1980. 89 p. : ill. ; 26 cm. Bibliography: p. [84]-86. Includes index.   ISBN 0-87959-094-7   LC Card 80-622235   DDC 091 19
1. Manuscripts - Texas - Austin - Exhibitions. 2. Ranuzzi family - Library - Exhibitions. 3. Ranuzzi Cospi, Ferdinando Vincenzo Antonio, 1658-1726 - Library - Exhibitions. 4. Libraries, Private - Italy - Bologna - Exhibitions. 5. Texas. University at Austin. Humanities Research Center - Exhibitions. I. Texas. University at Austin. Humanities Research Center. II. Title. III. Title: Ranuzzi collection.
Z6621.T372 R358 Z881.A935

Z'iednani Derzhavy Ameryky. see United States.

ZIMBABWE - FOREIGN RELATIONS - UNITED STATES.
United States. Congress. House. Committee on Foreign Affairs. Rhodesian sanctions, should the United States lift them? . Washington , 1980. iii, 80 p. ;   LC Card 80-601130   DDC 327.7306891 19
KF27 .F6 1979j

ZIMBABWE - POLITICS AND GOVERNMENT - 1979-1980.
McGovern, George Stanley, 1922- Impressions of southern Africa . Washington , 1979. v, 38 p. ;   LC Card 80-601034   DDC 327.68073 19
DT747.U6 M33

ZIMBABWE - POLITICS AND GOVERNMENT - 1980.
Baker, Pauline H. The birth of Zimbabwe . Washington , 1980. v, 21 p. :   LC Card 80-602587   DDC 968.91/04 19
DT962.8 .B34

United States. Congress. House. Committee on Foreign Affairs. Rhodesian sanctions, should the United States lift them? . Washington , 1980. iii, 80 p. ;   LC Card 80-601130   DDC 327.7306891 19
KF27 .F6 1979j

United States. Congress. House. Committee on Foreign Affairs. Subcommittee on Africa. Results of the recent elections in Zimbabwe . Washington , 1980. iii, 101 p. ;   LC Card 80-602533   DDC 324.96891/04 19
KF27 .F625 1980

United States. Congress. Senate. Committee on Foreign Relations. Rhodesia . Washington , 1980. iii, 59 p. ;   LC Card 80-601055   DDC 968.91/04 19
KF26 .F6 1979ab

Zimmerman, Alan. (joint author) Ross, Judith, 1947- Wisconsin public library building survey for handicapped accessibility /. Madison, WI [1979] 16, 2 p. ;   LC Card 80-621510   DDC 727/.8/04209775 19
Z711.92.P5 R67

ZIMMERMAN, DON ALAN, 1940-
United States. Congress. Senate. Committee on Labor and Human Resources. Nomination . Washington , 1980. ii, 14 p. ;   LC Card 80-602910   DDC 353.0085/2 19
KF26 .L27 1980c

Zimmerman, Joseph Francis, 1928- Gleason, Eugene J. Executive dominance in New York State. [Albany, 1974] 53 p.   LC Card 78-64398
NYPL [JLF 80-538]

Zimmerman, Larry J., 1947- The Future of South Dakota's past /. Vermillion, S.D. , 1981. p. cm.   LC Card 81-14812   DDC 978.3/01 19
E78.S63 F87

ZINC CHLORIDE.
Hill, S. D. Electrowinning of zinc from zinc chloride in monopolar and bipolar fused-salt cells /. Washington [1981] p. cm.   LC Card 80-607820   DDC 622 s 669/.52 19
TN23 .U43 TN796

ZINC - ELECTROMETALLURGY.
Cole, Ernest R. Insoluble anodes for electrowinning zinc and other metals /. Washington [1981] p. cm.   LC Card 80-607823   DDC 622 s 669/.52 19
TN23 .U43 TN796

Hill, S. D. Electrowinning of zinc from zinc chloride in monopolar and bipolar fused-salt cells /. Washington [1981] p. cm.   LC Card 80-607820   DDC 622 s 669/.52 19
TN23 .U43 TN796

ZINC - METALLURGY.
Behavior of cadmium during roasting of zinc concentrate /. Washington, D.C. [1981] p. cm.   LC Card 80-607819   DDC 622 s 669/.5 19
TN23 .U43 TN796

Hebble, T. L. (Terry L.) Recovery of principal metal values from electrolytic zinc waste /. Avondale, MD [1981] p. cm.   LC Card 81-10044   DDC 622 s 669/.52 19
TN23 .U43 TN796

ZINC ORES - ALASKA - DRENCHWATER CREEK REGION.
Nokleberg, Warren J. Stratiform zinc-lead deposits in the Drenchwater Creek area, Howard Pass quadrangle, northwestern Brooks Range, Alaska /. Menlo Park, CA , 1981. p. cm.   LC Card 81-607994   DDC 553.4/4/097987 19
TN483.A64 N64

Zinder (H.) and Associates, inc. Report to the New Mexico Energy and Minerals Department of storage and alternative options for increasing the availability of natural gas. Socorro, N.M. : New Mexico Energy Institute at New Mexico Institute of Mining & Technology, [1979] 61, [61] p. : map ; 28 cm. Cover title: Final report, storage and alternative options for increasing the availability of natural gas. "March 1979."   LC Card 80-622030   DDC 333.8/23311/09789 19
1. Gas, Natural - New Mexico. 2. Energy policy - New Mexico. 3. Gas as fuel. I. New Mexico. Energy and Minerals Dept. II. New Mexico Energy Institute at New Mexico Institute of Mining & Technology. III. Title. IV. Title: Final report, storage and alternative options for increasing the availability of natural gas. V. Title: Storage and alternative options for increasing the availability of natural gas.
TN881.N6 Z52 1979

Zink, Richard. Soil survey of Keya Paha County, Nebraska. [Washington, D.C.?] , 1980. ix, 224 p., 62 folded p. of plates :   LC Card 81-600561   DDC 631.4/7/782725 19
S599.N2 S63

Zinn, Charles J. How our laws are made / by Charles J. Zinn ; presented by Mr. Lesinski. Washington : U. S. Govt. Print. Off. : for sale by the Supt. of Docs., U. S. Govt. Print. Off., 1959. v, 34 p. ; 24 cm. (Document - 86th Congress, 1st session, House of Representatives . no. 156) LC Card 80-110570   DDC 328.73/077 19
1. Legislation - United States. I. Title.
KF4945.Z9 Z5 1959

Zinn, Clyde Dale. Systems analysis of the Texas gulf coast geopressured resources : final report /

by C. Dale Zinn ; prepared for Texas Energy Advisory Council, Energy Development Fund. [Austin] : The Council, 1979. v, 33 p. ; 28 cm. (Report - Texas Energy Development Fund . #EDF-020) LC Card 80-620765 DDC 333.8/8/097641 19
1. Geothermal engineering - Texas. 2. Geothermal resources - Texas. 3. Geothermal resources - Mexico, Gulf of. 4. Geothermal resources - Mexico, Gulf of. 5. System analysis. I. Texas. Energy Development Fund. II. Series: Texas. Energy Development Fund. Report - Texas Energy Advisory Council, Energy Development Fund , #EDF-020. III. Title.
TJ280.7 .Z58

ZIONISTS - UNITED STATES - BIOGRAPHY.
Urofsky, Melvin I. A voice that spoke for justice . Albany , 1981. p. cm.
0-87395-538-2 LC Card 81-5676 DDC 296.8/346/0924 B 19
BM755.W53 U76

ZIP CODE - UNITED STATES.
United States. Congress. House. Committee on Government Operations. Subcommittee on Government Information and Individual Rights. U. S. Postal Service Plan for nine-digit zip code . Washington , 1980. v, 462 p. : LC Card 81-601386 DDC 383/.145 19
KF27 .G6628 1980a

United States. Congress. Senate. Committee on Governmental Affairs. Subcommittee on Energy, Nuclear Proliferation, and Federal Services. Nine-digit zip codes . Washington , 1981. iii, 274 p. : LC Card 81-610629 DDC 383/.145 19
KF26 .G6728 1980d

ZIRCONIUM - CORROSION.
Riley, W. D. (William D.) Effect of ferric ion on corrosion resistance of zirconium in HCl-AlCl$_3$ environment /. Avondale, Md. , 1981. p. cm. LC Card 81-607817 DDC 622 s 620.1/8935223 19
TN23 .U43 TA480.Z65

Zissis, George John, 1922- Environmental Research Institute of Michigan. Infrared Information and Analysis (IRIA) Center. The infrared handbook /. Washington , 1978. ca. 1600 p. in various pagings : LC Card 77-90786
TA1570 .E56 1978 **NYPL [JSE 80-1602]**

Zone operations report. North Carolina. State Highway Patrol. 1964-74 (incomplete). [Raleigh] **NYPL [JLM 80-855]**

Zone-rated military mail. United States Postal Service. Board of Governors. Action of the Governors under 39 U. S. C. [Washington] [1977?] 802 p. in various pagings.
NYPL [*XME-9307]

ZONING, EMISSION DENSITY - LAW AND LEGISLATION - UNITED STATES.
American Society of Planning Officials. Legal issues of emission density zoning /. Research Triangle Park, N.C. , 1978. vi, 136 p. ; LC Card 79-601742 DDC 344.73/046342 19
KF3812.5.E55 A94

ZONING - ILLINOIS.
County growth management regulation . Urbana, Ill. , c1979. v, 112, [109] p. : LC Card 79-54714 DDC 352.9/6/09773 19
HT169.72.I3 C68

Smith, R. Marlin. A Guide for municipal zoning administration with forms /. Urbana-Champaign, Ill. , 1972. 136 p. ;
NYPL [JLF 81-263]

ZONING LAW - ARKANSAS.
Wright, Robert R. Zoning law in Arkansas . Little Rock, Ark. , c1980. 60 p. ; LC Card 80-84888 DDC 346.76704/5 347.670645 19
KFA4058 .W73

ZONING LAW - DISTRICT OF COLUMBIA.
United States. Congress. Senate. Committee on Governmental Affairs. Subcommittee on Governmental Efficiency and the District of Columbia. Resolution to disapprove Location of chanceries amendment act of 1979 . Washington , 1980. iv, 98 p. ; LC Card 80-602103 DDC 346.75304/5 19
KF26 .G6735 1979i

Zoning law in Arkansas . Wright, Robert R. Little Rock, Ark. , c1980. 60 p. ; LC Card 80-84888 DDC 346.76704/5 347.670645 19
KFA4058 .W73

ZONING LAW - MICHIGAN.
Hotaling, Robert B. Michigan townships planning and zoning handbook/. East Lansing (27 Kellogg Center for Continuing Education, MSU, East Lansing 48824) , 1980. xii, 208 p. : LC Card 80-620046 DDC 346.77404/5 347.740645 19
KFM4658 .H67

ZONING LAW - UNITED STATES.
National Institute of Law Enforcement and Criminal Justice. Corruption in land use and building regulation . [Washington, D.C.] , 1979. 2 v. ; LC Card 79-604180
HT169.7 .N35 1979

Wallace School of Community Service and Public Affairs. Bureau of Governmental Research and Service. The development standards document, with section-by-section explanation. [Eugene] [1979] 172 p. ; LC Card 80-624205 DDC 346.7304/5 347.30645 19
HD205 1979 .W34

Zoning map, Whitemarsh Township, Montgomery Co., Pennsylvania . Whitemarsh Township (Pa.) Board of Township Supervisors. [Lafayette Hill, Pa.] [1959] 1 map : LC Card 81-690184
G3824.W584G44 1959 .W4

ZONING - NEW YORK (CITY)
New York (City). Board of Estimate and Apportionment. In the matter of the establishment of a new "use district" to be known as the "retail district" . New York [1929?] ii, 90 p. : **NYPL [JLG 80-226]**

ZONING - UNITED STATES.
National Institute of Law Enforcement and Criminal Justice. Corruption in land use and building regulation . [Washington, D.C.] , 1979. 2 v. ; LC Card 79-604180
HT169.7 .N35 1979

Rahenkamp, Sachs, Wells, and Associates. Innovative zoning: a local officials guidebook /. [Washington] , 1977. 28 p.:
NYPL [*XME-8967]

ZONING - VIRGINIA.
Virginia. Dept. of Housing and Community Development. Status of local planning in Virginia, 1979 /. Richmond, Va. [1979] 55 p. : LC Card 80-622615 DDC 352.9/6/025755 19
HT167.5.V8 V53 1979

ZOOGEOGRAPHY - ALASKA - MAPS.
Alaska Interagency Fish and Wildlife Team. Wildlife atlas . [s.l.] , 1976. 30 leaves : LC Card 79-625526 DDC 912/.159909798
G1531.D4 A45 1976

ZOOLOGY - MISSOURI - PICTORIAL WORKS.
Schwartz, Charles Walsh. Wildlife drawings /. Jefferson City, Mo. , c1980. 122 p. : LC Card 81-621407 DDC 599 19
QL46 .S395

ZOOLOGY - NORTH DAKOTA.
Steinhaus, Virginia S. A list of vertebrates of northcentral North Dakota /. Grand Forks, N.D. [1979] 29 p. : LC Card 80-622454 DDC 596.09784 19
QL197 .S85

Steinhaus, Virginia S. A list of vertebrates of northwestern North Dakota /. Grand Forks, N.D. [1979] 28 p. ; LC Card 80-622453 DDC 596.09784/7 19
QL197 .S86

Steinhaus, Virginia S. A list of vertebrates of southcentral North Dakota /. Grand Forks, N.D. [1979] 30 p. ; LC Card 80-622452 DDC 596.09784 19
QL197 .S87

Steinhaus, Virginia S. A list of vertebrates of southeastern North Dakota /. Grand Forks, N.D. [1979] 29 p. : LC Card 80-622451 DDC 596.09784 19
QL197 .S88

ZOONOSES - PREVENTION - CONGRESSES.
National Cancer Institute Symposium on Biohazards and Zoonotic Problems of Primate Procurement, Quarantine, and Research, Frederick Cancer Research Center, 1975. Biohazards and zoonotic problems of primate procurement, quarantine, and research . [Bethesda, Md.] 1975. 137 p. : LC Card 76-600529 DDC 614.4/3 19
RA641.P7 N37 1975

ZOOPLANKTON - MASSACHUSETTS - SALEM.
Ichthyoplankton found in Beverly-Salem harbor, March 1975 through February 1976 . [Boston] , 1977. 85 p. : LC Card 79-621673 DDC 597/.03/90916345 19
QL628.M4 I25

ZOSTERA MARINA.
Surficial sediments and seagrasses of eastern Great South Bay, N.Y. /. Stony Brook, N.Y. , 1978. ii, 30 p. : LC Card 80-620917 DDC 551.46/146 19
GC383 .S87

Zukofsky, Louis, 1904-1978.
"A".
Ahearn, Barry. Zukofsky's "A" . Berkeley , c1982. p. cm. ISBN 0-520-04378-2 LC Card 81-13000 DDC 811/.52 19
PS3549.U47 A6833

Zukofsky's "A" . Ahearn, Barry. Berkeley , c1982. p. cm. ISBN 0-520-04378-2 LC Card 81-13000 DDC 811/.52 19
PS3549.U47 A6833

Zupan, Jeffrey M. Pushkarev, Boris. Urban rail in America . Bloomington , c1981. p. cm. ISBN 0-253-37555-X LC Card 81-47293 DDC 388.4/2/0973 19
HE4451 .P87

Zuvekas, Clarence. Agricultural development in Haiti : an assessment of sector problems, policies, and prospects under conditions of severe soil erosion / prepared for USAID/Haiti by Clarence Zuvekas, Jr. Washington, D.C. : Agency for International Development, [1978] xiv, 355 p. : ill. ; 28 cm. "May 1978." Bibliography: p. [345]-355. LC Card 80-601532 DDC 338.1/097294 19
1. Rural development - Haiti. 2. Agriculture - Economic aspects - Haiti. I. United States. AID Mission to Haiti. II. Title.
HD1841 .Z69

Zwank, Phillip J., 1944- Reduced recruitment in Utah mule deer relative to winter condition / by Phillip J. Zwank. [Salt Lake City] : Utah State Division of Wildlife Resources, [1979] ix, 80 p. : ill. ; 28 cm. (Publication - Utah State Division of Wildlife Resources ; no. 79-11) Originally presented as the author's thesis, Utah State University, 1978. Bibliography: p. 61-64. LC Card 80-621214 DDC 333.95/5 s 599.73/57 19
1. Mule deer - Reproduction. 2. Mule deer - Wintering. 3. Mammal populations - Utah. 4. Mammals - Reproduction. 5. Mammals - Wintering. 6. Mammals - Utah. I. Series: Utah. Division of Wildlife Resources. Publication , no. 79-11. II. Title.
SK453 .A25 no. 79-11 QL737.U55

Zymelman, Manuel. Forecasting manpower demand / by Manuel Zymelman. [Washington, D.C.] : Education Dept. of the World Bank, [1980] ii, 105 p. : ill. ; 28 cm. "July 1980." LC Card 80-146379 DDC 331.12/3/0724 19
1. Employment forecasting - Mathematical models. I. Title.
HD5701.55 .Z95

Zytowski, Donald G. Sex-fair interest measurement . Washington , 1978, 1979 printing. xvii, 169 p. : LC Card 79-602075 DDC 153.9/4 19
HF5381.5 .S4

Zywen, Mark A. Pennsylvania. Local Government Commission. Cable television in the Commonwealth of Pennsylvania, analysis and recommendations. Harrisburg, PA [1979] 109, [7] p. : LC Card 80-622151
HE8700.7.C6 P45 1979